Reverse
Acronyms, Initialisms &
Abbreviations Dictionary

Explore your options!

Gale databases are offered in a variety of formats

™ The information in this Gale publication is also available in some or all of the formats described here. Your Gale Representative will be happy to fill you in. Call toll-free 1-800-877-GALE.

GALE

GaleNet

A number of Gale databases are now available on GaleNet, our new online information resource accessible through the Internet. GaleNet features an easy-to-use end-user interface, the powerful search capabilities of BRS/SEARCH retrieval software and ease of access through the World Wide Web.

Diskette/Magnetic Tape

Many Gale databases are available on diskette or magnetic tape, allowing systemwide access to your most-used information sources through existing computer systems. Data can be delivered on a variety of mediums (DOS-formatted diskettes, 9-track tape, 8mm data tape) and in industry-standard formats (comma-delimited, tagged, fixed-field).

CD-ROM

A variety of Gale titles are available on CD-ROM, offering maximum flexibility and powerful search software.

Online

For your convenience, many Gale databases are available through popular online services, including DIALOG, NEXIS, DataStar, ORBIT, OCLC, Thomson Financial Network's I/Plus Direct, HRIN, Prodigy, Sandpoint's HOOVER, the Library Corporation's NLightN and Telebase Systems.

ISSN 0270-4404

Reverse Acronyms, Initialisms & Abbreviations Dictionary

A Companion Volume to *Acronyms, Initialisms & Abbreviations Dictionary*, with Terms Arranged Alphabetically by Meaning of Acronym, Initialism, or Abbreviation

Covering: Aerospace, Associations, Banking, Biochemistry, Business, Data Processing, Domestic and International Affairs, Economics, Education, Electronics, Genetics, Government, Information Technology, Internet, Investment, Labor, Law, Medicine, Military Affairs, Pharmacy, Physiology, Politics, Religion, Science, Societies, Sports, Technical Drawings and Specifications, Telecommunications, Trade, Transportation, and Other Fields

25th Edition

Volume 3

Part 3

P-Z

Mary Rose Bonk,
Editors

Pamela Dear,
Associate Editor

GALE

DETROIT · LONDON

Editor: Mary Rose Bonk

Associate Editor: Pamela Dear

Contributing Editors: Mildred Hunt

Data Entry Manager: Eleanor M. Allison
Data Entry Coordinator: Kenneth Benson

Production Director: Mary Beth Trimper
Production Assistant: Deborah Milliken

Graphic Services Manager: Barbara J. Yarrow
Macintosh Artist: Gary Leach

Manager, Technical Support Services: Theresa A. Rocklin
Programmer: Charles Beaumont

Library of Congress Catalog Card Number 84-643188
ISBN 0-7876-2455-1 (Volume 1 Complete)
ISBN 0-7876-2456-X (Part 1: A-F only)
ISBN 0-7876-2457-8 (Part 2: G-O only)
ISBN 0-7876-2458-6 (Part 3: P-Z only)
ISSN 0270-4404

Printed in the United States of America

Contents

Gale's publications in the acronyms and abbreviations field include:

Acronyms, Initialisms & Abbreviations Dictionary series:

Acronyms, Initialisms & Abbreviations Dictionary (Volume 1). A guide to acronyms, initialisms, abbreviations, and similar contractions, arranged alphabetically by abbreviation.

Acronyms, Initialisms & Abbreviations Dictionary Supplement (Volume 2). An interedition supplement in which terms are arranged alphabetically both by abbreviation and by meaning.

Reverse Acronyms, Initialisms & Abbreviations Dictionary (Volume 3). A companion to Volume 1 in which terms are arranged alphabetically by meaning of the acronym, initialism, or abbreviation.

Acronyms, Initialisms & Abbreviations Dictionary Subject Guide series:

Computer & Telecommunications Acronyms (Volume 1). A guide to acronyms, initialisms, abbreviations, and similar contractions used in the field of computers and telecommunications in which terms are arranged alphabetically both by abbreviation and by meaning.

Business Acronyms (Volume 2). A guide to business-oriented acronyms, initialisms, abbreviations, and similar contractions in which terms are arranged alphabetically both by abbreviation and by meaning.

International Acronyms, Initialisms & Abbreviations Dictionary series:

International Acronyms, Initialisms & Abbreviations Dictionary (Volume 1). A guide to foreign and international acronyms, initialisms, abbreviations, and similar contractions, arranged alphabetically by abbreviation.

Reverse International Acronyms, Initialisms & Abbreviations Dictionary (Volume 2). A companion to Volume 1, in which terms are arranged alphabetically by meaning of the acronym, initialism, or abbreviation.

Periodical Title Abbreviations series:

Periodical Title Abbreviations: By Abbreviation (Volume 1). A guide to abbreviations commonly used for periodical titles, arranged alphabetically by abbreviation.

Periodical Title Abbreviations: By Title (Volume 2). A guide to abbreviations commonly used for periodical titles, arranged alphabetically by title.

New Periodical Title Abbreviations (Volume 3). An interedition supplement in which terms are arranged alphabetically both by abbreviation and by title.

User's Guide

The following examples illustrate possible elements of entries in *RAIAD:*

```
              ①              ②       ③    ④
Force Aerienne Tactique [Tactical Air Force] [French] (NATG) ......................FATAC

                         ⑤                  ⑥
Multiple-Mirror Telescope [Mount Hopkins, AZ] [Jointly operated by
Smithsonian Institution and the University of Arizona] [Astronomy].......................MMT
                         ⑦                                              ⑧
```

①   Meaning or Phrase

②   English Translation

③   Language (for non-English entries)

④   Source code (Allows you to verify entries or find additional information. Decoded in the List of Selected Sources)

⑤   Location or Country of origin (Provides geographic identifiers for airports, colleges and universities, libraries, military bases, political parties, radio and television stations, and others)

⑥   Sponsoring organization

⑦   Subject category (Clarifies entries by providing appropriate context)

⑧   Acronym, Initialism, or Abbreviation

The completeness of a listing is dependent upon both the nature of the term and the amount of information provided by the source. If additional information becomes available during future research, an entry is revised.

Arrangement of Entries

Terms are arranged in alphabetical order, according to the meaning of the acronym, initialism, or abbreviation. If a particular translation has more than one initialism representing it, the various choices are then arranged alphabetically. Thus:

> Liquid Nitrogen...LIN
> Liquid Nitrogen...LN

Articles, conjunctions, prepositions, etc., generally are not considered in the alphabetizing:

> Master Switch...MS
> Master *of* Textile Chemistry...MTC
> Not Less Than...NLT
> Not *in* Line *of* Duty...NLD

List of Selected Sources

Each of the sources included in the following list contributed at least 50 terms. It would be impossible to cite a source for every entry because the majority of terms are sent by outside contributors, are uncovered through independent research by the editorial staff, or surface as miscellaneous broadcast or print media references.

For sources used on an ongoing basis, only the latest edition is listed. For most of the remaining sources, the edition that was used is cited. The editors will provide further information about these sources upon request.

Unless further described in an annotation, the publications listed here contain no additional information about the acronym, initialism, or abbreviation cited.

(AABC)   *Catalog of Abbreviations and Brevity Codes.* Washington, DC: U.S. Department of the Army, 1981. [Use of source began in 1969]

(AAG)   *Aerospace Abbreviations Glossary.* Report Number AG60-0014. Prepared by General Dynamics/Astronautics. San Diego, CA: 1962.

(AAGC)   *Acronyms and Abbreviations in Government Contracting.* 2d ed. By Patricia A. Tobin and Joan Nelson Phillips. Washington, DC: George Washington University, 1997.

(AAMN)   *Abbreviations and Acronyms in Medicine and Nursing.* By Solomon Garb, Eleanor Krakauer, and Carson Justice. New York, NY: Springer Publishing Co., 1976.

(ABBR)   *Abbreviations: The Comprehensive Dictionary of Abbreviations and Letter Symbols.* Vol. 1 C. By Edward Wall. Ann Arbor, MI: The Pierian Press, 1984.

(AC)   *Associations Canada 1995/96.* Edited by Ward McBurney. Toronto, Canada: Canadian Almanac & Directory Publishing Co. Ltd., 1995.

(ACII)   *"Acronym and Initials Index."* 7 February 1996. <http://www.ioi.ie/~readout/cl.html> (7 November 1996).

(AD)   *Abbreviations Dictionary.* 8thed. By Ralph De Sola. Boca Raton, FL: CRC Press, 1992.

(ADA)   *The Australian Dictionary of Acronyms and Abbreviations.* 2nd ed. Compiled by David J. Jones. Leura, NSW, Australia: Second Back Row Press Pty. Ltd., 1981.

(ADDR)   *Army Dictionary and Desk Reference.* By Tim Zurick. Harrisburg, PA: Stackpole Books, 1992.

(AEBS)   *Acronyms in Education and the Behavioral Sciences.* By Toyo S. Kawakami. Chicago, IL: American Library Association, 1971.

(AEE)   *American Educators' Encyclopedia.* By Edward L. Dejnozka and David E. Kapel. Westport, CT: Greenwood Press, 1991.

(AF)   *Reference Aid: Abbreviations in the African Press.* Arlington, VA: Joint Publications Research Service, 1979.

(AFIT)   *Compendium of Authenticated Systems and Logistics*. Washington, DC: Air Force Institute of Technology, 1984.

(AFM)   *Air Force Manual of Abbreviations*. Washington, DC: U.S. Department of the Air Force, 1975. [Use of source began in 1969]

(AIA)   *Aviation Insurance Abbreviations, Organisations and Institutions*. By M.J. Spurway. London, England: Witherby & Co. Ltd., 1983.

(AIE)   *Acronyms and Initialisms in Education*. 6th ed. Compiled by John Hutchins. Norwich, England: Librarians of Institutes and Schools of Education, 1995.

(ANA)   *"Abbreviations" - U.S. Navy Dictionary*. 3rd revision. Washington DC: DCP, 1989.

(APTA)   *Australian Periodical Title Abbreviations*. Compiled by David J. Jones. Leura, NSW, Australia: Second Back Row Press Pty. Ltd., 1985.

(ARC)   *Agricultural Research Centres: A World Directory of Organizations and Programmes*. 2 vols. Edited by Nigel Harvey. Harlow, Essex, England: Longman Group, 1983.
         A world guide to official, educational, industrial, and independent research centers which support research in the fields of agriculture, veterinary medicine, horticulture, aquaculture, food science, forestry, zoology, and botany.

(ARCH)   *Dictionary of Architecture and Construction*. Edited by Cyril M. Harris. New York, NY: McGraw-Hill, Inc., 1975.

(ASF)   *Guide to Names and Acronyms of Organizations, Activities, and Projects*. By Food and Agriculture Organization of the United Nations. Fishery Information, Data, and Statistics Service and U.S. National Oceanic and Atmospheric Administration. Aquatic Sciences and Fisheries Information System Reference Series, Number 10, 1982. n.p.

(BABM)   *Bailliere's Abbreviations in Medicine.* 5th ed. By Edwin B. Steen. London, England: Bailliere Tindall, 1984.

(BARN)   *The Barnhart Abbreviations Dictionary*. Edited by Robert K. Barnhart. New York, NY: John Wiley & Sons, Inc., 1995.

(BI)   *British Initials and Abbreviations*. 3rd ed. By Ian H. Wilkes. London, England: Leonard Hill Books, 1971.

(BIB)   *Bibliotech*. Ottawa, Canada: National Library of Canada, 1988-89.

(BJA)   *Biblical and Judaic Acronyms*. By Lawrence Marwick. New York, NY: Ktav Publishing House, Inc., 1979.

(BRI)   *Book Review Index*. 1997 Cumulation. Edited by Beverly Baer. Detroit, MI: Gale Research, 1998.

(BROA)   *Broadcasting and Cable Yearbook 1997*. 2 vol. New Providence, NJ: R.R. Bowker, 1997.

(BTTJ)   *Breaking Through Technical Jargon: A Dictionary of Computer and Automation Acronyms*. By Mark S. Merkow. New York, NY: Van Nostrand Reinhold, 1990.

(BUR)   *Computer Acronyms and Abbreviations Handbook*. Tokyo, Japan: Burroughs Co. Ltd., 1978.

(BYTE)   *Byte: The Small Systems Journal*. Peterborough, NH: McGraw-Hill Information Systems, Inc., 1987-89.

(CAAL)   *CAAL COMOPTEVFOR Acronym and Abbreviation List*. Norfolk, VA: (CAAL-U) Operational Test and Evaluation Force, 1981.

(CB)   *Centres & Bureaux: A Directory of Concentrations of Effort, Information and Expertise*. Edited by Lindsay Sellar. Beckenham, Kent, England: CBD Research Ltd., 1987.
          A guide to British organizations which include the words "centre" or "bureau" in their names. Entries include name and address; telephone and telex numbers; chief official; and a description of the purposes, activities, and services of the organization.

(CDAI)   *Concise Dictionary of Acronyms and Initialisms*. By Stuart W. Miller. New York, NY: Facts on File Publications, 1988.

(CDE)   *The Computer Desktop Encyclopedia*. By Alan Freedman. New York, NY: AMACOM, 1996.

(CDI)   *The Cancer Dictionary*. By Roberta Altman and Michael Sarg, M.D. New York, NY: Facts on File, 1992.

(CED)   *Current European Directories*. 2nd ed. Edited by G.P. Henderson. Beckenham, Kent, England: CBD Research, 1981.

(CET)   *Communications-Electronics Terminology*. AFM 11-1. Vol. 3. U.S. Department of the Air Force, 1973.

(CINC)   *A CINCPAC Glossary of Commonly Used Abbreviations and Short Titles*. By Ltc. J.R. Johnson. Washington, DC: 1968.

(CMD)   *Complete Multilingual Dictionary of Computer Terminology*. Compiled by Georges Nania. Chicago, IL: National Textbook Co., 1984.
          Computer-related terms in Spanish, French, Italian, Portuguese, and English. Indexes in French, Italian, Spanish, and Portuguese are also provided.

(CNC)   *American National Standard Codes for the Representation of Names of Countries, Dependencies, and Areas of Special Sovereignty for Information Interchange*. U.S. National Bureau of Standards. Washington, DC: Government Printing Office, 1986. [Use of source began in 1977]
          These standard codes, approved by the International Organization for Standardization and the American National Standards Institute, are used in the international interchange of data in many fields.

(CPH)   *The Charles Press Handbook of Current Medical Abbreviations*. 3rd ed. Philadelphia, PA: The Charles Press Publishers, Inc., 1991.

(CRD)   *Computer-Readable Databases: A Directory and Data Sourcebook*. 6th ed. Edited by Kathleen Young Marcaccio. Detroit, MI: Gale Research, 1990.
          A guide to online databases, offline files available in various magnetic formats, and CD-ROM files. Entries include producer name, address, telephone number, description of coverage, vendors, and contact person.

(CROSS)   *Cross-Border Links: A Directory of Organizations in Canada, Mexico, and the United States*. Edited by Ricardo Hernandez and Edith Sanchez. Albuquerque, NM: Inter-Hemispheric Education Resource Center, 1992.

(CSR)	*Computer Science Resources: A Guide to Professional Literature.* Edited by Darlene Myers. White Plains, NY: Knowledge Industry Publications, Inc., 1981.
	Covers several types of computer-related literature including journals, technical reports, directories, dictionaries, handbooks, and university computer center newsletters. Five appendices cover career and salary trends in the computer industry, user group acronyms, university computer libraries, and trade fairs and shows.
(CTT)	*Corporate TrendTrac.* Edited by A. Dale Timpe. Detroit, MI: Gale Research, 1988-89.
	Covers mergers and acquisitions, stock exchange listings and suspensions, company name changes, bankruptcies, liquidations, and reorganizations.
(DA)	*Dictionary of Aviation.* By R. J. Hall and R. D. Campbell. Chicago, IL: St. James Press, 1991.
(DAS)	*Dictionary of Abbreviations and Symbols.* By Edward Frank Allen. London, England: Cassell and Co. Ltd., 1949.
(DAVI)	*The Davis Book of Medical Abbreviations: A Deciphering Guide.* By Sarah Lu Mitchell-Hatton. Philadelphia, PA: F. A. Davis Co., 1991.
(DBA)	*Directory of British Associations.* Edited by G. P. Henderson and S. P. A. Henderson. Beckenham, Kent, England: CBD Research, Ltd., 1990.
(DBQ)	*A Dictionary of British Qualifications.* London, England: Kogan Page Ltd., 1985.
(DCTA)	*Dictionary of Commercial Terms and Abbreviations.* By Alan E. Branch. London, England: Witherby & Co. Ltd., 1984.
(DD)	*The Financial Post Directory of Directors 1997.* Toronto, Canada: The Financial Post, 1996.
(DEN)	*Dictionary of Electronics and Nucleonics.* By L.E.C. Hughes, R. W. B. Stephens and L. D. Brown. New York, NY: Barnes & Noble, 1969.
(DFIT)	*Dictionary of Finance and Investment Terms.* 4th ed. Edited by John Downes and Jordan Elliot Goodman. Hauppauge, NY: Barron's Educational Series, 1995.
(DGA)	*Dictionary of Graphic Arts Abbreviations.* By L. W. Wallis. Rockport, MA: Rockport Publishers, Inc., 1986.
(DHSM)	*Dictionary of Health Services Management.* 2nd ed. By Thomas C. Timmreck. Owings Mills, MD: Rynd Communications, 1987.
(DI)	*The Dictionary of Initials-What They Mean.* Compiled and edited by Harriette Lewis. Kingswood, Surrey, England: Paper Fronts Elliot Right Way Books, 1983.
(DICI)	*The Dictionary of Initials.* By Betsy M. Parks. Secaucus, NJ: Citadel Press, 1981.
(DIT)	*Dictionary of Informatics Terms in Russian and English.* By G. S. Zhdanov, E. S. Kolobrodov, V. A. Polushkin, and A. I. Cherny. Moscow: Nauka, 1971.
(DLA)	*Bieber's Dictionary of Legal Abbreviations.* 3rd ed. By Mary Miles Prince. Buffalo, NY: William S. Hein & Co., 1988.

(DMA)   *Dictionary of Military Abbreviations: British, Empire, Commonwealth.* By B. K. C. Scott. Hastings, East Sussex, England: Tamarisk Books, 1982.

(DMAA)   *Dictionary of Medical Acronyms and Abbreviations.* 3rd ed. Edited by Stanley Jablonski. Philadelphia, PA: Hanley & Belfus, Inc., 1998.

(DMC)   *Webster's New World Dictionary of Media and Communications.* Revised ed. By Richard Weiner. New York, NY: Macmillan, 1996.

(DNAB)   *Dictionary of Naval Abbreviations.* 3rd ed. Compiled and edited by Bill Wedertz. Annapolis, MD: Naval Institute Press, 1984.

(DOAD)   *The Dictionary of Advertising.* Edited by Laurence Urdang. Lincolnwood, IL: NTC Business Books, 1986.

(DOG)   *A Dictionary of Genetics.* 5th ed. By Robert C. King and William D. Stansfield. New York, NY: Oxford University Press, 1997.

(DOGT)   *"List of Acronyms."* <http://www.em.doe.gov/rtc1994/loa.html> (5 March 1997).

(DOM)   *The Dictionary of Multimedia: Terms & Acronyms.* By Brad Hansen. Wilsonvillee, OR: Franklin, Beedle & Associates, 1997.

(DOMA)   *Dictionary of Military Abbreviations.* By Norman Polmar, Mark Warren, and Eric Wertheim. Annapolis, MD: Naval Institute Press, 1994.

(DS)   *Dictionary of Shipping International Trade Terms and Abbreviations.* 3rd ed. By Alan E. Branch. London, England: Witherby & Co. Ltd., 1986.

(DSA)   *Dictionary of Sigla and Abbreviations to and in Law Books before 1607.* By William Hamilton Bryson. Charlottesville, VA: University Press of Virginia, 1975.

(DSUE)   *A Dictionary of Slang and Unconventional English.* 8th ed. By Eric Partridge. New York, NY: Macmillan Publishing Co., 1984.

(DUND)   *Directory of United Nations Databases and Information Services.* 4th ed. Compiled by the Advisory Committee for the Coordination of Information Systems. New York, NY: United Nations, 1990.
         A guide to computerized databases and information systems/services. Entries include sponsoring organization, year established, type, scope, coverage, timespan, and contact information.

(DWSG)   *Defense Weapon Systems Glossary.* By David Trotz. Piscataway, NJ: Target Marketing, 1992.

(EA)   *Encyclopedia of Associations.* 29th ed. Vol. 1, National Organizations of the U.S. Edited by Carol A. Schwartz and Rebecca L. Turner. Detroit, MI: Gale Research, 1995 (and supplement 1995) [Use of source began in 1960]
         A guide to trade, professional, and other nonprofit associations that are national and international in scope and membership and that are headquartered in the United States. Entries include name and address; telephone and telex number; chief official; and a description of the purpose, activities, and structure of the organization.

(EAAP)   *Encyclopedia of Associations: Association Periodicals*. 3 vols. Edited by Denise M. Allard and Robert C. Thomas. Detroit, MI: Gale Research, 1987.
> A directory of publications issued by all types of national nonprofit organizations in the United States. Entries include title and organization name, address, telephone number; description of periodical, frequency of publication, and price.

(EAIO)   *Encyclopedia of Associations: International Organizations*. 29th ed. Edited by Linda Irvin. Detroit, MI: Gale Research, 1995. [Use of source began in 1985]
> A guide to trade, professional, and other nonprofit associations that are national or international in scope and membership and that are headquartered outside the United States. Entries include name and address; principal foreign language name; telephone and telex number; chief official; and a description of the purpose, activities, and structure of the organization.

(ECED)   *The European Communities Encyclopedia and Directory 1992*. London, England: Europa Publications Ltd., 1991; distributed in U.S. by Gale Research, Detroit, MI.
> A comprehensive guide to the European Communities. Entries explain widely-used acronyms and include address, telephone, telex, fax numbers and chief officers for EC-level organizations.

(ECII)   *Electronics, Computers and Industrial Instrumentation Abbreviations and Acronyms*. Edited by Sergio Sobredo. Miami, FL: Sergio Sobredo Technical Services, 1986.

(ECON)   *The Economist*. London, England: The Economist Newspaper Ltd., 1997. [Use of source began in 1988]

(EDAC)   *Dictionary of Educational Acronyms, Abbreviations, and Initialisms*. 2nd ed. Edited by James C. Palmer and Anita Y. Colby. Phoenix, AZ: Oryx Press, 1985.

(EE)   *Eastern Europe and the Commonwealth of Independent States 1992*. London, England: Europa Publications Ltd., 1992; distributed in U.S. by Gale Research, Detroit, MI.

(EECA)   *Dictionary of Electrical, Electronics, and Computer Abbreviations*. By Phil Brown. London, England: Buttersworth, 1985.

(EG)   *Environmental Glossary*. 4th ed. Edited by G. William Frick and Thomas F.P. Sullivan. Rockville, MD: Government Institutes, Inc., 1986.

(EGAO)   *Encyclopedia of Governmental Advisory Organizations*. 9th ed. Edited by Donna Batten. Detroit, MI: Gale Research, 1994-95 (and supplement, 1995). [Use of source began in 1975]
> A reference guide to permanent, continuing, and ad hoc U.S. presidential advisory committees, interagency committees, and other government-related boards, panels, task forces, commissions, conferences, and other similar bodies serving in a consultative, coordinating, advisory, research, or investigative capacity. Entries include name and address, telephone number, designated federal employee, history, recommendation and findings of the committee, staff size, publications, and subsidiaries. Also includes indexes to personnel, reports, federal agencies, presidential administration, and an alphabetical and keyword index.

(EMRF)   *The St. James Encyclopedia of Mortgage & Real Estate Finance*. By James Newell, Albert Santi, and Chip Mitchell. Chicago, IL: St. James Press, 1991.

(EPA)   *Glossary of EPA Acronyms*. Washington, DC: Environmental Protection Agency, 1987.

(ERG)   *Environmental Regulatory Glossary*. 5th ed. Edited by G. William Frick and Thomas F. P. Sullivan. Rockville, MD: Government Institutes, Inc., 1990.

(EY)   *The Europa World Year Book 1992*. London: Europa Publications Ltd., 1992. distributed in U.S. by Gale Research, Detroit, MI.
         An annual survey containing detailed information about the political, economic, statistical, and commercial situation of the regions and countries covered.

(FAAC)   *Contractions Handbook*. Changes. U.S. Department of Transportation. Federal Aviation Administration, 1993. [Use of source began in 1969]

(FAAL)   *Location Identifiers*. U.S. Department of Transportation. Federal Aviation Administration. Air Traffic Service, 1982.

(FEA)   *The Far East and Australasia 1987*. 18th ed. London, England: Europa Publications Ltd., 1986; distributed in U.S. by Gale Research, Detroit, MI.
         An annual survey containing detailed information about the political, economic, statistical, and commercial situation of the regions and countries covered.

(FFDE)   *The Facts on File Dictionary of Environmental Science*. By L. Harold Stevenson and Bruce Wyman. New York, NY: Facts on File, 1991.
         Defines terms from disciplines as diverse as biology, chemistry, geology, physics, engineering, meteorology, social science, medicine, and economics.

(GAAI)   *"Glossary of Abbreviations, Acronyms, and Initialisms."* 17 February 1998.
         <http://www.em.doe.gov/idb97/acropdf.html

(GAVI)   *"Glossary of Aviation Acronyms and Abbreviations."*
         <http://olias.arc.nasa.gov/AFO_Acronyms_.html> (5 March 1997).

(GEA)   *Government Economic Agencies of the World: An International Directory of Governmental Organisations Concerned with Economic Development and Planning*. A Keesing's Reference Publication. Edited by Alan J. Day. Harlow, Essex, England: Longman Group Ltd., 1985.
         Covers over 170 countries and territories. Two introductory sections for each area cover economic data and prevailing economic and political conditions. Individual entries provide title, address, and names of chief officials of each agency. Current activities and financial structure of each agency are also detailed. An index of agency officials is provided.

(GFGA)   *Guide to Federal Government Acronyms*. Edited by William R. Evinger. Phoenix, AZ: The Oryx Press, 1989.

(GNE)   *The Green Encyclopedia*. By Irene Franck and David Brownstone. New York, NY: Prentice Hall General Reference, 1992.

(GPO)   *Style Manual*. Washington, DC: Government Printing Office, 1984. Terms are included in Chapter 24, Foreign Languages.

(GRD)   *Government Research Directory*. 8th ed. Edited by Joseph M. Palmisano. Detroit, MI: Gale Research, 1994. (and supplement, 1994).
         A descriptive guide to U.S. government research and development centers, institutes, laboratories, bureaus, test facilities, experiment stations, data collection and analysis centers, and grants management and research coordinating offices in agriculture, business, education, energy, engineering, environment, the humanities, medicine, military science, and basic applied sciences.

(HCT)   *Health Care Terms.* 2nd ed. By Vergil N. and Debora A. Slee. St. Paul, MN: Tringa Press, 1991.

(HGAA)   *The Handy Guide to Abbreviations and Acronyms for the Automated Office.* By Mark W. Greenia. Seattle, WA: Self-Counsel Press Inc., 1986.

(IAA)   *Index of Acronyms and Abbreviations in Electrical and Electronic Engineering.* Compiled by Buro Scientia. New York, NY: VCH Publishers, 1989.

(IBMDP)   *IBM Data Processing Glossary.* 6th ed. White Plains, NY: IBM Corp., 1977.

(ICAO)   *Aircraft Type Designators.* 13th ed. International Civil Aviation Organization, August, 1981.

(ICDA)   *Designators for Aircraft Operating Agencies, Aeronautical Authorities and Services.* 49th ed. International Civil Aviation Organization, June, 1982.
Document also includes telephony designators and postal and telegraphic addresses of government civil aviation authorities.

(ICLI)   *Location Indicators.* 51st ed. International Civil Aviation Organization, February, 1987.
Document also contains addresses of flight information centers.

(IDOE)   *The Illustrated Dictionary of Electronics.* 6th ed. By Stan Gibilisco. New York, NY: TAB Books, 1994.

(IEEE)   *IEEE Standard Dictionary of Electrical and Electronics Terms.* Edited by Frank Jay. New York, NY: The Institute of Electrical and Electronics Engineers, Inc., 1977, 1984.
Includes definitions for thousands of electrical and electronics terms. Each entry includes a numeric source code.

(IIA)   *Index of Initials and Acronyms.* Compiled by Richard Kleiner. New York, NY: Auerbach Publishers, 1971.

(IID)   *Information Industry Directory.* 15th ed. Edited by Annette Novallo. Detroit, MI: Gale Research, 1995. (and supplement, 1995).
An international guide to computer-readable databases, database producers, and publishers, online vendors and time-sharing companies, telecommunications networks, and many other information systems and services. Entries include name and address, telephone number, chief official, and a detailed description of the purpose and function of the system or service.

(ILCA)   *Index to Legal Citations and Abbreviations.* By Donald Raistrick. Abingdon, Oxfordshire, England: Professional Books Ltd., 1981.

(IMH)   *International Marketing Handbook.* 2nd ed. Edited by Frank Bair. Detroit, MI: Gale Research, 1985.
An in-depth guide to commercial and trade data on 142 countries of the world. Features include a list of European trade fairs and a report on growth markets in Western Europe.

(INF)   *Infantry.* Fort Benning, GA: U.S. Army Infantry Training School, 1996. [Use of source began in 1983]

(IRC)   *International Research Centers Directory 1992-93.* 6th ed. Edited by Annette Piccirelli. Detroit, MI: Gale Research, 1991.
A world guide to government, university, independent, nonprofit, and commercial research and development centers, institutes, laboratories, bureaus, test facilities,

experiment stations, and data collection and analysis centers, as well as foundations, councils, and other organizations which support research.

(IRUK)   *Industrial Research in the United Kingdom*. 12th ed. Harlow, Essex, England: Longman Group UK Ltd., 1987.
> A guide to all groups conducting or funding research relevant to British industrial development. Entries include name, address, telephone and telex numbers; chief officials; and scope of activities.

(IT)   *Information Today: The Newspaper for Users and Producers of Electronic Information Services*. Medford, NJ: Learned Information Inc., 1988-89.

(ITD)   *International Tradeshow Directory*. 5th ed. Frankfurt, Germany: M + A Publishers for Fairs, Exhibitions and Conventions Ltd., 1989.
> A guide to trade fairs and exhibitions throughout the world. Entries include event name, dates, frequency, location, description of purpose, profile of exhibitors and attendees.

(IYR)   *The 1989-92 International Yacht Racing Rules*. London, England: International Yacht Racing Union, 1989.

(KSC)   *A Selective List of Acronyms and Abbreviations*. Compiled by the Documents Department, Kennedy Space Center Library, 1971, 1973.

(LAIN)   *Latest Intelligence: An International Directory of Codes Used by Government, Law Enforcement, Military, and Surveillance Agencies*. By James E. Tunnell. Blue Ridge Summit, PA: TAB BOOKS, 1990.

(LCCP)   *MARC Formats for Bibliographic Data*. Appendix II. Washington, DC: Library of Congress, 1982.

(LCLS)   *Symbols of American Libraries*. 14th ed. Edited by the Enhanced Cataloging Division. Washington, DC: Library of Congress, 1992. [Use of source began in 1980]

(LWAP)   *Legal Words and Phrases: Speed Abbreviations*. By Joel Larus. Boston, MA: Aurico Publishing, 1965.

(MAE)   *Medical Abbreviations and Eponyms*. By Sheila B. Sloane. Philadelphia, PA: W.B. Saunders Co., 1985.

(MAH)   *Medical Abbreviations Handbook*. 2nd ed. Oradell, NJ: Medical Economics Co., Inc., 1983.

(MCD)   *Acronyms, Abbreviations, and Initialisms*. Compiled by Carl Lauer. St. Louis, MO: McDonnell Douglas Corp., 1989. [Use of source began in 1969]

(MDG)   *Microcomputer Dictionary and Guide*. By Charles J. Sippl. Champaign, IL: Matrix Publishers, Inc., 1975.
> A listing of definitions for over 5,000 microelectronics terms. Seven appendices.

(MEDA)   *Medical Acronyms*. 2nd ed. By Marilyn Fuller Delong. Oradell, NJ: Medical Economic Books, 1989.

(MENA)   *The Middle East and North Africa 1987*. 33rd ed. London, England: Europa Publications Ltd., 1986; distributed in U.S. by Gale Research, Detroit, MI.
> An annual survey containing detailed information about the political, economic, statistical, and commercial situation of the regions and countries covered.

(MHDB)   *McGraw-Hill Dictionary of Business Acronyms, Initials, and Abbreviations*. By Jerry M. Rosenberg. New York, NY: McGraw-Hill, Inc., 1992.

(MHDI)   *McGraw-Hill Dictionary of Information Technology and Computer Acronyms, Initials, and Abbreviations*. By Jerry M. Rosenberg. New York, NY: McGraw-Hill, Inc., 1992.

(MHDW)   *McGraw-Hill Dictionary of Wall Street Acronyms, Initials, and Abbreviations*. By Jerry M. Rosenberg. New York, NY: McGraw-Hill, Inc., 1992.

(MSA)   *Military Standard Abbreviations for Use on Drawings, and in Specifications, Standards, and Technical Documents*. MIL-STD-12D. U.S. Department of Defense, 1981. [Use of source began in 1975]

(MSC)   *Annotated Acronyms and Abbreviations of Marine Science Related Activities*. 3rd ed. Revised by Charlotte M. Ashby and Alan R. Flesh. Washington, DC: U.S. Department of Commerce. National Oceanographic and Atmospheric Administration. Environmental Data Service. National Oceanographic Data Center, 1976, 1981.

(MUGU)   *The Mugu Book of Acronyms and Abbreviations*. Missile Range, California: Management Engineering Office, 1963, 1964.

(NADA)   *The New American Dictionary of Abbreviations*. By Mary A. De Vries. New York, NY: Signet, 1991.

(NASA)   *Space Transportation System and Associated Payloads: Glossary, Acronyms, and Abbreviations*. Washington, DC: U.S. National Aeronautics and Space Administration, 1985.

(NATG)   *Glossary of Abbreviations Used in NATO Documents*. AAP 15(B), n.p., 1979. [Use of source began in 1976]

(NCC)   *NCC The National Centre for Information Technology. Guide to Computer Aided Engineering, Manufacturing and Construction Software*. Manchester, England: NCC Publications. The National Computing Centre Ltd., 1985.
   Includes software classifications and descriptions, names and addresses of suppliers, processor manufacturers, and operating systems.

(NFD)   *The NSFRE Fund-Raising Dictionary*. Edited by Barbara R. Levy. New York, NY: John Wiley & Sons, Inc., 1996.

(NFPA)   *Standard for Fire Safety Symbols/NFPA170*. Quincy, MA: National Fire Protection Association, 1994.

(NG)   *NAVAIR Glossary of Unclassified Common-Use Abbreviated Titles and Phrases*. NAVAIRNOTE 5216 AIR-6031, n.p., July, 1969.

(NGC)   *Catalogue of the National Gallery of Canada*. Compiled by National Gallery of Canada. Ottawa, Canada: National Gallery of Canada, 1998.

(NHD)   *The New Hacker's Dictionary*. Edited by Eric Raymond. Cambridge, MA: MIT Press, 1991.

(NITA)   *Dictionary of New Information Technology Acronyms*. 2nd ed. By Michael Gordon, Alan Singleton, and Clarence Rickards. London, England: Kogan Page, Ltd., 1986.

(NLC)   *Symbols of Canadian Libraries*. 12th ed. National Library of Canada. Minister of Supply and Services Canada, 1987.

(NOAA)   *NOAA Directives Manual.* 66-13 Acronyms. 1977.

(NQ)   *NASDAQ Company Directory.* New York, NY: National Association of Securities Dealers, Inc., 1990. [Use of source began in 1983]
> Entries include company name, SIC code, contact person's name, title, address, and telephone number.

(NRCH)   *A Handbook of Acronyms and Initialisms.* Washington, DC: U.S. Nuclear Regulatory Commission. Division of Technical Information and Document Control, 1985.

(NTCM)   *NTC's Mass Media Dictionary.* R. Terry Ellmore. Lincolnwood, IL: National Textbook Co., 1991.

(NUCP)   *A Dictionary of Nuclear Power and Waste Management with Abbreviations and Acronyms.* Foo-Sun Lau. Letchworth, England: Research Studies Press, Ltd., 1987.

(NVT)   *Naval Terminology.* NWP3. Rev. B. U.S. Department of the Navy. Office of the Chief of Naval Operations, 1980. [Use of source began in 1974]
> Includes a section on definitions of naval terminology.

(OA)   *Ocran's Acronyms: A Dictionary of Abbreviations and Acronyms Used in Scientific and Technical Writing.* By Emanuel Benjamin Ocran. London, England: Routledge & Kegan Paul Ltd., 1978.

(OAG)   *Official Airline Guide Worldwide Edition.* Oak Brook, IL: Official Airlines Guide, Inc., 1984. [Use of source began in 1975]

(OCD)   *Oxford Classical Dictionary.* 2nd ed. Edited by N.G. Hammond and H.H. Scullard. London, England: Oxford University Press, 1970.

(OCLC)   *OCLC Participating Institutions Arranged by OCLC Symbol.* Dublin, OH: OCLC, 1981.

(ODBW)   *The Oxford Dictionary for the Business World.* New York, NY: Oxford University Press, Inc., 1993.

(OICC)   *Abbreviations and Acronyms.* Des Moines, IA: Iowa State Occupational Information Coordinating Committee, 1986.

(OLDSS)   *Online Database Search Services Directory.* 2nd ed. Edited by Doris Morris Maxfield. Detroit, MI: Gale Research, 1988.
> Provides detailed descriptions of the online information retrieval services offered by libraries, private information firms, and other organizations in the United States and Canada. Entries include name and address, telephone number, and key contact, as well as online systems accessed, frequently searched databases, and access hardware.

(OPSA)   *"Official Postal Service Abbreviations."* <http://www.usps.gov/ncsc/lookups/abbr_suffix.txt> (17 December 1996).

(OSI)   *OSI Standards and Acronyms.* 3rd ed. Compiled by Adrian V. Stokes. United Kingdom: Stokes, 1991.

(PAZ)   *Parenting A to Z.* By Irene M. Franck and David M. Brownstone. New York, NY: HarperCollins Publishers, Inc., 1996.

(PCM)   *PC Magazine.* New York, NY: Ziff-Davis Publishing Co., 1997. [Use of source began in 1987]

(PD)   *Political Dissent: An International Guide to Dissident, Extra-Parliamentary, Guerrilla and Illegal Political Movements.* A Keesing's Reference Publication. Compiled by Henry W. Degenhardt. Edited by Alan J. Day. Harlow, Essex, England: Longman Group, 1983.
        Includes the history and aims of approximately 1,000 organizations, with details of their leaderships.

(PDAA) *Pugh's Dictionary of Acronyms and Abbreviations: Abbreviations in Management, Technology and Information Science.* 5th ed. By Eric Pugh. Chicago, IL: American Library Association, 1987.

(PGP)   *Peterson's Graduate Programs in the Humanities, Arts & Social Sciences.* 31st ed. Princeton, NJ: Peterson's 1997.

(PPE)   *Political Parties of Europe.* 2 vols. Edited by Vincent E. McHale. The Greenwood Historical Encyclopedia of the World's Political Parties. Westport, CT: Greenwood Press, 1983.
        One of a series of reference guides to the world's significant political parties. Each guide provides concise histories of the political parties of a region and attempts to detail the evolution of ideology, changes in organization, membership, leadership, and each party's impact upon society.

(PPW)   *Political Parties of the World.* 2nd ed. A Keesing's Reference Publication. Compiled and edited by Alan J. Day and Henry W. Degenhardt. Harlow, Essex, England: Longman Group, 1980, 1984.
        Covers historical development, structure, leadership, membership, policy, publications, and international affiliations. For each country, an overview of the current political situation and constitutional structure is provided.

(PS)   *Popular Science.* New York, NY: Times-Mirror Magazines, Inc., 1995. [Use of source began in 1992]

(RCD)   *Research Centers Directory.* 19th ed. Edited by Thomas J. Cichonski. Detroit, MI: Gale Research, 1994. [Use of source began in 1986]
        A guide to university-related and other nonprofit research organizations carrying on research in agriculture, astronomy and space sciences, behavioral and social sciences, computers and mathematics, engineering and technology, physical and earth sciences and regional and area studies.

(RDA)   *Army RD and A Magazine.* Alexandria, VA: Development, Engineering, and Acquisition Directorate, Army Materiel Command, 1997. [Use of source began in 1979]

(ROG)   *Dictionary of Abbreviations.* By Walter T. Rogers. London, England: George Allen & Co. Ltd., 1913; reprinted by Gale Research, 1969.

(SAA)   *Space-Age Acronyms, Abbreviations and Designations.* 2nd ed. By Reta C. Moser. New York, NY: IFI/Plenum, 1969.

(SAG)   *Stock Abbreviation Guide.* New York, NY: Associated Press. [Database]

(SDI)   *Report to the Congress on the Strategic Defense Initiative.* U.S. Department of Defense. Strategic Defense Initiative Organization, April, 1987.

(SEIS) *Seismograph Station Codes and Characteristics.* Geological Survey. Circular 791. By Barbara B. Poppe, Debbi A. Naab, and John S. Derr. Washington, DC: U.S. Department of the Interior, 1978.

(SLS) *World Guide to Scientific Associations and Learned Societies/Internationales Verzeichnis Wissenschaftlicher Verbande und Gesellschaften.* 4th ed. Edited by Barbara Verrel. New York, NY: K.G. Saur, 1984.
>A directory of more than 22,000 societies and associations in all fields of science, culture, and technology. International, national, and regional organizations from 150 countries are also included.

(SPSG) *Security Owner's Stock Guide.* New York, NY: Standard & Poor's Corp., 1994. [Use of source began in 1988]

(SRA) *State and Regional Associations of the United States.* 9th ed. Edited by Tracey E. Chirico, Buck J. Downs and John J. Russell. Washington, DC: Columbia Books, Inc., 1997.

(SSD) *Space Station Directory and Program Guide.* Edited and compiled by Melinda Gipson, Jane Glass, and Mary Linden. Arlington, VA: Pasha Publications Inc., 1988.

(TAG) *Transportation Acronym Guide 1996.* U.S. Department of Transportation. Washington, DC: Bureau of Transportation Statistics, 1996.

(TDOB) *The Dictionary of Banking.* By Charles J. Woelfel. Chicago, IL: Probus Publishing Company, 1994.

(TEL) *Telephony's Dictionary.* 2nd ed. By Graham Langley. Chicago, IL: Telephony Publishing Corp., 1986.
>Includes definitions for U.S. and international telecommunications terms. Ten appendices.

(TNIG) *Telecommunications, Networking and Internet Glossary.* By George S. Machovec. Chicago, IL: American Library Association, 1993.

(TOCD) *The Official Catholic Directory 1997.* New Providence, NJ: P.J. Kenedy & Sons, 1997.

(TSPED) *Trade Shows and Professional Exhibits Directory.* 2nd ed. Edited by Robert J. Elster. Detroit, MI: Gale Research, 1987. [Use of source began in 1986]
>A guide to scheduled events providing commercial display facilities including conferences, conventions, meetings, fairs and festivals, etc. Entries include name of trade show; sponsor name, address, and telephone number; attendance figures; principal exhibits; special features; publications; and date and location of shows.

(TSSD) *Telecommunications Systems and Services Directory.* 4th ed. (and supplement). Edited by John Krol. Detroit, MI: Gale Research, 1989. [Use of source began in 1985]
>An international descriptive guide to telecommunications organizations, systems, and services. Entries include name and address, telephone number, chief official, and a description of the purposes, technical structure, and background of the service or system.

(USDC) *"Glossary of Acronyms".* U.S. Department of Commerce. <http://www.pmel.noaa.gov/pubs/acronym.html> (5 March 1997).

(USGC) *"U.S. Government Commonly Used Abbreviations and Acronyms."* <http://www.fed.gov/hptext/infohwy/gov_acro.html> (5 March 1997).

(VNW) *Words of the Vietnam War.* By Gregory R. Clark. Jefferson, NC: McFarland and Co., Inc., 1990.

(VRA)   *VRA Special Bulletin. No. 2, 1987: Standard Abbreviaitons for Image Descriptions for Use in Fine Arts Visual Resources Collections.* Compiled by Nancy S. Schuller. Austin, TX: Visual Resources Association, 1987.

(WDAA)   *Webster's New World Dictionary of Acronyms and Abbreviations.* By Auriel Douglas and Michael Strumpf. New York, NY: Webster's New World, 1989.

(WDMC)   *Webster's New World Dictionary of Media and Communications.* Revised and updated ed. By Richard Weiner. New York, NY: Webster's New World, 1996.

(WGA)   *Webster's Guide to Abbreviations.* Springfield, MA: Merriam-Webster Inc., 1985.

(WYGK)   *HR Words you Gotta Know!* By William R. Tracey. New York: AMACOM, 1994.

Reverse
Acronyms, Initialisms &
Abbreviations Dictionary

P-Z

P & F Ind $1 Pfd [*NASDAQ symbol*] (TTSB) .... PFINP
P & F Industries, Inc. [*Associated Press*] (SAG) .... P & F
P & F Industries, Inc. [*NASDAQ symbol*] (NQ) .... PFIN
P/DAUM Information Services, Vancouver, British Columbia [*Library symbol National Library of Canada*] (BIB) .... BVAPDA
P G Energy $2.25 Dep Pfd [*NASDAQ symbol*] (TTSB) .... PGWCZ
P. G. Wodehouse Society (EA) .... PGWS
P. J. Allman Fan Club (EA) .... PJAFC
P. K. Le Roux Dam [*South Africa*] [*Seismograph station code, US Geological Survey*] (SEIS) .... PKR
P/L Experiment Test System [*NASA*] (GFGA) .... PETS
P. M. Musser Public Library, Muscatine, IA [*Library symbol Library of Congress*] (LCLS) .... IaMu
P. R. Mallory & Co., Burlington, MA [*Library symbol Library of Congress*] (LCLS) .... MBurPRM
P. S. Ross & Partners, Montreal, PQ, Canada [*Library symbol Library of Congress*] (LCLS) .... CaQMPSR
P. S. Ross & Partners, Montreal, Quebec (NLC) .... QMPSR
P. W. Lown Institute. Brandeis University. Studies and Texts (BJA) ..... LownInST
P1 [*Code*] for Multigroup [*Method*] [*Nuclear energy*] (NRCH) P1MG
P6 Rover Owners Club (EAIO) P6ROC
PA Computers & Telecommunications [*Information service or system*] (IID) .... PACTEL
Pa-An [*Myanmar*] [*Airport symbol*] (OAG) .... PAA
Pa-An [*Myanmar*] [*ICAO location identifier*] (ICLI) .... VBPA
Paarieto-Occipital [*Medicine*] (DMAA) .... PO
Paauilo, HI [*FM radio station call letters*] (RBYB) .... KILU
Paauilo, HI [*FM radio station call letters*] (RBYB) .... KNUQ-FM
PAB Bankshares, Inc. [*AMEX symbol*] (SAG) .... PAB
PAB Bankshares, Inc. [*Associated Press*] (SAG) .... PAB Bk
Pabst Blue Ribbon [*Beer*] .... PBR
Pac Ed Systems Corp. [*Vancouver Stock Exchange symbol*] .... PKD
Pac Engo Materials [*Vancouver Stock Exchange symbol*] .... PEG
Pac G&E 5%cmRed1stA Pfd [*AMEX symbol*] (TTSB) .... PCGPrE
Pac Rim Holding [*NASDAQ symbol*] (SPSG) .... PRIM
Pac Rim Holding Corp. [*Associated Press*] (SAG) .... PacRim
Pac Telesis Fin I 7.56%'TOPrS' [*NYSE symbol*] (TTSB) .... PACPrT
PACAF [*Pacific Air Forces*] Jungle Survival School (AFM) .... PJSS
Pacasmayo [*Peru*] [*ICAO location identifier*] (ICLI) .... SPYO
PACCAR, Inc. [*Associated Press*] (SAG) .... Pacar
PACCAR, Inc. [*NASDAQ symbol*] (NQ) .... PCAR
Pace Car Society [*Defunct*] (EA) .... PCS
Pace College, New York, NY [*Library symbol Library of Congress*] (LCLS) .... NNPC
Pace Co., Houston, TX [*Library symbol Library of Congress*] (LCLS) .... TxHPC
Pace Health Management Systems, Inc. [*Associated Press*] (SAG) .... PaceHlt
Pace Health Management Systems, Inc. [*NASDAQ symbol*] (SAG) .... PCES
PACE Health Mgmt [*NASDAQ symbol*] (TTSB) .... PCES
Pace Setter (MHDI) .... PS
Pace University (GAGS) .... Pace U
Pace University, Law Library, White Plains, NY [*Library symbol Library of Congress*] (LCLS) .... NNPC-L
Pace University, Law Library, White Plains, NY [*OCLC symbol*] (OCLC) .... VZL
Pace University Library, Union List of Serials, New York, NY [*OCLC symbol*] (OCLC) .... VPU
Pace University, New York, NY [*OCLC symbol*] (OCLC) .... VZP
Pace University, Pleasantville, Pleasantville, NY [*OCLC symbol*] (OCLC) .... VZU
Pace University Westchester, Pleasantville, NY [*Library symbol Library of Congress*] (LCLS) .... NPleP
Paced Sequential Memory Task (PDAA) .... PSMT
Pacem in Maribus [*Secondary name for the International Ocean Institute*] (MSC) .... PIM
Pacemaker [*Medicine*] (DMAA) .... PM
Pacemaker Wire [*Cardiology*] (DAVI) .... PMW
Pacemaker-Induced Ventricular Rate [*Cardiology*] (CPH) .... PIVR
Pacer .... P
Pacer Technology [*Associated Press*] (SAG) .... PacTec
Pacer Technology [*NASDAQ symbol*] (NQ) .... PTCH
Pace-Setting Potential [*Physiology*] .... PSP
PACFLT [*Pacific Fleet*] Enlisted Personnel Distribution Manual (CINC) .... PEDMAN
Pachaco Lake [*California*] [*Seismograph station code, US Geological Survey*] (SEIS) .... PCL
Pachella [*Sudan*] [*ICAO location identifier*] (ICLI) .... HSPA
Pachena Industries Ltd. [*Vancouver Stock Exchange symbol*] .... PHA
Pachiza [*Peru*] [*ICAO location identifier*] (ICLI) .... SPZH
Pacht, Ross et Al, Los Angeles, CA [*OCLC symbol*] (OCLC) .... PRL

Pachuca [*Mexico ICAO location identifier*] (ICLI) .... MMPC
Paci Press, Lodi, NJ [*Library symbol Library of Congress*] (LCLS) .... NjLP
Paci Press, Lodi, NJ [*Library symbol*] [*Library of Congress*] (LCLS) .... NjLPP
Pacific .... PAC
Pacific (AFM) .... PAC
Pacific [*Record label*] [*France*] .... Pac
Pacific .... PACF
Pacific .... PACIF
Pacific 10 Conference (EA) PAC-10
Pacific Acoustic Research Kaneohe-Alaska [*Navy*] .... PARKA
Pacific Advanced Media Studies [*Australia*] .... PAMS
Pacific Aeronautical Library .... PAL
Pacific Aerospace & Electronics, Inc. [*Associated Press*] (SAG) .... PacA & E
Pacific Aerospace & Electronics, Inc. [*Associated Press*] (SAG) .... PcA&E
Pacific Aerospace & Electronics, Inc. [*NASDAQ symbol*] (SAG) .... PCTH
Pacific Aerospace Index (DIT) .... PAI
Pacific Aerospace Rescue and Recovery Center [*Air Force*] .... PARRC
Pacific Affairs [*A publication*] (BRI) .... Pac A
Pacific Agricultural Cooperative for Export [*Corte Madera, CA*] (EA) .... PACE
Pacific Air Boats Ltd. [*Canada ICAO designator*] (FAAC) .... PAB
Pacific Air Charter, Inc. [*ICAO designator*] (FAAC) .... PRC
Pacific Air Combat Operations Staff .... PACOPS
Pacific Air Command [*Air Force*] .... PAC
Pacific Air Command, United States Army .... PACUSA
Pacific Air Express [*ICAO designator*] (FAAC) .... PCF
Pacific Air Force Operations (MCD) .... PACOPS
Pacific Air Forces .... PACAF
Pacific Air Forces .... PAF
Pacific Air Forces Base Command .... PACAFBASECOM
Pacific Air Forces Communications Network (SAA) .... PAFCOMNET
Pacific Air Forces Defense Network (SAA) .... PAFDEFNET
Pacific Air Forces Operations Analysis .... PACAF-OA
Pacific Air Forces Operations Analysis Office [*Hickam Air Force Base, HI*] .... PACAF-OA
Pacific Air Lines .... PAL
Pacific Air Rescue Center [*or Command*] (CINC) .... PARC
Pacific Airlift Management Office [*Military*] .... PAMO
Pacific Airlines Holding Co. [*Vietnam*] [*ICAO designator*] (FAAC) .... PIC
Pacific Alaska Airlines [*Air carrier designation symbol*] .... PAIX
Pacific Alaska Airlines [*ICAO designator*] (FAAC) .... PAK
Pacific Alternate Command Element (CINC) .... PACE
Pacific Amber Resources [*VS, Exchange Symbol*] (TTSB) .... PCR
Pacific America Container Express (MHDB) .... PACE
Pacific American Income Shares, Inc. [*Associated Press*] (SAG) .... PacAS
Pacific American Income Shares, Inc. [*NYSE symbol*] (SPSG) .... PAI
Pacific American Institute (EA) .... PAI
Pacific American Steamship Association [*Later, AIMS*] .... PASA
Pacific American Steamship Association [*Later, AIMS*] (EA) .... PASSA
Pacific American Tankship Association [*Defunct*] (EA) .... PATA
Pacific Am'n Inc. Shrs [*NYSE symbol*] (TTSB) .... PAI
Pacific & Arctic Railway (MHDB) .... P & AR
Pacific and Asian Affairs Council .... PAAC
Pacific and Asian Linguistics Institute [*University of Hawaii*] .... PALI
Pacific and Far East Federation of Engineering Societies .... PFEFES
Pacific and Mountain States [*MARC geographic area code Library of Congress*] (LCCP) .... n-usp-
Pacific and Southeast Asia (DNAB) .... PSEA
Pacific & Yukon Region, Canadian Wildlife Service, Environment Canada [*Service Canadien de la Faune de la Region du Pacifique et du Yukon, Environnement Canada*] Delta, British Columbia [*Library symbol National Library of Canada*] (NLC) .... BDECW
Pacific Animated Imaging [*NASDAQ symbol*] (TTSB) .... PAID
Pacific Animated Imaging Corp. [*Associated Press*] (SAG) .... PacAni
Pacific Animated Imaging Corp. [*NASDAQ symbol*] (SAG) .... PAID
Pacific Aqua Foods Ltd. [*Toronto Stock Exchange symbol*] .... PAF
Pacific Area Airways and Air Communications (IAA) .... PACAACS
Pacific Area Communications Message Traffic Control Unit (IAA) .... PACTCU
Pacific Area Communications System (MCD) .... PACS
Pacific Area Communicatios Network (SAA) .... PACN
Pacific Area Cooperative Renewable Energy Development [*University of Hawaii*] .... PACRED
Pacific Area Ground Environment Electronic Installation Agency (CINC) .... PACGEEIA
Pacific Area Movement Priority Agency [*Military*] .... PAMPA
Pacific Area Newspaper Publishers Association (EAIO) .... PANPA
Pacific Area Senior Officer Logistics Seminar (MCD) .... PASOLS

Pacific Area Standards Congress [*American National Standards Institute*]..... PASC
Pacific Area Trading and Investment Area .... PATIA
Pacific Area Travel Association [*San Francisco, CA*] .... PATA
Pacific Armies Look Exercise .... PALEX
Pacific Armies Management .... PAM
Pacific Armies Management Seminar .... PAMS
Pacific Arts Association (EA) .... PAA
Pacific Asia Tech [*Vancouver Stock Exchange symbol*] .... PFT
Pacific Asia Travel Association (EA) .... PATA
Pacific/Asian American Mental Health Research Center [*University of Illinois at Chicago*] [*Research center*] (RCD) .... P/AAMHRC
Pacific Asian American Women Writers West (EA) .... PAAWWW
Pacific Association of Collegiate Registrars and Admission Officers .... PACRAO
Pacific Association of Quantity Surveyors [*Australia*] .... PAQS
Pacific Atoll Cratering Experiment [*Military*] (DNAB) .... PACE
Pacific Automation Products (IAA) .... PAP
Pacific Ballet Theatre .... PBT
Pacific Bank NA [*Associated Press*] (SAG) .... PacifBnk
Pacific Bank NA [*NASDAQ symbol*] (SPSG) .... PBSF
Pacific Bantam Austin Club (EA) .... PBAC
Pacific Barrier Patrol [*Western seaward extension of the DEW Line*] [*Obsolete*] .... BARPAC
Pacific Barrier RADAR (MCD) .... PACBAR
Pacific Basin Blk Shipng Wrrt [*NASDAQ symbol*] (TTSB) .... PBBWF
Pacific Basin Bulk [*NASDAQ symbol*] (TTSB) .... PBBSF
Pacific Basin Bulk Shippers Ltd. [*Associated Press*] (SAG) .... PacBB
Pacific Basin Bulk Shippers Ltd. [*Associated Press*] (SAG) .... PacBBS
Pacific Basin Bulk Shippers Ltd. [*NASDAQ symbol*] (SAG) .... PBBSF
Pacific Basin Bulk Shippers Ltd. [*NASDAQ symbol*] (SAG) .... PBBWF
Pacific Basin Development Corp. [*Vancouver Stock Exchange symbol*] .... PBD
Pacific Basin Development Council (EA) .... PBDC
Pacific Basin Economic Council (FEA) .... PBEC
Pacific Beach, WA [*Location identifier FAA*] (FAAL) .... NIX
Pacific Bible College [*California*] .... PBC
Pacific Bible College of Azusa [*California*] .... PBCA
Pacific Bible Institute of Fresno [*California*] .... PBIF
Pacific Biological Station [*Department of Fisheries and Oceans*] [*Canada Research center*] (RCD) .... PBS
Pacific Biological Station, Fisheries and Oceans Canada [*Station Biologique du Pacifique, Peches et Oceans Canada*] **Nanaimo, British Columbia** [*Library symbol National Library of Canada*] (NLC) .... BNP
Pacific Biometrics, Inc. [*Associated Press*] (SAG) .... PacBio
Pacific Biometrics, Inc. [*Associated Press*] (SAG) .... PacBiom
Pacific Biometrics, Inc. [*NASDAQ symbol*] (SAG) .... PBMI
Pacific Broadcasting Association (EAIO) .... PBA
Pacific Capital Bancorp [*NASDAQ symbol*] (SAG) .... PABN
Pacific Capital Bancorp [*Associated Press*] (SAG) .... PacCapB
Pacific Car and Foundry .... PACCAR
Pacific Car Demurrage Bureau, San Francisco CA [*STAC*] .... PCD
Pacific Cassiar Ltd. [*Toronto Stock Exchange symbol*] .... PFL
Pacific Central NOTAM [*Notice to Airmen*] **Facility** [*Military*] .... PCNF
Pacific Christian College, Fullerton, CA [*Library symbol Library of Congress*] (LCLS) .... CFIP
Pacific Christian College, Fullerton, CA [*OCLC symbol*] (OCLC) .... CPC
Pacific City, OR [*Location identifier FAA*] (FAAL) .... PFC
Pacific Class Catamaran Association (EA) .... PCCA
Pacific Coast [*Railroad*] (MHDB) .... PACC
Pacific Coast Airlines [*ICAO designator*] (FAAC) .... PQA
Pacific Coast Apparel Co., Inc. [*NASDAQ symbol*] (SAG) .... ACAJ
Pacific Coast Apparel Co., Inc. [*Associated Press*] (SAG) .... PcCAp
Pacific Coast Apparel Co., Inc. [*Associated Press*] (SAG) .... PcCApp
Pacific Coast Canned Pear Service (EA) .... PCCPS
Pacific Coast Coin Exchange .... PCCE
Pacific Coast Coordinator of Naval Logistics .... PACORNALOG
Pacific Coast Coordinator of Naval Logistics .... PCCNL
Pacific Coast Electrical Association .... PCEA
Pacific Coast Federation of Fishermen's Associations (EA) .... PCFFA
Pacific Coast Forest Research Information Network [*Later, WESTFORNET*] [*Forest Service*] (IID) .... PACFORNET
Pacific Coast Garment Manufacturers [*Later, AAMA*] (EA) .... PCGM
Pacific Coast Hockey League [*Later, Western Hockey League*] (EA) .... PCHL
Pacific Coast Intercollegiate Yacht Racing Association .... PCIYRA
Pacific Coast International [*A publication*] (ILCA) .... Pac Coast Int
Pacific Coast Law Journal [*A publication*] (DLA) .... P Coast LJ
Pacific Coast Law Journal [*A publication*] (DLA) .... Pac Coast LJ
Pacific Coast Law Journal [*San Francisco*] [*A publication*] (DLA) .... Pacific CLJ
Pacific Coast Law Journal [*A publication*] (DLA) .... PCLJ
Pacific Coast League [*Baseball*] .... PCL
Pacific Coast Marine Firemen, Oilers, Watertenders, and Wipers Association .... MFOW
Pacific Coast Marine Firemen, Oilers, Watertenders, and Wipers Association [*Also known as Marine Firemen's Union*] (EA) .... MFU
Pacific Coast Oyster Growers Association (EA) .... PCOGA
Pacific Coast Paper Box Manufacturers' Association (EA) .... PCPBMA
Pacific Coast Railroad [*AAR code Terminated*] .... PC
Pacific Coast Stock Exchange [*Later, PSE*] .... P
Pacific Coast Stock Exchange [*Later, PSE*] (EA) .... PCSE
Pacific Coast Tariff Bureau .... PCTB
Pacific Coast Tariff Bureau, San Francisco CA [*STAC*] .... PCT
Pacific Coastal Airline [*Canada ICAO designator*] (FAAC) .... PCO
Pacific Coastal Marine Productivity [*Marine science*] (OSRA) .... PACICOM
Pacific College, Fresno, CA [*Library symbol Library of Congress*] (LCLS) .... CFP
Pacific Command [*Military*] (GFGA) .... PAC
Pacific Command [*Military*] .... PACCOM
Pacific Command [*Military*] .... PACOM

Pacific Command [*Department of Defense*] (BARN) .... PC
Pacific Command Air Defense Analysis Facility (CINC) .... PADAF
Pacific Command Blood Program Office [*Military*] (DNAB) .... PACOMBPO
Pacific Command Detachment [*Military*] (DNAB) .... PACOMDET
Pacific Command Electronic Intelligence Center (MCD) .... PEC
Pacific Command Electronic Warfare (CINC) .... PACOMEW
Pacific Command Emergency Procedures (CINC) .... PACOMEP
Pacific Command Frequency Allocation and Uses (CINC) .... PAU
Pacific Command Intelligence School (CINC) .... PACOMINTS
Pacific Command Joint Medical Regulating Office (DNAB) .... PACOMJRO
Pacific Command, North Vietnam Air Defense Analysis and Coordinating Group (CINC) .... NADAC
Pacific Command Operations Liaison Office [*Army*] (AABC) .... POLO
Pacific Command Ship .... PCS
Pacific Communications Area [*Air Force*] (MCD) .... PCA
Pacific Communications Division [*Military*] .... PCD
Pacific Communications Group .... PACOM
Pacific Communications Net [*Air Force*] .... PN
Pacific Communications Network [*Computer science*] (TNIG) .... PACCOM
Pacific Communications Network [*Air Force*] (IAA) .... PCN
Pacific Communities Hospital Library, Newport, OR [*Library symbol*] [*Library of Congress*] (LCLS) .... OrNepH
Pacific Comox Resources [*Vancouver Stock Exchange symbol*] .... PCM
Pacific Concerns Resource Center (EA) .... PCRC
Pacific Concord Resources Corp. [*Vancouver Stock Exchange symbol*] .... PCV
Pacific Conservatory of the Performing Arts .... PCPA
Pacific Crest Capital [*Associated Press*] (SAG) .... PacCrst
Pacific Crest Capital [*NASDAQ symbol*] (SAG) .... PCCI
Pacific Crest Trail .... PCT
Pacific Cruise Conference [*Formerly, TPPC*] [*Defunct*] (EA) .... PCC
Pacific Cypress Minerals Ltd. [*Vancouver Stock Exchange symbol*] .... PCY
Pacific Dance Association (EA) .... PDA
Pacific Data System (IAA) .... PDS
Pacific Daylight Saving Time (KSC) .... PDST
Pacific Daylight Time .... PDT
Pacific Defence Reporter [*A publication*] .... Pacif Defence Reporter
Pacific Defense College (CINC) .... PDC
Pacific Democrat Union (EAIO) .... PDU
Pacific Dermatologic Association (EA) .... PDA
Pacific Division [*Military*] .... PACD
Pacific Division [*Military*] .... PACDIV
Pacific Division Naval Facilities Engineering Command .... PACNAVFACENGCOM
Pacific Division Transport Control Center .... PTCC
Pacific Dunlop Ltd. [*Associated Press*] (SAG) .... PacDunl
Pacific Dunlop Ltd. [*NASDAQ symbol*] (NQ) .... PDLP
Pacific Dunlop Ltd. (MHDW) .... PDLPY
Pacific Dunlop Ltd. ADR [*NASDAQ symbol*] (TTSB) .... PDLPY
Pacific East Asia Cargo Airline, Inc. [*Philippines*] [*ICAO designator*] (FAAC) .... PEC
Pacific Economic Community (FEA) .... PEC
Pacific Economic Cooperation Conference (DOMA) .... PECC
Pacific Electric Railway [*AAR code*] .... PE
Pacific Electronic Security Division [*Military*] .... PESD
Pacific Electronics Trade Show .... PETS
Pacific Energy Development Program [*Fiji*] [*United Nations*] .... PEDP
Pacific Engineering Production Company (AAGC) .... PEPCOM
Pacific Ent $4.36 Pfd [*AMEX symbol*] (TTSB) .... PETPrA
Pacific Ent $4.40 Pfd [*AMEX symbol*] (TTSB) .... PETPrB
Pacific Ent $4.50 Pfd [*AMEX symbol*] (TTSB) .... PETPrC
Pacific Ent $4.75 Pfd [*AMEX symbol*] (TTSB) .... PETPrD
Pacific Enterprises [*Associated Press*] (SAG) .... PacEnt
Pacific Enterprises [*Associated Press*] (SAG) .... PcEn
Pacific Enterprises [*AMEX symbol*] (SAG) .... PET
Pacific Enterprises [*NYSE symbol*] (SPSG) .... PET
Pacific Environmental Group [*Marine science*] (MSC) .... PEG
Pacific Equatorial Ocean Dynamics .... PEQUOD
Pacific Equatorial Ocean Dynamics [*Project*] [*USA*] [*Marine science*] (OSRA) .... PEQUOD
Pacific Exchange [*System*] [*Military*] (AFM) .... PACEX
Pacific Exchange Network [*Marine science*] (OSRA) .... PEN
Pacific Exchange Network (USDC) .... PEN
Pacific Exploratory Mission-West [*Western Pacific tropospheric chemistry experiment*] (USDC) .... PEM-West
Pacific Exploratory Mission-West [*Western Pacific Tropospheric Chemistry Experiment*] [*Marine science*] (OSRA) .... PEM-West
Pacific Express Holdings Ltd. [*New Zealand*] [*ICAO designator*] (FAAC) .... PXH
Pacific Far East Line .... PFEL
Pacific Film Archives, University Art Museum, Berkeley, CA [*Library symbol Library of Congress*] (LCLS) .... CBPF
Pacific Fisheries Development Foundation [*Defunct*] (EA) .... PFDF
Pacific Fisheries Technologists [*An association*] .... PFT
Pacific Fishery Information Network [*Database*] [*National Marine Fisheries Service*] .... PacFIN
Pacific Fishery Management Council (EA) .... PFMC
Pacific Fleet .... PACFLT
Pacific Fleet Advance Headquarters [*Guam*] .... PACADV
Pacific Fleet Advance Headquarters Division (DNAB) .... PACADIV
Pacific Fleet Audio-Visual Command (DNAB) .... PFAVC
Pacific Fleet Augmentation Plan [*Navy*] (NVT) .... PACFLAP
Pacific Fleet Calls [*Radio call signs*] .... PACCALL
Pacific Fleet Combat Camera Group (DNAB) .... PFCCG
Pacific Fleet Command .... PACFLTCOM
Pacific Fleet Command Operational Control Center (DNAB) .... PACCOMOPCONCEN
Pacific Fleet Communications Instructions .... PACCOM
Pacific Fleet Mobile Photographic Group (DNAB) .... PFMPG

Pacific Fleet Mobile Photographic Unit (MUGU) .... PACFLTMOPHOTOU
Pacific Fleet Propulsion Examining Board (DNAB) .... PACFLTPROPEXAMBD
Pacific Forest Industries (EA) .... PFI
Pacific Forest Research Centre [*Canada*] (ARC) .... PFRC
Pacific Forest Research Centre, Agriculture Canada [*Centre de Recherches Forestieres du Pacifique, Agriculture Canada*] **Victoria, British Columbia** [*Library symbol National Library of Canada*] (NLC) .... BVIF
Pacific Forward Area Support Team (DNAB) .... PACFAST
Pacific Forward Area Support Team Detachment (DNAB) .... PACFASTDET
Pacific Forward Area Support Team Representative (DNAB) .... PACFASTREP
Pacific Fruit Express Co. [*AAR code*] .... PFE
Pacific Fruit Growers Express .... PFGX
Pacific Gamefish Foundation (EA) .... PGF
Pacific Gamefish Research Foundation [*Later, PORF*] (EA) .... PGRF
Pacific Gas & El 5 1/2% Pfd [*AMEX symbol*] (TTSB) .... PCGPrB
Pacific Gas & El 5% Pfd [*AMEX symbol*] (TTSB) .... PCGPrC
Pacific Gas & El 5% Pfd [*AMEX symbol*] (TTSB) .... PCGPrD
Pacific Gas & El 6% Pfd [*AMEX symbol*] (TTSB) .... PCGPrA
Pacific Gas & El 4.36% Pfd [*AMEX symbol*] (TTSB) .... PCGPrI
Pacific Gas & El 4.50% Pfd [*AMEX symbol*] (TTSB) .... PCGPrH
Pacific Gas & El 4.80% Pfd (TTSB) .... PCGPrG
Pacific Gas & El 6.30% Pfd [*AMEX symbol*] (TTSB) .... PCGPrZ
Pacific Gas & El 6.57% Pfd [*AMEX symbol*] (TTSB) .... PCGPrY
Pacific Gas & El 7.04% Pfd [*AMEX symbol*] (TTSB) .... PCGPrU
Pacific Gas & El 7.44% Pfd [*AMEX symbol*] (TTSB) .... PCGPrQ
Pacific Gas & El 6.875% Pfd [*AMEX symbol*] (TTSB) .... PCGPrX
Pacific Gas & Elec [*NYSE symbol*] (TTSB) .... PCG
Pacific Gas and Electric [*Rock music group*] .... PG & E
Pacific Gas & Electric Co. [*Associated Press*] (SAG) .... PacGE
Pacific Gas & Electric Co. [*AMEX symbol*] (SPSG) .... PCG
Pacific Gas & Electric Co. [*NYSE symbol*] (SAG) .... PCG
Pacific Gas & Electric Co. .... PG & E
Pacific Gas & Electric Co. [*Associated Press*] (SAG) .... PGE
Pacific Gas & Electric Co., San Francisco, CA [*Library symbol Library of Congress*] (LCLS) .... CSfPG
Pacific Gateway Exchange, Inc. [*NASDAQ symbol*] (SAG) .... PGEX
Pacific Gateway Prop [*AMEX symbol*] (TTSB) .... PGP
Pacific Gateway Properties [*Associated Press*] (SAG) .... PacGate
Pacific Gateway Properties [*Formerly, Perini Investment Properties, Inc.*] [*AMEX symbol*] (SPSG) .... PGP
Pacific Geoscience Centre [*Research center*] (RCD) .... PGC
Pacific Great Eastern Railway Co. [*Nicknames: Prince George Eventually, Please Go Easy*] [*Later, British Columbia Railway*] [*AAR code*] .... PGE
Pacific Grove, CA [*FM radio station call letters*] .... KAZU
Pacific Grove, CA [*FM radio station call letters*] .... KOCN
Pacific Grove Public Library, Pacific Grove, CA [*Library symbol Library of Congress*] (LCLS) .... CPg
Pacific Gulf Properties [*Associated Press*] (SAG) .... PacGulf
Pacific Gulf Properties [*AMEX symbol*] (TTSB) .... PAG
Pacific Gulf Properties, Inc. [*Associated Press*] (SAG) .... PacGul
Pacific Gulf Properties, Inc. [*AMEX symbol*] (SAG) .... PAG
Pacific Harbour [*Fiji*] [*Airport symbol*] (OAG) .... PHR
Pacific Hawaiian Products Co. [*Later, PHP Co.*] .... PHP
Pacific Headquarters, Pearl Harbor, Hawaii [*Navy*] .... PACHEDPEARL
Pacific Herring Packers Association (EA) .... PHPA
Pacific Historical Review [*A publication*] (BRI) .... PHR
Pacific Hospital of Long Beach, Long Beach, CA [*Library symbol Library of Congress*] (LCLS) .... CLobP
Pacific Hurricane Centers [*National Weather Service*] .... PHC
Pacific Industrial Property Association (EA) .... PIPA
Pacific Information Exchange [*Information service or system*] (IID) .... PIE
Pacific Inland Tariff Bureau .... PITB
Pacific Inland Tariff Bureau, Portland OR [*STAC*] .... PIB
Pacific Institute for Research and Evaluation [*Research center*] (RCD) .... PIRE
Pacific Institute of Bio-Organic Chemistry .... PIBC
Pacific Institute of Geography .... PIG
Pacific Insurance Conference .... PIC
Pacific Integrated Automatic Command and Control System [*Military*] (DNAB) .... PIACCS
Pacific Integrated Automatic Communications Systems [*Military*] .... PIACS
Pacific Intelligence Center (DNAB) .... PACINTCEN
Pacific Intelligence Center (MCD) .... PIC
Pacific International Services Corp. [*Associated Press*] (SAG) .... PacIntl
Pacific International Services Corp. [*NASDAQ symbol*] (NQ) .... PISC
Pacific International Trapshooting Association (EA) .... PITA
Pacific Investment Trust [*Finance*] [*British*] .... PIT
Pacific Ionospheric Scatter (CINC) .... PACSCAT
Pacific Island Aviation, Inc. [*Mariana Islands*] [*ICAO designator*] (FAAC) .... PSA
Pacific Island Network [*Marine science*] (OSRA) .... PIN
Pacific Island Network (USDC) .... PIN
Pacific Islands Association (EA) .... PIA
Pacific Islands Development Program [*East-West Center*] [*Research center*] (RCD) .... PIDP
Pacific Islands Ecosystems [*Springfield, VA*] [*Department of the Interior No longer available online*] [*Information service or system*] .... PIE
Pacific Islands Marine Resources Information System [*Marine science*] (OSRA) .... PIMRIS
Pacific Islands Monthly [*A publication*] .... Pacif Is Mon
Pacific Islands News Association [*Australia*] .... PINA
Pacific Islands Society of the United Kingdom and Ireland (EAIO) .... PISUKI
Pacific Kenridge [*Vancouver Stock Exchange symbol*] .... PKE
Pacific Launch Operations [*NASA*] .... PLO
Pacific Launch Operations Office [*NASA*] .... PLOO
Pacific Law Journal [*A publication*] (ILCA) .... PLJ
Pacific Law Magazine [*A publication*] (DLA) .... Pac Law Mag
Pacific Law Magazine [*A publication*] (DLA) .... Pacific Law Mag
Pacific Law Magazine [*A publication*] (DLA) .... PLM
Pacific Law Reporter [*San Francisco*] [*A publication*] (DLA) .... Pac Law Reptr
Pacific Law Reporter [*A publication*] (DLA) .... PLR
Pacific Legal Foundation (EA) .... PLF
Pacific Legal News [*A publication*] (DLA) .... Pac Leg N
Pacific Logging Congress (EA) .... PLC
Pacific Logistic Operations - Streamline [*Army*] .... PALOS
Pacific Lumber Exporters Association (EA) .... PLEA
Pacific Lumber Inspection Bureau (EA) .... PLIB
Pacific Lutheran University (GAGS) .... Pac Luth U
Pacific Lutheran University, Parkland, WA [*Library symbol Library of Congress*] (LCLS) .... WaPlP
Pacific Magazines and Printing Ltd. [*Commercial firm Australia*] .... PMP
Pacific Mail (ROG) .... PM
Pacific Marine Center [*National Oceanic and Atmospheric Administration*] .... PMC
Pacific Marine Environmental Laboratory [*Seattle, WA*] [*National Oceanic and Atmospheric Administration*] (GRD) .... PMEL
Pacific Marine Fisheries Commission [*Later, PSMFC*] (EA) .... PMFC
Pacific Marine Training Institute, North Vancouver, BC, Canada [*Library symbol Library of Congress*] (LCLS) .... CaBNvPM
Pacific Marine Training Institute, North Vancouver, British Columbia [*Library symbol National Library of Canada*] (NLC) .... BNVPM
Pacific Maritime Association (EA) .... PMA
Pacific Medical Center (BABM) .... PMC
Pacific Medical Center, Seattle, WA [*Library symbol*] [*Library of Congress*] (LCLS) .... WaSPaM
Pacific Merchant Shipping Association (AD) .... PMSA
Pacific Merchant Shipping Association (NADA) .... PMSA
Pacific Meteorological Network (AAG) .... PACMETNET
Pacific Micronesian Line (AD) .... PML
Pacific Minesearch Ltd. [*Vancouver Stock Exchange symbol*] .... PFM
Pacific Missile Center [*Marine science*] (DNAB) .... PACMISCEN
Pacific Missile Center [*Marine science*] (MSC) .... PMC
Pacific Missile Range [*Later, WTR*] (MUGU) .... PACMISRAN
Pacific Missile Range [*Later, WTR*] .... PMR
Pacific Missile Range Detachment [*Obsolete*] (MUGU) .... PMRDET
Pacific Missile Range Facility [*Obsolete*] .... PACMISRANFAC
Pacific Missile Range Facility [*Obsolete*] (MSC) .... PMRF
Pacific Missile Range Facility [*Obsolete*] (MUGU) .... PMRFAC
Pacific Missile Range Facility Detachment [*Obsolete*] (DNAB) .... PACMISRANFACDET
Pacific Missile Range Facility Representative [*Obsolete*] (DNAB) .... PACMISRANFACREP
Pacific Missile Range / Naval Missile Center (SAA) .... PMR/NMC
Pacific Missile Range Representative [*Obsolete*] (MUGU) .... PMRR
Pacific Missile Range Study Group [*Obsolete*] .... PMRSG
Pacific Missile Range Tracking Facility [*Obsolete*] (MUGU) .... PMRTF
Pacific Missile Test Center [*Navy*] .... PACMISTESTCEN
Pacific Missile Test Center [*Point Mugu, CA*] [*Navy*] .... PMTC
Pacific Missile Test Center Liaison Office [*Navy*] (DNAB) .... PACMISTESTCEN LO
Pacific Mobile Depot Activity Maintenance Team (CINC) .... PMDAMT
Pacific Molasses (AD) .... P/M
Pacific Motor Boat Club (AD) .... PMBC
Pacific Motor Tariff Bureau (AD) .... PMTB
Pacific Motor Tariff Bureau (NADA) .... PMTB
Pacific Motor Tariff Bureau, Inc., Oakland CA [*STAC*] .... PMB
Pacific Mountain Network [*Television*] .... PMN
Pacific Mountain Network Association (AD) .... PMNA
Pacific National [*ICAO designator*] (AD) .... ZE
Pacific National Exchange Vancouver [*Vancouver*] (AD) .... PNE
Pacific National Exhibition [*Vancouver*] (AD) .... PNE
Pacific National Exhibition Home Show [*Southex Exhibitions*] (TSPED) .... PNE
Pacific National Financial Corp. [*Toronto Stock Exchange symbol Vancouver Stock Exchange symbol*] .... PNF
Pacific Naval Construction Force (DNAB) .... PACNAVCONSTFOR
Pacific Naval Construction Force (DNAB) .... PACNCF
Pacific Naval Laboratories (AD) .... PNL
Pacific Navigation Systems (AD) .... PNS
Pacific/North American [*Sector*] [*Marine science*] (OSRA) .... PNA
Pacific/North American [*Sector*] (USDC) .... PNA
Pacific North Atlantic [*Marine science*] (OSRA) .... PNA
Pacific Northern [*Airline*] (AD) .... PN
Pacific Northern Airlines (AD) .... PNA
Pacific Northern Gas Ltd. [*Toronto Stock Exchange symbol Vancouver Stock Exchange symbol*] .... PNG
Pacific Northern Naval Coastal Frontier .... PNNCF
Pacific Northwest .... PNW
Pacific Northwest Ballet .... PNB
Pacific Northwest Bibliographic Center [*Library network*] .... PNBC
Pacific Northwest Bibliographic Center, Seattle, WA [*Library symbol Library of Congress*] (LCLS) .... WaSB
Pacific Northwest Bird and Mammal Society [*Later, SNUB*] (EA) .... PNBMS
Pacific Northwest Booksellers Association (AD) .... PNBA
Pacific Northwest Canadian Studies Consortium [*University of Oregon*] .... PNWCSC
Pacific Northwest Division/Battelle Memorial Institute (AD) .... PNWD/BMI
Pacific Northwest Environmental Research Laboratory [*Environmental Protection Agency*] (MSC) .... PNERL
Pacific Northwest Grain and Feed Association (EA) .... PNGFA
Pacific Northwest Heather Society [*Later, NAHS*] (EA) .... PNHS
Pacific Northwest International Trade Council (AD) .... PNITC
Pacific Northwest International Trade Council (NADA) .... PNITC
Pacific Northwest Laboratory [*Department of Energy*] [*Richland, WA*] .... PNL
Pacific Northwest Laboratory [*AEC*] .... PNWL

Pacific Northwest Library Association ... PNLA
Pacific Northwest Loggers Association (EA) ... PNLA
Pacific Northwest National Laboratory ... PNNL
Pacific Northwest Outport [*MTMC*] (TAG) ... PNW
Pacific Northwest Regional Commission [*Department of Commerce*] ... PNRC
Pacific Northwest Regional Health Science Library [*Library network*] ... PNRHSL
Pacific Northwest Regional Visibility Experiment using Natural Tracers [*Marine science*] (OSRA) ... PREVENT
Pacific Northwest River Basin Commission ... PNRBC
Pacific Northwest River Basins Commission [*Water Resources Council*] [*Terminated, 1981*] (NOAA) ... PNWRBC
Pacific Northwest Ski Association (EA) ... PNSA
Pacific Northwest Trade Association ... PNTA
Pacific Northwest Writers' Conference ... PNWC
Pacific NW Regional Visibility EXperiment using Natural Tracers (USDC) ... PREVENT
Pacific Ocean [*MARC geographic area code Library of Congress*] (LCCP) ... p-----
Pacific Ocean ... PAC
Pacific Ocean ... PacO
Pacific Ocean ... PO
Pacific Ocean Area [*World War II*] ... POA
Pacific Ocean Areas Headquarters Pearl Harbor ... POAHEDPEARL
Pacific Ocean Biological Survey Program [*Smithsonian Institution*] (GFGA) ... POBSP
Pacific Ocean Division [*Army Corps of Engineers*] ... POD
Pacific Ocean Division Engineers (CINC) ... PODE
Pacific Ocean Perch ... POP
Pacific Ocean Region ... POR
Pacific Ocean Research Foundation (EA) ... PORF
Pacific Ocean Ship (NASA) ... POS
Pacific Ocean Stations Program (SAA) ... POSP
Pacific Oceanic Fisheries Investigations (NOAA) ... POFI
Pacific Oceanographic Equipment Evaluation Range (NOAA) ... POEER
Pacific Oceanographic Group [*British Columbia*] (AD) ... POG
Pacific Oceanographic Laboratories [*Later, Pacific Marine Environmental Laboratory*] ... POL
Pacific Orchid Society of Hawaii (EA) ... POS
Pacific Orient Express (WDAA) ... POE
Pacific Overseas Air Technical Service Command ... POATSC
Pacific Passenger Services (AD) ... PPS
Pacific Peace Fund (EA) ... PPF
Pacific Peacemaker Project [*Defunct*] (EA) ... PPP
Pacific Petroleum (AD) ... PP
Pacific Petroleums Ltd., Calgary, AB, Canada [*Library symbol Library of Congress*] (LCLS) ... CaACP
Pacific Physician Services (SPSG) ... PPSI
Pacific Physician Services, Inc. [*Associated Press*] (SAG) ... PacPhy
Pacific Physician Services, Inc. [*NASDAQ symbol*] (SAG) ... PPSI
Pacific Plate Motion Experiment (NASA) ... PPME
Pacific Power and Light (AD) ... PP&L
Pacific Power & Light Co., Portland, OR [*Library symbol Library of Congress*] (LCLS) ... OrPPL
Pacific Press Library, Vancouver, British Columbia [*Library symbol National Library of Canada*] (NLC) ... BVAPP
Pacific Proving Ground [*AEC*] ... PPG
Pacific Railroad Society (EA) ... PRS
Pacific Range Electromagnetic Platform (AAG) ... PREP
Pacific Range Electromagnetic Signature Studies [*or System*] [*Military*] (NG) ... PRESS
Pacific Range Instrumentation Satellite (MUGU) ... PRIS
Pacific Region [*USTTA*] (TAG) ... PAC
Pacific Region Library, Public Works Canada [*Bibliotheque de la Region du Pacifique, Travaux Publics Canada*] **Vancouver, British Columbia** [*Library symbol National Library of Canada*] (NLC) ... BVAPWP
Pacific Regional Advisory Service [*South Pacific Bureau for Economic Co-Operation*] (EY) ... PRAS
Pacific Regional Branch of the International Council on Archives (EAIO) ... PARBICA
Pacific Rehab/Sports Medicine [*NASDAQ symbol*] (TTSB) ... PRHB
Pacific Rehabilitation & Sports Medicine, Inc. [*Associated Press*] (SAG) ... PacRehab
Pacific Rehabilitation & Sports Medicine, Inc. [*NASDAQ symbol*] (SAG) ... PRHB
Pacific Reporter [*A publication*] (DLA) ... P
Pacific Reporter [*A publication*] (DLA) ... Pac
Pacific Reporter [*Commonly cited as P*] [*A publication*] (DLA) ... Pac R
Pacific Reporter [*Commonly cited as P*] [*A publication*] (DLA) ... Pac Rep
Pacific Reporter [*A publication*] (DLA) ... Pac Repr
Pacific Reporter [*A publication*] (DLA) ... Pacif Rep
Pacific Reporter [*A publication*] (DLA) ... Pacific Rep
Pacific Reporter [*A publication*] (DLA) ... PR
Pacific Reporter, Second Series [*A publication*] (DLA) ... P 2d
Pacific Reporter, Second Series [*West*] [*A publication*] (AAGC) ... P2d
Pacific Reporter, Second Series [*A publication*] (DLA) ... Pac 2d
Pacific Representative for Commander Naval Surface Reserve Force (DNAB) ... PACREPCOMNAVSURFRES
Pacific Representative of the Chief of Naval Reserve (DNAB) ... PACREPNAVRES
Pacific Requisition Control Office [*Navy*] ... PRCO
Pacific Res & Engineering Unit [*AMEX symbol*] (TTSB) ... PXE.U
Pacific Research & Engineering Corp. [*Associated Press*] (SAG) ... PacR & E
Pacific Research & Engineering Corp. [*AMEX symbol*] (SAG) ... PXE
Pacific Research Institute for Information Systems and Management [*University of Hawaii at Manoa*] [*Research center*] (RCD) ... PRIISM
Pacific Research Institute for Public Policy (EA) ... PRI
Pacific Research Institute for Public Policy (EA) ... PRIPP
Pacific Research Office (CINC) ... PRO
Pacific Reserve Fleet ... PACRESFLT
Pacific Ridge Resources [*Vancouver Stock Exchange symbol*] ... PCF
Pacific Rim Energy [*Vancouver Stock Exchange symbol*] ... PIM
Pacific Rim Interactive Multimedia Computing [*Australia*] ... PRIMCOM
Pacific Rim Interactive Multi-Media Technology ... PRIMTEC
Pacific Rim Mining Corp. [*Vancouver Stock Exchange symbol*] ... PFG
Pacific Rocket Society (EA) ... PRS
Pacific Salmon Commission (EA) ... PSC
Pacific Scatter Communications System [*Air Force*] (CET) ... PSCS
Pacific School of English [*Australia*] ... PSE
Pacific School of Religion, Berkeley, CA [*Library symbol Library of Congress*] (LCLS) ... CBPac
Pacific Science Association (EA) ... PSA
Pacific Science Board [*National Academy of Sciences*] ... PSB
Pacific Science Center ... PSC
Pacific Science Council ... PSC
Pacific Scientific [*NYSE symbol*] (TTSB) ... PSX
Pacific Scientific Co. [*Associated Press*] (SAG) ... PacSci
Pacific Scientific Co. [*NYSE symbol*] (SPSG) ... PSX
Pacific Seabird Group (EA) ... PSG
Pacific Seafood Processors Association (EA) ... PSPA
Pacific Securities Depository Trust Co. ... PSDTC
Pacific Security Region ... PSR
Pacific Semiconductors, Inc. (MCD) ... PSI
Pacific Semiconductors, Inc., Culver City, CA [*Library symbol Library of Congress*] (LCLS) ... CCuP
Pacific Sentinel Gold [*NASDAQ symbol*] (TTSB) ... PSGVF
Pacific Sentinel Gold Corp. [*Associated Press*] (SAG) ... PacSen
Pacific Sentinel Gold Corp. [*NASDAQ symbol*] (SAG) ... PSGV
Pacific South Coast Freight Bureau ... PSCFB
Pacific South Coast Freight Bureau, San Francisco CA [*STAC*] ... PSC
Pacific, Southern & Western Railroad [*Nickname: Play Safe and Walk*] ... PS & W
Pacific Southern Naval Coastal Frontier ... PSNCF
Pacific Southwest Airlines [*ICAO designator*] (OAG) ... PS
Pacific Southwest Airlines ... PSA
Pacific Southwest Airlines [*Air carrier designation symbol*] ... PSAX
Pacific Southwest Forest and Range Experiment Station [*Berkeley, CA*] [*Department of Agriculture*] (GRD) ... PSW
Pacific Southwest Forest and Range Experiment Station [*Berkeley, CA*] (SAA) ... PSWFRES
Pacific Southwest Forest and Range Experiment Station, Berkeley, CA [*OCLC symbol*] (OCLC) ... AGP
Pacific Southwest Railway Museum Association [*Later, SDRM*] (EA) ... PSRMA
Pacific Southwest Regional Medical Library [*Library network*] ... PSRMLS
Pacific Special Activities Area [*Military*] ... PSAA
Pacific Standard Time ... PST
Pacific Star Communication [*Vancouver Stock Exchange symbol*] ... PS
Pacific Stars and Stripes Alumni Association (EA) ... PSSAA
Pacific State Hospital, Pomona, CA [*Library symbol Library of Congress*] (LCLS) ... CPomP
Pacific States Marine Fisheries Commission ... PSMFC
Pacific Steam Navigation Co. (MHDW) ... PSNC
Pacific Stock Exchange (EA) ... PSE
Pacific Stratus Investigation [*Marine science*] (OSRA) ... PSI
Pacific Studies [*A publication*] (BRI) ... Pac S
Pacific Studies Center (EA) ... PSC
Pacific Submarine Direct Support Element Coordinator (DNAB) ... PACSUBDSEC
Pacific Sulfur Investigation [*Marine science*] (OSRA) ... PSI
Pacific Sulfur/Stratus Investigation (USDC) ... PSI
Pacific Summer Time ... PST
Pacific Sunwear of Calif [*NASDAQ symbol*] (TTSB) ... PSUN
Pacific Sunwear of California, Inc. [*Associated Press*] (SAG) ... PacSun
Pacific Sunwear of California, Inc. [*NASDAQ symbol*] (SAG) ... PSUN
Pacific Technical Operations Area [*Military*] ... PACTOA
Pacific Telecommunications Council (EA) ... PTC
Pacific Telephone & Telegraph Co., Los Angeles, CA [*Library symbol Library of Congress*] (LCLS) ... CLPT
Pacific Telesis (NITA) ... PACTEL
Pacific Telesis Group [*NYSE symbol*] (SPSG) ... PAC
Pacific Telesis Group [*Associated Press*] (SAG) ... PacTel
Pacific Telesis Group Financing I [*NYSE symbol*] (SAG) ... PAC
Pacific Telesis Group Financing I [*Associated Press*] (SAG) ... PacT
Pacific Telesis Group Financing II [*NYSE symbol*] (SAG) ... PAC
Pacific Telesis Group Financing II [*Associated Press*] (SAG) ... PacT
Pacific Test Range (MUGU) ... PTR
Pacific Theater of Operations [*World War II*] ... PTO
Pacific Time ... PT
Pacific Trade and Development Conference [*OPTAD*] (FEA) ... PTDC
Pacific Trade Union Community [*Australia*] (EAIO) ... PTUC
Pacific Trans-Ocean Resources Ltd. [*Toronto Stock Exchange symbol*] ... PTX
Pacific Transport of Heat and Salt [*Canada-Japan-USA*] [*Marine science*] (OSRA) ... PATHS
Pacific Transportation Terminal Command [*Army*] ... PTTC
Pacific Triangle Information Services [*Information service or system*] (IID) ... PTIS
Pacific Tsunami Observation Program [*Marine science*] (OSRA) ... PacTOP
Pacific Tsunami Observation Program (USDC) ... PacTOP
Pacific Tsunami Warning Center [*National Weather Service*] (MSC) ... PTWC
Pacific Tuna Conference ... PTC
Pacific Tuna Development Foundation (EA) ... PTDF
Pacific Underwater Test Range (SAA) ... PUTR
Pacific Unicorn [*Vancouver Stock Exchange symbol*] ... PUC
Pacific Union Club, San Francisco, CA [*Library symbol Library of Congress*] (LCLS) ... CSfPUC
Pacific Union College (GAGS) ... Pac Union C
Pacific Union College [*Angwin, CA*] ... PUC

Pacific Union College, Angwin, CA [*Library symbol Library of Congress*] (LCLS) .... CAngP
Pacific Union College, Angwin, CA [*OCLC symbol*] (OCLC) .... CPU
Pacific University (GAGS) .... Pac U
Pacific University, Forest Grove, OR [*OCLC symbol*] (OCLC) .... OPU
Pacific University, Forest Grove, OR [*Library symbol Library of Congress*] (LCLS) .... OrFP
Pacific Utilization Research Center [*Marine science*] (MSC) .... PURC
Pacific Vending Technology Ltd. [*Vancouver Stock Exchange symbol*] .... PVT
Pacific Vocational Institute, Burnaby, BC, Canada [*Library symbol Library of Congress*] (LCLS) .... CaBBPVI
Pacific Vocational Institute Library [*UTLAS symbol*] .... PVI
Pacific Vocational Institute, Maple Ridge, BC, Canada [*Library symbol Library of Congress*] (LCLS) .... CaBMrP
Pacific Vocational Institute, Maple Ridge, British Columbia [*Library symbol Obsolete National Library of Canada*] (NLC) .... BMRP
Pacific War Council [*World War II*] .... PWC
Pacific War Time (IAA) .... PWT
Pacific War Veterans of America [*Defunct*] .... PWVA
Pacific Western Airlines Ltd. [*Canada ICAO designator*] (OAG) .... PW
Pacific Western Airlines Ltd. [*Toronto Stock Exchange symbol Vancouver Stock Exchange symbol*] .... PWA
Pacific Whale Foundation (EA) .... PWF
Pacific Winter Time (IAA) .... PWT
Pacifica: Australian Theological Studies [*A publication*] (APTA) .... Pac
Pacifica Foundation (EA) .... PF
Pacific-Antarctic Ridge [*Geology*] .... PAR
PacifiCare Health Sys'A' [*NASDAQ symbol*] (TTSB) .... PHSYA
PacifiCare Health Sys'B' [*NASDAQ symbol*] (TTSB) .... PHYSB
PacifiCare Health Systems, Inc. [*Associated Press*] (SAG) .... PacifC
PacifiCare Health Systems, Inc. [*Cypress, CA*] [*NASDAQ symbol*] (NQ) .... PHSY
Pacific-Asia Resources Center [*Japan*] (EAIO) .... PARC
Pacific-Asian Treaty Organization (NADA) .... PATO
PacifiCorp [*Associated Press*] (SAG) .... Pacf
PacifiCorp [*Associated Press*] (SAG) .... Pacif
PacifiCorp [*Associated Press*] (SAG) .... PacifCp
Pacificorp [*Associated Press*] (SAG) Pcfcp25
Pacificorp [*Associated Press*] (SAG) Pcfcp35
Pacificorp [*NYSE symbol*] (SAG) .... PCQ
Pacificorp [*NYSE symbol*] (SAG) .... PCX
PacifiCorp [*NYSE symbol*] (SPSG) .... PPW
PacifiCorp 5% Pfd [*AMEX symbol*] (TTSB) .... PPWPr
PacifiCorp $1.98 cm Pfd [*NYSE symbol*] (TTSB) .... PPWPrE
PacifiCorp 8.55%'QUIDS' [*NYSE symbol*] (TTSB) .... PCX
PacifiCorp 8.375% 'QUIDS' [*NYSE symbol*] (TTSB) .... PCQ
Pacificorp Capital [*Associated Press*] (SAG) .... PcCap
Pacificorp Capital [*NYSE symbol*] (SAG) .... PPW
Pacific's Electronics Acquisition Service (NITA) .... PEAS
Pacific-Sierra Research Corp. .... PSR
Pacific-Texas [*Pipeline*] .... PACTEX
Pacificulture Foundation (EA) .... PCF
Pacifistische Socialistische Partij [*Pacific Socialist Party*] [*Political party Netherlands*] .... PSP
Pacing and Cardiac Electrophysiology Retrieval System [*Intermedics, Inc.*] [*Information service or system*] (IID) .... PACERS
Pacing Impulse [*Cardiology*] (DAVI) .... PI
Pacing Item (MCD) .... PI
Pacing Item Evaluation (MCD) .... PIE
Pacis Amico, Persecutionis Osore, Joanne Lockio Anglo [*Pseudonym used by John Locke*] .... PAPOILA
Pack [*JETDS*] .... P
Pack (AAG) .... PK
Pack File Indexer (NITA) .... PFI
Pack for Domestic Use .... PKDOM
Pack for Overseas .... PKSEA
Pack Howitzer [*Marine Corps*] .... PKHOW
Pack Memorial Public Library, Asheville, NC [*Library symbol Library of Congress*] (LCLS) .... NcA
Pack Memorial Public Library, Sondley Reference Library, Asheville, NC [*Library symbol Library of Congress*] (LCLS) .... NcA-S
Pack Quickly [*Humorous interpretation for Parti Quebecois*] [*Canada*] .... PQ
Pack Unit [*Single title, multiple orders*] [*Publishing*] [*British*] .... PU
Pack Up and Fade Out [*End of military exercise*] [*British*] (DSUE) .... PUFO
Pack Year [*Cigarettes*] (MEDA) .... PY
Pack Years [*of cigarette consumption*] (DAVI) .... PY
Package [*Shipping*] (MCD) .... PK
Package [*Shipping*] (AFM) .... PKG
Package .... PKG
Package (WDMC) .... pkg
Package (WDMC) .... pkge
Package .... PKGE
Package Attitude Control [*NASA*] .... PAC
Package Carrier Committee (EA) .... PCC
Package Computer-Aided Design [*Computer science*] .... PCAD
Package Control [*or Controller*] .... PC
Package Control Number .... PCN
Package Data System [*NASA*] .... PDS
Package Design Council [*New York, NY*] (EA) .... PDC
Package Designation and Description File (DOMA) .... PDD
Package for Architectural Computer Evaluation (PDAA) .... PACE
Package for Online Programming [*Computer science*] (CDE) .... POP
Package Freighter [*Shipping*] .... PF
Package Height [*Freight*] .... P HGT
Package Information Form (IAA) .... PIF

Package Insert [*Instructional leaflet distributed with certain prescription drugs*] [*Also, PPI*] .... PI
Package Irradiation Plant [*Nuclear energy*] (NUCP) .... PIP
Package Operating System (PDAA) .... PACOS
Package Programs of London (NITA) .... PPL
Package Sequence Number .... PSN
Package Size Proneness [*Marketing*] .... PSP
Package Size Unspecified .... PSU
Package Test Power Supply .... PTPS
Package Transfer Unit .... PTU
Package Turn In (MCD) .... PTI
Package Will Follow [*Birthday-card notation*] .... PWF
Packaged (IAA) .... PKGD
Packaged Assembly Circuit .... PAC
Packaged CRAM [*Card Random-Access Memory*] Executive [*NCR Corp.*] [*Computer science*] .... PACE
Packaged Disaster Hospital [*Public Health Service*] .... PDH
Packaged Electronic Circuit [*Computer science*] (IAA) .... PEC
Packaged Gas Pressure System .... PGPS
Packaged Ice Association (EA) .... PIA
Packaged Interchangeable Electronic System .... PIES
Packaged Liquid Air-Augmented (IAA) .... PLARA
Packaged Liquid Air-Augmented Rocket (MCD) .... PLAAR
Packaged Liquid Missile .... PLM
Packaged Liquid Propellant System .... PLPS
Packaged Optimization Control [*Engineering*] .... POC
Packaged POL [*Petroleum, Oils and Lubricants*] (DOMA) .... PKG-POL
Packaged Ventilation Kit [*Civil Defense*] .... PVK
Packages Delivered Quick [*Allegheny Airlines service*] .... PDQ
Packaging .... PKGNG
Packaging and Industrial Films Association [*British*] (DBA) .... PIFA
Packaging, Crating, Handling, and Transportation [*Shipping*] (CINC) .... PCH & T
Packaging, Crating, Handling, and Transportation [*Shipping*] (AABC) .... PCHT
Packaging Development Plan .... PDP
Packaging Distributors Association [*British*] (DBA) .... PDA
Packaging Education Foundation (EA) .... PEF
Packaging Engineering Data System (AFM) .... PEDS
Packaging, Handling, and Storage (MCD) .... PHS
Packaging, Handling, Storage, and Transportation [*Shipping*] .... PHS & T
Packaging, Handling, Storage, and Transportation [*Shipping*] .... PHST
Packaging Information Record (MCD) .... PIR
Packaging Institute [*Later, PI/USA*] (EA) .... PI
Packaging Institute International [*Later, IoPP*] (EA) .... PI/INT'L
Packaging Institute, United States of America [*Later, PI/INT'L*] (EA) .... PI/USA
Packaging Machinery Manufacturers Institute (EA) .... PMMI
Packaging, Preservation, and Transportation .... PP & T
Packaging Requirements for Optimum Malfunction Isolation by Systematic Substitution (IAA) .... PROMISS
Packaging Research [*NASDAQ symbol*] (TTSB) .... PRCA
Packaging Research Corp. [*Associated Press*] (SAG) .... PackRs
Packaging Research Corp. [*Associated Press*] (SAG) .... PackRsh
Packaging Research Corp. [*NASDAQ symbol*] (SAG) .... PRCA
Packaging Research Wrrt [*NASDAQ symbol*] (TTSB) .... PRCAW
Packaging Science and Technology Abstracts [*International Food Information Service*] [*Germany Information service or system*] .... PSTA
Packaging Shipping Procedures .... PSP
Packaging, Storage, and Containerization Center [*DARCOM*] (MCD) .... PS & CC
Packard Automobile Classics (EA) .... PAC
Packard Bell Computer Corp. (IAA) .... PBCC
Packard Data Bank (EA) .... PDB
Packard Truck Organization [*Defunct*] (EA) .... PTO
Packards International Motor Car Club (EA) .... PIMCC
Packard's Radioimmunoassay System [*Medicine*] (DMAA) .... PRIAS
Packed (IAA) .... PKD
Packed Bed Reactor .... PBR
Packed by Carrier .... PBC
Packed by Owner .... PBO
Packed Cell [*Hematology*] (MAE) .... PC
Packed Cell Volume [*Hematology*] (CPH) .... PCV
Packed Computational (IAA) .... PCMP
Packed Encoding Rules (ACII) .... PER
Packed Lunches [*School meals*] [*British*] .... P
Packed Main Parachute .... PMP
Packed Memory [*Computer science*] (IAA) .... PAC
Packed Powder (WGA) .... PKD PDR
Packed Red Blood Cells [*Medicine*] .... PRBC
Packed Red Cell [*Hematology*] (MAE) .... PRC
Packed Snow on Runway [*NWS*] (FAAC) .... PSR
Packed Snow on Runway - Patchy [*Aviation*] (DNAB) .... PSR-P
Packed Switched Data .... PSD
Packed Tape Assembly .... PACTA
Packed under Federal Inspection .... PUFI
Packed Weight .... PW
Packer (WGA) .... PKR
Packer .... PKR
Packers and Stockyards .... P & S
Packers and Stockyards Administration [*Department of Agriculture*] .... P & SA
Packet .... PKT
Packet Adapter [*Telecommunications*] (IAA) .... PA
Packet Assembler/Disassembler [*Switching technique*] [*Computer science*] .... PAD
Packet Assembly Disassembly (NITA) .... PAD
Packet Autopiloted Cruiseway .... PAC
Packet Channel Interface Module [*Telecommunications*] .... PCIM
Packet + Circuit (MHDI) .... PACUIT
Packet Communications, Inc. .... PCI

Packet Communications Unit ... PCU
Packet Data Processing Facility (MCD) ... PDPF
Packet Data Satellites [*Telecommunications*] (TSSD) ... PDS
Packet Exchange Protocol [*Computer science*] (CDE) ... PEP
Packet Exchange Protocol [*Computer science*] (TNIG) ... PXP
Packet Internet Groper [*Computer program*] (PCM) ... PING
Packet Layer Protocol [*Computer science*] (TNIG) ... PLP
Packet Level Procedure [*or Protocol*] [*Computer programming*] (PCM) ... PLP
Packet Multiplexer ... PMX
Packet Network Adaptor (NITA) ... PNA
Packet Network Service Centre (NITA) ... PNSC
Packet of Accelerated Christian Education [*Educational material marketed by fundamentalist company, Accelerated Christian Education*] ... PACE
Packet Protocol Extension ... PPX
Packet Radio Network [*Telecommunications*] (OSI) ... PRN
Packet Radio Network ... PRNET
Packet Radio Unit ... PRU
Packet (Receive) ... P(R)
Packet Satellite [*Telecommunications*] ... PACSAT
Packet (Send) ... P(S)
Packet Switch Data System [*Information retrieval*] (IID) ... PSDS
Packet Switch Level Interface ... PSLI
Packet Switch Stream [*British*] [*Computer science*] (TNIG) ... PS
Packet Switched Data Network [*Telecommunications*] ... PSDN
Packet Switched Data Service [*Telecommunications*] (TEL) ... PSDS
Packet Switched Network ... PSN
Packet Switched Public Data Network [*Computer science*] (TNIG) ... PSPDN
Packet Switched System (NITA) ... PSS
Packet Switching [*Telecommunications*] ... PS
Packet Switching Exchange [*Telecommunications*] ... PSE
Packet Switching Node ... PSN
Packet Switching Processor ... PSP
Packet Switching Service [*Telecommunications Information service or system British*] (IID) ... PSS
Packet Switching Unit ... PSU
Packet SwitchStream [*British Telecommunications Plc*] [*London*] [*Information service or system*] (IID) ... PSS
Packet Terminal (NITA) ... PT
Packet Transfer Engine [*Newbridge Networks Corp.*] ... PTE
Packet Transport Equipment [*Computer science*] (PCM) ... PTE
Packetized Ensemble Protocol [*Computer science*] ... PEP
Packets per Second [*Computer science*] (PCM) ... PPS
Packet-Switching Data Network [*Computer science*] (DOM) ... PSDN
Packing (DS) ... Pkg
Packing and Allocation for a COMPOOL [*Communications Pool*] **Kaleidoscope** (SAA) ... PACK
Packing and Packaging Manual (MCD) ... P & PM
Packing and Preservation ... P & P
Packing, Crating, and Handling [*Shipping*] (AFM) ... PC & H
Packing, Crating, and Handling [*Shipping*] ... PCH
Packing Factor (EECA) ... PF
Packing Fraction (EECA) ... PF
Packing House [*Freight*] ... PKNG HSE
Packing Instruction (DS) ... Pkg instr
Packing List ... PL
Packing, Postage, and Insurance [*Shipping*] ... PPI
Packing Sheet (MCD) ... PS
Packing-House Products [*Food industry*] ... PHP
Packmaster [*Army*] (WGA) ... PKM
Packmaster [*Army*] ... Pkmr
Packs of Cigarettes Smoked ... PKS
Packs per Day [*Cigarettes*] [*Medicine*] ... p/d
Packs per Day [*Cigarettes*] [*Medicine*] ... PPD
Pack-Up Kit (MCD) ... PUK
Packwood Clarion, Packwood, IA [*Library symbol Library of Congress*] (LCLS) ... IaPwdC
Pacoima, CA [*Location identifier FAA*] (FAAL) ... PAI
PACOM [*Pacific Command*] **Air Defense Ground Environment Requirements Committee** (CINC) ... PADGERC
PACOM [*Pacific Command*] **Air Target Materials Review Group** (CINC) ... PATMRG
PACOM [*Pacific Command*] **Data Systems Center** (MCD) ... PDSC
PACOM [*Pacific Command*] **Executive Intelligence Summary** (MCD) ... PEILS
PACOM [*Pacific Command*] **Priority Number** (CINC) ... PPRI
PACOM [*Pacific Command*] **Reconnaissance Priority List** (CINC) ... PRPL
PACOM [*Pacific Command*] **Tactical Target Materials Catalog** (CINC) ... PTTMC
PACOM [*Pacific Command*] **Utilization and Redistribution Agency** ... PURA
PACOM [*Pacific Command*] **Warning Intelligence** [*Army*] ... PWI
Pacte Democratica per Catalunya [*Democratic Pact for Catalonia*] [*Spain Political party*] (PPE) ... PDC
Pacto [*Ecuador*] [*ICAO location identifier*] (ICLI) ... SETO
Pacto de Alianza de Centro [*Chile*] [*Political party*] (EY) ... PAC
Pacvest Capital, Inc. [*Toronto Stock Exchange symbol*] ... PVC
Pad (SAA) ... P
Pad (MCD) ... PD
Pad Abort [*NASA*] (KSC) ... PA
Pad Abort Measuring System [*NASA*] (KSC) ... PAMS
Pad and Boom [*Refueling*] [*Aerospace*] (MSA) ... P/B
Pad Automatic Data Equipment (PDAA) ... PADE
Pad Control Center [*NASA*] (NASA) ... PCC
Pad Coordinator [*NASA*] ... PC
Pad Emergency Air Pack [*NASA*] (KSC) ... PEAP
Pad Facility Controls [*Aerospace*] (AAG) ... P/FACCTL
Pad Journal Bearing ... PJB
Pad Mechanic [*Aerospace*] ... PM
Pad Safety in Blockhouse ... PSBH
Pad Safety Officer [*Aerospace*] (MCD) ... PSO
Pad Safety Plan ... PSP
Pad Safety Report [*NASA*] ... PSR
Pad Safety Supervision [*Aerospace*] (AAG) ... PSS
Pad Terminal Connection Room [*NASA*] ... PTCR
Padampur [*India*] [*ICAO location identifier*] (ICLI) ... VEPP
Padang [*Indonesia*] [*Airport symbol*] (OAG) ... PDG
Padang Sidempuan/Aek Godang [*Indonesia*] [*ICAO location identifier*] (ICLI) ... WIME
Padang/Tabing [*Indonesia*] [*ICAO location identifier*] (ICLI) ... WIMG
Padangpandjang [*Sumatra*] [*Seismograph station code, US Geological Survey*] (SEIS) ... PPI
Padded Sample Collection Bag [*NASA*] ... PSCB
Padder [*Capacitor*] [*Electronics*] ... PAD
Padding ... PDG
Paddington Railway Station (ROG) ... P
Paddle (DS) ... P
Paddle Steamer (ADA) ... PS
Paddle Steamer Preservation Society [*British*] (BI) ... PSPS
Paddle-Wheel Steamer [*Shipping*] (ROG) ... PWS
Paddy's Market Stallholders' Association [*Australia*] ... PMSA
Paderborn [*Germany Airport symbol*] (OAG) ... PAD
Paderborn/Lippstadt [*Germany ICAO location identifier*] (ICLI) ... EDLP
Paderewski Foundation [*Defunct*] (EA) ... PF
Padlock (AAG) ... PL
Padova [*Italy ICAO location identifier*] (ICLI) ... LIPP
Padova [*Italy ICAO location identifier*] (ICLI) ... LIPU
Padova [*Italy*] [*Seismograph station code, US Geological Survey*] (SEIS) ... PAD
Padre Island National Seashore [*National Park Service designation*] ... PAIS
Padre Resources [*Vancouver Stock Exchange symbol*] ... PRS
Padstow [*Town in England*] ... PAD
Paducah [*Kentucky*] [*Airport symbol*] (OAG) ... PAH
Paducah [*Kentucky*] [*Airport symbol*] (AD) ... PUK
Paducah & Illinois Railroad [*AAR code*] ... PI
Paducah Community College, Paducah, KY [*Library symbol Library of Congress*] (LCLS) ... KyPadC
Paducah Gaseous Diffusion Plant [*Department of Energy*] [*Paducah, KY*] (GAAI) ... PAD
Paducah Gaseous Diffusion Plant ... PGDP
Paducah Gaseous Diffusion Plant (DOGT) ... PGDP
Paducah Junior College [*Kentucky*] ... PJC
Paducah Junior College, Paducah, KY [*OCLC symbol*] (OCLC) ... KPC
Paducah, KY [*Location identifier FAA*] (FAAL) ... CNG
Paducah, KY [*Location identifier FAA*] (FAAL) ... FIO
Paducah, KY [*FM radio station call letters*] ... WDDJ
Paducah, KY [*Television station call letters*] ... WDKA
Paducah, KY [*AM radio station call letters*] ... WDXR
Paducah, KY [*FM radio station call letters*] (RBYB) ... WGCF-FM
Paducah, KY [*Television station call letters*] ... WKPD
Paducah, KY [*FM radio station call letters*] ... WKYQ
Paducah, KY [*AM radio station call letters*] ... WKYX
Paducah, KY [*AM radio station call letters*] ... WPAD
Paducah, KY [*Television station call letters*] ... WPSD
Paducah Public Library, Paducah, KY [*Library symbol Library of Congress*] (LCLS) ... KyPad
Paea [*Society Islands*] [*Seismograph station code, US Geological Survey*] (SEIS) ... PAE
Paediatric [*or Paediatrics*] ... PAED
Paediatric Surgery ... PS
Paedophile Information Exchange [*British*] (ILCA) ... PIE
Paekryoungdo Beach [*South Korea ICAO location identifier*] (ICLI) ... RKSE
Paekryoungdo Site [*South Korea ICAO location identifier*] (ICLI) ... RKSP
Paeoniflorigenone [*Biochemistry*] ... PFG
Pafco Financial Holdings Ltd. [*Toronto Stock Exchange symbol*] ... PFH
PAFEC Interactive Graphics System [*PAFEC Ltd.*] [*Software package*] (NCC) ... PIGS
Pagadian [*Philippines*] [*Airport symbol*] (OAG) ... PAG
Pagadian, Zamboanga Del Sur [*Philippines*] [*ICAO location identifier*] (ICLI) ... RPWP
Pagan/Occult/Witchcraft Special Interest Group (EA) ... POW-SIG
Paganella [*Italy ICAO location identifier*] (ICLI) ... LIVP
Pagans Against Nukes [*British*] (DI) ... PAN
Pagans for Peace Network [*Canada*] (EAIO) ... P4P
Pagas Airlines [*ICAO designator*] (AD) ... YP
Page (ODBW) ... p
Page (WDMC) ... p
Page ... P
Page [*or Pagination*] [*Online database field identifier*] ... PG
Page (WDMC) ... pg
Page (VRA) ... pg
Page [*Arizona*] [*Airport symbol*] (OAG) ... PGA
Page 1 [*Also, P-1*] (WDMC) ... p-1
Page Address Field ... PAF
Page Address Register ... PAR
Page America Group, Inc. [*Associated Press*] (SAG) ... PageAm
Page America Group, Inc. [*AMEX symbol*] (SPSG) ... PGG
Page and Adams' Code [*1912*] [*A publication*] (DLA) ... P & A
Page and Item Number ... PIN
Page and Line (IAA) ... PGLN
Page, AZ [*AM radio station call letters*] ... KPGE
Page, AZ [*FM radio station call letters*] ... KXAZ
Page Buffer (NITA) ... PB
Page Change Notice (MCD) ... PCN
Page Communications Engineers, Inc. [*Canada*] (MCD) ... PCE

Page Composition Random Access Memory (NITA) .... PCRAM
Page Control Block [Computer science] (IBMDP) .... PCB
Page Control Register .... PCR
Page Data Register .... PDR
Page Description Communications [Microsoft Corp.] (PCM) .... PDC
Page Description Language [Computer graphics] .... PDL
Page Down [Computer science] (CDE) .... PgDn
Page Element Data Base [Printing] (DGA) .... PEDB
Page Fault (IAA) .... PF
Page Fault Frequency [Computer science] (MHDI) .... PFF
Page Footing (BUR) .... PF
Page Formatter (MDG) .... PF
Page Frame Table (BUR) .... PFT
Page Generation [or Generator] (PDAA) .... PAGE
Page Heading (BUR) .... PH
Page Layout System [Graphic arts] (DGA) .... PLS
Page Layout Terminal [Graphic arts] (DGA) .... PLT
Page Length Field .... PLF
Page Level Availability Time Test [Computer science] .... PLATT
Page Map Address Register .... PMAR
Page Map Address Table [NASA] (NASA) .... PMAT
Page Map Table [NASA] (HGAA) .... PMT
Page Map Table Address Register [NASA] (HGAA) .... PMTA
Page Map Table Entry [NASA] (IAA) .... PMTE
Page Memorial Library, Aberdeen, NC [Library symbol] [Library of Congress] (LCLS) .... NcAbd
Page, OK [Location identifier FAA] (FAAL) .... PGO
Page on Contracts [A publication] (DLA) .... Page Contr
Page on Divorce [A publication] (DLA) .... Page Div
Page One [Broadcasting] (WDMC) P-1
Page Park Center Elementary School, Rockford, IL [Library symbol] [Library of Congress] (LCLS) .... IRoPpE
Page Petroleum Ltd. [Toronto Stock Exchange symbol] (SPSG) .... PGE
Page Printer (NVT) .... PP
Page Printer Control Block [Computer science] .... PPCB
Page Printer Control System [Computer science] .... PPCS
Page Printer Spooling System [Computer science] .... PPSP
Page Printing System [Honeywell, Inc.] [Computer science] .... PPS
Page Processing System (NITA) .... PPS
Page Public Library, Page, AZ [Library symbol Library of Congress] (LCLS) .... AzP
Page Reader Input System with Editing (NVT) .... PRISE
Page Reference Distribution Function [Computer science] (IAA) .... PRDF
Page Replacement Algorithm [Computer science] (MHDI) .... PRA
Page Revision Log (NASA) .... PRL
Page Send-Receive [Teletypewriter] .... PSR
Page Survival Index (PDAA) .... PSI
Page Table [Computer science] (IBMDP) .... PGT
Page Table [Computer science] (IAA) .... PT
Page Table Address [Computer science] (IAA) .... PTA
Page Table Base [Computer science] (IAA) .... PTB
Page Table Entry .... PTE
Page Table Word [Computer science] (IAA) .... PTW
Page Table Word Associative Memory [Computer science] (IAA) .... PTWAM
Page Up [Computer science] (BARN) .... PgUp
Page View Terminal [A video terminal that displays a full page] (WDMC) .... PVT
Page View Terminal [Typography] [Videotex terminal] .... PVT
Pageable Link-Pack Area .... PLPA
Pageable Partition Queue Area [Computer science] .... PPQA
Pageable System Queue Area [Computer science] (MCD) .... PSQA
Pagecorp, Inc. [Toronto Stock Exchange symbol] .... PGO
Paged Memory Management Unit [Computer chip] (BYTE) .... PMMU
Paged Memory-Management Unit (AD) .... pmmu
Page-Directory Base Register [Computer science] (BYTE) .... PDBR
Page-Directory Entry [Computer science] (BYTE) .... PDE
Page-End Character [Computer science] .... PE
Pageland, SC [FM radio station call letters] .... WMAP
Page-Oriented Holograph Memory [Computer science] .... POHM
Page-per-Minute [Computer science] (PCM) .... PPM
Page-Replacement Algorithm and Control Logic [Computer science] .... PRACL
Page-Replacement Algorithm and Control Logic (AD) .... pracl
Pages (WDMC) .... Pp
Pages (WDMC) .... pp
Pages .... PP
Pages Bleues Informatisees [Commission of the European Communities] [Information service or system] (CRD) .... PABLI
Pages from the Past [Later, PIR] [An association] (EA) .... PP
Pages, Inc. [Associated Press] (SAG) .... Pages
Pages, Inc. [NASDAQ symbol] (SAG) .... PAGZ
Pages per Hour .... PPH
Pages Per Inch (AD) .... pp/in
Pages Per Inch (AD) .... ppi
Pages Per Inch (WDMC) .... ppi
Pages per Inch [Publishing] .... PPI
Pages per Minute [Printer technology] .... PPM
Pages per Year [Facetious criterion for determining insignificance of Supreme Court Justices] [Proposed by University of Chicago professor David P. Currie] .... PPY
Page's Three Early Assize Rolls, County of Northumberland [Surtees Society Publications, Vol. 88] [A publication] (ILCA) .... Pag
Page's Three Early Assize Rolls, County of Northumberland [Surtees Society Publications, Vol. 88] [A publication] (DLA) .... Page
Paget Foundation for Paget's Disease of Bone and Related Disorders [Formerly, Paget's Disease Foundation (PDF)] (PAZ) .... PFPDBRD
Paget Resources Ltd. [Vancouver Stock Exchange symbol] .... PAG
Paget-Gorman Sign System (AIE) .... PGSS

Paget's Disease [Medicine] .... PD
Paget's Disease Foundation (EA) .... PDF
Paget's Judicial Puzzles [A publication] (DLA) .... Pag Jud Puz
Paghman [Afghanistan] [ICAO location identifier] (ICLI) .... OAPG
Paging and Area Warning .... P & AW
Paging and Area Warning (MCD) .... PA
Paging Area Memory Space [Computer science] (IAA) .... PAMS
Paging Control Unit [Telecommunications] (TEL) .... PCU
Paging Network [NASDAQ symbol] (SPSG) .... PAGE
Paging Network, Inc. [Associated Press] (SAG) .... Paging
Paging Network Inc. [Associated Press] (SAG) .... PagingN
Paging Partners [NASDAQ symbol] (TTSB) .... PPAR
Paging Partners Corp. [Associated Press] (SAG) .... Paging
Paging Partners Corp. [Associated Press] (SAG) .... PagingP
Paging Partners Corp. [NASDAQ symbol] (SAG) .... PPAR
Paging Partners Wrrt [NASDAQ symbol] (TTSB) .... PPARW
Pagnall [England] .... PAGN
Pago Pago [Samoa] [Airport symbol] (OAG) .... PPG
Pago Pago, AQ [Location identifier FAA] (FAAL) .... LOG
Pago Pago, AQ [Location identifier FAA] (FAAL) .... PPG
Pago Pago, AS [FM radio station call letters] .... KSBS
Pago Pago, AS [Television station call letters] KVZK-2
Pago Pago, AS [Television station call letters] KVZK-4
Pago Pago, AS [Television station call letters] KVZK-5
Pago Pago/International, Tutuila Island [American Samoa] [ICAO location identifier] (ICLI) .... NSTU
Pagoda .... Pag
Pagosa Springs [Colorado] [Seismograph station code, US Geological Survey Closed] (SEIS) .... PGS
Pagosa Springs, CO [AM radio station call letters] .... KPAG
Pagosa Springs, CO [FM radio station call letters] .... KRQS
Pagurian Corp. [Toronto Stock Exchange symbol] .... PGC
Pahaquarry [New Jersey] [Seismograph station code, US Geological Survey] (SEIS) .... PQN
Pahlavi [MARC language code Library of Congress] (LCCP) .... pal
Pahlavi [Iran] [Airport symbol] (AD) .... PHV
Pahoa [Hawaii] [Seismograph station code, US Geological Survey Closed] (SEIS) .... PAH
Pahoa, HI [Location identifier FAA] (FAAL) .... POA
Pahokee, FL [Location identifier FAA] (FAAL) .... PHK
Pahrock Range [Nevada] [Seismograph station code, US Geological Survey] (SEIS) .... PRN
Pahrump, NV [FM radio station call letters] .... KFBI
Pahute Mesa [Nevada] [Seismograph station code, US Geological Survey Closed] (SEIS) LO2
Pahute Mesa [Nevada] [Seismograph station code, US Geological Survey Closed] (SEIS) .... PMN
Paid .... PD
Paid (WDMC) .... pd
Paid (ODBW) .... pd
Paid by Agent [Business term] (DCTA) .... PBA
Paid Circulation Council [Later, ASCMP] .... PCC
Paid Educational Leave (AIE) .... PEL
Paid Educational Services [British] .... PES
Paid in Advance (WDMC) .... PIA
Paid Land Diversion Program [Department of Agriculture] (GFGA) .... PLD
Paid on Delivery (AD) .... pod
Paid Pensioner Recruiter [British military] (DMA) .... PPR
Paid Personal Holiday .... PPH
Paid Service Indication [Telecommunications] (TEL) .... PSI
Paid This Year [In stock listings of newspapers] .... P
Paid This Year, Dividend Omitted, Deferred, or No Action Taken at Last Dividend Meeting [Investment term] (DFIT) I
Paid Time Off (NFD) .... PTO
Paid Up [Insurance] (ODBW) .... pu
Paid Up [Insurance] (EY) .... PU
Paid-during-Service [Billing] .... PDS
Paid-In Capital [Finance] (MHDW) .... PIC
Paid-Up Policy [Insurance] (DSUE) .... PUP
Paige's New York Chancery Reports [A publication] (DLA) .... Pai
Paige's New York Chancery Reports [A publication] (DLA) .... Pai Ch
Paige's New York Chancery Reports [A publication] (DLA) .... Paige
Paige's New York Chancery Reports [1828-45] [A publication] (DLA) .... Paige Ch
Paige's New York Chancery Reports [A publication] (DLA) .... Paige Ch Rep
Paige's New York Chancery Reports [A publication] (DLA) .... Paige's Ch
Pail .... PL
Pailton [British ICAO location identifier] (ICLI) .... EGBP
Paimiut, AK [Location identifier FAA] (FAAL) .... PMU
Pain [Medicine] .... P
Pain & Burning [Medicine] (DMAA) .... P&B
Pain and Suffering (DAVI) .... P & S
Pain Control Unit .... PCU
Pain Disability Index [Medicine] (DMAA) .... PDI
Pain Dysfunction Syndrome [Medicine] (AAMN) .... PDS
Pain in the Ass .... PITA
Pain Intensity Differences [Medicine] .... PID
Pain Management Program [Neurology] (DAVI) .... PMP
Pain, Pallor, Pulse Loss, Paresthesia, Paralysis [Medicine] (MEDA) .... PPPPP
Pain Rating Index .... PRI
Pain Rehabilitation Center (AD) .... PRC
Pain Relief Level [Medicine] .... PREL
Pain Sensitivity Range [Biometrics] .... PSR
Pain Threshold .... PT
Paine and Duer's Practice [A publication] (DLA) .... Paine & D Pr
Paine College, Augusta, GA [Library symbol Library of Congress] (LCLS) .... GAuP

Paine College, Warren A. Candler Library, Augusta, GA [*OCLC symbol*] (OCLC) ... PNE
Paine Webber Gp Stk Index Sec [*AMEX symbol*] (TTSB) ... SIS
Paine Webber Group [*AMEX symbol*] (SAG) ... DLY
Paine Webber Group [*AMEX symbol*] (SAG) ... FCW
Paine Webber Group [*AMEX symbol*] (SAG) ... HCW
Paine Webber Group [*AMEX symbol*] (SAG) ... HPW
Paine Webber Group [*NYSE symbol*] (TTSB) ... PWJ
Paine Webber Group [*AMEX symbol*] (SAG) ... SIS
Paine, Webber, Jackson & Curtis [*Later, Paine Webber, Inc.*] ... PWJC
Paine Webber Premier Tax Free Income [*Associated Press*] (SAG) ... PainWP
Paine's United States Circuit Court Reports [*A publication*] (DLA) ... Pa
Paine's United States Circuit Court Reports [*A publication*] (DLA) ... Pai
Paine's United States Circuit Court Reports [*A publication*] (DLA) ... Paine
Paine's United States Circuit Court Reports [*A publication*] (DLA) ... Paine CC
Paine's United States Circuit Court Reports [*A publication*] (DLA) ... Paine CCR
Paine's United States Circuit Court Reports [*A publication*] (DLA) ... Paine Cir Ct R
Painesville, OH [*Location identifier FAA*] (FAAL) ... PVZ
Painesville, OH [*AM radio station call letters*] ... WBKC
PaineWebber Group [*Associated Press*] (SAG) ... PWDY
PaineWebber Group [*Associated Press*] (SAG) ... PWDY496
PaineWebber Group [*NYSE symbol*] (SAG) ... PWP
PaineWebber Group [*Associated Press*] (SAG) ... PWUSJ
PaineWebber Group [*AMEX symbol*] (SAG) ... PWY
PaineWebber Group, Inc. [*Associated Press*] (SAG) ... PainWeb
PaineWebber Group, Inc. [*Associated Press*] (SAG) ... PWHK
PaineWebber Group, Inc. [*NYSE symbol*] (SPSG) ... PWJ
PaineWebber Group, Inc. [*Associated Press*] (SAG) ... PWSPMid
PaineWebber Group, Inc. [*Associated Press*] (SAG) ... PWUSD
PaineWebber Premier High Income Trust [*Associated Press*] (SAG) ... PWPHIT
PaineWebber Premier Insured Municipal Income Fund [*Associated Press*] (SAG) ... PWPIM
PaineWebber Premium High Income [*NYSE symbol*] (SPSG) ... PHT
PaineWebber Premium Insured Municipal Income [*NYSE symbol*] (SPSG) ... PIF
Painful Tonic Seizure (AAMN) ... PTS
Paint (MSA) ... PNT
Paint ... PNT
Paint (AD) ... pnt
Paint (VRA) ... pt
Paint and Wallpaper Association of America [*Later, NDPA*] (EA) ... PWAA
Paint, Body, and Equipment [*Automotive engineering*] ... PBE
Paint, Body, and Equipment Association (EA) ... PBEA
Paint Filter Liquids Test [*Environmental science*] (FFDE) ... PFLT
Paint Hills [*Canada*] [*Airport symbol*] (OAG) ... YNC
Paint Manufacture and Allied Trades' Association [*British*] (BI) ... PMATA
Paint on Tangent (IAA) ... POT
Paint, Pesticide Chemicals, and Solvents ... PPS
Paint Research Association [*British*] ... PRA
Paint Research Institute [*Defunct*] (EA) ... PRI
Paint Research Station [*British*] (BI) ... PRS
Paint Spray Outfit ... PSO
Painted ... PNTD
Painted (AD) ... pntd
Painted (VRA) ... ptd
Painted (AAG) ... PTD
Painted Base (AAG) ... PB
Painted Metal (AD) ... pmet
Painted Soda Bottles Collectors Association (EA) ... PSBCA
Painter (AD) ... pntr
Painter ... PNTR
Painter (ADA) ... PR
Painter ... PTR
Painter (VRA) ... ptr
Painter/Apprentice Painter (AAG) ... P/AP
Painter Creek, AK [*Location identifier FAA*] (FAAL) ... IPK
Painter Creek, AK [*Location identifier FAA*] (FAAL) ... PCE
Painter Metal (AAG) ... PMET
Painters' Registration Board [*Western Australia*] ... PRB
Painting (ROG) ... PAINT
Painting ... PAINT
Painting (VRA) ... ptg
Painting and Decorating Contractors of America (EA) ... PDCA
Painting Brushmakers' Provident Society [*A union*] [*British*] ... PBPS
Painting Machine ... PM
Painting System ... PS
Paintmakers Association [*British*] (DBA) ... PA
Paints and Oil (AD) ... p & o
Paints and Oil ... P & O
Paintstick (VRA) ... ptst
Paintsville, KY [*AM radio station call letters*] ... WKLW
Paintsville, KY [*FM radio station call letters*] ... WKLW-FM
Paintsville, KY [*AM radio station call letters*] ... WSIP
Paintsville, KY [*FM radio station call letters*] ... WSIP-FM
Pair (IAA) ... P
Pair (KSC) ... PR
Pair (AD) ... pr
Pair (ODBW) ... pr
Pair Attraction Inventory [*Premarital, marital, and family counseling test*] [*Psychology*] ... PAI
Pair Distribution Function [*Physical chemistry*] ... PDF
Pair Feeding (DMAA) ... PF
Pair Inter Langues [*Bourg La Reine, France*] (EAIO) ... PIL
Pair Natural Orbital Configuration Interaction [*Atomic physics*] ... PNO-CI
Pair Orthogonalized Lowdin [*Physics*] ... POL
Pair Selected Ternary [*Computer science*] ... PST
Pair Shield Video (NITA) ... PSV
Paired [*for or against*] [*Votes in Congress*] ... P
Paired Associate Learning Subtest [*Speech and language therapy*] (DAVI) ... PALS
Paired Associates [*Psychometrics*] ... PA
Paired Comparisons [*Education*] (EDAC) ... PC
Paired Cone Pigments [*Vision physiology*] ... PCP
Paired Hands Test [*Education*] (EDAC) ... PHT
Paired Helical Filaments [*Neuroanatomy*] [*Term coined by Dr. Robert Terry to describe the components of neurofibrillary tangles in the brains of Alzheimer's Disease patients*] ... PHF
Paired Perpendicular Keratotomy [*Procedure to correct astigmatism*] ... PPK
Paired Selected Ternary (IAA) ... PST
Paired Wire [*Telecommunications*] (TEL) ... PRW
Paired-Associates Learning [*Task*] [*Psychology*] ... PAL
Paired-Ion Chromatography ... PIC
Paired-Pulse Facilitation [*Neurophysiology*] ... PPF
Pairgain Technologies [*NASDAQ symbol*] (SAG) ... PAIR
Pairgain Technologies [*Associated Press*] (SAG) ... PairTch
Pairpoint Cup Plate Collectors of America (EA) ... PCPCA
Pairs ... PRS
Pairwise Correlated Generalized Valence Bond [*Physics*] ... PCGVB
PAIS Foreign Language Index (NITA) ... PAIS FLI
Paisajes Espanoles SA [*Spain ICAO designator*] (FAAC) ... PAE
Paise [*Monetary unit*] [*India*] ... P
Paisley Branch, Bruce County Public Library, Ontario [*Library symbol National Library of Canada*] (NLC) ... OPAI
Paissa [*Costa Rica*] [*ICAO location identifier*] (ICLI) ... MRPI
Paissa [*Costa Rica*] [*ICAO location identifier*] (ICLI) ... MRPS
Paita [*Peru*] [*ICAO location identifier*] (ICLI) ... SPIT
Pajamas ... PJ
Pajamas [*Slang*] ... PJ's
Pajaro Valley Historical Association, Watsonville, CA [*Library symbol*] [*Library of Congress*] (LCLS) ... CWatsHi
Pak Lay [*Laos*] [*Airport symbol*] (AD) ... PKY
Pak [*or Phak*] **Mai** [*New Party*] [*Political party*] ... PM
Pakatoa [*New Zealand*] [*Airport symbol*] (AD) ... ZED
Pakenham Township Public Library, Ontario [*Library symbol National Library of Canada*] (BIB) ... OPT
Pakistan [*MARC geographic area code Library of Congress*] (LCCP) ... a-pk--
Pakistan [*ANSI three-letter standard code*] (CNC) ... PAK
Pakistan (VRA) ... Pak
Pakistan [*IYRU nationality code*] [*MARC country of publication code Library of Congress*] (LCCP) ... pk
Pakistan [*ANSI two-letter standard code*] (CNC) ... PK
Pakistan Army ... PA
Pakistan Army Education Corps [*British military*] (DMA) ... PAEC
Pakistan Army Medical Corps ... PAMC
Pakistan Army Ordnance Corps [*British military*] (DMA) ... PAOC
Pakistan Army Physical Training Corps [*British military*] (DMA) ... PAPTC
Pakistan Association of Special Libraries (NITA) ... PASLIB
Pakistan Atomic Research Reactor ... PARR
Pakistan Australia Association of Western Australia ... PAAWA
Pakistan Australia Friendship Association [*Australia*] ... PAFA
Pakistan Bar Journal [*A publication*] (DLA) ... Pak Bar J
Pakistan Broadcasting Corp. (IMH) ... PBC
Pakistan Committee for Democracy and Justice [*Defunct*] (EA) ... PCDJ
Pakistan Council of Scientific and Industrial Research ... PCSIR
Pakistan Criminal Law Journal [*A publication*] (DLA) ... Pak Crim LJ
Pakistan Democratic Front ... PDF
Pakistan Democratic Party [*Political party*] (PD) ... PDP
Pakistan Institute of Nuclear Science and Technology ... PINSTECH
Pakistan International Airlines Corp. [*ICAO designator*] (FAAC) ... PIA
Pakistan Investment Fd [*NYSE symbol*] (TTSB) ... PKF
Pakistan Investment Fund [*NYSE symbol*] (SPSG) ... PKF
Pakistan Investment Fund, Inc. [*Associated Press*] (SAG) ... PakisInv
Pakistan Islamic Front [*Pakistan*] [*Political party*] (ECON) ... PIF
Pakistan Law Reports [*India*] [*A publication*] (DLA) ... Pak LR
Pakistan Law Reports [*A publication*] (DLA) ... PLR
Pakistan Law Reports, Dacca Series [*A publication*] (DLA) ... Dacca
Pakistan Law Reports, Dacca Series [*A publication*] (DLA) ... PLR Dacca
Pakistan Law Reports, Karachi Series [*A publication*] (DLA) ... Kar
Pakistan Law Reports, Karachi Series [*1947-53*] [*A publication*] (DLA) ... PLR Kar
Pakistan Law Reports, Lahore Series [*A publication*] (DLA) ... Lah
Pakistan Law Reports, Lahore Series [*1947-55*] [*A publication*] (DLA) ... PLR Lah
Pakistan Law Reports, West Pakistan Series [*A publication*] (DLA) ... PLRWP
Pakistan Law Reports, West Pakistan Series [*A publication*] (DLA) ... WP
Pakistan Law Review [*A publication*] (DLA) ... Pak L Rev
Pakistan Law Review [*A publication*] (DLA) ... PLR
Pakistan Liberation Army (PD) ... PLA
Pakistan Liberation Movement [*Political party*] (PD) ... PLM
Pakistan Medical Research Council ... PMRC
Pakistan Minerals Development Corp. (AD) ... PMDC
Pakistan Muslim League [*Political party*] ... PML
Pakistan Narcotics Control Board ... PNCB
Pakistan National Alliance (PD) ... PNA
Pakistan National Congress [*Political party*] ... PNC
Pakistan National League [*Political party*] ... PNL
Pakistan National Party [*Political party*] (PD) ... PNP
Pakistan National Scientific and Documentation Center [*Later, PASTIC*] ... PANSDOC
Pakistan National Scientific and Documentation Center, Karachi, Pakistan [*Library symbol Library of Congress*] (LCLS) ... PkKP
Pakistan National Scientific and Technical Documentation Center (AD) ... PNSTDC

Pakistan National Scientific and Technology Documentation Centre (NITA) ... PANSDOC
Pakistan Naval Ship (AD) ... PNS
Pakistan Navy ... PN
Pakistan People's Party [*Political party*] (PD) ... PPP
Pakistan Press Association (AD) ... PPA
Pakistan Press Association (NADA) ... PPA
Pakistan Press International ... PPI
Pakistan Railways (DCTA) ... PR
Pakistan Science Foundation ... PSF
Pakistan Scientific and Technological Information Center [*Formerly, PANSDOC*] [*Quaid-I-Azan University Campus Islamabad, Pakistan*] ... PASTIC
Pakistan Standard (IAA) ... PS
Pakistan Standards Institution (IAA) ... PSI
Pakistan Students' Association of America ... PSAA
Pakistan Supreme Court Law Quarterly [*Lahore, Pakistan*] [*A publication*] (DLA) ... Pak Sup Ct Q
Pakistan Transport Workers' Federation ... PTWF
Pakistani Air Force ... PkAF
Pak-Man Resources, Inc. [*Vancouver Stock Exchange symbol*] ... PAC
Pakokku [*Myanmar*] [*Airport symbol*] (OAG) ... PKK
Pakokku [*Myanmar*] [*ICAO location identifier*] (ICLI) ... VBPU
Paksane [*Laos*] [*ICAO location identifier*] (ICLI) ... VLPK
Pakse [*Laos*] [*Airport symbol*] (AD) ... PKZ
Pakse [*Laos*] [*ICAO location identifier*] (ICLI) ... VLPS
PAL Aerolineas SA de CV [*Mexico ICAO designator*] (FAAC) ... LPA
PAL [*Permissive Action Link*] **Management Control Team** [*Army*] (AABC) ... PMCT
PAL Reading Service, Toronto, ON, Canada [*Library symbol*] [*Library of Congress*] (LCLS) ... CaOTPAL
PAL Reading Service, Toronto, Ontario [*Library symbol National Library of Canada*] (NLC) ... OTPAL
Pala [*Chad*] [*ICAO location identifier*] (ICLI) ... FTTP
Pala [*Chad*] [*Airport symbol*] (AD) ... PLF
Palace (ROG) ... P
Palace ... PAL
Palace (VRA) ... pala
Palace ... PALC
Palach Press Ltd. [*British*] (EAIO) ... PPL
Palacios [*Texas*] [*ICAO location identifier*] (ICLI) ... KPSX
Palacios, TX [*FM radio station call letters*] (RBYB) ... KKOS-FM
Palacios, TX [*Location identifier FAA*] (FAAL) ... PSX
Paladin Fuel Technology [*Vancouver Stock Exchange symbol*] ... PAN
Palaemontes-Lightening Hormone ... PLH
Palaeobotany ... PALAEOB
Palaeography ... PALAEOG
Palaeontology ... PALAEONT
Palaeozoic Axial Zone [*Geophysics*] ... PAZ
Palair Macedonian [*Yugoslavia*] [*ICAO designator*] (FAAC) ... PMK
Palamedes [*of Gorgias*] [*Classical studies*] (OCD) ... Pal
Palangkaraya [*Indonesia*] [*Airport symbol*] (OAG) ... PKY
Palangkaraya/Panarung [*Indonesia*] [*ICAO location identifier*] (ICLI) ... WRBP
Palapye [*Botswana*] [*ICAO location identifier*] (ICLI) ... FBPY
Palascia [*Italy ICAO location identifier*] (ICLI) ... LIBL
Palate (DMAA) ... pal
Palatine [*or Palatinate*] [*Genealogy*] ... PAL
Palatine Public Library District, Palatine, IL [*Library symbol Library of Congress*] (LCLS) ... IPal
Palatines to America (EA) ... PTA
Palatka, FL [*FM radio station call letters*] ... WFKS
Palatka, FL [*FM radio station call letters*] ... WHIF
Palatka, FL [*AM radio station call letters*] ... WIYD
Palatka, FL [*AM radio station call letters*] ... WPLK
Palau [*Palau Islands*] [*Seismograph station code, US Geological Survey Closed*] (SEIS) ... PLA
Palau [*ANSI three-letter standard code*] (CNC) ... PLW
Palau [*ANSI two-letter standard code*] (CNC) ... PW
Palaung State Liberation Army [*Myanmar*] [*Political party*] (EY) ... PSLA
Palaung State Liberation Organization [*Myanmar*] [*Political party*] (EY) ... PSLO
Palaw [*Myanmar*] [*ICAO location identifier*] (ICLI) ... VBPW
Palazzo (VRA) ... pala
Pale (ADA) ... P
Pale Soft Exudative [*Pork*] ... PSE
Pale Yellow Candle [*Baltic coffee-house*] [*London*] (DSUE) ... PYC
Palembang [*Indonesia*] [*Airport symbol*] (OAG) ... PLM
Palembang Sector [*Indonesia*] [*ICAO location identifier*] (ICLI) ... WIPZ
Palembang/Sultan Mahmud Badaruddin II [*Indonesia*] [*ICAO location identifier*] (ICLI) ... WIPP
Palenque [*Mexico*] [*Airport symbol*] (AD) ... PGM
Paleobioclimatic Operator ... PBO
Paleobotany (BARN) ... paleob
Paleoclimate Modeling Intercomparison Project [*Marine science*] (OSRA) ... PMIP
Paleoecologic ... PALEOECOL
Paleogeographic ... PALEOGEOG
Paleography (ROG) ... PAL
Paleography ... paleog
Paleolithic (VRA) ... Paleol
Paleontologic ... PALEONT
Paleontological Research Institution (EA) ... PRI
Paleontological Society (EA) ... PS
Paleontology ... PAL
Paleontology ... paleon
Paleopathology Association ... PA
Paleopathology Association (EA) ... PPA
Paleosecular Variation [*Geology*] ... PSV
Paleozoic [*Period, era, or system*] [*Geology*] ... PAL
Palermo [*California*] [*Seismograph station code, US Geological Survey*] (SEIS) ... PAM
Palermo [*Italy*] [*Airport symbol*] (OAG) ... PMO
Palermo/Boccadifalco [*Italy ICAO location identifier*] (ICLI) ... LICP
Palermo/Punta Raisi [*Italy ICAO location identifier*] (ICLI) ... LICJ
Palermo Resources, Inc. [*Vancouver Stock Exchange symbol*] ... PMO
Palestine ... PAL
Palestine (VRA) ... Pale
Palestine Affairs [*New York*] [*A publication*] (BJA) ... PA
Palestine Aid Society of America (EA) ... PAS
Palestine Arab Delegation (EA) ... PAD
Palestine Armed Struggle Command (PD) ... PASC
Palestine Broadcasting Service (BJA) ... PBS
Palestine Congress of North America [*Defunct*] (EA) ... PCNA
Palestine Economic Commission ... PEC
Palestine Economic Council for Development and Reconstruction (ECON) ... PECDAR
Palestine Economic Development and Reconstruction Agency (ECON) ... PEDRA
Palestine Endowment Funds [*Later, PEF Israel Endowment Funds*] (EA) ... PEF
Palestine Exploration Fund ... PEF
Palestine Exploration Fund. Quarterly Statement [*London*] [*A publication*] (BJA) ... PEFQS
Palestine Exploration Fund. Quarterly Statement [*London*] [*A publication*] (BJA) ... PEFQST
Palestine Human Rights Campaign (EA) ... PHRC
Palestine Human Rights Information Center (EA) ... PHRIC
Palestine Information Office (EA) ... PIO
Palestine Israelite Colonisation Association ... PICA
Palestine Liberation Army ... PLA
Palestine Liberation Front [*Political party*] (PD) ... PLF
Palestine Liberation Organization [*Political party*] (PD) ... PLO
Palestine National Council (PD) ... PNC
Palestine National Front [*Political party*] (PD) ... PNF
Palestine National Liberation Movement [*Political party*] (BJA) ... PNLM
Palestine Red Crescent (AD) ... PRC
Palestine Rejection Front (BJA) ... PRF
Palestine Research and Educational Center (EA) ... PREC
Palestine Solidarity Committee [*Defunct*] (EA) ... PSC
Palestine Study Group (EA) ... PSG
Palestine Symphonic Choir Project (EA) ... PSCP
Palestine, TX [*FM radio station call letters*] ... KLIS
Palestine, TX [*AM radio station call letters*] ... KNET
Palestine, TX [*FM radio station call letters*] ... KYYK
Palestine, TX [*Location identifier FAA*] (FAAL) ... PSN
[*The*] **Palestine Year Book** [*New York*] [*A publication*] (BJA) ... PYB
Palestiner Komunistische Partei [*Palestine Communist Party*] [*Political party*] (BJA) ... PKP
Palestinian Authority [*Political movement*] (ECON) ... PA
Palestinian Ceramic Chronology [*200BC-70AD*] [*A publication*] (BJA) ... PCC
Palestinian Communist Party [*Political party*] (PD) ... PCP
Palestinian Interim Self-Government Authority [*Proposed*] (ECON) ... PISGA
Palestinian National Authority [*Political party*] (ECON) ... PNA
Palestinian Popular Struggle Front [*Political party*] (BJA) ... PPSF
Palestinian Talmud (BJA) ... TP
Palette (VRA) ... pal
Paletwa [*Myanmar*] [*ICAO location identifier*] (ICLI) ... VBPE
Paley on Principal and Agent [*3rd ed.*] [*1833*] [*A publication*] (DLA) ... Pal Ag
Paley on Principal and Agent [*A publication*] (DLA) ... Paley Ag
Paley on Principal and Agent [*3rd ed.*] [*1833*] [*A publication*] (DLA) ... Paley Princ & Ag
Paley on Summary Convictions [*10th ed.*] [*1953*] [*A publication*] (DLA) ... Pal Conv
PALFED, Inc. [*Associated Press*] (SAG) ... Palfed
PALFED, Inc. [*NASDAQ symbol*] (NQ) ... PALM
Palgrave's Proceedings in Chancery [*A publication*] (DLA) ... Palg Ch
Palgrave's Proceedings in Chancery [*A publication*] (DLA) ... Palgrave
Palgrave's Rise and Progress of the English Commonwealth [*1832*] [*A publication*] (DLA) ... Palg Rise & Prog
Palgrave's Rise and Progress of the English Commonwealth [*A publication*] (DLA) ... Palg Rise Etc
Palgrave's Rise and Progress of the English Commonwealth [*A publication*] (DLA) ... Palgrave
Pali [*MARC language code Library of Congress*] (LCCP) ... pli
Pali Text Society (EA) ... PTS
PALINET and Union Library Catalogue of Pennsylvania [*Philadelphia, PA*] [*Library network*] ... PALINET/ULC
PALINET [*Pennsylvania Area Library Network*] **Central, Philadelphia, PA** [*OCLC symbol*] (OCLC) ... QIP
Paling Fence ... PF
Palio Air Service [*Italy ICAO designator*] (FAAC) ... PLS
Palisade Diabase [*Geology*] ... PD
Palisade Junior-Senior High School, Palisade, CO [*Library symbol Library of Congress*] (LCLS) ... CoPalJS
Palisade Public Library, Palisade, CO [*Library symbol Library of Congress*] (LCLS) ... CoPal
Palisades [*New York*] [*Seismograph station code, US Geological Survey*] (SEIS) ... PAL
Palisades Free Library, Palisades, NY [*Library symbol Library of Congress*] (LCLS) ... NPals
Palisades Newspapers, Englewood, NJ [*Library symbol Library of Congress*] (LCLS) ... NjEnPa
Palisades Nuclear Power Station (NRCH) ... PNPS
Palisades Plant [*Nuclear energy*] (NRCH) ... PP
Palisades Printing Corp., Cliffside Park, NJ [*Library symbol Library of Congress*] (LCLS) ... NjClpP

Pall Corp. [*Associated Press*] (SAG) ... PallCp
Pall Corp. [*NYSE symbol*] (SAG) ... PLL
Pall Corp., Glen Cove, NY [*Library symbol Library of Congress*] (LCLS) ... NGlcP
Pall Mall Gazette [*A publication*] ... PMG
Pall Mall Money Management [*Investment group*] [*British*] ... PMMM
Palladium [*Chemical element*] (ROG) ... PA
Palladium [*Chemical element*] ... Pd
Palladium Print (VRA) ... PAPT
Palladium-Nickel (EECA) ... PALLNIC
Pallet [*Spacelab*] [*NASA*] (NASA) ... P
Pallet [*Freight*] ... PALL
Pallet [*Building construction*] ... PLL
Pallet (NATG) ... PLLT
Pallet (AABC) ... PLT
Pallet Coolant Loop (NASA) ... PCL
Pallet Torque Hook ... PTH
Pallet Transporter Unit [*Military*] (CAAL) ... PTU
Pallet Truck (DCTA) ... PT
Pallet Utility Support Structure [*NASA*] (MCD) ... PUSS
Palleted Automated Transport (PDAA) ... PAT
Palletized Inertial Navigation System [*Military*] (LAIN) ... PINS
Palletized Load System [*Army*] (RDA) ... PLS
Palletized Night Attack System ... PNAS
Palletizing Optimization Potential (AD) ... POP
Pallet-Only Mode [*NASA*] (NASA) ... POM
Pallet-Size Container (MCD) ... PALCON
Palliative Care Foundation [*Canada*] (EAIO) ... PCF
Palliative Care Service ... PCS
Palliative Care Unit [*Medicine*] (CPH) ... PCU
Palliser Regional Library, Moose Jaw, Saskatchewan [*Library symbol National Library of Canada*] (NLC) ... SMJP
Palliser Regional Library, Moose Jaw, SK, Canada [*Library symbol Library of Congress*] (LCLS) ... CaSMJP
Pallor (KSC) ... PAL
Pallotine Missionary Sisters Queen of Apostles Prov (TOCD) ... SAC
Pallottine House of Studies ... PHS
Palm and Cycad Societies of Australia ... PCSA
Palm Bay, FL [*FM radio station call letters*] ... WEJF
Palm Bay, FL [*FM radio station call letters*] ... WWIA
Palm Beach [*Diocesan abbreviation*] [*Florida*] (TOCD) ... PMB
Palm Beach Atlantic College, West Palm Beach, FL [*Library symbol*] [*Library of Congress*] (LCLS) ... FWpbC
Palm Beach County Public Library System, West Palm Beach, FL [*Library symbol Library of Congress*] (LCLS) ... FWpbP
Palm Beach County Utility Corp. [*Toronto Stock Exchange symbol*] ... PBU
Palm Beach, FL [*Television station call letters*] ... WFGC
Palm Beach, FL [*AM radio station call letters*] ... WPBR
Palm Beach, FL [*FM radio station call letters*] ... WRMF
Palm Beach International Airport [*FAA*] (TAG) ... PBI
Palm Beach Junior College [*Lakeworth, FL*] ... PBJC
Palm Beach Junior College, Lake Worth, FL [*OCLC symbol*] (OCLC) ... EFM
Palm Beach Junior College, Lake Worth, FL [*Library symbol Library of Congress*] (LCLS) ... FLwP
Palm Beach Junior College, North Campus Library, Lake Worth, FL [*OCLC symbol*] (OCLC) ... EFN
Palm Beach Psychotherapy Training Center (EA) ... PBPTC
Palm City, FL [*FM radio station call letters*] ... WCNO
Palm Desert, CA [*FM radio station call letters*] ... KEZN
Palm Desert, CA [*FM radio station call letters*] ... KHCS
Palm Fatty Acid Distillate [*Organic chemistry*] ... PFAD
Palm Harbor Homes [*NASDAQ symbol*] (TTSB) ... PHHM
Palm Harbor Homes, Inc. [*Associated Press*] (SAG) ... PalmHH
Palm Harbor Homes, Inc. [*NASDAQ symbol*] (SAG) ... PHHM
Palm Island [*Queensland*] [*Airport symbol*] (AD) ... PCE
Palm Island [*Windward Islands, West Indies*] [*Airport symbol*] (AD) ... TTD
Palm Leaf [*Reaction*] [*Medicine*] ... PL
Palm Society [*Later, IPS*] (EA) ... PS
Palm Springs [*California*] [*Airport symbol*] (OAG) ... PSP
Palm Springs, CA [*AM radio station call letters*] ... KCMJ
Palm Springs, CA [*AM radio station call letters*] (RBYB) ... KDES
Palm Springs, CA [*FM radio station call letters*] ... KDES-FM
Palm Springs, CA [*Television station call letters*] ... KESQ
Palm Springs, CA [*Television station call letters*] ... KMIR
Palm Springs, CA [*FM radio station call letters*] ... KPLM
Palm Springs, CA [*FM radio station call letters*] ... KPSC
Palm Springs, CA [*AM radio station call letters*] ... KPSI
Palm Springs, CA [*FM radio station call letters*] ... KPSI-FM
Palm Springs, CA [*Location identifier FAA*] (FAAL) ... PSP
Palm Springs Golf 'Unit' [*NASDAQ symbol*] (TTSB) ... PSGCU
Palm Springs Public Library, Palm Springs, CA [*OCLC symbol*] (OCLC) ... CPG
Palm Springs Public Library, Palm Springs, CA [*Library symbol Library of Congress*] (LCLS) ... CPs
Palm Springs Savings Bank [*Associated Press*] (SAG) ... PlmSSB
Palm Springs Savings Bank [*Palm Springs, CA*] [*NASDAQ symbol*] (NQ) ... PSSB
Palm Springs Svgs Bk [*NASDAQ symbol*] (TTSB) ... PSSB
Palma [*Spain ICAO location identifier*] (ICLI) ... LECP
Palma [*Mallorca Island*] [*Airport symbol*] (OAG) ... PMI
Palma De Mallorca [*Spain ICAO location identifier*] (ICLI) ... LEPA
Palma de Mallorca Balearic Islands, Spain (AD) ... PMI
Palmar [*Costa Rica*] [*Airport symbol*] (AD) ... PMZ
Palmar Sur [*Costa Rica*] [*ICAO location identifier*] (ICLI) ... MRPM
Palmar Sweat Index (EDAC) ... PSI
Palmar Wireless [*NASDAQ symbol*] (SAG) ... PWIR
Palmaria [*Italy ICAO location identifier*] (ICLI) ... LIQP
Palmaris Longus (DMAA) ... Pl
Palmarito [*Venezuela*] [*Airport symbol*] (OAG) ... PTM
Palmarito, Apure [*Venezuela ICAO location identifier*] (ICLI) ... SVPT
Palmdale/Air Force Plant No. 42 [*California*] [*ICAO location identifier*] (ICLI) ... KPMD
Palmdale, CA [*AM radio station call letters*] ... KUTY
Palmdale, CA [*Location identifier FAA*] (FAAL) ... PMD
Palmdale, CA (NASA) ... PMDL
Palmdale Final Assembly [*NASA*] (NASA) ... PFA
Palmdale/Lancaster [*California*] [*Airport symbol*] (OAG) ... PMD
Palmdale/Lancaster [*California*] **Fox** [*Airport symbol*] (OAG) ... WJF
Palmer [*Alaska*] [*ICAO location identifier*] (ICLI) ... PAAQ
Palmer [*Alaska*] [*Seismograph station code, US Geological Survey*] (SEIS) ... PMR
Palmer, AK [*Location identifier FAA*] (FAAL) ... FGS
Palmer, AK [*FM radio station call letters*] (RBYB) ... KEEN
Palmer, AK [*Location identifier FAA*] (FAAL) ... PAQ
Palmer - Arctic Valley [*Alaska*] [*Seismograph station code, US Geological Survey*] (SEIS) ... PMS
Palmer College of Chiropractic, Davenport, IA [*Library symbol Library of Congress*] (LCLS) ... IaDaP
Palmer Drought Index ... PDI
Palmer Drought Severity Index [*Meteorology*] ... PDSI
Palmer Drug Abuse Program (DMAA) ... PDAP
Palmer Industries Ltd. [*Vancouver Stock Exchange symbol*] ... PMD
Palmer, MA [*Location identifier FAA*] (FAAL) ... PMX
Palmer Physical Laboratory [*Princeton University*] (MCD) ... PPL
Palmer Public Library, Palmer, AK [*Library symbol Library of Congress*] (LCLS) ... AkPal
Palmer Public Library, Palmer, IA [*Library symbol Library of Congress*] (LCLS) ... IaPal
Palmer Skin Conductance ... PSC
Palmer Wireless [*Associated Press*] (SAG) ... PlmrW
Palmer Wireless 'A' [*NASDAQ symbol*] (TTSB) ... PWIR
Palmer-Houston [*Alaska*] [*Seismograph station code, US Geological Survey*] (SEIS) ... PWA
Palmerola [*Honduras*] [*ICAO location identifier*] (ICLI) ... MHPA
Palmer's Assizes at Cambridge [*England*] [*A publication*] (DLA) ... Pal
Palmer's Assizes at Cambridge [*England*] [*A publication*] (DLA) ... Palm
Palmer's Assizes at Cambridge [*England*] [*A publication*] (DLA) ... Palmer
Palmer's Company Law [*22nd ed.*] [*1976*] [*A publication*] (DLA) ... Palm Comp L
Palmer's Company Precedents [*17th ed.*] [*1956-60*] [*A publication*] (DLA) ... Palm Comp Prec
Palmer's Company Precedents [*16 eds.*] [*1877-1952*] [*A publication*] (DLA) ... Palmer Co Prec
Palmer's English King's Bench Reports [*1619-29*] [*A publication*] (DLA) ... Pal
Palmer's English King's Bench Reports [*1619-29*] [*A publication*] (DLA) ... Palm
Palmer's English King's Bench Reports [*A publication*] (DLA) ... Palmer
Palmer's Law of Wreck [*1843*] [*A publication*] (DLA) ... Palm Wr
Palmer's Practice in the House of Lords [*1830*] [*A publication*] (DLA) ... Palm Pr Lords
Palmer's Private Companies [*41st ed.*] [*1950*] [*A publication*] (DLA) ... Palmer Pr Comp
Palmer's Reports [*53-60 Vermont*] [*A publication*] (DLA) ... Pal
Palmer's Reports [*53-60 Vermont*] [*A publication*] (DLA) ... Palm
Palmer's Reports [*53-60 Vermont*] [*A publication*] (DLA) ... Palmer
Palmer's Shareholders [*34th ed.*] [*1936*] [*A publication*] (DLA) ... Palm Sh
Palmerston North [*New Zealand*] [*ICAO location identifier*] (ICLI) ... NZPM
Palmerston North [*New Zealand*] [*Airport symbol*] (OAG) ... PMR
Palmetto, FL [*AM radio station call letters*] ... WBRD
Palmico County Library, Bayboro, NC [*Library symbol Library of Congress*] (LCLS) ... NcBy
Palmira [*Bolivia*] [*ICAO location identifier*] (ICLI) ... SLPM
Palmistry (ADA) ... PALM
Palmitoyl Carnitine [*Biochemistry*] ... PC
Palmitoyl Homocysteine [*Biochemistry*] ... PHC
Palmitoyl Hydrolyzed Animal Protein [*Organic chemistry*] ... PHAP
Palmitoyl-Protein Thioesterase [*An enzyme*] ... PPT
Palmoplantar Keratoderma [*Dermatology*] ... PPK
Palmoplantar Keratosis [*Medicine*] (DMAA) ... PPK
Palmoplantar Pustulosis [*Medicine*] (DMAA) ... PPP
Palms ... PLMS
Palmyra [*Syria*] [*ICAO location identifier*] (ICLI) ... OSPR
Palmyra [*Syria*] [*Airport symbol*] (AD) ... TDM
Palmyra, MO [*FM radio station call letters*] ... KICK
Palmyra, NY [*FM radio station call letters*] ... WZXV
Palmyra, PA [*FM radio station call letters*] (RBYB) ... WNCE-FM
Palmyra, Palymra Island [*Line Islands*] [*ICAO location identifier*] (ICLI) ... PLPA
Palmyrene (BJA) ... Palm
Palo [*Philippines*] [*Seismograph station code, US Geological Survey*] (SEIS) ... PLP
Palo Alto - Branner [*California*] [*Seismograph station code, US Geological Survey Closed*] (SEIS) ... PAC
Palo Alto, CA [*AM radio station call letters*] ... KDFC
Palo Alto, CA [*Location identifier FAA*] (FAAL) ... PAO
Palo Alto City Library, Palo Alto, CA [*Library symbol Library of Congress*] (LCLS) ... CPa
Palo Alto College, San Antonio, TX [*Library symbol*] [*Library of Congress*] (LCLS) ... TxSaPA
Palo Alto Medical Research Foundation [*Research center*] (RCD) ... PAMRF
Palo Alto Research Center [*Xerox Corp.*] ... PARC
Palo Alto Social Background Inventory [*Psychology*] ... PASBI
Palo Verde [*Costa Rica*] [*ICAO location identifier*] (ICLI) ... MRPE
Palo Verde Junior College [*California*] ... PVJC
Palo Verde Nuclear Generating Station (NRCH) ... PVNGS
Palo Verde Valley District Library, Blythe, CA [*Library symbol Library of Congress*] (LCLS) ... CBl
Paloemeu/Vincent Fajks [*Surinam*] [*ICAO location identifier*] (ICLI) ... SMPA

Paloh/Liku [*Indonesia*] [*ICAO location identifier*] (ICLI) .... WIOH
Paloma Petroleum Ltd. [*Toronto Stock Exchange symbol*] .... PAL
Palomar [*California*] [*Seismograph station code, US Geological Survey*] (SEIS) .... PLM
Palomar Capital [*Vancouver Stock Exchange symbol*] .... PO
Palomar College, San Marcos, CA [*OCLC symbol*] (OCLC) .... CPD
Palomar College, San Marcos, CA [*Library symbol Library of Congress*] (LCLS) .... CSmarP
Palomar Med Tech [*NASDAQ symbol*] (TTSB) .... PMTI
Palomar Medical Technologies [*Associated Press*] (SAG) .... PalmrMd
Palomar Medical Technologies [*NASDAQ symbol*] (SAG) .... PMTI
Palomar Mountain Observatory (AD) .... pmo
Palomar Observatory Sky Survey [*NASA*] .... POSS
Palomar Sky Survey [*NASA*] .... PSS
Palomares Road [*California*] [*Seismograph station code, US Geological Survey*] (SEIS) .... PLC
Palomar-Leiden Survey .... PLS
Palomero Toluqueno [*Race of maize*] .... P-T
Palomino Horse Association (EA) .... PHA
Palomino Horse Breeders of America (EA) .... PHBA
Palomino Pony Registry .... PPR
Palomino Rabbit Co-Breeders Association (EA) .... PRCA
Palos Heights Public Library, Palos Heights, IL [*Library symbol Library of Congress*] (LCLS) .... IPhe
Palos Park Public Library, Palos Park, IL [*Library symbol Library of Congress*] (LCLS) .... IPpa
Palos Verdes [*California*] [*Seismograph station code, US Geological Survey Closed*] (SEIS) .... PVR
Palos Verdes Library District, Palos Verdes Estates, CA [*Library symbol Library of Congress*] (LCLS) .... CPv
Palouse Silt Loam [*Agronomy*] .... PSL
Palpable [*Medicine*] .... PALP
Palpation [*Medicine*] (DMAA) .... palp
Palpation, Percussion, and Auscultation [*Medicine*] .... PP & A
Palpation, Percussion, and Auscultation [*Medicine*] .... PPA
Palpitation [*Cardiology*] (DAVI) .... palp
Palpitation [*Medicine*] .... PALPI
Palpitation [*Medicine*] .... palpit
Palpitation, Percussion, and Auscultation (AD) .... pp & a
Palpitation, Percussion, Auscultation (AD) .... ppa
Palpus [*Arthropod anatomy*] .... PLP
Palu [*Indonesia*] [*Airport symbol*] (OAG) .... PLW
Palu/Mutiara [*Indonesia*] [*ICAO location identifier*] (ICLI) .... WAML
Paludonus [*Pierre de la Palu*] [*Deceased, 1342*] [*Authority cited in pre-1607 legal work*] (DSA) .... Palud
Palus Nebularum [*Lunar area*] .... PN
Palus Putretudinis [*Lunar area*] .... PP
Palytoxin [*Organic chemistry*] .... PTX
Pam and Peter Fisher [*Commercial firm British*] .... P & P
PAM [*Payload Assist Module*] **Atlas-Centaur Class Spacecraft** (NASA) .... PAM-A
PAM [*Payload Assist Module*] **Delta Class Spacecraft** (NASA) .... PAM-D
PAM Transportation Services, Inc. [*Associated Press*] (SAG) .... PAM
PAM Transportation Services, Inc. [*NASDAQ symbol*] (NQ) .... PTSI
P.A.M. Transportation Svcs [*NASDAQ symbol*] (TTSB) .... PTSI
Pama [*Burkina Faso*] [*ICAO location identifier*] (ICLI) .... DHEP
Pama [*Burkina Faso*] [*Airport symbol*] (OAG) .... XPA
Pamatai [*French Polynesia*] [*Geomagnetic observatory code*] .... PPT
Pambwa [*Papua New Guinea*] [*Airport symbol*] (OAG) .... PAW
PAMCAM, Inc., South Plainfield, NJ [*Library symbol Library of Congress*] (LCLS) .... NjSopP
Pamela's Political Action Committee [*Nickname of "Democrats for the '80's," a committee founded by Pamela Harriman*] .... PamPAC
Pamida Holdings [*AMEX symbol*] (TTSB) .... PAM
Pamida Holdings Corp. [*AMEX symbol*] (SPSG) .... PAM
Pamida Holdings Corp. [*Associated Press*] (SAG) .... PamHld
Pamiers/Les Pujols [*France ICAO location identifier*] (ICLI) .... LFDJ
Pamitoyl-Oleoylphosphatidylcholine [*Biochemistry*] .... POPC
Pamlico Technical Institute, Alliance, NC [*Library symbol Library of Congress*] (LCLS) .... NcAlP
Pamol [*Malaysia*] [*Airport symbol*] (OAG) .... PAY
Pamol [*Malaysia*] [*ICAO location identifier*] (ICLI) .... WBKP
Pamorex Minerals, Inc. [*Toronto Stock Exchange symbol*] .... PMX
Pamour, Inc. [*Toronto Stock Exchange symbol*] .... PAM
Pampa [*Record label*] [*Brazil*] .... Pam
Pampa, TX [*AM radio station call letters*] .... KGRO
Pampa, TX [*FM radio station call letters*] .... KOMX
Pampa, TX [*Location identifier FAA*] (FAAL) .... PPA
Pampero [*River Plate gale*] [*Nautical term*] (DSUE) .... PAMP
Pamphlet .... P
Pamphlet (AFM) .... PAM
Pamphlet (WDMC) .... pam
Pamphlet [*Freight*] .... PAMPH
Pamphlet .... PM
Pamphlet (MSA) .... PMFLT
Pamphlet (DLA) .... PMPH
Pamphlet .... PPH
Pamphlet (AD) .... pph
Pamphlet Laws [*A publication*] (DLA) .... PL
Pamphlet Laws, Acts [*A publication*] (DLA) .... Pamph Laws
Pamphlet Laws, Acts [*A publication*] (DLA) .... Pamphl Laws
Pamplico, SC [*FM radio station call letters*] .... WMXT
Pamplona [*Spain*] [*Airport symbol*] (OAG) .... PNA
Pamplona/Noain-Pamplona [*Spain ICAO location identifier*] (ICLI) .... LEPP
Pamrapo Bancorp [*NASDAQ symbol*] (TTSB) .... PBCI
Pamrapo Bancorp, Inc. [*Associated Press*] (SAG) .... Pamrapo
Pamrapo Bancorp, Inc. [*NASDAQ symbol*] (NQ) .... PBCI
Pan African Association of Neurological Sciences (EAIO) .... PAANS
Pan African Freedom Movement for East, Central, and Southern Africa [*Superseded in 1963 by the liberation committee of the Organization of African Unity*] (PD) .... PAFMECSA
Pan African Institute for Development (EAIO) .... PAID
Pan Air, Inc. [*ICAO designator*] (FAAC) .... PAX
Pan Am Corp. [*AMEX symbol*] (SAG) .... PAA
Pan Am Corp. [*Associated Press*] (SAG) .... PanAmC
Pan Am Makes the Going Great [*Title of ballet choreographed by George Balanchine, taken from Pan American World Airways' slogan*] [*Pronounced "pam-ti-guh-guh"*] .... PAMTGG
Pan Am Weather Systems [*FAA designator*] (FAAC) .... XPA
Pan Amer Silver [*NASDAQ symbol*] (TTSB) .... PAASF
Pan America Climate Studies [*Marine science*] (OSRA) .... PACS
Pan American Allergy Society (EA) .... PAAS
Pan American Association of Educational Credit Institutions [*See also APICE*] (EAIO) .... PAAECI
Pan American Association of Educational Credit Institutions [*Bogota, Colombia*] (EAIO) .... PAECI
Pan American Basketball Confederation [*See also CPB*] (EAIO) .... PABC
Pan American Cancer Cytology Society [*Defunct*] (EA) .... PACCS
Pan American Center for Geographical Studies and Research [*See also CEPEIGE*] (EAIO) .... PACGSR
Pan American College [*Texas*] .... PAC
Pan American Commission of Tampa (EA) .... PACT
Pan American Council of International Committee of Scientific Management .... PACCIOS
Pan American Development Foundation (EA) .... PADF
Pan American Federation of Associations of Medical Schools [*See also FEPAFEM*] [*Caracas, Venezuela*] (EAIO) .... PAFAMS
Pan American Federation of Engineering Societies .... PFES
Pan American Foundation [*Defunct*] (EA) .... PAF
Pan American Grace Airways, Inc. [*Also, PANAGRA*] .... PAGA
Pan American Grace Airways, Inc. [*Also, PAGA*] .... PANAGRA
Pan American Health and Education Foundation (EA) .... PAHEF
Pan American Health Organization (EA) .... PAHO
Pan American Health Organization, Documentation Center, Division of Family Health, Washington, DC [*Library symbol Library of Congress*] (LCLS) .... DPAHO-FH
Pan American Health Organization, Pan American Sanitary Bureau, Washington, DC [*Library symbol Library of Congress*] (LCLS) .... DPAHO
Pan American Highway Congresses (EA) .... PAHC
Pan American Hockey Federation [*Winnipeg, MB*] (EAIO) .... PAHF
Pan American Implant Association (EA) .... PAIA
Pan American Institute of Geography and History [*Research center Mexico*] (IRC) .... PAIGH
Pan American Institute of Mining, Engineering, and Geology [*Defunct*] .... PAIMEG
Pan American Institute of Naval Engineering (EAIO) .... IPEN
Pan American Liaison Committee of Women's Organizations (EA) .... PALCO
Pan American Medical Association [*Also known as Association Medica Pan Americana*] (EA) .... PAMA
Pan American Medical Women's Alliance (EA) .... PAMWA
Pan American Minerals Corp. [*Toronto Stock Exchange symbol Vancouver Stock Exchange symbol*] .... PAA
Pan American Odontological Association (EA) .... PAOA
Pan American Oil Corp., Research Library, Tulsa, OK [*Library symbol Library of Congress*] (LCLS) .... OkTPA
Pan American Railway Congress Association .... PARCA
Pan American Round Tables in the USA [*Defunct*] (EA) .... PART
Pan American Sanitary Bureau .... PASB
Pan American Sanitary Conference .... PASC
Pan American Sanitary Organization .... PASO
Pan American Satellite [*Greenwich, CT*] [*Telecommunications service*] (TSSD) .... PanAmSat
Pan American Silver Corp. [*NASDAQ symbol*] (SAG) .... PAASF
Pan American Silver Corp. [*Associated Press*] (SAG) .... PanASlv
Pan American Society for Chemotherapy of Tuberculosis [*See also SAQT*] [*Buenos Aires, Argentina*] (EAIO) .... PASCT
Pan American Society of the United States (EA) .... PASUS
Pan American Sports Organization [*See also ODEPA*] [*Mexico City, Mexico*] (EAIO) .... PASO
Pan American Standards Commission [*See also COPANT*] (EAIO) .... PASC
Pan American Taekwondo Union (EA) .... PATU
Pan American Tung Research and Development League [*Defunct*] (EA) .... PATRDL
Pan American Union [*Central organ and permanent secretariat of the OAS*] .... PAU
Pan American Union of Baptist Men [*Defunct*] (EA) .... PAUBM
Pan American University, Edinburg, TX [*Library symbol Library of Congress*] (LCLS) .... TxEdP
Pan American University, Library, Edinburg, TX [*OCLC symbol*] (OCLC) .... TPN
Pan American Women's Association (EA) .... PAWA
Pan American World Airways Communications System .... PANAMAC
Pan American World Airways, Inc. [*See also PAA, PAN-AM, PN*] [*ICAO designator*] (MCD) .... PA
Pan American World Airways, Inc. [*See also PA, PAN-AM, PN*] .... PAA
Pan American World Airways, Inc. [*See also PA, PAA, PN*] .... PAN-AM
Pan American Zebu Association [*Later, IZBA*] (EA) .... PAZA
Pan Atlantic Re, Inc. (MHDW) .... PNRE
Pan Canadian Petroleum Ltd., Calgary, Alberta [*Library symbol National Library of Canada*] (NLC) .... ACPP
Pan Central Explorations Ltd. [*Toronto Stock Exchange symbol*] .... PAX
Pan European Survey [*A publication*] .... PES
Pan Europeenne Air Service [*France ICAO designator*] (FAAC) .... PEA

Pan Head [*Screw Head*] (ECII) ... PH
Pan Head [*Design engineering*] ... PNH
Pan Head Steel (IAA) ... PHS
Pan Hellenic Society Inventors of Greece in USA [*Defunct*] (EA) ... PHSIG
Pan Jao [*Afghanistan*] [*ICAO location identifier*] (ICLI) ... OAPJ
Pan Malayan Islamic Party ... PMIP
Pan Malaysian Air Transport [*ICAO designator*] (FAAC) ... PMA
Pan Metal [*formerly, Patton Morgan*] **Corp.** [*Ammunition manufacturer*] ... PMC
Pan Pacific and Southeast Asia Women's Association (AD) ... PPSAWA
Pan Pacific and Southeast Asia Women's Association (NADA) ... PPSAWA
Pan Pacific and Southeast Asia Women's Association of the USA (EA) ... PPSEAWA-USA
Pan Pacific Centers [*Defunct*] (EA) ... PPC
Pan Pacific Institute [*Flinders University, Australia*] ... PPI
Pan Pacific Petroleum [*Vancouver Stock Exchange symbol*] ... PPP
Pan Pacific Public Relations Federation [*Thailand*] [*Defunct*] ... PPPRF
Pan Salicornia Zone [*Ecology*] ... PS
Pan Stock Line Station (MCD) ... PSLS
Pan World Ventures, Inc. [*Vancouver Stock Exchange symbol*] ... PWD
Pana, IL [*FM radio station call letters*] ... WXKO
Panaca, NV [*FM radio station call letters*] ... KLNR
Panache Resources, Inc. [*Vancouver Stock Exchange symbol*] ... PNP
Panaco, Inc. [*NASDAQ symbol*] (SAG) ... PANA
Panaco, Inc. [*Associated Press*] (SAG) ... Panaco
Panaf Airways Ltd. [*Gambia*] [*ICAO designator*] (FAAC) ... PAF
Pan-African Documentation and Information System [*Economic Commission for Africa*] [*United Nations*] (IID) ... PADIS
Pan-African Federation of Agricultural Trade Unions (EA) ... PAFATU
Pan-African Network for a Geological Information System [*UNESCO*] (DUND) ... PANGIS
PanAfrican News Agency (EAIO) ... PANA
Pan-African Ornithological Congress ... PAOC
Pan-African Resource Center (EA) ... PARC
Pan-African Rinderpest Campaign [*Organization of African Unity*] ... PARC
Pan-African Socialist Union [*Southern Rhodesia*] ... PASU
Pan-African Telecommunications (BARN) ... PANAFTEL
PanAfrican Telecommunications Union (EAIO) ... PATU
Panafrican Union of Science and Technology ... PUST
Pan-African Women's Organization [*Commercial firm*] (NADA) ... PAWO
Pan-African Youth Movement (EA) ... PYM
Pan-Africanist Congress [*South Africa*] ... PAC
Panagarh [*India*] [*ICAO location identifier*] (ICLI) ... VEPH
Panagjuriste [*Bulgaria*] [*Geomagnetic observatory code*] ... PAG
Panair [*Spain ICAO designator*] (FAAC) ... PNR
Panair do Brasil, SA ... PAB
Panair International SRL [*Italy ICAO designator*] (FAAC) ... PIT
Panama [*Panama*] [*ICAO location identifier*] (ICLI) ... MPPC
Panama [*Panama*] [*ICAO location identifier*] (ICLI) ... MPZL
Panama [*MARC geographic area code Library of Congress*] (LCCP) ... ncpn--
Panama [*ANSI two-letter standard code*] (CNC) ... PA
Panama [*ANSI three-letter standard code*] (CNC) ... PAN
Panama (VRA) ... Pan
Panama (ODBW) ... Pan
Panama [*MARC country of publication code Library of Congress*] (LCCP) ... pn
Panama Air Lines ... PANAIR
Panama Air Traffic Control Area ... PATCA
Panama Basin ... PB
[*The*] **Panama Canal** ... PANCAN
[*The*] **Panama Canal** ... PC
Panama Canal Authority ... PCA
Panama Canal Commission [*Independent government agency*] ... PCC
Panama Canal Commission Acquisition Regulation (AAGC) ... PAR
Panama Canal Co. [*Superseded by Panama Canal Commission*] ... PANCANCO
Panama Canal Co. [*Superseded by Panama Canal Commission*] ... PCC
Panama Canal Department ... PCD
Panama Canal Zone [*Panama*] [*Airport symbol*] (AD) ... PCZ
Panama Canal Zone Library-Museum, Balboa Heights, CZ [*Library symbol Library of Congress*] (LCLS) ... CznBh
Panama City [*Florida*] [*Airport symbol*] (OAG) ... PFN
Panama City [*Panama*] [*Airport symbol*] (OAG) ... PTY
Panama City Beach, FL [*FM radio station call letters*] ... WAKT
Panama City Beach, FL [*AM radio station call letters*] ... WDLP
Panama City Beach, FL [*AM radio station call letters*] ... WKGC
Panama City Beach, FL [*FM radio station call letters*] ... WPCF
Panama City Beach, FL [*Television station call letters*] ... WPCT
Panama City, FL [*Location identifier FAA*] (FAAL) ... PAM
Panama City, FL [*Location identifier FAA*] (FAAL) ... TYF
Panama City, FL [*Television station call letters*] ... WFSG
Panama City, FL [*FM radio station call letters*] ... WFSW
Panama City, FL [*FM radio station call letters*] ... WFSY
Panama City, FL [*AM radio station call letters*] ... WGNE
Panama City, FL [*FM radio station call letters*] ... WILN
Panama City, FL [*Television station call letters*] ... WJHG
Panama City, FL [*FM radio station call letters*] ... WJTF
Panama City, FL [*FM radio station call letters*] ... WKGC
Panama City, FL [*AM radio station call letters*] ... WLTG
Panama City, FL [*Television station call letters*] ... WMBB
Panama City, FL [*FM radio station call letters*] ... WPAP
Panama City, FL [*FM radio station call letters*] ... WPFM
Panama City, FL [*Television station call letters*] ... WPGX
Panama City [*Panama*] **Paitilla Airport** [*Airport symbol*] (OAG) ... PAC
Panama City/Tyndall Air Force Base [*Florida*] [*ICAO location identifier*] (ICLI) ... KPAM
Panama Defense Forces [*Later, Public Forces*] ... PDF
Panama, Honduras, and Liberia [*Acronym used to refer to merchant ships operating under "flags of convenience"*] ... PANHONLIB
Panama, Liberia, and Honduras [*Acronym used to refer to merchant ships operating under "flags of convenience"*] ... PANLIBHON
Panama/Paitilla, Marco A. Gelabert [*Panama*] [*ICAO location identifier*] (ICLI) ... MPMG
Panama Public Forces ... FPP
Panama Red [*Variety of marijuana*] ... PR
Panama Sea Frontier ... PANSEAFRON
Panama Sea Frontier ... PSF
Panama-Liberia-Honduras-Costa Rica ... PANLIBHONCO
Panamanian Committee for Human Rights (EA) ... PCHR
Panamanian Public Force (AD) ... PPF
Panamanian Society of Engineers and Architects (IAA) ... SPEA
Panama-Red Marijuana (AD) ... Pr
PanAmerican Association of Biochemical Societies (EA) ... PAABS
Pan-American Association of Ophthalmology (EA) ... PAAO
Pan-American Association of Oto-Rhino-Laryngology and Broncho-Esophagology [*Mexico City, Mexico*] (EAIO) ... PAAORLBE
Panamerican Badminton Confederation (EAIO) ... PBC
Panamerican Beverages [*Commercial firm Associated Press*] (SAG) ... PanaBev
Panamerican Beverages [*NYSE symbol*] (SPSG) ... PB
Panamerican Beverages 'A' [*NYSE symbol*] (TTSB) ... PB
Pan-American Biodeterioration Society (EA) ... PABS
Pan-American Coffee Bureau [*Defunct*] (EA) ... PACB
Pan-American Congress ... PAC
Panamerican Cultural Circle (EA) ... PCC
Pan-American Festival Association (EA) ... PAFA
Pan-American Ground Training Unit ... PAGTU
PanAmerican League Against Rheumatism [*Canada*] (EAIO) ... PANLAR
Panamerican/Panafrican Association (EA) ... PPA
Pan-American Pharmaceutical and Biochemical Federation ... PPBF
Pan-American Progressive Consumers Alliance [*Later, NPCA*] (EA) ... PAPCA
Pan-American Treaty Series [*A publication*] (DLA) ... Pan-Am TS
Pan-American Union of Karatedo Organizations [*Later, PUKO*] (EA) ... PAUKO
Pan-American Union of Karatedo Organizations (EA) ... PUKO
Pan-American Weightlifting Confederation (EA) ... PAWC
Pan-American Weightlifting Confederation (EA) ... PAWLC
Pan-American World Airways (NADA) ... PAWA
Pan-American World Airways [*Stock exchange symbol*] (AD) ... PN
PanAmSat Corp. [*Associated Press*] (SAG) ... PnASat
PanAmSat Corp. [*NASDAQ symbol*] (SAG) ... SPOT
Panarcadian Federation of America (EA) ... PFA
Panarctic Oils Ltd., Calgary, AB, Canada [*Library symbol Library of Congress*] (LCLS) ... CaACPO
PanArctic Oils Ltd., Calgary, Alberta [*Library symbol National Library of Canada*] (NLC) ... ACPO
Panarea [*Lipari Islands*] [*Seismograph station code, US Geological Survey*] (SEIS) ... PLI
Panarim Resources, Inc. [*Vancouver Stock Exchange symbol*] ... PRM
Panart [*Record label*] [*Cuba, USA*] ... Pnt
Pan-Asia News Agency Ltd. [*Also, PANASIA*] [*Hong Kong*] ... PANA
Pan-Asia News Agency Ltd. [*Also, PANA*] [*Hong Kong*] ... PANASIA
Pan-Asian Newspaper Alliance [*Also, PANANEWS*] (NADA) ... PANA
Pan-Asian Newspaper Alliance [*Also, PANA*] (NADA) ... PANANEWS
Panasonic Energy Corp. [*Vancouver Stock Exchange symbol*] ... PEC
Panasystolic Murmur [*Cardiology*] (DAVI) ... PSM
Panatech Res & Dev [*NASDAQ symbol*] (TTSB) ... PNTC
Panatech Research & Development Corp. [*Associated Press*] (SAG) ... Pantch
Panatech Research & Development Corp. [*NASDAQ symbol*] (NQ) ... PNTC
Pan-Atlantic Steamship Corp. (MHDW) ... P-A
Panatlas Energy, Inc. [*Toronto Stock Exchange symbol*] ... PA
Panavia New Aircraft Project (MCD) ... PANNAP
Panavia SA [*ICAO designator*] (FAAC) ... PNV
Panax Pharmaceutical [*NASDAQ symbol*] (TTSB) ... PANX
Panax Pharmaceutical Co. Ltd. [*Associated Press*] (SAG) ... Panax
Panax Pharmaceutical Co. Ltd. [*Associated Press*] (SAG) ... PanaxP
Panax Pharmaceutical Company Ltd. [*NASDAQ symbol*] (SAG) ... PANX
Panax Pharmaceutical Unit [*NASDAQ symbol*] (TTSB) ... PANXU
Panax Pharmaceutical Wrrt [*NASDAQ symbol*] (TTSB) ... PANXW
Pancake ... PNCK
Pancake Torquer Motor (SAA) ... PTM
PanCana Minerals [*Toronto Stock Exchange symbol*] ... PCN
PanCanadian Petroleum [*TS, Exchange Symbol*] (TTSB) ... PCP
PanCanadian Petroleum Ltd. [*Toronto Stock Exchange symbol Vancouver Stock Exchange symbol*] ... PCP
PanCanadian Petroleum Ltd., Calgary, AB, Canada [*Library symbol Library of Congress*] (LCLS) ... CaACPP
Pancho's Mexican Buffet [*NASDAQ symbol*] (TTSB) ... PAMX
Pancho's Mexican Buffet, Inc. [*NASDAQ symbol*] (NQ) ... PAMX
Pancho's Mexican Buffet, Inc. [*Associated Press*] (SAG) ... PancMx
Panchromatic (DEN) ... PAN
Panchromatic [*Photography*] (WDMC) ... pan
Panchromatic (VRA) ... panchr
Panchromatic Film (ADA) ... PF
Pancontinental Oil Ltd. [*Toronto Stock Exchange symbol*] ... PNO
Pancreas-Specific Protein [*Medicine*] (DMAA) ... PASP
Pancreastatin [*Biochemistry*] ... PST
Pancreatectomized [*Medicine*] ... PX
Pancreatic Divisum [*Medicine*] ... PD
Pancreatic Dorsal Duct [*Anatomy*] ... PDD
Pancreatic Duct [*Anatomy*] ... PD
Pancreatic Function Test [*Medicine*] ... PFT
Pancreatic Insufficiency [*Gastroenterology*] ... PI
Pancreatic Juice Protein [*Medicine*] (DMAA) ... PJP

Pancreatic Lipase [*Medicine*] (DMAA) ..... PI
Pancreatic Oncofetal Antigen [*Immunochemistry*] ..... POA
Pancreatic Polypeptide [*Biochemistry*] ..... PP
Pancreatic Polypeptide [*Medicine*] (DMAA) ..... PPY
Pancreatic Secretory Trypsin Inhibitor [*Medicine*] (DMAA) ..... PSTI
Pancreatic Secretory Trypsin Inhibitor [*Biochemistry*] ..... PSTI
Pancreatic Spasmolytic Peptide [*Biochemistry*] ..... PSP
Pancreatic Suppression Test [*Medicine*] (AAMN) ..... PST
Pancreatic Trypsin Inhibitor [*Biochemistry*] ..... PTI
Pancreatic Ventral Duct [*Anatomy*] ..... PVD
Pancreaticobiliary Ductal Union [*Anatomy*] ..... PBDU
Pancreatitis-Associated Protein [*Medicine*] (DMAA) ..... PAP
Pancreozymin [*Also, CCK*] [*Endocrinology*] ..... PZ
Pancreozymin-Cholecystokinin [*Endocrinology*] (MAE) ..... PZ-CCK
Pancretan Association of America (EA) ..... PAA
Pancretan Association of America (EA) ..... PCAA
Pancuronium [*A muscle relaxant*] ..... P
Pancuronium [*A muscle relaxant*] ..... Pc
Pancuronium Bromide [*A muscle relaxant*] (DAVI) ..... PCB
Pancyprian Association of America [*Defunct*] (EA) ..... PAA
Panda Project [*NASDAQ symbol*] (TTSB) ..... PNDA
[*The*] **Panda Project, Inc.** [*Associated Press*] (SAG) ..... PandaPrj
[*The*] **Panda Project, Inc.** [*NASDAQ symbol*] (SAG) ..... PNDA
Pandamatenga [*Botswana*] [*ICAO location identifier*] (ICLI) ..... FBPA
Pandectae Florentinae [*A publication*] (DSA) ..... P Flo
Pandectae Florentinae [*A publication*] (DSA) ..... P Florent
Pandectae Florentinae [*A publication*] (DSA) ..... Pand Flo
Pandectae Florentinae [*A publication*] (DSA) ..... Pandect Flor
Pandectae (Pisanae) Florentinae [*A publication*] (DSA) ..... Pi
Pandectes Periodiques [*A publication*] (ILCA) ..... PP
Pandects [*A publication Authority cited in pre-1607 legal work*] (DSA) ..... P
[*The*] **Pandects** [*A publication*] (DLA) ..... Pand
Pandemokratiki Agrotikon Metapon Ellados [*Pan-Democratic Agrarian Front of Greece*] [*Political party*] (PPE) ..... PAME
Pandering [*FBI standardized term*] ..... PAND
P&F Indus'A' [*NASDAQ symbol*] (TTSB) ..... PFINA
Pandick Computerized Typesetting (NITA) ..... PACT
Pandie Pandie [*Australia Airport symbol Obsolete*] (OAG) ..... PDE
Pandjang (AD) ..... Pnd
Pan-Dodecanesian Association of America "Xanthos O Philikos" (EA) ..... PAAXOP
Pandora [*Costa Rica*] [*ICAO location identifier*] (ICLI) ..... MRPD
Panegyricus [*of Pliny the Younger*] [*Classical studies*] (OCD) ..... Pan
Panegyricus [*of Isocrates*] [*Classical studies*] (OCD) ..... Paneg
Panel (NFPA) ..... P
Panel (VRA) ..... p
Panel (AD) ..... pnl
Panel (KSC) ..... PNL
Panel Bridge (MUGU) ..... PNLBRG
Panel Call Indicator ..... PCI
Panel Data Interface [*Computer science*] (IAA) ..... PDI
Panel Electronic Circuit (EECA) ..... PEC
Panel Input ..... PI
Panel Jack ..... PJ
Panel Left [*Nuclear energy*] (NRCH) ..... PL
Panel Maintenance (IAA) ..... PM
Panel Marking Kit ..... PMK
Panel Meter (IEEE) ..... PM
Panel Monitor (MHDI) ..... PAM
Panel of American Women (EA) ..... PAW
Panel of Americans [*Defunct*] (EA) ..... POA
Panel of Consultants for the Performing Arts [*of CFC*] ..... PCPA
Panel of Experts on Climatic Change [*WMO*] (MSC) ..... PECC
Panel of Experts on Environmental Management (GNE) ..... PEEM
Panel of Experts on Environmental Pollution [*WMO*] (MSC) ..... PEEP
Panel of Experts on Fish Utilization [*FAO*] (ASF) ..... PEFU
Panel of Meteorological Aspects of Ocean Affairs [*Marine science*] (OSRA) ..... MAOA
Panel on Alternate Approaches to Graduate Education (EA) ..... PAAGE
Panel on Education and Training [*COSATI*] ..... PET
Panel on Educational Terminology [*Office of Education*] ..... PET
Panel on Inflight Scientific Experiments [*NASA*] ..... POISE
Panel on International Procurement in the Technology Age (AAGC) ..... PIPTA
Panel on International Programs and International Cooperation in Oceans Affairs [*Department of State*] (NOAA) ..... PIPICO
Panel on International Programs and International Organizations [*US State Department*] (USDC) ..... PIPICO
Panel on Oceanography ..... POO
Panel on Operational Meteorological Satellites ..... POMS
Panel on the Acquisition, Transmission, and Processing of Hydrological Data [*Marine science*] (MSC) ..... SAPHYDATA
Panel on the Environment [*of President's Science Advisory Committee*] ..... POE
Panel Point [*Technical drawings*] ..... PP
Panel Point (AD) ..... pp
Panel Power Distribution (MCD) ..... PPD
Panel Publishers (DLA) ..... PANPUB
Panel Receptacle ..... PR
Panel Review Board [*NASA*] (KSC) ..... PRB
Panelboard [*National Electrical Code*] (IEEE) ..... pnlbd
Paneled (WGA) ..... PAN
Panel-Information-Air Operation ..... PIA
Panelized Building Systems Council (EA) ..... PBSC
Panellinion Sosialistikon Kinema [*Pan-Hellenic Socialist Movement*] [*Greek Political party*] (PPE) ..... PASOK
Panel-Mounted Display (MCD) ..... PMD
Panel-Mounted Electronic Voltmeter ..... PMEV
Panel-Mounted Microfilm Reader ..... PMMR
Panels Per Facing [*Outdoor advertising*] (WDMC) ..... PPF
Panendoscopy [*Medicine*] ..... panendo
PanEnergy Corp. [*NYSE symbol*] (TTSB) ..... PEL
Panepirotic Federation of America and Canada [*Later, PFACA*] (EA) ..... PFAC
Panepirotic Federation of America, Canada, and Australia (EA) ..... PFACA
Pan-Ethnic Republican Party of Australia [*Political party*] ..... PERP
Paneuropa-Union [*Paneuropean Union*] (EAIO) ..... PEU
Pangenesis Related [*Protein chemistry*] ..... PR
Pangkal Pinang [*Indonesia*] [*ICAO location identifier*] (ICLI) ..... WIKK
Pangkalan Bun/Iskandar [*Indonesia*] [*ICAO location identifier*] (ICLI) ..... WRBI
Pangkalanbuun [*Indonesia*] [*Airport symbol*] (OAG) ..... PKN
Pangkalpinang [*Indonesia*] [*Airport symbol*] (OAG) ..... PGK
Pangnirtung [*Canada*] [*Airport symbol*] (OAG) ..... YXP
Pangnirtung, NT [*ICAO location identifier*] (ICLI) ..... CYXP
Pango Gold Mines Ltd. [*Toronto Stock Exchange symbol*] ..... PGD
Pangola Stunt Virus [*Plant pathology*] ..... PASV
Pangu Pati [*Papua New Guinea*] [*Political party*] (PPW) ..... PP
Panguitch [*Utah*] [*Airport symbol*] (OAG) ..... PNU
Panguna [*Solomon Islands*] [*Seismograph station code, US Geological Survey*] (SEIS) ..... PAA
Panhandle ..... PNHDL
Panhandle [*NWS*] (FAAC) ..... PNHDL
Panhandle & Santa Fe Railway Co. ..... P & SF
Panhandle & Santa Fe Railway Co. [*AAR code*] ..... PSF
Panhandle Community Unit, School District 2, Raymond IL [*Library symbol Library of Congress*] (LCLS) ..... IRaySD
Panhandle Eastern Corp. [*Associated Press*] (SAG) ..... PanEC
Panhandle Eastern Corp. [*Toronto Stock Exchange symbol*] ..... PNE
Panhandle Eastern Pipe Line Co. [*NYSE symbol*] (SPSG) ..... PEL
Panhandle Royalty Co. [*NASDAQ symbol*] (SAG) ..... PANR
Panhandle Royalty Co. [*Associated Press*] (SAG) ..... PanRoyl
Panhandle Rty [*NASDAQ symbol*] (TTSB) ..... PANRA
Panhandle State College, Goodwell, OK [*Library symbol Library of Congress*] (LCLS) ..... OkGoP
Panhandling [*FBI standardized term*] ..... PANH
Panic Attack [*Medicine*] (MEDA) ..... PA
Panic Attack Sufferers' Support Groups (EA) ..... PASS
Panic Bar [*Technical drawings*] ..... PB
Panic Bolt ..... PANB
Panic in Quebec [*Humorous interpretation for Parti Quebecois*] [*Canada*] ..... PQ
Panicum Mosaic Virus [*Plant pathology*] ..... PANMV
Panicum Mosaic Virus ..... PMV
Panimavida [*Chile*] [*Seismograph station code, US Geological Survey Closed*] (SEIS) ..... PAN
Pan-Indian Ocean Science Association (NOAA) ..... PIOSA
Pan-Iranist Party [*Political party*] (PPW) ..... PIP
Panis [*Bread*] [*Pharmacy*] (ROG) ..... PAN
Panjab Code [*India*] [*A publication*] (DLA) ..... Panj C
Panjabi [*MARC language code Library of Congress*] (LCCP) ..... pan
Panjgur [*Pakistan*] [*ICAO location identifier*] (ICLI) ..... OPPG
Panjgur [*Pakistan*] [*Airport symbol*] (OAG) ..... PJG
Panjim [*India*] [*Airport symbol*] (AD) ..... PAG
Pankhurst's Jurisprudence [*A publication*] (DLA) ..... Pank Jur
Pankypria Ergatiki Omospondia [*Pancyprian Federation of Labour*] [*The "Old Trade Unions" Cyprus*] ..... PEO
Pankypria Omospondia Anexartiton Syntechnion [*Pancyprian Federation of Independent Trade Unions*] [*Cyprus*] ..... POAS
Panleukopenia Virus [*Medicine*] (MAE) ..... PLV
Pan-Macedonian Association (EA) ..... PMA
Panna [*India*] [*Airport symbol*] (AD) ..... PNA
Panno Type (VRA) ..... PNTYP
Pannonhalmi Szent Benedek Rend Kozponti Konyvtara, Pannonhalma, Hungary [*Library symbol Library of Congress*] (LCLS) ..... HuPaB
Panoche, CA [*Location identifier FAA*] (FAAL) ..... PXN
Panola College, Carthage, TX [*Library symbol Library of Congress*] (LCLS) ..... TxCarP
Panorama (VRA) ..... PANA
Panorama Air Tour, Inc. [*ICAO designator*] (FAAC) ..... PAH
Panorama Flight Service [*ICAO designator*] (FAAC) ..... AFD
Panorama Resources Ltd. [*Vancouver Stock Exchange symbol*] ..... PMA
Panoramic ..... PAM
Panoramic (MSA) ..... PAN
Panoramic (IAA) ..... PANOR
Panoramic Camera ..... PC
Panoramic Cockpit Control and Display System (MCD) ..... PCCADS
Panoramic Control and Display System (MCD) ..... PCADS
Panoramic Design Technique ..... PDT
Panoramic Office Planning ..... POP
Panoramic RADAR ..... PANAR
Panoramic Stereo Rectification ..... PSR
Panormitanus [*Nicholas de Tudeschis*] [*Deceased, 1445*] [*Authority cited in pre-1607 legal work*] (DSA) ..... Pan
Panormitanus [*Nicholas de Tudeschis*] [*Deceased, 1445*] [*Authority cited in pre-1607 legal work*] (DSA) ..... Panor
Pan-Pacific and South-East Asia Women's Association [*Tokyo, Japan*] (EAIO) ..... PPSEAWA
Pan-Pacific Editing and Communication Experiment by Satellite (NITA) ..... PEACESAT
Pan-Pacific Education and Communication Experiments by Satellites [*University of Hawaii*] [*NASA*] ..... PEACESAT
Pan-Pacific Educational and Cultural Exchange by Satellite Program [*University of Hawaii, Manoa*] [*Research center*] (RCD) ..... PEACESAT
Pan-Pacific Surgical Association (EA) ..... PPSA

Panretinal Photocoagulation [*Ophthalmology*] ... PRP
Pan-Rhodian Society of America (EA) ... PRSA
Panshanger [*British ICAO location identifier*] (ICLI) ... EGLG
Pan-Somali Nationalist Movement [*Political party*] ... PNM
Pansophic Institute [*Defunct*] (EA) ... PI
Panstwowe Zaklady Lotnicze [*Poland ICAO designator*] (FAAC) ... PZL
Pantaloons (DSUE) ... PANTS
Pantan Resources [*Vancouver Stock Exchange symbol*] ... PQR
Pantanal Linhas Aereas Sul-Matogrossenses SA [*Brazil*] [*ICAO designator*] (FAAC) ... PTN
Pantelleria [*Italy ICAO location identifier*] (ICLI) ... LICG
Pantelleria [*Italy*] [*Airport symbol*] (OAG) ... PNL
Pantera International (EA) ... PI
Pantex Plant [*Department of Energy*] [*Amarillo, TX*] (GAAI) ... PANT
Pantex Site ... Pantex
Pantex Site Environmental Impact Statement ... Pantex EIS
Pantheon [*Record label*] [*France, etc.*] ... Pan
Panther Mines Ltd. [*Vancouver Stock Exchange symbol*] ... PTH
Panthere Rose [*France*] [*An association Defunct*] (EAIO) ... PR
Pantnagar [*India*] [*Airport symbol*] (AD) ... PGH
Pantograph (KSC) ... PANT
Pantograph Optical Projection System (IEEE) ... POPS
Pantomime ... PANTO
Pantomime [*British*] [*Slang*] (WDMC) ... panto
Pantomine ... pant
Pantone Color Institute (EA) ... PCI
Pantone Matching System [*Printing*] ... PMS
Pantone Open Color Environment [*Joint venture between Pantone, Inc. and LightSource Computer Images*] [*Computer science*] (PCM) ... POCE
Panton-Valentine [*Leukocidin*] [*Bacteriology*] (DAVI) ... P-V
Panton-Valentine Leukocidin ... P-VL
Pantorama Industries, Inc. [*Toronto Stock Exchange symbol*] ... PTA
Pantothenic Acid (DMAA) ... PA
Pantropical [*Botany*] ... pantrop
Pantry (MSA) ... PAN
Pantry ... PNTRY
Pants Down [*At a disadvantage*] [*Slang*] (DSUE) ... PD
Pantyffynnon [*British depot code*] ... PFN
Panvalet Access Method (IAA) ... PAM
Panzer Abwehr Kanone [*Cannon Against Armor*] [*German antitank gun*] ... PAK
Panzerbrechend [*Armor-Piercing*] [*German military - World War II*] ... PZ
Panzer-Division [*Armored Division*] [*German military*] ... PZDV
Panzerkampfwagen [*German tank*] [*World War II*] ... PZKPFW
Panzerkampfwagen [*German tank*] [*World War II*] ... PZKW
Panzerwagen [*Tank*] [*German military - World War II*] ... PWG
Pa-O National Army [*Myanmar*] [*Political party*] (EY) ... PNA
Pa-O National Organization [*Myanmar*] [*Political party*] (EY) ... PNO
Paoli, IN [*AM radio station call letters*] ... WSEZ
Paoli, IN [*FM radio station call letters*] ... WUME
Paoli News, Paoli, IN [*Library symbol Library of Congress*] (LCLS) ... InPaN
Paoli Public Library, Paoli, IN [*Library symbol Library of Congress*] (LCLS) ... InPa
Paoli Republican, Paoli, IN [*Library symbol Library of Congress*] (LCLS) ... InPaR
Paonia, CO [*FM radio station call letters*] ... KVNF
Paonia Public Library, Paonia, CO [*Library symbol Library of Congress*] (LCLS) ... CoPao
Paotow [*Republic of China*] [*Seismograph station code, US Geological Survey*] (SEIS) ... PAO
Papa [*Phonetic alphabet*] [*International*] (DSUE) ... P
Papa [*Pope*] [*Latin*] ... P
Papa [*Pope*] ... PP
Papa [*Father*] [*Latin*] (AD) ... Pp
Papa Johns International, Inc. [*Associated Press*] (SAG) ... PapaJohn
Papa Johns International, Inc. [*Associated Press*] (SAG) ... PapJohn
Papa Johns International, Inc. [*NASDAQ symbol*] (SAG) ... PZZA
Papa John's Intl [*NASDAQ symbol*] (TTSB) ... PZZA
Papa Westray [*Scotland*] [*Airport symbol*] (OAG) ... PPW
Papa Westray [*Orkney Islands, Scotland*] [*Airport symbol*] (AD) ... WEN
Papain [*An enzyme*] ... PAP
Papair Terminal SA [*Haiti*] [*ICAO designator*] (FAAC) ... HMP
Papal Volunteers for Latin America [*Defunct*] ... PAVLA
Papanicolaau Class I [*Biochemistry*] (DAVI) ... CL1
Papanicolaou [*diagnosis, smear, stain, or test*] [*Gynecology*] (DAVI) ... PAP
Papanicolaou [*Diagnosis, smear, stain, or test*] [*Medicine*] ... PAP
Papanicolaou Cancer Research Institute [*University of Miami*] [*Research center*] ... PCRI
Papaver Poppy [*Botany*] (ROG) ... PAPAV
Papaya Mosaic Virus [*Plant pathology*] ... PAPMV
Papaya Mosaic Virus ... PMV
Papaya Ringspot Virus [*Plant pathology*] ... PRSV
Papaya Ringspot Virus ... PRV
Papeete [*French Polynesia*] [*Seismograph station code, US Geological Survey*] (SEIS) ... PPT
Papeete [*French Polynesia*] [*Airport symbol*] (OAG) ... PPT
Papeete [*Orstom*] [*Society Islands*] [*Seismograph station code, US Geological Survey*] (SEIS) ... THT
Papeete, Society Islands [*Airport*] (AD) ... PPT
Papenoo [*Society Islands*] [*Seismograph station code, US Geological Survey*] (SEIS) ... PPN
Paper ... P
Paper (WGA) ... PA
Paper (VRA) ... pa
Paper (DSUE) ... PAP
Paper ... PPR
Paper ... PPR
Paper Advance (BUR) ... PA
Paper Agents Association [*British*] (DBA) ... PAA
Paper and Foil [*Capacitor*] (DEN) ... PF
Paper and Twine Association (EA) ... PTA
Paper Bag Institute (EA) ... PBI
Paper Bag Manufacturers' Association of South Australia ... PBMASA
[*The*] **Paper Bag Players** (EA) ... PBP
Paper Base (MSA) ... PB
Paper Book of Laurence, J., in Lincoln's Inn Library [*A publication*] (DLA) ... LPB
Paper Bound [*Books*] (ROG) ... PAP
Paper Chemistry [*Institute of Paper Chemistry*] [*Appleton, WI Bibliographic database*] ... PAPERCHEM
Paper Chromatography ... PC
Paper Converters Association [*Defunct*] (EA) ... PCA
Paper Copy ... PC
Paper Core (IAA) ... PC
Paper Crepe Tape ... PCT
Paper Cup and Container Institute [*Later, SSI*] (EA) ... PCCI
Paper Distribution Centers ... PDC
Paper Distribution Council (EA) ... PDC
Paper Electrophoresis [*Medicine*] (MAE) ... PE
Paper Equilibrium Tester (BARN) ... PET
Paper, Flat Tape ... PFT
Paper Flow Group [*Nuclear Regulatory Commission*] (GFGA) ... PFG
Paper Gain (MHDW) ... PG
Paper Impact Printing (HGAA) ... PIP
Paper Industries Research Association (NADA) ... PIRA
Paper Industry Federation (NADA) ... PIF
Paper Industry Management Association (EA) ... PIMA
Paper Industry Technical Association [*British*] (EAIO) ... PITA
Paper Insulated ... PI
Paper Life Ltd. [*British*] ... PL
Paper Loss (MHDW) ... PL
Paper Makers Advertising Association (EA) ... PMAA
Paper Makers' Allied Trades Association [*British*] (DBA) ... PMATA
Paper Manifesting System ... PMS
Paper Marketing Council of Queensland [*Australia*] ... PMCQ
Paper Mill Fourdrinier Wire Cloth Manufacturers Association [*Later, FWC*] (EA) ... PMFWCMA
Paper Mill Wire Cloth Manufacturers' Association (DGA) ... PMWCMA
Paper Mould and Dandy Roll Makers' Union (DGA) ... PMDRMU
Paper Napkin Association ... PNA
Paper Negative (VRA) ... PRNG
Paper or Cloth [*Freight*] ... PC
Paper or Paperboard [*Freight*] ... P PBD
Paper or Pulpboard [*Freight*] ... P PLPBD
Paper Pail Association [*Defunct*] (EA) ... PPA
Paper Plate Association [*Later, SSI*] (EA) ... PPA
Paper, Printing, and Binding [*Publishing*] ... PP & B
Paper, Printing, and Binding (AD) ... pp&b
Paper, Printing, Publishing [*Department of Employment*] [*British*] ... PPP
Paper Profit ... PP
Paper Publications Society [*Amsterdam, Netherlands*] (EA) ... PPS
Paper Radioimmunosorbent Test [*Analytical biochemistry*] ... PRIST
Paper Sack Development Association [*British*] (BI) ... PSDA
Paper Shipping Sack Manufacturers Association (EA) ... PSSMA
Paper Shipping-Containers Buyers Group ... PSCBG
Paper Society for the Overseas Blind [*Defunct*] (EA) ... PSOB
Paper Stationery and Tablet Manufacturers Association [*Later, PCA*] (EA) ... PSTMA
Paper Stock Institute of America (EA) ... PSI
Paper Stock Institute of America (EA) ... PSIA
Paper Stock Record (DGA) ... PSR
Paper Surface Efficiency (DGA) ... PSE
Paper Tape ... PT
Paper Tape Accessory (MHDI) ... PTA
Paper Tape and Transmission Code ... PTTC
Paper Tape Code on Eight Levels (NITA) ... PTT/8
Paper Tape Controller (NITA) ... PAPTC
Paper Tape Half-Duplex ... PTH
Paper Tape Oriented Operating System ... PTOS
Paper Tape Perforator [*or Punch*] ... PTP
Paper Tape Punch (ECII) ... PTP
Paper Tape Reader ... PR
Paper Tape Reader ... PTR
Paper Tape Reader Punch [*Computer science*] (IAA) ... PTRP
Paper Tape Selectric Composer (DGA) ... PTSC
Paper Tape Sender ... PTS
Paper Tape Software Package (NITA) ... PTSP
Paper Tape Splicing Equipment ... PTSE
Paper Tape System [*Computer science*] (IAA) ... PTS
Paper Tape-to-Magnetic Tape Conversion System (DIT) ... PTS
Paper Title [*Business term*] ... PT
Paper Towel Association [*British*] (BI) ... PTA
Paper Towel Dispenser [*Technical drawings*] ... PTD
Paper Towel Receptor [*Technical drawings*] ... PTR
Paper Trade Golfing Society [*British*] ... PTGS
Paper Trooper [*One who salvaged paper for war effort*] [*World War II*] ... PT
Paper Wrapper (ADA) ... PW
Paperback (WGA) ... P
Paperback (CDAI) ... PB
Paperback ... PBK
Paperback Original [*Award for best original paperback books of the year*] ... PORGIE
Paperboard (MSA) ... PBD
Paperboard [*Freight*] ... PPRBD

Paperboard (AD) ... pprbd
Paperboard ... PPRBD
Paperboard Butter Chip Association ... PBCA
Paperboard Industries Corp. [*Toronto Stock Exchange symbol*] ... PB
Paperboard Packaging Council (EA) ... PPC
Paperbound Books in Print [*A publication*] ... PBIP
Paper-Braided Jute (IAA) ... PBJ
PaperClip Imaging Software [*NASDAQ symbol*] (TTSB) ... PCLP
Paperclip Imaging Software, Inc. [*Associated Press*] (SAG) ... PapclS
Paperclip Imaging Software, Inc. [*NASDAQ symbol*] (SAG) ... PCLP
Paperclip Imaging Softw'r Wrrt [*NASDAQ symbol*] (TTSB) ... PCLPW
Paper-Core Quad Trunk (PDAA) ... PCQT
Papered (ROG) ... PPD
Papergram System [*Military*] (CAAL) ... PGS
Paper-Insulated, Lead-Covered Cable [*Telecommunications*] ... PILC
Paperleg [*A favored student*] [*Teen slang*] ... PL
Paperless Electronic Payment [*Business term*] ... PEP
Paperless Entry Processing User Group [*Defunct*] (CSR) ... PEP
Paperless Item Processing System [*Banking*] ... PIPS
Paperless Ordering Placement [*System*] (DOMA) ... POP
Papermaker [*MARC relator code*] [*Library of Congress*] (LCCP) ... ppm
Papermakers Felt Association (EA) ... PFA
Papermakers' Woven Felt Association (DGA) ... PWFA
Papers and Discussions. Victorian Institute of Engineers [*Australia A publication*] ... Pap & Disc Vic Inst Eng
Papers and Proceedings. Royal Society of Tasmania [*A publication*] ... Pap & Proc Roy Soc Tas
[*The*] **Papers of Andrew Jackson, Hermitage, TN** [*Library symbol Library of Congress*] (LCLS) ... THerP
Papers on English Language and Literature [*A publication*] ... PELL
Papers Per Hour [*News*] (WDMC) ... pph
Papers under Consideration ... PUC
Paper-Substrate Room-Temperature Phosphorescence [*Analytical chemistry*] ... PS-RTP
Paperweight Collectors' Association (EA) ... PCA
Paperwork Reduction Act (GFGA) ... PRA
Paphos [*Cyprus*] [*ICAO location identifier*] (ICLI) ... LCPH
Paphos [*Cyprus*] [*Airport symbol*] (OAG) ... PFO
Papi [*Aemilius*] **Papinianus** [*Deceased, 212*] [*Authority cited in pre-1607 legal work*] (DSA) ... Papi
Papier Mache (VRA) ... pm
Papiertechnische Stiftung [*Database producer*] ... PTS
Papilla [*Optic*] [*Medicine*] ... P
Papilla [*Medicine*] ... pap
Papilla Diameter [*Medicine*] ... pd
Papillary Carninoma of Thyroid [*Medicine*] (DMAA) ... PACT
Papillary Collecting Duct [*Medicine*] (DMAA) ... PCD
Papillary Distance ... PD
Papillary Eccrine Adenoma [*Oncology*] ... PEA
Papillary, Marginal, Attached [*With reference to gingivae*] [*Dentistry*] ... PMA
Papillary or Nodular Hyperplasia [*Medicine*] ... PN
Papillate [*A type of seed*] [*Botany*] ... P
Papilloma Virus, Polyoma Virus, Vacuolating Virus ... PAPOVA
Papillomas [*Medicine*] (DMAA) ... Paps
Papillomavirus ... PV
Papillon Airways [*ICAO designator*] (AD) ... HI
Papillon Club of America (EA) ... PCA
Papillon-Lefevre Syndrome [*Medicine*] (DMAA) ... PLS
Papiri Milanesi [*A publication*] (OCD) ... PMilan
Papirius Justus [*Flourished, 2nd century*] [*Authority cited in pre-1607 legal work*] (DSA) ... Papi
Pappaband [*Hard Cover*] [*German*] (AD) ... Ppb
Pappenheimer Bodies [*Hematology*] (DAVI) ... PAPP
Papua [*New Guinea*] (BARN) ... Pap
Papua Besena [*Papua New Guinea*] [*Political party*] (FEA) ... PB
Papua New Guinea [*MARC geographic area code Library of Congress*] (LCCP) ... a-pp--
Papua New Guinea [*IYRU nationality code*] (IYR) ... KP
Papua New Guinea [*Aircraft nationality and registration mark*] (FAAC) ... P2
Papua New Guinea [*ANSI two-letter standard code*] (CNC) ... PG
Papua New Guinea [*ANSI three-letter standard code*] (CNC) ... PNG
Papua New Guinea [*MARC country of publication code Library of Congress*] (LCCP) ... pp
Papua New Guinea Banking Corp. ... PNG
Papua New Guinea Institute of Chemistry ... PNGI
Papua New Guinea Line (AD) ... PNGL
Papua Nueva Guinea [*Papua New Guinea*] [*Spanish*] (AD) ... PNG
Papuan Infantry Battalion ... PIB
Papuan National Alliance [*Political party*] (PPW) ... PANAL
Papuan-Australian [*MARC language code Library of Congress*] (LCCP) ... paa
Papular Acrodermatitis of Childhood ... PAC
Papun [*Myanmar*] [*Airport symbol*] (OAG) ... PPU
Papun [*Myanmar*] [*ICAO location identifier*] (ICLI) ... VBPP
Papworth [*England*] ... PAPW
Papyri Durani (BJA) ... PDur
Papyri Graecae Magicae [*A publication*] (OCD) ... PGM
Papyri Iandanae [*A publication*] (OCD) ... PIand
Papyri Lundenses [*A publication*] (OCD) ... PLund
Papyri Osloenses [*A publication*] (OCD) ... POsl
Papyrus (BJA) ... Pap
Papyrus (VRA) ... pap
Papy's Reports [*5-8 Florida*] [*A publication*] (DLA) ... Papy
Par Amitie [*By Favor*] [*French*] ... PA
Par Autorite [*By Authority*] [*French*] ... PA
Par Exchange Rate [*Business term*] ... PER
Par Leadership Training Foundation [*Defunct*] (EA) ... PLTF
Par Selling (MHDB) ... PS
PAR Technology [*NYSE symbol*] (TTSB) ... PTC
PAR Technology Corp. [*Associated Press*] (SAG) ... ParTch
PAR Technology Corp. [*NYSE symbol*] (SPSG) ... PTC
Par Value [*Finance*] ... PV
Par Voie Telegraphique [*By Telegraph*] [*French*] ... PVT
Para [*Chemistry*] ... p
Para [*Monetary unit*] [*Former Yugoslavia*] ... P
Para 1 [*Unipara - having borne one child*] (DAVI) ... p1
Para Legal Association [*British*] (DBA) ... PLA
Para-Acetamidobenzoic Acid [*Biochemistry*] ... PAABA
Para-Acetamidohippuric Acid [*Biochemistry*] ... PAAHA
Para-Aminobenzensulfonamide [*Antibiotic*] ... PABS
Para-Aminobenzoate (DMAA) ... PAB
Para-Aminobenzoic Acid [*Also, PABA*] [*Biochemistry*] ... PAB
Para-Aminobenzoic Acid [*Also, PAB*] [*Biochemistry*] ... PABA
Para-Aminoclonidine [*Biochemistry*] ... PAC
Para-Aminohippurate [*Clearance Test*] [*Urology*] (DAVI) ... PAH
Para-Aminohippurate Clearance [*Chemical chemistry*] (AAMN) ... Cpah
Para-Aminohippuric [*Biochemistry*] ... PAH
Para-Aminohippuric Acid ... PAHA
Para-Aminophenol [*Organic chemistry*] ... PAP
Para-Aminopropiophenone [*Pharmacology*] ... PAPP
Para-Aminosalicylic [*Acid*] [*Organic chemistry*] ... PAS
Para-Aminosalicylic Acid [*Organic chemistry*] ... PASA
Para-Aminosalicylic Acid and Isonicotinic Acid Hydrazide (BARN) ... PAS-INAH
Para-Aminosalicylic Acid Calcium Salt [*Pharmacology*] ... PAC
Para-Aminosalicylic Acid Crystallized with Ascorbic Acid [*Organic chemistry*] (MAE) ... PAS-C
Para-Amps (EA) ... PA
Para-Aortic Lymph Node [*Anatomy*] (DAVI) ... PALN
Para-Azoxyanisole [*Organic chemistry*] ... PAA
Para-Bandit Target ... PBT
Para-(Benzyloxy)phenol [*Organic chemistry*] ... PBP
Parabola [*Mathematics*] (IAA) ... PARAB
Parabola [*Mathematics*] ... PRB
Parabolic (IAA) ... PARA
Parabolic (IAA) ... PARABOL
Parabolic ... PRBLC
Parabolic Aluminized Reflector [*Lamp*] ... PAR
Parabolic Aluminized Reflector [*A spotlight*] (WDMC) ... PAR
Parabolic Collimator Mirror ... PCM
Parabolic Corner Reflector ... PACORE
Parabolic Equation ... PE
Parabolic Microwave Reflector ... PMR
Parabolic Radius Gage (MCD) ... PRG
Parabolic Reflector Antenna ... PRA
Parabolized Navier-Stokes Modeling (MCD) ... PNS
Paraboloid ... PRBD
Para-bromophenacyl Bromide [*Organic chemistry*] ... PBPB
Paraburdoo [*Western Australia*] [*Airport symbol*] (AD) ... PAF
Paraburdoo [*Australia Airport symbol*] (OAG) ... PBO
Paracas [*Peru*] [*Seismograph station code, US Geological Survey Closed*] (SEIS) ... PCS
Paracel Islands [*MARC geographic area code Library of Congress*] (LCCP) ... aopf--
Paracel Islands [*ANSI three-letter standard code*] (CNC) ... PAR
Paracel Islands [*MARC country of publication code Library of Congress*] (LCCP) ... pf
Paracel Islands [*ANSI two-letter standard code*] (CNC) ... PI
Paracelsian, Inc. [*Associated Press*] (SAG) ... Parcls
Paracelsian, Inc. [*Associated Press*] (SAG) ... Parclsn
Paracelsian, Inc. [*NASDAQ symbol*] (SAG) ... PRLN
Paracelsian Inc. Wrrt [*NASDAQ symbol*] (TTSB) ... PRLNW
Paracelsus Healthcare Corp. [*Associated Press*] (SAG) ... Paracels
Paracelsus Healthcare Corp. [*NYSE symbol*] (SAG) ... PLS
Paracentesis [*Medicine*] (MAE) ... para
Paracentesis [*Medicine*] ... paracent
Paracentesis and Suction [*Medicine*] ... P & S
Paracentesis Fluid [*Medicine*] (DAVI) ... PCEN
Paracervical Block [*Anesthesiology*] ... PCB
Paracervical Ganglion [*Anatomy*] ... PCG
Paracetamol and Methionine [*Pain-relief drug*] ... PAMETON
Parachinar [*Pakistan*] [*ICAO location identifier*] (ICLI) ... OPPC
Para-Chloroaniline [*Organic chemistry*] ... PCA
Para-Chlorobenzoic Acid [*Organic chemistry*] ... PCBA
Para-Chlorobenzonitrile [*Organic chemistry*] ... PCBN
Para-Chlorobenzotrifluoride [*Organic chemistry*] ... PCBTF
Para-Chlorobenzyl Chloride [*Organic chemistry*] ... PCBC
Para-Chloromercuribenzoate [*Organic chemistry*] ... PCMB
Para-Chloromercuriphenyl Sulfonate [*or Sulfonic Acid*] [*Organic chemistry*] ... PCMS
Para-Chloromercuriphenylsulfonic Acid [*Organic chemistry*] ... PCMPS
Para-Chloro-meta-cresol [*Organic chemistry*] ... PCMC
Para-Chloro-meta-xylenol [*Organic chemistry*] ... PCMX
Para-Chloro-ortho-nitroaniline [*Also, PCONA*] [*Organic chemistry*] ... PCON
Para-Chloro-ortho-nitroaniline [*Also, PCON*] [*Organic chemistry*] ... PCONA
Para-Chlorophenol [*Organic chemistry*] ... PCP
Para-Chlorophenoxyacetic Acid [*Organic chemistry*] ... PCPA
(Para-Chlorophenoxy)propionic Acid [*Organic chemistry*] ... PCPP
Para-Chlorophenylacetic Acid [*Organic chemistry*] ... PCPA
Para-Chlorophenylalanine [*Biochemistry*] ... PCPA
Para-Chlorophenylthio [*Organic chemistry*] ... PCPT
Para-Chlorotoluene [*Organic chemistry*] ... PCT

Parachute (NASA) ... CHUTE
Parachute ... PAR
Parachute ... PARA
Parachute (AFM) ... PRCHT
Parachute (AD) ... prcht
Parachute Altitude Recognition System (MCD) ... PARS
Parachute Altitude Wind Sensor ... PAWS
Parachute and Cable Defence [*British military*] ... PAC
Parachute and Cable Defence [*British military*] (DMA) ... PACD
Parachute Association of Ireland (EAIO) ... PAI
Parachute Battalion [*Army*] ... PARABAT
Parachute Club of America [*Later, USPA*] (EA) ... PCA
Parachute Course Administrative Unit [*Military British*] (INF) ... PCAU
Parachute Drop Glider ... PDG
Parachute Facility (NASA) ... PF
Parachute Flare (NVT) ... PF
Parachute Fragmentation Bomb [*Air Force*] ... FRP
Parachute Fragmentation Bomb [*Air Force*] ... PARAFRAG
Parachute Infantry [*Military*] ... PARATROOPS
Parachute Infantry Battalion [*Army*] ... PIB
Parachute Infantry Regiment [*Military*] ... PIR
Parachute Jump Instructor [*Military British*] (INF) ... PJI
Parachute Jumping Activities [*Aviation*] (FAAC) ... PAJA
Parachute Jumping Exercise ... PJE
Parachute Landing Fall [*Military*] ... PLF
Parachute Location Aid (MCD) ... PLA
Parachute Low-Altitude Delivery [*Air Force*] ... PLAD
Parachute Low-Altitude Delivery System [*Military*] ... PLADS
Parachute Medical Rescue Service (EA) ... PMRS
Parachute Mine [*British military*] (DMA) ... PM
Parachute Opening Proximity Sensor (MCD) ... POPS
Parachute Paraglider Building [*NASA*] (KSC) ... PPB
Parachute Radio Transmitter [*Telecommunications*] (IAA) ... PRT
Parachute Refurbishment Building [*NASA*] (NASA) ... PRB
Parachute Refurbishment Facility [*NASA*] (NASA) ... PRF
Parachute Retrorocket Airdrop System (MCD) ... PRADS
Parachute Rigger [*Navy*] (KSC) ... PR
Parachute Rigger, First Class [*Navy*] ... PR1
Parachute Rigger, Second Class [*Navy*] ... PR2
Parachute Rigger, Third Class [*Navy*] ... PR3
Parachute Status Report [*Army*] (AABC) ... PSR
Parachute Study Group (EA) ... PSG
Parachute Subsystem [*NASA*] (NASA) ... PS
Parachute Subsystem Sequence Controller [*NASA*] (SAA) ... PSSC
Parachute Supported Radio Relay ... PSRR
Parachute Test Vehicle ... PTV
Parachute Training School [*British military*] (DMA) ... PTS
Parachute-Braked Landing [*Military*] (IAA) ... PBL
Parachutist [*Army skill qualification identifier*] (INF) ... P
Parachutist [*British military*] (DMA) ... Pa
Parachutist (AD) ... prchst
Parachutist Badge [*Military decoration*] ... Prcht Bad
Parachutust Adjustable Equipment Bag [*Army*] (VNW) ... PAE
Paracomp Technology, Inc. [*Vancouver Stock Exchange symbol*] ... PCZ
Paracortex (DMAA) ... PC
Paracortical Hyperplasia [*Oncology*] ... PC
Para-Coumaric Acid [*Organic chemistry*] ... PCA
Para-Cresol Methylhydroxylase [*An enzyme*] ... PCMH
Parade ... PDE
Parade [*Record label*] ... Pde
Paradental ... PARDENTL
Para-Dichlorobenzene [*Insecticide for moths, etc.*] ... PDB
Paradigm (WGA) ... PDG
Paradigm Medical Industries, Inc. [*Associated Press*] (SAG) ... ParaMed
Paradigm Medical Industries, Inc. [*Associated Press*] (SAG) ... ParMd
Paradigm Medical Industries, Inc. [*NASDAQ symbol*] (SAG) ... PMED
Paradigm Publishing Ltd. [*British*] ... PP
Paradigm Technology [*NASDAQ symbol*] (TTSB) ... PRDM
Paradigm Technology, Inc. [*Associated Press*] (SAG) ... Pardgm
Paradigm Technology, Inc. [*NASDAQ symbol*] (SAG) ... PRDM
Para-(Dimethylamino)benzaldehyde [*Organic chemistry*] ... PDAB
Para-Dimethylaminophenylazopyridine [*An indicator*] [*Chemistry*] ... PAMA
Paradise ... PRDS
Paradise Air (Pvt) Ltd. [*Sri Lanka*] [*FAA designator*] (FAAC) ... RPI
Paradise Airways, Inc. [*FAA designator*] (FAAC) ... PAI
Paradise, CA [*Television station call letters*] ... KCVU
Paradise, CA [*FM radio station call letters*] ... KHSL
Paradise, CA [*AM radio station call letters*] ... KKXX
Paradise, CA [*FM radio station call letters*] (RBYB) ... KZAP
Paradise, Inc. [*Associated Press*] (SAG) ... Paradl
Paradise, Inc. [*NASDAQ symbol*] (SAG) ... PARF
Paradise Island Airlines, Inc. [*ICAO designator*] (FAAC) ... PDI
Paradise, NV [*Television station call letters*] ... KBLR
Paradise, NV [*AM radio station call letters*] ... KNUU
Paradise Regained [*A publication*] (AD) ... PR
Paradise Valley, AZ [*FM radio station call letters*] (RBYB) ... KBUQ-FM
Paradise Valley Public Library, Alberta [*Library symbol National Library of Canada*] (NLC) ... APV
Paradise Valley Public Library, Paradise Valley, AB, Canada [*Library symbol*] [*Library of Congress*] (LCLS) ... CaAPv
Paradox Application Language [*ANSA*] [*Computer science*] ... PAL
Paradox, Paradox, CO [*Library symbol*] [*Library of Congress*] (LCLS) ... Copx
Paradoxical Pulse [*Medicine*] (DMAA) ... PP
Paradoxical Sleep ... PS
Paraendocrine Syndrome [*Endocrinology*] ... PES
Para-(Ethoxybenzylidene)aminobenzonitrile [*Also, EBCA*] [*Organic chemistry*] ... PEBAB
Parafascicular Nucleus [*Neuroanatomy*] ... PF
Parafascicular Thalamotomy [*Medicine*] ... PFT
Paraffin [*Chemistry*] (DAVI) ... par
Paraffin Bath [*Medicine*] ... PB
Paraffin, Olefin, Naphthene, Aromatic (AD) ... pona
Paraffined Carton Research Council [*Later, Paperboard Packaging Council*] ... PCRC
Paraffins, Olefins, Naphthenes, Aromatics ... PONA
Para-Fluorophenylalanine [*Biochemistry*] ... PFA
Paragigantocellularis [*Neuroanatomy*] ... PGi
Paraglider Research Vehicle [*NASA*] ... PARASEV
Paraglider Research Vehicle [*NASA*] (MCD) ... PARESEV
Paraglider Research Vehicle [*NASA*] (KSC) ... PARSEV
Paraglossa of Labium [*Entomology*] ... PGL
Paragnostic Information Retrieval [*Parapsychology*] ... PIR
Paragon Group [*NYSE symbol*] (TTSB) ... PAO
Paragon Group, Inc. [*NYSE symbol*] (SAG) ... PAO
Paragon Group, Inc. [*Associated Press*] (SAG) ... ParagGg
Paragon Group, Inc. [*Associated Press*] (SAG) ... ParagGp
Paragon Petroleum Ltd. [*Toronto Stock Exchange symbol*] ... PGN
Paragon Resources Ltd. [*Vancouver Stock Exchange symbol*] ... PAR
Paragon Trade Brands [*Associated Press*] (SAG) ... ParagTr
Paragon Trade Brands [*NYSE symbol*] (SPSG) ... PTB
Paragould [*Arkansas*] [*Seismograph station code, US Geological Survey*] (SEIS) ... PGA
Paragould, AR [*AM radio station call letters*] ... KDRS
Paragould, AR [*FM radio station call letters*] ... KLQZ
Paragould, AR [*Location identifier FAA*] (FAAL) ... PGR
Paragould, AR [*Location identifier FAA*] (FAAL) ... PZX
Paragraph (ADA) ... P
Paragraph (AAG) ... PAR
Paragraph (WDMC) ... par
Paragraph (AFM) ... PARA
Paragraph Completion Method [*Education*] (EDAC) ... PCM
Paraguana/Josefa Camejo Internacional, Falcon [*Venezuela ICAO location identifier*] (ICLI) ... SVJC
Paraguay ... Par
Paraguay ... PARA
Paraguay [*or Paraguayan*] (WDAA) ... PARAG
Paraguay [*ANSI three-letter standard code*] (CNC) ... PRY
Paraguay [*ANSI two-letter standard code*] (CNC) ... PY
Paraguay [*IYRU nationality code*] [*MARC country of publication code Library of Congress*] (LCCP) ... py
Paraguay [*MARC geographic area code Library of Congress*] (LCCP) ... s-py--
Paraguay Committee for Human Rights [*British*] ... PCHR
Paraguay Watch (EA) ... PW
Paraguayan Communist Party ... PCP
Paraguayan People's Documentation Center [*Mestre, Italy*] (EAIO) ... PPDC
Parah (BJA) ... Par
Para-Hexadecylaminobenzoate [*Clinical chemistry*] ... PHB
Para-Hydroxybenzoate [*Organic chemistry*] ... PHB
Para-Hydroxybenzoate Hydroxylase [*An enzyme*] ... PHBH
Para-Hydroxybenzoic Acid [*Organic chemistry*] ... PHBA
Para-Hydroxybenzoic Acid Hydrazide [*Organic chemistry*] ... PAHBAH
Para-Hydroxymercuribenzoate [*Biochemistry*] ... PHMB
Para-Hydroxymercuribenzoate [*Biochemistry*] (MAE) ... PMB
Para-Hydroxymercuriphenylsulfonate [*Organic chemistry*] ... PHMS
Para-Hydroxytriamterene [*Biochemistry*] ... PHTAT
Para-Hydroxytriamterene Sulfate [*Biochemistry*] ... PHTATS
Parainfluenza Virus ... PIV
Para-iodoclonidine [*Biochemistry*] ... PIC
Paraiso [*California*] [*Seismograph station code, US Geological Survey*] (SEIS) ... PRS
Para-Isopropylphenyl(iminodiacetic Acid) ... PIPIDA
Para-Isothiocyanatephenethylamine [*Biochemistry*] ... PIP
Parakou [*Benin*] [*ICAO location identifier*] (ICLI) ... DBBP
Parakou [*Benin*] [*Airport symbol*] (OAG) ... PKO
Paralegal Program [*Association of Independent Colleges and Schools specialization code*] ... P
Paralemniscal Tegmental Field [*Neuroanatomy*] ... PTF
Paralipomenon [*Old Testament book*] [*Douay version*] ... PAR
Parallactic Angle ... X
Parallax ... P
Parallax ... PAR
Parallax (AAG) ... PRLX
Parallax Aircraft Parking Aid (PDAA) ... PAPA
Parallax and Refraction (AD) ... p & r
Parallax and Refraction (IAA) ... PAR
Parallax and Refraction ... PR
Parallax Developments [*Vancouver Stock Exchange symbol*] ... PLX
Parallax in Altitude [*Navigation*] ... P in A
Parallax in Altitude [*Navigation*] ... PINA
Parallax Second [*Unit of interstellar-space measure*] ... PARSEC
Parallax Second [*Unit of interstellar-space measure*] ... PC
Parallel ... P
Parallel (KSC) ... PAR
Parallel (WDMC) ... par
Parallel (WDAA) ... PARA
Parallel ... PARL
Parallel (MSA) ... PRL
Parallel Access Multiple Distribution (PDAA) ... PAMD
Parallel Addressable Multiplexer [*Telecommunications*] (IAA) ... PAMUX
Parallel Alternate Curriculum (EDAC) ... PAC

Parallel and Novel Architectures [British]	PNA
Parallel Applications Programme [British]	PAP
Parallel Architecture Extended [Computer science]	PAX
Parallel Architecture for Networking Gateways Linking OSI Systems (NITA)	PANGLOSS
Parallel Architecture Research and Evaluation Tool [Computer science]	PARET
Parallel Bar Noise Maker [Antiacoustic torpedo device]	PBNM
Parallel Blade Damper (OA)	PBD
Parallel by Bit	PBB
Parallel by Character	PBC
Parallel Cascade Processor (IEEE)	PCP
Parallel Circular Plate (IEEE)	PCP
Parallel Communications Link	PCL
Parallel Communications Link Receiver (NITA)	PCLR
Parallel Cutter Mechanism	PCM
Parallel Data Adapter	PDA
Parallel Data Communicator (AAG)	PDC
Parallel Data Controller	PDC
Parallel Data Query [Computer science] (CDE)	PDQ
Parallel Data Transmission	PDT
Parallel Detection Polychromator [Instrumentation]	PDP
Parallel Digital Computing System	PDCS
Parallel Digital Input/Output	PDIO
Parallel Digital-to-Analog Converter	PARDAC
Parallel Distributed Processing [A simulation of mental processes]	PDP
Parallel [Detection] Electron Energy Loss Spectroscopy	PEELS
Parallel Element Processing Ensemble [Burroughs Corp.] (BUR)	PEPE
Parallel Fiber [Neuroanatomy]	PF
Parallel Filter System	PFS
Parallel Fold	PF
Parallel Fourier Transform (MCD)	PFT
Parallel Gap Soldering	PGS
Parallel Gap Welding	PGW
Parallel Hardware Processing Language [1977] [Computer science] (CSR)	PHPL
Parallel Head Disk	PHD
Parallel Hybrid Vehicle	PHV
Parallel Inference Machine [Computer science]	PIM
Parallel Inference Multiprocessor Operating System [Computer science]	PIMOS
Parallel Injection Readout (IAA)	PIR
Parallel Input [Computer science] (BUR)	PI
Parallel Input	PIN
Parallel Input/Output	PIO
Parallel Input/Output Control System (NITA)	PIOCS
Parallel Input-Output Unit [Computer science] (IEEE)	PIOU
Parallel Instruction Control Unit	PICU
Parallel Instruction Execution [Computer science] (BUR)	PIE
Parallel Instruction Queue	PIQ
Parallel Interface Element	PIE
Parallel Interface Extender [Computer science] (IAA)	PIX
Parallel Interface/Timer [Motorola, Inc.]	PI/T
Parallel Line Communication Adaptor (NITA)	PLCA
Parallel Mass Spectrometer	PMS
Parallel Memory Address Counter [Computer science]	PMAC
Parallel Memory-to-Memory Bus	PMMB
Parallel Microprogrammed Processor [Computer science]	PMP
Parallel Modular Signal Processor	PMSP
Parallel Multiple Incremental Computer	PMIC
Parallel Multiplexer Interface Adapter (MCD)	PMIA
Parallel Network Digital Computer (IEEE)	PNDC
Parallel Optical Computer	POC
Parallel Output [Computer science] (BUR)	PO
Parallel Output	POT
Parallel Output Platform	POP
Parallel Path Counter [Electronics] (IAA)	PPC
Parallel Pattern Processor	PPP
Parallel Peripheral Interface [Computer science]	PPI
Parallel Petroleum [NASDAQ symbol] (TTSB)	PLLL
Parallel Petroleum Corp. [Associated Press] (SAG)	ParPet
Parallel Petroleum Corp. [NASDAQ symbol] (NQ)	PLLL
Parallel Processing Automata (PDAA)	PPA
Parallel Processing Machine [Computer science] (IAA)	PPM
Parallel Processing System [Computer science] (MDG)	PPS
Parallel Processor	PP
Parallel Push Pull (IAA)	PPP
Parallel Quadrature Mirror Filter (PDAA)	PQMF
Parallel Random Access Machine [Computer science]	PRAM
Parallel Resistance (IDOE)	R_p
Parallel Rod Oscillator	PRO
Parallel Single [Outdoor advertising] (NTCM)	PS
Parallel Slit Map (OA)	PSM
Parallel Strand Lumber	PSL
Parallel Switch Control (MCD)	PSC
Parallel Swivel Joint	PSJ
Parallel to Serial (NITA)	PS
Parallel to Serial Converter (MCD)	P/S
Parallel to Serial Converter	PSC
Parallel Transfer Disk [Computer science]	PTD
Parallel Transmission Unit (AAG)	PTU
Parallel Tubular Array [Cytology]	PTA
Parallel Tuned Series Stabilized (IAA)	PTSS
Parallel Undocumented Development (PDAA)	PUD
Parallel Virtual Machine [Software package]	PVM
Parallel With (IAA)	PW

Parallel Working System	PWS
Parallel-Flow Condenser [Air conditioning systems]	PFC
Parallel-Flow Film Cooling	PFFC
Parallel-In Parallel-Out [Telecommunications] (TEL)	PIPO
Parallel-In Serial-Out [Telecommunications] (TEL)	PISO
Parallel-Line Equal Space [Medicine] (DMAA)	PLES
Parallelogram [Geometry] (ADA)	PAR
Parallelogram [Geometry] (ROG)	PARM
Parallel-Serial Scan Design [Electronics]	PSSD
Parallel-Shaft Speed Reducer	PSSR
Parallel-Tuned Parallel-Stabilized (IAA)	PTPS
Paralysie Generale [General Paralysis] [Medicine French]	PG
Paralysis Agitans	PA
Paralysis Agitans Juvenilis [Medicine] (DMAA)	PAJ
Paralysis Cure Research Foundation (EA)	PCRF
Paralytic Brachial Neuritis [Medicine] (MAE)	PBN
Paralytic Shellfish Poisoning [Marine biology]	PSP
Paralyzed Academic Investigator's Disease Syndrome [Medicine] (DMAA)	PAIDS
Paralyzed Veterans of America (EA)	PVA
Paralyzing Dose [Pharmacology] (DAVI)	PD
Paramagnetic Resonance (IAA)	PMR
Paramagnetic Scheromak	PS
Paramaribo [Suriname] [Geomagnetic observatory code]	PAB
Paramaribo [Surinam] [Airport symbol] (OAG)	PBM
Paramaribo [Surinam] [ICAO location identifier] (ICLI)	SMPB
Paramaribo [Surinam] [ICAO location identifier] (ICLI)	SMPM
Paramaribo [Suriname] [Airport symbol]	ZOG
Paramaribo/Kwatta [Surinam] [ICAO location identifier] (ICLI)	SMKW
Paramaribo/Zandery [Surinam] [ICAO location identifier] (ICLI)	SMZY
Paramaribo/Zorg en Hoop [Surinam] [ICAO location identifier] (ICLI)	SMZO
Paramaribo [Surinam] Zorg En Hoop Airport [Airport symbol] (OAG)	ORG
Paramark Enterprises, Inc. [Associated Press] (SAG)	ParamrkE
Paramark Enterprises, Inc. [Associated Press] (SAG)	Prmk
Paramark Enterprises, Inc. [NASDAQ symbol] (SAG)	TJCI
Paramax Electronics, Montreal, Quebec [Library symbol National Library of Canada] (BIB)	QMPAE
Paramecin [A protozoan toxin]	P
Paramedian Pontine Reticular Formation [Neuroanatomy]	PPRF
Paramedic Jumpers	PJ's
Paramedical	PARMEDL
Para-Menthane Hydroperoxide [Organic chemistry]	PMHP
Parameter	PAR
Parameter (KSC)	PARAM
Parameter [Computer science]	PARM
Parameter [Computer science]	PM
Parameter (ECII)	PRM
Parameter (AAG)	PRMTR
Parameter Adaptive Model Reference System	PAMRS
Parameter Adjusting Mechanism	PAM
Parameter Analysis of Respiration Agents Considering Operations Motivation Protection and Time Model (MCD)	PARACOMPT
Parameter Checkout [Computer science] (IAA)	PC
Parameter Checkout Engineer [Computer science] (IAA)	PCE
Parameter Count [Computer science]	PCOUNT
Parameter Entity Symbol Translator [Elstree Computing Ltd.] [Software package] (NCC)	PEST
Parameter Estimation by Sequential Testing [Computer]	PEST
Parameter Group Identifier [Computer science] (TNIG)	PGI
Parameter Identification [Communications]	PID
Parameter Identifier [Computer science] (TNIG)	PI
Parameter Input Tape (IAA)	PIT
Parameter Inventory Display System (DNAB)	PIDS
Parameter Processing System (CAAL)	PPS
Parameter Related Internal Standard Method [Statistical procedure]	PRISM
Parameter Sensitive Frequency Assignment Method (MCD)	PSFAM
Parameter Test Control Program [Computer science] (IAA)	PTCP
Parameter Test Program (SAA)	PTP
Parameter Test Setup	PTS
Parameterized Post-Newtonian [Gravity]	PPN
Parameters from Group Contribution [Equation of state]	PFGC
Parameters: US Army War College Quarterly [A publication] (BRI)	Parameters
Paramethoxyamphetamine (AD)	pma
Paramethoxyamphetamine	PMA
Para-Methoxytoluene [Organic chemistry]	PMT
Para-Methylstyrene [Organic chemistry]	PMS
Parametric Aircraft Performance Program (MCD)	PAPP
Parametric Amplifier	PA
Parametric Amplifier (NATG)	PAM
Parametric Amplifier	PAR
Parametric Amplifier	PARAMP
Parametric Amplifier Converter	PAC
Parametric Amplifier System	PAS
Parametric Array Doppler SONAR (PDAA)	PADS
Parametric Artificial Talker	PAT
Parametric Cubic [Computer science] (OA)	PC
Parametric Defense Coverage	PDC
Parametric Design Analysis (RDA)	PDA
Parametric Earth Model [Geodynamics]	PEM
Parametric Empirical Bayes [Statistics]	PEB
Parametric Industry (IAA)	PI
Parametric Integer Linear Program [Computer science]	PILP
Parametric Monotone Decreasing Ratio [Statistics]	PMDR
Parametric Quantron [Physics]	PQ
Parametric Ruled Surface (MCD)	PRS

Parametric Semiconductor Amplifier .... PSA
Parametric Sound Amplifier [*Blaupunkt*] .... PSA
Parametric Synthesis [*Computer science*] .... PARASYN
Parametric Synthesis [*Computer science*] .... PARSYN
Parametric Technical [*NASDAQ symbol*] (TTSB) .... PMTC
Parametric Technology Corp. [*Associated Press*] (SAG) .... ParmTch
Parametric Technology Corp. [*NASDAQ symbol*] (NQ) .... PMTC
Parametric Test Synthesis [*Computer science*] .... PATSY
Parametrized Post-Keplerian [*Physics*] .... PPK
Parametrized Post-Newtonian [*Physics*] .... PPN
Paramilitary (AD) .... pm
Paramilitary Specialists (AD) .... pm specialists
Paramonga [*Peru*] [*ICAO location identifier*] (ICLI) .... SPPG
Paramount Financial [*NASDAQ symbol*] (TTSB) .... PARA
Paramount Financial Corp. [*NASDAQ symbol*] (SAG) .... PARA
Paramount Financial Corp. [*Associated Press*] (SAG) .... Paramnt
Paramount Financial Corp. [*Associated Press*] (SAG) .... Paramt
Paramount Financial Wrrt [*NASDAQ symbol*] (TTSB) .... PARAW
Paramount Funding Corp. [*Toronto Stock Exchange symbol*] .... PF
Paramount Home Video .... PHV
Paramount Pictures Corp., Research Department, Los Angeles, CA [*Library symbol Library of Congress*] (LCLS) .... CLPP
Paramount Resources, Inc. [*Vancouver Stock Exchange symbol*] .... PAO
Paramount Resources Ltd. [*Toronto Stock Exchange symbol*] .... POU
Paramp Pump Klystron .... PPK
Paramus Historical and Preservation Society, Ridgewood, NJ [*Library symbol Library of Congress*] (LCLS) .... NjRwPHi
Paramus Public Library, Paramus, NJ [*Library symbol Library of Congress*] (LCLS) .... NjPar
Paramyxovirus .... PMV
Parana (AD) .... Pr
Parana [*Argentina*] [*Airport symbol*] (OAG) .... PRA
Parana [*Brazil*] [*Airport symbol*] (AD) .... PXA
Parana/Gral Urquiza [*Argentina ICAO location identifier*] (ICLI) .... SAAP
Paranagua [*Brazil*] [*Airport symbol*] (OAG) .... PNG
Paranagua [*Brazil*] [*Airport symbol*] (AD) .... PRU
Paranagua [*Brazil ICAO location identifier*] (ICLI) .... SBPG
Paranaiba [*Brazil*] [*Airport symbol*] (OAG) .... PBB
Paranavai [*Brazil*] [*Airport symbol*] (AD) .... PVI
Paraneoplastic Encephalomyelitis [*Medicine*] (DMAA) .... PNEM
Paraneoplastic Neurodegenarative Syndrome [*Medicine*] .... PNS
Para-Nitroaniline [*Organic chemistry*] .... PNA
Para-Nitroaniline-o-sulfonic Acid [*Organic chemistry*] .... PNASA
Para-Nitroblue Tetrazolium .... PNBT
Para-Nitrochlorobenzene [*Organic chemistry*] .... PNCB
Para-Nitro-ortho-anisidine [*Organic chemistry*] .... PNOA
Para-Nitro-ortho-toluidine [*Organic chemistry*] .... PNOT
Para-Nitro-o-toluidine [*Organic chemistry*] .... PNOT
Para-Nitrophenol [*or Nitrophenyl*] [*Organic chemistry*] .... PNP
Para-Nitrophenyl Acetate [*Organic chemistry*] .... PNPA
Para-Nitrophenyl Diphenyl Phosphate [*Organic chemistry*] .... PNDP
Para-Nitrophenyl Diphenyl Phosphate [*Organic chemistry*] .... PNPDPP
Para-Nitrophenyl Laurate [*Organic chemistry*] .... PNPL
Para-Nitrophenyl Nitronyl Nitroxide .... P-NPNN
Para-Nitrophenyl Phosphate [*Organic chemistry*] .... PNPP
((Para-Nitrophenyl)azo)salicylic Acid [*A dye*] [*Organic chemistry*] .... PNBAS
Para-Nitrophenyl-Beta-Galactosidase [*An enzyme*] (DAVI) .... PNP
Para-Nitrophenylglycerine [*Biochemistry*] .... PNPG
Para-Nitrophenylsulfate [*Pharmacology*] (DAVI) .... P-NPS
Para-Nitrotoluene [*Organic chemistry*] .... PNT
Para-Nitrotoluene-ortho-sulfonic Acid [*Organic chemistry*] .... PNTOS
Paranoia [*Psychology*] .... Pa
Paranoia Obvious [*Psychology*] .... PaO
Paranoia Subtle [*Psychology*] .... PaS
Paranoid [*Psychiatry*] (DAVI) .... Par
Paranoid Ideation (DAVI) .... PI
Paranoid Personality Disorder (AD) .... PPD
Paranormal Metal Bending .... PMB
Paraoxonase [*An enzyme*] .... PON
Paraparau [*Bolivia*] [*ICAO location identifier*] (ICLI) .... SLPP
Paraparaumu [*New Zealand*] [*ICAO location identifier*] (ICLI) .... NZPP
Parapat [*Sumatra*] [*Seismograph station code, US Geological Survey*] (SEIS) .... PSI
Paraphenylene Diisocyanate [*Organic chemistry*] .... PPDI
Paraphenylene Vinylene [*Organic chemistry*] .... PPV
Para-Phenylenediamine [*Organic chemistry*] .... PPD
Para-Phenylenediamine [*Organic chemistry*] .... PPDA
Paraphrase (ADA) .... PAR
Paraphrase (BARN) .... para
Paraplegic .... para
Paraplegic and Quadriplegic Association of New South Wales [*Australia*] .... PARAQUAD
Paraplegic and Quadriplegic Association of New South Wales [*Australia*] .... PQANSW
Paraplegic and Quadriplegic Association of Queensland [*Australia*] .... PQAQ
Paraplegic and Quadriplegic Association of South Australia .... PQASA
Paraplegic and Quadriplegic Association of Victoria [*Australia*] .... PQAV
Paraplegic and Quadriplegic Association of Western Australia .... PQAWA
Parapsychological Association (EA) .... PA
Parapsychological Services Institute (EA) .... PSI
Parapsychology .... PARAPSYCH
Parapsychology Foundation (EA) .... PF
Parapsychology Institute of America (EA) .... PIA
Pararescue .... PARSQ
Parashah (BJA) .... P
Parasi [*Solomon Islands*] [*Airport symbol*] (OAG) .... PRS
Parasite Tubing Method (PDAA) .... PTM
Parasite-Induced Erythrocyte Surface Antigen [*Immunology*] .... PIESA
Parasites and Ova [*Gastroenterology*] (DAVI) .... P & O
Parasitic (IAA) .... PARAS
Parasitic Disease Drug Service (MAE) .... PDDS
Parasitic Encephalitis Meningitis [*Medicine*] .... PEM
Parasitized Red Blood Cell [*Medicine*] .... PRBC
Parasitological Society of Southern Africa (EAIO) .... PARSA
Parasitology [*Medicine*] (DMAA) .... parasit
Parasitology .... PARASITOL
Parasitophorous Vacuole Membrane [*Malaria*] .... PVM
Paraskevi [*Lesbos*] [*Greece*] [*Seismograph station code, US Geological Survey*] (SEIS) .... PRK
Parasternal Line [*Anatomy*] (MAE) .... PSL
Parasympathetic [*Division of autonomic nervous system*] [*Neurolgoy*] (DAVI) .... parasym
Parasympathetic Division [*of autonomic nervous system*] [*Neurology*] (DAVI) .... parasym div
Parasympathetic Nervous System (AD) .... pns
Parasympathetic Nervous System .... PNS
Para-Terphenyl [*Organic chemistry*] .... PT
Para-tertiary-butylbenzaldehyde [*Organic chemistry*] .... PTBB
Para-tertiary-butylbenzoic Acid [*Organic chemistry*] .... PTBBA
Para-tertiary-butyltoluene [*Organic chemistry*] .... PTBT
Parathion (GNE) .... DNTP
Parathormone [*Medicine*] (MAE) .... PTH
Parathy Roidectomy [*Medicine*] (DMAA) .... para
Parathymosin (DMAA) .... PTMS
Parathyroid [*Medicine*] .... PT
Parathyroid Extract [*Medicine*] .... PTE
Parathyroid Fever [*Medicine*] (CPH) .... PTF
Parathyroid Gland [*Medicine*] (DMAA) .... PTG
Parathyroid Hormone [*Endocrinology*] .... PARATHORMONE
Parathyroid Hormone [*Endocrinology*] .... PTH
Parathyroid Hormone Secretion Rate [*Endocrinology*] (MAE) .... PTHS
Parathyroid Hormone-Like Peptide [*Endocrinology*] .... PTH-LP
Parathyroid Hormone-Related Protein [*Biochemistry*] .... PTHrP
Parathyroid Secretory Protein [*Biochemistry*] .... PSP
Parathyroidectomy [*Medicine*] .... PTx
Parathyroidectomy and Autotransplantation [*Medicine*] (BABM) .... PTXA
Parathyroidectomy and Autotransplantation [*Endocrinology*] (DAVI) .... PTXA
Paratid Midle [*Band protein*] (DMAA) .... Pm
Para-Tolualdehyde [*Organic chemistry*] .... PTAL
Para-Toluene Sulfonylisocyanate [*Organic chemistry*] .... PTSI
Para-Toluenesulfonic Acid .... PTS
Para-Toluenesulfonic Acid [*Organic chemistry*] .... PTSA
Para-Toluidine-meta-sulfonic Acid [*Also, PTMSA*] [*Organic chemistry*] .... PTMS
Para-Toluidine-meta-sulfonic Acid [*Also, PTMS*] [*Organic chemistry*] .... PTMSA
Paratransit Vehicle .... PTV
Paratyphoid A [*Medicine*] (DAVI) .... Para-A
Paratyphoid B [*Medicine*] (DAVI) .... Para-B
Paratyphoid C [*Medicine*] (DAVI) .... Para-C
Paravane [*Anti-moored-mine device*] (KSC) .... PARV
Paravane [*Anti-moored-mine device*] [*Obsolete*] .... PV
Paravane and Stores Crane [*Engineering*] .... PARVSTRCRA
Paravant Computer Systems, Inc. [*Associated Press*] (SAG) .... Paravnt
Paravant Computer Systems, Inc. [*Associated Press*] (SAG) .... Parvnt
Paravant Computer Systems, Inc. [*NASDAQ symbol*] (SAG) .... PVAT
Paraventricular [*Neuroanatomy*] (MAE) .... PV
Paraventricular Hypothalmic Nucleus [*Neuroanatomy*] .... PVH
Paraventricular Nucleus [*Brain anatomy*] .... PVN
Paravertebral Sympathetic Ganglion [*Neuroanatomy*] .... PVSG
Paravisual Director [*British*] .... PVD
Parawing Precision Aerial Delivery System (MCD) .... PPADS
Paraxial Magnification (SAA) .... PM
Paraxial-Ray Imaging Spectro Microscope .... PRISM
Paray Le Monial [*France ICAO location identifier*] (ICLI) .... LFGN
Parc National de la Boucle de la Pendjari [*Penjari River Bend National Park*] [*French*] [*Dahamey*] (AD) .... PNBP
Parc National de la Boucle du Baoule [*Baoule River Bend National Park*] [*French*] [*Mali*] (AD) .... PNBB
Parc Saint-Maur [*France*] [*Later, CLF*] [*Geomagnetic observatory code*] .... PSM
Parcel .... PAR
Parcel .... PCL
Parcel Air Lift [*US Postal Service*] .... PAL
Parcel Business Machine System (NITA) .... PBMS
Parcel Concentration Office [*British*] .... PCO
Parcel Delivery Van .... PDV
Parcel Mail Vans [*British railroad term*] .... PMV
Parcel Post .... PP
Parcel Post (AD) .... pp
Parcel Post Association [*Later, PSA*] (EA) .... PPA
Parcel Post, Insured [*Shipping*] .... PPI
Parcel Post Insured (AD) .... ppi
Parcel Receipt (AD) .... pr
Parcel Receipt [*Shipping*] .... PR
Parcel Shippers Association (EA) .... PSA
Parcel Sorting Machine [*Freight*] (DCTA) .... PSM
Parcel Ticket [*Freight*] .... PT
Parcelas .... PARC
Parcels (MSA) .... PLS
Parchment (VRA) .... parc
Parchment (ADA) .... PARCH
Parchment (ROG) .... PARCHM
Parchment .... PARCHT

Parchment (MSA) ... PCHT
Parchment Community Library, Parchment, MI [*Library symbol Library of Congress*] (LCLS) ... MiPar
Parcplace Systems, Inc. [*Associated Press*] (SAG) ... ParcPplce
Parcplace Systems, Inc. [*NASDAQ symbol*] (SAG) ... PARQ
ParcPlace-Digitalk [*NASDAQ symbol*] (TTSB) ... PARQ
Pardessus' Lois Maritimes [*A publication*] (DLA) ... Pard Lois Mar
Pardessus' Traites des Servitudes [*A publication*] (DLA) ... Pard Serv
Pardon (ADA) ... P
Pardon My Jumping In [*E-Mail discussion*] ... PMJI
Paregoric [*Slang*] ... PG
Parenchyma [*Botany*] ... P
Parenchymal Hepatic Resection Rate [*Medicine*] ... PHRR
Parenchymatous Bundle Sheath [*Botany*] ... PBS
Parent (CPH) ... P
Parent Advisory Committee [*Migrant education*] (AEE) ... PAC
Parent Advisory Council (EDAC) ... PAC
Parent Advocacy Coalition for Educational Rights [*Minnesota*] (EDAC) ... PACER
Parent and Child Center [*Project Head Start*] ... PCC
Parent as a Teacher Inventory [*Psychology*] ... PAAT
Parent Assisted Instruction in Reading and Spelling (AIE) ... PAIRS
Parent Attitude Research Instrument [*A questionnaire*] ... PARI
Parent Attitude Scale ... PAS
Parent Attitude Toward Child Experssiveness Scale (EDAC) ... PACES
Parent Care (EA) ... PC
Parent Cells ... PC
Parent Compound Handbook [*Later, Ring Systems Handbook*] [*American Chemical Society*] ... PCH
Parent Cooperative Pre-Schools International (EA) ... PCPI
Parent Council for Deaf Education [*Australia*] ... PCDE
Parent Country National (PDAA) ... PCN
Parent Daily Telephone Report [*Education*] (EDAC) ... PDR
Parent Diabetes Opinion Survey [*Test*] ... PDOS
Parent Education Follow Through Program (EDAC) ... PEFTP
Parent Effectiveness Training [*A course of study*] ... PET
Parent Effectiveness Training Course [*Australia*] ... PETC
Parent Egg Seed ... PES
Parent Indicator Code (DNAB) ... PIC
Parent Loans to Undergraduate Students [*Later, ALAS*] [*Department of Education*] ... PLUS
Parent Locator Service [*A service of the Office of Child Support Enforcement (OCSE)*] (PAZ) ... PLS
Parent Mass Peak ... PMP
Parent Offspring [*Genetics*] ... P:O
Parent Operating Service (MCD) ... POS
Parent Organization Designator (MCD) ... POD
Parent Problem-Solving Instrument (EDAC) ... PPSI
Parent Readiness Evaluation of Preschoolers [*Child development test*] ... PREP
Parent Rule Point (MCD) ... PRP
Parent Squadron Base [*Military*] (NVT) ... PARENTSQ
Parent Support Network [*Australia*] ... PSN
Parent Symptom Questionnaire [*Medicine*] (DMAA) ... PSQ
Parent to Parent, Inc. [*Australia*] ... PTP
Parent Training and Information [*Centers*] [*Established under the Individuals with Disabilities Education Act (IDEA)*] (PAZ) ... PTI
Parent Very Disturbed [*Pediatrics*] (DAVI) ... PVD
Parent-Adult-Child [*Transactional analysis*] ... P-A-C
Parental ... P
Parental Acceptance-Rejection Questionnaire [*Psychology*] ... PARQ
Parental Advisory (WDMC) ... PA
Parental Alliance for Choice in Education (AIE) ... PACE
Parental Bonding Instrument ... PBI
Parental Control [*Channel lockout*] [*Video technology*] ... PC
Parental Diagnostic Questionnaire [*Speech evaluation test*] ... PDQ
Parental Ditype [*Genetics*] ... PD
Parental Generation (MAE) ... P_1
Parental Generation [*Medicine*] (DMAA) ... Pi
Parental Guidance [*Pediatrics*] (DAVI) ... PG
Parental Guidance Recommended [*Movie rating*] [*Australia*] ... PGR
Parental Guidance Suggested [*Later, PG*] [*Movie rating*] ... GP
Parental Guidance Suggested [*Formerly, GP*] [*Some material may not be suitable for preteenagers Movie rating*] ... PG
Parental Guidance Suggested [*Now: Parents Strongly Cautioned. Some material may be inappropriate for children under 13*] [*Movie rating*] ... PG-13
Parental Investment [*Biology*] ... PI
Parental Involvement in Education ... Apple PIE
Parental Involvement Project (AIE) ... PIP
Parental Kidnapping Prevention Act (BARN) ... PKPA
Parental Recommendation [*Movie rating*] (CDAI) ... PR
Parent-Child Activity Rating Scale [*Education*] (EDAC) ... PCAR
Parenteral ... PARENT
Parenteral and Enteral Nutrition [*Gastroenterology*] (DAVI) ... PEN
Parenteral Drug Association (EA) ... PDA
Parenteral Nutrition [*Medicine*] ... PN
Parentheses (NTCM) ... PARENS
Parenthesis ... PAR
Parenthesis (WDMC) ... par
Parenthesis (WDMC) ... paren
Parenthesis [*or Parentheses*] (AFM) ... PAREN
Parent-Infant Traumatic Stress (DAVI) ... PITS
Parenting, Education, and Political Involvement [*Jack and Jill of America*] ... PEP
Parenting in a Nuclear Age (EA) ... PINA
Parenting in a Nuclear Age (EA) ... PNA
Parenting Stress Index [*Psychology*] ... PSI
Parent-Metabolite Ratio [*Medicine*] (MEDA) ... P/M
Parent-Offspring Conflict ... POC
Parents Active for Vision Education [*An association*] (EA) ... PAVE
Parents, Administrators, Community, Teachers, and Students [*School-community groups*] ... PACTS
Parents Against Middle-Aged Discrimination [*British*] (DI) ... PAMAD
Parents Against Molesters (EA) ... PAM
Parents Against Subliminal Seduction [*Defunct*] (EA) ... PASS
Parents' Alliance to Protect Our Children (EA) ... PAPOC
Parents and Alumni Committee Involved for Youth [*Brown University*] ... PACIFY
Parents and Cataract Kids [*An association*] (PAZ) ... PACK
Parents and Children's Equality [*An association*] (PAZ) ... PACE
Parents and Citizens Guide [*A publication*] ... Parents Cit Guide
Parents and Friends Association of Western Australia ... PFAWA
Parents and Teachers Against Violence in Education (EA) ... PTAVE
Parents Anonymous (EA) ... PA
Parents Anonymous Lifeline [*British*] (DI) ... PAL
Parents' Association ... PA
Parents Campaign for Handicapped Children and Youth (EA) ... PCHCY
Parents' Charter (AIE) ... PC
Parents, Children, and Teachers (AIE) ... PACT
Parents' Choice [*A publication*] (BRI) ... Par Ch
Parents' Choice [*A publication*] ... Par Ch
Parents' Choice Foundation (EA) ... PCF
Parents' Confidential Statement [*Education*] ... PCS
Parents' Confidential Statement of the College Scholarship Service [*Education*] (IIA) ... PCS-CSS
Parents Educational Resource Center ... PERC
Parents, Educators and Environmentalists to Save Anchoives [*An association*] ... PEETSA
Parents, Families, and Friends of Lesbians and Gays (PAZ) ... FLAG
Parents for Orthodoxy in Parochial Education [*Group opposing sex education in schools*] ... POPE
Parents for Private Adoption [*Defunct*] (EA) ... PPA
Parents for Quality Education [*Defunct*] (EA) ... PQE
Parents for Torah for All Children [*Program for learning disabled children*] ... P'TACH
Parents Helping Parents [*An association*] (EA) ... PHP
Parents League of American Students of Medicine Abroad [*Defunct*] (EA) ... PLASMA
Parents Magazine [*A publication*] (BRI) ... Par
Parents' Magazine Press ... PMP
Parents' Music Resource Center (EA) ... PMRC
Parents' Music Resource Network (EA) ... PMRN
Parents' National Educational Union [*British*] ... PNEU
Parents of Adult Jewish Singles ... PAJES
Parents of Diabetics ... POD
Parents of Down's Syndrome (EA) ... PODS
Parents of Down's Syndrome Children (EA) ... PODSC
Parents of Galactosemic Children [*An association*] ... PGC
Parents of Gays (EA) ... POG
Parents of Large Families ... POL
Parents of Large Families (AD) ... polf
Parents of Missing Children [*Australia*] ... PMC
Parents of Multiple Births Associations of Canada ... POMBA
Parents of Murdered Children [*Later, POMC*] (EA) ... PMC
Parents of Murdered Children (EA) ... POMC
Parents of Near Drownings [*An association*] (EA) ... POND
Parents of Premature and High Risk Infants International (EA) ... PPHRII
Parents of Punkers (EA) ... POP
Parents of Suicides (EA) ... PS
Parents of Surrogate-Borne Infants and Toddlers in Verbal Exchange (EA) ... POSITIVE
Parents Opposed to Opting Out [*An association*] (AIE) ... POO
Parents Opposed to Sex and Sensitivity Education [*An association*] ... POSSE
Parents Opposed to Sex Education ... POSE
Parents Reaching Out [*An association*] (EA) ... PRO
Parents Rights (EA) ... PR
Parents Rights Organization (EA) ... PRO
Parents' Section of the Alexander Graham Bell Association for the Deaf (EA) ... PS
Parents Sharing Custody (EA) ... PSC
Parents United (EA) ... PU
Parents Who Care [*An association*] (NADA) ... PWC
Parents without Partners (EA) ... PWP
Parentship for World Mission (NADA) ... PWM
Parent-Teacher Association ... PTA
Parent-Teacher Group ... PTG
Parent-Teacher Questionnaire (DMAA) ... PTQ
Parent-Teacher-Student Association [*Nickname: "Pizza"*] ... PTSA
Parent-to-Parent Information on Adoption Services [*British*] (DI) ... PPIAS
Parexel International Corp. [*Associated Press*] (SAG) ... Parexel
Parexel International Corp. [*NASDAQ symbol*] (SAG) ... PRXL
PAREXEL Intl [*NASDAQ symbol*] (TTSB) ... PRXL
Parge and Core [*Construction*] ... P & C
Pariaqueductal Grey Matter [*Neurology*] (DAVI) ... PAG
Pari-Cachoeira [*Brazil*] [*Airport symbol*] (AD) ... PCH
Parietal Cell Antibodies [*Immunology*] ... PCA
Parietal Cell Antibody [*Immunology*] (DAVI) ... PARIET
Parietal Cell Autoantibody [*Immunology*] ... PCaab
Parietal Cell Vagotomy [*Medicine*] (AAMN) ... PCV
Parietal Electrode Placement in Electroencephalography [*Medicine*] (DMAA) ... P
Parieto-Occipital [*Anatomy*] (AAMN) ... PO
Parimutuel Betting System ... PBS
Parintins [*Brazil*] [*Airport symbol*] (AD) ... PIN
Paris [*France ICAO location identifier*] (ICLI) ... LFFF

Paris [*France ICAO location identifier*] (ICLI) .... LFPS
Paris [*France ICAO location identifier*] (ICLI) .... LFYX
Paris [*France*] [*Airport symbol*] (OAG) .... PAR
Paris [*Texas*] [*Airport symbol*] (OAG) .... PRX
Paris and Fonblanque's Medical Jurisprudence [*A publication*] (DLA) .... Par & Fonb Med Jur
Paris & Mount Pleasant Railroad (IIA) .... P & MP
Paris, AR [*FM radio station call letters*] .... KERX
Paris Bourse [*The French stock exchange*] .... PB
Paris, Brussels, Koln [*Cologne*], Amsterdam, London [*High-speed rail network*] (ECON) .... PBKAL
Paris Business Forms, Inc. [*Associated Press*] (SAG) .... ParisBu
Paris Business Forms, Inc. [*Burlington, NJ*] [*NASDAQ symbol*] (NQ) .... PBFI
Paris Carnegie Public Library, Paris, IL [*Library symbol Library of Congress*] (LCLS) .... IPar
Paris Carnegie Public Library, Paris, IL [*Library symbol*] [*Library of Congress*] (LCLS) .... IParP
Paris, Centre Meteorologique [*France ICAO location identifier*] (ICLI) .... LFPW
Paris [*France*] **Charles De Gaulle Airport** [*Airport symbol*] (OAG) .... CDG
Paris/Charles-De-Gaulle [*France ICAO location identifier*] (ICLI) .... LFPG
Paris Commission [*See also CP*] (EAIO) .... PARCOM
Paris Community Hospital, Paris, IL [*Library symbol Library of Congress*] (LCLS) .... IParH
Paris Corp. [*NASDAQ symbol*] (TTSB) .... PBFI
Paris Foreign Mission Society (TOCD) .... mep
Paris Foreign Mission Society (TOCD) .... MEP
Paris Gestion Informatique [*Paris Informatics Administration*] [*France*] [*Information service or system*] (IID) .... PGI
Paris Granite .... PG
Paris Group [*See also GP*] [*France*] (EAIO) .... PG
Paris, ID [*Location identifier FAA*] (FAAL) .... BBH
Paris, IL [*Location identifier FAA*] (FAAL) .... PRG
Paris, IL [*FM radio station call letters*] .... WACF
Paris, IL [*AM radio station call letters*] .... WPRS
Paris Interbank Offered Rank (ODBW) .... PIBOR
Paris International Aviation and Space Salon (MCD) .... PIASS
Paris/Issy-Les-Moulineaux [*France ICAO location identifier*] (ICLI) .... LFPI
Paris Junior College [*Texas*] .... PJC
Paris Junior College, Paris, TX [*Library symbol Library of Congress*] (LCLS) .... TxParC
Paris, KY [*FM radio station call letters*] .... WGKS
Paris, KY [*AM radio station call letters*] .... WYGH
Paris/Le Bourget [*France ICAO location identifier*] (ICLI) .... LFPB
Paris, Lyons, and Mediterranean Railway (ROG) .... PLMR
Paris, ON [*Television station call letters*] CIII
Paris Opera Ballet .... POB
Paris/Orly [*France ICAO location identifier*] (ICLI) .... LFPO
Paris [*France*] **Orly Airport** [*Airport symbol*] (OAG) .... ORY
Paris - Parc St. Maur [*France*] [*Seismograph station code, US Geological Survey*] (SEIS) .... PAR
Paris Procurement Field Office .... PPFO
Paris Public Library, Ontario [*Library symbol National Library of Canada*] (NLC) .... OPAR
Paris Public Library, Paris, ON, Canada [*Library symbol*] [*Library of Congress*] (LCLS) .... CaOPar
Paris Publications, Inc. .... PP
Paris, TN [*Location identifier FAA*] (FAAL) .... PHT
Paris, TN [*Location identifier FAA*] (FAAL) .... TIQ
Paris, TN [*FM radio station call letters*] .... WAKQ
Paris, TN [*AM radio station call letters*] .... WMUF
Paris, TN [*FM radio station call letters*] .... WMUF-FM
Paris, TN [*AM radio station call letters*] .... WTPR
Paris, TX [*FM radio station call letters*] .... KBUS
Paris, TX [*AM radio station call letters*] .... KGDD
Paris, TX [*FM radio station call letters*] .... KOYN
Paris, TX [*AM radio station call letters*] .... KPLT
Paris, TX [*FM radio station call letters*] .... KPLT-FM
Paris, TX [*Location identifier FAA*] (FAAL) .... PRX
Paris Union School District, Paris, IL [*Library symbol*] [*Library of Congress*] (LCLS) .... IParSD
Pariser-Parr-Pople [*Physical chemistry*] .... PPP
Parish (ROG) .... P
Parish .... PA
Parish .... PAR
Parish Church [*British*] (ROG) .... PC
Parish Church (AD) .... Pr Ch
Parish Council .... PC
Parish Line R. R. [*AAR code*] .... PL
Parish Priest .... PP
Parish Register .... PR
Parish Visitors of Mary Immaculate [*Roman Catholic women's religious order*] .... PVMI
Parish Will Case [*A publication*] (DLA) .... Par WC
Parisi Spanish Proficiency Test (EDAC) .... PSPT
Parisiensis Nomina Anatomica [*Paris Anatomical Nomenclature*] [*Medicine*] .... PNA
Paris-Moulineaux [*France*] [*Airport symbol*] (OAG) .... JDP
Parity [*Obstetrics*] (DAVI) .... P
Parity [*Atomic physics*] .... P
Parity (ADA) .... PAR
Parity [*Gynecology and obstetrics*] (DAVI) .... para
Parity (IAA) .... PTY
Parity BIT [*Binary Digit*] [*Data communications*] (IAA) .... PB
Parity BIT [*Binary Digit*] [*Data communications*] .... PBIT
Parity BIT [*Binary Digit*] **Test** .... PBT
Parity Check [*Computer science*] (IAA) .... PC
Parity Check [*Data communications*] (TEL) .... PCHK
Parity Check Matrix (MCD) .... PCM
Parity Error .... PE
Parity Error Rate .... PER
Parity Index [*EEO*] .... PI
Parity Odd .... PO
Parity Price (MHDW) .... PP
Parity Switch .... PS
Parity Violating Energy Difference [*Physical chemistry*] .... PVED
Parity Violation Energy Difference [*Physics*] .... PVED
Park .... P
Park [*Postal Service standard*] (OPSA) .... PARK
Park (VRA) .... pk
Park (DD) .... Pk
Park [*or Parking*] .... PK
Park .... PRK
Park Avenue Elementary School, North Merrick, NY [*Library symbol*] [*Library of Congress*] (LCLS) .... NNmPE
Park City, UT [*FM radio station call letters*] .... KPCW
Park College, Parkville, MO [*Library symbol Library of Congress*] (LCLS) .... MoParkC
Park County Public Library, Bailey, CO [*Library symbol Library of Congress*] (LCLS) .... CoBai
Park. Dower [*1819*] [*A publication*] (DLA) .... Park Dow
Park Electrochemical [*NYSE symbol*] (TTSB) .... PKE
Park Electrochemical Corp. [*Associated Press*] (SAG) .... ParkEl
Park Electrochemical Corp. [*NYSE symbol*] (SPSG) .... PKE
Park Elementary School, Hutchinson, MN [*Library symbol*] [*Library of Congress*] (LCLS) .... MnHuPES
Park Elementary School, North Bellmore, NY [*Library symbol Library of Congress*] (LCLS) .... NNbePE
Park Falls, WI [*Location identifier FAA*] (FAAL) .... PKF
Park Falls, WI [*FM radio station call letters*] .... WCQM
Park Falls, WI [*FM radio station call letters*] .... WHBM
Park Falls, WI [*Television station call letters*] .... WLEF
Park Falls, WI [*AM radio station call letters*] .... WNBI
Park Forest Public Library, Park Forest, IL [*Library symbol Library of Congress*] (LCLS) .... IPf
Park Forest South Public Library, Park Forest South, IL [*Library symbol Library of Congress*] (LCLS) .... IPfs
Park Gallatin Hereford Association (EA) .... PGHA
Park High School, Livingston, MT [*Library symbol*] [*Library of Congress*] (LCLS) .... MtLvHS
Park Hill [*California*] [*Seismograph station code, US Geological Survey*] (SEIS) .... PKH
Park Hill North Junior High School, Kansas City, MO [*Library symbol Library of Congress*] (LCLS) .... MoKPh
Park Hill North Junior High School, Kansas City, MO [*Library symbol*] [*Library of Congress*] (LCLS) .... MoKPhJH
Park Hill School District, Kansas City, MO [*Library symbol*] [*Library of Congress*] (LCLS) .... MoKPhSD
Park Hills, MO [*AM radio station call letters*] .... KFMO
Park Home Residents Guild [*British*] (DBA) .... PHRG
Park Management Library, Manitoba Department of Natural Resources, Winnipeg, Manitoba [*Library symbol National Library of Canada*] (NLC) .... MWPNR
Park Meditech [*NASDAQ symbol*] (TTSB) .... PMDTF
Park Meditech, Inc. [*Associated Press*] (SAG) .... ParkMed
Park Meditech, Inc. [*NASDAQ symbol*] (SAG) .... PMDT
Park Museum Reference Library, Providence, RI [*Library symbol Library of Congress*] (LCLS) .... RPPM
Park National Corp. [*Associated Press*] (SAG) .... ParkNatl
Park National Corp. [*AMEX symbol*] (SAG) .... PRK
Park National Corp. [*AMEX symbol*] (TTSB) .... PRK
Park Ohio Industries [*Associated Press*] (SAG) .... ParkOh
Park Ohio Industries [*NASDAQ symbol*] (SAG) .... PKOH
Park Ranger (AD) .... PR
Park Rapids Area High School, Park Rapids, MN [*Library symbol*] [*Library of Congress*] (LCLS) .... MnParH
Park Rapids Middle School, Park Rapids, MN [*Library symbol*] [*Library of Congress*] (LCLS) .... MnParM
Park Rapids, MN [*FM radio station call letters*] .... KDKK
Park Rapids, MN [*AM radio station call letters*] .... KPRM
Park Rapids, MN [*Location identifier FAA*] (FAAL) .... PKD
Park Restoration and Improvement Program [*National Park Service*] .... PRIP
Park Reverse Neutral [*Automotive engineering*] .... PRN
Park, Reverse, Neutral, Drive, Low [*Automotive term for automatic gearshift indicator in cars; pronounced "prindle"*] .... PRNDL
Park Ridge Center (EA) .... PRC
Park Ridge Hospital, Medical Library, Rochester, NY [*Library symbol Library of Congress*] (LCLS) .... NRPH
Park Ridge Hospital, Medical Library, Rochester, NY [*OCLC symbol*] (OCLC) .... VQX
Park Ridge, IL [*FM radio station call letters*] .... WMTH
Park Ridge Public Library, Park Ridge, IL [*Library symbol*] [*Library of Congress*] (LCLS) .... Ipark
Park School Early Childhood Center, Westbury, NY [*Library symbol*] [*Library of Congress*] (LCLS) .... NWePSE
Park Synagogue, Cleveland, OH [*Library symbol Library of Congress*] (LCLS) .... OClP
Park View Health Center, Winnebago, WI [*Library symbol Library of Congress*] (LCLS) .... WWiP
Park View Intermediate School, Pasadena, TX [*Library symbol*] [*Library of Congress*] (LCLS) .... TxPPvI

Park West Hospital, Knoxville, TN [*Library symbol Library of Congress*] (LCLS) .... TKPH
Parke County Recorder's Office, Rockville, IN [*Library symbol Library of Congress*] (LCLS) .... InRvCR
Parke, Davis & Co. [*Research code symbol*] CI
Parke, Davis & Co. [*Research code symbol*] .... CN
Parke, Davis & Co. [*Research code symbol*] .... EA
Parke, Davis & Co. [*Great Britain*] [*Research code symbol*] .... INF
Parke, Davis & Co. [*Research code symbol*] .... PAA
Parke, Davis & Co. [*Research code symbol*] .... SN
Parke, Davis & Co., Detroit, MI [*Library symbol Library of Congress*] (LCLS) .... MiDPD
Parke, Davis & Co., Research Library, Ann Arbor, MI [*Library symbol Library of Congress*] (LCLS) .... MiAaP
Parke-Bernet [*Later, SPB*] [*Manhattan art auction house*] .... PB
Parked Aircraft Intrusion Detector (PDAA) .... PAID
Parked Aircraft Security System (PDAA) .... PASS
Parke-Davis [*Commercial firm*] (DAVI) .... PD
Parker Aircraft Corp. (MCD) .... PAC
Parker & Parsley Petrol [*NYSE symbol*] (TTSB) .... PDP
Parker & Parsley Petroleum [*Associated Press*] (SAG) .... ParkPar
Parker & Parsley Petroleum [*NYSE symbol*] (SAG) .... PDP
Parker, AZ [*AM radio station call letters*] .... KLPZ
Parker, AZ [*FM radio station call letters*] (RBYB) .... KVEZ-FM
Parker, AZ [*FM radio station call letters*] .... KWFH
Parker, CA [*Location identifier FAA*] (FAAL) .... PKE
Parker Chiropractic Resource Foundation (EA) .... PCRF
Parker College of Chiropractic, Dallas, TX [*Library symbol*] [*Library of Congress*] (LCLS) .... TxDaPCC
Parker Drilling [*NYSE symbol*] (TTSB) .... PKD
Parker Drilling Co. [*Associated Press*] (SAG) .... ParkDrl
Parker Drilling Co. [*NYSE symbol*] (SPSG) .... PKD
Parker Historical Society of Clay County, Spencer, IA [*Library symbol*] [*Library of Congress*] (LCLS) .... IaSpeHi
Parker on Arbitration [*1820*] [*A publication*] (DLA) .... Park Arb
Parker on the Laws of Shipping and Insurance [*England*] [*A publication*] (DLA) .... Parker
Parker Public Library, Parker, SD [*Library symbol Library of Congress*] (LCLS) .... SdPa
Parker-Coltrane Political Action Committee [*Defunct*] (EA) .... PCPAC
Parker-Hannifin [*NYSE symbol*] (TTSB) .... PH
Parker-Hannifin Corp. [*Associated Press*] (SAG) .... ParkHn
Parker-Hannifin Corp. [*NYSE symbol*] (SPSG) .... PH
Parkerized [*Metallurgy*] [*Tradename*] .... PARK
Parker's California Digest [*A publication*] (DLA) .... Park Dig
Parker's Criminal Reports [*New York*] [*A publication*] (DLA) .... PCR
Parker's English Exchequer Reports [*A publication*] (DLA) .... Par
Parker's English Exchequer Reports [*1743-67*] [*A publication*] (DLA) .... Park
Parker's English Exchequer Reports [*1743-67*] [*A publication*] (DLA) .... Park Exch
Parker's English Exchequer Reports [*A publication*] (DLA) .... Parker
Parker's English Exchequer Reports (Revenue Cases) [*A publication*] (DLA) .... Park Rev Cas
Parker's Insurance [*8 eds.*] [*1787-1842 England*] [*A publication*] (DLA) .... Park Ins
Parkers Marsh Natural Area [*Virginia*] (AD) .... PMNA
Parker's New Hampshire Reports [*A publication*] (DLA) .... Park
Parker's New Hampshire Reports [*A publication*] (DLA) .... Park NH
Parker's New Hampshire Reports [*A publication*] (DLA) .... Parker
Parker's New York Criminal Cases [*1823-68*] [*A publication*] (DLA) .... Park
Parker's New York Criminal Cases [*A publication*] (DLA) .... Park Cr Cas
Parker's New York Criminal Cases [*A publication*] (DLA) .... Park Crim (NY)
Parker's New York Criminal Reports [*A publication*] (DLA) .... P Cl R
Parker's New York Criminal Reports [*A publication*] (DLA) .... Par
Parker's New York Criminal Reports [*A publication*] (DLA) .... Park CR
Parker's New York Criminal Reports [*A publication*] (DLA) .... Park Cr Rep
Parker's New York Criminal Reports [*A publication*] (DLA) .... Park Crim L
Parker's New York Criminal Reports [*A publication*] (DLA) .... Park Crim R
Parker's New York Criminal Reports [*A publication*] (DLA) .... Park Crim Rep
Parker's New York Criminal Reports [*6 vols.*] [*A publication*] (DLA) .... Parker
Parker's New York Criminal Reports [*A publication*] (ILCA) .... Parker Cr Cas
Parker's New York Criminal Reports [*A publication*] (ILCA) .... Parker Cr Cas (NY)
Parker's New York Criminal Reports [*A publication*] (ILCA) .... Parker Cr R
Parker's New York Criminal Reports [*A publication*] (ILCA) .... Parker Cr R (NY)
Parker's New York Criminal Reports [*A publication*] (DLA) .... Parker's Cr R
Parker's New York Criminal Reports [*A publication*] (DLA) .... Parker's Crim R
Parker's New York Criminal Reports [*A publication*] (DLA) .... Parker's Crim Rep (NY)
Parker's Practice in Chancery [*A publication*] (DLA) .... Park Ch
Parker's Practice in Chancery [*A publication*] (DLA) .... Park Pr Ch
Parkers Prairie High School, Parkers Prairie, MN [*Library symbol*] [*Library of Congress*] (LCLS) .... MnPapH
Parkersburg [*West Virginia*] [*Airport symbol*] (OAG) .... PKB
Parkersburg Community College, Parkersburg, WV [*Library symbol Library of Congress*] (LCLS) .... WvPC
Parkersburg, WV [*Location identifier FAA*] (FAAL) .... PKB
Parkersburg, WV [*AM radio station call letters*] .... WADC
Parkersburg, WV [*FM radio station call letters*] .... WHCM
Parkersburg, WV [*AM radio station call letters*] .... WKYG
Parkersburg, WV [*AM radio station call letters*] .... WLTP
Parkersburg, WV [*Television station call letters*] .... WTAP
Parkersburg, WV [*FM radio station call letters*] .... WVPG
Parkersburg, WV [*FM radio station call letters*] .... WXIL
Parkersburg, WV [*FM radio station call letters*] .... WXKX
Parkervision, Inc. [*Associated Press*] (SAG) .... Parkrvsn
Parkervision, Inc. [*NASDAQ symbol*] (SAG) .... PRKR
ParkerVision Inc. [*NASDAQ symbol*] (TTSB) .... PRKR
Parkes [*Australia Airport symbol*] (OAG) .... PKE
Parkes' History of Court of Chancery [*1828*] [*A publication*] (DLA) .... Park Hist Ch
Parkes-Tidbinbilla Interferometer [*Astronomy*] .... PTI
Parkfield Array [*California*] [*Seismograph station code, US Geological Survey*] (SEIS) .... PKF
Parkfield Downhole Digital Seismic Network [*Seismology*] .... DDSN
Parking .... PARK
Parking (KSC) .... PKG
Parking .... PRKG
Parking Enforcement Aide (ECON) .... PEA
Parking Orbit [*NASA*] .... PO
Parking Orbit Injection [*NASA*] .... POI
Parking Orbit Rendezvous [*NASA*] (MCD) .... POR
Parking Patrol Officer .... PPO
Parking Place [*Traffic sign*] [*British*] .... P
Parkinson Support Groups of America (EA) .... PSGA
Parkinsonism [*Medicine*] (DMAA) .... PKN
Parkinsonism Dementia [*Medicine*] .... PD
Parkinsonism-Dementia Complex of Guam [*Medicine*] (DMAA) .... PDG
Parkinson's Disease [*Medicine*] .... PD
Parkinson's Disease Association of Victoria [*Australia*] .... PDAV
Parkinson's Disease Foundation (EA) .... PDF
Parkinson's Disease Society [*British*] .... PDS
Parkinson's Educational Program - USA (EA) .... PEP/USA
Parkland College, Champaign, IL [*OCLC symbol*] (OCLC) .... IAQ
Parkland College, Champaign, IL [*Library symbol Library of Congress*] (LCLS) .... IChamP
Parkland Industries Ltd. [*Toronto Stock Exchange symbol*] .... PKI
Parkland On-Line Information Systems [*Computer science*] (DMAA) .... POIS
Parkland Regional Library, Dauphin, Manitoba [*Library symbol National Library of Canada*] (NLC) .... MDP
Parkland Regional Library, Dauphin, MB, Canada [*Library symbol Library of Congress*] (LCLS) .... CaMDaP
Parkland Regional Library, Lacombe, AB, Canada [*Library symbol Library of Congress*] (LCLS) .... CaALaP
Parkland Regional Library, Lacombe, Alberta [*Library symbol National Library of Canada*] (NLC) .... ALAP
Parkland Regional Library, Yorkton, Saskatchewan [*Library symbol National Library of Canada*] (NLC) .... SYP
Parkland Regional Library, Yorkton, SK, Canada [*Library symbol Library of Congress*] (LCLS) .... CaSYP
Parklane Technologies, Inc. [*Vancouver Stock Exchange symbol*] .... PKL
Parklawn Health Library Computer Center [*Department of Health and Human Services*] (GFGA) .... PCC
Parklawn Health Library, Rockville, MD [*OCLC symbol*] (OCLC) .... HNP
Park-Neutral Switch [*Automotive engineering*] .... PNS
Park-Neutral-Drive-Low-Reverse (AD) .... P-N-D-L-R
Park-Ohio Indus [*NASDAQ symbol*] (TTSB) .... PKOH
Park-Ohio Industries, Inc. [*Associated Press*] (SAG) .... ParkOh
Park-Ohio Industries, Inc. [*NASDAQ symbol*] (NQ) .... PKOH
Park-Reverse-Neutral-Drive-Low [*Automobile transmissions*] .... PRNDL
Parks [*Alaska*] [*Airport symbol*] (OAG) .... KPK
Parks [*Commonly used*] (OPSA) .... PARKS
Parks, AK [*Location identifier FAA*] (FAAL) .... KPK
Parks & Recreation [*A publication*] (BRI) .... P&R
Parks and Recreation Girls Service .... PARGS
Parks and Renewable Resources, Fisheries Branch, La Ronge, SK, Canada [*Library symbol*] [*Library of Congress*] (LCLS) .... CaSLrPRF
Parks Canada, Auyuittuq National Park, Pangnirtung, NT, Canada [*Library symbol Library of Congress*] (LCLS) .... CaNWPPCA
Parks Canada [*Parcs Canada*] **Churchill, Manitoba** [*Library symbol National Library of Canada*] (NLC) .... MCPC
Parks Canada, Churchill, MB, Canada [*Library symbol Library of Congress*] (LCLS) .... CaMChPC
Parks Canada, Fort Langley National Historic Park, BC, Canada [*Library symbol*] [*Library of Congress*] (LCLS) .... CaBFlPC
Parks Canada, Fort Walsh National Historic Park, Maple Creek, SK, Canada [*Library symbol Library of Congress*] (LCLS) .... CaSMcPCF
Parks Canada, Grasslands National Park, Val Marie, SK, Canada [*Library symbol Library of Congress*] (LCLS) .... CaSVmPCG
Parks Canada, Klondike Historic Site, Dawson City, YT, Canada [*Library symbol Library of Congress*] (LCLS) .... CaYDPCK
Parks Canada, Kluane National Park, Haines Junction, YT, Canada [*Library symbol Library of Congress*] (LCLS) .... CaYHjPCK
Parks Canada, Lower Fort Garry National Historic Park, Selkirk, MB, Canada [*Library symbol Library of Congress*] (LCLS) .... CaMSePCL
Parks Canada, Nahanni National Park, Fort Simpson, NT, Canada [*Library symbol Library of Congress*] (LCLS) .... CaNWFsPCN
Parks Canada, National Historic Park, Coteau-du-lac, PQ, Canada [*Library symbol*] [*Library of Congress*] (LCLS) .... CaQClPC
Parks Canada, National Historic Sites, Whitehorse, YT, Canada [*Library symbol Library of Congress*] (LCLS) .... CaYWPCN
Parks Canada, Prairie Region Library, Archaeology Subsection Office, Winnipeg, MB, Canada [*Library symbol Library of Congress*] (LCLS) .... CaMWPCPA
Parks Canada, Prairie Region Library, Historic Resources Conservation SubsectionOffice, Winnipeg, MB, Canada [*Library symbol Library of Congress*] (LCLS) .... CaMWPCPH
Parks Canada, Prairie Regional Office, Winnipeg, MB, Canada [*Library symbol*] [*Library of Congress*] (LCLS) .... CaMWIAP
Parks Canada, Prince Albert National Park, Waskesiu Lakes, SK, Canada [*Library symbol Library of Congress*] (LCLS) .... CaSWaPCP
Parks Canada [*Parcs Canada*] **Revelstoke, British Columbia** [*Library symbol National Library of Canada*] (NLC) .... BRPC

Parks Canada, Riding Mountain National Park, Wasagaming, MB, Canada
[*Library symbol Library of Congress*] (LCLS) .... CaMWaPCR
Parks Canada, Ste. Foy, PQ, Canada [*Library symbol*] [*Library of Congress*]
(LCLS) .... CaQQPC
Parks Canada, Wood Buffalo National Park, Fort Smith, NT, Canada [*Library symbol Library of Congress*] (LCLS) .... CaNWFSPCW
Parks Canada [*Parcs Canada*] Yellowknife, Northwest Territories [*Library symbol National Library of Canada*] (NLC) .... NWYPC
Parks Canada, Yellowknife, NT, Canada [*Library symbol Library of Congress*] (LCLS) .... CaNWYPC
Parks College of Aeronautical Technology, East St. Louis, IL [*Library symbol Library of Congress*] (LCLS) .... IEsP
Parks College of Saint Louis University, Cahokia, IL [*Library symbol*] [*Library of Congress*] (LCLS) .... ICahP
Parks Elementary School, Pasadena, TX [*Library symbol*] [*Library of Congress*] (LCLS) .... TxPPE
Parks Library, Ministry of Parks, Victoria, British Columbia [*Library symbol National Library of Canada*] (NLC) .... BVILPHP
Parks, Recreation and Cultural Affairs Administration [*New York City*] ...... PRCA
Parks Residents Environmental Action Group [*Australia*] .... PREAG
Parks Service, Environment Canada [*Service des Parcs, Environnement Canada*], Quebec [*Library symbol National Library of Canada*] (BIB) .... QQCPQ
Parkside Elementary School, Marshall, MN [*Library symbol*] [*Library of Congress*] (LCLS) .... MnMarPE
Parkside Petroleum, Inc. [*Toronto Stock Exchange symbol Vancouver Stock Exchange symbol*] .... PRK
Parksville, BC [*AM radio station call letters*] (RBYB) .... CKCI
Parkvale Financial [*NASDAQ symbol*] (TTSB) .... PVSA
Parkvale Financial Corp. [*Associated Press*] (SAG) .... ParkvF
Parkvale Financial Corp. [*NASDAQ symbol*] (NQ) .... PVSA
Parkview Episcopal Hospital, Pueblo, CO [*Library symbol Library of Congress*] (LCLS) .... CoPPE
Parkville Elementary School, Great Neck, NY [*Library symbol Library of Congress*] (LCLS) .... NGrnPE
Parkville, MO [*FM radio station call letters*] .... KGSP
Parkway [*Commonly used*] (OPSA) .... PARKWAY
Parkway [*Commonly used*] (OPSA) .... PARKWY
Parkway (MSA) .... PKWAY
Parkway (KSC) .... PKWY
Parkway .... PKWY
Parkway .... PKY
Parkway (DD) .... Pky
Parkway (MCD) .... PKY
[*The*] Parkway Co. [*Associated Press*] (SAG) .... Parkwy
[*The*] Parkway Co. [*NASDAQ symbol*] (NQ) .... PKWY
Parkway Elementary School, East Meadow, NY [*Library symbol Library of Congress*] (LCLS) .... NEmPE
Parkway Elementary School, Plainview, NY [*Library symbol Library of Congress*] (LCLS) .... NPIPwE
Parkways [*Commonly used*] (OPSA) .... PARKWAYS
Parkways [*Commonly used*] (OPSA) .... PKWYS
Parkwood Hospital Services, London, Ontario [*Library symbol National Library of Canada*] (BIB) .... OLPHS
Parlake Resources Ltd. [*Toronto Stock Exchange symbol*] .... PLR
Parlamento Latinoamericano [*Latin American Parliament - LAP*] [*Bogota, Colombia*] (EAIO) .... PLA
Parlando [*Music*] (ROG) .... PARLO
Parlar Resources Ltd. [*Vancouver Stock Exchange symbol*] .... PLA
Parlex Corp. [*Associated Press*] (SAG) .... Parlex
Parlex Corp. [*NASDAQ symbol*] (NQ) .... PRLX
Parliament .... PARL
Parliament .... PARLT
Parliament .... Plt
Parliament House Book [*Scotland*] [*A publication*] (DLA) .... PHB
Parliament National Organisations and Public Offices [*British*] .... PNOPO
Parliamentarians for World Order (EA) .... PWO
Parliamentary .... PARLTY
Parliamentary .... PARLY
Parliamentary Association for Euro-Arab Cooperation (EA) .... PAEAC
Parliamentary Bill [*British*] (ROG) .... PB
Parliamentary Borough .... PARLB
Parliamentary Cases [*House of Lords Reports*] [*A publication*] (DLA) .... Parl Cas
Parliamentary Cases [*A publication*] (DLA) .... PC
Parliamentary Centre for Foreign Affairs and Foreign Trade, Ottawa, ON, Canada [*Library symbol*] [*Library of Congress*] (LCLS) .... CaOOPCF
Parliamentary Centre for Foreign Affairs and Foreign Trade [*Centre Parlementaire pour les Affaires Etrangeres et le Commerce Exterieur*], Ottawa, Ontario [*Library symbol National Library of Canada*] (NLC) .... OOPCF
Parliamentary Commissioner for Administration [*British*] .... PCA
Parliamentary Commissioner for Administrative Investigations [*Western Australia*] .... PCAI
Parliamentary Conservative Party [*British*] (BARN) .... PCP
Parliamentary Council of the European Movement .... PCEM
Parliamentary Counsel's Office [*Australia*] .... PCO
Parliamentary Criminal Justice Committee [*Queensland, Australia*] .... PCJC
Parliamentary Democratic Party [*Myanmar*] [*Political party*] .... PDP
Parliamentary Education for Teacher Education [*Australia*] .... PETE
Parliamentary Group for World Government .... PGWG
Parliamentary History of England [*Pre-1803*] [*A publication*] (DLA) .... Parl Hist Eng
Parliamentary Human Rights Group (EAIO) .... PHRG
Parliamentary Information Technology Committee [*Political communications*] [*British*] .... PITCOM
Parliamentary Labour Party [*British*] .... PLP
Parliamentary Liaison Group for Alternative Energy Strategies [*British*] .... PARLIGAES

Parliamentary Liaison Officer (ADA) .... PLO
Parliamentary Library of Victoria, Parliament House, Melbourne, V, Australia [*Library symbol Library of Congress*] (LCLS) .... AuMP
Parliamentary Library, Parliament House, Adelaide, SA, Australia [*Library symbol Library of Congress*] (LCLS) .... AuAP
Parliamentary Library, Parliament House, Hobart, TAS, Australia [*Library symbol Library of Congress*] (LCLS) .... AuHP
Parliamentary Library, Parliament House, Sydney, NSW, Australia [*Library symbol Library of Congress*] (LCLS) .... AuSP
Parliamentary Lobby Journalists [*British*] .... PLJ
Parliamentary Office of Science and Technology [*British*] .... POST
Parliamentary Officer [*Australia*] .... PO
Parliamentary On-Line Information System [*House of Commons Library*] [*Bibliographic database*] [*Information service or system*] [*British*] (IID) ...... POLIS
Parliamentary On-Line Library Study [*Atomic Energy Authority*] [*British*] .... POLLS
Parliamentary Papers [*A publication British*] .... PP
Parliamentary Private Secretary [*British*] .... PPS
Parliamentary Question [*British*] .... PQ
Parliamentary Register [*England*] [*A publication*] (DLA) .... Parl Reg
Parliamentary Remuneration Tribunal [*New South Wales, Australia*] .... PRT
Parliamentary Report [*British*] .... PR
Parliamentary Research Services [*British*] .... PRS
Parliamentary Retiring Allowances Trust [*Australia*] .... PRAT
Parliamentary Secretary [*British*] .... PS
Parliamentary Select Committee on Agriculture [*British*] .... PSCA
Parliamentary Standing Committee on Broadcasting [*Australia*] .... PSCB
Parliamentary Under Secretary [*British*] .... PUS
Parliment Place Elementary School, North Babylon, NY [*Library symbol*] [*Library of Congress*] (LCLS) .... NNbPE
Parlin Memorial Library, Everett, MA [*Library symbol Library of Congress*] (LCLS) .... MEvP
Parlin Public Library, Canton, IL [*OCLC symbol*] (OCLC) .... IEL
Parlin-Ingersoll Public Library, Canton, IL [*Library symbol Library of Congress*] (LCLS) .... ICan
Parlophone [*Record label*] [*Great Britain, Italy, Australia, etc.*] .... P
Parlor .... PRLR
Parlor Maid .... PM
Parlor Snake [*Slang for "to escort visitors around post"*] .... PS
Parlux Fragrances [*NASDAQ symbol*] (TTSB) .... PARL
Parlux Fragrances, Inc. [*NASDAQ symbol*] (NQ) .... PARL
Parlux Fragrances, Inc. [*Associated Press*] (SAG) .... Parlux
Parma [*Italy ICAO location identifier*] (ICLI) .... LIMP
Parma Byzantine [*Diocesan abbreviation*] [*Ohio*] (TOCD) .... PRM
Parma, OH [*AM radio station call letters*] .... WCCD
Parma Public Library, Parma, ID [*Library symbol*] [*Library of Congress*] (LCLS) .... IdPar
Parmac Mines [*Vancouver Stock Exchange symbol*] .... PMI
Parmelia (AD) .... pmla
Parmenides [*of Plato*] [*Classical studies*] (OCD) .... Prm
Parnaiba [*Brazil*] [*Airport symbol*] (OAG) .... PHB
Parnaiba [*Brazil ICAO location identifier*] (ICLI) .... SBPB
Parnassus: Poetry in Review [*A publication*] (BRI) .... Parnassus
Parnelli Jones [*Race car driver*] .... PJ
Parochial .... PAR
Parochial (ROG) .... PAROCH
Parochial Antiquities [*A publication*] (DLA) .... Par Ant
Parochial Church Council [*Church of England*] .... PCC
Parochial Clergy Association [*British*] (DBA) .... PCA
Parochial School .... PS
Parodies Done Quirkily [*Humorous translation of Peter Schickele's PDQ Bach*] .... PDQ
Parodorum Epicorum Graecorum Reliquiae [*A publication*] (OCD) .... Parod Epic Gr Rel
Parole and Probation Compact Administrators Association (EA) .... PPCAA
Parole Board [*Australian Capital Territory*] .... PB
Parole Board of South Australia .... PBSA
Parole Board of the Northern Territory [*Australia*] .... PBNT
Parole Evidence Rule [*Legal shorthand*] (LWAP) .... PER
Parole Officer (AD) .... P/O
Parole Officer .... PO
Parole Violator .... PV
Parolees, Law-Enforcement Assist Student Education [*Project to reduce drug abuse among junior and senior high school students in California*] .... PLEASE
Paromomycin-Vancomycin [*Blood agar*] [*Microbiology*] .... PV
Paros [*Greece*] [*ICAO location identifier*] (ICLI) .... LGPA
Paros [*Greece*] [*Airport symbol*] (OAG) .... PAS
Parosteal Osteosarcoma [*Oncology*] (DAVI) .... POS
Parotid Flow Rate [*otorhinolaryngology*] (DAVI) .... PFR
Parotid Gland [*Medicine*] (DMAA) .... PG
Parotid Hormone [*Biochemistry*] .... PH
Paroxypropione [*or Paraoxypropiophenone*] [*Endocrinology*] .... POP
Paroxysmal [*Medicine*] .... PAROX
Paroxysmal Atrial [*or Auricular*] Fibrillation [*Medicine*] (MAE) .... PAF
Paroxysmal Atrial [*or Auricular*] Fibrillation [*Medicine*] (MAE) .... PAFIB
Paroxysmal Atrial [*or Auricular*] Tachycardia [*Medicine*] (MAE) .... PAT
Paroxysmal Atrial [*or Auricular*] Tachycardia [*Medicine*] .... PATC
Paroxysmal Cold Hemoglobinuria [*Medicine*] .... PCH
Paroxysmal Depolarizing Shift [*Physiology*] .... PDS
Paroxysmal Dyspnea on Exertion [*Medicine*] .... PDE
Paroxysmal Junctional Tachycardia [*Cardiology*] .... PJT
Paroxysmal Junctional-Ventricular Tachycardia [*Medicine*] (MEDA) .... PJVT
Paroxysmal Localized Hyperhidrosis [*Dermatology*] (DAVI) .... PLH
Paroxysmal Nocturnal Dyspnoea (AD) .... pnd
Paroxysmal Nocturnal Dyspnea [*Medicine*] .... PND

Paroxysmal Nocturnal Hemoglobinuria [*Medicine*] ... PNH
Paroxysmal Nocturnal Hemoglobinuria (AD) ... pnh
Paroxysmal Nodal Tachycardia [*Cardiology*] ... PNT
Paroxysmal Superaventricular Tachycardia [*Medicine*] (MEDA) ... PST
Paroxysmal Supraventricular Tachycardia [*Cardiology*] (DAVI) ... PST
Paroxysmal Supraventricular Tachycardia [*Cardiology*] ... PSVT
Paroxysmal Tachycardia [*Cardiology*] ... PT
Paroxysmal Ventricular Tachycardia [*Medicine*] ... PVT
Parque Nacional Canaima [*Canaima National Park*] [*Venezuela*] (AD) ... PNC
Parque Nacional El Avila [*El Avila National Park*] [*Spanish*] (AD) ... PNEA
Parque Nacional Guatopo [*Guatopo National Park*] [*Venezuela*] [*Spanish*] (AD) ... PNG
Parque Nacional Henri Pittier [*Henri Pittier National Park*] [*Venezuela*] [*Spanish*] (AD) ... PNHP
Parque Nacional Iguazu [*Iguazu National Park*] [*Spanish*] (AD) ... PNI
Parque Nacional Ordesa [*Ordesa National Park*] [*Spanish*] (AD) ... PNO
Parque Nacional Sierra Nevada [*Sierra Nevada National Park*] [*Venezuela*] [*Spanish*] (AD) ... PNSN
Parque Nacional Tijuca [*Tijuca National Park*] [*Brazil*] [*Portuguese*] (AD) ... PNT
Parquet (BARN) ... para
Parquet Floor Layers' Trade Society [*A union*] [*British*] ... PFLTS
Parquet Resources, Inc. [*Toronto Stock Exchange symbol*] ... PQT
Parr Terminal Railroad [*AAR code*] ... PRT
Parr Terminal Railroad (MHDW) ... PTR
Parris Island, SC [*FM radio station call letters*] ... WOCW
Parris Island, South Carolina [*Marine Corps*] ... PISC
Parrita [*Costa Rica*] [*ICAO location identifier*] (ICLI) ... MRPR
Parrot Society (EA) ... PS
Parrott Rifle ... PR
Parrsboro Shore Historical Society, Parrsboro, Nova Scotia [*Library symbol National Library of Canada*] (BIB) ... NSPSH
Parrsboro Shore Historical Society, Parrsboro, NS, Canada [*Library symbol*] [*Library of Congress*] (LCLS) ... CaNSPaSH
Parry Sound [*Canada*] [*Airport symbol*] (OAG) ... YPD
Parry Sound, ON [*FM radio station call letters*] ... CKLP
Parry Sound Public Library, Ontario [*Library symbol National Library of Canada*] (NLC) ... OPS
Parry Sound Public Library, Parry Sound, ON, Canada [*Library symbol Library of Congress*] (LCLS) ... CaOPs
Pars Affecta [*The Part Affected*] [*Pharmacy*] ... PAR AFF
Pars Distalis [*Medicine*] ... PD
Pars Planus Lensectomy [*Ophthalmology*] (DAVI) ... PPL
Pars Systems (CRS) [*ICAO designator*] (FAAC) ... PRS
Parsabad/Moghan [*Iran*] [*ICAO location identifier*] (ICLI) ... OITP
PARSEC [*Parallax Second*] [*Unit of interstellar-space measurement*] ... PC
Parsec (IDOE) ... pc
PARSEC [*Parallax Second*] [*See PARSEC*] ... ps
Parsec Research Control Language [*Pronounced "parkul"*] [*Parsec Reseach Robotics*] ... PaRCL
Parser and Extensible Compiler [*Programming language*] (CSR) ... PARSEC
Parser Assembly Language [*Computer science*] ... PAL
Parshall, ND [*Location identifier FAA*] (FAAL) ... PSH
Parsimonious and Penurious (AD) ... p & p
Parsippany-Troy Hills, NJ [*AM radio station call letters*] ... WXMC
Parsley Latent Virus [*Plant pathology*] ... PARLV
Parsley Rhabdovirus [*Plant pathology*] ... PRV
Parsnip Mosaic Virus [*Plant pathology*] ... PARMV
Parsnip Virus 3 [*Plant pathology*] ... PARV3
Parsnip Yellow Fleck Virus [*Plant pathology*] ... PYFV
Parson ... P
Parsons [*Kansas*] [*Airport symbol*] (OAG) ... PPF
Parsons Active Ring-Around Miss Indicator ... PARAMI
Parsons Airways Northern Ltd. [*Canada ICAO designator*] (FAAC) ... FAP
Parsons' Answer to the Fifth Part of Coke's Reports [*A publication*] (DLA) ... Pars Ans
Parsons' Commentaries on American Law [*A publication*] (DLA) ... Par Am Law
Parsons' Commentaries on American Law [*A publication*] (DLA) ... Par Am Law Comm
Parsons' Decisions [*2-7 Massachusetts*] [*A publication*] (DLA) ... Par Dec
Parsons' Decisions [*2-7 Massachusetts*] [*A publication*] (DLA) ... Pars Dec
Parsons' Essays on Legal Topics [*A publication*] (DLA) ... Par Ess
Parsons, KS [*AM radio station call letters*] ... KLKC
Parsons, KS [*FM radio station call letters*] ... KLKC-FM
Parsons, KS [*Location identifier FAA*] (FAAL) ... PPF
Parsons Language Sample ... PLS
Parsons' Law by Hughes [*A publication*] (DLA) ... Par L
Parsons' Laws of Business [*A publication*] (DLA) ... Par Laws Bus
Parsons Mountain [*South Carolina*] [*Seismograph station code, US Geological Survey*] (SEIS) ... PRM
Parsons' Notes and Bills [*A publication*] (DLA) ... Par N & B
Parsons on Bills and Notes [*A publication*] (DLA) ... Par Bills & N
Parsons on Bills and Notes [*A publication*] (DLA) ... Pars Bills & N
Parsons on Contracts [*A publication*] (DLA) ... Par Cont
Parsons on Contracts [*A publication*] (DLA) ... Pars Cont
Parsons on Costs [*A publication*] (DLA) ... Par Costs
Parsons on Marine Insurance [*A publication*] (DLA) ... Pars Mar Ins
Parsons on Marine Insurance and General Average [*A publication*] (DLA) ... Par Mar Ins
Parsons on Maritime Law [*A publication*] (DLA) ... Par Mar L
Parsons on Maritime Law [*A publication*] (DLA) ... Pars Mar Law
Parsons on Mercantile Law [*A publication*] (DLA) ... Par Merc Law
Parsons on Mercantile Law [*A publication*] (DLA) ... Pars Merc Law
Parsons on Partnership [*1889*] [*A publication*] (DLA) ... Par Part
Parsons on Shipping and Admiralty [*A publication*] (DLA) ... Pars Shipp & Adm
Parsons on the Law of Shipping and Admiralty [*A publication*] (DLA) ... Par Adm
Parsons on the Law of Shipping and Admiralty [*A publication*] (DLA) ... Par Sh & Adm
Parsons on the Rights of a Citizen of the United States [*A publication*] (DLA) ... Par Rights Cit
Parsons on Wills [*1854*] [*A publication*] (DLA) ... Par Wills
Parsons Passive Miss Distance Indicating System (SAA) ... PARAMIS
Parsons' Reports [*65-66 New Hampshire*] [*A publication*] (DLA) ... Par
Parsons School of Design, New York, NY [*Library symbol Library of Congress*] (LCLS) ... NNParS
Parsons' Select Equity Cases [*1842-51*] [*Pennsylvania*] [*A publication*] (DLA) ... Par Eq Cas
Parsons' Select Equity Cases [*Pennsylvania*] [*A publication*] (DLA) ... Par Eq Cases
Parsons' Select Equity Cases [*Pennsylvania*] [*A publication*] (DLA) ... Par R
Parsons' Select Equity Cases [*1842-51*] [*Pennsylvania*] [*A publication*] (DLA) ... Pars
Parsons' Select Equity Cases [*1842-51*] [*Pennsylvania*] [*A publication*] (DLA) ... Pars Eq Cas
Parsons' Select Equity Cases [*Pennsylvania*] [*A publication*] (DLA) ... Pars S Eq Cas
Parsons' Select Equity Cases [*Pennsylvania*] [*A publication*] (DLA) ... Pars Sel Eq Cas (PA)
Parsons' Select Equity Cases [*Pennsylvania*] [*A publication*] (DLA) ... Parsons'
Parsons State Hospital, Parsons, KS [*Library symbol Library of Congress*] (LCLS) ... KParSH
Parsons, TN [*AM radio station call letters*] ... WKJQ
Parsons, TN [*FM radio station call letters*] ... WKJQ-FM
Part (WDMC) ... p
Part ... P
Part (BARN) ... par
Part (AAG) ... PRT
Part [*of a deck*] (DS) ... pt
Part [*Online database field identifier*] ... PT
Part (DAVI) ... pt
Part and Assembly Description Language [*Computer science*] ... PADL
Part and Component Evaluation Report [*NASA*] ... PACER
Part Bunkers [*Shipping*] (DS) ... ptB
Part Called [*Stock exchange term*] (MHDB) ... PT CL
Part Called [*Stock exchange term*] (SPSG) ... PTCLD
Part Card [*Computer science*] (IAA) ... PC
Part Card Change Notice (KSC) ... PCCN
Part Card Procurement Change Notice (KSC) ... PCPCN
Part Control Number (AAG) ... PCN
Part Control Number Request (AAG) ... PCNR
Part Damaged (ROG) ... PD
Part Exchange (WDAA) ... PT EX
Part Failure Rate ... PFR
Part Fill In and Ram [*Construction*] ... PFI & R
Part II of the Year Books [*A publication*] (DLA) ... First Pt Edw III
Part Information Correlation Key ... PICK
Part Load Specific Fuel Consumption [*Gas turbine*] ... PLSFC
Part Manufacturing Design ... PMD
Part Number (AD) ... P/N
Part Number (AD) ... pn
Part Number ... PN
Part Number Index (MCD) ... PNI
Part Number Specification (MCD) ... PNS
Part Of (KSC) ... P/O
Part of (AD) ... p/o
Part Paid (AD) ... pp
Part Paid [*Business and trade*] ... PP
Part Paid [*Business term*] ... PTPD
Part Program Manager ... PPM
Part Redeemed [*Stock exchange term*] (SPSG) ... PTRD
Part Reference Designator ... PRD
Part Requirement Card ... PRC
Part Stress Analysis (MCD) ... PSA
Part Surface (IAA) ... PS
Part Task Trainer (MCD) ... PTT
Part Throttle [*Engines*] ... PT
Part Throttle Acceleration [*Engines*] (EG) ... PTA
Part Throttle Deceleration [*Engines*] (EG) ... PTD
Part Throttle Reheat [*Aviation*] (OA) ... PTR
Part Through Crack [*Alloy tension*] ... PTC
Part Time Legislature ... PTL
Part Time Operation (DA) ... PTO
Part Total [*Earnings less than weekly benefit amount*] [*Unemployment insurance*] (OICC) ... PT
Part VII of the Year Books [*A publication*] (DLA) ... First Pt H VI
Partacoona [*Australia Seismograph station code, US Geological Survey*] (SEIS) ... PNA
Partai Demokrasi Indonesia [*Indonesian Democratic Party*] [*Political party*] (PPW) ... PDI
Partai Katolik Indonesia [*Catholic Party of Indonesia*] [*Political party*] ... PKI
Partai Kebang-Saan Demokratik Brunei [*Brunei National Democratic Party*] [*Political party*] (EY) ... PKDB
Partai Komunis Indonesia [*Communist Party of Indonesia*] [*Political party*] ... PKI
Partai Kristen Indonesia [*Christian Party of Indonesia*] [*Political party*] ... PKI
Partai Muslimin Indonesia [*Indonesian Muslim Party*] [*Political party*] (AD) ... PMI
Partai Nasionalis Indonesia [*Nationalist Party of Indonesia*] [*Political party*] ... PNI
Partai Perpaduan Kebang-Saan Brunei [*Brunei National United Party*] [*Political party*] (EY) ... PPKB
Partai Persatuan Pembangunan [*United Development Party*] [*Indonesia*] [*Political party*] (PPW) ... PPP
Partai Pesaka Bumiputra Bersatu [*United Traditional Bumiputra Party*] [*Malaysia*] [*Political party*] (PPW) ... PPBB

Partai Socialis Indonesia [*Socialist Party of Indonesia*] .... PSI
Partbook [*Music*] .... PTBK
Partei der Arbeit [*Labor Party*] [*Switzerland Political party*] (PPE) .... PdA
Partei der Deutschsprachigen Belgier [*Party of German-Speaking Belgians*] [*Political party*] (PPW) .... PDB
Partei des Demokratischen Sozialismus [*Party of Democratic Socialism*] [*Germany Political party*] (EAIO) .... PDS
Partei Freier Buerger [*Free Citizens' Party*] [*Germany Political party*] (PPW) .... PFB
Partei fuer Deutschland und Europa [*Party for Germany and Europe*] [*Germany Political party*] (PPW) .... PDE
Partei fuer Renten-, Steuer-, und Soziale Gerechtigkeit [*Party for Equitable Pensions, Taxation, and Social Services*] [*Germany Political party*] (PPW) .... PRS
Parteijargon [*Party Language*] [*German*] .... PJ
Partenavia [*Airplane code*] Pn6
Partenavia Construzioni Aeronautiche SpA [*Italy ICAO aircraft manufacturer identifier*] (ICAO) .... PN
Partes Aequales [*Equal Parts*] [*Pharmacy*] .... P AE
Partes Aequales [*Equal Parts*] [*Pharmacy*] .... P AEQ
Partes Aequales [*Equal Parts*] [*Pharmacy*] .... PART AEQ
Partes Aequales [*Equal Parts*] [*Pharmacy*] (ROG) .... PART AEQUAL
Partes Aequales [*Equal Parts*] [*Pharmacy*] .... PE
Partes Aequales [*Equal Parts*] [*Pharmacy*] .... PT AEQ
Partes Dolentes [*Painful Parts*] [*Pharmacy*] .... PART DOLENT
Partheite [*A zeolite*] .... PAR
Parthenius [*First century BC*] [*Classical studies*] (OCD) .... Parth
Parthian [*Language, etc.*] .... P
Parti Affectae [*To the Affected Part*] [*Pharmacy*] .... PA
Parti Affectae Applicandus [*Apply to the Affected Part*] [*Pharmacy*] .... PAA
Parti Africain de l'Independance [*African Independence Party*] [*Senegal*] [*Political party*] (PPW) .... PAI
Parti Africain pour l'Independance des Masses [*African Party for the Independence of the Masses*] [*Senegal*] [*Political party*] (PPW) .... PAIM
Parti Bansa Dayak Sarawak [*Malaysia*] [*Political party*] (FEA) .... PBDS
Parti Bersatu Sabah [*Malaysia*] [*Political party*] (ECON) .... PBS
Parti Chretien-Social [*Christian Social Party*] [*Luxembourg*] [*Political party*] (PPW) .... PCS
Parti Communiste [*Communist Party*] [*Luxembourg*] [*Political party*] (PPW) .... PC
Parti Communiste Algerien [*Algerian Communist Party*] [*Political party*] .... PCA
Parti Communiste Canadien (Marxiste-Leniniste) [*Marxist-Leninist Communist Party of Canada*] [*Political party*] .... PCC (M-L)
Parti Communiste de Belgique [*Communist Party of Belgium*] [*See also KPB*] [*Political party*] (PPE) .... PCB
Parti Communiste de Guadeloupe [*Communist Party of Guadeloupe*] [*Political party*] (PPW) .... PCG
Parti Communiste de Luxembourg [*Communist Party of Luxembourg*] [*Political party*] (PPE) .... PCL
Parti Communiste du Dahomey [*Communist Party of Dahomey*] [*Benin*] [*Political party*] .... PCD
Parti Communiste Francais [*French Communist Party*] [*Political party*] (PPW) .... PCF
Parti Communiste Internationaliste [*Internationalist Communist Party*] [*France Political party*] (PPE) .... PCI
Parti Communiste Libanais [*Lebanese Communist Party*] [*Political party*] (PPW) .... PCL
Parti Communiste Marocain [*Moroccan Communist Party*] [*Political party*] .... PCM
Parti Communiste Martiniquais [*Communist Party of Martinique*] [*Political party*] (PPW) .... PCM
Parti Communiste Marxiste-Leniniste [*Marxist-Leninist Communist Party*] [*France Political party*] (PPW) .... PCML
Parti Communiste Marxiste-Leniniste Francais [*French Marxist-Leninist Communist Party*] [*Dissolved, 1978*] [*Political party*] (PPW) .... PCMLF
Parti Communiste Reunionnais [*Communist Party of Reunion*] [*Political party*] (PPW) .... PCR
Parti Communiste Revolutionnaire - Marxiste-Leniniste [*Revolutionary Marxist-Leninist Communist Party*] [*France Political party*] (PPW) .... PCRML
Parti Communiste Suisse [*Communist Party of Switzerland*] [*Political party*] (PPE) .... PCS
Parti Communiste Tunisien [*Tunisian Communist Party*] [*Political party*] (PD) .... PCT
Parti Comorien pour la Democratie et le Progres [*Political party*] (EY) .... PCDP
Parti Congolais du Travail [*Congolese Labor Party*] [*Political party*] (PPW) .... PCT
Parti Conservateur Chretien-Social [*Conservative Christian-Social Party*] [*Switzerland Political party*] (PPE) .... PCCS
Parti d'Action Paysanne [*Farmers Actions Party*] [*Burkina Faso*] [*Political party*] .... PAP
Parti Dahomeen de l'Unite [*Dahomean Unity Party*] [*Benin*] [*Political party*] .... PDU
Parti de la Convergence pour les Libertes et l'Integration [*Burkina Faso*] [*Political party*] (EY) .... PCLI
Parti de la Federation Africaine [*African Federation Party*] [*Political party*] .... PFA
Parti de la Liberte du Citoyen [*Belgium Political party*] (EY) .... PLC
Parti de la Liberte et du Progres [*Party of Liberty and Progress*] [*See also PVV*] [*Belgium*] (PPE) .... PLP
Parti de la Revolution Populaire [*People's Revolutionary Party*] [*Zaire*] [*Political party*] (PD) .... PRP
Parti de la Revolution Populaire du Benin [*Benin People's Revolutionary Party*] [*Political party*] (PD) .... PRPB
Parti de la Revolution Socialiste [*Party of Socialist Revolution*] [*Benin*] [*Political party*] .... PRS
Parti de la Revolution Socialiste [*Party of Socialist Revolution*] [*Senegal*] [*Political party*] .... PRS
Parti de la Solidarite du Peuple [*Cameroon*] [*Political party*] (EY) .... PSP
Parti de la Solidarite Nationale [*Party of National Solidarity*] [*Luxembourg*] [*Political party*] (PPE) .... PSN
Parti de l'Action [*Party of Action*] [*Morocco*] [*Political party*] (PPW) .... PA
Parti de l'Avant-Garde Socialiste [*Socialist Vanguard Party*] [*Algeria*] [*Political party*] (PD) .... PAGS
Parti de Liberation Kanak [*New Caledonia*] [*Political party*] (EY) .... PALIKA
Parti de l'Independance et de la Liberte [*Party for Independence and Liberty*] [*Congo*] [*Political party*] .... PIL
Parti de l'Independance et du Travail [*Party of Independence and Labor*] [*Senegal*] [*Political party*] (PPW) .... PIT
Parti de l'Unite Congolaise [*Congolese Unity Party*] [*Political party*] .... PUC
Parti de l'Unite du Peuple Gabonais [*Political party*] (EY) .... PUP
Parti de l'Unite et de la Communaute Belgo-Congolaise [*Political party*] .... UCBC
Parti de l'Unite Nationale [*Party of National Unity*] [*Haiti*] [*Political party*] (PPW) .... PUN
Parti de l'Unite Nationale [*National Unity Party*] [*Congo*] .... PUNA
Parti de l'Unite Nationale Gabonaise [*Party for Gabonese National Unity*] [*Political party*] .... PUNGA
Parti de l'Unite Populaire [*Tunisia*] [*Political party*] (EY) .... PUP
Parti de Solidarite Senegalaise [*Senegalese Solidarity Party*] [*Political party*] .... PSS
Parti Democrate Chretien [*Christian Democratic Party*] [*Burundi*] [*Political party*] .... PDC
Parti Democrate et Social Chretien [*Zaire*] [*Political party*] (EY) .... PDSC
Parti Democrate Francais [*French Democratic Party*] [*Political party*] (PPW) .... PDF
Parti Democrate Populaire [*Popular Democratic Party*] [*France Political party*] (PPE) .... PDP
Parti Democrate Unifie [*Unified Democratic Party*] [*Name replaced by Section Voltaique de Rassemblement Burkina Faso*] [*Political party*] .... PDU
Parti Democrate-Chretien Suisse [*Christian Democratic Party of Switzerland*] [*Political party*] (PPE) .... PDC
Parti Democratico da Angola [*Democratic Party of Angola*] [*Political party*] .... PDA
Parti Democratique [*Democratic Party*] [*Luxembourg Political party*] (EAIO) .... PD
Parti Democratique Chretien d'Haiti [*Political party*] (EY) .... PDCH
Parti Democratique Chretien Malgache [*Malagasy Christian Democratic Party*] [*Political party*] (PPW) .... UDECMA-KMPT
Parti Democratique Dahomeen [*Dahomey Democratic Party*] [*Political party*] .... PRD
Parti Democratique de Guinee [*Democratic Party of Guinea*] [*Political party*] (PPW) .... PDG
Parti Democratique de la Cote-D'Ivoire [*Democratic Party of the Ivory Coast*] [*Political party*] (PPW) .... PDCI
Parti Democratique de la Haute Volta-Rassemblement Democratique Africain [*Democratic Party of Upper Volta-African Democratic Rally*] .... PDHV-RDA
Parti Democratique de l'Independance [*Democratic Independence Party*] [*Morocco*] [*Political party*] .... PDI
Parti Democratique des Populations Togolaises [*Togolese Democratic People's Party*] [*Political party*] .... PDPT
Parti Democratique Gabonais [*Gabonese Democratic Party*] [*Political party*] (PPW) .... PDG
Parti Democratique Malgache [*Malagasy Democratic Party*] .... PDM
Parti Democratique Progressif [*Algeria*] [*Political party*] (EY) .... PDR
Parti Democratique Senegalais [*Senegalese Democratic Party*] [*Political party*] (PPW) .... PDS
Parti Democratique Senegalais - Renovation [*Senegalese Democratic Party - Reform*] [*Political party*] .... PDS-R
Parti des Classes Moyennes [*Middle Class Party*] [*Luxembourg*] [*Political party*] (PPE) .... PCM
Parti des Democrates Camerounais [*Political party*] (EY) .... PDC
Parti des Forces Nouvelles [*New Forces Party*] [*France Political party*] (PPW) .... PFN
Parti des Nationalistes du Dahomey [*Dahomean Nationalists Party*] [*Political party*] .... PND
Parti des Paysans, Artisans, et Bourgeois [*Farmers', Artisans', and Burghers' Party*] [*Switzerland Political party*] (PPE) .... PAB
Parti des Reformes et de la Liberte de Wallonie [*Belgium Political party*] (PPW) .... PRLW
Parti d'Interets Congolais [*Party for Congolese Interests*] [*Political party*] .... PARTICO
Parti Dolonti Applicandum [*Apply to Painful Part*] [*Pharmacy*] (ROG) .... PDA
Parti d'Opposition Congolais [*Congolese Opposition Party*] [*Political party*] .... POC
Parti du Congres de l'Independance de Madagascar [*Party of the Congress for Malagasy Independence*] .... PCIM
Parti du Mouvement Populaire de la Cote Francaise des Somalis [*Popular Movement Party of French Somaliland*] [*Political party*] .... PMP
Parti du Peuple [*People's Party*] [*Burundi*] [*Political party*] .... PP
Parti du Progres Economique et Social des Independants Congolais Luluabourg [*Party for Economic and Social Progress of the Congolese Independents in Luluabourg*] [*Political party*] .... PESIC
Parti du Progres et du Socialisme [*Party of Progress and Socialism*] [*Morocco*] [*Political party*] (PPW) .... PPS
Parti du Progres Social [*Burkina Faso*] [*Political party*] (EY) .... PPS
Parti du Regroupement Africain [*African Regroupment Party*] [*Niger*] [*Political party*] (PD) .... PRA
Parti du Regroupement Africain [*African Regroupment Party*] [*Banned, 1974 Burkina Faso*] [*Political party*] .... PRA
Parti du Renouveau Democratique [*Benin*] [*Political party*] (EY) .... PRD
Parti du Travail [*Labor Party*] [*Switzerland Political party*] (PPE) .... PdT
Parti du Travail de Belgique [*Belgian Labour Party*] [*Political party*] (EY) .... PTB
Parti du Travail du Burkina [*Burkina Faso*] [*Political party*] (EY) .... PTB
Parti d'Union Socialiste des Musulmans Mauritaniens [*Party for Socialist Unity of Moslems of Mauritania*] [*Political party*] .... PUSMM
Parti d'Unite Arabe Islamique-Democratique [*Algeria*] [*Political party*] (EY) .... PUAID
Parti d'Unite Katangaise [*Katanga Unity Party*] [*Political party*] .... PUK
Parti Ecologiste [*Ecologist Party*] [*Belgium*] (PPW) .... Ecolo
Parti Ecologiste pour le Progres [*Burkina Faso*] [*Political party*] (EY) .... PEP

Parti Evangelique Populaire [*Popular Protestant Party*] [*Switzerland Political party*] (PPE) ... PEP
Parti Feministe du Canada ... PFC
Parti Gabonais du Progres [*Political party*] (EY) ... PGP
Parti Gerakan Rakyat Malaysia [*People's Action Party of Malaysia*] [*Political party*] (PPW) ... PGRM
Parti Independantiste [*Quebec*] ... PI
Parti Independantiste de l'Unite Guyanaise [*Pro-Independence Party of Guyanese Unity*] [*Political party*] (PPW) ... PIUG
Parti Islam se Malaysia [*Islamic Party of Malaysia*] [*Political party*] (PPW) ... PAS
Parti Ivoirien des Travailleurs [*Ivorian Workers' Party*] [*The Ivory Coast*] [*Political party*] (EY) ... PIT
Parti Kadazan Asli Sabah [*Malaysia*] [*Political party*] (FEA) ... PKAS
Parti Kongres Sarawak [*Malaysia*] [*Political party*] (EY) ... PKS
Parti Liberal [*Liberal Party (1974-1979)*] [*Belgium Political party*] (PPE) ... PL
Parti Liberal Democrate et Pluraliste [*Belgium Political party*] (PPW) ... PLDP
Parti Liberal Progressiste [*Liberal Progressive Party*] [*Morocco*] [*Political party*] (PPW) ... PLP
Parti Liberal Suisse [*Liberal Party of Switzerland*] [*Political party*] (PPE) ... PLS
Parti Liberal-Democrate [*Cameroon*] [*Political party*] (EY) ... PLD
Parti Mauricien Social-Democrate [*Mauritian Social Democratic Party*] [*Political party*] (PPW) ... PMSD
Parti Nasionalis Malaysia [*Political party*] (FEA) ... NASMA
Parti National Caledonien [*Caledonian National Party*] [*Political party*] (PPW) ... PNC
Parti National Democrate [*Morocco*] [*Political party*] (EY) ... PND
Parti National d'Haiti [*National Party of Haiti*] [*Political party*] ... PNH
Parti National du Progres [*National Progress Party*] [*Congo*] [*Political party*] ... PNP
Parti National du Travail [*Haiti*] [*Political party*] (EY) ... PNT
Parti National du Travail [*Benin*] [*Political party*] (EY) ... PNT
Parti National Liberal [*National Liberal Party*] [*Lebanon*] [*Political party*] (PPW) ... PNL
Parti National Lumumba [*Lumumba National Party*] [*Political party*] ... PANALU
Parti National Populaire [*National Popular Party*] [*Canada Political party*] (PPW) ... PNP
Parti National Populaire Guyanais [*French Guiana*] [*Political party*] (EY) ... PNPG
Parti National pour la Democratie et le Developpement [*Benin*] [*Political party*] (EY) ... PNDD
Parti National pour la Solidarite et le Developpement [*Algeria*] [*Political party*] (EY) ... PNSD
Parti National Progressiste [*Haiti*] [*Political party*] (EY) ... PNP
Parti National Progressiste d'Haiti [*National Progressive Party of Haiti*] [*Political party*] ... PNPH
Parti National Voltaique [*Voltaic National Party*] [*Political party*] ... PNV
Parti Nationale Africain [*African National Party*] [*Chad*] [*Political party*] ... PNA
Parti Nationale pour la Developpement du Tchad [*National Party for the Development of Chad*] ... PNDT
Parti Nationaliste [*Canada*] ... PN
Parti Nationaliste Occitan [*Occitanian Nationalist Party*] [*France Political party*] (PPE) ... PNO
Parti Nationaliste Progressiste Revolutionnaire [*Haiti*] [*Political party*] (EY) ... PANPRA
Parti Oubanguien de l'Independance [*Ubangi Independence Party*] [*Political party*] ... POI
Parti Ouvrier Belge [*Belgian Workers' Party*] [*Later, Belgian Socialist Party*] [*Political party*] (PPE) ... POB
Parti Ouvrier et Paysan du Congo [*Congolese Workers' and Peasants' Party*] [*Zaire*] [*Political party*] ... POP
Parti Ouvrier Socialiste Luxembourgeois [*Luxembourg Socialist Workers' Party*] (EAIO) ... POSL
Parti Ouvrier-Progressiste [*Canada*] ... POP
Parti Pekerja-Pekerja Malaysia [*Workers' Party of Malaysia*] [*Political party*] (PPW) ... PPM
Parti Perdapuan Kebangsaan Ra'ayat Brunei [*Brunei People's National United Party*] [*Political party*] (EY) ... PERKARA
Parti Pesaka Bumiputera Bersatu Sarawak [*United Bumiputra Party*] [*Malaysia*] [*Political party*] (FEA) ... PBB
Parti Populaire des Ueles [*Ueles People's Party*] [*Political party*] ... PPU
Parti Populaire Djiboutien [*Djibouti People's Party*] [*Political party*] (PPW) ... PPD
Parti Populaire Europeen [*European Peoples' Party - EPP*] (EAIO) ... PPE
Parti Populaire Francais [*French Popular Party*] [*Political party*] (PPE) ... PPF
Parti Populaire Senegalais [*Senegalese People's Party*] [*Political party*] (PPW) ... PPS
Parti Populaire Syrien [*Syrian People's Party*] [*Political party*] (BJA) ... PPS
Parti pour la Liberation du Peuple [*People's Liberation Party*] [*Senegal*] [*Political party*] (PPW) ... PLP
Parti pour l'Avancement de la Democratie en Ituri [*Party for Democratic Advancement in Ituri*] [*Political party*] ... PADI
Parti pour le Rassemblement Democratique des Mahorais [*Mayotte*] [*Political party*] (EY) ... PRDM
Parti Progressiste Dahomeen [*Dahomey Progressive Party*] [*Political party*] ... PPD
Parti Progressiste Democratique Guadeloupeen [*Political party*] (EY) ... PPDG
Parti Progressiste Katangais [*Political party*] ... PPK
Parti Progressiste Martiniquais [*Progressive Party of Martinique*] [*Political party*] (PPW) ... PPM
Parti Progressiste Nigerien [*Nigerian Progressive Party*] [*Political party*] ... PPN
Parti Progressiste Soudanais [*Sudanese Progressive Party*] [*Political party*] ... PPS
Parti Progressiste Tchadien [*Progressive Party of Chad*] [*Political party*] ... PPT
Parti Quebecois [*Quebec separatist political party*] ... PQ
Parti Radical [*Radical Party*] [*France*] [*Political party*] (EAIO) ... RAD
Parti Radical-Democratique Suisse [*Radical Democratic Party of Switzerland*] [*Political party*] (PPE) ... PRD
Parti Rakyat Jati Sarawak [*Sarawak Native People's Party*] [*Malaysia*] [*Political party*] (PPW) ... PAJAR
Parti Reformateur Liberal [*Liberal Reform Party*] [*Belgium Political party*] (PPW) ... PRL
Parti Republicain [*Republican Party*] [*France Political party*] (PPW) ... PR
Parti Republicain [*Republican Party*] [*Reunion*] [*Political party*] (EY) ... PR
Parti Republicain [*Republican Party*] [*Martinique*] [*Political party*] (PPW) ... PR
Parti Republicain [*Republican Party*] [*New Caledonia*] [*Political party*] (FEA) ... PR
Parti Republicain Caledonien [*New Caledonia*] [*Political party*] (FEA) ... PRC
Parti Republicain de la Cote d'Ivoire [*Republicaqn Party of the Ivory Coast*] [*Political party*] (EY) ... PRCI
Parti Republicain de la Liberte [*Republican Party for Liberty*] [*France Political party*] (PPE) ... PRL
Parti Republicain de la Liberte [*Republican Party for Liberty*] [*Burkina Faso*] [*Political party*] ... PRL
Parti Republicain du Peuple Camerounais [*Political party*] (EY) ... PRPC
Parti Republicain du Progres [*Republican Progress Party*] [*Central Africa*] [*Political party*] (PD) ... PRP
Parti Republicain Modere Haitien [*Political party*] (EY) ... PRMH
Parti Republicain Progressif [*Algeria*] [*Political party*] (EY) ... PRP
Parti Republicain Radical et Radical-Socialiste [*France*] [*Political party*] (ECED) ... R
Parti Republicain Social du Senegal [*Social Republican Party of Senegal*] [*Political party*] ... PRESS
Parti Revolutionnaire du Peuple Tunisien [*Revolutionary Party of the Tunisian People*] [*Political party*] (PD) ... PRPT
Parti Social d'Education des Masses Africaines [*African Party for Social Education of the Masses*] [*Burkina Faso*] ... PSEMA
Parti Social Democrate de Madagascar et des Comores [*Social Democratic Party of Madagascar and Comores*] ... PSD
Parti Social Francais [*French Social Party*] [*Political party*] (PPE) ... PSF
Parti Social pour le Progres [*Tunisia*] [*Political party*] (EY) ... PSP
Parti Social-Democrate [*Algeria*] [*Political party*] (EY) ... PSD
Parti Social-Democrate [*Social Democratic Party*] [*France Political party*] (PPW) ... PSD
Parti Social-Democratie [*Benin*] [*Political party*] (EY) ... PSD
Parti Socialiste [*Socialist Party*] [*Belgium Political party*] (PPW) ... PS
Parti Socialiste Autonome [*Autonomous Socialist Party*] [*France Political party*] (PPE) ... PSA
Parti Socialiste Caledonien [*New Caledonia*] [*Political party*] (FEA) ... PSC
Parti Socialiste Camerounais [*Cameroon Socialist Party*] [*Political party*] ... PSC
Parti Socialiste Centrafricain [*Central African Socialist Party*] [*Political party*] (PD) ... PSC
Parti Socialiste de la Nouvelle Caledonie [*Socialist Party of New Caledonia*] [*Political party*] (PPW) ... PSNC
Parti Socialiste Democratique [*Cameroon*] [*Political party*] (EY) ... PSD
Parti Socialiste des Comores [*Socialist Party of Comoros*] [*Political party*] (EY) ... PASOCO
Parti Socialiste des Ouvriers et Paysans [*Socialist Party of Workers and Peasants*] [*France Political party*] ... PSOP
Parti Socialiste - Federation de la Reunion [*Reunion Federation of the Socialist Party*] [*Political party*] (PPW) ... PS
Parti Socialiste Guyanais [*Guiana Socialist Party*] [*Political party*] (PPW) ... PSG
Parti Socialiste Ivoirien [*Ivorian Socialist Party*] [*The Ivory Coast*] [*Political party*] (EY) ... PSI
Parti Socialiste Mauricien [*Mauritian Socialist Party*] [*Political party*] (EY) ... PSM
Parti Socialiste Monegasque [*Monaco Socialist Party*] [*Political party*] (PPW) ... PSM
Parti Socialiste Polynesien [*Polynesian Socialist Party*] [*Political party*] (PPW) ... PSP
Parti Socialiste Suisse [*Social Democratic Party of Switzerland*] [*Political party*] (PPE) ... PSS
Parti Socialiste Unifie [*Unified Socialist Party*] [*France Political party*] (PPW) ... PSU
Parti Social-Liberal [*Algeria*] [*Political party*] (EY) ... PSL
Parti Solidaire Africain [*African Solidarity Party*] [*Congo*] [*Political party*] ... PSA
Parti Sosialis Rakyat Malaya [*People's Socialist Party of Malaya*] ... PSRM
Parti Soudanais Progressiste [*Sudanese Progressive Party*] [*Political party*] ... PSP
Parti Togolais du Progres [*Party for Togolese Progress*] ... PTP
Parti Travailliste Congolais [*Congolese Labor Party*] [*Political party*] ... PTC
Partia e Punes e Shqiperise [*Party of Labor of Albania - PLA*] [*Political party*] (PPW) ... PPS
Partia e Punes e Shqiperise [*Labor Party of Albania*] [*Formerly, PKSh*] [*Political party*] (PPE) ... PPSh
Partia Fashismit e Shqiperise [*Fascist Party of Albania*] [*Political party*] (PPE) ... PFSh
Partia Komuniste e Shqiperise [*Communist Party of Albania*] [*Later, PPSh*] [*Political party*] (PPE) ... PKSh
Partia Popullore [*Popular Party*] [*Albania*] [*Political party*] (PPE) ... PP
Partia Socialiste e Shqiperise [*Socialist Party of Albania*] [*Political party*] (EAIO) ... PSS
Partial [*Astronomy*] ... P
Partial (MSA) ... PART
Partial (VRA) ... part
Partial Acceptance and Takeover Date [*Telecommunications*] (TEL) ... PATO
Partial Annealing Zone [*Geology*] ... PAZ
Partial Anomalous Pulmonary Venous Connection (MAE) ... PAPVC
Partial Anomalous Pulmonary Venous Return ... PAPVR
Partial Application [*Military*] (AFIT) ... PA
Partial Autocorrelation Function [*Statistics*] ... PACF
Partial Automatic Translation Technique ... PATT
Partial Background Investigation [*Army*] ... PBI
Partial Body Neutron Activation [*Radiology*] ... PBNA
Partial Bony Impaction [*Orthopedics*] (DAVI) ... PBI

Partial Bulkhead (DS)	PBH
Partial Carriage Return (IAA)	PCR
Partial Crystal Control (IEEE)	PCC
Partial Delivery Injection [Materials science]	PDI
Partial Descriptive Method	PDM
Partial Differential Equation	PDE
Partial Differential Equation Language [Computer science]	PDEL
Partial Differential Equation Language [Computer science] (CSR)	PDELAN
Partial Discharge [High-voltage testing] (IEEE)	PD
Partial Double Error Detecting (NITA)	PDED
Partial Double Error Detection	PDED
Partial Energy Service [Electric power]	PES
Partial Expiratory Flow-Static Recoil Curve [Physiology] (MAE)	PEFSR
Partial Expiratory Flow-Volume [Physiology]	PEFV
Partial Function (IAA)	PF
Partial Gum [Philately]	PG
Partial Hepectomy [Medicine]	PHX
Partial Ileal Bypass [Medicine]	PIB
Partial Initial Decision [Nuclear energy] (NRCH)	PID
Partial Least Squares	PLS
Partial Line Down (NITA)	PLD
Partial Line Up (NITA)	PLU
Partial Lipodystrophy [Medicine]	PLD
Partial Loss [Insurance]	PL
Partial Lunar Orbit [Planetary science]	PLO
Partial Matrix Multiply (IAA)	PMM
Partial Metric System (MCD)	PMS
Partial Mission Capability Factor	PMCF
Partial Mobilization Expansion Plan [Army] (GFGA)	PAM
Partial Neglect of Differential Overlap [Physics]	PNDO
Partial Network Control Center	PNCC
Partial Niche Separation	PNS
Partial Nodular Transformation (DMAA)	PNT
Partial Nonprogressing Stroke (CPH)	PNS
Partial Nuclear Test Ban Treaty (AD)	PNTBT
Partial Ossicular Replacement Prosthesis	PORP
Partial Oxidation [Organic chemistry]	POX
Partial Parenteral Nutrition [Medicine] (DMAA)	PPN
Partial Pay [Air Force]	P/P
Partial Pay Card	PPC
Partial Preliminary Logistic Evaluation	PPLE
Partial Pressure (MAE)	P
Partial Pressure	PP
Partial Pressure Carbon Dioxide	PPCO2
Partial Pressure in Arterial Blood [Medicine] (DAVI)	P_A
Partial Pressure of Carbon Dioxide (AAMN)	pCO_2
Partial Pressure of Nitrogen [Medicine] (DAVI)	P_{N2}
Partial Pressure of Oxygen (DAVI)	PO
Partial Pressure of Oxygen (AAMN)	PO_2
Partial Pressure of Oxygen (CAAL)	PPO_2
Partial pressure of oxygen at 50% hemoglobin saturation [Medicine]	P_{50}
Partial Pressure of Venous Oxygen [Hematology] (CPH)	PvO_2
Partial Pressure of Water Vapor [Chemistry] (DAVI)	Ph_2O
Partial Pressure Sensor	PPS
Partial Product (IAA)	PP
Partial Program	PP
Partial Prothrombin Time [Hematology]	PPT
Partial Rank Correlation Coefficient [Nuclear energy] (NUCP)	PRCC
Partial Reaction of Degeneration	PRD
Partial Reaction of Degeneration (AD)	prd
Partial Reinforcement [Training]	PRF
Partial Remission [Medicine] (CDI)	PM
Partial Remission [Medicine]	PR
Partial Responders [to medication]	PR's
Partial Response [Oncology]	PR
Partial Response [Medicine] (DAVI)	PR
Partial Response Coding (IEEE)	PRC
Partial Response Maximum Likelihood [Computer science]	PRML
Partial Response Method	PRM
Partial Response Signalling (NITA)	PRS
Partial Retention of Diatomic Differential Overlap [Physics]	PRDDO
Partial Seismic Intrusion Device (MCD)	PSID
Partial Sequential Probability Ratio Test (PDAA)	PSPRT
Partial Shipment Number [DoD]	PSN
Partial Small Bowel Obstruction [Medicine] (MEDA)	PSBO
Partial Source Data Automation (NVT)	PSDA
Partial Symmetry	PARSYM
Partial Tension [Medicine] (DAVI)	P
Partial Test-Ban Treaty	PTBT
Partial Thermochemical Remanent Magnetization	PTCRM
Partial Thermoremanent Magnetization [Geophysics]	PTRM
Partial Thromboplastin Time [Hematology]	PTT
Partial Thromboplastin Time with Kaolin [Hematology]	PTTK
Partial Total Loss [Insurance] (DS)	PTL
Partial Water Vapor Pressure [Meteorology] (BARN)	e
Partial Wave Dispersing Relation	PWDR
Partial Weight Bearing [Medicine]	PWB
Partial Yield Spectroscopy (MCD)	PYS
Partial Zona Dissection [In-vitro fertilization] (PAZ)	PZD
Partial Zonal Drilling [In vitro fertilization] [Medicine] (BARN)	PZD
Partially	PRTLY
Partially Acidulated Rock Phosphate (OA)	PARP
Partially Allocated Quotas [Ocean fishery management]	PAQ
Partially Blinded Soldiers' Association of Australia	PBSAA
Partially Conserved Axial Current [Electronics] (IAA)	PCAC

Partially Conserved Axial-Vector Current	PCAC
Partially Conserved Baryon Current (IEEE)	PCBC
Partially Conserved Vector Current (IAA)	PCVC
Partially Delactosed Whey (OA)	PDW
Partially Delactosed Whey Powder (OA)	PDWP
Partially Functional Neutrophil (DMAA)	PFN
Partially Hearing (AIE)	PtHg
Partially Hydrogenated Menhaden Oil [Food science]	PHMO
Partially Hydrogenated Soybean Oil [Cooking fat]	PHSO
Partially Incinerated Compound [Furnace technology]	PIC
Partially Knocked Down [Consignment] [Shipping] (DS)	PKD
Partially Mission Capable [Maintenance and supply]	PMC
Partially Mission Capable Both [Maintenance and supply] (MCD)	PMCB
Partially Mission Capable Maintenance [Maintenance and supply] (MCD)	PMCM
Partially Mission Capable Supply [Maintenance and supply] (MCD)	PMCS
Partially Occupied Molecular Orbitals [Physical chemistry]	POMO
Partially Ordered Set (OA)	POS
Partially Ordered Set (HGAA)	POSET
Partially Oriented Yarns	POY
Partially Oxidized Tetracyanoplatinate Compound [Inorganic, one-dimensional conductor]	POTCP
Partially Reflecting Mirror	PRM
Partially Regulated Module	PRM
Partially Relaxed Fourier Transform [Mathematics]	PRFT
Partially Sighted (AIE)	PS
Partially Sighted Society [British]	PSS
Partially Smooth Water Area (DS)	PSWA
Partially Smutted [Plant pathology]	PS
Partially Synergistic [Pharmacology]	PS
Partially Tested (IAA)	PT
Partially Underground [Military]	PUG
Partially Unfolded Form [Biochemistry]	PUF
Partially Yttria-Stabilized Zirconia [Industrial ceramics]	PYSZ
Partially-Balanced Incomplete Block (PDAA)	PBIB
Partially-Hydrolyzed Polyacrylamide [Well drilling technology]	PHPA
Partially-Stabilized Zirconia [Ceramics]	PSZ
Participacion Democratica de Tzquierda [Chile] [Political party] (EY)	PDD
Participant Instrumentation Package (MCD)	PIP
Participant Instrumentation Package	PIP
Participant Record Advice	PRA
Participate (AABC)	PART
Participate (FAAC)	PTCP
Participate but Do Not Initiate [Investment term]	PNI
Participate in Archeology	PIT
Participating [Health insurance] (GHCT)	PAR
Participating [or Participation] (DLA)	Partic
Participating [Business term]	Ptc
Participating Activity [Responsible for standardization efforts] [DoD]	PA
Participating Agency Service Agreement (GNE)	PASA
Participating and Assertive Consumer Training [Health education]	PACT
Participating College Correspondence Course (MUGU)	PCCC
Participating Field Activity [DoD]	PFA
Participating Interest Contingency Agreement	PICA
Participating Irredeemable Preference [Shares]	PIP
Participating Jurisdiction	PJ
Participating Manager	PARM
Participating Preferred Stock (MHDW)	PPS
Participating Provider [Health insurance] (DMAA)	PAR
Participating Research Teams [Department of Energy]	PRT
Participating Test Organization [Air Force]	PTO
Participating Unit (NVT)	PU
Participation Certificate	PC
Participation Enriches Science, Music, and Art Organizations [Orlando, Florida]	PESO
Participation in Architectural Layout (PDAA)	PARTIAL
Participation Interest Purchase [FNMA] (EMRF)	PIP
Participation Systems, Inc. [Electronics Communications Co.] [Winchester, MA] [Telecommunications] (TSSD)	PSI
Participation-Achievement-Reward (PDAA)	PAR
Participative Management by Objectives (AD)	pmbo
Participative Teams (MCD)	PT
Participative Work Design	PWD
Participatory Anthropic Principle [Term coined by authors John Barrow and Frank Tipler in their book, "The Anthropic Cosmological Principle"]	PAP
Participial [Grammar]	PARTIC
Participial Adjective [Grammar]	PA
Participle [Grammar]	P
Participle [Grammar]	PART
Participle [Grammar] (WGA)	PPL
Participle [Grammar]	PPLE
Particle (IAA)	PART
Particle	PARTIC
Particle Accelerator Science and Technology (IAA)	PASAT
Particle Accelerators in High Earth Orbit [Proposed]	PAHEO
Particle Aiding Replication of Adenovirus [Virology]	PARA
Particle Analysis and Data Reduction [Environmental Protection Agency] (GFGA)	PADRE
Particle Analysis Cameras for the Shuttle [NASA]	PACS
Particle Beam Fusion Accelerator	PBFA
Particle Bed Reactor [Department of Energy]	PBR
Particle Board (VRA)	parti bd
Particle Board [Technical drawings]	PBD
Particle Concentration Fluorescence Immunoassay	PCFIA
Particle Count Monitoring Device (KSC)	PCMD

Particle Counting Immunoassay ... PACIA
Particle Counting System ... PCS
Particle Desorption Mass Spectrometry ... PDMS
Particle Distribution Function ... PDF
Particle Doppler Shift Spectrometer (PDAA) ... PDSS
Particle Electrostatic Thruster ... PET
Particle Environmental Monitor (MCD) ... PEM
Particle [*or Proton*] **Flux Density** ... PFD
Particle Impact Analyzer [*Astrophysics*] ... PIA
Particle Impact Noise Detection ... PIND
Particle in Cell [*Gas solid*] ... PIC
Particle [*or Proton*]-Induced X-Ray Emission ... PIXE
Particle Integration (CAAL) ... PI
Particle Measuring Systems [*Aerosol measurement device*] ... PMS
Particle/Neutral Beam (MCD) ... PNB
Particle Orientation Interferometer [*ASD*] ... POINTER
Particle Physics and Astronomy Research Council [*British*] ... PPARC
Particle Reduction Oven ... PRO
Particle Size Analog Computer (IAA) ... PARSAC
Particle Size Analogue Computer (PDAA) ... PARSAC
Particle Size Analyzer ... PSA
Particle Size Distribution ... PSD
Particle Size Distribution Analysis [*Statistics*] ... PSDA
Particle Size Monitor [*Instrumentation*] ... PSM
Particle Transfer Device ... PTD
Particle Transport Time (MAE) ... PTT
Particle-Beam Weapon ... PB
Particle-Beam Weapon ... PBW
Particleboard ... PTLBD
Particleboard/Plywood ... PB/P
Particle-Density [*Forensic science*] ... PD
Particle-Enhanced Turbidometric Immunoassay [*Clinical chemistry*] ... PETIA
Particle-Induced Visual Sensations ... PIVS
Particle-Oriented Paper (IAA) ... POP
Particles and Fields Subsatellite [*NASA*] (KSC) ... P & FS
Particles and Fields Subsatellite [*NASA*] ... PFS
Particles and Fields Subsatellite [*Telecommunications*] (OA) ... PFSS
Particles and Gases Working Group [*NASA*] (NASA) ... PGWG
Particles per Cubic Centimeter ... PPCC
Particles per Inch ... PPI
Particle-Sizing Interferometer (MCD) ... PSI
Particular ... PART
Particular ... PARTIC
Particular (ROG) ... PARTR
Particular Average ... P/AV
Particular Average ... PA
Particular [*Named*] **Port** [*British*] (ROG) ... PP
Particulars ... PARLARS
Particulate and/or Dissolved Organic Carbon [*Chemistry*] ... PDOC
Particulate Biogenic Silica [*Environmental science*] ... PBS
Particulate Combined Amino Acid [*Marine biology*] ... PCAA
Particulate Component (DMAA) ... PC
Particulate Data Reduction (EPA) ... PADRE
Particulate Data Reduction (EPA) ... PDR
Particulate Instrumentation by LASER Light Scattering (PDAA) ... PILLS
Particulate Matter ... PM
Particulate Matter [*Less than 10 microns*] ... PM10
Particulate Matter of 10 Microns in Diameter or Smaller [*BTS*] (TAG) ... PM-10
Particulate Methane Monooxygenase [*Biochemistry*] ... PMMO
Particulate Nitrogen [*Chemistry*] ... PN
Particulate Organic Carbon ... POC
Particulate Organic Concentration [*Environmental science*] ... POC
Particulate Organic Matter [*Environmental chemistry*] ... POM
Particulate Organic Nitrogen ... PON
Particulate Organic Phosphorus ... POP
Particulate Polycyclic Organic Matter (AD) ... ppom
Particulate Solid Research Institute ... PSRI
Particulate Total Nitrogen [*Analytical chemistry*] ... PTN
Particulates, Condensables, and Solubles [*In gases*] ... PCS
Particuliere Participatiemaatschappy [*Private Joint Stock Company*] [*Dutch*] ... PPM
Partido Accion Democratica [*Democratic Action Party*] [*El Salvador*] [*Political party*] (PPW) ... PAD
Partido Accion Popular [*Popular Action Party*] [*Peru*] [*Political party*] ... PAP
Partido Accion Popular [*Popular Action Party*] [*Ecuador*] [*Political party*] ... PAP
Partido Africano da Independencia da Guine e do Cabo Verde [*African Party for the Independence of Guinea and Cape Verde*] [*Political party*] (PPW) ... PAIGC
Partido Amplio de Izquierda Socialista [*Chile*] [*Political party*] (EY) ... PAIS
Partido Andalucista [*Spain*] [*Political party*] (ECED) ... PA
Partido Aragones Independiente [*Spain Political party*] (EY) ... PAI
Partido Aragones Regionalista [*Aragonese Regional Party*] [*Spain Political party*] (PPW) ... PAR
Partido Arnulfista [*Panama*] [*Political party*] (EY) ... PA
Partido Autentico Constitucional [*Authentic Constitutional Party*] [*El Salvador*] [*Political party*] ... PAC
Partido Autentico de la Revolucion Mexicana [*Authentic Party of the Mexican Revolution*] [*Political party*] (PPW) ... PARM
Partido Autentico Institucional Salvadoreno [*Salvadoran Authentic Institutional Party*] [*Political party*] (PPW) ... PAIS
Partido Autentico Institucional Salvadoreno [*Salvadoran Authentic Institutional Party*] [*Political party*] (EY) ... PAISA
Partido Barrientista Autentico [*Bolivia*] [*Political party*] (PPW) ... PBA
Partido Colorado [*Colorado Party*] [*Uruguay*] [*Political party*] (PPW) ... PC
Partido Comunista Chileno [*Communist Party of Chile*] [*Political party*] (PD) ... PCC
Partido Comunista Cubano [*Communist Party of Cuba*] [*Political party*] (PPW) ... PCC
Partido Comunista de Argentina [*Communist Party of Argentina*] [*Political party*] (PD) ... PCA
Partido Comunista de Bolivia [*Communist Party of Bolivia*] [*Political party*] (PPW) ... PCB
Partido Comunista de Chile [*Chilean Communist Party*] [*Political party*] (EY) ... PCCh
Partido Comunista de Espana [*Communist Party of Spain*] [*Political party*] (PPE) ... PCE
Partido Comunista de Espana - Reconstituido [*Reconstituted Spanish Communist Party*] [*Political party*] (PD) ... PCE-R
Partido Comunista de Espana Unificado [*Unified Communist Party of Spain*] [*Political party*] (PPW) ... PCEU
Partido Comunista de Euzkadi/Euzkadiko Partidu Komunista [*Basque Communist Party*] (PPW) ... EPK
Partido Comunista de Honduras [*Communist Party of Honduras*] [*Political party*] (PD) ... PCH
Partido Comunista de los Pueblos de Espana [*Communist Party of the Peoples of Spain*] [*Political party*] (EY) ... PCPE
Partido Comunista de Nicaragua [*Communist Party of Nicaragua*] [*Political party*] (PD) ... PCN
Partido Comunista de Portugal, Marxista-Leninista [*Marxist-Leninist Communist Party of Portugal*] [*Political party*] (PPE) ... PCP M-L
Partido Comunista del Pais Valenciano [*Spain Political party*] (EY) ... PCPV
Partido Comunista do Brasil [*Communist Party of Brazil*] [*Pro-Albanian*] [*Political party*] (PPW) ... PCB
Partido Comunista do Brasil [*Communist Party of Brazil*] [*Political party*] (PPW) ... PCdoB
Partido Comunista Dominicano [*Dominican Communist Party*] [*Dominican Republic*] [*Political party*] (PPW) ... PCD
Partido Comunista dos Trabalhadores Portugueses [*Portuguese Workers' Communist Party*] [*Political party*] (PPW) ... PCTP
Partido Comunista Ecuatoriano [*Communist Party of Ecuador*] [*Political party*] (PPW) ... PCE
Partido Comunista Marxista-Leninista de Bolivia [*Marxist-Leninist Communist Party of Bolivia*] [*Political party*] (PPW) ... PCB-ML
Partido Comunista Mexicano [*Mexican Communist Party*] [*Political party*] (PPW) ... PCM
Partido Comunista Obrero de Espana [*Communist Workers' Party of Spain*] [*Political party*] (PPW) ... PCOE
Partido Comunista Paraguayano [*Paraguayan Communist Party*] [*Political party*] (PD) ... PCP
Partido Comunista Peruano [*Peruvian Communist Party*] [*Political party*] (PPW) ... PCP
Partido Comunista Portugues [*Portuguese Communist Party*] [*Political party*] (PPE) ... PCP
Partido Comunista Puertorriqueno [*Puerto Rican Communist Party*] [*Political party*] (PPW) ... PCP
Partido Comunista Revolucionario [*Revolutionary Communist Party*] [*Peru*] [*Political party*] (PPW) ... PCR
Partido Comunista Salvadoreno [*Salvadoran Communist Party*] [*Political party*] (PPW) ... PCS
Partido Comunista Venezolana [*Venezuelan Communist Party*] [*Political party*] (PPW) ... PCV
Partido Conservador [*Conservative Party*] [*Ecuador*] [*Political party*] (PPW) ... PC
Partido Conservador [*Conservative Party*] [*Nicaragua*] [*Political party*] (EY) ... PC
Partido Conservador Colombiano [*Conservative Party of Colombia*] [*Political party*] (PPW) ... PCC
Partido Conservador Nicaraguense [*Nicaraguan Conservative Party*] [*Political party*] (PPW) ... PCN
Partido Conservador Tradicional [*Traditionalist Conservative Party*] [*Nicaragua*] [*Political party*] ... PCT
Partido Conservador Unido [*Chilean Catholic political party*] ... PCU
Partido Cristao Social Democratico [*Christian Social Democratic Party*] [*Portugal Political party*] (PPE) ... PCSD
Partido da Democracia Cristao [*Christian Democratic Party*] [*Portugal Political party*] (PPW) ... PDC
Partido da Direita Portuguesa [*Party of the Portuguese Right*] [*Political party*] (PPE) ... PDP
Partido da Social Democracia Brasiliera [*Brazilian Social Democratic Party*] [*Political party*] (EY) ... PSDB
Partido de Accion Democrata [*Democratic Action Party*] [*Spain Political party*] (PPW) ... PAD
Partido de Accion Nacional [*Nicaragua*] [*Political party*] (EY) ... PAN
Partido de Accion Popular [*Popular Action Party*] [*Panama*] [*Political party*] (PPW) ... Papo
Partido de Accion Socialista [*Socialist Action Party*] [*Costa Rica*] [*Political party*] (PPW) ... PAS
Partido de Accion Socialista [*Party of Socialist Action*] [*Spain Political party*] (PPW) ... PASOC
Partido de Accion Socialista de Honduras [*Political party*] (EY) ... PASOH
Partido de Conciliacion Nacional [*National Reconciliation Party*] [*El Salvador*] [*Political party*] (PPW) ... PCN
Partido de Integracion de America Central [*Nicaragua*] [*Political party*] (EY) ... PIAC
Partido de Integracion Democrata [*Democratic Integration Party*] [*Argentina Political party*] (PPW) ... PID
Partido de Integracion Nacional [*National Integration Party*] [*Peru*] [*Political party*] (PPW) ... Padin
Partido de la Izquierda Revolucionaria [*Party of the Revolutionary Left*] [*Bolivia*] [*Political party*] (PPW) ... PIR

Partido de la Liberacion Dominicana [*Dominican Liberation Party*] [*Dominican Republic*] [*Political party*] (PPW) ... PLD
Partido de la Resistencia Nicaraguense [*Political party*] (EY) ... PRN
Partido de la Revolucion Boliviana [*Bolivian Revolutionary Party*] [*Political party*] (AD) ... PRB
Partido de la Revolucion Democratica [*Mexico Political party*] (EY) ... PRD
Partido de la Revolucion Nacional [*Party of the National Revolution*] [*Bolivia*] [*Political party*] (PPW) ... PRN
Partido de la Revolucion Socialista [*Party of the Socialist Revolution*] [*Cuba*] [*Political party*] ... PRS
Partido de la Union Republicana Socialista [*Socialist Republican Union Party*] [*Bolivia*] ... PURS
Partido de Liberacion Nacional [*National Liberation Party*] [*El Salvador*] [*Political party*] (EY) ... PLN
Partido de los Democratas Melillenses [*Spanish North Africa*] [*Political party*] (MENA) ... PDM
Partido de los Pobres [*Poor People's Party*] [*Mexico Political party*] (PD) ... PLP
Partido de los Trabajadores [*Paraguay*] [*Political party*] (EY) ... PT
Partido de Orientacion Popular [*Popular Orientation Party*] [*El Salvador*] [*Political party*] (PPW) ... POP
Partido de Reconciliacion Democratica Nacional [*Party of National Democratic Reconciliation*] [*Guatemala*] [*Political party*] ... PRDN
Partido de Reconstrucao Nacional [*Brazil Political party*] (EY) ... PRN
Partido de Renovacion Democratica [*Democratic Renewal Party*] [*Costa Rica*] [*Political party*] (PPW) ... PRD
Partido de Renovacion Puertorriqueno [*Puerto Rican Renewal Party*] [*Political party*] (EY) ... PRP
Partido de Representacao Popular [*Brazil Political party*] ... PRP
Partido de Trabajadores Espanoles [*Spanish Workers' Party*] [*Political party*] (PPE) ... PTE
Partido de Unidad Nacional Conservadora [*Nicaragua*] [*Political party*] (EY) ... PUNC
Partido de Unificacion Anticomunista [*Anti-Communist Unification Party*] [*Guatemala*] [*Political party*] (PPW) ... PUA
Partido de Unificacion Revolucionaria [*Party of Revolutionary Unification*] [*Guatemala*] [*Political party*] ... PUR
Partido de Union Nacional del Sahara [*Western Sahara*] [*Political party*] ... PUNS
Partido de Veteranos Civiles [*Civilian Veterans' Party*] [*Dominican Republic*] [*Political party*] (PPW) ... PVC
Partido del Frente Cardenista de Reconstruccion Nacional [*Mexico Political party*] (EY) ... PFCRN
Partido del Progreso de Guinea Ecuatorial [*Progressive Party of Equatorial Guinea*] [*Political party*] (EY) ... PPGE
Partido del Pueblo de Panama [*Panamanian People's Party*] [*Political party*] (PPW) ... PPP
Partido del Pueblo Mexicano [*Mexican People's Party*] [*Political party*] (PPW) ... PPM
Partido Democracia Cristiana [*Christian Democratic Party*] [*Guatemala*] [*Political party*] (PPW) ... PDC
Partido Democracia Cristiana Guatemalteca [*Guatemalan Christian Democratic Party*] [*Political party*] (PPW) ... PDCG
Partido Democrata [*Democratic Party*] [*Chile*] [*Political party*] ... PD
Partido Democrata [*Democratic Party*] [*Costa Rica*] [*Political party*] (PPW) ... PD
Partido Democrata Cristiano [*Christian Democratic Party*] [*Peru*] [*Political party*] (PPW) ... PDC
Partido Democrata Cristiano [*Christian Democratic Party*] [*Paraguay*] [*Political party*] (PPW) ... PDC
Partido Democrata Cristiano [*Christian Democratic Party*] [*Costa Rica*] [*Political party*] (PPW) ... PDC
Partido Democrata Cristiano [*Christian Democratic Party*] [*Honduras*] [*Political party*] (PPW) ... PDC
Partido Democrata Cristiano [*Christian Democratic Party*] [*Bolivia*] [*Political party*] (PPW) ... PDC
Partido Democrata Cristiano [*Christian Democratic Party*] [*Panama*] [*Political party*] (PPW) ... PDC
Partido Democrata Cristiano [*Christian Democratic Party*] [*El Salvador*] [*Political party*] ... PDC
Partido Democrata de Confianza Nacional [*Nicaragua*] [*Political party*] (EY) ... PDC
Partido Democrata Liberal [*Liberal Democratic Party*] [*Spain Political party*] (EY) ... PDL
Partido Democrata Popular [*Popular Democratic Party*] [*Spain Political party*] (PPW) ... PDP
Partido Democrata Popular [*Popular Democratic Party*] [*Dominican Republic*] [*Political party*] (PPW) ... PDP
Partido Democrata Socialista [*Socialist Democratic Party*] [*Panama*] [*Political party*] (PPW) ... PDS
Partido Democratico Arubano [*Democratic Party of Aruba*] [*Political party*] (EY) ... PDA
Partido Democratico Cristao [*Christian Democratic Party*] [*Brazil Political party*] ... PDC
Partido Democratico Cristiano [*Christian Democratic Party*] [*Argentina Political party*] (PPW) ... PDC
Partido Democratico Cristiano [*Christian Democratic Party*] [*Chile*] [*Political party*] (PPW) ... PDC
Partido Democratico de Cooperacion Nacional [*Democratic Party of National Cooperation*] [*Guatemala*] [*Political party*] ... PDCN
Partido Democratico de Guinea Ecuatorial [*Democratic Party of Equatorial Guinea*] [*Political party*] (EY) ... PDGE
Partido Democratico Nacional [*National Democratic Party*] [*Chile*] [*Political party*] ... PDN
Partido Democratico Nacional [*National Democratic Party*] [*Venezuela Political party*] ... PDN
Partido Democratico para o Progresso [*Democratic Progressive Party*] [*Guinea-Bissau*] [*Political party*] (EY) ... PDP
Partido Democratico Revolucionario Hondureno [*Revolutionary Democratic Party of Honduras*] [*Political party*] ... PDRH
Partido do Centro Democratico Social [*Party of the Social Democratic Center*] [*Portugal Political party*] (PPE) ... CDS
Partido dos Socialistas de Galicia [*Spain Political party*] (EY) ... PS de G
Partido Ecologista Mexicano [*Political party*] (EY) ... PEM
Partido Ecuatoriano Socialista [*Ecuadorean Socialist Party*] [*Political party*] ... PES
Partido Espanol Nacional Sindicalista [*Political party*] [*Spain*] ... PENS
Partido Estadista Republicano [*Puerto Rico*] [*Political party*] ... PER
Partido Federacion Nacional Velasquista [*National Velasquista Federation*] [*Ecuador*] [*Political party*] (PPW) ... FNV
Partido Federalista Nacionalista Popular [*Panama*] [*Political party*] (EY) ... PFNP
Partido Feminista de Espana [*Feminist Party of Spain*] [*Political party*] (PPW) ... PFE
Partido Guatemalteco del Trabajo [*Guatemalan Labor Party*] [*Political party*] (PD) ... PGT
Partido Independente [*Independent Party*] [*Costa Rica*] [*Political party*] ... PI
Partido Independentista Puertorriqueno [*Puerto Rican Independence Party*] [*Political party*] (PPW) ... PIP
Partido Independiente de la Clase Obrera [*Panama*] [*Political party*] (EY) ... PICO
Partido Indio de Bolivia [*Political party*] ... PIB
Partido Intransigente [*Intransigent Party*] [*Argentina Political party*] (PD) ... PI
Partido Izquierda Democratica [*Democratic Left Party*] [*Political party*] (EAIO) ... PID
Partido Komunista ng Pilipinas [*Communist Party of the Philippines*] [*Political party*] (PPW) ... PKP
Partido Laborista [*Labor Party*] [*Panama*] [*Political party*] (PPW) ... Pala
Partido Laborista Agrario [*Panama*] [*Political party*] (EY) ... PLA
Partido Liberacion Nacional [*National Liberation Party*] [*Costa Rica*] [*Political party*] (PPW) ... PLN
Partido Liberal [*Nicaragua*] [*Political party*] (EY) ... Pali
Partido Liberal [*Liberal Party*] [*Paraguay*] [*Political party*] (PPW) ... PL
Partido Liberal [*Liberal Party*] [*Honduras*] [*Political party*] ... PL
Partido Liberal [*Liberal Party*] [*Colombia*] [*Political party*] (EY) ... PL
Partido Liberal [*Liberal Party*] [*Peru*] [*Political party*] (EY) ... PL
Partido Liberal [*Liberal Party*] [*Panama*] [*Political party*] (PPW) ... PL
Partido Liberal [*Liberal Party*] [*Portugal Political party*] (PPE) ... PL
Partido Liberal [*Liberal Party*] [*Spain Political party*] (PPE) ... PL
Partido Liberal Autentico [*Panama*] [*Political party*] (EY) ... PLA
Partido Liberal Constitucionalista [*Constitutionalist Liberal Party*] [*Nicaragua*] [*Political party*] (PPW) ... PLC
Partido Liberal de Cataluna [*Liberal Democratic Party of Catalonia*] [*Political party*] (PPW) ... PDLC
Partido Liberal de Honduras [*Liberal Party of Honduras*] [*Political party*] (PPW) ... PLH
Partido Liberal Independiente [*Independent Liberal Party*] [*Nicaragua*] [*Political party*] (PPW) ... PLI
Partido Liberal Independiente de Unidad Nacional [*Nicaragua*] [*Political party*] (EY) ... PLIUN
Partido Liberal Nacionalista [*Nationalist Liberal Party*] [*Nicaragua*] ... PLN
Partido Liberal Radical [*Radical Liberal Party*] [*Paraguay*] [*Political party*] (PPW) ... PLR
Partido Liberal Radical [*Radical Liberal Party*] [*Ecuador*] [*Political party*] (PPW) ... PLR
Partido Liberal Radical Autentico [*Authentic Liberal Radical Party*] [*Paraguay*] [*Political party*] (PD) ... PLRA
Partido Liberal Teete [*Teete Liberal Party*] [*Paraguay*] [*Political party*] (PPW) ... PLT
Partido Liberal Unificado [*Unified Liberal Party*] [*Paraguay*] [*Political party*] (PPW) ... PLU
Partido Libertador [*Liberating Party*] [*Brazil Political party*] ... PL
Partido Mariateguista Revolucionario [*Peru*] [*Political party*] (EY) ... PMR
Partido Marxista Leninista de Nicaragua [*Political party*] (EY) ... PLMN
Partido Mexicano de los Trabajadores [*Mexican Workers' Party*] [*Political party*] (PPW) ... PMT
Partido Mexicano Socialista [*Political party*] (EY) ... PMS
Partido Nacional [*National Party*] [*Honduras*] [*Political party*] (PPW) ... PN
Partido Nacional [*National Party*] [*Uruguay*] [*Political party*] (PPW) ... PN
Partido Nacional [*National Party*] [*Dominican Republic*] [*Political party*] ... PN
Partido Nacional [*National Party*] [*Spain*] [*Political party*] (AD) ... PN
Partido Nacional Ceuti [*Ceuta National Party*] [*Political party*] (PPW) ... PNC
Partido Nacional Conservador [*Nicaragua*] [*Political party*] (EY) ... PNC
Partido Nacional Conservador de Honduras [*National Conservative Party of Honduras*] [*Political party*] ... PNCH
Partido Nacional Cristiano [*National Christian Party*] [*Colorado Political party*] (EY) ... PNC
Partido Nacional de Democracia Centrista [*Chile*] [*Political party*] (EY) ... PNDC
Partido Nacional Democratico [*National Democratic Party*] [*Dominican Republic*] [*Political party*] ... PND
Partido Nacional Democratico [*National Democratic Party*] [*Costa Rica*] [*Political party*] (PPW) ... PND
Partido Nacional Guevarista [*Ecuador*] [*Political party*] (PPW) ... PNG
Partido Nacional Hondureno [*Honduran National Party*] [*Political party*] ... PNH
Partido Nacional Independiente [*National Independent Party*] [*Costa Rica*] [*Political party*] (PPW) ... PNI
Partido Nacional Republicano [*National Republican Party*] [*Paraguay*] [*Political party*] ... PNR
Partido Nacional Republicano [*National Republican Party*] [*Portugal Political party*] (PPE) ... PNR
Partido Nacional Revolucionario [*National Revolutionary Party*] [*Venezuela Political party*] ... PNR
Partido Nacional Velasquista [*National Velasquista Party*] [*Ecuador*] [*Political party*] (PPW) ... PNV
Partido Nacionalista Ceuti [*Political party*] (EY) ... PNC
Partido Nacionalista de los Trabajadores [*Argentina Political party*] (EY) ... PNT

Partido Nacionalista de Melilla - Asociacion Pro Melilla [*Political party*] (EY) ... PNM-Aprome
Partido Nacionalista de Mexicano [*Nationalist Party of Mexico*] [*Political party*] ... PNM
Partido Nacionalista del Pueblo [*Bolivia*] [*Political party*] (PPW) ... PNP
Partido Nacionalista Espanol de Melilla - Asociacion pro Melilla [*Spanish North Africa*] [*Political party*] (MENA) ... PNEM-APROME
Partido Nacionalista ng Pilipinas [*Philippine Nationalist Party*] [*Political party*] (EY) ... PNP
Partido Nacionalista Popular [*Popular Nationalist Party*] [*Panama*] [*Political party*] (PPW) ... PNP
Partido Nacionalista Renovador [*Nationalist Renewal Party*] [*Guatemala*] [*Political party*] (PPW) ... PNR
Partido Nacionalista Revolucionario [*Revolutionary Nationalist Party*] [*Ecuador*] [*Political party*] (PPW) ... PNR
Partido Nacionalista Vasco [*Basque Nationalist Party*] [*Spain Political party*] (PPE) ... PNV
Partido Nashonal di Pueblo [*National People's Party*] [*Netherlands Antilles*] [*Political party*] (EY) ... PNP
Partido ng Bayan [*Party of the Nation*] [*Philippines*] [*Political party*] ... PNB
Partido ng Masang Pilipino [*Political party*] (EY) ... PMP
Partido Nuevo Progresista [*New Progressive Party*] [*Puerto Rico*] [*Political party*] (PPW) ... PNP
Partido Obrero de Unificacion Marxista [*Workers' Party of Marxist Unification*] [*Former USSR*] (LAIN) ... POUM
Partido Obrero Marxista Revolucionario/Partido Socialista de los Trabajadores [*Marxist Revolutionary Workers' Party/Socialist Workers' Party*] [*Peru*] [*Political party*] (PPW) ... POMR/PST
Partido Obrero Revolucionaria Trotskista Posadista [*Bolivia*] [*Political party*] (PPW) ... PORTP
Partido Obrero Revolucionario [*Revolutionary Workers Party*] [*Bolivia*] [*Political party*] (PPW) ... POR
Partido Obrero Revolucionario [*Revolutionary Workers Party*] [*Peru*] [*Political party*] ... POR
Partido Obrero Revolucionario [*Revolutionary Workers Party*] [*Argentina Political party*] ... POR
Partido Obrero Revolucionario Marxista-Partido Socialista de los Trabajadores [*Peru*] [*Political party*] (EY) ... PORM-PST
Partido Obrero Revolucionario-Combate [*Revolutionary Struggle Workers' Party*] [*Bolivia*] [*Political party*] (PPW) ... PORC
Partido Obrero y Campesino de Mexico [*Mexico Political party*] ... POCM
Partido Operario de Unidade Socialista [*Workers' Party for Socialist Unity*] [*Portugal Political party*] (PPW) ... POUS
Partido Panamenista [*Panamanian Party*] [*Political party*] (PPW) ... PP
Partido Panamenista Autentico [*Panama*] [*Political party*] (EY) ... PPA
Partido Panamenista Republicano [*Panama*] [*Political party*] (EY) ... PPR
Partido para a Renovacao Social [*Party for Social Renovation*] [*Guinea-Bissau*] [*Political party*] (EY) ... PRS
Partido Patriotico Arubano [*Aruban Patriotic Party*] [*Netherlands Antilles*] [*Political party*] (PPW) ... PPA
Partido Patriotico Nobo [*New Patriotic Party*] [*Aruba*] [*Political party*] (EY) ... PPN
Partido Patriotico Revolucionario [*Mexico Political party*] (EY) ... PPR
Partido Peronista Autentico [*Authentic Peronist Party*] [*Argentina Political party*] (EY) ... PPA
Partido Popular [*Popular Party*] [*Spain Political party*] (PPE) ... PP
Partido Popular Cristiano [*Christian Popular Party*] [*Peru*] [*Political party*] (PPW) ... PPC
Partido Popular Democratica Cristiana [*Popular Christian Democratic Party*] [*Spain Political party*] (PPE) ... PPDC
Partido Popular Democratico [*Popular Democratic Party*] [*Puerto Rico*] [*Political party*] (PPW) ... PPD
Partido Popular Democratico [*Popular Democratic Party of Puerto Rico*] [*Spanish*] (BARN) ... PPD
Partido Popular Salvadoreno [*Salvadoran Popular Party*] [*Political party*] (PPW) ... PPS
Partido Popular Social Cristiano Autentico [*Political party*] (EY) ... PPSCA
Partido Popular Socialista [*Popular Socialist Party*] [*Argentina Political party*] (PPW) ... PPS
Partido Popular Socialista [*Popular Socialist Party*] [*Mexico Political party*] ... PPS
Partido Populista [*Populist Party*] [*Argentina Political party*] ... PP
Partido por la Democracia [*Democratic Party*] [*Chile*] [*Political party*] (EY) ... PPD
Partido Progreso Nacional [*National Progress Party*] [*Costa Rica*] [*Political party*] (PPW) ... PPN
Partido Proletariano Revolucionario [*Proletarian Revolutionary Party*] [*Portugal Political party*] (PPW) ... PPR
Partido Proletario de Mexico [*Proletarian Party of Mexico*] [*Political party*] (AD) ... PPM
Partido Quisqueyano Democrata [*Quisqueyan Democratic Party*] [*Dominican Republic*] [*Political party*] (PPW) ... PQD
Partido Radical [*Radical Party*] [*Spain Political party*] (PPE) ... PR
Partido Radical [*Radical Party*] [*Chile*] [*Political party*] ... PR
Partido Radical Liberal [*Radical Liberal Party*] [*Ecuador*] [*Political party*] ... PRL
Partido Reformista [*Reformist Party*] [*Dominican Republic*] [*Political party*] (PPW) ... PR
Partido Reformista Democratico [*Democratic Reformist Party*] [*Spain Political party*] (PPW) ... PRD
Partido Regionalista de Cantabria [*Spain Political party*] (EY) ... PRC
Partido Renovacion Patriotica [*Honduras*] [*Political party*] (EY) ... PRP
Partido Republicano [*Republican Party*] [*Ecuador*] [*Political party*] (EY) ... PR
Partido Republicano [*Republican Party*] [*Panama*] [*Political party*] (EY) ... PR
Partido Republicano Brasileiro [*Brazil Political party*] (EY) ... PRB
Partido Republicano Calderonista [*Calderonista Republican Party*] [*Costa Rica*] [*Political party*] (PPW) ... PRC
Partido Republicano Evolucionista [*Republican Evolutionist Party*] [*Portugal Political party*] (PPE) ... PRE
Partido Republicano Nacional [*National Republican Party*] [*Costa Rica*] [*Political party*] ... PRN
Partido Republicano Portugues [*Portuguese Republican Party*] [*Political party*] (PPE) ... PRP
Partido Revolucionario [*Revolutionary Party*] [*Guatemala*] [*Political party*] (PPW) ... PR
Partido Revolucionario Autentico [*Authentic Revolutionary Party*] [*Bolivia*] [*Political party*] (PPW) ... PRA
Partido Revolucionario Autentico Rios [*Bolivia*] [*Political party*] (PPW) ... PRAR
Partido Revolucionario Comunista [*Brazil Political party*] (EY) ... PRC
Partido Revolucionario de Izquierda Nacional Gueiler [*Revolutionary Party of the National Left - Gueiler Wing*] [*Bolivia*] [*Political party*] (PPW) ... PRING
Partido Revolucionario de la Izquierda Nacional Laboral [*Political party*] (PPW) ... PRIN-L
Partido Revolucionario de la Izquierda Nacional Moller [*Bolivia*] [*Political party*] (PPW) ... PRINM
Partido Revolucionario de la Izquierda Nacionalista [*National Leftist Revolutionary Party*] [*Bolivia*] [*Political party*] (PPW) ... PRIN
Partido Revolucionario de los Trabajadores [*Workers' Revolutionary Party*] [*Argentina Political party*] (PD) ... PRT
Partido Revolucionario de los Trabajadores [*Workers' Revolutionary Party*] [*Uruguay*] [*Political party*] (PD) ... PRT
Partido Revolucionario de los Trabajadores [*Workers' Revolutionary Party*] [*Peru*] [*Political party*] (PPW) ... PRT
Partido Revolucionario de los Trabajadores [*Revolutionary Workers' Party*] [*Costa Rica*] [*Political party*] (EY) ... PRT
Partido Revolucionario de los Trabajadores Centroamericanos [*Revolutionary Party of Central American Workers*] [*El Salvador*] [*Political party*] (PD) ... PRTC
Partido Revolucionario de los Trabajadores Centroamericanos - Seccion de Hondur as [*Revolutionary Party of Central American Workers - Honduras*] [*Political party*] ... PRTC-H
Partido Revolucionario de los Trabajadores de Bolivia Romero [*Bolivia*] [*Political party*] (PPW) ... PRTBR
Partido Revolucionario de Trabajadores [*Revolutionary Worker's Party*] [*Colorado Political party*] (EY) ... PRT
Partido Revolucionario de Trabajadores Bolivianos [*Bolivian Workers' Revolutionary Party*] [*Political party*] (PD) ... PRTB
Partido Revolucionario de Unification Democratica [*Revolutionary Party of Democratic Unification*] [*El Salvador*] ... PRUD
Partido Revolucionario de Union Civico [*Revolutionary Party for Civic Union*] [*Costa Rica*] [*Political party*] ... PRUC
Partido Revolucionario Democratico [*Democratic Revolutionary Party*] [*Panama*] [*Political party*] (PPW) ... PRD
Partido Revolucionario Dominicano [*Dominican Revolutionary Party*] [*Dominican Republic*] [*Political party*] (PPW) ... PRD
Partido Revolucionario Dominicano Autentico [*Dominican Republic*] [*Political party*] ... PRADA
Partido Revolucionario Febrerista [*Febrerista Revolutionary Party*] [*Paraguay*] [*Political party*] (PPW) ... PRF
Partido Revolucionario Hondureno [*Honduras Revolutionary Party*] [*Political party*] (PPW) ... PRH
Partido Revolucionario Institucional [*Party of the Institutionalized Revolution*] [*Mexico Political party*] ... PRI
Partido Revolucionario Obrerista y Clandestino de Union Popular [*Mexico Political party*] (EY) ... PROCUP
Partido Revolucionario Popular [*Popular Revolutionary Party*] [*Portugal Political party*] (PPE) ... PRP
Partido Revolucionario Socialista [*Mexico Political party*] (EY) ... PRS
Partido Riojano [*Spain Political party*] (EY) ... PR
Partido Roldosista Ecuatoriano [*Ecuador*] [*Political party*] (EY) ... PRE
Partido Social Conservador Colombiano [*Colombian Social Conservative Party*] [*Political party*] (EY) ... PSC
Partido Social Cristiano [*Social Christian Party*] [*Bolivia*] [*Political party*] ... PSC
Partido Social Cristiano [*Social Christian Party*] [*Guatemala*] [*Political party*] (PPW) ... PSC
Partido Social Cristiano [*Social Christian Party*] [*Ecuador*] [*Political party*] (PPW) ... PSC
Partido Social Democrata [*Social Democratic Party*] [*Bolivia*] [*Political party*] (PPW) ... PSD
Partido Social Democrata [*Social Democratic Party*] [*Spain Political party*] (PPE) ... PSD
Partido Social Democrata [*Social Democratic Party*] [*Mexico Political party*] (PPW) ... PSD
Partido Social Democratico [*Social Democratic Party*] [*Brazil Political party*] ... PSD
Partido Social Democratico [*Social Democratic Party*] [*Nicaragua*] [*Political party*] (PPW) ... PSD
Partido Social Democratico [*Social Democratic Party*] [*El Salvador*] [*Political party*] ... PSD
Partido Social Democratico Independente [*Independent Social Democratic Party*] [*Portugal Political party*] (PPE) ... PSDI
Partido Social Progresista [*Social Progressive Party*] [*Brazil Political party*] ... PSP
Partido Socialcristiano Nicaraguense [*Nicaraguan Social Christian Party*] [*Political party*] ... PSC
Partido Socialcristiano Nicaraguense [*Nicaraguan Social Christian Party*] [*Political party*] (PPW) ... PSCN
Partido Socialdemocracia [*Social Democratic Party*] [*Chile*] [*Political party*] (EY) ... PSD
Partido Socialdemocrata de Guinea Ecuatorial [*Social Democratic Party of Equatorial Guinea*] [*Political party*] (EY) ... PSGE
Partido Socialista [*Socialist Party*] [*Uruguay*] [*Political party*] ... PS
Partido Socialista [*Socialist Party*] [*Chile*] [*Political party*] ... PS
Partido Socialista Aponte [*Bolivia*] [*Political party*] (PPW) ... PSA
Partido Socialista Argentino [*Socialist Party of Argentina*] [*Political party*] ... PSA

Partido Socialista de Catalunya [*Catalan Socialist Party*] [*Spain Political party*] (PPE) ... PSC
Partido Socialista de Euskadi [*Basque Socialist Party*] [*Spain Political party*] (EY) ... PSE
Partido Socialista de Honduras [*Honduran Socialist Party*] [*Political party*] ... PASOH
Partido Socialista de los Trabajadores [*Socialist Workers' Party*] [*Mexico Political party*] (PPW) ... PST
Partido Socialista de los Trabajadores [*Socialist Workers Party*] [*Panama*] [*Political party*] (EY) ... PST
Partido Socialista de los Trabajadores [*Socialist Workers' Party*] [*Colombia*] [*Political party*] (PPW) ... PST
Partido Socialista de Melilla [*See also PSOE*] [*Spanish North Africa*] [*Political party*] (MENA) ... PSME
Partido Socialista de Melilla - Partido Socialista Obrero Espanol [*Political party*] (EY) ... PSME-PSOE
Partido Socialista del Pais Valenciano [*Spain Political party*] (EY) ... PSPV
Partido Socialista del Peru [*Socialist Party of Peru*] [*Political party*] (PPW) ... PSP
Partido Socialista del Pueblo de Ceuta [*Political party*] (EY) ... PSPC
Partido Socialista Democratico [*Social Democratic Party*] [*Argentina Political party*] (PPW) ... PSD
Partido Socialista Democratico [*Social Democratic Party*] [*Guatemala*] [*Political party*] (PD) ... PSD
Partido Socialista Ecuatoriano [*Ecuadorean Socialist Party*] [*Political party*] (PPW) ... PSE
Partido Socialista Galego - Esquerda Galega [*Spain Political party*] (EY) ... PSG-EG
Partido Socialista Nicaraguense [*Nicaraguan Socialist Party*] [*Political party*] (PPW) ... PSN
Partido Socialista Obrero Espanol [*Spanish Socialist Workers' Party*] [*See also PSME*] [*Political party*] (PPE) ... PSOE
Partido Socialista Popular [*Popular Socialist Party*] [*Peru*] [*Political party*] (PPW) ... PSP
Partido Socialista Popular [*Popular Socialist Party*] [*Spain Political party*] (PPE) ... PSP
Partido Socialista Popular [*Popular Socialist Party*] [*Pre-1965*] [*Cuba*] [*Political party*] (PPW) ... PSP
Partido Socialista Portuguesa [*Portuguese Socialist Party*] [*Political party*] (PPE) ... PS
Partido Socialista Portuguesa [*Portuguese Socialist Party*] [*Political party*] (PPW) ... PSP
Partido Socialista Revolucionario [*Revolutionary Socialist Party*] [*Mexico Political party*] (PPW) ... PSR
Partido Socialista Revolucionario [*Revolutionary Socialist Party*] [*Peru*] [*Political party*] (PPW) ... PSR
Partido Socialista Revolucionario [*Revolutionary Socialist Party*] [*Portugal Political party*] (PPE) ... PSR
Partido Socialista Revolucionario Ecuatoriano [*Socialist Revolutionary Party of Ecuador*] [*Political party*] (PPW) ... PSRE
Partido Socialista Revolucionario (Marxista-Leninista)/Movimiento de Izquierda Revolucionaria [*Revolutionary Socialist Party (Marxist-Leninist)/ Mi litant Movement of the Revolutionary Left*] [*Peru*] [*Political party*] (PPW) ... PSR-ML/MIR
Partido Socialista Tito Atahuichi [*Bolivia*] [*Political party*] (PPW) ... PSTA
Partido Socialista Unificado [*Socialist Unification Party*] [*Argentina Political party*] (PPW) ... PSU
Partido Socialista - Uno [*Socialist Party - One*] [*Also, PS-1 Bolivia*] [*Political party*] (PPW) ... PS
Partido Socialista - Uno [*Socialist Party - One*] [*Also, PS Bolivia*] [*Political party*] (PD) ... PS-1
Partido Socialista Uruguayo [*Uruguayan Socialist Party*] [*Political party*] (PD) ... PSU
Partido Tercera Republica [*Chile*] [*Political party*] (EY) ... PTR
Partido Trabajador [*Mexico Political party*] (EY) ... PT
Partido Trabalhista Brasileiro [*Brazilian Labor Party*] [*Political party*] (PPW) ... PTB
Partido Trabalhista Nacional [*National Workers' Party*] [*Brazil*] ... PTN
Partido Unidad Social Cristiana [*Costa Rica*] [*Political party*] (EY) ... PUSC
Partido Unido de la Revolucion Socialista Cubana [*Cuba*] [*Political party*] (EY) ... PURSC
Partido Unido Social Democratico [*United Social-Democratic Party*] [*Guinea-Bissau*] [*Political party*] (EY) ... PUSD
Partido Unificado Mariateguista [*Peru*] [*Political party*] (EY) ... PUM
Partido Union Boliviana [*Bolivian Unity Party*] [*Political party*] (PPW) ... PUB
Partido Union Democratica [*Guatemala*] [*Political party*] ... PUD
Partido Union Federal [*Federal Union Party*] [*Argentina Political party*] ... PUF
Partido Union Nacional [*National Union Party*] [*Costa Rica*] [*Political party*] ... PUN
Partido Union Patriotica [*Patriotic Union Party*] [*Dominican Republic*] [*Political party*] (PPW) ... PUP
Partido Union Revolucionaria [*Cuba*] ... PUR
Partido Unionista Centro Americana [*Nicaragua*] [*Political party*] (EY) ... PUCA
Partidual Nationale Crestine [*National Christian Party*] [*Romania*] [*Political party*] (PPE) ... PNC
Partidul Comunist Roman [*Romanian Communist Party*] [*Political party*] (PPE) ... PCR
Partidul Muncitoresc Roman [*Romanian Workers' Party*] [*Political party*] ... PMR
Partidul National Liberal [*National Liberal Party*] [*Romania*] [*Political party*] (PPE) ... PNL
Partidul National Poporului [*National People's Party*] [*Romania*] [*Political party*] (PPE) ... PNP
Partidul National-Democratic [*National Democratic Party*] [*Romania*] [*Political party*] (PPE) ... PND
Partidul Socialist Unitar [*Unitary Socialist Party*] [*Romania*] [*Political party*] (PPE) ... PSU
Partiia Sotsialistov Revolyutsionerov [*Socialist Revolutionary Party*] [*Russian Political party*] (PPE) ... SR
Partij Nationalistische Republiek [*Nationalist Republic Party*] [*Surinam*] [*Political party*] (PPW) ... PNR
Partij van de Arbeid [*Labor Party*] [*Netherlands Political party*] (PPE) ... PvdA
Partij van de Arbeid van Belgiee/Parti du Travail de Belgique [*Belgian Labor Party*] [*Political party*] (PPW) ... PvdA/PTA
Partij van de Vrijheid [*Party of Freedom*] [*Netherlands Political party*] (PPE) ... PvdV
Partij voor Vrijheid en Vooruitgang [*Freedom and Progress Party*] [*See also PLP*] [*Belgium*] [*Political party*] (PPW) ... PVV
Partim [*In Part*] ... P
Parting Line [*Castings*] (AAG) ... PL
Parting Post Calls (MCD) ... PPC
Partis [*A Part*] [*Pharmacy*] ... PART
Partisan Prohibition Historical Society (EA) ... PPHS
Partisan Review [*A publication*] (BRI) ... PR
Partit Comunista Obrero de Catalunya [*Communist Workers' Party of Catalonia*] [*Political party*] (PPW) ... PCOC
Partit dels Socialistes de Catalunya [*Party of Socialists of Catalonia*] [*Political party*] (PPW) ... PSC-PSOE
Partit Democrata d'Andorra [*Andorran Democratic Party*] [*Political party*] (PPW) ... PDA
Partit Nazzjonalista [*Nationalist Party*] [*Malta*] [*Political party*] (EAIO) ... PN
Partit Socialista Unificat de Catalunya [*Unified Socialist Party of Catalonia*] [*Spain Political party*] (PPE) ... PSUC
Partita Liberale Giovani Somali [*Somali Liberal Youth Party*] [*Political party*] ... PLGS
Partition [*Ballistics*] ... PART
Partition (WGA) ... Pn
Partition (AD) ... pn
Partition ... PRTN
Partition (KSC) ... PTN
Partition Affinity Ligand Assay [*Analytical microbiology*] ... PALA
Partition Coefficient ... PC
Partition Factor (NRCH) ... PF
Partition Function, Particle [*Symbol*] [*IUPAC*] ... q
Partition Function, Particle [*Symbol*] [*IUPAC*] ... z
Partition Function, System [*Symbol*] [*IUPAC*] ... Q
Partition Function, System [*Symbol*] [*IUPAC*] ... Z
Partition Specification Table (MHDI) ... PST
Partition Table [*Computer science*] (IAA) ... PT
Partition with Self Substitution Property (IAA) ... PSSP
Partitionable SIMD/MIMD [*Single Instruction, Multiple Data/Multiple Instruction, Multiple Data*] (MCD) ... PASM
Partitioned Access Method [*Computer science*] ... PAM
Partitioned Content Addressable Memory ... PCAM
Partitioned Data Set [*or System*] [*Computer science*] (NASA) ... PDS
Partitioned Emulation Program [*Computer science*] (BUR) ... PEP
Partitioned Libraries Management System (MHDI) ... PLMS
Partitioned Sequence Access Method ... PSAM
Partitioned-Pipe Mixer [*Engineering*] ... PPM
Partitiones Oratoriae [*of Cicero*] [*Classical studies*] (OCD) ... Part Or
Partitioning Industry Association [*British*] (DBA) ... PIA
Partitis Vicibus [*In Divided Parts*] [*Pharmacy*] ... PART VIC
Partitive Analytical Forecasting (PDAA) ... PAF
Partito Anti-Reformista [*Anti-Reform Party*] [*Malta*] [*Political party*] (PPE) ... PAR
Partito Comunista Italiano [*Italian Communist Party*] [*Political party*] ... PCI
Partito Comunista Marxista-Leninista [*Marxist-Leninist Communist Party*] [*San Marino*] [*Political party*] (PPE) ... PCML
Partito Comunista (Marxista-Leninista) de Italia [*Communist Party of Italy (Marxist-Leninist)*] [*Political party*] (PPE) ... PC(ML)I
Partito Comunista Sammarinese [*Communist Party of San Marino*] [*Political party*] (PPE) ... PCS
Partito Comunista Unificado de Italia [*Unified Communist Party of Italy*] [*Political party*] (PPE) ... PCUI
Partito d'Azione [*Action Party*] [*Italy Political party*] (PPE) ... Pd'A
Partito de Azione de Sardegna [*Sardinian Action Party*] [*Italy Political party*] (PPW) ... PAS
Partito della Democrazia Cristiana [*Christian Democrat Party*] [*Italy Political party*] (EY) ... DC
Partito della Democrazia Cristiana [*Christian Democratic Party*] [*Italy Political party*] ... PDC
Partito Democratica Italiana [*Italian Democratic Party*] [*Political party*] (PPE) ... PDI
Partito Democratico Cristiano Sammarinese [*Christian Democratic Party of San Marino*] [*Political party*] (PPE) ... PDCS
Partito Democratico della Sinistra [*Democratic Party of the Left*] [*Formerly, Italian Communist Party*] [*Political party*] (EY) ... PDS
Partito Democratico Italiano di Unita Monarchica [*Italian Democratic Party of Monarchical Unity*] [*Political party*] (PPE) ... PDIUM
Partito Democratico Nazionalista [*Democratic Nationalist Party (1921-1926)*] [*Malta*] [*Political party*] (PPE) ... PDN
Partito Democratico Populare [*Popular Democratic Party*] [*San Marino*] [*Political party*] (PPE) ... PDP
Partito di Democrazia Socialista [*Socialist Democracy Party*] [*San Marino*] [*Political party*] (PPW) ... PDS
Partito di Unita Proletaria per il Comunismo [*Democratic Party of Proletarian Unity for Communism*] [*Italy Political party*] (PPE) ... PdUP
Partito Liberale Italiano [*Italian Liberal Party*] [*Political party*] (PPW) ... PLI
Partito Monarchico [*Monarchist Party*] [*Italy Political party*] (PPE) ... PM
Partito Monarchico Popolare [*Popular Monarchist Party*] [*Italy Political party*] (PPE) ... PMP
Partito Nazionale Fascista [*National Fascist Party*] [*Italy Political party*] (PPE) ... PNF
Partito Nazionale Monarchico [*National Monarchist Party*] [*Italy Political party*] (PPE) ... PNM

Partito Nazionale Unito Africa [*National Party of United Africans*] [*Somalia*] [*Political party*] .... PNUA
Partito Populare Somalo [*Somali People's Party*] .... PPS
Partito Radicale [*Radical Party*] [*Founded, 1955*] [*Italy*] [*Political party*] (PPE) .... PR
Partito Repubblicano Italiano [*Italian Republican Party*] [*Political party*] (PPW) .... PRI
Partito Republicano Sammarinese [*Republican Party*] [*San Marino*] [*Political party*] (EY) .... PRS
Partito Socialista Autonomo [*Autonomous Socialist Party*] [*Switzerland Political party*] (PPW) .... PSA
Partito Socialista dei Lavoratori Italiani [*Socialist Party of Italian Workers*] [*Political party*] (PPE) .... PSLI
Partito Socialista Democratico Indipendente Sammarinese [*Independent Social Democratic Party of San Marino*] [*Political party*] (PPE) .... PSDIS
Partito Socialista Democratico Italiano [*Italian Social Democratic Party*] [*Political party*] .... PSDI
Partito Socialista Democratico Sammarinese [*Social Democratic Party of San Marino*] [*Political party*] (PPE) .... PSDS
Partito Socialista Italiano [*Italian Socialist Party*] [*Political party*] (PPE) .... PSI
Partito Socialista Italiano di Unita Proletaria [*Italian Socialist Party of Proletarian Unity (1945-1947)*] [*Political party*] (PPE) .... PSIUP
Partito Socialista Sammarinese [*Socialist Party of San Marino*] [*Political party*] (PPE) .... PSS
Partito Socialista: Sezione Italiana del Internazionale Socialista [*Socialist Party: Italian Section of International Socialism*] [*Political party*] (PPE) ..... PSSIIS
Partito Socialista Somalo [*Somali Socialist Party*] [*Political party*] (PPE) .... PSS
Partito Socialista Unificato [*Unified Socialist Party*] [*Italy Political party*] (PPE) .... PSU
Partito Socialista Unitario [*Socialist Unity Party*] [*Italy Political party*] (PPE) .... PSU
Partito Socialista Unitario de Lavoratori Italiani [*Unitary Socialist Party of Italian Workers*] [*Political party*] (PPE) .... PSULI
Partitu Populare Corsu [*Corsica*] [*Political party*] (PD) .... PPC
Partiya Litsom k Derevne [*The Party Face to Face with the Countryside*] [*Given name popular in Russia after the Bolshevik Revolution*] .... PARLIKDER
Partizanim-Chayalim-Chalutzim (BJA) .... PACHACH
Part-Length Control Element Assembly [*Nuclear energy*] (NRCH) .... PLCEA
Part-Length Control Element Drive Mechanism [*Nuclear energy*] (NRCH) .... PLCEDM
Partly [*NWS*] (FAAC) .... PTLY
Partly Filled Out [*Questionnaire*] .... PFO
Partly Soluble (WGA) .... P Sol
Partly Soluble [*Chemistry*] (DAVI) .... P sol
Partner (ADA) .... PART
Partner .... PRTNR
Partner (ROG) .... PTNR
Partner .... PTR
Partner Airlines [*Former USSR*] [*FAA designator*] (FAAC) .... PRR
Partner Relationship Inventory [*Marital relations test*] [*Psychology*] .... PRI
Partner Violence Screen [*Health*] .... PVS
PartnerRe Ltd. [*Associated Press*] (SAG) .... PartnerR
PartnerRe Ltd. [*NASDAQ symbol*] (SAG) .... PTRE
PartnerRe Ltd [*NASDAQ symbol*] (TTSB) .... PTREF
Partner-Resisted Exercise [*Army*] (INF) .... PRE
Partners for Livable Places (EA) .... PLP
Partners in Change Program [*Department of Labor*] .... PIC
Partners in Friendship (EA) .... PIF
Partners in Harmony, World Family of John Denver (EA) .... PHWFJD
Partners in Politics (EA) .... PP
Partners in Progress [*Government*] [*Civil rights*] .... PIP
Partners in Transition [*Poland, Czechoslovakia, and Hungary*] (ECON) .... PIT
Partners In Transition [*Poland, Czech, Hungary - called the Visegrad Trio*] .... PITS
Partners of the Americas (EA) .... PA
Partners Oil & Mining [*Vancouver Stock Exchange symbol*] .... PTO
Partners Perferred Yield III [*Associated Press*] (SAG) ParPf3
Partners Preferred Yield [*Associated Press*] (SAG) .... ParPfd
Partners Preferred Yield [*AMEX symbol*] (SAG) .... PYA
Partners Preferred Yield II [*Associated Press*] (SAG) ParPf2
Partners Preferred Yield II [*AMEX symbol*] (SAG) .... PYB
Partners Preferred Yield III [*AMEX symbol*] (SAG) .... PYC
Partners Preferred Yld'A' [*AMEX symbol*] (TTSB) .... PYA
Partners Preferred Yld'A' II [*AMEX symbol*] (TTSB) .... PYB
Partners Preferred Yld'A' III [*AMEX symbol*] (TTSB) .... PYC
Partnership .... P
Partnership (ADA) .... PARTN
Partnership [*Legal shorthand*] (LWAP) .... PARTSHIP
Partnership .... PRTNRSHP
Partnership (ROG) .... PTNRSHIP
Partnership Approach to Health (MEDA) .... PATH
Partnership for a Drug Free America (EA) .... DFA
Partnership for a New Generation of Vehicles .... PNGV
Partnership for a New Generation of Vehicles [*Collaboration of government and industry*] .... PNGV
Partnership for Environmental Technology Education [*Nonprofit organization of 400 community colleges*] .... PETE
Partnership for Long Term Care .... PLTC
Partnership for Over-Regulated Kar [*Humorous description of government-auto industry technology research program*] .... PORK
Partnership for Peace [*An organization of non-member countries which have established military cooperation with NATO*] (ECON) .... PFP
Partnership for Productivity International (EA) .... PFP
Partnership for Productivity International (EA) .... PFPI
Partnership for Rural Improvement [*Washington*] (EDAC) .... PRI
Partnerships Data Net [*Defunct*] (EA) .... PDN
Partners-in-Mission [*Church of England*] .... PIM

Parts .... PTS
Parts Accountability Technique (MCD) .... PAT
Parts Acquisition Group .... PAG
Parts Allocation Chart (MCD) .... PAC
Parts Allocation Requirements Technique .... PART
Parts Analysis Summary Sheet .... PASS
Parts and Assemblies Locator [*ADP/CES*] .... PAL
Parts and Componenets Manual (IAA) .... PACM
Parts and Data Record System (MCD) .... PADR
Parts and Design Language (NITA) .... PADL
Parts and Materials Accountability Control .... PAMAC
Parts and Supply Requisition (IAA) .... PSR
Parts and Tool Disposition (SAA) .... P & TD
Parts and Tool Disposition (IAA) .... PATD
Parts Application Handbook .... PAH
Parts Application Information [*Manufacturing*] .... PAI
Parts Application Reliability Data (IEEE) .... PARD
Parts Approval Request (MCD) .... PAR
Parts Assembly and Reuse Tool Set [*Computer software*] [*Digitalk, Inc.*] (PCM) .... PARTS
Parts Assembly Order (IAA) .... PAO
Parts Authorization List (KSC) .... PAL
Parts Breakdown .... PB
Parts Breakdown Structure .... PBS
Parts by Weight (IEEE) .... PBW
Parts by Weight (WDAA) .... PBWT
Parts Catalog (KSC) .... PC
Parts Change Notice (MCD) .... PCN
Parts, Components, Subassemblies .... PCS
Parts Control Area [*NASA*] (KSC) .... PCA
Parts Control Automated Support System [*Database*] .... PCASS
Parts Control Board .... PCB
Parts Control System [*DoD*] .... PCS
Parts Data Processing System [*Bell Telephone*] .... PDPS
Parts Deletion List (MSA) .... PDL
Parts Difference List (MCD) .... PDL
Parts Disposal Area (MCD) .... PDA
Parts Dissection Information System .... PDIS
Parts Documentation List (MCD) .... PDL
Parts Drawing Approval Request (MCD) .... PDAR
Parts Early Warning System (IAA) .... PEWS
Parts Engineering Support .... PES
Parts for Direct Discrete Analog Input/Output (MCD) .... PDDAIO
Parts for Import Cars Coalition [*Defunct*] (EA) .... PICC
Parts, Hybrids, and Packaging (MCD) .... PHP
Parts Identification Service .... PIS
Parts Installation and Removal Record [*NASA*] (KSC) .... PIRR
Parts Just in Time .... PJIT
Parts Kit .... PRTKT
Parts List .... PL
Parts List Assembly Order (MCD) .... PLAO
Parts List Change Notice (MCD) .... PLCN
Parts List Item Sequence Number (MCD) .... PLISN
Parts List Only (MCD) .... PLO
Parts List Page (KSC) .... PLP
Parts Listing Used On-Line Technique [*Computer science*] (IAA) .... PLUOT
Parts Load List .... PLL
Parts Logistics Analysis Network .... PLAN
Parts Manufacturer Approval [*FAA*] (MCD) .... PMA
Parts Manufacturing Associates (AD) .... PMA
Parts Manufacturing Workmanship .... PMW
Parts Master File (MCD) .... PMF
Parts Material List .... PML
Parts Material Requirements File .... PMR
Parts, Materials, and Packaging (MCD) .... PMP
Parts, Materials, and Processes (MCD) .... PMP
Parts Per .... PP
Parts per Billion .... PPB
Parts per Billion (AD) .... ppb
Parts per Billion 10 (IDOE) .... ppb
Parts per Cubic Centimeter (IAA) .... PPCC
Parts per Cubic Inch (WDAA) .... P IN^3
Parts per Hundred .... PPH
Parts per Hundred Million .... PPHM
Parts per Hundred of Asphalt [*Chemical technology*] .... PHA
Parts per Hundred of Rubber [*Chemical technology*] .... PHR
Parts Per Hundred Parts of Mix (AD) .... pphpm
Parts Per Hundred Parts of Rubber (AD) .... pphr
Parts per Million (IEEE) .... P/M
Parts per Million .... PPM
Parts Per Million (AD) .... ppm
Parts per Million .... ppm
Parts per Million (IDOE) .... ppm
Parts per Million by Volume [*Marine science*] (OSRA) .... ppmv
Parts per Million by Volume .... PPMV
Parts per Million by Weight (MCD) .... PPMW
Parts per Million Carbon [*Automotive engineering*] .... PPMC
Parts per Minute (MCD) .... PPM
Parts per Quadrillion .... PPQ
Parts per Quarter Note [*Computer science*] (PCM) .... PPQN
Parts per Square Inch (WDAA) .... P IN^2
Parts per Thousand (DNAB) .... PPT
Parts per Thousand (IDOE) .... ppt
Parts Per Thousand (GNE) .... ppth
Parts per Trillion [*Marine science*] (OSRA) .... ppt

Parts per Trillion ... PPT
Parts per Trillion by Volume ... PPTV
Parts per Weight ... PPW
Parts Preference Code [*Military*] (AFIT) ... PPC
Parts Provisioning Document ... PPD
Parts Provisioning System (KSC) ... PPS
Parts Quality Assurance ... PQA
Parts Release Card (KSC) ... PRC
Parts Release Order ... PRO
Parts Reliability Improvement Program ... PRIP
Parts Reliability Information Center [*NASA*] ... PRINCE
Parts Reliability Information Center/Apollo Parts Information Center [*NASA*] ... PRINCE/APIC
Parts Replacement Request (KSC) ... PRR
Parts Requirement List (KSC) ... PRL
Parts Requirement Notice (KSC) ... PRN
Parts Screening Program ... PSP
Parts Shipper ... PS
Parts Source [*NASDAQ symbol*] (TTSB) ... ACEP
Parts Source, Inc. (The) [*NASDAQ symbol*] (SAG) ... ACEP
Parts Source, Inc. (The) [*Associated Press*] (SAG) ... PartsS
Parts Specification Management for Reliability ... PSMR
Parts Test Information List (KSC) ... PTIL
Parts Tool Requirements File ... PTR
Parts Transfer Form (SAA) ... PTF
Parts Transfer Record (SAA) ... PTR
Parts Usage Maintenance Program [*Computer science*] (IAA) ... PUMP
Parts Used [*Medicine*] ... PU
Part-Throttle Unlock [*Automotive engineering*] ... PTU
Part-Time [*Employment*] ... P-T
Part-Time, Intermittent, Temporary [*Nuclear energy*] ... PIT
Part-Time Job ... PTJ
Part-Time Work Experience Program [*Texas*] (EDAC) ... PT-WEX
Party ... P
Party (AAG) ... PTY
Party ... PTY
Party City [*NASDAQ symbol*] (TTSB) ... PCTY
Party City Corp. [*NASDAQ symbol*] (SAG) ... PCTY
Party City Corp. [*Associated Press*] (SAG) ... PrtyCty
Party Election Broadcast [*British*] (BARN) ... PEB
Party for Democratic Prosperity [*Macedonia*] [*Political party*] ... PDP
Party for National Order [*Turkey Political party Defunct*] (MENA) ... PNO
Party for Peace and Democracy [*South Korea*] [*Political party*] ... PPD
Party for the Autonomy of Gibraltar [*Political party*] (PPW) ... PAG
Party Identity [*Telecommunications*] (TEL) ... PTI
Party Notified (IAA) ... PN
Party of Catalan Communists [*Political party*] (PPW) ... PCC
Party of Democratic Action [*Bosnia-Herzegovina*] [*Political party*] (EY) ... PDA
Party of Democratic Action of Kosovo-Metohija [*Serbia*] [*Political party*] (EY) ... PDA-KM
Party of Democratic Action of the Sandjak [*Serbia*] [*Political party*] (EY) ... PDA-S
Party of Democratic Reform [*Slovenia*] [*Political party*] (EY) ... PDR
Party of Democratic Socialism [*Germany Political party*] ... PDS
Party of Labor of Albania [*Political party*] (PPW) ... PLA
Party of Popular Yemenite Unity [*Political party*] (PD) ... PPYU
Party of the Civic Alliance [*Romania*] [*Political party*] (EY) ... PCA
Party of the Democratic Left of Slovakia [*Former Czechoslovakia*] [*Political party*] (EY) ... PDLS
Party of the Democratic Revolution [*Mexico Political party*] ... PRD
Party on Scientific and Technical Research Policy [*European community*] (MHDB) ... PREST
Party Raayat [*Leftist organization in Singapore*] ... PR
Party Socialiste Revolutionnaire [*Socialist Revolutionary Party*] [*Lebanon*] [*Political party*] (PPW) ... PSR
Party Test [*Telecommunications*] (TEL) ... PTT
Party to Exemption [*RSPA*] (TAG) ... PTE
Party to Expose the Petrov Conspiracy [*Australia Political party*] ... PTETPC
Party-Line Adapter Board [*Telecommunications*] (MHDI) ... PLAB
Paruima [*Guyana*] [*ICAO location identifier*] (ICLI) ... SYPR
Parve [*or Pareve*] [*In food labeling, indicates food is kosher and can be used with either meat or dairy products*] ... P
Parvus [*Small*] [*Pharmacy*] ... PARV
Parys [*South Africa*] [*ICAO location identifier*] (ICLI) ... FAPY
Parys [*South Africa*] [*Seismograph station code, US Geological Survey*] (SEIS) ... PRY
Pasadena [*California*] [*Seismograph station code, US Geological Survey*] (SEIS) ... PAS
Pasadena, CA [*AM radio station call letters*] ... KAZN
Pasadena, CA [*FM radio station call letters*] ... KPCC
Pasadena, CA [*AM radio station call letters*] ... KPPC
Pasadena, CA [*AM radio station call letters*] ... KRLA
Pasadena, CA [*FM radio station call letters*] ... KROQ
Pasadena, CA [*AM radio station call letters*] (RBYB) ... KXPA-AM
Pasadena City College [*California*] ... PCC
Pasadena City College, Pasadena, CA [*OCLC symbol*] (OCLC) ... CPA
Pasadena City College, Pasadena, CA [*Library symbol Library of Congress*] (LCLS) ... CPCiC
Pasadena Elementary School, Plainview, NY [*Library symbol Library of Congress*] (LCLS) ... NPIPE
Pasadena Energy [*Vancouver Stock Exchange symbol*] ... PDA
Pasadena Foundation for Medical Research [*California*] ... PFMR
Pasadena High School, Pasadena, TX [*Library symbol*] [*Library of Congress*] (LCLS) ... TxPPH
Pasadena Historical Society, Pasadena, CA [*Library symbol*] [*Library of Congress*] (LCLS) ... CPHi
Pasadena Independent School District, Pasadena, TX [*Library symbol*] [*Library of Congress*] (LCLS) ... TxPISD
Pasadena Independent School District, Professional Library, Pasadena, TX [*Library symbol*] [*Library of Congress*] (LCLS) ... TxPISD-P
Pasadena Online Information Network [*Pasadena Public Library*] (OLDSS) ... POINT
Pasadena Public Library, Newfoundland [*Library symbol National Library of Canada*] (NLC) ... NFPA
Pasadena Public Library, Pasadena, CA [*Library symbol Library of Congress*] (LCLS) ... CP
Pasadena Public Library, Pasadena, CA [*OCLC symbol*] (OCLC) ... CPP
Pasadena Public Library, Pasadena, NF, Canada [*Library symbol Library of Congress*] (LCLS) ... CaNfPa
Pasadena Public Library, Pasadena, TX [*Library symbol Library of Congress*] (LCLS) ... TxP
Pasadena, TX [*FM radio station call letters*] (RBYB) ... KFTG
Pasadena, TX [*AM radio station call letters*] ... KIKK
Pasadena, TX [*FM radio station call letters*] ... KKBQ
Pasadena, TX [*AM radio station call letters*] ... KLVL
Pasaje [*Ecuador*] [*ICAO location identifier*] (ICLI) ... SEPS
Pascack Historical Society and Museum, Park Ridge, NJ [*Library symbol Library of Congress*] (LCLS) ... NjParkHi
Pascack Publications Corp., Park Ridge, NJ [*Library symbol Library of Congress*] (LCLS) ... NjParkP
Pascack Valley Community Life, Westwood, NJ [*Library symbol Library of Congress*] (LCLS) ... NjWewP
Pascagoula, MS [*Location identifier FAA*] (FAAL) ... PAC
Pascagoula, MS [*Location identifier FAA*] (FAAL) ... PGL
Pascagoula, MS [*FM radio station call letters*] ... WKNN
Pascagoula, MS [*FM radio station call letters*] ... WXYK
Pascagoula-Moss Point, MS [*AM radio station call letters*] ... WZZJ
Pascal [*Symbol*] [*SI unit of pressure*] ... Pa
Pascal/MT Users Group [*Defunct*] (EA) ... MTPUG
Pascal Second ... PA S
Pascal Source File [*Computer science*] ... PAS
PASCAL Subset for Application in Test Computers (NITA) ... PASSAT
PASCAL Users' Group [*Defunct*] (EA) ... PUG
Pascal-Suttle Test [*Psychology*] (DAVI) ... PST
Pascha [*Easter*] [*Church calendars*] (ROG) ... PASCH
Paschal [*Easter Term*] [*Legal term*] (DLA) ... Pasc
Paschal [*Easter Term*] [*Legal term*] (DLA) ... Pasch
Paschale Tempore [*Easter Time*] [*Latin*] ... PT
Paschal's Reports [*25, 28-31 Texas*] [*A publication*] (DLA) ... Pasc
Paschal's Reports [*28-31 Texas*] [*Supplement to Vol. 25*] [*A publication*] (DLA) ... Paschal
Paschal's Texas Digest of Decisions [*A publication*] (DLA) ... Pasch Dig
Paschal's United States Constitution, Annotated [*A publication*] (DLA) ... Paschal's Ann Const
Paschen-Back Effect [*Spectroscopy*] ... PBE
Pasco [*Washington*] [*Airport symbol*] (OAG) ... PSC
Pasco County Library System, New Port Richey, FL [*Library symbol*] [*Library of Congress*] (LCLS) ... FNprP
Pasco Public Library, Pasco, WA [*Library symbol Library of Congress*] (LCLS) ... WaPa
Pasco, WA [*Television station call letters*] ... KEPR
Pasco, WA [*FM radio station call letters*] ... KEYW
Pasco, WA [*AM radio station call letters*] (RBYB) ... KFLD
Pasco, WA [*FM radio station call letters*] ... KGDN
Pasco, WA [*FM radio station call letters*] ... KOLU
Pasco, WA [*Location identifier FAA*] (FAAL) ... PSC
Pascoe Nally International [*British*] ... PNI
Pasco-Hernando Community College, North Campus Learning Resources Center, Brooksville, FL [*Library symbol*] [*Library of Congress*] (LCLS) ... FBroPH
Paseo ... PSO
Pasicrisie Luxembourgeoise [*Luxembourg Law Reports*] [*A publication*] (ILCA) ... Pas Lux
Pasifik Satelit Nusantara (PT) [*Associated Press*] (SAG) ... PasifSat
Pasifik Satelit Nusantara (PT) [*NASDAQ symbol*] (SAG) ... PSNR
Pasighat [*India*] [*Airport symbol*] (AD) ... IXT
Pasighat [*India*] [*ICAO location identifier*] (ICLI) ... VEPG
Pasni [*Pakistan*] [*ICAO location identifier*] (ICLI) ... OPPI
Pasni [*Pakistan*] [*Airport symbol*] (OAG) ... PSI
Paso Canoas [*Costa Rica*] [*ICAO location identifier*] (ICLI) ... MRPC
Paso De Indios [*Argentina ICAO location identifier*] (ICLI) ... SAVP
Paso De Los Libres [*Argentina*] [*Airport symbol*] (OAG) ... AOL
Paso De Los Libres [*Argentina ICAO location identifier*] (ICLI) ... SARL
Paso Fino Horse Association (EA) ... PFHA
Paso Fino Owners and Breeders Association [*Later, PFHA*] (EA) ... PFOBA
Paso Robles [*California*] [*Airport symbol*] (AD) ... PRB
Paso Robles, CA [*FM radio station call letters*] ... KDDB
Paso Robles, CA [*FM radio station call letters*] (RBYB) ... KNCR
Paso Robles, CA [*AM radio station call letters*] ... KPRL
Paso Robles, CA [*Location identifier FAA*] (FAAL) ... PRB
Paso Robles Public Library, Paso Robles, CA [*Library symbol Library of Congress*] (LCLS) ... CPr
Pasochoa [*Ecuador*] [*ICAO location identifier*] (ICLI) ... SEOA
Pasokan Rakyat Kalimantan Utara [*North Kalimantan People's Forces*] [*Malaya*] ... PARAKU
Paspalum Striate Mosaic Virus [*Plant pathology*] ... PSMV
Pasqua Hospital, Regina, Saskatchewan [*Library symbol National Library of Canada*] (NLC) ... SRGH
Pasqua Hospital, Regina, SK, Canada [*Library symbol Library of Congress*] (LCLS) ... CaSRGH

Pasquotank-Camden Library, Elizabeth City, NC [*Library symbol Library of Congress*] (LCLS) .... NcElcP
Pass [*Postal Service standard*] (OPSA) .... PASS
Pass Card Reader [*Telecommunications*] (TEL) .... PCR
Pass Down the Line [*Book*] [*Navy*] (MUGU) .... PDL
Pass Lake Resources Ltd. [*Vancouver Stock Exchange symbol*] .... PLJ
Pass Slip Stitch Over [*Knitting*] .... PSSO
Pass Time [*Military*] .... PST
Pass to Air Defense RADAR [*Aviation*] (FAAC) .... PADRA
Passage (AABC) .... PAS
Passage [*Maps and charts*] (KSC) .... PASS
Passage (DD) .... Pass
Passage [*Commonly used*] (OPSA) .... PASSAGE
Passage .... PSE
Passage [*NWS*] (FAAC) .... PSG
Passage [*Postal Service standard*] (OPSA) .... PSGE
Passage Free (ROG) .... PF
Passage, Power, and Passenger [*Evaluation of labor progress*] [*Obstetrics*] (DAVI) .... PPP
Passage Reading Test [*Education*] (EDAC) .... PRT
Passaic Byzantine [*Diocesan abbreviation*] [*New Jersey*] (TOCD) .... PSC
Passaic Citizen, Passaic, NJ [*Library symbol Library of Congress*] (LCLS) .... NjPasC
Passaic County Clerk, Paterson, NJ [*Library symbol Library of Congress*] (LCLS) .... NjPatCoC
Passaic County Historical Society, Paterson, NJ [*Library symbol Library of Congress*] (LCLS) .... NjPatPHi
Passaic Public Library, Passaic, NJ [*Library symbol Library of Congress*] (LCLS) .... NjPas
Passaic River Coalition (EA) .... PRC
Passaic Township Public Library, Stirling, NJ [*Library symbol Library of Congress*] (LCLS) .... NjSt
Passamaquoddy Bay (AD) .... Quoddy
Passamaquoddy Ferry & Navigation Co. [*AAR code*] .... PFN
Passband Tuning .... PBT
Passbook [*Banking*] .... PB
Passed [*Examination*] .... P
Passed .... PD
Passed (ODBW) .... pd
Passed (ROG) .... PSD
Passed a Territorial Army Course in Staff Duties [*British*] .... TSC
Passed Assistant Engineer [*British*] .... PAE
Passed Assistant Paymaster [*British*] .... PAPM
Passed Ball .... PB
Passed, but Not Advanced .... PNA
Passed Flying College [*British*] .... PFC
Passed Midshipman .... PM
Passed Motion .... PM
Passed School of Instruction [*of Officers*] [*British*] .... PS
Passed Separately [*Military*] .... PASEP
Passed Staff College [*British*] .... PSC
Passed the Final Examination of the Advanced Class [*Military College of Science*] [*British*] .... PAC
Passed to the Adjacent Sector .... PAS
Passed Urine [*Medicine*] .... PU
Passenger (KSC) .... PASS
Passenger (DCTA) .... PASSR
Passenger (AFM) .... PAX
Passenger (AFM) .... PSGR
Passenger .... PSSGNR
Passenger Acceptance and Load Accumulation [*Aviation*] .... PALA
Passenger Acceptance and Load Control [*Aviation*] .... PALC
Passenger Address System [*Aviation*] (DA) .... PA
Passenger Agent .... PA
Passenger Airbag Disable .... PAD
Passenger Airlift Contract [*Military*] .... PAXCON
Passenger Airlines Reservation System .... PARS
Passenger and Baggage Processing Committee [*IATA*] (DS) .... PBPC
Passenger and Immigration Lists [*A publication*] .... P & I
Passenger and Immigration Lists Bibliography [*A publication*] .... PILB
Passenger and Immigration Lists Index [*A publication*] .... PILI
Passenger and Immigration Lists Index [*A publication*] .... PLI
Passenger Automated Selection System (ADA) .... PASS
Passenger Car Equivalence [*TRB*] (TAG) .... PCE
Passenger Car Motor Oil .... PCMO
Passenger Carrying Vehicle [*Military*] (GFGA) .... PCV
Passenger Certificate [*Shipping*] (DS) .... PC
Passenger Control Liaison Office [*or Officer*] [*Army*] (AABC) .... PCLO
Passenger Control Point [*Army*] (AABC) .... PCP
Passenger Control Unit (MCD) .... PCU
Passenger Control Vehicle (WDAA) .... PCV
Passenger Facility Charge [*Airports*] .... PFC
Passenger Form and Procedures Committee [*IATA*] (DS) .... PFPC
Passenger Information Display .... PID
Passenger Information System .... PIS
Passenger Legal Liability [*Insurance*] (AIA) .... PLL
Passenger Liability [*Insurance*] (BARN) .... PL
Passenger Liaison Office [*Military*] (AABC) .... PLO
Passenger Motor Vehicle .... PMV
Passenger Motor Vehicle Labour Adjustment Training Arrangements [*Australia*] .... PMV-LATA
Passenger Motor Vehicle Manufacturing Plan [*Australia*] .... PMVMP
Passenger Name Check-In (MCD) .... PNC
Passenger Name List [*Travel industry*] .... PNL
Passenger Name Record [*Airlines*] .... PNR

Passenger Protective Breathing Equipment [*Aviation*] (DA) .... PPBE
Passenger Reservation Center [*Army*] .... PRC
Passenger Reservation Request (NVT) .... PRR
Passenger Ride Quality Apparatus [*Public transportation*] .... PRQA
Passenger Routing and Information System [*FTA*] (TAG) .... PARIS
Passenger Service .... PS
Passenger Service Improvement Corp. .... PSIC
Passenger Service Manager [*Travel industry*] .... PSM
Passenger Service Supervisor [*Travel industry*] .... PSS
Passenger Service Systems [*Airlines*] .... PSS
Passenger Services Conference [*IATA*] (DS) .... PSC
Passenger Ship .... PA
Passenger Shipping Association [*British*] (DBA) .... PSA
Passenger Standing Route Order [*Army*] (AABC) .... PSRO
Passenger Steamer .... PS
Passenger Traffic [*MTMC*] (TAG) .... PT
Passenger Traffic Management System [*Army*] .... PASTRAM
Passenger Traffic Manager .... PTM
Passenger Transfer Vehicle [*Airport transportation*] .... PTV
Passenger Transport .... PT
Passenger Transport Authorities [*British*] .... PTA
Passenger Transport Executive [*British*] .... PTE
Passenger Transport Vehicle .... PTV
Passenger Vehicle Operation Association Ltd. [*British*] (BI) .... PVOA
Passenger-Miles Traveled [*DOE*] (TAG) .... PMT
Passenger-Reserved Air Freight .... PRAF
Passengers' Luggage in Advance [*Railway*] (ROG) .... PLA
Passengers' Risk (ROG) .... PR
Passeport International [*International Passport*] [*An association France*] (EAIO) .... PI
Pass-Fail [*System*] (MAE) .... P/F
Passiflora Latent Virus [*Plant pathology*] .... PALV
Passim [*Everywhere*] [*Latin*] .... PASS
Passing Aid System (IAA) .... PAS
Passing Exercise (DOMA) .... PASSEX
Passing Scene Display .... PSD
Passing Scene Display System .... PSDS
Passing Scuttle .... PS
Passing Showers [*Meteorology*] .... P
Passing Stop Sign [*Traffic offense charge*] .... SS
Passing Stopped School Bus [*Traffic offense charge*] .... PSSB
Passing Title [*Real estate*] .... PT
Passing Window (MSA) .... PW
[*The*] Passionate Pilgrim [*Poetry*] (BARN) .... Pilgr
[*The*] Passionate Pilgrim [*Shakespearean work*] .... PP
Passionfruit Woodiness Virus [*Plant pathology*] .... PWV
Passionist Academic Institute, Chicago, IL [*Library symbol Library of Congress*] (LCLS) .... ICPas
Passionist Academic Institute, Chicago, IL [*OCLC symbol*] (OCLC) .... JAQ
Passipoverus [*Flourished, 13th century*] [*Authority cited in pre-1607 legal work*] (DSA) .... Pas
Passivate [*Metallurgy*] (IAA) .... PASS
Passivate [*Metallurgy*] .... PSVT
Passive (WDAA) .... PAS
Passive .... PASS
Passive .... PSIV
Passive Acoustic Classification (NVT) .... PAC
Passive Acoustic Detection [*Military*] (CAAL) .... PAD
Passive Acoustic Target [*Military*] .... PAT
Passive Acoustic Torpedo [*Military*] .... PAT
Passive Active Detection and Location (IEEE) .... PADLOC
Passive/Active Reporting Ocean Surveillance System [*Navy*] (NVT) .... PAROSS
Passive Activity Loss [*Investment term*] (DFIT) .... PAL
Passive Advanced Sonobuoy .... PADS
Passive Aggressive (DMAA) .... PA
Passive Air Defense [*British*] .... PAD
Passive Air Navigation Device .... PAND
Passive Airborne Detection and Ranging (MSA) .... PAADAR
Passive Airborne Detection and Ranging .... PADAR
Passive Airborne Time-Difference Intercept [*Navy*] .... PATI
Passive and Active Control of Space Structures .... PASCOSS
Passive and Active Interface Test [*Electronic warfare*] .... PACIT
Passive and Active Signal Digital Correlator Analyzer (MCD) .... PANDORA
Passive and Remote Crosswind Sensor (MCD) .... PRCS
Passive Angle Track (NVT) .... PAT
Passive Annual Heat Storage [*Housing technology*] .... PAHS
Passive Antidrown Device (DWSG) .... PADD
Passive Antisubmarine Warfare Environmental Protection System [*Navy*] (NATG) .... PASWEPS
Passive Artillery Locating System - Ground Based (MCD) .... PALS-G
Passive Attitude Control Experimental [*Satellite*] .... PACE
Passive Automatic Nighttime Tracking Investigation and Evaluation Studies [*DoD*] .... PANTIES
Passive Avoidance Reaction [*Medicine*] (DMAA) .... PAR
Passive Chemical Ionization Mass Spectrometry .... PACIMS
Passive Communications Satellite .... PACSAT
Passive Containment System [*Nuclear energy*] (NRCH) .... PCS
Passive Correlation and Ranging .... PACOR
Passive Correlation and Ranging Station (IAA) .... PACOR
Passive Count Monitoring Device (KSC) .... PCMD
Passive Countermeasure .... PCM
Passive Countermeasures (MSA) .... PACM
Passive Cutaneous Anaphylaxis [*Immunochemistry*] .... PCA
Passive Data Collection .... PDC
Passive Data Memory Unit .... PDMU

Passive Defense Group (MUGU) ... PDG
Passive Defense Handbook [*Navy*] (MCD) ... PDH
Passive Defense Recovery Force (MUGU) ... PDRF
Passive Detection [*Electronics*] ... PD
Passive Detection and Location [*Air Force*] (IAA) ... PADLOC
Passive Detection and Location of Countermeasures [*Air Force*] ... PADLOC
Passive Detection and Location of Countermeasures [*Air Force*] (IAA) ... PADLOCC
Passive Detection and Ranging [*Electronics*] (IAA) ... PADAR
Passive Detection System (NVT) ... PDS
Passive Direction Finding ... PDF
Passive Dosimeter Experiment (KSC) ... PDX
Passive Driving Periscope [*Military*] (PDAA) ... PDP
Passive Electromagnetic System (IAA) ... PES
Passive Electronic Advanced Receiver (MCD) ... PEART
Passive Electronics Countermeasures [*Military*] (NG) ... PECM
Passive Electronics Warfare (NG) ... PEW
Passive Equipment Cabinet [*Military*] (CAAL) ... PEC
Passive Exercise [*Physical Therapy*] (DAVI) ... Pas Ex
Passive Filtration Unit ... PFU
Passive Foreign Investment Company [*IRS*] ... PFIC
Passive Geodetic Earth-Orbiting Satellite [*NASA*] ... PAGEOS
Passive Geodetic Satellite [*NASA*] ... PGS
Passive Gravity Stabilization ... PGS
Passive Hemagglutination [*Immunology*] ... PHA
Passive Hemagglutination Technique [*Immunology*] ... PHT
Passive Heymann Nephritis [*Medicine*] (DMAA) ... PHN
Passive Hyperpolarizing Potential [*Neurochemistry*] ... PHP
Passive Identification/Detection and Direction (MCD) ... PIDD
Passive Identification/Direction Finding Equipment (MCD) ... PI/DE
Passive Immune Hemolysis (PDAA) ... PIH
Passive Immunological Agglutination ... PIA
Passive Infrared ... PIR
Passive Infrared Confirming Sensor (MCD) ... PIRCS
Passive Infrared Guidance System [*DoD*] ... PIGS
Passive Infrared Intrusion Detector (NVT) ... PIRID
Passive Infrared Night Equipment (MCD) ... PINE
Passive Infrared Seeker ... PIRS
Passive Infrared System ... PIS
Passive Integrated Transponder ... PIT
Passive Intercept Tracking System ... PITS
Passive Line Monitor [*Datapoint*] ... PLM
Passive Low Pass (IAA) ... PLP
Passive Lunar Marker ... PLM
Passive Measurement Program ... PMP
Passive Microelectronic Element ... PME
Passive Microwave Imaging System [*NASA*] ... PMIS
Passive Microwave Intercept Receiver Display ... PMIRD
Passive Microwave Radiometer Satellite (PDAA) ... PAMIRASAT
Passive Multichannel Microwave Radiometer [*NASA*] ... PMMR
Passive Navigation Device ... PND
Passive Night Vision Devices [*Army*] (AABC) ... PNVD
Passive Optical Satellite Surveillance [*System*] (NATG) ... POSS
Passive Optical Scan Tracker (MCD) ... POST
Passive Optical Seeker Technique ... POST
Passive Participle ... PP
Passive Participle (AD) ... pp
Passive RADAR Surveillance [*Military*] (CAAL) ... PRS
Passive Radiation Countermeasure [*Military*] ... PRCM
Passive Radio Frequency Acquisition System ... PARFAS
Passive Range of Motion [*Medicine*] ... PROM
Passive Ranging [*Military*] (LAIN) ... PR
Passive Ranging Doppler ... PARDOP
Passive Ranging Interferometer Sensor ... PRAIS
Passive Ranging on Submarines [*Navy*] ... PAROS
Passive Ranging RADAR ... PRR
Passive Satellite Attitude Control ... PSAC
Passive Satellite Communications Research Terminal (SAA) ... PSCRT
Passive Satellite Research Terminal ... PSRT
Passive Seismic Experiment [*NASA*] ... PSE
Passive Seismic Experiments Package [*NASA*] ... PSEP
Passive Solar Foundation [*Defunct*] (EA) ... PSF
Passive Solar Industries Council (EA) ... PSIC
Passive Solar Institute [*Defunct*] (EA) ... PSI
Passive Solar Products Association (EA) ... PSPA
Passive SONAR Tracking System ... PSTS
Passive Thermal Control ... PTC
Passive Thermal Control Section [*NASA*] (NASA) ... PTCS
Passive Thermal Control System (NASA) ... PTCS
Passive Track [*Military*] (CAAL) ... PT
Passive Track-On-Jam ... PTOJ
Passive Ultrasonic Sensor (PDAA) ... PUS
Passive Underwater Fire Control Feasibility Study ... PUFFS
Passive Underwater Fire Control Feasibility System ... PUFFS
Passive-Active Data Simulation ... PADS
Passive-Active Range Determination ... PARADE
Passive-Active Surveillance System (MCD) ... PASS
Passive-Aggressive Index [*Psychology*] ... PAI
Passive-Cavity Aerosal Spectrometer Probe [*Meteorology*] ... PCASP
Passive-Income Generator [*Investment term*] ... PIG
Passive-Ranging Interferometer Sensor (AD) ... prais
Passo Dei Giovi [*Italy ICAO location identifier*] (ICLI) ... LIMV
Passo Del Brennero [*Italy ICAO location identifier*] (ICLI) ... LIVB
Passo Della Cisa [*Italy ICAO location identifier*] (ICLI) ... LIMT
Passo Della Porretta [*Italy ICAO location identifier*] (ICLI) ... LIQD
Passo Fundo [*Brazil*] [*Airport symbol*] (OAG) ... PFB
Passo Fundo/Lauro Kurtz [*Brazil ICAO location identifier*] (ICLI) ... SBPF
Passo Resia [*Italy ICAO location identifier*] (ICLI) ... LIVE
Passo Rolle [*Italy ICAO location identifier*] (ICLI) ... LIVR
Passover (BARN) ... Pass
Passport (AABC) ... PSPT
Passport Control Officer [*British*] ... PCO
Passport Office [*Department of State*] ... PO
Passport to Knowledge [*Children's computer program sponsored by NASA and NSF*] ... PTK
Password [*Computer science*] ... PASSWD
Password [*Computer science*] ... PW
Password Authentication Protocol [*Computer science*] (PCM) ... PAP
Past (WDMC) ... p
Past ... P
Past Assistant Deputy Grand Treasurer [*Freemasonry*] ... PADGT
Past Assistant Grand Director of Ceremonies [*Freemasonry*] (ROG) ... PAGDC
Past Chief Patriarch [*Freemasonry*] ... PCP
Past Commander ... PC
Past Dental History ... PDH
Past Deputy Provincial Grand Master [*Freemasonry*] ... PDPGM
Past District Deputy Grand Master [*Freemasonry*] ... PDDGM
Past Due ... PD
Past Due Date ... PDD
Past Global Changes [*Marine science*] (OSRA) ... PAGES
Past Grand [*Freemasonry*] ... PG
Past Grand Chaplain [*Freemasonry*] ... PGCh
Past Grand Commander [*Freemasonry*] (ROG) ... PGC
Past Grand Deacon [*Freemasonry*] ... PGD
Past Grand Junior Deacon [*Freemasonry*] ... PGJD
Past Grand Junior Warden [*Freemasonry*] (ROG) ... PGJW
Past Grand Master [*Freemasonry*] ... PGM
Past Grand Orient [*Freemasonry*] (ROG) ... PGO
Past Grand Senior Deacon [*Freemasonry*] ... PGSD
Past Grand Senior Warden [*Freemasonry*] ... PGSW
Past Grand Sword Bearer [*Freemasonry*] (ROG) ... PGSB
Past Grand Treasurer [*Freemasonry*] ... PGT
Past Grand Warden [*Freemasonry*] ... PGW
Past History [*Medicine*] ... PH
Past History [*Medicine*] (MAE) ... PHx
Past History (DAVI) ... Px
Past in Review (EA) ... PIR
Past in Review [*Later, PIR*] (EA) ... PR
Past Master [*Freemasonry*] ... PM
Past Master, Knights of Malta [*Freemasonry*] (ROG) ... PMKM
Past Medical History ... PMH
Past Medical History (AD) ... pmh
Past Medical History (DAVI) ... PMHx
Past [*or Previous*] **Medical Illness** ... PMI
Past Menstrual Period [*Medicine*] ... PMP
Past Participle ... PP
Past Participle (WDMC) ... pp
Past Participle (AD) ... pple
Past Patriarch [*Freemasonry*] (ROG) ... PP
Past Performance and Present Posture (AAG) ... PPPP
Past Performance Information Management System [*Army*] ... PPIMS
Past President ... PP
Past President of the Faculty of Architects and Surveyors [*British*] (DBQ) ... PPFAS
Past President of the Institution of Highway Engineers [*British*] (DI) ... PPInstHE
Past President of the Institution of Structural Engineers [*British*] (DI) ... PPIStructE
Past President of the Royal Academy [*British*] (EY) ... PPRA
Past President of the Royal Institute of British Architects (EY) ... PPRIBA
Past President of the Royal Society of Arts [*British*] (DI) ... PPRSA
Past President of the Society of Industrial Artists and Designers [*British*] (DI) ... PPSIAD
Past Pro-Grand Junior Warden [*Freemasonry*] (ROG) ... PPGJW
Past Pro-Grand Organist [*Freemasonry*] (ROG) ... PPGO
Past Pro-Grand Orient [*Freemasonry*] (ROG) ... PPGO
Past Pro-Grand Pursuivant [*Freemasonry*] (ROG) ... PPGP
Past Pro-Grand Sword Bearer [*Freemasonry*] (ROG) ... PPGSB
Past Pro-Grand Warden [*Freemasonry*] (ROG) ... PPGW
Past Pro-Junior Warden [*Freemasonry*] (ROG) ... PPJW
Past Provincial Grand Master [*Freemasonry*] ... PPGM
Past Provincial Grand Senior [*Freemasonry*] (ROG) ... PPGSN
Past Provincial Grand Senior Warden [*Freemasonry*] ... PPGSW
Past Royal Grand Cross [*Freemasonry*] (ROG) ... PRGC
Past Savio Movement [*Defunct*] (EA) ... PSM
Past Senior Grand Deacon [*Freemasonry*] ... PSGD
Past Senior Grand Warden [*Freemasonry*] ... PSGW
Past Shakedown Availability [*Military*] ... PSA
Past Social History (CPH) ... PSH
Past Start Date ... PSD
Past Supreme Grand Master [*Freemasonry*] ... PSGM
Past Surgical History [*Medicine*] (DMAA) ... PSH
Past Tense [*Grammar*] (BARN) ... pa t
Past Tense ... PT
Past Vice-President ... PV-P
Past Worthy Patriarch ... PWP
Past Z ... PZ
Pastaza [*Ecuador*] [*ICAO location identifier*] (ICLI) ... SEPA
Paste ... P
Paste ... PST
Paste (VRA) ... pst

Paste Down Ends [Graphic arts] (DGA) .... PDE
Paste Grain [Bookbinding] .... PG
Paste Up (ADA) .... PU
Pasteboard (DGA) .... P
Pasteboard (VRA) .... pstbd
Paste-Down [Album] [Photography] (ROG) .... PD
Pastel (VRA) .... ps
Pastel Food [Vancouver Stock Exchange symbol] ...... PLF
Pastel Society [British] .... PS
Pastel Society of America (EA) .... PSA
Pasteurella [Genus of bacteria] .... P
Pasteurella [Genus of bacteria] .... PAST
Pasteurizing [Freight] .... PSTZG
Pastillus [A Lozenge, Troch, Pastil] [Pharmacy] (ROG) . PAST
Pasto [Colombia] [Airport symbol] (OAG) .... PSO
Pasto [Colombia] [Seismograph station code, US Geological Survey] (SEIS) .... PSO
Pasto/Antonio Narino [Colorado ICAO location identifier] (ICLI) ...... SKPS
Pastor .... P
Pastor .... PR
Pastor .... PSTR
Pastor Pastorum [Shepherd of the Shepherds] [Latin] (ROG) . PP
Pastoral .... PSTL
Pastoral Board of South Australia .... PBSA
Pastoral Epistles (BJA) .... Past
Pastoralists and Graziers' Association of Western Australia ..... PGAWA
Pastorate .... PAST
Pastors' Anonymous Recovery-Directed Order for Newness [Rehabilitation program for troubled clergymen] [Defunct] ..... PARDON
Pastry (MSA) .... PST
Pastrycooks, Bakers, Biscuitmakers, and Allied Trades Union [Australia] ..... PBBATU
Pastural Zone [Agriculture] .... PZ
Pasture Canyon [Utah] [Seismograph station code, US Geological Survey Closed] (SEIS) .... PST
Pasture Protection Boards' Association of New South Wales [Australia] .... PPBANSW
Pasuquin [Philippines] [Seismograph station code, US Geological Survey] (SEIS) ..... PIP
Pataca [Monetary unit] [Macau] .... PT
Patagonia [Region of South America] (ROG) .... PATA
Patapsco & Back Rivers Railroad Co. [AAR code] ...... PBR
Pataskala Public Library, Pataskala, OH [Library symbol Library of Congress] (LCLS) .... OPat
Patch and Test Facility .... PTF
Patch on Mortgages [1821] [A publication] (DLA) ..... Pat Mort
Patch Output Converter (IAA) .... POC
Patch Panel (NASA) .... P/P
Patch Survey and Switching Unit (MCD) .... PSSU
Patch Unit Radio [Bell System] .... PUR
Patchboard (MSA) .... PCHBD
Patchboard Programming System .... PPS
Patches of Shallow Fog not Deeper Than Two Meters [NWS] (FAAC) ... MIFG
Patching Central [Army] (AABC) .... PATCENT
Patchogue Library, Patchogue, NY [Library symbol Library of Congress] (LCLS) .... NPat
Patchogue, NY [AM radio station call letters] .... WALK
Patchogue, NY [FM radio station call letters] .... WALK-FM
Patchogue, NY [FM radio station call letters] .... WBLI
Patchogue, NY [AM radio station call letters] .... WLIM
Patchy [Meteorology] (DA) .... PTCHY
Patchy White Matter Lesion [Medicine] .... PWML
PATCLASS [Pergamon ORBIT InfoLine, Inc.] [No longer available online] [Information service or system] (CRD) ...... PATC
Patellar Inhibition Test [Neurology] (DAVI) .... PIT
Patellar Tendon [Anatomy] .... PT
Patellar Tendon Bearing [Medicine] .... PTB
Patellar-Tendon Supracondylar [Anatomy] .... PTS
Patellofemoral Joint [Anatomy] (DAVI) .... PF
Patellofemoral Joint Reaction [Physiology] .... PFJR
Patellofemoral Pain Syndrome [Medicine] (DMAA) .... PFPS
Patellofemoral Stress Syndrome [Medicine] .... PFSS
Patent .... P
Patent (KSC) .... PAT
Patent (AAGC) .... Pat
Patent .... PATNT
Patent (ROG) .... PATT
Patent Abstracts Bibliography [NASA] .... PAB
Patent Abstracts Section, Official Gazette [Federal government] [A publication] ...... PASG
Patent and Copyright Office, Department of Consumer and Corporate Affairs [Bureau des Brevets et du Droit d'Auteur, Ministere de la Consommation et des Corporations] Ottawa, Ontario [Library symbol National Library of Canada] (NLC) ...... OOSP
Patent and Copyright Office, Ottawa, ON, Canada [Library symbol Library of Congress] (LCLS) .... CaOOSP
Patent & Legal Library, DuPont Canada, Inc., Mississauga, Ontario [Library symbol National Library of Canada] (NLC) ..... OMDCPL
Patent and Trade Mark Institute of Canada .... PTIC
Patent and Trademark Office [Formerly, PO] [Department of Commerce] .... PTO
[United States] Patent and Trademark Office (AAGC) ... PTO
Patent and Trademark Office Board of Patent Appeals and Interferences (AAGC) ...... PTO Board
Patent and Trademark Office Society (EA) .... PTOS
Patent Applicant Service (NITA) .... PAS
Patent Assignee (NITA) .... PA

Patent Associated Literature .... PAL
Patent Attorneys' Professional Standards Body [Australia] ...... PAPSB
Patent Cases [A publication] (DLA) .... PC
Patent Classification (NITA) .... PC
Patent Classification Number [Database terminology] (NITA) CL
Patent Committee (MCD) .... PC
Patent Compensation Board [Energy Research and Development Administration] ..... PCB
Patent Cooperation Treaty [World Intellectual Property Organization, 1978] .... PCT
Patent, Copyright, and Trade Mark Cases [United States] [A publication] (DLA) ..... Pt Copyright & TM Cas
Patent Depository Library [Designated by the Patent and Trademark Office] ...... PDL
Patent, Design, and Trade Mark Review [India] [A publication] (DLA) ...... Pat Des & TM Rev
Patent Documentation Group (DIT) .... PDG
Patent Ductus [Cardiology] (MAE) .... PD
Patent Ductus Arteriosus [Cardiology] .... PDA
Patent Examining Procedure (IAA) .... PEP
Patent Examining System .... PES
Patent Family Service/Patent Register Service [Database] [International Patent Documentation Center] [Information service or system] (CRD).... PFS/PRS
Patent Foramen Ovale [Cardiology] .... PFO
Patent Glazing Contractors Association [British] (DBA) . PGCA
Patent Information Exploitation [Canadian Patent Office] . PIE
Patent Inventor Service (NITA) .... PIS
Patent Journal, Including Trademarks and Models [South Africa] [A publication] (DLA) .... Pat J
Patent Law (NITA) .... PATLAW
Patent Law Review [A publication] (DLA) .... Pat L Rev
Patent Law Review [A publication] (DLA) .... Pat Law Rev
Patent Law Review [A publication] (DLA) .... Pat LR
Patent Law Review [A publication] (DLA) .... PLR
Patent Licensing Bulletin Board [U.S. Department of Commerce] (BARN) ... PLBB
Patent Location (NITA) .... PL
Patent Log Reading [Navigation] .... PLR
Patent Medicine (WDAA) .... PAT MED
Patent Number (NITA) .... PN
Patent Office (DLA) .... Pat Off
Patent Office [Later, PTO] [Department of Commerce] . PO
Patent Office and Industrial Property and Copyright Department [British] .... POIPCD
Patent Office Board of Appeals (IAA) .... POBA
Patent Office [later, PTO] Classification System ...... POCS
Patent Office [later, PTO] Data Retrieval System [Department of Commerce] .... PODRS
Patent Office Journal [India] [A publication] (DLA) .... Pat Off J
Patent Office Journal [India] [A publication] (DLA) .... POJ
Patent Office Library (AD) .... POL
Patent Office Professional Association (EA) .... POPA
Patent Office Reports [A publication] (DLA) .... Pat Off Rep
Patent Office Reports [A publication] (DLA) .... POR
Patent Office Society (EA) .... POS
Patent Office Techniques of Mechanized Access and Classification [Automation project, shut down in 1972] ...... POTOMAC
Patent Online Information System [Database] [Japan] ... PATOLIS
Patent Pending .... PATPEND
Patent Pending (IAA) .... PP
Patent Rolls [British] .... PAT
Patent Royalties (AAGC) .... PARO
Patent Search [Computer science] .... PATSEARCH
Patent Search Documentation (NITA) .... PSD
Patent Search System (NITA) .... PATSEARCH
Patent Search System [Pergamon] [Database] [Computer science] [British] ..... PSS
Patent Security Category Review List (AAGC) .... PSCRL
Patent, Trademark, and Copyright Institute [Franklin Pierce College] (IID) ..... PTC
Patent, Trademark, and Copyright Journal (Bureau of National Affairs) [A publication] (DLA) .... Pat Trademark & Copyright J (BNA)
Patent, Trademark, and Copyright Journal of Research and Education [A publication] (DLA) ...... Idea
Patent, Trademark, and Copyright Journal of Research and Education [A publication] (DLA) .... Pat TM & Copyr J of R & Educ
Patented .... PATD
Patented (IAA) .... PTD
Patented Steel Wire Bureau [British] (BI) .... PSWB
Patented Uniform Lateral Stability Element .... PULSE
Patentee (NITA) .... PT
Patentee/Company Code (NITA) .... PC
Patent-Online-System [Bertelsmann Datenbankdienste GmbH] [Database] ...... PATOS
Patents (NITA) .... PA
Patents Advisory Committee [British] .... PAC
Patents, Decisions of the Commissioner and of United States Courts [A publication] (DLA) .... Dec Comm'r Pat
Pater [Father] [Latin] .... P
Pater Patriae [The Father of His Country] [Latin] .... PP
Paternal Grandfather (DAVI) .... PGR
Paternal Grandmother (DAVI) .... PGM
Paternal Grandmother (MEDA) .... PGM
Paternal Half Sister (OA) .... PHS
Paternal Origin [Medicine] (DMAA) .... pat
Paternal Sex Ratio Gene [Genetics] .... psr
Paternal Sister Dam (OA) .... PSD
Paternally Contributing [Genetics] (DAVI) .... P
Paterson [Diocesan abbreviation] [New Jersey] (TOCD) . PAT

Paterson [*New Jersey*] [*Airport symbol*] (AD) ... PNJ
Paterson [*New Jersey*] [*Seismograph station code, US Geological Survey*] (SEIS) ... PNJ
Paterson and Murray's Reports [*1870-71*] [*New South Wales*] [*A publication*] (DLA) ... Pat & Mr
Paterson Candy International [*British*] ... PCI
Paterson Free Public Library, Paterson, NJ [*Library symbol Library of Congress*] (LCLS) ... NjPat
Paterson, NJ [*Location identifier FAA*] (FAAL) ... JPJ
Paterson, NJ [*Location identifier FAA*] (FAAL) ... PNJ
Paterson, NJ [*AM radio station call letters*] ... WPAT
Paterson, NJ [*FM radio station call letters*] ... WPAT-FM
Paterson, NJ [*Television station call letters*] ... WXTV
Paterson on the Game Laws [*1861*] [*A publication*] (DLA) ... Pat Game L
Paterson on the Game Laws [*A publication*] (DLA) ... Paterson
Paterson on the Liberty of the Subject [*A publication*] (DLA) ... Paterson
Paterson Zochonis [*Commercial firm*] [*British*] ... PZ
Paterson's Abridgment of Poor Law Cases [*1857-63*] [*A publication*] (DLA) ... Pat Abr
Paterson's Appeal Cases [*A publication*] (ILCA) ... Paters App
Paterson's Compendium of English and Scotch Law [*A publication*] (DLA) ... Pat Comp
Paterson's Compendium of English and Scotch Law [*A publication*] (DLA) ... Paters Comp
Paterson's Compendium of English and Scotch Law [*A publication*] (DLA) ... Paterson
Paterson's Law and Usages of the Stock Exchange [*A publication*] (DLA) ... Paterson
Paterson's Licensing Acts Annual [*A publication*] (DLA) ... Pat Licens
Paterson's New South Wales Reports [*A publication*] (DLA) ... Pater
Paterson's Scotch Appeal Cases [*A publication*] (DLA) ... Pat App Cas
Paterson's Scotch Appeal Cases [*A publication*] (DLA) ... Pat HL Sc
Paterson's Scotch Appeal Cases [*A publication*] (DLA) ... Pater
Paterson's Scotch Appeal Cases [*A publication*] (DLA) ... Pater Ap Cas
Paterson's Scotch Appeal Cases [*A publication*] (DLA) ... Pater App
Paterson's Scotch Appeal Cases [*A publication*] (DLA) ... Paterson
Paterson's Scotch Appeal Cases [*A publication*] (DLA) ... Paterson Sc App Cas
Paterson's Scotch Appeals, House of Lords [*A publication*] (DLA) ... Pat
Path [*Postal Service standard*] (OPSA) ... PATH
Path [*Commonly used*] (OPSA) ... PATHS
Path (GAVI) ... PTH
Path Control [*Computer science*] (IBMDP) ... PC
Path Controller (NITA) ... PC
Path Extension Ratio (MCD) ... PER
Path Fault Secure (MHDI) ... PFS
Path Finder [*British military*] (DMA) ... PF
Path Independent Protocol ... PIP
Path Information Unit [*Computer science*] ... PIU
Path, Length of Arc [*Symbol*] [*IUPAC*] ... s
PATH [*Program for Appropriate Technology in Health*] **Library, Seattle, WA** [*Library symbol*] [*Library of Congress*] (LCLS) ... WaSPATH
Path Loss [*Communications*] ... PL
Path Loss, Downlink [*Communications*] ... PLd
Path Loss, Uplink [*Communications*] ... PLu
Path of Steepest Ascent [*Statistical design of experiments*] ... PSA
Path Selection Algorithm [*Telecommunications*] (TEL) ... PSA
Path Setup [*Telecommunications*] (TEL) ... PSU
Path Verification ... PV
Pathankot [*India*] [*Airport symbol*] (AD) ... IXP
Pathankot [*India*] [*ICAO location identifier*] (ICLI) ... VIPK
Pathe [*Record label*] [*France*] ... Pat
Pathe-Vox [*Record label*] [*France*] ... PaV
Pathfinder [*Aircraft*] ... PFDR
Pathfinder [*Army skill qualification identifier*] (INF) ... Y
Pathfinder Association (EAIO) ... PA
Pathfinder Badge [*Military decoration*] (GFGA) ... PFDBAD
Pathfinder Badge [*Military decoration*] (AABC) ... PfdrBad
Pathfinder Community Library, Baldwin, MI [*Library symbol Library of Congress*] (LCLS) ... MiBal
Pathfinder Force [*British RADAR designation which became overall synonym for RADAR*] [*Military*] ... PFF
Pathfinder Fund (EA) ... PF
Pathfinder Industries Ltd. [*Formerly, Pathfinder Financial Corporation*] [*Toronto Stock Exchange symbol*] ... PFC
Pathfinder Navigation Training Unit [*Military*] ... PFNTU
Pathfinder Regional Library Service System, Montrose, CO [*Library symbol*] [*Library of Congress*] (LCLS) ... CoMoP
Pathfinder Regional Library Service System, Montrose, CO [*OCLC symbol*] (OCLC) ... DMP
Pathfinder Test Vehicle [*NASA*] (MCD) ... PTV
PathoGenesis Corp. [*Associated Press*] (SAG) ... PathoG
PathoGenesis Corp. [*NASDAQ symbol*] (SAG) ... PGNS
Pathogenesis Related [*Biology*] ... PR
Pathologic Stage ... PS
Pathological (MSA) ... PATHOL
Pathological Human Serum [*Serology*] ... PHS
Pathological Internet Use ... PIU
Pathological (Surgical) Staging [*For Hodgkin's Disease*] ... PS
Pathologically Eclectic Rubbish Lister ... PERL
Pathologist ... PTHLGST
Pathology (AAMN) ... PA
Pathology (AABC) ... PATH
Pathology ... PATH
Pathology [*Medical specialty*] (DHSM) ... PTH
Pathology Laboratory [*Test*] ... PAL
Pathology On-Line Logging and Reporting System [*Computer science*] (PDAA) ... POLARS
Pathology Practice Association (EA) ... PPA
Pathology Services Accreditation Board [*Victoria, Australia*] ... PSAB
Pathology Transcription Unit ... PTU
Pathology Work Group (GNE) ... PWG
Pathonic Network, Inc. [*Toronto Stock Exchange symbol*] ... PHC
Pathovar [*Microbiology*] ... pv
Pathtechnics Ltd. [*Vancouver Stock Exchange symbol*] ... PAH
Pathway-Exposure Factor [*Environmental chemistry*] ... PEF
Pathways to Independence [*An association*] (EA) ... PTI
Patiala [*India*] [*ICAO location identifier*] (ICLI) ... VIPL
Patiala and East Punjab States Union ... PEPSU
Patience T'ai Chi Association (EA) ... PTCA
Patient ... P
Patient ... PA
Patient ... PAT
Patient (AABC) ... PNT
Patient ... PT
Patient Accounting, Census, and Statistics ... PACS
Patient Administration Information System [*Army*] (AABC) ... PADMIS
Patient Administration System [*British*] ... PAS
Patient Advise and Consent Encounter ... PACE
Patient Advocacy Legal Service [*An association Defunct*] (EA) ... PALS
Patient Advocates for Advanced Cancer Treatments ... PAACT
Patient Airlift Center [*Aeromedical evacuation*] ... PAC
Patient Appointments and Scheduling [*Medicine*] (DMAA) ... PAS
Patient as Customer Evaluation Survey ... PACES
Patient Assesment Instrument [*Medicine*] (DMAA) ... PAI
Patient Assesment Program [*Medicine*] (DMAA) ... PAP
Patient Automatic Data Recording Equipment (IEEE) ... PADRE
Patient Care Aide [*or Assistant*] (DAVI) ... PCA
Patient Care Algorithm System [*Medicine*] (DMAA) ... PCAS
Patient Care and Services (DMAA) ... PACS
Patient Care Associate [*Medicine*] ... PSA
Patient Care Audit (HCT) ... PCA
Patient Care Coordinator [*Medicine*] ... PCC
Patient Care Information System (IID) ... PCIS
Patient Care Manager ... PCM
Patient Care Publications ... PCP
Patient Care System [*Army*] (AABC) ... PACAS
Patient Care System ... PCS
Patient Care Unit (HCT) ... PCU
Patient Census ... PACENS
Patient Census Report ... PNTCENS
Patient Charge Ratio ... PCR
Patient Complains Of [*Medicine*] ... PCO
Patient Computer Medical Record ... PCMR
Patient Contact Record [*Medicine*] (DMAA) ... PCR
Patient Data Automation ... PDA
Patient Data Management ... PDM
Patient Data Management Systems [*Medical records*] (DAVI) ... PDMS
Patient Data System [*Pharmacology*] (DAVI) ... PDS
Patient Decontamination Site [*Army*] (INF) ... PDS
Patient Education (DAVI) ... pt ed
Patient Education Total Quality Improvement [*Medicine*] (DMAA) ... PETQI
Patient Escorted by Police (DMAA) ... PEBP
Patient Evaluation Center (DAVI) ... PEC
Patient Evaluation Grid [*Medicine*] (DMAA) ... PEG
Patient Evaluation Rating Scale [*Medicine*] (DMAA) ... PERS
Patient Examined by Doctor (DMAA) ... PED
Patient Focused Care [*Medicine*] ... PFC
Patient Information Leaflet [*Pharmacy*] ... PIL
Patient Infosystems, Inc. [*NASDAQ symbol*] (SAG) ... PATI
Patient Infosystems, Inc. [*Associated Press*] (SAG) ... PatInfo
Patient Load Factor (AFM) ... PLF
Patient Management Categories [*Medicine*] (MEDA) ... PMC
Patient Management Category (HCT) ... PCM
Patient Management Computer Stimulation (DMAA) ... PMCS
Patient Management Problem [*Gerontology*] ... PMP
Patient Medical Information System (OA) ... PMIS
Patient Medication Instruction ... PMI
Patient Outcome Research Team (PCM) ... PORT
Patient Package Insert [*Also, PI*] [*Instructional leaflet distributed with certain prescription drugs*] ... PPI
Patient Package Insert [*Pharmacy*] (DAVI) ... PPI
Patient Record Form ... PRF
Patient Record Information for Education Requirements [*Computer science*] ... PRIMER
Patient Relations [*Medicine*] ... PR
Patient Relations (DAVI) ... PR
Patient Resident Assessment Profile [*Geriatrics*] ... PRAP
Patient Review Tribunal [*Queensland, Australia*] ... PRT
Patient Satisfaction Questionnaire [*Medicine*] (DMAA) ... PSQ
Patient Self-Determination Act ... PSDA
Patient Support Associate [*Medicine*] ... PCA
Patient Symptom Diary ... PSD
Patient Treatment File [*Medicine*] (DMAA) ... PTF
Patient Unit Assistant [*Medicine*] (DMAA) ... PUA
Patient [*or Person*] **with** [*AIDS*] **Acquired Immunodeficiency Syndrome** [*Immunology*] (DAVI) ... PWA
Patient-Controlled Analgesia ... PCA
Patient-Controlled Epidural Analgesia ... PCEA
Patient-Identified Physicians Survey [*Department of Health and Human Services*] (GFGA) ... PIPS

Patient-Operated Selected Mechanisms (AD) .... posm
Patient-Operated Selector Mechanism [*Pronounced "possum"*] .... POSM
Patient's Advocate [*Medicine*] (DMAA) .... PA
Patients' Aid Society .... PAS
Patient's Daughter [*Also, Pt DTR*] (DAVI) .... Pt Dhgtr
Patient's Daughter [*Also, Pt Dhgtr*] (DAVI) .... PT DTR
Patients Encountered at [*Primary*] Health Care Centers .... PHCC
Patients Experience of the Relationship with the Therapist Method .... PERT
Patient's Interests [*Medicine*] .... PI
Patient's Interests (DAVI) .... PI
Patients Protection Law Commission (AD) .... PPLC
Patients' Rights Organization (EA) .... PRO
Patient's Serum [*Medicine*] .... PS
Patient's Time (DAVI) .... PAT/TM
Patillas, PR [*AM radio station call letters*] .... WEXS
Patina (VRA) .... pat
Patina Oil & Gas [*NYSE symbol*] (TTSB) .... POG
Patina Oil & Gas 7.125% Pfd [*NYSE symbol*] (TTSB) .... POGPr
Patina Oil & Gas Wrrt [*NYSE symbol*] (TTSB) .... POG.WS
Patino N. V. [*Toronto Stock Exchange symbol*] .... PNV
Patio .... PAT
Patlex Corp. [*Associated Press*] (SAG) .... Patlex
Patlex Corp. [*NASDAQ symbol*] (SAG) .... PTLX
Patna [*India*] [*Airport symbol*] (OAG) .... PAT
Patna [*India*] [*ICAO location identifier*] (ICLI) .... VEPT
Patna Law Journal [*India*] [*A publication*] (DLA) .... Pat LJ
Patna Law Journal [*India*] [*A publication*] (ILCA) .... PLJ
Patna Law Reporter [*India*] [*A publication*] (DLA) .... Pat L Reptr
Patna Law Reporter [*India*] [*A publication*] (DLA) .... PLR
Patna Law Reports [*India*] [*A publication*] (DLA) .... Pat LR
Patna Law Times [*India*] [*A publication*] (DLA) .... Pat LT
Patna Law Times [*India*] [*A publication*] (DLA) .... PLT
Patna Law Weekly [*A publication*] (DLA) .... Pat LW
Patna Law Weekly [*India*] [*A publication*] (DLA) .... PLW
Patna Weekly Notes [*India*] [*A publication*] (ILCA) .... PWN
Pato Branco [*Brazil*] [*Airport symbol*] (OAG) .... PTO
Patoka Public Library, Patoka, IL [*Library symbol Library of Congress*]
(LCLS) .... IPat
Paton Lyall Tosh [*Rock music group*] .... PILOT
Paton on Insurance [*1962*] [*A publication*] (DLA) .... Pat Ins
Paton on Stoppage in Transitu [*1859*] [*A publication*] (DLA) .... Pat St Tr
Paton's Scotch Appeal Cases [*Craigie, Stewart, and Paton*] [*A publication*]
(DLA) .... Pat App Cas
Paton's Scotch Appeal Cases [*A publication*] (DLA) .... Pat HL Sc
Paton's Scotch Appeal Cases [*A publication*] (DLA) .... Paton App Cas
Paton's Scotch Appeal Cases [*A publication*] (DLA) .... Paton Sc App Cas
Paton's Scotch Appeal Cases, House of Lords [*A publication*] (DLA) .... Pat
Patras [*Greece*] [*Seismograph station code, US Geological Survey*] (SEIS) ...... PAT
Patreksfjordur [*Iceland*] [*ICAO location identifier*] (ICLI) .... BIPA
Patreksfjordur [*Iceland*] [*Airport symbol*] (OAG) .... PFJ
Patres [*Fathers*] [*Latin*] .... PP
Patres Amplissimi [*Cardinals*] [*Latin*] .... PPAA
Patres Conscripti [*Senators*] [*Latin*] .... PC
Patres Conscripti [*Senators*] [*Latin*] (ROG) .... PPC
Patrexes of the Panopticon (EA) .... POP
Patria [*Cuba ICAO location identifier*] (ICLI) .... MUPT
Patria [*Peru*] [*ICAO location identifier*] (ICLI) .... SPIR
Patria Roja [*Red Fatherland*] [*Peru*] (PD) .... PR
Patriarch [*Greek Church*] (ROG) .... PAT
Patriarch .... PATR
Patriarch Athenagoras National Institute (EA) .... PANI
Patrice Lumumba Coalition (EA) .... PLC
Patrick Air Force Base [*Florida*] .... PAB
Patrick Air Force Base [*Florida*] .... PAFB
Patrick Air Force Base [*Florida*] (KSC) .... PAT
Patrick Auxiliary Air Force Base [*Florida*] (SAA) .... PAAFB
Patrick Henry Foundation [*Liberty, NY*] (EA) .... PHF
Patrick Indus [*NASDAQ symbol*] (TTSB) .... PATK
Patrick Industries, Inc. [*NASDAQ symbol*] (NQ) .... PATK
Patrick Industries, Inc. [*Associated Press*] (SAG) .... PatrkInd
Patrick Petroleum Co. [*NASDAQ symbol*] (SAG) .... PPCB
Patrick Shaw's Justiciary Cases [*1819-31*] [*Scotland*] [*A publication*]
(DLA) .... P Shaw
Patrick Shaw's Justiciary Cases [*1819-31*] [*Scotland*] [*A publication*]
(DLA) .... Shaw P
Patrick's Election Cases [*1824-49*] [*Upper Canada*] [*A publication*]
(DLA) .... Patr Elect Cas
Patrick's Election Cases [*Canada*] [*A publication*] (DLA) .... Patrick El Cas
Patriot Advanced Capability [*Missile technology*] [*Military*] (PS) .... PAC
Patriot Air Defense Information Language [*Army*] .... PADIL
Patriot Airlines, Inc. [*ICAO designator*] (FAAC) .... PAA
Patriot Amer Hospitality [*NYSE symbol*] (TTSB) .... PAH
Patriot American Hospitality, Inc. [*NYSE symbol*] (SAG) .... PAH
Patriot American Hospitality, Inc. [*Associated Press*] (SAG) .... PatrAH
Patriot Antimissile Capability [*Army*] .... PAC
Patriot Arm Decoy [*Weaponry*] (DWSG) .... PAD
Patriot Arm Fire Unit [*Weaponry*] (MCD) .... PAFU
Patriot Bank [*NASDAQ symbol*] (TTSB) .... PBIX
Patriot Bank Corp. (PA) [*Associated Press*] (SAG) .... PatriotB
Patriot Bank Corp. (PA) [*NASDAQ symbol*] (SAG) .... PBIX
Patriot Communications Model (MCD) .... PATCOM
PATRIOT [*Phased Array Tracking to Intercept Target*] Field Army Support
Center [*Army*] .... PFASC
Patriot Field Report [*Army*] .... PFR
Patriot Integration and Test System [*Army*] .... PITS

Patriot Maintenance Facility [*Army*] .... PMF
Patriot National Bank CT [*Associated Press*] (SAG) .... PatrNBk
Patriot National Bank CT [*NASDAQ symbol*] (SAG) .... PNBK
Patriot Natl Bk [*NASDAQ symbol*] (TTSB) .... PNBK
Patriot Organizational Maintenance Trainer [*Army*] .... POMT
Patriot Project Office [*Army*] .... PPO
Patriot Steering Committee .... PSC
Patriot Tactical Operations Simulator [*Army*] .... PTOS
Patriotic (ROG) .... PATR
Patriotic American Youth Society .... PAYS
Patriotic Burmese Forces [*World War II*] .... PBF
Patriotic Catholic Association [*Name given to nationalized Catholic Church in
China*] .... PCA
Patriotic Coalition for Democracy [*Political group*] [*Guyana*] .... PCD
Patriotic Education, Inc. (EA) .... PEI
Patriotic Front [*Zimbabwe*] [*Political party*] (PPW) .... PF
Patriotic Front - Zimbabwe African People's Union [*Political party*]
(PD) .... PF-ZAPU
Patriotic Funds Council of Victoria [*Australia*] .... PFCV
Patriotic Liberation Army [*Myanmar*] (PD) .... PLA
Patriotic Majority [*An association*] (EA) .... PM
Patriotic Order Sons of America (EA) .... POSA
Patriotic Party [*British*] .... PP
Patriotic People's Front [*Hungary Political party*] .... PPF
Patriotic Union of Kurdistan [*Iraq*] [*Political party*] (PD) .... PUK
Patriotikon Metopon [*Patriotic Front*] [*Greek Cyprus*] [*Political party*] (PPE) ...... PM
Patriots Information Network [*Defunct*] (EA) .... PIN
Patriots of Fort McHenry (EA) .... PFM
Patriotyczny Ruch Odrodzenia Narodowego [*Patriotic Movement for National
Rebirth*] [*Poland*] (EY) .... PRON
Patrol [*or Assistance*] [*or Program*] [*Military*] .... MEDCAP
Patrol [*Designation for all US military aircraft*] .... P
Patrol .... PAT
Patrol [*or Patrolman*] (AABC) .... PTL
Patrol Advanced Surveillance System (MCD) .... PASS
Patrol Aircraft (NATG) .... PA
Patrol Aircraft Service Unit .... PASU
Patrol Aircraft Service Unit .... PATSU
Patrol Air-Cushion Vehicle [*Also called Hovercraft*] [*Navy*] .... PACV
Patrol Airship Concept Evaluation .... PACE
Patrol Amphibian Plane .... PAP
Patrol Analysis Recording System [*British*] .... PARS
Patrol and Escort Aircraft [*Lighter-than-Air*] [*Navy symbol*] (MUGU) .... ZP
Patrol Antisubmarine Warfare Development Group .... PATASWDEVGRU
Patrol Base [*Army*] (VNW) .... PB
Patrol Boat [*Navy symbol*] .... PB
Patrol Boat .... PTL
Patrol Boat [*Coast Guard symbol*] (DNAB) .... WYTM
Patrol Boat, Air Cushion (MCD) .... PBA
Patrol Boat, Fast [*British military*] (DMA) .... PBF
Patrol Boat, Fast, Guided Weapon [*British military*] (DMA) .... PBFG
Patrol Boat, Hydrofoil (MCD) .... PBH
Patrol Boat, River [*Navy symbol*] .... PBR
Patrol Boat Roadstead [*Navy*] .... PBR
Patrol Bomber .... PB
Patrol Bomber [*Navy designation for Catalina aircraft*] .... PBY
Patrol Bomber, Four-Engine, Landplane [*Navy symbol*] .... VPB(HL)
Patrol Bomber, Four-Engine, Seaplane [*Navy symbol*] .... VPB(HS)
Patrol Bomber, Two-Engine, Landplane [*Navy symbol*] .... VPB(ML)
Patrol Bomber, Two-Engine, Seaplane [*Navy symbol*] .... VPB(MS)
Patrol Car [*British military*] (DMA) .... PC
Patrol Combatant [*Gunboat*] [*Navy symbol*] .... PG
Patrol Combatant Missile Hydrofoil Squadron (DNAB) .... PMHRON
Patrol Combatant Missile Hydrofoil Squadron Mobile Logistics Support
Group (DNAB) .... PMHRON MLSG
Patrol Combatant Support Ship [*Navy symbol*] .... AGHS
Patrol Craft .... PC
Patrol Craft [*Self-propelled*] [*Navy symbol*] .... YP
Patrol Craft Combat Direction System [*Navy*] (SAA) .... PCCDS
Patrol Craft (Fast) [*Navy symbol*] .... PCF
Patrol Craft (Hydrofoil) [*Navy symbol*] .... PCH
Patrol Craft Sailors Association (EA) .... PCSA
Patrol Craft Tender [*Navy symbol*] .... AGP
Patrol Diagnosis (NITA) .... PADIA
Patrol Emergency Officer [*Nuclear energy*] (NRCH) .... PEO
Patrol Escort [*Patrol Craft Escort*] [*Navy symbol*] .... PCE
Patrol Force .... PATFOR
Patrol Gunboat [*Navy symbol*] (NATG) .... PGB
Patrol Gunboat (Hydrofoil) [*Navy symbol*] .... PGH
Patrol Gunboat, Motorized [*Navy symbol*] (VNW) .... PG
Patrol Hydrofoil [*Missile*] (HGAA) .... PHF
Patrol Hydrofoil Guided Missile [*Navy*] (DNAB) .... PHGM
Patrol Hydrofoil Missile [*Navy symbol*] .... PHM
Patrol Hydrofoil Missile Ship [*Navy/NATO*] .... PHMS
Patrol Input Device (MCD) .... PID
Patrol Inspector [*Immigration and Naturalization Service*] .... PI
Patrol Land [*Aviation*] .... PL
Patrol Locator System [*Army*] .... PLS
Patrol Log Observations [*Aviation*] (DSUE) .... PLOB
Patrol/Mine Countermeasure Craft [*British*] .... PMC
Patrol Operations Report .... POR
Patrol Plane [*Navy symbol*] .... VP
Patrol Plane Commander .... PPC
Patrol Plane Navigator (DNAB) .... PPN
Patrol Plane Navigator/Communicator (DNAB) .... PPNC

Patrol Rescue Escort [*Patrol Craft Escort Rescue*] [*Navy symbol*] .... PCER
Patrol Seaplane .... PSP
Patrol Search Plane [*Navy designation for Mariner aircraft*] .... PBM
Patrol Seismic Intrusion Detector [*or Device*] [*DoD*] .... PSID
Patrol Service [*British military*] (DMA) .... PS
Patrol Service Gunnery Instructor [*Officer's rating*] [*British Royal Navy*] .... P
Patrol Ship (CINC) .... PS
Patrol Squadron .... PATRON
Patrol Squadron [*Navy symbol*] .... VP
Patrol [*Lighter-than-Air*] **Squadron** [*Navy symbol*] .... ZPRON
Patrol Torpedo Boat [*Later, PTF*] [*Navy symbol*] .... PT
Patrol Torpedo Boat, Fast [*Formerly, PT*] [*Navy symbol*] .... PTF
Patrol Torpedo Plane [*Navy symbol*] .... VPT
Patrol Vessel .... PV
Patrol Vessel, Eagle [*Eagle boat*] [*Navy symbol Obsolete*] .... PE
Patrol Vessel, Escort (Control) [*180 feet*] [*Navy symbol Obsolete*] .... PCE(C)
Patrol Vessel, Frigate [*Navy symbol*] .... PF
Patrol Vessel, Motor Gunboat [*Navy symbol Obsolete*] .... PGM
Patrol Vessel, Motor Torpedo Boat, Submarine Chaser [*Navy symbol*] .... PTC
Patrol Vessel, River Gunboat [*Navy symbol*] .... PR
Patrol Vessel, Submarine Chaser [*Navy symbol*] .... PC
Patrol Vessel, Submarine Chaser (Control) [*136 feet*] [*Navy symbol Obsolete*] .... PCS
Patrol Vessel, Yacht [*Navy symbol*] .... PY
Patrol Vessel, Yacht, Coastal [*Navy symbol Obsolete*] .... PYC
Patrol Vessels [*Navy symbol*] (MUGU) .... PP
Patrol Wing [*Later, Fleet Air Wing*] .... PATWING
Patrol Wing [*later, Fleet Air Wing*] **Atlantic Fleet** .... PATWINGLANTFLT
Patrol Wing [*Later, Fleet Air Wing*] **Detachment** (DNAB) .... PATWINGDET
Patrol Wing [*later, Fleet Air Wing*] **Scouting Force** .... PATWINGSCOFOR
Patrol Zone Area (MCD) .... PZA
Patrol-Bombing Plane [*Navy symbol*] .... VPB
Patrol-Bombing Squadron .... PATBOMRON
Patrolmen's Benevolent Association .... PBA
Patrologia Graeca [*J. P. Migne*] [*Paris*] [*A publication*] (BJA) .... MPG
Patrologia Graeca (BJA) .... PatrolGr
Patrologia Latina [*J. P. Migne*] [*Paris*] [*A publication*] (BJA) .... MPL
Patrologia Latina (BJA) .... PatrolLat
Patrologia Syriaca (BJA) .... PS
Patrologiae Cursus. Series Graeca [*A publication*] (OCD) .... PG
Patrologiae Cursus. Series Latina [*A publication*] (OCD) .... PL
Patron .... P
Patron .... PATR
Patron of Husbandry .... P of H
Patrons of Northwest Civic Cultural and Charitable Organizations .... PONCHO
Patrons of the Arts in the Vatican Museum (EA) .... PAVM
Patsy Cline International Fan Club (EA) .... PCIFC
Patsy Montana Fan Club (EA) .... PMFC
Pattani [*Thailand*] [*Airport symbol*] (OAG) .... PAN
Pattani [*Thailand*] [*ICAO location identifier*] (ICLI) .... VTSK
Pattani People's Movement [*Thailand*] [*Political party*] .... PPM
Pattani United Liberation Organization [*Thailand*] [*Political party*] (PD) .... PULO
Patten Corp. [*NYSE symbol*] (SPSG) .... PAT
Patten Corp. [*Associated Press*] (SAG) .... Patten
Patten Free Library, Bath, ME [*Library symbol Library of Congress*] (LCLS) .... MeBath
Patten Recognition Technology (NITA) .... PRT
Patter-Evoked Retinal Response [*neurology and ophthalmology*] (DAVI) .... PERR
Pattern .... P
Pattern .... PAT
Pattern (MDG) .... PATN
Pattern (AAG) .... PATT
Pattern .... PTTRN
Pattern 14 Rifle [*Made in the US for Great Britain, beginning in 1914*] .... P 14
Pattern Analysis [*Test*] .... PA
Pattern Analysis Test [*Army*] .... PAT
Pattern and Plastic Tool Builders Association [*Defunct*] (EA) .... PPTBA
Pattern Articulation Unit [*Computer science*] .... PAU
Pattern Card Makers' Society [*British*] (BI) .... PCMS
Pattern Correspondence Index .... PCI
Pattern Delayed-Response [*Ophthalmology*] .... PDR
Pattern Description Language .... PADEL
Pattern Disruption Point [*Medicine*] (DMAA) .... PDP
Pattern Error Analysis .... PEA
Pattern Flight [*Also, P/FLT*] (MUGU) .... P/F
Pattern Flight [*Also, P/F*] (MUGU) .... P/FLT
Pattern for Analysis, Decision, Action, and Learning .... PADAL
Pattern Generation Language [*Computer science*] .... PAGAN
Pattern Information Processing System .... PIPS
Pattern Jury Instructions [*A publication*] .... PJI
Pattern Learning Parser .... PLP
Pattern Makers Association of New York (EA) .... PMANY
Pattern Makers' League of North America (EA) .... PML
Pattern Makers Union (NADA) .... PMU
Pattern Makers Union (AD) .... PMU
Pattern of Cockpit Indication .... PCI
Pattern Recognition (BUR) .... PR
Pattern Recognition and Information Correlations [*Police crime-detection computer*] .... PATRIC
Pattern Recognition Feedback Control System [*Computer science*] (IAA) .... PRFCS
Pattern Recognition Information Synthesis Modeling [*Market analysis*] .... PRISM
Pattern Recognition Interpretation and Correlation (CET) .... PATRIC
Pattern Recognition Society (EA) .... PRS
Pattern Recognition System .... PRS
Pattern Recognition System Application Evaluation (IAA) .... PARSAVAL
Pattern Recognition Technique .... PRT
Pattern Reversal Evoked Potential .... PREP
Pattern Reversal Visual Evoked Potential .... PRVEP
Pattern Transformation Memory .... PTM
Pattern Transformation Memory System .... PTMS
Pattern Visual Evoked Potential [*neurology*] (DAVI) .... PVEP
Pattern Weavers' Society [*A union*] [*British*] (DCTA) .... PWS
Pattern-Contingent Chromatic Aftereffects .... PCCA
Patterned Elicitation Syntax Test [*Educational test*] .... PEST
Patterned Epitaxial Technology (IEEE) .... PET
Patternmaker [*Navy rating*] .... PM
Patternmaker (WGA) .... PTRNMKR
Patternmaker, First Class [*Navy rating*] PM1
Patternmaker, Second Class [*Navy rating*] PM2
Patternmaker, Ship Repair [*Navy rating*] .... PMSR
Patternmaker, Third Class [*Navy rating*] PM3
Patternmaking (WGA) .... PATMKG
Patterns of Care Study [*Roentgenography*] .... PCS
Pattern-Shift Visual Evoked Response [*Medicine*] (MEDA) .... PSVER
Patterson Aviation Co. [*ICAO designator*] (FAAC) .... ETL
Patterson, CA [*FM radio station call letters*] .... KOSO
Patterson, CA [*FM radio station call letters*] .... KZMS
Patterson Dental [*NASDAQ symbol*] (TTSB) .... PDCO
Patterson Dental Co. [*Associated Press*] (SAG) .... PattDntl
Patterson Dental Co. [*NASDAQ symbol*] (SAG) .... PDCO
Patterson Energy [*NASDAQ symbol*] (TTSB) .... PTEN
Patterson Energy, Inc. [*Associated Press*] (SAG) .... PatEng
Patterson Energy, Inc. [*NASDAQ symbol*] (SAG) .... PTEN
Patterson Experimental Array (MCD) .... PEA
Patterson, LA [*Location identifier FAA*] (FAAL) .... PTN
Patterson Library, Westfield, NY [*Library symbol*] [*Library of Congress*] (LCLS) .... NWef
Patterson, NY [*FM radio station call letters*] (RBYB) .... WAXB-FM
Patterson, NY [*FM radio station call letters*] (RBYB) .... WVYB
Patterson-Harker Method [*Physics*] .... PHM
Pattersonville, NY [*FM radio station call letters*] .... WPGL
Pattetico [*Pathetically*] [*Music*] (ROG) .... PATO
Patti Page Appreciation Society (EA) .... PPAS
Pattijoki [*Finland ICAO location identifier*] (ICLI) .... EFRH
Pattison's Missouri Digest [*A publication*] (DLA) .... Pat Dig
Patton, Jr., and Heath's Reports [*Virginia Special Court of Appeals*] [*A publication*] (DLA) .... P & H
Patton, Jr., and Heath's Reports [*Virginia Special Court of Appeals*] [*A publication*] (DLA) .... P Jr & H
Patton, Jr., and Heath's Reports [*Virginia Special Court of Appeals*] [*A publication*] (DLA) .... Pat & H
Patton, Jr., and Heath's Reports [*Virginia*] [*A publication*] (DLA) .... Patt & H
Patton, Jr., and Heath's Reports [*Virginia*] [*A publication*] (DLA) .... Patt & H (VA)
Patton, Jr., and Heath's Reports [*Virginia*] [*A publication*] (DLA) .... Patt & Heath R
Patton, Jr., and Heath's Reports [*Virginia Special Court of Appeals*] [*A publication*] (DLA) .... Patton & H
Patton, Jr., and Heath's Reports [*Virginia Special Court of Appeals*] [*A publication*] (DLA) .... Patton & H (VA)
Patton, Jr., and Heath's Reports [*Virginia*] [*A publication*] (DLA) .... Patton & Heath
Patton, PA [*FM radio station call letters*] .... WBRX
Patton Society (EA) .... PS
Patton State Hospital, Patton, CA [*Library symbol Library of Congress*] (LCLS) .... CPtSH
Patuxent River [*Maryland*] (MCD) .... PAX
Patuxent River [*Navy*] (MCD) .... PTR
Patuxent River, MD [*Location identifier FAA*] (FAAL) .... NHK
Patuxent River, MD [*Location identifier FAA*] (FAAL) .... NUI
Patuxent River, MD [*Location identifier FAA*] (FAAL) .... PXT
Patuxent River/Patuxent River Naval Air Station [*Maryland*] [*ICAO location identifier*] (ICLI) .... KNHK
Pau [*France*] [*Airport symbol*] (OAG) .... PUF
Pau/Pont-Long-Uzein [*France ICAO location identifier*] (ICLI) .... LFBP
Pauahi [*Hawaii*] [*Seismograph station code, US Geological Survey*] (SEIS) .... PUH
Pauk [*Myanmar*] [*Airport symbol*] (OAG) .... PAU
Pauk [*Myanmar*] [*ICAO location identifier*] (ICLI) .... VBPK
Pauken [*Kettledrums*] .... PKN
Paul (BJA) .... Pl
Paul and Lisa (EA) .... P & L
Paul Andrew Dawkins Children's Project (EA) .... PADCP
Paul Anka Fan Club (EA) .... PAFC
Paul B. Elder Co. [*Research code symbol*] .... HPEK
Paul Bunyan Elementary School, Bemidji, MN [*Library symbol*] [*Library of Congress*] (LCLS) .... MnBemPE
Paul Claudel Society (EA) .... PCS
Paul D. Camp Community College, Franklin, VA [*Library symbol Library of Congress*] (LCLS) .... ViFraPC
Paul D. Schreiber High School, Port Washington, NY [*Library symbol*] [*Library of Congress*] (LCLS) .... NPtwSH
Paul Harris Stores [*NASDAQ symbol*] (TTSB) .... PAUH
Paul Harris Stores [*NASDAQ symbol*] (SAG) .... PAUH
Paul Harris Stores [*Associated Press*] (SAG) .... PHarris
Paul Kagan Associates, Inc. [*Information service or system Telecommunications*] (IID) .... PKA
Paul McCartney Fan Club [*British*] (EAIO) .... WFC
Paul Otchakovsky-Laurens [*Publishing imprint, named for imprint editor*] .... POL
Paul Quinn College [*Texas*] .... PQC
Paul Quinn College, Waco, TX [*OCLC symbol*] (OCLC) .... PQC
Paul Quinn College, Waco, TX [*Library symbol Library of Congress*] (LCLS) .... TxWPQ

Paul Revere [*NYSE symbol*] (SPSG) .... PRL
Paul Revere Associated Yeoman (AD) .... PRAY
Paul Revere Corp. [*Associated Press*] (SAG) .... PRevere
Paul Smiths College [*New York*] .... PSC
Paul Smiths College, Library, Paul Smiths, NY [*OCLC symbol*] (OCLC) .... VNF
Paul Smiths College, Paul Smiths, NY [*Library symbol Library of Congress*] (LCLS) .... NPsP
Paul Smith's, NY [*FM radio station call letters*] .... WPSA
Paul, Weiss, Rifkind, Wharton & Garrison, Law Library, New York, NY [*Library symbol Library of Congress*] (LCLS) .... NNPaul
Paul-Bunnell [*Test*] [*Immunology*] (AAMN) .... PB
Paul-Bunnell-Davidsohn [*Test*] [*Immunology*] .... PBD
Paulding County Carnegie Public Library, Paulding, OH [*Library symbol Library of Congress*] (LCLS) .... OP
Paulding, OH [*FM radio station call letters*] .... WERT
Paulding, OH [*FM radio station call letters*] (RBYB) .... WKSD-FM
Pauli Exclusion Principle [*Physics*] .... PEP
Pauli Spin Operator [*Physics*] .... PSO
Pauli Spin Susceptibility [*Physics*] .... PSS
Paulin [*H.*] **& Co. Ltd.** [*Toronto Stock Exchange symbol*] .... PAP
Pauline Fathers (TOCD) .... OSPPE
Pauline Fathers (TOCD) .... osppe
Pauline Fathers and Brothers (TOCD) .... SSP
Pauline Fathers and Brothers, Society of St. Paul for the Apostolate of Communications (TOCD) .... ssp
Pauline Johnson College, Brantford, ON, Canada [*Library symbol Library of Congress*] (LCLS) .... CaOBrtP
Pauline Johnson College, Brantford, Ontario [*Library symbol National Library of Canada*] (NLC) .... OBRP
Pauline Pinkney International Fan Club (EA) .... PPIFC
Pauling Bond Order [*Physical chemistry*] .... PBO
Paulingite [*A zeolite*] .... PAU
Paulist Bible Pamphlet Series [*Glen Rock, NJ*] [*A publication*] (BJA) .... PBPS
Paulist Fathers (TOCD) .... CSP
Paulist Fathers (TOCD) .... csp
Paulist League (EA) .... PL
Paulist Library, San Francisco, CA [*Library symbol Library of Congress*] (LCLS) .... CSfPaul
Pauli-Weisskopf Equation [*Physics*] .... PWE
Paullina Free Public Library, Paullina, IA [*Library symbol Library of Congress*] (LCLS) .... IaPau
Paullina Times, Paullina, IA [*Library symbol Library of Congress*] (LCLS) .... IaPauT
Paullum [*A Little*] [*Pharmacy*] .... PAUL
Paulo Afonso [*Brazil*] [*Airport symbol*] (OAG) .... PAV
Paulo Afonso [*Brazil ICAO location identifier*] (ICLI) .... SBUF
Pauloff Harbor/Sanak Island, AK [*Location identifier FAA*] (FAAL) .... KPH
Paul's Scarlet Rose [*Plant cell line*] .... PSR
Pauls Valley, OK [*FM radio station call letters*] .... KGOK
Pauls Valley, OK [*AM radio station call letters*] .... KVLH
Pauls Valley, OK [*Location identifier FAA*] (FAAL) .... PVJ
Paulson Cap [*NASDAQ symbol*] (TTSB) .... PLCC
Paulson Capital Corp. [*Associated Press*] (SAG) .... Paulson
Paulson Capital Corp. [*NASDAQ symbol*] (SAG) .... PLCC
Paul-Son Gaming [*NASDAQ symbol*] (TTSB) .... PSON
Paul-Son Gaming Corp. [*Associated Press*] (SAG) .... PaulSon
Paul-Son Gaming Corp. [*NASDAQ symbol*] (SAG) .... PSON
Paulus de Castro [*Deceased, 1441*] [*Authority cited in pre-1607 legal work*] (DSA) .... Pau de Cast
Paulus de Castro [*Deceased, 1441*] [*Authority cited in pre-1607 legal work*] (DSA) .... Paul de Cast
Paulus de Castro [*Deceased, 1441*] [*Authority cited in pre-1607 legal work*] (DSA) .... Paul de Castr
Paulus de Liazaris [*Deceased, 1356*] [*Authority cited in pre-1607 legal work*] (DSA) .... P
Paulus de Liazaris [*Deceased, 1356*] [*Authority cited in pre-1607 legal work*] (DSA) .... P de L
Paulus de Liazaris [*Deceased, 1356*] [*Authority cited in pre-1607 legal work*] (DSA) .... Pau
Paulus de Liazaris [*Deceased, 1356*] [*Authority cited in pre-1607 legal work*] (DSA) .... Pau de La
Paulus de Liazaris [*Deceased, 1356*] [*Authority cited in pre-1607 legal work*] (DSA) .... Paul Liaz
Paulus Hungarus [*Deceased, 1242*] [*Authority cited in pre-1607 legal work*] (DSA) .... Pau Hunga
Paulus Hungarus [*Deceased, 1242*] [*Authority cited in pre-1607 legal work*] (DSA) .... Pau Hungar
Paulus Leonius [*Flourished, 16th century*] [*Authority cited in pre-1607 legal work*] (DSA) .... Pau Leon
Paulus Ruinus de Montepico [*Flourished, 15th century*] [*Authority cited in pre-1607 legal work*] (DSA) .... Pau de Montep
Pausanias [*Second century AD*] [*Classical studies*] (OCD) .... Paus
Pause/Still [*Video technology*] .... P/S
Paused Program [*Computer science*] .... P
Pauxillum [*A Little*] [*Pharmacy*] .... PAUX
Pauzhetka [*Former USSR Seismograph station code, US Geological Survey*] (SEIS) .... PAU
Paved Concrete Track [*Railways*] .... PACT
Paved Surface [*Aviation*] (DA) .... P
Paveh [*Iran*] [*ICAO location identifier*] (ICLI) .... OICP
Pavement .... PAVMT
Pavement [*Technical drawings*] .... PVMT
Pavement Classification Number [*Aviation*] (DA) .... PCN
Pavement Condition Index [*Aviation*] (DA) .... PCI
Pavement Depth Factor (ADA) .... PDF
Pavement Management System [*Australia*] .... PMS
Pavement Marking Demonstration Program [*Federal Highway Administration*] .... PMDP
Pavements and Soil Trafficability Information Analysis Center [*Army Corps of Engineers*] (IID) .... PSTIAC
Pavia [*Italy*] [*Seismograph station code, US Geological Survey*] (SEIS) .... PAV
Pavilion (ROG) .... P
Pavilion .... PAV
Pavilion (VRA) .... pavl
Pavillon Albert Prevost, Montreal, Quebec [*Library symbol National Library of Canada*] (NLC) .... QMIAP
Pavillon des Arts, Universite du Quebec, Montreal, Quebec [*Library symbol National Library of Canada*] (NLC) .... QMUQPA
Paving .... PAVE
Paving [*Technical drawings*] .... PV
Paving Brick Institute .... PBI
Pavlikeny [*Bulgaria*] [*Seismograph station code, US Geological Survey*] (SEIS) .... PVL
Pavlovsk [*Later, LNN*] [*Former USSR Geomagnetic observatory code*] .... SLU
Pavo [*Constellation*] .... Pav
Paw Paw Public Library, Paw Paw, IL [*Library symbol Library of Congress*] (LCLS) .... IPp
Paw Paw Public Library, Paw Paw, MI [*Library symbol Library of Congress*] (LCLS) .... MiPaw
Paw Paw School System, Paw Paw, IL [*Library symbol Library of Congress*] (LCLS) .... IPpS
Pawan Hans Ltd. [*India*] [*ICAO designator*] (FAAC) .... PHE
Pawcatuck, CT [*FM radio station call letters*] (RBYB) .... WKCD
Pawhuska, OK [*AM radio station call letters*] (RBYB) .... KOMH-AM
Pawhuska, OK [*AM radio station call letters*] (RBYB) .... KRIG
Pawhuska, OK [*FM radio station call letters*] (RBYB) .... KTGP-FM
Pawley's Island, SC [*FM radio station call letters*] .... WDAI
Pawley's Island, SC [*FM radio station call letters*] .... WSEA
Pawling Lattice Test Rig [*United Nuclear Co.*] .... PLATR
Pawling Research Reactor .... PRR
Pawn [*Chess*] .... P
Pawn to King Four [*Standard opening to a game of chess. Pawn is moved to the fourth square in front of the king*] P-K4
Pawnbroker .... PB
Pawnbroker .... PWNBKR
Pawnbrokers' Association of the City of New York (EA) .... PACNY
Pawnee City, NE [*Location identifier FAA*] (FAAL) .... PWE
Paws with a Cause [*An association*] (EA) .... PWC
Pawtucket Public Library, Pawtucket, RI [*Library symbol Library of Congress*] (LCLS) .... RPaw
Pawtucket, RI [*Location identifier FAA*] (FAAL) .... SFZ
Pawtucket, RI [*AM radio station call letters*] (RBYB) .... WPNW
Pawtucket-Woonsocket [*Rhode Island*] [*Airport symbol*] (AD) .... SFZ
Pax [*Peace*] [*Latin*] .... P
Pax Christi Institute (TOCD) .... PCJ
Pax Christi International (EAIO) .... PCI
Pax Christi International (EA) .... PXI
Pax Christi - USA (EA) .... PC-USA
Pax Romana, International Catholic Movement for Intellectual and Cultural Affairs [*See also MIIC*] [*Geneva, Switzerland*] (EAIO) .... ICMICA
Pax Romana, International Movement of Catholic Students [*See also MIEC*] [*Fribourg, Switzerland Paris, France*] (EAIO) .... IMCS
Pax Romana, Mouvement International des Etudiants Catholiques [*Pax Romana, International Movement of Catholic Students - IMCS*] [*Paris, France*] (EAIO) .... MIEC
Pax Romana, Mouvement International des Intellectuels Catholiques [*Pax Romana, International Catholic Movement for Intellectual and Cultural Affairs - ICMICA*] [*Geneva, Switzerland*] (EAIO) .... MIIC
Pax Tibi cum Sanctis [*Peace to Thee with the Saints*] [*Latin*] .... PTCS
Pax World Foundation (EA) .... PWF
Paxar Corp. [*Associated Press*] (SAG) .... Paxar
Paxar Corp. [*NYSE symbol*] (SAG) .... PXR
Paxson [*Alaska*] [*Seismograph station code, US Geological Survey*] (SEIS) .... PAX
Paxson Communications 'A' [*AMEX symbol*] (TTSB) .... PXN
Paxson Communications Corp. [*Associated Press*] (SAG) .... PaxsnC
Paxson Communications Corp. [*AMEX symbol*] (SAG) .... PXN
Paxton [*Record label*] [*Great Britain*] .... Pax
Paxton Carnegie Library, Paxton, IL [*Library symbol Library of Congress*] (LCLS) .... IPax
Paxton Community Hospital, Paxton, IL [*Library symbol Library of Congress*] (LCLS) .... IPaxH
Paxton, IL [*FM radio station call letters*] .... WPXN
Pay .... P
Pay Actual Computer Time .... PACT
Pay Adjustment Authorization .... PAA
Pay Adjustment Document [*Army*] .... PADOC
Pay Adjustment Voucher [*Military*] .... PAV
Pay and Allowances .... P & A
Pay and Allowances Accrue From [*Air Force*] .... PALCRU
Pay and Allowances Chargeable .... PANDLCHAR
Pay and Records Office [*British military*] (DMA) .... PRO
Pay and Subsistence of Naval Personnel [*Budget appropriation title*] .... P & SNP
Pay and Supply [*Coast Guard*] .... P & S
Pay and Supply [*Coast Guard*] .... PANDS
Pay and Supply Instruction [*Coast Guard*] .... P & SI
Pay As You Earn .... PAYE
Pay As You Enter .... PAYE
Pay as You Go [*US Congress*] .... PAYGO
Pay Board .... PB
Pay by Phone [*Business term*] .... PBP
Pay Clerk .... PC

Pay Clerk	PCLK
Pay Date	PDate
Pay Department [*Army British*] (ROG)	PD
Pay Dirt	PD
Pay Entry Base Date	PEBD
Pay for Skills [*Human resources*] (WYGK)	PFS
Pay Grade	PG
Pay Group	PG
Pay in Kind Preferred Stock (TDOB)	PIK
Pay No Attention to the Man Behind the Curtain [*Computer hacker terminology*] (NHD)	PNAMBIC
Pay on Delivery [*Shipping*]	POD
Pay on Return [*Business term*]	POR
Pay One Price	POP
Pay Order of Withdrawal	POW
Pay Packets Deficiency [*British*]	PPD
Pay/Personnel Administrative Support System (NVT)	PASS
Pay/Personnel Administrative Support System Manual (DNAB)	PASSMAN
Pay Readjustment Act [*1942*]	PRA
Pay Record	PAREC
Pay Record Access	PRA
Pay Records and Health Records	PAHEL
Pay, Subsistence, and Transportation [*Military*]	PS & T
Pay, Subsistence, and Transportation [*Military*]	PSANDT
Pay, Subsistence, and Transportation, Navy	PS & TN
Pay Supply Depot (WDAA)	PSD
Pay Television	PTV
Pay Tone [*Telecommunications*] (TEL)	PT
Paya Lebar [*Singapore*] [*ICAO location identifier*] (ICLI)	WSAP
Payable (ROG)	PABLE
Payable	PAYABL
Payable after Death [*Insurance*] (ADA)	PAD
Payable on Death [*Insurance*]	POD
Payable on Death (AD)	pod
Payable on Receipt [*Business term*]	POR
Payam (Air Center Service) [*Iran*] [*FAA designator*] (FAAC)	IRP
Pay-As-You-Go	PAYG
Pay-Back Period [*Finance*]	PBP
Paychex, Inc. [*Associated Press*] (SAG)	Paychx
Paychex, Inc. [*NASDAQ symbol*] (NQ)	PAYX
Payco American Corp. [*NASDAQ symbol*] (NQ)	PAYC
Payco American Corp. [*Associated Press*] (SAG)	Payco
Payee	P
Payee TIN [*Taxpayer Identification Number*] **Perfection File** [*IRS*]	PTPF
Payerne [*Switzerland ICAO location identifier*] (ICLI)	LSMP
Payette, ID [*AM radio station call letters*]	KIOV
Payette, ID [*FM radio station call letters*] (RBYB)	KQXR
Payette Public Library, Payette, ID [*Library symbol*] [*Library of Congress*] (LCLS)	IdPay
Paying Agent [*Legal term*] (DLA)	PA
Paying and Collecting Area (AFM)	P & CA
Paying Guest	PG
Paying Teller [*Banking*]	PT
Paying Their Own Way	POW
Payless Cashways [*NYSE symbol*] (TTSB)	PCS
Payless Cashways, Inc. [*Associated Press*] (SAG)	PayCsh
Payless Cashways, Inc. [*NYSE symbol*] (SPSG)	PCS
Payless ShoeSource [*NYSE symbol*] (TTSB)	PSS
Payless ShoeSource, Inc. [*Associated Press*] (SAG)	PaylSh
Payless ShoeSource, Inc. [*NYSE symbol*] (SAG)	PSS
Payload	PAYLD
Payload [*NASA*] (KSC)	PL
Payload [*NASA*]	PLD
Payload Aboard, Caution in Descent [*NASA*]	PLACID
Payload Accommodation/Carrier Support Center [*NASA*] (SSD)	PA/CSC
Payload Accommodations Handbook [*NASA*] (NASA)	PAH
Payload Accommodations Studies [*NASA*] (NASA)	PAS
Payload Accomodations Equipment [*NASA*] (SSD)	PAE
Payload Activity Planner [*NASA*]	PAP
Payload Adapter Ring	PAR
Payload and General Support Computer [*NASA*]	PGSC
Payload Assist Module [*NASA*] (MCD)	PAM
Payload Assist Module - Atlas Class Spacecraft (MCD)	PAM-A
Payload Assist Module - Delta Class Spacecraft (MCD)	PAM-D
Payload Attach Equipment [*NASA*] (SSD)	PAE
Payload Attachment Fitting [*NASA*]	PAF
Payload Avionics Test Station [*NASA*] (SSD)	PATS
Payload Bay [*NASA*] (MCD)	PLB
Payload Bay Door [*NASA*] (NASA)	PBD
Payload Bay Door [*NASA*] (MCD)	PLBD
Payload Bay Door Forward [*NASA*] (MCD)	PBDF
Payload Bay Door Mechanism [*NASA*] (NASA)	PBDM
Payload Bay Kit [*NASA*] (NASA)	PBK
Payload Bay Liner [*NASA*] (MCD)	PBL
Payload Center Operations Team [*NASA*] (MCD)	PCOT
Payload Certification Review (SSD)	PCR
Payload Changeout Room [*NASA*] (NASA)	PCR
Payload Checkout Room [*NASA*] (NASA)	PCR
Payload Checkout System [*NASA*] (NASA)	PCS
Payload Checkout Unit [*NASA*] (MCD)	PCU
Payload Command [*NASA*] (MCD)	PAYCOM
Payload Command Decoder Subunit [*NASA*] (KSC)	PCDS
Payload Command Decoder Unit [*NASA*] (NASA)	PCDU
Payload Common Communication Equipment [*NASA*] (NASA)	PCCE
Payload Configuration Control Board [*NASA*] (MCD)	PCCB
Payload Control and Checkout [*NASA*] (NASA)	PCC
Payload Control Facility [*NASA*] (MCD)	PCF
Payload Control Processor [*NASA*]	PCP
Payload Control Supervisor [*NASA*] (MCD)	PCS
Payload Cost Tradeoff Optimization [*NASA*] (NASA)	PCTO
Payload Data [*NASA*] (MCD)	PAYDAT
Payload Data Interleaver [*NASA*] (NASA)	PDI
Payload Data Interleaver [*NASA*] (MCD)	PLDI
Payload Data Interleaver System [*NASA*] (MCD)	PDIS
Payload Deployment and Retrieval Mechanism [*NASA*]	PDRM
Payload Deployment and Retrieval Subsystem [*NASA*] (NASA)	PD & RS
Payload Deployment and Retrieval System [*NASA*] (GFGA)	PDRS
Payload Deployment and Retrieval System Simulation [*NASA*] (SSD)	PDRSS
Payload Deployment and Retrieval System Test Article [*NASA*] (NASA)	PDRSTA
Payload Diameter	PD
Payload Distribution Panel [*NASA*] (MCD)	PDP
Payload Distribution Plan	PDP
Payload Effects Follow-On Study [*NASA*] (NASA)	PEFO
Payload Ejection Mechanism	PEM
Payload Enclosure Assembly (MCD)	PEA
Payload Engineering Data Base [*NASA*] (SSD)	PEDB
Payload Environmental Transportation System [*NASA*] (NASA)	PETS
Payload Feedback [*NASA*] (MCD)	PFB
Payload Flight Control Facility [*NASA*] (MCD)	PFCF
Payload Flight Test Article [*NASA*] (MCD)	PFTA
Payload Forward [*NASA*] (MCD)	PF
Payload Forward Bus [*NASA*] (MCD)	PFB
Payload Function [*NASA*] (MCD)	PF
Payload Function Key [*NASA*] (MCD)	PFK
Payload Ground Handling Mechanism [*NASA*] (MCD)	PGHM
Payload Ground Operation Requirements [*NASA*] (NASA)	PGOR
Payload Ground Operation Requirements Study [*NASA*] (MCD)	PGORS
Payload Ground Operations Contractor [*NASA*] (SSD)	PGOC
Payload Ground Requirements Working Group [*NASA*] (NASA)	PGRWG
Payload Ground Support Equipment [*NASA*] (MCD)	PGSE
Payload Ground Support Systems [*NASA*] (NASA)	PLGSS
Payload Handling [*NASA*] (NASA)	PLH
Payload Handling Panel [*NASA*] (MCD)	PHP
Payload Handling Station [*NASA*] (MCD)	PHS
Payload Hazardous Report (NASA)	PHR
Payload Insertion Device (NASA)	PID
Payload Installation and Deployment Aid [*NASA*] (NASA)	PIDA
Payload Integration Bay [*NASA*] (KSC)	PIB
Payload Integration Center [*NASA*] (MCD)	PIC
Payload Integration Committee [*NASA*] (NASA)	PIC
Payload Integration Contractor (MCD)	PIC
Payload Integration Equipment [*NASA*] (MCD)	PIE
Payload Integration Facility [*NASA*] (KSC)	PIF
Payload Integration Library System [*NASA*] (SSD)	PILS
Payload Integration Plan [*NASA*] (NASA)	PIP
Payload Integration Task Group [*NASA*] (NASA)	PITG
Payload Integration Test Set [*NASA*] (MCD)	PITS
Payload Interface Adapter [*NASA*] (SSD)	PIA
Payload Interface Plan [*NASA*] (NASA)	PIP
Payload Interrogator [*NASA*] (MCD)	PI
Payload Interrogator [*NASA*] (MCD)	PLI
Payload Launch Module	PLUM
Payload Launch Readiness Verification [*NASA*] (MCD)	PLRV
Payload Local Area Network [*NASA*] (SSD)	PLAN
Payload Management [*NASA*] (MCD)	PLDM
Payload Management [*NASA*] (NASA)	PLM
Payload Management [*NASA*] (NASA)	PM
Payload Mass Ratio	PMR
Payload Mating Dolly [*NASA*]	PLMD
Payload Mating Dolly [*NASA*]	PMD
Payload Midbody [*NASA*] (MCD)	PM
Payload Mission Integration Contract (MCD)	PMIC
Payload Module Decoder [*NASA*]	PMD
Payload Monitoring [*NASA*] (NASA)	PLM
Payload Monitoring and Control [*NASA*] (NASA)	PMC
Payload Officer [*NASA*] (MCD)	PLO
Payload Operations Center [*NASA*] (NASA)	POC
Payload Operations Contractor [*NASA*] (SSD)	PLOC
Payload Operations Control Center [*NASA*] (NASA)	POCC
Payload Operations Division [*NASA*] (MCD)	POD
Payload Operations Office [*NASA*]	POO
Payload Operations Support Team [*NASA*] (MCD)	POST
Payload Optimized Program [*NASA*] (KSC)	POP
Payload Ordnance Processing Area (NASA)	POPA
Payload Pointing System (SSD)	PPS
Payload Position Data	PPD
Payload Power Switch	PPS
Payload Preparation Room [*VAFB*] [*NASA*] (MCD)	PPR
Payload Processing Facility [*Air Force*] (NASA)	PPF
Payload Requirements Document (NASA)	PLRD
Payload Retention Mechanism [*NASA*] (NASA)	PRM
Payload Retention Subsystem [*NASA*] (NASA)	PRS
Payload Sensor (GFGA)	PL/SNSR
Payload Service Area [*NASA*] (NASA)	PSA
Payload Service Equipment [*NASA*] (MCD)	PSE
Payload Shroud (MCD)	PS
Payload Signal Processor [*NASA*] (MCD)	PLSP
Payload Signal Processor [*NASA*] (NASA)	PSP
Payload Specialist [*NASA*] (MCD)	PS

Payload Specialist Panel [*NASA*] (NASA) .... PSP
Payload Specialist Station [*NASA*] (NASA) .... PSS
Payload Specialist Station Panel [*NASA*] (MCD) .... PSSP
Payload Spin Test Facility (MCD) .... PSTF
Payload Station [*NASA*] (MCD) .... PS
Payload Station Distribution Panel [*NASA*] (MCD) .... PSDP
Payload Structure Fuel [*Ratio*] .... PSF
Payload Support [*NASA*] (MCD) .... PLDS
Payload Support [*NASA*] (NASA) .... PS
Payload Support Avionics [*NASA*] (NASA) .... PSA
Payload Support Equipment [*NASA*] (MCD) .... PSE
Payload Support Plan [*NASA*] (MCD) .... PSP
Payload Support Structure (SSD) .... PLSS
Payload Support System [*NASA*] (MCD) .... PSS
Payload Systems [*NASA*] (MCD) .... PLS
Payload Systems Operating Procedures [*NASA*] (NASA) .... PSOP
Payload Terminal Connector Room [*NASA*] (MCD) .... PTCR
Payload Test Facility [*VAFB*] [*NASA*] (MCD) .... PTF
Payload Test Set [*NASA*] (NASA) .... PTS
Payload Timing Buffer [*NASA*] (NASA) .... PTB
Payload Transportation System [*NASA*] (MCD) .... PTS
Payload Umbilical Mast (NASA) .... PLUM
Paymaster [*Military*] (ROG) .... P
Paymaster [*Military British*] (ROG) .... PAYM
Paymaster .... PAYMR
Paymaster [*Military British*] (ROG) .... PAYMTR
Paymaster (WGA) .... PAYR
Paymaster .... PM
Paymaster .... PMR
Paymaster (AD) .... Pmr
Paymaster [*Navy British*] .... (S)
Paymaster General (AD) .... PmG
Paymaster General [*Navy*] .... PMG
Paymaster in Chief [*Navy British*] (ROG) .... CHP
Paymaster, Marine Corps .... PAYMARCORPS
Paymaster Sergeant [*Marine Corps*] .... PMSGT
Paymaster Sergeant .... PS
Paymaster-Captain [*Navy British*] .... PC
Paymaster-Commander [*Navy British*] (DMA) .... P Cr
Paymaster-Commander [*Navy British*] .... PC
Paymaster-Lieutenant [*Navy British*] .... PL
Paymaster-Lieutenant-Commander [*Navy British*] .... PLC
Paymaster-Rear-Admiral [*Navy British*] .... PRA
Paymaster-Sub-Lieutenant [*Navy British*] .... PSL
Payment .... PAYMT
Payment .... PAYT
Payment (AFM) .... PMT
Payment (AD) .... pmt
Payment (WDMC) .... pt
Payment .... PT
Payment .... Pymt
Payment .... PYMT
Payment (DCTA) .... PYT
Payment after Closing [*Insurance*] .... PAC
[*The*] Payment Analysis Report [*Dun & Bradstreet Credit Services*] [*Information service or system*] (CRD) .... PAR
Payment and Telecommunication Services Corp. [*New York, NY Telecommunications Defunct*] (TSSD) .... PATS
Payment Authority [*Business term*] .... P/A
Payment by Results [*Payment system*] .... PBR
Payment Center (MHDB) .... PC
Payment for Public Use [*Canada*] .... PPU
Payment in Kind .... PIK
Payment in Lieu .... PIL
Payment in Lieu of Taxes .... PILOT
Payment in Lieu of Taxes Act .... PILTA
Payment in Lieu of Taxes Program [*Department of the Interior*] .... PILT
Payment in Part [*Business term*] .... PIP
Payment Option Election (MCD) .... POE
Payment Outstanding Suspense Accounts (NATG) .... POSA
Payment Outstanding Suspense Accounts (AD) .... posa
Payment-in-Kind Securities [*Investment term*] (DFIT) .... PIK Securities
Payments and Progress (AD) .... p&p
Payments and Progress Committee [*NATO*] (NATG) .... P and P
Payne and Ivamy's Carriage by Sea [*10th ed.*] [*1976*] [*A publication*] (DLA) .... Pay & Iv Carr
Payne Theological Seminary, Wilberforce, OH [*OCLC symbol*] (OCLC) .... OPT
Payne Theological Seminary, Wilberforce, OH [*Library symbol Library of Congress*] (LCLS) .... OWibfP
Payne Whitney Clinic, New York, NY [*Library symbol Library of Congress*] (LCLS) .... NNPaW
Payne Whitney Suicide Prevention Program [*New York Hospital*] (EA) .... PWSPP
Paynesville Elementary & Middle School, Paynesville, MN [*Library symbol*] [*Library of Congress*] (LCLS) .... MnPvEM
Paynesville, High School, Paynesville, MN [*Library symbol*] [*Library of Congress*] (LCLS) .... MnPvHS
Paynesville Historical Society, Paynesville, MN [*Library symbol*] [*Library of Congress*] (LCLS) .... MnPvHi
Paynesville Hospital, Medical Staff Library, Paynesville, MN [*Library symbol*] [*Library of Congress*] (LCLS) .... MnPvH
Paynesville, MN [*FM radio station call letters*] .... KZPK
Paynesville Public Library, Paynesville, MN [*Library symbol*] [*Library of Congress*] (LCLS) .... MnPv
Payola (AD) .... p-ola
Pay-on-Answer [*Telecommunications British*] .... POA

Pay-on-Receipt (AD) .... p-o-r
Payout Time [*Business term*] .... PT
Pay-per-Transaction [*Agreement between video cassette rental stores and owners of film rights*] .... p-p-t
Pay-per-View [*Pay-television service*] .... PPV
Pay-Per-View (AD) .... ppv
Pay-Raise Commission (AD) .... PRC
Payroll (AD) .... P/R
Payroll (AD) .... pr
Payroll .... PR
Payroll and Accounting, Personnel Management, Manpower Utilization [*Air Force*] .... PAPERMAN
Payroll Audit (AD) .... pra
Payroll Audit, Indexing, and Expiration .... PIE
Payroll Auditor [*Insurance*] .... PRA
Payroll Automation for Department of Agriculture .... PADA
Payroll Deduction .... PRD
Payroll Deduction Authorization (MCD) .... PDA
Payroll Earnings Record Keeping .... PERK
Payroll Journal [*Accounting*] .... PRJ
Payroll Savings Plan (GFGA) .... PSP
Payroll Section .... PRSEC
Payroll/Stock Ownership Plan .... PAYSOP
Payroll Tax (ADA) .... PRT
Pay-Roll Tax Rulings [*Australia A publication*] .... PT Rulings
Payroll-Based Stock Option Plan [*Human resources*] (WYGK) .... PAYSOP
Pays d'Europe Centrale et Orientale (ECON) .... PECO
Pays D'Europe Centrale et Orientale .... PECOS
Paysandu [*Uruguay*] [*Airport symbol*] (OAG) .... PDU
Paysandu/Aeropuerto Deptal [*Uruguay*] [*ICAO location identifier*] (ICLI) .... SUPU
Payson, AZ [*AM radio station call letters*] .... KMOG
Payson, AZ [*FM radio station call letters*] .... KRIM
Payson, UT [*FM radio station call letters*] .... KTCE
Payton Ventures [*Vancouver Stock Exchange symbol*] .... PYV
Paz De Ariporo [*Colombia*] [*Airport symbol*] (OAG) .... PZA
Pb-based Lanthanum-doped Zirconate Titanates .... PLZT
PBX Resources [*Vancouver Stock Exchange symbol*] .... PBX
PC DOCS Gp Intl. [*NASDAQ symbol*] (TTSB) .... DOCSF
PC DOCS Group International [*NASDAQ symbol*] (SAG) .... DOCS
PC DOCS Group International [*Associated Press*] (SAG) .... PC DOCS
PC Financial Network (PCM) .... PCFN
PC Quote [*AMEX symbol*] (TTSB) .... PQT
PC Quote, Inc. [*Associated Press*] (SAG) .... PC Quote
PC Quote, Inc. [*AMEX symbol*] (SAG) .... PQT
PC Resource [*A publication*] .... PCR
PC Satellite Network .... PCSN
PC Service Source [*NASDAQ symbol*] (TTSB) .... PCSS
PC Service Source, Inc. [*Associated Press*] (SAG) .... PC Svc
PC Service Source, Inc. [*NASDAQ symbol*] (SAG) .... PCSS
PC [*Personal Computer*] Tools for Windows (PCM) .... PCTWin
PCA International, Inc. [*Associated Press*] (SAG) .... PCA Int
PCA International, Inc. [*NASDAQ symbol*] (NQ) .... PCAI
PCA Intl [*NASDAQ symbol*] (TTSB) .... PCAI
PCBoard Programming Language [*Clark Development Co.*] (PCM) .... PPL
PCC Group [*NASDAQ symbol*] (TTSB) .... PCCG
PCC Group, Inc. [*Associated Press*] (SAG) .... PCC Gp
PCC Group, Inc. [*NASDAQ symbol*] (SAG) .... PCCG
PCD, Inc. [*Associated Press*] (SAG) .... PCD
PCD, Inc. [*NASDAQ symbol*] (SAG) .... PCDI
PCD Inc. [*NASDAQ symbol*] (TTSB) .... PCDI
PCH Post Career [*Vancouver Stock Exchange symbol*] .... PCH
P-Channel Depletion-Load Triode Inverter .... PDLT
P-Channel Junction Field-Effect Transistor (IDOE) .... PFET
PCI Services [*NASDAQ symbol*] (TTSB) .... PCIS
PCI Services, Inc. [*Associated Press*] (SAG) .... PCI Sv
PCI Services, Inc. [*NASDAQ symbol*] (SAG) .... PCIS
PCIA Expansion Bus [*Computer science*] .... PEB
PCI-toPCI Bridge Board (ACII) .... PPBB
PCL Industries Ltd. [*Toronto Stock Exchange symbol*] .... PCI
PCM [*Punch Card Machine*] Master Unit [*Computer science*] (GFGA) .... PCMMU
P-Com, Inc. [*NASDAQ symbol*] (SAG) .... PCMS
P-Com, Inc. [*Associated Press*] (SAG) .... P-Com
PCR [*Polymerase Chain Reaction*] Amplification of Specific Alleles [*Genetics*] .... PASA
PCT Holdings [*NASDAQ symbol*] (TTSB) .... PCTH
PCT Holdings, Inc. [*NASDAQ symbol*] (SAG) .... PCTH
PCT Holdings, Inc. [*Associated Press*] (SAG) .... PCTHold
PCTE Added Common Tools (NITA) .... PACT
PDG Environmental [*NASDAQ symbol*] (TTSB) .... PDGE
PDG Environmental, Inc. [*Associated Press*] (SAG) .... PDG En
PDG Environmental, Inc. [*NASDAQ symbol*] (SAG) .... PDGE
PDG Remediation [*NASDAQ symbol*] (TTSB) .... PDGS
PDG Remediation, Inc. [*Associated Press*] (SAG) .... PDG
PDG Remediation, Inc. [*NASDAQ symbol*] (SAG) .... PDGS
PDG Remediation Wrrt [*NASDAQ symbol*] (TTSB) .... PDGSW
PDK Labs [*NASDAQ symbol*] (TTSB) .... PDKL
PDK Labs $0.49 Cv'A' Pfd [*NASDAQ symbol*] (TTSB) .... PDKLP
PDK Labs, Inc. [*Associated Press*] (SAG) .... PDK
PDK Labs, Inc. [*NASDAQ symbol*] (SAG) .... PDKL
PDK Labs Wrrt'C' [*NASDAQ symbol*] (TTSB) .... PDKLM
P-Doped Semiconductor [*Photovoltaic energy systems*] .... p
PDQ Air Service, Inc. [*ICAO designator*] (FAAC) .... PDQ
PDS Financial [*NASDAQ symbol*] (TTSB) .... PDSF
PDS Financial Corp. [*Associated Press*] (SAG) .... PDS Fin
PDS Financial Corp. [*NASDAQ symbol*] (SAG) .... PDSF

PDT, Inc. [*Associated Press*] (SAG) .... PDT
PDT, Inc. [*NASDAQ symbol*] (SAG) .... PDTI
PE Ben Oilfield Services Ltd. [*Toronto Stock Exchange symbol*] .... PBN
Pea Early-Browning Virus [*Plant pathology*] .... PEBV
Pea Enation Mosaic Virus [*Plant pathology*] .... PEMV
Pea Green Mottle Virus [*Plant pathology*] .... PGMV
Pea Growing Research Organisation Ltd. [*British*] (BI) .... PGRO
[*A*] **Pea in the Pod, Inc.** [*NASDAQ symbol*] (SAG) .... APOD
Pea Leafroll Virus [*Plant pathology*] .... PELRV
Pea Mild Mosaic Virus [*Plant pathology*] .... PMMV
Pea Ridge National Military Park .... PERI
Pea Seed-Borne Mosaic Virus .... PsbMV
Pea Seed-Borne Mosaic Virus [*Plant pathology*] .... PSMV
Pea Streak Virus [*Plant pathology*] .... PESV
Peabody Conservatory of Music, Baltimore, MD [*Library symbol Library of Congress*] (LCLS) .... MdBPC
Peabody Developmental Gross Motor Scale .... PDGMS
Peabody Historical Society, Peabody, MA [*Library symbol Library of Congress*] (LCLS) .... MPeaHi
Peabody Individual Achievement Test [*Education*] .... PIAT
Peabody Institute, Danvers, MA [*Library symbol Library of Congress*] (LCLS) .... MDaP
Peabody Institute of Johns Hopkins University, Conservatory Library, Baltimore, MD [*OCLC symbol*] (OCLC) .... JHP
Peabody Institute of the City of Baltimore [*Maryland*] .... PICB
Peabody Institute of The Johns Hopkins University (GAGS) .... Peabody Inst
Peabody Institute, Peabody, MA [*Library symbol Library of Congress*] (LCLS) .... MPeal
Peabody Intellectual Performance Scale [*Education*] .... PIPS
Peabody Language Development Kit: Preschool (EDAC) .... PLDK-P
Peabody Language Development Kits [*Education*] .... PLDK
Peabody Law Review [*A publication*] (DLA) .... Peab L Rev
Peabody Library, Columbia City, IN [*Library symbol Library of Congress*] (LCLS) .... InColc
Peabody Mathematics Readiness Test [*Educational test*] .... PMRT
Peabody Museum (AD) .... PM
Peabody Museum of Archaeology and Ethnology [*Harvard University*] [*Research center*] (RCD) .... PEAMUSE
Peabody Museum of Archeology and Ethnology (AD) .... PMAE
Peabody Museum of Natural History (AD) .... PMNH
Peabody Museum of Natural History (NADA) .... PMNH
Peabody Museum of Salem (AD) .... PMS
Peabody Museum of Salem, Salem, MA [*Library symbol Library of Congress*] (LCLS) .... MSaP
Peabody Picture Vocabulary Test [*Education*] .... PPVT
Peabody Picture Vocabulary Test - Revised [*Education*] .... PPVT-R
Peabody Short Line R. R. [*Army*] .... PSL
Peace Action Center [*Defunct*] (EA) .... PAC
Peace Action Network (EA) .... PAN
Peace Activists East and West Coordinating Committee (EA) .... PAEWCC
Peace Air Togo [*ICAO designator*] (FAAC) .... PCT
Peace and Common Security [*Defunct*] (EA) .... PACS
Peace and Freedom Party [*Political party*] (DLA) .... PF
Peace and Freedom Party (EA) .... PFP
Peace and Prosperity Issue [*Politics*] .... P & P
Peace and Quiet .... P & Q
Peace and Quiet (AD) .... p & q
Peace and Reconciliation Inter-Schools Movement (AIE) .... PRISM
Peace and Solidarity Alliance (EA) .... PSA
Peace Brigades International (EA) .... PBI
Peace Centers Foundation [*Later, UDC*] (EA) .... PCF
Peace College, Raleigh, NC [*Library symbol Library of Congress*] (LCLS) .... NcRP
Peace Commissioner [*Ireland*] .... PC
Peace Corps (EA) .... PC
Peace Corps, Information Services Division, Washington, DC [*Library symbol*] [*Library of Congress*] (LCLS) .... DPC
Peace Corps Partnership Program (EA) .... PCPP
Peace Corps Physician .... PCP
Peace Corps School Partnership Program [*Later, PCPP*] (EA) .... SPP
Peace Corps Volunteer .... PCV
Peace Development Fund (EA) .... PDF
Peace Education Network (EA) .... PEN
PEACE [*Program for Emergency Assistance, Cooperation, and Education*] **for Guatemala** (EA) .... PG
Peace Garden Project [*Later, NPG*] (EA) .... PGP
Peace, Health, and Prosperity .... PH and P
Peace Library System, Peace River, AB, Canada [*Library symbol*] [*Library of Congress*] (LCLS) .... CaAPrPLS
Peace Library System, Peace River, Alberta [*Library symbol National Library of Canada*] (NLC) .... APRPLS
Peace Mission Movement (EA) .... PMM
Peace Movement of Ethiopia (EA) .... PME
Peace Movement Study Group [*Colgate University*] (EA) .... PMSG
Peace Museum (EA) .... PM
Peace Officer Standards and Training .... POST
Peace Officers Association of California (AD) .... POAC
Peace Officers Association of Georgia (AD) .... POAG
Peace Officers Research Association of California .... PORAC
Peace on Earth [*Australia Political party*] .... POE
Peace on Earth Research Center .... PERC
Peace PAC (EA) .... PP
Peace Pledge Union [*British*] .... PPU
Peace Research Abstracts (NITA) .... PRA
Peace Research and Education Project .... PREP
Peace Research Institute [*Later, Institute for Policy Studies*] (EA) .... PRI
Peace Research Institute - Dundas [*Canada*] (IRC) .... PRI-D
Peace Research Laboratory [*Later, LPRL*] [*An association*] (EA) .... PRL
Peace Research Network [*Later, PSA*] (EA) .... PRN
Peace Research Organization Fund .... PROF
Peace Resource Project (EA) .... PRP
Peace River [*Canada*] [*Airport symbol*] (OAG) .... YPE
Peace River, AB [*Television station call letters*] CFRN-2
Peace River, AB [*FM radio station call letters*] CKUA-5
Peace River, AB [*AM radio station call letters*] .... CKYL
Peace River, AB [*ICAO location identifier*] (ICLI) .... CYPE
Peace River Municipal Library, Alberta [*Library symbol National Library of Canada*] (NLC) .... APRM
Peace River Municipal Library, Peace River, AB, Canada [*Library symbol*] [*Library of Congress*] (LCLS) .... CaAPrM
Peace Science Society (International) (EA) .... PSS-I
Peace Science Society (International) .... PSS(Int)
Peace Studies Association (EA) .... PSA
Peace Tax Campaign [*Australia*] .... PTC
Peace through Education Project [*An association*] .... PTE
Peace through Law Education Fund (EA) .... PTLEF
Peace War Headquarters (NATG) .... PWHQ
Peaceful Alternatives to the Atlantic Pact .... PAAP
Peaceful Beginnings (EA) .... PB
Peaceful Nuclear Explosion .... PNE
Peaceful Nuclear Explosion (AD) .... pne
Peaceful Nuclear Explosions Treaty [*Officially, Treaty on Underground Nuclear Explosions for Peaceful Purposes*] .... PNET
Peaceful Uses of Military Forces .... PUMF
Peacekeeper in Minuteman Silos (DWSG) .... PIMS
Peacekeeper Rail Garrison [*Cancelled 1991*] [*Air Force*] (DOMA) .... PRG
Peace-Keeping Operation (MCD) .... PKO
Peacetime Acquisition Objective [*DoD*] (AFIT) .... PAO
Peacetime Aerial Reconnaissance Program [*Military*] (NVT) .... PARPRO
Peacetime Airborne Reconnaissance (AFM) .... PAR
Peacetime Contingency Operation [*Army*] (ADDR) .... PCO
Peacetime Establishment [*Military*] (NATG) .... PE
Peacetime Force Material Assets [*Navy*] (AFIT) .... PTFMA
Peacetime Force Materiel Objective [*Army*] .... PTFMO
Peacetime Force Materiel Procurement Objective [*Army*] .... PTFMPO
Peacetime Force Materiel Requirements [*Army*] .... PTFMR
Peacetime Force Materiel Requirements - Acquisition [*Army*] (AABC) .... PTFMR-A
Peacetime Force Materiel Requirements - Retention [*Army*] (AABC) .... PTFMR-R
Peacetime Intelligence Plan, Allied Central Europe [*NATO*] .... PIPACE
Peacetime Losses [*Military*] .... PTL
Peacetime Manpower Allocation Requirements Plan (CINC) .... PMARP
Peacetime Operating Assets [*DoD*] (AFIT) .... POA
Peacetime Operating Level (AFM) .... PTOL
Peacetime Operating Stock [*Military*] (CINC) .... POS
Peacetime Operating Stock [*Military*] .... PTOS
Peacetime Operating Stock Requirement [*Military*] (AFIT) .... POSR
Peacetime Planning Factors .... PPF
Peacetime Rate Factor [*Military*] (AABC) .... PTRF
Peacetime Replacement Factor [*Military*] .... PTRF
Peacetime Requirements and Procedures [*Strategic Air Command*] (MUGU) .... PREP
Peacetime Stockage Objective [*DoD*] (AFIT) .... PSO
Peacetime Subcontract .... PSC
Peacetime Support Period [*DoD*] .... PTSP
Peach Bottom Atomic Power Station (NRCH) .... PBAPS
Peach Bottom High-Temperature Gas-Cooled Reactor .... PB-HTGR
Peach Rosette Mosaic Virus [*Plant pathology*] .... PRMV
Peach Springs, AZ [*Location identifier FAA*] (FAAL) .... PGS
Peach Tree Valley [*California*] [*Seismograph station code, US Geological Survey*] (SEIS) .... PTV
Peach Yellow Leaf Roll [*Plant pathology*] .... PYLR
Peachey on Marriage Settlements [*1860*] [*A publication*] (DLA) .... Pea MS
Peachland Museum, British Columbia [*Library symbol National Library of Canada*] (NLC) .... BPEM
Peachland Museum, Peachland, BC, Canada [*Library symbol*] [*Library of Congress*] (LCLS) .... CaBPEM
Peacoat Locker .... PLKR
Peacock [*Philately*] .... pck
Peacock H.E. and Son (Thorney) Ltd. [*British*] [*FAA designator*] (FAAC) .... PCK
Peak (IDOE) .... P
Peak .... P
Peak [*Maps and charts*] .... PK
Peak Aboriginal Community Organisation [*Australia*] .... PACO
Peak Accelerometer Recorder (IEEE) .... PAR
Peak Acid Output [*Physiology*] .... PAO
Peak Airway Pressure [*Physiology*] .... PAP
Peak Airway Pressure [*Medicine*] (DAVI) .... PAW
Peak Amplitude [*Medicine*] (DMAA) .... PA
Peak and Northern Footpaths Society [*British*] (DBA) .... PNFS
Peak Annual Funding (NASA) .... PAF
Peak Area Ratio [*Chromatographic analysis*] .... PAR
Peak Aviation, PLC [*British*] [*FAA designator*] (FAAC) .... PEK
Peak Blood Pressure [*Cardiology*] (DAVI) .... PBP
Peak Bone Mass [*Medicine*] (DMAA) .... PBM
Peak Capacity .... PC
Peak Cathode Current .... PCC
Peak Centerline Temperature [*Nuclear energy*] (NRCH) .... PCT
Peak Cladding Temperature [*Nuclear energy*] (NRCH) .... PCT
Peak Clipping Amplifier .... PCA
Peak Design Heat Loss (PDAA) .... PDHL
Peak Detector .... PD

Peak Distribution Analyzer ..... PDA
Peak Dose Rate [*Radiation*] (AAG) ..... PDR
Peak Effective Power ..... PEP
Peak Ejection Rate [*Cardiology*] ..... PER
Peak Electrode Current ..... PEC
Peak Electron Volts ..... peV
Peak Energy Product ..... PEP
Peak Envelope Power [*Telecommunications*] ..... PEP
Peak Envelope Voltage [*Telecommunications*] (TEL) ..... PEV
Peak Exercise (DMAA) ..... Pex
Peak Expiration Rate [*Medicine*] ..... PER
Peak Expiratory Flow [*Pulmonary function*] ..... PEF
Peak Expiratory Flow/Peak Inspiratory Flow Rate [*Medicine*] (DAVI) ..... PEFR/PIFR
Peak Expiratory Flow Rate ..... PEFR
Peak Expiratory Flow Rate [*Medicine*] (DMAA) ..... PERF
Peak Expiratory Velocity [*Medicine*] (DMAA) ..... PEV
Peak Flow [*Medicine*] ..... PF
Peak Flow Gauge [*Medicine*] (AAMN) ..... PFG
Peak Flow Meter [*Medicine*] (AAMN) ..... PFM
Peak Flow Rate [*or Reading*] [*Medicine*] ..... PFR
Peak Flow Velocity [*Cardiology*] ..... PFV
Peak Follower Circuit ..... PFC
Peak Forward Voltage (IAA) ..... PFV
Peak Frequency ..... PF
Peak Heart Rate [*Cardiology*] ..... PHR
Peak Height Ratio ..... PHR
Peak Height Velocity (DMAA) ..... PHV
Peak Hour Factor [*Transportation*] ..... PHF
Peak Identification Computer ..... PIC
Peak Inspiratory Flow [*Medicine*] (AAMN) ..... PIF
Peak Inspiratory Flow Rate [*Medicine*] ..... PIFR
Peak Inspiratory Pressure [*Medicine*] (DAVI) ..... PIP
Peak Inspiratory Pressure [*Medicine*] (DAVI) ..... PMax
Peak Instantaneous Airborne Count (DA) ..... PIAC
Peak Intensity Ratio [*Spectroscopy*] ..... PIR
Peak Inverse Voltage [*RADAR*] ..... PIV
Peak Kilovolts ..... PkV
Peak Left Ventricular [*Pressure*] [*Cardiology*] ..... PLV
Peak Local Mean Error (MCD) ..... PLME
Peak Loss (IAA) ..... PL
Peak Negative Pressure [*Medicine*] (DAVI) ..... PNP
Peak Nucleate Boiling Flux ..... PNBF
Peak Operated Valve (MCD) ..... POV
Peak Operating Voltage ..... POV
Peak Overpressure [*Nuclear energy*] (NRCH) ..... POP
Peak Overshoot Ratio (IAA) ..... POR
Peak Pain Intensity Difference Score [*Medicine*] (DMAA) ..... PPID
Peak Phrenic Nerve Activity [*Medicine*] ..... PPNA
Peak Power (IAA) ..... PP
Peak Power (IDOE) ..... P_p
Peak Power Control [*Telecommunications*] (TEL) ..... PPC
Peak Power Frequency ..... PPF
Peak Power Meter ..... PPM
Peak Pressure ..... PP
Peak Production Rate ..... PPR
Peak Program Meter [*Television*] ..... PPM
Peak Program Meter (AD) ..... ppm
Peak Pulse Height Analysis ..... PPHA
Peak Pulse Power ..... PPP
Peak Radiated Power (CET) ..... PRP
Peak Rated Voltage (IAA) ..... PRV
Peak Reactive Hyperemia Blood Flow [*Hematology*] (MAE) ..... PRHBF
Peak Reading Digital Voltmeter ..... PRDV
Peak Recording Accelerograph [*Accelerometer*] (IEEE) ..... PRA
Peak Reserve Voltage (IAA) ..... PRV
Peak Reserve Working Voltage ..... PRWV
Peak Reverse Voltage ..... PRV
Peak Selector Memory [*Computer science*] ..... PSM
Peak Serum Concentration [*Immunology*] (DAVI) ..... CPmax
Peak Sideband Power (DEN) ..... PSP
Peak Systolic Gradient [*Medicine*] (MAE) ..... PSG
Peak Tanning Hours [*Supposedly occurring between 10am and 2pm*] [*See also BROTS, SROTS*] ..... PTH
Peak Technologies Group, Inc. [*NASDAQ symbol*] (SAG) ..... PEAK
Peak Technologies Group, Inc. [*Associated Press*] (SAG) ..... PeakTch
Peak Technologies Grp [*NASDAQ symbol*] (TTSB) ..... PEAK
Peak Transient Reverse Voltage [*Electronics*] (IAA) ..... PTRV
Peak Twitch Tension [*Physiology*] ..... PTT
Peak Underpressure [*Nuclear energy*] (NRCH) ..... PUP
Peak Value [*Computer science*] ..... pK
Peak Visibility Factor ..... PVF
Peak Voltage (IDOE) ..... E_p
Peak Voltage (IDOE) ..... E_{pk}
Peak Volts Alternating Current (KSC) ..... PVAC
Peak Watt Rating [*Electrical engineering*] ..... PWR
Peak Work Capacity ..... PWC
Peake on the Law of Evidence [*A publication*] (DLA) ..... Peake Ev
Peake's Additional Cases Nisi Prius [*170 English Reprint*] [*1795-1812*] [*A publication*] (DLA) ..... Pea (2)
Peake's Additional Cases Nisi Prius [*1795-1812*] [*A publication*] (DLA) ..... Peake Add Cas
Peake's Additional Cases Nisi Prius [*170 English Reprint*] [*England*] [*A publication*] (DLA) ..... Peake NP Add Cas
Peake's Additional Cases Nisi Prius [*170 English Reprint*] [*England*] [*A publication*] (DLA) ..... Peake NP Add Cas (Eng)
Peake's Cases [*1790-1812*] [*A publication*] (DLA) ..... Peake
Peake's English Nisi Prius Cases [*170 English Reprint*] [*A publication*] (DLA) ..... Peake NP
Peake's English Nisi Prius Cases [*170 English Reprint*] [*1790-1812*] [*A publication*] (DLA) ..... Peake NP Cas
Peake's English Nisi Prius Cases [*170 English Reprint*] [*A publication*] (DLA) ..... Peake NP Cas (Eng)
Peake's English Nisi Prius Cases [*1790-1812*] [*A publication*] (DLA) ..... PNP
Peake's English Nisi Prius Reports [*1790-1812*] [*A publication*] (DLA) ..... Pea
Peake's English Nisi Prius Reports [*Vol. 2*] [*A publication*] (DLA) ..... Pea Add Cas
Peak-to-Average Ratio [*Telecommunications*] ..... PAR
Peak-to-Peak (MCD) ..... PK/PK
Peak-to-Peak ..... PP
Peak-to-Peak [*Nuclear energy*] ..... PTP
Peak-to-Peak Heights [*Spectrometry*] ..... PPH
Peak-to-Peak Noise [*Instrumentation*] ..... PPN
Peak-to-Peak Voltage (IDOE) ..... $E_{pk\text{-}pk}$
Peak-to-Peak Voltage (IDOE) ..... $E_{p\text{-}p}$
Peak-to-Valley ..... P/V
Peak-to-Valley ..... PTV
Peak-to-Valley Variation (MCD) ..... PTVV
Peak-to-Zero (IAA) ..... PZ
Peale Museum, Baltimore, MD [*Library symbol Library of Congress*] (LCLS) ..... MdBPM
Peanut Advisory Board (EA) ..... PAB
Peanut Agglutinin [*Immunology*] ..... PNA
Peanut and Nut Salters Association [*Later, PBNPA*] (EA) ..... PNSA
Peanut Butter [*Brand name of the Red Wing Co.*] ..... PB
Peanut Butter and Jelly ..... PB and J
Peanut Butter and Jelly ..... PBJ
Peanut Butter and Jelly Sandwich (TAG) ..... PBJ
Peanut Butter and Nut Processors Association (EA) ..... PBNPA
Peanut Butter Manufacturers Association [*Later, PBNPA*] (EA) ..... PBMA
Peanut Butter Sandwich and Cookie Manufacturers Association [*Later, PBNPA*] (EA) ..... PBSCMA
Peanut Clump Virus [*Plant pathology*] ..... PCV
Peanut Flour ..... PF
Peanut Hull Flour ..... PHF
Peanut Leafspot [*Plant pathology*] ..... PL
Peanut Lectin [*Immunochemistry*] ..... PNL
Peanut Mottle Virus [*Plant pathology*] ..... PEMOV
Peanut Mottle Virus ..... PMV
Peanut Pals (EA) ..... PP
Peanut Stunt Virus ..... PSV
Peanut Yellow Mottle Virus [*Plant pathology*] ..... PYMV
Peanut-Butter Sandwich (AD) ..... p-nut butter
Peanut-Butter Sandwich (AD) ..... pnutbutsan
Peanut-Butter Sandwich (AD) ..... pnutbutwich
Peapod Dinghy ..... PEDIN
Pear Tree Wood (VRA) ..... pearwd
Pearce [*Australia ICAO location identifier*] (ICLI) ..... APPE
Pearce Sys Intl [*NASDAQ symbol*] (TTSB) ..... PRCEC
Pearce's Reports in Dearsley's English Crown Cases [*A publication*] (DLA) ..... Pearce CC
Pearl (VRA) ..... prl
Pearl Air Services (U) Ltd. [*Uganda*] [*ICAO designator*] (FAAC) ..... PBY
Pearl Airways Compagne Haitienne [*Haiti*] [*ICAO designator*] (FAAC) ..... HPA
Pearl City, HI [*AM radio station call letters*] ..... KIFO
Pearl City, HI [*FM radio station call letters*] ..... KUCD
Pearl Hall Elementary School, South Houston, TX [*Library symbol*] [*Library of Congress*] (LCLS) ..... TxShoPE
Pearl Harbor, Hawaii ..... PH
Pearl Harbor History Associates (EA) ..... PHHA
Pearl Harbor Naval Shipyard ..... PHNS
Pearl Harbor Naval Shipyard (DOGT) ..... PHNS
Pearl Harbor Navy Yard [*Later, Pearl Harbor Naval Shipyard*] ..... PHNY
Pearl Harbor, Oahu Island [*Hawaii*] [*ICAO location identifier*] (ICLI) ..... PHNC
Pearl Harbor Survivors Association (EA) ..... PHSA
Pearl Harbor Training Facility [*Navy*] ..... PHTF
Pearl Island [*Myanmar*] [*ICAO location identifier*] (ICLI) ..... VBPI
Pearl, MS [*AM radio station call letters*] ..... WJNT
Pearl, MS [*FM radio station call letters*] ..... WVIV
Pearl Necklace Polymer [*Organic chemistry*] ..... PNP
Pearl River Junior College [*Poplarville, MS*] ..... PRJC
Pearl River Public Library, Pearl River, NY [*Library symbol Library of Congress*] (LCLS) ..... NPr
Pearl River Valley Railroad Co. [*AAR code*] ..... PRV
Pearl S. Buck Birthplace Foundation (EA) ..... PSBBF
Pearl S. Buck Birthplace Foundation, Inc. (EA) ..... PBBFI
Pearl S. Buck Birthplace Museum, Hillsboro, WV [*Library symbol Library of Congress*] (LCLS) ..... WvHB
Pearl S. Buck Foundation (EA) ..... PSBF
Pearle Systems Ltd. [*Associated Press*] (SAG) ..... PerleSys
Pearlitic Malleable Iron (MCD) ..... PMI
Pearsall, TX [*AM radio station call letters*] ..... KVWG
Pearsall, TX [*FM radio station call letters*] ..... KVWG-FM
Pearson Aircraft [*ICAO designator*] (AD) ..... YE
Pearson Aviation Corp. [*ICAO designator*] (FAAC) ..... PCR
Pearson, GA [*FM radio station call letters*] (RBYB) ..... WPNG-FM
Pearson Universal Random Generator ..... PURGE
Pearson's Common Pleas [*Pennsylvania*] [*A publication*] (DLA) ..... Pearson
Pearson's Reports [*1850-80*] [*Pennsylvania*] [*A publication*] (DLA) ..... Pears
Pearson's Reports [*1850-80*] [*Pennsylvania*] [*A publication*] (DLA) ..... Pears (PA)
Peasants' and Workers' Party [*India*] [*Political party*] (PPW) ..... PWP
Peasants' National Unity [*Afghanistan*] [*Political party*] (EY) ..... PNU

Pease Community Christian School, Pease, MN [*Library symbol*] [*Library of Congress*] (LCLS) .... MnPeC
Pease Oil & Gas [*NASDAQ symbol*] (TTSB) .... WPOG
Pease Oil & Gas $1 Cv'A'Pfd [*NASDAQ symbol*] (TTSB) .... WPOGP
Pease Oil & Gas Co. [*Associated Press*] (SAG) .... Pease
Pease Oil & Gas Co. [*Associated Press*] (SAG) .... PeaseOG
Pease Oil & Gas Co. [*Associated Press*] (SAG) .... PseOG
Pease Oil & Gas Co. [*NASDAQ symbol*] (SAG) .... WPOG
Peat (ROG) .... P
Peat, Marwick, and Mitchell, Chicago, IL [*Library symbol Library of Congress*] (LCLS) .... ICPMM
Peat, Marwick & Partners, Ottawa, Ontario [*Library symbol National Library of Canada*] (NLC) .... OOPMP
Peat, Marwick & Partners, Toronto, Ontario [*Library symbol National Library of Canada*] (NLC) .... OTPM
Peat, Marwick et Associes, Montreal, PQ, Canada [*Library symbol Library of Congress*] (LCLS) .... CaQMPM
Peat Marwick McLintock [*Accounting firm*] [*British*] .... PMM
Peat, Marwick, Mitchell et Cie., Montreal, Quebec [*Library symbol National Library of Canada*] (NLC) .... QMPM
Peat Moss Association (EA) .... PMA
Peat Producers Association [*British*] (EAIO) .... PPA
Peat Producers Association of the United States (EA) .... PPAUS
Pebas [*Peru*] [*ICAO location identifier*] (ICLI) .... SPEB
Pebble [*Jewelry*] (ROG) .... PEB
Pebble Beach, CA [*FM radio station call letters*] .... KSPB
Pebble Gold Resources [*Vancouver Stock Exchange symbol*] .... PEB
Pebble Springs Nuclear Plant (NRCH) .... PSNP
Pebble-Bed Reactor [*Nuclear energy*] .... PBR
Pebble-Bed Reactor Experiment [*Nuclear energy*] .... PBRE
Pebbles [*Quality of the bottom*] [*Nautical charts*] .... P
PEC Israel Economic [*NYSE symbol*] (TTSB) .... IEC
PEC Israel Economic Corp. [*Associated Press*] (SAG) .... PEC
PEC Israel Economic Corp. Ltd. [*NYSE symbol*] (SAG) .... IEC
Pechichal [*Ecuador*] [*ICAO location identifier*] (ICLI) .... SEPE
Pechiney ADS [*NYSE symbol*] (TTSB) .... PY
Pechiney-Progil [*France*] [*Research code symbol*] .... HC
Pechiney-Ugine-Kuhlmann [*France*] [*Commercial firm*] .... PUK
Pecixe [*Guinea-Bissau*] [*ICAO location identifier*] (ICLI) .... GGPC
Peck (IAA) .... PCK
Peck (AAG) .... PK
Peck (DMAA) .... pk
Peck, MI [*Location identifier FAA*] (FAAL) .... ECK
Peckham Road [*California*] [*Seismograph station code, US Geological Survey*] (SEIS) .... PKC
Peck's Reports [*24-30 Illinois*] [*A publication*] (DLA) .... Peck
Peck's Reports [*7 Tennessee*] [*1921-24*] [*A publication*] (DLA) .... Peck
Peck's Reports [*7 Tennessee*] [*A publication*] (DLA) .... Peck (Tenn)
Peck's Reports, Illinois Supreme Court Reports [*11-22, 24-30*] [*A publication*] (DLA) .... Peck (Ill)
Peck's Trial (Impeachment) [*A publication*] (DLA) .... Peck Tr
Peckwell's English Election Cases [*1802-06*] [*A publication*] (DLA) .... Peck
Peckwell's English Election Cases [*A publication*] (DLA) .... Peck El Cas
Peckwell's English Election Cases [*1802-06*] [*A publication*] (DLA) .... Peck Elec Cas
Peckwell's English Election Cases [*A publication*] (DLA) .... Peckw
Pecky (WGA) .... PKY
Peclet Number [*IUPAC*] .... Pe
PECO En Cap Tr I 8.72% 'TOPrS' [*NYSE symbol*] (TTSB) .... PEPrY
PECO Energy [*Formerly, Philadelphia Electric Co.*] [*NYSE symbol*] (SPSG) .... PE
PECO Energy [*Associated Press*] (SAG) .... PECO
PECO Energy, $3.80 Pfd [*NYSE symbol*] (TTSB) .... PEPrA
PECO Energy, $4.30 Pfd [*NYSE symbol*] (TTSB) .... PEPrB
PECO Energy, $4.40 Pfd [*NYSE symbol*] (TTSB) .... PEPrC
PECO Energy, $4.68 Pfd [*NYSE symbol*] (TTSB) .... PEPrD
PECO Energy Dep Pfd [*NYSE symbol*] (TTSB) .... PEPrF
PECO Energy L.P. MIPS'A' [*NYSE symbol*] (TTSB) .... PEPrZ
Pecos City, TX [*Location identifier FAA*] (FAAL) .... PEQ
Pecos National Monument .... PECO
Pecos Resources [*Vancouver Stock Exchange symbol*] .... PES
Pecos, TX [*AM radio station call letters*] .... KIUN
Pecos, TX [*FM radio station call letters*] (RBYB) .... KKLY-FM
Pecos, TX [*FM radio station call letters*] .... KPTX
[*The*] **Pecos Valley Southern Railway Co.** [*AAR code*] .... PVS
Pecsi Tudomanyegyetem, Pecs, Hungary [*Library symbol Library of Congress*] (LCLS) .... HuPE
Pectate Lyase [*An enzyme*] .... PL
Pectin Acid Lyase [*An enzyme*] .... PAL
Pectin Methylesterase [*Also, PE*] [*An enzyme*] .... PME
Pectin transeliminase [*or Pectate Lyase*] [*An enzyme*] .... PTE
Pectinesterase [*Also, PME*] [*An enzyme*] .... PE
Pectoral [*Anatomy*] (ROG) .... P
Pectoral [*Lungs and Chest*] [*Medicine*] (ROG) .... PEC
Pectoralis Major [*Anatomy*] .... PM
Pectori [*To the Chest*] [*Pharmacy*] .... PECT
Peculiar [*Astronomy*] .... p
Peculiar (ROG) .... PECUL
Peculiar (AD) .... pq
Peculiar and Nonstandard Items (AAG) .... PNS
Peculiar Facility Change (AAG) .... PFC
Peculiar Ground Support Equipment [*DoD*] .... PGSE
Peculiar Meter .... PM
Peculiar Support Equipment [*NASA*] (NASA) .... PSE
Peculiar Test Equipment .... PTE
Pecuniary (ROG) .... PECUY
Pedagogic Algorithmic Language [*Computer science*] .... PAL
Pedagogic Automatic Computer (IEEE) .... PAC
Pedagogischer Austauschdienst [*Pedagogical Exchange Service*] [*German*] .... PAD
Pedagogue .... PED
Pedal .... PED
Pedal Artery .... PEDA
Pedal Blood Vessel .... PBV
Pedal Branch of Columellar [*Muscle*] .... PBC
Pedal Excretory Cell .... PEC
Pedal Furrow .... PF
Pedal Ganglion .... PG
Pedal Groove .... PG
Pedal Mode Ergometer .... PME
Pedal Power .... PP
Pedal Pulse .... PP
Pedal Sinus .... PS
Pedal Steel Guitar Association (EA) .... PSGA
Pedco Energy Ltd. [*Vancouver Stock Exchange symbol*] .... PCE
Peddie School, Hightstown, NJ [*Library symbol Library of Congress*] (LCLS) .... NjHigP
Peddler [*or Peddling*] [*FBI standardized term*] .... PED
Pedernales [*Venezuela*] [*Airport symbol*] (OAG) .... PDZ
Pedestal (IAA) .... PD
Pedestal (VRA) .... pdstl
Pedestal (AAG) .... PED
Pedestal [*Freight*] .... PEDSTL
Pedestal Sight Manipulation Test (IAA) .... PSMT
Pedestal-Mounted Manipulator [*Nuclear energy*] (NRCH) .... PMM
Pedestal-Mounted Stinger [*Army*] .... PMS
Pedestrian (WDAA) .... P
Pedestrian .... PED
Pedestrian League of America [*Later, APA*] (EA) .... PLA
Pedestrians Association [*British*] (DBA) .... PA
Pedestrians Association for Road Safety [*British*] (DI) .... PARS
Pedetemptim [*Gradually*] [*Pharmacy*] .... PEDET
Pediatric [*or Pediatrics*] .... PD
Pediatric .... PEDRTC
Pediatric .... PEDTRC
Pediatric Acquired Immune Deficiency Syndrome [*Medicine*] .... PAIDS
Pediatric AIDS [*Acquired Immune Deficiency Syndrome*] **Coalition** (EA) .... PAC
Pediatric AIDS Foundation (PAZ) .... PAF
Pediatric Allergy [*Medicine*] (DMAA) .... PdA
Pediatric Allergy .... PDA
Pediatric Association of Black French-Speaking Africa (EAIO) .... PABFSA
Pediatric Cardiology [*Medical specialty*] (DHSM) .... PDC
Pediatric Critical Care Medicine (DMAA) .... PCCM
Pediatric Drug Surveillance [*Program*] (DAVI) .... PeDS
Pediatric Drug Surveillance Program (BABM) .... PeDS
Pediatric Early Elementary Examination [*Child development test*] [*Psychology*] .... PEEX
Pediatric Emergency Department (DMAA) .... PED
Pediatric Emergency Room (DAVI) .... Per
Pediatric Endocrinology [*Medical specialty*] (DHSM) .... PDE
Pediatric Examination of Educational Readiness [*Child development test*] .... PEER
Pediatric Examination of Educational Readiness at Middle Childhood [*Child development test*] [*Psychology*] .... PEERAMID
Pediatric Hematology-Oncology [*Medical specialty*] (DHSM) .... PHO
Pediatric Intensive Care Unit [*Medicine*] .... PICU
Pediatric Liver Research Foundation [*Defunct*] (EA) .... PLRF
Pediatric Medical Special Care (DMAA) .... PMSC
Pediatric Nephrology [*Medical specialty*] (DHSM) .... PNP
Pediatric Nurse Practitioner .... PNP
Pediatric Nutrition Surveillance System [*Centers for Disease Control*] (DAVI) .... PNSS
Pediatric Orthopaedic Society of North America (EA) .... POSNA
Pediatric Pneumogram [*Radiology*] (DAVI) .... PPG
Pediatric Radiology [*Medical specialty*] (DHSM) .... PDR
Pediatric Research and Training Center [*University of Connecticut*] [*Research center*] (RCD) .... PRTC
Pediatric Risk of Mortality [*Medicine*] .... PRISM
Pediatric Services of Amer [*NASDAQ symbol*] (TTSB) .... PSAI
Pediatric Services of America, Inc. [*Associated Press*] (SAG) .... Pediatric
Pediatric Services of America, Inc. [*NASDAQ symbol*] (SAG) .... PSAI
Pediatric Surgery [*Medical specialty*] (DHSM) .... PDS
Pediatric Surgery [*Medicine*] (DMAA) .... PdS
Pediatric Surgery (DAVI) .... PS
Pediatric Urine Collector [*Medicine*] .... PUC
Pediatrician .... PED
Pediatric-Modified Diagnosis-Related Group (HCT) .... PM-DRG
Pediatrics (DMAA) .... Pd
Pediatrics (DAVI) .... PE
Pediatrics (AABC) .... PED
Pediatrics [*Medicine*] (DHSM) .... PEDI
Pediatrics .... PEDS
Pediatrix Medical Group [*NASDAQ symbol*] (TTSB) .... PEDX
Pediatrix Medical Group, Inc. [*NASDAQ symbol*] (SAG) .... PEDX
Pediatrix Medical Group, Inc. [*Associated Press*] (SAG) .... PtrixMd
Pedicel Length [*Botany*] .... PEDL
Pedicel Pubescence [*Botany*] .... PDPUB
Pediment (VRA) .... pedm
Pedlary (ROG) .... PED
Pedology .... PEDOL
Pedregulho/Estreito [*Brazil ICAO location identifier*] (ICLI) .... SBET

Pedro Afonso [*Brazil*] [*Airport symbol*] (AD) ... PAB
Pedro Aguirre Cerda [*Antarctica*] [*Seismograph station code, US Geological Survey Closed*] (SEIS) ... PED
Pedro Bay [*Alaska*] [*Airport symbol*] (OAG) ... PDB
Pedro Dome [*Alaska*] [*Seismograph station code, US Geological Survey Closed*] (SEIS) ... PJD
Pedro Ximenez [*A blending sherry*] ... PX
Pedro Ximenez Viejo [*A blending sherry*] ... PXV
Pedunculopontine Nucleus (DMAA) ... PPN
Pedunculopontine Tegmentum [*Neurology*] ... PPT
Pee Dee Belemnite [*An isotopic standard for oxygen and carbon*] ... PDB
Peebles, OH [*Location identifier FAA*] (FAAL) ... PZO
Peekskill Financial [*NASDAQ symbol*] (TTSB) ... PEEK
Peekskill Financial Corp. [*NASDAQ symbol*] (SAG) ... PEEK
Peekskill Financial Corp. [*Associated Press*] (SAG) ... Peekskill
Peekskill, NY [*FM radio station call letters*] ... WHUD
Peekskill, NY [*AM radio station call letters*] ... WLNA
Peeler ... PELR
Peeples and Stevens' Reports [*80-97 Georgia*] [*A publication*] (DLA) ... Peeples & Stevens
Peer Attitudes Toward the Handicapped Scale [*Psychology*] (EDAC) ... PATH
Peer Attitudes Toward the Handicapped Scale [*Educational testing*] ... PATHS
Peer Code Review (IAA) ... PCR
Peer Evaluation Program [*College of American Pathologists*] ... PEP
Peer Nomination Inventory [*Psychology*] ... PNI
Peer Nomination Inventory of Depression [*Child development test*] [*Psychology*] ... PNID
Peer of Ireland (ROG) ... IP
Peer Review ... PR
Peer Review Improvement Act of 1982 ... PRIA
Peer Review Organization [*Medicare*] ... PRO
Peer Review Oversight Group [*National Institutes of Health*] ... PROG
Peer Role-Taking Questionnaire [*Psychology*] (EDAC) ... PRTQ
Peere-Williams' English Chancery and King's Bench Cases [*1695-1736*] [*A publication*] (DLA) ... Peere Wms
Peere-Williams' English Chancery Reports [*1695-1736*] [*A publication*] (DLA) ... P Wms
Peere-Williams' English Chancery Reports [*1695-1736*] [*A publication*] (DLA) ... P Wms (Eng)
Peere-Williams' English Chancery Reports [*1695-1736*] [*A publication*] (DLA) ... PW
Peere-Williams' English Chancery Reports [*A publication*] (DLA) ... Will P
Peere-Williams' English Chancery Reports [*A publication*] (DLA) ... Williams
Peere-Williams' English Chancery Reports [*1695-1736*] [*A publication*] (DLA) ... Williams P
Peere-Williams' English Chancery Reports [*1695-1736*] [*A publication*] (DLA) ... Wms P
Peere-Williams' English Chancery Reports [*A publication*] (DLA) ... Wms Peere
Peerless [*Record label*] [*USA, Mexico*] ... Peer
Peerless Carpet Corp. [*Toronto Stock Exchange symbol*] ... PRG
Peerless Manufacturing Co. [*Associated Press*] (SAG) ... PeerMf
Peerless Manufacturing Co. [*NASDAQ symbol*] (NQ) ... PMFG
Peerless Mfg [*NASDAQ symbol*] (TTSB) ... PMFG
Peerless Motor Car Club (EA) ... PMCC
Peerless Systems Corp. [*Associated Press*] (SAG) ... PrissSys
Peerless Systems Corp. [*NASDAQ symbol*] (SAG) ... PRLS
Peerless Tube Co. [*AMEX symbol*] (SPSG) ... PLS
Peg [*Telecommunications*] (IAA) ... P
Peg Count [*Telecommunications*] (TEL) ... PC
Pega Capital Resources Ltd. [*Toronto Stock Exchange symbol*] ... PGA
Pegasus [*Constellation*] ... Peg
Pegasus [*Constellation*] ... Pegs
Pegasus Communications Corp. [*Associated Press*] (SAG) ... PegaCm
Pegasus Communications Corp. [*NASDAQ symbol*] (SAG) ... PGTV
Pegasus Gold [*AMEX symbol*] (TTSB) ... PGU
Pegasus Gold, Inc. [*Associated Press*] (SAG) ... PegGld
Pegasus Gold, Inc. [*AMEX symbol Toronto Stock Exchange symbol*] ... PGU
Pegasus Hava Tasimaciligi AS [*Turkey*] [*ICAO designator*] (FAAC) ... PGT
Pegasystems, Inc. [*NASDAQ symbol*] (SAG) ... PEGA
Pegasystems, Inc. [*Associated Press*] (SAG) ... Pegasys
Pegboard [*Freight*] ... PGBD
Peggy Lee Fan Club and Archives [*Later, OOPLFC & A*] (EA) ... PLFC & A
Pegu [*Myanmar*] [*ICAO location identifier*] (ICLI) ... VBPG
Pehpei [*Republic of China*] [*Seismograph station code, US Geological Survey*] (SEIS) ... PEH
Pehuajo [*Argentina*] [*Airport symbol*] (OAG) ... PEH
Pehuajo/Comodoro P. Zanni [*Argentina ICAO location identifier*] (ICLI) ... SAZP
Peierls-Nabarro Force [*Physics*] ... PNF
Peine [*Chile*] [*Seismograph station code, US Geological Survey Closed*] (SEIS) ... PEI
Peine/Eddesse [*Germany ICAO location identifier*] (ICLI) ... EDVP
Peipeinimaru, Tinian Island [*Mariana Islands*] [*ICAO location identifier*] (ICLI) ... PGWT
Peipeinimaru, TT [*Location identifier FAA*] (FAAL) ... TNI
Pejepscot Historical Society, Brunswick, ME [*Library symbol Library of Congress*] (LCLS) ... MeBP
Pekanbaru [*Indonesia*] [*Airport symbol*] (OAG) ... PKU
Pekanbaru [*Indonesia*] [*ICAO location identifier*] (ICLI) ... WIBB
Pekin Community High School District No. 30, Pekin, IL [*Library symbol Library of Congress*] (LCLS) ... IPekC
Pekin Community High School, Pekin, IL [*OCLC symbol*] (OCLC) ... IQV
Pekin, IL [*FM radio station call letters*] ... WBNH
Pekin, IL [*FM radio station call letters*] ... WCIC
Pekin, IL [*FM radio station call letters*] ... WGLO
Pekin, IL [*AM radio station call letters*] ... WVEL
Pekin, IL [*FM radio station call letters*] ... WXCL
Pekin Memorial Hospital, Pekin, IL [*Library symbol Library of Congress*] (LCLS) ... IPekH
Pekin Public Library, Pekin, IL [*OCLC symbol*] (OCLC) ... IEW
Pekin Public Library, Pekin, IL [*Library symbol Library of Congress*] (LCLS) ... IPek
Peking [*Republic of China*] [*Seismograph station code, US Geological Survey*] (SEIS) ... BJI2
Peking [*China*] [*Airport symbol*] (AD) ... PEK
Peking [*Republic of China*] [*Seismograph station code, US Geological Survey*] (SEIS) ... PEK
Peking Municipality [*China, Mainland*] [*MARC geographic area code Library of Congress*] (LCCP) ... a-cc-pe
Peking Review [*A publication*] (AD) ... PR
Pekingese Club of America (EA) ... PCA
Pekoe [*Tea trade*] (ROG) ... PEK
Pelabuhan Ratu [*Indonesia*] [*ICAO location identifier*] (ICLI) ... WIIR
Pelagius [*Deceased, 1232*] [*Authority cited in pre-1607 legal work*] (DSA) ... P
Pelagius [*Deceased, 1232*] [*Authority cited in pre-1607 legal work*] (DSA) ... Pe
Pelagius [*Deceased, 1232*] [*Authority cited in pre-1607 legal work*] (DSA) ... Pel
Pelagius [*Deceased, 1232*] [*Authority cited in pre-1607 legal work*] (DSA) ... Pl
Pelagius [*Deceased, 1232*] [*Authority cited in pre-1607 legal work*] (DSA) ... Pla
Pelaneng [*Lesotho*] [*ICAO location identifier*] (ICLI) ... FXPG
Pelaneng [*Lesotho*] [*Airport symbol*] (OAG) ... PEL
Pelangi Air Sdn. Bhd. [*Malaysia*] [*FAA designator*] (FAAC) ... PEG
Pelargonium Flower Break Virus [*Plant pathology*] ... PFBV
Pelargonium Leaf Curl Virus [*Plant pathology*] ... PLCV
Pelargonium Line Pattern Virus [*Plant pathology*] ... PLPV
Pelargonium Vein Clearing Virus [*Plant pathology*] ... PVCV
Pelargonium Zonate Spot Virus [*Plant pathology*] ... PZSV
Peldehue [*Chile*] [*Seismograph station code, US Geological Survey*] (SEIS) ... PEL
Pele Defense Fund (EA) ... PDF
Pelee Island Public Library, Ontario [*Library symbol National Library of Canada*] (NLC) ... OPIS
Pelerinage a Notre Dame de Beauraing [*An association*] (EAIO) ... PNDB
Pelger Muet Anomaly [*Laboratory science*] (DAVI) ... PELG
Pelham, GA [*Television station call letters*] ... WABW
Pelham Grenville Wodehouse [*British humorist, 1881-1975*] ... PG
Pelham Public Library, Pelham, NY [*Library symbol Library of Congress*] (LCLS) ... NPel
Pelican [*Alaska*] [*Airport symbol*] (OAG) ... PEC
Pelican Man's Bird Sanctuary (EA) ... PMBS
Pelican Mountain School, Desmarais, Alberta [*Library symbol National Library of Canada*] (BIB) ... ADESPS
Pelican Narrows Public Library, Saskatchewan [*Library symbol National Library of Canada*] (NLC) ... SPN
Pelican Rapids High School, Pelican Rapids, MN [*Library symbol*] [*Library of Congress*] (LCLS) ... MnPerH
Pelican Rapids, MN [*FM radio station call letters*] ... KBOT
Pelita Air Service PT [*Indonesia*] [*ICAO designator*] (FAAC) ... PAS
Pell City, AL [*Location identifier FAA*] (FAAL) ... PLR
Pell City, AL [*AM radio station call letters*] ... WFHK
Pella Chronicle, Pella, IA [*Library symbol Library of Congress*] (LCLS) ... IaPeCh
Pella, IA [*FM radio station call letters*] (RBYB) ... KAZR-FM
Pella, IA [*FM radio station call letters*] ... KCUI
Pella, IA [*FM radio station call letters*] ... KFMG
Pella, IA [*Location identifier FAA*] (FAAL) ... PEA
Pella Public Library, Pella, IA [*Library symbol Library of Congress*] (LCLS) ... IaPe
Pellagra Preventive (AD) ... pp
Pellagra Preventive [*Factor*] [*See also PPF*] [*Biochemistry*] ... PP
Pellagra Preventive Factor [*See also PP*] [*Biochemistry*] ... PPF
Pellagra-Preventive Factor (AD) ... P-P
Pellagra-Preventive Factor (AD) ... p-p factor
Pellet Clad Interaction [*Nuclear energy*] (NRCH) ... PCI
Pellet Size ... PS
Pellet Warhead ... PWH
Pellet-Fired Appliance [*Heating system*] ... PFA
Pellin-Broca Prism [*Physics*] ... PBP
Pellissippi Stat Technical Community College, Knoxville, TN [*Library symbol*] [*Library of Congress*] (LCLS) ... TKPT
Pello [*Finland ICAO location identifier*] (ICLI) ... EFPE
Pellston [*Michigan*] [*Airport symbol*] (OAG) ... PLN
Pellston, MI [*Location identifier FAA*] (FAAL) ... EPE
Pellston, MI [*Location identifier FAA*] (FAAL) ... PLN
Pellston Public Library, Pellston, MI [*Library symbol Library of Congress*] (LCLS) ... MiPel
Pelly Bay [*Canada*] [*Airport symbol*] (OAG) ... YUF
Pelly Bay, NT [*ICAO location identifier*] (ICLI) ... CYBB
Pelly Bay, NT [*ICAO location identifier*] (ICLI) ... CYUF
Pelon Nuevo [*Costa Rica*] [*ICAO location identifier*] (ICLI) ... MRPN
Pelopidas [*of Plutarch*] [*Classical studies*] (OCD) ... Pel
Pelorus ... PLRS
Pelorus Stand ... PLRSTN
Pelotas [*Brazil*] [*Airport symbol*] (OAG) ... PET
Pelotas [*Brazil ICAO location identifier*] (ICLI) ... SBPK
Pelsart Resources ADR [*NASDAQ symbol*] (TTSB) ... PELRY
Pelsart Resources NL [*NASDAQ symbol*] (NQ) ... PELR
Pelsart Resources NL [*Associated Press*] (SAG) ... Pelsart
Peltier Effect Diffusion Separation [*Physical chemistry*] ... PEDS
Peltier's Orleans Appeals [*1917-23*] [*A publication*] (DLA) ... Pelt
Peltier's Orleans Appeals Decisions [*Louisiana*] [*A publication*] (DLA) ... Plt
Pelusium Line [*Nile delta*] [*Geology*] ... PL
Pelvic and Rectal [*Medicine*] ... P & R
Pelvic Exam under Anesthesia [*Medicine*] ... PEUA
Pelvic Flexion Contracture [*Orthopedics*] (DAVI) ... PFC
Pelvic Floor Exercise (DMAA) ... PFE

Pelvic Inflammatory Disease [*Medicine*] ... PID

Pelvic Lymph Node [*Gynecology*] (DAVI) ... PLN

Pelvic Rock [*Orthopedics*] (DAVI) ... PR

Pelvic Sonoangiography [*Medicine*] (DMAA) ... PSAG

Pelvis and Legs Elevating [*Pilot seat*] ... PALE

Pem Air [*ICAO designator*] (AD) ... PD

PEMA Item Baseline List [*Army*] (AABC) ... PIBL

PEMA Policy and Guidance [*Military*] (AABC) ... PPG

PEM-AIR Ltd. [*Canada ICAO designator*] (FAAC) ... PEM

PEMARS [*Procurement of Equipment and Missiles, Army Management and AccountingReporting System*] **Accounting and Reporting Control Point** [*Army*] ... PARCP

Pematang Siantar/Gunung Pamela [*Indonesia*] [*ICAO location identifier*] (ICLI) ... WIMR

Pemba [*Mozambique*] [*ICAO location identifier*] (ICLI) ... FQPB

Pemba [*Tanzania*] [*ICAO location identifier*] (ICLI) ... HTPE

Pemba [*Mozambique*] [*Airport symbol*] (OAG) ... POL

Pemba Island [*Tanzania*] [*Airport symbol*] (OAG) ... PMA

Pemberton, BC [*FM radio station call letters*] ... CISP

Pemberton Exploration [*Vancouver Stock Exchange symbol*] ... PBE

Pemberton Houston Willoughby Investment Corp. [*Toronto Stock Exchange symbol Vancouver Stock Exchange symbol*] ... PHW

Pemberton Museum, British Columbia [*Library symbol National Library of Canada*] (NLC) ... BPEMM

Pemberton Museum, Pemberton, BC, Canada [*Library symbol*] [*Library of Congress*] (LCLS) ... CaBPEMM

Pemberton, NJ [*FM radio station call letters*] ... WBZC

Pemberton's Judgments and Orders [*A publication*] (DLA) ... Pemb Judg

Pemberton's Practice in Equity by Way of Revivor and Supplement [*1867*] [*A publication*] (ILCA) ... Pemb Eq

Pembina [*North Dakota*] [*ICAO location identifier*] (ICLI) ... KPMB

Pembina, ND [*Television station call letters*] ... KNRR

Pembina, ND [*Location identifier FAA*] (FAAL) ... PMB

Pembina Resources Ltd. [*Toronto Stock Exchange symbol*] ... PPL

Pembroke [*Canada*] [*Airport symbol*] (OAG) ... YTA

Pembroke College [*Oxford and Cambridge Universities*] (ROG) ... PEMB

Pembroke County Day School, Kansas City, MO [*Library symbol Library of Congress*] (LCLS) ... MoKPC

Pembroke Hill School, Kansas City, MO [*Library symbol*] [*Library of Congress*] (LCLS) ... MoKPHS

Pembroke Imperial Yeomanry [*British military*] (DMA) ... PIY

Pembroke, NH [*Location identifier FAA*] (FAAL) ... PBR

Pembroke, ON [*Television station call letters*] ... CHRO

Pembroke, ON [*AM radio station call letters*] ... CHVR

Pembroke, ON [*FM radio station call letters*] (RBYB) ... CHVR-FM

Pembroke Public Library, Ontario [*Library symbol National Library of Canada*] (NLC) ... OPEM

Pembroke Public Library, Pembroke, ON, Canada [*Library symbol Library of Congress*] (LCLS) ... CaOPem

Pembroke State College [*North Carolina*] ... PSC

Pembroke State University, Pembroke, NC [*Library symbol Library of Congress*] (LCLS) ... NcPeS

Pembroke Welsh Corgi Club of America (EA) ... PWCCA

Pembroke Yeomanry [*British military*] (DMA) ... Pem Yeo

Pembroke Yeomanry [*British military*] (DMA) ... PY

Pembroke Yeomanry Cavalry [*British military*] (DMA) ... PYC

Pembrokeshire [*County in Wales*] (ROG) ... PEM

Pembrokeshire [*County in Wales*] ... PEMB

Pembrokeshire [*County in Wales*] ... PEMBS

Pemo [*Congo*] [*ICAO location identifier*] (ICLI) ... FCPO

Pemphigus Vulgaris [*Dermatology*] ... PV

Pen [*Sports*] ... P

Pen (VRA) ... pe

PEN American Center (EA) ... PEN

Pen and Brush Club (EA) ... PBC

Pen and Brush, Inc. (EA) ... PBI

Pen and Ink (VRA) ... pe/i

Pen and Ink ... PI

Pen and Pocket Blade Forgers' and Smithers' Protective Society [*A union*] [*British*] ... PPBFSPS

Pen and Pocket Knife Cutters' Association [*A union*] [*British*] ... PPKCA

Pen Application Development System [*Computer software*] [*Slate Corp.*] (PCM) ... PADS

Pen Center USA West (EA) ... PCUSAW

PEN [*Poets, Playwrights, Essayists, Editors, and Novelists*] **Club of PuertoRico** (EA) ... PENCPR

Pen Fancier's Club (EA) ... PFC

Pen Friends [*Defunct*] (EA) ... PF

Pen Input to Computer and Scanned Screen Output [*Computer science*] (PDAA) ... PICASSO

Pen Interconnect [*NASDAQ symbol*] (TTSB) ... PENC

Pen Interconnect, Inc. [*NASDAQ symbol*] (SAG) ... PENC

Pen Interconnect, Inc. [*Associated Press*] (SAG) ... PenInt

Pen Interconnect, Inc. [*Associated Press*] (SAG) ... PenInter

Pen Interconnect Wrrt [*NASDAQ symbol*] (TTSB) ... PENCW

Pen Plotter Emulation Program [*Computer science*] (MHDI) ... PPEP

Pen Record (SAA) ... PR

Pen Recorder Output (SAA) ... PRO

Pen User Interface [*Computer science*] ... PUI

Penal Code [*A publication*] (DLA) ... PC

Penal Code [*A publication*] (DLA) ... Pen C

Penal Reform League Monthly Record [*1909-12*] [*A publication*] (DLA) ... Pen Ref League M Rec

Penal Reform League Quarterly Record [*1912-20*] [*A publication*] (DLA) ... Pen Ref League Q Rec

Penal Reformer [*1934-39*] [*A publication*] (DLA) ... Pen Ref

Penal Servitude ... PS

Penalties in Minutes [*Hockey*] ... PIM

Penalty Appeals Officer [*IRS*] ... PAO

Penalty Assessment Criteria [*Environmental Protection Agency*] ... PAC

Penalty Cost Model ... PCM

Penalty Minutes [*Hockey*] ... PM

Penang [*Malaysia*] [*Airport symbol*] (OAG) ... PEN

Penang (AD) ... Png

Penang [*Malaysia*] [*ICAO location identifier*] (ICLI) ... WMKP

Penarth Research International Ltd. [*British*] ... PRIL

Penas [*Bolivia*] [*Seismograph station code, US Geological Survey*] (SEIS) ... PNS

Penault's Prerosti de Quebec [*A publication*] (DLA) ... Pen P

Pence [*Monetary unit*] [*British*] ... p

Penciclovir [*Antiherpetic*] ... PCV

Pencil (MSA) ... PCL

Pencil (VRA) ... pl

Pencil Beam Antenna ... PBA

Pencil Beam RADAR ... PBR

Pencil Industry Export Association [*Defunct*] (EA) ... PIEA

Pencil Makers Association (EA) ... PMA

Pencil Note on Back [*Philately*] ... pnob

Pencil Tube (MDG) ... P

Pencil Tube ... PT

Pencil Writing on Back [*Deltiology*] ... PWB

Pencillin (AD) ... pnc

Pencrude Resources, Inc. [*Vancouver Stock Exchange symbol*] ... PNC

Pend Oreille County Library District, Newport, WA [*Library symbol*] [*Library of Congress*] (LCLS) ... WaNe

Pend Oreille Valley Railroad (AD) ... POV

Pendant [*Jewelry*] (ROG) ... PEDT

Pendant (ROG) ... Pend

Pendant (VRA) ... pend

Pendant Drop Method ... PDM

Pendant-Drop Melt Extraction [*Metal fiber technology*] ... PDME

Pendeli [*Greece*] [*Geomagnetic observatory code*] ... PEN

Pendens [*Weighing*] [*Pharmacy*] ... PEND

Pendentive (VRA) ... pndnt

Pender County Library, Burgaw, NC [*Library symbol Library of Congress*] (LCLS) ... NcBurgP

Pender County Library, Hampstead Branch Library, Hampstead, NC [*Library symbol*] [*Library of Congress*] (LCLS) ... NcBurgP-H

Pender Harbour, BC [*FM radio station call letters*] ... CIPN

Pender Island [*British Columbia*] [*Seismograph station code, US Geological Survey*] (SEIS) ... PIB

Pending ... PEND

Pending ... PND

Pending (AFM) ... PNDG

Pending (AD) ... pndg

Pending Availability ... PA

Pending Contractual Matters (NRCH) ... PCM

Pending Work Release Order (MCD) ... PWRO

Pendle Hill Library, Wallingford, PA [*Library symbol Library of Congress*] (LCLS) ... PWalPH

Pendleton [*Oregon*] [*Airport symbol*] (OAG) ... PDT

Pendleton [*Oregon*] [*Seismograph station code, US Geological Survey*] (SEIS) ... PNO

Pendleton and Fall Creek Township Public Library, Pendleton, IN [*Library symbol Library of Congress*] (LCLS) ... InPen

Pendleton Community Hospital, Pendleton, OR [*Library symbol Library of Congress*] (LCLS) ... OrPeCH

Pendleton, IN [*FM radio station call letters*] ... WEEM

Pendleton, OR [*FM radio station call letters*] ... KRBM

Pendleton, OR [*AM radio station call letters*] ... KTIX

Pendleton, OR [*AM radio station call letters*] ... KUMA

Pendleton, OR [*FM radio station call letters*] ... KUMA-FM

Pendleton, OR [*FM radio station call letters*] ... KWHT

Pendleton Times, Pendleton, IN [*Library symbol Library of Congress*] (LCLS) ... InPenT

Pendoro [*Indonesia*] [*ICAO location identifier*] (ICLI) ... WIPQ

Pendular ... PNDLR

Pendular Eye-Tracking Test [*Medicine*] (DMAA) ... PETT

Pendulous Axis [*Accelerometer*] (IEEE) ... PA

Pendulous Gyro Accelerometer ... PGA

Pendulous Gyro Integrating Accelerometer (IAA) ... PGIA

Pendulous Integrating Gyro ... PIG

Pendulous Integrating Gyro Accelerometer ... PIGA

Pendulous Integrating Gyro Unit ... PIGU

Pendulous Reference Axis [*Accelerometer*] (IEEE) ... PRA

Penederm, Inc. [*NASDAQ symbol*] (SAG) ... DERM

Penederm, Inc. [*Associated Press*] (SAG) ... Penedrm

Penelec Capital Ltd. [*NYSE symbol*] (SAG) ... PEC

Penelec Capital Ltd. [*Associated Press*] (SAG) ... Penelc

Penelec Capital L.P. 'MIPS' [*NYSE symbol*] (TTSB) ... PECPrZ

Penetanguishene Public Library, Ontario [*Library symbol National Library of Canada*] (BIB) ... OPEN

Penetrant Test [*Nuclear energy*] (NRCH) ... PT

Penetrate (AABC) ... PENT

Penetrate Dorfman [*FBI investigation of Teamster leader Allen Dorfman*] ... PENDORF

Penetrate Gray Electronics Markets [*FBI "sting" operation, 1982, where employees of Japanese computer firms were caught trying to obtain proprietary information illegally from IBM Co.*] ... PENGEM

Penetrating Cell ... PC

Penetrating Keratoplasty [*Ophthalmology*] (DAVI) ... PK

Penetrating Keratoplasty [*Ophthalmology*] .... PKP
Penetrating Wound .... PENW
Penetration (AFM) .... PEN
Penetration Aid [*Weaponry*] .... PENAID
Penetration Aids Deployment [*Weaponry*] (DWSG) .... PAD
Penetration Aids Deployment Concept (SAA) .... PAC
Penetration Aids/Strike System (NG) .... PASS
Penetration Augmented Munition .... PAM
Penetration Diameter [*Military*] .... P/D
Penetration Evaluation [*Military*] (NVT) .... PENVAL
Penetration for Tactical Aircraft [*Air Force*] .... PENTAC
Penetration Fracture (IAA) .... PF
Penetration Index (IAA) .... PI
Penetration of Radiation Through Aperture Simulation (PDAA) .... PORTAS
Penetration RADAR .... PENRAD
Penetration Report [*National Security Agency*] .... PENREP
Penetration Room Filtration [*Nuclear energy*] (NRCH) .... PRF
Penetration Room Ventilation System [*Nuclear energy*] (IEEE) .... PRVS
Penetration Survivability Assessment Model (MCD) .... PENSAM
Penetration Test (NATG) .... PT
Penetration Test Vehicle [*Aerospace*] .... PTV
Penetration Zone (Radius) (MCD) .... PZ(R)
Penetrator, High-Explosive, Incendiary (MCD) .... PHEI
Penfield High School Library, Penfield, NY [*OCLC symbol*] (OCLC) .... RXD
Pengelly Mines Ltd. [*Vancouver Stock Exchange symbol*] .... PEY
Penghu [*Hokoto*] [*Republic of China*] [*Seismograph station code, US Geological Survey*] (SEIS) .... PNG
Pengo [*Monetary unit in Hungary until 1946*] .... P
Peng-Robinson [*Equation of state*] .... PR
Pengrowth Gas Income Fund Trust Units [*Toronto Stock Exchange symbol*] .... PGF
Penguin Modern Classics [*Book publishing*] .... PMC
Penhold Public Library, Alberta [*Library symbol National Library of Canada*] (NLC) .... AP
Penicillin .... P
Penicillin [*Antibiotic*] .... PCN
Penicillin [*Antibiotic*] .... PEN
Penicillin [*Medicine*] (DMAA) .... Pen
Penicillin [*Antibiotic*] .... PENIC
Penicillin .... PNC
Penicillin Aluminum Monostearate [*Antibiotic*] .... PAM
Penicillin G [*Antibacterial agent*] .... PenG
Penicillin G [*Medicine*] (DMAA) .... PNG
Penicillin G Benzathine [*Pharmacology*] (DAVI) .... DBED
Penicillin in Beeswax [*Medicine*] (DMAA) .... PBO
Penicillin in Beeswax and Oil [*Medicine*] (DMAA) .... PBO
Penicillin, Oil, Beeswax [*Medicine*] .... POB
Penicillin Skin Test [*Immunology*] .... PenST
Penicillin, Streptomycin, and Tetracycline [*Antibiotics*] (MAE) .... PST
Penicillin V Postassium [*An antibiotic*] (DAVI) .... Pen VK
Penicillin V Potassium [*Medicine*] (DMAA) .... PVK
Penicillin V Potassium [*Biochemistry*] (MAE) .... PVP
Penicillinase-Producing Neisseria gonorrhoeae .... PPNG
Penicillin-Binding Protein [*Biochemistry*] .... PBP
Penicillin-Nonsusceptible S. Pneumoniae [*Clinical chemistry*] .... PNSP
Penicillin-Resistant S. Pneumoniae [*Clinical chemistry*] .... PRSP
Penicillin-Sensitive Enzymes [*Biochemistry*] .... PSE
Penicillium roqueforti [*Toxin*] [*Medicine*] .... PR
Penicilloyl Polylysine [*Pharmacology*] .... PPL
Penicillum Camelinum [*A Camel's-Hair Brush*] [*Pharmacy*] .... Penic Cam
Penile Erection [*Medicine*] (DMAA) .... PE
Penile-Brachial Index [*Medicine*] (DAVI) .... PBI
Peninsula .... PEN
Peninsula [*Maps and charts*] .... PEN
Peninsula .... penin
Peninsula [*Alaska*] [*Seismograph station code, US Geological Survey*] (SEIS) .... PNL
Peninsula Airways [*ICAO designator*] (AD) .... KS
Peninsula Airways, Inc. [*ICAO designator*] (FAAC) .... PEN
Peninsula College, Port Angeles, WA [*Library symbol Library of Congress*] (LCLS) .... WaPoP
Peninsula Community Library, Traverse City, MI [*Library symbol Library of Congress*] (LCLS) .... MiTP
Peninsula Drafting Management Association .... PDMA
Peninsula Elementary School, Lawrence, NY [*Library symbol Library of Congress*] (LCLS) .... NLawPE
Peninsula Enrichment Program for Bright Needy Children [*Queensland, Australia*] .... PEPBNC
Peninsula Library System [*Belmont, CA*] [*Library network*] .... PLS
Peninsula Library System, Belmont, CA [*Library symbol Library of Congress*] (LCLS) .... CBelmP
Peninsula Library System, Belmont, CA [*OCLC symbol*] (OCLC) .... CZP
Peninsula Petroleum Corp. [*Vancouver Stock Exchange symbol*] .... PPU
Peninsula Public Library, Lawrence, NY [*Library symbol Library of Congress*] (LCLS) .... NLaw
Peninsula Terminal Co. [*AAR code*] .... PT
Peninsula Trust Bank [*NASDAQ symbol*] (TTSB) .... PNTB
Peninsula Trust Bank, Inc. [*Associated Press*] (SAG) .... PeninTst
Peninsula Trust Bank, Inc. [*NASDAQ symbol*] (SAG) .... PNTB
Peninsular & Occidental Steamship Co. (AD) .... P & O
Peninsular & Oriental Steam Navigation Co. [*Steamship line*] .... P & O
Peninsular & Oriental Steam Navigation Co. [*Steamship line*] .... P & OSNCo
Peninsular & Oriental (Steam Navigation) Co. Ltd. (ROG) .... P & OC
Peninsular Base Section [*Military*] .... PBS
Peninsular Base Section [*Military*] .... PENBASE
Peninsular Chemresearch [*Calgon Corp.*] .... PCR
Peninsular/Oriental Steam Nav [*LO Symbol*] (TTSB) .... PORL
Penitent .... PEN
Penitentiary (WDAA) .... PEN
Penitentiary .... PENIT
Penn America Group [*NASDAQ symbol*] (SAG) .... PAGI
Penn America Group [*Associated Press*] (SAG) .... PennAm
Penn Central Transportation Co. [*Subsidiary of Penn Central Corp.*] [*Absorbed into Consolidated Rail Corp.*] [*AAR code*] .... PC
Penn Central Transportation Co. .... PCTC
Penn Engineering & Manufacturing Corp. [*Associated Press*] (SAG) .... PenEM
Penn Engineering & Manufacturing Corp. [*Associated Press*] (SAG) .... PenEMA
Penn Engineering & Manufacturing Corp. [*AMEX symbol*] (SPSG) .... PNN
Penn Engr & Mfg [*AMEX symbol*] (TTSB) .... PNN
Penn Engr & Mfg'A' [*AMEX symbol*] (TTSB) .... PNN.A
Penn Enterprises, Inc. [*Associated Press*] (SAG) .... PennEn
Penn Enterprises, Inc. [*NYSE symbol*] (SAG) .... PNT
Penn Hall Junior College [*Pennsylvania*] [*Closed, 1973*] .... PHJC
Penn National Gaming [*NASDAQ symbol*] (TTSB) .... PENN
Penn National Gaming, Inc. [*NASDAQ symbol*] (SAG) .... PENN
Penn National Gaming, Inc. [*Associated Press*] (SAG) .... PenNGm
Penn Octane [*NASDAQ symbol*] (TTSB) .... POCC
Penn Octane Corp. [*Associated Press*] (SAG) .... PennOct
Penn Octane Corp. [*NASDAQ symbol*] (SAG) .... POCC
Penn Pwr & Lt 4.40% Pfd [*NYSE symbol*] (TTSB) .... PPLPrA
Penn Pwr & Lt 4.50% Pfd [*NYSE symbol*] (TTSB) .... PPLPrB
Penn State Microoxidation Test [*Analytical chemistry*] .... PeSMoT
Penn State TRIGA [*Training Reactor, Isotopes General Atomic*] **Reactor** .... PSTR
Penn State University Automatic Digital Computer .... PENNSTAC
Penn Telecom, Inc. [*Gibsonia, PA*] (TSSD) .... PTI
Penn Traffic [*NYSE symbol*] (TTSB) .... PNF
Penn Traffic Co. [*Associated Press*] (SAG) .... PennTr
Penn Traffic Co. [*NYSE symbol*] (SAG) .... PNF
Penn Treaty American [*Associated Press*] (SAG) .... PennTrty
Penn Treaty American [*NASDAQ symbol*] (TTSB) .... PTAC
Penn Treaty American Corp. [*Associated Press*] (SAG) .... PenTrt
Penn Treaty American Corp. [*NASDAQ symbol*] (NQ) .... PTAC
Penn Valley Junior College, Kansas City, MO [*Library symbol Library of Congress*] (LCLS) .... MoKP
Penn Virginia [*NASDAQ symbol*] (TTSB) .... PVIR
Penn Virginia Corp. [*Associated Press*] (SAG) .... PennVa
Penn Virginia Corp. [*NASDAQ symbol*] (NQ) .... PVIR
Penn West Petroleum Ltd. [*Toronto Stock Exchange symbol*] .... PWT
Penn Yan, NY [*Location identifier FAA*] (FAAL) .... PYA
Penn Yan, NY [*AM radio station call letters*] .... WYLF
Penn Yan Public Library, Penn Yan, NY [*Library symbol Library of Congress*] (LCLS) .... NPy
Penna Enterprises [*NYSE symbol*] (TTSB) .... PNT
Penna RE Inv Tr SNI [*AMEX symbol*] (TTSB) .... PEI
Penn-America Group [*NASDAQ symbol*] (TTSB) .... PAGI
Pennant (MSA) .... PNNT
Pennant [*British naval signaling*] .... PT
Pennant Resources Ltd. [*Toronto Stock Exchange symbol*] .... PNR
Penncorp Financial Group [*Associated Press*] (SAG) .... Pencp
Penncorp Financial Group [*Associated Press*] (SAG) .... PencpFn
PennCorp Financial Group [*NYSE symbol*] (SPSG) .... PFG
PennCorp Finl $3.375 Pfd [*NYSE symbol*] (TTSB) .... PFGPr
Penner Serotype-O [*Laboratory science*] (DAVI) .... PEN-O
Penneshaw [*Australia Airport symbol*] (OAG) .... PEA
Pennewill's Delaware Reports [*A publication*] (DLA) .... Pe R
Pennewill's Delaware Reports [*A publication*] (DLA) .... Pen
Pennewill's Delaware Reports [*A publication*] (DLA) .... Penn
Pennewill's Delaware Reports [*A publication*] (DLA) .... Penn Del
Pennewill's Delaware Reports [*17-23 Delaware*] [*1897-1909*] [*A publication*] (DLA) .... Penne
Pennewill's Delaware Reports [*A publication*] (DLA) .... Pennew
Pennewill's Delaware Supreme Court Reports [*1897-1909*] [*A publication*] (DLA) .... Pennewill
Penney [*J. C.*] **Co., Inc.** [*NYSE symbol*] (SPSG) .... JCP
Penney [*J. C.*] **Co., Inc.** [*Associated Press*] (SAG) .... Penney
Penney (J.C.) [*NYSE symbol*] (TTSB) .... JCP
PennFed Financial Services, Inc. [*Associated Press*] (SAG) .... PennFed
PennFed Financial Services, Inc. [*NASDAQ symbol*] (SAG) .... PFSB
PennFed Financial Svcs [*NASDAQ symbol*] (TTSB) .... PFSB
PennFirst Bancorp [*Associated Press*] (SAG) .... PennBc
PennFirst Bancorp [*Associated Press*] (SAG) .... PennBcp
PennFirst Bancorp [*NASDAQ symbol*] (SAG) .... PWBC
Pennhurst State School and Hospital, Spring City, PA [*OCLC symbol*] (OCLC) .... PHP
Penni(a) [*Penny or Pence*] [*Monetary unit*] [*Finland*] (GPO) .... p
Pennichuck Corp. [*Associated Press*] (SAG) .... Penchk
Pennichuck Corp. [*NASDAQ symbol*] (SAG) .... PNNW
Pennie, Edmonds, Morton, Taylor & Adams, New York, NY [*Library symbol Library of Congress*] (LCLS) .... NNPennie
Pennilane Development [*Vancouver Stock Exchange symbol*] .... PLA
Penning Ionization Electron Spectroscopy .... PIES
Penning Ionization Gauge (IAA) .... PIG
Penning Ionization Spectroscopy (PDAA) .... PIS
Pennington County Extension Office, Thief River Falls, MN [*Library symbol*] [*Library of Congress*] (LCLS) .... MnTPC
Pennington Gap, VA [*Location identifier FAA*] (FAAL) .... LQV
Pennington Gap, VA [*Location identifier FAA*] (FAAL) .... PTG
Pennington Gap, VA [*AM radio station call letters*] .... WSWV
Pennington Gap, VA [*FM radio station call letters*] .... WSWV-FM
Pennington's New Jersey Reports [*2, 3 New Jersey*] [*A publication*] (DLA) .... Pen

Pennington's New Jersey Reports [*2, 3 New Jersey*] [*A publication*] (DLA) ... Pen NJ
Pennington's New Jersey Reports [*A publication*] (DLA) ... Penn
Pennington's New Jersey Reports [*2, 3 New Jersey*] [*A publication*] (DLA) ... Penning
Pennington's Stores Ltd. [*Toronto Stock Exchange symbol*] ... PNS
Penns Grove Record, Penns Grove, NJ [*Library symbol Library of Congress*] (LCLS) ... NjPegR
Pennsauken Resume, Pennsauken, NJ [*Library symbol Library of Congress*] (LCLS) ... NjPenP
Pennsuco, FL [*FM radio station call letters*] ... WFHQ
Pennsuco, FL [*FM radio station call letters*] (RBYB) ... WIRP-FM
Pennsylvania [*MARC geographic area code Library of Congress*] (LCCP) ... n-us-pa
Pennsylvania (DLA) ... P
Pennsylvania [*Postal code*] ... PA
Pennsylvania (ODBW) ... Pa
Pennsylvania [*MARC country of publication code Library of Congress*] (LCCP) ... pau
Pennsylvania ... PENN
Pennsylvania (ODBW) ... Penn
Pennsylvania (ODBW) ... Penna
Pennsylvania ... PENNA
Pennsylvania Academy of the Fine Arts ... PAFA
Pennsylvania Academy of the Fine Arts, Philadelphia, PA [*Library symbol Library of Congress Obsolete*] (LCLS) ... PPAFA
Pennsylvania Administrative Code [*A publication*] (DLA) ... PA Admin Code
Pennsylvania Advanced Reactor ... PAR
Pennsylvania & Atlantic Railroad Co. (IIA) ... P & A
Pennsylvania & Atlantic Railroad Co. [*Absorbed into Consolidated Rail Corp.*] [*AAR code*] ... PAUT
Pennsylvania Animal Network [*Coalition operated by Trans-Species Unlimited*] ... PAN
Pennsylvania Area Library Network ... PALINET
Pennsylvania Area Library Network, Philadelphia, PA [*OCLC symbol*] (OCLC) ... TQQ
Pennsylvania Area Library Network, Philadelphia, PA [*OCLC symbol*] (OCLC) ... TQR
Pennsylvania Association for Retarded Children (EDAC) ... PARC
Pennsylvania Association of Notaries (EA) ... PAN
Pennsylvania Avenue Development Corp. [*Washington, DC*] [*Federal corporatio n*] ... PADC
Pennsylvania Ballet ... PB
Pennsylvania Bank Cases [*A publication*] (DLA) ... PA Bk Cas
Pennsylvania Bar Association. Reports [*A publication*] (DLA) ... PA BA
Pennsylvania Bar Brief [*A publication*] (DLA) ... PA B Brief
Pennsylvania Bulletin [*A publication*] (DLA) ... PA Admin Bull
Pennsylvania Bureau of Municipal Research (MCD) ... PBMR
Pennsylvania Central Railroad (ROG) ... PCRR
Pennsylvania Coal Mining Association (EA) ... PCMA
Pennsylvania College of Optometry (GAGS) ... Penn C Opt
Pennsylvania College of Optometry, Philadelphia, PA [*Library symbol Library of Congress*] (LCLS) ... PPPCO
Pennsylvania Common Pleas Reporter [*A publication*] (DLA) ... PA Com Pl
Pennsylvania Common Pleas Reporter [*A publication*] (DLA) ... PA CP
Pennsylvania Commonwealth Court Reports [*A publication*] (DLA) ... PA C
Pennsylvania Commonwealth Court Reports [*A publication*] (DLA) ... PA Cmwlth
Pennsylvania Commonwealth Court Reports [*A publication*] (DLA) ... PA Commw
Pennsylvania Commonwealth Court Reports [*A publication*] (DLA) ... PA Commw Ct
Pennsylvania Commonwealth Reports [*A publication*] (AAGC) ... Pa Commw
Pennsylvania Commuter Airlines [*Airline code*] ... EB
Pennsylvania Commuter Airlines, Inc. [*ICAO designator*] (FAAC) ... ALO
Pennsylvania Comprehensive Mathematics Plan (EDAC) ... PCMP
Pennsylvania Comprehensive Reading Program (EDAC) ... PCRP
Pennsylvania Consolidated Statutes [*A publication*] (DLA) ... PA Cons Stat
Pennsylvania Consolidated Statutes, Annotated [*A publication*] (DLA) ... PA Cons Stat Ann
Pennsylvania Consolidated Statutes, Annotated [*A publication*] (DLA) ... Pa CSA
Pennsylvania Consolidated Statutes, Annotated (Purdon) [*A publication*] (DLA) ... PA Cons Stat Ann (Purdon)
Pennsylvania Corporation Reporter [*A publication*] (DLA) ... Corp
Pennsylvania Corporation Reporter [*A publication*] (DLA) ... Corp Rep
Pennsylvania Corporation Reporter [*A publication*] (DLA) ... Corp Rep (PA)
Pennsylvania Corp. Reporter [*A publication*] (DLA) ... PA Corp
Pennsylvania Corp. Reporter [*A publication*] (DLA) ... PA Corp R
Pennsylvania Corp. Reporter [*A publication*] (DLA) ... PA Corp Rep
Pennsylvania Corp. Reporter [*A publication*] (DLA) ... PCR
Pennsylvania Corporation Reporter [*A publication*] (DLA) ... Penn Corp Rep
Pennsylvania County Court Reports [*A publication*] (DLA) ... Co CR
Pennsylvania County Court Reports [*A publication*] (DLA) ... Co Ct Rep
Pennsylvania County Court Reports [*A publication*] (DLA) ... County Court
Pennsylvania County Court Reports [*A publication*] (DLA) ... County Court R
Pennsylvania County Court Reports [*A publication*] (DLA) ... County Court Rep
Pennsylvania County Court Reports [*A publication*] (DLA) ... PA CC
Pennsylvania County Court Reports [*A publication*] (DLA) ... PA CC Reps
Pennsylvania County Court Reports [*A publication*] (DLA) ... PA CCR
Pennsylvania County Court Reports [*A publication*] (DLA) ... PA Co Ct
Pennsylvania County Court Reports [*A publication*] (DLA) ... PA Co Ct R
Pennsylvania County Court Reports [*A publication*] (DLA) ... PA County Ct
Pennsylvania County Court Reports [*A publication*] (DLA) ... PA CR
Pennsylvania County Court Reports [*A publication*] (DLA) ... PCR
Pennsylvania County Court Reports [*A publication*] (DLA) ... Penn Co Ct Rep
Pennsylvania Courts, Decisions in Workmen's Compensation Cases [*A publication*] (DLA) ... PA C Dec WCC
Pennsylvania Department of Environmental Resources ... PADER
Pennsylvania Department of Environmental Resources (DOGT) ... PADER
Pennsylvania Department of Environmental Resources, Bureau of Topographic and Geologic Survey, Harrisburg, PA [*Library symbol*] [*Library of Congress*] (LCLS) ... PharER-T
Pennsylvania Department of Labor and Industry Decisions [*A publication*] (DLA) ... PA Dep L & I Dec
Pennsylvania Department Reports [*A publication*] (DLA) ... PA Dep Rep
Pennsylvania District and County Reports [*A publication*] (DLA) ... D & CC
Pennsylvania District and County Reports [*A publication*] (DLA) ... DC
Pennsylvania District and County Reports [*A publication*] (DLA) ... Dist & Co Rep
Pennsylvania District and County Reports [*A publication*] (DLA) ... PA D & C
Pennsylvania District and County Reports [*A publication*] (DLA) ... PA D & C Rep
Pennsylvania District and County Reports [*A publication*] (DLA) ... PA Dist & C Rep
Pennsylvania District and County Reports [*A publication*] (DLA) ... PA Dist & Co R
Pennsylvania District and County Reports [*A publication*] (DLA) ... PA Dist & Co Repts
Pennsylvania District and County Reports [*A publication*] (DLA) ... Penn Dist & Co Rep
Pennsylvania District and County Reports, Second Series [*A publication*] (DLA) ... DC 2d
Pennsylvania District and County Reports, Second Series [*A publication*] (DLA) ... PA D & C 2d
Pennsylvania District and County Reports, Third Series [*A publication*] (DLA) ... PA D & C 3d
Pennsylvania District Reporter [*A publication*] (DLA) ... PA Dist
Pennsylvania District Reporter [*A publication*] (DLA) ... PA Dist R
Pennsylvania District Reports [*A publication*] (DLA) ... Dist R
Pennsylvania District Reports [*A publication*] (DLA) ... Dist Reports
Pennsylvania District Reports [*A publication*] (DLA) ... Dist Reps
Pennsylvania District Reports [*A publication*] (DLA) ... District
Pennsylvania District Reports [*A publication*] (DLA) ... District Reps
Pennsylvania District Reports [*A publication*] (DLA) ... PA Dist Rep
Pennsylvania District Reports [*A publication*] (DLA) ... PA DR
Pennsylvania District Reports [*A publication*] (DLA) ... Penn Dist Rep
Pennsylvania Dutch Folk Culture Society (EA) ... PDFCS
Pennsylvania Economy League, Inc., Eastern Division, Philadelphia, PA [*Library symbol Library of Congress*] (LCLS) ... PPPE
Pennsylvania Electric Association ... PEA
Pennsylvania Farm Museum of Landis Valley, Lancaster, PA [*Library symbol Library of Congress*] (LCLS) ... PLLVM
Pennsylvania Fiduciary Reporter [*A publication*] (DLA) ... PA Fid
Pennsylvania Fiduciary Reporter [*A publication*] (DLA) ... PA Fiduc
Pennsylvania Gas & Water Co. [*Associated Press*] (SAG) ... PenG
Pennsylvania Gas & Water Co. [*NASDAQ symbol*] (SAG) ... PGWC
Pennsylvania German Society [*Later, TPGS*] (EA) ... PGS
[*The*] **Pennsylvania German Society** (EA) ... TPGS
Pennsylvania Grade Crude Oil Association (EA) ... PGCOA
Pennsylvania Higher Education Assistance Agency (EDAC) ... PHEAA
Pennsylvania Historical and Museum Commission, Division of Archives and Manuscript, Harrisburg, PA [*Library symbol*] [*Library of Congress*] (LCLS) ... PHarH-Ar
Pennsylvania Historical and Museum Commission, Harrisburg, PA [*Library symbol Library of Congress*] (LCLS) ... PHarH
Pennsylvania Horticultural Society, Philadelphia, PA [*Library symbol Library of Congress*] (LCLS) ... PPHor
Pennsylvania Hospital, Philadelphia, PA [*Library symbol Library of Congress*] (LCLS) ... PPPH
Pennsylvania Industrial Chemical Corp. [*Trademark*] ... PICCO
Pennsylvania International Raceway [*Auto racing*] ... PIR
Pennsylvania Law Journal [*A publication*] (DLA) ... PA Law J
Pennsylvania Law Journal [*Philadelphia*] [*A publication*] (DLA) ... PA Law Jour
Pennsylvania Law Journal [*A publication*] (DLA) ... PA LJ
Pennsylvania Law Journal [*A publication*] (DLA) ... Penn Law Jour
Pennsylvania Law Journal [*A publication*] (DLA) ... Penn LJ
Pennsylvania Law Journal [*A publication*] (DLA) ... Penna Law Journal
Pennsylvania Law Journal [*A publication*] (DLA) ... Penna LJ
Pennsylvania Law Journal [*A publication*] (DLA) ... PLJ
Pennsylvania Law Journal Reports [*1842-52*] [*A publication*] (DLA) ... PA LJ
Pennsylvania Law Journal Reports, Edited by Clark [*A publication*] (DLA) ... Clark
Pennsylvania Law Journal Reports, Edited by Clark [*1842-52*] [*A publication*] (DLA) ... Penn LJR
Pennsylvania Law Record [*A publication*] (DLA) ... PA L Rec
Pennsylvania Law Record [*Philadelphia*] [*A publication*] (DLA) ... Penn L Rec
Pennsylvania Law Record [*Philadelphia*] [*A publication*] (DLA) ... PLR
Pennsylvania Law Review [*A publication*] (DLA) ... Penn L Rev
Pennsylvania Law Series [*A publication*] (DLA) ... PA L Ser
Pennsylvania Law Series [*A publication*] (DLA) ... PA Law Ser
Pennsylvania Law Series [*A publication*] (DLA) ... PA LS
Pennsylvania Learning Resources Association (EDAC) ... PLRA
Pennsylvania Legal Gazette [*A publication*] (DLA) ... Penn LG
Pennsylvania Legal Gazette Reports (Campbell) [*A publication*] (DLA) ... Penn LG
Pennsylvania Legislative Reference Bureau, Harrisburg, PA [*Library symbol Library of Congress*] (LCLS) ... P-LR
Pennsylvania Legislative Service (Purdon) [*A publication*] (DLA) ... PA Legis Serv
Pennsylvania Military Academy (AD) ... PMC
Pennsylvania Military College ... PMC
Pennsylvania Miscellaneous Reports [*A publication*] (DLA) ... PA Misc
Pennsylvania Motor Truck Association, Inc., Harrisburg PA [*STAC*] ... PMT
Pennsylvania Muscle Institute [*University of Pennsylvania*] [*Research center*] (RCD) ... PMI
Pennsylvania Natural Diversity Inventory [*Bureau of Forestry*] [*Harrisburg*] [*Information service or system*] (IID) ... PNDI

Pennsylvania, New Jersey, Delaware .... PENJERDEL
Pennsylvania New York Central Transportation Co. (AD) .... PNYCTC
Pennsylvania, Ohio, New York Baseball League (IIA) .... PONY
Pennsylvania Personnel and Guidance Association (AD) .... PPGA
Pennsylvania Power and Light (AD) .... PP&L
Pennsylvania Power & Light Co. [*Associated Press*] (SAG) .... PaPL
Pennsylvania Power & Light Co. (IAA) .... PPAL
Pennsylvania Power & Light Co. [*NYSE symbol*] (SPSG) .... PPL
Pennsylvania Prison Society (AD) .... PPS
Pennsylvania Public Library Film Center, University Park, PA [*OCLC symbol*] (OCLC) .... PFC
Pennsylvania Public Service Commission Annual Report [*A publication*] (DLA) .... PA PSC
Pennsylvania Public Service Commission Decisions [*A publication*] (DLA) .... PA PSC Dec
Pennsylvania Railroad Co. [*AAR code Obsolete*] .... PRR
Pennsylvania Railroad Technical and Historical Society (EA) .... PRTHS
Pennsylvania Real Estate Investment Trust [*AMEX symbol*] (SPSG) .... PEI
Pennsylvania Real Estate Investment Trust [*Associated Press*] (SAG) .... PenRE
Pennsylvania Record [*A publication*] (DLA) .... PA Rec
Pennsylvania Rehabilitation Center, Johnstown, PA [*OCLC symbol*] (OCLC) .... PIR
Pennsylvania Reports [*A publication*] (AAGC) .... Pa
Pennsylvania Reports [*A publication*] (DLA) .... PA Rep
Pennsylvania Reports (Penrose and Watts) [*A publication*] (DLA) .... PR
[*The*] **Pennsylvania Research & Economic Partnership Network** [*Computer science*] (TNIG) .... PREPnet
Pennsylvania Resources and Information Center for Special Education [*Montgomery County Intermediate Unit*] [*King of Prussia*] [*Information service or system*] (IID) .... PRISE
Pennsylvania School for the Deaf, Philadelphia, PA [*OCLC symbol*] (OCLC) .... PIN
Pennsylvania Science and Engineering Foundation .... PSEF
Pennsylvania State College of Optometry .... PSCO
Pennsylvania State Data Center [*Middletown*] [*Information service or system*] (IID) .... PSDC
Pennsylvania State Library, Harrisburg, PA [*Library symbol Library of Congress*] (LCLS) .... P
Pennsylvania State Reports [*A publication*] (DLA) .... PA St
Pennsylvania State Reports [*A publication*] (DLA) .... PA St R
Pennsylvania State Reports [*A publication*] (DLA) .... PA State
Pennsylvania State Reports [*A publication*] (DLA) .... PA State R
Pennsylvania State Reports [*A publication*] (DLA) .... Pen St R
Pennsylvania State Reports [*A publication*] (DLA) .... Penn
Pennsylvania State Reports [*A publication*] (DLA) .... Penn R
Pennsylvania State Reports [*A publication*] (DLA) .... Penn Rep
Pennsylvania State Reports [*A publication*] (DLA) .... Penn St
Pennsylvania State Reports [*A publication*] (ILCA) .... Penn St R
Pennsylvania State Reports [*A publication*] (DLA) .... Penn St Rep
Pennsylvania State Reports [*A publication*] (DLA) .... Penn Stat
Pennsylvania State Reports [*A publication*] (DLA) .... Penn State Rep
Pennsylvania State Reports [*A publication*] (DLA) .... Penna R
Pennsylvania State Reports [*A publication*] (DLA) .... Penna SR
Pennsylvania State Reports [*A publication*] (DLA) .... Penna St
Pennsylvania State Reports [*A publication*] (DLA) .... Penna State Rep
Pennsylvania State Reports [*A publication*] (DLA) .... PSR
Pennsylvania State Trials (Hogan) [*A publication*] (DLA) .... PA St Tr
Pennsylvania State University (GAGS) .... Penn St U
Pennsylvania State University .... PSU
Pennsylvania State University, Agricultural Library, University Park, PA [*Library symbol Library of Congress*] (LCLS) .... PSt-A
Pennsylvania State University, Allentown Campus, Allentown, PA [*Library symbol Library of Congress*] (LCLS) .... PSt-All
Pennsylvania State University, Altoona Campus, Altoona, PA [*Library symbol Library of Congress*] (LCLS) .... PSt-Alt
Pennsylvania State University at Harrisburg (GAGS) .... Penn St U Harrisburg
Pennsylvania State University, Beaver Campus, Monaca, PA [*Library symbol Library of Congress*] (LCLS) .... PSt-Be
Pennsylvania State University, Behrend Campus, Erie, PA [*Library symbol Library of Congress*] (LCLS) .... PSt-E
Pennsylvania State University, Berks Campus, Wyomissing, PA [*Library symbol Library of Congress*] (LCLS) .... PSt-B
Pennsylvania State University Breazeale Nuclear Reactor [*Research center*] (RCD) .... PSBR
Pennsylvania State University, Capitol Campus, Middletown, PA [*Library symbol Library of Congress*] (LCLS) .... PSt-Ca
Pennsylvania State University, Capitol Campus, Middletown, PA [*OCLC symbol*] (OCLC) .... UVC
Pennsylvania State University, Commonwealth Campuses, University Park, PA [*OCLC symbol*] (OCLC) .... UPC
Pennsylvania State University, Delaware Campus, Chester, PA [*Library symbol Library of Congress*] (LCLS) .... PSt-De
Pennsylvania State University, DuBois Campus, DuBois, PA [*Library symbol Library of Congress*] (LCLS) .... PSt-D
Pennsylvania State University, Fayette Campus, Uniontown, PA [*Library symbol Library of Congress*] (LCLS) .... PSt-F
Pennsylvania State University, Hazelton Campus, Hazelton, PA [*Library symbol Library of Congress*] (LCLS) .... PSt-H
Pennsylvania State University Ionosphere Research Laboratory .... PSU/IRL
Pennsylvania State University, King of Prussia Graduate Center, King of Prussia,PA [*Library symbol Library of Congress*] (LCLS) .... PSt-KP
Pennsylvania State University, McKeesport Campus, McKeesport, PA [*Library symbol Library of Congress*] (LCLS) .... PSt-McK
Pennsylvania State University, Mont Alto Campus, Mont Alto, PA [*Library symbol Library of Congress*] (LCLS) .... PSt-MA
Pennsylvania State University, New Kensington Campus, New Kensington, PA [*Library symbol Library of Congress*] (LCLS) .... PSt-NK
Pennsylvania State University, Off-Campus Libraries [*Library symbol*] [*Library of Congress*] (LCLS) .... PSt-X
Pennsylvania State University, Ogontz Campus, Abington, PA [*Library symbol Library of Congress*] (LCLS) .... PSt-O
Pennsylvania State University Press (DGA) .... PSUP
Pennsylvania State University Radio Astronomy Observatory .... PSURAO
Pennsylvania State University Reactor (NRCH) .... PSR
Pennsylvania State University Reactor .... PSUR
Pennsylvania State University, School of Nursing, Allegheny General Hospital, Pittsburgh, PA [*Library symbol Library of Congress*] (LCLS) .... PSt-PiN
Pennsylvania State University, Schuylkill Campus, Schuylkill Haven, PA [*Library symbol Library of Congress*] (LCLS) .... PSt-Sk
Pennsylvania State University, Scranton Campus, Scranton, PA [*Library symbol Library of Congress*] (LCLS) .... PSt-S
Pennsylvania State University, Shenango Valley Campus, Sharon, PA [*Library symbol Library of Congress*] (LCLS) .... PSt-SV
Pennsylvania State University, University Park (USDC) .... PSU
Pennsylvania State University, University Park, PA [*Library symbol Library of Congress*] (LCLS) .... PSt
Pennsylvania State University, University Park, PA [*OCLC symbol*] (OCLC) .... UPM
Pennsylvania State University, Wilkes-Barre Campus, Wilkes-Barre, PA [*Library symbol Library of Congress*] (LCLS) .... PSt-WB
Pennsylvania State University, Worthington Scranton Campus, Dunmore, PA [*Library symbol Library of Congress*] (LCLS) .... PSt-WS
Pennsylvania State University, York Campus, York, PA [*Library symbol Library of Congress*] (LCLS) .... PSt-Y
Pennsylvania State's Agricultural Progress Days (TSPED) .... APD
Pennsylvania Statutes, Annotated [*A publication*] (DLA) .... PA Stat Ann
Pennsylvania Statutes, Annotated (Purdon) [*A publication*] (DLA) .... PA Stat Ann (Purdon)
Pennsylvania Superior Court Reports [*A publication*] (DLA) .... PA S
Pennsylvania Superior Court Reports [*A publication*] (DLA) .... PA Super
Pennsylvania Superior Court Reports [*A publication*] (DLA) .... PA Super Ct
Pennsylvania Superior Court Reports [*A publication*] (DLA) .... PA Superior Ct
Pennsylvania Superior Court Reports [*A publication*] (DLA) .... Penn Super
Pennsylvania Superior Court Reports [*A publication*] (DLA) .... Supr Ct
Pennsylvania Supreme Court Cases (Sadler) [*A publication*] (DLA) .... PA Cas
Pennsylvania Supreme Court Reports [*1845-date*] [*A publication*] (DLA) .... PA
Pennsylvania Technical Assistance Program [*Pennsylvania State University*] [*University Park, PA*] .... PENNTAP
Pennsylvania Transportation Institute [*Pennsylvania State University*] [*Research center*] (RCD) .... PTI
Pennsylvania Union List of Serials .... PAULS
Pennsylvania University Museum .... PUM
Pennsylvania Workmen's Compensation Board Decisions [*A publication*] (DLA) .... PA WC Bd Dec
Pennsylvania-Jersey-Maryland [*Electric power pool*] .... PJM
Pennsylvanian [*Period, era, or system*] [*Geology*] .... PENN
Pennsylvania-Ontario Transportation Co. [*AAR code*] .... POT
Pennsylvania-Ontario-New York League [*Old baseball league*] .... PONY
Pennsylvania-Reading [*Seashore Lines*] (AD) .... P-R
Pennsylvania-Reading Seashore Lines [*Absorbed into Consolidated Rail Corp.*] .... PRS
Pennsylvania-Reading Seashore Lines [*Absorbed into Consolidated Rail Corp.*] [*AAR code*] .... PRSL
Pennsylvania-Reading Seashore Lines [*Absorbed into Consolidated Rail Corp.*] .... PRSS
Pennsylvania's Regional Instruction System for Education [*Network of colleges and universities*] .... PRISE
Pennwalt Corp., King Of Prussia, PA [*Library symbol Library of Congress*] (LCLS) .... PKpP
Pennwalt Corp., Lucidol Division, Buffalo, NY [*Library symbol Library of Congress*] (LCLS) .... NBuPL
Pennwalt Corp., Pharmaceutical Division, Library, Rochester, NY [*OCLC symbol*] (OCLC) .... VQY
Pennwalt Corp., Pharmaceutical Division Research Library, Rochester, NY [*Library symbol Library of Congress*] (LCLS) .... NRPP
Pennwood Savings Bank [*Associated Press*] (SAG) .... Pennwd
Pennwood Savings Bank [*NASDAQ symbol*] (SAG) .... PWBK
Penny [*Nail size*] .... D
Penny (ODBW) .... p
Penny .... P
Penny .... PNY
Penny Cyclopoedia [*British A publication*] (ROG) .... PC
Penny Resistance (EA) .... PR
Penny Stock [*Investment term*] .... PS
Pennypacker's Pennsylvania Colonial Cases [*A publication*] (DLA) .... Penny
Pennypacker's Pennsylvania Colonial Cases [*A publication*] (DLA) .... Pennyp Col Cas
Pennypacker's Pennsyulvania Colonial Cases [*A publication*] (DLA) .... Penny Col Cas
Pennypacker's Unreported Pennsylvania Cases [*A publication*] (DLA) .... Penn
Pennypacker's Unreported Pennsylvania Cases [*A publication*] (DLA) .... Penny
Pennypacker's Unreported Pennsylvania Cases [*A publication*] (DLA) .... Pennyp
Pennypacker's Unreported Pennsylvania Cases [*A publication*] (DLA) .... Pennyp (PA)
Pennysaver Publishing Co., Lake Hiawatha, NJ [*Library symbol Library of Congress*] (LCLS) .... NjLhP
Pennysylvania-Ohio-Maryland League [*Old baseball league*] .... POM
Pennyweight [*Measurement*] (DAVI) .... dwt
Pennyweight .... PWT

Pennyworth [*British*] (ROG) ... PENNORTH
Pennzoil Co. [*Associated Press*] (SAG) ... Pennzol
Pennzoil Co. [*NYSE symbol Toronto Stock Exchange symbol*] (SPSG) ... PZL
Pennzoil Co., Exploration Library, Houston, TX [*OCLC symbol*] (OCLC) ... PNZ
Pennzoil Exploration Library, Houston, TX [*Library symbol Library of Congress*] (LCLS) ... TxHPen
Pennzoil Louisiana and Texas Offshore [*Oil industry group*] ... PLATO
Pennzoil Offshore Gas Operators (AD) ... POGO
Pennzoil United, Inc., Shreveport, LA [*Library symbol Library of Congress*] (LCLS) ... LsHUP
Penobscot Marine Museum (EA) ... PMM
Penobscot Marine Museum, Searsport, ME [*Library symbol Library of Congress*] (LCLS) ... MeSepPM
Penobscot Shoe [*AMEX symbol*] (TTSB) ... PSO
Penobscot Shoe Co. [*Associated Press*] (SAG) ... Penob
Penobscot Shoe Co. [*AMEX symbol*] (SPSG) ... PSO
Penology ... PENOL
Penrhyn [*Cook Islands*] [*ICAO location identifier*] (ICLI) ... NCPY
Penril Corp. [*Associated Press*] (SAG) ... Penril
Penril Data Communication Networks [*NASDAQ symbol*] (SPSG) ... PNRL
Penril DataComm Ntwks [*NASDAQ symbol*] (TTSB) ... PNRL
Penrod [*Nevada*] [*Seismograph station code, US Geological Survey Closed*] (SEIS) ... PNR
Penrose and Watts' Pennsylvania Reports [*1829-32*] [*A publication*] (DLA) ... P & W
Penrose and Watts' Pennsylvania Reports [*1829-32*] [*A publication*] (DLA) ... Pen & W
Penrose and Watts' Pennsylvania Reports [*A publication*] (DLA) ... Penn Rep
Penrose and Watts' Pennsylvania Reports [*1829-32*] [*A publication*] (DLA) ... Penr & W
Penrose Division, Ongwanada Hospital, Kingston, Ontario [*Library symbol National Library of Canada*] (NLC) ... OKOH
Penrose Hospital, Webb Memorial Library, Colorado Springs, CO [*Library symbol Library of Congress*] (LCLS) ... CoCP-M
Penrose Public Library, Colorado Springs, CO [*Library symbol Library of Congress*] (LCLS) ... CoC
Penrose Public Library, Colorado Springs, CO [*Library symbol*] [*Library of Congress*] (LCLS) ... CoCPP
Penrose Resources Corp. [*Vancouver Stock Exchange symbol*] ... PRC
Penruddocke's Short Analysis of Criminal Law [*2nd ed.*] [*1842*] [*A publication*] (DLA) ... Penr Anal
Penryn [*England*] ... PENR
Pensacola [*Florida*] [*Seismograph station code, US Geological Survey Closed*] (SEIS) ... PEN
Pensacola [*Florida*] [*Airport symbol*] (OAG) ... PNS
Pensacola Christian College, Pensacola, FL [*Library symbol*] [*Library of Congress*] (LCLS) ... FPeCC
Pensacola, FL [*Location identifier FAA*] (FAAL) ... NDP
Pensacola, FL [*Location identifier FAA*] (FAAL) ... NEO
Pensacola, FL [*Location identifier FAA*] (FAAL) ... NPA
Pensacola, FL [*Location identifier FAA*] (FAAL) ... NUN
Pensacola, FL [*Location identifier FAA*] (FAAL) ... PKZ
Pensacola, FL [*AM radio station call letters*] ... WBSR
Pensacola, FL [*AM radio station call letters*] ... WCOA
Pensacola, FL [*Television station call letters*] ... WEAR
Pensacola, FL [*Television station call letters*] ... WHBR
Pensacola, FL [*Television station call letters*] ... WJTC
Pensacola, FL [*FM radio station call letters*] ... WMEZ
Pensacola, FL [*FM radio station call letters*] ... WOWW
Pensacola, FL [*FM radio station call letters*] ... WPCS
Pensacola, FL [*AM radio station call letters*] ... WRNE
Pensacola, FL [*Television station call letters*] ... WSRE
Pensacola, FL [*AM radio station call letters*] ... WSWL
Pensacola, FL [*FM radio station call letters*] ... WTKX-FM
Pensacola, FL [*FM radio station call letters*] ... WUWF
Pensacola, FL [*AM radio station call letters*] ... WVTJ
Pensacola, FL [*FM radio station call letters*] ... WWRO
Pensacola, FL [*FM radio station call letters*] (RBYB) ... WYCL-FM
Pensacola, FL [*AM radio station call letters*] (RBYB) ... WZNO
Pensacola, Florida (AD) ... Pncla
Pensacola Junior College [*Florida*] ... PJC
Pensacola Junior College, Pensacola, FL [*Library symbol Library of Congress*] (LCLS) ... FPeC
Pensacola Junior College, Pensacola, FL [*Library symbol Library of Congress*] (LCLS) ... FPeJC
Pensacola Junior College, Pensacola, FL [*OCLC symbol*] (OCLC) ... FPJ
Pensacola/Pensacola Naval Air Station [*Florida*] [*ICAO location identifier*] (ICLI) ... KNPA
Pensacola Public Library, Pensacola, FL [*Library symbol Library of Congress*] (LCLS) ... FPe
Pensacola/Regional [*Florida*] [*ICAO location identifier*] (ICLI) ... KPNS
Pensacola-Tallahassee [*Diocesan abbreviation*] [*Florida*] (TOCD) ... PT
Pensamiento Cristiano. Tribuna de Exposicion del Pensamiento Evangelico [*Cordoba, Argentina*] [*A publication*] (BJA) ... PensCr
Pension ... PNSN
Pension Administration Plan [*Insurance*] ... PAP
Pension and Profit Sharing (Prentice-Hall, Inc.) [*A publication*] (DLA) ... Pens & Profit Sharing (P-H)
Pension and Retirement Annuity System ... PRAS
Pension and Welfare (WDMC) ... P & W
Pension and Welfare [*Payments made to talent unions for the benefit of performers*] (WDMC) ... P&W
Pension and Welfare Benefit Programs [*Labor-Managment Services Administration*] (IAA) ... PAWBP
Pension and Welfare Benefit Programs [*Labor-Management Services Administration*] ... PWBP
Pension and Welfare Benefits Administration [*Department of Labor*] ... PWBA
Pension Appeals Board [*Canada*] ... PAB
Pension Benefit Guaranty Corp. [*Government agency*] ... PBGC
Pension Decisions [*Department of the Interior*] [*A publication*] (DLA) ... Pen Dec
Pension for Wounds [*Navy British*] (ROG) ... PW
Pension Fund ... PF
Pension Fund Association [*Japan*] (ECON) ... PFA
Pension Fund Property Unit Trust [*British*] ... PFPUT
Pension Mortgage [*British*] ... PM
Pension Opportunities for Workers' Expanded Retirement [*Plan proposed in 1991 by the Department of Labor*] ... POWER
Pension Plan ... PP
Pension Portability Act of 1992 (WYGK) ... PPA
Pension Protection Act (GFGA) ... PPA
Pension Real Estate Association (EA) ... PREA
Pension Reporter [*Bureau of National Affairs*] [*A publication*] (DLA) ... Pension Rep
Pension Reporter (Bureau of National Affairs) [*A publication*] (DLA) ... Pens Rep (BNA)
Pension Research Council (EA) ... PRC
Pension Review Board [*Canada*] ... PRB
Pension Rights Center [*Washington, DC*] (EA) ... PRC
Pension Trustee (DLA) ... PT
Pension Valuation Factor ... PVF
Pensioner Party of Australia [*Political party*] ... PPA
Pensioners' Employment Bureau [*British*] ... PEB
Pensioners for Peace International (EAIO) ... PPI
Pensioners-Combined Pensioners Association of Victoria [*Australia*] ... PCPAV
Pensions for Professionals, Inc. ... PFP
Pensions for Technical Professionals [*An association*] ... PTP
Pensions Management Institute [*British*] (EAIO) ... PMI
Pensions Research Accountants Group (MHDB) ... PRAG
Penske Car [*Racing model*] ... PC
Penske Motorsports [*NASDAQ symbol*] (TTSB) ... SPWY
Penske Motorsports, Inc. [*Associated Press*] (SAG) ... PenskeM
Penske Motorsports, Inc. [*NASDAQ symbol*] (SAG) ... SPWY
Pensky-Martens Closed Cup [*Flash point test*] ... PMCC
Penson Elementary School, Grovedale, Alberta [*Library symbol National Library of Canada*] (BIB) ... AGPES
Penta Users Group (EA) ... PUG
Pentaacetylglucose [*Laundry bleach activator*] ... PAG
Pentaborane [*Rocket fuel*] ... PB
Pentabromochlorocyclohexane [*Flame retardant*] [*Organic chemistry*] ... PBCCH
Pentabromoethylbenzene [*Flame retardant*] [*Organic chemistry*] ... PBEB
Pentachloraniline [*Organic chemistry*] ... PCA
Pentachloroanisole [*Organic chemistry*] ... PCA
Pentachlorocyclohexene [*Organic chemistry*] ... PCCH
Pentachlorodioxin [*Organic chemistry*] ... PCDD
Pentachloronitrobenzene [*Agricultural fungicide*] ... PCNB
Pentachlorophenate [*A topical antibacterial*] (DAVI) ... PCP
Pentachlorophenol [*Also, PCP*] [*Wood preservative*] [*Organic chemistry*] (TEL) ... P
Pentachlorophenol [*Wood preservative*] [*Organic chemistry*] ... PCP
Pentachlorothioanisole [*Organic chemistry*] ... PCTA
Pentacostal Assemblies of Canada ... PAOC
Pentadecanoic Acid [*Organic chemistry*] ... PDA
Pentadecylbenzene [*Organic chemistry*] ... PDB
Pentadecylcatechol [*An allergen*] ... PDC
Pentadecylphenol [*Organic chemistry*] ... PDP
Pentaerythritol [*Organic chemistry*] ... PET
Pentaerythritol Tetraniconitate [*Niceritrol*] [*Pharmacology*] (DAVI) ... PETN
Pentaerythritol Tetranitrate [*Also, PETN*] [*Explosive, vasodilator*] ... PET
Pentaerythritol Tetranitrate [*Also, PET*] [*Explosive, vasodilator*] ... PETN
Pentaerythritol Tetranitrate [*An explosive and a vasodilator*] [*Cardiology*] (DAVI) ... PTEN
Pentaerythritol Triacrylate [*Organic chemistry*] ... PETA
Pentaethylene Glycol Dodecyl Ether [*Organic chemistry*] ... PEGDE
Pentaethylenehexamine [*Organic chemistry*] ... PEHA
Pentaeythrol (IAA) ... PE
Pentafluorobenzyl [*Organic radical*] ... PFB
Pentafluorobenzyl Bromide [*Organic chemistry*] ... PFB
Pentafluorobenzylhydroxylamine Hydrochloride [*Analytical biochemistry*] ... PFBHA
Pentafluoroiodosylbenzene [*Organic chemistry*] ... PFIB
Pentafluorophenylhydrazine [*Organic chemistry*] ... PFPH
Pentafluoropropionate [*or Pentafluoropropionyl*] [*Organic chemistry*] ... PFP
Pentafluoropropionic Anhydride [*Organic chemistry*] ... PFPA
Pentafluoropropionyl Imidazole [*Organic chemistry*] ... PFPI
Pentaflurobenzoyl Chloride [*Organic chemistry*] ... PFBC
Pentagastrin (DMAA) ... PG
Pentagon ... PENT
Pentagon ... PNT
Pentagon (AD) ... Pnt
Pentagon (MSA) ... PNTGN
Pentagon Annex (AD) ... Pnt Anx
Pentagon Computer Operations Support (MCD) ... PECOS
Pentagon Consolidated Telecommunications System (MCD) ... PCTS
Pentagon Counterintelligence Force ... PCF
Pentagon English [*Pseudotechnical language*] ... PENTENG
Pentagon Liaison Office (MCD) ... PLO
Pentagon Telecommunications Center (MCD) ... PTC
Pentagram [*One billion metric tons*] ... Pg
Pentair, Inc. [*Associated Press*] (SAG) ... Pentair
Pentair, Inc. [*NYSE symbol*] (TTSB) ... PNR

Pentair, Inc. [*NASDAQ symbol*] (NQ) .... PNTA
Pentameter .... PENT
Pentamethyldiethylenetriamine [*Organic chemistry*] .... PMDT
Pentamethylene Diguanidine [*Organic chemistry*] .... PMDG
Pentamethyl(hydroxy)chromane [*Organic chemistry*] .... PMC
Pentaploidy [*State of having five sets of chromosomes*] [*Genetics*] (DAVI) 5n
Pentateuch (BJA) .... Pent
Pentateuch (VRA) .... pentu
Pentazocine [*An analgesic*] .... PEN
Pentech International [*NASDAQ symbol*] (TTSB) .... PNTK
Pentech International, Inc. [*Associated Press*] (SAG) .... Pentch
Pentech International, Inc. [*NASDAQ symbol*] (NQ) .... PNTK
Pentecost .... PENT
Pentecostal .... PENTE
Pentecostal Assemblies of the World (EA) .... PA of W
Pentecostal Coalition for Human Rights [*Defunct*] (EA) .... PCHR
Pentecostal Fellowship of North America (EA) .... PFNA
Pentecostal World Conference [*Emmetten, Switzerland*] (EA) .... PWC
Penteli [*Greece*] [*Seismograph station code, US Geological Survey*] (SEIS) .... PTL
Pentelic (VRA) .... Pentl
Penthouse (DD) .... PH
Penthouse .... PH
Penthouse Entertainment Network [*Cable television system*] .... PET
Penticton [*British Columbia*] [*Seismograph station code, US Geological Survey*] (SEIS) .... PNT
Penticton [*Canada*] [*Airport symbol*] (OAG) .... YYF
Penticton, BC [*Television station call letters*] CHKL-1
Penticton, BC [*FM radio station call letters*] .... CIGV
Penticton, BC [*FM radio station call letters*] .... CJMG
Penticton, BC [*AM radio station call letters*] .... CKOR
Penticton, BC [*ICAO location identifier*] (ICLI) .... CYYF
Penticton Museum and Archives, British Columbia [*Library symbol National Library of Canada*] (NLC) .... BPM
Penticton Museum and Archives, Penticton, BC, Canada [*Library symbol Library of Congress*] (LCLS) .... CaBPM
Penticton Public Library, British Columbia [*Library symbol National Library of Canada*] (NLC) .... BP
Penticton Public Library, Penticton, BC, Canada [*Library symbol Library of Congress*] (LCLS) .... CaBP
Pentland Group plc [*LO Symbol*] (TTSB) .... PNDL
Pentobarbital [*Organic chemistry*] .... PB
Pentobarbital [*Sedative*] .... PEN
Pentobarbital-Chlorpromazine-Alcohol Group [*Medicine*] .... PCAG
Pentode [*Electronics*] (OA) .... P
Pentode (DEN) .... PEN
Pentode (AAG) .... PENT
Pentose Cycle [*Biochemistry*] (MAE) .... PC
Pentosenucleic Acid [*Biochemistry*] .... PNA
Pentose-Phosphate Pathway [*Metabolism*] .... PPP
Pentothal [*Anesthetic*] (AAMN) .... Pent
[*Sodium*] **Pentothal** [*An anesthetic*] (DAVI) .... PTL
Pentwater, MI [*FM radio station call letters*] (RBYB) .... WEWM
Pentwater Township Library, Pentwater, MI [*Library symbol Library of Congress*] (LCLS) .... MiPen
Pentyl [*Biochemistry*] .... Pe
Pentyl-alpha-pyrone [*Organic chemistry*] .... PAP
Pentylenetetrazole [*CNS stimulant*] .... PTZ
Penuelas [*Puerto Rico*] [*Seismograph station code, US Geological Survey*] (SEIS) .... PNP
Penuelas, PR [*AM radio station call letters*] .... WPPC
Penultimate Digit Storage [*Telecommunications*] (TEL) .... PDS
Penultimate Profit [*Investment term*] (DFIT) .... PPP
PENWEST Ltd. [*Bellevue, WA*] [*NASDAQ symbol*] (NQ) .... PENW
PENWEST Ltd. [*Associated Press*] (SAG) .... Penwst
Penwith [*England*] .... PENW
Penza [*Former USSR ICAO location identifier*] (ICLI) .... UWPP
Penzance [*City in England*] (ROG) .... PENZ
Penzance (AD) .... Pnz
Penzance [*British depot code*] .... PZ
Penzance [*England*] [*Airport symbol*] (OAG) .... PZE
Penzance/Eastern Green [*British ICAO location identifier*] (ICLI) .... EGHK
Peony [*Horticulture*] .... P
People .... P
People .... PEO
People .... PPL
People Against Cancer .... PAC
People Against Chlordane (EA) .... PAL
People Against Dioxins in Sanitary Products [*An association Australia*] .... PADS
People Against Displacement (NADA) .... PAD
People Against Gangsterism and Drugs [*South Africa*] .... PAGAD
People Against Lenient Sentences [*An association Australia*] .... PALS
People Against Loneliness [*British*] (DI) .... PALS
People Against Racism [*Civil rights organization*] .... PAR
People Against Racism in Education .... PARE
People Against Racist Terror (EA) .... PART
People Against Rape (EA) .... PAR
People Against Telephone Terrorism and Harassment (EA) .... PATTH
People Against Tobacco Smoke (EA) .... PATS
People Against Toxic Chemical Hazards [*An association Australia*] .... PATCH
People Against Unconstitutional Sex Education .... PAUSE
People Can't Memorize Computer Industry Acronyms (PS) .... PCMCIA
People Concerned about MIC [*Methyl Isocyanate*] (EA) .... PCAMIC
People Emerging Against Corrupt Establishments [*Underground military newspaper*] .... PEACE
People Express [*ICAO designator*] (AD) .... PE
People First Corp. [*Associated Press*] (SAG) .... PeopFst
People First Corp. [*NASDAQ symbol*] (SAG) .... PFKY
People First International (EA) .... PFI
People, Food and Land Foundation (EA) .... PFLF
People for a Change [*An association Defunct*] (EA) .... PC
People for a Change (EA) .... PFAC
People for a United India and World Peace (EA) .... PUIWP
People for Energy Progress [*Defunct*] (EA) .... PEP
People for Life (EA) .... PFL
People for Life (EA) .... PL
People for Nuclear Disarmament Australia [*An association*] .... PNDA
People for Prison Alternatives [*An association*] (AD) .... PPA
People for Prison Alternatives [*An association*] (NADA) .... PPA
People for Rehabilitating and Integrating the Disabled through Education [*New York City*] .... PRIDE
People for Self Management [*An association*] (NADA) .... PSM
People for the American Way (EA) .... PAW
People for the American Way (EA) .... PFAW
People for the Enjoyment of Eyeballing Knees [*Group opposing below-the-knee fashions introduced in 1970*] .... PEEK
People for the Ethical Treatment of Animals (EA) .... PETA
People Gas Light Co., Chicago, IL [*Library symbol Library of Congress*] (LCLS) .... ICPG
People, Goods, and Services Urban System [*Texas*] [*FHWA*] (TAG) .... PEGASUS
People Helping People, Inc., Brantford, Ontario [*Library symbol National Library of Canada*] (NLC) .... OBPH
People, Ideas, Resources, Objectives [*Management strategy*] (DHSM) .... PIRO
People in Need [*Food program sponsored by family of kidnapped heiress, Patricia Hearst, 1974*] .... PIN
People Like Us (IIA) .... PLU
People Living With HIV/AIDS [*Human Immunodeficiency Virus / Acquired Immune Deficiency Syndrome*] [*Australia*] .... PLWHA
People Meter [*TV ratings measuring device*] [*Advertising*] .... PM
People of America Responding to Educational Needs of Today's Society (EA) .... PARENTS
People of the Earth [*Also, RAN*] (EA) .... POE
People of the State of New York (AD) .... POSNY
People Opposed to Pornography in Schools [*Group opposing sex education in schools*] .... POPS
People Organized and Working for Economic Rebirth [*Program for black economic development*] [*Later, Nationway Ventures International Ltd.*] .... POWER
People Organized to Stop Rape of Imprisoned Persons (EA) .... POSRIP
People Persecuted by Pablo Escobar [*Colombia*] (ECON) .... PEPE
People Persecuted by Pablo Escobar .... PEPES
People Refreshment House Association [*British*] (BI) .... PRHA
People Taking Action .... PTA
People That Love [*Of television's "PTL Club"*] [*Facetious translations: "Pass the Loot" and "Pay the Lady"*] .... PTL
People to People Citizen Ambassador Program (EA) .... PPCAP
People to People International (EA) .... PTP
People to People International (EAIO) .... PTPI
People to People Music Committee (EA) .... PPMC
People, Topics, Opinions [*A publication British*] .... PTO
People United for Rural Education (EA) .... PURE
People United to Fight Frustrations (EA) .... PUFF
People United to Save Humanity [*In organization name "Operation PUSH"*] .... PUSH
People with AIDS Coalition (EA) .... PWA
People with Arthritis Can Exercise [*Medical program*] .... PACE
People with Disabilities .... PWD
People-Animals-Love (EA) .... PAL
People-Powered Vehicle [*Recreational vehicle powered by pedaling*] .... PPV
People-Powered Vehicle (AD) .... ppv
Peoples [*Internet language*] [*Computer science*] .... ppls
People's Action Movement [*Nevis*] [*Political party*] (PPW) .... PAM
People's Action Party [*Singapore*] [*Political party*] (PPW) .... PAP
People's Action Party [*Papua New Guinea*] [*Political party*] (EY) .... PAP
People's Action Party [*Malaya*] [*Political party*] .... PAP
People's Action Team [*South Vietnam*] .... PAT
People's Alliance [*Althydubandalag*] [*Iceland*] [*Political party*] (PPW) .... PA
People's Alliance Party [*Solomon Islands*] [*Political party*] (PPW) .... PAP
People's Alliance to Reform, Transform and Improve Everything (EA) .... PARTIE
People's Anti-War Mobilization (EA) .... PAM
People's Army Congress .... PAC
People's Army of Vietnam .... PAVN
Peoples Bancorp [*NASDAQ symbol*] (TTSB) .... PEBO
Peoples Bancorp [*Dekalb County*] [*Associated Press*] (SAG) .... PeopBcp
Peoples Bancorp (Dekalb County) [*NASDAQ symbol*] (SAG) .... PFDC
Peoples Bancorp, Inc. (Ohio) [*Associated Press*] (SAG) .... PeBcCH
Peoples Bancorp, Inc. (Ohio) [*NASDAQ symbol*] (SAG) .... PEBO
Peoples Bancorp(IN) [*NASDAQ symbol*] (TTSB) .... PFDC
Peoples Bancshares, Inc. [*NASDAQ symbol*] (SAG) .... PBKB
Peoples Bancshares, Inc. [*Associated Press*] (SAG) .... PBshBrc
Peoples Banctrust [*NASDAQ symbol*] (TTSB) .... PBTC
Peoples BancTrust Co. [*Associated Press*] (SAG) .... PeopBcT
Peoples BancTrust Company Inc. [*NASDAQ symbol*] (SAG) .... PBTC
People's Bank [*Bridgeport, CT*] [*NASDAQ symbol*] (NQ) .... PBCT
Peoples Bank [*Catawba, NC*] [*NASDAQ symbol*] (NQ) .... PEBK
Peoples Bank [*Catawba, NC*] [*Associated Press*] (SAG) .... PeopBk
Peoples Bank [*Bridgeport, CT*] [*Associated Press*] (SAG) .... PeopCT
People's Bank 8.5% Cv 'A' Pfd [*NASDAQ symbol*] (TTSB) .... PBCTP
Peoples Bank Corp. Indianapolis [*Associated Press*] (SAG) .... PeoBkIN
Peoples Bank Corp. (Indianapolis, IN) [*NASDAQ symbol*] (SAG) .... PPLS
Peoples Bank Indianapolis [*NASDAQ symbol*] (TTSB) .... PPLS
People's Bank of China (ECON) .... PBC

People's Bank of China ... PBoC
People's Bicentennial [*later, Business*] **Commission** ... PBC
People's Caretakers' Council [*Rhodesian*] ... PCC
People's Center for Housing Change (EA) ... PCHC
People's Choice TV [*NASDAQ symbol*] (TTSB) ... PCTV
Peoples Choice TV Corp. [*NASDAQ symbol*] (SAG) ... PCTV
Peoples Choice TV Corp. [*Associated Press*] (SAG) ... PeopChc
People's Christian Coalition [*Later, Sojourners*] (EA) ... PCC
Peoples Coalition for Peace and Justice [*Defunct*] ... PCPJ
People's Committee for Libyan Students (EA) ... PCLS
People's Community Civic League (EA) ... PCCL
People's Conference [*India*] [*Political party*] (PPW) ... PC
People's Democracy [*Ireland*] [*Political party*] ... PD
People's Democracy of Laos [*Political party*] (VNW) ... PDL
People's Democratic [*Saint Christopher and Nevis*] [*Political party*] (EY) ... PDP
People's Democratic Force [*The Bahamas*] [*Political party*] (EY) ... PDF
People's Democratic Movement [*Turks and Caicos Islands*] [*Political party*] (PPW) ... PDM
People's Democratic Movement [*Papua New Guinea*] [*Political party*] (FEA) ... PDM
People's Democratic Movement [*Guyana*] [*Political party*] (EY) ... PDM
People's Democratic Organisation for Independence and Socialism [*Senegambia*] [*Political party*] ... PDOIS
People's Democratic Party [*Sudan*] [*Political party*] ... PDP
People's Democratic Party [*South Korea Political party*] (EY) ... PDP
People's Democratic Party [*Netherlands Antilles*] [*Political party*] (EY) ... PDP
People's Democratic Party [*Sierra Leone*] [*Political party*] (EY) ... PDP
People's Democratic Party of Afghanistan [*Political party*] (PPW) ... PDPA
People's Democratic Republic of Ethiopia ... PDRE
People's Democratic Republic of Laos ... PRPL
People's Democratic Republic of Yemen [*Political party*] ... PDRY
People's Democratic Republic of Yemen [*ANSI two-letter standard code*] (CNC) ... YD
People's Democratic Republic of Yemen [*ANSI three-letter standard code*] (CNC) ... YMD
People's Dispensary for Sick Animals [*British*] ... PDSA
Peoples Energy [*NYSE symbol*] (TTSB) ... PGL
Peoples Energy Corp. [*Associated Press*] (SAG) ... PeopEn
Peoples Energy Corp. [*NYSE symbol*] (SPSG) ... PGL
Peoples Federal Savings Bank of DeKalb City [*NASDAQ symbol*] (NQ) ... PFDC
Peoples Financial Corp. [*Associated Press*] (SAG) ... PeopFin
Peoples Financial Corp. [*NASDAQ symbol*] (SAG) ... PFFC
Peoples First [*NASDAQ symbol*] (TTSB) ... PFKY
People's Forces of 25 April [*Portugal*] (PD) ... FP-25
People's Front for Democracy and Justice [*Formerly, EPLF*] [*Eritrea*] [*Political party*] (ECON) ... PFDJ
People's Front of the Liberation Tigers [*Sri Lanka*] [*Political party*] (EY) ... PFLT
Peoples Gas, Light & Coke Co., Chicago, IL [*OCLC symbol*] (OCLC) ... IDC
People's Heritage Financial Group, Inc. [*Associated Press*] (SAG) ... PeopHrt
People's Heritage Financial Group, Inc. [*NASDAQ symbol*] (NQ) ... PHBK
Peoples Heritage Finl Gr [*NASDAQ symbol*] (TTSB) ... PHBK
Peoples Holding [*NASDAQ symbol*] (TTSB) ... PHCO
Peoples Holding Co. [*Associated Press*] (SAG) ... PeopHld
Peoples Holding Co. [*NASDAQ symbol*] (SAG) ... PHCO
People's Institute for Survival and Beyond (EA) ... PISB
People's Involvement Corp. (EA) ... PIC
Peoples Jewellers Ltd. [*Toronto Stock Exchange symbol*] ... PCJ
People's Law School [*Defunct*] (EA) ... PLS
People's Legal Advisor [*Utica, NY*] [*A publication*] (DLA) ... Peo L Adv
People's Liberation [*Revolutionary group*] [*Turkey*] ... HK
People's Liberation Armed Forces [*National Liberation Front*] [*North Vietnam*] (VNW) ... PLAF
People's Liberation Army [*National Liberation Front*] [*North Vietnam*] (VNW) ... PLA
People's Liberation Army [*India*] (PD) ... PLA
People's Liberation Army [*China*] ... PLA
People's Liberation Army Air Force ... PLAAF
People's Liberation Army Navy ... PLAN
People's Liberation Army of Namibia [*Political party*] (PPW) ... PLAN
People's Liberation Forces [*Ethiopia*] [*Political party*] (AF) ... PLF
People's Liberation Movement [*Montserrat*] [*Political party*] (PPW) ... PLM
Peoples Liberation Organization (NADA) ... PLO
People's Liberation Organization of Tamil Eelam [*Sri Lanka*] [*Political party*] ... PLOT
People's Liberation Organization of Tamil Eelam [*Sri Lanka*] [*Political party*] ... PLOTE
People's Liberation Party [*Pakistan*] ... PLP
People's Lobby (EA) ... PL
People's Mandate Committee (EA) ... PMC
People's Medical Society (EA) ... PMS
People's Message System [*For Apple II computers*] [*Electronic bulletin board*] ... PMS
People's Music Network for Songs of Freedom and Struggle (EA) ... PMN/SFS
People's National Congress [*Guyana*] (PD) ... PNC
People's National Movement [*Trinidad and Tobago*] [*Political party*] (PD) ... PNM
People's National Party [*Ghana*] [*Political party*] (PPW) ... PNP
People's National Party [*Jamaica*] [*Political party*] (PPW) ... PNP
People's News Agency [*An association*] (EA) ... PNA
People's News Service [*British*] ... PNS
Peoples of the World [*A publication*] ... POW
Peoples of the World: Western Europeans [*A publication*] ... POW:WE
Peoples Oil Ltd. [*Vancouver Stock Exchange symbol*] ... PPS
People's Party [*Spain Political party*] (ECON) ... PP
People's Party [*Halkci Partisi*] [*Turkey Political party*] (PPW) ... PP
People's Party of Arunachal Pradesh [*India*] [*Political party*] (PPW) ... PPAP
Peoples Party of Pakistan (NADA) ... PPP
Peoples Party of Pakistan [*Political party*] (AD) ... PPP
People's Patriotic Party [*Myanmar*] [*Political party*] (PD) ... PPP
People's Peace and Prosperity Party [*Defunct*] (EA) ... PPPP
People's Police Force ... PPF
People's Political Party [*St. Vincent*] [*Political party*] (PPW) ... PPP
People's Press Printing Society [*British*] ... PPPS
People's Progress Party [*Papua New Guinea*] [*Political party*] (PPW) ... PPP
People's Progressive Party [*Gambia*] [*Political party*] (PPW) ... PPP
People's Progressive Party [*Guyana*] [*Political party*] (PD) ... PPP
People's Progressive Party [*Mauritania*] [*Political party*] (EY) ... PPP
People's Progressive Party [*Solomon Islands*] [*Political party*] (PPW) ... PPP
People's Progressive Party [*Anguilla*] [*Political party*] (PPW) ... PPP
People's Progressive Party of Guyana [*Political party*] ... PPPG
People's Redemption Council [*Liberia*] (PD) ... PRC
People's Redemption Party [*Nigeria*] [*Political party*] (PPW) ... PRP
People's Reform Party [*Philippines*] [*Political party*] (EY) ... PRP
Peoples' Reports [*77-97 Georgia*] [*A publication*] (DLA) ... Peoples
People's Republic of Benin (AD) ... PRB
People's Republic of China [*License plate code assigned to foreign diplomats in the US*] ... CY
People's Republic of China [*Mainland China*] ... PRC
People's Republic of China Army (MCD) ... PRCA
People's Republic of Kampuchea [*From 1979 to 1989*] [*Formerly, Cambodia*] [*Later, SOC*] (PD) ... PRK
People's Republic of South Yemen (BJA) ... PROSY
People's Republic of the Congo ... PRC
People's Republican Party [*Turkey Political party*] ... NRP
People's Revolutionary Army [*Grenada*] ... PRA
People's Revolutionary Government [*Grenada*] (PD) ... PRG
People's Revolutionary League of Ghana [*Political party*] (PPW) ... PRELOG
People's Revolutionary Party [*Benin*] [*Political party*] ... PRP
People's Revolutionary Party [*North Vietnam*] [*Political party*] ... PRP
People's Revolutionary Party of Kungleipak [*India*] [*Political party*] (PD) ... Prepak
People's Revolutionary Union - Marxist-Leninist [*Turkey*] (PD) ... TKP-ML
People's Rights Enforced Against Riots and Murder [*Vigilante group in New Jersey*] ... PRE-ARM
People's Savings Bank of Brockton [*Brockton, MA*] [*NASDAQ symbol*] (NQ) ... PBKB
Peoples Savings Bank of Brockton [*Associated Press*] (SAG) ... PSBBrc
People's Savings Financial Corp. [*Formerly, People's Savings Bank New Britain*] [*NASDAQ symbol*] (NQ) ... PBNB
People's Savings Financial Corp. [*Associated Press*] (SAG) ... PeoSvFn
People's Self-Defense Force [*South Vietnamese militia force*] (VNW) ... PSDF
People's Supreme Assembly [*Yemen*] [*Political party*] (PPW) ... PSA
Peoples Svgs Finl [*NASDAQ symbol*] (TTSB) ... PBNB
Peoples Telephone Co. [*Associated Press*] (SAG) ... PeopleTel
Peoples Telephone Co. [*AMEX symbol*] (SAG) ... PHO
Peoples Telephone Co. [*NASDAQ symbol*] (TTSB) ... PTEL
People's Telephone Co., Inc. [*Associated Press*] (SAG) ... PeopTel
People's Telephone Co., Inc. [*NASDAQ symbol*] (NQ) ... PTEL
People's Translation Service (EA) ... PTS
People's United Front [*Bangladesh*] [*Political party*] ... PUF
People's United Front [*Papua New Guinea*] [*Political party*] (PPW) ... PUF
People's United Party [*Belize*] [*Political party*] (PPW) ... PUP
[*The*] **People's Voice** [*Pre-World War II publication of Adam Clayton Powell, Jr., and Charlie Buchanan*] ... PV
Peoplesoft, Inc. [*Associated Press*] (SAG) ... Peopsft
Peoplesoft, Inc. [*NASDAQ symbol*] (SAG) ... PSFT
People-to-People Committee for the Handicapped (EA) ... PPCH
People-to-People Sports Committee (EA) ... PTPSC
People-to-People Tennis Committee (EA) ... PPTC
Peoria [*Diocesan abbreviation*] [*Illinois*] (TOCD) ... PEO
Peoria [*Illinois*] [*Airport symbol*] (OAG) ... PIA
Peoria & Eastern Railway [*Absorbed into Consolidated Rail Corp.*] [*AAR code*] ... PAE
Peoria and Pekin Union [*Railroad*] (AD) ... P & PU
Peoria & Pekin Union Railway Co. [*AAR code*] ... PPU
Peoria Board of Trade (EA) ... PBT
Peoria Heights Public Library, Peoria Heights, IL [*OCLC symbol*] (OCLC) ... IDT
Peoria Heights Public Library, Peoria Heights, IL [*Library symbol Library of Congress*] (LCLS) ... IPh
Peoria Historical Society, Peoria, IL [*Library symbol Library of Congress*] (LCLS) ... IPHi
Peoria, IL [*Location identifier FAA*] (FAAL) ... GZX
Peoria, IL [*Location identifier FAA*] (FAAL) ... PJR
Peoria, IL [*TV station call letters*] (RBYB) ... WAOE-TV
Peoria, IL [*FM radio station call letters*] ... WBGE
Peoria, IL [*FM radio station call letters*] ... WCBU
Peoria, IL [*FM radio station call letters*] ... WECU
Peoria, IL [*Television station call letters*] ... WEEK
Peoria, IL [*Television station call letters*] ... WHOI
Peoria, IL [*AM radio station call letters*] ... WIRL
Peoria, IL [*AM radio station call letters*] ... WMBD
Peoria, IL [*Television station call letters*] ... WMBD-TV
Peoria, IL [*FM radio station call letters*] ... WMXP
Peoria, IL [*AM radio station call letters*] ... WOAM
Peoria, IL [*AM radio station call letters*] ... WPEO
Peoria, IL [*FM radio station call letters*] ... WSWT
Peoria, IL [*Television station call letters*] ... WTVP
Peoria, IL [*FM radio station call letters*] ... WWCT
Peoria Kindergarten Primary Training School, Peoria, IL [*Library symbol Library of Congress*] (LCLS) ... IPK
Peoria Masonic Temple, Peoria, IL [*Library symbol Library of Congress*] (LCLS) ... IPM

Peoria Public Library, Peoria, AZ [*Library symbol*] [*Library of Congress*] (LCLS) ... AzPe
Peoria Public Library, Peoria, IL [*Library symbol Library of Congress*] (LCLS) ... IP
Peoria Record Club [*Record label*] ... PRCC
Peoria Terminal Co. [*AAR code*] ... PTC
Peotone, IL [*Location identifier FAA*] (FAAL) ... EON
Peotone Township Library, Peotone, IL [*Library symbol Library of Congress*] (LCLS) ... IPe
Pep Boys - Manny, Moe & Jack [*NYSE symbol*] (SPSG) ... PBY
Pep Boys-Man,Mo,Ja [*NYSE symbol*] (TTSB) ... PBY
Pep Boys-Manny, Moe & Jack [*Associated Press*] (SAG) ... PepBoy
Pep Pill [*Slang*] ... PP
Pepa [*Zaire*] [*ICAO location identifier*] (ICLI) ... FZRJ
Peperomia and Exotic Plant Society (EA) ... PEPS
Peperomia Society [*Later, PEPS*] (EA) ... PS
Pepino Latent Virus [*Plant pathology*] ... PELV
Pepino Mosaic Virus [*Plant pathology*] ... PEPMV
Pepitilla [*Race of maize*] ... PEP
Peppa Resources [*Vancouver Stock Exchange symbol*] ... PPA
Pepper (DICI) ... P
Pepper and Lewis' Digest of Laws [*Pennsylvania*] [*A publication*] (DLA) ... P & L Dig Laws
Pepper and Lewis' Digest of Laws [*Pennsylvania*] [*A publication*] (DLA) ... Pepper & L Dig
Pepper and Lewis' Digest of Laws [*Pennsylvania*] [*A publication*] (DLA) ... Pepper & L Dig Laws
Pepper Community [*Later, IPC*] ... PCC
Pepper Dust [*An adulterating element*] ... PD
Pepper Mottle Virus ... PeMV
Pepper Mottle Virus [*Plant pathology*] ... PEPMOV
Pepper Veinal Mottle Virus [*Plant pathology*] ... PVMV
Pepperdine University (GAGS) ... Pepperdine U
Pepperdine University, Law Library, Malibu, CA [*OCLC symbol*] (OCLC) ... CPF
Pepperdine University, Malibu, CA [*Library symbol Library of Congress*] (LCLS) ... CMalP
Pepperdine University, Malibu, CA [*OCLC symbol*] (OCLC) ... CPE
Pepperdine University School of Law (DLA) ... PEPUSL
Pepperell, AL [*AM radio station call letters*] (RBYB) ... WTLM-AM
Peppermint (DSUE) ... PEP
Pepsi Cola Puerto Rico Bottling [*Associated Press*] (SAG) ... PepsiPR
Pepsi Cola Puerto Rico Bottling [*NYSE symbol*] (SAG) ... PPO
PepsiCo Inc. [*NYSE symbol*] (SPSG) ... PEP
PepsiCo, Inc. [*Associated Press*] (SAG) ... PepsiC
PepsiCo, Inc., Research Library, Long Island, NY [*Library symbol Library of Congress*] (LCLS) ... NLicP
Pepsi-Cola Bottlers Association (EA) ... PCBA
Pepsi-Cola Puerto Rico Bott'B' [*NYSE symbol*] (TTSB) ... PPO
Pepsin A [*Medicine*] (MAE) ... PPS
Pepsin Inhibitor (OA) ... PI
Pepsin Pancreatin Digest [*Food protein digestibility assay*] ... PPD
Pepsinogen [*Medicine*] (MEDA) ... PG
Pepsinogen A (DMAA) ... PGA
Peptic Ulcer [*Medicine*] ... PU
Peptic Ulcer Disease ... PUD
Peptidase (DMAA) ... Pep
Peptidase A [*An enzyme*] ... PEPA
Peptidase C [*An enzyme*] ... PEPC
Peptidase D [*An enzyme*] ... PEPD
Peptidase S [*An enzyme*] ... PEPS
Peptide [*Biochemistry*] ... PEP
Peptide Absorption ... PA
Peptide Acid [*Organic chemistry*] ... PAC
Peptide Growth Factor [*Biochemistry*] ... PGF
Peptide Nucleic Acid [*Biochemistry*] ... PNA
Peptide Recognition Protein [*Biochemistry*] ... PRP
Peptide Separation [*Biochemistry*] ... PEP-SEP
Peptide Supply Factor [*Biochemistry*] ... PSF
Peptidoglycan [*Biochemistry*] ... PG
Peptidyl-Alpha-Hydroxyglycine Alpha-Amidating Lysine Phase Alteration Plane [*Medicine*] (DMAA) ... PAL
Peptidylglutamyl-Peptide Hydrolyzing [*Biochemistry*] ... PGPH
Peptidylprolyl Cis-Trans Isomerase [*An enzyme*] ... PPIase
Peptone, Glucose Yeast Extract [*Medium*] [*Medicine*] (BABM) ... PGYE
Peptone, Glucose Yeast Extract [*Medium*] [*Biochemistry*] (DAVI) ... PGYE
Peptone Yeast Extract [*Medium*] [*Microbiology*] (DAVI) ... PYE
Peptone-Starch-Dextrose [*Microbiology*] (MAE) ... PSD
Peptone-Yeast Glucose Maltose Agar [*Microbiology*] (MAE) ... PYGM
Peptone-Yeast-Glucose [*Medium*] [*Microbiology*] ... PYG
Pequot Lakes Elementary School, Pequot Lakes, MN [*Library symbol*] [*Library of Congress*] (LCLS) ... MnPelE
Pequot Lakes High School, Pequot Lakes MN [*Library symbol*] [*Library of Congress*] (LCLS) ... MnPelH
Pequot Lakes, MN [*FM radio station call letters*] ... KTIG
Pequot Library Association, Southport, CT [*Library symbol Library of Congress*] (LCLS) ... CtSoP
Per (WDMC) ... p
Per (IDOE) ... P
Per ... P
Per ... PR
Per Abdomen ... PA
Per Acre Rental (WDAA) ... PAR
Per Adresse [*Care Of*] [*German*] ... PA
Per Annum [*By the Year*] [*Latin*] ... PA
Per Annum [*By the Year*] [*Latin*] ... PER AN
Per Annum [*By the Year*] [*Latin*] ... PER ANN
Per Auguri [*Used on visiting cards to express congratulations, birthday wishes, etc.*] [*Italian*] ... PA
Per Calendar Month [*Business term*] (ADA) ... PCM
Per Calendar Month [*Business term*] (ODBW) ... pcm
Per Call Rate [*Telecommunications*] (IAA) ... PCR
Per Capita [*By the Individual*] [*Latin*] ... Per Cap
Per Capita Disposable Income [*Economics*] ... PCDI
Per Centum [*By the Hundred*] [*Latin*] ... PC
Per Centum [*By the Hundred*] [*Latin*] ... PERCENT
Per Column Inch [*Publishing*] ... PCI
Per Compass (IAA) ... PC
Per Condoglianza [*Used on visiting cards to express condolence*] [*Italian*] ... PC
Per Contra [*On the Other Side*] [*Latin*] ... Per con
Per Copia Conforme [*True Copy*] [*Italian*] ... PCC
Per Diem [*By the Day*] [*Latin*] ... PD
Per Diem [*By the Day*] [*Latin*] (ODBW) ... pd
Per Diem [*By the day*] [*Latin*] (WDMC) ... pd
Per Diem [*By the Day*] [*Latin*] (NOAA) ... PERDA
Per Diem Supplement (AAGC) ... PD Supp
Per Diem, Travel and Transportation Allowance Committee for Departments of the Army, Navy, and Air Force ... PDC
Per Diliquium [*By Deliquescence*] [*Pharmacy*] (ROG) ... PD
Per Dozen (WDAA) ... P/DOZ
Per Employee per Annum ... PEPA
Per Example ... PEX
Per Exchange Rate [*Finance*] (MHDW) ... PER
Per Gross Ton [*Shipping*] ... PGT
Per Gyro Compass [*Navigation*] ... PGC
Per Hour (IAA) ... PH
Per Hundred Million (NASA) ... PHM
Per Inquiry [*Advertising*] ... PI
Per Inquiry (WDMC) ... pi
Per Man Hour (WDAA) ... PMH
Per Million ... PM
Per Minute (IAA) ... PM
Per Month ... PM
Per Order (WDMC) ... PO
Per Os [*By Mouth*] [*Latin*] (AD) ... po
Per Os [*By Mouth*] [*Pharmacy*] ... PO
Per Person (AD) ... pp
Per Person, Double Occupancy (AD) ... ppdo
Per Person Interview Value [*Marketing*] (WDMC) ... PPIV
Per Person, Single Occupancy (AD) ... ppso
Per Pound [*Freight*] ... PLB
Per Power of Attorney [*Business term*] ... PPA
Per Price [*Business term*] ... PR
Per Procura [*By Proxy*] [*Latin*] ... ppa
Per Procuration [*Business term*] ... PPRO
Per Procurationem [*By Proxy, By the Action Of*] [*Legal term*] [*Latin*] (BARN) ... per pro
Per Procurationem [*By Proxy, By the Action Of*] [*Legal term Latin*] ... PER PROC
Per Procurationem [*By Proxy, By the Action Of*] [*Legal term Latin*] ... PP
Per Pupil Cost (AFM) ... PPC
Per Pupil Limitation (AFM) ... PPL
Per Pupil Operating Cost (ADA) ... PPOC
Per Rectum [*Through the rectum*] [*Pharmacology*] (DAVI) ... p rec
Per Rectum [*By the Rectum*] [*Latin*] (AD) ... pr
Per Rectum [*Medicine*] ... PR
Per Second (AAMN) ... PS
Per Ship ... PS
Per Speculum [*Medicine*] ... PS
Per Square Foot (ADA) ... PSF
Per Square Inch (ADA) ... PSI
Per Square Meter per Annum ... PSMPA
Per Standard Compass [*Navigation*] ... PSC
Per Steering Compass [*Navigation*] (DNAB) ... PSTCO
Per Steering Compass [*Navigation*] ... PSTGC
Per Task Data Area [*Computer science*] (BYTE) ... PTDA
Per Thousand Members per Year (DMAA) ... PTMPY
Per Truck ... PT
Per Unit (EECA) ... PU
Per Unit Monthly (DNAB) ... PUM
Per Urethra [*Medicine*] ... PU
Per Vaginam [*Medicine*] ... PV
Per Week ... PW
Per Week (ODBW) ... pw
Peracetic Acid [*Organic chemistry*] ... PAA
Peracta Operatione Emetici [*When the Operation of the Emetic is Finished*] [*Pharmacy*] (ROG) ... PER OP EMET
Peralta Oaks Research Center (AD) ... PORC
Peralto Resources Corp. [*Vancouver Stock Exchange symbol*] ... PLS
Perambulator [*British*] ... PRAM
Perambulator (AD) ... pram
Perbonate Unit [*Analytical biochemistry*] ... PU
Perceived Instrumentality of the College Test ... PICT
Perceived Level [*Noise*] ... PL
Perceived Noise ... PN
Perceived Noise Decibels ... PNdB
Perceived Noise Decibels (AD) ... pndb
Perceived Noise Level ... PNL
Perceived Noise Level, Tone Corrected ... PNLT
Perceived Outcome Potential (MHDI) ... POP
Perceived Quality of Life [*Medicine*] (DMAA) ... PQOL
Percent (WDMC) ... pc
Percent [*or Percentage*] (IAA) ... PC

Percent [*or Percentage*] ... PCT
Percent Adherence Index ... PAI
Percent Cortical Area [*Neurology*] ... PCA
Percent Defective Allowable (MHDB) ... PDA
Percent Deviation from the Median ... PDM
Percent Full Scale (KSC) ... PFS
Percent Hydrogen (SSD) ... pH
Percent Labeled Mitosis [*Cytology*] ... PLM
Percent Milli (NRCH) ... PCM
Percent Modern Carbon [*In atmosphere*] ... PMC
Percent of Crenated Red Blood Cells on Differential Count [*Hematology*] (DAVI) ... CRENA%
Percent of Females Reproductively Active [*Ecology*] ... PFRA
Percent of Males Reproductively Active [*Ecology*] ... PMRA
Percent Rated Wattage ... PRW
Percent Recovery [*Plant pathology*] ... PR
Percent Similarity Index ... PSI
Percent Time Active (CAAL) ... PTA
Percent Unaccounted For ... PUF
Percent Utilization [*Anesthesiology*] ... PU
Percentage [*Used instead of "average"*] [*Baseball*] ... PCT
Percentage Activity [*Measurement*] (DAVI) ... PA
Percentage Increase in Loss [*Statistics*] ... PIL
Percentage Mean Squared Error [*Statistics*] ... PMSE
Percentage Median Bias [*Statistics*] ... PMBIAS
Percentage of Completion Method (AAGC) ... PCM
Percentage of Successful Collisions [*Obstetrics*] ... PSC
Percentage of the Predicted Normal Value [*Indicated by the percent sign preceding the symbol*] [*Laboratory science*] (DAVI) ... %X
Percentage Quartile Deviation [*Statistics*] ... PQD
Percentage Quartile Deviation Median Bias [*Statistics*] ... PQDMB
Percentage Quota System (AD) ... PQS
Percentage Rates ... PR
Percentage Variance [*Statistics*] ... PVAR
Percentile ... P
Percentile Rank ... PR
Percentile Rank (AD) ... pr
Percept and Concept Cognition Test [*Psychology*] ... PCCT
Perception ... PCPT
Perception of Light ... PL
Perception of Ward [*Scales*] [*Psychology*] ... POW
Perception Schedule ... PS
Perceptions, Inc. (EA) ... PI
Perceptions of Developmental Skills Profile [*Education*] (EDAC) ... PODS
Perceptions of Parental Role Scales ... PPRS
Perceptron, Inc. [*Associated Press*] (SAG) ... Percptr
Perceptron, Inc. [*NASDAQ symbol*] (SAG) ... PRCP
Perceptual ... P
Perceptual Alternatives Laboratory [*University of Louisville*] [*Research center*] (RCD) ... PAL
Perceptual Isolation ... PI
Perceptual Maze Test [*Psychology*] ... PMT
Perceptual Performance (AD) ... pp
Perceptual Quotient [*Education*] (AEE) ... QP
Perceptual Respresentation System [*Memory*] ... PRS
Perceptual Speed [*A factor ability*] [*Psychology*] ... P
Perceptual Speed (Test) [*Psychology*] ... PS
Perceptual-Communicative Disorder [*Education*] (EDAC) ... PCD
Perch ... P
Percheron Horse Association of America (EA) ... PHAA
Perchloric Acid [*Inorganic chemistry*] ... PCA
Perchloride [*Chemistry*] (ROG) ... PERCHLOR
Perchloroethylene [*Also, TCE*] [*Dry cleaning*] ... P
Perchloroethylene [*Organic chemistry*] ... PCE
Perciconia circinata [*A toxin-producing fungus*] ... PC
Perclose, Inc. [*NASDAQ symbol*] (SAG) ... PERC
Perclose, Inc. [*Associated Press*] (SAG) ... Perclose
Percolator (DSUE) ... PERC
Per-Command Course (MCD) ... PCC
Percon, Inc. [*Associated Press*] (SAG) ... Percon
Percon, Inc. [*NASDAQ symbol*] (SAG) ... PRCN
Percuss and Vibrate [*Medicine*] (DAVI) ... P & V
Percussion ... P
Percussion (AAG) ... PERC
Percussion [*Medicine*] (DAVI) ... PERCUSS
Percussion and Ausculation [*Medicine*] (DHSM) ... PERCUSS & AUSC
Percussion and Auscultation [*Medicine*] ... P & A
Percussion and Postural Drainage ... P & PD
Percussion, Auscultation, and Fremitus [*Medicine*] ... PA & F
Percussion Note [*Physiology*] ... PN
Percussion Note (AD) ... pn
Percussion, Palpation, and Auscultation [*Medicine*] (DAVI) ... PP & A
Percussion, Vibration, and Drainage [*Medicine*] (DAVI) ... PVD
Percussion, Vibration and Suction [*Medicine*] (DAVI) ... PVS
Percussion Welding ... PEW
Percussive Arc Welder ... PAW
Percussive Arts Society (EA) ... PAS
Percussive Arts Society International Convention [*Percussive Arts Society*] ... PASIC
Percussive Butt Welder ... PBW
Percutaneous [*Medicine*] (AAMN) ... pcut
Percutaneous Abscess and Fluid Drainage [*Medicine*] (DMAA) ... PAFD
Percutaneous Abscess Drainage [*Surgery*] (DAVI) ... PAD
Percutaneous Aortic Balloon Valvuloplasty [*Medicine*] (HCT) ... PABV
Percutaneous Automated Diskectomy [*Neurology*] (DAVI) ... PAD
Percutaneous Balloon Aortic Valvuloplasty [*Cardiology*] (CPH) ... PBAV
Percutaneous Balloon Pulmonary Valvuloplasty [*Medicine*] (DMAA) ... PBPV
Percutaneous Biliary Drainage [*Gastroenterology*] (DAVI) ... PBD
Percutaneous Biopsy [*Medicine*] (CPH) ... PCB
Percutaneous Bladder Aspiration [*Urology*] (DAVI) ... PBA
Percutaneous Carotid Arteriogram [*Medicine*] (MAE) ... PCA
Percutaneous Cholangiography [*Medicine*] ... PTC
Percutaneous Cholecystostomy [*Medicine*] ... PC
Percutaneous Drain [*Surgery*] (DAVI) ... PD
Percutaneous Endoscopic Gastrostomy [*Medicine*] (CPH) ... PEG
Percutaneous Endoscopic Jejunostomy [*Medicine*] (DMAA) ... PEJ
Percutaneous Epidural Nerve Stimulator [*neurology*] (DAVI) ... PENS
Percutaneous Intraaortic Balloon Counterpulsation [*Catheter*] [*Medicine*] (DMAA) ... PIBC
Percutaneous Needle Aspiration Biopsy [*Medicine*] ... PNAB
Percutaneous Needle Lung Aspiration [*Medicine*] (DMAA) ... PNLA
Percutaneous Nephrostomy (DAVI) ... PCN
Percutaneous Nephrostomy Tube [*Nephrology*] (DAVI) ... PNT
Percutaneous Stone Manipulation [*Medicine*] ... PCSM
Percutaneous Transhepatic Biliary Drainage [*Medicine*] ... PTBD
Percutaneous Transhepatic Biliary Drainage - Enteric Feeding [*Medicine*] (DAVI) ... PTBD-EF
Percutaneous Transhepatic Cholangiogram [*Medicine*] ... PTC
Percutaneous Transhepatic Cholangioscopy [*Medicine*] ... PTCS
Percutaneous Transhepatic Gallbladder Drainage [*Medicine*] ... PTGBD
Percutaneous Transhepatic Selective Portography [*Roentgenography*] ... PTP
Percutaneous Transluminal Angioplasty [*Medicine*] ... PTA
Percutaneous Transluminal Aortic Valvuloplasty [*Cardiology*] (CPH) ... PTAV
Percutaneous Transluminal Balloon Angioplasty [*Cardiology*] (DMAA) ... PTBA
Percutaneous Transluminal Coronary Angioplasty [*Medicine*] ... PTCA
Percutaneous Transluminal Coronary Recanalization [*Cardiology*] (DMAA) ... PTCR
Percutaneous Transluminal Coronary Rotational Ablation [*Cardiology*] (DMAA) ... PTCRA
Percutaneous Transluminal Dilatation [*Medicine*] (DMAA) ... PTD
Percutaneous Transluminal Renal Angioplasty [*Medicine*] (DMAA) ... PTRA
Percutaneous Transvenous Mitral Valvotomy [*Cardiology*] ... PTMV
Percutaneous Ultrasonic Lithotripsy [*Medicine*] ... PUL
Percutaneous Ultrasonic Nephrolithotripsy [*Nephrology*] [*Radiology*] (DAVI) ... PUNL
Percutaneous Umbilical Blood [*Pediatrics*] (CPH) ... PUB
Percutaneous Umbilical Blood Sampling [*Medicine*] ... PUBS
Percutaneous Umbilical Cord Sampling [*Also, Cordocentesus*] [*Medical test*] (PAZ) ... PUBS
Percutaneously Inserted Spinal Cord Electrical Stimulation [*Medicine*] (DMAA) ... PISCES
Percutaneously-Introduced Cardiopulmonary Support System [*Medicine*] ... PCPS
Percy Township Branch, Northumberland County Public Library, Warkworth, Ontario [*Library symbol National Library of Canada*] (BIB) ... OWARNP
Perdant par Knockout [*Losing by a Knockout*] [*French*] ... PKO
Perdasdefogu [*Italy ICAO location identifier*] (ICLI) ... LIEP
Perdendo [*or Perdendosi*] [*Softer and Slower Music*] ... PERD
Perdendo [*or Perdendosi*] [*Softer and Slower Music*] ... PERDEN
Pere [*Father*] [*French*] ... P
Pere Marquette Memorial Association (EA) ... PMMA
Pere Marquette Railroad ... PM
Pere Marquette Residential Center, Grafton, IL [*Library symbol Library of Congress*] (LCLS) ... IGrafPM
Pere Marquette Youth Center, Edwardsville, IL [*Library symbol*] [*Library of Congress*] (LCLS) ... IEdMC
Peregrine Capital Myanmar ... PCM
Peregrine Fund (EA) ... PF
Peregrine Petroleum [*Vancouver Stock Exchange symbol*] ... PGR
Peregrinus Fabius [*Authority cited in pre-1607 legal work*] (DSA) ... Pereg
Pereira [*Colombia*] [*Airport symbol*] (OAG) ... PEI
Pereira/Matecana [*Colorado ICAO location identifier*] (ICLI) ... SKPE
Perennial [*Botany*] ... per
Perennial [*Botany*] ... prnnl
Perennial Allergic Rhinitis [*Medicine*] ... PAR
Perennial Plant Association (EA) ... PPA
Perennial Rye Grass [*Immunology*] ... PRG
Perera's Select Decisions [*Ceylon*] [*A publication*] (DLA) ... Per
Perez Self-Concept Inventory [*Psychology*] (EDAC) ... PSCI
Perfect ... PERF
Perfect ... PERF
Perfect ... PF
Perfect Crystal Technology (IAA) ... PCT
Perfect Diffuser [*Optics*] ... PD
Perfect Digital Invariant (OA) ... PDI
Perfect Hard Disk [*Century Data Systems*] [*Computer science*] ... PhD
Perfect Initials [*Philately*] ... PI
Perfect Master [*Freemasonry*] ... PM
Perfect Ream (DGA) ... PERF RM
Perfect Shuffle (MHDI) ... PS
Perfect Title [*Business term*] ... PT
PerfectData Corp. [*NASDAQ symbol*] (NQ) ... PERF
PerfectData Corp. [*Associated Press*] (SAG) ... Perfdta
Perfect-Gas Isentropic Decompression [*Engineering*] ... PID
Perfection Requires Individual Defect Elimination ... PRIDE
Perfectly Stirred Reactor ... PSR
Perfil de Evaluacion del Comportamiento [*Standardized test of elementary through high school students' behavior at school, at home, and with peers*] ... PEC

Perfins Club (EA)	PC
Perfluorinated Ion-Exchange Polymer [Organic chemistry]	PFIEP
Perfluorinated Polyether [Organic chemistry]	PFPE
Perfluoroalkoxy [Organic chemistry]	PFA
Perfluoroalkyl Ether [Organic chemistry]	PFAE
Perfluorocarbon [Organic chemistry]	PFC
Perfluorocarbon [Marine science] (OSRA)	PFC
Perfluorochemical [Organic chemistry]	PFC
Perfluorocytylbromide (DMAA)	PFOB
Perfluorodecalin [Organic chemistry]	PFD
Perfluorodecanoic Acid [Organic chemistry]	PFDA
Perfluoroisobutene [Organic chemistry]	PFIB
Perfluoroisobutylene [Organic chemistry] (MAE)	PFIB
Perfluorokerosene [Heat transfer agent]	PFK
Perfluorooctanoic Acid [Organic chemistry]	PFOA
Perfluorooctyl Bromide [Organic chemistry]	POB
Perforate [or Perforator]	PERF
Perforated Backup Plate	PBUP
Perforated Insignia [Philately]	PERFINS
Perforated Metal Export Groups [British] (DBA)	PMEG
Perforated Steel Planking (SAA)	PSP
Perforated Steel Plate (VNW)	PSP
Perforated Steel Plating (DNAB)	PSP
Perforated Tape [Computer science] (IAA)	PT
Perforated Tape and Transmission Code [Telecommunications] (IAA)	PTTC
Perforated Tape Reader	PTR
Perforated Tape Subsystem [Computer science] (IAA)	PTS
Perforateur Honeywell Bull (IAA)	P
Perforating Wound	PERFW
Perforation	P
Perforation (DSUE)	PERF
Perforation (WDMC)	perf
Perforator (IAA)	PERFR
Perforator (DEN)	PFR
Perform (ROG)	PERFM
Performance [Army] (INF)	P
Performance (DA)	PER
Performance (KSC)	PERF
Performance (VRA)	perf
Performance	PERFCE
Performance	PERFORM
Performance (WGA)	PFCE
Performance (MSA)	PRFM
Performance Acceptance Test (SAA)	PAT
Performance Accountability and Improvement Report	PAIR
Performance Advantage Kit [Personal computers]	PAK
Performance Advantage with Cummins Electronics [Automotive engineering]	PACE
Performance Alertness (AEBS)	PA
Performance Analysis	PA
Performance Analysis and Control	PAC
Performance Analysis and Design [Nuclear energy] (NRCH)	PAD
Performance Analysis and Design Synthesis [Computer program] [NASA]	PADS
Performance Analysis and Prediction Study (PDAA)	PAPS
Performance Analysis and Review	PAR
Performance Analysis and Test Histories (KSC)	PATH
Performance Analysis Display System (NITA)	PADS
Performance Analysis Model (MCD)	PAM
Performance Analysis of Networks, Electrical	PANE
Performance Analysis Reliability Reporting (DNAB)	PARR
Performance Analysis Routine [Computer science]	PAR
Performance Analysis Subsystem [Military] (CAAL)	PASS
Performance Analysis Workstation [Computer science]	PAW
Performance and Compatibility Requirements	P & CR
Performance and Compatibility Requirements	PACR
Performance and Control (SSD)	P & C
Performance and Cost Analysis Model (MCD)	PERCAM
Performance and Cost Evaluation	PACE
Performance and Demand Analyser (PDAA)	PANDA
Performance and Failure Assessment Monitor (MCD)	PAFAM
Performance and Improved Reliability	PAIR
Performance and Integration Retrofit	PAIR
Performance and Interface [Specification] [NASA] (NASA)	P & I
Performance and Operational [Test or reports]	P & O
Performance and Operations Requirements Document [NASA] (NASA)	PORD
Performance and Resources (NASA)	P & R
Performance Appraisal Report [Nuclear energy] (NRCH)	PAR
Performance Appraisal Required [Civil Service]	PA
Performance Appraisal Team [Nuclear energy] (NRCH)	PAT
Performance Assesment Battery [Medicine] (DMAA)	PAB
Performance Assessment (DOGT)	PA
Performance Assessment and Appraisal System	PAAS
Performance Assessment and Workload Evaluation (GAVI)	PAWES
Performance Assessment in Reading [Educational test]	PAIR
Performance Assessment Logic	PAL
Performance Assessment Monitoring (MCD)	PAM
Performance Assessment of Geological Isolation System [Nuclear energy] (NUCP)	PAGIS
Performance Assessment of Syntax: Elicited and Spontaneous [Educational test]	PASES
Performance Assessment Report [Small Cities Community Development Block Grant] [Department of Housing and Urban Development] (GFGA)	PAR
Performance Assured Certification	PAC
Performance Audit Inspection [Environmental Protection Agency] (GFGA)	PAI

Performance Audit Inspection (GNE)	PAI
Performance Augmentation Ring (MCD)	PAR
Performance Based Method [Environmental Protection Agency] [Analytical chemistry]	PBM
Performance Buffet Limit (GAVI)	PHIBUF
Performance Capability Measure (IAA)	PCM
Performance Certification Component [SQT] (MCD)	PCC
Performance Code	PC
Performance Coding System	PERCOS
Performance Contract (OICC)	PC
Performance Correlation Technique	PCT
Performance Criteria and Test Methods Task	PC/TM
Performance Criteria Categories (MCD)	PCC
Performance Data Base (GAVI)	PDB
Performance Data Book (NASA)	PDB
Performance Data Computer	PDC
Performance Data Computer System (MCD)	PDCS
Performance Data Services, Inc. [Falls Church, VA] [Software manufacturer]	PDSI
Performance Demonstration (MCD)	PD
Performance Demonstration Test	PDT
Performance Effectiveness [or Evaluation] Program [Navy]	PEP
Performance Efficiency Factor (AFIT)	PEF
Performance Efficiency Test [Employee screening and placement test]	PET
Performance Evaluation and Information Reduction (IAA)	PEIR
Performance Evaluation and Trend Analysis (NASA)	PETA
Performance Evaluation Board [NASA] (MCD)	PEB
Performance Evaluation Group (CINC)	PEG
Performance Evaluation Model	PEM
Performance Evaluation of Amplifiers from a Remote Location	PEARL
Performance Evaluation Procedure [Joint Commission on Accreditation of Hospitals] (DHSM)	PEP
Performance Evaluation Report [DoD]	PER
Performance Evaluation Reporting System [DoD]	PERS
Performance Evaluation Review Technique	PERT
Performance Evaluation Support Office	PESO
Performance Evaluation Team [Nuclear energy] (NRCH)	PET
Performance Evaluation Test	PET
Performance Evaluation, Test, and Simulation [Air Force]	PET & S
Performance Executive Airlines Ltd. [British ICAO designator] (FAAC)	PZY
Performance Factor	PF
Performance Fitness Examination [Military] (DNAB)	PFE
Performance Flight Certification [NASA] (NASA)	PFC
Performance Food Group [Commercial firm Associated Press] (SAG)	PerFood
Performance Food Group [NASDAQ symbol] (SAG)	PFGC
Performance Ford Club of America (EA)	PFCA
Performance Funding System [Department of Housing and Urban Development] (GFGA)	PFS
Performance Handicap Racing Formula [Sailing]	PHRF
Performance History	PH
Performance Improvement	PI
Performance Improvement Tests	PIT
Performance Incentive Contracting (AAGC)	PIC
Performance Index	PI
Performance Indicator (MCD)	PI
Performance Intelligence Quotient [Psychology] (DMAA)	PIQ
Performance Intensity (MAE)	PI
Performance Levels of a School Program Survey [Teacher evaluation test]	PLSPS
Performance Management and Evaluation	PME
Performance Management and Recognition System (MCD)	PMARS
Performance Management and Recognition System	PMRS
Performance Management Association (EAIO)	PMA
Performance Management Computer (PDAA)	PMC
Performance Management Operations Manual [NASA] (NASA)	PMOM
Performance Management Operations Network [NASA] (NASA)	PMON
Performance Management Package [NASA] (NASA)	PMP
Performance Management Software (IAA)	PMS
Performance Management System	PMS
Performance Measurement Baseline (MCD)	PMB
Performance Measurement Facility (IAA)	PMF
Performance Measurement Joint Executive Group (DOMA)	PMJEG
Performance Measurement Report [NASA] (NASA)	PMR
Performance Measurement System [Nuclear Regulatory Commission] (MCD)	PMS
Performance Measurement System/Department of Defense	PMS/DOD
Performance Measuring Tool (MCD)	PMT
Performance Monitor [NASA] (NASA)	PM
Performance Monitor Annunciation Driver [NASA] (MCD)	PMAD
Performance Monitor Annunciation Panel [NASA] (MCD)	PMAP
Performance Monitor Annunciator [NASA] (MCD)	PMA
Performance Monitor/Fault Locator [Military] (CAAL)	PM/FL
Performance Monitor Function [NASA] (NASA)	PMF
Performance Monitor Unit [Communications]	PMU
Performance Monitor Unit (AD)	pmu
Performance Monitoring Equipment (NVT)	PME
Performance Monitoring Receiver	PMR
Performance Monitoring System [Fort Belvoir, VA] [Army] (NASA)	PMS
Performance Number	PN
Performance Objectives (OICC)	PO
Performance of Commercial Activities [OMB Circular] (AAGC)	A-76
Performance, Operating and Maintenance Standards for Electronic Equipment (NG)	POMSEE
Performance Optimization Code	POC

Performance Optimization with Enhanced RISC [*Reduced Instruction Set Computer*] (PCM) .... POWER
Performance Program Statement [*Australia*] .... PPS
Performance Qualification (ACII) .... PQ
Performance Qualification Requirement .... PQR
Performance Qualification Test (MCD) .... PQT
Performance Rating (OICC) .... PR
Performance Rating System (OICC) .... PRS
Performance Ratio (AAG) .... PR
Performance Records for Optimizing System Design (IAA) .... PROSD
Performance Registry International .... PRI
Performance Related Gift [*Business Management*] .... PRG
Performance Report (AFM) .... PR
Performance Requirement .... PR
Performance, Requirements, Practices [*Military*] .... PRP
Performance Review for Operating Programs (BUR) .... PROP
Performance Review of Base Supply Effectiveness [*Air Force*] (AFM) .... PROBE
Performance Risk Index Number (NG) .... PRIN
Performance Scales Intelligence Quotient (EDAC) .... PSIO
Performance Score .... PS
Performance Shaping Factor [*Engineering*] .... PSF
Performance Shaping Parameters (IEEE) .... PSP
Performance Share Plan [*Human resources*] (WYGK) .... PSP
Performance Specification Tree .... PST
Performance Standard .... PS
Performance Standard Sheet .... PSS
Performance Standardization Branch Instruction (SAA) .... PSBI
Performance Standards Program .... PSP
Performance Status [*Rehabilitation*] (DAVI) .... PS
Performance Summary Report (NG) .... PSR
Performance Support System [*Human resources*] (WYGK) .... PSS
Performance Systems International, Inc. [*Associated Press*] (SAG) .... PerfSys
Performance Systems International, Inc. .... PSI
Performance Systems International, Inc. [*NASDAQ symbol*] (SAG) .... PSIX
Performance Technical Survey Report .... PTSR
Performance Technologies [*NASDAQ symbol*] (TTSB) .... PTIX
Performance Technologies, Inc. [*Associated Press*] (SAG) .... PerfTech
Performance Technologies, Inc. [*NASDAQ symbol*] (SAG) .... PTIX
Performance Technology [*Human resources*] (WYGK) .... PT
Performance Test .... PT
Performance Test Chamber (MCD) .... PTC
Performance Test Code .... PTC
Performance Test Model (OA) .... PTM
Performance Tracking System .... PTS
Performance Units Plan (MHDB) .... PUP
Performance Update Program [*Air Force*] (DOMA) .... PUP
Performance Verification System .... PVS
Performance Verification Test .... PVT
Performance Versus Intensity Function for Phonetically Balanced Words (MEDA) .... PI-PB
Performance Warehouse Association (EA) .... PWA
Performance Work Standard (AAGC) .... PWO
Performance Work Standard .... PWS
Performance Work Statement [*DoD*] .... PWS
Performance-Based Adult Vocational Education (EDAC) .... PAVE
Performance-Based Evaluation Instrument (EDAC) .... PBEI
Performance-Based Exposure Control Limit [*Environmental science*] .... PBECL
Performance-Based Incentive System (AAGC) .... PBIS
Performance-Based Management (AAGC) .... PBM
Performance-Based Measurement System [*Environmental Protection Agency*] .... PBMS
Performance-Based Organization .... PBO
Performance-Based Pay .... PBP
Performance-Based Payment System .... PBPS
Performance-Based Service Contracting (AAGC) .... PBSC
Performance-Based Teacher Education (OICC) .... PBTE
Performance-Measuring Equipment (AD) .... pme
Performance-Oriented Infantry Qualification Test (INF) .... POIQT
Performance-Oriented Packaging [*for hazardous materials*] .... POP
Performance-Oriented Packing Standard .... POPS
Performance-Related Pay [*Business term*] (ECON) .... PRD
Performance-Related Pay (ECON) .... PRP
Performance-Related Remuneration (ADA) .... PRR
Performax's Personal Matrix System (DMAA) .... PPMS
Performed (ROG) .... PERFD
Performer .... P
Performer [*MARC relator code*] [*Library of Congress*] (LCCP) .... prf
Performer Design Sheet .... PDS
Performer Diploma (PGP) .... PD
Performer Quotient [*TV-performer rating*] .... PQ
Performic Acid-Schiff Reaction [*Medicine*] (MAE) .... PFAS
Performing (ROG) .... PFRMG
Performing and Captive Animals Defence League [*British*] (BI) .... PADL
Performing and Visual Arts Society (EA) .... PAVAS
Performing Animal Welfare Society (EA) .... PAWS
Performing Artists for Nuclear Disarmament (EA) .... PAND
Performing Artists Network [*Electronic network*] .... PAN
Performing Arts [*US Copyright Office class*] .... PA
Performing Arts Biography Master Index [*A publication*] .... PABMI
Performing Arts Center for Health [*New York University/Bellevue Hospital, New York, NY*] [*Superseded by Center for Dance Medicine -CDM*] .... PACH
Performing Arts, Culture, and Entertainment [*Proposed cable television system*] .... PACE
Performing Arts Directory [*A publication*] .... PAD

Performing Arts for Crisis Training [*In association name, PACT Training*] (EA) .... PACT
Performing Arts Foundation (EA) .... PAF
Performing Arts Journal [*A publication*] .... PAJ
Performing Arts Journal [*A publication*] (BRI) .... Per A J
Performing Arts Medicine .... PAM
Performing Arts/Omaha [*Nebraska*] .... PA/O
Performing Arts Repertory Theater .... PART
Performing Arts Study Unit (EA) .... PASU
Performing Organization (NITA) .... PO
Performing Right Society [*British*] .... PRS
Performing Rights Organization [*Formerly, BMI-Canada Ltd.*] [*Canada*] .... PRO
Performing Rights Organization of Canada [*See also SDE*] .... PROC
Performing Scale [*Medicine*] (MAE) .... PS
Perfumania, Inc. [*Associated Press*] (SAG) .... Perfum
Perfumania, Inc. [*NASDAQ symbol*] (SAG) .... PRFM
Perfumery Importers Association [*Defunct*] (EA) .... PIA
Perfusion [*Cardiology*] (DAVI) .... Q
Perfusion Fixation [*Histology*] .... PF
Perfusion Fluid [*Medicine*] (DMAA) .... PF
Perfusion Pressure [*Cardiology*] (DAVI) .... PP
Perfusion Program Directors Council [*Cardiology*] (DAVI) .... PPDC
Perfusion Rate [*Cardiology*] (DAVI) .... PR
Perfusionist [*Medicine*] (DAVI) .... P
Perfusionist [*Medicine*] (HCT) .... PERF
Pergamino [*Parchment*] [*Spanish*] (AD) .... pno
Pergamino [*Argentina ICAO location identifier*] (ICLI) .... SAAN
Pergamon Compact Solution [*CD-ROM publisher*] (IT) .... PCS
Pergamon Financial Data Services [*Pergamon Orbit Infoline Ltd.*] [*British Information service or system*] (IID) .... PFDS
Pergamon Holding Foundation [*Liechtenstein*] .... PHF
Pergamon International Information Corp. [*Information service or system*] (IID) .... PIIC
Pergamon Press, Inc. .... PPI
Pergamon Press, Inc., Fairview Park, Elmsford, NY [*Library symbol Library of Congress*] (LCLS) .... PmP
Pergamon Professional and Financial Services [*Commercial firm British*] .... PPFS
Pergerakan Guerilja Rakyat Sarawak [*Sarawak People's Guerrilla Forces*] [*Malaya*] .... PGRS
Pergola [*Classified advertising*] (ADA) .... PERG
Perham Elementary School, Perham, MN [*Library symbol*] [*Library of Congress*] (LCLS) .... MnPhE
Perham, MN [*FM radio station call letters*] (RBYB) .... KPRW-FM
Perham Public Library, Perham, MN [*Library symbol*] [*Library of Congress*] (LCLS) .... MnPhP
Perhaps (ROG) .... PER
Perhaps .... PERH
Perhaps...Kids Meeting Kids Can Make a Difference (EA) .... PKMKCMD
Periadenitis Mucosa Necrotica Recurrens [*Medicine*] .... PMNR
Periadenitis Mucosa Necrotica Recurrens (AD) .... pmnr
Perials of the Sea (MHDB) .... POTS
Perianth .... P
Periapical [*Anatomy*] (DAVI) .... PA
Periapical [*Dentistry*] .... PERIAP
Periaqueductal Gray Matter [*Brain anatomy*] .... PAG
Periarteriolar Lymphocyte Sheath (AAMN) .... PALS
Periarteritis [*Medicine*] (DMAA) .... PA
Periarteritis Nodosa [*Also, PN*] [*Medicine*] .... PAN
Periarteritis [*or Polyarteritis*] Nodosa [*Also, PAN*] [*Medicine*] .... PN
Peribrachialis [*Anatomy*] .... PB
Peribrachialis Nuclei [*Neurology*] .... PBN
Peribronchial Fibrosis [*Medicine*] .... PBF
Pericardial Effusion [*Cardiology*] (DAVI) .... PE
Pericardial Fluid [*Cardiology*] (DAVI) .... PARC
Pericardial Fluid [*Medicine*] (DMAA) .... PF
Pericardial Friction Rub [*Medicine*] (MEDA) .... PFR
Pericardial Tamponade [*Medicine*] (DMAA) .... PT
Pericarditis [*Avian pathology*] .... PC
Pericardium [*Medicine*] .... P
Pericardium Wall [*Medicine*] .... PW
Pericentral .... PC
Pericentriolar Material [*Biochemistry*] .... PCM
Pericles [*Shakespearean work*] .... Per
Pericles [*of Plutarch*] [*Classical studies*] (OCD) .... Per
Pericles, Prince of Tyre [*A publication*] (AD) .... PPT
Pericom Semiconductor Corp. [*Associated Press*] (SAG) .... Pericom
Pericom Semiconductor Corp. [*NASDAQ symbol*] (SAG) .... PRCM
Pericope (VRA) .... peric
Pericruciate Association [*Cortex, of cat*] .... PCA
Pericynthion [*Perilune, or low point, in lunar orbit*] .... PC
Periderm [*Botany*] .... PD
Peri-Dinaphthalene [*A fluorophore*] [*Organic chemistry*] .... PERYLENE
Peridinin-Chlorophyll-Protein [*Botany*] .... PCP
Peridot [*Jewelry*] (ROG) .... PEDT
Peridural Artery [*Medicine*] (DMAA) .... PA
Perigean Range (AD) .... Pn
Perigean Range .... PN
Perigee (KSC) .... PER
Perigee .... PERI
Perigee (BARN) .... perig
Perigee Altitude (NASA) .... HP
Perigee Kick Motor (MCD) .... PKM
Perigee Motor Firing [*Aerospace*] (MCD) .... PMF
Perigee-Apogee Satellite [*Aerospace*] .... PAS
Perigee-Apogee Stage [*Aerospace*] .... PAS

Perigee-Apogee System [Aerospace] .... PAS
Perigeniculate Nucleus [Anatomy] .... PGN
Perigeux/Bassillac [France ICAO location identifier] (ICLI) .... LFBX
Perihelion Distance [Astronomy] (BARN) .... Q
Perilymph Fistula [Medicine] .... PLF
Perilymphatic Fistula [Medicine] (DMAA) .... PLF
Perilymphatic Fistula Syndrome [Medicine] (DMAA) .... PLFS
Perim [People's Democratic Republic of Yemen] [ICAO location identifier] (ICLI) .... ODAP
Perimeter .... P
Perimeter (AABC) .... PERI
Perimeter (KSC) .... PERIM
Perimeter Acquisition RADAR (MSA) .... PACR
Perimeter Acquisition RADAR [Army] .... PAR
Perimeter Acquisition RADAR Attack Characterization System (MCD) .... PARACS
Perimeter Acquisition RADAR Attack Characterization System [Army] .... PARCS
Perimeter Acquisition RADAR Building [Army] (AABC) .... PARB
Perimeter Acquisition RADAR Data Processor [Army] (AABC) .... PARDP
Perimeter Acquisition RADAR Simulation [Missile system evaluation] (RDA) .... PARSIM
Perimeter Acquisition RADAR [Characterization] System (MCD) .... PARS
Perimeter Airlines [ICAO designator] (AD) .... UW
Perimeter Array Antenna (PDAA) .... PARAN
Perimeter Array RADAR (MCD) .... PAR
Perimeter Aviation Ltd. [Canada ICAO designator] (FAAC) .... PAG
Perimeter Defense System (MCD) .... PDS
Perimeter Surveillance (LAIN) .... PS
Perimeter Ventures Ltd. [Vancouver Stock Exchange symbol] .... PVU
Perimeter-Insulated Raised Floor [Residential construction] .... PIRF
Perimortem (DAVI) .... PERI/M
Perinatal Clinical Research Center [Case Western Reserve University] [Research center] (RCD) .... PCRC
Perinatal Injury [Neonatology] (DAVI) .... PI
Perinatal Mortality [Medicine] .... PNM
Perinatal Mortality Rate [Medicine] .... PMR
Perinatal Telencephalic Leukoencephalopathy [Medicine] .... PTL
Perineal [Gynecology] (MAE) .... per
Perineal [Anatomy] (DAVI) .... peri
Perineal Pad [Gynecology] (MAE) .... perpad
Perini Corp. [AMEX symbol] (SPSG) .... PCR
Perini Corp. [Associated Press] (SAG) .... PeriniC
Perini Corp. [Associated Press] (SAG) .... PernC
Perini Corp. Dep Cv Exch Pfd [AMEX symbol] (TTSB) .... PCRPr
Perinuclear Anti-Neutrophilic Cytoplasmic Antibody [Medicine] (DMAA) .... P-ANCA
Periochae [of Livy] [Classical studies] (OCD) .... Per
Period .... P
Period (AABC) .... PD
Period [Record label] .... Per
Period .... PER
Period (VRA) .... per
Period .... PRD
Period Contract .... PC
Period Contract Acceptance .... PCA
Period Contract Request .... PCR
Period End Date (MCD) .... PED
Period Ending .... PE
Period Hours (IAA) .... PH
Period of Incapacity for Work (DI) .... PIW
Period of Interest (MCD) .... POI
Period of Onset [Medicine] .... PO
Period of Performance (MCD) .... POP
Period of Reduced Melting [Climatology] .... PRM
Period of Service [Military] .... POS
Period Order Quantity (PDAA) .... POQ
Period per Second (IAA) .... PPS
Period Pulse Train .... PPT
Period Tapering (IAA) .... PT
Period to Discharge [Medicine] (DAVI) .... PTD
Periodate Lysine-Paraformaldehyde .... PLP
Periodic (AFM) .... PDIC
Periodic (AAG) .... PE
Periodic (AAMN) .... per
Periodic (MSA) .... PERD
Periodic Acid [Inorganic chemistry] .... PA
Periodic Acid Mixed Diamine (OA) .... PAMD
Periodic Acid/Schiff [A stain] .... PA/S
Periodic Acid Schiff Procedure (DOG) .... PAS procedure
Periodic Acid - Silver Methenamine [Biological stain] .... PASM
Periodic Acid-Schiff Technique [Medicine] (DMAA) .... PAST
Periodic Acid-Schiff with Phenylhydrazine Interposition [A stain] .... PAPS
Periodic Acid-Thiocarbohydrazide-Silver Proteinate [Test] [Cytology] .... PA-TCH-SP
Periodic Aircraft Reconditioning Cycle (DNAB) .... PARC
Periodic Alternating Nystagmus [Ophthalmology] .... PAN
Periodic and Random Deviation .... PARD
Periodic Armaments Planning System (MCD) .... PAPS
Periodic Arrays of Pinning Sites [Solid state physics] .... PAPS
Periodic Bond Chain (IAA) .... PBC
Periodic Confidence Test .... PCT
Periodic Conformance Inspection (MCD) .... PCI
Periodic Current Reversal [Electrochemistry] .... PCR
Periodic Depot Level Maintenance .... PDLM
Periodic Duty (IAA) .... PD
Periodic Environmental Test .... PET
Periodic Error Integrating Controller .... PEIC
Periodic Evaluation Test .... PET
Periodic Health Examination .... PHE
Periodic Incremental Release [Physiology] .... PIR
Periodic Information Briefing (MCD) .... PIB
Periodic Inspection [Military] (AFM) .... PI
Periodic Inspection Control [Military] (IAA) .... PIC
Periodic Inspection Turn-Around Time [Military] (AFIT) .... PETAT
Periodic Intelligence Report (NATG) .... PERINTREP
Periodic Intelligence Report .... PERINTREPT
Periodic Intelligence Report .... PIR
Periodic Intelligence Review [Supreme Allied Commander, Atlantic] (NATG) .... PIR
Periodic Intelligence Summary [Army] (AABC) .... PERINTSUM
Periodic Interim Payment Program [Medicare] (GFGA) .... PIP
Periodic Lateralized Epileptiform Discharge [Medicine] (MAE) .... PLED
Periodic Leg Movement (DMAA) .... PLM
Periodic List of Data [Computer science] .... PLOD
Periodic Log System .... PLS
Periodic Logistical Report .... PLR
Periodic Maintenance (AFM) .... PM
Periodic Maintenance Information Cards (MCD) .... PMIC
Periodic Maintenance Requirements Manual [Navy] .... PMRM
Periodic Maintenance Team .... PMT
Periodic Motor Vehicle Inspection (PDAA) .... PMVI
Periodic Motor Vehicle Inspection (AD) .... pmvi
Periodic Operation Report .... POR
Periodic Order Quantity (AD) .... poq
Periodic Permanent Magnet .... PPM
Periodic Permanent Magnet Focusing (IAA) .... PPM
Periodic Personnel Report .... PPR
Periodic Personnel Report [Military] (AABC) .... PPREPT
Periodic Personnel Strength Report [Army] (AABC) .... PPSR
Periodic Programs Termination [Computer science] .... PPT
Periodic Pulse Metering [Telecommunications] (TEL) .... PPM
Periodic Reevaluation Tests .... PRT
Periodic Reliability Evaluation Test (MCD) .... PRET
Periodic Report (IAA) .... PR
Periodic Reversal (IAA) .... PR
Periodic Reverse Current (IAA) .... PRC
Periodic Self-Test [Computer science] .... PST
Periodic Short Pulse (MAE) .... PSP
Periodic Significant Scheduled Tasks [NASA] (NASA) .... PSST
Periodic Syndrome [Medicine] .... PS
Periodic Test [Nuclear energy] (NRCH) .... PT
Periodical (ROG) .... PER
Periodical .... PERI
Periodical and Book Association of America (EA) .... PBAA
Periodical Control System [Libraries] .... PCS
Periodical Directories and Bibliographies [A publication] .... PDB
Periodical Directories and Bibliographies Master Index [A publication] .... PDBMI
Periodical Enquiry Acquisition and Registration Locally (NITA) .... PEARL
Periodical Guide for Computerists [Applegate Computer Enterprises] [Information service or system Defunct] (IID) .... PGFC
Periodical Holdings in the Library of the School of Medicine [Washington University School of Medicine] [Library network] .... PHILSOM
Periodical Holdings List [Libraries] .... PHL
Periodical Index Term (NITA) .... PI
Periodical On-Line Keyword Access [Computer science] (PDAA) .... POLKA
Periodical Press Gallery [US Senate] .... PPG
Periodical Publication in Harvard Science Libraries .... PPHSL
Periodical Publications [British Library shelf designation] .... PP
Periodical Publishers Association [Later, MCA] (EA) .... PPA
Periodical Publishers' Service Bureau (NADA) .... PPSB
Periodical Publishers' Service Bureau (AD) .... PPSB
Periodical Source Index [A publication] .... PERS
Periodical Title Abbreviations [A publication] .... PTA
Periodical Title Abbreviations: by Abbreviation [A publication] .... PTA-A
Periodical Title Abbreviations: by Title [A publication] .... PTA-T
Periodical Writers Association of Canada .... PWAC
Periodically Elevated Electronic Kibitzer .... PEEK
Periodically Replenished Magma Chambers [Geology] .... PRMC
Periodicals Automation, Rand Library .... PEARL
Periodicals Data System (NITA) .... PDS
Periodicals in South African Libraries (NITA) .... PISAL
Periodicals Institute (EA) .... PI
Periodicals Publishing Record [Alberta Public Affairs Bureau] [Canada Information service or system] (CRD) .... PPR
Periodicity (DMAA) .... per
Periodogram (DMAA) .... PER
Periodonist .... PRDNTST
Periodontal Disease Clinical Research Center [State University of New York at Buffalo] [Research center] (RCD) .... PDCRC
Periodontal Disease Index [Dentistry] (DMAA) .... PDI
Periodontal Disease-Associated Microbiotae [Dentistry] .... PDAM
Periodontal Ligament [Dentistry] .... PDL
Periodontics and Restorative Dentistry .... PRD
Periodontist [Dentistry] (DAVI) .... perio
Periods of European History [A publication] .... PEH
Perioperative [Medicine] (DMAA) .... PO
Perioperative Myocardial Infarction [Medicine] (DMAA) .... PMI
Periosteal Bone Apposition Rate [Laboratory science] (DAVI) .... R_{pba}
Periosteal Fibroblast [Medicine] (DMAA) .... PF
Periostitis Ossificans Toxica [Medicine] (DMAA) .... POT
Peripheral (DAVI) .... P

Peripheral	PERIF
Peripheral	PRPHL
Peripheral Access Lattices	PAL
Peripheral Adapter Module	PAM
Peripheral Address Field	PAF
Peripheral Airway Obstruction [*Medicine*] (DMAA)	PAO
Peripheral Airways [*Medicine*] (DMAA)	PAW
Peripheral Allocation Table (NITA)	PAT
Peripheral Anterior Synechia [*Ophthalmology*]	PAS
Peripheral Arterial Disease [*Medicine*]	PAD
Peripheral Arteriosclerotic Occlusive Disease [*Medicine*] (MAE)	PAOD
Peripheral Assignment Table (CMD)	PAT
Peripheral Automatic Channel Emulator [*Computer science*]	PACE
Peripheral Autonomous Control (NITA)	PAC
Peripheral Basement Membrane [*Medicine*] (DMAA)	PBM
Peripheral Blood [*Medicine*] (AAMN)	PB
Peripheral Blood Cells [*Medicine*]	PBC
Peripheral Blood Leukocyte [*or Lymphocyte*] [*Hematology*]	PBL
Peripheral Blood Leukocyte [*Medicine*] (PDAA)	PPL
Peripheral Blood Monomuclear Cell [*Hematology*] (DAVI)	PBMNC
Peripheral Blood Mononuclear [*Cells*] [*Hematology*]	PBM
Peripheral Blood Mononuclear Cell [*Medicine*] (DMAA)	PMNC
Peripheral Blood Mononuclear Cells [*Hematology*]	PBMC
Peripheral Buffer	PB
Peripheral Bus Computer [*Bell System*]	PBC
Peripheral Cell	PC
Peripheral Circulatory Assist [*Medicine*]	PCA
Peripheral Circulatory Failure [*Medicine*] (DMAA)	PCF
Peripheral Command Indicator	PCI
Peripheral Component Interconnect [*Telecommunications*] (PCM)	PCI
Peripheral Component Interface (PCM)	PCI
Peripheral Computer System (IAA)	PCS
Peripheral Control (BUR)	PC
Peripheral Control Computer	PCC
Peripheral Control Element	PCE
Peripheral Control Program	PCP
Peripheral Control Pulse [*Computer science*]	PCP
Peripheral Control Routine (CMD)	PCR
Peripheral Control Terminal	PCT
Peripheral Control Unit (CMD)	PCU
Peripheral Controller (NITA)	PC
Peripheral Controller Enclosure (NITA)	PCE
Peripheral Controller Interface	PCI
Peripheral Coronary Pressure [*Cardiology*] (AAMN)	PCP
Peripheral Data Transfer [*Telecommunications*] (IAA)	PDT
Peripheral Device (BUR)	PD
Peripheral Equipment (AAG)	PE
Peripheral Equipment Functional Test (CAAL)	PEFT
Peripheral Equipment Test Set	PETS
Peripheral Equipment Tester [*Computer science*] (BUR)	PET
Peripheral Event Processor [*Computer science*]	PEP
Peripheral Fixed Shim [*Nuclear energy*] (NRCH)	PFS
Peripheral Graphics, Inc.	PGI
Peripheral Hyperalimentation (Solution) [*Medicine*]	PHA
Peripheral Input/Output (NITA)	PIO
Peripheral Input Tape [*Computer science*]	PIT
Peripheral Integrated Off-Line Utility System (SAA)	PIOUS
Peripheral Interchange Program [*Computer science*]	PIP
Peripheral Interface [*Computer science*] (PCM)	PI
Peripheral Interface Adapter [*Computer science*]	PIA
Peripheral Interface and Program Interrupt Translator (PDAA)	PIPIT
Peripheral Interface Controller [*Computer science*]	PIC
Peripheral Interface Device [*Computer science*] (EECA)	PID
Peripheral Interface Element [*Computer science*] (IAA)	PIE
Peripheral Interface Module	PIM
Peripheral Interface Programmer [*Circuit*] [*Computer science*]	PIP
Peripheral Interface Tests (MCD)	PIT
Peripheral Intravenous [*Line*] [*Pharmacology*] (DAVI)	PIV
Peripheral Iridectomy [*Medicine*]	PI
Peripheral Jet (AAG)	PJ
Peripheral Jet (Flat-Bottom)	PJF
Peripheral Jet (Skegs)	PJS
Peripheral Light Detection (DMAA)	PLD
Peripheral Light Loss	PLL
Peripheral Mononuclear Cell [*Cytology*]	PMC
Peripheral Nerve [*Anatomy*]	PN
Peripheral Nerve Conduction [*Neurology*] (DAVI)	PNC
Peripheral Nerve Injury [*Medicine*]	PNI
Peripheral Nerve Stimulator [*Medicine*] (MAE)	PNS
Peripheral Nervous System [*Medicine*]	PNS
Peripheral Nervous System (AD)	pns
Peripheral Neuroepithelioma [*Medicine*] (DMAA)	PNET
Peripheral Neuropathy [*Medicine*]	PN
Peripheral Neuropathy [*Medicine*]	PNP
Peripheral Nucleated Cell (AAMN)	PNC
Peripheral On-Line-Oriented Function [*Computer science*] (AD)	poof
Peripheral Parenteral Nutrition [*Medicine*] (DAVI)	PPN
Peripheral Performance Test (CAAL)	PPT
Peripheral Processing Unit [*Computer science*]	PPU
Peripheral Processor [*Computer science*]	PP
Peripheral Processor Saturation (MHDI)	PPSAT
Peripheral Processor System [*Computer science*] (IAA)	PPS
Peripheral Pulmonary Artery Stenosis [*Medicine*] (DMAA)	PPAS
Peripheral Pulses Palpable Both Legs [*Medicine*] (DMAA)	PPPBL
Peripheral Resistance [*Medicine*]	PR

Peripheral Resistance (AD)	pr
Peripheral Resistance Unit [*Medicine*]	PRU
Peripheral Shim Rod [*Nuclear energy*] (NRCH)	PSR
Peripheral Shock [*Psychology*]	PS
Peripheral Subsystem Interface [*Computer science*] (IAA)	PSI
Peripheral Switching Unit (NITA)	PSW
Peripheral T-Cell Lymphoma [*Oncology*]	PTCL
Peripheral T-Cell Lymphoma [*Oncology*]	PTL
Peripheral [*Vein*] Total Parenteral Nutrition [*Gastroenterology*] (DAVI)	PTPN
Peripheral Total Resistance [*Medicine*] (MAE)	PTR
Peripheral Ultra-Low Power Processor (PDAA)	PULPP
Peripheral Unit [*Computers*] (MSA)	PU
Peripheral Unit Processor [*Computer science*]	PUP
Peripheral Universal Processor (NITA)	PUP
Peripheral Vascular [*Medicine*]	PV
Peripheral Vascular Disease [*Medicine*]	PVD
Peripheral Vascular Insufficiency [*Medicine*]	PVI
Peripheral Vascular Occlusion [*Medicine*] (DAVI)	PVO
Peripheral Vascular Occlusive Disease [*Medicine*]	PVOD
Peripheral Vascular Resistance [*Cardiology*]	PVR
Peripheral Vascular Surgery [*Cardiology*] (DAVI)	PVS
Peripheral Vasoconstriction [*Medicine*]	PVC
Peripheral Vein [*Anatomy*]	PV
Peripheral Vein Plasma [*Cardiology*] (MAE)	PVP
Peripheral Venous Pressure [*Cardiology*]	PVP
Peripheral Vessel [*Cardiology*] (MAE)	PV
Peripheral Vision Command Indicator	PVCI
Peripheral Visual Field [*Optics*]	PVF
Peripheral White Blood Cells [*Medicine*]	PWBC
Peripheral Zone [*Botany*] [*Anatomy*]	PZ
Peripheral-Blood Stem-Cell [*Biochemistry Medicine*]	PBSC
Peripherally Synapsing Interneuron [*Neurology*]	PSI
Peripherally-Inserted Central Catheter [*Medicine*]	PICC
Peripherie Controller [*Computer science*] (IAA)	PIC
Peripherin (DMAA)	PRPH
Periphery (KSC)	PERIPH
Periphery Access Processor [*Computer science*] (IAA)	PAP
Periphonics Corp. [*NASDAQ symbol*] (SAG)	PERI
Periphonics Corp. [*Associated Press*] (SAG)	Periphn
Periplanone A [*Biochemistry*]	pA
Periplasmic Binding Protein [*Biochemistry*]	PBP
Periplus Maris Euxini [*of Arrian*] [*Classical studies*] (OCD)	Peripl M Eux
Periportal [*Anatomy*]	PP
Periproct [*Invertebrate anatomy*]	PP
Perirenal [*Nephrology*]	PR
Periscope	PE
Periscope	PERI
Periscope (KSC)	PERIS
Periscope Azimuth Error Indicator	PAEI
Periscope Bombsight Stabilizer	PBS
Periscope Depth (IAA)	PD
Periscope Depth Range [*SONAR*]	PDR
Periscope Detection RADAR (NG)	PDR
Periscope Simulation System [*Navy*]	PSS
Periscope Television Camera [*Telecommunications*] (IAA)	PTC
Periscope Viewer/Controller (MCD)	PVC
Periscope Visual Scene Generation	PVSG
Periscopic Concave [*Ophthalmology*]	PCc
Periscopic Convex [*Ophthalmology*]	PCx
Periscopic Convex [*Ophthalmology*] (DAVI)	PCx
Perishability Code [*Military*] (AFIT)	PYC
Perishable	P
Perishable (WGA)	PERSH
Perishable Agricultural Commodities Act, 1930	PACA
Perishable Sheet Metal Tool (MCD)	PSMT
Perishable Subsistence Automated Supply System [*DoD*]	PSASS
Perishables Tariff Bureau, Atlanta GA [*STAC*]	PTB
Peristaltic Charge-Coupled Device (IEEE)	PCCD
Peristent Muellerian Duct Syndrome [*Medicine*] (DMAA)	PMDS
Peristimulus Time [*Neurophysiology*]	PST
Peristimulus Time Histogram	PSTH
Peristyle (VRA)	pstyl
Perito Moreno [*Argentina*] [*Airport symbol*] (OAG)	PMQ
Perito Moreno [*Argentina ICAO location identifier*] (ICLI)	SAWP
Peritoneal Carcinomatosis [*Oncology*]	PCA
Peritoneal Cell (DMAA)	PC
Peritoneal Dialysis [*Medicine*]	PD
Peritoneal Dialysis Fluid [*Medicine*] (DMAA)	PDF
Peritoneal Dialysis System [*nephrology*] (DAVI)	PDS
Peritoneal Exudate [*Medicine*]	PE
Peritoneal Exudate Cells [*Hematology*]	PEC
Peritoneal Exudate Lymphocytes [*Hematology*]	PEL
Peritoneal Exudate Macrophage [*Hematology*]	PEM
Peritoneal Fluid (DAVI)	PERI
Peritoneal Fluid [*Medicine*] (MAE)	PF
Peritoneal Macrophage [*Immunology*] (AAMN)	PM
Peritoneal Mast Cell	PMC
Peritoneal Ovum Sperm Transfer [*Medicine*]	POST
Peritoneojugular Shunt [*Medicine*] (DMAA)	PJS
Peritoneovenous Shunt [*Medicine*]	PVS
Peritonsillar Abscess [*Medicine*]	PTA
Peritronics Med [*Vancouver Stock Exchange symbol*]	POM
Peritus in Sacred Liturgy [*Roman Catholic*]	PERSACLIT
Perivalvular Leakage [*Medicine*] (DMAA)	PVL
Perivenous Encephalomyelitis [*Neurology*] (DAVI)	PVE

Periventricular Gray [*Neurobiology*] .... PVG
Periventricular Hemorrhage [*Medicine*] .... PVH
Periventricular Leukomalacia [*Medicine*] .... PVL
Periventricular Leukomalacia Complex [*Medicine*] .... PLC
Periventricular White-Matter Radiolucency [*Medicine*] .... PWMR
Perjury [*FBI standardized term*] .... PERJ
Perjury (ROG) .... PERJY
Perkin Elmer Corp. .... PE
Perkin-Elmer [*NYSE symbol*] (TTSB) .... PKN
Perkin-Elmer Corp. (MCD) .... PEC
Perkin-Elmer Corp. [*Associated Press*] (SAG) .... PerkEl
Perkin-Elmer Corp. [*NYSE symbol*] (SPSG) .... PKN
Perkin-Elmer Processor [*Computer*] .... PEP
Perkin-Elmer Robot Language .... PERL
Perkin-Elmer Solvent Optimization System [*Chemistry*] .... PESOS
Perkins & Squier [*Paper manufacturer*] .... P & S
Perkins, Coie, Stone, Olsen & Williams, Seattle, WA [*Library symbol Library of Congress*] (LCLS) .... WaSPe
Perkins Family Rest L.P. [*NYSE symbol*] (TTSB) .... PFR
Perkins Family Restaurants Ltd. [*Associated Press*] (SAG) .... PerkF
Perkins Family Restaurants Ltd [*NYSE symbol*] (SPSG) .... PFR
Perkins Nuclear Station (NRCH) .... PNS
Perkins on Conveyancing [*A publication*] (DLA) .... Perk
Perkins on Pleading [*A publication*] (DLA) .... Perk
Perkins' Profitable Book (Conveyancing) [*A publication*] (DLA) .... Perk
Perkins' Profitable Book (Conveyancing) [*A publication*] (DLA) .... Perk Pr Bk
Perkins School for the Blind, Watertown, MA [*Library symbol Library of Congress*] (LCLS) .... MWatP
Perkinston Junior College [*Mississippi*] .... PJC
Perkiomen Airways [*ICAO designator*] (AD) .... RY
Perle System [*NASDAQ symbol*] (TTSB) .... PERLF
Perle Systems Ltd. [*Scarborough, ON*] [*NASDAQ symbol*] (NQ) .... PERL
Perley Hospital, Ottawa, ON, Canada [*Library symbol Library of Congress*] (LCLS) .... CaOOPH
Perley Hospital, Ottawa, Ontario [*Library symbol National Library of Canada*] (NLC) .... OOPH
Perlite Institute (EA) .... PI
Perlsucht Bacillary Emulsion [*Medicine*] .... PBE
Perlsucht Tuberculin Original [*Medicine*] (MAE) .... PTO
Perlsucht Tuberculin Rest [*Medicine*] (MAE) .... PTR
Perma Fix Enviro Svcs [*NASDAQ symbol*] (TTSB) .... PESI
Perma Fix Environmental Services [*Associated Press*] (SAG) .... PerF
Perma Fix Environmental Services [*Associated Press*] (SAG) .... PermF
Perma Fix Environmental Services [*Associated Press*] (SAG) .... PermFix
Perma Fix Environmental Services [*NASDAQ symbol*] (SAG) .... PESI
Permaculture International [*Australia*] .... PI
Perma-Fix Envir'l Svcs Wrrt [*NASDAQ symbol*] (TTSB) .... PESIW
Perma-Fix Envir'l Svcs Wrrt'B' [*NASDAQ symbol*] (TTSB) .... PESIZ
Permanens Rector [*Permanent Rector*] .... PR
Permanent [*Inks*] (DGA) .... P
Permanent .... PERM
Permanent (ROG) .... PERMT
Permanent (IAA) .... PMNT
Permanent Abeyance [*FDA*] .... PA
Permanent Address (ROG) .... PA
Permanent Air Force [*Australia*] .... PAF
Permanent and International Committee of Underground Town Planning and Construction .... PICUTPC
Permanent and Total [*Disability*] [*Medicine*] .... P & T
Permanent Appointment .... PA
Permanent Artificial Lighting (IEEE) .... PAL
Permanent Ballast (DS) .... PB
Permanent Bancorp [*NASDAQ symbol*] (SAG) .... PERM
Permanent Bancorp [*Associated Press*] (SAG) .... PermBcp
Permanent Bench Mark .... PBM
Permanent Board for Review of the Enlisted Rating Structure .... PBRERS
Permanent Board for Review of the Enlisted Retention Program .... PBRERP
Permanent Budget Account .... PBA
Permanent Building Societies Registrar [*New South Wales, Australia*] .... PBSR
Permanent Bunkers .... PB
Permanent Bureau of International Congresses for the Sciences of Genealogy and Heraldry (EA) .... PBICSGH
Permanent Central Opium Board (United Nations) .... PCOB(UN)
Permanent Change of Assignment [*Army*] .... PCA
Permanent Change of Duty [*Navy*] (DNAB) .... PCOD
Permanent Change of Station [*Army*] .... PCS
Permanent Charities Committee of the Entertainment Industries (EA) .... PCCEI
Permanent Commission and International Association on Occupational Health (EAIO) .... PCIAOH
Permanent Commission for the Conservation and Exploitation of the Maritime Resources of the South Pacific .... PCCEMRSP
Permanent Commission for the South Pacific (WDAA) .... PCSP
Permanent Commission of the International Fisheries Convention .... PCIFC
Permanent Committee for International Eucharistic Congresses (EA) .... PCIEC
Permanent Committee for the International Veterinary Congresses IVC
Permanent Committee of Geographical Names [*Later, BGN*] .... PCGN
Permanent Committee on Industrial Property [*World Intellectual Property Organization*] [*Switzerland Information service or system*] (IID) .... PCIPI
Permanent Committee on Patent Information [*World Intellectual Property Organization*] [*Information service or system*] (IID) .... PCPI
Permanent Congress of Trade Union Unity of Latin American Workers [*See also CPUSTAL*] [*Mexico City, Mexico*] (EAIO) .... PCTUULAW
Permanent Consultative Committee .... PCC
Permanent Control Narcotics Board .... PCNB
Permanent Control Number (MCD) .... PCN
Permanent Council of the International Convention of Stresa on Cheeses (EAIO) .... PCICS
Permanent Council of the Organization of American States .... PCOAS
Permanent Court of Arbitration [*See also CPA*] [*Hague, Netherlands*] (EAIO) .... PCA
Permanent Court of International Justice Annual Reports [*A publication*] (DLA) .... PCIJ Ann R
Permanent Court of International Justice Cases [*A publication*] (DLA) .... PCIJ
Permanent Cruiser Service [*British military*] (DMA) .... PCS
Permanent Deactivation .... PD
Permanent Diability Rating Board (DMAA) .... PDRB
Permanent Disability Retired List .... PDRL
Permanent Durable Quality [*Paper*] .... PDQ
Permanent Duty Assignment [*Air Force*] (AFM) .... PDA
Permanent Duty Location .... PDL
Permanent Duty Station [*Air Force*] (AFM) .... PDS
Permanent Echo [*RADAR*] .... PE
Permanent Employee (DSUE) .... PERM
Permanent Entry Number [*Computer science*] .... PEN
Permanent Entry Permit After Entry .... PEPAE
Permanent Entry Visa .... PEV
Permanent Error (IAA) .... PE
Permanent Executive Committee of the Inter-American Council for Education, Science, and Culture .... PECIACESC
Permanent Executive Committee of the Inter-American Economic and Social Council .... PECIAECOSOC
Permanent Executive Secretariat of the Andres Bello Convention [*See also SECAB*] (EAIO) .... PESABC
Permanent Factory Repairable (MCD) .... PFR
Permanent Families for Children [*Defunct*] (EA) .... PFC
Permanent Family File [*Navy*] (NG) .... PFF
Permanent Field Training Site .... PFTS
Permanent File Name .... PFN
Permanent Fireman .... PF
Permanent Force [*Canadian Militia before 1940*] .... PF
Permanent Frost .... PERMAFROST
Permanent Full-Time (GFGA) .... PFT
Permanent Full-Time Equivalent (GFGA) .... PFTE
Permanent General Assembly of National Olympic Committees .... PGA-NOC
Permanent Glow [*Telecommunications*] (TEL) .... PG
Permanent Grade .... PG
Permanent Grade (DNAB) .... PRM GR
Permanent Health Insurance [*British*] .... PHI
Permanent Income Hypothesis [*Economics*] .... PIH
Permanent Income Theory [*Econometrics*] .... PIT
Permanent International Altaistic Conference (EA) .... PIAC
Permanent International Association of Navigation Congresses [*Brussels, Belgium*] (EAIO) .... PIANC
Permanent International Association of Road Congresses [*See also AIPCR*] [*Paris, France*] (EAIO) .... PIARC
Permanent International Bureau of Analytical Chemistry of Human and Animal Food .... PIBAC
Permanent International Bureau of Motorcycle Manufacturers .... PIBMM
Permanent International Commission for the Proof of Small-Arms (EAIO) .... PICPSA
Permanent International Committee for Genetic Congresses .... PICGC
Permanent International Committee of Mothers .... PICM
Permanent Joint Board on Defense [*US, Canada*] .... PJBD
Permanent Labourers' Mutual Protective Association [*A union*] [*British*] .... PLMPA
Permanent Logical Link [*Telecommunications*] .... PLL
Permanent Loop Junctor (NITA) .... PLJ
Permanent Magnet (AD) .... p-m
Permanent Magnet [*Loudspeaker*] .... PM
Permanent Magnet Association (IAA) .... PMA
Permanent Magnet Generator .... PMG
Permanent Magnet Latch Valve .... PMLV
Permanent Magnet Motor (IAA) .... PMM
Permanent Magnet Producers Association [*Later, MMPA*] (EA) .... PMPA
Permanent Magnet Speaker .... PMS
Permanent Magnet Tester [*Memory*] [*Bell Laboratories*] (IAA) .... PMT
Permanent Magnet Twistor [*Memory*] [*Bell Laboratories*] .... PMT
Permanent Magnet Users Association [*Defunct*] (EA) .... PERMU
Permanent Magnetic Field .... PMF
Permanent Magnetic Movable Coil .... PMMC
Permanent Mailing Address .... PMA
Permanent Manned Orbital Station (AAG) .... PMOS
Permanent Manned Presence (SSD) .... PMP
Permanent Manual System (AD) .... PMS
Permanent Manufacturing Information (MSA) .... PMI
Permanent Married Quarters [*Canadian Forces*] .... PMQ
Permanent Mass Layoffs and Plant Closings Program [*Bureau of Labor Statistics*] .... PMLPC
Permanent Memory with Semi-Elastic Range (MCD) .... PMSE
Permanent Military Force (ADA) .... PMF
Permanent Mission of the United States of America to the Organization of American States (AD) .... PMUSAOAS
Permanent Mold Casting Mold (MCD) .... PMCM
Permanent Nordic Committee on Food and Nutrition [*Copenhagen, Denmark*] (EAIO) .... PNCFN
Permanent Officer of the Day [*or Deck*] [*Navy*] .... POOD
Permanent Orbital Station [*NASA*] (IAA) .... POS
Permanent Pacemaker [*Cardiology*] (MAE) .... PPM
Permanent Paranormal Object .... PPO
Permanent Partial [*Dentistry*] (MAE) .... PP

Permanent Partial Disability [*Dentistry*] (MAE)	PPD
Permanent Part-Time (ADA)	PPT
Permanent Part-Time Employment	PPTE
Permanent Part-Time Work	PPTW
Permanent Party [*Military*]	PP
Permanent Party (AD)	pp
Permanent Party Personnel (MCD)	PPP
Permanent Pasture [*Agriculture*]	PP
Permanent Pay Record [*Military*]	PPR
Permanent Personal Registration [*Voting*] (BARN)	PPR
Permanent Planning Group [*Military British*]	PPG
Permanent Press (ADA)	PP
Permanent Professor	PP
Permanent Recording Traffic [*Telecommunications*] (IAA)	PRT
Permanent Regional Bureau of the Middle East Committee for the Affairs of the Blind [*Riyadh, Saudi Arabia*] (EAIO)	PRBMECAB
Permanent Regular Commissions [*Army British*]	PRC
Permanent Representation to North Atlantic Council [*NATO*] (NATG)	PERMREP
Permanent Residence	PERMR
Permanent Restricted Area [*Former USSR*] (NATG)	PRA
Permanent Scratch File [*Computer science*]	PSCR
Permanent Secretariat of the Central American Common Market	PSCACM
Permanent Secretariat of the General Treaty on Central American Economic Integration (EAIO)	PSGTCAEI
Permanent Secretariat of the Hemispheric Congress (EA)	PSHC
Permanent Secretariat of the South American Agreement on Narcotic Drugs and Psychotropic Substances (EAIO)	PSSAANDPS
Permanent Secretary	PS
Permanent Section of Microbiological Standardization (MCD)	PSMS
Permanent Service for Mean Sea Level [*of the Federation of Astronomical and Geophysical Data Analysis Services*] [*Birkenhead, Merseyside, England*] (EAIO)	PSMSL
Permanent Shift of Hearing	PSH
Permanent Signal [*Telecommunications*] (TEL)	PS
Permanent Signal Detection [*Telecommunications*] (TEL)	PSD
Permanent Signal Finder	PSF
Permanent Sort Number [*Computer science*]	PSN
Permanent Space Based Logistics System	PSBLS
Permanent Split Capacitor (IAA)	PSC
Permanent Staff Instructor [*Military British*]	PSI
Permanent Stay [*in hospital*] [*British*]	P
Permanent Supplementary Artificial Lighting (IAA)	PSAL
Permanent Supplementary Artificial Lighting of Interiors (IEEE)	PSALI
Permanent System Control Number (MCD)	PSCN
Permanent Threshold Shift [*Hearing evaluation*]	PTS
Permanent Total Disability [*Medicine*]	PTD
Permanent Under Secretary [*British*]	PUS
Permanent Unit Code (NG)	PUC
Permanent Virtual Circuit	PVC
Permanent Vision Loss [*Medicine*] (DMAA)	PVL
Permanent Wants Directory [*A publication*]	PWD
Permanent Ware Institute [*Defunct*] (EA)	PWI
Permanent Water Ballast (DS)	PWB
Permanent Way Institution [*Fleet, Hampshire, England*] (EAIO)	PWI
Permanent Wood Foundation [*Building term*]	PWF
Permanent Working Group (NATG)	PWG
Permanent Working Staff [*NATO*] (NATG)	PWX
Permanent-Equity Pension Plan [*Human resources*] (WYGK)	PEPP
Permanently	PERMLY
Permanently Associated [*Telecommunications*] (TEL)	PA
Permanently Blind	PB
Permanently Grounded [*Aircraft classification letter*]	G
Permanently Lubricated Drivetrain	PLD
Permanently Manned Capability (SSD)	PMC
Permanently Medically Unfit	PMU
Permanently Mounted User Set [*Computer science*] (ADA)	PMUS
Permanently Separated from Duty Station [*Military*]	PSDS
Permanently Unfit for Military Service [*British*]	PUMS
Permanently Unfit for Naval Service [*British*]	PUNS
Permanently Unfit for Service [*Military*] (ADA)	PUS
Permeability	PERM
Permeability	PERMB
Permeability Factor	PF
Permeability Index [*Clinical chemistry*]	PI
Permeability Invariant	PERMINVAR
Permeability Quotient	PQ
Permeability Quotient (AD)	pq
Permeability Transition [*Biochemistry*]	PT
Permeability-Tuned Oscillator (IAA)	PTO
Permeable Base Transistor [*Electronics*]	PBT
Permeance (IDOE)	P
Permeance (IAA)	PR
Permeance Coefficient (IAA)	PC
Per-Member Payment (AD)	pmp
Permian [*Period, era, or system*] [*Geology*]	PERM
Permian Basin Royalty Trust [*NYSE symbol*] (SPSG)	PBT
Permian Basin Royalty Trust [*Associated Press*] (SAG)	Prmian
Permian Basin Rty Tr [*NYSE symbol*] (TTSB)	PBT
Permian Resources Ltd. [*Vancouver Stock Exchange symbol*]	PMN
Permian/Triassic [*A geological period boundary*]	P/Tr
Permian-Triassic Boundary [*Geology*]	PTB
Permissible Accumulated Dose	PAD
Permissible Contamination Limits [*Nuclear energy*] (NRCH)	PCL
Permissible Error (ADA)	PE

Permissible Exposure Level	PEL
Permissible Exposure Limit [*OSHA*]	PEL
Permissible Individual Maximum Pressure (SAA)	PIMP
Permissible Operating Distance [*Army*] (AFIT)	POD
Permissible Working Stress	S
Permission (AABC)	PER
Permission (MSA)	PERM
Permission (FAAC)	PMSN
Permission Granted [*Military*]	PERGRA
Permission, Limited Information, Specific Suggestions, and Intensive Therapy [*Occupational therapy*]	PLISSIT
Permission Not Granted [*Military*]	PERNOGRA
Permission to Photocopy (MCD)	PPC
Permission to Take Classes [*Education*]	PTC
Permissive Action Link [*Army*]	PAL
Permissive Action Link Cypher System (MCD)	PALCS
Permissive Action Link Report [*Army*] (AABC)	PALR
Permissive Action Link System [*Army*]	PALS
Permissive Arming and Protection System [*AEC*]	PAPS
Permissive Arming Line [*or Link*]	PAL
Permissive Low-Pressure Alarm (IEEE)	PLPA
Permissive Reassignment [*Air Force*] (AFM)	PR
Permit (FAAC)	PMT
Permit Assistance Team [*Environmental Protection Agency*] (GFGA)	PAT
Permit by Rule [*Pollution control*]	PBR
Permit Compliance System [*Environmental Protection Agency*] (GFGA)	PCS
Permit Imprint Collectors Society (EA)	PICS
Permit Office [*British*] (ROG)	PO
Permit to Fly [*Aviation*] (AIA)	PTF
Permits and State Programs Division [*Environmental Protection Agency*] (GFGA)	PSPD
Permits Division [*Environmental Protection Agency*] (GFGA)	PD
Permitted Flying Route [*Aviation*] (DA)	PFR
Permittivity [*Physics*] (BARN)	e
Permixtus [*Mixed*] [*Pharmacy*] (ROG)	PERMIXT
Permodalan Nasional Bank [*Malaysia*]	PNB
Permutation (NITA)	P
Permutation (DSUE)	PERM
Permutation Indexed Literature of Technology (IEEE)	PILOT
Permuted Formula Index [*Molecular formula indexing*]	PERDEX
Permuted on Subject Headings [*Indexing technique*]	POSH
Permuted on Subject Headings (AD)	posh
Permuterm Subject Index [*Institute for Scientific Information*] [*A publication*] (IID)	PSI
Pernicious Anemia [*Hematology*]	PA
Pernicious Anemia-Like Syndrome and Immunoglobulin Deficiency [*Hematology*] (AAMN)	PA-LS-ID
Perofskite [*CIPW classification*] [*Geology*]	pf
Peroneus Brevis [*Muscle*] [*orthopedics*] (DAVI)	PB
Peroneus Longus [*Muscle*] [*Orthopedics*] (DAVI)	PL
Peronne/Saint-Quentin [*France ICAO location identifier*] (ICLI)	LFAG
Perouges/Meximieux [*France ICAO location identifier*] (ICLI)	LFHC
Peroxidase [*Also, POD*] [*An enzyme*]	PO
Peroxidase [*Also, PO*] [*An enzyme*]	POD
Peroxidase [*Also, PO, POD*] [*An enzyme*]	PX
Peroxidase Stain [*Biochemistry*] (DAVI)	PEROX
Peroxidase-Antiperoxidase [*Immunochemistry*]	PantiP
Peroxidase-Antiperoxidase [*Immunochemistry*]	PAP
Peroxidase-Glucose Oxidase [*Also, GOD-POD*] [*Enzyme mixture*]	PGO
Peroxide	PEROX
Peroxide Assisted Leach [*Ore processing*]	PAL
Peroxide Number [*Hydrocarbon fuel specifications*]	PN
Peroxide Silicate [*Detergent and bleach*]	PERSIL
Peroxide Value [*Food analysis*]	PV
Peroxisomal Bifunctional Enzyme (DMAA)	PBFE
Peroxisomal Integral Membrane Protein [*Biochemistry*]	PIMP
Peroxisomal Integral Membrane Protein [*Biochemistry*]	PxIMP
Peroxisome Assembly Factor [*Biochemistry*]	PAF
Peroxisome Proliferator [*Biochemistry*]	PP
Peroxisome Proliferator Response Element [*Biochemistry*]	PPRE
Peroxisome Proliferator-Activated Receptor [*Genetics*]	PPAR
Peroxyacetyl Nitrate [*Lacrimator*]	PAN
Peroxybenzoyl Nitrate [*Lacrimator*]	PBzN
Peroxylaminedisulfonate [*Organic chemistry*]	PADS
Peroxypropionyl Nitrate [*Organic chemistry*]	PPN
Perpendicular (AAG)	PERP
Perpendicular (VRA)	perp
Perpendicular Diffraction Delay Line (PDAA)	PDDL
Perpendicular Ocean Platform [*Oceanography*]	POP
Perpendicular Ocean Platform (AD)	pop
Perpendicular Vegetation Index [*Botany*]	PVI
Perpendicular-to-Orbit Plane [*Aerospace*] (KSC)	POP
Perpetrator (WDAA)	PERP
Perpetual (ADA)	PERP
Perpetual (DLA)	Perpet
Perpetual Bank Federal Savings Bank [*Associated Press*] (SAG)	PerpBnk
Perpetual Bank Federal Savings Bank [*NASDAQ symbol*] (SAG)	PERT
Perpetual Convertible or Redeemable Note [*Economics*]	PCORN
Perpetual Curate	PC
Perpetual Inventory Control System	PICS
Perpetual Inventory File (DNAB)	PIF
Perpetual Midwest Financial [*NASDAQ symbol*] (TTSB)	PMFI
Perpetual Midwest Financial, Inc. [*Associated Press*] (SAG)	PerMdw
Perpetual Midwest Financial, Inc. [*NASDAQ symbol*] (SAG)	PMFI
Perpetual Motion Poetry Machine	PMPM

Perpetual Savings Bank FSB (MHDW) ... PASB
Perpetual State Bank (North Carolina) [*NASDAQ symbol*] (SAG) ... PSTB
Perpetual Storage, Inc., Salt Lake City, UT [*Library symbol Library of Congress*] (LCLS) ... Psl
Perpetual Traveller (ECON) ... PT
Perpetual Vice-President-Member Pickwick Club [*From "The Pickwick Papers" by Charles Dickens*] ... PVPMPC
Perpetuation of Unit Documentation Number (MCD) ... PUDN
Perpetuus [*Uninterrupted*] [*Latin*] ... P
Perpex Peristaltic Pump ... PPP
Perpignan [*France*] [*Airport symbol*] (OAG) ... PGF
Perpignan/Rivesaltes [*France ICAO location identifier*] (ICLI) ... LFMP
Perpustakaan Museum Pusat, Jakarta, Indonesia [*Library symbol Library of Congress*] (LCLS) ... IeDP
Perquimans County Library, Hertford, NC [*Library symbol Library of Congress*] (LCLS) ... NcHf
Perquisite ... PERK
Perquisites (MHDB) ... perks
Perrault's Conseil Superieur [*Canada*] [*A publication*] (DLA) ... Per CS
Perrault's Conseil Superieur [*Canada*] [*A publication*] (DLA) ... Perrault
Perrault's Prevoste de Quebec [*A publication*] (DLA) ... Per P
Perrault's Prevoste de Quebec [*A publication*] (DLA) ... Perrault
Perrault's Quebec Reports [*A publication*] (DLA) ... Perrault
Perrigo Co. [*Associated Press*] (SAG) ... Perrigo
Perrigo Co. [*NASDAQ symbol*] (SPSG) ... PRGO
Perrine, FL [*Location identifier FAA*] (FAAL) ... PRR
Perris [*California*] [*Seismograph station code, US Geological Survey*] (SEIS) ... PEC
Perris [*California*] [*Seismograph station code, US Geological Survey Closed*] (SEIS) ... PRR
Perris Public Library, Perris, CA [*Library symbol Library of Congress*] (LCLS) ... CPer
Perron Gold Mines [*Vancouver Stock Exchange symbol*] ... PGM
Perroni, Martin, O'Reilly [*Commercial firm*] ... PMO
Perrot Memorial Library, Old Greenwich, CT [*Library symbol Library of Congress*] (LCLS) ... CtOg
Perrot Memorial Library, Old Greenwich, CT [*OCLC symbol*] (OCLC) ... PEM
Perry and Davison's English King's Bench Reports [*1838-41*] [*A publication*] (DLA) ... Per & Dav
Perry and Davison's English King's Bench Reports [*A publication*] (DLA) ... Perry & D
Perry and Davison's English King's Bench Reports [*A publication*] (DLA) ... Perry & D (Eng)
Perry and Davison's English Queen's Bench Reports [*1834-44*] [*A publication*] (DLA) ... P & D
Perry and Knapp's English Election Cases [*1833*] [*A publication*] (DLA) ... P & K
Perry and Knapp's English Election Cases [*A publication*] (DLA) ... Perry & K
Perry and Knapp's English Election Cases [*A publication*] (DLA) ... Perry & Kn
Perry and Knapp's English Election Reports [*1838*] [*A publication*] (DLA) ... Per & Kn
Perry Basin [*Utah*] [*Seismograph station code, US Geological Survey*] (SEIS) ... PBU
Perry County District Library, New Lexington, OH [*Library symbol Library of Congress*] (LCLS) ... ONIP
Perry County Financial [*NASDAQ symbol*] (TTSB) ... PCBC
Perry County Financial Corp. [*NASDAQ symbol*] (SAG) ... PCBC
Perry County Financial Corp. [*Associated Press*] (SAG) ... PerryCF
Perry County Recorder's Office, Cannelton, IN [*Library symbol Library of Congress*] (LCLS) ... InCanCR
Perry Ellis [*Fashion designer, 1940-86*] ... PE
Perry, FL [*Location identifier FAA*] (FAAL) ... FPY
Perry, FL [*FM radio station call letters*] ... WNFK
Perry, FL [*AM radio station call letters*] ... WPRY
Perry, GA [*Location identifier FAA*] (FAAL) ... BEP
Perry, GA [*AM radio station call letters*] ... WPGA
Perry, GA [*FM radio station call letters*] ... WPGA-FM
Perry, GA [*Television station call letters*] ... WPGA-TV
Perry, IA [*AM radio station call letters*] ... KDLS
Perry, IA [*FM radio station call letters*] ... KDLS-FM
Perry, IA [*Location identifier FAA*] (FAAL) ... PRO
Perry Island, AK [*Location identifier FAA*] (FAAL) ... PYL
Perry Junior/Senior High School Library, Perry, NY [*OCLC symbol*] (OCLC) ... RXE
Perry Memorial Hospital, Princeton, IL [*Library symbol Library of Congress*] (LCLS) ... IPriPH
Perry Normal School, Boston, MA [*Library symbol Library of Congress*] (LCLS) ... MBPKN
Perry Nuclear Power Plant (NRCH) ... PNPP
Perry, OK [*AM radio station call letters*] ... KASR
Perry, OK [*FM radio station call letters*] ... KASR-FM
Perry, OK [*AM radio station call letters*] (RBYB) ... KVCS-AM
Perry, OK [*FM radio station call letters*] (RBYB) ... KVCS-FM
Perry on Trusts [*A publication*] (DLA) ... Per Tr
Perry Township Public Library Emsdale, Ontario [*Library symbol National Library of Canada*] (NLC) ... OEPT
Perry-Link Cubmarine [*A submersible vehicle*] ... PLC
Perry's English Insolvency Cases [*1831*] [*A publication*] (DLA) ... Perry Ins
Perry's Oriental Cases [*Bombay*] [*A publication*] (DLA) ... Per Or Cas
Perry's Oriental Cases [*Bombay*] [*A publication*] (DLA) ... Perry
Perry's Oriental Cases [*Bombay*] [*A publication*] (DLA) ... Perry OC
Perry's Oriental Cases [*Bombay*] [*A publication*] (DLA) ... PO Cas
Perry's Victory and International Peace Memorial National Monument ... PEVI
Perryton, TX [*AM radio station call letters*] ... KEYE
Perryton, TX [*FM radio station call letters*] ... KEYE-FM
Perryton, TX [*Location identifier FAA*] (FAAL) ... PYX
Perryville, MO [*FM radio station call letters*] ... KBDZ
Persae [*of Aeschylus*] [*Classical studies*] (OCD) ... Pers
Persan-Beaumont [*France ICAO location identifier*] (ICLI) ... LFPA
Persatuan Geologi Malaysia [*Geological Society of Malaysia*] (EAIO) ... PGM
Persatuan Rakyat Malaysian Sarawak [*Political party*] (EY) ... PERMAS
PERSCOM [*Personnel Command*] **Acquisition Accession Board** [*Army*] (INF) ... PAAB
Persepolis/Marvdasht [*Iran*] [*ICAO location identifier*] (ICLI) ... OISP
Persepolis Texts (BJA) ... PT
PerSeptive Biosystems [*NASDAQ symbol*] (TTSB) ... PBIO
PerSeptive Biosystems, Inc. [*NASDAQ symbol*] (SAG) ... PBIO
PerSeptive Biosystems, Inc. [*Associated Press*] (SAG) ... PerSptv
PerSeptive Biosystems, Inc. [*Associated Press*] (SAG) ... PSptv
PerSeptive Biosystems Wrrt [*NASDAQ symbol*] (TTSB) ... PBIOZ
PerSeptive Tech II Corp. [*NASDAQ symbol*] (SAG) ... PTCC
PerSeptive Technologies II Corp. [*Associated Press*] (SAG) ... PerSep
Perseus [*Constellation*] ... Per
Perseus [*Constellation*] ... Pers
Perseverance (ROG) ... PERSEVCE
Perseverance Society of Carpenters and Joiners [*A union*] [*British*] ... PSCJ
Perseverate [*Psychology*] ... p
Pershing [*Missile*] (GFGA) ... PSG
Pershing 1 [*Missile*] (GFGA) ... P1
Pershing 1a [*Missile*] (GFGA) ... P1a
Pershing Audio Reproduction System (PDAA) ... PARS
Pershing II [*Army*] ... PII
Pershing Instant Comment [*Donaldson, Lufkin & Jenrette*] [*Database*] ... PIC
Pershing Physical Deception Device [*Army*] ... PPDD
Pershing Project Manager ... PPM
Pershing Project Manager's Office (RDA) ... PPMO
Pershing Public School, Plummer, MN [*Library symbol*] [*Library of Congress*] (LCLS) ... MnPluS
Pershing Rifles [*Honorary military organization*] ... PR
Pershing Survivability Evaluation Program [*Military*] (MCD) ... PERSEP
Persia [*Obsolete*] ... PER
Persia (VRA) ... Per
Persia [*Obsolete*] ... PERS
Persia and Iraq Command [*World War II*] ... PAIC
Persia and Iraq Force [*World War II*] ... PAIF
Persia and Iraq Force [*World War II*] (DMA) ... PAIFORCE
Persian (DLA) ... P
Persian Bicolor and Calico Society (EA) ... PBCS
Persian Gulf [*MARC geographic area code Library of Congress*] (LCCP) ... ap----
Persian Gulf (MCD) ... PG
Persian Gulf Command [*World War II*] ... PGC
Persian Gulf Requirements and Capabilities [*Military*] ... PERCAP
Persian Gulf Service Command ... PGSC
Persian Leather [*Bookbinding*] (DGA) ... PERS
Persian, Modern [*MARC language code Library of Congress*] (LCCP) ... per
Persian, Old [*MARC language code Library of Congress*] (LCCP) ... peo
Persimmon ... P
Persist (FAAC) ... PRST
Persistence [*Medicine*] ... P
Persistence of Vision - Ray [*Computer program*] ... POV
Persistency Rater [*LIMRA*] ... PR
Persistent Antiradiation Missile (MCD) ... PARM
Persistent Atrial Standstill [*Medicine*] (DMAA) ... PAS
Persistent Chemical Agent Gas ... GP (Gas)
Persistent Chemical Agent Stimulant ... PCAS
Persistent Chemical Agent Stimulant/Chemical Agent Disclosure Solution [*Army*] ... PCAS/CADS
Persistent Corpus Luteum [*Medicine*] ... PCL
Persistent Early Curvature ... PEC
Persistent Estrus [*Endocrinology*] ... PE
Persistent Fat Retention [*Syndrome*] ... PFR
Persistent Fetal Circulation [*Medicine*] ... PFC
Persistent Generalized Lymphadenopathy [*Medicine*] ... PGL
Persistent Hepatitis [*Medicine*] ... PH
Persistent Hyperinsulinemic Hypoglycemia of Infancy [*Medicine*] ... PHHI
Persistent Hyperplastic Primary Vitreous [*Ophthalmology*] ... PHPV
Persistent Hypertrophic Vitreous [*Ophthalmology*] (DAVI) ... PHV
Persistent Information Space Architecture [*Computer science*] ... PISA
Persistent Internal Polarization ... PIP
Persistent Interstitial Pulmonary Emphysema [*Medicine*] (DMAA) ... PIPE
Persistent Mentoposterior [*A fetal position*] [*Obstetrics*] ... PMP
Persistent Neonatal Myasthenia Gravis [*Medicine*] (DAVI) ... PNMG
Persistent Object Management System (NITA) ... POMS
Persistent Occipit Posterior [*A fetal position*] [*Obstetrics*] ... POP
Persistent Occipito-Posterior (AD) ... pop
Persistent Organic Pollutant ... POP
Persistent Organic Pollutant [*Environmental science*] ... POP
Persistent Photoconductivity [*Physics*] ... PPC
Persistent Pulmonary Hypertension [*Medicine*] ... PPH
Persistent Pulmonary Hypertension of the Newborn [*Medicine*] ... PPHN
Persistent Spectral Hole-Burning [*Spectroscopy*] ... PSHB
Persistent Standoff Target Marker (MCD) ... PSTM
Persistent Tease [*Slang Bowdlerized version*] ... PT
Persistent Tolerant Infection ... PTI
Persistent Truncus Arteriosus [*Medicine*] (MAE) ... PTA
Persistent Universal Resource Locator [*Computer science*] ... PURL
Persistent Vegetative State [*Medicine*] ... PVS
Persisting Galactorrhea-Amenorrhea Syndrome [*Medicine*] (DMAA) ... PGAS
Persius [*34-62AD*] [*Classical studies*] (OCD) ... Pers
Person ... P
Person ... PER
Person (WDMC) ... per

.... (.)	PERS
....lore Place [Library cataloguing] (DGA)	PSON
...fore Place [Library cataloguing] (DGA)	PBP
...ounty Public Library, Roxboro, NC [Library symbol Library of ...ongress] (LCLS)	NcRox
...son in Addition to Crew [Sailing]	PAC
Person in Column One [1980 census]	PICO
Person Inheriting Parents' Property [Lifestyle classification British]	Pippy
Person of Opposite Sex Sharing Living Quarters (AD)	posslq
Person of Restricted Growth [Slang term used to describe a person of limi ted cultural awareness] [Lifestyle classification]	Porg
Person of Special Importance [British military] (DMA)	PSI
Person of the Opposite Sex in Same Living Quarters (AD)	posslq
Person Perception Questionnaire [Psychology] (EDAC)	PPQ
Person Technical Institute, Roxboro, NC [Library symbol Library of Congress] (LCLS)	NcRoxP
Person to Person [Telecommunications] (TEL)	P
Person to Person [Word processing]	P-P
Person to Person: Collect and Special Instruction [Telecommunications] (TEL)	PPCS
Person Who Has Everything [Lifestyle classification]	Pwhe
Person with AIDS [Acquired Immune Deficiency Syndrome] [Medicine]	PWA
Person With AIDS-Related Complex (CPH)	PWARC
Person Years [After radiation exposure]	PY
Persona Non Grata [Unacceptable Person] [Latin]	PNG
Persona Non Grata [An Unacceptable Person] [Latin] (AD)	png
Personal (DA)	P
Personal	PERS
Personal (WDMC)	pers
Personal	PERSL
Personal	PRSNL
Personal (FAAC)	PSNAL
Personal (ROG)	PSONAL
Personal Access Code	PAC
Personal Accident [Insurance] (AIA)	PA
Personal Accident Insurance	PAI
Personal Account (WDAA)	P/A
Personal Accounting Management	PAM
Personal Acquaintance Service	PAS
Personal Activities of Daily Living (DMAA)	PADL
Personal Address Book [MAPI - Mail Applications Program Interface] [Microsoft Corp.] [Computer science]	PAB
Personal Adjustment and Role Skills Scale [Medicine] (DMAA)	PARS
Personal Adjustment Inventory [Psychology]	PAI
Personal Affairs (AFM)	PA
Personal Analog Computer	PAC
Personal Ancestry File [Computer science] (PCM)	PAF
Personal and Family Survival [Civil Defense]	PFS
Personal & Organizational Security Handbook [A publication]	POSH
Personal Appearance	PA
Personal Applications Manager [Hewlett-Packard Co.]	PAM
Personal Area Network [Computer science]	PAN
Personal Arms and Equipment [Army] (ADDR)	PAE
Personal Article Floater [Air baggage insurance]	PAF
Personal Articulation Device [Facetious term for pre-word-processing equipment]	PAD
Personal Assets Line	PAL
Personal Assistance Service Worker [Medicine] (DMAA)	PASW
Personal Assistant [British]	PA
Personal Attitude Survey (EDAC)	PAS
Personal Attribute Inventory for Children (EDAC)	PAIC
Personal Attributes Questionnaire	PAQ
Personal Audit [Psychological testing]	PA
Personal Auto Policy [Insurance]	PAP
Personal Bibliographic Software, Inc. [Information service or system] (IID)	PBS
Personal Call (OA)	PC
Personal Card [Containing person's name, address, age, description, job, habits, haunts, movements] [Used in Belfast, Northern Ireland]	P (Card)
Personal Card File	PCF
Personal Care	PC
Personal Care Aide [or Assistant or Attendant]	PCA
Personal Care Assessment Instrument [Australia]	PCAI
Personal Care Clinic (DAVI)	PCC
Personal Care Residence (DAVI)	PCR
Personal Care Subsidy [Australia]	PCS
Personal Cash Allowance	PCA
Personal Code Calling (NITA)	PCC
Personal Communication Device [FTA] (TAG)	PCD
Personal Communications Controller (NITA)	PCC
Personal Communications Network [British]	PCN
Personal Communications Programme [British]	PCP
Personal Communications Report [FutureComm Publications, Inc. [Information service or system Defunct] (CRD)	PCR
Personal Communications Service [Provided by Personal Communications Network]	PCS
Personal Communications Services [Telecommunications]	PCS
Personal Communications System	PCS
Personal Composition System (DGA)	PCS
Personal Computer	PC
Personal Computer (WDMC)	pc
Personal Computer - Annual Energy Outlook Forecasting Model [Department of Energy] (GFGA)	PC-AEO
Personal Computer Board Panel Assembly (DWSG)	PCBPA
[The] Personal Computer Book	TPCB
Personal Computer Coprocessor	PCC
Personal Computer Disk Operating System [IBM's version of Microsoft program]	PC-DOS
Personal Computer Extended Technology [Computer bus]	PCET
Personal Computer Gridded Interactive Display and Diagnostic System [Marine science] (OSRA)	PCGRIDS
Personal Computer Gridded Interactive Display and Diagnostic System (USDC)	PCGRIDS
Personal Computer Information Service (NITA)	PCIS
Personal Computer, Instrument Product	PCIP
Personal Computer Instruments Bus (NITA)	PCIB
Personal Computer / Interactive Executive (HGAA)	PC/IX
Personal Computer Interface [Varitronics Systems, Inc.]	PCI
Personal Computer Local Network Interface Module (TSSD)	PC-LNIM
Personal Computer Management Association [Orange, CA] [Commercial firm Information service or system] (EA)	PCMA
Personal Computer Memory Card International Association (PCM)	PCMCIA
Personal Computer Modification Program	PCMOD
Personal Computer Network [Telecommunications]	PCN
Personal Computer Network Program (HGAA)	PCNP
Personal Computer News (NITA)	PCN
Personal Computer Query Tool [Military software package] (INF)	PCQT
Personal Computer Read-Only Memory	PC-ROM
Personal Computer Response Analysis Program	PCRAP
Personal Computer/Technology (HGAA)	PC/T
Personal Computer Wide Area Network Interface Module (TSSD)	PC-WNIM
Personal Computer World Show [Montbuild Ltd.] (TSPED)	PCW
Personal Computer-Disk Operating System (DOM)	PC-DOS
Personal Computer-Junior (NITA)	PCjr
Personal Computer-Software Interest Group (EA)	PCSIG
Personal Computing Conference (MHDI)	PERCOMP
Personal Computing System	PCS
Personal Computing Systems Architecture	PCSA
Personal Conferencing Specification [Telecommunications] (CDE)	PCS
Personal Consumption Expenditure	PCE
Personal Copier [In product name, PC-10] [Canon Inc.]	PC
Personal Corporation (BARN)	PC
Personal Correction	PC
Personal Data System (NITA)	PDS
Personal Data Transmitter [From the movie "Aliens"]	PDT
Personal Decision Series (HGAA)	PDS
Personal Defense Weapon [Army] (INF)	PDW
Personal Deposit Account [Banking]	PDA
Personal Description Questionnaire	PDQ
Personal Design Workstation (DGA)	PDW
Personal Development Program (MCD)	PDP
Personal Development Study [Psychology]	PDS
Personal Diagnositics, Inc. [Associated Press] (SAG)	PerDia
Personal Digital Assistant (ECON)	PDA
Personal Digital Assistant [Computer science]	PDA
Personal Disposable Income [Economics]	PDI
Personal Disposable Income [Economics]	Yp
Personal Dust Exposure Monitor (PDAA)	PDEM
Personal Earning and Benefit Estimate Statement [Social Security Administration]	PEBES
Personal Education Counseling (DNAB)	PEC
Personal Effectiveness Inventory (AIE)	PEL
Personal Effectiveness Training (MCD)	PET
Personal Effects	PE
Personal Effects	PEREF
Personal Effects Coverage [Insurance]	PEC
Personal Effects Distribution Center	PEDC
Personal Effects Floater [Insurance]	PEF
Personal Electronic Aid for Maintenance [Military]	PEAM
Personal Electronic Transaction Computer (NITA)	PET
Personal Electronic Transactor [Computer] [Commodore Business Machines]	PET
Personal Emergency Response System [Telecommunications]	PERS
Personal Employee Profiling [Information service or system] (IID)	PEP
Personal Employee Time (DHSM)	PET
Personal Engineering Computer User's Society [Defunct] (EA)	PECUS
Personal Equipment	PE
Personal Equipment and Rescue/Survivable Lowdown (MCD)	PEARL
Personal Equipment Data [Computer science] (IAA)	PED
Personal Equity Plan [Finance]	PEP
Personal Exemption Phase-Out [Income tax]	PEP
Personal Exercise Programmer	PEP
Personal Expense Money [Army]	PERSEXP
Personal Experience Questionnaire [Psychology]	PEQ
Personal Exposure Level [or Limit]	PEL
Personal Exposure Monitor [Environmental chemistry]	PEM
Personal, Fatigue, and Delay [Work measurement factors]	PFD
Personal Filing System [Data-base program] [Software Publishing Corp.]	PFS
Personal Finance Center [Information service or system]	PFC
Personal Financial Planning (ADA)	PFP
Personal Financial Record [Army] (AABC)	PFR
Personal Financial Specialist	PFS
Personal Flotation Device [Life jacket]	PFD
Personal Fouls [Basketball]	PF
Personal Freedom Outreach (EA)	PFO
Personal Guidance Base (AIE)	PGB
Personal Handy Phone [Telecommunications]	PHP
Personal Handyphone System [Telecommunications]	PHS
Personal Health Costs [Medicine] (DMAA)	PHC
Personal Health Survey [Psychology]	PHS
Personal History [Medicine] (AAMN)	PH

Personal History of Depressive Disorders (MEDA) .... PHDD
Personal Holding Company [*Generic term*] .... PHC
Personal Hygiene (MCD) .... PH
Personal Hygiene Facility [*NASA*] (NASA) .... PHF
Personal Hygiene Kit (MCD) .... PHK
Personal Hygiene Subsystem [*NASA*] (KSC) .... PHS
Personal Identification .... PI
Personal Identification Code [*Banking*] .... PIC
Personal Identification Device (MHDI) .... PID
Personal Identification Name (NITA) .... PIN
Personal [*or Private*] **Identification Number** [*Banking*] .... PIN
Personal Identification Project [*Computer science*] .... PIP
Personal Illumination Marker [*Military*] (INF) .... PIM
Personal Income .... PI
Personal Income Tax .... PIT
Personal Information Appliance [*Telecommunications*] (PCM) .... PIA
Personal Information Briefing [*of returning POW's*] [*Air Force*] .... PIB
Personal Information Manager .... PIM
Personal Information Manager [*Computer science*] .... PIM
Personal Information Network [*Indesys, Inc.*] [*Telecommunications service*] (TSSD) .... PIN
Personal Information Retrieval System .... PIRS
Personal Injury [*Insurance*] .... PI
Personal Injury Accident [*British police term*] .... PI
Personal Injury Commentator [*A publication*] (DLA) .... Pers Inj Comment'r
Personal Injury Law Journal [*A publication*] (DLA) .... Pers Inj LJ
Personal Injury Notice (AAG) .... PIN
Personal Innovation Program .... PIP
Personal Intelligent Communicator [*Computer science*] (PCM) .... PIC
Personal Interactive Electronics [*Apple Computer Inc.*] .... PIE
Personal Internet Connection [*Fee-based accounts*] .... PIC
Personal Interview Record .... PIR
Personal Investment [*A publication*] (ADA) .... PI
Personal Investment Authority [*British*] (ECON) .... PIA
Personal LAN (NITA) .... PLAN
Personal LASER Printer [*Computer science*] .... PLP
Personal Level Encryption [*Computer science*] .... PLE
Personal Library Software [*Commercial firm*] .... PLS
Personal Lines .... P/L
Personal Local Area Network [*Telecommunications*] (OSI) .... PLAN
Personal Locator Beacon [*Military*] (AFM) .... PLB
Personal Mailing System (HGAA) .... PMS
Personal Management Information System [*Computer science*] (IAA) .... PMIS
Personal Managers Association [*British*] (DBA) .... PMA
Personal Member of the Baptist Union [*British*] .... PMBU
Personal Member of the Congregational Union [*British*] .... PMCU
Personal Money Allowance .... PMA
Personal Name (NITA) .... PN
Personal Names from Cuneiform Inscriptions of the Cassite Period (BJA) .... CPN
Personal Names from Cuneiform Inscriptions of the Cassite Period [*A publication*] (BJA) .... PN
Personal Navigation .... P-NAV
Personal Number Calling [*Telecommunications*] .... PNC
Personal Objectives and Goals (MCD) .... POGO
Personal Opinion Message [*Western Union*] (IIA) .... POM
Personal Orientation Dimensions [*Personality development test*] [*Psychology*] .... POD
Personal Orientation Inventory [*Psychology*] .... POI
Personal Outlook Inventory [*Employment test*] .... POI
Personal Paid Days Off .... PPDO
Personal Plane Service [*Aircraft restoration firm*] [*British*] .... PPS
Personal Portable Computer .... PPC
Personal Portable Shopper [*Computer science*] .... PPS
Personal Preference Kit [*Small bag in which astronauts are allowed to take personal mementos*] .... PPK
Personal Preference Scale [*Psychology*] .... PPS
Personal Prelatures [*Diocesan abbreviation*] (TOCD) .... PP
Personal Printer Data Stream [*IBM Corp.*] (PCM) .... PPDS
Personal Printer Series [*IBM Corp.*] .... PPS
Personal Printing System [*Computer science*] .... PPS
Personal Process Service (LAIN) .... PPS
Personal Producing General Agent [*Insurance*] .... PPGA
Personal Productivity Center .... PPC
Personal Programmable Calculator (MHDI) .... PPC
Personal Property .... PP
Personal Property [*Legal shorthand*] (LWAP) .... PPROP
Personal Property Consignment Instruction Guide (MCD) .... PPCIG
Personal Property Floater [*Insurance*] .... PPF
Personal Property Floater [*Insurance*] (AD) .... ppf
Personal Property Government Bill of Lading (DNAB) .... PPGBL
Personal Property Policy [*Insurance*] .... PPP
"Personal Property Shipping Information" [*Pamphlet*] **Is Applicable** [*Military*] (AABC) .... PPSIA
Personal Property Shipping Office [*Military*] .... PPSO
Personal Property Tax (MHDW) .... PPT
Personal Property Traffic Management Regulation .... PPTMR
Personal Property Transit Time Guide [*MTMC*] (TAG) .... PPTTG
Personal Property Transportation Officer .... PPTO
Personal Protection Squad [*of the London Metropolitan Police*] .... PPS
Personal Protective Armor Association (EA) .... PPAA
Personal Protective Clothing (GNE) .... PPC
Personal Protective Device [*Toxicology*] .... PPD
Personal Protective Equipment [*General Motors Corp.*] .... PPE
Personal Questionnaire Rapid Scaling Technique [*Personality development test*] [*Psychology*] .... PQRST
Personal Radiation Dosimeter (KSC) .... PRD
Personal Radiation Monitor .... PRM
Personal Radio Communications System [*General Electric Co.*] .... PRCS
Personal Radio Operators Federation [*Defunct*] (EA) .... PROF
Personal Radio Operators International Federation [*Formerly, ARC*] (EA) .... PRO-IF
Personal Radio Steering Group [*Ann Arbor, MI*] [*Telecommunications service*] (TSSD) .... PRSG
Personal Rapid Transit [*Computer-guided transit system*] .... PRT
Personal Rapid Transit System [*Computer-guided transit system*] .... PRTS
Personal Reaction Blank [*Psychology*] (DAVI) .... PRB
Personal Reaction Index [*Interpersonal skills and attitudes test*] .... PRI
Personal Record of School Experiences (EDAC) .... PROSE
Personal Recording System .... PRS
Personal Reflection on Family Life and Employment Stressors [*Psychology*] .... PROFILES
Personal Relations Survey [*Managerial skills test*] .... PRS
Personal Report of Confidence as a Speaker [*Psychology*] .... PRCS
Personal Report of Public Speaking Apprehension (EDAC) .... PRPSA
Personal Rescue Enclosure (NASA) .... PRE
Personal Resources Questionnaire (DMAA) .... PRQ
Personal Responsibility Education Process .... PREP
Personal Responsibility in Daily Effort [*Military Airlift Command's acronym for the Zero Defects Program*] .... PRIDE
Personal Rest and Delay [*Air Force*] (AFM) .... PR & D
Personal Retrieval of Information by Microcomputer and Terminal Ensemble .... PRIMATE
Personal Rights Association [*British*] (BI) .... PRA
Personal Secretary (DCTA) .... P/SEC
Personal Secretary (DCTA) .... PS
Personal Security Clearance File .... PSCF
Personal Security File Number [*British Secret Service*] .... PF
Personal Security Preview [*Psychology*] (DAVI) .... PSP
Personal Sequential-Inference Machine [*Computer science*] .... PSI
Personal Service Agreements (MCD) .... PSA
Personal Service Corporation (TDOB) .... PSC
Personal Service Income .... PSI
Personal Services and Dependents' Services Support System [*Navy*] (DNAB) .... PERSERVDEPSERVS
Personal Services Department [*Navy British*] .... PSD
Personal Signaling System .... PSS
Personal Silicon Foundry (IAA) .... PSF
Personal Skills .... PS
Personal Skills Map [*Career effectiveness test*] .... PSM
Personal Social and Moral Education (AIE) .... PSME
Personal Social Services Council [*British*] (DI) .... PSSC
Personal Staff Officer [*Australia*] .... PSO
Personal Statement Analyzer (HGAA) .... PSA
Personal Success Program .... PSP
Personal Supercomputer [*Culler Scientific Systems Corp.*] .... PSC
Personal Survival .... PS
Personal System [*IBM computer introduced in 1987*] .... PS
Personal System/2 [*IBM Corp.*] PS/2
Personal Technology Research [*Commercial firm*] .... PTR
Personal Time [*Employment*] .... P/T
Personal Time Off (DAVI) .... PTO
Personal Trade [*Marketing and retail terminology referring to customers*] .... PT
Personal Transfer Capsule .... PTC
Personal Transportation [*Navy*] .... PERSTRAN
Personal Transporter .... PT
Personal Typesetting Workstation (DGA) .... PTW
Personal Typing Centre (NITA) .... PTC
Personal Typography System (DGA) .... PTS
Personal Use Radio Advisory Committee [*FCC Defunct*] (TSSD) .... PURAC
Personal Value Questionnaire [*Navy*] .... PVQ
Personal Values Abstract [*Scale*] .... PVA
Personal Values Inventory [*Psychology*] .... PVI
Personal Verifier Terminal (DA) .... PVT
Personal Videoconferencing Station [*Widcom, Inc.*] [*Los Gatos, CA*] [*Telecommunications service*] (TSSD) .... PVS
Personal Videoconferencing System (NITA) .... PVS
Personal Watercraft .... PWC
Personal Watercraft Industry Association (EA) .... PWIA
Personal Word Processor (WDMC) .... PWP
Personal Workstation 2 [*Computer hardware*] [*Unisys Corp.*] (PCM) PW2
Personalcomputer Literaturnachweis [*Datendienst Weiss*] [*Database*] .... PCLN
Personal-E Mailbox [*Computer software*] (PCM) .... PEM
Personalised System of Induction (AIE) .... PSI
Personalistic Discussion Group - Eastern Division (EA) .... PDG
Personality and Individual Differences [*A publication*] .... PID
Personality and Personal Illness Questionnaire (AD) .... PPIQ
Personality and Personal Illness Questionnaires [*Psychology*] .... PPI
Personality Completion Test [*Psychology*] .... PCT
Personality Data Base .... PDB
Personality Evaluation Form [*Psychology*] .... PEF
Personality Factor .... PF
Personality Factor Questionnaire (MAE) .... PFQ
Personality Inventory [*Psychology*] .... PI
Personality Inventory for Children [*Psychology*] .... PIC
Personality, Matter, Energy, Space, Time [*Colon classification, S. R. Ranganathan*] [*Library science*] .... PMEST
Personality, Matter, Energy, Space, Time (AD) .... pmest
Personality Organization and Stability [*Eysenck*] [*Psychology*] .... P

uotient [*Psychology*] .... PQ
Quotient (AD) .... pq
ality Rating Scale [*Psychology*] .... PRS
onality Record [*Psychological testing*] .... PR
ersonality Research Center [*University of Texas at Austin*] [*Research center*] (RCD) .... PRC
Personality Research Form [*Psychology*] .... PRF
Personality-Profile Exam .... PEP
Personalized Aerobics for Cardiovascular Enhancement .... PACE
Personalized Array Translator (IEEE) .... PAT
Personalized Automotive Security System [*In product name, PASS-Key*] [*Delco Electronics*] [*Automotive engineering*] .... PASS
Personalized System of Instruction .... PSI
Personally Owned Vehicle .... POV
Personal'naia Elektronnaia Vychislitel'naia Mashina [*Personal Computer*] [*Russian*] .... PEVM
Personenkraftwagen [*Automobile*] [*German*] .... PKW
Personennamen der Texte aus Ugarit [*A publication*] (BJA) .... PNU
Person-Miles of Travel [*FHWA*] (TAG) .... PMT
Personnel .... P
Personnel (KSC) .... PER
Personnel (AFM) .... PERS
Personnel (DD) .... pers
Personnel .... PRSNNL
Personnel (FAAC) .... PSNL
Personnel Access Control Accountability System [*NASA*] (MCD) .... PACAS
Personnel Accounting Level [*Air Force*] (AFM) .... PAL
Personnel Accounting Machine Installation .... PAMI
Personnel Accounting Symbol [*Air Force*] (AFM) .... PAS
Personnel Accounting System [*Marine Corps*] .... PAS
Personnel Accreditation Institute (EA) .... PAI
Personnel Action Center [*Army*] (INF) .... PAC
Personnel Action Code .... PAC
Personnel Action Memorandum [*Military*] .... PAM
Personnel Action Memorandum [*Military*] .... PERAM
Personnel Actions and Records Directorate [*Military Personnel Center*] (AABC) .... PARD
Personnel Activity Report [*Office of Management and Budget*] .... PAR
Personnel Activity Request .... PAR
Personnel Activity Sequence (AAG) .... PAS
Personnel Address Listing (SAA) .... PAL
Personnel Administration Section [*Library Administration Division of ALA*] .... PAS
Personnel Administrative Services Agency [*Army*] .... PASA
Personnel Administrator [*American Society for Personnel Administration*] [*A publication Information service or system*] .... PA
Personnel Advancement Requirement [*Navy*] (NVT) .... PAR
Personnel Air-Cushion Vehicle .... PACV
Personnel Airlock [*Nuclear energy*] (NRCH) .... PAL
Personnel Allocation Plan [*Navy*] .... PAP
Personnel Allotment Voucher [*Army*] .... PAV
Personnel and Accounting Integrated Data [*System*] [*Veterans Administration*] .... PAID
Personnel and Administration [*Army*] (AABC) .... P & A
Personnel and Administration Assistance Team, Atlantic [*Navy*] (DNAB) .... PAATLANT
Personnel and Administration Assistance Team, Pacific [*Navy*] (DNAB) .... PAATPAC
Personnel and Administration Center [*Army*] (AABC) .... PAC
Personnel and Administration, Combat Development Activity [*Army*] (AABC) .... PACDA
Personnel and Administrative Assistance Team [*Navy*] (NVT) .... PAAT
Personnel and Control Room Building [*Nuclear energy*] (NRCH) .... PCRB
Personnel and Equipment Modification List [*Air Force*] .... P & EML
Personnel and Equipment Working [*Aviation*] (FAAC) .... PAEW
Personnel and Logistics Systems Group [*Army*] (AABC) .... PALSG
Personnel and Pay [*Project*] [*Navy*] .... PERSPAY
Personnel and Separation Command (DNAB) .... PERSEPCOMD
Personnel and Service Area [*Nuclear energy*] (NRCH) .... PSA
Personnel and Training [*Military*] (MUGU) .... P & T
Personnel and Training Command .... PERS & TRACOMD
Personnel and Training Research Center [*Air Force*] .... PTRC
Personnel Applied Research Unit [*Canadian military*] .... PARU
Personnel Area (NRCH) .... PA
Personnel Armor System for Ground Troops (RDA) .... PASGT
Personnel Assignment Survey (MCD) .... PAS
Personnel Assistance and Audit Team [*Military*] .... PAAT
Personnel Assistance Center [*Military*] (INF) .... PAC
Personnel Assistance Center Noncommissioned Officer (INF) .... PACNCO
Personnel Assistance Point [*Army*] (AABC) .... PAP
Personnel Assistance Team [*Military*] .... PAT
Personnel Assistance Teams [*Military*] .... PATS
Personnel Augmentation List [*Military*] .... PAL
Personnel Authentication Identification System (MCD) .... PAIS
Personnel Authorization Table [*Air Force*] .... PAT
Personnel Automated Data System [*TIMMS*] [*Navy*] .... PADS
Personnel Availability Model (PDAA) .... PAM
Personnel/Burden Carrier Manufacturers Association [*Defunct*] (EA) .... PBC
Personnel Capabilities System [*Jet Propulsion Laboratory, NASA*] .... PCS
Personnel Carrier [*A vehicle*] .... PC
Personnel Casualty Report [*Military*] (NVT) .... PERCASREPT
Personnel Casualty Report [*Navy*] (ANA) .... PERS CASREP
Personnel Center .... PERSCEN
Personnel Change of Station .... PCS
Personnel Command [*Army*] (MCD) .... PERCOM
Personnel Command [*Army*] (INF) .... PersCom
Personnel Command [*Army*] (DOMA) .... PRESCOM
Personnel Compensation and Benefits (GFGA) .... PC & B
Personnel Consultancy Services Ltd. [*British*] .... PCS
Personnel Contamination Instrumentation .... PERCI
Personnel Continuity .... PCON
Personnel Control [*Military*] .... PERSCON
Personnel Control Center [*Air Force*] (AFM) .... PCC
Personnel Control Facility [*Army*] (AABC) .... PCF
Personnel Coordination Center [*Army*] .... PCC
Personnel Daily Summary [*Army*] (AABC) .... PDS
Personnel Data Card .... PDC
Personnel Data System [*Air Force*] .... PDS
Personnel Data System - Airmen [*Air Force*] .... PDS-A
Personnel Data System - Airmen (Interim) [*Air Force*] (AFM) .... PDS-A(I)
Personnel Data System - Civilian [*Air Force*] (AFM) .... PDS-C
Personnel Data System - Officers [*Air Force*] (AFM) .... PDS-O
Personnel Data System - Planning [*Air Force*] (AFM) .... PDSP
Personnel Database Application (MCD) .... PDBA
Personnel Database Application / Student Instructor Performance Module (DNAB) .... PDBA/SIPM
Personnel Decontamination Station (MCD) .... PDS
Personnel Delivery System .... PDS
Personnel Department .... PD
Personnel Department [*Marine Corps*] .... PERSD
Personnel Deployment and Distribution Management System [*Military*] (AABC) .... PERDDIMS
Personnel Deployment Report [*Military*] .... PERSDEP
Personnel Despatch and Reception Centre [*British military*] (DMA) .... PDRC
Personnel Development .... PD
Personnel Development and Education (MCD) .... PDE
Personnel Distribution [*Army*] .... PD
Personnel Distribution Command .... PDC
Personnel Electronic Record Management System [*Army*] (RDA) .... PERMS
Personnel Emergency Estimator Capability .... PEEC
Personnel, Enlisted [*or Enlisted Personnel Division*] [*Coast Guard*] .... PE
Personnel Equipment [*Air Force*] (AFM) .... PE
Personnel Equipment Data [*Army*] (IAA) .... PED
Personnel Equipment Data Analysis .... PEDA
Personnel Equivalent [*DoD*] .... PE
Personnel Exchange Program [*Military*] (NVT) .... PEP
Personnel Functional Assessment [*Of the Army Acquisition Corps*] (RDA) .... PFA
Personnel Group of America [*Associated Press*] (SAG) .... PersGp
Personnel Group of America [*NYSE symbol*] (SAG) .... PGA
Personnel Hazards Associated with Space Radiation [*Satellite*] .... PHASR
Personnel History Questionnaire (MHDB) .... PHQ
Personnel Identification Device [*Navy*] (IAA) .... PID
Personnel Identification Feature [*Navy*] (NVT) .... PIF
Personnel in an Awaiting Training Status [*Air Force*] (AFM) .... PATS
Personnel Increment Number (DOMA) .... PIN
Personnel Information Communication [*or Control*] System [*Computer science*] .... PICS
Personnel Information Roster [*Military*] .... PIR
Personnel Information System [*Army*] .... PERSINS
Personnel Information System (MHDB) .... PERSIS
Personnel Information System [*Army*] (AABC) .... PINS
Personnel Information Systems Command [*Army*] (AABC) .... PERSINSCOM
Personnel Information Systems Directorate [*Military Personnel Center*] (AABC) .... PERSINSD
Personnel Inquiry/Death/Occupational Illness [*Report*] (DNAB) .... PID
Personnel Interface Processor (MCD) .... PIP
Personnel Inventory Analysis [*Army*] .... PIA
Personnel Inventory Management System [*AT & T*] .... PIMS
Personnel Inventory Report [*Army*] (AABC) .... PERSIR
Personnel Investigations Center .... PIC
Personnel Journal Index [*Personnel Journal*] [*Information service or system*] (CRD) .... PJI
Personnel Laboratory [*Air Research and Development Command*] [*Air Force*] (AAG) .... PL
Personnel Landing Boat [*Navy symbol Obsolete*] .... LBP
Personnel Letdown Device .... PLD
Personnel Liaison Officer, Chief of Staff, Army (AABC) .... PLOCSA
Personnel Licensing and Training [*ICAO*] (AIA) .... PEL
Personnel Loss Rate Planning Factors (MCD) .... PLRPF
Personnel Management [*A publication*] .... Pers Man
Personnel Management [*NASDAQ symbol*] (TTSB) .... TPMI
Personnel Management Advisor (NOAA) .... PMA
Personnel Management and Accounting Card Processing System (MCD) .... PERMACAPS
Personnel Management and Accounting Card Processor [*Military*] .... PERMACAP
Personnel Management and Training Research Statistical Data System [*Navy*] (DNAB) .... PERSRSCHSYSTM
Personnel Management Assistance .... PMA
Personnel Management Assistance System [*Military*] (AABC) .... PERMAS
Personnel Management Authorization Document [*Army*] .... PMAD
Personnel Management Centre [*British*] (ODBW) .... PMC
Personnel Management Development Directorate [*Military Personnel Center*] (AABC) .... PMDD
Personnel Management Division [*Environmental Protection Agency*] (GFGA) .... PMD
Personnel Management Evaluation [*Marine science*] (OSRA) .... PME
Personnel Management Evaluation (USDC) .... PME
Personnel Management Evaluation System [*Department of Labor*] .... PMES
Personnel Management for Executives [*Military*] (RDA) .... PME
Personnel Management, Inc. [*Associated Press*] (SAG) .... PersnMg
Personnel Management, Inc. [*NASDAQ symbol*] (SAG) .... TPMI

Personnel Management Information (IAA) .... PMI
Personnel Management Information Center [Navy] (NVT) .... PERMIC
Personnel Management Information Center [Air Force] (AFM) ...... PMIC
Personnel Management Information System .... PMIS
Personnel Management Manual [A publication] (ADA) .... PMM
Personnel Management Officer [Army] (INF) .... PMO
Personnel Management Series [Civil Service Commission] .... PMS
Personnel Management Specialist (GFGA) .... PMS
Personnel Management System [Air Force] (AFM) .... PMS
Personnel Management Team .... PMT
Personnel Manning Assistance Report (DNAB) .... PERSMAR
Personnel Master File [Army] (AABC) .... PMF
Personnel Mobility Support System [Military] .... PMSS
Personnel Mobilization Center [Military] .... PMC
Personnel Navigant .... PN
Personnel Network [Army] .... PERSNET
Personnel Neutron Threshold Detector (IEEE) .... PNTD
Personnel Objectives Monitoring Operation .... POMO
Personnel Occurrence Report [RAF] [British] .... POR
Personnel of the Naval Shore Establishment [Report] (NG) ...... PONSE
Personnel Office [Kennedy Space Center Directorate] (NASA) ...... PO
Personnel Officer [Air Force] .... PERSO
Personnel Officer [Navy] .... PERSOF
Personnel Officer .... PO
Personnel Officers of Research and Development Agencies .... PORDA
Personnel on Station Date [Army] (AABC) .... POSD
Personnel On-Site Integration (SAA) .... POSI
Personnel Operations Center .... POC
Personnel, Operations, Maintenance (MCD) .... POM
Personnel Orbit Transfer Vehicle (MCD) .... POTV
Personnel/Payroll System .... PPS
Personnel Performance Problems Inventory [Test] .... PPPI
Personnel Performance Profile .... PPP
Personnel Planning Data [Navy] .... PPD
Personnel Planning Data Book [Navy] .... PPDB
Personnel Planning Information .... PPI
Personnel Planning Information Report (MCD) .... PPIR
Personnel Pool of America [An association] (AD) .... PPA
Personnel Practice Bulletin [A publication] .... Pers Prac B
Personnel Priority Designator [Military] (AFM) .... PPD
Personnel Priority Model (MCD) .... PPM
Personnel Processing (MUGU) .... PERP
Personnel Processing [Army] .... PERSPROC
Personnel Processing Group [Army] .... PPG
Personnel Processing Squadron .... PPS
Personnel Profile - Age by Grade [Army] .... PPAG
Personnel Program Manager [Navy] .... PPM
Personnel Program Review Committee [Military] .... PPRC
Personnel Protection and Communication Services [British] (AD) ...... PPCS
Personnel Psychology [A publication] (BRI) .... Per Psy
Personnel Qualification Record [Military] (INF) .... PQR
Personnel Qualification Roster [Military] (AABC) .... PQR
Personnel Qualification Standard (AD) .... PQS
Personnel Qualification Standards [Military] (NVT) .... PQS
Personnel Reaction Blank [Psychology] .... PRB
Personnel Readiness Capability Program [Navy] (DNAB) ...... PRCP
Personnel Readiness Center [Air Force] .... PRC
Personnel Readiness Date [Army] (AABC) .... PRD
Personnel Readiness File [Army] (AABC) .... PRF
Personnel Readiness System [Air Force] .... PRS
Personnel Reception Centre [British military] (DMA) .... PRC
Personnel Record Information Systems for Management .... PRISM
Personnel Records Branch [Army] (AABC) .... PRB
Personnel Records Division [Army] (AABC) .... PRD
Personnel Recovery Center [Military] .... PRC
Personnel Related Information System for Management (NITA) ...... PRISM
Personnel Relations Officer [for Shore Stations] [Navy] .... PRO
Personnel Reliability Program [Air Force] .... PRP
Personnel Reporting Code [Army] (AABC) .... PRC
Personnel Reporting Unit .... PERSRU
Personnel Requirements Branch (MUGU) .... PRB
Personnel Requirements Data (AAG) .... PRD
Personnel Requirements Generator .... PRG
Personnel Requirements Information System Methodology (NVT) ...... PRISM
Personnel Requirements Report [Army] .... PRR
Personnel Rescue Service [NASA] (NASA) .... PRS
Personnel Rescue System [NASA] (MCD) .... PRS
Personnel Research Activity [Later, NPTRL] [Navy] .... PRA
Personnel Research Activity, San Diego [California] [Navy] ...... PRASD
Personnel Research Activity, Washington, DC [Obsolete Navy] ...... PRAW
Personnel Research and Development Center [Office of Personnel
  Management] (GRD) .... PRDC
Personnel Research and Development Laboratory [Navy] (MCD) ...... PRDL
Personnel Research Board of the Army, Adjutant General .... PRBA(AG)
Personnel Research Branch [Army] (MCD) .... PRB
Personnel Research Division [Navy] (MCD) .... PRD
Personnel Research Field Activity, Washington [Navy] (MUGU) ...... PRFAW
Personnel Research, Inc. [Information service or system] (IID) ...... PRI
Personnel Research Institute Test (AEBS) .... PRI
Personnel Research Laboratory [Lackland Air Force Base, TX] ...... PRL
Personnel Research Section [Army] .... PRS
Personnel Research Staff [Department of Agriculture] .... PRS
Personnel Research Test [Military] .... PRT
Personnel Resources (EA) .... PR
Personnel Resources Data .... PRD

Personnel Resources Group [Military] .... PRG
Personnel Response and Evaluation System for Target Obscuration
  [Military] (RDA) .... PRESTO
Personnel Restraint Equipment (SAA) .... PRE
Personnel Review Board (AD) .... PRB
Personnel Section [of an air staff; also, officer in charge of this section] [Air
  Force] A-1
Personnel Section [of an Army or Marine Corps division general staff, or
  Marine brigade or aircraft wing general staff; also, the officer in charge of
  this section] G-1
Personnel Section [of a joint military staff; also, the officer in charge of this
  section] J-1
Personnel Section [Military] S-1
Personnel Security and Surety Program [Military] (ADDR) ...... PSSP
Personnel Security Clearance .... PCL
Personnel Security Investigation [Military] .... PSI
Personnel Security Officer [Military] .... PSO
Personnel Security Questionnaire .... PSQ
Personnel Selection Inventory [Test] .... PSI
Personnel Selection Officer [British military] (DMA) .... PSO
Personnel Separation Center .... PERSSEPCENT
Personnel Service Center [or Company] [Military] (INF) ...... PSC
Personnel Service Company [Army] (AABC) .... PSAC
Personnel Service Support [Army] (DOMA) .... PSS
Personnel Service Support Directorate (DOMA) .... PSSD
Personnel Services Division [Army] .... PSD
Personnel Services Organisation [Australia] .... PSO
Personnel Shipment Ready Date [Army] (AABC) .... PSRD
Personnel Simulation On-Line [Department of State] [Computer
  program] .... PERSON
Personnel Skill Levels (AAG) .... PSL
Personnel Specialities and Record Inventory (SAA) .... PSRI
Personnel Squadron .... PERS
Personnel Squadron .... PSQ
Personnel Staff Noncommissioned Officer [Military] .... PSNCO
Personnel Staffing Specialist (GFGA) .... PSS
Personnel Standardization and Evaluation Team [Military] ...... PERSET
Personnel Status Change (KSC) .... PSC
Personnel Status Report [Military] .... PERSTAT
Personnel Status Report [Military] .... PERSTATREP
Personnel Status Report [Military] .... PSR
Personnel Structure and Accounting System [Army] .... PERSACS
Personnel Structure and Composition System [Military] ... PERSACS
Personnel Subsystem [Army] .... PS
Personnel Subsystem [Air Force] (AFM) .... PSS
Personnel Subsystem Cost .... PSC
Personnel Subsystem Development Plan .... PSDP
Personnel Subsystem Elements [Army] (AABC) .... PSE
Personnel Subsystem Group (SAA) .... PSG
Personnel Subsystem Manager [Army] (AABC) .... PSM
Personnel Subsystem Process [Army] (AABC) .... PSP
Personnel Subsystem Products [Army] (AABC) .... PSPR
Personnel Subsystem Team [Military] (AFIT) .... PST
Personnel Subsystem Test and Evaluation [Military] .... PSTE
Personnel Supervision and Management Division of ASTSECNAV's Office
  [Absorbed into SECP, 1944] .... PS & M
Personnel Support Activity (DOMA) .... PSA
Personnel Support Detachment (DOMA) .... PSD
Personnel Support of Contingency Operations [Military] ...... PERSCO
Personnel Support System [Army] (AABC) .... PSS
Personnel Survey Control Officer [Military] (AABC) .... PSCO
Personnel System [or Subsystem] Development (AAG) .... PSD
Personnel System Staff Officer .... PERSSO
Personnel System Staff Officer .... PESSO
Personnel Systems Management [Air Force] (AFM) .... PSM
Personnel Test Battery .... PTB
Personnel Tests for Industry .... PTI
Personnel Tests for Industry - Oral Directions Test .... PTI-ODT
Personnel, Training and Force Development [Army] .... PTFD
Personnel Training and Training Devices Analysis Report (MCD) ...... PTTDAR
Personnel Transaction Identifier [Air Force] (AFM) .... PTI
Personnel Transaction Register by Originator [Military] (AABC) ...... PTRO
Personnel Transaction Summary by Originator [Military] (AABC) ...... PTSO
Personnel Transaction Summary by Type Transaction [Military] (AABC) ..... PTST
Personnel Transfer Capsule [Undersea technology] .... PTC
Personnel Transport Carrier .... PTC
Personnel, Utility [British military] (DMA) .... PU
Personnel Utilization Sheet .... PUS
Personnel Vehicle Radar (LAIN) .... PVR
Personnel Working File (DOMA) .... PWF
Personnelman [Navy rating] .... PN
Personnelman, First Class [Navy rating] PN1
Personnelman, Second Class [Navy rating] PN2
Personnelman, Third Class [Navy rating] PN3
Persons (WDMC) .... pers
Persons at One Time .... PAOT
Persons in Need of Supervision [Classification for delinquent children] ...... PINS
Persons of Opposite Sex Sharing Living Quarters [Bureau of the
  Census] .... POSSLQ
Persons of the Opposite Sex Sharing Living Quarters (AD) ...... potossiq
Persons on Board (AD) .... pob
Persons on Board [Aviation] .... POB
Persons Responsive to Educational Problems (EA) .... PREP
Persons Using [Television] (WDMC) .... PU
Persons Using Radio [Radio ratings] (WDMC) .... PUR

...g Television [*Television ratings*] ..... PUT
...ing Television (WDMC) ..... PUT
... Viewing Television [*Television ratings*] (NTCM) ..... PVT
...on-to-Person Accelerated Xerography [*Office technology*] [*British*] ..... PAX
...erson-Years of Observation [*Medicine*] ..... PYO
Person-Years-at-Risk [*After radiation exposure*] (FFDE) ..... PYAR
Perspective (WDAA) ..... PERS
Perspective [*Record label*] ..... Persp
Perspective (MSA) ..... PERSP
Perspective (VRA) ..... persp
Perspective control [*Photography*] ..... PC
Perspective Inversion Algorithm [*Computer science*] ..... PIA
Perspective Study of World Agricultural Development [*FAO*] [*United Nations*] (MSC) ..... PSWAD
Perspectives on Political Science [*A publication*] (BRI) ..... Pers PS
Perspectives - United States of America [*History course*] ..... PERUSA
Per-Square-Inch Gauge (AAGC) ..... PSIG
Perstetur [*Continue*] [*Pharmacy*] (ROG) ..... P
Perstetur [*Let It Be Continued*] [*Pharmacy*] ..... PT
Persuasion [*Novel by Jane Austen*] ..... P
Persutuan Perpustakaan Malaysia [*Library Association of the Federation of Malaysia*] (AD) ..... PPM
Persutuan Perpustakaan Singapura [*Library Association of Singapore*] (AD) ..... PPS
PERT [*Program Evaluation and Review Technique*] **Analysis Report** (KSC) ..... PAR
PERT [*Program Evaluation and Review Technique*] **and Cost Correlation Technique** ..... PACCT
PERT [*Program Evaluation and Review Technique*] **Associated Cost Control** [*Computer science*] (IAA) ..... PACC
PERT [*Program Evaluation and Review Technique*] **Automated Graphical Extension** (KSC) ..... PAGE
PERT [*Program Evaluation and Review Technique*] **Cost Performance Measurement** ..... PCPM
PERT [*Program Evaluation and Review Technique*] **Event Report** ..... PER
PERT [*Program Evaluation and Review Technique*] **Life Cycle Unified System** (IAA) ..... PLU
PERT [*Program Evaluation and Review Technique*] **Lifecycle Unified System** ..... PLUS
PERT [*Program Evaluation and Review Technique*] **Orientation and Training Center** ..... POTC
Pertain (AABC) ..... PERT
Pertaining To (NVT) ..... PERTO
Perth [*Australia ICAO location identifier*] (ICLI) ..... APGF
Perth [*Australia ICAO location identifier*] (ICLI) ..... APPP
Perth [*Australia ICAO location identifier*] (ICLI) ..... APPR
Perth [*Australia ICAO location identifier*] (ICLI) ..... APRF
Perth [*Australia Airport symbol*] (OAG) ..... PER
Perth [*Australia Seismograph station code, US Geological Survey Closed*] (SEIS) ..... PER
Perth [*Postcode*] (ODBW) ..... PH
Perth [*Scotland*] [*Airport symbol*] (AD) ..... PSL
Perth Amboy Free Public Library, Perth Amboy, NJ [*Library symbol Library of Congress*] (LCLS) ..... NjPera
Perth Chamber of Commerce [*Western Australia*] ..... PCC
Perth Courier, Ontario [*Library symbol National Library of Canada*] (NLC) ..... OPC
Perth Courier, Perth, ON, Canada [*Library symbol Library of Congress*] (LCLS) ..... CaOPC
Perth/International [*Australia ICAO location identifier*] (ICLI) ..... APPH
Perth/Jandakot [*Australia ICAO location identifier*] (ICLI) ..... APJT
Perth Market Authority [*Australia*] ..... PMA
Perth Museum, Ontario [*Library symbol National Library of Canada*] (NLC) ..... OPM
Perth Museum, Perth, ON, Canada [*Library symbol Library of Congress*] (LCLS) ..... CaOPM
Perth Muslim Association [*Australia*] ..... PMA
Perth Public Library, Ontario [*Library symbol National Library of Canada*] (NLC) ..... OP
Perth/Scone [*British ICAO location identifier*] (ICLI) ..... EGPT
Perth Stock Exchange [*Australia*] ..... PSE
Perth Theatre Trust [*Australia*] ..... PTT
Perthshire [*County in Scotland*] ..... PERTHS
Pertinent Data Quest (MCD) ..... PDQ
Pertubohan Kebangsaan Melayu Singapura [*Singapore Malays' National Organization*] [*Political party*] (FEA) ..... PKMS
Pertubuhan Bumiputera Bersatu Sarawak [*United Sarawak National Association*] [*Malaysia*] [*Political party*] (FEA) ..... PBBS
Perturbation Molecular Orbital [*Theory*] ..... PMO
Perturbation Theory [*Physical chemistry*] ..... PT
Perturbation Transport [*NASA*] ..... PERTRAN
Perturbative Configuration Interaction [*Based on*] **Localized Orbitals** [*Quantum mechanics*] ..... PCILO
Perturbed Angular Correlation ..... PAC
Perturbed Angular Distribution [*Nuclear physics*] ..... PAD
Perturbed Hard Chain Theory [*Equation of state*] ..... PHCT
Perturbed-Anisotropic-Chain Theory [*Chemistry*] ..... PACT
Perturbed-Hardness Chain [*Molecular thermodynamics*] ..... PHC
Pertussis [*Whooping cough*] ..... PERT
Pertussis Toxin [*Pharmacology*] ..... PT
Pertussis Toxin [*Pharmacology*] ..... PTX
Peru [*International civil aircraft marking*] (ODBW) ..... OB
Peru [*ANSI two-letter standard code*] (CNC) ..... PE
Peru [*MARC country of publication code Library of Congress*] (LCCP) ..... pe
Peru [*ANSI three-letter standard code*] (CNC) ..... PER
Peru [*IYRU nationality code*] (IYR) ..... PU
Peru [*MARC geographic area code Library of Congress*] (LCCP) ..... s-pe--
Peru and Miami County Public Library, Peru, IN [*Library symbol Library of Congress*] (LCLS) ..... InPer
Peru Consolidated Community School District 124, Peru, IL [*Library symbol Library of Congress*] (LCLS) ..... IPerSD
Peru/Grisson Air Force Base [*Indiana*] [*ICAO location identifier*] (ICLI) ..... KGUS
Peru, IL [*FM radio station call letters*] ..... WLRZ
Peru, IN [*Location identifier FAA*] (FAAL) ..... GUS
Peru, IN [*AM radio station call letters*] ..... WARU
Peru, IN [*FM radio station call letters*] ..... WARU-FM
Peru, IN [*Location identifier FAA*] (FAAL) XXX
Peru, NY [*FM radio station call letters*] ..... WXLU
Peru Public Library, Peru, IL [*Library symbol Library of Congress*] (LCLS) ..... IPer
Peru Solidarity [*An association*] (EA) ..... PS
Peru State College Library, Peru, NE [*OCLC symbol*] (OCLC) ..... NBP
Peru State College, Peru, NE [*Library symbol Library of Congress*] (LCLS) ..... NbPerS
Peru Tribune, Peru, IN [*Library symbol Library of Congress*] (LCLS) ..... InPerT
Perugia [*Italy ICAO location identifier*] (ICLI) ..... LIRZ
Perugia [*Italy*] [*Seismograph station code, US Geological Survey*] (SEIS) ..... PRG
Perusahaan PT IndoSatADS [*NYSE symbol*] (TTSB) ..... IIT
Perusal (ROG) ..... PERL
Perused (ROG) ..... PERD
Perusing (ROG) ..... PERUG
Perustuslaillinen Kansanpuolue [*Constitutional People's Party*] [*Finland Political party*] (PPE) ..... PKP
Peruvian ..... PERUV
Peruvian American Association (EA) ..... PAA
Peruvian Heart Association (EA) ..... PHA
Peruvian Inca Orchid Dog Club of America (EA) ..... PIODCA
Peruvian Paso Half-Blood Association [*Later, PPPBR*] (EA) ..... PPHBA
Peruvian Paso Horse Registry of North America (EA) ..... PPHRNA
Peruvian Paso Part-Blood Registry (EA) ..... PPPBR
Pervasive Developmental Disorder [*Medicine*] ..... PDD
Pervasive Developmental Disorder, Not Otherwise Specified ..... PDD/NOS
Pervert [*or Perverted*] [*FBI standardized term*] ..... PERV
Perylene [*Organic chemistry*] (AAMN) ..... Pe
Pesahim (BJA) ..... Pes
Pescadero [*California*] [*Seismograph station code, US Geological Survey*] (SEIS) ..... PSD
Pescara [*Italy ICAO location identifier*] (ICLI) ..... LIBP
Pescara [*Italy*] [*Airport symbol*] (OAG) ..... PSR
Peseta [*Monetary unit*] [*Spain and Latin America*] ..... P
Peseta [*Monetary unit*] [*Andorra and Spain*] (BARN) ..... Ps
Peseta [*Monetary unit*] [*Spain and Latin America*] ..... PST
Peseta [*Monetary unit*] [*Spain and Latin America*] ..... PT
Peseta [*Monetary unit*] [*Spain and Latin America*] ..... PTA
Pesewa [*Monetary unit*] [*Ghana*] ..... P
Peshawar [*Pakistan*] [*ICAO location identifier*] (ICLI) ..... OPPS
Peshawar [*Pakistan*] [*Seismograph station code, US Geological Survey Closed*] (SEIS) ..... PES
Peshawar [*Pakistan*] [*Airport symbol*] (OAG) ..... PEW
Peshawar [*Pakistan*] [*Seismograph station code, US Geological Survey*] (SEIS) ..... PSH
Pesher (BJA) ..... P
Pesher [*or Commentary on Nahum*] **from Qumran. Cave Four** (BJA) 4QpNah
Pesher [*or Commentary on Psalm 37*] **from Qumran. Cave Four** (BJA) 4QpPs37
Pesher [*or Commentary on Micah*] **from Qumran. Cave One** (BJA) 1QpMi
Pesher [*or Commentary on Nahum*] **from Qumran. Cave One** (BJA) 1QpNah
Peshitta (BJA) ..... P
Peshitta [*Syriac translation of the Bible*] (BJA) ..... Pesh
Peshtigo, WI [*FM radio station call letters*] ..... WJMR
Pesikta de-Rav Kahana (BJA) ..... PdRK
Pesikta de-Rav Kahana (BJA) ..... Pesik
Pesikta de-Rav Kahana (BJA) ..... Pesikt
Pesikta Rabbati (BJA) ..... PesiktR
Pesikta Rabbati (BJA) ..... PesR
Pesikta Rabbati (BJA) ..... PR
Peso [*Monetary unit*] [*Spain and Latin America*] ..... P
Pessus [*Pessary*] [*Pharmacy*] ..... PESS
Pest Articles News Summaries [*Commonwealth Mycological Institute*] [*Kew, England*] [*A publication*] ..... PANS
Pest Control Association (NADA) ..... PCA
Pest Control Association of New South Wales [*Australia*] ..... PCANSW
Pest Control Licensing Committee [*New South Wales, Australia*] ..... PCLC
Pest Control Literature Documentation [*Derwent Publications Ltd.*] [*Bibliographic database*] [*Information service or system*] (IID) ..... PESTDOC
Pest Control Operator ..... PCO
Pest Infestation Laboratory [*Agricultural Research Council*] (PDAA) ..... PIL
Pest Management Research Information System [*Agriculture Canada*] [*Information service or system*] (IID) ..... PRIS
Pestalozzi-Froebel Teachers College [*Illinois*] ..... PFTC
Pestalozzi-Froebel-Verband [*Pestalozzi-Froebel Association*] ..... PFV
Peste des Petits Ruminants [*Rinderpest-like disease*] [*Veterinary medicine*] ..... PPR
Peste des Petits Ruminants Virus [*Rinderpest-like disease*] [*Veterinary medicine*] ..... PPRV
Pesticide ..... PESTIC
Pesticide ..... PST
Pesticide Analysis Retrieval and Control System (NITA) ..... PARCS
Pesticide and Industrial Chemicals Research Center [*Public Health Service*] (GRD) ..... PICRC
Pesticide Assessment Guideline [*Environmental Protection Agency*] ..... PAG
Pesticide Data Program [*Environmental Protection Agency*] ..... PDP
Pesticide Document Management System [*Environmental Protection Agency*] (GFGA) ..... PDMS
Pesticide Documentation (NITA) ..... PESTDOC

Pesticide Education and Action Project (EA) .... PEAP
Pesticide Enforcement Management System (NITA) .... PEMS
Pesticide Enforcement Policy Statement [*Environmental Protection Agency*] .... PEPS
Pesticide Evaluation Summary Tabulation .... PEST
Pesticide Information Profiles (GNE) .... PIP
Pesticide Ingredient Review Program [*Chemical Specialties Manufacturers Association*] .... PIR
Pesticide Policy Advisory Committee [*Environmental Protection Agency*] .... PPAC
Pesticide Producers Association [*Defunct*] (EA) .... PPA
Pesticide Product Information System [*Environmental Protection Agency*] (GFGA) .... PPIS
Pesticide Registration [*Environmental Protection Agency*] .... PR
Pesticide Research Laboratory and Graduate Study Center [*Pennsylvania State University*] [*Research center*] (RCD) .... PRL
Pesticide Residue Analysis Information Service [*British*] .... PRAIS
Pesticide Safety Team Network (GNE) .... PSTN
Pesticides Abstracts (NITA) .... PESTAB
Pesticides Action Network (EA) .... PAN
Pesticides Action Network, North America (GNE) .... PAN NA
Pesticides Advisory Committee [*Tasmania, Australia*] .... PAC
Pesticides and Toxic Substances Division [*Environmental Protection Agency*] (GFGA) .... PTSD
Pesticides Documentation Bulletin .... PDBU
Pesticides in Groundwater Strategy [*Environmental Protection Agency*] (GFGA) .... PIGS
Pesticides Information Center [*National Agricultural Library*] [*Terminated, 1969*] .... PIC
Pesticides Office [*Environmental Protection Agency*] .... PO
Pesticides Regulation Division (NADA) .... PRD
Pesticides Regulation Division (AD) .... PRD
Pesticides Safety Precautions Scheme [*British*] .... PSPS
Pet Animal Welfare Scheme [*British*] (DI) .... PAWS
Pet Food Institute (EA) .... PFI
Pet Food Manufacturers Association [*British*] (DBA) .... PFMA
Pet Food Manufacturers' Association of Australia .... PFMAA
Pet Food Warehouse [*Commercial firm Associated Press*] (SAG) .... PetFood
Pet Food Warehouse [*NASDAQ symbol*] (SAG) .... PFWA
Pet, Inc., Corporate Information Center, St. Louis, MO [*OCLC symbol*] (OCLC) .... PET
Pet, Inc., St. Louis, MO [*Library symbol*] [*Library of Congress*] (LCLS) .... MoSPI
Pet Industry Distributors Association (EA) .... PIDA
Pet Industry Joint Advisory Council (EA) .... PIJAC
Pet Lovers Association (EA) .... PLA
Pet Owners' Protective Association .... POPA
Pet Population Control (AD) .... PPC
Pet Practice [*NASDAQ symbol*] (TTSB) .... VETS
[*The*] **Pet Practice, Inc.** [*Associated Press*] (SAG) .... PetPrac
[*The*] **Pet Practice, Inc.** [*NASDAQ symbol*] (SAG) .... VETS
Pet Pride (EA) .... PP
Pet Producers of America (EA) .... PPA
Pet Professional Retailers Organization [*Defunct*] (EA) .... PetPRO
Pet Services, Unlimited [*Commercial firm*] (EA) .... PSU
Pet Switchboard [*Defunct*] (EA) .... PS
Pet Trade and Industry Association (EAIO) .... PTIA
Pet Trade and Industry Exhibition [*British*] (ITD) .... PTIE
Peta [*A prefix meaning multiplied by 10^{15}*] [*SI symbol*] .... P
Peta [*Bolivia*] [*ICAO location identifier*] (ICLI) .... SLPT
Petajoule (ADA) .... PJ
Petal Length [*Botany*] .... PTLEN
Petal, MS [*FM radio station call letters*] .... WMFM
Petaluma & Santa Rosa Railroad Co. [*AAR code*] .... PSR
Petaluma, CA [*AM radio station call letters*] .... KTOB
Petaluma Free Public Library, Petaluma, CA [*Library symbol Library of Congress*] (LCLS) .... CPe
Petameter (IDOE) .... Pm
Petauke [*Zambia*] [*ICAO location identifier*] (ICLI) .... FLPE
Petawawa Canadian Forces Base, ON [*ICAO location identifier*] (ICLI) .... CYWA
Petawawa National Forestry Institute [*Canadian Forestry Service*] [*Research center*] (RCD) .... PNFI
Petawawa National Forestry Institute, Canadian Forestry Service, Environment Canada [*Institut Forestier National Petawawa, Service Canadien des Forets, Environnement Canada*] **Chalk River, Ontario** [*Library symbol National Library of Canada*] (NLC) .... OCKE
Petawawa Village and Township Union Public Library, Ontario [*Library symbol National Library of Canada*] (NLC) .... OPEV
Petco Animal Supplies [*NASDAQ symbol*] (SAG) .... PETC
Petco Animal Supplies [*Associated Press*] (SAG) .... PetcoAn
Pete Duel - Clube da Amizade do Universo [*Pete Duel Universal Friendship Club - PDUFC*] (EAIO) .... PDCAU
Pete Duel Universal Friendship Club (EAIO) .... PDUFC
Pete Shelley Fan Club/Harmony in My Head (EA) .... PSFC/HIMH
Peter [*Phonetic alphabet*] [*World War II*] (DSUE) .... P
Peter [*New Testament book*] .... P
Peter [*New Testament book*] .... Pet
Peter [*New Testament book*] .... Pt
Peter Bent Brigham Hospital [*Boston*] .... PBBH
Peter Breck Fan Club (EA) .... PBFC
Peter Burwash International Special Tennis Programs (EA) .... PBISTP
Peter Collins Publishing [*British*] .... PCP
Peter Duel Remembrance Club (EA) .... PDRC
Peter King [*Afro-jazz band*] .... PK
Peter Lougheed Centre, Calgary General Hospital, Alberta [*Library symbol National Library of Canada*] (BIB) .... ACPLC
Peter Miller Apparel Group, Inc. [*Toronto Stock Exchange symbol*] .... PMP
Peter Noone Just a Little Bit Better Promotion Club (EA) .... PNJALBB
Peter Peregrinus Ltd. [*Publisher*] .... PPL
Peter Symonds School Cadet Corps [*British military*] (DMA) .... PSSCC
Peter Warlock Society (EA) .... PWS
Peter White Public Library, Marquette, MI [*Library symbol Library of Congress*] (LCLS) .... MiMarq
Peter Whyte Gallery, Banff, AB, Canada [*Library symbol Library of Congress*] (LCLS) .... CaABPWG
Peter Wilcock Library, Charles Camsell General Hospital, Edmonton, Alberta [*Library symbol National Library of Canada*] (NLC) .... AECCH
Peterborough [*Postcode*] (ODBW) .... PE
Peterborough [*Canada*] [*Airport symbol*] (OAG) .... YPQ
Peterborough Board of Education [*UTLAS symbol*] .... PBS
Peterborough Centennial Museum and Archives, Ontario [*Library symbol National Library of Canada*] (BIB) .... OPETCM
Peterborough (Conington) [*British ICAO location identifier*] (ICLI) .... EGSF
Peterborough Historical Society, Peterborough, NH [*Library symbol Library of Congress*] (LCLS) .... NhPHi
Peterborough, NH [*FM radio station call letters*] .... WNHQ
Peterborough, NH [*AM radio station call letters*] (RBYB) .... WRPT-AM
Peterborough, ON [*FM radio station call letters*] .... CFFF
Peterborough, ON [*Television station call letters*] .... CHEX-TV
Peterborough, ON [*Television station call letters*] CIII-27
Peterborough, ON [*AM radio station call letters*] .... CKPT
Peterborough, ON [*FM radio station call letters*] .... CKQM
Peterborough, ON [*AM radio station call letters*] .... CKRU
Peterborough, ON [*FM radio station call letters*] .... CKWF
Peterborough Public Library, Ontario [*Library symbol National Library of Canada*] (NLC) .... OPETP
Peterborough Public Library, Peterborough, ON, Canada [*Library symbol Library of Congress*] (LCLS) .... CaOPeTP
Peterborough Royal Foxhound Show Society [*British*] (DBA) .... PRFSS
Peterborough/Sibson [*British ICAO location identifier*] (ICLI) .... EGSP
Peterhead/Longside [*British ICAO location identifier*] (ICLI) .... EGPS
Peters' Condensed Reports, United States Supreme Court [*A publication*] (DLA) .... Pet Cond
Peters' Condensed United States Circuit Court Reports [*A publication*] (DLA) .... Pet Cir CR
Peters' Condensed United States Circuit Court Reports [*A publication*] (DLA) .... Pet Cond Rep
Peters' Condensed United States Reports [*A publication*] (DLA) .... Cond R
Peters' Condensed United States Reports [*A publication*] (DLA) .... Cond Rep
Peters' Condensed United States Reports [*A publication*] (DLA) .... Cond Rep US
Peters' Condensed United States Reports [*A publication*] (DLA) .... Condensed Rep
Peters' Condensed United States Reports [*A publication*] (DLA) .... US Cond Rep
Peters' Prince Edward Island Reports [*1850-72*] [*Canada*] [*A publication*] (DLA) .... Pet
Peters' United States Circuit Court Reports [*A publication*] (DLA) .... PCC
Peters' United States Circuit Court Reports [*A publication*] (DLA) .... Pet
Peters' United States Circuit Court Reports [*A publication*] (DLA) .... Pet CC
Peters' United States Circuit Court Reports [*A publication*] (DLA) .... Peters CC
Peters' United States Digest [*A publication*] (DLA) .... Pet Dig
Peters' United States District Court Reports, Admiralty Decisions [*A publication*] (DLA) .... PAD
Peters' United States District Court Reports, Admiralty Decisions [*A publication*] (DLA) .... Pet
Peters' United States District Court Reports, Admiralty Decisions [*A publication*] (DLA) .... Pet Ad
Peters' United States District Court Reports, Admiralty Decisions [*A publication*] (DLA) .... Pet Ad Dec
Peters' United States District Court Reports, Admiralty Decisions [*A publication*] (DLA) .... Pet Ad R
Peters' United States District Court Reports, Admiralty Decisions [*A publication*] (DLA) .... Pet Adm
Peters' United States District Court Reports, Admiralty Decisions [*A publication*] (DLA) .... Peters' Ad
Peters' United States District Court Reports, Admiralty Decisions [*A publication*] (DLA) .... Peters' Adm Dec
Peters' United States District Court Reports, Admiralty Decisions [*A publication*] (DLA) .... Peters' Adm R
Peters' United States District Court Reports, Admiralty Decisions [*A publication*] (DLA) .... Peters Adm Rep
Peters' United States District Court Reports, Admiralty Decisions [*A publication*] (DLA) .... Peters' Admiralty Dec
Peters' United States District Court Reports, Admiralty Decisions (Appendix) [*A publication*] (DLA) .... Pet Adm App
Peters' United States District Courts Reports, Admiralty Decisions [*A publication*] (DLA) .... Peters Adm
Peter's United States Reports [*1828-42*] [*A publication*] (AAGC) .... Pet
Peters' United States Supreme Court Reports [*26-41 United States*] [*A publication*] (DLA) .... P
Peters' United States Supreme Court Reports [*26-41 United States*] [*A publication*] (DLA) .... Pet
Peters' United States Supreme Court Reports [*26-41 United States*] [*A publication*] (DLA) .... Pet SC
Peters' United States Supreme Court Reports [*26-41 United States*] [*A publication*] (DLA) .... Peters
Peters' United States Surpeme Court Reports [*26-41 United States*] [*A publication*] (DLA) .... PSCUS
Peters Valley [*New Jersey*] [*Seismograph station code, US Geological Survey Closed*] (SEIS) .... PVN
Petersburg [*Alaska*] [*Seismograph station code, US Geological Survey*] (SEIS) .... PSA
Petersburg [*Alaska*] [*Airport symbol*] (OAG) .... PSG
Petersburg, AK [*FM radio station call letters*] .... KFSK

...burg, AK [*AM radio station call letters*] .... KRSA

...rsburg, AK [*Location identifier FAA*] (FAAL) .... PSG

...etersburg, IL [*FM radio station call letters*] .... WLUJ

Petersburg, IN [*FM radio station call letters*] .... WFPC

Petersburg Long Distance [*Commercial firm Associated Press*] (SAG) .... PetrLng

Petersburg Long Distance [*NASDAQ symbol*] (SAG) .... PLDI

Petersburg Long Distance [*NASDAQ symbol*] (TTSB) .... PLDIF

Petersburg National Battlefield .... PETE

Petersburg, NJ [*FM radio station call letters*] .... WJSE

Petersburg Press, Petersburg, AK [*Library symbol Library of Congress*] (LCLS) .... AkPP

Petersburg Press-Dispatch, Petersburg, IN [*Library symbol Library of Congress*] (LCLS) .... InPetPD

Petersburg Public Library, Petersburg, AK [*Library symbol Library of Congress*] (LCLS) .... AkP

Petersburg Public Library, Petersburg, VA [*Library symbol Library of Congress*] (LCLS) .... ViPet

Petersburg, VA [*Location identifier FAA*] (FAAL) .... PTB

Petersburg, VA [*AM radio station call letters*] .... WGCV

Petersburg, VA [*FM radio station call letters*] .... WPLZ

Petersburg, VA [*Television station call letters*] .... WRIC

Petersburg, VA [*FM radio station call letters*] .... WSOJ

Petersburg, VA [*FM radio station call letters*] .... WVST

Petersburg, WV [*Location identifier FAA*] (FAAL) .... PWQ

Petersburg, WV [*FM radio station call letters*] .... WELD

Petersdorff on Bail [*1824*] [*A publication*] (DLA) .... Pet Bail

Petersdorff's Abridgment [*A publication*] (DLA) .... Pet Ab

Petersdorff's Abridgment [*1660-1823*] [*A publication*] (DLA) .... Pet Abr

Petersdorff's Abridgment [*A publication*] (DLA) .... Petersd Ab

Petersdorff's Law of Nations [*A publication*] (DLA) .... Pet L Nat

Petersdorff's Master and Servant [*1876*] [*A publication*] (DLA) .... Pet M & S

Petersen, Ross, Schloerb & Seidel, Library, Chicago, IL [*Library symbol Library of Congress*] (LCLS) .... ICPRS

Petersen's Photographic Magazine [*A publication*] (BRI) .... Pet PM

Petersfield Oil & Minerals [*Vancouver Stock Exchange symbol*] .... PTF

Peterson [*Alabama*] [*Seismograph station code, US Geological Survey*] (SEIS) .... PTR

Peterson, J. Robert, New York NY [*STAC*] .... PJR

Peterson Patriot, Peterson, IA [*Library symbol Library of Congress*] (LCLS) .... IaPetP

Petervin Information Associates [*Also, an information service or system*] (IID) .... PIA

Petes Brewing Co. [*Associated Press*] (SAG) .... Petes

Petes Brewing Co. [*NASDAQ symbol*] (SAG) .... WIKD

Pet-Facilitated Psychotherapy [*Psychiatry*] .... PFP

Pet-Facilitated Therapy [*Psychiatry*] .... PFT

Petgrave's Principal and Agent [*1857*] [*A publication*] (DLA) .... Petg Pr & Ag

Petheram's Discovery by Interrogations [*1864*] [*A publication*] (DLA) .... Peth Dis

Peticolas' Texas Digest [*A publication*] (DLA) .... Pet Dig

Petihta (BJA) .... Pet

Petiole [*Botany*] .... P

Petiole Gland Pairs, Number Of [*Botany*] .... PEGLN

Petit Brooke, or Brooke's New Cases, English King's Bench [*1515-58*] [*A publication*] (DLA) .... Petit Br

Petit Mal [*Epilepsy*] .... PM

Petite (WGA) .... P

Petite Ensemble Model (MCD) .... PEM

Petite Vitesse [*Goods train*] [*French*] .... PV

Petites Soeurs de Jesus [*Little Sisters of Jesus*] [*Italy*] (EAIO) .... PSJ

Petites Soeurs de la Sainte-Famille [*Little Sisters of the Holy Family*] [*Sherbrooke, PQ*] (EAIO) .... PSSF

Petites Soeurs de l'Assumption [*Little Sisters of the Assumption - LSA*] [*Paris, France*] (EAIO) .... PSA

Petition .... PET

Petition .... PETITN

Petition .... PETN

Petition Denied .... PDN

Petition [*or Proposal*] **for Rule Making** (NRCH) .... PRM

Petition Granted (DNAB) .... PGR

Petition Pending .... PPNDG

Petition to United States Supreme Court for Writ of Certiorari Granted [*Legal term*] (DLA) .... Cert Granted

Petitioner .... PETNR

Petitioner .... PETR

Petitions for Patent Waiver .... PPW

Petoskey, MI [*AM radio station call letters*] .... WJML

Petoskey, MI [*FM radio station call letters*] .... WKLZ

Petoskey, MI [*FM radio station call letters*] .... WLXT

Petoskey, MI [*AM radio station call letters*] .... WMBN

Petoskey Public Library, Petoskey, MI [*Library symbol Library of Congress*] (LCLS) .... MiPet

Petpetual State Bank [*North Carolina*] [*Associated Press*] (SAG) .... PerpSB

Petriburgensis [*Signature of the Bishops of Peterborough*] [*Latin*] (ROG) .... PETRIBURG

Petrie Stores Corp. [*Associated Press*] (SAG) .... Petrie

Petrie Stores Corp. [*NYSE symbol*] (SPSG) .... PST

Petrified Forest National Park .... PEFO

Petrified Forest National Park, Painted Desert Library, Holbrook, AZ [*Library symbol Library of Congress*] (LCLS) .... AzHP

Petrified Wood Society (EA) .... PWS

Petrine [*Of, or relating to, Peter the Apostle or Peter the Great*] .... PET

Petrine [*Of, or relating to, Peter the Apostle or Peter the Great*] (BJA) .... Ptr

Petro Union [*NASDAQ symbol*] (TTSB) .... PTRUQ

Petro Union, Inc. [*Associated Press*] (SAG) .... PetroUn

Petro Union, Inc. [*NASDAQ symbol*] (SAG) .... PTRU

Petro-Canada .... PC

Petro-Canada [*NYSE symbol*] (SAG) .... PCZ

Petro-Canada .... PEC

Petro-Canada [*Associated Press*] (SAG) .... PetroC

Petro-Canada [*Associated Press*] (SAG) PetroC2

Petro-Canada, Calgary, AB, Canada [*Library symbol Library of Congress*] (LCLS) .... CaACPC

Petro-Canada, Calgary, Alberta [*Library symbol National Library of Canada*] (NLC) .... ACPC

Petro-Canada Exploration, Calgary, AB, Canada [*Library symbol Library of Congress*] (LCLS) .... CaACPCE

Petro-Canada Installm't Vtg [*NYSE symbol*] (TTSB) .... PCZPP

Petro-Canada International Assistance Corp. .... PCIAC

Petro-Canada, Ottawa, Ontario [*Library symbol National Library of Canada*] (NLC) .... OOPEC

Petro-Canada Products, Inc. [*Toronto Stock Exchange symbol Vancouver Stock Exchange symbol*] .... PPB

Petro-Canada, Research Laboratory, Calgary, AB, Canada [*Library symbol Library of Congress*] (LCLS) .... CaACPCR

Petro-Canada Variable Vtg [*NYSE symbol*] (TTSB) .... PCZ

Petrocel Industries, Inc. [*Vancouver Stock Exchange symbol*] .... PEI

Petrochemical Corp. of Singapore .... PCS

Petrochemical Energy Group (EA) .... PEG

Petrochemical Investing Corp. .... PIC

PetroCorp [*NASDAQ symbol*] (TTSB) .... PETR

Petrocorp, Inc. [*NASDAQ symbol*] (SAG) .... PETR

Petrocorp, Inc. [*Associated Press*] (SAG) .... Petrocp

Petroflame International [*Vancouver Stock Exchange symbol*] .... PFA

Petroglyph (VRA) .... petrgly

Petrogold Financial Corp. [*Vancouver Stock Exchange symbol*] .... PGG

Petrographic .... PETROG

Petrography .... PETROGR

Petrol [*British Waterways Board sign*] .... P

Petrol Dealers' Association [*British*] .... PDA

Petrol Injection [*British*] .... PI

Petrol Pump Manufacturers Association [*British*] (DBA) .... PPMA

Petrol Railhead .... PRH

Petrol Retailers' Association [*British*] .... PRA

Petrol Tractor [*British*] .... PT

Petrolatum (WGA) .... PET

Petroleos de Portugal, EP [*Portuguese Petroleum Co.*] .... PETROGAL

Petroleos Mexicanos [*Spanish*] (AD) .... PM

Petroleos Mexicanos [*Mexico ICAO designator*] (FAAC) .... PMX

Petroleum .... PET

Petroleum (DD) .... Pet

Petroleum [*Chemistry*] (DAVI) .... petr

Petroleum (AABC) .... PETRL

Petroleum .... PETRO

Petroleum .... PETRO

Petroleum .... PETROL

Petroleum Abstracts Information Services [*University of Tulsa*] [*Oklahoma*] [*Information service or system*] (IID) .... PAIS

Petroleum Abstracts Search Service [*Online information service*] .... PASS

Petroleum Administration Act [*Canada*] .... PAA

Petroleum Administration for Defense [*Abolished, 1954*] .... PAD

Petroleum Administration for Defense District [*Department of Energy*] .... PADD

Petroleum Administration for War [*World War II*] .... PAW

Petroleum Administrative Board [*Terminated, 1936*] .... PAB

Petroleum Advisory Committee [*of Organization for Economic Cooperation and Development*] [*Terminated, 1976*] (EGAO) .... PAC

Petroleum and Fuel .... P & F

Petroleum and Gas Industry Communications Emergency Plan [*FCC*] .... PAGICEP

Petroleum & Resources [*NYSE symbol*] (TTSB) .... PEO

Petroleum & Resources Corp. [*NYSE symbol*] (SPSG) .... PEO

Petroleum & Resources Corp. [*Associated Press*] (SAG) .... PetRs

Petroleum and Water Logistics [*Army*] (RDA) .... PWL

Petroleum and Water Systems [*Army*] (RDA) .... PWS

Petroleum Association for Conservation of the Canadian Environment .... PACE

Petroleum Data System [*University of Oklahoma*] [*Databank*] (IID) .... PDS

Petroleum Data System [*Petroleum Information Corp.*] [*Information service or system*] (IID) .... PDS

Petroleum Degrading [*Agent*] .... PETRODEG

Petroleum Development [*NASDAQ symbol*] (TTSB) .... PETD

Petroleum Development Corp. [*NASDAQ symbol*] (NQ) .... PETD

Petroleum Development Corp. [*Associated Press*] (SAG) .... PetDv

Petroleum Distribution System - Korea [*Army*] (MCD) .... PDSK

Petroleum Division, Saskatchewan Research Council, Regina [*Library symbol National Library of Canada*] (BIB) .... SRRCP

Petroleum Economist [*London*] [*A publication*] (BJA) .... PE

Petroleum Electric Power Association [*Later, EUIPA*] (EA) .... PEPA

Petroleum Electric Supply Association [*Defunct*] (EA) .... PESA

Petroleum/Energy Business News Index [*American Petroleum Institute*] [*New York, NY Bibliographic database*] .... P/E NEWS

Petroleum Engineer .... PE

Petroleum Equipment Contractors Association (EA) .... PECA

Petroleum Equipment Institute (EA) .... PEI

Petroleum Equipment Suppliers Association (EA) .... PESA

Petroleum Ether Insoluble Oxidized Fatty Acid [*Food science*] .... PIOFA

Petroleum Ether-Soluble Lipid .... PSL

Petroleum Exploration Society of Great Britain .... PESGB

Petroleum Gas and Revenue Tax [*Canada*] .... PGRT

Petroleum Geo Services [*Associated Press*] (SAG) .... PetrlGeo

Petroleum Geo Services [*NASDAQ symbol*] (SAG) .... PGSA

Petroleum Geo-Svcs A/S ADS [*NASDAQ symbol*] (TTSB) .... PGSAY

Petroleum Handling Equipment (MCD) ... PHE
Petroleum Heat & Power Corp. [*Associated Press*] (SAG) ... PtHeat
Petroleum Heat & Pwr'A' [*NASDAQ symbol*] (TTSB) ... HEAT
Petroleum Helicopter, Inc. [*Associated Press*] (SAG) ... PtHel
Petroleum Helicopters [*NASDAQ symbol*] (TTSB) ... PHELK
Petroleum Helicopters de Colombia SA [*ICAO designator*] (FAAC) ... PHC
Petroleum Helicopters, Inc. [*NASDAQ symbol*] (NQ) ... PHEL
Petroleum Helicopters, Inc. (MCD) ... PHI
Petroleum Helicopters, Inc. [*ICAO designator*] (FAAC) ... PHM
Petroleum Helicopters (Vtg) [*NASDAQ symbol*] (TTSB) ... PHEL
Petroleum Incentives Administration [*Canada*] ... PIA
Petroleum Incentives Program [*Canada*] ... PIP
Petroleum Incentives Program, Energy, Mines and Resources Canada [*Programmes d'Encouragement Petrolier, Energie, Mines et Ressources Canada*] **Ottawa, Ontario** [*Library symbol National Library of Canada*] (NLC) ... OOPI
Petroleum Industry Advisory Committee [*British*] ... PIAC
Petroleum Industry Electrical Association [*Later, ENTELEC*] (EA) ... PIEA
Petroleum Industry Electrotechnical Association (IAA) ... PIEA
Petroleum Industry Local Authority Reporting (PDAA) ... PILAR
Petroleum Industry Research Foundation (NADA) ... PIRF
Petroleum Industry Research Foundation (EA) ... PIRINC
Petroleum Industry Security Council (EA) ... PISC
Petroleum Industry War Council ... PIWC
Petroleum Information Bureau ... PIB
Petroleum Information Corp. (IID) ... PI
Petroleum Intersectional Command [*Army*] (AABC) ... POLIC
Petroleum Intersectional Service [*Army*] ... POLIS
Petroleum Labor Policy Board [*Abolished, 1936*] ... PLPB
Petroleum Logistical Data - Pacific Command (CINC) ... PLD-PACOM
Petroleum Marketers Association of America (EA) ... PMAA
Petroleum Marketers Association of America ... PPMA
Petroleum Marketing Education Foundation (EA) ... PMEF
Petroleum Marketing Management [*Petroleum Marketers Association of America*] [*A publication*] ... PMM
Petroleum Marketing Monthly [*Department of Energy Information service or system*] (CRD) ... PMM
Petroleum Marketing Practices Act ... PMPA
Petroleum Material Requirements Plan (MCD) ... PMRP
Petroleum Monitoring Agency [*Ministry of Energy, Mines, and Resources*] [*Canada*] ... PMA
Petroleum Network [*Distribution and interdiction model*] (MCD) ... PETRONET
Petroleum, Oil, and Lubricants [*Military*] ... POL
Petroleum, Oil, and Lubrication Installation Damage Report (AD) ... poldamr
Petroleum, Oils, and Lubricants Capabilities (MCD) ... POLCAP
Petroleum Operating Agreement (CINC) ... POA
Petroleum Philatelic Society International (EAIO) ... PETROPHIL
Petroleum Pipehead ... PPH
Petroleum Planning Committee [*Obsolete NATO*] (NATG) ... PPC
Petroleum Point ... PP
Petroleum Pool Pacific Coast ... PPPC
Petroleum Press Service ... PPS
Petroleum Production Division (AD) ... PPD
Petroleum Production Pioneers (AD) ... PPP
Petroleum Production Survey [*Bureau of Mines*] ... PPS
Petroleum Products Exchange Data Clearing House (NITA) ... PETROEX
Petroleum Quality Assurance ... PQA
Petroleum Quality Assurance Representative ... PQAR
Petroleum Recovery Institute [*Research center*] (RCD) ... PRI
Petroleum Refining Engineer ... PRE
Petroleum Refining Laboratory [*Pennsylvania State University*] (MCD) ... PRL
Petroleum Research Fund ... PRF
Petroleum Reserves [*Navy*] ... PETRES
Petroleum Reserves Office [*or Officer*] ... PETRESO
Petroleum Resources Communications Foundation [*Canada*] ... PRCF
Petroleum Revenue Tax [*British*] ... PRT
Petroleum Safety Data [*American Petroleum Institute*] ... PSD
Petroleum Section [*Allied Force Headquarters*] ... PETSEC
Petroleum Security Subcommittee [*of Foreign Petroleum Supply Committee*] [*Terminated, 1976*] (EGAO) ... PSSC
Petroleum Supply Monthly [*Database*] [*Department of Energy Information service or system*] (CRD) ... PSM
Petroleum Test Laboratory Accreditation Program ... PTLAP
Petroleum Testing Laboratory ... PTL
Petroleum Warfare Department [*Ministry of Fuel and Power*] [*British World War II*] ... PWD
Petroleum Week [*A publication*] ... PW
Petroleum-Oil-and-Lubricants (AD) ... pol
Petrolia Oil & Gas [*Vancouver Stock Exchange symbol*] ... PEO
Petrolina [*Brazil*] [*Airport symbol*] (OAG) ... PNZ
Petrolina [*Brazil ICAO location identifier*] (ICLI) ... SBPL
Petrolite Corp. [*Associated Press*] (SAG) ... Petrlte
Petrolite Corp. [*NASDAQ symbol*] (NQ) ... PLIT
Petrolite Irradiation Reactor ... PIR
Petrologic Petroleum [*Vancouver Stock Exchange symbol*] ... PTP
Petrology ... PETROL
Petromac Energy, Inc. [*Vancouver Stock Exchange symbol*] ... PTM
Petromet Resouces Ltd. [*Associated Press*] (SAG) ... Petromt
Petromet Resources [*NASDAQ symbol*] (TTSB) ... PNTGF
Petromet Resources Ltd. [*Toronto Stock Exchange symbol*] ... PNT
Petromet Resources Ltd. [*NASDAQ symbol*] (NQ) ... PNTG
Petrominerals Corp. [*Associated Press*] (SAG) ... Petrmn
Petrominerals Corp. [*NASDAQ symbol*] (NQ) ... PTRO
Petronius [*First century AD*] [*Classical studies*] (OCD) ... Petron
Petronius' [*Titus*] **Arbiter, Satyricon, Etc.** [*A publication*] (DLA) ... Petron Satyric
Petropavlovsk [*Kazakhstan*] [*Seismograph station code, US Geological Survey*] (SEIS) ... PET
Petropolis [*St. Petersburg*] [*Imprint*] [*Latin*] (ROG) ... PETROPOL
Petropolis/Pico do Couto [*Brazil ICAO location identifier*] (ICLI) ... SBPI
Petroquin Resources Ltd. [*Vancouver Stock Exchange symbol*] ... PEQ
Petrostates Resource Corp. [*Vancouver Stock Exchange symbol*] ... PSR
Petro-Sun International, Inc. [*Toronto Stock Exchange symbol*] ... PTS
Petro-Sun International, Inc., Longueuil, PQ, Canada [*Library symbol*] [*Library of Congress*] (LCLS) ... CaQLoPS
Petro-Sun International, Inc., Longueuil, Quebec [*Library symbol National Library of Canada*] (NLC) ... QLPS
Petrotech, Inc. [*Toronto Stock Exchange symbol*] ... PET
Petro-Tex Chemical Corp., Research Library, Houston, TX [*Library symbol Library of Congress*] (LCLS) ... TxHPT
Petrotex Resources [*Vancouver Stock Exchange symbol*] ... PTT
Petrovskoye [*Former USSR ICAO location identifier*] (ICLI) ... UKHE
Petrox Energy & Mineral Corp. [*Toronto Stock Exchange symbol*] ... PEM
Petrozavodsk Commodity Exchange [*Russian Federation*] (EY) ... PCE
Petrus [*Authority cited in pre-1607 legal work*] (DSA) ... Pet
Petrus Aretinus [*Flourished, 1088-91*] [*Authority cited in pre-1607 legal work*] (DSA) ... Pet Aret
Petrus Belluga [*Flourished, 1446-68*] [*Authority cited in pre-1607 legal work*] (DSA) ... Petr Bellug
Petrus Boaterius [*Flourished, 1285-1321*] [*Authority cited in pre-1607 legal work*] (DSA) ... P Bo
Petrus Brito [*Flourished, 13th century*] [*Authority cited in pre-1607 legal work*] (DSA) ... PB
Petrus Calvelli [*Flourished, 14th century*] [*Authority cited in pre-1607 legal work*] (DSA) ... P Cal
Petrus Calvelli [*Flourished, 14th century*] [*Authority cited in pre-1607 legal work*] (DSA) ... P Cl
Petrus Crispanus [*Authority cited in pre-1607 legal work*] (DSA) ... Pe Cri
Petrus de Ancharano [*Deceased, 1416*] [*Authority cited in pre-1607 legal work*] (DSA) ... P de Ancha
Petrus de Ancharano [*Deceased, 1416*] [*Authority cited in pre-1607 legal work*] (DSA) ... Pe de Ancar
Petrus de Ancharano [*Deceased, 1416*] [*Authority cited in pre-1607 legal work*] (DSA) ... Pe de Anch
Petrus de Ancharano [*Deceased, 1416*] [*Authority cited in pre-1607 legal work*] (DSA) ... Pe de Ancha
Petrus de Ancharano [*Deceased, 1416*] [*Authority cited in pre-1607 legal work*] (DSA) ... Pet de Anch
Petrus de Bellapertica [*Deceased, 1308*] [*Authority cited in pre-1607 legal work*] (DSA) ... P de B
Petrus de Bellapertica [*Deceased, 1308*] [*Authority cited in pre-1607 legal work*] (DSA) ... P de Bp
Petrus de Bellapertica [*Deceased, 1308*] [*Authority cited in pre-1607 legal work*] (DSA) ... Pe
Petrus de Bellapertica [*Deceased, 1308*] [*Authority cited in pre-1607 legal work*] (DSA) ... Pe de Bel
Petrus de Bellapertica [*Deceased, 1308*] [*Authority cited in pre-1607 legal work*] (DSA) ... Pe de Belper
Petrus de Bellapertica [*Deceased, 1308*] [*Authority cited in pre-1607 legal work*] (DSA) ... Pe de Bepe
Petrus de Bellapertica [*Deceased, 1308*] [*Authority cited in pre-1607 legal work*] (DSA) ... Pe de Blpti
Petrus de Bellapertica [*Deceased, 1308*] [*Authority cited in pre-1607 legal work*] (DSA) ... Peca
Petrus de Bellapertica [*Deceased, 1308*] [*Authority cited in pre-1607 legal work*] (DSA) ... Pet
Petrus de Bellapertica [*Deceased, 1308*] [*Authority cited in pre-1607 legal work*] (DSA) ... Pet de Bel
Petrus de Bellapertica [*Deceased, 1308*] [*Authority cited in pre-1607 legal work*] (DSA) ... Pet de Bellap
Petrus de Bellapertica [*Deceased, 1308*] [*Authority cited in pre-1607 legal work*] (DSA) ... Pet de Belper
Petrus de Benintendis [*Flourished, 16th century*] [*Authority cited in pre-1607 legal work*] (DSA) ... Petr de Benint
Petrus de Orfila [*Deceased, 1307*] [*Authority cited in pre-1607 legal work*] (DSA) ... P de Orfi
Petrus de Salinis [*Flourished, 13th century*] [*Authority cited in pre-1607 legal work*] (DSA) ... P de Sal
Petrus de Salinis [*Flourished, 13th century*] [*Authority cited in pre-1607 legal work*] (DSA) ... P Salin
Petrus de Salinis [*Flourished, 13th century*] [*Authority cited in pre-1607 legal work*] (DSA) ... Pe de Sal
Petrus de Sampsone [*Flourished, 1246-58*] [*Authority cited in pre-1607 legal work*] (DSA) ... P de Sam
Petrus de Sampsone [*Flourished, 1246-58*] [*Authority cited in pre-1607 legal work*] (DSA) ... P de Samp
Petrus de Sampsone [*Flourished, 1246-58*] [*Authority cited in pre-1607 legal work*] (DSA) ... Pe de Samp
Petrus de Sampsone [*Flourished, 1246-58*] [*Authority cited in pre-1607 legal work*] (DSA) ... Pet de Sam
Petrus de Sampsone [*Flourished, 1246-58*] [*Authority cited in pre-1607 legal work*] (DSA) ... Pet de Samp
Petrus Filipi [*Authority cited in pre-1607 legal work*] (DSA) ... Pe Fi
Petrus Filipi [*Authority cited in pre-1607 legal work*] (DSA) ... Pe Fili
Petrus Gregorius [*Deceased, 1617*] [*Authority cited in pre-1607 legal work*] (DSA) ... Pet Greg
Petrus Gregorius [*Deceased, 1617*] [*Authority cited in pre-1607 legal work*] (DSA) ... Petr Greg
Petrus Hispanus [*Authority cited in pre-1607 legal work*] (DSA) ... P
Petrus Hispanus [*Authority cited in pre-1607 legal work*] (DSA) ... Pe
Petrus Hispanus [*Authority cited in pre-1607 legal work*] (DSA) ... Pe His

Petrus Jacobi [*Flourished, 14th century*] [*Authority cited in pre-1607 legal work*] (DSA) ... Pe Ja
Petrus Lombardi [*Flourished, 1154-59*] [*Authority cited in pre-1607 legal work*] (DSA) ... P Lom
Petrus Morini [*Authority cited in pre-1607 legal work*] (DSA) ... Pe Mo
Petrus Morini [*Authority cited in pre-1607 legal work*] (DSA) ... Pe Mori
Petrus Nunius de Avendano [*Flourished, 16th century*] [*Authority cited in pre-1607 legal work*] (DSA) ... Petr Nuni
Petrus Peckius (Ziricaeus) [*Deceased, 1589*] [*Authority cited in pre-1607 legal work*] (DSA) ... Pet Peck Zir
Petrus Piccoli de Monteforte [*Flourished, 14th century*] [*Authority cited in pre-1607 legal work*] (DSA) ... Pet de Mont
Petrus Piccoli de Monteforte [*Flourished, 14th century*] [*Authority cited in pre-1607 legal work*] (DSA) ... PP
Petrus Ravennas [*Flourished, 1468-1508*] [*Authority cited in pre-1607 legal work*] (DSA) ... Pe Rave
Petrus Ravennas [*Flourished, 1468-1508*] [*Authority cited in pre-1607 legal work*] (DSA) ... Petr Rave
Petrus Rigaldi [*Flourished, 14th century*] [*Authority cited in pre-1607 legal work*] (DSA) ... Pe Rigal
Petrusville [*South Africa*] [*ICAO location identifier*] (ICLI) ... FAPV
Pets Are Worth Safeguarding [*An association*] ... PAWS
Petsmart, Inc. [*NASDAQ symbol*] (SAG) ... PETM
Petsmart, Inc. [*Associated Press*] (SAG) ... PetsMrt
Petticoat Peeping [*From one girl to another, in reference to dress disarrangement*] ... PP
Pettigrew Regional Library, Plymouth, NC [*Library symbol Library of Congress*] (LCLS) ... NcPlyP
Petty ... PTTY
Petty Cash (WDMC) ... p/c
Petty Cash (WDMC) ... pc
Petty Cash ... PC
Petty Cash Book [*Business term*] ... PCB
Petty Cash Voucher (MCD) ... PCV
Petty Larceny ... PL
Petty Office First Class [*Military*] (AD) ... PO 1/C
Petty Office Second Class [*Military*] (AD) ... PO 2/C
Petty Office Third Class [*Military*] (AD) ... PO 3/C
Petty Officer [*Navy*] ... PO
Petty Officer Air Fitter [*British military*] (DMA) ... POAF
Petty Officer Aircrewman [*British military*] (DMA) ... POACMN
Petty Officer Airman [*British military*] (DMA) ... POA
Petty Officer Caterer [*British military*] (DMA) ... POCA
Petty Officer Control Electrician [*British military*] (DMA) ... POCEL
Petty Officer Cook [*British military*] (DMA) ... POCK
Petty Officer Electrician (Air) [*British military*] (DMA) ... POEL(A)
Petty Officer Electrician (Air Weapon) [*British military*] (DMA) ... POEL(AW)
Petty Officer Enroute Training [*Navy*] (NVT) ... POET
Petty Officer, First Class [*Navy*] ... E6
Petty Officer, First Class [*Navy*] ... PO1
Petty Officer in Charge [*Navy*] (NVT) ... POIC
Petty Officer Marine Engineering Mechanic [*British military*] (DMA) ... POMEM
Petty Officer Medical Assistant [*British military*] (DMA) ... POMA
Petty Officer of the Watch [*Navy*] (NVT) ... POOW
Petty Officer of the Watch [*Navy*] ... POW
Petty Officer on Watch [*Military*] (AD) ... POoW
Petty Officer Ordnance Electrician [*British military*] (DMA) ... POOEL
Petty Officer Physical Trainer [*British military*] (DMA) ... POPT
Petty Officer Radio Electrician (Air) [*British military*] (DMA) ... POREL(A)
Petty Officer, Second Class [*Navy*] ... E5
Petty Officer, Second Class [*Navy*] ... PO2
Petty Officer Steward [*British military*] (DMA) ... POSTD
Petty Officer Stores Accountant [*British military*] (DMA) ... POSA
Petty Officer Telegraphist Special (DSUE) ... POTS
Petty Officer, Third Class [*Navy*] ... E4
Petty Officer, Third Class [*Navy*] ... PO3
Petty Officer WREN [*Women's Royal Naval Service*] **Air Fitter** [*British military*] (DMA) ... POWRENAF
Petty Officer WREN [*Women's Royal Naval Service*] **Cinema Operator** [*British military*] (DMA) ... POWRENCINE
Petty Officer WREN [*Women's Royal Naval Service*] **Cook** [*British military*] (DMA) ... POWRENCK
Petty Officer WREN [*Women's Royal Naval Service*] **Dental Hygienist** [*British military*] (DMA) ... POWRENDHYG
Petty Officer WREN [*Women's Royal Naval Service*] **Dental Surgery Assistant** [*British military*] (DMA) ... POWRENDSA
Petty Officer WREN [*Women's Royal Naval Service*] **Meteorological Observer** [*British military*] (DMA) ... POWRENMET
Petty Officer WREN [*Women's Royal Naval Service*] **Motor Transport Driver** [*British military*] (DMA) ... POWRENMT
Petty Officer WREN [*Women's Royal Naval Service*] **Photographer** [*British military*] (DMA) ... POWRENPHOT
Petty Officer WREN [*Women's Royal Naval Service*] **Quarters Assistant** [*British military*] (DMA) ... POWRENQA
Petty Officer WREN [*Women's Royal Naval Service*] **(RADAR)** [*British military*] (DMA) ... POWREN(R)
Petty Officer WREN [*Women's Royal Naval Service*] **Radio Electrician** [*British military*] (DMA) ... POWRENREL
Petty Officer WREN [*Women's Royal Naval Service*] **Radio Supervisor (Morse)** [*British military*] (DMA) ... POWRENRS(M)
Petty Officer WREN [*Women's Royal Naval Service*] **Steward** [*British military*] (DMA) ... POWRENSTD
Petty Officer WREN [*Women's Royal Naval Service*] **Stores Accountant** [*British military*] (DMA) ... POWRENSA
Petty Officer WREN [*Women's Royal Naval Service*] **Stores Assistant (Clothes)** [*British military*] (DMA) ... POWRENS(C)
Petty Officer WREN [*Women's Royal Naval Service*] **Stores Assistant (Stores)** [*British military*] (DMA) ... POWRENS(S)
Petty Officer WREN [*Women's Royal Naval Service*] **Stores Assistant (Victualling)** [*British military*] (DMA) ... POWRENS(V)
Petty Officer WREN [*Women's Royal Naval Service*] **Telephonist** [*British military*] (DMA) ... POWRENTEL
Petty Officer WREN [*Women's Royal Naval Service*] **Training Support Assistant** [*British military*] (DMA) ... POWRENTSA
Petty Officer WREN [*Women's Royal Naval Service*] **Weapon Analyst** [*British military*] (DMA) ... POWRENWA
Petty Officer WREN [*Women's Royal Naval Service*] **Welfare Worker** [*British military*] (DMA) ... POWRENWW
Petty Officer WREN [*Women's Royal Naval Service*] **Writer (General)** [*British military*] (DMA) ... POWRENWTR(G)
Petty Officer WREN [*Women's Royal Naval Service*] **Writer (Pay)** [*British military*] (DMA) ... POWRENWTR(P)
Petty Officer Writer [*British military*] (DMA) ... POWTR
Petty Officers Advanced Leadership School [*Navy*] (MUGU) ... POALS
Petty Officer's Guide [*A publication Navy*] ... POG
Petty Officer's Military Academy [*Navy*] ... POMA
Petty Session Division [*Legal term*] (DLA) ... PSD
Petty Sessional Court [*British*] (ROG) ... PSC
Petty Sessions (DLA) ... PS
Petty Sessions Cases [*1875-98*] [*Ireland*] [*A publication*] (DLA) ... Millin
Petty Theft ... PT
Petunia Asteroid Mosaic Virus [*Plant pathology*] ... PAMV
Petunia Lovers of the World ... PLOW
Petunia Vein Clearing Virus [*Plant pathology*] ... PEVCV
Peugeot Owners' Club (EA) ... POC
Peugeot Renault Volvo [*Automobile joint project partners*] ... PRV
Peugot Societe Anonyme [*Peugeot Co. Ltd.*] [*French*] ... PSA
Peutz-Jeghers Syndrome [*Oncology*] ... PJS
Pewter (VRA) ... pew
Pewter (MSA) ... PWTR
Pewter Collectors Club of America (EA) ... PCCA
Peyer's Patch [*Immunology*] ... PP
P'Eylim-American Yeshiva Student Union (EA) ... PAYSU
Peyote ... P
Peyresourde-Balestas [*France ICAO location identifier*] (ICLI) ... LFIP
Pezamerica Resources Corp. [*Vancouver Stock Exchange symbol*] ... PZC
Pezaris Electronics Co., Montreal, Quebec [*Library symbol National Library of Canada*] (NLC) ... QMPE
Pezaris Electronics Co., Research Library, Montreal, PQ, Canada [*Library symbol Library of Congress*] (LCLS) ... CaQMPE
PezCorona Gold Corp. [*Vancouver Stock Exchange symbol*] ... PCG
Pezenas-Nizas [*France ICAO location identifier*] (ICLI) ... LFNP
Pezgold Resource Corp. [*Vancouver Stock Exchange symbol*] ... PEZ
Pfarrer [*Pastor*] [*German*] (EY) ... PFR
Pfaudler Technical Library, Rochester, NY [*Library symbol Library of Congress*] (LCLS) ... NRP
Pfeiffer College, Misenheimer, NC [*Library symbol Library of Congress*] (LCLS) ... NcMiP
Pfeiffer Vacuum Technology AG [*Associated Press*] (SAG) ... PfeifVac
Pfeiffer Vacuum Technology AG [*NYSE symbol*] (SAG) ... PV
Pfeifferella [*Genus of bacteria*] ... Pf
Pfennig [*Penny*] [*Monetary unit*] [*German*] ... PF
Pfennig [*Penny*] [*Monetary unit*] [*German*] ... PFG
Pferdsfeld [*Germany ICAO location identifier*] (ICLI) ... EDSP
PFF Bancorp [*NASDAQ symbol*] (TTSB) ... PFFB
PFF Bancorp, Inc. [*NASDAQ symbol*] (SAG) ... PFFB
PFF Bancorp, Inc. [*Associated Press*] (SAG) ... PFFBcp
Pfizer Canada, Inc., Medical Library, Kirkland, PQ, Canada [*Library symbol*] [*Library of Congress*] (LCLS) ... CaQKiPC
Pfizer, Inc. [*Research code symbol*] ... P
Pfizer, Inc. [*Research code symbol*] ... PA
Pfizer, Inc. [*NYSE symbol*] (SPSG) ... PFE
Pfizer, Inc. [*Associated Press*] (SAG) ... Pfizer
Pfizer, Inc., New York, NY [*Library symbol Library of Congress*] (LCLS) ... NNCP
Pfizer, Inc., Research Center Library, Easton, PA [*Library symbol Library of Congress*] (LCLS) ... PEP
Pfizer Ltd. [*Great Britain*] [*Research code symbol*] ... GS
Pfizer Ltd. [*Great Britain*] [*Research code symbol*] ... UK
PG & E Capital I [*AMEX symbol*] (SAG) ... PCG
PG & E Capital I [*Associated Press*] (SAG) ... PGECap
PG & E Corp. Holdings Co. [*NYSE symbol*] (SAG) ... PCG
PG & E Corp. Holdings Co. [*Associated Press*] (SAG) ... PG & E Cp
PG Energy, Inc. [*Associated Press*] (SAG) ... PGEner
PG Energy, Inc. [*NASDAQ symbol*] (SAG) ... PGWC
PG&E Cap I 7.90%'QUIPS' [*AMEX symbol*] (TTSB) ... PCGPrCA
PGI, Inc. [*AMEX symbol*] (SPSG) ... PGA
PGR. Press Gallery Report [*A publication*] (ADA) ... PGR
Phaedo [*of Plato*] [*Classical studies*] (OCD) ... Phd
Phaedrus [*of Plato*] [*Classical studies*] (OCD) ... Phdr
Phaeochromocytoma [*Medicine*] (BABM) ... PCC
Phaeochromocytoma [*Pheochromocytoma*] [*Endocrinology*] (DAVI) ... phaeo
Phage and the Origins of Molecular Biology ... PATOOMB
Phagocyte Glycoprotein [*Biochemistry*] ... PGP
Phagocytosis and Killing Function [*Immunology*] (AAMN) ... PKF
Phagocytosis Promoting Factor [*Immunology*] (DAVI) ... PPF
Phakic-Aphakic [*Ophthalmology*] (MAE) ... PA
Phakoemulsification [*Ophthalmology*] (DAVI) ... PE
Phalaborwa [*South Africa*] [*Airport symbol*] (OAG) ... PHW

Phalaborwa/Hendrik Van Eck [*South Africa*] [*ICAO location identifier*] (ICLI) ... FAPH
Phalange (WDAA) ... PHAL
Phalangeal Bracket [*i.e., cup handle*] [*Slang*] ... PB
Phalangeal Osteoarthritis [*Medicine*] ... POA
Phalanx (WDAA) ... PHAL
Phalen's Criminal Cases [*A publication*] (DLA) ... Phal CC
Phallacidin [*Biochemistry*] ... Ph
Phalloidin Tetramethylrhodamine [*Biochemistry*] ... PDTMR
Phalsbourg/Bourscheid [*France ICAO location identifier*] (ICLI) ... LFQP
Phamaceutical Manufacturers Association of Canada ... PMAC
Phamis, Inc. [*NASDAQ symbol*] (SAG) ... PHAM
Phamis, Inc. [*Associated Press*] (SAG) ... Phamis
Phan Thiet [*South Vietnam*] [*Airport symbol*] (AD) ... PHH
Phantom (IAA) ... PH
Phantom (MSA) ... PHM
Phantom Circuit [*Telecommunications*] (TEL) ... PH
Phantom Class Racing Association (EA) ... PCRA
Phantom II [*Model of automobile*] ... PII
Phantom Phanatics Society (EA) ... PPS
Phantom Range Pod (MCD) ... PRP
Phantom-Glass [*Theater term*] (DSUE) ... PHANT
Phaplu [*Nepal*] [*ICAO location identifier*] (ICLI) ... VNPL
Pharma Patch plc [*NASDAQ symbol*] (TTSB) ... SKINY
Pharmaceutical (WDAA) ... PHAR
Pharmaceutical ... PHARM
Pharmaceutical ... PHARMCL
Pharmaceutical ... PHARML
Pharmaceutical Advertising Council [*New York, NY*] (EA) ... PAC
Pharmaceutical and Healthcare Industries News Database [*PJB Group Publications Ltd.*] [*Information service or system*] (IID) ... PHIND
Pharmaceutical and Toxicological Research Institute [*Ohio State University*] [*Research center*] (RCD) ... PTRI
Pharmaceutical Benefit Manager [*or Management*] [*Managed health care*] ... PBM
Pharmaceutical Benefits Pricing Authority [*Australia*] ... PBPA
Pharmaceutical Card System (MCD) ... PCS
Pharmaceutical Chemist ... Ph C
Pharmaceutical Chemist [*British*] ... PharC
Pharmaceutical Chemist (MEDA) ... Pharm C
Pharmaceutical Chemistry (WDAA) ... PHARM CHEM
Pharmaceutical Council of Western Australia ... PCWA
Pharmaceutical Documentation [*British*] [*Patents retrieval system Derwent Publications*] (NITA) ... FARMDOC
Pharmaceutical Education Advisory Committee [*Australia*] ... PEAC
Pharmaceutical Evaluation Report [*Australia*] ... PER
Pharmaceutical Information Control System (DIT) ... PICS
Pharmaceutical Ingredients Asia [*Conference*] ... PHIA
Pharmaceutical Ingredients U.S. ... PhIUS
Pharmaceutical Journal [*A publication*] (ROG) ... P JI
Pharmaceutical Journal Formulary (ROG) ... PJF
Pharmaceutical Literature Documentation [*Derwent Publications Ltd.*] [*British Information service or system*] (IID) ... RINGDOC
Pharmaceutical Manufacturers Association (EA) ... PMA
Pharmaceutical Manufacturers Association Foundation (IAA) ... PMAF
Pharmaceutical Manufacturers Association of Canada ... PMAC
Pharmaceutical Marketing Services [*NASDAQ symbol*] (SPSG) ... PMRX
Pharmaceutical Marketing Services, Inc. [*Associated Press*] (SAG) ... PhrmMkt
Pharmaceutical Mktg Svcs [*NASDAQ symbol*] (TTSB) ... PMRX
Pharmaceutical News Index [*UMI/Data Courier*] [*Information service or system A publication*] ... PNI
Pharmaceutical Partners for Better Healthcare (ECON) ... PPBH
Pharmaceutical Price Regulation Scheme [*British*] ... PPRS
Pharmaceutical Product Development, Inc. [*Associated Press*] (SAG) ... PharmP
Pharmaceutical Product Development, Inc. [*NASDAQ symbol*] (SAG) ... PPDI
Pharmaceutical Product Devlpmt [*NASDAQ symbol*] (TTSB) ... PPDI
Pharmaceutical Research and Manufacturers of America ... PhRMA
Pharmaceutical Research and Testing [*Public Health Service*] (GRD) ... PRT
Pharmaceutical Resources [*NYSE symbol*] (SPSG) ... PRX
Pharmaceutical Resources, Inc. [*Associated Press*] (SAG) ... PhmRes
Pharmaceutical Sales Representative ... PSR
Pharmaceutical Society (NADA) ... PS
Pharmaceutical Society of Great Britain ... PSGB
Pharmaceutical Society of Great Britain, London, United Kingdom [*Library symbol Library of Congress*] (LCLS) ... UkLPh
Pharmaceutical Society of Great Britain, Scottish Department, Edinburgh, United Kingdom [*Library symbol Library of Congress*] (LCLS) ... UkEPh
Pharmaceutical Society of Ireland (BI) ... PSI
Pharmaceutical Wholesalers Association [*Later, DWA*] ... PWA
Pharmacia AB [*Sweden*] [*Research code symbol*] ... Ph
Pharmacia AB [*Commercial firm*] (MHDW) ... PHABY
Pharmacia & Upjohn [*NYSE symbol*] (TTSB) ... PNU
Pharmacia & Upjohn AB [*Commercial firm*] [*Sweden*] ... P&U
Pharmacia & Upjohn, Inc. [*Associated Press*] (SAG) ... PharUpj
Pharmacia & Upjohn, Inc. [*NYSE symbol*] (SAG) ... PNU
Pharmaciae Baccalaureus [*Bachelor of Pharmacy*] ... Phar B
Pharmaciae Doctor [*Doctor of Pharmacy*] ... Phar D
Pharmaciae Doctor [*Doctor of Pharmacy*] (DAVI) ... PhD
Pharmaciae Magister [*Master of Pharmacy*] ... Phar M
Pharmaciae Magister [*Master of Pharmacy*] (DAVI) ... PhM
Pharmacist [*or Pharmacy*] ... PHARM
Pharmacist ... PHRMST
Pharmacists Against Drug Abuse (EA) ... PADA
Pharmacists for Life (EA) ... PFL
Pharmacists in Ophthalmic Practice (EA) ... PIOP
Pharmacists in Ophthalmic Practice [*Later, PIOP*] (EA) ... POP
Pharmacist's Mate [*Navy rating*] ... PHM
Pharmacist's Mate, Dental Prosthetic Technician [*Navy rating*] ... PHMDP
Pharmacogenic Confusional Syndrome [*Medicine*] (DMAA) ... PCS
Pharmacokinetic ... PK
Pharmacokinetic Drug Monitoring Services [*Medicine*] (DMAA) ... PDMS
Pharmacologic Autonomic Block [*Medicine*] (DMAA) ... PAB
Pharmacological (MSA) ... PHARMACOL
Pharmacological Sciences Program [*Bethesda, MD*] [*National Institute of General Medical Sciences*] (GRD) ... PSP
Pharmacology [*Medicine*] (DMAA) ... PC
Pharmacology ... PHAR
Pharmacology ... PHARM
Pharmacology ... PHARMAC
Pharmacology, Clinical [*Medical specialty*] (DHSM) ... PA
Pharmacology Equivalent Name ... PEN
Pharmaco-Medical Documentation, Inc. [*Information service or system*] (IID) ... PMD
Pharmacopaeia Edinensis [*Edinburgh Pharmacopoeia*] [*A publication*] (ROG) ... PE
Pharmacopeia Inc. [*NASDAQ symbol*] (TTSB) ... PCOP
Pharmacopeia Nederlandsche [*Netherlands Pharmacopoeia*] ... PNed
Pharmacopeia of the United States ... PUS
Pharmacopoeia ... P
Pharmacopoeia ... Ph
Pharmacopoeia (ROG) ... PHAR
Pharmacopoeia Britannica [*British Pharmacopoeia*] ... PB
Pharmacopoeia Germanica [*German Pharmacopoeia*] ... PG
Pharmacopoeia Germanica [*German Pharmacopeia*] (MAE) ... PhG
Pharmacopoeia Internationalis [*International Pharmacopoeia*] (DAVI) ... PhI
Pharmacopoeia Internationalis [*International Pharmacopoeia*] ... PI
Pharmacopoeia of India [*A publication*] ... Ind P
[*The*] **Pharmacopoeia of Japan** [*A publication*] ... Jap P
Pharmacy [*or Pharmacist*] (MSA) ... PHAR
Pharmacy (DD) ... Pharm
Pharmacy ... PHARM
Pharmacy and Chemistry Technician [*Navy*] ... PCT
Pharmacy and Therapeutics ... P & T
Pharmacy Benefit Managers (ECON) ... PBM
Pharmacy Board of New South Wales [*Australia*] ... PBNSW
Pharmacy Board of Queensland [*Australia*] ... PBQ
Pharmacy Board of South Australia ... PBSA
Pharmacy Board of Victoria [*Australia*] ... PBV
Pharmacy College Admission Test ... PCAT
Pharmacy College Admissions Test (GAGS) ... PCAT
Pharmacy Corps [*Army*] ... PC
Pharmacy Director ... PD
Pharmacy Dispenser [*British military*] (DMA) ... PD
Pharmacy Equivalent Name [*Medicine*] (DMAA) ... PEN
Pharmacy Restructuring Authority [*Australia*] ... PRA
Pharmacy Services Administrative Organization ... PSAO
Pharmacy, Supply, and Administration (DOMA) ... PS & A
Pharmacyclics, Inc. [*NASDAQ symbol*] (SAG) ... PCYC
Pharmacyclics, Inc. [*Associated Press*] (SAG) ... Phmcyc
Pharma-Dokumentationsring [*Pharma Documentation Ring*] [*Information service or system*] (IID) ... PDR
Pharma-Dokumentations-Service [*Pharma Documentation Service*] [*Information service or system*] (IID) ... PDS
PharmChem Laboratories [*NASDAQ symbol*] (SPSG) ... PCHM
Pharmchem Laboratories, Inc. [*Associated Press*] (SAG) ... PharLb
Pharmhouse Corp. [*Associated Press*] (SAG) ... Phrmhse
Pharmhouse Corp. [*NASDAQ symbol*] (SAG) ... PHSE
Phar-Mor, Inc. [*Associated Press*] (SAG) ... PharMor
Phar-Mor, Inc. [*Associated Press*] (SAG) ... PhMor
Phar-Mor, Inc. [*NASDAQ symbol*] (SAG) ... PMOR
Phar-Mor Wrrt [*NASDAQ symbol*] (TTSB) ... PMORW
Pharmos Corp. [*NASDAQ symbol*] (SAG) ... PARS
Pharmos Corp. [*Associated Press*] (SAG) ... PharmoS
Pharos-Tribune, Logansport, IN [*Library symbol Library of Congress*] (LCLS) ... InLogPT
Pharr, TX [*AM radio station call letters*] ... KVJY
Pharyngitis ... PHY
Pharyngoconjunctival Fever [*Medicine*] ... PCF
Pharyngoconjunctival Fever (DAVI) ... PCF
Pharyngoesophageal [*Medicine*] ... PE
Pharynx [*Anatomy*] (DAVI) ... Phx
Phase (WDMC) ... ph
Phase (KSC) ... PH
Phase [*Computer science*] ... PHSE
Phase Address System ... PAS
Phase Adjusting Hub ... PAH
Phase Advance Pulse ... PAP
Phase Alternate Line (NITA) ... PAL
Phase Alternation Line [*West German color television system*] ... PAL
Phase Alternation Line Delay (IEEE) ... PAL-D
Phase Alternation Line Simple [*TV decoding system*] ... PALS
Phase Amplitude Monopulse (PDAA) ... PHAM
Phase and Frequency Locked Loop [*Telecommunications*] (IAA) ... PFLL
Phase Angle (IAA) ... PA
Phase Angle Error ... PAE
Phase Angle Voltmeter ... PAV
Phase Angle Voltmeter ... PAVM
Phase Array System ... PAS
Phase Change Material ... PCM
Phase Change Materials [*Solar energy*] ... PCM
Phase Code (NITA) ... PC

Phase Coherent (CET) ... PC
Phase Combining System [*Trademark*] [*A solubilizer in scintillation counting*] ... PCS
Phase Comparison Sinusoidal Frequency Shift Keying ... PCSFSK
Phase Compensator System ... PCS
Phase Conjugate Mirror ... PCM
Phase Constant (IAA) ... PHCONST
Phase Contrast Microscopy ... PCM
Phase Control (IAA) ... PC
Phase Control Keyboard ... PCK
Phase Conversion and Step-Down (MSA) ... PHCV-SD
Phase Data Recorder (KSC) ... PDR
Phase Delay Rectifier ... PDR
Phase Demodulation Unit ... PDU
Phase Discriminator ... PD
Phase Displacement (IAA) ... PDM
Phase Elapsed Time (NASA) ... PET
Phase Encoding [*Magnetic tape recording*] [*Computer science*] (MDG) ... PE
Phase Engineering Report ... PER
Phase Frequency Distortion [*Telecommunications*] (IAA) ... PFD
Phase Image of Poly(diethylsiloxane) [*Organic chemistry*] ... PDES
Phase Invariant Signature Algorithm [*Chemistry*] (DAVI) ... PISA
Phase Inversion Formulation [*Chemistry*] ... PIF
Phase Inversion Temperature [*Physical Chemistry*] ... PIT
Phase Keying Technique ... PKT
Phase Line ... PL
Phase Linear Interferometer Experiment (MCD) ... PLIE
Phase Lock Automatic Tuned Circuit Adjustment [*Telecommunications*] ... PATCA
Phase Lock Demodulator ... PLD
Phase Lock Doppler Tracking [*System*] (MUGU) ... PHLODOT
Phase Lock Frequency ... PLF
Phase Lock Loop Receiver ... PLLR
Phase Lock Receiving System ... PLRS
Phase Locked Arrays [*Physics*] ... PLA
Phase Margin Performance Measure [*Manual control system*] ... PMPM
Phase Match (IAA) ... PM
Phase Meter ... PHM
Phase Modulation [*Radio data transmission*] (DEN) ... PHM
Phase Modulation [*Radio data transmission*] ... PM
Phase Modulation (AD) ... p-m
Phase Modulation Generator ... PMG
Phase Name (NITA) ... PN
Phase Nulling LASER Gyroscope ... PNLG
Phase of the Moon [*Astronomy*] (NHD) ... POM
Phase Pushing Factor ... PPF
Phase Reversal Keying [*Computer science*] (IAA) ... PRK
Phase Review Package (MCD) ... PRP
Phase Sensitive Rectifier (NITA) ... PSR
Phase Separation ... PS
Phase Sequence Logic (IAA) ... PSL
Phase Sequence Relay ... PSR
Phase Shift (MSA) ... PSH
Phase Shift Keyed Modulation (NITA) ... PSKM
Phase Shift Keying [*Computer science*] ... PSK
Phase Shifter Driver ... PSD
Phase Space Theory [*Physical chemistry*] ... PST
Phase Stabilized Ammonium Nitrate (MCD) ... PSAN
Phase Time Modulation ... PTM
Phase Tracking Loop (MCD) ... PTL
Phase Transfer [*Physical chemistry*] ... PT
Phase Transfer Catalysis [*Physical chemistry*] ... PTC
Phase Transfer Function (MCD) ... PTF
Phase Type (NITA) ... PT
Phase Variable Canonical Form (PDAA) ... PVCF
Phase Velocity ... PHV
Phase Volume Ratio [*Physical chemistry*] ... PVR
Phase Zero ... PZ
Phase Zero Defense ... PZD
Phase Zero Program ... PZP
Phase-Alternation System [*A color TV format*] [*Also, phase alternate each line*] (WDMC) ... PAL
Phase-Amplitude Modulation ... PAM
Phase-Change [*Physics*] ... PC
Phased Array Analysis System ... PAAS
Phased Array Antenna ... PAA
Phased Array Antenna System ... PAAS
Phased Array Antenna Technology Investigation ... PAATI
Phased Array Control Electronics ... PACE
Phased Array Module ... PAM
Phased Array RADAR ... PAR
Phased Array RADAR and Divers Integrated Semiconductor Elements (PDAA) ... PARADISE
Phased Array RADAR Detection System (PDAA) ... PARDS
Phased Array RADAR Operational Simulation [*Army*] (AABC) ... PHAROS
Phased Array Sector Scanner [*Instrument for measuring ultrasound*] [*Trademark of General Electric Co.*] ... PASS
Phased Array Tracking to Intercept of Target [*Air defense system unit*] [*Army*] (RDA) ... PATRIOT
Phased Array Warning System ... PAWS
Phased Control Technique (PDAA) ... PACT
Phased Development Shuttle [*NASA*] (KSC) ... PDS
Phased Equipment Modernization [*Army*] (AABC) ... PEM
Phased Knee Rehabilitation (DMAA) ... PKR
Phased Loading Entry [*Computer science*] ... PLE
Phased Maintenance (MCD) ... PM
Phased Maintenance Availability [*Navy*] (DOMA) ... PMA
Phased Maintenance Checklist (MCD) ... PMC
Phased Maintenance During Overhaul ... PMDO
Phased Program Construction (IAA) ... PPC
Phased Project Planning [*NASA*] (KSC) ... PPP
Phased Provisioning Code (NASA) ... PPC
Phase-Delay Keying [*Computer science*] ... PDK
Phase-Exchange Keying [*Computer science*] (IEEE) ... PEK
Phase-In ... PI
Phase-In, Phase-Out (MCD) ... PIPO
Phase-Locked Automatic Frequency Control [*Telecommunications*] ... PAFC
Phase-Locked Control Loop [*NASA*] (IAA) ... PLCL
Phase-Locked Detector (IAA) ... PLD
Phase-Locked Discriminator (IAA) ... PLD
Phase-Locked Loop [*NASA*] ... PLL
Phase-Locked Loop with Decision Feedback [*NASA*] (IAA) ... PLLDF
Phase-Locked Oscillator ... PLO
Phase-Modulated Telemetry Transmission ... PMTT
Phase-Modulated Transmission ... PMT
Phase-Out ... PO
Phaser/Subarray ... P/S
Phase-Resolved Fluorescence Spectroscopy ... PRFS
Phase-Resolved Fluoroimmunoassay ... PRFIA
Phase-Response Curve ... PRC
Phase-Sensitive Anodic Stripping Voltammetry ... PSASV
Phase-Sensitive Converter ... PSC
Phase-Sensitive Demodulator [*or Detector*] ... PSD
Phase-Sensitive Modulator (MCD) ... PSM
Phase-Sensitive Voltmeter ... PSVM
Phase-Sensitive Voltmeter (IDOE) ... psvm
Phase-Shift ... PS
Phase-Shift Driver (CET) ... PHD
Phase-Shift Driver (MSA) ... PSHD
Phase-Shift Keying MODEM ... PSKM
Phase-Shift Keying - Pulse Code Modulation ... PSK-PCM
Phase-Shift Modal Interference ... PSMI
Phase-Shifter, Electronic ... PSE
Phase-Shifter Module ... PSM
Phase-Splitter (MSA) ... PHSP
Phase-System Switching [*Physical chemistry*] ... PSS
Phasing System [*Telecommunications*] (OA) ... PS
Phaungbyin [*Myanmar*] [*ICAO location identifier*] (ICLI) ... VBPB
PHC, Inc. [*Associated Press*] (SAG) ... PHC
PHC, Inc. [*Associated Press*] (SAG) ... PHC Inc
PHC, Inc. [*NASDAQ symbol*] (SAG) ... PIHC
PHC Inc.'A' [*NASDAQ symbol*] (TTSB) ... PIHC
PHC Inc. Wrrt [*NASDAQ symbol*] (TTSB) ... PIHCW
Phear's Rights of Water [*1859*] [*A publication*] (DLA) ... Phear Wat
Pheasant and Waterfowl Society of Australia ... PWSA
Pheasant Trust (EA) ... PT
Phelps Community Library, Redbridge, Ontario [*Library symbol National Library of Canada*] (NLC) ... ORP
Phelps Dodge [*NYSE symbol*] (TTSB) ... PD
Phelps Dodge Corp. [*NYSE symbol*] (SPSG) ... PD
Phelps Dodge Corp. [*Associated Press*] (SAG) ... PhelpD
Phenacetin [*Acetophenetidin*], Aspirin, Caffeine [*Pharmacology*] ... PAC
Phenacetin [*Acetophenetidin*], Aspirin, Deoxyephedrine [*Pharmacology*] ... PAD
Phenadoxone Hydrochloride [*An analgesic and hypnotic*] [*Pharmacy*] (DAVI) ... CB_{11}
Phenanthrene [*Organic chemistry*] (AAMN) ... Ph
Phenanthrene Amino Alcohol [*Organic chemistry*] ... PAA
Phenanthroimidazole [*Organic chemistry*] ... PI
Phenanthrylacetamide [*Organic chemistry*] ... PAA
Phenate-Hexamine Goggle [*British World War I anti-poison-gas helmet*] ... PHG
Phenazine Ethosulfate [*Biochemistry*] ... PEX
Phenazine Methosulfate [*Biochemistry*] ... PMS
Phenazine Methosulphate (AD) ... pms
Phencyclidine [*An anesthetic*] ... P
Phencyclidine Palmitate [*Organic chemistry*] (DAVI) ... PCP
Phenelzine (DMAA) ... PLZ
Phenethyl Alcohol [*Organic chemistry*] ... PEA
Phenethyl Propionate [*Insect attractant*] [*Organic chemistry*] ... PEP
Phenethylbiguanide [*or Phenformin*] [*Pharmacology*] (DAVI) ... DBI
Phenethylbiguanide [*Same as PEDG*] [*Antidiabetic compound*] ... PEBG
Phenethyldiguanide [*Same as PEBG*] [*Antidiabetic compound*] ... PEDG
Phenetic Coefficient of Variation ... PCV
Pheney's New Term Reports [*England*] [*A publication*] (DLA) ... Pheney Rep
Phenformin [*An oral hypoglycemic*] [*Obsolete*] (DAVI) ... PBI
Pheniminooxazolidinone [*Pharmacology*] ... PIO
Phenindione [*or Phenylindandione*] [*Anticoagulant*] ... PID
Phenix City, AL [*FM radio station call letters*] ... WGSY
Phenix City, AL [*AM radio station call letters*] ... WPNX
Phenix Society (EA) ... PS
Phenobarbital [*A drug*] ... PB
Phenobarbital [*A drug*] ... PHENO
Phenobarbital [*A Drug*] (DAVI) ... PHENOB
Phenobarbital [*A drug*] (DAVI) ... phenobarb
Phenobarbital and Belladonna [*A drug regimen*] ... P & B
Phenobarbital and Belladonna [*Medicine*] (DMAA) ... P&B
Phenododecinium [*or Phenoxyethyldimethyl-dodecylammonium*] **Bromide** [*Antiseptic*] ... PDDB
Phenol Alcohol [*Chemistry*] (DAVI) ... PA
Phenol Coefficient (IIA) ... PC
Phenol Enhanced Reassociation Technique [*Clinical chemistry*] ... PERT
Phenol Red ... PR

Phenol/Resorcinol/Formaldehyde [*Plastics technology*] ... PRF
Phenol Sector Group [*European Council of Chemical Manufacturers Federations*] [*Belgium*] (EAIO) ... PSG
Phenol Sulfotransferase [*An enzyme*] ... PST
Phenol-Acetic Acid-Urea [*Medicine*] (DMAA) ... PAU
Phenol-Formaldehyde [*Organic chemistry*] ... PF
Phenolfurfural [*Organic chemistry*] ... PFF
Phenol-Hydroquinone [*Photography*] (AD) ... p-q
Phenolic (AAG) ... PHEN
Phenolic Foam Manufacturers Association [*British*] (DBA) ... PFMA
Phenolic Glass Laminate ... PGL
Phenolic Heavy Oil ... PHO
Phenolic Molding Compound ... PMC
Phenolic Nylon ... PN
Phenolic Nylon with Microballoon ... PNM
Phenolphthalein [*Chemical indicator*] ... P
Phenolphthalein in Paraffin [*Emulsion*] ... PAP
Phenol-Soluble Acidic Nuclear Protein [*s*] [*Biochemistry*] ... PSANP
Phenolsulfonephthalein [*Chemical indicator*] ... PSP
Phenomena Induced by Charged Particle Beams ... PICPAB
Phenomenally Speedy Ordinary [*Photographic plates*] (ROG) ... PS
Phenomenological Systems, Inc. ... PSI
Phenomenon (BARN) ... phenom
Phenomenon of Man [*Project*] (EA) ... POM
Phenotemperature Normogram [*Phenology*] ... PTN
Phenothiazine [*A drug*] (DAVI) ... PHENTH
Phenotype [*Microbiology*] (DAVI) ... PHEN
Phenotype ... pheno
Phenoxyacetic Acid [*Organic chemistry*] ... POA
Phenoxybenzamine [*Also, POB*] [*Adrenergic blocking agent*] ... PBZ
Phenoxybenzamine [*Later, PBZ*] [*Adrenergic blocking agent*] ... POB
Phentolamine [*Antiadrenergic*] ... PA
Pheny(ethyl)malonamide [*Organic chemistry*] ... PEMA
Phenyl [*Organic chemistry*] ... Ph
Phenyl Acid Phosphate [*Organic chemistry*] ... PAP
Phenyl Glycidyl Ether [*Organic chemistry*] ... PGE
Phenyl Isocyanate [*Organic chemistry*] ... PI
Phenyl Methylcarbamate [*Organic chemistry*] ... PNMC
Phenyl Phosphorodiamidate [*Fertilizer technology*] ... PPDA
Phenylacetic Acid [*Organic chemistry*] ... PAA
Phenylalanin [*An amino acid*] (DAVI) ... PHA
Phenylalanine [*One-letter symbol*] [*Also, Phe*] ... F
Phenylalanine [*Medicine*] (MEDA) ... PHA
Phenylalanine [*Also, F*] [*An amino acid*] ... Phe
Phenylalanine [*Also, F*] [*An amino acid*] (DOG) ... phe
Phenylalanine (MAE) ... PHIA
Phenylalanine Ammonia-Lyase [*An enzyme*] ... PAL
Phenylalanine and Methotrexate [*Antineoplastic drug regimen*] (DAVI) ... PF
Phenylalanine Hydroxylase [*An enzyme*] ... PAH
Phenylalanine Mustard (AAMN) ... PAM
Phenylalanine mustard [*Melphalan*], Fluorouracil, Tamoxifen [*Antineoplastic drug regimen*] ... PFT
Phenylalanine-Lysine-Vasopressin (MAE) ... PLV
Phenyl(aminoethyl)sulfide [*Biochemistry*] ... PAES
Phenylaminotetrazole [*Psychology*] ... PAT
Phenylarsine Oxide ... PAO
Phenylazobenzyloxycarbonyl [*Biochemistry*] ... Pz
Phenyl-beta-naphthylamine [*Organic chemistry*] ... PBNA
Phenylbiguanide [*Biochemistry*] ... PBG
Phenylbiphenylyloxadiazole [*Analytical biochemistry*] ... PBD
Phenylboronate Agarose [*Biochemistry*] (DAVI) ... PBA
Phenylboronic Acid [*Organic chemistry*] ... PBA
Phenylbutazone (DAVI) ... BUTE
Phenylbutazone [*Organic chemistry*] (DAVI) ... BZ
Phenylbutazone [*Anti-inflammatory compound*] ... PBZ
Phenyl(butyl)nitrone [*Organic chemistry*] ... PBN
Phenylbutyric Acid [*Organic chemistry*] ... PBA
Phenylcarboxylic Acid [*Chemistry*] (DAVI) ... PCA
Phenylchlorocarbene [*Organic chemistry*] ... PCC
Phenylchlorodiazirine [*Organic chemistry*] ... PCD
(Phenylcyclohexyl)methylpiperidine [*Organic chemistry*] ... PCMP
(Phenylcyclohexyl)piperidine [*or Phencyclidine*] [*Anesthetic A street drug*] ... PCP
Phenylcyclopropanemethylamine [*Organic chemistry*] ... PCMA
Phenyldichlorarsine [*A war gas*] ... PD
Phenyl-Dichlorophosphine (PDAA) ... PDP
Phenyldiethanolamine [*Organic chemistry*] ... PDEA
Phenyldimethyltriazine [*Organic chemistry*] (AAMN) ... PDT
Phenyldiphenyloxadiazole [*Organic chemistry*] (MAE) ... PPD
Phenyldodecane [*Organic chemistry*] ... PDD
Phenylene Ether Copolymer [*Organic chemistry*] ... PEC
Phenylenediamine [*Chemistry*] ... PDA
Phenylephrine ... PE
Phenylephrine [*Medicine*] (DMAA) ... PHE
Phenylethanolamine [*Organic chemistry*] ... PEA
Phenylethanolamine N-Methyltransferase (DMAA) ... PENT
Phenylethanolamine N-Methyltransferase [*An enzyme*] ... PNMT
Phenylethanolaminotetralin [*Organic chemistry*] ... PEAT
Phenylethylamine [*Biochemistry*] ... PEA
(Phenyl)(ethyl)ethanolamine [*Organic chemistry*] ... PEEA
(Phenylethyl)phenylacetoxypiperidine [*Organic chemistry*] ... PEPAOP
(Phenylethyl)Phenyltetrahydropyridine [*Organic chemistry*] ... PEPTP
(Phenylethyl)phenyltetrahydropyridine [*Organic chemistry*] ... PETP
(Phenylethyl-propylamino)hydroxytetralin [*Biochemistry*] ... PPHT
Phenylethyl(thiogalactoside) [*Organic chemistry*] ... PETG
Phenyl-gamma-aminobutyric Acid [*Tranquilizer*] ... P-GABA
Phenyl-gamma-aminobutyric Acid [*Tranquilizer*] ... PhGABA
Phenylglycine [*An amino acid*] ... Phgly
Phenylglycine Acid Chloride [*Biochemistry*] (AAMN) ... PG-AC
Phenylhydantoin [*Pharmacology*] (CPH) ... PHT
Phenylhydroquinone [*Organic chemistry*] ... PHQ
Phenylisopropyladenosine [*Biochemistry*] ... PIA
Phenylisopropylhydrazine [*Pharmacology*] ... PIH
Phenylisothiocyanate [*Organic chemistry*] ... PITC
Phenylisothiocyanate [*Organic chemistry*] ... PTC
Phenylketonuria [*Congenital metabolism disorder*] [*Medicine*] ... PKU
Phenyl(mercapto)oxadiazole [*Reagent*] ... PMODA
Phenylmercuric Acetate [*Also, PMAC*] [*Herbicide and fungicide*] ... PMA
Phenylmercuric Acetate [*Also, PMA*] [*Herbicide and fungicide*] ... PMAC
Phenylmercuric Chloride [*Antiseptic*] ... PMC
Phenylmercuric Hydroxide [*Organic chemistry*] ... PMH
Phenylmercuric Nitrate [*Antiseptic*] ... PMN
(Phenylmercury)dodecenyl Succinate [*Antimicrobial agent*] ... PMDS
(Phenyl)(methyl)ethanolamine [*Organic chemistry*] ... PMEA
Phenylmethylisoxazole [*Organic chemistry*] ... PMI
Phenyl(methyl)pyrazolone [*An organic pigment*] ... PMP
Phenylmethylsulfonyl Fluoride [*Analytical chemistry*] ... PMSF
Phenylpropanol [*A drug*] (DAVI) ... PHENYL
Phenylpropanolamine (AD) ... ppa
Phenylpropanolamine [*Organic chemistry*] ... PPA
Phenylpropanolamine [*Organic chemistry*] ... PPL
Phenylpropanolamine(hydrochloride) [*Also, PPH, PPM*] [*Decongestant*] ... PPA
Phenylpropanolamine(hydrochloride) [*Also, PPA, PPM*] [*Decongestant*] ... PPH
Phenylpropanolamine(hydrochloride) [*Also, PPA, PPH*] [*Decongestant*] ... PPM
(Phenylpyridyl)diphenyltriazine [*Analytical chemistry*] ... PPDT
Phenylpyruvic Acid [*Organic chemistry*] ... PPA
Phenylpyruvic Acid Positive [*Biochemistry*] (DAVI) ... PPA pos
Phenylsulfonylacetophenone ... PSAP
Phenyltetrahydropyridine [*Biochemistry*] ... PTP
Phenylthiocarbamide [*or Phenylthiocarbamyl*] [*Organic chemistry*] ... PTC
Phenylthiohydantoin [*Organic chemistry*] ... PTH
Phenylthiourea [*Organic chemistry*] ... PTU
(Phenyl)triazolinedione [*Organic chemistry*] ... PTAD
Phenyltriazolinedione [*Organic chemistry*] ... PTD
Phenyltrichlorosilane [*Organic chemistry*] ... PTCS
Phenyltrimethylammonium [*Also, PTM, PTMA*] [*Organic chemistry*] ... PTA
Phenyltrimethylammonium [*Also, PTA, PTMA*] [*Organic chemistry*] ... PTM
Phenyltrimethylammonium [*Also, PTA, PTM*] [*Organic chemistry*] ... PTMA
Phenyltrimethylammonium Perbromide [*Organic chemistry*] ... PTAP
Phenyl(vinyl)imidazolidinethione [*Organic chemistry*] ... PVIZT
Phenylxylylethane [*Organic chemistry*] ... PXE
Phenytoin [*Pharmacology*] (DAVI) ... PT
Phenytoin [*Anticonvulsant*] ... PTN
Pheochromocytoma [*Oncology*] ... PC
Pheochromocytoma [*Oncology*] ... PCC
Pheochromocytoma [*Oncology*] ... PHEO
Pheochromocytoma, Thyroid Carcinoma Syndrome [*Oncology*] (MAE) ... PTC
Pheophytin [*Biochemistry*] ... PHE
P-heptyl-p-hydroxy Benzoate [*A preservative used in the making of American and British beer*] ... PHPHB
Pheripheral Exchange Synchronization (IAA) ... PESY
Pheromone and Receptor Transcription Factor [*Genetics*] ... PRTF
Pheromone Biosynthesis-Activating Neuropeptide [*Biochemistry*] ... PBAN
Pheromonebinding Proteins [*Biochemistry*] ... PBP
Phetchaburi/Maruk [*Thailand*] [*ICAO location identifier*] (ICLI) ... VTBM
Phetchaburi/Tha Yang [*Thailand*] [*ICAO location identifier*] (ICLI) ... VTBJ
PHH Aviation Systems, Inc. [*ICAO designator*] (FAAC) ... XAS
PHH Corp. [*NYSE symbol Toronto Stock Exchange symbol*] (SPSG) ... PHH
Phi Beta Kappa [*Honorary society*] ... PBK
Phi Chi Medical Fraternity (EA) ... PCMF
Phi Delta Kappa [*Fraternity*] ... PDK
Phi Epsilon Kappa [*Fraternity*] ... PEK
Phi Gamma Nu [*Fraternity*] ... PGN
Phi Kappa Phi [*Honor society*] (AEE) ... PKP
Phi Kappa Sigma [*Fraternity*] ... PKS
Phi Kappa Tau [*Fraternity*] ... PKT
Phi Lambda Kappa [*Fraternity*] ... PLK
Phi Lambda Upsilon [*Fraternity*] ... PLU
Phiala [*Bottle*] [*Pharmacy*] ... PH
Phiala [*Bottle*] [*Pharmacy*] ... PHIAL
Phiala Prius Agitata [*Having First Shaken the Bottle*] [*Pharmacy*] ... PPA
Phiala Prius Agitate [*Bottle Having First Been Shaken*] [*Latin*] (AD) ... ppa
Phil Collins Fan Club (EA) ... PCFC
Phil Esposito Foundation [*Defunct*] (EA) ... PEF
Phila Suburban [*NYSE symbol*] (TTSB) ... PSC
Philadelphia [*Branch in the Federal Reserve regional banking system*] (BARN) ... C
Philadelphia [*Pennsylvania*] [*Mint mark, when appearing on US coins*] ... P
Philadelphia [*Chromosome*] ... Ph'
Philadelphia [*Diocesan abbreviation*] [*Pennsylvania*] (TOCD) ... PH
Philadelphia [*Pennsylvania*] [*Seismograph station code, US Geological Survey Closed*] (SEIS) ... PHI
Philadelphia [*Pennsylvania*] ... PHIL
Philadelphia (ODBW) ... Phil
Philadelphia [*Pennsylvania*] ... PHILA
Philadelphia (ROG) ... PHILADA
Philadelphia (ROG) ... PHILADEL
Philadelphia ... Philly
Philadelphia [*Pennsylvania*] [*Airport symbol*] ... PHL
Philadelphia & Norfolk Steamship [*AAR code*] ... PNS
Philadelphia & Reading Railway ... P & R
Philadelphia & Western Railroad [*AAR code Terminated*] ... PW

Philadelphia Association for Clinical Trials (DAVI) .... PACT
Philadelphia Bar Association, Philadelphia, PA [*Library symbol Library of Congress*] (LCLS) .... PPB
[*The*] Philadelphia Belt Line Railroad Co. [*AAR code*] .... PBL
Philadelphia, Bethlehem & New England Railroad Co. [*AAR code*] .... PBNE
Philadelphia Bible Institute [*Pennsylvania*] .... PBI
Philadelphia Board of Public Education, Pedagogical Library, Philadelphia, PA [*Library symbol Library of Congress*] (LCLS) .... PPPL
Philadelphia Chromosome (MAE) .... Ph¹
Philadelphia Chromosome .... Ph¹c
Philadelphia City Institute Branch Free Library, Philadelphia, PA [*Library symbol Library of Congress Obsolete*] (LCLS) .... PPPCity
Philadelphia City Planning Commission, Philadelphia, PA [*Library symbol Library of Congress*] (LCLS) .... PPCPC
Philadelphia College of Art Library, Philadelphia, PA [*Library symbol Library of Congress*] (LCLS) .... PPPCA
Philadelphia College of Osteopathic Medicine .... PCOM
Philadelphia College of Osteopathic Medicine, Philadelphia, PA [*Library symbol Library of Congress*] (LCLS) .... PPCO
Philadelphia College of Osteopathy [*Pennsylvania*] .... PCO
Philadelphia College of Pharmacy and Science [*Pennsylvania*] .... PCPS
Philadelphia College of Pharmacy and Science (GAGS) .... Phila C Pharmacy
Philadelphia College of Pharmacy and Science, Philadelphia, PA [*OCLC symbol*] (OCLC) .... PCP
Philadelphia College of Pharmacy and Science, Philadelphia, PA [*Library symbol Library of Congress*] (LCLS) .... PPPCPh
Philadelphia College of Textiles and Science, Philadelphia, PA [*OCLC symbol*] (OCLC) .... PCT
Philadelphia College of Textiles and Science, Philadelphia, PA [*Library symbol Library of Congress*] (LCLS) .... PPPTe
Philadelphia College of the Bible, Philadelphia, PA [*Library symbol Library of Congress*] (LCLS) .... PPPSB
Philadelphia Consol Hldg [*NASDAQ symbol*] (TTSB) .... PHLY
Philadelphia Consolidated Holding [*Commercial firm Associated Press*] (SAG) .... PhilCon
Philadelphia Consolidated Holding [*NASDAQ symbol*] (SAG) .... PHLY
Philadelphia Contract Management District (SAA) .... PACMD
Philadelphia County Medical Society, Philadelphia, PA [*Library symbol Library of Congress Obsolete*] (LCLS) .... PPCM
Philadelphia Dance Alliance .... PDA
Philadelphia Dance Company .... PHILDANCO
Philadelphia Department of Records, Philadelphia, PA [*Library symbol*] [*Library of Congress*] (LCLS) .... PPDR
Philadelphia Depository Trust Co. .... PDTC
Philadelphia Electric Co., Philadelphia, PA [*Library symbol Library of Congress*] (LCLS) .... PPPEC
Philadelphia Fellowship Commission, Philadelphia, PA [*Library symbol Library of Congress Obsolete*] (LCLS) .... PPFC
Philadelphia Flyers Fan Club (EA) .... PFFC
Philadelphia General Hospital Laboratories, Philadelphia, PA [*Library symbol Library of Congress Obsolete*] (LCLS) .... PPGenH
Philadelphia General Hospital, Philadelphia, PA [*Library symbol Library of Congress*] (LCLS) .... PPGH
Philadelphia Group (DNAB) .... PHILAGRP
Philadelphia Housing Association, Philadelphia, PA [*Library symbol Library of Congress Obsolete*] (LCLS) .... PPPHA
Philadelphia Industrial Development Corp. .... PIDC
Philadelphia/International [*Pennsylvania*] [*ICAO location identifier*] (ICLI) .... KPHL
Philadelphia International Convention Center [*Pennsylvania*] .... PICC
Philadelphia Journalism Review [*A publication*] .... PJR
Philadelphia Law Journal [*A publication*] (DLA) .... Phila LJ
Philadelphia Legal Intelligencer [*Pennsylvania*] [*A publication*] (DLA) .... Phila Leg Int
Philadelphia Legal Intelligencer [*Pennsylvania*] [*A publication*] (DLA) .... Philadelphia Leg Int
Philadelphia, MS [*AM radio station call letters*] .... WHOC
Philadelphia, MS [*FM radio station call letters*] .... WWSL
Philadelphia Museum of Art (AD) .... PMA
Philadelphia Museum of Art, College of Art, Philadelphia, PA [*Library symbol Library of Congress Obsolete*] (LCLS) .... PPPM-I
Philadelphia Museum of Art, Philadelphia, PA [*Library symbol Library of Congress*] (LCLS) .... PPPM
Philadelphia Musical Academy .... PMA
Philadelphia Naval Shipyard (AD) .... PNS
Philadelphia/North Philadelphia [*Pennsylvania*] [*ICAO location identifier*] (ICLI) .... KPNE
Philadelphia [*Pennsylvania*] North Philadelphia [*Airport symbol*] (OAG) .... PNE
Philadelphia Ordnance Depot [*Military*] (AAG) .... PHOD
Philadelphia, PA [*Location identifier FAA*] (FAAL) .... CQH
Philadelphia, PA [*Location identifier FAA*] (FAAL) .... GLC
Philadelphia, PA [*AM radio station call letters*] .... KYW
Philadelphia, PA [*Television station call letters*] .... KYW-TV
Philadelphia, PA [*Location identifier FAA*] (FAAL) .... MUV
Philadelphia, PA [*Location identifier FAA*] (FAAL) .... MYY
Philadelphia, PA [*Location identifier FAA*] (FAAL) .... PDP
Philadelphia, PA [*Location identifier FAA*] (FAAL) .... PNE
Philadelphia, PA [*FM radio station call letters*] .... WBEB
Philadelphia, PA [*Television station call letters*] .... WCAU
Philadelphia, PA [*AM radio station call letters*] .... WDAS
Philadelphia, PA [*FM radio station call letters*] .... WDAS-FM
Philadelphia, PA [*AM radio station call letters*] (RBYB) .... WFIL
Philadelphia, PA [*FM radio station call letters*] .... WFLN
Philadelphia, PA [*Television station call letters*] .... WGBS
Philadelphia, PA [*AM radio station call letters*] .... WGMP
Philadelphia, PA [*AM radio station call letters*] .... WHAT

Philadelphia, PA [*FM radio station call letters*] .... WHYY
Philadelphia, PA [*FM radio station call letters*] .... WIOQ
Philadelphia, PA [*AM radio station call letters*] .... WIP
Philadelphia, PA [*FM radio station call letters*] .... WJJZ
Philadelphia, PA [*FM radio station call letters*] .... WKDU
Philadelphia, PA [*FM radio station call letters*] .... WMGK
Philadelphia, PA [*FM radio station call letters*] .... WMMR
Philadelphia, PA [*AM radio station call letters*] (RBYB) .... WNWR
Philadelphia, PA [*FM radio station call letters*] .... WOGL
Philadelphia, PA [*FM radio station call letters*] .... WPEB
Philadelphia, PA [*AM radio station call letters*] .... WPEN
Philadelphia, PA [*Television station call letters*] .... WPHL
Philadelphia, PA [*AM radio station call letters*] (RBYB) .... WPHT-AM
Philadelphia, PA [*TV station call letters*] (RBYB) .... WPSG-TV
Philadelphia, PA [*Television station call letters*] .... WPVI
Philadelphia, PA [*FM radio station call letters*] .... WRTI
Philadelphia, PA [*AM radio station call letters*] .... WTEL
Philadelphia, PA [*Television station call letters*] .... WTXF
Philadelphia, PA [*AM radio station call letters*] .... WURD
Philadelphia, PA [*FM radio station call letters*] .... WUSL
Philadelphia, PA [*FM radio station call letters*] .... WWDB
Philadelphia, PA [*FM radio station call letters*] .... WXPN
Philadelphia, PA [*FM radio station call letters*] .... WXTU
Philadelphia, PA [*Television station call letters*] .... WYBE
Philadelphia, PA [*FM radio station call letters*] .... WYSP
Philadelphia, PA [*FM radio station call letters*] .... WYXR
Philadelphia, PA [*AM radio station call letters*] .... WZZD
Philadelphia, PA [*Location identifier FAA*] (FAAL) .... XZY
Philadelphia Public Library (AD) .... PPL
Philadelphia Pulmonary Neoplasm Research Project (AD) .... PNRP
Philadelphia Quartermaster Center [*Merged with Defense Clothing and Textile Supply Center*] [*Military*] .... PQMC
Philadelphia Quartermaster Depot [*Military*] .... PQMD
Philadelphia Quartz Co., Valley Forge, PA [*Library symbol Library of Congress*] (LCLS) .... PVfP
Philadelphia Reading Test [*Education*] .... PRT
Philadelphia Regular Exchange Tea Total Young Belles Lettres Universal Experimental Bibliographical Association To Civilize Humanity [*From Edgar Allan Poe essay "How to Write a Blackwood Article"*] .... PRETTYBLUEBATCH
Philadelphia Reports [*Pennsylvania*] [*A publication*] (DLA) .... Ph Rep
Philadelphia Reports [*A publication*] (DLA) .... Phil
Philadelphia Reports [*Pennsylvania*] [*A publication*] (DLA) .... Phil (PA)
Philadelphia Reports [*Pennsylvania*] [*A publication*] (DLA) .... Phil R
Philadelphia Reports [*Pennsylvania*] [*A publication*] (DLA) .... Phil Rep
Philadelphia Reports [*Pennsylvania*] [*A publication*] (DLA) .... Phila
Philadelphia Reports [*Pennsylvania*] [*A publication*] (DLA) .... Phila (PA)
Philadelphia Reports [*Pennsylvania*] [*A publication*] (DLA) .... Phila Reports
Philadelphia Reports [*Pennsylvania*] [*A publication*] (DLA) .... Philad
Philadelphia Reports [*Pennsylvania*] [*A publication*] (DLA) .... Philada R
Philadelphia Reports [*Pennsylvania*] [*A publication*] (DLA) .... Philada Rep
Philadelphia Reports [*Pennsylvania*] [*A publication*] (DLA) .... Philadelphia Rep
Philadelphia Reports [*Pennsylvania*] [*A publication*] (DLA) .... PR
Philadelphia Service Center [*IRS*] .... PSC
Philadelphia Signal Corps Procurement District [*Army*] .... PSCPD
Philadelphia Stock Exchange (CDAI) .... PE
Philadelphia Stock Exchange .... PHILEX
Philadelphia Stock Exchange .... PHLX
Philadelphia Stock Exchange .... PSE
Philadelphia Suburban Corp. [*Associated Press*] (SAG) .... PhilSub
Philadelphia Suburban Corp. [*NYSE symbol*] (SPSG) .... PSC
Philadelphia Suburban Transportation [*AAR code*] .... PST
Philadelphia Textile Institute .... PTI
Philadelphia Transportation Co., Philadelphia, PA [*Library symbol Library of Congress Obsolete*] (LCLS) .... PPPR
Philadelphia Tuberculosis and Health Association, Philadelphia, PA [*Library symbol Library of Congress Obsolete*] (LCLS) .... PPPHC
Philadelphia Ukrainian [*Diocesan abbreviation*] [*Pennsylvania*] (TOCD) .... PHU
Philadelphia War Tax Resistance (EA) .... PWTR
Philadelphia, Wilmington & Baltimore Railroad .... PW & B
Philadelphia-Baltimore Stock Exchange [*Later, Philadelphia-Baltimore-WashingtonStock Exchange*] .... PBSE
Philadelphia-Baltimore-Washington Stock Exchange [*Later, Philadelphia Stock Exchange*] .... PBWSE
Philalethes Society (EA) .... PS
Philander Smith College [*Little Rock, AR*] .... PSC
Philanthropic (ROG) .... PHILANTHR
Philanthropic Advisory Service .... PAS
Philanthropic and Educational Organization [*Facetious translation "Pop Eats Out"*] .... PEO
Philanthropic Roundtable (EA) .... PR
Philanthropic Society of House Carpenters and Joiners [*A union*] [*British*] .... PSHCJ
Philanthropical (BJA) .... philan
Philanthropy .... philn
Philatelic Association of Government Employees .... PAGE
Philatelic Esperanto League [*See also ELF*] [*Solna, Sweden*] (EAIO) .... PEL
Philatelic Foundation (EA) .... PF
Philatelic Friends Exchange Circuit (EA) .... PFEC
Philatelic Hobbies for the Wounded (EA) .... PHW
Philatelic Literature Association [*Later, APRL*] (EA) .... PLA
Philatelic Literature Review [*A publication*] .... Phil Lit R
Philatelic Music Circle (EA) .... PMC
Philatelic Press Club [*Later, IPPC*] .... PPC
Philatelic Research Society .... PRS

Philatelic Sales Branch [*Later, PSD*] [*US Postal Service*] ..... PSB
Philatelic Sales Division [*Formerly, PSB*] [*US Postal Service*] ..... PSD
Philatelic Sales Unit ..... PSU
Philatelic Societies' Record [*A publication British*] ..... PSR
Philatelic Society of New South Wales [*Australia*] ..... PSNSW
Philatelic Traders' Society Ltd. [*British*] (BI) ..... PTS
Philatelic-Numismatic Combination [*or Commemorative*] ..... PNC
Philately ..... philat
Philbrook Art Center Library, Tulsa, OK [*OCLC symbol*] (OCLC) ..... OUM
Philbrook Art Center, Tulsa, OK [*Library symbol*] [*Library of Congress*] (LCLS) ..... OkTPh
Philco Automatic Circuit Tester ..... PACT
Philco Corp. (IAA) ..... PC
Philco Electronic Module ..... PEM
Philco Epoxy Transistor (IAA) ..... PET
Philco Houston Operations (SAA) ..... PHO
Philco Resources [*Vancouver Stock Exchange symbol*] ..... PRL
Philco-Ford Corp., Western Development Laboratories, Palo Alto, CA [*Library symbol Library of Congress*] (LCLS) ..... CPaP
Philebus [*of Plato*] [*Classical studies*] (OCD) ..... Phlb
Phileleftheron Demokratikon Kendron [*Liberal Democratic Union*] [*Greek*] (PPE) ..... PDK
Phileleftheron Demokratikon Komma [*Liberal Democratic Party*] [*Greek Political party*] (PPE) ..... PDK
Phileleftheron Komma [*Liberal Party*] [*Greek Political party*] (PPE) ..... PK
Philemon [*New Testament book*] ..... Phil
Philemon [*New Testament book*] ..... Philem
Philemon [*New Testament book*] ..... Phlm
Philemon [*New Testament book*] (BJA) ..... Phm
Philharmonia [*Record label*] ..... Phil
Philharmonic ..... PHIL
Philharmonic Hall (NADA) ..... PH
Philharmonic Orchestra [*Music*] ..... PO
Philharmonic Orchestra of Florida (AD) ..... POF
Philharmonic Society (WDAA) ..... PHIL SOC
Philip C. Jessup International Law Moot Court Competition (EAIO) ..... PCJILMCC
Philip C. Jessup International Law Moot Court Competition (EA) ..... PJILMCC
Philip Environmental [*NASDAQ symbol*] (SAG) ..... PENV
Philip Environmental [*NYSE symbol*] (TTSB) ..... PEV
Philip Environmental [*NYSE symbol*] (SAG) ..... PEV
Philip Environmental [*Commercial firm Associated Press*] (SAG) ..... PhilEnv
Philip Jose Farmer Society (EA) ..... PJFS
Philip K. Dick [*Science fiction writer*] ..... PKD
Philip K. Dick Society [*Defunct*] (EA) ..... PKDS
Philip Michael Thomas [*Co-star in TV series "Miami Vice"*] ..... PMT
Philip Morris Companies, Inc. [*NYSE symbol*] (SPSG) ..... MO
Philip Morris Companies, Inc. [*Associated Press*] (SAG) ..... PhilMr
Philip Morris Cos. [*NYSE symbol*] (TTSB) ..... MO
Philip Morris, Inc. ..... PM
Philip Morris Research Center, Richmond, VA [*Library symbol Library of Congress*] (LCLS) ..... ViRPM
Philip, SD [*Location identifier FAA*] (FAAL) ..... PHP
Philipp Brothers Ltd. [*Commercial firm*] ..... Philbro
Philippi, WV [*FM radio station call letters*] ..... WQAB
Philippians [*New Testament book*] (BJA) ..... Ph
Philippians [*New Testament book*] ..... Phil
Philippine Aid Plan ..... PAP
Philippine Air Force ..... PAF
Philippine Air Lines ..... PAL
Philippine Air Lines, Inc. [*ICAO designator*] (FAAC) ..... PAL
Philippine Airlines [*ICAO designator*] (AD) ..... PR
Philippine Army ..... PA
Philippine Association (EA) ..... PA
Philippine Ballet Theater (ECON) ..... PBT
Philippine Base [*Army World War II*] ..... FILBAS
Philippine Broadcasting Service (NADA) ..... PBS
Philippine Campaign Medal ..... PCM
Philippine Christian College (AEBS) ..... PCC
Philippine Civil Affairs Unit [*Army unit which supplied emergency subsistence after end of Japanese dominance*] [*World War II*] ..... PCAU
Philippine Code [*A publication*] (DLA) ..... Philippine Co
Philippine Collectors Society (EA) ..... PCS
Philippine Contingent [*Military*] ..... PHILCON
Philippine Cultural League [*Australia*] ..... PCL
Philippine Defense Ribbon [*Military decoration*] ..... PDR
Philippine Democratic Party [*Pilipino Lakas Ng Bayan*] [*Political party*] (PPW) ..... PDP
Philippine Eagle Airlines [*FAA designator*] (FAAC) ..... EAL
Philippine Expeditionary Force to Korea [*United Nations*] ..... PEFTOK
Philippine Forces, Vietnam ..... PFV
Philippine Global Communications, Inc. [*Manila*] [*Telecommunications*] ..... PHILCOM
Philippine Heart Center for Asia (PDAA) ..... PHCA
Philippine Independence Ribbon [*Military decoration*] ..... PIR
Philippine International Law Journal [*A publication*] (DLA) ..... Phil ILJ
Philippine International Law Journal [*A publication*] (DLA) ..... Phil Int LJ
Philippine International Law Journal [*Manila, Philippines*] [*A publication*] (DLA) ..... Philippine Internat LJ
Philippine International Law Journal [*A publication*] (DLA) ..... Philippine Int'l LJ
Philippine Island Reports [*A publication*] (DLA) ..... Phil
Philippine Island Reports [*A publication*] (DLA) ..... PI Rep
Philippine Island Reports [*A publication*] (DLA) ..... PR
Philippine Islands (WDAA) ..... PHIL I
Philippine Islands Public Service Commission Reports [*A publication*] (DLA) ..... PIPSCR
Philippine Islands Public Utility Commission Reports [*A publication*] (DLA) ..... PIPUCR
Philippine Labour Relations Journal [*A publication*] (DLA) ..... Phil Lab Rel J
Philippine Law Journal [*Manila*] [*A publication*] (DLA) ..... Phil LJ
Philippine Law Journal [*A publication*] (DLA) ..... Philippine LJ
Philippine Law Journal [*A publication*] (ILCA) ..... PLJ
Philippine Law Review [*A publication*] (DLA) ..... Phil L Rev
Philippine Law Review [*A publication*] (DLA) ..... Philippine L Rev
Philippine L-D Tel Pfd GDS [*NYSE symbol*] (TTSB) ..... PHIPrA
Philippine Liberation Ribbon [*Military decoration*] ..... PLR
Philippine Long D Tel ADS [*NYSE symbol*] (TTSB) ..... PHI
Philippine Long Distance Telephone Co. [*NYSE symbol*] (SAG) ..... PHI
Philippine Long Distance Telephone Co. [*Associated Press*] (SAG) ..... PhILD
Philippine Long Distance Telephone Co. ..... PLDT
Philippine Mahogany Association [*Defunct*] (EA) ..... PMA
Philippine Military Liaison Officer (DNAB) ..... PMLO
Philippine National Bank (AD) ..... PNB
Philippine National Line (AD) ..... PNL
Philippine National Oil Co. (AD) ..... PNOC
Philippine National Railways (DS) ..... PNR
Philippine Natural Gum ..... PNG
Philippine Navy ..... PN
Philippine Presidential Unit Citation Badge [*Military decoration*] ..... PHILPUC
Philippine Reports [*A publication*] (DLA) ..... Philippine
Philippine Republic Presidential Unit Citation [*Military decoration*] ..... PRPUC
Philippine Republic Presidential Unit Citation Emblem [*Military decoration*] ..... PRPUCE
Philippine Research Reactor (SAA) ..... PRR
Philippine Resource Center [*An association*] (EA) ..... PRC
Philippine Sea Frontier ..... PHILSEAFRON
Philippine Sea Frontier ..... PSF
Philippine Standards Association (IAA) ..... PSA
Philippine Statehood USA Movement [*An association*] (EA) ..... PSUSAM
Philippine Sugar Association [*Later, PSC*] (EA) ..... PSA
Philippine Sugar Commission (EA) ..... PSC
Philippine War Damage Commission [*Post-World War II*] ..... PWDC
Philippine Yearbook of International Law [*Manila, Philippines*] [*A publication*] (DLA) ..... Phil Yb Int'l L
Philippines [*MARC geographic area code Library of Congress*] (LCCP) ..... a-ph--
Philippines [*IYRU nationality code*] [*MARC country of publication code Library of Congress*] (LCCP) ..... ph
Philippines [*ANSI two-letter standard code*] (CNC) ..... PH
Philippines (AFM) ..... PHIL
Philippines (VRA) ..... Phil
Philippines ..... Philip
Philippines (BARN) ..... Philipp
Philippines [*ANSI three-letter standard code*] (CNC) ..... PHL
Philippines Alien Property Administration ..... PAPA
Philippines Aquatic Sciences and Fisheries Information System [*Marine science*] (OSRA) ..... PASFIS
Philippines Civil Liberties Union (PD) ..... ULC
Philippines News Agency (NADA) ..... PNA
Philippines News Agency (AD) ..... PNA
Philippines News Service ..... PNS
Philippines Overseas Employment Administration (PDAA) ..... POEA
Philippines Relief and Trade Rebilitation Administration (AD) ..... PRATRA
Philippus [*Flourished, 13th century*] [*Authority cited in pre-1607 legal work*] (DSA) ..... Ph
Philippus [*Flourished, 13th century*] [*Authority cited in pre-1607 legal work*] (DSA) ..... Phi
Philippus Decius [*Deceased circa 1537*] [*Authority cited in pre-1607 legal work*] (DSA) ..... Phil Dec
Philippus Franchus [*Deceased, 1471*] [*Authority cited in pre-1607 legal work*] (DSA) ..... Philip Fran
Philippus Francus [*Deceased, 1471*] [*Authority cited in pre-1607 legal work*] (DSA) ..... Phili Fran
Philippus Pudericus [*Authority cited in pre-1607 legal work*] (DSA) ..... Phus Plu
Philips [*Holland & International*] [*Record label*] ..... Phi
Philips & Du Pont Optical Co. [*Wilmington, DE*] ..... PDO
Philips Assembler Language (IAA) ..... PAL
Philips Automated Laboratory Management System (NITA) ..... PALM
Philips Automatic Sequence Calculator ..... PASCAL
Philips Aviation Services [*Netherlands ICAO designator*] (FAAC) ..... PHI
Philips Business Systems (NITA) ..... PBS
Philips Car Systems ..... PCS
Philips Electronics NV [*Formerly, Philips NV*] [*NYSE symbol*] (SPSG) ..... PHG
Philips Electronics NV Holding Co. [*Associated Press*] (SAG) ..... PhilipsEl
Philips Engineering and Development System (NITA) ..... PEDS
Philips International Telecommunications Training Center (IAA) ..... PITTC
Philips Inventory Control Technique [*Computer science*] (IAA) ..... PHICT
Philips Inventory Control Technique [*Computer science*] (IAA) ..... PICT
Philips Load and Go (NITA) ..... PHLAG
Philips Minigroove [*Record label*] ..... PhM
Philips Optical Language (IAA) ..... POL
Philips Petroleum Co., Exploration and Production Library, Bartlesville, OK [*Library symbol*] [*Library of Congress*] (LCLS) ..... OkBP-NR
Philips Question Answering System (NITA) ..... PHILQA
Philips Research Laboratories (NITA) ..... PRL
Philips Research Laboratories, Eindhoven, Netherlands [*Library symbol Library of Congress*] (LCLS) ..... NeEinP
Philips Roxane [*Commercial firm*] (DAVI) ..... P-R
Philips Roxane Laboratories [*Research code symbol*] ..... CSAG
Philipsburg, PA [*Location identifier FAA*] (FAAL) ..... PSB
Philipsburg, PA [*AM radio station call letters*] ..... WPHB
Philipsburg, PA [*FM radio station call letters*] ..... WPHB-FM

Philipsburg, PA [*FM radio station call letters*] (RBYB) ... WUBZ-FM
Philipsburg/Prinses Juliana, Sint Maarten Island [*Netherlands Antilles*] [*ICAO location identifier*] (ICLI) ... TNCM
Philipsburg State General Hospital, Philipsburg, PA [*Inactive*] [*OCLC symbol*] (OCLC) ... PHI
Philips-Duphar NV [*Netherlands*] [*Research code symbol*] ... DU
Phillimore's Civil and Canon Law [*A publication*] (DLA) ... Phil Civ & Can Law
Phillimore's Ecclesiastical Judgments [*A publication*] (DLA) ... Phil Ecc
Phillimore's Ecclesiastical Judgments [*1867-75*] [*A publication*] (DLA) ... Phil Ecc Judg
Phillimore's Ecclesiastical Judgments [*1867-75*] [*England*] [*A publication*] (DLA) ... Phil Jud
Phillimore's Ecclesiastical Judgments [*1867-75*] [*A publication*] (DLA) ... Phil Judg
Phillimore's Ecclesiastical Judgments [*1867-75*] [*A publication*] (DLA) ... Phill Ecc Judg
Phillimore's Ecclesiastical Judgments [*1867-75*] [*A publication*] (DLA) ... Phillim Eccl
Phillimore's English Ecclesiastical Cases Tempore Lee [*A publication*] (DLA) ... Cas T Lee
Phillimore's English Ecclesiastical Law [*2 eds.*] [*1873, 1895*] [*A publication*] (DLA) ... Phil Ecc
Phillimore's English Ecclesiastical Law [*2 eds.*] [*1873, 1895*] [*A publication*] (DLA) ... Phil Ecc Law
Phillimore's English Ecclesiastical Law [*A publication*] (DLA) ... Phillim Ecc Law
Phillimore's English Ecclesiastical Reports [*A publication*] (DLA) ... Ph
Phillimore's English Ecclesiastical Reports [*A publication*] (DLA) ... Phil
Phillimore's English Ecclesiastical Reports [*1809-21*] [*A publication*] (DLA) ... Phil Ecc
Phillimore's English Ecclesiastical Reports [*1809-21*] [*A publication*] (DLA) ... Phil Ecc R
Phillimore's English Ecclesiastical Reports [*1809-21*] [*A publication*] (DLA) ... Phill Ecc R
Phillimore's English Ecclesiastical Reports [*1809-21*] [*A publication*] (DLA) ... Phillim
Phillimore's English Ecclesiastical Reports [*1809-21*] [*A publication*] (DLA) ... Phillim Eccl
Phillimore's International Law [*A publication*] (DLA) ... Phil Int Law
Phillimore's International Law [*A publication*] (DLA) ... Phillim Int Law
Phillimore's Introduction to the Roman Law [*A publication*] (DLA) ... Phil Int Rom Law
Phillimore's Law of Domicil [*A publication*] (DLA) ... Phil Dom
Phillimore's Law of Domicil [*A publication*] (DLA) ... Phillim Dom
Phillimore's Private Law among the Romans [*A publication*] (DLA) ... Phil Rom Law
Phillip Leff Memorial Library, Beulaville, NC [*Library symbol Library of Congress*] (LCLS) ... NcBlv
Phillip Resources, Inc. [*Vancouver Stock Exchange symbol*] ... PHP
Phillipps' Famous Cases in Circumstantial Evidence [*A publication*] (DLA) ... Phil Fam Cas
Phillipps' State Trials [*A publication*] (DLA) ... Ph St Tr
Phillipps' State Trials [*Prior to 1688*] [*A publication*] (DLA) ... Phil St Tr
Phillips Academy, Andover, MA [*Library symbol Library of Congress*] (LCLS) ... MAnP
Phillips Airlines [*ICAO designator*] (AD) ... PP
Phillips and Drew Fund Management [*England*] [*British*] ... PDFM
Phillips Business Information, Inc. (IID) ... PBI
Phillips Cables Ltd. [*Toronto Stock Exchange symbol*] ... PCL
Phillips Cables Ltd., Vancouver, BC, Canada [*Library symbol Library of Congress*] (LCLS) ... CaBVaPC
Phillips Cables Ltd., Vancouver, British Columbia [*Library symbol National Library of Canada*] (NLC) ... BVAPC
Phillips County Library, Malta, MT [*Library symbol*] [*Library of Congress*] (LCLS) ... MtMa
Phillips' English Chancery Reports [*1841-49*] [*A publication*] (DLA) ... Ph
Phillips' English Chancery Reports [*1841-49*] [*A publication*] (DLA) ... Ph Ch
Phillips' English Chancery Reports [*1841-49*] [*A publication*] (DLA) ... Phil
Phillips' English Chancery Reports [*1841-49*] [*A publication*] (DLA) ... Phill
Phillips' English Chancery Reports [*1841-49*] [*A publication*] (DLA) ... Phill Ch
Phillips' English Chancery Reports [*1841-49*] [*A publication*] (DLA) ... Phill Ch (Eng)
Phillips' English Chancery Reports [*1841-49*] [*A publication*] (DLA) ... Phillips
Phillips' English Election Cases [*1780-81*] [*A publication*] (DLA) ... Ph
Phillips' English Election Cases [*1780-81*] [*A publication*] (DLA) ... Phil
Phillips' English Election Cases [*1780-81*] [*A publication*] (DLA) ... Phil El Cas
Phillips' English Election Cases [*1780-81*] [*A publication*] (DLA) ... Phill
Phillips' English Election Cases [*1780-81*] [*A publication*] (DLA) ... Phillips
Phillips Exeter Academy, Exeter, NH [*Library symbol Library of Congress*] (LCLS) ... NhExP
Phillips Gas [*NYSE symbol*] (SPSG) ... PGC
Phillips Gas [*Associated Press*] (SAG) ... PhlpGs
Phillips Gas 9.32% Pfd [*NYSE symbol*] (TTSB) ... PGCPr
Phillips' Grandeur of the Law [*A publication*] (DLA) ... Phil Grand
Phillips Head (DAC) ... PH
Phillips Head [*Screw*] ... PHH
Phillips Head [*Screw*] ... PHLH
Phillips' Illinois Reports [*152-245 Illinois*] [*A publication*] (DLA) ... Phil
Phillips' Illinois Reports [*152-245 Illinois*] [*A publication*] (DLA) ... Phill
Phillips' Illinois Reports [*152-245 Illinois*] [*A publication*] (DLA) ... Phillips
Phillips [*R.H.*], Inc. [*Associated Press*] (SAG) ... PhilRH
Phillips [*R.H.*], Inc. [*NASDAQ symbol*] (SAG) ... RHPS
Phillips Ionization Gauge ... PIG
Phillips' Law of Copyright Designs [*A publication*] (DLA) ... Phil Cop
Phillips Michigan City Flying Service, Inc. [*ICAO designator*] (FAAC) ... PHL
Phillips' North Carolina Equity Reports [*A publication*] (DLA) ... Phil Eq
Phillips' North Carolina Equity Reports [*A publication*] (DLA) ... Phill
Phillips' North Carolina Equity Reports [*A publication*] (DLA) ... Phill Eq (NC)
Phillips' North Carolina Equity Reports [*A publication*] (DLA) ... Phillips
Phillips' North Carolina Law Reports [*A publication*] (DLA) ... Phil
Phillips' North Carolina Law Reports [*A publication*] (DLA) ... Phil Law
Phillips' North Carolina Law Reports [*A publication*] (DLA) ... Phil NC
Phillips' North Carolina Law Reports [*A publication*] (DLA) ... Phill
Phillips' North Carolina Law Reports [*A publication*] (DLA) ... Phill L (NC)
Phillips' North Carolina Law Reports [*A publication*] (DLA) ... Phillips
Phillips on Evidence [*A publication*] (DLA) ... Ph Ev
Phillips on Evidence [*A publication*] (DLA) ... Phil Ev
Phillips on Evidence, Notes by Cowen, Hill, and Edwards [*A publication*] (DLA) ... Phil Ev Cow & H & Edw Notes
Phillips on Insurance [*A publication*] (DLA) ... Phil Ins
Phillips on Insurance [*A publication*] (DLA) ... Phill Ins
Phillips on Lunatics [*1858*] [*A publication*] (DLA) ... Phil Insan
Phillips on Lunatics [*1858*] [*A publication*] (DLA) ... Phil Lun
Phillips on Mechanics' Liens [*A publication*] (DLA) ... Phil Mech Liens
Phillips on Patents [*A publication*] (DLA) ... Phil Pat
Phillips Petroleum [*NYSE symbol*] (TTSB) ... P
Phillips Petroleum Co. [*NYSE symbol*] (SPSG) ... P
Phillips Petroleum Co. [*Associated Press*] (SAG) ... PhilPet
Phillips Petroleum Co. [*Toronto Stock Exchange symbol*] ... PLP
Phillips Petroleum Co., Exploration and Product Library, Bartlesville, OK [*OCLC symbol*] (OCLC) ... ONR
Phillips Petroleum Co., Research and Development Department, Bartlesville, OK [*Library symbol Library of Congress*] (LCLS) ... OkBP
Phillips Petroleum Co., Research and Development Department, Bartlesville, OK [*OCLC symbol*] (OCLC) ... OPS
Phillips Petroleum Load and Go [*System*] ... PHLAG
Phillips Petroleum Load and Go System (DNAB) ... PHLAGS
Phillips Post Processor ... P3
Phillips' Studii Legalis Ratio [*A publication*] (DLA) ... Phil St Leg R
Phillips' Treatise on Insurance [*A publication*] (DLA) ... Phil
Phillips' United States Practice [*A publication*] (DLA) ... Phil US Pr
Phillips University (GAGS) ... Phillips U
Phillips University, Enid, OK [*Library symbol Library of Congress*] (LCLS) ... OkEP
Phillips University, Graduate Seminary, Enid, OK [*Library symbol Library of Congress*] (LCLS) ... OkEG
Phillips University, Graduate Seminary Library, Enid, OK [*OCLC symbol*] (OCLC) ... OKG
Phillips University, Zollars Memorial Library, Enid, OK [*OCLC symbol*] (OCLC) ... OKZ
Phillips, WI [*Location identifier FAA*] (FAAL) ... PBH
Phillipsburg Free Public Library, Phillipsburg, NJ [*Library symbol Library of Congress*] (LCLS) ... NjPh
Phillipsburg, KS [*AM radio station call letters*] ... KKAN
Phillipsburg, KS [*FM radio station call letters*] ... KQMA
Phillipsburg, KS [*Location identifier FAA*] (FAAL) ... PHG
Phillipsite [*A zeolite*] ... PHI
Phillips(R.H.)Inc. Wrrt [*NASDAQ symbol*] (TTSB) ... RHPSW
Phillips-Van Heusen [*NYSE symbol*] (TTSB) ... PVH
Phillips-Van Heusen Corp. [*Associated Press*] (SAG) ... PhlVH
Phillips-Van Heusen Corp. [*NYSE symbol*] (SPSG) ... PVH
Phillnathean Society (EA) ... PS
Philo, CA [*FM radio station call letters*] ... KZYX
Philo Judaeus [*First century AD*] [*Classical studies*] (OCD) ... Philo
Philo Township Public Library, Philo, IL [*Library symbol Library of Congress*] (LCLS) ... IPhil
Philoctetes [*of Sophocles*] [*Classical studies*] (OCD) ... Phil
Philodemus [*First century BC*] [*Classical studies*] (OCD) ... Phld
Philolexian Society (EA) ... PS
Philological Quarterly [*A publication*] (BRI) ... PQ
Philological Society (EAIO) ... PS
Philologische Untersuchungen [*A publication*] (OCD) ... Phil Unters
Philologische Wochenschrift [*A publication*] (OCD) ... Phil Wochenschr
Philologus [*A publication*] (OCD) ... Philol
Philologus. Supplement [*A publication*] (OCD) ... Philol Suppl
Philology ... PHIL
Philology ... PHILOL
Philomathean Society (EA) ... PS
Philomathematicus [*Lover of Mathematics*] (ROG) ... PHILOMATH
Philomathes [*Lover of Learning*] (ROG) ... PHILOM
Philo-Phobe [*Psychological testing*] ... PP
Philopoemen [*of Plutarch*] [*Classical studies*] (OCD) ... Phil
Philosopher of Chiropractic ... Ph C
Philosopher's Index Retrieval System (NITA) ... PIRS
Philosopher's Information Retrieval System [*Bowling Green State University*] ... PIRS
Philosophia Patrum [*A publication*] (BJA) ... PHP
Philosophiae Baccalaureus [*Bachelor of Philosophy*] ... PB
Philosophiae Baccalaureus [*Bachelor of Philosophy*] ... Ph B
Philosophiae Doctor [*Doctor of Philosophy*] ... PD
Philosophiae Doctor [*Doctor of Philosophy*] [*Facetious translation: Piled Higher and Deeper*] ... Ph D
Philosophiae Doctor [*Doctor of Philosophy*] [*See also Ph D*] [*Latin*] ... Phil D
Philosophic Society for the Study of Sport (EA) ... PSSS
Philosophical Classics [*A publication*] ... PC
Philosophical Library [*A publication*] ... PL
Philosophical Research Society (EA) ... PRS
Philosophical Research Society, Los Angeles, CA [*Library symbol Library of Congress*] (LCLS) ... CLPhil
Philosophical Review [*A publication*] (BRI) ... Phil R
Philosophical Society [*British*] (DBA) ... PhS
Philosophical Transactions. Royal Society of London [*A publication*] ... PTRS

Philosophie Informationsdienst [*Philosophy Information Service*] [*University of Dusseldorf*] [*Information service or system*] (IID) ... PHI
Philosophies, Ancient and Modern [*A publication*] ... PAM
Philosophy (WGA) ... PHI
Philosophy ... PHIL
Philosophy (DD) ... Phil
Philosophy (EY) ... PHILOS
Philosophy Documentation Center (EA) ... PDC
Philosophy in Chiropractic ... Phil C
Philosophy of Education Society (EA) ... PES
Philosophy of Science Association (EA) ... PSA
Philosophy, Politics, and Economics (AD) ... ppe
Philosophy, Politics, Economics [*Oxford University*] ... PPE
Philostratus [*Second century AD*] [*Classical studies*] (OCD) ... Philostr
Philpot, KY [*FM radio station call letters*] ... WBIO
Phipps Bend Nuclear Plant (NRCH) ... PBNP
Phipson on Evidence [*12th ed.*] [*1976*] [*A publication*] (DLA) ... Phip Ev
Phipson's Digest, Natal Reports [*South Africa*] [*A publication*] (DLA) ... Phip
Phipson's Reports, Natal Supreme Court [*South Africa*] [*A publication*] (DLA) ... Phip
Phitsanulok [*Thailand*] [*ICAO location identifier*] (ICLI) ... VTPP
Phitsanulok/Sarit Sena [*Thailand*] [*ICAO location identifier*] (ICLI) ... VTPS
Phitsanuloke [*Thailand*] [*Airport symbol*] (OAG) ... PHS
Phleborrheogram [*Hematology*] (DAVI) ... PRG
Phleomycin [*Biochemistry*] ... PLM
Phleum Mottle Virus [*Plant pathology*] ... PHMOV
Phleum Mottle Virus ... PhMV
Phlogopite-Peridotite Solidus [*Geology*] ... PPS
Phloretin [*Biochemistry*] ... PHLO
Phnom Penh [*Cambodia*] [*Airport symbol*] (OAG) ... PNH
Phnom-Penh [*Cambodia*] [*ICAO location identifier*] (ICLI) ... VDPP
Phobia Clinic (EA) ... PC
Phobia Society of America [*Later, ADAA*] (EA) ... PSA
Phocine Distemper Virus ... PDV
Phoenician (BJA) ... P
Phoenician (BJA) ... Phoen
Phoenician ... PHON
Phoenissae [*of Euripides*] [*Classical studies*] (OCD) ... Phoen
Phoenix [*Constellation*] ... Phe
Phoenix [*Constellation*] ... Phoe
Phoenix [*Arizona*] [*Airport symbol*] (OAG) ... PHX
Phoenix 2000 Airtaxi Ltd. [*Hungary ICAO designator*] (FAAC) ... PHX
Phoenix Ability Survey System [*Test*] ... PASS
Phoenix Air Defense Sector (SAA) ... PHADS
Phoenix Air Service GmbH [*Germany ICAO designator*] (FAAC) ... PAM
Phoenix Airborne Missile ... PAM
Phoenix Airborne Missile Control System ... PAMCS
Phoenix Airline Services, Inc. [*ICAO designator*] (FAAC) ... WDY
Phoenix Airways (Pfy) [*South Africa*] [*FAA designator*] (FAAC) ... PHO
[*The*] **Phoenix and the Turtle** [*Shakespearean work*] ... PhT
Phoenix Aviation [*British ICAO designator*] (FAAC) ... PLP
Phoenix, AZ [*Location identifier FAA*] (FAAL) ... DVT
Phoenix, AZ [*Television station call letters*] ... KAET
Phoenix, AZ [*AM radio station call letters*] ... KASA
Phoenix, AZ [*Television station call letters*] ... KASW
Phoenix, AZ [*FM radio station call letters*] ... KBAQ
Phoenix, AZ [*FM radio station call letters*] ... KESZ
Phoenix, AZ [*FM radio station call letters*] ... KFLR
Phoenix, AZ [*AM radio station call letters*] ... KFYI
Phoenix, AZ [*AM radio station call letters*] ... KHEP
Phoenix, AZ [*FM radio station call letters*] (RBYB) ... KHTC
Phoenix, AZ [*AM radio station call letters*] ... KIDR
Phoenix, AZ [*AM radio station call letters*] ... KISO
Phoenix, AZ [*FM radio station call letters*] ... KJZZ
Phoenix, AZ [*FM radio station call letters*] ... KKLT
Phoenix, AZ [*FM radio station call letters*] ... KNAI
Phoenix, AZ [*FM radio station call letters*] ... KNIX
Phoenix, AZ [*Television station call letters*] ... KNXV
Phoenix, AZ [*AM radio station call letters*] ... KOOL
Phoenix, AZ [*FM radio station call letters*] ... KOOL-FM
Phoenix, AZ [*AM radio station call letters*] ... KOY
Phoenix, AZ [*Television station call letters*] ... KPAZ
Phoenix, AZ [*FM radio station call letters*] ... KPHF
Phoenix, AZ [*Television station call letters*] ... KPHO
Phoenix, AZ [*AM radio station call letters*] ... KPHX
Phoenix, AZ [*AM radio station call letters*] (RBYB) ... KPXQ-AM
Phoenix, AZ [*Television station call letters*] ... KSAZ-TV
Phoenix, AZ [*AM radio station call letters*] ... KSUN
Phoenix, AZ [*AM radio station call letters*] ... KTAR
Phoenix, AZ [*Television station call letters*] ... KTVK
Phoenix, AZ [*Television station call letters*] ... KTVW
Phoenix, AZ [*Television station call letters*] ... KUTP
Phoenix, AZ [*AM radio station call letters*] ... KVVA
Phoenix, AZ [*FM radio station call letters*] ... KYOT-FM
Phoenix, AZ [*FM radio station call letters*] ... KZON
Phoenix, AZ [*Location identifier FAA*] (FAAL) ... PQO
Phoenix, AZ [*Location identifier FAA*] (FAAL) ... RSZ
Phoenix Canada Oil Co. Ltd. [*Toronto Stock Exchange symbol*] ... PCO
Phoenix College, Phoenix, AZ [*Library symbol*] [*Library of Congress*] (LCLS) ... AzPhC
Phoenix Contract Management District (SAA) ... PXCMD
Phoenix Duf & Phelps Corp. [*Associated Press*] (SAG) ... PhxDffP
Phoenix Duff & Phelps [*NASDAQ symbol*] (TTSB) ... DUF
Phoenix Duff & Phelps Corp. [*NYSE symbol*] (SAG) ... DUF
Phoenix Duff & Phelps Corp. [*Associated Press*] (SAG) ... PhxDfP
Phoenix Duff & Phelps Corp. [*Associated Press*] (SAG) ... PhxDuffP
Phoenix Duff/Phelphs $1.50 Cv Pfd [*NYSE symbol*] (TTSB) ... DUFPr
Phoenix Flight Operations Ltd. [*Canada ICAO designator*] (FAAC) ... XPX
Phoenix Global [*Vancouver Stock Exchange symbol*] ... PGB
Phoenix Gold International, Inc. [*NASDAQ symbol*] (SAG) ... PGLD
Phoenix Gold International, Inc. [*Associated Press*] (SAG) ... PhxGold
Phoenix Gold Intl [*NASDAQ symbol*] (TTSB) ... PGLD
Phoenix Gold Mines Ltd. [*Toronto Stock Exchange symbol*] ... PXG
Phoenix House Foundation (EA) ... PHF
Phoenix International Raceway ... PIR
Phoenix/Luke Air Force Base [*Arizona*] [*ICAO location identifier*] (ICLI) ... KLUF
Phoenix Missile System ... PMS
Phoenix Network [*AMEX symbol*] (TTSB) ... PHX
Phoenix Network, Inc. [*AMEX symbol*] (SPSG) ... PHX
Phoenix Network, Inc. [*Associated Press*] (SAG) ... PhxNet
Phoenix, NY [*FM radio station call letters*] (RBYB) ... WRDS-FM
Phoenix, OR [*FM radio station call letters*] (RBYB) ... KAKT-FM
Phoenix, OR [*AM radio station call letters*] (RBYB) ... KAPL
Phoenix, OR [*FM radio station call letters*] ... KROG
Phoenix, OR [*AM radio station call letters*] ... KTMT
Phoenix Precision Instrument Co. ... PPI
Phoenix Project [*An association*] (EA) ... PP
Phoenix Public Library (AD) ... PPL
Phoenix Public Library, Phoenix, AZ [*Library symbol Library of Congress*] (LCLS) ... AzPh
Phoenix Re Corp. [*NASDAQ symbol*] (NQ) ... PXRE
Phoenix Resource Companies, Inc. [*AMEX symbol*] (SAG) ... PHN
Phoenix Resource Companies, Inc. [*Associated Press*] (SAG) ... PhnxRs
Phoenix [*Arizona*] **Scottsdale** [*Airport symbol*] (OAG) ... SCF
Phoenix Shannon Ltd. [*NASDAQ symbol*] (SAG) ... PHNX
Phoenix Shannon Ltd. [*Associated Press*] (SAG) ... PhnxShn
Phoenix Shannon plc ADR [*NASDAQ symbol*] (TTSB) ... PHNXY
Phoenix/Sky Harbor International [*Arizona*] [*ICAO location identifier*] (ICLI) ... KPHX
Phoenix Technologies [*NASDAQ symbol*] (TTSB) ... PTEC
Phoenix Technologies Ltd. [*Associated Press*] (SAG) ... PhnxTc
Phoenix Technologies Ltd. [*NASDAQ symbol*] (NQ) ... PTEC
Phoenix Theatre [*Defunct*] (EA) ... PT
Phoenix Weapons System ... PWS
Phoenixville, PA [*AM radio station call letters*] ... WPHE
Pholbe Phillips Editions [*Publisher*] [*British*] ... PPE
Phon [*Unit of loudness level*] ... P
Phon [*Unit of loudness level*] (IAA) ... PN
Phone (IAA) ... P
Phone (MDG) ... PH
Phone ... PH
Phone (KSC) ... PHN
Phone Center Staffing and Sizing Program [*Telecommunications*] (TEL) ... PSSP
Phone Line ... PL
Phone Line Formatter ... PLF
Phone Line Interface [*IBM Corp.*] (PCM) ... PLI
Phone Order [*Medicine*] ... P/O
Phonemic Spelling Council [*Defunct*] (EA) ... PSC
Phonetel Technologies [*Commercial firm Associated Press*] (SAG) ... Phonetel
Phonetel Technologies [*NASDAQ symbol*] (TTSB) ... PNTL
Phonetel Technologies, Inc. [*NASDAQ symbol*] (NQ) ... PNTL
Phonetic Alphabet Association (DGA) ... PAA
Phonetically Balanced [*With reference to word lists*] ... PB
Phonetically Balanced (Kindergarten) [*Speech and language therapy*] (DAVI) ... PB (k)
Phonetics ... PHON
Phonetics (ROG) ... PHONET
Phong Savanh [*Laos*] [*ICAO location identifier*] (ICLI) ... VLPV
Phonocardiogram [*Cardiology*] ... PCG
Phonocardiogram [*Cardiology*] (DAVI) ... Phono
Phonocardiogram [*Cardiology*] ... PKG
Phonocardiogram Amplifier [*Cardiology*] ... PA
PhonoCardioScan [*Cardiology*] ... PCS
Phonogram [*British military*] (DMA) ... P/N
Phonogram (ROG) ... PHON
Phonograph (AAG) ... PHON
Phonograph (MSA) ... PHONO
Phonograph ... PHONO
Phonograph Manufacturers Association (EA) ... PMA
Phonographic Performance Ltd. [*British*] ... PPL
Phonography ... PHONOG
Phonologic Programming Deficit Syndrome (DMAA) ... PPDS
Phonological Acquisition Device (DAVI) ... PAD
Phonology ... PHONOL
Phonon Side-Band Hole [*Spectroscopy*] ... PSBH
Phony Peach Bacteria [*Plant pathology*] ... PP
Phooey on Everything, Tomorrow's Saturday [*Bowdlerized version*] ... POETS
Phoolbagh [*India*] [*Airport symbol*] (AD) ... IPG
Phopholipase B [*An enzyme*] (DAVI) ... PLB
Phorbol [*Organic chemistry*] ... PHR
Phorbol Diacetate [*Organic chemistry*] ... PDA
Phorbol Dibenzoate [*Organic chemistry*] ... PDBz
Phorbol Dibutyrate [*Also, PDBu*] [*Organic chemistry*] ... PDB
Phorbol Dibutyrate [*Also, PDB*] [*Organic chemistry*] ... PDBu
Phorbol Didecanoate [*Organic chemistry*] ... PDD
Phorbol Monomyristate [*Organic chemistry*] ... PM
Phorbol Myristate Acetate [*Also, PTA, TPA*] [*Organic chemistry*] ... PMA
Phorbol Tetradecanoyl Acetate [*Also, PMA, TPA*] [*Organic chemistry*] ... PTA
Phormio [*of Terence*] [*Classical studies*] (OCD) ... Phorm
Phosgene [*Organic chemistry*] ... CG

Phosphatase [*An enzyme*] (DHSM) ... PTASE
Phosphate [*One-letter symbol*] [*Biochemistry*] ... p
Phosphate ... Ph
Phosphate (KSC) ... PHOS
Phosphate Adsorption Index [*Analytical chemistry*] ... PAI
Phosphate Buffer ... PB
Phosphate Carrier Compound ... PCC
Phosphate Chemicals Export Association (EA) ... PCEA
Phosphate Chemicals Export Association (EA) ... PHOSCHEM
Phosphate Clearance [*Organic chemistry*] (DAVI) ... C_P
Phosphate Clearance [*Medicine*] (MAE) ... Cp
Phosphate Cycle [*Chemistry*] (MAE) ... PC
Phosphate Dehydrogenase ... PD
Phosphate Dehydrogenase (MAE) ... PDH
Phosphate Dextrose (DAVI) ... PD
Phosphate Ester Base (PDAA) ... PEB
Phosphate Excretion Index [*Biochemistry*] (DAVI) ... PEI
Phosphate Excretion Rate [*Laboratory Science*] (DAVI) ... U_pV
Phosphate, Inorganic [*Chemistry*] ... Pi
Phosphate Mining Corp. of Christmas Island (EY) ... PMCI
Phosphate Rock [*Petrology*] ... PR
Phosphate Rock Institute [*Defunct*] (EA) ... PRI
Phosphate to Oxygen (BARN) ... P/O
Phosphate-Binding Protein [*Biochemistry*] ... PBP
Phosphate-Buffered Saline ... PBS
Phosphate-Buffered Saline Azide [*Culture medium*] ... PBSA
Phosphate-Buffered Sodium (MAE) ... PBS
Phosphate-Citrate-Dextrose Polycystic Disease (MAE) ... PCD
Phosphate-Eliminating Enzyme (DMAA) ... PEE
Phosphate-Saline [*A buffer*] [*Cell culture*] ... PS
Phosphate-Saline-Glucose [*A buffer*] [*Cell culture*] ... PSG
Phosphatidic Acid [*Biochemistry*] ... PA
Phosphatidyl ... Ptd
Phosphatidylcholine [*Lecithin*] [*Biochemistry*] ... PC
Phosphatidylcholine [*Biochemistry*] ... PtcD
Phosphatidyl(dimethyl)ethanolamine [*Biochemistry*] ... PDE
Phosphatidylethanolamine [*Biochemistry*] ... PE
Phosphatidylethanolamine Methyltransferase [*An enzyme*] ... PEMT
Phosphatidylglycerol ... PG
Phosphatidylglycerol [*Test used to determine fetal lung maturity*] (DAVI) ... PHG
Phosphatidylinositol [*Also, PtdIns*] [*Biochemistry*] ... PI
Phosphatidylinositol [*Also, PI*] [*Biochemistry*] ... PtdIns
Phosphatidylinositol Glycan [*Biochemistry*] ... PIG
Phosphatidylinositol Phosphate [*Biochemistry*] ... PIP
Phosphatidylinositol Transfer Protein [*Biochemistry*] ... PITP
Phosphatidylinositol-Specific Phospholipase C [*Biochemistry*] ... PIPLC
Phosphatidylmonomethylethanolamine [*Biochemistry*] ... PME
Phosphatidylserine [*Biochemistry*] ... PS
Phosphatidylserine [*Biochemistry*] ... PtdS
Phosphinothricin [*Organic chemistry*] ... PPT
Phosphinothricin Acetyl Transferase [*An enzyme*] ... PAT
Phosphoadenosine Diphosphosulfate [*Phosphoadenosyl-Phosphosulfate*] [*Biochemistry*] (DAVI) ... PAPS
Phosphoadenosine Phosphate [*Biochemistry*] ... PAP
Phosphoadenosine Phosphosulfate [*Also, APPS*] [*Biochemistry*] ... PAPS
Phosphoadenylyl Sulfate [*Biochemistry*] ... PAPS
Phosphoarginine [*Biochemistry*] ... PA
Phosphocholine [*Biochemistry*] ... PC
Phosphocholine [*Biochemistry*] ... PCh
Phosphocreatine [*Also, PCr*] [*Creatine phosphate; see CP*] [*Biochemistry*] ... PC
Phosphocreatine [*Also, CP, PC*] [*Biochemistry*] ... PCr
Phosphocreatine to Inorganic Phosphate Ratio ... Pcr/Pi
Phosphodiester [*Organic chemistry*] ... PD
Phosphodiesterase [*An enzyme*] ... PDE
Phosphodiesterase (DMAA) ... PDIE
Phosphodiesterase Inhibitor [*Biochemistry*] ... PDEI
Phosphodiesterase-Activating Factor [*Medicine*] (DMAA) ... PAF
Phosphoenolopyruvate Carboxykinase [*An enzyme*] ... PEPCK
Phosphoenolpyruvate [*Biochemistry*] ... PEP
Phosphoenolpyruvate Carboxykinase [*An enzyme*] ... PEPCK
Phosphoenolpyruvate Carboxylase [*An enzyme*] ... PEPC
Phosphoethanolamine [*Organic chemistry*] ... PEA
Phosphofructokinase [*An enzyme*] ... PFK
Phosphofructokinase, Muscle Type [*Medicine*] (DMAA) ... PFKM
Phosphogalactose Uridyltransferase [*Known as Galactose-1-phosphate Uridyl yltransferase*] [*An enzyme*] ... PGUT
Phosphoglucoisomerase [*An enzyme*] ... PGI
Phosphoglucomutase [*An enzyme*] ... PGM
Phosphogluconate [*Biochemistry*] ... PG
Phosphogluconate Dehydrogenase [*Organic chemistry*] (MAH) ... PDG
Phosphogluconate Dehydrogenase [*Also, PGDH*] [*An enzyme*] ... PGD
Phosphogluconate Dehydrogenase [*Also, PGD*] [*An enzyme*] ... PGDH
Phosphoglyceraldehyde Dehydrogenase [*An enzyme*] (MAE) ... PGD
Phosphoglycerate Kinase [*An enzyme*] ... PGK
Phosphoglycerate Mutase A (DMAA) ... PGMA
Phosphoglycerate Mutase B (DMAA) ... PGMB
Phosphoglyceric Acid [*Biochemistry*] ... PGA
Phosphoglyceromutase [*An enzyme*] ... PGAM
Phosphoglycolate Phosphatase [*An enzyme*] ... PGP
Phosphoglycolipid ... PGL
Phosphoglycolohydroxamate [*Biochemistry*] ... PGH
Phosphogypsum [*Inorganic chemistry*] ... PG
Phosphohexose Isomerase [*An enzyme*] ... PHI
Phosphoinositidase C [*An enzyme*] ... PIC
Phospholamban [*Biochemistry*] ... PLB
Phospholamban [*Biochemistry*] ... PLN
Phospholemman [*Biochemistry*] ... PLM
Phospholipase A [*An enzyme*] (DAVI) ... PLA
Phospholipase A_2 [*An enzyme*] ... PLA_2
Phospholipase C [*An enzyme*] ... PLC
Phospholipase D [*An enzyme*] ... PLD
Phospholipid [*Biochemistry*] ... PL
Phospholipid Transfer Protein [*Biochemistry*] ... PLTP
Phospholysine C [*Biochemistry*] ... PLC
Phosphomannose Isomerase [*An enzyme*] (MAE) ... PMI
Phosphomolybdic Acid [*Organic chemistry*] ... PMA
Phosphomonoester [*Biochemistry*] ... PME
Phosphonitrilic Chloride [*Inorganic chemistry*] ... PNC
Phosphonitrilic Fluoroelastomer [*Synthetic rubber*] ... PNF
Phosphonoacetic Acid [*Antiviral compound*] ... PAA
Phosphonoacetyl-L-Aspartate [*Biochemistry*] ... PALA
Phosphonoacetyl-L-Ornithine [*Biochemistry*] ... PALO
Phosphonoformic Acid [*Antiviral compound*] ... PFA
Phosphonylmethoxyethyladenine [*Antiviral*] ... PMEA
Phosphonylmethoxypropyladenine ... PMPA
(Phosphonylmethoxypropyl)adenine [*Antiviral*] ... PMPA
Phosphopentomutase [*An enzyme*] ... PPM
Phosphopyridoxal [*Medicine*] (DMAA) ... Py
Phosphopyruvate Hydratase [*An enzyme*] ... PPH
Phosphor Bronze (BARN) ... ph bz
Phosphor Bronze ... PHBRZ
Phosphor Bronze ... PhosBro
Phosphor Coated Paper ... PCP
Phosphoramide Mustard [*Antineoplastic drug*] ... PM
Phosphorescence-Microwave Double Resonance ... PMDR
Phosphorescent (KSC) ... PHOS
Phosphoribomutase [*An enzyme*] (MAE) ... PRM
Phosphoribose Diphosphate [*Biochemistry*] ... PPRibP
Phosphoribose Isomerase [*An enzyme*] (MAE) ... PRI
Phosphoribosyl ... PB
Phosphoribosyl Anthranilate Isomerase ... PRAI
Phosphoribosyl-5 Amino-Imidazole-Carboxamide (BABM) ... ALCAR
Phosphoribosylamine ... PRA
Phosphoribosylpyrophosphate [*Biochemistry*] ... PRPP
Phosphoribosyltransferase [*Also, PRTase*] [*An enzyme*] ... PRT
Phosphoribosyltransferase [*Medicine*] (MEDA) ... PRTase
Phosphoric Acid (ECON) ... PA
Phosphoric Acid Anodized (PDAA) ... PPA
Phosphoric Acid Fuel Cell [*Energy source*] ... PAFC
Phosphoric Acid-Resistant ... PAR
Phosphoric Acid-Sensitive ... PAS
Phosphoric Residue [*As substituent on nucleoside*] [*Biochemistry*] ... p
Phosphorodiamidic Anhydride [*Organic chemistry*] (DAVI) ... DPDA
Phosphoroimmunoassays ... PIA
Phosphorotioate Oligonucleotide [*Biochemistry*] ... PON
Phosphorous Excretion Index [*Medicine*] (MEDA) ... PEI
Phosphorous Propellant System (KSC) ... PPS
Phosphorous-Doped Vapor-Deposited Oxide (IAA) ... PVX
Phosphorus [*Chemical element*] ... P
Phosphorus [*Chemical symbol is P*] ... PHOS
Phosphorus Enhanced Diffusion (IAA) ... PED
Phosphorus Excretion Index [*Biochemistry*] (DAVI) ... PEI
Phosphorus Spot [*Urine Test*] [*Chemistry*] (DAVI) ... PHOS-S
Phosphorus Utilization Efficiency [*Ecology*] ... PUE
Phosphorus Vanadium Oxide [*Inorganic chemistry*] ... PVO
Phosphorus-Dissolving Bacteria [*Microbiology*] ... PDB
Phosphorus-Solubilizing Bacteria [*Microbiology*] ... PSB
Phosphoryl Triamide [*Organic chemistry*] ... PTA
Phosphorylase B Kinase [*An enzyme*] (MAE) ... PBK
Phosphorylase Kinase [*An enzyme*] ... PhK
Phosphorylase-Rupturing [*Biochemistry*] ... PR
Phosphorylated Monester [*Organic chemistry*] ... PME
Phosphorylcholine [*Biochemistry*] ... PC
Phosphorylcholine-Binding Myeloma Protein [*Medicine*] (DMAA) ... PC-BMP
Phosphorylribose Pyrophosphate [*Biochemistry*] ... PRPP
Phosphosilicate Glass (IEEE) ... PSG
Phosphotransacetylase [*An enzyme*] ... PTA
Phosphotransferase System [*Organic chemistry*] ... PTS
Phosphotungstic Acid [*Inorganic chemistry*] ... PTA
Phosphotungstic Acid-Hematoxylin [*A stain*] ... PTAH
Phosphotungstomolybdic Acid [*Inorganic chemistry*] ... PTMA
Phosphotyrosine-Binding [*Biochemistry*] ... PTB
Phot [*Electronics*] (DEN) ... PH
Phot Document Sensor [*Electronics*] (IAA) ... PDS
Photius [*Ninth century AD*] [*Classical studies*] (OCD) ... Phot
Photo Aperture Card (SAA) ... PAC
Photo Aperture Card Program (SAA) ... PACP
Photo Aperture Card System (SAA) ... PACS
Photo Area and Location System (NASA) ... PALS
Photo Articulation Test ... PAT
Photo Butt Line (MSA) ... PBL
Photo Compact Disk [*Eastman Kodak Co.*] (PCM) ... PCD
Photo Control [*NASDAQ symbol*] (TTSB) ... PHOC
Photo Control Corp. [*NASDAQ symbol*] (NQ) ... PHOC
Photo Data Analysis System [*Navy*] ... PDAS
Photo Data Quantizer ... PDQ
Photo Ditector (EECA) ... PD
Photo Electric Portable Probe Reader (IAA) ... PEPPRE
Photo Engravers & Electrotypers Ltd. [*Toronto Stock Exchange symbol*] ... PHE
Photo Exploitation Group ... PEG

Photo Finishing Institute [*Defunct*] (EA) .... PFI
Photo Flash Battery .... PFB
Photo Glow Tube .... PGT
Photo Image Processor (MCD) .... PIP
Photo Index and Cataloging System (NASA) .... PICS
Photo Intelligence Brief (AFM) .... PIB
Photo Intelligence Requirements Review Board [*Military*] .... PIRRB
Photo International [*Defunct*] (EAIO) .... PI
Photo Interpretation Brief (MCD) .... PIB
Photo Interpretation Console (IAA) .... PIC
Photo Interpretation Officer [*Air Force*] .... PIO
Photo Interpretation Report [*Air Force*] (AFM) .... PIR
Photo Interpreter .... PI
Photo Interpretive Program (BUR) .... PIP
Photo Lab Usage Reporting (MCD) .... PLUR
Photo Marketing Association (AD) .... PMA
Photo Marketing Association International (EA) .... PMA
Photo Marketing Magazine [*A publication*] (EAAP) .... PM
Photo Master (MCD) .... PM
Photo Mural (VRA) .... photmur
Photo Optic System .... POS
Photo Optical Cable Controlled Submersible (PDAA) .... PHOCAS
Photo Peak Analysis (IEEE) .... PPA
Photo Processing Interpretation Facility .... PPIF
Photo Quality (PCM) .... PQ
Photo RADAR Intelligence .... PRI
Photo Reconnaissance [*ICAO designator*] (FAAC) .... PR
Photo Resist Spinner .... PRS
Photo Roentgen Unit (IAA) .... PRUNIT
Photo Scale Reciprocal (DNAB) .... PSR
Photo Selective Metal Deposition .... PSMD
Photo Services Industrial Ltd. [*British*] .... PSI
Photo Systems Controller Console (KSC) .... PSCC
Photo Target Detection System .... PTDS
Photo Triangulation Party [*Military*] .... PHOTRIPART
Photo Type [*Deltiology*] .... PHO/TY
Photo Voltaic Relay (NITA) .... PVR
Photoabsorption Spectroscopy [*Chemistry*] .... PAS
Photoacid Generator .... PAG
Photoacoustic [*Spectroscopy*] .... PAC
Photoacoustic Raman Spectroscopy .... PARS
Photoacoustic Spectrometry [*Also, OAS*] .... PAS
Photoactivated Fluorescence Molecules [*Analytical biochemistry*] .... PAF
Photoactive Compound [*Chemistry*] .... PAC
Photoactive Pigment Electrophotography (IEEE) .... PAPE
Photoactive Yellow Protein [*Biochemistry*] .... PYP
Photoallergenic [*Response*] [*Medicine*] .... PA
Photo-Anodic Engraving (PDAA) .... PAE
Photocell .... PC
Photocell Emitter (IAA) .... PCE
Photochemical Aerosol-Forming Potential of Polluted Air [*Environmental chemistry*] .... PAFP
Photochemical Hole Burning [*Spectrometry*] .... PHB
Photochemical Machining [*Desktop manufacturing*] .... PCM
Photo-Chemical Machining Institute (EA) .... PCMI
Photochemical System .... PS
Photochemotherapy with Ultraviolet A [*Oncology*] .... PUVA
Photochromic Liquid Crystal Polymer [*Organic chemistry*] .... PLCP
Photochromic Microimage [*Microfiche*] .... PCMI
Photochromic Microimage (IAA) .... POMI
Photochromic Microimage System (IAA) .... PCMI
Photochromic Microreproduction (DIT) .... PCMR
Photocomm, Inc. [*NASDAQ symbol*] (NQ) .... PCOM
Photocomm, Inc. [*Associated Press*] (SAG) .... Photcm
Photocomposition Input Option (NITA) .... PIO
Photoconductive Decay [*Semiconductor material*] .... PCD
Photoconductive Relay (IEEE) .... PCR
Photoconductive Resonance [*Physics*] .... PCR
Photoconductive, Semiconductive Device .... PSD
Photoconductive Thermoplastic [*Materials science*] .... PT
Photoconductor .... PC
Photoconductor Lamp (IAA) .... PL
Photo-Control Corp. [*Associated Press*] (SAG) .... PhotoC
Photocopy (MSA) .... PHOC
Photocounting .... PC
Photo-Data Card [*Trademark*] [*Computer science*] .... PDC
Photo-Digital Store .... PDS
Photodiode .... PD
Photodiode .... PDIO
Photodiode Amplifier .... PA
Photodiode Array [*Instrumentation*] .... PDA
Photodiode Array Detector [*Spectrophotometry*] .... PDAD
Photodiode Array Processing (MCD) .... PAP
Photodiode Array Spectrophotometer (USDC) .... PDAS
Photodiode Array Spectrophotometer [*Marine science*] (OSRA) .... PDAS
Photodiode Detector [*Instrumentation*] .... PTD
Photodischarge Spectroscopy (MCD) .... PDS
Photodissociation Dye LASER .... PDL
Photodissociation Mass Spectrometry .... PDMS
Photodissociation [*or Photodominated*] **Region** [*Galactic science*] .... PDR
Photodynamic Therapy [*Oncology*] .... PDT
Photoelastic Modulator [*Instrumentation*] .... PEM
Photoelectric .... PE
Photoelectric (MSA) .... PELEC
Photoelectric Alignment Collimator (IAA) .... PEAC
Photoelectric Auto Collimator .... PEAC
Photoelectric Cell .... PEC
Photoelectric Counter Chronometer (IAA) .... PCC
Photoelectric Intravenous Angiography [*Medicine*] (DMAA) .... PIA
Photoelectric Keyboard .... PKB
Photo-Electric Portable Probe Reader (PDAA) .... PEPPER
Photoelectric Potential .... PEP
Photoelectric Scanner .... PES
Photoelectric Scanning [*Electronics*] (ECII) .... PES
Photoelectric Tape Reader .... PTR
Photoelectric Transducer (PDAA) .... PET
Photoelectric Web Guide .... PWG
Photoelectric Work Function .... PWF
Photoelectric Yield .... PEY
Photoelectroanalytical Chemistry .... PEAC
Photoelectrochemical Cell [*Energy conversion device*] .... PEC
Photoelectrochromic [*Chemistry*] .... PEC
Photoelectromagnetic .... PEM
Photoelectron (IAA) .... PE
Photoelectron Diffraction [*Spectroscopy*] .... PHD
Photoelectron Emission [*Also, OSEE*] .... PEE
Photoelectron Extended X-Ray Absorption Fine Structure .... PEXAFS
Photoelectron Layer .... PEL
Photoelectron Microscopy .... PEM
Photoelectron Spectromicroscope .... PESM
Photoelectron Spectroscopy .... PES
Photo-Electron Spectroscopy of Inner-Shell (PDAA) .... PESIS
Photo-Electron Spectroscopy of Outer-Shell (PDAA) .... PESOS
Photoelectron Yield Spectroscopy (MCD) .... PEYS
Photoelectron Yield Spectroscopy .... PYS
Photo-Electro-Nystagmography [*Medicine*] .... PENG
Photoelectrophoresis .... PEP
Photoemission [*Physics*] .... PE
Photoemission Diode .... PED
Photoemission Effect .... PEE
Photoemission Electron Microscope .... PEEM
Photoemission Electron Microscopy (MCD) .... PEEM
Photoemission Electron Microscopy [*Medicine*] (DMAA) .... PhEEM
Photoemission Microscope .... PEM
Photoemission of Adsorbed Xenon [*Physics*] .... PAX
Photoemission Scintillation (MCD) .... PS
Photoemission Spectroscopy .... PES
Photoemission Tube .... PET
Photoengraving (VRA) .... PHENG
Photoetching (VRA) .... PHET
Photoferroelectric Effect [*Physics*] .... PFE
Photoflash (AAG) .... PHOFL
Photoflash Relay .... PFR
Photoformed Ceramic Modules [*Du Pont process for making microconductors*] .... PCM
Photoformed Ceramic Substrates [*Du Pont process for making microconductors*] .... PCS
Photofragment Excitation [*Spectroscopy*] .... PHOFEX
Photofragment Spectroscopy .... PFS
Photogenic (VRA) .... PHGNDWG
Photogram (VRA) .... PHGRM
Photogrammetric Circulatory Survey (PDAA) .... PHOCIS
Photogrammetric Facility [*Army*] .... PF
Photogrammetric Instrumentation (AAG) .... P-I
Photogrammetric Ocean Survey Equipment .... POSE
Photogrammetric Programming Language [*Computer science*] (PDAA) .... PPL
Photogrammetric Target System [*Air Force*] .... PTS
Photogrammetric Triangulation System [*Air Force*] (IAA) .... PTS
Photogrammetry .... PG
Photogrammetry Branch, New Brunswick Department of Lands and Mines, Fredericton,New Brunswick [*Library symbol National Library of Canada*] (NLC) .... NBFLM
Photogrammetry Division, Nova Scotia Research Foundation, Halifax, Nova Scotia [*Library symbol Obsolete National Library of Canada*] (NLC) .... NSHRP
Photograph .... PHOT
Photograph (AAG) .... PHOTO
Photograph (VRA) .... photo
Photographer [*British military*] (DMA) .... Pho
Photographer [*Navy rating British*] .... PHOT
Photographer .... PHOTOGR
Photographer [*MARC relator code*] [*Library of Congress*] (LCCP) .... pht
Photographer's Airman Apprentice [*Navy*] .... PHAA
Photographers Association of America [*Later, Professional Photographers of America*] .... PAA
Photographer's Mate [*Navy rating*] .... PH
Photographer's Mate [*Navy rating Obsolete*] .... PHOM
Photographer's Mate, Combat Aircrewman [*Navy rating Obsolete*] .... PHOAC
Photographer's Mate, First Class [*Navy rating*] PH1
Photographer's Mate, Second Class [*Navy rating*] PH2
Photographer's Mate, Third Class [*Navy rating*] PH3
Photographers' Telegraph Association .... PTA
Photographic .... PHOTOG
Photographic Abstracts [*Pergamon*] [*Database*] .... PHOTABS
Photographic Administrators, Inc. (EA) .... PAI
Photographic and Reproduction Unit .... PARU
Photographic Art and Science Foundation (EA) .... PASF
Photographic Bulletin (MCD) .... PHB
Photographic Cabinet Makers' Society [*A union*] [*British*] .... PCMS
Photographic Camera Control System (KSC) .... PCCS

Photographic Change (MCD) .... PHC
Photographic Collectors Club of Great Britain (DBA) .... PCCGB
Photographic Credit Institute (EA) .... PCI
Photographic Dealers' Association [*British*] (BI) .... PDA
Photographic Effect (MAE) .... PE
Photographic Equipment and Materials (NATG) .... PEM
Photographic Equipment Management Control System .... PEMCONS
Photographic Exercise (AD) .... podex
Photographic Exploitation Products (MCD) .... PEP
Photographic Historical Society (EA) .... PHS
Photographic Image Conversion by Tonal Masking Procedures (MCD) .... PICTOMAP
Photographic Importers Association [*British*] (BI) .... PIA
Photographic Industry Council [*Defunct*] (EA) .... PIC
Photographic Industry Marketing Association [*Australia*] .... PIMA
Photographic Information Condensing System (DNAB) .... PICS
Photographic Instrument Repairing Associates [*British*] (DBA) .... PIRA
Photographic Instrumentation Data Recording System (MCD) .... PIDRS
Photographic Intelligence [*Military*] .... PHOTINT
Photographic Intelligence Report [*Military*] .... PIR
Photographic Intelligenceman [*Navy rating*] .... PT
Photographic Intelligenceman, First Class [*Navy rating*] PT1
Photographic Intelligenceman, Second Class [*Navy rating*] PT2
Photographic Intelligenceman, Third Class [*Navy rating*] PT3
Photographic Interpretation Center (MCD) .... PIC
Photographic Interpretation Section .... PIS
Photographic Interpretation Technique .... PIT
Photographic Interpretation Unit [*Marine Corps*] .... PIU
Photographic Interpreter .... PI
Photographic Inventory and Accountancy System .... PIAS
Photographic Laboratories Working Group [*Range Commanders Council*] [*White Sands Missile Range, NM*] .... PLWG
Photographic Laboratory Specialist [*Navy*] .... LB
Photographic Manufacturers and Distributors Association (EA) .... PMDA
Photographic Materials Specialty Group of the American Institute for Conservation of Historic and Artistic Works (EA) .... AIC/PMG
Photographic Mechanical Equipment Repair [*Course*] (DNAB) .... PHER
Photographic Micro-Image (AD) .... pmi
Photographic Microimage Master [*Reprography*] .... PMI
Photographic Press Review [*A publication British*] .... PPR
Photographic Processing Cells (AFM) .... PPC
Photographic Program Office [*NASA*] (KSC) .... PPO
Photographic Projection Plan Position Indicator (DEN) .... PPPPI
Photographic Reconnaissance .... PHR
Photographic Reconnaissance [*Military*] (MCD) .... PR
Photographic Reconnaissance and Exploitation Management Support System (MCD) .... PREMSS
Photographic Reconnaissance and Interpretation (NATG) .... PRI
Photographic Reconnaissance Capability [*When suffix to Navy aircraft designation*] .... P
Photographic Reconnaissance Equipment Advisory Group [*Military*] .... PREAG
Photographic Reconnaissance Interpretation Section [*Squadron*] IntelligenceCenter [*JICPOA*] .... PRISIC
Photographic Reconnaissance System .... PRS
Photographic Reconnaissance System Analysis by Computer .... PRESAC
Photographic Reconnaissance Unit [*Aircraft*] [*Marine Corps*] .... PRU
Photographic Recorder .... PR
Photographic Retrieval from Optical Disk .... PROD
Photographic Science Laboratory [*Navy*] .... PSL
Photographic Service .... PS
Photographic Society International (EA) .... PSI
Photographic Society of America (EA) .... PSA
Photographic Society of Ireland (BI) .... PSI
Photographic Squadron [*Navy*] .... PHOTRON
Photographic Squadron .... PS
Photographic Squadron [*Navy symbol*] .... VD
Photographic Squadron (Heavy) [*Navy symbol*] (NVT) .... VAP
Photographic Tasks and Equipment [*NASA*] .... PTE
Photographic Technical Advisory Board [*American National Standards Institute*] .... PTAB
Photographic Technology Laboratory (KSC) .... PTL
Photographic Training Centre [*British*] (CB) .... PTC
Photographic Triangulation Group, Atlantic [*Military*] (DNAB) .... PHOTOTRIGULANT
Photographic Triangulation Group, Pacific [*Military*] (DNAB) .... PHOTOTRIGUPAC
Photographic Type Composition (ADA) .... PTC
Photographic Vision [*Filter*] .... PV
Photographic Zenith Tube .... PZT
Photographical Historical Society of Canada .... PHSOC
Photographically Stored Information Analog Comparator .... PHOSIAC
Photographic-Spatial Volume (SAA) .... PSV
Photography .... PHOTOGR
Photography in Community Self-Development [*Program of Master Photo Dealers and Finishers Association*] .... PICS
Photography Program [*Association of Independent Colleges and Schools specialization code*] .... PH
Photogravure (VRA) .... PGRV
Photogravure [*Philately*] .... Photo
Photohydrodynamic [*Astrophysics*] .... PHD
Photoinduced Charge Transfer [*Electrochemistry*] .... PCT
Photo-Induced Electrochromism .... PIE
Photoinduced Electron Transfer .... PET
Photoinduced Transient Spectroscopy .... PITS
Photoinduced Tunnel Current .... PITC
Photointerpretation [*or Photointerpreter*] .... PI
Photointerpretation Department [*Military*] .... PID
Photointerpretation Squadron [*Military*] .... INTERPRON
Photointerpreter (IAA) .... PI
Photoionization [*Physical chemistry*] .... PI
Photoionization Detector .... PID
Photoionization Mass Spectrometry .... PIMS
Photoion-Photoelectron Coincidence [*Spectroscopy*] .... PIPECO
Photo-Island Grid .... PIG
Photojet Edge Sensor .... PES
Photojet Edge Sensor .... PJES
Photojournalist (DNAB) .... PH/JO
Photolettering (DGA) .... PL
Photo-Litho Reproducers' Association [*British*] (BI) .... PLRA
Photolithographic (VRA) .... PHLITHO
Photolithographic .... PHOTOLITH
Photolithographic Process (IAA) .... PLP
Photolocator (MCD) .... PL
Photoluminescence .... PL
Photoluminescence Excitation [*Physics*] .... PLE
Photoluminescence Yield [*Spectroscopy*] .... PLY
Photoluminescent Thermometer .... PLT
Photomagnetoelectric .... PME
Photomagnetoelectric Effect (IAA) .... PME
Photomap .... PMAP
Photomechanical (VRA) .... PTMC
Photomechanical Transfer [*Negative paper*] [*Eastman Kodak*] .... PMT
Photometer, Automated Universal Distribution Gonielectric Type .... PAUDGET
Photometer System (KSC) .... PS
Photometric Determination of Equilibrium Constants [*Computer science*] .... PHODEC
Photometric Instrument for Biological Optical Sections .... PHOBOS
Photometric Sunspot Index .... PSI
Photometry .... PHOTOM
Photomontage (VRA) .... photomon
Photomultiplier .... PM
Photomultiplier (IAA) .... PTM
Photomultiplier Detector Unit (KSC) .... PDU
Photomultiplier Tube [*Electronics*] .... PMT
Photomultiplier Tubes (AD) .... pmt
Photon Absorption Densitometry [*Medicine*] (DMAA) .... PAD
Photon Activation Analysis .... PAA
Photon Adjoint with Neutron (PDAA) .... PAWN
Photon Barrier [*Astrophysics*] .... PB
Photon Correlation Spectroscopy .... PCS
Photon Counting Array [*Instrumentation*] .... PCA
Photon Detector Assembly (MCD) .... PDA
Photon Dynamics [*NASDAQ symbol*] (TTSB) .... PHTN
Photon Dynamics, Inc. [*Associated Press*] (SAG) .... Photon
Photon Dynamics, Inc. [*NASDAQ symbol*] (SAG) .... PHTN
Photon Echo [*Spectroscopy*] .... PE
Photon Flow Integrating (IAA) .... PFI
Photon Flux Integration (IAA) .... PFI
Photon Scanning Tunnelling Microscope .... PSTM
Photon Stimulated Desorption [*For analysis of surfaces*] .... PSD
Photon Stimulated Desorption (Mass Spectroscopy) (MCD) .... PSD(MS)
Photon Target Scoring System (AAG) .... PTSS
Photon Tunneling Microscope .... PTM
Photonburst Mass Spectrometry .... PBMS
Photon-Counting Microspectrophotometer .... PMSP
Photon-Coupled Pair (IEEE) .... PCP
Photon-Coupled Transistor (IEEE) .... PCT
Photonic Array Processor [*Device for manipulating light beams in an optical computer*] .... PAP
Photonic Bandgap [*Physics*] .... PBG
Photonic Multichannel Analyzer .... PMA
Photon-Induced Dissociation [*For spectral studies*] .... PID
Photons for Atomic and Molecular Processes and Universal Studies [*Physics*] .... PAMPUS
Photonuclear Data Center [*National Institute of Standards and Technology*] .... PDC
Photo-Optical Recorder Tracker .... PORT
Photo-Optical Recorder Tracker (AD) .... port
Photo-Optical Surveillance Subsystem .... POSS
Photo-Optical Terrain Simulator (MUGU) .... POTS
Photo-Peak Analysis (AD) .... ppa
Photophoretic Force [*Pressure exerted by light*] .... PPF
Photophoretic Spectroscopy .... PPS
Photo-Plastic-Recording .... PPR
Photoplethysmography [*Medicine*] .... PPG
Photopolarimeter Radiometer [*Instrumentation*] .... PPR
Photopolarimeter Spectrometer .... PPS
Photopolymers Lithograph Plate .... PPLP
Photo-Processing Interpretation Facility (AD) .... ppif
Photoradiation Therapy [*Oncology*] .... PRT
Photoreacting [*or Photoreactivation*] [*Biochemistry*] .... PR
Photoreactivating .... PRE
Photoreactivating Light .... PRL
Photoreactivity (DMAA) .... PHR
Photoreceptor .... Ph
Photoreceptor Membrane [*Of the eye*] .... PRM
Photoreconnaissance [*Aircraft designation*] .... F
Photorecorder .... PR
Photorefractive [*Optics*] .... PR
Photorefractive Information Storage Materials Consortium (CDE) .... PRISM
Photorefractive Keratectomy [*Ophtholmology*] .... PRK
Photorefractive Volume Holographic Storage .... PVHS
Photoresist .... PR

Photoresponse Nonuniformity ..... PRNU
Photo-Selective Copper Reduction [*For circuit board manufacture*] ..... PSCR
Photosensitive Cell (IEEE) ..... PSC
Photosensitive Epilepsy ..... PSE
Photosensitive Membrane Light Modulator ..... PMLM
Photosensitivity Dermatitis [*Medicine*] (DMAA) ..... PD
Photosensitivity Dermatitis and Actinic Reticuloid Syndrome [*Medicine*] (DMAA) ..... PD/AR
Photoshop File [*Computer science*] ..... pad
Photostat (BJA) ..... Ph
Photostat (NTCM) ..... STAT
Photostimulated Desorption Ion Angular Distribution [*Surface analysis*] ..... PSDIAD
Photostimulated Luminescence [*Physics*] ..... PSL
Photosynthesis/Respiration [*Biochemistry*] ..... P/R
Photosynthetic Carbon Oxidation [*Plant metabolism*] ..... PCO
Photosynthetic Carbon Reduction [*Plant metabolism*] ..... PCR
Photosynthetic Gas Exchanger (SAA) ..... PSGE
Photosynthetic Oxygenation Illuminated by Solar Energy ..... POISE
Photosynthetic Panel [*i.e., leaf*] [*Slang*] ..... PP
Photosynthetic Unit ..... PSU
Photosynthetically Active Photon Flux Density [*Botany*] ..... PPFD
Photosynthetically Active Radiation ..... PAR
Photosystems ..... PS
Phototheque, National Film Board [*Phototheque, Office National du Film Ottawa, Ontario* [*Library symbol National Library of Canada*] (NLC) ..... OOICP
Phototherapeutic Keratectomy [*Ophthalmology*] ..... PTK
Phototherapy [*Medicine*] ..... PT
Photothermal Deflection ..... PTD
Photothermal Deflection Spectroscopy (MCD) ..... PDS
Photothermal Spectroscopy ..... PTS
Phototoxity [*Medicine*] ..... PT
Photo-Transferred Thermoluminescence (PDAA) ..... PTTL
Phototransistor (NRCH) ..... PT
Phototransistor (IEEE) ..... PXSTR
Phototransistor Amplifier ..... PTA
Phototransmission System [*Telecommunications*] (IAA) ..... PTS
Phototropic Energy Transfer ..... PET
Phototropic Energy Transfer Technique ..... PETT
Phototropism [*Botany*] ..... P
Phototube (KSC) ..... PHOTUB
Phototube ..... PHT
Phototype Environment Buoy (PDAA) ..... PEB
Photo-Type Traveling Wave Tube (NG) ..... PTWT
Phototypesetting (DGA) ..... PTS
Phototypesetting and Composing [*AT & T*] ..... PHOTAC
Phototypesetting Automatic Controller (DGA) ..... PAC
Photovoltaic ..... PV
Photovoltaic Cell (IAA) ..... PVC
Photovoltaic Power Supply ..... PPS
Photovoltaic System ..... PVS
Photovoltaic/Thermal ..... PV/T
Photovoltaic Transient Analysis Computer Program ..... PVTAP
Photran Corp. [*NASDAQ symbol*] (TTSB) ..... PTRN
Photronic Labs [*Associated Press*] (SAG) ..... PhotrIn
Photronics, Inc. [*NASDAQ symbol*] (NQ) ..... PLAB
PHP Healthcare [*NYSE symbol*] (TTSB) ..... PPH
PHP Healthcare Corp. [*Associated Press*] (SAG) ..... PHP
PHP Healthcare Corp. [*NYSE symbol*] (SPSG) ..... PPH
Phrae [*Thailand*] [*Airport symbol*] (OAG) ..... PRH
Phrae [*Thailand*] [*ICAO location identifier*] (ICLI) ..... VTCP
Phrase (ADA) ..... PH
Phrase ..... PHR
Phrase Structure (WGA) ..... PS
Phrase Structure and Dependency Parser (DIT) ..... PSDP
Phrase Structure Rule [*Linguistics*] ..... P
Phrase-Structure Grammar [*Computer science*] ..... PSG
Phreakers, Hackers, and Laundry Service Employees [*East Coast group of computer trespassers raided by the FBI*] ..... PHALSE
Phrenicon Metabolic Monitoring System ..... PMMS
Phrenology ..... PHREN
Phrenomena: an Annual Review [*A publication*] (APTA) ..... Phr
Phthalate Dioxygenase [*An enzyme*] ..... PDO
Phthalic Acid Esters [*Organic chemistry*] ..... PAE
Phthalic Anhydride [*Organic chemistry*] ..... PA
Phthalocyanine [*Organic chemistry*] ..... Pc
Phthaloyl [*Also, Phth*] [*Organic chemistry*] ..... Pht
Phthaloyl [*Also, Pht*] [*Organic chemistry*] ..... Phth
Phuket [*Thailand*] [*Airport symbol*] (OAG) ..... HKT
Phuket [*Thailand*] [*Airport symbol*] (AD) ..... PKC
Phuket [*Thailand*] [*ICAO location identifier*] (ICLI) ..... VTSP
Phuket Marine Biological Center [*Marine science*] (MSC) ..... PMBC
Phulbani [*India*] [*ICAO location identifier*] (ICLI) ..... VEPN
Phu-Lien [*Kien-An*] [*Vietnam*] [*Seismograph station code, US Geological Survey*] (SEIS) ..... PLV
Phuoc Long [*Vietnam*] [*Airport symbol*] (AD) ..... VSO
Phuquoc [*South Vietnam*] [*Airport symbol*] (AD) ..... PQC
Phuquoc [*Viet Nam*] [*ICAO location identifier*] (ICLI) ..... VVPQ
Phycobilisome [*Biochemistry*] ..... PBS
Phycoerythrin [*Biochemistry*] ..... PE
Phycoerythrobilin [*Biochemistry*] ..... PEB
Phycological Society of America (EA) ..... PSA
PhyCor, Inc. [*NASDAQ symbol*] (SPSG) ..... PHYC
PhyCor, Inc. [*Associated Press*] (SAG) ..... PhyCor
Phycourobilin [*Biochemistry*] ..... PUB

Phylacteries [*or Tefillin*] from Qumran. Cave One (BJA) 1QPhyl
Phylaxis Society (EA) ..... PS
Phyllis Dorothy James White [*In name P. D. James*] [*Author*] ..... PD
Phyllis Meyer Library, Fulton, IN [*Library symbol Library of Congress*] (LCLS) ..... InFu
Phylloquinone [*Vitamin K*] [*Also, PMQ*] [*Biochemistry*] ..... K
Phyllosticta maydis [*A toxin-producing fungus*] ..... PM
Phylloxera Board of South Australia ..... PBSA
Phylogenetic Species Concept [*Biology*] ..... PSC
Phylogenic Analysis Using Parsimony [*Biology*] ..... PAUP
Phylogeny Inference Package [*Botany*] ..... PHYLIP
Phymatotrichum omnivorum [*A fungus*] ..... PO
PhyMatrix Corp. [*NASDAQ symbol*] (TTSB) ..... PHMX
PhyMatrix Corp. [*NASDAQ symbol*] (SAG) ..... PHMX
PhyMatrix Corp. [*Associated Press*] (SAG) ..... PhyMatr
Physalaemin [*Biochemistry*] ..... Phy
Physalaemin-Like Immunoreactivity [*Medicine*] ..... PSLI
Physalis Mosaic Virus [*Plant pathology*] ..... PHMV
Physeptone [*A narcotic substitute*] ..... Phi
Physica [*of Aristotle*] [*Classical studies*] (OCD) ..... Ph
Physical ..... PHY
Physical (AFM) ..... PHYS
Physical ..... PHYSCL
Physical Activity (MCD) ..... PA
Physical Address Extension ..... PAX
Physical and Chemical (AAG) ..... P & C
Physical and Engineering Sciences Division [*Army Research Office*] ..... P & ESI
Physical and Mathematical Sciences Research Paper (IEEE) ..... PMSRP
Physical and Mental Impairment of Function Evaluation [*Medicine*] (DMAA) ..... PAMIE
Physical and Recreational Training [*Navy British*] ..... P & RT
Physical and Recreational Training Instructor [*British military*] (DMA) ..... PRTI
Physical Aptitude Examination (AFM) ..... PAE
Physical Block Number ..... PBN
Physical Blowing Agent [*Plastics technology*] ..... PBA
Physical Capacities Evaluation [*Test of hand skills*] ..... PCE
Physical Capacity, Upper Extremities, Lower Extremities, Hearing, Eyes, and Psychiatric System (DNAB) ..... PULHES
Physical Coal Cleaning [*Fuel technology*] ..... PCC
Physical Combat Proficiency Test [*Army*] ..... PCPT
Physical Condition, Upper Extremity Function, Lower Extremity Function, Sensory and Communication Abilities, Excretory Control, Social Support [*A neurological disability profile*] ..... PULSES
Physical Configuration Audit [*Military, NASA*] ..... PCA
Physical Configuration Inspection (AFIT) ..... PCI
Physical Configuration Item [*Military*] ..... PCI
Physical Constant Test Reactor [*Nuclear energy*] ..... PCTR
Physical Control System ..... PCS
Physical Control Zone (NASA) ..... PCZ
Physical Correlate Theory [*Psychophysics*] ..... PCT
Physical Correlation Analysis Program [*Military*] ..... PCAP
Physical Custody [*of Records*] (MHDB) ..... PHYCUS
Physical Damage [*Insurance*] ..... PD
Physical Damage Division [*Navy*] ..... PDD
Physical Defense Division [*Army*] ..... PDD
Physical Development (IAA) ..... PD
Physical Device Address [*Computer science*] (IBMDP) ..... PDA
Physical Device Table (NITA) ..... PDT
Physical Disabilities ..... PD
Physical Disabilities Fieldwork Performance Report [*Occupational therapy*] ..... PDFWPR
Physical Disabilities Special Interest Section [*American Occupational Therapy Association*] ..... PDSS
Physical Disability (CPH) ..... Phys Dis
Physical Disability Appeals Board [*Military*] (AFM) ..... PDAB
Physical Disqualification [*Military*] (DNAB) ..... PHYSQUAL
Physical Distribution (ADA) ..... PD
Physical Distribution Management ..... PDM
Physical Education ..... PE
Physical Education ..... PEd
Physical Education (WGA) ..... PHY ED
Physical Education ..... PHYS ED
Physical Education (Association) [*British*] ..... PE(A)
Physical Education Association of Ireland (EAIO) ..... PEAI
Physical Education Director ..... PE Dir
Physical Education Program ..... PEP
Physical Education Public Information [*Film*] ..... PEPI
Physical Efficiency Index [*Medicine*] (DMAA) ..... PEI
Physical Efficiency Indx [*Medicine*] (DAVI) ..... PEI
Physical Electronics and Physical Acoustics Group [*MIT*] (MCD) ..... PEPAG
Physical Electronics Facility (MCD) ..... PEF
Physical, Emotional, Mental, Safety [*Model for charting procedure*] [*Medicine*] ..... PEMS
Physical Engineer ..... Phys Eng
Physical Equipment Table ..... PET
Physical Estimation and Attraction Scales ..... PEAS
Physical Evaluation [*Medicine*] (MAE) ..... PE
Physical Evaluation Board [*Military*] ..... PEB
Physical Evaluation Board Hospital [*Military*] ..... PEBH
Physical Evaluation Board Liaison Officer [*Air Force*] (AFM) ..... PEBLO
Physical Examination ..... PE
Physical Examination (MAE) ..... PEx
Physical Examination ..... PHYSEXAM
Physical Examination ..... PX
Physical Examination Rate [*Military*] (AFM) ..... PER

Physical File System (IAA) .... PFS
Physical Fitness Index .... PFI
Physical Fitness Officer [*British military*] (DMA) .... PFO
Physical Fitness Test .... PFT
Physical Fitness Uniform [*Army*] (INF) .... PFU
Physical Habitat Simulation Model [*Ecology*] .... PHABSIM
Physical Input-Output [*Computer science*] (IAA) .... PIO
Physical Input-Output Control System [*Computer science*] (BUR) .... PIOCS
Physical Intrusion Detection System (DWSG) .... PIDS
Physical Inventory (NRCH) .... PI
Physical Inventory Taking (MHDB) .... PIT
Physical Jerks [*Exercise*] [*Slang British*] (DSUE) .... PJ's
Physical Logical Description (MHDI) .... PLD
Physical Master Tape (IAA) .... PMT
Physical Medicine [*Medical officer designation*] [*British*] .... P/M
Physical Medicine (CPH) .... Phys Med
Physical Medicine .... PM
Physical Medicine and Rehabilitation .... PM & R
Physical Medicine and Rehabilitation (AD) .... pm & r
Physical Medicine and Rehabilitation .... PM&R
Physical Medicine and Rehabilitation Service .... PMRS
Physical Medium Attachment [*Telecommunications*] (OSI) .... PMA
Physical Medium Attachment (NITA) .... PMA
Physical Medium Dependent [*Computer science*] .... PMD
Physical Medium Dependent Layer [*Telecommunications*] (OSI) .... PMD
Physical Memory Address .... PMA
Physical Memory Level .... PML
Physical Memory Manager [*Computer science*] (PCM) .... PMM
Physical, Mental, Social, Religious [*"Fourfold Life" symbol of American Youth Foundation*] .... PMSR
Physical Message Type [*Communications*] .... PMT
Physical Metallurgy Branch .... PMB
Physical Metallurgy Division, Energy, Mines and Resources Canada [*Division dela Metallurgie Physique, Energie, Mines et Ressources Canada*] **Ottawa, Ontari o** [*Library symbol National Library of Canada*] (NLC) .... OOMP
Physical Mock-Up .... PMU
Physical Mockup (AD) .... pmu
Physical Modelling Extension (NITA) .... PMX
Physical Movement of Spacecraft (SAA) .... PMOS
Physical Oceanographic Real-Time System (USDC) .... PORTS
Physical Oceanographic Real-Time System [*Marine science*] (OSRA) .... PORTS
Physical Organization Table (HGAA) .... POT
Physical Performance Evaluation System [*Army*] .... PPES
Physical Profile .... PP
Physical Profile (AD) .... pp
Physical Profile Serial Code [*Military*] .... PPSC
Physical Properties .... PP
Physical Properties (AD) .... pp
Physical Properties Laboratory [*Oklahoma State University*] [*Research center*] (RCD) .... PPL
Physical Property Data Service [*Institution of Chemical Engineers*] [*Databank*] [*Information service or system*] (IID) .... PPDS
Physical Quality of Life Index [*Overseas Development Council*] .... PQLI
Physical Readiness Program [*Navy*] (DNAB) .... PRP
Physical Readiness Training [*Army*] (INF) .... PRT
Physical Reconditioning Exercises [*Orthopedics*] (DAVI) .... PRE
Physical Record [*Computer science*] .... PHR
Physical Record [*Computer science*] .... PR
Physical Record Length [*Computer science*] (MHDI) .... PLENG
Physical Record Unit (NITA) .... PRU
Physical Research Unit (IAA) .... PRU
Physical Review Council [*DoD*] .... PRC
Physical Science (WDAA) .... PHYS SC
Physical Science for Nonscience Students .... PSNS
Physical Science Study Committee [*National Science Foundation*] .... PSSC
Physical Science Study Group .... PSSG
Physical Sciences .... PS
Physical Sciences and Engineering Library, McGill University, Montreal, Quebec [*Library symbol National Library of Canada*] (NLC) .... QMME
Physical Sciences Center .... PSC
Physical Sciences Committee [*Terminated, 1977*] [*NASA*] (EGAO) .... PSC
Physical Sciences Laboratory [*University of Wisconsin - Madison, New Mexico State University*] [*Research center*] .... PSL
Physical Sciences Laboratory [*Bethesda, MD*] [*National Institutes of Health*] (GRD) .... PSL
Physical Sciences Research Papers [*Air Force*] (MCD) .... PSRP
Physical Sciences Research Program [*North Carolina State University*] [*Research center*] (RCD) .... PSR
Physical Security (MCD) .... PHYSEC
Physical Security .... PS
Physical Security Equipment [*Army*] (RDA) .... PSE
Physical Security Equipment Agency [*Army*] .... PSEA
Physical Security Evaluation Procedure [*US Army Construction Engineering Research Laboratory*] (RDA) .... PSEP
Physical Security/Intrusion Detection System (MCD) .... PS/IDS
Physical Security/Pilferage Code (MCD) .... PSC
Physical Security / Pilferage Code .... PSPC
Physical Security Requirements Assessment Methodology [*Civil Engineering Research Laboratory*] [*Navy*] (RDA) .... PSRAM
Physical Security Subsystem .... PSS
Physical Self Maintenance Scale .... PSMS
Physical, Sensitivity, Intellectual [*Biorhythmics*] .... PSI
Physical Sequential (HGAA) .... PS
Physical Service Access Point [*Telecommunications*] (OSI) .... PhSAP
Physical Signalling (NITA) .... PLS
Physical Status [*Medicine*] .... PS
Physical Teardown (MCD) .... PT
Physical Teardown (MCD) .... PTD
Physical Teardown .... PTEAR
Physical Teardown and Evaluation (MCD) .... PT & E
Physical Teardown and Evaluation Review (MCD) .... PT & ER
Physical Teardown and Evaluation Review (MCD) .... PTER
Physical Teardown and Maintenance (MCD) .... PTM
Physical Teardown and Maintenance Allocation Review (MCD) .... PTEAR
Physical Teardown and Maintenance Evaluation [*Army*] .... PT & ME
Physical Teardown - Logistics Demonstration (MCD) .... PT-LD
Physical Therapist (DMAA) .... Phys Ther
Physical Therapist .... PT
Physical Therapist in Independent Practice (GFGA) .... PTIP
Physical Therapist Technician .... PTT
Physical Therapy (AABC) .... PHYSTER
Physical Therapy [*or Therapist*] .... PT
Physical Therapy Assistant .... PTA
Physical Therapy Doctor .... PhTD
Physical Therapy Technician [*Navy*] .... PHT
Physical Training [*Military*] .... PT
Physical Training and Welfare [*British military*] (DMA) .... PT & W
Physical Training Instructor [*British*] .... PTI
Physical Transaction Block .... PTB
Physical Unit [*Computer science*] (IBMDP) .... PU
Physical Unit Block [*Computer science*] .... PUB
Physical Unit Directory [*Computer science*] (MHDI) .... PUD
Physical Unit of Information [*Computer science*] (IAA) .... PUI
Physical Vapor Deposition [*Coating technology*] .... PVD
Physical Vapor Transport [*Materials processing*] .... PVT
Physical Vapor Transport of Organic Solutions [*Materials processing*] .... PVTOS
Physical Vulnerability [*Number*] (NATG) .... PV
Physical Vulnerability Data Sheets (MCD) .... PVDS
Physical Vulnerability Division [*Air Force*] .... PVD
Physical Vulnerability Technical Memorandum (MCD) .... PVTM
Physical Work Capacity .... PWC
Physical Year .... PY
Physical-Chemical System (SAA) .... PCS
Physically Controlled Space [*Military*] (GFGA) .... PCS
Physically Dangerous (DNAB) .... PHDAN
Physically Handicapped (OICC) .... PH
Physically Handicapped and Able Bodied [*Charitable organization*] [*British*] .... PHAB
Physically Handicapped in Science (BABM) .... PHIS
Physically Handicapped in Science (DAVI) .... PHIS
Physically Impaired .... PI
Physically or Otherwise Health Impaired .... POHI
Physically Qualified .... PQ
Physically Qualified Except .... PQX
Physically Restricted Status [*Military*] .... PRS
Physically-Challenged Assistance Program [*Chrysler Motors Corp.*] [*Detroit, MI*] [*Information service or system*] (IID) .... P-CAP
Physical-Technical Institute [*Former USSR*] .... PTI
Physican Reviewer (MEDA) .... PR
Physician .... PHY
Physician .... PHYS
Physician .... PHYS
Physician .... PHYSN
Physician Advisor (HCT) .... PA
Physician and Sports Medicine [*A publication*] .... PSM
Physician Computer Network [*NASDAQ symbol*] (SPSG) .... PCNI
Physician Computer Ntwk [*NASDAQ symbol*] (TTSB) .... PCNI
Physician Corp. of Amer [*NASDAQ symbol*] (TTSB) .... PCAM
Physician Corp. of America [*NASDAQ symbol*] (SAG) .... PCAM
Physician Corp. of America [*Associated Press*] (SAG) .... PhysCpA
Physician Insurers Association of America .... PIAA
Physician of Record (DAVI) .... POR
Physician Payment Reform .... PPR
Physician Payment Review Commission .... PPRC
Physician Practice Management .... PPM
Physician Relations Department (DMAA) .... PRD
Physician Reliance Network [*NASDAQ symbol*] (TTSB) .... PHYN
Physician Reliance Network, Inc. [*NASDAQ symbol*] (SAG) .... PHYN
Physician Reliance Network, Inc. [*Associated Press*] (SAG) .... PhysRel
Physician Reservists in Medical Universities and Schools [*Military*] .... PRIMUS
Physician Resources Group, Inc. [*Associated Press*] (SAG) .... PhysRs
Physician Resources Group, Inc. [*NYSE symbol*] (SAG) .... PRG
Physician Sales & Service [*NASDAQ symbol*] (TTSB) .... PSSI
Physician Sales & Service, Inc. [*Associated Press*] (SAG) .... PhySale
Physician Sales & Service, Inc. [*NASDAQ symbol*] (SAG) .... PSSI
Physician Support Systems [*NASDAQ symbol*] (TTSB) .... PHSS
Physician Support Systems, Inc. [*NASDAQ symbol*] (SAG) .... PHSS
Physician Support Systems, Inc. [*Associated Press*] (SAG) .... PhysSup
Physician Task Force on Hunger in America [*Defunct*] (EA) .... PTFHA
Physician-Assisted Suicide .... PAS
Physician-Hospital Organization .... PHO
Physician-Hospital Organization [*Information service or system*] (HCT) .... PHO
Physician-Owned Laboratory (HCT) .... POL
Physicians Against the Death Penalty (EA) .... PADP
Physicians and Surgeons (DAVI) .... P & S
Physician's Assistant .... PA
Physician's Assistant-Certified (WGA) .... PA-C
Physicians Association for Anthroposophical Medicine (EA) .... PAAM
Physicians Committee for Responsible Medicine (EA) .... PCRM

Physicians Communications Service [*Fisher-Stevens, Inc.*] [*Merged into BRS/COLLEAGUE*] ... PHYCOM
Physicians Computer Network [*NASDAQ symbol*] (SAG) ... PCNI
Physicians Computer Network [*Associated Press*] (SAG) ... PhyCpt
Physicians' Continued Competence Assessment Program [*Medicine*] (DMAA) ... PCCAP
Physicians Corp. of America (ECON) ... PCA
Physician's Current Procedural Terminology ... CPT
Physician's Data Query [*NIH*] ... PDQ
Physicians Data Query: Cancer Information File [*Database*] ... PDQC
Physicians Data Query: Directory File [*Database*] ... PDQD
Physicians Data Query: Protocol File [*Database*] ... PDQP
Physicians' Desk Reference [*Also, an information service or system A publication*] ... PDR
Physicians Education Network (EA) ... PEN
Physicians Equity Services ... PES
Physicians for a Violence-Free Society ... PVFS
Physicians for Automotive Safety [*Defunct*] (EA) ... PAS
Physicians for Choice (EA) ... PFC
Physicians for Human Rights (EA) ... PHR
Physicians for Research in Cost-Effectiveness (EA) ... PRICE
Physicians for Social Responsibility (EA) ... PSR
Physicians for the Prevention of Nuclear War (NADA) ... PPNW
Physicians for the Prevention of Nuclear War (AD) ... PPNW
Physicians Forum (EA) ... PF
Physician's Health Plan ... PHP
Physicians Health Services ... PHS
Physicians Health Services, Inc. [*NASDAQ symbol*] (SAG) ... PHSV
Physicians Health Services, Inc. [*Associated Press*] (SAG) ... PhysicHlt
Physicians' Health Study ... PHS
Physicians Health Svcs'A' [*NASDAQ symbol*] (TTSB) ... PHSV
Physicians Insur Ohio [*NASDAQ symbol*] (TTSB) ... PICOA
Physicians Insurance Co. of Ohio [*Associated Press*] (SAG) ... PhysIn
Physicians Insurance Co. of Ohio [*NASDAQ symbol*] (NQ) ... PICO
Physicians Insurance Medical Co. (BABM) ... PIMCO
Physicians Insurance Medical Co. (DAVI) ... PIMCO
Physician's Journal Update [*Television program*] ... PJU
Physicians National Housestaff Association [*Defunct*] ... PNHA
Physician's Office laboratory ... POL
Physician's Payment Review Commission (HCT) ... PhysPRC
Physician's Payment Review Commission ... PhysPRC
Physician's Questionnaire (AAMN) ... PQ
Physicians Radio Network ... PRN
Physicians Resource Group [*NYSE symbol*] (TTSB) ... PRG
Physicians Who Care (EA) ... PWC
Physicians's Corporation [*Medicine*] (DMAA) ... PC
Physicist ... Fis
Physicist [*or Physics*] (ADA) ... PHYS
Physicist ... PHYST
Physicochemical Hydrodynamics [*A publication*] ... PCH
Physico-Chemical Measurements Unit [*British*] ... PCMU
Physics [*Secondary school course*] [*British*] ... P
Physics ... PHY
Physics (DD) ... Phys
Physics Abstracts [*Institution of Electrical Engineers*] [*Information service or system A publication*] (CRD) ... PA
Physics Achievement Test ... PAT
Physics and Astronomy Classification Scheme ... PACS
Physics and Astronomy Programs [*NASA*] ... PAP
Physics and Chemistry Experiment ... PACE
Physics Briefs [*Physikalische Berichte*] [*American Institute of Physics Database*] [*Information service or system*] (IID) ... PB
Physics Department ... PD
Physics, Engineering, and Chemistry (AAG) ... PEC
Physics International ... PI
Physics of Control (IAA) ... POC
Physics of Failure in Electronics [*A publication*] (MCD) ... PFE
Physics Online Information System [*Computer science*] (PDAA) ... PHYLIS
Physics Post-Doctoral Information Pool [*American Institute of Physics*] (PDAA) ... PPIP
Physics Today [*A publication*] (BRI) ... Phys Today
Physikalisch Technische Bundesanstalt (ACII) ... PTB
Physikalisch-Technische Reichsanstalt ... PTR
Physikalisch-Technische-Werkstatten [*Roentgenology*] ... PTW
Physio-Control, Information Center, Redmond, WA [*Library symbol*] [*Library of Congress*] (LCLS) ... WaRedPC
Physio-Control Intl [*NASDAQ symbol*] (TTSB) ... PHYS
Physiognomonica [*of Aristotle*] [*Classical studies*] (OCD) ... Phgn
Physiognomy [*Slang*] (DSUE) ... PHYSIOG
Physiognomy [*Slang*] (DSUE) ... PHYSOG
Physiographic ... PHYSIOG
Physiologic Dead Space in Percent of Tidal Volume [*Medicine*] (DAVI) ... V_DV_T
Physiologic Rest Position [*Medicine*] (DMAA) ... PRP
Physiologic Shunt Flow [*Total venous admixture*] [*Medicine*] (DAVI) ... Qsp
Physiological ... PHYL
Physiological (MSA) ... PHYSIOL
Physiological (AFM) ... PHYSL
Physiological Aging Rate ... PAR
Physiological and Psychological Effects of NBC [*Nuclear, Biological, and Chemical Warfare*] **and Extended Operations** [*Army study project*] (INF) ... P^{2NBC2}
Physiological Data Monitor ... PDM
Physiological Data Monitoring System ... PDMS
Physiological Ecology ... PE
Physiological Evaluation of Primates ... PEP
Physiological Flow Model [*For simulating medical conditions*] ... PFM
Physiological Full Value ... PFV
Physiological Hyaluronidase Inhibitor [*Biochemistry*] ... PHI
Physiological Learning Aptitude (KSC) ... PLA
Physiological Measurement Group ... PMG
Physiological Monitoring System (SAA) ... PMS
Physiological Research Laboratories [*University of California at San Diego*] [*Research center*] ... PRL
Physiological Saline [*Pharmacology*] (DAVI) ... PhyS
Physiological Saline Solution [*Physiology*] ... PSS
Physiological Simulation Benchmark Experiment ... PHYSBE
Physiological Training Flight [*Air Force*] ... PHGLTF
Physiological Workload Index [*Aviation*] ... PWI
Physiologically Active Polyunsaturated Fatty Acid [*Nutrition*] ... PAPUFA
Physiologically Based Pharmacokinetics [*Biochemistry*] ... PBPK
Physiology [*Medical Officer designation*] [*British*] ... P
Physiology (DMAA) ... PHY
Physiology ... PHYS
Physiology (DAVI) ... Physio
Physiology (ROG) ... PHYSIOL
Physiology ... PHYSY
Physiology and Biomedical Engineering [*Program*] (DAVI) ... PBME
Physiology and Biomedical Engineering Program (BABM) ... PBME
Physiology of Chimpanzees in Orbit [*NASA*] ... POCO
Physiometrix, Inc. [*Associated Press*] (SAG) ... Physmet
Physiometrix, Inc. [*NASDAQ symbol*] (SAG) ... PHYX
Physiometrix Inc. [*NASDAQ symbol*] (TTSB) ... PHYX
Physiotherapists Board [*Australian Capital Territory*] ... PB
Physiotherapists' Board of Queensland [*Australia*] ... PBQ
Physiotherapists' Board of South Australia ... PBSA
Physiotherapists' Registration Board [*New South Wales, Australia*] ... PRB
Physiotherapists' Union of Employees [*Australia*] ... PUE
Physiotherapy [*Medicine*] ... PHYSIO
Physiotherapy [*Medicine*] (DMAA) ... physio
Physiotherapy [*Medicine*] ... PT
Physitest Normalise Canadien [*Canadian Standardized Test of Fitness - CSTF*] ... PNC
Physocyanin [*Biochemistry*] ... PC
Phytane [*Organic chemistry*] ... Ph
Phytoalexin [*Plant pathology*] ... PA
Phytochemical Society of Europe (EA) ... PSE
Phytochemical Society of North America (EA) ... PSNA
Phytogeography (BARN) ... Phytogeog
Phytohemagglutinin [*Immunology*] ... PHA
Phytohemagglutinin [*Immunology*] (AAMN) ... PHY
Phytohemagglutinin Antigen [*A skin test for cellular based immunity*] (DAVI) ... PHA
Phytohemagglutinin M [*Immunology*] (MAE) ... PHA-M
Phytohemagglutinin Stimulated Leukocyte Conditioned Medium ... PHALCM
Phytohemagglutinin-Stimulated Lymphocyte [*Medicine*] (DMAA) ... PHAL
Phytopathology ... PHYTOPATH
Phytophthora [*A fungus*] ... P
Phytophthora Cinnamoni [*A fungus*] ... PC
Phytophthora Citricola [*A fungus*] ... Pci
Phytophthora Megasperma F. Sp. Glycinea [*A fungus*] ... PMG
Phytophthora Megasperma F.Sp Medicaginia [*A fungus*] ... PMM
Phytophthora Megasperma Glycinea [*A fungus*] ... Phg
Phytophthora Megasperma Var. Sojae [*A fungus*] ... PMS
Phytophthora Parasitica [*A fungus*] ... PP
Phytoplankton Biochemical Oxygen Demand [*Oceanography*] ... PBOD
Phytoplankton Dissolved Oxygen Deficit [*Oceanography*] ... PDOD
Phytylmenaquinone [*Vitamin K*] [*Also, K*] [*Biochemistry*] ... PMQ
Phytylmenaquinone (DMAA) ... PMQ
Pi Alpha Alpha (EA) ... PAA
PI Edit's Macro Language [*Iliad Group*] [*Computer science*] ... PML
Pi Kappa Alpha [*Fraternity*] ... PKA
Pi Kappa Delta [*Society*] ... PKD
Pi Kappa Lambda [*Society*] ... PKL
Pi Omicron National Sorority (EA) ... PIO
Pi Tau Sigma [*Society*] ... PTS
PIA Merchandising Services, Inc. [*Associated Press*] (SAG) ... PIA Mer
PIA Merchandising Services, Inc. [*NASDAQ symbol*] (SAG) ... PIAM
PIA Merchandising Svcs [*NASDAQ symbol*] (TTSB) ... PIAM
Pia Societas Missionum [*Fathers of the Pious Society of Missions, Pallottini*] [*Roman Catholic religious order*] ... PSM
Pia Societas Sancti Francisci Xaverii pro Exteris Missionibus [*St. Francis Xavier Foreign Mission Society*] [*Xaverian Missionary Fathers*] [*Roman Catholic religious order*] ... SX
Pia Zadora Fan Club (EA) ... PZFC
Piacenza [*Italy*] [*Seismograph station code, US Geological Survey Closed*] (SEIS) ... PCN
Piacenza/San Damiano [*Italy ICAO location identifier*] (ICLI) ... LIMS
Piae Memoriae [*Of Pious Memory*] [*Latin*] ... PM
Piagetian Logical Operations Test (EDAC) ... PLOT
Piaggio Rinaldo [*Industria Aeronautiche & Meccaniche SpA*] [*Italy ICAO aircraft manufacturer identifier*] (ICAO) ... P
Pian Rosa [*Italy ICAO location identifier*] (ICLI) ... LIMH
Piangendo [*Plaintive*] [*Music*] ... PIANG
Pianissimo [*Very Softly*] [*Music*] ... P
Pianissimo [*Very Softly*] [*Music*] ... PIANISS
Pianissimo [*Very Softly*] [*Music*] (ROG) ... PMO
Pianissimo [*Very Softly*] [*Italian*] [*Music*] (AD) ... pmo
Pianissimo [*Very Softly*] [*Music*] (ODBW) ... pp
Pianissimo [*Very Softly*] [*Music*] ... PP
Pianississimo [*As Softly As Possible*] [*Music*] ... PPP

Pianistic and Orchestral Orgasm [*Music*] (AD) .... p & oo
Pianists Foundation of America [*Defunct*] (EA) .... PFA
Piano [*Musical instrument*] .... P
Piano [*Softly*] [*Music*] .... P
Piano [*Softly*] [*Music*] .... PIA
Piano [*Music*] .... PNO
Piano (AD) .... pno
Piano .... PNO
Piano Manufacturers Association International (EA) .... PMAI
Piano Nobile (VRA) .... pn nb
Piano Technicians Guild (EA) .... PTG
Piano Trade Suppliers' Association [*British*] (BI) .... PTSA
Piano Type Hinge .... PH
Pianoforte [*Soft, then Loud*] [*Music*] .... PF
Pianoforte [*Soft, then Loud*] [*Music*] .... PFTE
Pianoforte Action Makers' Labour Protection Union [*British*] .... PAMLPU
Pianoforte, Harmonium, and American Organ Makers' Union [*British*] .... PHAOMU
Pianoforte Keymakers' Union [*British*] .... PKU
Pianoforte Manufacturers and Distributors Association [*British*] (DBA) .... PMDA
Pianoforte Manufacturers' Association Ltd. [*British*] (BI) .... PMA
Pianoforte Polishers' Trade Society [*A union*] [*British*] .... PPTS
Pianoforte Publicity Association [*British*] (BI) .... PPA
Pianoforte Tuners' Association [*British*] (DBA) .... PTA
Piano-Shaped Object .... PSO
Piarco, Trinidad [*Trinidad and Tobago*] [*ICAO location identifier*] (ICLI) .... TTZP
Piarist Fathers (TOCD) .... schp
Piarist Fathers (TOCD) .... SchP
Pias [*Peru*] [*ICAO location identifier*] (ICLI) .... SPIS
Piaster [*Monetary unit*] [*Spain, Republic of Vietnam, and some Middle Eastern countries*] .... P
Piaster [*Monetary unit*] [*Spain, Republic of Vietnam, and some Middle Eastern countries*] .... PA
Piaster [*Monetary unit*] [*Spain, Republic of Vietnam, and some Middle Eastern countries*] .... PI
Piaster [*Monetary unit*] [*Spain, Republic of Vietnam, and some Middle Eastern countries*] .... PIAS
Piaster [*Monetary unit*] [*Spain, Republic of Vietnam, and some Middle Eastern countries*] (IMH) .... PT
Piaster Expenditure Control Working Group [*Military*] .... PECWG
Piatt County Schools Film Library, Monticello, IL [*Library symbol*] [*Library of Congress*] (LCLS) .... IMontF
Piazza (VRA) .... pl
Pibor [*Sudan*] [*ICAO location identifier*] (ICLI) .... HSPI
Pic Heron Bay Band Public Library, Heron Bay, Ontario [*Library symbol National Library of Canada*] (BIB) .... OHBP
Pic Prospectors [*Vancouver Stock Exchange symbol*] .... PIK
Pica [*Typography*] (ADA) .... P
Pica [*Typography*] [*Also, P*] (WDMC) .... p
Pica [*Typography*] (WDMC) .... PC
Pica [*Typesetting*] [*Also called pie*] (WDMC) .... pi
Picatinny Arsenal [*New Jersey*] [*Later, Armament Development Center*] [*Army*] .... PA
Picatinny Arsenal [*New Jersey*] [*Later, Armament Development Center*] [*Army*] .... PTA
Picatinny Arsenal Detonation Trap Number 1 [*Army*] (AABC) PDT-1
Picatinny Research Center [*Picatinny Arsenal*] (AD) .... PRC
Picayune, MS [*Location identifier FAA*] (FAAL) .... PCU
Picayune, MS [*AM radio station call letters*] .... WRJW
Picayune, MS [*FM radio station call letters*] .... WZRH
Piccadilly Cafeterias [*NYSE symbol*] (TTSB) .... PIC
Piccadilly Cafeterias, Inc. [*NYSE symbol*] (SPSG) .... PIC
Piccadilly Cafeterias, Inc. [*Associated Press*] (SAG) .... PicCafe
Piccadilly Resources Ltd. [*Vancouver Stock Exchange symbol*] .... PDY
Piccadilly Saloon [*London*] (DSUE) .... PIC
Piccola Missione per il Sordomuti [*Little Mission for the Deaf-Mute - LMDM*] [*Rome, Italy*] (EAIO) .... PMS
Piccole Apostole della Carita [*Ponte Lambro, Italy*] (EAIO) .... PADC
Piccolo [*Music*] (ROG) .... PIC
Piccolo .... PICC
Pichincha [*Ecuador*] [*ICAO location identifier*] (ICLI) .... SEPI
Pick (IAA) .... P
Pick Inverse Voltage [*Electronics*] (ECII) .... PIV
Pick Off, Circuit .... POC
Pick Publishing Corporation, New York, NY [*Library symbol Library of Congress*] (LCLS) .... PpC
Pick Resources Guide [*ALLM Books*] [*England*] [*Information service or system*] (IID) .... PRG
Pick Resources Guide/International [*ALLM Books*] [*Information service or system*] (IID) .... PRG/I
Pick Up [*Business term*] .... PU
Pick Up and Delivery [*Business term*] .... P & D
Pick Up and Delivery [*Business term*] .... PU & D
Pick Up and Delivery [*Business term*] .... PUD
Pick Up Cargo (AFM) .... PC
Pick Up Zone [*Shipping*] .... PZ
Pick Your Own [*Fruits and vegetables*] (DSUE) .... PYO
Pickaway County District Public Library, Circleville, OH [*Library symbol Library of Congress*] (LCLS) .... OCirP
Picked Cold, Rolled, and Annealed [*Metallurgy*] (ROG) .... PCR & A
Picked Ports .... PP
Pickens County Library, Easley, SC [*Library symbol Library of Congress*] (LCLS) .... ScEa
Pickens, MS [*FM radio station call letters*] .... WLTD
Pickens, MS [*FM radio station call letters*] (RBYB) .... WYJS-FM
[*The*] **Pickens Railroad Co.** [*Later, PICK*] [*AAR code*] .... PIC
[*The*] **Pickens Railroad Co.** [*Formerly, PIC*] [*AAR code*] .... PICK
Pickens, SC [*Location identifier FAA*] (FAAL) .... LQK
Pickens, SC [*AM radio station call letters*] .... WTBI
Picker .... PKR
Pickering College, Newmarket, ON, Canada [*Library symbol*] [*Library of Congress*] (LCLS) .... CaONeP
Pickering College, Newmarket, Ontario [*Library symbol National Library of Canada*] (NLC) .... ONEP
Pickering Public Library, Ontario [*Library symbol National Library of Canada*] (NLC) .... OPIC
Pickering Public Library, Pickering, ON, Canada [*Library symbol Library of Congress*] (LCLS) .... CaOPic
Pickering's English Statutes [*A publication*] (DLA) .... Pick Stat
Pickering's Massachusetts Reports [*18-41 Massachusetts*] [*A publication*] (DLA) .... P
Pickering's Massachusetts Reports [*18-41 Massachusetts*] [*A publication*] (DLA) .... Pick (Mass)
Pickering's Massachusetts Supreme Judicial Court Reports [*1822-39*] [*A publication*] (DLA) .... Pick
Picket Boat [*Navy*] .... PB
Picket Ships [*Navy*] .... PS
Pickford, MI [*FM radio station call letters*] .... WADW
Pickford Projective Pictures [*Psychology*] .... PPP
Pickle Lake [*Canada*] [*Airport symbol*] (OAG) .... YPL
Pickle Lake, ON [*FM radio station call letters*] .... CBQP
Pickle Lake, ON [*ICAO location identifier*] (ICLI) .... CYPL
Pickle Packers International (EA) .... PPI
Pickle Pat Public Library, Pickle Lake, Ontario [*Library symbol National Library of Canada*] (NLC) .... OPLP
Pickled and Oiled .... P & O
Pickled and Oiled (AD) .... p & o
Pickled, Cold-Rolled, and Close-Annealed [*Metal*] .... PCRCA
Pickled-in-Jar [*Food technology*] .... PIJ
Pickles and Sauces Association [*British*] (DBA) .... PSA
Pickle's Reports [*85-108 Tennessee*] [*A publication*] (DLA) .... Pickle
Picknick Dam [*TVA*] .... PD
Pickpocket .... PP
Pickpocket (AD) .... pp
Pickpocket and Confidence [*Police term*] .... PP & C
Picks Per Inch [*Weaving*] (DICI) .... ppi
Pickup and Deposit .... P/D
Pick-Up Car .... PUC
Pickup Trucks, Vans, and Four-Wheel-Drive Vehicles [*Initialism used as title of a publication*] .... PV 4
Pick-Up Walker (MEDA) .... PUW
Pickup Zone [*Military*] (INF) .... PZ
Pickup-Zone Control Officer [*Military*] (INF) .... PZCO
Pickup-Zone Release Point .... PRP
Pickwick [*Refers to an inferior quality cigar*] (DSUE) .... PICK
Picnic Basket Porphyrin [*Organic chemistry*] .... PBP
Pico [*A prefix meaning divided by one trillion*] [*SI symbol*] .... p
Pico Glass Pellet .... PGP
PICO Holdings, Inc. [*NASDAQ symbol*] (SAG) .... PICO
PICO Holdings, Inc. [*Associated Press*] (SAG) .... PICO Hld
Pico Island [*Azores*] [*Airport symbol*] (OAG) .... PIX
Pico, Pico Island [*Portugal ICAO location identifier*] (ICLI) .... LPPI
Pico Products [*AMEX symbol*] (TTSB) .... PPI
Pico Products, Inc. [*Associated Press*] (SAG) .... PicoPd
Pico Products, Inc. [*AMEX symbol*] (SPSG) .... PPI
Pico Resources [*Vancouver Stock Exchange symbol*] .... POS
Pico Ribonucleic Acid Virus .... PICORNAVIRUS
Picoampere [*One trillionth of an ampere*] .... pA
Picocoulomb [*One trillionth of a coulomb*] .... pC
Picocurie [*Also, pCi*] [*One trillionth of a curie*] .... pC
Picocurie (IDOE) .... pc
Picocurie [*Also, pC*] [*One trillionth of a curie*] .... pCi
Picocuries per Liter [*Measure of radioactivity*] .... pCi/L
Picofarad .... pF
Picofarad (MDG) .... PUFF
Picogram [*Measurement*] (DAVI) .... pcg
Picogram [*One trillionth of a gram*] .... pg
Picohenry [*One trillionth of a henry*] .... PH
Picojoule [*Logic gate efficiency measure*] (MDG) .... PJ
Picolinaldehyde Nicotinoylhydrazone [*Reagent*] .... PANH
Picoliter [*One trillionth of a liter*] (MAE) .... pl
Picom Insurance [*NASDAQ symbol*] (TTSB) .... PICM
PICOM Insurance Co. [*NASDAQ symbol*] (SAG) .... PICM
PICOM Insurance Co. [*Associated Press*] (SAG) .... PICOM
Picometer [*One trillionth of a meter*] .... pm
Picomole [*One trillionth of a mole*] (WGA) .... pmol
Picomole [*One trillionth of a mole*] (DAVI) .... pmole
Picomoler [*One trillionth of a mole*] (AAMN) .... pM
Piconewton [*Unit of force*] .... pN
Picopicogram [*One trillionth of one trillionth of a gram*] .... PPG
Picos [*Brazil*] [*Airport symbol*] (AD) .... PIC
Picosecond [*One trillionth of a second*] .... ps
Picosecond [*One trillionth of a second*] .... PSEC
Picosecond [*Alternative of preferred ps*] (IDOE) .... psec
Picot [*Crochet*] (ROG) .... P
Picota [*Peru*] [*ICAO location identifier*] (ICLI) .... SPAP
Picovolt (IDOE) .... pV
Picowatt .... pW
Picowatt Power (CET) .... PWP
Picowatt Psophometric (IAA) .... PWP
Picowatts, Psophometrically Weighted .... pWp

Picowatts, Psophometrically Weighted at a Point of Zero Reference Level ... pW0p
Picric Acid Turbidity Test ... PAT
Picroindigocarmine-Nuclear Fast Red [*A biological stain*] ... PIC-NF
Picrotoxin [*Biochemistry*] ... Pic
Picrotoxin [*Biochemistry*] ... PTX
Picrylated Guinea Pig Albumin [*Immunochemistry*] ... PicGPA
Pictograph (VRA) ... pictg
Pictographic Self-Rating Scale [*Psychology*] (AEBS) ... PSRS
Picton Gazette, Ontario [*Library symbol National Library of Canada*] (NLC) ... OPIG
Picton Gazette, Picton, ON, Canada [*Library symbol Library of Congress*] (LCLS) ... CaOPiG
Picton Public Library, Ontario [*Library symbol National Library of Canada*] (NLC) ... OPI
Pictor [*Constellation*] ... Pic
Pictor [*Constellation*] ... Pict
Pictorial (WDAA) ... PIC
Pictorial (ROG) ... PICT
Pictorial and Artifact Retrieval and Information System [*Canadian Heritage Information Network*] [*Information service or system*] ... PARIS
Pictorial Cancellation Society [*Defunct*] (EA) ... PCS
Pictorial Deviation Indicator (AAG) ... PDI
Pictorial Dictionary of Ancient Rome [*A publication*] (OCD) ... Pict Dict Rome
Pictorial Display (MCD) ... PD
Pictorial Eleven [*Later, PES*] [*An association*] (EA) ... PE
Pictorial Eleven Society [*Formerly, PE*] [*PCS*] [*Absorbed by*] (EA) ... PES
Pictorial Encoding Language [*Computer science*] (IEEE) ... PENCIL
Pictorial End-Papers [*Publishing*] ... PEP
Pictorial Engineering and Research Laboratory ... PERL
Pictorial Information Digitizer [*Computer science*] (DIT) ... PID
Pictorial Navigation Display (OA) ... PND
Pictorial Navigation Indicator [*Aviation*] (DA) ... PNI
Pictorial Photographers of America (EAIO) ... PPA
Pictorial Position Indicator ... PPI
Pictorial Reasoning Test [*Job screening test*] ... PRT
Pictorial Study of Values [*Psychology*] ... PSV
Pictorial Test of Intelligence [*Education*] ... PTI
Pictorialized Scatter Diagram [*Botany*] ... PSD
Pictou Advocate, Nova Scotia [*Library symbol National Library of Canada*] (NLC) ... NSPA
Pictou Advocate, Pictou, NS, Canada [*Library symbol*] [*Library of Congress*] (LCLS) ... CaNSPA
Pictou Regional Vocational School, Nova Scotia [*Library symbol National Library of Canada*] (NLC) ... NSPRV
Pictou Regional Vocational School, St. John's, NF, Canada [*Library symbol Library of Congress*] (LCLS) ... CaNfSPRV
Pictou-Antigonish Regional Library, New Glasgow, Nova Scotia [*Library symbol National Library of Canada*] (NLC) ... NSNGP
Pictou-Antigonish Regional Library, New Glasgow, NS, Canada [*Library symbol Library of Congress*] (LCLS) ... CaNSNgP
Picture (MDG) ... PC
Picture ... PCT
Picture (AABC) ... PIC
Picture ... PIC
Picture ... PIX
Picture Agency Council of America (EA) ... PACA
Picture Algorithms-Subroutine Orientated (NITA) ... PICASO
Picture and Frame Institute [*Defunct*] (EA) ... PFI
Picture and Resume [*Theatre slang*] ... P & R
Picture and Sound World Organization ... PSWO
Picture Animal Top Star of the Year [*or Performing Animal Television Star of the Year*] [*American Humane Association award*] ... PATSY
Picture Archival and Communication System ... PACS
Picture Archiving and Communication System Data Base (DMAA) ... PACS DB
Picture Arrangement Test ... PAT
Picture Articulation and Screening Test ... PALST
Picture Building System (NITA) ... PBS
Picture Butte Public Library, Alberta [*Library symbol National Library of Canada*] (NLC) ... APB
Picture Control Oscilloscope (IAA) ... PCO
Picture Description Instruction [*Telecommunications*] ... PDI
Picture Description Language [*Computer science*] (MHDI) ... PDL
Picture Description Test (PDAA) ... PDT
Picture Element [*Single element of resolution in image processing*] (IBMDP) ... PEL
Picture Element [*Single element of resolution in image processing*] ... PIXEL
Picture File [*Computer science*] ... pcs
Picture File Format [*Computer science*] (BTTJ) ... PIC
Picture File Format [*Computer science*] (BTTJ) ... PICT
Picture Frustration [*Study*] (MAE) ... PF
Picture Identification Test [*Psychology*] ... PIT
Picture Impressions Test [*Psychology*] ... PIT
Picture Interactive Computer System (IAA) ... PIC
Picture Level Benchmark [*Computer science*] (CDE) ... PLB
Picture Line-Up Generator [*Television*] ... PLUGE
Picture Netwok International, Ltd. ... PNI
Picture Network International [*Commercial firm Information service or system*] ... PNI
Picture Object Table (MHDI) ... POT
Picture Peace [*Defunct*] (EA) ... PP
Picture per Second (IAA) ... PICSEC
Picture Personality Test for Indian South Africans ... PPT-ISA
Picture Postcard ... PPC
Picture Postcard (AD) ... ppc
Picture Ratio (IAA) ... PR
Picture Rocks, PA [*Location identifier FAA*] (FAAL) ... PIX
Picture Story Language Test ... PSLT
Picture Story Test Blank [*Psychology*] ... PSTB
Picture System 2 [*Evans & Sutherland Computer Corp.*] (MCD) ... PS2
Picture Tel Corp. [*NASDAQ symbol*] (TTSB) ... PCTL
Picture Telegraphy [*Telecommunications*] (IAA) ... PT
Picture Telephone [*Telecommunications*] (EECA) ... PICTEL
Picture Vocational Interest Questionnaire for Adults [*Vocational guidance test*] ... PVI
Picture World Test [*Psychology*] ... PWT
Picture-by-Picture [*Television technology*] (PS) ... PBP
Pictured Rocks National Lakeshore [*National Park Service designation*] ... PIRO
Picture-in-a-Picture [*Multi-Vision Products*] [*Video technology*] ... PIP
Picture-outside-Picture [*Television technology*] (PS) ... POP
Picturephone Meeting Service [*AT & T*] ... PMS
Pictures [*Slang*] (WDMC) ... pic
Pictures of Specific Syndromes and Unknown Malformations [*Database*] ... POSSUM
Pictures per Minute (NTCM) ... PPM
Pictures per Second (WDAA) ... PPS
Pictures Per Second (AD) ... pps
PictureTel Corp. [*NASDAQ symbol*] (NQ) ... PCTL
PictureTel Corp. [*Associated Press*] (SAG) ... PicTel
Pie ... P
Pie De Palo [*Argentina*] [*Seismograph station code, US Geological Survey*] (SEIS) ... PPA
Pie Filling Institute [*Defunct*] (EA) ... PFI
Pie Zeses [*May You Live Piously*] [*Italian*] ... PZ
Piebald ... PB
Piece (AAG) ... PC
Piece (VRA) ... pc
Piece [*Numismatics*] ... PCE
Piece Goods Buyers Association [*Defunct*] (EA) ... PGBA
Piece Identification Number ... PIN
Piece Mark ... PCMK
Piece of Data [*Computer science*] (NHD) ... POD
Piece Part Specification (MCD) ... PPS
Pieces ... PCS
Piece-Wise Application of Radiation through the Electromagnetic-Pulse Simulator (PDAA) ... PARTES
Piecewise Markov Process (PDAA) ... PMP
Piecewise Parabolic Method [*Mathematical model of fluid flow*] ... PPM
Piecewise-Linear (IAA) ... PWI
Piecewise-Linear ... PWL
Piecewise-Sinusoidal Reaction Matching Technique [*Antenna*] [*Navy*] ... PSRMT
Piecework Linear ... PWL
Pied [*Foot*] [*French*] ... P
Pied Carre [*Square Foot*] [*French*] ... pc
Pied Cube [*Cubic Foot*] [*French*] ... pc
Piedmont ... PDMNT
Piedmont Airlines, Inc. [*ICAO designator*] (FAAC) ... PDT
Piedmont, AL [*AM radio station call letters*] ... WPID
Piedmont and Northern Railroad (AD) ... P & N
Piedmont & Northern Railway Co. [*AAR code*] ... PN
Piedmont Aviation, Inc. [*Air carrier designation symbol*] ... PAI
Piedmont Aviation, Inc. [*ICAO designator*] (OAG) ... PI
Piedmont Bancgroup [*Associated Press*] (SAG) ... PiedBGp
Piedmont Bancorp [*AMEX symbol*] (TTSB) ... PDB
Piedmont Bancorp, Inc. [*AMEX symbol*] (SAG) ... PDB
Piedmont Bancorp, Inc. [*Associated Press*] (SAG) ... PiedBcp
Piedmont Bancorp, Inc. [*Associated Press*] (SAG) ... PiedmBc
Piedmont BankGroup, Inc. [*NASDAQ symbol*] (NQ) ... PBGI
Piedmont College, Demorest, GA [*Library symbol Library of Congress*] (LCLS) ... GDemP
Piedmont Elementary School, Duluth, MN [*Library symbol*] [*Library of Congress*] (LCLS) ... MnDuPE
Piedmont Health Survey of the Elderly [*Department of Health and Human Services*] (GFGA) ... PHSE
Piedmont Hospital, Atlanta, GA [*Library symbol Library of Congress*] (LCLS) ... GAPie
Piedmont Management Co., Inc. [*NASDAQ symbol*] (NQ) ... PMAN
Piedmont Managment Co., Inc. [*Associated Press*] (SAG) ... PiedMg
Piedmont Mining Co., Inc. [*NASDAQ symbol*] (NQ) ... PIED
Piedmont Mining Co., Inc. [*Associated Press*] (SAG) ... PiedMn
Piedmont, MO [*AM radio station call letters*] ... KPWB
Piedmont, MO [*FM radio station call letters*] ... KPWB-FM
Piedmont National Wildlife Refuge [*Georgia*] (AD) ... PNWR
Piedmont Natl Gas [*NYSE symbol*] (TTSB) ... PNY
Piedmont Natural Gas Co., Inc. [*Associated Press*] (SAG) ... PiedNG
Piedmont Natural Gas Co., Inc. [*NYSE symbol*] (SPSG) ... PNY
Piedmont Technical College, Greenwood, SC [*Library symbol Library of Congress*] (LCLS) ... ScGrwP
Piedmont Technical College, Greenwood, SC [*OCLC symbol*] (OCLC) ... SPT
Piedmont Triad International Airport [*FAA*] (TAG) ... GSO
Piedmont Triad Library Council [*Library network*] ... PTLC
Piedmont Virginia Community College, Learning Resources Center, Charlottesville,VA [*Library symbol Library of Congress*] (LCLS) ... ViCP
Piedmonte Foods [*NASDAQ symbol*] (TTSB) ... PIFI
Piedmontese Association of the United States (EA) ... PAUS
Piedra Del Aguila [*Argentina ICAO location identifier*] (ICLI) ... SAVA
Piedras Negras [*Mexico ICAO location identifier*] (ICLI) ... MMPG
Piedras Negras [*Mexico*] [*Airport symbol*] (AD) ... PDS
Pieksamaki [*Finland ICAO location identifier*] (ICLI) ... EFPK
Pielago [*Ship's rigging*] (ROG) ... PIO
Piemonte Foods, Inc. [*Associated Press*] (SAG) ... Piemnt
Piemonte Foods, Inc. [*NASDAQ symbol*] (NQ) ... PIFI

Piena Pelle [*Full Leather*] [*Italian*] (AD) .... pp
Pier 1 Imports [*NYSE symbol*] (SPSG) .... PIR
Pier 1 Imports, Inc. [*Associated Press*] (SAG) .... Pier 1
Pier and Span Junction Set (MCD) .... PSJS
Pier to House [*Classified advertising*] (ADA) .... P/H
Pier to Pier (ADA) .... P/P
Pierce (MSA) .... PRC
Pierce Bland and Form Die (MSA) .... PBFD
Pierce Brosnan Fan Club (EA) .... PBFC
Pierce County Law Library, Tacoma, WA [*Library symbol*] [*Library of Congress*] (LCLS) .... WaTPL
Pierce County Library, Tacoma, WA [*Library symbol Library of Congress*] (LCLS) .... WaTPC
Pierce County Medical Library, Tacoma, WA [*Library symbol Library of Congress*] (LCLS) .... WaTPM
Pierce Die .... PCDI
Pierce District Library, Pierce, ID [*Library symbol*] [*Library of Congress*] (LCLS) .... IdPi
Pierce Elementary School, Pierce, ID [*Library symbol*] [*Library of Congress*] (LCLS) .... IdPiES
Pierce Ferry [*Arizona*] [*Seismograph station code, US Geological Survey Closed*] (SEIS) .... PFA
Pierce Mountain [*Vancouver Stock Exchange symbol*] .... PMU
Pierce on Railroad Law [*A publication*] (DLA) .... Pierce RR
Pierce Shell .... PCSH
Pierce Template .... PCTP
Pierce-Arrow Society (EA) .... PAS
Pierce-Blank Die (MCD) .... PBD
Pierce-Blank Die (Class B) (MCD) .... PBCB
Pierce-Blank Tool (MCD) .... PBT
Pierced [*Quilting*] .... P
Pierced Aluminum Plank [*Technical drawings*] .... PAP
Pierced Steel Planking [*Military*] .... PSP
Pierce's Disease [*Plant pathology*] .... PD
Pierce's Disease Bacterium [*Plant pathology*] .... PDB
Pierce's Perpetual Code [*1943*] [*A publication*] (DLA) .... PPC
Pierceton and Washington Township Library, Pierceton, IN [*Library symbol Library of Congress*] (LCLS) .... InPi
Piercing Pagoda [*NASDAQ symbol*] (TTSB) .... PGDA
Piercing Pagoda, Inc. [*NASDAQ symbol*] (SAG) .... PGDA
Piercing Pagoda, Inc. [*Associated Press*] (SAG) .... PiercPag
Pier-Harris Self-Concept Scale (EDAC) .... PHSCS
Piermont Public Library, Piermont, NY [*Library symbol Library of Congress*] (LCLS) .... NPie
Pierpont [*South Carolina*] [*Seismograph station code, US Geological Survey*] (SEIS) .... PPS
[*The*] **Pierpont Morgan Library** (BJA) .... PML
Pierpont Morgan Library, New York, NY [*Library symbol Library of Congress*] (LCLS) .... NNPM
Pierpont, SD [*FM radio station call letters*] .... KDSD
Pierre [*South Dakota*] [*Airport symbol*] (OAG) .... PIR
Pierre Allain [*Lightweight rock-climbing boot named after its designer*] .... PA
Pierre Arpels [*Jewelry designer*] .... PA
Pierre Cardin [*Fashion designer*] .... PC
Pierre de la Palu [*Deceased, 1342*] [*Authority cited in pre-1607 legal work*] (DSA) .... Pe de Pal
Pierre Elliott Trudeau [*Canadian prime minister*] [*Acronymic designation considered derogatory*] .... PET
Pierre Fauchard Academy (EA) .... PFA
Pierre, Rapid City & Northwestern Railroad [*Nickname: Plenty Rough Country and No Women*] .... PRC & NW
Pierre, SD [*AM radio station call letters*] .... KCCR
Pierre, SD [*AM radio station call letters*] .... KGFX
Pierre, SD [*FM radio station call letters*] .... KGFX-FM
Pierre, SD [*FM radio station call letters*] .... KLXS
Pierre, SD [*Television station call letters*] .... KPRY
Pierre, SD [*Television station call letters*] .... KTSD-TV
Pierrelatte [*France ICAO location identifier*] (ICLI) .... LFHD
Piers Plowman [*Middle English poem*] .... PP
Piers-Harris Children's Self-Concept Scale [*Child development test*] [*Psychology*] .... PHCSC
Pierson Press, Pierson, IA [*Library symbol Library of Congress*] (LCLS) .... IaPierP
Pierz Public Library, Pierz, MN [*Library symbol*] [*Library of Congress*] (LCLS) .... MnPi
Piestany [*Former Czechoslovakia*] [*ICAO location identifier*] (ICLI) .... LKPP
Piestany [*Former Czechoslovakia*] [*Airport symbol*] (OAG) .... PZY
Piet Retief [*South Africa*] [*ICAO location identifier*] (ICLI) .... FAPF
Pietas Tutissima Virtus [*Piety Is the Safest Virtue*] [*Motto of Ernst, Margrave of Brandenburg (1583-1613)*] [*Latin*] .... PTV
Pietermaritzburg [*South Africa*] [*ICAO location identifier*] (ICLI) .... FAPM
Pietermaritzburg [*South Africa*] [*Seismograph station code, US Geological Survey Closed*] (SEIS) .... PIE
Pietermaritzburg [*South Africa*] [*Airport symbol*] (AD) .... PTL
Pietermaritzburg [*South Africa*] [*Seismograph station code, US Geological Survey*] (SEIS) .... PTM
Pietermaritzburg [*South Africa*] [*Airport symbol*] (OAG) .... PZB
Pietersburg [*South Africa*] [*ICAO location identifier*] (ICLI) .... FAPB
Pietersburg [*South Africa*] [*ICAO location identifier*] (ICLI) .... FAPI
Pietersburg [*South Africa*] [*Airport symbol*] (OAG) .... PTG
Pieve Di Cadore [*Italy*] [*Seismograph station code, US Geological Survey Closed*] (SEIS) .... PDC
Pieze [*Unit of pressure*] .... pz
Piezo Resistive [*Automotive electronics*] .... PR
Piezoelectric .... PZE
Piezoelectric Field-Effect Transistor (PDAA) .... PI-FET
Piezoelectric Mount (IAA) .... PZM
Piezoelectric Power Generation .... PEPG
Piezoelectric Power Generation .... PPG
Piezoelectric Resonating Device .... PRD
Piezoelectric Transducer [*or Translator*] .... PZT
Piezoelectric Zirconate Titanate .... PZT
Piezoelectric-Crystal Unit (IEEE) .... CU
Piezoelectric-Oscillator Self-Tuned [*Electric system*] .... POST
Piezojunction Sensor .... PJS
Pig Health Control Association [*British*] .... PHCA
Pig Improvement Co. [*British*] (ECON) .... PIC
Pig Industry Consultative Group [*Queensland, Australia*] .... PICG
Pig Industry Development Authority [*British*] (BI) .... PIDA
Pig Iron .... PI
Pig Kidney [*Medicine*] (DMAA) .... PK
Pig Research and Development Corp. [*Australia*] .... PRDC
Pigeon (ADA) .... PGN
Pigeon Bay [*South Carolina*] [*Seismograph station code, US Geological Survey*] (SEIS) .... PBS
Pigeon District Library, Pigeon, MI [*Library symbol Library of Congress*] (LCLS) .... MiPi
Pigeon Trainer [*Navy*] .... PI
Piggott, AR [*FM radio station call letters*] (RBYB) .... KBOA
Piggyback (IAA) .... PB
Piggyback Experiment .... PBE
Piggyback Tape [*or Twistor*] [*Computer science*] .... PBT
Pigin Signed English .... PSE
Pigment (MSA) .... PGMT
Pigment (BARN) .... pig
Pigment Epithelium [*of the retina*] .... PE
Pigment Epithelium-Derived Factor [*Medicine*] (DMAA) .... PEDF
Pigment Volume .... PV
Pigment Volume Concentration .... PVC
Pigment-Binder Ratio [*Weight*] .... PBR
Pigmented Emulsified Creosote .... PEC
Pigmented Villonodular Synovitis [*Also, PVS*] [*Medicine*] .... PVNS
Pigmented Villonodular Synovitis [*Also, PVNS*] [*Medicine*] .... PVS
Pigmentum [*Paint*] [*Pharmacy*] .... PIGM
Pigott and Rodwell's English Registration Appeal Cases [*1843-45*] [*A publication*] (DLA) .... Pig & R
Pigott and Rodwell's Reports in Common Pleas [*1843-45*] [*A publication*] (DLA) .... P & R
Pigott's Common Recoveries [*3 eds.*] [*1739-92*] [*A publication*] (DLA) .... Pig
Pigott's Foreign Judgments [*3rd ed.*] [*1908-09*] [*A publication*] (DLA) ...... Pig Judg
Pigott's Recoveries [*England*] [*A publication*] (DLA) .... Pig Rec
Pigs (ROG) .... P
Pigtail (MSA) .... PGT
Pigue [*Argentina ICAO location identifier*] (ICLI) .... SAZE
Piikajarvi [*Finland ICAO location identifier*] (ICLI) .... EFPI
Piissimus [*Most Holy*] [*Latin*] .... PP
Pikangikum Band Library, Ontario [*Library symbol National Library of Canada*] (BIB) .... OPB
Pike [*Postal Service standard*] (OPSA) .... PIKE
Pike [*Commonly used*] (OPSA) .... PIKES
Pike .... PK
Pike and Eel [*A pub at Cambridge University*] [*British*] (DSUE) .... P & E
Pike and Fischer's Administrative Law [*A publication*] (DLA) .... P & F
Pike and Fischer's Administrative Law [*A publication*] (DLA) ..... Pike & F Adm Law
Pike and Fischer's Administrative Law [*A publication*] (DLA) .... Pike & Fischer Admin Law
Pike and Fischer's Administrative Law Reporter, Second Series [*A publication*] (DLA) .... Ad L 2d
Pike and Fischer's Administrative Law Reporter, Second Series [*A publication*] (ILCA) .... Ad L 2d(P & F)
Pike and Fischer's Federal Rules Service [*A publication*] (DLA) .... P & F
Pike and Fischer's Federal Rules Service [*A publication*] (DLA) .... Pike & F Fed Rules Service
Pike and Fischer's OPA Price Service [*A publication*] (DLA) .... P & F
Pike and Fischer's Radio Regulation Reporter [*A publication*] (DLA) .... P & F Radio Reg
Pike and Fischer's Radio Regulations [*A publication*] (DLA) .... RR
Pike County Free Public Library, Waverly, OH [*Library symbol Library of Congress*] (LCLS) .... OWaP
Pike Fry Rhabdovirus .... PFR
Pike-Amite Library System, McComb, MS [*Library symbol Library of Congress*] (LCLS) .... MsMc
Pike's History of the House of Lords [*A publication*] (DLA) .... Pike H of L
Pikes Peak Community College, Colorado Springs, CO [*Library symbol*] [*Library of Congress*] (LCLS) .... CoCEP
Pikes Peak Community College, Colorado Springs, CO [*OCLC symbol*] (OCLC) .... COE
Pikes Peak Library District [*Internationally recognized computerized library system*] .... PPLD
Pike's Reports [*1-5 Arkansas*] [*A publication*] (DLA) .... Pike
Piketon, OH [*FM radio station call letters*] (RBYB) .... WXZQ-FM
Pikeville College, Pikeville, KY [*Library symbol Library of Congress*] (LCLS) .... KyPikC
Pikeville, KY [*FM radio station call letters*] .... WDHR
Pikeville, KY [*FM radio station call letters*] .... WJSO
Pikeville, KY [*Television station call letters*] .... WKPI
Pikeville, KY [*AM radio station call letters*] .... WLSI
Pikeville, KY [*AM radio station call letters*] .... WPKE
Pikeville National [*NASDAQ symbol*] (TTSB) .... PKVL
Pikeville National Corp. [*Associated Press*] (SAG) .... Pikeville
Pikeville National Corp. [*NASDAQ symbol*] (NQ) .... PKVL

Pikeville, TN [*AM radio station call letters*] ..... WUAT
Pikunas Adult Stress Inventory [*Psychology*] ..... PASI
Pikunas Graphoscopic Scale [*Personality development test*] [*Psychology*] ..... PGS
Pikwitonei Granulite Domain [*Geology*] ..... PGD
Pilansberg [*South Africa*] [*ICAO location identifier*] (ICLI) ..... FAPN
Pilar [*Argentina*] [*Seismograph station code, US Geological Survey*] (SEIS) ..... PIL
Pilar [*Argentina ICAO location identifier*] (ICLI) ..... SACI
Pilar [*Paraguay*] [*ICAO location identifier*] (ICLI) ..... SGPI
Pilarcitos Creek [*California*] [*Seismograph station code, US Geological Survey*] (SEIS) ..... PCC
Pilaster [*Technical drawings*] ..... P
Pilaster (VRA) ..... pil
Pilatus Britten-Norman Ltd. [*British ICAO designator*] (FAAC) ..... PBN
Pilatus Flugzeugwerke AG [*Switzerland ICAO aircraft manufacturer identifier*] (ICAO) ..... PL
Pile ..... PL
Pile for Producing Power and Plutonium [*Nuclear energy*] (NRCH) ..... PIPPAP
Pilgrim Airlines [*ICAO designator*] (AD) ..... PM
Pilgrim Amer Bk & Thrift [*NYSE symbol*] (TTSB) ..... PBS
Pilgrim America Prime Rate Trust [*Associated Press*] (SAG) ..... PilgAPr
Pilgrim America Prime Rate Trust [*NYSE symbol*] (SAG) ..... PPR
Pilgrim America Prime Rt [*NYSE symbol*] (TTSB) ..... PPR
Pilgrim American Bank & Thrift Fund, Inc. [*NYSE symbol*] (SAG) ..... PBS
Pilgrim American Bank & Thrift Fund, Inc. [*Associated Press*] (SAG) ..... PilgAmer
Pilgrim Edward Doty Society (EA) ..... PEDS
Pilgrim Fellowship (EA) ..... PF
Pilgrim Holdings Ltd. [*Vancouver Stock Exchange symbol*] ..... PPI
Pilgrim Hospital, West Brentwood, NY [*Library symbol Library of Congress*] (LCLS) ..... NWebPH
Pilgrim Power Station (NRCH) ..... PS
Pilgrim Prime Rate Trust [*Associated Press*] (SAG) ..... PilgPrm
Pilgrim Prime Rate Trust [*NYSE symbol*] (SPSG) ..... PPR
Pilgrim Regional Banc Shares, Inc. [*Associated Press*] (SAG) ..... PilgRg
Pilgrim Regional Bank Shares, Inc. [*NYSE symbol*] (SPSG) ..... PBS
Pilgrim Society (EA) ..... PS
Pilgrim Society, Plymouth, MA [*Library symbol Library of Congress*] (LCLS) ..... MPIPS
Pilgrim's Pride [*NYSE symbol*] (TTSB) ..... CHX
Pilgrim's Pride Corp. [*NYSE symbol*] (SPSG) ..... CHX
Pilgrims Pride Corp. [*Associated Press*] (SAG) ..... PilgPr
[*The*] **Pilgrim's Progress** [*Bunyan*] (BARN) ..... Pilgr
Piling (MSA) ..... PLG
Pill Addicts Anonymous (EA) ..... PAA
Pill Box Antenna ..... PBA
Pill Counter [*Medicine*] (DMAA) ..... PC
Pillager Public School, Pillager, MN [*Library symbol*] [*Library of Congress*] (LCLS) ..... MnPilS
Pillar [*Buoy*] ..... P
Pillar (MSA) ..... PLR
Pillar of Fire Church (IIA) ..... POF
Pillared Interlayered Clays [*Catalysis technology*] ..... PILC
Pillared Interlayered Montmorillonite [*Catalysis technology*] ..... PILM
Pillars Bay [*Alaska*] [*Airport symbol*] (AD) ..... PBY
Pillius Medicinensis [*Flourished, 1165-1207*] [*Authority cited in pre-1607 legal work*] (DSA) ..... Pi
Pillius Medicinensis [*Flourished, 1165-1207*] [*Authority cited in pre-1607 legal work*] (DSA) ..... Pi M
Pillow Block ..... PLBLK
Pillowtex Corp. [*Associated Press*] (SAG) ..... Pilowtex
Pillowtex Corp. [*NYSE symbol*] (SPSG) ..... PTX
Pillowtex Corp. [*NYSE symbol*] (TTSB) ..... PTX
Pills Anonymous [*Later, DA*] [*An association*] (EA) ..... PA
Pillsbury Co., Minneapolis, MN [*Library symbol*] [*Library of Congress*] (LCLS) ..... MnMP
Pilon [*Cuba ICAO location identifier*] (ICLI) ..... MUPL
Pilot ..... P
Pilot (WGA) ..... PIL
Pilot (AFM) ..... PLT
Pilot Action Request ..... PAR
Pilot Aerial Survival System (PDAA) ..... PASS
Pilot Airborne Recovery Device [*A balloon-parachute*] ..... PARD
Pilot Approval [*Automotive project management*] ..... PA
Pilot Back Up Control ..... PIBOL
Pilot Back Up Control ..... PIBUC
Pilot Balloon Observation ..... PIBAL
Pilot Balloon Soundings ..... PIBALS
Pilot Boll Weevil Eradication Experiment [*Department of Agriculture*] ..... PBWEE
Pilot Butte Junior High School, Bend, OR [*Library symbol*] [*Library of Congress*] (LCLS) ..... OrBePJ
Pilot Bypass Filter (IAA) ..... PBF
Pilot Club International (EA) ..... PCI
Pilot Control and Display Panel ..... PCDP
Pilot Control Console ..... PCC
Pilot Control Panel ..... PCP
Pilot Control System (MCD) ..... PCS
Pilot Controlled Lighting (FAAC) ..... PCL
Pilot Controller Glossary [*Aviation*] (FAAC) ..... P/CG
Pilot Controller Integration (IEEE) ..... PCI
Pilot Decision Making [*Aviation*] (DA) ..... PDM
Pilot Direction Indicator [*Electronic communications*] ..... PDI
Pilot District Project [*Office of Economic Opportunity*] [*Defunct*] (EA) ..... PDP
Pilot Dogs (EA) ..... PD
Pilot Equalizer (IAA) ..... PE
Pilot Error ..... PE
Pilot Error Correction (IAA) ..... PEC
Pilot Flying (GAVI) ..... PF
Pilot Generator (IAA) ..... PG
Pilot Geriatric Arthritis Program [*Medicine*] (DMAA) ..... PGAP
Pilot Guide Dog Foundation (EA) ..... PGDF
Pilot House ..... PH
Pilot in Booster Loop (SAA) ..... PIBOL
Pilot in Command [*Navy*] (DOMA) ..... PIC
Pilot Indicator Unit [*Aviation*] (IAA) ..... PIU
Pilot Information Display Panel ..... PIDP
Pilot Information File [*Army*] ..... PIF
Pilot Information Office ..... PIO
Pilot Information Utilization ..... PIU
Pilot Instructor Training [*Aviation*] (FAAC) ..... PIT
Pilot International (EA) ..... PI
Pilot Item (MCD) ..... PI
Pilot Knob [*California*] [*Seismograph station code, US Geological Survey*] (SEIS) ..... PLT
Pilot Laboratories Corp. [*Vancouver Stock Exchange symbol*] ..... PLC
Pilot Landing Aid Television / Visual Landing Aid [*System*] (DNAB) ..... PLAT/VLA
Pilot Landing and Takeoff System (IIA) ..... PLATS
Pilot Light (MSA) ..... PLT LT
Pilot Location Indicator ..... PLI
Pilot Machine (NITA) ..... PIM
Pilot Make Busy (IEEE) ..... PMB
Pilot Map Display System ..... PMDS
Pilot Mortar Fire ..... PMF
Pilot Motor (MSA) ..... PM
Pilot Mount, MB [*ICAO location identifier*] (ICLI) ..... CWPO
Pilot Navigator (IAA) ..... PN
Pilot Night Vision System [*Army*] (MCD) ..... PNVS
Pilot Not Flying (GAVI) ..... PNF
Pilot Ocean Data System (MCD) ..... PODS
Pilot Officer (AD) ..... P/O
Pilot Officer [*British military*] (DMA) ..... Plt Off
Pilot Officer ..... PO
Pilot on Board (AD) ..... pob
Pilot Operational Equipment (MCD) ..... POE
Pilot Opinion Rating ..... POR
Pilot Overhaul Provisioning Review ..... POPR
Pilot Overhaul Provisioning Review (AD) ..... popr
Pilot Parachute Mortar Pyrotechnic Cartridge (SAA) ..... PPMPC
Pilot Parents (EA) ..... PP
Pilot Performance Description Record ..... PPDR
Pilot Performance Evaluation System [*Air Force*] ..... PPES
Pilot Plant Meat Irradiator ..... PPMI
Pilot Point [*Alaska*] [*Airport symbol*] (OAG) ..... PIP
Pilot Point, AK [*Location identifier FAA*] (FAAL) ..... UGB
Pilot, Pressure Regulator (MCD) ..... PPR
Pilot Production Model [*Military*] (CAAL) ..... PPM
Pilot Pulse Amplitude ..... PPA
Pilot Punch ..... PP
Pilot Qualified in Model (NVT) ..... PQM
Pilot Radiation Observation Experiment [*Marine science*] (OSRA) ..... PROBE
Pilot Radiation Observation Experiment (USDC) ..... PROBE
Pilot Rating ..... PR
Pilot Records of Achievement in Schools Evaluation (AIE) ..... PRAISE
Pilot Repair/Overhaul [*Military*] ..... PR/O
Pilot Repair Overhaul and Provisioning (MUGU) ..... PROP
Pilot Report [*Pertaining to meteorological conditions*] [*FAA*] ..... PIREP
Pilot Reports [*Marine science*] (OSRA) ..... PIREPS
Pilot Request (SAA) ..... PIR
Pilot Requests Forecast [*Aviation*] (FAAC) ..... PIRFC
Pilot Research Moored Array in the Tropical Atlantic [*Proposed project*] [*Marine science*] (OSRA) ..... PIRATA
Pilot Rock Public Library, Pilot Rock, OR [*Library symbol*] [*Library of Congress*] (LCLS) ..... OrPrK
Pilot Run Item Master Schedule Committee (IAA) ..... PRIMSCO
Pilot Secure Voice Project [*NATO Integrated Communications System*] (NATG) ..... PSVP
Pilot Self-Briefing Terminal [*Aviation*] (FAAC) ..... PSBT
Pilot Signal Selector Adaptor (SAA) ..... PSSA
Pilot Station [*Nautical charts*] ..... PIL STA
Pilot Station [*Alaska*] [*Airport symbol*] (OAG) ..... PQS
Pilot Stop Filter (IAA) ..... PF
Pilot [*or Public*] **Switched Digital Data Service** [*Telecommunications*] (TEL) ..... PSDDS
Pilot Systems Operator ..... PSO
Pilot Test Unit [*Air Force*] ..... PTU
Pilot to Dispatcher ..... PTD
Pilot Tone Phase Shift Keying [*Computer science*] (IAA) ..... PTPSK
Pilot Training [*Air Force*] ..... PLTTNG
Pilot Training Rate [*Navy*] ..... PTR
Pilot Training Squadron [*Air Force*] ..... PLTTNGSq
Pilot Training Squadron [*Air Force*] ..... PTS
Pilot Training Wing [*Air Force*] ..... PTW
Pilot Under Training [*Aviation*] (DA) ..... pU/T
Pilot Vessel ..... PV
Pilot Warning Indicator [*or Instrument*] [*Aviation*] ..... PWI
Pilot Weapons System Officer ..... PWSO
Pilot Weather Briefing [*Aviation*] (FAAC) ..... PWB
Pilot Wire (MSA) ..... PW
Pilot Wire Regulator ..... PWR
Pilotage Charts [*Air Force*] ..... PC
Pilot-Controlled Instrument Landing [*Aviation*] (NASA) ..... PCIL
Pilot-Controlled Visual Landing [*Aviation*] (NASA) ..... PCVL

Piloted Low-Speed Test [*Aerospace*] ..... PILOT
Pilot-Helicopter [*Navy British*] ..... Ph
Pilothouse ..... PLTHS
Pilot-Induced Deceleration ..... PID
Pilot-Induced Oscillation ..... PIO
Piloting of Office Documentation Architecture (NITA) ..... PODA
Pilot-Integrated Cockpit (AAG) ..... PIC
Pilotless Aerial Target [*Navy*] ..... KD
Pilotless Aircraft ..... P/A
Pilotless Aircraft [*Navy*] (IAA) ..... PAC
Pilotless Aircraft Development Laboratory [*Navy*] ..... PADL
Pilotless Aircraft Division [*Navy*] ..... PAD
Pilotless Aircraft Program (NG) ..... PAP
Pilotless Aircraft Research Division [*Later, Applied Materials and Physics Division*] [*Langley Research Center*] ..... PARD
Pilotless Aircraft Research Station [*NASA*] ..... PARS
Pilotless Aircraft Unit ..... PAU
Pilotless Airplane (AD) ..... P-plane
Pilotless Bomber [*Air Force*] ..... PB
Pilotless Intercepter [*Air Force*] ..... PI
Pilotless Plane ..... PP
Pilotless Target Aircraft [*Military*] ..... PTA
Pilot-LOS [*Line of Sight*] **Landing Aid Television** (NG) ..... PLAT
Pilot-Operated Relief Valve [*Nuclear energy*] (NRCH) ..... PORV
Pilot-Operated Solenoid Valve [*Nuclear energy*] (IAA) ..... POSV
Pilot-Operated Temperature Control Valve ..... PTCV
Pilots Advisory Service ..... PAS
Pilots and Passengers Association [*Defunct*] (EA) ..... PPA
Pilot's Attack Sight [*British*] ..... PAS
Pilots Automatic Telephone Weather Answering Service ..... PATWAS
Pilot's Discrete Encoder ..... PDE
Pilot's Display Control Panel ..... PDCP
Pilot's Display Recorder ..... PDR
Pilot's Display Unit (MCD) ..... PDU
Pilot's Electronic Eyelevel Presentation [*British*] ..... PEEP
Pilot's Employment Agency ..... PEA
Pilots for Christ International (EA) ..... PCI
Pilot's Horizontal Display [*Aviation*] (CAAL) ..... PHD
Pilots International Association (EA) ..... PIA
Pilot's Night Vision Sensor ..... PNVS
Pilot's Operating Handbook [*Aviation*] (DA) ..... POH
Pilot's Power Tool ..... PPT
Pilot's Projected-Display Indicator (AD) ..... ppdi
Pilots Radio Manual ..... PRM
Pilots Rights Association (EA) ..... PRA
Pilots Universal Sighting System ..... PUSS
Pilot-to-Forecaster Service (NOAA) ..... PTFS
Pilot-to-Metro Service ..... PMSV
Pilot-under-Instruction [*Navy*] ..... PUI
Pilot-Vehicle Interface [*Search technology*] ..... PVI
Pilsener Lager (DSUE) ..... PILS
Pilula [*Pill*] [*Pharmacy*] ..... PIL
Pilula [*Pill*] [*Pharmacology*] (DAVI) ..... Pil
Pim on Feudal Tenures [*A publication*] (DLA) ..... Pim Ten
Pima College, Tucson, AZ [*Library symbol Library of Congress*] (LCLS) ..... AzTPC
Pima Regional Library Service [*Library network*] ..... PRLS
Pimaga [*Papua New Guinea*] [*Airport symbol*] (OAG) ..... PMP
Pimco Advisors Ltd. [*NYSE symbol*] (SAG) ..... PA
Pimco Advisors Ltd. [*Associated Press*] (SAG) ..... PimcoAd
PIMCO Advisors'A' [*NYSE symbol*] (TTSB) ..... PA
Pimco Commercial Mortgage [*Associated Press*] (SAG) ..... PimCom
PIMCO Commercial Mortgage Security Trust [*NYSE symbol*] (SPSG) ..... PCM
PIMCO Comml Mtg Sec Tr [*NYSE symbol*] (TTSB) ..... PCM
Pimeria Alta Historical Society Museum, Nogales, AZ [*Library symbol Library of Congress*] (LCLS) ..... AzNPHi
Pi-Meson (BARN) ..... pion
Pimperne [*England*] ..... PIMP
Pin and Pellet Assay System [*Nuclear energy*] (NRCH) ..... PAPAS
Pin, Clip, and Fastener Association [*Later, PCFS*] (EA) ..... PCFA
Pin, Clip, and Fastener Services (EA) ..... PCFS
Pin Hole [*Eye examination*] (CPH) ..... PH
Pin Jointed Framework ..... PJF
Pin Number (AAG) ..... P/N
Pinal County Public Library, Florence, AZ [*Library symbol Library of Congress*] (LCLS) ..... AzFlCo
Pinane Hydroperoxide [*Organic chemistry*] ..... PHP
Pinar Del Rio [*Cuba ICAO location identifier*] (ICLI) ..... MUPR
Pinar del Rio (AD) ..... PR
Pinatype (VRA) ..... PITYP
Pinawa Public Library, Manitoba [*Library symbol National Library of Canada*] (NLC) ..... MP
Pinawa Public Library, Pinawa, MB, Canada [*Library symbol Library of Congress*] (LCLS) ..... CaMP
Pinch Biopsy [*Medicine*] (MEDA) ..... PB
Pinch Design Method [*Heat exchange design*] ..... PDM
Pinch Hitter [*Baseball*] ..... PH
Pinch Runner [*Baseball*] ..... PR
Pinchas Troester Library, Congregation B'nai Israel, London, ON, Canada [*Library symbol Library of Congress*] (LCLS) ..... CaOLPT
Pinchas Troester Library, Congregation B'Nai Israel, London, Ontario [*Library symbol National Library of Canada*] (NLC) ..... OLPT
Pinchbeck [*Jewelry*] (ROG) ..... PB
Pincher Creek, AB [*ICAO location identifier*] (ICLI) ..... CWPC
Pincher Creek Public Library, Alberta [*Library symbol National Library of Canada*] (NLC) ..... APC
Pinch-Off Voltage ..... POV
Pinchoff Voltage (IDOE) ..... V_p
Pinckney Community Public Library, Pinckney, MI [*Library symbol Library of Congress*] (LCLS) ..... MiPin
Pinckneyville, IL [*FM radio station call letters*] (RBYB) ..... WCCZ
Pinconning, MI [*FM radio station call letters*] (RBYB) ..... WMJK
Pindamonhangaba/Visaba [*Brazil ICAO location identifier*] (ICLI) ..... SBPW
Pindar [*518-438BC*] [*Classical studies*] (OCD) ..... Pind
Pine [*Commonly used*] (OPSA) ..... PINE
Pine (VRA) ..... pn
PINE [*Postal Service standard*] (OPSA) ..... PNE
Pine ..... PNE
Pine Bark ..... PB
Pine Bark Mixed with Clay Loam Soil ..... PS
Pine Bark Mixed with Peat ..... PP
Pine Bark Mixed with Weblite and Peat ..... PW
Pine Bell Mines [*Vancouver Stock Exchange symbol*] ..... PNL
Pine Bluff [*Arkansas*] [*Airport symbol Obsolete*] (OAG) ..... PBF
Pine Bluff and Jefferson County Public Library, Pine Bluff, AR [*Library symbol Library of Congress*] (LCLS) ..... ArPb
Pine Bluff, AR [*FM radio station call letters*] (RBYB) ..... KANX-FM
Pine Bluff, AR [*Television station call letters*] ..... KASN
Pine Bluff, AR [*AM radio station call letters*] ..... KCAT
Pine Bluff, AR [*AM radio station call letters*] ..... KCLA
Pine Bluff, AR [*FM radio station call letters*] ..... KIPR
Pine Bluff, AR [*AM radio station call letters*] ..... KOTN
Pine Bluff, AR [*AM radio station call letters*] ..... KPBA
Pine Bluff, AR [*FM radio station call letters*] ..... KPBQ
Pine Bluff, AR [*FM radio station call letters*] ..... KUAP
Pine Bluff, AR [*Television station call letters*] ..... KVTN
Pine Bluff, AR [*AM radio station call letters*] ..... KYDE
Pine Bluff, AR [*FM radio station call letters*] ..... KZYP
Pine Bluff Arsenal [*Army*] (AABC) ..... PBA
Pine Bluff Cotton Exchange [*Defunct*] (EA) ..... PBCE
Pine Bluff/Grider Field [*Arkansas*] [*ICAO location identifier*] (ICLI) ..... KPBF
Pine Canyon [*California*] [*Seismograph station code, US Geological Survey*] (SEIS) ..... PNC
Pine Castle-Sky Lake, FL [*AM radio station call letters*] ..... WAJL
Pine Cay [*Turks and Caicos Islands*] [*ICAO location identifier*] (ICLI) ..... MBPI
Pine Cay [*British West Indies*] [*Airport symbol Obsolete*] (OAG) ..... PIC
Pine Channel Gold [*Vancouver Stock Exchange symbol*] ..... PCD
Pine City Elementary School, Pine City, MN [*Library symbol*] [*Library of Congress*] (LCLS) ..... MnPcE
Pine City High School, Pine City, MN [*Library symbol*] [*Library of Congress*] (LCLS) ..... MnPcH
Pine City, MN [*AM radio station call letters*] ..... WCMP
Pine City, MN [*FM radio station call letters*] ..... WCMP-FM
Pine City Pubic Library, Pine City, MN [*Library symbol*] [*Library of Congress*] (LCLS) ..... MnPc
Pine County Historical Reference Library, Askov, MN [*Library symbol*] [*Library of Congress*] (LCLS) ..... MnAsHi
Pine Creek Railroad [*An association*] (EA) ..... PCR
Pine Crest Resources [*Vancouver Stock Exchange symbol*] ..... PNQ
Pine Forest Regional Library, Richton, MS [*Library symbol Library of Congress*] (LCLS) ..... MsRi
Pine Grosbeak [*Ornithology*] ..... PG
Pine Hill School, Miles City, MT [*Library symbol*] [*Library of Congress*] (LCLS) ..... MtMcPh
Pine Hills, FL [*AM radio station call letters*] (RBYB) ..... WQTM-AM
Pine Hills, FL [*AM radio station call letters*] (RBYB) ..... WWZN
Pine Island Center, FL [*AM radio station call letters*] (RBYB) ..... WTLQ-AM
Pine Island Centre, FL [*AM radio station call letters*] ..... WDCQ
Pine Lodge Correctional Center, Resident Library, Medical Lake, WA [*Library symbol Library of Congress*] (LCLS) ..... WaMeP-R
Pine Lodge Correctional Center, Staff Library, Medical Lake, WA [*Library symbol Library of Congress*] (LCLS) ..... WaMeP
Pine Manor College, Chestnut Hill, MA [*Library symbol Library of Congress*] (LCLS) ..... MChP
Pine Manor College, Chestnut Hill, MA [*OCLC symbol*] (OCLC) ..... PMA
Pine Manor Junior College (AD) ..... PMJC
Pine Mountain [*Oregon*] [*Seismograph station code, US Geological Survey*] (SEIS) ..... PMT
Pine Mountain, GA [*Location identifier FAA*] (FAAL) ..... PIM
Pine Mountain Observatory ..... PMO
Pine Pass [*British Columbia*] [*Seismograph station code, US Geological Survey Closed*] (SEIS) ..... PPC
Pine Point Mines Ltd. [*Toronto Stock Exchange symbol Vancouver Stock Exchange symbol*] ..... PPT
Pine River Elementary School, Pine River, MN [*Library symbol*] [*Library of Congress*] (LCLS) ..... MnPrE
Pine River High School, Pine River, MN [*Library symbol*] [*Library of Congress*] (LCLS) ..... MnPrH
Pine River Public Library, Pine River, MN [*Library symbol*] [*Library of Congress*] (LCLS) ..... MnPrP
Pine Siskin [*Ornithology*] ..... PS
Pine Tar [*Medicine*] ..... PT
Pine Technical Institute Learning Resource Center, Pine City, MN [*Library symbol*] [*Library of Congress*] (LCLS) ..... MnPcT
Pine Valley Explorers [*Vancouver Stock Exchange symbol*] ..... PVE
Pineal Recess [*Neuroanatomy*] ..... PR
Pineal Stalk [*Neuroanatomy*] ..... PS
Pineapple Growers Association of Hawaii (EA) ..... PGAH
Pineapple Research Institute, Honolulu, HI [*Library symbol Library of Congress*] (LCLS) ..... HHP
Pineapple Research Institute of Hawaii (EA) ..... PRI

Pinebluff Public Library, Pinebluff, NC [*Library symbol Library of Congress*] (LCLS) ... NcPb
Pinedale [*Wyoming*] [*Seismograph station code, US Geological Survey Closed*] (SEIS) ... Pl
Pinedale [*Wyoming*] [*Seismograph station code, US Geological Survey Closed*] (SEIS) ... PIN
Pinedale, WY [*FM radio station call letters*] (RBYB) ... KPIN-FM
Pinedale, WY [*Location identifier FAA*] (FAAL) ... PNA
Pinedo (AD) ... Pndo
Pinehouse Lake, SK [*FM radio station call letters*] ... CFNK
Pinehurst [*North Carolina*] [*Airport symbol*] (OAG) ... SOP
Pinehurst, NC [*AM radio station call letters*] ... WIOZ
Pinehurst-Kingston Library, Pinehurst, ID [*Library symbol*] [*Library of Congress*] (LCLS) ... IdPin
Pinellas Area Office [*Energy Research and Development Administration*] ... PAO
Pinellas Park, FL [*AM radio station call letters*] ... WHNZ
Pinellas Park, FL [*AM radio station call letters*] ... WMTX
Pinellas Park Public Library, Pinellas Park, FL [*Library symbol Library of Congress*] (LCLS) ... FPi
Pinellas Plant [*Department of Energy*] [*Largo, FL*] (GAAI) ... PINELLAS
Pineridge Capital [*Vancouver Stock Exchange symbol*] ... PRE
Pinerola [*Italy*] [*Seismograph station code, US Geological Survey*] (SEIS) ... PNI
Pines [*Commonly used*] (OPSA) ... PINES
Pines ... PNES
Pines (AD) ... Pnes
Pines ... PNES
Pinetree Software Canada Ltd. [*Vancouver Stock Exchange symbol*] ... PSW
Pineville, KY [*AM radio station call letters*] ... WANO
Pineville, KY [*FM radio station call letters*] ... WRIL
Pineville, LA [*AM radio station call letters*] ... KTLD
Pineville, WV [*Location identifier FAA*] (FAAL) ... VPX
Pineville, WV [*AM radio station call letters*] ... WWYO
Pinewood East Elementary School, Monticello, MN [*Library symbol*] [*Library of Congress*] (LCLS) ... MnMcPE
Pinewood Nematode ... PWN
Pinewood West Elementary School, Monticello, MN [*Library symbol*] [*Library of Congress*] (LCLS) ... MnMcPW
Ping Intercept Passive Ranging SONAR [*Military*] ... PIPRS
Pingdong (North) [*China*] [*ICAO location identifier*] (ICLI) ... RCSQ
Pingdong (South) [*China*] [*ICAO location identifier*] (ICLI) ... RCDC
Pingrey's Treatise of Chattel Mortgages [*A publication*] (DLA) ... Ping Chat Mortg
Pin-Grid Arrays ... PGA
Pin-Grid-Array [*Motorola, Inc.*] ... PGA
Pinguis [*Fat, Grease*] [*Latin*] (DAVI) ... ping
Pinhole Occulter Facility (SSD) ... POF
Pininfarina [*Automotive coachworks*] ... PF
Pinion (MSA) ... PIN
Pinion End ... PE
Pinion Gear Drive ... PGD
Pink ... P
Pink (ROG) ... PI
Pink [*Electrical wiring*] ... PNK
Pink Bollworm [*Cotton pest*] ... PB
Pink Bollworm [*Cotton pest*] ... PBW
Pink Pages Publication [*Vancouver Stock Exchange symbol*] ... PNK
Pink Puffer [*Emphysema*] (MAE) ... PP
Pink Sheet [*Investment term*] ... PS
Pinkerton's, Inc. [*Associated Press*] (SAG) ... Pinktn
Pinkerton's, Inc. [*NASDAQ symbol*] (SAG) ... PKTN
Pink-Eyed Dilution [*Medicine*] (DMAA) ... PED
Pink-Eyed, Tan-Hooded Rat [*Medicine*] (DMAA) ... PETH
Pinkham Creek [*Montana*] [*Seismograph station code, US Geological Survey Closed*] (SEIS) ... PNK
Pinkish [*Philately*] ... pnksh
Pinlebu [*Myanmar*] [*ICAO location identifier*] (ICLI) ... VBPL
Pinnacle [*Alaska*] [*Seismograph station code, US Geological Survey*] (SEIS) ... PCA
Pinnacle Banc Group [*NASDAQ symbol*] (TTSB) ... PINN
Pinnacle Banc Group, Inc. [*NASDAQ symbol*] (SAG) ... PINN
Pinnacle Bank [*Associated Press*] (SAG) ... PinnclBk
Pinnacle Bank [*AMEX symbol*] (SAG) ... PLE
Pinnacle Bank [*AMEX symbol*] (TTSB) ... PLE
Pinnacle Bank Group, Inc. [*Associated Press*] (SAG) ... PinBG
Pinnacle Financial Services [*Associated Press*] (SAG) ... PinclFn
Pinnacle Financial Services, Inc. [*Associated Press*] (SAG) ... PinclF
Pinnacle Financial Services, Inc. [*NASDAQ symbol*] (NQ) ... PNFI
Pinnacle Financial Svcs [*NASDAQ symbol*] (TTSB) ... PNFI
Pinnacle Micro [*NASDAQ symbol*] (TTSB) ... PNCL
Pinnacle Micro, Inc. [*Associated Press*] (SAG) ... PinclM
Pinnacle Micro, Inc. [*Associated Press*] (SAG) ... PinclMic
Pinnacle Micro, Inc. [*NASDAQ symbol*] (NQ) ... PNCL
Pinnacle Mountain [*Alaska*] [*Seismograph station code, US Geological Survey*] (SEIS) ... PNN
Pinnacle Systems [*NASDAQ symbol*] (TTSB) ... PCLE
Pinnacle Systems, Inc. [*NASDAQ symbol*] (SAG) ... PCLE
Pinnacle Systems, Inc. [*Associated Press*] (SAG) ... PinnSyst
Pinnacle Virtual File System [*Pinnacle Micro, Inc.*] [*Computer science*] (PCM) ... PVFS
Pinnacle West Capital [*NYSE symbol*] (TTSB) ... PNW
Pinnacle West Capital Corp. [*Associated Press*] (SAG) ... PinWst
Pinnacle West Capital Corp. [*NYSE symbol*] (SPSG) ... PNW
Pinnacles National Monument ... PINN
Pinnacles National Monument [*California*] (AD) ... PNM
Pinney's Wisconsin Reports [*A publication*] (DLA) ... Pin (Wis)
Pinney's Wisconsin Reports [*A publication*] (DLA) ... Pin Wis R
Pinney's Wisconsin Reports [*A publication*] (DLA) ... Pinn
Pinney's Wisconsin Reports [*A publication*] (DLA) ... Pinney
Pinney's Wisconsin Reports [*A publication*] (DLA) ... Pinney (sv)
Pinney's Wisconsin Supreme Court Reports [*1839-52*] [*A publication*] (DLA) ... Pin
Pinnule ... P
Pinon, NM [*Location identifier FAA*] (FAAL) ... PIO
Pinosylvin Methyl Ether [*Organic chemistry*] ... PME
Pin-Pack Test Board ... PPTB
Pinpoint (MAE) ... PP
Pinpoint [*Pupils*] [*Ophthalmology*] (DAVI) ... PP
Pinpoint Assignment Instructions [*Army*] (INF) ... PPAI
Pinpoint Retail Solutions [*Associated Press*] (SAG) ... PinptRtl
Pinprick [*Medicine*] (DMAA) ... PP
PINS [*Portable Inertial Navigation System*] **Alignment Console** ... PINSAC
Pins and Plaster [*Orthopedics*] (DAVI) ... P & P
Pint ... P
Pint ... PT
Pint (WDMC) ... pt
Pint (ODBW) ... pt
Pintle [*Design engineering*] ... PTL
Pinto Horse Association of America (EA) ... PtHA
Pinto Malartic [*Vancouver Stock Exchange symbol*] ... PMG
Pints Per Hundred Parts of Mix (AD) ... pphpm
Pinworm [*Gastroenterology*] (DAVI) ... PINWOR
Pinxit [*He, or She, Painted It*] [*Latin*] ... PINX
Pinxit [*He, or She, Painted It*] [*Latin*] (ROG) ... PINXT
Pinxit [*He, or She, Painted It*] [*Latin*] (ROG) ... PIX
Pinxit [*He, or She, Painted It*] [*Latin*] ... PNXT
Pinxit [*He or She Painted It*] [*Latin*] (AD) ... pnxt
Pinxit [*He, or She, Painted It*] [*Latin*] ... PXT
Pion Generator for Medical Irradiation [*Radiology*] ... PIGMI
Pioneer (AABC) ... PION
Pioneer ... PNR
Pioneer (AD) ... Pnr
Pioneer ... PNR
Pioneer Airlines, Inc. [*ICAO designator*] (FAAC) ... PIO
Pioneer Airways [*ICAO designator*] (AD) ... JB
Pioneer America Society (EA) ... PAS
Pioneer and Ammunition ... P & A
Pioneer and Demolition Section [*Army*] ... P & D
Pioneer and Demolition Section [*Army*] ... P & DSEC
[*The*] **Pioneer & Fayette Railroad Co.** [*AAR code*] ... PF
Pioneer Automobile Touring Club (EA) ... PATC
Pioneer Citizens Band Association (IAA) ... PCBA
Pioneer Civil Labour Unit [*British*] ... PCLU
Pioneer Clubs (EA) ... PC
Pioneer Commercial Funding Corp. [*NASDAQ symbol*] (SAG) ... PCFC
Pioneer Commercial Funding Corp. [*Associated Press*] (SAG) ... PioneerC
Pioneer Commercial Funding Corp. [*Associated Press*] (SAG) ... PionrC
Pioneer Community College Library, Kansas City, MO [*Library symbol*] [*Library of Congress*] (LCLS) ... MoKPi
Pioneer Companies, Inc. [*NASDAQ symbol*] (SAG) ... PIONA
Pioneer Companies, Inc. [*Associated Press*] (SAG) ... PionCos
Pioneer Corps [*British military*] (DMA) ... PC
Pioneer Cos. 'A' [*NASDAQ symbol*] (TTSB) ... PIONA
Pioneer Dairymen's Club of America (EA) ... PDCA
Pioneer Electron ADR [*NYSE symbol*] (TTSB) ... PIO
Pioneer Electronic Corp. [*NYSE symbol*] (SPSG) ... PIO
Pioneer Electronic Corp. [*Associated Press*] (SAG) ... PionrEl
Pioneer Financial Services, Inc. [*NYSE symbol*] (SPSG) ... PFS
Pioneer Financial Services, Inc. [*Associated Press*] (SAG) ... PionF
Pioneer Financial Services, Inc. [*Associated Press*] (SAG) ... PionFS
Pioneer Financial Svcs [*NYSE symbol*] (TTSB) ... PFS
Pioneer Fraternal Association (EA) ... PFA
Pioneer Ground Data System ... PGDS
Pioneer Group [*NASDAQ symbol*] (TTSB) ... PIOG
Pioneer Group Home, Tacoma, WA [*Library symbol Library of Congress*] (LCLS) ... WaTP
[*The*] **Pioneer Group, Inc.** [*NASDAQ symbol*] (NQ) ... PIOG
[*The*] **Pioneer Group, Inc.** [*Associated Press*] (SAG) ... PionGp
Pioneer Hi-Bred International [*NYSE symbol*] (SAG) ... PHB
Pioneer Hi-Bred International [*Associated Press*] (SAG) ... PionHiB
Pioneer Hi-Bred International, Inc., Des Moines, IA [*Library symbol Library of Congress*] (LCLS) ... IaDmPH
Pioneer Hi-Bred Intl [*NYSE symbol*] (TTSB) ... PHB
Pioneer Image Converter System [*NASA*] ... PICS
Pioneer Interest Shares [*Formerly, Mutual of Omaha Interest Shares, Inc.*] [*NYSE symbol*] (SPSG) ... MUO
Pioneer Interest Shares [*Associated Press*] (SAG) ... PionInt
Pioneer Interest Shs [*NYSE symbol*] (TTSB) ... MUO
Pioneer Jupiter Orbit [*NASA*] ... PJO
Pioneer Memorial Hospital, Heppner, OR [*Library symbol Library of Congress*] (LCLS) ... OrHepPM
Pioneer Memorial Hospital Library, Prineville, OR [*Library symbol*] [*Library of Congress*] (LCLS) ... OrPrH
Pioneer Memorial Museum, Salt Lake City, UT [*Library symbol Library of Congress*] (LCLS) ... USIP
Pioneer Metals Corp. [*Toronto Stock Exchange symbol Vancouver Stock Exchange symbol*] ... PSM
Pioneer Ministries (EA) ... PM
Pioneer Mission Operations Center [*NASA*] ... PMOC
Pioneer Multi-County Library, Norman, OK [*OCLC symbol*] (OCLC) ... OKM
Pioneer Multi-County Library, Norman, OK [*Library symbol Library of Congress*] (LCLS) ... OkN
Pioneer Off-Line Data-Processing System [*NASA*] ... POLDPS

Pioneer Railcorp [*NASDAQ symbol*] (TTSB) .... PRRR
Pioneer Railcorp [*NASDAQ symbol*] (SAG) .... PRRR
Pioneer Standard Electronics [*Associated Press*] (SAG) .... PionStd
Pioneer Station Training Facility [*NASA*] .... PSTF
Pioneer Std Electr [*NASDAQ symbol*] (TTSB) .... PIOS
Pioneer Television and Electronic Technicians Society [*Defunct*] (EA) .... PTETS
Pioneer Venus [*Spacecraft*] .... PV
Pioneer Venus Gas Chromatograph [*NASA*] .... PVGC
Pioneer Venus Orbiter [*NASA*] .... PVO
Pioneer Venus Orbiter Ultraviolet Spectrometer [*NASA*] .... PVOUVS
Pioneer Women/Na'amat, the Women's Labor Zionist Organization of America [*Later, MWWV*] (EA) .... PW-NWLZOA
Pioneer Women, the Women's Labor Zionist Organization of America [*Later, PW-MWLZOA*] (EA) .... PW-WLZOA
Pioneer Youth of America (EA) .... PYA
Pioneering Research Laboratory [*Massachusetts*] [*Army*] .... PRL
Pioneers' Association of South Australia .... PASA
Pioneer-Standard Electronics, Inc. [*Associated Press*] (SAG) .... PionStd
Pioneer-Standard Electronics, Inc. [*NASDAQ symbol*] (NQ) .... PIOS
Pioner Railcorp [*Associated Press*] (SAG) .... PioRail
Pious Disciples of the Divine Master (TOCD) .... PDDM
Pious Society Daughters of St. Paul (TOCD) .... FSP
Pious Society of Missionaries of St. Charles [*Later, CS*] [*Roman Catholic men's religious order*] .... PSSC
Pious Society of Our Lady of the Most Holy Trinity (EA) .... PSOLMHT
Pious Society of Our Lady of the Most Holy Trinity (TOCD) .... SLT
Pious Society of the Daughters of Saint Paul [*See also FSP*] [*Rome, Italy*] (EAIO) .... PSDSP
Pious Union of Our Mother of Good Counsel [*See also SMBC*] [*Genazzano, Italy*] (EAIO) .... PUMGC
Pious Union of Prayer (EA) .... PUP
Pious Union of St. Joseph for Dying Sinners [*Later, PUSJD*] (EA) .... PUSJDS
Pious Union of St. Joseph for the Dying [*Defunct*] (EA) .... PUSJD
Pip [*Phonetic alphabet*] [*Pre-World War II*] (DSUE) .... P
PIPA [*Pulsed Integrating Pendulous Accelerometer*] **Pulse Integrator** .... PPI
Pipe .... P
Pipe [*Freight*] .... PI
Pipe Analysis Log [*Gas well*] .... PAL
Pipe and Tobacco Council of America [*Defunct*] (EA) .... PTC
Pipe Break [*Nuclear energy*] (NRCH) .... PB
Pipe Break Air Piping System (IEEE) .... PBAPS
Pipe Break Automatic Protective System (IEEE) .... PBAPS
Pipe Collectors Club of America [*Defunct*] (EA) .... PCCA
Pipe Collectors International [*Later, PCCA*] (EA) .... PCI
Pipe Fabrication Institute (EA) .... PFI
Pipe Fittings Manufacturers Association [*Later, APFA*] (EA) .... PFMA
Pipe Flow (PDAA) .... PIFL
Pipe Jacking Association [*British*] (DBA) .... PJA
Pipe Joint Record (DNAB) .... PJR
Pipe Line Contractors Association (EA) .... PLCA
Pipe Line Contractors Association, International (EA) .... PLCAI
Pipe Line Insurance Managers Conference [*Defunct*] (EA) .... PLIMC
Pipe Lines Act [*Town planning*] [*British*] .... PL
Pipe or Tubing [*Freight*] .... PITU
Pipe Plug .... PPG
Pipe Plug Producers Council (EA) .... PPPC
Pipe Rail (AAG) .... PR
Pipe Roll Society (EA) .... PRS
Pipe Rolls [*British*] .... P
Pipe Size (BARN) .... PS
Pipe Sizing Program - Air (DNAB) .... PIPSAR
Pipe Sizing Program - Sprinkling (DNAB) .... PIPSPK
Pipe Sizing Program - Steam (DNAB) .... PIPSST
Pipe Sleeve .... PSL
Pipe Springs National Monument .... PISP
Pipe Stress Analysis (PDAA) .... PSA
Pipe Tap (MSA) .... PT
Pipe Test Insert [*Liquid Metal Engineering Center*] [*Energy Research and Development Administration*] (IEEE) .... PTI
Pipe Tobacco Council (EA) .... PTC
Pipe Ventilated .... PV
Pipe Ventilated, Forced Draught .... PVFD
Pipe Ventilated, Induced Draught .... PVID
Pipefitter [*Navy*] .... FP
Pipeline .... PL
Pipeline (AD) .... ppl
Pipeline .... PPLN
Pipeline Authority [*Australia*] .... PA
Pipeline Burst SRAM [*Static Random-Access Memory*] [*Computer science*] .... PB SRAM
Pipeline Element (NITA) .... PLE
Pipeline End Manifold (PDAA) .... PLEM
Pipeline Expanding Polymer .... PEP
Pipeline Girth Joint .... PGJ
Pipeline Induction Heat [*Industrial firm*] [*British*] .... PIH
Pipeline Outfit, Petroleum (MCD) .... POP
Pipeline Processor (IAA) .... PP
Pipeline Time [*Army*] .... PLT
Pipeline under the Ocean [*British project*] [*World War II*] .... PLUTO
Pipelined Vector Processor (NITA) .... PVP
Pipelines Authority of South Australia .... PASA
Pipe-Major [*British military*] (DMA) .... P/Maj
Piper [*Airplane code*] .... Pag
Piper Aircraft Corp. [*ICAO aircraft manufacturer identifier*] (ICAO) .... PA
Piper Aircraft Corp. .... PAC
Piper City Public Library, Piper City, IL [*Library symbol Library of Congress*] (LCLS) .... IPip
Piper Jaffray Companies [*NYSE symbol*] (SPSG) .... PJC
Piper Jaffray Cos. Inc. [*NYSE symbol*] (TTSB) .... PJC
Piper Jaffray, Inc. [*Associated Press*] (SAG) .... PiperJaf
Piper, Jr., H. E., Philadelphia PA [*STAC*] .... PJH
Piper Owner Society (EA) .... POS
Piper Pressurised Prop-Jet [*Airplane code*] .... Pah
Piperacillin [*An antibiotic*] .... PIP
Piperazinediethanesulfonic Acid [*A buffer*] .... PIPES
Piperidinedicarboxylic Acid [*Organic chemistry*] .... PDA
Piperidinocyclohexanecarbonitrile [*Organic chemistry*] .... PCC
Piperidinomethylcyclohexane [*Organic chemistry*] .... PMC
Piperidino-Pyrimidine [*Biochemistry*] (MAE) .... PDP
Piperonyl Butoxide [*Organic chemistry*] .... PB
Pipers Guild (EA) .... PG
Pipers to After Coming Head [*Obstetrics*] (DAVI) .... PACH
PIPES Buffer with Calcium and Magnesium .... PCM
Pipestone Cental High School, Pipestone, MN [*Library symbol*] [*Library of Congress*] (LCLS) .... MnPpHS
Pipestone, MN [*FM radio station call letters*] .... KISD
Pipestone, MN [*AM radio station call letters*] .... KLOH
Pipestone, MN [*Location identifier FAA*] (FAAL) .... PQN
Pipestone National Monument .... PIPE
Pipestone Petroleums, Inc. [*Toronto Stock Exchange symbol Vancouver Stock Exchange symbol*] .... PIE
Pipette [*Chemistry*] .... PPE
Piping .... PP
Piping and Filter Gallery [*Nuclear energy*] (NRCH) .... PFG
Piping and Instrumentation [*Nuclear energy*] (NRCH) .... P & I
Piping and Instrumentation [*Nuclear energy*] (IAA) .... PAI
Piping and Instrumentation Diagram [*or Design or Drawing*] [*Calcomp Ltd. Software package*] [*Nuclear energy*] (NRCH) .... P & ID
Piping and Instrumentation Diagram [*Engineering*] .... P & ID
Piping and Instrumentation Diagram [*or Design*] [*Nuclear energy*] (IAA) .... PAID
Piping and Valve Test Insert [*Nuclear energy*] (NRCH) .... PVTI
Piping Cost and Weight Analysis Program (DNAB) .... PIPCST
Piping Efficiency Program .... PEP
Piping Instrumentation and Operating Gallery [*Nuclear energy*] (NRCH) .... POG
Piping Load [*Nuclear energy*] (NRCH) .... PL
Pipon and Collier's Military Law [*3rd ed.*] [*1865*] [*A publication*] (DLA) .... Pip & C Mil L
Pippa Passes, KY [*FM radio station call letters*] .... WOAL
Piqua Nuclear Power Facility .... PNPF
Piqua, OH [*FM radio station call letters*] .... WCLR
Piqua, OH [*AM radio station call letters*] .... WPTW
Pique; Inclusions [*Diamond clarity grade*] .... P
PIRA International [*British*] (EAIO) .... PIRAI
Piracaba [*Brazil ICAO location identifier*] (ICLI) .... SBPR
Piracununga/Campo Fontenelle [*Brazil ICAO location identifier*] (ICLI) .... SBYS
Pirada [*Guinea-Bissau*] [*ICAO location identifier*] (ICLI) .... GGPR
Pirandello Society (EA) .... PS
Pirandello Society of America (EA) .... PSA
Pirapora [*Brazil*] [*Airport symbol*] (AD) .... PPR
Pirates Gold Corp. [*Vancouver Stock Exchange symbol*] .... PIT
Pirchei Agudath Israel (EA) .... PAI
Pirelli Active Safety System .... PASS
Piriform Cortex (DMAA) .... PC
Pirke Avot (BJA) .... PA
Pirmasens [*Germany ICAO location identifier*] (ICLI) .... EDIV
Pirmasens [*Federal Republic of Germany*] [*Seismograph station code, US Geological Survey*] (SEIS) .... PIR
Pirmasens Missile Repair Activity [*Germany Army*] .... PIMRA
Pirmasens/Zweibruecken [*Germany ICAO location identifier*] (ICLI) .... EDRZ
Piroxicam [*Anti-inflammatory*] .... PX
Pisa [*Italy ICAO location identifier*] (ICLI) .... LIRP
Pisa [*Italy*] [*Seismograph station code, US Geological Survey Closed*] (SEIS) .... PIS
Pisa [*Italy*] [*Airport symbol*] (OAG) .... PSA
Pisatin Demethylase [*An enzyme*] .... PDA
Piscataqua Pioneers (EA) .... PP
Piscataway, NJ [*FM radio station call letters*] .... WVPH
Pisces [*Constellation*] .... Pisc
Pisces [*Constellation*] .... Psc
Pisces Austrinus [*Constellation*] .... PsA
Pisces Austrinus [*Constellation*] .... PscA
Pisces Society of America .... PSA
Piscivorous .... PIS
Pisco [*Peru*] [*ICAO location identifier*] (ICLI) .... SPSO
Pishin [*Pakistan*] [*ICAO location identifier*] (ICLI) .... OPPN
Piskei Din Shel Batei ha-Din ha-Rabaniyim be-Yisrael (BJA) .... PDR
Piskei Din Shel Bet ha-Mishpat ha-'Elyon le-Yisrael (BJA) .... PD
Pismo Beach, CA [*FM radio station call letters*] .... KWBR
Pisosecond (IAA) .... PS
Pistachio Growers' Association [*Australia*] .... PGA
Pistol (MSA) .... PSTL
Pistol Expert .... PE
Pistol Petroleum [*Vancouver Stock Exchange symbol*] .... PIL
Pistol Prize Money [*British military*] (DMA) .... PPM
Pistol Sharpshooter [*Army*] .... PS
Piston [*Automotive engineering*] .... PIST
Piston (MSA) .... PSTN
Piston and Pin Standardization Group [*Later, NEPMA*] (EA) .... PPSG
Piston Arrestment Gas Entrapment System [*SPRINT launch cell*] [*Army*] (AABC) .... PAGE
Piston Operated Transducer .... POT

Piston Position Indicator ... PPI
Piston Ring Manufacturers Group [*Later, NEPMA*] (EA) ... PRMG
Piston Shock Tunnel ... PST
Piston Valve [*Automotive engineering*] ... PV
Piston-Driven Compaction (MCD) ... PDC
Piston-Hand Control Clutch (DNAB) ... P-HCC
Piston's Mauritius Reports [*A publication*] (DLA) ... Pist
Piston's Mauritius Reports [*A publication*] (DLA) ... Piston
Piston-Supported Upper Bearing ... PSUB
Pisum Virus [*Plant pathology*] ... PV
Piszkesteto [*Hungary*] [*Seismograph station code, US Geological Survey*] (SEIS) ... PSZ
Pit Border [*Paleobotany*] ... PB
Pit Membrane [*Paleobotany*] ... PM
Pit Rib Meristem [*Botany*] ... PRM
Pit Tub and Mine Car Manufacturers' Association [*British*] (BI) ... PTMCA
Pitalito [*Colorado ICAO location identifier*] (ICLI) ... SKPI
Pitcairn [*MARC country of publication code Library of Congress*] (LCCP) ... pc
Pitcairn [*MARC geographic area code Library of Congress*] (LCCP) ... popc--
Pitcairn Cierva Autogiro [*Aeronautics*] ... PCA
Pitcairn Islands [*ANSI three-letter standard code*] (CNC) ... PCN
Pitcairn Islands [*ANSI two-letter standard code*] (CNC) ... PN
Pitcairn Islands Study Group (EA) ... PISG
Pitcairn's Ancient Criminal Trials [*Scotland*] [*A publication*] (DLA) ... Pitc Crim Tr
Pitcairn's Criminal Trials [*1488-1624*] [*Scotland*] [*A publication*] (DLA) ... Pitc
Pitcairn's Criminal Trials [*3 Scotland*] [*A publication*] (DLA) ... Pitc Tr
Pitch [*or Pitcher*] [*Baseball*] ... P
Pitch [*Technical drawings*] ... P
Pitch (IDOE) ... P
Pitch ... PCH
Pitch and Putt Union of Ireland (EAIO) ... PPUI
Pitch and Roll Attitude (IAA) ... PRA
Pitch and Roll Channel Assembly (MCD) ... PRCA
Pitch and Yaw Engine (MCD) ... PAYE
Pitch Angle ... PA
Pitch Angle Distribution ... PAD
Pitch Attitude Command/Attitude Hold [*Aviation*] (MCD) ... PACAH
Pitch Attitude Hold [*Aviation*] (MCD) ... PAH
Pitch Augmentation Control System (PDAA) ... PACS
Pitch Axis [*Aerospace*] (AAG) ... X-X
Pitch Axis Definition ... PAD
Pitch Boundary Indicator (MCD) ... PBI
Pitch Centering Torquer (SAA) ... PCT
Pitch Channel ... PC
Pitch Circle [*Technical drawings*] ... PC
Pitch Circle Diameter [*Technical drawings*] (IAA) ... PCD
Pitch Circle Diameter [*Technical drawings*] (IAA) ... PD
Pitch Control (KSC) ... PC
Pitch Control Assembly (MCD) ... PCA
Pitch Control Motor ... PCM
Pitch Control System (MCD) ... PCS
Pitch Cycle (DNAB) ... PC
Pitch Diameter ... PD
Pitch Down (MCD) ... PD
Pitch Error Amplifier ... PEA
Pitch Fibre Pipe Association of Great Britain (BI) ... PEPA
Pitch Follow-Up Amplifier ... PFA
Pitch Follow-Up Amplifier ... PFUA
Pitch Follow-Up Motor ... PFM
Pitch Follow-Up Motor ... PFUM
Pitch Follow-Up Operation ... PFO
Pitch Follow-Up Operation ... PFUO
Pitch Follow-Up System ... PFS
Pitch Follow-Up System ... PFUS
Pitch, Hit, and Throw [*Youth competition sponsored by professional baseball*] ... PHT
Pitch Impregnation Carbonization (MCD) ... PIC
Pitch Integrated Flight Control Module (MCD) ... PIFCM
Pitch Limit Switch ... PLS
Pitch Line (MSA) ... PL
Pitch Lock Actuator (MCD) ... PLA
Pitch Mark [*Shipfitting*] ... PM
Pitch Mark [*Shipfitting*] (AAG) ... PMK
Pitch Mark (AD) ... pmk
Pitch Microwave System ... PMS
Pitch or Yaw ... P/Y
Pitch Over ... P/O
Pitch Phase Detector ... PPD
Pitch Power Valve (IAA) ... PPV
Pitch Precession Amplifier ... PPA
Pitch Precession Torquer ... PPT
Pitch Rate Command (MCD) ... PRC
Pitch Rate/Moment Ratio [*Automotive engineering*] ... PRMR
Pitch Ratio ... PR
Pitch Ratio Adjust Device (MCD) ... PRAD
Pitch Ratio Controller (MCD) ... PRC
Pitch Response Operator ... PRO
Pitch/Roll (MCD) ... P/R
Pitch, Roll, Azimuth Reference System (NG) ... PRARS
Pitch/Roll Rate Changer Assembly (MCD) ... PRRC
Pitch Servo Drive ... PSD
Pitch Starting Synchro Assembly ... PSSA
Pitch Steering Error ... PSE
Pitch Thrust Vector (KSC) ... PTV
Pitch Thrust Vector Control (KSC) ... PTVC
Pitch Trim (MCD) ... PT
Pitch Trim Adjustment ... PTA
Pitch Trim Angle ... PTA
Pitch Trim Compensator ... PTC
Pitch Trim Controller (MCD) ... PTC
Pitch-Depitch (AAG) ... PDP
Pitcher Mountain [*New Hampshire*] [*Seismograph station code, US Geological Survey*] (SEIS) ... PNH
Pitching Moment [*Physics*] ... PM
Pitch-Orthogonal Thrust ... POT
Pitch-Synchronous Digital Feature Extraction System (PDAA) ... PDFES
Pitch-Yaw-Roll (AAG) ... P-Y-R
Pitea [*Sweden ICAO location identifier*] (ICLI) ... ESNP
Pith [*Botany*] ... P
Pithiviers [*France ICAO location identifier*] (ICLI) ... LFFP
Pitisci's Lexicon [*A publication*] (DLA) ... Pitisc Lex
Pitkin County Public Library, Aspen, CO [*Library symbol Library of Congress*] (LCLS) ... CoAs
Pitless Adapter Division of Water Systems Council (EA) ... PAD
Pitman Examination Institute [*British*] ... P
Pitman on Principal and Surety [*1840*] [*A publication*] (DLA) ... Pit Sur
Pitman on Principal and Surety [*A publication*] (DLA) ... Pitm Prin & Sur
Pitman-Moore Co. [*Research code symbol*] ... P
Pitman-Moore Co. [*Research code symbol*] ... S
Pitney Bowes [*NYSE symbol*] (TTSB) ... PBI
Pitney Bowes $2.12 Cv Pref [*NYSE symbol*] (TTSB) ... PBIPr
Pitney Bowes Credit Corp. ... PBCC
Pitney Bowes Management Services ... PBMS
Pitney-Bowes, Inc. ... PB
Pitney-Bowes, Inc. [*NYSE symbol*] (SPSG) ... PBI
Pitney-Bowes, Inc. [*Associated Press*] (SAG) ... PitnB
Pitney-Bowes, Inc. [*Associated Press*] (SAG) ... PitnyBw
Pitocin [*Trademark of Parke, Davis & Co. for Oxytocin, a labor-inducing drug*] ... Pit
Pitometer-Log [*Engineering*] ... PTMTLG
Pitot/Static Tube (MCD) ... PS
Pitressin [*Trademark of Parke, Davis & Co. for Vasopressin, an antidiuretic hormone*] ... Pit
Pitt Interpretive Language [*Computer science*] (DIT) ... PIL
Pitt Meadows, BC [*ICAO location identifier*] (ICLI) ... CYPK
Pitt Press Mathematical Series [*A publication*] ... PPMS
Pitt Press Series [*A publication*] ... PPS
Pitt Technical Institute, Greenville, NC [*Library symbol Library of Congress*] (LCLS) ... NcGrP
Pitt-DesMoines Inc. [*AMEX symbol*] (TTSB) ... PDM
Pitten [*Austria*] [*Seismograph station code, US Geological Survey*] (SEIS) ... PIA
Pittencrieff Communic [*NASDAQ symbol*] (TTSB) ... PITC
Pittencrieff Communications [*NASDAQ symbol*] (SAG) ... PITC
Pittencrieff Communications [*Commercial firm Associated Press*] (SAG) ... Pitencr
Pitting Corrosion (PDAA) ... PC
Pittosporum Vein Yellowing Virus [*Plant pathology*] ... PVYV
Pitts & W Va RR SBI [*AMEX symbol*] (TTSB) ... PW
Pitt's Bankruptcy Acts [*A publication*] (DLA) ... Pitt Bank
Pitt's County Court Practice [*A publication*] (DLA) ... Pitt CC Pr
[*The*] **Pittsburg & Shawmut Railroad Co.** ... P & S
[*The*] **Pittsburg & Shawmut Railroad Co.** [*AAR code*] ... PS
Pittsburg, CA [*AM radio station call letters*] ... KATD
Pittsburg, KS [*AM radio station call letters*] ... KKOW
Pittsburg, KS [*FM radio station call letters*] ... KKOW-FM
Pittsburg, KS [*Television station call letters*] ... KOAM
Pittsburg, KS [*AM radio station call letters*] ... KPHN
Pittsburg, KS [*FM radio station call letters*] ... KRPS
Pittsburg, KS [*Location identifier FAA*] (FAAL) ... PTS
Pittsburg State University (GAGS) ... Pittsburg St U
Pittsburg State University, Pittsburg, KS [*OCLC symbol*] (OCLC) ... KFP
Pittsburg State University, Pittsburg, KS [*Library symbol Library of Congress*] (LCLS) ... KPT
Pittsburg, TX [*FM radio station call letters*] ... KXAL
Pittsburgh [*Pennsylvania*] [*Seismograph station code, US Geological Survey Closed*] (SEIS) ... PIT
Pittsburgh [*Pennsylvania*] [*Airport symbol*] ... PIT
Pittsburgh Academy of Medicine, Pittsburgh, PA [*Library symbol Library of Congress*] (LCLS) ... PPiAM
Pittsburgh, Allegheny & McKees Rocks Railroad Co. [*AAR code*] ... PAM
[*The*] **Pittsburgh & Lake Erie Railroad Co.** ... P & LERR
[*The*] **Pittsburgh & Lake Erie Railroad Co.** [*AAR code*] ... PLE
Pittsburgh & Ohio Valley Railway Co. [*AAR code*] ... POV
Pittsburgh & West Virginia Railroad ... P & WV
Pittsburgh & West Virginia Railroad [*Associated Press*] (SAG) ... PitWVa
Pittsburgh & West Virginia Railroad [*AMEX symbol*] (SPSG) ... PW
Pittsburgh & West Virginia Railroad [*AAR code*] ... PWV
Pittsburgh Ballet Theatre ... PBT
Pittsburgh Byzantine [*Diocesan abbreviation*] [*Pennsylvania*] (TOCD) ... PBR
Pittsburgh, Chartiers & Youghiogheny Railway Co. [*AAR code*] ... PCY
Pittsburgh Coal Mining Institute of America (EA) ... PCMIA
Pittsburgh Commerce Institute ... PC
Pittsburgh - Des Moines, Inc. [*AMEX symbol*] (SPSG) ... PDM
Pittsburgh Energy Research Center [*Later, PETC*] [*Energy Research and Development Administration*] ... PERC
Pittsburgh Energy Technology Center [*Formerly, PERC*] [*Department of Energy Pittsburgh, PA*] (GRD) ... PETC
Pittsburgh Festival of Contemporary Music [*Record label*] ... PFCM
Pittsburgh, Fort Wayne & Chicago Railway Co. (IIA) ... PFT
Pittsburgh/Greater Pittsburgh [*Pennsylvania*] [*ICAO location identifier*] (ICLI) ... KPIT
Pittsburgh Home Finl [*NASDAQ symbol*] (TTSB) ... PHFC

Pittsburgh Interpretive [*or Interactive*] **Language** [*Computer science*] (IAA) ..... PIL
Pittsburgh Law Review [*A publication*] (DLA) ..... Pittsb L Rev
Pittsburgh Legal Journal [*Pennsylvania*] [*A publication*] (DLA) ..... Leg J
Pittsburgh Legal Journal [*Pennsylvania*] [*A publication*] (DLA) ..... Leg Jour
Pittsburgh Legal Journal [*Pennsylvania*] [*A publication*] (DLA) ..... P Leg J
Pittsburgh Legal Journal [*Pennsylvania*] [*A publication*] (DLA) ..... P Leg Jour
Pittsburgh Legal Journal [*Pennsylvania*] [*A publication*] (DLA) ..... Pgh Leg Journal
Pittsburgh Legal Journal [*A publication*] (DLA) ..... Pitt LJ
Pittsburgh Legal Journal [*Pennsylvania*] [*A publication*] (DLA) ..... Pitts Leg J
Pittsburgh Legal Journal [*Pennsylvania*] [*A publication*] (DLA) ..... Pitts Leg Jour
Pittsburgh Legal Journal [*A publication*] (DLA) ..... Pitts LJ
Pittsburgh Legal Journal [*Pennsylvania*] [*A publication*] (DLA) ..... Pittsb Leg J
Pittsburgh Legal Journal [*Pennsylvania*] [*A publication*] (DLA) ..... Pittsb Leg J (PA)
Pittsburgh Legal Journal [*Pennsylvania*] [*A publication*] (DLA) ..... Pittsb LJ
Pittsburgh Legal Journal [*Pennsylvania*] [*A publication*] (DLA) ..... Pittsburgh Leg J
Pittsburgh Legal Journal [*Pennsylvania*] [*A publication*] (DLA) ..... Pittsburgh Leg Journal
Pittsburgh Legal Journal [*Pennsylvania*] [*A publication*] (DLA) ..... PLJ
Pittsburgh Legal Journal, New Series [*Pennsylvania*] [*A publication*] (DLA) ..... Pitts Leg J (NS)
Pittsburgh Legal Journal, New Series [*A publication*] (DLA) ..... Pitts LJ (NS)
Pittsburgh Legal Journal, New Series [*Pennsylvania*] [*A publication*] (DLA) ..... Pittsb Leg J NS
Pittsburgh Legal Journal, New Series [*Pennsylvania*] [*A publication*] (DLA) ..... PLJ NS
Pittsburgh Legal Journal, Old Series [*A publication*] (DLA) ..... Pittsb Leg J (OS)
Pittsburgh, McKeesport & Youghiogheny [*AAR code*] ..... PMKY
Pittsburgh Mining and Safety Research Center [*Bureau of Mines*] ..... PMSRC
Pittsburgh Mining Technology Center [*Department of Energy*] (GRD) ..... PMTC
Pittsburgh Naval Reactor (AD) ..... PNR
Pittsburgh Naval Reactors Office [*Energy Research and Development Administration*] ..... PNR
Pittsburgh Naval Reactors Office [*Department of Energy*] [*West Mifflin, PA*] (GAAI) ..... PNRO
Pittsburgh Opera Co. (AD) ..... POC
Pittsburgh, PA [*Location identifier FAA*] (FAAL) ..... AGC
Pittsburgh, PA [*Location identifier FAA*] (FAAL) ..... CCZ
Pittsburgh, PA [*Location identifier FAA*] (FAAL) ..... GPB
Pittsburgh, PA [*Location identifier FAA*] (FAAL) ..... GUT
Pittsburgh, PA [*Location identifier FAA*] (FAAL) ..... HFE
Pittsburgh, PA [*First station to broadcast a baseball game, August 5, 192 1*] [*AM radio station call letters*] ..... KDKA
Pittsburgh, PA [*Television station call letters*] ..... KDKA-TV
Pittsburgh, PA [*AM radio station call letters*] ..... KQV
Pittsburgh, PA [*Location identifier FAA*] (FAAL) ..... LXB
Pittsburgh, PA [*Location identifier FAA*] (FAAL) ..... MMJ
Pittsburgh, PA [*Location identifier FAA*] (FAAL) ..... PFS
Pittsburgh, PA (DLA) ..... Pitt
Pittsburgh, PA (DLA) ..... Pitts
Pittsburgh, PA (DLA) ..... Pittsb
Pittsburgh, PA [*Location identifier FAA*] (FAAL) ..... SAQ
Pittsburgh, PA [*Location identifier FAA*] (FAAL) ..... TQW
Pittsburgh, PA [*FM radio station call letters*] ..... WAMO
Pittsburgh, PA [*AM radio station call letters*] (RBYB) ..... WAMO-AM
Pittsburgh, PA [*FM radio station call letters*] ..... WBZZ
Pittsburgh, PA [*AM radio station call letters*] ..... WDSY
Pittsburgh, PA [*FM radio station call letters*] (RBYB) ..... WDSY-FM
Pittsburgh, PA [*FM radio station call letters*] ..... WDUQ
Pittsburgh, PA [*FM radio station call letters*] ..... WDVE
Pittsburgh, PA [*AM radio station call letters*] ..... WJAS
Pittsburgh, PA [*FM radio station call letters*] (RBYB) ..... WJJJ-FM
Pittsburgh, PA [*FM radio station call letters*] ..... WLTJ
Pittsburgh, PA [*FM radio station call letters*] (RBYB) ..... WNRQ
Pittsburgh, PA [*FM radio station call letters*] ..... WORD
Pittsburgh, PA [*Television station call letters*] ..... WPGH
Pittsburgh, PA [*AM radio station call letters*] ..... WPIT
Pittsburgh, PA [*FM radio station call letters*] ..... WPTS
Pittsburgh, PA [*Television station call letters*] ..... WPTT
Pittsburgh, PA [*Television station call letters*] ..... WPXI
Pittsburgh, PA [*FM radio station call letters*] ..... WQED
Pittsburgh, PA [*Television station call letters*] ..... WQED-TV
Pittsburgh, PA [*Television station call letters*] ..... WQEX
Pittsburgh, PA [*FM radio station call letters*] ..... WRCT
Pittsburgh, PA [*FM radio station call letters*] ..... WSHH
Pittsburgh, PA [*AM radio station call letters*] ..... WTAE
Pittsburgh, PA [*Television station call letters*] ..... WTAE-TV
Pittsburgh, PA [*FM radio station call letters*] ..... WVTY
Pittsburgh, PA [*AM radio station call letters*] ..... WWSW
Pittsburgh, PA [*FM radio station call letters*] ..... WWSW-FM
Pittsburgh, PA [*FM radio station call letters*] ..... WYEP
Pittsburgh, PA [*AM radio station call letters*] ..... WYJZ
Pittsburgh Penguins Booster Club (EA) ..... PPBC
Pittsburgh Plate Glass [*Commercial firm*] ..... PPG
Pittsburgh Pneumonia Agent [*Microbiology*] ..... PPA
Pittsburgh Public Library (AD) ..... PPL
Pittsburgh Regional Library Center [*Chatham College*] [*Pittsburgh, PA*] [*Library network*] ..... PRLC
Pittsburgh Regional Library Center, Pittsburgh, PA [*OCLC symbol*] (OCLC) ..... TQS
Pittsburgh Regional Library Center, Pittsburgh, PA [*OCLC symbol*] (OCLC) ..... TQT
Pittsburgh Regional Library Center - Union List, Pittsburgh, PA [*OCLC symbol*] (OCLC) ..... QPR
Pittsburgh Reporter [*Pennsylvania*] [*A publication*] (DLA) ..... Pittsb R (PA)
Pittsburgh Reports [*A publication*] (DLA) ..... Pitts
Pittsburgh Reports [*Pennsylvania*] [*A publication*] (DLA) ..... Pitts R
Pittsburgh Reports [*A publication*] (DLA) ..... Pitts Rep
Pittsburgh Reports [*Pennsylvania*] [*A publication*] (DLA) ..... Pitts Rep (PA)
Pittsburgh Reports [*A publication*] (DLA) ..... Pittsb
Pittsburgh Reports [*1853-73*] [*Pennsylvania*] [*A publication*] (DLA) ..... PR
Pittsburgh Reports, Edited by Crumrine [*A publication*] (DLA) ..... Crumrine
Pittsburgh Research-Based Instructional Supervising Model (EDAC) ..... PRISM
Pittsburgh Retrieval System (NITA) ..... PIRETS
Pittsburgh Sleep Quality Index ..... PSQI
Pittsburgh Supercomputing Center [*National Science Foundation Research center*] (RCD) ..... PSC
Pittsburgh Superconducting Center [*Pennsylvania*] (GRD) ..... PSC
Pittsburgh Superconducting Center Network ..... PSCNET
Pittsburgh Theological Seminary, Pittsburgh, PA [*OCLC symbol*] (OCLC) ..... PKT
Pittsburgh Theological Seminary, Pittsburgh, PA [*Library symbol Library of Congress*] (LCLS) ..... PPiPT
Pittsburgh, Youngstown & Ashland Railway Co. (IIA) ..... PYA
Pittsburgh Youth Ballet ..... PYB
Pittsburgh-Des Moines Corp. [*Associated Press*] (SAG) ..... PitDsm
Pittsdown, Crooked Island [*Bahamas*] [*ICAO location identifier*] (ICLI) ..... MYCP
Pittsfield [*Massachusetts*] [*Airport symbol*] (AD) ..... PSF
Pittsfield, IL [*Location identifier FAA*] (FAAL) ..... PPQ
Pittsfield, IL [*AM radio station call letters*] ..... WBBA
Pittsfield, IL [*FM radio station call letters*] ..... WBBA-FM
Pittsfield, IL [*FM radio station call letters*] ..... WIPA
Pittsfield, MA [*Location identifier FAA*] (FAAL) ..... EIF
Pittsfield, MA [*Location identifier FAA*] (FAAL) ..... PSF
Pittsfield, MA [*AM radio station call letters*] ..... WBEC
Pittsfield, MA [*FM radio station call letters*] ..... WBEC-FM
Pittsfield, MA [*AM radio station call letters*] ..... WBRK
Pittsfield, MA [*FM radio station call letters*] ..... WRCZ
Pittsfield, MA [*AM radio station call letters*] ..... WUHN
Pittsfield, MA [*FM radio station call letters*] ..... WUPE
Pittsfield, ME [*Location identifier FAA*] (FAAL) ..... BUP
Pittsfield, ME [*FM radio station call letters*] ..... WPBC
Pittsfield Public Library, Pittsfield, IL [*Library symbol Library of Congress*] (LCLS) ..... IPit
Pittsford, MI [*FM radio station call letters*] ..... WPCJ
Pittsford Township Library, Pittsford, MI [*Library symbol Library of Congress*] (LCLS) ..... MiPit
Pittsford-Medon High School Library, Pittsford, NY [*OCLC symbol*] (OCLC) ..... RXF
Pittsford-Sutherland High School Library, Pittsford, NY [*OCLC symbol*] (OCLC) ..... RXG
Pittston Brinks Grp [*NYSE symbol*] (TTSB) ..... PZB
Pittston Burlington Group [*NYSE symbol*] (TTSB) ..... PZX
[*The*] **Pittston Co.** [*Associated Press*] (SAG) ..... PitstnMn
[*The*] **Pittston Co.** [*Associated Press*] (SAG) ..... PitstnSvc
Pittston Minerals Group [*NYSE symbol*] (SPSG) ..... PZM
Pittston, PA [*AM radio station call letters*] ..... WARD
Pittston, PA [*AM radio station call letters*] (RBYB) ..... WKQV-AM
Pittston, PA [*FM radio station call letters*] ..... WWSH
Pittston Services Group [*Formerly, The Pittston Co.*] [*NYSE symbol*] (SPSG) ..... PZS
Pittway Corp. [*Associated Press*] (SAG) ..... Pittway
Pittway Corp. [*Associated Press*] (SAG) ..... Pittwy
Pittway Corp. [*Associated Press*] (SAG) ..... PittwyA
Pittway Corp. [*AMEX symbol*] (SPSG) ..... PRY
Pittway Corp.'A' [*AMEX symbol*] (TTSB) ..... PRY.A
Pituitary [*Endocrinology*] (AAMN) ..... PIT
Pituitary Adenylate Cyclase Activating Polypeptide [*Biochemistry*] ..... PACAP
Pituitary Adenylyl Cyclase-Activating Polypeptide [*Endocrinology*] ..... PACAP
Pituitary Adrenotrophic Hormone [*Endocrinology*] ..... PATH
Pituitary Gonadotropin [*Endocrinology*] (MAE) ..... PG
Pituitary Growth Hormone [*Endocrinology*] ..... PGH
Pituitary Opioid Peptide [*Medicine*] (DMAA) ..... POP
Pituitary Resistance to Thyroid Hormone [*Medicine*] (DMAA) ..... PRTH
Pituitary Stalk [*Neuroanatomy*] ..... PS
Pituitary-Adrenal [*Endocrinology*] (DAVI) ..... PA
Pityriasis [*Dermatology*] ..... PR
Pityriasis Lichenoides et Varioliformis Acuta [*Dermatology*] (MAE) ..... PLEVA
Pityriasis Rosea [*Dermatology*] (MAE) ..... PR
Pityriasis Rubra Pilaris [*Dermatology*] (MAE) ..... PRP
Piu Forte [*A Little Louder*] [*Music*] ..... PF
Piu Pianissimo [*Very Very Softly*] [*Italian*] [*Music*] (AD) ..... ppp
Piu Piano [*More Softly*] [*Music*] ..... PP
Piu Piu Piu Pianissimo [*Very, Very, Very Softly*] [*Italian*] [*Music*] (AD) ..... pppp
Piura [*Peru*] [*Airport symbol*] (OAG) ..... PIU
Piura/Capitan Concha [*Peru*] [*ICAO location identifier*] (ICLI) ..... SPUR
Pius [*Dutiful*] [*Latin*] ..... P
Piute Reservoir [*Utah*] [*Seismograph station code, US Geological Survey*] (SEIS) ..... PUU
Piva [*Solomon Islands*] [*Seismograph station code, US Geological Survey Closed*] (SEIS) ..... PIV
Pivot [*Automotive engineering*] ..... PIV
Pivot (MSA) ..... PVT
Pivot, AB [*Television station call letters*] CHAT-1
Pivot Ambulating Crutchless Orthosis [*Medicine*] ..... PACO
Pivotal Unknowables ..... PUKS
Pivoted Door (AAG) ..... PD
Pivoted Window (AAG) ..... PW
Pixar [*NASDAQ symbol*] (TTSB) ..... PIXR
PIXEL Block Mode [*Computer science*] (BYTE) ..... PBM
PIXEL [*Picture Element*] **per Inch** [*Computer science*] (PCM) ..... PPI
Pixel per Line [*Computer science*] (IAA) ..... PPL

PIXEL-Processing [*Computer science*] ... PP
Pixels Per Inch [*Computer graphics*] (WDMC) ... ppi
Pixley on Auditors [*8th ed.*] [*1901*] [*A publication*] (DLA) ... Pix Aud
PixTech, Inc. [*NASDAQ symbol*] (SAG) ... PIXT
PixTech, Inc. [*Associated Press*] (SAG) ... PixTech
Pizaz European [*British*] [*FAA designator*] (FAAC) ... PIZ
Pizza ... PZ
Pizza and Pasta Association [*British*] (DBA) ... PAPA
Pizza Inn [*NASDAQ symbol*] (TTSB) ... PZZI
Pizza Inn, Inc. [*Associated Press*] (SAG) ... PizzaInn
Pizza Inn, Inc. [*NASDAQ symbol*] (SAG) ... PZZI
Pizza Patio Ltd. [*Vancouver Stock Exchange symbol*] ... PZZ
Pizzeria ... PZA
Pizzicato [*Plucked*] [*Music*] ... PIZZ
PJ America, Inc. [*Associated Press*] (SAG) ... PJ Amer
PJ America, Inc. [*NASDAQ symbol*] (SAG) ... PJAM
PKA [*Professional Karate Association*] **Fighters Association** [*Defunct*] (EA) ... PKAFA
PKU [*Phenylketonuria*] **Parents** (EA) ... PKU-P
Pkynocytes [*Hematology*] (DAVI) ... KYKN
PL/M Extended [*Programming language*] (CSR) ... PLMX
PLA [*Public Library Association*] **Alternative Education Programs Section** ... PLA AEPS
PLA [*Public Library Association*] **Armed Forces Library Section** ... PLA AFLS
PLA [*Public Library Association*] **Audiovisual** ... PLA AV
PLA [*Public Library Association*] **Audiovisual Committee** ... PLA AVC
PLA [*Public Library Association*] **Community Information Section** ... PLA CIS
PLA [*Public Library Association*] **Legislative Committee** ... PLA LC
PLA [*Public Library Association*] **Marketing of Public Library Services Section** ... PLA MPLSS
PLA [*Public Library Association*] **Metropolitan Libraries Section** ... PLA MLS
PLA [*Public Library Association*] **Public Library Systems Section** ... PLA PLSS
PLA [*Public Library Association*] **Small and Medium-Sized Libraries Section** ... PLA SMLS
Place [*Investment term*] ... PL
Place ... PL
Place ... PL
Place (ODBW) ... pl
Place (DD) ... Pl
Place (VRA) ... pl
Place (ADA) ... PLA
Place [*Commonly used*] (OPSA) ... PLACE
Place Accepted for Enlistment ... PAFE
Place Accumulator in Indicators (IAA) ... PAI
Place Address in Index Register (SAA) ... PAX
Place Bearing/Distance [*Way point*] (GAVI) ... PBD
Place Before Subject [*Library cataloguing*] (DGA) ... PBS
Place Complement of Address in Index Register (SAA) ... PAC
Place Decrement in Index ... PDX
Place from Which Ordered to Active Duty [*Military*] ... PFWOAD
Place Identification/Characteristics and Area/Distance and Direction [*Bureau of the Census*] ... PICADAD
Place in Inactive File [*Army*] ... PIF
Place Index in Address (SAA) ... PXA
Place Index in Decrement ... PXD
Place Indicator in Accumulators (SAA) ... PIA
Place Names Committee [*Victoria, Australia*] ... PNC
Place of Acceptance [*Business term*] (DCTA) ... POA
Place of Acceptance (AD) ... poa
Place of Birth ... PLOB
Place of Birth ... POB
Place of Death (MAE) ... POD
Place of Delivery [*Shipping*] (DS) ... POD
Place of Discharge ... POD
Place of Last Entered Active Duty [*Military*] ... PLEAD
Place of Publication Class Number (NITA) ... PN
Place of Publisher (NITA) ... PP
Place of Work and Migration Sample [*Bureau of the Census*] (GFGA) ... POW/MIG
Place Resources Corp. [*Toronto Stock Exchange symbol*] ... PLG
Place to Go (IAA) ... PTG
Placebo [*Medicine*] ... P
Placebo [*Medicine*] ... pbo
Placebo [*Medicine*] ... PL
Placebo [*Medicine*] ... PLA
Placebo [*Medicine*] ... PLAC
Placebo Group [*Medicine*] ... PG
Placebo Treated [*Medicine*] ... PT
Placed off Hire ... POH
Placed under Observation [*Medicine*] ... PUO
Placement Contracting Officer [*Army*] (AABC) ... PCO
Placement Revision Request ... PRR
Placement Route and Patch [*Computer science*] (IAA) ... PRP
Place-Name ... PN
Placename Survey of the US (EA) ... PNSUS
Placenta, Ovary, Uterus [*Medicine*] ... POU
Placental Alkaline Phosphatase [*An enzyme*] ... PLAP
Placental Basement Membrane [*Medicine*] (DMAA) ... PBM
Placental Lactogen [*Endocrinology*] ... PL
Placental Lactogenic Hormone (DMAA) ... PLH
Placental Luteinizing Hormone-Releasing Factor [*Endocrinology*] ... pLRF
Placental Protein [*Gynecology*] ... PP
Placental Residual Blood Volume [*Medicine*] (DMAA) ... PRBC
Placental Residual Blood Volume [*Medicine*] (DMAA) ... PRBV
Placental Residual Blood Volume [*Hematology*] (MAE) ... PRBV
Placentia District Library, Placentia, CA [*Library symbol Library of Congress*] (LCLS) ... CPl
Placentia, NF [*Television station call letters*] ... CBNT-2
Placentia Public Library, Newfoundland [*Library symbol National Library of Canada*] (NLC) ... NFP
Placentia Public Library, Placentia, NF, Canada [*Library symbol Library of Congress*] (LCLS) ... CaNfP
Placentinus [*Deceased, 1192*] [*Authority cited in pre-1607 legal work*] (DSA) ... P
Placentinus [*Deceased, 1192*] [*Authority cited in pre-1607 legal work*] (DSA) ... Pla
Placentinus [*Deceased, 1192*] [*Authority cited in pre-1607 legal work*] (DSA) ... Plac
Placer Development Library, Vancouver, BC, Canada [*Library symbol Library of Congress*] (LCLS) ... CaBVaP
Placer Development Library, Vancouver, British Columbia [*Library symbol National Library of Canada*] (NLC) ... BVAP
Placer Development Ltd. [*Toronto Stock Exchange symbol Vancouver Stock Exchange symbol*] ... PDL
Placer Development Ltd. [*AMEX symbol*] (SPSG) ... PLC
Placer Dome [*Associated Press*] (SAG) ... PlcrD
Placer Dome, Inc. [*NYSE symbol Toronto Stock Exchange symbol Vancouver Stock Exchange symbol*] (SPSG) ... PDG
Placer Dome, Inc. [*Associated Press*] (SAG) ... PlacerD
Placerville, CA [*Location identifier FAA*] (FAAL) ... HNW
Placerville, CA [*FM radio station call letters*] ... KZSA
Placerville, CA [*Location identifier FAA*] (FAAL) ... PVF
Places, Organizations, Things, Biographics, Intangibles ... POTBI
Placid, Louisiana Land and Exploration, Amerada Hess, Getty, and Marathon [*Oil-and gas-holding bloc in Alaska*] ... PLAGM
Placid Oil Co., Exploration Library, Dallas, TX [*OCLC symbol*] (OCLC) ... DPO
Placid Oil Co. Exploration Library, Dallas, TX [*Library symbol Library of Congress*] (LCLS) ... TxDaPO
Placidyl [*Ethchlorvynol*] [*A hypnotic and sedative*] (DAVI) ... PL DYL
Placita ... PLA
Placita Anglo-Normannica Cases (Bigelow) [*A publication*] (DLA) ... Pl Ang-Norm
Placita Coronae [*Pleas of the Crown*] [*Latin Legal term*] (DLA) ... Pl C
Placita de Quo Warranto, Record Commission [*England*] [*A publication*] (DLA) ... PQW
Placita Generalia [*Latin A publication*] (DLA) ... Plac Gen
Placita Parliamentaria [*Latin A publication*] (DLA) ... Pl Par
Placita Parliamentaria [*Latin A publication*] (DLA) ... Pla Par
Placitorum Abbreviatio [*Latin A publication*] (DLA) ... Plac Abbrev
Placitum [*or Placita*] [*Agreeable, Agreed Upon*] [*Latin*] [*Legal term*] (DLA) ... P
Placitum [*or Placita*] [*Agreeable, Agreed Upon*] [*Latin*] [*Legal term*] (DLA) ... PLA
Plagioclase [*Lunar geology*] ... Pl
Plagioclase [*Lunar geology*] ... Plag
Plaid (ADA) ... PLD
Plaid Cymru [*Welsh national liberation party*] [*Political party*] ... PC
Plain (MSA) ... PL
Plain [*Commonly used*] (OPSA) ... PLAIN
Plain ... PLN
Plain ... PLN
Plain Abdominal Radiograph [*Medicine*] (DMAA) ... PAR
Plain Bond Copier [*Pitney Bowes*] ... PBC
Plain Clothes Gratuity [*British military*] (DMA) ... PCG
Plain Deckle Edges [*Graphic arts*] (DGA) ... PDE
Plain Edges [*Graphic arts*] (DGA) ... PE
Plain End [*Lumber*] (DAC) ... PE
Plain English Campaign [*British*] (DBA) ... PEC
Plain Face [*Construction*] ... PF
Plain Language [*As opposed to coded message*] [*Military*] ... PL
Plain Language Address [*Telecommunications*] (TEL) ... PLA
Plain Language Address Directory ... PLAD
Plain Ol' Country Boy ... POCB
Plain Old Balloon Angioplasty [*Cardiology*] [*Facetious*] ... POBA
Plain Old Telephone [*Bell System's basic model*] ... POT
Plain Old Telephone Service [*or System*] [*Humorous term for Long Lines Department of AT & T See also PANS*] ... POTS
Plain Old Telephone Service (AD) ... pots
Plain Paper Copier [*Electrophotography*] ... PPC
Plain Paper Optimized Printing [*Canon*] [*Computer science*] ... P-POP
Plain Plaster Cornice [*Construction*] ... PPC
Plain Talk (EA) ... PT
Plain Test (MCD) ... PT
Plain Washer [*Automotive engineering*] ... PL/WA
Plain Washer (MSA) ... PW
Plaine Des Jarres [*South Vietnam*] ... PDJ
Plaine Des Lacs [*New Caledonia*] [*ICAO location identifier*] (ICLI) ... NWWS
Plainedge High School, North Massapequa, NY [*Library symbol*] [*Library of Congress*] (LCLS) ... NNomPH
Plainedge Public Library, Seaford, NY [*Library symbol Library of Congress*] (LCLS) ... NSeaP
Plainfield Courier-News, Bridgewater, NJ [*Library symbol Library of Congress*] (LCLS) ... NjBriCN
Plainfield, IN [*FM radio station call letters*] ... WXIR
Plainfield News, Nashua, IA [*Library symbol Library of Congress*] (LCLS) ... IaNasPN
Plainfield, NJ [*AM radio station call letters*] ... WERA
Plainfield Public Library, Guilford Township and Hendricks County Historical Collection, Plainfield, IN [*Library symbol Library of Congress*] (LCLS) ... InPla-Hi
Plainfield Public Library, Plainfield, IN [*Library symbol Library of Congress*] (LCLS) ... InPla
Plainfield Public Library, Plainfield, NJ [*Library symbol Library of Congress*] (LCLS) ... NjPla

Plainfield Times, Plainfield, NJ [*Library symbol Library of Congress*] (LCLS) ... NjPlaT
Plainfield, VT [*FM radio station call letters*] ... WGDR
Plains [*Commonly used*] (OPSA) ... PLAINES
Plains [*Commonly used*] (OPSA) ... PLAINS
Plains ... PLNS
Plains (MCD) ... PLNS
Plains and Peaks Public Library System, Limon, CO [*Library symbol Library of Congress*] (LCLS) ... CoLimP
Plains Cotton Growers (EA) ... PCG
Plains Health Centre, Health Sciences Library, Regina, SK, Canada [*Library symbol Library of Congress*] (LCLS) ... CaSRHS
Plains Petroleum Co. [*Vancouver Stock Exchange symbol*] ... PPD
Plains Public Library, Plains, MT [*Library symbol*] [*Library of Congress*] (LCLS) ... MtP
Plains Public School Library, Plains, MT [*Library symbol*] [*Library of Congress*] (LCLS) ... MtPPS
Plains Resources [*AMEX symbol*] (TTSB) ... PLX
Plains Resources, Inc. [*Associated Press*] (SAG) ... PlnRsc
Plains Resources, Inc. [*AMEX symbol*] (SPSG) ... PLX
Plains Tribal Council of Assam [*India*] [*Political party*] (PPW) ... PTCA
Plains, TX [*FM radio station call letters*] (RBYB) ... KPHS-FM
Plains, TX [*FM radio station call letters*] ... KPLN-FM
Plainsong and Mediaeval Music Society (EA) ... PMMS
Plaint [*Legal term*] (ROG) ... PLT
Plaintiff ... P
Plaintiff [*Legal shorthand*] (LWAP) ... P
Plaintiff ... PLF
Plaintiff ... PLFF
Plaintiff [*Legal term*] (ROG) ... PLTF
Plaintiff ... PLTFF
Plaintiff [*Legal term*] (ROG) ... PTF
Plaintree Systems [*NASDAQ symbol*] (TTSB) ... LANPF
Plaintree Systems Inc. [*NASDAQ symbol*] (SAG) ... LANP
Plaintree Systems, Inc. [*Associated Press*] (SAG) ... Plaintr
Plainview, NY [*FM radio station call letters*] ... WPOB
Plainview, TX [*FM radio station call letters*] (RBYB) ... KHDY-FM
Plainview, TX [*AM radio station call letters*] ... KKYN
Plainview, TX [*FM radio station call letters*] ... KKYN-FM
Plainview, TX [*AM radio station call letters*] ... KVOP
Plainview, TX [*FM radio station call letters*] ... KWLD
Plainview, TX [*Location identifier FAA*] (FAAL) ... PVW
Plainview-Old Bethpage Middle School, Plainview, NY [*Library symbol*] [*Library of Congress*] (LCLS) ... NPIBM
Plainview-Old Bethpage Public Library, Plainview, NY [*Library symbol Library of Congress*] (LCLS) ... NPI
Plainview-Old Bethpage Senior High School, Plainview, NY [*Library symbol Library of Congress*] (LCLS) ... NPISH
Plainville, KS [*FM radio station call letters*] (RBYB) ... KFIX-FM
Plaisance [*Mauritius*] [*Geomagnetic observatory code*] ... PLS
Plaited Cordage Manufacturers Association [*British*] (BI) ... PCMA
Plamondon Public Library, Alberta [*Library symbol National Library of Canada*] (NLC) ... APL
Plamondon Public Library, Plamondon, AB, Canada [*Library symbol*] [*Library of Congress*] (LCLS) ... CaAPl
Plan (CPH) ... P
Plan (NASA) ... PLN
Plan Account Number File [*IRS*] ... PANF
Plan Analysis and Modeling System (MHDB) ... PAMS
Plan Case Control File [*IRS*] ... PCCF
Plan Characteristics File [*IRS*] ... PCF
Plan Filing Cabinet ... PFC
Plan for Action (MCD) ... PFA
Plan for Action by Citizens in Education ... PACE
Plan for Long-Range Technical Requirements ... PLTR
Plan for Maintenance [*Navy*] ... PFM
Plan for Navy Satellite Communications Plan ... PNSCP
Plan for Use (DNAB) ... PFU
Plan Handling and RADAR Operating System [*Aviation*] (DA) ... PHAROS
Plan Identification Number (DOMA) ... PID
Plan Identification Number (AFM) ... PIN
Plan Name and Address File [*IRS*] ... PNAF
Plan of Action (NASA) ... POA
Plan of Action and Milestones (NVT) ... POA & M
Plan of Action for Challenging Times (EA) ... PACT
Plan of Instruction ... POI
Plan of Intended Movement (MUGU) ... PIM
Plan of Launch Azimuth [*Aerospace*] (AAG) ... PLA
Plan of Service (OICC) ... POS
Plan of Service Automated Reporting System [*Employment and Training Administration*] [*Department of Labor*] ... POSARS
Plan of the Day ... POD
Plan Organization Index File [*IRS*] ... POIF
Plan, Organize, Direct, Coordinate, Control [*Principles of management*] ... PODCC
Plan Position Data Display ... PPDD
Plan Position Indicator (AD) ... ppi
Plan Position Indicator Mode [*Computer science*] (ADA) ... PPI
Plan Position Landing (DEN) ... PPL
Plan Position Presentation ... PPP
Plan Positional Plot Indicator ... PPPI
Plan Profile ... PP
Plan, Rehearse, Edit, and Psych [*Public speaking preparation technique*] ... PREP
Plan Repeater Indicator (IAA) ... PRI
Plan Speed Indicator [*Military*] ... PSI
Plan to Clear [*Aviation*] (FAAC) ... PTC
Plan Value Work Accounting (MCD) ... PVWA
Plan Video Display (NITA) ... PVD
Plan View (MSA) ... PV
Plan [*or Planned*] **View Display** [*RADAR*] (AFM) ... PVD
Plan View Display (GAVI) ... PVD
Plan, Year, and Age [*Insurance designations*] ... PYA
Planar (MSA) ... PLNR
Planar Array Antenna ... PAA
Planar Chromatography ... PLC
Planar Combat Problem ... PCP
Planar Deformation Feature [*Geology*] ... PDF
Planar Distributed Function Generator (PDAA) ... PDFG
Planar Epitaxial Passivated ... PEP
Planar Epitaxial Tuning Varactor ... PETV
Planar Gas Discharge (MCD) ... PGD
Planar Laser Induced Fluorescence ... PLIF
Planar Metallization with Polymer (IAA) ... PMP
Planar Oxygen Sensor ... POS
Planar Postive Column (IAA) ... PPC
Planar Radial Peaking Factor [*Network analysis*] (IEEE) ... PRPF
Planar Random Composite (MCD) ... PRC
Planar Randomly Reinforced Fiber Composite ... PRRFC
Planar Rider System ... PRS
Planar Silicon Photoswitch (IEEE) ... PSPS
Planar Silicon Power Transistor ... PSPT
Planar Systems [*Commercial firm Associated Press*] (SAG) ... PlanarSy
Planar Systems [*NASDAQ symbol*] (SAG) ... PLNR
Planar Tube ... PLT
Planar Turbulence Amplifier (IEEE) ... PTA
Planar Wing Module (MCD) ... PWM
Planck Constant [*Symbol*] [*IUPAC*] ... h
Planck Function [*Symbol*] [*IUPAC*] ... Y
Plan-Do Intergration [*Medicine*] (DMAA) ... PDI
Plan-Do-Check-Act [*Medicine*] (DMAA) ... PDCA
Plane (MSA) ... PLN
Plane Captain (MUGU) ... P/C
Plane Captain Designated [*or Designation*] (DNAB) ... PCDESIG
Plane Change (MCD) ... PC
Plane Circular Aperture ... PCA
Plane Commander ... PC
Plane Disagreement [*Telecommunications*] (TEL) ... PD
Plane Frame [*Camutek*] [*Software package*] (NCC) ... PF
Plane Grating Spectrograph ... PGS
Plane Guard (NVT) ... PLG
Plane Handler [*Navy*] ... PH
Plane of Vibration ... POV
Plane Paper Copier (IAA) ... PPC
Plane Parallel ... PP
Plane Polarized [*Telecommunications*] (TEL) ... PP
Plane Position Indicator [*RADAR*] ... PPI
Plane Strain Plastometer ... PSP
Plane Stress Analysis and Plot [*Computer science*] ... PSAP
Plane Swivel Joint ... PSJ
Plane Transport System (DA) ... PTS
Planed ... P
Planed All Round (DAC) ... PAR
Planed and Square-Edge (DAC) ... pse
Planed and Square-Jointed (DAC) ... psj
Planed Four Sides [*Technical drawings*] (DAC) ... P4S
Planed One Edge [*Technical drawings*] (DAC) ... P1E
Planed One Side [*Technical drawings*] (DAC) ... P1S
Planed One Side and Two Edges [*Technical drawings*] (DAC) ... P1S2E
Planed, Tongued, and Grooved (DAC) ... PTG
Planemasters Services, Inc. [*ICAO designator*] (FAAC) ... PMS
Plane-Polarized Wave ... PPW
Planer Fixture ... PLRF
Planet (MSA) ... PLNT
Planet Drum Foundation (EA) ... PDF
Planet Hollywood International, Inc. [*NASDAQ symbol*] (SAG) ... PHII
Planet Hollywood International, Inc. [*Associated Press*] (SAG) ... PlanHlly
Planet Hollywood Intl'A' [*NASDAQ symbol*] (TTSB) ... PHII
Planet in Field of View [*NASA*] ... PIFOV
Planet in View [*NASA*] ... PIV
Planet Polymer Technologies [*NASDAQ symbol*] (TTSB) ... POLY
Planet Polymer Technologies, Inc. [*Associated Press*] (SAG) ... PlPolyT
Planet Polymer Technologies, Inc. [*NASDAQ symbol*] (SAG) ... POLY
Planet Scan Platform [*NASA*] (KSC) ... PSP
Planet Sensor Output ... PSO
Planeta Rica [*Colombia*] [*Airport symbol*] (AD) ... PLC
Planetary (MSA) ... PLNTY
Planetary Association for Clean Energy (EA) ... PACE
Planetary Atmosphere (SAA) ... P/A
Planetary Atmosphere Experimental [*or Experiments*] **Test** [*NASA*] ... PAET
Planetary Boundary Layer [*Aerospace*] ... PBL
Planetary Citizens (EA) ... PC
Planetary Entry Capsule [*Aerospace*] ... PEC
Planetary Entry Parachute Program [*NASA*] ... PEPP
Planetary Entry Radiation Facility [*Langley Research Center*] [*NASA*] (PDAA) ... PERF
Planetary Ephemeris Program (IEEE) ... PEP
Planetary Exploration Plan [*NASA*] ... PEP
Planetary Explorer [*NASA*] ... PE
Planetary Gear Drive ... PGD
Planetary Gearhead Motor [*Aerospace*] ... PGM
Planetary Horizon Platform [*Aerospace*] ... PHP

Planetary Initiative for the World We Choose (EA) .... PIWWC
Planetary Landing Observation Package [Aerospace] .... PLOP
Planetary Liquid-Cooled Brake [Off-highway equipment] .... PLCB
Planetary Manned Space Flight Network [Aerospace] (MCD) ...... PMSFN
Planetary Microbiological Assay [Aerospace] .... PMA
Planetary Mission [NASA] (NASA) .... PM
Planetary Observation Geometry and Science Instrument Sequence
  Program [Aerospace] .... POGASIS
Planetary Office (IAA) .... PO
Planetary Operations Analysis Area [NASA] .... POAA
Planetary Orbit .... PO
Planetary Orbit Determination (IEEE) .... PLOD
Planetary Orbiter Error Analysis Study Program .... POEAS
Planetary Physical Processes Laboratory (SSD) .... PPPL
Planetary Programs [NASA] .... PP
Planetary Quarantine [NASA] .... PQ
Planetary Quarantine Plan [NASA] .... PQP
Planetary RADAR [Equipment box] .... PR
Planetary Radio Astronomy .... PRA
Planetary Rocket Launcher Platform (AAG) .... PRLP
Planetary Rocket Ocean Platform .... PROP
Planetary Rotation Engine (IAA) .... PRE
Planetary Rotation Machine (IAA) .... PLM
Planetary Scan System [or Subsystem] .... PSS
Planetary Society (EA) .... PS
[The] Planetary Society .... TPS
Planetary Space Vehicle [NASA] (NASA) .... PSV
Planetary Spectroscopy Telescope (SSD) .... PST
Planetary Surface (IAA) .... PS
Planetary Vehicle [NASA] .... PV
Plane-Wave Born Approximation .... PWBA
Plane-Wave Orbital [Physics] .... PWO
Plane-Wave Spectrum .... PWS
Planification de l'Emploi [Canadian Jobs Strategy - CJS] .... PE
Planification d'Urgence Canada [Emergency Planning Canada - EPC] .... PUC
Plank (AAG) .... PLK
Planking and Strutting [Construction] .... P & S
Plankinton City Library, Plankinton, SD [Library symbol Library of
  Congress] (LCLS) .... SdPl
Plank-on-Edge .... POE
Plank-on-Edge Buoy (AD) .... poe buoy
Plankton Rate Processes in Oligotrophic Oceans [Cooperative research
  project] .... PRPOOS
Plannar Wing Weapon (MCD) .... PWW
Planned (DA) .... plnd
Planned Action with Constant Evaluation [Computer science] ..... PACE
Planned Active Duty Date [Military] .... PADD
Planned Aids for Cross-Culture Knowledge, Action and Growth in
  Effectiveness .... PACKAGE
Planned Amortization Class [Investment term] (DFIT) .... PAC
Planned Amortization Credit [Investment term] (ECON) .... PAC
Planned Approach to Community Health .... PATCH
Planned Arrival and Departure System [FAA] (TAG) .... PADS
Planned Attack on Nine Inner Cities [to build education parks] ... PANIC
Planned Availability Concept (MHDI) .... PAC
Planned Completion Date (TEL) .... PCD
Planned Component Replacement [Predictive maintenance schedule] .... PCR
Planned Data to Transportation [DoD] .... PDT
Planned Depot Level Maintenance (MCD) .... PDLM
Planned Derated Hours [Electronics] (IEEE) .... PDH
Planned Derating [Electronics] (IEEE) .... PD
Planned District Craft [Navy symbol] .... YTX
Planned Event Discrepancy Notification [NASA] (KSC) .... PEDN
Planned Experience for Effective Relating .... PEER
Planned Flight Data [Aviation] (DA) .... PFD
Planned Giving Today [A publication] .... PGT
Planned Incremental Modernization (DOMA) .... PIM
Planned Insurance Coverage .... PIC
Planned Interdependency Incentive Method .... PIIM
Planned Labor Application [Military] (AFIT) .... PLA
Planned Landing Area [NASA] .... PLA
Planned Life Extension [Pershing] (MCD) .... PLE
Planned Lifetime Advocacy Network .... PLAN
Planned Logistics Analysis and Evaluation Technique [Air Force] .... PLANET
Planned Maintenance [Contract Data Research] [Software package]
  (NCC) .... PLANMAN
Planned Maintenance Plan (MCD) .... PMP
Planned Maintenance Requirements .... PMR
Planned Maintenance System [SNMMS] .... PMS
Planned Maintenance System for Surface Missile Ships .... PMS/SMS
Planned Maintenance System for Surface Missile Ships (AD) ..... PMSSMS
Planned Missile System .... PMS
Planned Obsolescence (MHDB) .... PO
Planned Outage Factor [Electronics] (IEEE) .... POF
Planned Outage Hours [Electronics] (IEEE) .... POH
Planned Parenthood .... PP
Planned Parenthood Federation of America (EA) .... PPFA
Planned Parenthood Federation of America, Inc., Katharine Dexter
  McCormick Library, New York, NY [Library symbol Library of Congress]
  (LCLS) .... NNPPFA
Planned Parenthood League (AD) .... PPL
Planned Parenthood of Alameda, San Francisco, San Francisco, CA
  [Library symbol Library of Congress] (LCLS) .... CSfPP
Planned Parenthood of Billings, Billings, MT [Library symbol] [Library of
  Congress] (LCLS) .... MtBilPP

Planned Parenthood of Mercer Area, Trenton, NJ [Library symbol Library of
  Congress] (LCLS) .... NjTPP
Planned Parenthood of Nashville, Nashville, TN [Library symbol Library of
  Congress] (LCLS) .... TNPP
Planned Parenthood of New York City, Inc., Abraham Stone Memorial
  Library, Margaret Sanger Center, New York, NY [Library symbol Library
  of Congress] (LCLS) .... NNPPNYC
Planned Parenthood of Northeast Texas, Dallas, TX [Library symbol Library
  of Congress] (LCLS) .... TxDaPP
Planned Parenthood of Rochester and Monroe County, Rochester, NY
  [Library symbol Library of Congress] (LCLS) .... NRPlanP
Planned Parenthood of Southeast Pennsylvania, Philadelphia, PA [Library
  symbol Library of Congress] (LCLS) .... PPPlanP
Planned Parenthood - World Population [Later, PPFA] (EA) ...... PPWP
Planned Position Indicator Readout (NVT) .... PPIRO
Planned Preventive Maintenance (IEEE) .... PPM
Planned Procurement Guide .... PPG
Planned Product Improvement P2I
Planned Program Accomplishment (GNE) .... PPA
Planned Program Product Improvement [Army] .... P_3I
Planned Quality Assurance Program [Navy] .... PQAP
Planned Regulatory Action [Federal government] (GFGA) .... PRA
Planned Release of Selected and Modified Organisms [British] ... PROSAMO
Planned Requirements (DNAB) .... P/R
Planned Requirements - Bureau Directed .... PRB
Planned Requirements, Conversion (NG) .... PRC
Planned Requirements, Outfitting [Navy] (NG) .... PRO
Planned Residential Development .... PRD
Planned Restricted Availability [Military] (NVT) .... PRA
Planned Restricted Availability [Navy] (ANA) .... PRAV
Planned Retirement Income Program [Institute of Financial Management] .... PRIP
Planned Standard Equipment [Navy] (AFIT) .... PLNSTD
Planned Standard Programming [Computer science] .... PSP
Planned Start Installation [Telecommunications] (TEL) .... PSI
Planned Systems Schedule (AAG) .... PSS
Planned Unit Development [Housing] .... PUD
Planned Urban Development .... PUD
Planned Value of Work Accomplished .... PVWA
Planned Value of Work Scheduled (MCD) .... PVWS
Planned Variations Demonstration [HUD] .... PVD
Planned-Amortization-Class Bond [Investment term] .... PAC
Planner .... PLNR
Planners for Equal Opportunity [Defunct] (EA) .... PEO
Planners Network (EA) .... PN
Planners Referral Service [Information service or system] (IID) .. PRS
Planning .... P
Planning (DLA) .... Plan
Planning .... PLAN
Planning .... PLNG
Planning (MCD) .... PLNN
Planning [Aircraft classification letter] .... Z
Planning Action Directive [Military] (AFIT) .... PAD
Planning Action Request [NASA] (MCD) .... PAR
Planning, Activation, Modification [Army reorganization] .... PAM
Planning Activity Report .... PAR
Planning Advisory Committee (OICC) .... PAC
Planning Advisory Service (GNE) .... PAS
Planning Aid for Retail Information System [IBM Corp.] .... PARIS
Planning, Analysis, and Integration .... PA & I
Planning Analysis Evaluation System .... PAES
Planning and Analysis Division [Environmental Protection Agency] (GFGA) .... PAD
Planning and Analysis for Uncertain Situations (MHDI) .... PAUS
Planning and Budgeting [Military] (AFIT) .... P & B
Planning and Compensation Reports [British] .... P & CR
Planning and Compensation Reports [British A publication] (DLA) .... Plan & Comp
Planning and Conservation League (EA) .... PCL
Planning and Control Guide .... PCG
Planning and Control Made Easy (PDAA) .... PACE
Planning and Control Memorandum [Army] .... PCM
Planning and Control Techniques .... PCT
Planning and Coordinating Committee for Environmental Studies [National
  Research Council] .... PCCES
Planning and Development Library, City of Ottawa, Ontario [Library symbol
  National Library of Canada] (BIB) .... OOCPB
Planning and Engineering for Repair and Alteration [Navy] .... PERA
Planning and Estimating (AAG) .... P & E
Planning and Estimating (IAA) .... PAE
Planning and Forecasting (MCD) .... P & F
Planning and Implementing Vocational Readiness in Occupational
  Therapy .... PIVOT
Planning and Management Division [Environmental Protection Agency]
  (GFGA) .... PMD
Planning and Operations .... P & O
Planning and Operations Division [Military] .... P & O Div
Planning and Operations Management Team (MCD) .... POMT
Planning and Organization .... P & O
Planning and Policy Guidance (MCD) .... PPG
Planning and Programming Guidance [Army] (AABC) .... PPG
Planning and Programming Guidance (AD) .... ppg
Planning and Research Library, Technical Services Branch, Ontario Police
  Commission, Toronto, Ontario [Library symbol National Library of
  Canada] (NLC) .... OTOPCT
Planning and Review (MCD) .... P & R
Planning and Role Setting for Public Libraries [Public Library Association]
  [A publication] .... PRSPL

Planning and Scheduling ... PS
Planning and Scheduling Document Record [*NASA*] (NASA) ... PSDR
Planning and Scheduling Session ... PASS
Planning and Scheduling System (NASA) ... PASS
Planning and the Black Community (EA) ... PBC
Planning and Timing [*of Investments*] ... PT
Planning Appeals Board. Reports [*A publication*] ... PABR
Planning Assistance (EA) ... PA
Planning Assistance, Inc., New York, NY [*Library symbol Library of Congress*] (LCLS) ... NNPlan
Planning Assistance Through Technical Evaluation of Relevance Numbers [*RAND Corp.*] ... PATTERN
Planning Associates for Computers and Telecommunications (NITA) ... PACTEL
Planning Automation and Control for Evaluating Requirements ... PACER
Planning Board ... PB
Planning Board European Inland Surface Transport [*Army*] (AABC) ... PBEIST
Planning Board for Ocean Shipping [*Army NATO*] ... PBOS
Planning Branch, Saskatchewan Department of Highways and Transportation, Regina,Saskatchewan [*Library symbol National Library of Canada*] (NLC) ... SRHP
Planning Card (AAG) ... PC
Planning Card Index (AAG) ... PCI
Planning Career Goals [*Vocational guidance test*] ... PCG
Planning Change Board (AAG) ... PCB
Planning Change Notice ... PCN
Planning Change Notice Request ... PCNR
Planning Change [*or Check*] **Request** (AAG) ... PCR
Planning Committee [*International Organization for Standardization*] (IEEE) ... PLACO
Planning Concept (MCD) ... PC
Planning Configuration List ... PCL
Planning Consultancy Ltd. (NITA) ... PCL
Planning, Control, and Decision Evaluation System [*IBM Corp.*] ... PLANCODE
Planning Control Sheet ... PCS
Planning Coordination Conference [*NATO*] (NATG) ... PCC
Planning Data Sheet (KSC) ... PDS
Planning Data Systems [*Information service or system*] (IID) ... PDS
Planning Department Library, Regional Municipality of Ottawa-Carleton, Ottawa, Ontario [*Library symbol National Library of Canada*] (NLC) ... OORM
Planning Development Library, Greater Vancouver Regional District, Vancouver, British Columbia [*Library symbol National Library of Canada*] (NLC) ... BVAPD
Planning Development Program (OICC) ... PDP
Planning Directive (NG) ... PD
Planning Document ... PD
Planning Economics Group, Boston [*Information service or system*] (IID) ... P/E
Planning Element System Report (NATG) ... PESR
Planning Engineers Desktop Computer Users Group (EA) ... PEDCUG
Planning Estimate ... PE
Planning Estimate Handbook (SAA) ... PEH
Planning, Evaluation, and Reporting [*Education-improvement system*] ... PER
Planning Evaluation Technique (MCD) ... PLANET
[*The*] **Planning Exchange Database** [*Pergamon InfoLine*] [*Database*] [*Information service or system*] (IID) ... PLANEX
Planning Executives Institute [*Later, PF*] ... PEI
Planning Exercise [*Military*] (NVT) ... PLANEX
Planning Factors Development (MCD) ... PFD
Planning Factors File (MCD) ... PFF
Planning Factors Management (MCD) ... PFM
Planning Factors Management Office ... PFMO
Planning for Better Family Living [*UN Food and Agriculture Organization*] ... PBFL
Planning for Higher Education [*A publication*] ... Plan Higher Ed
Planning Forum (EA) ... PF
Planning Grant Program ... PGP
Planning Group [*DoD*] ... PG
Planning Guidance Memorandum (DOMA) ... PGM
Planning Guide [*HUD*] ... PG
Planning Information Office, City of Halifax, Nova Scotia [*Library symbol National Library of Canada*] (NLC) ... NSHPI
Planning Library & Resource Centre, Calgary, Alberta [*Library symbol National Library of Canada*] (NLC) ... ACPL
Planning Library and Resource Centre, City of Calgary, Calgary, AB, Canada [*Library symbol Library of Congress*] (LCLS) ... CaACPL
Planning Library, Charlottetown, PE, Canada [*Library symbol Library of Congress*] (LCLS) ... CaPCPL
Planning Library, Charlottetown, Prince Edward Island [*Library symbol National Library of Canada*] (NLC) ... PCPL
Planning, Management, Evaluation (AD) ... pme
Planning Management Information System (AD) ... PMIS
Planning/Management Team [*NASA*] (MCD) ... PMT
Planning, Measurements & Evaluation Section [*Public Library Association*] [*American Library Association*] ... PLMES
Planning Ministers' Conference [*Australia*] ... PMC
Planning Network ... PLANNET
Planning Objective Coordinator ... POC
Planning Objectives ... PO
Planning Operation With Enabling Resources ... POWER
Planning Operational Gaming Experiment [*Game*] ... POGE
Planning, Organizing, Staffing, Coordinating, Reporting, and Budgeting [*Management*] ... POSCORB
Planning, Organizing, Staffing, Directing, Coordinating, Reporting, and Budgeting [*Principles of management*] ... POSDCORB
Planning Package [*NASA*] (NASA) ... PP
Planning Parts List ... PPL
Planning Permission (AD) ... pp
Planning Production Data Sheet ... PPDS
Planning, Programming, and Budgeting Management Information System [*Army*] ... PPBMIS
Planning, Programming, and Budgeting System [*Army*] ... PPBS
Planning, Programming, and Execution System [*Army*] (AAGC) ... PPES
Planning, Programming, Budgeting, and Execution System [*Army*] (RDA) ... PPBES
Planning Purpose ... PP
Planning Purpose Proposal ... PPP
Planning Purpose Quote ... PPQ
Planning Record Sheet ... PRS
Planning Reference ... PR
Planning References (AAG) ... PR's
Planning Release Record (AAG) ... PRR
Planning Requirements List (MCD) ... PRL
Planning, Research and Development Division, Alberta Attorney General, Edmonton,Alberta [*Library symbol National Library of Canada*] (NLC) ... AEPRD
Planning Research & Systems Ltd. [*British*] ... PRS
Planning Research Corp. [*Telecommunications service*] (TSSD) ... PRC
Planning Research Corporation [*Marine science*] (OSRA) ... PRC
Planning Research Corporation (USDC) ... PRC
Planning Resident Order (KSC) ... PRO
Planning Sciences ADS [*NASDAQ symbol*] (TTSB) ... PLNSY
Planning Sciences International [*Associated Press*] (SAG) ... PlanSci
Planning Sciences International [*NASDAQ symbol*] (SAG) ... PLNS
Planning Section Library, Calgary Police Service, Alberta [*Library symbol National Library of Canada*] (NLC) ... ACPS
Planning Status of Committed Engineering Changes (SAA) ... PSCEC
Planning Study (AAG) ... PS
Planning Summary Sheets (AAG) ... PSS
Planning Systems Generator ... PSG
Planning Test List ... PTL
Planning the Australian Capital Territory Together ... PACTT
Planning through Retrieval of Information for Management Extrapolation ... PRIME
Planning Tracking System (MCD) ... PTS
Planning Tracking Unit (MCD) ... PTU
Planning, Training, and Checkout System [*NASA*] (MCD) ... PTCS
Planning Work Package (MCD) ... PWP
Planning-Organization-Staffing-Directing-Coordinating-Reporting-Budgeting g (AD) ... posdcorb
Planning-Programming Guidance Memo [*Navy*] ... PPGM
Planning-Programming-Budgeting [*System*] [*Army*] ... P-P-B
Planning-Programming-Budgeting-Accounting System (AD) ... PPBAS
Plano, IL [*FM radio station call letters*] ... WSPY
Plano Public Library, Plano, TX [*Library symbol Library of Congress*] (LCLS) ... TxPlao
Plano, TX [*AM radio station call letters*] (RBYB) ... KAAM
Plan-Paper Copier (AD) ... ppc
Plans ... PL
Plans, Analysis, and Evaluation Division [*Army*] (MCD) ... PAED
Plans and Analysis ... P & A
Plans and Combat Operations ... P & CO
Plans and Operations Automated Storage Program [*Military*] ... POASP
Plans and Operations Division [*War Department*] [*World War II*] ... P & O
Plans and Operations for the Safeguard Communications Command [*Army*] (RDA) ... P & OSCC
Plans and Policies ... P & P
Plans and Programs ... P & P
Plans and Reports Improvement Memorandum [*Military*] (CAAL) ... PRIM
Plans and Requirements Review ... PRR
Plans and Training [*Military*] (IIA) ... P & T
Plans and Training Division [*Military*] ... P & T Div
Plans Division [*Military*] ... PD
Plans for the Employment of Naval and Air Forces of the Associated Powers in theEastern Theatre in the Event of War with Japan ... PLENAPS
Plans Officer ... PLO
Plans, Specifications, and Estimates [*Construction*] ... PS & E
Plant ... PLNT
Plant ... PLT
Plant Acquisition and Construction Equipment [*Nuclear energy*] (NRCH) ... PACE
Plant Air Package (IAA) ... PAP
Plant Alarm and Display System [*Nuclear energy*] (NRCH) ... PADS
Plant Alarms Sum (ECII) ... PAS
Plant and Capital Equipment (MCD) ... PACE
Plant and Facilities ... P & F
Plant and Office Layout (MCD) ... POLO
Plant and Soil Science Research Station [*Southern Illinois University at Carbondale*] [*Research center*] (RCD) ... PLSSRS
Plant Appropriation Request Simulation (IAA) ... PARSIM
Plant Automation Communication System [*IBM Corp.*] ... PACS
Plant Biological Institute [*University of Saskatchewan*] [*Canada*] ... PBI
Plant Biotechnology Institute [*National Research Council of Canada*] [*Research center*] (RCD) ... PBI
Plant Biotechnology Institute, National Research Council Canada [*Institut de Biotechologie des Plantes, Conseil National de Recherches Canada*], Saskatoon,Saskatchewan [*Library symbol Obsolete National Library of Canada*] (NLC) ... SSP
Plant Breeders' Rights ... PBR
Plant Breeding Abstracts [*A publication*] ... PBA
Plant Breeding Institute [*British*] ... PBI
Plant Breeding Research Forum [*Defunct*] (EA) ... PBRF
Plant Cell Suspension Cultures [*Biotechnology*] ... PCSC
Plant City, FL [*AM radio station call letters*] ... WFNS
Plant Clearance Contracting Officer [*DoD*] ... PCCO

Plant Clearance Officer [*DoD*] ... PCO
Plant Clearance Order ... PCO
Plant Component Test Facility [*Nuclear energy*] ... PCTF
Plant Computer (NRCH) ... PC
Plant Computer System (NRCH) ... PCS
Plant Control Interface ... PCI
Plant Control Room [*Nuclear energy*] (IAA) ... PCR
Plant Control System [*Nuclear energy*] (NRCH) ... PCS
Plant Data Acquisition System (NRCH) ... PDAS
Plant Data Handling and Display System [*Nuclear energy*] (NRCH) ... PDH & DS
Plant Data System [*Nuclear energy*] (NRCH) ... PDS
Plant Design and Management System [*Computer Aided Design Centre*] [*Software package*] (NCC) ... PDMS
Plant Design Factor [*Nuclear energy*] (NRCH) ... PDF
Plant Design Flood [*Nuclear energy*] (GFGA) ... PDF
Plant Engineer Mechanical (AAG) ... PEM
Plant Engineering (AAG) ... PE
Plant Engineering Agency ... PEA
Plant Engineering and Maintenance (MCD) ... PE & M
Plant Engineering and Maintenance (NASA) ... PEM
Plant Engineering Check Sheet (AAG) ... PECS
Plant Engineering Inspection (AAG) ... PEI
Plant Engineering Job Order (AAG) ... PEJO
Plant Engineering Maintenance Order ... PEMO
Plant Engineering Order ... PEO
Plant Engineering Shop Order (AAG) ... PESO
Plant Engineering Work Order (MCD) ... PEWO
Plant Engineering Work Release (AAG) ... PEWR
Plant Equipment (MCD) ... PE
Plant Equipment Codes [*DoD*] ... PEC
Plant Equipment Operator [*Nuclear energy*] (NRCH) ... PEO
Plant Equipment Package [*DoD*] ... PEP
Plant Equipment Packages Management Information System (MCD) ... PEPMIS
Plant Experimentation (PDAA) ... PLEX
Plant Extrusion (OA) ... PE
Plant Gene Resources of Canada [*See also RPC*] ... PGRC
Plant Genetic Materials ... PGM
Plant Growth Regulator ... PGR
Plant Growth Regulator Society of America (EA) ... PGRSA
Plant Growth Substance ... PGS
Plant Growth Unit [*NASA*] (MCD) ... PGU
Plant Health and Seeds Inspectorate [*Ministry of Agriculture, Fisheries, and Food*] [*British*] ... PHSI
Plant Height [*Botany*] ... PH
Plant Information Network [*Fish and Wildlife Service*] [*Ceased operation*] (IID) ... PIN
Plant Instrumentation Program ... PIP
Plant Introduction [*Botany*] ... PI
Plant Location Assistance Nationwide Network ... PLANN
Plant Makeup [*Nuclear energy*] (NRCH) ... PMU
Plant Manager Instruction [*Nuclear energy*] (NRCH) ... PMI
Plant Modelling System Program (PDAA) ... PMSP
Plant Monitoring and Control [*IBM Corp.*] ... PM & C
Plant Monitoring and Control - Host Interface [*IBM Corp.*] ... PM & C-HI
Plant Monitoring and Information System [*Nuclear energy*] (NRCH) ... PMIS
Plant Monitoring System [*Nuclear energy*] (NRCH) ... PMS
Plant Nitrogen in Grain [*Harvest nitrogen index*] ... PNG
Plant Nitrogen Purge System (IEEE) ... PNPS
Plant Normal [*Nuclear energy*] (NRCH) ... PN
Plant Nuclear Protection System (IAA) ... PNPS
Plant Operating Guide (DNAB) ... POG
Plant Operating System [*Nuclear energy*] (NRCH) ... POS
Plant Operations Review Committee [*Nuclear energy*] (NRCH) ... PORC
Plant Parasitic Systems ... PPS
Plant Patent Act [*1930*] ... PPA
Plant Pathogenic Bacteria Committee (EA) ... PPBC
Plant Performance Evaluation Activity [*Military*] (DNAB) ... PPEA
Plant Pest Control Division [*of ARS, Department of Agriculture*] ... PPC
Plant Pest Control Division (AD) ... PPCD
Plant Physiology Laboratory (SSD) ... PPL
Plant Process Computer ... PPC
Plant Protease Test (MAE) ... PPT
Plant Protection ... PP
Plant Protection and Quarantine Programs [*Department of Agriculture*] (IMH) ... PPQ
Plant Protection Society of Western Australia [*Australia*] ... PPSWA
Plant Protection System [*Nuclear energy*] (NRCH) ... PPS
Plant Quality Assurance ... PQA
Plant Quality Assurance Director [*Nuclear energy*] (NRCH) ... PQAD
Plant Quarantine Division [*of ARS, Department of Agriculture*] ... PQ
Plant Quarantine Division (AD) ... PQD
Plant Quarantine Inspection House (AD) ... PQIH
Plant Records Center [*of the American Horticultural Society*] (IID) ... PRC
Plant Recovery [*Nuclear energy*] (NRCH) ... PR
Plant Report ... PR
Plant Representative Officer (MCD) ... PRO
Plant Research Institute, Burnley [*Victoria*] [*State*] (EERA) ... VPRI
Plant Research Library, Biosystematics Research Institute, Agriculture Canada [*Bibliotheque de Recherches sur les Vegetaux, Institut de Recherches Biosystematiques, Agriculture Canada*] **Ottawa, Ontario** [*Library symbol National Library of Canada*] (NLC) ... OOAGB
Plant Resources of South-East Asia [*A publication*] ... PROSEA
Plant Response Fertilization [*Agriculture*] ... PRF
Plant Review Board [*Nuclear energy*] (NRCH) ... PRB
Plant Safety Bureau ... PSB
Plant Science Seminar [*Later, ASP*] ... PSS
Plant Sciences Data Center [*Formerly, Plant Records Center*] [*American Horticultural Society*] [*Mt. Vernon, VA*] ... PSDC
Plant Service Building [*Nuclear energy*] (NRCH) ... PSB
Plant Service Water Pump (IEEE) ... PSWP
Plant Services Maintenance (PDAA) ... PLASMA
Plant Stress [*Horticulture*] ... PS
Plant, Technology, and Safety Management (HCT) ... PTSM
Plant Test Date [*Telecommunications*] (TEL) ... PTD
Plant Test Number [*Telecommunications*] (TEL) ... PTN
Plant Transportation Advisory Committee ... PTAC
Plant Uncoupling Mitochondrial Protein [*Biochemistry*] ... PUMP
Plant Unit ... PU
Plant Variety Protection ... PVP
Plant Variety Protection Act [*1970*] ... PVPA
Plant Variety Protection Office [*Department of Agriculture*] ... PVPO
Plant Variety Rights Office [*Ministry of Agriculture, Fisheries, and Food*] [*British*] ... PVRO
Plant Vent Stack [*Nuclear energy*] (NRCH) ... PVS
Plantagenet [*Genealogy*] (ROG) ... PL
Plantago Mottle Virus [*Plant pathology*] ... PIMV
Plantago Severe Mottle Virus [*Plant pathology*] ... PISMV
Plantago Virus 4 [*Plant pathology*] ... PIV4
Plantain Virus X [*Plant pathology*] ... PIVX
Plantar [*Related to the sole of the foot*] (DAVI) ... PL
Plantar Fasciaitis [*Medicine*] ... PF
Plantar Flexion [*Medicine*] ... PF
Plantar Flexion [*Medicine*] (BABM) ... plant-flex
Plantar Flexion [*Orthopedics*] (DAVI) ... plant-flex
Plantar Wart [*Orthopedics*] (DAVI) ... PW
Plantas Medicinales [*Ministerio de Sanidad y Consumo*] [*Spain Information service or system*] (CRD) ... PLAMED
Plantation Key, FL [*FM radio station call letters*] ... WCTH
Plantation Key, FL [*FM radio station call letters*] ... WFKZ
Plantation Workers' International Federation [*Later, IFPAAW*] ... PWIF
Plant-Available Water [*Botany*] ... PAW
Plantelet Clumps [*Hematology*] (DAVI) ... PL-CLP
Plant-Growth-Promoting Rhizobacteria ... PGPR
Planting Council (EA) ... PC
Plant-in-Place ... PIP
Plant-in-Place Records ... PIPR
Plantronics, Inc. [*Associated Press*] (SAG) ... Plantron
Plantronics, Inc. [*NYSE symbol*] (SPSG) ... PLT
Plants and Gardens News [*A publication*] ... P & G News
Plant-Unique Analysis [*Nuclear energy*] (NRCH) ... PUA
Plantwax [*A fungicide*] ... Px
Plantwide Failure Reporting (MCD) ... PWFR
Planuebergang [*Grade Crossing*] [*German military - World War II*] ... PV
Planum Temporale [*Brain anatomy*] ... PT
Plan-View Size (PDAA) ... PVS
Plaque (MSA) ... PLQ
Plaque Index [*Dentistry*] ... PI
Plaque Neutralization [*Dentistry*] (DMAA) ... PN
Plaque Reduction Neutralization Test [*Immunochemistry*] ... PRNT
Plaque-Forming Cell [*Immunochemistry*] ... PFC
Plaque-Forming Cell Response [*Immunochemistry*] (OA) ... PFCR
Plaque-Forming Factor (PDAA) ... PFF
Plaque-Forming Unit [*Immunochemistry*] ... PFU
Plaquemines Parish Library, Buras, LA [*Library symbol Library of Congress*] (LCLS) ... LBuP
Plaridel, Bulacan [*Philippines*] [*ICAO location identifier*] (ICLI) ... RPUX
Plas Speed Indicator (IAA) ... PSI
Plaser Light [*Vancouver Stock Exchange symbol*] ... PLH
Plasma ... P
Plasma ... pl
Plasma Adsorption [*Medicine*] (DMAA) ... PA
Plasma Aldosterone [*Endocrinology*] ... PA
Plasma Aldosterone Concentration [*Hematology*] (DMAA) ... PAC
Plasma Amine Oxidase [*Hematology*] (DMAA) ... PAO
Plasma and High Energy Physics (IAA) ... PAHEP
Plasma & Materials Technologies [*NASDAQ symbol*] (TTSB) ... PMAT
Plasma & Materials Technologies, Inc. [*Associated Press*] (SAG) ... Plasma
Plasma & Materials Technologies, Inc. [*NASDAQ symbol*] (SAG) ... PMAT
Plasma Arc Chamber ... PAC
Plasma Arc Cutting [*Welding*] ... PAC
Plasma Arc System ... PAS
Plasma Arc Tunnel ... PAT
Plasma Arc Welding ... PAW
Plasma Arc-augmented Laser Welding ... PALW
Plasma Atomic Absorption System [*Spectrometry*] ... PLAAS
Plasma Beat Wave Accelerator [*Physics*] ... PBWA
Plasma Beta-Wave Accelerator [*Plasma physics*] ... PBWA
Plasma Catecholamine [*Biochemistry*] ... PCA
Plasma Cell [*Oncology*] ... PC
Plasma Cell Dyscracia with Polyneuropathy, Organomegaly, Endocrinopathy, Monoclonal Protein [*M-protein*], Skin changes [*Medicine*] (DAVI) ... POEMS
Plasma Cell Dyscrasia [*Medicine*] ... PCD
Plasma Cell Dyscrasias of Unknown Significance [*Medicine*] ... PCDUS
Plasma Cell Labeling Index [*Medicine*] (DMAA) ... PCLI
Plasma Cell Leukemia [*Oncology*] ... PCL
Plasma Chamber Evacuation Subsystem (MCD) ... PCE
Plasma Chemical Vapor Deposition ... PCVD
Plasma Chromatography ... PC
Plasma Chromatography Mass Spectroscopy ... PCMS

Plasma Clearance Rate [*Medicine*] (DMAA) ... PCR
Plasma Clot Diffusion Chamber [*Medicine*] (DMAA) ... PCDC
Plasma Confinement Experiment [*Physics*] ... PCX
Plasma Creatinine (DAVI) ... P_{cr}
Plasma Defect [*Hematology*] (DAVI) ... PD
Plasma Defect [*Medicine*] (MAE) ... PD
Plasma Deposited (IAA) ... PD
Plasma Desorption [*of ions for analysis*] ... PD
Plasma Desorption Mass Spectroscopy ... PDMS
Plasma Diagnostic Base ... PDB
Plasma Diagnostics Package [*NASA*] ... PDP
Plasma Display ... PD
Plasma Display (MCD) ... PDS
Plasma Display Panel [*Computer science*] ... PDP
Plasma Display Processor [*Computer science*] ... PDP
Plasma Display Terminal [*Computer science*] ... PDT
Plasma Display Touch Panel [*Computer science*] ... PDTP
Plasma Dynamics and Gaseous Discharge Laboratory [*MIT*] (MCD) ... PDGDL
Plasma Electron Beam (PDAA) ... PEB
Plasma Electron Profiles, Symmetric Integrals (MCD) ... PEPSI
Plasma Emission [*Spectrophotometry*] ... PE
Plasma Equivalent Unit [*Medicine*] (DMAA) ... PEU
Plasma Exchange [*Medicine*] ... PE
Plasma Factor (DMAA) ... PF
Plasma Fibronectin [*Biochemistry*] ... PFN
Plasma Gastrin [*Endocrinology*] (AAMN) ... PG
Plasma Generator System ... PGS
Plasma Glucose [*Hematology*] ... PG
Plasma Growth Hormone [*Hematology*] (MAE) ... PGH
Plasma Heating Obtained by Energetic Neutral Injection Experiment (IEEE) ... PHOENIX
Plasma Homovanillic Acid [*Biochemistry*] ... PHVA
Plasma Immunoreactive Insulin [*Hematology*] (MAE) ... P-IRI
Plasma Immunoreactive Secretion [*Medicine*] (DMAA) ... PIRS
Plasma Inorganic Iodine [*Clinical chemistry*] (MAE) ... PII
Plasma Insulin Activity [*Clinical chemistry*] ... PIA
Plasma Insulin Concentration [*Clinical chemistry*] ... PIC
Plasma Iron [*Hematology*] ... PI
Plasma Iron Transport [*Hematology*] ... PIT
Plasma Iron Transport [*or Turnover*] **Rate** [*Hematology*] ... PITR
Plasma Iron Turnover [*Hematology*] (DAVI) ... PIT
Plasma Jet (AAG) ... PJ
Plasma Lactic Dehydrogenase [*An enzyme*] (AAMN) ... PLDH
Plasma Level Monitoring [*Medicine*] (DMAA) ... PLM
Plasma Light Source ... PLS
Plasma Membrane [*Cytology*] ... PM
Plasma Membrane Vesicle [*Cytology*] ... PMV
Plasma Norepinephrine [*Medicine*] (DMAA) ... PNE
Plasma Oncotic Pressure [*Medicine*] (MAE) ... POP
Plasma Osmotic Pressure [*Medicine*] ... POP
Plasma Osmotic Pressure (AD) ... pop
Plasma Physics and Environmental Perturbation (NASA) ... PPEP
Plasma Physics Laboratory [*Also known as PPPL*] ... PPL
Plasma Postheparin Lipolytic Activity [*Clinical chemistry*] ... PHLA
Plasma Potassium [*Biochemistry*] (DAVI) ... P_K
Plasma Power Generator ... PPG
Plasma Power Supply ... PPS
Plasma Propulsion Laboratory (MCD) ... PPL
Plasma Protein ... PP
Plasma Protein Fraction [*Hematology*] ... PPF
Plasma Protein Isolate [*Food technology*] ... PPI
Plasma [*or Proserum*] **Prothrombin Conversion Accelerator** [*Factor VII*] [*Also, SPCA Hematology*] ... PPCA
Plasma Prothrombin Conversion Accelerator (AD) ... ppca
Plasma Prothrombin Conversion Factor (AD) ... ppcf
Plasma Quad [*Instrumentation*] ... PQ
Plasma Recognition Factor Activity [*Hematology*] (AAMN) ... PRFA
Plasma Renin Activity [*Hematology*] ... PRA
Plasma Renin Activity [*Medicine*] (AD) ... pra
Plasma Renin Concentration [*Hematology*] ... PRC
Plasma Renin Substrate [*Hematology*] ... PRS
Plasma Rotating Electrode Process [*Metallurgy*] ... PREP
Plasma Sciences and Applications (IAA) ... PSAA
Plasma Sodium [*Organic chemistry*] (DAVI) ... PNa
Plasma Source Ion Implantation ... PSSI
Plasma Spray Unit ... PSU
Plasma Spray Welder ... PSW
Plasma Spraying [*Welding*] ... PSP
Plasma Therm [*NASDAQ symbol*] (TTSB) ... PTIS
Plasma Thermocouple Reactor [*Nuclear energy*] (NRCH) ... P-T
Plasma Thromboplastin Antecedent [*Factor XI*] [*Hematology*] ... PTA
Plasma Thromboplastin Component [*Factor IX*] [*Also, CF Hematology*] ... PTC
Plasma Thromboplastin Component [*Medicine*] (DMAA) ... PTH
Plasma Thromboplastin Factor [*Factor VIII*] [*Also, AHF, AHG, TPC Hematology*] ... PTF
Plasma Transferred Arc [*Metallurgy*] ... PTA
Plasma Triglyceride [*Hematology*] (DAVI) ... PG
Plasma Urea Nitrogen (AAMN) ... PUN
Plasma Vapor Deposition (IAA) ... PVD
Plasma Vaporization Process ... PVP
Plasma Varactor Phase Shifter ... PVPS
Plasma Volume [*Medicine*] ... PV
Plasma Volume [*Laboratory science*] (DAVI) ... V_p
Plasma Wave Guide Switch (IAA) ... PWS
Plasma Wave Instrument [*Physics*] ... PWI
Plasma Wave Source [*Physics*] ... PWS
Plasma Wave System [*Instrumentation*] ... PWS
Plasma-Arc Machining [*Manufacturing term*] ... PAM
Plasma-Assisted Chemical Etching [*Metallurgy*] ... PACE
Plasma-Assisted Chemical Vapor Deposition [*Coating technology*] ... PACVD
Plasma-Coupled Device ... PCD
Plasma-Covered Antenna ... PCA
Plasmacrit Test [*Medicine*] ... PCT
Plasmacytoid Lymphocyte [*Hematology*] (DAVI) ... PLMT
Plasmacytoma [*Medicine*] ... PC
Plasmacytoma [*Medicine*] ... PCT
Plasmacytoma Growth Factor [*Oncology*] ... PCT-GF
Plasmacytoma Repressor Factor [*Cytology*] ... PRF
Plasma-Derived Serum ... PDS
Plasma-Developed Resist Processing [*Lithography*] ... PDR
Plasma-Enhanced Chemical Vapor Deposition [*Coating technology*] ... PECVD
Plasma-Enhanced Metalorganic Chemical Vapor Deposition [*Coating technology*] ... PE-MOCVD
Plasma-Glucose Disappearance Rate [*Hematology*] (MAE) ... PGDR
Plasma-Glucose Tolerance Rate [*Hematology*] (MAE) ... PGTR
Plasma-Injection Vacuum Energy Diverter ... PIVED
Plasma-Iron Disappearance [*Hematology*] (MAE) ... PID
Plasma-Iron Disappearance Time [*Hematology*] (MAE) ... PIDT
Plasmalemma [*Cytology*] ... PM
Plasma-Materials Interactions (MCD) ... PMI
Plasmapheresis [*Hematology*] ... PP
Plasma-Therm, Inc. [*Associated Press*] (SAG) ... PlasThrm
Plasma-Therm, Inc. [*NASDAQ symbol*] (NQ) ... PTIS
Plasmatron Inert Gas (SAA) ... PIG
Plasmid Chloramphenicol Acetyltransferase [*An enzyme*] ... pCAT
Plasmid Maintenance Sequence [*Genetics*] ... PMS
Plasmid Stanley Cohen [*Molecular biology*] ... pSC
Plasmin Prothrombin Conversion Factor [*Factor V*] [*Hematology*] ... PPCF
Plasminogen [*An enzyme*] (DAVI) ... PLG
Plasminogen Activator [*Biochemistry*] ... PA
Plasminogen Activator Activity [*Biochemistry*] ... PAA
Plasminogen Binding [*Hematology*] ... PB
Plasminogen Proactivator [*Hematology*] ... PPA
Plasminogen-Activator Inhibitor [*Biochemistry*] ... PAI
Plasminogen-Like [*Medicine*] (DMAA) ... PLGL
Plasmodium [*Biology*] (MAE) ... P
Plasmodium [*The malarial parasite*] [*Infectious diseases*] (DAVI) ... Pl
Plasmodium Berghei Anka [*Bacteriology*] ... PbA
Plasmon Surface Polariton [*Physics*] ... PSP
Plaster (WGA) ... PL
Plaster (VRA) ... pla
Plaster (AAG) ... PLAS
Plaster Master (MSA) ... PM
Plaster of Paris ... POP
Plaster of Paris (AD) ... pop
Plaster of Paris ... PP
Plasterboard ... PBD
Plasterer (ADA) ... PLSTR
Plasterer (WGA) ... PLSTRER
Plasterers' Friendly Society [*A union*] [*British*] ... PFS
Plastering ... PLST
Plaster-Molded Cornice [*Construction*] ... PMC
Plastic ... PLAS
Plastic (VRA) ... plas
Plastic (AAG) ... PLSTC
Plastic and Metal Products Manufacturers Association (EA) ... PMPMA
Plastic Apply Template (MCD) ... PAT
Plastic Assault Boat [*Navy*] ... PAB
Plastic Bag Association (EA) ... PBA
Plastic Ball Grid Arrays ... PBGA
Plastic Bath Manufacturers Association [*British*] (DI) ... PBMA
Plastic Bonded Explosive ... PBX
Plastic Bonded Starter Mix ... PBSM
Plastic Bottle Feeder ... PBF
Plastic Bottle Institute (EA) ... PBI
Plastic Chip Carrier (NITA) ... PLCC
Plastic Clad Plastic [*Materials science*] ... PCP
Plastic Coated Silica (NITA) ... PCS
Plastic Connector Backing Shell ... PCBS
Plastic Connector Shell ... PCS
Plastic Container Manufacturers Institute [*Defunct*] (EA) ... PCMI
Plastic Core ... PC
Plastic Die [*Tool*] (AAG) ... PLDI
Plastic Dielectric Capacitor ... PDC
Plastic Energy Absorption in Compression Unit (IEEE) ... PEACU
Plastic Engine Technology Corp. [*Toronto Stock Exchange symbol*] ... PLW
Plastic Explosive (NATG) ... PE
Plastic Food Container Association [*Defunct*] ... PFCA
Plastic Fuel Tank ... PFT
Plastic Houseware Manufacturers Association ... PHMA
Plastic Igniter Cord (IAA) ... PIC
Plastic Impregnated Laminate ... PIL
Plastic Insulated Cable (IAA) ... PIC
Plastic Insulated Conductor ... PIC
Plastic Insulated Wire ... PIW
Plastic Jacket ... PJ
Plastic Laboratory [*Princeton University*] (MCD) ... PL
Plastic Laminate [*Technical drawings*] ... PLAM
Plastic Laminating Mold (MCD) ... PLM
Plastic Leaded Chip Carrier [*Computer science*] ... PLCC

Plastic Leadless Chip Carrier [Computer technology] (PCM) ...... PLCC
Plastic Limit [IEEE] ...... PL
Plastic Master [Tool] (AAG) ...... PLMS
Plastic Media Blasting [Coating technology] ...... PMB
Plastic Mock-Up Assembly ...... PMA
Plastic Mold (MCD) ...... PM
Plastic Optical Fiber [Automotive electronics] ...... POF
Plastic Pin Grid Array (PCM) ...... PPGA
Plastic Pipe and Fittings Association (EA) ...... PPFA
Plastic Pipe Manufacturers Society [British] (DBA) ...... PPMS
Plastic Products Manufacturers Association [Later, Plastic and Metal
    Products Manufacturers Association] (EA) ...... PPMA
Plastic Quad Flat Package [Computer science] (PCM) ...... PQFP
Plastic Radial Grating ...... PRG
Plastic Roller Conveyor ...... PRC
Plastic Shipping Container Institute (EA) ...... PSCI
Plastic Soft Materials Manufacturers Association (EA) ...... PSMMA
Plastic Surgery [Medicine] ...... PL
Plastic Surgery [Medicine] ...... PS
Plastic Surgery [Medicine] ...... PSurg
Plastic Surgery Educational Foundation (EA) ...... PSEF
Plastic Surgery Research Council (EA) ...... PSRC
Plastic to Metal Seal ...... PMS
Plastic Training Cartridge [Army] (INF) ...... PTC
Plastic Tube ...... PT
Plastic Viscosity ...... PV
Plastic Waste Processor (DWSG) ...... PWP
Plastic Wire Guide ...... PWG
Plastic-Clad Silica [Optics] ...... PCS
Plastic-Encapsulated Microcircuit [Telecommunications] ...... PEM
Plasticity Index [Soil] (DICI) ...... PF
Plasticity Number (AAG) ...... PN
Plasticity Retention Index [Rubber test method] ...... PRI
Plasticized Transparent [Flexography] (DGA) ...... PT
Plasticized White Phosphorus ...... PWP
Plastic-Lined Pipe ...... PLP
Plastics and Rubber Institute [Institution of the Rubber Industry and Pla stics
    Institute] [Formed by a merger of] (EAIO) ...... PRI
Plastics: Computer Aided Materials Selector [Rapra Technology Ltd.]
    [Information service or system] (CRD) ...... PLASCAMS
Plastics Education Foundation (EA) ...... PEF
Plastics Engineers Association [Defunct] (EA) ...... PEA
Plastics in Construction Council [Later, CCS] ...... PCC
Plastics in Construction Council [Later, CCS] (EA) ...... PICC
Plastics Industries Association [Ireland] ...... PIA
Plastics Industry Notes [Later, CIN] ...... PIN
Plastics Institute (NADA) ...... PI
Plastics Institute of America (EA) ...... PIA
Plastics Machinery Distributors Association [British] (EAIO) ...... PMDA
Plastics Pipe Institute (EA) ...... PPI
Plastics Recycling Foundation (EA) ...... PRF
Plastics Research Laboratory [MIT] (MCD) ...... PRL
Plastics Technical Evaluation Center [Dover, NJ] [Army] ...... PLASTEC
Plastics Technical Evaluation Center [Military] ...... PTEC
Plastics Technology [A publication] ...... PT
Plastid [Botany] ...... P
Plastid [Botany] ...... pl
Plastid Isolation Column System [Analytical chemistry] ...... PICS
Plasti-Fab Ltd. [Toronto Stock Exchange symbol] ...... PFB
Plasti-Fab Ltd., Calgary, AB, Canada [Library symbol Library of Congress]
    (LCLS) ...... CaACPF
Plasti-Fab Ltd., Calgary, Alberta [Library symbol National Library of Canada]
    (NLC) ...... ACPF
Plasti-Line [NASDAQ symbol] (TTSB) ...... SIGN
Plasti-Line, Inc. [Associated Press] (SAG) ...... PlastLn
Plasti-Line, Inc. [NASDAQ symbol] (NQ) ...... SIGN
Plastochron Index [Botany] ...... PI
Plastocyanin ...... Pc
Plastocyanin ...... PCY
Plastoquinone [Biochemistry] ...... PQ
Plate [Electron tube] [Technical drawings] ...... P
Plate (IDOE) ...... P
Plate (KSC) ...... PL
Plate (VRA) ...... plat
Plate ...... PLT
Plate (ROG) ...... PTE
Plate and Cylinder Production (DGA) ...... P & CP
Plate Block [Philately] ...... PB
Plate Block [Philately] ...... PL-BL
Plate Block of Four [Philately] PB4
Plate Circuit (DEN) ...... PC
Plate Control Wedge [Printing technology] ...... PCW
Plate Count Agar [Microbiology] ...... PCA
Plate Current [Electronics] (IAA) ...... PLCURR
Plate Dissipation ...... PD
Plate Dissipation [Electronics] (IAA) ...... PLDISS
Plate Glass ...... PG
Plate Glass ...... PLGL
Plate Glass [Freight] ...... PLT GL
Plate Glass Association [British] (BI) ...... PGA
Plate Heat Exchanger [Chemical engineering] ...... PHE
Plate Heat Exchanger [Chemical Engineering] (DNAB) ...... PHER
Plate Number Coil [Philately] ...... PNC
Plate Number Coil (AD) ...... pnc
Plate Number Society [Defunct] (EA) ...... PNS

Plate Power (IAA) ...... PP
Plate Power (IDOE) ...... P_p
Plate Printers, Die Stampers, and Engravers [Union] (AD) ...... PPDSE
Plate Pulse (IAA) ...... PP
Plate Resistance (IDOE) ...... R_p
Plate Sunk [Printing] (DGA) ...... PS
Plate to Plate (DEN) ...... P to P
Plate Volage (IDOE) ...... V_p
Plate Voltage (IDOE) ...... E_p
Plateau [Board on Geographic Names] ...... PLAT
Plateau Length ...... PL
Plated (IAA) ...... PL
Plated (MSA) ...... PLD
Plated ...... PLTD
Plated Interconnecting Matrix ...... PIM
Plated through Hole ...... PTH
Plated Wire Memory ...... PWM
Plate-Glazed [Paper] ...... PG
Platelet [Hematology] (MAE) ...... pl
Platelet [Hematology] ...... PLAT
Platelet [Hematology] ...... PLT
Platelet Activating Factor (DMAA) ...... PTAF
Platelet Activating Factor Receptor (DMAA) ...... PTAFR
Platelet Activation-Dependent Granulocyte External Membrane Protein
    [Biochemistry] ...... PADGEM
Platelet Adhesiveness [Hematology] ...... PA
Platelet Adhesiveness Plasma [Hematology] (DMAA) ...... PAPF
Platelet Aggregate Ratio [Hematology] ...... PAR
Platelet Aggregation Factor [Hematology] ...... PAF
Platelet Aggregation Profiler [Hematology] ...... PAP
Platelet Alkaline Phosphatase [An enzyme] ...... PAP
Platelet Associated Activity [Pharmacology] ...... PAA
Platelet Concentrate [Hematology] ...... PC
Platelet Concentration [hematology] (DAVI) ...... PCON
Platelet Count [Hematology] ...... PC
Platelet Count [Hematology] ...... PCT
Platelet Deaggregation [Hematology] ...... PD
Platelet Defect [Hematology] (MAE) ...... PLD
Platelet Distribution Width [Hematology] ...... PDW
Platelet Factor [Hematology] ...... PF
Platelet Factor 3 Availability [Hematology] (DAVI) PF3a
Platelet Granule Extract [Hematology] (MAE) ...... PGE
Platelet Immunofluorescence Test [Analytical biochemistry] ...... PIFT
Platelet Lactogen [Hematology] (DMAA) ...... PL
Platelet Microsome [Medicine] (DMAA) ...... PM
Platelet Neutralization Procedure [Medicine] (MEDA) ...... PNP
Platelet Peroxidase [An enzyme] ...... PPO
Platelet Phosphohexokinase ...... PHK
Platelet Radioactive Antiglobulin Test [Hematology] (DAVI) ...... PRAT
Platelet Suspension Immunofluorescence Test [Medicine] (DMAA) ...... PSIFT
Platelet Uptake Index [Clinical chemistry] ...... PUI
Platelet-Activating Factor [Hematology] ...... PAF
Platelet-Aggregation Factor Inhibitor [Medicine] (DMAA) ...... PAFI
Platelet-Associated Complement [Medicine] (DMAA) ...... PAC
Platelet-Associated Immunoglobulin [Hematology] ...... PAIg
Platelet-Associated Immunoglobulin G [Hematology] ...... PAIgG
Platelet-Derived Growth Factor [Endocrinology] (DAVI) ...... PDFG
Platelet-Derived Growth Factor [Medicine] ...... PDGF
Platelet-Derived Growth Factor [Genetics] ...... PDGF
Platelet-Derived Growth Factor [Medicine] (DMAA) ...... PDGFA
Platelet-Derived Growth Factor Receptor [Genetics] ...... PDGFR
Platelet-Derived Wound-Healing Factor [Biochemistry] ...... PDWHF
Platelet-Endothelial Cell Adhesion Molecule [Cytology] ...... PECAM
Platelet-Free Plasma [Hematology] ...... PFP
Platelet-Poor Blood [Hematology] (MAE) ...... PPB
Platelet-Poor Plasma [Hematology] ...... PPP
Platelet-Rich Plasma [Hematology] ...... PRP
Platelet-Rich Plasma, citrated [Hematology] ...... cPRP
Platelets [Hematology] (DAVI) ...... PLATL
Platemakers Educational and Research Institute [Later, IAP] ...... PERI
Plate-Motion Vector [Geology] ...... PMV
Plateresque (VRA) ...... Pltrsq
Plates [Classical studies] (OCD) ...... PLS
Plates for Beam Forming (DEN) ...... PBF
Plates on Elastic Foundations [Structures & Computers Ltd.] [Software
    package] (NCC) ...... PLONEF
Platform (DCTA) ...... P
Platform (SSD) ...... PF
Platform (NASA) ...... PFM
Platform (KSC) ...... PLAT
Platform (AAG) ...... PLATF
Platform ...... PLTFM
Platform (AAG) ...... PTFM
Platform Assembly (MCD) ...... PA
Platform Check Subsystem ...... PCSS
Platform Control ...... PLC
Platform Control Center [NASA] (SSD) ...... PCC
Platform/Crane (DCTA) ...... PC
Platform Electron Card [Electronics] (OA) ...... PEC
Platform Electronic Package ...... PEP
Platform Electronics Assembly (KSC) ...... PEA
Platform Evaluation Program ...... PEP
Platform for Internet Content Selection [Computer science] ...... PICS
Platform for Internet Content Selection [Computer science] ...... PICS
Platform for Internet Content Selection [Computer science] ...... PICS

Platform for Internet Content Selection ... PICS
Platform for Internet Content Selection [*Computer science*] ... PICS
Platform for Internet Content Specification [*Computer science*] ... PICS
Platform for Internnet Content Selection [*Computer science*] ... PICS
Platform Functional Specification [*Computer science*] ... PFS
Platform Independent File Format [*Computer science*] ... PDF
Platform Mission Control Center [*NASA*] ... PMCC
Platform Observables Subassembly ... PLATO
Platform of Opportunity Program [*National Oceanic and Atmospheric Administration*] (MSC) ... POO
Platform Position Computer ... PPC
Platform Position Equipment ... PPE
Platform Position Unit ... PPU
Platform Position Unit (AD) ... ppu
Platform Sensor Package ... PSP
Platform Shock Attenuation and Realignment System (MCD) ... PSAR
Platform (Sided) (DCTA) ... PS
Platform Specific Driver [*Computer science*] ... PSD
Platform Support Center [*NASA*] (SSD) ... PSC
Platform Transmitter Terminal [*Satellite-based tracking system*] ... PTT
Platform-Mounted Nuclear Plant (NRCH) ... PMNP
Plating ... PLTG
Plating ... PLTG
Plating Fixture (AAG) ... PTFX
Platinized Titanium Anode ... PTA
Platinol [*Cis-Platinum*] [*Antineoplastic drug regimen*] (DAVI) ... PACE
Platinol [*Cisplatin*], Adriamycin, Cyclophosphamide [*Antineoplastic drug regimen*] ... PAC
Platinol [*Cisplatin*], Bleomycin, Vinblastine [*Antineoplastic drug regimen*] ... PBV
Platinol [*Cis-Platinum*] **Cyclophosphamide, Vindesine** [*Antineoplastic drug regimen*] (DAVI) ... PCE
Platinol [*Cisplatin*], Vinblastine, Bleomycin [*Antineoplastic drug regimen*] ... PVB
Platinova Resources Ltd. [*Toronto Stock Exchange symbol*] ... PVA
Platinum [*Chemistry*] (ROG) ... PL
Platinum [*Chemical symbol is Pt*] (AAG) ... PLAT
Platinum [*Chemistry*] (ROG) ... PLATN
Platinum [*Metal*] (VRA) ... platn
Platinum [*Chemical element*] ... Pt
Platinum [*Alaska*] [*Airport symbol*] (OAG) ... PTU
Platinum, AK [*Location identifier FAA*] (FAAL) ... PTU
Platinum Cobalt Unit [*Water analysis*] ... pcu
Platinum Communication System [*Vancouver Stock Exchange symbol*] ... PNU
Platinum Compensating Lead Wire (PDAA) ... PCLW
Platinum Diamminodichloride [*Cisplatin and cis-platinum*] [*Antineoplastic drug*] (DAVI) ... PDD
Platinum Entertainment [*NASDAQ symbol*] (TTSB) ... PTET
Platinum Group Element [*Chemistry*] ... PGE
Platinum Group Metal [*In meteorites*] ... PGM
Platinum Group Nugget [*In meteorites*] ... PGN
Platinum Print (VRA) ... PTPT
Platinum Resistance Thermometer ... PRT
Platinum Software [*NASDAQ symbol*] (TTSB) ... PSQL
Platinum Software Corp. [*Associated Press*] (SAG) ... PlatSoft
Platinum Software Corp. [*NASDAQ symbol*] (SAG) ... PSQL
Platinum Technology [*NASDAQ symbol*] (SPSG) ... PLAT
Platinum Technology, Inc. [*Associated Press*] (SAG) ... PlatTc
Platinum Temperature Probe ... PTP
Platinumsmiths Association of New York (EA) ... PANY
Plato [*Fourth century BC*] [*Classical studies*] (OCD) ... Pl
Platonic ... PLAT
Platoon (NATG) ... PL
Platoon ... PLAT
Platoon [*British military*] (DMA) ... Pln
Platoon [*Military*] (AABC) ... PLT
Platoon ... PLTN
Platoon Anti-Tank (SAA) ... PAT
Platoon Combat Skills [*Army*] (INF) ... PCS
Platoon Command Center [*Army*] ... PCC
Platoon Command Post [*Military*] (RDA) ... PCP
Platoon Early Warning System (RDA) ... PEWS
Platoon Gunnery Trainer (DOMA) ... PGT
Platoon Leader [*Military*] (INF) ... PL
Platoon Leader [*Military*] ... PLATLDR
Platoon Leader's Class [*Army*] ... PLC
Platoon Leaders Unit [*Marine Corps*] ... PLU
Platoon Patrol Base [*Military*] (VNW) ... PPB
Platoon/Section [*Army*] ... P/S
Platoon/Section Command Post ... P/S CP
Platoon Sector Indicator [*Army*] ... PSI
Platoon Sergeant ... E7
Platoon Sergeant [*Marine Corps*] ... PLSGT
Platoon Sergeant [*Army*] (AABC) ... PSG
Platoon Sergeant [*Military*] ... PSGT
Platoon Truck [*British*] ... PT
Platoon Weapons [*British military*] (DMA) ... PW
Platoon Weapons Instructor [*British military*] (DMA) ... PWI
Platt National Park ... PLAT
Platt National Park [*Oklahoma*] (AD) ... PNP
Platt on Leases [*1841*] [*A publication*] (DLA) ... Pl L
Platt on Leases [*A publication*] (DLA) ... Platt
Platt on Leases [*1847*] [*A publication*] (DLA) ... Platt Leas
Platt on the Law of Covenants [*1829*] [*A publication*] (DLA) ... Platt
Platt on the Law of Covenants [*A publication*] (DLA) ... Platt Cov
Platte Technical Community College, Columbus, NE [*Library symbol Library of Congress*] (LCLS) ... NbCoC
[*The*] **Platters Fan Club** (EA) ... TPFC
Platteville Public Library, Platteville, CO [*Library symbol Library of Congress*] (LCLS) ... CoPl
Platteville Public Library, Platteville, CO [*Library symbol*] [*Library of Congress*] (LCLS) ... CoPIP
Platteville, WI [*Location identifier FAA*] (FAAL) ... PVB
Platteville, WI [*AM radio station call letters*] (RBYB) ... WPVL
Platteville, WI [*FM radio station call letters*] (RBYB) ... WPVL-FM
Platteville, WI [*FM radio station call letters*] ... WSUP
Platt's Oilgram News Service ... PONS
Platt's Oilgram Price Service ... POPS
Plattsburg/Plattsburg Air Force Base [*New York*] [*ICAO location identifier*] (ICLI) ... KPBG
Plattsburgh [*New York*] [*Airport symbol*] (OAG) ... PLB
Plattsburgh [*New York*] [*Seismograph station code, US Geological Survey*] (SEIS) ... PNY
Plattsburgh Air Force Base [*New York*] (AAG) ... PLAFB
Plattsburgh, NY [*Location identifier FAA*] (FAAL) ... FQV
Plattsburgh, NY [*Location identifier FAA*] (FAAL) ... PBG
Plattsburgh, NY [*Location identifier FAA*] (FAAL) ... PLB
Plattsburgh, NY [*Location identifier FAA*] (FAAL) ... VAL
Plattsburgh, NY [*FM radio station call letters*] (RBYB) ... WBTZ-FM
Plattsburgh, NY [*FM radio station call letters*] (RBYB) ... WCEL-FM
Plattsburgh, NY [*FM radio station call letters*] ... WCFE
Plattsburgh, NY [*Television station call letters*] ... WCFE-TV
Plattsburgh, NY [*AM radio station call letters*] ... WEAV
Plattsburgh, NY [*FM radio station call letters*] ... WGFB
Plattsburgh, NY [*AM radio station call letters*] ... WIRY
Plattsburgh, NY [*FM radio station call letters*] (RBYB) ... WKOL
Plattsburgh, NY [*FM radio station call letters*] ... WPLT
Plattsburgh, NY [*AM radio station call letters*] (RBYB) ... WZBZ
Plattsburgh Public Library, Plattsburgh, NY [*Library symbol Library of Congress*] (LCLS) ... NPla
Plattsmouth, NE [*AM radio station call letters*] ... KOTD
Plattsmouth, NE [*FM radio station call letters*] ... KOTD-FM
Plattsmouth, NE [*Location identifier FAA*] (FAAL) ... PMV
Plattsmouth Public Library, Plattsmouth, NE [*Library symbol Library of Congress*] (LCLS) ... NbPl
Platyschisma Shale Member [*Geology*] ... PSM
Platz [*Square*] [*German*] (EY) ... PL
Platz (VRA) ... pl
Plauen [*German Democratic Republic*] [*Seismograph station code, US Geological Survey*] (SEIS) ... PLN
Plausible Conflict Situations [*Army*] ... PCS
Plausible Deniability ... PD
Plautus [*Third century BC*] [*Classical studies*] (OCD) ... Plaut
Plaxton's Canadian Constitutional Decisions [*A publication*] (DLA) ... Plaxton
Play By Play Toys & Novelties, Inc. [*NASDAQ symbol*] (SAG) ... PBYP
Play By Play Toys & Novelties, Inc. [*Associated Press*] (SAG) ... PlayBy
Play Co. Toys [*Associated Press*] (SAG) ... PlayCo
Play Company Toys [*NASDAQ symbol*] (SAG) ... PLCO
Play Co. Toys & Entertainment Corp. [*Associated Press*] (SAG) ... Play Co
Play Co. Toys & Entertainment Corp. [*Associated Press*] (SAG) ... PlayCo
Play Co. Toys & Entertainment Corp. [*NASDAQ symbol*] (SAG) ... PLCO
Play Co. Toys & Entmt [*NASDAQ symbol*] (TTSB) ... PLCO
Play Co. Toys & Entmt Wrrt [*NASDAQ symbol*] (TTSB) ... PLCOW
Play or Pay (ROG) ... PP
Play Schools Association (EA) ... PSA
Play Skills Inventory ... PSI
Play Units for Severely Handicapped (EDAC) ... PUSH
Playa Blanca [*Costa Rica*] [*ICAO location identifier*] (ICLI) ... MRPB
Playas [*Ecuador*] [*ICAO location identifier*] (ICLI) ... SEPL
Playback (KSC) ... PB
Playback (NASA) ... PLBK
Playback Verifier (MCD) ... PV
Playboy Club of London ... PCL
Playboy Enterprises Cl'B' [*NYSE symbol*] (TTSB) ... PLA
Playboy Enterprises, Inc. ... PEI
Playboy Enterprises, Inc. [*NYSE symbol*] (SPSG) ... PLA
Playboy Enterprises, Inc. [*Associated Press*] (SAG) ... Playby
Playboy Enterprises'A'(vtg) [*NYSE symbol*] (TTSB) ... PLAA
Playboys Enterprises [*Associated Press*] (SAG) ... PlaybyA
Playboys Enterprises [*Associated Press*] (SAG) ... PlaybyB
Play-by-Play (WDMC) ... PBP
Play-By-Play Toys&Novelties [*NASDAQ symbol*] (TTSB) ... PBYP
Played Matches [*Cricket*] (ROG) ... PLD
Player Assessment Device ... PAD
Player/Missile [*Atari computers*] ... P/M
Player of the Decade [*Sports*] ... POTD
Player Piano Group (EAIO) ... PPG
Player Resources, Inc. [*Vancouver Stock Exchange symbol*] ... PYR
Player Trade Society [*A union*] [*British*] ... PTS
Player Unit Component (MCD) ... PUC
Players International [*NASDAQ symbol*] (TTSB) ... PLAY
Players International Corp. [*Associated Press*] (SAG) ... Players
Players International, Inc. [*NASDAQ symbol*] (NQ) ... PLAY
Players League [*Major league in baseball, 1890*] ... P
Players League [*Major league in baseball, 1890*] ... PL
Players' Union [*Football*] [*British*] ... PU
Playground and Recreation Association of Queensland [*Australia*] ... PRAQ
Playground and Recreation Association of Victoria [*Australia*] ... PRAV
Playgroup Association of New South Wales [*Australia*] ... PANSW
Playgroup Association of South Australia ... PASA
Playgroup Association of the Northern Territory [*Australia*] ... PATNT
Playgroup Association of Western Australia ... PATWA

Playing Card Collectors' Association (EA) ... PCCA

Playing to Win (EA) ... PTW

Playitas [*Nicaragua*] [*Seismograph station code, US Geological Survey*] (SEIS) ... PYT

Playon Chico [*Panama*] [*Airport symbol*] (OAG) ... PYC

Plays and Players Club, Philadelphia, PA [*Library symbol Library of Congress Obsolete*] (LCLS) ... PPPlay

Playtex Products [*NYSE symbol*] (SPSG) ... PYX

Playtex Products, Inc. [*Associated Press*] (SAG) ... PlaytxPd

Plaza (VRA) ... pl

Plaza (ADA) ... PLA

Plaza [*Commonly used*] (OPSA) ... PLAZA

Plaza ... PLZ

Plaza (AD) ... Plz

Plaza (MCD) ... PLZ

Plaza [*Commonly used*] (OPSA) ... PLZA

Plaza Elementary School, Baldwin, NY [*Library symbol Library of Congress*] (LCLS) ... NbaldPE

Plaza y Janes [*Publisher*] [*Spain*] ... P & J

PLC Capital LLC 'A' 'MIPS' [*NYSE symbol*] (TTSB) ... PLPrM

PLC Capital LLC, Inc. [*NYSE symbol*] (SAG) ... PL

PLC Capital LLC, Inc. [*Associated Press*] (SAG) ... PLC

PLC Systems [*AMEX symbol*] (SPSG) ... PLC

PLC Systems [*Associated Press*] (SAG) ... PLC Sys

PLD Telekom, Inc. [*Associated Press*] (SAG) ... PLD Tele

PLD Telekom, Inc. [*NASDAQ symbol*] (SAG) ... PLDI

Plea Side (ROG) ... PS

Pleading and Practice Cases [*1837-38*] [*England*] [*A publication*] (DLA) ... Pl & Pr Cas

Pleadings [*Legal shorthand*] (LWAP) ... PL

Pleadings [*Legal term*] (ROG) ... PLEADGS

Pleak Memorial Library/Hobart Historical Society, Hobart, IN [*Library symbol*] [*Library of Congress*] (LCLS) ... InHobHi

Pleak Memorial Library/Hobart Historical Society, Hobart, IN [*Library symbol Library of Congress*] (LCLS) ... InHoHi

Pleas of the Crown [*A publication*] (DLA) ... PC

Pleasant ... P

Pleasant ... PLSNT

Pleasant Grove, UT [*FM radio station call letters*] ... KPGR

Pleasant Harbor [*Alaska*] [*Airport symbol*] (OAG) ... PTR

Pleasant Hope, MO [*FM radio station call letters*] (RBYB) ... KZBE

Pleasant Saturday Evenings ... PSE

Pleasant Sunday Afternoons ... PSA

Pleasant Sunday Evenings (ROG) ... PSE

Pleasant Valley [*California*] [*Seismograph station code, US Geological Survey*] (SEIS) ... PEV

Pleasanton, TX [*AM radio station call letters*] ... KBOP

Pleasanton, TX [*Location identifier FAA*] (FAAL) ... PEZ

Pleasantview Elementary School, Sauk Rapids, MN [*Library symbol*] [*Library of Congress*] (LCLS) ... MnSrPE

Pleasantville, NJ [*FM radio station call letters*] ... WMID

Pleasantville, NJ [*AM radio station call letters*] ... WOND

Please (AFM) ... PLS

Please ... PLZ

Please (MDG) ... PSE

Please Call Back [*International telex abbreviation*] (WDMC) ... RSVP

Please Draw Quickly [*Initialism used as title of TV series*] ... PDQ

Please Exchange ... PX

Please Follow Up ... PFU

Please Furnish (NOAA) ... PLFUR

Please Furnish Transportation Requests (NOAA) ... PLFTR

Please Mind Your Own Business ... PMYOB

Please Mind Your Own Business (AD) ... pmyob

Please Note [*Copyediting*] (WDMC) ... P/N

Please Note (AD) ... pn

Please Note ... PN

Please Omit Flowers (AD) ... pof

Please Pay (ROG) ... PP

Please Return ... PR

Please See Me ... PSM

Please Turn Over [*the page*] ... PTO

Please Turn Over (WDMC) ... pto

Please Wait Awhile [*Humorous interpretation for Pacific Western Airlines Corp.*] ... PWA

Pleasonton, TX [*FM radio station call letters*] ... KBUC

Pleasure (ROG) ... PL

Pleasure Horse Club of America (EA) ... PHCA

Pleasure Navigation International Joint Committee [*See also CINP*] [*The Hague, Netherlands*] (EAIO) ... PNIC

Pleaters, Stitchers, and Embroiderers Association (EA) ... PSEA

Plebeian (WGA) ... PLEB

Plebiscitum [*A Decree of the People*] [*Latin*] (DLA) ... PLEB

Pleckstrin-Homology [*Domain*] [*Biochemistry*] ... PH

Pledged Account Mortgage ... PAM

Pledges/Cost (WDMC) ... P/C

Pledges/Cost [*Fundraising*] (WDMC) ... p/c

Pleiade [*Record label*] [*France*] ... Ple

Pleiades Foundation for Peace [*Later, PFPSE*] (EA) ... PFP

Pleiades Foundation for Peace and Space Education (EA) ... PFPSE

Pleiku [*South Vietnam*] [*Airport symbol*] (AD) ... PXU

Pleiku/Cu-Hanh [*Viet Nam*] [*ICAO location identifier*] (ICLI) ... VVPK

Pleinsbachian [*Geology*] ... P

Plenipotentiary ... PLEN

Pleno Titulo [*With Full Title*] [*Latin*] ... PT

Plentiful Foods [*Department of Agriculture*] [*A publication*] ... PF

Plenty Tough [*Slang*] ... PT

Plenty Trouble [*Slang*] ... PT

Plentywood, MT [*AM radio station call letters*] ... KATQ

Plentywood, MT [*FM radio station call letters*] ... KATQ-FM

Plentywood, MT [*Location identifier FAA*] (FAAL) ... PWD

Plenum Air Tread [*Army amphibian vehicle*] ... PAT

Plenum Air Tread, Amphibious [*Army vehicle*] ... PATA

Plenum Bleed Duct [*Hovercraft*] ... PBD

Plenum Chamber ... PC

Plenum Chamber Burning ... PCB

Plenum Fill Experiment [*Nuclear energy*] (NRCH) ... PFE

Plenum Publishing [*NASDAQ symbol*] (TTSB) ... PLEN

Plenum Publishing Corp. [*NASDAQ symbol*] (NQ) ... PLEN

Plenum Publishing Corp. [*Associated Press*] (SAG) ... Plenum

Plerocercoid Growth Factor [*Endocrinology*] ... PGF

Plesetsk [*Satellite launch complex*] [*Former USSR*] ... PLE

Pleshenitzi [*Formerly, Minsk*] [*Former USSR Geomagnetic observatory code*] ... MNK

Plessey Assessment Services (NITA) ... PAS

[*The*] **Plessey Co. Ltd.** (MCD) ... PL

Plessey Electronic Payroll (DEN) ... PEP

Plessey Scientific-Atlanta Multistar System (NITA) ... PSAMS

Plessisville, PQ [*AM radio station call letters*] ... CKTL

Plessisville, PQ [*FM radio station call letter*] (RBYB) ... CKYQ-FM

Plethysmograph Pressure [*Measurement*] [*Medicine*] (DAVI) ... PP

Plettenberg [*South Africa*] [*Airport symbol*] (OAG) ... PBZ

Plettenberg Bay [*South Africa*] [*ICAO location identifier*] (ICLI) ... FAPG

Plettenberg Bay [*South Africa*] [*Airport symbol*] (AD) ... PBS

Pleural [*Medicine*] (MAE) ... pl

Pleural Effusion [*Medicine*] ... PE

Pleural Fluid [*Medicine*] (DMAA) ... PF

Pleural Fluid [*Medicine*] (DAVI) ... PLEU

Pleural Fluid [*Medicine*] (MAE) ... Pleur Fl

Pleural Ganglion [*Medicine*] ... PLG

Pleural Pressure [*Medicine*] ... PP

Pleural Sclerite [*Entomology*] ... PS

Pleuropneumonia [*Veterinary medicine*] (DSUE) ... PLEURO

Pleuropneumonia Organisms [*Bacteriology*] ... PPO

Pleuropneumonia-Like Organism (AD) ... pplo

Pleuropneumonia-Like Organisms [*Bacteriology*] ... PPLO

Plexiglass (VRA) ... plexg

Plexus [*Medicine*] ... PLX

Plexus Corp. [*Associated Press*] (SAG) ... Plexus

Plexus Corp. [*NASDAQ symbol*] (NQ) ... PLXS

Plexus Resources Corp. [*Toronto Stock Exchange symbol*] ... PXS

Plexus Visibility Score [*Medicine*] ... PVS

Pli Premier Jour Officiel [*Official First Day Cover - OFDC*] [*Canada Post Corp.*] ... PPJO

Pliers (MSA) ... PLR

Pliers and Wrench [*Combination tool*] ... PLENCH

Plimoth Plantation, Inc., Plymouth, MA [*Library symbol Library of Congress*] (LCLS) ... MPIP

Plimsoll Line [*Shipping*] (DAS) ... PL

Pliocene Research, Interpretations and Synoptic Mapping [*Climatology*] ... PRISM

PLM Equipment Growth Fund I Ltd. [*AMEX symbol*] (SPSG) ... GFX

PLM Equipment Growth Fund II Ltd. [*AMEX symbol*] (SPSG) ... GFY

PLM Equipment Growth Fund III Ltd. [*AMEX symbol*] (SPSG) ... GFZ

PLM International [*AMEX symbol*] (TTSB) ... PLM

PLM International, Inc. [*AMEX symbol*] (SPSG) ... PLM

Ploecker-Lee-Kesler [*Equation of state*] ... PLK

Ploermel-Loyat [*France ICAO location identifier*] (ICLI) ... LFRP

Plonia Technica ... PT

Ploshchad [*Square*] [*Russian*] (EY) ... PL

Plot Board (KSC) ... PB

Plot File Import Utility [*IBM Corp.*] ... PFIU

Plot Function [*Computer science*] ... PF

Plot Plan Drawing (SAA) ... PPD

Plot Points [*Computer science*] ... PP

Plot Position Indicator ... PPI

Plot Titles [*Test*] [*Psychology*] ... PT

Plotter [*British military*] (DMA) ... P

Plotter (MSA) ... PLTR

Plotter Display System (DNAB) ... PDS

Plotting ... PLOT

Plotting and RADAR ... PR

Plotting Board Operator (MUGU) ... PBO

Plotting Board Plot (MUGU) ... PBP

Plotting Data Distributor (MCD) ... PDD

Plotting Display (IAA) ... PD

Plotting Display Control Unit ... PDCU

Plotting Display Subchannel Data Distributor (MCD) ... PDSDD

Plotting Equipment [*JETDS nomenclature*] [*Military*] (CET) ... PT

Plotting System ... PS

Plough, Inc., Memphis, TN [*Library symbol Library of Congress*] (LCLS) ... TMPI

Plough, Sweeper, and Blower (DA) ... PSB

Plovdiv [*Bulgaria*] [*ICAO location identifier*] (ICLI) ... LBPD

Plow Creek Commune Library, Tiskilwa, IL [*Library symbol Library of Congress*] (LCLS) ... ITisP

Plow Snow [*NWS*] (FAAC) ... PLW

Plowden on Usury [*A publication*] (DLA) ... Pl U

Plowden's Criminal Conversation Trials [*A publication*] (DLA) ... Pl Cr Con Tr

Plowden's English King's Bench Commentaries [*or Reports*] [*A publication*] (DSA) ... Com

Plowden's English King's Bench Commentaries [*or Reports*] [*1550-80*] [*A publication*] (DLA) ... Pl
Plowden's English King's Bench Commentaries [*or Reports*] [*1550-80 England*] [*A publication*] (DLA) ... Pl Com
Plowden's English King's Bench Commentaries [*or Reports*] [*A publication*] (DLA) ... Plow
Plowden's English King's Bench Commentaries [*or Reports*] [*A publication*] (DLA) ... Plowd
Plow-Furrow-Cover [*Waste*] (DICI) ... PFC
Plowright Tissue Culture Vaccine [*Against rinderpest*] ... PTCV
Plowshare Advisory Committee [*AEC*] ... PAC
Plow-Steel Rope ... PSR
PLRS/JTIDS [*Position Location Reporting System/Joint Tactical Information Distribution System*] **Hybrid** (MCD) ... PJH
PLRS/JTIDS [*Position Location Reporting System/Joint Tactical Information Distribution System*] **Hybrid Interface** ... PJHI
Plucky Little King [*Used by Western diplomats in Amman in reference to King Hussein of Jordan*] ... PLK
Plug ... P
Plug (AAG) ... PL
Plug (AAG) ... PLG
Plug and Jack Set ... PJS
Plug and Play [*Microsoft Corp.*] [*Computer auto-configuration system*] (PCM) ... PNP
Plug and Play (PCM) ... PnP
Plug Care [*Computer science*] (IAA) ... PC
Plug Cock (AAG) ... PC
Plug Compatible [*Computer science*] (BUR) ... PC
Plug Compatible Computer (ADA) ... PCC
Plug Compatible Ethernet ... PCE
Plug Compatible Mainframe [*Computer science*] ... PCM
Plug Compatible Mainframe Manufacturer (NITA) ... PCMM
Plug Compatible Manufacturer [*Computer science*] ... PCM
Plug Compatible Memory ... PCM
Plug Compatible Module [*Computer science*] (IAA) ... PCM
Plug Compatible Peripheral [*Computer science*] (EECA) ... PCP
Plug Handling Fixture (NRCH) ... PHF
Plug/Jack Patch Cord ... PJPC
Plug Patch Cord ... PPC
Plugboard ... PB
Plugboard (MSA) ... PLBD
Plug-Flow Membrane Reactor [*Chemical engineering*] ... PFMR
Plug-Flow Reactor [*Engineering*] ... PFR
Pluggable Unit (SAA) ... PLU
Pluggable Unit (SAA) ... PU
Plugged Telescoping Catheter [*Clinical chemistry*] ... PTC
Plugging Back [*Computer science*] (IAA) ... PB
Plugging Switch (IEEE) ... PLS
Plugging Temperature Indicator [*Nuclear energy*] (NRCH) ... PTI
Plug-In Amplifier ... PIA
Plug-In Blank ... PIB
Plug-In Electronics ... PIE
Plug-In Extension ... PIE
Plug-In Instrument (IAA) ... PI
Plug-In Inventory Control System [*Bell System*] ... PICS
Plug-In Inventory Control System/Detailed Continuing Property Record [*Telecommunications*] (TEL) ... PICS/DCPR
Plug-In Module (MCD) ... PIM
Plug-In Module Assembly (MCD) ... PIMA
Plug-In Relay ... PIR
Plug-In Unit ... PIU
Plug-In Unit Mounting Panel ... PIUMP
Plug-In Valve ... PIV
Plug-Type Receptacle ... PTR
Plum Brook Reactor [*Nuclear energy*] ... PBR
Plum Brook Reactor Facility [*Lewis Research Center*] ... PBRF
Plum Creek Library System, Worthington, MN [*Library symbol Library of Congress*] (LCLS) ... MnWoP
Plum Creek Timber Co., Inc. [*NYSE symbol*] (SPSG) ... PCL
Plum Creek Timber Co., Inc. [*Associated Press*] (SAG) ... PlumCrk
Plum Creek Timber L.P. [*NYSE symbol*] (TTSB) ... PCL
Plum Island Animal Disease Center [*Formerly, PIADL*] ... PIADC
Plum Island Animal Disease Laboratory [*of ARS, Department of Agriculture*] [*Later, PIADC*] ... PIADL
Plum Pox Virus [*Plant pathology*] ... PPV
Plumas County Free Library, Quincy, CA [*Library symbol Library of Congress*] (LCLS) ... CQCL
Plumbeotype (VRA) ... PLTYP
Plumber (WGA) ... PLBR
Plumber ... PLMBR
Plumbers and Builders Merchants Association [*Australia*] ... PBMA
Plumbers and Drainers' Examination and Licensing Board [*Queensland, Australia*] ... PDELB
Plumbers and Pipefitters [*Union*] (AD) ... PPF
Plumbers, Gasfitters, and Drainers Registration Board [*Victoria, Australia*] ... PGDRB
Plumbers' Merchants Association [*British*] (BI) ... PMA
Plumbing (WGA) ... PLBG
Plumbing ... PLBG
Plumbing (AAG) ... PLMB
Plumbing (WGA) ... PLMG
Plumbing Advisory Board [*South Australia*] ... PAB
Plumbing and Deck Drain (MSA) ... P & DD
Plumbing and Drainage Institute (EA) ... PDI
Plumbing and Piping Industry Council (NADA) ... PPIC
Plumbing and Piping Industry Council (AD) ... PPIC
Plumbing Brass Institute [*Later, PMI*] (EA) ... PBI
Plumbing Fixture Manufacturers Association [*Defunct*] (EA) ... PFMA
Plumbing Industry Progress and Education Fund ... PIPE
Plumbing Manufacturers Institute (EA) ... PMI
Plumbing Mart [*Vancouver Stock Exchange symbol*] ... PLB
Plumbing Supervisor/Specialist (AAG) ... PS/S
Plumbing Trade Union (NADA) ... PTU
Plumbing Trades Union [*British*] ... PTU
Plumbing-Heating-Cooling Information Bureau (EA) ... PHCIB
Plumbum [*Lead*] [*Chemical element*] ... Pb
Plumbum [*Lead*] [*Pharmacy*] ... PLUMB
Plume [*Numismatics*] ... PL
Plume Data Analysis of Advanced Propellants (MCD) ... PDAAP
Plume Exposure Pathway [*Nuclear emergency planning*] ... PEP
Plume Interaction Experiment [*Army*] (RDA) ... PIE
Plume RADAR Frequency Interference Code (MCD) ... PRFIC
Plume Radiation Intensity Measurement (MUGU) ... PRIM
Plume Suppression System [*Combustion technology*] ... PSS
Plume Visibility Model [*Environmental Protection Agency*] (GFGA) ... PLUVUE
Plume-Induced Flow Separation ... PIFS
Plumeria Society of America (EA) ... PSA
Plummer Public Hospital, Sault Ste. Marie, ON, Canada [*Library symbol Library of Congress*] (LCLS) ... CaOStMPH
Plummer Public Hospital, Sault Ste. Marie, Ontario [*Library symbol National Library of Canada*] (NLC) ... OSTMPH
Plummer Public Library, Plummer, ID [*Library symbol*] [*Library of Congress*] (LCLS) ... IdPlu
Plumptre on Contracts [*2nd ed.*] [*1897*] [*A publication*] (DLA) ... Plum Contr
Pluna [*Airline flight code*] (ODBW) ... PU
Plunger (MSA) ... PLGR
Plunger Actuated Indexer ... PAI
Plunger Snap Switch ... PSS
Pluperfect [*Grammar*] ... PLUP
Pluperfect [*Grammar*] ... PLUPF
Plural ... PL
Plural (ODBW) ... pl
Plural (WDMC) ... plu
Plural ... PLU
Plural ... PLUR
Pluripotent Hematopoietic Stem Cells [*Cytology*] ... PHSC
Pluripotent Myeloid Stem Cell [*Cytology*] (MAE) ... PMSC
Pluripotent Progenitor [*Cytology*] ... PPP
Pluripotent Stem Cell [*Cytology*] ... PSC
Plus [*More*] ... P
Plus ... PS
Plus Minus [*More or less*] ... PM
Plus or Minus (MSA) ... P or M
Plus or Minus ... PORM
Plus or Minus (AD) ... porm
Plus Programming Language [*Computer science*] ... PPL
Plus-X-Reversal ... PXR
Plutarch [*First century AD*] [*Classical studies*] (OCD) ... Plut
Plutchnik [*Geriatric rating scale*] (DMAA) ... PLUT
Pluto Fast Flyby [*NASA*] (PS) ... PFF
Pluto-Charon System [*Planetary science*] ... PCS
Pluton Industries Ltd. [*Vancouver Stock Exchange symbol*] ... PTN
Plutona-Molybdenum CERMET [*Ceramic Metal Element*] (NASA) ... PMC
Plutonium [*Chemical symbol is Pu*] (AAG) ... PLU
Plutonium [*Chemical element*] ... Pu
Plutonium Air Transportable [*Nuclear energy*] (NRCH) ... PAT
Plutonium Canister Decontamination Cell [*Nuclear energy*] (NRCH) ... PCDC
Plutonium Chloride ... PuCl
Plutonium Concentrator Concentrate [*Nuclear energy*] (NRCH) ... PCC
Plutonium Concentrator Distillate [*Nuclear energy*] (NRCH) ... PCD
Plutonium Contaminated Material ... PCM
Plutonium Decontamination Emergency Team [*Army*] ... PLUCON
Plutonium Dioxide ... PuO2
Plutonium Equipment Transfer Area [*Nuclear energy*] (NRCH) ... PETA
Plutonium Equipment Warm Shop [*Nuclear energy*] (NRCH) ... PEWS
Plutonium Finishing Plant ... PFP
Plutonium Finishing Plant Environmental Impact Statement ... PFP EIS
Plutonium Maintenance and Operating Gallery [*Nuclear energy*] (NRCH) ... PMOG
Plutonium Organic Recycle [*Nuclear energy*] (NRCH) ... POR
Plutonium Preparation Area [*Nuclear energy*] (GFGA) ... PPA
Plutonium Process Cell [*Nuclear energy*] (NRCH) ... PPC
Plutonium Product Cell [*Nuclear energy*] (NRCH) ... PPC
Plutonium Product Filter Room [*Nuclear energy*] (NRCH) ... PPFR
Plutonium Product Loadout [*Nuclear energy*] (NRCH) ... PPL
Plutonium Product Shipping Preparation Station [*Nuclear energy*] (NRCH) ... PPSPS
Plutonium Product Storage [*Nuclear energy*] (NRCH) ... PPS
Plutonium Product Storage Vault [*Nuclear energy*] (NRCH) ... PPSV
Plutonium [*Loop-Testing*] **Reactor** [*British*] (DEN) ... PLUTO
Plutonium Reclamation Facility [*Nuclear energy*] ... PRF
Plutonium Recovery Modification Project [*Department of Energy*] ... PRMP
Plutonium Recycle Acid [*Nuclear energy*] (NRCH) ... PRA
Plutonium Recycle Critical Facility [*Nuclear energy*] ... PRCF
Plutonium Recycle Test Reactor [*Nuclear energy*] ... PRTR
Plutonium Rework Cell [*Nuclear energy*] (NRCH) ... PRC
Plutonium Rework Sample Cell [*Nuclear energy*] (NRCH) ... PRSC
Plutonium Stripper Feed [*Nuclear energy*] (NRCH) ... PSF
Plutonium Stripping Concentrate [*Nuclear energy*] (NRCH) ... PSC
Plutonium Stripping Concentration Distillate [*Nuclear energy*] (NRCH) ... PSCD
Plutonium Uranium Extraction [*Nuclear energy*] ... PUREX

Plutonium, Uranium, Thorium Assembly Reactivity Code .... PLUTHARCO
Plutonium Utilization Program [*Nuclear Regulatory Commission*] (NRCH) ...... PUP
Plutonium Waste Handling Area [*Nuclear energy*] (NRCH) .... PWHA
Plutonium-Contaminated Liquid [*Nuclear energy*] (NUCP) .... PCL
Plutonyl Nitrate [*Inorganic chemistry*] .... PUN
Plutus [*of Aristophanes*] [*Classical studies*] (OCD) .... Plut
Pluvius Policy [*Insurance against rain*] .... PP
Ply Gem Industries Inc. [*NYSE symbol*] (TTSB) .... PGI
Ply Rating [*Tires*] (NATG) .... PR
Ply-Gem, Inc. [*NYSE symbol*] (SAG) .... PGI
Ply-Gem, Inc. [*Associated Press*] (SAG) .... PlyGem
Plymouth [*British ICAO location identifier*] (ICLI) .... EGRP
Plymouth [*Postcode*] (ODBW) .... PL
Plymouth [*England*] [*Airport symbol*] (OAG) .... PLH
Plymouth [*Record label*] .... Ply
Plymouth [*England*] .... PLYM
Plymouth Audioconferencing Network [*Plymouth Polytechnic*] [*Plymouth, England*] [*Telecommunications*] (TSSD) .... PACNET
Plymouth Barracuda/Cuda Owners Club (EA) .... PB/COC
Plymouth/Blackburne [*Montserrat Island*] [*ICAO location identifier*] (ICLI) ..... TRPM
Plymouth Brethren (ROG) .... PB
Plymouth Financial [*Vancouver Stock Exchange symbol*] .... PLM
Plymouth, IN [*FM radio station call letters*] .... WLTA
Plymouth, IN [*AM radio station call letters*] .... WTCA
Plymouth, IN [*FM radio station call letters*] (RBYB) .... WZOC-FM
Plymouth, MA [*Location identifier FAA*] (FAAL) .... PYM
Plymouth, MA [*AM radio station call letters*] .... WPLM
Plymouth, MA [*FM radio station call letters*] .... WPLM-FM
Plymouth Marine Laboratory [*Natural Environment Research Council*] [*British Information service or system*] (IID) .... PML
Plymouth, MI [*FM radio station call letters*] .... WSDP
Plymouth (Mount Wise) [*British ICAO location identifier*] (ICLI) .... EGDB
Plymouth, NC [*Location identifier FAA*] (FAAL) .... PMZ
Plymouth, NC [*AM radio station call letters*] .... WPNC
Plymouth, NC [*FM radio station call letters*] .... WPNC-FM
Plymouth, NH [*FM radio station call letters*] .... WPCR
Plymouth, NH [*AM radio station call letters*] .... WPNH
Plymouth, NH [*FM radio station call letters*] .... WPNH-FM
Plymouth Owners Club (EA) .... POC
Plymouth Public Library, Plymouth, IN [*Library symbol Library of Congress*] (LCLS) .... InPly
Plymouth Public Library, Plymouth, MA [*Library symbol Library of Congress*] (LCLS) .... MPl
Plymouth/Roborough [*British ICAO location identifier*] (ICLI) .... EGHD
Plymouth Rock Fanciers Club (EA) .... PRFC
Plymouth Rock Foundation (EA) .... PRF
Plymouth Rubber Cl'B' [*AMEX symbol*] (TTSB) .... PLR.B
Plymouth Rubber Co., Inc. [*AMEX symbol*] (SPSG) .... PLR
Plymouth Rubber Co., Inc. [*Associated Press*] (SAG) .... PlyR
Plymouth Rubber'A'vtg [*AMEX symbol*] (TTSB) .... PLR. A
Plymouth State College (GAGS) .... Plymouth St C
Plymouth State College of the University of New Hampshere, Plymouth, NH [*OCLC symbol*] (OCLC) .... PSM
Plymouth State College of the University of New Hampshire, Plymouth, NH [*Library symbol Library of Congress*] (LCLS) .... NhPlS
Plymouth Subarea Channel [*NATO*] (NATG) .... PLYMCHAN
Plymouth, WI [*AM radio station call letters*] .... WJUB
Plymouth, WI [*FM radio station call letters*] .... WXER
Plympton [*England*] .... PLYMP
Plymtree [*England*] .... PLYMT
Plywood (BARN) .... plwd
Plywood (VRA) .... ply
Plywood .... PLY
Plywood (AAG) .... PLYWD
Plywood .... PLYWD
Plywood [*Technical drawings*] .... PWD
Plywood Research Foundation (EA) .... PRF
PM Air, Inc. [*ICAO designator*] (FAAC) .... PAZ
PM Industries, Inc. [*Vancouver Stock Exchange symbol*] .... PMS
PM [*Product Management*] **Materiel Systems Assessment** (RDA) .... PMSA
PMA Communications, Inc. [*Boston, MA*] (TSSD) .... PMAC
PMC Capital [*AMEX symbol*] (TTSB) .... PMC
PMC Capital, Inc. [*AMEX symbol*] (SPSG) .... PMC
PMC Commercial Tr [*AMEX symbol*] (TTSB) .... PCC
PMC Commercial Trust [*AMEX symbol*] (SAG) .... PCC
PMC Commercial Trust [*Associated Press*] (SAG) .... PMC CT
PMC Corp. [*Toronto Stock Exchange symbol*] .... PFN
PMC Technologies Ltd. [*Vancouver Stock Exchange symbol*] .... PMT
P-Methylstyrene [*Plastics*] .... PMS
PMI Group [*NYSE symbol*] (TTSB) .... PMA
PMI Group, Inc. [*NYSE symbol*] (SAG) .... PMA
PMI Group, Inc. [*Associated Press*] (SAG) .... PMI Gp
PMR Corp. [*Associated Press*] (SAG) .... PMR Cp
PMR Corp. [*NASDAQ symbol*] (SAG) .... PMRP
PMT Services [*Associated Press*] (SAG) .... PMT Svc
PMT Services [*NASDAQ symbol*] (SAG) .... PMTS
PNC Bank Corp. [*NYSE symbol*] (SPSG) .... PNC
PNC Bank Corp. [*NYSE symbol*] (TTSB) .... PNC
PNC Bank Cp $1.60 Cv C Pfd [*NYSE symbol*] (TTSB) .... PNCPrC
PNC Bank Cp $1.80 Cv D Pfd [*NYSE symbol*] (TTSB) .... PNCPrD
Pneumatic .... PN
Pneumatic (AAG) .... PNEU
Pneumatic (AD) .... pneu
Pneumatic .... PNEUM
Pneumatic Air Saw .... PAS
Pneumatic All-Terrain Amphibian (IEEE) .... PATA
Pneumatic Analog Computer .... PAC
Pneumatic Antishock Garment [*Roentgenology*] .... PASG
Pneumatic Auxiliary Console (AAG) .... PAC
Pneumatic Checkout Rack (KSC) .... PCR
Pneumatic Checkout Unit (AAG) .... PCU
Pneumatic Circuit Indicator .... PCI
Pneumatic Control Assembly (NASA) .... PCA
Pneumatic Control Distributors (KSC) .... PCD
Pneumatic Control Regulator (KSC) .... PCR
Pneumatic Control System [*Gas chromatography*] .... PCS
Pneumatic Control Valve .... PCV
Pneumatic Damping Control .... PDC
Pneumatic Distribution System .... PDS
Pneumatic End to End .... PETE
Pneumatic Energy Detector with Remote Optics .... PEDRO
Pneumatic Equalization [*Tube*] [*Otorhinolaryngology*] (DAVI) .... PE
Pneumatic Explosion Generator .... PEG
Pneumatic Float .... PF
Pneumatic Float Bridge .... PFB
Pneumatic Float Bridge .... PFBRG
Pneumatic Function Controller .... PFC
Pneumatic Ground Group .... PGG
Pneumatic Hydraulic Test Console (KSC) .... PHTC
Pneumatic Lead Cutter .... PLC
Pneumatic Limit Switch .... PLS
Pneumatic Operated Piston (ECII) .... POP
Pneumatic Power Subsystem (NASA) .... PPS
Pneumatic Pressure Generator (MCD) .... PNEUG
Pneumatic Reading System .... PRS
Pneumatic Regulation Unit (AAG) .... PRU
Pneumatic Retinopathy [*Ophthalmology*] .... PR
Pneumatic Scale Corp. [*Stock exchange symbol*] (AD) .... PNU
Pneumatic Sensor Assembly .... PSA
Pneumatic Supply Subsystem (AAG) .... PSS
Pneumatic Suspension [*Automotive engineering*] .... PS
Pneumatic System .... PS
Pneumatic [*or Pressure*] **System Automatic Regulator** (AAG) .... PSAR
Pneumatic [*or Pressure*] **System Manifold Regulator** [*or Manual*] (AAG) ..... PSMR
Pneumatic Telescope Mast .... PTM
Pneumatic Temperature Control .... PTC
Pneumatic Test Console .... PTC
Pneumatic Test Sequencer (AFM) .... PTS
Pneumatic Test Set (KSC) .... PTS
Pneumatic Tube [*Technical drawings*] .... PT
Pneumatic Tube System .... PTS
Pneumatically Operated Disconnect (KSC) .... POD
Pneumatically Operated Equipment (AAG) .... POE
Pneumatically Operated Valve .... POV
Pneumatically-Released Pilot (DNAB) .... PRP
Pneumatics Control Panel (AAG) .... PCP
Pneumatosis Cystoides Intestinorum [*Medicine*] (AAMN) .... PCI
Pneumatosis Intestinalis [*Medicine*] .... PI
Pneumocconiosis [*Medicine*] (AD) .... pneumoccon
Pneumocystic Pneumonia [*Medicine*] (DAVI) .... PCP
Pneumocystis Carinii Pneumonia [*Microbiology*] .... PCP
Pneumoencephalogram [*Medicine*] .... PEG
Pneumoencephalography [*Medicine*] (CPH) .... PNE
Pneumograph (AD) .... pneumog
Pneumomediastinum [*Medicine*] (AAMN) .... PM
Pneumonia [*Medicine*] .... PN
Pneumonia [*Medicine*] (MAE) .... pneu
Pneumonia (WDAA) .... PNEUM
Pneumonia Virus of Mice .... PVM
Pneumonoultra-Microscopicsilicovolcanoconiosis [*Medicine*] (AD) .... pneumonoultra
Pneumotaxic Center [*Medicine*] (DAVI) .... PNC
Pneumotaxic Center (BABM) .... PNC
Pneumothorax [*Medicine*] .... PNEUMO
Pneumothorax [*Medicine*] .... PNX
Pneumothorax [*Medicine*] (AD) .... pnx
Pneumothorax [*Medicine*] .... PT
Pneumothorax [*Medicine*] (AAMN) .... PTX
Pneumothorax [*Medicine*] .... PX
Pneumotoxic Center (AAMN) .... PC
P-Nitrophenyl-B-Galactoside [*Chemistry*] (MAE) .... PNPG
PNP [*Positive-Negative-Positive*] **Transistor Magnetic Logic** (IEEE) .... PTML
PNPN [*Positive-Negative-Positive-Negative*] **Transistor Magnetic Logic** (IAA) .... PTML
PNR Food Industries Ltd. [*Toronto Stock Exchange symbol*] .... EAT
Pnuematically-Impacted Stabilized Earth .... PISE
Po [*Burkina Faso*] [*ICAO location identifier*] (ICLI) .... DHCP
Po [*Upper Volta*] [*Airport symbol*] (AD) .... PUP
Poa Semilatent Virus .... PSLV
Poale Agudath Israel of America (EA) .... PAI
Poblacion [*Population*] [*Spanish*] (AD) .... pob
Pocahontas, AR [*AM radio station call letters*] .... KPOC
Pocahontas, AR [*FM radio station call letters*] .... KPOC-FM
Pocahontas Fed Svg& L A Ark [*NASDAQ symbol*] (TTSB) .... PFSL
Pocahontas Federal Savings & Loan Association [*NASDAQ symbol*] (SAG) .... PFSL
Pocahontas Federal Savings & Loan Association [*Associated Press*] (SAG) .... PochFdl
Pocahontas, IA [*Location identifier FAA*] (FAAL) .... POH

Pocahontas Record Democrat, Pocahontas, IA [Library symbol Library of Congress] (LCLS) .... IaPocR
Pocatalico, WV [FM radio station call letters] .... WRVZ
Pocatello [Idaho] [Airport symbol] (OAG) .... PIH
Pocatello, ID [Television station call letters] .... KISU
Pocatello, ID [FM radio station call letters] .... KMGI
Pocatello, ID [FM radio station call letters] .... KPKY
Pocatello, ID [Television station call letters] .... KPVI
Pocatello, ID [AM radio station call letters] .... KSEI
Pocatello, ID [AM radio station call letters] .... KWIK
Pocatello, ID [FM radio station call letters] .... KZBQ-FM
Pocatello Public Library, Pocatello, ID [Library symbol] [Library of Congress] (LCLS) .... IdP
Pocatello Regional Medical Center, Medical Library, Pocatello, ID [Library symbol] [Library of Congress] (LCLS) .... IdPH
Pocatello Regional Medical Center, Pocatello, ID [Library symbol] [Library of Congress] (LCLS) .... IdPM
POCC [Payload Operations Control Center] Automated Computer Network .... PACNET
POCC [Payload Operations Control Center] Experiments Timeline System [Ground Data Systems Division and Spacelab] [NASA] (NASA) .... PETS
Pocillum [Little Cup] [Pharmacy] (ROG) .... POCIL
Pocillum [Little Cup] [Pharmacy] .... Pocill
Pockels Langmuir Adam Wilson McBain Trough [Surface film balance] .... PLAWM Trough
Pockels Readout Optical Modulator .... PROM
Pocket (MSA) .... PKT
Pocket (AD) .... pock
Pocket Book .... PB
Pocket Books (AD) .... Pocket Bks
Pocket Checklist (MCD) .... PCL
Pocket Computer .... PC
Pocket Dosimeter-High (MCD) .... PDH
Pocket Dosimeter-Low (MCD) .... PDL
Pocket Edition (WDAA) .... PE
Pocket Internet Explorer [Microsoft Corp.] [Computer science] .... PIE
Pocket Knife Ancillary Workers' Association [A union] [British] .... PKAWA
Pocket Oxford Dictionary [A publication] .... POD
Pocket Panel [Automotive engineering] .... P/PNL
Pocket Select Language [Burroughs Corp.] .... PSL
Pocket Submarine (NATG) .... SSZ
Pocket Testament League (EA) .... PTL
Pocketpiece [A. C. Nielsen Co.] [Rating report] (NTCM) .... PP
Pock-Forming Unit .... PFU
Poco [Somewhat] [Music] .... P
Poco [Somewhat] [Music] .... PO
Poco a Poco [Little by Little] [Music] .... P a P
Poco Forte [Rather Loud] [Music] .... PF
Poco Petroleums Ltd. [Toronto Stock Exchange symbol] .... POC
Pocock on Costs [1881] [A publication] (DLA) .... Poc Costs
Pocomoke City, MD [AM radio station call letters] .... WDMV
Pocomoke City, MD [FM radio station call letters] .... WKHI
Pocomoke City, MD [FM radio station call letters] (RBYB) .... WKHW-FM
Pocono Airlines, Inc. [ICAO designator] (FAAC) .... POC
Pocono Mountain Vacation Bureau (AD) .... PMVB
Pocos De Caldas [Brazil] [Airport symbol] (OAG) .... POO
Pocos De Caldas [Brazil ICAO location identifier] (ICLI) .... SBPC
Poculum [Cup] [Pharmacy] .... POC
Poculum [Cup] [Pharmacy] (ROG) .... POCUL
Poculum [Cup] (AD) .... pocul
Pocumtuck Valley Memorial Association, Deerfield, MA [Library symbol Library of Congress] (LCLS) .... MDeeP
Pod Air Conditioner (AAG) .... PAC
Pod Cooling Unit (AAG) .... PCU
Pod Tail Section .... PTS
Podiatrist .... PDTRST
Podiatrist (AD) .... podia
Podiatrists' Board of Queensland [Australia] .... PBQ
Podiatrists' Registration Board [New South Wales, Australia] .... PRB
Podiatry (DAVI) .... POD
Podiatry Association [British] (DBA) .... PA
Podiatry Bibliographical Society [Defunct] (EA) .... PBS
Podium (VRA) .... pdm
Podkamennaya [Former USSR Geomagnetic observatory code] .... POD
Podkamennaya Tunguska [Former USSR ICAO location identifier] (ICLI) .... UNKT
Podor [Senegal] [ICAO location identifier] (ICLI) .... GOSP
Podor [Senegal] [Airport symbol] (OAG) .... POD
Poe & Brown [NASDAQ symbol] (SAG) .... POBR
Poe & Brown [Commercial firm Associated Press] (SAG) .... PoeBwn
Poe Foundation (EA) .... PF
Poe on Pleading and Practice [A publication] (DLA) .... Poe Pl
Poe Studies Association (EA) .... PSA
Poenitentia [Penance] [Latin] (ADA) .... POENIT
Poesoegroenoe [Surinam] [ICAO location identifier] (ICLI) .... SMPG
Poet Laureate .... PL
Poet Laureatus Caesareus [Imperial Poet Laureate] [Latin] (ROG) .... PLC
Poet of the New Generation [Term used to describe poets writing for entertainment value] (ECON) .... PONG
Poet, Printer, Publisher, Publican, and Player [Nickname given to William Oxberry (fl. 1784-1824)] .... 5P's
Poetae Latini Minores [A publication] (OCD) .... PLM
Poetae Lyrici Graeci [A publication] (OCD) .... PLG
Poetae Melici Graeci [A publication] (OCD) .... Poet Mel Gr
Poetarum Philosophorum Graecorum Fragmenta [A publication] (OCD) .... PPF
Poetarum Romanorum Veterum Reliquiae [A publication] (OCD) .... Poet Rom Vet

Poetic Allusion Watch .... PAW
Poetica [of Aristotle] [Classical studies] (OCD) .... Poet
Poetical (AD) .... poet
Poetics Today [A publication] (BRI) .... Poetics T
Poetry (AD) .... po
Poetry [A publication] (BRI) .... Poet
Poetry Criticism [A publication] .... PC
Poetry Criticism (AD) .... poecrit
Poetry League of America (EA) .... PLA
Poetry London [A publication British] .... PL
Poetry Project (EA) .... PP
Poetry Society [British] .... PS
Poetry Society of America (EA) .... PSA
Poetry Therapy Institute (EA) .... PTI
Poetry Treasury [An association Defunct] (EA) .... PT
Poets and the Pub [Programme] [Australia] .... PATP
Poets and Writers (EA) .... PW
Poets International Organisation [Bangalore, India] (EAIO) .... PIO
Poets, Playwrights, Editors, Essayists, and Novelists [AccountingPANANEWS] (NADA) .... PEN
Poets' Union of New South Wales [Australia] .... PUNSW
Pogo Fan Club and Walt Kelly Society (EA) .... PFCWTS
Pogo Producing [NYSE symbol] (TTSB) .... PPP
Pogo Producing Co. [Associated Press] (SAG) .... PogoPd
Pogo Producing Co. [NYSE symbol] (SPSG) .... PPP
Pogonion (DMAA) .... Pog
Pogonomyrinex Occidentalis [A genus of ants] .... Pogo
Pohai Sea and Area [China, Mainland] [MARC geographic area code Library of Congress] (LCCP) .... a-ccp-
Pohang (AD) .... Poh
Pohang [South Korea ICAO location identifier] (ICLI) .... RKTH
Pohang Iron & Steel ADS [NYSE symbol] (TTSB) .... PKX
Pohang Iron & Steel Co. (ECON) .... POSCO
Pohang Iron & Steel Co., Ltd. [NYSE symbol] (SAG) .... PKX
Pohang Iron & Steel Co., Ltd. [Associated Press] (SAG) .... Pohang
Pohenegamook, PQ [FM radio station call letters] CFVD-2
Pohjanmaan Lento OY [Finland ICAO designator] (FAAC) .... PLF
Poids Moliculaire [Molecular Weight] [French] (AD) .... pm
Poikilocyte [or Poikilocytosis] [Medicine] (MAE) .... poik
Poincare-Lighthill-Kuo [Method] .... PLK
Poinsettia Cryptic Virus [Plant pathology] .... PCRV
Point [Lacrosse position] .... P
Point (IDOE) .... P
Point .... PNT
Point (WGA) .... PO
Point [Commonly used] (OPSA) .... POINT
Point (WDMC) .... pt
Point .... PT
Point (ODBW) .... pt
Point (DD) .... Pt
Point .... PT
Point [Maps and charts] .... PT
Point after Touchdown [Football] .... PAT
Point Air Defense System .... PADS
Point, Area, and Line Source Air Quality Model [Environmental Protection Agency] (GFGA) .... PAL
Point, Area, and Line Source with Deposition and Settling of Pollutants [Air quality model] [Environmental Protection Agency] (GFGA) .... PALDS
Point Arguello Launch Complex .... PALC
Point Arguello Launch Site (AAG) .... PALS
Point Arguello Range Safety Impact Predictor (MUGU) .... PARSIP
Point Baker, AK [Location identifier FAA] (FAAL) .... KPB
Point Barrow [Alaska] [ICAO location identifier] (ICLI) .... PAPB
Point Barrow [Alaska] [Later, BRW] [Seismograph station code, US Geological Survey] [Closed] (SEIS) .... PTB
Point Barrow, AK [Location identifier FAA] (FAAL) .... NFV
Point Barrow, AK [Location identifier FAA] (FAAL) .... VIR
Point Beach Nuclear Plant (NRCH) .... PBNP
Point by Point .... PBP
Point Calculation Worksheet [Army] (INF) .... PCW
Point Comfort & Northern Railway Co. [AAR code] .... PCN
Point Comfort, TX [FM radio station call letters] (RBYB) .... KAJI
Point Contact (IDOE) .... PC
Point Cook [Australia ICAO location identifier] (ICLI) .... AMPC
Point Credit Accounting and Reporting System (AFM) .... PCARS
Point Defense .... PD
Point Defense Missile System [NATO] (NATG) .... PDMS
Point Defense Surface Missile System .... PDSMS
Point Delay Fuze [Army] .... PD
Point Density Analysis [Mathematics] .... PDA
Point Detonating [Projectile] .... PD
Point Detonating Fuse (IAA) .... PDF
Point Detonating Fuze [Army] .... PDF
Point Detonating Self-Destroying [Projectile] .... PDSD
Point Detonating Super-Quick Fuze (NATG) .... PDSQ
Point, Digital, Qualifier [In automobile name Opel PDQ] .... PDQ
Point Director Array .... PDA
Point Distribution Model (DMAA) .... PDM
Point Edward Public Library, Ontario [Library symbol National Library of Canada] (NLC) .... OPED
Point Focusing and Centering [Optics] .... PFC
Point Foundation (EA) .... PF
Point Hope [Alaska] [Airport symbol] (OAG) .... PHO
Point Indicating Machine (IAA) .... PIM
Point Initiating .... PI

Point Initiating, Base Detonating Projectile [*Army*] ... PIBD
Point Initiating Fuze ... PIF
Point Insulating ... PI
Point Judith, RI [*Location identifier FAA*] (FAAL) ... PJI
Point Lay [*Alaska*] [*Airport symbol*] (OAG) ... PIZ
Point Lay, AK [*Location identifier FAA*] (FAAL) ... PIZ
Point Leamington Public Library, Newfoundland [*Library symbol National Library of Canada*] (NLC) ... NFPL
Point Leamington Public Library, Point Leamington, NF, Canada [*Library symbol Library of Congress*] (LCLS) ... CaNfPL
Point Loma College [*California*] ... PLC
Point Loma College, San Diego, CA [*OCLC symbol*] (OCLC) ... CPT
Point Loma College, San Diego, CA [*Library symbol Library of Congress*] (LCLS) ... CSdP
Point Loma Nazarene College (GAGS) ... Point Loma C
Point Lookout, MO [*FM radio station call letters*] (RBYB) ... KCOZ
Point Lookout, MO [*FM radio station call letters*] ... KSMS
Point Missile Defense System (DNAB) ... PMDS
Point Mugu, CA [*Location identifier FAA*] (FAAL) ... NRE
Point Mugu, CA [*Location identifier FAA*] (FAAL) ... RRG
Point Mugu Naval Air Station [*California*] [*ICAO location identifier*] (ICLI) ... KNTD
Point Of Action (EECA) ... POA
Point of Aim [*Military*] ... PA
Point of Application [*Medicine*] (MAE) ... POA
Point of Basal Convergence ... PBC
Point of Beginning ... POB
Point of Beginning (AD) ... pob
Point of Business ... POB
Point of Care [*Medicine*] ... POC
Point of Closest Approach ... PCA
Point of Compliance (FFDE) ... POC
Point of Compound Curve (KSC) ... PCC
Point of Contact (AABC) ... POC
Point of Contact (AD) ... poc
Point of Control and Observation [*Telecommunications*] (OSI) ... PCO
Point of Curve [*Technical drawings*] ... PC
Point of Departure ... POD
Point of Discharge (GFGA) ... POD
Point of Entry [*Accounts*] ... POE
Point of Equal Time [*Aviation*] ... PET
Point of Exit ... POX
Point of Exposure [*Environmental Protection Agency*] (ERG) ... POE
Point of Frog [*Electronics*] (MSA) ... PF
Point of Impact (AFM) ... PI
Point of Impact ... POI
Point of Intended Movement [*Military*] ... PIM
Point of Interception [*Navigation*] ... PI
Point of Interception (GNE) ... POI
Point of Interface [*Telecommunications*] ... POI
Point of Intersection ... PI
Point of Maximal Impulse [*Medicine*] ... PMI
Point of Maximum Impulse (AD) ... pmi
Point of Maximum Intensity ... PMI
Point of Minimum Radius (IAA) ... PMR
Point of No Return (AD) ... PN
Point of No Return (AD) ... pnr
Point of No Return [*Aviation*] ... PNR
Point of Possible Collision [*Navigation*] ... PPC
Point of Presence [*Telecommunications*] (PCM) ... PoP
Point of Presence [*Telecommunications*] (DOM) ... POP
Point of Purchase [*Advertising*] ... POP
Point of Reverse Curve (MSA) ... PRC
Point of Safe Return (MCD) ... PSR
Point of Sale ... PoS
Point of Sale (AD) ... pos
Point of Sale (ODBW) ... POS
Point of Service ... POS
Point of Service [*Health plan option*] ... POS
Point of Service Option ... POS
Point of Shipment ... P/S
Point of Spiral Tangent (KSC) ... PST
Point of Subjective Equality [*Psychology*] ... PSE
Point of Switch ... PS
Point of Symmetry ... PS
Point of tangency (AD) ... pot
Point of Tangency ... PT
Point of Total Assumption (MCD) ... PTA
Point of Turn [*Navigation*] ... PT
Point of Use ... POU
Point of Vertical Curve ... PVC
Point of Vertical Intersection ... PVI
Point of Vertical Tangent ... PVT
Point of View ... POV
Point of Weapon Release [*Military*] ... PWR
Point of Zero Charge [*Electrochemistry*] ... PZC
Point Park College, Pittsburgh, PA [*Library symbol Library of Congress*] (LCLS) ... PPiPP
Point Park College, Pittsburgh, PA [*Inactive*] [*OCLC symbol*] (OCLC) ... PTP
Point Pelee National Park [*Ontario, Canada*] (AD) ... PPNP
Point Pelee National Park, Parks Canada [*Parc National de la Pointe-Pelee, Parcs Canada*] **Leamington, Ontario** [*Library symbol National Library of Canada*] (NLC) ... OLEI
Point per Inch (IAA) ... PPI
Point Pleasant, NJ [*FM radio station call letters*] ... WADB
Point Pleasant, NJ [*FM radio station call letters*] (RBYB) ... WRAT-FM
Point Pleasant, WV [*AM radio station call letters*] ... WBGS
Point Pleasant, WV [*FM radio station call letters*] ... WBYG
Point Position Data ... PPD
Point Response Function [*Of a telescope*] ... PRF
Point Retreat, AK [*Location identifier FAA*] (FAAL) ... PRT
Point Reyes [*California*] [*Seismograph station code, US Geological Survey Closed*] (SEIS) ... PRC
Point Reyes, CA [*Location identifier FAA*] (FAAL) ... PYE
Point Reyes National Seashore [*National Park Service designation*] ... PORE
Point Saline [*Grenada*] [*ICAO location identifier*] (ICLI) ... TGPY
Point Shipping Co. [*Steamship*] (MHDW) ... PSC
Point Source Ambient Monitoring [*Environmental Protection Agency*] (GFGA) ... PSAM
Point Source Monitoring [*Environmental Protection Agency*] (GFGA) ... PSM
Point Source Range (IAA) ... PSR
Point Sparger [*Engineering*] ... PS
Point Spread [*In visual cortex*] ... PS
Point Spread Function ... PSF
Point Spread Junction (IAA) ... PSJ
Point Sur, CA [*Location identifier FAA*] (FAAL) ... NNZ
Point Surface Origin ... PSO
Point Target Data Base (SAA) ... PTDB
Point Target Weapon ... PTW
Point Weather Warning ... PWW
PointCast Business Network ... PBN
PointCast Network [*Computer science*] ... PCN
Point-Contact Photo-Voltaic [*Solar cells*] ... PCPV
Point-Contact Transistor [*Electronics*] (IAA) ... PCT
Pointe Claire Public Library [*UTLAS symbol*] ... PCC
Pointe Claire Public Library, Pointe Claire, PQ, Canada [*Library symbol Library of Congress*] (LCLS) ... CaQPOC
Pointe Coupee Parish Library, New Roads, LA [*Library symbol Library of Congress*] (LCLS) ... LNewr
Pointe Molloy [*Kerguelen Islands*] [*Seismograph station code, US Geological Survey*] (SEIS) ... PMK
Pointe Noire (AD) ... PNe
Pointe Noire [*Congo*] [*Airport symbol*] (OAG) ... PNR
Pointe-A-Pitre [*Guadeloupe*] [*Airport symbol*] (OAG) ... PTP
Pointe-A-Pitre/Le Raizet, Guadeloupe [*French Antilles*] [*ICAO location identifier*] (ICLI) ... TFFR
Pointe-Claire Public Library [*Bibliotheque Publique de Pointe-Claire*] **Quebec** [*Library symbol National Library of Canada*] (NLC) ... QPOC
Pointed (WGA) ... PTD
Pointed Soft Point [*Ammunition*] ... PSP
Pointed Soft Point Bullet ... PSP
Pointe-Noire [*Congo*] [*ICAO location identifier*] (ICLI) ... FCPP
Pointer (MCD) ... PNTR
Pointer [*Computer science*] ... PTR
Pointer & Spruill Library, Raleigh, NC [*Library symbol*] [*Library of Congress*] (LCLS) ... NcRPS
Pointer Game (AEBS) ... PG
Pointer/Tracker (MCD) ... P/T
Pointing and Attitude Control System [*Aerospace*] (NASA) ... PACS
Pointing and Stabilization Platform Element [*Army*] (MCD) ... POISE
Pointing and Tracking Demonstration Unit (MCD) ... PTDU
Pointing and Tracking Scope ... PTS
Pointing Device Adapter [*Computer science*] ... PDA
Pointing Error Sensor (MCD) ... PES
Pointing Reference System (KSC) ... PRS
Pointing-Control System [*Aerospace*] ... PCS
Point-in-Space (MCD) ... PINS
Point-of-Failure [*Computer science*] (IBMDP) ... POF
Point-of-Last-Environment [*Computer science*] (IBMDP) ... POLE
Point-of-Origin Device (IEEE) ... POD
Point-of-Origin Device (AD) ... pod
Point-of-Purchase [*Advertising*] (WDMC) ... POP
Point-of-Purchase Advertising (AD) ... pop advertising
Point-of-Purchase Advertising Institute [*Fort Lee, NJ*] (EA) ... POPAI
Point-of-Sale [*Retail*] (WDMC) ... p-o-s
Point-of-Sale [*Retail*] (WDMC) ... POS
Point-of-Sale System (AD) ... P-O-S S
Point-of-Sale Terminal (AD) ... pos terminal
Point-of-Sale Terminal [*Business term*] ... POST
Point-of-Sale Transaction ... POST
Point-of-Service [*Human resources*] (WYGK) ... POS
Point-of-Service Plan [*Insurance*] (PAZ) ... POS
Point-of-Service System (AD) ... P-O-S S
Point-of-Use/Point-of-Entry [*Water standards*] (FFDE) ... POU/POE
Point-of-View (AD) ... p-o-v
Point-Positioning Data Base [*Cartography*] (RDA) ... PPDB
Points [*Commonly used*] (OPSA) ... POINTS
Points [*Postal Service standard*] (OPSA) ... PTS
Points ... PTS
Points Against [*Football*] ... PA
Points and Lines [*Military*] (CAAL) ... P & L
Points For [*Football*] ... PF
Points of Call Airlines Ltd. [*Canada ICAO designator*] (FAAC) ... PTS
Points per Game (WGA) ... PPG
Points Per Inch (WDMC) ... ppi
Points to Consider ... PTC
Point-to-Point [*Air Force*] ... P/P
Point-to-Point [*Robotics*] [*Telecommunications*] ... PTP
Point-to-Point Correlation [*Graphing*] ... PPC
Point-to-Point Protocol [*Computer science*] (PCM) ... PPP
Point-to-Point Radio [*FAA designator*] (CET) ... P

Point-to-Point System (IAA) ... PPS
Point-to-Point Tunneling Protocol [*Microsoft Corp.*] ... PPTP
Point-to-Point Tunneling Protocol [*Computer science*] ... PPTP
Poipu, HI [*FM radio station call letters*] ... KSRF
Poise [*Unit of dynamic viscosity*] ... P
Poise Distribution Amplifier (AFM) ... PDA
Poiseuille [*Unit of dynamic viscosity*] ... PI
Poison ... P
Poison ... POI
Poison (AAMN) ... POIS
Poison (AD) ... pois
Poison Control Center ... PCC
Poison Control Data Base [*Database*] ... PCDB
Poison Control Information Center ... PCIC
Poison Ivy [*Campers' slang*] ... PI
Poison Prevention Packaging Act ... PPPA
Poison-Boltzmann Equation [*Physical chemistry*] ... PBE
Poisoning [*FBI standardized term*] ... POIS
Poisoning Surveillance and Epidemiology Branch [*Defunct*] (EA) ... PSEB
Poisonous Plant Research Laboratory [*Agricultural Research Service*] [*Research center*] (RCD) ... PPRL
Poisons Advisory Committee [*Australia*] ... PAC
Poisson Probability Distribution Function [*Mathematics*] ... PPDF
Poisson Probability Frequency Function [*Mathematics*] ... PPFF
Poitiers [*France*] [*Airport symbol*] (OAG) ... PIS
Poitiers/Biard [*France ICAO location identifier*] (ICLI) ... LFBI
Pokemouche, NB [*FM radio station call letters*] (RBYB) ... CKRO-FM
Pokeweed Antiviral Protein [*Immunochemistry*] ... PAP
Pokeweed Mitogen [*Genetics*] ... PWM
Pokeweed Mitogen-Stimulated Spleen-Cell-Conditioned Medium [*For growing cells*] ... PWMSCM
Pokeweed Mosaic Virus [*Plant pathology*] ... POKMV
Pokhara [*Nepal*] [*Airport symbol*] (OAG) ... PKR
Pokhara [*Nepal*] [*ICAO location identifier*] (ICLI) ... VNPK
Pokhvala Knige [*A publication*] ... PK
POL [*Petroleum, Oil, and Lubricants*] **Installations Damage Report** (NATG) ... POLDAM
Pola [*Yugoslavia*] [*Seismograph station code, US Geological Survey Closed*] (SEIS) ... POL
Pola Resources Ltd. [*Vancouver Stock Exchange symbol*] ... POR
Polacca [*Ship's rigging*] (ROG) ... POL
Polamerican Law Journal [*A publication*] (DLA) ... Polam LJ
Poland [*MARC geographic area code Library of Congress*] (LCCP) ... e-pl--
Poland [*MARC country of publication code Library of Congress*] (LCCP) ... pl
Poland [*ANSI two-letter standard code*] (CNC) ... PL
Poland [*ANSI three-letter standard code*] (CNC) ... POL
Poland (VRA) ... Pol
Poland [*IYRU nationality code*] (IYR) ... PZ
Poland [*License plate code assigned to foreign diplomats in the US*] ... QW
Poland [*International civil aircraft marking*] (ODBW) ... SP
Poland and Hungary Assistance for Economic Restructuring [*EC*] (ECED) ... PHARE
Poland China Record Association (EA) ... PCRA
Poland Spring, ME [*Television station call letters*] ... WMTW
Poland Watch Center [*Defunct*] (EA) ... PWC
Poland's Digest of the Military Laws of the United States [*A publication*] (DLA) ... Pol Mil Dig
Poland's Law of Trade Marks [*A publication*] (DLA) ... Pol Tr Mar
Polanyi Society (EA) ... PS
Polar (AD) ... pol
Polar Adjectives Test (AEBS) ... PAT
Polar Air Cargo, Inc. [*FAA designator*] (FAAC) ... PAC
Polar Air Co. [*Russian Federation*] [*ICAO designator*] (FAAC) ... JPC
Polar and Auroral Dynamics [*Meteorology*] ... PAD
Polar Atlantic [*American air mass*] ... PA
Polar Automatic Weather Station (NG) ... PAWS
Polar Auxin Transport [*Botany*] ... PAT
Polar Avia [*ICAO designator*] (AD) ... JW
Polar Beacon Experiments and Auroral Research (AD) ... Polar BEAR
Polar Bear Association (EA) ... PBA
Polar Bear Club - USA (EA) ... PBC-USA
Polar Bear Club - Winter Swimmers [*Later, PBC-USA*] (EA) ... PBC-WS
Polar Branch, Research Environmental Science Division [*Army*] ... PBRESD
Polar Cap Absorption ... PCA
Polar Cap Absorption Event ... PCAE
Polar Cap Disturbance (DNAB) ... PCD
Polar Circling Balloon Observatory ... POCIBO
Polar Circulation Index [*Climatology*] ... PCI
Polar Component [*Food science*] ... PC
Polar Continental [*American air mass*] ... PC
Polar Continental Shelf Project [*Canada*] ... PSCP
Polar Coordinates Navigation System ... PCNS
Polar Crane [*Nuclear energy*] (NRCH) ... PC
Polar DAAC [*Distributed Active Archive Center*] **Advisory Group** [*Marine science*] (OSRA) ... PoDAG
Polar DAAC [*Distributed Active Archive Center*] **Advisory Group** (USDC) ... PoDAG
Polar Distance [*Navigation*] ... P
Polar Distance [*Navigation*] ... PD
Polar Experiment ... POLEX
Polar Experiment in the Northern Hemisphere (MSC) ... POLEX-NORTH
Polar Experiment in the Southern Hemisphere (MSC) ... POLEX-SOUTH
Polar Express Corp. [*Associated Press*] (SAG) ... PolarE
Polar Express Corp. [*NASDAQ symbol*] (SAG) ... POLR
Polar Express Corp. [*Associated Press*] (SAG) ... PolrEx
Polar Express Wrrt'B' [*NASDAQ symbol*] (TTSB) ... POLRW
Polar Flattening [*Symbol*] [*Physics*] ... f
Polar Front [*Climatology*] ... PF
Polar Front Jet Stream (ADA) ... PFJ
Polar Front Zone [*Marine science*] (MSC) ... PFZ
Polar Gas Library, Toronto, ON, Canada [*Library symbol Library of Congress*] (LCLS) ... CaOTPG
Polar Gas Library, Toronto, Ontario [*Library symbol National Library of Canada*] (NLC) ... OTPG
Polar Geophysical Institute [*Murmansk Region*] [*Russia*] ... PGI
Polar Ice Core Drilling Office [*National Science Foundation*] (MSC) ... PICO
Polar Icebreaker Canadian Design Group ... PICDG
Polar International Airlines, Inc. [*ICAO designator*] (FAAC) ... POL
Polar Ionospheric Beacon ... PIB
Polar Ionospheric Beacon Satellite [*NASA*] ... PIBS
Polar Ionospheric Trough ... PIT
Polar Lipid Fatty Acid [*Biochemistry*] ... PLFA
Polar Lipid Fraction [*Biochemistry*] ... PLF
Polar Maritime Air Colder than Underlying Surface (AD) ... mPk
Polar Meteorological Satellite (SSD) ... PMS
Polar Night Jet Stream (ADA) ... PNJ
Polar Operational Environmental Satellite (USDC) ... POES
Polar Operational Meteorological Satellite (USDC) ... POMS
Polar Operational Meteorological Satellite [*Marine science*] (OSRA) ... POMS
Polar Orbiting Environmental Satellite ... POES
Polar Orbiting Geophysical Observatories [*Marine science*] (OSRA) ... POGO
Polar Orbiting Geophysical Observatory [*NASA*] ... POGO
Polar Orbiting Lunar Observatory [*Satellite*] ... POLO
Polar Orbiting Platform (SSD) ... POP
Polar Orbiting Satellite [*Marine science*] (OSRA) ... POS
Polar Orbiting Satellite (USDC) ... POS
Polar Orbiting Satellite System - University of Michigan [*Designed by engineering students*] ... POSSUM
Polar Ozone Aerosol Measurement ... POAM
Polar Pacific [*American air mass*] ... PP
Polar Radius of Earth [*Symbol*] ... B
Polar Reflection Faraday Effect ... PRFE
Polar Regions Award (IAA) ... PRA
Polar Research and Development Center [*Army*] ... PRDC
Polar Research Board [*National Academy of Sciences*] ... PRB
Polar Research Laboratory [*USA*] [*Marine science*] (OSRA) ... PRL
Polar Satellite Launch Vehicle ... PSLV
Polar Science Center [*University of Washington*] [*Research center*] (RCD) ... PSC
Polar Stratospheric Cloud [*Meteorology*] ... PSC
Polar Stratospheric Telescope ... POST
Polar Subsurface Sounder (SSD) ... PSS
Polar to Analog (KSC) ... P/A
Polar to Cartesian ... P-C
Polar to Rectangular (SAA) ... PTR
Polar Track Structure [*Aviation*] (FAAC) ... PTS
Polaravia OY [*Finland ICAO designator*] (FAAC) ... PLV
Polaris Accelerated Change Operation [*Missiles*] ... PACO
Polaris Accelerated Flight [*Chamber*] [*Missiles*] ... PAF
Polaris Acceleration Test [*Military*] (SAA) ... PAT
Polaris Cargo Resupply Ship [*Navy symbol*] (DNAB) ... AK-FBM
Polaris Control and Information Center [*Missiles*] ... PC & IC
Polaris Correction [*Missiles*] ... Q
Polaris Documentation Control [*Missiles*] ... PDC
Polaris Energy [*Vancouver Stock Exchange symbol*] ... PLY
Polaris Engineering Technical Service [*Missiles*] ... PETS
Polaris Evaluation Missile ... PEM
Polaris Executive Plan [*British*] ... PEPLAN
Polaris Industrial Team [*Missiles*] ... PIT
Polaris Industries [*NYSE symbol*] (TTSB) ... PII
Polaris Industries, Inc. [*NYSE symbol*] (SAG) ... PII
Polaris Industries, Inc. [*Associated Press*] (SAG) ... Polaris
Polaris Integrated Test Team [*Missiles*] ... PITT
Polaris Material Office [*Missiles*] ... PMO
Polaris Material Office, Atlantic Fleet [*Missiles*] ... PMOLANT
Polaris Material Office, Pacific Fleet [*Missiles*] ... PMOPAC
Polaris Missile Assembly Facility ... PMAF
Polaris Missile Facility [*Military*] (IAA) ... PMF
Polaris Missile Facility ... POMF
Polaris Missile Facility, Atlantic (AD) ... POMFLANT
Polaris Missile Facility, Atlantic Fleet ... POMFLANT
Polaris Missile Facility, Pacific (AD) ... POMPAC
Polaris Missile Facility, Pacific Fleet ... PMFPAC
Polaris Missile Facility, Pacific Fleet ... POMFPAC
Polaris Missile Office ... PMO
Polaris Missile System ... PMS
Polaris Operation Support Task Group [*Missiles*] ... POST
Polaris Operational Performance Surveillance Engineering Report [*Missiles*] ... POPSER
Polaris Operational Readiness Instrumentation [*Missiles*] ... PORI
Polaris Standard [*Missiles*] ... PS
Polaris Star Tracker [*Missiles*] ... PST
Polaris Systems Officer [*British military*] (DMA) ... PSO
Polaris Tactical Missile ... PTM
Polaris Target Card Computing System [*Missiles*] ... PTCCS
Polaris Task Group [*Missiles*] ... PTG
Polaris Technical Information Bulletin [*Missiles*] ... POTIB
Polaris Tender Management Computer [*Missiles*] ... PTMC
Polaris-Poseidon Intelligence Digest (MCD) ... PPID
Polarity (MSA) ... PLRT
Polarity (AAG) ... PO
Polarity (AD) ... po

Polarity [*or Polarize*] (KSC) ... POL
Polarity [*or Polarize*] (IAA) ... POLAR
Polarity (AD) ... polar
Polarity Coincidence Correlator ... PCC
Polarity Correlation Function (IAA) ... PKF
Polarity Health Institute (EA) ... PHI
Polarity Reversal Unit [*Electrochemistry*] ... PRU
Polarity Scale [*Psychology*] ... PS
Polarity Selector (IAA) ... PS
Polarizable Point Charge [*Model for the water molecule*] ... PPC
Polarization ... P
Polarization (MSA) ... PLZN
Polarization and Directionality of the Earth's Reflectances [*Instrumentation*] ... POLDER
Polarization Angle (AD) ... polang
Polarization Angle [*Telecommunications*] ... POLANG
Polarization Approximation [*Physical chemistry*] ... PA
Polarization Beam Splitter ... PBS
Polarization Diversity Array ... PDA
Polarization Diversity LIDAR ... PDL
Polarization Modulated Electron Nuclear Double Resonance [*Spectroscopy*] ... PM-ENDOR
Polarization Modulation (MCD) ... PM
Polarization-Maintaining [*Optical Film*] ... PM
Polarization-Modulation Laser-Scanning Microscopy ... PM-LSM
Polarization-Preserving Fiber ... PPF
Polarize (MSA) ... PLZ
Polarized Field Frequency Relay (IAA) ... PFR
Polarized Frequency Relay ... PFR
Polarized Infrared Absorption Spectroscopy ... PIRAS
Polarized Light ... PL
Polarized Light Microscopy ... PLM
Polarized Orbital Approximation (PDAA) ... POA
Polarized Platen Viewer (OA) ... PPV
Polarized Relay (IAA) ... PR
Polarized Return-to-Zero Recording [*Computer science*] (IBMDP) ... RZ(P)
Polarized Total Internal Reflection Fluorescence Microscopy ... PTIRFM
Polarized Zeeman Atomic Absorption ... PZAA
Polarizer-Compensator-Analyzer (PDAA) ... PCA
Polar-Motion Analysis by Radio Interferometric Surveying [*Geodetic measuring facilities*] ... POLARIS
Polarographic Analyzer ... PA
Polaroid (VRA) ... PLRD
Polaroid Color Pack Camera ... PCP
Polaroid Corp. [*Associated Press*] (SAG) ... Polaroid
Polaroid Corp. [*NYSE symbol*] (SPSG) ... PRD
Polaroid Corp., Cambridge, MA [*Library symbol Library of Congress*] (LCLS) ... MCP
Polaroid Corp. Library, Cambridge, MA [*Library symbol*] [*Library of Congress*] (LCLS) ... MCPC
Polaroid Stereoscopic Chroncyclegraph ... PSC
Polaromicrotribrometry [*Analytical chemistry*] ... PMT
Polar-Orbiting Operational Environmental Satellite (USDC) ... POES
Polar-orbiting Operational Environmental Satellite [*Marine science*] (OSRA) ... POES
Polaska Rzeczpospolita Ludowa [*Polish People's Republic*] (AD) ... Pol Rze Lud
Pole ... P
Pole [*Unit of measurement*] ... PO
Pole Amplitude Modulation (IEEE) ... PAM
Pole Broken [*Telecommunications*] (TEL) ... PBR
Pole Cat [*Slang*] ... PK
Pole Cell [*Insect embryology*] ... PC
Pole Fittings [*JETDS nomenclature*] [*Military*] (CET) ... PF
Pole Mountain [*Wyoming*] [*Seismograph station code, US Geological Survey Closed*] (SEIS) ... PMW
Pole Piece (DEN) ... PP
Pole Position [*Automobile racing*] ... PP
Pole Vault ... PV
Polemic (AD) ... polem
Pole-Mounted Amplifier ... PMA
Polen [*Poland*] [*Norwegian*] (AD) ... Pol
Poles, Italians, Greeks, and Slavs ... PIGS
Polestar Exploration, Inc. [*Vancouver Stock Exchange symbol*] ... PSE
Polet [*Former USSR*] [*FAA designator*] (FAAC) ... POT
Pol-Fly [*Poland ICAO designator*] (FAAC) ... PFL
Polhemus Navigational Sciences, Inc. (MCD) ... PNSI
Police ... PLC
Police ... POL
Police Academy ... PA
Police Accident Report [*NHTSA*] (TAG) ... PAR
Police Administration Building ... PAB
Police Aerial Reinforcement [*or Resupply*] **Unit** [*Thailand*] (CINC) ... PARU
Police Agent (WDAA) ... PA
Police and Citizens' Youth Club [*Australia*] ... P & CYC
Police and Criminal Evidence Act [*1964*] [*British*] ... PACE
Police and Firemen's Insurance Association (EA) ... PFIA
Police and Prison Civil Rights Union [*Founded in 1989*] [*South Africa*] (ECON) ... POPCRU
Police Appeal Board [*South Australia*] ... PAB
Police Association of New South Wales [*Australia*] ... PANSW
Police Association of South Australia ... PASA
Police Association of Tasmania [*Australia*] ... PAT
Police Association of the Northern Territory [*Australia*] ... PANT
Police Association (Victoria) [*Australia*] ... PA(V)
Police Athletic League ... PAL
Police Attendance Line ... PAL
Police Aviation Services [*British ICAO designator*] (FAAC) ... PLC
Police Board of New South Wales [*Australia*] ... PBNSW
Police Burgh ... PB
Police Car ... P/C
Police Car Collectors Association (EA) ... PCCA
Police Chiefs Spouses - Worldwide [*An association*] (EA) ... PCSW
Police Code [*INTERPOL*] ... POLCOD
Police College (AD) ... Pol Col
Police Commissaire [*Interpol*] [*British*] (AD) ... Pol Com
Police Commissioner (WGA) ... PC
Police Commissioner (AD) ... Pol Com
Police Commissioner's Office ... PCO
Police Complaint Authority [*British*] ... PCA
Police Court [*British*] (ROG) ... PC
Police Court (DLA) ... Po Ct
Police Court Mission [*British*] (ROG) ... PCM
Police Department ... PD
Police Discipline Board [*New South Wales, Australia*] ... PDB
Police Education Advisory Council [*New South Wales, Australia*] ... PEAC
Police Executive Research Forum (EA) ... PERF
Police Federation [*London*] (AD) ... Pol Fed
Police Federation Newsletter [*A publication*] (DLA) ... Pol Fedn Newsl
Police Federation Newsletter [*A publication*] (ILCA) ... Police Fedn Newsl
Police Federation of Australia and New Zealand ... PFANZ
Police Field Force (CINC) ... PFF
Police Force of the Northern Territory [*Australia*] ... PFNT
Police Forces [*British*] ... PF
Police Forces [*British*] ... PFC
Police Foundation (EA) ... PF
Police Foundation [*Washington, D.C.*] (AD) ... Pol Found
Police Foundation Institute (NADA) ... PFI
Police History Society [*British*] (DBA) ... PHS
Police Information Network [*San Francisco Bay area, California*] ... PIN
Police Insignia Collector's Association (EA) ... PICA
Police Insignia Collectors Association [*British*] (DBA) ... PICA
Police Journal [*A publication*] (ILCA) ... Pol J
Police Justice ... PJ
Police Justice's Court [*A publication*] (ILCA) ... Police J Ct
Police Law Quarterly [*A publication*] (DLA) ... Pol LQ
Police Law Quarterly [*A publication*] (ILCA) ... Police LQ
Police Magistrate ... PM
Police Management Association [*Defunct*] (EA) ... PMA
Police Marksman Association (EA) ... PMA
Police Mutual Assurance Society [*British*] ... PM
Police Mutual Assurance Society [*British*] ... PMAS
Police National Computer [*British*] ... PNC
Police National Computer Unit [*British*] ... PNCU
Police Officer ... PO
Police Officer, Female ... POF
Police Officer, Male ... POM
Police Officer Student Training (AD) ... POST
Police Officers (AD) ... POs
Police Officers' Association [*British*] (BI) ... POA
Police Officers Research Association (AD) ... PORA
Police Officers Research Association (NADA) ... PORA
Police Operations Systems Support System Elementary ... POSSE
Police Petty Officer (DNAB) ... PPO
Police Protective League (NADA) ... PPL
Police Protective League (AD) ... PPL
Police Requirements Support Unit [*Home Office*] [*British*] ... PRSU
Police Sergeant [*Scotland Yard*] ... PS
Police Superannuation Board [*Australia*] ... PSB
Police Training Centre [*British*] ... PTC
Police Training Foundation ... PTF
Police War Reserve [*British*] (DAS) ... PWR
Police-Constable [*Scotland Yard*] ... PC
Police-FBI Fencing, Incognito [*Phony fencing ring operated by Washington, DC, law enforcement agents during 1976 to identify and arrest area thieves*] ... PFF Inc
Policewoman (ODBW) ... PW
Policies Allotment Board [*Navy*] (DNAB) ... PAB
Policies and Procedures Guide (SAA) ... PPG
Policies, Systems, and Procedures ... PSP
Policy (AFM) ... PLCY
Policy ... PLCY
Policy ... POL
Policy (DLA) ... Pol'y
Policy Advisory Center ... PAC
Policy Advisory Committee [*National Cancer Institute*] [*Department of Health and Human Services*] (GFGA) ... PAC
Policy Advisory Committee [*Office of Economic Opportunity*] ... PAC
Policy Alternatives for the Caribbean and Central America (EA) ... PACCA
Policy Analysis and Resource Allocation [*Department of State*] ... PARA
Policy Analysis for California Education [*Research center*] (RCD) ... PACE
Policy Analysis Staff [*Environmental Protection Agency*] (GFGA) ... PAS
Policy Analyst (GNE) ... PA
Policy and External Affairs Staff [*Environmental Protection Agency*] (GFGA) ... PEAS
Policy and Grants Division [*Environmental Protection Agency*] (GFGA) ... PGD
Policy and Procedure Governing the Use of Nicknames [*Army*] (AABC) ... POPGUN
Policy and Regulations Division, Information Resources Management Service (AAGC) ... KMP
Policy Board (OICC) ... PB

Policy Control (ADA) .... PC
Policy Coordination Council [*Marine science*] (OSRA) .... PCC
Policy Coordination Council (USDC) .... PCC
Policy Coordination Group (DOGT) .... PCG
Policy Determination (GNE) .... PD
Policy Determination Committee (AAG) .... PDC
Policy Development and Research .... PD & R
Policy Formulation Division (AAGC) .... PFD
Policy Group on Scientific Information [*Marine science*] (MSC) .... POGSI
Policy Guidance Council (DOMA) .... PGC
Policy Improvement Program .... PIP
Policy Information Center [*Department of Health and Human Services Information service or system*] (IID) .... PIC
Policy Integration Program .... PIP
Policy Land Use Zone [*Australian Capital Territory*] .... PLUZ
Policy Liaison Division (AAGC) .... PLD
Policy Loan .... PL
Policy Management Systems [*Associated Press*] (SAG) .... PlcyMg
Policy Management Systems [*NYSE symbol*] (SPSG) .... PMS
Policy Memorandum [*Military*] .... PM
Policy Mgmt Systems [*NYSE symbol*] (TTSB) .... PMS
Policy, Planning and Implementation Unit .... PPIU
Policy Planning Council [*U.S. Department of State*] (BARN) .... PPC
Policy Plans and National Security Council Affairs .... PPNSCA
Policy Processing Sheet [*Insurance*] .... PPS
Policy Proof of Interest .... PPI
Policy Proof of Interest (AD) .... ppi
Policy Research and Analysis .... PRA
Policy Research Group [*Australian Labor Party*] .... PRG
Policy Review (MCD) .... PR
Policy Review Committee [*Terminated, 1981*] [*National Security Council*] (EGAO) .... PRC
Policy Review Committee Intelligence [*Military*] .... PRCI
Policy Signing and Accounting Centre [*Insurance firm*] [*British*] .... PSAC
Policy Statement .... PS
Policy Statements [*Australian Broadcasting Tribunal*] [*A publication*] .... POS
Policy Status Report [*Insurance*] .... PSR
Policy Studies Institute [*Research center British*] (IRC) .... PSI
Policy Studies Journal [*A publication*] (BRI) .... Pol Stud J
Policy Studies Organization (EA) .... PSO
Policy Target Adjustment Factor (MEDA) .... PTAF
Policy-Framework Paper (ECON) .... PFP
Policyholders Protective Association of America (EA) .... PPA
Policyowner Attitude Survey Service [*LIMRA*] .... PASS
Polio Society (EA) .... PS
Polio Vaccine .... PV
Poliokeawe [*Pali*] [*Hawaii*] [*Seismograph station code, US Geological Survey*] (SEIS) .... PWH
Poliomyelitis [*Medicine*] .... PM
Poliomyelitis [*Medicine*] .... POLIO
Poliomyelitis [*Medicine*] (AD) .... polio
Poliomyelitis Welfare Association of South Australia .... PWASA
Poliovirus .... PV
Poliovirus Type 1, Maloney .... PV-1(M)
Poliovirus Type 2, Lansing .... PV-2(L)
POLISARIO [*Frente Popular para la Liberacion de Saguia El Hamra y Rio De Oro*] [*Popular Front for the Liberation of Saguia El Hamra and Rio De Oro Morocco*] (PD) .... PF
Polise-Air [*Russian Federation*] [*ICAO designator*] (FAAC) .... PMR
Polish (AAG) .... POL
Polish [*MARC language code Library of Congress*] (LCCP) .... pol
Polish Academy of Sciences .... PAS
Polish Air Force Veterans Association (EA) .... PAFVA
Polish Alma Mater of America (EA) .... PAMA
Polish American Congress (EA) .... PAC
Polish American Folk Theatre .... PAFT
Polish American Historical Association (EA) .... PAHA
Polish American Immigration and Relief Committee (EA) .... PAIRC
Polish American Librarians Association (EA) .... PALA
Polish American Workmen's Aid Fund (EA) .... PAWAF
Polish Americans for the Statue of Liberty [*Defunct*] (EA) .... PASL
Polish Army Veterans Association of America (EA) .... PAVA
Polish Assistance, Inc. (EA) .... PAI
Polish Association of America [*Later, NFLI*] (EA) .... PAA
Polish Astronautical Society [*See also PTA*] .... PAS
Polish Beneficial Association (EA) .... PBA
Polish Canadian Librarians Association .... PCLA
Polish Community in Australia .... PCA
Polish Council of Unity in the United States [*Defunct*] (EA) .... PCUUS
Polish Ex-Servicemen's Association [*Australia*] .... PEA
Polish Falcons of America (EA) .... PFA
Polish Genealogical Society (EA) .... PGS
Polish Helsinki Watch Committee (EAIO) .... PHWC
Polish Historical Military Society (EA) .... PHMS
Polish Independent Student Association (EA) .... PISA
Polish Institute of Art and Sciences in America, Inc., Research Library, New York, NY [*Library symbol*] [*Library of Congress*] (LCLS) .... NNPIA
Polish Institute of Arts and Sciences in Canada, Montreal, PQ, Canada [*Library symbol Library of Congress*] (LCLS) .... CaQMPI
Polish Institute of Arts and Sciences in Canada [*Institut Polonais des Arts et des Sciences au Canada*] **Montreal, Quebec** [*Library symbol National Library of Canada*] (NLC) .... QMPI
Polish Institute of Arts and Sciences of America (EA) .... PIASA
Polish Institute of Hydrology and Meteorology .... PIHM
Polish Legion of American Veterans (NADA) .... PLAV
Polish Legion of American Veterans, USA (EA) .... PLAV
Polish Legion of American Veterans, USA , Ladies Auxiliary (EA) .... PLAVA
Polish Legion of American Veterans, USA, Ladies Auxiliary (EA) .... PLAVLA
Polish Military History Society of America (EA) .... PMHSA
Polish Museum of America (EA) .... PMA
Polish National Alliance of the United States of North America (EA) .... PNA
Polish National Union of America (EA) .... PNUA
Polish Nobility Association (EA) .... PNA
Polish Notation [*Mathematics*] .... PN
Polish Ocean Lines (AD) .... POL
Polish People's Republic .... PPR
Polish POW Camps Philatelic Study Group (EA) .... PPCPSG
Polish Red Cross Society .... PRCS
Polish Register [*Polish ship classification society*] (DS) .... PR
Polish Resettlement Corps [*British military*] (DMA) .... PRC
Polish Roman Catholic Union of America (EA) .... PRCUA
Polish Roman Catholic Union of America, Chicago, IL [*Library symbol Library of Congress*] (LCLS) .... ICPRCU
Polish Sea League of America (EA) .... PSLA
Polish Singers Alliance of America (EA) .... PSAA
Polish Social and Cultural Association [*British*] (EAIO) .... PSCA
Polish Social Democratic Union [*Political party*] .... PSDU
Polish Socialist Alliance of the United States of America (EA) .... PSAUSA
Polish Telephones & Microwave Corp. [*Associated Press*] (SAG) .... PolishTel
Polish Telephones & Microwave Corp. [*Associated Press*] (SAG) .... PolTel
Polish Telephones & Microwave Corp. [*NASDAQ symbol*] (SAG) .... PTMC
Polish Tels & Microwave Corp. [*NASDAQ symbol*] (TTSB) .... PTMC
Polish Tels & Microwave Wrrt [*NASDAQ symbol*] (TTSB) .... PTMCW
Polish Underground Movement (1939-1945) Study Trust (EA) .... PUMST
Polish Union of America (EA) .... PUA
Polish Union of the United States of North America (EA) .... PUUSNA
Polish Union Printers Association [*Chicago*] .... PUPA
Polish United Workers' Party [*See also PZPR*] [*Political party*] (PD) .... PUWP
Polish Western Association of America (EA) .... PWAA
Polish Women's Alliance of America (EA) .... PWAA
Polish Women's Association [*Australia*] .... PWA
Polish Workers' Aid Fund [*Defunct*] (EA) .... PWAF
Polish Workers' Party .... PWP
Polish Workers Task Force (EA) .... PWTF
Polish Yearbook of International Law [*Warsaw*] [*A publication*] (DLA) .... Pol YB Int'l L
Polish Yearbook of International Law [*Warsaw*] [*A publication*] (DLA) .... Pol Yb of Internat L
Polish-American Guardian Society (EA) .... PAGS
Polish-American Information Bureau [*Later, PATIB*] (EA) .... PAIB
Polish-American Numismatic Association (EA) .... PANA
Polish-American Travel Information Bureau (EA) .... PATIB
Polished [*Freight*] .... PLSHD
Polished (VRA) .... pol
Polished Buckram (DGA) .... PB
Polished Buckram (DGA) .... POL BKM
Polished Plate Glass [*Technical drawings*] (DAC) .... PPGL
Polished Surface Technique (IEEE) .... PST
Polished-Stone Value (PDAA) .... PSV
Polishing .... POLSG
Polishing Tool Kit .... PTK
Polish-Russian Union (NADA) .... PRU
Polish-US Economic Council (EA) .... PUSEC
Polistes Wasp Venom [*Laboratory science*] (DAVI) .... PWV
Polite .... POL
Politica [*of Aristotle*] [*Classical studies*] (OCD) .... Pol
Political .... POL
Political (EY) .... POLIT
Political (AD) .... polit
Political (AFM) .... POLTL
Political Action Caucus [*Superseded by LPAC*] (EA) .... PAC
Political Action Committee [*Generic term*] .... PAC
Political Action Committee .... PAC
Political Action Committee for Cable Television (NTCM) .... PACCT
Political Action Committee for Engineers and Scientists .... PACES
Political Action Teams .... PAT
Political Adviser (AD) .... Pol Ad
Political Adviser (AD) .... polad
Political Adviser .... POLAD
Political and Economic Planning [*A British organization*] [*Later, Policy Studies Institute*] .... PEP
Political & Economic Risk Consultancy [*Commercial firm*] [*Hong Kong*] .... PERC
Political and Social Reform Movement [*British*] .... PSR
Political Asylum Project [*Defunct*] (EA) .... PAP
Political Bureau [*of USSR*] .... POLITBUREAU
Political Campaign Institute [*Commercial firm*] (EA) .... PCI
Political Code [*A publication*] (ILCA) .... PC
Political Code [*A publication*] (DLA) .... Pol C
Political Code [*A publication*] (DLA) .... Pol Code
Political Committee (AD) .... pol com
Political Committee at Senior Level [*NATO*] (NATG) .... SPC
Political Consultative Committee [*Warsaw Pact*] .... PCC
Political Consultative Council (CINC) .... PCC
Political Correctness .... PC
Political Critic (AD) .... polcrit
Political Directorate [*Allied German Occupation Forces*] .... DPOL
Political Division [*Geography*] .... P
Political Economy (AD) .... pol econ
Political Economy Research Center [*Research center*] (RCD) .... PERC

Political, Environmental, Social, and Technological [*Business term*] (ODBW) ... PEST
Political Exercise [*International relations game*] ... POLEX
Political Freedom Movement [*British*] ... PFM
Political Information System [*Databank of political strategist Richard Wirthlin*] ... PINS
Political Institutions Simulation [*Game*] ... POLIS
Political Intelligence Department [*British World War II*] ... PID
Political Officer [*NATO*] ... PO
Political Party Broadcast [*Television*] [*British*] ... PPB
Political Party Democrats 66 [*Netherlands*] [*Political party*] (EAIO) ... DPP
Political Plugola (AD) ... p-p-ola
Political Prisoners (AD) ... pols
Political Products Manufacturers Association (EA) ... PPMA
Political Research Quarterly [*A publication*] (BRI) ... Pol Res Q
Political Resource Directory [*A publication*] ... PRD
Political Rights Defense Fund [*Defunct*] (EA) ... PRDF
Political Risk Letter [*Database*] [*Frost & Sullivan, Inc.*] [*Information service or system*] (CRD) ... PRL
Political Risk Review [*A publication*] (EAAP) ... PRR
Political Science (AD) ... pol sci
Political Science ... poli sci
Political Science (DD) ... PolSc
Political Science (AD) ... poly sci
Political Science Quarterly [*A publication*] (ILCA) ... Pol Sci Quar
Political Science Quarterly [*A publication*] (BRI) ... PSQ
Political Science Reviewer [*A publication*] (BRI) ... PSR
Political Studies Association [*British*] ... PSA
Political Studies Association of the United Kingdom ... PSAUK
Political Survey Officers [*Navy*] ... PSO
Political Victory Fund [*National Rifle Association*] ... PVF
Political Warfare ... POLWAR
Political Warfare (AD) ... polwar
Political Warfare Advisory Directorate ... POLWARADDIR
Political Warfare Coordination Committee [*London*] [*World War II*] ... PWCC
Political Warfare Executive [*World War II*] ... PWE
Political World Union (EA) ... PWU
Politically Correct ... PC
Politically Correct ... Poco
Politically Motivated Violence (ADA) ... PMV
Politically Simulated World [*Computer-assisted political science game*] ... PSW
Political-Military Interdepartmental Group (AD) ... PMIG
Politicheskoe Byuro [*Political Bureau of the Central Committee*] [*Russian*] (AD) ... Politburo
Politicheskoe Byuro [*Political Bureau of USSR*] ... POLITBURO
Politician ... POL
Politician (AD) ... poli
Politician in the Penitentiary (AD) ... pol in the pen
Politicians (AD) ... pols
Politico-Military Affairs [*U.S. Department of State*] (BARN) ... PMA
Politics [*A publication*] ... Polit
Politieke Partij Democraten 66 [*Political Party Democrats 66*] [*Netherlands*] (EAIO) ... PPD
Politieke Partij Radikalen [*Radical Political Party*] [*Netherlands Political party*] (PPE) ... PPR
Politiki Aneksartitos Parataksis [*Independent Political Front*] [*Greek Political party*] (PPE) ... PAP
Polizei Pistole [*Police Pistol*] [*Walther Waffenfabrik, German arms manufacturer*] ... PP
Polizei Pistole Kriminal [*Pistol suitable for undercover police or detective use*] [*Walther Waffenfabrik, German arms manufacturer*] ... PPK
Polizia Ferroviaria [*Railroad Police*] [*Italian*] (AD) ... POLFER
Polizia Stradale [*Highway Police*] [*Italian*] (AD) ... POLSTRADA
Polizza di Carico [*Bill of Lading*] [*Shipping*] [*Italian*] ... P/C
Polk Audio [*AMEX symbol*] (SAG) ... PKA
Polk Audio [*NASDAQ symbol*] (TTSB) ... POLK
Polk Audio [*Associated Press*] (SAG) ... PolkAud
Polk Audio, Inc. [*Baltimore, MD*] [*NASDAQ symbol*] (NQ) ... POLK
Polk Audio, Inc. [*Associated Press*] (SAG) ... PolkAu
Polk City Community Library, Polk City, IA [*Library symbol Library of Congress*] (LCLS) ... IaPolc
Polk Community College, Winter Haven, FL [*Library symbol Library of Congress*] (LCLS) ... FWhP
Polk County Biomedical Consortium [*Library network*] ... PCBC
Polk County Enterprise, Livingston, TX [*Library symbol Library of Congress*] (LCLS) ... TxLivP
Polk County High School, Benton, TN [*Library symbol Library of Congress*] (LCLS) ... TBeP
Polk County Library, Crookston, MN [*Library symbol Library of Congress*] (LCLS) ... MnCr
Polk County Public Library, Columbus, NC [*Library symbol Library of Congress*] (LCLS) ... NcCol
Polk State School and Hospital, Polk, PA [*OCLC symbol*] (OCLC) ... PHO
Polk Street Elementary School, Franklin Square, NY [*Library symbol*] [*Library of Congress*] (LCLS) ... NFsPE
Polka [*Music*] ... P
Polka Lovers Klub of America (EA) ... POLK of A
Poll/Final [*Computer science*] (TNIG) ... P/F
Pollable Data Terminal [*Bell System*] ... PDT
Pollack's Ohio Unreported Judicial Decisions Prior to 1823 [*A publication*] (DLA) ... Ohio Unrep Jud Dec
Pollack's Ohio Unreported Judicial Decisions Prior to 1823 [*A publication*] (ILCA) ... Poll
Polled Access Circuit ... PAC
Polled Access Network ... PAN
Pollen [*Botany*] ... P
Pollen Accumulation Rate [*Botany*] ... PAR
Pollen Adherence Factor [*Immunology*] (DMAA) ... PAF
Pollen Body [*Botany*] ... PB
Pollen Equivalent [*Immunology*] ... PE
Pollen Grain [*Botany*] ... PG
Pollen Grain Trajectory [*Botany*] ... PGT
Pollen Index (WDAA) ... POL IND
Pollen Index (AD) ... pol ind
Pollen Mass [*Botany*] ... PM
Pollen Mother Cell [*Botany*] ... PMC
Pollen/Ovule Ratio [*Botany*] ... P/O
Pollen Tube [*Botany*] ... PT
Pollensa [*Spain ICAO location identifier*] (ICLI) ... LEPO
Pollex [*An Inch*] [*Pharmacy*] ... POLL
Pollexfen's English King's Bench Reports [*1669-85*] [*A publication*] (DLA) ... Pol
Pollexfen's English King's Bench Reports [*1669-85*] [*A publication*] (ILCA) ... Poll
Pollexfen's English King's Bench Reports [*1669-85*] [*A publication*] (ILCA) ... Pollex
Pollexfen's English King's Bench Reports [*1669-85*] [*A publication*] (ILCA) ... Pollexf
Pollexfen's English King's Bench Reports [*1669-85*] [*A publication*] (ILCA) ... Pollexfen
Polling (IAA) ... POL
Pollo Tropical [*Commercial firm Associated Press*] (SAG) ... PolloTrp
Pollo Tropical [*NASDAQ symbol*] (SAG) ... POYO
Pollock and Maitland's History of English Common Law [*A publication*] (DLA) ... P & M
Pollock and Maitland's History of English Common Law [*A publication*] (DLA) ... P & MHEL
Pollock and Maitland's History of English Common Law [*A publication*] (DLA) ... Pollock & Maitl
Pollock on Contracts [*A publication*] (DLA) ... Pol Cont
Pollock on the Power of Courts to Compel the Production of Documents [*A publication*] (DLA) ... Pol Prod Doc
Pollock on the Production of Documents [*A publication*] (DLA) ... Poll Prod
Pollock's Digest of the Laws of Partnership [*A publication*] (DLA) ... Pol Dig Part
Pollock's Digest of the Laws of Partnership [*A publication*] (DLA) ... Pol Part
Pollock's Practice of the County Courts [*A publication*] (ILCA) ... Poll CC Pr
Poll-Tax Rolls [*British*] ... PT
Pollutant Mass Rate [*Environmental science*] (GFGA) ... PMR
Pollutant Response in Marine Animals [*Marine science*] (MSC) ... PRIMA
Pollutant Standards Index [*Environmental Protection Agency*] ... PSI
Polluter Pays Principle ... PPP
Pollution ... PLLTN
Pollution ... POL
Pollution (AD) ... poll
Pollution ... POLLUT
Pollution ... POLTN
Pollution ... POLUT
Pollution Abatement and Control ... PAC
Pollution Abatement and Environmental Control Technology [*Army*] (AABC) ... PAECT
Pollution Abatement Operations Center (MCD) ... PAOC
Pollution and Overpopulation ... POP
Pollution Characterization by Absorption on Spectroscopy (SSD) ... POLCATS
Pollution Control (MHDB) ... PC
Pollution Control Equipment (GFGA) ... PCE
Pollution Control Guidance Document ... PCGD
Pollution Control Guide [*A publication*] (DLA) ... Poll Contr Guide
Pollution Control Guide (Commerce Clearing House) [*A publication*] (DLA) ... Pollution Cont Guide (CCH)
Pollution Control Report [*Navy*] ... PCR
Pollution Control Revenue ... PCR
Pollution Control Revenue Bond [*Environmental Protection Agency*] ... PCRB
Pollution Control Valve (IEEE) ... PCV
Pollution Generation Multiplier from Output Table (PDAA) ... PGMOT
Pollution Hazard Assessment System [*Environmental science*] ... PHAS
Pollution Incident Reporting System [*Coast Guard*] ... PIRS
Pollution Information Project (NITA) ... PIP
Pollution Liability Agreement Among Tanker Owners [*Insurance*] (DS) ... PLATO
Pollution Liability Insurance and Risk Retention Act (GFGA) ... PLIRRA
Pollution Liability Insurance Association [*Defunct*] (EA) ... PLIA
Pollution Minimum ... PM
Pollution Monitoring Satellite ... PMS
Pollution Prevention Act [*1990*] ... PPA
Pollution Prevention Information Clearinghouse [*Environmental Protection Agency*] ... PPIC
Pollution Prevention Information Exchange System [*Environmental science*] ... PIES
Pollution Prevention Office [*Environmental Protection Agency*] ... PPO
Pollution Prevention Research Center [*North Carolina State University*] [*Research center*] (RCD) ... PPRC
Pollution Quotient ... PQ
Pollution Reduction by Information and Control Technology ... PREDICT
Pollution Report (GNE) ... POLREP
Pollution Research and Control Corp. [*Associated Press*] (SAG) ... PolRs
Pollution Research and Control Corp. [*Associated Press*] (SAG) ... PolutRs
Pollution Research and Control Corp. [*NASDAQ symbol*] (SAG) ... PRCC
Pollution Resh & Ctl CA [*NASDAQ symbol*] (TTSB) ... PRCC
Pollution Transfer Program [*Marine science*] (MSC) ... PTP
Pollution-Monitoring Satellite (AD) ... pms
Polly Woodside Maritime Museum [*Australia*] ... PWMM
Polnippon [*Poland ICAO designator*] (FAAC) ... PLN
polnisch [*Polish*] [*German*] (AD) ... poln

Polo Aviation Ltd. [*British*] [*FAA designator*] (FAAC) .... CUK
Polo, IL [*Location identifier FAA*] (FAAL) .... PLL
Polo, IL [*FM radio station call letters*] .... WLLT
Polo Laico Liberali-Repubblicani Federalisti [*Italy*] [*Political party*]
  (ECED) .... PLI F
Polocrosse Association of Australia .... PAA
Poloidal Divertor Experiment [*Princeton University*] .... PDX
Poloidal Field (MCD) .... PF
Polonais [*Polish*] [*French*] (AD) .... Polon
Polonium [*Chemical element*] .... Po
Polonium [*Chemical symbol is Po*] (AAG) .... POL
Polonus Philatelic Society (EA) .... PPS
Polska Agencja Prasowa [*Polish Press Agency*] .... PAP
Polska Akademia Nauk [*Polish Academy of Sciences*] [*Also, an information
  service or system*] (IID) .... PAN
Polska Partia Robotnicza [*Polish Workers' Party*] [*Political party*] ..... PPR
Polska Partia Socialno-Demokratyczna [*Polish Social-Democrat Party*]
  [*Political party*] .... PPSD
Polska Partia Socjalistyczna [*Polish Socialist Party*] .... PPS
Polska Partia Socjalistyczna - Frakcja Rewolucyjna [*Polish Socialist Party -
  Revolutionary Faction*] [*Political party*] (PPE) .... PPS-FR
Polska Partia Socjalistyczna - Wolnosc, Rownosc, Niepodleglosc [*Polish
  Socialist Party - Freedom, Equality, Independence*] [*Political party*]
  (PPE) .... PPS-WRN
Polska Unia Socjaldemokratyczna [*Polish Social Democratic Union*] [*Political
  party*] .... PUSD
Polska Zjednoczona Partia Robotnicza [*Polish United Workers' Party -
  PUWP*] [*Political party*] (PPW) .... PZPR
Polski Osrodek Spoleczno-Kulturalny [*Polish Social and Cultural Association
  - PSCA*] (EAIO) .... POSK
Polski Osrodek Spoleczno-Kulturalny Posk [*Polish Social and Cultural
  Association - PSCA*] (EAIO) .... POSKP
Polskie Koleje Panstwowe [*Polish State Railways*] .... PKP
Polskie Linie Lotnicze [*Poland*] [*ICAO designator*] (FAAC) .... LOT
Polskie Radio [*Polish Radio*] (AD) .... PR
Polskie Stronnictwo Ludowe [*Polish Peasant Party*] [*Political party*] (PPE) ..... PSL
Polskie Stronnictwo Ludowe-Lewica [*Polish Peasant Party-Left (1913-1920)*]
  [*Political party*] (PPE) .... PSL-Lewica
Polskie Stronnictwo Ludowe-Nowe Wyzwolenie [*Polish Peasant Party-New
  Liberation*] [*Political party*] (PPE) .... PSL-NW
Polskie Stronnictwo Ludowe-Piast [*Polish Peasant Party-Piast*] [*Political
  party*] (PPE) .... PSL-Piast
Polskie Stronnictwo Ludowe-Wyzwolenie [*Polish Peasant Party-Liberation*]
  [*Political party*] (PPE) .... PSL-Wyzwolenie
Polskie Stronnictwo-Lewica [*Polish Peasant Party-Left (1947-1949)*] [*Political
  party*] (PPE) .... PSL-Lewica
Polskie Zaklady Lotnicze [*Poland ICAO aircraft manufacturer identifier*]
  (ICAO) .... PO
Polson City Library, Polson, MT [*Library symbol*] [*Library of Congress*]
  (LCLS) .... MtPol
Polson, MT [*AM radio station call letters*] .... KERR
Polson, MT [*Location identifier FAA*] (FAAL) .... PLS
Polson's Law of Nations [*1848*] [*A publication*] (DLA) .... Pol Law of Nat
Polson's Law of Nations [*1848*] [*A publication*] (DLA) .... Pols Nat
Polstead [*British ICAO location identifier*] (ICLI) .... EGSJ
Polwarth Sheepbreeders' Association of Australia .... PSAA
Poly Harnstoff Dispersion [*Organic chemistry*] .... PHD
Poly Methyl Methacrylate Association [*European Council of Chemical
  Manufacturers Federations*] [*Brussels, Belgium*] (EAIO) .... PMMA
Poly Methyl Methacrylate Producers Association [*Belgium*] (EAIO) .... PMMAPA
Poly (Phenylenevinylene) [*Organic chemistry*] .... PPV
Poly(A)-Binding Protein .... PABP
Polyacenequinone Radical [*Organic chemistry*] .... PAQR
Polyacetal [*Organic chemistry*] .... PA
Polyacrylamide [*Also, PAAM, PAM*] [*Organic chemistry*] .... PAA
Polyacrylamide [*Also, PAA, PAM*] [*Organic chemistry*] .... PAAM
Polyacrylamide [*Also, PAA, PAAM*] [*Organic chemistry*] .... PAM
Polyacrylamide Gel [*Analytical chemistry*] .... PAG
Polyacrylamide Gel Electrophoresis [*Analytical chemistry*] ...... PAGE
Polyacrylamide-Hydrazide [*Organic chemistry*] .... PAAH
Poly(Acrylamidomethyl Propane) Sulphonic Acid [*Organic chemistry*] ...... PAMPS
Polyacrylic [*Organic chemistry*] .... PA
Polyacrylic Acid [*Organic chemistry*] .... PAA
Polyacrylonitrile [*Organic chemistry*] .... PAN
Polyacrylonitrile .... PAN
Poly(acryloylpyrrolidine) [*Organic chemistry*] .... PAP
Polyadenylated .... PolyA
Polyadenylic Acid [*Biochemistry*] (MAE) .... poly(A)
Poly(adipicanhydride) [*Organic chemistry*] .... PADA
Poly(alkyl Sulfone) [*Organic chemistry*] .... PAS
Polyalkylene Glycol [*Organic chemistry*] .... PAG
Polyalkyleneoxide [*Organic chemistry*] .... PAO
Polyalkylmethacrylate (IAA) .... PAMA
Polyalphaolefin [*Organic chemistry*] .... PAO
Poly-alpha-olefin [*Organic chemistry*] .... PAOL
Polyaluminum Chloride [*Inorganic chemistry*] .... PAC
Polyamide [*Organic chemistry*] .... PA
Polyamide Nucleic Acid [*Biochemistry*] .... PNA
Polyamide-Imide [*Organic chemistry*] .... PAI
Polyamidoamine [*Organic chemistry*] .... PAMAM
Polyaminosiloxane [*Organic chemistry*] .... PAS
Polyaminotriazole [*Organic chemistry*] .... PAT
Polyanhydride [*Organic chemistry*] .... PA
Polyanionic Cellulose [*Organic chemistry*] .... PAC
Polyanthos, New Orleans, LA [*Library symbol Library of Congress*] (LCLS) .... LNPo

Polyaperture Device [*NASA*] (KSC) .... PAD
Poly-a-polymerase [*An enzyme*] .... PAP
Polyarlterephthalate [*Organic chemistry*] .... PAT
Polyarteritis [*Medicine*] .... PA
Polyarteritis Nodosa [*Medicine*] .... PAN
Polyarteritis Nodosa [*Rheumatology*] (DAVI) .... PN
Polyarthrite Chronique Evolutive [*Chronic Evolutive Polyarthritis*] [*Medicine
  French*] .... PCE
Polyarthritis [*Medicine*] (DMAA) .... PA
Polyarylamid [*Organic chemistry*] .... PARA
Polyarylate [*Resin*] .... PAR
Polyarylether [*Organic chemistry*] .... PAE
Polyaryletherketone [*Organic chemistry*] .... PAEK
Polyarylsulfone [*Organic chemistry*] .... PAS
Polyarylsulfone [*Organic chemistry*] .... PASU
Polyaspartic Acid [*Biochemistry*] .... PAA
Polyaspartic Ester [*Organic chemistry*] .... PAE
Polybay Tier .... PBT
Polybenzamide [*Organic chemistry*] .... PBA
Polybenzene [*Organic chemistry*] .... PB
Polybenzimidazole [*Organic chemistry*] (NATG) .... PBI
Polybenzimidazolone [*Organic chemistry*] .... PBIL
Polybenzothiazole [*Organic chemistry*] .... PBT
Poly(benzyl Glutamate) [*Organic chemistry*] .... PBG
Polybenzyl-L-glutamate [*Biochemistry*] .... PBLG
Poly-Beta-Hydroxybutyrate (DMAA) .... PBHB
Poly(bis(chloromethyl)oxetane) [*Organic chemistry*] .... PBCMO
Polybius [*Second century BC*] [*Classical studies*] (OCD) ..... Polyb
Polybromated Biphenyls [*Organic chemistry*] (DAVI) .... PBBs
Polybrominated Biphenyl [*Flame retardant, toxic chemical*] ...... PBB
Polybrominated-Biphenyl [*AD*] .... PPB
Polybromostyrene [*Organic chemistry*] .... PBRS
Polybutadiene [*Organic chemistry*] .... PBD
Poly(butadiene-acrylic Acid) [*Organic chemistry*] .... PBAA
Poly(butadiene-acrylonitrile) [*Organic chemistry*] .... PBAN
Poly(butadiene-malic Acid) [*A polymer*] .... PBDMA
Polybutene [*Organic chemistry*] .... PBE
Poly(butenesulfone) [*Organic chemistry*] .... PBS
Poly(butoxycarbonyloxystyrene) [*Organic chemistry*] .... PBOCST
Polybutyl Acrylate [*Organic chemistry*] .... PBA
Poly(butyl Isocyanate) [*Organic chemistry*] .... PBIC
Polybutyl Methacrylate [*Organic chemistry*] .... PBMA
Polybutylene [*Organic chemistry*] .... PB
Polybutylene Terephthalate [*Organic chemistry*] .... PBT
Polybutylene Terephthalate [*Organic chemistry*] .... PBTP
Polycaprolactone [*Organic chemistry*] .... PCL
Polycarbonate [*Organic chemistry*] .... PC
Polycarbosilane [*Organic chemistry*] .... PC
Polycationized Ferritin [*Biochemistry*] .... PCF
Polychemotherapy [*Oncology*] .... PCT
Polychlorinated Benzodioxin [*Organic chemistry*] .... PCBD
Polychlorinated Biphenyl [*Organic chemistry*] .... PCB
Polychlorinated Diaromatic Hydrocarbon [*Organic chemistry*] ..... PCDH
Polychlorinated Dibenzo (BARN) .... PCD
Polychlorinated Dibenzodioxin [*Organic chemistry*] .... PCDD
Polychlorinated Dibenzodioxins [*Automotive emissions*] [*Organic
  chemistry*] .... PCDD
Polychlorinated Dibenzofuran [*Organic chemistry*] .... PCDF
Polychlorinated Dibenzofurans [*Automotive emissions*] [*Organic
  chemistry*] .... PCDF
Polychlorinated Naphthalene [*Organic chemistry*] .... PCN
Polychlorinated Terphenyl [*Pesticide*] .... PCT
Polychlorobenzene .... PCB
Polychloro(chloromethylsulfonamido)diphenyl Ether [*Insectproofing agent
  for wool*] .... PCSD
Polychloroethylene (BARN) .... PCE
Polychloroprene [*Organic chemistry*] .... PCP
Polychloroterphenyl [*Organic chemistry*] .... PCT
Polychlorotrifluoroethylene [*Organic chemistry*] .... PCTFE
Polychlorotrifluoroethylene [*Lubricants*] .... PCTFE
Polychlorstyrene [*Organic chemistry*] .... PCLST
Polychromasia [*Hematology*] (DAVI) .... POLYC
Polychromatic Color Removal [*Printing technology*] .... PCR
Polychromatic Optical Thickness Fringe (OA) .... POTF
Polychrome (VRA) .... plyc
Polychrome Methylene Blue .... PMB
Polyclonal Antibody [*Immunochemistry*] .... PAB
Polyclonal B Cell Activation [*Hematology*] .... PCBA
Polyclonal B Cell Activator [*Hematology*] .... PBA
Polyclonal Gammopathy Identified [*Immunology*] (DAVI) ...... PLCL
Polyclonal Rheumatoid Factor [*Medicine*] (DMAA) .... PRF
Polycom Inc. [*NASDAQ symbol*] (TTSB) .... PLCM
Polycom, Inc. [*NASDAQ symbol*] (SAG) .... PLCM
Polycom, Inc. [*Associated Press*] (SAG) .... Polycom
Polycore Composite Construction [*Automotive engineering*] ...... PCC
Polycrystal Isolation (IAA) .... PCI
Polycrystalline Alumina .... PCA
Polycrystalline Cubic Boron Nitrite .... PCBN
Polycrystalline Diamond (ECON) .... PCD
Polycrystalline Diamond Compact [*Well drilling technology*] ...... PDC
Polycrystalline Diamond Compact Drill Bit .... PDC
Polycrystalline Lead Zirconate Titanate [*Piezoelectricity*] .... PZT
Polycrystalline Silicon [*Photovoltaic energy systems*] .... p-Si
Polycrystalline Silicon Self-Aligned [*Photovoltaic energy systems*] (MHDI) .... PSA
Polycultural Institution of America .... PIA

Polycyclic Aromatic Amine [*Organic chemistry*] ... PAA
Polycyclic Aromatic Compound [*Organic chemistry*] ... PAC
Polycyclic [*or Polynuclear*] **Aromatic Hydrocarbon** [*Organic chemistry*] ... PAH
Polycyclic Aromatic Hydrocarbon ... PAH
Polycyclic Aromatic Hydrocarbons [*Automotive emissions*] [*Organic chemistry*] ... PAH
Polycyclic Aromatic Ketone [*Organic chemistry*] ... PAK
Polycyclic Hydrocarbon (DMAA) ... PCH
Polycyclic Organic Matter (AD) ... pom
Polycyclic Organic Matter ... POM
Polycystic Disease [*of kidneys*] [*Medicine*] ... PCD
Polycystic Kidney [*Medicine*] (DMAA) ... PCK
Polycystic Kidney Disease [*Medicine*] ... PCKD
Polycystic Kidney Disease [*Medicine*] ... PKD
Polycystic Kidney Research Foundation (PAZ) ... PKR
Polycystic Lipomembranous Osteodysplasia [*Medicine*] (DMAA) ... PLO
Polycystic Liver Disease [*Medicine*] (DMAA) ... PLD
Polycystic Ovarian Disease [*Medicine*] ... PCOD
Polycystic Ovarian Disease [*Medicine*] ... POD
Polycystic Ovarian Syndrome [*Also, POS*] [*Gynecology*] ... PCOS
Polycystic Ovarian Syndrome [*Also, PCOS*] [*Gynecology*] ... POS
Polycystic Ovary [*Gynecology*] ... PCO
Polycythemia Rubra Vera [*Medicine*] ... PRV
Polycythemia Vera [*Also, PV*] [*Hematology*] ... PCV
Polycythemia Vera [*Also, PCV*] [*Hematology*] ... PV
Polycythemia Vera Study Group (MEDA) ... PVSG
Polycytidylic Acid [*Biochemistry*] (DMAA) ... poly-C
Polydactyly-Imperforate Anus-Vertebral Anomalies [*Syndrome*] [*Medicine*] (DMAA) ... PIAVA
Polydenosine Diphosphate-Ribose Polymerase (DMAA) ... PPRP
Polydex Pharmaceuticals [*NASDAQ symbol*] (TTSB) ... POLXF
Polydex Pharmaceuticals Ltd. [*NASDAQ symbol*] (NQ) ... POLX
Polydex Pharmaceuticals Ltd. [*Associated Press*] (SAG) ... Polydex
Polydiacetylene [*Organic chemistry*] ... PDA
Polydicyclopentadiene [*Organic chemistry*] ... PDCPD
Polydimethyl Phenylene Oxide [*Organic chemistry*] ... PDMPO
Poly(dimethylacrylamide) [*Organic chemistry*] ... PDA
Polydimethylsiloxane [*Organic chemistry*] ... PDMS
Polydimethylsiloxane [*Organic chemistry*] ... PDS
Polydioxanone [*Organic chemistry*] ... PDS
Polydipsia [*Medicine*] (DAVI) ... poly
Poly-DL-alanine Poly-L-lysine [*Biochemical analysis*] ... PAL
Polydor & Deutsche Grammophon [*Record label*] [*Germany, Europe, etc.*] ... Pol
Polydor/Deutsche-Grammophon Variable Microgroove [*Record label*] [*Germany*] ... PV
Polyelectrolyte [*Organic chemistry*] ... PE
Polyester ... PET
Polyester (VRA) ... plyes
Polyester ... POLY
Polyester ... POLYEST
Polyester Oriented Yarn (DICI) ... POY
Polyestercarbonate [*Organic chemistry*] ... PEC
Polyestradiol Phosphate [*Endocrinology*] ... PEP
Polyether Block Amide [*Plastics technology*] ... PEBA
Polyether Ketone Ketone ... PEKK
Polyether Polyurethane Urea [*Organic chemistry*] ... PEUU
Polyetheretherketone (DMAA) ... PEEK
Polyetherimide ... PEI
Polyetherketone [*Organic chemistry*] ... PEEK
Polyetherketone [*Organic chemistry*] ... PEK
Polyetherketoneketone [*Materials science*] ... PEKK
Polyethersulfone [*Organic chemistry*] ... PES
Polyethersulfone [*Organic chemistry*] ... PESU
Poly(ethyl Acrylate) [*Organic chemistry*] ... PEA
Poly(ethyl L-Glutamate) [*Organic chemistry*] ... PELG
Polyethyl Methacrylate [*Organic chemistry*] ... PEMA
Polyethylene [*Organic chemistry*] ... PE
Polyethylene [*Organic chemistry*] (IAA) ... PET
Polyethylene [*Organic chemistry*] ... POLTHN
Polyethylene (DEN) ... POLY
Polyethylene (AD) ... poly
Polyethylene Bottle (AD) ... poly bot
Polyethylene Expanded Video Longitudinal Cable (MCD) ... PEVL
Polyethylene Foam ... PEF
Polyethylene Glycol [*Organic chemistry*] ... PEG
Polyethylene Glycol [*Organic chemistry*] ... PG
Polyethylene Glycol Adipate [*Organic chemistry*] ... PEGA
Polyethylene Glycol Succinate [*Organic chemistry*] ... PEGS
Polyethylene Glycol-Adenosine Deaminase [*A modified enzyme*] ... PEG-ADA
Polyethylene Insulated Conductor [*Telecommunications*] ... PIC
Polyethylene Isopthalate [*Organic chemistry*] ... PEIS
Polyethylene Naphthalate [*Organic chemistry*] ... PEN
Poly(ethylene oxide) [*Acronym is trade name owned by Seitetsu Kagaku Co.*] ... PEO
Poly(ethylene Oxide) [*Trademark*] ... POLYOX
Polyethylene Powder ... PEP
Polyethylene Sodium Sulfonate [*Anticoagulant*] ... PES
Polyethylene Sulfonic Acid [*Organic chemistry*] (MAE) ... PSA
Poly(ethylene Terephthalate) [*Organic chemistry*] ... PET
Poly(ethylene Terephthalate) [*Organic chemistry*] ... PETP
Polyethylene Tetrachloride [*Organic chemistry*] (IAA) ... PETC
Polyethylene-Chlorotrifluoroethylene [*Organic chemistry*] ... PECTFE
Polyethylene-High Density [*Organic chemistry*] ... PEHD
Polyethyleneoxide [*Organic chemistry*] ... PEOX
Polyethylenetetrafluoroethylene [*Organic chemistry*] ... PETFE
Polyethylenimine [*Organic chemistry*] ... PEI
Polyfactorial Study of Personality [*Psychology*] (AEBS) ... PFSP
Polyfactorial Study of Personality [*Psychology*] ... PSP
Polyfluorinated Polyether [*Lubricants, polymers*] ... PFPE
Poly(fluoroalkoxyphosphazene) [*Organic chemistry*] ... PFAP
Polyfurfuryl Alcohol [*Organic chemistry*] ... PFA
Polygalacturonase [*An enzyme*] ... PG
Polygalacturonase [*An enzyme*] ... PGase
Polygalacturonase-Inhibiting Protein [*Biochemistry*] ... PGIP
Polygamy [*FBI standardized term*] ... POLY
Poly-Gel Mitigator ... PGM
Polyglandular Autoimmune Syndrome [*Medicine*] (DMAA) ... PGA
Polyglutaraldehyde [*Organic chemistry*] ... PGL
Poly(glyceryl Methacrylate) [*Organic chemistry*] ... PGMA
Polyglycidal Methacrylate-Ethyl Acrylate [*Organic chemistry*] (PDAA) ... PGMA-EA
Polyglycine [*Biochemistry*] ... PG
Polyglycolic Acid [*Organic chemistry*] (RDA) ... PGA
Polygon-MODE [*Mid-Ocean Dynamics Experiment*] [*Soviet-US cooperative undersea weather exploration*] ... POLYMODE
PolyGram NV [*NYSE symbol*] (SPSG) ... PLG
PolyGram NV [*Associated Press*] (SAG) ... Polygr
Polygraph (AD) ... polyg
Polyguanylic Acid [*Biochemistry*] (DMAA) ... poly-G
Polygyros [*Greece*] [*Seismograph station code, US Geological Survey*] (SEIS) ... PLG
Polyhedra Derived Virus ... PDV
Polyhedra Molecular Demonstration Model ... PMDM
Poly(heptadiester) [*Organic chemistry*] ... PHDE
Poly(hexyl Isocyanate) [*Organic chemistry*] ... PHIC
Polyhexyl Methacrylate [*Organic chemistry*] ... PHMA
Poly-Hexylthiophene [*Organic chemistry*] ... PHT
Polyhydroxyalkanoate [*Organic chemistry*] ... PHA
Poly(hydroxybenzoate) [*Organic chemistry*] ... PHB
Polyhydroxybutyrate [*Organic chemistry*] ... PHB
Poly(hydroxybutyrate-Valerate) [*Organic chemistry*] ... PHBV
Poly(hydroxyethyl Methacrylate) [*Organic chemistry*] ... PHEMA
Poly(hydroxypropylglutamine) [*Organic chemistry*] ... PHPG
Poly(hydroxystearic Acid) [*Organic chemistry*] ... PHA
Polyhydroxystearic Acid [*Organic chemistry*] ... PHSA
Poly(hydroxystyrene) [*Organic chemistry*] ... PHOST
Polyhydroxystyrene [*Also, PHOST*] [*Organic chemistry*] ... PHS
Polyimide [*Organic chemistry*] ... PI
Polyimide Composite Material ... PCM
Polyimidesulfone [*Organic chemistry*] ... PISU
Poly(iminoethylene) [*Organic chemistry*] ... PIE
Polyinosinic Acid [*Biochemistry*] (DMAA) ... poly-I
Polyinosinic Polycytidylic Acid (BARN) ... poly I:C
Polyisobutylene [*Organic chemistry*] ... PIB
Polyisocyanurate Insulation Manufacturers Association (EA) ... PIMA
Polyisohexylcyanoacrylate [*Antibacterial*] ... PIHCA
Polyisoprene [*Organic chemistry*] ... PI
Polyisothianaphthene [*Organic chemistry*] ... PITN
Polyketide Synthase [*An enzyme*] ... PKS
Polylactic Acid [*Organic chemistry*] (RDA) ... PLA
Polylacticco-Glycolic Acid [*Organic chemistry*] ... PLGA
Poly-L-arginine [*Biochemistry*] ... PLA
Poly(L-glutamic Acid) [*Organic chemistry*] ... PGA
Poly-L-lysine [*Also, PLL*] [*Biochemical analysis*] ... PL
Poly-L-lysine [*Also, PL*] [*Biochemistry*] ... PLL
Poly-L-ornithine ... PLO
PolyMedica Industries [*AMEX symbol*] (TTSB) ... PM
PolyMedica Industries, Inc. [*AMEX symbol*] (SAG) ... PM
PolyMedica Industries, Inc. [*Associated Press*] (SAG) ... Polymed
Poly(mellitic Dianhydride Methacrylate) [*Organic chemistry*] ... PMDM
Polymer (VRA) ... plym
Polymer (AD) ... poly
Polymer Adhesive ... PA
Polymer Dispersed Liquid Crystal [*Physical chemistry*] ... PDLC
Polymer Ejection for Noise Suppression ... PENS
Polymer Electrolyte Membrane [*Fuel technology*] ... PEM
Polymer Glass Sealant ... PGS
Polymer Grid Triode [*Imaging technology*] ... PGT
Polymer Group [*NYSE symbol*] (TTSB) ... PGH
Polymer Group, Inc. [*NYSE symbol*] (SAG) ... PGH
Polymer Group, Inc. [*Associated Press*] (SAG) ... PolyGp
Polymer International (NS), Inc. [*Toronto Stock Exchange symbol*] ... PI
Polymer Jell Material ... PJM
Polymer Materials [*Deutsches Kunststoff-Institut*] [*Germany Information service or system*] (CRD) ... POLYMAT
Polymer Matrix Composite [*Materials science*] ... PMC
Polymer Microdevice Laboratory [*Case Western Reserve University*] [*Research center*] (RCD) ... PML
Polymer of Ribose Phosphate [*Organic chemistry*] (MAE) ... PRP
Polymer Optical Fiber [*Telecommunications*] ... POF
Polymer Permeation Analyzer ... PPA
Polymer Products Development Center (AD) ... PPDC
Polymer Research Corp. of America [*Associated Press*] (SAG) ... PolyRs
Polymer Research Corp. of America [*NASDAQ symbol*] (NQ) ... PROA
Polymer Research Institute [*Polytechnic Institute of New York*] [*Research center*] (RCD) ... PRI
Polymer Research Institute [*University of Massachusetts*] [*Research center*] (RCD) ... PRI
Polymer Resh America [*NASDAQ symbol*] (TTSB) ... PROA
Polymer Thick Film ... PTF
Polymerase [*An enzyme*] ... POL

Polymerase [*Deoxyribonucleic Acid*] [*Formerly, RIDP*] [*An enzyme*] .... RDDP
Polymerase [*Deoxyribonucleic Acid*] [*Later, RDDP*] [*An enzyme*] .... RIDP
Polymerase Alpha (DMAA) .... POLA
Polymerase Chain Reaction [*Genetics*] .... PCR
Polymerase-Inducing Unit .... PIU
Polymer-Cement Concrete (KSC) .... PCC
Polymer-Clad Silica [*Chemistry*] .... PCS
Polymer-Coated Erythromycin [*An antibiotic*] (DAVI) .... PCE
Polymer-Concrete (KSC) .... PC
Polymer-Dispersed Liquid Crystal [*Electronics*] .... PDLC
Polymeric Aluminum Silicate Sulfate [*Inorganic chemistry*] .... PASS
Polymeric Carrier Delivery System [*Nuclear energy*] (NUCP) .... PCD
Polymeric Fatty Acid [*Food science*] .... PFA
Polymeric Immunoglobulin [*Medicine*] (DMAA) .... PIG
Polymeric Immunoglobulin Receptor [*Biochemistry*] .... PIGR
Polymeric Membrane .... PM
Polymeric Triglyceride [*Food science*] .... PT
Polymer-Immobilised Clusters of the Noble Metals [*Catalytic chemistry*] .... PCNM
Polymer-Impregnated Concrete (KSC) .... PIC
Polymerised Cashew Nut Shell Liquid (PDAA) .... PCNSL
Polymerizable Oligomer (OA) .... PO
Polymerization of Monomer Reactants [*Organic chemistry*] .... PMR
Polymerized and Oxidized Material [*Food science*] .... POM
Polymerized Grass Extract [*Immunology*] .... PGR
Polymerized Human Serum Albumin [*Biochemistry*] .... PHSA
Polymerized Ragweed [*Immunology*] .... PRW
Polymerized Trimethyldihydroquinoline [*Organic chemistry*] .... PTDQ
Polymerized Water (AD) .... polywater
Poly(metal Phosphinate) [*Organic chemistry*] .... PMP
Polymethacrylic [*Organic chemistry*] .... PM
Poly(methyl Acrylate) [*Organic chemistry*] .... PMA
Poly(methyl Isopropenyl Ketone) [*Organic chemistry*] .... PMIPK
Poly(Methyl Isopropenyl Ketone) [*Organic chemistry*] .... PMIPK
Poly(methyl L-Glutamate) [*Organic chemistry*] .... PMLG
Poly(methyl Methacrylate) [*Also, PMMA*] [*Organic chemistry*] .... PMM
Poly(methyl Methacrylate) [*Also, PMM*] [*Organic chemistry*] .... PMMA
Polymethyl Methacrylate [*Dentistry*] (DAVI) .... PMMA
Poly(methyl Methacrylate Peroxide) [*Organic chemistry*] .... PMMAP
Polymethylbenzene [*Organic chemistry*] .... PMB
Polymethylenepolyphenyl Polyisocyanate [*Organic chemistry*] .... PMPPI
Polymethylgalacturonase [*An enzyme*] .... PMG
Polymethylhydrosiloxane [*Organic chemistry*] .... PMHS
Poly(methyl-Hydrostyrene) [*Organic chemistry*] .... PMHS
Polymethylmethacrylate (AD) .... pmma
Poly(methylpentene) [*Organic chemistry*] .... PMP
Polymethylstyrene [*Organic chemistry*] .... PMS
Polymixin-B Sulfate/Bacitracin/Neomycin [*Antibacterial regime*] .... PBN
Polymonochlorotrifluorethyle [*Organic chemistry*] (IAA) .... PCTFE
Polymonochlorotrifluoroethylene (IDOE) .... Kel-f
Polymorph [*Hematology*] .... PM
Polymorphic [*Biology*] .... P
Polymorphic Amplifiable Restriction (Endonuclease) Fragment [*Genetics*] .... PARF
Polymorphic Programming Language [*1971*] [*Computer science*] (CSR) .... PPL
Polymorphic Reticulosis [*Ophthalmology*] (DAVI) .... PMR
Polymorphism Information Content [*Medicine*] (DMAA) .... PIC
Polymorphonuclear [*Leukocyte*] [*Hematology*] (DAVI) .... PM
Polymorphonuclear [*Hematology*] .... PMN
Polymorphonuclear [*Leukocyte*] [*Hematology*] (DAVI) .... polymorph
Polymorphonuclear Basophilic [*Leucocytes*] [*Hematology*] .... PMB
Polymorphonuclear Eosinophile [*Hematology*] .... PME
Polymorphonuclear Granulocyte [*Hematology*] (DAVI) .... PMNG
Polymorphonuclear Leukocyte [*Hematology*] .... PML
Polymorphonuclear Leukocyte [*Hematology*] .... PMNL
Polymorphonuclear Leukocyte (AD) .... pmnl
Polymorphonuclear Leukocyte [*Hematology*] .... POLY
Polymorphonuclear Leukocytes [*Hematology*] (DAVI) .... POLPS
Polymorphonuclear Neutrophil (AD) .... pmn
Polymorphonuclear Neutrophil (DMAA) .... PMNN
Polymorphonuclear Neutrophil Granulocyte [*Hematology*] (DAVI) .... poly
Polymorphonuclear Neutrophilic [*Hematology*] .... PMN
Polymorphonuclear Segmented Neutrophils [*Hematology*] (DAVI) .... polys (segs)
Polymorphonucleocyte [*Hematology*] (CPH) .... PMN
Polymorphous (AD) .... polymorph
Polymorphous Light Eruption [*Medicine*] .... PMLE
Polymorphous Posterior Corneal Dystropy [*Medicine*] (DMAA) .... PPCD
Polymusic [*Record label*] .... Polym
Polymyalgia Rheumatica [*Medicine*] .... PMR
Polymyositis [*Medicine*] .... PM
Polymyositis/Dermatomyositis [*Rheumatology*] (DAVI) .... PM/DM
Polymyositis Ossificans Progressiva [*Medicine*] (DMAA) .... POP
Polymyxin [*An antibiotic*] (DAVI) .... P
Polymyxin B [*An antibiotic*] .... PB
Polynesia (AD) .... Poly
Polynesia (VRA) .... Polyn
Polynesia .... POLYN
Polynesia [*MARC geographic area code Library of Congress*] (LCCP) .... pops--
Polynesian Airline Operations Ltd. [*Western Samoa*] [*ICAO designator*] (FAAC) .... PAO
Polynesian Airlines [*Airline code*] [*Australia*] .... PH
Polynesian Air-Ways [*ICAO designator*] (FAAC) .... PLA
Polynesian Cultural Center (EA) .... PCC
Polyneuropathy [*Medicine*] .... P
Polyneuropathy Associated with Organomegaly Endocrine Disorders, Myeloma, and Skin Modifications .... POEMS
Poly-N-isopropylacrylamide [*Organic chemistry*] .... PNIPAAM
Poly-N-Isopropylacrylamide [*Organic chemistry*] .... PNIPAM
Polynomial Discriminant Method (PDAA) .... PDM
Polynomial Error Protection Code [*Computer science*] .... PEPC
Polynomial Generator Checker (IAA) .... PGC
Polynomial Operations [*Air Force*] .... POLOPS
Polynomial Propogation Time Immediate Language [*Computer science*] (MHDI) .... PIML
Polynomial Regression (IAA) .... POLREG
Polynomial Solution (IAA) .... PLS
Polynomial Time (IAA) .... P
Polynominal Error Protection (MCD) .... PEP
Polynuclear Aromatic [*Organic chemistry*] .... PNA
Polynuclear Aromatic Hydrocarbon [*Environmental chemistry*] .... PNAH
Polynuclear Hydrocarbon (DMAA) .... PNH
Polynuclear Organic Matter (FFDE) .... POM
Polynucleotide Kinase [*An enzyme*] .... PNK
Poly(octyl Isocyanate) [*Organic chemistry*] .... POIC
Polyoctyl Methacrylate [*Organic chemistry*] .... POMA
Polyolefin [*Organic chemistry*] .... PO
Polyolefin Elastomers [*Plastics*] .... POE
Polyolefin Plastomer [*Organic chemistry*] .... POP
Polyoma Virus .... PV
Polyoma Virus [*Medicine*] (DMAA) .... Py
Polyoma Virus .... PyV
Polyoma-Like Particle [*Genetics*] .... PLP
Poly-Ortho-methylstyrene [*Organic chemistry*] .... POMS
Polyostotic Fibrous Dysplasia [*Medicine*] (DMAA) .... PFD
Polyoxometalate [*Organic chemistry*] .... POM
Polyoxyethylene (AD) .... poe
Polyoxyethylene [*Organic chemistry*] .... POE
Polyoxyethylene Monostearate [*Organic chemistry*] .... POEMS
Polyoxyethyleneoxypropylene [*Organic chemistry*] .... POEOP
Poly(oxymethylene) [*Organic chemistry*] .... POM
Polyoxymethylene (AD) .... pom
Polyoxypropylenediamine [*Organic chemistry*] .... POPDA
Poly(para-benzamide) [*Organic chemistry*] .... PPB
Poly(para-Methylstyrene) [*Organic chemistry*] .... PPMS
Poly(para-phenylene) [*Organic chemistry*] .... PPP
Poly(para-phenylene Sulfide) [*Organic chemistry*] .... PPS
Polypentene [*Organic chemistry*] .... PPE
Polypeptide [*Biochemistry*] .... PP
Polypeptide Growth Factor [*Endocrinology*] (DAVI) .... PPGF
Poly(perfluorobutyl Acrylate) [*Organic chemistry*] .... PFBA
Polyphagia [*Medicine*] (DAVI) .... poly
Polyphagous [*Biology*] .... P
Polyphase .... PYPH
Polyphase Corp. [*AMEX symbol*] (SPSG) .... PLY
Polyphase Corp. [*AMEX symbol*] (TTSB) .... PLY
Polyphase Induction Motor .... PIM
Polyphase Instrument Corp. [*Associated Press*] (SAG) .... Polyph
Polyphenol Oxidase [*An enzyme*] .... PPO
Poly(phenolformaldehyde) [*Organic chemistry*] .... PPF
Polyphenylene Ether Plastic [*Materials science*] .... PPE
Polyphenylene Oxide [*Organic chemistry*] .... PPO
Polyphenylene Oxide (AD) .... ppo
Polyphenylene Sulfide Plastic .... PPS
Polyphenylene Sulfide Sulfone [*Organic chemistry*] .... PPSS
Polyphenylene Sulfone [*Organic chemistry*] .... PSU
Polyphenylene Sulfone Plastic .... PPSU
Poly(phenylenebibenzimidazole) [*Organic chemistry*] .... PBI
Poly(phenyleneterephthalamide) [*Organic chemistry*] .... PPDT
Polyphenylether (IEEE) .... PPE
Polyphenylmethylsiloxane [*Organic chemistry*] .... PPMS
Polyphenylquinoxaline [*Resin*] .... PPQ
Polyphenylquinoxaline (AD) .... ppq
Polyphon [*Record label*] [*Denmark, etc.*] .... Pol
Polyphoretic Phosphate [*Organic chemistry*] (DAVI) .... PPP
Polyphosphate [*Inorganic chemistry*] (AAMN) .... PP
Polyphosphate Ester [*Inorganic chemistry*] .... PPE
Polyphosphonate [*Organic chemistry*] .... PPN
Polyphosphonositides .... PPI
Poly(phosphoric Acid) [*Inorganic chemistry*] .... PPA
Polyphthalate-Polycarbonate .... PPC
Polyphthalimide [*Organic chemistry*] .... PPI
Polyporus sulphureus [*A fungus*] .... Ps
Polyposis Coli [*Medicine*] (DMAA) .... PC
Poly-P-Phenylene Benzobesthiazole .... PBZT
Poly(p-phenylene Benzobisoxazole) (RDA) .... PBO
Polypropyl Methacrylate [*Organic chemistry*] .... PPMA
Polypropylene [*Organic chemistry*] .... PP
Poly(propylene Glycol) [*Organic chemistry*] .... PPG
Poly(propylene Oxide) [*Organic chemistry*] .... PPO
Polypropylene Oxide Plastic .... PPOX
Polypropylene-Paper-Polypropylene [*Biochemistry*] .... PPP
Polyptic (VRA) .... plypt
Polypurine Tract [*Genetics*] .... PPT
Polypyrrole [*Photovoltaic energy systems*] .... PP
Polyquinazolotriazole [*Organic chemistry*] .... PQT
Polyquinoxaline [*Organic chemistry*] .... PQ
Polyribitol Phosphate [*Organic chemistry*] .... PRP
Polyribosylribitol Phosphate Conjugated to Tetanus Toxoid [*Medicine*] .... PRP-T
Polyribosylribitol Phosphate-Diptheria Toxoid [*Medicine*] .... PRP-D
Polysar Ltd. [*Toronto Stock Exchange symbol Vancouver Stock Exchange symbol*] .... PY

Polysar Ltd., Sarnia, ON, Canada [*Library symbol Library of Congress*] (LCLS) .... CaOSP
Polysar Ltd., Sarnia, Ontario [*Library symbol National Library of Canada*] (NLC) .... OSP
Polysexual (AD) .... polysex
Polysialic Acid [*Organic chemistry*] .... PSA
Polysilicic Acid [*Organic chemistry*] .... PSA
Polysilicon Dielectric Polysilicon [*Organic chemistry*] (IAA) .... PDP
Polysilicon Diode (IAA) .... PSD
Polysomnogram [*Medicine*] (MAE) .... PSG
Polysonic Wind Tunnel (MCD) .... PSWT
Polystation Doppler Tracking System (MCD) .... POLYDOP
Polysteel Building Systems Ltd. [*Toronto Stock Exchange symbol*] .... PBS
Polystyrene (VRA) .... plyst
Polystyrene [*Organic chemistry*] .... PS
Polystyrene Base (DGA) .... PB
Polystyrene, Deuterated [*Organic chemistry*] .... PSD
Polystyrene Dielectric Capacitor .... PDC
Polystyrene, Hydrogenous [*Organic chemistry*] .... PSH
Polystyrene Latex (PDAA) .... PSL
Polystyrene Latex Sphere .... PLS
Polystyrene Packaging Council (EA) .... PSPC
Poly(styrene peroxide) [*Organic chemistry*] .... PSP
Poly(styrene-Divinylbenzene) [*Organic chemistry*] .... PSDVB
Polystyrene-Divinylbenzene Copolymer [*Organic chemistry*] .... PSVD
Poly(styrenesulfonate) [*Organic chemistry*] .... PSS
Polystyrene-Tube Radioimmunoassay [*Medicine*] (DMAA) .... PTRIA
Polysulfone [*Also, PSO*] [*Organic chemistry*] .... PS
Polysulfone [*Organic chemistry*] .... PSF
Polysulfone [*Also, PS*] [*Organic chemistry*] .... PSO
Polysulfone Hollow Fiber [*Filtration membrane*] .... PSHF
Polysulphide Rubber Compound (PDAA) .... PRC
Polysulphide Rubber Compound (AD) .... prc
Poly(t-Butyl Isopropenyl Ketone) [*Organic chemistry*] .... PTBIPK
Poly(t-Butyl Vinyl Ketone) [*Organic chemistry*] .... PTBVK
Polytechnic (AIE) .... P
Polytechnic (AD) .... Poly
Polytechnic (AD) .... poly
Polytechnic .... POLY
Polytechnic Academic Registrars' Group (AIE) .... PARG
Polytechnic Institute of Brooklyn [*Later, PINY*] (MCD) .... PIB
Polytechnic Institute of Brooklyn Aeronautical Laboratory (MCD) .... PIBAL
Polytechnic Institute of Brooklyn, Microwave Research Institute (IEEE) .... PIBMRI
Polytechnic Institute of New York .... PINY
Polytechnic Institute of New York, Brooklyn, NY [*Library symbol Library of Congress*] (LCLS) .... NBPol
Polytechnic Institute of New York, Long Island Graduate Center, Farmingdale, NY [*Library symbol Library of Congress*] (LCLS) .... NBPol-G
Polytechnic Institute of New York Weber Research Institute [*Farmingdale, NY*] .... POLY-WRI
Polytechnic Institute of Puerto Rico .... PIPR
[*The*] Polytechnic of Central London .... PCL
Polytechnic of North London, School of Librarianship, London, England [*OCLC symbol*] (OCLC) .... PNL
Polytechnic of the South Bank [*London, England*] .... PSB
Polytechnic Personnel Officers Group (AIE) .... PPOG
Polytechnic Research & Development Co. (AAG) .... PRD
Polytechnic University (GAGS) .... Poly U
Polytechnical (BARN) .... polytech
Polytechnical Documentation (NITA) .... POLYDOC
Polytechnics and Colleges Computer Committee (AIE) .... PCCC
Polytechnics and Colleges Funding Council [*British*] .... PCFC
Poly(tertiary-butylstyrene) [*Organic chemistry*] .... PtBS
Polytetrafluoroethylene [*Teflon*] .... PFTE
Polytetrafluoroethylene [*Organic chemistry*] .... PTFE
Polytetrafluoroethylene (DAVI) .... TFE
Polytetrahydrofuran [*Organic chemistry*] .... PTHF
Polytetramethylene Ether Glycol [*Organic chemistry*] .... PTMEG
Poly(tetramethylene Terephthalate) [*Organic chemistry*] .... PTMT
Polythermalex (IAA) .... PTX
Polythiazide [*Organic chemistry*] .... PTX
Poly(thienylenevinylene) [*Organic chemistry*] .... PTV
Polythiophene [*Organic chemistry*] .... PT
Polythiophene [*Organic chemistry*] .... Pth
Polythymidylic Acid [*Biochemistry*] (DMAA) .... poly-T
Poly(tolyquinoxaline) [*Organic chemistry*] .... PTQ
Polytranslation Analysis and Programming (IEEE) .... POLYTRAN
Polytrifluorochloroethene (BARN) .... PTFCE
Polytrifluorochloroethylene [*Organic chemistry*] .... PCFE
Poly(trimethylsilyl-propyne) [*Organic chemistry*] .... PTMSP
Polyunsaturated Fatty Acid [*Nutrition*] .... PUFA
Polyunsaturated/Saturated [*Fatty acid ratio*] .... P/S
Polyurethane (VRA) .... plyur
Polyurethane [*Also, PUR*] [*Organic chemistry*] .... PU
Polyurethane [*Also, PU*] [*Organic chemistry*] .... PUR
Polyurethane Division, Society of the Plastics Industry (EA) .... PDSPI
Polyurethane Film [*Plastics technology*] .... PUF
Polyurethane Foam .... PF
Polyurethane Foam .... PUF
Polyurethane Foam Association (EA) .... PFA
Polyurethane Manufacturers Association (EA) .... PMA
Polyurethane Recycle and Recovery Council [*Plastics recycling research*] .... PURRC
Polyuria [*Medicine*] (DAVI) .... poly

Polyuridylic Acid [*Biochemistry*] (MAE) .... poly(U)
Polyvalance Pneumococcal Polysaccharides [*A vaccine for patients with splenectomies*] [*Medicine*] (DAVI) .... PPS
Polyvalent Surface Immunoglobulin [*Immunology*] .... PV SIg
Polyvalent Tolerance (BABM) .... PT
Polyvalent Tolerance [*Immunology*] .... PVT
Polyvinyl (VRA) .... plyvn
Polyvinyl (AD) .... poly
Polyvinyl (WGA) .... PV
Polyvinyl Acetate [*Organic chemistry*] (IAA) .... PVA
Poly(vinyl Acetate) [*Organic chemistry*] .... PVAC
Poly(vinyl Acetate) [*Organic chemistry*] .... PVAE
Poly(vinyl Alcohol) [*Also, PVAL*] [*Organic chemistry*] .... PVA
Poly(vinyl Alcohol) [*Also, PVA*] [*Organic chemistry*] .... PVAL
Polyvinyl Bromide (PDAA) .... PVBr
Polyvinyl Butyl Ether [*Organic chemistry*] .... PVBE
Poly(vinyl Butyral) [*Safety glass laminating material*] [*Organic chemistry*] .... PVB
Polyvinyl Carbazol (IAA) .... PVC
Poly(vinyl Chloride) [*Organic chemistry*] .... PVC
Polyvinyl Chloride-Coated Fabric (PDAA) .... PVCCF
Poly(vinyl Cinnamate) [*Organic chemistry*] .... PVCN
Polyvinyl Ether [*Organic chemistry*] .... PVE
Polyvinyl Ethyl Ether [*Organic chemistry*] .... PVEE
Poly(vinyl Fluoride) [*Organic chemistry*] .... PVF
Polyvinyl Formal [*Organic chemistry*] .... PVF
Polyvinyl Formal [*Organic chemistry*] .... PVFM
Polyvinyl Hexyl Ether [*Organic chemistry*] .... PVHE
Poly(vinyl Isobutyl Ether) [*Organic chemistry*] .... PVI
Poly(vinyl Methyl Ether) [*Organic chemistry*] .... PVM
Poly(vinyl Methyl Ether) [*Organic chemistry*] .... PVME
Polyvinyl Methyl Ketone [*Organic chemistry*] (DICI) .... PVMK
Poly(vinyl Nitrate) [*Organic chemistry*] .... PVN
Polyvinylcarbazol [*Organic chemistry*] (IEEE) .... PVK
Polyvinylchloride Acetate [*Organic chemistry*] .... PVCA
Poly(vinylidene Chloride) [*Organic chemistry*] .... PVDC
Poly(vinylidene Difluoride) [*Organic chemistry*] .... PVDF
Poly(vinylidene Fluoride) [*Organic chemistry*] .... PVDF
Poly(vinylidene Fluoride) [*Organic chemistry*] .... PVF_2
Polyvinylpyridine-N-Oxide [*Organic chemistry*] .... PVNO
Poly(vinylpyridinium) Dichromate [*Organic chemistry*] .... PVPDC
Poly(vinylpyrrolidone) [*Organic chemistry*] .... PVP
Poly(vinylpyrrolidone) Iodine Complex .... PVP-I
Polyvinylsulfonate [*Organic chemistry*] .... PVS
Poly(vinyltoluene) [*Organic chemistry*] .... PVT
Polyvision Corp. [*AMEX symbol*] (SAG) .... PLI
Polyvision Corp. [*Associated Press*] (SAG) .... Polyvisn
Polyvision Corp. [*Associated Press*] (SAG) .... Polyvsn
Poly(xylenyl ether) [*Organic chemistry*] .... PXE
Polyzoa [*Quality of the bottom*] [*Nautical charts*] .... Po
POM [*Program Objective Memorandum*] **Preparation Instructions** [*Military*] ..... PPI
Pomacocha [*Peru*] [*ICAO location identifier*] (ICLI) .... SPPM
Pomalaa [*Indonesia*] [*Airport symbol*] (OAG) .... PUM
Pomariorio [*Tuamotu Archipelago*] [*Seismograph station code, US Geological Survey*] (SEIS) .... PMO
POMCUS [*Prepositioning of Materiel Configured to Unit Sets*] **Objective Levels** [*Military*] .... POMOL
Pomegranate Guild of Judaic Needlework (EA) .... PGJN
Pomeranian (AD) .... pom
Pomeranian Dog (DSUE) .... POM
Pomeridiano [*Afternoon*] [*Italian*] (AD) .... pom
Pomeridianus [*In the Afternoon*] [*Pharmacy*] .... POMERID
Pomeroy Computer Resources [*NASDAQ symbol*] (TTSB) .... PMRY
Pomeroy Computer Resources, Inc. [*NASDAQ symbol*] (SAG) .... PMRY
Pomeroy Computer Resources, Inc. [*Associated Press*] (SAG) .... Pomeroy
Pomeroy Elementary School, Pasadena, TX [*Library symbol*] [*Library of Congress*] (LCLS) .... TxPPoE
Pomeroy Herald, Pomeroy, IA [*Library symbol Library of Congress*] (LCLS) .... IaPomH
Pomeroy on Civil Remedies [*A publication*] (DLA) .... Pom Rem
Pomeroy on Civil Remedies and Remedial Rights [*A publication*] (DLA) .... Pom Rem & Rem Rights
Pomeroy on Code Remedies [*A publication*] (DLA) .... Pom Code Rem
Pomeroy on Contracts [*A publication*] (DLA) .... Pom Contr
Pomeroy on Municipal Law [*A publication*] (DLA) .... Pom Mun Law
Pomeroy on Specific Performance of Contracts [*A publication*] (DLA) .... Pom Spec Perf
Pomeroy Public Library, Pomeroy, IA [*Library symbol Library of Congress*] (LCLS) .... IaPom
Pomeroy's Constitutional Law of the United States [*A publication*] (DLA) .... Pom Const Law
Pomeroy's Equity Jurisprudence [*A publication*] (DLA) .... Pom Eq Jur
Pomeroy's Equity Jurisprudence [*A publication*] (DLA) .... Pom Eq Juris
Pomeroy's Reports [*73-128 California*] [*A publication*] (DLA) .... Pomeroy
Pominex Ltd. [*Toronto Stock Exchange symbol*] .... PER
Pomio [*New Britain*] [*Seismograph station code, US Geological Survey Closed*] (SEIS) .... PNB
Pommy [*British*] (ODBW) .... Pom
Pomologic (AD) .... pomol
Pomological (AD) .... pom
Pomology .... POMOL
Pomona [*California*] [*Airport symbol*] (AD) .... JPO
Pomona [*California*] [*Seismograph station code, US Geological Survey Closed*] (SEIS) .... POM
Pomona, CA [*AM radio station call letters*] .... KMNY
Pomona, CA [*AM radio station call letters*] .... KTSJ

Pomona, CA [*AM radio station call letters*] (RBYB) ... KWPA-AM
Pomona, CA [*Location identifier FAA*] (FAAL) ... POM
Pomona Elementary School, Grand Junction, CO [*Library symbol Library of Congress*] (LCLS) ... CoGjPE
Pomona, NJ [*FM radio station call letters*] ... WLFR
Pomona Public Library, Pomona, CA [*Library symbol Library of Congress*] (LCLS) ... CPom
Pomona Public Library, Pomona, CA [*OCLC symbol*] (OCLC) ... PFO
Pompano Airways [*ICAO designator*] (AD) ... MG
Pompano Beach, FL [*Location identifier FAA*] (FAAL) ... PMP
Pompano Beach, FL [*FM radio station call letters*] ... WMXJ
Pompano Beach, FL [*AM radio station call letters*] ... WRBD
Pompano Beach, FL [*AM radio station call letters*] ... WWNN
Pompeii [*Italy*] [*Seismograph station code, US Geological Survey Closed*] (SEIS) ... PMP
Pompeiiana, Inc. (EA) ... PI
Pompeius [*of Plutarch*] [*Classical studies*] (OCD) ... Pomp
Pompey (AD) ... Pomp
Pom-Pom (AD) ... pom
Pom-Pom [*Gun*] ... PP
Pompon [*Horticulture*] ... Pom
Pomposo [*Grandly*] [*Music*] (ROG) ... POMP
Pompton Lakes, NJ [*AM radio station call letters*] ... WGHT
Ponape [*Caroline Islands*] [*Airport symbol*] (OAG) ... PNI
Ponape Island [*Caroline Islands*] [*ICAO location identifier*] (ICLI) ... PTPN
Ponca City [*Oklahoma*] [*ICAO location identifier*] (ICLI) ... KPNC
Ponca City [*Oklahoma*] [*Seismograph station code, US Geological Survey*] (SEIS) ... PCO
Ponca City [*Oklahoma*] [*Airport symbol*] (OAG) ... PNC
Ponca City, OK [*Location identifier FAA*] (FAAL) ... AYQ
Ponca City, OK [*FM radio station call letters*] ... KIXR
Ponca City, OK [*FM radio station call letters*] ... KLOR
Ponca City, OK [*FM radio station call letters*] ... KLVV
Ponca City, OK [*FM radio station call letters*] ... KPNC
Ponca City, OK [*Location identifier FAA*] (FAAL) ... PER
Ponca City, OK [*Location identifier FAA*] (FAAL) ... PNC
Ponca City, OK [*AM radio station call letters*] ... WBBZ
Ponca City Public Library, Ponca City, OK [*Library symbol Library of Congress*] (LCLS) ... OkPo
Ponce [*Diocesan abbreviation*] [*Puerto Rico*] (TOCD) ... PCE
Ponce [*Puerto Rico*] [*Seismograph station code, US Geological Survey*] (SEIS) ... PON
Ponce [*Puerto Rico*] [*Airport symbol*] (OAG) ... PSE
Ponce De Leon ... PDL
Ponce/Mercedita [*Puerto Rico*] [*ICAO location identifier*] (ICLI) ... TJPS
Ponce, PR [*AM radio station call letters*] ... WEUC
Ponce, PR [*FM radio station call letters*] ... WEUC-FM
Ponce, PR [*FM radio station call letters*] ... WIOC
Ponce, PR [*AM radio station call letters*] ... WISO
Ponce, PR [*Television station call letters*] ... WKPV
Ponce, PR [*AM radio station call letters*] ... WLEO
Ponce, PR [*FM radio station call letters*] ... WOQI
Ponce, PR [*AM radio station call letters*] ... WPAB
Ponce, PR [*AM radio station call letters*] ... WPRP
Ponce, PR [*Television station call letters*] ... WQTO
Ponce, PR [*FM radio station call letters*] ... WRIO
Ponce, PR [*Television station call letters*] ... WSTE
Ponce, PR [*Television station call letters*] ... WSUR
Ponce, PR [*Television station call letters*] ... WTIN
Ponce, PR [*Television station call letters*] ... WVOZ
Ponce, PR [*FM radio station call letters*] ... WZAR
Ponce, PR [*AM radio station call letters*] ... WZBS
Ponce School of Medicine (GAGS) ... Ponce Sch Med
Ponceau Red [*Biological stain*] ... PR
Poncebank [*NYSE symbol*] (SAG) ... PBK
PONCEBANK [*NYSE symbol*] (TTSB) ... PBK
Poncebank [*Associated Press*] (SAG) ... Poncebk
Ponchong [*Tea trade*] (ROG) ... P HONG
Poncius Blegerii [*Flourished, 14th century*] [*Authority cited in pre-1607 legal work*] (DSA) ... Pon Ble
Pond [*Maps and charts*] ... P
Pond [*Pound*] [*Monetary unit*] [*Afrikaans*] ... pd
Pond Inlet [*Canada*] [*Airport symbol*] (OAG) ... YIO
Pond Inlet, NT [*ICAO location identifier*] (ICLI) ... CYIO
Ponder Industries [*NASDAQ symbol*] (TTSB) ... PNDR
Ponder Industries, Inc. [*NASDAQ symbol*] (SAG) ... PNDR
Ponder Industries, Inc. [*Associated Press*] (SAG) ... Ponder
Ponder Oils Ltd. [*Toronto Stock Exchange symbol*] ... PON
Ponderal Index [*Measurement*] (DAVI) ... PI
Pondere [*By Weight*] [*Latin*] ... P
Pondere [*By Weight*] [*Latin*] ... POND
Pondere [*By Weigh*] [*Latin*] (AD) ... pond
Ponderosa Pine or Sugar Pine [*Lumber*] ... PPSP
Ponderosa Pine Woodwork Association [*NWWDA*] [*Absorbed by*] (EA) ... PPW
Ponderosa Pine Woodwork Association [*NWWDA*] [*Absorbed by*] ... PPWA
Ponderosa Ventures, Inc. [*Vancouver Stock Exchange symbol*] ... PDV
Ponderosus [*Heavy*] [*Pharmacy*] ... POND
Pondoland (AD) ... Pondo
Pondus [*Weight*] [*Latin*] (MAE) ... p
Pondus Civile [*Civil (Avoirdupois) Weight*] [*Pharmacy*] (ROG) ... PC
Pondus Medicinale [*Medicinal Weight*] [*Pharmacy*] (ROG) ... PM
Poneloya [*Nicaragua*] [*Seismograph station code, US Geological Survey*] (SEIS) ... PYN
Ponendum [*To Be Placed*] [*Latin*] ... P
Poney Explorations Ltd. [*Vancouver Stock Exchange symbol*] ... PXL
Ponggaluku [*Indonesia*] [*ICAO location identifier*] (ICLI) ... WAAL
Pongola [*South Africa*] [*ICAO location identifier*] (ICLI) ... FAPL
Pongtuk [*Cambodia*] [*ICAO location identifier*] (ICLI) ... VDPT
Poni Curavit [*Caused to Be Placed*] [*Latin*] ... PC
Poni Iussit [*Ordered to Be Placed*] [*Latin*] ... PI
Ponies of Britain [*An association*] (DBA) ... PofB
Ponoka Public Library, Alberta [*Library symbol National Library of Canada*] (NLC) ... APO
Pons/Avy [*France ICAO location identifier*] (ICLI) ... LFCP
Ponta Delgada [*Azores*] [*Seismograph station code, US Geological Survey*] (SEIS) ... PDA
Ponta Delgada [*Portugal*] [*Airport symbol*] (OAG) ... PDL
Ponta Delgada, Sao Miguel Island [*Portugal ICAO location identifier*] (ICLI) ... LPPD
Ponta Do Ouro [*Mozambique*] [*ICAO location identifier*] (ICLI) ... FQPO
Ponta Grossa [*Brazil*] [*Airport symbol*] (OAG) ... PGZ
Ponta Grossa [*Brazil ICAO location identifier*] (ICLI) ... SBGS
Ponta Pora [*Brazil*] [*Airport symbol*] (OAG) ... PMG
Ponta Pora/Internacional [*ICAO location identifier*] (ICLI) ... SBPP
Pontarlier [*France ICAO location identifier*] (ICLI) ... LFSP
Ponte Vedra Beach, FL [*FM radio station call letters*] (RBYB) ... WTLK-FM
Pontefract Volunteer Rifles [*British military*] (DMA) ... PVR
Ponteix, SK [*Television station call letters*] ... CBCP-3
Pontevedra (AD) ... Pont
Pontiac [*Automotive engineering*] ... PONT
Pontiac (AD) ... Ponti
Pontiac, IL [*Location identifier FAA*] (FAAL) ... PNT
Pontiac, IL [*FM radio station call letters*] ... WJEZ
Pontiac, IL [*AM radio station call letters*] ... WPOK
Pontiac, MI [*Location identifier FAA*] (FAAL) ... PTK
Pontiac Motor Division [*General Motors Corp.*] ... PMD
Pontiac Public Libraries, Pontiac, MI [*Library symbol Library of Congress*] (LCLS) ... MiPon
Pontiac-Oakland Club International (EA) ... POCI
Pontiac-William Holliday School District 105, Fairview Heights, IL [*Library symbol Library of Congress*] (LCLS) ... IFhPSD
Pontianak [*Indonesia*] [*Airport symbol*] (OAG) ... PNK
Pontianak Sector [*Indonesia*] [*ICAO location identifier*] (ICLI) ... WIOZ
Pontianak/Supadio [*Indonesia*] [*ICAO location identifier*] (ICLI) ... WIOO
Pontifex [*Bishop*] [*Latin*] ... P
Pontifex [*Bishop*] [*Latin*] (WGA) ... PONT
Pontifex Maximus [*Supreme Pontiff*] [*Latin*] ... PM
Pontifex Maximus [*Supreme Pontiff*] [*Latin*] (AD) ... Pont Max
Pontifica Opera di Assistenza [*Pontifical Relief Organization*] ... POA
Pontifical Association of the Holy Childhood (EA) ... PAHC
Pontifical College Josephinum [*Worthington, OH*] ... PCJ
Pontifical College Josephinum, Worthington, OH [*Library symbol Library of Congress*] (LCLS) ... OWorP
Pontifical College Josephinum, Worthington, OH [*OCLC symbol*] (OCLC) ... PCJ
Pontifical Commission for Migrants and Itinerant Peoples [*See also PCMT*] [*Vatican City, Vatican City State*] (EAIO) ... PCMIP
Pontifical Council for Culture [*Vatican City*] (EAIO) ... PCC
Pontifical Institute for Foreign Missions (TOCD) ... PIME
Pontifical Institute for Foreign Missions (TOCD) ... pime
Pontifical Institute for Mission Extension [*Roman Catholic men's religious order*] ... PIME
Pontifical Institute of Mediaeval Studies [*Canada*] (IRC) ... PIMS
Pontifical Institute of Mediaeval Studies, University of Toronto, Ontario [*Library symbol National Library of Canada*] (NLC) ... OTIM
Pontifical Institute of Mediaeval Studies, University of Toronto, Toronto, ON, Canada [*Library symbol Library of Congress*] (LCLS) ... CaOTIM
Pontifical Mission for Palestine (EA) ... PMP
Pontifical Missionary Union [*Later, PMUPR*] [*See also OPM*] (EA) ... PMU
Pontifical Missionary Union of Priests and Religious (EA) ... PMUPR
Pontificia Commissione Migrazioni e Turismo [*Pontifical Commission for Migrants and Itinerant Peoples - PCMIP*] [*Vatican City, Vatican City State*] (EAIO) ... PCMT
Pontificia Universidade Catolica [*Rio de Janeiro*] ... PUC
Pontificiae Universitatis Gregorianae Liber Annuus [*Rome*] [*A publication*] (BJA) ... GregLA
Pontificum [*Of the Popes*] [*Latin*] ... PP
Pontine Gaze Center [*Eye anatomy*] ... PGC
Pontine Nuclei [*Neuroanatomy*] ... PN
Pontine Reticular Formation [*Neurophysiology*] ... PRF
Pontius [*Authority cited in pre-1607 legal work*] (DSA) ... Pon
Pontius Family Association (EA) ... PFA
Pontius Guillelmi [*Authority cited in pre-1607 legal work*] (DSA) ... PG
Pontivy [*France ICAO location identifier*] (ICLI) ... LFED
Ponto-Geniculate-Occipital [*Electroencephalography*] ... PGO
Pontoise/Cormeilles-En-Vexin [*France ICAO location identifier*] (ICLI) ... LFPT
Pontoon (AD) ... pon
Pontoon (AAG) ... PON
Pontoon (WGA) ... Pont
Pontoon [*Navy symbol*] (DNAB) ... YWN
Pontoon Air Cushion Kit [*Army*] (RDA) ... PACK
Pontoon Assembly Depot (NVT) ... PAD
Pontoon Assembly Detachment ... PAD
Pontoon Barge [*Navy symbol*] (DNAB) ... YWN
Pontoon Bridge (AD) ... PonBrg
Pontoon Bridge (MUGU) ... PONBRG
Pontoon Bridge (AD) ... pont b
Pontoon Dock ... PD
Pontoon Salvage Vessel [*Navy symbol*] ... YSP
Pontoon Stowage Barge [*Navy symbol Obsolete*] ... YPK
Pontotoc, MS [*AM radio station call letters*] ... WSEL

Pontotoc, MS [*FM radio station call letters*] ... WSEL-FM
Pont-Saint-Esprit [*France ICAO location identifier*] (ICLI) ... LFND
Pont-Saint-Vincent [*France ICAO location identifier*] (ICLI) ... LFSV
Pont-Sur-Yonne [*France ICAO location identifier*] (ICLI) ... LFGO
Pontypool Road [*Welsh depot code*] ... PPRD
Pony and Zebra (AD) ... pobra
Pony Baseball (EA) ... PB
Pony Club Association of Queensland [*Australia*] ... PCAQ
Pony Club Association of South Australia ... PCASA
Pony Club Association of Victoria [*Australia*] ... PCAV
Pony Club Association of Western Australia ... PCAWA
Pony Express Historical Association (EA) ... PEHA
Pony of the Americas Club (EA) ... POAC
Pony Riding for the Disabled Association [*Australia*] ... PRDA
Ponza [*Italy ICAO location identifier*] (ICLI) ... LIQZ
Poodle Club of America (EA) ... PCA
Poodle Dog (AD) ... pood
Pooh Property Trust [*A.A. Milne estate*] [*British*] ... PPT
Pool ... P
Pool Control Error (IAA) ... PCE
Pool Cooling and Purification System [*Nuclear energy*] (NRCH) ... PCPS
Pool Critical Assembly [*Nuclear reactor*] ... PCA
Pool Density [*Pisciculture*] ... PD
Pool Energy Services [*NASDAQ symbol*] (TTSB) ... PESC
Pool Energy Services Co. [*NASDAQ symbol*] (SAG) ... PESC
Pool Energy Services Co. [*Associated Press*] (SAG) ... PoolEn
Pool Exercise Program [*Arthritis Foundation*] ... PEP
Pool Frequency [*Pisciculture*] ... PF
Pool Maintenance Module [*Telecommunications*] (TEL) ... PMM
Pool Operational Module [*Telecommunications*] (TEL) ... POM
Pool Promoters Association [*British*] (BI) ... PPA
Pool Repair Cycle Time (MCD) ... PRCT
Pool Temperature [*Nuclear energy*] (NRCH) ... PT
Pool Test Reactor [*Nuclear energy*] ... PTR
Pool Training Reactor [*Nuclear energy*] ... PTR
Poole (AD) ... Poo
Poole, Aberley, Worthington, and Nolen [*Four early residents of Pawn, Oregon. The city derives its name from the initial letters of their surnames*] ... PAWN
Pooled Analytical Stereoplotter System (PDAA) ... PASS
Pooled Development Funds [*Economics*] ... PDF
Pooled Human Serum [*Hematology*] (DMAA) ... PHS
Pooled Mixed Lymphocyte Culture [*Clinical chemistry*] ... PMLC
Pooled Normal Serum (PDAA) ... PNS
Pooled Platelet Concentrate [*Medicine*] (MEDA) ... PPC
Pooled Superannuation Trust ... PST
Poona [*India*] [*Airport symbol*] (OAG) ... PNQ
Poona [*India*] [*Seismograph station code, US Geological Survey*] (SEIS) ... POO
Poop [*Portion of a ship*] ... P
Poop and Bridge [*of a ship*] (DS) ... PB
Poop and Forecastle [*of a ship*] (DS) ... PF
Poop, Bridge, and Forecastle [*of a ship*] (DS) ... PBF
Poop Deck [*Naval engineering*] ... PDK
Poor Acquisition Data (AAG) ... PAD
Poor Bloody Infantry [*British military slang*] ... PBI
Poor Bloody Observer [*British World War I military slang*] (DSUE) ... PBO
Poor Clare Missionary Sisters (TOCD) ... MC
Poor Clare Nuns of the Holy Eucharist [*Roman Catholic religious order*] ... PCHE
Poor Clares [*Roman Catholic women's religious order*] ... PC
Poor Clares of Perpetual Adoration [*Roman Catholic women's religious order*] ... PCPA
Poor Clares of St. Colette [*Roman Catholic women's religious order*] ... PCC
Poor Classes [*British*] (DSUE) ... PC
Poor Clergy Relief Corp. [*British*] (BI) ... PCRC
Poor Clergy Relief Society [*British*] ... PCRS
Poor Clerks Regular of the Mother of God of the Pious Schools [*Rome, Italy*] (EAIO) ... PCRMGPS
Poor Condition [*Medicine*] (DMAA) ... PC
Poor Coordination [*Medicine*] (DMAA) ... PC
Poor Handmaids of Jesus Christ [*Ancilla Domini Sisters*] [*Roman Catholic religious order*] ... PHJC
Poor Health (DAVI) ... PH
Poor Law [*A publication*] (DLA) ... PL
Poor Law and Local Government Magazine [*A publication*] (DLA) ... Poor L & Local Gov't
Poor Law Board ... PLB
Poor Law Commissioner [*A publication*] (DLA) ... PL Com
Poor Law Commissioners [*British*] ... PLC
Poor Law Guardian [*British*] ... PLG
Poor Law Magazine [*1858-1930*] [*Scotland*] [*A publication*] [*A publication*] (DLA) ... PL Mag
Poor Law Magazine [*A publication*] (DLA) ... PLM
Poor Law Office (ROG) ... PLO
Poor Law Union [*British*] ... PLU
Poor Little Old Me Syndrome [*British*] ... PLOME
Poor Man's Optical Landing System ... POMOLA
Poor Metabolism [*Medicine*] ... PM
Poor Miserable Soul [*Medical slang*] ... PMS
Poor Miserable Soul (AD) ... pms
Poor Precordial R-Wave Progression [*Cardiology*] ... PPRWP
Poor Rate [*British*] (ROG) ... PR
Poor Richard Club, Philadelphia, PA [*Library symbol Library of Congress Obsolete*] (LCLS) ... PPPRC
Poor R-Wave Progression [*On electrocardiogram*] [*Cardiology*] (DAVI) ... PRWP
Poor Sisters of Jesus Crucified and the Sorrowful Mother [*Roman Catholic religious order*] ... CJC
Poor Sisters of Nazareth (TOCD) ... PSN
Poor Sisters of St. Joseph (TOCD) ... PSSJ
Poor Skiing Conditions ... P
Poor Standing [*Moody's bond rating*] ... Caa
Poor Transmission [*Telecommunications*] (TEL) ... PTR
Poore's Federal and State Constitution [*A publication*] (DLA) ... Poore Const
Poorly Characterized Phase [*Mineralogy*] ... PCP
Poorly Differentiated [*Medicine*] ... PD
Poorly Differentiated Lung Cancer [*Medicine*] (DMAA) ... PDLC
Poorly Differentiated Lymphatic [*or Lymphocytic*] **Lymphoma** [*Oncology*] ... PDLL
Poorly Differentiated Lymphocytic [*Oncology*] ... PDL
Poorly Differentiated Lymphocytic-Diffuse [*Oncology*] (DMAA) ... PDLD
Poorly Differentiated Lymphocytic-Nodular [*Oncology*] (DMAA) ... PDLN
Poorly Differentiated Lymphoma, Diffuse [*Oncology and pathology*] (DAVI) ... PLDD
Poorly Graphitized Carbon [*Physical chemistry*] ... PGC
Poorly Organized, Unstable Personality [*Eysenck*] [*Psychology*] ... P
Pop Corn [*Crochet*] ... pc
Pop Festivals [*Public-performance tariff class*] [*British*] ... LPF
Pop Warner Football (EA) ... PWF
Pop Your Seat Belt, Open the Window, Get Out [*Automobile safety*] ... POGO
Popayan [*Colombia*] [*Airport symbol*] (OAG) ... PPN
Popayan, Colombia (AD) ... Popa
Popayan/Guillermo Leon Valencia [*Colorado ICAO location identifier*] (ICLI) ... SKPP
Popcorn Institute (EA) ... PI
Popcorn Processors Association [*Later, PI*] ... PPA
Pope ... P
Pope and Martyr [*Church calendars*] ... PM
Pope & Talbot [*NYSE symbol*] (TTSB) ... POP
Pope and Talbot [*Steamship*] (MHDW) ... PT
Pope & Talbot, Inc. [*NYSE symbol*] (SPSG) ... POP
Pope & Talbot, Inc. [*Associated Press*] (SAG) ... PopeTal
Pope and Young Club (EA) ... PYC
Pope County Library, Russellville, AR [*Library symbol*] [*Library of Congress*] (LCLS) ... ArRu
Pope on Customs and Excise [*11th ed.*] [*1828*] [*A publication*] (DLA) ... Pope Cust
Pope on Lunacy [*A publication*] (DLA) ... Pope Lun
Pope Resources Ltd. [*Associated Press*] (SAG) ... PopeRes
Pope Resources Ltd. [*NASDAQ symbol*] (SPSG) ... POPEZ
Pope Resources L.P. [*NASDAQ symbol*] (TTSB) ... POPEZ
Pope Valley Holding [*Vancouver Stock Exchange symbol*] ... PVH
Pope Vanoy [*Alaska*] [*Airport symbol*] (OAG) ... PVY
Popham's English King's Bench Reports [*1592-1627*] [*A publication*] (DLA) ... Pop
Popham's English King's Bench Reports [*1592-1627*] [*A publication*] (DLA) ... Poph
Popham's English King's Bench Reports [*79 English Reprint*] [*1592-1626*] [*A publication*] (DLA) ... Popham
Popham's Insolvency Act of Canada [*A publication*] (DLA) ... Poph Insol
Poplar (VRA) ... plr
Poplar Bluff [*Missouri*] [*Airport symbol*] (OAG) ... POF
Poplar Bluff, MO [*Location identifier FAA*] (FAAL) ... FDI
Poplar Bluff, MO [*FM radio station call letters*] ... KAHR
Poplar Bluff, MO [*FM radio station call letters*] ... KJEZ
Poplar Bluff, MO [*FM radio station call letters*] ... KKLR
Poplar Bluff, MO [*AM radio station call letters*] ... KLID
Poplar Bluff, MO [*FM radio station call letters*] ... KLUH
Poplar Bluff, MO [*FM radio station call letters*] ... KOKS
Poplar Bluff, MO [*Television station call letters*] ... KPOB
Poplar Bluff, MO [*AM radio station call letters*] ... KWOC
Poplar Bluff, MO [*FM radio station call letters*] ... KZMA
Poplar Bluff, MO [*Location identifier FAA*] (FAAL) ... POF
Poplar Grove National Cemetery ... POGR
Poplar Mosaic Virus [*Plant pathology*] ... POPMV
Poplarville, MS [*AM radio station call letters*] ... WRPM
Poplarville, MS [*FM radio station call letters*] ... WZKX
Poplarville Public Library, Poplarville, MS [*Library symbol Library of Congress*] (LCLS) ... MsPop
Popliteal (AD) ... pop
Popliteal (DMAA) ... Pop
Popliteal [*Artery*] [*Anatomy*] (AAMN) ... POP
Popliteal [*Anatomy*] ... POPLIT
Popliteal (AD) ... poplit
Popliteal Lymph Node [*Anatomy*] ... PLN
Popliteal Tendon [*Anatomy*] ... PT
Popocatepetl [*Mexico*] [*Seismograph station code, US Geological Survey*] (SEIS) ... PPM
Popokabaka [*Zaire*] [*ICAO location identifier*] (ICLI) ... FZCP
Popolo Italiano, Atlantic City, NJ [*Library symbol Library of Congress*] (LCLS) ... NjAcPI
Popondetta [*New Guinea*] [*Airport symbol*] (AD) ... PNG
Popondetta [*Papua New Guinea*] [*Airport symbol*] (OAG) ... PNP
Popondetta [*Papua New Guinea*] [*Seismograph station code, US Geological Survey Closed*] (SEIS) ... POP
Poppa (AD) ... Pop
Poppet (AD) ... pop
Poppet [*Engineering*] ... PPT
Popping [*Mining engineering*] ... POP
Poppleton-Allen Sales Aptitude Test ... PASAT
Poppy Advisory and Control Board [*Tasmania, Australia*] ... PACB
Poprad/Tatry [*Former Czechoslovakia*] [*ICAO location identifier*] (ICLI) ... LKTT

Popski's Private Army [*Commando force led by Vladimir Peniakoff*] [*World War II*] .... PPA
Poptun [*Guatemala*] [*ICAO location identifier*] (ICLI) .... MGPP
Popular (AD) .... pop
Popular (WDMC) .... pop
Popular .... POP
Popular Art (AD) .... pop art
Popular Concerts [*Public-performance tariff class*] [*British*] .... LP
Popular Concerts (AD) .... pops
Popular Creek Public Library District, Streamwood, IL [*Library symbol*] [*Library of Congress*] (LCLS) .... IStw
Popular Cult .... PC
Popular Culture Association (EA) .... PCA
Popular Democratic Coalition [*Ecuador*] [*Political party*] (PPW) .... CPD
Popular Democratic Front [*Jordan*] [*Political party*] .... PDF
Popular Democratic Front for the Liberation of Palestine .... PDFLP
Popular Democratic Party [*Puerto Rico*] [*Political party*] .... PDP
[*A*] **Popular Dictionary of Australian Slang** [*A publication*] .... PDAS
Popular Edition [*Publishing*] .... POP ED
Popular Flying Association [*British*] .... PFA
Popular Forces [*ARVN*] .... PF
Popular Front for Armed Resistance [*Pakistan*] .... PFAR
Popular Front for the Liberation of Ahvaz [*Iran*] .... PFLA
Popular Front for the Liberation of Oman [*Political party*] (PD) .... PFLO
Popular Front for the Liberation of Oman and the Arabian Gulf [*Political party*] (PD) .... PFLOAG
Popular Front for the Liberation of Palestine [*Political party*] (PD) .... PFLP
Popular Front for the Liberation of Palestine - General Command [*Political party*] (PD) .... PFLP-GC
Popular Front of Estonia [*Political party*] .... PFE
Popular Front Party [*Ghana*] [*Political party*] (PPW) .... PFP
Popular Library of Art [*A publication*] .... PLA
Popular Low-Power Schottky [*Electronics*] (MCD) .... PLS
Popular Luxury [*Coined by Thomas Hine, design critic for the Philadelphia Inquirer, to describe the period from the mid-1950's to the mid-1960's*] .... Populuxe
Popular Magazine Review Online [*EBSCO Subscription Services*] [*Information service or system*] .... PMRO
Popular Monthly Law Tracts [*1877-78*] [*A publication*] (DLA) .... Pop Mo L Tr
Popular Movement Against the European Community (ECON) .... PM
Popular Music (AD) .... pop music
Popular Music and Society [*A publication*] (BRI) .... PMS
Popular Nationalist Party [*Panama*] [*Political party*] (PD) .... PNP
Popular New Titles from Abroad [*Book acquisition program for libraries*] .... PONTA
Popular News and Review [*A publication*] .... PNR
Popular Party [*European political movement*] (ECON) .... PP
Popular Power Package (IAA) .... PPP
Popular Priced Dress Manufacturers Group [*Later, AMA*] (EA) .... PPDMG
Popular Psychiatry (AD) .... pop psych
Popular Response [*Rorschach*] [*Psychology*] .... P
Popular Rotocraft Association (EA) .... PRA
Popular Science [*A publication*] (AD) .... Pop Sci
Popular Science Monthly [*A publication*] (ROG) .... POP SCI MO
Popular Self-Defense Force [*Local armed units protecting Vietnamese hamlets*] .... PSDF
Popular Struggle Front [*Palestine*] [*Political party*] (PD) .... PSF
Popular Unity of Chile [*Political party*] .... PUC
Popular Unity Party [*Bangladesh*] [*Political party*] (PPW) .... PUP
Populare [*Record label*] [*Romania*] .... Pop
Populated Place [*Board on Geographic Names*] .... PPL
Population .... P
Population (AAG) .... POP
Population (AD) .... pop
Population (WDMC) .... pop
Population (ODBW) .... pop
Population .... Popn
Population Action Council (EA) .... PAC
Population Association of America (EA) .... PAA
Population at Risk (FFDE) .... PAR
Population Biology .... PB
Population Biology/Physiological Ecology [*Program*] [*National Science Foundation*] .... PBPE
Population Census .... PC
Population Census Report (OICC) .... PCR
Population Clearing House and Information System (NITA) .... PCHIS
Population Communication (EA) .... PC
Population Communications International [*An association*] (EA) .... PCI
Population Concern [*British*] (EAIO) .... PC
Population Council (EA) .... PC
Population Council, New York, NY [*Library symbol Library of Congress*] (LCLS) .... NNPopC
Population Crisis Committee (EA) .... PCC
Population Crisis Committee, Washington, DC [*Library symbol Library of Congress*] (LCLS) .... DPopC
Population Density (NRCH) .... PD
Population Distribution (NRCH) .... PD
Population Division [*Bureau of the Census*] (OICC) .... POP
Population Division and Housing and Household Economics Statistics Division [*Bureau of the Census*] [*Also, an information service or system*] (IID) .... HHESD
Population Documentation Center [*Food and Agriculture Organization*] [*United Nations Information service or system*] (IID) .... PDC
Population Doubling .... PD
Population Doubling Level [*Cytology*] .... PDL
Population Doubling Time [*Cytology*] .... PDT

Population Drainage Area [*Civil Defense*] .... PDA
Population Dynamics, Seattle, WA [*Library symbol Library of Congress*] (LCLS) .... WaSPoD
Population Equivalent (FFDE) .... PE
Population Explosion (AD) .... popex
Population Growth Estimation .... PGE
Population Growth Rate .... PGR
Population Housing Census (OICC) .... PHC
Population Information Documentation System for Africa .... PIDSA
Population Information Network [*UNESCO*] .... POPINFORM
Population Information On-Line [*Bibliographic database*] (IID) .... POPLINE
Population Information Program [*Later, CCP*] (EA) .... PIP
Population Information System [*UNESCO*] .... POPINS
Population Institute (EA) .... PI
Population Institute, Washington, DC [*Library symbol Library of Congress*] (LCLS) .... DPopI
Population Online (NITA) .... POPLINE
Population Paper Listing [*US Census Bureau*] [*A publication*] .... PPL
Population Planning (DAVI) .... PP
Population Planning Associates [*Medicine*] (DAVI) .... PPA
Population Planning Associates (BABM) .... PPA
Population Post-stimulus Time Histogram [*Statistics*] .... PPSTH
Population Protection and Resources Management [*Military British*] .... PPRM
Population Reference Bureau (EA) .... PRB
Population Reference Bureau, Washington, DC [*Library symbol Library of Congress*] (LCLS) .... DPopR
Population Renewal Office (EA) .... PRO
Population Research Center [*University of Chicago*] [*Research center*] (RCD) .... PRC
Population Research Laboratory [*University of Alberta*] [*Research center*] (RCD) .... PRL
Population Research Service [*Information service or system*] (IID) .... PRS
Population Resource Center (EA) .... PRC
Population, Resources, and Environment Program [*American Association for the Advancement of Science*] .... PREP
Population Sample (MAE) .... PS
Population Size [*Symbol*] (MAE) .... N
Population size [*Statistics*] (DAVI) .... N
Population Studies and Training Center [*Brown University*] [*Research center*] (RCD) .... PS & TC
Population Studies Center [*University of Michigan*] [*Research center*] (RCD) .... PSC
Population Viability Analysis [*Biology*] .... PVA
Population-Environment Balance (EA) .... PEB
Populist Conservative [*Wing of the Republican Party represented by Congressmen Gingrich, Kemp, and Lott*] .... POP-CON
Populist Party of America [*Political party*] (EA) .... PP
Populus [*People*] [*Latin*] .... P
Populus Romanus [*The Roman People*] [*Latin*] .... PR
Pop-Up Bottom Seismograph [*Marine science*] (MSC) .... PUBS
Pop-Up Pore Pressure Instrument [*Oceanography*] .... PUPPI
Por Favor [*Please*] [*Portuguese*] .... PF
Por Orden [*By Order*] [*Spanish*] .... PO
Porangatu [*Brazil*] [*Airport symbol*] (AD) .... PGT
Porbandar [*India*] [*Airport symbol*] (OAG) .... PBD
Porbandar [*India*] [*ICAO location identifier*] (ICLI) .... VAPR
Porcelain .... P
Porcelain (AAG) .... PORC
Porcelain (AD) .... porc
Porcelain Enamel [*Technical drawings*] .... PE
Porcelain Enamel Bath [*Classified advertising*] (ADA) .... PEB
Porcelain Enamel Bath and Basin [*Classified advertising*] (ADA) .... PEB & B
Porcelain Enamel Institute (EA) .... PEI
Porcelain Fused to Metal [*Dentistry*] .... PFM
Porcelain on Steel Council [*Defunct*] (EA) .... PSC
Porcelain Pavers (DICI) .... PP
Porcelain-Enamelled Metal Substrate (EECA) .... PEMS
Porch (WGA) .... PCH
Porch (VRA) .... pch
Porch Index [*Psychiatry*] (DAVI) .... PI
Porch Index of Communicative Ability [*Psychology*] .... PICA
Porch Index of Communicative Ability in Children [*Psychology*] .... PICAC
Porcine Brain Natriuretic Peptide [*Biochemistry*] .... PBNP
Porcine Calcitonin [*Biochemistry*] (AAMN) .... PCT
Porcine Cerebral Microvascular [*Cell line*] .... PCMV
Porcine Cirovirus .... PCV
Porcine Follicle Stimulating Hormone [*Endocrinology*] .... PFSH
Porcine Follicular Fluid [*Endocrinology*] .... PFF
Porcine Growth Hormone [*Biochemistry*] .... PGH
Porcine Pancreatic Elastase [*An enzyme*] .... PPE
Porcine Pancreatic Lipase [*An enzyme*] .... PPL
Porcine Parathyroid Hormone [*Endocrinology*] .... pPTH
Porcine Parvovirus [*Veterinary science*] (DMAA) .... PPV
Porcine Platelet-Derived Growth Factor [*Biochemistry*] .... PPDGF
Porcine Somatotropin [*Gene-spliced animal hormone*] [*Monsanto Co.*] .... PST
Porcine Stress Syndrome [*Veterinary medicine*] .... PSS
Porcine Transforming Growth Factor .... pTGF
Porcine Zona Pellucida [*Experimental animal contraceptive*] .... PZP
Porcupine Campus, Northern College of Applied Arts and Technology, South Porcupine, Ontario [*Library symbol National Library of Canada*] (NLC) .... OSPNC
Porcupine Creek, AK [*Location identifier FAA*] (FAAL) .... PCK
Pore Diameter .... PD
Pore Forming Protein [*Biochemistry*] .... PFP
Pore Free (IAA) .... PF

Pore Gradient Electrophoresis .... PGE
Pore Size Distribution .... PSD
Pore Volume [*Geology*] .... PV
Pores per Inch .... ppi
Porga [*Benin*] [*ICAO location identifier*] (ICLI) .... DBBO
Porgera [*Papua New Guinea*] [*Airport symbol*] (OAG) .... RGE
Pori [*Finland ICAO location identifier*] (ICLI) .... EFPO
Pori [*Finland*] [*Airport symbol*] (OAG) .... POR
PORI [*Polaris Operational Readiness Instrumentation*] **Operational Test System** [*Missiles*] .... POTS
Porifera (AD) .... Por
Pork Council of Australia .... PCA
Pork Industry Handbook [*A publication*] .... PIH
Pork Sandwich (AD) .... porksan
Pork Sandwich (AD) .... porkwich
Porkkala [*Finland*] [*Seismograph station code, US Geological Survey*] (SEIS) .... PKK
Porlamar [*Venezuela*] [*Airport symbol*] (OAG) .... PMV
Porlock Society (EA) .... PS
Pornofilm (AD) .... porno
Pornographer (AD) .... porno
Pornographic (AD) .... porn
Pornographic Biography (AD) .... pornobio
Pornographic Cassette (AD) .... pornette
Pornographic Magazine (AD) .... porno mag
Pornographic Magazines (AD) .... pornzines
Pornographic Motion Picture (AD) .... pornofilm
Pornographic Motion Picture Film (AD) .... pornfilm
Pornographic Novel (AD) .... pornovel
Pornographic Novelist (AD) .... pornovelist
Pornographic Squad (AD) .... Porn Squad
Pornography (DSUE) .... PORN
Pornography (DSUE) .... PORNO
Pornovision [*Television*] .... PV
Poro Point, La Union [*Philippines*] [*ICAO location identifier*] (ICLI) .... RPXP
Porogi [*Waterfall*] [*Russian*] (AD) .... Por
Porokeratosis Punctata Palmaris et Plantaris [*Medicine*] (DMAA) .... PPPP
Porosity (AD) .... por
Porous Clay Heterostructure [*Materials science*] .... PCH
Porous Electrode Electrostatic Precipitation .... PEEP
Porous Friction Surface [*Airfield pavement*] .... PFS
Porous Layer, Open Tubular Column [*Gas chromatography*] .... PLOT
Porous Media Research Institute [*University of Waterloo*] [*Research center*] (RCD) .... PMRI
Porous Polyurethane Foam [*Also, PUF*] [*Plastics technology*] .... PPF
Porous Polyurethane Foam [*Also, PPF*] [*Plastics technology*] .... PUF
Porous Silicon [*Physics*] .... PS
Porous Tungsten Ionizer .... PTI
Porous Tungsten Plug .... PTP
Porous Tungsten Vaporizer .... PTV
Porous-Coated Anatomical [*Prosthesis*] .... PCA
Porphobilinogen [*Clinical chemistry*] .... PBG
Porphobilinogen Deaminase [*An enzyme*] .... PBGD
Porphobilinogen Deaminase [*Clinical chemistry*] (MAE) .... PD
Porphobilinogen - Quantitative [*Genetics*] (DAVI) .... PBG-QN
Porphobilinogen Synthase [*Medicine*] (DMAA) .... PBG-S
Porphyria, Chester Type (DMAA) .... PORC
Porphyria Cutanea Tarda [*Disease*] [*Medicine*] .... PCT
Porphyrin [*Medicine*] (DAVI) .... P
Porphyrin Biosynthetic Pathway [*Biochemistry*] (AAMN) .... PBP
Porphyrin-Quinone [*Photochemistry*] .... P-Q
Porphyrins [*Chemistry*] (DAVI) .... PROPH
Porphyry (VRA) .... porph
Porphyry [*Third century AD*] [*Classical studies*] (OCD) .... Porph
Porpoise Rescue Foundation (EA) .... PRF
Porquis Junction [*Ontario*] [*Airport symbol*] (AD) .... YQJ
Porrentruy [*Switzerland ICAO location identifier*] (ICLI) .... LSZY
Porsche Cars North America, Inc. .... PCNA
Porsche Club of America (EA) .... PCA
Porsche Dual-Function Transmission [*Automotive engineering*] .... PDF
Porsche Experimental Prototype [*Automotive engineering*] .... PEP
Porsche Flug Motor [*Automotive engineering*] .... PFM
Porsche Owners Club (EA) .... POC
Port [*Maps and charts*] .... P
Port [*Commonly used*] (OPSA) .... PORT
Port .... PRT
Port .... PRT
Port .... PT
Port (ODBW) .... pt
Port (WDMC) .... pt
Port Activities Report [*Navy*] .... PACREP
Port Adelaide [*South Australia*] (AD) .... Port Ade
Port Agency [*Army*] .... PA
Port Air Materiel Office .... PAMO
Port Alberni [*Vancouver Island, British Columbia*] (AD) .... Port Ald
Port Alberni, BC [*AM radio station call letters*] .... CJAV
Port Alexander [*Alaska*] (AD) .... Port Alex
Port Alexander [*Alaska*] [*Airport symbol*] (AD) .... POX
Port Alfred [*Formerly, Crozet*] [*South Africa*] [*Geomagnetic observatory code*] .... CZT
Port Alfred [*South Africa*] [*ICAO location identifier*] (ICLI) .... FAPA
Port Allegany, PA [*FM radio station call letters*] .... WHKS
Port Allen, LA [*AM radio station call letters*] (RBYB) .... WPFC
Port Alsworth [*Alaska*] [*Airport symbol*] (OAG) .... PTA
Port Amenities Liaison Officer [*British*] (DSUE) .... PALO
Port and Ocean Engineering Under Arctic Conditions International Committee (EAIO) .... POAC
Port and Starboard .... P & S
Port Angeles [*Washington*] [*Airport symbol*] (OAG) .... CLM
Port Angeles Coast Guard Air Station [*Washington*] [*ICAO location identifier*] (ICLI) .... KNOW
Port Angeles, WA [*Location identifier FAA*] (FAAL) .... CLM
Port Angeles, WA [*AM radio station call letters*] .... KAPY
Port Angeles, WA [*AM radio station call letters*] .... KONP
Port Angeles, WA [*Location identifier FAA*] (FAAL) .... NOW
Port Angeles Western Railroad (IIA) .... PAW
Port Antisubmarine Officer [*Navy*] .... PA/SO
Port Antonio [*Jamaica*] (AD) .... Port Ant
Port Antonio [*Jamaica*] [*Airport symbol*] (OAG) .... POT
Port Arthur (AD) .... Port Art
Port Arthur, TX [*AM radio station call letters*] .... KALO
Port Arthur, TX [*FM radio station call letters*] .... KHYS
Port Arthur, TX [*Television station call letters*] .... KJAC
Port Arthur, TX [*FM radio station call letters*] .... KLTN
Port Arthur, TX [*AM radio station call letters*] .... KOLE
Port Au Choix, NF [*AM radio station call letters*] .... CFNW
Port Au Port West School/Public Library, Newfoundland [*Library symbol National Library of Canada*] (NLC) .... NFPW
Port Au Port West School/Public Library, Port Au Port West, NF, Canada [*Library symbol Library of Congress*] (LCLS) .... CaNfPw
Port Augusta [*Australia Airport symbol*] (OAG) .... PUG
Port Augusta [*South Australia*] [*Airport symbol*] (AD) .... UBK
Port Austin Township Library, Port Austin, MI [*Library symbol Library of Congress*] (LCLS) .... MiPa
Port Authorities Queensland [*Australia*] .... PAQ
Port Authority [*Western Australia*] .... PA
Port Authority of New York [*Later, PANYNJ*] .... PANY
Port Authority of New York and New Jersey [*Formerly, PANY*] .... PANYNJ
Port Authority of New York and New Jersey Library, New York, NY [*OCLC symbol*] (OCLC) .... YPA
Port Authority of New York and New Jersey, New York, NY [*Library symbol Library of Congress*] (LCLS) .... NNPA
Port Authority Trans-Hudson [*New York*] .... PATH
Port Autonome d'Abidjan [*The Ivory Coast*] (EY) .... PAA
Port Autonome de San Pedro [*The Ivory Coast*] (EY) .... PASP
Port Bailey [*Alaska*] [*Airport symbol*] (OAG) .... KPY
Port Bailey, AK [*Location identifier FAA*] (FAAL) .... KPY
Port Berge [*Madagascar*] [*ICAO location identifier*] (ICLI) .... FMNG
Port Berge [*Madagascar*] [*Airport symbol*] (OAG) .... WPB
[*The*] **Port Bienville Railroad** [*AAR code*] .... PBVR
Port Blair [*Andaman Islands*] [*Airport symbol*] (OAG) .... IXZ
Port Blair [*Andaman Islands*] [*Seismograph station code, US Geological Survey*] (SEIS) .... PBA
Port Blair [*India*] [*ICAO location identifier*] (ICLI) .... VEPB
Port Blair [*India*] [*ICAO location identifier*] (ICLI) .... VOPB
Port Call [*Army*] .... PC
Port Call Control Number [*Army*] (AABC) .... PCCN
Port [*or Anchorage*] **Capacity Report** [*Navy*] (NVT) .... PORTREP
Port Carling Public Library, Ontario [*Library symbol National Library of Canada*] (BIB) .... OPORC
Port Charges Operator (DNAB) .... PCOP
Port Charges Paid by Commercial Operator (DNAB) .... PCOP
Port Charges Paid by Foreign Government (DNAB) .... PCGOV
Port Charges Paid by United States Army, Navy, or Air Force (DNAB) .... PCUS
Port Charlotte, FL [*FM radio station call letters*] .... WEEJ
Port Charlotte, FL [*FM radio station call letters*] (RBYB) .... WFSN-FM
Port Charlotte, FL [*AM radio station call letters*] (RBYB) .... WKII
Port Charlotte, FL [*FM radio station call letters*] .... WVIJ
Port Check BIT [*Binary Digit*] [*Telecommunications*] (TEL) .... PCB
Port Chester Public Library, Port Chester, NY [*Library symbol Library of Congress*] (LCLS) .... NPtc
Port Chicago (AD) .... Port Chi
Port Clarence [*Alaska*] [*Airport symbol*] (OAG) .... KPC
Port Clarence, AK [*Location identifier FAA*] (FAAL) .... KPC
Port Clinton, OH [*Location identifier FAA*] (FAAL) .... PCW
Port Clinton, OH [*FM radio station call letters*] .... WXKR
Port Colborne Public Library, Ontario [*Library symbol National Library of Canada*] (NLC) .... OPCPL
Port Colborne Public Library, Port Colborne, ON, Canada [*Library symbol Library of Congress*] (LCLS) .... CaOPoC
Port Command Area [*Telecommunications*] (TEL) .... PCM
Port Command Store [*Telecommunications*] (TEL) .... PCS
Port Commissioners Workers' Union [*India*] .... PCWU
Port Committee (NATG) .... PC
Port Communications Area [*Telecommunications*] (TEL) .... PCA
Port Control [*Telecommunications*] (TEL) .... PC
Port Control Diagnostic [*Telecommunications*] (TEL) .... PCD
Port Control Office .... PORCO
Port Control Store [*Telecommunications*] (TEL) .... PCS
Port Control System [*Telecommunications*] (TEL) .... PCS
Port Coquitlam Public Library, British Columbia [*Library symbol National Library of Canada*] (NLC) .... BPC
Port Coquitlam Public Library, Port Coquitlam, BC, Canada [*Library symbol Library of Congress*] (LCLS) .... CaBPc
Port Dalhousie [*Ontario, Canada*] (AD) .... Port Dal
Port Detachment [*British military*] (DMA) .... P Det
Port Director .... PD
Port Director .... PORDIR
Port Dover Centennial Public Library, Ontario [*Library symbol National Library of Canada*] (NLC) .... OPD

Port Dover Centennial Public Library, Port Dover, ON, Canada [*Library symbol Library of Congress*] (LCLS) ... CaOPd
Port Dry Out [*Nuclear energy*] (NUCP) ... PDO
Port Du [*Carriage Forward*] [*French*] ... PD
Port Dues ... PD
Port Elgin Branch, Bruce County Public Library, Ontario [*Library symbol National Library of Canada*] (NLC) ... OPOEB
Port Elgin Branch Library, Port Elgin, ON, Canada [*Library symbol*] [*Library of Congress*] (LCLS) ... CaOPteOEB
Port Elgin, ON [*AM radio station call letters*] ... CFPS
Port Elizabeth [*South Africa*] [*Airport symbol*] (OAG) ... PLZ
Port Elizabeth [*South Africa*] (AD) ... Port Liz
Port Elizabeth [*New Jersey*] (AD) ... Port Liz
Port Elizabeth/H. F. Verwoerd [*South Africa*] [*ICAO location identifier*] (ICLI) ... FAPE
Port Emergency Planning Group [*NATO*] (NATG) ... PEPG
Port Engineer (DNAB) ... PE
Port Everglades Belt Line Railway [*AAR code Obsolete*] ... PEBL
Port Everglades Railway [*AAR code*] ... PER
Port Ewen Free Library, Port Ewen, NY [*Library symbol Library of Congress*] (LCLS) ... NPte
Port Expander Unit ... PEU
Port Fidalgo [*Alaska*] [*Seismograph station code, US Geological Survey*] (SEIS) ... FID
Port Flag [*Navy British*] ... PO
Port Francqui [*Zaire*] [*Airport symbol*] (AD) ... PFR
Port Fuel Injector [*Automotive engines*] ... PFI
Port Gauthier [*Ivory Coast*] [*ICAO location identifier*] (ICLI) ... DIPG
Port Gentil [*Gabon*] [*ICAO location identifier*] (ICLI) ... FOOG
Port Gentil [*Gabon*] [*Airport symbol*] (OAG) ... POG
Port Gibson, MS ... WKPG
Port Graham, AK [*Location identifier FAA*] (FAAL) ... PGM
Port Group [*Telecommunications*] (TEL) ... PG
Port Group Control [*Telecommunications*] (TEL) ... PGC
Port Group Highway [*Telecommunications*] (TEL) ... PGH
Port Group Highway Timeslot [*Telecommunications*] (TEL) ... PGHTS
Port Group Interface [*Telecommunications*] (TEL) ... PGI
Port Harcourt [*Nigeria*] [*ICAO location identifier*] (ICLI) ... DNPO
Port Harcourt [*Nigeria*] [*Airport symbol*] (OAG) ... PHC
Port Hardy [*British Columbia*] [*Seismograph station code, US Geological Survey*] (SEIS) ... PHC
Port Hardy [*Canada*] [*Airport symbol*] (OAG) ... YZT
Port Hardy, BC [*AM radio station call letters*] ... CFNI
Port Hardy, BC [*ICAO location identifier*] (ICLI) ... CYZT
Port Harrison [*Canada*] [*Airport symbol*] (OAG) ... YPH
Port Hastings Museum and Archives, Nova Scotia [*Library symbol National Library of Canada*] (NLC) ... NSPHM
Port Hawkesbury, NS [*AM radio station call letters*] ... CIGO
Port Health Officer ... PHO
Port Hedland [*Australia ICAO location identifier*] (ICLI) ... APHH
Port Hedland [*Australia ICAO location identifier*] (ICLI) ... APPA
Port Hedland [*Australia ICAO location identifier*] (ICLI) ... APPD
Port Hedland [*Australia Airport symbol*] (OAG) ... PHE
Port Heiden [*Alaska*] [*Seismograph station code, US Geological Survey Closed*] (SEIS) ... PHA
Port Heiden [*Alaska*] [*Airport symbol*] (OAG) ... PTH
Port Heiden, AK [*Location identifier FAA*] (FAAL) ... PDN
Port Heiden, AK [*Location identifier FAA*] (FAAL) ... PTH
Port Heiden, AK [*Location identifier FAA*] (FAAL) ... XPH
Port Henry, NY [*FM radio station call letters*] ... WMNM
Port Hueneme, CA [*AM radio station call letters*] ... KTRO
Port Hueneme, CA [*Location identifier FAA*] (FAAL) ... NTD
Port Huron [*Michigan*] [*ICAO location identifier*] (ICLI) ... KPHN
Port Huron [*Michigan*] [*Airport symbol*] (AD) ... PHN
Port Huron & Detroit Railroad Co. [*AAR code*] ... PHD
Port Huron Junior College [*Michigan*] ... PHJC
Port Huron, MI [*Location identifier FAA*] (FAAL) ... EYP
Port Huron, MI [*Location identifier FAA*] (FAAL) ... PHN
Port Huron, MI [*FM radio station call letters*] (RBYB) ... WGRT-FM
Port Huron, MI [*AM radio station call letters*] ... WHLS
Port Huron, MI [*FM radio station call letters*] ... WNFA
Port Huron, MI [*FM radio station call letters*] ... WORW
Port Huron, MI [*AM radio station call letters*] ... WPHM
Port Huron, MI [*FM radio station call letters*] ... WSAQ
Port Huron, MI [*FM radio station call letters*] ... WSGR
Port Identification [*Telecommunications*] (TEL) ... PID
Port Import/Export Reporting Service [*Journal of Commerce, Inc.*] [*Information service or system*] ... PIERS
Port Isabel, TX [*FM radio station call letters*] ... KVPA
Port Jackson Sydney [*Sydney, New South Wales, Australia*] (AD) ... Port Jack
Port Jefferson Elementary School, Port Jefferson, NY [*Library symbol Library of Congress*] (LCLS) ... NPjES
Port Jefferson Free Library, Port Jefferson, NY [*Library symbol Library of Congress*] (LCLS) ... NPj
Port Jefferson Station-Terryville Public Library, Port Jefferson Station, NY [*Library symbol Library of Congress*] (LCLS) ... NPjs
Port Jersey [*AAR code*] ... PJR
Port Jervis Free Public Library, Port Jervis, NY [*Library symbol Library of Congress*] (LCLS) ... NPtjer
Port Jervis, NY [*AM radio station call letters*] ... WDLC
Port Jervis, NY [*FM radio station call letters*] ... WRPJ
Port Jervis, NY [*FM radio station call letters*] ... WTSX
Port Lavaca, TX [*AM radio station call letters*] ... KGUL
Port Lavaca, TX [*FM radio station call letters*] (RBYB) ... KILE-AM
Port Lavaca, TX [*FM radio station call letters*] ... KPLV
Port Lavaka, TX [*Location identifier FAA*] (FAAL) ... PKV
Port Liaison Officer ... PLO
Port Light ... PLT
Port Lincoln [*Australia Airport symbol*] (OAG) ... PLO
Port Line [*Steamship*] (MHDW) ... PL
Port Liner Terms Charges [*Shipping*] (DS) ... PLTC
Port Lions [*Alaska*] [*Airport symbol*] (OAG) ... ORI
Port Loko [*Sierra Leone*] [*ICAO location identifier*] (ICLI) ... GFPO
Port Macquarie [*Australia Airport symbol*] (OAG) ... PQQ
Port Macquarie [*New South Wales*] [*Airport symbol*] (AD) ... PTR
Port Management Association of Eastern and Southern Africa (EA) ... PMAESA
Port Matilda, PA [*FM radio station call letters*] ... WIKN
Port McNicoll Public Library, Ontario [*Library symbol National Library of Canada*] (NLC) ... OPMN
Port McNicoll Public Library, Port McNicoll, ON, Canada [*Library symbol Library of Congress*] (LCLS) ... CaOPmn
Port Menier [*Canada*] [*Airport symbol*] (OAG) ... YPN
Port Menier, PQ [*ICAO location identifier*] (ICLI) ... CYPN
Port Meteorological Office [*National Weather Service*] ... PMO
Port Moller [*Alaska*] [*Seismograph station code, US Geological Survey*] (SEIS) ... PMA
Port Moller [*Alaska*] [*Airport symbol*] (OAG) ... PML
Port Moller Air Force Station [*Alaska*] [*ICAO location identifier*] (ICLI) ... PAPM
Port Moller, AK [*Location identifier FAA*] (FAAL) ... PML
Port Moller, AK [*Location identifier FAA*] (FAAL) ... PPX
Port Moody Public Library, British Columbia [*Library symbol National Library of Canada*] (NLC) ... BPMP
Port Moody Public Library, Port Moody, BC, Canada [*Library symbol Library of Congress*] (LCLS) ... CaBPmP
Port Moody Station Museum, British Columbia [*Library symbol National Library of Canada*] (NLC) ... BPMM
Port Moody Station Museum, Port Moody, BC, Canada [*Library symbol*] [*Library of Congress*] (LCLS) ... CaBPMM
Port Moresby [*Papua New Guinea*] [*ICAO location identifier*] (ICLI) ... AYPY
Port Moresby (AD) ... P Mor
Port Moresby [*Papua New Guinea*] [*Seismograph station code, US Geological Survey*] (SEIS) ... PMG
Port Moresby [*Papua New Guinea*] [*Airport symbol*] (OAG) ... POM
Port Neches, TX [*AM radio station call letters*] ... KUHD
Port Nelson, Exuma Island [*Bahamas*] [*ICAO location identifier*] (ICLI) ... MYRP
Port Nicholson (AD) ... P Nic
Port Nicholson [*Wellington, New Zealand*] (AD) ... Port Nick
Port Number [*Telecommunications*] (TEL) ... PT
Port Objective for Real-Time Systems [*Marine science*] (OSRA) ... PORTS
Port Objective for Real-Time Systems (USDC) ... PORTS
Port of Aerial Debarkation [*Air Force*] ... PAD
Port of Aerial Embarkation [*Air Force*] ... PAE
Port of Aerial Embarkation [*Air Force*] ... POAE
Port of Arrival ... POA
Port of Baltimore (AD) ... PoB
Port of Bristol Authority [*British*] ... PBA
Port of Call ... POC
Port of Debarkation [*Navy*] ... PD
Port of Debarkation [*Military*] ... POD
Port of Debarkation (AD) ... pod
Port of Delivery [*Shipping*] ... POD
Port of Departure (AD) ... pod
Port of Destination [*MARAD*] (TAG) ... POD
Port of Discharge [*Navy*] ... POD
Port of Embarkation [*Military*] ... P of E
Port of Embarkation [*Military*] ... PE
Port of Embarkation [*Shipping*] ... POE
Port of Embarkation (DFIT) ... POE
Port of Entry [*Shipping*] ... POE
Port of Entry [*Immigration*] (DAVI) ... PofE
Port of Geelong Authority [*Victoria, Australia*] ... PGA
Port of Houston World Trade Center, Houston, TX [*Library symbol Library of Congress*] (LCLS) ... TxHPH
Port of Loading [*Shipping*] ... POL
Port of London (ROG) ... P of L
Port of London Authority [*British*] ... PLA
Port of Miami (AD) ... PoM
Port of New Orleans (AD) ... PNO
Port of New York Authority [*Later, PANYNJ*] ... PNYA
Port of New York Authority [*Later, PANYNJ*] ... PONYA
Port of Palm Beach District [*AAR code*] ... PPBD
Port of Portland Library, Portland, OR [*Library symbol Library of Congress*] (LCLS) ... OrPP
Port of Refuge [*Shipping*] ... POR
Port of Service (AD) ... PoS
Port of Spain (AD) ... PoS
Port Of Spain [*Trinidad and Tobago*] [*Airport symbol*] (OAG) ... POS
Port of Support File (DOMA) ... POSF
Port of The Dalles (AD) ... P o TD
Port Officer ... PO
Port Operations Officer (DS) ... POO
Port Operations, Transport and Integrated Accountancy (MHDB) ... PORTIA
Port or Starboard ... P/S
Port Orford Public Library, Port Orford, OR [*Library symbol Library of Congress*] (LCLS) ... OrPto
Port Outwardbound, Starboard Homewardbound [*Refers to shaded cabins of British naval officers in the Far East*] ... POSH
Port Perry High School, Ontario [*Library symbol National Library of Canada*] (NLC) ... OPPP

Port Perry High School, Port Perry, ON, Canada [*Library symbol Library of Congress*] (LCLS) .... CaOPpP
Port Phillip (AD) .... P Php
Port Phillip [*Melbourne, Victoria, Australia*] (AD) .... Port Phil
Port Phillip Conservation Council [*Australia*] .... PPCC
Port Pipe (ADA) .... PP
Port Pirie [*Australia Airport symbol*] (OAG) .... PPI
Port Pirie (AD) .... PPr
Port Postal Office (AFM) .... PPO
Port Rexton, NF [*Television station call letters*] CBNT-1
Port Richmond [*Staten Island, New York*] (AD) .... Port Rich
Port Rowan Public Library, Ontario [*Library symbol National Library of Canada*] (NLC) .... OPR
Port Rowan Public Library, Port Rowan, ON, Canada [*Library symbol Library of Congress*] (LCLS) .... CaOPr
Port Royal [*Jamaica*] [*Seismograph station code, US Geological Survey*] (SEIS) .... PRJ
Port Royal, SC [*FM radio station call letters*] (RBYB) .... WHBZ
Port Safety and Security [*USCG*] (TAG) .... PSS
Port Said [*Egypt*] [*ICAO location identifier*] (ICLI) .... HEPS
Port Said [*Egypt*] [*Airport symbol*] (AD) .... PSD
Port St. Joe, FL [*FM radio station call letters*] .... WMTO
Port St. Joe, FL [*FM radio station call letters*] .... WPBH
Port St. Johns [*South Africa*] [*ICAO location identifier*] (ICLI) .... FAPJ
Port St. Lucie, FL [*AM radio station call letters*] .... WPSL
Port Saunders Public Library, Newfoundland [*Library symbol National Library of Canada*] (NLC) .... NFPS
Port Saunders Public Library, Port Saunders, NF, Canada [*Library symbol Library of Congress*] (LCLS) .... CaNfPS
Port Security .... PS
Port Security Detachment [*Military*] (GFGA) .... PSD
Port Security Harbor Defense (DOMA) .... PSHD
Port Security Station [*Coast Guard*] .... PSSTA
Port Security Unit [*Coast Guard*] (DOMA) .... PSU
Port Services Office [*or Officer*] (DNAB) .... PSO
Port Sharing Unit (IAA) .... PSU
Port Side Abreast (DNAB) .... P/AB
Port Side Light (IAA) .... PSLT
Port Side Out, Starboard Side Home [*British slang*] (AD) .... posdsplt
Port Stanley [*Falkland Islands*] [*Seismograph station code, US Geological Survey Closed*] (SEIS) .... PSF
Port Stanley [*Falkland Islands*] [*Airport symbol*] .... PSY
Port Stephens [*Australia Airport symbol*] (OAG) .... PTE
Port Storage Area [*Telecommunications*] (TEL) .... PSA
Port Storage Utility [*Telecommunications*] (TEL) .... PSU
Port Store [*Telecommunications*] (TEL) .... PS
Port Strobe [*Telecommunications*] (TEL) .... PS
Port Sudan [*Sudan*] [*ICAO location identifier*] (ICLI) .... HSSP
Port Sudan (AD) .... Port Sud
Port Sudan [*Sudan*] [*Airport symbol*] (OAG) .... PZU
Port Sulphur, LA [*AM radio station call letters*] .... KAGY
Port Sulphur, LA [*FM radio station call letters*] (RBYB) .... KKND-FM
Port Sulphur, LA [*FM radio station call letters*] (RBYB) .... KLJZ
Port [*or Anchorage*] Summary Report [*Navy*] (NVT) .... PORTSUM
Port Support Activity (DOMA) .... PSA
Port Swettenham [*Malaysia*] (AD) .... Port Swett
Port Talbot [*Wales*] (AD) .... Port Talb
Port Talbot Railway [*Wales*] .... PT
Port Task Force .... PTF
Port Terminal Railroad Association .... PTRA
Port Tewfik [*Egypt*] (AD) .... Port Tew
Port to Port [*Shipping*] (DS) .... P to P
Port Townsend Public Library, Port Townsend, WA [*Library symbol*] [*Library of Congress*] (LCLS) .... WaPt
Port Townsend Railroad, Inc. [*Formerly, PTS*] [*AAR code*] .... PTRR
Port Townsend Railroad, Inc. [*Later, PTRR*] [*AAR code*] .... PTS
Port Transportation Officer .... PTO
Port Utilities [*AAR code*] .... PUCC
Port Utilization Committee .... PUC
Port Vila [*New Hebrides*] [*Seismograph station code, US Geological Survey*] (SEIS) .... PVC
Port Vila [*Vanuata*] [*Airport symbol*] (OAG) VLI
Port Visit [*Navy*] (NVT) .... PTVST
Port Walter, AK [*Location identifier FAA*] (FAAL) .... PWR
Port War Signal Station [*British military*] (DMA) .... PWSS
Port Washington [*Long Island, New York*] (AD) .... Port Wash
Port Washington Public Library, Port Washington, NY [*Library symbol Library of Congress*] (LCLS) .... NPtw
Port Washington, WI [*AM radio station call letters*] .... WGLB
Port Washington, WI [*FM radio station call letters*] .... WGLB-FM
Port Wellen [*Ontario, CAN*] (AD) .... Port Wel
Port Wells [*Alaska*] [*Seismograph station code, US Geological Survey*] (SEIS) .... PWL
Port Williams [*Alaska*] [*Airport symbol*] (OAG) .... KPR
Port Williams, AK [*Location identifier FAA*] (FAAL) .... KPR
Port Workers' Committee [*British*] .... PWC
Porta Hepatis [*Anatomy*] .... PH
Porta Systems [*AMEX symbol*] (TTSB) .... PSI
Porta Systems Corp. [*Associated Press*] (SAG) .... PortSys
Porta Systems Corp. [*AMEX symbol*] (SPSG) .... PSI
Porta Westfalica [*Germany ICAO location identifier*] (ICLI) .... EDVY
Portable [*JETDS nomenclature*] .... P
Portable (KSC) .... PORT
Portable (AD) .... port
Portable (DNAB) .... PRTL

Portable (AABC) .... PTBL
Portable Acoustic Collection Equipment (MCD) .... PACE
Portable Acoustic Doppler Detector .... PADD
Portable Acoustic Monitoring System .... PAMS
Portable Acoustic Tracking System for Divers (MCD) .... PATS
Portable Aircraft Calibration Tracker [*NASA*] .... PACT
Portable Aircraft Condition Evaluator Recorder .... PACER
Portable Air-Launched Missile Telemetry Acquisition System (MCD) .... PATAS
Portable Alpha Monitor .... PAM
Portable and Extensible Data Management System (IAA) .... PEDMS
Portable Annotation Unit [*Military*] (CAAL) .... PAU
Portable Arc Furnace .... PAF
Portable Arc Melting Furnace .... PAMF
Portable Arm Control Console (KSC) .... PACC
Portable Arming System Trainer (MCD) .... PAST
Portable Array for Numerical Data Acquisition [*Instrumentation*] .... PANDA
Portable Assisted Study Sequence Program [*California*] (EDAC) .... PASS
Portable Automated Mesonet [*Meteorology*] .... PAM
Portable Automated Remote Inspection System [*Failure Analysis Associates*] (RDA) .... PARIS
Portable Automatic Data Recording Equipment .... PADRE
Portable Automatic Weather Observing Station (MCD) .... PAWOS
Portable Automatic Weather Station (MUGU) .... PAWS
Portable Beacon and Scoring Unit (MCD) .... PBSU
Portable BIT [*Binary Digit*] Map [*Computer science*] .... PBM
Portable Cable Checker .... PCC
Portable Camera-Transmitter .... PCT
Portable Cesium Beam Time Standard .... PCBTS
Portable Cesium Irradiator .... PCI
Portable Cesium Time Standard .... PCTS
Portable Checkout Unit .... PCU
Portable Chest X-Ray (CPH) .... PCXR
Portable Code Processor .... PCP
Portable Coded LASER Target .... PCLT
Portable Commercial Test Equipment (NASA) .... PCTE
Portable Common Test Environment [*British*] .... PCTE
Portable Common Tools Environment (IAA) .... PCTE
Portable Communications System .... PCS
Portable Compass Indicator .... PCI
Portable Computer .... PC
Portable Computer and Community Association .... PCCA
Portable Computer Memory Card Industry Association (DOM) .... PCMCIA
Portable Computer Unit .... PCU
Portable Conference Telephone [*Bell Laboratories*] .... PCT
Portable Conformable Mask [*Microlithography*] .... PCM
Portable Data Acquisition System (MCD) .... PDAS
Portable Data Acquisition System .... PODAS
Portable Data Carrier .... PDC
Portable Data Communications [*British*] .... PDC
Portable Data Loader [*Aviation*] .... PDL
Portable Data Processing System .... PODAPS
Portable Data Store [*Computer science*] (PDAA) .... PODS
Portable Data System (MCD) .... PDS
Portable Detector and Cueing System .... PDECS
Portable Diagnostic Analyzer (SSD) .... PDA
Portable Dictionary 1 [*English/Japanese electronic dictionary*] [*Sanyo Electric*] PD1
Portable Differential Magnetometer .... PDM
Portable Digital Strain Indicator .... PDSI
Portable Distributed Objects [*Next*] .... PDO
Portable Diver Monitoring System .... PMDS
Portable Document File [*Computer science*] (PCM) .... PDF
Portable Document Format [*Computer science*] .... PDF
Portable Document Format [*Computer science*] .... pdf
Portable Drilling Rig Manufacturers Association [*Defunct*] (EA) .... PDRMA
Portable Duress Sensor (MCD) .... PDS
Portable Earth Terminal [*NASA*] .... PET
Portable Educational Tools Environment (AIE) .... PETE
Portable Electric Tool Manufacturers' Association [*British*] (BI) .... PETMA
Portable Electronic Runway Lighting (PDAA) .... PERL
Portable Electronic Telephone .... PET
Portable Electronic Traffic Analyzer [*British*] .... PETA
Portable Electronic Translator .... PET
Portable Electronic Typewriter Interface [*Applied Creative Technology, Inc.*] .... PETI
Portable Electronics Test Equipment (DNAB) .... PETE
Portable Emergency Thermal Environment .... PETE
Portable Encoder/Illustrator [*Facetious term for pre-word-processing equipment*] .... PENCIL
Portable Energy Provision (SSD) .... PEP
Portable Engine Test Stand (MCD) .... PETS
Portable Environmental Control System [*NASA*] .... PECS
Portable Environmental Measuring System .... PEMS
Portable Equipment Test Chamber (MCD) .... PETC
Portable Executable .... PE
Portable Executable File [*Computer science*] .... PE
Portable Field Recording System [*NASA*] (KSC) .... PFRS
Portable Field Trainer/Evaluator (MCD) .... PFTE
Portable Flame Thrower [*Army*] .... PFT
Portable Foot Restraint (NASA) .... PFR
Portable Fresnel-Lens Optical-Landing System (NG) .... PFLOLS
Portable Gas LASER .... PGL
Portable Ground Station .... PGS
Portable Heat Rejection System .... PHRS
Portable High-Potential Tester .... PHPT

Portable Image Display System (NASA) .... PIDS
Portable Imaging Computer .... PIC
Portable Inertial Guidance System .... PIGS
Portable Inertial Navigation System .... PINS
Portable Inflatable Recompression Chamber (MCD) .... PIRC
Portable Information Evaluation .... PIE
Portable Injection Kit .... PIK
Portable Injection Molding Kit .... PIMK
Portable Instantaneous Display and Analysis Spectrometer ... PIDAS
Portable Instrumentation Package [Military] (CAAL) .. PIP
Portable Insulin Dosage-Regulating Apparatus [Medicine] ... PIDRA
Portable Integrated Maintenance Information System ... PIMIS
Portable Intelligence Maintenance Aid [Army] (DOMA) .. PIMA
Portable Interactive Computing Object .... PiCO
Portable Interface Bond Detector (IAA) .... PIBD
Portable Keyboard .... PKB
Portable Laboratory Salinometer .... PLS
Portable Landing Light System (PDAA) .... PLLS
Portable LASER Range-Finder .... PLR
Portable Life Support Stretcher Unit [Military] (CAAL) ... PLSSU
Portable Life Support System [or Subsystem] [NASA] ... PLSS
Portable Lightweight Upper Air Sounding System (MCD) ... PLUS
Portable Low-Power [Reactor] (NRCH) .... PL
Portable Magnetic Tape .... PMT
Portable Magnetometer [NASA] .... PM
Portable Maintenance Access Terminal [Computer science] ... PMAT
Portable Maintenance Aid [Army] .... PMA
Portable Medium Power Plant [Nuclear energy] (NRCH) .. PM
Portable Memory Unit [Computer science] .... PMU
Portable Microfiche Reader [DASA Corp.] .... PMR
Portable Mine Neutralization System (MCD) .... POMINS
Portable Molding Kit .... PMK
Portable Monitoring Set (MCD) .... PMS
Portable Navigation System .... PNS
Portable Network Graphic [Computer science] (PCM) ... PNG
Portable Network Graphics [Computer science] (PCM) .. PNG
Portable Network Graphics [Computer science] (DOM) .. PNG
Portable Nursing Unit Terminal .... PNUT
Portable Ocean Platform Motion Instrumentation Package [Marine science] (MSC) ... POPMIP
Portable Oceanographic Survey System (MCD) .... POSS
Portable Operating System Interface Exchange .... POSIX
Portable Operating System Interface for Computer Environments (AAGC) ... POSIX
Portable Operating System Interface for Unix [Computer science] (PCM) ... POSIX
Portable Operating System Specification [IEEE] ...... POSIX
Portable Operating Systems for Computer Environments (AD) ... POSIX
Portable Optic-Electronic Tracker (PDAA) .... POET
Portable Orders Entry Terminal (IAA) .... POET
Portable Outdoor Toilet (AD) .... pot
Portable Outside Toilet [A unit of mobility equipment] [Military] ... POT
Portable Oxygen System (MCD) .... POS
Portable Perishable Tool System (MCD) .... PPTS
Portable Personal Computer (DGA) .... PPC
Portable Personal Shopper .... PPS
Portable Pix Map [Computer science] .... PPM
Portable Plotting Package [Nuclear energy] (NRCH) ... P3
Portable Plotting Package [Nuclear energy] (NRCH) ... PPP
Portable Pneumatic Checkout Equipment (KSC) .... PPCE
Portable Power Equipment Manufacturers Association (EA) ... PPEMA
Portable Propagation Recorder [Bell System] .... PPR
Portable Public Address System (MCD) .... PPAS
Portable Purge Equipment [NASA] .... PPE
Portable RADAR Equipment .... PRE
Portable Radiation Thermometer .... PRT
Portable Radio Telephone .... PRT
Portable Range-Finder/Illuminator .... PRFI
Portable Rechargeable Battery Association .... PRBA
Portable Rectilinear Scanning Device .... PRSD
Portable Remote Telecommunications System (DOMA) .... PORTS
Portable Remote Terminal .... PRT
Portable Rod-and-Frame Test (EDAC) .... PRFT
Portable Router Template (MCD) .... PRT
Portable Router Tool .... PRT
Portable Sanitation Association (EA) .... PSA
Portable Seismic Recorder .... PSR
Portable Seismic Recording System .... PSRS
Portable, Self-Contained, Instrument Package .... PORTAPAK
Portable Sensor Verifier (AAG) .... PSV
Portable Service Processor (IEEE) .... PSP
Portable Ship Instrumentation Package .... POSIP
Portable Simulation System (MCD) .... PSS
Portable Sound Analyzer .... PSA
Portable Standard List Processing [Computer science] ... PSL
Portable Surface Supported Diving System (PDAA) ..... PSSDS
Portable Tactual Performance Test [Child development test] [Psychology] ... P-TPT
Portable Tape Recorder .... PTR
Portable Telemetry Ground Station .... PTGS
Portable Tele-Transaction Computer [Telxon] .... PTC
Portable Temperature Control (KSC) .... PTC
Portable Test Equipment (AAG) .... PTE
Portable Test Unit .... PTU
Portable Toilet (AD) .... portalet

Portable Toxic Vapor Detector .... PTVD
Portable Traffic Monitor [Telecommunications] (TEL) . PTM
Portable Underwater Tracking Transducer .... PUTT
Portable Vapor Detector .... PVD
Portable Vehicle Analyzer [Auto repair] [Electronics] ... PVA
Portable Vehicular Ramp [MTMC] (TAG) .... PVR
Portable Video Tape Recorder .... PVTR
Portable Voice Communications System .... PVCS
Portable Water (AD) .... pot w
Portable Water Coolant Circulator .... POWACO
Portable Wear Metal Analyzer [Air Force] .... PWMA
Portable Welding Machine .... PWM
Portable Word Processor .... CTAC
Portable Word Processor .... PWP
Portable X-Ray Unit .... PXU
Portacaval [Medicine] .... PC
Portacaval Anastomosis [Animal model of chronic liver disease] ... PCA
Portacaval Bypass [Cardiology] (DMAA) .... PCB
Portacaval Shunt [Medicine] .... PCS
Portacaval Transposition [Medicine] (MAE) .... PCT
PortaCom Wireless [VS, Exchange Symbol] (TTSB) ...... PCW
Portage (BARN) .... por
Portage [Alaska] [Seismograph station code, US Geological Survey] (SEIS) ... PTE
Portage County District Library, Hiram, OH [Library symbol Library of Congress] (LCLS) ... OHirP
Portage Creek [Alaska] [Airport symbol] (OAG) .... PCA
Portage Free Public Library, Portage, WI [Library symbol Library of Congress] (LCLS) ... WP
Portage, IN [AM radio station call letters] .... WNDZ
Portage Industries Corp. [Associated Press] (SAG) ... Portage
Portage Industries Corp. [AMEX symbol] (SPSG) .... PTG
Portage La Prairie, MB [AM radio station call letters] ... CFRY
Portage La Prairie, MB [Television station call letters] ... CHMI
Portage La Prairie, MB [ICAO location identifier] (ICLI) ... CYPG
Portage La Prairie Public Library, Portage La Prairie, MB, Canada [Library symbol Library of Congress] (LCLS) ... CaMPlp
Portage Lake District Library, Houghton, MI [Library symbol Library of Congress] (LCLS) ... MiHP
Portage Lake District Library, Houghton, MI [Library symbol] [Library of Congress] (LCLS) ... MiHPL
Portage, MI [FM radio station call letters] .... WFAT
Portage, MI [AM radio station call letters] (RBYB) .. WNWN
Portage, MI [FM radio station call letters] .... WRKR
Portage, PA [AM radio station call letters] .... WZGO
Portage, PA [FM radio station call letters] .... WZGO-FM
Portage Plains Regional Library, Portage La Prairie, Manitoba [Library symbol National Library of Canada] (NLC) ... MPLP
Portage Press, Portage, IN [Library symbol Library of Congress] (LCLS) ... InPorP
Portage Public Library, Portage, MI [Library symbol Library of Congress] (LCLS) ... MiPor
Portage Public Schools, Portage, MI [OCLC symbol] (OCLC) ... EXP
Portage Public Schools, Portage, MI [Library symbol Library of Congress] (LCLS) ... MiPorPS
Portage Township Schools, Portage, IN [Library symbol Library of Congress] (LCLS) ... InPorS
Portage, WI [FM radio station call letters] (RBYB) .. WBKY-FM
Portage, WI [FM radio station call letters] .... WDDC
Portage, WI [FM radio station call letters] .... WPDR
Portage, WI [FM radio station call letters] .... WUSX
Portageville [Missouri] [Seismograph station code, US Geological Survey Closed] (SEIS) ... PTG
Portageville, MO [AM radio station call letters] .... KMIS
Portal (VRA) .... ptl
Portal Blood Flow [Physiology] .... PBF
Portal Cirrhosis [Medicine] (DMAA) .... PC
Portal Fibrosis [Medicine] .... PF
Portal Hypertension [Medicine] .... PHT
Portal of Entry [Bacteriology] .... P of E
Portal Pressure Gradient [Medicine] (DMAA) .... PPG
Portal Systemic Encephalopathy [Medicine] .... PSE
Portal Tract [Anatomy] .... PT
Portal Tributary Blood Flow [Physiology] .... PTBF
Portal Vein [Anatomy] .... PV
Portal Vein Inflow [Physiology] .... PVI
Portal Vein Thrombosis [Physiology] .... PVT
Portal Venous Flow [Physiology] .... PVF
Portal Venous Pressure [Physiology] .... PVP
Portal Venous Velocity [Physiology] .... PVV
Portales, NM [FM radio station call letters] .... KENW
Portales, NM [Television station call letters] ...... KENW-TV
Portales, NM [AM radio station call letters] .... KSEL
Portales, NM [FM radio station call letters] .... KSEL-FM
Portales, NM [Location identifier FAA] (FAAL) .... PRZ
Portales Public Library, Portales, NM [Library symbol Library of Congress] (LCLS) ... NmP
Portalon [Costa Rica] [ICAO location identifier] (ICLI) ... MRPL
Portal-to-Portal Act of 1947 (WYGK) .... PTPA
Portametric Voltmeter Bridge .... PVB
Port-Au-Prince [Haiti] [ICAO location identifier] (ICLI) ... MTEG
Port-Au-Prince [Haiti] [Airport symbol] (OAG) .... PAP
Port-Au-Prince/Internacional [Haiti] [ICAO location identifier] (ICLI) ... MTPP
Port-Aux-Francais [Formerly, Kerguelen] [France] [Geomagnetic observatory code] ... KGL
Port-Aux-Francais [Kerguelen Islands] [Seismograph station code, US Geological Survey Closed] (SEIS) ... PAF

Portavideo [*Vancouver Stock Exchange symbol*] .... PMM
Port-Cartier, PQ [*AM radio station call letters*] .... CIPC
Port-De-Paix [*Haiti*] [*ICAO location identifier*] (ICLI) .... MTPX
Portec, Inc. [*NYSE symbol*] (SPSG) .... POR
Portec, Inc. [*Associated Press*] (SAG) .... Portec
Ported Coax Cable Sensor [*Military*] (DWSG) .... PCCS
Ported Pressure Switch [*Automotive engineering*] .... PPS
Ported Vacuum Switch [*Automotive engineering*] .... PVS
Ported-Coax Intrusion Sensor [*Military*] (INF) .... PINTS
Porte-Oceane [*Record label*] [*France*] .... POc
Porter (DSUE) .... PORT
Porter .... PRTR
Porter County Herald, Hebron, IN [*Library symbol Library of Congress*] (LCLS) .... InHebPH
Porter County Recorder's Office, Valparaiso, IN [*Library symbol Library of Congress*] (LCLS) .... InValCR
Porter House [*Initials often used as a pattern on clothing designed by this firm*] .... PH
Porter McLeod National Retail [*NASDAQ symbol*] (SAG) .... PMNR
Porter McLeod National Retail [*Associated Press*] (SAG) .... PrtMcled
Porter McLeod Natl Retail [*NASDAQ symbol*] (TTSB) .... PMNR
Porter Memorial Hospital, Physicians' Library, Denver, CO [*Library symbol Library of Congress*] (LCLS) .... CoDPo-M
Porter Need Satisfaction Questionnaire (EDAC) .... PNSQ
Porter/Novelli [*A public relations firm*] [*New York, NY*] (WDMC) .... P/N
Porter Public Library, Westlake, OH [*OCLC symbol*] (OCLC) .... OPW
Porter Wagoner International Fan Club [*Defunct*] (EA) .... PWIFC
Porterfield Airplane Club (EA) .... PAC
Porter-Phelps-Hunting Foundation, Hadley, MA [*Library symbol*] [*Library of Congress*] (LCLS) .... MHadP
Porter's Alabama Reports [*A publication*] (DLA) .... Port (Ala)
Porter's Alabama Reports [*A publication*] (DLA) .... Port Ala R
Porter's Alabama Reports [*A publication*] (DLA) .... Porter
Porter's Alabama Reports [*A publication*] (DLA) .... Porter (Ala)
Porter's Alabama Reports [*A publication*] (DLA) .... Porter R
Porter's Alabama Reports [*A publication*] (DLA) .... Porter's Ala R
Porter's Alabama Reports [*A publication*] (DLA) .... Porter's R
Porter's Alabama Reports [*A publication*] (DLA) .... Porter's Repts
Porter's Alabama Supreme Court Reports [*1834-39*] [*A publication*] (DLA) .... Port
Porter's Indiana Reports [*3-7 Indiana*] [*A publication*] (DLA) .... Port
Porter's Indiana Reports [*3-7 Indiana*] [*A publication*] (DLA) .... Porter
Porter's Laws of Insurance [*A publication*] (DLA) .... Port Ins
Porter-Silber Chromogen [*Medicine*] (MAE) .... PS
Porter-Silber Chromogen [*Medicine*] (MAE) .... PSC
Porterville, CA [*FM radio station call letters*] .... KIOO
Porterville, CA [*Television station call letters*] .... KKAG
Porterville, CA [*AM radio station call letters*] .... KTIP
Porterville, CA [*Location identifier FAA*] (FAAL) .... PTV
Porterville Public Library, Porterville, CA [*Library symbol Library of Congress*] (LCLS) .... CPor
Porterville State Hospital, Porterville, CA [*Library symbol Library of Congress*] (LCLS) .... CPorH
Porteus Maze Test [*Medicine*] (MAE) .... PMT
Portfolio [*A publication*] .... PF
Portfolio (WGA) .... PORT
Portfolio Evaluation Plan [*Australia*] .... PEP
Portfolio Insurance [*Finance*] .... PI
Portimao [*Portugal ICAO location identifier*] (ICLI) .... LPPM
Portion .... P
Portion .... POR
Portion (ROG) .... PORTN
Portion Control [*Food service*] .... PC
Portland [*British ICAO location identifier*] (ICLI) .... EGDP
Portland [*Diocesan abbreviation*] [*Oregon*] (TOCD) .... P
Portland [*Oregon*] [*Airport symbol*] (OAG) .... PDX
Portland [*Maine*] [*Seismograph station code, US Geological Survey Closed*] (SEIS) .... POR
Portland (AD) .... Por
Portland [*Diocesan abbreviation*] [*Maine*] (TOCD) .... PRT
Portland [*Oregon*] [*Seismograph station code, US Geological Survey*] (SEIS) .... PTD
Portland [*Australia Airport symbol*] (OAG) .... PTJ
Portland [*Maine*] [*Airport symbol*] (OAG) .... PWM
Portland Air Defense Sector (SAA) .... POADS
Portland & Ogdensburgh Railroad .... P & O
Portland Branch, Rideau Lakes Union Library, Ontario [*Library symbol National Library of Canada*] (BIB) .... OPRL
Portland Cement .... PC
Portland Cement [*Technical drawings*] (DAC) .... PORT CEM
Portland Cement Association (EA) .... PCA
Portland Cement Concrete .... PCC
Portland City Archives, Portland, OR [*Library symbol Library of Congress*] (LCLS) .... OrP-A
Portland Community College, Portland, OR [*Library symbol Library of Congress*] (LCLS) .... OrPPC
Portland District Library, Portland, MI [*Library symbol Library of Congress*] (LCLS) .... MiPtl
Portland General Corp. [*NYSE symbol*] (SPSG) .... PGN
Portland General Corp. [*Associated Press*] (SAG) .... PortGC
Portland General Electric Co. [*NYSE symbol*] (SAG) .... PGB
Portland General Electric Co. [*Associated Press*] (SAG) PortG35
Portland General Electric Co., Library, Portland, OR [*OCLC symbol*] (OCLC) .... PGE
Portland General Electric Co., Portland, OR [*Library symbol Library of Congress*] (LCLS) .... OrPGE
Portland Genl Corp. [*NYSE symbol*] (TTSB) .... PGN
Portland Genl Elec 8.25% 'QUIDS' [*NYSE symbol*] (TTSB) .... PGB
Portland Grain Exchange (EA) .... PGE
Portland, IN [*Location identifier FAA*] (FAAL) .... PLD
Portland, IN [*FM radio station call letters*] (RBYB) .... WBSJ-FM
Portland, IN [*AM radio station call letters*] .... WPGW
Portland, IN [*FM radio station call letters*] .... WPGW-FM
Portland/International [*Oregon*] [*ICAO location identifier*] (ICLI) .... KPDX
Portland/International Jetport [*Maine*] [*ICAO location identifier*] (ICLI) .... KPWM
Portland, Maine (AD) .... P Me
Portland, ME [*Location identifier FAA*] (FAAL) .... GCS
Portland, ME [*Location identifier FAA*] (FAAL) .... PWM
Portland, ME [*FM radio station call letters*] .... WBLM
Portland, ME [*Television station call letters*] .... WCSH
Portland, ME [*FM radio station call letters*] .... WCSO
Portland, ME [*AM radio station call letters*] .... WGAN
Portland, ME [*Television station call letters*] .... WGME
Portland, ME [*AM radio station call letters*] .... WLOB
Portland, ME [*FM radio station call letters*] .... WMEA
Portland, ME [*FM radio station call letters*] .... WMGX
Portland, ME [*AM radio station call letters*] .... WPOR
Portland, ME [*FM radio station call letters*] .... WPOR-FM
Portland, ME [*Television station call letters*] .... WPXT
Portland, ME [*AM radio station call letters*] .... WZAN
Portland Motor Boat Club [*Oregon*] (AD) .... PMBC
Portland Opera Association [*Oregon*] (AD) .... POA
Portland, OR [*Location identifier FAA*] (FAAL) .... GPO
Portland, OR [*Location identifier FAA*] (FAAL) .... IAP
Portland, OR [*Television station call letters*] .... KATU
Portland, OR [*AM radio station call letters*] .... KBBT
Portland, OR [*AM radio station call letters*] .... KBNP
Portland, OR [*FM radio station call letters*] .... KBOO
Portland, OR [*AM radio station call letters*] .... KBPS
Portland, OR [*FM radio station call letters*] .... KBPS-FM
Portland, OR [*FM radio station call letters*] .... KBVM
Portland, OR [*AM radio station call letters*] .... KEX
Portland, OR [*FM radio station call letters*] .... KGON
Portland, OR [*Television station call letters*] .... KGW
Portland, OR [*FM radio station call letters*] .... KINK
Portland, OR [*AM radio station call letters*] .... KKEY
Portland, OR [*AM radio station call letters*] (RBYB) .... KKPZ
Portland, OR [*FM radio station call letters*] .... KKRZ
Portland, OR [*FM radio station call letters*] .... KKSN
Portland, OR [*Television station call letters*] .... KNMT
Portland, OR [*Television station call letters*] .... KOIN
Portland, OR [*FM radio station call letters*] .... KOPB
Portland, OR [*Television station call letters*] .... KOPB-TV
Portland, OR [*AM radio station call letters*] (RBYB) .... KOTK
Portland, OR [*AM radio station call letters*] .... KPDQ
Portland, OR [*FM radio station call letters*] .... KPDQ-FM
Portland, OR [*Television station call letters*] .... KPTV
Portland, OR [*FM radio station call letters*] .... KRRC
Portland, OR [*FM radio station call letters*] .... KUFO
Portland, OR [*FM radio station call letters*] .... KUPL-FM
Portland, OR [*AM radio station call letters*] .... KWJJ
Portland, OR [*FM radio station call letters*] .... KWJJ-FM
Portland, OR [*AM radio station call letters*] .... KXL
Portland Oregonian [*A publication*] (AD) .... PO
Portland Port Authority [*Australia*] .... PPA
Portland Problem Behavior Checklist (EDAC) .... PPBC
Portland Problem Behavior Checklist - Revised [*Educational test*] .... PPBC-R
Portland Public Docks (AD) .... PPD
Portland Public Library, Portland, ME [*Library symbol Library of Congress*] (LCLS) .... MeP
Portland Public Library, Portland, ME [*OCLC symbol*] (OCLC) .... PPN
Portland Public School District, Portland, OR [*Library symbol Library of Congress*] (LCLS) .... OrPPS
Portland Railroad .... PORT
Portland Society for Calligraphy (EA) .... PSC
Portland State University (GAGS) .... Portland St U
Portland State University .... PSU
Portland State University, Portland, OR [*Library symbol Library of Congress*] (LCLS) .... OrPS
Portland Terminal Co. [*AAR code*] .... PTM
Portland Terminal R. R. Co. [*Formerly, Northern Pacific Terminal R. R.*] [*AAR code*] .... NPT
Portland, TN [*AM radio station call letters*] .... WQKR
Portland Traction Co. [*AAR code*] .... PRTD
Portland, TX [*FM radio station call letters*] .... KRAD
Portland University. Law Review [*A publication*] (DLA) .... Port UL Rev
Portland University. Law Review [*A publication*] (DLA) .... Portland UL Rev
Portmadoc (AD) .... Pmd
Portmanteau (DSUE) .... PORT
Portneuf Library District, Chubbuck, ID [*Library symbol*] [*Library of Congress*] (LCLS) .... IdChP
Porto [*Portugal ICAO location identifier*] (ICLI) .... LPPR
Porto [*Serro Do Pilar*] [*Portugal*] [*Seismograph station code, US Geological Survey*] (SEIS) .... PTO
Porto Alegre [*Sao Tome*] [*ICAO location identifier*] (ICLI) .... FPPA
Porto Alegre [*Brazil*] [*Airport symbol*] (OAG) .... POA
Porto Alegre/Canoas [*Brazil ICAO location identifier*] (ICLI) .... SBCO
Porto Alegre/Salgado Filho [*Brazil ICAO location identifier*] (ICLI) .... SBPA
Porto Alfonso [*Brazil*] [*Airport symbol*] (AD) .... PXX
Porto Amboim [*Angola*] [*ICAO location identifier*] (ICLI) .... FNPA
Porto Amboin [*Angola*] [*Airport symbol*] (OAG) .... PBN

Porto Amelia [*Mozambique*] [*Airport symbol*] (AD) ... POL
Porto Cannone [*Italy*] [*Seismograph station code, US Geological Survey*] (SEIS) ... PTC
Porto De Moz [*Brazil ICAO location identifier*] (ICLI) ... SBMZ
Porto D'Ischia [*Italy*] [*Seismograph station code, US Geological Survey Closed*] (SEIS) ... PDI
Porto Heli [*Greece*] [*ICAO location identifier*] (ICLI) ... LGHL
Porto Murtinho [*Brazil*] [*Airport symbol*] (AD) ... PMJ
Porto Nacional [*Brazil*] [*Airport symbol*] (AD) ... PNB
Porto Nacional [*Brazil ICAO location identifier*] (ICLI) ... SBPN
Porto Santo [*Portugal*] [*Airport symbol*] (OAG) ... PXO
Porto Santo, Porto Santo Island [*Portugal ICAO location identifier*] (ICLI) ... LPPS
Porto Seguro [*Brazil*] [*Airport symbol*] (OAG) ... BPS
Porto Seguro [*Brazil*] [*Airport symbol*] (AD) ... ORO
Porto Velho [*Brazil*] [*Airport symbol*] (OAG) ... PVH
Porto Velho [*Brazil ICAO location identifier*] (ICLI) ... SBPH
Porto Velho [*Brazil ICAO location identifier*] (ICLI) ... SBPV
Port-Of-Spain/Piarco, Trinidad [*Trinidad and Tobago*] [*ICAO location identifier*] (ICLI) ... TTPP
Port-Of-Spain/Port-Of-Spain, Trinidad [*Trinidad and Tobago*] [*ICAO location identifier*] (ICLI) ... TTPS
Portoroz [*Former Yugoslavia*] [*ICAO location identifier*] (ICLI) ... LYPZ
Portoviejo [*Ecuador*] [*Airport symbol*] (OAG) ... PVO
Portoviejo [*Ecuador*] [*ICAO location identifier*] (ICLI) ... SEPV
Portrait ... POR
Portrait ... PORT
Portrait (AD) ... port
Portrait (VRA) ... ptrt
Ports [*Commonly used*] (OPSA) ... PORTS
Ports [*Postal Service standard*] (OPSA) ... PRTS
Ports ... PRTS
Ports and Beaches (NATG) ... PB
Ports and Beaches and Inland Waterways Transports [*Military*] (NATG) ... PB/IWT
Ports and Inland Waterways ... PIW
Ports and Waterways ... PW
Ports and Waterways Safety Act (GFGA) ... PWSA
Ports Canada ... PCA
Ports Canada ... PRTC
Ports Canada, Ottawa, ON, Canada [*Library symbol*] [*Library of Congress*] (LCLS) ... CaOOPOR
Ports Canada, Ottawa, Ontario [*Library symbol National Library of Canada*] (NLC) ... OOPOR
Ports of New South Wales Journal [*A publication*] ... Ports NSW Jl
Port(s) of Support (DOMA) ... POS
Ports [*Harbors*] **Performance Indicator** [*Australia*] ... PPI
Ports Report File (MCD) ... PORTSREP
Portsmouth [*England*] [*Airport symbol*] (AD) ... PME
Portsmouth [*City in England*] ... PORTS
Portsmouth [*County borough in England*] ... PORTSM
Portsmouth [*New Hampshire*] [*Airport symbol*] (AD) ... PSM
Portsmouth & Sunderland Newspapers Ltd., Portsmouth, Hants, United Kingdom [*Library symbol Library of Congress*] (LCLS) ... UkPS
Portsmouth Athenaeum, Portsmouth, NH [*Library symbol Library of Congress*] (LCLS) ... NhPoA
Portsmouth Bank Shares [*NASDAQ symbol*] (TTSB) ... POBS
Portsmouth Bank Shares [*Associated Press*] (SAG) ... PortsBk
Portsmouth Bank Shares, Inc. [*NASDAQ symbol*] (NQ) ... POBS
Portsmouth Bank Shares, Inc. [*Associated Press*] (SAG) ... PortBk
Portsmouth Gaseous Diffusion Plant (DOGT) ... PORTS
Portsmouth Gaseous Diffusion Plant [*Department of Energy*] [*Portsmouth, OH*] (GAAI) ... PORTS
Portsmouth Naval Shipyard [*New Hampshire*] ... PNS
Portsmouth Naval Shipyard [*New Hampshire*] ... PNSY
Portsmouth, NH [*Location identifier FAA*] (FAAL) ... PSM
Portsmouth, NH [*FM radio station call letters*] ... WHEB
Portsmouth, NH [*AM radio station call letters*] (RBYB) ... WTMN
Portsmouth, OH [*Location identifier FAA*] (FAAL) ... PMH
Portsmouth, OH [*AM radio station call letters*] ... WNXT
Portsmouth, OH [*FM radio station call letters*] ... WNXT-FM
Portsmouth, OH [*FM radio station call letters*] ... WOHP
Portsmouth, OH [*FM radio station call letters*] ... WOSP
Portsmouth, OH [*FM radio station call letters*] ... WPAY
Portsmouth, OH [*FM radio station call letters*] ... WPAY-FM
Portsmouth, OH [*Television station call letters*] ... WPBO
Portsmouth, OH [*Television station call letters*] ... WUXA
Portsmouth/Pease Air Force Base [*New Hampshire*] [*ICAO location identifier*] (ICLI) ... KPSM
Portsmouth Priory, Portsmouth, RI [*Library symbol Library of Congress*] (LCLS) ... RPorP
Portsmouth Public Library, Portsmouth, OH [*Library symbol Library of Congress*] (LCLS) ... OPosm
Portsmouth Public Library, Portsmouth, VA [*Library symbol Library of Congress*] (LCLS) ... ViPo
Portsmouth, RI [*FM radio station call letters*] ... WJHD
Portsmouth, VA [*Location identifier FAA*] (FAAL) ... PVG
Portsmouth, VA [*Television station call letters*] ... WAVY
Portsmouth, VA [*Television station call letters*] ... WGNT
Portsmouth, VA [*AM radio station call letters*] (RBYB) ... WGPL-AM
Portsmouth, VA [*AM radio station call letters*] ... WPCE
Portsmouth, VA [*AM radio station call letters*] ... WPMH
Portsmouth, VA [*AM radio station call letters*] ... WSVY
Portugais [*Portuguese*] [*French*] (AD) ... Portug
Portugal [*MARC geographic area code Library of Congress*] (LCCP) ... e-po--
Portugal [*IYRU nationality code*] ... P
Portugal ... PG
Portugal (ODBW) ... Pg
Portugal [*MARC country of publication code Library of Congress*] (LCCP) ... po
Portugal [*NATO*] ... PO
Portugal (AD) ... Por
Portugal (VRA) ... Port
Portugal (ODBW) ... Port
Portugal ... PORT
Portugal [*ANSI three-letter standard code*] (CNC) ... PRT
Portugal [*ANSI two-letter standard code*] (CNC) ... PT
Portugal Fund [*NYSE symbol*] (SPSG) ... PGF
Portugal Fund [*Associated Press*] (SAG) ... Portugl
Portugal Telecom ADS [*NYSE symbol*] (TTSB) ... PT
Portugal Telecom SA [*Associated Press*] (SAG) ... PortglT
Portugal Telecom SA [*NYSE symbol*] (SAG) ... PT
Portugalia, Companhia Portuguesa de Transportes Aeros SA [*Portugal ICAO designator*] (FAAC) ... PGA
Portugese Air Force [*ICAO designator*] (FAAC) ... AFP
Portugese Overseas Province (AD) ... POP
Portugiesisch [*Portuguese*] [*German*] (AD) ... port
Portuguese (ODBW) ... Pg
Portuguese [*Language, etc.*] ... PG
Portuguese [*Language, etc.*] (DLA) ... Po
Portuguese [*MARC language code Library of Congress*] (LCCP) ... por
Portuguese ... POR
Portuguese (AD) ... Por
Portuguese (ODBW) ... Port
Portuguese (ROG) ... PTG
Portuguese Air Force ... PAF
Portuguese American Progressive Club of New York (EA) ... PAPCNY
Portuguese China (AD) ... Port Chi
Portuguese Communist Party ... PCP
Portuguese Continental Union of the United States of America (EA) ... PCU
Portuguese Cultural Centre of Melbourne [*Victoria, Australia*] ... PCCM
Portuguese East Africa [*Mozambique*] ... PEA
Portuguese Government Trade Office (EA) ... PGTO
Portuguese Guinea [*Guinea-Bissau*] [*MARC geographic area code Library of Congress*] (LCCP) ... f-pg--
Portuguese Guinea [*Guinea-Bissau*] [*MARC country of publication code Library of Congress*] (LCCP) ... pg
Portuguese India (AD) ... Port Ind
Portuguese Language Development Group [*Modern Language Association of America*] (AEBS) ... PLDG
Portuguese National Tourist Office (EA) ... PNTO
Portuguese Navy ... PNY
Portuguese Navy [*ICAO designator*] (FAAC) ... PON
Portuguese Pharmacopoeia [*A publication*] ... Port P
Portuguese Popular Democrats ... PPD
Portuguese Timor [*a-io (Indonesia) used in records cataloged after April 1980*] [*MARC geographic area code Library of Congress*] (LCCP) ... a-pt--
Portuguese Timor (AD) ... Port Tim
Portuguese Timor [*io (Indonesia) used in records cataloged after January 1978*] [*MARC country of publication code Library of Congress*] (LCCP) ... pt
Portuguese Trade Commission (EA) ... PTC
Portuguese Water Dog Club of America (EA) ... PWDCA
Portuguese West Africa [*Angola*] ... PWA
Port-Vila/Bauerfield [*Vanuatu*] [*ICAO location identifier*] (ICLI) ... NVVV
Port-Wine Stain ... PWS
Porvenir [*Panama*] [*Airport symbol*] (OAG) ... PVE
Porvenir [*Chile*] [*Airport symbol*] (AD) ... WPR
Porvenir/Capitan Fuentes Martinez [*Chile*] [*ICAO location identifier*] (ICLI) ... SCFM
Porvoo [*Finland*] [*Seismograph station code, US Geological Survey Closed*] (SEIS) ... PRV
POS Pilot Plant Corp., Saskatoon, SK, Canada [*Library symbol Library of Congress*] (LCLS) ... CaSSPP
POS Pilot Plant Corp., University of Saskatchewan Campus, Saskatoon, Saskatchewan [*Library symbol National Library of Canada*] (NLC) ... SSPP
Posa Piano [*Handle with Care*] [*Shipping*] [*Italian*] ... PP
Posadas [*Argentina*] [*Airport symbol*] (OAG) ... PSS
Posadas [*Argentina ICAO location identifier*] (ICLI) ... SARP
Poseidon Automatic Cable Tester [*Missiles*] (DNAB) ... PACT
Poseidon [*Missile*] **Communication Improvement Program** [*Navy*] ... PCIP
Poseidon Design Information Memo [*Missiles*] ... PODIM
Poseidon Information Retrieval System [*Missiles*] ... PIRS
Poseidon Random Access Memory [*Missiles*] ... PRAM
Poseidon Random-Access Memory (AD) ... Pram
Poseidon Software Working Group [*Missiles*] ... POSWG
Poseidon Technical Information Bulletin [*A publication*] (AD) ... POTIB
Poseidon Test Analysis Software Working Group [*Missiles*] ... POTASWG
Poseidon Undersea Launching System (NOAA) ... PULS
Pos-Escrito [*Postscript*] [*Portuguese*] ... PS
Posey County News, Poseyville, IN [*Library symbol Library of Congress*] (LCLS) ... InPosN
Posey's Unreported Cases [*Texas*] [*A publication*] (ILCA) ... Posey
Posey's Unreported Cases [*Texas*] [*A publication*] (DLA) ... Posey Unrep Cas
Posey's Unreported Cases [*Texas*] [*A publication*] (DLA) ... Tex Unrep Cas
Posigrade Rocket Motor (NASA) ... PRM
Position ... P
Position (WGA) ... PN
Position (AD) ... pn
Position (IAA) ... PON
Position (KSC) ... POS
Position (AD) ... pos
Position (WDMC) ... pos
Position (AD) ... posit

Position (NVT) ... POSIT
Position (AFM) ... POSN
Position (AD) ... posn
Position ... PSN
Position ... PSTN
Position Adjusting Type ... PAT
Position Analog Unit [*Manufacturing term*] ... PAU
Position Analysis Questionnaire ... PAQ
Position and Altitude Monitor (MCD) ... PAM
Position and Azimuth Determining System [*Aviation*] ... PADS
Position and Homing Indicator ... PHI
Position and Homing Inertial Navigator ... PHIN
Position and Intended Movement [*or Maneuver*] (NATG) ... PIM
Position and Pay Management [*Army*] (AABC) ... PPM
Position and Proper Motion [*Catalog of star positions*] ... PPM
Position and Time-Resolved Ion Counting [*Detector*] ... PATRIC
Position and Velocity ... PAV
Position and Velocity Computer ... PVC
Position and Velocity Extraction ... PAVE
Position and Velocity Tracking (IAA) ... PAV
Position and Velocity Tracking ... PAVT
Position Angle [*Astronomy*] ... PA
Position Approximate [*Nautical charts*] ... PA
Position, Attitude, Trajectory-Control [*Aerospace*] (AAG) ... PAT-C
Position Bearing and Distance Indicator (MCD) ... PBDI
Position Classification (GFGA) ... PC
Position Classification Field Office ... PCFO
Position Classification Standard [*Civil Service*] ... PCS
Position Computer (IAA) ... POCO
Position Control Number (AFM) ... PCN
Position Control System ... PCS
Position Correct (CAAL) ... POSCOR
Position, Course, and Speed ... PCS
Position Depth Charge ... PDC
Position Description ... PD
Position Dilution of Position [*Navigation systems*] ... PDOP
Position Dilution of Precision ... PDOP
Position Display Parallax Corrected ... PDPC
Position Distribution Report [*DoD*] ... PDR
Position Document ... PD
Position Doubtful [*Nautical charts*] ... PD
Position Effect [*Parapsychology*] ... PE
Position Encoding Module (CAAL) ... PEM
Position Error ... PE
Position Error Correction (DA) ... PEC
Position Failure ... PF
Position Feedback (MCD) ... PFB
Position Field Classification Officer ... PFCO
Position Finder [*British military*] (DMA) ... PF
Position Finding Instrument (DS) ... PFI
Position Fixing Device (ADA) ... PFD
Position Fixing Navigation System (AABC) ... PFNS
Position Guide (MCD) ... PG
Position in Miles (MCD) ... PIM
Position Independent Code [*Telecommunications*] (TEL) ... PIC
Position Indicating General Measuring Instrument ... PIGMI
Position Indicating Probe (IEEE) ... PIP
Position Indicating Radio Beacon ... PIRB
Position Indicator [*Army*] ... PI
Position Indicator ... PIN
Position Indicator System ... PIS
Position Initialization (GAVI) ... POS INIT
Position Iterative Operation ... PIO
Position Keeper ... PK
Position Keeping Computer ... PKC
Position Launch [*Search mode wherein X signifies the launch mode number*] (MCD) ... PLX
Position Launch/Bearing Only Launch ... PLBOL
Position Line [*Navigation*] ... PL
Position Location [*DoD*] ... PL
Position Location and Aircraft Communication Equipment ... PLACE
Position Location and Communications Experiment [*NASA*] ... PLACE
Position Location and Navigation System ... PLANS
Position Location and Reporting System [*Military*] (INF) ... PLARS
Position Location Post Processor (MCD) ... PLPP
Position Location, Reporting, and Control of Tactical Aircraft [*Military*] ... PLRACTA
Position Location Reporting System [*Military*] ... PLRS
Position Location Reporting System/Tactical Information Distribution Systems [*Military*] (RDA) ... PLRS/TIDS
Position Location System [*Army*] ... PLS
Position Management Program ... PMP
Position Modulator (NRCH) ... POM
Position/Navigation [*System*] [*Military*] (INF) ... POS/NAV
Position Number (ADA) ... PN
Position Number [*Military*] (ADDR) ... POSNO
Position of Earth Satellite in Digital Display (MCD) ... POESID
Position of Germany [*British World War II*] ... POG
Position of Responsibility (ADA) ... POR
Position Offered ... PO
Position Operational, Meteorological Aircraft Report ... POMAR
Position Paper (MCD) ... PP
Position Pennant [*Navy British*] ... PN
Position Record (NASA) ... PR
Position Reference (GAVI) ... POS REF
Position Register (IAA) ... PR
Position Relief Briefing Observed [*Aviation*] (FAAC) ... PRBO
Position Report [*Air Force*] ... POREP
Position Report [*Air Force*] ... PR
Position Report [*Aviation*] (FAAC) ... PSNRP
Position Report Printout ... PRP
Position Reports ... POSITREPS
Position Sensitive Light Detector (IAA) ... PSD
Position Sensor (MCD) ... PSNSR
Position Subject to Return of Incumbent [*Aviation*] (FAAC) ... PSRI
Position Subject to Rotating Shifts [*Aviation*] (FAAC) ... PSRS
Position Track RADAR ... PTR
Position Vacant (ADA) ... PV
Position Value ... PV
Position Velocity-Time ... PVT
Position Wanted [*Employment*] ... PW
Positional Alcohol Nystagmus [*Physiology*] ... PAN
Positional Nystagmus [*Physiology*] (MAE) ... PN
Positional Tolerancing ... PT
Position-Determining Equipment ... PDE
Position-Determining System ... PDS
Position-Effect Variegation [*Genetics*] ... PEV
Position-Effect Variegation [*Genetics*] [*Botany*] ... PEV
Positioner ... PSNR
Positioner Antenna and Solar Panel [*NASA*] ... PA/SP
Positioner Layout and Cell Evaluator [*Robotics*] ... PLACE
Position-Event-Time ... PET
Positioning and Locating System [*Aviation*] (PDAA) ... PALS
Positioning and Navigation System ... PANS
Positioning and Orientation ... P & O
Positioning and Surveying System (MCD) ... PASS
Positioning Arm Disk ... PAD
Positioning Devices [*JETDS nomenclature*] [*Military*] (CET) ... TG
Positioning Orbital Propulsion System (MCD) ... POPS
Positioning Reporting Recording System (RDA) ... PRRS
Positioning-Head Drum (DNAB) ... PHD
Position-Navigation-Time ... PNT
Positions Equipment Task Summary (AAG) ... PETS
Position-Sensitive Proportional Counter [*Instrumentation*] ... PSPC
Position-Sensitive Proportional Detector [*For X-ray diffraction*] ... PSPD
Position-Specific Antigen ... PS
Positive [*Crystal*] ... p
Positive (IAA) ... P
Positive (AFM) ... POS
Positive (IDOE) ... pos
Positive (AD) ... pos
Positive (AD) ... posit
Positive ... POSIT
Positive (AAG) ... POST
Positive Acknowledgment and Retransmission [*Telecommunications*] (IAA) ... PAR
Positive Action Through Holistic Evaluation Program (EDAC) ... PATHE
Positive Addiction [*Self-improvement method developed by William Glasser, MD*] ... PA
Positive Airway Pressure (MAE) ... PAP
Positive and Negative Syndrome Scale [*Medicine*] (DMAA) ... PANSS
Positive Arming Link [*Military*] (DNAB) ... PAL
Positive Attitude ... PA
Positive Attitudinal Reinforcement [*In George Lee Walker novel "The Chronicles of Doodah"*] ... PAR
Positive Channel [*Telecommunications*] (IAA) ... PCH
Positive Channel Metal Oxide Semiconductor (NITA) ... P-MOS
Positive Chemical Ionization Mass Spectroscopy ... PCIMS
Positive Column (IAA) ... PC
Positive Concatenation Structures [*Mathematics*] ... PCS
Positive Conducting [*Electronics*] (IAA) ... P
Positive Continuous Engagement [*Automotive engineering*] ... PCE
Positive Continuous Ullage Control ... PCUC
Positive Control ... PC
Positive Control Area ... PCA
Positive Control Bombardment System [*Air Force*] ... PCBS
Positive Control Communication ... PCC
Positive Control Communications System ... PCCS
Positive Control Document (MCD) ... PCD
Positive Control Line ... PCL
Positive Control Route [*Aviation*] (OA) ... PCR
Positive Control Zone (DNAB) ... PCZ
Positive Controlled Airspace ... PCA
Positive Crankcase Ventilation [*For automotive antipollution systems*] ... PCV
Positive Definitive Successive Over-Relaxation (PDAA) ... PDSOR
Positive Displacement ... PD
Positive Displacement [*Engineering*] ... PDISPL
Positive Displacement ... POSDSPLT
Positive Displacement (AD) ... posdsplt
Positive Displacement Blower ... PDB
Positive Displacement Mechanical [*or Metering*] **Pump** ... PDMP
Positive Displacement Pump ... PDP
Positive Displacement Pump-Constant Volume Sampler (ERG) ... PDP-CVS
Positive Displacement Unit [*Mechanical pumps*] ... PDU
Positive Electron (AD) ... positron
Positive Electron ... POSITRON
Positive End Expiratory Pressure [*Medicine*] ... PEEP
Positive End-Airway Pressure [*Medicine*] (DMAA) ... PEAP
Positive Energy [*Vancouver Stock Exchange symbol*] ... PEP
Positive Engagement Clutch ... PEC

Positive Expected Value	PEV
Positive Expiratory Pressure Plateau [*Medicine*] (MAE)	PEPP
Positive Expulsion (SAA)	PE
Positive Expulsion Bladder	PEB
Positive Expulsion Device	PED
Positive Feedback Circuit	PFC
Positive Flight Termination (MUGU)	PFT
Positive Fuel Stop	PFS
Positive Grid Oscillator	PGO
Positive High-Angle of Attack	PHAA
Positive Hostile Aircraft Identification	PHAID
Positive Hostile Identification Device [*Air Force*]	PHID
Positive Identification (ECII)	IP
Positive Identification and Direction Equipment	PI/DE
Positive Identification Feature	PI
Positive Identification Feature (MCD)	PIF
Positive Identification RADAR Advisory Zone (NVT)	PIRAZ
Positive Immittance Converter (PDAA)	PIC
Positive Immittance Inverter (IEEE)	PII
Positive Impedance Converter (IAA)	PIC
Positive Infinitely Variable	PIV
Positive Input - Negative Output [*Computer science*]	PINO
Positive Intelligence (LAIN)	PI
Positive Interlace [*Television*]	PI
Positive Ion Accelerator	PIA
Positive Ion Chamber	PIC
Positive Ion Cluster Composition Analyzer [*Instrumentation*]	PICCA
Positive Ion Neutral Injector [*Nuclear energy*] (NUCP)	PINI
Positive Ion Source	PIS
Positive Joint Mobilization [*Medicine*] (DMAA)	PJM
Positive Locator Aid to Navigation	PLAN
Positive Lock Fastener	PLF
Positive Logic Level	PLL
Positive Low Angle of Attack	PLAA
Positive Matte Technique (AD)	pmt
Positive Mental Attitude (AD)	pma
Positive Mental Attitude	PMA
Positive/Negative	P/N
Positive Negative Positive (AD)	pnp
Positive Neutral Finder [*Automotive engineering*]	PNF
Positive Noninterfering [*Alarm system*]	PNI
Positive Noninterfering (AD)	pni
Positive Occipital Sharp Transients of Sleep [*On electroencephalogram*] [*Neurology*] (DAVI)	POSTS
Positive on Negative (AD)	p-on-n
Positive Opening Fin (MCD)	POF
Positive Peer Control	PPC
Positive Peer Culture (AD)	PPC
Positive Personnel Identity Verification (PDAA)	PPIV
Positive Predictive Value [*Experimentation*]	PPV
Positive Pregnancy and Parenting Fitness (EA)	PPPF
Positive Pressure (MAE)	pos pr
Positive Pressure (CPH)	Pos Press
Positive Pressure Breathing [*Aerospace*]	PPB
Positive Pressure Breathing System [*Aerospace*]	PPBS
Positive Pressure Paradox	PPP
Positive Pressure Ventilation [*Medicine*]	PPV
Positive Regulatory Domain [*Genetics*]	PRD
Positive Resistor (AD)	posistor
Positive Response Television [*Associated Press*] (SAG)	PosResp
Positive Response Television [*NASDAQ symbol*] (SAG)	PRTV
Positive Review [*A publication*] (ROG)	POS R
Positive Rolandic Spikes [*Neurology*] (DAVI)	PRS
Positive Self-Image [*Psychology*]	PSI
Positive Spike Pattern (MAE)	PSP
Positive Start Voltage	PSV
Positive Support Review, Inc. [*Telecommunications service*] (TSSD)	PSR
Positive Target Control [*Aviation*] (FAAC)	PTC
Positive Temperature Coefficient	PTC
Positive Temperature Coefficient Resistance [*Materials science and technology*]	PTCR
Positive Termination Rate [*Job Training and Partnership Act*] (OICC)	PTR
Positive Transmitter Control	PTC
Positive Turnaround Control Point (MCD)	PTCP
Positive Value (DA)	PS
Positive Volume (IEEE)	PV
Positive Vorticity Advection [*NWS*] (FAAC)	PVA
Positive Wave in Children [*Neurophysiology*]	Pc
Positive Women [*An association Australia*]	PW
Positive-Channel Metal-Oxide Semiconductor [*Electronics*] (IAA)	PCHMOS
Positive-Channel Metal-Oxide Semiconductor [*Telecommunications*] (TEL)	PMOS
Positive-Intrinsic-Negative [*or P-Type Intrinsic N-Type*]	PIN
Positively Vet [*British*] (BARN)	PV
Positive-Negative Ambivalent Quotient (AD)	pnavq
Positive-Negative Ambivalent Quotient [*Psychology*]	PNAvQ
Positive-Negative Metal Transistor [*Electronics*] (IAA)	PNMT
Positive-Negative Positive-Negative (AD)	pnpn
Positive-Negative Pressure Respiration (AD)	pnpr
Positive-Negative Pressure Respiration	PNPR
Positive-Negative Selection [*Genetic engineering technique*]	PNS
Positive-Negative-Intrinsic-Positive [*Electron device*] (MSA)	PNIP
Positive-Negative-Positive [*Transistor*]	PNP
Positive-Negative-Positive-Negative [*Transistor*] (MUGU)	PNPN
Positive-on-Negative (IAA)	PONN

Positives and Deposition (DGA)	PD
Positives and Etching (DGA)	PE
Positivism (ROG)	POSIT
Positraction [*Automotive engineering*]	P/TRAC
Positron [*Also called positive electron*] [*Symbol Physics*] (DAVI)	E+
Positron (AD)	posit
Positron Annihilation Spectroscopy (MCD)	PAS
Positron Annihilation Spectroscopy for Chemical Analysis	PASCA
Positron Computed Tomography	PCT
Positron Corp. [*NASDAQ symbol*] (SAG)	POSI
Positron Corp. [*Associated Press*] (SAG)	Positr
Positron Corp. [*Associated Press*] (SAG)	Positron
Positron Corp. Wrrt [*NASDAQ symbol*] (TTSB)	POSIW
Positron Electron Proton [*Physics*]	PEP
Positron Emission Transaxial Tomography [*Also, PETT*] (PAZ)	PET scan
Positron Emission Transaxial [*or Transverse*] Tomography [*Roentgenography*]	PETT
Positron Intensity Accumulator (MCD)	PIA
Positron-Electron Project [*High-energy accelerator*]	PEP
Positron-Electron Tandem Ring Accelerator [*Nuclear*]	PETRA
Positron-Emission Tomography	PET
Poso [*Indonesia*] [*Airport symbol*] (OAG)	PSJ
Poso/Kasigunou [*Indonesia*] [*ICAO location identifier*] (ICLI)	WAMP
Posorja [*Ecuador*] [*ICAO location identifier*] (ICLI)	SEPO
Posse School, Inc., Kendal Green, MA [*Library symbol Library of Congress Obsolete*] (LCLS)	MKgP
Possessed (ROG)	POSSED
Possession [*or Possessive*] (WGA)	POS
Possession [*or Possessive*] (AFM)	POSS
Possession (AD)	poss
Possession (WGA)	POSSN
Possession	POSSON
Possessive (WDMC)	poss
Possessive (AD)	posses
Possessive Pronoun (AD)	pos pron
Possibility (AD)	pos
Possible	Po
Possible	POSS
Possible (WDMC)	poss
Possible (FAAC)	PSBL
Possible Carotid Artery System [*Medicine*]	PCAS
Possible Criminal Informant	PCI
Possible Jobs [*Test*] [*Psychology*]	PJ
Possible Nuclear Test Site [*Pronounced "peanuts"*] [*Air Force intelligence*]	PNUTS
Possible Nuclear Underground Test	PNUT
Possible Parliamentary Question [*Australia*]	PPQ
Possible Submarine (NVT)	POSSUB
Possible Vertebral-Basilar System [*Medicine*] (BABM)	PVBS
Possible Vertebral-Basilar System [*Cardiology*] (DAVI)	PVBS
Possibly (VRA)	posb
Possibly (WDMC)	posb
Possis Medical [*NASDAQ symbol*] (TTSB)	POSS
Possis Medical, Inc. [*NASDAQ symbol*] (NQ)	POSS
Possis Medical, Inc. [*Associated Press*] (SAG)	Possis
Possum Growers and Breeders Association (EA)	PGBA
Post [*After*] [*Latin*]	P
Post [*Surgery laboratory work*] (DAVI)	P
Post Abortion Syndrome	PAS
Post Acceleration (IAA)	PDA
Post Adjudicative Review [*Social Security Administration*] (OICC)	PAR
Post Adjutant	PA
Post Alloy Diffused Transistor [*Electronics*] (IAA)	PDT
Post Alloy Diffusion (IAA)	PAD
Post Amplifier	PA
Post and Girder [*Lumber*] (DAC)	P & G
Post and Rail	P & R
Post and Telecommunications Service (IAA)	PTS
Post and Telegraphy [*Telecommunications*] (IAA)	PT
Post and Wire (ADA)	P & W
Post Attach Requirements (AAG)	PAR
Post Aurem [*Behind the Ear*] [*Pharmacy*]	POST AUR
Post Aurem [*Behind the Ear*] [*Latin*] (AD)	post aur
Post Award Action	PAA
Post Award Conference (MCD)	PAC
Post Award Contract	PAC
Post Biblical Hebrew [*Language, etc.*] (BJA)	PBH
Post Boost Control System [*Aerospace*]	PBCS
Post Boost Vehicle [*Missiles*] (AFM)	PBV
Post Boost Vehicle Propulsion [*Missiles*] (MCD)	PBVP
Post Card (ROG)	PC
Post Card [*Philately*]	PC
Post Card Distributors Association	PCDA
Post Card Manufacturers Association [*Defunct*] (EA)	PCMA
Post Checkout	PCO
Post Christum Natum [*After the Birth of Christ*] [*Latin*]	P Chr N
Post Christum Natum [*After the Birth of Christ*] [*Latin*] (ROG)	PCN
Post Cibos [*After Meals*] [*Latin*] [*Pharmacy*] (DAVI)	PC
Post Cibum [*After Meals*] [*Pharmacy*]	PC
Post Column Method [*Chromatography*]	PCM
Post Commander [*Military*]	PC
Post Commercial Action Plan [*International Trade Administration*]	PCAP
Post Conference List	PCL
Post Conference Provisioning Tape (MCD)	PCPT

Post Consulatum [After the Consulate] [Latin] .... PC
Post Consumer Waste (EG) .... PCW
Post Coronary Care Unit .... P-CCU
Post Dated (WDAA) .... PD
Post D-Day Logistic Support [Army] (AABC) .... PDDLS
Post Defense Force .... PDF
Post Deployment Software Support Real-Time Interactive Simulation
    System .... PRISS
Post Design Services [British] (RDA) .... PDS
Post Detection Filter [Telecommunications] (TEL) .... PDF
Post Detection Integration (MCD) .... PDI
Post Detection Processor [Military] (CAAL) .... PDP
Post Detection Pulse Compression [Military] (CAAL) .... PDPC
Post Dialing Delay [Telecommunications] (TEL) .... PDD
Post Diluvium [After the Flood] [Latin] (ROG) .... PD
Post Eagle Publishing Co., Clifton, NJ [Library symbol Library of Congress]
    (LCLS) .... NjClifPE
Post Engineer [Army] (AABC) .... PE
Post Engineer Request .... PER
Post Exchange [Marine Corps] .... PE
Post Exchange [Military] .... PX
Post Experience Vocational Education (AIE) .... PEVE
Post Falls Public Library, Post Falls, ID [Library symbol Library of
    Congress] (LCLS) .... IdPf
Post Fire Evaluation [Military] (CAAL) .... PFE
Post Flight (AFIT) .... P/F
Post Flight Analysis .... PFA
Post Flight Data Analysis .... PFDA
Post Flight Evaluation .... PFE
Post Flight Inspection [Air Force] .... PO
Post Flight Processor .... PFP
Post Graduate Certificate of Education .... PGCE
Post Graduate Intelligence Program (DOMA) .... PGIP
Post Hoc Least Significant Difference [Statistics] .... PLSD
Post Hospital [Army] .... PHosp
Post Implementation Review .... PIR
Post Indicator Valve .... PIV
Post Infection Fatigue Syndrome [Medicine] .... PIFS
Post Junior College [Connecticut] .... PJC
Post Landing [NASA] (KSC) .... PL
Post Landing and Safing [NASA] (NASA) .... PLS
Post Launch and Instrumentation Message [NASA] (IAA) .... PLIM
Post Launch Information Message [NASA] (KSC) .... PLIM
Post Launch Memorandum Report .... PLMR
Post Launch Phase .... PLP
Post Laundry [Army] .... PL
Post Loading Test (NG) .... PLT
Post Loss-of-Coolant Accident Protection [Nuclear energy] (NRCH) .... PLOCAP
Post Maintenance Check (MCD) .... PMC
Post Maintenance Check Flight (MCD) .... PMCF
Post Manufacturing Checkout (KSC) .... PMC
Post Mark Collectors Club (EA) .... PMCC
Post Mast Message (IAA) .... PMM
Post Master's Certificate (PGP) .... PMC
Post M-Day Deployment List [Military] (AABC) .... PMDL
Post Meridiem [After Noon] [Latin] .... PM
Post Meridiem [After noon] [Latin] (AD) .... pm
Post Meridiem [Afternoon] [Latin] (WDMC) .... pm
Post Mobilization Individual Training and Support (MCD) .... PMITS
Post Mortem [After Death] [Latin] .... PM
Post Mortem (AD) .... pm
Post Mortem (AD) .... post
Post Mortem (AD) .... post-mort
Post Mortem Core Dump [Computer science] .... PMCD
Post Mortem Dump [Computer science] .... PMD
Post Mortem Interval [Forensics] [Medicine] .... PMI
Post Mortem Tape Dump [Computer science] .... PMTD
Post Nickel Strike (PDAA) .... PNS
Post Obitum [After Death] [Latin] .... post-obit
Post of Duty .... POD
Post of Duty File .... PODF
Post of the Corps .... POC
Post Office .... PO
Post Office (NITA) .... PO
Post Office (WDMC) .... po
Post Office (VRA) .... post ofc
Post Office Advisory Committee [British] .... POAC
Post Office Advisory Council (AD) .... POAC
Post Office Agents' Association [Australia] .... POAA
Post Office Ambulance Centre [British] (DI) .... POAC
Post Office and Civil Service Committee [US Senate] [Obsolete] .... PO & CS
Post Office Box .... POB
Post Office Clerks' Association [A union] [Northern Ireland] .... POCA
Post Office Controlling Officers' Association [A union] [British] .... POCOA
Post Office Corps [British military] (DMA) .... POC
Post Office Counters Ltd. [British] .... POC
Post Office Department [Canada] .... PO
Post Office Department [Later, United States Postal Service] .... POD
Post Office Department Board of Contract Appeals (AFIT) .... PODBCA
Post Office Directory .... POD
Post Office Electrical Engineer (IAA) .... POEE
Post Office Engineering Department (IAA) .... POED
Post Office Engineering Federation [A union] [British] .... POEF
Post Office Engineering Union [British] .... POEU
Post Office Facsimile [British] .... POSTFAX

Post Office Gazette [British A publication] (DCTA) .... POGaz
Post Office Guide [Book of regulations] [British] .... POG
Post Office Insurance Society [British] (DI) .... POIS
Post Office Investigation/Intelligence Department [British] (DI) .... POID
Post Office Library, Ottawa, ON, Canada [Library symbol Library of
    Congress] (LCLS) .... CaOOPO
Post Office Management and Service Improvement Program
    [Obsolete] .... POMSIP
Post Office Management Staffs Association [A union] [British] (DCTA) .... POMSA
Post Office National Users' Council [British] .... PONUC
Post Office Order .... POO
Post Office Plan .... POP
Post Office Position Indicator [A form of long-range position indicator]
    [British] .... POPI
Post Office Position Indicator [British] (AD) .... popi
Post Office Preferred (DCTA) .... POP
Post Office Processing Utility Subsystem [Telecommunications] (TEL) .... POPUS
Post Office Protocol [Telecommunications] .... POP
Post Office Protocol 3 [Electronic mail] POP3
Post Office Radio Interference Service [British] (DI) .... PORIS
Post Office Radio Interference Station (AD) .... PORIS
Post Office Regional Employees' Association [Defunct] (EA) .... POREA
Post Office Research Station (AD) .... PORS
Post Office Return .... POR
Post Office Rifles [Military British] (ROG) .... POR
Post Office Savings Bank .... POSB
Post Office Savings Department (AD) .... POSD
Post Office Scheme [Regulations] [British] .... POS
Post Office Senior Staff Negotiating Council [British] .... POSSNC
Post Office Staff Superannuation Fund [British] (DI) .... POSSF
Post Office Telecommunications [British] .... POT
Post Office Users Coordination Committee [British] .... POUCC
Post Office Users' National Council [British] (ILCA) .... POUNC
Post Office Work Unit [Computer performance measure] [British
    Telecom] .... POWU
Post Operation Data Analysis Facility .... PODAF
Post Orbit [NASA] .... PO
Post Overhaul Reaction Safeguard Examination [Navy] (NVT) .... PORSE
Post Overhaul Upkeep Period .... POUP
Post Pagado [Postage Paid] [Shipping] [Spanish] .... PP
Post Partum [Afterbirth] [Latin] (AD) .... post part
Post Partum [Afterbirth] [Latin] (AD) .... pp
Post Partum [After Birth] [Latin] (ADA) .... PP
Post Pill Galactorrhea-Amenorrhea [Medicine] .... PPGA
Post Placement and Training Support Program for People with Disabilities
    [Australia] .... PP/TSD
Post Position [Racing] .... PP
Post Processing .... PP
Post Production Service (AAG) .... PPS
Post Production Support (MCD) .... PPS
Post Production Test .... PPT
Post Properties [NYSE symbol] (TTSB) .... PPS
Post Properties, Inc. [Associated Press] (SAG) .... PostPr
Post Properties, Inc. [Associated Press] (SAG) .... PostPrp
Post Properties, Inc. [NYSE symbol] (SPSG) .... PPS
Post Quartermaster [Marine Corps] .... PQM
Post Reditum ad Populum [of Cicero] [Classical studies] (OCD) .... Red Pop
Post Reditum in Senatu [of Cicero] [Classical studies] (OCD) .... Red Sen
Post Request .... PR
Post Roman Conditam [After the Founding of Rome] [Latin] .... PRC
Post Script: Essays in Film and the Humanities [A publication]
    (BRI) .... Post Script
Post Scriptum [Written Afterwards, Postscript] [Latin] .... PS
Post Sending Delay .... PSD
Post Shakedown Availability .... PSA
Post Singulas Sedes Liquidas [After Every Loose Stool] [Pharmacy]
    (ROG) .... POST SING SED LIQ
Post Stall Gyration (MCD) .... PSG
Post Strike Emergency Reporting .... POSTER
Post Strike Reconnaissance List [Military] (CINC) .... PSRL
Post, Telegraph and Telephone Authority (NITA) .... PTT
Post, Telephon und Telegraphenbetriebe [Switzerland
    Telecommunications] .... PTT
Post, Telephone, and Telegraph [Telecommunications] (IAA) .... PTT
Post Telephone or Telex (NITA) .... PTT
Post Ten Tumblers [Pseudonym used by William Maginn] .... PTT
Post Town .... PT
Post, TX [AM radio station call letters] .... KPOS
Post, TX [FM radio station call letters] .... KPOS-FM
Post und Telegraphenverwaltung [Postal and Telegraph Administration]
    [Austria Telecommunications] .... PTT
Post Urbem Conditam [After the Building of the City of Rome] [Latin] .... PUC
Post Village .... PV
Post War World Council [Defunct] (EA) .... PWWC
Posta Kutusu [Postbox] [Turkish] (EY) .... PK
Postacceptance Modification .... PAM
Post-Accident Containment Venting [Nuclear energy] (NRCH) .... PACV
Post-Accident Environment [Nuclear energy] (IEEE) .... PAE
Post-Accident Heat Removal [Nuclear energy] .... PAHR
Post-Accident Monitoring [Nuclear energy] (NRCH) .... PAM
Post-Accident Monitoring System [Nuclear energy] (NRCH) .... PAMS
Post-Accident Radioactivity Depletion [Nuclear energy] (NRCH) .... PARD
Post-Accident Radioactivity Removal [Nuclear energy] (NRCH) .... PARR
Post-Accident Sampling Systems [Nuclear energy] .... PASS
Postacoustic Spectroscopy .... PAS

Post-Activation Diffusion (IEEE) ... PAD
Postadoption Center for Education and Research ... PACER
Post-Adoption Centre [*British*] (CB) ... PAC
Postage ... P
Postage (AD) ... post
Postage (ROG) ... POSTE
Postage (WGA) ... PSTG
Postage and Handling [*Shipping*] ... P/H
Postage and Handling (WDMC) ... P&H
Postage and Insurance ... P & I
Postage and Insurance (ILCA) ... Post & Ins
Postage and Packing [*Shipping*] ... P & P
Postage and Registration (DLA) ... Post & Reg
Postage Due ... PD
Postage Forward Parcels [*Shipping*] ... PFP
Postage Free (ROG) ... PF
Postage Paid [*Shipping*] ... PP
Postage Paid (AD) ... pp
Postage Paid Impression [*Freight*] (DCTA) ... PPI
Postage Prepaid in Money ... PPM
Postagram [*British military*] (DMA) ... P/G
Postal (AFM) ... PSTL
Postal ... PSTL
Postal Address Reader Indexer System (PDAA) ... PARIS
Postal Analysis Response and Reporting System [*Computer system designed to track mail through the US Postal Service*] [*R. R. Donnelley & Sons Co.*] ... PARRS
Postal and Courier Communications [*British*] ... PCC
Postal and Telegraphic Censorship [*Telecommunications*] (IAA) ... PTC
Postal Answer Line [*US Postal Service automated telephone information service*] ... PAL
Postal Assistant (DCTA) ... PA
Postal Bulletin [*A publication*] ... POB
Postal Business Training Centre [*British*] ... PBTC
Postal Church Service ... PCS
Postal Clerk [*Navy rating*] ... PC
Postal Clerk, First Class [*Navy rating*] ... PC1
Postal Clerk, Second Class [*Navy rating*] ... PC2
Postal Clerk, Third Class [*Navy rating*] ... PC3
Postal Commemorative Society (EA) ... PCS
Postal Concentration Center [*Army*] ... PCC
Postal [*Service*] **Contracting Manual** [*A publication*] (AAGC) ... PCM
Postal Contracting Manual [*Postal Service*] ... POCM
Postal [*Service*] **Contracting Manual Circular** (AAGC) ... PCMC
Postal District ... PD
Postal Efficiency Plan (SAA) ... PEP
Postal Employees Salary Increase Act of 1960 ... PESIA
Postal Finance and Supply Office (AFM) ... PFSO
Postal Finance Officer [*Army*] ... PFO
Postal Headquarters [*British*] ... PHQ
Postal History Society (EA) ... PHS
Postal History Society of Canada (EA) ... PHSC
Postal History Society of New Zealand [*Auckland*] (EA) ... PHSNZ
Postal History Society of Ontario [*Later, PHSC*] (EA) ... PHSO
Postal History Society of the Americas (EA) ... PHS of A
Postal History Study Group (EA) ... PHSG
Postal Inspection Service ... PIS
Postal Inspectors' Association [*A union*] [*British*] ... PIA
Postal Instruction (IAA) ... PI
Postal Laws and Regulations [*Later, Postal Manual*] ... PL & R
Postal Laws and Regulations (IAA) ... PLAR
Postal Laws and Regulations [*Later, Postal Manual*] (IAA) ... POAR
Postal Manual ... PM
Postal Money Order [*Military*] ... PMO
Postal Note (ADA) ... PN
Postal Officer (DCTA) ... PO
Postal Order ... PO
Postal Orders (AD) ... POs
Postal Rate Commission [*Federal government*] ... PRC
Postal Reform League (IAA) ... PRL
Postal Regulating Detachment [*Military*] ... PRD
Postal Regulations (DLA) ... PR
Postal Reorganization Act (AD) ... PRA
Postal Reorganization Act of 1970 (AAGC) ... PRA
Postal Satsang [*An association*] (EA) ... PS
Postal Savings System [*Terminated, 1966*] ... PSS
Postal Security Device [*Computer science*] ... PSD
Postal Separation System (SAA) ... PSS
Postal Service [*US*] ... PS
Postal Service Board of Contract Appeals (AAGC) ... PSBCA
Postal Service Center (AFM) ... PSC
Postal Service Manual [*A publication*] ... POSMA
Postal Service Manual [*A publication*] (AFM) ... PSM
Postal Service Representative [*British*] (DCTA) ... PSR
Postal Supervisory Officers' Association [*Australia*] ... PSOA
Postal, Telegraph, and Telephone Administration (NATG) ... PTT
Postal, Telegraph, and Telephone International [*See also IPTT*] [*Geneva, Switzerland*] (EAIO) ... PTTI
Postal Telegraph Cable ... PTC
Postal Telegraph Clerks' Association [*A union*] [*British*] ... PTCA
Postal Telegraph Co. [*Terminated*] ... PT
Postal Union of the Americas and Spain [*See also UPAE*] [*Montevideo, Uruguay*] (EAIO) ... PUAS
Postal Union of the Americas, Spain, and Portugal [*Uruguay*] (EAIO) ... PUASP
Postal Vehicle Service ... PVS
Postal Wire [*Telecommunications*] (IAA) ... PW
Postalloy Diffusion Technique (IAA) ... PADT
Postalloy Diffusion Transistor ... PADT
Post-Anesthesia Care Unit (MEDA) ... PACU
Postanesthesia Recovery Room [*Medicine*] (DAVI) ... PARR
Postanesthesia [*or Postanesthetic*] **Room** [*Medicine*] ... PAR
Postanesthetic Recovery [*Medicine*] ... PAR
Postanesthetic Recovery Unit [*Medicine*] ... PARU
Post-Apollo Space Electrophoresis [*European Space Agency*] ... PASE
Post-Attack Command and Control System [*Military*] ... PACCS
Post-Attack Command and Control System/Airborne Data Automation [*Military*] ... PACCS/ADA
Post-Attack Command Control Squadron [*Air Force*] ... PACCSq
Post-Attack Communication System ... PACS
Post-Attack Intelligence ... PAINT
Post-Attack Intercontinental Link ... PAIL
Post-Attack Mobilization of the United States Army ... PAMUSA
Post-Attack Resource Management System (MCD) ... PARM
Post-Augustan (AD) ... post-Aug
Post-Aural [*Medicine*] (DMAA) ... PA
Postauricular Myogenic [*Medicine*] (DMAA) ... PAM
Postavailability Trials ... PAT
Post-Boost Propulsion System [*Aerospace*] ... PBPS
Postbuckled Rectangular Plate ... PRP
Postburn Day [*Medicine*] (DMAA) ... PBD
Postcapillary Venule [*Medicine*] (DMAA) ... PCV
Postcard (WDMC) ... pc
Postcard (ODBW) ... pc
Postcard ... PC
Postcard (BJA) ... Pcd
Postcard (VRA) ... PSCD
Postcard Club Federation [*Defunct*] (EA) ... PCF
Postcard Collector's Club of America [*Defunct*] (EA) ... PCCA
Postcard History Society (EA) ... PHS
Postcard Traders' Association [*British*] (DBA) ... PTA
Postcardiotomy Syndrome [*Medicine*] ... PCS
Postcaval [*or Portacaval*] **Shunt** [*Medicine*] ... PCS
Postcheckout Operations ... PCO
Post-Chlorinated (IAA) ... PC
Postcode (ADA) ... PC
Postcoital [*Medicine*] ... PC
Postcoital [*Medicine*] (DMAA) ... PC
Postcoital Bleeding [*Medicine*] (DMAA) ... PCB
Postcoital Test [*Medicine*] (DAVI) ... PCT
Post-Colonial Literatures and Languages Centre [*Macquarie University*] [*Australia*] ... PCLLRC
Post-Compression Remodeling [*Medicine*] (DMAA) ... PCR
Postconstruction Availability (NVT) ... PCA
Post-Construction Permit [*Nuclear energy*] (NRCH) ... PCP
Post-Consumer Recycle [*or Reclaim*] [*Plastics industry*] ... PCR
Postconsumer Recycled Content [*Plastics technology*] ... PRC
Post-Consumer Resin [*Plastic recycling*] ... PCR
Post-Contract Implementation Report (AAGC) ... PCIR
Postconviction Remedy ... PCR
Post-Coronary Care Unit [*Cardiology*] (DAVI) ... PCU
Postdated ... PD
Post-Deflection Accelerator (DEN) ... PDA
Post-Delivery Availability [*Military*] (NVT) ... PDA
Post-Delivery Test and Trial Team (MCD) ... PDTTT
Post-Delivery Test and Trials [*Military*] (CAAL) ... PDT & T
Post-Deployment Software System (MCD) ... PDSS
Post-Depositional Remanent Magnetization [*Geophysics*] ... PDRM
Post-Design Analysis ... PDA
Postdetrital Remanent Magnetization [*Geophysics*] ... PDRM
Post-Development Maintainability Logistics Review (MCD) ... PDMLR
Post-Diapause Eclosion Time [*Entomology*] ... PDET
Postdilution Hemofiltration [*Medicine*] ... PDHF
Postdoctorate ... PD
Post-Drug Potentiation ... PDP
Postdural Puncture Headache [*Medicine*] (DMAA) ... PDPH
Poste De La Baleine [*Quebec*] [*Seismograph station code, US Geological Survey*] (SEIS) ... PBQ
Poste e Telegrafi [*Post and Telegraph Service*] [*Italy*] ... PT
Poste Recommandee [*Registered Post*] ... PR
Poste-Avion [*Airmail*] [*French*] ... PAV
Posted County Price [*Agriculture*] ... PCP
Posted Price (MENA) ... pp
Posted to Geographics ... PT GEO
Postejaculatory Interval [*Physiology*] ... PEI
Postelectrophoresis Relaxation ... PER
Postemergence [*Weed control*] ... POST
Posten [*Sentry*] [*German military*] ... P
Post-Enumeration Survey [*Bureau of the Census*] ... PES
[*The*] **Poster** [*A publication*] (ROG) ... POST
Poster (VRA) ... post
Poster Society (EA) ... PS
Posterior ... P
Posterior (MAE) ... PO
Posterior ... post
Posterior [*Spanish*] (AD) ... post
Posterior (AD) ... poster
Posterior Airway Space [*Medicine*] (DMAA) ... PAS
Posterior Anterior [*Medicine*] ... PA
Posterior Aorta ... PA
Posterior Area of [*Loose*] **Skin** ... PAS

Posterior Auditory Field .... PAF
Posterior Axillary Line [*Medicine*] .... PAL
Posterior Basal Body [*Botany*] .... PBB
Posterior Bite Wing [*Dentistry*] .... PBW
Posterior Carotid Foramen [*Anatomy*] .... PCF
Posterior Cerebral Artery [*Brain anatomy*] .... PCA
Posterior Cervical [*Medicine*] (DMAA) .... PC
Posterior Chamber [*Ophthalmology*] .... PC
Posterior Chamber - Intraocular Lens [*Ophthalmology*] .... PC-IOC
Posterior Chamber Intraocular Lens [*Ophthalmology*] (DAVI) .... PCIOL
Posterior Chamber Lens [*Ophthalmology*] (DAVI) .... PCL
Posterior Circumflex [*Artery*] [*Anatomy*] (DAVI) .... PC
Posterior Commissure [*Neuroanatomy*] .... PC
Posterior Communicating [*Artery*] [*Medicine*] (DMAA) .... PCOM
Posterior Communicating Artery [*Anatomy*] .... PCA
Posterior Concave Side .... PCS
Posterior Corneal Deposit [*Ophthalmology*] (MAE) .... PCD
Posterior Cortex [*Medicine*] (DMAA) .... PC
Posterior Cranial Fossa [*Anatomy*] (MAE) .... PCF
Posterior Cricoarytenoid [*A muscle of the larynx*] .... PCA
Posterior Cruciate Ligament [*Anatomy*] .... PCL
Posterior Deltoid [*Myology*] .... PD
Posterior Descending Artery [*Anatomy*] (DAVI) .... PDA
Posterior Diameter (AD) .... post d
Posterior Digestive [*Gland*] .... PD
Posterior Fontanelle [*Anatomy*] (DAVI) .... PF
Posterior Fossa Extra-Axial Arachnoid Cyst [*Medicine*] (DAVI) .... PFEAAC
Posterior Fossa Tumor [*Anatomy*] (MAE) .... PFT
Posterior Hyaloid Membrane [*Eye anatomy*] .... PHM
Posterior Inferior Cerebal Artery [*Cardiology*] (DAVI) .... PICA
Posterior Inferior Cerebellar Artery [*Anatomy*] .... PICA
Posterior Inferior Communicating Artery [*Cardiology*] (DAVI) .... PICA
Posterior Internal Cerebral Artery [*Cardiology*] (DAVI) .... PICA
Posterior Lateral Line Lobe [*Of electric fishes*] .... PLLL
Posterior Latissimus Dorsi [*Anatomy*] .... PLD
Posterior Leaf Mitral Valve [*Cardiology*] (DMAA) .... PLMV
Posterior Left Atrial Wall [*Cardiology*] .... PLA
Posterior Left Ventricle [*Anatomy*] (DAVI) .... PLV
Posterior Left Ventricular Wall [*Cardiology*] .... PLV
Posterior Lip Nerve (DAVI) .... PLN
Posterior Lung Fiber [*Medicine*] (DMAA) .... PLF
Posterior Medial Collateral Ligament [*Anatomy*] .... PMCL
Posterior Medial Corner of Knee [*Sports medicine*] .... PMC
Posterior Middle Suprasylvian Area [*Anatomy*] .... PMSA
Posterior Mitral Leaflet [*Cardiology*] .... PM
Posterior Mitral Leaflet [*Cardiology*] .... PML
Posterior Mitral Valve Leaflet [*Anatomy*] (AAMN) .... PMVL
Posterior Myocardial Infarction [*Medicine*] (DMAA) .... PMI
Posterior Nasal Spine [*Medicine*] (DMAA) .... PNS
Posterior Odds Processing [*Weather forecasting*] [*National Science Foundation*] .... POP
Posterior Papillary Muscle [*Image on transesophageal echocardiography*] [*Cardiology*] (DAVI) .... PPM
Posterior Parietal Cortex [*Neuroanatomy*] .... PP
Posterior Parietal Cortex [*Brain anatomy*] .... PPC
Posterior Pituitary [*Medicine*] .... PP
Posterior Pole Plasm [*Insect embryology*] .... PPL
Posterior Polymorphous Dystrophy [*Neurology*] (DAVI) .... PPD
Posterior Polymorphous Dystrophy of the Cornea [*Ophthalmology*] (DAVI) .... PPMD
Posterior Probability [*Computations*] .... POSTP
Posterior Repair [*Gynecology*] (DAVI) .... PR
Posterior Ridge .... PR
Posterior Root [*Medicine*] (DMAA) .... PR
Posterior Sacroiliac Spine [*Anatomy*] (DAVI) .... PSIS
Posterior Sagittal Diameter [*Anatomy*] (MAE) .... Post Sag D
Posterior Sagittal Index [*Anatomy*] (AAMN) .... PSI
Posterior Spinal Fusion [*Medicine*] (DAVI) .... PSF
Posterior Subcapsular Cataractous Plaque [*Ophthalmology*] (DAVI) .... PSCP
Posterior Subcapsular Cataracts [*Ophthalmology*] .... PSC
Posterior Subcapsular Plaque [*Ophthalmology*] (DAVI) .... psp
Posterior Superior Iliac Spine [*Posterosuperior iliac spine*] [*Anatomy*] (DAVI) .... PSI
Posterior Tibial [*Anatomy*] .... PT
Posterior Tibial [*Pulse*] [*Medicine*] (DAVI) .... PTA
Posterior Tibial Pulse [*Cardiology*] (DAVI) .... PTP
Posterior Trabeculae Carneae [*Heart anatomy*] .... PTC
Posterior Urethral Valve [*Medicine*] (DMAA) .... PUV
Posterior Vaginal Wall [*Medicine*] (DMAA) .... PVW
Posterior Ventral Microtubule [*Anatomy*] .... PVM
Posterior Vitreous Detachment [*Ophthalmology*] .... PVD
Posterior Vitreous Face [*Ophthalmology*] (DAVI) .... PVF
Posterior Wall [*Medicine*] .... PW
Posterior Wall Excursion [*Anatomy*] (DMAA) .... PWE
Posterior Wall Infarct [*Anatomy*] (MAE) .... PWI
Posterior Wall of Bronchus Intermedius [*Anatomy*] .... PWBI
Posterior Wall of Left Ventricle [*Anatomy*] (AAMN) .... PWLV
Posterolateral Dendrite [*Neurology*] .... PLD
Posterolateral Rotation Instability [*Sports medicine*] .... PLRI
Posteromedial Hypothalamus [*Medicine*] (DMAA) .... PMH
Posteromedial Release [*Orthopedics*] (DAVI) .... PMR
Posteromedial Rotation Instability [*Sports medicine*] .... PMRI
Postes, Telegraphes, et Telediffusion [*Post, Telegraph, and Telephone*] [*General Post Office Facetious translation: Prostitution Telematique et Telephonique*] [*France*] .... PTT
Poste's Translation of Gaius [*A publication*] (ILCA) .... Poste's Gai
Poste's Translation of Gaius [*A publication*] (DLA) .... Poste's Gaius Inst
Post-Execution Reporting (MHDI) .... PER
Post-Exercise Discussion [*NATO*] (NATG) .... PXD
Postexposure [*Medicine*] .... PE
Postexposure Baking [*Microlithography*] .... PEB
Postexposure Prophylaxis [*Medicine*] .... PEP
Postextrasystolic Potentiation [*Cardiology*] .... PES
Postextrasystolic Potentiation [*Medicine*] (DMAA) .... PESP
Post-Fielding Review [*DoD*] .... PFR
Post-Fielding Training Analysis .... PFTA
Post-Fielding Training Effectiveness Analysis .... PFTEA
Postfinal Acceptance Trials [*Navy*] (NVT) .... POSTFAT
Postflight Checklist (MCD) .... PFC
Postgamma Proteinuria [*Medicine*] (MAE) .... PGP
Postganglionic [*Medicine*] (MEDA) .... postgangl
Postganglionic [*Neurology*] (DAVI) .... postgangl
Postglacial Fault [*Biology*] .... PGF
Postgonococcal Urethritis [*Medicine*] .... PGU
Postgraduate [*Refers to courses or students*] [*Slang*] .... PG
Postgraduate and Research Students' Association [*Australian National University*] .... PARSA
Postgraduate Center for Mental Health (EA) .... PCMH
Postgraduate Center for Psychotherapy [*Later, Postgraduate Center for Mental Health*] (EA) .... PCP
Post-Graduate Certificate (PGP) .... PGC
Postgraduate Committee in Medicine [*Australia*] .... PCM
Postgraduate Committee in Veterinary Science [*Australia*] .... PGCVS
Postgraduate Diploma [*Australia*] .... PGDip
Postgraduate Diploma (PGP) .... Postgraduate D
Postgraduate Diploma in Agricultural Science [*Australia*] .... PGDipAgrSc
Postgraduate Diploma in Agriculture .... PostgradDipAgr
Postgraduate Diploma in Arts [*Australia*] .... PGDipA
Postgraduate Diploma in Development Technology [*Australia*] .... PGDipDevTech
Postgraduate Diploma in Educational Studies [*Australia*] .... PGDipEdSt
Postgraduate Diploma in Educational Studies (Industrial Arts) .... PostGradDipEdStud(IndArts)
Postgraduate Diploma in Forest Science [*Australia*] .... PGDipForSc
Postgraduate Diploma in Irrigation Engineering Management [*Australia*] .... PGDipIEM
Postgraduate Diploma in Management Studies [*Australia*] .... PGDipMgtSt
Postgraduate Diploma in Mathematics and Mathematics Education [*Australia*] .... PGDipMath & MathEd
Postgraduate Diploma in Physiotherapy [*Australia*] .... PGDipPhysio
Postgraduate Diploma in Science [*Australia*] .... PGDipSc
Postgraduate Federation in Veterinary Science [*Australia*] .... PGFVS
Postgraduate Medical Education Committee [*University of Queensland, Australia*] .... PMEC
Postgraduate Medical Institute (AD) .... Postgrad Med Inst
Postgraduate Year .... PGY
Post-Harvest Documentation Service [*Kansas State University*] (IID) .... PHDS
Posthemorrhagic Hydrocephalus [*Neurology*] (DAVI) .... PHH
Post-Heparin Esterase [*Medicine*] (MAE) .... PHE
Postheparin Lipolytic Activity [*Medicine*] (DMAA) .... PHLA
Post-Heparin Phospholipase [*Medicine*] (MAE) .... PHP
Postheparin Plasma (DAVI) .... PHP
Postherpetic Neuragia [*Medicine*] .... PHN
Postherpetic Neuralgia [*Medicine*] (DAVI) .... PHN
Post-Holiday Movie .... PHM
Posthospital Care [*Medicine*] .... PHC
Post-Hostilities Planning Committee [*Navy World War II*] .... PHPC
Post-Hostilities Planning Staff [*World War II*] .... PHPS
Post-Hostilities Planning Subcommittee of the Chiefs of Staff Committee [*World War II*] .... PHP
Posthumous .... POSTH
Posthumous (AD) .... posth
Posthumously .... PSTH
Posthypnotic Suggestion [*Psychology*] .... PHS
Posthypnotic Suggestion [*Psychiatry*] (DAVI) .... PHS
Posthypoxic Intention Myoclonus [*Medicine*] (DMAA) .... PHIM
Post-Imperative Negative Variation [*Medicine*] (DMAA) .... PINV
Postimpressionist Movement [*Art*] .... PI
Postinfective Chronic Fatigue Syndrome [*Medicine*] (DMAA) .... PICFS
Postinflammatory Corticoid [*Medicine*] .... PC
Postinflammatory Corticoid [*Medicine*] .... PIC
Posting Data Transfer [*Air Force*] (AFM) .... PDT
Postinhibitory Rebound [*Physiology*] .... PIR
Postinjection Propulsion Subsystem [*NASA*] .... PIPS
Postinoculation [*Medicine*] .... PI
Post-Insertion Deorbit Preparation [*NASA*] (MCD) .... PDP
Postinspiratory Pressure [*Medicine*] (DAVI) .... PIP
Postipankki [*National savings bank*] [*Finland*] .... PSP
Post-Irradiation Examination [*Nuclear energy*] (NRCH) .... PIE
Post-Irradiation Experiment [*Nuclear energy*] (NRCH) .... PIE
Post-Irradiation Open Test Assembly [*Nuclear energy*] (NRCH) .... PIOTA
Postischemic [*Medicine*] .... PI
Postjunctional Membrane .... PJM
Post-Landing Survival System [*NASA*] .... PLSS
Postlanding Vent [*or Ventilation*] [*Apollo*] [*NASA*] .... PLV
Post-Landing Vent Control [*NASA*] (KSC) .... PLVC
Post-LANDSAT Advanced Concept Evaluation (MCD) .... PLACE
Post-Launch Analysis of Compliance [*NASA*] .... PLAC
Postlethwaite's Dictionary of Trade and Commerce [*A publication*] (DLA) .... Postl Dict
Postlude (AD) .... postl

Postlumbar Interbody Fusion [*Neurology*] (DAVI) ..... PLIF
Post-Lumbar Puncture Headache [*Medicine*] (DMAA) ..... PLPH
Post-Maastricht Tension [*European community*] (ECON) ..... PMT
Postmaintenance Inspection Pilot ..... PMIP
Postmammillary Caudal Magnocellular Nuclei [*Neuroanatomy*] ..... PCM
Postman (DCTA) ..... PMN
Postman, Higher Grade [*British*] (DI) ..... PHG
Postman's Delivery Office (DCTA) ..... PDO
Postman's Federation [*A union*] [*British*] ..... PF
Postmark [*Deltiology*] ..... PM
Postmark ..... PMK
Postmark (AD) ..... pmk
Post-Market Trading ..... PMT
Post-Marketing Surveillance ..... PMS
Postmasburg [*South Africa*] [*ICAO location identifier*] (ICLI) ..... FAPT
Postmastectomy Pain Syndrome [*Medicine*] (DMAA) ..... PMPS
Postmaster ..... PM
Postmaster ..... PM
Postmaster (DCTA) ..... PMR
Postmaster General ..... PMG
Postmaster General (AD) ..... PmG
Postmeiotic Segregation [*Genetics*] ..... PMS
Postmenopausal [*Gynecology*] (DAVI) ..... PM
Post-Menopausal Bleeding [*Medicine*] (AD) ..... pmb
Postmenopausal Bleeding [*Medicine*] ..... PMB
Post-Menopausal Estrogen and Progestin Intervention [*Medicine*] (BARN) ..... PEPI
Postmenopausal Estrogen Progestin Interventions ..... PEPI
Postmenopausal Estrogen/Progestin Interventions ..... PEPI
Postmenopausal Estrogen Therapy [*Gynecology*] (CPH) ..... PME
Postmenopausal Osteoporosis [*Medicine*] ..... PMO
Postmenopausal Palpable Ovary [*Gynecology*] ..... PMPO
Postmenopausal Syndrome [*Medicine*] ..... PMS
Post-Menopausal Syndrome [*Medicine*] (AD) ..... pms
Post-Merger Syndrome [*Business term*] ..... PMS
Postmitochondrial Supernatant [*Medicine*] (MAE) ..... PMS
Postmitochondrial Supernatant [*Medicine*] (DMAA) ..... PSM
Postmodern ..... POMO
Postmodernist [*Architecture*] ..... PM
Postmolded Plastic Chip Carrier [*Computer science*] ..... PPCC
Postmortem (AAMN) ..... POST
Postmortem Aging [*of meat*] ..... PA
Post-Mortem Debugger [*Computer science*] (PCM) ..... PMD
Post-Mortem Dumps (AD) ..... pmd
Postmortem Human Kidney [*Cells*] ..... PHK
Post-Mortem Survival [*Parapsychology*] ..... PMS
Postmyocardial Infarction [*Syndrome*] [*Medicine*] ..... PMI
Postmyocardial Infarction Syndrome [*Medicine*] (DMAA) ..... PMIS
Postnasal [*Otorhinolaryngology*] (DAVI) ..... PN
Postnasal Drainage [*Medicine*] ..... PD
Postnasal Drainage [*or Drip*] [*Medicine*] ..... PND
Postnasal Drip [*Medicine*] (AD) ..... pnd
Postnatal [*Medicine*] ..... PN
Postnatal Clinic ..... PNC
Postnatal Days ..... PND
Postnatal Depression [*Medicine*] (ECON) ..... PND
Postnatal Infection [*Medicine*] ..... PNI
Postnuclear Fraction [*Biochemical tissue analysis*] ..... PNF
Postnuclear Supernatant ..... PNS
Postnumeric Encoding Technique [*US Postal Service*] ..... POSTNET
Posto Telefonico Pubblico [*Public Telephone*] [*Italy*] ..... PTP
Post-Occupancy Evaluation ..... POE
Postoperational Analysis Critique and Exercise Report [*Military*] (CAAL) ..... PACER
Post-Operations Evaluation (MCD) ..... POE
Postoperative [*Medicine*] ..... PO
Postoperative (AD) ..... p-o
Post-Operative (AD) ..... p-op
Postoperative [*Medicine*] ..... POP
Postoperative [*Medicine*] ..... POSTOP
Post-Operative (AD) ..... post-op
Postoperative Care [*Medicine*] ..... POC
Postoperative Day [*Medicine*] ..... POD
Postoperative Destruct System (MCD) ..... PODS
Postoperative Diagnosis [*Medicine*] ..... PODx
Postoperative Endophthalmitis [*Ophthalmology*] ..... POE
Postoperative Exercise [*Medicine*] (DAVI) ..... POE
Postoperative Low Cardiac Output [*Medicine*] (DMAA) ..... PLCO
Postoperative Respiratory Therapy (DAVI) ..... PORT
Postoperative Suprachoroidal Hemorrhage [*Medicine*] ..... PSCH
Post-Operative Treatment [*Medicine*] (DMAA) ..... POT
Postoral Ciliary [*Gland*] ..... POC
Postovulatory Follicle [*Endocrinology*] ..... POF
Postpaid ..... pp
Postpaid ..... PPD
Postpaid (WDMC) ..... ppd
Post-Painted Parts ..... PPP
Postparotid Basic Protein (DMAA) ..... PPb
Postpartum [*Medicine*] ..... P
Postpartum [*Medicine*] (CPH) ..... PP
Postpartum Amenorrhea [*Medicine*] ..... PPA
Postpartum Day [*Obstetrics*] (DAVI) ..... PPD
Postpartum Depression (PAZ) ..... PPD
Post-Partum Hemorrhage [*Medicine*] (AD) ..... pph
Postpartum Hemorrhage [*Medicine*] ..... PPH
Postpartum Psychosis [*Obstetrics*] [*Psychiatry*] (DAVI) ..... PPP
Postpartum Renal Failure [*Medicine*] (DMAA) ..... PPRF
Postpartum Sterilization [*Gynecology*] (DAVI) ..... PPS
Postpartum Sterilization [*Medicine*] ..... PPS
Postpartum Support, International (EA) ..... PSI
Postpartum Tubal Ligation [*Medicine*] ..... PPTL
Postpass ..... PP
Postpass Message ..... PPM
Postpay Coin Telephone [*Telecommunications*] (TEL) ..... PO
Postperfusion Syndrome [*Medicine*] ..... PPS
Postperfusion Syndrome [*Cardiology*] (DAVI) ..... PPS
Postpericardiotomy Syndrome [*Medicine*] (DMAA) ..... PPS
Post-Pill Amenorrhea [*Medicine*] (MEDA) ..... PPA
Post-Pill Galactorrheamenorrhea [*Medicine*] (AD) ..... ppga
Post-Polio Muscular Atrophy [*Medicine*] (AD) ..... ppma
Post-Polio Sequelae [*Medicine*] ..... PPS
Post-Polio Syndrome [*Medicine*] (AD) ..... p-ps
Post-Poliomyelitis Muscular Atrophy [*Medicine*] ..... PPMA
Postpolycythemia Myeloid Metaplasia [*Medicine*] (AAMN) ..... PPMM
Postponed ..... PP
Postponed Accounting System [*Banking*] ..... PAS
Post-Postscriptum [*Further Postscript*] [*Latin*] ..... PPS
Postprandial [*After Meals*] [*Pharmacy*] ..... PP
Postprandial Blood Sugar [*Clinical chemistry*] ..... PPBS
Postprandial Plasma Glucose [*Endocrinology*] (DAVI) ..... PPPG
Postprocessor [*Computer science*] ..... POSTP
Postprocessor [*Computer science*] ..... POSTPRO
Postprocessor [*Computer science*] (IAA) ..... PP
Postprocessor Call Library [*Computer science*] (IAA) ..... PPLB
Post-Program Monitoring ..... PPM
Post-Proline Cleaving Enzyme [*Biochemistry*] ..... PPCE
Postpulmonary Complications ..... PPC
Postpump Syndrome [*Medicine*] (MAE) ..... PPS
Post-Qualification Education (PDAA) ..... PQE
Post-Qualification Education (AD) ..... pqe
Postradiation Dysplasia [*Medicine*] ..... PRD
Post-Resuscitation ..... PR
Post-Retirement Benefits (AAGC) ..... PRB
Posts and Telegraphs Industrial Workers' Union [*India*] ..... PTIWU
Posts and Timbers [*Technical drawings*] ..... P & T
Posts, Camps, and Stations [*Military*] ..... PC & S
Posts, Camps, and Stations [*Military*] ..... PCS
Post's Reports [*42-64 Missouri*] [*A publication*] (DLA) ..... Post
Post's Reports [*23-26 Michigan*] [*A publication*] (DLA) ..... Post
Post-Schistosomal Liver Cirrhosis [*Medicine*] ..... PSLC
Post-Scram Reactivity Monitor [*Nuclear energy*] (NRCH) ..... PSRM
PostScript [*Adobe printer language*] ..... PS
PostScript [*Computer science*] ..... ps
PostScript and LASERJet-Type [*LASER printer*] ..... PCL
PostScript Printer Description [*Computer science*] (PCM) ..... PPD
Postscripta [*Postscripts*] [*Latin*] ..... PSS
Postsecondary Education Planning Commission [*Florida*] (EDAC) ..... PEPC
Postsecondary Education Statistics Division [*Department of Education*] (GFGA) ..... PESD
Postsecondary Education Task Force on Energy Management [*Canada*] ..... PETFEM
Postsecondary Longitudinal Studies Program [*Department of Education*] (GFGA) ..... PLS
Post-Separation Employment ..... PSE
Post-Shoring-Polyethylene [*Method of constructing underground homes*] ..... PSP
Postshunt Encephalopathy [*Medicine*] ..... PSE
Post-Sinusoidal Resistance ..... PSR
Post-Sleep Activity ..... PSA
PostSparKasse [*Post Office Savings Bank*] [*Austria*] ..... PSK
Postspinal Headache (AAMN) ..... PSH
Poststenotic [*Medicine*] (DMAA) ..... PST
Poststimulatory Auditory Adaptation ..... PSAA
Post-Stimulus Histogram [*Psychometrics*] ..... PSH
Post-Stimulus Time ..... PST
Poststimulus Time Histiogram [*Medical statistics*] ..... PSTH
Poststimulus Time Histogram [*Medicine*] (DMAA) ..... PTSH
Post-Storage Checkout [*NASA*] (KSC) ..... PSC
Poststreptococcal Acute Glomerulonephritis [*Medicine*] ..... PSAGN
Post-Streptococcal Glomerulonephritis [*Medicine*] ..... PSGN
Post-Surgical Pain [*Medicine*] ..... PSP
Postsurgical, Tumor, Nodes, and Metastases [*Classifications for postsurgical resection pathological staging of cancer*] [*Oncology*] (DAVI) ..... pTNM
Postsurgical Unit (DAVI) ..... PSU
Postsynaptic Current [*Neurophysiology*] ..... PSC
Postsynaptic Density [*Neurophysiology*] ..... PSD
Postsynaptic Membrane [*Neurology*] ..... PSM
Postsynaptic Potential [*Neurophysiology*] ..... PSP
Post-Synchronization (AD) ..... post-sync
Post-Tensioned Concrete [*Technical drawings*] ..... PTC
Post-Tensioning Institute [*Defunct*] (EA) ..... PTI
Post-Test Analysis [*NASA*] (NASA) ..... PTA
Posttetanic Potentiation [*Neurophysiology*] ..... PTP
Post-Tetanic Potentiation [*Neurology*] ..... PTP
Post-Township ..... P-TWP
Post-Transfusion Hepatitis [*Medicine*] ..... PTH
Post-Transfusion Liver Disease [*Medicine*] ..... PTLD
Posttransfusion Mononucleosis [*Medicine*] ..... PTM
Post-Transfusion Purpura [*Medicine*] ..... PTP
Post-Traumatic Amnesia [*Medicine*] ..... PTA
Posttraumatic Borderline Personality Disorder [*Medicine*] (DMAA) ..... PTBPD

Posttraumatic Brain Syndrome [*Medicine*] (DMAA) ... PTBS
Posttraumatic Fibromyalgia Syndrome [*Medicine*] (DMAA) ... PTFS
Posttraumatic Progressive Myelopathy [*Neurology*] (DAVI) ... PTPM
Post-Traumatic Stress [*Medicine*] ... PTS
Post-Traumatic Stress Disorder [*Psychiatry*] ... PTSD
Posttraumatic Stress Syndrome [*Medicine*] (DMAA) ... PTSS
Post-Traumatic Stress System [*Medicine*] ... PTSS
Post-Treatment Resource Program [*Medicine*] ... PTRP
Post-Trip Review ... PTR
Posttuning Drift ... PTD
Post-Turnover Change [*Nuclear energy*] (NRCH) ... PTC
Postulate-Based Permuted Subject Indexing (PDAA) ... POPSI
Postural Drainage [*Medicine*] (MAE) ... PD
Postural Drainage and Clapping [*Medicine*] (DAVI) ... PD & C
Postural Drainage and Percussion [*Medicine*] (DAVI) ... PD & P
Posture Foundation [*Initialism is used in brand of sneaker shoe, PF Flyers*] ... PF
Postvaccination ... PV
Postvasectomy Specimen [*Urology*] (DAVI) ... PVAS
Post-Vietnam Psychiatric Syndrome ... PVNPS
Post-Vietnam Syndrome ... PVS
Postville Herald, Postville, IA [*Library symbol Library of Congress*] (LCLS) ... IaPosH
Postville Public Library, Postville, IA [*Library symbol Library of Congress*] (LCLS) ... IaPos
Postviral Fatigue Syndrome [*Medicine*] (DMAA) ... PVFS
Post-Virgil ... PV
Postvoiding [*Medicine*] (MAE) ... PV
Postvoiding Cystogram [*Medicine*] (MAE) ... PVC
Postvoiding Residual [*Medicine*] ... PVR
Postwar ... PW
Postwar Planning [*World War II*] ... PWP
Post-War Scientific Collaboration [*British*] ... PWSC
Postweaning Diarrhea Syndrome [*Medicine*] (DMAA) ... PWDS
Post-Weld Heat Treatment [*Nuclear energy*] (NRCH) ... PWHT
Post-Write Disturb (IAA) ... PWD
Potable ... POT
Potable and Sanitary Water System [*Nuclear energy*] (NRCH) ... PSWS
Potable Water (KSC) ... POTW
Potable Water [*Nuclear energy*] (NRCH) ... PW
Potable Water Intake ... PWI
Potable Water System (KSC) ... PWS
Potash (AD) ... pot
Potash and Phosphate Institute (EA) ... PPI
Potash Co. of America, Inc. [*Toronto Stock Exchange symbol*] ... PCA
Potash Corp. of Saskatchewan [*Canada*] ... PCS
Potash Corp. of Saskatchewan [*NYSE symbol*] (SPSG) ... POT
Potash Corp. of Saskatchewan, Inc. [*Associated Press*] (SAG) ... Potash
Potash Corp. Saskatchewan [*NYSE symbol*] (TTSB) ... POT
Potash Export Association (EA) ... PEA
Potash Institute [*Later, PPI*] (EA) ... PI
Potash Institute of North America [*Later, PPI*] (EA) ... PINA
Potash, Oil, and Wheat Country [*Saskatoon, Saskatchewan*] (AD) ... POW Country
Potassa [*Chemistry*] (MAE) ... pot
Potasse et Engrais Chimiques ... PEC
Potassium [*Chemical element*] ... K
Potassium [*Chemical symbol is K*] ... POT
Potassium [*An element*] (DAVI) ... potass
Potassium Aluminum Sulfate (AD) ... potash alum
Potassium Aminopropylamide [*Organic chemistry*] ... KAPA
Potassium Bromide [*An anticonvulsant and sedative*] (DAVI) ... KBr
Potassium Channel Opener [*Vasodilator*] ... PCO
Potassium Dideuterium Phosphate ... KDP
Potassium [*Kalium*] **Dihydrogen Phosphate** [*Inorganic chemistry*] ... KDP
Potassium, Glucose, and Insulin (MAE) ... PGI
Potassium Gold Cyanide [*Inorganic chemistry*] ... PGC
Potassium Hemoglobinate [*Organic chemistry*] (DAVI) ... K hgb
Potassium Hemoglobinate (AAMN) ... KHb
Potassium Hexafluorozirconate [*Inorganic chemistry*] ... PFZ
Potassium Hydroxide [*Organic chemistry*] ... KOH
Potassium Iodide (AAMN) ... KI
Potassium Lithium Niobate (PDAA) ... PLN
Potassium Metasilicate [*CIPW classification*] [*Geology*] ... ks
Potassium Permanganate [*Pharmacology*] (DAVI) ... KMnO
Potassium Picrate Active Substances [*Measure of detergent content of water*] ... PPAS
Potassium [*Chemical symbol: K*], Rare-Earth Elements, and Phosphorus [*Acronym used to describe crust material brought from the moon by astronauts*] ... KREEP
Potassium, Sodium Chloride, Sodium Lactate [*Solution*] (AAMN) ... PSL
Potassium, Sodium Chloride, Sodium Lactate Solution (BABM) ... PSL SOL
Potassium, Sodium Chloride, Sodium Lactate Solution [*Pharmacology*] (DAVI) ... PSL sol
Potassium Solubility Product [*Biochemistry*] (DAVI) ... Ksp
Potassium Sorbate [*Food additive*] ... PS
Potassium Tantalate Niobate (MCD) ... KTN
Potassium Thiocyanate [*Broth*] [*A reagent*] [*Pharmacology*] (DAVI) ... KSCN
Potassium Thiocyanate [*or KSCN*] [*Organic chemistry*] (DAVI) ... SCN
Potassium Turbo-Alternator ... KTA
Potassium, Urine 24 Hour [*Biochemistry*] (DAVI) ... K24H
Potassium-Adsorption-Ratio ... PAR
Potassium-Containing Minimal Capacitation Medium [*Medicine*] (BABM) ... K-MCM
Potassium-Excretion Rate [*Medicine*] (DAVI) ... U_kV
Potassium-Plasma [*Biochemistry*] (DAVI) ... K-PL
Potassium-Urine [*Spot*] [*Biochemistry*] (DAVI) ... K-SPT
Potato (ROG) ... POT
Potato Agar [*Microbiology*] ... PA
Potato Association of America (EA) ... PAA
Potato Aucuba Mosaic Virus [*Plant pathology*] ... PAUMV
Potato Black Ringspot Virus [*Plant pathology*] ... PBRV
Potato Carrot Agar [*Culture Media*] ... PCA
Potato Chip Institute, International [*Later, PC/SFA*] (EA) ... PCI
Potato Chip Manufacturers [*British*] (DBA) ... PCMA
Potato Chip/Snack Food Association [*Formerly, NPCI, PCI*] [*Later, SFA*] ... PC/SFA
Potato Curly Top Disease [*Plant pathology*] ... PCT
Potato Cyst Nematode [*Plant pathology*] ... PCN
Potato Dextrose Agar [*Culture media*] ... PDA
Potato Dextrose Broth [*Microbiology*] ... PDB
Potato Eaters (EA) ... PE
Potato Extract-Glucose-Thiamine Hydrochloride [*Growth medium*] ... PGT
Potato Futures Market [*Finance*] ... PFM
Potato Growers' Association of New South Wales [*Australia*] ... PGANSW
Potato Growers' Association of Western Australia ... PGAWA
Potato Growers of Australia ... PGA
Potato Industry Council (Western Australia) ... PIC(WA)
Potato Industry Trust Fund Committee [*Western Australia*] ... PITFC
Potato Kallikrein Inhibitor [*Medicine*] (DMAA) ... PKI
Potato Leafroll Virus ... PLRV
Potato Marketing Authority [*Australia*] ... PMA
Potato Marketing Board [*British*] ... PMB
Potato Merchants' Association [*Australia*] ... PMA
Potato Mop-Top Virus [*Plant pathology*] ... PMTV
Potato Processing Waste ... PPW
Potato Processors' Association [*Australia*] ... PPA
Potato Processors Association [*British*] (DBA) ... PPA
Potato Spindle Tuber Disease ... PSTD
Potato Spindle Tuber Viroid [*Plant pathology*] ... PSTVd
Potato Spindle Tuber Virus ... PSTV
Potato Tuber Peroxidase [*An enzyme*] ... PTP
Potato Virus A [*Plant pathology*] ... PVA
Potato Virus M [*Plant pathology*] ... PVM
Potato Virus S [*Plant pathology*] ... PVS
Potato Virus T [*Plant pathology*] ... PVT
Potato Virus X [*Plant pathology*] ... PVX
Potato Virus Y ... PVY
Potato Yellow Dwarf Virus [*Plant pathology*] ... PYDV
Potatoes (AD) ... potats
Potato-Tomato (AD) ... pomato
Potchefstroom [*South Africa*] [*ICAO location identifier*] (ICLI) ... FAPS
Poteau Junior College [*Oklahoma*] ... PJC
Poteau, OK [*FM radio station call letters*] ... KOMS
Poteau, OK [*AM radio station call letters*] ... KPRV
Poteau, OK [*FM radio station call letters*] ... KZBB
Poteau, OK [*Location identifier FAA*] (FAAL) ... RKR
Potency Factor (GNE) ... PF
Potency Ratio [*Medicine*] (DMAA) ... PR
Potentate ... POT
Potential (AFM) ... POT
Potential (AD) ... pot
Potential (WDMC) ... pot
Potential (AAMN) ... POTEN
Potential (IDOE) ... V
Potential Abnormality of Glucose Tolerance [*Medicine*] ... PotAGT
Potential Acquisition Valuation Method [*Management*] ... PAV
Potential Acuity Meter [*Instrumentation*] ... PAM
Potential AIDS [*Acquired Immune Deficiency Syndrome*] **Victim** ... PAV
Potential Area of Danger [*Navigation*] ... PAD
Potential Barrier Method (IAA) ... PBM
Potential Benefit Factor (OA) ... PBF
Potential Binding Level [*Of natural waters for metal ions*] ... PBL
Potential Complications [*Medicine*] (DMAA) ... PC
Potential Conflict Forecasts [*Army*] ... PCF
Potential Contractor Program (MCD) ... PCP
Potential Current Transformer ... PCT
Potential Determining Ions ... PDI
Potential Difference [*Electricity*] (ROG) ... DP
Potential Difference [*Electricity*] ... PD
Potential Difference [*Electronics*] (IAA) ... POTDIF
Potential Difference [*in Volts*] (DMAA) ... U
Potential Difference [*Symbol*] ... V
Potential Energy ... PE
Potential Energy [*Symbol*] [*IUPAC*] ... V
Potential Energy Source [*Physiology*] ... PES
Potential Enviromental Concentration [*Pollution technology*] ... PEC
Potential Evapotranspiration [*Hydrology*] ... ETP
Potential Evapotranspiration (DICI) ... PE
Potential Evapotranspiration ... PET
Potential Excess [*of stock*] [*DoD*] ... PE
Potential Excess Report ... PER
Potential for Foster Parenthood Scale [*Psychology*] ... PFPS
Potential for Successful Performance [*Test*] ... PSP
Potential Gas Committee ... PGC
Potential Hijacker [*Airline notation*] ... QQ
Potential Host Institures List [*European Commission*] ... PHIL
Potential Icing Category [*Meteorology*] (DA) ... PIC
Potential Leaf Area [*Botany*] ... PLA
Potential Long Supply Utilization Screening (NATG) ... PLUS
Potential Military Relevance ... PMR
Potential Mixed Layer Depth ... POTMLD

Potential Natural Vegetation (GNE) ... PNV
Potential Network Access Facility ... PNAF
Potential Offender Identification Program ... POIP
Potential Officer [*British military*] (DMA) ... PO
Potential Officer Material [*British military*] (DMA) ... POM
Potential Ozone Depleter ... POD
Potential Points of Collision [*Navigation*] ... PPC
Potential Problem Report [*Navy*] (CAAL) ... PPR
Potential Rating Index by ZIP [*Zone Improvement Plan*] **Market** [*Advertising*] ... PRIZM
Potential Repository Zone [*Nuclear waste storage*] ... PRZ
Potential Requirements File (NITA) ... PRF
Potential Selected Item List (MCD) ... PSIL
Potential Single Point Failures [*NASA*] (KSC) ... PSPF
Potential Source List (MCD) ... PSL
Potential Surface Analysis (ADA) ... PSA
Potential Switch ... PSW
Potential to Emit (GNE) ... PTE
Potential Toxic Area (NASA) ... PTA
Potential Transformer ... PT
Potential Variation Mixed Basis [*Photovoltaic energy systems*] ... PVMB
Potential Viewer [*Television ratings*] (NTCM) ... PV
Potential Volume Change ... PVC
Potential Vorticity [*Meteorology*] [*Fluid mechanics*] ... PV
Potential Years of Life Lost [*Medicine*] (DMAA) ... PYLL
Potential-Energy Distribution Function [*Physical chemistry*] ... PEDF
Potential-Energy Function [*Physical chemistry*] ... PEF
Potential-Energy Surface [*Chemical kinetics*] ... PES
Potentially Compensable Event (DICI) ... PCE
Potentially Contaminated Area (DNAB) ... PCA
Potentially Critical Failures ... PCF
Potentially Exempt Transfer (ODBW) ... PET
Potentially Exempt Transfer (ODBW) ... PET
Potentially Lethal Arrhythmia [*Medicine*] (DMAA) ... PLA
Potentially Lethal Damage [*Medicine*] ... PLD
Potentially Lethal Damage Repair [*Medicine*] ... PLDR
Potentially Reportable Deficiency [*Nuclear energy*] (NRCH) ... PRD
Potentially Responsible Party [*Environmental Protection Agency*] ... PRP
Potentiometer [*Automotive engineering*] ... P/MTR
Potentiometer (DEN) ... PM
Potentiometer [*or Potentiometric*] ... POT
Potentiometer (IDOE) ... pot
Potentiometer (AD) ... pot
Potentiometer Slidewire ... PSW
Potentiometer Strip Chart ... PSC
Potentiometer Synchro ... PS
Potentiometer Tapping Kit ... PTK
Potentiometers (AD) ... pots
Potentiometric Electrometer (IAA) ... POTELECTROMET
Potentiometric Immunoassay [*Clinical chemistry*] ... PIA
Potentiometric Ionophore Modulated Immunoassay [*Electrochemistry*] ... PIMIA
Potentiometric Voltmeter ... PVM
Potentional Performance Capability (IAA) ... PPC
Potentionmetric Voltmeter Bridge (IAA) ... PVB
Potenza [*Italy ICAO location identifier*] (ICLI) ... LIBZ
Potere Battericida del Sangue [*Bactericidal Property of the Blood*] [*Medicine*] ... PBS
Potez [*Etablissements Henri Potez*] [*France ICAO aircraft manufacturer identifier*] (ICAO) ... PZ
Potgietersrus [*South Africa*] [*ICAO location identifier*] (ICLI) ... FAPP
Pothier on Partnership [*A publication*] (DLA) ... Poth Part
Pothier on the Law of Obligations [*A publication*] (DLA) ... Poth Ob
Pothier on the Law of Obligations [*A publication*] (DLA) ... Poth Obl
Pothier on the Law of Obligations [*A publication*] (DLA) ... Poth Oblig
Pothier. Procedure Civile [*A publication*] (DLA) ... Poth Proc Civ
Pothier's Contracts [*A publication*] (DLA) ... Poth Cont
Pothier's Pandectae Justinianeae, Etc. [*A publication*] (DLA) ... Pothier Pand
Pothier's Pandects [*A publication*] (DLA) ... Poth Pand
Pothier's Treatise on Maritime Contracts [*A publication*] (DLA) ... Poth Mar Cont
Pothier's Treatise on the Contract of Sale [*A publication*] (DLA) ... Poth Cont Sale
Pothier's Treatise on the Contract of Sale [*A publication*] (DLA) ... Poth Contr Sale
Potion ... Pot
Potlatch Corp. [*Formerly, PFI*] [*NYSE symbol*] (SPSG) ... PCH
Potlatch Corp. [*Associated Press*] (SAG) ... Potltch
Poto [*Peru*] [*ICAO location identifier*] (ICLI) ... SPOP
Potomac Annex [*Navy*] ... POTANN
Potomac Antique Tools and Industries Association (EA) ... PATINA
Potomac Appalachian Trail Club (EA) ... PATC
Potomac Edison [*NYSE symbol*] (SAG) ... PEQ
Potomac Edison [*Associated Press*] (SAG) ... PotEd25
Potomac Edison 8.00% 'QUIDS' [*NYSE symbol*] (TTSB) ... PEQ
Potomac El Pwr$3.89'91 Pfd [*NYSE symbol*] (TTSB) ... POMPrA
Potomac Elec Pwr $2.44 Cv Pfd [*NYSE symbol*] (TTSB) ... POMPr
Potomac Elec Pwr $3.37cm'87 Pfd [*NYSE symbol*] (TTSB) ... POMPrH
Potomac Electric Power Co. ... PEPC
Potomac Electric Power Co. ... PEPCO
Potomac Electric Power Co. [*NYSE symbol*] (SPSG) ... POM
Potomac Electric Power Co. [*Associated Press*] (SAG) ... PotEl
Potomac Electric Power Co. [*Associated Press*] (SAG) ... PotmEl
Potomac Electric Pwr [*NYSE symbol*] (TTSB) ... POM
Potomac Horse Fever Agent ... PHFA
Potomac Institute [*Defunct*] (EA) ... PI
Potomac Naval River Command (MCD) ... PNRC
Potomac Pacific Engineering, Inc. ... PPE
Potomac Public Library, Potomac, IL [*Library symbol Library of Congress*] (LCLS) ... IPot
Potomac River Fisheries Commission [*Maryland and Virginia*] (NOAA) ... PRFC
Potomac River Naval Command [*Washington, DC*] ... PRNC
Potomac State College [*of West Virginia University*] ... PSC
Potomac State College, Keyser, WV [*Library symbol Library of Congress*] (LCLS) ... WvKP
Potomac-Cabin John, MD [*AM radio station call letters*] ... WCTN
Potosi [*Bolivia*] [*Airport symbol*] (AD) ... POI
Potosi [*Bolivia*] [*ICAO location identifier*] (ICLI) ... SLPO
Potosi, MO [*FM radio station call letters*] ... KHCR
Potosi, MO [*AM radio station call letters*] ... KYRO
Potosina del Aire SA de CV [*Mexico ICAO designator*] (FAAC) ... PSN
Potplant Growers Association [*British*] (DBA) ... PPGA
Potrerillos [*Chile*] [*Airport symbol*] (AD) ... RER
Potrero [*Cattle Ranch*] [*Spanish*] (AD) ... potr
Potrero Grande [*Costa Rica*] [*ICAO location identifier*] (ICLI) ... MRPG
Potsdam [*Germany*] [*Later, NGK*] [*Seismograph station code, US Geological Survey*] (SEIS) ... POT
Potsdam [*New York*] [*Seismograph station code, US Geological Survey*] (SEIS) ... PTN
Potsdam, NY [*Location identifier FAA*] (FAAL) ... PTD
Potsdam, NY [*FM radio station call letters*] ... WAIH
Potsdam, NY [*AM radio station call letters*] ... WPDM
Potsdam, NY [*FM radio station call letters*] ... WSNN
Potsdam, NY [*FM radio station call letters*] ... WTSC
Potsdam Public Library, Potsdam, NY [*Library symbol Library of Congress*] (LCLS) ... NPot
Potsmokers Anonymous (EA) ... PA
Potter & Brumfield, Inc. (IAA) ... PAB
Potter Distilleries Ltd. [*Toronto Stock Exchange symbol Vancouver Stock Exchange symbol*] ... PTD
Potter Instrument Coordinated Measuring Machine ... PICOMM
Potter on Corporations [*A publication*] (DLA) ... Pott Corp
Potteries Motor Traction Co. [*British*] ... PMT
Potter's Edition of Dwarris on Statutes [*A publication*] (DLA) ... Pot Dwar
Potter's Edition of Dwarris on Statutes [*A publication*] (DLA) ... Pott Dwarris
Potters Financial [*NASDAQ symbol*] (TTSB) ... PTRS
Potters Financial Corp. [*Associated Press*] (SAG) ... PottrFinl
Potters Financial Corp. [*NASDAQ symbol*] (SAG) ... PTRS
Potter's Reports [*4-7 Wyoming*] [*A publication*] (DLA) ... Potter
Potters Savings & Loan Co. [*Associated Press*] (SAG) ... PotrSvg
Potters Savings & Loan Co. [*NASDAQ symbol*] (SAG) ... PTRS
Potters' Society of Australia ... PSA
Pottery ... POT
Pottery (AD) ... pott
Pottery (VRA) ... ptry
Pottery [*Freight*] ... PTRY
Pottery and Glass Wholesalers Association (NADA) ... PGWA
Pottery Cache (BJA) ... pc
[*The*] **Pottery of Palestine from the Earliest Times to the End of the EarlyBronze Age** [*A publication*] (BJA) ... PPEB
Potting Mold (MCD) ... PM
Pottle [*Unit of measure*] (ROG) ... POT
Potton Technical Industries, Mansonville, PQ, Canada [*Library symbol Library of Congress*] (LCLS) ... CaQMaPTI
Potton Technical Industries, Mansonville, Quebec [*Library symbol National Library of Canada*] (NLC) ... QMPTI
Potts Camp, MS [*FM radio station call letters*] (RBYB) ... WCNA
Potts Junction [*Guam*] [*Seismograph station code, US Geological Survey*] (SEIS) ... PJG
Pott's Law Dictionary [*3rd ed.*] [*1815*] [*A publication*] (DLA) ... Pot LD
Potts' Law Dictionary [*3rd ed.*] [*1815*] [*A publication*] (DLA) ... Potts LD
Pottstown, PA [*Location identifier FAA*] (FAAL) ... PTW
Pottstown, PA [*AM radio station call letters*] ... WPAZ
Pottsville Free Public Library, Pottsville, PA [*OCLC symbol*] (OCLC) ... POT
Pottsville Free Public Library, Pottsville, PA [*Library symbol*] [*Library of Congress*] (LCLS) ... PPo
Pottsville, PA [*FM radio station call letters*] ... WAVT
Pottsville, PA [*AM radio station call letters*] ... WPAM
Pottsville, PA [*AM radio station call letters*] ... WPPA
Pottsville, PA [*Location identifier FAA*] (FAAL) ... ZER
Potus [*A Drink*] [*Pharmacy*] ... POT
Pouce [*Inch*] [*French*] ... P
Pouce Coupe Public Library, British Columbia [*Library symbol National Library of Canada*] (NLC) ... BPOC
Pouce Coupe Public Library, Pouce Coupe, BC, Canada [*Library symbol*] [*Library of Congress*] (LCLS) ... CaBPOC
Pouch Cove Public Library, Newfoundland [*Library symbol National Library of Canada*] (NLC) ... NFPC
Pouch Cove Public Library, Pouch Cove, NF, Canada [*Library symbol Library of Congress*] (LCLS) ... CaNfPc
Poughkeepsie [*New York*] [*Airport symbol*] (OAG) ... POU
Poughkeepsie, NY [*Location identifier FAA*] (FAAL) ... POU
Poughkeepsie, NY [*Location identifier FAA*] (FAAL) ... PWL
Poughkeepsie, NY [*FM radio station call letters*] (RBYB) ... WALQ
Poughkeepsie, NY [*AM radio station call letters*] ... WEOK
Poughkeepsie, NY [*AM radio station call letters*] ... WKIP
Poughkeepsie, NY [*FM radio station call letters*] (RBYB) ... WNSX-FM
Poughkeepsie, NY [*FM radio station call letters*] ... WPDH
Poughkeepsie, NY [*FM radio station call letters*] ... WRHV
Poughkeepsie, NY [*FM radio station call letters*] ... WRNQ
Poughkeepsie, NY [*FM radio station call letters*] ... WSPK
Poughkeepsie, NY [*Television station call letters*] ... WTBY
Poughkeepsie, NY [*FM radio station call letters*] ... WVKR

[*The*] Poughkeepsie Savings Bank FSB [*Poughkeepsie, NY*] [*NASDAQ symbol*] (NQ) .... PKPS
[*The*] Poughkeepsie Savings Bank FSB [*Associated Press*] (SAG) .... PoughSv
Poughkeepsie Svgs Bank [*NASDAQ symbol*] (TTSB) .... PKPS
Pouilloux [*France*] [*Seismograph station code, US Geological Survey*] (SEIS) .... POU
Pouilly-Maconge [*France ICAO location identifier*] (ICLI) .... LFEP
Poultney, VT [*AM radio station call letters*] .... WVNR
Poultry [*Freight*] .... PLTRY
Poultry .... PLTY
Poultry (AD) .... poul
Poultry .... POUL
Poultry Advisory Board [*Queensland, Australia*] .... PAB
Poultry Advisory Board (Queensland) [*Australia*] .... PAB(Q)
Poultry and Egg Institute of America (EA) .... PEIA
Poultry and Egg National Board [*Later, AEB*] (EA) .... PENB
Poultry and Egg Situation .... PES
Poultry Breeders of America (EA) .... PBA
Poultry Byproduct Meal .... PBPM
Poultry Disease Research Center [*University of Georgia*] [*Research center*] (RCD) .... PDRC
Poultry Education Association [*British*] (BI) .... PEA
Poultry Farmers' Association of Western Australia .... PFAWA
Poultry Feather Meal [*Fisheries*] .... PFM
Poultry Husbandry Adviser [*Ministry of Agriculture, Fisheries, and Food*] [*British*] .... PHA
Poultry Industry Investigation Officer [*Australia*] .... PIIO
Poultry Industry Manufacturers Council [*Defunct*] (EA) .... PIMCO
Poultry Industry Trust Fund [*Australia*] .... PITF
Poultry Marketing Guide .... PMG
Poultry Meat Industry Committee [*New South Wales, Australia*] .... PMIC
Poultry Producers' Association of Western Australia .... PPAWA
Poultry Products Inspection Act (GFGA) .... PPIA
Poultry Publishers Association (EA) .... PPA
Poultry Research Centre [*of the Agricultural Research Council*] [*British*] (ARC) .... PRC
Poultry Science Association (EA) .... PSA
Poultrymen's Cooperative Association (EA) .... PCA
Poultry-Related Antigens [*Immunology*] .... PAg
Poum [*New Caledonia*] [*ICAO location identifier*] (ICLI) .... NWWJ
Pound [*Libra*] [*Unit of weight*] .... lb
Pound (IDOE) .... P
Pound (ROG) .... PD
Pound (MAE) .... pnd
Pound Avoirdupois (BARN) .... lb av
Pound Calorie (WDAA) .... LB CAL
Pound Centigrade Unit .... PCU
Pound Troy .... LBT
Pound, VA [*FM radio station call letters*] .... WDXC
Poundal [*Unit of force*] .... pdl
Poundal Seconds per Square Foot .... PDL S/FT²
Poundals per Square Foot .... PDL/FT²
Pounder (MSA) .... PDR
Pounder [*Gun*] .... PR
Pound-Force per Hour (MCD) .... PHR
Pound-Force per Inch (MSA) .... LBIN
Pound-Force per Second .... LBF-S
Pound-Force per Square Foot (IAA) .... PSF
Pound-Force per Square Inch (WDAA) .... LBF/IN²
Pound-Force per Square Inch (IAA) .... PSI
Pound-Force Seconds per Square Foot .... LBF S/FT²
Pounds [*As measurement of total stress*] [*Aerospace*] (AAG) .... P
Pounds, Force (MCD) .... LBF
Pounds, Mass (MCD) .... LBM
Pounds of Mass per Second per Square Inch LBM/S-IN2
Pounds per Brake Horsepower .... PBHP
Pounds per Capita per Day (AAG) .... PCD
Pounds per Cubic Foot .... LB/FT³
Pounds per Cubic Foot .... PCF
Pounds per Cubic Inch .... LB/IN³
Pounds per Cubic Yard .... LB/YD³
Pounds per Foot .... LB/FT
Pounds per Foot-Hour .... LB/(FT H)
Pounds per Foot-Second .... LB/(FT S)
Pounds per Gallon .... LB/GAL
Pounds per Gallon .... ppg
Pounds per Horsepower .... PHP
Pounds per Horsepower-Hour .... LB/(HP H)
Pounds per Hour .... LB/H
Pounds per Hour (AAG) .... PHR
Pounds per Hour (NG) .... PPH
Pounds Per Hour (AD) .... pph
Pounds per Hour per Pound (SAA) .... PPH/LB
Pounds per Inch [*Lubrication load*] .... PPI
Pounds per Lineal Foot [*Technical drawings*] .... PFL
Pounds per Minute (AAG) .... LB/M
Pounds per Minute .... LB/MIN
Pounds per Minute .... PM
Pounds per Minute .... PPM
Pounds Per Minute (AD) .... ppm
Pounds per Second .... LB/S
Pounds Per Second (AD) .... pps
Pounds per Second (AAG) .... PPS
Pounds per Square Foot .... LB/FT²
Pounds per Square Foot (IDOE) .... psf

Pounds per Square Foot .... PSF
Pounds per Square Inch .... LB/IN²
Pounds per Square Inch (IDOE) .... psi
Pounds per Square Inch [*Marine science*] (OSRA) .... psi
Pounds per Square Inch .... PSI
Pounds per Square Inch (AAG) .... S
Pounds per Square Inch Absolute (IAA) .... PSI
Pounds per Square Inch Absolute .... PSIA
Pounds per Square Inch, Absolute [*Marine science*] (OSRA) .... psia
Pounds per Square Inch Absolute (IDOE) .... psia
Pounds per Square Inch, Differential [*Marine science*] (OSRA) .... psid
Pounds per Square Inch Differential (MCD) .... PSID
Pounds per Square Inch Gauge .... PSIG
Pounds per Square Inch, Gauge [*Marine science*] (OSRA) .... psig
Pounds per Square Inch Gauge (IDOE) .... psig
Pounds per Square Inch Sealed (NASA) .... PSIS
Pounds per Square Yard .... LB/YD²
Pounds per Thousand Barrels [*Petroleum technology*] .... PTB
Pounds Pressure .... PP
Pounds [*Libra in Latin*] Static Thrust (DOMA) .... lbst
Pounds Thrust [*NASA*] (KSC) .... LBT
Pounds-Out-the-Door [*Measure of industrial production*] .... POD
Pour [*For*] [*French*] .... P
Pour Condoler [*To Offer Sympathy*] [*French*] .... PC
Pour Copie Conforme [*Certified True Copy*] [*French*] .... PCC
Pour Dire Adieu [*To Say Farewell*] [*On visiting cards*] [*French*] .... PDA
Pour l'Amenagement et le Renouveau Institutionel et Social [*France Political party*] .... PARIS
Pour Point [*Petroleum characteristic*] .... PP
Pour Prendre Conge [*To Take Leave*] [*French*] (AD) .... p p c
Pour Prendre Conge [*To Take Leave*] [*French*] .... PPC
Pour Remercier [*To Express Thanks*] [*French*] .... PR
Pour Rendre Visite [*To Make a Call*] [*French*] .... PRV
Poura [*Burkina Faso*] [*ICAO location identifier*] (ICLI) .... DHCR
Poured Concrete Wall Contractors Association (EA) .... PCWCA
Poured-On, Passed-Over [*Bowdlerized version*] .... POPO
Pouvoir Hydrogene [*Hydrogen Power*] [*Negative logarithm of effective H ion concentration Chemistry*] .... pH
Poverty Advisory Group .... PAG
Poverty Budget Share [*Bureau of the Census*] (GFGA) .... PBS
Poverty Datum Line .... PDL
Poverty Law Reporter [*Commerce Clearing House*] [*A publication*] (DLA) .... Pov L Rep
Poverty Lawyers for Effective Advocacy .... PLEA
Povolzhskii Region, RSFSR [*MARC geographic area code Library of Congress*] (LCCP) .... e-urp-
Povungnituk [*Canada*] [*Airport symbol*] (OAG) .... YPX
Powassan and District Union Public Library, Powassan, Ontario [*Library symbol National Library of Canada*] (NLC) .... OPDU
Powassan Encephalitis [*Medicine*] .... POW
Powder .... PDR
Powder [*Navy*] .... POW
Powder [*England*] .... POWD
Powder (AD) .... powd
Powder (KSC) .... PWD
Powder [*Pharmacy*] (DAVI) .... pwdr
Powder Actuated Tool Manufacturers' Institute (EA) .... PATMI
Powder Bed (DAVI) .... PB
Powder Board (DAVI) .... PB
Powder Coating Institute (EA) .... PCI
Powder Diffraction File (DICI) .... PDF
Powder Diffraction Search-Match System [*International Data Center*] .... PDSM
Powder Injection Molding [*Metallurgy*] .... PIM
Powder Melting Process [*Physics*] .... PMP
Powder Metal Industries Association [*Australia*] .... PMIA
Powder Metal Industries Federation .... PMIF
Powder Metallurgy .... PM
Powder Metallurgy Equipment Association (EA) .... PMEA
Powder Passing .... PWDP
Powder Science and Technology Research Association [*Norway*] (EAIO) .... POSTEC
Powder X-Ray Diffraction .... PXRD
Powdered .... POWD
Powdered [*Freight*] .... PWDRD
Powdered Activated Carbon [*Adsorbent*] .... PAC
Powdered Activated Carbon Treatment [*For wastewater*] [*E. I. Du Pont De Nemours & Co., Inc.*] .... PACT
Powdered Extract [*Pharmacy*] .... PE
Powdered Metal Cathode .... PMC
Powdered Metal Part .... PMP
Powell Air Ltd. [*Canada ICAO designator*] (FAAC) .... PWL
Powell. Conveyancing [*1810*] [*A publication*] (ILCA) .... Pow Conv
Powell Cycle Registry (EA) .... PCR
Powell Indus [*NASDAQ symbol*] (TTSB) .... POWL
Powell Industries, Inc. [*Associated Press*] (SAG) .... Powell
Powell Industries, Inc. [*NASDAQ symbol*] (NQ) .... POWL
Powell on Contracts [*A publication*] (DLA) .... Pow Cont
Powell on Evidence [*10th ed.*] [*1921*] [*A publication*] (DLA) .... Pow Ev
Powell on Mortgages [*6th ed.*] [*1826*] [*A publication*] (DLA) .... Pow Mort
Powell on Mortgages [*A publication*] (DLA) .... Pow Mortg
Powell on the Law of Inland Carriers [*A publication*] (DLA) .... Pow Inl Car
Powell River [*Canada*] [*Airport symbol*] (OAG) .... YPW
Powell River, BC [*AM radio station call letters*] .... CHQB
Powell River District Libraries, British Columbia [*Library symbol National Library of Canada*] (NLC) .... BPRD

Powell River District Libraries, Powell, BC, Canada [*Library symbol Library of Congress*] (LCLS) .... CaBPrD
Powell River District Public Library Association, British Columbia [*Library symbol National Library of Canada*] (NLC) .... BPRDP
Powell River District Public Library, Powell River, BC, Canada [*Library symbol*] [*Library of Congress*] (LCLS) .... CaBPrDP
Powell River Historical Museum, British Columbia [*Library symbol National Library of Canada*] (NLC) .... BPORH
Powell River Historical Museum, Powell River, BC, Canada [*Library symbol Library of Congress*] (LCLS) .... CaBPorH
Powell Sport Wagon Registry (EA) .... PSWR
Powell, TN [*AM radio station call letters*] .... WQBB
Powell, WY [*FM radio station call letters*] .... KLZY
Powell, WY [*AM radio station call letters*] .... KPOW
Powell, WY [*Location identifier FAA*] (FAAL) .... POY
Powell's Essay upon the Learning of Devises, Etc. [*A publication*] (DLA) .... Pow Dev
Powell's Inland Carriers [*2nd ed.*] [*1861*] [*A publication*] (DLA) .... Pow Car
Powell's Lane Elementary School, Westbury, NY [*Library symbol*] [*Library of Congress*] (LCLS) .... NWePLE
Powell's Law of Appellate Proceedings [*A publication*] (DLA) .... Pow App Proc
Power [*Symbol*] [*IUPAC*] .... P
Power .... POW
Power (AD) .... pow
Power .... PW
Power (KSC) .... PWR
Power (IDOE) .... pwr
Power .... PWR
Power Amplifier .... PA
Power Amplifier Assembly .... PAA
Power Amplifier Device [*or Driver*] .... PAD
Power Amplifier Klystron .... PAK
Power Amplifier Neutralizing Capacitor (DEN) .... PANC
Power Analysis Report [*Automobile testing*] .... PAR
Power and Communication Contractors Association (EA) .... PCCA
Power and Heat Rejection Kit [*NASA*] .... PHRK
Power and Light (IAA) .... PAL
Power and Lighting (MSA) .... P & L
Power and Signal List [*Telecommunications*] (TEL) .... PSL
Power and Temperature Monitor Unit (KSC) .... PTMU
Power and Water Authority [*Northern Territory, Australia*] .... PAWA
Power and Water Authority [*Northern Territory, Australia*] .... PWA
Power Apparatus and Systems (MCD) .... PAS
Power Approach [*Aerospace*] .... PA
Power Ascension Testing (IEEE) .... PAT
Power Assist Lathe .... PAL
Power Assist Module [*NASA*] .... PAM
Power Bias Panel .... PBP
Power Boat Association of Victoria [*Australia*] .... PBAV
Power Boiler .... PB
Power Box (IAA) .... PB
Power Brake [*Automotive engineering*] .... P/BRK
Power Brakes [*Automotive engineering*] .... PB
Power Breakfast Syndrome [*Suffered by late-risers forced to attend breakfast meetings*] .... PBS
Power Breeder Reactor (AAG) .... PBR
Power Builder [*Computer software*] (CDE) .... PB
Power Building (NATG) .... PBD
Power Burst Facility [*Nuclear energy*] .... PBF
Power by Wire [*Flight control*] .... PBW
Power Cartesian (IAA) .... PC
Power Cathode Follower .... PCF
Power Change Request [*NASA*] (NASA) .... PCR
Power Circuit (IAA) .... PC
Power Circuit Breaker (MSA) .... PCB
Power Component (IAA) .... PC
Power Conditioning Assembly .... PCA
Power Conditioning Brass Board (MCD) .... PCBB
Power Conditioning Equipment .... PCE
Power Conditioning Group (MCD) .... PCG
Power Conditioning, Switching, and Control .... PCSC
Power Conditioning System .... PCS
Power Conditioning Unit .... PCU
Power Contactor .... PC
Power Control [*System*] (NG) .... PC
Power Control .... POC
Power Control and Distribution .... PCD
Power Control Assembly (NASA) .... PCA
Power Control Box (NASA) .... PCB
Power Control Console [*Diving apparatus*] .... PCC
Power Control Device [*Nuclear energy*] (NRCH) .... PCD
Power Control Lever (DNAB) .... PCL
Power Control Linkage Assembly .... PCLA
Power Control List (MCD) .... PCL
Power Control Mission (NASA) .... PCM
Power Control One [*Hydraulic*] (MCD) PC1
Power Control Panel [*Aerospace*] (AAG) .... PCP
Power Control Room [*Nuclear energy*] .... PCR
Power Control Technologies [*NYSE symbol*] (TTSB) .... ATP
Power Control Technologies, Inc. [*NYSE symbol*] (SAG) .... ATP
Power Control Technologies, Inc. [*Associated Press*] (SAG) .... PwCtlT
Power Control Two [*Hydraulic*] (MCD) PC2
Power Control Unit .... PCU
Power Controller Unit Assembly (IEEE) .... PCUA
Power Conversion (CET) .... P-C

Power Conversion and Distribution System .... PCDS
Power Conversion Distributor .... PCD
Power Conversion Equipment (DNAB) .... PCE
Power Conversion Equipment Test Facility [*Nuclear energy*] .... PCETF
Power Conversion Products Council [*Later, PCPCI*] (EA) .... PCPC
Power Conversion Products Council International (EA) .... PCPCI
Power Conversion Room .... PCR
Power Conversion System .... PCS
Power Conversion Test Facility (SAA) .... PCTF
Power Conversion Unit (IEEE) .... PCU
Power Cooling Mismatch Accident [*Nuclear energy*] (NUCP) .... PCMA
Power Cord (BARN) .... pc
Power Corp. of Canada [*Toronto Stock Exchange symbol Vancouver Stock Exchange symbol*] .... POW
Power Crane and Shovel Association (EA) .... PCSA
Power Density Exceeding a Specified Level over an Area with an Assigned Frequency Band (IEEE) .... PODAF
Power Density Imbalance Limit (IAA) .... POIL
Power Density Meter .... PDM
Power Density Spectra (IEEE) .... PDS
Power Development Engineer (IAA) .... PWRDEVELENGR
Power Diffraction File (NITA) .... PDF
Power Diffraction Search and Match System (PDAA) .... PDSMS
Power Directional Relay .... PDR
Power Dissipation Index (IAA) .... PDI
Power Distribution .... PD
Power Distribution and Control .... PDC
Power Distribution and Control System [*or Subsystem*] [*NASA*] (NASA) .... PDCS
Power Distribution and Control Unit .... PDCU
Power Distribution Assembly (KSC) .... PDA
Power Distribution Box (NASA) .... PDB
Power Distribution Cubiale (NATG) .... PDC
Power Distribution Panel .... PDP
Power Distribution Specification (IAA) .... PDS
Power Distribution System [*or Subsystem*] .... PDS
Power Distribution Trailer (NATG) .... PDT
Power Distribution Unit (AAG) .... PDU
Power Distributor (KSC) .... PWD
Power Divider (IAA) .... PD
Power Dividing Network [*Telecommunications*] (LAIN) .... PDN
Power Doubler (IAA) .... PD
Power Drain Protection [*Automotive engineering*] .... PDP
Power Drive System .... PDS
Power Drive Unit (MCD) .... PDU
Power Driven (IAA) .... PD
Power Driver Decontamination Apparatus (NATG) .... PDDA
Power Engineering Society .... PES
Power Engineering Society of the Institute of Electrical and Electronic Engineers (ITD) .... IEEE/PES
Power Engineering Specification .... PES
Power Equipment [*Military*] (IAA) .... PE
Power Equipment [*JETDS nomenclature*] [*Military*] (CET) .... PU
Power Evaluation Program .... PEP
Power Excursion Accident [*Nuclear energy*] (NUCP) .... PEA
Power Explorations, Inc. [*Toronto Stock Exchange symbol*] .... PWR
Power Extension Package (MCD) .... PEP
Power Extension Plant (MCD) .... PEP
Power Factor [*Radio*] .... PF
Power Factor (IDOE) .... pf
Power Factor Capacitor [*Radio*] (IAA) .... PFC
Power Factor Corrector (MCD) .... PFC
Power Factor Corrector Capacitor [*Radio*] (IAA) .... PFCC
Power Factor Indicator (IAA) .... PFI
Power Factor Meter .... PFM
Power Fail Automatic Restart [*Computer science*] .... PFAR
Power Fail Recovery System [*Computer science*] (MDG) .... PFR
Power Fail/Restart (NITA) .... PF/R
Power Fail/Restart .... PFR
Power Failure (FAAC) .... PWRNO
Power Failure Indicator [*NASA*] (KSC) .... PFI
Power Failure Release .... PFR
Power Fastenings Association [*British*] (DBA) .... PFA
Power Financial Corp. [*Toronto Stock Exchange symbol*] .... PWF
Power Flux Density [*Telecommunications*] (TEL) .... PFD
Power Flying Control Unit [*Aviation*] (DA) .... PFCU
Power Focus [*Photography*] .... PF
Power for Level Flight [*Aeronautics*] .... PLF
Power for Underwater Logistics and Living .... PULL
Power Frame [*Telecommunications*] (TEL) .... PF
Power, Fulcrum, Weight .... PFW
Power Gain .... PG
Power Gain Antenna .... PGA
Power Gate [*Electronics*] (OA) .... PG
Power Generating Assembly (KSC) .... PGA
Power Generation (MCD) .... PG
Power Generation Control Complex [*Nuclear energy*] (NRCH) .... PGCC
Power Generation, Distribution, and Control Subsystem (MCD) .... PGDCS
Power Generation Group [*Nuclear Regulatory Commission*] (NRCH) .... PGG
Power Generation Satellite (HGAA) .... PGS
Power Generation System [*or Subsystem*] .... PGS
Power Generator Section (KSC) .... PGS
Power Generator Unit (IAA) .... PGU
Power Grid Tube .... PGT
Power Hybrid Microcircuit .... PHM
Power Indicator (IAA) .... PI

Power Industry Computer Applications (MCD) ... PICA
Power Industry Computer Applications Conference (MCD) ... PICAC
Power Industry Laboratory Association [*Defunct*] (EA) ... PILA
Power Information Center [*Interagency Advanced Power Group*] [*DoD Washington, DC*] ... PIC
Power Information Network [*Computer science*] ... PIN
Power Injection ... PI
Power Input ... PI
Power Input Panel ... PIP
Power Integrated Circuit [*Computer science*] ... PIC
Power Integration Unit (SSD) ... PIU
Power Intelligence (DNAB) ... PINT
Power Intercept Unit [*Military*] (CAAL) ... PIU
Power Interface Unit (MCD) ... PIU
Power Interlock (IAA) ... PI
Power Jets Memorandum ... PJM
Power Jets Report ... PJR
Power Level ... PWL
Power Level Indicator ... PLI
Power Lever Angle ... PLA
Power Lever Angle Position (MCD) ... PLAP
Power Lever Control (MCD) ... PLC
Power Limiting Valve ... PLV
Power Line (IAA) ... PL
Power Line Carrier ... PLC
Power Line Carrier Communication (PDAA) ... PLCC
Power Line Communications ... PLC
Power Line Harmonic Radiation ... PLHR
Power Line Impedance Network ... PLIN
Power Line Modulation (AABC) ... PLM
Power Line Radiation [*Radioscience*] ... PLR
Power Line Transient (IEEE) ... PLT
Power Loading (IAA) ... PL
Power Loading Control (IAA) ... PLC
Power Locks (BARN) ... PL
Power Loom Carpet Weavers' and Textile Workers' Union [*British*] ... PLCWTWU
Power Management and Distribution (NASA) ... PMAD
Power Management Inventory [*Test*] ... PMI
Power Management Profile [*Test*] ... PMP
Power Management System ... PMS
Power Marketing Administration [*Department of Energy*] ... PMA
Power Metal Grid (PDAA) ... PMG
Power Microwave Tube ... PMT
Power Module (MCD) ... PM
Power Monitor (IAA) ... PWRMON
Power Monitor Relay ... PMR
Power of Attorney ... PA
Power of Attorney ... POA
Power of Attorney (AD) ... PoA
Power of Authority ... P/A
Power of Hydrogen (IAA) ... PH
Power of Influence Test [*Psychology*] ... POIT
Power of World Wide Energy Resources [*In organization name "Natural POWWER"*] (EA) ... POWWER
Power on Clear (MHDI) ... POC
Power on Clear [*Navy Navigation Satellite System*] (DNAB) ... POCL
Power On - Clock On [*Aerospace*] ... POCO
Power On/Off Protection ... POP
Power Open Association [*Computer science*] (CDE) ... POA
Power Open Environment [*Computer science*] ... POE
Power Operational Support Equipment ... POSE
Power Oscillator [*Electronics*] ... PO
Power Oscillator (AD) ... po
Power Outlet Box ... POB
Power Output ... PO
Power Pack Charger ... PPC
Power Package ... PP
Power Package (MSA) ... PPKG
Power Panel (IAA) ... PWRPNL
Power PC [*Personal Computer*] **Reference Platform** [*Configuration standard*] (PCM) ... PReP
Power People ... PP
Power per Cubic Foot ... PCF
Power per Square Inch ... PSI
Power Plan (IAA) ... PP
Power Planning Modeling Application Procedure [*Environmental Protection Agency*] (GFGA) ... PPMAP
Power Plant ... PP
Power Plant (IAA) ... PWRPLT
Power Plant Automation ... PPA
Power Plant Bulletin (MCD) ... PPB
Power Plant Change (NVT) ... PPC
Power Plant Frame [*Mazda Miata*] [*Connecting engine and transmission to final drive*] ... PPF
Power Plant Laboratory (MUGU) ... PPL
Power Plant Operating ... PPO
Power Plant Siting Program [*Environmental Protection Agency*] (GFGA) ... PPSP
Power Play [*Hockey*] ... PP
Power Pole (NASA) ... PP
Power Processing Unit (MCD) ... PPU
Power Radio Frequency [*Telecommunications*] (IAA) ... PRF
Power Range [*Nuclear energy*] (NRCH) ... PR
Power Range Detector (IEEE) ... PRD
Power Range Monitor (IEEE) ... PRM
Power Rating ... PR
Power Ratio ... PR
Power Reactant Storage [*or Supply*] **and Distribution** [*NASA*] (NASA) ... PRSD
Power Reactant Storage and Distribution System (MCD) ... PRSDS
Power Reactant Storage Assembly [*NASA*] (MCD) ... PRSA
Power Reactant Subsystem [*NASA*] (NASA) ... PRS
Power Reactor and Nuclear Fuel Development Corp. [*Japan*] (PDAA) ... PNC
Power Reactor Demonstration Program ... PRDP
Power Reactor Development Programme Evaluation Committee [*Canada*] (HGAA) ... PRDPEC
Power Reactor Inherently Safe Module [*Nuclear energy*] ... PRISM
Power Reactor Innovation Small Module [*Nuclear energy*] ... PRISM
Power Recovery Turbine ... PRT
Power Reflection Coefficient [*of RADAR signals*] ... PRC
Power Regulating and Control Unit (CET) ... PRCU
Power Regulation and Control Unit (AD) ... prcu
Power Relay Satellite ... PRS
Power Remote Control Panel (AAG) ... PRCP
Power Requirement Data ... PRD
Power Research Library of Contemporary Art [*University of Sydney, Australia*] ... PRLCA
Power Restored (FAAC) ... PWROK
Power Return ... PR
Power, Rodwell, and Drew's English Election Cases [*1847-56*] [*A publication*] (DLA) ... Pow R & D
Power, Rodwell, and Drew's English Election Cases [*1847-56*] [*A publication*] (DLA) ... PR & D
Power, Rodwell, and Drew's English Election Cases [*A publication*] (DLA) ... PR & D El Cas
Power Saw Association [*British*] (BI) ... PSA
Power Saw Manufacturers Association [*Later, CSMA*] (EA) ... PSMA
Power Section (NG) ... P/S
Power Semiconductor (IAA) ... PWRSEMICOND
Power Separation Filter (IAA) ... PSF
Power/Sequence Interface Unit (MCD) ... PSIU
Power Series (IAA) ... PS
Power Servo Amplifier (KSC) ... PSA
Power Servo Assembly (MCD) ... PSA
Power/Signal Distribution Assembly ... P/SDA
Power Signal-to-Noise Ratio ... PSNR
Power Source ... PS
Power Source Logic ... PSL
Power Spectra [*Neurophysiology*] ... PS
Power Spectral [*or Spectrum*] **Density** ... PSD
Power Spectrum Distribution [*Electronics*] ... PSD
Power Spectrum Equalization [*Electronics*] ... PSE
Power Sprayer and Duster Council (EA) ... PSDC
Power Standing Wave Ratio ... PSWR
Power Static Inverter (NASA) ... PSI
Power Station (MCD) ... PS
Power Steering [*Automotive engineering*] ... P/STRG
Power Steering [*Automobile ads*] ... PS
Power Steering and Brakes [*Automotive engineering*] (IIA) ... PS & B
Power Steering Pressure Switch [*Automotive engineering*] ... PSPS
Power Strapping Machine ... PSM
Power Subsystem Group [*NASA*] (MCD) ... PSG
Power Supplies [*JETDS nomenclature*] [*Military*] (CET) ... PP
Power Supply ... PS
Power Supply (IAA) ... PWRSUP
Power Supply and Control Gear ... PSCG
Power Supply and Multiplexer Unit [*Telecommunications*] (TSSD) ... PSMU
Power Supply Assembly ... PSA
Power Supply Calibrator ... PSC
Power Supply Control Group [*Military*] (CAAL) ... PSCG
Power Supply Control Unit (CET) ... PSCU
Power Supply Engineering and Construction [*Nuclear energy*] (NRCH) ... PSE & C
Power Supply / Frequency Converter (DWSG) ... PS/FC
Power Supply/Fuel Cell (MCD) ... PS/FC
Power Supply Kit ... PSK
Power Supply Manufacturers Association [*British*] (DBA) ... PSMA
Power Supply Module (MHDI) ... PSM
Power Supply Rejection Ratio (IAA) ... PSRR
Power Supply Section ... PSS
Power Supply Subsystem (IAA) ... PSS
Power Supply Unit (MSA) ... PSU
Power Switchboard ... PSWBD
Power Switching Amplifier ... PSA
Power Switching and Logic ... PS & L
Power Switching Assembly ... PSA
Power Switching Distribution Unit ... PSDU
Power Switching Unit (MCD) ... PSU
Power System Communications (IAA) ... PSC
Power System Communications (IAA) ... PSCC
Power System Engineering (MCD) ... PSE
Power System Instrumentation and Measurement (MCD) ... PSIM
Power System Module ... PSM
Power System Optimization Program [*Computer science*] ... PSOP
Power System Planning ... PSP
Power System Relaying (MCD) ... PSR
Power System Synthesizer ... PSS
Power Takeoff [*Automotive engineering*] ... PTO
Power Test Fail ... PTF
Power Test Operations (MCD) ... PTO
Power Testing Code (MCD) ... PTC
Power Tool Institute (EA) ... PTI

Power Train (AABC) ... PWTN
Power Transfer (KSC) ... PT
Power Transfer Assembly (IAA) ... PTA
Power Transfer Coefficient ... PTC
Power Transfer Switch ... PTS
Power Transfer Unit ... PTU
Power Transformation Weighting Method [Mathematics] ... PTWM
Power Transformers (MCD) ... PTR
Power Transient Suppressor (IEEE) ... PTS
Power Transmission Council ... PTC
Power Transmission Distributors Association (EA) ... PTDA
Power Transmission Line (OA) ... PTL
Power Transmission Representatives Association (EA) ... PTRA
Power Transport Equipment ... PTE
Power Unit ... PU
Power Unit (IAA) ... PWRU
Power Upgrade Program ... PUP
Power Utility Pak [Computer software] [Jwalk and Associates] (PCM) ... PUP
Power Vacuum Module [Automotive engineering] ... PVM
Power Wagon [Military vehicle] ... PW
Power Windows [Automobile ads] ... PW
Power Wirewound Resistor ... PWR
Power Wirewound Resistor ... PWWR
Power-Assist System [Motorcycle steering] ... PAS
Power-Assisted Brakes ... PAB
Power-Assisted Steering [Automotive feature] ... PAS
Power-Assisted Storage Equipment (IEEE) ... PASE
PowerCerv Corp. [NASDAQ symbol] (SAG) ... PCRV
PowerCerv Corp. [NASDAQ symbol] (TTSB) ... PCRV
PowerCerv Corp. [Associated Press] (SAG) ... PowrCrv
Power-Cooling Mismatch [Nuclear energy] ... PCM
Power-Dependent Insertion Limit [Nuclear energy] (NRCH) ... PDIL
Power-Deployed Reserve Parachute (MCD) ... PRP
Power-Driven ... PDVN
Powered (IAA) ... PWD
Powered Air Purifying Respirator (ERG) ... PAPR
Powered All the Way ... PAW
Powered Balloon [System] ... POBAL
Powered Battle Armor [A computer game] (PCM) ... PBA
Powered Causeway Section [Military] (CAAL) ... PCS
Powered Descent Initiation [Aerospace] ... PDI
Powered Disposal Bomb Pod (AAG) ... PDBP
Powered Flight (NASA) ... PF
Powered Return to Launch Site [NASA] (MCD) ... PRTLS
Powered Thermocouple Reference Junction ... PTRJ
Powered Ultralight Manufacturers Association [Defunct] (EA) ... PUMA
Powered Underwater Research Vehicle [Navy] ... PURV
Power-Enrichment Vacuum Regulator [Automotive engineering] ... PEVR
Powerful Permutation Procedure [Meteorology] ... PPP
Powerful Radio Galaxy [Cosmology] ... PRG
Powerful Resource for Information and System Management [Computer science] (IAA) ... PRISM
Powergan PLC [Associated Press] (SAG) ... PwgnADS
Powergan PLC [Associated Press] (SAG) ... PwgnIntr
Powergem Resources Corp. [Vancouver Stock Exchange symbol] ... PWG
Powergen PLC [NYSE symbol] (SAG) ... PWG
PowerGen PLC ADS [NYSE symbol] (TTSB) ... PWG
PowerGen PLC Interim ADS [NYSE symbol] (TTSB) ... PWG.PP
Power-Generating Fusion Reaction ... PGFR
Powerhouse ... PH
Powerhouse (MSA) ... PWRH
Powerhouse Exhaust Facility (IAA) ... PEF
Powerhouse Resources [NASDAQ symbol] (TTSB) ... PHKWE
Powerhouse Resources, Inc. [NASDAQ symbol] (SAG) ... PHKW
Powerhouse Resources, Inc. [Associated Press] (SAG) ... PwrhsRs
Power-Loss Factor (IDOE) ... F_p
Power-Mate Corp. (IAA) ... PMC
Power-On Reset [Electronics] ... PORS
Power-On Self Test [IBM-PC feature] ... POST
Power-Operated ... PO
Power-Operated (AD) ... po
Power-Operated ... POPD
Power-Operated Gun Turret ... POGT
Power-Operated Relief Valve [Nuclear energy] (NRCH) ... PORV
Powerplant and Industrial Fuel Use Act of 1978 ... PIFUA
Power-Plant and Process Design Management System [Computer science] ... PDMS
Powerplant Performance Analysis ... PPA
Powerplant Specific Weight ... PSW
Power-Play Goal [Hockey] ... PPG
PowerPoint [Computer science] (PCM) ... PPT
Power-Proportioning Temperature Programmer (IAA) ... PPTP
Powers' Reports, New York Surrogate Court [A publication] (DLA) ... Pow Surr
Powers' Reports, New York Surrogate Court [A publication] (DLA) ... Powers
Powers' Reports, New York Surrogate Court [A publication] (DLA) ... Power's Sur
[The] Powers That Be [E-Mail discussion] ... TPTB
Power-Specific (MCD) ... PS
Power-Specific Biological Activity [Engine emissions testing] ... PSBA
Power-Steering Pressure Sensor [Automotive engineering] ... PSPS
Powertrain Control Module [Automotive engineering] ... PCM
Powertrain Control Signal [Automotive engineering] ... PTCS
Powertrain Input Signal [Automotive engineering] ... PTIS
Powertrain Operations [Auto manufacturer corporate structure] ... PTO
Powertrain Product Engineering [Automotive] ... PTPE
Powerwave Technologies, Inc. [Associated Press] (SAG) ... Powrwv

Powerwave Technologies, Inc. [NASDAQ symbol] (SAG) ... PWAV
Powhatan [Arkansas] [Seismograph station code, US Geological Survey] (SEIS) ... POW
Powlesland & Mason [Railway] [Wales] ... PM
Powszechny Bank Gospodarczy [Poland] ... PBG
Powys Self-Help Trust [British] ... PSHT
Powys Society (EA) ... PS
Powys Society of North America (EA) ... PSNA
Pox Battery, Acute [Biochemistry] (DAVI) ... POX-AC
Poynette, WI [AM radio station call letters] ... WIBU
Poynter on Marriage and Divorce [2nd ed.] [1824] [A publication] (DLA) ... Poynt M & D
Poynting Vector [Electromagnetism] (DEN) ... P
Poynting Vector [Symbol] [Electromagnetism] (DEN) ... S
Poza Rica [Mexico ICAO location identifier] (ICLI) ... MMPA
Poza Rica [Mexico] [Airport symbol] (OAG) ... PAZ
Poznan [Poland] [Airport symbol] (OAG) ... POZ
Poznan [Poland] (AD) ... Poz
Poznan/Lawica [Poland ICAO location identifier] (ICLI) ... EPPO
Pozzolan Aggregate Mixture (OA) ... PAM
PP & L Resources, Inc. [Associated Press] (SAG) ... PP&L Res
PP & L Resources, Inc. [NYSE symbol] (SAG) ... PPL
PP&L Resources [NYSE symbol] (TTSB) ... PPL
PPC Oil & Gas Corp. [Toronto Stock Exchange symbol] ... PPC
PPG Indus [NYSE symbol] (TTSB) ... PPG
PPG Industries, Inc. [Formerly, Pittsburgh Plate Glass Co.] [Associated Press] (SAG) ... PPG
PPG Industries, Inc., Coatings and Resins Division, Allison Park, PA [OCLC symbol] (OCLC) ... PPG
PPG Industries, Inc., Glass Research Center, Information Services Library, Pittsburgh, PA [Library symbol Library of Congress] (LCLS) ... PPiPPG
PPT Vision [NASDAQ symbol] (TTSB) ... PPTV
PPT Vision, Inc. [Associated Press] (SAG) ... PPT Vis
PPT Vision, Inc. [NASDAQ symbol] (SAG) ... PPTV
PQ Corp. [Formerly, Philadelphia Quartz Co.] ... PQ
PR [Public Relations] Committee for Licensing and Registration (EA) ... PCLR
PR Newswire [PR Newswire, Inc.] [Information service or system] (IID) ... PRN
Praca [Plaza] [Portuguese] (AD) ... Pr
Prachakorn Thai [Thai Citizens Party] [Political party] ... PT
Prachin Buri [Thailand] [ICAO location identifier] (ICLI) ... VTBI
Prachin Buri/Watthana Nakhon [Thailand] [ICAO location identifier] (ICLI) ... VTBW
Prachuap Khiri Khan [Thailand] [ICAO location identifier] (ICLI) ... VTBP
Prachuap Khiri Khan/Hua Hin [Thailand] [ICAO location identifier] (ICLI) ... VTPH
Prachuap Khiri Khan/Pran Buri [Thailand] [ICAO location identifier] (ICLI) ... VTBN
Practical ... P
Practical (DLA) ... Prac
Practical ... PRACL
Practical (AD) ... pract
Practical (ROG) ... PRACT
Practical Absolute Cavity Radiometer (PDAA) ... PACRAD
Practical Algorithm to Receive Information Coded in Alphanumeric [Information retrieval] ... PATRICIA
Practical Allergy Research Foundation (EA) ... PARF
Practical Annual Capacity [FAA] ... PANCAP
Practical Application of Mid-Points for Exponential Regression ... PAMPER
Practical Approach to Chemical Information Retrieval ... PACIR
Practical Bomb Rack Adapter (NG) ... PBRA
Practical Computer Solutions (NITA) ... PCS
Practical Data Manager [Hitachi Ltd.] [Japan] ... PDM
Practical Engineering Applications Software (NITA) ... PEAS
Practical Engineering Paperwork ... PEP
Practical Exercise ... PE
Practical Factors ... P/F
Practical Guide Series (ACII) ... PGS
Practical Intelligence ... P
Practical Job Training (MCD) ... PJT
Practical Lawyer [A publication] (DLA) ... Pract Law
Practical Nurse ... PN
Practical Nurse's Education ... PNE
Practical Nurse's Education (AD) ... pne
Practical Nursing Student (DAVI) ... PNS
Practical Ordered Program (OA) ... POP
Practical Policy Test [Psychology] ... PPT
Practical Quantification Limit [Metallurgy] ... POL
Practical Quantitation Level [Environmental chemistry] (ERG) ... PQL
Practical Quantitation Limit [Environmental chemistry] ... PQL
Practical Register in Chancery [England] [A publication] (DLA) ... PR Ch
Practical Register in Chancery [1 vol.] [A publication] (DLA) ... Pr Reg Ch
Practical Register in the Bail Court [A publication] (DLA) ... Pr Reg BC
Practical Register in the Common Pleas [1705-42] [A publication] (DLA) ... Pr Reg CP
Practical Register in the Common Pleas [England] [A publication] (DLA) ... Pract Reg
Practical Register in the Common Pleas [A publication] (DLA) ... PRCP
Practical Research into Organizational Behavior and Effectiveness (EDAC) ... PROBE
Practical Satellites ... PRACSATS
Practical Storage Life ... PSL
Practical Test Standards [FAA] (TAG) ... PTS
Practical, Unpretentious, Nomographic Computer ... PUNC
Practice (AABC) ... PRAC
Practice ... PRAC
Practice (AD) ... prac
Practice (AD) ... pract
Practice [Legal shorthand] (LWAP) ... PRACT

Practice Act [*A publication*] (DLA) ..... Prac Act
Practice Amendment (AAG) ..... PA
Practice Bomb Contained (NG) ..... PBC
Practice Cases [*A publication*] (DLA) ..... PC
Practice Cases, in the King's Bench [*England*] [*A publication*] (DLA) ..... Pr CKB
Practice Depth Charge ..... PDC
Practice Extraction and Report Language [*Facetious translation: Pathologically Eclectic Rubbish Lister*] [*Computer science*] (NHD) ..... PERL
Practice Guided Weapon (MCD) ..... PGW
Practice Instrument Landing (ADA) ..... PIL
Practice Landing Approach [*Aviation*] ..... PLA
Practice Limpet Assembly Modular [*Navy*] (CAAL) ..... PLAM
Practice Multiple Bomb (MCD) ..... PMB
Practice Multiple Bomb Rack (NG) ..... PMBR
Practice of the High Court of Chancery [*A publication*] (DLA) ..... Pr HC Ch
Practice Precautionary Landing Approach [*Aviation*] ..... PPLA
Practice Reports [*Various jurisdictions*] [*A publication*] (DLA) ..... Pr
Practice Reports [*Quebec*] [*A publication*] (DLA) ..... Pr R
Practice Reports [*Ontario*] [*A publication*] (DLA) ..... Pr R
Practice Reports [*England*] [*A publication*] (DLA) ..... Pr Rep
Practice Reports [*Ontario*] [*A publication*] (DLA) ..... Pr Rep
Practice Reports [*A publication*] (DLA) ..... Prt Rep
Practice Reports [*1848-1900*] [*Upper Canada*] [*A publication*] (DLA) ..... PRUC
Practice Training Index ..... PRI
Practising Law Institute (EA) ..... PLI
Practitioner ..... PRACT
Practitioner (AD) ..... pract
Practitioner ..... PRACTNR
Practitioner's Handbooks [*A publication*] ..... PH
Prader-Labhart-Willi Syndrome [*Medicine*] (DMAA) ..... PLWS
Prader-Willi [*Syndrome*] [*Medicine*] (AAMN) ..... P-W
Prader-Willi Chromosome Region [*Medicine*] (DMAA) ..... PWCR
Prader-Willi Syndrome Association (EA) ..... PWS
Prado [*Brazil*] [*Airport symbol*] (AD) ..... PDO
Prado Explorations Ltd. [*Toronto Stock Exchange symbol*] ..... PDX
Praecipitatus [*Precipitated*] [*Pharmacy*] ..... PPT
Praed Street Irregulars (EA) ..... PSI
Praefatio [*Latin*] (OCD) ..... praef
Praegitzer Industries [*NASDAQ symbol*] (TTSB) ..... PGTZ
Praegitzer Industries, Inc. [*NASDAQ symbol*] (SAG) ..... PGTZ
Praegitzer Industries, Inc. [*Associated Press*] (SAG) ..... Praegtzr
Praemissis Praemittendis [*Omitting Preliminaries, To Whom It May Concern*] [*Latin*] ..... PP
Praenomen (AD) ..... praen
Praeparata [*Prepared*] [*Pharmacy*] (ROG) ..... PPT
Praeparatio Evangelica [*of Eusebius*] [*Classical studies*] (OCD) ..... Praep Evang
Praepositus [*Deceased, 1509*] [*Authority cited in pre-1607 legal work*] (DSA) ..... Praepo
Praepositus [*Deceased, 1509*] [*Authority cited in pre-1607 legal work*] (DSA) ..... Prepo
Praepositus [*Deceased, 1509*] [*Authority cited in pre-1607 legal work*] (DSA) ..... Prepos
Praepter Propter [*Approximately*] [*Pharmacy*] ..... PP
Praesens [*Present Tense*] [*Latin*] ..... praes
Praeter Propter [*About, Nearly*] [*Latin*] (ROG) ..... PR PR
Praeteritum [*Past Tense*] [*Latin*] ..... praet
Praeventivpille [*Dano-Norwegian*] [*Contraceptive pill*] (AD) ..... p-pille
Pragmatic (AD) ..... prag
Prague [*Former Czechoslovakia*] [*Airport symbol*] (OAG) ..... PRG
Prague Institute of Advanced Studies ..... PIAS
Praha [*Former Czechoslovakia*] [*ICAO location identifier*] (ICLI) ..... LKAA
Praha [*Prague*] [*Czechoslovakia*] [*Seismograph station code, US Geological Survey*] (SEIS) ..... PRA
Praha/Ruzyne [*Former Czechoslovakia*] [*ICAO location identifier*] (ICLI) ..... LKPR
Praia [*Cape Verde Islands*] [*Airport symbol*] (OAG) ..... RAI
Praia/Praia, Santiago Island [*Cape Verde*] [*ICAO location identifier*] (ICLI) ..... GVPR
Praia Verde [*Portugal ICAO location identifier*] (ICLI) ..... LPPV
Prairie (AD) ..... Pr
Prairie ..... PR
Prairie (MCD) ..... PR
Prairie [*Commonly used*] (OPSA) ..... PRAIRIE
Prairie [*Commonly used*] (OPSA) ..... PRARIE
Prairie [*Commonly used*] (OPSA) ..... PRR
Prairie Agricultural Machinery Institute [*Canada*] ..... PAMI
Prairie Agricultural Machinery Institute, Humboldt, Saskatchewan [*Library symbol National Library of Canada*] (NLC) ..... SHPA
Prairie Agricultural Machinery Institute, Humboldt, SK, Canada [*Library symbol Library of Congress*] (LCLS) ..... CaSHPA
Prairie Association of Publishers Education Representatives [*Canada*] ..... PAPER
Prairie Chicken Foundation (EA) ..... PCF
Prairie City News, Prairie City, IA [*Library symbol Library of Congress*] (LCLS) ..... IaPcN
Prairie County Library, Terry, MT [*Library symbol*] [*Library of Congress*] (LCLS) ..... MtT
Prairie Crocus Regional Library, Rivers, Manitoba [*Library symbol National Library of Canada*] (NLC) ..... MRIP
Prairie Crocus Regional Library, Rivers, MB, Canada [*Library symbol Library of Congress*] (LCLS) ..... CaMRiP
Prairie District Library, Mountain Home, ID [*Library symbol*] [*Library of Congress*] (LCLS) ..... IdMhP
Prairie Du Chien, WI [*Location identifier FAA*] (FAAL) ..... PDC
Prairie du Chien, WI [*AM radio station call letters*] ..... WPRE
Prairie du Chien, WI [*FM radio station call letters*] ..... WPRE-FM
Prairie Farm Assistance Act ..... PFAA
Prairie Farm Rehabilitation Administration [*Canada*] ..... PFRA
Prairie Farm Rehabilitation Administration, Agriculture Canada [*Administration du Retablissement Agricole des Prairies, Agriculture Canada*] **Regina, Saskatchewan** [*Library symbol National Library of Canada*] (NLC) ..... SRRE
Prairie Fiction Collection, Alberta Culture [*UTLAS symbol*] ..... PFC
Prairie Flying Service (1976) Ltd. [*Canada ICAO designator*] (FAAC) ..... PFS
Prairie Grove, AR [*FM radio station call letters*] ..... KDAB
[A] Prairie Home Companion [*National Public Radio program*] ..... PHC
Prairie Island Nuclear Generating Plant (NRCH) ..... PINGP
Prairie Migratory Bird Research Centre, Canadian Wildlife Service, Environment Canada [*Centre de Recherches sur les Oiseaux Migrateurs des Prairies, Service Canadien de la Faune, Environnement Canada*] **Saskatoon, Saskatchewan** [*Library symbol National Library of Canada*] (NLC) ..... SSECW
Prairie Oil Royalties Co. Ltd. [*AMEX symbol Toronto Stock Exchange symbol*] (SPSG) ..... POY
Prairie Print Makers [*Defunct*] (EA) ..... PPM
Prairie Provinces [*MARC geographic area code Library of Congress*] (LCCP) ..... n-cnp-
Prairie Regional Laboratory, National Research Council, Saskatoon, SK, Canada [*Library symbol Library of Congress*] (LCLS) ..... CaSSP
Prairie Regional Office, Parks Canada [*Bureau Regional des Pres, Parcs Canada*] **Winnipeg, Manitoba** [*Library symbol National Library of Canada*] (NLC) ..... MWIAP
Prairie Religious Library Association ..... PRLA
Prairie Schooner [*A publication*] (BRI) ..... PS
Prairie State College, Learning Center, Chicago Heights, IL [*Library symbol Library of Congress*] (LCLS) ..... IChP
Prairie Swine Centre [*University of Saskatchewan*] [*Canada*] (IRC) ..... PSC
Prairie View Agricultural and Mechanical College, Prairie View, TX [*Library symbol Library of Congress*] (LCLS) ..... TxPvC
Prairie View Agricultural and Mechanical University (GAGS) ..... Prairie View A&M U
Prairie View School, Sandwich, IL [*Library symbol Library of Congress*] (LCLS) ..... ISanP
Prairie View, TX [*FM radio station call letters*] ..... KPVU
Prairie Woods Elementary School, New London, MN [*Library symbol*] [*Library of Congress*] (LCLS) ..... MnNIPES
Prairiefire Rural Action (EA) ..... PRA
Prairies Service [*Record series prefix*] [*Canada*] ..... PS
Praise the Lord [*Of television's "PTL Club"*] [*Facetious translations: "Pass the Loot" and "Pay the Lady"*] ..... PTL
Praise the Lord Anyway ..... PTLA
Praja Socialist Party [*India*] [*Political party*] (PPW) ..... PSP
Prakrit [*MARC language code Library of Congress*] (LCCP) ..... pra
Pralidoxime [*Pharmacology*] (DAVI) ..... PAM
Pralidoxime Chloride [*Pharmacology*] (DAVI) ..... PAM
Pralidoxime Methiodide [*Biochemistry*] ..... PAM
Prambanam (VRA) ..... Pram
Prandium [*dinner*] [*Latin*] (AD) ..... prand
Prandium [*Dinner*] [*Pharmacy*] ..... PRAND
Prandtl Number [*IUPAC*] ..... Pr
Prang-Mark Society (EA) ..... PMS
Prapat/Sibisa [*Indonesia*] [*ICAO location identifier*] (ICLI) ..... WIMP
Praseodymium [*Chemical element*] ..... Pr
Praseodymium Barium Copper Oxide [*Inorganic chemistry*] ..... PBCO
Praslin Island [*Seychelles Islands*] [*Airport symbol*] (OAG) ..... PRI
Prater on Husband and Wife [*2nd ed.*] [*1836*] [*A publication*] (DLA) ..... Pra H & W
Prater's Cases on Conflict of Laws [*A publication*] (DLA) ..... Pra Cas
Pratica Di Mare [*Italy ICAO location identifier*] (ICLI) ..... LIRE
Prato [*Italy*] [*Seismograph station code, US Geological Survey*] (SEIS) ..... PRT
Pratt & Lambert, Inc. ..... P & L
Pratt & Lambert United, Inc. [*NYSE symbol*] (SAG) ..... PLU
Pratt & Lambert United, Inc. [*Associated Press*] (SAG) ..... PratLm
Pratt and Mackenzie on Highways [*21st ed.*] [*1967*] [*A publication*] (DLA) ..... Pratt High
Pratt & Whitney [*Aircraft*] ..... P & W
Pratt & Whitney Aircraft (KSC) ..... P & WA
Pratt & Whitney Aircraft (MCD) ..... PWA
Pratt & Whitney Aircraft (AAG) ..... PWAC
Pratt & Whitney Aircraft Ltd., Longueuil, Quebec [*Library symbol National Library of Canada*] (NLC) ..... QLOU
Pratt & Whitney Aircraft Ltd., Mississauga, ON, Canada [*Library symbol Library of Congress*] (LCLS) ..... CaOMPW
Pratt & Whitney Aircraft Ltd., Mississauga, Ontario [*Library symbol National Library of Canada*] (NLC) ..... OMPW
Pratt & Whitney Aircraft, Longueuil, PQ, Canada [*Library symbol Library of Congress*] (LCLS) ..... CaQLoU
Pratt & Whitney Canada, Inc. [*ICAO designator*] (FAAC) ..... PWC
Pratt & Whitney Engine Program [*Aviation*] (NG) ..... PEP
Pratt & Whitney Engineering Division ..... PW/ED
Pratt Hotel Corp. [*AMEX symbol*] (SPSG) ..... PHC
Pratt Hotel Corp. [*Associated Press*] (SAG) ..... PratHtl
Pratt Institute (GAGS) ..... Pratt Inst
Pratt Institute, Brooklyn, NY [*Library symbol Library of Congress*] (LCLS) ..... NBP
Pratt Institute, Brooklyn, NY [*OCLC symbol*] (OCLC) ..... VZQ
Pratt Institute Center for Community and Environmental Development [*Research center*] (RCD) ..... PICCED
Pratt Junior College [*Kansas*] ..... PJC
Pratt, KS [*FM radio station call letters*] ..... KGLS
Pratt, KS [*AM radio station call letters*] ..... KWLS
Pratt, KS [*Location identifier FAA*] (FAAL) ..... PTT
Pratt on Friendly Societies [*15th ed.*] [*1931*] [*A publication*] (DLA) ..... Pratt Fr Soc
Pratt on Savings Banks [*6th ed.*] [*1845*] [*A publication*] (DLA) ..... Pratt Sav B
Pratt on Sea Lights [*2nd ed.*] [*1858*] [*A publication*] (DLA) ..... Pratt SL

Pratt on the Property Tax Act [*A publication*] (DLA) ..... Pratt Prop T
Pratt's Contraband-of-War Cases [*1861*] [*A publication*] (DLA) ..... Pr Cont
Pratt's Contraband-of-War Cases [*A publication*] (DLA) ..... Pratt
Pratt's Contraband-of-War Cases [*A publication*] (DLA) ..... Pratt Cont
Pratt's Edition of Bott on the Poor Laws [*A publication*] (DLA) ..... Pratt PL
Pratt's Law of Benefit Building Societies [*A publication*] (DLA) ..... Pratt BS
Pratt's Statutes Establishing Courts of Request [*A publication*] (DLA) ..... Pratt Cts Req
Pratt's Supplement to Bott's Poor Laws [*1833*] [*A publication*] (DLA) ..... Pratt
Prattsburgh Railroad (AD) ..... PRAT
Prattsburgh Railway Corp. [*AAR code*] ..... PRC
Prattville, AL [*AM radio station call letters*] (RBYB) ..... WIQR
Prattville, AL [*FM radio station call letters*] ..... WXFX
Pratylenchus penetrans [*A nematode*] ..... Pp
Prausnitz-Kuestner [*Reaction*] [*Immunology*] ..... PK
Prausnitz-Kunstner [*Reaction or Transfer Test*] [*Medicine*] (DAVI) ..... PK
Pravitel'stvennaya Komissiya po Raketam Dalnego Deistviya [*State Commission for the Study of the Problems of Long-Range Rockets*] [*Former USSR*] ..... PKRDD
Praxair, Inc. [*Associated Press*] (SAG) ..... Praxair
Praxair, Inc. [*NYSE symbol*] (SPSG) ..... PX
Praxis Almae Curiae Cancellariae (Brown) [*A publication*] (DLA) ..... Prax Can
Praxis Resources Ltd. [*Vancouver Stock Exchange symbol*] ..... PXR
Praxis Technologies Corp. [*Toronto Stock Exchange symbol*] ..... PXT
Pray while Aloft [*Humorous interpretation for Pacific Western Airlines Corp.*] ..... PWA
Prayer ..... PR
Prayer Book ..... PB
Prayer Book Society [*British*] (DBA) ..... PBS
Prayer of Manasses [*Apocrypha*] (BJA) ..... PrMan
[*The*] **Prayer of Manasses, King of Judah** [*Apocrypha*] ..... PR of MAN
[*The*] **Prayer of Nabonidus from Qumran. Cave Four** (BJA) 4QPrNab
Prayers (ROG) ..... PRS
Prayers for Life (EA) ..... PL
Praying for Corporal [*Private First Class desirous of promotion, or female in wartime desirous of a boyfriend*] ..... PFC
Prazosin [*A vasodilator*] ..... PRAZ
Prazosin [*A vasodilator*] ..... PZ
PRD Electronics, Inc., Information Center Library, Syosset, NY [*Library symbol Library of Congress*] (LCLS) ..... NSyoP
Pre Coded Originating Mail Processor (PDAA) ..... POMP
Pre Departure Clearance (GAVI) ..... PDC
Pre Phase-In ..... PPI
Pre Phase-Out ..... PPO
Pre/Post Sleep Activity (NASA) ..... PSA
Pre-1920 [*Deltiology*] ..... P
Pre-Academic Learning Inventory [*Child development test*] ..... PAL
Preacademic Training Student [*Military*] ..... PATS
Preacher ..... PR
Preacher General ..... PG
Preacher's Kid [*Slang*] ..... PK
Pre-Achilles Fat Pad [*Medicine*] (DMAA) ..... PAFP
Pre-Action Calibration [*Gunnery*] (NVT) ..... PAC
Preadmission Assessment Form [*Health Care Financing Administration*] ..... PAF
Pre-Admission Certification [*Medicine*] (MEDA) ..... PAC
Preadmission Review (WYGK) ..... PAR
Preadmission Screening ..... PAS
Pre-Admission Screening [*Medicine*] (MEDA) ..... PAS
Preadmission Screening and Annual Resident Review [*Medicare*] ..... PASARR
Preadmission Testing ..... PAT
Preadsorb-Dilute-Shake [*Phage growth method*] ..... PDS
Preadvisory Data (KSC) ..... PAD
Prealbumin [*Biochemistry*] ..... PA
Prealbumin [*Biochemistry*] ..... PAB
Prealbumin Globulin [*Biochemistry*] (OA) ..... PAG
Preamble (ILCA) ..... Pr
Preamble ..... PRL
Preamplifier ..... PA
Preamplifier (AAG) ..... PREAMP
Preamplifier Extension Plug ..... PEP
Preamplifier Limited Infrared (IAA) ..... PLIP
Preamplifier Module Assembly ..... PMA
Pre-Apprenticeship Allowance ..... PAA
Preapproved ..... PA
Preapproved Loan [*Business term*] ..... PAL
Prearm ..... PA
Prearranged Fire ..... PAF
Prearranged Payments [*Business term*] ..... PAP
Prearranged Transfers ..... PAT
Pre-Arrangement Interment Association of America [*Later, PAA*] (EA) ..... PIAA
Pre-Arrangement Interment Exchange of America [*Later, PIAA*] ..... PIEA
Prearrival Inspection ..... PAI
Prearrival Inspection Procedure ..... PIP
Preassembled Cable in Pipe ..... PCP
Pre-Assigned Multiple Access [*Telecommunications*] (LAIN) ..... PAMA
Preatomized Fuel [*Trademark*] [*Petroferm product*] ..... PAF
Pre-Authorization Order ..... PO
Preauthorized Automatic Transfer Scheme [*Banking*] ..... PATS
Preauthorized Check Plan [*Insurance*] ..... PAC
Pre-Authorized Chequing [*Canada*] ..... PAC
Preauthorized Chequing [*Canadian term for an electronic funds transfer*] (NFD) ..... PAC
Preavailability ..... PA
Preaward Survey [*To determine a contractor's capability*] [*DoD*] ..... PAS
Preaward Survey Monitor [*DoD*] ..... PASM
Preaward Survey Review Board [*DoD*] ..... PASRB
Prebed Care [*Medicine*] (MAE) ..... PBC
Prebendary ..... PREB
Prebent ..... PRBNT
Preble County District Library, Camden Branch, Camden, OH [*Library symbol Library of Congress*] (LCLS) ..... OCamd
Preble County District Library, Eaton, OH [*Library symbol Library of Congress*] (LCLS) ..... OEP
Preble. Digest, Patent Cases [*A publication*] (DLA) ..... Preb Dig
Preble. Digest, Patent Cases [*A publication*] (DLA) ..... Preb Pat Cas
Preburner [*NASA*] (NASA) ..... PB
Preburner Oxidizer Pump (MCD) ..... POP
Preburner Valve Actuator [*NASA*] (NASA) ..... PVA
Precambrian [*Period, era, or system*] [*Geology*] ..... PREC
Precambrian Paleobiology Research Group ..... PPRG
Precambrian Shield Resources Ltd. [*Toronto Stock Exchange symbol*] ..... PCB
Precancel Stamp Society (EA) ..... PSS
Precanceled Envelope Collectors Club (EA) ..... PECC
Precancelled [*Philately*] ..... Pr
Precarrier ..... PC
Precast ..... PC
Precast (AAG) ..... PRCST
Precast (AD) ..... prcst
Precast Concrete [*Technical drawings*] ..... PCC
Precast Concrete Frame Association [*British*] (DBA) ..... PCFA
Precast Concrete Manufacturers' Association of New South Wales [*Australia*] ..... PCMANSW
Precast Concrete Manufacturers' Association of Victoria [*Australia*] ..... PCMAV
Precast Flooring Federation [*British*] (DBA) ..... PFF
Precastable Autoclaved Lightweight Concrete [*Residential construction*] ..... PALC
Precaution [*ICAO designator*] (FAAC) ..... PRCTN
Precaution Category [*For clinical laboratories*] ..... PC
Precautions, Limitations, and Setpoints [*Nuclear energy*] (NRCH) ..... PLS
Precede (FAAC) ..... PRECD
Precedence (AABC) ..... PREC
Precedence Charting System (IAA) ..... PCS
Precedence Diagraming Method (MCD) ..... PDM
Precedence Manual In / Manual Out (DNAB) ..... PMI/MO
Precedence Network In-Dialing [*Telecommunications*] (TEL) ..... P-NID
Precedence Rating [*Military*] (AFIT) ..... PR
Precedence Work Item ..... PWI
Precedent, Action, and Result ..... PAR
Precedent Analysis by Nearest Neighbor Discriminant Analysis ..... PANNDA
Precedents in Chancery [*A publication*] (DLA) ..... PC
Precedents in Chancery, Edited by Finch [*1689-1723*] [*England*] [*A publication*] (DLA) ..... Ch Pre
Precedents in Chancery, Edited by Finch [*A publication*] (DLA) ..... Finch Prec
Precedents in Chancery, Edited by Finch [*1689-1722*] [*England*] [*A publication*] (DLA) ..... Pr Ch
Precedents in Chancery, Edited by Finch [*A publication*] (DLA) ..... Pre Ch
Precedents in Chancery, Edited by Finch [*24 English Reprint*] [*1689-1722*] [*A publication*] (DLA) ..... Prec in Ch
Precedents in Chancery, Edited by Finch [*24 English Reprint*] [*A publication*] (DLA) ..... Prec in Ch (Eng)
Precedents of Private Acts of Parliament [*A publication*] (DLA) ..... PPAP
Preceding ..... P
Preceding ..... PREC
Preceding Preparatory Interval [*Psychometrics*] ..... PPI
Precentor (ROG) ..... PREC
[*The*] **Precentor and Prebendary of Alton Borealis in the Church of Sarum** [*Pseudonym used by Arthur Ashley Sykes*] ..... TPAPOABITCOS
Precertification to Verify Necessary Treatment ..... PREVENT
Pre-Chamber [*Automotive engineering*] ..... PC
Pre-Chamber Ignition [*Automotive engineering*] ..... PCI
Precharge ..... PRCH
Precheck Verification [*NASA*] (NASA) ..... PCV
Pre-Choice [*Advertising*] (WDMC) ..... pre
Precinct ..... PCT
Precinct ..... PRE
Precio Maximo de Venta al Publico [*Maximum Price Charged the Public*] [*Spanish*] (AD) ..... pmvp
Precious (VRA) ..... prec
Precious (ROG) ..... PREC
Precious Metal ..... PM
Precious Metal Adder (Cost) (MCD) ..... PMA
Precious Metal Anode ..... PMA
Precious Metal Indicator Code ..... PMIC
Precious Metal Plating (AD) ..... pmp
Precious Metal Tip (IAA) ..... PMT
Precious Metals Area Representative [*DoD*] (AFIT) ..... PMAR
Precious Metals Master File [*DoD*] (AFIT) ..... PMMF
Precious Metals Recovery Program [*DoD*] (AFIT) ..... PMRP
Precipitable Water Vapor ..... PWV
Precipitat Prepared [*Laboratory science*] (DAVI) ..... ppt
Precipitate (AD) ..... ppt
Precipitate (MSA) ..... PPT
Precipitate [*Laboratory science*] (DAVI) ..... precip
Precipitate Reduction Sinter [*Metal*] (DICI) ..... PRS
Precipitated ..... PPTD
Precipitated (AD) ..... pptd
Precipitated Calcium Carbonate [*Inorganic chemistry*] ..... PCC
Precipitate-Free Zone (MCD) ..... PFZ
Precipitation (DAVI) ..... pcpn
Precipitation (WGA) ..... PPN
Precipitation ..... PPTN

Precipitation (AD) .... pptn
Precipitation .... PRECIP
Precipitation and Off-Path Scattered Interference [*Report*] [*FCC*] .... POPSI
Precipitation from Homogeneous Solution [*Catalyst preparation process*] .... PFHS
Precipitation Hardening .... PH
Precipitation Identifier Information Not Available [*NWS*] (FAAC) .... PWINO
Precipitation Series Algorithm (USDC) .... PSA
Precipitation Series Algorithm [*Marine science*] (OSRA) .... PSA
Precipitation Static .... P
Precipitation Thin-Layer Chromatography [*Medicine*] (DMAA) .... PTLC
Precipitation with a Compressed Fluid Antisolvent [*Chemical engineering*] .... PCA
Precipitation-Efficiency Index .... PEI
Precipitation-Evaporation .... P-E
Precipitin [*Test*] [*Immunology*] .... PRCPTN
PRECIS Project, Aurora High School, Ontario [*Library symbol National Library of Canada*] (NLC) .... OAUHS
PRECIS Word (NITA) .... PW
Precise Access Block Diagram .... PABD
Precise Access Diagram .... PAD
Precise Acquisition System .... PAS
Precise and Accurate Time and Time Interval [*An experiment aboard the Spacelab*] [*NASA*] (PDAA) .... PATTI
Precise Angle Indicator .... PAI
Precise Automated Tracking System (PDAA) .... PATS
Precise Block Diagram .... PBD
Precise Code [*Computer science*] (RDA) .... P
Precise Hybrid Elements for Nonlinear Operation (IEEE) .... PHENO
Precise Hybrid Elements for Nonlinear Operations (IAA) .... PHENOS
Precise Installation Position .... PIP
Precise Integrated Navigation System [*Offshore Systems of Vancouver*] .... PINS
Precise Integrated Navigation System [*Navy*] (DOMA) .... PINS
Precise LASER Distance Measuring Instrument .... PLDMI
Precise Navigation .... PNAV
Precise Participant Location .... PPL
Precise Participant Location-Identification [*Navigation*] .... PPLI
Precise Personnel Assignment System [*Marine Corps*] (GFGA) .... PREPAS
Precise Position Location Information .... PPLI
Precise Positioning Service [*Military*] .... PPS
Precise Range and Range-Rate Experiment .... PRARE
Precise Ship Motion Instrument .... PSMI
Precise Time and Time Interval (AFM) .... PTTI
Precise Tone Generator [*Telecommunications*] (TEL) .... PTG
Precisely Guided Reentry Test Vehicle (SAA) .... PGRVT
Precision (MSA) .... PRCN
Precision (AABC) .... PREC
Precision .... PRECSN
Precision Acquisition of Vehicle Entry Phased Array Warning System .... PAVE PAWS
Precision Adaptive Sub-Band Coding [*Electronics*] .... PASC
Precision Aerial Delivery System .... PADS
Precision Aerial Display System .... PADS
Precision Aerobatics Model Pilots Association (EA) .... PAMPA
Precision Aim Technique [*for helicopters*] [*Army*] (RDA) .... PAT
Precision Aim-Technique Heliborne Antitank [*Gun system concept*] [*Ballistic Research Laboratory*] (RDA) .... PATHAT
Precision Air-Bearing Floor (SSD) .... PABF
Precision Aircraft Armament Control Experiment (RDA) .... PAACE
Precision Aircraft Control Technology (MCD) .... PACT
Precision Aircraft Reference .... PAR
Precision Airlines [*ICAO designator*] (AD) .... RP
Precision Alignment Gyrocompass .... PAG
Precision Altimeter Techniques Study .... PATS
Precision Altitude and Landing Monitor [*Aircraft location*] .... PALM
Precision Analog Computing Equipment .... PACE
Precision and Accuracy Reporting System [*Environmental Protection Agency*] (GFGA) .... PARS
Precision Aneroid Barometer (DNAB) .... PAB
Precision Angle (IAA) .... PA
Precision Annotated Retrieval Display [*System*] [*Computer science*] .... PARD
Precision Antenna Display System (IAA) .... PADS
Precision Anti-Radiation Missile [*Military*] (PDAA) .... PARM
Precision Approach Airfield RADAR [*Aviation*] (IAA) .... PAAR
Precision Approach and Landing System (NASA) .... PALS
Precision Approach Interferometer RADAR (MCD) .... PAIR
Precision Approach Lighting System [*Aviation*] (FAAC) .... PALS
Precision Approach Path Indicator [*FAA*] (TAG) .... PAPI
Precision Approach Path Indicator [*Aviation*] (FAAC) .... PAPI
Precision Approach RADAR [*Aviation*] .... PAR
Precision Approach RADAR Training System (MCD) .... PARTS
Precision Approach - UNICOM [*Aviation*] .... PAU
Precision Architecture [*Hewlett-Packard Co.*] [*Computer science*] .... PA
Precision Artwork Language [*Computer science*] .... PAL
Precision Askania Range System of Electronic Timing (MUGU) .... PARSET
Precision Askania Range Target Acquisition and Control (MUGU) .... PARTAC
Precision Autocollimating Solar Sensor .... PASS
Precision Automated Tracking System [*FAA*] (TAG) .... PATS
Precision Automatic Noise Figure Indicator .... PANFI
Precision Axis (KSC) .... PRA
Precision Bombing Range [*Army*] .... PBR
Precision Cast Parts, Portland, OR [*Library symbol*] [*Library of Congress*] (LCLS) .... OrPPCP
Precision Casting Standard (MCD) .... PCS
Precision Castparts [*NYSE symbol*] (TTSB) .... PCP
Precision Castparts Corp. [*NYSE symbol*] (SPSG) .... PCP
Precision Castparts Corp. (MHDW) .... PCST
Precision Castparts Corp. [*Associated Press*] (SAG) .... PrecCst
Precision Chiropractic Research Society [*Also known as Spinal Stress Research Society*] (EA) .... PCRS
Precision Clearing Agent (DNAB) .... PCA
Precision Components, Inc. [*Addison, IL*] [*Telecommunications service*] (TSSD) .... PCI
Precision Condenser Microphone .... PCM
Precision Control [*Computer programming*] (BYTE) .... PC
Precision Course Direction [*Aerospace*] (MCD) .... PCD
Precision Delay Line .... PDL
Precision Delivery Glider System .... PDGS
Precision Depth Digitizer [*Oceanography*] .... PDD
Precision Depth Recorder .... PDR
Precision Device [*British military*] (DMA) .... PD
Precision Distance Measuring Equipment [*FAA*] (TAG) .... DME/P
Precision Distance Measuring Equipment (MCD) .... PDME
Precision Doppler VHF Omni-Range (PDAA) .... PDVOR
Precision Drill Jig .... PDJ
Precision Drill Jig Bushing .... PDJB
Precision Drilling (1987) Ltd. [*Toronto Stock Exchange symbol*] .... PD
Precision Drilling Corp. [*NYSE symbol*] (SAG) .... PDS
Precision Drilling Corp. [*Associated Press*] (SAG) .... PrecDr
Precision Drive Axis (KSC) .... PDA
Precision Drop Glider [*Army*] .... PDG
Precision Earth-Pointing System (MCD) .... PEPSY
Precision Echo Sounder Recorder .... PESR
Precision Elastic Limit .... PEL
Precision Electromagnetic Ram [*Denne Developments*] (PS) .... PEMRam
Precision Emitter Location Strike System [*Air Force*] .... PELSS
Precision Emitter Location System [*Air Force*] (MCD) .... PELS
Precision Encoding and Pattern Recognition Device [*Computer science*] .... PEPR
Precision Fathometer Recorder [*Raytheon Co.*] .... PFR
Precision Frequency Distribution Amplifier .... PFDA
Precision Frequency Multivider (KSC) .... PFM
Precision Frequency Source .... PFS
Precision Gas Products [*Commercial firm*] .... PGP
Precision Gear Train Tools and Test .... PGTTT
Precision Gimbal Experiment .... PGE
Precision Graphic Recorder .... PGR
Precision Ground [*Electronics*] (IAA) .... PG
Precision Guided Maneuvering Re-Entry Vehicle (PDAA) .... PGMARV
Precision Guided Missile .... PGM
Precision Guided Mortar Munition .... PGMM
Precision Guided Reentry Vehicle .... PGRV
Precision Gunnery System [*Army training device*] (INF) .... PGS
Precision Gunnery Training System [*Army*] (INF) .... PGTS
Precision High Dose .... PHD
Precision Hover Sensor (PDAA) .... PHS
Precision In Line [*Electronics*] (EECA) .... PIL
Precision Indicator of the Meridian .... PIM
Precision Infrared Tracking .... PIRT
Precision Infrared Triangulation .... PIRT
Precision Insertion Loss Measurement Set (IAA) .... PILMS
Precision Inspection Request (IAA) .... PIR
Precision Instrument (NVT) .... PI
Precision Instrument Landing System .... PILS
Precision Instrument Mount .... PIM
Precision Instrumentation RADAR .... PIR
Precision Integrator for Meteorological Echoes (IEEE) .... PRIME
Precision Intelligence Augmentation System .... PIAS
Precision Interactive Operation [*Computer science*] .... PIO
Precision Iterative Operation (IAA) .... PIO
Precision LASER Designator (RDA) .... PLD
Precision LASER Tracking System (NASA) .... PLTS
Precision Lightweight Global-Positioning-Satellite Receiver .... PLGR
Precision Lightweight GPS [*Global Positioning System*] **Receiver** [*Army*] (INF) .... PLGR
Precision Lightweight GPS [*Global Positioning System*] **Receiver** [*Navigation systems*] .... PLGR
Precision Lightweight GPS Receiver .... PLGR
Precision Loading and Utilization System (AAG) .... PLUS
Precision Location and Tracking System (PDAA) .... PLATS
Precision Location Strike System [*Air Force*] .... PLSS
Precision Long-Range Tracking RADAR .... PRELORT
Precision Machining Commercialization (MCD) .... PMC
Precision Management of Concordville, Inc. [*Media, PA*] (TSSD) .... PMC INC
Precision Manned Bomber .... PMB
Precision Measurements Association (EA) .... PMA
Precision Measurements Equipment Laboratory [*NASA*] .... PMEL
Precision Measuring Equipment (AFM) .... PME
Precision Measuring Equipment Laboratory (NADA) .... PMEL
Precision Measuring Equipment Laboratory (AD) .... PMEL
Precision Measuring Subsystem (KSC) .... PMSS
Precision Mechanisms in Sodium [*Nuclear energy*] (NRCH) .... PMIS
Precision Metalforming Association (EA) .... PMA
Precision Mirror Calorimeter (AD) .... pmc
Precision Missile Tracking System [*Military*] (IAA) .... PMTS
Precision Monolithics Inc (NITA) .... PMI
Precision Navigation Ambiguity Resolution .... PNAV
Precision Navigation Project .... PNP
Precision Optical Tracking System (KSC) .... POTS
Precision Optics Corp. [*NASDAQ symbol*] (SAG) .... POCI
Precision Optics Corp. [*Associated Press*] (SAG) .... PrcOptCp
Precision Optics Mass [*NASDAQ symbol*] (TTSB) .... POCI

Precision Optimized Measurement Time [*Spectroscopy*] ... PROMT
Precision Orbit Determination (MCD) ... POD
Precision Oscillator Crystal ... POC
Precision Photomechanical Corp. ... PPC
Precision Plan Position Indicator ... PPPI
Precision Pointing Control System [*Engineering*] ... PPCS
Precision Position Locator System [*Army*] ... PPLS
Precision Positioning Service ... PPS
Precision Potentiometer Manufacturers Association [*Later, Variable Resistive Components Institute*] (EA) ... PPMA
Precision Power Supply ... PPS
Precision Pressure Balance ... PPB
Precision Quartz Crystal ... PQC
Precision Radiation Thermometer ... PRT
Precision Range Information Analysis for Missiles (MCD) ... PRIAM
Precision Range Integrated Maneuver Exercise [*Army*] (RDA) ... PRIME
Precision Ranging System ... PRS
Precision Recording (Optical) of Fingerprints ... PROOF
Precision Recovery Including Maneuvering Entry [*Air Force*] ... PRIME
Precision Reduction Laboratory (AFM) ... PRL
Precision Remote Bathythermograph ... PRBT
Precision Response Corp. [*Associated Press*] (SAG) ... PrecRes
Precision Response Corp. [*NASDAQ symbol*] (SAG) ... PRRC
Precision RISC [*Reduced Instruction Set Computer*] **Organization** ... PRO
Precision Rotary Stripper ... PRS
Precision Runway Monitor [*FAA*] (TAG) ... PRM
Precision Spot Positioning ... PSP
Precision Standard [*NASDAQ symbol*] (TTSB) ... PCSN
Precision Standard, Inc. [*NASDAQ symbol*] (NQ) ... PCSN
Precision Standard, Inc. [*Associated Press*] (SAG) ... PrecStd
Precision Systems [*NASDAQ symbol*] (TTSB) ... PSYS
Precision Systems, Inc. [*Associated Press*] (SAG) ... PrecSy
Precision Systems, Inc. [*NASDAQ symbol*] (SAG) ... PSYS
Precision Teaching ... PT
Precision Technology, Inc. (AAG) ... PTI
Precision Time Fuze ... PT
Precision Timing System ... PTS
Precision Torque Measuring System (NASA) ... PTMS
Precision Transform [*Eastman Kodak Co.*] [*Computer science*] (PCM) ... PT
Precision Transmitter Receiver ... PTR
Precision Underwater Navigation ... PUN
Precision Valley Aviation [*ICAO designator*] (FAAC) ... PRE
Precision Variable Delay Line ... PVDL
Precision Velocity Update (MCD) ... PVU
Precision Verification Team ... PVT
Precision Verification Test (MCD) ... PVT
Precision VHF [*Very High-Frequency*] **Omnidirectional Range** (IAA) ... PVOR
Precision VHF Omnirange ... PVOR
Precision Voltage Reference (MDG) ... PVR
Precision Welding-Head ... PWH
Precision-Acrobatics (DOMA) ... PA
Precision-Guided Munition (MCD) ... PGM
Precite [*Supra, Cited Before*] [*French*] (ILCA) ... Prec
Preclinical Literature Information System [*Computer science*] ... PLIS
Pre-Combat Inspection (INF) ... PCI
Precombustor Oxidizer Valve (KSC) ... PCOV
Pre-Command Course [*Military*] ... PCC
Precommissioning [*Military*] ... PRECOM
Precommissioning [*Military*] (NVT) ... PRECOMG
Precommissioning Detail [*Navy*] (NVT) ... PRECOMDET
Precommissioning Detail [*Navy*] ... PRECOMMDET
Precommissioning School [*Navy*] ... PRECOMMSCOL
Precommissioning Unit [*Navy*] (DNAB) ... PRECOMUNIT
Precommit Track Time [*DoD*] ... PCTT
Precompetitive Research and Development ... PRD
Precompressor Cooling (MCD) ... PCC
Precomputed Altitude ... PA
Precomputed Loan ... precomp
Pre-Conditioned Air System [*Aviation*] (DA) ... PCA
Preconditioned Conjugate Gradient ... PCG2
Preconditioning [*Medicine*] (DMAA) ... PC
Preconditioning Interim Operating Management Recommendation [*Nuclear energy*] (NRCH) ... PCIOMR
Preconfiguration Unit Load ... PUL
Preconscious ... PCS
Preconscious Activity Scale (EDAC) ... PAS
Preconstruction Operating Instruction [*Environmental Protection Agency*] ... PCOI
Preconstruction Requirement [*Environmental Protection Agency*] ... PR
Precontract Cost Letter [*Navy*] (NG) ... PCCL
Precontractual Authorization ... PCA
Pre-Coordinate Indexing System ... PRECIS
Precordia [*Anatomy*] ... PC
Precordial Acceleration Tracing [*Medicine*] (DMAA) ... PACT
Pre-Counseling Inventory [*Psychology*] ... PCI
Precracked Charpy V-Notch (PDAA) ... PCVN
Precursor above the Horizon Sensor [*Strategic Defense Initiative*] ... PATHS
Precursor Active Galaxies ... PAG
Precursor Fluid [*Medicine*] (MEDA) ... PF
Precursor-Messenger Ribonucleic Acid ... pre-mRNA
Predator and Rodent Control [*US Fish and Wildlife Service*] (IIA) ... PARC
Predators Present [*Ecology*] ... P
Predecease (ROG) ... PREDECE
Predecessor (KSC) ... PRE
Predecessors and Defunct Companies (NITA) ... PDC
Predefined Command (MCD) ... PDC
Predefined Input Control Sequence (MCD) ... PICS
Predelivery Acceptance Test [*NASA*] ... PDA
Pre-Delivery Inspection (DCTA) ... PDI
Predelivery Test (MCD) ... PDT
Predella (VRA) ... prdl
Predemonstration Fusion Device ... PDFD
Predeparture Check [*Aviation*] (AIA) ... PDC
Pre-Departure Clearance [*FAA*] (TAG) ... PDC
Predeployment ... PD
Predeployment Inspection [*Navy*] (NVT) ... PDI
Predesign and Systems Analysis [*NASA*] (KSC) ... PDSA
Predesignated High-Interest Tactical Area [*Navy*] (NVT) ... PHITAR
Predesigned [*or Priority*] **High-Interest Tactical Air Prediction** [*Acoustic forecast*] (MCD) ... PHITAP
Predetection Combining (IAA) ... PDC
Predetection Recording ... PDR
Predetermined Demand Rate ... PDR
Predetermined Motion Time Standards [*Management*] (IAA) ... PMTS
Predetermined Motion Time Systems [*Management*] ... PMTS
Pre-Determined Motion-Time [*Management*] (PDAA) ... PMT
Pre-Determined Route [*Aviation*] (DA) ... PDR
Predetermined Time Value (IEEE) ... PTV
Predialyzed Human Albumin [*Medicine*] (MAE) ... PDA
Predialyzed Human Serum [*Medicine*] (MAE) ... PDS
Predicasts Abstract Terminal System [*Computer science*] ... PATS
Predicasts Overview of Markets and Technology [*Predicasts, Inc.*] [*Cleveland, OH Bibliographic database*] ... PTS PROMT
Predicasts Overview of Markets and Terminology (NITA) ... PROMT
Predicasts Overviews of Marketing and Technology [*Business database*] ... PROMT
Predicasts Terminal Systems [*Predicasts, Inc.*] [*Cleveland, OH Database*] ... PTS
Predicasts Time Series [*Series of databases*] [*Predicasts, Inc. Cleveland, OH*] ... PTS
Predicate ... P
Predicate ... PRED
Predictable Model Guidance Scheme (OA) ... PMGS
Predictable System Performance (SAA) ... PSP
Predicted [*NASA*] (KSC) ... P/D
Predicted ... PRED
Predicted Blood Volume [*Medicine*] ... PBV
Predicted Cardia Output [*Medicine*] (DMAA) ... PCO
Predicted Comparative Failure Probability ... PCFP
Predicted Drift Angle [*Navigation*] ... PDA
Predicted Environmental Concentration (DCTA) ... PEC
Predicted Fire Weapon ... PFW
Predicted Fire Weapon System [*Army*] ... PFWS
Predicted First-Year Average [*Law school*] ... PFYA
Predicted Four Hour Sweat Rate (PDAA) ... P4SR
Predicted Grade [*IRS*] ... PG
Predicted Ground Speed [*Navigation*] ... PGS
Predicted Impact (MCD) ... PI
Predicted Impact Point [*Aerospace*] (AAG) ... PIP
Predicted Intercept Contour ... PIC
Predicted Intercept Point ... PIP
Predicted Intercept Range [*Military*] (CAAL) ... PIR
Predicted Manning System [*Military*] ... PMS
Predicted Maximum Heart Rate [*Medicine*] (DMAA) ... PMHR
Predicted No Effect Concentration [*Environmental technology*] ... PNEC
Predicted Operational Environment [*Military*] (CAAL) ... POE
Predicted Orbit ... PROR
Predicted Period-of-Effect [*Meteorology*] ... PPE
Predicted Propagation Correction (PDAA) ... PPC
Predicted Quarterly Demand ... PQD
Predicted Range Against Target [*Military*] (NVT) ... PRAT
Predicted Range for Electrooptical Systems [*Military*] (CAAL) ... PREOS
Predicted Range of the Day [*Military*] (NVT) ... PRD
Predicted Rate [*Medicine*] (DAVI) ... PR
Predicted Repair Level (MCD) ... PRL
Predicted Residual Sum of Squares ... PRESS
Predicted Site Acquisition Data [*NASA*] ... PSAD
Predicted Site Acquisition Table [*NASA*] ... PSAT
Predicted SONAR Range [*Military*] (NVT) ... PSR
Predicted Speech Intelligibility Computer (IAA) ... PSICOMP
Predicted Wave Signaling ... PWS
Prediction (AFM) ... PRED
Prediction Analysis Techniques ... PAT
Prediction and Allocation ... P & A
Prediction and Optimization of Failure Rate (MHDB) ... PROF
Prediction Error Filter [*Wave frequency and phase modifier*] ... PEF
Prediction Error Transform (PDAA) ... PET
Prediction Interval Initiation Date (DNAB) ... PIID
Prediction Marker Generator ... PMG
Prediction of Contingency Maintenance and Parts Requirements (MCD) ... PRECOMP
Prediction of Radiation Effects by Digital Computer Techniques ... PREDICT
Prediction Program [*NASA*] ... PRDX
Prediction, Simulation, Adaptation, Decision [*Computer science*] ... PSAD
Predictive Accuracy [*Medicine*] (DMAA) ... PA
Predictive Aircraft Maintenance System ... PAMS
Predictive Analysis and Crash Testing [*Automotive safety research*] ... PACT
Predictive Analyzer [*Computer science*] (DIT) ... PA
Predictive Emission Monitoring System [*Environmental science*] ... PEMS
Predictive Influence Function [*Statistics*] ... PIF
Predictive Linguistic Constraint ... PLC
Predictive Maintenance ... PDM

Predictive Multisensor Correlation	PMC
Predictive Period LASER (KSC)	PPL
Predictive Proportional Guidance	PPG
Predictive Proportional Navigation	PPN
Predictive Saccades [Ophthalmology]	PS
Predictive Smooth Pursuit [Ophthalmology]	PSP
Predictor [British military] (DMA)	P
Predictor Display Technique	PDT
Predictor Frame Memory	PFM
Predilute	PD
Predischarge Education Program [DoD]	PREP
Predischarge Graded Exercise Test [Cardiology] (DAVI)	PDGXT
Predischarge Remedial Education Program [For servicemen]	PREPS
Predischarge Utilization Review [Medicine]	PDUR
Predisposing, Reinforcing, and Enabling Causes in Educational Diagnosis and Evaluation [Occupational therapy]	PRECEDE
Predneaziatskii Sbornik Voprosy Khattologii i Khurritologii [A publication] (BJA)	PASb
Prednisolone [Endocrinology]	P
Prednisolone Glucose Tolerance Test [Medicine] (DMAA)	PGTT
Prednisolone, Oncovin [Vicristine], L-Asparaginase [Antineoplastic drug regimen] (DAVI)	POLE
, Prednisone [Vincristine] [Antineoplastic drug regimen]	BOP
, Prednisone [Vincristine] [Antineoplastic drug regimen]	MOPr
Prednisone [Also, PDN, Pr, Pred, Pro] [Endocrinology] [Antineoplastic drug]	P
Prednisone [Also, P, Pr, Pred, Pro] [Endocrinology] [Antineoplastic drug]	PDN
Prednisone [Also, P, PDN, Pred, Pro] [Endocrinology] [Antineoplastic drug]	Pr
Prednisone [Also, P, PDN, Pr, Pro] [Endocrinology] [Antineoplastic drug]	Pred
Prednisone (DMAA)	PRED
Prednisone [Also, P, PDN, PR, Pred] [Antineoplastic drug, Endocrinology]	Pro
Prednisone, ara-C [Cytarabine], Thioguanine, Cyclophosphamide, Oncovin [Vincristine] [Antineoplastic drug regimen]	PATCO
Prednisone, Methotrexate, Fluorouracil, Adriamycin, Cyclophosphamide [Antineoplastic drug regimen]	PM-FAC
Prednisone, Methotrexate with Leucovorin, Adriamycin, Cyclophosphamide, Epipodophyllin [Etoposide, VP-16] [Antineoplastic drug regimen]	Pro-MACE
Prednisone, Oncovin [Vincristine], Cytarabine, Adriamycin [Antineoplastic drug regimen]	POCA
Prednisone, Oncovin [Vincristine] Cytosine Arabinoside, Cyclophospham ide, and Adriamycin [Antineoplastic drug regimen] (DAVI)	POACH
Prednisone, Oncovin [Vincristine], Methotrexate, Purinethol [Mercaptopurine] [Antineoplastic drug regimen]	POMP
Predocketed Application (NRCH)	PDA
Predocketed Construction (NRCH)	PDC
Predocketed Special Project (NRCH)	PDS
Predominant [National Weather Service] (FAAC)	PDMT
Predominant Interest Agency (AAGC)	PIA
Predominant Interest Installation (AAGC)	PII
Predominately Black Colleges and Universities	PBCU
Predominately Minority Colleges and Universities	PMCU
Predominating Organism (AAMN)	PO
Preduzece Soko [Former Yugoslavia] [ICAO aircraft manufacturer identifier] (ICAO)	PS
Pre-Eclampsia [Medicine]	PE
Pre-Eclamptic Toxemia [Medicine]	PET
Pre-Edge X-Ray Absorption [For study of solids]	PEXA
Preedited Interpreter (IAA)	PRINT
Pre-Edited Interpretive System [Computer science]	PRINT
Preedited Region [Genetics]	PER
Pre-Ejection Period [Cardiology]	PEP
Pre-Ejection Period Index [Cardiology]	PEPI
Pre-Ejection Period/Left Ventricular Ejection Time [Medicine] (MEDA)	PEP/LVET
Pre-Ejection Period to Ejection Period [Cardiology] (DAVI)	PEP/EP
Pre-Embossed Rigid Magnetic Media [Computer science]	PERM
Pre-Emphasis Circuit (OA)	PC
Pre-Employment Program	PEP
Pre-Employment Training (OICC)	PET
Pre-Emption [Telecommunications] (TEL)	PE
Pre-Emption (ROG)	PRE-EMPTN
Pre-Emptive Right (MHDW)	PER
Preexcitation Syndrome [Cardiology]	PES
Pre-Expanded Bin (DNAB)	PEB
Prefabricated	PFAB
Prefabricated [Technical drawings]	PFB
Prefabricated (KSC)	PREFAB
Prefabricated Aluminium Scaffold Manufacturers Association [British] (DBA)	PASMA
Prefabricated Bituminous Surfacing	PBS
Prefabricated Surfacing Aluminum	PSA
Prefac Enterprises, Inc. [Toronto Stock Exchange symbol]	PRF
Preface (ROG)	PFCE
Preface	PREF
Preface (WDMC)	pref
Preface (ROG)	PREFCE
Prefatory (WDMC)	pre
Prefect	PRE
Prefect-Apostolic [Roman Catholic]	PA
Prefect-Apostolic [Roman Catholic]	PREF-AP
Prefecture	PREF
Prefecture	preft
Preference	PF
Preference (AAG)	PFCE
Preference [or Preferred] (AFM)	PREF

Preference Equity Redemption Cumulative Stock (ECON)	PERCS
Preference for Duty	PD
Preferential Arrival Route [Aviation] (DA)	PAR
Preferential Departure [Aviation] (DA)	PDAR
Preferential Departure and Arrival Route [FAA] (TAG)	PDAR
Preferential Departure Route [FAA] (TAG)	PDR
Preferential Planning List	PPL
Preferential Trade Arrangements [ASEAN] (IMH)	PTA
Preferential Treatment (OICC)	PT
Preferred	P
Preferred	PF
Preferred (AAG)	PFD
Preferred [Stock exchange term] (SPSG)	PR
Preferred (WDMC)	pre
Preferred	PREF
Preferred (KSC)	PREF
Preferred (WDAA)	PREFD
Preferred and Well Qualified [Candidate designation]	PWQ
Preferred Arrival Date (AFM)	PAD
Preferred Body Temperature [Physiology]	PBT
Preferred Capital Stock [Investment term]	PCS
Preferred Delivery Date (AFM)	PDD
Preferred Equipment Package [Automotive retailing]	PEP
Preferred Flights, Inc. [Canada ICAO designator]	EMS
Preferred Hotels Association [Also known as Preferred Hotel Worldwide] (EA)	PHA
Preferred Income Fund [NYSE symbol] (SPSG)	PFD
Preferred Income Fund [Associated Press] (SAG)	PfdInco
Preferred Income Management Fund [NYSE symbol] (SPSG)	PFM
Preferred Income Management Fund, Inc. [Associated Press] (SAG)	PfIMF
Preferred Income Mgmt Fund [NYSE symbol] (TTSB)	PFM
Preferred Income Opportunity Fund [NYSE symbol] (SAG)	PFO
Preferred Income Opportunity Fund [Associated Press] (SAG)	PrfIOF
Preferred Income Oppt Fd [NYSE symbol] (TTSB)	PFO
Preferred Item List (RDA)	PIL
Preferred Lenders Program [Small Business Administration]	PLP
Preferred Measurement Hardware List [NASA] (NASA)	PMHL
Preferred Mechanical Parts List [NASA] (NASA)	PMPL
Preferred National Land Rights Model [Australia]	PNLRM
Preferred Networks [NASDAQ symbol] (TTSB)	PFNT
Preferred Overseas Shore Duty	POS
Preferred Parts and Materials List [NASA]	PPML
Preferred Parts Index	PPI
Preferred Parts List	PPL
Preferred Parts List System (MCD)	PPLS
Preferred Pharmacy Program	PPP
Preferred Policyholders' Discount [British] (BARN)	PPD
Preferred Procurement Number Selector Code [Military] (AFIT)	PPNSC
Preferred Provider [Medicine] (DMAA)	PP
Preferred Provider Arrangement [Information service or system] (HCT)	PPA
Preferred Provider Arrangement	PPA
Preferred Resources, Inc. [Vancouver Stock Exchange symbol]	PFR
Preferred Sea Duty	PSD
Preferred Semiconductor Circuit [Electronics] (IAA)	PSC
Preferred Speech Interference Level	PSIL
Preferred Spelling (WDAA)	PFD SP
Preferred Stock [Investment term] (DFIT)	PFD
Preferred Stock [Investment term]	PFRD
Preferred Stock [Investment term]	PS
Preferred Stock Advisory Committee [New Deal]	PSAC
Preferred Storage Area (MCD)	PSA
Preferred Target Point (KSC)	PTP
Preferred Vision Provider	PVP
Preferred-Provided Organization [Insurance] (AD)	PPO
Preferred-Provider Option [Insurance]	PPO
Preferred-Provider Organization [Insurance]	PPO
Prefetch [Computer science]	PF
Prefilled Clutch Hydraulic Actuation [Automotive Products, Inc.] [Automotive engineering]	PFCH
Prefinished [Technical drawings]	PFN
Pre-First Article Test	PFAT
Prefix [Indicating a private radiotelegram]	P
Prefix (ROG)	PFX
Prefix [Indicating a private radiotelegram] (BUR)	PR
Prefix	PRE
Prefix (WDMC)	pre
Prefix (AAG)	PREF
Prefix Storage Area [Computer science] (OA)	PSA
Preflight	PF
Preflight (KSC)	PREFLT
Preflight Acceptance Checkout Equipment	PACE
Preflight Acceptance Checkout Equipment for Spacecraft	PACE-S/C
Preflight Acceptance Checkout Equipment-Launch Vehicle	PACE/LV
Pre-Flight Certification Test	PFCT
Preflight Console (MCD)	PFC
Preflight Data Insertion Program (NVT)	PDIP
Preflight Heat Exchanger [NASA] (KSC)	PHE
Pre-Flight Information Bulletin [Aviation] (DA)	PIB
Preflight Integration of Munitions and Electronic Systems (MCD)	PRIMES
Preflight Operation Division [NASA]	POD
Preflight Operations Procedure (MCD)	POP
Preflight Qualification	PFQ
Preflight Review [NASA] (KSC)	PFR
Preflight School [Military]	PFS
Preflight School [Military]	PREFLTSCOL

Preflight Team [*Air Force*] (AFM) ... PFT
Preflight Test Bus (MCD) ... PFTB
Preflight Test Set (DNAB) ... PTS
Preflight Tool (MCD) ... PFT
Preflight Verification Test (NASA) ... PVT
Prefocus ... PRFCS
Prefocused ... PREF
Preform In-Mold Surfacing [*Plastics technology*] ... PIMS
Preformed ... PREFMD
Preformed [*Technical drawings*] ... PRF
Preformed Beams [*SONAR*] ... PFB
Preformed Line Product (IAA) ... PLP
Preformed Road Markings [*Road markings embedded in the pavement rather than painted on street's surface*] ... PRM
Pre-Freshman and Cooperative Education for Minorities in Engineering ... PREFACE
Prefrontal Cortex [*Anatomy*] ... PFC
Preganglionic [*Anatomy*] ... pregang
P-Register [*Computer science*] ... P
Pregnancy [*or Pregnant*] ... PREG
Pregnancy [*or Pregnant*] (AAMN) ... PREGN
Pregnancy Advisory Service [*British*] ... PAS
Pregnancy and Infant Loss Center (EA) ... PILC
Pregnancy at Term [*Gynecology*] ... PAT
Pregnancy Counselling Service [*Australia*] ... PCS
Pregnancy Crisis Centre [*Australia*] ... PCC
Pregnancy Discrimination Act [*An amendment to Title VII of the Civil Rights Act of 1964*] (PAZ) ... PDA
Pregnancy Discrimination Act of 1978 (WYGK) ... PDA
Pregnancy Induced [*Gynecology*] ... PI
Pregnancy, Labor and Delivery (DAVI) ... PLD
Pregnancy Rate [*Medicine*] ... PR
Pregnancy Support Service (Tasmania) [*Australia*] ... PSS(T)
Pregnancy Urine [*Medicine*] ... PU
Pregnancy Urine Hormone [*Endocrinology*] ... PUH
Pregnancy Zone Protein (AAMN) ... PZ
Pregnancy Zone Protein ... PZP
Pregnancy-Associated [*Gynecology*] (MAE) ... PA
Pregnancy-Associated alpha-Glycoprotein [*Gynecology*] ... PAG
Pregnancy-Associated Plasma Protein ... PAPP
Pregnancy-Associated Prostaglandin Synthetase Inhibitor [*Endocrinology*] ... PAPSI
Pregnancy-Induced Hypertension [*Gynecology*] ... PIH
Pregnancy-Specific Beta-1-Glycoprotein [*Medicine*] (DMAA) ... PSbetaG
Pregnancy-Specific beta-Glycoprotein [*Gynecology*] ... PSBG
Pregnancy-Specific Glycoprotein [*Biochemistry*] ... PSG
Pregnanediol [*Biochemistry*] ... PD
Pregnanediol [*Biochemistry*] ... P-DIOL
Pregnanediol Glucuronide [*Endocrinology*] ... PDG
Pregnanediol Glucuronide [*Endocrinology*] ... PG
Pregnant ... PG
Pregnant (DMAA) ... pg
Pregnant Guppy [*Reference to Boeing 377 aircraft*] (SAA) ... PG
Pregnant Mare's Serum [*Endocrinology*] ... PMS
Pregnant Mare's Serum (AD) ... pms
Pregnant Mare's Serum Gonadotrophin (AD) ... pmsg
Pregnant Mare's Serum Gonadotrophin [*Endocrinology*] ... PMSG
Pregnant Mare's Urine [*Veterinary medicine*] (BARN) ... PMU
Pregnant Urban Professional [*Terminology used in "The Yuppie Handbook"*] [*Lifestyle classification*] ... Puppie
Pregnant without Permission [*Military World War II*] ... PWOP
Pregnenolone [*Endocrinology*] ... PREG
Pregnenolone Binding Protein [*Endocrinology*] ... PBP
Pregnenolone Carbonitril [*Pharmacology*] (DAVI) ... PCN
Preheat ... PHT
Preheater (KSC) ... PHR
Preheating, Falling-Film, Rising-Film [*Sections of a concentrator*] [*Chemical engineering*] ... PFR
Prehistoric Society (EA) ... PS
Prehistory [*or Prehistoric*] (BARN) ... prehis
Prehistory [*or Prehistoric*] (WDAA) ... PREHIST
Pre-Homeobox [*Genetics*] ... PHB
Pre-Hospital Arrest Survival Evaluation [*Cardiology study*] ... PHASE
Prehospital Care Provider [*Health insurance*] (DMAA) ... PHCP
Preimplantation Embryo ... PIE
Pre-Impregnated Glass Fibers [*Fiberglass production*] ... PREPREG
Preinactivation Material Inspection [*Military*] (NVT) ... PIMI
Preincubation Mixture ... PM
Preinduction [*Medicine*] ... PI
Pre-Induction Training ... PIT
Preinfarction Angina [*Cardiology*] (DMAA) ... PIA
Preinfarction Syndrome [*Cardiology*] ... PIS
Preinitiation Complex [*Genetics*] ... PIC
Preinsert Sequencing ... PIS
Preinserted ... PINSTD
Pre-Inspection Acceptance (SAA) ... PIA
Preinstallation Acceptance ... PIA
Preinstallation Calibration (KSC) ... PIC
Preinstallation Checkout (NASA) ... PIC
Preinstallation Test [*NASA*] (KSC) ... PIT
Preinterservice Data Exchange Program ... PIDEP
Preiss Byron Multimedia [*NASDAQ symbol*] (TTSB) ... CDRM
Preiss (Byron) Multimedia Co., Inc. [*Associated Press*] (SAG) ... BPreis
Preiss Byron Multimedia Wrrt [*NASDAQ symbol*] (TTSB) ... CDRMW
Preiss [*Byron*] **Multimedia Co., Inc.** [*NASDAQ symbol*] (SAG) ... CDRM
Preiss [*Byron*] **Multimedia Co., Inc.** [*Associated Press*] (SAG) ... PreissM
Prejudice (AABC) ... PREJ
Prekindergarten School, Roosevelt, NY [*Library symbol*] [*Library of Congress*] (LCLS) ... NRoosPK
Preknock Pulse ... PKP
Prelaunch (NASA) ... PL
Prelaunch Automatic Checkout Equipment [*NASA*] ... PACE
Prelaunch Channel Number [*NASA*] (IAA) ... PCN
Prelaunch Checkout Plan [*NASA*] (KSC) ... PLCOP
Prelaunch Hazard Area (MUGU) ... PHA
Prelaunch, Launch, and Ascent Procedures [*NASA*] (IAA) ... PLAP
Prelaunch Monitor [*NASA*] (KSC) ... PLM
Prelaunch Operations Plan [*NASA*] (NASA) ... POP
Prelaunch Status Simulator ... PLSS
Prelaunch Survival Probability (CINC) ... PLSP
Prelaunch Wind Profile (SAA) ... PWP
Preliminary ... P
Preliminary (KSC) ... PLM
Preliminary ... PRE
Preliminary ... PREL
Preliminary (AFM) ... PRELIM
Preliminary (ROG) ... PRELIMY
Preliminary (VRA) ... prelm
Preliminary Acceptance (KSC) ... PA
Preliminary Acceptance Trials [*Navy*] ... PAT
Preliminary Advisory Data (MCD) ... PAD
Preliminary Airworthiness Evaluations ... PAE
Preliminary Allowance Equipage List [*Military*] (CAAL) ... PAEL
Preliminary Allowance List [*Military*] (DNAB) ... PAL
Preliminary Allowance Parts List [*Military*] (CAAL) ... PAPL
Preliminary Allowance Quantity [*Military*] (CAAL) ... PAQ
Preliminary Amplifier (IAA) ... PA
Preliminary Amplifier (IAA) ... PRE
Preliminary Analysis Group (NATG) ... PAG
Preliminary Annual Engineering Plan [*Military*] (AFIT) ... PAEP
Preliminary Approval for Service Use [*Military*] ... PASU
Preliminary Army Evaluation (MCD) ... PAE
Preliminary Army Planning and Program Guidance Memorandum (MCD) ... PAPPGM
Preliminary As-Built [*Nuclear energy*] (NRCH) ... PAB
Preliminary Assessment (ERG) ... PA
Preliminary Assessment and Site Inspection [*Environmental Protection Agency*] (FFDE) ... PA/SI
Preliminary Assessment Information Rule [*Environmental Protection Agency*] ... PAIR
Preliminary Authority to Proceed (NASA) ... PATP
Preliminary Automated Ground Environment ... PAGE
Preliminary Basis of Issue Plan [*Military*] (MCD) ... PBOIP
Preliminary Breakdown ... PB
Preliminary Change Letter [*Navy*] (NG) ... PCL
Preliminary Change Transmittal (AAG) ... PCT
Preliminary Command and Sequencing [*Viking lander mission*] [*NASA*] ... PC & S
Preliminary Commitment (IMH) ... PC
Preliminary Communications [*Military*] (NVT) ... PRECOMM
Preliminary Communications Search [*Military*] (NVT) ... PRECOM
Preliminary Component Specification ... PCS
Preliminary Configuration Control Number (AAG) ... PCCN
Preliminary Configuration Management Plan (MCD) ... PCMP
Preliminary Contract Change Proposal [*NASA*] (KSC) ... PCCP
Preliminary Contract Work Breakdown Structure (MCD) ... PCWBS
Preliminary Cost Proposal (MCD) ... PCP
Preliminary Data Report ... PDR
Preliminary Data Requirements (NASA) ... PDR
Preliminary Definition Plan (NASA) ... PDP
Preliminary Design ... PD
Preliminary Design Acceptance (NRCH) ... PDA
Preliminary Design Activity (LAIN) ... PDA
Preliminary Design and Development (MCD) ... PDD
Preliminary Design Approval [*or Authorization*] (NRCH) ... PDA
Preliminary Design Assessment [*Nuclear energy*] (NRCH) ... PDA
Preliminary Design Phase ... PDP
Preliminary Design Proposal (MCD) ... PDP
Preliminary Design Report (NRCH) ... PDR
Preliminary Design Review (NASA) ... PDR
Preliminary Design Review Commercial (MCD) ... PDRC
Preliminary Development Model ... PDM
Preliminary Diagnosis [*Medicine*] (DAVI) ... prelim diag
Preliminary Diagnostic Clinic ... PDC
Preliminary Draft Environmental Statement (NRCH) ... PDES
Preliminary Draft Equipment Publication (MCD) ... PDEP
Preliminary Draft Manuscript ... PDM
Preliminary Draft Presidential Memo ... PDPM
Preliminary Encapsulated Inert Test Vehicle (MCD) ... PEITV
Preliminary Engineering Change Memorandum [*Air Force*] (CET) ... PECM
Preliminary Engineering Change Proposal ... PECP
Preliminary Engineering Configuration List ... PECL
Preliminary Engineering Inspection [*NASA*] (KSC) ... PEI
Preliminary Engineering Parts List ... PEPL
Preliminary Engineering Report (KSC) ... PER
Preliminary Engineering Reports (MUGU) ... PERS
Preliminary Engineering Technical Proposal ... PETP
Preliminary Environmental Assessment (MCD) ... PEA
Preliminary Equipment Component Index [*or Inventory*] ... PECI
Preliminary Evaluation ... PE
Preliminary Evaluation [*Orbit identification*] ... PREL

Preliminary Evaluation Team	PET
Preliminary Examination Team [*NASA*]	PET
Preliminary Exploitation (MCD)	PE
Preliminary Failure Analysis Report [*NASA*] (KSC)	PFAR
Preliminary Final Draft Manuscript	PFDM
Preliminary Flight Appraisal Test (MCD)	PFAT
Preliminary Flight Certification [*NASA*]	PFC
Preliminary Flight Motor (MCD)	PFM
Preliminary Flight Rating [*Air Force*]	PFR
Preliminary Flight Rating Test	PFRT
Preliminary Flight Readiness Test [*NASA*] (KSC)	PFRT
Preliminary Flight Test Memo	PFTM
Preliminary Flight Test Report	PFTR
Preliminary Flightweight Demonstration Test Motor (MCD)	PFDTM
Preliminary Functional Description (CINC)	PFD
Preliminary Government-Furnished Equipment List (MCD)	PGFEL
Preliminary Group Assembly Parts List	PGAPL
Preliminary Guaranteed Minimum Price	PGMP
Preliminary Handbook of Operations and Service Instructions	PHOSI
Preliminary Hardware Design Review	PHDR
Preliminary Hazard Analyses (NASA)	PHA
Preliminary Imagery Nomination File (MCD)	PIN
Preliminary Impact Engineering Change Proposal (MCD)	PIECP
Preliminary Incubation (OA)	PI
Preliminary Information Pamphlet	PIP
Preliminary Injunction [*Legal term*] (HGAA)	PI
Preliminary Inquiry Officer (DNAB)	PIO
Preliminary Inspection (MCD)	PI
Preliminary Instruction Book	PIB
Preliminary Interface Control Drawing	PICD
Preliminary Interface Revision Notice [*NASA*] (KSC)	PIRN
Preliminary Investigation (NASA)	PI
Preliminary Issue	PI
Preliminary Joint Operation Procedure (KSC)	PJOP
Preliminary Landing Site (NASA)	PLS
Preliminary Leaf [*Bibliography*]	PL
Preliminary Life-Cycle Cost Estimate	PLCCE
Preliminary List of Design Changes	PLDC
Preliminary Logistics Evaluation	PLE
Preliminary Maintainability and Spare Parts	PMSP
Preliminary Maintenance Allocation Chart (MCD)	PMAC
Preliminary Maintenance Analysis Report [*Aerospace*] (AAG)	PMAR
Preliminary Maintenance Engineering Analysis Requirement (MCD)	PMEAR
Preliminary Maintenance Inspection (MCD)	PMI
Preliminary Management Plan (AD)	PMP
Preliminary Master Government-Furnished Equipment List (MCD)	PMGFEL
Preliminary Materials List [*NASA*]	PML
Preliminary Materials Review	PMR
Preliminary Materials Review Board	PMRB
Preliminary Materials Review Group [*NASA*] (KSC)	PMRG
Preliminary Mid-Ocean Dynamics Experiment [*Marine science*] (MSC)	PREMODE
Preliminary Mission Profile (MCD)	PMP
Preliminary Natural Resources Survey (GNE)	PNRS
Preliminary Negotiation Reports	PNR
Preliminary Network Plan (SSD)	PNP
Preliminary Notification (NRCH)	PN
Preliminary Notification [*Nuclear energy*] (NRCH)	PNO
Preliminary Number Deflator [*Empirical mathematics*] (ECON)	PND
Preliminary Operating and Maintenance Instructions [*Aerospace*] (AAG)	POMI
Preliminary Operating and Maintenance Manual [*Military*] (AABC)	POMM
Preliminary Operating Safety Analysis [*Nuclear energy*] (NRCH)	POSA
Preliminary Operational Capability [*Military*] (AFIT)	POC
Preliminary Operations Requirements Review [*NASA*] (NASA)	PORR
Preliminary Orbit Determination Method [*Computer*] [*NASA*]	PODM
Preliminary Overhaul Work Package (DNAB)	POWP
Preliminary Pages [*Frontmatter*] [*Publishing*]	prelims
Preliminary Parts List	PPL
Preliminary Performance Design Requirements	PP/DR
Preliminary Personnel Requirements Analysis [*Navy*]	PPRA
Preliminary Phase Correction (IAA)	PPC
Preliminary Pile Assembly (IAA)	PPA
Preliminary Pollutant Limit Value (MCD)	PPLV
Preliminary Power Laboratory (IAA)	PPL
Preliminary Process Potential Index	PPPI
Preliminary Program and Budget Guidance	PPBG
Preliminary Program Management Network [*Military*]	PPMN
Preliminary Project Design Description (NRCH)	PPDD
Preliminary Project Development Plan [*NASA*]	PPDP
Preliminary Publication Revision Notice	PPRN
Preliminary Qualification Test (MCD)	PQT
Preliminary Quantitative Analysis	PQA
Preliminary Quantitative Material Requirements (MCD)	PQMR
Preliminary Reference Earth Model [*Geology*]	PREM
Preliminary Reference Trajectory [*NASA*] (KSC)	PRT
Preliminary Regional Experiment for STORM [*Stormscale Operational and Research Meteorology*] [*Marine science*] (OSRA)	PRE-STORM
Preliminary Regional Experiment for STORM [*Stormscale Operational and Research Meteorology*] (USDC)	PRE-STORM
Preliminary Repair Level Decision Analysis Model (PDAA)	PRAM
Preliminary Report	PR
Preliminary Required Operational Capability [*Military*]	PROC
Preliminary Requirements Model [*NASA*]	PRM
Preliminary Requirements Review [*NASA*] (KSC)	PRR
Preliminary Review [*Army*]	PR
Preliminary Rifle Instruction [*Military*]	PRI
Preliminary Safety Analysis [*NASA*] (SSD)	PSA
Preliminary Safety Analysis Report	PSAR
Preliminary Safety Information Document [*Nuclear energy*] (NRCH)	PSID
Preliminary Scholastic Aptitude/National Merit Scholarship Qualifying Test (PAZ)	PSAT/NMSQT
Preliminary Scholastic Aptitude Test	PSAT
Preliminary Science Meeting [*NASA*]	PSSM
Preliminary Specification Change Notice [*NASA*] (NASA)	PSCN
Preliminary Study	PS
Preliminary System Design Description [*Nuclear energy*] (NRCH)	PSDD
Preliminary System of Requirements	PSOR
Preliminary System Operational Concept (MCD)	PSOC
Preliminary System Package Plan	PSPP
Preliminary System Safety Engineering Plan	PSSEP
Preliminary Systems Engineering Design	PSED
Preliminary Task Plan (MCD)	PTP
Preliminary Technical Development Plan (AFM)	PTDP
Preliminary Technical Report (MCD)	PRETCHREP
Preliminary Technical Report [*Army*] (AABC)	PRETECHREP
Preliminary Technical Report	PTR
Preliminary Technical Survey Report [*Military*] (AFIT)	PTSR
Preliminary Test Information (KSC)	PTI
Preliminary Test Report [*NASA*] (KSC)	PTR
Preliminary Tool and Facility Analysis (MCD)	PTFA
Preliminary Training Effectiveness Analysis	PTEA
Preliminary Value Engineering Program Plan (MCD)	PVEPP
Preliminary Work Statement (MCD)	PWS
Preliminary Working Paper (AAGC)	PWP
Preliminary-Breath-Test [*Device used by police to determine whether or not a driver is legally intoxicated*]	PBT
Preload Indicating	PLI
Preload Indicating Washer	PLIW
Preload Washer	PLW
Prelude [*Music*] (ROG)	PREL
Premakeready [*Graphic arts*] (DGA)	P/M/R
Premanagement Orientation Program [*LIMRA*]	POP
Premanufacture Notification [*Environmental Protection Agency*]	PMN
Premanufacture Notification Form [*Environmental Protection Agency*] (GFGA)	PMNF
Pre-Manufacturing Notice [*Government regulations*]	PMN
Premarital Counseling Kit [*Psychology*]	PCK
Pre-Marital Inventory (AD)	PMI
Premarital Personal and Relationship Evaluation	PREPARE
Premark International, Inc. [*NYSE symbol*] (SPSG)	PMI
Premark International, Inc. [*Associated Press*] (SAG)	Premerk
Premark Intl [*NYSE symbol*] (TTSB)	PMI
Premarket Approval Application [*Food and Drug Administration*]	PMA
Premarket Notification [*Requirement for introducing new chemicals into the EEC*]	PMN
Pre-Mate Readiness Review [*NASA*] (KSC)	PMRR
Premate Verification/System Test [*NASA*] (KSC)	PV/ST
Prematriculation Immunization Requirement	PIR
Prematriculation Program in Medical Education (DMAA)	PRIME
Premature [*Medicine*]	PREM
Premature [*Infant*] (DAVI)	premie
Premature Anti-Fascist [*World War II designation used by Army Counterintelligence Department*]	PAF
Premature Atrial Beat [*Cardiology*] (AAMN)	PAB
Premature Atrial Contraction [*Medicine*]	PAC
Premature Atrial Stimulus [*Medicine*] (DMAA)	PAS
Premature Auricular Contraction [*Cardiology*] (AAMN)	PAC
Premature Baby [*Medical slang*] (WDAA)	PREEMIE
Premature Baby Unit [*National Health Service*] [*British*] (DI)	PBU
Premature Beat [*Medicine*] (CPH)	PB
Premature Birth, Live Infant [*neonatology*] (DAVI)	PBLI
Premature Chromosome Condensation [*Genetics*]	PCC
Premature Dead Female Child (DAVI)	PDFC
Premature Dead Male Child (DAVI)	PDMC
Premature Engine Removal Rate (AAG)	PERR
Premature Junctional Beat [*Cardiology*]	PJB
Premature Junctional Contractions [*Cardiology*] (DMAA)	PJC
Premature Living Female Child [*Neonatology*] (DAVI)	PLFC
Premature Living Male Child [*Neonatology*] (DAVI)	PLMC
Premature Nodal Beat [*Cardiology*] (DAVI)	PNB
Premature Nodal Contraction (AD)	pnc
Premature Nodal Contraction [*Cardiology*]	PNC
Premature Onset of Labor [*Obstetrics*] (DAVI)	POL
Premature Release [*Telecommunications*] (TEL)	PR
Premature Removal Rate	PRR
Premature [*or Prolonged*] Rupture of Fetal Membrane [*Gynecology*] (MAE)	PRFM
Premature [*or Prolonged*] Rupture of Membranes [*Gynecology*] (MAE)	PRM
Premature [*or Prolonged*] Rupture of Membranes [*Gynecology*]	PROM
Premature Separation Switch (SAA)	PSS
Premature Spontaneous Rupture of Bag of Waters [*Medicine*] (MEDA)	PSRBOW
Premature Spontaneous Rupture of Bag of Waters [*Obstetrics*] (DAVI)	PSRBOW
Premature Start [*Yacht racing*] (IYR)	PMS
Premature Tricuspid Closure [*Medicine*] (DMAA)	PTC
Premature Ventricular Beat [*Cardiology*]	PVB
Premature Ventricular Contraction [*Cardiology*]	PVC
Premature Ventricular Extrasystole [*Cardiology*] (AAMN)	PVE
Premature Ventricular Systole [*Cardiology*] (MAE)	PVS

Premature Voluntary Release [*British military*] (DMA) .... PVR
Premature Vulcanization Inhibitor (MCD) .... PVI
Premature-Removal Period (MCD) .... PRP
Premdor, Inc. [*Toronto Stock Exchange symbol*] .... PDI
Premdor, Inc. [*NYSE symbol*] (SPSG) .... PI
Premdor, Inc. [*Associated Press*] (SAG) .... Premdr
Premedical Student (WDAA) .... PREMED
Pre-Medical Student Assessment Test (EDAC) .... PMSAT
Premenos Technology [*NASDAQ symbol*] (TTSB) .... PRMO
Premenos Technology Corp. [*NASDAQ symbol*] (SAG) .... PRMO
Premenos Technology Corp. [*Associated Press*] (SAG) .... PrmosT
Premenstrual Asthma [*Medicine*] (DAVI) .... MPA
Premenstrual Dysphoric Disorder [*Proposed psychiatric diagnosis*] .... PDD
Premenstrual Dysphoric Disorder [*Medicine*] .... PMDD
Premenstrual Dysphoric Disorder [*Gynecology*] (DMAA) .... PMDD
Pre-Menstrual Syndrome [*Medicine*] (AD) .... pms
Premenstrual [*Stress*] **Syndrome** [*Medicine*] .... PMS
Premenstrual Tension [*Medicine*] .... PMT
Premenstrual Tension [*Medicine*] (AD) .... pmt
Pre-Menstrual Tension Advisory Service [*British*] .... PMTAS
Premenstrual Tension Syndrome [*Medicine*] .... PMTS
Premiair [*Norway*] [*FAA designator*] (FAAC) .... VKG
Pre-Midshipmen School .... PMS
Premier (ROG) .... PREM
Premier .... PREM
Premier Automobiles Ltd. [*India*] .... PAL
Premier Bancorp, Inc. [*NASDAQ symbol*] (NQ) .... PRBC
Premier Bancorp, Inc. [*Associated Press*] (SAG) .... PrmrBc
Premier Bankshares [*NASDAQ symbol*] (TTSB) .... PBKC
Premier Bankshares [*Associated Press*] (SAG) .... PremBksh
Premier Bankshares Corp. [*NASDAQ symbol*] (NQ) .... PBKC
Premier Bankshares Corp. [*Associated Press*] (SAG) .... PrmBn
Premier Commercial Bank Ltd. [*Nigeria*] .... PCB
Premier Cruise Lines .... PCL
Premier Farnell $1.35 Pref ADS [*NYSE symbol*] (TTSB) .... PFPPr
Premier Farnell PLC [*NYSE symbol*] (SAG) .... PFP
Premier Farnell PLC [*Associated Press*] (SAG) .... PrmFar
Premier Farnell PLC ADS [*NYSE symbol*] (TTSB) .... PFP
Premier Financial Bancorp, Inc. [*NASDAQ symbol*] (SAG) .... PFBI
Premier Financial Bancorp, Inc. [*Associated Press*] (SAG) .... PremFin
Premier Financial Services [*Associated Press*] (SAG) .... PremFn
Premier Financial Services, Inc. [*Freeport, IL*] [*NASDAQ symbol*] (NQ) .... PREM
Premier Financial Svcs [*NASDAQ symbol*] (TTSB) .... PREM
Premier Finl Bancorp [*NASDAQ symbol*] (TTSB) .... PFBI
Premier Industrial Corp. [*NYSE symbol*] (SPSG) .... PRE
Premier Industrial Corp. [*Associated Press*] (SAG) .... PremrIn
Premier Laser Systems, Inc. [*Associated Press*] (SAG) .... PLas
Premier Laser Systems, Inc. [*NASDAQ symbol*] (SAG) .... PLSI
Premier Laser Systems, Inc. [*Associated Press*] (SAG) .... PrLas
Premier Laser Systems, Inc. [*Associated Press*] (SAG) .... PrmLasr
Premier Laser Systems Wrrt'A' [*NASDAQ symbol*] (TTSB) .... PLSIW
Premier Laser Systems Wrrt'B' [*NASDAQ symbol*] (TTSB) .... PLSIZ
Premier Laser Systems'A' [*NASDAQ symbol*] (TTSB) .... PLSIA
Premier Parks [*NASDAQ symbol*] (TTSB) .... PARK
Premier Parks, Inc. [*NASDAQ symbol*] (SAG) .... PARK
Premier Parks, Inc. [*Associated Press*] (SAG) .... PrmPks
Premier Radio Network [*Associated Press*] (SAG) .... PrmRad
Premier Radio Network [*NASDAQ symbol*] (SAG) .... PRNI
Premiere (WDMC) .... prem
Premiere Radio Networks [*NASDAQ symbol*] (TTSB) .... PRNI
Premiere Radio Networks 'A' [*NASDAQ symbol*] (TTSB) .... PRNIA
Premiere Radio Networks, Inc. [*Associated Press*] (SAG) .... PrRadA
Premiere Technologies [*NASDAQ symbol*] (TTSB) .... PTEK
Premiere Technologies, Inc. [*Associated Press*] (SAG) .... PremT
Premiere Technologies, Inc. [*NASDAQ symbol*] (SAG) .... PTEK
Premier's Commission on Future Health Care for Albertans, Edmonton, Alberta [*Library symbol National Library of Canada*] (BIB) .... AEPCF
Premier's Office, Province of New Brunswick, Fredericton, New Brunswick [*Library symbol National Library of Canada*] (NLC) .... NBFPO
Premillennial Tension .... PMT
Premis Corp. [*NASDAQ symbol*] (SAG) .... PMIS
Premis Corp. [*Associated Press*] (SAG) .... Premis
Premises (ROG) .... PREMES
Premises (DSUE) .... PREMS
Premises (ROG) .... PRES
Premises Distribution System [*AT & T Corp.*] .... PDS
Pre-Mission Calibration (PDAA) .... PMC
Premission Documentation Change [*NASA*] (KSC) .... PDC
Premisys Communications [*Associated Press*] (SAG) .... Prmisy
Premisys Communications [*NASDAQ symbol*] (SAG) .... PRMS
Premium .... PM
Premium (ODBW) .... pm
Premium (AD) .... pm
Premium (WDMC) .... prem
Premium (AFM) .... PREM
Premium .... PRM
Premium Advertising Association of America [*Later, PMAA*] (EA) .... PAAA
Premium Air Shuttle, Ltd. [*Nigeria*] [*FAA designator*] (FAAC) .... EMI
Premium and Dispersion Credits [*Insurance*] .... PDC
Premium Audit .... PRA
Premium Bond (ODBW) .... PB
Premium Merchandising Club of New York (EA) .... PMC
Premium Notice Ordinary [*Insurance*] .... PNO
Premium Quality (MUGU) .... PQ
Premium Quality Zinc .... PQZ
Premium Savings Bond [*British*] (DCTA) .... PSB
Premium Transportation Authorization (AAG) .... PTA
Premium Unleaded Petrol .... PULP
Premodeling Data Output [*Environmental Protection Agency*] .... PREMOD
Premodulation (NASA) .... PREMOD
Premodulation Processing Equipment .... PPE
Premodulation Processor .... PMP
Premodulation Processor - Deep Space - Data .... PDD
Premodulation Processor - Deep Space - Voice .... PDV
Premodulation Processor - Near Earth Data (KSC) .... PND
Premolar [*Dentistry*] .... P
Premolar [*Dentistry*] .... PM
Premolar [*Dentistry*] (AD) .... pm
Premolar Hypodontia, Hyperhidrosis, Canities Prematura [*Syndrome*] [*Medicine*] (DMAA) .... PHC
Premolded [*Technical drawings*] (MSA) .... PRMLD
Premolded Expansion Joint [*Technical drawings*] .... PEJ
Premont, TX [*FM radio station call letters*] .... KMFM
Premote Hemodynamics and Metabolism in an Orbiting Satellite (KSC) .... PHAMOS
Premotor Cortex [*Neuroanatomy*] .... PMC
Prenatal .... prenat
Prenatal Care [*Medicine*] (DMAA) .... PC
Prenatal Care [*Obstetrics*] (DAVI) .... PNC
Prenatal Clinic [*Obstetrics*] (DAVI) .... PNC
Prenatal Diagnosis [*Medicine*] .... PND
Prenatal Vitamins (DAVI) .... PNV
Prenegotiation Memorandum (AAGC) .... PM
Prenegotiation Position (MCD) .... PNP
Prenegotiation Position Memorandum (AAGC) .... PPM
Prenex Normal Form [*Logic*] .... PNF
Prenodal Contraction [*Cardiology*] (DAVI) .... PNC
Pre-Normative Requirements for Intelligent Actuation & Measurements (ACII) .... PRIAM
Prensa Independiente Mexicana Sociedad Anonima [*Press agency*] [*Mexico*] .... PIMSA
Prensa Latina, Angencia Informativa Latinoamericana [*Press agency*] [*Cuba*] .... PRELA
Prensa Venezolana [*Press agency*] [*Venezuela*] .... PEVE
Prentice Hall Canada, Inc., Scarborough, Ontario [*Library symbol National Library of Canada*] (NLC) .... OTPHC
Prentice Hall Press [*Publisher*] .... PHP
Prentice-Hall Federal Taxes [*Database*] (IT) .... PHFTX
Prentice-Hall, Inc. [*Publishers*] .... P-H
Prentice-Hall Information Network [*Prentice-Hall Information Services*] [*Information service or system*] (IID) .... PHINet
Prentice-Hall International [*Publisher*] .... PHI
Prentice-Hall New York Estate Tax Reports [*A publication*] (DLA) .... P-H NYETR
Prentice-Hall Unreported Trust Cases [*A publication*] (DLA) .... P-H Unrep Tr Cas
Prentice's Proceedings in an Action [*2nd ed.*] [*1880*] [*A publication*] (DLA) .... Pren Act
Prentiss, MS [*Location identifier FAA*] (FAAL) .... PYT
Prentiss, MS [*FM radio station call letters*] .... WJDR
Prentiss Normal and Industrial Institute [*Mississippi*] .... PNII
Prentiss Properties Trust [*NYSE symbol*] (SAG) .... PP
Prentiss Properties Trust [*Associated Press*] (SAG) .... PrentPr
Preoccupied [*Biology, taxonomy*] .... preocc
Preoperational (MCD) .... PO
Pre-Operational Common Age List .... POCAL
Preoperational Inspection Services Engineering (IAA) .... POISE
Preoperational Maintenance Plan .... PMP
Preoperational Monitoring Program [*Nuclear energy*] (NRCH) .... PMP
Pre-Operational Peculiar Age List .... POPAL
Preoperational Readiness Inspection (MCD) .... PORI
Pre-Operational Support [*Military*] .... PRE-OPS
Preoperational Test [*Nuclear energy*] (NRCH) .... PT
Preoperative [*Surgery*] (DAVI) .... pre
Preoperative [*Medicine*] .... PREOP
Preoperative Diagnosis [*Medicine*] .... PODx
Preoperative Testing Center .... PTC
Preoptic [*Area of the brain*] .... PO
Preoptic Anterior Hypothalamic Area [*Medicine*] (DMAA) .... POA-HA
Preoptic Area [*of the brain*] .... POA
Pre-Optimization Linearization of Undulation and Detection of Errors (PDAA) .... PRELUDE
Preoral Ciliary [*Gland*] .... PRC
Pre-Oriented Yarn (AD) .... poy
Pre-Overhaul Inspection (MCD) .... POI
Preoverhaul Test Requirement Outline .... PTRO
Preoverhaul Tests [*Navy*] (NVT) .... POTS
Preoverhaul Tests and Inspections [*Navy*] (NVT) .... POT & I
Pre-Oxidation Gettering of the Other Side (PDAA) .... POGO
Prepaid .... PP
Prepaid .... PPD
Prepaid (WDMC) .... ppd
Prepaid Accountable Care Term [*Medicine*] (DMAA) .... PACT
Prepaid Dental Plan [*Insurance*] (MCD) .... PPD
Prepaid Expense [*Finance*] (MHDW) .... PE
Prepaid Group Practice [*Insurance*] .... PGP
Prepaid Group Practice [*Insurance*] (DHSM) .... PPGP
Prepaid Health Plan [*Insurance*] .... PHP
Pre-Paid Legal Services, Inc. [*AMEX symbol*] (SPSG) .... PPD
Pre-Paid Legal Services, Inc. [*Associated Press*] (SAG) .... PrpdLg
Pre-Paid Legal Svcs [*AMEX symbol*] (TTSB) .... PPD
Prepaid Ticket Advice [*Travel industry*] .... PTA

Preparation [*or Preparatory*] ... PREP
Preparation (WDMC) ... prep
Preparation ... PREP
Preparation ... PREPN
Preparation for Overseas Movement [*Military*] ... POM
Preparation for Overseas Movement (AD) ... pom
Preparation for Use ... PFU
Preparation Meetings [*Quakers*] ... PM
Preparation of Overseas Replacement [*Military*] (RDA) ... POR
Preparation of Replacements for Oversea Movement [*MTMC*] (TAG) ... POR
Preparation, Operation, Maintenance, Shipboard Electronics Equipment (AD) ... pomsee
Preparation through Acceptance ... PTA
Preparative Flag [*Navy British*] ... PP
Preparative Layer Chromatography ... PLC
Preparative Quencher [*Spectroscopy*] ... PQ
Preparative Quencher Stopped Flow [*Spectroscopy*] ... PQSF
Preparatory (ROG) ... PPATY
Preparatory (VRA) ... prep
Preparatory (WDMC) ... prep
Preparatory Academy for the Royal Academy of Dramatic Art [*British*] (BI) ... PARADA
Preparatory Commission ... PC
Preparatory Commission for International Refugee Organization ... PCIRO
Preparatory Commission of the United Nations Organization ... PRECO
Preparatory Committee ... PC
Preparatory Committee [*United Nations Committee on Environment and Development*] ... PrepCom
Preparatory Committee for the International Medical Commission for Health and Human Rights (EAIO) ... IMC
Preparatory Interval [*Psychometrics*] ... PI
Preparatory Investment Protection [*For the consortia which invested in deep sea mining*] ... PIP
Preparatory Marksmanship Training [*Military*] (INF) ... PMT
Preparatory School ... PREPSCOL
Preparatory School Alumnus [*Lifestyle classification*] ... Preppy
Prepare (AFM) ... PREP
Prepare (WDMC) ... prep
Prepare (ROG) ... PREPE
Prepare (FAAC) ... PRP
Prepare Chassis ... PCH
Prepare, Explain, Show, Observe, Supervise [*Formula*] [*LIMRA*] ... PESOS
Prepare Final Acceptance Trials [*Navy*] (NVT) ... PREFAT
Prepare Fleet Rehabilitation and Modernization Overhaul [*Navy*] (NVT) ... PREFRAM
Prepare for Board of Inspection and Survey [*Navy*] (NVT) ... PREINSURV
Prepare for Shipyard Overhaul [*Navy*] (NVT) ... PREOVHL
Prepare Inactivation [*Navy*] (NVT) ... PREINACT
Prepare Master Tape ... PMT
Prepare Postshakedown Availability [*Navy*] (NVT) ... PREPPSA
Prepare Reply ... PR
Prepared (MAE) ... ppd
Prepared ... PREPD
Prepared Hessian Surfacing [*Air Force*] ... PHS
Prepared Message ... PM
Preparedness and Industrial Planning ... PIP
Preparedness for Emergency Plant Pest Action [*In Animal and Plant Health Inspection Service publication PEPPA Pot*] ... PEPPA
Preparedness of Resources in Mission Evaluation (SAA) ... PRIME
Preparedness Staff [*Environmental Protection Agency*] (GFGA) ... PS
Prepared-on-Premises Flavor (AD) ... popf
Preparer ... PRPRR
Preparer Inventory File [*IRS*] ... PIF
Preparing ... PREPG
Preparing Activity [*Responsible for Federal document and study projects*] ... PA
Preparing for AIDS/HIV Vaccine Evaluation [*National Institutes of Health project*] ... PAVE
Preparing, Providing [*Pharmacy*] (ROG) ... PP
Prepayment Coin Telephone [*Telecommunications*] (TEL) ... PRE
Pre-Pearl Harbor Dad [*A humorous wartime degree*] ... PH D
Preplanned Product Improvement [*DoD*] ... P^3I
Pre-Planned Product Improvement (DOMA) ... P^3I
Preplanned Product Improvement [*DoD*] (MCD) ... PPPI
Preplanned Reconnaissance Pacific (CINC) ... PRERECPAC
Pre-Planned Training System (PDAA) ... PPTS
Preplant Inc. [*Herbicides*] [*Agriculture*] ... PPI
Prepleading Investigation [*Law*] ... PPI
Preposition [*Industrial engineering*] ... PP
Preposition ... PR
Preposition ... PREP
Preposition (WDMC) ... prep
Preposition (AABC) ... PREPOS
Prepositional Phrase (BYTE) ... PP
Prepositional Procurement Package (DOMA) ... PPP
Prepositioned Equipment Requirements List [*Navy*] (MCD) ... PERL
Prepositioned Instruction [*DoD*] ... PI
Prepositioned Material Configured in Unit Sets (AD) ... pomcus
Prepositioned Material Receipt Card [*DoD*] ... PMRC
Pre-Positioned Material Receipt Document ... PPMRD
Prepositioned Material Receipt Documents (MCD) ... PMRD
Pre-Positioned Materiel Receipt Card ... PPMRC
Prepositioned Receipt Card (AABC) ... PPRC
Prepositioned Stock (NG) ... PPS
Prepositioned Storage [*Army*] (AABC) ... PREPOSTOR
Prepositioned War Reserve Equipment [*Army*] ... PWRE
Prepositioned War Reserve Interrogation and Readiness Reporting (MCD) ... PIRR
Prepositioned War Reserve Material Requirements [*Navy*] (MCD) ... PWREMR
Prepositioned War Reserve Material Stocks [*Navy*] (MCD) ... PWREMS
Prepositioned War Reserve Materiel (MCD) ... PWRM
Prepositioned War Reserve Materiel Requirement (NVT) ... PWRMR
Prepositioned War Reserve Materiel Requirement Balance (AFIT) ... PWRMRB
Prepositioned War Reserve Materiel Stock (NVT) ... PWRMS
Prepositioned War Reserve Requirements [*Army*] (NG) ... PWRR
Prepositioned War Reserve Requirements for Medical Facilities [*Army*] (AABC) ... PWRR-MF
Prepositioned War Reserve Stocks [*Army*] ... PPWRS
Prepositioned War Reserve Stocks [*Army*] ... PWRS
Prepositioned War Reserve Stocks for Medical Facilities [*Army*] (AABC) ... PWRS-MF
Prepositioned War Reserves [*Army*] ... PPWR
Prepositioning [*Ship*] [*Navy*] (DOMA) ... PREPRO
Prepositioning of Materiel Configured to Unit Sets [*Army*] (AABC) ... POMCUS
Prepositus Hypoglossi [*Neuroanatomy*] ... PrH
Pre-Pottery Neolithic B Period [*Paleontology*] ... PPNB
Pre-Pottery Neolithic C Phase [*Paleontology*] ... PPNC
Pre-Power-Dependent Insertion Limit [*Nuclear energy*] (NRCH) ... PPDIL
Prepped Out Beyond Belief [*Book title*] ... POB^2
Pre-Pre-Delivery Inspection [*Automotive project management*] ... PPDI
Prepregnancy [*Medicine*] ... PP
Preprimary Evaluation and Training ... PET
Preprinted ... PP
Preprints on Precision Measurement and Fundamental Constants [*National Institute of Standards and Technology*] ... PPMFC
Pre-Problem Training Situation (SAA) ... PPTS
Preprocessing Center [*NASA*] (NASA) ... PPC
Preprocessor ... PP
Preprocessor [*Computer*] [*Coast Guard*] ... PREPRO
Pre-Processor Utility (NITA) ... PPU
Preproduction (KSC) ... PP
Preproduction Engineering ... PPE
Preproduction Evaluation (NG) ... PPE
Preproduction Model [*Military*] (AFIT) ... PREPROD
Pre-production Part Index ... PPI
Preproduction Proposal Evaluation ... PPE
Preproduction Qualification Test [*Army*] ... PPQT
Pre-Production Qualification Test and Evaluation [*Army*] ... PPQT & E
Preproduction Reliability Design Review [*Navy*] (CAAL) ... PRDR
Preproduction Test [*Army*] ... PPT
Preproduction Unit (MCD) ... PPU
Preproenkephalin [*Biochemistry*] ... PPE
Pre-Professional Skill Test (EDAC) ... P-PST
Preprogram Definition Phase ... PPDP
Preprogrammed Self-Instruction [*Computer science*] (IEEE) ... PSI
Preprogrammed Vehicles (MCD) ... PPV
Preprophase Band [*Cytology*] ... PPB
Pre-Proposal Conference (MCD) ... PPC
Preprotachykinin [*Biochemistry*] ... PPT
Preprototype (SAA) ... PPT
Preprototype Demonstration ... PDP
Preprototype Demonstration ... PPD
Prepublication ... prepub
Prequalification Prototype (KSC) ... PQP
Prequalified [*NASA*] (KSC) ... PREQUAL
Pre-Qualified Offsets Supplier ... PQOS
Pre-Qualified Offsets Supplier Status ... PQOSS
Pre-Ranger Course [*Army*] (INF) ... PRC
Pre-Raphaelite ... PR
Pre-Reading Assessment Inventory [*Education*] (EDAC) ... PRAI
Prereading Expectancy Screening Scale [*Educational test*] ... PRESS
Pre-Recorded Announcement and Boarding Music Reproducer ... PRAM
Prereduced, Anaerobically Sterilized [*Microbiology*] ... PRAS
Prerefund Audit [*IRS*] ... PRA
Prerefunded Municipal Note [*Investment term*] (DFIT) ... PRE-RE
Prerelease Orientation Program [*Reformatory program*] ... PROP
Prerequisite (WGA) ... PREREQ
Pre-Retirement Association [*British*] (DI) ... PRA
Pre-Retirement Education (AIE) ... PRE
Preretro Update Display ... PRD
Preretro Update Display ... PUD
Prerigor Pressurization [*Meat processing*] ... PRP
Prerogative Court (DLA) ... Pr Co
Prerogative Court (DLA) ... Prer
Prerogative Court, New Jersey (DLA) ... Prerog Ct
Prerogative Court of Canterbury [*English court previously having jurisdiction over wills*] ... PCC
Prerogative Court of York [*English court previously having jurisdiction over wills*] ... PCY
Pres Prudente [*Brazil*] [*Airport symbol*] (OAG) ... PPB
Presa Benito Juarez [*Mexico*] [*Seismograph station code, US Geological Survey*] (SEIS) ... PBJ
Presa Del Infiernillo [*Mexico*] [*Seismograph station code, US Geological Survey Closed*] (SEIS) ... PIM
Presa Malpaso [*Mexico*] [*Seismograph station code, US Geological Survey*] (SEIS) ... PMM
Pre-Sargonic (BJA) ... PSarg
Presbyopia [*Ophthalmology*] ... P
Presbyopia [*Ophthalmology*] ... Pb
Presbyopia [*Ophthalmology*] ... PR
Presbyopia (AD) ... Pr

Presbyter [*Elder*] [*Latin*] (AD) ... Pr
Presbyteri Oratorii [*Oratorians*] [*Roman Catholic religious order*] ... PO
Presbyteri Sancti Sulpicii [*Sulpicians*] [*Roman Catholic men's religious order*] ... PSS
Presbyterian ... P
Presbyterian (ROG) ... PR
Presbyterian ... PRES
Presbyterian ... PRESB
Presbyterian ... PRESBY
Presbyterian and Reformed Renewal Ministries International [*Formerly, PCC*] (EA) ... PRR
Presbyterian and Reformed Renewal Ministries International (EA) ... PRRM
Presbyterian Association of Musicians (EA) ... PAM
Presbyterian Charismatic Communion [*Later, PRR*] [*An association*] (EA) ... PCC
Presbyterian Church House [*British*] (BI) ... PCH
Presbyterian Church Library, Cleveland, MS [*Library symbol Library of Congress*] (LCLS) ... MsCleP
Presbyterian Church of Eastern Australia ... PCEA
Presbyterian, Church of England [*Military*] (ROG) ... EP
Presbyterian Church of England ... PC of E
Presbyterian Church of England Chaplain [*Navy British*] ... Pres C of E Ch
Presbyterian College, Clinton, SC [*Library symbol Library of Congress*] (LCLS) ... ScClP
Presbyterian College, Montreal, PQ, Canada [*Library symbol Library of Congress*] (LCLS) ... CaQMPC
Presbyterian College, Montreal, Quebec [*Library symbol National Library of Canada*] (NLC) ... QMPC
Presbyterian Educational Association of the South [*Defunct*] (EA) ... PEAS
Presbyterian Evangelical Coalition (EA) ... PEC
Presbyterian Evangelistic Fellowship [*Defunct*] (EA) ... PEF
Presbyterian Foundation [*Australia*] ... PF
Presbyterian Health, Education, and Welfare Association (EA) ... PHEWA
Presbyterian Historical Society (EA) ... PHS
Presbyterian Historical Society, Philadelphia, PA [*Library symbol Library of Congress*] (LCLS) ... PPPrHi
Presbyterian Historical Society, Philadelphia, PA [*OCLC symbol*] (OCLC) ... PRE
Presbyterian Hunger Program (EA) ... PHP
Presbyterian Inland Mission ... PIM
Presbyterian Interracial Council (EA) ... PIC
Presbyterian Lay Committee (EA) ... PLC
Presbyterian Medical Center, Doctors' Library, Denver, CO [*Library symbol Library of Congress*] (LCLS) ... CoDPM-M
Presbyterian Men (EA) ... PM
Presbyterian, Methodist, and United Board [*British military*] (DMA) ... PMUB
Presbyterian Peace Fellowship (EA) ... PPF
Presbyterian Reformed Church of Australia ... PRCA
Presbyterian Renewal Ministries (EA) ... PRM
Presbyterian Saint Luke's Hospital, Chicago, IL [*Library symbol Library of Congress*] (LCLS) ... ICSL
Presbyterian Theological Seminary, Omaha, NE [*Library symbol Library of Congress*] (LCLS) ... NbOP
Presbyterian University of Pennsylvania, Scheie Eye Institute Library, Philadelphia, PA [*Library symbol Library of Congress*] (LCLS) ... PPPres
Presbyterians for Biblical Concerns (EA) ... PBC
Presbyterians for Democracy and Religious Freedom (EA) ... PDRF
Presbyterians for Lesbian/Gay Concerns (EA) ... PLGC
Presbyterians Pro-Life [*An association*] (EA) ... PPL
Presbyterians United for Biblical Concerns [*Later, PBC*] (EA) ... PUBC
Presbyterorum Ordinis [*Decree on the Ministry and Life of Priests*] [*Vatican II document*] ... PO
Presbytery ... PRESBY
Presbytery (VRA) ... presby
Preschool ... PRSCHL
Preschool and Early Primary Skills Survey [*Child development test*] ... PEPSS
Preschool and Kindergarten Interest Descriptor [*Educational test*] ... PRIDE
Preschool and Primary Nowicki-Strickland Internal-External Control Scale (EDAC) ... PPNS-IE
Preschool Behavior Questionnaire ... PBQ
Preschool Education Program [*Sesame Street TV program*] ... PEP
Preschool Embedded Figures Test [*Child development test*] ... PEFT
Preschool Interpersonal Problem Solving Test ... PIPS
Preschool Inventory (EDAC) ... PSI
Preschool Language Assessment Instrument [*Child development test*] ... PLAI
Preschool Language Scale [*Child development test*] ... PLS
Preschool Playgrounds Association [*British*] ... PPA
Preschool Play-Group Association [*British*] (DI) ... PPGA
Preschool Self-Concept Picture Test [*Psychology*] ... PSCPT
Prescott [*Arizona*] [*Airport symbol*] (OAG) ... PRC
[*The*] **Prescott & Northwestern Railroad Co.** [*AAR code*] ... PNW
Prescott, AR [*AM radio station call letters*] ... KTPA
Prescott, AZ [*FM radio station call letters*] ... KAHM
Prescott, AZ [*FM radio station call letters*] ... KGCB
Prescott, AZ [*AM radio station call letters*] ... KNOT
Prescott, AZ [*FM radio station call letters*] ... KNOT-FM
Prescott, AZ [*Television station call letters*] ... KUSK
Prescott, AZ [*AM radio station call letters*] ... KYCA
Prescott, AZ [*Location identifier FAA*] (FAAL) ... PRC
Prescott Builders Association (EA) ... PBA
Prescott City-Yavapai County Library, Prescott, AZ [*Library symbol Library of Congress*] (LCLS) ... AzPr
Prescott College, Prescott, AZ [*Library symbol Library of Congress*] (LCLS) ... AzPrP
Prescott Development Corp. [*Vancouver Stock Exchange symbol*] ... PDC
Prescott Public Library, Ontario [*Library symbol National Library of Canada*] (NLC) ... OPRE
Prescott Valley, AZ [*FM radio station call letters*] ... KDTK
Prescott Valley, az [*FM radio station call letters*] (RBYB) ... KKLD-FM
Prescott Valley, AZ [*FM radio station call letters*] ... KPPV
Prescott Valley, AZ [*AM radio station call letters*] ... KQNA
Prescreening Developmental Questionnaire [*Child development test*] ... PDQ
Prescribe (AABC) ... PRESB
Prescribed Action Link [*DoD*] ... PAL
Prescribed Concentration of Alcohol (ADA) ... PCA
Prescribed Goods (General) Order ... PGGO
Prescribed Load List [*Vehicle maintenance operation*] [*Army*] ... PLL
Prescribed Loan Optimization Model [*Army*] (AABC) ... PLOM
Prescribed Nuclear Load [*Military*] (AABC) ... PNL
Prescribed Nuclear Stockage [*Military*] (AABC) ... PNS
Prescribed Payments System (ADA) ... PPS
Prescribed Period [*Social Security Administration*] (OICC) ... PP
Prescribed Right to Income and Maximum Equity ... PRIME
Prescribed Tumor Lethal Dose [*Oncology*] ... PTLD
Prescribing ... P
Prescription (MSA) ... PRESCR
Prescription ... PRESCR
Prescription (AAMN) ... Ps
Prescription Athletic Turf [*Trademark for an artificial turf*] ... PAT
Prescription Drug ... PD
Prescription Drug Marketing Act [*1987*] ... PDMA
Prescription Drug Maximum Allowable Cost ... PDMAC
Prescription Drug Plan [*Insurance*] (WYGK) ... PDP
Prescription Drug Program [*Health insurance*] (GHCT) ... PDP
Prescription Drug User Fee Act ... PDUFA
Prescription Footwear Association (EA) ... PFA
Prescription Only Medicine [*British*] ... POM
Prescription Pricing Authority (PDAA) ... PPA
Prescription Rate Carryover [*Health insurance*] (GHCT) ... PRC
Prescription Television ... RxTV
Prescription-Event Monitoring ... PEM
Prescriptive Analysis for Curriculum Evaluation [*Vocational guidance*] ... PACER
Prescriptive Math Inventory ... PMI
Prescriptive Objective Reference Testing [*Vocational guidance*] ... PORT
Prescriptive Parent Programming [*Education*] ... PPP
Prescriptive Program Plan [*Education*] ... PPP
Prescriptive Reading Inventory ... PRI
Prescriptive Reading Performance Test [*Educational test*] ... PRPT
Pre-Sea Trial Audit (MCD) ... PSTA
Pre-Season Predictor Model [*Television ratings*] (NTCM) ... PSP
Preselect Heading (NG) ... PSH
Preselected Alternate Master-Slave [*Telecommunications*] (TEL) ... PAMS
Pre-Selection English Test [*Australia*] ... PSET
Presely Cos. 'A' [*NYSE symbol*] (TTSB) ... PDC
Presence ... PRES
Presence and Amplitude Detector ... PAD
Presence or Absence ... P/A
Presending Pause (NITA) ... PSP
Presensitized Photoplate ... PSP
Present ... P
Present ... PR
Present (AAG) ... PRES
Present (ROG) ... PREST
Present (WGA) ... PRS
Present [*NWS*] (FAAC) ... PRSNT
Present [*Legal term*] (ROG) ... PSNT
Present Address Unknown ... PAU
Present Again (ADA) ... PA
Present Atmospheric Level ... PAL
Present BIT [*Binary Digit*] [*Computer science*] ... P
Present Complaint [*Medicine*] ... PC
Present Duty Assignment Option [*Military*] ... PDA
Present for Duty ... PFD
Present Illness [*Medicine*] ... PI
Present Indication [*Aviation*] (IAA) ... PRIND
Present Level [*Aviation*] (FAAC) ... PLVL
Present Longititude [*Aviation*] (FAAC) ... PLONG
Present Medical Illness ... PMI
Present Next Digit ... PND
Present Not for Duty [*Military*] ... PNFD
Present Not for Duty (AD) ... pnfd
Present Pain Intensity ... PPI
Present Participle [*Grammar*] ... PP
Present Participle [*Grammar*] ... PPR
Present Participle (AD) ... ppr
Present Participle (WGA) ... PR P
Present Participle [*Grammar*] (WDAA) ... PRES PART
Present Position [*Military*] ... PP
Present Position (AD) ... pp
Present Position (GAVI) ... PPOS
Present Position (AD) ... ppsn
Present Position [*Aviation*] (FAAC) ... PPSN
Present Position Indicator [*Aviation*] ... PPI
Present Practice Waste Load (DICI) ... PPWL
Present Pupil (AIE) ... PP
Present Serviceability Index (IEEE) ... PSI
Present Serviceability Rating [*FHWA*] (TAG) ... PSR
Present State Examination [*Medicine*] (DMAA) ... PSE
Present University Research Efforts [*Database*] [*Harperson Data Services*] ... PURE
Present Value [*Finance*] ... PV
Present Value Analysis (MCD) ... PVA

Present Value Cash Flow [*Finance*] .... PVCF
Present Value Index (TDOB) .... PVI
Present Value Interest Factor [*Finance*] .... PVIF
Present Value Interest Factor of an Annuity [*Real estate*] .... PVIFA
Present Value of Annual Charges .... PVAC
Present Value Service [*LIMRA*] .... PVS
Present Worth [*Economics*] .... PW
Present Worth Expenditures [*Telecommunications*] (TEL) .... PWE
Present Worth Factor [*Real estate*] .... PWF
Present Worth of All Future Revenue Requirements [*Finance*] .... PWAFRR
Present Worth of Annual Charges [*Pronounced "p-wack"*] [*Bell System*] .... PWAC
Presentation [*Gynecology*] .... Pr
Presentation (VRA) .... presen
Presentation Brothers (TOCD) .... FPM
Presentation Brothers [*See also FPM*] (EAIO) .... PB
Presentation College, Aberdeen, SD [*Library symbol Library of Congress*] (LCLS) .... SdAbP
Presentation Context Identifier [*Computer science*] (TNIG) .... PCI
Presentation Equipment for Slow Scan RADAR .... PRESSAR
Presentation Graphic Feature [*Computer science*] .... PGF
Presentation Label [*Publishing*] .... P/L
Presentation Level Protocol [*AT & T Videotex System*] .... PLP
Presentation Level Video (PCM) .... PLV
Presentation Loss Rate (MCD) .... PLR
Presentation Manager [*Computer science*] .... PM
Presentation of Information for Maintenance and Operation [*DoD*] .... PIMO
Presentation of Technical Information Group (SAA) .... PTIG
Presentation of the Blessed Virgin Mary [*Roman Catholic women's religious order*] .... PBVM
Presentation of the Blessed Virgin Mary Sisters (TOCD) .... PBVM
Presentation Portfolio (VRA) .... PORT
Presentation Protocol Control Information [*Telecommunications*] .... PPCI
Presentation Protocol Data Unit [*Computer science*] (TNIG) .... PPDU
Presentation Protocol Machine [*Telecommunications*] (OSI) .... PPM
Presentation Quotient [*Business Term*] .... PQ
Presentation Service Access Point [*Telecommunications*] (OSI) .... PSAP
Presentation Service Data Unit [*Telecommunications*] (OSI) .... PSDU
Presentation Services [*Computer science*] (IBMDP) .... PS
Presentation Services for Data Management (MHDB) .... PSDM
Present-Barrel-Equivalent .... PBE
Present-Day Preachers [*A publication*] .... PDPR
Present-Day Primers [*A publication*] .... PDP
Pre-Sentence Investigation (OICC) .... PSI
Preservation .... PRESERV
Preservation (BARN) .... presv
Preservation (AABC) .... PRSVN
Preservation (MSA) .... PSVTN
Preservation Action (EA) .... PA
Preservation and Conservation [*IFLA Core Program*] .... PAC
Preservation and Packaging Data Sheet [*DoD*] .... PPDS
Preservation and Reformatting Section [*Committee of Association for Library Collections and Technical Services*] .... PARS
Preservation & Reformatting Section [*Association for Library Collections and Technical Services*] [*American Library Association*] .... PARS
Preservation, Handling, Storage, Packaging, and Shipping (NRCH) .... PHSPS
Preservation Method .... PVMTD
Preservation of Capital [*Investment term*] .... POC
Preservation of Library Materials Section [*Resources and Technical Services Division*] [*American Library Association*] .... PLMS
Preservation of Location Uncertainty [*Strategy for protecting missiles*] [*Military*] .... PLU
Preservation of Our Femininity and Finances [*Women's group opposing below-the-knee fashions introduced in 1970*] .... POOFF
Preservation of the Rights of Prisoners [*An association British*] .... PROP
Preservation, Packaging, Packing, and Marking .... PPP & M
Preservation Research and Testing Office [*Library of Congress*] (EA) .... PRTO
Preservation Security Manager .... PSM
Preservation Services Fund .... PSF
Preservative (AAG) .... PRSRV
Preservative (MSA) .... PSVTV
Preserve (MSA) .... PSV
Preserve American Patriotic Holidays Committee (EA) .... PATH
Preserve Our Presidential Sites (EA) .... POPS
Preserved .... PRES
Preserved Context Index System [*British Library*] [*London, England*] [*Information service or system*] .... PRECIS
Preservice Inspection [*Nuclear energy*] (NRCH) .... PSI
Pre-Service Teacher Education Program [*National Science Foundation*] .... PSTEP
Preserving .... PRSV
Preserving Individual Cultures and Knowledge in Lands Everywhere [*An association*] .... PICKLE
Preset .... P
Preset Spin Echo Technique .... PRESET
Preshaving (MSA) .... PRE-S
Preshipment Inspection [*International trade*] .... PSI
Presho Public Library, Presho, SD [*Library symbol Library of Congress*] (LCLS) .... SdPr
Presidencia R. Saenz Pena [*Argentina ICAO location identifier*] (ICLI) .... SARS
Presidency (ROG) .... PR
President .... P
President (EY) .... PRES
President .... PRES
President (ODBW) .... Pres
President (DD) .... pres
President .... PRES'T
President (ROG) .... PSDT
President Benjamin Harrison Foundation (EA) .... PBHF
President Benjamin Harrison Memorial Home, Indianapolis, IN [*Library symbol Library of Congress*] (LCLS) .... InIBHM
President Casinos [*NASDAQ symbol*] (TTSB) .... PREZ
President Casinos, Inc. [*Associated Press*] (SAG) .... PresCasn
President Directeur General [*President Director General*] [*French*] .... PDG
President Falconer's Scotch Session Cases [*1744-51*] [*A publication*] (DLA) .... Pr Falc
President Falconer's Scotch Session Cases (Gilmour and Falconer) [*1681-86*] [*A publication*] (DLA) .... Pres Falc
President Mines [*Vancouver Stock Exchange symbol*] .... PDT
President of the British Academy .... PBA
President of the Canteen Committee [*Military British*] .... PCC
President of the Faculty of Architects and Surveyors [*British*] (DBQ) .... PFAS
President of the Geographical Society [*British*] (ROG) .... PGS
President of the Geological Society [*British*] .... PGS
President of the Linnaean Society [*British*] .... PLS
President of the Mess Committee [*Military British*] .... PMC
President of the Meteorological Society [*British*] .... PMS
President of the Miniature Society [*British*] (DI) .... PMS
President of the Privy Council [*Canada*] .... PPC
President of the Royal Academy [*British*] .... PRA
President of the Royal Architectural Institute of Canada (NGC) .... PRAIC
President of the Royal Canadian Academy .... PRCA
President of the Royal Canadian Academy of Arts (NGC) .... PRCA
President of the Royal College of Physicians [*British*] .... PRCP
President of the Royal College of Preceptors [*British*] (ROG) .... PRCP
President of the Royal College of Surgeons [*British*] .... PRCS
President of the Royal Entomological Society [*British*] .... PRES
President of the Royal Geographical Society [*British*] .... PRGS
President of the Royal Hibernian Academy [*British*] .... PRHA
President of the Royal Institute of British Architects .... PRIBA
President of the Royal Institute of Oil Painters [*British*] .... PROI
President of the Royal Institute (of Painters in Water Colours) [*British*] (ROG) .... PRI
President of the Royal Institution (London) (ROG) .... PRI
President of the Royal Irish Academy .... PRIA
President of the Royal Scottish Academy .... PRSA
President of the Royal Scottish Water Colour Society .... PRSW
President of the Royal Society [*British*] .... PRS
President of the Royal Society for the Promotion of Health [*British*] .... PRSH
President of the Royal Society of Edinburgh .... PRSE
President of the Royal Society of Painter-Etchers and Engravers [*British*] .... PRE
President of the Royal Society of Painters in Water Colours [*British*] .... PRWS
President of the Royal Ulster Academy of Arts .... PRUAA
President of the Society of Antiquaries [*British*] .... PSA
President of the Society of Industrial Artists [*British*] .... PSIA
President of the Society of Marine Artists [*British*] .... PSMA
President of the United Mineworkers .... PUM
President of the United States .... POTUS
President of the United States .... PUS
President of the Zoological Society [*British*] .... PZS
President on Board Civil Aircraft (FAAC) EXEC-1
President Regimental Institutes [*British*] .... PRI
President Riverboat Casinos [*NASDAQ symbol*] (SAG) .... PREZ
Presidente Prudente [*Brazil*] [*Airport symbol*] (AD) .... PPB
Presidente Prudente [*Brazil ICAO location identifier*] (ICLI) .... SBDN
Presidente Roque Saenz Pena [*Argentina*] [*Airport symbol*] (AD) .... PRQ
Presidential (WGA) .... PRESDL
Presidential Academic Fitness Award [*Department of Education*] (GFGA) .... PAFA
Presidential and Democratic Party Victory Fund (EA) .... PDPVF
Presidential Appointee Subject .... PAS
[*A*] **Presidential Classroom for Young Americans** (EA) .... APCYA
Presidential Decision Directive .... PDD
Presidential Decision Memorandum [*Jimmy Carter Administration*] .... PDM
Presidential Determination .... PD
Presidential Directive .... PD
Presidential Directives/National Security Council .... PD/NSC
Presidential Election Campaign Fund Act of 1966 .... PECFA
Presidential Emergency Action Direction System (MCD) .... PEADS
Presidential Emergency Action Document .... PEAD
Presidential Emergency Board .... PEB
Presidential Ethics Commission (NADA) .... PECUSA
Presidential Executive Interchange Program [*Federal government*] .... PEIP
Presidential Exemption [*Environmental Protection Agency*] .... PE
Presidential Libraries Office (NADA) .... PLO
Presidential Life [*NASDAQ symbol*] (TTSB) .... PLFE
Presidential Life Corp. [*NASDAQ symbol*] (NQ) .... PLFE
Presidential Life Corp. [*Associated Press*] (SAG) .... PresLf
Presidential Management Improvement Award .... PMIA
Presidential Management Incentives [*Office of Management and Budget*] .... PMI
Presidential Management Intern Program [*Executive Office of the President*] (GFGA) .... PMIP
Presidential Medal of Freedom [*Military decoration*] (AABC) .... PM of F
Presidential Medal of Freedom (AD) .... PMF
Presidential Medal of Freedom [*Military decoration*] (GFGA) .... PMOF
Presidential Medal of Honour [*Botswana*] .... PH
Presidential Memo .... PM
Presidential Proclamation (AAGC) .... Pres Proc
Presidential Proclamation .... PRESPROC
Presidential Protective Division [*US Secret Service*] .... PPD
Presidential Realty Corp. [*AMEX symbol*] (SPSG) .... PDL
Presidential Realty Corp. [*Associated Press*] (SAG) .... PresR
Presidential Review Directive (USDC) .... PRD

Presidential Review Memorandum [*Jimmy Carter Administration*] .... PRM
Presidential Rlty Cl'A' [*AMEX symbol*] (TTSB) .... PDL A
Presidential Rlty Cl'B' [*AMEX symbol*] (TTSB) .... PDL B
Presidential Service Badge [*Military decoration*] (AABC) .... PSvcBad
Presidential Special Representative (BARN) .... PSR
Presidential Studies Quarterly [*A publication*] (BRI) .... Pres SQ
Presidential Survivability Support System .... PSSS
Presidential Unit Citation [*Military decoration*] .... PUC
Presidential Unit Emblem [*Military decoration*] (AABC) .... PUE
Presidential Young Investigator Program [*National Science Foundation*] .... PYI
Presidential's Hundred Tab [*Military*] PRES100
President's Advisor for Science .... PAS
President's Advisory Committee for Women [*Terminated, 1980*] (EGAO) .... PACFW
President's Advisory Committee on Government Organization [*Abolished, 1961*] .... PACGO
President's Advisory Committee on Labor-Management Policy [*Abolished, 1973*] .... PCLMP
President's Advisory Committee on Management Improvement [*Terminated, 1973*] .... PACMI
President's Advisory Panel on Timber and the Environment .... PAPTE
President's Advisory Staff on Scientific Information Management .... PASSIM
President's Air Quality Advisory Board [*Environmental Protection Agency*] .... PAQAB
President's Appalachian Regional Commission .... PARC
Presidents Association [*New York, NY*] (EA) .... PA
President's Budget (DOMA) .... PB
President's Certificate of Merit [*Military decoration*] (AFM) .... PCM
Presidents Club [*Commercial firm*] (EA) .... PC
President's Commission on Americans Outdoors .... PCAO
President's Commission on Campus Unrest (EA) .... PCCU
President's Commission on Income Maintenance Programs (EA) .... PCIMP
President's Commission on Obscenity and Pornography (DGA) .... PCOP
President's Commission on Personnel Interchange [*Later, President's Commission on Executive Exchange*] .... PCPI
President's Commission on the Status of Women .... PCSW
President's Commisssion on Environmental Quality (GNE) .... PCEQ
President's Committee for Traffic Safety (EA) .... PCTS
President's Committee on Consumer Interests [*Terminated, 1971*] .... PCCI
President's Committee on Economic Security [*New Deal*] .... PCES
President's Committee on Employment of the Handicapped [*Washington, DC*] .... PCEH
President's Committee on Equal Employment Opportunity [*Later, OFCCP*] [*Department of Labor*] .... PCEEO
President's Committee on Mental Retardation [*Washington, DC*] .... PCMR
President's Committee on Migratory Labor [*Terminated, 1964*] .... PCML
President's Committee on Science and Technology .... PCST
President's Committee on Scientists and Engineers [*Expired, 1958*] .... PCSE
President's Conference Committee .... PCC
President's Council of Advisers on Science and Technology [*1989*] .... PCAST
President's Council on Aging [*Inactive*] .... PCA
President's Council on Integrity and Efficiency (AAGC) .... PCIE
President's Council on Integrity and Efficiency in Government (EPA) .... PCIE
President's Council on Management Improvement [*Executive Office of the President*] (GFGA) .... PCMI
President's Council on Physical Fitness [*Later, PCPFS*] (KSC) .... PCOPF
President's Council on Physical Fitness [*Later, PCPFS*] .... PCPF
President's Council on Physical Fitness and Sports (EGAO) .... PCPFS
President's Council on Sustainable Development [*1993*] .... PCSD
President's Council on Youth Fitness (EA) .... PCYF
President's Council on Youth Opportunity [*Defunct*] (EA) .... PCOYO
President's Daily Brief .... PDB
Presidents' Day National Committee (EA) .... PDNC
President's Economy Program .... PEP
President's Emergency Relief Organization (NADA) .... PERO
President's Environmental Merit Award Program [*Environmental Protection Agency*] .... PEMAP
President's Export Council (AAGC) .... PEO
President's Family is Aboard Aircraft (FAAC) EXEC-1F
President's Foreign Intelligence Advisory Board (AFM) .... PFIAB
President's Hundred Tab [*Military decoration*] (AABC) .... PHTab
President's Intelligence Checklist [*Daily report prepared by CIA*] .... PICKLE
President's Intelligence Oversight Board (DOMA) .... PIOB
President's Interagency Committee on Export Expansion [*Absorbed by President's Export Council in 1979*] (EGAO) .... PICEE
President's Management Council (AAGC) .... PMC
President's Management Improvement Council (AD) .... PMIC
President's National Advisory Committee (AD) .... PNAC
President's National Advisory Committee (NADA) .... PNAC
President's National Crime Commission (NADA) .... PNCC
President's National Crime Commission (AD) .... PNCC
President's Organization for Unemployment Relief (AD) .... POUR
Presidents' Professional Association [*Later, Presidents Association*] (EA) .... PPA
President's Re-Employment Agreement [*New Deal*] .... PRA
President's Reorganization Project [*Carter Administration*] [*Executive Office of the President*] (GFGA) .... PRP
President's Science Advisory Committee [*Terminated, 1973*] [*Executive Office of the President*] .... PSAC
President's Scientific Advisory Committee Panel on Oceanography [*Marine science*] (MSC) .... PSACPOO
President's Soviet Protocol Committee [*World War II*] .... PSPC
President's Special Representative and Adviser on African, Asian, and Latin American Affairs [*Department of State*] .... PSRAAALAA
President's Task Force on Urban Renewal (EA) .... PTFUR
President's Urban and Regional Policy Group [*Terminated, 1978*] (EGAO) .... URPG
President's Veterans Program [*Employment*] .... PVP
President's War Relief Control Board [*World War II*] .... PWRCB
Presidents-Directeurs Generaux .... P-DGs
Presiding Bishop [*Episcopal Church*] .... PB
Presiding Bishop's Fund for World Relief (EA) .... PBF/WR
Presiding Elder .... PE
Presiding Judge .... PJ
Presiding Officers' Review and Advisory Group [*Commonwealth Parliament*] [*Australia*] .... PORAG
Presiding Probate Judge [*British*] (ROG) .... PJ
Presidio of Monterey [*Military*] (AABC) .... PMRY
Presidio of San Francisco [*Military*] (AABC) .... PSF
Presidio Oil Co. [*Associated Press*] (SAG) .... Presd
Presidio Oil Co. [*AMEX symbol*] (SPSG) .... PRS
Presidio, TX [*Location identifier FAA*] (FAAL) .... PRS
Presley Companies [*Associated Press*] (SAG) .... Presly
Presley Co. [*NYSE symbol*] (SPSG) .... PDC
Presley Labs [*Vancouver Stock Exchange symbol*] .... PL
Presley-ites Fan Club (EA) .... PFC
Presov [*Czechoslovakia*] [*Airport symbol*] (AD) .... POV
Prespeech Assessment Scale [*Occupational therapy*] .... PSAS
Prespin Automatic Dynamic Alignment .... PADA
Presque Isle [*Maine*] [*Airport symbol*] (OAG) .... PQI
Presque Isle County Library, Rogers City, MI [*Library symbol Library of Congress*] (LCLS) .... MiRog
Presque Isle, ME [*Location identifier FAA*] (FAAL) .... PQI
Presque Isle, ME [*Television station call letters*] .... WAGM
Presque Isle, ME [*FM radio station call letters*] .... WBPW
Presque Isle, ME [*AM radio station call letters*] .... WEGP
Presque Isle, ME [*FM radio station call letters*] .... WMEM
Presque Isle, ME [*Television station call letters*] .... WMEM-TV
Presque Isle, ME [*FM radio station call letters*] .... WOZI
Presque Isle, ME [*FM radio station call letters*] (RBYB) .... WQHR-FM
Presque Isle, ME [*FM radio station call letters*] .... WUPI
Presque Isle/Presque Isle [*Maine*] [*ICAO location identifier*] (ICLI) .... KPQI
Presquile National Wildlife Refuge [*Virginia*] (AD) .... PNWR
Press [*Publishing*] .... P
Press (AD) .... Pr
Press .... PRS
Press (MSA) .... PRS
Press Advertisement Managers' Association (DGA) .... PAMA
Press Agent .... PA
Press and Publications Administration [*China*] .... PPA
Press and Union League Club of San Francisco, San Francisco, CA [*Library symbol Library of Congress*] (LCLS) .... CSfPr
Press Association Ltd. (IID) .... PA
Press Club (NTCM) .... PC
Press Complaints Commission (ECON) .... PCC
Press Computer System (DGA) .... PCS
Press Control, Inc. .... PCI
Press Council [*British*] .... PC
Press Division [*Environmental Protection Agency*] (GFGA) .... PD
Press, Doon, IA [*Library symbol Library of Congress*] (LCLS) .... IaDooP
Press Fit .... PRFT
Press Fit Socket .... PFS
Press Gallery [*US Senate*] .... PG
Press Independence and Critical Ability (NTCM) .... PICA
Press Lots of Keys to Abort [*Computer term*] .... PLOKTA
Press Night .... PN
Press on Regardless [*Automotive marathon*] .... POR
Press Packed .... PP
Press Pressure (SSD) .... PP
Press Publishing Co., Atlantic City, NJ [*Library symbol Library of Congress*] (LCLS) .... NjAcP
Press Relations Wire [*Commercial firm*] (EA) .... PRW
Press Release .... PR
Press Revise (DGA) .... PR
Press Secretary (ILCA) .... PS
Press Test [*Psychology*] .... PT
Press to Start (KSC) .... PS
Press to Transmit .... PTT
[*The*] **Press Trust of India** .... PTI
Press Union of Liberia .... PUL
Press Wireless [*A radio service for the transmission of news*] .... PREWI
Pressboard (MSA) .... PBD
Press-Button Signalling (PDAA) .... PBS
Pressed (AAG) .... PRSD
Pressed .... PRSSD
Pressed Brick Makers' Association Ltd. [*British*] (BI) .... PBMA
Pressed Felt Manufacturers' Association [*British*] (BI) .... PFMA
Pressed Glassmakers Society [*British*] (DBA) .... PGS
Pressed Metal Institute [*Later, AMSA*] .... PMI
Pressed Notch Depth (PDAA) .... PND
Pressed Plutonium Oxide .... PPO
Presser (MSA) .... PRSR
Presser Foot .... PRFT
Pressfeeder [*Printing*] .... Prsfdr
Pressing .... PRSG
Pressing .... PRSNG
Pressing and Distribution (WDMC) .... P & D
Pressing Direction .... PRD
Pressman (AABC) .... PRSMN
PressNet Environmental Reports [*Information service or system*] (IID) .... PER

Pressor Dose [Medicine] .... PD
Pressoreceptor [Laboratory science] (DAVI) .... PR
Press-Radio Bureau (NTCM) .... PRB
Presstek, Inc. [Associated Press] (SAG) .... Prestek
Presstek, Inc. [NASDAQ symbol] (NQ) .... PRST
Press-to-Talk (IDOE) .... PTT
Press-to-Test Light .... PTTL
Pressure [or p] [Symbol IUPAC] .... P
Pressure .... PR
Pressure (FAAC) .... PRES
Pressure (MCD) .... PRESS
Pressure Absolute [AGA] (TAG) .... PSIA
Pressure Actuated [Switch] .... PA
Pressure Alarm [Nuclear energy] (NRCH) .... PA
Pressure Alarm, High-Limit [Nuclear energy] (NRCH) .... PAHL
Pressure Alpha Center (MCD) .... PAC
Pressure Altitude (GAVI) .... HPRES
Pressure Altitude [Aviation] .... PA
Pressure Altitude Variation [Aviation] .... PAV
Pressure Ambient (NASA) .... PAMB
Pressure and Temperature Control (KSC) .... PTC
Pressure Angle (MSA) .... PA
Pressure Anomaly Difference (PDAA) .... PAD
Pressure Area [Medicine] .... PA
Pressure Assembled Thyristor .... PAT
Pressure at the Airway Opening [Medicine] (DAVI) .... Pawo
Pressure at the Body Surface [Medicine] (DAVI) .... Pbs
Pressure Bias Modulation (MCD) .... PBM
Pressure Boundary Subsystem [Nuclear energy] (NRCH) .... PBS
Pressure Breathing .... PB
Pressure Breathing Assistor [Medicine] .... PBA
Pressure Chamber .... PC
Pressure Check Range .... PCR
Pressure Compensator Over-Ride (PDAA) .... PCOR
Pressure Concentration Temperature .... PCT
Pressure Control Distributor (KSC) .... PCD
Pressure Control System .... PCS
Pressure Control Unit (MCD) .... PCU
Pressure Control Unit, Atlas (MCD) .... PCUA
Pressure Control Unit Sequencer (AAG) .... PCUSEQ
Pressure [or Pressurizer] Control Valve (AAG) .... PCV
Pressure [or Pressurized] Control Valve (IAA) .... PV
Pressure Controller [Nuclear energy] .... PC
Pressure Cycling Switch [Automotive engineering] .... PCS
Pressure, Diastolic [Cardiology] .... Pd
Pressure Die Casting [Commercial firm British] .... PDC
Pressure Difference Recording Controller .... PDRC
Pressure Differential Monitoring Valve .... PDMV
Pressure Differential Scanning Calorimetry [Analytical technique] .... PDSC
Pressure Differential Switch (IAA) .... PDIS
Pressure Disconnect Valve (MCD) .... PDV
Pressure Distillate (IAA) .... PD
Pressure Distribution Panel (AAG) .... PDP
Pressure Distribution Unit .... PDU
Pressure Drop (KSC) .... PD
Pressure Enclosure (MCD) .... PE
Pressure, End-Systole [Cardiology] .... Pes
Pressure Environmental Equipment (NVT) .... PEE
Pressure Equalization [Tube] [Otorhinolaryngology] (DAVI) .... PE
Pressure Equalization [Tubes or Equalizing] [Otorhinolaryngology] (DAVI) .... PET
Pressure Equalization System [Nuclear energy] (NUCP) .... PES
Pressure Equalizing [Tube] [Otorhinolaryngology] (DAVI) .... PE
Pressure Falling Rapidly [NWS] (FAAC) .... PRESFR
Pressure Fan (AAG) .... PF
Pressure Fed Booster (NASA) .... PFB
Pressure Fed Launch Vehicle [NASA] (KSC) .... PFLV
Pressure Fed Liquid (KSC) .... PRFL
Pressure Feedback Exhaust [Automotive engineering] .... PFE
Pressure Flow Meter .... PFM
Pressure for Economic and Social Toryism [Tory Reform Group] [British] (DI) .... PEST
Pressure Function Controller .... PFC
Pressure Garment Assembly .... PGA
Pressure, Gas, Start, Turbine, Auxiliary Pump-Drive Assembly [Pronounced "pigstap"] .... PGSTAP
Pressure Gas Umbilical (KSC) .... PGU
Pressure Gas Welding .... PGW
Pressure Gauge (KSC) .... PG
Pressure Gradient from Alveolus to Airway Opening [Medicine] (DAVI) .... P(A-awo)
Pressure, Hydraulic Unit .... PHU
Pressure Ignition Rocket (NATG) .... PIR
Pressure in the Airway [level to be specified] (DAVI) .... Paw
Pressure Indicating Alarm [Engineering] .... PIA
Pressure Indicating Alarm Switching [Engineering] .... PIAS
Pressure Indicator [Nuclear energy] .... PI
Pressure Indicator Controller .... PIC
Pressure Indicator Recorder (ECII) .... PIR
Pressure Indicator Recorder Controller (ECII) .... PIRC
Pressure Inductor (IAA) .... PRESSDUCTOR
Pressure Jump [NWS] (FAAC) .... PRJMP
Pressure Length Loop (DMAA) .... PLL
Pressure Level Recorder .... PLR
Pressure Line of Position [Air Force] .... PLOP
Pressure Lubrication Unit .... PLU

Pressure, Manifold .... PM
Pressure Measurement Package .... PMP
Pressure Measuring Unit (KSC) .... PMU
Pressure Model Static and Transient Launch Configuration (SAA) .... PSTL
Pressure Modulation Radiometer .... PMR
Pressure Monitoring Module [Mechanical engineering] .... PRM
Pressure Multiplier [Nuclear energy] (NRCH) .... PM
Pressure Noise Level (MCD) .... PNL
Pressure of Carbon Dioxide (HGAA) .... pCO_2
Pressure of Inspiration [Medicine] .... Pi
Pressure of Inspiration [Medicine] (DAVI) .... Pi
Pressure on Expiration [Medicine] .... Pe
Pressure on Space [Publishing] (DGA) .... POS
Pressure Oscillation (IAA) .... PO
Pressure Oxidation .... P-OX
Pressure Pattern (MCD) .... PP
Pressure Plane Joint .... PPJ
Pressure Plane Swivel Joint .... PPSJ
Pressure Pulse Contour [Cardiac computer] (PDAA) .... PPC
Pressure Rate Product [In treadmill test] .... PRP
Pressure Ratio .... PR
Pressure Ratio Acceleration Control [Gas turbine engine] .... PRAC
Pressure Ratio Limiter (MCD) .... PRL
Pressure Recorder (NRCH) .... PR
Pressure Recorder Controller [Nuclear energy] (NRCH) .... PRC
Pressure Reducing Station .... PRS
Pressure Reducing [or Regulation or Relief] Valve .... PRV
Pressure Regulation Exhaust .... PRX
Pressure Regulator (KSC) .... PR
Pressure Remanent Magnetization .... PRM
Pressure Response Cell [For chemical kinetic studies] .... PRC
Pressure Response Spectrum [Nuclear energy] (NRCH) .... PRS
Pressure Rise per Stage (MCD) .... PRPS
Pressure Rise Rate [Nuclear energy] (NRCH) .... PRR
Pressure Rising Rapidly [NWS] (FAAC) .... PRESRR
Pressure Safety Valve .... PSV
Pressure [or Propellant] Seal .... PS
Pressure Seal (NASA) .... PSL
Pressure Sealing Zipper .... PSZ
Pressure Sensitive Adhesive [Trademark] .... PSA
Pressure Sensitive Identification .... PSI
Pressure Sensitive Manufacturers Association [British] (DBA) .... PSMA
Pressure Sensitive Tape Council (EA) .... PSTC
Pressure Sensor .... PS
Pressure Sine Wave Generator .... PSWG
Pressure Static Probe Assembly (MCD) .... PSPA
Pressure Status Unit (AAG) .... PSU
Pressure Suit Assembly .... PSA
Pressure Suit Circuit (KSC) .... PSC
Pressure Suit Conditioning Assembly (MCD) .... PSCA
Pressure Support Ventilation [Medicine] (DAVI) .... PSV
Pressure Suppression Test Facility [Nuclear energy] (IEEE) .... PSTF
Pressure Switch .... PS
Pressure Switch Assembly (NASA) .... PSA
Pressure Switch, High [Nuclear energy] (NRCH) .... PSH
Pressure Switch Joint .... PSJ
Pressure Switch Manifold [Automotive transmissions] .... PSM
Pressure Switching Alarm [Engineering] .... PSA
Pressure System Automatic Regulator (IAA) .... PSAR
Pressure System Control (AAG) .... PSC
Pressure, Systolic [Cardiology] .... Ps
Pressure Technology Corp. of America .... PTCA
Pressure/Temperature (KSC) .... P/T
Pressure, Temperature, Level, and Flow [Chemical engineering] .... PTLF
Pressure Temperature Test Set (DWSG) .... PTTS
Pressure Test (AAG) .... PT
Pressure Test Barrel .... PTB
Pressure Test Equipment (MCD) .... PTE
Pressure Test Gauge .... PTG
Pressure Test Record .... PTR
Pressure Test Station (DNAB) .... PTS
Pressure Time Fuel System [Cummins Engine Co., Inc.] .... PT
Pressure to Clutch Engage [Aerospace] (AAG) .... PCE
Pressure to Horizontal Locks [Missiles] (AAG) .... PHL
Pressure to Vertical Locks .... PVL
Pressure, Torque, and Load .... PTL
Pressure Transducer (KSC) .... PT
Pressure Transducer Assembly .... PTA
Pressure Transducer Calibration System .... PTCS
Pressure Transducer Calibrator .... PTC
Pressure Transfer Gauge .... PTG
Pressure Transmitter (NRCH) .... PT
Pressure Transmitter Recorder (ECII) .... PTR
Pressure Transmural [Pretaining to an airway or blood vessel] [Medicine] (DAVI) .... Ptm
Pressure Tube Reactor Experiment [Nuclear energy] (NUCP) .... PTRE
Pressure Tube to Spool Piece [Nuclear energy] (NRCH) .... PT/SP
Pressure Tubing .... PT
Pressure/Vacuum .... P/V
Pressure Vacuum Chamber .... PVC
Pressure Vacuum System .... PVS
Pressure Velocity .... PV
Pressure, Vent, and Vacuum .... PVV
Pressure Vessel (MSA) .... PV
Pressure Vessel for Human Occupancy [Deep-sea diving] .... PVHO

Pressure Vessel Manufacturers Association (EA) .... PVMA
Pressure Vessel Material .... PVM
Pressure Vessel Research Committee [*National Institute of Standards and Technology*] .... PVRC
Pressure Vessel Thermal Shock (PDAA) .... PVTS
Pressure Volume Compensator (KSC) .... PVC
Pressure, Volume, Temperature .... PVT
Pressure Wave Supercharger [*Automotive engineering*] .... PWS
Pressure Wave Velocity [*Cardiology*] .... PWV
Pressure-Acoustic-Magnetic [*Minesweeping system*] (DNAB) .... PAM
Pressure-Actuated Valve (NASA) .... PAV
Pressure-Assisted Sintering [*Forging*] [*Automotive engineering*] .... PAS
Pressure-Control Ventilation [*Medicine*] (DMAA) .... PCV
Pressure-Controlled Intermittent Coronary Sinus Occlusion [*Medicine*] (DMAA) .... PICSO
Pressure-Gradient Single-Ended [*Microphone*] (DEN) .... PGS
Pressure-Indicating Switch [*Nuclear energy*] (NRCH) .... PIS
Pressure-Induced Intracranial Focal Ischemia [*Medicine*] .... PIFI
Pressure-Modulated Radiometer (AD) .... pmr
Pressure-Operated Initiator (MCD) .... POI
Pressure-Operated Switch (IAA) .... POS
Pressure-Operated Valve (MCD) .... POV
Pressure-Proof [*Technical drawings*] .... PP
Pressure-Proof (AD) .... pp
Pressure-Retaining Amphipod Trap [*Deep-sea biology*] .... PRAT
Pressure-Sensitive .... P-S
Pressure-Sensitive Devices (MCD) .... PSD
Pressure-Sensitive Label .... PSL
Pressure-Sensitive Tape .... PST
Pressure-Swing Adsorption [*Chemical engineering*] .... PSA
Pressure-Temperature Composition .... PTX
Pressure-Tolerant Electronics (IEEE) .... PTE
Pressure-Transmitting Medium [*Engineering*] .... PTM
Pressure-Treated Wood .... PTW
Pressure-Tube Reactor [*Nuclear energy*] .... PTR
Pressure-Tube Superheat Reactor [*Nuclear energy*] .... PTSR
Pressure-Type Window .... PTW
Pressure-Volume .... P-V
Pressurised Gas-Cooled Water Reactor [*Nuclear energy*] (NUCP) .... PGWR
Pressurization Control Panel [*NASA*] (KSC) .... PCP
Pressurization Events Trainer .... PET
Pressurization Systems Regulator Manifold (AAG) .... PSRM
Pressurization Valve .... PV
Pressurize (MSA) .... PRSRZ
Pressurized Air Compressor (DNAB) .... PRESAIR
Pressurized Air Starter System (MCD) .... PASS
Pressurized Air Subsystem .... PAS
Pressurized Ballistic Range [*NASA*] .... PBR
Pressurized Cabin Hydraulic Leakage Tester (DWSG) .... PCHLT
Pressurized Concrete Reactor Vessel [*Nuclear energy*] .... PCRV
Pressurized Deuterium Reactor [*Nuclear energy*] .... PDR
Pressurized Fluid-Bed [*Chemical engineering*] .... PFB
Pressurized Fluidized-Bed Combustion .... PFBC
Pressurized Fluidized-Bed Hydroretorting [*Chemical engineering*] .... PFH
Pressurized Heavy Water Reactor [*Nuclear energy*] .... PHWR
Pressurized Heavy Water-Moderated and Cooled Reactor [*Nuclear energy*] (IAA) .... PHWR
Pressurized Inert Gas Metal Arc (KSC) .... PIGMA
Pressurized Membrane Container .... PMC
Pressurized Module (SSD) .... PM
Pressurized Relief Tank (NRCH) .... PRT
Pressurized Sonobuoy Launch Tube [*Navy*] (CAAL) .... PSLT
Pressurized Sphere Injection (DNAB) .... PSI
Pressurized Stone Groundwood [*Pulp and paper technology*] .... PGW
Pressurized Subcritical Experiment [*Nuclear energy*] .... PSE
Pressurized Tank [*Liquid gas carriers*] .... P
Pressurized Thermal Shock [*Nuclear energy*] .... PTS
Pressurized Water .... PW
Pressurized Water Ractor - Full Length Emergency Cooling Heat Transfer [*Nuclear energy*] (PDAA) .... PWR-FLECHT
Pressurized Zone Microphone .... PZM
Pressurized-Water Reactor [*Nuclear energy*] .... PWR
Pressurizer (NRCH) .... PZR
Pressurizer Level (IEEE) .... PL
Pressurizer Level Control System [*Nuclear energy*] (GFGA) .... PZR LCS
Pressurizer Overpressure Protection System [*Nuclear energy*] (IEEE) .... POP
Pressurizer Overpressure Protection System [*Nuclear energy*] (NRCH) .... POPS
Pressurizer Pressure Control System [*Nuclear energy*] (GFGA) .... PZR PCS
Pressurizing (KSC) .... PRESIG
Prestaged Ammunition Loading System [*Army*] (RDA) .... PALS
Pre-Stamped Envelope .... PSE
Prestart (AAG) .... PRE-ST
Prestart Panel [*Aerospace*] (AAG) .... PSP
Pre-Startup Safety Review [*Chemical engineering*] .... PSSR
Prestel Advanced Network Design Architecture .... PANDA
Prestel Users Group (NITA) .... PUG
Prestige .... PRSTG
Prestige Bancorp, Inc. [*NASDAQ symbol*] (SAG) .... PRBC
Prestige Bancorp, Inc. [*Associated Press*] (SAG) .... PresBnc
Prestige Financial [*NASDAQ symbol*] (TTSB) .... PRFN
Prestige Financial Corp. [*Associated Press*] (SAG) .... PrestFn
Prestige Financial Corp. [*NASDAQ symbol*] (SAG) .... PRFN
Prestissimo [*Very Fast*] [*Music*] (ROG) .... PRESTMO
Prestissimo [*Very Fast*] [*Music*] (ROG) .... PRESTO
Pre-Stock Unit Equipment [*Military British*] .... PUE
Preston [*Postcode*] (ODBW) .... PR
Preston [*Cuba*] [*Airport symbol*] (AD) .... PST
Preston and Blackburn/Samlesbury [*British ICAO location identifier*] (ICLI) .... EGNG
Preston Carnegie Library, Preston, ID [*Library symbol*] [*Library of Congress*] (LCLS) .... IdPre
Preston Commercial and Technical Information Service (NITA) .... PCTIS
Preston, ID [*AM radio station call letters*] .... KACH
Preston, ID [*FM radio station call letters*] .... KKEX
Preston Microfilming Services Ltd., Toronto, ON, Canada [*Library symbol Library of Congress*] (LCLS) .... PmS
Preston, MN [*AM radio station call letters*] .... KFIL
Preston, MN [*FM radio station call letters*] .... KFIL-FM
Preston on Conveyancing [*5th ed.*] [*1819-29*] [*A publication*] (DLA) .... Pres Conv
Preston on Conveyancing [*A publication*] (DLA) .... Prest Conv
Preston on Estates [*3rd ed.*] [*1829*] [*A publication*] (DLA) .... Pres Est
Preston on Estates [*A publication*] (DLA) .... Prest Est
Preston on Legacies [*1824*] [*A publication*] (DLA) .... Pres Leg
Preston on Merger [*A publication*] (DLA) .... Pres Mer
Preston on Merger [*A publication*] (DLA) .... Prest Merg
Preston R. R. [*AAR code*] .... PRES
Preston School of Industry, Ione, CA [*Library symbol Library of Congress*] (LCLS) .... CIoP
Preston, Thorgrimson, Shidler, Gates & Ellis, Seattle, WA [*Library symbol*] [*Library of Congress*] (LCLS) .... WaSPTS
Preston Times, Preston, IA [*Library symbol Library of Congress*] (LCLS) .... IaPreT
Prestonburg Community College, Prestonsburg, KY [*Library symbol*] [*Library of Congress*] (LCLS) .... KyPrbC
Preston's Abstracts of Title [*2nd ed.*] [*1823-24*] [*A publication*] (DLA) .... Pres Abs
Prestonsburg, KY [*AM radio station call letters*] .... WDOC
Prestonsburg, KY [*AM radio station call letters*] .... WPRT
Prestonsburg, KY [*FM radio station call letters*] .... WQHY
Prestonsburg, KY [*FM radio station call letters*] .... WXKZ
Prestressed Ceramic RADOME .... PCR
Prestressed Concrete (BARN) .... PC
Prestressed Concrete (ADA) .... PSC
Prestressed Concrete Association [*British*] (DBA) .... PCA
Prestressed Concrete Institute (EA) .... PCI
Prestressed Concrete Pressure Vessel .... PCPV
Prestressed Concrete Reactor Vessel [*Nuclear energy*] .... PCRV
Prestrike (SAA) .... PR/S
Pre-Strike Surveillance/Reconnaissance System (MCD) .... PRESSURS
Prestwick [*British ICAO location identifier*] (ICLI) .... EGPK
Prestwick [*British ICAO location identifier*] (ICLI) .... EGQQ
Prestwick [*Scotland*] [*Airport symbol*] (AD) .... PIK
Prestwick BAE [*British ICAO designator*] (FAAC) .... PWK
Presumed Finding of Death [*DoD*] .... PFOD
Presumed Ocular Histoplasmosis Syndrome [*Ophthalmology*] .... POHS
Presumptive [*Grammar*] .... PRES
Presumptive Disability [*Title XVI*] [*Social Security Administration*] (OICC) .... PD
Presumptive Hematopoietic Stem Cell .... PSC
Presunrise Authority .... PSA
Presunrise Service Authority (NTCM) .... PSA
Presurgery Coagulation Profile [*Hematology and surgery*] (DAVI) .... P-SURG
Presurgical Coagulation Evaluation [*Medicine*] (DAVI) .... PSCE
Presynaptic Action Potential [*Neurochemistry*] .... pAP
Presynchronization .... Presync
Presystolic Gallop [*Cardiology*] .... PSG
Presystolic Murmur [*Cardiology*] .... PM
Presystolic Murmur [*Medicine*] (AD) .... pm
Presystolic Murmur [*Cardiology*] .... PSM
Pretax Earnings [*Employment*] .... PTE
Pretchabun/Lom Sak [*Thailand*] [*ICAO location identifier*] (ICLI) .... VTPL
Pretectal [*Neuroanatomy*] .... PT
Preterit [*Past tense*] [*Grammar*] (ROG) .... PRET
Preterit [*Past tense*] [*Grammar*] .... pt
Preterm Foundation [*Australia*] .... PF
Preterm Labor [*Obstetrics*] (DAVI) .... PTL
Preterm Milk [*Medicine*] .... PTM
Pretest [*Advertising*] (WDMC) .... pre
Pre-Test Laboratory (DNAB) .... PTL
Pretesting Orientation Exercises [*US Employment Service*] [*Department of Labor*] .... POE
Pretesting Orientation on the Purpose of Testing [*US Employment Service*] [*Department of Labor*] .... POPT
Pretibial Edema [*Medicine*] (DAVI) .... PTE
Pretibial Myxedema [*Medicine*] (DMAA) .... PM
Pretoria [*South Africa*] [*ICAO location identifier*] (ICLI) .... FAHQ
Pretoria [*South Africa*] [*ICAO location identifier*] (ICLI) .... FAPR
Pretoria [*South Africa*] [*Seismograph station code, US Geological Survey*] (SEIS) .... PRE
Pretoria [*South Africa*] (ROG) .... PRET
Pretoria Theological Series [*A publication*] (BJA) .... PRTS
Pretoria/Wonderboom [*South Africa*] [*ICAO location identifier*] (ICLI) .... FAWB
Pretoria-Witwatersrand [*South Africa*] .... PWV
Pretransfusion Serologic Testing .... PTST
Pretransmission Precautionary Answer to Nature's Call [*Especially before a long program*] [*Television*] .... PTP
Pretransmit Receiving .... PTR
Pretransplant Blood Transfusion [*Medicine*] .... PTBT
Pre-Treatment Anxiety [*Medicine*] (DMAA) .... PTA
Pretreatment Implementation Review Task Force [*Environmental Protection Agency*] (EPA) .... PIRT
Pretreatment Permitting and Enforcement Tracking System [*Environmental Protection Agency*] (ERG) .... PPETS

Pretreatment Standards for Existing Sources [*Environmental Protection Agency*] .... PSES
Pretreatment Standards for New Indirect Sources [*Environmental Protection Agency*] .... PSNS
Pretrial Intervention (BARN) .... PTI
Pre-Trial Investigation (DNAB) .... PTI
Pre-Trial Release (OICC) .... PTR
Pretrial Services Resource Center (EA) .... PSRC
Pre-Trip Inspection [*Shipping*] .... PTI
Pretty Amazing New Services (NITA) .... PANS
Pretty Damn Good .... PDG
Pretty Damn Quick .... PDQ
Pretty Darn Quick (TAG) .... PDQ
Pretty Good Privacy [*Telecommunications*] .... PGP
Pretty Good Stuff [*Liquor*] .... PGS
Pretty Important Person .... PIP
Pretty Poor [*Slang Bowdlerized version*] .... PP
Pretty Poor Planning .... PPP
Pretty Things Fan Club (EA) .... PTFC
Pretty Tough Lawyer [*Refers to Melvin Belli, attorney for Tammy and Jim Bakker of the PTL Club*] .... PTL
Pretty Young Thing [*In song title from the Michael Jackson album "Thriller"*] .... PYT
Pretuned Module [*Telecommunications*] (IAA) .... PTM
Pre-Turbo Pressure .... PTP
Pre-University Orbital Information Tracker Equipment and Recorder (PDAA) .... POINTER
Pre-Urban Professional [*Acronym coined by TeenAge magazine to describe its typical reader*] [*Lifestyle classification*] .... Pup
Prevail (FAAC) .... PVL
Prevailing Visibility .... PV
Prevailing Wage (MHDW) .... PW
Prevailing Wage Rate [*US Employment Service*] [*Department of Labor*] .... PWR
Prevailing-In Torque [*Automotive engineering*] .... PIT
Prevailing-Out Torque [*Automotive engineering*] .... POT
Prevalence of Gingivitis [*Dentistry*] (DAVI) .... PMA
Prevalent (FAAC) .... PVLT
Prevalve .... PREVLV
Prevalve (NASA) .... PV
Prevent (AAG) .... PVNT
Preventative .... PREVT
Preventative Cyclic Retransmission [*Telecommunications*] (TEL) .... PCR
Preventative Medicine (DAVI) .... PVMed
Prevention (DAVI) .... PR
Prevention .... PREV
Prevention .... PRVNTN
Prevention and Detection of Illegal Entry [*Military*] (DNAB) .... PADIE
Prevention and Removal of Corrosion and Scale [*Engineering*] .... PRCS
Prevention Detention [*Scotland Yard*] .... PD
Prevention of Blindness [*Medicine*] (MAE) .... POB
Prevention of Blindness (AD) .... pob
Prevention of Cruelty to Animals Society Member (DSUE) .... POCTA
Prevention of Deterioration Center [*Defunct*] (EA) .... PDC
Prevention of Fraud Investments Act [*British*] .... PFIA
Prevention of Oil Pollution Act [*1971*] .... POPA
Prevention of Over-Radiation [*Military*] .... POOR
Prevention of Significant Deterioration [*Environmental Protection Agency*] .... PSD
Prevention of Stripping Equipment (NATG) .... PSE
Prevention of Terrorism Act [*British*] (ECON) .... PTA
Prevention of Violence (DICI) .... PV
Prevention Research Center [*Pacific Institute for Research and Evaluation*] [*Research center*] (RCD) .... PRC
Prevention Routiere Internationale [*International Road Safety Organization*] [*Luxembourg*] (EAIO) .... PRI
Preventive .... PRNTV
Preventive .... PRVNTV
Preventive Action Engineer (NASA) .... PAE
Preventive Aggressive Device [*Restraint*] [*Medicine*] .... PAD
Preventive Dentistry (DAVI) .... PD
Preventive Enforcement Patrol [*New York City police*] .... PEP
Preventive Health Behavior [*Medicine*] (DMAA) .... PHB
Preventive Intervention Research Center for Child Health [*Yeshiva University*] [*Research center*] (RCD) .... PIRC
Preventive Maintenance .... PM
Preventive Maintenance (AD) .... pm
Preventive Maintenance Agreement .... PMA
Preventive Maintenance and Repair [*Aviation*] (MCD) .... PMR
Preventive Maintenance Checks and Services [*for Army vehicles*] (INF) ..... PMCS
Preventive Maintenance Contract (AD) .... pmc
Preventive Maintenance, Daily (MCD) .... PMD
Preventive Maintenance Division [*Air Force*] .... PMD
Preventive Maintenance Inspection (AFM) .... PMI
Preventive Maintenance Instruction (NASA) .... PMI
Preventive Maintenance Management Program .... PMMP
Preventive Maintenance Plan (KSC) .... PMP
Preventive Maintenance Procedure [*Nuclear energy*] (NRCH) .... PMP
Preventive Maintenance, Repair, and Operational Services (ODBW) .... PROS
Preventive Maintenance System .... PMS
Preventive Maintenance Time (MCD) .... PMT
Preventive Maintenance Welding (PDAA) .... PMW
Preventive Material .... PM
Preventive Medicine [*Also, PVNTMED*] (AFM) .... PM
Preventive Medicine (DAVI) .... PrevMed
Preventive Medicine (MAE) .... PRM
Preventive Medicine [*Also, PM*] .... PVNTMED
Preventive Medicine Unit [*Navy*] (NVT) .... PMU

Preventive Medicine Unit .... PREMEDU
Preventive Medicine Unit .... PREVMEDU
Preventive Officer [*British*] (ROG) .... PO
Preventive Operational Maintenance and Repair [*Military*] (NVT) .... POMAR
Preverbal Assessment-Intervention Profile [*Test*] .... PAIP
Preveza [*Greece*] [*ICAO location identifier*] (ICLI) .... LGPZ
Preveza/Lefkas [*Greece*] [*Airport symbol*] (OAG) .... PVK
Preview .... P
Preview .... P/V
Preview (MSA) .... PRVW
Preview and Graphics Editing [*Computer science*] (MHDI) .... PAGE
Preview Monitor [*A TV monitor*] [*Filmmaking*] (WDMC) .... PV
Previous (AFM) .... PREV
Previous Abnormality of Glucose Tolerance .... PrevAGT
Previous Applicants Need Not Reapply [*Civil Service*] .... PANNR
Previous Element Coding .... PEC
Previous Endorsement(s) Guaranteed [*Banking*] .... PEG
Previous Highroller, on a Budget [*Lifestyle classification*] .... Phob
Previous History [*Medicine*] .... PH
Previous Medical Illness (CPH) .... PMI
Previous Menstrual Period [*Medicine*] .... PMP
Previous Menstrual Period [*Medicine*] (AD) .... pmp
Previous Operating Time (AFIT) .... PT
Previous Orders [*Military*] .... PO
Previous Orders (AD) .... po
Previous Processor Mode .... PPM
Previous Program Selection [*In-car entertainment*] [*Electronics*] .... PREV
Previous Psychiatric History (MEDA) .... PPHx
Previous Question [*Parliamentary law*] .... PQ
Previous Question (AD) .... pq
Previous Result Negative (IAA) .... PRN
Previous Signaling Element Phase Shift Keying [*Computer science*] (IAA) .... PSPSK
Previous to Appearance in MEDLINE [*Latham, NY*] [*Bibliographic database*] .... PRE-MED
Previously Complied With .... PCW
Previously Not Available [*Army*] (AABC) .... PNVAL
Previously-Taxed Income .... PTI
Previtamin D3 [*A precursor to vitamin D3*] (DAVI) .... PreD$_3$
Prevocational [*Education*] (DAVI) .... pre-voc
Prevulcanization Inhibitor .... PVI
Prey [*Zoology*] .... P
PRF [*Pulse Repetition Frequency*] Ranging Doppler RADAR .... PRADOR
PRI Automation [*Associated Press*] (SAG) .... PRI Auto
PRI Automation [*NASDAQ symbol*] (SAG) .... PRIA
Price [*Economics*] .... P
Price (BARN) .... pc
Price [*Utah*] [*Seismograph station code, US Geological Survey*] (SEIS) .... PCU
Price [*Online database field identifier*] .... PR
Price (ODBW) .... pr
Price .... PRC
Price [*Utah*] [*Airport symbol*] (OAG) .... PUC
Price Adjusted Rates of Exchange [*Monetary conversion rate*] (ECON) .... PARE
Price Adjusted Single Sampling (PDAA) .... PASS
Price Adjusting Sampling Plan (PDAA) .... PASP
Price Adjustment Board .... PAB
Price Agreement Bulletin .... PAB
Price Analysis and Review Technique for Spares .... PARTS
Price Analysis File (AFIT) .... PAF
Price Analysis Sheet .... PAS
Price Analyst .... PA
Price and Availability .... P & A
Price and Availability List (CINC) .... PAL
Price and Budgeting (MCD) .... P & B
Price and Delivery Quotations .... PDQ
Price and Delivery Request .... P & DR
Price and Item Display [*British*] .... PAID
Price and Management Data .... PAMD
Price and Management Data Section [*of a stock list*] [*Navy*] .... PAMDS
Price and Stewart's Trade Mark Cases [*A publication*] (DLA) .... Price & St
Price [*T. Rowe*] Associates, Inc. [*Associated Press*] (SAG) .... PriceTR
Price Commission [*Cost of Living Council*] .... PC
Price Communications [*AMEX symbol*] (TTSB) .... PR
Price Communications Corp. [*AMEX symbol*] (SAG) .... PR
Price Communications Corp. [*Associated Press*] (SAG) .... PrcCm
Price Control Cases [*A publication*] (DLA) .... PC
Price Control Council (NADA) .... PCC
Price/Cost .... P/C
Price/Costco, Inc. [*NASDAQ symbol*] (SPSG) .... PCCW
Price Costco, Inc. [*Associated Press*] (SAG) .... PriceCst
Price Decontrol Board [*Post-World War II*] .... PDB
Price Decontrol Board [*Post-World War II*] [*A publication*] (DLA) .... PDC
Price Description Record [*Computer science*] (IBMDP) .... PDR
Price [*or Profit*]/Earnings Ratio [*Relation between price of a company's stock and its annual net income*] .... P/E
Price Earnings Ratio [*Investment term*] (DFIT) .... PE
Price Earnings Ratio [*Relation between price of a company's stock and its annual net income*] .... PER
Price Enterprises [*NASDAQ symbol*] (TTSB) .... PREN
Price Enterprises, Inc. [*NASDAQ symbol*] (SAG) .... PREN
Price Enterprises, Inc. [*Associated Press*] (SAG) .... PriceEnt
Price Escalation Estimated Rates .... PEER
Price Ex-Dividend [*Stock market*] .... PXD
Price History System (MCD) .... PHS
Price in Effect [*Military*] .... PIE

Price Index Numbers for Current Cost Accounting [*Service in Information and Analysis*] [*British Information service or system*]   (IID) ..... PINCCA
Price Level [*Economics*] ..... PL
Price List ..... PL
Price List ..... PRLST
Price Look-Up   (IAA) ..... PLU
Price Master File   (MCD) ..... PMF
Price Negotiation Memorandum   (MCD) ..... PNM
Price Not Available   (DNAB) ..... PNA
Price on Acts Relating to Real Estate [*A publication*]   (DLA) ..... Price R Est
Price on Application [*Business term*]   (ADA) ..... POA
Price on Maritime Liens [*1940*] [*A publication*]   (DLA) ..... Price Liens
Price on Request ..... POR
Price per Copy [*of books*] ..... PC
Price. Procedural Regulation [*United States*] [*A publication*]   (DLA) ..... PPR
Price Received ..... PR
Price Redetermination [*Economics*] ..... PR
Price Redetermination Contract   (SAA) ..... PRC
Price Redetermination/Service Reallocation   (AAGC) ..... PR/SR
Price Reduced [*of a book*] ..... PR
Price REIT [*NYSE symbol*]   (TTSB) ..... RET
Price REIT, Inc. [*Associated Press*]   (SAG) ..... PrcREI
Price REIT, Inc. [*NYSE symbol*]   (SAG) ..... RET
Price Signal Code [*Military*]   (AABC) ..... PSC
Price Spreading [*Business term*] ..... PS
Price Stabilization Corp. ..... PRISCO
Price/Stern/Sloan Publishers, Inc. ..... P/S/S
Price, UT [*FM radio station call letters*] ..... KARB
Price, UT [*AM radio station call letters*] ..... KOAL
Price, UT [*FM radio station call letters*] ..... KPRQ
Price, UT [*AM radio station call letters*] ..... KRPX
Price, UT [*Location identifier FAA*]   (FAAL) ..... PUC
Price Variation Clause   (DS) ..... pvc
Price, Waterhouse & Co. Library, Vancouver, BC, Canada [*Library symbol Library of Congress*]   (LCLS) ..... CaQMPW
Price, Waterhouse & Co., Vancouver, British Columbia [*Library symbol National Library of Canada*]   (NLC) ..... BVAPW
Price Waterhouse Energy Solutions ..... PWES
Price Waterhouse Financial Solutions ..... PWFS
Price-Adjusted Rate Preferred [*Investment term*]   (MHDW) ..... PAR
Priced   (AD) ..... prcd
Priced Aerospace Ground Equipment List ..... PAGEL
Priced Exhibit   (MCD) ..... PE
Priced Ground Support Equipment List   (AAG) ..... PGSEL
Priced Parts List   (NASA) ..... PPL
Priced Provisioned Item List   (MCD) ..... PPIL
Priced Spare Parts [*Military*]   (AFIT) ..... PSP
Priced Spare Parts List ..... PSPL
Priced Spare Parts List Revision ..... PSPLR
Price-Level-Adjusted Accounting   (ADA) ..... PLA
Price-Level-Adjusted Deposit ..... PLAD
Price-Level-Adjusted Mortgage ..... PLAM
Price-Lifting Operation [*Business term*]   (ECON) ..... PLO
Pricellular Corp. [*AMEX symbol*]   (SAG) ..... PC
Pricellular Corp. [*Associated Press*]   (SAG) ..... Pricell
PriCellular Corp. 'A' [*AMEX symbol*]   (TTSB) ..... PC
Price-Pottenger Nutrition Foundation   (EA) ..... PPNF
Prices and Incomes Board [*British*] ..... PIB
Prices Current ..... PC
Prices Current   (WDMC) ..... pc
Price's English Exchequer Reports [*1814-24*] [*A publication*]   (DLA) ..... Pr
Price's English Exchequer Reports [*1814-24*] [*A publication*]   (DLA) ..... Pr Exch
Price's English Exchequer Reports [*1814-24*] [*A publication*]   (DLA) ..... Pri
Price's English Exchequer Reports [*A publication*]   (DLA) ..... Price
Price's English Mining Commissioners' Cases [*A publication*]   (DLA) ..... Pri
Price's English Mining Commissioners' Cases [*A publication*]   (DLA) ..... Price
Price's English Practice Cases [*1830-31*] [*A publication*]   (DLA) ..... Price PC
Price's English Practice Cases [*A publication*]   (DLA) ..... Price Pr Cas
Price's General Practice [*A publication*]   (DLA) ..... Price Gen Pr
Price's Mining Cases [*A publication*]   (DLA) ..... Price Min Cas
Price's Notes of Points of Practice, English Exchequer Cases [*A publication*]   (DLA) ..... Price Notes PP
Price's Notes of Practice Cases in Exchequer [*1830-31*] [*England*] [*A publication*]   (DLA) ..... Price Notes PC
Prices Paid Index [*Economics*] ..... PPI
Price's Precipitation Reaction [*Medicine*] ..... PPR
Price-Sales Ratio [*Economics*] ..... PSR
Price-Tag Awareness [*See also PTS*] ..... PTA
Price-Tag Shock [*See also PTA*] ..... PTS
Price-to-Book Value Ratio [*Investment term*]   (DFIT) ..... PBR
Priceville, AL [*AM radio station call letters*] ..... WJRA
Prichard, AL [*AM radio station call letters*] ..... WKSJ
Prichard, AL [*AM radio station call letters*] ..... WLPR
Pricing and Acceptability Claims Processing System [*Health insurance*]   (GHCT) ..... P & A
Pricing Evaluation for Audit Technique [*Finance*] ..... PEAT
Pricing Instructions Memorandum   (MCD) ..... PIM
Pricing Review to Intensify Competitive Environment [*Computer science*] ..... PRICE
Pricing Work Statement   (MCD) ..... PWS
Prickett's Reports [*1 Idaho*] [*A publication*]   (DLA) ..... Prickett
Pride ..... PRD
Pride and Prejudice [*Novel by Jane Austen*] ..... P & P
Pride Automotive Gp [*NASDAQ symbol*]   (TTSB) ..... LEAS
Pride Automotive Gp Wrrt [*NASDAQ symbol*]   (TTSB) ..... LEASW

Pride Automotive Group, Inc. [*NASDAQ symbol*]   (SAG) ..... LEAS
Pride Automotive Group, Inc. [*Associated Press*]   (SAG) ..... PrideA
Pride Automotive Group, Inc. [*Associated Press*]   (SAG) ..... PrideAto
Pride Companies Ltd. [*NYSE symbol*]   (SPSG) ..... PRF
Pride Companies Ltd. [*Associated Press*]   (SAG) ..... Pride
Pride Co. $2.60cm Cv L.P. [*NYSE symbol*]   (TTSB) ..... PRF
Pride, Efficiency, Dedication, Reliability, and Order   (DNAB) ..... PEDRO
Pride, Hustle, and Drive ..... PHD
Pride, Integrity, Guts [*Police alternative for the appellation applied to police by radical groups*] ..... PIG
Pride, Loyalty, Integrity, Capability, Knowledge   (DNAB) ..... PLICK
Pride of Newark [*Feigenspan beer*] ..... PON
Pride of the Navy Yard   (DNAB) ..... PONY
Pride Petroleum Services, Inc. [*NASDAQ symbol*]   (CTT) ..... PRDE
Pride Petroleum Services, Inc. [*Associated Press*]   (SAG) ..... PrdePt
Pride Petroleum Svcs [*NASDAQ symbol*]   (TTSB) ..... PRDE
Pride Resources Ltd. [*Vancouver Stock Exchange symbol*] ..... PDE
Pride Users' Association [*Defunct*]   (EA) ..... PUA
Prideaux and Cole's English Reports [*4 New Sessions Cases*] [*A publication*]   (DLA) ..... P & C
Prideaux and Cole's English Reports [*4 New Sessions Cases*] [*1850-51*] [*A publication*]   (DLA) ..... Prid & C
Prideaux and Cole's English Reports [*4 New Sessions Cases*] [*1850-51*] [*A publication*]   (DLA) ..... Prid & Co
Prideaux's Directions to Churchwardens [*10th ed.*] [*1835*] [*A publication*]   (DLA) ..... Prid Ch W
Prideaux's Forms and Precedents in Conveyancing [*24th ed.*] [*1952*] [*A publication*]   (DLA) ..... Prid Conv
Prideaux's Judgments and Crown Debts [*4th ed.*] [*1854*] [*A publication*]   (DLA) ..... Prid Judg
Pridie [*The Day Before*] [*Latin*] ..... P
Pridie [*The Day Before*] [*Latin*] ..... PRID
Pridie Kalendas [*The Day before the Calends*] [*Latin*] ..... PK
Pridie Kalendas [*The Day before the Calends*] [*Latin*] ..... PRK
Pridie Nonas [*The Day before the Nones*] [*Latin*] ..... PRN
Priest ..... P
Priest ..... PR
Priest [*California*] [*Seismograph station code, US Geological Survey*]   (SEIS) ..... PRI
Priest ..... PRST
Priest and Martyr [*Church calendars*] ..... PM
Priest, CA [*Location identifier FAA*]   (FAAL) ..... ROM
Priest Confessor ..... PC
Priest, Confessor, and Doctor   (ROG) ..... PC & D
Priest Lake Community Library, Priest River, ID [*Library symbol*] [*Library of Congress*]   (LCLS) ..... IdPrP
Priest River Library, Priest River, ID [*Library symbol*] [*Library of Congress*]   (LCLS) ..... IdPr
Priest Vicar ..... PV
Priest-in-Charge [*Church of England*] ..... P-in-C
Priestly Fraternity of St. Peter   (TOCD) ..... FSSP
Priestly Source [*Biblical scholarship*] ..... P
Priests and Brothers of the Congretation of Holy Cross   (TOCD) ..... csc
Priests Eucharistic League   (EA) ..... PEL
Priests for Equality   (EA) ..... PFE
Priests of the Congregation of Holy Cross   (TOCD) ..... CSC
Prilled ..... PU
Prilled Urea [*A fertilizer*] ..... PU
Prima Energy [*NASDAQ symbol*]   (TTSB) ..... PENG
Prima Energy Corp. [*NASDAQ symbol*]   (NQ) ..... PENG
Prima Energy Corp. [*Associated Press*]   (SAG) ..... PrimaE
Prima Leben und Sparen [*Quality Living and Saving*] [*Brand name and discount store chain in West Germany and US*] ..... PLUS
Prima Luce [*Early in the Morning*] [*Pharmacy*] ..... PRIM LUC
Primacord Interstage ..... PI
Primadonna Resorts [*NASDAQ symbol*]   (TTSB) ..... PRMA
Primadonna Resorts, Inc. [*Associated Press*]   (SAG) ..... Primadn
Primadonna Resorts, Inc. [*NASDAQ symbol*]   (SAG) ..... PRMA
Prim-Air Aps [*Denmark ICAO designator*]   (FAAC) ..... PIR
Primal Therapy ..... PT
Primapun [*Indonesia*] [*ICAO location identifier*]   (ICLI) ..... WAKN
Primaquine [*Antimalarial*] ..... Pq
Primarily Primates [*An association*]   (EA) ..... PP
Primark Corp. [*NYSE symbol*]   (SPSG) ..... PMK
Primark Corp. [*Associated Press*]   (SAG) ..... Primrk
Primary   (DAVI) ..... I⁰
Primary   (IDOE) ..... P
Primary ..... P
Primary   (NASA) ..... PR
Primary   (KSC) ..... PRI
Primary   (IDOE) ..... pri
Primary   (AFM) ..... PRIM
Primary Academic Sentiment Scale [*Child development test*] ..... PASS
Primary Access Method [*Sperry UNIVAC*] ..... PAM
Primary Account Number [*Business term*] ..... PAN
Primary Acquired Melanosis [*Oncology*] ..... PAM
Primary Acquired Sideroblastic Anemia [*Medicine*] ..... PASA
Primary Action Office [*or Officer*] [*Army*] ..... PAO
Primary Address Code   (AFM) ..... PAC
Primary Adhesively Bonded Structural Technology [*Aviation*] ..... PABST
Primary Administrative Contracting Officer [*Military*]   (AFIT) ..... PACO
Primary Adrenocortical Micronodular Dysplasia [*Medicine*]   (DMAA) ..... PAMD
Primary Adrenocortical Nodular Dysplasia [*Endocrinology*]   (DMAA) ..... PAND
Primary Aeronautical Designation   (DNAB) ..... PA
Primary Aerospace Vehicle [*or Aircraft*] ..... PA
Primary Aerospace Vehicle [*or Aircraft*] Inventory ..... PAI

Primary Affective Disorder [*Psychiatry*] (DAVI) .... PAD
Primary Affective Witzelsucht [*Medicine*] (CPH) .... PAW
Primary Afferent Depolarization [*Electrophysiology*] .... PAD
Primary Afferent Depolarization (PDAA) .... PAMIRASAT
Primary African Green Monkey Kidney [*Cells*] .... PAGMK
Primary Air Force Specialty .... PAFS
Primary Air Force Specialty Code .... PAFSC
Primary Air Inlet Muffler (MCD) .... PAIM
Primary Aircraft Authorized [*Air Force*] .... PAA
Primary Aircraft Training System (MCD) .... PATS
Primary Alerting System .... PAS
Primary Ambulatory Care Center [*Medicine*] (DMAA) ...... PACC
Primary Amenorrhea [*Gynecology*] (MAE) .... PA
Primary Amoebic Meningitis [*or Meningoencephalitis*] [*Medicine*] ...... PAM
Primary Amoebic Meningoencephalitis [*Medicine*] .... PAME
Primary Anemia [*Medicine*] .... PA
Primary Angioplasty in Myocardial Infarction [*Cardiology study*] .... PAMI
Primary Ascent System [*Aerospace*] (NASA) .... PAS
Primary Atypical Pneumonia [*Medicine*] .... PAP
Primary Auditory Visual Experience [*National Visitor Center*] ...... PAVE
Primary Auxiliary Area [*Nuclear energy*] (NRCH) .... PAA
Primary Auxiliary Building [*Nuclear energy*] (NRCH) ...... PAB
Primary Auxiliary Memory [*Unit*] [*Computer science*] (MCD) ...... PAM
Primary Avionics Software System (NASA) .... PASS
Primary Bank [*NASDAQ symbol*] (SAG) .... PETE
Primary Bank [*Associated Press*] (SAG) .... PrimaryB
Primary Bibliography (DGA) .... PRIM BIB
Primary Biliary Cirrhosis [*Medicine*] .... PBC
Primary Billet (DNAB) .... PRI BIL
Primary Block Number [*Computer science*] .... PBN
Primary Buffer [*Chemistry*] .... PB
Primary Bus [*Computer science*] (CAAL) .... PB
Primary Calibration System .... PCS
Primary Cancer Site [*Oncology*] .... PCS
Primary Carbon Assimilation [*Botany*] .... PCA
Primary Care Block Grant .... PCBG
Primary Care Case Management [*Medicine*] (DMAA) ...... PCCM
Primary Care Case Manager [*Medicine*] (DMAA) .... PCCM
Primary Care Center [*Health care*] (HCT) .... PCC
Primary Care Clinic (DAVI) .... PCC
Primary Care Extender [*Insurance*] (DMAA) .... PRIMEX
Primary Care Manager (HCT) .... PCM
Primary Care Network [*Medical insurance*] .... PCN
Primary Care Nursing .... PCN
Primary Care Organization Consortium [*Health insurance*] (DMAA) ...... PCOC
Primary Care Organization Network [*Health insurance*] (DMAA) .... PCON
Primary Care Physician .... PCP
Primary Care Unit [*Medicine*] (DMAA) .... PCU
Primary Carpet Backing .... PCB
Primary Category Code (NITA) .... PCC
Primary Center .... PC
Primary Central Alarm Station [*Nuclear energy*] (NRCH) ...... PCAS
Primary Certified Reference Material [*Nuclear energy*] (NRCH) ...... PCRM
Primary Checkpoint File .... PCF
Primary Chemotherapy-Radiotherapy [*Oncology*] .... PCR
Primary Chicken Kidney [*Cell line*] .... PCK
Primary Ciliary Dyskinesia [*Medicine*] .... PCD
Primary Circuit (MCD) .... PC
Primary Clock Pulse Generator .... PCPG
Primary Closure [*Medicine*] (DMAA) .... PC
Primary Code .... PC
Primary Code Modulation [*Computer science*] (IAA) ...... PCM
Primary Command Point [*Military*] (CAAL) .... PCP
Primary Commercial Blanket Bond [*Insurance*] .... PCBB
Primary Communications Research Centre [*University of Leicester*]
  [*Canada*] .... PCRC
Primary Communications-Oriented (IAA) .... PCO
Primary Communications-Oriented System (IEEE) .... PCOS
Primary Conditioning Solution .... PCS
Primary Containment Isolation System [*Nuclear energy*] (NRCH) ...... PCIS
Primary Containment Vessel .... PCV
Primary Contracting Officer (MCD) .... PCO
Primary Contributor .... PC
Primary Control (MCD) .... PC
Primary Control Assembly [*Nuclear energy*] (NRCH) ...... PCA
Primary Control Inventory Control Point [*Navy*] .... PCICP
Primary Control Program [*Computer science*] .... PCP
Primary Control Rod Drive Mechanism [*Nuclear energy*] (NRCH) ...... PCRDM
Primary Control Rod Driveline [*Nuclear energy*] (NRCH) ...... PCRD
Primary Control Rod System [*Nuclear energy*] (NRCH) ...... PCRS
Primary Control Ship [*Navy*] .... PCS
Primary Control Unit (IAA) .... PCU
Primary Control Unit, Hydraulics (AAG) .... PCU/HDR
Primary Control Vessel (DNAB) .... PCV
Primary Coolant Activity [*Nuclear energy*] (NRCH) ...... PCA
Primary Coolant Line (NASA) .... PCL
Primary Coolant Loop (NASA) .... PCL
Primary Coolant Pump [*Nuclear energy*] (NRCH) .... PCP
Primary Coolant System (MSA) .... PCS
Primary Cooling Water [*Reactor*] .... PCW
Primary Cosmic Radiation .... PCR
Primary CRITICOMM [*Critical Intelligence Communications System*] Relay
  Station (CET) .... PCRS
Primary Cross-Connection Point (NITA) .... PCP
Primary Current Distribution [*Electroplating*] .... PCD

Primary Data Bus [*Computer science*] .... PDB
Primary Data User Station [*Computer science*] (PDAA) ...... PDUS
Primary Degenerative Cerebral Disease [*Medicine*] (DMAA) ...... PDCD
Primary Degenerative Dementia [*Medicine*] .... PDD
Primary Demographic Report [*A. C. Nielsen Co.*] (NTCM) ...... PDR
Primary Diagnosis [*Medicine*] .... PRDIAG
Primary Earnings per Share (TDOB) .... PEPS
Primary Education (AIE) .... PE
Primary Education [*A publication*] .... Primary Ed
Primary Education Program [*Child development test*] ...... PEP
Primary Effusion Lymphoma [*Oncology*] .... PEL
Primary Electricity .... PE
Primary Emission Neuron Activation (IEEE) .... PENA
Primary Enrichment Medium [*Microbiology*] .... PEM
Primary Environmental Prediction System .... PEPS
Primary Environmental Processing Systems [*Navy*] (GFGA) ...... PEPS
Primary Expense Account .... PEA
Primary Failed Part (DNAB) .... PFP
Primary Familial and Congenital Polycythemia [*Medicine*] ...... PFCP
Primary Feedback Element (IAA) .... PFE
Primary Fibrinolysin [*Medicine*] (DMAA) .... PF
Primary Fibromyalgia Syndrome [*Medicine*] (DMAA) ...... PFS
Primary Flash Distillate [*Chemical technology*] .... PFD
Primary Flight Control .... PFC
Primary Flight Control [*on an aircraft carrier*] [*Navy*] ...... PRI-FLY
Primary Flight Control Display .... PFCD
Primary Flight Control System [*NASA*] (MCD) .... PFCS
Primary Flight Display .... PFD
Primary Flight System (NASA) .... PFS
Primary Flow Control System [*Nuclear energy*] (NRCH) ...... PFCS
Primary Focus Feed [*Satellite communications*] .... PFF
Primary Freon Loop (NASA) .... PFL
Primary Frequency Generator .... PFG
Primary Frequency Supply [*Telecommunications*] (TEL) ...... PFS
Primary Guidance and Navigation System [*Apollo*] [*NASA*] ...... PGNS
Primary Guidance, Navigation, and Control System [*or Subsystem*] [*Apollo*]
  [*NASA*] (MCD) .... PGNCS
Primary Guidance Subsystem (MCD) .... PGS
Primary Health Care .... PHC
Primary Health Centre [*British*] .... PHC
Primary Heat Transport System [*Nuclear energy*] (NRCH) ...... PHTS
Primary Hepatic Carcinoma [*Medicine*] .... PHC
Primary Hepatocellular Carcinoma [*Oncology*] (DAVI) ...... PHC
Primary Hepatocellular Carcinoma [*Medicine*] (DMAA) ...... PHCC
Primary High-Voltage Power Supply .... PHVPS
Primary Human Amnion [*Biology*] (BARN) .... PHA
Primary Human Fetal Glial [*Cytology*] .... PHFG
Primary Hyperparathyroidism .... PH
Primary Hyperparathyroidism (MAE) .... PHP
Primary Hyperparathyroidism .... PHPT
Primary Immunodeficiency Disease [*Medicine*] .... PID
Primary Immunodeficiency Syndrome [*Medicine*] (DMAA) ...... PIDS
Primary Indicating Position (IAA) .... PIP
Primary Indicating Position Data Logger (IEEE) .... PIP
Primary Industry and Energy .... PIE
Primary Industry Bank of Australia Ltd. (ADA) .... PIBA
Primary Infarction [*Medicine*] .... PI
Primary Influent Treatment System .... PITS
Primary Initiatives in Mathematics Education (AIE) ...... PRIME
Primary Input (IAA) .... PI
Primary Inspection Agency [*Federal Manufactured Housing Construction and
  Safety Standards*] [*Department of Housing and Urban Development*]
  (GFGA) .... PIA
Primary Insurance Account [*Social Security Administration*] (OICC) ...... PIA
Primary Insurance Amount .... PIA
Primary Intelligence Requirement [*Military*] (INF) ...... PIR
Primary Intracerebral Hemorrhage (CPH) .... PIH
Primary Inventory Control Activity (MCD) .... PICA
Primary Irritant Contact Dermatitis [*Medicine*] (DMAA) ...... PICD
Primary Irritation Evaluation Program .... PIEP
Primary Irritation Indices [*for skin*] .... PII
Primary Key [*Computer science*] (PCM) .... PK
Primary Kidney Fold .... PKF
Primary Knock-on-Atom (MCD) .... PKA
Primary Landing Site (MCD) .... PLS
Primary Language Record [*Education*] (AIE) .... PLR
Primary Lateral Sclerosis [*Medicine*] (DMAA) .... PLS
Primary Layer Depth [*Military*] (CAAL) .... PLD
Primary Leadership Course [*Army*] .... PLC
Primary Leadership Development Course [*Army*] (INF) ...... PLDC
Primary Leading [*Photography*] (DGA) .... PL
Primary Learning Network [*Computer science*] (IAA) ...... PLN
Primary Level Field Activity [*Defense Supply Agency*] ...... PLFA
Primary Life Support System [*or Subsystem*] (NASA) ...... PLSS
Primary Line of Sight [*Sextants*] .... PLOS
Primary Liver Cell Cancer [*Oncology*] .... PLCC
Primary Location Code [*Computer science*] .... PLC
Primary Long-Distance Carrier [*Telephone service*] ...... PLDC
Primary Loss Expectancy [*Insurance*] .... PLE
Primary Loss Retention [*Insurance*] .... PLR
Primary Market [*Investment term*] .... PM
Primary Market Area .... PMA
Primary Measurement Instrument .... PMI
Primary Mediastinal Germ-Cell Tumor [*Medicine*] (DMAA) ...... PMGCT
Primary Medical Care for the Uniformed Services [*DoD*] ...... PRIMUS

Primary Medical Group [*Insurance*] (DMAA) ... PMG
Primary Mental Abilities [*Test*] [*Education*] ... PMA
Primary Mental Abilities Test [*Education*] ... PMAT
Primary Mental Health Project (AD) ... PMHP
Primary Mesenchyme Cell [*Cytology*] ... PMC
Primary Metropolitan Statistical Area [*Census Bureau*] ... PMSA
Primary Military Occupational Code (AD) ... PMOSC
Primary Military Occupational Specialty [*Army*] ... PMOS
Primary Military Occupational Specialty Code [*Army*] (AABC) ... PMOSC
Primary Mission Area [*Military*] (CAAL) ... PRMAR
Primary Mission Equipment ... PME
Primary Mission Gross Weight ... PMGW
Primary Mission Readiness ... PMR
Primary Monkey Kidney [*Physiology*] ... PMK
Primary Motivation [*Psychology*] (DAVI) ... PM
Primary Munition ... PM
Primary Myelodysplastic Syndrome [*Medicine*] (DMAA) ... PMDS
Primary Myeloproliferative Disease [*Medicine*] ... PMD
Primary Myocardial Disease [*Medicine*] ... PMD
Primary Navigation Display (GAVI) ... PND
Primary Navigation, Guidance and Control System (KSC) ... PNGCS
Primary Navigation Reference (AAG) ... PNR
Primary Navigation System ... PNGS
Primary Navy Enlisted Classification [*Code*] ... PNEC
Primary Navy Officer Billet Classification and Navy Enlisted Classification ... PRINOBC/NEC
Primary Next of Kin [*Army*] (AABC) ... PNOK
Primary Noncommissioned Officer Course [*Army*] (INF) ... PNCOC
Primary Nonferrous Smelter Order [*Environmental Protection Agency*] ... PNFSO
Primary Nuclear Airlift Force ... PNAF
Primary Open-Angle Glaucoma [*Ophthalmology*] ... POAG
Primary Operand Unit (IAA) ... PROP
Primary Operating Stock [*DoD*] ... POS
Primary Operating System (IEEE) ... POS
Primary Operation ... POP
Primary Optic Afferents ... POA
Primary Optic Atrophy ... POA
Primary Optical Area (AD) ... poa
Primary Order Dial (NITA) ... PRIMORDIAL
Primary Organization Element (NOAA) ... POE
Primary Output (IAA) ... PO
Primary Ovarian Failure [*Gynecology*] (DMAA) ... POF
Primary Oxygen System ... POS
Primary Pacific Secure Voice Communications [*Navy*] (CAAL) ... PRIPACSEVOCAM
Primary Paraffin Sulfonate [*Organic chemistry*] ... PPS
Primary Part Failure (DNAB) ... PPF
Primary Party Organization [*Politics*] ... PPO
Primary Pattern Generator [*Bell Laboratories*] ... PPG
Primary Payload [*NASA*] (NASA) ... P/PL
Primary Personal Interest [*Personnel study*] ... PPI
Primary Plant Mineralized Water (IAA) ... PPMW
Primary Power Control (MCD) ... PPC
Primary Power Standard ... PPS
Primary Power System [*Nuclear energy*] (NRCH) ... PPS
Primary Pressure [*Nuclear energy*] (NRCH) ... PP
Primary Pressure Standard ... PPS
Primary Pressure Vessel (MCD) ... PPV
Primary Private Practice Income [*Medicine*] (MAE) ... PPPI
Primary Private Practice Insurance [*Medicine*] (DMAA) ... PPPI
Primary Producers (ADA) ... PP
Primary Producers' Cooperative Society (AD) ... PPCS
Primary Producers Union (AD) ... PPU
Primary Production Required [*Resource management*] ... PRR
Primary Products Promotion [*Australia*] ... PPP
Primary Progress Assessment Chart [*Psychology*] ... PPAC
Primary Propulsion Branch [*Manned Spacecraft Center*] ... PPB
Primary Propulsion System [*Spacecraft*] ... PPS
Primary Protection System [*Computer science*] ... PPS
Primary Public Safety Answering Point (DMAA) ... PSAP
Primary Pulmonary Hypertension [*Medicine*] ... PPH
Primary Rabbit Kidney [*Medicine*] (DMAA) ... PRK
Primary Rabbit Kidney [*Medicine*] (DMAA) ... PRK
Primary RADAR (DA) ... PR
Primary RADAR (FAAC) ... PRIRA
Primary Ranging Test (OA) ... PRT
Primary Rat Kidney [*Cells*] ... PRK
Primary Rate, Inc. ... PRI
Primary Rate Interface (PCM) ... PRI
Primary Raynaud's Phenomenon [*Medicine*] ... PRP
Primary Recovery Ship [*NASA*] ... PRS
Primary Recovery Site [*NASA*] (KSC) ... PRS
Primary Reference [*Automobile fuel*] (DICI) ... PR
Primary Reference Fuel [*Automotive engineering*] ... PRF
Primary Reference Material [*Medicine*] (MAE) ... PRM
Primary Reference Material [*Library science*] (DAVI) ... PRM
Primary Replacement Unit ... PRU
Primary Report of Aircraft Mishap [*Army*] (DOMA) ... PRAM
Primary Representational System (EDAC) ... PRS
Primary Rescue Site [*NASA*] (NASA) ... PRS
Primary Resistance (IDOE) ... R_p
Primary Resistance (IDOE) ... R_{pri}
Primary Reviewing Authority ... PRA
Primary Rhesus Monkey Kidney (AAMN) ... PMK
Primary Routing Center [*Telecommunications*] (TEL) ... PRC
Primary Sampling System [*Nuclear energy*] (NRCH) ... PSS
Primary Sampling Unit [*Statistics*] ... PSU
Primary School (ADA) ... PS
Primary School Staff Relations [*Project*] (AIE) ... PSSR
Primary School Teachers and Science [*Project*] (AIE) ... PSTS
Primary Sclerosing Cholangitis [*Medicine*] ... PSC
Primary Secondary Impedance (IAA) ... PRISSECIMP
Primary/Secondary Peace Education Network [*Later, PEN*] (EA) ... PSPEN
Primary Self-Concept Inventory [*Psychology*] (EDAC) ... PSCI
Primary Shield Water (DNAB) ... PSW
Primary Smog Product (PDAA) ... PSP
Primary Sodium Pump [*Nuclear energy*] (NRCH) ... PSP
Primary Sodium Pump Guard Vesel [*Nuclear energy*] (NRCH) ... PSPGV
Primary Specialty Skill Identifier [*Military*] (AABC) ... PSSI
Primary Staff Action Officer [*Military*] ... PSAO
Primary Standardization Office [*Military*] (AABC) ... PSO
Primary Standards Laboratory ... PSL
Primary Supply Point [*Military*] (AFM) ... PSP
Primary Support Point [*Military*] (AFM) ... PSP
Primary Surge Tank [*Nuclear energy*] (NRCH) ... PST
Primary Surveillance RADAR ... PSR
Primary Tactical Radio Circuit (IAA) ... PRITAC
Primary Target [*Army*] ... PT
Primary Target [*Military*] ... PTGT
Primary Target Area [*Military*] ... PTA
Primary Target Line [*Military*] ... PTL
Primary Target Point [*NASA*] ... PTP
Primary Teaching Certificate [*Australia*] ... PTC
Primary Technical Course [*Military*] ... PTC
Primary Thickening Meristem [*Botany*] ... PTM
Primary Trainer [*Aircraft*] ... PT
Primary Training Centre [*British military*] (DMA) ... PTC
Primary Trait System (EDAC) ... PTS
Primary Tungsten Association [*British*] (EAIO) ... PTA
Primary Type Battery [*JETDS nomenclature*] [*Military*] (CET) ... BA
Primary Valve ... PV
Primary Ventricular Fibrillation (CPH) ... PVF
Primary Visual Cortex [*Anatomy*] ... PVC
Primary Vocational Interest [*Personnel study*] ... PVI
Primary Voice Alert System [*NORAD*] (MCD) ... PVAS
Primary [*or Push*] **Wave** [*Earthquakes*] ... P
Primary Waveform Generator [*Telecommunications*] (TEL) ... PWFG
Primary Weapons and Equipment ... PWE
Primary Winding (IAA) ... PRI
Primary Work Code (SSD) ... PWC
Primary Zone [*Military*] ... PZ
Primase (DMAA) ... PRIM
Primate ... PRIM
Primate Calicivirus ... PCV
Primate Chorionic Gonadotropin [*Medicine*] (DMAA) ... PCG
Primate Equilibrium Platform ... PEP
Primate Information Center [*University of Washington*] [*Seattle, WA*] ... PIC
Primate Research Center ... PRC
Primate Research Institute [*New Mexico State University*] [*Hollman, NM*] ... PRI
Primate Society of Great Britain (DBA) ... PSGB
Primate T-Lymphotropic Viruses ... PTLV
Primate Vaccine Evaluation Network ... PVEN
Prime (AAG) ... PRM
Prime ... PRM
Prime Air, Inc. [*ICAO designator*] (FAAC) ... PRM
Prime Air, Inc. [*FAA designator*] (FAAC) ... TRZ
Prime Assets Ratio ... PAR
Prime [*or Principal*] **Associate Contractor** (MCD) ... PAC
Prime Bancorp [*NASDAQ symbol*] (TTSB) ... PSAB
Prime Bancorp, Inc. [*Associated Press*] (SAG) ... PrmBcp
Prime Bancorp, Inc. [*NASDAQ symbol*] (CTT) ... PSAB
Prime Candidate Alloy (MCD) ... PCA
Prime Capital Corp. [*NASDAQ symbol*] (SAG) ... PMCP
Prime Capital Corp. [*Associated Press*] (SAG) ... PrimeCp
Prime Ceiling Incentive ... PCI
Prime Compatible Set (PDAA) ... PCS
Prime Computer Inc., Corporation Library, Framingham, MA [*OCLC symbol*] (OCLC) ... PRI
Prime Condition Aircraft ... PCA
Prime Contract End Item (MCD) ... PCEI
Prime Contract Termination (AAG) ... PCT
Prime Contracting Officer (SAA) ... PCO
Prime Contractor ... PC
Prime Contractor Furnished Equipment (MCD) ... PCFE
Prime Cost ... PC
Prime Disjunctive Normal Form (PDAA) ... PDNF
Prime Driver ... PD
Prime Energy [*NASDAQ symbol*] (SAG) ... PNRG
Prime Energy [*Associated Press*] (SAG) ... PrmEgy
Prime Equipment ... PE
Prime Equities International [*NASDAQ symbol*] (SAG) ... PEZV
Prime Equities International [*Associated Press*] (SAG) ... PrimEq
Prime Equities Intl [*NASDAQ symbol*] (TTSB) ... PEZVF
Prime Factor Transform (IAA) ... PFT
Prime Focus Universal Extragalactic Instrument [*Astronomy*] ... PFUEI
Prime Function (NASA) ... PF
Prime Group Engineer (AAG) ... PGE
Prime Hard Wheat ... PHW
Prime Hospitality [*NYSE symbol*] (SPSG) ... PDQ
Prime Hospitality Corp. [*Associated Press*] (SAG) ... PrmHsp

Prime Implicant Solution (IAA) .... PIS
Prime Interest Rate [*Banking*] .... PI
Prime Intermediate Maintenance Activity .... PIMA
Prime Inventory Control Point (DNAB) .... PICP
Prime Item Development (MCD) .... PID
Prime Item Development Specification .... PIDS
Prime Item Fabrication Specification .... PIFS
Prime Level Code .... PLC
Prime Macro-Assembler (NITA) .... PMA
Prime Management Group, Inc. [*NASDAQ symbol*] (SAG) .... PMGI
Prime Management Group, Inc. [*Associated Press*] (SAG) .... PrimeMg
Prime Medical Services [*NASDAQ symbol*] (TTSB) .... PMSI
Prime Medical Services, Inc. [*NASDAQ symbol*] (NQ) .... PMSI
Prime Medics [*NASDAQ symbol*] (SAG) .... PMSI
Prime Medics [*Associated Press*] (SAG) .... PrmeMd
Prime Minister .... PM
Prime Minister's Country Task Force [*Australia*] .... PMCTF
Prime Ministers of England [*A publication*] .... PME
Prime Minister's Office .... PMO
Prime Minister's Question [*British*] (BARN) .... PMQ
Prime Minister's Science Council [*Australia*] .... PMSC
Prime Mission Electronic Equipment [*NASA*] (KSC) .... PMEE
Prime Mission Project [*Military*] .... PMP
Prime Mission Vehicle (MCD) .... PMV
Prime Motor Inns Ltd. [*NYSE symbol*] (SPSG) .... PMP
Prime Motor Inns Ltd. [*Associated Press*] (SAG) .... PrMLtd
Prime Motor Inns L.P. [*NYSE symbol*] (TTSB) .... PMP
Prime Mover (AD) .... p mvr
Prime Mover (MCD) .... PM
Prime Mover [*Technical drawings*] .... PMVR
Prime Mover Control [*Valve*] .... PMC
Prime Network Software Package [*Prime Computer, Inc.*] .... PRIMENET
Prime Operating System [*Prime Computer, Inc.*] .... PRIMOS
Prime Power Brass Board (MCD) .... PPBB
Prime Power Distribution .... PPD
Prime Power Unit .... PPU
Prime Quality [*Slang*] .... P and Q
Prime RADAR Digitizer (IAA) .... PRD
Prime Residential [*NYSE symbol*] (TTSB) .... AAH
Prime Residential, Inc. [*NASDAQ symbol*] (SAG) .... PRES
Prime Residential, Inc. [*Associated Press*] (SAG) .... PrimeRsd
Prime Resources Corp. [*Vancouver Stock Exchange symbol*] .... PMR
Prime Responsible Authority (IAA) .... PRA
Prime Retail [*NASDAQ symbol*] (TTSB) .... PRME
Prime Retail 8.5%Ptc Cv'B'Pfd [*NASDAQ symbol*] (TTSB) .... PRMEP
Prime Retail, Inc. [*NASDAQ symbol*] (SAG) .... PRME
Prime Retail, Inc. [*Associated Press*] (SAG) .... PrmRetl
Prime Retail, Inc. [*Associated Press*] (SAG) .... PrmRtl
Prime Select (MCD) .... PS
Prime Sponsor .... PS
Prime Stock Number .... PRISN
Prime Subframe (MCD) .... PSF
Prime System Indicator .... PSI
Prime Time Access Rule [*Television*] .... PTAR
Prime Time Entertainment Network [*Television broadcasting*] .... PTEN
Prime Time Performer [*In book title, "Vitale: Just Your Average Bald, One-Eyed Basketball Wacko Who Beat the Ziggy and Became a PTP'er"*] .... PTP'er
Prime Time School Television [*Defunct*] (EA) .... PTST
Prime Time Sunday [*TV program*] .... PTS
Prime Underwriting Facility [*Banking*] .... PUF
PRIME Users Group (EA) .... PUG
Prime Vendor Support [*Army*] .... PVS
Prime Vertical .... PV
Prime Western [*Zinc*] .... PW
Primed Lymphocyte Typing [*Hematology*] .... PLT
Primed Oscillator Expendable Transponder [*Military*] (CAAL) .... POET
PrimeEnergy Corp. [*NASDAQ symbol*] (SPSG) .... PNRG
PRIMENET Node Controller (NITA) .... PNC
Primer (IAA) .... PRI
Primer (MSA) .... PRMR
Primer Binding Site [*Genetics*] .... PBS
Primeras Lineas Uruguayas de Navegacion Aerea [*Uruguayan National Airlines*] .... PLUNA
Primeras Lineas Uruguayas de Navegacion Aerea [*Uruguay*] [*ICAO designator*] (FAAC) .... PUA
Primer-Dependent Deoxynucleic Acid Polymerase Index [*Medicine*] (DMAA) .... PDPI
Primeros Puestos del Deporte Espanol [*Ministerio de Cultura*] [*Spain Information service or system*] (CRD) .... DESP
Prime's Online Graduate Opportunities (NITA) .... POGO
PrimeSource Corp. [*Associated Press*] (SAG) .... PrimeSrc
PrimeSource Corp. [*NASDAQ symbol*] (SAG) .... PSRC
Primex Forest Industries Ltd. [*Toronto Stock Exchange symbol Vancouver Stock Exchange symbol*] .... PXF
Primex Technologies, Inc. [*Associated Press*] (SAG) .... Primex
Primex Technologies, Inc. [*NASDAQ symbol*] (SAG) .... PRMX
Primghar Public Library, Primghar, IA [*Library symbol Library of Congress*] (LCLS) .... IaPri
Primidone [*Antiepileptic drug*] .... PRM
Primipara [*Obstetrics*] (DAVI) .... I-Para
Primipara [*Woman bearing first child*] [*Medicine*] (MAE) .... Para
Primipara [*Woman bearing first child*] [*Medicine*] (AAMN) .... PRIMIP
Primipara [*Woman bearing first child*] [*Obstetrics*] (DAVI) .... PRIMP
Primitive .... P
Primitive .... PR
Primitive .... PRIM
Primitive Art Society of Chicago (EA) .... PASC
Primitive Baptist .... PB
Primitive Baptist Library, Elon College, NC [*Library symbol Library of Congress*] (LCLS) .... NcElonP
Primitive Endoderm [*Cytology*] .... PE
Primitive Equation .... PE
Primitive Helium Mantle [*Geology*] .... PHEM
Primitive [*Fetal*] **Hemoglobin** .... HbP
Primitive Methodist [*A publication*] .... PRIM METH
Primitive Methodist Quarterly Review [*A publication*] (ROG) .... PMQ
Primitive Methodists (ROG) .... PM
Primitive Neuroectodermal Tumor [*Oncology*] .... PNET
Primitive Yolk Sac [*Embryology*] .... PYS
Primo Mane [*Early in the Morning*] [*Pharmacy*] .... PRIM M
Primordial Black Hole [*Astrophysics*] .... PBH
Primordial Density Fluctuation [*Cosmology*] .... PDF
Primordial Germ Cell .... PGC
Primordial Hot Mantle Plume (PDAA) .... PHMP
Primrose League [*British*] (DI) .... PL
Primrose Technology Corp. [*Vancouver Stock Exchange symbol*] .... PTE
Primus [*First*] [*Latin*] .... P
Primus Telecommunications Group, Inc. [*Associated Press*] (SAG) .... PrimusT
Primus Telecommunications Group, Inc. [*NASDAQ symbol*] (SAG) .... PRTL
Prince .... P
Prince .... PR
Prince (AD) .... Pr
Prince .... PRNC
Prince Albert [*South Africa*] [*ICAO location identifier*] (ICLI) .... FAPC
Prince Albert [*Canada*] [*Airport symbol*] (OAG) .... YPA
Prince Albert Coat [*Slang*] .... PA
Prince Albert National Park, Parks Canada [*Parc National Prince Albert, ParcsCanada*] **Waskesiu Lakes, Saskatchewan** [*Library symbol National Library of Canada*] (NLC) .... SWPCP
Prince Albert RADAR Laboratory .... PARL
Prince Albert, SK [*FM radio station call letters*] .... CFMM
Prince Albert, SK [*Television station call letters*] .... CIPA
Prince Albert, SK [*AM radio station call letters*] .... CKBI
Prince Albert, SK [*Television station call letters*] .... CKBI-TV
Prince Albert, SK [*ICAO location identifier*] (ICLI) .... CYPA
Prince Albert Victor's Own [*British military*] (DMA) .... PAVO
Prince Albert Victor's Own Cavalry [*British military*] (DMA) .... PAVOC
Prince Albert's Guard [*British military*] (DMA) .... PAG
Prince Albert's Light Infantry [*Military unit*] [*British*] .... PALI
Prince Albert's Own [*Military unit*] [*British*] .... PAO
Prince Albert's Volunteer Guards [*British military*] (DMA) .... PAVG
Prince Charles Hospital [*Australia*] .... PCH
Prince Consort (IIA) .... PC
Prince Consort's Own [*Military unit*] [*British*] .... PCO
Prince Edward Air Ltd. [*Canada ICAO designator*] (FAAC) .... CME
Prince Edward Island [*Canada*] [*MARC geographic area code Library of Congress*] (LCCP) .... n-cn-pi
Prince Edward Island [*Canadian province*] [*Postal code*] .... PE
Prince Edward Island [*Canadian province*] .... PEI
Prince Edward Island [*Canada MARC country of publication code Library of Congress*] (LCCP) .... pic
Prince Edward Island (DLA) .... Pr Edw I
Prince Edward Island (DLA) .... Pr Edw Isl
Prince Edward Island Department of Education, Charlottetown, PE, Canada [*Library symbol Library of Congress*] (LCLS) .... CaPCE
Prince Edward Island Department of Education, Charlottetown, Prince Edward Island [*Library symbol National Library of Canada*] (NLC) .... PCE
Prince Edward Island Department of Municipal Affairs, Charlottetown, PE, Canada [*Library symbol Library of Congress*] (LCLS) .... CaPCMA
Prince Edward Island Department of Municipal Affairs, Charlottetown, Prince Edward Island [*Library symbol National Library of Canada*] (NLC) .... PCMA
Prince Edward Island Food Technology Centre, Information Centre, Charlottetown, PE, Canada [*Library symbol*] [*Library of Congress*] (LCLS) .... CAPCFT
Prince Edward Island Libraries, Charlottetown, PE, Canada [*Library symbol Library of Congress*] (LCLS) .... CaPC
Prince Edward Island Provincial Library [*UTLAS symbol*] .... PEI
Prince Edward Island Provincial Library, Charlottetown, Prince Edward Island [*Library symbol National Library of Canada*] (NLC) .... PC
Prince Edward Island Reports [*Canada*] [*A publication*] (DLA) .... Pr Edw I
Prince Edward Island Reports [*Canada*] [*A publication*] (DLA) .... Pr Edw Isl
Prince Edward Island Reports (Haviland's) [*A publication*] (DLA) .... PEI
Prince Edward Island Reports (Haviland's) [*1850-1914*] [*A publication*] (DLA) .... PEI Rep
Prince Edward Island Revised Statutes [*Canada*] [*A publication*] (DLA) .... PEI Rev Stat
Prince Edward Island Statutes [*Canada*] [*A publication*] (DLA) .... PEI Stat
Prince Frederick, MD [*FM radio station call letters*] .... WMJS
Prince George [*Canada*] [*Airport symbol*] (OAG) .... YXS
Prince George, BC [*FM radio station call letters*] .... CBYG
Prince George, BC [*Television station call letters*] .... CIFG
Prince George, BC [*FM radio station call letters*] .... CIRX
Prince George, BC [*AM radio station call letters*] .... CJCI
Prince George, BC [*FM radio station call letters*] (RBYB) .... CKKN
Prince George, BC [*AM radio station call letters*] .... CKPG
Prince George, BC [*Television station call letters*] .... CKPG-TV
Prince George, BC [*ICAO location identifier*] (ICLI) .... CYXS
Prince George Public Library, British Columbia [*Library symbol National Library of Canada*] (NLC) .... BPG

Prince George Public Library, Prince George, BC, Canada [*Library symbol Library of Congress*] (LCLS) .... CaBPG
Prince George's County Memorial Library, Hyattsville, MD [*Library symbol Library of Congress*] (LCLS) .... MdHyP
Prince Line [*Steamship*] (MHDW) .... PL
Prince Line Ltd. [*Steamship*] (MHDW) .... PLL
Prince of Jerusalem [*Freemasonry*] .... PJ
Prince of Wales (AD) .... P o W
Prince of Wales .... POW
Prince of Wales [*Military unit*] [*British*] .... PW
Prince of Wales' Dragoon Guards [*Military British*] (ROG) .... PWDG
Prince of Wales' Island (ROG) .... PWI
Prince of Wales Northern Heritage Centre, Government of the Northwest Territories, Yellowknife, Northwest Territories [*Library symbol National Library of Canada*] (NLC) .... NWYWNH
Prince [*or Princess*] **of Wales' Own** [*Military unit*] [*British*] (DMA) .... POWO
Prince of Wales' Own [*Military unit*] [*British*] .... PWO
Prince of Wales' Own Royal [*Military unit*] [*British*] .... PWOR
Prince of Wales' Royal [*Military unit*] [*British*] .... PWR
Prince of Wales Royal Indian Military College [*British military*] (DMA) .... PWRIMC
Prince of Wales' Volunteer Service [*British*] .... PWVS
Prince of Wales' Volunteers [*Military unit*] [*British*] .... PWV
Prince Patrick Island [*Canada*] .... PPI
Prince Regent (ROG) .... PR
Prince Rupert [*Canada*] [*Airport symbol*] (OAG) .... YPR
Prince Rupert [*Canada*] [*Airport symbol Obsolete*] (OAG) .... ZSW
Prince Rupert, BC [*AM radio station call letters*] .... CFPR
Prince Rupert, BC [*AM radio station call letters*] .... CHTK
Prince Rupert, BC [*ICAO location identifier*] (ICLI) .... CYPR
Prince Rupert Public Library, British Columbia [*Library symbol National Library of Canada*] (NLC) .... BPR
Prince Rupert Public Library, Prince Rupert, BC, Canada [*Library symbol Library of Congress*] (LCLS) .... CaBPR
Prince Rupert Regional Archives, Prince Rupert, British Columbia [*Library symbol National Library of Canada*] (NLC) .... BPRA
Prince William County Public Library, Manassas, VA [*Library symbol Library of Congress*] (LCLS) .... ViManCo
Prince William Forest Park [*National Park Service designation*] .... PRWI
Prince William Sound Community College [*Alaska*] .... PWSCC
Princeps [*First Edition*] [*French*] .... P
Prince's New Mexico Laws [*A publication*] (DLA) .... Prince NML
[*The*] **Prince's Youth Business Trust** [*British*] .... PYBT
Princess (ROG) .... P
Princess (ROG) .... PCSS
Princess (ROG) .... PSS
Princess Air [*British ICAO designator*] (FAAC) .... PRN
Princess Anne, MD [*FM radio station call letters*] .... WESM
Princess Anne, MD [*FM radio station call letters*] .... WOLC
Princess Charlotte of Wales [*Military unit*] [*British*] .... PCW
Princess Kitty Fan Club (EA) .... PKFC
Princess Louise's Sutherland and Argyll Highlanders [*Military British*] (ROG) .... PL
Princess Mary's Royal Air Force Nursing Service [*British*] .... PMRAFNS
Princess of Wales' Own [*Military unit*] [*British*] (ROG) .... PSWO
Princess Patricia of Connaught's Light Infantry [*Military unit*] [*Canada*] .... PPCLI
Princess Patricia's Canadian Light Infantry (AD) .... PPCLI
Princess Pat's [*Princess Patricia of Connaught's Light Infantry*] [*Military unit*] [*Canada*] .... PP
Princess Royal's [*Military unit*] [*British*] .... PR
Princess Royal's Dragoon Guards [*Military unit*] [*British*] (ROG) .... PRDG
Princess Ventures [*Vancouver Stock Exchange symbol*] .... PRV
Princess Victoria's Royal Irish Fusiliers [*Military British*] (ROG) .... PV
Princeton [*New Jersey*] [*Airport symbol Obsolete*] (OAG) .... PCT
Princeton [*New Jersey*] [*Seismograph station code, US Geological Survey*] (SEIS) .... PRIN
Princeton Accelerator Laboratory .... PAL
Princeton Air Link .... PAL
Princeton American [*NASDAQ symbol*] (TTSB) .... PELT
Princeton American Corp. [*Associated Press*] (SAG) .... PrinAm
Princeton and District Museum and Archives, Princeton, British Columbia [*Library symbol National Library of Canada*] (NLC) .... BPPM
Princeton Applied Research Corp. [*Princeton University*] .... PAR
Princeton Applied Research Corp. .... PARC
Princeton Aviation [*ICAO designator*] (AD) .... PN
Princeton Aviation Corp. [*ICAO designator*] (FAAC) .... PCN
Princeton Azimuthally-Varying-Field Cyclotron .... PAVFC
Princeton, BC [*AM radio station call letters*] .... CIOR
Princeton, BC [*ICAO location identifier*] (ICLI) .... CYDC
Princeton Community Library, Princeton, MN [*Library symbol*] [*Library of Congress*] (LCLS) .... MnP
Princeton Daily Clarion, Princeton, IN [*Library symbol Library of Congress*] (LCLS) .... InPrC
Princeton Datafilm, Inc., Princeton, NJ [*Library symbol Library of Congress*] (LCLS) .... PriD
Princeton Dental Management Corp. [*NASDAQ symbol*] (SAG) .... PDMC
Princeton Dental Management Corp. [*Associated Press*] (SAG) .... PrnDn
Princeton Dental Management Corp. [*Associated Press*] (SAG) .... PrnDnt
Princeton Dental Mgmt [*NASDAQ symbol*] (TTSB) .... PDMC
Princeton Dental Mgmt Wrrt [*NASDAQ symbol*] (TTSB) .... PDMCW
Princeton Electronic Products, Inc. [*NASDAQ symbol*] (NQ) .... PELT
Princeton Electronic Products, Inc. (IAA) .... PEP
Princeton Experiment Package [*NASA*] .... PEP
Princeton High School, Princeton, MN [*Library symbol*] [*Library of Congress*] (LCLS) .... MnPH
Princeton, IL [*AM radio station call letters*] .... WZOE

Princeton, IL [*FM radio station call letters*] .... WZOE-FM
Princeton, IN [*AM radio station call letters*] .... WRAY
Princeton, IN [*FM radio station call letters*] .... WRAY-FM
Princeton, IN [*FM radio station call letters*] .... WSJD
Princeton Junction, NJ [*FM radio station call letters*] .... WWPH
Princeton Junior High School, Princeton, MN [*Library symbol*] [*Library of Congress*] (LCLS) .... MnPJ
Princeton, KY [*AM radio station call letters*] .... WAVJ
Princeton, KY [*FM radio station call letters*] (RBYB) .... WAVJ-FM
Princeton, KY [*AM radio station call letters*] .... WPKY
Princeton Large Torus [*Nuclear reactor*] .... PLT
Princeton, ME [*Location identifier FAA*] (FAAL) .... PNN
Princeton Media Group, Inc. [*NASDAQ symbol*] (SAG) .... PMGI
Princeton Media Group, Inc. [*Associated Press*] (SAG) .... PrinceM
Princeton Microfilm Corp. .... PMC
Princeton Microfilm Corporation, Princeton, NJ [*Library symbol Library of Congress*] (LCLS) .... PmC
Princeton, MN [*AM radio station call letters*] .... WQPM
Princeton, MN [*FM radio station call letters*] .... WQPM-FM
Princeton National Bancorp [*NASDAQ symbol*] (SAG) .... PNBC
Princeton National Bancorp [*Associated Press*] (SAG) .... PrincNtl
Princeton Natl Bancorp [*NASDAQ symbol*] (TTSB) .... PNBC
Princeton, NJ [*AM radio station call letters*] .... WHWH
Princeton, NJ [*FM radio station call letters*] .... WPRB
Princeton North Elementary School, Princeton, MN [*Library symbol*] [*Library of Congress*] (LCLS) .... MnPNE
Princeton Packet, Inc., Princeton, NJ [*Library symbol Library of Congress*] (LCLS) .... NjPP
Princeton Particle Accelerator (IAA) .... PPA
Princeton Plasma Physics Laboratory [*Also known as PPL - Plasma Physics Laboratory*] [*Princeton, NJ*] [*Department of Energy*] .... PPPL
Princeton Polymer Laboratories .... PPL
Princeton Public Library, Princeton, IN [*Library symbol Library of Congress*] (LCLS) .... InPr
Princeton Public Library, Princeton, NJ [*Library symbol Library of Congress*] (LCLS) .... NjPPP
Princeton Reference Design (MCD) .... PRD
Princeton Resources Corp. [*Vancouver Stock Exchange symbol*] .... PTC
Princeton Shopping News, Princeton, NJ [*Library symbol Library of Congress*] (LCLS) .... NjPS
Princeton South Elementary School, Princeton, MN [*Library symbol*] [*Library of Congress*] (LCLS) .... MnPSE
Princeton Theological Seminary, Princeton, NJ [*Library symbol Library of Congress*] (LCLS) .... NjPT
Princeton Theological Seminary, Princeton, NJ [*OCLC symbol*] (OCLC) .... PTS
Princeton Time Sharing Services, Inc. .... PTSS
Princeton University (GAGS) .... Princeton U
Princeton University .... PU
Princeton University Device Physics Laboratory [*New Jersey*] .... PU-DPL
Princeton University, Gest Library, Princeton, NJ [*Library symbol Library of Congress*] (LCLS) .... NjP-G
Princeton University Observatory [*New Jersey*] .... PUO
Princeton University, Office of Population Research, Princeton, NJ [*Library symbol Library of Congress*] (LCLS) .... NjP-Pop
Princeton University, Pennsylvania University, Army Avionics Research (PDAA) .... PPAAR
Princeton University Press (DGA) .... PUP
Princeton University, Princeton, NJ [*Library symbol Library of Congress*] (LCLS) .... NjP
Princeton University, Princeton, NJ [*Inactive*] [*OCLC symbol*] (OCLC) .... PUL
Princeton University, Princeton Special Collection, Princeton, NJ [*Library symbol*] [*Library of Congress*] (LCLS) .... NjP-SC
Princeton University Research Center [*Marine science*] (MSC) .... PURC
Princeton University Solid State and Materials Laboratory [*New Jersey*] .... PSSL
Princeton, WV [*FM radio station call letters*] .... WAEY
Princeton, WV [*FM radio station call letters*] .... WKMY
Princeton, WV [*AM radio station call letters*] .... WPVO
Princeton-Pennsylvania Accelerator [*Closed, 1972*] [*AEC*] .... PPA
Princeton-Pennsylvania Proton Accelerator [*Closed, 1972*] [*AEC*] (IAA) .... PPA
Princeville [*Hawaii*] [*Airport symbol*] (OAG) .... HPV
Princeville Airways [*ICAO designator*] (AD) .... WP
Princeville Airways, Inc. [*ICAO designator*] (FAAC) .... PRI
Principal .... P
Principal .... PP
Principal (ROG) .... PPAL
Principal .... Pr
Principal [*Principal*] [*Spanish*] (AD) .... pral
Principal .... PRIN
Principal .... PRIN
Principal .... PRINC
Principal Administrative Contracting Officer (AAGC) .... PACO
Principal Administrative Officer .... PAO
Principal Administrative Officers Committee [*Chiefs of Staff*] [*World War II*] .... PAOC
Principal Air Aide-de-Camp [*RAF*] [*British*] .... PAADC
Principal Ammunition Technical Officer [*British military*] (DMA) .... PATO
Principal and Interest [*Banking*] (ADA) .... P & I
Principal and Interest [*Finance*] (DFIT) .... P&I
Principal Appreciation Conversion Security [*Finance*] .... PACS
Principal Armament Supply Officer [*British military*] (DMA) .... PASO
Principal Assistant (NOAA) .... PA
Principal Assistant County Architect [*British*] .... PACA
Principal Assistant Responsible for Contracting [*Army*] .... PARC
Principal Assistant Secretary .... PAS
Principal Assistant Secretary (Priority) .... PAS(PR)

Principal Associate Contractor (MCD) .... PAC
Principal Axes .... PA
Principal Beach Master [RAF] [British] .... PBM
Principal Borehole (AD) .... prb
Principal Business Activity (GFGA) .... PBA
Principal Care Provider [For a patient] (DAVI) .... PCP
Principal Careers Officer (AIE) .... PCO
Principal Chaplain (ADA) .... PC
Principal Chaplain [Navy British] .... Pch
Principal Civil Service Pension Scheme [British] .... PCSPS
Principal Clerk of Session .... PCS
Principal Clinical Medical Officer [British] .... PCMO
Principal Coast Officer [Customs] [British] (ROG) .... PCO
Principal Colonial Medical Officer [British] .... PCMO
Principal Commonwealth Supply Committee [World War II] .... PCSC
Principal Component .... PC
Principal Component Analysis .... PCA
Principal Component Analysis with Varimax Rotation .... PCAV
Principal Components Regression .... PCR
Principal Conductor of the Works [Freemasonry] .... PCW
Principal Contracting Officer [Air Force] .... PCO
Principal Control Authority (NATG) .... PCA
Principal Co-Ordinates Analysis .... PCoA
Principal Coordinating Scientist [NASA] (KSC) .... PCS
Principal Decision Authority (DOMA) .... PDA
Principal Deputy Assistant Secretary of Defense .... PDASD
Principal Deputy for Acquistion [Army] (RDA) .... PDA
Principal Development Activity [Navy] .... PDA
Principal Development Authority (MCD) .... PDA
Principal Diagonal Artery [Anatomy] (DAVI) .... PDA
Principal Direction of Fire [Military] .... PDF
Principal Direction of Force [Mechanical engineering] .... PDOF
Principal Display Panel [Packaging] .... PDP
Principal Distance [Graphic arts] (OA) .... PD
Principal Distribution Depot [DoD] .... PDD
Principal DOD Executive (AAGC) .... PDA
Principal DOD [Department of Defense] Executive .... PDE
Principal Duty [Military] .... PDY
Principal Engineer (AAG) .... PE
Principal Error Axis for Position .... PEAP
Principal Error Axis for Velocity .... PEAV
Principal Exchange-Rate-Linked Securities [Investment term] .... PERLS
Principal Executive Officer [Civil Service] [British] .... PEO
Principal Hazardous Constituent (GNE) .... PHC
Principal House Officer [Australia] .... PHO
Principal Industry Activity [IRS] .... PIA
Principal, Interest, Taxes, Energy, and Maintenance [Real estate] .... PITY-EM
Principal, Interest, Taxes, Insurance [Real estate] .... PITI
Principal Investigator (MCD) .... PI
Principal Keeper [Slang for a warden] .... PK
Principal Locating Point [Automotive engineering] .... PLP
Principal Maintenance Inspector (NASA) .... PMI
Principal Matron [Navy British] .... PM
Principal Medical Officer .... PMO
Principal Military Landing Officer (AD) .... PMLO
Principal Military Landing Offices [British] .... PMLO
Principal Musician [Marine Corps] .... PRINMUS
Principal Naval Liaison Officer [British] .... PNLO
Principal Naval Overseer [British] .... PNO
Principal Naval Transport Officer [British military] (DMA) .... PNTO
Principal Neo-Tech, Inc. [Toronto Stock Exchange symbol] .... PNI
Principal Neutralizing Determinant [Immunology] .... PND
Principal Neutralizing Domain [Medicine] .... PND
Principal Nursing Officer .... PNO
Principal of Pedagogy [Academic degree] .... PeP
Principal Officer [Foreign Service] .... PO
Principal Officer of Aircraft Equipment [Ministry of Aircraft Production] [British World War II] .... POAE
Principal Only (DFIT) .... PO
Principal Only Strip [Mortgage security] .... PO
Principal Operating Component .... POC
Principal Operating Component (AD) .... poc
Principal Ordnance Mechanical Engineer [British military] (DMA) .... POME
Principal Organic Hazardous Constituent [Environmental chemistry] .... POHC
Principal Outer Membrane Protein .... POMP
Principal Period of Maintenance (AAGC) .... PPM
Principal Point .... PP
Principal Port Authority [British] (ROG) .... PPA
Principal Priority Officer .... PPO
Principal Private Residence [Income tax] [British] .... PPR
Principal Private Secretary [British] .... PPS
Principal Probate Registry (DLA) .... PPR
Principal Problem Strategy Questionnaire (EDAC) .... PPSQ
Principal Professional and Technology Officer [British] .... PPTO
Principal Profile Forms [Soil classification] .... PPF
Principal Project Designer [Engineering project management] .... PPD
Principal Public Library [Library network] .... PRO
Principal Quality Engineers [British] (RDA) .... PQE
Principal Quantum Number [Atomic physics] (DEN) .... n
Principal Quantum Number [Atomic physics] .... PQN
Principal Regional Office for Asia and the Pacific [UNESCO] .... PROAP
Principal Register [Computer science] .... PR
Principal Responsible Party .... PRP
Principal Roman Catholic Chaplain [Navy British] .... PRCCh
Principal Scientific Officer [British] .... PSO

Principal Sea Transport Officer .... PSTO
Principal Sojourner [Freemasonry] (ROG) .... PS
Principal Staff Element [Defense Supply Agency] .... PSE
Principal Staff Officer [British military] (DMA) .... PSO
Principal Subject [In a sonata or rondo] [Music] (ROG) .... PS
Principal Subordinate Command (NATG) .... PSC
Principal Unit Security Officer (AAG) .... PUSO
Principal Veterinary Officer (ROG) .... PVO
Principal Veterinary Surgeon [British] .... PVS
Principal Visiting Officer [Australia] .... PVO
Principal Welfare Officer [Navy British] .... PWO
Principal Wireless Telegraphy Officer (IAA) .... PWTO
Principality (ROG) .... PRIN
Principally (ROG) .... PRIN
Principe [Principe] [ICAO location identifier] (ICLI) .... FPPR
Principia [Elements] [Latin] (ROG) .... PRIN
Principia College, Elsah, IL [OCLC symbol] (OCLC) .... IBP
Principia College, Elsah, IL [Library symbol Library of Congress] (LCLS) .... IEIsP
Principle (ROG) .... PPLE
Principle (ROG) .... PRIN
Principle (VRA) .... prin
Principle .... PRINC
Principle Directorate of Guided Weapons [British] (SAA) .... PDGW
Principle Management Facility (MCD) .... PMF
Principle of Adding [New math] .... PA
Principle of Limit Design .... PLD
Principle of Multiplying [New math] .... PM
Principle of the Alphabet Literacy System [Software] [IBM Corp.] .... PALS
Principle of the Equivalent Generator .... PEG
Principle Warfare Officer [British] .... PWO
Principles and Applications of Value Engineering .... PAVE
Principles of Adult Learning Scale (EDAC) .... PALS
Principles of Radiation and Contamination Control [Nuclear energy] .... PORACC
Principos Activos [Ministerio de Sanidad y Consumo] [Spain Information service or system] (CRD) .... PACTIV
Prindle Class Association (EA) .... PCA
Prineville, OR [FM radio station call letters] .... KIJK
Prineville, OR [AM radio station call letters] .... KRCO
Prinicipal-Teacher Interaction Study (EDAC) .... PTI
Prins and Conderlag's Reports [Ceylon] [A publication] (ILCA) .... Prins & Conderlag
Prins Christian Sund [Greenland] [ICAO location identifier] (ICLI) .... BGPC
Prins Recycling [NASDAQ symbol] (TTSB) .... PRNS
Prins Recycling Corp. [Associated Press] (SAG) .... PrinsRec
Prins Recycling Corp. [NASDAQ symbol] (SAG) .... PRNS
Prinsburg Public Schools, Prinsburg, MN [Library symbol] [Library of Congress] (LCLS) .... MnPrbPS
Print [Film] [Also, P] (WDMC) .... p
Print .... P
Print [or Printed] (NTCM) .... PR
Print (VRA) .... pr
Print (ECII) .... PR
Print (MSA) .... PRT
Print (MSA) .... PT
Print Active Computer Tables (SAA) .... PACT
Print Advertising Association [Defunct] (EA) .... PAA
Print Alphanumerically [Computer science] (MDG) .... PRA
Print Alphanumerically (AD) .... pra
Print and Advertising [Marketing] (ECON) .... P & A
Print and Drawing Council of Canada [1976] (NGC) .... PDCC
Print and Search Processor [Computer science] .... PANDS
Print Area Reader (DGA) .... PAR
Print Business Opportunities [A publication] (EAAP) .... PBO
Print Club (EA) .... PC
Print Collectors' Club [British] (DBA) .... PCC
Print Command [Computer science] (IAA) .... PC
Print Command Register .... PCR
Print Contrast (DGA) .... PC
Print Contrast Scale (IEEE) .... PCS
Print Contrast Signal [Computer science] .... PCS
Print Contrast System (BUR) .... PCS
Print Control Language (NITA) .... PCL
Print Control Unit (SAA) .... PCU
Print Council of America (EA) .... PCA
Print Cycle [Computer science] (IAA) .... PC
Print Definition Language [Computer science] (EECA) .... PDL
Print Down Module .... PDM
Print Illegal and Trace .... PIT
Print Image (IAA) .... PI
Print Load Analyzer .... PLA
Print Matrix (IAA) .... PM
Print Measurement Bureau [Founded in 1971] [Also the name of a database] [Canada] .... PMB
Print Numerically (DEN) .... PRN
Print Octal (DEN) .... PRO
Print of Curve (IAA) .... PC
Print on Metal (DGA) .... POM
Print Out [Computer science] (IAA) .... PRP
Print Out Effect .... POE
Print Pattern Generator (IAA) .... PPG
Print Position Counter .... PPC
Print Positions .... PP
Print Positions per Line [Computer science] (MHDI) .... PPL
Print Quality Enhancement Technology [IBM] (PCM) .... PQET
Print Quality Improvement [Advanced photo system] .... PQI
Print Quality Monitor [Computer science] (IAA) .... PQM

Print Queue Processor [*Computer science*] ... PQUE
Print Register (IAA) ... PR
Print Restore [*Computer science*] (MHDB) ... PR
Print Scan [*Computer science*] (IAA) ... PS
Print Screen [*Computer keyboard*] ... PrtSc
Print under Glaze [*Ceramics*] ... PUG
Printed [*or Printer*] ... PR
Printed (DGA) ... PRTD
Printed (VRA) ... prtd
Printed ... PTD
Printed and Fired Circuit ... PAF
Printed Board Assembly (IAA) ... PBA
Printed Card (IAA) ... PC
Printed Circuit ... PC
Printed Circuit [*Computer science*] (IAA) ... PRCCT
Printed Circuit (IAA) ... PRINCIR
Printed Circuit Assembly [*Telecommunications*] (TEL) ... PCA
Printed Circuit Board [*Automotive engineering*] ... PC/BRD
Printed Circuit Board (MCD) ... PCB
Printed Circuit Board Assembly (MCD) ... PCBA
Printed Circuit Board Configuration List (MCD) ... PCBCL
Printed Circuit Board Repair (MCD) ... PCBR
Printed Circuit Board Socket ... PCBS
Printed Circuit Card ... PCC
Printed Circuit Conference ... PCC
Printed Circuit Design Interface (NITA) ... PCDI
Printed Circuit Generator ... PCG
Printed Circuit Interconnection Federation [*British*] (DBA) ... PCIF
Printed Circuit Keyboard ... PCK
Printed Circuit Keyboard ... PCKB
Printed Circuit Lamp ... PCL
Printed Circuit Patchboard ... PCP
Printed Circuit Soldering Equipment ... PCSE
Printed Control Unit [*Military*] (GFGA) ... PCU
Printed Information Distribution (SAA) ... PRINFO
Printed Judgments of Sind, by Candy and Birdwood [*India*] [*A publication*] (DLA) ... Candy
Printed Matter Only (AD) ... pmo
Printed Minutes of Evidence [*A publication*] (DLA) ... Pr Min
Printed on Recycled Paoer (AD) ... PORP
Printed Paper Mat Institute (EA) ... PPMI
Printed Paper Rate [*British*] (ILCA) ... PPR
Printed Paper Rate (AD) ... ppr
Printed Planning Parts List ... PPPL
Printed Side Down [*Graphic arts*] (DGA) ... PSD
Printed Side Up [*Graphic arts*] (DGA) ... PSU
Printed Text ... PT
Printed Wire Assembly [*Computer science*] ... PWA
Printed Wiring (MSA) ... PW
Printed Wiring and Electronic Assemblies [*NASA*] ... PWEA
Printed Wiring Board ... PWB
Printed Wiring Board (DOMA) ... PWB
Printed Wiring Board Assembly (MCD) ... PWBA
Printed Wiring Cards [*Telecommunications*] ... PWC
Printed Wiring Laboratory (MCD) ... PWL
Printed Wiring Master ... PWM
Printed Wiring Master Drawing (NASA) ... PWMD
Printed-Circuit Board (IDOE) ... pcb
Printer [*Navy*] ... PI
Printer [*Computer science*] (IAA) ... PR
Printer ... PRINTR
Printer [*Computer science*] ... PRN
Printer ... PRNTR
Printer [*Computer science*] (MDG) ... PRT
Printer [*MARC relator code*] [*Library of Congress*] (LCCP) ... prt
Printer ... PRTR
Printer [*Navy*] (DGA) ... PRTR
Printer (MSA) ... PTR
Printer Access Protocol (BYTE) ... PAP
Printer Action Table [*Computer science*] (HGAA) ... PAT
Printer Command Language [*Hewlett Packard*] [*Computer science*] ... PCL
Printer Communications Adapter ... PCA
Printer Control ... PC
Printer Control ... PRC
Printer Control Language ... PCL
Printer Control Option (SAA) ... PCO
Printer Direction Optimizer (BUR) ... PDO
Printer Driver ... PD
Printer Driver ... PRD
Printer Dump ... PRD
Printer Dump (AD) ... prd
Printer Font ASCII [*Computer science*] (CDE) ... PFA
Printer Font Binary [*Computer science*] (CDE) ... PFB
Printer Font Metrics [*Computer science*] (CDE) ... PFM
Printer Interface Cartridge [*Epson America, Inc.*] ... PIC
Printer Job Language [*Computer science*] ... PJL
Printer, Lithographer [*Navy*] ... PRTRL
Printer, Lithographer, and Multilith Operator [*Navy*] ... PRLTRL & M
Printer of Plates [*MARC relator code*] [*Library of Congress*] (LCCP) ... pop
Printer, Offset Process [*Navy*] ... PRTRM
Printer Output [*Computer science*] (CDE) ... printout
Printer Output Microfilm ... POM
Printer Page [*Computer science*] ... PP
Printer Page Description [*Computer science*] ... PPD
Printer/Plotter (NASA) ... P/P
Printer/Plotter System (MCD) ... PPS
Printer Storage System [*Computer science*] (MHDI) ... PSS
Printer Terminal ... PT
Printer-Emulation Package [*Software*] ... PEP
Printers' Charitable Corp. (DGA) ... PCC
Printers' Costing Association [*British*] (BI) ... PCA
Printer's Devil (ROG) ... PD
Printer's Error ... PE
Printers' Estimating and Costing System (DGA) ... PECS
Printers Integrated Management System (DGA) ... PIMS
Printers' Managers and Overseers Association (AD) ... PM & OA
Printers' Medical Aid and Sanatoria Association [*British*] (BI) ... PMASA
Printers' Pension Corp. (DGA) ... PPC
Printers' Provident Association (DGA) ... PPA
Print-Handicapped Radio, Australian Capital Territory ... PHRACT
Printing (ROG) ... PNTG
Printing (WDMC) ... print
Printing ... PRINTG
Printing (MSA) ... PRNTG
Printing (AFM) ... PRTG
Printing ... PTG
Printing (WDMC) ... ptg
Printing Accountants Club (EA) ... PAC
Printing Advisory and Management Service (DGA) ... PAMS
Printing and Allied Trades Christian Association (DGA) ... PATCA
Printing and Allied Trades Employers' Federation. News [*A publication*] ... PATEFA News
Printing and Binding [*Publishing*] ... P & B
Printing and Information Technology Division (NITA) ... PIT
Printing and Publishing Services, Victoria [*Australia*] ... PPSV
Printing, Bookbinding, and Kindred Trades' Overseers Association [*British*] (BI) ... PBKTOA
Printing Brokerage Association (EA) ... PBA
Printing Character [*Computer science*] ... PCHAR
Printing Control Officer [*Air Force*] (AFM) ... PCO
Printing Corp. of America ... PCA
Printing Cylinder (DGA) ... PC
Printing Cylinder (DGA) ... PTG CYL
Printing Equipment Education Trust [*British*] ... PEET
Printing Estimators and Production Men's Club [*New York, NY*] (EA) ... PEPMC
Printing Executive Register (DGA) ... PER
Printing Historical Society [*British*] ... PHS
Printing House Square (DGA) ... PHS
Printing Impressions [*A publication*] (DGA) ... PI
Printing Industries of America (EA) ... PIA
Printing Industries of Metropolitan New York ... PIMNY
Printing Industry Computer Associates, Inc. ... PICA
Printing Industry Credit Exchange/PIA [*of the Printing Industries of America*] [*Defunct*] (EA) ... PICE/PIA
Printing Industry Institute [*A graphic arts training school*] ... PII
Printing Industry Language for Operations of Typesetting ... PILOT
Printing Industry Management Association (DGA) ... PIMA
Printing Industry Research Association (NADA) ... PIRA
Printing Institute, Philadelphia, PA [*Library symbol Library of Congress Obsolete*] (LCLS) ... PPPrI
Printing Management Information Systems ... PMIS
Printing Mechanism (IAA) ... PM
Printing, Packaging, and Allied Trades Research Association ... PATRA
Printing, Packaging, and Allied Trades Research Association (AD) ... PPATRA
Printing, Paper, and Binding [*Publishing*] (WDMC) ... PPB
Printing Platemakers Association [*Later, GPA*] ... PPA
Printing Request (MCD) ... PR
Printing Resources Management Information System (DNAB) ... PRMIS
Printing Response-Time Monitor ... PRTM
Printing Systems Division (NITA) ... PSD
Printing Technical School (DGA) ... PTS
Printing Trades Alliance [*British*] (DBA) ... PTA
Printing World [*A publication*] (DGA) ... PW
Printing-Out Paper ... POP
Printout ... PO
Printout (MSA) ... PTOUT
Printout Microfilm (NITA) ... POM
Print-Punch [*Computer science*] (BUR) ... PP
Print-Punch Editor [*Computer science*] (SAA) ... PPE
Printronix, Inc. [*Associated Press*] (SAG) ... Prtronx
Printronix, Inc. [*NASDAQ symbol*] (NQ) ... PTNX
Printronix Inc. [*NASDAQ symbol*] (TTSB) ... PTNX
Print-to-Point [*Telecommunications*] (IAA) ... PTP
Prinzmetal's Angina [*Cardiology*] (DAVI) ... PMA
Prioirty Access Timer [*Telecommunications*] (OSI) ... PAT
Prion Protein (DMAA) ... PRNP
Prion Protein [*Biochemistry*] ... PrP
Prior ... PR
Prior Active Air Force Commissioned Service ... PAAFCS
Prior Active Air Force Enlisted Service ... PAAFES
Prior Active Army Commissioned Service ... PAACS
Prior Active Army Enlisted Service ... PAAES
Prior Active Coast Guard Commissioned Service ... PACGCS
Prior Active Coast Guard Enlisted Service ... PACGES
Prior Active Foreign Commissioned Service ... PAFCS
Prior Active Foreign Enlisted Service (DNAB) ... PAFES
Prior Active Marine Corps Commissioned Service ... PAMCCS
Prior Active Marine Corps Enlisted Service ... PAMCES
Prior Active National Guard Commissioned Service ... PANGCS
Prior Active National Guard Enlisted Service ... PANGES

Prior Active Navy Enlisted Service PANES
Prior Endorsement Guaranteed (HGAA) PEG
Prior Fiscal Year (AFIT) PFY
Prior Immobilization and Positioning [*Roentgenology*] PIP
Prior Informed Consent [*For use of pesticides*] PIC
Prior Lien [*Business term*] (MHDW) Pr Ln
Prior Menstrual Period [*Gynecology*] (DAVI) PMP
Prior Notice Required (AD) pnr
Prior Notice Required (AFM) PNR
Prior Operating Budget Year [*Military*] (AFIT) POBY
Prior Other Active Commissioned Service [*Military*] POACS
Prior Other Active Enlisted Service [*Military*] POAES
Prior Permission PP
Prior Permission Only (AFM) PPO
Prior Permission Only (AD) ppo
Prior Permission Required (AD) ppr
Prior Permission Required (FAAC) PPR
Prior Preferred Stock PPS
Prior Quarter Liability [*IRS*] PQL
Prior Record Variable [*Criminal sentencing*] PRV
Prior Service [*Military*] PS
Prior Service Training [*US Army Reserve*] (INF) PST
Prior to Admission [*Medicine*] PA
Prior to Admission [*Medicine*] PTA
Prior to Arrival [*Medicine*] (MAE) PTA
Prior to Birth [*Medicine*] PTB
Prior to Discharge [*Medicine*] (MAE) PTD
Prior to Expiration of Term of Service [*Reenlistments*] [*Military*] PETS
Prior to Overseas Movement [*DoD*] POM
Prior to Program [*Medicine*] (MAE) PTP
Prior to Surgery (DAVI) PTS
Prior Treatment [*Medicine*] PT
Prior Year (AABC) PY
Prior Year Notice [*IRS*] PYNC
Prior Year Overhead (AAGC) PYO
Prior Year Refund Information File [*IRS*] PRIF
Prior Year Report PYR
Prior Year's Return [*IRS*] PYR
Priorities Allotment Board PAB
Priorities and Allocations (MUGU) P & A
Priorities and Allocations Manual [*Army*] (AABC) PAM
Priorities Exploitation Group PEG
Priorities for ELINT Guidance (MCD) PEG
Priorities in School Mathematics Project (EDAC) PRISM
Priority [*Telecommunications*] (TEL) P
Priority (AFM) PRI
Priority [*Telecommunications*] PRIO
Priority PRTY
Priority A (MCD) PA
Priority Abatement Areas [*Environment*] (GNE) PAA
Priority Access Control Enabled [*Telecommunications*] PACE
Priority Action Report (AAG) PAR
Priority Action Request (AAG) PAR
Priority Activities in Cancer Education PACE
Priority Admission to Nursery Schools (AIE) PANS
Priority Aggregate PA
Priority Air Transport [*Army*] (FAAC) PAT
Priority Air Travel [*Army*] PAT
Priority Aircraft Subsystem Suitability Intensive Review (MCD) PASS-IN-REVIEW
Priority Area Children (AIE) PAC
Priority Assignment Base (MCD) PAB
Priority Aviation Co., Inc. [*ICAO designator*] (FAAC) BCK
Priority Baggage (DNAB) PRIBAG
Priority Based Assessment of Foot Additives [*Medicine*] (DMAA) PAFA
Priority Data Reduction PDR
Priority Decision System (NITA) PDS
Priority Defense Items Information System PDIIS
Priority Delayed Weather [*NWS*] (FAAC) PDW
Priority Delivery Date (AFM) PDD
Priority Delivery Date/Required Delivery Date (AFM) PDD/RDD
Priority Designator [*Army*] PD
Priority Directive PD
Priority Disassembly and Inspection Report PDIR
Priority Distribution System [*Military*] (AFM) PDS
Priority Energy Policy [*Environmental Protection Agency*] PEP
Priority for Allocation/Application of COMSEC Equipment Resources (MCD) PACER
Priority Foreign Country [*International trade*] (ECON) PFC
Priority Group PG
Priority Improved Management Effort (KSC) PRIME
Priority Improvement Effort [*DoD*] PRIME
Priority Improvement Management Effort Base Engineering Emergency Force [*Air Force*] (DOMA) PRIME BEEF
Priority Improvement Management Effort Readiness in Base Services [*Air Force*] (DOMA) PRIME RIBS
Priority Information Requirement [*Military intelligence*] (INF) PIR
Priority Intelligence Requirement [*Military*] (INF) PIR
Priority Interrupt (IEEE) PI
Priority Interrupt Control Unit [*Computer science*] (MDG) PICU
Priority Interrupt Controller PIC
Priority Low-Use Minimal PLUM
Priority Management Effort [*Army*] PRIME
Priority Management Evaluation [*Navy*] PRIME
Priority Memory Access PMA
Priority Memory Address (NITA) PMA
Priority Message Precedence [*Telecommunications*] (ADDR) PP
Priority Monitor Report PMR
Priority National Intelligence Estimate [*CIA*] (LAIN) PNIE
Priority National Intelligence Objectives (MCD) PNIO
Priority Network In-Dial / Network Out-Dial (DNAB) PNID/NOD
Priority of Fire [*Military*] (INF) POF
Priority of Movements [*Military British*] POM
Priority Operational Objective [*Military*] POO
Priority Order Output System [*Japan*] (DIT) POOS
Priority Oriented Demand Assignment [*Computer science Telecommunications*] PODA
Priority Output Writers Execution Processor [*Computer science*] (IAA) POWER
Priority Output Writers, Execution Processors, and Input Readers (MHDI) POWER
Priority Output Writes Execution Process [*Computer science*] (IAA) POWER
Priority Parts Quality Review PPQR
Priority Placement Certificate [*Military*] (AFM) PPC
Priority Placement Program (DOMA) PPP
Priority Problem Analysis Report [*Military*] (DNAB) PPAR
Priority Problem Areas (MCD) PPA
Priority Processor PP
Priority Rate Limiting (MCD) PRL
Priority Receiving with Inter-Departmental Efficiency [*Computer science*] PRIDE
Priority Reconnaissance Exploitation List (CINC) PREL
Priority Regular World Day PRWD
Priority Regulation PR
Priority Repair Induction [*Code*] PRI
Priority Requirement for Information (AFM) PRI
Priority Requirement Objective List (AFM) PROL
Priority Research Objectives for Vietnam Operations Support PROVOST
Priority Resolver PR
Priority Routine Organizer for Computer Transfers and Operations and Transfers PROCTOT
Priority Routine Organizer for Computer Transfers and Operations of Registers PROCTOR
Priority Selection Table [*Computer science*] (IBMDP) PST
Priority Selection Table Extension [*Computer science*] (IBMDP) PST-E
Priority Specific Air Information Request [*Defense Mapping Agency*] (MCD) PSAIR
Priority Standardization Effort [*Army*] (AABC) PSE
Priority Strike Program PSP
Priority System Change Request PSCR
Priority Telegram PT
Priority Ventures [*Vancouver Stock Exchange symbol*] PVS
Prior-Lien Bond [*Business*] (MHDB) PLB
Prior-Participating Preferred [*Stock*] (MHDW) PPP
Priory P
Priory PR
Priory Cell PRC
Priscianus [*Authority cited in pre-1607 legal work*] (DSA) Pri
Priscilla Presley Fan Club [*Defunct*] (EA) PPFC
Prism PR
Prism (MSA) PSM
Prism Adaptation Test [*Ophthalmology*] PAT
Prism and Cover (Test) [*Ophthalmology*] P & C
Prism Cover Test [*Ophthalmology*] (CPH) PCT
Prism Diopter PD
Prism Entertainment [*AMEX symbol*] (TTSB) PRZ
Prism Entertainment Corp. [*Associated Press*] (SAG) PrismEnt
Prism Entertainment Corp. [*AMEX symbol*] (SPSG) PRZ
Prism Group [*Associated Press*] (SAG) Prism
Prism Group [*NASDAQ symbol*] (SAG) PRSM
Prism Group [*NASDAQ symbol*] (TTSB) PRSMC
PRISM [*Personnel Record Information System for Management*] **Information RetrievalLanguage** [*Computer science*] (PDAA) PIRL
Prism Resources Ltd. [*Vancouver Stock Exchange symbol*] PRR
Prism Solutions [*Associated Press*] (SAG) PrismS
Prism Solutions [*NASDAQ symbol*] (SAG) PRZM
Prism Solutions [*NASDAQ symbol*] (TTSB) PRZM
Prismacolor (VRA) prsmc
Prismatic Coefficient [*Boat design*] Cp
Prismatic Joint (IAA) P
Prismatic Tank [*Liquid gas carriers*] pr
Prism-Mirror-Prism [*For electron microscopy*] PMP
Prison PRI
Prison (ROG) PRIS
Prison Atheist League of America (EA) PALA
Prison Commission [*British*] PRICOM
Prison Families Anonymous (EA) PFA
Prison Fellowship International (EA) PFI
Prison Fellowship Ministries (EA) PF
Prison Fellowship Ministries (EA) PFM
Prison Fellowship of Australia PFA
Prison Industries [*Industries conducted in English prisons*] PRINDUS
Prison Industries Reorganization Administration [*Terminated, 1940*] PIRA
Prison Law Reporter [*A publication*] (ILCA) Prison L Reptr
Prison Law Reporter [*A publication*] (DLA) Prison L Rptr
Prison Mission Association (EA) PMA
Prison Officers' Association [*A union*] [*British*] (DCTA) POA
Prison Officer's Club (AD) POC
Prison Pen Pals (EA) PPP
Prison Research Education Action Project (EA) PREAP
Prison Service Establishment (AIE) PSE

Prison Service Journal [*A publication*] (DLA) ... Prison Serv J
Prison Ship [*Navy symbol*] (DNAB) ... YWN
Prison Visitors' Association (NADA) ... PVA
Prison Wardens Association (NADA) ... PWA
Prison-Acquired Lymphoproliferative Syndrome [*Medicine*] (DMAA) ... PALS
Prison-Ashram Project (EA) ... PAP
Prisoner [*Military*] ... P
Prisoner ... PNR
Prisoner (AFM) ... PRIS
Prisoner Aid and Rehabilitation Society (NADA) ... PARS
Prisoner Detention System ... PDS
Prisoner identification number assigned to Oscar Wilde in Reading Gaol [*Used as pseudonym*] ... C33
Prisoner of Conscience (BJA) ... PC
Prisoner of Mother England [*Nineteenth-century convict in penal colony of Australia, now a nickname for any Australian*] ... POME
Prisoner of War [*Also, PW*] ... POW
Prisoner of War (AD) ... pow
Prisoner of War [*Also, POW*] ... PW
Prisoner of War Cage ... PWC
Prisoner of War Camp ... PWC
Prisoner of War/Civilian Internees/Detainees (MCD) ... PW/CI/DET
Prisoner of War Command ... PWC
Prisoner of War Compound ... PWC
Prisoner of War Enclosure ... PWE
Prisoner of War Information Bureau [*Post-World War II*] ... PWIB
Prisoner of War Information Center (DOMA) ... PWIC
Prisoner of War Information System (DOMA) ... PWIS
Prisoner of War Interrogation ... PWI
Prisoner of War of Japan ... POW(J)
Prisoner of Watergate (AD) ... P o W
Prisoner of Zion (BJA) ... PZ
Prisoner under Detention (ADA) ... PUD
Prisoner-at-Large ... PAL
Prisoner-Initiated Review ... PIR
Prisoners Accelerated Creative Exposure [*An association*] ... PACE
Prisoners' Aid Association of New South Wales [*Australia*] ... PAANSW
Prisoners' Aid Society [*Australia*] ... PAS
Prisoners' Barracks (ADA) ... PB
Prisoner's Dilemma [*Psychology*] ... PD
Prisoners of Conscience [*File of persons imprisoned for political or religious beliefs kept by Amnesty International*] ... POC
Prisoners of War and Displaced Persons Directorate [*Allied German Occupation Forces*] ... DPOW
Prisoners of War Executive [*Branch of SHAEF*] [*World War II*] ... PWX
Prisoners' Right of Privacy [*British*] (DI) ... PROP
Prisoner's Rights Union (EA) ... PRU
Prisoner's Union [*Later, PRU*] (EA) ... PU
Prisonnier de Guerre [*Prisoner of War - POW*] [*French*] ... PG
Pristane [*Organic chemistry*] ... Pr
Pristane/Phytane Ratio [*Environmental science*] ... Pr/Ph
Pristina [*Former Yugoslavia*] [*ICAO location identifier*] (ICLI) ... LYPR
Pristina [*Former Yugoslavia*] [*Airport symbol*] (OAG) ... PRN
Pritchard, BC [*Television station call letters*] (RBYB) ... CHKM-1
Pritchard's Admiralty Digest [*3rd ed.*] [*1887*] [*A publication*] (DLA) ... Pr Adm Dig
Pritchard's Admiralty Digest [*3rd ed.*] [*1887*] [*A publication*] (DLA) ... Pritch Adm Dig
Pritchard's Divorce and Matrimonial Causes [*3rd ed.*] [*1874*] [*A publication*] (DLA) ... Pritch M & D
Pritchard's Quarter Sessions [*A publication*] (DLA) ... Pritch Quar Sess
Pritikin Health Association of Australia ... PHA
Privacy Act ... PA
Privacy Act (MCD) ... PVA
Privacy Act Coordinator [*Navy*] (DNAB) ... PAC
Privacy Act Statement (NRCH) ... PAS
Privacy Commission ... PC
Privacy Protection Study Commission [*Government commission*] ... PPSC
Privacy-Enhanced Mail [*Software package*] ... PEM
Privatdozent [*Tutor*] [*German*] ... PD
Private [*Marine Corps*] ... E1
Private ... P
Private (DLA) ... pr
Private ... PRI
Private ... PRIV
Private (ROG) ... PRIVE
Private [*British military*] (DMA) ... Prt
Private (VRA) ... prv
Private [*British*] ... PTE
Private [*Military*] (AFM) ... PVT
Private (DD) ... Pvt
Private ... PVT
Private ... PVTE
Private 2 [*Army*] ... E2
Private Access to Court Electronic Records (AAGC) ... PACER
Private Account [*Banking*] ... PA
Private Activity Bond (AAGC) ... PAB
Private Acts of the State of Tennessee [*A publication*] (DLA) ... Tenn Priv Acts
Private Agencies Collaborating Together (EA) ... PACT
Private Aircraft Inspection Reporting System (PDAA) ... PAIRS
Private Aircraft Reporting System [*FAA*] (PDAA) ... PARS
Private Alarm Signalling System ... PASS
Private and Executive Secretary's Diploma (AIE) ... PESD
Private and Local Laws [*A publication*] (DLA) ... P & L Laws
Private and Special Laws [*A publication*] (DLA) ... Sp St
Private Architect [*British*] ... PA
Private Automatic Branch Exchange [*Telecommunications*] (DEN) ... PABX
Private Automatic Computer Exchange [*Telecommunications*] ... PACX
Private Automatic Exchange [*Telecommunications*] ... PAX
Private Automatic Loudspeaking Exchange [*Telecommunications*] (IAA) ... PALX
Private Automatic Switching System [*Telecommunications*] ... PASS
Private Automatic Telegraph Branch Exchange [*Telecommunications*] ... PATBX
Private Automatic Telegraph Exchange (PDAA) ... PATX
Private Automatic Telex Branch Exchange (NITA) ... PATBX
Private Automatic Telex Exchange (NITA) ... PATX
Private Boxes and Bags ... PBB
Private Branch Exchange [*Telecommunications*] ... PBX
Private Branch Exchange Final Selector [*Telecommunications*] (IAA) ... PBXFS
Private Brand Proneness [*Marketing*] ... PBP
Private Business [*Slang British*] ... PB
Private Businesses Association of Australia ... PBAA
Private Carrier Conference [*of ATA*] (EA) ... PCC
Private Channel Television ... PCTV
Private Child Care Provider (EDAC) ... PCCP
Private Circuit Control Module [*Telecommunications*] (TEL) ... PCCM
Private Circuit Digital Data Service [*Telecommunications*] (TEL) ... PCDDS
Private Circuit-Switching Network [*Telecommunications*] (OSI) ... PCSN
Private Citizen, Inc. [*An association*] (EA) ... PCI
Private Collection (VRA) ... prv coll
Private College Admissions Center [*Later, NAAPHE*] ... PCAC
Private Communications Association [*Later, NCA*] ... PCA
Private Communications Technology [*Microsoft Corp.*] [*Computer science*] ... PCT
Private Communications Technology [*Computer science*] ... PCT
Private Companies Practice Section ... PCPS
Private Concerns [*An association Defunct*] (EA) ... PC
Private Contract [*Tea trade*] (ROG) ... PC
Private Corporation ... PC
Private Database Service (NITA) ... PDS
Private Detective ... PD
Private Development Corp. of the Philippines ... PDCP
Private Diagnostic Clinic ... PDC
Private Digital Exchange ... PDX
Private Doctors of America [*Defunct*] (EA) ... PDA
Private Doctors' Society of South Australia ... PDSA
Private Duty Nurse (DAVI) ... PDN
Private E-1 [*Army*] ... PV1
Private E-2 [*Army*] ... PV2
Private Electronic Exchange [*Telecommunications*] (IAA) ... PEX
Private Employment Agency (OICC) ... PEA
Private Examination (WDAA) ... PX
Private Exchange (IAA) ... PRIVX
Private Exchange ... PX
Private Export Funding Corp. (IMH) ... PEFC
Private Export Funding Corp. ... PEFCO
Private Express Statutes (DICI) ... PES
Private Eye Writers of America [*An association*] ... PWA
Private Finance Initiative [*British*] ... PFI
Private First Class [*Marine Corps*] ... E2
Private First Class [*Army*] ... E3
Private, First Class [*Army*] ... PFC
Private Forestry Association of Tasmania [*Australia*] ... PFAT
Private Forestry Council [*Australia*] ... PFC
Private Grocers' Merchandising Association [*British*] (BI) ... PGMA
Private Health Plan Option [*Medicare*] (GFGA) ... PHPO
Private Hospital Supplementary Charges (ADA) ... PHSC
Private Hospitals' Association of Queensland [*Australia*] ... PHAQ
Private Hospitals' Association of Victoria [*Australia*] ... PHAV
Private Hospitals' Association of Western Australia ... PHAWA
Private Hotel ... PH
Private Housing Finance [*A publication*] (DLA) ... Priv Hous Fin
Private Industry Council [*Generic term for group that helps provide job training*] ... PIC
Private Input/Output [*Telecommunications*] (TEL) ... PIO
Private Institution [*British*] ... PI
Private Intelligent Networker (NITA) ... PIN
Private International Law [*A publication*] (DLA) ... Int Private Law
Private Investigator ... PI
Private Investment Co. for Asia SA ... PICA
Private Islands Unlimited (EA) ... PIU
Private Jet Expeditions, Inc. [*ICAO designator*] (FAAC) ... PJE
Private Jet Services AG [*Sweden ICAO designator*] (ICDA) ... PP
Private Label [*Business term*] ... PL
Private Label Manufacturers Association (EA) ... PLMA
Private Label Merchandiser [*USCG*] (TAG) ... PLM
Private Legislation Reports [*Scotland*] [*A publication*] (DLA) ... PLR
Private Libraries Association [*British*] ... PLA
Private Line ... PL
Private Line Assured Service [*Telecommunications*] (TEL) ... PLAS
Private Line Carrier [*Telecommunications*] (IAA) ... PLC
Private Line Carrier Divided Ringing [*Telecommunications*] (IAA) ... PLCDR
Private Line Interface ... PLI
Private Line Service ... PLS
Private Line Telephone ... PLF
Private Line Telephone ... PLT
Private Line Teletypewriter ... PLT
Private Line Teletypewriter [*Telecommunications*] (IAA) ... PLTTY
Private Line Teletypewriter Service [*Telecommunications*] (TEL) ... PLITTY
Private Line Teletypewriter Service (NITA) ... PLTTY
Private Local Area Network [*Racal LAN Systems, Inc.*] [*Boca Raton, FL*] (TSSD) ... PLANET
Private Mail Bag ... PMB

Private Mailing Card [*Deltiology*] .... PMC
Private Management Domain [*Computer science*] (TNIG) .... PMD
Private Management Domain [*Telecommunications*] (OSI) .... PRMD
Private Manual Branch Exchange [*Communications*] .... PMBX
Private Manual Branch Exchange (AD) .... pmbx
Private Manual Exchange (AD) .... pmx
Private Manual Exchange .... PMX
Private Market Value [*Investment term*] (DFIT) .... PMV
Private Medical Communication .... PMC
Private Medical Doctor (DAVI) .... PMD
Private Message Switching [*Telecommunications British*] .... PRIMEX
Private Meter Check [*Telecommunications*] (TEL) .... PMC
Private Microwave [*System*] .... PMW
Private Mortgage Insurance [*Insurance of mortgages by private insurers*] .... PMI
Private Mortgage Insurance (AD) .... pmi
Private Motor Vehicle (DNAB) .... PMV
Private Network Communication Systems (MCD) .... PNCS
Private New Capital Expenditure .... PNCE
Private Non-Profit .... PNP
Private Office [*Documents issued by the Secretary General, NATO*] (NATG) .... PO
Private Packet Exchange .... PPX
Private Parliamentary Secretary [*British*] (AD) .... pps
Private Passenger .... P/P
Private Patient [*Medicine*] .... PP
Private Patient [*Medicine*] (DMAA) .... PVT
Private Patients' Plan [*British*] .... PPP
Private Physician .... PMd
Private Pilot's Licence [*British*] .... PPL
Private Pilot's Licence/Helicopters [*British*] (AIA) .... PPL/H
Private Planning Association of Canada .... PPAC
Private Plants and Naval Activities .... PP & NA
Private Posting Box .... PPB
Private Practice [*Chiropody*] [*British*] .... PP
Private Practice Dental Delivery System .... PPDDS
Private Practice Section [*American Physical Therapy Association*] (EA) .... PPS
Private Property [*Military*] .... PP
Private Property (AD) .... pp
Private Property [*Military*] (DNAB) .... PRIV PROP
Private Proprietary Homes for Adults .... PPHA
Private Purchasing Tariff [*British*] .... PPT
Private Radio Bureau [*FCC*] (NTCM) .... PRB
Private Road [*Maps and charts*] [*British*] (ROG) .... PR
Private Satellite Network, Inc. [*New York, NY*] [*Telecommunications*] (TSSD) .... PSN
Private Schools Association [*British*] .... PSA
Private Screenings [*Cable TV programming service*] .... PS
Private Secretary .... PS
Private Secretary to the King [*British*] .... PSK
Private Secretary's Certificate [*British*] (DI) .... PSC
Private Sector Adjustment Factor [*Banking*] .... PSAF
Private Sector Council (EA) .... PSC
Private Sector Initiative Program [*Department of Labor*] .... PSIP
Private Sector Liquidity .... PSL
Private Security Advisory Council [*Terminated, 1977*] [*Department of Justice*] (EGAO) .... PSAC
Private Security Liaison Council (EA) .... PSLC
Private Security Program [*Association of Independent Colleges and Schools specialization code*] .... PS
Private Siding [*Rail*] [*Shipping*] (DS) .... PS
Private Siding and Collected One End .... PS & C
Private Siding and Delivered One End .... PS & D
Private Siding to Private Siding .... PS to PS
Private Siding to Station .... PS to S
Private Source Funds (DNAB) .... PSF
Private Statutes [*Legal term*] (DLA) .... Pr Stat
Private Switching Network Service [*Telecommunications*] .... PRISNET
Private Telecommunication Network [*Telecommunications*] (OSI) .... PTN
Private Telecommunication Network Exchange [*Telecommunications*] (OSI) .... PTNX
Private Telecommunications Systems [*Radio-Suisse Ltd.*] [*Switzerland Telecommunications*] .... PTS
Private Telegraph and Telephone Service [*Telecommunications*] (IAA) .... PTTS
Private Terms .... PT
Private Tombs at Thebes [*Oxford*] [*A publication*] (BJA) .... PTT
Private Trade Entity .... PTE
Private Training College for the Disabled (AIE) .... PTCD
Private Treaty Wool Merchants' Association of South Australia .... PTWMASA
Private Treaty Wool Merchants' Association of Victoria [*Australia*] .... PTWMAV
Private Treaty Wool Merchants' Association of Western Australia .... PTWMAWA
Private Truck Council of America (EA) .... PTCA
Private Trust [*Includes testamentary, investment, life insurance, holding title, etc.*] [*Legal term*] (DLA) .... P
Private Trust [*Includes testamentary, investment, life insurance, holding title, etc.*] [*Legal term*] (DLA) .... P Tr
Private Varnish [*Privately owned railroad cars*] .... PV
Private Venture .... P
Private Viewdata System [*Computer science*] .... PVS
Private Virtual Circuit [*Telecommunications*] .... PVC
Private Voluntary Organization .... PVO
Private Wagon Federation [*British*] (DBA) .... PWF
Private Wine Buyers' Society [*British*] (BI) .... PWB
Private Wire (NATG) .... PW
Private Wire Service .... PWS
Private Wire System (AAG) .... PWS
Private Write Area [*NASA*] (NASA) .... PWA
Privatefoeretagarnas Partioganisation i Finland [*Finnish Private Entrepreneurs' Party*] [*Political party*] (PPE) .... PPF
Private-Label and Generic Brands .... PLG
Privately Bonded .... PB
Privately Developed Item (AAGC) .... PDI
Privately Financed Consumption (MHDW) .... PFC
Privately Maintained [*Nautical charts*] .... Priv Maintd
Privately Owned (AFM) .... PO
Privately Owned Automobile .... POA
Privately Owned Conveyance [*Army*] .... POC
Privately Owned Conveyance (AD) .... poc
Privately Owned Firearm (MCD) .... POF
Privately Owned/Government Operated (GFGA) .... POGO
Privately Owned Motor Vehicle (NATG) .... POMV
Privately Owned Vehicle (NVT) .... POV
Privately Owned Vehicle (AD) .... pov
Privately Printed (AD) .... pp
Privately Printed (WDMC) .... pp
Privately Printed .... PP
Privately-Owned Open Air-Braked [*Railway wagons*] (PDAA) .... POA
Privately-Owned Sewage Treatment Facility .... PSTF
Private-Sector Development (ECON) .... PSD
Privative .... PRIV
Privatization Council [*New York, NY*] (EA) .... PC
Privatization Investment Fund Trust Units [*Toronto Stock Exchange symbol*] .... PIF
Priviledged Information (SAA) .... PI
Privilege .... PRIV
Privilege Car [*on a train*] [*Theatre slang*] .... PC
Privileged Architecture Library Code .... PAL
Privileged Character [*A favored student*] [*Teen slang*] .... PC
Privileges and Elections Subcommittee [*US Senate*] .... P & E
Privileges and Immunities [*Legal shorthand*] (LWAP) .... P & I
Privilegia Londini [*A publication*] (DLA) .... Priv Lond
Privy (ROG) .... P
Privy Council [*or Councillor*] [*British*] .... PC
Privy Council Appeals [*England*] [*A publication*] (DLA) .... Priv C App
Privy Council Appeals [*England*] [*A publication*] (DLA) .... Priv Counc App
Privy Council Cases [*British*] .... PCC
Privy Council Decisions [*India*] [*A publication*] (DLA) .... PCI
Privy Council Decisions [*India*] [*A publication*] (DLA) .... Priv Counc DI
Privy Council Judgments [*India*] [*A publication*] (DLA) .... PC Judg
Privy Council Judgments [*1829-69*] [*India*] [*A publication*] (DLA) .... Pershad
Privy Council Office [*British*] .... PCO
Privy Council Reports [*A publication*] (DLA) .... P Cl R
Privy Councillor (Canada) .... PC(C)
Privy Councillor, England (ROG) .... PCE
Privy Councillor, Ireland (ROG) .... PCI
Privy Seal [*British*] .... PS
Prix de Cession de Base [*Basic Wholesale Price*] [*French*] .... PCB
Prize [*or Prizeman*] [*British*] (ROG) .... PRI
Prize Cases [*1914-22*] [*England*] [*A publication*] (DLA) .... P Cas
Prize Cases [*A publication*] (DLA) .... Pr C
Prize Cases (Trehearn and Grant) [*England*] [*A publication*] (DLA) .... P Cas
Prize Court (DLA) .... PC
Prize Court Reports [*South Africa*] [*A publication*] (DLA) .... Prize CR
Prize Money .... PM
Prize Ring [*Boxing*] .... PR
Prizes and Awards Committee (ACII) .... P&A
Prizzi [*Italy ICAO location identifier*] (ICLI) LICX
Pro [*For*] [*Latin*] .... P
Pro Air Service [*ICAO designator*] (FAAC) .... PSZ
Pro Anno [*For the Year*] [*Latin*] .... PA
Pro Applicatione [*To Be Applied*] [*Pharmacy*] (ROG) .... PA
Pro Archia [*of Cicero*] [*Classical studies*] (OCD) .... Arch
Pro Athletes Outreach (EA) .... PAO
Pro Balbo [*of Cicero*] [*Classical studies*] (OCD) .... Balb
Pro Caecina [*of Cicero*] [*Classical studies*] (OCD) .... Caecin
Pro Caelio [*of Cicero*] [*Classical studies*] (OCD) .... Cael
Pro Capillis [*For the Hair*] [*Pharmacy*] .... PRO CAPILL
Pro Cluentio [*of Cicero*] [*Classical studies*] (OCD) .... Clu
Pro Computer Services (NITA) .... PCS
Pro Cornelio de Maiestate [*of Cicero*] [*Classical studies*] (OCD) .... Corn
Pro Defendente [*On Behalf of Defendant*] [*Latin Legal term*] (DLA) .... pd
Pro Dose [*For a Dose*] [*Pharmacy*] .... PRO DOS
Pro Ecclesia Foundation (EA) .... PEF
Pro Female [*International Bowhunting Organization*] [*Class Equipment*] .... PF
Pro Flacco [*of Cicero*] [*Classical studies*] (OCD) .... Flac
Pro Fonteio [*of Cicero*] [*Classical studies*] (OCD) .... Font
Pro Forma [*As a Matter of Form*] [*Latin*] (WGA) .... pf
Pro Grand Master [*Freemasonry*] .... PRO GM
Pro Haec Vice [*For This Turn*] [*Latin*] (ROG) .... PHV
Pro Independence Movement [*Puerto Rico*] .... PIM
Pro Ligario [*of Cicero*] [*Classical studies*] (OCD) .... Lig
Pro Loco et Tempore [*For the Place and Time*] [*Latin*] (ROG) .... PRO LOC et TEM
Pro Male Fingers [*International Bowhunting Organization*] [*Class equipment*] .... PMF
Pro Male Release [*International Bowhunting Organization*] [*Class equipment*] .... PMR
Pro Marcello [*of Cicero*] [*Classical studies*] (OCD) .... Marcell
Pro Maria Committee (EA) .... PMC
Pro Media Foundation (EA) .... PMF
Pro Memoria [*In Remembrance*] [*Latin*] .... PM
Pro Mense [*Per Month*] [*Latin*] .... PM
Pro Mille [*Per Thousand*] [*Latin*] .... PM

Pro Milone [*of Cicero*] [*Classical studies*] (OCD) ..... Mil
Pro Mundi Vita [*Brussels, Belgium*] [*Defunct*] (EAIO) ..... PMV
Pro Murena [*of Cicero*] [*Classical studies*] (OCD) ..... Mur
Pro Musica [*Record label*] ..... APM
Pro Parte [*In Part*] [*Latin*] ..... pp
Pro Plancio [*of Cicero*] [*Classical studies*] (OCD) ..... Planc
Pro Querente [*For the Plaintiff*] [*Latin Legal term*] (DLA) ..... pq
Pro Querente [*For the Plaintiff*] [*Latin*] (ILCA) ..... Pro Quer
Pro Quinctio [*of Cicero*] [*Classical studies*] (OCD) ..... Quinct
Pro Rabirio Postumo [*of Cicero*] [*Classical studies*] (OCD) ..... Rab Post
Pro Rata ..... PR
Pro Rata Aetatis [*According to Age*] [*Pharmacy*] ..... P RAT AETAT
Pro Rate Distribution [*Clause*] [*Insurance*] ..... PRD
Pro Ratione Aetatis [*According to Age*] [*Pharmacy*] (ROG) ..... P RAT AET
Pro Ratione Aetatis [*In Proportion to Age*] [*Latin*] (AD) ..... p rat aet
Pro Ratione Aetatis [*In Proportion to Age*] [*Latin*] (MAE) ..... p rat aetat
Pro Ratione Aetatis [*According to Age*] [*Pharmacy*] ..... PRO RAT AET
Pro Re Nata [*Whenever Necessary*] [*Pharmacy*] ..... PRN
Pro Recto [*Rectal*] [*Pharmacy*] ..... PRO RECT
pro recto [*By rectum*] [*Latin*] [*Pharmacy*] (DAVI) ..... pro rect
Pro Rege Deiotaro [*of Cicero*] [*Classical studies*] (OCD) ..... Deiot
Pro Roscio Comoedo [*of Cicero*] [*Classical studies*] (OCD) ..... QRosc
Pro Sanctity Movement (EA) ..... PSM
Pro Scauro [*of Cicero*] [*Classical studies*] (OCD) ..... Scaur
Pro Seniors [*International Bowhunting Organization*] [*Class Equipment*] ..... PSR
Pro Sestio [*of Cicero*] [*Classical studies*] (OCD) ..... Sest
Pro Sexto Roscio Amerino [*of Cicero*] [*Classical studies*] (OCD) ..... Rosc Am
Pro Sight Technology ..... PST
PRO Specification (NITA) ..... PROSPEC
Pro Stock Owners Association (EA) ..... PSOA
Pro Sulla [*of Cicero*] [*Classical studies*] (OCD) ..... Sull
Pro Tempore [*For the Time Being*] [*Latin*] ..... PRO TEM
Pro Tempore [*For the Time Being*] [*Latin*] ..... PT
Pro Tempore et Loco [*For the Time and Place*] [*Latin*] (ROG) ..... PRO TEM et LOC
Pro Usu Externo [*For External Use*] [*Pharmacy*] ..... PRO US EXT
Proactinium (IDOE) ..... Pa
Proactivator [*Medicine*] ..... PA
Proactive Inhibition [*Psychology*] ..... PI
Proactive Interference (EDAC) ..... PI
Proactive Rehabilitation of Outside Plant Using Heuristic Expert Techniques [*GTE computer software*] ..... PROPHET
ProActive Technologies, Inc. [*Associated Press*] (SAG) ..... ProActiv
ProActive Technologies, Inc. [*AMEX symbol*] (SAG) ..... PTE
Proactive TMDE Support (RDA) ..... PTS
Pro-Active World Suspension [*Automotive engineering*] ..... PAWS
ProAir Services [*ICAO designator*] (AD) ..... SZ
Pro-Am Bowfishing Association ..... PABA
Pro-American Forum [*Defunct*] (EA) ..... PAF
Proanthocyanidin (Assay) [*Analytical chemistry*] ..... PA
Probabilistic Analysis of Risk (KSC) ..... PAR
Probabilistic Automatic Pattern Analyzer [*Computer science*] ..... PAPA
Probabilistic Budgeting and Forward Costing (MCD) ..... POBCOST
Probabilistic Budgeting and Forward Costing ..... PROBCOST
Probabilistic Decision Algorithm [*Artificial intelligence job performance aid*] [*Army*] ..... PDA
Probabilistic Information Processing ..... PIP
Probabilistic Materials System (PDAA) ..... PROMATS
Probabilistic Potential Theory (PDAA) ..... PPT
Probabilistic Risk Assessment [*Computer-based technique for accident prediction*] ..... PR
Probabilistic Risk Assessment [*Computer-based technique for accident prediction*] ..... PRA
Probabilistic Safety Analysis (NRCH) ..... PSA
Probabilistic Safety Study [*Nuclear energy*] (NRCH) ..... PSS
Probabilities Recall Optimizing the Employment of Calibration Time (KSC) ..... PROTECT
Probability [*or Probability Ratio*] [*Statistics*] ..... P
Probability (PCM) ..... Pb
Probability [*NWS*] (FAAC) ..... PRBLTY
Probability (KSC) ..... PROB
Probability 40 Percent [*ICAO*] (FAAC) PROB40
Probability Based Matching and Self-Trained Interpretive and Retrieval Systems [*Database*] [*John Wiley & Sons, Inc.*] [*Information service or system*] (CRD) ..... PBM/STIRS
Probability Based-Matched [*Database search techniques*] ..... PBM
Probability Density [*Statistics*] (IAA) ..... PD
Probability Density Distribution [*Statistics*] ..... PDD
Probability Density Function [*Statistics*] ..... PDF
Probability Discrete Automata (IEEE) ..... PDA
Probability Distribution Analyzer [*Statistics*] ..... PDA
Probability Distribution Function [*Statistics*] ..... PDF
Probability Distribution Subprogram [*Computer science*] (BUR) ..... PDS
Probability Forecasting [*Computer program*] [*Bell System*] ..... PROBFOR
Probability Mass Function (IAA) ..... PMF
Probability of a Kill Given a Hit [*Military*] (DNAB) ..... PKH
Probability of Acceptance (KSC) ..... PA
Probability of Acceptance ..... P(ACC)
Probability of Acceptance (IAA) ..... POA
Probability of Acquisition [*Military*] ..... PA
Probability of Acquisition [*Military*] ..... PACQI
Probability of Command Shutdown (MCD) ..... PCS
Probability of Consequence Factor ..... PCF
Probability of Correct Selection [*Statistics*] ..... PCS
Probability of Crew Survival (AAG) ..... PCS
Probability of Damage (MCD) ..... PD
Probability of Death [*Biology*] ..... PD
Probability of Detection ..... PD
Probability of Detection (USDC) ..... POD
Probability of Detection (AD) ..... pod
Probability of Detection [*Marine science*] (OSRA) ..... POD
Probability of Detection [*Navy*] (NVT) ..... PROBDET
Probability of Detection and Conversion [*Military*] ..... PDC
Probability of Detection and Verification [*Military*] (CAAL) ..... PDV
Probability of Detection Conversion and Kill [*for an interceptor system*] [*Military*] ..... Pdck
Probability of Detection, Evaluation, and Transfer (MCD) ..... PDET
Probability of Equal Regressive Slopes [*Statistics*] ..... P(ES)
Probability of Failure (NASA) ..... PF
Probability of Failure on Demand (ACII) ..... PFD
Probability of Failure, Performance [*NASA*] (SAA) ..... PFP
Probability of Failure, Stress [*NASA*] (SAA) ..... PFS
Probability of Failure, Vehicle [*NASA*] (SAA) ..... PFV
Probability of False Alarm [*DoD*] ..... PFA
Probability of False Alarm [*Criminology*] (LAIN) ..... PFA
Probability of Having a Space ..... PHS
Probability of Hit [*Military*] (MCD) ..... PH
Probability of Hit to Probability of Kill (INF) ..... PHPK
Probability of Incurring Estimated Costs [*Military*] (MCD) ..... PICOST
Probability of Incurring Estimated Costs [*Military*] ..... PIECOST
Probability Of Intercept (LAIN) ..... POI
Probability of Kill (MCD) ..... PK
Probability of Kill Single Shot (MCD) ..... PKSS
Probability of Launch on Time (MCD) ..... PLOT
Probability of Leakage through Overlay ..... PLO
Probability of Leakage through Underlay ..... PLU
Probability of Mission Abort [*Navy*] (ANA) ..... PMA
Probability of Mission Success [*Aerospace*] (AAG) ..... PMS
Probability of No Covariate Effect [*Statistics*] ..... P(COV)
Probability of Not Having a Space ..... PNS
Probability of Severe Hail (USDC) ..... POSH
Probability of Severe Hail [*Marine science*] (OSRA) ..... POSH
Probability of Single Shot Engagement Kill [*Military*] ..... PSEK
Probability of Single Shot Kill [*Of a guided missile*] ..... PSSK
Probability of Spurious Fire [*Military*] (CAAL) ..... PSF
Probability of Successful Engagement [*Military*] (CAAL) ..... PSE
Probability of Survival [*Automotive componant analysis*] ..... POS
Probability of Survival (MCD) ..... PS
Probability of Track [*Military*] ..... PTK
Probability Outgoing Quality Limit (PDAA) ..... POQL
Probability Proportional to Aggregate Size [*Statistics*] ..... PPAS
Probability Proportional to Size [*Statistics*] ..... PPS
Probability Reliability Sequential Tests (MCD) ..... PRST
Probability Sample File [*Human Relations Area Files*] [*Information retrieval*] ..... PSF
Probability Sampling Unit (WDMC) ..... PSU
Probability State Variable [*Statistics*] ..... PSV
Probability Unit [*Statistics*] ..... PROBIT
Probable ..... Pr
Probable ..... prob
Probable Allergic Rhinitis [*Medicine*] (DAVI) ..... PAR
Probable Causal Relationship [*Medicine*] (MEDA) ..... PCR
Probable Cause [*Legal term*] ..... PC
Probable Cause of Failure (MCD) ..... PCOF
Probable Diagnosis (DAVI) ..... PDX
Probable Error [*Statistics*] ..... PE
Probable Error of Measurement ..... PEM
Probable Error Radial [*Statistics*] (IAA) ..... PER
Probable Line of Deployment [*Army*] (AABC) ..... PLD
Probable Maximum Flood [*Nuclear energy*] (NRCH) ..... PMF
Probable Maximum Flooding (AD) ..... pmf
Probable Maximum Hurricane (AD) ..... pmh
Probable Maximum Hurricane [*Nuclear energy*] (NRCH) ..... PMH
Probable Maximum Loss [*Insurance*] ..... PML
Probable Maximum Loss (AD) ..... pml
Probable Maximum Precipitation [*Nuclear energy*] (NRCH) ..... PMP
Probable Maximum Surge [*Nuclear energy*] (NRCH) ..... PMS
Probable Maximum Winter Precipitation [*Nuclear energy*] (NRCH) ..... PMWP
Probable Missed Approach per Arrival [*Aviation*] (PDAA) ..... PMA/ARR
Probable Submarine (NVT) ..... PROBSUB
Probable Ultimate Net Cost [*Accounting*] ..... PUNC
Probably ..... PROB
Probably (VRA) ..... prob
Probably Disappointed Again (PCM) ..... PDA
Probably Secure Operating System (MHDB) ..... PSOS
Probably Won't Arrive [*Humorous interpretation for Pacific Western Airlines Corp.*] ..... PWA
Probate ..... P
Probate ..... PRO
Probate [*Legal term*] (DLA) ..... Prob
Probate and Admiralty Division Law Reports [*A publication*] (DLA) ..... Prob & Adm Div
Probate and Divorce [*Legal*] [*British*] ..... P & D
Probate and Divorce Cases [*1865-75*] [*England*] [*A publication*] (DLA) ..... LRP & D
Probate and Divorce, English Law Reports [*A publication*] (DLA) ..... Prob & Div
Probate and Matrimonial [*Legal*] [*British*] ..... P & M
Probate and Matrimonial (AD) ..... p&m
Probate and Matrimonial Cases [*A publication*] (DLA) ..... Prob & Mat
Probate Code [*A publication*] (DLA) ..... Prob C
Probate Court (DLA) ..... P Ct
Probate Court [*British*] (ROG) ..... PC
Probate Court Act [*A publication*] (DLA) ..... PC Act

Probate Court Reporter [*Ohio*] [*A publication*] (DLA) .... Prob Ct Rep
Probate Division, English Law Reports [*A publication*] (DLA) .... Prob Div
Probate, Divorce, and Admiralty [*British*] (DLA) .... PDA
Probate, Divorce, and Admiralty Division [*Legal*] [*British*] (ROG) .... PDAD
Probate, Divorce, and Admiralty Divisional Court [*England*] (DLA) ...... PD Div'l Ct
Probate Judge .... PJ
Probate Practice Act [*A publication*] (DLA) .... Prob Pr Act
Probate Reports [*A publication*] (DLA) .... PR
Probate Reports [*A publication*] (DLA) .... Prob R
Probate Reports [*A publication*] (DLA) .... Prob Rep
Probate Reports, Annotated [*A publication*] (DLA) .... Prob Rep Ann
Probation [*or Probationer*] .... PRO
Probation [*FBI standardized term*] .... PROB
Probation [*Legal term*] (DLA) .... Probat
Probation and Parole Law Reports [*A publication*]
 (DLA) .... Probation & Parole L Rep
Probation and Parole Law Summaries [*A publication*]
 (DLA) .... Probation & Parole L Summ
Probation and Rehabilitation of Airmen [*Air Force*] (AFM) .... PRA
Probation and Rehabilitation of Airmen (AD) .... pra
Probation Journal [*A publication*] (DLA) .... Prob J
Probation Journal [*A publication*] (ILCA) .... Probat J
Probation Officer (AD) .... P/O
Probation Officer .... PO
Probation Officers and Volunteers in Corrections [*Victoria, Australia*] .... POVC
Probationary [*British military*] (DMA) .... Proby
Probationary Acting Radio Electrical Artificer [*British military*] (DMA) .... P/AREA
Probationary Aircraft Artificer 3rd Class [*British military*] (DMA) P/AA3
Probationary Aircraft Artificer, Acting, 2nd Class [*British military*]
 (DMA) P/AAA2
Probationary Control Electrical Artificer 3rd Class [*British military*]
 (DMA) P/CEA3
Probationary Control Electrical Artificer, Acting, 2nd Class [*British military*] (DMA) P/ACEA2
Probationary Electrical Artificer (Air) 3rd Class [*British military*]
 (DMA) .... P/EA(A)3
Probationary Marine Engineering Artificer [*British military*] (DMA) .... P/MEA
Probationary Marine Engineering Artificer, Acting, 2nd Class [*British military*] (DMA) P/AMEA2
Probationary Medical Assistant [*British military*] (DMA) .... PMA
Probationary Ordnance Electrical Artificer 3rd Class [*British military*]
 (DMA) P/OEA3
Probationary Ordnance Electrical Artificer, Acting, 2nd Class [*British military*] (DMA) P/AOEA2
Probationary Radio Electrical Artificer [*British military*] (DMA) .... P/REA
Probe [*Missile vehicle type symbol*] .... N
Probe (MSA) .... P
Probe Aerodynamic Center [*NASA*] .... PAC
Probe Aerodynamic Upper [*NASA*] (MCD) .... PAU
Probe Drill Guidance System .... PDGS
Probe Entry Site [*Instrumentation*] .... PES
Probe Ephemeris Tape .... PET
Probe Heater Motor Controller [*NASA*] (MCD) .... PHMC
Probe Ministries International (EA) .... PMI
PROBE [*Program Optimization and Budget Evaluation*] **Staff Support System**
 [*Military*] PS3
PROBE [*Program Optimization and Budget Evaluation*] **Steering Committee**
 [*Military*] .... PSC
Probe Systems, Inc. .... PSI
Probe Velocity Transducer (KSC) .... PVT
Probe-Microphone Real Ear Measurement [*Audiology*] .... PREM
Probes for the International Quiet Solar Year [*OSS*] .... PIQSY
Probing Lensing Anomalies Network [*Astronomy*] .... PLANET
Problem .... PROB
Problem Accountability Record (NASA) .... PAR
Problem Action Center [*NASA*] (NASA) .... PAC
Problem Action Control Center [*NASA*] (NASA) .... PACC
Problem Action Log (AAG) .... PAL
Problem Action Record (KSC) .... PAR
Problem Action Request (NASA) .... PAR
Problem Action Team [*NASA*] (NASA) .... PAT
Problem Analysis (NASA) .... P/A
Problem Analysis and Recommended Action (IAA) .... PARA
Problem Analysis and Resolution .... PAR
Problem Analysis and Response Program (IAA) .... PAR
Problem Analysis by Logical Approach .... PABLA
Problem Analysis Report (MCD) .... PAR
Problem and Change Tracking Directory System .... PCTDS
Problem Appraisal Scales [*Personality development test*] [*Psychology*] .... PAS
Problem Areas in Diabetes [*Scale*] [*Medicine*] (DMAA) .... PAID
Problem Assessment Engineering (NASA) .... PAE
Problem Control and Contact Unit [*IRS*] .... PCC
Problem Control and Display .... PCD
Problem Data System (MCD) .... PDS
Problem Definition [*Army*] .... PD
Problem Definition/Solution .... PD/S
Problem Descriptor System .... PDS
Problem Descriptor System/Matrix Generation [*Programming language*]
 [*1965*] (CSR) .... PDS/MAGEN
Problem Determination Aid (EECA) .... PDA
Problem Determination Aid [*Computer science*] (MDG) .... PDAID
Problem Documentation Number (AAG) .... PDN
Problem Driver Pointer System [*NHTSA*] (TAG) .... PDPS
Problem Equipment Indicator Reports (MCD) .... PEIR
Problem, Etiology, Signs, and Symptoms [*Medicine*] (DMAA) .... PESS

Problem/Failure Report .... PFR
Problem Identification and Analysis Report [*Military*] (CAAL) .... PIAR
Problem Identification and Correction [*DoD*] (AFIT) .... PIAC
Problem Identification Program (MCD) .... PIP
Problem Input (SAA) .... PI
Problem Input Preparation [*Computer science*] (BUR) .... PIP
Problem Investigation and Repair Record [*NASA*] (KSC) .... PIRR
Problem Language Analyzer [*Computer science*] .... PLAN
Problem Oriented System .... POS
Problem Program Efficiency (IEEE) .... PPE
Problem Program Evaluator .... PPE
Problem Program Monitor (IAA) .... PPM
Problem Report (MCD) .... PR
Problem Report Squawk Sheet [*NASA*] (NASA) .... PRSS
Problem Reporting and Corrective Action (MCD) .... PRACA
Problem Reporting and Corrective Action (NASA) .... PRCA
Problem Reporting and Resolution .... PRR
Problem Reporting and Resolution System [*Military*] (CAAL) .... PRRS
Problem Reproducer Equipment (SAA) .... PRE
Problem Resolution Coordinator [*IRS*] .... PRC
Problem Resolution Office [*IRS*] .... PRO
Problem Resolution Program [*IRS*] .... PRP
Problem Resolution Tasking System [*Army*] (INF) .... PRT
Problem Solution Engineering [*Programming language*] [*Computer science*]
 (CSR) .... PROSE
Problem Solving Process .... PSP
Problem Specification .... PS
Problem Specification Language .... PSL
Problem Statement [*Computer science*] (IAA) .... PS
Problem Statement Analyzer [*Computer science*] (IAA) .... PSA
Problem Statement Language [*Computer science*] (IAA) .... PSL
Problem Statement Language/Problem Specification Analyzer [*Computer science*] .... PSL/PSA
Problem Status and Summary Report [*NASA*] (KSC) .... PSSR
Problem Status Report (MCD) .... PSR
Problem Status Report Analysis (SAA) .... PSRA
Problem Tracking and Change Control [*Computer science*] .... PT/CC
Problem Trend Evaluation (MCD) .... PTE
Problemata [*of Aristotle*] [*Classical studies*] (OCD) .... Pr
Probleme der Agyptologie [*A publication*] (BJA) .... PA
Problem-Etiology-Signs [*or Symptoms*] [*Nursing*] .... PES
Problem-Focused Research Applications [*of ASRA*] [*National Science Foundation*] .... PFRA
Problem-Knowledge Coupler (DMAA) .... PKC
Problem-Objective-Approach-Response [*System of planning patient care*]
 [*Medicine*] .... POAR
Problem-Oriented Basic Research [*National Science Foundation*] .... POBR
Problem-Oriented Language [*Computer science*] .... POL
Problem-Oriented Language (AD) .... pol
Problem-Oriented Language for Analytical Chemistry [*Computer science*]
 (PDAA) .... POLAC
Problem-Oriented Language Generator [*Computer science*] (BUR) .... POLGEN
Problem-Oriented Language Organizer [*Computer science*] (PDAA) .... POLO
Problem-Oriented Medical Information System [*Computerized patient-management system*] .... PROMIS
Problem-Oriented Medical Record .... POMR
Problem-Oriented Records [*Medicine*] .... POR
Problem-Oriented Routine (IEEE) .... POR
Problem-Oriented System of Charting (AAMN) .... POSC
Problems of Reconstruction [*British World War II*] .... RP
Problems-Objectives-Methods-Evaluation [*Planning method*] .... POME
Problem-Solving and Inference Machine (IAA) .... PSI
Problem-Solving Information [*Apparatus*] .... PSI
Problem-Solving Instructional Material [*National Science Foundation project*] .... PSIM
Problem-Solving Interpreter [*Computer language*] .... PSI
Problem-Solving Language .... PSL
Probucol [*Anticholesteremic*] .... P
Probyn on Land Tenure [*4th ed.*] [*1881*] [*A publication*] (DLA) .... Prob LT
Procaer SpA [*Italy ICAO aircraft manufacturer identifier*] (ICAO) .... PC
Procainamide [*Cardiac depressant*] .... PA
Procainamide-Hydroxylamine (DMAA) .... PAHA
Procambial Strand [*Botany*] .... PS
, Procarbazine [*Vincristine*] [*Antineoplastic drug regimen*] .... MOP
Procarbazine [*Also, PC, PCB, Pr*] [*Antineoplastic drug*] .... P
Procarbazine [*Also, P, PCB, Pr*] [*Antineoplastic drug*] .... PC
Procarbazine [*Also, P, PC, Pr*] [*Antineoplastic drug*] .... PCB
Procarbazine [*Antineoplastic drug*] (DAVI) .... PCZ
Procarbazine [*Also, P, PC, PCB*] [*Antineoplastic drug*] .... Pr
Procarbazine [*Antineoplastic drug*] (DAVI) .... Procarb
Procarbazine, Alanine Nitrogen Mustard [*L-Phenylanine mustard, L-PAM*],
 Velban [*Vinblastine*] [*Antineoplastic drug regimen*] .... PAVe
Procarbazine, CCNU [*Lomustine*], Vincristine [*Antineoplastic drug regimen*]
 (DAVI) .... PCV
Procarbazine, Hydroxyurea, Radiotherapy Protocol (DAVI) .... PHRT
Procarbazine, Ifosfamide, Methotrexate [*Antineoplastic drug regimen*] .... PRIME
Procarbazine, Methotrexate, Adriamycin, Cyclophosphamide, Etoposide,
 Mustargen [*Nitrogen mustard*], Oncovin , Procarbazine, Prednisone
 [*Vincristine*] [*Antineoplastic drug regimen*] .... PROMACE-MOPP
Procarbazine, Oncovin [*Vincristine*], CCNU [*Lomustine*] [*Antineoplastic drug regimen*] .... POC
Procarbazine, Oncovin [*Vincristine*], Cyclophosphamide, CCNU [*Lomustine*]
 [*Antineoplastic drug regimen*] .... POCC
, Procarbazine, Prednisone [*Vincristine*] [*Antineoplastic drug regimen*] .... BOPP
Procaterol [*Pharmacology*] .... PRC

Procedural Approach to the Composition of Essays [*In book title*] .... PACE
Procedural Change Directive (KSC) .... PCD
Procedural Control Language [*1971*] [*Computer science*] (CSR) .... PCL
Procedural Information Pamphlet .... PIP
Procedural Language (PCM) .... PL
Procedural Language for Integrity Constraints [*Computer science*] (MHDI) .... PLIC
Procedural Language Implementing Analog Techniques [*Computer science*] (IEEE) .... PLIANT
Procedural Language Processor .... PLP
Procedural Nomenclature (MCD) .... PNOM
Procedural Regulations [*Civil Aeronautics Board*] .... PR
Procedural Support Data .... PSD
Procedure .... P
Procedure (AAG) .... PCDR
Procedure (ROG) .... PCEDURE
Procedure (AABC) .... PRO
Procedure (AAG) .... PROC
Procedure (AFM) .... PROCD
Procedure (ROG) .... PROCDRE
Procedure .... PROCED
Procedure Base Register (IAA) .... PBR
Procedure Change Control Action Form (AAG) .... PCCAF
Procedure Change Notice .... PCN
Procedure Change Request [*NASA*] .... PCR
Procedure Committee Change Authorization Form (AAG) .... PCCAF
Procedure Completion Sheet [*NASA*] (MCD) .... PCS
Procedure Definition Language [*Computer science*] (BUR) .... PDL
Procedure Definition Processor [*Computer science*] .... PDP
Procedure Definition Processor (NITA) .... PDP
Procedure Distribution List (MCD) .... PDL
Procedure Documentation [*Computer science*] (MHDB) .... PRODOC
Procedure for Automatic Testing (IAA) .... PAT
Procedure Library [*Computer science*] .... PL
Procedure Library [*Computer science*] .... PROCLIB
Procedure Library Mathematics [*Computer science*] (IAA) .... PLMATH
Procedure of Questionable Usefulness [*Medicine*] (CPH) .... POQU
Procedure Qualification Record [*Nuclear energy*] (NRCH) .... PQR
Procedure Review Board [*Nuclear energy*] (NRCH) .... PRB
Procedure Review Committee (AAG) .... PRC
Procedure Review Group [*Nuclear energy*] (NRCH) .... PRG
Procedure Review Section [*Social Security Administration*] .... PRS
Procedure Sign .... PRESIGN
Procedure Sign [*Military*] (AABC) .... PROSIGN
Procedure Sign [*Military*] (IAA) .... PROSIN
Procedure Sign [*Military*] .... PROSINE
Procedure Signal [*Navy*] .... PROSIG
Procedure Turn [*Aviation*] (FAAC) .... PT
Procedure Turn [*FAA*] (TAG) .... PT
Procedure Turn [*ICAO*] (FAAC) .... PTN
Procedure Validation Report (AAG) .... PVR
Procedure Value Analysis (PDAA) .... PVA
Procedure Word .... PROWORD
Procedure Work Log System (IAA) .... PROWL
Procedure-Oriented Language [*Computer science*] .... POL
Procedures, Alternatives, Indications, and Complications [*Medicine*] (DMAA) .... PAIC
Procedures and Analysis .... P & A
Procedures and Relationships for the Operation of Manual Stations and Spaces (DNAB) .... PROMSS
Procedures Authorized Task (MCD) .... PAT
Procedures Committee [*Institute of Electrical and Electronics Engineers*] (IEEE) .... PROCOM
Procedures Development Simulator (KSC) .... PDS
Procedures Evaluation [*DoD*] .... PE
Procedures for Air Navigation Services [*ICAO*] .... PANS
Procedures for Air Navigation Services - Meteorology (IEEE) .... PANSMET
Procedures for Instrument Calibration .... PIC
Procedures for Inventory Control Afloat [*Navy*] .... PICA
Procedures for Long Supply Assets Utilization Screening [*DoD*] .... PLUS
Procedures for the Control of Air Traffic (SAA) .... PCAT
Procedures Manual (IEEE) .... PM
Procedures Review [*DoD*] .... PR
Proceed [*ICAO designator*] (FAAC) .... PCD
Proceed (AFM) .... PROCD
Proceed by First Available Government Transportation [*Military*] .... PROFAGTRANS
Proceed Directly on Course [*Aviation*] (FAAC) .... PDDC
Proceed Immediately - Report for Purpose Indicated [*Military*] .... PROIMREP
Proceed in Time Report Not Later Than [*Hour and/or date indicated*] [*Military*] .... PROTIMEREP
Proceed on Duty Assigned [*Military*] .... PRODUTAS
Proceed On or About (MUGU) .... PROBOUT
Proceed Ship, Command Station Reporting Duty or Purpose Indicated [*Military*] .... PROREP
Proceed to a Port in Continental United States [*Military*] .... PROUS
Proceed to Port in Which Unit is Located [*Navy*] (DNAB) .... PROPORICH
Proceed to Select [*Telecommunications*] (TEL) .... PTS
Proceed to Send [*Telecommunications*] (TEL) .... PTS
Proceed Without Delay Report Duty or Purpose Indicated [*Military*] .... PROWDELREP
Proceeding on Course [*Aviation*] (FAAC) .... POC
Proceedings (IAA) .... P
Proceedings (ROG) .... PCEEDGS
Proceedings (IAA) .... PR
Proceedings .... PROC
Proceedings (WDMC) .... proc
Proceedings .... PROCS
Proceedings. American Society of International Law [*A publication*] (DLA) .... Proc Amer Soc of Internat L
Proceedings and Ordinances of the Privy Council, Edited by Sir Harry Nicolas [*A publication*] (DLA) .... Nicolas
Proceedings. Electrical Association of Australia [*A publication*] .... Proc Elec Assoc Aust
Proceedings. Electrical Association of New South Wales [*Australia A publication*] .... Proc Elec Assoc NSW
Proceedings. Engineering Association of New South Wales [*Australia A publication*] .... Proc Eng Assoc NSW
Proceedings. Fordham Corporate Law Institute [*A publication*] (DLA) .... Fordham Corp Inst
Proceedings in Chancery [*A publication*] (DLA) .... Proc Ch
Proceedings in English King's Council [*1392-93*] [*A publication*] (DLA) .... Graves
Proceedings in Print [*A bibliographic publication*] .... PIP
Proceedings. Institution of Radio Engineers of Australia [*A publication*] .... Proc Instn Radio Eng Aust
Proceedings. Microscopical Society of Victoria [*Australia A publication*] .... Proc Microscopical Soc Vic
Proceedings of Court of Appeal of Maryland [*In American Legal Records, 1*] [*A publication*] (DLA) .... Bond MD App
Proceedings of the Cambridge Philological Society [*A publication*] (OCD) .... PCPS
Proceedings of the Conference. Indian Society of International Law [*New Delhi, India*] [*A publication*] (DLA) .... Pro Indian Soc of Internat L
Proceedings of the Institute of Electrical Engineers [*A publication*] (IAA) .... PROCIEE
Proceedings of the Society for Experimental Biology and Medicine [*A publication*] .... PSEBM
Proceedings. Royal Society of Queensland [*Australia A publication*] .... Proc Roy Soc Qld
Proceedings. Royal Society of Victoria [*Australia A publication*] .... Proc Roy Soc Vic
Proceedings. Scientific Society. University of Adelaide [*A publication*] .... Proc Sci Soc Univ Adel
Proceedings. Society of Chemical Industry of Victoria [*Australia A publication*] .... Proc Soc Chem Indust Vic
Proceedings, Uniform Law Conference of Canada [*A publication*] (DLA) .... Unif L Conf
Proceedings. Western Australian Institution of Engineers [*A publication*] .... Proc WA Instn Eng
Procept, Inc. [*NASDAQ symbol*] (SAG) .... PRCT
Procept, Inc. [*Associated Press*] (SAG) .... Procept
Procerebral Lobe [*Neuroanatomy*] .... PC
Process (AFM) .... PRCS
Process (AD) .... prcs
Process .... PRCS
Process (VRA) .... proc
Process (AABC) .... PROC
Process Accessible Segment Table .... PAST
Process Action Request .... PAR
Process Action Team [*Army*] (RDA) .... PAT
Process Allocator [*Telecommunications*] (TEL) .... PA
Process Analysis Team .... PAT
Process Analytical Chemistry .... PAC
Process Analytical Instrument .... PAI
Process and Effluent Radiological Monitoring and Sampling System [*Nuclear energy*] (NRCH) .... PERMSS
Process and Effluent Radiological Monitoring System [*Nuclear energy*] (NRCH) .... PERMS
Process and Experiment Automation Real-Time Language [*Computer science*] .... PEARL
Process and Indoctrinate Recruits .... PIR
Process & Instrument Design (ACII) .... PID
Process and Instrumentation Diagram [*Engineering*] (NRCH) .... P & ID
Process and Manufacturing Engineering (NRCH) .... PME
Process and Test Control [*Pendar Technical Association Ltd.*] [*Software package*] (NCC) .... PROTECON
Process and Test Language .... PTL
Process Assembler Language .... PAL
Process Assembly Case Evaluator Routine [*Computer science*] .... PACER
Process Audit List (MCD) .... PAL
Process Automation (CMD) .... PA
Process Automation & Computer Systems .... PACS
Process Automation Interface (IAA) .... PAI
Process Automation Monitor [*Texas Instruments, Inc.*] .... PAM
Process Automation Monitor/Disc Version (NITA) .... PAM/D
Process Automation Monitor/Disk Version [*Texas Instruments, Inc.*] .... PAMD
Process Average Quality .... PAQ
Process Basic (ECII) .... PB
Process Branch Indicator .... PBI
Process Bulletin .... PB
Process Capability Laboratory .... PCL
Process Chain Evaluation Model (IEEE) .... PCEM
Process Characterization Analysis Package (MHDI) .... PCAR
Process Chemistry .... PC
Process Chemistry Cell (NRCH) .... PCC
Process Communication Monitor [*Telecommunications*] (IAA) .... PCM
Process Communication Supervisor (IAA) .... PCS
Process Communications Link (ECII) .... PCL
Process Compiler [*Computer science*] (IAA) .... PROCOMP
Process Computer (NRCH) .... PC

Process Computer [*Computer science*] ... PROCOMP
Process Computer System (NRCH) ... PCS
Process Control (DEN) ... PC
Process Control Analyzer ... PCA
Process Control and Sequencing Language [*Computer science*] (IAA) ... PROSEL
Process Control Block ... PCB
Process Control Computer ... PCC
Process [*or Processor*] **Control Element** [*Computer science*] (IAA) ... PCE
Process Control Executive (MHDI) ... PCX
Process Control Interface ... PCI
Process Control Language [*Texas Instruments, Inc.*] [*Computer science*] (IAA) ... PCL
Process Control Language [*Texas Instruments, Inc.*] ... PCLA
Process Control Language (NITA) ... PROCOL
Process Control Module [*Telecommunications*] (TEL) ... PCM
Process Control Operating System ... PCOS
Process Control Oriented Language [*Computer science*] (IAA) ... PROCOL
Process Control Processor (IEEE) ... PCP
Process Control Program [*Nuclear energy*] (NRCH) ... PCP
Process Control Sheet [*Nuclear energy*] (NRCH) ... PCS
Process Control System ... PCS
Process Data (NITA) ... PD
Process Data Processing (IAA) ... PDP
Process Demonstration Unit [*Chemical engineering*] ... PDU
Process Descriptor [*Telecommunications*] (IAA) ... PD
Process Descriptor Base [*Telecommunications*] (TEL) ... PDB
Process Design Language [*Computer science*] (MHDI) ... PDL
Process Development Pile [*Nuclear energy*] ... PDP
Process Development Unit [*Chemical engineering*] ... PDU
Process Diagnostic [*Interpersonal skills and attitudes test*] ... PD
Process Display Data Base [*Computer science*] (ECII) ... PDB
Process Dynamics Recorder ... PDR
Process Engineering Database ... PEDB
Process Engineering Evaluation Techniques Package (PDAA) ... PEETPACK
Process Engineering Order ... PEO
Process Engineers and Constructors' Association [*Australia*] ... PECA
Process Environmental Analysis ... PEA
Process Equipment Accessory (MCD) ... PEA
Process Equipment Manufacturers Association (EA) ... PEMA
Process Evaluation and Information Reduction (IAA) ... PEIR
Process Evaluation Guide [*Graphic Communications Association*] ... PEG
Process Evaluation Test Vehicle ... PETV
Process Evaluation Tester ... PET
Process Execution Module (NITA) ... PEM
Process Flow Diagram (NRCH) ... PFD
Process Fuel Equivalent (MCD) ... PFE
Process Gas Chromatography ... PGC
Process Gas Consumers Group (EA) ... PGC
Process Hazard Analysis [*Engineering*] ... PHA
Process Hazard Analysis [*Environmental science*] ... PHA
Process Hazardous Review [*Environmental science*] ... PHR
Process Hazards Analysis [*Chemical engineering*] ... PHA
Process Heat Reactor Program [*Nuclear Regulatory Commission*] ... PHR
Process Holding Fixture (MCD) ... PHF
Process Identifier [*Computer science*] (PCM) ... PID
Process Image (NITA) ... PI
Process Inherent Ultimately Safe [*Nuclear reactor*] ... PIUS
Process Ink Gamut [*Printing technology*] ... PIG
Process Input Unit [*Computer science*] (BUR) ... PIU
Process Input-Output [*Computer science*] (ECII) ... PIO
Process Input-Output Subroutine Package [*Computer science*] (MHDI) ... PIOSP
Process Instrument Sheet ... PIS
Process Instrumentation [*Nuclear energy*] (NRCH) ... PI
Process Instrumentation System [*Nuclear energy*] (NRCH) ... PIS
Process Instruments Digital Communication System [*Beckman Industries*] ... PIDCOM
Process Intelligent Control [*A data processing system from LISP Machine, Inc.*] ... PICON
Process Interface Control ... PIC
Process Interface Unit ... PIU
Process Interrupt Status Word ... PISW
Process Layup Procedure ... PLP
Process Liquid Chromatography ... PLC
Process Management and Information System [*I. P. Sharp Associates Ltd.*] [*Software package*] (NCC) ... PROMIS
Process Management Information System (ACII) ... PMIS
Process Manager [*Marine science*] (OSRA) ... PM
Process Manager (USDC) ... PM
Process Manual ... PM
Process Measurement & Control Division (ACII) ... PMCD
Process Measurement Systems Ltd. (NITA) ... PMS
Process Monitoring and Control System ... PMCS
Process Monitoring and Control Systems (AD) ... pmcs
Process Monitoring and Display Software [*Computer science*] (ECII) ... PMDS
Process Monitoring Modules (ACII) ... PMM
Process Operating Management System [*Manufacturing*] ... POMS
Process Operating System [*Toshiba Corp.*] [*Japan*] ... POPS
Process Operator Console ... POC
Process Organization to Simplify Error Recovery (PDAA) ... POSER
Process Oriented Observation Program [*NORPAX*] (MSC) ... POOP
Process Page Table [*Telecommunications*] (TEL) ... PPT
Process Plan Association [*British*] (DS) ... PPA
Process Plant Association [*British*] (DBA) ... PPA
Process Quality Control System ... PQCS
Process Quality Measurement System [*Chemical process engineering*] ... PQMS
Process Radiation Monitor [*Nuclear energy*] (NRCH) ... PRM
Process Radiation Sampler [*Nuclear energy*] (NRCH) ... PRS
Process Requirements Drawing (MCD) ... PRD
Process Safety Incident Investigation [*Engineering*] ... PSII
Process Safety Management [*Chemical engineering*] ... PSM
Process Sampling System [*Nuclear energy*] (NRCH) ... PSS
Process Service Area (IAA) ... PSA
Process Sheet ... PS
Process Signal Former (IAA) ... PSF
Process Signal Interface Controller ... PSIC
Process Simulation Language [*Computer science*] (TEL) ... PSL
Process Solution (MCD) ... PS
Process Specification (AAGC) ... D SPEC
Process Specification ... PS
Process Specification Advance Change Notice (SAA) ... PSACN
Process Specification Departure (SAA) ... PSD
Process Standard Specification ... PSS
Process Status Longword [*Number*] [*Computer science*] (BYTE) ... PSL
Process Steering and Control Module [*Telecommunications*] (TEL) ... PSCM
Process Storage [*Computer science*] (IAA) ... PS
Process Storage Address Register [*Computer science*] (IAA) ... PSAR
Process Storage Data Register (IAA) ... PSDR
Process Subsystem [*Telecommunications*] (TEL) ... PS
Process Supercritical Fluid Chromatography ... PSFC
Process Switching Service (IAA) ... PSS
Process System Index ... PSI
Process Systems Engineering ... PSE
Process Systems, Inc. ... PSI
Process Systems Program ... PROSPRO
Process Technical Bulletin (MCD) ... PTB
Process Technology Department, Inco Ltd., Copper Cliff, Ontario [*Library symbol National Library of Canada*] (BIB) ... OCCIN
Process Unit Control Panel [*Computer science*] (IAA) ... PUCP
Process Validation Enterprise [*Army*] (RDA) ... PVE
Process Variable (IAA) ... PV
Process Variable Record ... PVR
Process Waste Treatment Plant [*Engineering*] ... PWTP
Process Water Cooler (MSA) ... PWC
Process Word (IAA) ... PWD
Process-Activation Table [*Computer science*] ... PAT
Processed ... PROCSD
Processed Apple and Pear Committee [*Victoria, Austria*] ... PAPC
Processed Apples Institute (EA) ... PAI
Processed Array Signal ... PAS
Processed Citation File ... PCF
Processed Commodities Inventory System [*Department of Agriculture*] (GFGA) ... PCIS
Processed Data Recorder ... PDR
Processed Directional Transmission [*Military*] (NVT) ... PDT
Processed Eucheuma Seaweed ... PES
Processed Food Industry Council [*Australia*] ... PFIC
Processed Language [*Computer science*] ... PROLAN
Processed Meats Committee [*Later, DPMC*] (EA) ... PMC
Processed Message File (MCD) ... PMF
Processed Payment Document (GFGA) ... PPD
Processed RADAR Display System (PDAA) ... PRDS
Processed Vegetable Growers Association [*British*] (DBA) ... PVGA
Processed Woodchip, Sawdust, and Woodflour Association [*British*] (BI) ... PWSWA
Processes and Materials (NASA) ... P & M
Processes and Resources of the Bering Sea Shelf [*University of Alaska*] ... PROBES
Processes of Science Test (AD) ... POST
Processing ... PRCESSN
Processing (IAA) ... PRCS
Processing (MSA) ... PRCSG
Processing ... PRCSG
Processing Amplifier (NTCM) ... Proc Amp
Processing and Communications Terminal (MCD) ... PACT
Processing and Control Element [*Computer science*] (IAA) ... PACE
Processing and Manufacturing in Space [*European Space Agency*] ... PAMIS
Processing and Spectral Control ... PSC
Processing and Staging Facility [*Solid rocket booster*] (NASA) ... PSF
Processing and Storage Facility [*NASA*] (NASA) ... PSF
Processing Center [*Telecommunications*] (TEL) ... PC
Processing Conditions [*Food*] (DICI) ... PC
Processing Control Number ... PCN
Processing Data Rate (IEEE) ... PDR
Processing Distribution and Control System ... PDCS
Processing Element [*of central processing unit*] ... PE
Processing Element Memory [*Computer science*] ... PEM
Processing Element Module [*Computer science*] (IAA) ... PEM
Processing Enhancing Protein [*Biochemistry*] ... PEP
Processing Figure Channel [*Electronics*] (ECII) ... PFC
Processing Information List [*Computer science*] ... PIL
Processing Libraries - Anecdotes, Facetia, Satire, Etc., Periodicals [*A publication*] ... PLAFSEP
Processing, Marketing, and Distribution ... PMD
Processing Modflow [*Computer program*] [*Scientific Software Group*] ... PM
Processing MODFLOW for Windows ... PMWIN
Processing Module [*Computer science*] ... PM
Processing Negativity [*Computer science*] ... PN
Processing of Indexing Terms ... PIT
Processing Office [*Bureau of the Census*] (GFGA) ... PO
Processing Option [*Computer science*] (MHDB) ... PROCOPT

Processing Overseas Replacement Training [*Military*] (VNW) ... POR
Processing Refabrication Experiment [*Nuclear energy*] (NRCH) ... PRE
Processing, Research, Inspection, and Marine Extension Program [*National Oceanic and Atmospheric Administration*] (MSC) ... PRIME
Processing Research Institute [*Carnegie Mellon University*] ... PRI
Processing Routines Aided by Graphics for Manipulation of Arrays (PDAA) ... PRAGMA
Processing Routines Aided by Graphics for Manipulation of Arrays (AD) ... pragma
Processing Sequence [*Computer science*] (MHDB) ... PROCSEQ
Processing Serial Number (MCD) ... PSN
Processing Service Centers [*Social Security Administration*] ... PSC
Processing Status Display [*NASA*] ... PSD
Processing Tax Board of Review Decisions [*United States Internal Revenue Bureau*] [*A publication*] (DLA) ... PTBR
Processing Tax Division [*United States Internal Revenue Bureau*] (DLA) ... PT
Processing Telecom Technologies (PCM) ... PTT
Processing Terminal Network Architecture [*Computer science*] (BUR) ... PNA
Processing Time ... PT
Processing Unit ... PROCU
Processing Unit [*Computer science*] ... PU
Processing Unit Cabinet [*Computer science*] ... PUC
Procession (ROG) ... PROC
Procession Register Clock ... PRC
Process-Model Based Controller (ACII) ... PMBC
Processor [*Computer science*] ... P
Processor [*Computer science*] (IAA) ... PR
Processor ... PRCSR
Processor [*or Processing*] ... PROC
Processor and Distribution Assembly [*Viking lander analysis equipment*] [*NASA*] ... PDA
Processor and Memory [*Computer science*] ... PAM
Processor Command Bus (NITA) ... PCB
Processor Common Communications System ... PCCS
Processor Common Input/Output System [*Computer science*] ... PCIOS
Processor Control Cards [*Computer science*] (IAA) ... PCC
Processor Control Console [*Telecommunications*] (TEL) ... PCC
Processor Control Program ... PCP
Processor Control Unit ... PCU
Processor Controlled Keying [*Computer science*] (DCTA) ... PCK
Processor Controller [*Computer science*] (MDG) ... PC
Processor Data Bus In (MHDI) ... PDBIN
Processor Data Monitor (NASA) ... PDM
Processor Defined Function ... PDF
Processor Direct Slot [*Computer science*] ... PDS
Processor Emergency Recovery Circuit [*Bell System*] ... PERC
Processor Enhancement Socket [*Computer science*] (PCM) ... PES
Processor in Memory [*Computer science*] ... PIM
Processor Independent NetWare [*Computer science*] ... PIN
Processor Input Channel (NVT) ... PIC
Processor Input-Output [*Computer science*] (MDG) ... PIO
Processor Interconnection Channel (NITA) ... PIC
Processor Interface [*Computer science*] (IAA) ... PI
Processor Interface Buffer [*Telecommunications*] (TEL) ... PIB
Processor Interface Module ... PIM
Processor Interrupts Enabled [*Computer science*] (MHDI) ... PINTE
Processor, Laptop Imagery Transmission Equipment (DOMA) ... PC-LITE
Processor Memory Enhancement ... PME
Processor Memory Switch [*Computer science*] (ECII) ... PMS
Processor Memory Switch Matrix ... PMSX
Processor Module (NITA) ... PM
Processor Monitoring Instrument [*Computer science*] (ADA) ... PMI
Processor Program State Control (NITA) ... PPSC
Processor Ready for Use [*Telecommunications*] (TEL) ... PRFU
Processor Request Flag [*Telecommunications*] (TEL) ... PRF
Processor Resource/Systems Manager [*Computer science*] (CDE) ... PR/SM
Processor Service Unit (ECII) ... PSU
Processor Simulation Language [*Computer science*] (PDAA) ... PROCSIM
Processor Speed Up [*Computer memory core*] ... PSU
Processor State Register ... PSR
Processor State Register Main [*Computer science*] ... PSRM
Processor State Register Utility [*Computer science*] ... PSRU
Processor Status ... PS
Processor Status Word ... PSW
Processor Storage Control Function ... PSCF
Processor System Modeling Language [*1976*] [*Computer science*] (CSR) ... PSML
Processor Tape Read ... PTR
Processor Technology Disk Operating System ... PTDOS
Processor Utility [*Telecommunications*] (TEL) ... PU
Processor Utility Monitor [*Telecommunications*] (TEL) ... PUM
Processor Utility Subsystem [*Telecommunications*] (TEL) ... PUS
Process-Oriented Contract Administration Services ... PROCAS
Process-Oriented Design (AD) ... pod
Process-Oriented Language [*Computer science*] (IEEE) ... POL
Process-Oriented Real-Time Algorithmic Language [*1978*] [*Computer science*] (CSR) ... PORTAL
Processors and Growers Research Organisation [*British*] (IRUK) ... PGRO
Processors, Memories, and Switches [*Programming language*] (CSR) ... PMS
Processors-Memories-Switches (AD) ... p-m-s
Processor-Upgradable Microcomputer Architecture [*DFI, Inc.*] (PCM) ... PUMA
Process-Reactive [*Scale*] [*Psychometrics*] ... PR
Prochlorperazine [*Antiemetic*] ... PCZ
Pro-Choice Defense League (EA) ... PCDL
Proclamation (DLA) ... Proc
Procoagulant Activity ... PCA
Procollagen [*Medicine*] (DMAA) ... PC
Procom Emerald [*Vancouver Stock Exchange symbol*] ... PMM
Procom Technology Inc. [*NASDAQ symbol*] (SAG) ... PRCM
Procom Technology Inc. [*Associated Press*] (SAG) ... ProcmT
Proconsul ... P
Proconsul ... PRC
Procopius [*Sixth century AD*] [*Classical studies*] (OCD) ... Procop
Procrastinators' Club of America (EA) ... PCA
Procrustes Target Analysis [*Marine science*] (OSRA) ... PTA
Procrustes Target Analysis (USDC) ... PTA
Procter & Gamble [*NYSE symbol*] (TTSB) ... PG
Procter & Gamble Co. ... P & G
Procter & Gamble Co. [*NYSE symbol*] (SPSG) ... PG
Procter & Gamble Co. [*Associated Press*] (SAG) ... ProctGm
Procter & Gamble Co., Cincinnati, OH [*Library symbol Library of Congress*] (LCLS) ... OCPG
Procter and Gamble Co., Health and Beauty Library, Cincinnati, OH [*Library symbol*] [*Library of Congress*] (LCLS) ... OCPG-H
Procter & Gamble Co., Ivorydale Technical Center, Cincinnati, OH [*Library symbol Library of Congress*] (LCLS) ... OCPG-I
Procter & Gamble Co., Miami Valley Laboratories, Cincinnati, OH [*Library symbol Library of Congress*] (LCLS) ... OCPG-Mv
Procter & Gamble Co., Sharon Woods Technical Center, Technical Library, Cincinnati, OH [*Library symbol Library of Congress*] (LCLS) ... OCPG-Sw
Procter & Gamble Co., Winton Hill Technical Center, Cincinnati, OH [*Library symbol Library of Congress*] (LCLS) ... OCPG-Wh
Proctolin-Like Bioactivity [*Neurobiology*] ... PLB
Proctolin-Like Immunoactivity [*Neurobiology*] ... PLI
Proctologist ... PR
Proctology ... PROCT
Proctology [*Gastroenterology*] (DAVI) ... PROCTO
Proctor ... PROC
Proctor & Gamble [*Commercial firm*] (NADA) ... PG
Proctor & Redfern Group, Don Mills, Ontario [*Library symbol National Library of Canada*] (NLC) ... OTPR
Proctor & Redfern Group, Toronto, ON, Canada [*Library symbol Library of Congress*] (LCLS) ... CaOTPR
Proctor Community Hospital, Peoria, IL [*Library symbol Library of Congress*] (LCLS) ... IPPH
Proctor Maple Research Center [*University of Vermont*] [*Research center*] (RCD) ... PMRC
Proctor, MN [*FM radio station call letters*] (RBYB) ... KUSZ
Proctor Senior High School, Proctor, MN [*Library symbol*] [*Library of Congress*] (LCLS) ... MnProSH
Proctorial System of Instruction (IEEE) ... PSI
Proctor's Bench and Bar of New York [*A publication*] (DLA) ... Proc B & B
Proctor's Practice [*A publication*] (DLA) ... Proc Pr
Proctor's Practice [*A publication*] (DLA) ... Proc Prac
Proctorville, OH [*FM radio station call letters*] ... WMEJ
Proctoscopy (AD) ... Pr
Proctoscopy [*Medicine*] ... PROCTO
Proctosigmoidoscopy [*Medicine*] (AD) ... PR
Proculus [*Flourished, 1st century*] [*Authority cited in pre-1607 legal work*] (DSA) ... Pro
Procurator Fiscal ... PF
Procure (AABC) ... PROC
Procurement ... PRCMNT
Procurement (MSA) ... PRCMT
Procurement (MSA) ... PROC
Procurement Accounting and Reporting System [*Navy*] (NVT) ... PARS
Procurement Acquisition Directive ... PAD
Procurement Action Management System (MCD) ... PAMS
Procurement Action System (MCD) ... PAS
Procurement Administrative Lead Time ... PALT
Procurement Agency (MCD) ... PA
Procurement Aging and Staging System [*Army*] (AABC) ... PASS
Procurement Aids Man [*Marine Corps*] ... PAM
Procurement Aids Noncommissioned Officer [*Marine Corps*] ... PANCO
Procurement Aircraft and Missiles, Navy [*An appropriation*] ... PAMN
Procurement and Assignment ... P & A
Procurement and Contract (IAA) ... PAC
Procurement and Contracting (AFM) ... P & C
Procurement and Contracts Division [*NASA*] ... PCD
Procurement and Contracts Management Division [*Environmental Protection Agency*] (GFGA) ... PCMD
Procurement and Distribution [*Military*] ... P & D
Procurement and Expedition ... P & E
Procurement and Inventory of Equipment System (DNAB) ... PIES
Procurement and Management Assistance [*Small Business Administration*] ... PMA
Procurement and Material ... PM
Procurement and Production [*Military*] ... P & P
Procurement and Production (AFIT) ... PAP
Procurement and Production Status System ... PAPS
Procurement and Subcontract Management [*NASA*] (NASA) ... P & SM
Procurement and Systems Acquisition Division (AAGC) ... PSAD
Procurement Appropriation, Army (MCD) ... PAA
Procurement Appropriation, Secondary (MCD) ... PAS
Procurement Appropriations [*Army*] (AABC) ... PA
Procurement, Army ... PA
Procurement Assistance Office (AAGC) ... PAO
Procurement Authorization ... PA
Procurement Authorization and Receiving Report [*NASA*] (KSC) ... PARR
Procurement Automated Data Document System [*Military*] (RDA) ... PADDS
Procurement Automated Integrated Requirements (MCD) ... PAIR

Procurement Automated Source System [Small Business Administration] [Washington, DC Information service or system] (IID) ... PASS
Procurement Center Representative [Small Business Administration] ... PCR
Procurement Change Order (MCD) ... PCO
Procurement Circular (AAGC) ... Proc Cir
Procurement Circular [Air Force] (AFIT) ... PROCCIR
Procurement Code Change Request (IAA) ... PCCR
Procurement Command [Army] ... PC
Procurement, Commitment, and Obligation Record [Navy] ... PC & OR
Procurement Committee (MCD) ... PMC
Procurement Committee ... PROCOM
Procurement Communication [Military] ... PC
Procurement Congressional Descriptive Summary [Army] (RDA) ... PCDS
Procurement Contracting Officer (AAGC) ... PCO
Procurement Control Document [NASA] (MCD) ... PCD
Procurement Control Number (AFM) ... PCN
Procurement Data ... PD
Procurement Data List ... PDL
Procurement Data Package [Military] (AABC) ... PDP
Procurement Data Reference ... PDR
Procurement Data Requirements Document (NASA) ... PDRD
Procurement Data Requirements List (NASA) ... PDRL
Procurement Data Sheet ... PDS
Procurement Defense Agencies [DoD] ... PDA
Procurement Description Data [DoD] ... PDD
Procurement Directive [Army] ... PD
Procurement District [Air Force] (AFIT) ... PD
Procurement Division ... PD
Procurement Division, Judge Advocate General, United States Army (DLA) ... JAGT
Procurement Document (NASA) ... PD
Procurement Document Change (NASA) ... PDC
Procurement Document Tracking System (MCD) ... PDTS
Procurement Drawing ... PD
Procurement Equipment Maintenance, Army (MCD) ... PEMA
Procurement, Equipment, Missiles, Army ... PEMA
Procurement Evaluation Panel [Air Force] (MCD) ... PEP
Procurement Executive [British] ... PE
Procurement Executives Association (AAGC) ... PEA
Procurement Field Office ... PFO
Procurement for Minimum Total Cost through Value Engineering and Reliability ... PROVER
Procurement History File [DoD] ... PHF
Procurement Information Center ... PIC
Procurement Information Circular (AAGC) ... PIC
Procurement Information Control System [NASA] ... PICS
Procurement Information Digest (AFM) ... PID
Procurement Information for Contracts [AFSC] ... PIC
Procurement Information Letter (MCD) ... PIL
Procurement Information Notice [Environmental Protection Agency] (ERG) ... PIN
Procurement Initiation Request (MCD) ... PIR
Procurement Inspection (MCD) ... PI
Procurement Instruction Identification Number [Army] (AABC) ... PIIN
Procurement Instrument Identification (NG) ... PII
Procurement Instrument Identification Number [Military] ... PIIN
Procurement Integration Quality Assurance (AAGC) ... PIQA
Procurement Intern Development Center (DNAB) ... PIDC
Procurement Item (NASA) ... PI
Procurement Item/Identification Description [DoD] ... PID
Procurement Justification [Navy] ... PJ
Procurement Lead Time [Army] ... PLT
Procurement Lead Time ... PROLT
Procurement Lead Time Requirement ... PLTR
Procurement Legal Division [Later, Office of General Counsel] [Navy] ... PLD
Procurement, Logistics, and Readiness Division (AAGC) ... PLRD
Procurement Management and Acquisition Control System [Social Security Administration] ... PM & ACS
Procurement Management Code [Military] (AFIT) ... PMC
Procurement Management Review [DoD] ... PMR
Procurement Management System (MCD) ... PROMS
Procurement Manual [US Postal Service] [A publication] (AAGC) ... PM
Procurement, Marine Corps [An appropriation] ... PMC
Procurement Method Coding [DoD] ... PMC
Procurement Methods Analyst (AFM) ... PMA
Procurement Methods and Practices (AD) ... PMP
Procurement Notice [NASA] (AAGC) ... PN
Procurement Objective (NVT) ... PO
Procurement of Aircraft and Missiles ... PAM
Procurement of Ammunition, Army (AABC) ... PAA
Procurement of Equipment and Missiles, Army Management and Accounting Reporting System (AABC) ... PEMARS
Procurement of Equipment and Munition Appropriations [Military] (AABC) ... PEMA
Procurement of Ordnance and Ammunition - Navy ... POAN
Procurement of Weapons and Tracked Combat Vehicles, Army (AABC) ... PWTCVA
Procurement of Weapons and Tracked Vehicles, Army (AABC) ... PWTVA
Procurement Office for Military Automotive Supplies ... POMAS
Procurement Officer [Military] ... PROCO
Procurement Officers Work Group (AAGC) ... POWG
Procurement Online Ordering System (MCD) ... POLO
Procurement Operations Information System (MCD) ... POIS
Procurement Package (AAGC) ... PP
Procurement Package Engineering Release (MCD) ... PPER
Procurement Plan (MCD) ... PP
Procurement Planning Officer ... PPO
Procurement Planning Schedule [DoD] ... PPS
Procurement Policy Board [ABA Public Contract Law Section] (AAGC) ... PPB
Procurement, Precedence of Supplies, Material and Equipment Committee [Joint Communications Board] ... PPSMEC
Procurement Problem Report (AD) ... PPR
Procurement Program Number [Military] ... PPN
Procurement Quality Assurance [Program] [DoD] ... PQA
Procurement Quality Assurance (AD) ... pqa
Procurement Quality Assurance Instruction ... PQAI
Procurement Quality Assurance Program [DoD] ... PQAP
Procurement Quality Control (IAA) ... PQC
Procurement Reallocation Notice ... PRN
Procurement Regulation [Military] ... PR
Procurement Regulation Directive [NASA] (NASA) ... PRD
Procurement Repair Parts List (AAG) ... PRPL
Procurement Request [or Requisition] ... PR
Procurement Request [Army] (IAA) ... PUR
Procurement Request Code [Military] (AFIT) ... PRC
Procurement [or Purchase] Request for Vendor Data (AAG) ... PRVD
Procurement Request Order Number [Army] (AABC) ... PRON
Procurement Requirements Document [NASA] (NASA) ... PRD
Procurement Requirements Package (MCD) ... PRP
Procurement Research Coordinating Counsel (AAGC) ... PRCC
Procurement Research Office [Army] ... PRO
Procurement Review Board (MCD) ... PRB
Procurement Review Team ... PRT
Procurement Round Table (EA) ... PRT
Procurement Seminar for Auditors [Army] ... PSA
Procurement Seminar for Project Management [Army] ... PSPM
Procurement Services Office ... PSO
Procurement Source Code (AFM) ... PSC
Procurement Specification (MCD) ... PS
Procurement Squadron ... PROS
Procurement Status Report (IEEE) ... PSR
Procurement Surveys Division [NASA] (MCD) ... PSD
Procurement Technical Assistance Cooperative Agreement Program [DoD] ... ProTACA
Procurement Technical Data File [DoD] ... PTDF
Procurement Work Directive [Army] (AABC) ... PWD
Procurers of Painted-Label Sodas [Defunct] (EA) ... POPS
Procureur Generaal [Public Attorney] [Dutch] (ILCA) ... PG
Procuring Activity [Military] ... PA
Procuring Contracting Office [or Officer] [Military] ... PCO
Procuring Contrast Offer ... PCO
Procyclic Acidic Repetitive Protein [Biochemistry] ... PARP
ProCyte Corp. [NASDAQ symbol] (NQ) ... PRCY
ProCyte Corp. [Associated Press] (SAG) ... Procyt
Procytox [Cyclophosphamide], Epipodophyllotoxin Derivative , Prednisolone [VM-26] [Antineoplastic drug regimen] ... PEP
Prodemca: Friends of the Democratic Center in the Americas [Defunct] (EA) ... PFDCCA
Pro-Dex, Inc. [NASDAQ symbol] (NQ) ... PDEX
ProDex, Inc. [Associated Press] (SAG) ... ProDex
Prodigy Internet ... PI
Produce ... PROD
Produce ... PROD
Produce Marketing Association [Newark, DE] (EA) ... PMA
Produce Packaging and Marketing Association [British] (DBA) ... PPMA
Produce Packaging Association [Later, PMA] (EA) ... PPA
Produce Packaging Development Association (AD) ... PPDA
Producer [Films, television, etc.] ... P
Producer ... PRODR
Producer ... PRODR
Producer Fixed Capital Formation (MCD) ... PFCF
Producer Price ... PP
Producer Price Index [Bureau of Labor Statistics] [Information service or system] ... PPI
Producer Subsidy Equivalent [OECD model for the study of farm-support policies in the EC, Japan, America, Canada, Australia, and New Zealand] ... PSE
Producers Commission Association (EA) ... PCA
Producers' Council [Later, CPMC] (EA) ... PC
Producers Distributing Corp. ... PRODISCO
Producers' Durable Equipment (GFGA) ... PDE
Producers Entertainment Group [NASDAQ symbol] (SAG) ... TPEG
Producers Entertainment Group Ltd. [Associated Press] (SAG) ... PrdEn
Producers Entertainment Group Ltd. [Associated Press] (SAG) ... PrdEnt
Producers Entertainment Grp [NASDAQ symbol] (TTSB) ... TPEG
Producers Entmt 8.50% Cv'A'Pfd [NASDAQ symbol] (TTSB) ... TPEGP
Producers Group (EA) ... PG
Producers Guild of America (EA) ... PGA
Producers Livestock Marketing Association [Later, IPLA] (EA) ... PLMA
Producers of Associated Components for Electronics (IAA) ... PACE
Producer's Reliability Risk ... PRR
Producibility Design Analysis Report (AAG) ... PDAR
Producibility Engineering and Planning [Army] (AABC) ... PEP
Producibility Evaluation Task [Army] (RDA) ... PET
Producing ... PRODNG
Producing Region [Agriculture] ... PR
Product ... P
Product [or Production] (AABC) ... PROD
Product (WDMC) ... prod
Product ... PRODT
Product Acceptance [Automotive engineering] ... PA

Product Acceptance & Research [*Commercial firm*] (WDMC) .... PAR
Product Acceptance Exceptions .... PASE
Product Acceptance Review (NASA) .... PAR
Product Acceptance Standard [*Automotive engineering*] .... PAS
Product Acceptance Test [*Advertising*] (DOAD) .... PAT
Product Acceptance Testing and Evaluation [*Marketing*] (MCD) .... PAT & E
Product Activity/Operational Code (MCD) .... PAO
Product Administration (HCT) .... PA
Product Administration and Contract Control (IAA) .... PACC
Product Analysis (IEEE) .... PA
Product and Marketing Planning (IAA) .... PMP
Product and Service Code (AAGC) .... PSC
Product and Support Requirements Request [*Computer science*] (IBMDP) .... PSRR
Product Application Bulletins [*A publication*] (EAAP) .... PAB
Product Assembly Document .... PAD
Product Assembly Drawing [*Automotive project management*] .... PAD
Product Assortment (MHDB) .... PA
Product Assurance (NASA) .... PA
Product Assurance Alert Notice (MCD) .... PAAN
Product Assurance & Development, British Columbia Packers Ltd., Vancouver, British Columbia [*Library symbol National Library of Canada*] (NLC) .... BVAPAD
Product Assurance and Test .... PA & T
Product Assurance Directorate [*Armament, Munitions, and Chemical Command*] [*Army*] .... PAD
Product Assurance Information Retrieval System [*Boeing*] .... PAIRS
Product Assurance Operations [*Army*] .... PAO
Product Assurance Plan [*Army*] (AABC) .... PAP
Product Assurance Program Management Operations Plan (MCD) .... PAPMOP
Product Assurance Survey .... PAS
Product Availability Search (MCD) .... PAS
Product Baseline (MCD) .... PBL
Product Change Information .... PCI
Product Change Proposal (MCD) .... PCP
Product Chassis Package .... PCP
Product Code (NITA) .... PC
Product Configuration Baseline (NASA) .... PCB
Product Configuration Documentation (AAGC) .... PCD
Product Configuration Identification (KSC) .... PCI
Product Control Center [*DoD*] .... PCC
Product Control Number (AFM) .... PCN
Product Control Register .... PR-CNTL
Product Co-Ordination Unit [*British Overseas Trade Board*] (DS) .... PCU
Product Cost Index .... PCI
Product Data Exchange Specification (NITA) .... PDES
Product Data Exchange using STEP [*Sequentially Timed Events Plotting*] .... PDES
Product Data Management .... PDM
Product Definition Data Interface (MCD) .... PDDI
Product Definition Database (MCD) .... PDDB
Product Definition Exchange Specification [*Army*] .... PDES
Product Departure Authorization .... PDA
Product Description Information Standards [*or System*] .... PDIS
Product Design [*Phase*] .... PD
Product Design & Development [*Radnor, PA*] [*A publication*] .... PD & D
Product Design Graphics System [*Prime Computer Ltd.*] [*Software package*] (NCC) .... PDGS
Product Design Minuteman Airborne Mechanical System (SAA) .... PDMAMS
Product Design Minuteman Mechanical System (IAA) .... PDMMS
Product Design Review [*Army*] .... PDR
Product Design Standard .... PDS
Product Development .... P/D
Product Development and Management Association [*Indianapolis, IN*] (EA) .... PDMA
Product Development Manual [*Automotive project management*] .... PDM
Product Development Process [*Automotive engineering*] .... PDP
Product Development Team [*Automotive project management*] .... PDT
Product Disaster Loans [*Small Business Administration*] .... PDL
Product Effectiveness Manual .... PEM
Product Engineering and Production (MCD) .... PEP
Product Engineering Control Center [*Telecommunications*] (TEL) .... PECC
Product Engineering Office .... PEO
Product Engineering Recommendation [*Automotive engineering*] .... PER
Product Engineering Services Office [*DoD*] .... PESO
Product Engineering Tribute to Excellence .... PETE
Product Group for the Western Pacific (EERA) .... WESTPAC
Product Identification Number .... PIN
Product Improved Compatibility Electronics (MCD) .... PICE
Product Improved Vulcan Air Defense System (MCD) .... PIVADS
Product Improvement (MCD) .... PI
Product Improvement (MCD) .... PIP
Product Improvement Bulletin .... PIB
Product Improvement Control Office (AFM) .... PICO
Product Improvement Joint Review [*Military*] .... PIJR
Product Improvement Management Information Report .... PRIMIR
Product Improvement Plan .... PIP
Product Improvement Program [*Military*] .... PIP
Product Improvement Proposal (MCD) .... PIP
Product Improvement Review .... PIR
Product Improvement Test .... PIT
Product Improvement Vulcan Air Defense (MCD) .... PIVAD
Product Improvement Working Group [*Military*] (AFIT) .... PIWG
Product Information Center [*AgriData Resources, Inc.*] [*Information service or system*] .... PIC
Product Information Memoranda .... PIM
Product Information Network [*McGraw-Hill Information Systems Co.*] [*Information service or system*] (IID) .... PIN
Product Information Release .... PIR
Product Information Specialist .... PIS
Product Information System (IAA) .... PRINSYS
Product Innovation and Design .... PID
Product Inspection Discrepancy Report (MCD) .... PIDR
Product Inspection Verification .... PIV
Product Introductory Presentation .... PIP
Product Inventory Electronically Recorded (PDAA) .... PIER
Product Inventory Level Estimator (PDAA) .... PILE
Product Liability [*Insurance*] .... PL
[*The*] **Product Liability Alliance** (EA) .... TPLA
Product Liability Common Defense [*Later, PLPD*] [*An association*] (EA) .... PLCD
Product Liability International [*A publication*] (DLA) .... Prod Liab Int'l
Product Liability Prevention [*Conference*] .... PLP
Product Liability Prevention and Defense [*An association*] (EA) .... PLPD
Product Liability Reporter [*Commerce Clearing House*] [*A publication*] (DLA) .... Prod Liab Rep
Product License .... PL
Product License Application [*FDA*] .... PLA
Product Life Cycle (ODBW) .... PLC
Product Limit Estimator (MHDB) .... PLE
Product Line Development .... PLD
Product Line Manager .... PLM
Product Line Organization .... PLO
Product Line Simulator .... PLS
Product Management Information System (AD) .... PMIS
Product Management System .... PMS
Product Manager, Army Communications System .... PM ACS
Product Manager's Office (RDA) .... PMO
Product Manufacturing Organization .... PMO
Product Measurement Facility (IAA) .... PMF
Product Moment Coefficient of Correlation [*Statistics*] .... R
Product Name (NITA) .... PN
Product of Activated Lymphocytes [*Medicine*] (DMAA) .... PAL
Product of Ambulatory Care [*Medicine*] (HCT) .... PAC
Product of Antigenic Recognition [*Immunochemistry*] .... PAR
Product of Incomplete Combustion [*Environmental Protection Agency*] (ERG) .... PIC
Product of Inertia (MCD) .... POI
Product of Sums (AD) .... pos
Product/Ore/Bulk/Oil Carrier [*Shipping*] (DS) .... PROBO
Product Oriented Procedures Evaluation (AD) .... POPE
Product Output Reporting System .... PORS
Product Performance Agreement Center [*Military*] .... PPAC
Product Planning Committee .... PPC
Product Positioning Time (AFM) .... PPT
Product Profile Information System [*Shell Oil Co.*] .... PPIS
Product Publication (IAA) .... PP
Product Quality Evaluation Plan [*Military*] (AABC) .... PQEP
Product Quality Improvement [*Program*] [*Chrysler Corp.*] .... PQI
Product Range Testing [*Business term*] .... PRT
Product Regional Center [*Department of Supply and Service*] [*Canada*] (IMH) .... PRC
Product Reliability and Maintainability .... PRAM
Product Reliability Validation Test (MCD) .... PRVT
Product Requirement Information Management System (MCD) .... PRIMS
Product Requirement Schedule (MCD) .... PRS
Product Research and Development [*Advertising*] (DOAD) .... PRD
Product Safety Advisory Council [*Consumer Product Safety Commission*] .... PSAC
Product Safety and Liability Reporter [*A publication*] (DLA) .... Prod Safety & Liab Rep
Product Safety and Liability Reporter [*A publication*] .... PSLR
Product Safety Association [*Defunct*] (EA) .... PSA
Product Safety Committee [*New South Wales, Australia*] .... PSC
Product Service (IAA) .... PS
Product Service Publication [*General Motors Corp.*] .... PSP
Product Software (MCD) .... PS
Product Specification (AAGC) .... C SPEC
Product Standards (MCD) .... PS
Product Support .... PS
Product Support Administration (MCD) .... PSA
Product Support Confidential (AAG) .... PSC
Product Support Engineering (MCD) .... PSE
Product Support Instructions (AAG) .... PSI
Product Support Manual (AAG) .... PSM
Product Support Organization .... PSO
Product Support Planning and Estimating (AAG) .... PSP & E
Product Support Procurement Summary (MCD) .... PSPS
Product Support Program (NG) .... PSP
Product Support Reports and Functions .... PSRF
Product Support Task Control (AAG) .... PSTC
Product Support Technician .... PST
Product Support Work Order .... PSWO
Product Team (AAGC) .... PT
Product Test (IAA) .... PT
Product Validation (MCD) .... PRODVAL
Product Verification Demonstration (MCD) .... PVD
Product Verification Inspection [*DoD*] .... PVI
Product Verification Specification .... PVS
Product Verification Test (MCD) .... PVT
Product Verification Test - Contractor (MCD) .... PVT-C
Product Work Authorization (NASA) .... PWA
Production [*of Energy*] .... P

Production (AFM) .... PDN
Production [*Economics*] .... Pn
Production (AAGC) .... Prod
Production (WDMC) .... prod
Production (DD) .... prod
Production (DOMA) .... PROD
Production .... PRODN
Production .... Prodn
Production .... PRODON
Production .... PRODUCTN
Production Acceleration Capacity [*Manufacturing*] .... PAC
Production Acceleration Insurance Program .... PAIP
Production Acceptance Inspection (IAA) .... PAI
Production Acceptance Review .... PAR
Production Acceptance Test [*NASA*] (KSC) .... PAT
Production Acceptance Test Procedure (MCD) .... PATP
Production Acceptance Test Requirement (MCD) .... PATR
Production Action Control Technique (SAA) .... PACT
Production Action Request (MCD) .... PAR
Production Adjustment .... PA
Production Adjustment Index [*Word processing*] .... PAI
Production Administration Deficiency Report [*DoD*] .... PADR
Production Advisers Consortium (NADA) .... PRODAC
Production Allocation and Requirements Technique (MHDB) .... PART
Production Allocation Program .... PAP
Production Analysis Control Technique [*Navy*] .... PACT
Production Analysis Report .... PAR
Production Analyzer (IAA) .... PRAN
Production and Application of Light (MCD) .... PAL
Production and Deployment [*Phase*] (DOMA) .... PROD/DEPL
Production and Deployment Phase [*Military*] (MCD) .... PD
Production and Distribution of Foodstuffs [*British*] .... PDF
Production and Maintenance Engineering Agent (MCD) .... PMEA
Production and Marketing Administration [*Department of Agriculture*] [*Functions dispersed, 1953*] .... PMA
Production and Operations Management Society (EA) .... POMS
Production and Procurement [*Military*] .... P & P
Production and Test Branch (IAA) .... PTB
Production Assembly Facility [*Manufacturing*] .... PAF
Production Assessment Test .... PAT
Production Assistance Report to Pricing [*DoD*] .... PARP
Production Assistant .... PA
Production Assurance Unit (MCD) .... PAU
Production, Augmentation, and Reliability (NG) .... PAR
Production Automated Riveting .... PAR
Production Automated Scheduling System (IEEE) .... PASS
Production Base (MCD) .... PB
Production Base Analysis (MCD) .... PBA
Production Base Modernization (MCD) .... PBM
Production Base Plan (MCD) .... PBP
Production Base Productivity Improvement through Manufacturing Technology (MCD) .... PBPITMT
Production Base Support [*Army*] (AABC) .... PBS
Production Baseline Set (MCD) .... PBLS
Production Broach (AAG) .... PDBH
Production Capability Review [*Army*] .... PCR
Production Certificate (MCD) .... PC
Production Change Number (KSC) .... PCN
Production Change Point .... PCP
Production Change Request (MCD) .... PCR
Production Check Equipment (MCD) .... PCE
Production Code Administration (BARN) .... PCA
Production Command [*Army*] .... PRODC
Production Common Digitizer .... PCD
Production Company [*Films, television, etc.*] .... PC
Production Compliance Audit [*Automotive emissions standards*] .... PCA
Production Compression Capability .... PCC
Production Confirmatory Test (MCD) .... PCT
Production Control (MCD) .... PC
Production Control (IAA) .... PRC
Production Control and Planning System (MCD) .... PCAPS
Production Control File Manager (IAA) .... PCFM
Production Control Information [*Software supplier*] [*Sheffield, England*] (NCC) .... PCI
Production Control Information System (NVT) .... PCIS
Production Control Monitoring System (NVT) .... PCMS
Production Control Priority List (MCD) .... PCPL
Production Control Quantometer .... PCQ
Production Control Record [*NASA*] (KSC) .... PCR
Production Control Section .... PCS
Production Control System (BUR) .... PCS
Production Control Work Order (MCD) .... PCWO
Production Costs .... PC
Production Data Package (MCD) .... PDP
Production Data Sheet (MCD) .... PDS
Production Date [*Computer science*] .... PDATE
Production Day [*Army*] (AABC) .... P (Day)
Production Decision Criteria .... PDC
Production Decision Criteria Matrix .... PDM
Production Department .... PD
Production Design Engineers .... PDE
Production Development Group (IAA) .... PDG
Production Director (NTCM) .... PD
Production Distribution Unit (AAG) .... PDU
Production Distribution Using Component Evaluation (IAA) .... PRODUCE
Production Drawing and Assembly Release Record (AAG) .... PDARR
Production Drawing Control .... PDC
Production EAGLE [*Elevation Angle Guidance Landing Equipment*] **Package** .... PEP
Production Efficiency Board [*British World War II*] .... PEB
Production Electronic Equipment Procurement Status Report .... PEEP
Production Eligibility Date (MUGU) .... PED
Production Emergency Redistribution Group .... PERG
Production Engine Remanufacturers Association (EA) .... PERA
Production Engine Remanufacturers Program [*Automotive engineering*] .... PER
Production Engineering .... PE
Production, Engineering and Logistics Information (AAGC) .... PELI
Production Engineering and Manufacturing Organization (AAG) .... PEMO
[*The*] **Production Engineering and Productivity Exhibition and Conference** [*British*] (ITD) .... PEP
Production Engineering Division [*Frankford Arsenal*] [*Philadelphia, PA*] .... PE
Production Engineering Division [*University of Wisconsin - Madison*] [*Research center*] (RCD) .... PED
Production Engineering Education and Research Center .... PEERC
Production Engineering Measure [*Army*] (MCD) .... PEM
Production Engineering Order .... PEO
Production Engineering Planning .... PEP
Production Engineering Productivity System [*Camtek Ltd.*] [*Software package*] .... PEPS
Production Engineering Research Association [*Research center British*] (IRC) .... PERA
Production Engineering Service .... PES
Production Engineering Specification (NG) .... PES
Production Entitlement Guarantee [*International Agricultural Trade Research Consortium*] (ECON) .... PEG
Production Environmental Tests .... PET
Production Equipment Agency [*Army*] .... PEQUA
Production Equipment Code [*Military*] .... PEC
Production Equipment Package .... PEP
Production Equipment Records Unit (IEEE) .... PERU
Production Equipment Redistribution Group [*Army*] .... PERG
Production Equipment Redistribution Inventory [*Army*] .... PERI
Production Equipment Reserve Inventory [*Navy*] (NG) .... PERI
Production Error Log (NITA) .... PEL
Production Estimate Card (MSA) .... PE CARD
Production Evaluation Missile [*Military*] (CAAL) .... PEM
Production Evaluation Surveillance Test .... PEST
Production Evaluation Test .... PET
Production Executive [*British*] .... PE
Production Executive Committee .... PEC
Production Executive of the War Cabinet [*World War II*] .... PX
Production Experimental Test (SAA) .... PET
Production Facilities (WDMC) .... pro-fax
Production Facility (NTCM) .... Pro-Fax
Production Flight Procedures Manual (MCD) .... PFPM
Production Flow Analysis (PDAA) .... PFA
Production Formulation, Accounting, and Cost System (MHDI) .... PROFACTS
Production Illustration (MSA) .... P/I
Production Image Generator (MCD) .... PIG
Production Implementation Program (AAG) .... PIP
Production Improvement Program [*Navy*] (NG) .... PIP
Production Improvement Verification Test .... PIVT
Production Information and Control System [*IBM Corp.*] [*Software package*] .... PICS
Production Information Processing System (IAA) .... PIPS
Production Information Stocks and Cost Enquiry System (MHDB) .... PISCES
Production Inspection Record .... PIR
Production Installation Group [*Military*] (CAAL) .... PIG
Production Instrumentation Package (NASA) .... PIP
Production Interval .... PI
Production Inventory Analysis (AAG) .... PIA
Production Inventory Control (MHDI) .... PIC
Production Inventory Control System .... PICS
Production Job Sheet .... PJS
Production Language .... PL
Production Lead Time .... PLT
Production Level Video .... PLV
Production Line Configured [*Military*] (CAAL) .... PLC
Production Line Maintenance [*Air Force*] .... PLM
Production Line Manufacturing .... PLM
Production List (AAG) .... PL
Production Management Action Group [*British*] .... PROMAG
Production Management System [*Safe Computing Ltd.*] [*Software package*] (NCC) .... PMS
Production [*or Product*] **Manager** .... PM
Production Master Scheduling System (PDAA) .... PROMAST
Production Men's Guild of the Dress Industry of New York City (EA) .... PMGDINYC
Production Missile Test Program .... PMTP
Production Mock-Up (AAG) .... PDMU
Production Mode .... PM
Production Mold (AAG) .... PDMO
Production Monitor (IAA) .... PM
Production Monitoring Test (NG) .... PMT
Production Music Libraries Association (EA) .... PMLA
Production Notice (KSC) .... PN
Production of Onshore Lower 48 Oil and Gas Model [*Department of Energy*] (GFGA) .... PROLOG
Production of Reliable Items Demands Excellence [*Navy*] (NG) .... PRIDE
Production Office Coordinator (WDMC) .... POC

Production Offset (AABC) ... PO
Production Offset Quantity [*Military*] ... POQ
Production Operational Capability ... POC
Production Operations Review Board [*NASA*] (NASA) ... PORB
Production Operators [*NASDAQ symbol*] (TTSB) ... PROP
Production Operators Corp. [*Associated Press*] (SAG) ... ProdOp
Production Operators Corp. [*NASDAQ symbol*] (NQ) ... PROP
Production Order (KSC) ... PO
Production Order Change (KSC) ... POC
Production Order Location and Reporting [*NASA*] (NASA) ... POLAR
Production Order Records (SAA) ... POR
Production Order Records Change Notice (KSC) ... PORCN
Production Order Request (SAA) ... POR
Production Orientated Draughting and Manufacturing (PDAA) ... PRODAM
Production Packing Depth Range (NG) ... PPDR
Production Part Pattern (MCD) ... PPP
Production Parts Breakdown (MCD) ... PPB
Production Parts Release (KSC) ... PPR
Production Pattern (AAG) ... PDPA
Production per Man-Hour ... PMH
Production Planning (IAA) ... PROP
Production Planning and Control [*Military*] (AABC) ... PP & C
Production Planning and Control ... PPC
Production Planning and Control System ... PPCS
Production Planning Change Request (SAA) ... PPCR
Production Planning Inventory Control System (PDAA) ... PPICS
Production Planning Memorandum ... PPM
Production Planning System [*TDS Business Systems Ltd.*] [*Software package*] (NCC) ... PPS
Production Possibility Frontier [*Economics*] ... PPF
Production Process Prove-Out Program ... P4
Production Processes ... PP
Production Program Library [*Social Security Administration*] ... PROGLIB
Production Progress Report (MCD) ... PPR
Production Prototype ... PPT
Production Qualification and Testing ... PQT
Production Qualification Test and Evaluation ... PQT & E
Production Qualification Test / Limited Operational Test ... PQT/LOT
Production Quality Assurance ... PQA
Production Quality Control ... PQC
Production Quotation Support ... PQS
Production Rate ... PR
Production Rate Index (OA) ... PRI
Production Reader Assembly (KSC) ... PRA
Production Readiness Assessment [*Army*] ... PRA
Production Readiness Master Plan ... PRMP
Production Readiness Plan ... PRP
Production Readiness Review ... PRR
Production Readiness Verification Testing (MCD) ... PRVT
Production Readjustments Committee [*WPB*] ... PRC
Production Recording System ... PRS
Production Records, Inc. (EA) ... PRI
Production Release System (MCD) ... PRS
Production Reliability Acceptance Test ... PRAT
Production Reliability Cost Improvement (DWSG) ... PRCI
Production Reliability Test ... PRT
Production Repair Order ... PRO
Production Request Design Review ... PRDR
Production Requirements [*Military*] (AFIT) ... PR
Production Requirements Plan ... PRP
Production Research Division, Esso Resources Canada Ltd., Calgary, Alberta [*Library symbol National Library of Canada*] (NLC) ... ACIPRD
Production Research Reports ... PRR
Production Reserve Policy ... PRP
Production Responsibilities Document (MCD) ... PRD
Production Review [*Automotive project management*] ... PR
Production, Reviewing, Organizing, and Monitoring of Performance Techniques (BUR) ... PROMPT
Production Run Tape ... PRT
Production Sample (AAG) ... PDSE
Production Sampling Test (IAA) ... PST
Production Schedule Completion Report [*DoD*] ... PSCR
Production Scheduling and Control (AAGC) ... PS&C
Production Scheduling and Control (IAA) ... PSC
Production Scheduling and Inventory Control ... PSIC
Production Special Testing Equipment (MCD) ... PSTE
Production Special Tooling (MCD) ... PST
Production Stock Item (MCD) ... PSI
Production Support and Equipment Replacement [*Military*] (AABC) ... PS & ER
Production Support Equipment Unit (MCD) ... PSEU
Production Support Group (NITA) ... PSG
Production Support Repair Plan (SAA) ... PSRP
Production Support Repair Unit (SAA) ... PSRU
Production Surveillance Test (MCD) ... PST
Production System Generator ... PSG
Production System Integration Area ... PSIA
Production System Simulator [*Computer science*] ... PROSIM
Production Systems Acceptance Branch [*Social Security Administration*] ... PSAB
Production Systems Acceptance Section [*Social Security Administration*] ... PSAS
Production Systems Management (IAA) ... PSM
Production Tabulating Form (AAG) ... PTF
Production Tape (AAG) ... PDTA
Production Techniques (MCD) ... PT
Production Temporary Facility Tool (SAA) ... PTFT
Production Test [*Military*] ... PT
Production Test Engineering Task Description (MCD) ... PTETD
Production Test Equipment (MCD) ... PTE
Production Test Plan (MCD) ... PTP
Production Test Procedure (NATG) ... PTP
Production Test Program Report ... PTPR
Production Test Record ... PTR
Production Test Requirements (KSC) ... PTR
Production Test Specification ... PTS
Production Training Indicator [*Computer science*] ... PTI
Production Type Test ... PTT
Production Unit (CAAL) ... PU
Production Unit Price Goals (MCD) ... PUPG
Production Upgrade Management Program (DNAB) ... PUMP
Production Urgency Committee [*WPB*] ... PUC
Production Validation [*Military*] (AABC) ... PV
Production Validation Test - Contractor (MCD) ... PVT-C
Production Validation Test - Government ... PVT-G
Production Work Order (MCD) ... PWO
Production-Equipment-Missile Agency [*Army*] ... PEMA
Production-Oriented Maintenance Organization (MCD) ... POMO
Production-Oriented Scheduling Techniques (MCD) ... POST
Production-Oriented Survey (MCD) ... POS
Productive Cost Management (ADA) ... PCM
Productive Cough [*Medicine*] (DMAA) ... PC
Productive Man Work Unit (AD) ... pmu
Productive Man-Hours per Month [*Navy*] (NG) ... PMH/M
Productive Rehabilitation Institute of Dallas for Ergonomics [*Research center*] (RCD) ... PRIDE
Productive Standard Hour (PDAA) ... PSH
Productive Standard Minute (MHDI) ... PSM
Productive Time [*Computer order entry*] ... PT
Productivity ... PRDCTVTY
Productivity and Technical Assistance Division [*Mutual Security Agency*] [*Abolished, 1953*] ... PTAD
Productivity Australia [*A publication*] ... Prod Aust
Productivity Communication Center [*Defunct*] (EA) ... PCC
Productivity Criteria Quotient ... PCQ
[*The*] **Productivity Effectiveness Program** [*Title of a pamphlet by Robert Gedaliah that describes sedentary exercises for desk-bound workers*] ... PEP
Productivity Enhancing Capital Investment [*DoD*] ... PECI
Productivity Enhancing Capital Investment Program (MCD) ... PECIP
Productivity Enhancing Incentive Fund (DNAB) ... PEIF
Productivity Environmental Preference Survey [*Test*] ... PEPS
Productivity Improvement and Control System (BUR) ... PICS
Productivity Improvement Program [*Office of Management and Budget*] (GFGA) ... PIP
Productivity Improvement Program [*Department of Labor*] ... PIP
Productivity Improvements for the Decade of the Eighties ... PRIDE
Productivity Increases, Quality Control, Robotization, and Savings [*Japanese formula for economic success*] (AD) ... pqrs
Productivity Index (IEEE) ... PI
Productivity Integrated Measurement System [*Army*] ... PRIMES
Productivity Investment Fund [*Program*] [*Air Force*] ... PIF
Productivity Measurement and Evaluation System (MCD) ... PMES
Productivity Measurement Experiment [*National Institute of Standards and Technology*] ... PROMEX
Productivity, Reliability, Availability, and Maintainability (AD) ... pram
Productivity, Reliability, Availability, and Maintainability Office [*Air Force*] ... PRAM
Productivity, Reliability, Availability, and Maintenance Program Office [*Air Force*] (DOMA) ... PRAMPO
Productivity Research and Extension Program [*North Carolina State University*] [*Research center*] (RCD) ... PREP
Productivity Research Division [*Office of Personnel Management*] (GRD) ... PRD
Productivity/Respiration [*Physiology*] ... P/R
Productivity Savings Reward (AAGC) ... PSR
Productivity Technologies Corp. [*NASDAQ symbol*] (SAG) ... PRAC
Productivity Technologies Corp. [*Associated Press*] (SAG) ... Product
Productivity Technologies Corp. [*Associated Press*] (SAG) ... Productv
Productivity Trend Evaluation System (MCD) ... PTES
Product-Moment Correlation Co-Efficient (DMAA) ... PMCC
Producto Material Neto [*Net Material Product*] [*Spain*] (AD) ... pmn
Producto Nacional Bruto [*Gross National Product*] [*Spanish*] (AD) ... pnb
Product-Quality-Routing-Service-Timing [*Industrial engineering*] ... PQRST
Products (AAGC) ... Prods
Products Administration Contract Control ... PACC
Products and Process Research and Development Support (DCTA) ... PPRDS
Products for Power [*Automotive components manufacturer*] ... PFP
Products List Circular [*Patents*] ... PLC
Products, Marketing, and Technology [*Bank Administration Institute*] [*A publication*] ... PMT
Products of Combustion (DICI) ... POC
Products of Conception [*Medicine*] (MEDA) ... POC
Products of Conception [*Obstetrics*] (DAVI) ... POC
Products of Sums (IAA) ... POS
Product-with-Purchase (WDMC) ... P-W-P
Product-with-Purchase (WDMC) ... p-w-p
Produto National Bruto [*Gross National Product*] [*Portugal*] (AD) ... PNB
Prodynorphin [*Biochemistry*] ... PDYN
Proeme [*Introduction to Coke's Institutes*] [*A publication*] (DLA) ... Inst Proem
Proenkephalin [*Biochemistry*] ... PENK
Pro-Fac Co-op 'A' Pfd [*NASDAQ symbol*] (TTSB) ... PFACP
Pro-Fac Cooperative, Inc. [*NASDAQ symbol*] (SAG) ... PFACP
Pro-Fac Cooperative, Inc. [*Associated Press*] (SAG) ... ProFac
Pro-Family Press Association [*Defunct*] (EA) ... PFPA

Profanity [*FBI standardized term*] ..... PROF
Profco Resources Ltd. [*Vancouver Stock Exchange symbol*] ..... PSO
Professeurs d'Economie Domestique des Universites Canadiennes [*Canadian University Teachers of Home Economics - CUTHE*] ..... PEDUC
Professinal Sports Care Management, Inc. [*NASDAQ symbol*] (SAG) ..... PSCM
Profession ..... P
Profession [*or Professional*] ..... PROF
Profession Related Intern-Mentorship Experience ..... PRIME
Professional [*Civil Service employees designation*] ..... P
Professional ..... PRO
Professional ..... PRO
Professional (ODBW) ..... pro
Professional ..... PROFESSL
Professional ..... PROFL
Professional Abstracts Registries [*Database Innovations, Inc.*] ..... PAR
Professional Accounting System for Schools (AIE) ..... PASS
Professional Activities for Continuing Education [*AEC*] ..... PACE
Professional Activities Group ..... PAG
Professional Activities Survey [*Medicine*] ..... PAC
Professional Activity Study [*Later, CPHA*] ..... PAS
Professional, Administrative, and Technical (OICC) ..... PAT
Professional, Administrative, Clerical, Technical, and Other (BARN) ..... PACTO
Professional Administrative Development [*Medicine*] ..... PAD
Professional, Administrative, Technical, and Clerical [*Bureau of Labor Statistics survey*] ..... PATC
Professional, Administrative, Technical, Clerical, and Other [*Bureau of Labor Statistics survey*] (DNAB) ..... PATCO
Professional Administrator [*Australia A publication*] ..... PA
Professional Administrator (DD) ..... PAdm
Professional Administrator [*A publication*] ..... Prof Admin
Professional Aeromedical Transport Association (EA) ..... PATA
Professional Agent [*Professional Insurance Agents*] [*A publication*] ..... PA
Professional Agrologist (DD) ..... PAg
Professional Air Traffic Controllers Organization [*Defunct*] (EA) ..... PATCO
Professional Airways Systems Specialists (EA) ..... PASS
Professional Amateur Sports Systems [*Cable-television network*] ..... PASS
Professional and Administrative (AAG) ..... P & A
Professional and Administrative Career Examination [*Formerly, FSEE*] [*Civil Service*] ..... PACE
Professional and Executive [*Employment register*] [*British*] ..... P/E
Professional and Executive Recruitment Service [*British*] ..... PER
Professional and Linguistic Assessment Board (AIE) ..... PLAB
Professional and Managerial Class [*British*] (DI) ..... PMC
Professional and Managerial Position Questionnaire [*Test*] ..... PMPQ
Professional and Occupational Licensing Directory [*A publication*] ..... POLD
Professional and Organizational Development [*In association name Professional and Organizational Development Network in Higher Education*] (EA) ..... POD
Professional and Scholarly Publishing Division [*Association of American Publishers*] (EDAC) ..... PSP
Professional and Statutory Board (AIE) ..... PSB
Professional and Technical Advisory Committee [*JCAH*] ..... PTAC
Professional and Technical Consultants Association (EA) ..... PATCA
Professional and Technical Programs, Inc. ..... PTPI
Professional and Technical Role Analyses [*Occupational therapy*] ..... PATRA
Professional and Technical Services Library, Transport Canada [*Bibliotheque des Services Professionnels et Techniques, Transports Canada*], Vancouver, British Columbia [*Library symbol National Library of Canada*] (NLC) ..... BVATPT
Professional and Technical Workers Aliyah [*British*] (BI) ..... PATWA
Professional and Technology [*Category*] [*British*] ..... P & T
Professional and Technology Officer [*British*] ..... PTO
Professional Apparel Association ..... PAA
Professional Application Creation Environment (NITA) ..... PACE
Professional Application Creation Environment (HGAA) ..... PACEO
Professional Application Development System [*Slate*] [*Computer science*] ..... PADS
Professional Archers Association (EA) ..... PAA
Professional Art Dealers Association of Canada ..... PADAC
Professional Arts Management Institute (EA) ..... PAMI
Professional Associate, Chartered Surveyors' Institution [*Later, ARICS*] ..... PASI
Professional Associate of the Royal Institution of Chartered Surveyors [*Canada*] (DD) ..... ARICS
Professional Association [*Telecommunications*] ..... PA
Professional Association of Alexander Teachers [*British*] (DBA) ..... PAAT
Professional Association of Canadian Theatres ..... PACT
Professional Association of Christian Educators (EA) ..... PACE
Professional Association of Consulting Engineers ..... PACE
Professional Association of Custom Clothiers (EA) ..... PACC
Professional Association of Diving Instructors (EA) ..... PADI
Professional Association of Health Care Office Managers ..... PAHCOM
Professional Association of Nursery Nurses [*British*] (DBA) ..... PANN
Professional Association of Pet Industries (EA) ..... PAPI
Professional Association of Resume Writers (EA) ..... PARW
Professional Association of Secretarial Services [*Later, NASS*] (EA) ..... PASS
Professional Association of Teachers [*British*] ..... PAT
Professional Association of Teachers [*British*] (DBA) ..... PAT
Professional Association of the Interstate Commerce Commission ..... PAICC
Professional Athletes International [*Later, NFLPA*] (EA) ..... PAI
Professional Audiovideo Retailers Association (EA) ..... PARA
Professional Audiovisual Education Study ..... PAVE
Professional Audit Review Team (AAGC) ..... PART
Professional Auto Group, Inc. ..... PAG
Professional Aviation Maintenance Association (EA) ..... PAMA
Professional Bancorp [*AMEX symbol*] (SPSG) ..... MDB
Professional Bancorp [*Associated Press*] (SAG) ..... PrfBcp
Professional Baseball Athletic Trainers Society (EA) ..... PBATS
Professional Basketball Writers' Association of America (EA) ..... PBWAA
Professional Bibliographic System [*Database manager package*] [*Personal Bibliographic Software, Inc. Ann Arbor, MI*] ..... PBS
Professional Bicycle Racers Association [*Defunct*] (EA) ..... PBRA
Professional Billiards Tour [*An association*] ..... PBT
Professional Bookmen of America [*Later, Pi Beta Alpha*] (EA) ..... PBA
Professional Books Ltd. (ILCA) ..... PB
Professional Bowhunters Society (EA) ..... PBS
Professional Bowlers Association of America (EA) ..... PBA
Professional Boxing Control Board [*Victoria, Australia*] ..... PBCB
Professional Bull Riders [*An association*] ..... PBR
Professional Business and Technical Management [*British*] [*An association*] (DBA) ..... ProfBTM
Professional Business Colleges of Australia ..... PBCA
Professional Capabilities Questionnaire [*Jet Propulsion Laboratory, NASA*] ..... PCQ
Professional Car Society (EA) ..... PCS
Professional Career Information Service [*Department of Labor*] ..... PCIS
Professional Careers Sourcebook [*A publication*] ..... PCS
Professional Certificate in Education ..... P Cert Ed
Professional Chess Association (EA) ..... PCA
Professional Classes Aid Council (AIE) ..... PCAC
Professional Coin Grading Service (BARN) ..... PCGS
Professional Comedians' Association (EA) ..... PCA
Professional Communication (MCD) ..... PC
Professional Compounding Centers of America ..... PCCA
Professional Conference Organizer ..... PCO
Professional Construction Estimators Association of America (EA) ..... PCEAA
Professional Continuing Education (DOMA) ..... PCE
Professional Convention Management Association [*Birmingham, AL*] (EA) ..... PCMA
Professional Corporation ..... PC
Professional Corporation Guide (Prentice-Hall, Inc.) [*A publication*] (DLA) ..... Prof Corp Guide (P-H)
Professional Council of Religious Education [*British*] (DBA) ..... PCFRE
Professional Currency Dealers Association (EA) ..... PCDA
Professional Cycling Association [*British*] (DBA) ..... PCA
Professional Dance Teachers Association (EA) ..... PDTA
Professional Dental Tech [*ECM, Symbol*] (TTSB) ..... PRO.EC
Professional Dental Technologies, Inc. [*AMEX symbol*] (SAG) ..... PRO
Professional Dental Technologies, Inc. [*Associated Press*] (SAG) ..... ProDnt
Professional Development (ADA) ..... PD
Professional Development Advisory Committee [*American Occupational Therapy Association*] ..... PDAC
Professional Development and Recruitment Career Program [*Military*] ..... PDRC
Professional Development Division [*American Occupational Therapy Association*] ..... PDD
Professional Development Education [*Military*] (RDA) ..... PDE
Professional Development Institute [*Canada*] ..... PDI
Professional Development League (EA) ..... PDL
Professional Development Program [*Military*] ..... PDP
Professional Development Program Improvement Center (EDAC) ..... PDPIC
Professional Development School ..... PDS
Professional Development Seminar (HGAA) ..... PDS
Professional Development System [*PC software*] [*Microsoft, Inc.*] (PCM) ..... PDS
Professional Digital [*Recording*] (NTCM) ..... PD
Professional Diploma [*Education*] (AEE) ..... PD
Professional Disc Golf Association ..... PDGA
Professional Disk Operating System [*Computer science*] ..... ProDOS
Professional Drag Racing Association (EA) ..... PDRA
Professional Driver Improvement Course ..... PDIC
Professional Drivers Association ..... PDA
Professional Drivers Council for Safety and Health ..... PROD
Professional Dyers Guild [*Defunct*] ..... PDG
Professional Education (AFM) ..... PE
Professional Education and Training for Research Librarianship Program (EDAC) ..... PETREL
Professional Education Libraries [*UTLAS symbol*] ..... PEL
Professional Education of the Media Specialist ..... PEMS
Professional Educational Development Corp. [*An association*] (EA) ..... PEDC
Professional Emphasis Group [*National Audience Board*] (NTCM) ..... PEG
Professional Employment Register [*British*] (ODBW) ..... PER
Professional Engineer ..... PE
Professional Engineer ..... PEng
Professional Engineer ..... PrEng
Professional Engineer ..... Prof Eng
Professional Engineer [*A publication*] ..... Prof Engr
Professional Engineering and Research Consultants ..... PERC
Professional Engineering Career Development Series [*Book series*] ..... PECDS
Professional Engineers Conference Board for Industry (EA) ..... PECBI
Professional Engineers in Industry ..... PEI
Professional Engineers in Private Practice ..... PEPP
Professional Engineers' Legislative Committee ..... PELC
Professional Engineers Ontario [*Canada*] (DD) ..... APEO
Professional Enhancement Project [*American Occupational Therapy Association*] ..... PEP
Professional Enrichment News [*Portuguese*] (BJA) ..... PEN
Professional Equestrian Instructors and Trainers Association [*Defunct*] (EA) ..... PEITA
Professional Examination Service ..... PES
Professional Experience Program [*Australia*] ..... PEP
Professional Express Courier Service, Inc. [*ICAO designator*] (FAAC) ..... PAD
Professional Farmers of America (EA) ..... PFA

Professional Filler System [*Military*] ... PROFFIS
Professional Film and Video Equipment Association (EA) ... PFVEA
Professional Fishermen's Association [*Tasmania, Australia*] ... PFA
Professional Football Referees Association (EA) ... PFRA
Professional Football Researchers Association (EA) ... PFRA
Professional Football Trainers (EA) ... PFT
Professional Football Writers of America (EA) ... PFWA
Professional Footballers' Association [*British*] (BI) ... PFA
Professional Fraternity Association (EA) ... PFA
Professional Geologist ... PG
Professional Geologist (DD) ... PGeol
Professional Geophysicist (DD) ... PGeoph
Professional Golf Club Repairmen's Association (EA) ... PGCRA
Professional Golfers Association (NADA) ... PGA
Professional Golfers' Association of America (EA) ... PGA
Professional Graphics Adapter [*IBM Corp.*] ... PGA
Professional Graphics Controller [*IBM Corp.*] ... PGC
Professional Graphics Language [*Software*] [*IBM Corp.*] (BYTE) ... PGL
Professional Grounds Management Society (EA) ... PGMS
Professional Group (MCD) ... PG
Professional Group - Antennas and Propagation ... PGAP
Professional Group Audio ... PGA
Professional Group - Automatic Control ... PGAC
Professional Group - Broadcast and Television Receivers ... PGBTR
Professional Group - Broadcast Transmission Systems ... PGBTS
Professional Group - Circuit Theory ... PGCT
Professional Group - Communications Systems ... PGCS
Professional Group - Component Parts ... PGCP
Professional Group - Education ... PGE
Professional Group Electronic Component Parts (IAA) ... PGECP
Professional Group - Electronic Devices ... PGED
Professional Group - Engineering Management ... PGEM
Professional Group - Human Factors in Electronics ... PGHFE
Professional Group - Industrial Electronics ... PGIE
Professional Group - Information Theory ... PGIT
Professional Group - Instrumentation ... PGI
Professional Group - Medical Electronics ... PGME
Professional Group - Microwave Theory and Techniques ... PGMTT
Professional Group - Military Electronics (MUGU) ... PGMIL
Professional Group - Military Electronics (AAG) ... PGMILE
Professional Group - Nuclear Science ... PGNS
Professional Group of Mathematical Symbol Jugglers (MUGU) ... PGMSJ
Professional Group on Aeronautical and Navigational Electronics ... PGANE
Professional Group on Electronic Computers [*IEEE*] ... PGEC
Professional Group on Engineering Writing and Speech [*Institute of Radio Engineers; now IEEE*] ... PGEWS
Professional Group on Instrumentation and Measurement [*National Bureau of Standards*] ... PGIM
Professional Group on Space Electronics and Telemetry (AAG) ... PGSET
Professional Group - Product Engineering and Production ... PGPEP
Professional Group - Production Techniques ... PGPT
Professional Group - Radio Frequency Interference ... PGRFI
Professional Group - Reliability and Quality Control ... PGRQC
Professional Group - Ultrasonic Engineering ... PGUE
Professional Group - Vehicular Communications ... PGVC
Professional Group-Quality Control (IAA) ... PGQC
Professional Group-Radio Telemetry and Remote Control (IAA) ... PGRTRC
Professional Group-Telemetry and Remote Control (IAA) ... PGTRC
Professional Guidance Systems, Inc. [*Information service or system*] (IID) ... PGS
Professional Guides Association of America (EA) ... PGAA
Professional Hairdressers' Association [*Australia*] ... PHA
Professional Handlers Association (EA) ... PHA
Professional Hi-Resolution Image Processing System [*TerraVision, Inc.*] (PCM) ... PHIPS
Professional Hockey Writers' Association (EA) ... PHWA
Professional Horsemen's Association of America (EA) ... PHA
Professional Horsemen's Association of America [*Later, PHA*] (EA) ... PHAA
Professional Hydrologist ... PH
Professional Image Computer (NITA) ... PIC
Professional Improvement Points Program [*Louisiana*] (EDAC) ... PIPS
Professional Indemnity [*Insurance*] ... PI
Professional Indemnity [*Insurance*] (ODBW) ... pi
Professional, Industrial and Commercial Updating [*Vocational training*] [*British*] ... PICKUP
Professional Institute for the American Management Association (OICC) ... PIAMA
Professional Institute of the Public Service of Canada [*See also IPFP*] ... PIPS
Professional Institute of the Public Service of Canada, Ottawa, ON, Canada [*Library symbol*] [*Library of Congress*] (LCLS) ... CaOOPIP
Professional Institute of the Public Service of Canada [*Institut Professionnel de la Fonction Publique du Canada*], Ottawa, Ontario [*Library symbol National Library of Canada*] (BIB) ... OOPIP
Professional Institutions Council for Conservation [*British*] ... PICC
Professional Instrument Course [*Aeronautics*] ... PIC
Professional Insurance Agents [*Alexandria, VA*] (EA) ... PIA
Professional Insurance Communicators of America (EA) ... PICA
Professional Insurance Mass-Marketing Association [*Bethesda, MD*] (EA) ... PIMA
Professional Insurance Mass-Marketing Association [*Bethesda, MD*] (EA) ... PIMMA
Professional Interfraternity Conference [*Later, PFA*] (EA) ... PIC
Professional Investor Report [*A publication*] (IT) ... PIR
Professional Karate Association [*Defunct*] (EA) ... PKA
Professional Knitwear Designers Guild ... PKDG
Professional Land Economist [*Canada*] (DD) ... PLE
Professional Landman [*Canada*] (DD) ... PLand
Professional Lawn Care Association of America (EA) ... PLCAA
Professional Legal Assistants (EA) ... PLA
Professional Legal Secretary [*National Association of Legal Secretaries*] [*Designation awarded by*] ... PLS
Professional Liability Insurance (DMAA) ... PLI
Professional Library Access and Information Delivery [*Information service or system*] (IID) ... PLAID
Professional Library, Board of Education for the Borough of East York, Toronto, Ontario [*Library symbol National Library of Canada*] (NLC) ... OTEYBE
Professional Library, Board of Education for the City of York, Toronto, Ontario [*Library symbol National Library of Canada*] (NLC) ... OTYBE
Professional Library, Edmonton Catholic School District, Edmonton, Alberta [*Library symbol National Library of Canada*] (NLC) ... AEPL
Professional Library Literature Acquisition Program ... PROLLAP
Professional Library, Metropolitan Separate School Board, Willowdale, Ontario [*Library symbol National Library of Canada*] (NLC) ... OTMSS
Professional Local Area Network (NITA) ... PLAN
Professional Management for Executives [*Army*] ... PME
Professional Manager (DD) ... PMgr
Professional/Managerial (WDMC) ... p/m
Professional Managers Association (EA) ... PMA
Professional Manufacturers' Agents (EA) ... PMA
Professional Mariners Alliance [*Defunct*] (EA) ... PMA
Professional Master of Business Administration (PGP) ... PMBA
Professional Master of Science in Accounting (PGP) ... PMSA
Professional Media Service Corp., Gardena, CA [*Library symbol*] [*Library of Congress*] (LCLS) ... CGarP
Professional Medical Film (AABC) ... PMF
Professional Military Comptroller School ... PMCS
Professional Military Education (AFM) ... PME
Professional Military Ethic (MCD) ... PME
Professional Motion Picture Equipment Association [*Later, PFVEA*] (EA) ... PMPEA
Professional Music Men, Inc. (EA) ... PMM
Professional Musicians' Club [*Australia*] ... PMC
Professional Numismatists' Association [*British*] (BI) ... PNA
Professional Numismatists Guild (EA) ... PNG
Professional Office System ... PROF
Professional Office System [*IBM Corp.*] ... PROFS
Professional Officer ... PO
Professional Officer [*A publication*] ... Prof Officer
Professional Officer Course [*AFROTC*] (AFM) ... POC
Professional Oglers of Female Figures [*Men's group opposing below-the-knee fashions introduced in 1970*] ... POOFF
Professional Operating System (NITA) ... POS
Professional Opportunities through Academic Partnership [*National War College*] ... PROTAP
Professional or Managerial (WDMC) ... POM
Professional Over-the-Road Drivers [*Part of Teamsters Union*] ... PROD
Professional Panhellenic Association [*Later, PFA*] (EA) ... PPA
Professional Paper ... PP
Professional Paper (AD) ... pp
Professional Performance of the Royal Northern College of Music [*British*] (DBQ) ... PPRNCM
Professional Personal Computer ... PPC
Professional Photographers of America (EA) ... PP of A
Professional Photographers of America [*Atlanta, GA*] (WDMC) ... PP of A
Professional Photographers of America (NADA) ... PPA
Professional Photographers of America (AD) ... PPA
Professional Photographers of Israel (PDAA) ... PPI
Professional Photographic Laboratories Association [*British*] (DBA) ... PPLA
Professional Picture Framers Association (EA) ... PPFA
Professional Pool Players Association [*Defunct*] (EA) ... PPPA
Professional Productivity Management System (HGAA) ... PPMS
Professional Programmers Association (EA) ... PPA
Professional Protector and Legal Defense Fund ... PPLDF
Professional Psychics United (EA) ... PPU
Professional Publishers Marketing Group (EA) ... PPMG
Professional Putters Association (EA) ... PPA
Professional Qualification Examination [*National Security Agency*] (EDAC) ... PQE
Professional Qualification Index (AFM) ... PQI
Professional Qualification Index (AD) ... pqi
Professional Qualification Test [*of the National Security Agency*] ... PQT
Professional Race Pilots Association [*Later, USARA*] (EA) ... PRPA
Professional Racing Organization of America [*Later, USCF*] (EA) ... PRO
Professional Radio and Electronics Institute of Australia ... PREIA
Professional Rate Training Course (DNAB) ... PRTC
Professional Reactor Operator Society (EA) ... PROS
Professional Reference Center [*Los Angeles County Office of Education*] [*Downey, CA*] [*Library network*] ... PRC
Professional Registration Boards of the Northern Territory [*Australia*] ... PRB
Professional Rehabilitation Workers with the Adult Deaf [*Later, ADARA*] (EA) ... PRWAD
Professional Relations Council [*American Chemical Society*] ... PRC
Professional Resellers Organization [*Defunct*] (EA) ... PRO
Professional Results in Daily Effort [*Strategic Air Command's acronym for the Zero Defects Program*] ... PRIDE
Professional Review Organization [*Medicare*] ... PRO
Professional Rights and Responsibilities ... PR & R
Professional Rodeo Cowboys Association (EA) ... PRCA
Professional Salespersons of America [*Defunct*] (EA) ... PSA
Professional School Photographers of America (EA) ... PSPA
Professional, Scientific, and Technical ... PST
Professional Secretaries International [*Kansas City, MO*] (EA) ... PSI

Professional Service Association (EA) .... PSA
Professional Service Corporation [Medicine] (HCT) .... PSC
Professional Service Dates [Formerly, ADBD] .... PSD
Professional Services Business Management Association [Later, PSMA]
(EA) .... PSBMA
Professional Services Council [Washington, DC] (EA) .... PSC
Professional Services Management Association [Alexandria, VA] (EA) ...... PSMA
Professional Services Section (BARN) .... PSS
Professional Skaters Guild of America (EA) .... PSGA
Professional Skating Association of Canada .... PSAC
Professional Ski Instructors of America (EA) .... PSIA
Professional Skills Alliance (EA) .... PSA
Professional Skills Development Program [Bureau of the Census]
(GFGA) .... PSDP
Professional Soccer Reporter's Association (EA) .... PSRA
Professional Specialty Group .... PSG
Professional Sports Care Management, Inc. [Associated Press] (SAG) .... ProSport
Professional Sports Care Mgmt [NASDAQ symbol] (TTSB) ...... PSCM
Professional Sports Photographers Association [British] (EAIO) .... PSPA
Professional Sports Teams Histories [A publication] .... PSTH
Professional Squash Coaches' Association of Victoria [Australia] .... PSCAV
Professional Staff [Associated Press] (SAG) .... ProfStaff
Professional Staff [NASDAQ symbol] (SAG) .... PSTF
Professional Staff Member [Congress] (DOMA) .... PSM
Professional Standards Review Council of America (EA) ..... PSRCA
Professional Standards Review Organization [Generic term for groups of
physicians who may review the policies and decisions of their
colleagues] .... PSRO
Professional Standards Review Organization (NADA) .... PSRO
Professional Stringers Association [Defunct] (EA) .... PSA
Professional Systems Division [American Institute of Architects Service Corp.]
[Information service or system] (IID) .... PSD
Professional Tattoo Artists Guild (EA) .... PTAG
Professional Tattooists Association of Australia .... PTAA
Professional Tax Planner .... PTP
Professional Teaching Practices Commission (OICC) .... PTPC
Professional Technical Group .... PTG
Professional Technical Group on Antennas and Propagation [of the
IEEE] .... PTGAP
Professional Technical Group on Electronic Computers [Later, IEEE
Computer Society] .... PTGEC
Professional Technical Group on Engineering Writing and Speech [of the
IEEE] .... PTGEWS
Professional, Technical, Managerial, and Administrative Staff .... PTMAS
Professional Tennis Coaches' Association [Australia] .... PTCA
Professional Tennis Registry, USA (EA) .... PTR
Professional Travel Film Directors Association [Later, Professional
Travelogue Sponsors - PTS] (EA) .... PTFDA
Professional Travelogue Sponsors (EA) .... PTS
Professional Truck Driver Institute of America (EA) .... PTDIA
Professional Trucking Services Association (EA) .... PTSA
Professional Turkey Calling Association of America (EA) ... PTCAA
Professional Video Productions, Inc. [Telecommunications service]
(TSSD) .... PVP
Professional Video Services Corp. [Telecommunications service] (TSSD) ...... PVS
Professional Video Services Corp. [Telecommunications service] (TSSD) .... PVSC
Professional Virgin (DSUE) .... PV
Professional Volunteer .... PV
Professional Walleye Trail .... PWT
Professional Women Bowlers Association [Later, LPBT] (EA) ...... PWBA
Professional Women in Construction (EA) .... PWC
Professional Women Photographers (EA) .... PWP
Professional Women Singers Association (EA) .... PWSA
Professional Women's Appraisal Association (EA) .... PWAA
Professional Women's Caucus (EA) .... PWC
Professional Writers of America (NADA) .... PWA
Professional-Amateur (WDAA) .... PRO-AM
Professional'naia Elektronnaia Vychislitel'naia Mashina [Professional
Computer] [Russian] .... PEVM
Professionals and Amateurs [Sports] (WDMC) .... pro-am
Professionals Coalition for Nuclear Arms Control (EA) .... PCNAC
Professionals for National Security [Defunct] (EA) ...... PNS
Professionals Insurance Co. Management Group [NASDAQ symbol]
(SAG) .... PICM
Professionals Insurance Co. Management Group [Associated Press]
(SAG) .... PICM Gp
Professionals - Nicaragua (EA) .... Pro-Nica
Professionals Organized for Women's Equal Rights [Feminist group] ...... POWER
Professionals, Owners, and Managers [A. C. Nielsen Co.] [Demographic
category] (NTCM) .... POM
Professionnel Air Systems [France ICAO designator] (FAAC) .... PSL
Professions and Occupations Sourcebook [A publication] ...... POS
Professionwide Pension Plan [American Chemical Society] ...... PWPP
Professor (EY) .... PROF
Professor (ODBW) .... Prof
Professor .... PROF
Professor Chen Wen-Chen Memorial Foundation (EA) .... CWCMF
Professor of Aerospace Studies [Air Force] (AFIT) .... PAS
Professor of Air Science [Air Force] .... PAS
Professor of Air Science and Tactics .... PAST
Professor of Military Science .... PMS
Professor of Military Science and Tactics .... PMS & T
Professor of Military Science and Tactics (MUGU) .... PMST
Professor of Moral Philosophy .... PMP
Professor of Naval Science .... PNS

Professor of Naval Science and Tactics [Naval ROTC] .... PNS & T
Professor of Sacred Scripture .... PSS
Professor Ordinarius [Ordinary Professor] [Latin] (ROG) .... PO
Professor Publicus [Public Professor] [Latin] (ROG) ..... PP
Professors of Curriculum (EA) .... PC
Proffatt on Notaries [A publication] (DLA) .... Prof Not
Proffatt on Private Corporations in California [A publication] (DLA) .... Prof Corp
Proffatt on Trial by Jury [A publication] (DLA) .... Prof Jur
Proffatt on Wills [A publication] (DLA) .... Prof Wills
Proffitt's, Inc. [NASDAQ symbol] (NQ) .... PRFT
Proffitt's, Inc. [Associated Press] (SAG) .... Proffitt
Proficiency .... P
Proficiency .... PRO
Proficiency .... PROFCY
Proficiency Analytical Testing [National Institute on Occupational Safety and
Health] .... PAT
Proficiency Data Card [Army] .... PDC
Proficiency Evaluation Review .... PER
Proficiency Examination Program (MCD) .... PEP
Proficiency Pay [Military] .... PROFP
Proficiency Pay [Military] .... PRO-PAY
Proficiency Pay Designator [Military] (AABC) .... PPD
Proficiency Rating Designator [Military] .... PRD
Proficiency Testing .... PT
Proficiency Testing Research (EA) .... PTR
Profile (KSC) .... PF
Profile (DAVI) .... PR
Profile (VRA) .... prof
Profile (GAVI) .... PROF
Profile .... Prof
Profile Analysis [Medicine] .... PA
Profile Analysis and Recording Control (PDAA) .... PARC
Profile Angle (MSA) .... PA
Profile Automobile League (EA) .... PAL
Profile Block (MCD) .... PB
Profile Descent (GAVI) .... PD
Profile for Open Systems Internetworking Technologies [Computer
science] (CDE) .... POSIT
Profile Ignition Pick-Up [Automotive engineering] ..... PIP
Profile Milling Machine .... PMM
Profile of Adaptation to Life - Clinical [Personality development test]
[Psychology] .... PAL-C
Profile of Adaptation to Life - Holistic [Personality development test]
[Psychology] .... PAL-H
Profile of Average Reflectivity .... PAR
Profile of DARCOM Environmental Quality (MCD) .... PDEQ
Profile of Mood States [A questionnaire] .... POMS
Profile of Mood States-Bipolar Form .... POMS-BI
Profile of Nonverbal Sensitivity [Psychology] .... PONS
Profile of Nonverbal Sensitivity (AD) .... pons
Profile of Phonology (AIE) .... PROPH
Profile Reliability (MCD) .... PR
Profile Resolution Obtained by Excitation (PDAA) ...... PROBE
Profile Telemetry of Upper Ocean Currents [Marine science] (OSRA) .... PROTEUS
Profile Telemetry of Upper Ocean Currents (USDC) ...... PROTEUS
Profile Template .... PT
Profiled Lightly Doped Drains (NITA) .... PLDD
Profiled Peristaltic Charge Coupled-Device [Computer science] (IAA) .... PPCCD
Profiler Triangle Analysis Package (USDC) .... PTAP
Profiler Triangle Analysis Package [Marine science] (OSRA) .... PTAP
Profilin (DMAA) .... PFN
Profiling ALACE [Autonomous Lagrangian Circulation Explorer] [Marine
science] (OSRA) .... PALACE
Profiling Current Meter [Oceanography] (MSC) .... PCM
Profiling Fixture .... PFFX
Profit .... P
Profit Analysis Model (MHDI) .... PAM
Profit and Loss [Accounting] .... P & L
Profit and Loss [Accounting] .... P/L
Profit and Loss Statement [Finance] (DFIT) .... P&L
Profit and Performance Planning (DCTA) .... PPP
Profit before Tax [Finance] (WDAA) .... PBT
Profit Center (MHDB) .... PC
Profit Commission on Renewal [Insurance] (AIA) .... PCOR
PROFIT Control Users Association (EA) .... PCUA
Profit Impact of Marketing Strategy .... PIMS
Profit Improvement Program .... PIP
Profit Making Organization .... PMO
Profit Margin (TDOB) .... PM
Profit Motivated [Housing] .... PM
Profit on Day One [Classification for new newspaper] ... PODO
Profit Option Plan [Retailing] .... POP
Profit Rate (WGA) .... PR
Profit Rating of Projects .... PROP
Profit Recovery Group International, Inc. (The) [NASDAQ symbol] (SAG) .... PRGX
Profit Recovery Group International, Inc. (The) [Associated Press]
(SAG) .... ProfRec
Profit Recovery Grp Intl [NASDAQ symbol] (TTSB) ...... PRGX
Profit Sharing [Business term] .... PS
Profit Sharing Council of America (EA) .... PSCA
Profit Sharing Plan [Business term] (MHDW) .... PSP
Profit Sharing Research Foundation (EA) .... PSRF
Profit Sharing Trust Fund .... PSTF
Profit Sharing Trustee (DLA) .... PST
Profit Simulation, Planning and Evaluation of Risk (MHDB) .... PROSPER

Profit Taking [*Investment term*] ... PT
Profit/Volume Ratio ... P/V
Profit/Volume Ratio ... PVR
Profitable Information by Design (MHDI) ... PRIDE
Profitable Information by Design through Phased Planning and Control (MHDB) ... PRIDE
Profit-and-Loss-Sharing Account [*Banking*] (IMH) ... PLS
Profit-Maximizing Price (MHDW) ... PMP
Profit-Related Pay [*Economics*] ... PRP
Proflavine [*An antiseptic*] ... PRO
Proflex Ltd. [*Vancouver Stock Exchange symbol*] ... PFX
Pro-Forma Statement (MHDI) ... PFS
Profound and Multiple Learning Difficulties (AIE) ... PMLD
Profound Sensitivity Syndrome [*Psychology*] ... PS^2
Profoundly Mentally Retarded ... PMR
Profoundly Retarded Multiply Handicapped (AIE) ... PRMH
PROFS [*Program for Regional Observing and Forecasting Services*] **Operational Weather Education and Research** [*Marine science*] (OSRA) ... POWER
PROFS [*Program for Regional Observing and Forecasting Services*] **Operational Weather Education and Research** (USDC) ... POWER
PROFS [*Program for Regional Observing and Forecasting Services*] **Operational Work Station** (USDC) ... POWS
PROFS [*Program for Regional Observing and Forecasting Services*] **Operational Work Station** [*Marine science*] (OSRA) ... POWS
Profunda Femoris Artery [*Anatomy*] (DAVI) ... PFA
Progenitor Genealogical Society (EA) ... PGS
Pro-German [*Prisoner of war term*] [*World War I*] (DSUE) ... PG
Progesterone [*A hormone*] ... P
Progesterone [*A hormone*] ... PRE
Progesterone [*Endocrinology*] (DAVI) ... prog
Progesterone Receptor [*Endocrinology*] ... PgR
Progesterone Receptor [*Endocrinology*] ... P-R
Progesterone Receptor Assay [*Clinical chemistry*] ... PRA
Progesterone Receptor Knockout [*Mouse strain*] ... PRKO
Progesterone Response Element [*Endocrinology*] ... PRE
Progesterone Withdrawal [*Endocrinology*] ... PW
Prognathism [*Dentistry*] (DAVI) ... prog
Prognose Compiler [*Computer science*] (IAA) ... PROCOM
Prognosen-Trends-Entwicklungen [*Forecasts-Trends-Developments*] [*Society for Business Information*] [*Information service or system*] (IID) ... PROGNO
Prognosis (AABC) ... PRGS
Prognosis [*or Prognostication*] (AAG) ... PROG
Prognosis (AAMN) ... PROGN
Prognosis [*Medicine*] (WGA) ... Px
Prognostic Nutrition Index [*Dietetics*] (DAVI) ... PNI
Prognostic Prediction Devices ... PPD
Prognostically Bad Sign During Pregnancy [*Obstetrics*] (MAE) ... PBSP
Program (KSC) ... P
Program [*Telecommunications*] ... PG
Program ... PGM
Program (NG) ... PM
Program (AFM) ... PRGM
Program ... PRGM
Program (KSC) ... PROG
Program Access ... PA
Program Accomplishment Year to Date Evaluation Reviews ... PAYERS
Program Account (NG) ... PA
Program Acquisition Cost (MCD) ... PAC
Program Acquisition Unit Cost (AAGC) ... PAUC
Program Action Directive (AFM) ... PAD
Program Action Officer [*Navy*] (CAAL) ... PAO
Program Action Request (SSD) ... PAR
Program Activation Task Force [*Military*] (AFIT) ... PATF
Program Activity Recording [*Computer science*] (IAA) ... PAR
Program Activity Structure ... PAS
Program Address ... PA
Program Address Counter [*Computer science*] (EECA) ... PAC
Program Address Register ... PAR
Program Address Storage (IEEE) ... PAS
Program Adjustment Committee ... PAC
Program Adjustment Request [*Navy*] ... PAR
Program Administrator (MCD) ... PA
Program Administrator's [*Progress*] **Report** [*DoD*] ... PAR
Program Advisory Board (MCD) ... PAB
Program Advisory Committee ... PAC
Program Affinity Grouping and Evaluation System ... PAGES
Program Agent (OICC) ... PA
Program Aid [*A publication*] ... PA
Program Aid Software Systems [*Computer science*] (IEEE) ... PASS
Program Allocation and Reimbursements (AFIT) ... PAR
Program Allocation Checker ... PAC
Program Allowance Schedule ... PAS
Program Alternative Simulation (IAA) ... PAS
Program Alternative Simulation System (KSC) ... PASS
Program Amount (NITA) ... PA
Program Analysis [*Computer science*] ... PA
Program Analysis Adaptable Control [*Computer science*] ... PAAC
Program Analysis and Evaluation ... PA & E
Program Analysis and Evaluation Model (IEEE) ... PAEM
Program Analysis and Resouces Evaluation (IAA) ... PARE
Program Analysis and Resources Review ... PARR
Program Analysis and Review ... PAR
Program Analysis and Review System (EDAC) ... PARS
Program Analysis Control and Evaluation [*Computer science*] (IAA) ... PACE
Program Analysis Division (AAGC) ... PAD
Program Analysis for Documentation [*Computer science*] ... PAD
Program Analysis for Resource Management ... PARM
Program Analysis Memorandum (MCD) ... PAM
Program Analysis of Service Systems [*Procedure to evaluate human service programs*] ... PASS
Program Analysis System (PDAA) ... PANSY
Program Analysis Team (KSC) ... PAT
Program and Budget Estimate (MCD) ... PABE
Program and Budget Guidance [*Army*] ... PBG
Program and Budget Planning ... PBP
Program and Budgeting System (OICC) ... PBS
Program and Cost Control System [*Army*] (RDA) ... PCCS
Program and File Analysis ... PFA
Program and Funds Control System (MCD) ... PFCS
Program and Policy Advisory Board [*UN Food and Agriculture Organization*] ... PPAB
Program Application Code (DNAB) ... PAC
Program Application Instructions [*Telecommunications*] (TEL) ... PA
Program Applique a la Selection et a la Compilation Automatique de la Litterature [*Centre National de la Recherche Scientifique-Informascience*] [*Bibliographic database*] ... PASCAL
Program Appraisal and Review (IEEE) ... PAR
Program Appraisal Report ... PAR
Program Approval Disposal and Redistribution [*Army*] (AABC) ... PADAR
Program Approval Document [*NASA*] (KSC) ... PAD
Program Archives, Canadian Broadcasting Corp. [*Archives des Emissions, Societe Radio-Canada*] **Toronto, Ontario** [*Library symbol National Library of Canada*] (NLC) ... OTBCP
Program as Broadcast [*Radio*] (DEN) ... P-as-B
Program as Recorded [*Radio*] (DEN) ... P-as-R
Program Assembly Card (NITA) ... PAC
Program Assessment (MCD) ... PA
Program Assessment Guide [*Department of Labor*] (OICC) ... PAG
Program Assessment Report [*or Review*] (MCD) ... PAR
Program Assessment Review Report [*Military*] (GFGA) ... PARR
Program Attention [*Computer science*] (IAA) ... PA
Program Attention Key [*Computer science*] ... PA
Program Attention Key [*Computer science*] (BUR) ... PAK
Program Attitude Test (IEEE) ... PAT
Program Audience Rating ... PAR
Program Authorization (AFM) ... PA
Program Authorization Control System (MCD) ... PACS
Program Authorization - Map [*Military*] (AFIT) ... PA-M
Program Authorized Credentials [*Computer science*] ... PAC
Program Automated Method [*Computer science*] ... PAM
Program Baseline (DOMA) ... PB
Program Block (IAA) ... PB
Program Board Panel ... PBP
Program Board Stowage ... PBS
Program Booking Center [*Telecommunications*] (TEL) ... PBC
Program Breakdown ... PB
Program Breakdown Structure [*Nuclear energy*] ... PBS
Program/Budget Accounting and Progress Reporting System [*Proposed*] [*Navy*] ... PBAPRS
Program Budget Accounting System [*Military*] (GFGA) ... PBAS
Program Budget Advisory Committee [*Army*] ... PBAC
Program Budget Committee [*Military*] ... PBC
Program Budget Decision [*DoD*] ... PBD
Program Budget Directive (MCD) ... PBD
Program Budget Document (MCD) ... PBD
Program Budget Execution Review [*Army*] ... PBER
Program Budget Manager (MCD) ... PBM
Program Budget System [*Military*] ... PROBUS
Program Budgeting (ADA) ... PB
Program Buffer Storage (IAA) ... PBS
Program Business Management (NASA) ... PBM
Program Calibration Area [*Computer science*] (DOM) ... PCA
Program Card [*Computer science*] (IAA) ... PC
Program Change ... PC
Program Change Action Notice (DNAB) ... PCAN
Program Change Analysis [*DoD*] ... PCA
Program Change Approval Document (DOMA) ... PCAD
Program Change Control Management (NASA) ... PCCM
Program Change Control System (NG) ... PCCS
Program Change Decision [*Army*] ... PCD
Program Change Factor ... PCF
Program Change Identification Number (NASA) ... PCIN
Program Change Integration (NASA) ... PCIN
Program Change Notice (MCD) ... PCN
Program Change Package (IAA) ... PCPS
Program Change Procedure ... PCP
Program [*or Project*] **Change Proposal** ... PCP
Program Change Request [*DoD*] ... PCR
Program Change Review Board [*NASA*] ... PCRB
Program Characteristics File [*Medicaid*] (GFGA) ... PCF
Program Check [*Computer science*] (IAA) ... PC
Program Check Interruption [*Computer science*] (MDG) ... PCI
Program Checkout Facility ... PCF
Program Committee [*UN Food and Agriculture Organization*] ... PC
Program Committee on Education for Mission (EA) ... PCEM
Program Communication Block ... PCB
Program Communications [*Military*] (AFIT) ... PC
Program Comparator ... PCO
Program Compiler [*Computer science*] (IEEE) ... PROCOMP

Program Complex File [Computer science] (MHDI) .... PCF
Program Composition Notation [Computer science] .... PCN
Program Configuration Control Board [NASA] (NASA) .... PCCB
Program Configuration Manager .... PCM
Program Continuity Memorandum [Military] .... PCM
Program Control .... PC
Program Control Block [Computer science] (BUR) .... PCB
Program Control Card (IAA) .... PCC
Program Control Contract Manager (MCD) .... PCCM
Program Control Counter .... PCC
Program Control Display System [NATO Air Defense Ground Environment] (NATG) .... PCD
Program Control Document (KSC) .... PCD
Program Control Facility .... PCF
Program Control Input (NASA) .... PCI
Program Control Number (AFM) .... PCN
Program Control Plan (AAG) .... PCP
Program Control Procedure [Nuclear energy] (NRCH) .... PCP
Program Control Register .... PCR
Program Control Report .... PCR
Program Control Table [Computer science] .... PCT
Program Control Unit [Computer science] .... PCU
Program Control Word .... PCW
Program Controller (NITA) .... PC
Program Coordination (IEEE) .... PC
Program Coordination Committee (SSD) .... PCC
Program Coordination Office (AAG) .... PCO
Program Coordination Staff [Environmental Protection Agency] (GFGA) .... PCS
Program Cost Estimate (AFM) .... PCE
Program Cost Management (MCD) .... PCM
Program Cost Status [Report] (MCD) .... PCS
Program Counter .... PC
Program Counter [Computer science] (IAA) .... PCR
Program Counter .... PCTR
Program Counter Store .... PCS
Program Counter Timer (IAA) .... PCT
Program Coupler Assembly (KSC) .... PCA
Program Cumulative Audience [Advertising] (DOAD) .... PCA
Program Data Cards (OICC) .... PDC
Program Data Coordinator (MCD) .... PDC
Program Data File .... PDF
Program Data Form [Army] .... PDF
Program Data Manager (MCD) .... PDM
Program Data Processing Section (AAG) .... PDPS
Program Data Processing System (IAA) .... PDPS
Program Data Requirement Plan [Nuclear Regulatory Commission] (NRCH) .... PDRP
Program Data Sheets [Army] (AABC) .... PDS
Program Data Source (BUR) .... PDS
Program Deceleration (KSC) .... PD
Program Decision Memorandum [Military] .... PDM
Program Decision Package [Military] .... PDP
Program Decoder .... PD
Program Definition and Management System (MCD) .... PDMS
Program Definition and Requirements Document (SSD) .... PDRD
Program Definition Block (NITA) .... PDB
Program Definition Data Sheet .... PDDS
Program Definition Phase [Army] .... PDP
Program Definition Phase Studies [Navy] .... PDPS
Program Demonstration and Development Division [ACTION] .... PDDD
Program Description and Requirements [NASA] (NASA) .... PDAR
Program Description Document [Military] (CAAL) .... PDD
Program Description Language (MCD) .... PDL
Program Design and Learning Tool (NITA) .... PD/LT
Program Design Data .... PDD
Program Design, Inc. [Commercial firm] .... PDI
Program Design Language (NASA) .... PDL
Program Design Review (MCD) .... PDR
Program Design Specification (CAAL) .... PDS
Program Developing Agency [Military] (CAAL) .... PDA
Program Development and Evaluation Division [Environmental Protection Agency] (GFGA) .... PDED
Program Development and Test Facility [Social Security Administration] .... PDTF
Program Development Executive (MHDI) .... PDX
Program Development Facility [Computer science] (MHDI) .... PDF
Program Development Increment Package [Military] .... PDIP
Program Development Paper (MCD) .... PDP
Program Development Plan [NASA] .... PDP
Program Development Plan (USDC) .... PDP
Program Development Review Committee [Navy] (CAAL) .... PDRC
Program Development Specialist .... PDS
Program Development System [Computer science] .... PDS
Program Development Tracking System [Computer science] .... PDTS
Program Device (KSC) .... PROGDEV
Program Device Librarian [Computer science] .... PDL
Program Dimension Drawing (MCD) .... PDD
Program Directive (NG) .... PD
Program Directive .... PDIR
Program Directive Document (RDA) .... PDD
Program Directive - Operations (KSC) .... PD-O
Program Director [Television] .... PD
Program Director for Automation [FAA] (TAG) .... ANA
Program Director for Navigation and Landing [FAA] (TAG) .... ANN
Program Director for Weather and Flight Service Stations [FAA] (TAG) .... ANW
Program Directors Flight Readiness Review [NASA] (KSC) .... PDFRR

Program Director's Review [NASA] (NASA) .... PDR
Program Discrepancy Report (IEEE) .... PDR
Program Distribution System .... PDS
Program Document Requirement (BUR) .... PDR
Program Documentation Generator [Computer science] (MHDI) .... PDG
Program Drum Recording .... PDR
Program Element (AFM) .... PE
Program Element Administrator [Navy] (NG) .... PEA
Program Element Breakdown [Computer science] (IAA) .... PEB
Program Element Code (AFM) .... PEC
Program Element Description .... PED
Program Element Descriptive Data (CAAL) .... PEDD
Program Element Descriptive Summary (CAAL) .... PEDS
Program Element Directive .... PED
Program Element Identifier [Military] (AFIT) .... PEID
Program Element Manager (MCD) .... PEM
Program Element Monitor (AFM) .... PEM
Program Element Number [Computer science] (KSC) .... PEN
Program Element Plan (AFIT) .... PEP
Program Element Plan Supplement .... PEPS
Program Element Summary .... PES
Program Element Summary Data [DoD] .... PESD
Program Element Summary Data Sheet [DoD] .... PESDS
Program Elements Activity Accounts (MCD) .... PEAA
Program Emphasis Statement [US Employment Service] [Department of Labor] .... PES
Program Endorsement Memorandum (AAGC) .... PEM
Program Engineering Management Network [Computer science] (RDA) .... PEMN
Program Environment Checkout System .... PECOS
Program Environment Control .... PEC
Program Error Correction Report .... PECR
Program Error Note [Computer science] .... PEN
Program Error Report (MHDI) .... PER
Program Estimating Equation .... PEE
Program Estimating Factor (AFM) .... PEF
Program Estimation Revaluation Technique [Computer science] (IAA) .... PERT
Program Evaluation (OICC) .... PE
Program Evaluation Analysis Plan (MCD) .... PEAP
Program Evaluation and Budget Committee [American Library Association] .... PEBCO
Program Evaluation and Field Operations Staff [Environmental Protection Agency] (GFGA) .... PEFOS
Program Evaluation and Methodology Division [General Accounting Office] [Federal government] (GFGA) .... PEMD
Program Evaluation and Review Technique [Computer science] .... PERT
Program Evaluation and Review Technique - Cost System (DNAB) .... PERT-CS
Program Evaluation and Review Technique/Critical Path Method [Computer science] (DOM) .... PERT/CPM
Program Evaluation and Review Technique - Network Automatic Plotting (SAA) .... PERT-NAP
Program Evaluation and Review Technique Simulation [Game] .... PERTSIM
Program Evaluation and Review Technique Task, Action, and Milestone Items .... PERT-TAM
Program Evaluation and Review Technique/Time Analyzer [Sperry UNIVAC] .... PERT/TIME
Program Evaluation and Review Technique with Cost .... PERTCO
Program Evaluation Center [Navy] (AFIT) .... PEC
Program Evaluation Division [Environmental Protection Agency] (GFGA) .... PED
Program Evaluation for Repetitive Manufacture (IEEE) .... PERM
Program Evaluation Group [Air Force] .... PEG
Program Evaluation Office [Army] .... PEO
Program Evaluation Procedure [Air Force] .... PEP
Program Evaluation Program [Air Force] (IAA) .... PEP
Program Evaluation Research Task (IEEE) .... PERT
Program Evaluation Team .... PET
Program Evaluator and Tester [Computer science] .... PET
Program Event Recording [Computer science] (MDG) .... PER
Program Execution Directive (AAG) .... PED
Program Execution Request .... PER
Program Execution Subdirective (AABC) .... PESD
Program Execution System .... PES
Program Executive Office [or Officer] .... PEO
Program Executive Office - Armored Systems Modernization [Army] (RDA) .... PEO-ASM
Program Executive Office - Field Artillery System [Army] (RDA) .... PEO-FAS
Program Executive Office - Intelligence and Electronic Warfare [Army] (RDA) .... PEO-IEW
Program Executive Office - Missile Defense [Military] (RDA) .... PEO-MD
Program Executive Officer, Global Protection Against Limited Strikes [Army] (RDA) .... PEO-GPALS
Program (Exercise) on Treadmill .... PT
Program File Processor .... PFP
Program Financial Plan (NASA) .... PFP
Program Financial Status Report (AAG) .... PFSR
Program Flying Training [Air Force] (AFM) .... PFT
Program for Acquiring Competence in Entrepreneurship (EDAC) .... PACE
Program for Administrative Traffic Reports On-Line [Computer program] [Bell System] .... PATROL
Program for Advanced Concepts in Electronic Design .... PACED
Program for Advancement of Industrial Technology [Canada] .... PAIT
Program for Afloat College Education [Navy] (NVT) .... PACE
Program for Alcohol Recovery .... PAR
Program for Algebraic Sequences Specifically of Input-Output Nature [Computer science] .... PASSION

Program for Alternative Fluorocarbon Toxicity Testing [*Environmental science*] .... PAFTT
Program for Analysis of Nonlinear Equilibrium and Stability [*NASA*] .... PANES
Program for Analysis of the World Ecosystem .... PAWE
Program for Analysis of Time Series (NASA) .... PATS
Program for Analysis, Reporting, and Maintenance [*Computer science*] .... PARMA
Program for Applied Research on Fertility Regulation [*Northwestern University*] [*Research center*] .... PARFR
Program for Appropriate Technology in Health (EA) .... PATH
Program for Assessing Youth Employment Skills [*Vocational guidance test*] .... PAYES
Program for Astronomical Research and Scientific Experiments Concerning Space .... PARSECS
Program for Automated Gated Evaluation [*Cardiology*] (DAVI) .... PAGE
Program for Automatic Coding Techniques [*Computer science*] .... PACT
Program for Automatic Finite Element Calculation (IAA) .... PAFEC
Program for Automation Retrieval Improvement by Feedback (NITA) .... PARIF
Program for Climate Model Diagnosis and Intercomparison [*Department of Energy*] .... PCMDI
Program for Collaborative Research in the Pharmaceutical Sciences [*University of Illinois at Chicago*] [*Information service or system*] (IID) .... PCRPS
Program for Cooperative Cataloging [*American Library Association*] .... PCC
Program for Elective Surgical Second Opinion [*Blue Cross/Blue Shield*] .... PRESSO
Program for EPS [*Electrical Power System*] Analysis and Rapid Look-Ahead [*NASA computer program*] .... PEARL
Program for European Traffic with Highest Efficiency and Unprecedented Safety (ECON) .... PROMETHEUS
Program for Evaluation of Ground Environment .... PEGE
Program for Evaluation of Rejects and Substitutions [*Computer science*] (IAA) .... PERS
Program for Export Market Development [*Canada*] .... PEMD
Program for Financed Insurance Techniques .... PROFIT
Program for Geographical Display (IAA) .... PGD
Program for Harmonized ATC [*Air Traffic Control*] Research in Europe (GAVI) .... PHARE
Program for Improved Contract Management [*Military*] (AFIT) .... PIC
Program for Increased Education [*Military*] .... PIE
Program for Information Managers [*Later, AIM*] [*An association*] .... PRIM
Program for In-Orbital Rendezvous [*Antisatellite system*] [*Air Force*] .... PRIOR
Program for Integrated Shipboard Electronics .... PRISE
Program for Interactive Multiple Process Simulation (PDAA) .... PIMP
Program for Learning in Accordance with Needs [*Westinghouse Learning Corp.*] .... PLAN
Program for Linguistic Analysis of Natural Plants (IEEE) .... PLANT
Program for Management Development [*Harvard Business School*] (DD) .... PMD
Program for Numeric Tool Operation [*Computer science*] .... PRONTO
Program for Operational Trajectories [*Marine science*] (OSRA) .... POT
Program for Operational Trajectories (USDC) .... POT
Program for Operational Transport and Dispersion (USDC) .... POTAD
Program for Operator Scheduling [*Bell System computer program*] .... POPS
Program for Optical System Design .... POSD
Program for Population Genetics [*Collaboration of US and China Groups*] .... PPG
Program for Rapid Earth-to-Space Trajectory Optimization [*NASA*] .... PRESTO
Program for Regional Observing and Forecasting Services [*Boulder, CO*] [*Department of Commerce*] (GRD) .... PROFS
Program for Research in Information Systems Engineering [*University of Michigan*] [*Research center*] (RCD) .... PRIZE
Program for Research on Objectives-Based Evaluation [*UCLA*] .... PROBE
Program for the Aging (OICC) .... PA
Program for the Analysis of Infrared Spectra [*Computer program*] [*Analytical chemistry*] .... PAIRS
Program for the Introduction and Adaptation of Contraceptive Technology (EA) .... PIACT
Program for the Rapid Estimation of Construction Requirements .... PRESCORE
Program for the Refinement of the Materiel Acquisition Process [*Army*] (AABC) .... PROMAP
Program for the Study of Crime and Delinquency [*Ohio State University*] [*Research center*] (RCD) .... PSCD
Program for the Study of the Future (EA) .... PSF
Program for the Vocational Training of Young People and their Preparation for Adult and Working Life [*EC*] (ECED) .... PETRA
Program Forecast Period [*Military*] (AFIT) .... PFP
Program Fraud Civil Remedies Act .... PFCRA
Program Function [*Computer science*] (IBMDP) .... PF
Program Generation Center [*Military*] (CAAL) .... PGC
Program Generation System [*Computer science*] (MDG) .... PGS
Program Generator (IAA) .... PG
Program Generic [*Computer science*] (TEL) .... PG
Program Guidance .... PG
Program Guidance and Review Committee [*Army*] (AABC) .... PGRC
Program Guidance Memorandum .... PGM
Program Hardware Interface Specification (CAAL) .... PHIS
Program Idea Quotient [*Home testing measurement*] (NTCM) .... PIQ
Program Identification Code (MUGU) .... PIC
Program Identification Number (MUGU) .... PIN
Program Impact Analysis Scenario .... PIAS
Program Implementation Guideline (EG) .... PIG
Program Implementation Plan (MCD) .... PIP
Program in Correctional Institutions (OICC) .... PCI
Program in Process [*Computer science*] (BUR) .... PIP
Program in Progress [*Computer science*] (IAA) .... PIP
Program Incident Report .... PIR
Program Independence, Modularity, Economy .... PRIME
Program Indicator (IEEE) .... PI
Program Indicator-Code [*Computer science*] (ECII) .... PICODE
Program Information .... PI
Program Information and Control System (MCD) .... PICS
Program Information Block (IAA) .... PIB
Program Information Briefing .... PIB
Program Information Center .... PIC
Program Information Control and Retrieval System (NASA) .... PICRS
Program Information Coordination and Review Service [*NASA*] (NASA) .... PICRS
Program Information Document [*NASA*] (MCD) .... PID
Program Information File .... PIF
Program Information Package (AAGC) .... PIP
Program Information Report [*Head Start Program*] [*Department of Health and Human Services*] (GFGA) .... PIR
Program Initialization Module [*Computer science*] (ECII) .... PIM
Program Initiation Agreement (SSD) .... PIA
Program Initiations and Commitments (AAG) .... PIC
Program Innovations (ADA) .... PI
Program Input-Output Cassette [*Computer science*] (IAA) .... PIOC
Program Instruction [*Computer science*] (BUR) .... PI
Program Instruction, Calibration [*Marine Corps*] .... PIC
Program Instruction Frequency Analyzer [*Telecommunications*] (IAA) .... PIFAL
Program Instruction Tape [*Computer science*] (IEEE) .... PIT
Program Instrumentation Requirements Document [*NASA*] .... PIRD
Program Instrumentation Summary Handbook [*NASA*] (KSC) .... PISH
Program Integrated Network .... PIN
Program Integrating Plan [*Computer science*] (IAA) .... PIP
Program Integration Manual .... PIM
Program Integration Plan .... PIP
Program Integrator [*Military*] (RDA) .... PI
Program Interface Control Plan (NASA) .... PICP
Program Interface Module .... PIM
Program Interrupt .... PI
Program Interrupt [*Computer science*] (IAA) .... PRI
Program Interrupt Control [*Computer science*] .... PIC
Program Interrupt Element [*Computer science*] (IAA) .... PIE
Program Interrupt Entry [*Computer science*] .... PIE
Program Interrupt Flag Register [*Computer science*] (IAA) .... PIFR
Program Interrupt Register [*Computer science*] (IAA) .... PIR
Program Interrupt Status Word (NITA) .... PISW
Program Interrupt Word .... PIW
Program Introduction .... PI
Program Introduction Document (NASA) .... PID
Program Issuances [*Assistance Payments Administration, HEW*] .... PI
Program Language Analyzer [*Computer science*] (IEEE) .... PLAN
Program Language for User's System (NITA) .... PLUS
Program Level (IAA) .... PL
Program Level Change Tape [*Computer science*] (IBMDP) .... PLC
Program Library [*Computer science*] .... PL
Program Library [*Computer science*] .... PLIB
Program Library Tape [*Computer science*] (IEEE) .... PLT
Program Library Update System .... PLUS
Program Life Requirement (NG) .... PLR
Program Life-Cycle Cost Estimate [*Army*] .... PLCCE
Program Line Number [*DoD*] .... PLN
Program Line Organization .... PLO
Program Listing Document (MCD) .... PLD
Program Lock-in Register (NITA) .... PLR
Program Logic [*Computer science*] (TEL) .... PL
Program Logic Network (NASA) .... PLN
Program Logical Address Space .... PLAS
Program Logistic Management Plan (MCD) .... PLMP
Program Logistics (NG) .... PROLOG
Program Logistics and Network Scheduling System (IEEE) .... PLANS
Program Logistics Master Schedule [*NASA*] (NASA) .... PLMS
Program Management and Operations Staff [*Environmental Protection Agency*] (GFGA) .... PMOS
Program Management and Performance Review .... PMPR
Program Management and Support Division [*Environmental Protection Agency*] (GFGA) .... PMSD
Program Management Board (AFM) .... PMB
Program Management Control .... PMC
Program [*or Project*] Management Control System [*Army*] .... PMCS
Program Management Course [*Army*] (RDA) .... PMC
Program Management Decision Brief [*Defense Systems Management College*] (DOMA) .... PMDB
Program Management Directive [*Air Force*] .... PMD
Program Management Documentation [*Army*] .... PMD
Program Management Facility [*NASA*] (MCD) .... PMF
Program Management Information System [*Army*] .... PMIS
Program Management Instruction .... PMI
Program Management Network (MCD) .... PMN
Program Management Office [*Environmental Protection Agency*] (GFGA) .... PMO
Program Management Office [*NASA*] (KSC) .... PMO
Program Management Office for Armored Systems Integration [*Army*] (RDA) .... PM-ASI
Program Management Phase-Out Plan [*Military*] (AFIT) .... PMPP
Program Management Plan [*NASA*] .... PMP
Program Management Planning and Scheduling [*Military*] (DNAB) .... PMPS
Program Management Responsibility (MCD) .... PMR
Program Management Responsibility Transfer (MCD) .... PMRT
Program Management Responsibility Transfer Date (AFIT) .... PMRTD
Program Management Responsibility Transfer Plan (AFIT) .... PMRTP
Program Management Simulation Exercise [*Aerospace*] .... PMSE
Program Management Staff [*Environmental Protection Agency*] (GFGA) .... PMS

Program Management Support [*Army*] .... PMS
Program Management Support Staff [*Environmental Protection Agency*] (GFGA) .... PMSS
Program Management System [*Computer science*] .... PMS
Program Management Unit [*Computer science*] (IAA) .... PMU
Program Manager [*or Management*] (MCD) .... PM
Program Manager (AD) .... pm
Program Manager Assistance Group [*Military*] (MCD) .... PMAG
Program Manager - Test, Measurement, and Diagnostic Systems [*Army*] .... PM TMDS
Program Manager's Guidance Memorandum .... PMGM
Program Manager's Integration Review [*NASA*] (NASA) .... PMIR
Program Manager's Preflight Review [*NASA*] (KSC) .... PMPFR
Program Manager's Review [*NASA*] (NASA) .... PMR
Program Manager's Support System [*Defense Systems Management College*] [*Fort Belvoir, VA*] (RDA) .... PMSS
Program Marginal Checking .... PMC
Program Master Milestone Schedule (MCD) .... PMMS
Program Master Schedule (MCD) .... PMS
Program Master Tape .... PMT
Program Measurement Information System [*Computer science*] (IAA) .... PMIS
Program Memorandum (MCD) .... PM
Program Method [*Computer science*] (IAA) .... PM
Program Milestone [*NASA*] (NASA) .... PM
Program Module Connection Diagram (MHDI) .... PMCD
Program Module Dictionary .... PMD
Program Monitor Panel .... PMP
Program Monitoring (MUGU) .... PM
Program Monitoring and Diagnosis .... PMD
Program Monitoring and Planning Techniques (IEEE) .... PROMPT
Program Monitoring System (MCD) .... PROMS
Program Network Diagram [*Telecommunications*] (TEL) .... PND
Program Notice (KSC) .... PN
Program Number [*Horse racing*] .... PN
Program Objective .... PO
Program Objective Memorandum/Budget Estimate Submission (MCD) .... POM/BES
Program Objective Memorandum Generator [*Military*] .... POMGEN
Program Objectives Change Proposal .... POCP
Program Objectives Change Request [*DoD*] .... POCR
Program Objectives Document (AAGC) .... POD
Program Objectives for Fiscal Year (DNAB) .... PO-FY
Program Objectives Memorandum [*Military*] .... POM
Program Obligation Plan (KSC) .... POP
Program of Action for Mediation, Arbitration, and Inquiry [*American Library Association*] .... PAMAI
Program of Active Cooling Effects and Requirements .... PACER
Program of Advanced Professional Development, University of Denver College of Law (DLA) .... PADUD
Program of Advanced Studies .... PAS
Program of Advanced Studies of Institution Building and Technical Assistance Methodologies [*MUCIA*] .... PASITAM
Program of All-Inclusive Care for the Elderly .... PACE
Program of Equal Employment Opportunity Evaluation Reports .... PEER
Program of Industry/Laboratory Projects [*National Research Council of Canada*] .... PILP
Program of Instruction .... POI
Program of Instrumentation (MUGU) .... PI
Program of Noncollegiate Sponsored Instruction (OICC) .... PONSI
Program of Operation [*Computer science*] .... PROGOFOP
Program of Research and Evaluation in Public Schools [*Mississippi State University*] [*Research center*] (RCD) .... PREPS
Program of Study (AEE) .... POS
Program of Surgical Control of Hyperlipidemia .... POSCH
Program of Technical Cooperation [*Organization of American States*] .... PTC
Program of Technology and Society [*Later, DTS*] (EA) .... PTS
Program of University Research .... PUR
Program Office [*Air Force*] (CET) .... PO
Program Office Directive .... POD
Program on Advanced Technology for the Highway .... PATH
Program on Criminal Justice and the Elderly (DICI) .... PCJE
Program on International Politics, Economics, and Security [*University of Chicago*] .... PIPES
Program on Long-Range Forecasting Research [*Marine science*] (OSRA) .... PLRE
Program on Short- and Medium-Range Weather Prediction Research [*Marine science*] (OSRA) .... PSMP
Program on the Promotion of Marine Sciences [*Marine science*] (OSRA) .... PROMAR
Program Operating Plan .... POP
Program Operation and Environment Transfer (SAA) .... POET
Program Operation Control Center [*Space science*] .... POCC
Program Operation Description .... POD
Program Operation Mode .... POM
Program Operation Mode (IAA) .... POMD
Program Operations and Management Office [*Environmental Protection Agency*] (GFGA) .... POMO
Program Operations Manual System [*Social Security Administration*] .... POMS
Program Operations Officer [*Social Security Administration*] .... POO
Program Operations Staff [*Environmental Protection Agency*] (GFGA) .... POS
Program Operations Support Staff [*Environmental Protection Agency*] (GFGA) .... POSS
Program Operations Vocational Education Unit (OICC) .... POVEU
Program Opportunity Notice [*Energy Research and Development Administration*] .... PON
Program Opportunity Notification (AD) .... PON
Program Optimization and Budget Evaluation [*Military*] .... PROBE
Program Optimizer (IAA) .... POGO
Program Order Sequence .... POS
Program Organization for Evaluation and Decision .... POED
Program Oriented Language [*Computer science*] (ECII) .... POL
Program Originator (AFM) .... PO
Program Package (MCD) .... PP
Program Package Document .... PPD
Program Paper .... PP
Program Parts Selection List .... PPSL
Program Performance (NASA) .... PP
Program Performance and Budget Execution Review System [*Army*] .... PPBERS
Program Performance Baseline (NASA) .... PPB
Program Performance Evaluator (NITA) .... PPE
Program Performance Measurement Systems (IEEE) .... PPMS
Program Performance Specification (CAAL) .... PPS
Program Plan and Budget Request (OICC) .... PPBR
Program Plan Budgeting (TDOB) .... PBB
Program Planning and Budget Execution System [*Army*] .... PPBES
Program Planning and Budgeting Staff [*Environmental Protection Agency*] (GFGA) .... PPBS
Program, Planning, and Budgeting System [*Johnson Administration*] [*Executive Office of the President*] (GFGA) .... PPBS
Program Planning and Control (AAG) .... PPC
Program Planning and Evaluation (AD) .... PP & E
Program Planning and Evaluation .... PPE
Program Planning and Review Staff [*Environmental Protection Agency*] (GFGA) .... PPRS
Program Planning and Status Assessment System [*Nuclear energy*] (NRCH) .... PPSAS
Program Planning Budget (NOAA) .... PPB
Program Planning Coordination Office [*United Nations*] .... PPC
Program Planning Directives [*NASA*] (KSC) .... PPD
Program Planning Document (NG) .... PPD
Program Planning Guide (OICC) .... PPG
Program Planning Report (IAA) .... PPR
Program Planning Summary (OICC) .... PPS
Program Planning System [*DoD*] .... PPS
Program Planning-Budgeting-Evaluation System Project (EA) .... PPBES
Program Planning-Budgeting-Evaluation System Project (EA) .... PPBESP
Program Policy Guidelines .... PPG
Program Policy Staff [*UN Food and Agriculture Organization*] .... PPS
Program Position Indicator .... PPI
Program Preferred Parts List .... PPPL
Program Printout (MCD) .... PPO
Program Problem Area .... PPA
Program Product [*Computer science*] .... PP
Program Production Library [*Computer science*] .... PPL
Program Progress Review .... PPR
Program, Project Management [*Army*] .... PPM
Program Proposal Request .... PPR
Program Protection Plan [*DoD*] (RDA) .... PPP
Program Pulse Generator (IEEE) .... PPG
Program Quality Review (AD) .... PQR
Program Random Process (PDAA) .... PRP
Program Rating Summary Report [*Television ratings*] (NTCM) .... PRS
Program Reader Assembly [*Computer science*] .... PRA
Program Reference Table .... PRT
Program Register [*Computer science*] (BUR) .... PR
Program Regulation Guide .... PRG
Program Release Notice [*NASA*] (NASA) .... PRN
Program Reliability Information System for Management [*Polaris*] .... PRISM
Program Reporting and Evaluation System for Total Operations [*AFSC*] .... PRESTO
Program Reporting, Organization, and Management Planning Technique (IAA) .... PROMPT
Program Representative Office (AAGC) .... PRO
Program Request Block (IAA) .... PRB
Program [*or Project*] **Requirement Data** [*NASA*] (KSC) .... PRD
Program Requirement Process Specification [*NASA*] (KSC) .... PRPS
Program Requirements (KSC) .... PR
Program Requirements Analysis Method .... PRAM
Program Requirements Change Board [*NASA*] (NASA) .... PRCB
Program Requirements Control Board [*NASA*] .... PRCB
Program Requirements Control Board Directive [*NASA*] (NASA) .... PRCBD
Program Requirements Document .... PRD
Program Requirements Handbook (MUGU) .... PRH
Program Requirements Package [*Computer science*] .... PRP
Program Requirements Review [*NASA*] (NASA) .... PRR
Program Requirements Summary (MUGU) .... PRS
Program Research and Development (IAA) .... PRAD
Program Research and Development Announcement [*Energy Research and Development Administration*] .... PRDA
Program Research in Integrated Multiethnic Education [*Defunct*] (EA) .... PRIME
Program Resource Advisory Committee [*TRADOC*] (MCD) .... PRAC
Program Resource Information System [*Department of Agriculture*] .... PRIS
Program, Resources, Objectives, Management [*Air Force Systems Command technique*] .... PROM
Program Rest Code (MCD) .... PRC
Program Review and Resources Management [*NASA*] .... PRRM
Program Review Board .... PRB
Program Review Committee (AFM) .... PRC
Program Review Control Board [*NASA*] (NASA) .... PRCB
Program Review Control Board Directive [*NASA*] (NASA) .... PRCBD
Program Review Group [*Military*] .... PRG

Program Review Panel [*Army*] (AABC) .... PRP
Program Review Team [*Navy*] (DNAB) .... PRT
Program Revision Intent .... PRI
Program Revision Report (KSC) .... PRR
Program Schedule Chart (NASA) .... PSC
Program Section [*Computer science*] (IAA) .... PS
Program Segment Prefix [*Computer science*] .... PSP
Program Selection Key [*Computer science*] (BUR) .... PSK
Program Sequence Control (NITA) .... PSC
Program Service Center [*Social Security Administration*] (OICC) .... PSC
Program Simulation (OICC) .... PS
Program Source [*Computer science*] (IAA) .... PS
Program Specification (MCD) .... PS
Program Specification Block [*IBM Corp.*] .... PSB
Program Specification Block Name [*Computer science*] (MHDB) .... PSBNAME
Program Staff Officer .... PSO
Program Standards Checker [*Computer science*] .... PSC
Program Start (KSC) .... PS
Program Stateword [*Computer science*] (IAA) .... PS
Program Station Basis [*Rating system*] (WDMC) .... PSB
Program Statistics and Data Systems .... PS & DS
Program Status [*Computer science*] (IAA) .... PS
Program Status Chart [*Computer science*] .... PSC
Program Status Documents [*Computer science*] .... PSD
Program Status Doubleword .... PSD
Program Status Doubleword Register [*Computer science*] (MHDB) ... PSDR
Program Status Information [*Computer science*] (MCD) .... PSI
Program Status Register .... PSR
Program Status Report [*or Review*] .... PSR
Program Status Review [*NASA*] (NASA) .... PSR
Program Status Table [*Computer science*] (IAA) .... PST
Program Status Table [*Computer science*] (IAA) .... PTAB
Program Status Word [*Computer science*] .... PSW
Program Status Word Register [*Computer science*] (MHDB) .... PSWR
Program Storage Unit [*Computer science*] (MDG) .... PSU
Program Storage Unit (NITA) .... PSU
Program Store [*Computer science*] (IEEE) .... PS
Program Structure Code (AFM) .... PSC
Program Study Authorization (KSC) .... PSA
Program Study Request (AAG) .... PSR
Program Summary (NG) .... PS
Program Summary Network (MCD) .... PSN
Program Summary Record [*Military*] (AFIT) .... PSR
Program Supply Interest (MCD) .... PSI
Program Support and Advanced Systems (SAA) .... PSAS
Program Support Communications Network (SSD) .... PSCN
Program Support Communications Requirements Document (SSD) .... PSCRD
Program Support Contract (SSD) .... PSC
Program Support Control System .... PSCS
Program Support Document (MUGU) .... PSD
Program Support Facility (USDC) .... PSF
Program Support Facility [*Marine science*] (OSRA) .... PSF
Program Support Handbook .... PSH
Program Support Inventory Control Point .... PSICP
Program Support Library (MCD) .... PSL
Program Support Management [*NASA*] (KSC) .... PSM
Program Support Plan [*NASA*] .... PSP
Program Support Plan Summary .... PSPS
Program Support Representative (NITA) .... PSR
Program Support Requirements (KSC) .... PSR
Program Support Requirements Document [*NASA*] (KSC) ...... PSRD
Program Support Staff [*Environmental Protection Agency*] (GFGA) .... PSS
Program Switching Center [*Computer science*] (IAA) .... PSC
Program Synchronization Table (CMD) .... PST
Program System Description (SAA) .... PSD
Program System Example (SAA) .... PROSE
Program System Package Plan .... PSPP
Program Systems Division [*Environmental Protection Agency*] (GFGA) .... PSD
Program Tape Preparation Unit .... PTPU
Program Task Planning (MCD) .... PTP
Program Technical Review (MCD) .... PTR
Program Technical Training (AFM) .... PTT
Program Temporary Fix [*Computer science*] .... PTF
Program Test and Operations Plan .... PTOP
Program Test System [*Computer science*] (IEEE) .... PTS
Program Test Tape [*Computer science*] (IEEE) .... PTT
Program Testing Information Bulletin (IAA) .... PTIB
Program Time Analyzer .... PTA
Program Time Base [*Military*] (AFIT) .... PTB
Program Timing and Maintenance [*Electronics*] (IAA) .... PTM
Program Timing and Miscellaneous [*Electronics*] .... PTM
Program to Analyse the Block System [*Computer science*] (PDAA) .... PABLOS
Program to Combat Racism [*British*] (DI) .... PCR
Program to Improve Management of Army Resources (AABC) .... PRIMAR
Program to Monitor Emerging Diseases .... ProMED
Program to Operate Simulated Trajectories .... POST
Program to Optimize Shuttle [*or Simulated*] Trajectories [*NASA*] (KSC) .... POST
Program to Program Communications (MHDI) .... PTOPC
Program to Realistically Evaluate Strategic Anti-Ballistic Missile Gaming Effectiveness [*Military*] (PDAA) .... PRESAGE
Program to Record Official Mail Point-to-Point Times [*Postal Service program*] .... PROMPT
Program Track Unit [*Telecommunications*] (LAIN) .... PTU
Program Transfer Interface .... PTI
Program Triple Store .... PTS

Program Trouble Memorandum [*NASA*] (IAA) .... PTM
Program Trouble Report [*NASA*] (KSC) .... PTR
Program Under Control (NITA) .... PUC
Program Unit Code [*Military*] (AFIT) .... PUC
Program Unit Counter .... PUNC
Program Unit Punch (SAA) .... PUP
Program Update Library .... PUL
Program Update Tape .... PUT
Program Usage Replenishment System .... PURS
Program Utility Routines [*Computer science*] .... PUR
Program Validation Services [*Computer science*] .... PVS
Program with Developing Institutions (EA) .... PDI
Program with Developing Institutions (EA) .... PWDI
Program Word [*Computer science*] (IAA) .... PW
Program Work Breakdown Structure (NASA) .... PWBS
Program Work Request .... PWR
Program Work Requirement (MCD) .... PWR
Program Work Statement (MCD) .... PWS
Program Year (AFM) .... PY
Programa de Cooperacion Tecnica [*Program of Technical Cooperation - PTC*] [*Organization of American States*] [*Washington, DC*] ...... PCT
Programa de Estudios Conjuntos sobre la Integracion Economica Latinoamericana [*Program of Joint Studies for Latin American Economic Integration*] (EAIO) .... ECIEL
Programa de las Naciones Unidas para el Desarrollo [*United Nations Development Program - UNDP*] [*Spanish*] (MSC) .... PNUD
Programa de las Naciones Unidas para el Medio Ambiente [*United Nations Environmental Programme Regional Office for Latin America*] (EAIO) ..... PNUMA
Programa Democratico [*Democratic Program*] [*Spain Political party*] (PPE) .... PD
Programa Latinoamericano de Cooperacion Energetica [*Latin American Energy Cooperation Program*] (EAIO) .... PLACE
Programa Mundial de Alimentos [*World Food Program*] [*Spanish*] (AD) .... PMA
Program-Aid Routine [*Computer science*] .... PAR
Program-Assisted Console Evaluation and Review [*Air Force*] .... PACER
Program-Based Budget Classification and Analysis System [*Pronounced "pib-kaz"*] [*Office of Management and Budget*] .... PBBCAS
Program-Controlled Computer (DIT) .... PCC
Program-Controlled Input-Output .... PCI/O
Program-Controlled Interruption [*Computer science*] (IBMDP) ... PCI
Program-Controlled Output (NASA) .... PCO
Program-Length Advertising [*Broadcasting*] (WDMC) .... PLA
Program-Length Commercial [*Television*] .... PLC
Programmable .... P
Programmable Actuator-Transducer [*Automotive engineering*] .... PAT
Programmable Algorithm Machine [*Computer science*] .... PAM
Programmable Algorithm Machine Assembly Language [*Computer science*] .... PAL
Programmable Algorithm Machine High-Level Language [*Computer science*] .... PHIL
Programmable Analogical Controller (NITA) .... PAC
Programmable Analogue Matched Filter (PDAA) .... PAMF
Programmable Armament Control Set (DOMA) .... PACS
Programmable Array Combinatorial Circuit (NITA) .... PACC
Programmable Array Logic [*Computer science*] (IEEE) .... PAL
Programmable Array Logic Assembler [*Computer science*] (IEEE) .... PALASM
Programmable Asynchronous Clustered Teleprocessing .... PACT
Programmable Asynchronous Dual Line Adapter .... PADLA
Programmable Asynchronous Line Adapter .... PASLA
Programmable Augmented Noise Source [*Military*] (CAAL) .... PANS
Programmable Automatic Comparator .... PAC
Programmable Automatic Transistor Tester (PDAA) .... PATT
Programmable Automation .... PA
Programmable Autonomously-Controlled Electrode [*Instrumentation*] .... PACE
Programmable Buffer Interface Card [*Computer science*] (NASA) .... PBIC
Programmable Buffer Interface Module (MCD) .... PBIM
Programmable Calculator [*Computer science*] (IAA) .... PROCAL
Programmable Character Generator .... PCG
Programmable Communication Processor .... PCP
Programmable Communications Adapter [*Computer science*] .... PCA
Programmable Communications Interface .... PCI
Programmable Communications Interface Unit .... PCIU
Programmable Communications Subsystem .... PCS
Programmable Computer .... PC
Programmable Controller (NITA) .... PC
Programmable Controller (ACII) .... PC
Programmable Data Acquisition System (IDOE) .... PDAS
Programmable Data Collection System [*Military*] (CAAL) ..... PDCS
Programmable Data Language (NITA) .... PDL
Programmable Data Processor (IAA) .... PDP
Programmable Data Station [*or System*] .... PDS
Programmable Data Terminal [*Digital Equipment Corp.*] (IEEE) .... PDT
Programmable Data Terminal Set [*Military*] (CAAL) .... PDTS
Programmable Delay Unit .... PDU
Programmable Diagnostic Unit [*TACOM*] [*Army*] (RDA) ...... PDU
Programmable Digital Autopilot (MCD) .... PDAP
Programmable Digital Controller (PDAA) .... PDC
Programmable Electronic Engine Control [*Automotive engineering*] ..... PEEC
Programmable Electronic System [*Engineering*] .... PES
[*A*] Programmable Emulator [*Hi-Q International*] [*Computer science*] (PCM) ..... APE
Programmable Equipment for Personnel Subsystem Simulation .... PEPSS
Programmable Extension Package (IAA) .... PEP
Programmable Format [*Perforating keyboard*] .... PF
Programmable Frequency Standard .... PFS
Programmable Front-End Processor [*Computer science*] ...... PFEP
Programmable Function (NITA) .... PF

Programmable Function Panel (NASA) .... PFP
Programmable Gain Amplifier (MCD) .... PGA
Programmable Gain Instrumentation Amplifier (IAA) ..... PGIA
Programmable Gate Array .... PGA
Programmable Graphics Processor .... PGP
Programmable Guidance Controller [Military] .... PGC
Programmable Hand-Held Calculator (RDA) .... PHHC
Programmable Host Access [Computer science] (IAA) ...... PHA
Programmable Image Feature Extractor [to provide real-time machine vision
   for the Martian Rover robot] [Jet Propulsion Laboratory] (BYTE) .... PIFEX
Programmable Implantable Medication System .... PIMS
Programmable Indicator Data Processor [Military] (CAAL) ..... PIDP
Programmable Industrial Controller (NITA) .... PiC
Programmable Input Buffer .... PIB
Programmable Integrated Control Equipment .... PICE
Programmable Integrated Processor (IEEE) .... PIP
Programmable Integrated Scripts for MIRROR [Management Information
   Reporting and review of Operational Resources Systems] [Computer
   Language] (PCM) .... PRISM
Programmable Interconnect Point [Computer science] ...... PIP
Programmable Interrupt Controller [Computer science] ..... PIC
Programmable Interval Clock (NASA) .... PIC
Programmable Interval Timer .... PIT
Programmable Keyboard and Display [Computer science] (NASA) ..... PKD
Programmable Line Adapter .... PLA
Programmable Line Controller (NITA) .... PLC
Programmable Link Adaptation System (MCD) .... PLAS
Programmable Logic Array [Computer science] .... PLA
Programmable Logic Control [Computer science] (IAA) ..... PC
Programmable Logic Control [Computer science] .... PLC
Programmable Logic Controller .... PLC
Programmable Logic Device .... PLD
Programmable Logic Sequencer [Computer science] .... PLS
Programmable Machine Control (IAA) .... PC
Programmable Machine Controller (NRCH) .... PMC
Programmable Machine Interface (MCD) .... PMI
Programmable Machine Tool Controller (IAA) .... PMC
Programmable Macro Logic (NITA) .... PML
Programmable Matched Filter (IAA) .... PMF
Programmable Matrix Controller (IAA) .... PMC
Programmable Memory Interface [Computer science] .... PMI
Programmable Microcomputer Module .... PMM
Programmable Miniature Message Terminal (MCD) .... PROMT
Programmable MODEM Interface [Computer science] (MCD) ..... PMI
Programmable Multiple Ion Monitor .... PROMIM
Programmable Multiple Position Machine (MCD) .... PMPM
Programmable Multiplex [Computer science] (TEL) .... PMUX
Programmable Network .... PN
Programmable Network Telecommunications Operating System .... PRONTO
Programmable Option Select [Computer science] .... POS
Programmable Patch System .... PPS
Programmable Peripheral Interface (MCD) .... PPI
Programmable Peripheral Interface Microcomputer (IAA) ..... PPIM
Programmable Peripheral Interface Unit .... PPIU
Programmable Power Supply .... PPS
Programmable Power Supply Unit (EECA) .... PPSU
Programmable Protocol Interface Board .... PPIB
Programmable Random Access Memory [Computer science] (IAA) ..... PRAM
Programmable Read Only Memory System [Computer science] .... PROMS
Programmable Read-Only Memory [Computer science] ..... PROM
Programmable, Realtime, Incoherent, Matrix, Optical Processor [Computer
   science] .... PRIMO
Programmable Remote Operation [Computer Devices, Inc.] ..... PRO
Programmable Robot Observer with Logical Enemy Response [Developed
   by Robot Defense Systems of Thornton, CO] .... PROWLER
Programmable Rotary Encoded Logic [Computer science] (MHDB) ..... PREL
Programmable Sample Changer [Spectroscopy] .... PSC
Programmable Sampling Network Switch .... PSNS
Programmable Scanning Receiver (DWSG) .... PSCR
Programmable Signal Data Processor (MCD) .... PSDP
Programmable Signal Processor (MCD) .... PSP
Programmable Signal Processor RADAR .... PSPR
Programmable Sound Generator [Chip] [Atari, Inc.] .... PSG
Programmable Switch [Computer science] (IAA) .... PS
Programmable Symbol Generator .... PSG
Programmable Synchronous/Asynchronous Receiver (IEEE) ..... PSAR
Programmable Synchronous/Asynchronous Transmitter (IEEE) ..... PSAT
Programmable Tapped Delay Line (PDAA) .... PTDL
Programmable Telecommunications Interface (MCD) .... PTCI
Programmable Temperature Controls .... PTC
Programmable Temperature Vaporizer .... PTV
Programmable Terminal [Computer science] .... PT
Programmable Terminal Communications Interface (MCD) ..... PTCI
Programmable Terminal Monitor/Operating System (NITA) ..... PTM/OS
Programmable Terminal Multiplexer [Texas Instruments, Inc.] ..... PTM
Programmable Terminal System [Computer science] (IAA) ..... PTS
Programmable Test Console .... PTC
Programmable Text Processor [Programming language] (CSR) ..... PTP
Programmable Threshold Detector (MCD) .... PTD
Programmable Timer Module .... PTM
Programmable Touch Panel [Electronics] .... PTP
Programmable Transformer Converter (MCD) .... PRTRNS
Programmable Translation Array .... PTA
Programmable Transversal Filter [SMP] .... PTF
Programmable Unijunction Transistor (IAA) .... PUJT

Programmable Unijunction Transistor .... PUT
Programmable Universal Direct Drive .... PUDD
Programmable Universal Manipulator (NITA) .... PUMA
Programmable Universal Manipulator for Assembly [General Motors Corp.
   assembly robot] .... PUMA
Programmable Universal Micro Accelerator [Computer science] (CDE) ..... PUMA
Programmable Variations Generator [Computer science] ..... PVG
Programmable Video Interface .... PVI
Programmable Weapons Release System (IEEE) .... PWRS
Programmatic and Technical Support [Army] .... PATS
Programmatic Center for Fire Research [National Institute of Standards and
   Technology] .... PCFR
Programmatic Environmental Impact Statement (NRCH) ..... PEIS
Programme Activity Center [Advisory Committee on Pollution of the Sea] ..... PAC
Programme and Project Management System [United Nations Development
   Programme] (DUND) .... PPMS
Programme Biologique Internationale [International Biological Program -
   IBP] (MSC) .... PBI
Programme d'Aide aux Athletes [Athlete Assistance Program] [Canada] ..... PAA
Programme de Recherche sur l'Amiante de l'Universite de Sherbrooke
   [Asbestos Research Program] [University of Sherbrooke Quebec]
   [Information service or system] (IID) .... PRAUS
Programme des Economies d'Energie dans l'Industrie Canadienne .... PEEIC
Programme du Pipeline des Iles de l'Arctique [Canada] ..... PPIA
Programme Elargi d'Assistance Technique [Expanded Program of Technical
   Assistance] [United Nations] .... PEAT
Programme for Alternative Fluorocarbon Toxicity Testing [British] .... PAFT
Programme for International Managers in Europe [Business program] ..... PRIME
Programme for Strategic and International Security Studies [Switzerland]
   (PDAA) .... PSIS
Programme Hydrologique International [International Hydrological Program -
   IHP] [UNESCO] (MSC) .... PHI
Programme International de Correlation Geologique [International Geological
   Correlation Programme - IGCP] (EAIO) .... PICG
Programme International sur la Securite des Substances Chimiques
   [International Programme on Chemical Safety] (EAIO) ..... PISSC
Programme National de Lutte Contre l'Abus de l'Alcool et des Drogues
   chez les Autochtones [Canada] .... PNLAADA
Programme National D'etude de la Dynamique du Climat [France] [Marine
   science] (OSRA) .... PNEDC
Programme National d'Etudes de la Dynamique du Climat (USDC) .... PNEDC
Programme of Mass Privatisation [Poland] (ECON) .... MPP
Programme of Policy Research in Engineering Science and Technology
   [British] .... PREST
Programme on Exchange and Transfer of Information (NITA) ..... POETRI
Programme on Exchange and Transfer of Information on Community
   Water Supply and Sanitation [International Reference Center for
   Community Water Supply and Sanitation] [Information service or system]
   (IID) .... POETRI
Programme Regional Oceanien de l'Environnement [South Pacific Regional
   Environmental Programme - SPREP] (EAIO) .... PROE
Programme Support and Development [British] .... PSD
Programmed Access/Security System [Card Key Systems] ..... PASS
Programmed Accounts Receivable Extra Service [Computer science] .... PAREX
Programmed Activity Transmission (MCD) .... PAT
Programmed Airline Reservation System .... PARS
Programmed Analysis Computer Transfer (KSC) .... PACT
Programmed Analysis for Value Engineers .... PAVE
Programmed Application Library [IBM Corp.] .... PAL
Programmed Appropriation Commitments - Fixed Asset Control System
   (PDAA) .... PAC-FACS
Programmed Arithmetic (IAA) .... PA
Programmed Audit Library .... PAL
Programmed Automated Replenishment Ordering System (IAA) ..... PAROS
Programmed Automatic Circuit Evaluator and Recorder ..... PACER
Programmed Automatic Circuit Tester .... PACT
Programmed Automatic Communications Equipment ...... PACE
Programmed Automatic Telemetry Evaluator .... PATE
Programmed Automatic Test Equipment .... PATE
Programmed Automatic Welding System .... PAWS
Programmed Book [Publishing] .... PROG BK
Programmed Cell Death [Cytology] .... PCD
Programmed Check (AAG) .... PC
Programmed Combustion [Ford Motor Co.] .... PROCO
Programmed Communications Support Program [Air Force] (AFM) ..... PCSP
Programmed Course, Home Nursing [Red Cross] .... PCHN
Programmed Cryptographic Facility [Computer science] ..... PCF
Programmed Data Processor .... PDP
Programmed Data Quantizer .... PDQ
Programmed Depot Level Maintenance [Air Force] .... PDLM
Programmed Depot Maintenance (MCD) .... PDM
Programmed Digital Automatic Control [Computer science] ..... PRODAC
Programmed Digital Logic .... PDL
Programmed Digital Processor .... PDP
Programmed Editor and Automated Resources for Learning ..... PEARL
Programmed Educational Package .... PREP
Programmed Electrical Stimulation [Neurophysiology] ..... PES
Programmed Electronic X-Ray Automatic Diffractometer (IAA) ..... PEXRA
Programmed Electronic X-Ray Automatic Diffractometer ..... PEXRAD
Programmed Electronics Pattern (PDAA) .... PREP
Programmed Exciter .... PE
Programmed Extended Time Sharing [Computer science] ..... PETS
Programmed Film Reader [System] .... PFR
Programmed Frequency Amplitude Modulation .... PFAM
Programmed Fuel Computer [Automotive engineering] ..... PFC

Programmed Fuel Injection [*Automotive engineering*] ... PGM-FI
Programmed Function Key (NITA) ... PFK
Programmed Function Keyboard [*Computer science*] ... PFK
Programmed Functional Indices for Laboratory Evaluation [*RAND Corp.*] ... PROFILE
Programmed Gain Control ... PGC
Programmed Individual Presentation (IAA) ... PIP
Programmed Inert Gas Multi-Electrode (PDAA) ... PIGME
Programmed Information [*Computer science*] ... PI
Programmed Initiations, Commitments, Obligations, and Expenditures [*AFSC*] ... PICOE
Programmed Input/Output ... PIO
Programmed Inquiry, Learning or Teaching [*Computer science*] ... PILOT
Programmed Instruction ... PI
Programmed Instruction for Management Education (HGAA) ... PRIM
Programmed Instruction for Management Education [*American Management Association*] ... PRIME
Programmed Instruction Language Learning [*Computer science*] ... PILL
Programmed Instruction Learning on Teaching [*A simplified programming language for computer-assisted instruction*] (EDAC) ... PILOT
Programmed Instruction Text ... PIT
Programmed Integrated System Maintenance (NG) ... PRISM
Programmed International Computer Environment [*International relations simulation game*] ... PRINCE
Programmed Introduction (MCD) ... PI
Programmed Language Enquiry System (NITA) ... PLANES
Programmed Language-Based Enquiry System ... PLANES
Programmed Learning Aid ... PLAID
Programmed Learning Textbook ... PLT
Programmed Learning under Supervision ... PLUS
Programmed Local Oscillator ... PLO
Programmed Logic Array (NITA) ... PLA
Programmed Logic for Automated Learning Operation [*Computer science*] (IAA) ... PLATO
Programmed Logic for Automatic Teaching [*or Training*] **Operations** [*University of Illinois*] [*Programming language*] ... PLATO
Programmed Math Tutorial [*National Science Foundation*] ... PMT
Programmed Mixture Ratio (KSC) ... PMR
Programmed Mode Switch (IAA) ... PMS
Programmed Multichannel Valve [*Chromatography*] ... PMCV
Programmed Multiline Controller ... PMLC
Programmed Multiple Development [*Analytical chemistry*] ... PMD
Programmed Numerical Control ... PNC
Programmed Operational Date (AFIT) ... POD
Programmed Operational Functional Appraisal [*Navy*] ... POFA
Programmed Operational Warshot Evaluation and Review ... POWER
Programmed Operational Warshot Evaluation and Review (AD) ... power
Programmed Operators and Primitives [*Computer science*] ... POP
Programmed Oscillator ... PO
Programmed Processor System ... PPS
Programmed RADAR Simulator (IAA) ... PRS
Programmed Rate Control (NITA) ... PRC
Programmed Reinforced Instruction Necessary to Continuing Education ... PRINCE
Programmed Reliability in Design Engineering ... PRIDE
Programmed Review of Information for Costing and Evaluation (MCD) ... PRICE
Programmed Review of Operator Functions - Elementary (DNAB) ... PROF-E
Programmed Reviewing, Ordering, and Forecasting Inventory Technique ... PROFIT
Programmed School Input (NVT) ... PSI
Programmed Sequential Control Language ... PSCL
Programmed Shutter and Aperture [*Photography*] (DICI) ... PSA
Programmed Single-Axis Mount [*Military camera*] ... PROSAM
Programmed Slip Differential [*Automotive engineering*] ... PSD
Programmed Symbols (MEDA) ... PS
Programmed System Evolution (MCD) ... PSE
Programmed Temperature Gas Chromatography ... PTGC
Programmed Test Input (MCD) ... PTI
Programmed Test Input System (MCD) ... PTIS
Programmed Thermal Desorber ... PTD
Programmed Transmission Control (BUR) ... PTC
Programmed Turn Phase ... PTP
Programmed-Temperature Vaporizing [*Analytical chemistry*] ... PTV
Programmer (AAG) ... PG
Programmer (AFM) ... PRGMR
Programmer ... PRGRMR
Programmer [*or Programming*] ... PROG
Programmer (ECII) ... PROGR
Programmer Advanced Debugging System [*Computer science*] ... PADS
Programmer Analyst Aptitude Test ... PAAT
Programmer and Probability Analyzer [*Computer science*] (IEEE) ... PAPA
Programmer and Timer ... PT
Programmer Appraisal Instrument [*Computer science*] (IEEE) ... PAI
Programmer Aptitude Competence Test System ... PACTS
Programmer Aptitude Test ... PAT
Programmer Assistance and Liaison [*Computer science*] (NRCH) ... PAL
Programmer Brain Damage [*Computer hacker terminology*] (NHD) ... PBD
Programmer Capacity ... PCAP
Programmer Exercised Autopilot Test (AAG) ... PEAT
Programmer Group (IAA) ... PG
Programmer in Charge of Records [*Computer science*] (IAA) ... PCR
Programmer Interface Unit (MCD) ... PIU
Programmer Operating Standards Technique ... POST
Programmer Productivity Technique (IAA) ... PPT
Programmer Reference Manual [*Computer science*] ... PRM
Programmer Support Environment [*Computer science*] (LAIN) ... PPSE
Programmer Test Station ... PTS
Programmer Training Center ... PTC
Programmer Trouble Report [*Nuclear energy*] (GFGA) ... PTR
Programmer Work Station ... PWS
Programmer-Oriented Graphics Operation (IEEE) ... POGO
Programmers Aid in Debugging [*Computer science*] (MHDI) ... PAID
Programmers' Analysis 'N' Development Aid (NITA) ... PANDA
Programmer's Automatic Testing System ... PATSY
Programmers Hierarchical Interactive Graphics Standards (NITA) ... PHIGS
Programmers Hierarchical Interactive Graphics System [*IBM Corp.*] ... PHIGS
Programmer's Imaging Kernel [*Computer science*] (BTTJ) ... PIK
Programmers Minimal Interface to Graphics (MCD) ... PMIG
Programmer's Paradise [*NASDAQ symbol*] (TTSB) ... PROG
Programmers Paradise, Inc. [*NASDAQ symbol*] (SAG) ... PROG
Programmers Paradise, Inc. [*Associated Press*] (SAG) ... ProgPar
Programmer's Utility Filing System (DIT) ... PUFS
Programmer's Workbench [*Microsoft, Inc.*] (PCM) ... PWB
Programmer's Workbench Memorandum Macros [*Computer science*] (MHDI) ... PWB/MM
Programmes Analysis Unit [*British*] (MCD) ... PAU
Programmes Directorate Committee [*British*] ... PDC
Programmes Library Update and Maintenance (PDAA) ... PLUM
Programminformationssystem Sozialwissenschaften [*Informationszentrum Sozialwissenschaften*] [*Germany Defunct Information service or system*] (CRD) ... PROFIS
Programming [*Computer science*] (IAA) ... PR
Programming (MSA) ... PRGMG
Programming ... PRGMNG
Programming ... PROGMG
Programming Analysis Consulting Education (IEEE) ... PACE
Programming and Instrumentation Environment [*Computer science*] ... PIE
Programming and Resources Management [*NASA*] (MCD) ... PRM
Programming Checklist (MCD) ... PCL
Programming Computer [*Computer science*] ... PROC
Programming Control Language [*Computer science*] (PCM) ... PCL
Programming Documentation Standards [*Computer science*] (WDAA) ... PDS
Programming in Logic [*Programing language*] [*1970*] ... PROLOG
Programming Interpersonal Curricula for Adolescents [*Learning model*] [*Education*] ... PICA
[*A*] **Programming Language** [*1960*] [*Computer science*] (CSR) ... APL
[*A*] **Programming Language** [*1963*] (CSR) ... MENTOR
Programming Language [*Computer science*] ... PL
Programming Language Committee [*CODASYL*] ... PLC
Programming Language / Edit [*Computer science*] (MHDI) ... PL/E
Programming Language for Allocation and Network Scheduling [*1975*] [*Computer science*] (CSR) ... PLANS
Programming Language for Automatic Checkout Equipment ... PLACE
Programming Language for Information Management System [*Computer science*] (MHDI) ... PLIMS
Programming Language for Interaction and Teaching [*1966*] [*Computer science*] ... PLANIT
Programming Language for Interactive Teaching [*Computer science*] (IAA) ... PLANT
Programming Language for Microprocessors (NITA) ... PL/M
Programming Language for System [*Computer science*] (IAA) ... PLS
Programming Language for UNIVAC [*Universal Automatic Computer*] **Systems** [*Computer science*] (CSR) ... PLUS
Programming Language for Users of MAVIS [*Microprocessor-Based Audio Visual Information System*] (PDAA) ... PLUM
Programming Language/Microcomputers [*Intel Corp.*] [*1973*] [*Computer science*] (CSR) ... PL/M
Programming Language Nineteen-Hundred [*Computer science*] ... PLAN
[*A*] **Programming Language Shared Variables** [*Computer science*] ... APLSV
[*A*] **Programming Language/Structured** [*Computer science*] (CSR) ... APL/S
[*A*] **Programming Language/University of Massachusetts** [*Computer science*] (CSR) ... APLUM
Programming Language, Version One [*Computer science*] (MCD) ... PL/1
Programming Languages for Machine Tools [*Conference*] ... PROLAMAT
Programming Languages for Numerically Controlled Machine Tools [*Conference*] [*Computer science*] (IAA) ... PROLAMAT
Programming Languages for the Zilog [*Computer science*] (CSR) ... PLZ
Programming Logic Manual ... PLM
Programming Managers Information System (MHDI) ... PROMISE
Programming Optimizing System (IAA) ... POS
Programming Panels and Decoding Circuits ... PPDC
Programming Panels and Decoding Circuits (NITA) ... PP-DC
Programming Plan (AFM) ... PP
Programming Program Strela [*Computer science*] ... PPS
Programming Request for Price Quotation [*Computer science*] ... PRPQ
Programming Script Language (PCM) ... PSL
Programming Services for Multimedia Industry Terminals [*IBM Corp.*] ... PSMIT
Programming Status Report [*Computer science*] ... PSR
Programming Support Monitor [*Texas Instruments, Inc.*] ... PSM
Programming Support Representative [*IBM Corp.*] ... PSR
Programming Support System (SAA) ... PSS
Programming System ... PS
Programming System Activity Log [*Computer science*] ... PSAL
Programming System with Symbolic Addresses [*Computer science*] (IAA) ... PROSA
Programming Tools and Information [*IBM Corp.*] [*Computer science*] ... PTI
Program-Planning-Budgeting ... PPB
Programs and Financial Management [*Navy*] ... P & FM
Programs Development Group (MUGU) ... PDG

Programs for Persons with Limited English-Speaking Ability [*Department of Labor*] ..... PLESA
Programs for Research on Romance Authors ..... PRORA
Programs for the Improvement of Practice [*Washington, DC Department of Education*] (GRD) ..... PIP
Programs in the Arts for Special Education Project (EDAC) ..... PASE
Programs, Materials, Techniques (AD) ..... pmt
Programs of Cooperation (MCD) ..... POC
Programs Research Unit (KSC) ..... PRU
Program-Sensitive Malfunction ..... PSM
Progranulocytes [*Hematology*] (DAVI) ..... P-GRN
Progres et Democratie Moderne [*Progress and Modern Democracy*] [*France Political party*] (PPE) ..... PDM
Progres Social Francais [*French Social Progress*] [*Political party*] (PPE) ..... PSF
Progreso [*Honduras*] [*ICAO location identifier*] (ICLI) ..... MHPE
Progreso y Futuro de Ceuta [*Political party*] (EY) ..... PFC
Progress [*South Africa*] [*ICAO location identifier*] (ICLI) ..... FAPZ
Progress (AABC) ..... PROG
Progress (DAVI) ..... progr
Progress Analysis Group [*Navy*] (MCD) ..... PAG
Progress Assessment Chart [*Psychology*] ..... PAC
Progress at NPL [*National Priorities List*] **Sites** [*A publication*] [*EPA*] ..... PNPLS
Progress Change Authority ..... PCA
Progress Control Clerk [*DoD*] ..... PCC
Progress Control Unit (KSC) ..... PCU
Progress Curve Report ..... PCR
Progress Financial Corp. [*Plymouth Meeting, PA*] [*NASDAQ symbol*] (NQ) ..... PFNC
Progress Financial Corp. [*Associated Press*] (SAG) ..... ProgFn
Progress Finl [*NASDAQ symbol*] (TTSB) ..... PFNC
Progress in Advanced Component Technology (IAA) ..... PACT
Progress in Technology [*Automotive industry*] ..... PT
[*The*] **Progress Interview** ..... TPI
Progress note [*Medical records*] (DAVI) ..... PN
Progress Payment Report (AAGC) ..... PPR
Progress Payments [*Military procurement*] ..... PP
Progress Performance Evaluation Panel [*Job Corps*] ..... P/PEP
Progress Presse Agentur GmbH [*Press agency*] [*Germany*] ..... PPA
Progress Report ..... PR
Progress Software [*NASDAQ symbol*] (SPSG) ..... PRGS
Progress Software Corp. [*Associated Press*] (SAG) ..... PrgSoft
Progress Summary Report ..... PSR
Progress Tests and Examinations ..... PT & E
Progress-Enterprise, Lunenburg, Nova Scotia [*Library symbol National Library of Canada*] (NLC) ..... NSLPE
Progress-Enterprise, Lunenburg, NS, Canada [*Library symbol*] [*Library of Congress*] (LCLS) ..... CaNSLuPE
Progressieve Surinaamse Volkspartij [*Progressive Suriname People's Party*] [*Political party*] (PPW) ..... PSV
Progressiewe Federale Party [*Progressive Federal Party*] [*South Africa*] [*Political party*] (PPW) ..... PFP
Progression of Disease [*Medicine*] ..... PD
Progressive ..... P
Progressive ..... PRO
Progressive [*A publication*] (BRI) ..... Prog
Progressive ..... PROGS
Progressive Accumulated Stress [*Psychiatry*] ..... PAS
Progressive Aerobic Circuit Exercise [*Fitness training*] ..... PACE
Progressive Aircraft Engine Repair ..... PAREN
Progressive Aircraft Reconditioning [*or Repair*] **Cycle** ..... PARC
Progressive Aircraft Repair [*or Rework*] ..... PAR
Progressive Alliance [*Defunct*] (EA) ..... PA
Progressive Alliance of Liberia [*Political party*] (PPW) ..... PAL
Progressive Angus Breeders Association ..... PABA
Progressive Animal Welfare Society (GNE) ..... PAWS
Progressive Arbeiders- en Landbouwersunie [*Progressive Workers' and Farm Laborers' Union*] [*Surinam*] [*Political party*] (PPW) ..... PALU
Progressive Architecture [*A publication*] (BRI) ..... Prog Arch
Progressive Augmentation by Dilating the Urethra Anterior [*Medicine*] (DMAA) ..... PADUA
Progressive Axemen's Association of Western Australia ..... PAAWA
Progressive Bank [*NASDAQ symbol*] (TTSB) ..... PSBK
Progressive Bank, Inc. [*Associated Press*] (SAG) ..... ProgBk
Progressive Bank, Inc. [*Pawling, NY*] [*NASDAQ symbol*] (NQ) ..... PSBK
Progressive Base Line Dimensioning (SAA) ..... PBLD
Progressive Bulbar Palsy [*Medicine*] (MEDA) ..... PBP
Progressive Care Unit [*Medicine*] ..... PCU
Progressive Citizens of America ..... PCA
Progressive Conservative [*Canada Political party*] ..... PC
Progressive Conservative Broadcasting Corp. [*Fictional version of the Canadian Broadcasting Corp.*] ..... PCBC
Progressive Conservative Party [*Australia Political party*] ..... PCP
Progressive Conservative Party [*Canada Political party*] (PPW) ..... PCP
Progressive Conservative Youth Federation of Canada ..... PCYF
Progressive Constitutionalist Party [*Malta*] [*Political party*] (PPE) ..... PCP
Progressive Corp. [*NYSE symbol*] (SPSG) ..... PGR
Progressive Corp. [*Associated Press*] (SAG) ..... ProgCp
Progressive Corp., Ohio [*NYSE symbol*] (TTSB) ..... PGR
Progressive Democratic Party [*Montserrat*] [*Political party*] (PPW) ..... PDP
Progressive Democratic Party [*St. Vincent*] [*Political party*] (PPW) ..... PDP
Progressive Democrats [*Ireland*] [*Political party*] ..... PD
Progressive Deterioration Scale ..... PDS
Progressive Education Association [*Defunct*] ..... PEA
Progressive Exercise Program ..... PEP
Progressive External Ophthalmoplegia ..... PEO
Progressive Form of Tick-Borne Encephalitis [*Medicine*] (DMAA) ..... PFTBE
Progressive Foundation (EA) ..... PF
Progressive Free Wave ..... PFW
Progressive French Polishers' Society [*A union*] [*British*] ..... PFPS
Progressive Hongkong Society [*Political party*] ..... PHS
Progressive Independent Party [*South Africa Political party*] (EY) ..... PIP
Progressive Inspection Plan [*Navy*] (NG) ..... PIP
Progressive Jewish Activism List [*An association*] ..... PJAL
Progressive Labor [*A faction of Students for a Democratic Society*] ..... PL
Progressive Labor Movement (BARN) ..... PLM
Progressive Labor Party (EA) ..... PLP
Progressive Labour Party [*Saint Lucia*] [*Political party*] (EAIO) ..... PLP
Progressive Learning Systems [*Potomac, MD*] (TSSD) ..... PLS
Progressive Liberal Party [*Bahamas*] [*Political party*] (PPW) ..... PLP
Progressive Librarians Guild [*American Library Association*] ..... PLG
Progressive Lowering of Temperature ..... PLT
Progressive Massive Fibrosis ..... PMF
Progressive Massive Fibrosis [*Medicine*] (AD) ..... pmf
Progressive Merger Procedure [*Econometrics*] ..... PMP
Progressive Mine Workers of America ..... PMW
Progressive Minerals [*Vancouver Stock Exchange symbol*] ..... PVM
Progressive Multifocal Leukoencephalopathy [*Oncology*] ..... PML
Progressive Muscle Relaxation Training [*Psychology*] ..... PMRT
Progressive Muscular Atrophy [*Medicine*] ..... PMA
Progressive Muscular Dystrophy [*Medicine*] ..... PMD
Progressive National Party [*Turks and Caicos Islands*] [*Political party*] (PPW) ..... PNP
Progressive Neuronal Degeneration of Childhood [*Medicine*] ..... PNDC
Progressive Nuclear Palsy [*Neurology*] (DAVI) ..... PNP
Progressive Onslaught to Stamp out Stock Errors [*Navy*] (NG) ..... POSSE
Progressive Order of the West [*Defunct*] (EA) ..... POW
Progressive Overload Program [*Weight training*] ..... POP
Progressive Party of America [*Third party in 1948 Presidential race*] ..... PPA
Progressive Patient Care ..... PPC
Progressive Patient Care (AD) ..... ppc
Progressive People's Party [*Sierra Leone*] [*Political party*] (EY) ..... PPP
Progressive People's Party [*Sudan*] [*Political party*] (EY) ..... PPP
Progressive People's Party [*Liberia*] [*Political party*] (PPW) ..... PPP
Progressive Perceptive Deafness [*Medicine*] ..... PPD
Progressive Pneumonia of Sheep ..... PPS
Progressive Policy Institute [*Research center*] (RCD) ..... PPI
Progressive Political Action Committee [*Defunct*] ..... PPAC
Progressive Political Action Committee [*Defunct*] (EA) ..... PROPAC
Progressive Postmyelitis Muscular Atrophy [*Medicine*] (DMAA) ..... PPMA
Progressive Proofs [*Graphic arts*] (DGA) ..... PROGS
Progressive Qualification Scheme [*British*] ..... PQS
Progressive Range of Motion [*Medicine*] ..... PROM
Progressive Refinement of Integrated Supply Management (AFM) ..... PRISM
Progressive Renal Failure [*Medicine*] (AAMN) ..... PRF
Progressive Republican League ..... PRL
Progressive Resistance ..... PR
Progressive Resistive Exercise [*Medicine*] ..... PRE
Progressive Retinal Atrophy [*Medicine*] (AD) ..... pra
Progressive Rework Plan ..... PRP
Progressive Rubella Panencephalitis [*Medicine*] ..... PRP
Progressive Science Series [*A publication*] ..... PSS
Progressive Series Modulator (IAA) ..... PSM
Progressive Shift Schedule Management Technology [*Automotive engineering*] ..... PROSMATEC
Progressive Socialist Party [*Lebanon*] [*Political party*] (BJA) ..... PSP
Progressive Socialist Party of Lebanon ..... PSPL
Progressive Society of Carpenters and Joiners [*A union*] [*British*] ..... PSCJ
Progressive Space Forum [*Defunct*] (EA) ..... PSF
Progressive Spinal Ataxia [*Medicine*] (DMAA) ..... PSA
Progressive Spinal Muscular Atrophy [*Medicine*] ..... PSMA
Progressive Student Network (EA) ..... PSN
Progressive Supranuclear Ophthalmoplegia (CPH) ..... PSO
Progressive Supranuclear Palsy [*Neurology*] ..... PSP
Progressive Symmetrical Erythrokeratoderma [*Medicine*] (DMAA) ..... PSEK
Progressive Systemic Sclerosis [*Medicine*] ..... PSS
Progressive Tax (MHDW) ..... PT
Progressive Union of Cabinet Makers [*British*] ..... PUCM
Progressive Unionist Party [*Northern Ireland*] [*Political party*] (PPW) ..... PUP
Progressive Wave Tube ..... PWT
Progressive Zionist Caucus (EA) ..... PZC
Progressive Zionist League-Hashomer Hatzair (EA) ..... PZL
Progressiven Organisationen der Schweiz [*Progressive Organizations of Switzerland*] [*Political party*] (PPE) ..... POCH
ProGroup, Inc. [*NASDAQ symbol*] (NQ) ..... PRGR
ProGroup, Inc. [*Associated Press*] (SAG) ..... Progrp
Prohibit ..... PROH
Prohibited ..... Prohib
Prohibited Area [*Followed by identification*] ..... P
Prohibited Telegrams ..... PT
Prohibition [*FBI standardized term*] ..... PROH
Prohibition National Committee (EA) ..... PNC
Prohormone Convertase [*Medicine*] (DMAA) ..... PC
Prohormone-Converting Endopeptidase ..... PCE
Proinsulin-Like Compound [*Endocrinology*] ..... PLC
Project (AFM) ..... PROJ
Project (VRA) ..... proj
Project ..... PROJ
Project '88: Americans for the Reagan Agenda [*Defunct*] (EA) P-88/ARA
Project Action Officer [*Air Force*] (AFIT) ..... PAO
Project Action Team [*Acquisition Reform*] (AAGC) ..... PAT

Project Activities Relationship Diagram (PDAA) ... PARD
Project Administration (MCD) ... PA
Project Administration Officer [*Military*] (AFIT) ... PAO
Project Advisory Committee (EGAO) ... PAC
Project Advisory Group [*Army*] ... PAG
Project Aerospace Plane (AAG) ... PAP
Project Analysis (MHDB) ... PA
Project Analysis and Control (IAA) ... PAC
Project Analysis and Control System (MHDI) ... PROJACS
Project Analysis Information System [*Agency for International Development*] ... PAIS
Project Approval Document [*NASA*] ... PAD
Project Archipel de Montreal, Centre de Documentation Project Archipel de Montreal, Centre de Documentation, Montreal, PQ, Canada [*Library symbol*] [*Library of Congress*] (LCLS) ... CaQMPA
Project Assignment Instruction (MCD) ... PAI
Project ASTIC [*UTLAS symbol*] ... ATC
Project Audit Report ... PAR
Project Authorization ... PA
Project Authorization Notice (MCD) ... PAN
Project Authorization Request (IAA) ... PAR
Project Blue Book [*An association*] (EA) ... PBB
Project Breakdown Structure [*Nuclear energy*] (NRCH) ... PBS
Project Breed Rescue Efforts and Education [*An association*] (EA) ... BREED
Project Censored (EA) ... PC
Project Change Board (AAG) ... PCB
Project Children (EA) ... PC
Project Choice, East St. Louis, IL [*Library symbol Library of Congress*] (LCLS) ... IEsPC
Project Concern International (EA) ... PCI
Project Concern's Options Service (EA) ... PCOS
Project Configuration Control Board [*Army*] (AABC) ... PCCB
Project Control (NASA) ... PC
Project Control and Administration [*NASA*] ... PC & A
Project Control Branch [*Social Security Administration*] ... PCB
Project Control Center ... PCC
Project Control Drawing (AAG) ... PCD
Project Control Drawing System (AAG) ... PCDS
Project Control Ledgers [*Navy*] (NG) ... PCL
Project Control Number (AAG) ... PCN
Project Control Office (MCD) ... PCO
Project Control Plan (IEEE) ... PCP
Project Control Room [*NASA*] (NASA) ... PCR
Project Control Sheet [*Computer science*] ... PCS
Project Control System [*Computer science*] ... PCS
Project Control Tool (BUR) ... PCT
Project Coordination and Liaison Administration (OICC) ... PCLA
Project Coordination Centre [*Defence Research Board*] [*Canada*] ... PCC
Project Coordination Staff [*NASA*] (KSC) ... PCS
Project Coordinator (NG) ... PC
Project Cost Control System ... PCCS
Project Cost Model [*Project Software Ltd.*] [*Software package*] (NCC) ... PCM
Project Cost Plan (NASA) ... PCP
Project Cost Record [*or Report*] [*NASA*] (KSC) ... PCR
Project Cuddle [*An association*] (EA) ... PC
Project Data Card ... PDC
Project Data Compliance Report (MCD) ... PDCR
Project Data Control (MCD) ... PDC
Project Data Index [*Jet Propulsion Laboratory, NASA*] ... PDI
Project Data Processing System (MCD) ... PDPS
Project Definition/Joint Validation (MCD) ... PD/JV
Project Definition Phase (NRCH) ... PDP
Project Design Flood (NRCH) ... PDF
Project Design Memo ... PDM
Project Development Brochure [*Military*] ... PDB
Project Development Plan ... PDP
Project Development Unit [*Chemical engineering*] ... PDU
Project Directive (NASA) ... PD
Project Document ... PD
Project Document List ... PDL
Project Engineer ... PE
Project Engineer ... PJE
Project Engineer ... PROJENGR
Project Engineer Evaluation Report (HGAA) ... PEER
Project Engineering Control ... PROJECT
Project Engineering Graphics System [*Computer Aided Design Centre*] [*Software package*] (NCC) ... PEGS
Project Engineering Guide (MCD) ... PEG
Project Engineering Memorandum ... PEM
Project Engineering Research Association system (NITA) ... PERA system
Project Engineering System ... PEGS
Project Equality (EA) ... PE
Project Equipment Inspection Record [*NASA*] (KSC) ... PEIR
Project Evaluation and Assistance, Civil Engineering [*Air Force*] ... PEACE
Project Evaluation and Control System (MCD) ... PECOS
Project Evaluation and Cost Optimization System (IAA) ... PECOS
Project Evaluation and Review Technique (DAC) ... PERT
Project Evaluation and Review with Graphic Output (IEEE) ... PERGO
Project for an Energy-Enriched Curriculum [*Department of Energy*] ... PEEC
Project for Evaluation and Treatment of Radioactive Waste [*Nuclear energy*] (NUCP) ... PETRA
Project for Historical Biobibliography [*A publication*] ... PHIBB
Project for Integrated Catalogue Automation [*Royal Netherlands Library*] [*Cataloging cooperative*] (IID) ... PICA
Project for Mathematical Development of Children [*National Science Foundation*] ... PMDC
Project for Public Spaces (EA) ... PPS
Project for Retraining of Employable Persons as Relates to EDP ... PREPARE
Project for the Advancement of Church Education ... PACE
Project for the Advancement of Coding Techniques ... PACT
Project for the Analysis of Technology Transfer [*NASA*] ... PATT
Project for the Oral History of Music in America ... POHMA
Project for Utilization and Redistribution of Materiel [*Air Force*] ... PURM
Project Friend (EA) ... PF
Project Funds Management Record (MCD) ... PFMR
Project Grant Information System ... PGIS
Project Group ... PG
Project Group, Inc. [*Advertising agency*] [*Acronym now used as official n ame of agency*] ... PGI
Project Handclasp (EA) ... PH
Project: Hearts and Minds [*An association*] (EA) ... PHAM
Project Identification [*Computer science*] ... PROJID
Project Impact Analysis (NASA) ... PIA
Project Impact Analysis Report (MCD) ... PIAR
Project Implementation Directive [*Air Force*] ... PID
Project Implementation Plan ... PIP
Project in Foreign Language Pedagogy (AIE) ... PIF
Project Independence Evaluation System [*Energy policy*] ... PIES
Project Independence Report ... PIR
Project: Individualized Reading and Mathematics Inter-District (EDAC) ... PIRAMID
Project Inform (EA) ... PI
Project Information Center ... PIC
Project Information Retrieval System [*HEW*] ... PIRS
Project Information Tracking System [*Environmental Protection Agency*] (GFGA) ... PITS
Project Initiation Period ... PIP
Project Instrumentation Plan [*NASA*] (GFGA) ... PIP
Project Interface Adapter (SSD) ... PIA
Project Intrex [*Massachusetts Institute of Technology*] (EA) ... PI
Project Jonah [*Defunct*] (EA) ... PJ
Project Labor Agreement (AAGC) ... PLA
Project Leader ... PL
Project Level Steering Committee (HGAA) ... PLSC
Project Lighthawk [*Later, LH*] (EA) ... PL
Project Line Organization ... PLO
Project Literacy US [*Joint project of American Broadcasting Co. and Public Broadcasting Service*] ... PLUS
Project Local [*Defunct*] (EA) ... PL
Project Logic Planning (IAA) ... PROLOG
Project Magic (EA) ... PM
Project Magic Wand [*Military*] (MCD) ... PMW
Project/Major Subcontractor Affected (MCD) ... P/MSA
Project Management and Budgeting ... PMB
Project Management and Production Team Technique [*Computer science*] ... PROMPT
Project Management Body of Knowledge ... PMBOK
Project Management Committee (AD) ... PMC
Project Management Course [*Army*] ... PMC
Project Management Division/Batelle Memorial Institute (AD) ... PMD/BMI
Project Management File (MCD) ... PMF
Project Management Institute (EA) ... PMI
Project Management Integrated System (NITA) ... PROMIS
Project Management Office [*Army*] (AABC) ... PMO
Project Management Professional ... PMP
Project Management Report ... PMR
Project Management Staff Officer [*Military*] (AFIT) ... PMSO
Project Management Staffing Practices Study [*Navy*] (NG) ... PMSPS
Project Management Support Office [*Army*] (RDA) ... PMSO
Project Management System [*IBM Corp.*] [*Computer science*] ... PMS
Project Management Team (ODBW) ... PMT
Project Management Work-Bench (NITA) ... PMW
Project Manager [*Military*] ... PJM
Project Manager [*Military*] ... PM
Project Manager [*Military*] ... PROJMGR
Project Manager, Advanced Attack Helicopter [*Military*] ... PM-AAH
Project Manager, Advanced Scout Helicopter [*Military*] ... PM-ASH
Project Manager, Air Systems Command [*Navy*] ... PMA
Project Manager, Aircraft Survivability Equipment [*Military*] ... PM-ASE
Project Manager, Antisubmarine Warfare Systems ... PROJMGRASWS
Project Manager, Army Container Oriented Distribution System (MCD) ... PMACODS
Project Manager Development (MCD) ... PMD
Project Manager Development Course [*Military*] (RDA) ... PMDC
Project Manager Development Program [*Army*] (RDA) ... PMDP
Project Manager, Electronics System Command [*Navy*] ... PME
Project Manager, Fleet Ballistic Missile [*Navy*] ... MFBMP
Project Manager, Fleet Ballistic Missile [*Navy*] ... PROJMGRFBM
Project Manager for Cannon Artillery Weapon Systems (RDA) ... PM-CAWS
Project Manager for Mines, Countermine, and Demolitions [*Army*] (RDA) ... PM-MCD
Project Manager for Night Vision/Reconnaissance Surveillance and Target Acquisition [*Military*] (RDA) ... PM NV/RSTA
Project Manager for Nuclear Munitions [*Army*] (RDA) ... PM-NUC
Project Manager for Selected Ammunition ... PMSA
Project Manager, General Purpose Vehicle (SAA) ... PM-GPV
Project Manager - Mobile Electric Power [*DoD*] ... PM-MEP
Project Manager, Navigation and Control [*Military*] ... PM-NAVCON
Project Manager, Night Vision (RDA) ... PMNV

Project Manager, Remotely Piloted Vehicle [Military] .... PM-RPV
Project Manager, Ships .... PMS
Project Manager, Surface Missile Systems [Navy] .... MSMSP
Project Manager, Surface Missile Systems [Navy] .... PROJMGRSMS
Project Manager Test Offices [Military] .... PMTO
Project Manager, Training Devices Engineering Management [Orlando, FL]
   [Army] .... PMT-EM
Project Manager, Utility Tactical Transport Aircraft System
   [Military] .... PM-UTTAS
Project Manager's System Assessment .... PMSA
Project Manufacturing Controller (MCD) .... PMC
Project Marketing Loan Facility [Australia] .... PMLF
Project Master Data File [For spacecraft] .... PMDF
Project Master Plan [Army] .... PMP
Project Mercury Technical History Program [NASA] .... PMTHP
Project Military Adviser (NATG) .... PMA
Project/Miscellaneous Change Board (MCD) .... P/MCB
Project Neighbor to Neighbor (EA) N2N
Project Network Analysis .... PNA
Project Network Technique (EECA) .... PNT
Project Nondesign Memo .... PNDM
Project Note .... PN
Project Notification and Review System [Department of Labor] .... PNRS
Project Number [Online database field identifier] [Computer science] .... PN
Project Objective Plan (NG) .... POP
Project of National Significance .... PNS
Project Office [or Officer] [Military] .... PO
Project Office Change Letter .... POCL
Project Office for Physical Security Equipment [Army] (RDA) .... POPSE
Project Office Memo .... POM
Project Officer's Group .... POG
Project Officers Interim Report [Air Force] (MCD) .... POIR
Project Officers Meeting .... POM
Project Officers Report (MCD) .... POR
Project on Corporate Responsibility (EA) .... PCR
Project on Equal Education Rights [Defunct] (EA) .... PEER
Project on Government Procurement (EA) .... PGP
Project on Information Processing (IEEE) .... PIP
Project on Information Technology and Education [Defunct] (EA) .... PITE
Project on Linguistic Analysis .... POLA
Project on Military Procurement [Later, PGP] (EA) .... PMP
Project on National Vocational Education Resources (EDAC) .... PONVER
Project on Scientific Information Exchange in Psychology [Superseded by
   Office of Communication] .... PSIEP
Project on Technology, Work, and Character (EA) .... PTWC
Project on the Improvement of College Teaching .... PICT
Project on the Status and Education of Women (EA) .... PSEW
Project on the Vietnam Generation [Later, II] (EA) .... PVG
Project Operating Work Statement [NASA] (NASA) .... POWS
Project Operation Support Division [NASA] .... POSD
Project Operations [Navy] (NVT) .... POPS
Project Operations Director (BARN) .... POD
Project Operations in Port [Navy] (NVT) .... POPSIPT
Project Optimization [Industrial engineering] .... PRO-OP
Project Optimization Procedure (IAA) .... POP
Project ORBIS (EA) .... PO
Project Order [DoD] .... PO
Project Order Action Request [Navy] (NG) .... POAR
Project Overcome (EA) .... PO
Project Parts Coordinator .... PPC
Project Performance Audit Report .... PPAR
Project Physics Course [National Science Foundation] .... PPC
Project Planning and Control (NG) .... PP & C
Project Planning and Control System [Social Security Administration] .... PPCS
Project Planning Centre for Developing Countries [Research center British]
   (IRC) .... PPC
Project Planning Directive (NG) .... PPD
Project Planning Technique (MCD) .... PPT
Project Priesthood (EA) .... PP
Project Priority List [Environmental Protection Agency] .... PPL
Project Procurement Instructions [Jet Propulsion Laboratory, NASA] .... PPI
Project Profile Manual .... PPM
Project, Programmer Number .... PPN
Project Progress Report (OICC) .... PPR
Project Proposal (KSC) .... PP
Project Public Information [Department of Education] (AEBS) .... PPI
Project Quality Assurance .... PQA
Project Quality Assurance Manager [Nuclear energy] (NRCH) .... PQAM
Project Quality Engineering .... PQE
Project Release (EA) .... PR
Project Report .... PR
Project Reporting Organization and Management Planning
   Technique .... PROMPT
Project Research Laboratory .... PRL
Project Return on Investment (MHDW) .... PROI
Project Review Board [NASA] (NASA) .... PRB
Project Rover (SAA) .... PR
Project Safe Run (EA) .... PSR
Project Safety Management .... PSM
Project Scan Record .... PSR
Project Schedule Plan (NASA) .... PSP
Project Slip .... PS
Project Software & Development, Inc. [Associated Press] (SAG) .... ProjSft
Project Software & Development, Inc. [NASDAQ symbol] (SAG) .... PSDI
Project Software & Dvlp [NASDAQ symbol] (TTSB) .... PSDI

Project Software Management Plan (SSD) .... PSMP
Project ST [Later, NSTA] (EA) .... PST
Project Standard Practice (DNAB) .... PSP
Project Starlight International (EA) .... PSI
Project Start [Milestone chart] .... PS
Project Stock [Military] (AABC) .... PS
Project Structured Analysis of LOGEX [Logistical Exercise] Methodology
   (MCD) .... PSALM
Project Study [British military] (DMA) .... PS
Project Summary Report (MCD) .... PSR
Project Summary Work Breakdown Structure .... PSWBS
Project Support Laboratory [Military] (CAAL) .... PSL
Project Systems Control (MCD) .... PSC
Project Team Head (MHDI) .... PTH
Project Technical Office [Military] (DNAB) .... PTO
Project Tibet (EA) .... PT
Project to Optimize Many Individual Numbers (SAA) .... PTOMAIN
Project to Research Objects Theories, Extraterrrestrials, and Unusual
   Sightings (EA) .... PROTEUS
Project Top Hat [Defunct] (EA) .... PTH
Project Tracking System [Environmental Protection Agency] (ERG) .... PTS
Project Transition [DoD] .... PROJTRNS
Project Transition [DoD] (OICC) .... PT
Project Trust (EAIO) .... PT
Project Type Organization (AAG) .... PTO
Project Unique Identification Code (AAGC) .... PUIC
Project Vietnam Orphans [British] (DI) .... PVO
Project VISIT - Vehicle Internal Systems Investigative Team (EA) .... VISIT
Project Volunteer (EA) .... PV
Project West Wing (MCD) .... PWW
Project Wolf USA (EA) .... PWUSA
Project Work Authorization .... PWA
Project Work Review [Army] (AFIT) .... PWR
Project Work Schedule [Computer science] .... PWS
Project Yedid [Defunct] (EA) .... PY
Projectavision $0.40 Cv'B'Pfd [NASDAQ symbol] (TTSB) .... PJTVP
Projectavision, Inc. [Associated Press] (SAG) .... Pjctvs
Projectavision, Inc. [Associated Press] (SAG) .... Pjctvsn
Projectavision, Inc. [NASDAQ symbol] (SAG) .... PJTV
Projectavision Inc. Wrrt [NASDAQ symbol] (TTSB) .... PJTVW
Projected Antisubmarine Classification and Location System
   (DNAB) .... PASCALS
Projected Automation Requirement .... PAR
Projected Average Progress (NG) .... PAP
Projected Benefit Obligation (TDOB) .... PBO
Projected Books, Inc. [Defunct] (EA) .... PBI
Projected Charge Density (PDAA) .... PCD
Projected Control Board .... PCB
Projected Data Display .... PDD
Projected Decision Date (NRCH) .... PD
Projected Decision Date (NRCH) .... PDD
Projected Display .... PD
Projected Duty Air Force Specialty Code (AFM) .... PDAFSC
Projected Engagement Scheduler [Military] (CAAL) .... PES
Projected Impact Point [Aviation] .... PIP
Projected Inactive Time [Computer science] .... PIT
Projected Manpower Requirements Account [Navy] .... PMRA
Projected Map Display .... PMD
Projected Map Display (AD) .... pmd
Projected Map Display Set (AD) .... pmds
Projected Map Display System .... PMDS
Projected Map Display Unit (DNAB) .... PMDU
Projected Map System (OA) .... PMS
Projected Operational Environment (NVT) .... POE
Projected Operational Logistics Analysis Requirements .... POLAR
Projected Program Objective (NG) .... PPO
Projected Rating .... PRORAT
Projected Requisition Authority [Army] (AABC) .... PRA
Projected Return on Open Office Facilities [Computer program] .... PROOF
Projected Rotation Date (NG) .... PRD
Projected Window (MSA) .... PW
Projectile (MSA) .... PJCTL
Projectile (AFM) .... PROJ
Projectile Airburst and Impact Location System .... PAILS
Projectile Development Establishment [British] .... PDE
Projectile Fragment .... PF
Projectile Measurement System [Computer science Army] .... PROMS
Projectile Pull and Drain [Machine] (MCD) .... PPD
Projection (MSA) .... PJTN
Projection and Integrated Standalone Monitor [Dolch Computer Systems]
   [Computer science] (PCM) .... PRISM
Projection by Reflection Optics of Xerographic Images (IEEE) .... PROXI
Projection Display Unit .... PDU
Projection Lens [Microscopy] .... PL
Projection Microradiography (IAA) .... PMR
Projection Neurons [Neuroanatomy] .... PN
Projection Plan Position Indicator .... PPPI
Projection Readout Indicator [Aviation] (OA) .... PRI
Projection Video Monitor .... PVM
Projection Weld Flange Nut .... PWFN
Projection Welding .... PW
Projection X-Ray Microscope .... PXM
Projective Assessment of Aging Method [Personality development test]
   [Psychology] .... PAAM
Projective Field Theory .... PFT

Projective Tests of Attitudes .... PTOA
Projector (MSA) .... PJTR
Projector [or Projection] .... PROJ
Projector (VRA) .... projt
Projector Charge .... PC
Projector Infantry, Antitank [British shoulder-controlled weapon] .... PIAT
Project-Oriented Management Information System .... PROMIS
Projects and Exports Policy [Board of Trade] [British] .... PEP
Projects for Continental Operations [World War II] .... PROCO
Projects Management Information System [UNESCO] (DUND) .... PMIS
Projects of Optimum Urgency and Feasibility .... POUF
Projects to Advance Creativity in Education [HEW] .... PACE
Projects with Industry Program [Department of Education] .... PWI
Projet des Francophones de l'Atlantique [Canada] .... PROFAT
Projet National de Coordination des Ressources dans le Domaine de la
    Statistiques et de l'Information Judiciaires [Canada] .... PNRC
Projets de Services Communautaires du Canada .... PSCC
Projets pour une Agriculture Ecologique [Ecological Agriculture Projects -
    EAP] [Sainte Anne De Bellevue, PQ] (EAIO) .... PAE
Prokininogenase [An enzyme] (MAE) .... PKA
Prolactin [Also, LTH, PRL] [Endocrinology] .... PR
Prolactin [Also, LTH, PR] [Endocrinology] .... PRL
Prolactin [Biochemistry] (DAVI) .... PROLAC
Prolactin Inhibiting Factor [Endocrinology] (DAVI) .... PIF
Prolactin Inhibitor [Endocrinology] .... PI
Prolactin Receptor [Biochemistry] .... PLR
Prolactin-Like Protein [Biochemistry] .... PLP
Prolactin-Release Inhibiting Factor [Also, PRIH] [Endocrinology] ...... PIF
Prolactin-Release Inhibiting Factor [Also, PIF] [Endocrinology] .... PRIH
Prolactin-Release Inhibiting Hormone [Endocrinology] .... PIH
Prolactin-Releasing Factor [Endocrinology] .... PRF
Prolactin-Releasing Hormone [Endocrinology] .... PRH
Prolapsed Intervertebral Disc [Medicine] .... PID
Prolapsing Mitral Valve [Cardiology] .... PMV
Prolate Spheroidal Wave Function (PDAA) .... PSWF
Proler International Corp. [Associated Press] (SAG) .... Proler
Proler International Corp. [NYSE symbol] (SPSG) .... PS
Proler Intl [NYSE symbol] (TTSB) .... PS
Proletarian (WDAA) .... PROLE
Proletarian Party .... PP
Proletarian Party of America (NADA) .... PPA
Proletarian Party of America [Political party] (AD) .... PPA
Pro-Life Action League (EA) .... PLAL
Pro-Life Direct Action League (EA) .... PLDAL
Pro-Life Nonviolent Action Project (EA) .... PLNAP
Pro-Life Nonviolent Action Project (EA) .... PNAP
Proliferating Angioendotheliomatosis .... PA
Proliferating Cell Nuclear Antigen [Cytology, immunology] .... PCNA
Proliferation [Biology] .... P
Proliferation Inhibitory Factor [Immunochemistry] .... PIF
Proliferation Regulatory Factor [Biochemistry] .... PRF
Proliferation-Associated Gene A (DMAA) .... PAGA
Proliferative [or Proliferation] .... Prolif
Proliferative Breast Disease [Medicine] .... PBD
Proliferative Diabetic Retinopathy [Ophthalmology] .... PDR
Proliferative Glomerulonephritis [Medicine] .... PGN
Proliferative Helper Cells [Immunology] .... PHC
Proliferative Kidney Disease [Medicine] (DMAA) .... PKD
Proliferative Retinopathy Photocoagulation .... PRP
Proliferative Vitreoretinopathy [Ophthalmology] .... PVR
Proliferative Vitreoretinopathy [Ophthalmology] (DAVI) ...... PVR
Proliferin [Biochemistry] .... PLF
Proliferin Related Protein [Biochemistry] .... PRP
Prolifers for Survival [Defunct] (EA) .... PS
Prolific Resources [Vancouver Stock Exchange symbol] .... POF
Proline [One-letter symbol; see Pro] .... P
Proline [Also, P] [An amino acid] .... Pro
Proline [An amino acid] (DOG) .... pro
Proline-Rich Domain [Genetics] .... PRD
Proline-Rich Protein [Biochemistry] .... PRP
Proline-Rich Protein [Biochemistry] .... PRR
Prolog and List Processing .... LOGLISP
Prolog Equation Solving System (BYTE) .... PRESS
Prolog Inference Engine [Computer science] .... PIE
Prologic Management Systems, Inc. [AMEX symbol] (SAG) .... PRC
Prologic Management Systems, Inc. [NASDAQ symbol] (SAG) .... PRLO
Prologic Management Systems, Inc. [Associated Press] (SAG) .... Prol
Prologic Management Systems, Inc. [Associated Press] (SAG) .... Prolog
Prologic Management Systems, Inc. [Associated Press] (SAG) .... Prologc
Prologic Management Systems, Inc. [Associated Press] (SAG) .... Prologic
PROLOGIC Mgmt Sys [NASDAQ symbol] (TTSB) .... PRLO
PROLOGIC Mgmt Sys Wrrt [NASDAQ symbol] (TTSB) .... PRLOW
Prologue .... PROL
Prolong Tablets [Pharmacy] .... PT
Prolongatus [Prolonged] [Latin] (DAVI) .... prolong
Prolonged Depolarizing Afterpotential [Neurophysiology] .... PDA
Prolonged Detention Care (CPH) .... PDC
Prolonged Elevated-Pollution Episode [Environmental Protection Agency] .... PEPE
Prolonged Fever of Unknown Origin [Medicine] (DMAA) .... PFUO
Prolonged Illness Coverage [Insurance] (PAZ) .... PIC
Prolonged Postictal Encephalopathy [Medicine] (DMAA) .... PPIE
Prolonged Premature Rupture of Membranes [Obstetrics] (DAVI) .... PPROM
Prolonged Reversible Ischemic Neurologic Deficit [Medicine] (DMAA) .... PRIND
Prolonged Rupture of Fetal Membranes [Obstetrics] (DAVI) .... PRFM
Prolonged Rupture of Membranes [Gynecology] (DAVI) .... PROM

Prolonged Sleep Apnea .... PSA
Prolonged Vacuum Exposure .... PVE
Prolonged-Action [Pharmacy] .... PA
Prolonged-Dwell Peritoneal Dialysis [Medicine] (DMAA) .... PDPD
Prolonged-Release [Pharmacy] .... PR
Prolotherapy Association (EA) .... PA
Prolyl [Biochemistry] .... Pro
Prolyl Endopeptidase .... PEP
Prolyl(leucyl)glycinamide [Biochemistry] .... PLG
Prolymphocyte [Hematology] (DAVI) .... P-LYM
Prolymphocytic Leukemia [Also, PLL] [Oncology] .... PL
Prolymphocytic Leukemia [Also, PL] [Oncology] .... PLL
PROM [Programmable Read-Only Memory] Memory Board .... PMB
PROM [Programmable Read-Only Memory] Programmer Board .... PPB
Promair Australia [Airline code] .... FB
Promark Software [Vancouver Stock Exchange symbol] ...... PRW
Prome [Myanmar] [Airport symbol] (OAG) .... PRU
Prome [Myanmar] [ICAO location identifier] (ICLI) .... VBPR
Pro-Melanin-Concentrating Hormone (DMAA) .... PMCH
Pro-Melanin-Concentrating Hormone-Like (DMAA) .... PMCHL
Promenade (DD) .... Pr
Promenade (DD) .... prom
Promenade (ODBW) .... prom
Promenade [Maps and charts] .... PROM
Promenade Deck [of a ship] (DS) .... PDK
Promenade Deck [of a ship] (DS) .... Prom dk
Promethean Technologies, Inc. [Vancouver Stock Exchange symbol] .... PTI
Prometheus Society (EA) .... ProSoc
Prometheus Society (EA) .... PS
Prometheus Vinctus [of Aeschylus] [Classical studies] (OCD) .... PV
Prometheus-Europe [Paris, France] (EAIO) .... PE
Promethium [Chemical symbol] .... Pm
Prominent .... PROM
Prominent Resources Corp. [Vancouver Stock Exchange symbol] .... PRN
Promise [Legal shorthand] (LWAP) .... PROM
Promise to Pay (MHDW) .... PTP
Promisee [Legal shorthand] (LWAP) .... PROMEE
Promisel & Korn, Inc. [Information service or system] (IID) .... P & KI
Promisor [Legal shorthand] (LWAP) .... PROMOR
Promissory [A publication] (DLA) .... Prom
Promissory (ROG) .... PROMY
Promissory Note [Business term] .... PN
Promissory Note (AD) .... pn
Promonocytes [hematology] (DAVI) .... P-MONO
Promontory .... PROM
Promontory Point [Utah] [Seismograph station code, US Geological Survey
    Closed] (SEIS) .... PPU
Promotable Second-Tier Debt [Economics] .... PSTD
Promote (AABC) .... PRM
Promote [or Promotion] (AFM) .... PROM
Promote and Develop Fishery Products Pertaining to American Fisheries
    Account [National Oceanic and Atmospheric Administration] (GFGA) .... P & D
Promote Our Wonderful Energy Resources (EA) .... POWER
Promote Real Independence for the Disabled and Elderly (EA) .... PRIDE
Promote Yard Performance Efficiency and Reliability (DNAB) .... PYPER
Promoted to Glory [Salvation Army] .... G
Promoter [Genetics] .... P
Promoting Achievement through Communications [Education] .... PAC
Promoting Aphasics' Communicative Competence [Medicine] (DMAA) .... PACC
Promoting Aphasics Communicative Effectiveness [Australia] .... PACE
Promoting Enduring Peace (EA) .... PEP
Promoting Intellectual Adaptation Given Experiential Transforming
    Project (EDAC) .... PIAGET
Promotion .... PROM
Promotion [Slang] (DSUE) .... PROMO
Promotion Appeal Board, Postal and Telecommunications Commission
    [Australia] .... PAB-PTC
Promotion Cooperative du Transport Individuel Publique [Public cars for
    private use to reduce traffic congestion] [Also known as TIP]
    [France] .... PROCOTIP
Promotion Director .... PD
Promotion Eligibility Date [Military] .... PED
Promotion Evaluation Pattern .... PEP
Promotion Industry Club (EA) .... PIC
Promotion List (DICI) .... PL
Promotion List Service Date [Air Force] .... PLSD
Promotion Management List [Pronounced "pemell"] [Air Force] .... PML
Promotion Marketing Association of America [New York, NY] (EA) .... PMAA
Promotion of Community and Cultural Awareness [Australia] .... PCCA
Promotion of Non-Executive Directors (ODBW) .... PRONED
Promotion of Social Education [British] (DI) .... POSE
Promotion Qualification Score [Military] .... PQS
Promotion Service Date .... PSD
Promotion Status (DNAB) .... PROM STAT
Promotion, Transfer, and Redundancy [Railway union agreement] [British]
    (ECON) .... PRT
Promotional Announcement (NTCM) .... Promo
Promotional Fare [Also, L, Q, V] [Airline fare code] .... K
Promotional Fare [Also, K, Q, V] [Airline fare code] L
Promotional Fare [Also, K, L, V] [Airline fare code] .... Q
Promotional Fare [Also, K, L, Q] [Airline fare code] V
Promotional Telephone Call [Marketing] (OICC) .... PTC
Promotions and Placements Referral System (MCD) .... PPRS
Promotions Appeal Board [Victoria, Australia] .... PAB
Prompt [i.e., the right side] [A stage direction] .... P

Prompt (ROG) .... PPT
Prompt Action to Telephone Inquiries (SAA) .... PATTI
Prompt Air, Inc. [*FAA designator*] (FAAC) .... PRT
Prompt Burst Experiments [*Nuclear energy*] (NRCH) .... PBE
Prompt Gamma Neutron Activation Analysis [*Analytical chemistry*] .... PGNAA
Prompt Gamma-Ray Activation Analysis .... PGAA
Prompt Mobilization Designation Withdrawn .... PMW
Prompt Ordering Plan .... POP
Prompt Payment [*OMB Circular*] (AAGC) A-125
Prompt Payment Act (AAGC) .... PPA
Prompt Payment Discount (AAGC) .... PPD
Prompt Radiation Analysis (MCD) .... PRA
Prompt Relief Trip [*Nuclear energy*] (NRCH) .... PRT
Prompt Response Insurance Delivery Express .... PRIDE
Prompt Side [*of a stage*] [*i.e., the right side A stage direction*] .... PS
Prompt-by-Example [*Computer science*] .... PBE
Promulgate (AABC) .... PROM
Promulgate .... PROML
Promulgators of Public Toilets in Public Parks (AD) .... PPTPP
Promus Hotel [*NYSE symbol*] (TTSB) .... PRH
Promus Hotel Corp. [*NYSE symbol*] (SAG) .... PRH
Promus Hotel Corp. [*Associated Press*] (SAG) .... PrmsH
Promyelocytic Leukaemia Protein [*Biochemistry*] .... PML
Promyelocytic Leukemia [*Medicine*] .... PML
Pronasale [*Anatomy*] .... PRN
Pronation [*Medicine*] .... PRO
Pronation .... PRON
Pronation/Lateral Rotation [*Fracture*] [*Orthopedics*] (DAVI) .... PLR
Pronator Quadratus [*Muscle*] [*Anatomy*] (DAVI) .... PQ
Pronator Teres [*Musle*] [*Orthopedics*] (DAVI) .... PT
Pronestyl [*Procainamide*] [*Bristol-Myers Squibb Co.*] [*Pharmacology*] (DAVI) .... P'STYL
ProNet, Inc. [*NASDAQ symbol*] (NQ) .... PNET
ProNet, Inc. [*Associated Press*] (SAG) .... Pronet
Pronominal [*Grammar*] (ROG) .... PR
Pronominal (ADA) .... PRON
Pronoun .... PR
Pronoun [*Grammar*] (WGA) .... PRO
Pronoun .... PRON
Pronounced .... PR
Pronounced .... PRON
Pronto Explorations Ltd. [*Vancouver Stock Exchange symbol*] .... PEX
Pronto Explorations Ltd. [*Toronto Stock Exchange symbol*] .... PRO
Pronuclear Oocyte and Sperm Transfer [*Embryology*] .... PROST
Pronuclei [*Embryology*] .... PN
Pronunciation (ROG) .... PRON
Pronunciation (WDMC) .... pron
Proodeftiki Parataxis [*Progressive Front*] [*Greek Cyprus*] [*Political party*] (PPE) .... PP
Prooemium (BJA) .... prooem
Proof [*Philately*] .... P
Proof .... PF
Proof (KSC) .... PRF
Proof (WDMC) .... prf
Proof (VRA) .... prf
Proof and Experimental Establishment [*British*] .... PEE
Proof and Experimental Establishments (RDA) .... P & EE
Proof and Experimental Test Establishment [*Canada*] (MCD) .... PETE
Proof Coins [*Numismatics*] .... PC
Proof Gallon [*Wines and spirits*] .... PG
Proof in Print .... PIP
Proof of Accounts .... POA
Proof of Analog Results through a Numerical Equivalent Routine [*Computer science*] .... PARTNER
Proof of Concept [*Army*] .... POC
Proof of Debt [*Business term*] (DCTA) .... POD
Proof of Delivery [*Shipping*] (DS) .... POD
Proof of Deposit [*Banking*] .... POD
Proof of Design (MCD) .... POD
Proof of Eligibility [*Medicine*] (DMAA) .... POE
Proof of Purchase .... POP
Proof of Purchase (WDMC) .... PROP
Proof Shot [*Ammunition*] .... PS
Proof Stress .... PS
Proof Test (AAG) .... PT
Proof Test Capsule [*NASA*] .... PTC
Proof Test Facility [*Nuclear energy*] .... PTF
Proof Test Model [*NASA*] .... PTM
Proof Test Orbiter [*NASA*] .... PTO
Proof Test Reactor [*Nuclear energy*] .... PTR
Proof Test Spacecraft [*NASA*] .... PT-S/C
Proofer [*Freight*] .... PRFR
Proofing [*Freight*] .... PRFG
Proofing, Inspection, and Quality Assurance [*Military*] .... PIQA
Proof-Of Principle [*Test*] .... POP
Proof-of-Concept Experiment [*Solar thermal conversion*] .... POCE
Proof-of-Concept Experiment Testbed [*Solar thermal conversion*] (MCD) .... POCET
Proofread (MSA) .... PRFRD
Proofreader [*MARC relator code*] [*Library of Congress*] (LCCP) .... pfr
Proofreaders Club of New York (EA) .... PCNY
Proofreading Tests of Spelling [*Educational test*] .... PRETOS
Proopiocortin [*Biochemistry*] .... POC
Pro-Opiolipomelanocortin [*Endocrinology*] .... proOLMC
Pro-Opiomelanocortin [*Endocrinology*] .... POMC
Proopiomelanocortin (DMAA) .... POMC
Prop (DS) .... P
Prop Forward .... PF
Propaganda (AABC) .... PGND
Propaganda (AFM) .... PROP
Propaganda Due [*Secret Italian Masonic organization, allegedly tied to the Roman Catholic church*] P-2
Propagate [*Botany*] .... Prop
Propagating Space Charge (PDAA) .... PSC
Propagation [*Military*] .... PRO
Propagation Distribution [*Broadcasting*] .... P
Propagation Loss .... PL
Propagation Loss (NVT) .... PROPLOSS
Propagation Loss Classification System [*Navy*] (NVT) .... PLCLAS
Propagation Prediction Report (SAA) .... PRO
Propair, Inc. [*Canada ICAO designator*] (FAAC) .... PRO
Propane .... PROPN
Propane [*Organic chemistry*] .... PRPNE
Propane Phosphonic Acid Anhydride [*Organic chemistry*] .... PPA
Propanediamine [*Organic chemistry*] .... PDA
Propane-Precipitated Asphalt [*Petroleum technology*] .... PPA
Propanethiol [*Organic chemistry*] .... PT
Propargyl(dideaza)folic Acid [*Biochemistry*] .... PDDF
Propellant (KSC) .... PROP
Propellant (NASA) .... PROPLT
Propellant (KSC) .... PRPLNT
Propellant (MSA) .... PRPLT
Propellant Acquisition Device (NASA) .... PAD
Propellant and Pressurant Loading System [*NASA*] (KSC) .... PPLS
Propellant Calibration Measuring Unit (KSC) .... PCMU
Propellant Control Unit (SAA) .... PCU
Propellant Delivery System .... PDS
Propellant Development & Characterization Subcommittee [*Joint Army, Navy, NASA, Air Force*] .... PDCS
Propellant Dispersion (KSC) .... PD
Propellant Dispersion System (MCD) .... PDS
Propellant Disposition Effects .... PDE
Propellant Drain Area (NASA) .... PDA
Propellant Engine Research Environmental Facility .... PEREF
Propellant, Explosive, and Pyrotechnic .... PEP
Propellant, Explosive, Pyrotechnic Pollution Abatement Research and Development (DNAB) .... PEPPARD
Propellant Expulsion and Storage Assembly .... PESA
Propellant Feed System .... PFS
Propellant Field System .... PFS
Propellant [*or Propulsion*] **Gas Supply Unit** .... PGSU
Propellant Gauging System .... PGS
Propellant Injector Tube Simulator (MCD) .... PITS
Propellant Inspection Building [*NASA*] (KSC) .... PIB
Propellant Isolation Valve .... PIV
Propellant Latching Solenoid Valve .... PLSV
Propellant Level Control Unit [*NASA*] (KSC) .... PLCU
Propellant Life Support and Ordnance [*NASA*] (KSC) .... PLSO
Propellant Loading [*NASA*] (KSC) .... PL
Propellant Loading and All Systems Test [*NASA*] (KSC) .... PLAST
Propellant Loading and Pressurization System [*NASA*] .... PLPS
Propellant Loading and Utilization (AAG) .... PLU
Propellant Loading and Utilization Group (AAG) .... PLUG
Propellant Loading Control Monitor [*NASA*] (KSC) .... PLCM
Propellant Loading Control System [*NASA*] (AAG) .... PLCS
Propellant Loading Data Transmission System [*NASA*] (KSC) .... PLDTS
Propellant Loading Exercise (MCD) .... PLX
Propellant Loading Sequencer (AAG) .... PLS
Propellant Loading System .... PLS
Propellant Loading Terminal Cabinet (AAG) .... PLTC
Propellant Management (KSC) .... PM
Propellant Mass Ratio (SAA) .... PMR
Propellant Monitor and Control (AFM) .... PMC
Propellant on Board at Takeoff .... POBATO
Propellant Pneumatic Control Panel (KSC) .... PPCP
Propellant Quantity Gauge [*or Gauging*] **System** [*Apollo*] [*NASA*] .... PQGS
Propellant Quantity Indicator (NASA) .... PQI
Propellant Quantity Measuring Device .... PQMD
Propellant Seal .... PSL
Propellant Slosh Dynamics .... PSD
Propellant Storage Depot [*NASA*] .... PSD
Propellant Storage Module [*NASA*] .... PSM
Propellant Supply (KSC) .... PS
Propellant Supply System [*or Subsystem*] .... PSS
Propellant System .... PS
Propellant Systems Cleaning Laboratory [*NASA*] (NASA) .... PSCL
Propellant Tank Flow .... PTF
Propellant Tanking Computer System (KSC) .... PTCS
Propellant Tanking Console (AAG) .... PTC
Propellant Toxicity Monitoring Devices (KSC) .... PTMD
Propellant Transfer .... PT
Propellant Transfer Operation (AFM) .... PTO
Propellant Transfer Pressurization System (KSC) .... PTPS
Propellant Transfer System .... PTS
Propellant Unit (NASA) .... PU
Propellant Utilization [*Aerospace*] .... PU
Propellant Utilization Acoustical Checkout (AAG) .... PUAC
Propellant Utilization and Gauging [*Apollo*] [*NASA*] .... PUG
Propellant Utilization and Gauging System [*Apollo*] [*NASA*] (KSC) .... PUGS
Propellant Utilization and Loading .... PUL
Propellant Utilization Checkout Kit (KSC) .... PUCK

Propellant Utilization Control System (KSC)	PUCS
Propellant Utilization Control Unit	PUCU
Propellant Utilization Data Translator (AAG)	PUDT
Propellant Utilization Exerciser	PUE
Propellant Utilization Loading System (AAG)	PULS
Propellant Utilization System	PUS
Propellant Utilization System Exerciser	PUSE
Propellant Utilization Time Trace	PUTT
Propellant Utilization Valve [NASA] (NASA)	PUV
Propellant Utilization Valve [NASA] (AAG)	PUVLV
Propellant Utilization Vehicle Electronic Package (MCD)	PUVEP
Propellant Valve Actuator (MCD)	PVA
Propellant Venting System	PVS
Propellant Weight Fraction (NATG)	PWF
Propellant-Actuated Device	PAD
Propellant-Actuated Valve	PAV
Propellant-Loading Control Unit [NASA] (IAA)	PLCU
Propellants and Explosives [Military] (AABC)	P & E
Propellants and Life Support Laboratory [NASA] (NASA)	PLSL
Propellants, Explosives, and Rocket Motors Establishment [British Ministry of Defense] [Research center] (RDA)	PERME
Propellants System Components Laboratory [Kennedy Space Center] [NASA]	PSCL
Propelled Ascent Mine	PRAM
Propelled Rapid Ascent Mine (MCD)	PRAM
Propeller	PROP
Propeller Change (MCD)	PRC
Propeller Club of the United States (EA)	PCUS
Propeller Horsepower	PHP
Propeller Order	PRO
Propeller Order Transmitter (OA)	POT
Propeller Pitch	PP
Propeller Revolution	PRV
Propeller Revolution Indicator System (MSA)	PRIS
Propeller Shaft Bearing Unit [Truck engineering]	PSBU
Propeller Shaft Rate [Navy] (CAAL)	PSR
Propeller STOL [Short Takeoff and Landing] Transport	PST
Propeller Torpedo [Boat]	PT
Propeller Twist [Genetics]	Prtw
Propeller-Excited Vibration (PDAA)	PEV
Propelling	PROPLING
Propensity to Consume (MHDW)	PTC
Proper [Heraldry]	PPR
Proper	PR
Proper	PROP
Proper	PM
Proper Motion [Astronomy] (BARN)	PM
Proper Return Port [Shipping]	PRP
Properly Driven Net	PDN
Pro-Personal Computer (NITA)	PPC
Properties and Installations	P & I
Properties of Electrolyte Solutions Data Center [National Institute of Standards and Technology]	PESDC
Properties of Irregular Parts System (MCD)	PIPS
Properties Research Laboratory [Purdue University] [Lafayette, IN]	PRL
Propertius [Roman poet, c. 29BC] [Classical studies] (ROG)	PROP
Property (AFM)	PPTY
Property (AD)	ppty
Property	PR
Property	PROP
Property (DD)	prop
Property	PROP
Property Accountability (MCD)	PROPER COUNT
Property Accountability Record System (NASA)	PARS
Property Accountability Task Force [Army] (MCD)	PATF
Property Action Order	PAO
Property Administrator [DoD]	PA
Property Advisory Group [British] (DCTA)	PAG
Property Agents International	PAI
Property and Accounting Technician [Navy]	PAT
Property and Compensation Reports [A publication] (DLA)	P & CR
Property and Compensation Reports [A publication] (DLA)	Prop & Comp
Property and Compensation Reports [A publication] (DLA)	Prop & Comp R
Property and Liability Information System	PALIS
Property Book [Army] (AABC)	PB
Property Book - Army Equipment Status Reporting System (AABC)	PB-AESRS
Property Book Officer [Army] (AABC)	PBO
Property Cap Tr [AMEX symbol] (TTSB)	PCT
Property Capital Trust [AMEX symbol] (SPSG)	PCT
Property Capital Trust [Associated Press] (SAG)	PropCT
Property/Casualty [Insurance]	P/C
Property Consultants Society [British] (DBA)	PCS
Property Control Branch [of Allied Military Government] [Post-World War II]	PCB
Property Control Office [of Allied Military Government] [Post-World War II]	PCO
Property Control System	PCS
Property Control Transaction Report	PCTR
Property Damage	PD
Property Damage and Public Liability [Insurance] (IIA)	PD & PL
Property Damage, Personal Liability [Insurance]	PDPL
Property Disposal Account [Military] (NG)	PDA
Property Disposal Agent [Military] (NG)	PDA
Property Disposal Contracting Officer [Military]	PDCO
Property Disposal Officer [Army]	PDO
Property Disposition [FHA] (EMRF)	PD
Property Disposition Authorization	PDA
Property Enterprise Trust [Investment term British] (ECON)	PET

Property Estimation Program [Utah Water Research Laboratory]	PEP
Property in Question	PIQ
Property Income Certificate [Investment term British]	PINC
Property Income Trust [Investment term]	PIT
Property Index [British police term]	PI
Property Inheritance Network Computer	PIN
Property Law Bulletin [A publication] (DLA)	Prop Law Bull
Property Lawyer [1826-30] [A publication] (DLA)	Prop Law
Property Lawyer, New Series [England] [A publication] (DLA)	Prop Law NS
Property Line [Real estate] (MSA)	PL
Property Loss Research Bureau (EA)	PLRB
Property Management (OICC)	PM
Property Management and Disposal Service [Abolished, 1973] [General Services Administration]	PMDS
Property Management Association of America (EA)	PMA
Property Management Association of America (EA)	PMAA
Property Management Exposition [Bachner Communications] (TSPED)	PMEXPO
Property Management Manual [NASA] (MCD)	PMM
Property Management Plan [Australia]	PMP
Property Management Regulation (AAGC)	PMR
Property Market Analysis [Consulting firm] [British]	PMA
Property Movement Order	PMO
Property Movement Request (MCD)	PMR
Property Owners Association of America [Defunct] (EA)	POAA
Property Owners' Association of New South Wales [Australia]	POANSW
Property Owners' Association of Queensland [Australia]	POAQ
Property Owners' Protection Association	POPA
Property Press (DLA)	PROPRE
Property Protection Area	PPA
Property Protection Insurance	PPI
Property Record for Equipment Servicing and Sharing (MCD)	PRESS
Property Recovery Section	PRS
Property Release Option Program [HUD]	PROP
Property Security Investment Trust [British]	PSIT
Property Services Agency [Department of the Environment] [British]	PSA
Property Services Agency Information on Construction and Architecture [Property Service Agency Library Service] [British Information service or system]	PICA
Property Tax (MHDW)	PT
Property Transfer [Real estate] (KSC)	PT
Property Unit Trust [Finance British]	PUT
Prophenoloxidase	proPO
Prophesy Development [Vancouver Stock Exchange symbol]	PPY
Prophet	PT
Prophet 21, Inc. [Associated Press] (SAG)	Proph21
Prophet 21, Inc. [NASDAQ symbol] (SAG)	PXXI
Prophet Resources Ltd. [Vancouver Stock Exchange symbol]	PPH
Propheter Construction Co., Inc. [ICAO designator] (FAAC)	PPA
Prophets and Kings (BJA)	PK
Prophylactic (AABC)	PRO
Prophylactic	PROPH
Prophylactic (DAVI)	prophy
Prophylactic Antibiotic	PA
Prophylactic Brain Irradiation [Oncology]	PBI
Prophylactic Cranial Irradiation [Oncology]	PCI
Prophylactic Whole Brain Radiation Therapy [Medicine] (DMAA)	PWBRT
Propidium Iodide [Fluorescent dye]	PI
Propionic [Bacteriology] (DAVI)	P
Propionic Acid (DMAA)	PA
Propionic Acid [Organic chemistry]	PRA
Propionyl CoA Carboxylase [An enzyme]	PCC
Propionyl Erythromycin Lauryl Sulfate [Antimicrobial agent]	PELS
Propionyl(dimethylamino)naphthalene [Organic chemistry]	PRODAN
Pro-Platelet Basic Protein (DMAA)	PPBP
Propodial Anlage [Zoology]	PAN
Propodial Mucus Gland [Zoology]	PMG
Propodial Sinus [Zoology]	PRS
Proponent	PPNT
Proponent Agency [Army]	PA
Proponent Evaluation (MCD)	PE
Proponent Sponsored Engineer Corps Training [Army Corps of Engineers]	PROSPECT
Proportion (ROG)	PPN
Proportion (AD)	ppn
Proportion (MSA)	PROPN
Proportion (ROG)	PROPON
Proportion in a Specific Class	P
Proportion Not in a Specific Class	Q
Proportional (IAA)	P
Proportional (KSC)	PROP
Proportional	PROPAL
Proportional	PROPL
Proportional	PA
Proportional Action (AAG)	PB
Proportional Band	PBW
Proportional Bandwidth (MCD)	PCI
Proportional Change Index [Occupational therapy]	PC
Proportional Counter [Instrumentation]	PD
Proportional Derivative (IAA)	PEL
Proportional Elastic Limit	PEGR
Proportional Exhaust Gas Recirculation [Engines]	PFA
Proportional Fluid Amplifier	PID
Proportional Integral Differential [Digital control-algorithm] (IAA)	PL
Proportional Limit	PN
Proportional Navigation (IAA)	PNAV
Proportional Navigation	

Proportional Part	PP
Proportional Plus Derivative (IAA)	PD
Proportional Plus Integral	PPI
Proportional Representation [in legislatures, etc.]	PR
Proportional Representation Society of Australia	PRSA
Proportional Spacing [Typography] (WDMC)	PS
Proportional Stock Density [Pisciculture]	PSD
Proportional to Absolute Temperature (IAA)	PAT
Proportional to Absolute Temperature (IAA)	PTAT
Proportional-Integral Derivative [Engineering]	PID
Proportional-Integral-Derivative (ACII)	PID
Proportional-Plus Integral [Digital control]	PI
Proportional-Plus Integral-Plus Derivative [Digital control algorithm]	PID
Proportionate Morbidity Ratio [Statistics] (DAVI)	PMR
Proportionate Mortality Rate [or Ratio]	PMR
Proportioning	PRPG
Proportioning and Bypass Valve	PBV
Proportioning Control Valve [Automotive brakes]	PCV
Proposal (AAG)	PROP
Proposal (MSA)	PRPSL
Proposal Analysis Report (AAGC)	PAR
Proposal Authorization	PA
Proposal Control Number (AAG)	PCN
Proposal Development (AAG)	PD
Proposal Development Group [Aerospace] (AAG)	PDG
Proposal Directive Plan of Action (MCD)	PDPOA
Proposal Equipment Packages (MCD)	PEP
Proposal Evaluation Form (AAG)	PEF
Proposal Evaluation Manager	PEM
Proposal Evaluation Panel (MCD)	PEP
Proposal Evaluation Plan [or Program] (MCD)	PEP
Proposal Evaluation Report (MCD)	PER
Proposal Exploitation Product	PEP
Proposal for Advanced Development Program	PADP
Proposal Identification Number (AAG)	PIN
Proposal Information Exchange [Military]	PIE
Proposal Instruction Package (MCD)	PIP
Proposal Management System	PMS
Proposals Outstanding	PO
Proposals Paper	PP
Propose (FAAC)	PPS
Proposed	PPSD
Proposed (AFM)	PROP
Proposed (MSA)	PRPSD
Proposed Advanced Development Objective [Army] (AABC)	PADO
Proposed Boundary Crossing Time [Aviation]	PBCT
Proposed Change	PC
Proposed Change Order (AFIT)	PCO
Proposed Change Point Line [NASA] (KSC)	PCPL
Proposed Development Approach [Navy]	PDA
Proposed Engineering Change Estimate	PECE
Proposed Extended Contract Work Breakdown Structure [Military]	PECWBS
Proposed Fabric Flammability Standard [Consumer Product Safety Commission]	PFF
Proposed Final Environmental Statement [Department of Energy]	PFES
Proposed Finding [Nuclear energy] (NRCH)	PF
Proposed International Nonproprietary Name [Drug research]	PINN
Proposed Letter of Agreement (MCD)	PLOA
Proposed MAPAD Change Letter (AAGC)	PMCL
Proposed Material Erection Schedule (MCD)	PMES
Proposed Material Need (MCD)	PMN
Proposed Material Ordering Guide (MCD)	PMOG
Proposed Military Improvement (CAAL)	PMI
Proposed MILSTRIP Change Letters	PMCL
Proposed Notice of Change	PNOC
Proposed Operating Plan and Budget (AD)	popb
Proposed Operating Program and Budget [Army]	POP & B
Proposed Partial Package Program (MUGU)	PPPP
Proposed Quality Material Development Objective (NATG)	PQMDO
Proposed Regulation	PR
Proposed Request	PR
Proposed Required Operational Capability [Military] (AABC)	PROC
Proposed Rule [Federal government] (GFGA)	PR
Proposed Sale of Securities (GFGA)	PSS
Proposed Specification Change Notice	PSCN
Proposed System Package Plan [Military]	PSPP
Proposed Technical Approach	PTA
Proposed Technical Development Plan	PTDP
Proposed Underwater Fire Control Feasibility Study (SAA)	PUFS
Proposed United States of America Standard	PUSAS
Proposed Units of Work	PUOW
Proposed Uses of Federal Funds [Health Planning and Resource Development Act of 1974]	PUFF
Proposition (ROG)	PPOSN
Proposition	PROP
Proposition Letter Formula	PLF
Proposition One [Defunct] (EA)	PO
Propositional Calculus [Logic]	PC
Propria Pecunia Dedicavit [With His Own Money He Offered It] [Latin] (ROG)	PPD
Propria Pecunia Posuit [Erected at His Own Expense] [Latin]	PPP
Propria Persona [In His or Her Own Person] [Latin]	PP
Propria Persona [In His or Her Own Person] [Latin] (WGA)	pro per
Propriano [France ICAO location identifier] (ICLI)	LFKO
Proprietary (ROG)	PROPR

Proprietary [Freight]	PROPTRY
Proprietary	PROPY
Proprietary (NFD)	Pty
Proprietary (DD)	Pty
Proprietary	PTY
Proprietary Articles Trade Association [British] (BI)	PATA
[The] Proprietary Association [Later, NDMA] (EA)	PA
Proprietary Association of Great Britain	PAGB
Proprietary Chapel [Church of England]	PRCH
Proprietary Computer Systems, Inc. [Information service or system] (IID)	PCS
Proprietary Crematoria Association [British] (DBA)	PCA
Proprietary Data Control Record (NASA)	PDCR
Proprietary Industries Association (AAGC)	PIA
Proprietary Information (SAA)	PI
Proprietary Information	PROPIN
Proprietary Information Protection	PIP
Proprietary Limited (ADA)	P/L
Proprietary Medicines Advisory Committee [Australia]	PMAC
Proprietary Medicines Association of Australia	PMAA
Proprietary Procurement Request (NG)	PPR
Proprietary Software Systems [Computer science] (IEEE)	PSS
Proprietary Support System [Computer science] (IAA)	PSS
Proprietor	PROP
Proprietor (EY)	PROPR
Proprietor of Copyright on a Composite Work	PCW
Proprietor of Copyright on a Work by a Corporate Body	PCB
Proprietor of Copyright on a Work Made for Hire	PWH
Proprietress (ROG)	PROPRSS
Proprioceptive Neuromuscular Facilitation [Neurology]	PNF
Proprioceptive Neuromuscular Facilitation (AD)	pnf
Propulsion (AAG)	P
Propulsion (AAG)	PROP
Propulsion	PROPUL
Propulsion (MSA)	PRPLN
Propulsion Alarm and Monitoring System (PDAA)	PALMS
Propulsion Analysis Trajectory Simulation [Computer program] [NASA]	PATS
Propulsion and Aeroballistics Research (SAA)	PAR
Propulsion and Associated Systems Test (MCD)	PAST
Propulsion and Auxiliary Control Console [NASA] (DNAB)	PACC
Propulsion and Auxiliary Control Electronic Enclosure (DNAB)	PACEE
Propulsion and Auxiliary Systems Department [David W. Taylor Naval Ship Research and Development Center]	PAS
Propulsion and Control Assembly	PACA
Propulsion and Electrical Operating System (IEEE)	PEOS
Propulsion and Power Division [Manned Spacecraft Center] [NASA]	PPD
Propulsion and Power Generation	PPG
Propulsion and Propellant Section [Picatinny Arsenal] [Dover, NJ]	PPS
Propulsion and Reaction Control Subsystem [NASA] (KSC)	P/RCS
Propulsion and Vehicle Engineering [A Marshall Space Flight Center laboratory] (MCD)	P & VE
Propulsion and Vehicle Engineering - Administrative [Marshall Space Flight Center Laboratory] (SAA)	P & VE-ADM
Propulsion and Vehicle Engineering - Advanced Flight Systems [Marshall Space Flight Center Laboratory] (SAA)	P & VE-F
Propulsion and Vehicle Engineering - Director [Marshall Space Flight Center Laboratory] (SAA)	P & VE-DIR
Propulsion and Vehicle Engineering - Engineering Materials [Marshall Space Flight Center Laboratory] (SAA)	P & VE-M
Propulsion and Vehicle Engineering - Nuclear Vehicle Projects [Marshall Space Flight Center Laboratory] (SAA)	P & VE-N
Propulsion and Vehicle Engineering - Program Coordination [Marshall Space FlightCenter Laboratory] (SAA)	P & VE-PC
Propulsion and Vehicle Engineering - Propulsion and Mechanics [Marshall Space Flight Center Laboratory] (SAA)	P & VE-P
Propulsion and Vehicle Engineering - Reliability [Marshall Space Flight Center Laboratory] (SAA)	P & VE-REL
Propulsion and Vehicle Engineering - Structures [Marshall Space Flight Center Laboratory] (SAA)	P & VE-S
Propulsion and Vehicle Engineering - Technical and Scientific Staff [Marshall Space Flight Center Laboratory] (SAA)	P & VE-TS
Propulsion and Vehicle Engineering - Vehicle Engineering [Marshall Space Flight Center Laboratory] (SAA)	P & VE-E
Propulsion and Vehicle Engineering - Vehicle Systems Integration [Marshall Space Flight Center Laboratory] (SAA)	P & VE-V
Propulsion Arming and Firing Unit [Military]	PAFU
Propulsion Assistance (DS)	PA
Propulsion Assistance Module (MCD)	PAM
Propulsion Auxiliaries Local Control Rack (DNAB)	PALCR
Propulsion Auxiliary Control Box (AAG)	PACOB
Propulsion Auxiliary Control Panel [NASA] (KSC)	PACP
Propulsion Contamination Effects Module (NASA)	PCEM
Propulsion [Ground] Control Box (AAG)	PCB
Propulsion Energy Management Study (MCD)	PEMS
Propulsion Engineering Officer (MCD)	PEO
Propulsion Environmental Chamber	PEC
Propulsion Evaluation Plan	PEP
Propulsion Examining Board [Navy] (NVT)	PEB
Propulsion Experimental Test (SAA)	PET
Propulsion Field Laboratory	PFL
Propulsion Flight Control Integration Technology (MCD)	PROFIT
Propulsion Gas Umbilical	PGU
Propulsion Integration Test Stand	PITS
Propulsion Laboratory [Army] (GRD)	PL
Propulsion Local Control Console (DNAB)	PLCC
Propulsion Memorandum	PM

Propulsion Module [*NASA*] (KSC) ... PM
Propulsion Multiplexer ... PMUX
Propulsion Operating Guide (DNAB) ... POG
Propulsion Power (KSC) ... PP
Propulsion Pressurization Subsystem ... PPS
Propulsion Range ... PR
Propulsion Research and Open Water Testing of Experimental Underwater Systems (MCD) ... PROTEUS
Propulsion Research Environmental Chamber ... PREC
Propulsion Research Environmental Facility ... PREF
Propulsion Research Laboratory ... PRL
Propulsion Section ... PS
Propulsion Subsystem Structure ... PSS
Propulsion Support System (KSC) ... PSS
Propulsion System Decision and Vibration Analysis (DNAB) ... PROVIB
Propulsion System Demonstrator [*Marine Corps*] (DOMA) ... PSD
Propulsion System Rocket Engine (MCD) ... PSRE
Propulsion System Test Bed [*for ABC helicopters*] (RDA) ... PSTB
Propulsion Systems Analysis Report (SAA) ... PSAR
Propulsion Systems Development Facility (KSC) ... PSDF
Propulsion Systems Integration Group [*NASA*] (NASA) ... PSIG
Propulsion Systems Laboratory [*USATACOM*] (RDA) ... PSL
Propulsion Technology Validation (MCD) ... PTV
Propulsion Test Article [*NASA*] (NASA) ... PTA
Propulsion Test Complex (KSC) ... PTC
Propulsion Test Instrumentation System (KSC) ... PTIS
Propulsion Test Vehicle ... PTV
Propulsion Test Vehicle Assembly [*NASA*] ... PTVA
Propulsion Test Vehicle Engineering [*NASA*] (MCD) ... PTVE
Propulsion Unit (KSC) ... PU
Propulsion Wind Tunnel Facility [*Arnold Air Force Base, TN*] [*Air Force*] ... PWT
Propulsive Coefficient ... PC
Propulsive Fluid Accumulator ... PROFAC
Propulsive Left Landing with Aerodynamic Maneuvering Entry (PDAA) ... PLAME
Propyl [*Organic chemistry*] ... Pr
Propyl Gallate [*Antioxidant*] [*Organic chemistry*] ... PG
Propyl Isome (OA) ... PI
Propylaeum (VRA) ... prpylm
Propylene Carbonate [*Organic chemistry*] ... PC
Propylene Glycol ... PG
Propylene Glycol Dibenzoate [*Organic chemistry*] ... PGDB
Propylene Glycol Dinitrate [*Organic chemistry*] ... PGDN
Propylene Glycol Monomethyl Ether Acetate [*Organic chemistry*] ... PGMEA
Propylene Oxide [*Organic chemistry*] ... PO
Propylenediamine [*Organic chemistry*] ... PDA
Propylenediaminetetraacetic Acid [*Organic chemistry*] ... PDTA
Propyleneurea [*Organic chemistry*] ... PU
Propylhydroxybenzyl Benzimidazole [*Organic chemistry*] (MAE) ... PHBB
Propyl(thio)uracil [*Biochemistry*] ... PPT
Propylthiouracil [*Also, PT, PTU*] [*Thyroid inhibitor*] ... PROP
Propylthiouracil [*Also, PROP, PTU*] [*Thyroid inhibitor*] ... PT
Propylthiouracil [*Also, PROP, PT*] [*Thyroid inhibitor*] ... PTU
Pro-Rata Distribution (AD) ... prd
Prorated Mental Age [*Psychology*] ... PMA
Proscenium [*Theater term*] (DSUE) ... PROS
Proscenium [*Theater term*] (WDAA) ... PROSC
Prose ... pr
Prosecuting Attorney ... PA
Prosecuting Attorney (DLA) ... Pros Atty
Prosecution (ROG) ... PROS
Prosecution (ROG) ... PROSECON
Prosecutor's Management Information System [*Law Enforcement Assistance Administration*] ... PROMIS
Proserpine [*Australia ICAO location identifier*] (ICLI) ... ABPN
Proserpine [*Australia Airport symbol*] (OAG) ... PPP
Prosody ... PROS
Prosoft I-Net Solutions, Inc. [*NASDAQ symbol*] (SAG) ... POSO
Prosoft I-Net Solutions, Inc. [*Associated Press*] (SAG) ... Prosoft
Prosopographia Attica [*A publication*] (OCD) ... Prosop Att
Prospair Ltd. [*British ICAO designator*] (FAAC) ... PRA
Prospect, AK [*Location identifier FAA*] (FAAL) ... ECD
Prospect Creek, AK [*Location identifier FAA*] (FAAL) ... PPC
Prospect Elementary School, Baldwin, NY [*Library symbol Library of Congress*] (LCLS) ... NBaldPrE
Prospect Group [*NASDAQ symbol*] (TTSB) ... PROS
[*The*] **Prospect Group, Inc.** [*New York, NY NASDAQ symbol*] (NQ) ... PROS
[*The*] **Prospect Group, Inc.** [*Associated Press*] (SAG) ... ProsGp
Prospect Heights Public Library District, Prospect Heights, IL [*Library symbol Library of Congress*] (LCLS) ... IProD
Prospect Heights Public Library District, Prospect Heights, IL [*OCLC symbol*] (OCLC) ... JAO
Prospect Hill [*Vole virus*] ... PH
Prospect Hill Millimeter Wave Observatory [*Waltham, MA*] [*Air Force*] ... PHMWO
Prospect Hill Virus [*Medicine*] (DMAA) ... PHV
Prospect School, Hempstead, NY [*Library symbol*] [*Library of Congress*] (LCLS) ... NHemPE
Prospect Street Hi Income [*NYSE symbol*] (TTSB) ... PHY
Prospect Street High Income Portfolio, Inc. [*NYSE symbol*] (SPSG) ... PHY
Prospect Street High Income Portfolio, Inc. [*Associated Press*] (SAG) ... ProsSt
Prospecting Authority [*Australia*] ... PA
Prospective Commanding Officer [*Navy*] ... PCO
Prospective Data Element [*Army*] (AABC) ... PDE
Prospective Decision Date (NRCH) ... PDD
Prospective Designated Overhaul Point (MCD) ... PDOP
Prospective Engineer Officer ... PEO
Prospective Evaluation of Radial Keratotomy [*for eye surgery*] ... PERK
Prospective Evaluation of Radial Keratotomy [*Protocol*] [*Ophthalmology*] (DAVI) ... PERK
Prospective Executive Officer ... PXO
Prospective Investigation of Pulmonary Embolism Diagnosis [*Medicine*] ... PIOPED
Prospective Loss ... PL
Prospective Parliamentary Candidate [*British*] ... PPC
Prospective Payment Assessment Commission [*Washington, DC*] (EGAO) ... PROPAC
Prospective Payment System [*For hospital care*] ... PPS
Prospective Pricing System [*Information service or system*] (HCT) ... PPS
Prospective Pricing System ... PPS
Prospective Randomized Amlodipine Survival Evaluation [*Medicine*] (DMAA) ... PRAISE
Prospective Randomized Milrinone Survival Evaluation [*Medicine*] ... PROMISE
Prospective Rate Setting Information System [*Medicine*] (DMAA) ... PRSIS
Prospective Reimbursement Plan [*Medicaid*] ... PRP
Prospective Reimbursement System [*Health insurance*] (GHCT) ... PRS
Prospective Supply Officer (DNAB) ... PSO
Prospectively (DLA) ... prosp
Prospectors Air [*Vancouver Stock Exchange symbol*] ... PRS
Prospectors' and Developers' Association [*Canada*] ... PDA
Prospectors and Developers Association of Canada (EAIO) ... PDAC
Prospectors and Mine Owners Association (EA) ... PMOA
Prospectors and Treasure Hunters Guild (EA) ... PATH
Prospectors Club [*Later, PCI*] ... PC
Prospectors Club International [*Defunct*] (EA) ... PCI
[*The*] **Prosperos** (EA) ... TP
Prosser [*Washington*] [*Seismograph station code, US Geological Survey*] (SEIS) ... PRW
Prosser Public Library, Bloomfield, CT [*Library symbol Library of Congress*] (LCLS) ... CtBl
Prosser, WA [*AM radio station call letters*] ... KARY
Prosser, WA [*FM radio station call letters*] ... KZXR
Prostacyclin Stimulating Plasma Factor [*Endocrinology*] ... PSPF
Prostaglandin [*Also, Pg*] [*Biochemistry*] ... PG
Prostaglandin A [*Biochemistry*] ... PGA
Prostaglandin Analog [*Biochemistry*] ... PGA
Prostaglandin B [*Biochemistry*] ... PGB
Prostaglandin C [*A prostoglandin endoperoxide*] [*Biochemistry*] (DAVI) ... PGC
Prostaglandin D [*Biochemistry*] ... PGD
Prostaglandin E [*Biochemistry*] ... PGE
Prostaglandin E, immunoreactive [*Biochemistry*] ... iPGE
Prostaglandin F [*Biochemistry*] ... PGF
Prostaglandin F and its Metabolite [*Dihydro-keto-prostaglandin*] [*Medicine*] (BABM) ... PGFM
Prostaglandin F and Its Metabolite [*Dihydroketoprostaglandin*] [*Endocrinology*] (DAVI) ... PGFM
Prostaglandin G [*A prostaglandin endoperoxide*] [*Biochemistry*] ... PGG
Prostaglandin H [*A prostaglandin endoperoxide*] [*Biochemistry*] ... PGH
Prostaglandin H Synthase [*An enzyme*] (GNE) ... PHS
Prostaglandin Hydrogen Synthase [*An enzyme*] ... PGHS
Prostaglandin I [*Biochemistry*] ... PGI
Prostaglandin Production ... PGP
Prostaglandin Synthase [*An enzyme*] ... PGS
Prostaglandin Synthetase [*An enzyme*] ... PS
Prostaglandin Synthetase Inhibitor (DMAA) ... PGSI
Prostaglandin X [*or Prostacyclin*] [*Biochemistry*] ... PGX
Prostaglandin-Like Substance [*Biochemistry*] (MAE) ... PLS
Prostate [*Anatomy*] (DAVI) ... pros
Prostate (CPH) ... prost
Prostate Cancer Cure Foundation Ltd. ... PCCF
Prostate Patient Outcomes Research Team ... PPORT
Prostate-Specific Acid Phosphatase [*An enzyme*] ... PSAcPh
Prostate-Specific Antigen [*Immunochemistry*] ... PSA
Prostatic (AAMN) ... PROSTAT
Prostatic Acid Phosphatase [*An enzyme*] ... PAP
Prostatic Carcinoma [*Medicine*] (DMAA) ... PC
Prostatic Echogram [*Medicine*] (AAMN) ... Pecho
Prostatic Fluid [*Medicine*] (DMAA) ... PF
Prostatic Hypertrophy [*Medicine*] (MAE) ... PH
Prostatic Massage [*Medicine*] ... PM
Prostatic Needle Biopsy [*Oncology*] (DAVI) ... PNB
Prostatic Secretory Protein (DMAA) ... PRPS
Prostatic Urethra [*Anatomy*] [*Urology*] (DAVI) ... PU
Prostatodynia [*Medicine*] ... PD
Prosthesis ... PROSTH
Prosthetic (AABC) ... PROS
Prosthetic ... PRSTC
Prosthetic and Orthotic [*Health insurance*] (GHCT) ... P&O
Prosthetic Distribution Center [*Veterans Administration*] ... PDC
Prosthetic Valve (Disk) Closing [*Cardiology*] ... PVC
Prosthetic Valve (Disk) Opening [*Cardiology*] ... PVO
Prosthetic Valve Echogram [*Cardiology*] ... PVE
Prosthetic Valve Endocarditis [*Medicine*] ... PVE
Prosthetic-Group Removing [*An enzyme*] (BABM) ... PR
Prosthetic-Group Removing [*Enzyme*] [*Biochemistry*] (DAVI) ... PR
Prosthetics and Orthotics Database [*University of Strathclyde*] [*Glasgow, Scotland*] [*Information service or system*] (IID) ... POD
Prosthetics Center [*Veterans Administration*] ... PC
Prosthetics Research Board ... PRB
Prosthion [*Medicine*] (MAE) ... PR
Prostitute (ADA) ... PRO
Prostitute (DSUE) ... PROS

Prostitute [*or Prostitution*] [*FBI standardized term*] ..... PROST
Prostitutes Anonymous (EA) ..... PA
Prostitutes of Los Angeles [*An association*] (AD) ..... POLA
Prostitutes of New York ..... PONY
Prostitutes' Union of Massachusetts ..... PUMA
Prostitutes United for Social and Sexual Integration [*British*] (DI) ..... PUSSI
Prostrate ..... PROS
Protactinium [*or Protoactinium*] [*Chemical element*] ..... Pa
Protagoras [*of Plato*] [*Classical studies*] (OCD) ..... Prt
Protamine Insulin ..... PI
Protamine Sulfate [*Biochemistry*] (DAVI) ..... PROSO
Protamine Zinc Insulin ..... PZI
Protease [*Chemistry*] ..... PR
Protease Inhibitor ..... Pi
Protease Nexin I [*Biochemistry*] ..... PNI
Protease Nexin II [*Biochemistry*] ..... PNII
Protease-Resistant Prion [*Medicine*] ..... PRP
Protease-Resistant Protein [*Microbiology*] ..... PrP
Protect [*or Protection*] (MSA) ..... PROT
Protect (MSA) ..... PTCT
Protect America's Children [*An association*] (EA) ..... PAC
Protect Each Other [*An association*] (NADA) ..... PEO
Protect Enable [*Computer science*] (PCM) ..... PE
Protect Life in All Nations (EA) ..... PLAN
Protect Our Nation's Youth [*Baseball league*] [*Name usually written Pony*] ..... PONY
Protect Our Pelican Society [*Later, PMBS*] (EA) ..... POPS
Protect Our Responsibilities Now [*Book title*] ..... PORN
Protect Our Wetlands and Duck Resources [*Department of the Interior*] [*Washington, DC*] ..... POWDR
Protect Status (MHDB) ..... PS
Protect the Planet [*Manual*] ..... PTP
Protect Your Environment [*Groups*] ..... PYE
Protectable Mobilization Reserve Materiel Objective [*Army*] (AABC) ..... PMRMO
Protectable Mobilization Reserve Materiel Requirements [*Army*] ..... PMRMR
Protected Air-Cooled Condenser [*Nuclear energy*] (NRCH) ..... PACC
Protected Area [*Nuclear energy*] (NRCH) ..... PA
Protected Bronchoalveolar Lavage [*Medicine*] (DMAA) ..... PBAL
Protected Cruiser [*Navy symbol Obsolete*] C
Protected Difference Fat (OA) ..... PDF
Protected Difference Milk (OA) ..... PDM
Protected Distribution System [*Military*] (GFGA) ..... PDS
Protected Employee Group [*Program*] ..... PEG
Protected Environment ..... PE
Protected Environment plus Prophylactic Antibiotics [*Oncology*] ..... PEPA
Protected Environment Unit [*Medicine*] ..... PEU
Protected Home Circle Life Insurance Society (EA) ..... PHCLIS
Protected Least Significant Difference (DMAA) ..... PLSD
Protected Location [*Shipping*] (DS) ..... PL
Protected Memory Address ..... PMA
Protected Message Exchange ..... PMX
Protected Partition Area [*Telecommunications*] (IAA) ..... PPA
Protected Queue Area [*Computer science*] (BUR) ..... PQA
Protected Specimen Brush [*Medicine*] ..... PSB
Protected Water Storage Tank [*Nuclear energy*] (NRCH) ..... PWST
Protected Wireline Distribution System (CET) ..... PWDS
Protecteur du Citoyen du Quebec, Ste.-Foy [*Library symbol National Library of Canada*] (BIB) ..... QSTFP
Protection ..... PROTEC
Protection ..... PROTECT
Protection Actual [*Probability for avoidance of ship*] ..... PROTA
Protection Against Limited Strikes [*Military defence system*] ..... PALS
Protection and Advocacy [*System*] [*To protect the rights of developmentally disabled persons*] ..... P & A
Protection and Advocacy for Mentally Ill Individuals Act [*1986*] ..... PAMII
Protection and Indemnity [*Insurance*] ..... P & I
Protection and Indemnity of Oil Pollution Indemnity Clause [*Insurance*] (DS) ..... PIOPIC
Protection Auxiliary Cabinet [*Nuclear energy*] (NRCH) ..... PAC
Protection Engineers Group [*United States Telephone Association*] [*Telecommunications*] ..... PEG
Protection Factor ..... PF
Protection in Evaluation Procedures ..... PEP
Protection of Children Against Sexual Exploitation Act of 1977 ..... POCASEA
Protection of Foreign Officials and Official Guests of the United States Act ..... POFOOGUSA
Protection of Offshore Energy Assets [*Navy*] (NVT) ..... POEA
Protection of Pupil Rights Amendment ..... PPRA
Protection of Reefs and Islands from Degradation and Exploitation ..... PRIDE
Protection One [*NASDAQ symbol*] (TTSB) ..... ALRM
Protection One, Inc. [*NASDAQ symbol*] (SAG) ..... ALRM
Protection One, Inc. [*Associated Press*] (SAG) ..... ProtectO
Protection, Rest, Ice, Compression, Evaluation [*Medicine*] ..... PRICE
Protection Survey Kit ..... PSK
Protection Water Quality Management ..... PWQM
Protective (AAG) ..... PROTCT
Protective ..... PRTCTV
Protective Action for Children's Television (NTCM) ..... PACT
Protective Action Guide [*Nuclear energy*] ..... PAG
Protective Antigen ..... PA
Protective Care Unit [*Medicine*] ..... PCU
Protective Climate [*Solar heating*] ..... PC
Protective Clothing Arrangement [*Telecommunications*] (TEL) ..... PCA
Protective Clothing Distributors Association [*British*] (DBA) ..... PCDA
Protective Coatings and Metalizing Process (DNAB) ..... PCAMP
Protective Connecting Arrangement [*Telecommunications*] (TEL) ..... PCA
Protective Cover (MCD) ..... PC
Protective Cover (AAG) ..... PRCR
Protective Device (BUR) ..... PD
Protective Equipment Decontamination Section [*Nuclear energy*] (NRCH) ..... PEDS
Protective Ground [*Electronics*] (IAA) ..... PG
Protective LASER Devices (MCD) ..... PLD
Protective Life Corp. [*NYSE symbol*] (SPSG) ..... PL
Protective Life Corp. [*Associated Press*] (SAG) ..... ProtLf
Protective Mobilization Plan ..... PMP
Protective Multiple Earthing [*Electricity*] ..... PME
Protective Multiple Earthing (AD) ..... pme
Protective Oceanic Device ..... POD
Protective Outfit Toxicological Microclimate Controlled (RDA) ..... POTMC
Protective Packaging, Inc. (AD) ..... PPI
Protective Reaction [*Bombing raid*] [*Vietnam*] ..... PR
Protective Security Attendant [*Australia*] ..... PSA
Protective Security Officer ..... PSO
Protective Security Service ..... PSS
Protective Serum Dilution ..... PSD
Protective Service ..... PS
Protective Shelter ..... PS
Protective Shielding Program ..... PSP
Protective Signature Service (MCD) ..... PSS
Protective Structures Development Center [*Military*] ..... PSDC
Protective Structures Division [*Office of Civil Defense*] ..... PSD
Protective Subsystem [*Military*] (INF) ..... PS
Protective Vehicle Division [*US Secret Service*] ..... PVD
Protective Zone ..... PZ
Protectively Located [*Plant layout*] ..... PL
Protectorate Regiment [*British military*] (DMA) ..... PR
Protein ..... P
Protein (MAE) ..... PR
Protein ..... Pro
Protein ..... PROT
Protein A Hemolytic Plaque Assay [*Medicine*] (DMAA) ..... PrA-HPA
Protein A Immobilized in Collodion Charcoal (DAVI) ..... PACC
Protein Advisory Group [*United Nations*] ..... PAG
Protein A-Gold Technique [*Medicine*] (DMAA) ..... pAg
Protein C [*Medicine*] (DMAA) ..... PC
Protein C (DMAA) ..... PROC
Protein C Cofactor (DMAA) ..... PCCF
Protein C Inhibitor [*Organic chemistry*] ..... PCI
Protein Catabolic Rate [*Biochemistry*] (DAVI) ..... PCR
Protein Convertase [*Medicine*] (DMAA) ..... PC
Protein Crystal Growth Facility (SSD) ..... PCGF
Protein Crystal Growth System ..... PCGS
Protein Crystal Growth Unit (SSD) ..... PCGU
Protein Data Bank [*Brookhaven National Laboratory*] [*Information service or system*] (CRD) ..... PDB
Protein Database ..... PRODASE
Protein Design Labs [*NASDAQ symbol*] (TTSB) ..... PDLI
Protein Design Labs [*Associated Press*] (SAG) ..... ProtDg
Protein Design Labs, Inc. [*NASDAQ symbol*] (SAG) ..... PDLI
Protein Diet (DMAA) ..... PD
Protein Dispersibility Index [*Analytical chemistry*] ..... PDI
Protein Disulfide-Isomerase [*An enzyme*] ..... PDI
Protein Efficiency Ratio [*Nutrition*] ..... PER
Protein Electrophoresis [*Biochemistry*] (DAVI) ..... PE
Protein Electrophoresis [*Medicine*] (DMAA) ..... PEP
Protein Electrophoresis [*Biochemistry*] (DAVI) ..... PRO EL
Protein Energy Malnutrition [*Medicine*] ..... PEM
Protein Engineering Research Institute [*Japanese governmental and industrial consortium*] [*Later, BERI*] ..... PERI
Protein Exchange [*Dietetics*] ..... Pro Ex
Protein Fat-Free [*Food technology*] ..... PFF
Protein Grain Products International (EA) ..... PGPI
Protein Granule ..... PG
Protein Identification Resource [*National Biomedical Research Foundation*] [*Georgetown University Medical Center*] [*Information service or system*] (IID) ..... PIR
Protein in Vitamin K Absence (AAMN) ..... PIVKA
Protein Induced by Vitamin K Absence and Antagonists (PDAA) ..... PNKA
Protein Information Resource Databases (DOG) ..... PIR databases
Protein Isoaspartyl Methyltransferase [*An enzyme*] ..... PIMT
Protein Kinase [*Also, PKase*] [*An enzyme*] ..... PK
Protein Kinase [*Also, PK*] [*An enzyme*] ..... PKase
Protein Kinase A [*An enzyme*] ..... PKA
Protein Kinase Activation Ratio [*Medicine*] (DMAA) ..... PKAR
Protein Kinase B [*An enzyme*] ..... PKB
Protein Kinase C [*An enzyme*] ..... PKC
Protein Kinase C (DMAA) ..... PRKC
Protein Kinase C Alpha (DMAA) ..... PRKCA
Protein Kinase Inhibitor [*Biochemistry*] ..... PKI
Protein Kinase K [*An enzyme*] ..... PKK
Protein Magnetic Resonance [*Medicine*] (MAE) ..... PMR
Protein Nitrogen Units [*Clinical chemistry*] ..... PNU
Protein, Oil, and Starch [*Pilot manufacturing plant established by the Canadian government*] ..... POS
Protein Phosphatase [*An enzyme*] ..... PP
Protein Phosphatase [*An enzyme*] ..... PrP
Protein Phosphatase 1 [*An enzyme*] PP1
Protein Phosphatase Alpha (DMAA) ..... PPPA
Protein Polymer Technol Wrrt [*NASDAQ symbol*] (TTSB) ..... PPTIW

Protein Polymer Technologies [*NASDAQ symbol*] (TTSB) .... PPTI
Protein Polymer Technologies, Inc. [*NASDAQ symbol*] (SAG) .... PPTI
Protein Polymer Technologies, Inc. [*Associated Press*] (SAG) .... ProtP
Protein Polymer Technologies, Inc. [*Associated Press*] (SAG) .... ProtPoly
Protein Preprolactin [*Biochemistry*] .... PPL
Protein, Quantity Not Sufficient [*Laboratory science*] (DAVI) .... PQNS
Protein Relaxation Enhancement (OA) .... PRE
Protein Rich Fraction [*Food analysis*] .... PRF
Protein S Beta (DMAA) .... PSB
Protein Separation Efficiency [*Food technology*] .... PSE
Protein Sequence Query .... PSQ
Protein Serine Kinase (DMAA) .... PSK
Protein Sparing Modified Fast .... PSMF
Protein Synthesis .... PS
Protein Truncation Test [*Analytical biochemistry*] .... PTT
Protein Tyrosine Phosphatase [*An enzyme*] .... PTP
Protein Tyrosine Phosphatase [*An enzyme*] .... PTPase
Protein, Vitamins, Minerals [*J. B. Williams Co. brand of liquid protein*] .... PVM
Proteinaceous Infectious Particle .... PRION
Proteinase (DMAA) .... PRTN
Proteinase Inhibitor [*Biochemistry*] .... PI
Proteinase Inhibitor Inducing Factor [*Biochemistry*] .... PIIF
Protein-Binding (MAE) .... PB
Protein-Bound [*Clinical chemistry*] (DAVI) .... PB
Protein-Bound Iodine [*Clinical chemistry*] .... PBI
Protein-Bound Iron (MAE) .... PB-Fe
Protein-Bound Thyroxine [*Endocrinology*] (DAVI) .... PBT_4
Protein-Calorie Malnutrition [*Medicine*] .... PCM
Protein-Calorie Undernutrition [*Medicine*] .... PCU
Protein-Carboxyl Methylase [*Medicine*] (BABM) .... PCM
Protein-Carboxyl Methylase [*Biochemistry*] (DAVI) .... PCM
Protein-Free .... PF
Protein-Free Hybridoma Medium .... PFHM
Protein-Losing Enteropathy [*Gastroenterology*] (DAVI) .... PLE
Protein-Polysaccharide [*Biochemistry*] (DAVI) .... PPL
Proteins, Vitamins, and Minerals [*Pharmacology*] (DAVI) .... PROVIMI
Proteins, Vitamins, and Minerals (BABM) .... PROVIMI
Protein-Tyrosine Kinase [*An enzyme*] .... PTK
Protein-Tyrosine Phosphatase C (DMAA) .... PTPC
Protein-Tyrosine Phosphatase Gamma (DMAA) .... PTPG
Protein-Tyrosine Phosphatase, Non-Receptor (DMAA) .... PTPN
Proteinuria [*Clinical chemistry*] .... P
Protein-Xanthophyll [*Alfalfa protein concentrate process*] .... PRO-XAN
Proteoglycan [*Biochemistry*] .... PG
Proteoglycans/Glyosaminoglyans .... PG/GAG
Proteoliaisin [*Biochemistry*] .... PLN
Proteolipid [*Biochemistry*] .... PLP
Proteolipid Protein [*Biochemistry*] .... PLP
Proteon, Inc. [*Associated Press*] (SAG) .... Proteon
Proteon, Inc. [*NASDAQ symbol*] (SPSG) .... PTON
Proteose-Yeast Castione Medium [*Microbiology*] (MAE) .... PYC
Protest .... PRO
Protest (ROG) .... PROT
Protestant .... P
Protestant (ADA) .... PR
Protestant .... PROT
Protestant .... PRTSTNT
Protestant Alliance [*British*] (DBA) .... PA
Protestant Big Sisters .... PBS
Protestant Church-Owned Publishers Association (EA) .... PCPA
Protestant Cinema Critics Guild [*Later, PCG*] (EA) .... PCCG
Protestant Cinema Guild [*Formerly, PCCG*] [*Defunct*] .... PCG
Protestant Episcopal .... PE
Protestant Episcopal Church (WDAA) .... PEC
Protestant Episcopal Church, Diocesan Library, Portland, OR [*Library symbol Library of Congress*] (LCLS) .... OrPD
Protestant Episcopal Theological Seminary in Virginia, Alexandria, VA [*Library symbol Library of Congress*] (LCLS) .... ViAlTh
Protestant Guild for the Blind (EA) .... PGB
Protestant Health and Human Services Assembly (EA) .... PHHSA
Protestant Health and Welfare Assembly [*Later, PHHSA*] (EA) .... PHWA
Protestant Lawyers Association of New York (EA) .... PLANY
Protestant Press Agency [*British*] .... PPA
Protestant Reformation Society (EA) .... PRS
Protestant School Board of Greater Montreal, Montreal, PQ, Canada [*Library symbol Library of Congress*] (LCLS) .... CaQMPSM
Protestant School Board of Greater Montreal, Quebec [*Library symbol National Library of Canada*] (NLC) .... QMPSB
Protestant Teachers Association (NADA) .... PTA
Protestant Teachers Association of New York City (EA) .... PTANYC
Protestant Truth Society [*British*] (DBA) .... PTS
Protestant Women of the Chapel .... PWOC
Protestants and Other Americans for Separation of Church and State (NADA) .... POAU
Protestants and Other Americans United [*for Separation of Church and State*] .... POAU
Protesting Unfair Marketing Practices [*Student legal action organization*] .... PUMP
Protet [*Protest*] [*French*] .... P
Proteus [*Genus of bacteria*] (MAE) .... P
Proteus [*Bacterium*] .... PROT
Proteus Air Systeme [*France ICAO designator*] (FAAC) .... PRB
Proteus Engine [*Hovercraft*] .... PE
Proteus Resources, Inc. [*Vancouver Stock Exchange symbol*] .... PRI
Proteus Vulgaris [*Bacterium*] .... PV
Prothonotary Apostolic .... PA
Prothoracic Gland [*Insect anatomy*] .... PG
Prothoracic Gland [*Insect anatomy*] .... PTG
Prothoracicotropic Hormone .... PTTH
Prothrombin [*Factor II*] [*Hematology*] .... Pro
Prothrombin [*Hematology*] .... PROTHROM
Prothrombin Activity [*Hematology*] .... PTA
Prothrombin and Proconvertin Control [*Hematology*] (DAVI) .... P & P/CT
Prothrombin Complex [*Hematology*] .... PTC
Prothrombin Complex Concentrates [*Hematology*] .... PCC
Prothrombin Consumption Index (PDAA) .... PCI
Prothrombin Consumption Time [*Hematology*] (DAVI) .... PCT
Prothrombin Conversion Factor [*Hematology*] .... PCF
Prothrombin, Proconvertin, Stuart Factor, Antihemophilic B Factor [*Blood coagulation factors*] [*Hematology*] .... PPSB
Prothrombin Time [*Hematology*] (CPH) .... PRO-X
Prothrombin Time [*Hematology*] (DAVI) .... PRTH
Prothrombin Time [*Hematology*] .... PT
Prothrombin Time [*Hematology*] (AAMN) .... PTT
Prothrombin Time Control [*Hematology*] (DAVI) .... PRTH-C
Prothrombin Time Control [*Hematology*] (DAVI) .... PT-CT
Prothrombin Time Fixing Agent (DMAA) .... PTFA
Prothrombin-Proconvertin [*Hematology*] .... PP
Prothymosin Alpha (DMAA) .... PTMA
Protinus [*Speedily*] [*Pharmacy*] .... PROT
Protium [*or Light hydrogen*] [*Chemical element*] (DAVI) .... H^1
Protivo-Voxdushnaia Oborona [*Antiaircraft Defense*] [*Former USSR*] .... PVO
Proto [*Linguistics*] .... P
Proto Yiddish (BJA) .... PY
Proto-Canaanite (BJA) .... PC
Protocatechuatedioxygenase [*An enzyme*] .... PCD
Protocol (DLA) .... Prot
Protocol [*A chemotherapy regimen including dactinomycin, doxorubicin, vincristine, cyclophosphamide, and radiation therapy*] (DAVI) T-2
Protocol Addressing Information [*Telecommunications*] (OSI) .... PAI
Protocol Computers Inc. (NITA) .... PCI
Protocol Control Information [*Telecommunications*] .... PCI
Protocol Converter (MCD) .... PC
Protocol Converter [*Electronics*] (ECII) .... PCV
Protocol Converter (DA) .... PROCON
Protocol Converter Concentrator [*Telecommunications*] (IAA) .... PCC
Protocol Converter for Native Equipment [*Telecommunications*] (IAA) .... PCNE
Protocol Data Query [*Database*] [*National Institutes of Health*] .... PDQ
Protocol Data Unit [*Telecommunications*] .... PDU
Protocol Data Unit [*Electronic communications*] .... PDU
Protocol Description Language [*Telecommunications*] (IAA) .... PDL
Protocol for Automotive Local Area Network .... PALMNET
Protocol for Specific Purpose .... PSP
Protocol Implementation Conformance Statement [*Computer science*] (TNIG) .... PICS
Protocol Implementation Review Committee [*National Institutes of Health*] .... PIRC
Protocol Internationale .... PI
Protocol Machine [*Computer science*] (TNIG) .... PM
Protocol on Privileges and Immunities of the European Economic Community [*A publication*] (DLA) .... Prot PI
Protocol on the Statute of the European Communities Court of Justice [*A publication*] (DLA) .... Prot CJ
Protocol Systems [*NASDAQ symbol*] (TTSB) .... PCOL
Protocol Systems, Inc. [*NASDAQ symbol*] (SAG) .... PCOL
Protocol Systems, Inc. [*Associated Press*] (SAG) .... ProtSy
Protocol-Independent Routing [*Computer science*] .... PIR
Protocollagen Proline Hydroxylase [*An enzyme*] (MAE) .... PPH
Proto-Indo-European [*Language*] (BARN) .... PIE
Proton [*A nuclear particle*] .... p
Proton Affinity [*Surface ionization*] .... PA
Proton Attenuation Procedure .... PAP
Proton Balance Equation .... PBE
Proton Beam Transport System .... PBTS
Proton Binding Energy .... PBE
Proton Elastic-Scattering Analysis .... PESA
Proton Electron Positron Colliding Beams (IAA) .... PEP
Proton Event .... PE
Proton Event Start Forecast [*Solar weather information*] .... PESTF
Proton Exchange Membrane [*Fuel technology*] (PS) .... PEM
Proton Exchange Membrane Fuel Cell [*Energy source*] .... PEMFC
Proton Flare Project (PDAA) .... PFP
Proton Induced Cascade [*Physics*] .... PIC
Proton Linear Accelerator .... PLA
Proton Magnetic Resonance .... PMR
Proton Motive Force [*Physics*] .... PMF
Proton Omnidirectional Detector (USDC) .... POD
Proton Omnidirectional Detector [*Marine science*] (OSRA) .... POD
Proton Polar Zone .... PPZ
Proton Reference Level [*Chemistry*] .... PRL
Proton Relaxation Enhancement [*Physics*] .... PRE
Proton Relaxation Rate .... PRR
Proton Resonance (IAA) .... PRES
Proton Storage Ring [*Nuclear physics*] .... PSR
Proton Synchrotron [*Nuclear energy*] .... PS
Proton Target Area .... PTA
Proton Vector Magnetometer (NOAA) .... PVM
Proton-Electron-Proton [*Nuclear physics*] .... PEP
Proton-Enhanced Diffusion .... PED
Proton-Induced X-Ray Analysis .... PIX
Protonotary Apostolic [*Roman Catholic*] .... PROTAP

Protonous Poly(ethylene oxide) [*Organic chemistry*] ... HPEO
Proton-Proton [*Nuclear physics*] ... PP
Protons on Protons and Electrons [*Physics*] ... POPAE
Protopan Chloride [*Medicine*] (BARN) ... PAM
Protoplasmic [*Freeze etching in microscopy*] ... P
Protoplasmic Fracture [*Freeze etching in microscopy*] ... PF
Protoplasmic Surface [*Freeze etching in microscopy*] ... PS
Protoporphyria [*Medicine*] ... PP
Protoporphyrin [*Biochemistry*] ... PP
Protoporphyrin [*Hematology*] ... PROTO
Proto-Semitic (BJA) ... PS
Protosolar Cloud [*Astronomy*] ... PSC
ProtoSource Corp. [*Associated Press*] (SAG) ... Proto
ProtoSource Corp. [*Associated Press*] (SAG) ... ProtoS
ProtoSource Corp. [*NASDAQ symbol*] (SAG) ... PSCO
ProtoSource Corp. Unit [*NASDAQ symbol*] (TTSB) ... PSCOU
ProtoSource Corp. Wrrt [*NASDAQ symbol*] (TTSB) ... PSCOW
Protosynthetic Indexing (NITA) ... PSI
Protosynthex Index ... PSI
Prototroch ... P
Prototype (AAG) ... P
Prototype ... PR
Prototype ... PROT
Prototype (KSC) ... PROTO
Prototype (IAA) ... PRTP
Prototype (IAA) ... PT
Prototype [*Designation for all US military aircraft*] ... Y
Prototype Advanced Indicator System (MCD) ... PAIS
Prototype Application Loop [*Nuclear energy*] (NRCH) ... PAL
Prototype Carrier Operational Test and Evaluation Site [*Military*] (CAAL) ... PCOTES
Prototype Closed-Loop Development Installation [*Nuclear energy*] (NRCH) ... PCLDI
Prototype Closed-Loop System [*Nuclear energy*] (NRCH) ... PCLS
Prototype Closed-Loop Test [*Nuclear energy*] (NRCH) ... PCLT
Prototype Communications Processor ... PCP
Prototype Demonstration ... PD
Prototype Development Associate ... PDA
Prototype Die Casting Service ... PDCS
Prototype Environmental Buoy [*Marine science*] (MSC) ... PEB
Prototype Evaluation Test ... PET
Prototype Fast Reactor ... PFR
Prototype Hydrofoil Gunboat ... PHG
Prototype Language for Economic Analysis [*Computer science*] (IID) ... PLEA
Prototype Large Breeder Reactor [*Also, NCBR*] [*Nuclear energy*] ... PLBR
Prototype Lunar Geologist Tool ... PLGT
Prototype Miniature Air-Launched System ... PMALS
Prototype Missile (NATG) ... YM
Prototype Nuclear Process ... PNP
Prototype Ocean Surveillance Terminal [*Navy*] (ANA) ... POST
Prototype On-Line Instrument System [*Computer science*] (NRCH) ... POIS
Prototype Optical Surveillance System ... POSS
Prototype Organic Power Reactor [*Nuclear energy*] ... POPR
Prototype Preliminary Flight Rating Test ... PPFRT
Prototype Production Evaluation (NG) ... PPE
Prototype Protein C Activator [*Biochemistry*] ... PCA
Prototype Qualification Test - Contractor (MCD) ... PQT-C
Prototype Qualification Test - Government (MCD) ... PQT-G
Prototype Qualification Test - Service Evaluation (MCD) ... PQT-SE
Prototype Qualification Testing (RDA) ... PQT
Prototype Real-Time Optical Tracker [*Computer science*] ... PRTOT
Prototype Regional Observation and Forecasting Service [*National Oceanic and Atmospheric Administration*] (GRD) ... PROFS
Prototype System Characteristics ... PSC
Prototype Systems Review ... PSR
Prototype Test Vehicle (MCD) ... PTV
Prototype Tracked Air-Cushion Vehicle ... PTACV
Prototype Validation Test (MCD) ... PVT
Prototype Validation Test - Contractor (MCD) ... PVT-C
Prototype Validation Test - Government ... PVT-G
Prototype Wave Height ... PWH
Prototype WWMCCS Intercomputer Network (MCD) ... PWIN
Prototypic Inlet Piping [*Nuclear energy*] (NRCH) ... PIP
Protractor (AAG) ... PROT
Protractor (MSA) ... PROTR
Protrepticus [*of Clemens Alexandrinus*] [*Classical studies*] (OCD) ... Protr
Protruded Intervertebral Disc [*Medicine*] ... PID
Protruded Intervertebral Disc [*Medicine*] ... PIVD
Protrusio Acetabuli [*Medicine*] (DMAA) ... PA
Proud to be Australian [*Political party*] ... PTBA
Proudhon's Domaine Public [*A publication*] (DLA) ... Proud Dom Pub
Proudman Oceanographic Laboratory [*UK*] [*Marine science*] (OSRA) ... POL
Prourokinase [*Thrombolytic*] [*An enzyme*] ... PUK
Proust Research Association (EA) ... PRA
Proutist Universal (EA) ... PU
Prouty's Reports [*61-68 Vermont*] [*A publication*] (DLA) ... Prouty
Prova di Restituzione Termica [*Italy*] [*Medicine*] ... PRT
Prova Elementi Combustibili [*An Italian fast reactor*] ... PEC
Provabilistic Information Processing [*Computer science*] (IAA) ... PIP
Provascular Tissue [*Botany*] ... PT
Prove in Plan (MCD) ... PIP
Proved ... PR
Proved ... PRO
Proved Name Registraton [*Advertising*] (DOAD) ... PNR
Proven Commercial Registration [*Advertising*] (WDMC) ... PCR
Proven Resources Ltd. [*Vancouver Stock Exchange symbol*] ... PVN
Provena Foods [*AMEX symbol*] (TTSB) ... PZA
Provena Foods, Inc. [*Associated Press*] (SAG) ... Prvena
Provena Foods, Inc. [*AMEX symbol*] (SPSG) ... PZA
Provenance (VRA) ... prov
Provencal [*Language, etc.*] ... PR
Provencal [*MARC language code Library of Congress*] (LCCP) ... pro
Provencal [*Language, etc.*] ... PROV
Provence [*France*] (ROG) ... PROV
Provence Aero Service [*France ICAO designator*] (FAAC) ... RPA
Proverb ... PROV
Proverbs [*Old Testament book*] (BJA) ... Pr
Proverbs [*Old Testament book*] (BJA) ... Pro
Proverbs [*Old Testament book*] ... Prov
Proverbs [*Old Testament book*] ... Prv
Provide (KSC) ... PROV
Provide Addict Care Today [*Later, NADAP*] ... PACT
Provide Repair Service [*Navy*] (NVT) ... PRS
Provided ... PROVD
Provided Chief of Mission Concurs [*Army*] ... PCMC
Provided No Military Objection Exists [*Army*] ... PNMO
Provided [*Following Named*] **Officers Have Not Departed Your Command** [*Amend Assignment Instructions as Indicated*] [*Army*] (AABC) ... PODUC
Provided Otherwise Qualified [*Military*] (AABC) ... POQ
Provided You Concur [*Army*] ... PUC
Providence [*Diocesan abbreviation*] [*Rhode Island*] (TOCD) ... PRO
Providence ... PRVDNC
Providence [*Rhode Island*] [*Airport symbol*] (OAG) ... PVD
Providence Air Charter [*ICAO designator*] (FAAC) ... PTL
Providence & Worcester Co. [*AAR code*] ... PW
Providence & Worcester Railroad Co. [*Associated Press*] (SAG) ... PrvWor
Providence and Worcester Railroad Co. [*NASDAQ symbol*] (NQ) ... PWRR
Providence & Worcester RR [*NASDAQ symbol*] (TTSB) ... PWRR
Providence Association of Ukrainian Catholics in America (EA) ... PAUCA
Providence Athenaeum, Providence, RI [*Library symbol Library of Congress*] (LCLS) ... RPA
Providence Bay Branch, Carnarvon Township Public Library, Ontario [*Library symbol National Library of Canada*] (NLC) ... OPBCT
Providence College (GAGS) ... Providence C
Providence College, Phillips Memorial Library, Providence, RI [*OCLC symbol*] (OCLC) ... PRC
Providence College, Providence, RI [*Library symbol Library of Congress*] (LCLS) ... RPPC
Providence Energy [*AMEX symbol*] (TTSB) ... PVY
Providence Energy Corp. [*Associated Press*] (SAG) ... PrvEng
Providence Energy Corp. [*AMEX symbol*] (SPSG) ... PVY
Providence Engineering Society, Providence, RI [*Library symbol Library of Congress*] (LCLS) ... RPEng
Providence Hospital, Everett, WA [*Library symbol Library of Congress*] (LCLS) ... WaEPH
Providence Hospital Library, Southfield, MI [*Library symbol*] [*Library of Congress*] (LCLS) ... MiSfP
Providence Hospital, Medford, OR [*Library symbol*] [*Library of Congress*] (LCLS) ... OrMePH
Providence Hospital, Medical Library and Learning Resource Center, Seattle, WA [*Library symbol Library of Congress*] (LCLS) ... WaSPM
Providence Hospital, Medical Library and Learning Resource Center, Seattle, WA [*Library symbol*] [*Library of Congress*] (LCLS) ... WaSPrM
Providence Hospital, Medical Library, Cincinnati, OH [*Library symbol Library of Congress*] (LCLS) ... OCPH
Providence Hospital, School of Nursing, Detroit, MI [*Library symbol Library of Congress*] (LCLS) ... MiDP
Providence, KY [*FM radio station call letters*] ... WHRZ
Providence Medical Center, Portland, OR [*Library symbol Library of Congress*] (LCLS) ... OrPPM
Providence Public Library (AD) ... PPL
Providence Public Library, Providence, RI [*Library symbol Library of Congress*] (LCLS) ... RP
Providence, RI [*Location identifier FAA*] (FAAL) ... ARJ
Providence, RI [*Location identifier FAA*] (FAAL) ... UNQ
Providence, RI [*AM radio station call letters*] ... WALE
Providence, RI [*FM radio station call letters*] ... WBRU
Providence, RI [*FM radio station call letters*] ... WDOM
Providence, RI [*FM radio station call letters*] ... WELH
Providence, RI [*AM radio station call letters*] ... WHJJ
Providence, RI [*FM radio station call letters*] ... WHJY
Providence, RI [*Television station call letters*] ... WJAR
Providence, RI [*AM radio station call letters*] ... WLKW
Providence, RI [*Television station call letters*] ... WNAC
Providence, RI [*AM radio station call letters*] (RBYB) ... WPMZ
Providence, RI [*Television station call letters*] ... WPRI
Providence, RI [*AM radio station call letters*] ... WPRO
Providence, RI [*FM radio station call letters*] ... WPRO-FM
Providence, RI [*AM radio station call letters*] ... WRCP
Providence, RI [*AM radio station call letters*] ... WRIB
Providence, RI [*Television station call letters*] ... WSBE
Providence, RI [*FM radio station call letters*] ... WWBB
Providence, RI [*FM radio station call letters*] ... WWLI
Providence - Saint Margaret Health Center, Kansas City, KS [*Library symbol Library of Congress*] (LCLS) ... KKcP
Providence/Theodore Francis Greene State [*Rhode Island*] [*ICAO location identifier*] (ICLI) ... KPVD
Providence Worcester Railroad Co. [*Associated Press*] (SAG) ... PrvWor
Providence Worcester Railroad Co. [*NASDAQ symbol*] (SAG) ... PWRR
Providencia [*Colombia*] [*Airport symbol*] (OAG) ... PVA

Providencia/Providencia [*Colorado ICAO location identifier*] (ICLI) ... SKPV
Providenciales [*Turks and Caicos Islands*] [*ICAO location identifier*] (ICLI) ... MBPV
Providenciales [*British West Indies*] [*Airport symbol*] (OAG) ... PLS
Provident American Corp. [*Norristown, PA*] [*NASDAQ symbol*] (NQ) ... PAMC
Provident American Corp. [*Associated Press*] (SAG) ... PrvAm
Provident Bancorp [*NASDAQ symbol*] (TTSB) ... PRBK
Provident Bancorp, Inc. [*NASDAQ symbol*] (SAG) ... PRBK
Provident Bancorp, Inc. [*Associated Press*] (SAG) ... ProvBcp
Provident Bankshares [*NASDAQ symbol*] (TTSB) ... PBKS
Provident Bankshares Corp. [*NASDAQ symbol*] (NQ) ... PBKS
Provident Bankshares Corp. [*Associated Press*] (SAG) ... PrvBksh
Provident Companies [*NYSE symbol*] (TTSB) ... PVT
Provident Companies Dep Pfd [*NYSE symbol*] (TTSB) ... PVTPr
Provident Companies, Inc. [*Associated Press*] (SAG) ... ProvCo
Provident Companies, Inc. [*NYSE symbol*] (SAG) ... PVT
Provident Financial Holdings, Inc. [*NASDAQ symbol*] (SAG) ... PROV
Provident Financial Holdings, Inc. [*Associated Press*] (SAG) ... ProvFinl
Provident Life Accident Insurance Co. of America [*NYSE symbol*] (SPSG) ... PVA
Provident Life & Accident Insurance Co. of America [*Associated Press*] (SAG) ... PrvLf
Provident Life & Accident Insurance Co. of America [*NYSE symbol*] (SPSG) ... PVB
Provident Medical Center, Chicago, IL [*Library symbol*] [*Library of Congress*] (LCLS) ... ICPrM
Provident Mutual Life Insurance Co., Philadelphia, PA [*Library symbol Library of Congress Obsolete*] (LCLS) ... PPProM
Provider Based Physician ... PBP
Provider Reimbursement Review Board [*Medicare*] ... PRRB
Providian Corp. [*Formerly, Capital Holding*] [*Associated Press*] (SAG) ... Providn
Providian Corp. [*Formerly, Capital Holding*] [*NYSE symbol*] (SAG) ... PVN
Providian LLC [*NYSE symbol*] (SAG) ... PVN
Providian LLC, Inc. [*Associated Press*] (SAG) ... PrvLLC
Providian LLC'MIPS' [*NYSE symbol*] (TTSB) ... PVNPrM
Providing Avenues for Continuing Encouragement [*Scholarship awarded by Fraternity of Recording Executives*] ... PACE
Providing Lifetime Activity for Youth ... PLAY
Providing Organization (DOMA) ... PROVORG
Providing Professional Development, Assessment, and Coordination of Competency-Based Education Project [*Illinois*] (EDAC) ... PACCE
Provigo, Inc. [*Toronto Stock Exchange symbol*] ... PGI
Province (ROG) ... PRO
Province ... PROV
Province ... PROVNC
Province de Quebec, Ministere des Affaires Sociales, Montreal, PQ, Canada [*Library symbol Library of Congress*] (LCLS) ... CaQMSa
Province du Canada-Francais, Archives de la Compagnie de Jesus, Quebec, PQ, Canada [*Library symbol Library of Congress*] (LCLS) ... CaQQACJ
Province Guard [*Cambodia*] (CINC) ... PG
Province Intelligence and Operations Coordination Center [*Vietnam*] (VNW) ... PIOCC
Province Laws (DLA) ... PRO L
Province of Alberta Law Library System, Edmonton, AB, Canada [*Library symbol Library of Congress*] (LCLS) ... CaAELL
Province of Alberta Law Library System, Edmonton, Alberta [*Library symbol National Library of Canada*] (NLC) ... AELL
Province of New Brunswick, Premier's Office, Fredericton, NB, Canada [*Library symbol Library of Congress*] (LCLS) ... CaNBFPO
Province of Ontario [*Canada*] ... PO
Province of Quebec Association of Architects [*1890, OAQ from 1974*] [*Canada*] (NGC) ... PQAA
Province Pacification Plan (CINC) ... PPP
Province Quebec [*Quebec*] [*Canadian province Postal code*] ... PQ
Province Senior Advisor [*Army*] (VNW) ... PSA
Provinces X Explorations [*Vancouver Stock Exchange symbol*] ... PXE
Provincetown [*Massachusetts*] [*Airport symbol*] (OAG) ... PVC
Provincetown, MA [*Location identifier FAA*] (FAAL) ... PVC
Provincetown, MA [*Location identifier FAA*] (FAAL) ... RZP
Provincetown, MA [*Location identifier FAA*] (FAAL) ... VQO
Provincetown, MA [*FM radio station call letters*] ... WOMR
Provincetown-Boston Airline [*ICAO designator*] (AD) ... PT
Provincetown-Boston Airlines, Inc. ... PBA
Provincial ... PROV
Provincial ... PRV
Provincial Archives and Records Service [*Canada*] ... PARS
Provincial Archives of Alberta, Edmonton, AB, Canada [*Library symbol Library of Congress*] (LCLS) ... CaAEPAA
Provincial Archives of Alberta, Edmonton, Alberta [*Library symbol National Library of Canada*] (NLC) ... AEPAA
Provincial Archives of Alberta, Historical Resource Library [*UTLAS symbol*] ... AHR
Provincial Archives of British Columbia, Victoria, British Columbia [*Library symbol National Library of Canada*] (NLC) ... BVIPA
Provincial Archives of Manitoba, Winnipeg, Manitoba [*Library symbol National Library of Canada*] (NLC) ... MWPA
Provincial Archives of Manitoba, Winnipeg, MB, Canada [*Library symbol Library of Congress*] (LCLS) ... CaMWPA
Provincial Archives of New-Brunswick [*Archives Provinciales du Nouveau-Brunswick*] **Fredericton, New Brunswick** [*Library symbol National Library of Canada*] (NLC) ... NBFA
Provincial Archives of Newfoundland and Labrador, St. John's, Newfoundland [*Library symbol National Library of Canada*] (NLC) ... NFSA
Provincial Archives, Victoria, BC, Canada [*Library symbol Library of Congress*] (LCLS) ... CaBViPA
Provincial Booksellers' Fairs Association [*British*] (DI) ... PBFA
Provincial Carters' and Motormen's Association [*A union*] [*British*] ... PCMA
Provincial Cities and Rural Highways Program [*Australia*] ... PCRH
Provincial Commissioner [*British government*] ... PC
Provincial Congress Committee ... PCC
Provincial Development Assistance Program [*Agency for International Development*] ... PDAP
Provincial Express, Inc. [*Canada ICAO designator*] (FAAC) ... PRV
Provincial Grand Director of Ceremonies [*Freemasonry*] ... PGDC
Provincial Grand Lodge [*Freemasonry*] ... PGL
Provincial Grand Master [*Freemasonry*] ... ProvGM
Provincial Grand Secretary [*Freemasonry*] ... PGS
Provincial Grand Sword-Bearer [*Freemasonry*] ... PGSB
Provincial Health Assistance Program [*Vietnam*] ... PHAP
Provincial Hospital Services Association [*British*] (DBA) ... PHSA
Provincial Institute of Mining ... PIM
Provincial Institute of Technology and Art ... PITA
Provincial Institute of Textiles ... PIT
Provincial Library of Manitoba, Winnipeg, MB, Canada [*Library symbol*] [*Library of Congress*] (LCLS) ... CaMPW
Provincial Library of Manitoba, Winnipeg, MB, Canada [*Library symbol Library of Congress*] (LCLS) ... CaMWP
Provincial Newspapers Association of Ireland (AD) ... PNAI
Provincial Planning Office, Newfoundland Department of Municipal Affairs, St. John's, Newfoundland [*Library symbol National Library of Canada*] (NLC) ... NFSMA
Provincial Public Health Nursing Services, Winnipeg, Manitoba [*Library symbol National Library of Canada*] (NLC) ... MWPPH
Provincial Public Health Nursing Services, Winnipeg, MB, Canada [*Library symbol Library of Congress*] (LCLS) ... CaMWPPH
Provincial Reconnaissance Unit [*Military*] ... PRU
Provincial Reference Library, St. John's, Newfoundland [*Library symbol National Library of Canada*] (NLC) ... NFSPR
Provincial Reference Library, St. John's, NF, Canada [*Library symbol Library of Congress*] (LCLS) ... CaNfSPR
Provincial/Regional Library Association Presidents [*Canada*] ... PRAP
Provincial Resource Centre for the Visually-Impaired, Vancouver, BC, Canada [*Library symbol*] [*Library of Congress*] (LCLS) ... CaBVaPVI
Provincial Resource Centre for the Visually-Impaired, Vancouver, British Columbia [*Library symbol National Library of Canada*] (NLC) ... BVAPVI
Provincial Sewerage Authorities Association of Victoria [*Australia*] ... PSAAV
Provincial Society of Spanish and Moroccan Leather Finishers [*A union*] [*British*] ... PSSMLF
Provincial Warning Center [*NATO*] (NATG) ... PWC
Provincial Wholesale Newspaper Distributors' Association [*British*] (BI) ... PWNDA
Provinciale [*Provincial*] [*Netherlands*] (EY) ... PROV
Provincial-Municipal Simulator [*Computer-based urban management system*] ... PROMUS
Proving for Production (MCD) ... PFP
Proving Ground [*Army*] ... PG
Proving Ground [*Navy*] ... PROV
Proving Ground Command [*Air Force*] ... PGC
Proving Grounds ... PROVGR
Provinical Reference and Resource Library, Newfoundland Public Library Services,St. John's, New Foundland [*Library symbol National Library of Canada*] (NLC) ... NFSG
Provision [*or Provisional*] (AFM) ... PROV
Provision ... PROVIS
Provision ... PROVSN
Provision Coordinate Schedule (MCD) ... PCS
Provision for Deferred Income Tax ... PDIT
Provision of Industrial Facilities [*Army*] (AABC) ... PIF
Provision of Production Facilities [*Military*] (AABC) ... PPF
Provisional ... P
Provisional Acceptable Means of Compliance (MCD) ... PAMC
Provisional Acceptance Date (NATG) ... PAD
Provisional Algal Assay Procedure [*Test measuring impact of chemicals on algal growth*] ... PAAP
Provisional Allowance ... PA
Provisional Approval for Service Use [*Navy*] (NVT) ... PASU
Provisional Base Defense Battalion [*Marine Corps*] (VNW) ... PBDB
Provisional Basic Military Requirements (NATG) ... PBMR
Provisional Battalion [*Military A publication*] (ROG) ... PB
Provisional Committee on Nomenclature of Viruses (DAVI) ... PCNV
Provisional Corps, Vietnam ... PROVCORPV
Provisional Costs ... PC
Provisional Cut [*Television*] (NTCM) ... PC
Provisional Frequency Board [*ITU*] ... PFB
Provisional Government of the Algerian Republic ... PGAR
Provisional International Civil Aviation Organization [*Later, ICAO*] ... PICAO
Provisional International Computation Center ... PICC
Provisional International Reference Preparation ... PIRP
Provisional International Standard ... PIS
Provisional Irish Republican Army ... PIRA
Provisional Legislative Council [*Hong Kong*] ... PLC
Provisional Light [*Navigation signal*] ... Prov
Provisional Maintenance Company [*Navy*] (DNAB) ... PROVMAINTCO
Provisional Medical Unit Self-Contained Company [*Navy*] (DNAB) ... PROVMUSTCO
Provisional Military Administrative Council [*Ethiopia*] [*Political party*] (PD) ... PMAC
Provisional Military Advisory Group ... PMAG
Provisional Military Assistance Advisory Group (CINC) ... PROVMAAG
Provisional Military Assistance Advisory Group, Korea (CINC) ... PROVMAAG-K
Provisional Military Demarcation Line (CINC) ... PMDL

Provisional Military Government [*Ethiopia*] ... PMG
Provisional National Defence Council [*Ghana*] (PD) ... PNDC
Provisional [*Program Management*] **Office** [*Army*] ... PMO
Provisional Operating Authorization [*for nuclear power plant*] ... POA
Provisional Operating License [*for nuclear power plant*] ... POL
Provisional Ordnance Group [*Military*] ... POG
Provisional Organization for European Inland Transportation [*World War II*] ... POEIT
Provisional Program Load Library Tape [*Computer science*] (MHDI) ... PPLLT
Provisional Program Management Office [*Army*] ... PPMO
Provisional Qualitative and Quantitative Personnel Requirements Information [*Army*] (AABC) ... PQQPRI
Provisional Reconnaissance Unit ... PRV
Provisional Relative Sunspot Number [*NASA*] ... PRSN
Provisional Revolutionary Government [*Political arm of the Vietcong*] (VNW) ... PRG
Provisional Revolutionary Government of South Vietnam (VNW) ... PRGVN
Provisional Sinn Fein [*Northern Ireland*] ... PSF
Provisional Sinn Fein [*Northern Ireland*] [*Political party*] (PPW) ... SF
Provisional Site Acceptance (NATG) ... PSA
Provisional Special Forces Co. (CINC) ... PSFC
Provisional System Feature [*Telecommunications*] (TEL) ... PSF
Provisional Technical Secretariat [*United Nations*] ... PTS
Provisional Tolerable Weekly Intake [*Toxicology*] ... PTWI
Provisional Troop Carrier Airborne Division ... PTCAD
Provisioned Item Order (MCD) ... PIO
Provisioning Action Control Evaluation [*Military*] (AFIT) ... PACE
Provisioning Automated Logistics Material System (MCD) ... PALMS
Provisioning Budget Forecast Procedure (MCD) ... PBFP
Provisioning Contract Control Number (NASA) ... PCCN
Provisioning Contracting Officer [*Military*] (AFIT) ... PCO
Provisioning Control Code [*Military*] (AFIT) ... PCC
Provisioning Data Check List [*NASA*] (KSC) ... PDCL
Provisioning Data Master Record (MCD) ... PDMR
Provisioning Description Data ... PDD
Provisioning Document ... PD
Provisioning Documentation and Effort [*Military*] (AFIT) ... PD & E
Provisioning Engineer ... PVE
Provisioning List (MCD) ... PL
Provisioning List Item Sequence Number (NASA) ... PLISN
Provisioning Master Data Record ... PMDR
Provisioning Master Record (MCD) ... PMR
Provisioning Numerical Listing/Index ... PNL/I
Provisioning Order (AFM) ... PO
Provisioning Order Obligating Document ... POOD
Provisioning Parts Breakdown ... PPB
Provisioning Parts List (AAG) ... PPL
Provisioning Parts List Index (MCD) ... PPLI
Provisioning Parts Schedule (MCD) ... PPS
Provisioning Parts Selection List (MCD) ... PPSL
Provisioning Performance Schedule (AFM) ... PPS
Provisioning Performance Schedule (MCD) ... PPSKED
Provisioning Policy Statement (MCD) ... PPS
Provisioning Preparedness Review [*Navy*] (CAAL) ... PPR
Provisioning Procedures [*Corps of Engineers*] ... PP
Provisioning Procurement Data ... PPD
Provisioning Program Plan (MCD) ... PPP
Provisioning Requirements Statement ... PRS
Provisioning Review Input Data Evaluation (MCD) ... PRIDE
Provisioning Sequence Number (MCD) ... PSN
Provisioning Supply Support Requests [*DoD*] ... PSSR
Provisioning Support Request [*Military*] (CAAL) ... PSR
Provisioning Team (AAG) ... PT
Provisioning Technical Documentation ... PTD
Provisioning Technical Documentation Data Selection Sheet [*NASA*] (NASA) ... PTDDSS
Provisioning Technical Working Group ... PTWG
Provisioning Technician ... PVT
Provisioning Transcript Documentation (MCD) ... PTD
Provisions (DLA) ... provns
Provisions ... PROVONS
Provisions of Following Reference Apply [*Army*] (AABC) ... PRAP
Provisions Stowage Assembly (NASA) ... PSA
Provisions Supply Office [*Military*] ... PSO
Proviso [*Contract clause*] (ROG) ... PROVO
Provo [*Utah*] [*Airport symbol*] (OAG) ... PVU
Provo Public Library, Provo, UT [*Library symbol Library of Congress*] (LCLS) ... UP
Provo, UT [*Location identifier FAA*] (FAAL) ... FFU
Provo, UT [*FM radio station call letters*] ... KBYU
Provo, UT [*Television station call letters*] ... KBYU-TV
Provo, UT [*AM radio station call letters*] ... KEYY
Provo, UT [*AM radio station call letters*] ... KOVO
Provo, UT [*AM radio station call letters*] ... KSRR
Provo, UT [*FM radio station call letters*] ... KXRK
Provo, UT [*Television station call letters*] (RBYB) ... KZAR-TV
Provo, UT [*FM radio station call letters*] ... KZHT
Provo, UT [*Location identifier FAA*] (FAAL) ... PVU
Provocateur (DSUE) ... PROVO
Provocation Dose [*Medicine*] (MEDA) ... PD
Provocative Concentration [*Immunology*] ... PC
Provocative Use Test [*Medicine*] (DMAA) ... PUT
Provost (WDAA) ... PR
Provost ... PRO
Provost ... PROV
Provost ... PRT
Provost Marshal [*Army*] ... PM
Provost Marshal General [*Army*] ... PMG
[*The*] **Provost Marshal General** [*Army*] ... TPMG
Provost Marshal General's School, United States Army ... PMGS
Provost Marshal's Office ... PMO
Provost Public Library, Alberta [*Library symbol National Library of Canada*] (NLC) ... APR
Provost-Sergeant ... PS
Proxicom Template Markup Language [*Computer science*] ... PTML
Proxim, Inc. [*NASDAQ symbol*] (SAG) ... PROX
Proxim, Inc. [*Associated Press*] (SAG) ... Proxim
Proxima Corp. [*Associated Press*] (SAG) ... Proxima
Proxima Corp. [*NASDAQ symbol*] (SAG) ... PRXM
Proxima Luce [*Day Before*] [*Latin*] (MAE) ... prox luc
Proximal ... Pr
Proximal (CPH) ... prox
Proximal Alveolar Region [*Medicine*] (DMAA) ... PAR
Proximal Articular Set Angle [*Orthopedics*] (DAVI) ... PASA
Proximal Convoluted Tubule [*of a nephron*] ... PCT
Proximal Femoral Focal Deficiency [*Orthopedics*] (DAVI) ... PFFD
Proximal Gastric Vagotomy [*Medicine*] ... PGV
Proximal Interphalangeal [*Joint*] ... PIP
Proximal Interphalangeal Joint [*Anatomy*] ... PIPJ
Proximal Main Pulmonary Artery [*Anatomy*] ... PMPA
Proximal Negative Response ... PNR
Proximal Over-Shoulder Strap [*Medicine*] ... POSS
Proximal Palmar Crease [*Anatomy*] ... PPC
Proximal Phalanx [*Anatomy*] ... PP
Proximal Sequence Element [*Genetics*] ... PSE
Proximal Spinal Muscular [*Medicine*] (DMAA) ... PSMA
Proximal Spinal Muscular Atrophy [*Medicine*] (DMAA) ... PSMA
Proximal Subungual Onychomycosis ... PSO
Proximal Third [*of bone*] [*Orthopedics*] (DAVI) ... P/3
Proximal Tibial Epiphysis [*Orthopedics*] (DAVI) ... PTE
Proximal Tubule Fluid [*Laboratory science*] (DAVI) ... PTF
Proxime Accessit [*Next in Order of Merit*] [*Latin*] ... PROX ACC
Proximity (AABC) ... PROX
Proximity Automatic Vehicle Monitoring (PDAA) ... PAVM
Proximity Computer (MCD) ... PXC
Proximity Defense Systems [*Military*] (INF) ... PDS
Proximity Detector ... PD
Proximity Effect Tunneling Spectroscopy (MCD) ... PETS
Proximity Fuze [*Bomb, rocket, or shell*] ... PF
Proximity Information, Range, and Disposition ... PIRAD
Proximity Instrumented Open Test Assembly [*Nuclear energy*] (NRCH) ... PIOTA
Proximity Operations Vehicle (SSD) ... POV
Proximity Optical Device (NASA) ... POD
Proximity Sensing Computer (MCD) ... PXSC
Proximity Sensing Head ... PSH
Proximity Sensor Test Facility [*Nuclear energy*] (NRCH) ... PSTF
Proximity Test Plug [*Nuclear energy*] (NRCH) ... PTP
Proximity Warning Device (MCD) ... PWD
Proximity Warning Indicator [*or Instrument*] [*Aviation*] ... PWI
Proximity Warning System (IAA) ... PWS
Proximo [*In Next Month*] [*Latin*] ... PROX
Proximo [*In Next Month*] [*Latin*] (ODBW) ... prox
Proximum [*Near*] [*Latin*] (MAE) ... p
Proxylem Tracheary Element [*Botany*] ... PTE
ProxyMed Inc. [*NASDAQ symbol*] (TTSB) ... PILL
ProxyMed, Inc. [*NASDAQ symbol*] (SAG) ... PILL
ProxyMed, Inc. [*Associated Press*] (SAG) ... Proxymd
Proxymed Pharmacy [*NASDAQ symbol*] (SAG) ... PILL
Proyecto Ambiental para Centro America [*Environmental Project for Central America*] [*Spanish*] (ECON) ... PACA
Proyecto de Desarrollo Nacional [*Project for National Development*] [*Chile*] (PPW) ... Proden
Prozone Phenomenon [*Immunology*] ... PZ
Prudent Laboratory Use System [*Health insurance*] (GHCT) ... PLUS
Prudent Limit of Endurance (NVT) ... PLE
Prudent No Added Salt [*Diet*] (DAVI) ... PNAS
Prudent Purchaser Arrangement [*Medical insurance*] ... PPA
Prudential Assurance Co. Ltd. [*Australia*] ... PAC
Prudential Grace Lines [*Steamship*] (MHDB) ... P-G
Prudential Insurance Co. of America, Business, Recreation, and Field Management Libraries, Los Angeles, CA [*Library symbol Library of Congress*] (LCLS) ... CLPI
Prudential Insurance Co. of America, Houston, TX [*Library symbol Library of Congress*] (LCLS) ... TxHPI
Prudential Portfolio Managers Ltd. [*British*] ... PPM
Prudential Property & Casualty Insurance Co., Holmdel, NJ [*OCLC symbol*] (OCLC) ... PRU
Prudential Property Services [*Prudential Group*] [*British*] ... PPS
Prudential Reinsurance Holdings, Inc. [*Associated Press*] (SAG) ... PrudRe
Prudential Reinsurance Holdings, Inc. [*NYSE symbol*] (SAG) ... RE
Prudential-Bache Capital Funding ... PBCF
Prudhoe Bay [*Arkansas*] [*Airport symbol*] (OAG) ... PUO
Prudhoe Bay, AK [*Location identifier FAA*] (FAAL) ... PUO
Prueba de Admisiones para Estudios Graduados (GAGS) ... PAEG
Prueba de Lectura y Lenguaje Escrito [*Standardized test of reading and writing in Spanish for students in grades 3 through 10*] ... PLLE
Pruhonice [*Czechoslovakia*] [*Seismograph station code, US Geological Survey*] (SEIS) ... PRU
Prune Belly Anomaly [*Medicine*] (DMAA) ... PBA
Prune Belly Syndrome [*Medicine*] (DMAA) ... PBS

Prune Brownline [*Plant pathology*] ..... PBL
Prune Dwarf Virus ..... PDV
Prune Extract Lactose Yeast Medium [*Microbiology*] ..... PLY
Prunedale, CA [*FM radio station call letters*] ..... KLVM
Prunus Necrotic Ringspot Virus ..... PNRSV
Pruritic Urticarial Papules and Plaques [*Dermatology*] (BARN) ..... PUPP
Pruritic Urticarial Papules and Plaques of Pregnancy [*Medicine*] ..... PUPPP
Prussia [*Obsolete*] ..... PRUS
Prussian [*Philately*] ..... Prus
Prussian Dollar [*Monetary unit*] (ROG) ..... PD
PRX [*Public Relations Exchange*] **International** (EA) ..... PRXI
Pryme Energy Resources [*Vancouver Stock Exchange symbol*] ..... PYE
Pryor, OK [*AM radio station call letters*] ..... KMYZ
Pryor, OK [*FM radio station call letters*] ..... KMYZ-FM
Przhevalsk [*Former USSR Seismograph station code, US Geological Survey*] (SEIS) ..... PRZ
PS Business Parks, Inc. [*AMEX symbol*] (SPSG) ..... PSB
PS Business Parks, Inc. [*Associated Press*] (SAG) ..... PSBP
PS Financial, Inc. [*Associated Press*] (SAG) ..... PS Fincl
PS Financial, Inc. [*NASDAQ symbol*] (SAG) ..... PSFI
PS Group, Inc. [*Associated Press*] (SAG) ..... PS Grp
PS Group, Inc. [*NYSE symbol*] (SPSG) ..... PSG
Psalm ..... PS
Psalm ..... PSA
Psalms [*Old Testament book*] ..... Ps
Psalms [*Old Testament book*] ..... Psa
Psalms [*Old Testament book*] ..... PSS
Psalms of Solomon [*Pseudepigrapha*] (BJA) ..... PsSol
Psalter (VRA) ..... pslt
PSC, Inc. [*Associated Press*] (SAG) ..... PSC
PSC, Inc. [*Formerly, Photographic Sciences Corp.*] [*NASDAQ symbol*] (NQ) ..... PSCX
PSE & G Capital Trust [*NYSE symbol*] (SAG) ..... PEG
PSE & G Capital Trust [*Associated Press*] (SAG) ..... PSEG
Pseudepigrapha (BJA) ..... Psdepgr
Pseudepigrapha (BJA) ..... Pseud
Pseudepigrapha (BJA) ..... Pseudep
Pseudo [*Classical studies*] (OCD) ..... PS
Pseudo Interrupt Device ..... PID
Pseudo Load Factor (IAA) ..... PLDF
Pseudo Machine Code [*Computer science*] (BUR) ..... PMC
Pseudo Noise Matched Filter (IAA) ..... PNMF
Pseudo Noise/Time Division Multiple Access (MCD) ..... PN/TDMA
Pseudo Spread Spectrum (MCD) ..... PSS
Pseudo Stow Document (DNAB) ..... PSD
Pseudoachondrodysplasia [*Medicine*] (DMAA) ..... PSACH
Pseudoadder Tree [*Computer science*] ..... PAT
Pseudoadiabatic Operation [*Chemical engineering*] ..... PO
Pseudoalcoholic Liver Lesions [*Medicine*] ..... PLL
Pseudoamniotic Fluid [*Gynecology*] ..... PAF
Pseudoaneurysm [*Medicine*] ..... PA
Pseudo-Archaic Forgery ..... PAF
Pseudo-Astronomy ..... PA
Pseudoautosomal Region [*Genetics*] ..... PAR
Pseudocholinesterase [*An enzyme*] (DAVI) ..... PC HE
Pseudocholinesterase [*Same as ACAH*] [*An enzyme*] ..... PCE
Pseudocleistogamous [*Botany*] ..... PCL
Pseudocode (AAG) ..... PC
Pseudoconditioning Control [*Neurophysiology*] ..... PC
Pseudoequivalent Service Rounds [*Military*] (NVT) ..... PESR
Pseudoexfoliation (DMAA) ..... PRX
Pseudoexfoliation (DMAA) ..... PSX
Pseudoextracellular Fluid [*for biocompatibility testing*] ..... PECF
Pseudofollicutitis Barbae [*Medicine*] ..... PFB
Pseudohomogeneous Axial Dispersion Model [*Fluid dynamics*] ..... PD
Pseudohyperbolic Particle [*Astrophysics*] ..... PHP
Pseudohypertrophic Muscular Dystrophy (CPH) ..... PHMD
Pseudohypoaldosteronism [*Medicine*] ..... PHA
Pseudohypoparathyroidism [*Endocrinology*] ..... PHOPT
Pseudohypoparathyroidism [*Endocrinology*] ..... PHP
Pseudo-Identification Feature (MCD) ..... PIF
Pseudoinfinite, Logarithmically Periodic ..... PILP
Pseudoinflammatory Fundus Disease [*Medicine*] (DMAA) ..... PFD
Pseudoisocyanine [*Organic chemistry*] ..... PIC
Pseudo-Isocytidine [*Antineoplastic compound*] ..... PIC
Pseudoline Control Block [*Computer science*] ..... PLCB
Pseudolumina [*Anatomy*] ..... PL
Pseudolymphocytic Choriomeningitis [*Medicine*] (DMAA) ..... PLC
Pseudomatrix Isolation ..... PMI
Pseudomembranous Colitis [*Medicine*] ..... PMC
Pseudomonas [*Bacterium*] (MAE) ..... Ps
Pseudomonas aeruginosa [*Bacterium*] ..... PA
Pseudomonas Exotoxin [*Bacterial toxin*] ..... PE
Pseudomonas Stutzeri [*Bacterium*] ..... PS
Pseudomonas Syringae PV Glycinea [*Plant pathology*] ..... PSG
Pseudomonas Syringae Syringae [*Plant pathology*] ..... Pss
Pseudomonic Acid [*Biochemistry*] ..... PSA
Pseudomyxoma Peritonei [*Medicine*] (DMAA) ..... PP
Pseudonoise ..... PN
Pseudonoise Generator ..... PNG
Pseudonurse Cells [*Cytology*] ..... PNC
Pseudonym (WGA) ..... PS
Pseudonym ..... PSEUD
Pseudonym [*Legal shorthand*] (LWAP) ..... PSEUDO
Pseudonyms and Nicknames Dictionary [*A publication*] ..... PND
Pseudopassive Array ..... PPA
Pseudophase Ion Exchange [*Chemistry*] ..... PPIE
Pseudophase Liquid Chromatography ..... PLC
Pseudo-Pinch Design Method [*Heat exchange design*] ..... PPDM
Pseudopregnancy [*Gynecology*] ..... PSP
Pseudoprogram (IAA) ..... PP
Pseudo-Pseudohypoparathyroidism [*Also, PPHP*] [*Endocrinology*] ..... PPHOPT
Pseudo-Pseudohypoparathyroidism [*Also, PPHOPT*] [*Endocrinology*] ..... PPHP
Pseudorabies Virus ..... PRV
Pseudorandom ..... PR
Pseudorandom Access Memory [*Computer science*] (IAA) ..... PRAM
Pseudorandom Binary Sequence [*Computer science*] ..... PRBS
Pseudorandom Binary Sequence Generator [*Computer science*] (NRCH) ..... PRBSG
Pseudorandom Frequency Modulated [*Computer science*] ..... PRFM
Pseudorandom Noise ..... PRN
Pseudorandom Number ..... PN
Pseudorandom Number ..... PRN
Pseudorandom Pulse ..... PRP
Pseudorandom Sequence ..... PRS
Pseudo-Range Correction ..... PRC
Pseudorelative Velocity ..... PRV
Pseudo-Renal Artery Syndrome [*Medicine*] (DMAA) ..... PRAS
Pseudoresident Reader (MHDB) ..... PRR
Pseudoresidual ..... PR
Pseudoresidual Plot Program ..... PRPP
Pseudosarcomatous Fasciitis [*Medicine*] ..... PSF
Pseudosingle Domain [*Behavior of grains in rocks*] [*Geophysics*] ..... PSD
Pseudostatic Random Access Memory [*Apple Computer Inc.*] ..... PSRAM
Pseudostatic Spontaneous Potential (IAA) ..... PSP
Pseudo-Steady-State Approximation [*Chemical engineering*] ..... PSSA
Pseudo-Synthetic Video (DOMA) ..... PSV
Pseudoterminal Bud [*Botany*] ..... PB
Pseudotumor Cerebri [*Medicine*] (AAMN) ..... PTC
Pseudotumor Cerebri Syndrome [*Medicine*] (DMAA) ..... PCS
Pseudovaginal Perineoscrotal Hypospadias [*Medicine*] ..... PPSH
Pseudoword Target [*Psychology*] ..... Pt
Pseudoxanthoma Elasticum [*Medicine*] ..... PXE
PSI Energy [*Associated Press*] (SAG) ..... PSI
PSI Energy, 4.16%cmPfd vtg [*NYSE symbol*] (TTSB) ..... PINPrB
PSI Energy, 4.32% Pfd [*NYSE symbol*] (TTSB) ..... PINPrC
PSI Energy, 7.15% Pfd [*NYSE symbol*] (TTSB) ..... PINPrD
PSI Energy, 7.44% Pfd [*NYSE symbol*] (TTSB) ..... PINPrK
PSI Energy, 6.875% Pfd [*NYSE symbol*] (TTSB) ..... PINPrJ
PSI Energy, Inc. [*NYSE symbol*] (SPSG) ..... PIN
Psi Quotient [*Parapsychology*] ..... PQ
PSICOR, Inc. [*NASDAQ symbol*] (NQ) ..... PCOR
PSICOR, Inc. [*Associated Press*] (SAG) ..... Psicor
Psilcybin [*Medicine*] (MEDA) ..... PCP
Psi-Mediated Instrumental Response [*Parapsychology*] ..... PMIR
PSINet, Inc. [*Associated Press*] (SAG) ..... PSINet
PSINet, Inc. [*NASDAQ symbol*] (SAG) ..... PSIX
PSINet Inc. [*NASDAQ symbol*] (TTSB) ..... PSIX
Psittacosis-Lymphogranuloma Venereum [*Medicine*] ..... P-LGV
Psittacosis-Lymphogranuloma Venereum Trachoma [*Microbiology*] ..... PLT
Pskov State Aviation Enterprise [*Former USSR*] [*FAA designator*] (FAAC) ..... PSW
PSM Technologies, Inc. [*Vancouver Stock Exchange symbol*] ..... PSY
Psoralens and Ultraviolet A [*Therapy*] [*Medicine*] ..... PUVA
Psoriasis Area and Severity Index [*Medicine*] ..... PASI
Psoriasis Association [*Australia*] ..... PA
Psoriasis Education and Research Centre [*University of Toronto*] [*Canada Research center*] (RCD) ..... PERC
Psoriasis Research Association (EA) ..... PRA
Psoriasis Research Institute (EA) ..... PRI
Psoriatic Arthritis (DAVI) ..... PsA
PSRO [*Professional Standards Review Organization*] **Hospital Discharge Data Set** ..... PHDDS
PSRO [*Professional Standards Review Organization*] **Management Information System** (DHSM) ..... PMIS
PST Vans [*NASDAQ symbol*] (TTSB) ..... PSTV
PST Vans, Inc. [*Associated Press*] (SAG) ..... PST Vn
PST Vans, Inc. [*NASDAQ symbol*] (SAG) ..... PSTV
Psychedelic Review [*A publication*] ..... PR
Psychemedics Corp. [*AMEX symbol*] (SAG) ..... PMD
Psychemedics Corp. [*Associated Press*] (SAG) ..... PsycCp
Psychiatric (MAE) ..... PS
Psychiatric ..... PSYCHC
Psychiatric ..... PSYCTRC
Psychiatric Aide (DAVI) ..... PA
Psychiatric Attitudes Battery [*Psychology*] ..... PAB
Psychiatric Case History Event System (PDAA) ..... PSyCHES
Psychiatric Chemistry ..... PSYCHEM
Psychiatric Deviate, Subtle (DAVI) ..... PdS
Psychiatric Diagnostic Interview [*Personality development test*] [*Psychology*] ..... PDI
Psychiatric Emergency Team ..... PET
Psychiatric Epidemiology Research Interview ..... PERI
Psychiatric Evaluation Form [*Psychology*] ..... PEF
Psychiatric Evaluation Form (DAVI) ..... PEF
Psychiatric Evaluation Profile [*Psychology*] (MAE) ..... PEP
Psychiatric Home Treatment Service (DAVI) ..... PHTS
Psychiatric Institute ..... PI
Psychiatric Institute of America [*For-profit network of private psychiatric hospitals*] (EA) ..... PIA
Psychiatric Military Duty ..... PMD

Psychiatric Military Officer ..... PMO
Psychiatric Nurse ..... PN
Psychiatric Nurses' Association of Canada ..... PNAC
Psychiatric Record (AD) ..... PR
Psychiatric Regional Hospital [*Health insurance*] (GHCT) ..... PRH
Psychiatric Rehabilitation Association [*British*] ..... PRA
Psychiatric Rehabilitation Team (EA) ..... PRT
Psychiatric Research Foundation ..... PRF
Psychiatric Review Technique Form [*Social Security Administration*] ..... PRTF
Psychiatric Services Officer [*Australia*] ..... PSO
Psychiatric Services Section [*of the American Hospital Association*] [*Later, SCSMHPS*] (EA) ..... PSS
Psychiatric Social Work in Mental Observation Wards [*British*] ..... PSWMOW
Psychiatric Social Work in Out-Patient Clinics [*British*] ..... PSWOPC
Psychiatric Social Work Training [*British*] ..... PSWT
Psychiatric Social Worker [*British*] ..... PSW
Psychiatric Status Schedules [*Psychology*] ..... PSS
Psychiatrist (DSUE) ..... PSYCH
Psychiatrist ..... PSYCH
Psychiatrists Against Psychiatric Abuse [*Canada*] (EAIO) ..... PAPA
Psychiatry ..... P
Psychiatry ..... PSY
Psychiatry ..... PSYCH
Psychiatry [*or Psychiatric*] (DAVI) ..... psychiat
Psychiatry ..... PSYCHY
Psychiatry ..... PSYCTRY
Psychiatry and Neurology ..... P & N
Psychiatry and Neurology (AD) ..... p & n
Psychiatry-Neurology (AD) ..... pn
Psychic (ROG) ..... PSYCH
Psychic Detective Bureau (EA) ..... PDB
Psychic Phenomena ..... PP
Psychic Science International Special Interest Group (EA) ..... PSISIG
Psychic Workers Association (NADA) ..... PWA
Psychic Zodiac ..... PZ
Psychical Research Foundation (EA) ..... PRF
Psycho-Acoustic Laboratory [*Harvard University*] (MCD) ..... PAL
Psychoacoustic Testing ..... PAT
Psycho-Acoustical Measuring System (PDAA) ..... PACMS
Psychoactive Substance Use Disorder ..... PSUD
Psychoaffective Disorder [*Psychiatry*] (DAVI) ..... PAD
Psychoanalysis [*or Psychoanalyst*] (DAVI) ..... PSAn
Psychoanalysis (DSUE) ..... PSYCHO
Psychoanalysis [*Medicine*] (DMAA) ..... psychoan
Psychoanalysis [*Medicine*] ..... PYA
Psychoanalyst ..... PA
Psychoanalytic Assistance Fund (EA) ..... PAF
Psychodevelopment Checklist [*Psychology*] (DAVI) ..... PC
Psychodevelopment Checklist [*Psychology*] (DAVI) ..... PDC
Psychodynamic ..... PD
Psychodynamics and Therapeutic Education ..... PATE
Psycho-Educational Battery [*Educational test*] ..... PEB
Psychoeducational Profile [*Test for autistic children*] ..... PEP
Psychoepistemological Profile [*Student personality test*] ..... PEP
Psychogalvanic Reflex [*or Response*] [*Psychology*] ..... PGR
Psychogalvanic Skin Resistance [*Otolaryngology*] ..... PGSR
Psychogalvanometer ..... PSG
Psychogenic Aspermia [*Medicine*] ..... PA
Psychogenic Nocturnal Polydipsia [*Medicine*] ..... PNP
PsychoHistory Forum (EA) ..... PF
Psychokinesis ..... PK
Psychokinesis on Living Targets ..... PK-LT
Psychokinetic Metal-Bending [*Parapsychology*] ..... PK-MB
Psycholinguistic Age [*Education*] ..... PLA
Psycholinguistic Rating Scale ..... PRS
Psychological (CINC) ..... PSY
Psychological (AFM) ..... PSYCHL
Psychological ..... PSYCHL
Psychological Abstracts Current Awareness Service (IID) ..... PACAS
Psychological Abstracts Direct Access Terminal ..... PADAT
Psychological Abstracts Information Services [*American Psychological Association*] ..... PAIS
Psychological Abstracts Information Services [*American Psychological Association*] (IID) ..... PsycINFO
Psychological Abstracts Reference Retrieval System [*Syracuse University*] ..... PARRS
Psychological Abstracts Search and Retrieval ..... PASAR
Psychological Abstracts Tape Edition Lease or Licensing ..... PATELL
Psychological Age ..... PA
Psychological and Medico-Legal Journal [*A publication*] (DLA) ..... Psych & MLJ
Psychological Audit for Interpersonal Relations [*Psychology*] ..... PAIR
Psychological Distress Inventory [*Student personality test*] ..... PDI
Psychological General Well Being [*Index*] (DMAA) ..... PGWB
Psychological Information (NITA) ..... PSYCINFO
Psychological Insight Test [*Psychometrics*] ..... PIT
Psychological Laboratories [*Harvard University*] (KSC) ..... PLR
Psychological Laboratory (MCD) ..... PL
Psychological Learning Aptitude (MCD) ..... PLA
Psychological Operation [*Military*] (CINC) ..... PO
Psychological Operation [*Military*] ..... PSYOP
Psychological Operations Automated Management Information System (MCD) ..... PAMIS
Psychological Operations Exploitation Team [*Vietnam*] ..... POET
Psychological Operations Group (DOMA) ..... POG
Psychological Operations Support Activity [*Military*] (MCD) ..... PSA
Psychological Operations Task Force [*Army*] (INF) ..... POTF
Psychological Problem [*Classification system used by doctors on Ellis Island to detain, re-examine, and possibly deny entry to certain immigrants*] X
Psychological Profile ..... PP
Psychological Research Associates ..... PRA
Psychological Response Classification System ..... PRCS
Psychological Saline Solution (BARN) ..... PSS
Psychological Sciences Division [*Office of Naval Research*] (DNAB) ..... PSY-SDIV
Psychological Screening Inventory [*Personality development test*] ..... PSI
Psychological Semantic Analysis (NITA) ..... PSA
Psychological Services Bureau (AEBS) ..... PSB
Psychological, Social, and Vocational [*Adjustment factors*] ..... PSV
Psychological Strategy Board [*Military*] (LAIN) ..... PSB
Psychological Stress Evaluator [*Lie detector*] ..... PSE
Psychological Studies Group [*Military*] (VNW) ..... PSG
Psychological Warfare ..... PSYWAR
Psychological Warfare ..... PW
Psychological Warfare Branch [*Allied Forces*] [*World War II*] ..... PWB
Psychological Warfare Division [*SHAEF*] [*World War II*] ..... PWD
Psychological Warfare Operations (DNAB) ..... PSY-OPS
Psychological Warfare Service [*Allied Forces*] [*World War II*] ..... PWS
Psychological Warfare Society [*Birmingham, England*] (EA) ..... PWS
Psychological Weapon [*Military*] (AFM) ..... PSYWPN
Psychologist ..... PSYC
Psychologists and Psychiatrists [*in service*] [*British*] ..... PP
Psychologists for Social Action [*Defunct*] (EA) ..... PSA
Psychologists for Social Responsibility (EA) ..... PsySR
Psychologists for the Ethical Treatment of Animals (EA) ..... PsyETA
Psychologists Interested in Religious Issues (EA) ..... PIRI
Psychologists Interested in the Advancement of Psychotherapy [*Later, APA*] (EA) ..... PIAP
Psychology ..... PSYC
Psychology (AFM) ..... PSYCH
Psychology (DD) ..... Psych
Psychology ..... PSYCHOL
Psychology ..... PSYCY
Psychology of Addictive Behaviors [*An association*] (EA) ..... PAB
Psychology Society (EA) ..... PS
Psychology Today [*A publication*] (BRI) ..... PT
Psychometric Behavior Checklist [*Psychology*] ..... PBC
Psychometric Colorimeter Chamber (MCD) ..... PCC
Psychometric Society (EA) ..... PS
Psychometrist [*Psychology*] ..... P
Psychomotor Development Index [*Bayley Scales of Infant Development*] ..... PDI
Psychoneuroimmunology ..... PNI
Psychoneuroimmunology (AD) ..... pni
Psychoneurologist ..... PN
Psychoneurotic [*Cases, patients, etc.*] ..... PN
Psychonomic Society (EA) ..... PS
Psychopath [*Psychiatry*] (DAVI) ..... psycho
Psychopath [*Psychiatry*] (DAVI) ..... psy-path
Psychopathic Deviate [*Psychology*] ..... Pd
Psychopathic Deviate Obvious [*Psychology*] ..... PdO
Psychopathic Deviate Subtle [*Psychology*] ..... PdS
Psychopathology (DAVI) ..... psychopathol
Psychophysical Timing Curve ..... PTC
Psychophysics [*Psychiatry*] (DAVI) ..... psychophys
Psychophysiological Information Acquisition, Processing, and Control System ..... PIAPACS
Psychophysiology [*Psychiatry*] (DAVI) ..... psychophysiol
Psychorotrophic Plate Count [*Bacteriology*] ..... PPC
Psychosocial Adjustment to Illness Scale [*Personality development test*] [*Psychology*] ..... PAIS
Psychosocial Pain Inventory [*Psychology*] ..... PSPI
Psycho-Social Rehabilitation International (EAIO) ..... PSRI
Psychosomatic (DAVI) ..... psy-som
Psychosomatic [*Medicine*] (DMAA) ..... PYM
Psychosomatic Inventory [*Psychology*] ..... PSI
Psychosomatic Medicine (DAVI) ..... PSMed
Psychosomatic Medicine [*Psychiatry*] (DAVI) ..... PsychosMed
Psychosomatic Medicine ..... PYM
Psychosurgery Review Board [*Victoria, Australia*] ..... PRB
Psychosynthesis Institute (EA) ..... PI
Psychosynthesis Research Foundation (EA) ..... PRF
Psychotherapy [*Psychiatry*] (DAVI) ..... psychother
Psychotherapy Outcome Research ..... POR
Psychotic ..... PS
Psychotic Depression [*Medicine*] ..... PD
Psychotic Deviate [*Psychiatry*] (DAVI) ..... PD
Psychotic Inpatient Profile [*Psychology*] ..... PIP
Psychotic Reaction Profile [*Psychology*] ..... PRP
Psynetics Foundation (EA) ..... PF
PSYOP [*Psychological Operation*] **Automated Terminal** (RDA) ..... PAT
PT Boats, Inc. (EA) ..... PTB
PT Boats, Inc. (EAIO) ..... PTBI
P.T. Telekomunikasi ADS [*NYSE symbol*] (TTSB) ..... TLK
P.T. Tri Polyta Indonesia ADS [*NYSE symbol*] (TTSB) ..... TPI
Ptarmigan Airways Ltd. [*Canada ICAO designator*] (FAAC) ..... PTA
Pterin [*Biochemistry*] ..... Ptn
Pterocephaliid-Ptychaspid [*Paleogeologic boundary*] ..... P/P
Pteropod/Foramifera [*Ratio in coastal waters*] ..... P/F
Pteropods [*Quality of the bottom*] [*Nautical charts*] ..... Pt
Pteroyl [*Biochemistry*] ..... Pte
Pteroyldiglutamic Acid [*Pharmacology*] ..... PDGA

Pteroylhexaglutamylglutamic [or Pteroylheptaglutamic] **Acid** [Biochemistry] .... PHGA
Pteroylmonoglutamic **Acid** [Folic acid] [Also, FA, PteGlu] [Biochemistry] .... PGA
Pteroylmonoglutamic **Acid** [Folic acid] [Also, FA, PGA] [Biochemistry] .... PteGlu
Pteroyltriglutamic **Acid** [Pharmacology] .... PTGA
Pterygoarthromyodysplasia Congenital [Medicine] (DMAA) .... PAMC
PTI Hldg Wrrt [NASDAQ symbol] (TTSB) .... PTIIW
PTI Holding [NASDAQ symbol] (TTSB) .... PTI Hold
PTI Holding, Inc. [Associated Press] (SAG) .... PTI Hold
PTI Holding, Inc. [Associated Press] (SAG) .... PTIHd
PTI Holding, Inc. [NASDAQ symbol] (SAG) .... PTII
Ptolemaeus Mathematicus [Second century AD] [Classical studies] (OCD) ...... Ptol
Ptolemaic (BJA) .... Ptol
PTP Resource Corp. [Formerly, Petrologic Petroleum Ltd.] [Vancouver Stock Exchange symbol] .... PT
PTS Marketing and Advertising Reference Service [Predicasts, Inc.] [Cleveland, OH] [Information service or system] (IID) .... MARS
PTS [Predicasts, Inc.] **New Product Announcements/Plus** [Information service or system] (IID) .... NPA
PTS [Predicasts] **Regional Business News** [Cleveland, OH] [Database] [Information service or system] (IID) .... RBN
Ptychodiscus brevis [An alga, the cause of the red tide] .... PB
Ptychodiscus brevis **Toxin** [Florida red-tide toxin] .... PBTX
P-Type Intrinsic N-Type [or Positive-Intrinsic-Negative] .... PIN
P-Type, N-Type, P-Type Transistor (NITA) .... PNP
Puale Bay [Alaska] [Seismograph station code, US Geological Survey] (SEIS) .... PUB
Puangchon Chao Thai [Thai Mass Party] [Thailand] [Political party] .... PCT
Pub Sv Colo, 8.40% Pfd [NYSE symbol] (TTSB) .... PSBPrB
Pub Sv Colo.,7.15% Pfd [NYSE symbol] (TTSB) .... PSRPrA
Pub Sv E&G 4.08% Pfd [NYSE symbol] (TTSB) .... PEGPrA
Pub Sv E&G 4.18% Pfd [NYSE symbol] (TTSB) .... PRGPrB
Pub Sv E&G 4.30% Pfd [NYSE symbol] (TTSB) .... PEGPrD
Pub Sv E&G 5.05% Pfd [NYSE symbol] (TTSB) .... PEGPrC
Pub Sv E&G 5.28% Pfd [NYSE symbol] (TTSB) .... PEGPrE
Pub Sv E&G 5.97% Pfd [NYSE symbol] (TTSB) .... PEGPrW
Pub Sv E&G 6.75% Pfd [NYSE symbol] (TTSB) .... PEGPrY
Pub Sv E&G 6.80% Pfd [NYSE symbol] (TTSB) .... PEGPrG
Pub Sv E&G 7.44% Pfd [NYSE symbol] (TTSB) .... PEGPrV
Pub Sv E&G 7.52% Pfd [NYSE symbol] (TTSB) .... PEGPrJ
Pub Sv of Colo.,4 1/4% Pfd [AMEX symbol] (TTSB) .... PSRPr
Pubblicazioni. Stazione Zoologica di Napoli [A publication] .... PSZN
Pubco Corp [Associated Press] (SAG) .... PubcoC
Pubco Corp. [NASDAQ symbol] (NQ) .... PUBO
Puberal Macromastia [Medicine] (DMAA) .... PM
Public (DSUE) .... PB
Public .... PUB
Public (WDMC) .... pub
Public .... PUB
Public (DD) .... Pub
Public (WGA) .... PUBL
Public Access by New Technology to Highly Elaborate Online Networks [Computer science] (PDAA) .... PANTHEON
Public Access **Catalogue** (ADA) .... PAC
Public Access **Control** .... PAC
Public Access Cordless Telephone Service [Australia] .... PACTS
Public Access Machine Readable Documents (NITA) .... PAMD
Public Access Message System .... PAMS
Public Access to Court Electronic Records .... PACER
Public Access Videotex .... PAV
Public **Accountant** .... PA
Public Accountants Registration Board [Australia] .... PARB
Public Accounts Committee [British government] .... PAC
Public **Act** .... PA
Public Action Coalition on Toys [Opposes sexist toys] .... PACT
Public Acts of the State of Tennessee [A publication] (DLA) .... Tenn Pub Acts
Public Address [Amplification equipment] [Communications] .... PA
Public Address Assembly [Ground Communications Facility, NASA] .... PADA
Public Address Intercom System (NRCH) .... PAIC
Public Address System (WDMC) .... PA
Public Address System .... PAS
Public Administered Whipping [Slang] .... PAW
Public **Administration** .... PA
Public **Administration** [A publication] .... Publ Admin
Public Administration Clearing House [1931-1956] .... PACH
Public Administration Review [A publication] (BRI) .... PAR
Public Administration **Service** (EA) .... PAS
Public Administration Service, Joint Reference Library, Chicago, IL [Library symbol Library of Congress] (LCLS) .... ICPA
Public Administration Times [A publication] (EAAP) .... PAT
Public **Advocate** (EA) .... PA
Public Advocate - Coalition of Public Interest Professionals (EA) .... PACPIP
Public **Affairs** .... PA
Public **Affairs** (DNAB) .... PUBAFF
Public Affairs and Information Program [Atomic Industrial Forum] (NRCH) .... PAIP
Public Affairs Assist Team [Hazardous substance emergency response] ...... PAAT
Public Affairs Center [Navy] (DNAB) .... PACEN
Public Affairs Center, Atlantic [Navy] (DNAB) .... PACENLANT
Public Affairs Center, Pacific [Navy] (DNAB) .... PACENPAC
Public Affairs Committee [Defunct] (EA) .... PAC
Public Affairs Coordinator [Nuclear energy] (NRCH) .... PAC
Public Affairs **Council** (EA) .... PAC
Public Affairs Council Education [An association] [Canadian] (NFD) .... PACE
Public Affairs Council for Education [Canada] .... PACE
Public Affairs Division [Military] (AABC) .... PAD

Public Affairs **Event** (NVT) .... PAE
Public Affairs Information, Inc. [Sacramento, CA] [Database producer] [Information service or system] .... PAI
Public Affairs Institute [Defunct] (EA) .... PAI
Public Affairs Office [NASA] .... PAO
Public Affairs Officer [Embassies] .... PAO
Public Affairs Program [of the American Friends Service Committee] (EA) ..... PAP
Public Affairs Ready Reserve Unit (DNAB) .... PUBAFFRRU
Public Affairs Research Council [Research center] (RCD) .... PAR
Public Against Violence [Former Czechoslovakia] [Political party] .... PAV
Public Agency Career Employment Maker [OEO project] .... PACEMAKER
Public Agency Risk Managers Association [San Jose, CA] (EA) .... PARMA
Public Agenda Foundation (EA) .... PAF
Public and Indian Housing [HUD] .... PIH
Public and Institutional Property [Insurance] .... PIP
Public and International Affairs [USCG] (TAG) .... PIA
Public and Local Acts of the Legislature of the State of Michigan [A publication] (DLA) .... Mich Pub Acts
Public and Private [Nongovernment] Schools [Public-performance tariff class] [British] .... PPS
Public and Private Transport .... PPT
Public **Archives** [of Canada] .... PA
Public Archives, Charlottetown, PE, Canada [Library symbol Library of Congress] (LCLS) .... CaPCA
Public Archives, Charlottetown, Prince Edward Island [Library symbol National Library of Canada] (NLC) .... PCA
Public Archives, Ethnic Archives of Canada, Ottawa, ON, Canada [Library symbol Library of Congress] (LCLS) .... CaOOAEA
Public Archives, Honolulu, HI [Library symbol Library of Congress] (LCLS) .... H-Ar
Public Archives, Manuscript Division, Ottawa, ON, Canada [Library symbol Library of Congress] (LCLS) .... CaOOAMS
Public Archives, National Film Archives, Ottawa, ON, Canada [Library symbol Library of Congress] (LCLS) .... CaOOANF
Public Archives of Canada .... PAC
Public Archives of Canada Library [UTLAS symbol] .... PAL
Public Archives of Canada, National Map Collection [UTLAS symbol] .... NMC
Public Archives of Canada, National Map Collection, Ottawa, ON, Canada [Library symbol Library of Congress] (LCLS) .... CaOOAMA
Public Archives of Canada, Ottawa, ON, Canada [Library symbol Library of Congress] (LCLS) .... CaOOA
Public Archives [Archives Publiques] Ottawa, Ontario [Library symbol National Library of Canada] (NLC) .... OOA
Public **Art Fund** (EA) .... PAF
Public Arts Advisory Council (NADA) .... PACC
Public **Assistance** .... PA
Public Assistance Director [Federal disaster planning] .... PAD
Public Assistance Information [A publication] .... PAI
Public Assistance Processing System .... PAPS
Public Assistance Program .... PAP
Public Assistance/Vocational Rehabilitation .... PA/VR
Public Authorities Superannuation Board [New South Wales, Australia] .... PASB
Public Authority Contribution [Australia] .... PAC
Public Awareness Committee [American Library Association] .... PAC
Public Awareness Program .... PAP
Public Bargaining Cases (Commerce Clearing House) [A publication] (DLA) .... Pub Bargaining Cas (CCH)
Public Benevolent Institution [Australia] .... PBI
Public Board of Inquiry .... PBOI
Public Brand Software (PCM) .... PBS
Public Broadcast Laboratory .... PBL
Public Broadcaster [Radio or TV station affiliated with NPR or PBS] .... Pubcaster
Public Broadcasting Environment Center [Corporation for Public Broadcasting] .... PBEC
Public Broadcasting Laboratory (NTCM) .... PBL
Public Broadcasting Service [Facetious translation: Primarily British Shows] (EA) .... PBS
Public Broadcasting System .... PBS
Public Buildings Administration [Functions transferred to PBS, 1949] .... PBA
Public Buildings Commission [Functions transferred to PBA, 1939] .... PBC
Public Buildings Service [of General Services Administration] .... PBS
Public Call Office (DAS) .... PCO
Public Choice Society (EA) .... PCS
Public **Citizen** (EA) .... PC
Public Citizen Health Research Group (EA) .... PCHRG
Public Citizen Litigation Group (EA) .... PCLG
Public Citizens Visitors Center [An association Defunct] (EA) .... PCVC
Public Coin Box [Telecommunications] (TEL) .... PCB
Public Communications Office .... PCO
Public Concern Foundation (EA) .... PCF
Public **Contract** .... PC
Public Contract Law Journal [A publication] (AAGC) .... P Contr LJ
Public Convenience and Necessity [Department of Transportation] .... PCN
Public Cryptography Study Group [Defunct] (EA) .... PCSG
Public Data Communications Network [Library science] .... PDCN
Public Data Network [Packet-switching network] [British Telecommunications Ltd. London] .... PDN
Public Debt Interest (ADA) .... PDI
Public Defender [Australia] .... PD
Public Defender (Legal Aid Office) [Australia] .... PD(LAO)
Public Defender's Office [Australia] .... PDO
Public Defender's Office (LAIN) .... PDO
Public Demographics, Inc. (IID) .... PDI
Public Dialup Internet Access List [Computer science] (CDE) .... PDIAL
Public Display of Affection [Slang] .... PDA
Public Dividend Capital (PDAA) .... PDC

Public Document Room (NRCH) .... PDR
Public Documents (ROG) .... PUB DOC
Public Documents Commission [*Government agency*] .... PDC
Public Documents Department [*Government Printing Office*] .... PDD
Public Domain .... PD
Public Domain Software on File [*Facts on File, Inc.*] [*Information service or system*] (IID) .... PDSOF
Public Education Association .... PEA
Public Education Fund Network (EA) .... PEF/NET
Public Education Needs Civic Involvement in Learning .... PENCIL
Public Education Religion Studies Center [*Defunct*] (EA) .... PERSC
Public, Educational, Government [*Cable television access channels*] (NTCM) .... PEG
Public Electronic Network [*Information service or system*] (IID) .... PEN
Public Employee Bargaining Reports (Commerce Clearing House) [*A publication*] (DLA) .... Pub Employee Bargaining Rep (CCH)
Public Employee Department (of AFL-CIO) (EA) .... PED
Public Employee Relations Library [*of International Personnel Management Association*] .... PERL
Public Employee Relations Reports [*A publication*] (DLA) .... Pub Employee Rel Rep
Public Employees Blanket Bond .... PEBB
Public Employees Retirement System (DICI) .... PERS
Public Employees Roundtable (EA) .... PER
Public Employment Office [*State Employee Security Agency*] (OICC) .... PEO
Public Employment Relations Board (EDAC) .... PERB
Public Employment Relations Commission (EDAC) .... PERC
Public Expenditure Survey [*British*] .... PES
Public Expenditure Survey Committee [*British*] (ODBW) .... PESC
Public Exposure Limit (MCD) .... PEL
Public Facility Loans .... PFL
Public Forecasts [*Symbol*] [*National Weather Service*] .... FP
Public Funding [*Finance*] (WDAA) .... PF
Public Gaol [*British*] .... PG
Public General Laws [*A publication*] (DLA) .... Pub Gen Laws
Public Hall [*Freemasonry*] (ROG) .... PUB HA
Public Hazards Office (NADA) .... PHO
Public Health .... PH
Public Health Act (DAS) .... PHA
Public Health Agency (DMAA) .... PHA
Public Health Bibliography .... PHB
Public Health Cancer Association of America [*Defunct*] (EA) .... PHCAA
Public Health Department .... PHD
Public Health Director .... PHD
Public Health Engineer .... PH Eng
Public Health Engineering Abstracts [*A publication*] .... PHEA
Public Health Foundation [*Information service or system*] (IID) .... PHF
Public Health Inspector [*British*] .... PHI
Public Health Inspectors' Registration Board [*British*] (BI) .... PHIRB
Public Health Laboratory Service [*British*] .... PHLS
Public Health Laboratory Service Board [*British*] .... PHLSB
Public Health Law .... PHL
Public Health Network [*Information service or system*] (IID) .... PHN
Public Health Nurse .... PHN
Public Health Nursing Division, Newfoundland Department of Health, St. John's, Newfoundland [*Library symbol National Library of Canada*] (NLC) .... NFSHPH
Public Health Reports [*A publication*] .... PHR
Public Health Research Institute (NADA) .... PHRI
Public Health Research Institute of the City of New York, Inc. [*Research center*] (RCD) .... PHRI
Public Health Risk Evaluation Data [*Environmental Safety*] .... PHRED
Public Health Service [*Department of Health and Human Services*] .... PHS
Public Health Service Acquisition Regulations [*Department of Health and Human Services*] (GFGA) .... PHSAR
Public Health Service Act (GFGA) .... PHSA
Public Health Service Building .... PHB
Public Health Service Publications .... PHSP
[*The*] **Public Historian** [*A publication*] .... Pub Hist
Public Holiday (DA) .... PH
Public House [*A drinking establishment*] [*British*] .... PH
Public House [*A drinking establishment*] [*British*] .... PUB
Public House (ODBW) .... pub
Public Houses [*Public-performance tariff class*] [*British*] .... P
Public Housing Administration [*or HHFA; disbanded 1965*] .... PHA
Public Housing Agencies (USGC) .... PHA
Public Housing Agency [*Department of Housing and Urban Development*] (GFGA) .... PHA
Public Housing Authorities Directors Association (EA) .... PHADA
Public Housing Development [*Department of Housing and Urban Development*] (GFGA) .... PHD
Public Housing Drug Elimination Act [*1988*] .... PHDEA
Public Information .... PI
Public Information Act .... PIA
Public Information Adviser [*NATO*] (NATG) .... PIA
Public Information Assist Team [*Environmental Protection Agency*] (ERG) .... PIAT
Public Information Center [*Nuclear energy*] (NRCH) .... PIC
Public Information Committee [*of the NATO Military Committee*] (NATG) .... PIC
Public Information Division [*Coast Guard symbol*] .... CPI
Public Information Division [*Army*] .... PID
Public Information in Rural Areas Technical Experiment (NITA) .... PIRATE
Public Information in Rural Areas Technology Experiment [*British Library*] (PDAA) .... PIRATE
Public Information Liaison Officer [*Military*] .... PILO
Public Information Office [*or Officer*] .... PIO
Public Information on Nuclear Energy Service [*American Nuclear Society*] .... PINES
Public Information Reference Unit [*Environmental Protection Agency*] (GFGA) .... PIRU
Public Interest [*A publication*] .... Pub Int
Public Interest Computer Association (EA) .... PICA
Public Interest Economics Center (EA) .... PIE-C
Public Interest Economics Foundation [*Defunct*] (EA) .... PIE
Public Interest Economics Foundation [*Defunct*] (EA) .... PIE-F
Public Interest Immunity Certificate [*British*] (ECON) .... PIIC
Public Interest Nongovernmental Organization .... PINGO
Public Interest Public Relations (EA) .... PIPR
Public Interest Research Group [*Formed by consumer-advocate Ralph Nader*] .... PIRG
Public Interest Satellite Association [*Defunct*] (EA) .... PISA
Public Interest Video Network/New Voices Radio (EA) .... PIVN
Public Intoxication Act [*Australia*] .... PIA
Public Investment Data System (MHDW) .... PIDS
Public Involvement Program (GNE) .... PIP
Public Key Cryptography .... PKC
Public Land Law Review [*A publication*] (DLA) .... Pub Land L Rev
Public Land Law Review Commission [*Terminated, 1970*] .... PLLRC
Public Land Mobile Service Data Base [*Comp Comm, Inc.*] [*Information service or system*] (CRD) .... PLMS
Public Land Order [*Interior*] .... PLO
Public Lands Appreciation Day [*A joint effort of Times Mirror Magazines and the Bureau of Land Management*] (PS) .... PLAD
Public Lands Appreciation Day .... PLAD
Public Lands Council (EA) .... PLC
Public Lands Foundation (EA) .... PLF
Public Lands Institute (EA) .... PLI
Public Law [*An act of Congress*] .... PL
Public Law (AAGC) .... Pub Law
Public Law Education Institute (EA) .... PLEI
Public Law Forum [*A publication*] (DLA) .... Pub LF
Public Law Review [*A publication*] .... PLR
Public Laws .... PULA
Public Laws of Rhode Island [*A publication*] (DLA) .... RI Pub Laws
Public Leadership Education Network (EA) .... PLEN
Public Lending Right [*Royalty for books borrowed from public libraries*] [*British*] .... PLR
Public Liability [*Business term*] .... PL
Public Liability and Property Damage [*Insurance*] .... PL & PD
Public Liability Company (DFIT) .... PLC
Public Libraries Automation Network [*California State Library*] [*Sacramento, CA*] .... PLAN
Public Libraries, Central Library, Merthyr-Tydfil, United Kingdom [*Library symbol Library of Congress*] (LCLS) .... UkMe
Public Libraries of Springfield and Greene County, Springfield, MO [*Library symbol Library of Congress*] (LCLS) .... MoSp
Public Library .... PL
Public Library Association (EA) .... PLA
Public Library Commission, Victoria, BC, Canada [*Library symbol Library of Congress*] (LCLS) .... CaBViLC
Public Library Data Service .... PLDS
Public Library Development Incentive Scheme [*British*] .... PLDIS
Public Library Development Plan [*American Library Association, Public Library Association*] .... PLDP
Public Library Entrepreneur of the Year Award [*Sponsored by Geac Computers Ltd.*] .... PLEYA
Public Library of Annapolis and Anne Arundel County, Annapolis, MD [*Library symbol Library of Congress*] (LCLS) .... MdAAC
Public Library of Brookline, Brookline, MA [*Library symbol Library of Congress*] (LCLS) .... MBr
Public Library of Charlotte and Mecklenburg County [*North Carolina*] .... PLCMC
Public Library of Charlotte and Mecklenburg County, Charlotte, NC [*Library symbol Library of Congress*] (LCLS) .... NcC
Public Library of Charlotte and Mecklenburg County, Charlotte, NC [*OCLC symbol*] (OCLC) .... NPC
Public Library of Cincinnati and Hamilton County, Cincinnati, OH [*Library symbol Library of Congress*] (LCLS) .... OC
Public Library of Cincinnati and Hamilton County, Cincinnati, OH [*OCLC symbol*] (OCLC) .... OCP
Public Library of Columbus and Franklin County, Columbus, OH [*OCLC symbol*] (OCLC) .... OCO
Public Library of Des Moines, Des Moines, IA [*OCLC symbol*] (OCLC) .... IOU
Public Library of Enid and Garfield County, Enid, OK [*OCLC symbol*] (OCLC) .... OEG
Public Library of Enid and Garfield County, Enid, OK [*Library symbol Library of Congress*] (LCLS) .... OkE
Public Library of Fort Wayne and Allen County, Fort Wayne, IN [*Library symbol Library of Congress*] (LCLS) .... InFw
Public Library of Knoxville and Knox County, Knoxville, TN [*Library symbol Library of Congress*] (LCLS) .... TKL
Public Library of Nashville and Davidson County, Nashville, TN [*Library symbol Library of Congress*] (LCLS) .... TN
Public Library of Natchez and Adams County, Natchez, MS [*Library symbol Library of Congress*] (LCLS) .... MsN
Public Library of Pine Bluff and Jefferson County, Pine Bluff, AR [*OCLC symbol*] (OCLC) .... APJ
Public Library of South Australia, Adelaide, SA, Australia [*Library symbol Library of Congress*] (LCLS) .... AuASA
Public Library of Steubenville and Jefferson County, Steubenville, OH [*Library symbol Library of Congress*] (LCLS) .... OSte

Public Library of the City of Somerville, Somerville, MA [Library symbol Library of Congress] (LCLS) .... MSo
Public Library of the District of Columbia, Martin Luther King Memorial Library, Washington, DC [Library symbol Library of Congress] (LCLS) ...... DWP
Public Library of Youngstown and Mahoning County, Youngstown, OH [Library symbol Library of Congress] (LCLS) .... OY
Public Library, Port Hope, ON, Canada [Library symbol Library of Congress] (LCLS) .... CaOPh
Public Library, Port Hope, Ontario [Library symbol National Library of Canada] (NLC) .... OPH
Public Library, St. James, MB, Canada [Library symbol Library of Congress] (LCLS) .... CaMStJ
Public Library, St. James-Assiniboia, Manitoba [Library symbol National Library of Canada] (NLC) .... MStJ
Public Library Services, Manitoba Department of Culture, Heritage and Recreation, Winnipeg, Manitoba [Library symbol National Library of Canada] (NLC) .... MWPL
Public Library, Sulphur Springs, AR [Library symbol Library of Congress] (LCLS) .... ArSuL
Public Library Systems Section [Public Library Association] .... PLSS
Public Light Bus [British] .... PLB
Public Lighting Commission .... PLC
Public Limited Co. [British] .... PLC
Public Links [Amateur golf] .... PUBLINX
Public Management Sources [A publication] .... PMS
Public Media Center (EA) .... PMC
Public Members Association of the Foreign Service (EA) .... PMAFS
Public Message Service [Western Union Corp.] .... PMS
Public Mobile Radio (WDMC) .... PMR
Public Network [Telecommunications] .... PN
Public Offender Counselors Association [Later, IAAOC] (EA) .... POCA
Public Offering [Investment term] .... PO
Public Offering Price (AD) .... POP
Public Office [British] (ROG) .... PO
Public Office of Information (MCD) .... POI
Public Official .... PO
Public Oil Co. (AD) .... POC
Public Opinion Laboratory [Northern Illinois University] [Research center] (RCD) .... POL
Public Opinion Location Library [The Roper Center for Public Opinion Research] [Information service or system] (CRD) .... POLL
Public Opinion Quarterly [A publication] (AD) .... POQ
Public Opinion Quarterly [A publication] (BRI) .... Pub Op Q
Public Opinion Research (AD) .... por
Public Order Act .... POA
Public Oversight Board .... POB
Public Packet Network [Computer science] (ODBW) .... PPN
Public Packet Switched [or Switching] **Network** [Telecommunications] .... PPSN
Public Packet Switching Service (NITA) .... PPSS
Public Papers of the President [A publication] (DLA) .... Pub Papers
Public Parks Advisory Committee [South Australia] .... PPAC
Public Participation Library, Regina, Saskatchewan [Library symbol National Library of Canada] (BIB) .... SRPP
Public Pension Offset [Federal Employees Retirement System] (GFGA) .... PPO
Public Personnel Association [Later, IPMA] (EA) .... PPA
Public Policy Affecting Women Task Force (EA) .... PPAW
Public Policy and Government Relations Council .... PPGRC
Public Policy Education Fund (EA) .... PPEF
Public Policy for Public Libraries Section [Public Library Association] [American Library Association] .... PPPLS
Public Policy Program [Australian National University] .... PPP
Public Policy Task Force [Defunct] (EA) .... PPTF
Public/Private Ventures [Philadelphia, PA] [Research center] (RCD) .... P/PV
Public Property .... PP
Public Quarters .... PQ
Public Radio in Mid-America (NTCM) .... PRIMA
Public Radio International .... PRI
Public Rangelands Improvement Act of 1978 .... PRIA
Public Record Office [British] .... PRO
Public Record Office, London, United Kingdom [Library symbol Library of Congress] (LCLS) .... UkLPR
Public Relations (AD) .... pr
Public Relations .... PR
Public Relations .... Pub Rel
Public Relations Advisory Committee .... PRAC
Public Relations Bulletin [American Bar Association A publication] (DLA) .... Pub Rel Bull
Public Relations Club (AD) .... PRC
Public Relations Consultants Association (EAIO) .... PRCA
Public Relations Exchange [Later, PRXI] (EA) .... PRE
Public Relations Foundation .... PRF
Public Relations Institute of Ireland (BI) .... PRI
Public Relations Journal [A publication] (BRI) .... Pub Rel J
Public Relations Office [or Officer] [Usually military] .... PRO
Public Relations Office of the Sugar Industry .... PROSI
Public Relations Personnel [Navy] .... PRP
Public Relations Policy Committee [NATO] (NATG) .... PRPC
Public Relations Section [Library Administration and Management Association] .... PRS
Public Relations Society of America (EA) .... PRSA
Public Relations Society of America Online Information Service (IID) .... PRLINK
Public Relations Student Society of America (EA) .... PRSSA
Public Release of Information and Transcripts [Student legal action organization] .... PRINT
Public Research and Development .... PR & D

Public Residential Facility .... PRF
Public Resolution (AAGC) .... Pub Res
Public Resolution Number [Congress] (ILCA) .... Pub Res No
Public Resources Association [Defunct] (EA) .... PRA
Public Resources Code [California] [A publication] (ILCA) .... Pub Res C
Public Responsibility .... PR
Public Responsibility in Medicine and Research (EA) .... PRIM & R
Public Revenue Education Council (EA) .... PREC
Public Risk and Insurance Management Association [Washington, DC] (EA) .... PRIMA
Public Roads Administration .... PRA
Public Roads Bureau .... PRB
Public Safety [FCC] (NTCM) .... P
Public Safety and Training Association (NADA) .... PSTA
Public Safety Answering Point [Telecommunications] (TEL) .... PSAP
Public Safety Officer .... PSO
Public Sale .... PS
Public School .... PS
Public School Bursars' Association [British] (BI) .... PSBA
Public School League [Sports] .... PSL
Public School System Blanket Bond [Insurance] .... PSSBB
Public School Word-Book [A publication] .... PSWB
Public Schools Athletic League .... PSAL
Public Sector and Broadcasting Union [Australia] .... PSBU
Public Sector Borrowing Requirement .... PSBR
Public Sector Debt Repayment [British] (ECON) .... PSDR
Public Sector Economics Research Centre [University of Leicester] [British] (CB) .... PSERC
Public Sector [or Service] **Employment** .... PSE
Public Sector Financial Deficit .... PSFD
Public Securities Association [Database producer] (EA) .... PSA
Public Security Investigation Agency [Japan] (CINC) .... PSIA
Public Servants' Housing and Finance Association [British] (BI) .... PSHFA
Public Service .... PS
Public Service 2000 Program [Canada] PS2000
Public Service Act .... PSA
Public Service Alliance of Canada [Labor union of federal government employees] .... PSAC
Public Service Alliance of Canada, Ottawa, ON, Canada [Library symbol Library of Congress] (LCLS) .... CaOOPSAC
Public Service Alliance of Canada [Alliance de la Fonction Publique du Canada] **Ottawa, Ontario** [Library symbol National Library of Canada] (NLC) .... OOPSAC
Public Service Announcement .... PSA
Public Service Answering Point .... PSAP
Public Service Association of South Australia .... PSASA
Public Service Board (NADA) .... PSB
Public Service Board Victoria [Australia] .... PSBV
Public Service Careers [Program] [Department of Labor] .... PSC
Public Service Careers Program [Department of Labor] .... PSCP
Public Service Commission [Usually, of a specific state] .... PSC
Public Service Commission [Usually, of a specific state] (DLA) ...... Pub Ser Comm
Public Service Commission, Baton Rouge, LA [Library symbol Library of Congress] (LCLS) .... LBrPS
Public Service Commission, Ottawa, ON, Canada [Library symbol Library of Congress] (LCLS) .... CaOOCS
Public Service Commission [Commission de la Fonction Publique] **Ottawa, Ontario** [Library symbol National Library of Canada] (NLC) .... OOCS
Public Service Commission Reports [A publication] (DLA) .... PSCR
Public Service Commission, Training Centres Libraries, Ottawa, ON, Canada [Library symbol Library of Congress] (LCLS) .... CaOOCSL
Public Service Co. .... PSC
Public Service Co. North Carolina [NYSE symbol] (SAG) .... PGS
Public Service Co. North Carolina [Associated Press] (SAG) .... PubSNC
Public Service Co. of Colorado [Associated Press] (SAG) .... PSCol
Public Service Company of Colorado [AMEX symbol] (SAG) .... PSR
Public Service Co. of Colorado [NYSE symbol] (SPSG) .... PSR
Public Service Co. of Colorado [Associated Press] (SAG) .... PSvCol
Public Service Co. of Colorado, Denver, CO [Library symbol Library of Congress] (LCLS) .... CoDP
Public Service Co. of New Mexico [NYSE symbol] (SPSG) .... PNM
Public Service Co. of New Mexico [Associated Press] (SAG) .... PSvNM
Public Service Elec & Gas Co. [NYSE symbol] (SAG) .... PEG
Public Service Electric & Gas Co. (CDAI) .... PEG
Public Service Electric & Gas Co. .... PSE & G
Public Service Electric & Gas Co. [Associated Press] (SAG) .... PSEG
Public Service Electric & Gas Co., Newark, NJ [Library symbol] [Library of Congress] (LCLS) .... NjNPSE
Public Service Electric & Gas Co., Newark, NJ [OCLC symbol] (OCLC) .... PSE
Public Service Enterprise Group, Inc. [NYSE symbol] (SPSG) .... PEG
Public Service Job (OICC) .... PSJ
Public Service Medal .... PSM
Public Service Obligation [Australia] .... PSO
Public Service Organisation [Government grant] [British] .... PSO
Public Service Research Council (EA) .... PSRC
Public Service Review [A publication] .... Publ Serv Rev
Public Service Satellite Consortium (EA) .... PSSC
Public Service Senior Executive Service [Australia] .... PSSES
Public Service Staff Relations Act [Canada] .... PSSRA
Public Service Staff Relations Board [Canada] .... PSSRB
Public Service Staff Relations Board, Ottawa, ON, Canada [Library symbol Library of Congress] (LCLS) .... CaOOPS
Public Service Staff Relations Board [Commission des Relations de Travail dans la Fonction Publique] **Ottawa, Ontario** [Library symbol National Library of Canada] (NLC) .... OOPS

Public Service Vehicle ... PSV
Public Service Workers' Trade Union Federation [*Ceylon*] ... PSWTUF
Public Services International [*See also ISP*] [*Ferney Voltaire, France*] (EAIO) ... PSI
Public Services Satellite ... PSS
Public Services Temporary Clerks' Association [*A union*] [*British*] ... PSTCA
Public Services Unit (EERA) ... PSU
Public Social Responsibility [*Unit of the Anglican Church of Canada General Synod*] ... PSR
Public Speaking and Humor Club (EA) ... PSHC
Public Statutes [*Legal term*] (DLA) ... PS
Public Statutes [*A publication*] (DLA) ... Pub St
Public Stenographer ... PS
Public Storage [*NYSE symbol*] (TTSB) ... PSA
Public Storage 10% cm'A'Pfd [*NYSE symbol*] (TTSB) ... PSAPrA
Public Storage 10%'E'Pfd [*NYSE symbol*] (TTSB) ... PSAPrE
Public Storage 8.25%Cv Pfd [*NYSE symbol*] (TTSB) ... PSAPrX
Public Storage 8.45%'H'Dep Pfd [*NYSE symbol*] (TTSB) ... PSAPrH
Public Storage 9.20% cm'B'Pfd [*NYSE symbol*] (TTSB) ... PSAPrB
Public Storage 9.50%'D'Pfd [*NYSE symbol*] (TTSB) ... PSAPrD
Public Storage 9.75% 'F' Pfd [*NYSE symbol*] (TTSB) ... PSAPrF
Public Storage 8.875% Dep Pfd [*NYSE symbol*] (TTSB) ... PSAPrG
Public Storage Adj Rt'C'Pfd [*NYSE symbol*] (TTSB) ... PSAPrC
Public Storage Canadian Properties [*Limited Partnership Units*] [*Toronto Stock Exchange symbol*] ... PSP
Public Storage Canadian Properties II [*Limited Partnership Units*] [*Toronto Stock Exchange symbol*] ... PSS
Public Storage Canadian Properties IIIa Ltd. [*Toronto Stock Exchange symbol*] ... PSH
Public Storage, Inc. [*NYSE symbol*] (SAG) ... PSA
Public Storage, Inc. [*Associated Press*] (SAG) ... PubSt
Public Storage, Inc. [*Associated Press*] (SAG) ... PubStrg
Public Storage Prop'A' X [*AMEX symbol*] (TTSB) ... PSL
Public Storage Prop'A' XI [*AMEX symbol*] (TTSB) ... PSM
Public Storage Prop'A' XII [*AMEX symbol*] (TTSB) ... PSN
Public Storage Prop'A' XIV [*AMEX symbol*] (TTSB) ... PSP
Public Storage Prop'A' XIX [*AMEX symbol*] (TTSB) ... PSY
Public Storage Prop'A' XV [*AMEX symbol*] (TTSB) ... PSQ
Public Storage Prop'A' XX [*AMEX symbol*] (TTSB) ... PSZ
Public Storage Prop'A'XVI [*AMEX symbol*] (TTSB) ... PSU
Public Storage Prop'A'XVII [*AMEX symbol*] (TTSB) ... PSV
Public Storage Prop'A'XVIII [*AMEX symbol*] (TTSB) ... PSW
Public Storage Properties IX [*Associated Press*] (SAG) ... PbSt9
Public Storage Properties IX, Inc. [*AMEX symbol*] (SAG) ... PSK
Public Storage Properties X, Inc. [*Associated Press*] (SAG) ... PbSt 10
Public Storage Properties X, Inc. [*AMEX symbol*] (SAG) ... PSL
Public Storage Properties XI, Inc. [*Associated Press*] (SAG) ... PbSt 11
Public Storage Properties XI, Inc. [*AMEX symbol*] (SAG) ... PSM
Public Storage Properties XII, Inc. [*Associated Press*] (SAG) ... PbSt 12
Public Storage Properties XII, Inc. [*AMEX symbol*] (SAG) ... PSN
Public Storage Properties XIV, Inc. [*Associated Press*] (SAG) ... PbSt14
Public Storage Properties XIV, Inc. [*AMEX symbol*] (SAG) ... PSP
Public Storage Properties XIX, Inc. [*Associated Press*] (SAG) ... PbSt19
Public Storage Properties XIX, Inc. [*AMEX symbol*] (SAG) ... PSY
Public Storage Properties XV [*AMEX symbol*] (SPSG) ... PSQ
Public Storage Properties XV, Inc. [*Associated Press*] (SAG) ... PbSt15
Public Storage Properties XVI [*AMEX symbol*] (SPSG) ... PSU
Public Storage Properties XVI, Inc. [*Associated Press*] (SAG) ... PbSt16
Public Storage Properties XVII, Inc. [*Associated Press*] (SAG) ... PbSt17
Public Storage Properties XVII, Inc. [*AMEX symbol*] (SAG) ... PSV
Public Storage Properties XVIII [*AMEX symbol*] (SPSG) ... PSW
Public Storage Properties XVIII, Inc. [*Associated Press*] (SAG) ... PbSt18
Public Storage Properties XX [*AMEX symbol*] (SPSG) ... PSZ
Public Storage Properties XX, Inc. [*Associated Press*] (SAG) ... PbSt20
Public Strategies Group, Inc. [*Consulting firm hired in 1993 to improve Minneapolis school district*] (ECON) ... PSG
Public Sustained Yield Unit [*Forestry*] ... PSYU
Public Sv E&G 7.40% cm Pfd [*NYSE symbol*] (TTSB) ... PEGPrI
Public Svc E&G Cap 8.00%'MIPS' [*NYSE symbol*] (TTSB) ... PEGPrX
Public Svc E&G Cap 9.375% 'MIPS' [*NYSE symbol*] (TTSB) ... PEGPrZ
Public Svc Enterpr [*NYSE symbol*] (TTSB) ... PEG
Public Svc New Mexico [*NYSE symbol*] (TTSB) ... PNM
Public Svc No Car [*NYSE symbol*] (TTSB) ... PGS
Public SvcColorado [*NYSE symbol*] (TTSB) ... PSR
Public Switched Data Network (NITA) ... PSDN
Public Switched Data Service [*Telecommunications*] ... PSDS
Public Switched Digital Service [*Computer science*] (TNIG) ... PSDS
Public Switched Network (BUR) ... PSN
Public Switched Telephone Circuits [*Telecommunications*] (TEL) ... PSTC
Public Switched Telephone Network ... PSTN
Public Technology, Inc. [*Research center*] (RCD) ... PTI
Public Telecommunications Facilities Program [*Department of Commerce*] ... PTFP
Public Telecommunications Financial Management Association (EA) ... PTFMA
Public Telecommunications Operator (NITA) ... PTO
Public Telecommunications Trust [*Proposed replacement for Corporation for Public Broadcasting*] ... PTT
Public Telephone Network (DA) ... PTN
Public Telephone Service [*or System*] [*Telecommunications*] (TEL) ... PTS
Public Television ... PTV
Public Television Library ... PTL
Public Telex Access Unit [*Telecommunications*] (OSI) ... PLTXAU
Public Tenants' Union of Victoria [*Australia*] ... PTUV
Public Tool Interface [*Computer science*] (ODBW) ... PTI
Public Transport (DA) ... PT
Public Transportation Facilities and Equipment Management System [*FHWA*] (TAG) ... PTMS
Public Trust Office [*Australia*] ... PTO
Public Trustee ... PT
Public Trustee Office (DLA) ... PTO
Public Understanding of Science Program (EDAC) ... PUOS
Public Urban Locator Service ... PULSE
Public Use Microdata Sample [*Bureau of the Census*] (GFGA) ... PUMS
Public Use Sample Helper (PDAA) ... PUSH
Public Utilities Advertising Association [*Later, PUCA*] (EA) ... PUAA
Public Utilities Board (NADA) ... PUB
Public Utilities Code [*A publication*] (DLA) ... Pub Util C
Public Utilities Commission ... PUC
Public Utilities Communicators Association [*Later, UCI*] [*New Castle, PA*] (EA) ... PUCA
Public Utilities Law Anthology [*A publication*] (DLA) ... Pub Util L Anthol
Public Utilities Panel [*EECE*] ... PUP
Public Utilities Regulatory Policy Act [*1978*] ... PURPA
Public Utilities Reports [*A publication*] (DLA) ... Pub U Rep
Public Utilities Reports [*A publication*] (DLA) ... Pub Util Rep
Public Utilities Reports [*A publication Information service or system*] (IID) ... PUR
Public Utilities Reports, New Series [*A publication*] (DLA) ... PUR (NS)
Public Utilities Reports, Third Series [*A publication*] (DLA) ... PUR 3d
Public Utilities Review Act [*1934*] ... PURA
Public Utility Co. ... PUC
Public Utility District [*Bonds*] ... PUD
Public Utility Holding Co. Act of 1935 ... PUHCA
Public Utility Research Center [*University of Florida*] [*Research center*] (RCD) ... PURC
Public Vehicle Operators' Association [*Later, CBRPT*] [*British*] (DI) ... PVOA
Public Voice for Food and Health Policy (EA) ... PVFHP
Public Volunteer ... PV
Public Voucher ... PV
Public Water Supply System (GFGA) ... PWSS
Public Water System (GFGA) ... PWS
Public Watering Place (ADA) ... PWP
Public Welfare ... PW
Public Windows Interface [*Computer science*] (PCM) ... PWI
Public Workers and Constructional Operatives' Union [*British*] ... PWCOU
Public Works ... PW
Public Works Administration [*All functions transferred to office of Federal Works Agency, 1943*] ... PWA
Public Works and Economic Development Act ... PWEDA
Public Works and Economic Development Association (EA) ... PWEDA
Public Works and Government Services Canada (ACII) ... PWGSC
Public Works Canada [*See also TPC*] ... PWC
Public Works Canada, Atlantic Regional Library, Halifax, NS, Canada [*Library symbol Library of Congress*] (LCLS) ... CaNSHPW
Public Works Canada, Ontario Regional Library, Toronto, ON, Canada [*Library symbol Library of Congress*] (LCLS) ... CaOTPWC
Public Works Canada [*Travaux Publics Canada*] **Ottawa, Ontario** [*Library symbol National Library of Canada*] (NLC) ... OOPW
Public Works Canada, Pacific Region Library, Vancouver, BC, Canada [*Library symbol*] [*Library of Congress*] (LCLS) ... CaBVaPWP
Public Works Canada, Quebec Region Library, Montreal, PQ, Canada [*Library symbol*] [*Library of Congress*] (LCLS) ... CaQMPWQ
Public Works Canada, Western Regional Library, Edmonton, AB, Canada [*Library symbol*] [*Library of Congress*] (LCLS) ... CaAEPWW
Public Works Center [*Navy*] ... PWC
Public Works Center [*Navy*] ... PWCEN
Public Works Center Activity Civil Engineer [*Navy*] (DNAB) ... PWCACE
Public Works Center, Atlantic [*Navy*] ... PWCLANT
Public Works Center Detachment [*Navy*] (DNAB) ... PWCDET
Public Works Center Management Information System [*Navy*] (DNAB) ... PWCMIS
Public Works Center Management System [*Navy*] ... PWCMS
Public Works Center, Pacific [*Navy*] ... PWCPAC
Public Works Department [*Navy*] ... PWD
Public Works Department (NADA) ... PWD
Public Works Department [*Navy*] ... PWDEPT
Public Works Developmental Management System [*Navy*] ... PWDMS
Public Works Emergency Housing Corp. [*New Deal*] ... PWEHC
Public Works Employment Act (AAGC) ... PWEA
Public Works Historical Society (EA) ... PWHS
Public Works Loan Board [*British*] ... PWLB
Public Works Management System [*Navy*] ... PWMS
Public Works of Art Projects [*New Deal*] ... PWAP
Public Works Officer [*Navy*] ... PWO
Public Works Planning (GFGA) ... PWP
Public Works Training Center [*Navy*] ... PWTC
Public Works Transportation Center (MCD) ... PWTC
Public Worship Regulation Act [*1874*] [*British*] (ROG) ... PWR
Publicacoes Tecnicas Internacionais Ltda. [*International Technical Publications Ltd.*] [*Information service or system*] (IID) ... PTI
Publically-Owned Treatment Works (DNAB) ... POTW
Publication (AFM) ... PUB
Publication (WDMC) ... pub
Publication [*or Published or Publisher*] (EY) ... PUBL
Publication ... PUBLCTN
Publication (MSA) ... PUBN
Publication Analysis Report (SAA) ... PAR
Publication Announcement ... PA
Publication Authority Form (AAG) ... PAF
Publication Automated Information Locator System [*Army*] ... PAILS
Publication Change Notice (MCD) ... PCN

Publication Change Request (MCD) .... PCR
Publication Contract Requirements .... PCR
Publication Control Sheet (MCD) .... PCS
Publication Date [*Online database field identifier*] .... PD
Publication Design and Ad Placement (DGA) .... PDAP
Publication Identification Number [*Military*] (INF) .... PIN
Publication Information Processing and Printing System .... PIPPS
Publication Information Register (IAA) .... PIR
Publication Instructions .... PI
Publication of the Modern Language Association of America (AD) .... PMLA
Publication Revision Request (AAG) .... PRR
Publication Series .... PUBS
Publication Standard .... PS
Publication Systems Associates, Inc. [*Information service or system*] (IID) .... PSA
Publication Text Management System (MCD) .... PTMS
Publication Type [*Online database field identifier*] .... PT
Publication Work Request (MCD) .... PWR
Publication Year [*Online database field identifier*] .... PY
Publications .... P
Publications (NITA) .... PB
Publications (MCD) .... PU
Publications (CDAI) .... PUBS
Publications Account Number [*DoD*] .... PAN
Publications Allowance List [*Military*] (CAAL) .... PAL
Publications. American Archaeological Expedition to Syria [*A publication*] (BJA) .... PAAES
Publications and Films Review Board [*Western Australia*] .... PFRB
Publications and Information Section, Mineral Development Division Library, Newfoundland Department of Mines and Energy, St. John's, Newfoundland [*Library symbol National Library of Canada*] (NLC) .... NFSMEM
Publications and Printing Office [*Army*] .... PPO
Publications and Technical Literature Research Section [*Environmental Protection Agency*] (IID) .... PTLRS
Publications Board [*Later, CFSTI, NTIS*] .... PB
Publications Bulletin .... PB
Publications Contract Coverage Schedule (MCD) .... PCCS
Publications Control Officer [*DoD*] .... PCO
Publications Data Request .... PDR
Publications Distribution Center [*Military*] (AFM) .... PDC
Publications Distribution Manager [*Military*] (AFM) .... PDM
Publications Distribution Officer [*Military*] .... PDO
Publications in Climatology (MCD) .... PC
Publications Indexed for Engineering [*A publication*] .... PIE
Publications International Ltd. .... PIL
Publications of the Institute for Research in Construction [*National Research Council of Canada*] [*Information service or system*] (IID) .... IRCPUBS
Publications Reference File [*Government Printing Office*] [*Database*] [*Washington, DC*] (MCD) .... PRF
Publications Requirements List (NG) .... PRL
Publications Requirements Manager [*DoD*] .... PRM
Publications Requirements Tables (AAG) .... PRT
Publications Special Assistance Team [*Military*] .... PUBSAT
Publications Standing Instruction (AAG) .... PSI
Publications Statistiques Hongroises [*Hungary*] .... PSH
Publications Supply Officer [*Military*] .... PSO
Public-General Hospital Section [*American Hospital Association*] (EA) .... PGHS
Publicist .... public
Publicity .... PUB
Publicity and Psychological Warfare .... P & PW
Publicity Man [*Slang*] .... PM
Publicity Man (AD) .... pm
Publicity Release (NTCM) .... PR
Publicity Security Officer [*Navy*] .... PSO
Publicker Indus [*NYSE symbol*] (TTSB) .... PUL
Publicker Industries, Inc. [*Associated Press*] (SAG) .... Publick
Publicker Industries, Inc. [*NYSE symbol*] (SPSG) .... PUL
Public-Key Encryption [*Microcomputer technology*] .... PKE
Publicly Available Price Cap Agreements (AAGC) .... PAPCAPS
Publicly Owned Treatment Works (EG) .... POTW
Public-Private Interface .... PPI
Public-Private Task Force .... PPTF
Publish (FAAC) .... PUBL
Publish Australia Group Enterprise .... PAGE
Publish or Perish [*Said of scholars, scientists, etc.*] .... P or P
Published (AABC) .... PUB
Published (WDMC) .... pub
Published (ROG) .... PUBD
Published (ROG) .... PUBLD
Published Data Tape [*A. C. Nielsen Co.*] [*A publication*] (WDMC) .... PDT
Published Internal Revenue Mimeograph [*A publication*] (DLA) .... IR-MIM
Published Price [*of a book*] .... PP
Publisher (NITA) .... PB
Publisher [*MARC relator code*] [*Library of Congress*] (LCCP) .... pbl
Publisher [*Online database field identifier*] .... PU
Publisher .... PUB
Publisher (WDMC) .... pub
Publisher .... PUBLR
Publisher .... PUBLR
Publisher Management System (NITA) .... PMS
Publisher/Vendor/Library Relations [*Committee of Association for Library Collections and Technical Services*] .... PVLR
Publishers' Accounts Clearing House [*British*] (BI) .... PACH
Publishers' Ad Club [*New York, NY*] (EA) .... PAC
Publishers' Alliance [*Defunct*] (EA) .... PA
Publishers' Association [*London, England*] (DIT) .... PA
Publishers' Binding (DGA) .... PB
Publisher's Binding (DGA) .... PUB BDG
Publisher's Central Bureau .... PCB
[*The*] **Publishers' Circular** [*A publication*] (ROG) .... PC
Publishers' Data Center, Inc. .... PDC
Publishers Data Service Corp. [*Monterey, CA*] .... PDSC
Publishers' Databases Ltd. [*Publishing consortium*] [*British*] .... PDL
Publisher's Directory [*Formerly, BPD*] [*A publication*] .... PD
Publishers Discount Option List .... PDOL
Publishers for Peace [*An association*] .... PFP
Publishers Information Bureau [*New York, NY*] (EA) .... PIB
Publishers' Information Card [*Later, IBIS*] [*British*] .... PIC
Publisher's Library Binding .... PLB
Publishers' Library Marketing Group [*Defunct*] (EA) .... PLMG
Publishers' Library Promotion Group [*Later, PLMG*] (EA) .... PLPG
Publishers Licensing Society (DGA) .... PLS
Publishers Marketing Association (EA) .... PMA
Publisher's Name [*Online database field identifier*] .... PB
Publisher's Name [*Online database field identifier*] .... PN
Publishers Newspaper Syndicate .... PNS
Publishers' Parcels Delivery Service (AD) .... PPDS
Publishers' Publicity Association (EA) .... PPA
Publishers Publicity Circle .... PPC
Publisher's Ream (DGA) .... PUB RM
Publishers' Trade List Annual .... PTLA
Publishers Weekly [*A publication*] (BRI) .... PW
Publishers Weekly [*A publication*] (WDMC) .... PW
Publishers' Weekly Announcements [*Title changed to Forthcoming Books*] [*A publication*] .... PWA
Publishing .... PBLSHNG
Publishing (DCTA) .... PUBLSHG
Publishing Center for Cultural Resources [*Defunct*] (EA) .... PCCR
Publishing Co. North Amer [*NASDAQ symbol*] (TTSB) .... PCNA
Publishing Co. of North America, Inc. (The) [*Associated Press*] (SAG) .... PbCoNA
Publishing Co. of North America, Inc. (The) [*NASDAQ symbol*] (SAG) .... PCNA
Publishing Employees Organizing Committee [*AFL-CIO*] .... PEOC
Publishing, Entertainment, Advertising, and Allied Fields Law Quarterly [*A publication*] (DLA) .... Pub Ent Advert & Allied Fields LQ
Publishing Interchange Language [*Computer science*] (CDE) .... PIL
Publishing Manufacturers Executive Association (EA) .... PMEA
Publishing Services [*American Library Association*] .... PS
Publishing Systems Group [*Later, CPSUG*] (EA) .... PSG
Publishing Technology Corp. [*Information service or system*] (IID) .... PTC
Pubococcygeus [*Muscle*] [*Anatomy*] .... PC
Pubococcygeus [*Muscle*] [*Anatomy*] (DAVI) .... PC
Pubococcygeus [*Muscle*] [*Anatomy*] (DAVI) .... PCG
Pubococcygeus [*Muscle*] (BABM) .... PCG
Pucacaca [*Peru*] [*ICAO location identifier*] (ICLI) .... SPCP
Pucallpa [*Peru*] [*Airport symbol*] (OAG) .... PCL
Pucallpa [*Peru*] [*ICAO location identifier*] (ICLI) .... SPCL
Puchase Request Order .... PRO
Puchuni [*Bolivia*] [*ICAO location identifier*] (ICLI) .... SLPU
Pucklechurch [*England*] .... PUCK
Pudasjarvi [*Finland ICAO location identifier*] (ICLI) .... EFPU
Pudding [*Phonetic alphabet*] [*Royal Navy World War I*] (DSUE) .... P
Pudding (BARN) .... pud
Pudendal [*Anatomy*] (MAE) .... pdl
Pudendal (DMAA) .... PUD
Pudgie's Chicken [*NASDAQ symbol*] (TTSB) .... PUDG
Pudgies Chicken, Inc. [*NASDAQ symbol*] (SAG) .... PUDG
Pudgies Chicken, Inc. [*Associated Press*] (SAG) .... Pudgie
Pudgies Chicken, Inc. [*Associated Press*] (SAG) .... Pudgies
Pudgies Chicken Wrrt [*NASDAQ symbol*] (TTSB) .... PUDGW
Puebla [*Mexico ICAO location identifier*] (ICLI) .... MMPB
Puebla [*Mexico*] [*Seismograph station code, US Geological Survey Closed*] (SEIS) .... PUE
Puebla Institute (EA) .... PI
Pueblo [*Diocesan abbreviation*] [*Colorado*] (TOCD) .... PBL
Pueblo [*Colorado*] [*Airport symbol*] (OAG) .... PUB
Pueblo Army Depot [*Colorado*] .... PAD
Pueblo Army Depot [*Colorado*] (AABC) .... PUAD
Pueblo Army Depot Activity (AABC) .... PUADA
Pueblo, Cambio, y Democracia - Partido Roldosista Popular [*People, Change, and Democracy - Popular Roldosista Party*] [*Ecuador*] [*Political party*] (PPW) .... PCD-PRP
Pueblo, CO [*FM radio station call letters*] .... KCCY
Pueblo, CO [*FM radio station call letters*] (RBYB) .... KCFP-FM
Pueblo, CO [*AM radio station call letters*] .... KCSJ
Pueblo, CO [*AM radio station call letters*] .... KDZA
Pueblo, CO [*FM radio station call letters*] (RBYB) .... KDZA-FM
Pueblo, CO [*FM radio station call letters*] .... KERP
Pueblo, CO [*AM radio station call letters*] .... KFEL
Pueblo, CO [*FM radio station call letters*] .... KGFT
Pueblo, CO [*AM radio station call letters*] .... KGHF
Pueblo, CO [*FM radio station call letters*] .... KKMG
Pueblo, CO [*FM radio station call letters*] .... KKPC
Pueblo, CO [*AM radio station call letters*] (RBYB) .... KKPC-AM
Pueblo, CO [*FM radio station call letters*] .... KNKN
Pueblo, CO [*Television station call letters*] .... KOAA
Pueblo, CO [*AM radio station call letters*] .... KRMX
Pueblo, CO [*AM radio station call letters*] .... KRRU
Pueblo, CO [*FM radio station call letters*] .... KTSC
Pueblo, CO [*Television station call letters*] .... KTSC-TV
Pueblo, CO [*FM radio station call letters*] .... KVUU
Pueblo, CO [*FM radio station call letters*] .... KYZX

Pueblo, CO [*Location identifier FAA*] (FAAL) .... PUB
Pueblo, CO [*Location identifier FAA*] (FAAL) .... TFR
Pueblo Community College, Pueblo, CO [*Library symbol*] [*Library of Congress*] (LCLS) .... CoPCC
Pueblo Depot Activity [*Colorado*] [*Army*] .... PUDA
Pueblo Memorial [*Colorado*] [*ICAO location identifier*] (ICLI) .... KPUB
Pueblo Regional Library, Pueblo, CO [*Library symbol Library of Congress*] (LCLS) .... CoP
Pueblo to People (EA) .... PTP
Pueblo Viejo [*Peru*] [*Seismograph station code, US Geological Survey Closed*] (SEIS) .... PVP
Puelches [*Argentina ICAO location identifier*] (ICLI) .... SAZU
Puella Americana Vallensis [*Valley Girl*] [*Teenaged girl who follows the fads, fashions, and slang originated among teenagers in California's San Fernando Valley*] .... PAV
Puerperal Ovarian-Vein Thrombophlebitis [*Medicine*] .... POVT
Puerta Galera [*Philippines*] [*Seismograph station code, US Geological Survey*] (SEIS) .... PGP
Puerto Armuellas [*Panama*] [*Airport symbol*] (AD) .... AML
Puerto Asis [*Colombia*] [*Airport symbol*] (OAG) .... PUU
Puerto Asis [*Colorado ICAO location identifier*] (ICLI) .... SKAS
Puerto Ayacucho [*Venezuela*] [*Airport symbol*] (OAG) .... PYH
Puerto Ayacucho, T. F. Amazonas [*Venezuela ICAO location identifier*] (ICLI) .... SVPA
Puerto Aysen [*Chile*] [*Airport symbol*] (AD) .... WPA
Puerto Barrios [*Guatemala*] [*ICAO location identifier*] (ICLI) .... MGPB
Puerto Barrios [*Guatemala*] [*Airport symbol*] (AD) .... PBR
Puerto Bermudez [*Peru*] [*ICAO location identifier*] (ICLI) .... SPEZ
Puerto Berrio [*Colombia*] [*Airport symbol*] (OAG) .... PBE
Puerto Bolivar/Riohacha [*Colorado ICAO location identifier*] (ICLI) .... SKPB
Puerto Cabello [*Venezuela*] [*Airport symbol*] (OAG) .... PBL
Puerto Cabello/Gral. Bartolome Salom Internacional, Carabobo [*Venezuela ICAO location identifier*] (ICLI) .... SVPC
Puerto Cabezas [*Nicaragua*] [*ICAO location identifier*] (ICLI) .... MNPC
Puerto Cabezas [*Nicaragua*] [*Airport symbol*] (AD) .... PUZ
Puerto Carreno [*Colombia*] [*Airport symbol*] (OAG) .... PCR
Puerto Carreno [*Colorado ICAO location identifier*] (ICLI) .... SKPC
Puerto Castilla [*Honduras*] [*ICAO location identifier*] (ICLI) .... MHCT
Puerto Cortes [*Honduras*] [*ICAO location identifier*] (ICLI) .... MHPU
Puerto Del Rosario/Fuerteventura [*Canary Islands*] [*ICAO location identifier*] (ICLI) .... GCFV
Puerto Deseado [*Argentina*] [*Airport symbol*] (OAG) .... PUD
Puerto Deseado [*Argentina ICAO location identifier*] (ICLI) .... SAWD
Puerto Escondido [*Mexico ICAO location identifier*] (ICLI) .... MMPS
Puerto Esperanza [*Peru*] [*ICAO location identifier*] (ICLI) .... SPEP
Puerto Inca [*Peru*] [*ICAO location identifier*] (ICLI) .... SPTI
Puerto Inirida [*Colombia*] [*Airport symbol*] (OAG) .... PDA
Puerto Jimenez [*Costa Rica*] [*ICAO location identifier*] (ICLI) .... MRPJ
Puerto Leguizamo [*Colombia*] [*Airport symbol*] (OAG) .... LQM
Puerto Lempira [*Honduras*] [*ICAO location identifier*] (ICLI) .... MHPL
Puerto Lempira [*Honduras*] [*Airport symbol*] (AD) .... PRS
Puerto Lopez [*Colombia*] [*Airport symbol*] (AD) .... PRM
Puerto Madryn [*Argentina ICAO location identifier*] (ICLI) .... SAVY
Puerto Maldonado [*Peru*] [*Airport symbol*] (AD) .... MDD
Puerto Maldonado [*Peru*] [*Airport symbol*] (OAG) .... PEM
Puerto Maldonado/Padre Aldamiz [*Peru*] [*ICAO location identifier*] (ICLI) .... SPTU
Puerto Montt [*Chile*] [*Airport symbol*] (OAG) .... PMC
Puerto Montt [*Chile*] [*ICAO location identifier*] (ICLI) .... SCTZ
Puerto Montt/Internacional El Tepual [*Chile*] [*ICAO location identifier*] (ICLI) .... SCTE
Puerto Obaldia [*Panama*] [*ICAO location identifier*] (ICLI) .... MPOA
Puerto Obaldia [*Panama*] [*Airport symbol*] (OAG) .... PUE
Puerto Ocopa [*Peru*] [*ICAO location identifier*] (ICLI) .... SPPA
Puerto Ordaz [*Venezuela*] [*Airport symbol*] (OAG) .... PZO
Puerto Paez [*Venezuela*] [*Airport symbol*] (AD) .... PPZ
Puerto Pinasco [*Paraguay*] [*ICAO location identifier*] (ICLI) .... SGPO
Puerto Plata [*Dominican Republic*] [*Airport symbol*] (OAG) .... POP
Puerto Plata/La Union [*Dominican Republic*] [*ICAO location identifier*] (ICLI) .... MDPP
Puerto Princesa [*Philippines*] [*Airport symbol*] (OAG) .... PPS
Puerto Princesa, Palawan [*Philippines*] [*ICAO location identifier*] (ICLI) .... RPVP
Puerto Rican [*Derogatory term*] .... PR
Puerto Rican American Insurance Co. (AD) .... PRAICO
Puerto Rican American Women's League .... PRAWL
Puerto Rican Association for Community Affairs (EA) .... PRACA
Puerto Rican Bar Association (EA) .... PRBA
Puerto Rican Board of Guardians [*Defunct*] (EA) .... PRBG
Puerto Rican Cement [*NYSE symbol*] (TTSB) .... PRN
Puerto Rican Cement Co., Inc. [*Associated Press*] (SAG) .... PR Cem
Puerto Rican Cement Co., Inc. [*NYSE symbol*] (SPSG) .... PRN
Puerto Rican Communist Party [*Political party*] .... PRCP
Puerto Rican Family Institute (EA) .... PRFI
Puerto Rican Independence [*Later, GPRG*] [*An association*] (EA) .... PRI
Puerto Rican Independence Party [*Political party*] (PD) .... PIP
Puerto Rican Legal Defense and Education Fund (EA) .... PRLDEF
Puerto Rican Migration Consortium (EA) .... PRMC
Puerto Rican Revolutionary Workers Organization (NADA) .... PRRWO
Puerto Rican Revolutionary Workers Organization .... PRWO
Puerto Rican Socialist Party [*Political party*] (PD) .... PSP
Puerto Rican Water Resources Authority .... PRWRA
Puerto Rico [*MARC geographic area code Library of Congress*] (LCCP) .... nwpr--
Puerto Rico [*Colombia*] [*Airport symbol*] (AD) .... PCC
Puerto Rico [*IYRU nationality code*] [*MARC country of publication code Library of Congress*] (LCCP) .... pr
Puerto Rico [*ANSI two-letter standard code*] (CNC) .... PR
Puerto Rico [*Postal code*] .... PR
Puerto Rico [*ANSI three-letter standard code*] (CNC) .... PRI
Puerto Rico [*Bolivia*] [*ICAO location identifier*] (ICLI) .... SLPR
Puerto Rico Air NAtional Guard [*FAA designator*] (FAAC) .... PNG
Puerto Rico Air National Guard .... PRANG
Puerto Rico Area Office [*AEC*] .... PRA
Puerto Rico Association (AD) .... PRA
Puerto Rico Association (NADA) .... PRA
Puerto Rico Cancer Center [*University of Puerto Rico*] [*Research center*] (RCD) .... PRCC
Puerto Rico Communications Authority .... PRCA
Puerto Rico, Decisiones [*A publication*] (DLA) .... PRD
Puerto Rico Economic Development Administration (NADA) .... PREDA
Puerto Rico Federal Reports [*A publication*] (DLA) .... PR Fed
Puerto Rico Federal Reports [*A publication*] (DLA) .... PRF
Puerto Rico Federal Reports [*A publication*] (DLA) .... Puerto Rico F
Puerto Rico Federal Reports [*A publication*] (DLA) .... Puerto Rico Fed
Puerto Rico Industrial Commission Decisions [*A publication*] (DLA) .... PRIC Dec
Puerto Rico Industrial Development Co. .... PRIDCO
Puerto Rico International Airlines, Inc. [*Prinair*] [*ICAO designator*] (OAG) .... PQ
Puerto Rico International Undersea Laboratory .... PRINUL
Puerto Rico Junior College .... PRJC
Puerto Rico Legal Project [*of the National Lawyers Guild*] (EA) .... PRLP
Puerto Rico Mainland US Statehood Students Association (EA) .... PRSSA
Puerto Rico National Airlines .... PRINAIR
Puerto Rico Nuclear Center .... PRNC
Puerto Rico Operations Area .... PROA
Puerto Rico Reactor (NRCH) .... PRR
Puerto Rico Reconstruction Administration [*Terminated, 1955*] .... PRRA
Puerto Rico Reports [*A publication*] (DLA) .... Puerto Rico
Puerto Rico Reports, Spanish Edition [*A publication*] (DLA) .... DPR
Puerto Rico Reports, Spanish Edition [*A publication*] (DLA) .... SPR
Puerto Rico Rum Institute [*Later, PRRPA*] .... PRRI
Puerto Rico Rum Producers Association [*Defunct*] (EA) .... PRRPA
Puerto Rico Socialist Party (NADA) .... PRSP
Puerto Rico Solidarity Committee (EA) .... PRSC
Puerto Rico Statehood Commission (EA) .... PRSA
Puerto Rico Supreme Court Reports [*A publication*] (DLA) .... PR
Puerto Rico Supreme Court Reports [*A publication*] (DLA) .... PRR
Puerto Rico Supreme Court Reports [*A publication*] (DLA) .... PRSCR
Puerto Rico Supreme Court Reports [*A publication*] (DLA) .... Puerto Rico Rep
Puerto Rico Tax Court Decisions [*A publication*] (DLA) .... PRTCD
Puerto Rico, USA Foundation (EA) .... PRUSAF
Puerto Suarez [*Bolivia*] [*Airport symbol*] (OAG) .... PSZ
Puerto Suarez [*Bolivia*] [*ICAO location identifier*] (ICLI) .... SLPS
Puerto Vallarta [*Mexico*] [*Airport symbol*] (OAG) .... PVR
Puerto Vallarta/Lic. Gustavo Dias Ordaz Internacional [*Mexico ICAO location identifier*] (ICLI) .... MMPR
Puerto Vallarta Taxi Aereo, SA de CV [*Mexico*] [*FAA designator*] (FAAC) .... TXV
Puerto Victoria [*Peru*] [*ICAO location identifier*] (ICLI) .... SPGT
Puerto Villa-Roel [*Bolivia*] [*ICAO location identifier*] (ICLI) .... SLPV
Puerto Williams [*Chile*] [*Airport symbol*] (AD) .... WPU
Puerto Williams/Guardia-Marina Zanartu [*Chile*] [*ICAO location identifier*] (ICLI) .... SCGZ
Puerto Yuca [*Bolivia*] [*ICAO location identifier*] (ICLI) .... SLKY
Puetzer [*Germany ICAO aircraft manufacturer identifier*] (ICAO) .... PU
Puffed [*Freight*] .... PFD
Puffendorf's Law of Nature and Nations [*A publication*] (DLA) .... Puf
Pug Dog Club of America (EA) .... PDCA
PUG Library Information Group (NITA) .... PUGLIG
Puget Sound (FAAC) .... PGTSND
Puget Sound [*Also, Puget Sound Naval Shipyard*] [*Washington*] .... PS
Puget Sound Freight Lines [*AAR code*] .... PSFL
Puget Sound General Hospital, Tacoma, WA [*Library symbol Library of Congress*] (LCLS) .... WaTPG
Puget Sound Naval Shipyard [*Bremerton, WA*] (MCD) .... PSNS
Puget Sound Naval Shipyard [*Bremerton, WA*] .... PSNSY
Puget Sound Naval Shipyard Material Laboratories [*Bremerton, WA*] .... PSNS-MATLABS
Puget Sound P&L [*NYSE symbol*] (TTSB) .... PSD
Puget Sound P&L 7.875% Pfd [*NYSE symbol*] (TTSB) .... PSDPr
Puget Sound P&L Adj Rt'B'Pfd [*NYSE symbol*] (TTSB) .... PSDPrB
Puget Sound Power & Light Co. [*NYSE symbol*] (SPSG) .... PSD
Puget Sound Power & Light Co. [*Associated Press*] (SAG) .... PugetP
Puget Sound Power & Light Co. [*Associated Press*] (SAG) .... PugtP
Puget Sound Power and Light Co., Bellevue, WA [*Library symbol Library of Congress*] (LCLS) .... WaBP
Puget Sound Tug & Barge [*AAR code*] .... PSTB
Pugilist .... PUG
Pugillus [*A Handful*] [*Pharmacy*] (ROG) .... P
Pugillus [*A Handful*] [*Pharmacy*] (ROG) .... PUG
Pugsley and Burbridge's New Brunswick Reports [*A publication*] (DLA) .... NBRP & B
Pugsley and Burbridge's New Brunswick Reports [*A publication*] (DLA) .... P & B
Pugsley and Burbridge's New Brunswick Reports [*17-20 New Brunswick*] [*A publication*] (DLA) .... Pugs & Bur
Pugsley and Burbridge's New Brunswick Reports [*17-20 New Brunswick*] [*A publication*] (DLA) .... Pugs & Burg
Pugsley and Trueman's New Brunswick Reports [*A publication*] (DLA) .... NBRP & T
Pugsley and Trueman's New Brunswick Reports [*A publication*] (DLA) .... P & T
Pugsley and Trueman's New Brunswick Reports [*A publication*] (DLA) .... Pugs & T
Pugsley and Trueman's New Brunswick Reports [*1882-83*] [*A publication*] (DLA) .... Pugs & Tru

Pugsley's New Brunswick Reports [*A publication*] (DLA) ... NBR Pug
Pugsley's New Brunswick Reports [*1876-93*] [*Canada*] [*A publication*] (DLA) ... NBR Pugs
Pugsley's New Brunswick Reports [*14-16 New Brunswick*] [*A publication*] (DLA) ... Pug
Pugsley's New Brunswick Reports [*14-16 New Brunswick*] [*A publication*] (DLA) ... Pugs
Pugwash Conferences on Science and World Affairs ... P-COSWA
Pugwash Etudiant du Canada ... PEC
Puisne Judge [*Australia*] ... PJ
Puivert [*France ICAO location identifier*] (ICLI) ... LFNW
Puka Puka [*French Polynesia*] [*ICAO location identifier*] (ICLI) ... NTGP
Pukalani, HI [*FM radio station call letters*] ... KMVI-FM
Pukapuka [*French Polynesia*] [*Airport symbol*] (OAG) ... PKP
Pukarua [*French Polynesia*] [*ICAO location identifier*] (ICLI) ... NTGQ
Pukarua [*French Polynesia*] [*Airport symbol*] (OAG) ... PUK
Pul. Przedsiebiorstwo Uslug Lotniczych [*Poland ICAO designator*] (FAAC) ... PUL
Pula [*Former Yugoslavia*] [*ICAO location identifier*] (ICLI) ... LYPL
Pula [*Monetary unit*] (ODBW) ... P
Pula [*Former Yugoslavia*] [*Airport symbol*] (OAG) ... PUY
Pulaski [*Virginia*] [*Seismograph station code, US Geological Survey Closed*] (SEIS) ... PUV
Pulaski Bank, A Savings Bank [*Associated Press*] (SAG) ... PulaskiB
Pulaski Bank, A Savings Bank [*NASDAQ symbol*] (SAG) ... PULB
Pulaski Bank A Svgs Bk MO [*NASDAQ symbol*] (TTSB) ... PULB
Pulaski County Public Library, Winamac, IN [*Library symbol Library of Congress*] (LCLS) ... InWina
Pulaski Furniture [*NASDAQ symbol*] (TTSB) ... PLFC
Pulaski Furniture Corp. [*NASDAQ symbol*] (NQ) ... PLFC
Pulaski Furniture Corp. [*Associated Press*] (SAG) ... PulaskF
Pulaski, NY [*FM radio station call letters*] ... WSCP
Pulaski, TN [*Location identifier FAA*] (FAAL) ... GZS
Pulaski, TN [*FM radio station call letters*] ... WINJ
Pulaski, TN [*AM radio station call letters*] ... WKSR
Pulaski, VA [*AM radio station call letters*] ... WBLB
Pulaski, VA [*FM radio station call letters*] ... WPSK
Pulaski, VA [*AM radio station call letters*] ... WPUV
Pulau Pioman [*Malaysia*] [*ICAO location identifier*] (ICLI) ... WMBT
Pulau-Weh [*Sumatra*] [*Seismograph station code, US Geological Survey Closed*] (SEIS) ... PWS
Puli Club of America (EA) ... PCA
Pulitzer Publishing [*NYSE symbol*] (TTSB) ... PTZ
Pulitzer Publishing Co. (MHDW) ... PLTZC
Pulitzer Publishing Co. [*NYSE symbol*] (SPSG) ... PTZ
Pulitzer Publishing Co. [*Associated Press*] (SAG) ... PultzPb
Pulkovo [*Former USSR Seismograph station code, US Geological Survey*] (SEIS) ... PUL
Pull (NFPA) ... P
Pull and Adjust [*Brace*] [*Medicine*] ... PA
Pull and Push Plate ... P & PP
Pull and Push Plate (AD) ... p & pp
Pull and Push Plate (IAA) ... PAPP
Pull and Push Plate ... PXPPL
Pull and Void (MCD) ... PV
Pull Back (NTCM) ... PB
Pull Box (AAG) ... PB
Pull Chain [*Technical drawings*] (DAC) ... PC
Pull Next Stitch Over [*Knitting*] (BARN) ... PNSO
Pull Out (IAA) ... PO
Pull Out of Hole (AD) ... poh
Pull Rod ... PLRD
Pull Switch ... PS
Pull Up Point ... PUP
Pull Up Push Over (NASA) ... PUPO
Pullbutton (AAG) ... PLB
Pulled Up [*Horse racing*] ... P
Pullenshope (Hendrina) [*South Africa*] [*ICAO location identifier*] (ICLI) ... FAHE
Puller (MSA) ... PLR
Pulletop Nature Reserve [*New South Wales*] (AD) ... PNR
Pulley (AAG) ... PUL
Pulley Drive (IAA) ... PD
Pulley End ... PE
Pulling Boat Hands (DMAA) ... PBH
Pulling on Attorneys and Solicitors [*3rd ed.*] [*1862*] [*A publication*] (DLA) ... Pull Att
Pulling on Mercantile Accounts [*1846*] [*A publication*] (DLA) ... Pull Acc
Pulling Whaleboat ... PWB
Pulling's Law of Mercantile Accounts [*A publication*] (DLA) ... Pull Accts
Pulling's Treatise on the Laws, Customs, and Regulations of the City and Port o f London [*A publication*] (DLA) ... Pull Laws & Cust Lond
Pulling's Treatise on the Laws, Customs, and Regulations of the City and Port ofLondon [*A publication*] (DLA) ... Pull Port of London
Pullman [*Washington*] [*Airport symbol*] (OAG) ... PUW
Pullman Memorial Hospital, Pullman, WA [*Library symbol*] [*Library of Congress*] (LCLS) ... WaPH
Pullman, MI [*Location identifier FAA*] (FAAL) ... PMM
Pullman, WA [*FM radio station call letters*] ... KHTR
Pullman, WA [*AM radio station call letters*] ... KQQQ
Pullman, WA [*FM radio station call letters*] ... KRLF
Pullman, WA [*AM radio station call letters*] ... KWSU
Pullman, WA [*Television station call letters*] ... KWSU-TV
Pullman, WA [*FM radio station call letters*] ... KZUU
Pullman, WA [*FM radio station call letters*] ... KZZL
Pullman, WA [*Location identifier FAA*] (FAAL) ... PUW
Pull-Out Harness ... POH
Pull-Over Enrichment [*Automotive engineering*] ... POE
Pull-Through [*Gun cleaning*] ... PT
Pulmentum [*Gruel Pulmonary*] [*Latin*] (MAE) ... pulm
Pulmocutaneous Exchange ... PCE
Pulmonary ... PUL
Pulmonary ... PULM
Pulmonary Alveolar Macrophage [*Attacks inhaled particles*] ... PAM
Pulmonary Alveolar Microlithiasis [*Medicine*] (MAE) ... PAM
Pulmonary Alveolar Proteinosis [*Medicine*] ... PAP
Pulmonary Angiography [*Medicine*] ... PA
Pulmonary Arterial Capillary Wedge Pressure [*Medicine*] (DMAA) ... PACWP
Pulmonary Arterial [*or Artery*] **Pressure** [*Medicine*] ... PAP
Pulmonary Arterial Vasconstrictor Substance [*Medicine*] ... PAVS
Pulmonary Arteriolar Resistance [*Medicine*] (MAE) ... PAR
Pulmonary Arteriovenous Fistula [*Medicine*] ... PAF
Pulmonary Arteriovenous Fistula [*Medicine*] ... PAVF
Pulmonary Arteriovenous Malformation [*Medicine*] (DMAA) ... PAVM
Pulmonary Artery [*Medicine*] ... PA
Pulmonary Artery Ballon Pump [*Medicine*] (DMAA) ... PABP
Pulmonary Artery Banding [*Cardiology*] ... PAB
Pulmonary Artery Catheter [*Medicine*] ... PAC
Pulmonary Artery Counter-Pulsation [*Cardiology*] (MAE) ... PACP
Pulmonary Artery Diastolic [*Pressure*] [*Cardiology*] ... PAD
Pulmonary Artery Diastolic Pressure [*Cardiology*] (AAMN) ... PADP
Pulmonary Artery End-Diastolic Pressure [*Cardiology*] ... PAEDP
Pulmonary Artery Hypertension [*Medicine*] ... PAH
Pulmonary Artery Hypotension [*Cardiology*] (DAVI) ... PAH
Pulmonary Artery Mean Pressure [*Medicine*] (MEDA) ... PAMP
Pulmonary Artery Occlusion [*Medicine*] (DMAA) ... PAO
Pulmonary Artery Occlusion Pressure [*Cardiology*] ... PAOP
Pulmonary Artery Pressure [*Cardiology*] ... PPA
Pulmonary Artery Pressure [*Medicine*] (DMAA) ... Ppa
Pulmonary Artery Stenosis [*Medicine*] ... PAS
Pulmonary Artery Systolic Pressure [*Medicine*] (DMAA) ... PASP
Pulmonary Artery Thromboembolectomy [*Cardiology*] (DAVI) ... PATE
Pulmonary Artery Wedge [*Pressure*] [*Cardiology*] (DAVI) ... PAW
Pulmonary Artery Wedge Pressure [*Cardiology*] ... PAW
Pulmonary Artery Wedge Pressure [*Medicine*] ... PAWP
Pulmonary Atresia [*Medicine*] ... PA
Pulmonary Atresia/Pulmonary Stenosis [*Cardiology*] (DAVI) ... PA/PS
Pulmonary Atresia with Intact Ventricular Septum [*Cardiology*] (DAVI) ... PAIVS
Pulmonary Blood Flow [*Medicine*] ... PBF
Pulmonary Blood Flow [*Medicine*] (DAVI) ... Qp
Pulmonary Blood Flow Redistribution [*Medicine*] ... PFR
Pulmonary Blood Volume [*Medicine*] ... PBV
Pulmonary Capillary [*Medicine*] ... PC
Pulmonary Capillary Blood Flow [*Medicine*] (DAVI) ... Qc
Pulmonary Capillary Blood Flow [*Cardiology*] (DAVI) ... Qpc
Pulmonary Capillary Blood Volume [*Cardiology*] (DAVI) ... V_c
Pulmonary Capillary Pressure [*Medicine*] (CPH) ... PCP
Pulmonary Capillary Protein Leakage [*Medicine*] (DMAA) ... PCPL
Pulmonary Capillary Wedge [*Medicine*] ... PCW
Pulmonary Capillary Wedge Pressure [*Medicine*] ... PCWP
Pulmonary Care Unit [*Medicine*] (DMAA) ... PCU
Pulmonary Clearance Delay [*Medicine*] ... PCD
Pulmonary Diffusion Capacity for Carbon Monoxide [*Medicine*] (DAVI) ... D_{CO}
Pulmonary Disease [*Medicine*] ... PD
Pulmonary Disease [*Medicine*] ... PUD
Pulmonary Ectopic Beat [*Cardiology*] ... PEB
Pulmonary Edema [*Medicine*] ... PE
Pulmonary Edema [*Medicine*] ... PEd
Pulmonary Edema Fluid [*Medicine*] (DMAA) ... PEF
Pulmonary Effusion [*Medicine*] ... PE
Pulmonary Embolism [*Medicine*] ... PE
Pulmonary Embolus [*Medicine*] (DAVI) ... PEM
Pulmonary Extravascular Water [*Medicine*] (DMAA) ... PEW
Pulmonary Extravascular Water Volume [*Physiology*] ... PEWV
Pulmonary Factor [*Medicine*] ... PF
Pulmonary Flow Rate [*Medicine*] (DAVI) ... PFR
Pulmonary Function [*Medicine*] (DMAA) ... PF
Pulmonary Function Score [*Physiology*] ... PFS
Pulmonary Function Test [*Medicine*] ... PFT
Pulmonary Hypertension [*Medicine*] (MAE) ... PH
Pulmonary Hypertension [*Cardiology*] (CPH) ... PHT
Pulmonary Incompetence [*Medicine*] ... PI
Pulmonary Indices [*Medicine*] ... PI
Pulmonary Infarction [*Medicine*] ... PI
Pulmonary Infiltration with Eosinophilia [*Medicine*] ... PIE
Pulmonary Intensive Care Unit [*Medicine*] ... PICU
Pulmonary Interstitial Edema [*Medicine*] (DAVI) ... PIE
Pulmonary Interstitial Emphysema [*Medicine*] ... PIE
Pulmonary Intervertebral Disc [*Medicine*] ... PI
Pulmonary Macrophages [*Medicine*] ... PM
Pulmonary Mean Pressure [*Medicine*] ... PMP
Pulmonary Mean Transit Time [*Medicine*] (MAE) ... PMTT
Pulmonary Resistance [*Cardiology*] (MAE) ... Rp
Pulmonary Sequestration ... PS
Pulmonary Stenosis [*Medicine*] ... PS
Pulmonary Stretch Receptors [*Medicine*] ... PSR
Pulmonary Surfactant Apoprotein [*Biochemistry*] ... PSAP
Pulmonary Thromboembolic Disease [*Medicine*] ... PTED
Pulmonary Thromboembolism [*Medicine*] ... PTE
Pulmonary Transit Time [*Physiology*] ... PTT
Pulmonary Tuberculosis [*Medicine*] ... PT
Pulmonary Valve Gradient [*Medicine*] (DMAA) ... PVG

Pulmonary Valve Opening [*Cardiology*] ... PO
Pulmonary Valve Stenosis [*Cardiology*] ... PVS
Pulmonary Valvotomy [*Cardiology*] ... PV
Pulmonary Vascular Disease [*Medicine*] ... PVD
Pulmonary Vascular Effect [*Physiology*] ... PVE
Pulmonary Vascular Resistance [*Physiology*] ... PVR
Pulmonary Vascular Resistance Index [*Medicine*] (DMAA) ... PVRI
Pulmonary Vascularity [*Medicine*] ... PV
Pulmonary Vein [*Medicine*] ... PV
Pulmonary Venous Congestion [*Medicine*] ... PVC
Pulmonary Venous Hypertension [*Medicine*] ... PVH
Pulmonary Venous Obstruction [*Medicine*] (DMAA) ... PVO
Pulmonary Venous Obstructive Disease [*Cardiology*] (DAVI) ... PVOD
Pulmonary Venous Occlusion [*Cardiology*] (DAVI) ... PVO
Pulmonary Venous Pressure [*Medicine*] (MAE) ... PI
Pulmonary Wedge Pressure [*Medicine*] ... PWP
Pulmonic Closure [*Medicine*] (MAE) ... PC
Pulmonic First Heart Sound [*Medicine*] (DAVI) ... P_1
Pulmonic First Sound [*Medicine*] (MEDA) ... P_1
Pulmonic Regurgitation [*Cardiology*] (DAVI) ... PR
Pulmonic Second Sound [*Medicine*] ... P_2
Pulmonic Valve [*Cardiology*] (DAVI) ... PV
Pulp and Paper Centre, University of British Columbia, Vancouver, British Columbia [*Library symbol National Library of Canada*] (NLC) ... BVAPPC
Pulp and Paper Industry Division [*Instrument Society of America*] ... PUPID
Pulp and Paper Machinery Manufacturers Association [*Later, APMA*] (EA) ... PPMMA
Pulp and Paper Manufacturers Association [*Later, PPMMA*] (EA) ... PPMA
Pulp and Paper Manufacturers' Federation of Australia ... PPMFA
Pulp and Paper Prepackaging Association [*Later, SSI*] (EA) ... PAPPA
Pulp and Paper Prepackaging Association [*Later, SSI*] ... PPPA
Pulp and Paper Research and Education Center [*Auburn University*] [*Research center*] (RCD) ... PPREC
Pulp and Paper Research Institute of Canada [*McGill University*] [*Research center*] (RCD) ... PAPRICAN
Pulp and Paper Research Institute of Canada ... PPRIC
Pulp and Paper Research Institute of Canada (AD) ... PPRICA
Pulp and Paper Research Institute of Canada, Pointe Claire, PQ, Canada [*Library symbol Library of Congress*] (LCLS) ... CaQMPp
Pulp and Paper Research Institute of Canada [*Institut Canadien de Recherches sur les Pates et Papiers*] **Pointe-Claire, Quebec** [*Library symbol National Library of Canada*] (NLC) ... QMPP
Pulp and Paper Research Institute of Canada, Vancouver Laboratory, Vancouver, BC, Canada [*Library symbol*] [*Library of Congress*] (LCLS) ... CaBVaPPR
Pulp and Paper Traffic League [*Defunct*] (EA) ... PPTL
Pulp Chemicals Association (EA) ... PCA
Pulp Grinding [*Freight*] ... PLP GRNDG
Pulp Manufacturers' Research League ... PMRL
Pulp, Paper, and Paperboard Export Association of the United States (EA) ... PPPEA
Pulp, Paper, and Paperboard Institute USA [*Later, API*] ... PPPI
Pulp, Paper, and Woodworkers of Canada ... PPWC
Pulp Refining Equipment Manufacturers Association (EA) ... PREMA
Pulp Testing [*Dentistry*] ... PT
Pulpboard ... PLPBD
Pulpboard (VRA) ... pulpbd
Pulpoaxial [*Dentistry*] ... PA
Pulpobuccoaxial [*Dentistry*] ... PBA
Pulpodistal [*Dentistry*] ... PD
Pulpolabial [*Dentistry*] ... PLa
Pulpolingual [*Dentistry*] ... PL
Pulpolinguoaxial [*Dentistry*] ... PLA
Pulpomesial [*Dentistry*] ... PM
Pulpomesioaxial [*Dentistry*] ... PMA
Pulpwash [*Byproduct of citrus processing*] ... PW
Pulpwood (VRA) ... pulpwd
Pulsar Energy/Resources [*Vancouver Stock Exchange symbol*] ... POE
Pulsar Wind Nebula [*Astronomy*] ... PWN
Pulsated, Overheated, Water Rocket [*Swiss space rocket*] ... POHWARO
Pulsatile Assist Device [*Cardiology*] ... PAD
Pulsatility Index [*Medicine*] ... PL
Pulsating Air System [*Automotive engineering*] ... PAS
Pulsating Arc (IAA) ... PA
Pulsating Current ... PC
Pulsating Current ... PCUR
Pulsating Electromagnetic Field ... PEMF
Pulsating Star ... PULSAR
Pulsating/Steady Visual Approach Slope Indicator [*Aviation*] (FAAC) ... PVASI
Pulsating Visual Approach Slope Indicator [*Aviation*] (FAAC) ... PLASI
Pulsating Water-Jet Lavager [*Medicine*] (RDA) ... PWJ
Pulsation (MSA) ... PLSN
Pulsational Magnetic Radiation [*Astronomy*] ... PMR
Pulsator (MSA) ... PLSR
Pulse ... P
Pulse (MSA) ... PLS
Pulse Acquisition RADAR [*Military*] (NG) ... PAR
Pulse Acquisition RADAR [*Military*] (MSA) ... PUAR
Pulse Amplifier ... PA
Pulse Amplifier/Symbol Generator ... PASG
Pulse Amplitude and Phase Modulation (PDAA) ... PAPM
Pulse Amplitude Code Modulation [*Electronics*] ... PACM
Pulse Amplitude Modulation [*Electronics*] ... PAM
Pulse Amplitude Modulation - Frequency Modulation [*Electronics*] ... PAM-FM
Pulse Analysis-Recording Information System ... PARIS
Pulse Analyzer Signal Generator ... PASG
Pulse and Respiration [*Medicine*] ... P & R
Pulse Averaging Discriminator ... PAD
Pulse Bancorp [*NASDAQ symbol*] (TTSB) ... PULS
Pulse Bancorp, Inc. [*NASDAQ symbol*] (SAG) ... PULS
Pulse Bancorp, Inc. [*Associated Press*] (SAG) ... PulseBcp
Pulse Beacon (KSC) ... PB
Pulse Beacon Impact Predictor (AAG) ... PBIP
Pulse Burst Modulation (IAA) ... PBM
Pulse Burst Period (PDAA) ... PBP
Pulse Burst Wave ... PBW
Pulse Burst Waveform ... PBWF
Pulse Cleaned [*Dust filtration*] ... PC
Pulse Code [*Telecommunications*] (IAA) ... PC
Pulse Code Adaptor (NITA) ... PCA
Pulse Code Modulated Ground Station ... PCMGS
Pulse Code Modulation [*Telecommunications*] (OSI) ... PCM
Pulse Code Modulation [*Telecommunications*] (IAA) ... PM
Pulse Code Modulation and Timing Electronics Assembly ... PCMTEA
Pulse Code Modulation and Timing Equipment (KSC) ... PCMTE
Pulse Code Modulation Data Handling System [*Telecommunications*] (IAA) ... PCMDHS
Pulse Code Modulation, Digital ... PCMD
Pulse Code Modulation Event ... PCME
Pulse Code Modulation - Frequency Modulation ... PCM-FM
Pulse Code Modulation/Frequency Shift Keying/Amplitude Modulation (SAA) ... PCM/FSK/AM
Pulse Code Modulation Master Unit [*Electronics*] (NASA) ... PCMMU
Pulse Code Modulation/Nonreturn to Zero (KSC) ... PCM/NRZ
Pulse Code Modulation - Phase-Shift ... PCM-PS
Pulse Code Modulation Pseudonoise [*Telecommunications*] (IAA) ... PCMPN
Pulse Code Modulation Shared (MCD) ... PCMS
Pulse Code Modulation Telemetry System (AAG) ... PCMTS
Pulse Code Modulation-Phase-Modulation (IAA) ... PCMPM
Pulse Comparator (AAG) ... PC
Pulse Comparator ... PCP
Pulse Compression ... PC
Pulse Compression/Expansion Unit ... PCEU
Pulse Compression Filter ... PCF
Pulse Compression Loop ... PCL
Pulse Compression Network ... PCN
Pulse Compression RADAR ... PCR
Pulse Compression Tube ... PCT
Pulse Controller ... PC
Pulse Count [*Telecommunications*] (TEL) ... PCT
Pulse Counter [*Computer science*] (MDG) ... PC
Pulse Counter Adapter ... PCA
Pulse Counter Chain ... PCC
Pulse Cytophotometry [*Hematology*] ... PCP
Pulse Data Modulation [*Computer science*] (IAA) ... PDM
Pulse Delay Binary Modulation (MCD) ... PDBM
Pulse Delay Device ... PDD
Pulse Delay Mechanism [*British military*] (DMA) ... PDM
Pulse Delay Time ... PDT
Pulse Delta Modulation (IEEE) ... PDM
Pulse Demodulation Analysis ... PDA
Pulse Detection Unit (NASA) ... PDU
Pulse Detector [*Spectroscopy*] ... PD
Pulse Distribution Amplifier ... PDA
Pulse Doppler ... PD
Pulse Doppler RADAR ... PDR
Pulse Doppler Seeker ... PDS
Pulse Doppler Single Target Track [*Military*] (CAAL) ... PDSTT
Pulse Driver ... PD
Pulse Duration ... PD
Pulse Duration Modulation [*Data transmission*] ... PDM
Pulse Duty Ratio ... PDR
Pulse Echo [*Materials research*] ... PE
Pulse Echo Pattern ... PEP
Pulse Echo Pattern Analyzer ... PEPA
Pulse Edge Discrimination (OA) ... PED
Pulse Effective Power [*Telecommunications*] (IAA) ... PEP
Pulse Eliminating Filter (IAA) ... PEF
Pulse Encoding [*Computer science*] ... PE
Pulse Envelop Correlation Air Navigation ... PECAN
Pulse Feedback [*Telecommunications*] (IAA) ... PF
Pulse Fourier Transform ... PFT
Pulse Frequency ... PF
Pulse Frequency (MDG) ... PFR
Pulse Frequency (IDOE) ... prt
Pulse Gate ... PG
Pulse Gate Binary Modulation (MCD) ... PGBM
Pulse Generator ... PG
Pulse Generator ... PGN
Pulse Generator Display ... PGD
Pulse Generator Display System ... PGDS
Pulse Group Repetition Frequency ... PGRF
Pulse Height Analysis [*Spectroscopy*] ... PHA
Pulse Height Analyzer System ... PHAS
Pulse Height Discrimination ... PHD
Pulse Height to Time Converter (OA) ... PHTC
Pulse Induction (ADA) ... PI
Pulse Inert Gas ... PIG
Pulse Input Proportional [*Electro-optical system*] ... PIP
Pulse Integrating Pendulum ... PIP

Pulse Integrating Pendulum Accelerometer	PIPA
Pulse Integrating Pendulum Assembly (NASA)	PIPA
Pulse Integration System	PIS
Pulse Intensity Modulation	PIM
Pulse Interference Blanker	PIB
Pulse Interference Eliminator [RADAR]	PIE
Pulse Interference Emitting (MCD)	PIE
Pulse Interference Separation and Blanking [RADAR]	PISAB
Pulse Interval Modulation	PIM
Pulse Jet Engine	PJE
Pulse Jitter Tester	PJT
Pulse Length (NVT)	PL
Pulse Length Error (MCD)	PLE
Pulse Level Detector (MCD)	PLD
Pulse Light Approach Slope Indicator (PDAA)	PLASI
Pulse Link Relay [Telecommunications] (TEL)	PLR
Pulse Link Repeater [Telecommunications] (TEL)	PLR
Pulse Mode Multiplex	PMM
Pulse Mode Multiplex (AD)	pmm
Pulse Mode Performance Model (KSC)	PMPM
Pulse Modulation	PM
Pulse Modulation (AD)	pm
Pulse Modulation Unit (NASA)	PMU
Pulse Modulator (IDOE)	PM
Pulse Morse Code Modulation (OA)	PMCM
Pulse Network (KSC)	PN
Pulse Nuclear Radiation (AAG)	PNR
Pulse Number Modulation	PNM
Pulse Omission Detector (MCD)	POD
Pulse Oriented Electrophoresis [Analytical biochemistry]	POE
Pulse Oscillator (IAA)	PO
Pulse Output	PO
Pulse Oximeter/End Tidal [Carbon Dioxide] [Medicine] (DAVI)	POET
Pulse Pair (IAA)	PP
Pulse Pair Repetition Frequency (MCD)	PPRF
Pulse per Second (IAA)	PS
Pulse Phase Modulation (DEN)	P-PH-M
Pulse Phase Modulation [Telecommunications] (IAA)	PPM
Pulse Plasma Accelerator	PPA
Pulse Plasma Thruster	PPT
Pulse Polarization Binary Modulation (MCD)	PPBM
Pulse Polarography [Analytical chemistry]	PP
Pulse Position Indicator (MCD)	PPI
Pulse Position Modulation [Radio data transmission]	PPM
Pulse Position Modulation (AD)	ppm
Pulse Power Module (RDA)	PPM
Pulse Pressure [Medicine]	PP
Pulse Quaternary Modulation	PQM
Pulse RADAR Intelligent Diagnostic Environment [US Army Missile Command] (RDA)	PRIDE
Pulse Radiation Effect	PRE
Pulse Ranging Navigation	PRN
Pulse Ranging Network (KSC)	PRN
Pulse Rate	PR
Pulse Rate Frequency (MUGU)	PRF
Pulse Rate Increase [Medicine]	PRI
Pulse Rate Indicator	PRI
Pulse Rate Modulation	PRM
Pulse Ratio (IEEE)	PR
Pulse Recurrence Frequency	PRF
Pulse Recurrence Frequency Discrimination [Telecommunications] (TEL)	PRFD
Pulse Recurrence Frequency Stagger (OA)	PRFS
Pulse Recurrence [or Repetition] Interval (NATG)	PRI
Pulse Recurrence [or Repetition] Period (CET)	PRP
Pulse Recurrence [or Repetition] Rate (MUGU)	PRR
Pulse Recurrence [or Repetition] Time (CET)	PRT
Pulse Regenerator	PR
Pulse Repetition Frequency [Computer science]	PRF
Pulse Repetition Frequency (IDOE)	prf
Pulse Repetition Frequency [Medicine] (DAVI)	PRP
Pulse Repetition Internal	PRI
Pulse Repetition Period [Computer science] (IAA)	PRP
Pulse Repetition Rate Modulation [Data transmission] [Computer science] (TEL)	PRRM
Pulse Resources [Vancouver Stock Exchange symbol]	PUL
Pulse Sciences, Inc.	PSI
Pulse Sense	PSE
Pulse Sensor (KSC)	PS
Pulse Sequence Generation [Instrumentation]	PSG
Pulse Shape Control Circuit (IAA)	PSC
Pulse Shape Discriminator	PSD
Pulse Shaper	PS
Pulse Shift Keying (CAAL)	PSK
Pulse Signal Generator (IAA)	PSG
Pulse Slope Modulation (IAA)	PSM
Pulse Stretcher	PS
Pulse Synchronized Contraction [In the vascular system] [Medicine]	PSC
Pulse Target Generator	PTG
Pulse Time Code	PTC
Pulse Time Modulation [Radio]	PTM
Pulse Time Multiplex	PTM
Pulse Time Multiplex (MSA)	PTMUX
Pulse Timer	PT
Pulse to Pulse	P-P

Pulse Torquing Assembly (KSC)	PTA
Pulse Train	PT
Pulse Train Jitter [Computer science] (IAA)	PTJ
Pulse Training Assembled Reactor [Nuclear energy] (NRCH)	PULSTAR
Pulse Transfer Function	PTF
Pulse Transformer (IAA)	PT
Pulse Transmission Logic (IAA)	PTL
Pulse Transmission Mode (MCD)	PTM
Pulse Transmission Time [Medicine] (DMAA)	PTT
Pulse Video Thermography [Nondestructive testing technique]	PVT
Pulse Voltage Converter (OA)	PVC
Pulse Voltammetry [Analytical chemistry]	PV
Pulse Volume Rate [Physiology]	PVR
Pulse Volume Recording [Medicine]	PVR
Pulse Wave Form	PWF
Pulse Wave Velocity	PWV
Pulse Width [RADAR]	PW
Pulse Width Modulation [Electronic instrumentation]	PWM
Pulse-Address MODEM	PAM
Pulse-Address Multiple Access [Satellite communications]	PAMA
Pulse-Air Feeder [Automotive engineering]	PAF
Pulse-Air Injection Reactor [Automotive engineering]	PAIR
Pulse-Amplitude Transmission System (PDAA)	PATSY
Pulse-Coded Optical Landing Aid [Aviation] (PDAA)	PCOLA
Pulse-Coded Processing System	PCPS
Pulse-Count Modulation (MSA)	PCTM
Pulsed Acoustic Doppler Wind Shear Sensing System (PDAA)	PADWSS
Pulsed Activation Doppler (MCD)	PAD
Pulsed Adsorption Bed [Process]	PAB
Pulsed Air Blast	PAB
Pulsed Amperometric Detection [Electroanalytical chemistry]	PAD
Pulsed Amplifier Tube	PAT
Pulsed Appendage Large Mobile Electromagnetic-Pulse Simulator (PDAA)	PALMES
Pulsed Argon Gas LASER	PAGL
Pulsed Argon LASER	PAL
Pulsed Avalanche Diode Oscillator [Telecommunications] (IEEE)	PAO
Pulsed Bridge Element [Telecommunications] (OA)	PBE
Pulsed Carrier without Any Modulation Intended to Carry Information (IEEE)	PO
Pulsed Coaxial Gun	PCG
Pulsed Column Test Rig [Chemical engineering]	PCTR
Pulsed Combustion Jet	PCJ
Pulsed Continuous Wave (IEEE)	PCW
Pulsed Doppler Cross-Sectional Echocardiography [Medicine] (DMAA)	PD-CSE
Pulsed Doppler Echocardiography [Medicine] (DMAA)	PDE
Pulsed Doppler Frequency Diversity (NG)	PDFD
Pulsed Doppler Ultrasonography [Radiology] (DAVI)	PDU
Pulsed Dye LASER	PDL
Pulsed Electromagnetic Energy [Diathermy] (CPH)	PEME
Pulsed Electron Beam (IEEE)	PEB
Pulsed Electron Beam Annealer [Photovoltaic energy systems]	PEBA
Pulsed Electron Beam Source (MCD)	PEBS
Pulsed Electrothermal (MCD)	PET
Pulsed Fast Neutron Analysis [for detection of explosives] (PS)	PFNA
Pulsed Field Electrophoresis [Analytical biochemistry]	PFE
Pulsed Field Gel Electrophoresis	PFGE
Pulsed Field Gradient [Electroanalytical chemistry]	PFG
Pulsed Field Gradient Gel Electrophoresis	PFGE
Pulsed Field Gradient Spin-Echo	PGSE
Pulsed Flame Combustor	PFC
Pulsed Gas Crymotography	PGC
Pulsed Gas LASER	PGL
Pulsed Gas Metal Arc (KSC)	PGMA
Pulsed Glide Path (IAA)	PGP
Pulsed Gradient Spin Echo [Physics]	PGSE
Pulsed High-Energy Radiographic Machine Emitting X-Rays	PHERMEX
Pulsed High-Frequency Electroporation [Analytical biochemistry]	PHFE
Pulsed Holograpy Development [Department of Energy]	PHD
Pulsed Illumination Source	PIS
Pulsed Integrating Pendulums [NASA] (QAA)	PIPS
Pulsed Intense Plasma for Exploratory Research	PIPER
Pulsed Ion Linear Accelerator	PILAC
Pulsed Ionization Chamber	PIC
Pulsed LASER Airborne Depth Sounding System [Naval Oceanographic Office]	PLADS
Pulsed LASER Annealing [Semiconductor technology]	PLA
Pulsed Laser Deposition [Coating technology]	PLD
Pulsed LASER Deposition [Coating technology]	PLD
Pulsed LASER Experiment	PLE
Pulsed LASER Interferometry	PLI
Pulsed LASER Oscillator	PLO
Pulsed LASER Remote Crosswind Sensor (MCD)	PLRC
Pulsed LASER System	PLS
Pulsed Light Generator	PLG
Pulsed Light Source	PLS
Pulsed Light Theodolite	PLT
Pulsed Locked Oscillator	PLO
Pulsed Magnetic Field System	PMFS
Pulsed Microwave Power	PMP
Pulsed Neodymium LASER	PNL
Pulsed Neutron Interrogation (PDAA)	PNI
Pulsed Neutron Interrogation (AD)	pni
Pulsed Photolysis LASER-Induced Fluorescence [Environmental science]	PPLIF

Pulsed Pinch Plasma Electromagnetic Engine (AAG) ...... PPPEE
Pulsed Positive Ion-Negative Ion Chemical Ionization [*Instrumentation*].... PPINICI
Pulsed Positive/Negative Ion Chemical Ionization ...... PPNICI
Pulsed Power Amplifier ...... PPA
Pulsed Power Circuit (IEEE) ...... PPC
Pulsed RADAR Transmitter ...... PRT
Pulsed Ruby LASER System ...... PRLS
Pulsed Sequential Access Relay [*Electronics*] (ECII) ...... PULSAR
Pulsed Single Photon Fluorescence Lifetime Instrumentation ...... PSPFLI
Pulsed Solid-State LASER Light Source ...... PSLLS
Pulsed Strain Gauge (IAA) ...... PSG
Pulsed Ultrasonic Blood Velocity Detector (AAMN) ...... PUVD
Pulsed Ultrasound Doppler Velocity Meter ...... PUDVM
Pulsed Uniform LASER-Stimulated Artificial Radiation [*Proposed acronymic designation for pulsars, in the event they are found to be artificially caused by intelligent life from outer space*] ...... PULSAR
Pulsed Universal Grid ...... PUG
Pulsed Xenon Arc ...... PXA
Pulsed Xenon Illuminator ...... PXI
Pulsed Xenon LASER ...... PXL
Pulsed Xenon Light Source ...... PXLS
Pulsed Xenon Light Source System ...... PXLSS
Pulsed Xenon Solar Simulator ...... PXSS
Pulsed Xenon System ...... PXS
Pulsed-Field Gel Electrophoresis (DMAA) ...... PFG
Pulse-Doppler Elevation Scan (PDAA) ...... PDES
Pulse-Doppler Non-Elevation Scan (PDAA) ...... PDNES
Pulse-Duration Commutator ...... PDC
Pulse-Duration Modulation - Frequency Modulation (CET) ...... PDM-FM
Pulse-Flow Coulometry ...... PFC
Pulse-Forming Machine ...... PFM
Pulse-Forming Network ...... PFN
Pulse-Frequency Distortion Analyzer ...... PFDA
Pulse-Frequency Diversity [*Electronics*] (NG) ...... PFD
Pulse-Frequency Modulation [*RADAR*] [*Telecommunications*] ...... PFM
Pulse-Height Resolution [*By photomultiplier tubes*] ...... PHR
Pulsejet ...... PJ
Pulse-Length Discriminator (IEEE) ...... PLD
Pulse-Length Modulation ...... PLM
Pulse-Modulated Coherent Doppler-Effect X-Band Pulse-Repetition Synthetic-Array Pulse Compression Side Lobe Planar Array ...... PUMCODOXPURSACOMLOPAR
Pulse-Modulated Communications System ...... PMCS
Pulse-Modulated Infrared Jammer ...... PMIJ
Pulse-Modulated Jammer ...... PMJ
Pulse-Modulated Wave [*Telecommunications*] (IAA) ...... PMW
Pulse-Modulator Tube ...... PMT
Pulse-Phased Radio Navigation System ...... PPRNS
Pulse-Rebalanced Strapdown Gyro (MCD) ...... PRSG
Pulse-Reflection Logic (IAA) ...... PRL
Pulses per Hour ...... PPH
Pulses Per Hour (AD) ...... pph
Pulses Per Inch (WDMC) ...... ppi
Pulses per Inch (CMD) ...... PPI
Pulses per Minute ...... PPM
Pulses per Minute (IDOE) ...... ppm
Pulses per Minute (MSA) ...... PPMIN
Pulses per Second [*Data transmission*] ...... PPS
Pulses per Second (IDOE) ...... pps
Pulses Per Second (AD) ...... pps
Pulses per Second [*Data transmission*] (DEN) ...... PS
Pulse-Spacing Modulation (ECII) ...... PSM
Pulse-Synthesized Advanced Conversion Equipment ...... PACE
Pulse-Taking Questionnaire ...... PTQ
Pulse-to-Cycle Fraction ...... PCF
Pulse-Type Phase Detector ...... PPD
Pulse-Width Coded ...... PWC
Pulse-Width Detector [*or Discriminator*] [*RADAR*] ...... PWD
Pulse-Width Encoder ...... PWE
Pulse-Width Modulated Audio Frequency (IAA) ...... PWMAF
Pulse-Width Modulation - Frequency Modulation [*RADAR*] ...... PWM-FM
Pulse-Width Multiplier (IEEE) ...... PWM
Pulsifer's Reports [*35-68 Maine*] [*A publication*] (DLA) ...... Pulsifer (ME)
Pulte Corp. [*NYSE symbol*] (SPSG) ...... PHM
Pulte Corp. [*Associated Press*] (SAG) ...... Pulte
Pulton. De Pace Regis [*A publication*] (DLA) ...... Pult
Pulton's Abridgment of the Statutes [*A publication*] (DLA) ...... P Abr
Pulverized (MSA) ...... PLVRZD
Pulverized ...... PULV
Pulverized Coal [*Fuel technology*] ...... PC
Pulverized Coal Combustion [*or Combustor*] ...... PCC
Pulverized Coal / Flue Gas Desulfurization [*Energy technology*] ...... PC/FGD
Pulverized Coal-Fired Plant ...... PCF
Pulverized Fuel ...... PF
Pulverized Fuel Ash (IEEE) ...... PFA
Pulverized Limestone Association (EA) ...... PLA
Pulvis [*Powder*] [*Pharmacy*] ...... PULV
Pulvis Conspersus [*Dusting Powder*] [*Pharmacy*] ...... PULV CONSPER
Pulvis Grossus [*Coarse Powder*] [*Pharmacy*] [*Latin*] (MAE) ...... pulv gros
Pulvis Patrum [*The Fathers' Powder (or Jesuits' Powder)*] [*Pharmacy*] (ROG) .... PP
Pulvis Subtilis [*Smooth Powder*] [*Pharmacy*] [*Latin*] (MAE) ...... pulv subtil
Pulvis Tenuis [*Very fine powder*] [*Latin*] (DMAA) ...... pulv tenu
Puma Technology, Inc. [*NASDAQ symbol*] (SAG) ...... PUMA
Puma Technology, Inc. [*Associated Press*] (SAG) ...... PumaT
Pumani [*Papua New Guinea*] [*Airport symbol*] (OAG) ...... PMN

Pumice [*Quality of the bottom*] [*Nautical charts*] ...... Pm
Pumice (AD) ...... pm
Pumice (MSA) ...... PMC
Pumice Institute of America (EA) ...... PIA
Pumiliotoxin B [*Organic chemistry*] ...... PTXB
Pump (AAG) ...... P
Pump (KSC) ...... PMP
Pump Actuator Set ...... PAS
Pump Algebra Tutor [*Computer program*] ...... PAT
Pump Bearing Test Facility [*Nuclear energy*] ...... PBTF
Pump Control Sensor ...... PCS
Pump Control Valve [*Hydraulics*] ...... PCV
Pump Discharge ...... PDISCH
Pump Distributors Association [*British*] (DBA) ...... PDA
Pump Drive Assembly ...... PDA
Pump Fed Liquid (KSC) ...... PUFL
Pump Horsepower ...... PHP
Pump, Hydraulic Ram, Hand-Driven (MSA) ...... PHRHD
Pump Jet Vehicle ...... PJV
Pump Optimizing Program ...... POP
Pump Seal Test Facility [*Nuclear energy*] (NRCH) ...... PSTF
Pump Unit (AAG) ...... PU
Pumped Dye LASER ...... PDL
Pumped Hydro Storage [*Power source*] ...... PHS
Pumped Tunnel Diode Transistor Logic ...... PTDTL
Pumped Two-Phase System (SSD) ...... PTPS
Pumping ...... PMPG
Pumping Mean Effective Pressure [*Automotive engine testing*] ...... PMEP
Pumping Station (NATG) ...... PS
Pump-Line-Nozzle ...... PLN
Pump-Motor Assembly ...... PMA
Pump-Out Facilities [*Nautical charts*] ...... P F
Pump-Priming (MHDB) ...... PP
Puna [*Ecuador*] [*ICAO location identifier*] (ICLI) ...... SEPU
Punch ...... P
Punch (KSC) ...... PCH
Punch ...... PNCH
Punch ...... PNCH
Punch (AD) ...... pnch
Punch ...... PUN
Punch Card (NITA) ...... PC
Punch Card Accounting System [*Computer science*] ...... PCAS
Punch Card Equipment [*Computer science*] (AFM) ...... PCE
Punch Card Machine [*Computer science*] ...... PCM
Punch Card Machine System [*Computer science*] ...... PCMS
Punch Card System (NITA) ...... PCS
Punch Driver ...... PD
Punch Driver Selectric ...... PDS
Punch Feed Read (CMD) ...... PFR
Punch Memory Parity Error [*Computer science*] (IAA) ...... PMPE
Punch Off [*Computer science*] (BUR) ...... PF
Punch On ...... PN
Punch Out [*Computer science*] (IAA) ...... PO
Punch Through [*Computer science*] (IAA) ...... PT
Punch through Varactor [*Computer science*] (IAA) ...... PTV
Punch-Die (MSA) ...... P-D
Punched Card [*Computer science*] ...... PC
Punched Card Accounting Machine [*Computer science*] ...... PCAM
Punched Card Control Unit [*Computer science*] (AABC) ...... PCCU
Punched Card Data Processing ...... PCDP
Punched Card Punch [*Computer science*] (IEEE) ...... PCP
Punched Card Reader [*Computer science*] (BUR) ...... PCR
Punched Card Requisition [*Computer science*] (MCD) ...... PCR
Punched Card System [*Computer science*] ...... PCS
Punched Card Unit (NITA) ...... PCU
Punched Card Utility [*Computer science*] ...... PCU
Punched Paper Tape [*Computer science*] ...... PPT
Punched Paper Tape Reader [*Computer science*] ...... PPTR
Punched Tape [*Computer science*] ...... PT
Punched Tape Block Reader [*Computer science*] ...... PTBR
Punched Tape Reader [*Computer science*] ...... PTR
Punched Tape Verifier [*Computer science*] ...... PTV
Puncheon [*Unit of measurement*] ...... PUN
Punching ...... PCHG
Punch-On [*Computer science*] (AD) ...... pn
Punch-Through Device (PDAA) ...... PThD
Punctuated Equilibrium [*Bacteriology*] ...... punceq
Punctuation ...... PUNC
Punctuation (ROG) ...... PUNCT
Punctum Proximum [*Near Point of vision*] [*Ophthalmology*] (DAVI) ...... P
Punctum Proximum [*Near Point*] [*Latin*] ...... PP
Punctum Remotum [*Far Point*] [*Latin*] ...... PR
Punctum Remotum [*Remote Point*] [*Latin*] (AD) ...... pr
Puncture (DAVI) ...... PUNC
Punctured Uniform Code [*Computer science*] (IAA) ...... PUC
Pune [*India*] [*ICAO location identifier*] (ICLI) ...... VAPO
Pungo National Wildlife Refuge [*North Carolina*] (AD) ...... PNWR
Punia [*Zaire*] [*ICAO location identifier*] (ICLI) ...... FZOP
Punia [*Zaire*] [*Airport symbol*] (AD) ...... PUN
Punic (BJA) ...... P
Punic (BJA) ...... Pu
Punica [*of Silius Italicus*] [*Classical studies*] (OCD) ...... Pun
Punishment (DSUE) ...... PUN
Punishment Quarters (AD) ...... pq
Punjab Cavalry [*British military*] (DMA) ...... PC

Punjab Frontier Force [*British military*] (DMA) .... PFF
Punjab High Court Cases [*India*] [*A publication*] (DLA) .... PHCC
Punjab Irregular Force [*British military*] (DMA) .... PIF
Punjab Irregular Frontier Force [*British military*] (DMA) .... PIFF
Punjab Law Reporter [*India*] [*A publication*] (DLA) .... PLJ
Punjab Law Reporter [*India*] [*A publication*] (DLA) .... PLR
Punjab Law Reporter, Jammu and Kashmir Section [*India*] [*A publication*] (DLA) .... PLRJ & K
Punjab Law Times [*India*] [*A publication*] (DLA) .... PLT
Punjab Light Horse [*British military*] (DMA) .... PLH
Punjab Record [*India*] [*A publication*] (DLA) .... PR
Punjab Record [*India*] [*A publication*] (DLA) .... Punj Rec
Punjab Regiment [*India*] [*Army*] .... Pu
Punjab Weekly Reporter [*India*] [*A publication*] (ILCA) .... PWR
Punjabi Muslim [*Pakistan*] .... PM
Punkt [*Point*] [*German military*] .... P
Puno [*Peru*] [*Seismograph station code, US Geological Survey*] (SEIS) .... PUN
Puno [*Peru*] [*ICAO location identifier*] (ICLI) .... SPNP
Puns Corps (EA) .... PC
Punt, Pass, and Kick [*Youth competition sponsored by professional football*] .... PPK
Punta [*Flamenco dance term*] .... PUN
Punta Alegre [*Cuba ICAO location identifier*] (ICLI) .... MUPA
Punta Arenas [*Chile*] [*Seismograph station code, US Geological Survey Closed*] (SEIS) .... PTA
Punta Arenas [*Chile*] [*Airport symbol*] (OAG) .... PUQ
Punta Arenas [*Chile*] [*ICAO location identifier*] (ICLI) .... SCCZ
Punta Arenas/Internacional Carlos Ibanez Del Campo [*Chile*] [*ICAO location identifier*] (ICLI) .... SCCI
Punta Burica [*Costa Rica*] [*ICAO location identifier*] (ICLI) .... MRPA
Punta Cana [*Dominican Republic*] [*ICAO location identifier*] (ICLI) .... MDPC
Punta Cana [*Dominican Republic*] [*Airport symbol*] (OAG) .... PUJ
Punta De Lomas [*Peru*] [*ICAO location identifier*] (ICLI) .... SPNA
Punta De Maisi [*Cuba ICAO location identifier*] (ICLI) .... MUMA
Punta De Talca [*Chile*] [*Seismograph station code, US Geological Survey*] (SEIS) .... PUT
Punta Del Este [*Uruguay*] [*Airport symbol*] (OAG) .... PDP
Punta Del Este/Aeropuerto Deptal de Maldonado [*Uruguay*] [*ICAO location identifier*] (ICLI) .... SUPE
Punta Gorda [*Florida*] [*Airport symbol*] (OAG) .... PGD
Punta Gorda [*Belize*] [*Airport symbol*] (OAG) .... PND
Punta Gorda [*British Honduras*] [*Airport symbol*] (AD) .... TGY
Punta Gorda, FL [*AM radio station call letters*] .... WCCF
Punta Gorda, FL [*FM radio station call letters*] .... WIKX
Punta Indio [*Argentina ICAO location identifier*] (ICLI) .... SAAI
Punta Penasco [*Mexico ICAO location identifier*] (ICLI) .... MMPE
Puntavia Air Services [*Djibouti*] [*FAA designator*] (FAAC) .... PTV
Punted Over [*Boating*] [*British*] (ROG) .... PO
Punter [*Football*] .... P
Puntilla Lake, AK [*Location identifier FAA*] (FAAL) .... PTI
Punxsutawney, PA [*AM radio station call letters*] .... WECZ
Punxsutawney, PA [*FM radio station call letters*] .... WPXZ
Pupakea [*Hawaii*] [*Seismograph station code, US Geological Survey Closed*] (SEIS) .... PUP
Pupil .... P
Pupil (DSUE) .... PUP
Pupil Behavior Inventory [*Psychology*] .... PBI
Pupil Behavior Rating Scale [*Psychology*] .... PBRS
Pupil Classroom Behavior Scale .... PCBS
Pupil Control Ideology Form [*Education*] (EDAC) .... PCI
Pupil Evaluation Inventory [*Education*] (EDAC) .... PEI
Pupil Evaluation Team [*Education*] .... PET
Pupil Nurse [*British*] (DI) .... PN
Pupil Observation Survey [*Education*] .... POS
Pupil Record of Educational Behavior [*Aptitude test*] .... PREB
Pupil Record of Educational Progress [*Education*] (AEBS) .... PREP
Pupil Registering and Operational Filing [*Computer science*] .... PROF
Pupil Services Expectation Questionnaire .... PSEQ
Pupil Services Fulfillment Questionnaire .... PSFQ
Pupil Teacher .... PT
Pupillary Distance [*Medicine*] .... pd
Pupil-Perceived Needs Assessment [*Education*] (EDAC) .... PPNA
Pupils Equal and React to Light and Accomodation [*Medicine*] .... PEARLA
Pupils Equal and Reactive to Light (DAVI) .... PERL
Pupils Equal, React to Light and Accommodation [*Medicine*] .... PERLA
Pupils Equal, Regular, and Reactive to Light (DAVI) .... PERL
Pupils Equal, Regular and Reactive to Light and Accommodation (DAVI) .... PERLA
Pupils Equal, Round and Reactive to Light (DAVI) .... PERRL
Pupils Equal, Round, and Reactive to Light and Accommodation (Directly and Consensually) (DAVI) .... PERRLA (DC)
Pupils Equal, Round, React to Light and Accommodation [*Medicine*] .... PERRLA
Pupils Equal, Round, Regular and Reactive to Light (DAVI) .... PERRL
Pupils Equal, Round, Regular, and Reactive to Light and Accommodation (DAVI) .... PERRLA
Pupils Round, Equal, React to Light and Accommodation [*Medicine*] (MAE) .... PRERLA
Pupils Round, Regular, and Equal [*Medicine*] (MAE) .... PRRE
Pupils, Tension, Media, Disc, Fundus [*Medicine*] .... PTMDF
Pupil-Teacher Ratio .... PTR
Puppeteers of America (EA) .... PA
Puppetry Guild of Australia .... PGA
Puppis [*Constellation*] .... Pup
Puppis [*Constellation*] .... Pupp
Purari [*Papua New Guinea*] [*Seismograph station code, US Geological Survey*] (SEIS) .... PUR
Purbeck [*District in England*] .... PURB
Purcellville Library, Purcellville, VA [*Library symbol Library of Congress*] (LCLS) .... ViPur
Purchase (DCTA) .... PCH
Purchase (ROG) .... PCHE
Purchase (WGA) .... PCHS
Purchase (AFM) .... PUR
Purchase .... PURCH
Purchase .... PURCH
Purchase and Resale Agreement [*Canada*] (BARN) .... PRA
Purchase and Sale [*Business term*] .... P & S
Purchase Card .... PC
Purchase Change Order (MCD) .... PCO
Purchase Description .... PD
Purchase Free Library, Purchase, NY [*Library symbol Library of Congress*] (LCLS) .... NPur
Purchase Information, Gifts, Loans, Exchanges Tracking [*Suggested name for the Library of Congress computer system*] .... PIGLET
Purchase Memo (MCD) .... PM
Purchase Methods Analyst .... PMA
Purchase of Telephone Services Contracts .... POTS
Purchase of Telephones and Services Program (AAGC) .... POTS
Purchase Order .... PO
Purchase Order Authorization (SAA) .... POA
Purchase Order Change Notice .... POCN
Purchase Order Change Number .... POCN
Purchase Order Change Order (AAG) .... POCO
Purchase Order Closeout (NASA) .... POC
Purchase Order Closeout (AAG) .... POCO
Purchase Order Contract .... POC
Purchase Order Deviation (KSC) .... POD
Purchase Order Information System (MCD) .... POIS
Purchase Order Item (KSC) .... POI
Purchase Order Receiving System (MCD) .... PORES
Purchase Order Request .... POR
Purchase Order Revision Request .... PORR
Purchase Order Scan .... PSCAN
Purchase Order Supplement .... POS
Purchase Outside Production (SAA) .... POP
Purchase, Outside Vendors .... POV
Purchase Parts Request (KSC) .... PPR
Purchase Power [*Commercial firm*] (EA) .... PP
Purchase Price .... PP
Purchase Price Control (AD) .... PPC
Purchase Rate Factor .... PRF
Purchase Request .... PR
Purchase Request Line Item [*DoD*] .... PRLI
Purchase Request/Military Interdepartmental Purchase Request (AFIT) .... PR/MIPR
Purchase Request Number .... PRN
Purchase Request Package [*Shipping*] (MCD) .... PRP
Purchase Requisition (NOAA) .... PUREQ
Purchase Requisition Change Supplement .... PRCS
Purchase Tax [*British*] .... PT
Purchase Transaction Analysis .... PTA
Purchased (AAG) .... P
Purchased (ROG) .... PCHD
Purchased Equipment .... PE
Purchased Gas Adjustment .... PGA
Purchased Input Concept Optimization with Suppliers [*Auto industry quality and cost management program*] .... PICOS
Purchased Labor (NASA) .... P/L
Purchased Materials Inspection .... PMI
Purchased on Assembly (KSC) .... POA
Purchased Part (AD) .... pp
Purchased Part Shortage Notice .... PPSN
Purchased Part Tab Card .... PPTC
Purchased Parts .... PP
Purchased Parts Equipment Notice (SAA) .... PPEN
Purchased Parts List .... PPL
Purchased Parts Material Requirements .... PPMR
Purchased Parts Requirement Notice (KSC) .... PPRN
Purchase-Money Mortgage [*Real estate*] .... PM
Purchase-Money Mortgage [*Real estate*] .... PMM
Purchaser (ROG) .... PCHR
Purchaser .... PCHSR
Purchaser Furnished Equipment (NATG) .... PFE
Purchases Journal [*Accounting*] .... PJ
Purchase-with-Purchase [*Sales promotion*] .... PWP
Purchasing .... PRCHNG
Purchasing .... PURC
Purchasing (DD) .... purch
Purchasing (ROG) .... PURCHG
Purchasing Agent .... PA
Purchasing Agents Association (NADA) .... PAA
Purchasing Agents of the Electronic Industry [*Rosedale, NY*] (EA) .... PAEI
Purchasing Agents of the Radio, Television, and Electronics Industries [*An association*] (IAA) .... PARTEI
Purchasing and Contracting .... P & C
Purchasing and Contracting [*Army*] (IAA) .... PAC
Purchasing and Contracting [*Army*] .... PC
Purchasing Approval Request (NRCH) .... PAR
Purchasing Department Specification (MSA) .... PDS
Purchasing Electronic Notebook (HGAA) .... PEN
Purchasing Internal Change Order (MCD) .... PICO

Purchasing Management Association of Canada ... PMAC
Purchasing Manager ... PM
Purchasing Office [*DoD*] (AFIT) ... PO
Purchasing Power Benefit (ADA) ... PPB
Purchasing Power Equivalent ... PPE
Purchasing Power of the Dollar (MHDW) ... PPD
Purchasing Power Parity [*Economics*] ... PPP
Purchasing Receipt [*Business term*] ... PUR
Purchasing, Receiving, and Payable System ... PREP
Purdon's Digest of Laws [*Pennsylvania*] [*A publication*] (DLA) ... Purd Dig
Purdon's Digest of Laws [*Pennsylvania*] [*A publication*] (DLA) ... Purd Dig Laws
Purdon's Pennsylvania Statutes [*A publication*] (DLA) ... PS
Purdue Center for Parallel and Vector Computing [*Purdue University*] [*Research center*] (RCD) ... ParVec
Purdue Interpretive Programming and Operating System (MCD) ... PINT
Purdue Laboratory for Applied Industrial Control [*Purdue University*] [*Research center*] (RCD) ... PLAIC
Purdue Master Attitude Scales [*Psychology*] ... PMAS
Purdue Mechanical Adaptability Test ... PMAT
Purdue Perceptual-Motor Survey [*Kephart Scale*] ... PPMS
Purdue Research Foundation [*Purdue University*] [*Research center*] (MCD) ... PRF
Purdue Student-Teacher Opinionaire [*Test*] ... PSTO
Purdue Teacher Evaluation Scale ... PTES
Purdue Teacher Opinionaire [*Test*] ... PTO
Purdue University ... PU
Purdue University (GAGS) ... Purdue U
Purdue University, Calumet Campus, Hammond, IN [*Library symbol Library of Congress*] (LCLS) ... InHamP
Purdue University, Calumet Campus, Hammond, IN [*Library symbol Library of Congress Obsolete*] (LCLS) ... InLP-Ham
Purdue University, Calumet Campus, Hammond, IN [*OCLC symbol*] (OCLC) ... IPC
Purdue University Fast FORTRAN [*Formula Translation*] **Translator** [*Computer science*] ... PUFFT
Purdue University, Lafayette, IN [*Library symbol Library of Congress*] (LCLS) ... InLP
Purdue University, Lafayette, IN [*OCLC symbol*] (OCLC) ... IPL
Purdue University, North Central Campus, Westville, IN [*Library symbol Library of Congress*] (LCLS) ... InWevP
Purdue University, North Central Campus, Westville, IN [*OCLC symbol*] (OCLC) ... IPN
Purdue University Reactor ... PUR
Purdue University Research (MCD) ... PUR
Purdue University-Calumet (GAGS) ... Purdue U (Calumet)
Purdy Treatment Center for Women, Gig Harbor, WA [*Library symbol Library of Congress*] (LCLS) ... WaGhP
Pure and Applied Chemistry [*IUPAC*] ... PAC
Pure and Vulcanized Rubber (IAA) ... PVR
Pure and Vulcanized Rubber Insulation ... P & VIR
Pure Atria Corp. [*NASDAQ symbol*] (SAG) ... PASW
Pure Atria Corp. [*Associated Press*] (SAG) ... PureAtria
Pure Car Carrier [*Shipping*] (DS) ... PCC
Pure Car Truck Carrier [*Shipping*] (DS) ... PCTC
Pure Clairvoyance [*Psychical research*] ... PC
Pure Direct Current [*Electronics*] (IAA) ... PDC
Pure Edge Dislocation ... PED
Pure Fluid Amplification ... PFA
Pure Fluid Encoder System ... PFES
Pure Fluid Impact Modulator ... PFIM
Pure Fluid System ... PFS
Pure Gold Resources, Inc. [*Toronto Stock Exchange symbol*] ... PUG
Pure Grain Alcohol ... PGA
Pure Gum [*of envelopes*] ... PG
Pure India Rubber [*Cables*] ... PIR
Pure Lemon Juice ... PLJ
Pure Mexican Cocaine (AD) ... pMc
Pure Milk Tablet (IIA) ... PMT
Pure Pancreatic Juice ... PPJ
Pure Peruvian Cocaine (AD) ... pPc
Pure Plutonium Oxide ... PPO
Pure Prairie League [*Musical group*] ... PPL
Pure Premium Rating Method [*Insurance*] ... PPRM
Pure Pulmonary Atresia [*Medicine*] (DMAA) ... PPA
Pure Random Search [*Optimization method*] ... PRS
Pure Red Cell Agenesis [*Hematology*] (MAE) ... PRCA
Pure Red Cell Aplasia [*Hematology*] ... PRCA
Pure Research Institute [*Later, BRINC*] (EA) ... PRI
Pure Screw Dislocation ... PSD
Pure Software [*NASDAQ symbol*] (TTSB) ... PRSW
Pure Software, Inc. [*NASDAQ symbol*] (SAG) ... PRSW
Pure Software, Inc. [*Associated Press*] (SAG) ... PureSf
Pure Tech International, Inc. [*Associated Press*] (SAG) ... PureTc
Pure Tech International, Inc. [*NASDAQ symbol*] (NQ) ... PURT
Pure Telepathy [*Psychical research*] ... PT
Pure Terephthalic Acid (DICI) ... PTA
Pure Time Sharing [*Computer science*] (IEEE) ... PTS
Pure Tone Average [*Otorhinolaryngology*] (DAVI) ... PTA
Pure Tone Average Threshold (DMAA) ... PTAT
Pure Ultrafiltration (DMAA) ... PUF
Pure Water Flux [*Engineering*] ... PWF
Pure Water Preservation Society [*British*] ... PWPS
Pure White Cell Aplasia [*Medicine*] (DMAA) ... PWCA
Pure World, Inc. [*Associated Press*] (SAG) ... PureWld
Pure World, Inc. [*NASDAQ symbol*] (SAG) ... PURW
Purebred Dairy Cattle Association (EA) ... PDCA
Purebred Hanoverian Association of American Breeders and Owners (EA) ... PHAABO
Pureed, Mechanical, Soft [*Diet*] (DAVI) ... PMS
Purepac, Inc [*NASDAQ symbol*] (SAG) ... PURE
Purepac, Inc. [*Associated Press*] (SAG) ... Purepac
PureTec Corp. [*NASDAQ symbol*] (TTSB) ... PURT
Purex Corp., Carson, CA [*Library symbol Library of Congress*] (LCLS) ... CCarsP
Purgative [*Medicine*] (ROG) ... PUR
Purgativus [*Cathartic, purgative*] [*Latin*] (MAE) ... purg
Purge (NASA) ... PGE
Purge (AAG) ... PRG
Purge Alarm [*Nuclear energy*] (NRCH) ... PA
Purge Control Valve (NASA) ... PCV
Purge Fan [*Nuclear energy*] (NRCH) ... PF
Purge Isolation [*Nuclear energy*] (NRCH) ... PI
Purge, Vent, and Drain (NASA) ... PV & D
Purge, Vent, Drain System (MCD) ... PVD
Purge, Vent, Repressurize, and Drain (NASA) ... PVRD
Purgeable Organic Analyzer ... POA
Purgeable Organic Carbon [*Chemistry*] ... POC
Purgeable Organic Halogen [*Chemistry*] (FFDE) ... POX
Purge-and-Trap [*Technique*] [*Environmental Protection Agency*] ... P & T
Purge-and-Trap [*Technique*] [*Environmental Protection Agency*] ... PaT
Purge-and-Trap Gas Chromatography [*Environmental Protection Agency*] ... PATGC
Purging (MSA) ... PRNG
Purichlor Technology Ltd. [*Vancouver Stock Exchange symbol*] ... PUR
Purification ... PRFCN
Purification ... PURIF
Purified [*Animal breeding*] ... P
Purified Brucella Protein [*Biochemistry*] (DAVI) ... PBP
Purified Concentrate ... PC
Purified Diphtheria Toxoid Precipitated by Aluminum Phosphate (AAMN) ... PTAP
Purified Extract of Brucella abortus ... PEBA
Purified Isophthalic Acid ... PIA
Purified Protein Derivative (AD) ... ppd
Purified Protein Derivative [*Tuberculin*] ... PPD
Purified Protein Derivative - Battey [*Tuberculin*] (AAMN) ... PPD-B
Purified Protein Derivative-Standard [*Tuberculin*] ... PPD-S
Purified Spleen Extract [*Medicine*] (DMAA) ... PSE
Purified Terephthalic Acid [*Organic chemistry*] ... PTA
Purifier (AAG) ... PUR
Purine [*Biochemistry*] ... Pu
[*A*] **Purine** [*Biochemistry*] ... Pur
[*A*] **Purine Nucleoside** [*Also, R*] ... Puo
[*A*] **Purine Nucleoside** [*One-letter symbol; see Puo*] ... R
Purine Nucleotide Phosphorylase [*An enzyme*] (DAVI) ... PNP
Purine Repressor [*Biochemistry*] ... PurR
Purine-Nucleoside Phosphorylase [*An enzyme*] ... PNP
Purinethol [*Mercaptopurine*] [*Also, M, MP*] [*Antineoplastic drug*] ... P
Purinethol, Oncovin, Methotrexate, Prednisone [*Medicine*] (MEDA) ... POMP
Purity [*of the Drug*] [*Pharmacy*] (ROG) ... PUR
Purity-Supreme [*Supermarkets*] ... PS
Purkinje Cell [*Neuroanatomy*] ... P
Purkinje Cell [*Neuroanatomy*] ... PC
Purkinje Cell Layer [*Cytology*] ... PCL
Purkinje Fiber [*Medicine*] (DMAA) ... PETT
Purkinje Fibers [*Cardiology*] (DAVI) ... PF
Purl [*Knitting*] ... P
Purl into Back of Stitch [*Knitting*] (WDAA) ... PB
Purley Library, Croydon, United Kingdom [*Library symbol Library of Congress*] (LCLS) ... UkCrP
Purlwise [*Knitting*] ... PW
Purnell Library Service [*Commercial firm*] ... PLS
Puromycin [*Trypanocide*] [*Antineoplastic drug*] ... PUR
Puromycin Aminonucleoside [*Biochemistry*] (OA) ... PA
Puromycin Aminonucleoside [*Medicine*] (DMAA) ... PAN
Puromycin Aminonucleoside [*Biochemistry*] ... PANS
Purple ... P
Purple ... PPL
Purple (AAG) ... PR
Purple (MSA) ... PRP
Purple (ROG) ... PU
Purple [*Philately*] ... pur
Purple Acid Phosphatase [*An enzyme*] ... PAP
Purple Agar Base [*Media*] [*Microbiology*] ... PAB
Purple Finch [*Ornithology*] ... PF
Purple Flower Gang (EA) ... PFG
Purple Heart [*Given to personnel wounded in military service*] [*Military decoration*] ... PH
Purple Indicating Light (MSA) ... PIL
Purple Loosestrife Task Force [*Defunct*] (EA) ... PLTF
Purple Martin Conservation Association (EA) ... PMCA
Purple Plum Association [*Defunct*] (EA) ... PPA
Purple Urine Bag Syndrome [*Medicine*] (DMAA) ... PUBS
Purple-K-Powder ... PKP
Purple's Statutes, Scates' Compilation [*A publication*] (DLA) ... Purple's St
Purplish Blue ... PB
Purplish Pink (AD) ... pPk
Purplish Red (AD) ... pR
Purplish Red ... PR
Purpose ... PPSE
Purpose (MSA) ... PRP
Purpose (AFM) ... PURP

Purpose and Activities (NITA) .... PA
Purpose Identification Code .... PIC
Purpose Identification Code - Month and Calendar Year of Detachment (DNAB) .... PIC-MOD
Purpose in Life [*Personality development test*] [*Psychology*] .... PIL
Purpose of Neighborhood Youth [*Foundation*] .... PONY
Purpose-Made [*Construction*] .... PM
Purpura Fulminans [*Medicine*] (DMAA) .... PETT
Purpura Fulminans (DMAA) .... PF
Purpura Hyperglobulinemia [*Medicine*] (DAVI) .... PH
Purpure [*Purple*] [*Heraldry*] .... P
Purpure [*Purple*] [*Heraldry*] .... PUR
Purpure [*Purple*] [*Heraldry*] (ROG) .... PURP
Purse Seine Vessel Owners Association (EA) .... PSVOA
Purse Seine Vessel Owners Marketing Association [*Later, PSVOA*] (EA) .... PSVOMA
Pursuance (ROG) .... PURSCE
Pursuant (AABC) .... PUR
Pursuant .... PURST
Pursuant to Authority Contained In [*Army*] .... PAC
Pursuant to Instructions Contained In (MUGU) .... PIC
Pursuing Our Italian Names Together (EA) .... POINT
Pursuit [*Airplane designation*] .... P
Pursuit (AABC) .... PUR
Pursuit .... PURS
Pursuit Deterrent Munition .... PDM
[*The*] **Pursuit of Happiness** [*Rock music group*] .... TPOH
Purus [*Pure*] [*Latin*] .... pur
Purus, Inc. [*NASDAQ symbol*] (SAG) .... PURS
Purus, Inc. [*Associated Press*] (SAG) .... Purus
Purvis' Collection of the Laws of Virginia [*A publication*] (DLA) .... Purv Coll
Pusan [*South Korea*] [*Seismograph station code, US Geological Survey Closed*] (SEIS) .... PUS
Pusan [*South Korea*] [*Airport symbol*] (OAG) .... PUS
Pusat Dokumentasi dan Informasi Ilmiah [*Indonesian Center for Scientific Documentation and Information*] [*Information service or system*] (IID) .... PDII
Pusat Dokumentasi Ilmiah Nasional (NITA) .... PDIN
Pusdiklat Perhubungan Udara/PLP [*Indonesia*] [*ICAO designator*] (FAAC) .... UDA
Push and Hold [*Push button*] .... PAH
Push and Latch [*Push button*] .... PAL
Push and Release [*Push button*] .... PAR
Push Button [*Automotive engineering*] .... P/BTN
Push Button .... PB
Push Button Unit (NITA) .... PBU
Push Down List [*Computer science*] (MHDI) .... PDL
Push Down List [*Computer science*] (IAA) .... PUDL
Push Down Memory [*Computer science*] .... PDM
Push Down Memory MODEM [*Computer science*] .... PDMM
Push Down Stack Automaton [*Computer science*] .... PSA
Push Fluids [*Medicine*] (DMAA) .... PETT
PUSH [*People United to Save Humanity*] **International Trade Bureau** (EA) .... PITB
Push Money [*Sales incentive*] .... PM
Push Off Early, Tomorrow's Saturday [*Bowdlerized version*] .... POETS
Push Off Quickly [*i.e., Be quick about it*] [*British*] .... POQ
Push Over Pull Up (NASA) .... POPU
Push Rod [*Mechanical engineering*] .... PRD
Push to Talk .... PTT
Push-Button Data Generator (IEEE) .... PBDG
Push-Button Indicator .... PBI
Push-Button Operation .... PBO
Push-Button Panel .... PBP
Push-Button Rotary Switch .... PBRS
Push-Button Selection Station .... PSS
Push-Button Station (IAA) .... PBSTA
Push-Button Switch .... PBS
Push-Button Switch .... PBSW
Push-Button Telephone .... PBT
Pushdown Automation [*Computer science*] (HGAA) .... PDA
Push-Effective Address [*Computer science*] (IEEE) .... PEA
Pusher [*Freight*] .... PSHR
Pusher Plane .... PP
Push-On, Pull-Off [*Computer science*] .... POPO
Push-Out Base (IAA) .... POB
Push-Pull [*Technical drawings*] .... PP
Push-Pull (AD) .... p-p
Push-Pull Amplifier (IAA) .... PPA
Push-Pull Bearing .... PPB
Push-Pull Output (DEN) .... PPO
Push-Pull Power (IAA) .... PPP
Push-Pull Power Amplifier (IAA) .... PPPA
Pushto [*MARC language code Library of Congress*] (LCCP) .... pus
Pustulotic Arthroosteitis [*Medicine*] (DMAA) .... PAO
Put [*In options listings of newspapers*] .... P
Put and Call [*Stock exchange term*] .... P & C
Put and Call [*Stock exchange term*] .... PAC
Put and Call Brokers and Dealers Association [*Inactive*] (EA) .... PCBDA
Put Away [*Papers*] [*British*] .... PA
Put It in Corporate Executives' Swimming Pools [*Waste management slang*] .... PICESP
Put of More [*Stock exchange term*] .... P/M
Put Out [*i.e., angry*] [*Bowdlerized version*] .... PO'd
Put Out [*i.e., angry*] [*Bowdlerized version*] .... PO'ed
Put to Sleep [*ASPCA terminology*] .... PTS
Put Word in String (SAA) .... PUTWS
Putao [*Myanmar*] [*Airport symbol*] (OAG) .... PBU
Putao [*Burma*] [*Airport symbol*] (AD) .... PUT
Putao [*Myanmar*] [*ICAO location identifier*] (ICLI) .... VBPT
Putative Neurotransmitter [*Biochemistry*] .... PN
Puterbaugh's Illinois Chancery Pleading [*A publication*] (DLA) .... Puter Ch
Puterbaugh's Illinois Common Law Pleading [*A publication*] (DLA) .... Puter Pl
Putnam Cal Inv Grade Muni [*AMEX symbol*] (TTSB) .... PCA
Putnam California Investment Grade [*Associated Press*] (SAG) .... PutnCA
Putnam California Investment Grade Municipal [*AMEX symbol*] (SPSG) .... PCA
Putnam Convertible Opportunities & Income Trust [*Associated Press*] (SAG) .... PCOIT
Putnam Convertible Opportunities & Income Trust [*NYSE symbol*] (SAG) .... PCV
Putnam County Community Unit, School District 535, Granville, IL [*Library symbol Library of Congress*] (LCLS) .... IGranPSD
Putnam County Library, Condit Branch, Putnam, IL [*Library symbol Library of Congress*] (LCLS) .... IHenn-P
Putnam County Library, Granville Branch, Granville, IL [*Library symbol Library of Congress*] (LCLS) .... IHenn-G
Putnam County Library, Hennepin Branch, Hennepin, IL [*Library symbol Library of Congress*] (LCLS) .... IHenn-H
Putnam County Library, Hennepin, IL [*Library symbol Library of Congress*] (LCLS) .... IHenn
Putnam County Library, Magnolia Branch, Magnolia, IL [*Library symbol Library of Congress*] (LCLS) .... IHenn-M
Putnam County Library, McNabb Branch, McNabb, IL [*Library symbol Library of Congress*] (LCLS) .... IHenn-Mc
Putnam County Library, Standard Branch, Standard, IL [*Library symbol Library of Congress*] (LCLS) .... IHenn-S
Putnam County Public Library, Cookeville, TN [*Library symbol Library of Congress*] (LCLS) .... TCoo
Putnam, CT [*Location identifier FAA*] (FAAL) .... PUT
Putnam, CT [*AM radio station call letters*] .... WINY
Putnam Cv Opp Inc. Tr [*NYSE symbol*] (TTSB) .... PCV
Putnam Dividend Income [*NYSE symbol*] (TTSB) .... PDI
Putnam Dividend Income [*NYSE symbol*] (SPSG) .... PDI
Putnam Dividend Income Fund [*Associated Press*] (SAG) .... PDIF
Putnam Hi Income Cv/Bd Fd [*NYSE symbol*] (TTSB) .... PCF
Putnam Hi Yield Muni [*NYSE symbol*] (TTSB) .... PYM
Putnam High Income Convertible & Bond Fund [*NYSE symbol*] (SPSG) .... PCF
Putnam High Income Convertible & Bond Fund [*Associated Press*] (SAG) .... PHICB
Putnam High Yield Municipal [*NYSE symbol*] (SPSG) .... PYM
Putnam High Yield Municipal Trust [*Associated Press*] (SAG) .... PHYM
Putnam Interm Gvt Income [*NYSE symbol*] (TTSB) .... PGT
Putnam Intermediate Government Income [*NYSE symbol*] (SPSG) .... PGT
Putnam Intermediate Government Income Trust [*Associated Press*] (SAG) .... PIGIT
Putnam Inv Grade Muni Tr [*NYSE symbol*] (TTSB) .... PGM
Putnam Inv Grade Muni Tr II [*NYSE symbol*] (TTSB) .... PMG
Putnam Inv Grade Muni Tr III [*AMEX symbol*] (TTSB) .... PML
Putnam Investment Grade Multiple Sectors III [*Associated Press*] (SAG) PIGMT3
Putnam Investment Grade Multiple Sectors III [*AMEX symbol*] (SPSG) .... PML
Putnam Investment Grade Municipal Trade II [*NYSE symbol*] (SPSG) .... PMG
Putnam Investment Grade Municipal Trust [*NYSE symbol*] (SPSG) .... PGM
Putnam Investment Grade Municipal Trust [*Associated Press*] (SAG) .... PIGM
Putnam Investment Grade Municipal Trust II [*Associated Press*] (SAG) PIGMT2
Putnam Managed Hi Yield Tr [*NYSE symbol*] (TTSB) .... PTM
Putnam Managed High Yield Trust [*Associated Press*] (SAG) .... PMHYT
Putnam Managed High Yield Trust [*NYSE symbol*] (SPSG) .... PTM
Putnam Managed Muni Income [*NYSE symbol*] (TTSB) .... PMM
Putnam Managed Municipal Income [*NYSE symbol*] (SPSG) .... PMM
Putnam Managed Municipal Income Trust [*Associated Press*] (SAG) .... PMMI
Putnam Master Income Tr [*NYSE symbol*] (TTSB) .... PMT
Putnam Master Income Trust [*Associated Press*] (SAG) .... PMIT
Putnam Master Income Trust [*NYSE symbol*] (SPSG) .... PMT
Putnam Master Interm Income [*NYSE symbol*] (TTSB) .... PIM
Putnam Master Intermediate Income Trust [*NYSE symbol*] (SPSG) .... PIM
Putnam Master Intermediate Income Trust [*Associated Press*] (SAG) .... PMIIT
Putnam Memorial Hospital, Medical Library, Bennington, VT [*Library symbol Library of Congress*] (LCLS) .... VtBennP
Putnam Muni Opport Tr [*NYSE symbol*] (TTSB) .... PMO
Putnam Municipal Opportunities Trust [*NYSE symbol*] (SPSG) .... PMO
Putnam Municipal Opportunities Trust [*Associated Press*] (SAG) .... PMOT
Putnam Museum, Davenport, IA [*Library symbol Library of Congress*] (LCLS) .... IaDaPM
Putnam New York Investment Grade [*Associated Press*] (SAG) .... PutNY
Putnam New York Investment Grade Municipal [*AMEX symbol*] (SPSG) .... PMN
Putnam North Westchester S.L.S., Yorktown Heights, NY [*Library symbol*] [*Library of Congress*] (LCLS) .... NYhP
Putnam NY Inv Grade Muni [*AMEX symbol*] (TTSB) .... PMN
Putnam Premier Income Tr [*NYSE symbol*] (TTSB) .... PPT
Putnam Premier Income Trust [*Associated Press*] (SAG) .... PPrIT
Putnam Premier Income Trust [*NYSE symbol*] (SPSG) .... PPT
Putnam Public Library, Nashville, MI [*Library symbol Library of Congress*] (LCLS) .... MiNas
Putnam Tax Free Health Care Fund [*Associated Press*] (SAG) .... PTFHC
Putnam Tax-Free Health Care Fund [*NYSE symbol*] (SPSG) .... PMH
Putnam Tax-Free Hlth Care Fd [*NYSE symbol*] (TTSB) .... PMH
Putnam-Northern Westchester BOCES [*Boards of Cooperative Educational Services*], Yorktown Heights, NY [*OCLC symbol*] (OCLC) .... YPW
Putnam's Proceedings before the Justice of the Peace [*A publication*] (DLA) .... Putnam
Putout [*Baseball*] .... PO
Putrescine [*Organic chemistry*] .... PUT
Putting Hubby Through [*College "degree" earned by some wives*] .... PHT

Putting Research into Educational Practice [*Information service of ERIC*] .... PREP
Putting Research into Educational Research .... PRER
Putting-On Voltage [*Doppler navigation*] (DEN) .... POV
Putumayo [*Ecuador*] [*ICAO location identifier*] (ICLI) .... SEPT
Putusibau/Pangsuma [*Indonesia*] [*ICAO location identifier*] (ICLI) .... WIOP
Puu Honuaula [*Hawaii*] [*Seismograph station code, US Geological Survey*] (SEIS) .... PHO
Puu Huluhulu [*Hawaii*] [*Seismograph station code, US Geological Survey Closed*] (SEIS) .... PHH
Puu Pili [*Hawaii*] [*Seismograph station code, US Geological Survey*] (SEIS) .... PPL
Puumala [*Vole virus*] .... PA
Puumala Virus .... PUV
Puyallup, WA [*AM radio station call letters*] .... KJUN
Puyallup, WA [*AM radio station call letters*] (RBYB) .... KKBY-AM
Puy-De-Dome [*France*] [*Seismograph station code, US Geological Survey Closed*] (SEIS) .... PDD
Puyo [*Ecuador*] [*ICAO location identifier*] (ICLI) .... SEPY
Puzzle Buffs International (EA) .... PBI
PVC [*Polyvinylchloride*] **Belting Manufacturers Association** [*Defunct*] (EA) .... PVCBMA
PVC Container [*NASDAQ symbol*] (TTSB) .... PVCC
PVC Container Corp. [*Associated Press*] (SAG) .... PVC
PVC Container Corp. [*Eatontown, NJ*] [*NASDAQ symbol*] (NQ) .... PVCC
PVF Capital [*NASDAQ symbol*] (TTSB) .... PVFC
PVF Capital Corp. [*NASDAQ symbol*] (SAG) .... PVFC
PVF Capital Corp. [*Associated Press*] (SAG) .... PVFCap
PWA Corp. [*Toronto Stock Exchange symbol Vancouver Stock Exchange symbol*] .... PWA
Pweto [*Zaire*] [*ICAO location identifier*] (ICLI) .... FZQC
PWG Capital Trust I [*Associated Press*] (SAG) .... PWG C
PWG Capital Trust I [*NYSE symbol*] (SAG) .... PWJ
PWRS [*Prepositioned War Reserve Stock*] **Interrogation and Readiness Reporting System** [*Navy*] .... PIRR
PXRE Corp. [*NASDAQ symbol*] (TTSB) .... PXRE
PXRE Corp. [*Associated Press*] (SAG) .... PXRE Cp
Pya [*Monetary unit*] [*Myanmar*] .... P
Pyatigorsk [*Former USSR Seismograph station code, US Geological Survey*] (SEIS) .... PYA
Pycnocline Scattering Layer (DNAB) .... PSL
Pyelonephritis [*Medicine*] (MAE) .... PN
Pygmy Fund (EA) .... PF
[*The*] **Pygmy Fund** (EA) .... TPF
Pyhasalmi [*Finland ICAO location identifier*] (ICLI) .... EFPY
Pyke's Lower Canada King's Bench Reports [*1809-10*] [*A publication*] (ILCA) .... Py R
Pyke's Lower Canada King's Bench Reports [*1809-10*] [*A publication*] (ILCA) .... Pyke
Pyke's Lower Canada King's Bench Reports [*1809-10*] [*A publication*] (ILCA) .... Pyke LC
Pyke's Lower Canada King's Bench Reports [*1809-10*] [*A publication*] (ILCA) .... Pyke's R
Pyke's Reports [*Canada*] [*A publication*] (DLA) .... PR
Pylon Electronic Development Co., Ltd., Lachine, PQ, Canada [*Library symbol*] [*Library of Congress*] (LCLS) .... CaQLaPED
Pylon Electronic Development Co. Ltd., Lachine, Quebec [*Library symbol National Library of Canada*] (NLC) .... QLPED
Pylon Electronic Development Co. Ltd., Ottawa, Ontario [*Library symbol National Library of Canada*] (NLC) .... OOPED
Pylon/Fin Movement .... P/FM
Pyloric Dilator [*Neuron*] .... PD
Pyloric Stenosis [*Medicine*] .... PS
Pyloroplasty and Vagotomy [*Medicine*] .... P & V
Pyng Tech [*Vancouver Stock Exchange symbol*] .... PYT
Pyoderma Gangrenosum [*Medicine*] .... PG
Pyogenic Abscess of the Liver [*Medicine*] (DMAA) .... PAL
Pyogenic Culture [*Medicine*] (MAE) .... PyC
Pyongtaek [*South Korea ICAO location identifier*] (ICLI) .... RKSG
Pyongyang [*North Korea*] [*Airport symbol*] (OAG) .... FNJ
Pyongyang [*Heizo*] [*North Korea*] [*Seismograph station code, US Geological Survey*] [*Closed*] (SEIS) .... PYO
Pyongyang [*North Korea ICAO location identifier*] (ICLI) .... ZKIA
Pyongyang [*North Korea ICAO location identifier*] (ICLI) .... ZKKK
Pyongyang/Sunan [*North Korea ICAO location identifier*] (ICLI) .... ZKPY
Pyralidae [*Entomology*] .... Pyr
Pyramid [*California*] [*Seismograph station code, US Geological Survey*] (SEIS) .... PYR
Pyramid (MSA) .... PYR
Pyramid (VRA) .... pyrm
Pyramid [*Freight*] .... PYRMD
Pyramid Air Lines [*Egypt*] [*ICAO designator*] (FAAC) .... PYR
Pyramid Element Designator .... PED
Pyramid Texts (BJA) .... PT
Pyramidal Decussation [*Neuroanatomy*] .... PD
Pyramidal Tract [*Anatomy*] .... PT
Pyramidal Tract [*Neuroanatomy*] .... Pyr
Pyramids [*Board on Geographic Names*] .... PYRS
Pyranose [*One-letter symbol*] [*Biochemistry*] .... p
Pyrazinamide [*Antibacterial compound*] .... PZA
Pyrazine [*Organic chemistry*] .... PZ
Pyrazofurin [*Antineoplastic drug*] .... PRZF
Pyrazofurin [*Antineoplastic drug regimen*] (DAVI) .... PRZF
Pyrene [*Organic chemistry*] (AAMN) .... Py
Pyrenebutyric Acid [*Organic chemistry*] .... PBA
Pyrenees [*France*] [*Seismograph station code, US Geological Survey*] (SEIS) .... PYF
Pyrenees Region [*MARC geographic area code Library of Congress*] (LCCP) .... ep----
Pyrenees-Orientales (AD) .... P-O
Pyrethrum [*Pellitory*] [*Pharmacology*] (ROG) .... PYRETH
Pyretic Tick-Borne Encephalitis [*Medicine*] (DMAA) .... PTBE
Pyrexia of Unknown Etiology [*Medicine*] .... PUE
Pyrexia [*fever*] **of Unknown Origin** [*Commonly called Trench Fever*] .... PUO
Pyrgos [*Greece*] [*Airport symbol*] (AD) .... PYR
Pyribenzamine [*Antihistamine*] [*Trademark*] .... PBZ
Pyridine [*Organic chemistry*] .... Py
Pyridine [*Organic chemistry*] .... PYR
Pyridine Aldoxime Methiodide [*Biochemistry*] .... PAM
Pyridine Aldoxime Methyl [*Pharmacology*] .... PAM
Pyridine Nucleotide [*Medicine*] (DMAA) .... PN
Pyridineacetic Acid [*Organic chemistry*] .... PAA
(Pyridinealdehyde)pyridylhydrazone [*Organic chemistry*] .... PAPH
Pyridinealdoxime Methochloride [*Organic chemistry*] .... PAMCl
Pyridine-Butadiene Rubber .... PBR
Pyridinethiol Oxide [*Pharmacology*] .... PTO
Pyridinium Bromide Perbromide [*Inorganic chemistry*] .... PBPB
Pyridinium Chlorochromate [*Organic chemistry*] .... PCC
Pyridinium Dichromate [*Organic chemistry*] .... PDC
Pyridinium Para-Toluenesulfonate [*Organic chemistry*] .... PPTS
Pyridinium(nitro)benzenesulfonate [*Organic chemistry*] .... PNBS
Pyridinium-para-Tosylate [*Organic chemistry*] .... PPTS
Pyridinylmethylethylene(hydrazinecarbothioamide) [*Organic chemistry*] .... PMHC
Pyridohomotropane [*Organic chemistry*] .... PHT
Pyridoxal [*Also, Pxl*] [*Biochemistry*] .... PL
Pyridoxal [*Also, PL*] [*Biochemistry*] .... Pxl
Pyridoxal Isonicotinoylhydrazone [*Biochemistry*] .... PINH
Pyridoxal Phosphate [*Also, PLP*] [*Biochemistry*] .... PALP
Pyridoxal Phosphate [*Also, PALP*] [*Biochemistry*] .... PLP
Pyridoxal Phosphate Effect [*Medicine*] .... PPE
Pyridoxamine [*Also, Pxm*] [*Biochemistry*] .... PM
Pyridoxamine [*Also, PM*] [*Biochemistry*] .... Pxm
Pyridoxamine Phosphate [*Biochemistry*] .... PMP
Pyridoxamine Phosphate [*or Pyridoxyl Phosphate*] [*Organic chemistry*] (DAVI) .... PyrP
Pyridoxine [*or Pyridoxol*] [*Also, Pxn*] [*Biochemistry*] .... PN
Pyridoxine [*Also, PN*] [*Biochemistry*] .... Pxn
Pyridoxine Hydrochloride [*Pharmacology*] (DAVI) .... B_6
Pyridoxine Kinase (DMAA) .... PNK
Pyridoxine Phosphate [*Biochemistry*] .... PNP
Pyridoxine-Deficient Diet (MAE) .... PDD
Pyridoxyl [*Biochemistry*] .... Pxy
Pyridoxyl (Pyridoxamine) Phosphate (BABM) .... PyrP
Pyridyl Oxide-N-tert-butylnitrone [*Organic chemistry*] .... POBN
(Pyridylazo)dimethylaniline [*Organic chemistry*] .... PADA
Pyridylazonaphthol [*An indicator*] [*Chemistry*] .... PAN
(Pyridylazo)resorcinol [*Organic chemistry*] .... PAR
(Pyridylcarbonylamino)tetrahydropyridine [*Biochemistry*] .... PATP
(Pyridyl)diphenyltriazine [*Analytical chemistry*] .... PDT
Pyridylethylamine [*Organic chemistry*] .... PEA
Pyridylethylcysteine [*Biochemistry*] .... PEC
Pyridylmercuric Acetate [*Fungicide*] [*Organic chemistry*] .... PMA
(Pyridyloxide)butylnitrone [*Organic chemistry*] .... POBN
Pyrimethamine-Quinine [*Organic chemistry*] (MAE) .... PQ
Pyrimethamine-Sulfadoxine [*Pharmacology*] (DAVI) .... PRM-SDX
Pyrimidine (DOG) .... Py
[*A*] **Pyrimidine** [*Biochemistry*] .... Pyr
Pyrimidine [*Single-letter symbol*] [*Genetics*] (DOG) .... Y
[*A*] **Pyrimidine Nucleoside** [*Also, Y*] .... Pyd
[*A*] **Pyrimidine Nucleoside** [*One-letter symbol; see Pyd*] .... Y
Pyrite [*CIPW classification*] [*Geology*] .... pr
Pyrite-Pyrrhotite-Magnetite [*Mineralogy*] .... PPM
Pyritization Index [*Geoscience*] .... PI
Pyro Ammonia (ROG) .... PA
Pyro Battery (KSC) .... PBAT
Pyro Continuity Verification Box [*NASA*] (NASA) .... PCVB
Pyro Substitute Monitor [*NASA*] (NASA) .... PSM
Pyroactuated Ball Valve .... PABV
Pyroair Tech [*Vancouver Stock Exchange symbol*] .... PYA
Pyrocap International [*ECM Symbol*] (TTSB) .... PYR.EC
Pyrocap International Corp. [*Associated Press*] (SAG) .... Pyr
Pyrocap International Corp. [*AMEX symbol*] (SAG) .... PYR
Pyrocap International Corp. [*Associated Press*] (SAG) .... Pyrocp
Pyrocatechol Violet [*Also, PV*] [*An indicator Chemistry*] .... PCV
Pyrocatechol Violet [*Also, PCV*] [*An indicator Chemistry*] .... PV
Pyrochromatogram [*Analytical chemistry*] .... PYCG
Pyroconvective Cooling .... PCC
Pyroelectric .... PE
Pyroelectric Quad Detector .... PQD
Pyroelectric Vidicon (PDAA) .... PEV
Pyrogallic Acid (ROG) .... PYRO
Pyrogallol Red [*Also, PR*] [*An indicator Chemistry*] .... PGR
Pyrogallol Red [*Also, PGR*] [*An indicator Chemistry*] .... PR
Pyrogen [*Medicine*] .... Py
Pyrogen Unit [*Biochemistry*] .... PYGN
Pyrogenic Exotoxin C [*Medicine*] .... PEC
Pyrographalloy Boron .... PGB
Pyrolysis Field Desorption Mass Spectrometry .... Py-FD-MS
Pyrolysis Fuel Oil [*Petroleum refining*] .... PFO
Pyrolysis Gas Analysis .... PGA
Pyrolysis Gas Chromatography .... PGC
Pyrolysis Gas Chromatography .... PYGC

Pyrolysis Gas Liquid Chromatography .... PGLC
Pyrolysis High-Resolution Mass Spectrometry .... Py-HRMS
Pyrolysis Mass Spectrometry .... Py-MS
Pyrolysis Time-Resolved Mass Spectrometry .... Py-TRMS
Pyrolysis to Gases and Liquids [Chemical processing] .... PTGL
Pyrolytic Boron Nitride [Inorganic chemistry] .... PBN
Pyrolytic Graphite (MCD) .... PG
Pyrolytic Release .... PR
Pyrolyzed Polyacrylonitrile [Organic chemistry] .... PPAN
Pyromaniac (WDAA) .... PYRO
Pyromellitic Acid [Organic chemistry] .... PMA
Pyromellitic Dianhydride [Organic chemistry] .... PMDA
Pyrometer (IEEE) .... PY
Pyrometer (AAG) .... PYR
Pyrometer [Engineering] .... PYROM
Pyrometric Cone Equivalent [Refractory industry] .... PCE
Pyronin Y [A biological dye] .... PY
Pyrophosphate [Chemistry] .... PP
Pyrophosphate [Scintiscanning] .... PYP
Pyrophosphate Index [Agronomy] .... PPI
Pyrophosphate, Inorganic [Chemistry] .... PPi
Pyrotechnic .... PYRO
Pyrotechnic Circuit Test Console (KSC) .... PCTC
Pyrotechnic Control Assembly [NASA] .... PCA
Pyrotechnic Countermeasure [Military] (SDI) .... PCM
Pyrotechnic Development Vehicle (PDAA) .... PDV
Pyrotechnic Devices Checker .... PDC
Pyrotechnic Devices Simulator (SAA) .... PDS
Pyrotechnic Electron Generator (MCD) .... PEG
Pyrotechnic Gyro (AAG) .... PG
Pyrotechnic Ignition Control (NASA) .... PIC
Pyrotechnic Initiator Capacitor (NASA) .... PIC
Pyrotechnic Initiator Controller (NASA) .... PIC
Pyrotechnic Initiator Unit (MCD) .... PIU
Pyrotechnic Installation Building [NASA] (KSC) .... PIB
Pyrotechnic Optical Plume Simulator (MCD) .... POPS
Pyrotechnic Outside Warning System (IEEE) .... POWS
Pyrotechnic Rocket Container .... PRC
Pyrotechnic Signal Manufacturers Association (EA) .... PSMA
Pyrotechnic Verification Test [NASA] (NASA) .... PVT
Pyrotechnical (ROG) .... PYROTECH
Pyrotechnical and Explosive [NASA] (KSC) .... P & E

Pyrotechnical Evaluation Range [Army] (RDA) .... PER
Pyrotechnics Arming Switch .... PAS
Pyrotechnics Circuit Simulator .... PCS
Pyrotechnics Guild International (EA) .... PGI
Pyrotechnics No-Voltage Test Set .... PNVTS
Pyroxene [Also, PYX] [A mineral] .... PX
Pyroxene [Also, PX] [A mineral] .... PYX
Pyroxene Gneisses [Agronomy] .... PYROX GN
Pyroxene Subgroup [Acmite, sodium metasilicate, potassium metasilicate, diopside, wollastonite, hypersthene] [CIPW classification Geology] .... P
Pyroxiline (VRA) .... pyrox
Pyrrhus [of Plutarch] [Classical studies] (OCD) .... Pyrrh
Pyrrolidine [Organic chemistry] .... PYRR
Pyrrolidinoethyl Chloride [Organic chemistry] .... PYRREC
Pyrrolidonecarboxylic Acid [Organic chemistry] .... PCA
Pyrroline-5-Carboxylate Reductase (DMAA) .... PYCR
Pyrrolinecarboxylic Acid [Biochemistry] .... PC
Pyrrolizidine Alkaloid [Toxicology] .... PA
Pyrrolnitrin [Antifungal antibiotic] .... PN
Pyrroloquinoline Quinone [Biochemistry] .... PQQ
Pyruvate [Biochemistry] .... PYR
Pyruvate [Organic chemistry] (DAVI) .... PYRUV
Pyruvate Carboxylase [An enzyme] (MAE) .... PC
Pyruvate Decarboxylase [An enzyme] .... PDC
Pyruvate Dehydrogenase (DMAA) .... PDF
Pyruvate Dehydrogenase [An enzyme] .... PDH
Pyruvate Dehydrogenase Complex [Also, PDHC] [Biochemistry] .... PDC
Pyruvate Dehydrogenase Complex [Biochemistry] .... PDHC
Pyruvate, Inosine, Glucose Phosphate, Adenine (AAMN) .... PIGPA
Pyruvate Kinase [An enzyme] .... PK
Pyruvate Kinase [An enzyme] (DAVI) .... PYRKIN
Pyruvate Kinase, Liver Type [Medicine] (DMAA) .... PKI
Pyruvate Oxidation Factor [Biochemistry] .... POF
Pyruvenol [Biochemistry] .... Prv
[Serum Glutamic] Pyruvic Transaminase [Also, SGPT] [An enzyme] (DAVI) ...... PT
Pythian [of Pindar] [Classical studies] (OCD) .... Pyth
Pythium [A fungus] .... PY
Pythium aphanidermatum [A fungus] .... PA
Pyxis [Constellation] .... Pyx
Pyxis [Constellation] .... Pyxi
Pyxis Corp. [Associated Press] (SAG) .... Pyxis
Pyxis Corp. [NASDAQ symbol] (SAG) .... PYXS

Q
By Meaning

Q Allowance List [*Aviation*] (DNAB) .... QAL
Q Band (IDOE) .... Q
Q Output (IDOE) .... Q
Q Steaks, Inc. [*NASDAQ symbol*] (SAG) .... QSTK
Q. Van Weytson on Average [*A publication*] (DLA) .... Q Van Weyt
Qabel Foundation (EA) .... QF
Qachas' Nek [*Lesotho*] [*ICAO location identifier*] (ICLI) ...... FXQN
Qacha's Nek [*Lesotho*] [*Airport symbol*] (OAG) .... UNE
Qades [*Afghanistan*] [*ICAO location identifier*] (ICLI) ...... OAQD
Qadmoniot [*Jerusalem*] (BJA) .... Qad
Qaisar [*Afghanistan*] [*ICAO location identifier*] (ICLI) ...... OAQR
Qaisumah [*Saudi Arabia*] [*Airport symbol*] (OAG) .... AQI
Qala-I-Naw [*Afghanistan*] [*ICAO location identifier*] (ICLI) .. OAQN
Qala-I-Nyazkhan [*Afghanistan*] [*ICAO location identifier*] (ICLI) .. OAQK
Qala-Nau [*Afghanistan*] [*Airport symbol Obsolete*] (OAG) .. LQN
QANTAS Airways Ltd. [*Australia*] (DS) .... QA
QANTAS Airways Ltd. [*Australia ICAO designator*] .... QF
Qantas Airways Ltd. [*Australia ICAO designator*] (FAAC) .... QFA
QANTAS Empire Airways Ltd. [*Later, QANTAS Airways Ltd.*] .. QEA
Qantas Flight Catering Centre [*Australia*] .... QFCC
Qara Qash [*Sinkiang province of China*] (AD) .... QQ
Qara Qum [*Sinkiang province of China*] (AD) .... QQ
Qarar (BARN) .... Q
Qarqin [*Afghanistan*] [*ICAO location identifier*] (ICLI) ...... OAQQ
Qasim [*Pakistan*] [*ICAO location identifier*] (ICLI) .... OPQS
Qatabanian (BJA) .... Qat
Qatar [*MARC geographic area code Library of Congress*] (LCCP) .. a-qa--
Qatar [*MARC country of publication code Library of Congress*] (LCCP) .. qa
Qatar [*IYRU nationality code*] [*ANSI two-letter standard code*] (CNC) .. QA
Qatar [*ANSI three-letter standard code*] (CNC) .... QAT
Qatar (AD) .... Qat
Qatar Air Cargo [*FAA designator*] (FAAC) .... QAC
Qatar Airways [*FAA designator*] (FAAC) .... QTR
Qatar Amiri Flight [*ICAO designator*] (FAAC) .... QAF
Qatar Amiri Flight [*Qatar*] [*ICAO designator*] (ICDA) ...... QX
Qatar General Petroleum Corp. .... QGPC
Qatar General Petroleum Organization (AD) .... QGPO
Qatar Monetary Agency (AD) .... QMA
Qatar Petroleum Co. (AD) .... QPC
Qatar Riyal [*Monetary unit*] (BJA) .... QR
Qatn [*South Arabia*] [*Airport symbol*] (OAG) .... XTN
Qayyum Moslem League [*Pakistan*] (PD) .... QML
Qazigund [*India*] [*ICAO location identifier*] (ICLI) .... VIQG
QC Explorations [*Vancouver Stock Exchange symbol*] ...... QC
QC Optics [*AMEX symbol*] (SAG) .... OPC
QC Optics [*Associated Press*] (SAG) .... QC Opt
QCF Bancorp [*NASDAQ symbol*] (TTSB) .... QCFB
QCF Bancorp, Inc. [*Associated Press*] (SAG) .... QCF Bc
QCF Bancorp, Inc. [*NASDAQ symbol*] (SAG) .... QCFB
QData Systems, Inc. [*Vancouver Stock Exchange symbol*] .. QD
QEP Co., Inc. [*Associated Press*] (SAG) .... QEP Co
QEP Co., Inc. [*NASDAQ symbol*] (SAG) .... QEPC
Qere (BJA) .... Q
Qere (BJA) .... Qr
Q-Factor (DEN) .... Q
Qi and Yin Deficiency (DMAA) .... QYD
QIAGEN [*NASDAQ symbol*] (SAG) .... QGEN
QIAGEN [*Associated Press*] (SAG) .... QIAGEN
Qiemo [*China*] [*Airport symbol*] (OAG) .... IQM
Qingdao [*China*] [*Airport symbol*] (OAG) .... TAO
Qingdao [*China*] [*ICAO location identifier*] (ICLI) .... ZSQD
Qinghaosu [*Antimalarial drug*] .... QHS
Qingquangang [*China*] [*ICAO location identifier*] (ICLI) ... RCMQ
Qingyang [*China*] [*Airport symbol*] (OAG) .... IQN
Qiqihar [*China*] [*ICAO location identifier*] (ICLI) .... ZYQQ
Qishn [*People's Democratic Republic of Yemen*] [*ICAO location identifier*]
(ICLI) .... ODAQ
QIT - Fer et Titane, Inc., Sorel, Quebec [*Library symbol National Library of
Canada*] (NLC) .... QSOCS
Qlogic Corp. [*NASDAQ symbol*] (SAG) .... QLGC
Qlogic Corp. [*Associated Press*] (SAG) .... Qlogic
QLT Photofherapeutics [*NASDAQ symbol*] (TTSB) .... QLTIF
Q-Med, Inc. [*Associated Press*] (SAG) .... Q Med
Q-Med, Inc. [*Clark, NJ*] [*NASDAQ symbol*] (NQ) .... QEKG
QMG Holdings, Inc. [*Toronto Stock Exchange symbol*] ..... QMG
QMS, Inc. [*NYSE symbol*] (SPSG) .... AQM

QMS, Inc. [*Associated Press*] (SAG) .... QMS
Q-Phase CW Signal [*Television*] (IDOE) .... QCW
QPQ Corp. [*Associated Press*] (SAG) .... QPQ
QPQ Corp. [*Associated Press*] (SAG) .... QPQ Cp
QPQ Corp. [*NASDAQ symbol*] (SAG) .... QPQQ
QPQ Corp. Wrrt [*NASDAQ symbol*] (TTSB) .... QPQQWX
QPX Minerals, Inc. [*Vancouver Stock Exchange symbol*] ... QPX
QSA Tech, Inc. [*Vancouver Stock Exchange symbol*] .... QST
QSound Labs [*NASDAQ symbol*] (TTSB) .... QSNDF
Qsound Labs, Inc. [*NASDAQ symbol*] (SAG) .... QSND
Qsound Labs, Inc. [*Associated Press*] (SAG) .... Qsound
QSR Ltd. [*NASDAQ symbol*] (SAG) .... QSRT
QSR Ltd [*NASDAQ symbol*] (TTSB) .... QSRTF
Q-Switch LASER .... QSL
Q-Switch Ruby LASER .... QRL
Q-Tags Test of Personality [*Psychology*] .... QTTP
Quaalude [*or Methaqualone*] [*A trademark*] [*Pharmacology*] (DAVI) .. Q
Quaalude (AD) .... quaal
Quaalude (AD) .... quad
Quaalude [*Methaqualone*] [*A trademark*] [*Pharmacology*] (DAVI) .. QUALOD
Quaaludes [*Methaqualone*] [*Pharmacology*] (DAVI) .... ludes
Quabbin [*Massachusetts*] [*Seismograph station code, US Geological Survey*]
(SEIS) .... QUA
Quacksalver (AD) .... quack
Quacksalvers (AD) .... quacks
Quackupuncture (AD) .... quackupunc
Quaco Historical and Library Society, St. Martins, NB, Canada [*Library
symbol*] [*Library of Congress*] (LCLS) .... CaNBSmQH
Quaco Historical and Library Society, St. Martins, New Brunswick [*Library
symbol National Library of Canada*] (NLC) .... NBSQH
Quad (IAA) .... Q
Quad Asynchronous Local Terminal Adapter [*Computer science*]
(MHDB) .... QUALTA
Quad Bus Transceiver (NITA) .... QBT
Quad Center [*Typography*] .... QC
Quad City Hldgs [*NASDAQ symbol*] (TTSB) .... QCHI
Quad City Holdings [*NASDAQ symbol*] (SAG) .... QCHI
Quad City Holdings [*Associated Press*] (SAG) .... QuadCty
Quad City Times, Davenport, IA [*Library symbol*] [*Library of Congress*]
(LCLS) .... IaDaQT
Quad City Times, Davenport, IA [*Library symbol Library of Congress*]
(LCLS) .... IaDQT
Quad Column [*Typesetting*] (WDMC) .... qc
Quad Crown [*Paper*] (DGA) .... QC
Quad Demy [*Paper*] (DGA) .... QD
Quad Driver Module [*Electronics*] .... QDM
Quad Flat Pack (NITA) .... QFP
Quad Foolscap [*Paper*] (DGA) .... Q CAP
Quad Foolscap [*Paper*] (DGA) .... QUAD CAP
Quad Imperial [*Paper*] (DGA) .... QI
Quad in Line [*Electronics Telecommunications*] (TEL) ..... QUIL
Quad In-Line .... QIL
Quad In-Line Package .... QUIP
Quad Left [*Typography*] .... QL
Quad Medium [*Paper*] (DGA) .... QM
Quad Pulse Output Module (ACII) .... QPAT
Quad Right [*Typography*] .... QR
Quad Royal [*Paper*] (DGA) .... QR
Quad Synchronous Adapter [*Perkin-Elmer*] .... QSA
Quad Systems Corp. [*NASDAQ symbol*] (SAG) .... QSYS
Quad Systems Corp. [*Associated Press*] (SAG) .... QuadSy
Quad-Cities Nuclear Information Center (AD) .... QCNIC
Quad-Cities Station [*Nuclear energy*] (NRCH) .... QCS
Quaddel Reaktion Zeit [*Wheal Reaction Time*] [*German*] .. QRZ
Quadex Users' Organization (EA) .... QUO
Quad-in-Line Package [*Computer science*] (IAA) .... QIP
Quad-Phase Amplitude Modulation System (AD) .... QAMS
Quad-Phase Shift Key [*Computer science*] (AD) .... qpsk
Quadpixel Data-Flow Manager [*Computer science*] .... QPDM
Quadra Logic Technologies [*Associated Press*] (SAG) ..... QLT
Quadra Logic Technologies, Inc. [*Vancouver Stock Exchange symbol Toronto
Stock Exchange symbol*] .... QLT
Quadra Logic Technologies, Inc. [*NASDAQ symbol*] (NQ) .. QLTI
Quadragesms [*Year Books of Edward III*] (ILCA) .... Quadr
Quadragesms [*Yearbooks of Edward III*] [*A publication*] (DLA) .. Quadr
Quadrajet Carburetor [*Automotive engineering*] .... Q/JET

Quadrajet Carburetor [*Automotive engineering*] ... QUAD
Quadrangle (AAG) ... QUAD
Quadrangle (AD) ... quad
Quadrangle ... QUAD
Quadrangle (ODBW) ... quad
Quadrans [*A Farthing*] [*Monetary unit*] [*British*] ... Q
Quadrans [*A Farthing*] [*Monetary unit*] [*British*] (ROG) ... QA
Quadrans [*A Farthing*] [*Monetary unit*] [*British*] (ROG) ... QR
Quadrant (MSA) ... QDRNT
Quadrant (AD) ... qdrnt
Quadrant ... QDRT
Quadrant [*A publication*] ... Quad
Quadrant (KSC) ... QUAD
Quadrant (DMAA) ... quad
Quadrant (AD) ... quad
Quadrant [*A publication*] ... Quadr
Quadrant Aimable Charge Warhead (MCD) ... QAC
Quadrant Continuous Wave ... QCW
Quadrant Continuous Wave (AD) ... qcw
Quadrant Electrometer (AD) ... qem
Quadrant Electrometer ... QEM
Quadrant Elevation ... QE
Quadrant Elevation (AD) ... qe
Quadrant Eleventh-Gram Second ... QES
Quadrant Pain [*Gastroenterology*] (DAVI) ... Qp
Quadrant Power Tilt (IEEE) ... QPT
Quadrant Transformer Assembly ... QTA
Quadrant Transformer Assembly (AD) ... qta
Quadrantal Correction (AD) ... QC
Quadrantectomy [*Medicine*] ... QU
Quadrantectomy, Axillary Dissection, Radiotherapy [*Oncology*] ... QUART
Quadraphonic ... QUAD
Quadraphonic (AD) ... quadrap
Quadraphonic Eight [*Tape cartridge format*] (NTCM) ... Q8
Quadraplegic Communications Group, Inc., Media and Information Services, Winnipeg, MB, Canada [*Library symbol*] [*Library of Congress*] (LCLS) ... CaMWQCG
Quadrat (AD) ... quad
Quadrate (AD) ... qua
Quadratic Assignment Problem [*Mathematics*] ... QAP
Quadratic Discriminant Analysis [*Mathematics*] ... QDA
Quadratic Dynamic Matrix Control ... QDMC
Quadratic Matrix Control [*Chemical engineering*] [*Computer science*] ... QDMC
Quadratic Performance Index ... QPI
Quadratic Performance Index (AD) ... qpi
Quadratic Programming [*Computer science*] (BUR) ... QP
Quadratic Programming Internal Model Control [*Chemical engineering*] [*Computer science*] ... QPIMC
Quadratic Residues (MHDB) ... QR
Quadratic Score Statistic [*Test*] ... QSS
Quadratic Sieve [*Computer science*] (BARN) ... QS
Quadratic Zeeman Effect [*Physics*] ... QZE
Quadratkilometer [*Square Kilometer*] [*German*] (AD) ... qkm
Quadratmeter [*Square Meter*] [*German*] (AD) ... qm
Quadrature ... QDRTR
Quadrature (NASA) ... QUAD
Quadrature Amplified Modulation (NITA) ... QAM
Quadrature Amplitude Modulation (AD) ... qam
Quadrature Amplitude Modulation ... QAM
Quadrature Amplitude Modulation (MCD) ... QTAM
Quadrature Amplitude Modulation (IEEE) ... QUAM
Quadrature Amplitude Shift Keying ... QASK
Quadrature Channel Phase-Locked Loop (IAA) ... QCPLL
Quadrature Double Sideband (MCD) ... QDSB
Quadrature Grid ... QG
Quadrature Grid (AD) ... qg
Quadrature Hybrid (IAA) ... QH
Quadrature Modulation ... QM
Quadrature Partial Response (NITA) ... QPR
Quadrature Partial-Response System [*Telecommunications*] (TEL) ... QPRS
Quadrature Phase and Amplitude Modulation (NITA) ... QPAM
Quadrature Phase Detection [*Physics*] ... QPD
Quadrature Phase Shift Key [*or Keying*] [*Telecommunications*] ... QPSK
Quadrature Rejection Frequency ... QRF
Quadrature Rejection Ratio ... QRR
Quadrature Sideband Amplitude Modulation [*Telecommunications*] ... QSAM
Quadrature-Amplitude Modulation (AD) ... quam
Quadrax Corp. [*Associated Press*] (SAG) ... Qdrax
Quadrax Corp. [*NASDAQ symbol*] (NQ) ... QDRX
Quadrax Corp. [*Associated Press*] (SAG) ... Quadrax
Quadrax Corp. Wrrt 'C' [*NASDAQ symbol*] (TTSB) ... QDRXZ
Quadrennial Defense Review [*Army*] ... QDR
Quadrennial Review of Military Compensation [*DoD*] ... QRMC
Quadriatic Arc Computer ... QUAC
Quadriceps [*Anatomy*] ... Q
Quadriceps [*Medicine*] (MEDA) ... quad
Quadriceps [*Muscle*] [*Anatomy*] (DAVI) ... quad
Quadriceps Active Displacement [*Sports medicine*] ... QAD
Quadriceps Exercise [*Orthopedics*] (DAVI) ... quad ex
Quadriceps Extension Exercise [*Orthopedics*] (DAVI) ... QEE
Quadriceps Jerk [*Neurology*] (DAVI) ... QJ
Quadrigeminal Plate Cistern [*Neurology*] (DAVI) ... QPC
Quadrilateral (WGA) ... QUAD
Quadrilateral Element Panel Method [*Aerospace propulsion*] ... QUADPAN
Quadrillion (AD) ... Q
Quadrillion ... QUAD
Quadrillion British Thermal Units (GNE) ... qBtu
Quadrillion BTU's [*Also known as "quads"*] ... Q
Quadripartite Agreed Materiel Development Objective [*Military*] ... QAMDO
Quadripartite Agreed Materiel Requirement [*Military*] ... QAMR
Quadripartite Agreed Plans of Engineering Design [*Military*] ... QAPED
Quadripartite Agreed Plans of Engineering Tests [*Military*] ... QAPET
Quadripartite Agreed Plans of Service Tests [*Military*] ... QAPST
Quadripartite Agreement ... QA
Quadripartite Agreements Committee [*Military*] ... QAC
Quadripartite Armaments Standardization Committee [*Military*] (AABC) ... QASC
Quadripartite Chemical, Biological, Radiological Standardization Committee [*Military*] (AABC) ... QCSC
Quadripartite Development Objective [*Military*] (AABC) ... QDO
Quadripartite Development Objective (AD) ... qdo
Quadripartite Electronic Standardization Committee [*Military*] (AABC) ... QElecSC
Quadripartite Engineer Standardization Committee [*Military*] (AABC) ... QEngrSC
Quadripartite Materiel and Agreements Committee [*Military*] (AABC) ... QMAC
Quadripartite Materiel Committee [*Military*] ... QMC
Quadripartite Mobility Standardization Committee [*Military*] (AABC) ... QMobSC
Quadripartite Nonmateriel Committee [*Military*] (AABC) ... QNMC
Quadripartite Quartermaster Standardization Committee [*Military*] (AABC) ... QQSC
Quadripartite Research Coordination Committee [*Military*] (AABC) ... QRCC
Quadripartite Research List [*Military*] (AABC) ... QRL
Quadripartite Standardisation Agreement List [*Australia*] ... QSAL
Quadripartite Standardization Agreement [*Military*] ... QSTAG
Quadripartite Standardization Agreements List [*Military*] ... QSAL
Quadripartite Standing Operating Procedures [*Military*] ... QSOP
Quadripartite Technical Procedures Committee [*Military*] (AABC) ... QTPC
Quadripartite Working Group [*Military*] ... QWG
Quadripartite Working Group for Combat Development [*American, Australian, British, and Canadian armies*] (AD) ... QWGCD
Quadripartite Working Group on Combat Developments (MCD) ... QWG/CD
Quadripartite Working Group on Electronic Warfare (MCD) ... QWG/EW
Quadripartite Working Group on Engineering (MCD) ... QWG/ENG
Quadripartite Working Group on Logistics [*Military*] (RDA) ... QWG/LOG
Quadripartite Working Group on Proofing Inspection Quality Assurance (MCD) ... QWG/PIQA
Quadripartite Working Group on Surveillance and Target Acquisition/Night Observation (MCD) ... QWG/STANO
Quadriphase Shift Keying (MCD) ... QSK
Quadriplegia (AD) ... quadrip
Quadriplegic [*Medicine*] (DMAA) ... quad
Quadriplegic ... Quad
Quadriplex (AD) ... quadplex
Quadriplexer ... QDXR
Quadripod Cane (AD) ... quad c
Quadriradial [*Genetics*] (DAVI) ... QR
Quadroon (AD) ... quadro
Quadrophonic (NITA) ... QUAD
Quadrophonic Stereo (AD) ... qs
Quadrophonic Stereo (WDAA) ... QS
Quadruped (AD) ... quadrup
Quadruped Walking Machine Program [*Army*] ... QWMP
Quadruple ... Q
Quadruple ... QUAD
Quadruple ... QUADR
Quadruple Expansion (DS) ... QE
Quadruple Expansion Engine ... Q
Quadruple Expansion Engine (AD) ... qee
Quadruple Flip-Flop (AD) ... qff
Quadruple Play (DEN) ... QP
Quadruple Screw (IAA) ... QS
Quadruple Strength ... XXXX
Quadruple Terminal Digits (AABC) ... QTD
Quadruple Thermoplastic (SAA) ... QT
Quadruple Turbo-Electric Vessel (DS) ... QTEV
Quadruple-Screw Motorship (AD) ... qsm
Quadruple-Screw Ship (AD) ... QSS
Quadruple-Screw Turbine Steamship (AD) ... qsts
Quadruplet (AD) ... quad
Quadruplet (ODBW) ... quad
Quadruplex [*Videotape recording*] (NTCM) ... QUAD
Quadruplicato [*Four Times as Much*] [*Pharmacy*] ... Quadrupl
Quadruplicato [*Four Times as Much*] [*Latin*] (AD) ... quadrupl
Quadrupole Flip-Flop [*Computer science*] ... QFF
Quadrupole Mass Analyzed Ion Kinetic Energy Spectroscopy ... QMIKES
Quadrupole Mass Spectrometer ... QMS
Quadrupole Residual Gas ... QRG
Quadrupole Residual Gas Analyzer ... QRGA
Quadrupole Residual Gas Analyzer (AD) ... qrga
Quadrupole Residual Gas Analyzer System ... QRGAS
Quadrupole Resonance ... QR
Quadrupole Resonance Response ... QRR
Quadrupole Screw Ship ... QSS
Quadrupole Splitting (OA) ... QS
Quae Vide [*Which See*] [*Plural form*] [*Latin*] ... QQ V
Quae Vide [*Which See*] [*Latin*] (AD) ... qqv
Quaere [*Inquire*] [*Latin*] ... Q
Quaere [*Query*] [*Latin*] ... QU
Quaere Legal Resources Ltd. [*UTLAS symbol*] ... LAW
Quaere Legal Resources Ltd., Toronto, Ontario [*Library symbol National Library of Canada*] (NLC) ... OTQL
Quaestiones Convivales [*of Plutarch*] [*Classical studies*] (OCD) ... Quaest Conv

Quaestiones Disputatae (BJA) .... QD
Quaestiones et Salutationes in Exodum [*Philo*] (BJA) .... QE
Quaestiones et Salutationes in Genesin [*Philo*] (BJA) .... QG
Quaestiones Graecae [*of Plutarch*] [*Classical studies*] (OCD) .... Quaest Graec
Quaestiones Naturales [*of Seneca the Younger*] [*Classical studies*] (OCD) .... QNat
Quaestiones Platonicae [*of Plutarch*] [*Classical studies*] (OCD) .... Quaest Plat
Quaestiones Romanae [*of Plutarch*] [*Classical studies*] (OCD) .... Quaest Rom
Quagmire (AD) .... quag
Quai [*Embankment*] [*French*] (AD) .... Q
Quai d'Orsay (AD) .... Qd'O
Quail Embryo Fibroblast [*Medicine*] (DMAA) .... QEF
Quail Pea Mosaic Virus [*Plant pathology*] .... QPMV
Quail Ridge Winery [*Vancouver Stock Exchange symbol*] .... QRW
Quail Unlimited (EA) .... QU
Quain and Ramstad Clinic, Bismarck, ND [*Library symbol Library of Congress*] (LCLS) .... NdBQ
Quais-LASER-Intensity Interferometer (AD) .... qlii
Quaker Action Group (AD) .... QAG
Quaker Center for Prisoner Support Activities (EA) .... QCPSA
Quaker Chemical [*NASDAQ symbol*] (TTSB) .... QCHM
Quaker Chemical Corp. [*NASDAQ symbol*] (NQ) .... QCHM
Quaker Chemical Corp. [*Associated Press*] (SAG) .... QuakCh
Quaker City Bancorp [*NASDAQ symbol*] (SAG) .... QCBC
Quaker City Bancorp [*Associated Press*] (SAG) .... QuakCty
Quaker Committee on Jails and Justice [*Canada*] .... QCJJ
Quaker Committee on Social Rehabilitation (NADA) .... QCSR
Quaker Committee on Social Rehabilitation (AD) .... QCSR
Quaker Council for European Affairs (EA) .... QCEA
Quaker Esperanto Society (EA) .... QES
Quaker Fabric [*NASDAQ symbol*] (TTSB) .... QFAB
Quaker Fabric Corp. [*NASDAQ symbol*] (SAG) .... QFAB
Quaker Fabric Corp. [*Associated Press*] (SAG) .... QuakFab
Quaker Line (AD) .... Q
Quaker Oats [*NYSE symbol*] (TTSB) .... OAT
Quaker Oats [*Trade name*] .... QO
Quaker Oats (AD) .... Quaker
Quaker Oats Co. [*NYSE symbol Toronto Stock Exchange symbol*] (SPSG) .... OAT
Quaker Oats Co. [*Toronto Stock Exchange symbol*] .... OAT
Quaker Oats Co. [*Associated Press*] (SAG) .... QuakrOat
Quaker Oats Co., Research Library, Barrington, IL [*Library symbol Library of Congress*] (LCLS) .... IBarQ
Quaker Oats Co., Research Library, Barrington, IL [*OCLC symbol*] (OCLC) .... IUQ
Quaker Oats Foundation (AD) .... QOF
Quaker Peace and Service (AD) .... Q P & S
Quaker Peace and Service [*An association*] (EAIO) .... QPS
Quaker Press (AD) .... Quaker
Quaker Resources Canada Ltd. [*Vancouver Stock Exchange symbol*] .... QRC
Quaker Resources, Inc. [*Vancouver Stock Exchange symbol*] .... QUK
Quaker State Corp. [*NYSE symbol*] (SPSG) .... KSF
Quaker State Corp. [*Associated Press*] (SAG) .... QuakSC
Quaker State Motor Oils (AD) .... QSMO
Quaker Theological Discussion Group (EA) .... QTDG
Quaker United Nations Office (EAIO) .... QUNO
Quakertown, PA [*Location identifier FAA*] (FAAL) .... UKT
Qualcomm, Inc. [*NASDAQ symbol*] (SPSG) .... QCOM
Qualcomm, Inc. [*Associated Press*] (SAG) .... Qualcom
QUALCOMM, Inc. Automatic Satellite Position Reporting .... QASPR
Qualcosa [*Something*] [*Italian*] (AD) .... qc
Qualification (AD) .... qlfyn
Qualification (AD) .... qual
Qualification (NG) .... QUAL
Qualification (ROG) .... QUALN
Qualification Acceptance Vibration Test [*NASA*] (NASA) .... QAVT
Qualification and Validation Board [*Army*] (RDA) .... QV
Qualification Approval (WDAA) .... QA
Qualification Approval Test (NATG) .... QAT
Qualification Card (AD) .... Q-card
Qualification Correlation Certification (AD) .... qcc
Qualification Correlation Certification .... QCC
Qualification Course .... QC
Qualification Course (AD) .... qc
Qualification Design Review [*NASA*] (MCD) .... QDR
Qualification Firings Alignment (DNAB) .... QFA
Qualification for Acceptance Thermal Testing [*NASA*] (NASA) .... QATT
Qualification Information and Test (AD) .... qit
Qualification Maintainability Inspection .... QMI
Qualification Motor (MCD) .... QM
Qualification, Operational Test, and Evaluation .... QOT & E
Qualification Proposal .... QP
Qualification Review Sheet (KSC) .... QRS
Qualification Site Approval [*NASA*] (NASA) .... QSA
Qualification Standards for Postal Field Service .... QSPS
Qualification Standards for Wage Board Positions .... QWBP
Qualification Status List (KSC) .... QSL
Qualification Test .... QT
Qualification Test and Evaluation [*Military*] .... QT & E
Qualification Test and Proof (IAA) .... QTPT
Qualification Test Model .... QTM
Qualification Test Plan [*NASA*] (NASA) .... QTP
Qualification Test Procedure .... QTP
Qualification Test Program .... QTP
Qualification Test Report .... QTR
Qualification Test Specification .... QTS
Qualification Test Unit .... QTU
Qualification Test Vehicle .... QTV
Qualification, Validation, and Certification Board [*Army*] (RDA) .... QVC
Qualifications and Standards Laboratory (WDAA) .... Q & SL
Qualifications Appraisal Panel (OICC) .... QAP
Qualifications Record (AEBS) .... QR
Qualifications Record (AD) .... qr
Qualifications-Based Selection [*Metallurgy*] .... QBS
Qualified (KSC) .... QLFD
Qualified (AD) .... qufyd
Qualified Associate of the Land Agents' Society [*British*] .... QALAS
Qualified Bidders (AD) .... qb
Qualified Bidders List .... QBL
Qualified Binary Grouping [*Computer science*] (IAA) .... QBG
Qualified Buyer .... QB
Qualified Designated Entities [*Independent counseling groups and churches involved with aiding aliens*] [*Immigration and Naturalization Service term*] .... QDE
Qualified Domestic Relations Order [*Court authorization for retirement distribution*] .... QDRO
Qualified Domestic Trust .... QDT
Qualified Export Manager [*American Society of International Executives*] [*Designation awarded by*] .... QEM
Qualified Film Producers List (AAGC) .... QFPL
Qualified Flight Instructor .... QFI
Qualified Flying Instructor .... QFI
Qualified for Deep Diving (AD) .... qdd
Qualified for Deep Diving Duties [*Navy British*] .... QDD
Qualified for Mobilization Ashore Only [*Navy*] .... QMAO
Qualified for Mobilization Ashore Only (AD) .... qmao
Qualified for Warrant Air Mechanic [*British military*] (DMA) .... QWAM
Qualified for Warrant Engineer [*British military*] (DMA) .... QWE
Qualified for Warrant Mechanician [*British military*] (DMA) .... QWM
Qualified Helicopter Instructor .... QHI
Qualified in Gunnery [*British military*] (DMA) .... QG
Qualified in Ordnance [*Obsolete Navy*] .... QO
Qualified in Small Arms [*British military*] (DMA) .... QSA
Qualified Indorsement (MHDB) .... QI
Qualified Instructor [*British military*] (DMA) .... QI
Qualified International Executive (AD) .... QIE
Qualified International Executive - Air Forwarding [*American Society of I nternational Executives, Inc.*] [*Designation awarded by*] .... QIE-AF
Qualified International Executive - Export Management [*American Society o f International Executives, Inc.*] [*Designation awarded by*] .... QIE-EM
Qualified International Executive - Forwarding [*American Society of Inter national Executives, Inc.*] [*Designation awarded by*] .... QIE-F
Qualified International Executive - Traffic Management [*American Society of International Executives, Inc.*] [*Designation awarded by*] .... QIE-TM
Qualified Logical Link Control [*Telecommunications*] .... QLLC
Qualified Majority Voting [*Napoleonic Code*] .... QMV
Qualified Manufacturers List [*DoD*] .... QML
Qualified Medicare Beneficiary .... QMB
Qualified Member of the Master Photographers Association [*British*] (DBQ) .... LMPA
Qualified Mental Health Professional .... QMHP
Qualified Mental Retardation Professional .... QMRP
Qualified Military Available .... QMA
Qualified Military Available (AD) .... qma
Qualified Mortgage Bond .... QMB
Qualified Non-Elective Contribution .... QNEC
Qualified Optician [*British*] .... QO
Qualified Parts and Suppliers List (MCD) .... QPSL
Qualified Parts List (AAG) .... QPL
Qualified Personal Residence Trust [*Investment term*] .... QPRT
Qualified Possession Source Investment Income [*IRS*] .... QPSII
Qualified Process Supplies (MCD) .... QPS
Qualified Processing Source .... QPS
Qualified Producers List (IAA) .... QPL
Qualified Productivity Aid for Computing (IAA) .... QPAC
Qualified Products List [*Military*] .... QPL
Qualified Products Lists and Sources .... QPL & S
Qualified Psychiatrist (MAE) .... QP
Qualified Radium Plaque Adaptometer Operator [*Navy*] .... QRPAO
Qualified Railroad Retirement Beneficiary .... QRRB
Qualified Real-Estate Valuer (AD) .... QRV
Qualified Repair Source (AFIT) .... QRS
Qualified Repair Source List (AFIT) .... QRSL
Qualified Sales Engineer of the Institute of Sales and Marketing Management [*British*] (DBQ) .... SEngFInstSMM
Qualified Scientists and Engineers (AD) .... qse
Qualified Scientists and Engineers .... QSE
Qualified Small Business Corp. .... QSBC
Qualified Source List [*NASA*] (NASA) .... QSL
Qualified Terminable Interest Property [*Plan*] [*Tax law*] .... Q-TIP
Qualified Terminable Interest Property Trust [*Investment term*] (DFIT) .... QTIP
Qualified Testing Officer [*British military*] (DMA) .... QTO
Qualified Thrift Lender .... QTL
Qualified Tuition Reduction [*IRS*] .... QTR
Qualified Vehicle Modifier .... QVM
Qualified Vendors List .... QVL
Qualified Verification Procedures List .... QVPL
Qualified Verification Testing [*NASA*] .... QVT
Qualified Verification Vibration Testing [*NASA*] (NASA) .... QVVT
Qualified Voluntary Employee Contribution .... QVEC
Qualifier [*Linguistics*] .... Q
Qualifier Type (NITA) .... QT
Qualify (AD) .... qlfy

Qualify (AD) .... qual
Qualifying (AD) .... qlfyg
Qualifying Certificate .... QC
Qualifying Certificate [Australia] .... QualCert
Qualifying Dividend Account .... QDA
Qualifying Examinations (AD) .... quals
Qualifying Facility [Electric power] .... QF
Qualifying Tests (AD) .... quals
Qualitate Qua [In the Capacity Of] [Latin] .... QQ
Qualitative .... QUAL
Qualitative (IDOE) .... qual
Qualitative Analysis (AD) .... qual anal
Qualitative Analysis (WDAA) .... QUAL ANAL
Qualitative Construction Requirement [Army] ...... QCR
Qualitative Development Requirement Information ...... QDRI
Qualitative Equipment Requirements [Army] (AABC) ...... QER
Qualitative Equipment Requirements (AD) .... qer
Qualitative Experimental Stress Tomography .... QUEST
Qualitative Incentive Procurement Service (AD) ...... QIPS
Qualitative Management Program [Army] (INF) ...... QMP
Qualitative Material Objective (AD) .... qmo
Qualitative Material Report .... QMR
Qualitative Material Requirement (AD) .... qmr
Qualitative Materiel Approach [Army] (AABC) ...... QMA
Qualitative Materiel Development Objective [Army] ...... QMDO
Qualitative Materiel Development Objective [Army] (AFIT) ...... QUMDO
Qualitative Materiel Objective [Army] (AABC) ...... QMO
Qualitative Materiel Requirement [Army] .... QMR
Qualitative Military Requirements [NATO] (NATG) ...... QMR
Qualitative Operational Requirement [Military] ...... QOR
Qualitative Operational Requirement (AD) .... qor
Qualitative Operational Requirements (AD) .... qopri
Qualitative Personnel Requirements [NASA] (KSC) ...... QPR
Qualitative Personnel Requirements Information [NASA] (MCD) ...... QPRI
Qualitative Personnel Requirements Inventory (MCD) ...... QPRI
Qualitative Point Average (WDAA) .... QPA
Qualitative Point Average (AD) .... qpa
Qualitative Requirements Information (AD) .... qri
Qualitative Requirements Information [Army] .... QRI
Qualitative Research Consultants Association (EA) ...... QRCA
Qualitative Research Requirement for Nuclear Weapons Effects
  Information (AABC) .... QRR
Qualitative Research Requirements Information [Army] ...... QRRI
Qualitative Simulation Algorithm [Mathematics] ...... QSIM
Qualite [Quality] [French] (ROG) .... QTE
Qualiton & MHV [Record label] [Hungary] .... Qual
Quality (IAA) .... Q
Quality (AFM) .... QLTY
Quality (AD) .... qlty
Quality .... QLTY
Quality (ODBW) .... qlty
Quality (DS) .... Qty
Quality (KSC) .... QUAL
Quality (AD) .... qual
Quality Acceptance (AD) .... QA
Quality Achievement Data System (NASA) ...... QUADS
Quality Achievement Factor (RDA) .... QAF
Quality Action Team [Industrial engineering] ...... QAT
Quality Adjusted Life Years .... QALY's
Quality Adjustment Factor (DMAA) .... QAF
Quality Analysis (IAA) .... QA
Quality and Productivity Improvement (AAGC) ...... Q/PI
Quality and Reliability .... Q & R
Quality and Reliability (IAA) .... QAR
Quality and Reliability Assessment Council ...... QRAC
Quality and Reliability Assurance .... Q & RA
Quality and Reliability Assurance (NG) .... QRA
Quality and Reliability Assurance Committee (AAGC) ...... QRAC
Quality and Reliability Assurance Laboratory [NASA] (KSC) ...... QRAL
Quality and Reliability Management [DoD] ...... QUARAM
Quality and Reliability Year .... QRY
Quality and Reliability Year (AD) .... qry
Quality and Resource Management .... QRM
Quality and Resource Management (HCT) .... QRM
Quality Answering System (AD) .... QAS
Quality Assessment (HCT) .... QA
Quality Assessment Coordinator (MEDA) .... QAC
Quality Assessment Director (MEDA) .... QAD
Quality Assessment Division [Higher Education Funding Council] (AIE) ...... QAD
Quality Association and Inspection Service [British] ...... QA + IS
Quality Assurance .... QA
Quality Assurance (AD) .... qa
Quality Assurance Acceptance Standard (IAA) ...... QAAS
Quality Assurance Ammunition Specialist [or Speciality] (MCD) ...... QAAS
Quality Assurance and Expert Systems [Computer science] ...... QAES
Quality Assurance and Operations [Nuclear Regulatory Commission]
  (GFGA) .... QA & O
Quality Assurance and Operations (IAA) .... QA & O
Quality Assurance and Reliability .... QA & R
Quality Assurance and Reliability Team .... QUART
Quality Assurance and Test Service (IAA) .... QATS
Quality Assurance and Utilization Review [Medicine] (DMAA) ...... QAUR
Quality Assurance Assistant [DoD] .... QAA
Quality Assurance Audit (MCD) .... QAA
Quality Assurance Board (AD) .... QAB

Quality Assurance Board (NADA) .... QAB
Quality Assurance Bulletin (AD) .... QAB
Quality Assurance Chart (MCD) .... QAC
Quality Assurance Check (AD) .... QAC
Quality Assurance Checklist (NRCH) .... QAC
Quality Assurance Code .... QAC
Quality Assurance Coding (AD) .... QAC
Quality Assurance Coordination Committee (DMAA) ...... QACC
Quality Assurance Coordinator [Environmental Protection Agency] (GFGA) .... QAC
Quality Assurance Corrective Action Document (NASA) ...... QACAD
Quality Assurance Criterion [Nuclear energy] (NRCH) ...... QAC
Quality Assurance Data .... QAD
Quality Assurance Data Summary (AD) .... QADS
Quality Assurance Data System .... QADS
Quality Assurance Department (AD) .... QAD
Quality Assurance Department Instruction (AD) ...... QADI
Quality Assurance Directive .... QAD
Quality Assurance Directorate [Materials] [British] ...... QAD
Quality Assurance Directorate (Materials) [British] ...... QAD(MATS)
Quality Assurance Division [Picatinny Arsenal] [Dover, NJ] ...... QAD
Quality Assurance Engineering .... QAE
Quality Assurance Environment Testing [Military] (CAAL) ...... QAET
Quality Assurance Evaluation Test (NG) .... QAET
Quality Assurance Evaluator [Military] .... QAE
Quality Assurance Field Activity .... QAFA
Quality Assurance Field Operations .... QAFO
Quality Assurance Forms Guide Manual (SAA) ...... QAFM
Quality Assurance Function .... QAF
Quality Assurance Group .... QAG
Quality Assurance Index (MCD) .... QAI
Quality Assurance Information Letter (MCD) ...... QAIL
Quality Assurance Inspection .... QAI
Quality Assurance Inspection Procedure .... QAIP
Quality Assurance Installation Review Group [Nuclear energy] (NRCH) ..... QAIRG
Quality Assurance Instruction (NRCH) .... QAI
Quality Assurance Interface Coordination Group (AD) ...... QAICG
Quality Assurance International .... QAI
Quality Assurance Laboratory .... QAL
Quality Assurance Laboratory Test Request (MCD) ...... QALTR
Quality Assurance Letter of Instructions .... QALI
Quality Assurance Management and Information System [Environmental
  Protection Agency] (GFGA) .... QAMIS
Quality Assurance Management Meeting [DoD] ...... QAMM
Quality Assurance Management Review [DoD] ...... QAMR
Quality Assurance Management Staff [Environmental Protection Agency]
  (GFGA) .... QAMS
Quality Assurance Manager .... QAM
Quality Assurance Manual .... QAM
Quality Assurance Monitor (HCT) .... QAM
Quality Assurance Monitor [Medical records] (DAVI) ...... QAM
Quality Assurance Monitoring (DMAA) .... QAM
Quality Assurance Monitoring Information System (AD) ...... QAMIS
Quality Assurance Office [Navy] .... QAO
Quality Assurance Officer [Environmental Protection Agency] (GFGA) ...... QAO
Quality Assurance Operating Plan .... QAOP
Quality Assurance Operating Procedure (AD) ...... QAOP
Quality Assurance Operation (AD) .... qao
Quality Assurance Operation .... QAO
Quality Assurance Outline .... QAO
Quality Assurance Overview Contractor (AD) ...... QAOC
Quality Assurance Package .... QAP
Quality Assurance Plan .... QAP
Quality Assurance Planning (AD) .... QAP
Quality Assurance Procedure .... QAP
Quality Assurance Procedures .... QUAP
Quality Assurance Professional (HCT) .... QAP
Quality Assurance Program [Nuclear energy] ...... QAP
Quality Assurance Program Index [Nuclear energy] (NRCH) ...... QAPI
Quality Assurance Program Plan [Nuclear energy] (NRCH) ...... QAPP
Quality Assurance Provision .... QAP
Quality Assurance Publications [Navy] .... QUAPS
Quality Assurance / Quality Control (FFDE) ...... QA/QC
Quality Assurance Reagent [Cardiology] (DAVI) ...... QAR
Quality Assurance Receipt Inspection [Military] (DNAB) ...... QARI
Quality Assurance Record .... QAR
Quality Assurance Record Center (MCD) .... QARC
Quality Assurance Record - Receiving (MCD) ...... QAR-R
Quality Assurance Record - Tooling (MCD) ...... QAR-T
Quality Assurance Report [A publication] (AD) ...... QAR
Quality Assurance Representative .... QAR
Quality Assurance Requirements (NRCH) .... QAR
Quality Assurance Responsible/Witness (MCD) ...... QAR
Quality Assurance Review Center [National Cancer Institute] ...... QARC
Quality Assurance Review Technique (MHDB) ...... QART
Quality Assurance/Risk Management (MEDA) ...... QA/RM
Quality Assurance, Sample, and Data Management ...... QASDM
Quality Assurance Service [Medicine] .... QAS
Quality Assurance Service [or Serviceability] Test [Nuclear energy] (NG) ..... QAST
Quality Assurance Service Test (PDAA) .... QUAST
Quality Assurance Spacecraft Acceptance Center (MCD) ...... QASAC
Quality Assurance Specialist [DoD] .... QAS
Quality Assurance Specialist, Ammunition Surveillance (MCD) ...... QASAS
Quality Assurance Standard Practice (MCD) ...... QASP
Quality Assurance Standards [Business] (DAVI) ...... QAS
Quality Assurance Surveillance Plan (NITA) ...... QASP

Quality Assurance System (AD)	QAS
Quality Assurance Systems Analysis Review (AD)	QASAR
Quality Assurance Systems List (IEEE)	QASL
Quality Assurance Team (MCD)	QAT
Quality Assurance Technical [Material] (DAVI)	QAT
Quality Assurance Technical Publications (AAG)	QATP
Quality Assurance Test and Inspection Plan [Military] (CAAL)	QUATIP
Quality Assurance Test and Inspection Procedures (MCD)	QATIP
Quality Assurance Test Procedure (AD)	QATP
Quality Assurance Unit	QAU
Quality Assurance Verification Procedures [Military] (DNAB)	QAVP
Quality at Work [Quality Decision Management] [Computer science] (PCM)	QAW
Quality Bakers of America Cooperative (EA)	QBA
Quality Bakers of America Cooperative (EA)	QBAC
Quality Basic-Oxygen Process (AD)	qbop
Quality Brands Associates of America [Defunct] (EA)	QBA
Quality Brands Associates of America (AD)	QBAA
Quality Brands Associates of America (NADA)	QBAA
Quality Buffy Coat [Hematology] (DAVI)	QBC
Quality Certificate	QC
Quality Characteristics List (MSA)	QCL
Quality Check Program [DoD]	QCP
Quality Checklist	QCL
Quality Chekd Dairy Products Association (EA)	QCDPA
Quality Circle [Labor-management team organized to increase industrial productivity]	QC
Quality Color Dithering Process [Computer science] (PCM)	QCDP
Quality Communications Circle (MCD)	QCC
Quality Completion Order (AD)	QCO
Quality Conformance Acceptance Inspection (MCD)	QCAI
Quality Conformance Inspection (MSA)	QCI
Quality Construction Master	QCM
Quality Continuation Plan [BMW manufacturer's warranty]	QCP
Quality Control [or Controller]	QC
Quality Control (WDMC)	qc
Quality Control (AD)	qc
Quality Control Analysis	QCA
Quality Control and Evaluation (MCD)	QCE
Quality Control and Inspection Department [Navy] (DNAB)	QCID
Quality Control and Performance Monitoring System (MCD)	QCPMS
Quality Control and Reliability (AD)	QC & R
Quality Control and Techniques (SAA)	QC & T
Quality Control and Techniques (IAA)	QCAT
Quality Control and Test (AD)	QC & T
Quality Control Board (MCD)	QCB
Quality Control Branch	QCB
Quality Control Bulletin (AD)	QCB
Quality Control Centre (NITA)	QCC
Quality Control Chain (IAA)	QCC
Quality Control Change Request (SAA)	QCCR
Quality Control Collection Analysis and Reporting System	QCCARS
Quality Control Committee (MCD)	QCC
Quality Control Council of America [Defunct] (EA)	QCCA
Quality Control Data	QCD
Quality Control Deficiency Report (AFM)	QCDR
Quality Control Departmental Instruction (AD)	QCDI
Quality Control Directive (MCD)	QCD
Quality Control Directive Supplement (SAA)	QCDSU
Quality Control Engineer (IAA)	QCENGR
Quality Control Engineering (AD)	QCE
Quality Control Engineers	QCE
Quality Control [Tabulating] Form (AAG)	QCF
Quality Control History Record	QCHR
Quality Control Index [Environmental Protection Agency] (GFGA)	QCI
Quality Control Information (AABC)	QCI
Quality Control Inspection	QCI
Quality Control Inspection Element (AFIT)	QCIE
Quality Control Inspection Procedure [Nuclear energy] (NRCH)	QCIP
Quality Control Level	QCL
Quality Control Manager	QCM
Quality Control Manual	QCM
Quality Control Officer (AAG)	QCO
Quality Control Officer [Military]	QLTYCONO
Quality Control Operating Procedure	QCOP
Quality Control Organization	QCO
Quality Control Planning Procedure (IAA)	QCPP
Quality Control Procedure	QCP
Quality Control Procedures Manual (SAA)	QCPM
Quality Control Property Clearance (SAA)	QCPC
Quality Control Reference [Analytical chemistry]	QCRS
Quality Control/Reliability (AD)	QC/R
Quality Control/Reliability	qcr
Quality Control/Reliability	QCR
Quality Control Reliability Investigator (SAA)	QCRI
Quality Control Report	QCR
Quality Control Representative [Military] (AABC)	QCR
Quality Control Review	QCR
Quality Control Room	QCR
Quality Control Select Vendor (MCD)	QCSEL
Quality Control Service Request (SAA)	QCSR
Quality Control Single Source Procurement (MCD)	QCSSP
Quality Control Standard (AAG)	QCS
Quality Control Stop Order (AD)	QCSO
Quality Control Survey (SAA)	QCS
Quality Control System	QCS
Quality Control Technology (WDAA)	QCT
Quality Control Test Engineering (SAA)	QCTE
Quality Control Test Report	QCTR
Quality Control Test Team [Military]	QCTT
Quality Control Verification Test Inspection (SAA)	QCVTI
Quality Cost System	QCS
Quality Courts Motels [Later, QM]	QCM
Quality Courts United [Later, QM] (EA)	QCU
Quality Criteria for Water (EG)	QCW
Quality Data and Reporting (MCD)	QDR
Quality Data Evaluation (MCD)	QDE
Quality Data Information and Control (NASA)	QUIC
Quality Data System (NASA)	QDS
Quality Deer Management Association	QDMA
Quality Deficiency Evaluation and Action System (MCD)	QDEAS
Quality Deficiency Record [DoD]	QDR
Quality Deficiency Report [DoD]	QDR
Quality Dining [NASDAQ symbol] (TTSB)	QDIN
Quality Dining, Inc. [NASDAQ symbol] (SAG)	QDIN
Quality Dining, Inc. [Associated Press] (SAG)	QualDin
Quality Dino Entertainment [Commercial firm Associated Press] (SAG)	QltyDin
Quality Dino Entertainment [NASDAQ symbol] (SAG)	RCOR
Quality Dino Entmt [NASDAQ symbol] (TTSB)	RCORF
Quality Education Data [Information service or system] (IID)	QED
Quality Education for Minorities (AD)	QEM
Quality Education for Minorities Project (EA)	QEM
Quality, Efficiency, Dependability (AD)	QED
Quality Electrical System Test (AD)	quest
Quality Electrical Systems Test [Interpreter]	QUEST
Quality Engineer [or Engineering]	QE
Quality Engineer (IAA)	QUALENGR
Quality Engineering and Assurance Division [Navy] (DNAB)	QEAD
Quality Engineering Bulletin [NASA]	QEB
Quality Engineering Diagnostic Laboratory (MCD)	QEDL
Quality Engineering Operations	QEO
Quality Engineering Operations (AD)	qeo
Quality Engineering Planning List (MCD)	QEPL
Quality Engineering Significant Control Points (MCD)	QESCP
Quality Engineering Significant Control Points (AD)	qescp
Quality Engineering Test Establishment [Department of National Defence] [Canada] (IRC)	QETE
Quality Evaluation (NG)	QE
Quality Evaluation and Engineering Laboratory [Navy]	QEEL
Quality Evaluation and Engineering Laboratory, Concord [California] [Navy]	QEEL/CO
Quality Evaluation and Engineering Laboratory, Keyport [Washington] [Naval Torpedo Station]	QE/K
Quality Evaluation Laboratory	QEL
Quality Evaluation Program [College of American Pathologists]	QEP
Quality Evaluation System Tests (NG)	QEST
Quality Examination Program (AFM)	QEP
Quality Excellence [Chrysler Corp.]	QE
Quality Expo TIME-International (ITD)	QET
Quality Factor	Q
Quality Factor (AD)	q
Quality Factor (AD)	qf
Quality Factor [Nuclear energy]	QF
Quality Food Centers [NASDAQ symbol] (TTSB)	QFCI
Quality Food Centers, Inc. [NASDAQ symbol] (NQ)	QFCI
Quality Food Centers, Inc. [Associated Press] (SAG)	QlFood
Quality Form [Nuclear energy] (NRCH)	QF
Quality Function Deployment [Automotive engineering]	QFD
Quality Function Development [Failure analysis]	QFD
Quality History Record [Nuclear energy] (NRCH)	QHR
Quality Improvement (HCT)	QI
Quality Improvement (AD)	qi
Quality Improvement Network (DMAA)	QIN
Quality Improvement Process [Quality control]	QIP
Quality Improvement Program (ACII)	QIP
Quality Improvement Project (HCT)	QIP
Quality Improvement through Cost Optimization (MHDB)	QUICO
Quality Improvement through Cost Optimization (AD)	quico
Quality in Education [Project] (AIE)	QET
Quality Increase (AABC)	QI
Quality Index	QI
Quality Indices (WDAA)	QI
Quality Indices (AD)	qi
Quality Information and Test [System]	QIT
Quality Information and Test System (WDAA)	QITS
Quality Information Center	QIC
Quality Information System (IAA)	QIS
Quality Inspection Criteria	QIC
Quality Inspection Criteria (AD)	qic
Quality Inspection Point (KSC)	QIP
Quality Insurance Chain (IAA)	QIC
Quality Insurance System (IAA)	QIS
Quality International Hotels (AD)	QIH
Quality Loss Factor [Manufacturing]	BTAC
Quality Low-Priced [Art series]	QLP
Quality Management (HCT)	QM
Quality Management	QM
Quality Management Approach [Business term]	QMA
Quality Management Board (DOMA)	QMB
Quality Management System	QMS
Quality Manual [A publication] (MCD)	QM

Quality Material Approach (AD) ... qma
Quality Memorandum ... QM
Quality Micro Systems [*Trademark*] ... QMS
Quality Monitoring Control System [*Military*] (CAAL) ... QMCS
Quality Monitoring System (MCD) ... QMS
Quality Motels (EA) ... QM
Quality of Care [*Medicine*] (DAVI) ... Q of C
Quality of Care Measurement [*Insurance*] (WYGK) ... QCM
Quality of Conformance ... QOC
Quality of Contact (DAVI) ... QOC
Quality of Design ... QOD
Quality of Life [*Program*] [*Army*] ... QOL
Quality of Life Index ... QLI
Quality of Life Index (AD) ... qli
Quality of Life Index [*Medicine*] (DMAA) ... QOLI
Quality of Living ... QL
Quality of Merit ... QM
Quality of Output [*Economics*] ... q
Quality of Patient Care [*Hospital administration*] (DAVI) ... QPC
Quality of School Life Scale [*Educational test*] ... QSL
Quality of Service [*Telecommunications*] (TEL) ... QOS
Quality of Service [*Telecommunications*] ... QoS
Quality of Urban Air Review Group [*British*] (ECON) ... QUARG
Quality of Well Being Index ... QWBI
Quality of Well-Being [*Medicine*] (DMAA) ... QWB
Quality of Work Life [*Anti-recession program of Ford Motor Co.*] ... QWL
Quality of Working Life (DAVI) ... QW
Quality of Working Life (AD) ... qwl
Quality of Working Life [*Labour Canada program*] ... QWL
Quality of Worklife Database [*Management Directions*] [*Information service or system*] (IID) ... QWLD
Quality Operating Instruction ... QOI
Quality Operating System ... QOS
Quality Paperback Book Club [*Trademark of Book-of-the-Month Club, Inc.*] ... QPB
Quality Paperback Book Club [*Trademark of Book-of-the-Month Club, Inc.*] (CDAI) ... QPBC
Quality Patient Care Scale [*Medicine*] (DMAA) ... QALPACS
Quality People ... QP
Quality per End Item (AD) ... qpei
Quality per Final Article (AD) ... qfa
Quality per Next Assembly (AD) ... qna
Quality Performance Chart (SAA) ... QPC
Quality Performance Instruction Sheet (AD) ... QPIS
Quality Planning and Administration (MCD) ... QPAA
Quality Planning Instruction Sheet (MCD) ... QPIS
Quality Planning Requirements Document [*NASA*] (NASA) ... QPRD
Quality Planning Specification [*NASA*] (NASA) ... QPS
Quality Practice Manual [*A publication*] ... QPM
Quality Product (IAA) ... QP
Quality Product Assurance ... QPA
Quality/Productivity Assessment (MCD) ... Q/PA
Quality Productivity Improvement (MCD) ... QPI
Quality Program Manager [*Nuclear energy*] (NRCH) ... QPM
Quality Program Plan (MCD) ... QPP
Quality Program Provision ... QPP
Quality Progress Review (MCD) ... QPR
Quality Qualified Military Availability (AD) ... qqma
Quality Quest System [*Vancouver Stock Exchange symbol*] ... QQS
Quality Readiness Review (MCD) ... QRR
Quality Recording Alarm [*Engineering*] ... QRA
Quality Reliability Assurance (AD) ... qra
Quality Reliability Consumption Reports ... QRCR
Quality Reliability Deployment [*Automotive engineering*] ... QRD
Quality Requirement (IAA) ... QR
Quality Requirement Discrepancy Notice (SAA) ... QRDN
Quality Response Rating Scales (EDAC) ... QRRS
Quality Review ... QR
Quality Review Bulletin [*A publication*] (DMAA) ... QRB
Quality Review File [*IRS*] ... QRF
Quality Review Management Information System [*IRS*] ... QMIS
Quality Review Organization (AD) ... QRO
Quality Salary Increase (AD) ... qsi
Quality Salary Increase (AFM) ... QSI
Quality Scheme for Ready Mixed Concrete (EAIO) ... QSRMC
Quality Search Procedure (AD) ... qsp
Quality Semiconductor [*NASDAQ symbol*] (TTSB) ... QUAL
Quality Semiconductor, Inc. [*NASDAQ symbol*] (SAG) ... QUAL
Quality Semiconductor, Inc. [*Associated Press*] (SAG) ... QualSemi
Quality, Service, Cleanliness [*McDonald's Hamburger stands motto*] ... QSC
Quality, Service, Cleanliness, and Value [*Formula for successful fast-food restaurants as taught by McDonald's Corp. at its Hamburger University*] ... QSCV
Quality Service Indicator ... QSI
Quality Stamp ... QSTAMP
Quality Standard ... QS
Quality Standard Inspection Criteria ... QSIC
Quality Standard Inspection Criteria (AD) ... qsic
Quality Standardization Agreements (MCD) ... QSTAG
Quality Statistics Report [*Nuclear energy*] (NUCP) ... QSR
Quality Status Review (MCD) ... QSR
Quality Step Increase (GFGA) ... QSI
Quality Stock ... QS
Quality Strike Reconnaissance ... QSR
Quality Surveillance [*Navy*] (DNAB) ... QS
Quality Surveillance Division [*Navy*] ... QSD
Quality System Review ... QSR
Quality Systems [*NASDAQ symbol*] (TTSB) ... QSII
Quality Systems Acquisition Technology [*Army*] (RDA) ... QSAT
Quality Systems, Inc. [*NASDAQ symbol*] (NQ) ... QSII
Quality Systems, Inc. [*Associated Press*] (SAG) ... QualSy
Quality Systems Management [*DoD*] ... QSM
Quality Technical Information Service (NITA) ... QUALTIS
Quality Technical Report (AD) ... QTR
Quality Technical Requirement (AD) ... QTR
Quality Technology Information Service [*Atomic Energy Authority*] [*British*] (IID) ... QUALTIS
Quality Test (AD) ... QT
Quality Test (AD) ... qt
Quality Test Plan [*Nuclear energy*] (NRCH) ... QTP
Quality Unit Pack ... QUP
Quality Unsatisfactory Material Report (MCD) ... QUMR
Quality Utilization Effectiveness Statistically Qualified ... QUEST
Quality Value Convenience Network, Inc. [*Television*] ... QVC
Quality Verification [*Nuclear energy*] (NRCH) ... QV
Quality Verification (AD) ... qv
Quality Verification Inspection ... QVI
Quality Verification Plan ... QVP
Quality Verification Report ... QVR
Quality Verification Surveillance (AD) ... QVS
Quality Verification Test (AD) ... qvt
Quality-Adjusted Life Expectancy [*Medicine*] (DMAA) ... QALE
Quality-Adjusted Life Year (DMAA) ... QALY
Quality-Adjusted Time without Symptoms and Toxicity [*Medicine*] (CDI) ... Q-TWIST
Quality-Assurance Department (AD) ... Qu-AD
Quality-Assurance Division (AD) ... Qu-AD
Quality-Assurance Field Operation (AD) ... qafo
Quality-Assurance Firing (AD) ... qaf
Quality-Assurance Liaison Division (AD) ... QALD
Quality-Control Data (AD) ... qcd
Quality-Control Information (AD) ... qci
Quality-Control Level (AD) ... qcl
Quality-Control Report (AD) ... QC Rept
Quality-Control Representative (AD) ... QC Rep
Quality-Control Standard (AD) ... QC Stand
Quality-Protein Maize ... QPM
Quality-Technology ... Q-TECH
QualMark Corp. [*NASDAQ symbol*] (TTSB) ... QMRK
Quan Zhou [*Republic of China*] [*Seismograph station code, US Geological Survey*] (SEIS) ... QZN
Quanah, Acme & Pacific Railroad (AD) ... QA & P
Quanah, Acme & Pacific Railway Co. [*AAR code*] ... QAP
Quanah, TX [*FM radio station call letters*] ... KIXC
Quanah, TX [*AM radio station call letters*] ... KVDL
Quandary Peak [*Colorado*] (AD) ... Quandary
Quanex Corp. [*NYSE symbol*] (SPSG) ... NX
Quanex Corp. [*Associated Press*] (SAG) ... Quanex
Quang Duc [*South Vietnam*] [*Airport symbol*] (AD) ... HOO
Quang Ngai [*Vietnam*] [*Airport symbol*] (AD) ... XNG
Quantek Corp. [*Trademark*] ... QC
Quantico, VA [*Location identifier FAA*] (FAAL) ... NYG
Quantification of Integrated Logistics Support ... QILS
Quantification of Uncertainty in Estimating Support Tradeoffs (PDAA) ... QUEST
Quantified Intrapersonal Decision-Making [*In book title*] ... QUID
Quantified Risk Analysis ... QRA
Quantifier Negation [*Principle of logic*] ... QN
Quantile-Quantile [*Computer science*] ... Q-Q
Quantimet Image Analyzing Computer (PDAA) ... QIAC
Quanti-Pirquet [*Reaction or test for tuberculin*] (AAMN) ... QP
Quanti-Pirquet (AD) ... q-P
Quantisizer (AD) ... qnt
Quantitas Duplex [*Double Quantity*] [*Pharmacy*] ... QT DX
Quantitative (DAVI) ... qt
Quantitative [*or Quantity*] ... QUANT
Quantitative Analysis [*Laboratory science*] (DAVI) ... quant anal
Quantitative and Qualitative Personnel Requirements (AD) ... qqpr
Quantitative and Qualitative Personnel Requirements ... QQPR
Quantitative and Qualitative Personnel Requirements Information [*Military*] ... QQPRI
Quantitative Assessment and Training Center (AD) ... QAT
Quantitative Autoradiography [*Medicine*] ... QAR
Quantitative Budget Analysis (MCD) ... QBA
Quantitative Buffy Coat [*Hematology*] (DAVI) ... QBC
Quantitative Buffy-Coat Analysis (MEDA) ... QBCA
Quantitative Chemiluminescence ... QC
Quantitative Command (AD) ... qc
Quantitative Command ... QC
Quantitative Competitive Polymerase Chain Reaction [*Analytical biochemistry*] ... QC-PCR
Quantitative Competive Polymerase Chain Reaction [*Genetics*] ... QC-PCR
Quantitative Computer Management (IEEE) ... QCM
Quantitative Computerized Tomography [*Biomedical engineering*] ... QCT
Quantitative Coronary Angiography [*Cardiology*] (DAVI) ... QCA
Quantitative Decision System (AD) ... QDS
Quantitative Descriptive Analysis ... QDA
Quantitative Design Objective ... QDO
Quantitative Differential Thermal Analysis ... QDTA
Quantitative Differential Thermal Analysis (AD) ... qdta
Quantitative (Electrophysiological) Battery [*Cardiology*] (DAVI) ... QB
Quantitative Environmental Science and Technology [*ULDECO Ltd.*] [*British*] (IRUK) ... QUEST

Quantitative Evaluation of Library Searching [*Spectra matching technique*] .... QELS
Quantitative Evaluative Device (AEBS) .... QED
Quantitative Evaluative Device (AD) .... qed
Quantitative Fibrinogen Assay [*Clinical chemistry*] .... QFA
Quantitative Flight Characteristics .... QFC
Quantitative Flight Characteristics (AD) .... qfc
Quantitative Flight Characteristics Criteria (AD) .... qfcc
Quantitative Flight Characteristics Criteria .... QFCC
Quantitative Fluorescence Image Analysis [*Medicine*] .... QFIA
Quantitative Immunoelectrophoresis Methods [*Analytical biochemistry*] .... QIE
Quantitative Immunofluorescence .... QIF
Quantitative Immunoglobulin [*Immunology*] (DAVI) .... QIG
Quantitative Infrared Analysis .... QIA
Quantitative Inhalation Challenge Apparatus [*Medicine*] (MAE) .... QUICHA
Quantitative Inhalation Challenge Apparatus [*Medicine*] (AD) .... quicha
Quantitative Intelligence Analysis Technique (PDAA) .... QUILT
Quantitative Leak Test .... QLT
Quantitative Leak Test (AD) .... qlt
Quantitative Methods .... QM
Quantitative Methods for Public Management [*Course*] .... QMPM
Quantitative Muscle Testing [*Medicine*] (MAE) .... QMT
Quantitative Oceanographic Data .... QOD
Quantitative Pharmaco-Electro-Encephalography [*Medicine*] (DMAA) .... QPEEG
Quantitative Physical Science .... QPS
Quantitative Physical Science (AD) .... qps
Quantitative Pilocarpine Ionophoresis Test .... QPIT
Quantitative Precipitation Forecast (NOAA) .... QPF
Quantitative Precipitation Forecast (AD) .... qpf
Quantitative Precipitation Ratio Forecasts [*National Weather Service*] .... QPRF
Quantitative Property-Property Relationship .... QPPR
Quantitative, Qualitative, Maintainability, and Reliability .... QQM & R
Quantitative Quality Characteristics .... QQC
Quantitative Restrictions [*International trade*] .... QR
Quantitative Sacroiliac Scintigraphy [*Orthopedics*] [*Radiology*] (DAVI) .... QSS
Quantitative Sensory Test [*Medicine*] (DMAA) .... QST
Quantitative Structural Design Criteria [*NASA*] .... QSDC
Quantitative Structure Activity Relationships [*National Institute on Drug Abuse*] .... QuSAR
Quantitative Structure-Activity Relationship [*Pharmacochemistry*] .... (Q)SAR
Quantitative Structure-Property Relationship .... QSPR
Quantitative Structure-Time-Activity Relationship [*Chemistry*] .... QSTAR
Quantitative Test (NITA) .... Qtest
Quantitative Trait Loci [*Genetics*] .... QTC
Quantitative Trait Loci [*Genetics*] .... QTL
Quantitative Understanding of Explosive Stimulus Transfer .... QUEST
Quantitative Utility Estimates for Science and Technology [*RAND Corp.*] .... QUEST
Quantitative Utility Evaluation Suggesting Targets for the Allocations of Resources (AD) .... questar
Quantitatively Based Management Information System .... QUBMIS
Quantity .... Q
Quantity [*Microeconomics*] (AD) .... Q
Quantity (GAVI) .... QNH
Quantity (AD) .... qnty
Quantity (AFM) .... QNTY
Quantity .... QT
Quantity (AD) .... qt
Quantity (WDMC) .... qt
Quantity (WDMC) .... qty
Quantity .... QTY
Quantity (AD) .... qty
Quantity (KSC) .... QTY
Quantity (KSC) .... QUAN
Quantity (AD) .... quant
Quantity at Captain's Option [*Shipping*] (DS) .... QCO
Quantity Desired as Requested [*Military*] .... QTYDESREQ
Quantity Desired or Requested (AD) .... qtydesreq
Quantity Discount Agreement (AD) .... qda
Quantity Discount Agreement .... QDA
Quantity Distance [*Explosives*] .... QD
Quantity Gauging System (NASA) .... QGS
Quantity Indicator (KSC) .... QI
Quantity Not Sufficient [*Pharmacy*] .... QNS
Quantity Not Sufficient (AD) .... qns
Quantity of Electric Charge (IAA) .... Q
Quantity of Electricity [*Symbol*] [*IUPAC*] .... Q
Quantity on Hand .... QOH
Quantity per Application (MCD) .... QPA
Quantity per Article (AD) .... qpa
Quantity per Assembly (AD) .... qpa
Quantity per Assembly (MCD) .... QPA
Quantity per End Item (MCD) .... QPEI
Quantity per Equipment/Component .... QPC
Quantity per Unit Pack (AD) .... qup
Quantity Planning Specification (NASA) .... QPS
Quantity Progress Report (AD) .... QPR
Quantity Requested .... QR
Quantity Required .... QR
Quantity Share [*Economics*] .... QS
Quantity Surveying .... QS
Quantity Surveyors Research and Information Group (AD) .... QSRIG
Quantity Unit Pack .... QUP
Quantization [*Telecommunications*] (IAA) .... QTZN
Quantized Amplitude Modulation (NITA) .... QUAM

Quantized Decision Detection (AD) .... qdd
Quantized Decision Detection .... QDD
Quantized Field Theory .... QFT
Quantized Field Theory (AD) .... qft
Quantized Frequency Modulation (AD) .... qfm
Quantized Frequency Modulation .... QFM
Quantized Frequency Modulation Repeater .... QFMR
Quantized Gate Video [*RADAR*] .... QGV
Quantized Gate Video (AD) .... qgv
Quantized High Y [*Picture resolution*] (NTCM) .... QHY
Quantized Pulse Modulation .... QPM
Quantized Pulse Position .... QPP
Quantized Pulse Position Modulation [*Telecommunications*] (IAA) .... QPPM
Quantized Pulsed Amplitude Modulation .... QPAM
Quantizer (MDG) .... QNT
Quantizer [*Telecommunications*] (IAA) .... QTZR
Quantizer, Analyzer, and Record Keeper [*Telecommunications*] (TEL) .... QUARK
Quantizer Threshold Spacing [*Telecommunications*] (MHDB) .... QTS
Quantock Marine Enterprises (AD) .... QME
[*Value of*] Quantum (IDOE) .... q
Quantum (AD) .... quant
Quantum Access, Inc. [*Database producer*] (IID) .... QA
Quantum Amplification by Stimulated Emission of Radiation .... QUASER
Quantum Amplification by Stimulated-Emission of Radiation (AD) .... quaser
Quantum Cascade [*LASER*] (ECON) .... QC
Quantum Chemistry Microcomputer Program Exchange .... QCMPE
Quantum Chemistry Program Exchange .... QCPE
Quantum Chromodynamics [*Nuclear physics*] .... QCD
Quantum Chromodynamics (AD) .... qcd
Quantum Chromodynamics [*Laboratory science*] (DAVI) .... QCD
Quantum Computer [*Physics*] .... QC
Quantum Conformal Fluctuation [*Theoretical physics*] .... QCM
Quantum Corp. [*NASDAQ symbol*] (NQ) .... QNTM
Quantum Corp. [*Associated Press*] (SAG) .... Quantum
Quantum Counter .... QC
Quantum Counter (AD) .... qc
Quantum Design, Inc. .... QD
Quantum Distribution Function .... QDF
Quantum Dot [*Solid state physics*] .... QD
Quantum Efficiency .... QE
Quantum Electrodynamics [*Theory*] .... QED
Quantum Electrodynamics (AD) .... qed
Quantum Electrodynamics Electron Volts (AD) .... qeev
Quantum Electronics and Applications (IAA) .... QEA
Quantum Electronics and Applications Society (MCD) .... QEAS
Quantum Electronics Council .... QEC
Quantum Emission Domain [*Spectral physics*] .... QED
Quantum Energy [*Vancouver Stock Exchange symbol*] .... QEC
Quantum Flavor Dynamics .... QFD
Quantum Hall Effect [*Physics*] .... QHE
Quantum Health Resources [*NASDAQ symbol*] (SPSG) .... QHRI
Quantum Health Resources, Inc. [*Associated Press*] (SAG) .... QuantHlt
Quantum Hlth Resources [*NASDAQ symbol*] (TTSB) .... QHRI
Quantum Information and Computing [*Consortium sponsored by DARPA*] .... QUIC
Quantum Key Distribution [*For encrypting communication*] .... QKD
Quantum League [*An association*] (EA) .... QL
Quantum Leap (WDAA) .... QL
Quantum Learning Sys [*NASDAQ symbol*] (TTSB) .... QLSI
Quantum Learning Systems, Inc. [*NASDAQ symbol*] (SAG) .... QLSI
Quantum Learning Systems, Inc. [*Associated Press*] (SAG) .... QuantLrn
Quantum Libet [*As Much as You Please*] [*Pharmacy*] .... Q Lib
Quantum Libet [*As Much as Is Desired*] [*Pharmacy*] .... QL
Quantum Libet [*As Much as You Like*] [*Latin*] (AD) .... ql
Quantum Mechanics (AD) .... qm
Quantum Mechanics .... QM
Quantum Nondemolition [*Method of measurement*] .... QND
Quantum Number .... QN
Quantum Placet [*As Much as You Please*] [*Pharmacy*] .... Q PL
Quantum Placet [*As Much as You Please*] [*Pharmacy*] .... QP
Quantum Placet [*At Discretion*] [*Latin*] (AD) .... qp
Quantum Point Contact [*Physics*] .... QPC
Quantum Quatra Die [*Every Fourth Day*] [*Latin*] (AD) .... qqd
Quantum Quatra Hora [*Every Four Hours*] [*Latin*] (AD) .... qqh
Quantum Readout System [*Method of measurement*] .... QRS
Quantum Rectum [*The Quantity Is Correct*] [*Pharmacy*] .... QR
Quantum Rectus [*Quantity is Correct*] [*Latin*] (AD) .... qr
Quantum Resources [*Vancouver Stock Exchange symbol*] .... QEC
Quantum Restaurant Group [*Associated Press*] (SAG) .... QuanRst
Quantum Restaurant Group, Inc. [*NYSE symbol*] (SPSG) .... KRG
Quantum Rice-Ramsperger-Kassel [*Chemical kinetics methodology*] .... QRRK
Quantum Satis [*Sufficient Quantity*] [*Latin*] .... qs
Quantum Scalar Irradiance [*Instrumentation*] .... QSI
Quantum Size Effect (PDAA) .... QSE
Quantum Sufficiat [*A Sufficient Quantity*] [*Pharmacy*] .... QUANT SUFF
Quantum Sufficiat Ad [*To a Sufficient Quantity*] [*Pharmacy*] .... QS AD
Quantum Sufficit [*A Sufficient Quantity*] [*Pharmacy*] (ADA) .... QS
Quantum Sufficit [*As Much as Suffices*] [*Latin*] (AD) .... qs
Quantum Sufficit [*As Much As Will Suffice*] [*Latin*] (MAE) .... qsuff
Quantum Suffit [*A Sufficient Quantity*] [*Pharmacy*] .... Quant Suff
Quantum Suffit [*Sufficient Quantity*] [*Latin*] (AD) .... quant suff
Quantum Switch (AD) .... Q-switch
Quantum Systems, Inc. .... QSI
Quantum Theory of LASERS .... QTL
Quantum Theory of Paramagnetism .... QTP
Quantum Theory of Paramagnetism (AD) .... qtp

Quantum Theory Project [*University of Florida*] [*Research center*] (RCD) .... QTP
Quantum Vis [*As Much as You Wish*] [*Pharmacy*] (ADA) .... QQV
Quantum Vis [*or Voleris*] [*As Much as You Wish*] [*Pharmacy*] .... QV
Quantum Well [*Physics*] .... QW
Quantum Well Infra-red Photodetectors .... QWIP
Quantum Yield (AD) .... qy
Quantum Yield .... QY
Quantum-Dot Cellular Automata [*Microelectronics*] .... QCA
QuantumLink [*Quantum Computer Services, Inc.*] [*Vienna, VA*] [*Information service or system*] (IID) .... Q-Link
Quantum-Well Infrared Photodetector [*Physics*] .... QUIP
Qu'Appelle [*Canadian river*] (ROG) .... QUAPP
Quaqtaq, PQ [*ICAO location identifier*] (ICLI) .... CUHA
Quaque [*Each*] [*Latin*] (AD) .... q
Quaque [*Each or Every*] [*Latin*] .... Q
Quaque [*Each or Every*] [*Pharmacy*] .... QQ
Quaque [*Each*] [*Latin*] (AD) .... qq
Quaque Aente Meridiem [*Every Morning*] [*Pharmacy*] .... QAM
Quaque Die [*Every Day*] [*Pharmacy*] .... QD
Quaque Hora [*Every Hour*] [*Latin Pharmacy*] (WGA) .... q hr
Quaque Hora [*Every Hour*] [*Pharmacy*] .... QH
Quaque Hora [*Every Hour*] [*Latin*] (AD) .... qh
Quaque Hora [*Every Hour*] [*Latin*] (AD) .... qq hor
Quaque Hora [*Every Hour*] [*Pharmacy*] .... QQ HOR
Quaque Hora [*Every Hour*] [*Pharmacy*] .... QQH
Quaque Hora Somni [*Every Hour of Sleep*] [*Pharmacy*] [*Latin*] (MAE) .... qhs
Quaque Mane [*Every Morning*] [*Latin*] (AD) .... qm
Quaque Matin [*Every Morning*] [*Pharmacy*] .... QM
Quaque Nocte [*Every Night*] [*Pharmacy*] .... QN
Quaque Nocte [*Every Night*] [*Latin*] (AD) .... qn
Quaque Otra Die [*Every Other Day*] [*Pharmacy*] .... QOD
Quaque Otra Hora [*Every Other Hour*] [*Pharmacy*] .... QOH
Quaque Otra Nocte [*Every Other Night*] [*Pharmacy*] .... QON
Quaque Post Meridiem [*Every night*] [*Latin*] [*Pharmacy*] (DAVI) .... QPM
Quaque Quarta Hora [*Every Fourth Hour*] [*Pharmacy*] .... QQH
Quaque Quartus Hora [*Every Fourth Hour*] [*Pharmacy*] Q4H
Quaque Secunda Hora [*Every Second Hour*] [*Pharmacy*] Q2H
Quaque Tertia Hora [*Every Third Hour*] [*Pharmacy*] Q3H
Quaquero [*Quaker*] [*Spanish*] (AD) .... Quaq
Quarantine (AD) .... Q
Quarantine (AD) .... quar
Quarantine (AABC) .... QUAR
Quarantine Document System [*Information retrieval*] [*NASA*] .... QDS
Quarantine Launch (AD) .... Q/L
Quarantine Maximum (AD) .... Q-max
Quarantine Officer in Charge [*Military*] (AD) .... QOIC
Quarantine Operations (AD) .... quaops
Quarantine Operations [*Military*] (NVT) .... QUAOPS
Quarantine Report [*HEW*] .... QR
Quarantine Station .... QS
Quare Executionem Non [*Wherefore Execution Should Not Be Issued*] [*Latin Legal term*] (DLA) .... QEN
Quark [*Physics*] .... Q
Quarles & Brady, Law Library, Milwaukee, WI [*Library symbol Library of Congress*] (LCLS) .... WMQ
Quarles' Tennessee Criminal Digest [*A publication*] (DLA) .... Quar Crim Dig
Quarmain [*United Arab Emirates*] [*ICAO location identifier*] (ICLI) .... OMAQ
Quarrel (ROG) .... QL
Quarrel (AD) .... ql
Quarry (KSC) .... QRY
Quarry .... QUAR
Quarry (AD) .... quarr
Quarry Masters' Association [*Australia*] .... QMA
Quarry Masters' Association of New South Wales [*Australia*] .... QMANSW
Quarry Products Training Council (AIE) .... QPTC
Quarry Tile (AD) .... qt
Quarry Tile [*Technical drawings*] .... QT
Quarry-Tile Base [*Technical drawings*] .... QTB
Quarry-Tile Base (AD) .... qtb
Quarry-Tile Floor (AD) .... qtf
Quarry-Tile Floor [*Technical drawings*] .... QTF
Quarry-Tile Roof [*Technical drawings*] .... QTR
Quarry-Tile Roof (AD) .... qtr
Quart (AD) .... q
Quart (WDMC) .... q
Quart .... Q
Quart .... QR
Quart (AFM) .... QT
Quart (IDOE) .... qt
Quart (ODBW) .... qt
Quart (AD) .... qt
Quart (AD) .... qu
Quart (WGA) .... QU
Quart Imperial (DNAB) .... QI
Quarta Pars [*One-Fourth Part*] [*Latin*] (AD) .... quar pars
Quarter (AD) .... q
Quarter (ODBW) .... q
Quarter (WDMC) .... q
Quarter .... Q
Quarter .... QR
Quarter (WDMC) .... qr
Quarter (AD) .... qr
Quarter (AD) .... qrt
Quarter (IAA) .... QRTR
Quarter (AD) .... qt
Quarter (AD) .... qtr
Quarter (ODBW) .... qtr
Quarter .... QTR
Quarter (AFM) .... QTR
Quarter (ADA) .... QU
Quarter (AD) .... qu
Quarter [*Business term*] .... QUAR
Quarter Amplitude Damped (ACII) .... QAD
Quarter Century Wireless Association (EA) .... QCWA
Quarter Die Sumendum [*To be taken four times a day*] [*Latin*] [*Pharmacy*] (DAVI) .... QDS
Quarter Distribution [*Parapsychology*] .... QD
Quarter Gallon (AD) .... quart
Quarter Half Circle (IAA) .... QHC
Quarter Inch Cartridge [*Computer science*] .... QIC
Quarter Ocean Net .... QON
Quarter Ocean Net (AD) .... qon
Quarter of Coverage [*Social Security Administration*] (OICC) .... QC
Quarter Orbit Magnetic Attitude Control .... QOMAC
Quarter Panel [*Automotive engineering*] .... Q/PNL
Quarter Racing Owners of America (EA) .... QROA
Quarter Scale Ground Vibration Test (MCD) .... QSGVT
Quarter Scale Model (MCD) .... QSM
Quarter Scale Model Vibration Testing (NASA) .... QSMVT
Quarter Section .... QS
Quarter Section (AD) .... qs
Quarter Sessions .... QS
Quarter Square Multiplier .... QSM
Quarter Wave .... QW
Quarter Wave (AD) .... qw
Quarter Window [*Automotive engineering*] .... Q/WDO
Quarter Word Designator [*Computer science*] .... Q
Quarterback [*Football*] .... Q
Quarterback [*Football*] .... QB
Quarterback (AD) .... qb
Quarterdeck [*i.e., "after castle," by analogy with FX - forecastle*] [*Navy British*] .... AX
Quarterdeck (AD) .... qd
Quarterdeck .... QD
Quarterdeck Anti-Virus Research Center .... QUARC
Quarterdeck Corp. [*NASDAQ symbol*] (SAG) .... QDEK
Quarterdeck Corp. [*NASDAQ symbol*] (TTSB) .... QDEK
Quarterdeck Corp. [*Associated Press*] (SAG) .... Quartrdk
Quarterdeck Expanded Memory Manager [*Computer science*] .... QEMM
Quarterdeck Office Systems [*NASDAQ symbol*] (SPSG) .... QDEK
Quartered .... QTD
Quartered (AD) .... qtd
Quartered Partition .... QP
Quarterfinals (WGA) .... QF
Quarter-Girth Measure (AD) .... qgm
Quarter-Inch Compatibility [*Format*] .... QIC
Quartering [*Military British*] .... Q
Quartering (AD) .... qrtg
Quarterly [*A periodical published four times a year*] (WDMC) .... q
Quarterly (ODBW) .... q
Quarterly .... Q
Quarterly (ODBW) .... qly
Quarterly [*A periodical published four times a year*] (WDMC) .... qr
Quarterly (ROG) .... QR
Quarterly .... QRLY
Quarterly (ROG) .... QRTLY
Quarterly (AD) .... qrtly
Quarterly (AD) .... qtly
Quarterly (ODBW) .... qtly
Quarterly .... Qtly
Quarterly (AFM) .... QTR
Quarterly .... QTRLY
Quarterly (AD) .... qu
Quarterly .... QUAR
Quarterly (ROG) .... QUARLY
Quarterly .... QUART
Quarterly (AD) .... Quart
Quarterly (AD) .... quart
Quarterly Acceptance List (AFIT) .... QAL
Quarterly Accession List .... QAL
Quarterly Advanced Training Schedule [*Navy*] (DNAB) .... QATS
Quarterly Bulletin. Institution of Engineers of Australia [*A publication*] .... Quart Bull Instn Eng Aust
Quarterly Business Outlook [*A publication*] (EAAP) .... QBO
Quarterly Compilation of Abstracts [*A publication*] .... QCA
Quarterly Control Contract Factor (MCD) .... QCF
Quarterly Credit .... QC
Quarterly Cumulative Index Medicus [*A publication*] .... QCIM
Quarterly Economic Review [*A publication*] (AD) .... QER
Quarterly Economic Review (ODBW) .... QER
Quarterly Force Revision [*Military*] (NVT) .... QFR
Quarterly Forecast Demand .... QFD
Quarterly Index [*A publication*] (AD) .... QI
Quarterly Index of Lubricant Sales [*Industry report*] .... QUILS
Quarterly Information Bulletin [*Navy*] (DNAB) .... QIB
Quarterly Intercession Paper [*A publication*] (ROG) .... QIP
Quarterly. Japan Commercial Arbitration Association [*A publication*] (DLA) .... Q Japan Com'l Arb Ass'n
Quarterly Journal of Inter-American Relations [*A publication*] (DLA) .... Qu Jour Int-Amer Rel

Quarterly Journal of Speech [*A publication*] (BRI) .... QJS
Quarterly Journal of Studies in Alcohol [*A publication*] (AD) .... QJSA
Quarterly Law Journal [*A publication*] (DLA) .... Qu LJ
Quarterly Law Journal [*Virginia*] [*A publication*] (DLA) .... Quar Law Journal
Quarterly Law Journal [*Virginia*] [*A publication*] (DLA) .... Quart LJ (VA)
Quarterly Law Review [*A publication*] (DLA) .... QL Rev
Quarterly Law Review [*A publication*] (DLA) .... Qu L Rev
Quarterly Law Review [*Virginia*] [*A publication*] (DLA) .... Quar L Rev
Quarterly Law Review [*Virginia*] [*A publication*] (DLA) .... Quart L Rev (VA)
Quarterly Management Bulletin [*A publication*] (DNAB) .... QMB
Quarterly Meetings [*Quakers*] .... QM
Quarterly Memorandum .... QM
Quarterly Meteorological Summary [*Navy*] (DNAB) .... QMS
Quarterly Moving Average .... QMA
Quarterly National Accounts (NITA) .... QNA
Quarterly Newsletter. American Bar Association [*A publication*] (DLA) .... QN
Quarterly Newsletter. Special Committee on Environmental Law [*A publication*] (DLA) .... Q Newl-Spec Comm Env L
Quarterly Noncompliance Report [*Environmental Protection Agency*] (GFGA) .... QNCR
Quarterly Notes (ILCA) .... QN
Quarterly Operating Report .... QOR
Quarterly Payment Demand on Legal Loan .... QPDOLL
Quarterly Printing Industry Business Indicator Report [*A publication*] (EAAP) .... QBIR
Quarterly Process Review .... QPR
Quarterly Production Progress Conference [*Navy*] (NG) .... QPPC
Quarterly Progress Report .... QPR
Quarterly Project Reliability Summary [*Navy*] (NG) .... QPRS
Quarterly Provisional Tax .... QPT
Quarterly Quality Assurance [*Environmental Protection Agency*] .... QQA
Quarterly Replenishment .... QR
Quarterly Report (OICC) .... QR
Quarterly Research Review .... QRR
Quarterly Review and Analysis .... QRA
Quarterly Review of Biology [*A publication*] (BRI) .... QRB
Quarterly Review of Doublespeak [*A publication*] .... QRD
Quarterly Review of Drilling Statistics [*American Petroleum Institute*] .... QRDS
Quarterly Review of Jurisprudence [*1887-88*] [*A publication*] (DLA) .... Q Rev Juris
Quarterly Review of the Rural Economy [*A publication*] .... Q Rev Rural Econ
Quarterly Statistical Report (NRCH) .... QSR
Quarterly Status Report .... QSR
Quarterly Stock List .... QSL
Quarterly Stock Status Report .... QSSR
Quarterly Summary Report .... QSR
Quarterly Surprise Security Inspection [*Navy*] (DNAB) .... QSSI
Quarterly Survey of Intentions [*Became Consumer Buying Expectations Survey*] [*Bureau of the Census*] .... QSI
Quarterly Technical Progress Report .... QTPR
Quarterly Technical Report .... QTR
Quarterly Technical Review [*Jet Propulsion Laboratory publication*] .... QTR
Quarterly Title List .... QTL
Quarterly Training Briefing [*Army*] (INF) .... QTB
Quarterly Weight Report (DNAB) .... QWR
Quarterly World Day .... QWD
Quarterly World Day (AD) .... qwd
Quartermaster [*Military*] .... Q
Quartermaster [*Military*] (VNW) .... QM
Quartermaster .... QMR
Quartermaster [*Military*] (AD) .... Qmr
Quartermaster [*British military*] (DMA) .... Qr Mr
Quartermaster (AD) .... Qrmr
Quartermaster (AD) .... qrtmstr
Quartermaster (ROG) .... QU
Quartermaster (ROG) .... QUARTM
Quartermaster Cataloging and Standardization Office [*Army*] .... QMC & SO
Quartermaster Center and School [*Army*] (RDA) .... QMC&S
Quartermaster Clerk [*Marine Corps*] .... QMC
Quartermaster Clerk [*Navy rating*] .... QMCLK
Quartermaster Corporal-Major [*British military*] (DMA) .... QMCM
Quartermaster Corps [*Army*] (WGA) .... QC
Quartermaster Corps (AAGC) .... QM
Quartermaster Corps [*Army*] .... QMC
Quartermaster Corps Regulations [*Army*] .... QMCR
Quartermaster Corps Technical Committee [*Army*] .... QMCTC
Quartermaster Data Processing Center [*Army*] .... QMDPC
Quartermaster Depot [*Army*] .... QMDEP
Quartermaster Emergency Operation Plan [*Army*] .... QEOP
Quartermaster Equipment and Parts Commodity Center [*Army*] .... QMEPCC
Quartermaster Fellows (AD) .... Q-fellows
Quartermaster, First Class [*Navy rating*] QM1
Quartermaster Food and Container Institute .... QMFCI
Quartermaster Food and Container Institute for the Armed Forces .... QFCI
Quartermaster Food and Container Institute for the Armed Forces .... QMFCIAF
Quartermaster General [*Military*] .... QG
Quartermaster General [*Military*] (GFGA) .... QM Gen
Quartermaster General [*Army*] .... QMG
[*The*] Quartermaster General [*Army*] .... TQMG
Quartermaster Industrial Mobilization Services Offices [*Army*] .... QMIMSO
Quartermaster Intelligence Agency [*Merged with Defense Intelligence Agency*] .... QMIA
Quartermaster Maintenance [*World War II*] .... Q(Maint)
Quartermaster Movements [*World War II*] .... Q(Mov)
Quartermaster of the Watch [*Navy*] (DNAB) .... QMOW
Quartermaster Officers' Reserve Corps [*Military*] .... QMORC

Quartermaster Operation [*Military*] .... QO
Quartermaster Operations [*World War II*] .... Q(Ops)
Quartermaster Petroleum Center [*Army*] (MUGU) .... QMPC
Quartermaster Petroleum Center, United States Army .... QMPCUSA
Quartermaster Purchasing Agency [*Army*] .... QMPA
Quartermaster Radiation Laboratory [*Army*] .... QMRL
Quartermaster Radiation Planning Agency [*Army*] .... QMRPA
Quartermaster Radiation Planning Agency (AD) .... QRPA
Quartermaster Radiation Planning Agency (NADA) .... QRPA
Quartermaster Research and Development Center [*or Command*] [*Natick, MA*] .... QRDC
Quartermaster Research and Development Evaluation Agency [*Army*] .... QRDEA
Quartermaster Research and Engineering [*Military*] (AD) .... QMR & E
Quartermaster Research and Engineering Center [*or Command*] [*Natick, MA*] .... QREC
Quartermaster Research and Engineering Command [*Army*] .... QMREC
Quartermaster Research and Engineering Field Evaluation Agency [*Merged with Troop Evaluation Test*] .... QMREFEA
Quartermaster Reserve Corps [*Military*] .... QMRC
Quarter-Master, Royal Marines [*Navy British*] (ROG) .... RMQM
Quartermaster School [*Army*] .... QMS
Quartermaster, Second Class [*Navy rating*] QM2
Quartermaster Sergeant [*Military*] (AD) .... Qm Sgt
Quartermaster Sergeant [*Military*] .... QMS
Quartermaster Sergeant [*Marine Corps*] .... QMSGT
Quartermaster Sergeant [*Military*] .... QS
Quartermaster Stores [*Military*] .... QMS
Quartermaster Supply Officer [*Army*] .... QMSO
Quartermaster Table of Organization and Equipment [*Units*] [*Military*] .... QMTOE
Quartermaster Technical Library, Fort Lee, VA [*Library symbol Library of Congress*] (LCLS) .... ViFiQ
Quartermaster, Third Class [*Navy rating*] QM3
Quartermaster Water-Repellent [*Military*] (AD) .... quarpel
Quartermaster Water-Repellent Clothing [*Military*] .... QUARPEL
Quartermaster-General of the Marine Corps .... QMGMC
Quartermaster-General to the Forces [*Military British*] .... QMGF
Quartermaster-General's Office [*Military British*] (ROG) .... QMGO
Quartermasters Association [*Later, ALA*] .... QMA
Quartermaster-Sergeant [*British military*] (DMA) .... QM Segt
Quartermaster-Sergeant Instructor [*British military*] (DMA) .... QMSI
Quartermaster-Trainee [*Navy*] (DNAB) .... QM-T
Quartermon Versor [*Symbol of a function*] [*Mathematics*] (ROG) .... U
Quartern (ROG) .... QU
Quarternary [*Geology*] .... Q
Quarternary Ammonium [*Chemistry*] .... QA
Quarternary Ammonium Compound [*Chemistry*] .... QAC
Quarternary Ethylaminoethyl [*Organic chemistry*] .... QEAE
Quarternote [*A publication*] (EAAP) .... QN
Quarternote Society (AD) .... QS
Quarter-Orbit Magnetic Attitude Control (PDAA) .... QMAC
Quarter-Plate (VRA) .... QRTR
Quarter-Round [*Technical drawings*] (DAC) .... QR
Quarters [*Officer's rating*] [*British Royal Navy*] .... Q
Quarters .... QRS
Quarters (AD) .... qrs
Quarters .... QT
Quarters .... QTRS
Quarters Allowance .... QA
Quarters Armourer [*British military*] (DMA) .... QA
Quarters Assistant [*British military*] (DMA) .... QA
Quarters Improvement Program (MCD) .... QIP
Quarters of Coverage [*Social Security Administration*] (GFGA) .... QC
Quarters Officer [*British military*] (DMA) .... QO
Quarters Rating [*British military*] (DMA) .... QR
Quarters, Subsistence, and Laundry [*Military*] .... QS & L
Quarters, Subsistence, and Laundry (AD) .... qs & l
Quarter-Square Multipliers (AD) .... qsm
Quarter-Wave Antenna (AD) .... qwa
Quarter-Wave Antenna .... QWA
Quarter-Wave Optical Thickness (WDAA) .... QWOT
Quarter-Wave Optical Thickness (AD) .... qwot
Quarter-Wave Plate (AD) .... qwp
Quarter-Wave Plate (AD) .... QWP
Quartet [*Music*] .... QT
Quartet [*Music*] .... QTT
Quartet (AD) .... quart
Quartette (AD) .... qtte
Quartette [*Music*] .... QTTE
Quartetto [*Quartet*] [*Music*] (ROG) .... QUART
Quartetto Italiano [*Italian Quartet*] [*Italian*] (AD) .... Quart Ital
Quartier de Securite Renforce [*Maximum Security Prison*] [*French*] (AD) .... QSR
Quartier General [*Headquarters*] [*French*] (AD) .... QG
Quartier Generale [*Headquarters*] [*Italian*] (AD) .... QG
Quartile (AD) .... q
Quartile .... Q
Quartile Deviation [*Statistics*] .... QD
Quartile Deviation (AD) .... qd
Quartile Variation [*Symbol*] (AD) .... Q
Quarto [*An eight-page, four-leaf book*] (WDMC) 4to
Quarto [*Bookbinding*] (WDMC) .... q
Quarto (AD) .... Q
Quarto [*Book from 25 to 30 centimeters in height*] .... Q
Quarto [*Book from 25 to 30 centimeters in height*] .... QTO
Quarto (AD) .... qto

Quarto Castello [*Italy*] [*Seismograph station code, US Geological Survey Closed*] (SEIS) .... QCI
Quarto Edition [*Shakespearean work*] .... Q
Quartoquadrillion (WDAA) .... Q
Quartos (WDAA) .... QQ
Quartos (AD) .... qq
Quarts (AD) .... qts
Quartus [*Fourth*] [*Pharmacy*] .... QUART
Quartus Foundation for Spiritual Research (EA) .... QFSR
Quartz [*CIPW classification*] [*Geology*] .... Q
Quartz (AAG) .... QTZ
Quartz (AD) .... qtz
Quartz (AD) .... Qz
Quartz (AD) .... qz
Quartz [*Quality of the bottom*] [*Nautical charts*] .... QZ
Quartz Aircraft Lamp .... QAL
Quartz Aircraft Lamp (AD) .... qal
Quartz Aircraft Landing Lamp (AD) .... qall
Quartz Aircraft Landing Lamp .... QALL
Quartz Creek Gold Mines (BC), Inc. [*Vancouver Stock Exchange symbol*] ...... QCG
Quartz Crystal .... QC
Quartz Crystal (AD) .... qc
Quartz Crystal Filter .... QCF
Quartz Crystal Frequency Oscillator .... QCFO
Quartz Crystal Microbalance .... QCM
Quartz Crystal Monitor .... QCM
Quartz Crystal Oscillator .... QCO
Quartz Crystal Unit .... QCU
Quartz Crystal Unit (AD) .... qcu
Quartz Crystal Unit Set (AD) .... qcus
Quartz Crystal Unit Set .... QCUS
Quartz Devices Conference and Exhibition .... QDC & E
Quartz Fiber Electrometer (WDAA) .... QFE
Quartz Fiber Electrometer (AD) .... qfe
Quartz Fiber Product (AD) .... qfp
Quartz Fiber Product .... QFP
Quartz Frequency Oscillator .... QFO
Quartz Frequency Oscillator (AD) .... qfo
Quartz Halogen .... QH
Quartz Helix .... QH
Quartz Helix (AD) .... qh
Quartz Horizontal Magnetometer (NOAA) .... QHM
Quartz Incandescent Lamp .... QIL
Quartz Incandescent Lamp (AD) .... qil
Quartz Insulation Part (AD) .... qip
Quartz Insulation Part .... QIP
Quartz Iodine .... QI
Quartz Iodine Crystal .... QIC
Quartz Iodine Lamp .... QIL
Quartz Iodine Lamp (AD) .... qil
Quartz Landing Lamp (AD) .... qll
Quartz Landing Lamp [*Aviation*] .... QLL
Quartz Manometer (ACII) .... QM
Quartz Metal Sealed Window (AD) .... qmsw
Quartz Metal Sealed Window .... QMSW
Quartz Metal Window .... QMW
Quartz Metal Window (AD) .... qmw
Quartz Mountain Gold Corp. [*Vancouver Stock Exchange symbol Toronto Stock Exchange symbol*] .... QZM
Quartz Mountain Gold Corp. (MHDW) .... QZMGF
Quartz Mountain State Park [*Oklahoma*] [*Seismograph station code, US Geological Survey*] (SEIS) .... QMO
Quartz/Phenolic .... Q/P
Quartz Pressure Transducer [*Telecommunications*] (IAA) .... QPT
Quartz Thermometer Sensor .... QTS
Quartz Wedge (AD) .... q-wedge
Quartz-Crystal Filter (AD) .... qcf
Quartz-Crystal Frequency Oscillator (AD) .... qcfo
Quartz-Crystal Oscillator (AD) .... qco
Quartz-Fayalite-Magnetite [*Geology*] .... QFM
Quartz-Halogen (AD) .... q-h
Quartz-Iodine Crystal (AD) .... qic
Quartz-Iron-Fayalite [*Geology*] .... QIF
Quartzite [*Lithology*] .... QTZ
Quartzite (AD) .... qtzt
Quartzite Granite [*Agronomy*] .... QUARTZ GR
Quartzitic (AD) .... qtzic
Quartz-Locked .... QL
Quartzose (AD) .... qtze
Quartzsite, AZ [*FM radio station call letters*] .... KBUX
Quartzsite Integrated Acoustic and Engine Test Site .... QIAET
Quarzazate [*Morocco*] [*ICAO location identifier*] (ICLI) .... GMMZ
QUASAR [*Quasi-Stellar*] [*Astronomy*] (IAA) .... QSO
Quasar [*Galaxy*] .... QSR
Quasar Satellite [*Proposed observatory in space*] .... QUASAT
Quashey (AD) .... Quash
Quasi [*Almost, As It Were*] [*Latin*] .... Q
Quasi [*Almost, As It Were*] [*Latin*] .... QU
Quasi [*As It Were*] [*Latin*] (AD) .... qu
Quasi Algorithm (OA) .... QA
Quasi Birth and Death [*Statistics*] .... QBD
Quasi Classical Trajetory [*Physical chemistry*] .... QCT
Quasi Contract [*Legal shorthand*] (LWAP) .... QK
Quasi Dicat [*As If One Should Say, or As Though One Should Say*] [*Latin*] .... QD
Quasi Dictum [*As If Said, or As Though It Had Been Said*] [*Latin*] .... QD

Quasi Dixisset [*As If One Had Said*] [*Latin*] .... QD
Quasi-Adiabatic Representation .... QAR
Quasi-Autonomous Local Government Organisation [*British*] (DI) .... QUALGO
Quasi-Autonomous Non-Governmental [*or National Governmental*] **Organisation** [*British*] .... QUANGO
Quasi-Autonomous Non-Governmental Organization (AD) .... quango
Quasi-Bidirectional (MHDI) .... QBD
Quasi-Biennial .... QB
Quasi-Biennial Oscillation [*Earth science*] .... QBO
Quasi-Biennial Oscillation [*Marine science*] (OSRA) .... QBO
Quasibiennial Stratospheric Oscillation (AD) .... qso
Quasi-Biennial Stratospheric Oscillation .... QSO
Quasiclassical Trajectory [*Chemical physics*] .... QCT
Quasi-Contract [*Business term*] .... QC
Quasi-Degenerate Many-Body Perturbation Theory [*Physics*] .... QDMBPT
Quasi-Direct Broadcast Satellite .... Q-DBS
Quasi-Elastic Light Scattering [*Also, QLS, QUELS*] [*Physics*] .... QELS
Quasi-Elastic Light Scattering [*Also, QELS, QUELS*] [*Physics*] .... QLS
Quasi-Elastic Light Scattering [*Also, QELS, QLS*] [*Physics*] .... QUELS
Quasi-Elastic Neutron Scattering [*Physics*] .... QENS
Quasi-Equilibrium Theory [*Physical chemistry*] .... QET
Quasi-Fermi Level .... QFL
Quasi-Fermi Level (AD) .... qfl
Quasi-Grain Boundary Free [*Photovoltaic energy systems*] .... QGBF
Quasi-Hydrostatic Pressure [*Physics*] .... QHP
Quasi-Inertial .... QI
Quasi-Lagrangian Model [*Marine science*] (OSRA) .... QLM
Quasi-Lagrangian Model (USDC) .... QLM
Quasi-LASER Machine (AD) .... qlm
Quasi-LASER Sequential Machine (AD) .... qlsm
Quasi-Linear Machine .... QLM
Quasi-Linear Sequential Machine .... QLSM
Quasi-Linear Sequential Machine .... QSM
Quasi-Linear Theory .... QLT
Quasi-Liquid Crystal [*Organic chemistry*] .... QLC
Quasi-Morphine Withdrawal Syndrome [*Medicine*] (DMAA) .... QMWS
Quasi-Official Agencies (AD) .... QOA
Quasi-Optical Circuit .... QOC
Quasi-Optical Technique .... QOT
Quasi-Optimal Rendezvous Guidance System .... QORGS
Quasiparticle [*Physics*] .... QP
Quasi-Peak .... QP
Quasi-Periodic Oscillation [*Astronomy*] .... QPO
Quasi-Phase-Matching [*Physics*] .... QPM
Quasi-Propulsive Coefficient (DS) .... QPC
Quasi-Public Company .... QPC
Quasi-Quadrennial .... QQ
Quasiquadrennial Oscillation [*Astronomy*] .... QQO
Quasi-Random Band Model .... QRBM
Quasi-Random Band Model (AD) .... qrbm
Quasi-Random Code Generator (AD) .... qrcg
Quasi-Random Code Generator (CET) .... QRCG
Quasi-Sensory Communication [*Parapsychology*] .... QSC
Quasi-Solid State Panel .... QSSP
Quasi-Solid-State Panel (AD) .... qssp
Quasi-Spectral Time Integration on Nested Grids .... QSTING
Quasistatic Compliance [*Measurement*] (DAVI) .... QSC
Quasi-Static Field (AD) .... qsf
Quasi-Static Field .... QSF
Quasistatic Pressure Volume [*Measurement*] (DAVI) .... QSPV
Quasi-Stationary Front .... QSF
Quasi-Stationary State Approximation .... QSSA
Quasi-Stationary-State Approximation (AD) .... qssa
Quasi-Steady Glide [*NASA*] .... QSG
Quasi-Steady State .... QSS
Quasi-Stellar [*Astronomy*] .... QUASAR
Quasi-Stellar Blue Galaxies (AD) .... qsbg
Quasi-Stellar Blue Galaxies (SAA) .... QSRS
Quasi-Stellar Blue Objects (AD) .... qsbo
Quasi-Stellar Galaxy (AD) .... qsg
Quasi-Stellar Galaxy .... QSG
Quasi-Stellar [*or QUASAR*] **Object** .... QSO
Quasistellar Object (AD) .... qso
Quasi-Stellar Radio (AD) .... quasar
Quasi-Stellar Radio Source .... QSR
Quasi-Stellar Radio Source .... QSRS
Quasi-Stellar Radio Sources (AD) .... qsrs
Quasi-Stellar Source (AD) .... qss
Quasi-Stellar Source .... QSS
Quasithermal Noise [*Plasma physics*] .... QTN
Quasi-Triennial .... QT
Quasi-Two-Dimensional .... QTD
Quasi-Very-Long-Baseline Interferometry .... QVLBI
Quasi-Wide Sense Stationary Uncorrelated Scattering (IAA) .... QWSSUS
Quasi-Wide-Sense-Stationary Uncorrelated Scattering (PDAA) .... QWSSUA
Quassar de Mexico SA de CV [*ICAO designator*] (FAAC) .... QUA
Quassia [*Pharmacology*] (ROG) .... QUASS
Quatar Fertilizer Co. (AD) .... QAFCO
Quater [*Four Times*] [*Pharmacy*] .... QUAT
Quater in Die [*Four Times a Day*] [*Pharmacy*] .... QD
Quater in Die [*Four Times a Day*] [*Latin*] (AD) .... qd
Quater in Die [*Four Times a Day*] [*Latin*] (AD) .... qid
Quater in Die [*Four Times a Day*] [*Pharmacy*] .... QID
Quaternary [*Period, era, or system*] [*Geology*] .... QUAT
Quaternary (AD) .... Quat

Quaternary (AD) ... quat
Quaternary Alluvium (AD) ... qal
Quaternary Ammonium Compound (AD) ... qac
Quaternary Ammonium Compound [*Chemistry*] (DAVI) ... QAC
Quaternary Ammonium Compound [*Class of antimicrobial agents*] ... QUAT
Quaternary Carrier [*Biochemistry*] ... QC
Quaternary Coherent Phase-Shift Keying ... QCPSK
Quaternary Differential Phase-Shift Keying (TEL) ... QDPSK
Quaternary Phase Shift Keying (NITA) ... QPSK
Quaternary Research Laboratory [*University of Michigan*] [*Research center*] (RCD) ... QRL
Quaternion (NASA) ... QUAT
Quatrefage's Angle [*Parietal Angle*] (DAVI) ... Q
Quatrefoil (VRA) ... qtfl
Quatrefoil [*Numismatics*] ... QUAT
Quattro Pro for Windows [*Borland International*] [*Computer science*] (PCM) ... QPW
Quattrovalvole [*Four valves per cylinder*] [*Italian*] ... QV
Quattuor [*Four*] [*Latin*] (AD) ... quat
Quattuor [*Four*] [*Latin*] (DAVI) ... QUAT
Quay (ROG) ... QU
Quay (ROG) ... QY
Quay (AD) ... Qy
Que Besa su Mano [*Who Kisses Your Hand*] [*Spanish*] (AD) ... QBSM
Que Besa Sus Manos [*Kissing Your Hands*] [*Spanish*] ... QBSM
Que Besa sus Pies [*Who Kisses Your Feet*] [*Spanish*] (AD) ... QBSP
Que Me - Comite Vietnam pour la Defense des Droits de l'Homme [*Que Me - Vietnam Committee on Human Rights*] (EAIO) ... QMCVDDH
Que Que [*Rhodesia*] (AD) ... QQ
Que Viva Mexico [*Long Live Mexico*] [*Spanish*] (AD) ... QVM
Que West Resources Ltd. [*Toronto Stock Exchange symbol*] ... QWR
Quebec [*MARC geographic area code Library of Congress*] (LCCP) ... n-cn-qu
Quebec [*Postal code*] (CDAI) ... PQ
Quebec [*Phonetic alphabet*] [*International*] (DSUE) ... Q
Quebec (AD) ... Q
Quebec (AD) ... Qbc
Quebec [*Canada*] (WDAA) ... QBC
Quebec [*Quebec*] [*Seismograph station code, US Geological Survey*] (SEIS) ... QCQ
Quebec (AD) ... QE
Quebec [*MARC country of publication code Library of Congress*] (LCCP) ... quc
Quebec [*Canadian province*] ... QUE
Quebec [*Canada*] (DD) ... Que
Quebec [*Canadian province*] (ODBW) ... Que
Quebec [*Canada*] [*Airport symbol*] (OAG) ... YQB
Quebec Aid for the Partially-Sighted, Montreal, PQ, Canada [*Library symbol*] [*Library of Congress*] (LCLS) ... CaQMAPS
Quebec Aid for the Partially-Sighted [*Aide aux Insuffisants Visuels du Quebec*] **Montreal, Quebec** [*Library symbol National Library of Canada*] (NLC) ... QMAPS
Quebec Airways Ltd. (MCD) ... QAL
Quebec and Ontario [*Canada*] (AD) ... Q & O
Quebec & Ontario Paper Co. Ltd., Thorold, Ontario [*Library symbol National Library of Canada*] (NLC) ... OTHOP
Quebec Appeal Cases [*Maritime Law Book Co. Ltd.*] [*Canada Information service or system*] (CRD) ... QAC
Quebec Archives, Montreal, PQ, Canada [*Library symbol Library of Congress*] (LCLS) ... CaQMQAr
Quebec Archives, Montreal, Quebec [*Library symbol National Library of Canada*] (NLC) ... QMQAR
Quebec Association for Children with Learning Disabilities, Montreal, PQ, Canada [*Library symbol Library of Congress*] (LCLS) ... CaQMACL
Quebec Association for Children with Learning Disabilities [*Association Quebecoise pour les Enfants Souffrant de Troubles d'Apprentissage*] **Montreal, Quebec** [*Library symbol National Library of Canada*] (NLC) ... QMACL
Quebec Association of Computer Users in Education [*Canada*] (EDAC) ... QACUE
Quebec Building Envelope Council (AC) ... QBEC
Quebec Bus Owners Association (AC) ... QBOA
Quebec Central Railway [*Canada*] (AD) ... QC Ry
Quebec Central Railway Co. [*AAR code*] ... QC
Quebec Central Railway Co. [*Canada*] (AD) ... QCRC
Quebec City (AD) ... QC
Quebec City, PQ [*Television station call letters*] ... CBVT
Quebec City, PQ [*Television station call letters*] ... CFAP
Quebec City, PQ [*Television station call letters*] ... CFCM
Quebec City, PQ [*Television station call letters*] ... CIVQ
Quebec City, PQ [*Television station call letters*] ... CKMI
Quebec Commission des Droits de la Personne, Montreal, PQ, Canada [*Library symbol Library of Congress*] (LCLS) ... CaQMQDP
Quebec Commission des Droits de la Personne, Quebec, PQ, Canada [*Library symbol Library of Congress*] (LCLS) ... CaQQCDP
Quebec dans le Monde [*An association*] (EAIO) ... AC
Quebec Family History Society, Pointe Claire, Quebec [*Library symbol National Library of Canada*] (BIB) ... QPOCQ
Quebec Federation of Historical Societies [*Canada*] (EAIO) ... QFHS
Quebec Fertilizer Manufacturers Association (AC) ... QFMA
Quebec Iron & Titanium Corp., Sorel, PQ, Canada [*Library symbol Library of Congress*] (LCLS) ... CaQSoIT
Quebec King's Bench Reports [*A publication*] (DLA) ... QRKB
Quebec Land Surveyor [*Canada*] (DD) ... QLS
Quebec Law [*A publication*] (DLA) ... QL
Quebec Law [*A publication*] (DLA) ... Que L
Quebec Law Reports ... QLR
Quebec Law Reports [*Canada*] [*A publication*] (DLA) ... Que LR
Quebec Law Reports [*Canada*] [*A publication*] (DLA) ... Quebec L (Can)
Quebec Library Association (AC) ... QLA
Quebec Library Association/Association des Bibliothecaires du Quebec [*Canada*] ... QLA/ABO
Quebec Library, Translation Bureau, Secretary of State Canada [*Bibliotheque de Quebec, Bureau des Traductions, Secretariat d'Etat*], Ste.-Foy, Quebec [*Library symbol National Library of Canada*] (NLC) ... QQSS
Quebec Medical Association (AC) ... QMA
Quebec Ministere de l'Education, Centrale des Bibliotheques, Montreal, PQ, Canada [*Library symbol Library of Congress*] (LCLS) ... CaQMECB
Quebec Ministere de l'Environnement, Quebec, PQ, Canada [*Library symbol Library of Congress*] (LCLS) ... CaQQEN
Quebec Ministere des Affaires Culturelles, Quebec, PQ, Canada [*Library symbol Library of Congress*] (LCLS) ... CaQQAC
Quebec Ministere des Affaires Intergouvernementales, Bibliotheque Administrative, Quebec, PQ, Canada [*Library symbol Library of Congress*] (LCLS) ... CaQQAI
Quebec Ministere du Tourisme, de la Chasse, et de la Peche, Montreal, PQ, Canada [*Library symbol Library of Congress*] (LCLS) ... CaQMTCP
Quebec, Montreal, Ottawa & Occidental [*Railway*] ... QMO & O
Quebec North Shore and Labrador Railway [*Canada*] (AD) ... QNS & L
Quebec Official Reports [*A publication*] (DLA) ... QOR
Quebec Official Reports [*A publication*] (DLA) ... QR
Quebec Official Reports, Court of Appeals [*A publication*] ... Que C A
Quebec Official Reports, King's Bench [*A publication*] (ILCA) ... LRKB
Quebec Official Reports, King's Bench [*A publication*] (DLA) ... Que KB
Quebec Official Reports, King's Bench [*Canada*] [*A publication*] (DLA) ... Queb KB
Quebec Official Reports, Queen's Bench [*1892-1900*] [*Canada*] [*A publication*] (DLA) ... Br
Quebec Official Reports, Queen's Bench [*A publication*] (DLA) ... Que QB
Quebec Official Reports, Superior Court [*A publication*] (DLA) ... Que SC
Quebec Official Reports, Superior Court [*A publication*] (DLA) ... Que Super
Quebec Official Reports, Superior Court [*A publication*] (DLA) ... SC
Quebec Order of Dentists [*Canada*] (AD) ... QOD
Quebec Pension Plan [*Canada*] ... QPP
Quebec Police Force [*Canada*] (AD) ... QPF
Quebec, PQ [*AM radio station call letters*] ... CBV
Quebec, PQ [*FM radio station call letters*] ... CBVE
Quebec, PQ [*FM radio station call letters*] ... CBV-FM
Quebec, PQ [*FM radio station call letters*] (RBYB) ... CHIK-FM
Quebec, PQ [*FM radio station call letters*] ... CHOI
Quebec, PQ [*AM radio station call letters*] ... CHRC
Quebec, PQ [*FM radio station call letters*] (RBYB) ... CION
Quebec, PQ [*FM radio station call letters*] ... CITF
Quebec, PQ [*FM radio station call letters*] ... CJMF
Quebec, PQ [*FM radio station call letters*] ... CKIA
Quebec, PQ [*FM radio station call letters*] ... CKRL
Quebec, PQ [*ICAO location identifier*] (ICLI) ... CYQB
Quebec Practice [*A publication*] (DLA) ... Que Pr
Quebec Practice [*Canada*] [*A publication*] (DLA) ... Quebec Pr (Can)
Quebec Practice Reports [*A publication*] (DLA) ... QPR
Quebec Practice Reports [*A publication*] (DLA) ... Que PR
Quebec Practice Reports [*A publication*] (DLA) ... Que Prac
Quebec Practice Reports [*1897-1943*] [*A publication*] (DLA) ... Queb Pr
Quebec Provincial Police [*Canada*] (AD) ... QPP
Quebec Queen's Bench Reports [*Canada*] [*A publication*] (DLA) ... LRQB
Quebec Queen's Bench Reports [*Canada*] [*A publication*] (DLA) ... QRQB
Quebec Rapports Judiciaires Officiels (Banc de la Reine, Cour Superieure) [*A publication*] (DLA) ... Que BR
Quebec Region Canadian University Press (AD) ... QRCUP
Quebec Region Library, Public Works Canada [*Bibliotheque de la Region du Quebec, Travaux Publics Canada*] **Montreal, Quebec** [*Library symbol National Library of Canada*] (NLC) ... QMPWQ
Quebec Regional Office, Employment and Immigration Canada [*Bureau Regional duQuebec, Emploi et Immigration Canada*] **Montreal, Quebec** [*Library symbol National Library of Canada*] (NLC) ... QMMIQ
Quebec Revised Judicial [*A publication*] (DLA) ... Que Rev Jud
Quebec Revised Statutes [*Canada*] [*A publication*] (DLA) ... Que Rev Stat
Quebec Securities Commission [*Canada*] (AD) ... QSC
Quebec Society for the Protection of Plants [*Canada*] (AD) ... QSPP
Quebec Standard Test [*Canada*] (AD) ... QST
Quebec Statutes [*Canada*] [*A publication*] (DLA) ... Que Stat
Quebec Sturgeon River Mines Ltd. [*Toronto Stock Exchange symbol*] ... QSR
Quebec Superior Court Reports [*A publication*] (DLA) ... QRSC
Quebec Supreme Court Reports [*A publication*] (DLA) ... CS
Quebec Symphony Orchestra [*Canada*] (AD) ... QSO
Quebec Tax Reporter (Commerce Clearing House) [*A publication*] (DLA) ... Que Tax Rep (CCH)
Quebec Teachers' Federation [*Canada*] (AD) ... QTF
Quebec Teaching Congress [*Canada*] (AD) ... QTC
Quebec Tourist Information Bureau [*Canada*] (AD) ... QTIB
Quebec White Anglo-Saxon Protestant ... QWASP
Quebec Zoological Society [*Canada*] (AD) ... QZS
Quebecair (AD) ... QBA
Quebecair (AD) ... QUE
Quebecair, Inc. [*Airlines*] [*ICAO designator*] (OAG) ... QB
Quebecair, Inc. [*Airlines*] ... QBA
Quebecois (AD) ... Que
Quebecor Cl'A' [*AMEX symbol*] (TTSB) ... PQB
Quebecor, Inc. [*AMEX symbol*] (SPSG) ... PQB
Quebecor, Inc. [*Toronto Stock Exchange symbol*] ... QBR
Quebecor, Inc. [*Associated Press*] (SAG) ... Quebcor
Quebecor Printing [*NYSE symbol*] (TTSB) ... PRW
Quebecor Printing, Inc. [*NYSE symbol*] (SAG) ... PRW
Quebecor Printing, Inc. [*Associated Press*] (SAG) ... QuebPr
Quebec-Telephone [*Toronto Stock Exchange symbol*] ... QT

Quebrada ... QBDA
Quebradillas, PR [*AM radio station call letters*] ... WKVN
Quebradillas, PR [*FM radio station call letters*] ... WQQZ
Quechan Indian Reservation (AD) ... QIR
Quechon Tribal Museum [*Yuma, Arizona*] (AD) ... QTM
Quechua (AD) ... Que
Quechua [*MARC language code Library of Congress*] (LCCP) ... que
Queckenstedt's Test [*Neurology*] (DAVI) ... QT
Queckenstedt-Stookey Test [*Neurology*] (DAVI) ... Q-S
Quecksilbersaeule [*Mercury Column*] [*German*] (AD) ... QS
Queen ... Q
Queen [*Chess*] ... Q
Queen [*Phonetic alphabet*] [*Pre-World War II*] [*World War II*] (DSUE) ... Q
Queen (ADA) ... QN
Queen (AD) ... Qn
Queen ... QN
Queen (AD) ... Qu
Queen ... QU
Queen [*Alaska*] [*Airport symbol Obsolete*] (OAG) ... UQE
Queen Alexandra's Imperial Military Nursing Service [*British*] (BARN) ... QA
Queen Alexandra's Imperial Military Nursing Service [*British*] ... QAIMNS
Queen Alexandra's Imperial Military Nursing Service Reserve [*British military*] (DMA) ... QAIMNSR
Queen Alexandra's Military Family Nursing Service [*British military*] (DMA) ... QAMFNS
Queen Alexandra's Own Gurkha Rifles [*British military*] (DMA) ... QAOGR
Queen Alexandra's Royal Air Force Nursing Service [*British*] (AD) ... QARAFNS
Queen Alexandra's Royal Army Nursing Corps [*British*] ... QARANC
Queen Alexandra's Royal Army Nursing Service [*British*] (AD) ... QARANC
Queen Alexandra's Royal Naval Nursing Service Reserve [*British military*] (DMA) ... QARNNSR
Queen Alexandra's Royal Navy Nursing Service [*British*] ... QARNNS
Queen Alia International Airport [*Jordan*] ... QAIA
Queen Anne (DLA) ... Ann
Queen Anne (DLA) ... Anne
Queen Anne's Bounty ... QAB
Queen Anne's County Free Library, Centreville, MD [*Library symbol Library of Congress*] (LCLS) ... MdCe
Queen Charlotte [*British Columbia*] [*Seismograph station code, US Geological Survey*] (SEIS) ... QCC
Queen Charlotte Airlines Ltd. ... QCA
Queen Charlotte Islands (AD) ... QC Isl
Queen Charlotte Islands ... QCI's
Queen Charlotte Islands Museum, Queen Charlotte, British Columbia [*Library symbol National Library of Canada*] (NLC) ... BQCM
Queen Consort [*British*] (ROG) ... QC
Queen Elizabeth (DLA) ... Eliz
Queen Elizabeth 2 [*Luxury liner*] ... QE 2
Queen Elizabeth Chemical Center [*British*] (AD) ... QECC
Queen Elizabeth College [*British*] ... QEC
Queen Elizabeth Hall [*London, England*] ... QEH
Queen Elizabeth Hospital, Charlottetown, PE, Canada [*Library symbol*] [*Library of Congress*] (LCLS) ... CaPCQEH
Queen Elizabeth Hospital, Charlottetown, Prince Edward Island [*Library symbol National Library of Canada*] (NLC) ... PCQEH
Queen Elizabeth Hospital, Montreal, PQ, Canada [*Library symbol Library of Congress*] (LCLS) ... CaQMQE
Queen Elizabeth Hospital, Montreal, Quebec [*Library symbol National Library of Canada*] (NLC) ... QMQE
Queen Elizabeth Hospital, Toronto, ON, Canada [*Library symbol*] [*Library of Congress*] (LCLS) ... CaOTQE
Queen Elizabeth Hospital, Toronto, Ontario [*Library symbol National Library of Canada*] (NLC) ... OTQE
Queen Elizabeth II Library, Memorial University of Newfoundland, St. John's, Newfoundland [*Library symbol National Library of Canada*] (NLC) ... NFSM
Queen Elizabeth Military Hospital [*Ministry of Defense*] [*British*] (PDAA) ... QEMH
Queen Elizabeth National Park [*Uganda*] (AD) ... QENP
Queen Elizabeth Park (AD) ... QEP
Queen Elizabeth Planetarium (AD) ... QEP
Queen Elizabeth Theatre [*Vancouver*] (AD) ... QET
Queen Elizabeth Way [*Canada*] ... QEW
Queen Elizabeth's Foundation for the Disabled [*British*] (AD) ... QEFD
Queen Elizabeth's Hospital School [*England*] ... QEH
Queen Elizabeth's Overseas Nursing Service [*British*] (DAVI) ... QEONS
Queen Elizabeth's Own [*British military*] (DMA) ... QEO
Queen Emma Summer Palace (AD) ... QESP
Queen Mary (DLA) ... M
Queen Mary College [*London*] ... QMC
Queen Mary College Industrial Research Ltd. [*Research center British*] (IRUK) ... QMC-IRL
Queen Mary Street School, Ottawa, Ontario [*Library symbol National Library of Canada*] (BIB) ... OOQM
Queen Mary Veterans Hospital, Montreal, PQ, Canada [*Library symbol Library of Congress*] (LCLS) ... CaQMQ
Queen Mary Veterans Hospital [*Hopital Reine-Marie (Anciens combattants)*] **Montreal, Quebec** [*Library symbol National Library of Canada*] (NLC) ... QMQ
Queen Mary's Army Auxiliary Corps [*The WAAC*] [*British*] ... QMAAC
Queen Mary's Own [*British military*] (DMA) ... QMO
Queen Mary's Regiment [*British military*] (DMA) ... QMR
Queen Mary's School Cadet Corps [*British military*] (DMA) ... QMSCC
Queen Mary's Yeomanry [*British military*] (DMA) ... QMY
Queen Mother [*British*] ... QM
Queen of Angels School of Nursing, Los Angeles, CA [*Library symbol Library of Congress*] (LCLS) ... CLQ
Queen of the Angels Seminary, San Fernando, CA [*Library symbol Library of Congress*] (LCLS) ... CSfeQ
Queen of the Rosary College, Fremont, CA [*Library symbol Library of Congress*] (LCLS) ... CFr
Queen Post (AD) ... qp
Queen Post ... QP
Queen Street Camera, Inc. [*Toronto Stock Exchange symbol*] ... QSC
Queen Street Mall and Valley Mall Advisory Committee [*Brisbane, Australia*] ... QSMVMAC
Queen Street Mental Health Centre, Toronto, ON, Canada [*Library symbol Library of Congress*] (LCLS) ... CaOTQSM
Queen Street Mental Health Centre, Toronto, Ontario [*Library symbol National Library of Canada*] (NLC) ... OTQSM
Queen Victoria [*British*] ... QV
Queen Victoria Museum [*Launceston, Tasmania*] (AD) ... QVM
Queen Victoria's Clergy Sustentation Fund [*British*] ... QVCSF
Queen Victoria's Own [*British military*] (DMA) ... QVO
Queen Victoria's Rifles [*Military unit*] [*British*] ... QVR
Queen Victoria's School [*British military*] (DMA) ... QVS
Queenie [*Phonetic alphabet*] [*Royal Navy World War I*] (DSUE) ... Q
Queens (AD) ... Qns
Queen's Aide-de-Camp [*Military British*] ... QADC
Queen's Award to Industry [*British*] (AD) ... QAI
Queen's Awards for Export [*British*] ... QAE
Queen's Awards Office [*British*] ... QAO
Queen's Bad Bargain [*Undesirable serviceman*] [*Slang British*] (DSUE) ... QBB
Queens Bar Bulletin [*United States*] [*A publication*] (DLA) ... Queens B Bull
Queen's Bays [*Later, QDG*] [*Military unit*] [*British*] ... QB
Queen's Bench [*Legal*] [*British*] ... QB
Queen's Bench Division [*Military unit*] [*British*] ... QBD
Queen's Bench Division, Law Reports [*A publication*] ... QBD
Queen's Bench Library [*Alberta*] [*UTLAS symbol*] ... LSE
Queen's Bench Reports [*Legal*] [*British*] ... QBR
Queen's Bench Reports [*A publication*] (AD) ... QBRs
Queen's Bench Reports, by Adolphus and Ellis, New Series [*A publication*] (DLA) ... QB
Queen's Bench Reports, by Adolphus and Ellis, New Series [*A publication*] (DLA) ... QBR
Queen's Bench Reports, Lower Canada [*A publication*] (DLA) ... QBLC
Queen's Bench Reports, Upper Canada [*A publication*] (DLA) ... QBUC
Queen's Bishop [*Chess*] ... QB
Queen's Bishop's Pawn [*Chess*] (IIA) ... QBP
Queens Borough Public Library [*New York, NY*] ... QBPL
Queens Borough Public Library, Jamaica, NY [*Library symbol Library of Congress*] (LCLS) ... NJQ
Queen's Bureau of Investigation [*British*] (AD) ... QBI
Queen's College [*Oxford and Cambridge Universities*] (ROG) ... QC
Queen's College (AD) ... Qns Coll
Queen's College [*Cambridge, Oxford*] (AD) ... QU
Queen's College Cadet Battalion [*Taunton*] [*British military*] (DMA) ... QCCB
Queens College, Charlotte, NC [*Library symbol Library of Congress*] (LCLS) ... NcCQ
Queens College, Flushing, NY [*Library symbol Library of Congress*] (LCLS) ... NFQC
Queens College, Flushing, NY [*OCLC symbol*] (OCLC) ... XQM
Queen's College, Ireland (ROG) ... QCI
Queen's College of Physicians, Ireland (ROG) ... QCPI
Queens College of The City University of New York (GAGS) ... Queens C (CUNY)
Queens College Press [*Australia*] (AD) ... QCP
Queen's College, St. John's, Newfoundland [*Library symbol National Library of Canada*] (NLC) ... NFSQ
Queen's College, St. John's, NF, Canada [*Library symbol Library of Congress*] (LCLS) ... CaNfSQ
Queen's Commendation for Brave Conduct [*British*] (AD) ... QCBC
Queens' Council Member of Parliament [*British*] (AD) ... QCMP
Queen's Counsel [*British*] ... QC
Queens County (AD) ... Q Co
Queens County Bancorp [*NASDAQ symbol*] (SAG) ... QCSB
Queens County Bancorp [*Associated Press*] (SAG) ... QueenCB
Queens County Bancorp [*Associated Press*] (SAG) ... QueenCtB
Queens County Bar Association. Bulletin [*United States*] [*A publication*] (DLA) ... Queens CBA Bull
Queens County Museum, Liverpool, Nova Scotia [*Library symbol National Library of Canada*] (NLC) ... NSLQCM
Queens County Museum, Liverpool, NS, Canada [*Library symbol*] [*Library of Congress*] (LCLS) ... CaNSLiQCM
Queen's Dragoon Guards [*Formerly, KDG, QB*] [*Military unit*] [*British*] ... QDG
Queen's Edinburgh Rifles [*British military*] (DMA) ... QER
Queens Educational and Social Team (AD) ... QUEST
Queen's Evidence [*British*] [*Legal term*] (BARN) ... QE
Queen's Fire Service Medal for Distinguished Service [*British*] ... QFSM
Queen's Fire Services Medal [*British*] (AD) ... QFSM
[*The*] **Queen's Flight** [*British ICAO designator*] (FAAC) ... TQF
Queen's Gallantry Medal [*British*] ... QGM
Queen's Gurkha Engineers [*British military*] (DMA) ... QGE
Queen's Gurkha Officer [*Military British*] ... QGO
Queen's Hall (AD) ... QH
Queen's Hall Orchestra ... QHO
Queen's Harbour Master [*British*] ... QHM
Queen's Hard Bargain [*Undesirable serviceman*] [*Slang British*] (DSUE) ... QHB
Queen's Honorary Chaplain [*British*] ... QHC
Queen's Honorary Dental Surgeon [*British*] ... QHDS
Queen's Honorary Nursing Sister [*British*] ... QHNS
Queen's Honorary Physician [*British*] ... QHP
Queen's Honorary Surgeon [*British*] ... QHS

Queen's Honorary Veterinarian [*British*] (AD) ... QHV
Queens Hospital Center, Jamaica, NY [*Library symbol Library of Congress*] (LCLS) ... NJQH
Queen's Institute of District Nursing [*British*] ... QIDN
Queens Intermediate School, Pasadena, TX [*Library symbol*] [*Library of Congress*] (LCLS) ... TxPQI
Queen's Intramural Law Journal [*1968-70*] [*Canada*] [*A publication*] (DLA) ... Queens Intra LJ
Queen's Intramural Law Journal [*A publication*] (DLA) ... Queen's Intramural LJ
Queen's Knight [*Chess*] ... QK
Queen's Knight [*Chess*] ... QKT
Queen's Knight [*Chess*] (IIA) ... QN
Queen's Knight's Pawn [*Chess*] (IIA) ... QKTP
Queen's Knight's Pawn [*Chess*] (IIA) ... QNP
Queen's Lancashire Regiment [*Military unit*] [*British*] ... QLR
Queen's Lancers [*Military unit*] [*British*] ... QL
Queen's Light Dragoons [*British military*] (DMA) ... QLD
Queen's Messenger [*British*] ... QM
Queens Moat Houses [*Hoteller*] [*British*] ... QMH
Queens Museum (AD) ... QM
Queen's Nursing Institute [*British*] ... QNI
Queen's Nursing Sister [*British*] (DAVI) ... QNS
Queen's Own [*Military unit*] [*British*] ... QO
Queen's Own Cameron Highlanders [*Military unit*] [*British*] ... QOCH
Queen's Own Corps of Guides [*British military*] (DMA) ... QOCG
Queen's Own Dorset and West Somerset Yeomanry [*British military*] (DMA) ... QOD & WSY
Queen's Own Dorsetshire Yeomanry [*British military*] (DMA) ... QODY
Queen's Own Hussars [*Military unit*] [*British*] ... QOH
Queen's Own Lowland Yeomanry [*Military unit*] [*British*] ... LY
Queen's Own Lowland Yeomanry [*Military unit*] [*British*] (DMA) ... QOLY
Queen's Own Mercian Yeomanry [*Military unit*] [*British*] ... QOMY
Queen's Own Nigeria Regiment [*British military*] (DMA) ... QONR
Queen's Own Oxfordshire Hussars [*British military*] (DMA) ... QOOH
Queen's Own Rifles [*Military unit*] [*British*] ... QOR
Queen's Own Rifles, Canada [*Military*] (ROG) ... QORC
Queen's Own Rifles of Canada Regimental Museum, Toronto, ON, Canada [*Library symbol Library of Congress*] (LCLS) ... CaOTQRM
[*The*] **Queen's Own Rifles of Canada Regimental Museum, Toronto, Ontario** [*Library symbol National Library of Canada*] (NLC) ... OTQRM
Queen's Own Royal [*Military unit*] [*British*] ... QOR
Queen's Own Royal Glasgow Imperial Yeomanry [*British military*] (DMA) ... QORGIY
Queen's Own Royal Glasgow Yeomanry [*British military*] (DMA) ... QORGY
Queen's Own Royal Regiment [*British military*] (DMA) ... QORR
Queen's Own Royal West Kent Regiment [*Military unit*] [*British*] ... QORWKR
Queen's Own Royal West Kent Regiment [*Military unit*] [*British*] ... RWK
Queen's Own Westminster Volunteer Rifles [*Military British*] (ROG) ... QOWVR
Queen's Own Worcestershire Hussars [*British military*] (DMA) ... QOWH
Queen's Own Yeomanry [*British military*] (DMA) ... QOY
Queens Park (AD) ... Qns Pk
Queen's Park Football Club (AD) ... QPFC
Queen's Park Harriers [*British*] (ROG) ... QPH
Queen's Park Ranger [*British*] (DI) ... QPR
Queen's Pawn [*Chess*] (ADA) ... QP
Queen's Pleasure [*British*] ... QP
Queen's Polar Medal [*British*] (AD) ... QPM
Queen's Police Medal [*British*] ... QPM
Queen's [*Victoria*] **Prime Ministers** [*A publication*] ... QPM
Queen's Printer [*British*] (AD) ... QP
Queens Public Library (AD) ... QPL
Queen's Quarterly [*A publication*] (BRI) ... Queens Q
Queen's Rangers [*British military*] ... QR
Queen's Regulation [*Military British*] ... QR
Queen's Regulations and Admiralty Instructions [*Obsolete Navy British*] ... QR & AI
Queen's Regulations and Orders for the Canadian Army ... QR & O (Can)
Queen's Regulations and Orders for the Royal Canadian Air Force ... QR Air
Queen's Regulations and Orders for the Royal Canadian Navy ... QRCN
Queen's Rifle Volunteer Brigade [*British military*] (DMA) ... QRVB
Queen's Rook [*Chess*] (ADA) ... QR
Queen's Rook's Pawn [*Chess*] (IIA) ... QRP
Queen's Row Spare ... QRS
Queen's Row Unit ... QRU
Queen's Row Unit Spare ... QRUS
Queen's Royal [*Military unit*] [*British*] ... QR
Queen's Royal Irish Hussars [*Military unit*] [*British*] ... QRIH
Queen's Royal Regiment [*Military unit*] [*British*] ... QRR
Queen's Royal Rifles [*British military*] (DMA) ... QRR
Queen's Scarf (ADA) ... QS
Queen's Scholar [*British*] ... QS
Queen's Serjeant [*Military British*] (ROG) ... QS
Queen's Service Medal [*British*] (AD) ... QSM
Queen's Service Medal [*British*] (AD) ... qsm
Queen's Service Order [*British*] (AD) ... QSO
Queen's Silver Jubilee Medal [*British*] (AD) ... QSJM
Queen's University [*Canada*] ... QU
Queen's University, Agnes Ethrington Art Centre, Kingston, ON, Canada [*Library symbol Library of Congress*] (LCLS) ... CaOKQA
Queen's University, Archives, Kingston, ON, Canada [*Library symbol Library of Congress*] (LCLS) ... CaOKQAR
Queen's University at Kingston Centre for International Relations [*Canada Research center*] (RCD) ... QCIR
Queen's University, Belfast [*Ireland*] ... QUB
Queen's University, Canadian Institute of Guided Ground Transport, Kingston, ON,Canada [*Library symbol*] [*Library of Congress*] (LCLS) ... CaOKQCI
Queen's University, Department of Geography, Kingston, ON, Canada [*Library symbol Library of Congress*] (LCLS) ... CaOKQG
Queen's University, Department of Geological Sciences, Kingston, ON, Canada [*Library symbol Library of Congress*] (LCLS) ... CaOKQGS
Queen's University, Douglas Library, Map Collection, Kingston, ON, Canada [*Library symbol Library of Congress*] (LCLS) ... CaOKQMA
Queen's University, Health Sciences Library, Kingston, ON, Canada [*Library symbol Library of Congress*] (LCLS) ... CaOKQH
Queen's University Highland Battalion [*British military*] (DMA) ... QUH
Queen's University Information Systems (NITA) ... QUIS
Queens University Interpretative Code (AD) ... QUICK
Queen's University Interrogation of Legal Language (NITA) ... QUILL
Queen's University Interrogation of Legal Literature [*Queen's University of Belfast*] [*Northern Ireland*] [*Information service or system*] (IID) ... QUILL
Queen's University, Ireland ... QUI
Queen's University, Kingston, ON, Canada [*Library symbol Library of Congress*] (LCLS) ... CaOKQ
Queen's University, Kingston, Ontario [*Library symbol National Library of Canada*] (NLC) ... OKQ
Queen's University, Law Library, Kingston, ON, Canada [*Library symbol Library of Congress*] (LCLS) ... CaOKQL
Queen's University Library (AD) ... QUL
Queen's University, McArthur College of Education, Kingston, ON, Canada [*Library symbol Library of Congress*] (LCLS) ... CaOKQM
Queen's University, Medical Library [*UTLAS symbol*] ... QUM
Queen's University of Belfast, Belfast, United Kingdom [*Library symbol Library of Congress*] (LCLS) ... UKBelQU
Queen's University of Dublin (AD) ... QUD
Queen's University Online Bibliographic Information Retrieval and Dissemination (NITA) ... QUOBIRD
Queen's Westminster Rifle Volunteers [*British military*] (DMA) ... QWRV
Queen's Westminster Rifles [*British military*] (DMA) ... QWR
Queensboro Bridge [*New York City*] (AD) ... QB
Queensborough Community College of the City University of New York, Bayside, NY [*Library symbol Library of Congress*] (LCLS) ... NBsdQ
Queensborough Community College of the City University of New York, Library, Bayside, NY [*OCLC symbol*] (OCLC) ... ZQC
Queensbury [*England*] [*Seismograph station code, US Geological Survey*] (SEIS) ... QMB
Queensbury, NY [*FM radio station call letters*] (RBYB) ... WNYQ-FM
Queensbury, NY [*FM radio station call letters*] (RBYB) ... WSRQ
Queensland [*Fever*] [*Medicine*] (BABM) ... Q
Queensland [*Airline code*] (AD) ... QL
Queensland (AD) ... Qld
Queensland (ODBW) ... Qld
Queensland (AD) ... Qnsd
Queensland [*Australia*] (BARN) ... Qnsld
Queensland [*Australia*] ... Queens
Queensland (AD) ... Queensl
Queensland [*MARC geographic area code Library of Congress*] (LCCP) ... u-at-qn
Queensland Academy of Space Sciences [*Australia*] ... QASS
Queensland Academy of Sport [*Australia*] ... QAS
Queensland Agricultural Bank [*Australia*] ... QAB
Queensland Air Museum Society [*Australia*] ... QAMS
Queensland Air Navigation Co. Ltd. [*Australia*] (ADA) ... QAN
Queensland Airlines Party Ltd. ... QAPL
Queensland Airlines Proprietary Ltd. [*Australia*] (AD) ... QAPL
Queensland Allergy and Hyperactivity Association [*Australia*] ... QAHA
Queensland Alumina Ltd. [*Australia*] (AD) ... QAL
Queensland Amateur Gymnastic Association [*Australia*] (AD) ... QAGA
Queensland Amateur Swimming Association [*Australia*] (AD) ... QASA
Queensland Amateur Wrestling Association [*Australia*] (AD) ... QAWA
Queensland Ambulance Service Board [*Australia*] ... QASB
Queensland Ambulance Transport Brigade [*Australia*] (AD) ... QATB
Queensland & Northern Territory Aerial Service [*Later, QANTAS Airways Ltd.*] [*Australia*] ... QANTAS
Queensland and Northern Territory Judgements Bulletin [*Australia A publication*] ... QNTJB
Queensland Art Gallery [*Australia*] ... QAG
Queensland Art Teachers' Association [*Australia*] ... QATA
Queensland Arts Council [*Australia*] ... QAC
Queensland Arts Movement [*Australia*] ... QAM
Queensland Association for Gifted and Talented Children [*Australia*] ... QAGTC
Queensland Association of Independent Legal Services [*Australia*] ... QAILS
Queensland Association of Industries for the Disabled [*Australia*] ... QAID
Queensland Association of Permanent Building Societies [*Australia*] ... QAPBS
Queensland Association of Personnel Services [*Australia*] (AD) ... QAPS
Queensland Australian Football League (AD) ... QAFL
Queensland Ballet [*Australia*] ... QB
Queensland Band Association [*Australia*] ... QBA
Queensland Barristers' Board [*Australia*] ... QBB
Queensland Baseball League [*Australia*] ... QBL
Queensland Beekeepers' Association [*Australia*] ... QBA
Queensland Blind Workers Union of Employees [*Australia*] ... QBWUE
Queensland Blinded Soldiers' Association [*Australia*] ... QBSA
Queensland Boating and Fisheries Patrol [*Australia*] ... QBFP
Queensland Book Depot [*Australia*] (AD) ... QBD
Queensland Bookbinders' Guild [*Australia*] ... QBG
Queensland Bowling Association [*Australia*] (AD) ... QBA
Queensland Braille Writing Association [*Australia*] ... QBWA
Queensland Bridge Association [*Australia*] ... QBA
Queensland Bureau of Emergency Services [*Australia*] ... QBES

Queensland Bush Children's Health Scheme [*Australia*] ... QBCHS
Queensland Bush Nursing Association [*Australia*] ... QBNA
Queensland Business and Industry Directory [*Australia A publication*] ... QBID
Queensland Butter Board [*Australia*] (AD) ... QBB
Queensland Cancer Fund [*Australia*] ... QCF
Queensland Cane Growers' Association [*Australia*] ... QCGA
Queensland Cane-Growers Council [*Australia*] (AD) ... QCGC
Queensland Chamber of Agricultural Societies [*Australia*] ... QCAS
Queensland Chamber of Industry [*Australia*] ... QCOI
Queensland Chamber of Mines [*Australia*] ... QCM
Queensland Chicken Meat Council [*Australia*] ... QCMC
Queensland Children's Research Foundation [*Australia*] ... QCRF
Queensland Cleaning Contractors Association [*Australia*] (AD) ... QCCA
Queensland Coal Associates [*Australia*] (AD) ... QCA
Queensland Coal Association [*Australia*] ... QCA
Queensland Coal Board [*Australia*] ... QCB
Queensland Coal Mining [*Australia*] (AD) ... QCM
Queensland Colliery Employees Union [*Australia*] (AD) ... QCEU
Queensland Colonial Association [*Australia*] ... QCA
Queensland Colostomy Association [*Australia*] ... QCA
Queensland Confederation of Industry [*Australia*] (AD) ... QCI
Queensland Conservation Council [*Australia*] (AD) ... QCC
Queensland Conveyancing Cases [*Australia A publication*] ... Q Conv R
Queensland Conveyancing Law and Practice [*A publication*] ... AQC
Queensland Cooperative Milling Association [*Australia*] (AD) ... QCMA
Queensland Cotton Corp. [*Australia*] ... QCC
Queensland Council of Finance Counsellors and Lease Brokers [*Australia*] ... QCFCLB
Queensland Council of State School Organisations [*Australia*] ... QCSSO
Queensland Council on the Ageing [*Australia*] ... QCOTA
Queensland Country Press Association [*Australia*] ... QCPA
Queensland Country Women's Association [*Australia*] (AD) ... QCWA
Queensland Cricket Association [*Australia*] (AD) ... QCA
Queensland Criminal Justice Commission [*Australia*] ... QCJC
Queensland Criminal Reports [*A publication*] ... QCAR
Queensland Croquet Association (AD) ... QCA
Queensland Crown Lands Law Reports [*A publication*] (DLA) ... Queensl Cr Lands LR
Queensland Cruising Yacht Club [*Australia*] ... QCYC
Queensland Cultural Centre Trust [*Australia*] ... QCCT
Queensland Dairyfarmers' Organisation [*Australia*] ... QDO
Queensland Dairymens Organisation [*Australia*] (AD) ... QDO
Queensland Dance Studio Proprietors' Association [*Australia*] ... QDSPA
Queensland Department of Forestry [*Australia*] ... QDF
Queensland Department of Forests [*Australia*] ... QDOF
Queensland Development Education Centre [*Australia*] ... QDEC
Queensland Distance Education College [*Australia*] ... QDEC
Queensland Dive Tourism Association of Australia ... QDTAA
Queensland Education Information Centre [*Australia*] ... QEIC
Queensland Egg Industry Council [*Australia*] ... QEIC
Queensland Electricity Supply Industry Superannuation Board [*Australia*] ... QESISB
Queensland Employers Federation [*Australia*] (AD) ... QEF
Queensland Environmental Program [*Australia*] (AD) ... QEP
Queensland Exporters' Association [*Australia*] ... QEA
Queensland Farmers and Graziers' Association [*Australia*] ... QFGA
Queensland Farmers' Federation [*Australia*] ... QFF
Queensland Fever [*Medicine*] (DAVI) ... Q
Queensland Film Development Office [*Australia*] ... QFDO
Queensland Fire Service [*Australia*] ... QFS
Queensland Fisheries Research Institute [*Australia*] (AD) ... QFRI
Queensland Fisheries Service [*Australia*] (AD) ... QFS
Queensland Fishing Industry Training Committee [*Australia*] ... QFITC
Queensland Flour Millers' Association [*Australia*] ... QFMA
Queensland Flower Growers' Association [*Australia*] ... QFGA
Queensland Food Industry Training Council [*Australia*] ... QFITC
Queensland Forest Service [*Australia*] ... QFS
Queensland Foundation for Local Government Engineering [*Australia*] ... QFLGE
Queensland Funeral Directors' Association [*Australia*] ... QFDA
Queensland Furniture Industry Training Committee [*Australia*] ... QFITC
Queensland Golf Union [*Australia*] ... QGU
Queensland Government Bureau of Emergency Services [*Australia*] ... QGBES
Queensland Government Mining Journal [*A publication*] ... Qd Govt Mining J
Queensland Government Tourist Bureau [*Australia*] (AD) ... QGTB
Queensland Grain Growers Association [*Australia*] (AD) ... QGGA
Queensland Graingrower [*A publication*] ... Qd Graingrower
Queensland Graingrowers' Association [*Australia*] ... QGA
Queensland Grains [*Australia Commercial firm*] ... QG
Queensland Guild of Furniture Manufacturers [*Australia*] ... QGFM
Queensland Gymnastic Association [*Australia*] ... QGA
Queensland Healthy Soil Society [*Australia*] ... QHSS
Queensland Herbarium Plant Specimen Data Base [*State*] [*Computer science*] (EERA) ... HERBRECS
Queensland Heritage [*A publication*] ... Q Her
Queensland Hide and Skin Industries Association [*Australia*] ... QHSIA
Queensland Historical Society [*Australia*] ... QHS
Queensland Historical Society. Journal [*A publication*] ... Q Hist Soc J
Queensland Horticultural Export Association [*Australia*] ... QHEA
Queensland Housing Commission [*Australia*] ... QHC
Queensland Immigration Control Association [*Australia*] ... QICA
Queensland Imperial Bushmen [*British military*] (DMA) ... QIB
Queensland Industrial Gazette [*A publication*] ... QIG
Queensland Industrial Relations Commission [*Australia*] ... QIRC
Queensland Industry [*A publication*] ... Qd Ind
Queensland Industry [*A publication*] ... Qld Ind
Queensland Institute for Educational Research [*Australia*] (AD) ... QIER
Queensland Institute of Architects [*Australia*] (AD) ... QIA
Queensland Institute of Medical Research [*Australia*] (AD) ... QIMR
Queensland Institute of Public Affairs [*Australia*] (AD) ... QIPA
Queensland Institute of Technology [*Australia*] (AD) ... QIT
Queensland Institute of Technology. Law Journal [*A publication*] ... QITLJ
Queensland Institute of Technology, North Quay, QLD, Australia [*Library symbol Library of Congress*] (LCLS) ... AuNqIT
Queensland Insurance [*Australia*] (AD) ... QI
Queensland Irish Association [*Australia*] ... QIA
Queensland Japan Chamber of Commerce and Industry [*Australia*] ... QJCCI
Queensland Justice of the Peace and Local Authorities' Journal [*A publication*] (DLA) ... Queens JP & Loc Auth Jo
Queensland Justice of the Peace. Reports [*A publication*] (DLA) ... Queensl JP Rep
Queensland Justice of the Peace. Reports [*A publication*] (DLA) ... Queensl JPR
Queensland Keep Fit Association [*Australia*] ... QKFA
Queensland Ladies Golf Union [*Australia*] ... QLGU
Queensland Law [*A publication*] (DLA) ... Queensl L
Queensland Law Society [*Australia*] (AD) ... QLS
Queensland Law Society. Journal [*A publication*] ... Qd Law Soc J
Queensland Law Society. Journal [*A publication*] ... QL Soc J
Queensland Law Society. Journal [*A publication*] (DLA) ... Queens L Soc'y J
Queensland Law Society. Journal [*A publication A publication*] (DLA) ... Queensl LSJ
Queensland Lawn Tennis Association [*Australia*] (AD) ... QLTA
Queensland Lawyer [*Australia A publication*] ... Qd L
Queensland Lawyer [*A publication*] ... Qld Law
Queensland Lawyer [*Australia*] [*A publication*] (DLA) ... Queens Law
Queensland Library Promotion Council [*Australia*] (AD) ... QLPC
Queensland Light Opera Co. [*Australia*] (AD) ... QLOC
Queensland Litter Research Association [*Australia*] ... QLRA
Queensland Littoral Society [*Australia*] (AD) ... QLS
Queensland Livestock Exporters' Association [*Australia*] ... QLSEA
Queensland Local Government Association [*Australia*] (AD) ... QLGA
Queensland Maritime Museum [*Australia*] ... QMM
Queensland Master Builders Association [*Australia*] (AD) ... QMBA
Queensland Master Painters Association [*Australia*] (AD) ... QMPA
Queensland Mathematical Sciences Council [*Australia*] ... QMSC
Queensland Meat Exporters' Association [*Australia*] ... QMEA
Queensland Mechanical Cane Harvesters' Association [*Australia*] ... QMCHA
Queensland Merino Stud Sheepbreeders' Association [*Australia*] ... QMSSA
Queensland Milk Board [*Australia*] ... QMB
Queensland Mining Council [*Australia*] ... QMC
Queensland Motor Industry Association [*Australia*] (AD) ... QMIA
Queensland Netball Association [*Australia*] ... QNA
Queensland Newsagents' Federation [*Australia*] ... QNF
Queensland Nursery Industry Association [*Australia*] ... QNIA
Queensland Nurses' Union of Employees [*Australia*] ... QNUE
Queensland Office of International Business [*Australia*] ... QOIB
Queensland Open Learning Project [*Australia*] ... QOLP
Queensland Opera Company [*Australia*] ... QOC
Queensland Parliamentary Commissioner for Administration. Investigations Report [*Australia A publication*] ... QPCAI Report
Queensland Parliamentary Library, Parliament House, Brisbane, QLD, Australia [*Library symbol Library of Congress*] (LCLS) ... AuBrP
Queensland People's Party [*Australia Political party*] ... QPP
Queensland Philatelic Council [*Australia*] ... QPC
Queensland Photolab Association [*Australia*] ... QPA
Queensland Police Academy [*Australia*] (AD) ... QPA
Queensland Police Club [*Australia*] ... QPC
Queensland Police Journal [*A publication*] ... Qd Police J
Queensland Police Union [*Australia*] ... QPU
Queensland Polynesian Association [*Australia*] (AD) ... QPA
Queensland Pork Producers' Organisation [*Australia*] ... QPPO
Queensland Press Ltd. [*Australia*] ... QPL
Queensland Producers' Federation [*Australia*] ... QPF
Queensland Professional Fishermens League [*Australia*] (AD) ... QPFL
Queensland Public Acts [*A publication*] (DLA) ... Queensl Acts
Queensland Public Acts [*A publication*] (DLA) ... Queensl Pub Acts
Queensland Purchasing and Sales [*Australia*] ... QPS
Queensland Quality Centre [*Australia*] ... QQC
Queensland Quarter Horse Association [*Australia*] ... QQHA
Queensland Railfast Express [*Australia*] (AD) ... QRX
Queensland Railways [*Australia*] (AD) ... QR
Queensland Raw Sugar Industry [*Australia*] ... QRSI
Queensland Research League [*Australia*] (AD) ... QRL
Queensland Retail Traders and Shopkeepers' Association [*Australia*] ... QRTSA
Queensland Rifle Association [*Australia*] (AD) ... QRA
Queensland Right to Life [*An association Australia*] ... QRTL
Queensland Road Transport Association [*Australia*] ... QRTA
Queensland Rose Society [*Australia*] ... QRS
Queensland Rubber Co. [*Australia*] (AD) ... QRC
Queensland Sales Representatives and Commercial Travellers' Guild [*Australia*] ... QSRTCG
Queensland Scholastic Aptitude Test [*Australia*] ... QSAT
Queensland Secondary Principals' Association [*Australia*] ... QSPA
Queensland Shopkeepers Association [*Australia*] (AD) ... QSA
Queensland Small Business Council [*Australia*] ... QSBC
Queensland Smallbore Rifle Association [*Australia*] ... QSRA
Queensland Soccer Federation [*Australia*] (AD) ... QSF
Queensland Society [*Australia*] (AD) ... QS
Queensland Society [*Australia*] (NADA) ... QS
Queensland Society for Crippled Children [*Australia*] ... QSCC
Queensland Society of Sugar Cane Technologists [*Australia*] (AD) ... QSSCT
Queensland Soft Drink Manufacturers' Association [*Australia*] ... QSDMA

Queensland Spastic Welfare League [*Australia*] .... QSWL
Queensland Specialist Contractors' Association [*Australia*] .... QSCA
Queensland Sport and Recreational Fishing Council [*Australia*] .... QSRFC
Queensland State Archives, Dutton Park, QLD, Australia [*Library symbol Library of Congress*] (LCLS) .... AuDpAr
Queensland State Library [*Australia*] (AD) .... QSL
Queensland State Reports [*A publication*] (DLA) .... Queens St R
Queensland State Reports [*A publication*] (DLA) .... Queensl R
Queensland State Reports [*Australia*] [*A publication*] (DLA) .... Queensl St R
Queensland State Reports [*Australia*] [*A publication*] (DLA) .... Queensl St Rep
Queensland State Reports [*A publication*] (DLA) .... SQT
Queensland Sugar Corp. [*Australia*] .... QSC
Queensland. Supreme Court. Reports [*A publication*] (DLA) .... Queensl SCR
Queensland Swimming Association [*Australia*] .... QSA
Queensland Symphony Orchestra [*Australia*] (AD) .... QSO
Queensland Table Tennis Association [*Australia*] .... QTTA
Queensland Teachers' Journal [*A publication*] .... Qd Teach J
Queensland Teachers Union [*Australia*] (AD) .... QTU
Queensland Tertiary Admissions Centre [*Australia*] (AD) .... QTAC
Queensland Tertiary Education Foundation [*Australia*] .... QTEF
Queensland Timber Board [*Australia*] (AD) .... QTB
Queensland Timber Board Union of Employees [*Australia*] .... QTBUE
Queensland Timber Importers and Exporters' Association [*Australia*] .... QTIEA
Queensland Timber Industry Training Council [*Australia*] .... QTITC
Queensland Times Proprietory Ltd., Ipswich, QLD, Australia [*Library symbol Library of Congress*] (LCLS) .... AuIpQT
Queensland Tobacco Leaf Marketing Board [*Australia*] .... QTLMB
Queensland Tourism Industry Authority [*Australia*] .... QTIA
Queensland Tourist and Travel Corp. [*Australia*] (AD) .... QTTC
Queensland Trades and Labor Council [*Australia*] (AD) .... QTLC
Queensland Transmission and Supply Corp. [*Australia*] .... QTSC
Queensland Trotting Board [*Australia*] (AD) .... QTB
Queensland Turf Club [*Australia*] (AD) .... QTC
Queensland Unit and Group Titles Law and Practice [*Australia A publication*] .... LQUT
Queensland United Graziers' Association [*Australia*] .... QUGA
Queensland University Aphasia and Language Test .... QUALT
Queensland University Libraries Office of Cooperation [*Australia*] .... QULOC
Queensland University of Technology. Law Journal [*A publication*] .... QUTLJ
Queensland Victoria Research Foundation [*Australia*] .... QVRF
Queensland Water Resources Commission [*Australia*] .... QWRC
Queensland Women's Historical Society [*Australia*] .... QWHS
Queensland Writers' Centre [*Australia*] .... QWC
Queensland Youth Orchestra [*Australia*] (AD) .... QYO
Queens-Midtown Tunnel (AD) .... QMT
Queenstake Resources [*TS Symbol*] (TTSB) .... QTR
Queenstake Resources Ltd. [*Toronto Stock Exchange symbol*] .... QTR
Queenston Gold Mines Ltd. [*Toronto Stock Exchange symbol*] .... QUE
Queenstown [*South Africa*] [*ICAO location identifier*] (ICLI) .... FAQT
Queenstown [*New Zealand*] [*ICAO location identifier*] (ICLI) .... NZQN
Queenstown [*Australia Airport symbol*] (OAG) .... UEE
Queenstown [*South Africa*] [*Airport symbol*] (AD) .... UTW
Queenstown [*New Zealand*] [*Airport symbol*] (AD) .... ZON
Queenstown [*New Zealand*] [*Airport symbol*] (OAG) .... ZQN
Queenstown Rifle Volunteers [*British military*] (DMA) .... QRV
Queensway [*Furniture store chain*] [*British*] .... Q
Queensway Studios [*Record label*] [*Great Britain*] .... Queens
Queensway-Carleton Hospital, Ottawa, ON, Canada [*Library symbol Library of Congress*] (LCLS) .... CaOQC
Queensway-Carleton Hospital, Ottawa, Ontario [*Library symbol National Library of Canada*] (NLC) .... OOQC
Queer [*Homosexual*] [*Slang*] (DSUE) .... Q
Queer (AD) .... q
Queer Fellows (AD) .... Q-fellows
Quekett Microscopical Club [*British*] (BI) .... QMC
Quelimane [*Mozambique*] [*ICAO location identifier*] (ICLI) .... FQQL
Quelimane [*Mozambique*] [*Airport symbol*] (OAG) .... UEL
Quellon/Ad Quellon [*Chile*] [*ICAO location identifier*] (ICLI) .... SCON
Quelquefois [*Sometimes*] [*French*] (AD) .... qqf
Quelques [*Some*] [*French*] (AD) .... qq
Quench (AD) .... q
Quench (IAA) .... Q
Quench Compensation Factor .... QCF
Quench Correction .... QC
Quench Frequency (DEN) .... QF
Quench Frequency (AD) .... qf
Quench Melt Growth [*Physics*] .... QMG
Quench Particle Collection Bomb (MCD) .... QPCB
Quench Polish Quench (PDAA) .... QPQ
Quench Spray Pump (IEEE) .... QSP
Quench Spray Subsystem (IEEE) .... QSS
Quenched (MSA) .... QNCH
Quenched and Tempered (AD) .... q & t
Quenched and Tempered (MCD) .... QT
Quenched Carbonaceous Composite [*Plasma technology*] .... QCC
Queneau-Schuhmann [*Lead process*] .... Q-S
Quenia [*Kenya*] [*Portuguese*] (AD) .... Que
Quensk [*Language of the Quains*] (AD) .... Qndk
Quentin (AD) .... Quen
Quentin E. Deverill [*Protagonist in TV series; initialism also used as title of the series*] .... QED
Quenu-Muret Sign [*Cardiology*] (DAVI) .... Q-M
Quepos [*Costa Rica*] [*Airport symbol*] (OAG) .... XQP
Quepos (La Managua) [*Costa Rica*] [*ICAO location identifier*] (ICLI) .... MRQP
Quercetin [*Botany*] .... Q
Quercus [*Oak*] [*Pharmacology*] (ROG) .... QUERC
Queretaro [*Mexico ICAO location identifier*] (ICLI) .... MMQT
Queretaro (AD) .... Qro
Queretaro (AD) .... Quer
Querner, J. L., San Antonio TX [*STAC*] .... QJL
Querulous (DAVI) .... quer
Querwellen [*of transverse seismic waves*] (BARN) .... Q
Query (WDMC) .... inq
Query [*Journalism*] [*Proofreading*] (WDMC) .... q
Query (ODBW) .... q
Query .... Q
Query (AD) .... qu
Query (AD) .... qy
Query [*Journalism*] [*Proofreading*] (WDMC) .... qy
Query .... QY
Query Analyzer (IEEE) .... QA
Query and Reporting Processor .... QRP
[*A*] **Query and Retrieval Interactive Utility System** [*Computer science*] (ADA) .... AQUARIUS
Query Author [*Proofreader's notation*] .... QA
Query Buffer [*Computer science*] (IAA) .... QB
Query by Example [*Data processing search method*] .... QBE
Query by Image Content [*Computer science*] .... QBIC
Query Complexity Degree (MHDB) .... QCD
Query Control Station (MCD) .... QCS
Query Evaluation and Search Technique .... QUEST
Query Fever [*Medicine*] (DAVI) .... Q
Query Fever (AD) .... Q fever
Query Formulation and Encoding .... QFE
Query Interactive Processor (IEEE) .... QUIP
Query Interpretation Program (SAA) .... QIP
Query Language [*1975*] (CSR) .... Q
Query Language [*Computer science*] (DIT) .... QL
Query Language (AD) .... ql
Query Language [*Computer science*] (MHDI) .... QUEL
Query Language/One [*Computer science*] (MHDI) QL/1
Query Language Processor [*Computer science*] .... QLP
Query Management Facility [*Database*] (BYTE) .... QMF
Query Message (WDAA) .... QM
Query Message (AD) .... qm
Query Module (MCD) .... QM
Query Normalization .... QN
Query on Business Objects [*Computer science*] (PCM) .... QuoBO
Query Online Terminal Assistance [*Computer science*] .... QUOTA
Query Processing (MCD) .... QP
Query Property Similarity (MHDI) .... QPS
Query/Response (MCD) .... Q/R
Query Response Communications Console .... QRCC
Query Similarity [*Computer science*] (MHDI) .... QS
Query System [*Computer science*] .... QS
Query, Update Entry, Search, Time Sharing [*Computer science*] (AD) .... QESTS
Query, Update Entry, Search, Time-Sharing System (NVT) .... QEST
Query-by-Forms [*Data processing search method*] .... QBF
Quesnel [*Canada*] [*Airport symbol*] (OAG) .... YQZ
Quesnel and District Museum, Quesnel, BC, Canada [*Library symbol*] [*Library of Congress*] (LCLS) .... CaBQM
Quesnel and District Museum, Quesnel, British Columbia [*Library symbol National Library of Canada*] (NLC) .... BQM
Quesnel, BC [*Television station call letters*] (RBYB) CITM-2
Quesnel, BC [*AM radio station call letters*] .... CKCQ
Quesnel, BC [*ICAO location identifier*] (ICLI) .... CYQZ
Quesnel Library, British Columbia [*Library symbol National Library of Canada*] (BIB) .... BQ
Quest Diagnostics, Inc. [*NYSE symbol*] (SAG) .... DGX
Quest Diagnostics, Inc. [*Associated Press*] (SAG) .... QstDiag
Quest Energy Corp. [*Vancouver Stock Exchange symbol*] .... QUY
Quest for Peace (EA) .... QP
Quest for Value Dual Fd [*NYSE symbol*] (TTSB) .... KFV
Quest for Value Fund [*NYSE symbol*] (SAG) .... KFV
Quest for Value Fund [*Associated Press*] (SAG) .... QstVC
Quest for Value Fund [*Associated Press*] (SAG) .... QstVl
Quest For Value Income Shrs [*NYSE symbol*] (TTSB) .... KFVPr
Quest International Resources Corp. [*NASDAQ symbol*] (SAG) .... QIXX
Quest International Resources Corp. [*Associated Press*] (SAG) .... QuestInt
Quest Intl Res [*NASDAQ symbol*] (TTSB) .... QIXXF
Quest Medical [*NASDAQ symbol*] (TTSB) .... QMED
Quest Medical, Inc. [*NASDAQ symbol*] (NQ) .... QMED
Quest Medical, Inc. [*Associated Press*] (SAG) .... QuestM
Questa Oil & Gas [*NASDAQ symbol*] (TTSB) .... QUES
Questa Oil & Gas Co. [*NASDAQ symbol*] (SAG) .... QUES
Questa Oil & Gas Co. [*Associated Press*] (SAG) .... Questa
Questar Corp. [*Associated Press*] (SAG) .... Questar
Questar Corp. [*NYSE symbol*] (SPSG) .... STR
QuesTech Inc. [*NASDAQ symbol*] (TTSB) .... QTEC
QuesTech, Inc. [*NASDAQ symbol*] (NQ) .... QTEC
QuesTech, Inc. [*Associated Press*] (SAG) .... Questch
[*The*] **Questers** (EA) .... TQ
Question (WDMC) .... inq
Question (WDMC) .... q
Question (AD) .... q
Question .... Q
Question (AD) .... qn
Question (WDMC) .... qn
Question (FAAC) .... QN
Question (AD) .... qstn

Question (WDAA) ... QSTN
Question ... QU
Question (AD) ... qu
Question (AD) ... ques
Question (WDMC) ... ques
Question (AAG) ... QUES
Question ... QUEST
Question ... QUESTN
Question (ROG) ... QUON
Question Analysis Transformation and Search [*Computer science*] ... QUANTRAS
Question Analysis Transformation and Search [*Data processing*] (AD) ... quantras
Question and Answer (WDMC) ... Q and A
Question and Answer (MSA) ... Q & A
Question and Answer (IAA) ... QAA
Question and Information Connection [*St. Louis Public Library*] (AD) ... QUIC
Question Answering System (MHDB) ... QUANSY
Question Mark (AABC) ... QUES
Question or Query (AAG) ... Q-QY
Question/Query (AD) ... q/qy
Question Standard (NATG) ... QS
Questionable (DAVI) ... quest
Questionable (ROG) ... QUONBLE
Questionable Activity Report [*Employment and Training Administration*] [*Department of Labor*] ... QAR
Questionable Corrective Task ... QCT
Questionable Corrective Task (AD) ... qct
Questionable Questionnaire (AD) ... qq
Questionable Questionnaires ... QQ
Question-Answering System ... QAS
Questioned [*Soundness of decision or reasoning in cited case questioned*] [*Used in Shepard's Citations*] [*Legal term*] (DLA) ... q
Questioned (AD) ... quest
Questioned Document (AD) ... qd
Questioned Document [*Criminology*] ... QD
Questioned Trade [*on a stock exchange*] ... QT
Questionnaire ... Q
Questionnaire (AD) ... qstnr
Questionnaire ... QU
Questionnaire (ADA) ... Questn
Questionnaire (AD) ... questn
Questionnaire Analysis Program (IAA) ... QUAP
Questionnaire Design Research Laboratory [*Department of Health and Human Services*] (GFGA) ... QDRL
Questionnaire for Students, Teachers, and Administrators (EDAC) ... QUESTA
Questionnaire Interpreter Program (IAA) ... QUIP
Questionnaire Service Co. [*Information service or system*] (IID) ... QSC
Questions ... QQ
Questions (WDMC) ... qq
Questions of Procedure for Ministers ... QPM
Questmont Mines [*Vancouver Stock Exchange symbol*] ... QST
Questron Technology [*Associated Press*] (SAG) ... Questron
Questron Technology [*NASDAQ symbol*] (SAG) ... QUST
Questron Technology [*NASDAQ symbol*] (TTSB) ... QUST
Quetico Provincial Park [*Ontario, Canada*] (AD) ... QPP
Quetta [*Pakistan*] [*Seismograph station code, US Geological Survey*] (SEIS) ... QUE
Quetta [*Pakistan*] [*Airport symbol*] (OAG) ... UET
Quetta/Samungli [*Pakistan*] [*ICAO location identifier*] (ICLI) ... OPQT
Quetzal [*Monetary unit*] [*Guatemala*] ... Q
Quetzalcoatlus Northropi [*Pterosaur, a model constructed for the Smithsonian Institution and referred to by these initials*] ... QN
Queue ... Q
Queue Control (NITA) ... QC
Queue Control Block [*Data processing*] (AD) ... qcb
Queue Control Block [*Computer science*] ... QCB
Queue Element [*Computer science*] ... QEL
Queue Element Area [*Computer science*] (IAA) ... QEA
Queue Empty (MHDI) ... QE
Queue Entry ... QE
Queue Executive Interface [*Computer science*] (MHDB) ... QXI
Queue Full ... QF
Queue Input/Output ... QIO
Queue Jump (AD) ... qjump
Queue Jump Command ... QJMP
Queue Length [*Telecommunications*] (TEL) ... QL
Queue Line Sharing Adapter [*Computer science*] ... QLSA
Queue Manager [*Computer science*] (CMD) ... QM
Queue Message [*Computer science*] (PCM) ... QMSG
Queue Modification Process ... QMOD
Queue Run-Time [*Computer science*] ... QRT
Queue Search Limit [*Computer science*] ... QSL
Queue Select [*Computer science*] ... QS
Queued Access Method [*Computer science*] ... QAM
Queued Access Method (AD) ... qam
Queued Indexed Access Memory [*Computer science*] (AD) ... qiam
Queued Indexed Access Memory [*Computer science*] (IAA) ... QIAM
Queued Indexed Sequential Access Method [*IBM Corp.*] [*Computer science*] ... QISAM
Queued Packet Synchronous Exchange [*Telecommunications*] (OSI) ... QPSX
Queued Sequential Access Method [*IBM Corp.*] [*Computer science*] ... QSAM
Queued Sequential Access Method (AD) ... qsam
Queued Telecommunication Access Method (AD) ... qtam
Queued Telecommunications Access Method [*IBM Corp.*] [*Computer science*] ... QTAM
Queued Terminal Access Method [*Computer science*] ... QTAM
Queued Transaction Handling [*Computer science*] ... QTH
Queued-Indexed Sequential-Access Method [*Computer science*] (AD) ... qisam
Queueing Matrix Evaluation (AD) ... qme
Queueing Matrix Evaluation (PDAA) ... QME
Queueing System (AD) ... QS
Queuing Theory [*Telecommunications*] ... QT
Queuing Time [*Telecommunications*] (TEL) ... QT
Quevedo [*Ecuador*] [*ICAO location identifier*] (ICLI) ... SEQE
Quezaltenango [*Guatemala*] [*ICAO location identifier*] (ICLI) ... MGQZ
Quezon City [*Philippines*] (AD) ... Q City
Quezon City (AD) ... QC
Quezon City [*Philippines*] [*Seismograph station code, US Geological Survey*] (SEIS) ... QCP
Quezon Memorial Park [*Philippines*] (AD) ... QMP
Quezon National Park [*Philippines*] (AD) ... QNP
Qui Bixit Annos [*Who Lived ___ Years*] [*Latin*] ... QBAN
Qui Nhon [*Vietnam*] (VNW) ... QNH
Qui Nhon [*South Vietnam*] [*Airport symbol*] (AD) ... UIH
Qui Nhon Support Command [*Vietnam*] ... QNSC
Qui Tam [*Who as Well*] [*Latin*] (ILCA) ... QT
Qui Vixit [*Who Lived*] [*Latin*] ... QV
Quibdo [*Colombia*] [*Airport symbol*] (OAG) ... UIB
Quibdo/El Carano [*Colorado ICAO location identifier*] (ICLI) ... SKUI
Quiberon [*France ICAO location identifier*] (ICLI) ... LFEQ
Quiche [*Guatemala*] [*ICAO location identifier*] (ICLI) ... MGQC
Quichua (AD) ... Quich
Quick (AD) ... q
Quick ... Q
Quick ... QCK
Quick (MSA) ... QIK
Quick (AD) ... qk
Quick Access Recording ... QAR
Quick Action Button [*Military*] (CAAL) ... QAB
Quick Action Shuttle ... QAS
Quick Airways Holland BV [*Netherlands ICAO designator*] (FAAC) ... QAH
Quick and Dirty [*Computer science*] ... Q & D
Quick and Dirty (AD) ... q & d
Quick and Dirty Operating System [*Microsoft Corp.*] (ECON) ... QDOS
Quick and Effective System to Enhance Retrieval [*Computer science*] ... QUESTER
Quick and Efficient System to Enhance Retrieval (AD) ... quester
Quick & Reilly Group [*NASDAQ symbol*] (TTSB) ... BQR
Quick & Reilly Group, Inc. [*NYSE symbol*] (SPSG) ... BQR
Quick & Reilly Group, Inc. [*Associated Press*] (SAG) ... QkReily
Quick Assembly [*Furniture*] ... QA
Quick Assembly (AD) ... qa
Quick Asset [*Finance*] ... QA
Quick Attach Kit ... QAK
Quick Attach-Detach [*Engine*] ... QAD
Quick Attach-Detach Kit ... QADK
Quick Attach-Detach-Kit (AD) ... qadk
Quick Basic Oxygen Process [*Steelmaking*] ... Q-BOP
Quick Batch (MHDI) ... QB
Quick Break (MSA) ... QB
Quick Break (AD) ... qb
[*The*] **Quick Brown Fox Jumped over the Fence** [*Typing exercise*] ... QBFJOTF
[*The*] **Quick Brown Fox Jumped over the Lazy Dogs** [*Typing exercise*] ... QBFJOTLD
Quick Change (AD) ... q/c
Quick Change (IAA) ... QC
Quick Change Boost Control [*Automotive engineering*] ... QCBC
Quick Change Real-Time (MHDI) ... QCRT
Quick Change Response [*System*] ... QCR
Quick Change Unit (MCD) ... QCU
Quick Changeover [*Manufacturing*] ... QCO
Quick Charge [*Airplane*] (IIA) ... QC
Quick Claim Deed (MHDB) ... QCD
Quick Cleaning (MSA) ... QC
Quick Code (NITA) ... QC
Quick Connect (AD) ... qc
Quick Connect ... QC
Quick Connect Coupling ... QCC
Quick Connect Handle ... QCH
Quick Connect Kit ... QCK
Quick Connect Relay ... QCR
Quick Connect Valve Coupler ... QCVC
Quick Control Dial [*Photography*] ... QCD
Quick Curl [*Refers to Barbie doll hair*] [*Doll collecting*] ... QC
Quick Decision Exercise [*Training simulation*] [*Army*] ... QDX
Quick Delivery (WDAA) ... QD
Quick Delivery (AD) ... qd
Quick Delivery Order ... QDO
Quick Dependable Communications ... QDC
Quick Detachable [*Weapon*] (AD) ... qd
Quick Detachable Communication (AD) ... qdc
Quick Diagnostic Debugging Program [*Computer science*] (MHDI) ... QDEBUG
Quick Die Change [*Automotive engineering*] ... QDC
Quick Disconnect ... QD
Quick Disconnect ... QDISC
Quick Disconnect Cap ... QDC
Quick Disconnect Circular Connector ... QDCC
Quick Disconnect Connector ... QDC
Quick Disconnect Handle ... QDH
Quick Disconnect Kit ... QDK
Quick Disconnect, Large ... QDL

Quick Disconnect, Miniature ... QDM
Quick Disconnect Nipple ... QDN
Quick Disconnect Pivot ... QDP
Quick Disconnect Series ... QDS
Quick Disconnect, Small ... QDS
Quick Disconnect Swivel ... QDS
Quick Disconnect Valve ... QDV
Quick Disconnect Valve (AD) ... qdv
Quick Disk Reformatter [*Vernon Buerg*] [*Computer utility tool*] (PCM) ... QDR
Quick Early Warning Test [*Medicine*] (MAE) ... QEW
Quick Editor [*Computer science*] (ECII) ... QED
Quick Electrolyte Analyzer [*Laboratory science*] (DAVI) ... QEA
Quick Engine Change (AD) ... qec
Quick Engine Change ... QEC
Quick Engine Change Assembly (NG) ... QECA
Quick Engine Change Kit (NG) ... QECK
Quick Engine Change Stand (NG) ... QECS
Quick Engine Change Unit ... QECU
Quick Engine-Change Unit (AD) ... qecu
Quick Erecting Antenna Mast [*Army*] (RDA) ... QEAM
Quick Erection Dome ... QED
Quick Estimate (AD) ... qe
Quick Exhaust Air Valve ... QEAV
Quick Exhaust Valve ... QEV
Quick Exhaust Valve (AD) ... qev
Quick Fix (MCD) ... QF
Quick Fix - Black Hawk ... QF-BH
Quick Fix Interference Reduction Capability (AFM) ... QFIRC
Quick Fix Program ... QFP
Quick Flashing (AD) ... Qk Fl
Quick Flashing Light [*Navigation signal*] ... QKFL
Quick FORTRAN [*Programming language*] [*1979*] ... QUICKTRAN
Quick Fortran [*Computer science*] (AD) ... quiktran
Quick FORTRAN [*Programming language*] [*1979*] (CSR) ... QWIKTRAN
Quick Fraction [*Reference to membrane potentials*] (DAVI) ... Q fract
Quick Freeze (AD) ... qf
Quick Freeze ... QF
Quick Hot-Swap [*Computer disk drive*] ... QHS
Quick Interactive Documentation System (WDAA) ... QUIDS
Quick Is Beautiful [*NASA project philosophy*] ... QIB
Quick Junction [*Electronics*] ... QJ
Quick Kinescope [*Film replay*] (NTCM) ... QK
Quick Law Systems (AD) ... QLS
Quick [*Flashing*] **Light** [*Navigation signal*] ... Q
Quick Like a Bunny ... QLAB
Quick Loading System (AD) ... QLS
Quick Look (KSC) ... Q/L
Quick Look (AD) ... ql
Quick Look Analysis Program ... QLAP
Quick Look and Checkout System ... QLCS
Quick Look Data Reference (NASA) ... QLDR
Quick Look Data Station [*NASA*] (KSC) ... QLDS
Quick Look Intermediate Tape ... QLIT
Quick Look (Report) ... QL(R)
Quick Look Station [*NASA*] (MCD) ... QLS
Quick Make-and-Break [*Contact*] (DEN) ... QMB
Quick Make-and-Break (AD) ... qmb
Quick Mechanical Disconnect Kit (AD) ... qmdk
Quick Mechanical Disconnect Kit ... QMDK
Quick Medical Reference [*Computer system*] ... QMR
Quick Modification Concept (MCD) ... QMC
Quick Neurological Screening Test ... QNST
Quick on System (AD) ... QOS
Quick Opening (AD) ... qo
Quick Opening [*Nuclear energy*] (NRCH) ... QO
Quick Outlet (WDAA) ... QO
Quick Picture Vocabulary Test [*Speech and language therapy*] (DAVI) ... QPVT
Quick Printing Management [*A publication*] (DGA) ... QPM
Quick Process (AD) ... qp
Quick Processing [*Chemicals*] ... QP
Quick Program Search (WDAA) ... QPS
Quick Prothrombin Time [*Hematology*] (DAVI) ... QPT
Quick Query Program ... QQP
Quick RAM [*Random Access Memory*] **Change** [*Computer science*] (IAA) ... QRC
Quick Reacting, Mobile Force [*Military NATO*] (NATG) ... QRMF
Quick Reaction ... QR
Quick Reaction (AD) ... qr
Quick Reaction Acquisition (MCD) ... QRA
Quick Reaction Aircraft (MCD) ... QRA
Quick Reaction Alert [*Military*] (AFM) ... QRA
Quick Reaction Alert (AD) ... qra
Quick Reaction Area (MCD) ... QRA
Quick Reaction Capability [*Military*] ... QRC
Quick Reaction Capability (AD) ... qrc
Quick Reaction Change (MCD) ... QRC
Quick Reaction Combat Capability (DOMA) ... QRCC
Quick Reaction Communications (MHDI) ... QRC
Quick Reaction Development ... QRD
Quick Reaction [*or Response*] **Estimate** ... QRE
Quick Reaction Force [*Military*] (CINC) ... QRF
Quick Reaction Grooming ... QRG
Quick Reaction Installation Capability (CET) ... QRIC
Quick Reaction Installation Capability (AD) ... qric
Quick Reaction Integration (NASA) ... QRI
Quick Reaction Integration Activity (NASA) ... QRIA
Quick Reaction Inventory Control Center [*Army*] (MCD) ... QRICC
Quick Reaction Operation (WDAA) ... QRO
Quick Reaction Operation (AD) ... qro
Quick Reaction Organization (WDAA) ... QRO
Quick Reaction Procurement System [*Army*] (AABC) ... QRPS
Quick Reaction Program [*Army*] ... QRP
Quick Reaction Sortie (NASA) ... QRS
Quick Reaction Space Laboratory [*NASA*] (NASA) ... QRSL
Quick Reaction Task (MCD) ... QRT
Quick Reaction Team [*Military*] ... QRT
Quick Receipt (AD) ... qr
Quick Recovery (DAVI) ... QR
Quick Recovery Defibrillator [*Cardiology*] (DAVI) ... QR
Quick Reference List ... QRL
Quick Release Valve ... QRV
Quick Relocate and Link ... QRL
Quick Replaceable Assembly ... QRA
Quick Response (AD) ... QR
Quick Response Capability [*Military*] ... QRC
Quick Response Controller (NITA) ... QRC
Quick Response Graphic (AD) ... qrg
Quick Response Graphic ... QRG
Quick Response Multicolor Copier (MCD) ... QRMC
Quick Response Proposal [*Navy*] ... QRP
Quick Response Services [*NASDAQ symbol*] (SAG) ... QRSI
Quick Response Services [*Commercial firm Associated Press*] (SAG) ... QuickRsp
Quick Response Targeting Program [*Lunar*] ... QRTP
Quick Search Procedure ... QSP
Quick Service ... QS
Quick Service Assistant (MCD) ... QSA
Quick Service Restaurant ... QSR
Quick Service Supervisor (MCD) ... QSS
Quick Set Compound ... QSC
Quick Strike Reconnaissance (MCD) ... QSR
Quick Supply Store [*Military*] (AABC) ... QSS
Quick Sweep [*Construction*] ... QS
Quick Tan [*Trademark of Plough, Inc.*] ... QT
Quick Test ... QT
Quick Test (AD) ... qt
Quick Test [*Medicine*] (DMAA) ... QT
Quick Text Editor ... QED
Quick Text Editor (WDAA) ... QTED
Quick Text Editor (AD) ... qted
Quick Transmission Change (MCD) ... QTC
Quick Turn Around Time (NITA) ... QTAT
Quick Turn Stock (AD) ... qts
Quick Turnaround Cell [*Engineering*] (RDA) ... QTC
Quick Update and Access Interlibrary Loans System ... QUAILLS
Quick View Plus (PCM) ... QVP
Quick Weight Loss (AD) ... qwl
Quick Weight Loss ... QWL
Quick Word Test [*Education*] (EDAC) ... QWT
Quick-Access Recording (AD) ... qar
Quick-Acting (AD) ... qa
Quick-Acting ... QA
Quick-Acting Choke [*Automotive engineering*] ... QAC
Quick-Acting Scuttle (AD) ... qas
Quick-Acting Water-Tight (DNAB) ... QAWT
Quick-Attach Kit (AD) ... qak
Quick-Attach-Detach (AD) ... qad
Quick-BASIC [*Beginner's All-Purpose Symbolic Instruction Code*] **Extended** [*Computer science*] (PCM) ... QBX
Quickborn [*Germany ICAO location identifier*] (ICLI) ... EDZQ
Quickbrew [*Brand of tea*] [*British*] ... QB
Quickchange [*Aviation*] ... QC
Quick-Change Real Time (AD) ... qcrt
Quick-Change Response (AD) ... qcr
Quick-Change Unit (AD) ... qcu
Quick-Connect Coupling (AD) ... qcc
Quick-Connect Handle (AD) ... qch
Quick-Connect Kit (AD) ... qck
Quick-Connect Valve Coupler (AD) ... qcvc
Quick-Connects Bulkhead Mounting (AD) ... qcbm
Quick-Connects for Bulkhead Mounting (PDAA) ... QCM
Quick-Disconnect (AD) ... q-d
Quick-Disconnect Cap (AD) ... qdc
Quick-Disconnect Circular Connection (AD) ... qdcc
Quick-Disconnect Handle (AD) ... qdh
Quick-Disconnect Kit (AD) ... qdk
Quick-Disconnect Nipple (AD) ... qdn
Quick-Disconnect Pivot (AD) ... qdp
Quick-Disconnect Series (AD) ... qds
Quick-Disconnect Swivel (AD) ... qds
Quick-Draw Graphics System (PDAA) ... QDGS
Quicken Financial Network (PCM) ... QFN
Quicken Interchange File [*Computer science*] (PCM) ... QIF
Quicken Small Business Expert [*Financial software*] ... QSBE
Quicker for Victory [*World War II*] ... Q4V
Quick-Exhaust Air Valve (AD) ... qeav
Quick-Firing [*Gun*] ... QF
Quick-Fit Sea (DNAB) ... QFS
Quick-Fix Interference-Reduction Capability (AD) ... qfirc
Quickie Strike (MHDB) ... QS
Quick-Inline Package (NITA) ... QUIP
Quick-Look Guide ... QLG

Quick-Look Intermediate Tape (AD) ... qlit
Quickly (AD) ... qkly
Quick-Make [*Contact*] (IAA) ... QM
Quick-Make, Quick-Break ... QMQB
Quick-Make Quick-Break (AD) ... qmqb
Quick-Opening Blowdown Valve [*Nuclear energy*] (NRCH) ... QOBV
Quick-Opening Device ... QOD
Quick-Opening Device (AD) ... qod
Quick-Reaction Dome (AD) ... qed
Quick-Release Valve (AD) ... qrv
Quick-Response Multicolor Printer (RDA) ... QRMP
Quick's Test [*For pregnancy or prothrombin*] [*Laboratory science*] (DAVI) ... QT
Quicksilver Data [*Information service or system*] (IID) ... QD
Quicksilver Messenger Service [*Pop music group*] ... QMS
Quick-Start Recording [*Video technology*] ... QSR
Quick-Strike Reconnaissance (AD) ... qsr
Quickturn Design Sys [*NASDAQ symbol*] (TTSB) ... QKTN
Quickturn Design System [*NASDAQ symbol*] (SAG) ... QKTN
Quickturn Design System [*Commercial firm Associated Press*] (SAG) ... Quicktr
Quid Pro Quid ... QPQ
Quidel Corp. [*NASDAQ symbol*] (SPSG) ... QDEL
Quidel Corp. [*Associated Press*] (SAG) ... Quidel
Quidel Corp. Wrrt [*NASDAQ symbol*] (TTSB) ... QDELW
Quien Sabe Ranch [*California*] [*Seismograph station code, US Geological Survey*] (SEIS) ... QSR
Quiescat in Pace [*May He, or She, Rest in Peace*] [*Latin*] ... QIP
Quiesce-at-End-of-Chain [*Computer science*] (IBMDP) ... QEC
Quiesce-Completed [*Computer science*] (IBMDP) ... QC
Quiescent [*Cytology*] ... Q
Quiescent ... QUIES
Quiescent Aerial [*or Antenna*] ... QA
Quiescent Aerial (AD) ... qa
Quiescent Carrier Telephony (AD) ... qct
Quiescent Carrier Telephony (WDAA) ... QCT
Quiescent Center [*Plant root growth*] ... QC
Quiescent Command/Service Module (MCD) ... QCSM
Quiescent Power Supply ... QPS
Quiescent Power Supply Current ... QPSC
Quiescent Push-Pull [*Electronics*] (DEN) ... QPP
Quiescit [*He Rests*] [*Latin*] ... Q
Quiet [*or sub rosa, as, "On the QT"*] ... QT
Quiet (AD) ... qt
Quiet Automatic Gain Control (AD) ... qagc
Quiet Automatic Gain Control (IAA) ... QAGC
Quiet Automatic Voltage Control [*Electronics*] (ECII) ... QAVC
Quiet Automatic Volume Control (AD) ... qavc
Quiet Automatic Volume Control ... QAVC
Quiet Birdmen [*An association*] (EA) ... QB
Quiet Cab (AD) ... Q-cab
Quiet, Clean, General Aviation Turbofan [*NASA*] ... QCGAT
Quiet, Clean, Short-Haul Experimental Engine [*NASA*] ... QCSEE
Quiet, Clean, Short-Haul Experimental Engine (DICI) ... QCSHEE
Quiet Communities Act (GFGA) ... QCA
Quiet Community Program [*Environmental Protection Agency*] (GFGA) ... QCP
Quiet Experimental Short Takeoff and Landing [*Program*] [*NASA*] ... QUESTOL
Quiet, Experimental, Short-Takeoff-and-Landing [*NASA*] (AD) ... questal
Quiet Extended Life (AD) ... qel
Quiet Extended Life ... QEL
Quiet Fast Boat [*Navy symbol*] ... QFB
Quiet Heavy Vehicle [*Automotive engineering*] ... QHV
Quiet Helicopter Program (RDA) ... QHP
Quiet Ionosphere (IAA) ... QI
Quiet Not a Number [*Computer programming*] (BYTE) ... QNaN
Quiet Propulsion Lift Technology [*NASA*] ... QPLT
Quiet Propulsion Lift Technology (AD) ... qplt
Quiet Radio Transmission (DNAB) ... QRT
Quiet Short-Haul Air Transportation System ... QSATS
Quiet Short-Haul Research Aircraft [*NASA*] ... QSRA
Quiet Short-Haul Research Aircraft (AD) ... qsra
Quiet Sleep [*Physiology*] ... QS
Quiet STOL [*Short Takeoff and Landing*] **Experimental Engine** [*Aviation*] (OA) ... QSEE
Quiet Sun Year ... QSY
Quiet Sun Year (AD) ... qsy
Quiet Takeoff and Landing (AD) ... qtol
Quiet Takeoff and Landing [*Aviation*] ... QTOL
Quiet-and-Short Takeoff and Landing (AD) ... qstol
Quieting Reflex [*In book title "Q-R: The Quieting Reflex" by Charles F. Stroebel*] ... QR
Quieting Response [*Medicine*] (DMAA) ... QR
Quiet-Short-Takeoff-and-Landing [*Airplane*] [*Japan*] ... QSTOL
Quiksilver, Inc. [*Costa Mesa, CA*] [*NASDAQ symbol*] (NQ) ... QUIK
Quiksilver, Inc. [*Associated Press*] (SAG) ... Quikslv
Quilate [*Carat*] [*Portuguese*] (AD) ... ql
Quill & Quire [*A publication*] (BRI) ... Quill & Q
Quill and Scroll Society (EA) ... QSS
Quillagua [*Chile*] [*Seismograph station code, US Geological Survey*] (SEIS) ... QUL
Quillayute, WA [*Location identifier FAA*] (FAAL) ... UIL
Quiller Press [*Publisher*] [*British*] ... Q
Quiller-Couch [*Sir Arthur, 1863-1944, English man of letters*] [*Letter used as pen name*] ... Q
Quillmana [*Peru*] [*Seismograph station code, US Geological Survey Closed*] (SEIS) ... QUM
Quillo Resources, Inc. [*Vancouver Stock Exchange symbol*] ... QLD
Quillwork (VRA) ... quilwk
Quilmes [*Argentina ICAO location identifier*] (ICLI) ... SADQ
Quilmes Ind(Quinsa)ADS [*NYSE symbol*] (TTSB) ... LQU
Quilpie [*Australia Airport symbol*] (OAG) ... ULP
Quilpue/Mil el Belloto [*Chile*] [*ICAO location identifier*] (ICLI) ... SCBL
Quilter's Newsletter Magazine [*A publication*] ... QN MAG
Quilting ... Q
Quimica [*Chemistry*] [*Spanish*] (AD) ... quim
Quimica de Portugal (AD) ... Quimigal
Quimper [*France*] [*Airport symbol*] (OAG) ... UIP
Quimper/Pluguffan [*France ICAO location identifier*] (ICLI) ... LFRQ
Quin on Banking [*1833*] [*A publication*] (DLA) ... Quin Bank
Quina [*Quinine*] [*Pharmacy*] (ROG) ... QU
Quina [*Quinine*] [*Pharmacy*] (ROG) ... QUIN
Quinacrine [*Fluorescent method*] [*Chromosome stain*] ... Q
Quinacrine Mustard [*Chromosome stain*] ... QM
Quinaldine Red [*Medicine*] (DMAA) ... QR
Quincemil [*Peru*] [*Airport symbol*] (AD) ... QUP
Quincemil [*Peru*] [*ICAO location identifier*] (ICLI) ... SPIL
Quincy (AD) ... Qcy
Quincy (AD) ... Quin
Quincy [*Illinois*] [*Airport symbol*] (OAG) ... UIN
Quincy, CA [*FM radio station call letters*] ... KNLF
Quincy, CA [*AM radio station call letters*] ... KPCO
Quincy, CA [*FM radio station call letters*] ... KQNC
Quincy, CA [*FM radio station call letters*] ... KSPY
Quincy College (AD) ... QC
Quincy College, Quincy, IL [*OCLC symbol*] (OCLC) ... IBQ
Quincy College, Quincy, IL [*Library symbol Library of Congress*] (LCLS) ... IQC
Quincy Division/General Dynamics (AD) ... QD/GD
Quincy, FL [*FM radio station call letters*] (RBYB) ... WTPS
Quincy, FL [*AM radio station call letters*] ... WWSD
Quincy, FL [*FM radio station call letters*] ... WXSR
Quincy Free Public Library, Quincy, IL [*Library symbol Library of Congress*] (LCLS) ... IQ
Quincy Historical Society, Quincy, MA [*Library symbol Library of Congress*] (LCLS) ... MQHi
Quincy, IL [*FM radio station call letters*] ... WGCA
Quincy, IL [*AM radio station call letters*] ... WGEM
Quincy, IL [*FM radio station call letters*] ... WGEM-FM
Quincy, IL [*Television station call letters*] ... WGEM-TV
Quincy, IL [*FM radio station call letters*] (RBYB) ... WMOS
Quincy, IL [*FM radio station call letters*] ... WQCY
Quincy, IL [*Television station call letters*] ... WQEC
Quincy, IL [*FM radio station call letters*] ... WQUB
Quincy, IL [*AM radio station call letters*] ... WTAD
Quincy, IL [*Television station call letters*] ... WTJR
Quincy Junior College (AD) ... QJC
Quincy, MA [*AM radio station call letters*] ... WJDA
Quincy Public Library, Quincy, IL [*OCLC symbol*] (OCLC) ... IDQ
Quincy Railroad Co. [*AAR code*] ... QRR
Quincy Railroad Co. [*Later, QRR*] [*AAR code*] ... QUI
Quincy, WA [*FM radio station call letters*] (RBYB) ... KTRQ-FM
Quincy, WA [*AM radio station call letters*] ... KWNC
Quincy, WA [*FM radio station call letters*] ... KWWW
Quincy Yacht Club (AD) ... QYC
Quincy's Massachusetts Reports [*A publication*] (DLA) ... Quin
Quincy's Massachusetts Reports [*A publication*] (DLA) ... Quincy
Quindar Scanning System (NASA) ... QSS
Quinella Exploration Ltd. [*Vancouver Stock Exchange symbol*] ... QUX
Quinhagak [*Alaska*] [*Airport symbol*] (OAG) ... KWN
Quinhagak, AK [*Location identifier FAA*] (FAAL) ... KWN
Quinhon [*Viet Nam*] [*ICAO location identifier*] (ICLI) ... VVQN
Quinhon Missionary Sisters of the Holy Cross (TOCD) ... QMHC
Quinic Acid [*Organic chemistry*] ... QA
Quinidine [*Pharmacology*] (DAVI) ... Q
Quinidine [*Pharmacology*] (DAVI) ... QUINID
Quinidine-N-oxide [*Organic chemistry*] ... QNO
Quininde [*Ecuador*] [*ICAO location identifier*] (ICLI) ... SEQN
Quinine [*Pharmacology*] (DAVI) ... QUININ
Quinine, Atabrine, Plasmoquine [*Treatment for malaria*] ... QAP
Quinine, Atebrin, Plasmoquine [*Medicine*] (AD) ... qap
Quinine-Colchicine [*Medicine*] (MAE) ... QC
Quinn River Valley [*Nevada*] [*Seismograph station code, US Geological Survey Closed*] (SEIS) ... QRV
Quinnex, Inc. [*FAA designator*] (FAAC) ... QNX
Quinnipiac College (AD) ... QC
Quinnipiac College, Hamden, CT [*Library symbol Library of Congress*] (LCLS) ... CtHamQ
Quinoid Dehydropteridine Reductase [*An enzyme*] (DAVI) ... QDPR
Quinoline Amino Alcohol [*Organic chemistry*] ... QAA
Quinoline Oxide [*Biochemistry*] (OA) ... QO
Quinoline Still Residue [*Coal tar technology*] ... QSR
(Quinolinesulfonyl)nitrotriazole [*Organic chemistry*] ... QSNT
Quinone [*An oxidizing agent*] [*Chemistry*] (DAVI) ... Q
Quinonemethide [*Organic chemistry*] ... QM
Quinoxaline Ladder Polymer [*Organic chemistry*] ... QLP
Quinquaginta [*Fifty*] [*Latin*] ... L
Quinque [*Five*] [*Latin*] (MAE) ... quinq
Quinque [*Five*] [*Latin*] ... V
Quinsigamond Community College [*Worchester, MA*] ... QCC
Quinsigamond Community College, Worcester, MA [*Library symbol Library of Congress*] (LCLS) ... MWQ
Quinsigamond Community College, Worcester, MA [*OCLC symbol*] (OCLC) ... WQC
Quinstar Resources [*Vancouver Stock Exchange symbol*] ... QUR

Quint [*Energy unit*] (FFDE) ... Q
Quint-A (AD) ... Q-A
Quintal (AD) ... q
Quintal [*Unit of weight*] ... Q
Quintal [*Hundred-weight*] [*Spanish*] (AD) ... Q1
Quintal [*Hundred-weight*] [*French*] (AD) ... qal
Quintal (AD) ... ql
Quintal [*Unit of weight*] ... QL
Quintal Metrico [*Metric Quintal*] [*Spain*] (AD) ... qm
Quintales [*Quintals*] [*Spanish*] (AD) ... qq
Quintana Roo (AD) ... Q Roo
Quintana Roo (AD) ... QR
Quintar [*Monetary unit*] [*Albania*] ... Q
Quintaux [*Quintals*] [*French*] (AD) ... qtaux
Quintaux [*Hundred-Weights*] [*French*] (AD) ... qx
Quintel Entertainment [*NASDAQ symbol*] (TTSB) ... QTEL
Quintel Entertainment, Inc. [*NASDAQ symbol*] (SAG) ... QTEL
Quintel Entertainment, Inc. [*Associated Press*] (SAG) ... Quintel
Quintel Industries Ltd. [*Vancouver Stock Exchange symbol*] ... QTL
Quinten (AD) ... Quin
Quintero [*Chile*] [*ICAO location identifier*] (ICLI) ... SCER
Quinterra Resources, Inc. [*Toronto Stock Exchange symbol Vancouver Stock Exchange symbol*] ... QUA
Quintessence of Dental Technology ... QDT
Quintet [*Music*] ... QNT
Quintet (AD) ... qnt
Quintet (AD) ... quin
Quintetto [*Quintet*] [*Music*] (ROG) ... QUINT
Quintiles Transnational [*NASDAQ symbol*] (TTSB) ... QTRN
Quintiles Transnational Corp. [*NASDAQ symbol*] (SAG) ... QTRN
Quintiles Transnational Corp. [*Associated Press*] (SAG) ... Quintiles
Quintilian [*First century AD*] [*Classical studies*] (OCD) ... Quint
Quintilian (AD) ... Quint
Quintilianus (AD) ... Quin
Quintilius (AD) ... Quin
Quintillian (AD) ... Quin
Quintino (AD) ... Quin
Quintius (AD) ... Quin
Quinto Mining [*Vancouver Stock Exchange symbol*] ... QU
Quintuple ... QUIN
Quintuple ... QUINT
Quintuple Screw (DS) ... QN
Quintuplet (AD) ... quin
Quintuplet [*Neonatology*] (DAVI) ... quint
Quintuplets (AD) ... quins
Quintuplicate (AD) ... quint
Quintuplicate (AD) ... quintupl
Quintus [*Fifth*] [*Latin*] ... Q
Quintus [*Fifth*] [*Latin*] (WGA) ... QUINT
Quintus [*Fifth*] [*Latin*] (AD) ... quint
Quintus Smyrnaeus [*Classical studies*] (OCD) ... Quint Smyrn
Quintus Tullius Cicero (AD) ... Q Cic
Quinuclidinol Atrolactate [*Organic chemistry*] ... QNA
Quinuclidinyl Benzilate [*Also, QNB*] [*Army symbol*] ... BZ
Quinuclidinyl Benzilate [*Also, BZ*] [*Hallucinogen*] ... QNB
Quipp, Inc. [*NASDAQ symbol*] (NQ) ... QUIP
Quipp, Inc. [*Associated Press*] (SAG) ... Quipp
Quire [*Measure of paper*] ... Q
Quire (AD) ... q
Quire [*Paper*] (WDMC) ... q
Quire [*Paper*] (WDMC) ... qr
Quire (AD) ... qr
Quire [*Measure of paper*] ... QR
Quirindi [*New South Wales*] [*Airport symbol*] (AD) ... QUI
Quirindi [*Australia Airport symbol Obsolete*] (OAG) ... UIR
Quis Rerum Divinarum Heres [*Philo*] (BJA) ... Her
Quisling [*World War II*] (AD) ... quis
Quisqualic Acid [*Biochemistry*] ... QA
Quisque [*Each, Every*] [*Pharmacy*] ... Q
Quisque [*Each, Every*] [*Pharmacy*] ... QQ
Quisqueya Airlines SA [*Haiti*] [*ICAO designator*] (FAAC) ... QAS
Quit Claim (WDAA) ... QC
Quit Claim (AD) ... qc
Quit for Domestic Reasons [*Unemployment insurance*] (OICC) ... DOM
Quitclaim [*Legal term*] (BARN) ... QC
Quit-Claim Deed (AD) ... qcd
Quite Bloody Impossible [*Slang*] (AD) ... qbi
Quite Bloody Impossible [*British slang, applied particularly to flying conditions*] ... QBI
Quitman County Library, Marks, MS [*Library symbol Library of Congress*] (LCLS) ... MsMar
Quitman, GA [*AM radio station call letters*] ... WSFB
Quitman, GA [*FM radio station call letters*] ... WSTI
Quitman, MS [*AM radio station call letters*] ... WBFN
Quitman, MS [*FM radio station call letters*] ... WYKK
Quitman, TX [*Location identifier FAA*] (FAAL) ... UIM
Quito [*Ecuador*] [*Seismograph station code, US Geological Survey Closed*] (SEIS) ... QUI
Quito [*Ecuador*] [*Airport symbol*] (OAG) ... UIO
Quito, Ecuador, Tracking Station [*NASA*] (NASA) ... QUI
Quito/Mariscal Sucre [*Ecudaor*] [*ICAO location identifier*] (ICLI) ... SEQU
Quiver (ROG) ... QUIV
Quivira National Wildlife Refuge [*Kansas*] (AD) ... QNWR
Quixote (AD) ... quix
Quixote Center (EA) ... QC
Quixote Corp. [*NASDAQ symbol*] (NQ) ... QUIX
Quixote Corp. [*Associated Press*] (SAG) ... Quixte
Quizno's Corp. [*NASDAQ symbol*] (TTSB) ... QUIZ
Quizno's Franchise Corp. [*NASDAQ symbol*] (SAG) ... QUIZ
Quizno's Franchise Corp. [*Associated Press*] (SAG) ... Quiznos
Qume Video Terminal (NITA) ... QVT
Qumran (BJA) ... Q
Qumran Literature (BJA) ... QL
Qumran Manuscripts (BJA) ... QM
Qunatitative Immuno-Electrophoresis (AD) ... qie
Quo Modo [*In What Manner*] [*Latin*] (AD) ... qm
Quo Modo [*In What Manner*] [*Latin*] ... QM
Quo Warranto [*Latin Legal term*] (DLA) ... Q WAR
Quoc-Lo [*Main national highway in South Vietnam*] (VNW) ... QL
Quod Deterius Potiori Insidiari Soleat [*Philo*] (BJA) ... Det
Quod Deus Immutabilis Sit [*Philo*] (BJA) ... Deus
Quod Deus Sit Immutabilis [*Philo*] (BJA) ... Immut
Quod Erat Demonstrandum [*That Which Was to Be Proved*] [*Latin*] (AD) ... qed
Quod Erat Demonstrandum [*Which was to be demonstrated*] [*Latin*] [*Mathematics*] (WDMC) ... QED
Quod Erat Demonstrandum [*Which Was the Thing to Be Proved*] [*Latin*] ... QED
Quod Erat Faciendum [*Which Was to Be Made, or Done*] [*Latin*] ... QEF
Quod Erat Faciendum [*That Which Was to Be Done*] [*Latin*] (AD) ... qef
Quod Erat Inveniendum [*That Which Was to Be Discovered*] [*Latin*] (AD) ... qei
Quod Erat Inveniendum [*Which Was to Be Found Out*] [*Latin*] ... QEI
Quod Est [*Which Is*] [*Latin*] ... QE
Quod Est [*Which Is*] [*Latin*] (AD) ... qe
Quod Omnis Probus Liber Sit [*of Philo*] (BJA) ... Prob
Quod Vide [*Which see*] [*Latin*] (WDMC) ... qqv
Quod Vide [*Which see*] [*Latin*] (WDMC) ... qv
Quod Vide [*or Videte*] [*Which See*] [*Latin*] ... QV
Quodlibet [*As You Please*] [*Latin*] (AD) ... quod
Quoin Hill [*Vanuatu*] [*ICAO location identifier*] (ICLI) ... NVVQ
Quokka (AD) ... quok
Quomodo Adulescens Poetas Audire Debeat [*of Plutarch*] [*Classical studies*] (OCD) ... Quomodo Adul
Quomodo Historia Conscribenda Sit [*of Lucian*] [*Classical studies*] (OCD) ... Hist Conscr
Quoniam Attachiamenta [*A publication*] (DLA) ... Quon Attach
Quonset Point [*Rhode Island*] (AD) ... Quon Pt
Quonset Point [*Navy*] ... QUP
Quonset Point/Quonset Point Naval Air Station [*Rhode Island*] [*ICAO location identifier*] (ICLI) ... KNCO
Quoque [*Every*] [*Latin*] (AD) ... qq
Quoque [*Also*] [*Pharmacy*] ... QQ
Quoque Library, Quoque, NY [*Library symbol Library of Congress*] (LCLS) ... NQ
Quorn Hounds ... QH
Quorom [*Of Which*] [*Latin*] (AD) ... quor
Quorum (DLA) ... Q
Quorum [*Of Which*] [*Pharmacy*] ... QUOR
Quorum (AD) ... quor
Quorum Health Group [*NASDAQ symbol*] (TTSB) ... QHGI
Quorum Health Group, Inc. [*NASDAQ symbol*] (SAG) ... QHGI
Quorum Health Group, Inc. [*Associated Press*] (SAG) ... QuorumH
Quorum Resource Corp. [*Vancouver Stock Exchange symbol*] ... QRM
Quota Club International [*Later, QI*] ... QCI
QUOTA [*Query Online Terminal Assistance*] **Input Processor** [*Computer science*] ... QUIP
Quota International (EA) ... QI
Quota Restriction ... QR
Quota Sample Survey (WDAA) ... QSS
Quota Source (AABC) ... QS
Quota Year [*Pisciculture*] ... QY
Quotation [*Investment term*] ... QN
Quotation (AD) ... qn
Quotation (AD) ... qotn
Quotation (AD) ... qtn
Quotation (WDAA) ... QTN
Quotation (ROG) ... QU
Quotation ... QUOT
Quotation (AD) ... quot
Quotation Estimate (MCD) ... QE
Quotation Information Center KK [*Nihon Keizai Shimbun, Inc.*] [*Information service or system*] (IID) ... QUICK
Quotation Request ... QR
Quotation Ticker [*Business term*] ... QT
Quote (AD) ... qot
Quote (AD) ... qte
Quote ... QTE
Quote Resources, Inc. [*Vancouver Stock Exchange symbol*] ... QUO
Quoted (WDAA) ... QTED
Quoted (AD) ... qted
Quoted Exhibit (SAA) ... QE
Quoted In [*or Quoting*] [*Legal term*] (DLA) ... quot
Quoted Price [*Investment term*] ... QP
Quotidie [*Daily*] [*Latin*] (AD) ... quot
Quotidie [*Every Day*] [*Latin*] (AD) ... quotid
Quotidie [*Daily*] [*Pharmacy*] ... QUOTID
Quotient (ADA) ... Q
Quotient ... QT
Quotient (MSA) ... QUOT
Quoties [*As Often as Needed*] [*Pharmacy*] ... QUOT
Quoties [*As often as necessary*] [*Latin*] [*Pharmacology*] (DAVI) ... quot
Quoties Opus Sit [*As Often as Necessary*] [*Pharmacy*] ... QUOT OP SIT
Quoties Opus Sit [*As often as necessary*] [*Latin*] [*Pharmacy*] (DAVI) ... quot os

Quoting (AD) .... qtg
Quran [*Koran*] [*Malay*] (AD) .... Qur
Qutdligssat [*Greenland*] [*ICAO location identifier*] (ICLI) .... BGQS
Qutdligssat [*Greenland*] [*Airport symbol*] (AD) .... QUN
Quthing [*Lesotho*] [*ICAO location identifier*] (ICLI) .... FXQG
Quujjuaq, PQ [*ICAO location identifier*] (ICLI) .... CYVP

Q-Value (AD) .... q-v
Qwest Commuter Corp. [*ICAO designator*] (FAAC) .... QCC
Qwestair [*Australia ICAO designator*] (FAAC) .... QWA
Q-Zar, Inc. [*NASDAQ symbol*] (SAG) .... QZAR
Q-Zar, Inc. [*Associated Press*] (SAG) .... Q-Zar
Q-Zar Inc. [*NASDAQ symbol*] (TTSB) .... QZARF

R
By Meaning

R. A. Bloch Cancer Foundation [*Formerly, Cancer Connection*] (EA) ... CC
R & B, Inc. [*Associated Press*] (SAG) ... R & B Inc
R & B, Inc. [*NASDAQ symbol*] (SPSG) ... RBIN
R & D Associates, Marina Del Rey, CA [*Library symbol Library of Congress*] (LCLS) ... CMdrR
R & E Research Associates, Palo Alto, CA [*Library symbol Library of Congress*] (LCLS) ... ResA
R & G Financial Corp. [*Associated Press*] (SAG) ... RG Fincl
R & G Financial Corp. [*NASDAQ symbol*] (SAG) ... RGFC
R. Austin Freeman Society (EA) ... RAFS
R Disc Operating System (NITA) ... RDOS
R. E. Blake [*Record label*] ... REB
R. F. Scientific, Inc. [*Telecommunications service*] (TSSD) ... RFS
R. J. Reynolds Tobacco Co. ... RJR
R. J. Sutton Fan Club (EA) ... RJSFC
R. K. Toaz Junior High School, Huntington, NY [*Library symbol Library of Congress*] (LCLS) ... NHuTJ
R. L. Polk & Co. of California, Los Angeles, CA [*Library symbol Library of Congress*] (LCLS) ... CLPoC
R. L. Thomas High School Library, Webster, NY [*OCLC symbol*] (OCLC) ... RXH
R. M. Hardy & Associates Ltd., Edmonton, AB, Canada [*Library symbol Library of Congress*] (LCLS) ... CaAERM
R. M. Hardy & Associates Ltd., Edmonton, Alberta [*Library symbol National Library of Canada*] (NLC) ... AERM
R. R. Bowker Co. [*Publisher*] ... RRB
R. R. Bowker Co., New York, NY [*Library symbol Library of Congress*] (LCLS) ... NNRRB
R. T. French Co., Library, Rochester, NY [*OCLC symbol*] (OCLC) ... VQZ
R. T. French Co., Rochester, NY [*Library symbol Library of Congress*] (LCLS) ... NRF
R. Thuber & Associates, Victoria, BC, Canada [*Library symbol Library of Congress*] (LCLS) ... CaBViT
R. W. Norton Art Foundation, Shreveport, LA [*Library symbol Library of Congress*] (LCLS) ... LShN
R. Warren [*Pseudonym used by Charles Ashton*] ... RW
RAAF [*Royal Australian Air Force*] **Welfare Trust Fund** [*Australia*] ... RWTF
RAB [*Radio Advertising Bureau*] **Instant Background** [*A publication*] ... IB
Raba Raba [*New Guinea*] [*Airport symbol*] (AD) ... RBF
Raba Raba [*Papua New Guinea*] [*Airport symbol*] (OAG) ... RBP
Rabalanakaia [*New Britain*] [*Seismograph station code, US Geological Survey*] (SEIS) ... RAL
Rabat [*Morocco*] [*Airport symbol*] (OAG) ... RBA
Rabat [*Morocco*] [*Seismograph station code, US Geological Survey*] (SEIS) ... RBA
Rabat/Sale [*Morocco*] [*ICAO location identifier*] (ICLI) ... GMME
Rabat Zaers [*Morocco*] [*Seismograph station code, US Geological Survey*] (SEIS) ... RBZ
Rabaul [*Papua New Guinea*] [*ICAO location identifier*] (ICLI) ... AYRB
Rabaul [*New Britain Island*] [*Airport symbol*] (OAG) ... RAB
Rabaul [*New Britain Island*] [*Seismograph station code, US Geological Survey*] (SEIS) ... RAB
Rabaul Volcano Observatory [*Papua New Guinea*] ... RVO
Rabba (BJA) ... R
Rabbanite (BJA) ... R
Rabbet (MSA) ... RAB
Rabbet [*Technical drawings*] ... RBT
Rabbi ... R
Rabbi ... RBB
Rabbi David Kimhi [*Biblical scholar, 1160-1235*] (BJA) ... RaDaK
Rabbi Moses ben Maimon [*Maimonides*] [*Jewish philosopher, 1135-1204*] ... RaM-BaM
Rabbi Moses ben Nahman [*Spanish Talmudist, 1195-1270*] (BJA) ... RAMBAN
Rabbi Moses Zacuto (BJA) ... RAMAZ
Rabbi Saadia Gaon [*Jewish scholar, 882-942*] (BJA) ... RSG
Rabbi Shlomo Yitzhaqi [*Medieval Jewish commentator*] ... RASHI
Rabbi Solomon Bar Isaac (BJA) ... RaSHI
Rabbinic [*Hebrew*] [*Language*] (BARN) ... Rabb
Rabbinic Center for Research and Counseling (EA) ... RCRC
Rabbinic Hebrew (BJA) ... RH
Rabbinic Supervisor (BJA) ... RS
Rabbinical ... RAB
Rabbinical ... RABB
Rabbinical Alliance of America (EA) ... RAA
Rabbinical Assembly (EA) ... RA
Rabbinical Council of America (EA) ... RCA
Rabbinical School (BJA) ... RS
Rabbinical Seminary (BJA) ... RS
Rabbit Alveolar Macrophage [*Clinical chemistry*] ... RAM
Rabbit Antibodies to Pig Ovary [*Immunology*] ... RAPO
Rabbit Antibody to Human Ovary [*Medicine*] (DMAA) ... RAHO
Rabbit Antidog Thymus Serum [*Immunology*] (MAE) ... RADTS
Rabbit Anti-Human [*Immunology*] ... RAH
Rabbit Anti-Human Glomerular Basement Membrane [*Immunology*] ... RaHGBM
Rabbit Anti-Human Thymocyte Globulin [*Immunology*] (AAMN) ... RAHTG
Rabbit Anti-Human Thymocyte Serum [*Immunology*] (OA) ... RAHTS
Rabbit Antimouse [*Hematology*] ... RAM
Rabbit Anti-Mouse Brain (PDAA) ... RAMB
Rabbit Antimouse Immunoglobulin G [*Immunology*] ... RAMIG
Rabbit Antimouse Thymocyte [*Immunology*] ... RAMT
Rabbit Antirat Lymphocyte Serum [*Immunology*] (MAE) ... RARLS
Rabbit Anti-Rat Thymocyte Serum [*Immunology*] (DMAA) ... RARTS
Rabbit Antithymocyte Globulin [*Immunochemistry*] ... RATG
Rabbit Aorta Contracting Substance [*TA_2 - see TA, Thromboxane*] [*Biochemistry*] ... RCS
Rabbit Aorta Contracting Substance-Releasing Factor [*Medicine*] (PDAA) ... RCS-RF
Rabbit Aortic Endothelial Cells ... RAEC
Rabbit Calicivirus Disease ... RCD
Rabbit Calicivirus Disease ... RCD
Rabbit Hemorrhagic Disease Virus ... RHDV
Rabbit Ileal Loop Test [*for enterotoxins*] ... RILT
Rabbit Kidney ... RK
Rabbit Kidney Vacuolating Virus ... RKV
Rabbit Oil & Gas [*Vancouver Stock Exchange symbol*] ... RAB
Rabbit Ovarian Antitumor Serum [*Medicine*] (DMAA) ... ROATS
Rabbit Reticulocyte Lysate [*Biochemistry*] ... RRL
Rabbit Serum Albumin [*Immunology*] ... RSA
Rabbit-Air AG, Zurich [*Switzerland ICAO designator*] (FAAC) ... RBB
Rabbit-Mouse Hybridomas [*Immunochemistry*] ... RMH
Rabbits Against Human Ovary [*Immunology*] ... RAHO
Rabbonim Aid Society ... RAS
Rabelais [*French author, 1494-1553*] (ROG) ... RAB
Raben & Sjogren [*Publisher*] [*Sweden*] ... R & S
Rabi [*Fiji*] [*ICAO location identifier*] (ICLI) ... NFFR
Rabi [*Fiji*] [*Airport symbol*] (OAG) ... RBI
Rabies Immune Globulin [*Immunology*] ... RIG
Rabies Immune Globulin, Human [*Immunology*] (MAE) ... RIGH
Rabies Post-Exposure Prophylaxis [*Medicine*] (DMAA) ... RPEP
Rabies Vector Species ... RVS
Rabies Virus ... RV
Rabkin and Johnson's Federal, Income, Gift, and Estate Taxation [*A publication*] (DLA) ... R & J
Raboche-Krest'ianskaia Krasnaia Armiia [*Workers' and Peasants' Red Army*] [*Redesignated Soviety Army*] [*Former USSR*] ... RKKA
RAC Financial Group, Inc. [*Associated Press*] (SAG) ... RAC Fin
RAC Financial Group, Inc. [*NASDAQ symbol*] (SAG) ... RACF
RAC Fin'l Grp [*NASDAQ symbol*] (TTSB) ... RACF
Racal Communications Processor [*Racal Datacom, Inc.*] ... RCP
Racal Electronic Design and Analysis by Computer (IAA) ... REDAC
Racal Electronic Optical System [*Software package*] [*Racal Imaging Systems*] ... REOS
Racal-Milgo, Inc., Miami, FL [*Library symbol Library of Congress*] (LCLS) ... FMME
Race Across America [*Annual cycling event*] ... RAAM
Race Car Club of America [*An association*] ... RCCA
Race Cargo Airlines [*Ghana*] [*ICAO designator*] (FAAC) ... ACE
Race, National Origin, and Sex (DNAB) ... RNS
Race Relations Act [*1976*] [*British*] (DCTA) ... RRA
Race Relations Advisory Committee [*Trades Union Congress*] [*British*] (DCTA) ... RRAC
Race Relations and Overseas Students Panel (AIE) ... RROSP
Race Relations Board [*Military*] (VNW) ... RRB
Race Relations Employment Advisory Service [*British*] ... RREAS
Race Relations/Equal Opportunity [*Military*] (AABC) ... RR/EO
Race Relations Information Center [*Defunct*] ... RRIC
Race Relations Law Reporter [*A publication*] (DLA) ... Race Rel L Rep
Race Relations Law Survey [*A publication*] (DLA) ... Rac Rel L Survey
Race Specific Incompatibility ... rsi
Race Track Chaplaincy of America (EA) ... RTCA
Race Walking Association [*British*] (DBA) ... RWA
Race Weight [*of a horse*] ... RW
Racecourse Association [*British*] (DBA) ... RCA
Racecourse Development Committee [*New South Wales*] ... RDC
Racecourses Development Board [*South Australia*] ... RDB

Racecourses Licences Board [*Victoria, Australia*] ... RLB
Racehorse Owners Association [*British*] (DBA) ... ROA
Racehorse Transporters Association [*British*] (DBA) ... RTA
Racemic [*Also, dl, rac*] [*Chemistry*] ... r
Racemic [*Also, dl, r*] [*Chemistry*] ... rac
Racer Resources Ltd. [*Vancouver Stock Exchange symbol*] ... RAC
Race-Relations Education Board [*Military*] (DNAB) ... RREB
Race-Relations Education Program [*Military*] (DNAB) ... RRE
Rach Sentence Completion Test [*Speech and language therapy*] (DAVI) ... RSCT
Rachel Carson Council (EA) ... RCC
Rachel Carson Homestead Association (EA) ... RCHA
Rachel Minke Fan Club (EA) ... RMFC
Rachgia [*Viet Nam*] [*ICAO location identifier*] (ICLI) ... VVRG
Rachidian Tooth ... RT
Rachmaninoff Society [*Record label*] ... RS
Racial and Ethnic Category [*Army*] (INF) ... REDCAT
Racial Attitudes and Consciousness Exam [*Two-part television program broadcast in 1989*] ... RACE
Racial Awareness Facilitator [*School*] [*Navy*] (NVT) ... RAF
Racial Awareness Facilitator Training [*Navy program*] ... RAFT
Racial Awareness Pilot Project [*University of Cincinnati*] ... RAPP
Racial Equality in Training Schemes (AIE) ... REITS
Racial Preservation Society [*British*] ... RPS
Racial Unconscious [*Psychiatry*] ... RUCS
Raciborz [*Poland*] [*Seismograph station code, US Geological Survey*] (SEIS) ... RAC
Racine County Institutions Medical Library, Racine, WI [*Library symbol Library of Congress*] (LCLS) ... WRacC
Racine County Law Library, Racine, WI [*Library symbol Library of Congress*] (LCLS) ... WRacCL
Racine Public Library, Racine, WI [*OCLC symbol*] (OCLC) ... WIR
Racine Public Library, Racine, WI [*Library symbol Library of Congress*] (LCLS) ... WRac
Racine Unified School District Number One, Racine, WI [*Library symbol Library of Congress*] (LCLS) ... WRacSD
Racine, WI [*Location identifier FAA*] (FAAL) ... HRK
Racine, WI [*Location identifier FAA*] (FAAL) ... RAC
Racine, WI [*AM radio station call letters*] ... WBJX
Racine, WI [*FM radio station call letters*] (RBYB) ... WEZY
Racine, WI [*Television station call letters*] ... WJJA
Racine, WI [*FM radio station call letters*] ... WKKV
Racine, WI [*AM radio station call letters*] ... WRJN
Racing ... RACG
Racing Fans Club of America (EA) ... RFCA
Racing, Gaming, and Liquor Commission [*Northern Territory, Australia*] ... RGLC
Racing Information Bureau [*British*] (CB) ... RIB
Racing Public Relations Association ... RPRA
Racing Research Fund [*Defunct*] (EA) ... RRF
Racing Service Center [*Motorcycle racing*] ... RSC
Rack ... RK
Rack Clearance Center [*Association of American Publishers*] ... RCC
Rack Controller Unit [*Computer science*] (PCM) ... RCU
Rack Entry Module (PDAA) ... REM
Rack Manufacturers Institute (EA) ... RMI
Rack Mounted (IAA) ... RM
Rack Register (MHDB) ... RKR
Rack Service Association (EA) ... RSA
Racketeer Influenced and Corrupt Organization Act (DFIT) ... RICO
Racketeer-Influenced and Corrupt Organizations [*Nickname of a 1970 law used by federal prosecutors to indict organized crime leaders*] ... RICO
Racketeering in Interstate Commerce (DICI) ... RICO
Rackham Arthritis Research Unit [*University of Michigan*] [*Research center*] (RCD) ... RARU
Racking Horse Breeders Association of America (EA) ... RHBA
Rack-Mount Extender (MHDI) ... RME
RACON [*RADAR Beacon*] ... R
RACON Station [*ITU designation*] (CET) ... RLB
Racotek, Inc. [*NASDAQ symbol*] (SAG) ... RACO
Racotek, Inc. [*Associated Press*] (SAG) ... Racotek
Racquet and Tennis Club, New York, NY [*Library symbol Library of Congress*] (LCLS) ... NNRT
Racquetball Association of Ireland (EAIO) ... RAI
Racquetball Manufacturers Association [*Defunct*] (EA) ... RMA
Rad [*Non-SI unit; preferred unit is Gy, Gray*] ... rd
Rada [*Sweden ICAO location identifier*] (ICLI) ... ESFR
Rada Electronic Industries Ltd. [*New York, NY NASDAQ symbol*] (NQ) ... RADI
Rada Electronics Industries [*NASDAQ symbol*] (TTSB) ... RADIF
Rada Electronics Industries Ltd. [*Associated Press*] (SAG) ... RadaElc
RADAR [*Navy symbol Obsolete British*] ... ASV
RADAR [*JETDS nomenclature*] ... P
RADAR ... Ra
RADAR ... RAD
RADAR (DEN) ... RD
RADAR (AAG) ... RDR
RADAR Absorption Noise and Clutter (NASA) ... RANC
RADAR Acoustic Sounding System [*National Oceanic and Atmospheric Administration*] ... RASS
RADAR Acquisition and Tracking System (MCD) ... RATS
RADAR Acquisition Tracking Probe for Active Calibration (DNAB) ... RATPAC
RADAR Acquisition Visual-Tracking Equipment ... RAVE
RADAR Address Counter ... RAC
RADAR Advanced Measurements Program for Analysis of Reentry Techniques [*ARPA - Raytheon*] ... RAMPART
RADAR Advisory [*Aviation*] (FAAC) ... RARAD
RADAR Advisory Service ... RAS
RADAR Aim Point ... RAP
RADAR Air Traffic Control Center [*Later, RATCF*] [*Navy*] ... RATCC
Radar Air Traffic Control Facilities [*FAA*] (TAG) ... RATCF
RADAR Aircraft Altitude (IAA) ... RAA
RADAR Alignment Designation Accuracy Test (MCD) ... RADAT
RADAR Alphanumeric Display Sub-System (PDAA) ... RADS
RADAR Altimeter (TEL) ... ALT
RADAR Altimeter [*Aviation*] (KSC) ... RA
RADAR Altimeter [*Aviation*] (SSD) ... RADALT
RADAR Altimeter [*Aviation*] (NASA) ... RALT
RADAR Altimeter and Altitude Warning System [*Military*] (CAAL) ... RAAWS
RADAR Altimeter and Doppler Velocity Sensor ... RADVS
RADAR Altimeter Equipment ... RAE
RADAR Altimeter Indicator (MCD) ... RAI
RADAR Altimeter Low-Altitude Control [*Military*] (CAAL) ... RALAC
RADAR Altimeter Low-Altitude Control System [*Military*] (NG) ... RALACS
RADAR Altimeter Target Simulator (MCD) ... RATS
RADAR Altimeter - Terrain Following RADAR (MCD) ... RA-TFR
RADAR Altimeter Warning Set (MCD) ... RAWS
RADAR Analog Digital Data and Control (KSC) ... RADAC
RADAR Analog Target Acquisition Computer ... RATAC
RADAR Analysis and Detection Unit (WDAA) ... RADU
RADAR Analysis and Development Unit [*National Severe Storms Forecast Center*] (NOAA) ... RADU
RADAR Analysis System (MCD) ... RADAN
RADAR and Air Communications ... R & AC
Radar and Algorithm Display Model [*Marine science*] (OSRA) ... RADS
Radar and Algorithm Display Model (USDC) ... RADS
RADAR and Optical Systems Code ... ROSCOE
RADAR and Television Aid to Navigation ... RATAN
RADAR and Warning Coordination [*Teletypewriter circuit*] ... RAWARC
RADAR Approach Aid [*Aviation*] (DA) ... RAD
RADAR Approach Control [*Air Force*] ... RAPCON
RADAR Approach Control Center (MCD) ... RAPCC
RADAR Area Correlation Guidance System (PDAA) ... RADAG
RADAR Area Correlator ... RAC
RADAR Arithmetic Processing Element [*Navy*] ... RAPE
RADAR Arrival Route [*Aviation*] (DA) ... RAR
RADAR Assembly Spares (NG) ... RAS
RADAR Attitude Sensing System (MCD) ... RASS
RADAR Augmentation Device ... RAD
RADAR Augmentation Reliability (MCD) ... RAR
RADAR Augmentation System (MCD) ... RAS
RADAR Automatic Data Transmission Assembly (IAA) ... RADATA
RADAR Automatic Target Detection [*Military*] (CAAL) ... RATD
RADAR Automatic Weather System ... RAWS
RADAR Azimuth Converter ... RAC
RADAR Beacon (IAA) ... RACON
Radar Beacon (IDOE) ... Racon
RADAR Beacon ... RADON
RADAR Beacon ... RB
RADAR Beacon (KSC) ... RDRBCN
RADAR Beacon [*Maps and charts*] ... YH
RADAR Beacon [*Maps and charts*] ... YK
RADAR Beacon Antenna ... RBA
RADAR Beacon, Forward Air Controller ... RABFAC
RADAR Beacon Forward Air Controller - Target Data Communicator (MCD) ... RABFAC-TDC
RADAR Beacon Sequencer ... RBS
RADAR Beacon Station (IAA) ... RBS
RADAR Beacon System ... RBS
RADAR Beacon Tracking Level [*FAA*] ... RBTL
RADAR Beacon Transponder ... RABET
RADAR Beam Sharpening ... RBS
RADAR Beam Sharpening Element ... RBSE
RADAR Blip Identification Message ... RBI
RADAR Bomb Directing Systems ... RBDS
RADAR Bomb Evaluation (MCD) ... RABVAL
RADAR Bomb Scoring ... RBS
RADAR Bomb Scoring Central (NG) ... RBSC
RADAR Bombardment System (NATG) ... RBS
RADAR Bombsight ... RBS
RADAR Boresight Range (KSC) ... RBR
RADAR Bright Display Equipment [*FAA*] ... RBDE
RADAR Calibration Sphere ... RCS
RADAR Calibration Target (MCD) ... RADCAT
RADAR Calibration Unit ... RCU
RADAR Chart Protector (DNAB) ... RCP
RADAR Cloud Detection Report [*NWS*] (FAAC) ... RCD
RADAR Cloud Detection Report No Echoes Observed [*NWS*] (FAAC) ... RCDNE
RADAR Cloud Detection Report Not Available [*NWS*] (FAAC) ... RCDNA
RADAR Cloud Detector Inoperative Due to Breakdown Until [*NWS*] (FAAC) ... RCDNO
RADAR Cloud Detector Inoperative Due to Maintenance Until [*NWS*] (FAAC) ... RCDOM
RADAR Collimator System ... RCS
RADAR Computer (MCD) ... RC
RADAR Computer Interaction Simulator ... RACIS
RADAR Conspicuous Object ... Ra (Conspic)
RADAR Control ... RADCON
RADAR Control (DEN) ... RC
RADAR Control Clouds ... RCC
RADAR Control Computer (MCD) ... RCC
RADAR Control Console [*Military*] (CAAL) ... RCC
RADAR Control Console Operator [*Military*] (CAAL) ... RCCO

RADAR Control Officer ... RCO
RADAR Control Panel (MCD) ... RCP
RADAR Control Room ... RCR
RADAR Control Ship ... RCS
RADAR Control Squadron ... RADCS
RADAR Control Trailer [*Military*] (AABC) ... RCT
RADAR Control Unit [*Military*] (CAAL) ... RCU
RADAR Control Van (NATG) ... RCV
RADAR Controlled Approach (NVT) ... RCA
RADAR Conversion Program ... RCP
RADAR Correlation Guidance Study ... RCGS
RADAR [*or Radio*] **Countermeasures** [*Military*] (AAG) ... RCM
RADAR Countermeasures and Deception [*Military*] (MCD) ... RADC
RADAR Countermeasures and Deception [*Military*] ... RADCM
RADAR Course-Directing Central [*Military*] ... RCDC
RADAR Course-Directing Control (MUGU) ... RCDC
RADAR Coverage Indication [*or Indicator*] ... RCI
RADAR Coverage Indicator (IAA) ... RCI
RADAR Coverage Penetration Analysis ... RACPAS
RADAR Coverage via Tactical Air Navigation (IAA) ... RATAC
RADAR Cross Section ... RCS
RADAR Cross Section ... RXS
RADAR Data ... RD
RADAR Data Converter (AFM) ... RADCON
RADAR Data Converter (MCD) ... RDC
RADAR Data Distribution Switchboard [*Military*] (CAAL) ... RDDS
RADAR Data Extractor (PDAA) ... RADEX
RADAR Data Plotting Board ... RDPB
RADAR Data Processing ... RDP
RADAR Data Processing Center [*Military*] ... RDPC
RADAR Data Processing Equipment (AABC) ... RDPE
RADAR Data Processing System ... RDPS
RADAR Data Transmission ... RADAT
RADAR Data Transmission and Assembly (IEEE) ... RADATA
RADAR Data-Transmission System (WDAA) ... RADATS
RADAR Decoy Balloon [*Air Force*] ... RDB
RADAR Departure [*Aviation*] (FAAC) ... RADEP
RADAR Departure Route [*Aviation*] (DA) ... RDR
RADAR Design Corp. ... RDC
RADAR Determination Satellite System [*Aviation*] (DA) ... RDSS
RADAR Diagnostic Report (IAA) ... RDR
RADAR Digital Probe ... RDP
RADAR Direction Finder [*or Finding*] (CET) ... RDF
RADAR Display ... RD
RADAR Display Console ... RDC
RADAR Display Distribution System (DWSG) ... RADDS
RADAR Display Equipment ... RDE
RADAR Display Room (IAA) ... RDR
RADAR Display Unit ... RDU
RADAR Distance Indicator ... RADIST
RADAR Distribution Switchboard ... RDS
RADAR Dome [*NASA*] ... RADOME
RADAR Dome Wind [*NWS*] (FAAC) ... RDWND
RADAR Doppler [*Missile-tracking system*] (AAG) ... RADOP
RADAR Doppler Automatic Navigator ... RADAN
RADAR Echo Augmentation Device ... READ
RADAR Echo Simulation Study [*or Subsystem*] ... RESS
RADAR Echoing Area ... REA
RADAR Effects Processor (MCD) ... REP
RADAR Effects Reactor ... RER
RADAR Electronic Scan Technique ... REST
RADAR Electronic Scan Test (IAA) ... REST
RADAR/Electro-Optical (MCD) ... RDR/EO
RADAR Electrooptical Area Correlation Tracker [*Military*] (CAAL) ... REACT
RADAR Emission Location Attack Control System ... RELACS
RADAR Engineering Design Objectives (NG) ... REDO
RADAR Environment Simulation (NATG) ... RES
RADAR Equipment Trailer (MCD) ... RET
RADAR Evaluation Branch [*ADC*] ... REB
RADAR Evaluation Pod [*Spacecraft*] ... REP
RADAR Evaluation Squadron [*Air Force*] ... RADAREVALSq
RADAR Evaluation Squadron [*Air Force*] ... RADES
RADAR Evaluation Squadron [*Military*] ... RES
RADAR Exercise (NVT) ... RADEX
RADAR Facsimile ... RAFAX
RADAR Field Gradient (IEEE) ... RFG
RADAR Film Viewer ... RFV
RADAR Filter Assembly ... RFA
RADAR Frequency (IAA) ... RF
RADAR Frequency/Infrared Frequency (IEEE) ... RF/IR
RADAR Frequency Interferometer (MCD) ... RFI
RADAR Frequency Target Discrimination System (MCD) ... RFTDS
RADAR Glider Positioning (IAA) ... RGP
RADAR Ground Stabilization ... RGS
RADAR Guidance (IAA) ... RG
RADAR Guided Weapon System (MCD) ... RGWS
RADAR Gunlaying (IAA) ... RGL
RADAR Height Indicator (CET) ... RHI
RADAR Home on Jam ... RHOJ
RADAR Homing and Warning (MCD) ... RHAW
RADAR Homing and Warning Receiver (MCD) ... RHAWR
RADAR Homing and Warning Receiver (MCD) ... RHWR
RADAR Homing and Warning System ... RHAWS
RADAR Homing Beacon [*Maps and charts*] (IAA) ... RHB
RADAR Homing Beacon [*Maps and charts*] ... YJ
RADAR Homing Bomb [*Air Force*] ... RHB
RADAR Homing Guidance Investigation (MCD) ... RHOGI
RADAR Horizon Distance (IAA) ... RHD
RADAR Identification and Direction System (NG) ... RAID
RADAR Identification Point (AFM) ... RIP
RADAR Impact Prediction System (CET) ... RIPS
RADAR Improvement Plan (NATG) ... RIP
RADAR Improvement Program ... RIP
RADAR Indicating Console [*FAA*] ... RIC
RADAR Inertial Altimeter ... RINAL
RADAR In-Flight Monitoring System ... RIMS
RADAR Information Service [*Aviation*] (DA) ... RIS
RADAR Input ... RI
RADAR Input Control ... RIC
RADAR Input Countermeasures Officer [*Air Force*] ... RICMO
RADAR Input Countermeasures Technician [*Air Force*] ... RICMT
RADAR Input Drum ... RID
RADAR Input Mapper ... RIM
RADAR Input Monitor (CET) ... RIM
RADAR Inputs Test ... RIT
RADAR Installed System Tester (KSC) ... RIST
RADAR Intelligence ... RADINT
RADAR Intelligence Information ... RII
RADAR Intelligence Map ... RIM
RADAR Intelligence Photo Producer ... RIPP
RADAR Intercept (IAA) ... RI
RADAR Intercept Calculator ... RIC
RADAR Intercept Control ... RIC
RADAR Intercept Event ... RIE
RADAR Intercept Officer [*Navy*] ... RIO
RADAR Interface Recorder (MCD) ... RIR
RADAR Interface Unit [*Military*] (CAAL) ... RIU
RADAR Interference (LAIN) ... RI
RADAR Intermittent (IEEE) ... RDRINT
RADAR Intermittent (MSA) ... RINT
RADAR/Jimsphere ... RJ
RADAR Keyboard Multiplexer [*Computer science*] (MHDI) ... RKM
RADAR Land Mass Simulation ... RLMS
RADAR Laydown Delivery (AFM) ... RLD
RADAR Line of Sight ... RLS
RADAR Lock-On ... RLO
RADAR Logic Unit (MCD) ... RLU
RADAR Low-Angle Drogue Delivery (AFM) ... RLADD
RADAR Maintenance and Test Control (MCD) ... RMTC
RADAR Maintenance Spares (NG) ... RMS
RADAR Manual System (DNAB) ... RMS
RADAR Map Matching ... RMM
RADAR Mapper ... RM
RADAR Mapper, Gap Filler (MSA) ... RMGF
RADAR Mapper Gapfiller ... RMG
RADAR Mapper, Long Range ... RML
RADAR Mapper, Long Range (MSA) ... RMLR
RADAR Mapping of Panama ... RAMP
RADAR Mapping Set [*or System*] ... RMS
RADAR Marker [*Military*] ... RAMARK
RADAR Masking Parameter (IAA) ... RAMP
RADAR Master Oscillator ... RMO
RADAR Material Office [*Navy*] (MCD) ... RMO
RADAR Message Conversion and Distribution (DA) ... RMCDE
RADAR Microwave Link (IEEE) ... RML
RADAR Microwave Link Repeater (FAAC) ... RMLR
RADAR Microwave Link Terminal (FAAC) ... RMLT
RADAR Missile (MUGU) ... RM
RADAR Modification Program (NG) ... RAMP
RADAR Monitor and Control Console [*Military*] (CAAL) ... RMCC
RADAR Navigation ... RADAN
RADAR Navigation (DNAB) ... RAN
RADAR Netting Station [*Military*] (AABC) ... RNS
RADAR Netting Unit [*Military*] (AABC) ... RNU
RADAR Not Functioning Properly [*Military*] (AFIT) ... RNFP
RADAR Observer ... RO
RADAR Observer License ... ROL
RADAR Observer Testing System ... ROTS
RADAR Ocean Reconnaissance Satellite (MCD) ... RORSAT
RADAR Ocean Surveillance Satellite (NVT) ... ROSAT
RADAR Ocean Wave Spectrometer ... ROWS
RADAR Off Target ... ROFT
RADAR on Target ... ROT
RADAR Operating Below Prescribed Standarad [*NWS*] (FAAC) ... ROBEPS
RADAR Operator (CET) ... RADOP
RADAR Operator ... RAO
RADAR Operator ... RO
RADAR Operator Mechanic (WDAA) ... ROM
RADAR/Optical Weapons [*Military*] ... RADOP
RADAR Optical Weapons (IEEE) ... RADOPWEAP
RADAR Order of Battle ... ROB
RADAR Order Switch ... ROS
RADAR Out of Battle (CET) ... ROB
RADAR Out of Commission for Parts [*ADC*] ... ROCP
RADAR Overheat Protection Unit (MCD) ... ROPU
RADAR Performance Analyzer ... RPA
RADAR Performance Figure (IAA) ... RPF
RADAR Performance Monitor ... RPM
RADAR Picket Combat Air Patrol (NVT) ... RAPCAP
RADAR Picket Destroyer [*Navy symbol Navy*] ... DDR

RADAR Picket Escort Ship [*Navy symbol*] ... DER
RADAR Picket Frigate [*Navy symbol*] (NVT) ... FFR
RADAR Picket Ship [*Navy symbol*] ... AGR
RADAR Picket Submarine [*Navy symbol*] ... SSR
RADAR Picket Submarine (Nuclear Powered) [*Navy symbol Obsolete*] ... SSRN
RADAR Planning Chart ... RPC
RADAR Planning Device ... RPD
RADAR Plot (DEN) ... RP
RADAR Plotting Board ... RPB
RADAR Plotting Sheet (OA) ... RPS
RADAR Position Symbol [*ICAO*] (FAAC) ... RPS
RADAR Power Programmer ... RPP
RADAR Precipitation Integrator [*National Weather Service*] ... RPI
RADAR Prediction Data Table (PDAA) ... RPDT
RADAR Prediction Device ... RPD
RADAR Prediction System (MCD) ... RAPS
RADAR Prediction Uncertainty ... RPU
RADAR Processing Center ... RPC
RADAR Processing Language [*Computer science*] (IEEE) ... RPL
RADAR Processor (CET) ... RAPR
Radar Product General (USDC) ... RPG
Radar Product General [*Marine science*] (OSRA) ... RPG
RADAR Proficiency Simulator ... RAPS
RADAR Programmable Signal Processor ... RPSP
RADAR Quality Control ... RQC
RADAR Radiation Receiver ... RRR
RADAR Range Gate ... RRG
RADAR Range Height Indicator Not Operating on Scan [*Meteorology*] (FAAC) ... RHINO
RADAR Range-Rate Error ... RRRE
RADAR Ranging System ... RRS
RADAR Recording and Analysis Equipment (DA) ... RRA
RADAR Reflective Balloon ... RRB
RADAR Reflectivity Measuring Facility ... RRMF
RADAR Reflector ... Ra Ref
RADAR Refraction (MCD) ... RADREF
RADAR Regulation Zone (DA) ... RRZ
RADAR Repeater Indicator Console ... RRIC
RADAR Report [*FAA*] ... RAREP
RADAR Research and Development Establishment (IAA) ... RRDE
RADAR Research Establishment [*British*] ... RRE
RADAR Responder Beacon ... RACON
RADAR Responder Beacon [*System*] (MUGU) ... REBECCA
RADAR Return Code ... RRC
RADAR Safety Beacon System (MCD) ... RSBS
RADAR Satellite [*Canada*] ... RADARSAT
RADAR Scan Converter [*Military*] (CAAL) ... RSC
RADAR Scanner ... RS
RADAR Scattering ... RS
RADAR Scope Interpretation (AAG) ... RSI
RADAR Scorer (MCD) ... RASCORE
RADAR Sea Clutter ... RSC
RADAR Sea State Analyzer [*Marine science*] (MSC) ... RASSAN
RADAR Search Equipment ... RSE
RADAR Seeker Simulator [*Military*] (CAAL) ... RSS
RADAR Selector (MCD) ... RS
RADAR Sensing System [*Military*] (CAAL) ... RSS
RADAR Service Area ... RSA
RADAR Set ... RS
RADAR Set Control ... RSC
RADAR Set Group [*HAWK missile*] (MCD) ... RSG
RADAR Ship Target Classification [*Military*] (CAAL) ... RSTC
RADAR Signal Generator (MCD) ... RSG
RADAR Signal Processor ... RSP
RADAR Signal Simulator ... RSS
RADAR Signalling Processing Equipment ... RSPE
RADAR Signature Analysis [*Air Force*] ... RSA
RADAR Significance Analysis Code ... RSAC
RADAR Significant Power Line ... RSPL
RADAR Simulator (CET) ... RS
RADAR Simulator (MSA) ... RSIM
RADAR Squadron [*Air Force*] ... RADRON
RADAR Squadron [*Air Force*] ... RADS
RADAR Start (CET) ... RS
RADAR Start (MSA) ... RST
RADAR Station ... Ra
RADAR Status History ... RSH
RADAR Storm Detection Unit ... RSDU
RADAR System Console [*Military*] (CAAL) ... RSC
RADAR System Controller [*Military*] (CAAL) ... RSC
RADAR System Development (IAA) ... RSD
RADAR System Test Station (MCD) ... RSTS
RADAR Systems Design Section ... RSDS
RADAR Systems Group [*of General Motors Corp.*] ... RSG
RADAR Systems Improvement Program (DWSG) ... RSIP
RADAR Systems Technician (MCD) ... RST
RADAR Target Acquisition (IAA) ... RATAC
RADAR Target Data Analog Processor (MCD) ... RTDAP
RADAR Target Data Processor (MCD) ... RTDP
RADAR Target Folder Viewer ... RTFV
RADAR Target Identification ... RTI
RADAR Target Identification Point (AFM) ... RTIP
RADAR Target Materiel (AFM) ... RTM
RADAR Target Measuring System (MCD) ... RTMS
RADAR Target Scatter [*RADAR program*] ... RATSCAT
RADAR Target Scattering Advanced Measurement System ... RAMS
RADAR Target Signature Analysis ... RTSA
RADAR Target Simulator ... RTS
RADAR Telephone Transmission System ... RTTS
RADAR Terminal Control ... RATCON
RADAR Terrain Analysis ... RTA
RADAR Terrain Avoidance ... RATAV
RADAR Test Set ... RTS
RADAR Test Station (MCD) ... RTS
RADAR Test System ... RTS
RADAR Threshold Lobe Limit (CET) ... RTL
RADAR Timing Unit ... RTU
RADAR Tracking Center [*or Control*] ... RTC
RADAR Tracking Error Measurement ... RTEM
RADAR Tracking Radiotelegraphy (IAA) ... RT
RADAR Tracking Station [*Military*] ... RTS
RADAR Tracking System ... RTS
RADAR Transmitter ... RDR XMTR
RADAR Transmitter (AAG) ... RDRSMTR
RADAR Transparency (MCD) ... RT
RADAR Triangle Navigation (IAA) ... RATRAN
RADAR Trigger (CET) ... R/T
RADAR Unit (MCD) ... RU
RADAR Vector ... RAVEC
RADAR Vector (SAA) ... RV
RADAR Vectoring Area [*Aviation*] (DA) ... RVA
RADAR Video Buffer ... RVB
RADAR Video Controller [*Military*] (CAAL) ... RVC
RADAR Video Data Processor ... RVDP
RADAR Video Digitizer ... RVD
RADAR Video Extractor ... RVE
RADAR Video Processor [*Military*] (CAAL) ... RVP
RADAR Video Recorder (NVT) ... RAVIR
RADAR Video Recorder ... RVR
RADAR Video Recorder Unit ... RVRU
RADAR Warning and Homing ... RWH
RADAR Warning Installation (NATG) ... RWI
RADAR Warning Receiver (MCD) ... RWR
RADAR Warning System (MCD) ... RWS
RADAR Warning Trainer (MCD) ... RWT
RADAR Weather Report (IAA) ... RAREP
RADAR Weather Report Equipment Inoperative Due to Breakdown [*NWS*] (FAAC) ... PPINO
RADAR Weather Report Equipment Inoperative Due to Maintenance [*NWS*] (FAAC) ... PPIOM
RADAR Weather Report Equipment No Echoes Observed [*NWS*] (FAAC) ... PPINE
RADAR Weather Report Equipment Operation REsumed [*NWS*] (FAAC) ... PPIOK
RADAR Weather Report Not Available [*NWS*] (FAAC) ... PPINA
RADAR Wind [*Upper air observation*] ... RAWIN
RADAR Wind [*Upper air observation*] ... RAWIND
Radar Wind Sounding [*Determination of winds by radar observation of a balloon*] [*Marine science*] (OSRA) ... RAWIN
RADAR Wind Sounding [*Upper air observation*] (MSA) ... RAWINDS
RADAR Wind Sounding and Radiosonde [*Upper air observation*] ... RAWINSONDE
RADAR Winds [*Upper air observation*] ... RAWINS
RADAR-Absorbent Material [*Aviation*] ... RAM
RADAR-Absorbing Coating [*Military*] (RDA) ... RACO
RADAR-Absorbing Material ... RAM
RADAR-Absorbing Paint [*Military*] (RDA) ... RAP
RADAR-Absorbing Primary Structure (MCD) ... RAPS
RADAR-Absorbing Structures ... RAS
RADAR-Aided Tracking Computer (WDAA) ... RATC
RADAR-Equipped Inertial Navigation System ... REINS
RADAR-IFF Data Processor (MCD) ... RIDP
RADAR-Intercept Operator ... RIO
RADARman (GFGA) ... RADM
RADARman [*Also, RDM*] [*Navy rating*] ... RD
RADARman [*Also, RD*] ... RDM
RADARman, First Class [*Navy rating*] ... RD1
RADARman, Seaman [*Navy rating*] ... RDSN
RADARman, Second Class [*Navy rating*] ... RD2
RADARman, Third Class [*Navy rating*] ... RD3
Radar's Reports [*138-163 Missouri*] [*A publication*] (DLA) ... Radar
RADAUS [*Radio-Austria AG*] **Data-Service** [*Telecommunications*] ... RDS
RADC [*Rome Air Development Center*] **Automatic Document Classification On-Line** [*Air Force Information service or system*] (IID) ... RADCOL
Radcliff, KY [*FM radio station call letters*] (RBYB) ... WASE
Radcliffe College, Archives, Cambridge, MA [*Library symbol Library of Congress*] (LCLS) ... MCR-Ar
Radcliffe College, Cambridge, MA [*Library symbol Library of Congress*] (LCLS) ... MCR
Radcliffe College, Schlesinger Library, Cambridge, MA [*Library symbol Library of Congress*] (LCLS) ... MCR-S
Radcliffe College, Schlesinger Library, Cambridge, MA [*OCLC symbol*] (OCLC) ... SLR
Radcliffe Resources Ltd. [*Vancouver Stock Exchange symbol*] ... RCF
Raddolcendo [*Gradually Softer*] [*Music*] ... RADDOL
Rad-Equivalent Therapy [*Radiology*] ... RET
Rader Aviation, Inc. [*ICAO designator*] (FAAC) ... GBR
Radet for Teknisk Terminologi [*Norwegian Council for Technical Terminology*] [*Oslo*] [*Information service or system*] (IID) ... RTT
Radfahrabteilung [*Bicycle Battalion*] [*German military - World War II*] ... R
Radford Army Ammunition Depot [*Virginia*] (MCD) ... RAAD

Radford Army Ammunition Plant (AABC) ... RAAP
Radford Army Ammunition Plant [*Virginia*] ... RAD
Radford Arsenal [*Army*] (AAG) ... RAD
Radford College, Radford, VA [*Library symbol Library of Congress*] (LCLS) ... ViRa
Radford College, Radford, VA [*OCLC symbol*] (OCLC) ... VRA
Radford Public Library, Radford, VA [*Library symbol Library of Congress*] (LCLS) ... ViRaP
Radford University (GAGS) ... Radford U
Radford, VA [*AM radio station call letters*] ... WRAD
Radford, VA [*FM radio station call letters*] ... WRIQ
Radford, VA [*FM radio station call letters*] ... WVRU
Radiac (IDOE) ... rad
Radiac [*Nucleonics*] ... RDC
RADIAC [*Radiation Detection, Indication, and Computation*] **Equipment** (NATG) ... RAD
RADIAC [*Radiation Detection, Indication, and Computation*] **Instrument System** ... RIS
Radial [*Followed by three digits; for use on instrument approach charts*] [*Aviation*] ... R
Radial ... RAD
Radial [*Commonly used*] (OPSA) ... RADIAL
Radial [*Commonly used*] (OPSA) ... RADIEL
Radial ... RADL
Radial (AAG) ... RADL
Radial (MSA) ... RDL
Radial Artery Pressure [*Medicine*] ... RP
Radial Basis Function [*Mathematics*] ... RBF
Radial Beam Traveling Wave Tube [*Electronics*] ... RBTWT
Radial Beam Tube [*Electronics*] ... RBT
Radial Blanket Assembly [*Nuclear energy*] (NRCH) ... RBA
Radial Collateral Ligament [*Anatomy*] ... RCL
Radial Compression Model [*Chromatography*] ... RCM
Radial Compression Separation System [*Chromatography*] ... RCSS
Radial Defect Examination (IEEE) ... RDE
Radial Distribution Function [*X-ray diffraction*] ... RDF
Radial Distribution Method ... RDM
Radial Fibers [*Ear anatomy*] ... RF
Radial Flow (AAG) ... RF
Radial Flow Reactor [*Chemical engineering*] ... RFR
Radial Flow Torr Deposition System (IEEE) ... RFTD
Radial Force Variation [*Automotive tire testing*] ... RFV
Radial Four-Valve Combustion [*Automotive engineering*] ... RFVC
Radial Glial Guide [*Neurology*] ... RG
Radial Immunodiffusion [*Analytical biochemistry*] ... RID
Radial Immunodiffusion [*Immunology*] (DAVI) ... RID
Radial Immunodiffusion Cerebrospinal Fluid [*or Colloidal Gold*] [*Immunology*] (DAVI) ... RIDCSF
Radial Inlet Manifold ... RIM
Radial Jerk [*Reflex*] [*Neurology*] (DAVI) ... RJ
Radial Keratoplasty [*Ophthalmology*] (DAVI) ... RK
Radial Keratotomy [*Ophthalmology*] ... RK
Radial Nerve Factor [*of sea urchin*] ... RNF
Radial Optical Tracking Theodolite (MUGU) ... RADCOT
Radial Photon Absorptiometry [*Chemistry*] (DAVI) ... RPA
Radial Probable Error (IEEE) ... RPE
Radial Pulse [*Medicine*] ... RP
Radial Pulse Line Accelerators (MCD) ... RADLAC
Radial Quantum Number ... RQN
Radial Sedan [*Class of racing cars*] ... RS
Radial Stress-Field [*Hypothesis describing forces in a sand-pile*] ... RSF
Radial Structure Function [*of solid catalysts*] ... RSF
Radial, Tangential, Normal ... RTN
Radial Time Base ... RTB
Radial Transmission Line ... RTL
Radial Tuned Suspension (ADA) ... RTS
Radial Wall Variation [*Tire design*] [*Automotive engineering*] ... RWV
Radial-Burning Pulse Motor (MCD) ... RPM
Radially Adjustable Facility Tube (IEEE) ... RAFT
Radially Distributed Annular Rocket Chamber ... RADARC
Radially Extended Linear Impeller Propulsion [*Submarine technology*] ... RELIP
Radian ... R
Radian [*Symbol*] [*SI unit of plane angle*] ... rad
Radian Corp., Austin, TX [*Library symbol Library of Congress*] (LCLS) ... TxAuR
Radian Corp. Library, Durham, NC [*Library symbol*] [*Library of Congress*] (LCLS) ... NcDurRa
Radian Energy Distribution ... RED
Radian Means per Second (NASA) ... RMS
Radiance [*Symbol*] [*IUPAC*] ... L
Radiance Spectral Distribution ... RSD
Radiancy ... R
Radians per Second ... RAD/S
Radians per Second Squared ... RAD/S^2
Radiant Augmented Special Test Apparatus (MCD) ... RASTA
Radiant Energy [*Symbol*] [*IUPAC*] ... Q
Radiant Energy Conversion ... REC
Radiant Exitance [*Symbol*] [*IUPAC*] ... M
Radiant Flash Pyrolysis Reactor [*Chemical engineering*] ... RFPR
Radiant Heat ... RH
Radiant Heat Pump ... RHP
Radiant Heat Temperature (NASA) ... RHT
Radiant Heating and Cooling Institute ... RHCI
Radiant Intensity [*Symbol*] [*IUPAC*] ... I
Radiant Intensity [*Symbol*] ... J
Radiant Intensity Measurements (MUGU) ... RIM
Radiant Intensity Measuring System ... RIMS
Radiant Power Measuring Instrument [*Geophysics*] ... RPMI
Radiata Pine Research Institute [*Australia*] ... RPRI
Radiated Emission (IEEE) ... RE
Radiated Simulation System (MCD) ... RSS
Radiated Susceptibility (IEEE) ... RS
Radiating Facility ... RADFAC
Radiating Site Target Acquisition System (MCD) ... RASTAS
Radiation ... R
Radiation (KSC) ... RAD
Radiation ... RADIAT
Radiation (AAG) ... RADN
Radiation Absorbed Dose [*Unit of measurement of radiation energy*] ... RAD
Radiation Absorbed Dose (DOG) ... rad
Radiation Absorbed Dose [*Unit of measurement of radiation energy*] (IAA) ... RD
Radiation Adaptive Compression Equipment ... RACE
Radiation Advisory Committee (GNE) ... RAC
Radiation Airborne Measurement Program ... RAMP
Radiation and Contamination Control ... RACC
Radiation and Dosimetry Services (NRCH) ... RADS
Radiation and Meteoroid Satellite [*NASA*] ... RMS
Radiation and Repair Engineering [*Nuclear energy*] (NRCH) ... R & RE
Radiation and Repair Engineering [*Nuclear energy*] (IAA) ... RARE
Radiation and Repair Engineering Facility [*Nuclear energy*] (NRCH) ... RAREF
Radiation Applications, Inc. ... RAI
Radiation Attenuation Measurement (CET) ... RAM
Radiation Automatic Casualty Assessment System [*Military*] ... RACAS
Radiation Biological Effectiveness (IAA) ... RBE
Radiation Biological Equivalent ... RBE
Radiation Biology Laboratory [*Smithsonian Institution*] ... RBL
Radiation Casualty [*Criteria for battlefield targets*] (MCD) ... RADCAS
Radiation/Chemical Technician (IEEE) ... RCT
Radiation Chemistry Data Center [*Notre Dame, IN*] [*Department of Commerce*] ... RCDC
Radiation Concentration Guide [*Formerly, MPC*] ... RCG
Radiation Constraints Panel [*NASA*] (MCD) ... RCP
Radiation Control Board (AAG) ... RCB
Radiation Control Center ... RADCC
Radiation Control Valve [*Nuclear energy*] (NRCH) ... RCV
Radiation Control Zone ... RCZ
Radiation Controlled Balloon [*Meteorology*] ... RACOON
Radiation Coordinating Council [*Environmental Protection Agency*] (GFGA) ... RCC
Radiation Counter Laboratories, Inc. ... RCL
Radiation Damage [*Nucleonics*] (OA) ... RD
Radiation Danger Zone (IAA) ... RDZ
Radiation Data Acquisition Chart ... RADATAC
Radiation Degradation Product ... RDP
Radiation Density Constant ... RDC
Radiation Detection ... RD
Radiation Detection Capability (MCD) ... RADEC
Radiation Detection, Indication, and Computation [*Radiological measuring instruments*] ... RADIAC
Radiation Dosimeter Satellite [*NASA*] ... RADOSE
Radiation Effect Research Institute ... RERI
Radiation Effects (AAG) ... RE
Radiation Effects Information Center [*Battelle Memorial Institute*] [*Defunct*] ... REIC
Radiation Effects Machine Analysis System (AAG) ... REMAS
Radiation Effects Mobile Laboratory ... REML
Radiation Effects on Network Systems ... RENS
Radiation Effects Reactor [*Nuclear energy*] ... RER
Radiation Effects Research Foundation [*Formerly, ABCC*] ... RERF
Radiation Emergency Area ... REA
Radiation Emergency Assistance Center/Training Site [*Department of Energy*] ... REAC/TS
Radiation Emergency Medical Preparedness and Assistance Network [*World health organization*] ... REMPAN
Radiation Equipment (NRCH) ... RE
Radiation Equipment and Accessories Corporation (SAA) ... REAC
Radiation Equivalent Man (IAA) ... REM
Radiation Equivalent Manikin Absorption ... REMAB
Radiation Equivalent Manikin Calibration ... REMCAL
Radiation Evaluation Loop [*Nuclear energy*] (NRCH) ... REL
Radiation Exclusion Plot [*Chart of actual or predicted fallout*] ... RADEX
Radiation Experience Data [*Food and Drug Administration*] [*Database*] ... RED
Radiation Exposure Evaluation Laboratory (DNAB) ... REEL
Radiation Exposure Guide ... REG
Radiation Exposure State (NATG) ... RES
Radiation Field Analyzer ... RFA
Radiation Flux Density ... RFD
Radiation Gasdynamics (PDAA) ... RGD
Radiation Guidance (MUGU) ... R/G
Radiation Hazard Effects (KSC) ... RHE
Radiation Hazards ... RADHAZ
Radiation Health Information Project [*Defunct*] (EA) ... RHIP
Radiation Homing (AAG) ... RH
Radiation Hybrid Mapping [*Biochemistry*] ... RH
Radiation Indicator [*Nuclear energy*] (NRCH) ... RI
Radiation Injury Claims Record (DNAB) ... RADINJCLRDS
Radiation Instrument Development Laboratory ... RIDL
Radiation Intelligence ... RINT
Radiation Intensity (AABC) ... RI
Radiation Laboratory (AAG) ... RADLAB
Radiation Laboratory ... RL
Radiation Leukemia Virus [*Medicine*] (DMAA) ... RadLV

Radiation Level [*Nuclear energy*] ... RL
Radiation Level Indicator ... RLI
Radiation Management Corp. (NRCH) ... RMC
Radiation Material Corp. ... RMC
Radiation Measurement ... RM
Radiation/Meteoroid [*NASA satellite*] ... R/M
Radiation Monitor (NRCH) ... RM
Radiation Monitoring Equipment ... RME
Radiation Monitoring Satellite (IAA) ... RMS
Radiation Monitoring System [*Nuclear energy*] (NUCP) ... RMS
Radiation Office [*Environmental Protection Agency*] ... RO
Radiation Oncology [*Medicine*] (DMAA) ... RaONC
Radiation Oncology Administrators [*Later, SROA*] (EA) ... ROA
Radiation Oncology Services (MEDA) ... RA
Radiation Physics Laboratory [*National Institute of Standards and Technology*] (MCD) ... RPL
Radiation Polarization Measurement ... RPM
Radiation Pressure ... RP
Radiation Protection ... RP
Radiation Protection Committee [*South Australia*] ... RPC
Radiation Protection Design Features (NRCH) ... RPDF
Radiation Protection Guide [*AEC*] ... RPG
Radiation Protection Officer [*NASA*] (NASA) ... RPO
Radiation Protection Plan [*Nuclear energy*] (NRCH) ... RPP
Radiation Protection Standards (SAA) ... RPS
Radiation Reaction [*Cells*] [*Medicine*] ... RR
Radiation Recorder Controller (NRCH) ... RRC
Radiation Related Eosinophilia [*Medicine*] (AAMN) ... RRE
Radiation Research Associates, Inc. (NRCH) ... RRA
Radiation Research Society (EA) ... RRS
Radiation Resistance Cable ... RRC
Radiation Response ... RR
Radiation Retinopathy [*Ophthalmology*] ... RR
Radiation Safety Advisor [*British*] (NUCP) ... RSA
Radiation Safety Booklet (DNAB) ... RSB
Radiation Safety Officer [*Nuclear energy*] (NRCH) ... RSO
Radiation Sensitive [*Physiology*] ... RS
Radiation Shielding Computer Codes [*Database*] [*Oak Ridge National Laboratory*] [*Department of Energy*] [*Information service or system*] (CRD) ... RSC
Radiation Shielding Information Center [*Department of Energy*] [*Oak Ridge, TN*] ... RSIC
Radiation Shielding Information Data Base [*Oak Ridge National Laboratory*] [*Department of Energy Information service or system*] (CRD) ... RSI
Radiation Signature Measurement ... RSM
Radiation Source (NRCH) ... RS
Radiation Special Test Apparatus (IAA) ... RASTA
Radiation Spectral Visual Data Distribution (IAA) ... RSVP
Radiation Spectral Visual Photometer ... RSVP
Radiation Subprogramme Data Center [*Marine science*] (MSC) ... RSDC
Radiation Surveillance Network [*Public Health Service*] ... RSN
Radiation Survey Meter [*NASA*] ... RSM
Radiation Test Model ... RTM
Radiation Therapy (DAVI) ... Rad Ther
Radiation Therapy [*Medicine*] (MAE) ... RATx
Radiation Therapy (DAVI) ... RoRx
Radiation Therapy [*Medicine*] ... RT
Radiation Therapy (DAVI) ... RTx
Radiation Therapy Oncology Group (EA) ... RTOG
Radiation Therapy Technician ... RTT
Radiation Therapy Technologist (HCT) ... RADTT
Radiation Therapy Treatment Planning [*Medicine*] (DMAA) ... RTTP
Radiation Tracking Transducer ... RTT
Radiation Transfer Index ... RTI
Radiation Usage Factor (MCD) ... RUF
Radiation Weapon (AAG) ... RW
Radiation Weapons Analysis Systems Group (SAA) ... RWASG
Radiation Work Permit [*Nuclear energy*] (NRCH) ... RWP
Radiation-Anneal Hardening [*Alloy*] ... RAH
Radiation-Driven Low-Mass X-Ray Binary [*Cosmology*] ... RD-LMXB
Radiation-Hardened Interfacing Amplifier ... RHIA
Radiation-Hardened Power Supply ... RHPS
Radiation-Induced Color Halo [*Physics*] ... RICH
Radiation-Induced Surface Effect ... RISE
Radiation-Induced Thermally Activated Depolarization [*Radiation dosimetry technique*] ... RITAD
Radiation-Leukemia-Protection (MAE) ... RLP
Radiation-Resistant ... RR
Radiation-Resistant Linear Circuit ... RRLC
Radiation-Resistant Wire ... RRW
Radiation-Sensing Field Effect Transistor [*Instrumentation*] ... RADFET
Radiative Energy Attenuation [*Analytical chemistry*] ... REA
Radiative Transfer Equation ... RTE
Radiative-Convective Model [*Meteorology*] ... RCM
Radiative-Convective-Atmospheric [*Meteorology*] ... RCA
Radiative-Convective-Photochemical [*Meteorology*] ... RCP
Radiatively Important Trace Gas ... RITG
Radiatively Important Trace Species [*Program*] (USDC) ... RITS
Radiatively Important Trace Substances ... RITS
Radiatively-Active Trace [*Analytical chemistry*] ... RAT
Radiator (AAG) ... RAD
Radiator ... RADTR
Radiator (MSA) ... RDTR
Radiator Fan Timer Module [*Cooling systems*] [*Automotive engineering*] ... RFTM
Radica Games [*NASDAQ symbol*] (TTSB) ... RADAF
Radica Games Ltd. [*NASDAQ symbol*] (SAG) ... RADA
Radica Games Ltd. [*Associated Press*] (SAG) ... RadicaG
Radical ... R
Radical ... RAD
Radical (IDOE) ... rad
Radical (ROG) ... RADIC
Radical Alliance [*British*] ... RadA
Radical Alliance of Social Service Workers (EA) ... RASSW
Radical Alternatives to Prison [*British*] ... RAP
Radical and Intense [*Extremely great*] [*Slang*] ... R & I
Radical Caucus in Psychiatry (EA) ... RCP
Radical Education [*A publication*] ... Radical Ed
Radical Education Dossier [*A publication*] ... Radical Ed Dossier
Radical Education Project [*Students for a Democratic Society*] ... REP
Radical Force (EA) ... RF
Radical Liberal ... RADIC-LIB
Radical Mastectomy [*Medicine*] ... RM
Radical Neck Dissection [*Medicine*] ... RND
Radical Philosophy Society [*British*] ... RPS
Radical Proverbs [*A publication*] ... RP
Radical Science Information Service [*News service attempting to interrelate radical politics and scientific issues*] ... RSIS
Radical Women (EA) ... RW
Radicalist International [*Defunct*] (EA) ... RI
Radically Tapered Antenna ... RTA
Radicofani [*Italy ICAO location identifier*] (ICLI) ... LIQR
Radii of Standard Parallels ... RSP
Radikale Venstre [*Radical Liberals*] [*Denmark Political party*] (PPE) ... RV
Radio ... R
Radio (WDAA) ... RA
Radio (AAG) ... RAD
Radio (IDOE) ... rad
Radio ... RDO
Radio (AABC) ... RDO
Radio Access Point (MCD) ... RAP
Radio Acoustic Ranging ... RAR
Radio Acoustic Sounding System ... RASS
Radio Activity Detection, Identification and Computation (IAA) ... RADIAC
Radio Adaptive Communications ... RAC
Radio Administration Plenipotentiary Conference ... RAPC
Radio Advertising Bureau [*New York, NY*] (EA) ... RAB
Radio Advisory Committee [*Corporation for Public Broadcasting*] (NTCM) ... RAC
Radio Aeronautica Mexicana, Sociedad Anonima ... RAMSA
Radio Aeronautica Paraguaya Sociedad Anonima (RAPSA) [*Paraguay*] [*ICAO designator*] (ICDA) ... XP
Radio Affiliate Replacement Plan [*Canadian Broadcasting Corporation*] ... RARP
Radio Aids and Facilities (IAA) ... RAFAC
Radio Aids to Marine Navigation Committee [*British*] ... RAMNAC
Radio Aids Training Flight [*British military*] (DMA) ... RATF
Radio Air Play ... RAP
Radio Airborne Teletype (MCD) ... RATT
Radio Allocations Study Organization (NTCM) ... RASO
Radio Altimeter ... RA
Radio Altitude (IAA) ... RALT
Radio Amateur Civil Emergency Service [*Civil defense*] ... RACES
Radio Amateur Emergency Network (IEEE) ... RAEN
Radio Amateur Megacycle Society (IAA) ... RAMS
Radio Amateur Old Timers' Association [*British*] (BI) ... RAOTA
Radio Amateur Satellite Corp. (EA) ... AMSAT
Radio Amateur Telecommunications Society (EA) ... RATS
Radio Amateurs Emergency Network (EECA) ... RAYNET
Radio Amplification by Stimulated Emission of Radiation ... RASER
Radio Amplification of Gamma Emissions [*Antiguerrilla weapon*] ... RAGE
Radio and Communication Facilities Inoperative ... RACFI
Radio and Communications Facilities Operative (IAA) ... RACFO
Radio and Electronic Component Manufacturers Association (IAA) ... RECMFA
Radio and Electronic Component Manufacturers' Federation ... RECMF
Radio and Electronic Engineer (IAA) ... RADELECTENG
Radio and Electronic Officers' Union [*British*] (DCTA) ... REOU
Radio and Electronics Engineering Association (IAA) ... REEA
Radio and Electronics Measurements Committee [*London, England*] (DEN) ... REMC
Radio and Electronics World Telecommunications (NITA) ... REWTEL
Radio and Hobbies Australia [*A publication*] ... Radio Hobbies Aust
Radio and Microwave Systems [*British*] ... RMS
Radio and Panel Section [*Navy*] ... R & P SEC
Radio and RADAR ... R/R
Radio and Space Research Station [*Later, Appleton Laboratory*] [*British*] (MCD) ... RSRS
Radio and Teletype Control Center ... RATTC
Radio and Television (NADA) ... RTNA
Radio and Television Aids to Navigation ... RATAN
Radio and Television Dealers' Association ... RTDA
Radio and Television Directors Guild [*Later, DGA*] ... RTDG
Radio and Television Executives' Society [*Later, IRTS*] ... RTES
Radio and Television Executives Society (NADA) ... RTES
Radio and Television Manufacturers Association [*Later, EIA*] ... RTMA
Radio and Television Research Council (EA) ... RTRC
Radio and Television Retailers' Association (NADA) ... RTRA
Radio Annoyance Level (OA) ... RAL
Radio Antenna ... RA
Radio Area of Dominant Influence [*Advertising*] (DOAD) ... RADI
Radio Association Defending Airwave Rights (EA) ... RADAR
Radio Astronomical Space System of Aperture Synthesis (MCD) ... RASSAS
Radio Astronomy Experiment Selection Panel ... RAES

Radio Astronomy Explorer [*Satellite*] .... RAE
Radio Astronomy Laboratory [*Research center*] (RCD) .... RAL
Radio Astronomy Observatory [*University of Michigan*] [*Research center*] .... RAO
Radio Astronomy Observatory [*University of Texas at Austin*] [*Research center*] (RCD) .... UTRAO
Radio Astronomy Satellite (IAA) .... RAS
Radio Attenuation Measurement [*Spacecraft for testing communications*] .... RAM
Radio Attenuation Measurement Project .... RAMP
Radio Audience Measurement (NTCM) .... RAM
Radio Audizioni Italiana-Televisione [*Italian Radio Broadcasting and Television Company*] .... RAI-TV
Radio Authority [*Government regulatory agency*] [*British*] .... RA
Radio Automated Facsimile and Reproduction .... RAFAR
Radio Battalion [*Marine Corps*] .... RADBN
Radio Beacon .... R/B
Radio Beacon Array .... RBA
Radio Beacon Guidance System (AAG) .... RBGS
Radio Beacon Station (IAA) .... RBS
Radio Beam Communications .... RBC
Radio Beam Communications Set .... RBCS
Radio Bearing (DEN) .... RB
Radio Berlin International .... RBI
Radio Brenner [*Radio network*] [*Germany*] .... RB
Radio Broadcast Data Service (WDMC) .... RBDS
Radio Broadcast Data System .... RBDS
Radio Broadcasting Data System .... RBDS
Radio Bureau of Canada .... RBC
Radio/Cable Switching Integration System (MCD) .... RCSIS
Radio Canada International .... RCI
Radio Car [*British*] .... RC
Radio Caracas Television [*Venezuela*] (EY) .... RCTV
Radio Chemical Center [*British*] (BARN) .... RCC
Radio Club Amsterdam Dx Certificate (IAA) .... RCADXC
Radio Club of America (EA) .... RCA
Radio Club of America .... RCOA
Radio Code (WDAA) .... RC
Radio Code Aptitude Area [*Military*] .... RC
Radio Code Aptitude Test .... RCAT
Radio Code Test, Speed of Response [*Military*] .... RCTSR
Radio Collectors of America (EA) .... RCA
Radio Command [*or Control*] (KSC) .... R/C
Radio Command Guidance (AAG) .... RCG
Radio Command Guidance System (IAA) .... RCGS
Radio Command Linkage (AAG) .... RCL
Radio Command System .... RCS
Radio Common Carrier .... RCC
Radio Common Channels .... RCC
Radio Communication Supervisor (IAA) .... RS
Radio Communications (MCD) .... RADCOM
Radio Communications and Electronic Engineers Association .... RCEEA
Radio Communications Center .... RCC
Radio Communications Equipment .... RCE
Radio Communications Instruction (MUGU) .... RCI
Radio Communications Link [*FAA*] (TAG) .... RCL
Radio Communications Monitoring Association (EA) .... RCMA
Radio Communications Set .... RCS
Radio Communications System [*Military*] (CAAL) .... RCS
Radio Compass .... RC
Radio Compass Station (IAA) .... RCSTN
Radio Component Manufacturers' Federation (IAA) .... RCMF
Radio Component Standardization Committee [*British*] .... RCSC
Radio Components (IAA) .... RC
Radio Control [*British military*] (DMA) .... R/C
Radio Control Equipment [*FAA*] (TAG) .... RCE
Radio Control Models and Electronics [*A publication*] .... RCM and E
Radio Control Operator .... RCO
Radio Control Panel [*Aviation*] .... RCP
Radio Control System .... RCS
Radio Controlled .... RC
Radio Controlled Aircraft Society of New South Wales [*Australia*] .... RCASNSW
Radio Corporation of America (NASA) .... RCA
Radio Corp. of America Communications (MCD) .... RCAC
Radio Corp. of America, Communications Systems Division, Camden, NJ [*Library symbol Library of Congress*] (LCLS) .... NjCaRD
Radio Corp. of America, Electron Tube Division, Engineering Section, Lancaster, PA [*Library symbol Library of Congress Obsolete*] (LCLS) .... PLRCAE
Radio Corp. of America, Electronics Division, Harrison, NJ [*Library symbol Library of Congress*] (LCLS) .... NjHarR
Radio Corp. of America, Laboratories Division, Princeton, NJ [*Library symbol Library of Congress*] (LCLS) .... NjPRCA
Radio Corp. of America, Missile and Surface Radar Division, Moorestown, NJ [*Library symbol Library of Congress*] (LCLS) .... NjMorR
Radio Corp. of America Victor (IAA) .... RCAVIC
Radio Corp. of America, West Coast Missile & Surface RADAR Division, Van Nuys, CA [*Library symbol Library of Congress*] (LCLS) .... CVnRCAM
Radio Correspondents Association (IAA) .... RCA
Radio Council of America (NADA) .... RCA
Radio Counter-Measures [*British military*] (DMA) .... RCM
Radio Countermeasures and Detection (IAA) .... RACMD
Radio Data System [*Telecommunications*] .... RDS
Radio Data System - Traffic Management Channel .... RDS-TMC
Radio Data System - Traffic Message Channel [*Traffic and highway management*] (ECON) .... RDS-TMS
Radio Day (CET) .... RADAY
Radio Detection and Location .... RADAL
Radio Detection and Ranging .... RADAR
Radio Detector .... RD
Radio Determination Satellite Service [*Geostar Corp.*] .... RDSS
Radio Digital Distance Magnetic Indicator (MCD) .... RDDMI
Radio Digital System [*Telecommunications*] (TEL) .... RDS
Radio Digital Terminal [*Bell System*] .... RDT
Radio Direction and Track .... RADAT
Radio Direction Finder [*or Finding*] (AABC) .... RDF
Radio Direction Finder Station .... RDFSTA
Radio Direction Finding Station [*ITU designation*] (CET) .... RG
Radio Directors' Guild [*Defunct*] (IAA) .... RDG
Radio Display Service .... RDS
Radio Distribution and Control Equipment [*Aviation*] (DA) .... RDCE
Radio Distribution Point (IAA) .... RDP
Radio Doppler Inertial .... RDI
Radio Duties - Special .... RS
Radio, Electrical, and Television Retailers' Association [*British*] .... RETRA
Radio Electrical Artificer [*British military*] (DMA) .... REA
Radio Electrical Mechanic [*British military*] (DMA) .... REM
Radio Electrical Mechanician [*British military*] (DMA) .... REMN
Radio Electrician .... RE
Radio Electrician [*Navy British*] .... REL
Radio Electrician .... RELE
Radio Electronic Combat [*Communications*] .... REC
Radio Electronic News Gathering (NTCM) .... RENG
Radio Electronic Warfare Service (MCD) .... REWS
Radio Electronics Television School (IAA) .... RETS
Radio Emergency Associated Citizens Teams [*Acronym alone is now used as official association name*] (EA) .... REACT
Radio Emergency Search Communications Unit .... RESCU
Radio Engineering Laboratories .... REL
Radio Engineering Unit (IAA) .... REU
Radio Equipment (IAA) .... RE
Radio Equipment Department [*British military*] (DMA) .... RED
Radio Executives Club (NTCM) .... REC
Radio Expenditure Report [*A publication*] (DOAD) .... RER
Radio Exploration Satellite (PDAA) .... REX
Radio Exploration Satellite [*Japan*] .... REXS
Radio Exposure (AAG) .... RE
Radio Exterior Espana (EY) .... REE
Radio Facility .... RF
Radio Facility Charts (MCD) .... RFC
Radio Facility Control Officer [*Military*] (IAA) .... RFCO
Radio Finger Printing [*Identification of wireless radio operators by individual keying characteristics*] .... RFP
Radio France (IAA) .... RF
Radio Free Europe .... RFE
Radio Free Europe/Radio Liberty (EA) .... RFE/RL
Radio Free Kabul [*British Defunct*] (EAIO) .... RFK
Radio Free People [*An association Defunct*] .... RFP
Radio Free Women [*Defunct*] (EA) .... RFW
Radio Frequency (GAVI) .... rf
Radio Frequency [*Transmission*] .... RF
Radio Frequency/Acoustic Firing Group [*Military*] (CAAL) .... RF/AFG
Radio Frequency Allocation (MCD) .... RFA
Radio Frequency Amplifier .... RFA
Radio Frequency and Electromagnetic-Interference [*Telecommunications*] .... RF/EMI
Radio Frequency Attenuator (MCD) .... RFA
Radio Frequency Attitude Sensor .... RFAS
Radio Frequency Authorizations [*Air Force*] .... RFA
Radio Frequency Automatic Test Equipment (MCD) .... RFATE
Radio Frequency Cables; Bulk [*JETDS nomenclature*] [*Military*] (CET) .... RG
Radio Frequency Carrier Shift (NVT) .... RFCS
Radio Frequency Chart (AAG) .... RFC
Radio Frequency Checkout (AAG) .... RFCO
Radio Frequency Choke (AAG) .... RFC
Radio Frequency Coil (IAA) .... RFC
Radio Frequency Command Generator (MCD) .... RFCG
Radio Frequency Communications .... RFC
Radio Frequency Compatibility .... RFC
Radio Frequency Compatibility Program .... RFCP
Radio Frequency Component Cable Assemblies [*JETDS nomenclature*] [*Military*] (CET) .... CG
Radio Frequency Connectors [*JETDS nomenclature*] [*Military*] (CET) .... UG
Radio Frequency Control Monitor [*Formerly, RFU*] (MCD) .... RFCM
Radio Frequency Controller [*Telecommunications*] (ECII) .... RFC
Radio Frequency Crystal .... RFC
Radio Frequency Data Link (MCD) .... RFDL
Radio Frequency Demodulator .... RFD
Radio Frequency Display (MCD) .... RFD
Radio Frequency Equipment Analyzer .... RFEA
Radio Frequency Expandable Decoy (DWSG) .... RFED
Radio Frequency Fault Detection .... RFFD
Radio Frequency Filter .... RFF
Radio Frequency Finder (NVT) .... RFF
Radio Frequency Fuze .... RFF
Radio Frequency Generator .... RFG
Radio Frequency Hazard (IAA) .... RADHAZ
Radio Frequency Head (IAA) .... RFH
Radio Frequency Heating .... RFH
Radio Frequency Horn Technique .... RFHT
Radio Frequency Identification .... RFID
Radio Frequency Identification .... RFID
Radio Frequency Impedance Probe .... RFIP

Radio Frequency Indicator	RFI
Radio Frequency Induction [Of plasmas]	RFI
Radio Frequency Integrated Circuit	RFIC
Radio Frequency Integrated Circuit	RFIC
Radio Frequency Interchange (MDG)	RFI
Radio Frequency Interface (MCD)	RFI
Radio Frequency Interference	RFI
Radio Frequency Interference Meter	RFIM
Radio Frequency Interference Tests (KSC)	RFIT
Radio Frequency Joint	RFJ
Radio Frequency Laboratories	RFL
Radio Frequency Leakage Detector	RFLD
Radio Frequency Lens	RFL
Radio Frequency Liaison Office [Navy] (DNAB)	RAFLO
Radio Frequency Management (NOAA)	RFM
Radio Frequency Management Office (MCD)	RFMO
Radio Frequency Monitoring [Military] (CAAL)	RFM
Radio Frequency Noise	RFN
Radio Frequency Noise Analyzer (DNAB)	RFNA
Radio Frequency Oscillator	RFO
Radio Frequency Plasma	RFP
Radio Frequency Propagation Program (NG)	RFPP
Radio Frequency Pulse (MCD)	RFP
Radio Frequency Receiver	RFR
Radio Frequency Relay	RFR
Radio Frequency Rotary Joint	RFRJ
Radio Frequency Saturation (IAA)	RFSAT
Radio Frequency Seal	RFS
Radio Frequency Shielded Enclosure	RFSE
Radio Frequency Signal Management System [Aviation] (GFGA)	RFSMS
Radio Frequency Simulation System (MCD)	RFSS
Radio Frequency Spectrum Management (LAIN)	RFSM
Radio Frequency Subsystem [NASA]	RFS
Radio Frequency Surveillance/Electronic Countermeasures (MCD)	RFS/ECM
Radio Frequency Surveillance Subsystem	RFSS
Radio Frequency Systems Test Facility (KSC)	RFSTF
Radio Frequency Test Console	RFTC
Radio Frequency Test Facility [Oak Ridge National Laboratory]	RFTF
Radio Frequency Test Set (AABC)	RFTS
Radio Frequency Tracking [Military] (MCD)	RF-TK
Radio Frequency Transformer (IAA)	RFT
Radio Frequency Transmission Line	RFTL
Radio Frequency Unit [Later, RFCM] (MCD)	RFU
Radio Frequency Update Link	RFUDL
Radio Frequency Voltmeter	RFVM
Radio Frequency Wave	RFW
Radio Frequency Wave Form	RFWF
Radio Grenada	RGda
Radio Guidance (AAG)	RG
Radio Guidance Operation (DNAB)	RGO
Radio Guidance Surveillance and Automatic Tracking (AAG)	RGSAT
Radio Guidance System	RGS
Radio Guide (IAA)	RG
Radio Hanoi [North Vietnam radio programming which targeted US troops in South Vietnam] (VNW)	VNA
Radio Historical Society of America (NTCM)	RHSA
Radio Hong Kong	RHK
Radio in American Sector [of Berlin] (SAA)	RIAS
Radio Industry [Telecommunications] (IAA)	RI
Radio Industry Council [British]	RIC
Radio Industry Zagreb [Former Yugoslavia]	RIZ
Radio Inertial (MCD)	RI
Radio Inertial (MSA)	RIN
Radio Inertial Guidance (AAG)	RIG
Radio Inertial Guidance System	RIGS
Radio Inertial Missile Equipment	RIME
Radio Inertial Monitoring Equipment (KSC)	RIME
Radio In-Flight Correction	RIFC
Radio Influence	RI
Radio Influence Level	RIL
Radio Influence Voltage	RIV
Radio Information Distribution System (MCD)	RIDS
Radio Information Office [National Audience Board] (NTCM)	RIO
Radio Information Service (WDAA)	RIS
Radio Information Test	RIT
Radio Inspector	RI
Radio Intelligence [Military] (IAA)	RADINT
Radio Intelligence [Military] (IAA)	RDOINT
Radio Intelligence Division [of the Federal Communications Commission]	RID
Radio Intercept Officer (MCD)	RIO
Radio Interference (MCD)	RI
Radio Interference Field Intensity [Meter] (NG)	RIFI
Radio Interference Field Intensity Meter	RIFIM
Radio Interference Filter	RIF
Radio Interference Guard	RIG
Radio Interference Level	RIL
Radio Interference Measuring System	RIMS
Radio Interference Service [Department of Trade] [British]	RIS
Radio Interior Communications	RADIC
Radio Launch Control System (IEEE)	RLC
Radio Launch Control System	RLCS
Radio Liberty [Board for International Broadcasting]	RL
Radio Liberty Committee [Later, RFE/RL] (EA)	RLC
Radio Link (OA)	RL
Radio Linked Telemetry System	RLTS

Radio Logic Routing Interface Unit (MCD)	RLRIU
Radio Magnetic Deviation Indicator (AAG)	RMDI
Radio Magnetic Indicator	RMI
Radio Maintenance Unit (DEN)	RMU
Radio Management Control (MCD)	RMC
Radio Management Panel (GAVI)	RMP
Radio Manufacturers Association [Later, Electronic Industries Association]	RMA
Radio Marker (IAA)	RM
Radio Marker Beacon	RMB
Radio Marker Station	RMS
Radio Marketing Bureau [British] (CB)	RMB
Radio Marti [Cuba]	RM
Radio Mast	R MAST
Radio Material Office [or Officer] [Navy] (IEEE)	RMO
Radio Material Officer (MCD)	RM
Radio Materials Co. (IAA)	RMC
Radio Merchandise Sales (IAA)	RMS
Radio Message (IAA)	RM
Radio Monitor	RM
Radio Monte Carlo [Monaco] (EY)	RMC
Radio Motor Patrol [New York police cars]	RMP
Radio Nacional de Cabo Verde [National Radio of Cape Verde] (EY)	RNCV
Radio National [Australian Broadcasting Corp.]	RN
Radio Naval Association [British]	RNA
Radio Navigation [Military] (EECA)	R/NAV
Radio Navigation [USCG] (TAG)	RADNAV
Radio Navigation	RN
Radio Navigation Point [Military] (MCD)	RNP
Radio Navigational Aids (NATG)	RNA
Radio Navigational Warning (WDAA)	RNW
Radio Network for Inter-American Telecommunications	RIT
Radio New Zealand	RNZ
Radio Noise (IAA)	RN
Radio Noise Burst Monitor (MCD)	RNBM
Radio Noise Figure (CET)	RNF
Radio Noise Interference Test	RNIT
Radio Noise Voltage	RNV
Radio Noncontingent	RNC
Radio Note [Military]	RADNOTE
Radio of Free Asia (NTCM)	ROFA
Radio Officers Union [British]	ROU
Radio On-Scene Report (WDMC)	ROSR
Radio Operated Auto Racing	ROAR
Radio Operational Intercom System (KSC)	ROIS
Radio Operator [Navy]	RADOP
Radio Operator (AAG)	RADOPR
Radio Operator	RO
Radio Operator (General) 1st Class [British military] (DMA)	RO1(G)
Radio Operator (General) 2nd Class [British military] (DMA)	RO2(G)
Radio Operator/Maintenance Driver	ROMAD
Radio Operator (Warfare) 1st Class [British military] (DMA)	RO1(W)
Radio Operator (Warfare) 2nd Class [British military] (DMA)	RO2(W)
Radio Operator's Aptitude Test [Military]	ROA
Radio Operator's Aptitude Test [Military]	ROAT
Radio, Optical, Inertial	ROI
Radio Optical Observatory	ROO
Radio or Computer Operated Mobile Platform [Army]	ROCOMP
Radio Orchestra	RO
Radio Orient (IAA)	RO
Radio Paging Association [British] (DBA)	RPA
Radio Phone (DS)	RP
Radio Phone Unit [Navy]	RPU
Radio Physics Laboratory (IAA)	RPL
Radio Physics Research	RPR
Radio Planning Board [Navy]	RADPLANBD
Radio Position Finding [A term for RADAR before early 1942]	RPF
Radio Position Fixing System [Aviation] (DA)	RPFS
Radio Positioning Land Station [ITU designation] (CET)	PL
Radio Positioning Mobile Station [ITU designation] [Telecommunications] (CET)	PO
Radio Production Executive (IAA)	RPE
Radio Program Standard [Australian Broadcasting Tribunal]	RPS
Radio Projects Management Office	RPMO
Radio Propagation Forecast	RADPROPCAST
Radio Propagation Unit [Army] (MCD)	RPU
Radio Proximity Fuze	RPF
Radio Quadrangle [Military]	RADIQUAD
Radio Range	RNG
Radio Range	RR
Radio Range Beacon (IAA)	RRB
Radio Range Station [ITU designation] (CET)	RLR
Radio Range Station Reported Unreliable [Message abbreviation]	RARU
Radio Readout	RDO
Radio Receiver Set	RRS
Radio Receptor (IAA)	RR
Radio Receptor Co.	RRC
Radio Recognition	RR
Radio Recording Spectrophotometer	RRS
Radio Regulations	RR
Radio Relay [Military]	RADREL
Radio Relay (CINC)	RR
Radio Relay Aircraft (CET)	RRA
Radio Relay Center (NATG)	RRC
Radio Relay Link (NATG)	RRL
Radio Relay Message Unit [Telecommunications] (TEL)	MUR

Radio Relay Pod ... RRP
Radio Relay Squadron [*Military*] (IAA) ... RADRELRON
Radio Relay Squadron ... RRS
Radio Relay Squadron [*Military*] (IAA) ... RRSQ
Radio Relay Station ... RRS
Radio Relay System ... RRS
Radio Relay Terminal ... RRT
Radio Remote Set (CAAL) ... RRS
Radio Repairman (IAA) ... RADREPMN
Radio Republic Indonesia (IAA) ... RRI
Radio Republic South Africa (IAA) ... RRSA
Radio Republik Indonesia [*Radio network*] ... RRI
Radio Research ... RR
Radio Research and Development Establishment (MCD) ... RRDE
Radio Research Board (DEN) ... RRB
Radio Research Board. Report. [*Australia*] [*A publication*] ... RRB Rept
Radio Research Co. ... RRC
Radio Research Coordination Officer [*Air Force*] ... RRCO
Radio Research Laboratory ... RRL
Radio Research Station [*British*] ... RRS
Radio Research Unit [*Army*] (AABC) ... RRU
Radio Review of Australia [*A publication*] ... Radio Rev Aust
Radio Ripple Proximity (IAA) ... RRP
Radio School (IAA) ... RS
Radio Section (IAA) ... RADSEC
Radio Section (IAA) ... RDOSEC
Radio Security Service [*British*] ... RSS
Radio Service (IAA) ... RDOSTN
Radio Service Code (IAA) ... RAC
Radio Set (IAA) ... RS
Radio Set Control Group ... RSCG
Radio Shack Computer Alumni Association (EA) ... RSCAA
Radio Simulation Patch Panel (CET) ... RSPP
Radio Simulator ... RS
Radio Society of Great Britain [*Potters Bar, Hertfordshire, England*] (EAIO) ... RSGB
Radio Solar Telescope Network (MCD) ... RSTN
Radio Spectrum Measurement System [*National Telecommunications and Information Administration*] ... RSMS
Radio Squadron, Mobile [*Military*] (IAA) ... RADRONMOB
Radio Squadron Mobile (MUGU) ... RSM
Radio Standards Laboratory [*National Institute of Standards and Technology*] ... RSL
Radio Station ... RADSTA
Radio Station [*Coast Guard*] ... RASTA
Radio Station [*Maps and charts*] ... RS
Radio Subsystem ... RSS
Radio Supernovae [*Astrophysics*] ... RSN
Radio Supervisor [*British*] ... RS
Radio Supervisor (Special) [*British military*] (DMA) ... RS(S)
Radio Supervisor (Warfare) [*British military*] (DMA) ... RS(W)
Radio Switch Panel ... RSP
Radio Switchboard (CAAL) ... RS
Radio Symphony Orchestra ... RSO
Radio Tanzania Zanzibar ... RTZ
Radio Technical Commission for Aeronautics (EA) ... RTCA
Radio Technical Commission for Marine Services (IAA) ... RTCMS
Radio Technical Commission for Maritime [*or Marine*] **Services** (TSSD) ... RTCM
Radio Technical Committee for Aeronautics (NTCM) ... RTC
Radio Technical Committee for Maritime services ... RCTM
Radio Technical New Entrant [*Telecommunications*] (OA) ... RTNE
Radio Technician ... RT
Radio Technician Selection Test [*Military*] ... RTST
Radio Tecnica Colombiana ... RTC
Radio Telefis Eireann [*Radio and television network*] [*Ireland*] ... RTE
Radio Telegraph (MSA) ... RTLG
Radio Telegraph Station ... R Sta
Radio Telegraphy ... RATG
Radio Telegraphy (ADA) ... RT
Radio Telemetry ... RTel
Radio Telephone (MSA) ... RT
Radio/Telephone Network [*Nuclear energy*] (GFGA) ... R/T Net
Radio Telephone/Teleprinter (INF) ... RATT
Radio Telephony (NTCM) ... RT
Radio Telephony (MSA) ... RTEL
Radio Telescope in Orbit (IEEE) ... RATIO
Radio Telescope Network ... RTN
Radio Teletype (IEEE) ... RADIT
Radio Teletypewriter (CET) ... RADTT
Radio Teletypewriter (IAA) ... RATT
Radio Televisao Portuguesa [*Portuguese Radio-Television System*] ... RTP
Radio Television de Andalucia [*Spain*] (EY) ... RTVA
Radio Television Hong Kong ... RTHK
Radio Television Luxembourgeoise [*Radio Television Luxembourg*] [*French*] ... RTL
Radio Television Madrid [*Spain*] (EY) ... RTVM
Radio Television Malaysia ... RTM
Radio/Television Repair Program [*Association of Independent Colleges and Schools specialization code*] ... RT
Radio/Television Services [*Washington State University*] [*Pullman*] [*Telecommunications service*] (TSSD) ... RTVS
Radio Television Seychelles ... RTS
Radio Television Tunisien [*Tunisian Radio and Television*] (AF) ... RTT
Radio Thailand (FEA) ... RTH
Radio Thrust Misalignment ... RTM
Radio Tower ... R TR
Radio Tower (IAA) ... RT
Radio Tracking (KSC) ... RT
Radio Tracking System Analyst (MUGU) ... RTSA
Radio Trades Examination Board [*British*] (BI) ... RTEB
Radio Trans-Europe ... RTE
Radio Transmission Control (NATG) ... RTC
Radio Transmission Control Panel (NATG) ... RTCP
Radio Transmission Facility ... RTF
Radio Transmission Frequency Measuring System ... RTFMS
Radio Transmitter (IAA) ... RDOTRANS
Radio Transmitter ... RT
Radio Trunk Extension (NATG) ... RTE
Radio Tuned Circuit (DEN) ... RTC
Radio Vatican [*Vatican State*] (PDAA) ... RV
Radio Vehicle (DEN) ... RV
Radio Voice of the Gospel (DICI) ... RVOG
Radio Warfare Establishment [*British military*] (DMA) ... RWE
Radio Wave Propagation ... RWP
Radio Weather Intercept Element ... RAWIE
Radio Wholesalers Federation [*British*] (BI) ... RWF
Radio Wire Broadcasting Network ... RTS
Radio Wire Integration [*Military*] ... RWI
Radio Working Party ... RWP
Radio Writers' Guild [*Later, WGA*] ... RWG
Radioactinium [*Nuclear physics*] (WGA) ... RdAc
Radioactive ... RA
Radioactive ... RAACT
Radioactive ... RADA
Radioactive Argon Processing System (NRCH) ... RAPS
Radioactive Carbon [*Key substance for determination of age of objects by measurement of radioactivity*] ... C^{14}
Radioactive Decay Law ... RDL
Radioactive Dentin Abrasion [*Dentistry*] ... RDA
Radioactive Detection and Measurement ... RADIAC
Radioactive Drain Header [*Nuclear energy*] (NRCH) ... RDH
Radioactive Fallout Study Program [*Canada*] ... RFSP
Radioactive Gaseous Effluent Monitoring System ... RAGEMS
Radioactive Illuminated Fire Control (MCD) ... RIFC
Radioactive Interference [*NASA*] ... RAI
Radioactive Iodinate Human Serum Albumin [*Clinical chemistry*] (AAMN) ... RIHSA
Radioactive Iodinated Serum Albumin [*Scan or Study*] [*Medicine*] (DAVI) ... RISA
Radioactive Iodine [*Medicine*] ... RAI
Radioactive Iodine Uptake [*Medicine*] ... RIU
Radioactive Iron [*Chemistry*] (DAVI) ... FE^{59}
Radioactive Isotope [*Roentgenology*] ... RAI
Radioactive Isotope-Powered Pulse Light Equipment (IEEE) ... RIPPLE
Radioactive Isotopic Venogram, Bilateral [*Nuclear Medicine*] (DAVI) ... RAD ISO VENO BILAT
Radioactive Lead [*or* Pb^{210}] [*Radiology*] (DAVI) ... RaD
Radioactive Lighting Rod [*Nuclear energy*] (NRCH) ... RLR
Radioactive Liquid Waste (IEEE) ... RALW
Radioactive Material ... RAM
Radioactive Materials Committee [*National Science Foundation*] (NUCP) ... RMC
Radioactive Materials Packaging [*Nuclear energy*] ... RAMPAC
Radioactive Materials Reference Manual (NRCH) ... RMRM
Radioactive Mineral (MAE) ... R
Radioactive Phosphorus (DAVI) ... P 32
Radioactive Scrap and Waste Facility ... RSWF
Radioactive Sodium Chemistry Loop ... RSCL
Radioactive Thermoelectric Generator [*Nuclear energy*] (NRCH) ... RTG
Radioactive Uptake [*Medicine*] (DMAA) ... RAU
Radioactive Uptake [*Radiology*] (DAVI) ... RU
Radioactive Waste ... RADWASTE
Radioactive Waste Campaign (EA) ... RWC
Radioactive Waste Consultation Task Force [*National Science Foundation*] (NUCP) ... RWCTF
Radioactive Waste Management ... RWM
Radioactive Waste Management Advisory Committee ... RWMAC
Radioactive Waste Management Center ... RWMC
Radioactive Waste Management Site ... RWMS
Radioactive Waste Reduction [*Nuclear energy*] (NRCH) ... RWR
Radioactive Waste System [*Nuclear energy*] (NRCH) ... RWS
Radioactive Waste Treatment System [*Nuclear energy*] (NUCP) ... RTS
Radioactive Waste Vent [*Nuclear energy*] (NRCH) ... RWV
Radioactivity Concentration Guide (KSC) ... RCG
Radioactivity Decay Constant ... RDC
Radioactivity Detection ... RAD
Radioactivity Environmental Monitoring [*Information service or system*] (IID) ... REM
Radioallergosorbent Test [*Immunochemistry*] ... RAST
Radioantigen-Binding Assay [*Medicine*] ... RABA
Radio-Austria AG ... RADAUS
Radiobeacon [*Maps and charts*] ... RBN
Radiobeacon Calibration Transmitter ... RCT
Radiobinding Assay [*Analytical chemistry*] ... RBA
Radiobiological Research Unit (IEEE) ... RRU
Radiobiology ... RADBIOL
Radiobiology ... RADIOBIOL
Radiocardiogram ... RKG
Radiochemical Centre [*United Kingdom*] (NRCH) ... RCC
[*The*] **Radiochemical Centre** [*British*] ... TRC

Radiochemical Co., Atomic Energy of Canada Ltd., [*Societe Radiochimique, L'Energie Atomique du Canada Ltee.*], Kanata, Ontario [*Library symbol National Library of Canada*] (NLC) .... OKAER
Radiochemical Gamma Activation Analysis .... RGAA
Radiochemical Inspectorate [*British*] (NUCP) .... RCI
Radiochemical Neutron Activation Analysis .... RNAA
Radiochemical Processing Plant [*Oak Ridge National Laboratory*] .... RPP
Radiochemistry .... RADCHM
Radiochemistry .... RADIOCHEM
Radiochemistry and Nuclear Engineering Research Laboratory [*National Environmental Research Center*] .... RNERL
Radiocommunication Failure Message [*Aviation*] .... RCF
Radiocommunication Failure Message [*Aviation*] (WDAA) .... RCFM
Radiocontrast Media [*Clinical chemistry*] .... RCM
Radio-Controlled (IDOE) .... RC
Radio-Controlled Aerial Target [*Military*] .... RCAT
Radio-Controlled Boat (IAA) .... RCB
Radio-Controlled Improvised Explosive Device [*Criminology*] (LAIN) .... RCEID
Radio-Controlled Mine [*Military*] .... RCM
Radio-Controlled Miniature Aerial Target [*Military*] (MCD) .... RCMAT
Radio-Controlled Ultraviolet Measurement Program (MUGU) .... RUMP
Radiodiffusion-Television Belge [*Belgian Radio Broadcasting and Television System*] .... RTB
Radiodiffusion-Television Belge - Institut des Services Comuns [*Belgian Radio Broadcasting and Television - Common Services Institute*] .... RTBISC
Radiodiffusion-Television Congolaise [*Congolese Radio and Television*] (AF) .... RTC
Radiodiffusion-Television de Djibouti .... RTD
Radiodiffusion-Television du Senegal [*Radio and television network*] [*Senegal*] .... RTS
Radiodiffusion-Television Francaise [*French Radio Broadcasting and Television System*] .... RTF
Radiodiffusion-Television Gabonaise [*Gabonese radio and television network*] .... RTG
Radiodiffusion-Television Guineenne [*Guinean radio and television network*] .... RTG
Radiodiffusion-Television Ivoirienne [*Ivory Coast Radio and Television*] (AF) .... RTI
Radiodiffusion-Television (Upper Volta) [*Radio and television network*] .... RTV
Radiodifusao Portuguesa [*State Broadcasting Service*] .... RDP
Radiodifusion Argentina al Exterior [*Broadcasting organization*] [*Argentina*] .... RAE
Radio-Echo Sounding [*Geophysics*] .... RES
Radio-Eireann [*Eire*] [*Record label*] .... RE
Radioelectrocardiograph (IAA) .... RCG
Radioelectrocardiograph .... RECG
Radioelectrocomplexing [*Clinical chemistry*] (AAMN) .... REC
Radioelectroencephalograph .... REEG
Radioelectromyograph .... REMG
Radio-Electronics-Television Manufacturers Association [*Later, Electronic Industries Association*] .... RETMA
Radioelektronnaya Razvedka [*Reconnaissance and Intelligence*] [*Soviet counterintelligence*] (LAIN) .... RER
Radioelektronnaya Zashchita [*Radioelectronic Defense*] [*Soviet counterintelligence*] (LAIN) .... REZ
Radioelektronnoye Podavleniye [*Radio Electronic Suppression*] [*Soviet counterintelligence*] (LAIN) .... REP
Radioencephalogram .... REG
Radioenzymatic Assay [*Analytical biochemistry*] .... REA
Radio-Frequency Glow Discharge [*Materials science*] .... RFGD
Radio-Frequency LINAC (SDI) .... RFL
Radio-Frequency Quadrupole [*Accelerator for subatomic physics study*] .... RFQ
Radiofrequency Resonance Absorption (MCD) .... RRAS
Radio-Frequency Shift (IEEE) .... RFS
Radio-Gas Chromatography .... RGC
Radiogas Monitor [*Nuclear energy*] (NRCH) .... RGM
Radiogram .... RAD
Radiogram (DEN) .... RG
Radiographer [*British military*] (DMA) .... R
Radiographer (HCT) .... RAD
Radiographers Registration Board [*Tasmania, Australia*] .... RRB
Radiographic Baseline [*Medicine*] (DMAA) .... RBI
Radiographic Contrast Media [*Chemistry*] (DAVI) .... RCM
Radiographic Inspection [*NASA*] (AAG) .... RADI
Radiographic Test [*Nuclear energy*] (NRCH) .... RT
Radiography (IAA) .... RADIOG
Radio-High-Performance Liquid Chromatography .... RHPLC
Radioimmunoassay [*Clinical chemistry*] .... RIA
Radioimmunoassay Double Antibody [*Test*] [*Clinical chemistry*] .... RIA-DA
Radio-Immunoassay Double Antibody [*Immunology*] (DAVI) .... RIA-DA
Radioimmunoconjugate .... RIC
Radioimmunoelectrophoresis [*Biochemistry*] (DAVI) .... radio-IEP
Radioimmunoguided Surgery [*Medicine*] .... RIGS
Radioimmunoprecipitation [*Clinical chemistry*] .... RIP
Radioimmunoprecipitation Assay [*Clinical chemistry*] .... RIPA
Radioimmunosorbent Assay [*Clinical chemistry*] .... RISA
Radioimmunosorbent Technique [*or Test*] [*Clinical chemistry*] .... RIST
Radioimmunotherapy [*Medicine*] .... RAIT
Radio-Influence Field (IEEE) .... RIF
Radio-Interference-Free Instrument .... RIFI
Radioiodide Uptake [*Endocrinology*] .... RAIU
Radioiodinated Fatty Acid [*Medicine*] (MAE) .... RIFA
Radioiodinated Rose Bengal [*Medicine*] (MAE) .... RIRB
Radioiodinated Serum Albumin [*Medicine*] .... RISA
Radioiodinated Triolein [*Medicine*] (MAE) .... RIT

Radioisotope .... RI
Radioisotope Detection .... RID
Radioisotope Electrogenerator (IAA) .... REG
Radioisotope Field Support .... RIFS
Radioisotope Heater Unit (NASA) .... RHU
Radioisotope Medicine .... RIM
Radioisotope Method [*Analytical chemistry*] .... RIM
Radioisotope Power Device .... RPD
Radioisotope Power Packages for Electricity [*Nuclear energy*] (NUCP) .... RIPPLE
Radio-Isotope Power Supply [*or System*] [*Nuclear energy*] (NG) .... RIPS
Radioisotope Process Development Laboratory [*ORNL*] .... RPDL
Radioisotope Thermoelectric Generator .... RTG
Radioisotope Transport Loop [*Nuclear energy*] (NRCH) .... RTL
Radioisotope-Excited X-Ray Analyzer (PDAA) .... REXA
Radioisotope-Powered Cardiac Pacemaker (MCD) .... RPCP
Radioisotope-Powered Prolonged Life Equipment (IEEE) .... RIPPLE
Radioisotopic Pathology [*Medical specialty*] (DHSM) .... RIP
Radioisotopic Power Generator [*Navy*] .... RPG
Radioisotopic Sand Tracer [*Marine science*] (MSC) .... RIST
Radio-Keith-Orpheum [*Motion picture production and exhibition firm, also active in broadcasting*] .... RKO
Radiola [*Record label*] [*Australia*] .... Rad
Radio-Labeled Monoclonal Antiglobulin [*Clinical chemistry*] .... RMA
Radiolaria [*Quality of the bottom*] [*Nautical charts*] .... Rd
Radiola-Telefunken [*Record label*] [*Australia*] .... RadT
Radiolocation (IAA) .... R
Radiolocation (IAA) .... RIL
Radiolocation .... RL
Radiolocation Land Station [*ITU designation*] .... LR
Radiolocation Mobile Station [*ITU designation*] .... MR
Radiologic .... RADLGC
Radiologic Contrast-Induced Renal Failure [*Medicine*] (DMAA) .... RCIRF
Radiologic Technologist .... RT
Radiological [*or Radiology*] (AAG) .... RADL
Radiological .... RADLGCL
Radiological (IAA) .... RDGL
Radiological Accident and Incident Control .... RAIC
Radiological Advisory Council of Queensland [*Australia*] .... RACQ
Radiological Affairs Safety Committee (DNAB) .... RASC
Radiological Affairs Support Office [*Obsolete Navy*] .... RASO
Radiological and Chemical Support [*Nuclear energy*] (NRCH) .... R & CS
Radiological and Environmental Sciences Laboratory [*Nuclear energy*] (NRCH) .... RESL
Radiological Assessment Coordinator [*Nuclear energy*] (NRCH) .... RAC
Radiological Assessment Team [*Nuclear energy*] (NRCH) .... RAT
Radiological Assistance Plan [*AEC*] .... RAP
Radiological Center .... RADLCEN
Radiological Control [*Military*] (AABC) .... RADCON
Radiological Control Area (MCD) .... RCA
Radiological Control Center [*Army*] (KSC) .... RADCC
Radiological Control Center [*Army*] .... RCC
Radiological Control Practices Evaluation (MCD) .... RCPE
Radiological Control Program [*Nuclear energy*] (NRCH) .... RCP
Radiological Defense [*To minimize the effect of nuclear radiation on people and resources*] .... RADDEF
Radiological Defense [*To minimize the effect of nuclear radiation on people and resources*] .... RADEF
Radiological Defense [*To minimize the effect of nuclear radiation on people and resources*] .... RADLDEF
Radiological Defense [*To minimize the effect of nuclear radiation on people and resources*] .... RD
Radiological Defense Laboratory [*NASA*] .... RADLDEFLAB
Radiological Defense Laboratory [*NASA*] (KSC) .... RDL
Radiological Defense Officer [*Civil defense*] .... RDO
Radiological Defense Warning System .... RDWS
Radiological Effluent and Environmental Technical Specifications [*Nuclear Regulatory Commission*] (NRCH) .... REETS
Radiological Emergency Assessment Center [*National Science Foundation*] (NUCP) .... REAC
Radiological Emergency Assistance Team [*AEC*] .... REAT
Radiological Emergency Communications System [*Nuclear energy*] (NRCH) .... RECS
Radiological Emergency Medical Team [*Military*] (AABC) .... REMT
Radiological Emergency Plan [*Nuclear energy*] (NRCH) .... REP
Radiological Emergency Response Coordination [*Nuclear energy*] (NRCH) .... RERC
Radiological Emergency Response Operation [*Nuclear energy*] (NRCH) ..... RERO
Radiological Emergency Response Planning (NRCH) .... RERP
Radiological Environmental Monitoring Program [*Nuclear energy*] (NRCH) .... REMP
Radiological Environmental Technical Specifications [*Nuclear energy*] (NRCH) .... RETS
Radiological Fallout [*Army*] .... RADFO
Radiological Fallout [*Army*] (AABC) .... RADLFO
Radiological Health (KSC) .... RH
Radiological Health Data .... RHD
Radiological Health Data and Reports [*A publication*] .... RHD & R
Radiological Health Laboratory .... RHL
Radiological Information Plot (NATG) .... RIP
Radiological Monitor [*or Monitoring*] [*Military*] .... RADLMON
Radiological Monitoring (AFM) .... RADMON
Radiological Monitoring .... RAMONT
Radiological Monitoring Assessment Prediction System (PDAA) .... RADMAP
Radiological Monitoring for Instructors [*Civil Defense*] .... RMI
Radiological Monitoring System .... RMS

Radiological North Sea Project [*British*] RANOSP
Radiological Officer RADLO
Radiological Operations [*Military*] (AABC) RADLOPS
Radiological Physics Center [*National Cancer Institute*] RPC
Radiological Prediction Fallout Plot RADFAL
Radiological Protection Service (DEN) RPS
Radiological Release Information System (MCD) RRIS
Radiological Repair Barge [*Non-self-propelled*] [*Navy symbol*] YRR
Radiological Research Accelorator Facility [*Department of Energy*] RARAF
Radiological Safety [*Military*] RADLSAFE
Radiological Safety [*Military*] RADSAFE
Radiological Safety Analysis Computer (MCD) RSAC
Radiological Safety Office [*or Officer*] (NASA) RSO
Radiological Safety Review [*Nuclear energy*] (NRCH) RSR
Radiological Sciences Unit [*Medicine*] (DMAA) RSU
Radiological Service Training Institute (DMAA) RSTI
Radiological Society of North America (EA) RSNA
Radiological Survey [*Military*] RADLSV
Radiological Survey Officer [*Military*] RADLSO
Radiological Survey Officer (IEEE) RADSO
Radiological Systems Microfilm Associates (EA) RSMA
Radiological Warfare RADLWAR
Radiological Warfare RADWAR
Radiological Warfare RW
Radiological Warhead RW
Radiological Weapons RW
Radiological-Chemical-Biological Warfare RCBW
Radiologically-Controlled Radiation Area (DNAB) RCRA
Radiologist RAD
Radiologist, Anesthesiologist, and Pathologist (HCT) RAPS
Radiologist-General R-G
Radiologist-Pediatric R-P
Radiologists, Anesthesiologists, Pathologists, and Physiatrists RAPP's
Radiologists Business Managers Association (EA) RBMA
Radiology [*or Radiologist*] (ADA) R
Radiology (DAVI) RA
Radiology [*or Radiologist*] (ADA) RAD
Radiology Radiol
Radiology RADLGY
Radiology RADY
Radiology (IAA) RDGY
Radiology Information System [*Computer science*] RIS
Radiology Management System RMS
Radiology Technician [*or Technologist*] (AAMN) RTech
Radiology Technologist (Nuclear Medicine) (DAVI) RT(NM)
Radiology Telephone Access (DAVI) RTA
Radioluminescent RL
Radioman [*Navy rating*] RM
Radioman (DOMA) RM
Radioman, First Class [*Navy rating*] RM1
Radioman, Second Class [*Navy rating*] RM2
Radioman Telegrapher [*Telecommunications*] (IAA) RMT
Radioman, Third Class [*Navy rating*] RM3
Radiomaritime Telex Letter RTL
Radiometeorograph Observation (IAA) RAOBS
Radiometer (NASA) RDMTR
Radiometer Performance Factor RPF
Radiometer Recording Titration System [*Experimentation*] RRTS
Radiometer/Scatterometer [*Sensor*] [*Meteorology*] RADSCAT
Radiometric Age Data Bank [*Geological Survey*] [*Information service or system Defunct*] (IID) RADB
Radiometric Area Correlation Guidance RACG
Radiometric Area Correlator (MCD) RAC
Radiometric Contrast Matching (MCD) RADCOM
Radiometric Homing Level Gauge RHLG
Radiometric Microbiological Assay RMA
Radiometric Moon Tracer RMT
Radiometric Neutron Activation Analysis RNAA
Radiometric Sextant Subsystem RMS
Radiometric Sun Tracer RST
Radion Access Unit [*Army*] RAU
Radionavigation land station using two separate loop antennas, and a single transmitter, and operating at a power of 150 watts or more [*ITU designation*] (CET) RL
Radionavigation Land Test (PDAA) RLT
Radio-Navigation Mobile RNM
Radionavigation Mobile Station [*ITU designation*] (CET) RO
Radio-Newsreel-Television Working Press Association (EA) RNTWPA
Radionic Association (EA) RA
Radionuclear Applications Laboratory [*Pennsylvania State University*] [*Research center*] (RCD) RNAL
Radionuclide [*Radiology*] RN
Radionuclide Angiography [*Medicine*] RNA
Radionuclide Cerebral Angiogram [*Cardiology*] (DAVI) RCA
Radionuclide Hysterosalpingogram [*Medicine*] RN-HSG
Radionuclide Imaging of the Inferior Vena Cava [*Medicine*] (DMAA) RIVC
Radionuclide Migration RNM
Radionuclide Perfusion Lung Scan RPLS
Radionuclide Superior Cavography [*Medicine*] (DMAA) RNSC
Radionuclide Venography [*Clinical chemistry*] (AAMN) RNV
Radionuclide Ventriculography [*Medicine*] RNV
Radionuclide Ventriculography [*Medicine*] (DMAA) RNVG
Radionuclide Ventriculography [*Cardiology*] (CPH) RVG
Radioopaque RO
Radiopaque Contrast Material (WGA) ROM
Radiophare Omnidirectionnel [*Omnidirectional Radio Beacon*] (NATG) RPO
Radiopharmaceutical Internal Dose Information Center [*Oak Ridge, TN*] [*Department of Energy*] (GRD) RIDIC
Radio-Photo Luminescent [*Dosimetry*] RPL
Radioprom & Orfei (Bulgaria) [*Record label*] Bulg
Radio-Quebec, Montreal, PQ, Canada [*Library symbol Library of Congress*] (LCLS) CaQMRQ
Radioreceptor [*Assay method*] [*Clinical chemistry*] RR
Radioreceptor Assay [*Clinical chemistry*] RRA
Radio's All-Dimension Audience Research (NTCM) RADAR
Radiosensitivity Test (AAMN) RST
Radiosonde Analysis and Verification Unit RAVU
Radiosonde and RAWIN [*Radar Wind Sounding*] [*Combined method*] [*Marine science*] (OSRA) RAWINSONES
Radiosonde Balloon RABAL
Radiosonde Balloon Wind Data [*Meteorology*] (FAAC) RABAL
Radiosonde Data Processor (IAA) RDP
Radiosonde Observation RAOB
Radiosonde Observation RASONDE
Radiosonde Observation (MUGU) RSO
Radiosonde Observation Data RADAT
Radiosonde Observation Freezing Levels [*NWS*] (FAAC) RAFRZ
Radiosonde Observation Icing At [*NWS*] (FAAC) RAICG
Radiosonde Observation Not Filed [*NWS*] (FAAC) RAFI
Radiosonde Report Already Sent in PIBAL [*Pilot Balloon Observation*] **Collection** [*Aviation*] (FAAC) RAPI
Radiosonde Station [*ITU designation*] (CET) WXR
Radiosondes Shipped From (NOAA) RASSH
Radiospare (IAA) RS
Radiotelegram R
Radiotelegram [*or Radiotelegraph*] RATG
Radiotelegram Service (IAA) RS
Radiotelegraph RTG
Radiotelegraph Communication (IAA) RTC
Radiotelegraphy RT
Radiotelemetric Theodolite RTT
Radiotelemetry and Remote Control (MCD) RTRC
Radiotelemetry Subsystem RTS
Radiotelephone RATEL
Radiotelephone RT
Radiotelephone RTF
Radiotelephone Communication (IAA) RTC
Radiotelephone Communication (IAA) RTCOMN
Radio-Telephone (High Frequency) [*Telecommunications*] (DS) RTh
Radio-Telephone (Medium Frequency) [*Telecommunications*] (DS) RTm
Radiotelephone Operator (AABC) RATELO
Radiotelephone Operator RTO
Radiotelephone Operator Maintenance Proficiency (DNAB) ROMP
Radio-Telephone (Very-High Frequency) [*Telecommunications*] (DS) RTv
Radiotelephony R/T
Radioteleprinter (DA) RTT
Radioteletype RATT
Radioteletype (IAA) RTT
Radioteletype (IAA) RTTY
Radioteletypewriter RTT
Radioteletypewriter (IAA) RTTW
Radioteletypewriter RTTY
Radioteletypewriter Set RTS
Radio-Television Belge de la Communaute Culturelle Francaise [*Broadcasting organization*] [*Belgium*] (EY) RTBF
Radio-Television Correspondents Association (EA) RTCA
Radiotelevision Dominicana [*Dominican Radio and Television*] [*Dominican Republic*] RTVD
Radiotelevision Espanola [*Spanish*] RTVE
Radio-Television Malgache [*Malagasy Radio and Television*] (AF) RTM
Radio-Television Marocaine [*Moroccan Radio and Television*] (AF) RTM
Radiotelevision Murciana [*Spain*] (EY) RTVMU
Radio-Television Nationale Congolaise RTNC
Radio-Television Nationale du Burundi (EY) RTNB
Radio-Television News Directors Association (EA) RTNDA
Radio-Television Scolaire [*French*] RTS
Radio-Television Singapore RTS
Radiotelevision Valencia [*Spain*] (EY) RTVV
Radiotherapist (MAE) Rad
Radiotherapy RADIO
Radiotherapy (AAMN) RT
Radiotherapy Analog Dosimetry RANDO
Radiothermokeratoplasty [*Ophthalmology*] (DAVI) RTKP
Radiothorium [*Nuclear physics*] (WGA) RdTh
Radioulnar Synostosis [*Medicine*] (DMAA) RUS
Radio-Winds (USDC) RAWINS
Radio-Winds and Radiosondes (USDC) RAWINSONES
Radish Mosaic Virus [*Plant pathology*] RAMV
Radish Yellow Edge Virus [*Plant pathology*] RYEV
RadiSys Corp. [*Associated Press*] (SAG) RadiSys
RadiSys Corp. [*NASDAQ symbol*] (SAG) RSYS
Radium [*Chemical symbol is Ra*] (KSC) R
Radium [*Chemical element*] Ra
Radium [*Chemical symbol is Ra*] RAD
Radium [*Record label*] [*France*] Radi
Radium Emanation (WDAA) RA EM
Radium Emanation RE
Radium Plaque Adaptometer [*Navy*] RPA
Radium Plaque Adaptometer Operator [*Navy*] RPAO
Radium Therapy [*Clinical chemistry*] (MAE) RT

Radius [*Symbol*] [*IUPAC*] ... r
Radius (AAG) ... RAD
Radius (IDOE) ... rad
Radius (AAG) ... RADS
Radius, Inc. [*Associated Press*] (SAG) ... Radius
Radius, Inc. [*NASDAQ symbol*] (SAG) ... RDUS
Radius of Action (AAG) ... RA
Radius of Action (CAAL) ... ROA
Radius of Curvature ... ROC
Radius of Curvature of Flattest Meridian of Apical Cornea [*Ophthalmology*] (DAVI) ... K
Radius of Gyration (AAG) ... r
Radius of Landing Site [*NASA*] (KSC) ... RLS
Radius of Safety (MCD) ... RS
Radius of Suspension ... ROS
Radius Vector Subroutine ... RVS
Radius-Ulna [*Medicine*] (MAE) ... Rad Ul
Radix [*Root*] [*Latin*] ... RAD
Radix (IDOE) ... rad
Radix Complement [*Mathematics*] ... RC
Radix Institute (EA) ... RI
Radix Point ... RXP
Radix Teachers Association (EA) ... RTA
Radixin (DMAA) ... RDX
Radnor Township, PA [*FM radio station call letters*] ... WYBF
Radnorshire [*County in Wales*] (ROG) ... RAD
Radnorshire [*County in Wales*] ... RADN
Radnorshire [*County in Wales*] (ROG) ... RADNORS
Rado Reef Resources [*Vancouver Stock Exchange symbol*] ... RAO
RADOME [*RADAR Dome*] **Antenna** (NVT) ... RADANT
RADOME [*RADAR Dome*], Antenna, and Radio Frequency [*Array*] [*Electronics*] ... RARF
RADOME [*RADAR Dome*] **Antenna Structure** ... RAS
RADOME [*RADAR Dome*] **Test Equipment** ... RTE
Radon [*Chemical element*] ... Rn
Radon Action Program (GNE) ... RAP
Radon Progeny Integrating Sampling Unit (GNE) ... RPISU
RADs [*Radiation Absorbed Doses*] **per Hour** (DEN) ... r/h
Radula Sinus ... RAS
Radular Sac ... RS
Radular Teeth ... RT
RADWASTE [*Radioactive Waste*] **Area** [*Nuclear energy*] (NRCH) ... RWA
RADWASTE [*Radioactive Waste*] **Building** [*Nuclear energy*] (NUCP) ... RWB
RADWASTE [*Radioactive Waste*] **Disposal System** [*Nuclear energy*] (NRCH) ... RWDS
RADWASTE [*Radioactive Waste*] **Process Cell** [*Nuclear energy*] (NRCH) ... RWPC
RADWASTE [*Radioactive Waste*] **Sample Station** [*Nuclear energy*] (NRCH) ... RWSS
RADWASTE [*Radioactive Waste*] **Solidification Facility** [*Nuclear energy*] (NRCH) ... RWSF
RADWASTE [*Radioactive Waste*] **Work Permit** [*Nuclear energy*] (NRCH) ... RWP
Radway Public Library, Alberta [*Library symbol National Library of Canada*] (NLC) ... ARAD
Radway Public Library, Radway, AB, Canada [*Library symbol*] [*Library of Congress*] (LCLS) ... CaARad
Radyr Junction [*Cardiff*] [*Welsh depot code*] ... RYR
Raeford, NC [*AM radio station call letters*] ... WMFA
RAF Benson, FTU [*British*] [*FAA designator*] (FAAC) ... BSO
Raf-Avia [*Latvia*] [*ICAO designator*] (FAAC) ... MTL
Raffles and Bingo Permits Board [*Victoria, Australia*] ... RBPB
Raff's Pension Manual [*A publication*] (DLA) ... Raff Pens Man
Rafha [*Saudi Arabia*] [*ICAO location identifier*] (ICLI) ... OERF
Rafha [*Saudi Arabia*] [*Airport symbol*] (OAG) ... RAH
RAF-HQSTC (Air Transport) [*British ICAO designator*] (FAAC) ... RRR
Rafique and Jackson's Privy Council Decisions [*India*] [*A publication*] (DLA) ... R & J
Rafsanjan [*Iran*] [*ICAO location identifier*] (ICLI) ... OIKR
Rafter Input Converter ... RIC
Rag Chewers' Club [*Amateur radio*] ... RCC
Rag Shops [*NASDAQ symbol*] (TTSB) ... RAGS
Rag Shops, Inc. [*NASDAQ symbol*] (SAG) ... RAGS
Rag Shops, Inc. [*Associated Press*] (SAG) ... RagShp
Raga [*Sudan*] [*ICAO location identifier*] (ICLI) ... HSRJ
Ragado Fino Virus ... RFV
Ragan (Brad) [*AMEX symbol*] (TTSB) ... BRD
Ragan [*Brad*], Inc. [*AMEX symbol*] (SPSG) ... BRD
Ragan [*Brad*], Inc. [*Associated Press*] (SAG) ... Ragan
Ragent Bancshrs 10% Cv'A'Pfd [*NASDAQ symbol*] (TTSB) ... RBNKP
Ragged [*NWS*] (FAAC) ... RGD
Ragged Left [*Typesetting*] (WDMC) ... rl
Ragged Left [*Printing*] (WDMC) ... RL
Ragged Red Fibers [*Muscle pathology*] ... RRF
Ragged Right [*Typography*] (BARN) ... rr
Ragland's California Superior Court Decisions [*A publication*] (DLA) ... Rag
Ragland's California Superior Court Decisions [*A publication*] (DLA) ... Rag Super Ct Dec (Calif)
Ragocyte [*Medicine*] (DMAA) ... RA
Ragsdale Senior High School, Jamestown, NC [*Library symbol*] [*Library of Congress*] (LCLS) ... NcJRS
Ragtime Society (EA) ... RS
Ragweed [*Medicine*] (DMAA) ... RAG
Ragweed [*Immunology*] ... RW
Ragweed Antigen [*Immunology*] ... RA
Ragweed Antigen E [*Immunology*] ... RWAGE
Raha [*Indonesia*] [*Airport symbol*] (OAG) ... RAQ
Raha/Sugi Manuru [*Indonesia*] [*ICAO location identifier*] (ICLI) ... WAAR
Rahim Organizational Conflict Inventories [*Interpersonal skills and attitudes test*] ... ROCI
Rahimyar Kahn [*Pakistan*] [*Airport symbol*] (AD) ... RYK
Rahimyarkhan [*Pakistan*] [*ICAO location identifier*] (ICLI) ... OPRK
Rahmana Litslan (BJA) ... RL
Rahrump, NV [*FM radio station call letters*] (RBYB) ... KXTE-FM
Rahway Public Library, Rahway, NJ [*Library symbol Library of Congress*] (LCLS) ... NjRah
Rahway Valley R. R. [*AAR code*] ... RV
Raiatea [*French Polynesia*] [*Airport symbol*] (OAG) ... RFP
Raiatea/Uturoa [*French Polynesia*] [*ICAO location identifier*] (ICLI) ... NTTR
Raibarelli/Fursatganj [*India*] [*ICAO location identifier*] (ICLI) ... VIRB
Raichur [*India*] [*ICAO location identifier*] (ICLI) ... VORR
RAID Assessment Mode (MCD) ... RAM
Raid Plotter ... RP
Raid/Reconnaissance Exercise [*Military*] (NVT) ... RECONEX
Raid Size Estimate ... RSE
Raider ... RDR
Raiding Squadron Royal Marines [*British military*] (DMA) ... RSRM
Raiding Support Regiment [*British Royal Marines*] [*World War II*] ... RSR
Rail (MSA) ... R
Rail (AAG) ... RL
Rail Air International Service (PDAA) ... RAIS
Rail and Canal ... R & C
Rail and Lake ... R & L
Rail and Ocean ... R & O
Rail and Water [*Shipping*] ... R & W
Rail and Water [*Shipping*] ... RW
Rail Archaeological Research Effort [*An association*] ... RARE
Rail Armed Guard Escort Service [*Military Traffic Management Command*] ... RAGES
Rail, Automatic Straightening, Intrinsically Controlled [*Railroad maintenance device*] [*British*] ... RASTIC
Rail, Canal, and Lake [*Transportation*] ... RC & L
Rail Cost Adjustment Factor [*Interstate Commerce Commission*] ... RCAF
Rail Diesel Car ... RDC
Rail Discharge Point Jet (NATG) ... RDPJ
Rail Discharge Point Mogas (NATG) ... RDPM
Rail Dynamics Laboratory ... RDL
Rail Gun Armature Plasma Investigation Device (PDAA) ... RAPID
Rail, Lake, and Rail ... RL & R
Rail Loading Point (NATG) ... RLP
Rail Mail Steamer ... RMS
Rail Makers' Association [*British*] (BI) ... RMA
Rail, Maritime, and Transport Union [*British*] (ECON) ... RMT
Rail Operations Center [*MTMC*] (TAG) ... ROC
Rail Rapid Transit [*TXDOT*] (TAG) ... RRT
Rail Security Service [*MTMC*] (TAG) ... RSS
Rail Services Planning Office [*Interstate Commerce Commission*] ... RSPO
Rail Steel Bar Association [*Later, SMA*] (EA) ... RSBA
Rail Surveillance Service [*Military Traffic Management Command*] ... RSS
Rail Tractor [*British*] ... RT
Rail Transfer System (KSC) ... RTS
Rail Transit [*BTS*] (TAG) ... RT
Rail Transport ... RT
Rail Transportation Officer [*Military*] ... RTO
Rail Travel Authorization [*Military*] ... RTA
Rail Travel Promotion Agency [*Defunct*] (EA) ... RTPA
RailAmerica, Inc. [*NASDAQ symbol*] (SAG) ... RAIL
RailAmerica, Inc. [*Associated Press*] (SAG) ... RailAm
RailAmerica Inc. Wrrt 'B' [*NASDAQ symbol*] (TTSB) ... RAILZ
Rail-Borne Crane [*British*] ... RBC
Railcar (MSA) ... RLCR
Railhead [*British military*] (DMA) ... RH
Railhead ... RHD
Railhead Officer [*Military Obsolete*] ... RHO
Railhead Ordnance Officer ... ROO
Railing (AAG) ... RLG
Railroad [*or Railway*] ... R
Railroad ... RR
Railroad ... RR
Railroad Accident/Incident Reporting System [*Department of Transportation*] ... RAIRS
Railroad Advancement through Information and Law Foundation ... RAIL
Railroad and Airline Wage Board [*Terminated, 1953*] ... RAWB
Railroad Bond [*Business term*] (MHDW) ... RB
Railroad Communication System ... RRCS
Railroad Construction and Maintenance Association [*Later, NRC/MAI*] (EA) ... RCMA
Railroad Crossing [*Telecommunications*] (TEL) ... RRX
Railroad Data Center [*Association of American Railroad*] (PDAA) ... RRDC
Railroad Employees' Department [*of AFL-CIO*] ... RED
Railroad Enthusiasts (EA) ... RRE
Railroad Equipment Trust Certificate ... RETC
Railroad Evangelistic Association (EA) ... REA
Railroad Financial Corp. [*Associated Press*] (SAG) ... RailFn
Railroad Freight Classification ... RFC
Railroad Inspection Reporting System [*BTS*] (TAG) ... RIRS
Railroad Insurance Association ... RIA
Railroad Insurance Underwriters [*Later, RTI*] (EA) ... RIU
Railroad Interdiction Mine [*DoD*] ... RIM
Railroad Labor Board Decisions [*A publication*] (DLA) ... RLB Dec
Railroad Operations Computer Simulation [*FTA*] (TAG) ... ROCSIM
Railroad Operations Control System (PDAA) ... ROCS

Railroad Public Relations Association (EA) .... RPRA
Railroad Record Club [*Commercial firm*] (EA) .... RRC
Railroad Reports [*A publication*] (DLA) .... RR Rep
Railroad Reports [*United States*] [*A publication*] (DLA) .... RRR
Railroad Research Information Service [*National Academy of Sciences*] [*Defunct*] .... RRIS
Railroad Retirement Act (GFGA) .... RRA
Railroad Retirement Board .... RRB
Railroad Retirement Tax [*IRS*] .... RRT
Railroad Retirement Tax [*IRS*] .... RRTA
Railroad Revitalization and Regulatory Reform Act [*1976*] .... RRRR
Railroad, Revitalization and Regulatory Reform Act of 1976 (AAGC) 4RAct
Railroad Station (VRA) .... RR sta
Railroad Station Historical Society (EA) .... RSHS
Railroad Telegraphers Union .... RTU
Railroad Transport (NATG) .... RRT
Railroad Transportation Insurers [*Defunct*] (EA) .... RTI
Railroad Tunnel [*Board on Geographic Names*] .... TNLR
Railroad Unemployment Insurance Act (GFGA) .... RUIA
Railroad Yardmasters of America (EA) .... RYA
Railroad Yardmasters of North America [*Absorbed by RYA*] (EA) .... RYNA
Railroadiana Collectors Association Inc. (EA) .... RCAI
Railroadians of America (EA) .... RROA
Railroads for National Defense [*MTMC*] (TAG) .... RND
Rails-to-Trails Conservancy (EA) .... RTC
Railtex, Inc. [*Associated Press*] (SAG) .... Railtex
Railtex, Inc. [*NASDAQ symbol*] (SAG) .... RTEX
Railton Owners Club (EA) .... ROC
Rail-Water [*Shipping*] .... RAWA
Rail-Water-Rail [*Shipping*] .... RAWARA
Rail-Water-Rail [*Shipping*] .... R-W-R
Railway (ROG) .... RAIL
Railway (AAG) .... RLWY
Railway .... RLWY
Railway .... RLY
Railway .... RW
Railway .... RWY
Railway (AFIT) .... RY
Railway Abidjan-Niger .... RAN
Railway Accounting Officers Association [*Later, AAR*] .... RAOA
Railway and Airline Supervisors Association [*AFL-CIO*] .... RASA
Railway and Canal Cases [*1835-55*] [*England*] [*A publication*] (DLA) .... NH & C
Railway and Canal Cases [*England*] [*A publication*] (DLA) .... R & C Ca
Railway and Canal Cases [*England*] [*A publication*] (DLA) .... R & C Cas
Railway and Canal Cases [*England*] [*A publication*] (DLA) .... R & Can Cas
Railway and Canal Cases [*1835-54*] [*A publication*] (DLA) .... R & CC
Railway and Canal Cases [*1835-54*] [*A publication*] (DLA) .... Rail Ca
Railway and Canal Cases [*England*] [*A publication*] (DLA) .... RR & Can Cas
Railway and Canal Cases [*1835-54*] [*A publication*] (DLA) .... RR & Cn Cas
Railway and Canal Cases [*England*] [*A publication*] (DLA) .... Ry & C Cas (Eng)
Railway and Canal Cases [*England*] [*A publication*] (DLA) .... Ry & Can Cas
Railway and Canal Historical Society [*British*] (BI) .... RCHS
Railway and Canal Traffic Cases [*England*] [*A publication*] (DLA) .... R & Can Tr
Railway and Canal Traffic Cases [*England*] [*A publication*] (DLA) .... R & Can Tr Cas
Railway and Canal Traffic Cases [*A publication*] (DLA) .... Rail & Can Cas
Railway and Canal Traffic Cases [*England*] [*A publication*] (DLA) .... Ry & C Traffic Cas (Eng)
Railway and Canal Traffic Cases [*A publication*] (DLA) .... Ry & Can Traf Ca
Railway and Canal Traffic Cases [*England*] [*A publication*] (DLA) .... Ry & Can Traffic Cas
Railway and Canal Traffic Cases (Neville) [*England*] [*A publication*] (DLA) .... R & C Tr Cas
Railway and Corporation Law Journal [*A publication*] (DLA) .... Railway & Corp Law J
Railway and Corporation Law Journal [*A publication*] (DLA) .... Ralw & Corp LJ
Railway and Corporation Law Journal [*A publication*] (DLA) .... Ry & Corp Law J
Railway and Corporation Law Journal [*A publication*] (DLA) .... Ry & Corp Law Jour
Railway and Corporation Law Journal [*A publication*] (DLA) .... Ry Corp Law Jour
Railway and Industrial Spring Association [*Later, RISRI*] .... RISA
Railway and Industrial Spring Research Institute [*Defunct*] (EA) .... RISRI
Railway and Locomotive Historical Society (EA) .... RLHS
Railway Association of Canada, Montreal, PQ, Canada [*Library symbol Library of Congress*] (LCLS) .... CaQMRA
Railway Association of Canada, Montreal, Quebec [*Library symbol National Library of Canada*] (NLC) .... QMRA
Railway Automotive Management Association [*Defunct*] (EA) .... RAMA
Railway Benevolent Institution [*British*] .... RBI
Railway, Canal, and Road Traffic Cases [*A publication*] (DLA) .... Traff Cas
Railway Cases [*A publication*] (DLA) .... Rail Cas
Railway Cases [*A publication*] (DLA) .... Railw Cas
Railway Cases [*A publication*] (DLA) .... RC
Railway Commission of Canada (DLA) .... Can RC
Railway Construction Engineer [*British military*] (DMA) .... RCE
Railway Correspondence and Travel Society [*British*] .... RCTS
Railway Development Association [*British*] .... RDA
Railway Development Society [*British*] (DBA) .... RDS
Railway Dock and Marine Grades Association [*A union*] [*British*] .... RDMGA
Railway Electric Supply Manufacturers Association [*Later, RSA*] .... RESMA
Railway Electrical and Mechanical Supply Association (IAA) .... REMSA
Railway Employers' Association Defence League [*British*] .... READL
Railway Engineering Maintenance Suppliers Association (EA) .... REMSA
Railway Enthusiasts' Club [*British*] (BI) .... REC
Railway Equipment and Publication Co., The, New York NY [*STAC*] .... REP
Railway Equipment Register .... RER
Railway Executive [*British*] .... RE
Railway Executive Committee [*British*] .... REC
Railway Express Agency [*Later, REA Express*] [*Defunct*] .... REA
Railway Fuel and Operating Officers Association [*Later, IAROO*] (EA) .... RF & OOA
Railway Inclusive Tour (DCTA) .... RIT
Railway Industry Association [*British*] (EAIO) .... RIA
Railway Industry Clearance Association (EA) .... RICA
Railway Information Bureau .... RIB
Railway Insurance Rating Bureau [*Defunct*] (EA) .... RIRB
Railway Invigoration Society [*British*] (BI) .... RIS
Railway Labor Executives' Association (EA) .... RLEA
Railway Labor's Political League .... RLPL
Railway Mail Service .... RMS
Railway Museum, Cranbrook, British Columbia [*Library symbol National Library of Canada*] (NLC) .... BCRR
Railway Museum of New South Wales [*Australia*] .... RMNSW
Railway Office [*British*] (ROG) .... RO
Railway Operating Department [*British military*] (DMA) .... ROD
Railway Patrolmen's International Union [*Later, BRAC*] (EA) .... RPU
Railway Pioneer Regiment [*British military*] (DMA) .... RPR
Railway Post Office .... RPO
Railway Preservation Society of Ireland (BI) .... RPSI
Railway Progress Institute (EA) .... RPI
Railway Security Agency [*South Vietnam government security*] (VNW) .... RSA
Railway Services Unit [*MTMC*] (TAG) .... RSU
Railway Signal and Communications Suppliers Association [*Later, RSS*] (EA) .... RSCSA
Railway Sorting Office .... RSO
Railway Station (ROG) .... RS
Railway Station Police Officer [*British*] .... RSPO
Railway Stations [*Public-performance tariff class*] [*British*] .... RYS
Railway Suboffice .... RSO
Railway Supervisors Association (NADA) .... RSA
Railway Supply Association (EA) .... RSA
Railway Supply Manufacturers Association [*Defunct*] (EA) .... RSMA
Railway Systems and Management Association [*Defunct*] (EA) .... RSMA
Railway Systems and Procedures Association [*Later, RSMA*] .... RSPA
Railway Systems Suppliers (EA) .... RSS
Railway Systems Suppliers (EA) .... RSSI
Railway Tank Wagon [*British military*] (DMA) .... RTW
Railway Telegraph and Telephone Appliance Association .... RTTAA
Railway Tie Association (EA) .... RTA
Railway Traffic Officer [*Military*] .... RTO
[*The*] **Railway Transfer Co. of the City of Minneapolis** [*AAR code*] .... RTM
Railway Transport Establishment [*British military*] (DMA) .... RTE
Railway Transportation Directorate, Transport Canada [*Direction du Transport Ferroviaire, Transports Canada*] **Ottawa, Ontario** [*Library symbol National Library of Canada*] (NLC) .... OOTRT
Railway Tyre and Axle Manufacturers Association [*British*] (BI) .... RTAMA
Railway Underwriter .... RU
Railway Wheel Association [*Defunct*] (EA) .... RWA
Railwaymen's Union of Malaya .... RUM
Rain [*Meteorology*] .... R
Rain [*ICAO*] (FAAC) .... RA
Rain and Hail Insurance Bureau [*Defunct*] (EA) .... RHIB
Rain and Snow [*Sleet*] [*Meteorology*] .... RASN
Rain and Snow [*Sleet*] [*Meteorology*] .... RS
Rain Erosion Coating .... REC
Rain Erosion Seed Test .... REST
Rain in Area (ADA) .... RIA
Rain Repellant and Surface Conditioner (PDAA) .... REPCON
Rain Showers [*Meteorology*] .... RASH
Rain Showers [*ICAO*] (FAAC) .... SHRA
Rain Umbrella [*An association*] (EA) .... RU
Rainbow .... RNBW
Rainbow Bridge National Monument .... RABR
Rainbow Cargo Express [*Ghana*] [*ICAO designator*] (FAAC) .... RBO
Rainbow City, AL [*AM radio station call letters*] .... WJBY
Rainbow Coalition [*Named for the 1984 political campaign of Rev. Jesse Jackson*] [*Later, NRCI*] (EA) .... RC
Rainbow Darter [*Ichthyology*] .... Rd
Rainbow Group [*Party group in the European Parliament*] (ECED) .... ARC
Rainbow Group [*European political movement*] (ECON) .... RBW
Rainbow Lake [*Canada*] [*Airport symbol*] (OAG) .... YOP
Rainbow Lake Municipal Library, Alberta [*Library symbol National Library of Canada*] (NLC) .... ARLM
Rainbow Lake Municipal Library, Rainbow Lake, AB, Canada [*Library symbol*] [*Library of Congress*] (LCLS) .... CaARIM
Rainbow Monument [*Utah*] [*Seismograph station code, US Geological Survey*] (SEIS) .... RMU
Rainbow Network Communications [*Floral Park, NY*] [*Telecommunications*] (TSSD) .... RNC
Rainbow Optical Landing System (PDAA) .... ROLS
Rainbow Technologies [*NASDAQ symbol*] (TTSB) .... RNBO
Rainbow Technologies, Inc. [*Associated Press*] (SAG) .... RainTc
Rainbow Technologies, Inc. [*NASDAQ symbol*] (NQ) .... RNBO
Rainbow Trout .... RBT
Rainbows for All God's Children [*Later, RFAGC*] (EA) .... RAGC
Rainbows for All God's Children (EA) .... RFAGC
Rainelle, WV [*Location identifier FAA*] (FAAL) .... RNL
Rainelle, WV [*FM radio station call letters*] (RBYB) .... WRLB-FM
Rainelle, WV [*AM radio station call letters*] .... WRRL
Rainelle, WV [*FM radio station call letters*] .... WRRL-FM
Rainer Foundation [*British*] (BI) .... RF
Rainerius [*Authority cited in pre-1607 legal work*] (DSA) .... Ra

Rainerius [*Authority cited in pre-1607 legal work*] (DSA) .... Rai
Rainerius [*Authority cited in pre-1607 legal work*] (DSA) .... Re
Rainerius de Forlivio [*Deceased, 1358*] [*Authority cited in pre-1607 legal work*] (DSA) .... Rane
Rainex Industries [*Formerly, Rainex Resources Ltd.*] [*Vancouver Stock Exchange symbol*] .... RXR
Rainfall [*NWS*] (FAAC) .... RNFL
Rainfed [*Agriculture*] .... RF
Rainforest Action Group [*Australia*] .... RAG
Rainforest Action Network (EA) .... RAN
Rainforest Alliance (EA) .... RA
Rainforest Cafe [*NASDAQ symbol*] (TTSB) .... RAIN
Rainforest Cafe, Inc. [*NASDAQ symbol*] (SAG) .... RAIN
Rainforest Cafe, Inc. [*Associated Press*] (SAG) .... RainCfe
Rainforest Foundation Australia .... RFA
Rainforest Information Centre [*Australia*] (EAIO) .... RIC
Rainform (MCD) .... RF
Rainform Compressed (MCD) .... RC
Rainform Expanded (MCD) .... RE
Rainform Message Processing (MCD) .... RMP
Rainier Energy Resources [*Vancouver Stock Exchange symbol*] .... RNY
Rainier School, Resident Library, Buckley, WA [*Library symbol Library of Congress*] (LCLS) .... WaBucR-R
Rainier School, Staff Library, Buckley, WA [*Library symbol Library of Congress*] (LCLS) .... WaBucR
Rainsville, AL [*AM radio station call letters*] .... WVSM
Raintight (MSA) .... RT
Rainwater Conductor (AAG) .... RWC
Rainwater Head .... RWH
Rainwater Pipe [*Construction*] .... RWP
Rainy River Community College, International Falls, MN [*Library symbol Library of Congress*] (LCLS) .... MnIfRC
Rainy River Community College, International Falls, MN [*OCLC symbol*] (OCLC) .... RRC
Rainy River Public Library, Ontario [*Library symbol National Library of Canada*] (NLC) .... ORAR
Raipur [*India*] [*Airport symbol*] (OAG) .... RPR
Raipur [*India*] [*ICAO location identifier*] (ICLI) .... VARP
Raise (AAG) .... RA
Raise Head of the Bed [*Medicine*] (DAVI) .... RHB
Raise Top (OA) .... RT
Raise-Bottom-Slightly [*Definition of a gentleman*] [*Slang British*] (DI) .... RBS
Raised (MSA) .... RSD
Raised Afterdeck [*of a ship*] (DS) .... RAD
Raised Black Letters [*Automobile tires*] .... RBL
Raised Deck [*of a ship*] (DS) .... R dk
Raised Face (MSA) .... RF
Raised Face Diameter (MSA) .... RFD
Raised Face Height (MSA) .... RFH
Raised Foredeck [*of a ship*] (DS) .... RFD
Raised Oil-Tight Manhole [*Shipfitting*] .... ROTMH
Raised Pavement Marker [*Highway design*] .... RPM
Raised Quarter Deck [*of a ship*] (DS) .... RQD
Raised Ranch [*Architecture*] (BARN) .... RR
Raised Shelter Deck (DS) .... RSD
Raised White Letters [*Tire design*] [*Automotive engineering*] .... RWL
Raisin Administrative Committee (EA) .... RAC
Raisin Bargaining Association (EA) .... RBA
Raising Achievements in Mathematics Project (AIE) .... RAMP
Raithby's English Statutes at Large [*A publication*] (DLA) .... Raith St
Raithby's Study of the Law [*A publication*] (DLA) .... Raith St
Rajahmundry [*India*] [*ICAO location identifier*] (ICLI) .... VORY
Rajaratam Revised Reports [*Ceylon*] [*A publication*] (DLA) .... Raj
Rajasthan Law Weekly [*India*] [*A publication*] (DLA) .... RLW
Rajasthani [*MARC language code Library of Congress*] (LCCP) .... raj
Rajawali Citra Televisi Indonesia (EY) .... RCTI
Rajbiraj [*Nepal*] [*Airport symbol Obsolete*] (OAG) .... RJB
Rajbiraj [*Nepal*] [*ICAO location identifier*] (ICLI) .... VNRB
Raji Airlines [*Pakistan*] [*ICAO designator*] (FAAC) .... RAJ
Rajkot [*India*] [*Airport symbol*] (OAG) .... RAJ
Rajkot [*India*] [*ICAO location identifier*] (ICLI) .... VARK
Rajneesh Foundation International (EA) .... RFI
Rajshahi [*Bangladesh*] [*Airport symbol*] (AD) .... RJH
Rajshahi [*Bangladesh*] [*ICAO location identifier*] (ICLI) .... VGRJ
Rakahanga [*Cook Islands*] [*ICAO location identifier*] (ICLI) .... NCRK
Rake Out, Wedge, and Point Flashings [*Construction*] .... ROW & PF
Rake Public Library, Rake, IA [*Library symbol Library of Congress*] (LCLS) .... IaRa
Rakhov [*Former USSR Seismograph station code, US Geological Survey Closed*] (SEIS) .... RAK
Rakops [*Botswana*] [*ICAO location identifier*] (ICLI) .... FBRK
RAL Marketing Group, Inc. [*Vancouver Stock Exchange symbol*] .... RMG
Ralcorp Holdings [*NYSE symbol*] (SAG) .... RAH
Ralcorp Holdings [*Associated Press*] (SAG) .... Ralcorp
Raleigh [*Diocesan abbreviation*] [*North Carolina*] (TOCD) .... R
Raleigh/Durham [*North Carolina*] [*Airport symbol*] .... RDU
Raleigh Energy [*Vancouver Stock Exchange symbol*] .... RLE
Raleigh Flying Service, Inc. [*ICAO designator*] (FAAC) .... RFA
Raleigh, NC [*Location identifier FAA*] (FAAL) .... LEI
Raleigh, NC [*AM radio station call letters*] .... WCLY
Raleigh, NC [*FM radio station call letters*] .... WCPE
Raleigh, NC [*FM radio station call letters*] .... WKIX
Raleigh, NC [*FM radio station call letters*] .... WKNC
Raleigh, NC [*Television station call letters*] .... WLFL
Raleigh, NC [*AM radio station call letters*] .... WLLE
Raleigh, NC [*AM radio station call letters*] .... WPJL
Raleigh, NC [*AM radio station call letters*] .... WPTF
Raleigh, NC [*FM radio station call letters*] .... WQDR
Raleigh, NC [*FM radio station call letters*] .... WRAL
Raleigh, NC [*Television station call letters*] .... WRAL-TV
Raleigh, NC [*Television station call letters*] (RBYB) .... WRAZ
Raleigh, NC [*AM radio station call letters*] (RBYB) .... WRBZ
Raleigh, NC [*FM radio station call letters*] .... WSHA
Raleigh/Raleigh-Durham [*North Carolina*] [*ICAO location identifier*] (ICLI) .... KRDU
Raleigh Research Reactor .... RRR
Raleigh-Edwards Tensile Impact Machine Pendulum .... RETIMP
Raleighvallen [*Surinam*] [*ICAO location identifier*] (ICLI) .... SMRA
Rallentando [*Gradually Slower*] [*Music*] .... RALL
Rallentando [*Gradually Slower*] [*Music*] (ROG) .... RALLEN
Rallentando [*Gradually Slower*] [*Music*] (ROG) .... RALLO
Ralls, TX [*AM radio station call letters*] .... KCLR
Rally for Democracy and National Unity [*Mauritania*] [*Political party*] (EY) .... RDNU
Rally for the Republic [*French Political party*] (ECON) .... RPF
Rally Point [*Air Force*] .... RP
Rally's Hamburgers [*NASDAQ symbol*] (TTSB) .... RLLY
Rally's, Inc. [*Associated Press*] (SAG) .... Rallys
Rally's, Inc. [*NASDAQ symbol*] (NQ) .... RLLY
Raloxifene Response Element [*Biochemistry*] .... RRE
Ralph L. Smith Mental Retardation Research Center [*University of Kansas*] [*Research center*] (RCD) .... MRRC
Ralph Lauren [*Fashion designer, 1939-*] .... RL
Ralph M. Parsons, Electronics Division, Pasadena, CA [*Library symbol Library of Congress*] (LCLS) .... CPRP
Ralph Mayer Center for Artists' Techniques [*University of Delaware*] [*Newark*] [*Information service or system*] (IID) .... RMCAT
Ralph Vaughan Williams [*British composer, 1872-1958*] .... RVW
Ralph Waldo Emerson [*Initials used as pseudonym*] .... RWE
Ralph Waldo Emerson Memorial Association (EA) .... RWEMA
Ralph Waldo Emerson Society (EA) .... RWES
Ralston Public Library, Alberta [*Library symbol National Library of Canada*] (NLC) .... AR
Ralston Public Library, Ralston, AB, Canada [*Library symbol*] [*Library of Congress*] (LCLS) .... CaAR
Ralston Public Library, Ralston, NE [*Library symbol Library of Congress*] (LCLS) .... NbRal
Ralston Purina Co., Corporate Library, St. Louis, MO [*OCLC symbol*] (OCLC) .... RRL
Ralston Ralston Purina Group [*Associated Press*] (SAG) .... RalsRP
Ralston-Purina Group [*NYSE symbol*] (SPSG) .... RAL
Raltech Scientific Services, Inc., Madison, WI [*Library symbol Library of Congress*] (LCLS) .... WMaR
Raluana Point [*New Britain*] [*Seismograph station code, US Geological Survey*] (SEIS) .... RPT
Ram .... R
RAM [*Radioactive Materials*] **Accident/Incident Database** [*Nuclear energy*] .... RAMAIDB
RAM Address Register .... RAAR
Ram Air Cushion [*Aerospace*] (AAG) .... RAC
Ram Air Freight, Inc. [*ICAO designator*] (FAAC) .... REX
Ram Air Rocket Engine .... RARE
Ram Air Temperature .... RAT
Ram Air Turbine (MCD) .... RAT
Ram Air Turbine System .... RATS
Ram Air-Driven Unit .... RADU
Ram Air-Inflated Drogue [*Military*] (CAAL) .... RAID
RAM and ROM (NITA) .... RAROM
Ram Effect [*Mechanical engineering*] (OA) .... RE
RAM [*Reliability, Availability, and Maintainability*] **Improvement of Selected Equipment** [*Military*] (MCD) .... RISE
RAM Input/Output Timer .... RIOT
Ram on Assets, Debts, and Incumbrances [*2nd ed.*] [*1837*] [*A publication*] (DLA) .... Ram Ass
Ram on Exposition of Wills of Landed Property [*1827*] [*A publication*] (DLA) .... Ram W
Ram on Facts [*A publication*] (DLA) .... Ram F
Ram Petroleums Ltd. [*Toronto Stock Exchange symbol*] .... RPL
RAM Plus Input/Output (NITA) .... RAMIO
RAM [*Reliability, Availability, and Maintainablity*] **Rationale Annex** [*Army*] .... RRA
RAM [*Reliability, Availability, and Maintainability*] **Rationale Report** [*Army*] .... RRR
Ramachandrier's Cases on Adoption [*1892*] [*India*] [*A publication*] (DLA) .... Ramachandrier A
Ramachandrier's Cases on Dancing Girls [*1892*] [*India*] [*A publication*] (DLA) .... Ramachandrier DG
Ramachandrier's Cases on Hindu Marriage Law [*1891*] [*India*] [*A publication*] (DLA) .... Ramachandrier HML
Ramagundam [*India*] [*ICAO location identifier*] (ICLI) .... VORG
Ramah, NM [*FM radio station call letters*] .... KTDB
Ram-Air Inflation Decelerator [*Munitions*] (RDA) .... RAID
Ramakrishna - Vivekananda Center (EA) .... RVC
Raman [*Turkey*] [*Seismograph station code, US Geological Survey*] (SEIS) .... RAM
Raman Forward-Scattering [*Physics*] .... RFS
Raman LASER .... RL
Raman LASER Source .... RLS
Raman Microprobe [*Spectrometer*] .... RMP
Raman Optical Activity [*Spectrometry*] .... ROA
Raman Scattering [*Spectroscopy*] .... RS
Raman Spectroscopy .... RS
Ramanathan's Reports [*Ceylon*] [*A publication*] (DLA) .... Ram
Ramanathan's Supreme Court Reports [*Ceylon*] [*A publication*] (ILCA) .... Ram Rep
Ramanathan's Supreme Court Reports [*Ceylon*] [*A publication*] (DLA) .... Ram SC

Raman-Induced Kerr Effect (PDAA) .... RIKE
Raman-Induced Kerr Effect Scattering [*Spectroscopy*] .... RIKES
Ramapo Catskill Library System [*Library network*] .... RCLS
Ramapo Catskill Library System, Middletown, NY [*Library symbol Library of Congress*] (LCLS) .... NMiR
Ramapo College of New Jersey, Mahwah, NJ [*Library symbol Library of Congress*] (LCLS) .... NjMahR
Ramapo College of New Jersey, Mahwah, NJ [*OCLC symbol*] (OCLC) .... RNJ
Ramapo Financial [*NASDAQ symbol*] (TTSB) .... RMPO
Ramapo Financial Corp. [*Associated Press*] (SAG) .... RamFin
Ramapo Financial Corp. [*NASDAQ symbol*] (NQ) .... RMPO
Ram-Augmented Interstellar Rocket (WDAA) .... RAIR
Rambler Exploration [*Vancouver Stock Exchange symbol*] .... RBR
Rambler Oil Co. [*Toronto Stock Exchange symbol*] .... RMB
Ramblers' Association [*British*] (DBA) .... RA
Ramco Gershenson Properties Trust [*Associated Press*] (SAG) .... RamcoG
Ramco Gershenson Properties Trust [*NYSE symbol*] (SAG) .... RPT
Ramco-Gershenson Prop Tr [*NYSE symbol*] (TTSB) .... RPT
RAMCON, Inc., Environmental Engineering Library, Memphis, TN [*Library symbol Library of Congress*] (LCLS) .... TMRI
Ramcor Resources, Inc. [*Vancouver Stock Exchange symbol*] .... RAM
Ramenskoye [*US prefix for Soviet-Russian developmental aircraft flown at the Ramenskoye test facility*] (DOMA) .... RAM
Ramey [*Puerto Rico*] [*ICAO location identifier*] (ICLI) .... TJFF
Ramingining [*Australia Airport symbol*] (OAG) .... RAM
Ramjet .... RJ
Ramjet (MSA) .... RMJ
Ramjet Addition (AAG) .... RJA
Ramjet Engine .... RJE
Ramjet Inlet System .... RIS
Ramjet Performance Analysis (MCD) .... RJPA
Ramjet Test Vehicle .... RJTV
Ramm Venture [*Vancouver Stock Exchange symbol*] .... RAV
Ramnad [*India*] [*ICAO location identifier*] (ICLI) .... VORM
Ramo Wooldridge [*Later, TRW, Inc.*] .... RW
Ramore Library, Ontario [*Library symbol National Library of Canada*] (BIB) .... ORA
Ramo-Wooldridge One-Pass Assembly Program (SAA) .... RAWOOP-SNAP
Ramo-Wooldridge-Thompson Corp. [*Later, TRW, Inc.*] (AAG) .... R/W
Ramp [*Postal Service standard*] (OPSA) .... RAMP
Ramp 66, Inc. [*ICAO designator*] (FAAC) .... PPK
Ramp Actuator .... RA
Ramp Check [*Aviation*] (FAAC) .... RMPCK
Ramp Craft Logistic [*Navy British*] .... RCL
Ramp Function Generator (IAA) .... RFG
Ramp Generator and Signal Converter (IEEE) .... RGSC
Ramp Gross Weight [*Aviation*] .... RGW
Rampage Resources Ltd. [*Vancouver Stock Exchange symbol*] .... RPG
Rampart [*Alaska*] [*Airport symbol*] (OAG) .... RMP
Rampart Institute (EA) .... RI
Rampart Resources Ltd. [*Vancouver Stock Exchange symbol*] .... RMP
Ramped Cargo Lighter .... RCL
Ramped Dump Barge .... RDB
Ramped Powered Lighter [*British military*] (DMA) .... RPL
Ram's Cases of Pleading and Evidence [*A publication*] (DLA) .... Ram Cas P & E
Ram's Science of Legal Judgment [*2nd ed.*] [*1834*] [*A publication*] (DLA) .... Ram Leg J
Ram's Science of Legal Judgment, Notes by Townshend [*A publication*] (DLA) .... Ram Leg Judgm (Towns Ed)
Ramsar [*Iran*] [*ICAO location identifier*] (ICLI) .... OINR
Ramsar [*Iran*] [*Airport symbol*] (AD) .... RZR
Ramsay Health Care [*NASDAQ symbol*] (TTSB) .... RHCI
Ramsay Health Care, Inc. [*NASDAQ symbol*] (NQ) .... RHCI
Ramsay's Appeal Cases [*Canada*] [*A publication*] (DLA) .... RAC
Ramsay's Appeal Cases [*Canada*] [*A publication*] (DLA) .... Ramsay App Cas
Ramsay's Appeal Cases [*Canada*] [*A publication*] (DLA) .... Ramsay App Cas (Can)
Ramsbottom Carbon Residue [*Analysis of petroleum products*] .... RCR
Ramsele [*Sweden ICAO location identifier*] (ICLI) .... ESUR
Ramseur Pilot Light Teaching System .... RPL
Ramsey and Morin's Montreal Law Reporter [*A publication*] (DLA) .... Ram & Mor
Ramsey County Medical Society, St. Paul, MN [*Library symbol Library of Congress*] (LCLS) .... MnSRM
Ramsey County Public Library, St. Paul, MN [*Library symbol Library of Congress*] (LCLS) .... MnSRC
Ramsey County Public Library, St. Paul, MN [*OCLC symbol*] (OCLC) .... RCL
Ramsey Elementary School, Montevideo, MN [*Library symbol*] [*Library of Congress*] (LCLS) .... MnMovRE
Ramsey Free Public Library, Ramsey, NJ [*Library symbol Library of Congress*] (LCLS) .... NjRam
Ramsey Health Care, Inc. [*Associated Press*] (SAG) .... Ramsay
Ramsey, IL [*FM radio station call letters*] .... WJLY
Ramsey, Kenneth J., Pittsburgh PA [*STAC*] .... RKJ
Ramsey's Quebec Appeal Cases [*A publication*] (DLA) .... Ram
Ramsey's Quebec Appeal Cases [*1873-86*] [*A publication*] (DLA) .... Rams App
Ramstein [*Germany ICAO location identifier*] (ICLI) .... EDAR
Ramstein [*Germany ICAO location identifier*] (ICLI) .... EDAX
Ramtron International Corp. [*Associated Press*] (SAG) .... Ramtrn
Ramtron International Corp. [*Associated Press*] (SAG) .... Ramtron
Ramtron International Corp. [*NASDAQ symbol*] (SAG) .... RMTR
Ramtron Int'l [*NASDAQ symbol*] (TTSB) .... RMTR
Ramus Infraorbitalis [*Anatomy*] .... RIO
Ramus Interventricularis [*First-order branch of coronary artery*] [*Medicine*] .... RIV
Ramus Supraorbitalis [*Anatomy*] .... RSO
Ranae [*Frogs*] [*of Aristophanes*] [*Classical studies*] (OCD) .... Ran
Ranau [*Malaysia*] [*Airport symbol*] (OAG) .... RNU
Ranau [*Malaysia*] [*ICAO location identifier*] (ICLI) .... WBKR
Rancagua/De La Independencia [*Chile*] [*ICAO location identifier*] (ICLI) .... SCRG
Ranch [*Commonly used*] (OPSA) .... RANCH
Ranch [*Commonly used*] (OPSA) .... RANCHES
Ranch .... RNCH
Ranch (MCD) .... RNCH
Ranch [*Commonly used*] (OPSA) .... RNCHS
[*The*] **Ranchero Club** (EA) .... TRC
Ranchers for Peace (EA) .... RP
Ranchi [*India*] [*Airport symbol*] (OAG) .... IXR
Ranchi [*India*] [*ICAO location identifier*] (ICLI) .... VERC
Ranching Heritage Association (EA) .... RHA
Ranchmen's Resources Ltd. [*Toronto Stock Exchange symbol*] .... RRL
Rancho .... RCH
Rancho Alegre [*Bolivia*] [*ICAO location identifier*] (ICLI) .... SLRH
Rancho Cordova, CA [*AM radio station call letters*] .... KSTE
Rancho Del Mar [*Costa Rica*] [*ICAO location identifier*] (ICLI) .... MRRM
Rancho Mirage, CA [*FM radio station call letters*] (RBYB) .... KMRJ-FM
Rancho Nuevo [*Costa Rica*] [*ICAO location identifier*] (ICLI) .... MRRN
Rancho Palos Verdes, CA [*Television station call letters*] .... KRPA
Rancho Santa Ana Botanic Garden, Claremont, CA [*Library symbol Library of Congress*] (LCLS) .... CCR
Rancho Seco Nuclear Generating Station (NRCH) .... RSNGS
Rand [*Monetary unit*] [*Botswana, Lesotho, South Africa, and Swaziland*] .... R
Rand and Furness on Poisons [*A publication*] (DLA) .... Rand & Fur Poi
Rand Cap [*NASDAQ symbol*] (TTSB) .... RAND
Rand Capital Corp. [*NASDAQ symbol*] (NQ) .... RAND
Rand Capital Corp. [*Associated Press*] (SAG) .... RandCa
Rand Corp., Santa Monica, CA [*Library symbol Library of Congress*] (LCLS) .... CStmoR
Rand Corp., Washington, DC [*Library symbol Library of Congress*] (LCLS) .... CStmoR-W
Rand Development Corp. (IAA) .... RDC
Rand Graduate Institute (AAGC) .... RGI
RAND Health Insurance Experiment [*Managed care study*] .... RHIE
Rand Information Systems Ltd. (NITA) .... RISL
Rand Intelligent Terminal Agent .... RITA
Rand Light Infantry [*British military*] (DMA) .... RLI
Rand McNally & Co., Chicago, IL [*Library symbol Library of Congress*] (LCLS) .... ICRand
Rand Merchant Bank [*South Africa*] .... RMB
Rand Rifles [*British military*] (DMA) .... RR
Randall Consolidated School, Bassett, WI [*Library symbol Library of Congress*] (LCLS) .... WBasR
Randall on Perpetuities [*A publication*] (DLA) .... Rand Perp
Randall's Edition of Peake on Evidence [*A publication*] (DLA) .... Rand Peak
Randall's Reports [*62-71 Ohio State*] [*A publication*] (DLA) .... Rand
Randers [*Denmark ICAO location identifier*] (ICLI) .... EKRD
Randers Group [*ECM Symbol*] (TTSB) .... RGI.EC
Randers Group, Inc. [*Associated Press*] (SAG) .... Rander
Randers Group, Inc. [*AMEX symbol*] (SAG) .... RGI
Randle Cliff RADAR (PDAA) .... RCR
Randolph Air Force Base [*Texas*] .... RAFB
Randolph Annual [*A publication*] (DLA) .... Rand Ann
Randolph Center, VT [*FM radio station call letters*] .... WVTC
Randolph County Recorder's Office, Winchester, IN [*Library symbol Library of Congress*] (LCLS) .... InWincCR
Randolph Hospital, Inc., Asheboro, NC [*Library symbol*] [*Library of Congress*] (LCLS) .... NcAsbH
Randolph on Commercial Paper [*A publication*] (DLA) .... Rand Com Paper
Randolph on Eminent Domain [*A publication*] (DLA) .... Rand Em Dom
Randolph Public Library, Asheboro, NC [*Library symbol Library of Congress*] (LCLS) .... NcAsbC
Randolph Technical Institute, Asheboro, NC [*Library symbol Library of Congress*] (LCLS) .... NcAsbR
Randolph, VT [*FM radio station call letters*] .... WCVR
Randolph, VT [*AM radio station call letters*] .... WWWT
Randolph-Macon College [*Virginia*] .... RMC
Randolph-Macon College, Ashland, VA [*Library symbol Library of Congress*] (LCLS) .... ViAsR
Randolph-Macon College, Ashland, VA [*OCLC symbol*] (OCLC) .... VRM
Randolph-Macon Woman's College [*Virginia*] .... RMWC
Randolph-Macon Woman's College, Lynchburg, VA [*Library symbol Library of Congress*] (LCLS) .... ViLRM
Randolph-Macon Woman's College, Lynchburg, VA [*OCLC symbol*] (OCLC) .... VLR
Randolph's Reports [*22-27 Virginia*] [*1821-28*] [*A publication*] (DLA) .... Rand
Randolph's Reports [*7-11 Louisiana*] [*A publication*] (DLA) .... Rand
Randolph's Reports [*21-56 Kansas*] [*A publication*] (DLA) .... Rand
Randolph-Sheppard Vendors of America (EA) .... RSVA
Random (DNAB) .... RAN
Random [*Sample or Specimen*] (DAVI) .... RAND
Random (WGA) .... RDM
Random .... RND
Random (MSA) .... RNDM
Random Access [*Computer science*] (AAG) .... RA
Random Access [*Computer science*] (MHDI) .... RAX
Random Access Allocation [*Computer science*] (IAA) .... RALLOC
Random Access and Correlation for Extended Performance [*Telecommunications*] .... RACEP
Random Access and Inquiry [*Computer science*] .... RAI
Random Access Array (NITA) .... RAA
Random Access Capability [*Microscopy*] .... RAC
Random Access Card Equipment [*Computer science*] (CDE) .... RACE
Random Access Communications System .... RACS
Random Access Computer (IIA) .... RAC

Random Access Computer Equipment ... RACE
Random Access Control Equipment (IEEE) ... RACE
Random Access Controller [*Computer science*] (IAA) ... RAC
Random Access Data (BUR) ... RAD
Random Access Delta Modulation ... RADEM
Random Access Device ... RAD
Random Access Disc (MCD) ... RAD
Random Access Discrete Address [*Army division-level battlefield radio communications system*] ... RADA
Random Access Discrete Address Communications System [*Army*] ... RADACS
Random Access Discrete Address System ... RADAS
Random Access Discrete Address System Simulator [*Army*] (IAA) ... RADSIM
Random Access Document Indexing and Retrieval ... RADIR
Random Access Dump and Reload (IAA) ... RADAR
Random Access Image Device [*Computer science*] (IAA) ... RAID
Random Access Indestructive Advanced Memory [*Computer science*] (MSA) ... RAIAM
Random Access Information Retrieval [*Computer science*] (IEEE) ... RAIR
Random Access Initializer [*Computer science*] (IAA) ... RAINIT
Random Access Interactive Debugger (IAA) ... RAID
Random Access Light Valve ... RALV
Random Access Logical File Handler (MCD) ... RALFH
Random Access Measurement [*System*] [*Computer science*] ... RAM
Random Access Measurement System [*Computer science*] ... RAMS
Random Access Mechanization of Phosphorus ... RAMP
Random Access Memorix Storage [*Computer science*] (IAA) ... RAMS
Random Access Memory [*Computer science*] ... RAM
Random Access Memory Accounting Computer [*Computer science*] (IAA) ... RAMAC
Random Access Memory Buffer [*Computer science*] ... RAMB
Random Access Memory Device [*Computer science*] ... RAMD
Random Access Memory Digital to Analog Converter [*Computer science*] (CDE) ... RAMDAC
Random Access Memory Module [*Computer science*] ... RAMM
Random Access Memory Store [*Computer science*] (TEL) ... RAMS
Random Access Metal-Oxide-Semiconductor Memory [*Computer science*] (IAA) ... RAMM
Random Access Method [*Computer science*] (WDAA) ... RAM
Random Access Method of Accounting and Control [*Computer science*] ... RAMAC
Random Access Method of Accounting and Control (NITA) ... RAMAC
Random Access Noiselike Signal Address [*Telecommunications*] (IAA) ... RANSAD
Random Access Nondestructive Advanced Memory [*Computer science*] ... RANDAM
Random Access Parallel Tape ... RAPTAP
Random Access Personnel Information Dissemination ... RAPID
Random Access Personnel Information Dissemination System [*Army*] (AABC) ... RAPIDS
Random Access Personnel Information Disseminatora (NITA) ... RAPID
Random Access Plan-Position Indicator [*Air Force*] ... RAPPI
Random Access Program [*Computer science*] ... RAP
Random Access Programming and Checkout Equipment ... RAPCOE
Random Access Projector ... RAP
Random Access Secure Communications Antijam Link ... RASCAL
Random Access Storage [*Computer science*] (IAA) ... RAS
Random Access Storage and Control [*Computer science*] ... RASTAC
Random Access Storage and Display [*Computer science*] ... RASTAD
Random Access Video Editing [*Computerized film editing*] ... RAVE
Random Access Viewer ... RAV
Random Access Viewing Equipment ... RAVE
Random Access-to-Random Access [*Computer science*] (IAA) ... RARA
Random Acess Index Edit [*Computer science*] (IAA) ... RAINDX
Random Age Replacement ... RAR
Random Amplified Polymorphic DNA [*Deoxyribonucleic Acid*] [*Genetics*] ... RAPD
Random Angle Modulation ... RAM
Random Barrage System [*Military*] ... RBS
Random Block Number [*Computer science*] ... RBN
Random Blood Smear [*Hematology*] (DAVI) ... RBS
Random Blood Sugar [*Medicine*] (MAE) ... RBS
Random Breath Testing (ADA) ... RBT
Random Chemistry Profile (DAVI) ... RCP
Random Close-Packed [*Granular physics*] ... RCP
Random Coefficient Model [*Mathematics*] ... RCM
Random Coincidence Monitor [*Beckman Instruments, Inc.*] [*Instrumentation*] ... RCM
Random Communication (IAA) ... RACOM
Random Communication Satellite ... RANCOM
Random Communication Satellite System ... RCSS
Random Digit Dialing [*Telecommunications*] ... RDD
Random Digit Sample (NTCM) ... RDS
Random Dimer Model [*Physics*] ... RDM
Random Disc File [*Computer science*] (IAA) ... RANDIS
Random Domain Library Screening [*Genetic laboratory technique*] ... RANDOLS
Random Dot Stereogram ... RDS
Random Double-Blind Trial [*Medicine*] (DMAA) ... RDB
Random Drift ... RD
Random Driver [*Nuclear energy*] (NRCH) ... RD
Random Dynamic Load ... RDL
Random Entry Memory (ADA) ... REM
Random Event Generator [*Psychology*] ... REG
Random Evolutionary Hits ... REH
Random Evolutionary Hits per Codon ... REHC
Random Evolutionary Operation ... REVOP
Random Filing System ... RFS
Random Force Field ... RFF
Random House AudioBooks [*Publisher*] ... RHAB
Random House Dictionary [*A publication*] ... RHD
[*The*] **Random House Dictionary of the English Language: Second Edition - Unabridged** [*A publication*] ... RHDEL-II
[*The*] **Random House Dictionary of the English Language: Second Edition - Unabridged** [*A publication*] ... RHD-II
Random House Encyclopedia [*A publication*] ... RHE
Random Input Describing Function [*Computer science*] ... RIDF
Random Input Sampling [*Computer science*] ... RIP
Random Interlace [*Television*] ... RI
Random Interval (AEBS) ... RI
Random Item File Locater ... RIFL
Random Lengths [*Lumber*] ... RL
Random Logic ... RL
Random Loose-Packed [*Granular physics*] ... RLP
Random Mass Storage [*Computer science*] ... RMS
Random Motion Simulator [*NASA*] (NASA) ... RMS
Random Multiple Access ... RMA
Random Navigation ... R-NAV
Random Noise Voltmeter ... RNV
Random Number ... R
Random Number (IEEE) ... RN
Random Number Generator [*Parapsychology*] ... RNG
Random Peptide Phage Display Library [*Biochemistry*] ... RPPDL
Random Phase Approximation ... RPA
Random Phase Model (OA) ... RPM
Random Procedure Information (WDAA) ... RPI
Random Pulse Generator [*Telecommunications*] (OA) ... RPG
Random Saccades [*Ophthalmology*] ... RS
Random Sequence Number (DNAB) ... RSN
Random Sequential Automaton (IAA) ... RSA
Random Signal Vibration Protector (PDAA) ... RSVP
Random Sine Vibration ... RSV
Random Smooth Pursuit [*Ophthalmology*] ... RSP
Random Spatial Phase Modulator ... RSPM
Random Splice [*Telecommunications*] (TEL) ... RS
Random Urine [*Urology*] (DAVI) ... URIN
Random Variable [*Statistics*] ... RV
Random Vibration Control ... RVC
Random Walk ... RW
Random Walk Advection and Dispersion Model [*Environmental Protection Agency*] (GFGA) ... RADM
Random Width and Length (DAC) ... R/W & L
Random Widths [*Lumber*] ... RW
Random-Dot Kinematogram [*For motion detection*] ... RDK
Randomization Analyser (IAA) ... RANDANAL
Randomized Clinical Trial [*Medicine*] ... RCT
Randomized Complete Block [*Statistical design*] ... RCB
Randomized Control Trial [*Statistics*] ... RCT
Randomized Controlled Clinical Trial [*Medicine*] (DMAA) ... RCCT
Randomized Controlled Field Trial [*Statistics*] ... RCFT
Randomized Intervention Analysis [*Experimental design*] ... RIA
Randomized Pattern Search (PDAA) ... RPS
Randomized Response Technique [*Statistics*] ... RRT
Randomized Trial [*Statistics*] ... RT
Random-Pulse RADAR System (AAG) ... RPRS
Random-to-Serial Converter ... RASER
Rand's Omnibus Calculator of the Kinetics of Earth Trajectories ... ROCKET
Randstrom Manufacturing Corp. [*Vancouver Stock Exchange symbol*] ... ROW
Randy Floyd Fan Club (EA) ... RFFC
Randy Travis Fan Club (EA) ... RTFC
Randy Wade Fan Club (EA) ... RWFC
Raney's Reports [*16-20 Florida*] [*A publication*] (DLA) ... Raney
Ranfurly Library Service [*An association*] (EAIO) ... RLS
Rangaire Corp. (MHDW) ... RANG
Range ... R
Range [*Aviation*] ... RA
Range (AAG) ... RG
Range [*Maps and charts*] (MDG) ... RGE
Range [*or Ranging*] (AAG) ... RNG
Range and Azimuth Only ... RAZON
Range and Bearing Launch [*Navy*] (CAAL) ... RBL
Range and Distance Measuring Equipment ... RDME
Range and Range Rate (IAA) ... RARR
Range and Range Rate ... RRR
Range and Safety (AAG) ... R & S
Range and Sensitivity Extending Resonator [*Electronics*] ... RASER
Range and True Bearing (IAA) ... RTB
Range and Zero [*NASA*] (KSC) ... R & Z
Range Applications Joint Program Office ... RAJPO
Range Area (NASA) ... RA
Range Assessment Mode (MCD) ... RAM
Range Assessor [*British military*] (DMA) ... RA
Range Automated Information System (KSC) ... RAIS
Range, Azimuth, and Elevation (MCD) ... RAE
Range, Azimuth, and Elevation ... RAZEL
Range, Azimuth, and Elevation Detection of Optical Targets ... RAEDOT
Range, Azimuth, Elevation, and Time ... RAET
Range Azimuth Indicator ... RAI
Range Bearing [*JETDS nomenclature*] ... S
Range Bearing Indicator (MCD) ... RBI
Range Betting Method ... RBM
Range Calibration Satellite (SAA) ... RCS
Range Change Method [*Aircraft*] ... RCM

Range Clearance [*NASA*] (KSC) .... R/C
Range Command [*NASA*] (NASA) .... RC
Range Commanders Council [*White Sands Missile Range*] (KSC) .... RCC
Range Commanders Council Meteorological Group [*White Sands Missile Range*] .... RCC/MG
Range Commanders Council Telemetry Group [*White Sands Missile Range, NM*] .... RCC/TG
Range Communications Component (MCD) .... RCC
Range Communications Control Center [*Military*] (MCD) .... RCCC
Range Communications Electronics Instructions [*NASA*] (KSC) .... RCEI
Range Communications Instruction (IAA) .... RCI
Range Communications Instructions [*NASA*] (KSC) .... RCI
Range Company (DNAB) .... RANGECO
Range Computer (IAA) .... RNGCOMP
Range Contractor [*NASA*] (KSC) .... RC
Range Control [*NASA*] (KSC) .... RC
Range Control Center [*NASA*] .... RCC
Range Control Office [*or Officer*] [*NASA*] (KSC) .... RCO
Range Control Station [*or System*] [*Army*] .... RCS
Range Correction .... RC
Range Cutoff (MCD) .... RCO
Range Data Distributive System [*Military*] .... RDDS
Range Data Measurement Subsystem (MCD) .... RDMS
Range Data Processor (MCD) .... RDP
Range Deflection Protractor [*Weaponry*] (INF) .... RDP
Range Destruct System .... RDS
Range Development (MUGU) .... RD
Range Development Officer (MUGU) .... RDO
Range Doppler Angle Angle (IAA) .... RDAA
Range Drone Data Control System [*Military*] (CAAL) .... RDDCS
Range Endurance Speed and Time [*Computer*] .... REST
Range Error Average (MUGU) .... REA
Range Error Detector .... RED
Range Error Function [*Aerospace*] (AAG) .... REF
Range Error Probable [*Military*] .... REP
Range Estimating and Evaluation Procedure [*Computer science*] .... REEP
Range Estimation Program (MCD) .... REP
Range Evaluation Missile .... REM
Range Extender Vehicle [*Gasoline-electric hybrid*] .... REV
Range Extender with Gain [*Bell System*] .... REG
Range Facility Control Officer [*Military*] (IAA) .... RFCO
Range Frequency Synthesizer .... RFS
Range from Entry Interface (NASA) .... REI
Range Gate Deception [*Military*] (LAIN) .... RGD
Range Gate Pull Off (NVT) .... RGPO
Range Gate Walk Off [*Military*] (LAIN) .... RGWO
Range Gated Filter .... RGF
Range Gated Receiver .... RGR
Range Geneaological Society, Buhl, MN [*Library symbol Library of Congress*] (LCLS) .... MnBulR
Range Group [*Military*] .... RANG
Range Illumination RADAR .... RIR
Range Information Display System (MCD) .... RIDS
Range Information System [*For aircraft*] (MCD) .... RIS
Range Instrumentation (MCD) .... RI
Range Instrumentation and Support Systems .... RISS
Range Instrumentation Conference (MUGU) .... RIC
Range Instrumentation Control System .... RICS
Range Instrumentation Coordination (KSC) .... RIC
Range Instrumentation Development Division (SAA) .... RIDD
Range Instrumentation Performance Evaluation (MUGU) .... RIPE
Range Instrumentation Planning Study [*AFSC*] .... RIPS
Range Instrumentation Ship .... RIS
Range Instrumentation Ship .... TAGM
Range Instrumentation Station .... RIS
Range Instrumentation Systems Office [*White Sands Missile Range*] .... RISO
Range Instruments Development (MCD) .... RID
Range Interference Detecting and Control .... RIDAC
Range Keeper Operator [*Navy*] .... RKO
Range Light (AAG) .... RALT
Range Location Velocity .... RLV
Range Maintenance Plan (MCD) .... RMP
Range Marks .... RM
Range, Maximum .... RMAX
Range Measurements Laboratory [*Air Force*] .... RML
Range Measuring System [*Air Force*] .... RMS
Range Meteorological Sounding System (MCD) .... RMSS
Range Modification System .... RMS
Range Monitoring and Control Subsystem (MCD) .... RMCS
Range of Incentive Effectiveness .... RIE
Range of Jamming .... ROJ
Range of Joint Motion [*Medicine*] (DMAA) .... ROJM
Range of Motion [*or Movement*] .... ROM
Range of Movement [*Medicine*] .... RM
Range of Spares (MCD) .... ROS
Range of the Day [*Military*] (CAAL) .... ROD
Range on Target .... ROT
Range on Target Signal .... ROTS
Range Only (CAAL) .... RO
Range Operation (AAG) .... RO
Range Operation Performance Summary .... ROPS
Range Operation Station .... ROS
Range Operational Monitoring and Control Center .... ROMACC
Range Operations Center [*Western Test Range*] (MCD) .... ROC
Range Operations Conference [*NASA*] (KSC) .... ROC
Range Operations Conference Circuit (MUGU) .... ROCC
Range Operations Control Center (MCD) .... ROCC
Range Operations Control System (SAA) .... ROCS
Range Operations Directorate [*White Sands Missile Range*] .... ROD
Range Operations Duty Officer (MUGU) .... RODO
Range Operations Instruction [*NASA*] (KSC) .... ROI
Range Operations Instruction [*NASA*] (MUGU) .... ROINST
Range Operations Monitor Analysis Center (MCD) .... ROMAC
Range Operations Monitoring and Control .... ROMAC
Range Operations Officer .... ROO
Range Operations Supervisor (MUGU) .... ROS
Range Optical Tracking Equipment (AAG) .... ROTE
Range Optical Tracking Instrument .... ROTI
Range Pad Service .... RPS
Range Planning Estimate (MUGU) .... RPE
Range Planning Office (MUGU) .... RPO
Range Positioning System .... RPS
Range Probable Error [*Formerly, Range Error Probable*] [*Air Force*] (NATG) .... RPE
Range Pulse .... RP
Range Rate (MCD) .... RNG RT
Range Rate (NASA) .... RR
Range Rate Error .... RRE
Range Rate Frequency Synthesizer .... RRFS
Range Rate Indicator .... RRI
Range Rate Search (MCD) .... RRS
Range Recorder [*NASA*] (IAA) .... RR
Range Remote Job Entry [*Telecommunications*] (OSI) .... RRJE
Range Ring Profile (MCD) .... RRP
Range Rover Register [*An association*] (EAIO) .... RRR
Range Safety [*NASA*] (KSC) .... RS
Range Safety Approval (MUGU) .... RSA
Range Safety Beacon [*NASA*] (AAG) .... RSB
Range Safety Command [*or Control*] [*NASA*] .... RSC
Range Safety Command Receiver [*NASA*] (KSC) .... RSCR
Range Safety Command Shutdown System (IAA) .... RSCSS
Range Safety Command System [*NASA*] (AAG) .... RSCS
Range Safety Data Coordinator (SAA) .... RSDC
Range Safety Destruct System .... RSDS
Range Safety Group [*Range Commanders Council*] [*White Sands Missile Range, NM*] .... RSG
Range Safety Impact Display System .... RASIDS
Range Safety Launch Approval (AFM) .... RSLA
Range Safety Officer [*Military*] .... RSO
Range Safety Officer / Missile Flight Safety Officer [*Military*] (SAA) .... RSO/MFSO
Range Safety Operational Plan (MUGU) .... RSOP
Range Safety Operations Requirement .... RSOR
Range Safety Receiving Station .... RSRS
Range Safety Report [*NASA*] (AAG) .... RSR
Range Safety Switch [*NASA*] (MCD) .... RSS
Range Safety System [*NASA*] .... RSS
Range Scheduling (MUGU) .... RSCH
Range Search and Track (MCD) .... RST
Range Selector .... RS
Range Setter (IAA) .... RS
Range Single Shot Probability [*Military*] .... RSSP
Range Slaving System .... RSS
Range Solar Panel .... RSP
Range Solar Panel Substrate .... RSPS
Range Sorting Program .... RSP
Range Squadron .... RANS
Range Support Directive (SAA) .... RSD
Range Support Operation .... RSO
Range Support Plan (MUGU) .... RSP
Range Surveillance .... R/S
Range Surveillance Aircraft (MCD) .... RNSAC
Range Technical Advisory Group .... RTAG
Range Telemetry Central [*Aerospace*] .... RTC
Range Time Data Editor [*NASA*] (KSC) .... RTDE
Range Time Decoder .... RTD
Range Time Signal .... RTS
Range Timing (AAG) .... RT
Range Timing System .... RTS
Range to Go .... RTG
Range to Ground (MCD) .... RTG
Range to Velocity [*Ratio of the RADAR platform*] .... R/V
Range Tower Transfer Assembly (KSC) .... RTTA
Range Track on Target [*Air Force*] .... RTOT
Range Tracker (KSC) .... RTK
Range Tracking .... RT
Range Training Officer (MCD) .... RTO
Range Transfer Unit (MCD) .... RTU
Range Unit .... RU
Range User .... RU
Range Users Handbook .... RUH
Range Utilization Resources and Allocation Listings (SAA) .... RURALS
Range While Search .... RWS
Range-Altitude Monitor .... RAM
Range-Drift Measuring Unit .... RDMU
Range-Extended Directionally-Controlled Antitank Missile (MCD) .... REDCAT
Range-Finder [*Gunnery*] .... RF
Rangefinder with Automatic Compensator [*Firearms*] .... RAC
Range-Gemini to Agena (SAA) .... RGA
Range-Height Converter (IAA) .... RHC
Range-Height Indicator [*RADAR*] .... RHI
Rangeilunda [*India*] [*ICAO location identifier*] (ICLI) .... VERN

Rangeland ... RNGLND
Rangely [*Colorado*] [*Seismograph station code, US Geological Survey*] (SEIS) ... RGC
Rangely Public Library, Rangely, CO [*Library symbol Library of Congress*] (LCLS) ... CoRa
Rangemile Ltd. [*British ICAO designator*] (FAAC) ... RGM
Range-Only Measurement of Trajectory and Recording ... ROMOTAR
Range-Only Multiple Aircraft Navigation System [*Air Force*] ... ROMANS
Range-Only RADAR [*Military*] (AABC) ... ROR
Ranger [*Army skill qualification identifier*] (INF) ... G
Ranger ... RGR
Ranger Antiarmor, Antipersonnel Weapon System [*Army*] (INF) ... RAAWS
Ranger Assessment Phase [*Army*] (INF) ... RAP
Ranger Battalions Association (EA) ... RBA
Ranger Battalions Association World War II (EA) ... RBA WWII
Ranger Fan Club (EA) ... RFC
Ranger Instructor [*Army*] (INF) ... RI
Ranger Junior College [*Texas*] ... RJC
Ranger Junior College, Ranger, TX [*Library symbol Library of Congress*] (LCLS) ... TxRaC
Ranger Oil Ltd. [*Associated Press*] (SAG) ... RangrO
Ranger Oil Ltd. [*NYSE symbol Toronto Stock Exchange symbol*] (SPSG) ... RGO
Ranger Regimental Association (EA) ... RRA
Ranger Rick's Nature Club (EA) ... RRNC
Ranger Tab [*Military decoration*] ... RgrT
Ranger Tab [*Military decoration*] ... RT
Ranger Training Brigade [*Fort Benning, GA*] [*Army*] (INF) ... RTB
Ranger Uranium Mines [*Commercial firm Australia*] ... RUM
Range-Rate Tracking System ... RRTS
Ranger-Parachutist [*Army skill qualification identifier*] (INF) ... V
Ranges, Ammunition, and Targets (MCD) ... RAT
Ranges and Space Ground Support (AAG) ... RSGS
Rangetaker [*British military*] (DMA) ... RT
Range-to-Target (NASA) ... RT
Ranging (IAA) ... RGN
Ranging Airborne LASER Tracker (MCD) ... RALT
Ranging and Processing Satellite (DA) ... RAPSAT
Ranging and Velocity Navigation ... RAVEN
Ranging Demodulator Assembly [*Deep Space Instrumentation Facility, NASA*] ... RDA
Ranging Gun [*British military*] (DMA) ... RG
Ranging Integration Location System ... RILS
Ranging Machine Gun [*British military*] (DMA) ... RMG
Ranging Noise Generator ... RNG
Ranging Tone Transfer Assembly ... RTTA
Rangiroa [*French Polynesia*] [*ICAO location identifier*] (ICLI) ... NTTG
Rangiroa [*French Polynesia*] [*Airport symbol*] (OAG) ... RGI
[*The*] **Rangkaian Komputer Malaysia** [*Computer science*] (TNIG) ... RangKoM
Rangoon [*Burma*] [*Seismograph station code, US Geological Survey Closed*] (SEIS) ... RAN
Rangoon [*City in Burma*] (ROG) ... RANG
Rangoon [*Burma*] [*Airport symbol*] (AD) ... RGN
Rangoon [*Myanmar*] [*Airport symbol*] (OAG) ... RGN
Rangoon Criminal Law Journal [*A publication*] (DLA) ... Rang Cr LJ
Rangoon Law Reports [*India*] [*A publication*] (DLA) ... Rang LR
Rangoon/Mingaladon [*Myanmar*] [*ICAO location identifier*] (ICLI) ... VBRR
Rangpur [*Bangladesh*] [*Airport symbol*] (AD) ... RAU
Ranitidine [*An antiulcer drug*] ... RAN
Rank ... R
Rank and File ... R & F
Rank Annihilation Factor Analysis [*Computer science*] ... RAFA
Rank Group PLC (The) [*NASDAQ symbol*] (SAG) ... RANK
Rank Group PLC (The) [*Associated Press*] (SAG) ... RankGrp
Rank Has Its Obligations [*Military slang*] ... RHIO
Rank Has Its Privileges [*Military slang*] ... RHIP
Rank Has Its Responsibilities [*Military slang*] ... RHIR
Rank Organisation ADR [*NASDAQ symbol*] (TTSB) ... RANKY
[*The*] **Rank Organisation Ltd.** [*NASDAQ symbol*] (NQ) ... RANK
Rank Organisation Ltd. [*Toronto Stock Exchange symbol*] ... RO
[*The*] **Rank Organisation PLC** [*Associated Press*] (SAG) ... RankOrg
Rank Xerox ... RX
Rank Xerox Ltd. [*Xerox subsidiary*] ... RXL
Rank Xerox Operating System [*Computer science*] (IAA) ... RXOS
Rankin Automotive Group, Inc. [*Associated Press*] (SAG) ... RankinA
Rankin Automotive Group, Inc. [*NASDAQ symbol*] (SAG) ... RAVE
Rankin Inlet [*Canada*] [*Airport symbol*] (OAG) ... YRT
Rankin Inlet, NT [*FM radio station call letters*] ... CBQR
Rankin Inlet, NT [*ICAO location identifier*] (ICLI) ... CYRT
Rankin on Patents [*1824*] [*A publication*] (DLA) ... Rank P
Rankine [*Temperature scale*] ... R
Rankine Cycle Air Turboaccelerator ... RATA
Rankine-Cycle Energy Recovery [*System*] [*Navy*] (DOMA) ... RACER
Rankine-Hugoniot [*Physics*] ... RH
Ranking and Spicer's Company Law [*11th ed.*] [*1970*] [*A publication*] (DLA) ... Rank & S Comp L
Ranking Index for Maintenance Expenditures (PDAA) ... RIME
Ranking, Spicer, and Pegler on Executorship [*21st ed.*] [*1971*] [*A publication*] (DLA) ... Rank S & P Exec
Ranks Hovis McDougall [*Commercial firm British*] (ECON) ... RHM
Rannikko- ja Sisaevesiliikenteen Tvoenantajaliitto [*Employers' Federation of Coastal and Inland Waterways Transportation*] [*Finland*] (EY) ... RASILA
Ranohira [*Madagascar*] [*ICAO location identifier*] (ICLI) ... FMSO
Ranong [*Thailand*] [*ICAO location identifier*] (ICLI) ... VTSR
Ransiki [*West Irian, Indonesia*] [*Airport symbol*] (AD) ... RSK
Ransiki/Abresso [*Indonesia*] [*ICAO location identifier*] (ICLI) ... WASC
Ransom Eli Olds [*Acronym used as name of automobile manufactured by Ransom E. Olds Co.*] ... REO
Ransom Resources Ltd. [*Vancouver Stock Exchange symbol*] ... RNS
Ransomville Free Library, Ransomville, NY [*Library symbol Library of Congress*] (LCLS) ... NRans
Rantasalmi [*Finland ICAO location identifier*] (ICLI) ... EFRN
Rantoul, IL [*AM radio station call letters*] ... WBAN
Rantoul, IL [*FM radio station call letters*] ... WLTM
Rantoul, IL [*FM radio station call letters*] (RBYB) ... WQQB-FM
Rantoul, IL [*FM radio station call letters*] ... WZNF
Rantoul Public Library, Rantoul, IL [*Library symbol Library of Congress*] (LCLS) ... IRant
Rantoul,IL [*AM radio station call letters*] (RBYB) ... WJCI-AM
Ranuna [*India*] [*ICAO location identifier*] (ICLI) ... VERA
Rao's Decisions on Hindu Law [*1893*] [*India*] [*A publication*] (DLA) ... Rao DHL
Raoul [*Raoul Island*] [*Seismograph station code, US Geological Survey*] (SEIS) ... RAO
Raoul d'Harcourt [*Deceased, 1307*] [*Authority cited in pre-1607 legal work*] (DSA) ... Ra de Hacur
Raoul Island [*New Zealand*] [*ICAO location identifier*] (ICLI) ... NZRN
Raoul Wallenberg Association [*See also RWF*] (EA) ... RWA
Raoul Wallenberg Committee of the United States (EA) ... RWCUS
Raoul Wallenberg Foreningen [*Raoul Wallenberg Association - RWA*] (EAIO) ... RWF
Rapalje and Lawrence's American and English Cases [*A publication*] (DLA) ... Rap & L
Rapalje and Lawrence's American and English Cases [*A publication*] (DLA) ... Rap & Law
Rapalje and Lawrence's American and English Cases [*A publication*] (DLA) ... Rapal & L
Rapalje and Lawrence's Law Dictionary [*A publication*] (DLA) ... Rap & L Law Dict
Rapalje and Lawrence's Law Dictionary [*A publication*] (DLA) ... Rapalje & L
Rapalje and Mack's Digest of Railway Law [*A publication*] (DLA) ... RM Dig
Rapalje on Contempt [*A publication*] (DLA) ... Rap Contempt
Rapalje on Larceny [*A publication*] (DLA) ... Rap Lar
Rapalje's Federal Reference Digest [*A publication*] (DLA) ... Rap Fed Ref Dig
Rapalje's New York Digest [*A publication*] (DLA) ... Rap NY Dig
Rapalje's Treatise on Witnesses [*A publication*] (DLA) ... Rap Wit
Rapaport Diamond Corp. [*Information service or system*] (IID) ... RDC
Rape [*Division in the county of Sussex*] [*British*] ... RA
Rape Crisis Center (EA) ... RCC
Rape Emergency Aid and Counseling for Her [*An association*] (NADA) ... REACH
Rape Methyl Ester [*Fuel technology*] ... RME
[*The*] **Rape of Lucrece** [*Shakespearean work*] ... Luc
Rapeseed Flour [*Food technology*] ... RF
Rapeseed Meal ... RSM
Rapeseed Protein Concentrate [*Food technology*] ... RPC
Rapeseed Protein Isolate [*Food technology*] ... RPI
Raphael Cumanus [*Deceased, 1427*] [*Authority cited in pre-1607 legal work*] (DSA) ... Raph Cum
Raphael Fulgosius [*Deceased, 1427*] [*Authority cited in pre-1607 legal work*] (DSA) ... Ra F
Raphael Fulgosius [*Deceased, 1427*] [*Authority cited in pre-1607 legal work*] (DSA) ... Ra Fulgo
Raphael Fulgosius [*Deceased, 1427*] [*Authority cited in pre-1607 legal work*] (DSA) ... Raph
Raphanus Virus [*Plant pathology*] ... RV
Raphe Nucleus [*Neuroanatomy*] ... R
Raphe Pallidus [*Anatomy*] ... RP
Rapid (AAG) ... RAP
Rapid [*Commonly used*] (OPSA) ... RAPID
Rapid ... RPD
Rapid (AAG) ... RPD
Rapid Access [*Film*] (DGA) ... RA
Rapid Access Blood Bank Information (MAE) ... RABBI
Rapid Access Data [*Xerox Corp.*] ... RAD
Rapid Access Data Drum (NITA) ... RAD
Rapid Access Data Retrieval Unit [*Computer science*] (PDAA) ... RADRU
Rapid Access Device ... RAD
Rapid Access Disk ... RAD
Rapid Access Drive (BUR) ... RAD
Rapid Access Drum (IAA) ... RAD
Rapid Access for Phoenix Intermodal Development ... RAPID
Rapid Access Loop ... RAL
Rapid Access Management Information System [*Computer science*] ... RAMIS
Rapid Access Parallel Tape [*Computer science*] (IAA) ... RAPTAP
Rapid Access Recording (IEEE) ... RAR
Rapid Access Storage (NITA) ... RAS
Rapid Access Tariff Expediting Service [*Journal of Commerce, Inc.*] [*Database*] ... RATES
Rapid Access to Literature Via Fragmentation Codes (NITA) ... RALF
Rapid Access to Sequential Block [*Computer science*] (PDAA) ... RASB
Rapid Access with Extensive Search [*Algorithm*] ... RAES
Rapid Accurate Polynomial Interpolation Device (IAA) ... RAPID
Rapid Acquisition and Identification System ... RAIDS
Rapid Acquisition by Sequential Estimation (IAA) ... RASE
Rapid Acquisition of Manufactured Parts [*Military*] ... RAMP
Rapid Acquisition of Spare Parts (DOMA) ... RASP
Rapid Action Change [*DoD*] ... RAC
Rapid Action Maintenance Engineering Change [*Navy*] (MCD) ... RAMEC
Rapid Action Minor Engineering Change ... RAMEC
Rapid Advancement in Reading [*Education*] ... RAIR
Rapid Aerospace Vehicle Evaluation System [*Grumman Corp.*] ... RAVES
Rapid Air [*France ICAO designator*] (FAAC) ... RAP

Rapid Alert Programmed, Power Management of RADAR Targets [Military] (PDAA) .... RAPPORT
Rapid Alerting and Identification Display (PDAA) .... RAID
Rapid Alphanumeric Digital Indicating Device .... RANDID
Rapid Alternating Movement .... RAM
Rapid American Withdrawal [Antiwar march sponsored by Vietnam Veterans Against the War] (EA) .... RAW
Rapid Amortization Mortgage .... RAM
Rapid Amplification of CDNA [Complementary Deoxyribonucleic Acid] Ends [Genetics] .... RACE
Rapid Amplification of Cloned Ends [Analytical biochemistry] .... RACE
Rapid Analysis of Products by Integrated Engineering Routines [Computer-assisted design] .... RAPIER
Rapid Analytical Block Aerial Triangulation System (PDAA) .... RABATS
Rapid Anastigmatic (Lens) [Photography] (ROG) .... RA
Rapid and Large Leakage (GNE) .... RLL
Rapid Application Development [Computer science] .... RAD
Rapid Area Distribution Support [Air Force] .... RADS
Rapid Area Maintenance [Air Force] .... RAM
Rapid Area Supply Support [Military] (AFM) .... RASS
Rapid Area Transportation Support [Air Force] (MCD) .... RATS
Rapid Assessment Program [Environmental evaluation strategy] .... RAP
Rapid Automated Problem Identification System [DoD] .... RAPIDS
Rapid Automatic Checkout Equipment .... RACE
Rapid Automatic Drill .... RAD
Rapid Automatic Malfunction Isolation System .... RAMIS
Rapid Automatic Sweep Equipment [Air Force] .... RASE
Rapid Availability of Information and Data for Safety [NASA] (KSC) .... RAIDS
Rapid Beam Deflector (WDAA) .... RBD
Rapid Bloom Offboard Chaff [Navy ship system] .... RBOC
Rapid Canadian Resource Corp. [Vancouver Stock Exchange symbol] .... RDR
Rapid Carbohydrate Utilization Test (PDAA) .... RCUT
Rapid Change (MCD) .... RC
Rapid Changing Environment (AAG) .... RCE
Rapid Circuit Etch .... RCE
Rapid City [South Dakota] [Airport symbol] (OAG) .... RAP
Rapid City [Diocesan abbreviation] [South Dakota] (TOCD) .... RC
Rapid City [South Dakota] [Seismograph station code, US Geological Survey] (SEIS) .... RCD
Rapid City/Ellsworth Air Force Base [South Dakota] [ICAO location identifier] (ICLI) .... KRCA
Rapid City Public Library, Rapid City, SD [OCLC symbol] (OCLC) .... RCP
Rapid City Public Library, Rapid City, SD [Library symbol Library of Congress] (LCLS) .... SdR
Rapid City Regional Library, Manitoba [Library symbol National Library of Canada] (NLC) .... MRA
Rapid City Regional Library, Rapid City, MB, Canada [Library symbol Library of Congress] (LCLS) .... CaMRa
Rapid City, SD [Location identifier FAA] (FAAL) .... ELR
Rapid City, SD [FM radio station call letters] .... KBHE
Rapid City, SD [Television station call letters] .... KBHE-TV
Rapid City, SD [Television station call letters] .... KCLO
Rapid City, SD [Television station call letters] .... KEVN
Rapid City, SD [FM radio station call letters] (RBYB) .... KFXS
Rapid City, SD [AM radio station call letters] .... KIMM
Rapid City, SD [FM radio station call letters] .... KIQK
Rapid City, SD [AM radio station call letters] .... KKLS
Rapid City, SD [FM radio station call letters] .... KKMK
Rapid City, SD [FM radio station call letters] .... KLMP
Rapid City, SD [AM radio station call letters] .... KOTA
Rapid City, SD [Television station call letters] .... KOTA-TV
Rapid City, SD [FM radio station call letters] .... KOUT
Rapid City, SD [FM radio station call letters] .... KTEQ
Rapid City, SD [AM radio station call letters] .... KTOQ
Rapid City, SD [Location identifier FAA] (FAAL) .... RAP
Rapid City, SD [Location identifier FAA] (FAAL) .... RCA
Rapid City, SD [Location identifier FAA] (FAAL) .... RUS
Rapid Combat Mapping Service [or System] [Military] .... RACOMS
Rapid Curing [Asphalt grade] .... RC
Rapid Cycling Bubble Chamber (IAA) .... RCBC
Rapid Data Transmission System for Requisitioning [Navy] .... RDTSR
Rapid Decompression Test .... RDT
Rapid Demolition Device .... RDD
Rapid Deployable Surveillance Systems [Military] (NVT) .... RDSS
Rapid Deployment Force [Military] .... RDF
Rapid Deployment Force - Army .... RDF-A
Rapid Deployment Force/Light Tank [Military] (MCD) .... RDF/LT
Rapid Deployment Imagery Terminal (DOMA) .... RDIT
Rapid Deployment Joint Task Force [Military] (RDA) .... RDJTF
Rapid Development Capability [Military] (NG) .... RDC
Rapid Digital Automatic Computing .... RADAC
Rapid Displacement Heating [Pulp and paper technology] .... RDH
Rapid Draft Letter (DNAB) .... RDL
Rapid Electrophoresis .... REP
Rapid Emergency Reconstitution Team [Military] .... RAPIER
Rapid Engineer Development, Heavy Operational Repair Squadron, Engineering [Air Force] (AFM) .... RED HORSE
Rapid Engineering Deployable, Heavy Operational Repair Squadron, Engineer [Air Force] (DOMA) .... RED HORSE
Rapid Erythrocyte Degeneration [Medicine] (DMAA) .... RED
Rapid Evaluation System (IAA) .... RES
Rapid Excavation and Maintenance System [for gas piping repair] [Military] .... REMS
Rapid Excavation and Mining [Project] [Bureau of Mines] .... REAM
Rapid Excess Disposal [Military] (AABC) .... RED
Rapid Execution and Combat Targeting [Air Force] .... RE ACT

Rapid Expansion of Supercritical Solution [Chemical engineering] .... RESS
Rapid Extinction Effect [Electrophysiology] .... REE
Rapid Eye Movement .... REM
Rapid Eye Movement Deprivation .... REMD
Rapid Eye Movement Period (PDAA) .... REMP
Rapid Eye Movement - Quiescent Period .... REM-Q
Rapid Eye Movement Sleep [Neurology] (DAVI) .... REMS
Rapid Eye Movement State .... REMS
Rapid Eye Movement-Movement Period .... REM-M
Rapid Fermentation Technique .... RFT
Rapid Filling Period [Cardiology] .... RFP
Rapid Filling Wave [Cardiology] .... RFW
Rapid Fire Artillery Support System (MCD) .... RFASS
Rapid Flow Analysis .... RFA
Rapid Fluorescent Focus Inhibition Test [Medicine] (MEDA) .... RFFIT
Rapid Force Projection Initiative .... RFPI
Rapid Force Projection Initiative / Enhanced Fiber Optic Guided Missile [Army] (INF) .... RFPI/EFOGM
Rapid Freeze Quench .... RFQ
Rapid Frequency Settling Time (IAA) .... RFST
Rapid Frozen Section [Pathology and surgery] (DAVI) .... RFS
Rapid Gradient Echo (DMAA) .... RAGE
Rapid Housing Payment System [Department of Housing and Urban Development] (GFGA) .... RHPS
Rapid Ignition Propagation (MCD) .... RIP
Rapid Information Technique for Evaluation .... RITE
Rapid Information Transmission System .... RITS
Rapid Infrared Forming Technique [Materials science] .... RIF
Rapid Infusion Pump [Chemotherapy] (DAVI) .... RIP
Rapid Installation Plan .... RIP
Rapid Insurance Valuation Language (IAA) .... RIVAL
Rapid Integrated Logistic Support System [Military] (AABC) .... RILS
Rapid Intervention Vehicle (DA) .... RIV
Rapid Isolation Valve [Analytical chemistry] .... RIV
Rapid Item Processor to Facilitate Complex Operations on Magnetic Tape Files [Computer science] .... RIPFCOMTF
Rapid Iterative Reanalysis for Automated Design [Computer program] .... RITREAD
Rapid Liquid Metal Embrittlement (MCD) .... RLME
Rapid Mass Transfer [Physics] .... RMT
Rapid Memory Reload (MCD) .... RMR
Rapid Message Preparation System (NATG) .... RAMPS
Rapid Micromedia Method [Analytical biochemistry] .... RMM
Rapid Movement Disorder [Neurology] (DAVI) .... RMD
Rapid Multiple Peptide System [Biotechnology] .... RaMPS
Rapid Multistream .... RMS
Rapid Munitions Assembly System (DWSG) .... RAMS
Rapid Omnidirectional Compaction [Materials technology] [Dow Chemical Co.] .... ROC
Rapid Optical Ocean Surveillance Testbed [Navy] (EECA) .... ROOST
Rapid Optics Fabrication Technology (MCD) .... ROFT
Rapid Passive Localization (MCD) .... RAPLOC
Rapid Passive Localization - Low-Ship Impact [Navy] (CAAL) .... RAPLOC-LSI
Rapid Passive Localization - Wide Aperture Array [Military] (CAAL) .... RAPLOC-WAA
Rapid Patent Service [Research Publications, Inc.] [Information service or system] (IID) .... RPS
Rapid Photo Screening .... RPS
Rapid Plasma Reagin [Card test for venereal disease] .... RPR
Rapid Plasma Reagin Card Test [Clinical chemistry] .... RPR-CT
Rapid Pole Line [A type of pole line construction] .... RPL
Rapid Power Reduction (IEEE) .... RPR
Rapid Processing [Film] (MAE) .... RP
Rapid Processing Mode [Medicine] (MAE) .... RPM
Rapid Prototyping/Evolutionary Design (MCD) .... RP/ED
Rapid Pull Through [Gastroenterology] .... RPT
Rapid Reaction, Deployable Command, Control, and Communications R2DC3
Rapid Reaction Forces [Army] (AABC) .... RRF
Rapid Recompression-High Pressure Oxygen [Medicine] (MAE) .... RR-HPO
Rapid Rectilinear .... RR
Rapid Reduction of Nitrogen Oxides [Automotive engineering] .... RAPRENOx
Rapid Reinforcement of NATO (MCD) .... RRN
Rapid Response Bibliography Service [Information retrieval] (AEBS) .... RRB
Rapid Response Interference Prediction Model (MCD) .... RRIPM
Rapid Retargeting and Precision Pointing [Strategic Defense Initiative] R2P2
Rapid Runway Repair .... RRR
Rapid Sampling Vertical Profiler [Oceanography] .... RSVP
Rapid Scanning of Spectra [Instrumentation] .... RSS
Rapid Sealift Acquisition Group [Navy] .... RAPSAG
Rapid Sequence Intravenous Pyelogram [Medicine] .... RSIVP
Rapid Serial Visual Presentation [Computer science] .... RSVP
Rapid Setting [Asphalt grade] .... RS
Rapid Single-Flux Quantum Circuit [Physics] .... RSFQ
Rapid Site Preparation .... RSP
Rapid Solidification Plasma Deposition [Metallurgy] .... RSPD
Rapid Solidification/Powder Metallurgy .... RS/PM
Rapid Solidification Process (MCD) .... RSP
Rapid Solidification Rate (IEEE) .... RSR
Rapid Solidification Technology [Metallurgy] .... RST
Rapid Speech Transition Index [Acoustics] .... RASTI
Rapid Surfactant Test [Medicine] (MEDA) .... RST
Rapid Telephone Access System (IAA) .... RTAS
Rapid Text Search [Computer science] (IT) .... REX
Rapid Thermal Annealing [Physics] .... RTA

Rapid Thermal Chemical Vapor Deposition [*Coating technology*] [*Semiconductor technology*] ... RTCVD
Rapid Thermal Decomposition in Solution [*Powder processing*] ... RTDS
Rapid Thermal Melt Processed [*Inorganic chemistry*] ... RTMP
Rapid Thermal Processing [*Semiconductor technology*] ... RTP
Rapid Thermal Processing Chemical Vapor Deposition [*Coating technology*] [*Semiconductor technology*] ... RTPCVD
Rapid Thorium-Uranium System [*Nuclear energy*] ... RAPTUS
Rapid Transit (IAA) ... RT
Rapid Transit and Electrical Power Systems ... RT & EPS
Rapid Transit Experimental [*Gas-turbine bus*] ... RTX
Rapid Transit System (DCTA) ... RTS
Rapid Transmission and Storage [*Goldmark Corp.*] [*TV system*] ... RTS
Rapid Tuning Magnetron ... RTM
Rapid Update Cycle (USDC) ... RUC
Rapid Update Cycle [*Marine science*] (OSRA) ... RUC
Rapid Ventricular Response [*Cardiology*] (DAVI) ... RVR
Rapid Virtual Reality (PCM) ... RVR
Rapidair [*ICAO designator*] (AD) ... MC
Rapid-American Corp. ... RA
Rapidata Interactive Text Editor (IEEE) ... RITE
Rapidate Interactive Debugger [*Computer science*] (MHDI) ... RID
Rapides Parish Library, Alexandria, LA [*Library symbol Library of Congress*] (LCLS) ... LAIR
Rapid-Fire ... RF
Rapid-Fire Gun ... RFG
Rapid-Hardening Portland Cement ... RHPC
Rapidly Adapting Lateral Position Handler ... RALPH
Rapidly Deployable Barge [*Military*] (MCD) ... RDB
Rapidly Deployable Medical Facilities ... RDMF
Rapidly Deployable Mobile SIGINT [*Signal Intelligence*] **System** (MCD) ... RDMSS
Rapidly Extensible Language System [*Computer science*] (CSR) ... REL
Rapidly Miscible Pool [*Medicine*] (MAE) ... RMP
Rapidly Moving Telescope [*Astronomy*] ... RMT
Rapidly Progressive Crescenting Glomerulonephritis [*Medicine*] (DMAA) ... RPCGN
Rapidly Progressive Glomerular Nephritis [*Medicine*] ... RPGN
Rapidly Progressive Glomerulonephritis [*Nephrology*] (DAVI) ... RPGN
Rapidly Solidified Materials ... RSM
Rapid-Onset-Rate [*Air Force*] (DOMA) ... ROR
Rapids ... RPDS
Rapids (MCD) ... RPDS
Rapids Commonly used (OPSA) ... RAPIDS
Rapids [*Real Time Automated Personnel Identification System*] **Program Office** ... RPO
Rapindik [*New Britain*] [*Seismograph station code, US Geological Survey Closed*] (SEIS) ... RAP
Rapp on the Bounty Laws [*A publication*] (DLA) ... Rapp Bount
Rappahannock Community College, North Campus, Warsaw, VA [*Library symbol Library of Congress*] (LCLS) ... ViWaR
Rappen [*Monetary unit*] [*Switzerland*] ... RP
Rapport: The Modern Guide to Books, Music & More [*A publication*] (BRI) ... Rapport
Rapports de la Cour de l'Echiquier [*Exchequer Court Reports*] [*Canada*] [*A publication*] (DLA) ... RC de l'E
Rapports de la Cour Supreme du Canada [*Database*] [*Federal Department of Justice*] [*Information service or system*] (CRD) ... RCS
Rapports de Pratique de Quebec [*Quebec Practice Reports*] [*Canada*] [*A publication*] (DLA) ... RPQ
Rapports Judiciaires [*Quebec Law Reports*] [*A publication*] (DLA) ... RJQ
Rapports Judiciaires de Quebec [*Quebec Law Reports*] [*Canada*] [*A publication*] (DLA) ... Rap Jud Quebec CS (Can)
Rapports Judiciaires de Quebec [*Quebec Law Reports*] [*Canada*] [*A publication*] (DLA) ... Rap Jud Quebec KB (Can)
Rapports Judiciaires de Quebec [*Quebec Law Reports*] [*Canada*] [*A publication*] (DLA) ... Rap Jud Quebec QB (Can)
Rapports Judiciaires de Quebec, Cour du Banc de la Reine [*Quebec Law Reports, Queen's Bench*] [*A publication*] (DLA) ... Rap Jud QBR
Rapports Judiciaires de Quebec, Cour du Banc du Roi [*Quebec Law Reports, King's Bench*] [*A publication*] (DLA) ... QRKB
Rapports Judiciaires de Quebec, Cour du Banc du Roi [*Quebec Law Reports, King's Bench*] [*A publication*] (DLA) ... RJQ BR
Rapports Judiciaires de Quebec, Cour Superieure [*Quebec Law Reports, Superior Court*] [*A publication*] (DLA) ... QRSC
Rapports Judiciaires de Quebec. Cour Superieure [*Quebec Law Reports, Superior Court*] [*A publication*] (DLA) ... Rap Jud QCS
Rapports Judiciaires de Quebec, Cour Superieure [*Quebec Law Reports, Superior Court*] [*A publication*] (DLA) ... RJQ CS
Rapports Judiciaires Officiels, Cour d'Appel [*1892-date*] [*Official Law Reports, Court of Appeal Quebec*] [*A publication*] (DLA) ... Que CA
Rapports Judiciaires Officiels, Cour du Banc du Roi [*ou de la Reine*] [*Official Law Reports, Court of King's, or Queen's, Bench Quebec*] [*A publication*] (DLA) ... Que CBR
Rapports Judiciaires Officiels, Cour Superieure [*Official Law Reports, Superior Court*] [*Quebec*] [*A publication*] (DLA) ... Que CS
Rapports Judiciaires Officiels de Quebec [*Quebec Official Law Reports*] [*A publication*] (ILCA) ... RJO
Rapports Judiciaires Officiels de Quebec, Cour du Banc du Roi [*Quebec Official Law Reports, King's Bench*] [*A publication*] (ILCA) ... RJOQ (BR)
Rapports Judiciaires Officiels de Quebec, Cour Superieure [*Quebec Official Law Reports, Superior Court*] [*A publication*] (ILCA) ... RJOQ (CS)
RAPRA Technology [*Formerly, Rubber and Plastics Research Association*] (EA) ... RAPRA
RAPRA Trade Names [*RAPRA Technology Ltd.*] [*Information service or system*] (IID) ... RAPTN
Rapsgate [*England*] ... RAPSG
Raptor Information Center (EA) ... RIC
Raptor Research Foundation (EA) ... RRF
Raptor Systems [*NASDAQ symbol*] (TTSB) ... RAPT
Raptor Systems, Inc. [*NASDAQ symbol*] (SAG) ... RAPT
Raptor Systems, Inc. [*Associated Press*] (SAG) ... RaptorS
Rare [*Numismatics*] ... R
Rare [*When applied to species*] [*Biology*] ... R
Rare and Endangered Native Plant Exchange (EA) ... RENPE
Rare Animal Relief Effort ... RARE
Rare Antigen/Antibody Resource Exchange Program [*American Association of Blood Banks*] ... RARE
Rare Bird Alert [*Linnaean Society*] (BARN) ... RBA
Rare Book and Special Collections Division [*Library of Congress*] ... RBSCD
Rare Books & Manuscript Librarianship [*American Library Association*] ... RBML
Rare Books and Manuscripts Section [*Association of College and Research Libraries*] ... RBMS
Rare Books Section [*Association of College and Research Libraries*] ... RBS
Rare Breeds Poultry Club of America (EA) ... RBPCA
Rare Breeds Survival Trust [*British*] ... RBST
Rare Disease Database [*National Organization for Rare Disorders*] [*Information service or system*] (IID) ... RDB
Rare Earth ... RE
Rare Earth Boride (PDAA) ... REB
Rare Earth Information Center (NITA) ... REIC
Rare Earth Metal [*Inorganic chemistry*] ... REM
Rare Earth Permanent Magnet ... REPM
Rare Earth Research Conference (EA) ... RERC
Rare Earth Transition Metal [*Computer science*] ... RETM
Rare Fruit Council [*Later, RFCI*] (EA) ... RFC
Rare Fruit Council International (EA) ... RFCI
Rare Fruit Council of Australia ... RFCA
Rare Gas Halogen [*Inorganic chemistry*] ... RGH
Rare Hospitality Intl., Inc. [*NASDAQ symbol*] (SAG) ... RARE
Rare Hospitality Intl., Inc. [*Associated Press*] (SAG) ... RareHosp
Rare Object Searches with Bolometers Underground [*Astrophysics*] ... ROSEBUD
Rare Poultry Society [*British*] ... RPS
Rare Records [*Record label*] ... Rar
Rare Tube Gas ... RTG
Rare-Earth Alloy ... REA
Rare-Earth Catalyst [*Automotive engineering*] ... REC
Rare-Earth Cobalt ... RAECO
Rare-Earth Device ... RED
Rare-Earth Element [*Chemistry*] ... REE
Rare-Earth Exchanged [*Faujasite, a zeolite*] ... REX
Rare-Earth Information Center (EA) ... RIC
Rare-Earth Iron Garnet (IAA) ... REIG
Rare-Earth LASER ... REL
Rare-Earth LASER Device ... RELD
Rare-Earth Oxide ... REO
Rare-Earth Oxysulfide ... REOS
Rarefied Gas Dynamics ... RGD
Rarefied Gas Field [*or Flow*] ... RGF
Rarefied Hypersonic Flow ... RHF
Rare-Gas Recovery [*Nuclear energy*] (NRCH) ... RGR
Rarely Reversed [*Decisions in law*] ... RR
Rarissime [*Very Rarely*] [*Latin*] (GPO) ... rr
Rarissimum [*Extremely Rare*] [*Latin*] ... rariss
Raritan Arsenal (AAG) ... RA
Raritan Bancorp [*NASDAQ symbol*] (TTSB) ... RARB
Raritan Bancorp [*Associated Press*] (SAG) ... RarintnBc
Raritan Bancorp [*Associated Press*] (SAG) ... RaritnBc
Raritan Bancorp, Inc. [*NASDAQ symbol*] (NQ) ... RARB
Raritan River Rail Road Co. [*AAR code*] ... RR
Raritan Valley Hospital, Greenbrook, NJ [*Library symbol Library of Congress*] (LCLS) ... NjGrbR
Rarity (WGA) ... RTY
Raro Occurrit [*Rarely Occurs*] [*Latin*] (ROG) ... RAR OCC
Raron [*Switzerland ICAO location identifier*] (ICLI) ... LSER
Rarotonga [*Cook Islands*] [*Airport symbol*] (OAG) ... RAR
Rarotonga [*Cook Islands*] [*Seismograph station code, US Geological Survey*] (SEIS) ... RAR
Ras Al Khaimah/International [*United Arab Emirates*] [*ICAO location identifier*] (ICLI) ... OMRK
Ras Al Khaymah [*United Arab Emirates*] [*Airport symbol*] (OAG) ... RKT
Ras Lanouf V 40 [*Libya*] [*ICAO location identifier*] (ICLI) ... HLNF
Ras Responsive Element [*Genetics*] ... RRE
Ras Shamra (BJA) ... RS
Ras Shamra Mythological Texts (BJA) ... RSMT
Ras-al-Khaima [*Trucial Oman*] [*Airport symbol*] (AD) ... RKT
Rascal Avionics Management System (MCD) ... RAMS
RASD [*Reference and Adult Services Division*] **Business Reference Services Section** ... RASD BRASS
RASD [*Reference and Adult Services Division*] **Collection Development and Evaluation Section** ... RASD CODES
RASD [*Reference and Adult Services Division*] **History Section** ... RASD HS
RASD [*Reference and Adult Services Division*] **Interlibrary Loan Committee** [*American Library Association*] ... RASD ILC
RASD [*Reference and Adult Services Division*] **Machine-Assisted Reference Section** ... RASD MARS
RASD Quarterly [*American Library Association A publication*] ... RQ
Rasheed (Rat) Leukemia Virus ... RaLV
Rasheed (Rat) Sarcoma Virus ... RaSV
Rasht [*Iran*] [*ICAO location identifier*] (ICLI) ... OIGG
Rasht [*Iran*] [*ICAO location identifier*] (ICLI) ... OIGT

Rasht [*Iran*] [*Airport symbol*] (OAG) ... RAS
Rashtriya Swayamsevak Sangh [*National Union of Selfless Servers*] [*Militant Hindu organization India*] ... RSS
Rashtriya Swayamseyak Sangh [*National Union of Selfless Servers*] [*Militant Hindu organization India*] (PD) ... RSSS
Ras-Nasrani [*Egypt*] [*ICAO location identifier*] (ICLI) ... HERN
Raspberry Bushy Dwarf Virus [*Plant pathology*] ... RBDV
Raspberry Island [*Alaska*] [*Seismograph station code, US Geological Survey*] (SEIS) ... RAI
Raspberry Ringspot Virus [*Plant pathology*] ... RRV
Raspberry Vein Chlorosis Virus [*Plant pathology*] ... RVCV
Rassemblement Arabique-Islamique [*Algeria*] [*Political party*] (EY) ... RAI
Rassemblement Chretien de Madagascar [*Christian Rally of Madagascar*] ... RCM
Rassemblement Constitutionnel Democratique [*Tunisia*] [*Political party*] (ECON) ... RCD
Rassemblement Democratique Africain [*Niger*] [*Political party*] (PD) ... RDA
Rassemblement Democratique Africain [*Ivory Coast*] [*Political party*] (PPW) ... RDA
Rassemblement Democratique Caledonien [*Caledonian Democratic Rally*] [*Political party*] (PPW) ... RDC
Rassemblement Democratique Centrafricain [*Central African Republic*] [*Political party*] ... RDC
Rassemblement Democratique Dahomeen [*Dahomean Democratic Rally*] ... RDD
Rassemblement Democratique du Ruanda [*Democratic Rally of Rwanda*] ... RADER
Rassemblement Democratique Nationaliste et Progressiste [*Progressive Nationalist and Democratic Assembly*] [*Haiti*] (PD) ... RDNP
Rassemblement Democratique pour l'Independance [*Quebec*] ... RDI
Rassemblement des Democrates Liberaux pour la Reconstruction Nationale [*Benin*] [*Political party*] (EY) ... RDI
Rassemblement des Democrates pour l'Avenir de la Reunion [*Rally of Democrats for the Future of Reunion*] [*Political party*] (PPW) ... RADAR
Rassemblement des Gauches Republicaines [*Assembly of the Republican Left*] [*France Political party*] ... RGR
Rassemblement des Jeunes Togolais [*Togolese Youth Rally*] ... RJT
Rassemblement des Jeunesses Democratiques Africaines [*Rally of African Democratic Youth*] ... RJDA
Rassemblement des Socialistes et des Democrates [*Rally of Socialists and Democrats*] [*Reunion*] [*Political party*] (PPW) ... RSD
Rassemblement des Travaillistes Mauriciens [*Mauritius*] [*Political party*] (EY) ... RTM
Rassemblement du Peuple Camerounais [*Camerounese People's Rally*] ... RAPECA
Rassemblement du Peuple Togolais [*Rally of the Togolese People*] [*Political party*] (PPW) ... RPT
Rassemblement Europeen de la Liberte [*European Liberty Rally*] [*France Political party*] (PPE) ... REL
Rassemblement Katangais [*Katanga Rally*] ... RK
Rassemblement Mahorais pour la Republique [*Mayotte Rally for the Republic*] [*Political party*] (PPW) ... RMPR
Rassemblement National [*Canada Political party*] (PPW) ... RN
Rassemblement National Arabe [*Arab National Rally*] [*Tunisia*] (PD) ... RNA
Rassemblement National Democratique [*National Democratic Rally*] [*Senegal*] [*Political party*] (PPW) ... RND
Rassemblement National Populaire [*National People's Rally*] [*France*] ... RNP
Rassemblement National pour la Democratie [*Benin*] [*Political party*] (EY) ... RND
Rassemblement Populaire Caledonien et Metropolitain [*Caledonian and Metropolitan Popular Rally*] [*Political party*] (PPW) ... RPCM
Rassemblement Populaire pour le Progres [*Popular Rally for Progress*] [*Djibouti*] [*Political party*] (PPW) ... RPP
Rassemblement Populaire pour l'Independance [*People's Rally for Independence*] [*Djibouti*] [*Political party*] (PPW) ... RPI
Rassemblement pour la Caledonie dans la Republique [*Popular Caledonian Rally for the Republic*] [*Political party*] (PPW) ... RPCR
Rassemblement pour la Culture et la Democratie [*Algeria*] [*Political party*] (EY) ... RCD
Rassemblement pour la Democratie et le Progres [*Mali*] [*Political party*] (EY) ... RDP
Rassemblement pour la Republique [*Rally for the Republic*] [*France Political party*] (ECON) ... RPR
Rassemblement pour la Republique [*Rally for the Republic*] [*Wallis and Futuna Islands*] [*Political party*] (PD) ... RPR
Rassemblement pour la Republique [*Rally for the Republic*] [*Martinique*] [*Political party*] (PPW) ... RPR
Rassemblement pour la Republique [*Rally for the Republic*] [*French Guiana*] [*Political party*] (PPW) ... RPR
Rassemblement pour la Republique [*Rally for the Republic*] [*Reunion*] [*Political party*] (PPW) ... RPR
Rassemblement pour la Republique [*Rally for the Republic*] [*Mayotte*] [*Political party*] (EY) ... RPR
Rassemblement pour la Republique [*Rally for the Republic*] [*French Polynesia*] [*Political party*] (PPW) ... RPR
Rassemblement pour le Salut National [*Rally for National Salvation*] [*Senegal*] (PD) ... RSN
Rassemblement pour l'Independance Nationale [*Quebec separatist party, 1960-1968*] [*Canada*] ... RIN
Rassemblement pout l'Unite Nationale [*Cameroon*] [*Political party*] (EY) ... RUN
Rassemblement Socialiste Progressiste [*Tunisia*] [*Political party*] (EY) ... RSP
Rastell's Abridgment of the Statutes [*A publication*] (DLA) ... Rast Abr
Rastell's Entries [*A publication*] (DLA) ... Ent
Rastell's Entries [*A publication*] (DSA) ... Ra
Rastell's Entries and Statutes [*England*] [*A publication*] (DLA) ... Rast
Rastell's Entries and Statutes [*A publication*] (DLA) ... Rast Ent
Rastell's Old Entries [*So cited in Rolle Abridgment*] [*A publication*] (DLA) ... Entries Antient
Rastell's Old Entries [*A publication*] (DLA) ... Old Ent
Raster Graphics, Inc. [*Associated Press*] (SAG) ... RasterG
Raster Graphics, Inc. [*NASDAQ symbol*] (SAG) ... RGFX
Raster Image Device Accelerator [*Printer technology*] ... RIDA
Raster Image File Format [*Computer science*] (BTTJ) ... RIFF
Raster Image Processor [*Printer technology*] ... RIP
Raster Image Processor System (PCM) ... RIPS
Raster Input Scanner (NITA) ... RIS
Raster Operation ... ROP
Raster Scan Display Generator (MCD) ... RSDG
Raster Suppression [*of color images*] ... RS
Raster-to-Vector Processor [*Computer graphics technology*] ... RVP
Rasurae [*Scrapings or Filings*] [*Latin*] (MAE) ... ras
Rat Aortic Smooth Muscle Cells ... rASMC
Rat Atrial Natriuretic Peptide [*Biochemistry*] ... rANP
Rat Basophilic Leukemia [*Cell line*] ... RBL
Rat Calcitonin Gene-Related Peptide [*Biochemistry*] ... rCGRP
Rat Chorionic Gonadotropin ... rCG
Rat der Europaeischen Industrieverbaende [*Council of European Industrial Federations*] ... REI
Rat der Gemeinden Europas [*Council of European Municipalities*] ... RGE
Rat Embryo Fibroblast [*Cells*] ... REF
Rat Embryo Tissue Culture ... RETC
Rat Growth Hormone [*Endocrinology*] ... RGH
Rat Hepatic Lectin [*Biochemistry*] ... RHL
Rat Hepatoma-Associated Virus ... RHAV
Rat Hypothalamus Growth Hormone-Releasing Factor [*Endocrinology*] ... rhGRF
Rat Insulinoma [*A cell line*] ... RIN
Rat Intrinsic Factor Concentrate ... RIFC
Rat Island [*Alaska*] [*Seismograph station code, US Geological Survey Closed*] (SEIS) ... RAT
Rat Kidney ... RK
Rat Liver Mitochondria (MAE) ... RLMD
Rat Lung-Conditioned Medium [*Culture media*] ... RLCM
Rat Mast Cell ... RMC
Rat Mast Cell Protease [*An enzyme*] ... RMCP
Rat Mast Cell Technique [*Allergy*] (DAVI) ... RMCT
Rat, Mouse, and Hamster Fanciers (EA) ... RMHF
Rat Osteosarcoma [*Cell line*] ... ROS
Rat Ovarian Hyperemia [*Test*] (MAE) ... ROH
Rat Prolactin [*Biochemistry*] ... rPRL
Rat Red Blood Cell ... RRBC
Rat Resources [*Vancouver Stock Exchange symbol*] ... RAT
Rat Sarcoma Virus ... RSV
Rat Seminal Vesicle ... RSV
Rat Serum Albumin [*Immunology*] ... RSA
Rat Skin Collagen ... RSC
Rat Spleen Cell [*Medicine*] (DMAA) ... RSC
Rat Stomach Strip [*Medicine*] (DMAA) ... RSS
Rat Thymus Antiserum [*Biochemistry*] (MAE) ... RATHAS
Rat Transforming Growth Factor [*Biochemistry*] ... RTGF
Rat Unit ... RU
Rat Urine Protein [*Biochemistry*] (DAVI) ... RUP
Rat Virus [*Immunology*] (MAE) ... RV
Ratanlal's Unreported Criminal Cases [*India*] [*A publication*] (DLA) ... Rat Unrep Cr
Ratchaburi [*Thailand*] [*ICAO location identifier*] (ICLI) ... VTBR
Ratchet [*Design engineering*] ... RCHT
Ratchet (AAG) ... RTC
Rate (DAVI) ... k
Rate ... R
Rate (AAG) ... RT
Rate Action (AAG) ... RA
Rate Adaptive Digital Subscriber Line (PCM) ... RADSL
Rate Analysis and Transportation Evaluation [*Student legal action organization*] ... RATE
Rate and Acceleration Measuring Pendulum (PDAA) ... RAMP
Rate and Free Gyro ... RFG
Rate and Position Sensor (IAA) ... RAPS
Rate and Rhythm [*of pulse*] ... R & R
Rate and Track Subsystem ... RATS
Rate Beacon (AAG) ... RB
Rate Center [*Telecommunications*] (TEL) ... RC
Rate Change Authorization (NVT) ... RCA
Rate Command ... RC
Rate Command Control System (AAG) ... RCCS
Rate Command System (AAG) ... RCS
Rate Constant [*Symbol*] [*Chemistry*] ... k
Rate Construction Unit [*Hypothetical basic currency unit*] (DCTA) ... RCU
Rate Damping (NASA) ... RTD
Rate Damping Control ... RDC
Rate Difference [*Toxicology*] ... RD
Rate Dumping (MCD) ... RTD
Rate Effect (IEEE) ... RE
Rate [*Loop*] **Gain** ... RG
Rate Grown ... RG
Rate Gyro Accelerometer Package (MCD) ... RGAP
Rate Gyro Assembly ... RGA
Rate Gyro Assembly - Left Solid Rocket Booster (MCD) ... RGAL
Rate Gyro Assembly - Orbiter (MCD) ... RGAO
Rate Gyro Assembly - Right Solid Rocket Booster (MCD) ... RGAR
Rate Gyro Electronics Assembly (MCD) ... RGEA
Rate Gyro Package ... RGP
Rate Gyro Redundancy Management Algorithm (NASA) ... RGRMA
Rate Gyro System ... RGS
Rate Gyroscope (KSC) ... RG

Rate Gyroscope Limit ... RGL
Rate Gyroscope Unit ... RGU
Rate Improvement Mortgage [*Banking*] ... RIM
Rate Input Form (NVT) ... RIF
Rate Integrating Gyro ... RIG
Rate/Limited (MCD) ... R/L
Rate Measuring Package (MCD) ... RMP
Rate Not Reported (DS) ... RNR
Rate of a Transfer Unit (IAA) ... RTU
Rate of Application ... RA
Rate of Approach (IIA) ... RA
Rate of Change ... RC
Rate of Climb [*Aviation*] ... R/C
Rate of Climb [*Aviation*] ... ROC
Rate of Convergence (IEEE) ... ROC
Rate of Descent [*Aviation*] (MCD) ... R/D
Rate of Descent (KSC) ... ROD
Rate of Dispersal Success [*Ecology*] ... RDS
Rate of Energy Loss ... REL
Rate of Exchange ... R of E
Rate of Exchange ... RE
Rate of Exchange [*Finance*] ... ROE
Rate of Fire [*In rounds per minute*] [*Military*] ... ROF
Rate of Flow [*Medicine*] (MAE) ... Rf
Rate of Information Throughput [*Computer science*] (BUR) ... RIT
Rate of Interest [*Economics*] ... R/I
Rate of Loss of Energy (IAA) ... RLE
Rate of Pay [*British military*] (DMA) ... ROP
Rate of Penetration [*Drilling technology*] ... ROP
Rate of Read ... ROR
Rate of Return (MCD) ... ROR
Rate of Return Method [*Insurance*] ... RRM
Rate of Return on Capital Employed (DS) ... RORCE
Rate of Rise of Restriking Voltage (IEEE) ... RRRV
Rate of Rise of Voltage [*Electronics*] (IAA) ... RRV
Rate of Speed (MCD) ... ROS
Rate of Turn ... ROT
Rate of Turntable ... ROTT
Rate of Turntable ... RTT
Rate Package (AAG) ... RP
Rate per Minute ... RPM
Rate Pressure Product [*Cardiology*] ... RPP
Rate Quoting System ... RQS
Rate Ratio ... RR
Rate Rebate [*British*] ... RR
Rate Sensing Package (AAG) ... RSP
Rate Sensor Assembly (MCD) ... RSA
Rate Signal Generator (AAG) ... RSG
Rate Stabilization and Control System (MCD) ... RRSCS
Rate Stabilization and Control System ... RSCS
Rate Stabilization Reserve [*Health insurance*] (GHCT) ... RSR
Rate Subsystem Analyst (MUGU) ... RSA
Rate Support Grant [*British*] ... RSG
Rate Switching Gyro (MCD) ... RSG
Rate to Be Agreed [*Business term*] (DCTA) ... RTBA
Rate Transmitter ... RT
Rate Variance Formula [*Air Force*] ... RVF
Rateable Value [*Property value*] [*British*] ... RV
Rate-Aided Manually Implemented Tracking (NATG) ... RAMIT
Rate-Aided Tracking Computer ... RATC
Rated ... RAT
Rated (IAA) ... RD
Rated Boost ... RB
Rated Breaking Strength (IAA) ... RBS
Rated Capacity Report [*Army*] ... RCR
Rated Continuous Working Voltage (IAA) ... RCWV
Rated Distribution and Training Management ... RDTM
Rated Duty (IAA) ... RD
Rated Exposure Unit [*Advertising*] (NTCM) ... REU
Rated Horsepower ... RHP
Rated Load ... RL
Rated Maximum Pressure (SAA) ... RMP
Rated Mobilization and Professional Resource (MUGU) ... RMPR
Rated Position Identifier (AFM) ... RPI
Rated Power Level (NASA) ... RPL
Rated Pressure (NATG) ... RP
Rated Pressure Ratio (EG) ... RPR
Rated Radius [*Automotive engineering*] ... RR
Rated Sail Area [*IOR*] [*Yacht racing*] ... RSA
Rated Same or Lower ... RS or L
Rated Time (IEEE) ... RT
Rated Voltage ... RV
Rate-Dependent Left Bundle Branch Block [*Medicine*] (DMAA) ... RDLBBB
Rate-Determining Step [*Chemical kinetics*] ... RDS
Rate-Invariant Path [*Economic theory*] ... RIP
Rate-Lock Standby [*FNMA*] (EMRF) ... RLS
Ratepayers' Association [*British*] (ILCA) ... RA
Ratepayers' Association of New South Wales [*Australia*] ... RANSW
Rates and Allotments [*Eight-Sheet Outdoor Advertising Association*] [*A publication*] ... R & A
Rate-Sensitive Assets (TDOB) ... RSA
Rate-Sensitive Liabilities (TDOB) ... RSL
Rathbun Memorial Library, East Haddam, CT [*Library symbol Library of Congress*] (LCLS) ... CtEhad
Rathkamp Matchcover Society (EA) ... RMS
Rathus Assertiveness Scale [*Psychology*] (EDAC) ... RAS
Rating (AABC) ... RAT
Rating (MUGU) ... RTG
Rating and Income Tax Reports [*England*] [*A publication*] (DLA) ... R & IT
Rating and Valuation Association [*British*] (DBA) ... RVA
Rating and Valuation Reporter [*A publication*] ... R & VR
Rating Board [*Medicine*] (MAE) ... RB
Rating Factor (IEEE) ... RF
Rating of Perceived Exertion ... RPE
Rating Pending ... RP
Rating Scale Unit [*Acoustics*] ... RSU
Rating Schedule [*Medicine*] (MAE) ... RS
Rating Sheet [*Psychometrics*] ... RS
Ratio ... R
Ratio (AAG) ... RAT
Ratio Actuator (MCD) ... RA
Ratio Adjust Device (MCD) ... RAD
Ratio Analysis Diagram [*Metallurgy*] ... RAD
Ratio Balance Panel ... RBP
Ratio Changers and Boosters Assembly (MCD) ... RCBA
Ratio Command (MCD) ... R/C
Ratio Correction Factor ... RCF
Ratio Detector (IAA) ... RD
Ratio of Charge to Mass [*Physics*] (DAVI) ... e/m
Ratio of Charges [*Health insurance*] (GHCT) ... ROC
Ratio of Charges to Costs ... RCC
Ratio of Decayed and Filled Surfaces [*Dentistry*] (MEDA) ... RDFS
Ratio of Decayed and Filled Teeth [*Dentistry*] (MEDA) ... RDFT
Ratio of Earth-to-Vehicle Radii ... REV
Ratio of Serum Alanine Aminotransterase to Serum Aspartate Aminotransferase [*Medicine*] (MEDA) ... ALT/AST
Ratio Test Set ... RTS
Ratio Transfer (IAA) ... RT
Ratio Transformer [*Unit*] ... RT
Ratioflug Luftfahrtunternehmen GmbH [*Germany ICAO designator*] (FAAC) ... RAT
Ration ... RA
Ration (IAA) ... RAT
Ration Accessory Convenience [*World War II*] ... RAC
Ration Allowance [*British military*] (DMA) ... RA
Ration Book ... RB
Ration Breakdown Point [*Military*] (AABC) ... RBP
Ration Cash Allowance [*British military*] (DMA) ... RCA
Ration Distributing Point [*Military*] ... RDP
Ration Lightweight-30 Day [*Military*] (RDA) ... RLW-30
Rational Activity Coefficient ... RAC
Rational Behavior Therapy ... RBT
Rational Behavior Therapy Center [*Psychology*] (DAVI) ... RBTC
Rational Expectations [*Economics*] ... RATEX
Rational Expectations [*Economics*] (ECON) ... RE
Rational Expectations Equilibrium [*Economics*] ... REE
Rational Expectations Hypothesis [*Economics*] ... REH
Rational FORTRAN [*Computer science*] ... RATFOR
Rational Number (MDG) ... R
Rational Recovery Systems (EA) ... RRS
Rational Self-Analysis [*Psychology*] (DHSM) ... RSA
Rational Self-Counseling [*Psychology*] (DHSM) ... RSC
Rational Software [*NASDAQ symbol*] (SAG) ... RATL
Rational Software [*Associated Press*] (SAG) ... RatnSft
Rational Therapy [*Short form for rational-emotive therapy*] ... RT
Rational Use of the Sea Floor Program [*National Oceanic and Atmospheric Administration*] (MSC) ... RUSEF
Rational-Emotive Psychotherapy [*Also known as R-EP, RT*] ... R-ET
Rationalist Association of New South Wales [*Australia*] ... RANSW
Rationalist Concept of Logic ... RCL
Rationalist Press Association [*British*] (EAIO) ... RPA
Rationalist Society of Australia ... RSA
Rationalization, Standardization, and Integration [*or Interoperability*] [*Program*] [*Army*] (INF) ... RSI
Rationing [*British*] ... R
Rations [*Military*] (AABC) ... RAT
Rations Not Available [*Military*] (AABC) ... RNA
Ratios for Automotive Executives [*Computer software*] ... RAES
Rat-Mannose-Binding Protein A ... R-MBP-A
Rat-Mannose-Binding Protein C ... R-MBP-C
Ratnagiri [*India*] [*ICAO location identifier*] (ICLI) ... VARG
Ratners Group PLC (MHDW) ... RATNY
Raton, NM [*FM radio station call letters*] ... KNJU
Raton, NM [*AM radio station call letters*] ... KRTN
Raton, NM [*FM radio station call letters*] ... KRTN-FM
Raton, NM [*Location identifier FAA*] (FAAL) ... MXR
Raton, NM [*Location identifier FAA*] (FAAL) ... RTN
Ratoon Stunting Disease [*of sugarcane*] ... RSD
Rattail [*Metallurgy*] ... RTTL
Rattan Manufacturers and Importers Association ... RMIA
Ratter and Dunnet Public Library, Warren, Ontario [*Library symbol National Library of Canada*] (NLC) ... OWRD
Rattigan's Leading Cases on Hindu Law [*A publication*] (DLA) ... Ratt LC
Rattigan's Select Hindu Law Cases [*A publication*] (DLA) ... Rat Sel Cas
Rattigan's Select Hindu Law Cases [*India*] [*A publication*] (DLA) ... Rattigan
Rattler Resources [*Vancouver Stock Exchange symbol*] ... RTA
Rattlesnake Hills [*Washington*] [*Seismograph station code, US Geological Survey*] (SEIS) ... RSW
Rattlesnake Hldg Co. [*NASDAQ symbol*] (TTSB) ... RTTL
[*The*] **Rattlesnake Holding Co., Inc.** [*Associated Press*] (SAG) ... Rattlsnk

[*The*] **Rattlesnake Holding Co., Inc.** [*NASDAQ symbol*] (SAG) ... RTTL
Rattlesnake Mountain [*Washington*] [*Seismograph station code, US Geological Survey*] (SEIS) ... RMW
Rattling Brook, NF [*FM radio station call letters*] ... CHOS
Rattus Exulans [*The Polynesian rat*] ... RE
Rattus Norvegicus [*The Norway or brown rat*] ... RN
Rattus Rattus [*The ship or black rat*] ... RR
Rauch Industries, Inc. [*Associated Press*] (SAG) ... Rauch
Rauch Industries, Inc. [*AMEX symbol*] (SPSG) ... RCH
Raudha [*South Arabia*] [*Airport symbol*] (AD) ... RXA
Raufarhofn [*Iceland*] [*ICAO location identifier*] (ICLI) ... BIRG
Raufarhofn [*Iceland*] [*Airport symbol*] (OAG) ... RFN
Rauma Oy [*Associated Press*] (SAG) ... Rauma
Rauma Oy [*Associated Press*] (SAG) ... RaumaOy
Rauma Oy [*NYSE symbol*] (SAG) ... RMA
Rauma Oy ADS [*NYSE symbol*] (TTSB) ... RMA
Raumbildentfernungsmesser [*Stereoscopic range-finder*] [*German military - World War II*] ... REM
Raumordnung, Stadtebau, Wohnungswesen, Bauwesen [*Fraunhofer Society*] [*Germany*] (IID) ... RSWB
Rauschenberg Overseas Cultural Interchange [*Retrospective exhibit of artist Robert Rauschenberg's work*] ... ROCI
Rauscher [*Murine*] **Leukemia Virus** ... RLV
Rauscher Murine Leukemia Virus [*Medicine*] (DMAA) ... RMLV
Rauscher Murine Leukemia Virus ... R-MuLV
Rautavaara [*Finland ICAO location identifier*] (ICLI) ... EFRA
Rauvai [*Tuamotu Archipelago*] [*Seismograph station code, US Geological Survey*] (SEIS) ... RUV
Rauwolfia Serpentina [*A plant, the root extract of which is used medicinally*] ... RS
Rav Tov Committee to Aid New Immigrants [*Later, RTIJRO*] (EA) ... RTCANI
Rav Tov International Jewish Rescue Organization (EA) ... RTIJRO
Ravan Fan Club [*Defunct*] (EA) ... RFC
Raven Air, Inc. [*ICAO designator*] (FAAC) ... RVA
Raven Air Ltd. [*British ICAO designator*] (FAAC) ... RVR
Raven Coloured Progressive Matrices [*Psychiatry*] (DAVI) ... RCPM
Raven Indus [*NASDAQ symbol*] (TTSB) ... RAVN
Raven Industries, Inc. [*Associated Press*] (SAG) ... Raven
Raven Industries, Inc. [*NASDAQ symbol*] (SAG) ... RAVN
Ravena, NY [*FM radio station call letters*] (RBYB) ... WABY-FM
Ravena, NY [*FM radio station call letters*] ... WEMX
Ravenel, SC [*FM radio station call letters*] ... WMGL
Ravenna Army Ammunition Plant (AABC) ... RVAAP
Ravenroc Resources Ltd. [*Vancouver Stock Exchange symbol*] ... RRC
Raven's Matrices [*Intelligence test*] ... RM
Raven's Proressive Matrices [*Psychiatry*] (DAVI) ... RPM
Ravensbos [*Netherlands*] [*Seismograph station code, US Geological Survey*] (SEIS) ... RSB
Ravensburg [*Federal Republic of Germany*] [*Seismograph station code, US Geological Survey*] (SEIS) ... RAV
Ravenswood Hospital Medical Center, Chicago, IL [*Library symbol Library of Congress*] (LCLS) ... ICRaH
Ravenswood, WV [*FM radio station call letters*] ... WFYZ
Ravenswood, WV [*AM radio station call letters*] ... WMOV
Ravenswood, WV [*FM radio station call letters*] ... WRZZ
Ravine, PA [*Location identifier FAA*] (FAAL) ... RAV
Ravns Storo [*Greenland*] [*ICAO location identifier*] (ICLI) ... BGRS
Raw Agricultural Commodity ... RAC
Raw Cooling Water [*Nuclear energy*] (NRCH) ... RCW
Raw Cycle Time (AAGC) ... RCT
Raw Data Recorder (NASA) ... RDR
Raw Data System ... RADS
Raw End (OA) ... RE
Raw Fat and Bone Processors Association [*British*] (BI) ... RFBPA
Raw Material ... RM
Raw Material and Purchase Parts (MCD) ... RM & PP
Raw Material Price Index (NITA) ... RAMPI
Raw Materials (MCD) ... RME
Raw Materials Board [*of the Reconstruction Finance Corp.*] ... RMB
Raw Materials Committee of the Commonwealth Supply Council [*British World War II*] ... RMCCSC
Raw Materials Department [*Ministry of Supply*] [*British*] ... RMD
Raw Materials Finance Department [*Ministry of Supply*] [*British*] ... RMF
Raw Materials Processing ... RMP
Raw RADAR Data Recorder ... RRDR
Raw Score [*Psychology*] ... X
Raw Service Water [*Nuclear energy*] (NRCH) ... RSW
Raw Statement of Intelligence Interest (MCD) ... RAWSII
Raw Stock ... RS
Raw Stock Material Requirements ... RSMR
Raw Type Write Submodule ... RTWS
Raw Umber and Maize Preservation Society [*An association*] ... RUMPS
Raw Water [*Nuclear energy*] ... RW
Raw Water Cooling ... RWC
Rawalakot [*Pakistan*] [*ICAO location identifier*] (ICLI) ... OPRT
Rawalpindi/Islamabad [*Pakistan*] [*Airport symbol Obsolete*] (OAG) ... RWP
Rawdon Resources Ltd. [*Vancouver Stock Exchange symbol*] ... RWN
Rawhide (MSA) ... RWHD
Rawhide (VRA) ... rwhi
Rawindsonde Observation [*Marine science*] (OSRA) ... RAOB
RAWINSONDE [*Radiosonde and RADAR Wind Sounding*] [*Upper air observation*] (NASA) ... RS
RAWINSONDE [*Radiosonde and RADAR Wind Sounding*] [*Upper air observation*] ... RW
Rawle on Covenants for Title [*A publication*] (DLA) ... Raw Cov
Rawle on Covenants for Title [*A publication*] (DLA) ... Rawle Cov
Rawle on the Constitution of the United States [*A publication*] (DLA) ... Raw Const
Rawle on the Constitution of the United States [*A publication*] (DLA) ... Rawle Const US
Rawle, Penrose, and Watts' Pennsylvania Reports [*1828-40*] [*A publication*] (DLA) ... Rawle Pen & W
Rawle, Penrose, and Watts' Pennsylvania Reports [*1828-40*] [*A publication*] (DLA) ... RP & W
Rawle, Penrose, and Watts' Pennsylvania Reports [*1828-40*] [*A publication*] (DLA) ... RPW
Rawle's Equity in Pennsylvania [*A publication*] (DLA) ... Raw Eq
Rawle's Pennsylvania Reports [*1828-35*] [*A publication*] (DLA) ... R
Rawle's Pennsylvania Reports [*5 vols.*] [*A publication*] (DLA) ... Raw
Rawle's Pennsylvania Supreme Court Reports [*1828-35*] [*A publication*] (DLA) ... Rawle
Rawlings Sporting Goods [*NASDAQ symbol*] (TTSB) ... RAWL
Rawlings Sporting Goods Company, Inc. [*NASDAQ symbol*] (SAG) ... RAWL
Rawlings Sporting Goods Co., Inc. [*Associated Press*] (SAG) ... Rawlings
Rawlins [*Wyoming*] [*Airport symbol*] (AD) ... RWL
Rawlins, WY [*Television station call letters*] ... KFNR
Rawlins, WY [*FM radio station call letters*] ... KIQZ
Rawlins, WY [*AM radio station call letters*] ... KRAL
Rawlins, WY [*Location identifier FAA*] (FAAL) ... RWL
Rawlinson's Municipal Corporations [*10th ed.*] [*1910*] [*A publication*] (DLA) ... Rawl Mun Corp
Rawson Memorial Library, Cass City, MI [*Library symbol Library of Congress*] (LCLS) ... MiCac
Rawson-Koenig [*NASDAQ symbol*] (TTSB) ... RAKO
Rawson-Koenig, Inc. [*NASDAQ symbol*] (NQ) ... RAKO
Rawson-Koenig, Inc. [*Associated Press*] (SAG) ... RawsnKo
Raxaul [*India*] [*ICAO location identifier*] (ICLI) ... VERL
Ray Coble Fan Club [*Defunct*] (EA) ... RCFC
Ray Control ... RC
Ray Control Electrode (IAA) ... RC
Ray Control Electrode (IAA) ... RCE
Ray Griff Fan Club (EA) ... RGFC
Ray Heatherton Irish Friends Club [*Defunct*] (EA) ... RHIFC
Ray Kirkland Fan Club (EA) ... RKFC
Ray Memorial Library, Franklin, MA [*Library symbol Library of Congress*] (LCLS) ... MFran
Ray of Hope [*An association*] (EA) ... ROH
Ray Price Fan Club (EA) ... RPFC
Ray Society (EA) ... RS
Rayaguda [*India*] [*ICAO location identifier*] (ICLI) ... VERG
Rayburn House Office Building [*Washington, DC*] (DLA) ... RHOB
Raychem Corp. [*Associated Press*] (SAG) ... Raycm
Raychem Corp. [*NYSE symbol*] (SPSG) ... RYC
Rayden on Divorce [*A publication*] (DLA) ... Rayden
Raydex Bonded Shield (NITA) ... RBS
Rayleigh Number [*IUPAC*] ... Ra
Rayleigh Quotient Iteration ... RQI
Rayleigh Radiation Law [*Physics*] ... RRL
Rayleigh Scattering of Moessbauer Resonance [*Physics*] ... RSMR
Rayleigh Wave [*Earthquakes*] ... Lr
Rayleigh Wave [*Seismology*] ... R
Rayleigh-Jeans Equation [*Physics*] ... RJE
Rayleigh-Ritz Method [*Physics*] ... RRM
Rayleigh-Schrodinger Perturbation Theory [*Physical chemistry*] ... RSPT
Raymac Oil Corp. [*Vancouver Stock Exchange symbol*] ... RYC
Raymond A. Sapp Memorial Library, Wyanet, IL [*Library symbol Library of Congress*] (LCLS) ... IWya
Raymond, Chabot, Martin, Pare, Montreal, PQ, Canada [*Library symbol*] [*Library of Congress*] (LCLS) ... CaQMRCM
Raymond, Chabot, Martin, Pare, Montreal, Quebec [*Library symbol National Library of Canada*] (NLC) ... QMRCM
[*The*] **Raymond Corp.** [*NASDAQ symbol*] (NQ) ... RAYM
Raymond Corp. [*Associated Press*] (SAG) ... Raymd
Raymond International, Inc., Houston, TX [*Library symbol Library of Congress*] (LCLS) ... TxHRa
Raymond James Financial, Inc. [*Associated Press*] (SAG) ... RJamFn
Raymond James Financial, Inc. [*NYSE symbol*] (SPSG) ... RJF
Raymond James Finl [*NYSE symbol*] (TTSB) ... RJF
Raymond Manufacturing Co. ... RMCO
Raymond, MS [*Location identifier FAA*] (FAAL) ... RYB
Raymond Public Library, Alberta [*Library symbol National Library of Canada*] (NLC) ... ARAY
Raymond Public Library, Raymond, MN [*Library symbol*] [*Library of Congress*] (LCLS) ... MnRa
Raymond, WA [*FM radio station call letters*] ... KSWW
Raymond Walters General and Technical College, Blue Ash, OH [*OCLC symbol*] (OCLC) ... ORW
Raymond Walters General and Technical College, Cincinnati, OH [*Library symbol Library of Congress*] (LCLS) ... OCRW
Raymond's Bill of Exceptions [*A publication*] (DLA) ... Ray B Ex
Raymond's Bill of Exceptions [*A publication*] (DLA) ... Raym B Ex
Raymond's Digested Chancery Cases [*A publication*] (DLA) ... Raym Ch Dig
Raymond's Reports [*81-89 Iowa*] [*A publication*] (DLA) ... Raymond
Raymondville, TX [*FM radio station call letters*] (RBYB) ... KBIC
Raymondville, TX [*AM radio station call letters*] ... KSOX
Raymondville, TX [*FM radio station call letters*] ... KSOX-FM
Raymundus de Pennafort [*Deceased, 1275*] [*Authority cited in pre-1607 legal work*] (DSA) ... R
Raymundus de Pennafort [*Deceased, 1275*] [*Authority cited in pre-1607 legal work*] (DSA) ... Ra

Raymundus de Pennafort [*Deceased, 1275*] [*Authority cited in pre-1607 legal work*] (DSA) ... Ray
Raymundus de Sabanacho [*Authority cited in pre-1607 legal work*] (DSA) ... R
Raymundus de Sabanacho [*Authority cited in pre-1607 legal work*] (DSA) ... Ray de Saba
Raymundus Fabri [*Flourished, 14th century*] [*Authority cited in pre-1607 legal work*] (DSA) ... Ra Fab
Raynaud's and Scleroderma Association Trust [*British*] (EAIO) ... RSAT
Raynaud's Association Trust (EA) ... RAT
Raynaud's Disease [*Medicine*] ... RD
Raynaud's Phenomenon [*Medicine*] ... RA
Raynaud's Phenomenon [*Medicine*] ... RP
Raynaud's Phenomenon, Esophageal Motor Dysfuntion, Sclerodactyly, and Telangiectasis Syndrome [*Medicine*] (DMAA) ... REST
Rayne, LA [*FM radio station call letters*] ... KCRL
Raynerius de Forlivio [*Deceased, 1358*] [*Authority cited in pre-1607 legal work*] (DSA) ... Ray
Raynerius de Forlivio [*Deceased, 1358*] [*Authority cited in pre-1607 legal work*] (DSA) ... Ray de For
Rayner's English Tithe Cases [*1575-1782*] [*A publication*] (DLA) ... Ray Ti Cas
Rayner's English Tithe Cases [*3 vols.*] [*A publication*] (DLA) ... Rayn
Rayner's English Tithe Cases [*1575-1782*] [*A publication*] (DLA) ... Rayn Ti Cas
Ray-Net Communications Systems, Inc. [*Vancouver Stock Exchange symbol*] ... RYT
Rayon (AAG) ... RA
Rayon ... RYN
Rayon and Cotton [*Freight*] ... RC
Rayong/Utapao [*Thailand*] [*ICAO location identifier*] (ICLI) ... VTBU
Rayonier Canada, Research Division, Vancouver, BC, Canada [*Library symbol Library of Congress Obsolete*] (LCLS) ... CaBVaRC
Rayonier, Inc. [*Associated Press*] (SAG) ... RaynrInc
Rayonier, Inc. [*NYSE symbol*] (SAG) ... RYN
Rayonier Timberlands Cl'A' [*NYSE symbol*] (TTSB) ... LOG
Rayonier Timberlands Ltd. [*Associated Press*] (SAG) ... RayTLP
Rayonier Timberlands LP [*NYSE symbol*] (SPSG) ... LOG
Rayon-Rayon Bias-Belted (PDAA) ... RR-BB
Ray-Path Distance (MUGU) ... RAYDIST
Raypath Resources Ltd. [*Vancouver Stock Exchange symbol*] ... RPH
Rayrock Yellowknife Resources, Inc. [*Toronto Stock Exchange symbol*] ... RAY
Rays ... R
Rays Initiating from a Point (MCD) ... RIP
Ray's Medical Jurisprudence of Insanity [*A publication*] (DLA) ... Ray Ins
Ray's Medical Jurisprudence of Insanity [*A publication*] (DLA) ... Ray Med Jur
Ray's Mental Pathology [*A publication*] (DLA) ... Ray Men Path
Rayside-Balfour Public Library, Azilda Branch, Azilda, ON, Canada [*Library symbol*] [*Library of Congress*] (LCLS) ... CaOARB
Rayside-Balfour Public Library, Chelmsford, ON, Canada [*Library symbol Library of Congress*] (LCLS) ... CaOCheRB
Rayskala [*Finland ICAO location identifier*] (ICLI) ... EFRY
Raytech Corp. [*NYSE symbol*] (SPSG) ... RAY
Raytech Corp. [*Associated Press*] (SAG) ... Raytc
Raytel Medical [*NASDAQ symbol*] (TTSB) ... RTEL
Raytel Medical Corp. [*Associated Press*] (SAG) ... Raytel
Raytel Medical Corp. [*NASDAQ symbol*] (SAG) ... RTEL
Raytheon Acoustic Telemetry and Control ... RATAC
Raytheon Advanced Battery Acquisition RADAR ... RABAR
Raytheon Airborne Microwave (MCD) ... RAM
Raytheon Airborne Microwave Platform [*Sky station*] ... RAMP
Raytheon Automated Digital Design System (PDAA) ... RADDS
Raytheon Automatic Drafting Artwork Compiler ... RADAC
Raytheon Automatic Test Equipment Language [*Computer science*] (CSR) ... RATEL
Raytheon Communications Equipment [*Citizens band radio*] ... RAY-COM
Raytheon Co. [*Associated Press*] (SAG) ... Raythn
Raytheon Co. [*NYSE symbol*] (SPSG) ... RTN
Raytheon Co., Goleta, CA [*Library symbol Library of Congress*] (LCLS) ... CGoR
Raytheon Co., Missile Systems Division Library, Bedford, MA [*Library symbol Library of Congress*] (LCLS) ... MBdR
Raytheon Co./Research Division ... RAY/RD
Raytheon Co., Wayland, MA [*Library symbol Library of Congress*] (LCLS) ... MWayR
Raytheon Controlled Inventory [*Computer science*] ... RAYCI
Raytheon Data Communications Network (NITA) ... RAYNET
Raytheon Data Systems Co. ... RDS
Raytheon Digital Automatic Computer (MUGU) ... RAYDAC
Raytheon Electronic Systems ... RES
Raytheon Manufacturing Co. (MCD) ... RMC
Raytheon Resistor [*Electro-optical control device*] ... RAYSISTOR
Raytheon Service Co. ... RSC
Raytheon Spectrum Analyzer ... RAYSPAN
Raytheon Telephone [*Citizens band radio*] ... RAY-TEL
Rayville, LA [*FM radio station call letters*] ... KTJC
Rayville, LA [*AM radio station call letters*] ... KXLA
Rayville, LA [*Location identifier FAA*] (FAAL) ... MRK
Raza Unida Party (EA) ... RUP
Razor Grinders' Protection Society [*A union*] [*British*] ... RGPS
Razor Hafters' Trade Protection Society [*A union*] [*British*] ... RHTPS
Razor Trade Federation [*A union*] [*British*] ... RTF
Razor Trade Forgers' Society [*A union*] [*British*] ... RTFS
[*The*] **Razorback Award** (IAA) ... TRA
Razoxane [*Medicine*] (DMAA) ... RAZ
Razzy Bailey Fan Club (EA) ... RBFC
R-B Rubber Products [*NASDAQ symbol*] (TTSB) ... RBBR
R-B Rubber Products, Inc. [*Associated Press*] (SAG) ... R-B Rub
R-B Rubber Products, Inc. [*NASDAQ symbol*] (SAG) ... RBBR
RBK NT Corp. [*Toronto Stock Exchange symbol*] ... RBK
RC Reid-Bicknell Eng. Ltd., Woodbridge, Ontario [*Library symbol National Library of Canada*] (NLC) ... OWRB
RCA Cable and Rockefeller Center Cable Pay-TV Program Service ... RCTV
RCA [*Radio Corp. of America*] **Consumer Electronics Library, Indianapolis, IN** [*OCLC symbol*] (OCLC) ... IMJ
RCA Corp. Communications ... RCC
RCA, Selectavision Video Disc Operations Library, Indianapolis, IN [*Library symbol Library of Congress*] (LCLS) ... InIRCA
RCA Victor Co. Ltd., Montreal, PQ, Canada [*Library symbol Library of Congress*] (LCLS) ... CaQMV
RCA Victor Co. Ltd., Montreal, Quebec [*Library symbol National Library of Canada*] (NLC) ... QMV
RCA Video Productions ... RVP
RCJ Resources Ltd. [*Vancouver Stock Exchange symbol*] ... RCJ
RCM Strategic Global Government Fund [*Associated Press*] (SAG) ... RCM Str
RCM Strategic Global Government Fund [*NYSE symbol*] (SAG) ... RCS
RCM Strategic Global Gvt Fund [*NYSE symbol*] (TTSB) ... RCS
RCM Technologies [*NASDAQ symbol*] (TTSB) ... RCMT
RCM Technologies, Inc. [*Associated Press*] (SAG) ... RCM
RCM Technologies, Inc. [*NASDAQ symbol*] (NQ) ... RCMT
RCM Technologies Wrrt'C' [*NASDAQ symbol*] (TTSB) ... RCMTZ
RCMP [*Royal Canadian Mounted Police*] **Crime Laboratory, Winnipeg, Manitoba** [*Library symbol National Library of Canada*] (NLC) ... MWRC
RCMP Headquarters [*Direction Generale de la GRC*] **Ottawa, Ontario** [*Library symbol National Library of Canada*] (NLC) ... OOR
RCMP [*Royal Canadian Mounted Police*] **Law Enforcement Reference Centre , Ottawa, Ontario** [*Centre de Documentation Policiere, Gendarmerie Royale du Canada*] [*Library symbol National Library of Canada*] (NLC) ... OOR
RCMP, Scientific Information Centre, Ottawa, ON, Canada [*Library symbol*] [*Library of Congress*] (LCLS) ... CaOORS
RCMP Scientific Information Centre [*Centre d'Information Scientifique de la GRC*] **Ottawa, Ontario** [*Library symbol National Library of Canada*] (NLC) ... OORS
RCRA [*Resource Conservation and Recovery Act*] **Administrative Action Tracking System** (ERG) ... RAATS
RCRA [*Resource Conservation and Recovery Act*] **Enforcement Division** [*Environmental Protection Agency*] (GFGA) ... RED
RCRA [*Resource Conservation and Recovery Act*] **Facility Assessment** ... RFA
RCRA [*Resource Conservation and Recovery Act*] **Facility Investigation** ... RFI
RCRA [*Resource Conservation and Recovery Act*] **Implementation Plan** [*Environmental Protection Agency*] (GFGA) ... RIP
RCS [*Reaction Control System*] **Module Forward** [*NASA*] (NASA) ... RMF
RCSB Financial [*NASDAQ symbol*] (TTSB) ... RCSB
RCSB Financial, Inc. [*Associated Press*] (SAG) ... RCSB
RCSB Financial, Inc. [*Associated Press*] (SAG) ... RCSB Fn
RCSB Finl 7% Perp Cv 'B' Pfd [*NASDAQ symbol*] (TTSB) ... RCSBP
Re Capital Corp. [*NASDAQ symbol*] (SAG) ... RCAP
Rea Gold [*AMEX symbol*] (TTSB) ... REO
Rea Gold Corp. [*Associated Press*] (SAG) ... ReaGld
Rea Gold Corp. [*Associated Press*] (SAG) ... ReaGold
Rea Gold Corp. [*NASDAQ symbol*] (SAG) ... REDGF
Rea Gold Corp. [*Toronto Stock Exchange symbol Vancouver Stock Exchange symbol*] ... REO
Reach and Frequency [*Advertising*] (WDMC) ... R & F
Reach Avalanche Photodiode (IAA) ... RAPD
Reach to Recovery (DAVI) ... R to R
Reacquire ... REACQ
REACT International (EA) ... RI
Reactance [*Measurement and physics*] (DAVI) ... X
Reactance [*Symbol*] [*IUPAC*] (AAG) ... X
Reactance Meter (IAA) ... RM
Reactant Service System ... RSS
Reactants Supply System [*NASA*] (KSC) ... RSS
Reaction (AAG) ... R
Reaction (MSA) ... RCTN
Reaction (AAG) ... REAC
Reaction [*Laboratory science*] (DAVI) ... rx
Reaction [*Medicine*] ... RXN
Reaction Access System [*Computer program*] ... REACCS
Reaction Augmentation System ... RAS
Reaction Bonded Silicon Nitride [*Materials science and technology*] ... RBSN
Reaction Center ... RC
Reaction Chamber ... RC
Reaction Control ... RC
Reaction Control Assembly ... RCA
Reaction Control Center (KSC) ... RCC
Reaction Control Engine ... RCE
Reaction Control Jet ... RCJ
Reaction Control Motor (IAA) ... RCM
Reaction Control System [*or Subsystem*] [*Steering system in spacecraft*] [*NASA*] ... RCS
Reaction Control System [*or Subsystem*] **Controller** [*Apollo*] [*NASA*] (NASA) ... RCSC
Reaction Coupling (IAA) ... RC
Reaction Cured Glass [*Ceramic technology*] ... RCG
Reaction Energy Profile ... REP
Reaction Engine Module [*NASA*] (KSC) ... REM
Reaction Injection Molding [*Plastics technology*] ... RIM
Reaction Jet Control [*NASA*] (NASA) ... RJC
Reaction Jet Device [*NASA*] (NASA) ... RJD
Reaction Jet Driver [*NASA*] (NASA) ... RJD
Reaction Jet Driver - Aft [*NASA*] (NASA) ... RJDA
Reaction Jet Driver - Forward [*NASA*] (NASA) ... RJDF
Reaction Jet/Engine Control [*NASA*] (NASA) ... RJ/EC

Reaction Jet OMS [*Orbital Maneuvering Subsystem*] **Driver** [*NASA*] (NASA) ... RJOD
Reaction Jet Pipe ... RJP
Reaction Jet System (KSC) ... RJS
Reaction Kinetic Analysis (PDAA) ... RKA
Reaction Mass ... RM
Reaction Motors Division (SAA) ... RMD
Reaction of Degeneration [*Physiology*] ... DeR
Reaction of Degeneration [*Physiology*] ... DR
Reaction of Degeneration [*Physiology*] ... RD
Reaction Product Imaging [*Chemistry*] ... RPI
Reaction Products Separator Tank [*Nuclear energy*] (NRCH) ... RPST
Reaction Rate Constant [*Chemistry*] (DAVI) ... k
Reaction Research Society (EA) ... RRS
Reaction Shot [*TV news*] (WDMC) ... reax
Reaction Time ... RT
Reaction Torque Temperature Sensitivity ... RTTS
Reaction Voltage ... RV
Reaction Wheel Assembly (MCD) ... RWA
Reaction Wheel Scanner ... RWS
Reaction Wheel Systems (AAG) ... RWS
Reaction with Distillation [*Koch Engineering Co.*] [*Chemical engineering*] ... RWD
Reaction Zone ... RZ
Reaction-Control Valve ... RCV
Reaction-Limited Cluster Aggregation ... RLCA
Reaction-Sintered Silicon Nitrate ... RSSN
Reaction-Yield-Detected Magnetic Resonance [*Also, RYDMR*] [*Spectroscopy*] ... RYDMAR
Reaction-Yield-Detected Magnetic Resonance [*Also, RYDMAR*] [*Spectroscopy*] ... RYDMR
Reactivate ... REACTVT
Reactive ... REAC
Reactive [*Laboratory science*] (DAVI) ... REC
Reactive Airway Disease [*Medicine*] (MAE) ... RAD
Reactive Airways Dysfunction Syndrome [*Medicine*] (DMAA) ... RADS
Reactive Atmosphere Process ... RAP
Reactive Bias Circuit (MCD) ... RBC
Reactive Chemical Vapor Deposition [*Coating technology*] ... RCVD
Reactive Current Sensing (MCD) ... RCS
Reactive Electronic Equipment Simulator (RDA) ... REES
Reactive Evaporation [*Coating technology*] ... RE
Reactive Factor (IAA) ... RF
Reactive Factor Meter ... RFM
Reactive Hydrocarbon [*Environmental science*] ... RHC
Reactive Hyperemia [*Medicine*] ... RH
Reactive Hyperemia Blood Flow [*Medicine*] (MAE) ... RHBF
Reactive Ion Beam Etching ... RIBE
Reactive Ion Etching [*Semiconductor technology*] ... RIE
Reactive Ion Plating [*Coating technology*] ... RIP
Reactive Kilovolt-Ampere ... RKVA
Reactive Load Factor (IAA) ... RLF
Reactive Loss (IAA) ... RL
Reactive Metals, Inc. Titanium Co. Extrusion Plant [*Department of Energy*] [*Ashtabula, OH*] (GAAI) ... RMI
Reactive Modulation Amplifier ... RMA
Reactive Organic Gas [*Environmental chemistry*] ... ROG
Reactive Oxygen Intermediate [*Biochemistry*] ... ROI
Reactive Oxygen Metabolites [*Biochemistry*] ... ROM
Reactive Oxygen Species ... ROS
Reactive Perfluoroalkyl Polymeric Surfactant [*Organic chemistry*] ... RPPS
Reactive Plasma Deposition ... RPD
Reactive Plume Model [*Environmental Protection Agency*] (GFGA) ... RPM
Reactive Protein [*Clinical chemistry*] (MAE) ... RP
Reactive Soil Pool [*Agriculture*] ... RSP
Reactive Stream Separation (MCD) ... RSS
Reactive System Sensitivity (IAA) ... RSS
Reactive Terminal Service [*International Telephone & Telegraph computer*] ... RTS
Reactive to Light [*Referring to the pupils of the eyes*] [*Ophthalmology*] (DAVI) ... RTL
Reactive Volt-Ampere ... VAR
Reactive Volt-Ampere Meter ... RVA
Reactive Voltmeter ... RVM
Reactivity Initiated Accident [*Nuclear energy*] (NRCH) ... RIA
Reactivity Measurement Facility [*Nuclear energy*] ... RMF
Reactivity Monitoring and Alarm System [*Nuclear energy*] (NRCH) ... RMAAS
Reactivity Surveillance Procedures [*Nuclear energy*] (NRCH) ... RSP
Reactivity Test Assembly [*Nuclear energy*] ... RTA
Reactivity-Adjusted Non-Methane Organic Gas [*Automotive emissions*] ... RANMOG
Reactor (IAA) ... RC
Reactor (AAG) ... REAC
Reactor Accident Calculation ... RAC
Reactor Accident Mitigation Project [*Nuclear energy*] (NUCP) ... RAMA
Reactor Alarm System (IEEE) ... RAS
Reactor Analysis and Safety [*Nuclear energy*] (NRCH) ... RAS
Reactor and Plant Integrated Dynamics [*Computer science*] (KSC) ... RAPID
Reactor and Vessel Instrumentation System [*Nuclear energy*] (NRCH) ... RVIS
Reactor Auxiliary Building [*Nuclear energy*] (NRCH) ... RAB
Reactor Auxiliary Building Normal Ventilation System [*Nuclear energy*] (NRCH) ... RABNVS
Reactor Auxiliary Cooling System [*Nuclear energy*] (NUCP) ... RACS
Reactor Building [*Nuclear energy*] (NRCH) ... RB
Reactor Building Closed Cooling Water [*Nuclear energy*] (NRCH) ... RBCCW
Reactor Building Cooling System [*Nuclear energy*] (NRCH) ... RBCS
Reactor Building Cooling Unit [*Nuclear energy*] (NRCH) ... RBCU
Reactor Building Cooling Water System (IEEE) ... RBCWS
Reactor Building Equipment Drain Tank [*Nuclear energy*] (NRCH) ... RBEDT
Reactor Building Exhaust System Isolation [*Nuclear energy*] (NRCH) ... RBESI
Reactor Building Heating System [*Nuclear energy*] (NRCH) ... RBHS
Reactor Building Hydrogen Purge Fan (IEEE) ... RBHPF
Reactor Building Protection [*Nuclear energy*] (NRCH) ... RBP
Reactor Building Spray [*Nuclear energy*] (NRCH) ... RBS
Reactor Building Sump [*Nuclear energy*] (IAA) ... RBS
Reactor Building Vent (IEEE) ... RBV
Reactor Building Vent Process Radiation Monitor [*Nuclear energy*] (NRCH) ... RBVPRM
Reactor Building Ventilation Isolation [*Nuclear energy*] (NRCH) ... RBVI
Reactor Cavity [*Nuclear energy*] (NRCH) ... RC
Reactor Cavity Cooling System [*Nuclear energy*] ... RCCS
Reactor Characterization Program [*Nuclear energy*] (NRCH) ... RCP
Reactor Closed Cooling [*Nuclear energy*] (NRCH) ... RCC
Reactor Compartment (MSA) ... RC
Reactor Compatibility Experiment [*Nuclear energy*] (NRCH) ... RCE
Reactor Containment Building [*Nuclear energy*] (NRCH) ... RCB
Reactor Containment Fan Cooler [*Nuclear energy*] (NRCH) ... RCFC
Reactor Control Room ... RCR
Reactor Coolant [*Nuclear energy*] (NRCH) ... RC
Reactor Coolant Bleed Holdup Tank [*Nuclear energy*] (NRCH) ... RCBHT
Reactor Coolant Bleed Tank [*Nuclear energy*] (NRCH) ... RCBT
Reactor Coolant Drain Tank [*Nuclear energy*] (NRCH) ... RCDT
Reactor Coolant Leakage Calculation (IEEE) ... RCLC
Reactor Coolant Letdown Cooler [*Nuclear energy*] (NRCH) ... RCLC
Reactor Coolant Loop [*Nuclear energy*] (NRCH) ... RCL
Reactor Coolant Pressure Boundary [*Nuclear energy*] (NRCH) ... RCPB
Reactor Coolant Pump [*Nuclear energy*] (NRCH) ... RCP
Reactor Coolant System [*Nuclear energy*] (NRCH) ... RCS
Reactor Coolant System Dose Equivalent (IEEE) ... RCSDE
Reactor Coolant Treatment System [*Nuclear energy*] (NRCH) ... RCTS
Reactor Cooling Water [*Nuclear energy*] (NRCH) ... RCW
Reactor Core (IEEE) ... RCO
Reactor Core Fan Cooling (Unit) (IEEE) ... RCFC(U)
Reactor Core Isolation Cooling [*Nuclear energy*] (NRCH) ... RCIC
Reactor Core Isolation Cooling System [*Nuclear energy*] (NRCH) ... RCICS
Reactor Cover Gas Monitor [*Nuclear energy*] (NRCH) ... RCGM
Reactor Deck Development Mock-Up [*Nuclear energy*] (NRCH) ... RDDM
Reactor Design from Thermal-Hydraulic Operating Parameters [*NASA*] ... REDTOP
Reactor Development and Technology [*Nuclear energy*] (MCD) ... RDT
Reactor Development Division [*of AEC*] ... RDD
[*The*] **Reactor Development Laboratory** [*UKAEA*] [*British*] ... RDL
Reactor Development Program [*Nuclear Regulatory Commission*] (NRCH) ... RDP
Reactor Drain Tank [*Nuclear energy*] (NRCH) ... RDT
Reactor Engineer Console ... REC
Reactor Environmental Test Apparatus (MCD) ... RETA
Reactor Equipment Ltd. [*Nuclear energy*] (NRCH) ... REL
Reactor Experimental [*Former USSR*] (DEN) ... REX
Reactor Feed Pump [*Nuclear energy*] (NRCH) ... RFP
Reactor Feed Pump Turbine [*Nuclear energy*] (NRCH) ... RFPT
Reactor Feedwater [*Nuclear energy*] (NRCH) ... RFW
Reactor Flight Demonstration ... RFD
Reactor for Physical and Technical Investigations [*Former USSR Nuclear energy*] ... RPT
Reactor Head Cooling [*Nuclear energy*] (NRCH) ... RHC
Reactor Heat Transport System (NRCH) ... RHTS
Reactor Instrument Penetration Valve (IEEE) ... RIP
Reactor Island [*Nuclear energy*] (NRCH) ... RI
Reactor Isolation Pressure Valve (IEEE) ... RIPV
Reactor Licensing [*Nuclear energy*] (NRCH) ... RL
Reactor Licensing Operating Procedure [*Nuclear energy*] (NRCH) ... RLOP
Reactor Low-Water Level (IEEE) ... RLWL
Reactor Maintenance, Assembly, and Disassembly ... R-MAD
Reactor Makeup Water [*Nuclear energy*] (NRCH) ... RMW
Reactor Makeup Water Storage [*Nuclear energy*] (NRCH) ... RMWS
Reactor Make-Up Water System [*Nuclear energy*] (IAA) ... RMWS
Reactor Makeup Water Tank [*Nuclear energy*] (NRCH) ... RMWT
Reactor Manual Control System [*Nuclear energy*] (NRCH) ... RMCS
Reactor Manufacturer [*Nuclear energy*] (NRCH) ... RM
Reactor Materials [*A publication*] ... RCM
Reactor Monitor System (IEEE) ... RMS
Reactor Monitoring and Control [*Nuclear energy*] (NRCH) ... RM & C
Reactor Monitoring and Control [*Nuclear energy*] (IAA) ... RMAC
Reactor Operator [*Nuclear energy*] (NRCH) ... RO
Reactor Physics Constants Center [*Argonne National Laboratory*] ... RPCC
Reactor Plant Control System [*Nuclear energy*] (NRCH) ... RPCS
Reactor Plant Designer [*Nuclear energy*] (NRCH) ... RPD
Reactor Plant Planning (DNAB) ... RPP
Reactor Plant Planning Year (DNAB) ... RPPY
Reactor Plant River Water Pump (IEEE) ... RPRWP
Reactor Plant Test (DNAB) ... RPT
Reactor Plant Test Section (DNAB) ... RPTS
Reactor Plant Test Support Organization (DNAB) ... RPTSO
Reactor Pressure [*Nuclear energy*] (NRCH) ... RP
Reactor Pressure Plus (NRCH) ... PR+
Reactor Pressure Vessel [*Nuclear energy*] (NRCH) ... RPV
Reactor Primary Loop ... RPL
Reactor Project [*Nuclear energy*] (NRCH) ... RP
Reactor Protection Actuating Signal [*Nuclear energy*] (NRCH) ... RPAS
Reactor Protection Control Rod System (IEEE) ... RPCRS
Reactor Protection Logic System (IEEE) ... RPLS
Reactor Protection System [*Nuclear energy*] (NRCH) ... RPS

Reactor Protective System Motor Generator (IEEE) ... RPSMG
Reactor Radiation Division [*National Institute of Standards and Technology*] ... RRD
Reactor Recirculating System (NRCH) ... RRS
Reactor Recirculation Cooling [*Nuclear energy*] (NRCH) ... RRC
Reactor Recirculation Motor Generator (IEEE) ... RRMG
Reactor Refueling Plug (NRCH) ... RRP
Reactor Refueling System (NRCH) ... RRS
Reactor Regulating System (NRCH) ... RRS
Reactor Research and Development ... RRD
Reactor Review and Audit Committee [*Oak Ridge National Laboratory*] ... RRAC
Reactor Safeguards (NRCH) ... RS
Reactor Safety Advisory Committee [*Canada*] (BARN) ... RSAC
Reactor Safety Commission [*Germany*] ... RSC
Reactor Safety Coordinator [*Nuclear energy*] (NRCH) ... RSC
Reactor Safety Research [*Nuclear energy*] ... RSR
Reactor Safety Study [*Nuclear energy*] ... RSS
Reactor Safety Study Methodology Application Program [*Nuclear energy*] (NRCH) ... RSSMAP
Reactor Service Building (NRCH) ... RSB
Reactor Shutdown System [*Nuclear energy*] (NRCH) ... RSS
Reactor Siting Index (NRCH) ... RSI
Reactor Standards Office [*Oak Ridge National Laboratory*] ... RSO
Reactor Steam Cycle ... RSC
Reactor Synthesis ... RSYN
Reactor System Outline [*Nuclear energy*] (NRCH) ... RSO
Reactor System with Interstage Product Removal [*Chemical engineering*] ... RSIPR
Reactor Thermal Power (IEEE) ... RTP
Reactor Trip [*Nuclear energy*] (NRCH) ... RT
Reactor Trip Override [*Nuclear energy*] (NRCH) ... RTO
Reactor Trip System [*Nuclear energy*] (NRCH) ... RTS
Reactor Turbine Generator Board [*Nuclear energy*] (NRCH) ... RTGB
Reactor Vessel [*Nuclear energy*] ... RV
Reactor Vessel Auxiliary Cooling System ... RVACS
Reactor Vessel Support System (IEEE) ... RVSS
Reactor Vessel Water Level Indication System (IEEE) ... RVLIS
Reactor Visual Range (HGAA) ... RVR
Reactor Water Cleanup [*Nuclear energy*] (NRCH) ... RWC
Reactor Water Cleanup [*Nuclear energy*] (NRCH) ... RWCU
Reactor Water Cleanup System [*Nuclear energy*] (NRCH) ... RWCS
Reactor Water Cleanup Unit [*Nuclear energy*] (IAA) ... RWCU
Reactor Work Permit (IEEE) ... RWP
Reactor-in-Flight Test [*NASA*] ... RIFT
Reactor-in-Flight Test/System [*NASA*] (AAG) ... RIFT/S
Reactors and Reactor Control (MCD) ... R & RC
Reactors and Reactor Control (IAA) ... RARC
Read (AAG) ... R
Read (AAG) ... RD
Read Access Key ... RAK
Read Address Counter ... RAC
Read after Write ... RAW
Read Alter Wire ... RAW
Read Amplifier ... RA
Read and Compute ... RC
Read and Destroy ... R & D
Read around Number ... RAN
Read around Ratio ... RAR
Read Backward ... RB
Read Bit Feedback [*Computer science*] (WDAA) ... RBF
Read Buffer ... RB
Read Channel Continue ... RCC
Read Channel Initialize ... RCI
Read Check [*Computer science*] (IAA) ... RDCHK
Read Clock (IAA) ... RC
Read Clock (IAA) ... RCL
Read Clutch Magnet (IAA) ... RCM
Read, Compute, Write (IAA) ... RCW
Read Criteria (SAA) ... RDCRIT
Read Data ... RD
Read Data Available ... RDA
Read Data Check (CMD) ... RDC
Read Delay (IAA) ... RD
Read Direct ... RD
Read Disconnect Delay [*Computer science*] (IAA) ... RDD
Read Drum (IAA) ... RDR
Read Emitter [*Computer science*] (IAA) ... RE
Read, Encode, Annotate, Ponder [*Reading improvement method*] ... REAP
Read Encode/Capture/Proof/Sort [*Computer science*] (MHDB) ... RECAPS
Read Error [*Computer science*] (IAA) ... RE
Read, Execute, Write [*Computer science*] (IAA) ... REW
Read for Data (IAA) ... RFD
Read Forward ... RF
Read in Bed - It's Terrific ... RIBIT
Read Interrupt Mask [*Computer science*] ... RIM
Read Least Significant Time [*Military*] ... RLST
Read Machine-Specific Register [*Computer science*] ... RDMSR
Read Major Line [*Computer science*] (IAA) ... RML
Read/Modify/Write ... R/M/W
Read Modify Write (NITA) ... RMW
Read/Mostly [*Computer science*] (TEL) ... R/M
Read Natural Childbirth Foundation (EA) ... RNCF
Read News [*Computer science*] (CDE) ... rn
Read Once, Write All [*Computer science*] ... ROWA
Read Only [*Computer science*] (IBMDP) ... RO
Read Only Back-Up Address Register [*Computer science*] (MHDB) ... ROBAR
Read Only Memory Automatic Design [*Computer science*] (MHDB) ... ROMAD
Read Only Nano Store (MHDB) ... RONS
Read Out Material [*Computer science*] (IAA) ... RM
Read Printer (NITA) ... RP
Read Printer ... RPR
Read Program Memory [*Computer science*] (MDG) ... RPM
Read, Punch, and Interpret ... RPI
Read Select (SAA) ... RDS
Read Strobe ... RDS
Read Symbol Table ... RST
Read Tape [*Computer science*] ... RT
Read Tape Binary [*Computer science*] (IEEE) ... RTB
Read Tape Decimal ... RTD
Read the Fabulous Manual [*Internet language*] [*Computer science*] ... RTFM
Read the Fascinating Manual [*You can substitute a common profane verbal adjective for the third word*] [*Internet*] ... RTFM
Read the Fine Manual [*Computer science*] (DOM) ... RTFM
Read the Flaming Manual [*Bowdlerized version*] (CDE) ... RTFM
Read the Frequently Asked Questions [*Computer hacker terminology*] (NHD) ... RTFAQ
Read the Manual ... RTM
Read Time Stamp Counter [*Computer science*] ... RDTSC
Read while Write [*Computer science*] (IAA) ... RWW
Read/Write (NITA) ... R/W
Read, Write and Compare (ECII) ... RWC
Read, Write, and Compute ... RWC
Read/Write Extend Delete ... RWED
Read/Write Register ... RWR
Readability (IAA) ... R
Readability Ease Assessment Device (MCD) ... READ
Readability, Strength, Modulation (IAA) ... RSM
Readability, Strength, Tone ... RST
Readable ... RDBL
Readable ... RDBL
Reader (NTCM) ... R
Reader (MSA) ... RDR
Reader Action Service [*ZIP code computer*] ... REACTS
Reader and Reader-Printer (PDAA) ... RRP
Reader Code ... RC
Reader Common Contact ... RCC
Reader Control Relay ... RCR
Reader Enrollment and Delivery System [*Library of Congress Washington, DC Information service or system*] (IID) ... READS
Reader Printer ... RP
Reader Punch ... RP
Reader Railroad [*AAR code*] ... RRR
Reader Service Card ... RSC
Reader/Sorter Processor ... RSP
Reader Stop [*Computer science*] (BUR) ... RS
Reader Tape [*Contact*] (MCD) ... RT
Reader Tape Contact ... RTC
Readers Admission System [*Online Public Access Catalog*] ... RAS
Reader's Comment Form (IBMDP) ... RCF
Reader's Digest [*A publication*] ... RD
Reader's Digest Assn'A' [*NYSE symbol*] (TTSB) ... RDA
Reader's Digest Assn'B' [*NYSE symbol*] (TTSB) ... RDB
Reader's Digest Association [*NYSE symbol*] (SPSG) ... RDA
Readers Digest Association [*NYSE symbol*] (SAG) ... RDB
Readers Digest Association [*Associated Press*] (SAG) ... RdrDB
Reader's Digest Association [*Associated Press*] (SAG) ... RdrDg
Reader's Digest of Canada Ltd., Montreal, PQ, Canada [*Library symbol Library of Congress*] (LCLS) ... CaQMRD
Reader's Digest of Canada Ltd., Montreal, Quebec [*Library symbol National Library of Canada*] (NLC) ... QMRD
Readers International [*Subscription book club*] [*British*] ... RI
Reader's Library [*A publication*] ... RL
Readers per Copy [*Newspapers and magazines*] ... RPC
Readers Union Rugby Union (NADA) ... RU
Reader-to-Advertiser Phone Inquiry Delivery System [*Chilton Corp.*] ... RAPID
Readex Microprint Corp., New York, NY [*Library symbol Library of Congress*] (LCLS) ... Readex
Readicare, Inc. [*AMEX symbol*] (SAG) ... RDI
ReadiCare, Inc. [*NASDAQ symbol*] (TTSB) ... RDIC
ReadiCare, Inc. [*Associated Press*] (SAG) ... RediCr
Readily Accessible Parts Information Directory [*Information service or system*] (IID) ... RAPID
Readily Operative Overhead Protection by Hippos [*Facetious proposal for protection against nuclear attack*] ... ROOPH
Readily-Oxidizable Carbon (PDAA) ... ROC
Read-In (DEN) ... RI
Read-In Counter ... RIC
Read-In Mode ... RIM
Readin', Ritin', and Rithmetic [*Also, RRR*] ... 3R's
Readin', Ritin', and Rithmetic [*Also, 3R's*] ... RRR
Readiness (MSA) ... RDNS
Readiness Action Proposal (MCD) ... RAP
Readiness Analysis Group ... RAG
Readiness and Emergency Action [*Red Cross Disaster Services*] ... R & EA
Readiness and Money (DNAB) ... RAM
Readiness Antisubmarine Warfare Carrier Air Wing [*Navy*] (NVT) ... RCVSG
Readiness Assessment Program [*Navy*] ... RAP
Readiness Attack Carrier Air Wing [*Navy*] (NVT) ... RCVW
Readiness Based Maintenance [*Army*] (DOMA) ... RBM
Readiness Capability [*Military*] ... REDCAPE

Readiness Category [*Military*] ... REDCAT
Readiness Command [*Army*] ... REDCOM
Readiness Condition [*Military*] ... RECON
Readiness Condition [*Military*] ... REDCON
Readiness Count ... R
Readiness Count (MCD) ... R (Count)
Readiness Data ... RD
Readiness Date ... RD
Readiness Enhancement Technology [*Military*] ... RET
Readiness Estimation System (MCD) ... RES
Readiness Evaluation Program for Avionics Intermediate Repair Simulation (MCD) ... REPAIRS
Readiness Exercise [*Navy*] (DOMA) ... READIEX
Readiness for Mobilization Evaluation (MCD) ... REMOBE
Readiness Forecast Authorization Equipment Data [*Air Force*] (AFM) ... RFAED
Readiness Group [*Military*] (AABC) ... RG
Readiness Improvement (MCD) ... READIMP
Readiness Improvement Program [*Military*] (CAAL) ... RIP
Readiness Improvement Status Evaluation (MCD) ... RISE
Readiness Improvement Summary Evaluation (MCD) ... RISE
Readiness Improvement through Correspondence Training (MCD) ... REDICORT
Readiness in Base Service [*Air Force*] (DOMA) ... RIBS
Readiness Index Factor ... RIF
Readiness Indicator Model (MCD) ... RIM
Readiness Information Access System (MCD) ... RIAS
Readiness Information System [*Army*] ... REIS
Readiness Initiative Team [*Military*] ... RIT
Readiness Intergrated Database ... RIDB
Readiness Management Assembly [*Military*] (INF) ... RMA
Readiness Management Information System [*Military*] (AABC) ... RMIS
Readiness Manager [*DARCOM*] [*Army*] ... RM
Readiness Objective Code [*Military*] (AABC) ... ROBCO
Readiness/Operational Evaluation (NVT) ... ROPEVAL
Readiness Patrol Squadron [*Navy*] (NVT) ... RVAW
Readiness Potential ... RP
Readiness Project Officer ... RPO
Readiness Rating ... REDRAT
Readiness Region [*Military*] ... RR
Readiness Removal Rate (DNAB) ... RRR
Readiness Reportable Code (DNAB) ... RRC
Readiness Reportable Status (NVT) ... RRS
Readiness Review (KSC) ... RR
Readiness Risk Index Number (NG) ... RRIN
Readiness Squadron (DNAB) ... RS
Readiness Standing Operating Procedures [*Military*] (INF) ... RSOP
Readiness Support Group Detachment (DNAB) ... READSUPPGRUDET
Readiness Task Force ... RTF
Readiness Training (MCD) ... REDTRAIN
Readiness Training Facility (DNAB) ... READTRAFAC
Readiness Training Squadron [*Military*] (NVT) ... RTS
Reading ... RDG
Reading [*British depot code*] ... RDG
Reading [*Pennsylvania*] [*Airport symbol*] (OAG) ... RDG
Reading (MSA) ... RDNG
Reading [*County borough in England*] ... READ
Reading [*Postcode*] (ODBW) ... RG
Reading Age [*Education*] (DAVI) ... RdA
Reading Age (BABM) ... RdA
Reading & Bates [*NYSE symbol*] (TTSB) ... RB
Reading & Bates $1.625 Cv Pfd [*NYSE symbol*] (TTSB) ... RBPr
Reading & Bates Corp. [*NYSE symbol*] (SPSG) ... RB
Reading & Bates Corp. [*Associated Press*] (SAG) ... RdgBate
Reading & Bates Corp. [*Associated Press*] (SAG) ... RdgBt
Reading and Comprehension in Chemistry ... RECOC
Reading and Mathematics Observation System (EDAC) ... RAMOS
Reading and Vocabulary Test [*Also, RVT*] [*Military*] ... RV
Reading and Vocabulary Test [*Also, RV*] [*Military*] ... RVT
Reading Association Sydney [*Australia*] ... RAS
Reading Attitude Imagination Technique (EDAC) ... RAIT
Reading Community Library, Reading, MI [*Library symbol*] [*Library of Congress*] (LCLS) ... MiRea
Reading Community Library, Reading, MI [*Library symbol Library of Congress*] (LCLS) ... MiRes
Reading Co. [*NASDAQ symbol*] (NQ) ... RDGC
Reading Co. [*Associated Press*] (SAG) ... Readg
Reading Co. Cl'A' [*NASDAQ symbol*] (TTSB) ... RDGCA
Reading Comprehension Interview (EDAC) ... RCI
Reading Development Continuum (AIE) ... RDC
Reading Disability ... RD
Reading Efficiency and Delinquency [*Program*] ... READ
Reading, English, and Communications [*Educational Resources Information Center (ERIC) Clearinghouse*] [*Indiana University*] (PAZ) ... CS
Reading Entertainment, Inc. [*NASDAQ symbol*] (SAG) ... RDGE
Reading Entertainment, Inc. [*Associated Press*] (SAG) ... ReadgE
Reading/Everyday Activities in Life [*Educational test*] ... R/EAL
Reading Free Vocational Interest Inventory [*Vocational guidance test*] ... R-FVII
Reading Grade Level ... RGL
Reading Is Fundamental (EA) ... RIF
Reading List ... RL
Reading Material for the Blind and Physically Handicapped [*Library of Congress Information service or system*] (CRD) ... BLND
Reading Matter Depth (DGA) ... RMD
Reading of Standard ... RS
Reading of Unknown ... RU
Reading, OH [*FM radio station call letters*] ... WMKV
Reading on Statute Law [*A publication*] (DLA) ... RSL
Reading, PA [*AM radio station call letters*] ... WEEU
Reading, PA [*AM radio station call letters*] ... WIOV
Reading, PA [*AM radio station call letters*] ... WRAW
Reading, PA [*FM radio station call letters*] ... WRFY
Reading, PA [*Television station call letters*] ... WTVE
Reading, PA [*FM radio station call letters*] ... WXAC
Reading Public Library, Reading, MA [*Library symbol Library of Congress*] (LCLS) ... MR
Reading Public Library, Reading, PA [*Library symbol Library of Congress*] (LCLS) ... PR
Reading Public Library, Reading, PA [*OCLC symbol*] (OCLC) ... RPL
Reading Quotient ... RdQ
Reading Reform Foundation (EA) ... RRF
Reading Research and Education Center [*Champaign, IL*] [*Department of Education*] (GRD) ... RREC
Reading Room Association Library, Gouveneur, NY [*Library symbol Library of Congress*] (LCLS) ... NGou
Reading Teacher [*A publication*] (BRI) ... RT
Reading Test ... RT
Reading, Writing and Arithmetic Development System (EDAC) ... REWARD
Reading-Ease [*Score*] [*Advertising*] ... RE
Readings: A Journal of Reviews and Commentary in Mental Health [*A publication*] (BRI) ... Readings
Readjusted ... READJ
Readjustment ... RDJ
Readjustment Assistance Act 74 for Vietnam Era Veterans (OICC) ... RAVE
Readjustment Pay [*Military*] ... READJP
Readmission [*Hospital administration*] (DAVI) ... readm
Read-Mostly Memory [*Computer science*] ... RMM
Read-Mostly Mode [*Computer science*] ... RMM
Read-Only Memory [*Computer memory*] [*Computer science*] ... ROM
Read-Only Memory Instruction Register [*Computer science*] (IAA) ... RIR
Read-Only Memory Module [*Computer science*] ... ROMM
Read-Only Memory Register [*Computer science*] (IAA) ... ROMR
Read-Only Memory Storage [*Computer science*] (IAA) ... ROMS
Read-Only Men [*On Board car window sign's version of the computer term, Read-Only Memory*] ... ROM
Read-Only Name Store (NITA) ... RONS
Read-Only Storage [*Computer science*] ... ROS
Read-Only Storage Address Register ... ROSAR
Read-Only Storage Data Register ... ROSDR
Read-Only Tag ... ROT
Read-Only Tape Handler ... ROTH
Read-Only Typing Reperforator (NITA) ... ROTR
Readout [*Computer science*] (IAA) ... RDO
Readout ... RDOUT
Readout (KSC) ... RO
Readout and Relay ... RR
Readout Matrix ... RM
Readout Memory (IEEE) ... ROM
Readout Technique ... RT
Read-Rite Corp. [*NASDAQ symbol*] (SPSG) ... RDRT
Read-Rite Corp. [*Associated Press*] (SAG) ... ReadRt
Read's Declarations and Pleadings [*A publication*] (DLA) ... Read Dec
Read's Declarations and Pleadings [*A publication*] (DLA) ... Read PL
Read-Write [*Computer science*] (MSA) ... R-W
Read-Write Memory [*Computer science*] (MCD) ... RWM
Read-Write Tape [*Computer science*] ... RWT
Read-Write Vertical Redundancy Check [*Computer science*] (IAA) ... RWVRC
Read-Write-Continue [*Computer science*] ... RWC
Read-Write-Initialize [*Computer science*] ... RWI
Read-Write-Verify [*Computer science*] ... RWV
Ready [*Broadcasting*] (WDMC) ... RDX
Ready ... RDY
Ready (AAG) ... RDY
Ready (DAVI) ... REDY
Ready Afloat Marine Amphibious Brigade (CINC) ... RAMAB
Ready Alert [*Navy*] (NVT) ... RA
Ready and Waiting [*or Willing*] [*Slang*] ... RAW
Ready Calendar ... RC
Ready Crew Building (NATG) ... RCB
Ready Duty (NVT) ... READU
Ready Extension Unit (MHDB) ... REU
Ready for Baseline (NASA) ... RFB
Ready for Data (IEEE) ... RFD
Ready for Delivery (MUGU) ... RFD
Ready for Duty ... RFD
Ready for Ferry [*Navy*] (NVT) ... RFF
Ready for Installation (MCD) ... RFI
Ready for Issue [*Military*] ... RFI
Ready for Next Message (IAA) ... RENM
Ready for Next Message ... RFNM
Ready for Occupancy (MCD) ... RFO
Ready for Operations [*Reporting system*] [*DoD*] ... REDOPS
Ready for Sea [*Navy*] ... RFS
Ready for Sea/Individual Ship Exercise (MCD) ... RFS/ISE
Ready for Sending [*Computer science*] (IAA) ... RFS
Ready for Service ... RFS
Ready for Takeoff [*Aviation*] ... RFTO
Ready for the World [*Rhythm and Blues recording group*] ... RFTW
Ready for Training [*Military*] ... RFT
Ready for Typesetter [*Publishing*] ... RFT
Ready Missile Test Facility [*Military*] (CAAL) ... RMTF
Ready Mixed Cement [*Commercial firm British*] ... RMC

Ready Mixed Concrete (ADA) .... RMC
Ready Money (ROG) .... RM
Ready Money Down [*Immediate payment*] .... RMD
Ready Operating Status (DNAB) .... ROS
Ready Qualified for Standby [*Military*] .... RQS
Ready Reckoner (DGA) .... RR
Ready Reference .... RR
Ready Reinforcement Personnel Section [*Air Force*] (AFM) .... RRPS
Ready Replacement Pilot .... RRP
Ready Reportable Status (MCD) .... RRS
Ready Reserve Agreement [*Navy*] (DOMA) .... RRA
Ready Reserve Fleet .... RRF
Ready Reserve Force [*Military*] .... RRF
Ready Reserve Force Working Group (DOMA) .... RRFWG
Ready Reserve Mobilization Reinforcement Pool [*Army*] .... RRMRP
Ready Reserve Mobilization Reinforcement System [*Army*] .... RRMRS
Ready Reserve of the Armed Forces .... RRAF
Ready Reserve Strategic Army Forces .... RRSTRAF
Ready Round Transporter (NATG) .... RRT
Ready Service (AAG) .... RS
Ready Service Magazine [*Military*] (DNAB) .... RSM
Ready Service Ring (NG) .... RSR
Ready Service Spares .... RSS
Ready, Soon, Now (Approach) [*Marketing*] .... RSN
Ready Spares Chassis .... RSCH
Ready Store Positive Maintenance Program (MCD) .... RSPMP
Ready to Eat [*Cereals*] .... RTE
Ready to Fire (MCD) .... RTF
Ready to Send [*Computer command*] (PCM) .... RTS
Ready to Use .... RTU
Ready Unit (NVT) .... READU
Ready Use [*British*] .... RU
Ready, Willing and Able [*Legal shorthand*] (LWAP) .... RWA
Ready-Access [*Telecommunications*] (TEL) .... RA
Ready-for-Use (NG) .... RFU
Readymade (VRA) .... rdymd
Ready-to-Assemble .... RTA
Ready-to-Drink [*Bottled and canned beverages*] .... RTD
Ready-to-Load Date [*At origin*] (DOMA) .... RLD
Ready-to-Sail Report [*Navy*] (NVT) .... READYREP
Ready-to-Wear [*Clothing*] .... RTW
Reagan Alumni Association (EA) .... RAA
Reagan Political Items Collectors (EA) .... RPIC
Reagent Array Analysis Method [*Analytical biochemistry*] .... RAAM
Reagent Grade .... RG
Reagent Grade Water .... RGW
Reagin Screen Test [*Medicine*] (MEDA) .... RST
Reagin Screen Test [*For syphilis*] [*Medicine*] (DAVI) .... RST
Reako Exploration [*Vancouver Stock Exchange symbol*] .... RXX
Real .... R
Real [*Mathematics*] .... Re
Real Americans Buy American Cars [*An association Defunct*] .... RABAC
Real and Not Corrected Input Data [*Computer science*] .... RANCID
Real Aperture RADAR .... RAR
Real Aviation Ltd. [*Ghana*] [*ICAO designator*] (FAAC) .... RLV
Real Beam Ground Map (MCD) .... RBGM
Real Circuit .... RC
Real Data System Element Model [*Computer science*] (MHDB) .... RDDSEM
Real de Minas Mine [*Vancouver Stock Exchange symbol*] .... RDN
Real Decisions Corp. [*Information service or system*] (IID) .... RDC
Real Estate .... RE
Real Estate Accounts Payable and Operating Reports .... REAPOR
Real Estate and Business Agents' Supervisory Board [*Western Australia*] .... REBASB
Real Estate and Space Management Information System (USDC) .... RSMIS
Real Estate and Space Management Information System [*Marine science*] (OSRA) .... RSMIS
Real Estate and Stock Institute of Victoria [*Australia*] .... RESIV
Real Estate Appraisal School [*Federal Home Loan Bank Board*] .... REAS
[*The*] **Real Estate Appraiser and Analyst** [*Society of Real Estate Appraisers*] [*A publication*] .... TREA & A
Real Estate Association of New South Wales [*Australia*] .... REANSW
Real Estate Aviation Chapter (EA) .... REAC
Real Estate Brokerage Council (EA) .... RBC
Real Estate Brokerage Council (EA) .... REBC
Real Estate Business [*Realtors National Marketing Institute*] [*A publication*] .... REB
Real Estate Comm. Library, Boise, ID [*Library symbol*] [*Library of Congress*] (LCLS) .... IdBRE
Real Estate Consulting Professional [*International College of Real Estate Consulting Professionals*] [*Designation awarded by*] .... RECP
Real Estate Cost Analysis Program .... RECAP
Real Estate Council .... REC
Real Estate Data, Inc. [*Information service or system*] (IID) .... REDI
Real Estate Educators Association [*Chicago, IL*] (EA) .... REEA
Real Estate Employers Federation of New South Wales [*Australia*] .... REEFNSW
Real Estate Fund of America .... REFA
Real Estate Information Network [*Database*] .... REIN
Real Estate Information Network [*National Association of Realtors*] [*Information service or system*] (IID) .... REINET
Real Estate Investing Letter [*Harcourt Brace Jovanovich, Inc.*] [*No longer available online*] [*Information service or system*] (CRD) .... REIL
Real Estate Investment Trust [*NYSE symbol*] (SAG) .... RCT
Real Estate Investment Trust [*Associated Press*] (SAG) .... REIT
Real Estate Investment Trust [*Pooled funds that invest in income-producing residential and commerical properties*] .... REIT
Real Estate Investment Trust of America (MHDW) .... REI
Real Estate Issues [*American Society of Real Estate Counselors*] [*A publication*] .... REI
Real Estate Law Institute (EA) .... RELI
Real Estate Law Report [*A publication*] (DLA) .... Real Est L Rep
Real Estate Leaders of America [*Montgomery, AL*] (EA) .... RELA
Real Estate Limited Partnership .... RELP
Real Estate Listing Service [*Database*] [*MDR Telecom*] [*Information service or system*] (CRD) .... RELS
Real Estate Management Information System (BUR) .... REMIS
Real Estate Mortgage Investment Conduit [*Federal National Mortgage Association*] .... REMIC
Real Estate Owned [*Banking*] .... REO
Real Estate Planning Report [*Military*] (AABC) .... REPR
Real Estate Program [*Association of Independent Colleges and Schools specialization code*] .... RE
Real Estate Record [*New York*] [*A publication*] (DLA) .... Real Est Rec
Real Estate Research Corp. .... RERC
Real Estate Salespersons' Association of Victoria [*Australia*] .... RESAV
Real Estate Salespersons' Association of Western Australia .... RESAWA
Real Estate Securities and Syndication Institute (EA) .... RESSI
Real Estate Settlement Procedures Act of 1974 .... RESPA
Real Estate Trainers Association, International (EA) .... RETAI
Real Fire Heating International Exhibition [*British*] (ITD) .... RFHI
Real Fourier Transform .... RFT
Real Gas .... RG
Real Goods Trading Corp. [*Associated Press*] (SAG) .... RealGd
Real Hazard Index .... RHI
Real Life (NHD) .... RL
Real Market Share [*Business term*] (MHDB) .... RMS
Real Memory Operating System [*Computer science*] (IAA) .... RMOS
Real Name [*British Library indexing for pseudonymous author*] .... RN
Real Number (DEN) .... RE
Real Part [*of complex number*] (DEN) .... RP
Real Program Value (CAAL) .... RPV
Real Property .... RP
Real Property [*Legal shorthand*] (LWAP) .... RPROP
Real Property Actions and Proceedings [*A publication*] (DLA) .... Real Prop Acts
Real Property Actions and Proceedings Law [*New York, NY A publication*] .... RPAPL
Real Property Administrator [*Building Owners and Managers Institute*] [*Designation awarded by*] .... RPA
Real Property Cases [*England*] [*A publication*] (DLA) .... Real Pr Cas
Real Property Cases [*1843-47*] [*A publication*] (DLA) .... Real Prop Cas
Real Property Cases [*1843-48*] [*England*] [*A publication*] (DLA) .... RPC
Real Property Commissioner's Report [*1832*] [*England*] [*A publication*] (DLA) .... RPC
Real Property Commissioner's Report [*1832*] [*England*] [*A publication*] (DLA) .... RPC Rep
Real Property Facilities [*Army*] (AABC) .... RPF
Real Property Industrial Fund .... RPIF
Real Property Installed Equipment [*Air Force*] (MCD) .... RPIE
Real Property Inventory [*Military*] .... RPI
Real Property Maintenance (DOMA) .... RPM
Real Property Maintenance Activities [*or Administration*] [*Army*] (AABC) .... RPMA
Real Property Management .... RPM
Real Property Management System (MCD) .... RPMS
Real Property, Probate, and Trust Journal [*A publication*] (DLA) .... Real Prop Prob & Trust J
Real Property Resource Review Board (AFM) .... RPRRB
Real Property Tax Law [*New York, NY A publication*] .... RPTL
Real Scene Focus Sensor (PDAA) .... RSFS
Real Soon Now [*Internet language*] [*Computer science*] .... RSN
Real Storage .... RS
Real Storage Management [*Computer science*] (IBMDP) .... RSM
Real Storage Page Table [*Computer science*] (BUR) .... RSPT
Real Time [*Computer*] [*Computer science*] .... RT
Real Time Developments [*Commercial firm British*] .... RTD
Real Time Geometry .... RTG
Real Time Operating System [*Computer science*] .... RTOS
Real Time Protocol [*Telecommunications*] (OSI) .... RTP
Real Time Scan [*Medicine*] (DMAA) .... RTS
Real Time Streaming Protocol (PCM) .... RTSP
Real Time Velocimeter System [*Army*] (RDA) .... RTVS
Real Wages [*Economics*] .... RW
Real World Computing Partnership [*Japan*] [*Agreement for conducting cooperative global research*] .... RWCP
Real World Interval (WDAA) .... RWI
Real World Problem Generation .... RWPG
Real World Reading Test (EDAC) .... RWRT
Real World Vehicular Rate .... RWVR
Real World Visual Display .... RWVD
Real Year Dollars (NASA) .... RYD
Real-Aerovias Brasil [*Brazilian international airline*] .... ABR
Real-Aerovias Brasil [*Brazilian international airline*] .... BIA
Realcap Holdings Ltd. [*Toronto Stock Exchange symbol*] .... REA
Realco, Inc. [*Associated Press*] (SAG) .... Realco
Realco, Inc. [*NASDAQ symbol*] (SAG) .... RLCO
Realco Inc. [*NASDAQ symbol*] (TTSB) .... RLCO
Realco Inc. Wrrt [*NASDAQ symbol*] (TTSB) .... RLCOW
Real-Fluid Isentropic Decompression [*Engineering*] .... RID
Real-Fluid Nonisentropic Decompression [*Engineering*] .... RND
Realigned .... RLGD
Realignment of Airdrop Activities (MCD) .... RADA
Realignment of Resources and Services (MCD) .... RORS

Realignment of Supply Activities (MCD) .... RASA
Realisations et Etudes Electronique [Computer manufacturer] [France] R2E
Realised Ultimate Reality Piton [Mountain climbing] .... RURP
Realistic Air Defense Engagement System [Army] (RDA) .... RADES
Realistic Battlefield Environment-Electronic [Military] (PDAA) .... REBEEL
Realistic, Equal, Active, for Life Women of Canada [An association] .... REAL
Realistic Job Preview .... RJP
Reality Interactive [NASDAQ symbol] (TTSB) .... RINT
Reality Interactive, Inc. [Associated Press] (SAG) .... Reality
Reality Interactive, Inc. [NASDAQ symbol] (SAG) .... RINT
Reality Interactive Unit [NASDAQ symbol] (TTSB) .... RINTU
Reality Interactive Wrrt [NASDAQ symbol] (TTSB) .... RINTW
Reality Orientation .... RO
Reality-Oriented Discussion .... R-O Dis
Realizable Value (ADA) .... RV
Realization (ROG) .... REALIZN
Realkatalog der Aegyptologie [A publication] (BJA) .... RK
Reallexikon der Aegyptischen Religionsgeschichte [Berlin] [A publication]
    (BJA) .... RaeRG
Reallexikon der Aegyptischen Religionsgeschichte [Berlin] [A publication]
    (BJA) .... RAR
Reallexikon der Assyriologie [Berlin] [A publication] (BJA) ..... RLA
Reallexikon der Assyriologie [Berlin] [A publication] (BJA) ..... RLAss
Reallexikon der Vorgeschichte [M. Ebert] [A publication] (BJA) ..... EbertRV
Reallexikon der Vorgeschichte [Berlin] [A publication] (BJA) ..... RLV
Reallexikon fuer Antike und Christentum [A publication] (OCD) ..... RAC
Reallocation Inventory (AFIT) .... RI
Really Here in Name Only [Education] [British] .... Rhino
Really Universal Computer-Aided Production System (PDAA) ..... RUCAPS
Real-Time Accumulator .... RTA
Real-Time Acquisition and Processing of Inflight Data .... RAPID
Real-Time Acquisitions Management and Bibliographic Order System
    [Suggested name for the Library of Congress computer system] .... RAMBO
Real-Time Adaptive Control .... RTAC
Real-Time Adaptive Control System [Military] (CAAL) .... RTACS
Real-Time Advanced Core and Thermohydraulic .... RETACT
Real-Time Analysis and Display System [Marine science] (OSRA) ..... RADS
Real-Time Analysis and Display System (USDC) .... RADS
Real-Time Analyzer [Electronics] .... RTA
Real-Time Application Program Interface to DISOSS (NITA) ..... RAPID
Real-Time Applications Interactive Debugger (MCD) .... RAID
Real-Time Atmospheric Compensation [Astronomy] .... RTAC
Real-Time Automated Personnel Identification System [DoD] .... RAPIDS
Real-Time [or Recording] Automatic Digital Optical Tracker .... RADOT
Real-Time Auxiliary Computing Facility [Apollo] [NASA] ..... RTACF
Real-Time Basic [Computer science] (MDG) .... RTE-B
Real-Time Batch Monitor [Xerox Corp.] .... RBM
Real-Time BIT [Binary Digit] Mapping .... RTBM
Real-Time Calling Standards [Chromatography] .... RTCS
Real-Time Captioning [for the deaf] .... RTC
Real-Time Casualty Assessment (MCD) .... RTCA
Real-Time Cell-Identification Processor (PDAA) .... RTCIP
Real-Time Cinetheodolite Data System .... RTCDS
Real-Time Clock [Computer science] (MCD) .... RTC
Real-Time Combined File [IRS] .... RTCF
Real-Time Command [Computer science] .... RTC
Real-Time Command Controller [Computer science] (NASA) ..... RTCC
Real-Time Communication System .... RTCS
Real-Time Communications [RCA] .... REALCOM
Real-Time Communications Control (NITA) .... RTCC
Real-Time Communications Processor (NASA) .... RTCP
Real-Time Composition System (NITA) .... RTCS
Real-Time Computation [Computer science] (IAA) .... RTC
Real-Time Computation System [Computer science] (IAA) ..... RTCS
Real-Time Computer .... RTC
Real-Time Computer Center [NASA] (NASA) .... RTCC
Real-Time Computer Command [NASA] (NASA) .... RTCC
Real-Time Computer Complex .... RCC
Real-Time Computer Complex [NASA] .... RTCC
Real-Time Computer Facility .... RTCF
Real-Time Computer System .... RTCS
Real-Time Conference [GEnie] [Telecommunications] .... RTC
Real-Time Control [Computer science] (MCD) .... RTC
Real-Time Control Area (NTCM) .... RTCA
Real-Time Control Program [Computer science] (IAA) .... RTCP
Real-Time Control Unit .... RTCU
Real-Time Counter [Computer science] .... RTC
Real-Time Data Acquisition .... REDAC
Real-Time Data Channel (IEEE) .... RTDC
Real-Time Data Distribution .... RTDD
Real-Time Data File (NOAA) .... RTDF
Real-Time Data Handling System .... RTDHS
Real-Time Data Manager (MCD) .... RDM
Real-Time Data System .... RTDS
Real-Time Data Translator .... RTDT
Real-Time Debug [Computer science] (MHDI) .... RTDBUG
Real-Time Debugging Aid .... RDA
Real-Time Decoder .... RTD
Real-Time Digital Data Acquisition System (PDAA) .... RTDDAS
Real-Time Digital Data Correction (MUGU) .... RTDDC
Real-Time Disk-Operating System [Computer science] .... RDOS
Real-Time Display .... RTD
Real-Time DSN [Deep Space Network] Monitor Software Assembly
    [NASA] .... RTMSW

Real-Time Electromagnetic Digitally Controlled Analyser and
    Processor .... REDCAP
Real-Time Electronic Access and Display [System] [Computer science] .... READ
Real-Time Engine (MCD) .... RTE
Real-Time Engine Simulation (MCD) .... RTES
Real-Time Event [Computer science] (IAA) .... RTE
Real-Time Event Monitor [Computer science] (IAA) .... REMON
Real-Time Event Monitor [Computer science] (IEEE) .... REMOS
Real-Time Executive [Computer science] .... RTE
Real-Time Executive [Computer science] (IAA) .... RTEX
Real-Time Executive .... RTX
Real-Time Executive Extended (PDAA) .... RTXE
Real-Time Executive Monitor [Computer science] (IAA) ..... RTMON
Real-Time Executive Routine [Computer science] .... REX
Real-Time Executive System [Computer science] (MHDI) ..... REX
Real-Time Executive System [SEMIS] .... RTES
Real-Time Executive System [SEMIS] (IAA) .... RXS
Real-Time Finance and Manpower Management Information System [Marine
    Corps] (MCD) .... REAL FAMMIS
Real-Time FORTRAN [Computer science] .... RTF
Real-Time Generation of Video .... RTGV
Real-Time Graphic Display .... RTGD
Real-Time Gross Settlement [Banking] (ECON) .... RTGS
Real-Time Hybrid System (NASA) .... RTHS
Real-Time Information Retrieval System .... RTIRS
Real-Time Information Retrieval System [Computer science] (HGAA) ..... RTIS
Real-Time Infrared [Spectroscopy] .... RTIR
Real-Time Input/Output (NITA) .... RTIO
Real-Time Input/Output Controller [Computer science] (IEEE) ..... RTI/OC
Real-Time Input/Output Interface Subsystem [Space Flight Operations
    Facility, NASA] .... RTIO
Real-Time Input-Output Transducer [or Translator] [Computer science] ..... RIOT
Real-Time Integrated Ticket Administration (NITA) .... RITA
Real-Time Interactive Processor (MCD) .... RTIP
Real-Time Interface [Computer science] .... RTI
Real-Time Interface [Computer science] (NASA) .... RTIF
[A] Real-Time Interface Coprocessor (BTTJ) .... ARTIC
Real-Time Interference [Computer science] (IAA) .... RTI
Real-Time Language [Computer science] (IEEE) .... RTL
Real-time Lens Error Correction [Computer science] (NTCM) ..... RLC
Real-Time Link [Computer science] (MHDI) .... RTL
Real-Time Management (MHDB) .... RTM
Real-Time Manufacturing Information Control System [Computer science]
    (MHDI) .... REMICS
Real-Time Memory System .... RTMS
Real-Time Metric .... RTM
Real-Time Minimal Byte Error Probability [Computer science] (MHDI) ..... RTMBEP
Real-Time Module (NITA) .... RTM
Real-Time Monitor [Systems Engineering Labs] .... RTM
Real-Time Multiplexer Display .... RTMD
Real-Time Multiprogramming Operating System [Computer science]
    (IEEE) .... RTMOS
Real-Time Multiprogramming System .... RTMS
Real-Time On-Scene Report (NTCM) .... ROSR
[The] Real-Time Operating System Nucleus [Computer science] (PCM) .... TRON
Real-Time Operation .... RTO
Real-Time Operations, Dispatching, and Scheduling [System] [TRW,
    Inc.] .... RODS
Real-Time Optical Alignment and Diagnostic System [Module] ...... ROADS
Real-Time Optical System (MCD) .... RTOS
Real-Time Optional Processing (NITA) .... RTOP
Real-Time Peripheral (IEEE) .... RTP
Real-Time Position (AAG) .... RTP
Real-Time Position Location Reporting System (MCD) .... RTPLRS
Real-Time Procedural Language [Computer science] (MDG) ..... RTPL
Real-Time Process Control .... RTPC
Real-Time Processing [Computer science] (IAA) .... RTP
Real-Time Processing System (NITA) .... RPS
Real-Time Profiler [Instrumentation] .... RTP
Real-Time Program [Computer science] (IAA) .... RTP
Real-Time Program Management .... RTPM
Real-Time Programming System [Computer science] (IEEE) ..... RPS
Real-Time Quality Control .... RTQC
Real-Time Quotes [Information retrieval] .... RTQ
Real-Time Readout .... RTR
Real-Time Readout .... RTRO
Real-Time Reconnaissance Cockpit Display System [or Subsystem] ...... RTRCDS
Real-Time Record (NTCM) .... RTR
Real-Time Record Interpreter (NTCM) .... RTRI
Real-Time Reliability (NITA) .... RTR
Real-Time Reporting System on Oceanic Conditions (SSD) ..... RTRSOC
Real-Time Rescheduling Subsystem .... RTRS
Real-Time Scheduling Display System .... RTSDS
Real-Time Scientific System .... RTSS
Real-Time Seismic Amplitude Measurement .... RSAM
Real-Time Signal Processor (MCD) .... RSP
Real-Time Signal Processor (NVT) .... RTSP
Real-Time Simulation .... RTS
Real-Time Simulation Facility [NASA] (MCD) .... RTSF
Real-Time Simulation Research System (WDAA) .... RTSRS
Real-Time Software [Computer science] (MHDI) .... RTSW
Real-Time Sonobuoy (MCD) .... RETS
Real-Time Statistical and Terminal Profile [IRS] .... RSTP
Real-Time Subroutines .... RTS
Real-Time Supply [NASA] (MCD) .... RTS

Real-Time Switching System ... RSS
Real-Time Synthetic Video (DOMA) ... RTSV
Real-Time System ... RTS
Real-Time Tactical Operating System (MCD) ... RTTOS
Real-Time Telecommunications Executive (IAA) ... RTEX
Real-Time Telemetry (IAA) ... RTT
Real-Time Telemetry Data (MCD) ... RTTD
Real-Time Telemetry Data System ... RTTDS
Real-Time Telemetry Processing System (PDAA) ... RTPS
Real-Time Telemetry System ... RTTS
Real-Time Television ... RTTV
Real-Time Temporal Logic [*Computer science*] ... RTTL
Real-Time Terminal Application Program System [*Computer science*] ... RTAPS
Real-Time Traffic Adaptive Signal Control [*FHWA*] (TAG) ... RT-TRACS
Real-Time Traffic Control System ... RT-TRACS
Real-Time Transient Model [*Computer science*] ... RTTM
Real-Time Ultrasound [*Medicine*] (DMAA) ... RTU
Real-Time Video ... RTV
Real-Time Video Processing ... RTVP
Real-Time Virtual Memeory [*Computer science*] (IAA) ... RTVM
Real-Time Virtual Operating System (NITA) ... RTVOS
Realtor ... RLTR
Realtor (WGA) ... Rltr
Realtors Land Institute (EA) ... RLI
Realtors National Marketing Institute [*Chicago, IL*] (EA) ... RNMI
Realty ... RLTY
Realty Income [*NYSE symbol*] (TTSB) ... O
Realty Income Corp. [*NYSE symbol*] (SAG) ... O
Realty Income Corp. [*Associated Press*] (SAG) ... RltyInco
Realty Refund SBI [*NYSE symbol*] (TTSB) ... RRF
Realty Refund Trust [*Associated Press*] (SAG) ... RltRef
Realty Refund Trust SBI [*NYSE symbol*] (SPSG) ... RRF
Ream (ADA) ... R
Ream ... RM
Ream (WDMC) ... rm
Ream Wrapped (WDMC) ... RW
Reamer [*Design engineering*] ... RMR
Reamfixture (MCD) ... RMF
Reao [*French Polynesia*] [*ICAO location identifier*] (ICLI) ... NTGE
Reao [*French Polynesia*] [*Airport symbol*] (OAG) ... REA
Reappoint (AFM) ... REAPT
Reappointed (WGA) ... REAPTD
Reappraisement Decisions [*A publication*] (DLA) ... RD
Rear ... R
Rear (AABC) ... RR
Rear Admiral [*Navy*] ... O8
Rear Admiral [*Also, RADM, RADML*] ... RA
Rear Admiral [*Also, RA, RADML*] (AAG) ... RADM
Rear Airfield Supply Organization [*Military*] ... RASO
Rear Area Combat Operations (INF) ... RACO
Rear Area Damage Control Center (AABC) ... RADCC
Rear Area Operations Center (MCD) ... RAOC
Rear Area Protection [*Military*] (AABC) ... RAP
Rear Area Protection Operations Extended (MCD) ... RAP-EX
Rear Area Security [*Army*] (AABC) ... RAS
Rear Area Security and Area Damage Control [*Military*] ... RASC/DC
Rear Area Security Control Center [*Military*] ... RASCC
Rear Area Security Controller [*Military*] ... RASC
Rear Area Types [*Military slang for rear support troops*] (VNW) ... RATS
Rear Artillery ... RA
Rear Axle [*Automotive engineering*] ... R/A
Rear Axle Weight [*Automotive engineering*] ... RAW
Rear Combat Vehicle/Communications Zone (MCD) ... RCV-COMMZ
Rear Combat Zone (NATG) ... RCZ
Rear Commodore [*Navy*] (NVT) ... RC
Rear Compressor Variable Vane ... RCVV
Rear Connection (MSA) ... RC
Rear Defence Locality [*British military*] (DMA) ... RDL
Rear Door [*Automotive engineering*] ... R/DR
Rear Door ... RD
Rear Echelon COMINT [*Communications Intelligence*] **System** [*Military*] (MCD) ... RECS
Rear Echelon Maintenance Combined Operation [*Military*] ... REMCO
Rear Engine, Front and Rear Drive [*Automotive design*] ... RFR
Rear Engine Power-Take-Off [*Automotive engineering*] ... REPTO
Rear Engine, Rear Drive [*Automotive engineering*] ... RR
Rear Face of Block [*Automotive engineering*] ... RFOB
Rear Floor [*Automotive engineering*] ... R/FLR
Rear Gunner [*British military*] (DMA) ... R/G
Rear Headrest ... RHR
Rear Lower Control Arm ... RLCA
Rear Maintenance Area [*Military British*] ... RMA
Rear Overhead [*TII*] (TAG) ... ROH
Rear Projection [*Television*] ... RP
Rear Projection Readout ... RPR
Rear Quarter [*Automotive engineering*] ... R/QTR
Rear Upper Control Arm ... RUCA
Rear Vacuum Break [*Automotive engineering*] ... RVB
Rear View (AAG) ... R/V
Rear View [*Technical drawings*] ... RV
Rear Vision Television [*Driver safety systems*] [*Automotive engineering*] ... RVTV
Rear Wheel Brake ... RWB
Rear Wheel Drive ... RWD
Rear Window [*Automotive engineering*] ... R/WDO
Rear Window Wiper [*Automotive engineering*] ... RWW
Rear-Admiral (Administration) Eastern Fleet [*British*] ... RA(A)EF
Rear-Admiral, Alexandria [*British*] ... RAL
Rear-Admiral Commanding [*British*] ... RAC
Rear-Admiral Commanding Combined Operational Bases (Western Approaches) [*British*] ... RACOB(WA)
Rear-Admiral Commanding Destroyers (British Pacific Fleet) ... RAD(BPF)
Rear-Admiral (Destroyers) [*Obsolete Navy British*] ... RA(D)
Rear-Admiral Fleet Train [*British Pacific Fleet*] ... RAFT
Rear-Admiral, Naval Air Stations [*British military*] (DMA) ... RANAS
Rear-Admiral of Aircraft Carriers [*Obsolete British*] ... RA(A)
Rear-Admiral of Aircraft Carriers, Eastern Fleet [*British*] ... RAACEF
Rear-Admiral of the United Kingdom [*Navy British*] (ROG) ... RAUK
Rearm and Refuel [*Military*] (VNW) ... REARF
Rearm, Resupply, Refuel [*Army*] ... R3
Rearrangement Induced Premeiotically [*Genetics*] ... RIP
Rearranging Sequence [*Genetics*] ... RS
Rear-Screen Projection (WDAA) ... RSP
Rearward Communications System (MDG) ... RCS
Rearward Launched Ballistic Missile ... RLBM
Rearward Launched Missile ... RLM
Rear-Wheel Antilock Brake System [*Automotive engineering*] ... RABS
Rearwin Club (EA) ... RC
Reason (ROG) ... REASN
Reason (AFM) ... RSN
Reason for Backlog [*Telecommunications*] (TEL) ... RFB
Reason for Change (MCD) ... RFC
Reason for Deficiency (SAA) ... READEF
Reason for Visit Classification [*Medicine*] (DHSM) ... RFVC
Reason Foundation (EA) ... RF
Reason to Believe (ECON) ... RTB
Reasonable (ROG) ... REAS
Reasonable Alternative (GNE) ... RA
Reasonable and Customary [*Refers to medical charges*] [*Insurance*] ... R & C
Reasonable Assumed [*or Assured*] **Resources** [*Minerals*] ... RAR
Reasonable Available Control Measures [*Environmental Protection Agency*] (GFGA) ... RACM
Reasonable Available Control Technology [*Environmental Protection Agency*] ... RACT
Reasonable Benefit Limit [*Superannuation*] ... RBL
Reasonable Benefit Multiple ... RBM
Reasonable Compensation Equivalent [*Medicine*] (DMAA) ... RCE
Reasonable Effort (GNE) ... RE
Reasonable Efforts Program [*Environmental Protection Agency*] (EPA) ... REP
Reasonable Factors Other than Age [*Equal Employment Opportunity Commission*] ... RFOA
Reasonable Man [*Legal shorthand*] (LWAP) ... RM
Reasonable Maximum Exposure [*Toxicology*] ... RME
Reasonable Prudent Man [*Legal shorthand*] (LWAP) ... RPM
Reasonable Transportation Control Measure (GNE) ... RTCM
Reasonably Expected as Safe [*Medicine*] (DMAA) ... REAS
Reasoning Factor [*or Ability*] [*Psychology*] ... R
Reasoning Module [*Computer science*] ... RM
Reasons to Believe [*An association*] (EA) ... RB
Reassemble (AAG) ... REASM
Reassemble (MSA) ... REASSEM
Reassembly (MSA) ... REASSY
Reassign (ROG) ... REASSN
Reassign (AABC) ... RSG
Reassign ... RSGN
Reassigned (ROG) ... REASSND
Reassignment ... RASGN
Reassignment (ROG) ... REASST
Reassignment ... RSGMT
Reassurance (ROG) ... REASSCE
Reassurance to Each [*To help families of the mentally ill*] ... REACH
Reaumur [*Temperature scale*] [*German*] ... R
Reaumur (ROG) ... REAUM
Reba McEntire International Fan Club (EA) ... RMIFC
Reba Resources Ltd. [*Vancouver Stock Exchange symbol*] ... REB
Rebabbit ... RBBT
Rebate [*Technical drawings*] ... RBT
Rebecca/Eureka [*Navigation*] (AIA) ... REB
Rebecca Eureka Beacon [*Navigation*] (IAA) ... REB
Rebel ... REB
Rebel Lee Fan Club (EA) ... RLFC
Reblooming Iris Society (EA) ... RIS
Rebounds [*Basketball, hockey*] ... R
Rebounds [*Basketball, hockey*] ... REB
Rebounds per Game [*Basketball, hockey*] ... RPG
Rebreathing [*Medicine*] (DAVI) ... rb
Rebreathing Ventilation [*Medicine*] (DAVI) ... $V_D$rb
Rebroadcast Link [*Aerial*] ... RBL
Rebuild America (EA) ... RA
Rebuild Los Angeles [*Commission established after 1992 riots*] (ECON) ... RLA
Rebuild Standard [*Marine Corps*] ... RS
Rebuilder ... RBLDR
Rebuilding Grade [*Automotive engineering*] [*Polymer Steel Corp.*] ... RG
Rebuilt (VRA) ... rblt
Rebuilt (DS) ... RBT
Rebuilt ... REB
Rebuilt [*Automotive advertising*] ... REBLT
Rebun [*Japan*] [*Airport symbol Obsolete*] (OAG) ... RBJ
Rebun [*Japan ICAO location identifier*] (ICLI) ... RJCR
Rebuttable Presumption Against Regulation [*of pesticides*] [*Environmental Protection Agency*] ... RPAR

Recalculated .... RECALC
Recall (MSA) .... RCL
Recall Finder .... RCF
Recallable Airborne Infrared Display .... RAID
Recalled to Active Duty .... REACDU
Recap and Movement Authorization [*NASA*] (NASA) .... RAMA
Recapitulation (AABC) .... RECAP
Recco Corp. [*Vancouver Stock Exchange symbol*] .... RCC
Receipt (ROG) .... R
Receipt .... RC
Receipt (AFM) .... RCPT
Receipt (IAA) .... RCT
Receipt .... REC
Receipt .... RECPT
Receipt .... RECPT
Receipt .... RECT
Receipt .... REPT
Receipt [*British naval signaling*] .... RRRRR
Receipt Account Title File [*Office of Management and Budget*] (GFGA) .... RAT
Receipt Acknowledged .... REACK
Receipt Acknowledged and Understood .... RECAU
Receipt and Despatch Unit [*Aircraft*] .... RDU
Receipt Authority Voucher .... RAV
Receipt Day (NRCH) .... RD
Receipt Delivery Control Unit [*Social Security Administration*] .... RDCU
Receipt, Excess, Adjustment, Due-In History File [*Army*] .... RAH
Receipt for [*or of*] **Classified Security Information** (AAG) .... RCSI
Receipt, Inspection, and Maintenance [*Military*] .... RIM
Receipt Inspection Checklist (DNAB) .... RICL
Receipt Inspection Form [*Military*] (DNAB) .... RIF
Receipt Inspection Segment (OA) .... RIS
Receipt of Change Notice .... RCN
Receipt of Classified Material (AAG) .... RCM
Receipt of Goods .... ROG
Receipt of Goods Received .... RGR
Receipt Pass (AAG) .... RP
Receipt, Storage, and Delivery [*Business term*] .... RS & D
Receipt, Storage, and Issue [*Army*] (AABC) .... RSI
Receipted (ROG) .... RECETED
Receipts [*Stock exchange term*] (SPSG) .... RCT
Receivable .... RCVBL
Receivable Accounts Data Entry and Retrieval [*Computer science*] (MHDI) .... RADAR
Receive (AFM) .... RCV
Receive .... RCV
Receive (IDOE) .... rcv
Receive (IDOE) .... RCV
Receive (NASA) .... RECV
Receive (NITA) .... RX
Receive and Process Complaints and Requests for Assistance, Advice, or Information Only [*Army*] (AABC) .... RPCRAAIO
Receive, Assemble, Maintain, Inspect, and Store (IAA) .... RAMIS
Receive Channel/Transmit Channel [*Telecommunications*] (MCD) .... RCH/TCH
Receive Clock (IAA) .... RCL
Receive Clock Pulse .... RCP
Receive Data and Acknowledge [*Telecommunications*] (OSI) .... RDA
Receive Data Register [*Computer science*] (MDG) .... RDR
Receive, First-In, First-Out [*Communications engineering*] .... RFIFO
Receive Format Generator .... RFG
Receive Hub [*Telegraph*] [*Telecommunications*] (TEL) .... RH
Receive Leg [*Telecommunications*] (TEL) .... RL
Receive Location (DOMA) .... R/L
Receive Logic Chassis .... RLC
Receive Not Ready [*Computer science*] (IEEE) .... RNR
Receive Only .... RO
Receive Only Link Eleven [*Naval datalink system*] [*British*] .... ROLE
Receive Processor .... RP
Receive Pulse On/Off Keyed (MCD) .... RPOOK
Receive Ready [*Computer science*] (IEEE) .... RR
Receive, Record, Display .... RRD
Receive Reference Equivalent [*Telecommunications*] (TEL) .... RRE
Receive Replenishment From [*Navy*] (NVT) .... RPL
Received (ODBW) .... r
Received (ODBW) .... rcd
Received .... RCD
Received (MSA) .... RCVD
Received .... RCVD
Received (DS) .... REC
Received (AAG) .... RECD
Received (ODBW) .... recd
Received (WDMC) .... recd
Received .... RECVD
Received but Did Not Return Questionnaire (AABC) .... RBDNRQ
Received Copy of Temporary Pay Record .... RCT
Received Data (IEEE) .... RD
Received for Duty .... RECDUT
Received for Duty under Instruction .... RECDUINS
Received for Temporary Additional Duty .... RECTAD
Received for Temporary Additional Duty under Instruction .... RECTADINS
Received for Temporary Duty .... RECTD
Received for Temporary Duty under Instruction .... RECTEMDUINS
Received for Treatment .... RECTREAT
Received in Connection with Fitting Out (DNAB) .... RECCFO
Received Line Signal Detector .... RLSD
Received [*Payment under Provisions of the*] **Mustering Out Payment Act** [*Military*] (DNAB) .... RECMOP
Received, Not Billed (AFM) .... RNB
Received Pronunciation [*of the English language*] .... RP
Received Signal Level [*Telecommunications*] (TEL) .... RSL
Received Solid [*Amateur radio*] .... R
Received Text (ROG) .... RT
Receive-Only Page Printer .... ROPP
Receive-Only Printer [*Computer science*] .... ROP
Receive-Only Tape Reperforator [*Computer science*] (IAA) .... ROTR
Receive-Only Typing Reperforator .... ROTR
Receive-Only Typing Reperforator - Series to Parallel .... ROTR-S/P
Receiver .... R
Receiver (IAA) .... RC
Receiver [*Telecommunications*] (ECII) .... RCR
Receiver .... RCV
Receiver (AAG) .... RCVR
Receiver (IDOE) .... RCVR
Receiver (IDOE) .... rcvr
Receiver (AAG) .... REC
Receiver .... RECR
Receiver (NASA) .... RECVR
Receiver (AAG) .... REVR
Receiver [*or Reception*] [*Radio*] (NATG) .... RX
Receiver Active Signal Processor [*Military*] (CAAL) .... RASP
Receiver and Data Processor (MCD) .... RDP
Receiver Attenuation .... RA
Receiver Autonomous Integrity Monitoring [*Computer software*] .... RAIM
Receiver Auxiliary (IAA) .... RA
Receiver Card .... RC
Receiver Control Unit (IAA) .... RCU
Receiver Cuts Out [*Telecommunications*] (TEL) .... RCO
Receiver Data from Unit Control (MCD) .... RDUC
Receiver/Exciter .... RE
Receiver/Exciter Ranging [*NASA*] .... RER
Receiver/Exciter Subsystem [*Deep Space Instrumentation Facility, NASA*] .... RCV
Receiver Holding Register .... RHR
Receiver Hopping Mode (IAA) .... RH
Receiver Impulse Characteristic (IAA) .... RIC
Receiver Incremental Tuning .... RIT
Receiver Interface .... RI
Receiver Interface Board [*Navy Navigation Satellite System*] (DNAB) .... RIB
Receiver Intermodulation [*Telecommunications*] (TEL) .... RIM
Receiver Measurement Adapter (MCD) .... RMA
Receiver, Mobile .... RM
Receiver Noise Figure .... RNF
Receiver Off the Hook .... R-O-H
Receiver Only [*Radio*] .... RONLY
Receiver [*or Relative*] **Operating Characteristics** [*Signal detection*] [*Graph for assessing diagnostic tests*] .... ROC
Receiver Processor Unit [*Electronics*] .... RPU
Receiver Protective Device (DEN) .... REPROD
Receiver Room [*Navy*] (CAAL) .... RR
Receiver Side Lobe Suppression (MCD) .... RSLS
Receiver Signal Element Timing (IAA) .... RSET
Receiver Site [*Nevada*] [*Seismograph station code, US Geological Survey Closed*] (SEIS) .... NYR
Receiver Station .... RS
Receiver Test Equipment .... RTE
Receiver Threshold Test (CET) .... RTT
Receiver/Transmitter [*Radio*] (KSC) .... R/T
Receiver/Transmitter Unit .... RTU
Receiver Waveform Simulation [*Telecommunications*] (OA) .... RWS
Receiver-Carrier Detector .... RCD
Receiver-Independent Exchange [*Navigation systems*] [*Data communications*] .... RINEX
Receiver-Off-Hook Tone Connecting Circuit .... ROTCC
Receivership [*or Bankruptcy*] [*Designation used with NYSE symbols*] (SPSG) .... Q
Receivership (LWAP) .... RECRSHIP
Receiver-Transmitter-Modulator .... RTM
Receive-Transmit [*Radio*] .... RT
Receiving (IAA) .... R
Receiving (AAG) .... RCG
Receiving (MSA) .... RCVG
Receiving .... RCVNG
Receiving .... RECVG
Receiving Agency Materiel Division [*Military*] .... RAMD
Receiving Ambient Function Test (PDAA) .... RAFT
Receiving and Inspection (KSC) .... R & I
Receiving and Inspection (IAA) .... RAI
Receiving and Inspection Test (IAA) .... RIT
Receiving Array Hydrophone .... RAH
Receiving, Assembly Maintenance, Inspection, Storage [*Military*] .... RAMIS
Receiving Barracks .... RECBKS
Receiving Basin for Off-Site Fuel [*Nuclear energy*] .... RBOF
Receiving Capability Out [*Aviation*] (FAAC) .... RCVNO
Receiving Depository Financial Institution .... RDFI
Receiving Hospital Field Station .... RHFS
Receiving Inspection (AAG) .... RI
Receiving Inspection and Preparation for Checkout (SAA) .... RIPCO
Receiving Inspection Data Status [*Report*] [*Nuclear energy*] (NRCH) .... RIDS
Receiving Inspection Detail Instruction [*NASA*] (NASA) .... RIDI
Receiving Inspection General Instruction [*NASA*] (NASA) .... RIGI
Receiving Inspection Instruction [*Nuclear energy*] (NRCH) .... RII
Receiving Inspection Operating Sheet (MCD) .... RIOS

Receiving Inspection Plan [*Nuclear energy*] (NRCH) .... RIP
Receiving Inspection Report .... RIR
Receiving Inspection Segment .... RIS
Receiving Memo .... RM
Receiving Objective Loudness Rating [*Telephones*] (IEEE) .... ROLR
Receiving Office [*or Officer*] .... RO
Receiving Operations Package [*DoD*] .... ROP
Receiving Order [*Business term*] (DCTA) .... RO
Receiving Proficiency Pay [*Military*] .... RPROP
Receiving Quality Control (IAA) .... RQC
Receiving Report (AAG) .... RR
Receiving Report Change (AAG) .... RRC
Receiving Report Change Notice (AAG) .... RRCN
Receiving Ship .... RECSHIP
Receiving Ship [*or Station*] .... RS
Receiving Ship [*Navy symbol*] (DNAB) .... YWN
Receiving, Shipping, and Storage (NASA) .... RS & S
Receiving Site Equipment [*NASA*] .... RSE
Receiving Station [*Military*] .... RECSTA
Receiving Stolen Goods .... RSG
Receiving Stolen Property .... RSP
Receiving Terminal (IAA) .... RT
Receiving Test (DNAB) .... RT
Receiving Tube .... RT
Receiving-Only Monitor .... ROMON
Receiving-Safing Facility [*NASA*] (MCD) .... RSF
Recemment Degorgee [*Recently Disgorged*] [*Refers to aging of wine*]
   [*French*] .... RD
Recency-Frequency-Monetary Value Ratio (NTCM) .... RFMVR
Recens [*Fresh*] [*Pharmacy*] .... REC
Recent [*Used to qualify weather phenomena*] .... RE
Recent (ROG) .... REC
Recent Advances in Manufacturing [*Information service or system*] (IID) ...... RAM
Recent College Graduates Survey [*Department of Education*] (GFGA) .... RCGS
Recent Crustal Movements [*Geology*] (NOAA) .... RCM
Recent Drizzle [*Meteorology*] (DA) .... REDZ
Recent Freezing Rain [*Meteorology*] (DA) .... REFRA
Recent Hail [*Meteorology*] (DA) .... REGR
Recent Law (DLA) .... REC L
Recent Laws in Canada [*A publication*] (DLA) .... Rec Laws
Recent Rain [*Meteorology*] (DA) .... RERA
Recent Shower [*Meteorology*] (DA) .... RESH
Recent Snow [*Meteorology*] (DA) .... RESN
Recent Thunderstorm (DA) .... RETS
Recent Vertical Crustal Movement [*Geology*] .... RVCM
Recentis [*Fresh*] [*Pharmacy*] (ROG) .... RECENT
Recently Acquired Income Deficiency Syndrome .... RAIDS
Recently Immigrated Professional Irish Legals [*Lifestyle classification*] ..... RIPILS
Recently Separated Veteran .... RSV
Recently Used Directory [*Computer science*] (MHDI) .... RUD
Receptacle (MSA) .... RCPT
Receptacle (WGA) .... REC
Receptacle .... RECP
Receptacle (AAG) .... RECPT
Recepter Interacting Domain [*Biochemistry*] .... RID
Reception (IAA) .... R
Reception (AABC) .... RCPT
Reception (MSA) .... RCPTN
Reception .... REC
Reception (ADA) .... RECEP
Reception (WGA) .... RECP
Reception (AAG) .... RECPT
Reception (IAA) .... RECT
Reception Automatic Picture Transmission (PDAA) .... RAPT
Reception Center [*Army*] .... RC
Reception Center [*Army*] (IAA) .... RECCEN
Reception Center [*Army*] .... Recp Cen
Reception Fair [*Radio logs*] .... RF
Reception Good [*Radio logs*] .... RG
Reception Nil [*Radio logs*] .... RN
Reception Node .... RN
Reception Poor [*Radio logs*] .... RP
Reception, Staging, Onward Movement and Integration [*Military*] (INF) .... RSOI
Reception Station .... RS
Reception Station System [*Army*] .... RESTAS
Receptionist (WGA) .... RECPST
Receptive Field [*of visual cortex*] .... RF
Receptive Language Age [*of the hearing-impaired*] .... RLA
Receptive One-Word Picture Vocabulary Test [*Educational test*] .... ROWPVT
Receptive-Expressive Observation [*Sensorimotor skills test*] .... REO
Receptor [*Biochemistry*] .... R
Receptor Affinity Distribution [*Biochemistry*] .... RAD
Receptor for Advanced Glycation End-Product [*Biochemistry*] .... RAGE
Receptor Mediated Endocytosis [*Biochemistry*] .... RME
Receptor Potential .... RP
Receptor Protein Tyrosine Phosphatase [*Biochemistry*] .... RPTP
Receptor Tyrosine Kinase [*Biochemistry*] .... RTK
Receptor-Affinity Chromatography .... RAC
Receptor-Associated Protein [*Biochemistry*] .... RAP
Receptor-Chemoeffector [*Biochemistry*] .... RC
Receptor-Chemoeffector Complex [*Biochemistry*] .... RCC
Receptor-Destroying Enzyme [*A neuraminidase*] [*Immunochemistry*] .... RDE
Receptor-Ligand Complex .... RL
Receptor-Mediated Permeabilizer [*Medicine*] .... RMP
Receptor-Operated Calcium Channel [*Physiology*] .... ROCC

Recertification (NASA) .... RECERT
Recess (MSA) .... REC
Recessed [*Electrical outlet symbol*] .... R
Recessed Annular Connector .... RAC
Recessed Selectromatic Terminal (NASA) .... RST
Recessive Dystrophic Epidermolysis Bullosa [*Also, EBDR*]
   [*Dermatology*] .... RDEB
Recessive Epidermolysis Bullosa Dystrophia-Hallopeaun Siemens
   [*Dermatology*] .... R-EBD-HS
Recessive X-Linked Ichthyosis [*Medicine*] .... RXLI
Recessive-Expressive Emergent Language Scores [*For the hearing-
   impaired*] .... REEL
Recharge (NASA) .... RECHG
Re-Chargeable Air-Breathing Apparatus (PDAA) .... RABA
Rechargeable Power Pack .... RPP
Recharged from Inversion Layer (PDAA) .... REFIL
Recharger .... RECHRG
Recherches Amerindiennes au Quebec, Montreal, PQ, Canada [*Library
   symbol*] [*Library of Congress*] (LCLS) .... CaQMRAQ
Recherches Amerindiennes au Quebec, Montreal, Quebec [*Library symbol*
   National Library of Canada*] (NLC) .... QMRAQ
Recherches sur l'Origine de l'Ecriture Cuneiforme [*A publication*] (BJA) .... REC
Recht [*Law*] [*German*] .... R
Recht der Arbeit [*Right to Work*] [*German*] (DLA) .... R Arb
Rechtsgeschichte [*German*] (ILCA) .... RG
Rechtspraak [*Case Law, Judicial Decisions*] [*Netherlands*] (ILCA) .... Rspr
Rechtsprechung [*Court Practice*] [*German*] (ILCA) .... Rspr
Rechtsprechung in Arbeitssachen [*Labor Court Reports*] [*German*]
   (ILCA) .... Rspr Arb
Rechtswissenschaft [*Jurisprudence*] [*German*] (ILCA) .... RW
Rechtswissenschaftliche Experten und Gutachter [*NOMOS Datapool*]
   [*Database*] .... REX
Recidivism [*or Recidivist*] (WDAA) .... RECID
Recife [*Brazil*] [*Airport symbol*] (OAG) .... REC
Recife [*Brazil ICAO location identifier*] (ICLI) .... SBRE
Recife/Guararapes [*Brazil ICAO location identifier*] (ICLI) .... SBRF
Recipe [*Take*] [*Latin*] [*Pharmacy*] (DAVI) .... R
Recipe [*Take*] [*Pharmacy*] .... R
Recipe .... REC
Recipe [*Used as a symbol for medical prescriptions*] .... Rx
Recipe Index [*A publication*] .... RI
Recipient [*MARC relator code*] [*Library of Congress*] (LCCP) .... rcp
Recipient .... RECIP
Recipient Agency [*Federal government*] (GFGA) .... RA
Recipient City (NITA) .... RC
Recipient Name (NITA) .... RN
Recipient Rights .... RR
Recipient Rights Adviser .... RA
Recipient Rights Officer .... RRO
Recipient State (NITA) .... RS
Recipient Type (NITA) .... RT
Recipient Value (GFGA) .... RV
Recipient's Serum [*In blood matching*] .... RS
Reciprocal (AAG) .... RECP
Reciprocal Asymmetrical [*Medicine*] (DMAA) .... RA
Reciprocal Cross Sterile Females [*Genetics*] .... RSF
Reciprocal Derivative Constant-Current Stripping Analysis [*Analytical
   electrochemistry*] .... RD-CCSA
Reciprocal Detection Latency .... RDL
Reciprocal Impedance Converter (PDAA) .... RIC
Reciprocal Ohm [*Unit of conductance*] .... mho
Reciprocal Ohmmeter [*Electronics*] (IAA) .... ROM
Reciprocal Thermal Efficiency (PDAA) .... RTE
Reciprocal Trade Agreement .... RTA
Reciprocate (AAG) .... RECIP
Reciprocating .... R
Reciprocating Aircraft Engine Type Designation System .... RAETDS
Reciprocating Cryogenic Refrigerator .... RCR
Reciprocating Gas-Fueled Engine .... RECIP
Reciprocating Steam (MCD) .... RS
Recirculate (AAG) .... RECIRC
Recirculate (NASA) .... RECRC
Recirculating [*Automotive engineering*] .... RECIR
Recirculating Ball [*Automotive engineering*] .... RB
Recirculating Cooler .... RC
Recirculating Dialyzate [*Artificial kidney dialysis system*] .... REDY
Recirculating Document Feeder (NITA) .... RDF
Recirculating Single Pass [*Medicine*] (BARN) .... RSP
Recirculation Actuation Signal [*Nuclear energy*] (NRCH) .... RAS
Recirculation Duct Assembly .... RDA
Recirculation Flow Control [*Nuclear energy*] (NRCH) .... RFC
Recirculation Flow Control System [*Nuclear energy*] (NRCH) .... RFCS
Recirculation Isolation Valve (NASA) .... RIV
Recirculation Pump Trip [*Nuclear energy*] (NRCH) .... RPT
Recirculation Spray Heat Exchanger [*Nuclear energy*] (NRCH) .... RSHX
Recirculation Valve (MCD) .... RV
Recirculative Fluid Flow .... RFF
Recirculatory Air (AAG) .... RA
Recital (ROG) .... RECL
Recitation .... RECIT
Recitative [*Music*] .... RECIT
Recite [*Swell Organ*] [*Music*] .... R
Recited (ROG) .... RECTD
Reciting .... RECG
Reciting (ROG) .... RECTG

Reckitt & Sons Ltd. [*Great Britain*] [*Research code symbol*] ... M
Reckson Associates Realty [*NYSE symbol*] (TTSB) ... RA
Reckson Associates Realty Corp. [*NYSE symbol*] (SAG) ... RA
Reckson Associates Realty Corp. [*Associated Press*] (SAG) ... Reckson
Reclaim (AABC) ... RCLM
Reclaim, Inc. [*Associated Press*] (SAG) ... Reclaim
Reclaim, Inc. [*NASDAQ symbol*] (SAG) ... ROOF
Reclaim Managers Association [*Defunct*] (EA) ... RMA
Reclaimed Wheat Grass Cover [*Agriculture*] ... RW
Reclaimed Wheat Grass/Shrub Cover [*Agriculture*] ... RS
Reclaiming ... RCLMG
Reclamation (WGA) ... REC
Reclamation ... RECL
Reclamation Control Officer [*Military*] (AFIT) ... RCO
Reclamation in Lieu of Procurement [*Navy*] (NG) ... RILOP
Reclamation Insurance Type [*Military*] (AFIT) ... RIT
Reclamation Order Control Number ... ROCN
Reclamation Program Control Officer [*Military*] (AFIT) ... RPCO
Reclamation Program Manager [*Military*] (AFIT) ... RPM
Reclamation Reform Act [*1982*] ... RRA
Reclearance in Flight [*Aviation*] (FAAC) ... RIF
Recleared [*Aviation*] (FAAC) ... RECLR
Reclined (MSA) ... RCLD
Reclining Chair (DAVI) ... R/C
Reclose ... RECL
Recluse ... R
Recluse Missionaries of Jesus and Mary [*Roman Catholic women's religious order*] ... RMJM
Recognisance (ROG) ... RECOGE
Recognisances (ROG) ... RECOGS
Recognised Investment Exchange [*British*] ... RIE
Recognised Professional Body [*Marketing of Investments Board Organising Committee, London Stock Exchange*] [*Finance*] ... RPB
Recognition [*Experimentation*] ... R
Recognition [*or Recognize*] (AAG) ... RECOG
Recognition and Control Processor [*Computer science*] (IBMDP) ... RCP
Recognition Awards for the Integration of Research and Education [*National Science Foundation*] ... RAIRE
Recognition Context [*Computer science*] (PCM) ... RC
Recognition Differential ... RD
Recognition Equipment, Inc. (IAA) ... REI
Recognition for Information Technology Achievement [*An award*] (PDAA) ... RITA
Recognition Memory [*Semionics Associates*] [*Computer science*] ... REM
Recognition, Reassurance, and Relaxation [*Military mental health technique*] (INF) ... 3R's
Recognition Signal [*Navy*] ... RECOGSIG
Recognition Structure [*Immunochemistry*] ... RS
Recognition Suppression Technique ... RST
Recognition Technologies Users Association (EA) ... RTUA
Recognizance ... RECOGN
Recognize All Potential (DNAB) ... RAP
Recognized Private Operating Agencies (NATG) ... RPOA
Recognized Rescue Center [*Navy*] (DNAB) ... RRC
Recognizing Exceptional Achievement in Community Help Award [*Association of Personal Computer User Groups*] (PCM) ... REACH
Recoil (MSA) ... RCL
Recoil Mechanism (AAG) ... RECMECH
Recoiling Structural Contour Map [*Surface analysis*] ... RSCM
Recoilless ... RCLS
Recoilless Gun (AABC) ... RCLG
Recoilless Launcher ... RCL
Recoilless Rifle (AABC) ... RCLR
Recoilless Rifle ... RR
Recombinant Alpha 1-Antitrypsin [*Biochemistry*] ... RAAT
Recombinant B-Cell Stimulatory Factor [*Biochemistry*] ... rBSF
Recombinant Bio-Catalysis, Inc. [*Commercial firm*] ... RBI
Recombinant Bovine Growth Hormone ... RBGH
Recombinant Circle Polymerase Chain Reaction [*Genetics*] ... RCPCR
Recombinant DNA [*Deoxyribonucleic Acid*] (MCD) ... RDNA
Recombinant DNA Advisory Committee [*National Institutes of Health*] ... RAC
Recombinant Follicle-Stimulating Hormone [*Endocrinology*] ... RFSH
Recombinant Human Erythropoietin [*Biochemistry*] ... rHuEPO
Recombinant Human Granulocyte, Colony Stimulating Factor [*Hematology*] ... RHG-CSF
Recombinant Human Growth Hormone [*Biochemistry*] ... RHGH
Recombinant Human Leukocyte Interferon A [*Pharmacology*] (DAVI) ... IFLrA
Recombinant Human Platelet Factor [*Biochemistry*] ... rhPF
Recombinant Immunoblot Assay [*Medicine*] ... RIBA
Recombinant Immunoblot Assay (DMAA) ... RIBA
Recombinant Inbred [*Genetics*] ... RI
Recombinant Interferon [*Biochemistry*] ... RIFN
Recombinant Interferon Gamma-Inducing Factor [*Biochemistry*] ... rIGIF
Recombinant Interleukin [*Immunotherapy*] ... RIL
Recombinant Interleukin Receptor Antagonist Protein [*Biochemistry*] ... RIRAP
Recombinant Macrophage Colony-Stimulating Factor [*Biochemistry*] ... RMCSF
Recombinant Migration Inhibitory Factor [*Biochemistry*] ... rMIF
Recombinant Porcine Somatotropin ... RPST
Recombinant Secretory Leukoprotease Inhibitor [*Biochemistry*] ... RSLPI
Recombinant Tissue Plasminogen Activator [*Biochemistry*] ... rtPA
Recombinant Tissue Plasminogen Activator (BARN) ... r-tPA
Recombinant Tissue-Type Plasminogen Activator [*Genetics*] (DAVI) ... RTPA
Recombinant Tumor Necrosis Factor [*Biochemistry*] ... RTNF
Recombinant Vaccinia Virus ... rVV
Recombination Frequency [*Genetics*] (DOG) ... RF
Recombination Signal Sequence [*Immunology*] ... RSS
Recombination-Activating Gene ... RAG
Recombiner Charcoal Adsorber [*Nuclear energy*] (NRCH) ... RECHAR
Recommend (KSC) ... RECM
Recommend (AAG) ... RECMD
Recommend (WDAA) ... RECOM
Recommend Repair Parts List ... RRPL
Recommend Transfer Of (NOAA) ... RECTR
Recommendation (MHDB) ... R
Recommendation (AFM) ... REC
Recommendation ... RECMN
Recommendation (DAVI) ... Recomm
Recommendation Approval Document (MCD) ... RAD
Recommendation for Acceptance (AAG) ... RFA
Recommended Area for Protection [*Australia*] ... RAP
Recommended Buy List ... RBL
Recommended Common Support Equipment List (MCD) ... RCSEL
Recommended Completion ... RECOMP
Recommended Concentration Guide [*Nuclear energy*] (NRCH) ... RCG
Recommended Course Indicator ... RCI
Recommended Daily Allowance [*Dietary*] ... RDA
Recommended Daily Dietary Allowance ... RDDA
Recommended Daily Intake [*Dietary*] ... RDI
Recommended Dietary Allowance (DAVI) ... RDA
Recommended Distribution of Effort [*Civil defense*] ... RDE
Recommended Duty Assignment (AFM) ... RDA
Recommended Exposure Limit ... REL
Recommended for Medal and Gratuity [*British*] ... RMG
Recommended for Re-Engagement [*British*] ... RR
Recommended Ground Zero [*Military*] (AABC) ... RGZ
Recommended Immediate Procurement Records (MCD) ... RIPR
Recommended Initial System Stockage ... RISS
Recommended International Nonproprietary Name [*Drug research*] ... RINN
Recommended Maintenance Operation Chart [*Army*] (AABC) ... RMOC
Recommended Maximum Contaminant Level [*Environmental Protection Agency*] ... RMCL
Recommended Operating Condition [*Computer science*] ... ROC
Recommended Peculiar Support Equipment List (MCD) ... RPSEL
Recommended Practice ... RP
Recommended Provisioning List ... RPL
Recommended Qualitative and Quantitative Personnel Requirements Information [*Military*] (MCD) ... RQQPRI
Recommended Retail Price ... RRP
Recommended Spare Parts List [*NASA*] ... RSPL
Recommended Spares and Spare Parts List ... RSSPL
Recommended Special Support Equipment List ... RSSEL
Recommended Standard [*Telecommunications*] (TEL) ... RS
Recommended Test Sequence Chart (MCD) ... RTSC
Recommended Vehicle Adjustment [*Military*] (AABC) ... REVA
Recommended Weight Limit [*Ergonmetrics*] ... RWL
Recommissioned (DS) ... Recmd
Recomp Algebraic Formula Translator [*Computer science*] ... RAFT
Recomp Computer Interpretive Program Expediter [*Computer science*] ... RECIPE
Recomp Users Group [*Computer science*] ... RUG
Recomplement ... RECOMP
Recompression ... RCMPRS
Recompression Thermonuclear ... RTN
Recomputation ... RECMPT
Recompute Last Fix [*Navy Navigation Satellite System*] (DNAB) ... RCMP
RECON Information System (MCD) ... RIS
Reconcentration (WDAA) ... RECON
Reconciliation (AABC) ... RECNCLN
Reconciliation ... RECON
Reconciliation and Purification Program [*Air Force*] ... RAPP
Reconciling Congregation Program (EA) ... RCP
Reconciling with Accounting and Finance Officer (AAGC) ... RFO
Recondition ... RCNDT
Recondition (WDAA) ... RECON
Recondition (AABC) ... RECOND
Reconditioned (DCTA) ... R
Reconditioned Sys [*NASDAQ symbol*] (TTSB) ... RESY
Reconditioned Sys Wrrt'B' [*NASDAQ symbol*] (TTSB) ... RESYZ
Reconditioned Systems, Inc. [*Associated Press*] (SAG) ... RecdSys
Reconditioned Systems, Inc. [*Associated Press*] (SAG) ... RecS
Reconfigurable Computer System Design Facility (MHDB) ... RCSDF
Reconfigurable EC System (MCD) ... RECS
Reconfigurable Electrical Test Stand (NASA) ... RETS
Reconfiguration [*Aviation*] (FAAC) ... RCON
Reconfiguration (NASA) ... RECONFIG
Reconfiguration and Fault Detection Unit ... RFDU
Reconfiguration Data Collection System [*or Subsystem*] (MCD) ... RDCS
Reconfiguration Maximum Theoretical Bandwidth ... RMTB
Reconfiguration System (MCD) ... RS
Reconfigured Integrated Two-Stage Liquefaction [*Chemical engineering*] ... RITSL
Reconnaisance Exploitation Report (MCD) ... RECCEXREP
Reconnaissance [*Designation for all US military aircraft*] ... R
Reconnaissance ... RCN
Reconnaissance (CINC) ... RECCE
Reconnaissance (NVT) ... RECCO
Reconnaissance ... RECN
Reconnaissance (NATG) ... RECON
Reconnaissance (AAG) ... RECONN
Reconnaissance Air Meet (DOMA) ... RAM
Reconnaissance Aircraft (DNAB) ... RA

Reconnaissance Aircraft Maintenance Van ... RAMVAN
Reconnaissance Airplane Company [*Army*] (VNW) ... RAC
Reconnaissance and Interdiction Detachment [*Army*] (DOMA) ... RAID
Reconnaissance and Operations Center (NATG) ... ROC
Reconnaissance and Radioelectronic Combat [*Military*] (INF) ... REC
Reconnaissance and Security [*Military*] (INF) ... R & S
Reconnaissance and Security Line ... RSL
Reconnaissance and Security Positions [*Military*] ... RSP
Reconnaissance and Surveillance (MCD) ... R & S
Reconnaissance and Survey Officer [*Military*] (AABC) ... RSO
Reconnaissance and Tactical Security [*Teams*] [*Military*] ... RATS
Reconnaissance Attack Helicopter ... RAH
Reconnaissance/Attack Navigator ... RAN
Reconnaissance Attack Squadron [*Navy*] ... COMRECONATKRON
Reconnaissance Attack Squadron [*Navy*] (DNAB) ... RECONATKRON
Reconnaissance Attack Squadron [*Navy*] (NVT) ... RVAH
Reconnaissance Attack Wing [*Navy*] ... COMRECONATKWING
Reconnaissance Attack Wing [*Navy*] (NVT) ... RAW
Reconnaissance Attack Wing [*Navy*] (DNAB) ... RECONATKWING
Reconnaissance Battalion [*Navy*] (DNAB) ... RECONBN
Reconnaissance Bomber ... RB
Reconnaissance by Fire [*Military*] (VNW) ... RBF
Reconnaissance by Orbiting Ship-Identification Equipment ... ROSIE
Reconnaissance Car [*British*] ... RC
Reconnaissance Cockpit Display ... RCD
Reconnaissance Commando Doughboy [*Military*] (AABC) ... RECONDO
Reconnaissance Co. [*Military*] ... RECONCO
Reconnaissance Duty Officer ... RDO
Reconnaissance, Electronic Warfare, and Naval Intelligence System ... RENS
Reconnaissance Electronic Warfare Special Operation and Naval Intelligence Processing (IAA) ... REWSONIP
Reconnaissance, Electronic Warfare, Special Operations, and Naval Intelligence Processing (MCD) ... RENSONIP
Reconnaissance, Electronic Warfare, Special Operations, and Naval Intelligence Processing Systems ... REWSON
Reconnaissance Electro-Optical Viewing System ... REVS
Reconnaissance Experimental [*British military*] (DMA) ... RE
Reconnaissance Fighter (MUGU) ... RF
Reconnaissance Force ... RF
Reconnaissance in Force [*Military*] (VNW) ... RIF
Reconnaissance Inspection [*Military*] (GFGA) ... RI
Reconnaissance Intelligence Technical Squadron ... RITS
Reconnaissance Intelligence Technical Squadron [*Air Force*] ... RITSq
Reconnaissance Long Range [*Army*] ... RCNLR
Reconnaissance Management System ... RMS
Reconnaissance Medium Range [*Army*] ... RENMR
Reconnaissance Officer ... RO
Reconnaissance Optique de Caracteres [*Optical Character Recognition*] [*French*] ... ROC
Reconnaissance/Reaction (MCD) ... RE ACT
Reconnaissance Reporting Facility ... RRF
Reconnaissance Reporting System ... RRS
Reconnaissance Satellite (NVT) ... RECSAT
Reconnaissance Satellite ... RS
Reconnaissance Satellite Summary (DNAB) ... RECSATSUM
Reconnaissance Scout Vehicle (MCD) ... RSV
Reconnaissance Seaplane [*Russian symbol*] ... ARK
Reconnaissance, Selection, and Occupation of Position [*Military*] ... RSOP
Reconnaissance Squadron [*Military*] ... RECSQUAD
Reconnaissance Squadron [*Military*] ... RS
Reconnaissance Strategic Missile ... RSM
Reconnaissance Strike Bomber ... RSB
Reconnaissance Strip [*Military*] (AFM) ... RS
Reconnaissance, Surveillance, and Target Acquisition [*Military*] (AABC) ... RESTA
Reconnaissance, Surveillance, and Target Acquisition Aircraft (MCD) ... RSTAA
Reconnaissance, Surveillance, and Target Acquisition/Battle Management Command, Control, and Communications (MCD) ... RSTA/BMC3
Reconnaissance, Surveillance, and Target Acquisition Center [*Fort Monmout h, NJ*] [*Army*] (MCD) ... RSTA
Reconnaissance, Surveillance, and Targeting Vehicle [*Military*] ... RST-V
Reconnaissance, Surveillance, Target Acquisition, and Engagement (MCD) ... RSTA & E
Reconnaissance System Officer (MCD) ... RSO
Reconnaissance Tactical Missile ... RTM
Reconnaissance Task Force (AFM) ... RTF
Reconnaissance Team [*Military*] (VNW) ... RT
Reconnaissance Technical Flight [*Air Force*] ... RTF
Reconnaissance Technical Group [*Air Force*] ... RTG
Reconnaissance Technical Group [*Air Force*] (AFM) ... RTGp
Reconnaissance Technical Squadron [*Air Force*] (CINC) ... RTS
Reconnaissance Technical Squadron [*Air Force*] (AFM) ... RTSq
Reconnaissance Training Group [*Air Force*] (AFM) ... RTGp
Reconnaissance Watch Officer (MCD) ... RWO
Reconnaissance Wing [*Military*] ... RW
Reconnaissance Zone ... RZ
Reconnaissance-Experimental Aircraft ... RX
Reconnaissance-Strike [*Military*] ... RS
Reconnoitre (WDAA) ... RECON
Reconquista [*Argentina*] [*Airport symbol*] (OAG) ... RCQ
Reconquista [*Argentina ICAO location identifier*] (ICLI) ... SATR
Reconsideration Denied (AAGC) ... recons denied
Reconsign ... R/C
Reconsignment (WDAA) ... RECON
Reconstitutable and Enduring Intelligence System ... REIS
Reconstitutable Emergency Communications System ... RECS
Reconstituted Ion Current [*Chromatography*] ... RIC
Reconstituted Sendai Virus Envelope [*Immunology*] ... RSVE
Reconstitution Site (NVT) ... RS
Reconstruct (AABC) ... RECONST
Reconstructed Communism Party [*Italy*] ... RC
Reconstructed Gas Chromatogram ... RGC
Reconstructed Ion Chromatogram ... RIC
Reconstruction (VRA) ... recon
Reconstruction (CPH) ... reconstr
Reconstruction and Development Program [*South Africa*] ... RDP
Reconstruction by Optimized Series Expansion [*Of large molecules*] ... ROSE
Reconstruction Committee [*British World War II*] ... R
Reconstruction Committee [*British World War II*] ... RC
Reconstruction Education for National Understanding [*An association*] (EA) ... RENU
Reconstruction Finance Corp. [*Abolished, 1957*] ... RFC
Reconstruction Finance Corporation Act [*Obsolete*] ... RFCA
Reconstruction Finance Corporation Mortgage Co. ... RFCMC
Reconstruction of Town and Country [*British World War II*] ... RTC
Reconstruction, Social Insurance [*British World War II*] ... R(SI)
Reconstruction, Workmen's Compensation [*British World War II*] ... R(W)
Reconstructionist Rabbinical College [*Pennsylvania*] ... RRC
Reconstructive ... RECNSTRCTV
Recontact Date [*Automotive retailing*] ... RCD
Reconveyance (ROG) ... RECONCE
Reconveyance (ROG) ... RECONVCE
Record ... R
Record ... RCD
Record (AFM) ... RCRD
Record (AAG) ... REC
Record ... REC
Record (WDMC) ... rec
Record Address (IAA) ... RA
Record and Playback Assembly (MCD) ... RPA
Record and Playback Subsystem (NASA) ... RPS
Record and Process Input Tables (IAA) ... RAPIT
Record and Report ... RAR
Record and Tape Exchange [*Defunct*] (EA) ... RATE
Record Archival Management System (HGAA) ... RAMS
Record Assigned System (MCD) ... RAS
Record Breeze, Lindenwold, NJ [*Library symbol Library of Congress*] (LCLS) ... NjLwR
Record Carrier (IAA) ... RC
Record Carrier Competition Act [*1981*] ... RCCA
Record Change [*or Changer*] (AAG) ... RC
Record Club of America [*Defunct*] ... RCOA
Record Code (IAA) ... RC
Record Collectors' Club (EA) ... RCC
Record Commissioner [*British*] (DLA) ... REC COM
Record Commissioners [*British*] (DLA) ... RC
Record Control Number [*Military*] (AFM) ... RCN
Record Control Word [*Computer science*] ... RCW
Record Count [*Computer science*] ... RC
Record Definition Field [*Computer science*] (BUR) ... RDF
Record Description [*Computer science*] ... RD
Record Element Specification [*Computer science*] ... RES
Record Evaluate and Control Time System (IAA) ... REACT
Record Evaluation System ... RES
Record Extraction, Manipulation, and Print ... REMAP
Record Format [*Computer science*] ... RECFM
[*The*] **Record Group** [*Funded by N. V. Philips*] ... TRG
Record Handling Electronics ... RHE
Record Identification Code [*Navy*] ... RIC
Record Identification Number ... RIN
Record Identity [*Military*] (AFIT) ... RID
Record Information Movement Study (KSC) ... RIMS
Record Input Subroutine ... RIS
Record Length ... RL
Record Length Register ... RLR
Record Librarian [*Medial records*] (DAVI) ... RL
Record Lock ... RLOCK
Record Maintenance Statistics (MHDB) ... RECMS
Record Management System ... RMS
Record Mark (BUR) ... RM
Record Number [*Online database field identifier*] ... RCN
Record Number [*Online database field identifier*] ... RECNUM
Record Number [*Online database field identifier*] ... RN
Record of Access/Eligibility [*DoD*] ... RACEL
Record of Acquisition (WDAA) ... ROA
Record of Changes (DNAB) ... ROC
Record of Comments (NASA) ... ROC
Record of Decision [*Environmental Protection Agency*] ... ROD
Record of Discussion (MCD) ... ROD
Record of Oral Language (ADA) ... ROL
Record of Performance ... ROP
Record of Personal Experience (AIE) ... RPE
Record of Procurement Action (MCD) ... RPA
Record of Production ... ROP
Record of Purchase (NRCH) ... ROP
Record of Trial [*Army*] (AABC) ... R/T
Record One Stop Association [*Defunct*] (EA) ... ROSA
Record Organization Based on Transposition (PDAA) ... ROBOT
Record Parallel (MCD) ... RCDP

Record, Parrsboro, Nova Scotia [*Library symbol National Library of Canada*] (NLC) .... NSPR
Record, Parrsboro, NS, Canada [*Library symbol*] [*Library of Congress*] (LCLS) .... CaNSPaR
Record, Paulsboro, NJ [*Library symbol Library of Congress*] (LCLS) .... NjPauR
Record Position (AAGC) .... RP
Record Processor [*Computer science*] (OA) .... RP
Record Rarities [*Record label*] .... RR
Record Retention Agreement [*IRS*] .... RRA
Record/Retirement .... R/R
Record/Retransmit (IEEE) .... R/R
Record Select Program [*Computer science*] .... RSP
Record Selection Expression (MHDI) .... RSE
Record Separator [*Control character*] [*Computer science*] .... RS
Record Sequence Number [*Computer science*] (IAA) .... RSN
Record, Springhill, Nova Scotia [*Library symbol National Library of Canada*] (NLC) .... NSSR
Record, Springhill, NS, Canada [*Library symbol*] [*Library of Congress*] (LCLS) .... CaNSSpR
Record Status Code [*Military*] (AABC) .... RSC
Record Status Indicator [*Military*] (AABC) .... RSI
Record Test Kit .... RTK
Record Time Compliance Order .... RTCO
Record Time Compliance Technical Order (AAG) .... RTCTO
Record Transfer .... RT
Record, Truro, Nova Scotia [*Library symbol National Library of Canada*] (NLC) .... NSTR
Record/Update .... R/U
Recordable LASER Videodisc [*Optical Disc Corp.*] (DOM) .... RLV
Recordak Automated Information Retrieval [*System*] .... RAIR
Recordari Facias Loquelam [*Have the Record Before the Court*] [*Latin*] [*Legal term*] (BARN) .... Re fa lo
Recordati [*Italy*] [*Research code symbol*] .... Rec
Recorded (WDAA) .... RECD
Recorded Acoustic Signal Target Repeater .... RASTR
Recorded Announcement [*Telecommunications*] (TEL) .... R/A
Recorded Announcement [*Telecommunications*] (TEL) .... RCAN
Recorded Information Service [*Telecommunications*] (TEL) .... RIS
Recorded Program (NTCM) .... REC
Recorded Program (IAA) .... RP
Recorded Time Signal .... RTS
Recorded Video Imaging (MCD) .... RVI
Recorded Voice Announcement [*Telecommunications*] (IBMDP) .... RVA
Recorder (ECII) .... R
Recorder (KSC) .... RCDR
Recorder (IAA) .... RD
Recorder .... REC
Recorder and Communications Control (NASA) .... R & CC
Recorder and Communications Control Panel (NASA) .... RCCP
Recorder Announcement (DNAB) .... ROA
Recorder Group Monitor .... RGM
Recorder on Demand .... ROD
Recorder Point (MCD) .... RP
Recorder Processor Viewer .... RPV
Recorder Publishing Co., Stirling, NJ [*Library symbol Library of Congress*] (LCLS) .... NjStR
Recorder Switch Unit .... RSU
Recorders [*JETDS nomenclature*] [*Military*] (CET) .... RO
Recorders-Reproducers [*JETDS nomenclature*] [*Military*] (CET) .... RD
Record-Herald and Tribune, Indianola, IA [*Library symbol Library of Congress*] (LCLS) .... IaIndianR
Record-Herald and Tribune, Indianola, IA [*Library symbol*] [*Library of Congress*] (LCLS) .... IaIndR
Recordimeter (NTCM) .... RM
Recording (MSA) .... RCDG
Recording (ECII) .... REC
Recording (WDMC) .... rec
Recording (IAA) .... RG
Recording Ammeter (MSA) .... RAMM
[*The*] Recording and Controlling of In-Transit Requisition System [*Army*] .... TRACIRS
Recording and Video Playback of Electronic Warfare Information .... REVIEW
Recording Annunciator (IAA) .... RA
Recording Completing [*Trunk*] [*Telecommunications*] (TEL) .... RC
Recording Control Panel .... RCP
Recording Controller [*Nuclear energy*] (NRCH) .... RC
Recording Demand (DEN) .... RD
Recording Demand Meter .... RDM
Recording Doppler Comparator [*Astronomy*] (OA) .... RDC
Recording Engineer [*MARC relator code*] [*Library of Congress*] (LCCP) .... rce
Recording for the Blind (EA) .... RFB
Recording for the Blind and Dyslexic .... RFB&D
Recording for the Blind and Dyslexic [*An association*] (PAZ) .... RFBD
Recording for the Blind, Bethesda, MD [*OCLC symbol*] (OCLC) .... RFB
Recording for the Blind, Inc., New York, NY [*Library symbol Library of Congress*] (LCLS) .... NNRB
Recording Industries Music Performance Trust Funds [*Later, MPTF*] (EA) .... RIMPTF
Recording Industry Association of America (EA) .... RIAA
Recording Infrared Tracking Instrument .... RIRTI
Recording Kilovolt-Ampere Meter (MSA) .... RKVAM
Recording Optical Spectrum Analyzer (MCD) .... ROSA
Recording Optical Tracking Instrument [*Missiles*] .... ROTI
Recording Secretary (WGA) .... rec sec
Recording Secretary .... RS

[*A*] Recording Stray Energy Monitor .... ARESTEM
Recording Tachometer (IEEE) .... RTM
Recording Varmeter (MSA) .... RVARM
Record-News, Mount Ayr, IA [*Library symbol Library of Congress*] (LCLS) .... IaMayrR
Records .... RCDS
Records Administration (MCD) .... RA
Records and Analysis Subsystem (TEL) .... RAS
Records and Archives Management Programme [*UNESCO*] .... RAMP
Records and Control .... R & C
Records and Reports .... R & R
Records Arrival Date [*Bell System*] (TEL) .... RAD
Records Association System - Standard Data Elements System (MCD) .... RAS-STADES
Records Check (AFM) .... RC
Records Communication Program [*Army*] .... RC
Records for Our Fighting Men [*Collected phonograph records during World War II*] .... RFOFM
Records Holding Area [*Military*] .... RHA
Records Issue Date [*Bell System*] (TEL) .... RID
Records Management Office [*or Officer*] [*Military*] (AFM) .... RMO
Records Management Society [*British*] (DBA) .... RMS
Records of the Past [*A publication*] (BJA) .... RP
Records Office [*or Officer*] [*Air Force*] (AFM) .... RO
Records per Sector [*Computer science*] .... RPS
Records Processing Center [*Veterans Administration*] .... RPC
Records, Racing, and Rallying [*Sporting aviation*] .... RRR
Records, Reports, and Control (AFM) .... RR & C
Records Repository [*Air Force*] (AFM) .... RRep
Records Review [*Air Force*] (AFM) .... RRev
Records Will Be Handcarried [*Army*] (AABC) .... RWBH
Records Will Not Be Handcarried [*Army*] (AABC) .... RWNBH
Recoton Corp. [*NASDAQ symbol*] (NQ) .... RCOT
Recoton Corp. [*Associated Press*] (SAG) .... Recoton
Recover [*or Recovery*] .... REC
Recover Processor Improvement (DWSG) .... RPI
Recoverable Booster Space System (IAA) .... RBSS
Recoverable Booster Support System .... RBSS
Recoverable Booster System .... RBS
Recoverable Drop Vehicle (MCD) .... RDV
Recoverable Interplanetary Space Probe (IAA) .... RISP
Recoverable Interplanetary Transport Approach .... RITA
Recoverable Item Breakdown .... RIB
Recoverable Item List .... RIL
Recoverable Item Program [*Marine Corps*] .... RIP
Recoverable Launch Vehicle Structure (KSC) .... RLVS
Recoverable Orbital Launch System .... ROLS
Recoverable Plasma Diagnostics Package (SSD) .... RPDP
Recoverable Repair Parts .... RRP
Recoverable Sparoair Probe (MUGU) .... RSP
Recoverable Test Bed Missile .... RTBM
Recovered .... R/C
Recovered Alcoholic Clergy Association (EA) .... RACA
Recovered Allied Military Personnel .... RAMP
Recovered Doppler Airborne Vector Scorer .... RDAVS
Recovered Materials Advisory Notice [*EPA*] (AAGC) .... RMAN
Recovered Polypropylene [*Organic chemistry*] .... RPP
Recovery (IAA) .... R
Recovery (MSA) .... RCVY
Recovery (NASA) .... RCY
Recovery (KSC) .... RECOV
Recovery .... RECOVY
Recovery .... RECVY
Recovery (AAG) .... RECY
Recovery Access Presentation System (GAVI) .... RAPS
Recovery Aids Material (MUGU) .... RAM
Recovery and Evacuation Program [*Marine Corps*] .... REP
Recovery and Modification Services (MCD) .... RAMS
Recovery and Overpayment Accounting and Reporting System [*Social Security Administration*] (GFGA) .... ROAR
Recovery, Assist, Secure, and Traverse System [*Navy*] .... RAST
Recovery Beacon .... RB
Recovery Beacon Antenna [*NASA*] (KSC) .... RBA
Recovery Beacon Evaluation .... REBE
Recovery Code .... RC
Recovery Command Post .... RCP
Recovery Communications Network .... RCN
Recovery Control Center .... RCC
Recovery Control Center, Atlantic (DNAB) .... RCCA
Recovery Control Center, Pacific (DNAB) .... RCCP
Recovery Control Group (IAA) .... RCG
Recovery Controller [*NASA*] (MCD) .... RC
Recovery Employing Storage Chute Used in Emergencies [*Inflatable aircraft wing*] .... RESCUE
Recovery Engineering [*NASDAQ symbol*] (TTSB) .... REIN
Recovery Engineering, Inc. [*Associated Press*] (SAG) .... RecvEng
Recovery Engineering, Inc. [*NASDAQ symbol*] (SAG) .... REIN
Recovery Equipment (IAA) .... RE
Recovery Exercise Module (MCD) .... REM
Recovery Forces .... RF
Recovery Forecast .... RF
Recovery Group [*Air Force*] .... RECGP
Recovery Improvement Program Reporting System .... RIPRS
Recovery, Inc. .... RI
Recovery Management Support [*Computer science*] .... RMS

Recovery Management Support Recorder (MHDI) .... RMSR
Recovery of Male Potency (EA) .... ROMP
Recovery Operating Plan [NASA] (IAA) .... ROP
Recovery Operations [NASA] .... RO
Recovery Operations Branch [NASA] (KSC) .... ROB
Recovery Operations Control Room [NASA] (KSC) .... ROCR
Recovery Phase (IEEE) .... RP
Recovery Pilot Plant (ACII) .... RPP
Recovery Quotient [Medicine] (DMAA) .... RQ
Recovery Reliability (MCD) .... RR
Recovery Room (BARN) .... Rec Rm
Recovery Room .... RR
Recovery Sequence Tester .... RST
Recovery Storage Unit [Military] .... RSU
Recovery Storage Unit Boot Test [Military] .... RSBT
Recovery Systems Track Site (IAA) .... RSTS
Recovery Task Unit .... RTU
Recovery Techniques Evaluation [NASA] (KSC) .... RTE
Recovery Temperature Ratio .... RTR
Recovery Termination Management [Computer science] .... RTM
Recovery Test Vehicle .... RTV
Recovery Time [Military] (AFIT) .... RT
Recovery Time (IDOE) .... t_r
Recovery Unit and Base Support Group [Air Force] .... RUBSG
Recovery Vehicle [NASA] (NASA) .... RV
Recovery Vessel [NASA] (NASA) .... RV
Recovery Zone (MCD) .... RZ
Recreation (MSA) .... RCN
Recreation .... RCRTN
Recreation .... REC
Recreation (AABC) .... RECR
Recreation .... RECRE
Recreation .... RECRN
Recreation Advisory Council [Bureau of Outdoor Recreation] .... RAC
Recreation Aide [Red Cross] .... RA
Recreation and Education for Multiple Sclerosis .... REFMS
Recreation and Public Purposes Act .... R & PP
Recreation and Welfare [Navy] .... RW
Recreation Assistant (MEDA) .... Rec Asst
Recreation Information Management System [Department of Agriculture Washington, DC Information service or system] (IID) .... RIM
Recreation Management Exhibition [British] (ITD) .... REC MAN
Recreation Managers' Association [British] (DBA) .... RMA
Recreation Research Demonstration Unit (RDA) .... RRDU
Recreation Resources Center [University of Wisconsin] [Research center] (RCD) .... RRC
Recreation Specialist (MEDA) .... Rec Spec
Recreation Supervisor [Red Cross] .... RS
Recreation Systems Analysis [Computer science] .... RECSYS
Recreation Technician (MEDA) .... Rec Tech
Recreation Vehicle Dealers Association of North America (EA) .... RVDA
Recreation Vehicle Industry Association (EA) .... RVIA
Recreation Vehicle Rental Association (EA) .... RVRA
Recreation-Active Vehicle .... RAV
Recreation-Active Vehicle 4-Wheel Drive RAV4
Recreational .... RCRTNL
Recreational Active Vehicle .... RAV
Recreational Active Vehicle [Toyota] [Concept car] .... RAV
Recreational Active Vehicle-Electric .... RAV-E
Recreational Boating Safety [USCG] (TAG) .... RBS
Recreational Coach and Equipment Association [Later, MHI] .... RCEA
Recreational Dive Planner .... RDP
Recreational, Entertainment, and Health Naturally Radioactive Products (NRCH) .... REHNRAP
Recreational Equipment Inc. [Commercial firm] .... REI
Recreational Fisheries Information Network [Database] [National Marine Fisheries Service] .... RecFIN
Recreational Industries Council on Exporting (EA) .... RICE
Recreational Industry Vehicle Association (IAA) .... RIVA
Recreational Pilot Certificate [Aviation] (DA) .... RPC
Recreational Scuba Training Council (EA) .... RSTC
Recreational Software Advisory Council .... RSAC
Recreational Software Advisory Council .... RSAC
Recreational Software Advisory Council on the Internet .... RSACI
Recreational Software Advisory Council on the Internet [Computer science] .... RSACi
Recreational Therapist [or Therapy] .... RT
Recreational Therapist Registered .... RTR
Recreational Vehicle [Formed by phonetic spelling of initials R and V] .... ARVEE
Recreational Vehicle (BARN) .... rec v
Recreational Vehicle (BARN) .... recvee
Recreational Vehicle .... RV
Recreational Vehicle Club Directors of America (EA) .... RVCDA
Recreational Vehicle Dealers Association of North America .... RVDANA
Recreational Vehicle Institute .... RVI
Recreations .... R
Recredited .... R/C
Recreo [Guatemala] [Seismograph station code, US Geological Survey] (SEIS) .... REC
Recruit [Army] E1
Recruit (ROG) .... R
Recruit .... RCT
Recruit (AFM) .... RECRT
Recruit Allocation Control System [Navy] (NVT) .... RACS
Recruit Depot [Navy] .... RDEP

Recruit Induction [Military] .... RI
Recruit Instruction [Navy] .... RI
Recruit Performance Test (OA) .... RPT
Recruit Reception Center .... RRC
Recruit Remedial Literacy Training Unit (DNAB) .... RRLTU
Recruit, Retrain, Reemploy Medics [Program] .... RMED
Recruit Roll [Navy] .... RR
Recruit Training Center .... RTC
Recruit Training Command (Women) (DNAB) .... RTC(W)
Recruit Training Regiment [Marine Corps] (DOMA) .... RTR
Recruiter .... RCRTR
Recruiter [British military] (DMA) .... Rec
Recruiter Assistance [or Assistant] Program [Navy] (DNAB) .... RAP
Recruiter Code Identification [Army] (AABC) .... RCID
Recruiter Identification Code [Military] .... RIC
Recruiter of the Month [Navy] (DNAB) .... ROM
Recruiter of the Quarter [Navy] (DNAB) .... ROQ
Recruiter-in-Charge (DNAB) .... RINC
Recruiting (AABC) .... RCTG
Recruiting .... RECRUIT
Recruiting Advertising Improvement Program [Navy] (DNAB) .... RAIP
Recruiting Advertising Management System [Navy] (DNAB) .... RAMS
Recruiting Aids Department [Navy] .... RAD
Recruiting Analysis Service [LIMRA] .... RAS
Recruiting Center .... RC
Recruiting Command Post .... RCP
Recruiting Command Support System [Navy] (DNAB) .... RCSS
Recruiting District Assistance Council [Navy] (DNAB) .... RDAC
Recruiting Enlisted Selection System [Military] (DNAB) .... RESS
Recruiting Main Station [Military] .... RMS
Recruiting Office [or Officer] [Navy] .... CRUIT
Recruiting Officer [Military] .... RO
Recruiting Operations Group [Military] .... ROG
Recruiting Publicity Center [Military] .... RPC
Recruiting Service .... RS
Recruiting Station .... CRUITSTA
Recruiting Station .... RS
Recruiting Station and Office of Naval Officer Procurement .... CRUITNOP
Recruiting Warrant .... RW
Recruitment and Assessment Services [British Civil Service] (ECON) .... RAS
Recruitment and Manning Organization [WSA] .... RMO
Recruitment and Placement (MCD) .... R & P
Recruitment and Training Program .... RTP
Recruitment for the Armed Forces [British] .... RF
Recruitment Surveys [Army British] .... RS
Recrystallization Controlled Rolling (PDAA) .... RCR
Recrystallization-Anneal (PDAA) .... RA
Recrystallized .... RECRYST
Rectal [or Rectum] [Medicine] .... R
Rectal (DAVI) .... rtl
Rectal Examination [Medicine] .... RE
Rectal Morphine Sulfate Suppository [Medicine] (DMAA) .... RMS
Rectal Sinus .... RS
Rectal Suppository [Medicine] .... RS
Rectal Temperature (DAVI) .... R/T
Rectangle (AAG) .... RECT
Rectangular Concrete Columns [Jacys Computing Services] [Software package] (NCC) .... RCC
Rectangular Coordinate Plotter .... RCP
Rectangular Guide (DEN) .... RG
Rectangular Hollow Section [Metal industry] .... RHS
Rectangular Hysteresis Loop (PDAA) .... RHL
Rectangular Midwater Trawl (ADA) .... RMT
Rectangular Module (IAA) .... RM
Rectangular Parallelepiped Resonant Method [Crystal elasticity] .... RPR
Rectangular Tank [Liquid gas carriers] .... r
Rectangular Tongue Terminal .... RTT
Rectangular Wave Modulation (IEEE) .... RWM
Rectangular Wave-Guide Assembly .... RWA
Rectification (IDOE) .... rect
Rectification [or Rectifier] (IAA) .... RECT
Rectification (ROG) .... RECTIFON
Rectificatus [Rectified] [Pharmacy] .... RECT
Rectified (IDOE) .... rect
Rectified Air Speed [Navigation] .... RAS
Rectified Alternating Current [Radio] .... RAC
Rectified Alternating Current (IDOE) .... rac
Rectified Alternating Current [Electronics] (ECII) .... RAC
Rectified Skew Orthomorphic (PDAA) .... RSO
Rectified Spirits (ROG) .... RS
Rectifier (IAA) .... R
Rectifier (IAA) .... RA
Rectifier (IEEE) .... REC
Rectifier (IDOE) .... rect
Rectifier .... RECTR
Rectifier Diode (IAA) .... RD
Rectifier Enclosure Unit [Power supply] [Telecommunications] (TEL) .... REU
Rectifier Power Unit .... RPU
Rectify (AAG) .... RECT
Rectifying Antenna [Microwave power transmission] .... RECTENNA
Rectifying-Demodulating Phonopneumograph [Medicine] .... RDP
Rectilineal [Geometry] (ROG) .... RECTIL
Rectilinear Polarization [Physics] (ECON) .... R
Recto (ROG) .... A
Recto [Also, RO] [Right-hand page] .... R

Recto [*Also, R*] ..... RO
Recto (BJA) ..... rto
Rectocolic Hemorrhage [*Medicine*] (DMAA) ..... RCH
Rector [*or Rectory*] ..... R
Rector ..... RECT
Rectourethral (DAVI) ..... RU
Rectovaginal [*Gynecology*] (DAVI) ..... RV
Rectovaginal Constriction [*Gynecology*] (DMAA) ..... RVC
Rectum [*Medicine*] ..... rect
Rectus [*Clockwise configuration*] [*See RS*] [*Biochemistry*] ..... (R)
Rectus [*Muscle*] [*Anatomy*] (DAVI) ..... R
Rectus [*Muscle*] [*Anatomy*] ..... RECT
Rectus Femoris [*A muscle*] [*Anatomy*] ..... RF
Rectus-Sinister [*Nomenclature system*] [*Biochemistry*] ..... RS
Recueil (BJA) ..... Rec
Recueil de Droit Fiscal Quebecois [*A publication*] (DLA) ..... RDFQ
Recueillis Temporaires [*Temporarily Taken In*] [*Of unadoptable children*] [*French*] ..... RT
Recuperative Catalytic Oxidation [*Chemical engineering*] ..... RCO
Recurrence [*Medicine*] ..... R
Recurrence [*or Recurrent*] [*Medicine*] (MAE) ..... rec
Recurrence [*or Recurrent*] [*Medicine*] ..... RECUR
Recurrence Rate ..... RR
Recurrent (MSA) ..... RCUR
Recurrent Aphthous Stomatitis [*Medicine*] ..... RAS
Recurrent Aphthous Ulceration [*Medicine*] ..... RAU
Recurrent Brief Depression [*Psychology*] (ECON) ..... RBD
Recurrent Change of Station (SAA) ..... RCS
Recurrent Change of Status (SAA) ..... RCS
Recurrent Chronic Dissecting Aneurysm [*Medicine*] (DMAA) ..... RCDA
Recurrent Deep Vein Thrombosis [*Medicine*] (DAVI) ..... RDVT
Recurrent Fault Analysis [*Telecommunications*] (TEL) ..... RFA
Recurrent Herpes Labialis [*Medicine*] (DMAA) ..... RHL
Recurrent Induced Malaria [*Medicine*] (DMAA) ..... RIM
Recurrent Intrahepatic Cholestasis of Pregnancy [*Obstetrics*] (DMAA) ..... RICP
Recurrent Intrahepatic Obstructive Jaundice [*Medicine*] (MAE) ..... RIOJ
Recurrent Intussusception ..... RI
Recurrent Laryngeal Nerve [*Medicine*] (MAE) ..... RLN
Recurrent Oral Ulcer [*Medicine*] (DMAA) ..... ROU
Recurrent Peak Forward Current ..... RPFC
Recurrent Spontaneous Psychokinesis [*Poltergeist*] [*Parapsychology*] ..... RSPK
Recurrent Ulcer of the Duodenal Bulb [*Medicine*] (DMAA) ..... RUD
Recurrent Upper Respiratory Tract Infection [*Medicine*] (ADA) ..... RURTI
Recurring (MCD) ..... REC
Recurring Cost (NASA) ..... RC
Recurring Digital Fibroma of Childhood [*Medicine*] (DMAA) ..... RDFC
Recurring Document Listing (MCD) ..... RDL
Recurring Nuisances Act [*British*] ..... RNA
Recurring Venous Thromboembolism [*Medicine*] (DMAA) ..... RVTE
Recursive Aided Inertial Navigation for Precision Approach and Landing [*NASA*] ..... RAINPAL
Recursive Digital Filter [*Computer science*] (IAA) ..... RDF
Recursive Equality Quadratic Program (PDAA) ..... REQP
Recursive Function Theory (IAA) ..... RFT
Recursive Least Square Lattice (DMAA) ..... RLSL
Recursive Least Squares [*Mathematics*] ..... RLS
Recursive Macroactuated Generator (MHDI) ..... RMAG
Recursive Monte Carlo Method ..... RMC
Recursive Queue Analyzer (IEEE) ..... RQA
Recursive Transition Network [*Language analysis*] (BYTE) ..... RTN
Recursive Vector Quantization [*Software compression program*] (PCM) ..... RVQ
Recursively Enumerable (IAA) ..... RE
Recyclable, Incineratable, Biodegradable [*Food packaging*] ..... RIB
Recycle Acid [*Nuclear energy*] (NRCH) ..... REA
Recycle Water [*Nuclear energy*] (NRCH) ..... REW
Recycling ..... RECYCLE
Recycling Advisory Council (GNE) ..... RAC
Recycling Industries [*NASDAQ symbol*] (TTSB) ..... RECY
Recycling Industries, Inc. [*NASDAQ symbol*] (SAG) ..... RECY
Recycling Industries, Inc. [*Associated Press*] (SAG) ..... Recycling
Recycling Isoelectric Focusing [*Preparative electrophoresis*] ..... RIEF
Recycling Legislation Action Coalition [*Defunct*] (EA) ..... RLAC
Recycling Sourcebook [*A publication*] ..... RSB
Recycling Valve ..... RV
Red ..... R
Red ..... RD
Red Air, SA [*Belgium*] [*FAA designator*] (FAAC) ..... VDO
Red and Black Horizontal Bands [*Navigation markers*] ..... RBHB
Red and Blue (KSC) ..... R & B
Red and Gold (Edges) [*Bookbinding*] (ROG) ..... R/G
Red and White Beacon [*Nautical charts*] ..... RWBN
Red and White Dairy Cattle Association (EA) ..... RWDCA
Red Andina de Informacion Comercial [*Andean Trade Information Network*] (EAIO) ..... RAIC
Red Angus Association of America (EA) ..... RAAA
Red Arrows Display Squadron [*British ICAO designator*] (FAAC) ..... SAK
Red Artillery Model [*Military*] ..... RAM
Red Badge of Courage (EA) ..... RBC
Red Ball Express [*Military*] ..... RBE
Red Bank Public Library, Red Bank, NJ [*Library symbol Library of Congress*] (LCLS) ..... NjRb
Red Bank, TN [*FM radio station call letters*] ..... WAWL
Red Bank, TN [*FM radio station call letters*] ..... WJTT
Red Baron Aviation, Inc. [*ICAO designator*] (FAAC) ..... RBN
Red Basic Intelligence File (MCD) ..... RBIF

Red Bay, AL [*AM radio station call letters*] ..... WRMG
Red Beacon [*Nautical charts*] ..... R Bn
Red Berkshire Swine Record Association (EA) ..... RBSRA
Red Blood Cell [*or Corpuscle*] [*Medicine*] ..... RBC
Red Blood Cell Adenosine Deaminase [*An enzyme*] (AAMN) ..... RBC-ADA
Red Blood Cell Cast [*Hematology*] (DAVI) ..... RBCC
Red Blood Cell Distribution Width Index [*Medicine*] (DMAA) ..... RDW
Red Blood Cell Fallout [*Hematology*] (DAVI) ..... RBC FO
Red Blood Cell Fragility [*Test*] [*Hematoloy*] (DAVI) ..... EFRAG
Red Blood Cell Mass [*in circulation*] ..... RBCM
Red Blood Cell Precursor Production Rate [*Hematology*] ..... RPR
Red Blood Cell Transketolase [*Medicine*] (PDAA) ..... RBCTK
Red Blood Cell Turnover Rate [*Hematology*] ..... RTR
Red Blood Cell Volume [*Hematology*] ..... RBCV
Red Blood Cells per High Power Field [*Hematology*] (MAE) ..... RBC/hpf
Red Blood Count [*Medicine*] ..... RBC
Red Bluff [*California*] [*Airport symbol*] (AD) ..... RBL
Red Bluff, CA [*FM radio station call letters*] ..... KALF
Red Bluff, CA [*AM radio station call letters*] ..... KBLF
Red Bluff, CA [*AM radio station call letters*] (RBYB) ..... KEGR
Red Bluff, CA [*Location identifier FAA*] (FAAL) ..... PBT
Red Bluff, CA [*Location identifier FAA*] (FAAL) ..... RBL
Red Bluff Elementary School, Pasadena, TX [*Library symbol*] [*Library of Congress*] (LCLS) ..... TxPRbE
Red Book [*Full name is "Drug Topics Red Book," a pharmacist's guide*] [*A publication*] ..... RB
Red Brick Systems [*NASDAQ symbol*] (TTSB) ..... REDB
Red Brick Systems, Inc. [*Associated Press*] (SAG) ..... RdBrick
Red Brick Systems, Inc. [*NASDAQ symbol*] (SAG) ..... REDB
Red Brigades [*Revolutionary group*] [*Italy*] ..... RB
Red Bud Public Library, Red Bud, IL [*Library symbol Library of Congress*] (LCLS) ..... IRb
Red Butte Canyon [*Utah*] [*Seismograph station code, US Geological Survey*] (SEIS) ..... RBU
Red Carpet Airlines, Inc. [*ICAO designator*] (ICDA) ..... UR
Red Carpet Clubs [*United Airlines' club for frequent flyers*] (EA) ..... RCC
Red Carpet Flying Service [*ICAO designator*] (AD) ..... MF
Red Cedar Shingle and Handsplit Shake Bureau [*Later, CSSB*] (EA) ..... RCSHSB
Red Cell [*or Corpuscle*] [*Hematology*] ..... RC
Red Cell Agglutination [*Hematology*] (DAVI) ..... RCA
Red Cell Aggregate [*or Aggregation*] [*Hematology*] ..... RCA
Red Cell Cast [*Hematology*] (MAE) ..... RC
Red Cell Count [*Hematology*] (MAE) ..... RCC
Red Cell Folate [*Hematology*] (AAMN) ..... RCF
Red Cell Immune Adherence [*Medicine*] (DMAA) ..... RCIA
Red Cell Iron Turnover Rate [*Hematology*] (MAE) ..... RCITR
Red Cell Mass [*Hematology*] ..... RCM
Red Cell Precursor Production Rate [*Hematology*] (DAVI) ..... RPPR
Red Cell Size Distribution Width [*Hematology*] ..... RDW
Red Cell Volume [*Hematology*] ..... RCV
Red China ..... RC
Red Clover Cryptic Virus [*Plant pathology*] ..... RCCV
Red Clover Mottle Virus [*Plant pathology*] ..... RCMV
Red Clover Necrotic Mosaic Virus [*Plant pathology*] ..... RCNMV
Red Clover Vein Mosaic Virus ..... RCVMV
Red Cross ..... RC
Red Cross Act ..... RCA
Red Cross and Red Crescent Youth [*Geneva, Switzerland*] ..... RCY
Red Cross Blood Center ..... RCBC
Red Cross Field Representative ..... RCFR
Red Cross International Committee ..... RCIC
Red Cross of Constantine (EA) ..... RCC
Red Data Books (GNE) ..... RDB
Red de Accion sobre Plaguicidas y Alternativas en Mexico [*Member of the Pesticide Action Network*] (CROSS) ..... RAPAM
Red de Educacion Popular Entre Mujeres Afiliada al Consejo de Educacion de A dultos de America Latino [*Women's Network of the Council for Adult Education in Latin American*] [*Ecuador*] (EAIO) ..... REPEM- CEAAL
Red de Mujeres del Consejo de Educacion de Adultos de Americana Latina [*Women's Network of the Council for Adult Education in Latin America - WN-CAELA*] [*Quito, Ecuador*] (EAIO) ..... RM-CEAAL
Red de Salud de las Mujeres Latinoamericanas y del Caribe [*Latin American and Caribbean Women's Health Network*] (EAIO) ..... RSMLC
Red Deer [*Canada*] [*Airport symbol Obsolete*] (OAG) ..... YQF
Red Deer, AB [*Television station call letters*] CFRN-6
Red Deer, AB [*FM radio station call letters*] ..... CIZZ
Red Deer, AB [*AM radio station call letters*] ..... CKGY
Red Deer, AB [*AM radio station call letters*] ..... CKRD
Red Deer, AB [*Television station call letters*] ..... CKRD-TV
Red Deer College, Alberta [*Library symbol National Library of Canada*] (NLC) ..... ARDC
Red Deer College, Red Deer, AB, Canada [*Library symbol Library of Congress*] (LCLS) ..... CaARDC
Red Deer Industrial, AB [*ICAO location identifier*] (ICLI) ..... CYQF
Red Deer Public Library, Alberta [*Library symbol National Library of Canada*] (NLC) ..... ARD
Red Deer Public Library, Red Deer, AB, Canada [*Library symbol Library of Congress*] (LCLS) ..... CaARd
Red Deer Regional Hospital Center, Red Deer, Alberta [*Library symbol National Library of Canada*] (NLC) ..... ARDRH
Red Devil [*Alaska*] [*Airport symbol*] (OAG) ..... RDV
Red Devils Parachute Display Team [*British ICAO designator*] (FAAC) ..... DEV
Red Documental [*Ministerio de Educacion Publica*] [*Chile*] [*Information service or system*] (CRD) ..... REDO
Red Earth Energy Ltd. [*Vancouver Stock Exchange symbol*] ..... REE

Red Edges ... RE
Red Flag Database [*Air Force*] (GFGA) ... RFDB
Red Flint Glazed [*Paper*] (DGA) ... RED FG
Red Fox Minerals [*Vancouver Stock Exchange symbol*] ... RFM
Red Fumes (NATG) ... RF
Red Fuming Nitric Acid ... RFNA
Red Green Blue [*Video monitor*] ... RGB
Red Green Blue Intensity [*Video monitor*] ... RGBI
Red, Green, Blue Monitor ... RGB monitor
Red, Green, Blue, Yellow [*Video monitor*] (IAA) ... RGBY
Red Heat (IAA) ... RH
Red Herring [*Investment term*] ... RH
Red Hill Community Unit, School District 10, Sumner, IL [*Library symbol Library of Congress*] (LCLS) ... ISumSD
Red Hill Marketing Group Ltd. [*Vancouver Stock Exchange symbol*] ... RDH
Red Hills Conservation Association (EA) ... RHCA
Red Hook Public Library, Red Hook, NY [*Library symbol Library of Congress*] (LCLS) ... NRed
Red Hook Public Library, Red Hook, NY [*Library symbol*] [*Library of Congress*] (LCLS) ... NRedL
Red Hot Concepts, Inc. [*Associated Press*] (SAG) ... RedHot
Red Hot Concepts, Inc. [*Associated Press*] (SAG) ... RedHt
Red Hot Concepts, Inc. [*NASDAQ symbol*] (SAG) ... RHCS
Red Hot Concepts Unit [*NASDAQ symbol*] (TTSB) ... RHCSU
Red Indicator Light ... RIL
Red Integrated Strategic Offensive Plan [*Army*] (AABC) ... RISOP
Red Integrated Tactical Operational Plan (CINC) ... RITOP
Red Interamericana de Telecomunicaciones [*Inter-American Telecommunication Network*] (NTCM) ... RIT
Red Internacional de American Latina [*International Telecommunication Network for Latin America*] (NTCM) ... RITAL
Red Kidney Bean ... RKB
Red Lake [*Canada*] [*Airport symbol*] (OAG) ... YRL
Red Lake & Sun Valley [*Vancouver Stock Exchange symbol*] ... RSV
Red Lake Buffalo Resources Ltd. [*Toronto Stock Exchange symbol*] ... RBF
Red Lake Falls Public Library, Red Lake Falls, MN [*Library symbol*] [*Library of Congress*] (LCLS) ... MnRlF
Red Lake, ON [*AM radio station call letters*] ... CKDR-5
Red Lake Public Library, Ontario [*Library symbol National Library of Canada*] (NLC) ... ORL
Red Lamp (IAA) ... RL
Red Latinoamericana de Documentacion en Educacion [*Latin American Education Documentation Network*] (PDAA) ... REDUC
Red Light Running [*NHTSA*] (TAG) ... RLR
Red Line Instrumentation (IAA) ... RLI
Red Lion Hotels [*NYSE symbol*] (TTSB) ... RL
Red Lion Hotels, Inc. [*NYSE symbol*] (SAG) ... RL
Red Lion Hotels, Inc. [*Associated Press*] (SAG) ... RLionH
Red Lion Inns Ltd. [*AMEX symbol*] (SPSG) ... RED
Red Lion Inns Ltd. [*Associated Press*] (SAG) ... RLionInn
Red Lion Inns L.P. [*AMEX symbol*] (TTSB) ... RED
Red Lion, PA [*AM radio station call letters*] ... WGCB
Red Lion, PA [*FM radio station call letters*] ... WGCB-FM
Red Lion, PA [*Television station call letters*] ... WGCB-TV
Red Lodge, MT [*FM radio station call letters*] ... KMXE
Red Lodge, MT [*Location identifier FAA*] (FAAL) ... RED
Red Marrow [*Hematology*] ... RM
Red Mexicana de Accion Frente al Libre Comercio [*Mexican Action Network on Free Trade*] (CROSS) ... RMALC
Red Nacional de los Ferrocariles Espanoles [*Spanish National Railways*] (EY) ... RENFE
Red Nucleus [*Brain anatomy*] ... RN
Red Nucleus, Magnocellular [*Division*] [*Hematology*] (DAVI) ... RNm
Red Oak Express, Red Oak, IA [*Library symbol Library of Congress*] (LCLS) ... IaRedoE
Red Oak, IA [*FM radio station call letters*] ... KCSI
Red Oak, IA [*Television station call letters*] ... KHIN
Red Oak, IA [*AM radio station call letters*] ... KOAK
Red Oak, IA [*Location identifier FAA*] (FAAL) ... RDK
Red Oak Public Library, Red Oak, IA [*Library symbol Library of Congress*] (LCLS) ... IaRedo
Red Oak Tannins [*in leaves*] ... ROT
Red, Orange, Yellow, Green, Blue, Indigo, Violet [*Primary Colors*] [*Mnemonic aid*] ... ROYGBIV
Red Panamericana de Informacion y Documentacion en Ingenieria Sanitaria y Ciencias del Ambiente [*Pan American Network for Information and Documentation in Sanitary Engineering and Environmental Sciences*] [*WHO*] [*United Nations*] (DUND) ... REPIDISCA
Red Pennant [*Navy British*] ... RD
Red Phosphorus [*Military*] (RDA) ... RP
Red Poll Cattle Club of America [*Later, ARPA*] (EA) ... RPCCA
Red Primary (IAA) ... R
Red Red Rose [*An association Defunct*] (EA) ... RRR
Red Reflex [*Ophthalmology*] (DAVI) ... RR
Red Resistance Front [*Netherlands Political party*] ... RRF
Red Resource Monitoring (MCD) ... RRM
Red Ringspot Virus [*of blueberry*] ... RRSV
Red River Army Depot [*Texas*] (AABC) ... RRAD
Red River Boys Fan Club [*Inactive*] (EA) ... RRBFC
Red River Community College [*UTLAS symbol*] ... RRC
Red River Community College, Learning Resources Centre, Winnipeg, MB, Canada [*Library symbol Library of Congress*] (LCLS) ... CaMWRR
Red River Community College, Library Technician Program, Winnipeg, MB, Canada [*Library symbol*] [*Library of Congress*] (LCLS) ... CaMWRRL
Red River/Grand Forks Air Force Base [*North Dakota*] [*ICAO location identifier*] (ICLI) ... KRDR
Red River Parish Library, Coushata, LA [*Library symbol Library of Congress*] (LCLS) ... LCouRR
Red River Settlement [*Canada*] ... RRS
Red River Valley & Western Railroad [*North Dakota*] ... RRV & W
Red River Valley Sugarbeet Growers Association (EA) ... RRVSGA
Red Rock Public Library, Ontario [*Library symbol National Library of Canada*] (NLC) ... ORR
Red Rock Public Library, Red Rock, ON, Canada [*Library symbol Library of Congress*] (LCLS) ... CaORr
Red Rocks, NF [*FM radio station call letters*] ... CKSS
Red Roof Inns [*NYSE symbol*] (TTSB) ... RRI
Red Roof Inns, Inc. [*Associated Press*] (SAG) ... RedRoof
Red Roof Inns, Inc. [*NYSE symbol*] (SAG) ... RRI
Red Sea and Area [*MARC geographic area code Library of Congress*] (LCCP) ... mr----
Red Sea Mission Team (EA) ... RSMT
Red Springs, NC [*AM radio station call letters*] ... WYRU
Red Star of Maximum Intensity of Metal [*Astronomy*] (BARN) ... K
Red Star of Prominent Titanium Oxide Intensity [*Astronomy*] (BARN) ... M
Red Status Timeline ... RSTL
Red Sucker Lake [*Canada*] [*Airport symbol*] (OAG) ... YRS
Red Sulfhydryl Reagent ... RSR
Red Supergiant [*Astronomy*] ... RSG
Red Suspender League (EA) ... RSL
Red Tag News Publications [*Later, RTNPA*] (EA) ... RTNP
Red Tag News Publications Association (EA) ... RTNPA
Red Tetrazolium [*Also, TPTZ, TTC*] [*Chemical indicator*] ... RT
Red under Gold Edges [*Books*] ... RGE
Red Venous Blood [*Hematology*] (MAE) ... RVB
Red Veterinary Petrolatum (MAE) ... RVP
Red Wing Collectors Society (EA) ... RWCS
Red Wing, MN [*AM radio station call letters*] ... KCUE
Red Wing, MN [*FM radio station call letters*] ... KWNG
Red Wing, MN [*Location identifier FAA*] (FAAL) ... RGK
Red Wing Public Library, Red Wing, MN [*Library symbol Library of Congress*] (LCLS) ... MnRw
Red Wings For'Em Club (EA) ... RWFC
Redactor (WGA) ... RED
Redactus in Pulverem [*Reduce to a Powder*] [*Pharmacy*] ... RED in PULV
Redaurum Red Lake Mines Ltd. [*Toronto Stock Exchange symbol*] ... RRK
Red-Banded Leaf Roller [*Entomology*] ... RBLR
Red-Bellied Woodpecker [*Ornithology*] ... RW
Redbook Assumption Cost Estimating Request ... RACER
Redbourne [*England*] ... REDB
Redbridge [*England*] ... REDBR
Redcliff [*Vanuatu*] [*ICAO location identifier*] (ICLI) ... NVSR
Redcliff [*Vanuatu*] [*Airport symbol*] (OAG) ... RCL
Redcliff Public Library, Alberta [*Library symbol National Library of Canada*] (NLC) ... ARE
Redcliff Public Library, Redcliff, AB, Canada [*Library symbol*] [*Library of Congress*] (LCLS) ... CaARe
Redcliff Public Library, Redcliff, CO [*Library symbol Library of Congress*] (LCLS) ... CoRe
Redcoat Air Cargo Ltd. [*British ICAO designator*] (ICDA) ... RY
Red-Cockaded Woodpecker ... RCW
Reddi Brake Supply [*NASDAQ symbol*] (TTSB) ... REDI
Reddi Brake Supply Corp. [*Associated Press*] (SAG) ... ReddiBrk
Reddi Brake Supply Corp. [*NASDAQ symbol*] (SAG) ... REDI
Reddick's Library, Ottawa, IL [*Library symbol Library of Congress*] (LCLS) ... IOt
Reddie's Inquiries in International Law [*2nd ed.*] [*1851*] [*A publication*] (DLA) ... Red Int L
Reddie's Law of Maritime Commerce [*1841*] [*A publication*] (DLA) ... Red Mar Com
Reddie's Researches in Maritime International Law [*1844-45*] [*A publication*] (DLA) ... Red Mar Int L
Reddie's Roman Law [*A publication*] (DLA) ... Red RL
Reddie's Science of Law [*2nd ed.*] [*A publication*] (DLA) ... Red Sc L
Redding [*California*] [*Airport symbol*] (OAG) ... RDD
Redding Aero Enterprises, Inc. [*FAA designator*] (FAAC) ... KLP
Redding, CA [*FM radio station call letters*] ... KFPR
Redding, CA [*Television station call letters*] ... KIXE
Redding, CA [*AM radio station call letters*] ... KLXR
Redding, CA [*FM radio station call letters*] ... KNCQ
Redding, CA [*AM radio station call letters*] ... KNRO
Redding, CA [*AM radio station call letters*] ... KQMS
Redding, CA [*Television station call letters*] ... KRCR
Redding, CA [*AM radio station call letters*] ... KRDG
Redding, CA [*FM radio station call letters*] ... KSHA
Redding, CA [*AM radio station call letters*] ... KVIP
Redding, CA [*FM radio station call letters*] ... KVIP-FM
Reddish [*Philately*] ... redsh
Reddish Orange ... RO
Reddish Purple ... RP
Reddy Memorial Hospital, Montreal, PQ, Canada [*Library symbol Library of Congress*] (LCLS) ... CaQMRM
Reddy Memorial Hospital, Montreal, Quebec [*Library symbol National Library of Canada*] (NLC) ... QMRM
Rede CONSISDATA de Servicos Integrados [*CONSISDATA Integrated Services Network*] [*Consultoria, Sistemas, e Processamento de Dados Ltda.*] [*Brazil*] [*Information service or system*] (CRD) ... RCSI
Rede Ferroviaria Federal Sociedade Anonima [*Federal Railway Corporation*] [*Brazil*] (EY) ... RFFSA
Redeem Our Country (EA) ... ROC
Redeemable [*Finance*] (ODBW) ... red

Redeemable Bond [*Investment term*] ... RB
Redeemable Listed Trust ... RLT
Redeemable Stock ... RS
Redeemed ... RED
Redeemer College, Ancaster, Ontario [*Library symbol National Library of Canada*] (NLC) ... OHRC
Redemption (DLA) ... Redem
Redemption Fee [*Finance*] ... R
Redemptionist Seminary, Oconomowoc, WI [*Library symbol Library of Congress*] (LCLS) ... WOccR
Redemptorist Fathers (TOCD) ... CSSR
Redemptorist Fathers (TOCD) ... cssr
Redeployment Day [*Military*] ... R (Day)
Redeployment Point [*Military*] (INF) ... RDP
Redeployment Report [*Military*] ... REDREP
Redesdale's Treatise upon Equity Pleading [*A publication*] (DLA) ... Redes Pl
Redesignate (AFM) ... REDSG
Redesigned Missile Tracking RADAR [*Army*] (AABC) ... RMTR
Redesigned Solid Rocket Booster ... RSRB
Redesigned Solid Rocket Motor ... RSRM
Redetermination ... R
Redevelopment Act (OICC) ... RA
Redevelopment Area Resident ... RAR
Redevelopment Land Agency [*Washington, DC*] ... RLA
Redeye Air Missile [*System*] (RDA) ... RAM
Redeye Launch Simulator (MCD) ... RELS
Redfed Bancorp [*NASDAQ symbol*] (SAG) ... REDF
Redfed Bancorp [*Associated Press*] (SAG) ... RedfedBc
Redfern Resources [*Vancouver Stock Exchange symbol*] ... RFR
Redfield and Bigelow's Leading Cases [*England*] [*A publication*] (DLA) ... Redf & B
Redfield and Bigelow's Leading Cases on Bills and Notes [*A publication*] (DLA) ... Red & Big Cas B & N
Redfield Carnegie Library, Redfield, SD [*Library symbol Library of Congress*] (LCLS) ... SdRe
Redfield on Carriers and Bailments [*A publication*] (DLA) ... Red Bail
Redfield on Carriers and Bailments [*A publication*] (DLA) ... Red Car
Redfield on Carriers and Bailments [*A publication*] (DLA) ... Redf Carr
Redfield on Railways [*A publication*] (DLA) ... Redf Railways
Redfield on the Law of Railroads [*A publication*] (DLA) ... Red RR
Redfield on the Law of Wills [*A publication*] (DLA) ... Red Wills
Redfield Public Library, Redfield, IA [*Library symbol Library of Congress*] (LCLS) ... IaRedf
Redfield, SD [*AM radio station call letters*] ... KQKD
Redfield, SD [*FM radio station call letters*] ... KQKD-FM
Redfield's American Railway Cases [*A publication*] (DLA) ... Red Am R Cas
Redfield's American Railway Cases [*A publication*] (DLA) ... Redf Am Railw Cas
Redfield's Leading American Railway Cases [*A publication*] (DLA) ... Red Am RR Cas
Redfield's Leading American Railway Cases [*A publication*] (DLA) ... Red Cas RR
Redfield's Leading American Railway Cases [*A publication*] (DLA) ... Red RR Cas
Redfield's Leading Cases on Wills [*A publication*] (DLA) ... Red Cas Wills
Redfield's Leading Cases on Wills [*A publication*] (DLA) ... Redf Wills
Redfield's New York Practice Reports [*A publication*] (DLA) ... Red Pr
Redfield's New York Surrogate Court Reports [*A publication*] (DLA) ... Redf Sur (NY)
Redfield's New York Surrogate Court Reports [*5 vols.*] [*A publication*] (DLA) ... Redf Surr (NY)
Redfield's New York Surrogate Reports [*A publication*] (DLA) ... Red
Redfield's New York Surrogate Reports [*A publication*] (DLA) ... Redf
Redfield's New York Surrogate Reports [*A publication*] (DLA) ... Redf (NY)
Redfield's New York Surrogate Reports [*A publication*] (DLA) ... Redf Surr
Redfield's Railway Cases [*England*] [*A publication*] (DLA) ... Redf R Cas
Redford Resources, Inc. [*Vancouver Stock Exchange symbol*] ... RDF
Red-Giant Branch [*Stellar physics*] ... RGB
Redgrave Information Resources Corp. [*Publisher*] ... RIR
Redgrave Information Resources Corp., Westport, CT [*Library symbol Library of Congress*] (LCLS) ... RiR
Red-Green ... RG
Redheads International (EA) ... RI
Redhill [*British ICAO location identifier*] (ICLI) ... EGGR
Redhill [*British ICAO location identifier*] (ICLI) ... EGKR
Redhill [*England*] [*Airport symbol*] ... KRH
Redhill [*International vehicle registration*] (ODBW) ... RH
Redhook Ale Brewery [*NASDAQ symbol*] (TTSB) ... HOOK
Redhook Ale Brewery, Inc. [*NASDAQ symbol*] (SAG) ... HOOK
Redhook Ale Brewery, Inc. [*Associated Press*] (SAG) ... RedhkA
Redifon Analog-Digital Computer [*British*] ... RADIC
Redig, SD [*Location identifier FAA*] (FAAL) ... REJ
Redigatur In Pulverent [*Let It Be Reduced to Powder*] [*Pharmacy*] (ROG) ... REDIG IN PULV
Redington's Reports [*31-35 Maine*] [*A publication*] (DLA) ... Red
Redington's Reports [*31-35 Maine*] [*A publication*] (DLA) ... Redington
Redirect [*Computer science*] (TNIG) ... RD
Rediscount [*Banking*] ... REDISC
Rediscount Rate ... RR
Redispatch Accepted (FAAC) ... RDSPA
Redistilled ... REDIST
Redistribution (AFM) ... REDISTR
Redistribution and Marketing (AFM) ... R & M
Redistribution Order [*Military*] (AFM) ... RDO
Redistribution Order [*Military*] (DNAB) ... RO
Redistribution Out/Redistribution In (CINC) ... RO/RI
Redlake Elementary School, Redlake, MN [*Library symbol*] [*Library of Congress*] (LCLS) ... MnRelE
Redlake High School, Redlake, MN [*Library symbol*] [*Library of Congress*] (LCLS) ... MnRelH
Redlands, CA [*AM radio station call letters*] (RBYB) ... KCAL
Redlands, CA [*FM radio station call letters*] ... KCAL-FM
Redlands, CA [*FM radio station call letters*] ... KUOR
Redlane [*England*] ... REDL
Redlaw Ind 2001 Wrrts [*AMEX symbol*] (TTSB) ... RDLWS
Redlaw Industries [*AMEX symbol*] (TTSB) ... RDL
Redlaw Industries [*AMEX symbol*] (SAG) ... RDL
Redlaw Industries [*Associated Press*] (SAG) ... Rdlw
Redlaw Industries, Inc. [*AMEX symbol Toronto Stock Exchange symbol*] (SPSG) ... RDL
Redlaw Industries, Inc. [*Associated Press*] (SAG) ... Redlaw
Redlaw Industries, Inc. [*Associated Press*] (SAG) ... Redlw
Redlich-Kwong [*Physics*] ... R-K
Redline (KSC) ... R/L
Redman and Lyon on Landlord and Tenant [*8th ed.*] [*1924*] [*A publication*] (DLA) ... R & LL & T
Redman Industries [*NASDAQ symbol*] (TTSB) ... RDMN
Redman Industries [*NASDAQ symbol*] (SAG) ... RDMN
Redman Industries [*Associated Press*] (SAG) ... Redman
Redman on Arbitration [*A publication*] (DLA) ... Redm Arb
Redman on Landlord and Tenant [*A publication*] (DLA) ... Redman
Redmond [*Oregon*] [*Airport symbol*] (OAG) ... RDM
Redmond, OR [*FM radio station call letters*] ... KLRR
Redmond, OR [*FM radio station call letters*] ... KSJJ
Redmond, OR [*Location identifier FAA*] (FAAL) ... RAW
Redmond Public Library, Redmond, OR [*Library symbol Library of Congress*] (LCLS) ... OrRed
Redmond, R. A., Los Angeles CA [*STAC*] ... RRA
Redmond Senior High School, Redmond, OR [*Library symbol*] [*Library of Congress*] (LCLS) ... OrRedHS
Rednik & Wolfe, Chicago, IL [*Library symbol*] [*Library of Congress*] (LCLS) ... ICRW
Redon/Bains-Sur-Oust [*France ICAO location identifier*] (ICLI) ... LFER
Redondo Beach, CA [*FM radio station call letters*] ... KFOX
Redondo Beach Public Library, Redondo Beach, CA [*Library symbol Library of Congress*] (LCLS) ... CRdb
Redondo Peak [*New Mexico*] [*Seismograph station code, US Geological Survey*] (SEIS) ... REDP
Redoubt [*Alaska*] [*Seismograph station code, US Geological Survey*] (SEIS) ... RDT
Redoubt Volcano [*Alaska*] [*Seismograph station code, US Geological Survey*] (SEIS) ... RED
Redox Chemiluminescence Detector [*Instrumentation*] [*Sievers*] ... RCD
Redox Potential [*Organic chemistry*] (DAVI) ... E
Redox Potential [*Symbol*] [*Organic chemistry*] (DAVI) ... E_h
Redpath Industries Ltd. [*Toronto Stock Exchange symbol*] ... RIN
Redrawn ... REDWN
Redruth [*England*] ... REDR
Redstone Army Airfield [*Huntsville, AL*] ... RAAF
Redstone Arsenal [*Huntsville, AL*] [*Army*] ... RA
Redstone Arsenal [*Huntsville, AL*] [*Army*] ... RSA
Redstone Arsenal Information Center [*Army*] ... RAIC
Redstone Arsenal Support Activity (MCD) ... RASA
Redstone Computer ... RECOMP
Redstone Resources, Inc. [*Toronto Stock Exchange symbol*] ... RR
Redstone Scientific Information Center [*Army*] ... RESIC
Redstone Scientific Information Center [*Army*] ... RSIC
Redstone Scientific Information Center, United States Army Missile Command, Redstone Arsenal, AL [*Library symbol Library of Congress*] (LCLS) ... ARaS
Redstone Technical Test Center [*Army*] (RDA) ... RTTC
Reduce [*Army*] ... Rd
Reduce (MSA) ... RDC
Reduce [*or Reduction*] (AAG) ... RED
Reduce Errors and Decrease Expense (DNAB) ... READE
Reduce Geography in No Time (SAA) ... REGENT
Reduce Operating Costs [*Air Force project*] ... ROC
Reduced (WDMC) ... red
Reduced (ROG) ... REDD
Reduced Acreage Program [*Agriculture*] ... RAP
Reduced Annual Income Deficiency Syndrome [*British*] ... RAIDS
Reduced Aperture (MCD) ... RA
Reduced Array of Inexpensive Drives [*Computer science*] ... RAID
Reduced Aspect Ratio ... RAR
Reduced Availability (MCD) ... RAV
Reduced Blast/Enhanced Radiation ... RB/ER
Reduced Capability (MCD) ... RC
Reduced Casualties and Mishaps ... RCM
Reduced Charge (AAG) ... RCHG
Reduced Chi-Square Statistic ... RCSS
Reduced Coenzyme A [*Biochemistry*] (DAVI) ... HS-CoA
Reduced Crude Conversion [*Petroleum refining*] ... RCC
Reduced Crude Desulfurization [*Petroleum refining*] ... RCD
Reduced Cuing ... RC
Reduced Delta Code Modulation [*Digital memory*] ... RDCM
Reduced Energy Consumption for Commercial Air Transportation (DICI) ... RECAT
Reduced Enrichment in Research and Test Reactions [*Department of Energy*] ... RERTR
Reduced Exoatmospheric Cross Section ... REX
Reduced Exposure Mining System ... REMS
Reduced Focal Length ... RFL
Reduced Frequency Response [*Telecommunications*] (OA) ... RFR
Reduced Friction Strut [*Suspension system*] [*Automotive engineering*] ... RFS

Reduced Function Computer [*Computer science*] ... RFC
Reduced Gluthathione [*Biochemistry*] (DAVI) ... GSH
Reduced Gravity Environment ... RGE
Reduced Haloperidol [*An antidepressant*] (DAVI) ... RH
Reduced Hard Pressure (MSA) ... RHP
Reduced Ignition Relay (MCD) ... RID
Reduced Injury Factor Baseball ... RIF
Reduced Inspection Quality Assurance Program ... RIQAP
Reduced Instruction Set Chip (NITA) ... RISC
Reduced Instruction Set Computer ... RISC
Reduced Instruction-Set Computing (PCM) ... RISC
Reduced Layer Formation (BARN) ... RLF
Reduced [*or Reduction*] **Level** ... RL
Reduced Magnetic Field [*Computer science*] (PCM) ... RMF
Reduced Material Condition (NVT) ... RMC
Reduced Material Condition Maintenance (MCD) ... RMCM
Reduced Methylene Blue [*Medicine*] (DMAA) ... MBH2
Reduced Operational Capability Program [*Navy*] (NVT) ... ROC
Reduced Operational Status [*Military*] ... ROS
Reduced Oxygen Concentration (MCD) ... ROC
Reduced Physical Fidelity (MCD) ... RPF
Reduced Product Verification [*DoD*] ... RPV
Reduced Quantity Generator (ERG) ... RQG
Reduced Range ... RR
Reduced Range Practice Rocket [*Army*] ... RRPR
Reduced Rate Contribution Clause [*Insurance*] ... RRCC
Reduced Residual Radiation ... RRR
Reduced/Short Takeoff and Landing [*Aircraft*] ... R/STOL
Reduced Smoke (MCD) ... RS
Reduced Smoke Rocket Motor (MCD) ... RSRM
Reduced Strength (MCD) ... RS
Reduced Takeoff and Landing [*Aviation*] ... RTOL
Reduced Tillage System [*Agriculture*] ... RT
Reduced to Apprentice Seaman [*Navy*] ... REDAS
Reduced Under Anesthesia [*Medicine*] (DMAA) ... RUA
Reduced Voltage (IAA) ... RV
Reduced Weight (DCTA) ... RW
Reduced-Excitation Inertial Reference Integrating Gyro ... RIRIG
Reduced-Instruction-Set Computer (DMAA) ... RISC
Reduced-Size Antenna Monopulse System ... RAMS
Reduced-Size Blueprint (NG) ... RSB
Reducer [*Photographic processing*] (DGA) ... R
Reducer (MSA) ... RDCR
Reducing (WGA) ... Rdg
Reducing (ROG) ... REDCN
Reducing Flame ... RF
Reducing Kernel Hilbert Space [*Electronics*] (OA) ... RKHS
Reducing Substance [*Laboratory science*] (DAVI) ... RS
Reducing Sugar ... RS
Reductase Test [*Biochemistry*] (DAVI) ... R
Reduction (MSA) ... RDCN
Reduction ... RDCTN
Reduction (ROG) ... RECTON
Reduction (ODBW) ... red
Reduction (WDMC) ... red
Reduction ... REDN
Reduction (KSC) ... REDUC
Reduction and Acquisition of Lunar Pulse Heights [*NASA*] (NASA) ... RALPH
Reduction and Oxidation ... REDOX
Reduction Gas Detector [*Instrumentation*] ... RGD
Reduction Gear [*or Gearbox*] (NG) ... RG
Reduction Gearbox Assembly (DNAB) ... RGA
Reduction Implementation Panel [*DoD*] ... RIP
Reduction in Benefit Limitation ... RIBLIM
Reduction in Force [*Military*] ... RIF
Reduction in Leadtime (MCD) ... RIL
Reduction in Paperwork (SAA) ... RIP
Reduction in Requirement [*Air Force*] (AFM) ... RIR
Reduction of Area ... RA
Reduction of Attitudes and Repressed Emotions [*Treatment given to sex offenders*] [*Psychology*] ... ROARE
Reduction of Electrical Demand Using Computer Equipment [*Energy management system designed by John Helwig of Jance Associates, Inc.*] ... REDUCE
Reduction of (Military) Budgets ... RO(M)B
Reduction of the Membrane Potential ... RMP
Reduction, Refinement, and Replacement [*Animal research*] ... 3R's
Reduction Tables ... RT
Reduction to Next Inferior Rank ... RNIR
Reduction Unlimited ... RUN
Reduction-Option Loan [*Banking*] ... ROL
Reductive Pentose Phosphate [*Photosynthesis cycle*] ... RPP
Reductive Photo Dehalogenation ... RPD
Redundancy [*Used in correcting manuscripts, etc.*] ... R
Redundancy (IAA) ... RDN
Redundancy (NASA) ... REDUN
Redundancy Adjustment of Probability (IEEE) ... RAP
Redundancy Check (IAA) ... RC
Redundancy Management (MCD) ... RM
Redundancy Management Control (MCD) ... RMC
Redundancy Management/Moding, Sequencing, and Control (MCD) ... RM/MS & C
Redundancy Management System [*NASA*] (MCD) ... RMS
Redundancy Payments Act [*1965*] [*British*] (DCTA) ... RPA
Redundancy Reduction (AAG) ... RR
Redundancy Status [*NASA*] (MCD) ... RS
Redundant (KSC) ... RED
Redundant (AAG) ... REDNT
Redundant Array of Independent Disks [*Computer science*] (CDE) ... RAID
Redundant Arrays of Inexpensive Disks [*Computer science*] ... RAID
Redundant Attitude Control System (MCD) ... RACS
Redundant Battery Charger (KSC) ... RBC
Redundant Churches Fund [*British*] (EAIO) ... RCF
Redundant Element Removal (IAA) ... RER
Redundant Gyro Monitor (NASA) ... RGM
Redundant Reconfigurable Digital Flight Control System (MCD) ... RRDFCS
Redundant Residue Number System (IEEE) ... RRNS
Redundant Set [*NASA*] (MCD) ... RS
Redundant Set Launch Sequencer (MCD) ... RSLS
Redundant System Monitor Model [*NASA*] (MCD) ... RSMM
Reduplication ... REDUPL
Redwar's Comments on Ordinances of the Gold Coast Colony [*1889-1909*] [*Ghana*] [*A publication*] (DLA) ... Red
Redwar's Comments on Ordinances of the Gold Coast Colony [*1889-1909*] [*Ghana*] [*A publication*] (DLA) ... Redwar
Redwater Public Library, Alberta [*Library symbol National Library of Canada*] (NLC) ... ARED
Redwater Public Library, Redwater, AB, Canada [*Library symbol*] [*Library of Congress*] (LCLS) ... CaARed
Redwing Airways, Inc. [*ICAO designator*] (FAAC) ... RWG
Redwing Resources, Inc. [*Vancouver Stock Exchange symbol*] ... RWG
Redwood (VRA) ... rdwd
Redwood City Public Library, Redwood City, CA [*Library symbol Library of Congress*] (LCLS) ... CRc
Redwood Empire Bancorp [*AMEX symbol*] (SPSG) ... REB
Redwood Empire Bancorp [*Associated Press*] (SAG) ... RedEm
Redwood Empire Bancorp [*Associated Press*] (SAG) ... RedEmp
Redwood Empire Bcp 7.80% Cv Pfd [*AMEX symbol*] (TTSB) ... REBPr
Redwood Falls Hospital, Redwood Falls, MN [*Library symbol*] [*Library of Congress*] (LCLS) ... MnRwfH
Redwood Falls, MN [*AM radio station call letters*] ... KLGR
Redwood Falls, MN [*FM radio station call letters*] ... KLGR-FM
Redwood Falls, MN [*Television station call letters*] ... KRWF
Redwood Falls, MN [*Location identifier FAA*] (FAAL) ... RWF
Redwood Falls Public Library, Redwood Falls, MN [*Library symbol*] [*Library of Congress*] (LCLS) ... MnRwf
Redwood Falls-Morton Junior Senior High School, Redwood Falls, MN [*Library symbol*] [*Library of Congress*] (LCLS) ... MnRwfJSH
Redwood Inspection Service (EA) ... RIS
Redwood Library and Athenaeum, Newport, RI [*Library symbol Library of Congress*] (LCLS) ... RNR
Redwood National Park ... REDW
Redwood Records Cultural and Educational Fund (EA) ... RRCEF
Redwood Region Logging Conference (EA) ... RRLC
Redwood Resources, Inc. [*Vancouver Stock Exchange symbol*] ... RDW
Redwood Trust [*NASDAQ symbol*] (TTSB) ... RWTI
Redwood Trust, Inc. [*Associated Press*] (SAG) ... Redwd
Redwood Trust, Inc. [*NASDAQ symbol*] (SAG) ... RWTI
Redwood Trust Wrrt [*NASDAQ symbol*] (TTSB) ... RWTIW
Redwood Valley, CA [*Location identifier FAA*] (FAAL) ... REW
Reebok International Ltd. [*NYSE symbol*] (SPSG) ... RBK
Reebok International Ltd. [*Associated Press*] (SAG) ... Reebok
Reebok Intl [*NYSE symbol*] (TTSB) ... RBK
Reebok Tennis Professional [*Shoes*] ... RTP
Reed and Carnrick [*Commercial firm*] (DAVI) ... R & C
Reed City, MI [*Location identifier FAA*] (FAAL) ... RCT
Reed City, MI [*AM radio station call letters*] ... WDEE
Reed City Public Library, Reed City, MI [*Library symbol Library of Congress*] (LCLS) ... MiRc
Reed College (GAGS) ... Reed C
Reed College, Portland, OR [*OCLC symbol*] (OCLC) ... ORC
Reed College, Portland, OR [*Library symbol Library of Congress*] (LCLS) ... OrPR
Reed International Ltd. [*Associated Press*] (SAG) ... ReedIntl
Reed International Ltd. [*NYSE symbol*] (SAG) ... RUK
Reed Intl P.L.C. ADS [*NYSE symbol*] (TTSB) ... RUK
Reed, John M., San Antonio TX [*STAC*] ... RJM
Reed Ltd., Technical Information Centre, Quebec, PQ, Canada [*Library symbol Library of Congress*] (LCLS) ... CaQQR
Reed Ltd., Toronto, ON, Canada [*Library symbol Library of Congress*] (LCLS) ... CaOTRL
Reed Ltd., Toronto, Ontario [*Library symbol National Library of Canada*] (NLC) ... OTRL
Reed on Bills of Sale [*A publication*] (DLA) ... Reed
Reed on Bills of Sale [*A publication*] (DLA) ... Reed BS
Reed on Railways as Carriers [*A publication*] (DLA) ... Reed Car
Reed Organ Society (EA) ... ROS
Reed Reactor Facility [*Reed College*] [*Research center*] (RCD) ... RRF
Reed Reference Electronic Publishing ... RREP
Reed Relay Scanner ... RRS
Reed Stenhouse Companies Ltd. [*Toronto Stock Exchange symbol*] ... RSS
Reed Stenhouse Investment Services [*British*] ... RSIS
Reed Switching Matrix ... RSM
Reed Valve [*Automotive engineering*] ... RV
Reede Gray Elementary School, Redwood Falls, MN [*Library symbol*] [*Library of Congress*] (LCLS) ... MnRwfGES
Reeds [*Music*] ... RDS
Reed's American Law Studies [*A publication*] (DLA) ... Reed Am LS
Reeds Jewelers [*NASDAQ symbol*] (TTSB) ... REED
Reeds Jewelers, Inc. [*Wilmington, NC*] [*NASDAQ symbol*] (NQ) ... REED
Reeds Jewelers, Inc. [*Associated Press*] (SAG) ... ReedJwl

Reed's Leading Cases on Statute of Frauds [*A publication*] (DLA) .... Reed Fraud
Reed's Pennsylvania Blackstone [*A publication*] (DLA) .... Reed PA Black
Reed's Practical Suggestions for the Management of Lawsuits [*A publication*] (DLA) .... Reed Pr Sug
Reedsburg, WI [*FM radio station call letters*] (RBYB) .... WBDL-FM
Reedsburg, WI [*FM radio station call letters*] .... WNFM
Reedsburg, WI [*AM radio station call letters*] .... WRDB
Reedsport, OR [*AM radio station call letters*] .... KDUN
Reedsport, OR [*FM radio station call letters*] .... KRBZ
Reedsport, OR [*FM radio station call letters*] .... KSYD
Reed-Sternberg Cell [*Medicine*] (MAE) .... RS
Reedsville, PA [*Location identifier FAA*] (FAAL) .... RVL
Re-Education (DAVI) .... re-ed
Reef .... RF
Reefed Parachute Canopy .... RPC
Reefer [*Military*] (DNAB) .... RFER
Reefing Hook .... RHK
Reel (DGA) .... R
Reel (MSA) .... RE
Reel .... RL
Reel and Wheel [*Freight*] .... RW
Reel Sequence [*Computer science*] .... RS
Reeling Machines [*JETDS nomenclature*] [*Military*] (CET) .... RL
Reels [*JETDS nomenclature*] [*Military*] (CET) .... RC
Reemployment Priority List [*DoD*] .... RPL
Reengus [*India*] [*ICAO location identifier*] (ICLI) .... VIRG
Reenlist [*Military*] (AFM) .... REENL
Re-Enlistment [*Army*] .... Reenlmt
Reenlistment Allowance [*Military*] .... RAL
Reenlistment Allowance [*Military*] (DNAB) .... REENL ALLOW
Reenlistment Allowance [*Military*] .... REENLA
Reenlistment and Separation [*Military*] (AFM) .... R & S
Reenlistment Bonus [*Military*] .... REENLB
Reenlistment Control Point (DOMA) .... RCP
Reenlistment Incentive Program (DNAB) .... RIP
Reenlistment Leave Travel Allowance [*Military*] .... RLTA
Reenlistment Qualification Test [*Military*] (MCD) .... RQT
Reenlistment Steering Group [*Military*] (MCD) .... RSG
Reentrant Data Processing .... REDAP
Reentrant Process Allocator [*Telecommunications*] (TEL) .... RPA
Reentrant Processor [*Telecommunications*] .... REP
Reentry [*Aerospace*] (KSC) .... R/E
Reentry .... REY
Reentry Advanced Fusing Test (IAA) .... RAFT
Reentry Air Data System (ADA) .... READS
Reentry Analysis and Modeling of Target Characteristics .... RAMTAC
Reentry Angle .... REA
Reentry Antenna Test .... RANT
Reentry Antimissile .... RAM
Reentry Attenuation Measurement [*NASA*] .... RAM
Reentry Body .... RB
Reentry Body .... REB
Reentry Body Assembly .... RBA
Reentry Body Building (IAA) .... REB
Reentry Body Coordination Committee .... RBCC
Reentry Control Electronics .... RCE
Reentry Control System [*Aerospace*] (AFM) .... RCS
Reentry Dynamics Program .... REDYP
Reentry Environment and Systems Technology .... REST
Reentry Environmental Systems Division [*General Electric Co.*] (MCD) .... RESD
Reentry Experiment .... REX
Reentry Flight Demonstration .... RFD
Reentry Heating Energies Analyzer [*Air Force*] .... RHEA
Reentry Measurement Program [*Military*] .... RMP
Reentry Measurement System .... REMS
Reentry Measurement System .... RMS
Reentry Measurement Vehicle [*Military*] .... RMV
Reentry Measurements Instrumentation Package .... RMIP
Reentry Module .... REM
Reentry Nose Tip [*Air Force*] .... RENT
Reentry Payload Launch Vehicle .... RPLV
Reentry Physics Program .... REP
Reentry RADAR Cross Section .... RRCS
Reentry Range .... RR
Reentry Rate Command [*NASA*] .... RRC
Reentry Reference Time [*NASA*] .... RRT
Reentry System (ADA) .... RES
Reentry System (AFM) .... RS
Reentry System Environmental Protection .... RESEP
Reentry System Technology [*Aerospace*] .... RST
Reentry System Test Program .... REST
Reentry Systems Department .... RSD
Reentry Systems Evaluation RADAR [*Aerospace*] .... RESER
Reentry Test Vehicle [*Air Force*] .... RTV
Reentry Vehicle [*Aerospace*] .... REV
Reentry Vehicle [*Aerospace*] .... RV
Reentry Vehicle and Ground Control [*NASA*] (KSC) .... RV/GC
Reentry Vehicle, Experimental [*Aerospace*] .... RVX
Reentry Vehicle Jamming Simulator [*Army*] .... RVJS
Reentry Vehicle Module [*NASA*] (KSC) .... RVM
Reentry Vehicle Nosetip [*Aerospace*] (MCD) .... RVNT
Reentry Vehicle Separation [*Aerospace*] (MUGU) .... RVS
Reentry Vehicle Simulator [*Aerospace*] (AAG) .... RVS
Reentry Vehicle Test and Observables [*Air Force*] .... RVTO
Reese Hospital and Medical Center, Chicago, IL [*OCLC symbol*] (OCLC) .... IHA
Reese, "Musik in the Middle Ages" [*A publication*] .... Remma
Rees-Stealy Medical Clinic, San Diego, CA [*Library symbol Library of Congress*] (LCLS) .... CSdRS
Re-Evaluation Deadline [*Rehabilitation*] (DAVI) .... Re-D
Reevaluation of Capital [*Business term*] (MHDB) .... ROC
Reeve Aleutian Airways, Inc. [*Air carrier designation symbol*] .... RAA
Reeve Aleutian Airways, Inc. [*ICAO designator*] (OAG) .... RV
Reeve Aleutian Airways, Inc. [*ICAO designator*] (FAAC) .... RVV
Reeve on Descents [*A publication*] (DLA) .... Reeve Des
Reeve on Domestic Relations [*A publication*] (DLA) .... Reeve Dom Rel
Reeve on the Law of Shipping [*A publication*] (DLA) .... Reeve Sh
Reeves Electronic Analog Computer .... REAC
Reeves Entertainment Group [*Television*] .... REG
Reeve's History of the English Law [*A publication*] (DLA) .... Reeve Eng L
Reeve's History of the English Law [*A publication*] (DLA) .... Reeve Eng Law
Reeve's History of the English Law [*A publication*] (DLA) .... Reeve Hist Eng Law
Reeve's History of the English Law [*A publication*] (DLA) .... Reeves HEL
Reeve's History of the English Law [*A publication*] (DLA) .... Reeves Hist Eng Law
Reeves MacDonald Mines [*Vancouver Stock Exchange symbol*] .... RV
REFAC Technology Develop [*AMEX symbol*] (TTSB) .... REF
Refac Technology Development Corp. [*AMEX symbol*] (SAG) .... REF
Refac Technology Development Corp. [*Associated Press*] (SAG) .... Refac
Refacer .... RFCR
Refectory (DSUE) .... REF
Refectory (DSUE) .... REFEC
Refectory (VRA) .... refty
Refer (EY) .... REF
Refer to Accepter [*Banking*] .... RA
Refer to Drawer [*Banking*] .... RD
Refer to Drawer Please Represent [*Business term*] (DCTA) .... RDPR
Referee [*Football*] .... R
Referee .... REF
Referee Stops Contest [*Amateur boxing*] .... RSC
Referees' Association [*British*] (DBA) .... RA
Referee's Decision [*Legal term*] (DLA) .... Ref Dec
Reference [*Online database field identifier*] .... RE
Reference [*Online database field identifier*] (NATG) .... REF
Reference (IDOE) .... ref
Reference .... REF
Reference (ROG) .... REFC
Reference [*Online database field identifier*] .... RF
Reference Address for Small Core Memory (IAA) .... RAS
Reference and Adult Services Division [*American Library Association*] (EA) .... RASD
Reference and Recreational Library (Stadacona), Canada Department of National Defence [*Bibliotheque de Consultation et de Lecture (Stadacona), Ministere de la Defense Nationale*] **Halifax, Nova Scotia** [*Library symbol National Library of Canada*] (NLC) .... NSHND
Reference & Research Book News [*A publication*] (BRI) .... R&R Bk N
Reference and Research Library Resources Systems [*New York State Library*] [*Albany*] [*Information service or system*] (IID) .... 3R's
Reference and Subscription Books Review Committee [*American Library Association*] .... RSBRC
Reference and User Services Association [*Formerly, RASD*] .... RUSA
Reference Areas Advisory Committee [*Victoria, Australia*] .... RAAC
Reference Attitude Display .... RAD
Reference Australia [*A publication*] .... Ref Aust
Reference Book of Corporate Managements [*Dun's Marketing Services*] [*Information service or system*] (CRD) .... RBCM
Reference Book Review [*A publication*] (BRI) .... Ref Bk R
Reference Breakdown Air Traffic Control Services Report (FAAC) .... REBAT
Reference Burst (LAIN) .... RB
Reference Burst Identification (LAIN) .... RBID
Reference Cavity .... RC
Reference Clock [*Telecommunications*] (TEL) .... RC
Reference Clock Trigger [*Telecommunications*] (IAA) .... RCT
Reference Color Space [*Computer science*] .... RCS
Reference Concentration .... RfC
Reference Concentration [*Toxicology*] .... RFC
Reference Concept Group (SSD) .... RCG
Reference Configuration (SSD) .... RC
Reference Configuration (SSD) .... REFCON
Reference Configuration Description (SSD) .... RCD
Reference Control Unit (MCD) .... RCU
Reference Control Unit Launch (MCD) .... RCUL
Reference Daily Intake [*FDA*] .... RDI
Reference Data and Bias (SAA) .... RDB
Reference Datum Height [*Aviation*] (DA) .... RDH
Reference Design Document (KSC) .... RDD
Reference Designation Index (MCD) .... RDI
Reference Designation Overflow Code (NASA) .... RDOC
Reference Designator (NASA) .... RD
Reference Designator Code (NASA) .... RDC
Reference Designator Number (MCD) .... REF/DES
Reference Dispatch (NOAA) .... REDIS
Reference Document .... RD
Reference Dose [*Environmental science*] .... RfD
Reference Drawing (NATG) .... RD
Reference Drawing Group [*NATO*] (NATG) .... RDG
Reference Equivalent [*Telecommunications*] (TEL) .... RE
Reference Equivalent Threshold Sound Pain [*or Pressure*] **Level** .... RETSPL
Reference Frequency [*Telecommunications*] (IAA) .... REFFREQ
Reference Frequency Unit [*Telecommunications*] (OA) .... RFU
Reference Fuel .... RF
Reference Gas Cell [*Instrumentation*] .... RGC

Reference Guide to American Literature [*A publication*] .... RGAL
Reference Guide to Short Fiction [*A publication*] .... RGSF
Reference Guides Series (ACII) .... RGS
Reference Indication Number .... RIN
Reference Interaction Site Model [*Chemical physics*] .... RISM
Reference Jet Transport .... RJT
Reference Librarian Enhancement System [*University of California*] [*Online microcomputer system*] .... REFLES
Reference Library .... RL
Reference Library Data Base .... RLDB
Reference Library, Government House [*Salle de Reference, Residence du Gouverneur-General*] **Ottawa, Ontario** [*Library symbol National Library of Canada*] (NLC) .... OOGH
Reference Library of Hispanic America [*A publication*] .... RCHA
Reference Line (AAG) .... REFL
Reference Line (IAA) .... RL
Reference Link Control Unit [*Telecommunications*] (TEL) .... RLCU
Reference List .... RL
Reference Manual (IAA) .... RM
Reference Mark (IAA) .... RM
Reference Material .... RM
Reference Materials Searching System (NITA) .... REFSEARCH
Reference Measuring Unit (MCD) .... RMU
Reference Measuring Unit Computer .... RMUC
Reference Memory [*Psychology*] .... RM
Reference Message (FAAC) .... REMES
Reference Message from Our Office (FAAC) .... ROMES
Reference Message from Your Office (FAAC) .... RUMES
Reference Method .... RM
Reference Method Item Identification [*DoD*] .... RMII
Reference Mission [*NASA*] (NASA) .... RM
Reference Mixture Radio (KSC) .... RMR
Reference My Talk Address [*Military*] (IAA) .... MTA
Reference Noise [*Telecommunications*] .... RN
Reference Noise Generator .... RNG
Reference Normal Serum [*Clincial chemistry*] (AAMN) .... RNS
Reference Number (CINC) .... REFNO
Reference Number .... RN
Reference Number Action Activity Code (MCD) .... RNAAC
Reference Number Category Code (MCD) .... RNCC
Reference Number Format Code (MCD) .... RNFC
Reference Number Mandatory Category Code [*DoD*] .... RNMCC
Reference Number Status Code (MCD) .... RNSC
Reference Number Variation Code (MCD) .... RNVC
Reference Optical Alignment .... ROA
Reference or Partial Description Method Reason Code (MCD) .... RPDMRC
Reference Oscillator [*Telecommunications*] (OA) .... RO
Reference Our Letter (NOAA) .... ROLET
Reference Our Memorandum (FAAC) .... ROMEMO
Reference Our Private Branch Exchange Message (SAA) .... ROPBX
Reference Our Requisition (NOAA) .... ROREQ
Reference Our Telephone Call (NOAA) .... ROPHO
Reference Our Telephone Conversation (FAAC) .... REFONE
Reference Our Telex (DS) .... ROT
Reference Overhaul Work Package (DNAB) .... ROWP
Reference Paper .... RP
Reference Papers [*Army*] (AABC) .... REFP
Reference Pattern (NATG) .... RP
Reference Point .... RP
Reference Point Foundation (EA) .... RPF
Reference Point Tracking .... RPT
Reference Preparation for Serum Proteins (DMAA) .... RPSP
Reference Private Branch Exchange Message (SAA) .... REPBX
Reference Publication (MCD) .... RP
Reference Pulse .... RP
Reference Quality Level (IEEE) .... RQL
Reference Radio .... RERAD
Reference Receiver .... RR
Reference Register [*Computer science*] .... RR
Reference Repository Location .... RRL
Reference Requisition (NOAA) .... REREQ
Reference Requisition from Our Office (FAAC) .... RORQN
Reference Roughness Index [*FHWA*] (TAG) .... RRI
Reference Safety Analysis Report [*Nuclear energy*] (NRCH) .... RESAR
Reference Satellite A (NASA) .... RSA
Reference Sensing Element (DNAB) .... RSE
Reference Sensing Element Amplifier .... RSEA
Reference Sequence Number [*Online bibliographies*] .... RSN
Reference Serum [*Clinical chemistry*] .... RS
[*The*] **Reference Service** [*Mead Data Central, Inc.*] [*Information service or system*] (IID) .... REFSRV
Reference Services Division [*of ALA*] [*Later, RASD*] (EA) .... RSD
Reference Services, Nova Scotia Provincial Library, Halifax, Nova Scotia [*Library symbol National Library of Canada*] (NLC) .... NSHPLX
Reference Services Review [*A publication*] (BRI) .... RSR
Reference Signal Generator .... RSG
Reference Sound Source .... RSS
Reference Stable Member Matrix (KSC) .... REFSMMAT
Reference Standard .... RS
Reference Standards Book [*Military*] .... RSB
Reference Standards Equipment [*Deep Space Instrumentation Facility, NASA*] .... RSE
Reference Standards Laboratory [*Deep Space Instrumentation Facility, NASA*] .... RSL
Reference Telegram (NATG) .... REFTEL
Reference Telegram from Your Office (FAAC) .... RUTEL
Reference Telephone Conversation (NOAA) .... REPHO
Reference Telephonic Power (DEN) .... RTP
Reference Temperature (IAA) .... REFTEMP
Reference Test Chart .... RTC
Reference Theta Pinch Reactor .... RTPR
Reference Trajectory [*NASA*] (KSC) .... RT
Reference Transfer Calibrator (OA) .... RTC
Reference Transmission Level Point [*Telecommunications*] .... RTLP
Reference Travel Order (NOAA) .... REFTO
Reference Update Review (SSD) .... RUR
Reference Velocity (GAVI) .... VREF
Reference Voltage .... RV
Reference Voltage [*Automotive engineering*] .... VREF
Reference Voltage (IDOE) .... V_{ref}
Reference Your .... REUR
Reference Your Dispatch .... REFURDIS
Reference Your Dispatch (NOAA) .... RUDIS
Reference Your Letter .... REFURLTR
Reference Your Letter (NOAA) .... RULET
Reference Your Memorandum (NOAA) .... RUMEM
Reference Your Memorandum (FAAC) .... RUMEMO
Reference Your Message [*Military*] (AABC) .... RYM
Reference Your Public Branch Exchange Message (SAA) .... RUPBX
Reference Your Radio .... REURAD
Reference Your Requisition (NOAA) .... RUREQ
Reference Your Telegram (WDAA) .... RYT
Reference Your Telegraph Wire Exchange [*Telecommunications*] (IAA) .... REYRTWX
Reference Your Telephone Call (NOAA) .... RUPHO
Reference Your Telex (WDAA) .... RYT
Reference Your TWX [*Teletypewriter communications*] (AAG) .... REURTWX
References (WGA) .... REFF
Reference-Voltage Generator .... RVG
Referendum .... REF
Referential Integrity [*Computer science*] (PCM) .... RI
REfernce Invoice (FAAC) .... REINV
Refernce Letter (FAAC) .... RELET
Referral Order [*Military*] (DNAB) .... RO
Referral Service Network Office .... RSNO
Referred (OICC) .... R
Referred .... REFD
Referred (BARN) .... rfrd
Referred Care [*Medicine*] .... RC
Referred-to-Input .... RTI
Referred-to-Output .... RTO
Referring Doctor [*Medicine*] (AAMN) .... ref doc
Referring Emergency Service for Consumers' Ultimate Enjoyment [*Service plan of Recreational Vehicle Dealers of America*] (EA) .... RESCUE
Referring Physician (DAVI) .... ref phys
REFF, Inc. [*Toronto Stock Exchange symbol*] .... RFF
Reffton Corp., Montgomery, AL [*Library symbol Library of Congress*] (LCLS) .... AMR
Refill [*of bract liquid*] [*Botany*] .... R
Refilled, Tapped, and Fractionated [*Rock formation*] [*Geology*] .... RTF
Refilling Point .... RP
Refined .... REFD
Refined (MSA) .... RFND
Refined Aeronautical Support Program (NG) .... RASP
Refined Bitumen Association [*British*] (DBA) .... RBA
Refined, Bleached, and Deodorized [*Vegetable oil technology*] .... RBD
Refined Gigabit System [*High purity hydrogen peroxide*] .... RGS
Refined Menhaden Oil [*Food science*] .... RMO
Refined Oil of Vitriol .... ROV
Refined Oil Products .... ROP
Refined Soybean Oil .... RSBO
Refined Sugar Association [*British*] (DBA) .... RSA
Refined Trajectory Analysis .... RETRAN
Refiner Mechanical Pulp [*Papermaking*] .... RMP
Refinery [*or Refining*] .... REF
Refinery .... REFY
Refinery .... RFNRY
Refinery Evaluation Modeling System [*Department of Energy*] (GFGA) .... REMS
Refining .... RFNG
Refining in Transit .... RIT
Reflect (NASA) .... RFL
Reflect Array Pulse Compressor (RDA) .... RAC
Reflectance .... R
Reflectance [*or Reflector*] (AAG) .... REFL
Reflectance, Fluorescence, Transmittance [*Densitometer*] [*Instrumentation*] .... RFT
Reflectance Units of Dirt Shade (PDAA) .... RUDS
Reflected .... REFLD
Reflected Electron Energy Loss Spectra .... REELS
Reflected High-Energy Electron Diffraction [*Spectroscopy*] .... RHEED
Reflected Light Photohead .... RLPH
Reflected P Wave [*Earthquakes*] .... PcP
Reflected S Wave [*Earthquakes*] .... ScS
Reflected Signal Indication [*Air Force*] .... RSI
Reflected-Reflected-Transmitted [*Wave mechanics*] .... RRT
Reflecting Satellite Communication Antenna .... RESCAN
Reflection [*Angle of*] .... R
Reflection [*or Reflector*] (IAA) .... REFL
Reflection (IAA) .... REFLEC

Reflection Absorption Infrared Spectroscopy [*Also, IRAS, IRRAS, RAIRS, RAIS*] ... RAIR
Reflection Absorption Infrared Spectroscopy [*Also, IRAS, IRRAS, RAIR, RAIS*] ... RAIRS
Reflection Absorption Infrared Spectroscopy [*Also, IRAS, IRRAS, RAIR, RAIRS*] ... RAIS
Reflection Anisotropy Microscopy ... RAM
Reflection Anisotropy Microscopy ... RAM
Reflection Coefficient Bridge ... RCB
Reflection Direction Finding ... RDF
Reflection Direction Finding, Low Angle (MCD) ... RDFL
Reflection Electron Diffraction [*For surface structure analysis*] ... RED
Reflection Electron Microscopy ... REM
Reflection High-Energy Electron Diffraction (DMAA) ... RHEED
Reflection Interference Contrast Microscopy ... RICM
Reflection Loss [*Telecommunications*] (TEL) ... RL
Reflection Modulation (IAA) ... RM
Reflection Phase Grating [*Acoustics*] ... RPG
Reflection Resources [*Vancouver Stock Exchange symbol*] ... REF
Reflections of Elvis Fan Club (EA) ... REFC
Reflective Electron Optical System ... REOS
Reflective High-Energy Electron Diffraction ... RHEED
Reflective Insulation [*Technical drawings*] ... RI
Reflective Memory System (NITA) ... RMS
Reflective Mossbauer Technique (PDAA) ... REMOTE
Reflective Raised Pavement Marker [*Highway design*] ... RRPM
Reflectivity Data Acquisition System ... RDAS
Reflectivity Measurements Pacific ... REMPAC
Reflectivity Measuring Facility ... RMF
Reflectone, Inc. [*Associated Press*] (SAG) ... Reflctn
Reflectone, Inc. [*Associated Press*] (SAG) ... Reflectn
Reflectone, Inc. [*NASDAQ symbol*] (NQ) ... RFTN
Reflector ... REF
Reflector [*or Reflected*] ... RFL
Reflector and Lighting Equipment Manufacturers (IAA) ... RLM
Reflector Antenna System ... RAS
Reflector Erosion Experiment [*NASA*] ... REX
Reflector Lamp ... R
Reflector Lamps Manufacturer (IAA) ... RLM
Reflector Moderated Reactor (AAG) ... RMR
Reflector Orbital Equipment ... ROE
Reflector Orbital Experiment (MCD) ... ROE
Reflector Support Truss ... RST
Reflector-cum-Periscope [*British military*] (DMA) ... RCP
Reflectors [*JETDS nomenclature*] [*Military*] (CET) ... RR
Reflex ... REFL
Reflex (MSA) ... RFLX
Reflex Anal Dilatation [*Medicine*] ... RAD
Reflex Digital Control ... RDC
Reflex Milk Ejection (OA) ... RME
Reflex Plasma Discharge ... RPD
Reflex Sympathetic Dystrophy [*Medicine*] ... RSD
Reflex Sympathetic Dystrophy Association (EA) ... RSDA
Reflex Sympathetic Dystrophy Syndrome [*Medicine*] (DMAA) ... RSDS
Reflexive ... R
Reflexive ... REFL
Reflight ... RF
Reflood Assist Bypass Valve [*Nuclear energy*] (NRCH) ... RABV
Reflux ... RE
Reform [*Judaism*] ... R
Reform, AL [*FM radio station call letters*] ... WTID
Reform Jewish Appeal (EA) ... RJA
Reform Judaism (BJA) ... RJ
Reform of Intermediate and Secondary Education (OICC) ... RISE
Reform of the Australian Taxation System [*1985*] [*A publication*] ... RATS
Reform the Armed Forces Movement [*Philippines*] ... RAM
Reformation ... REF
Reformatorische Politieke Federatie [*Reformist Political Federation*] [*Netherlands Political party*] (PPE) ... RPF
Reformatory (ROG) ... REFORM
Reformatory (AABC) ... RFTY
Reformed ... REF
Reformed (WGA) ... REFD
Reformed Church ... RC
Reformed Church in America (ROG) ... RCA
Reformed Church Women [*An association*] (EA) ... RCW
Reformed Episcopal [*Church*] ... RE
Reformed Episcopal Church ... RECH
Reformed Episcopal Seminary, Philadelphia, PA [*Library symbol Library of Congress Obsolete*] ... PPRETS
Reformed Ogboni Fraternity [*Nigeria*] ... ROF
Reformed Presbyterian ... RP
Reformed Presbyterian Church ... RPCH
Reformed Presbyterian Theological Seminary, Pittsburgh, PA [*Library symbol*] [*Library of Congress*] (LCLS) ... PPiRP
Reformed Presbyterian Theological Seminary, Pittsburgh, PA [*OCLC symbol*] (OCLC) ... PRP
Reformed Protestant Episcopal ... RPE
Reformed Spelling (BARN) ... Ref Sp
Reformed Spelling ... RS
Reformed Theological Seminary, Jackson, MS [*OCLC symbol*] (OCLC) ... MRT
Reformed Theological Seminary, Jackson, MS [*Library symbol Library of Congress*] (LCLS) ... MsJRT
Reformer's Book Shelf [*A publication*] ... RBS

Reforming Institutions to Guarantee Humane Treatment Standards [*Student legal action organization*] ... RIGHTS
Reformulated Gasoline ... RFG
Reformulated Gasoline Blendstock for Downstream Oxygenated Blending ... RBOB
Refounded National Party [*South Africa Political party*] (EAIO) ... RNF
Refracted Bottom-Reflected Ray ... RBR
Refracted Near Field [*Optics*] ... RNF
Refracted Surface-Reflected Ray ... RSR
Refraction ... R
Refraction (AAMN) ... RFR
Refractive Index [*Symbol*] [*Physics*] ... n
Refractive Index ... RI
Refractive Index Detector [*Instrumentation*] ... RID
Refractive Index Gradient [*Analytical chemistry*] ... RIG
Refractive Index Matched Anomalous Diffraction [*Light measurement*] ... RIMAD
Refractive Index Matching [*Coal technology*] ... RIM
Refractive Index Profile ... RIP
Refractive Index Sounding Central ... RISC
Refractive Index Sounding System ... RISS
Refractive Index Unit ... RIU
Refractive Modulus (IDOE) ... M
Refractories Association of Great Britain (BI) ... RAGB
[*The*] Refractories Institute (EA) ... TRI
Refractories Research Center [*Ohio State University*] [*Research center*] (RCD) ... RRC
Refractoriness under Load (IAA) ... RUL
Refractory ... REFR
Refractory (AAG) ... REFR
Refractory (MSA) ... RFRC
Refractory Anemia [*Medicine*] ... RA
Refractory Anemia, Erythroblastic [*Hematology*] (DAVI) ... RAEB
Refractory Anemia with Excess Myeloblast [*Hematology*] (MAE) ... RAEM
Refractory Anemia with Excess of Blasts [*Hematology*] ... RAEB
Refractory Anemia with Excess of Blasts in Transformation [*Hematology*] ... RAEB-T
Refractory Anemia with Ringed Sideroblasts [*Hematology*] ... RARS
Refractory Anemia with Ringed Sideroblasts [*Hematology*] ... RAS
Refractory Anemia without Excess of Blasts [*Hematology*] ... RAWEB
Refractory Ascites [*Medicine*] (DMAA) ... RA
Refractory Ceramic Fiber [*Materials science*] ... RCF
Refractory Girl [*A publication*] ... Ref Girl
Refractory Girl [*A publication*] ... Refr G
Refractory Grade Bauxite [*Geology*] ... RGB
Refractory Heavy Minerals [*In sands used for glass making*] ... RHM
Refractory Metal Sheet Program [*Navy*] (NG) ... RMSP
Refractory Metal-Oxide Semiconductor (IEEE) ... RMOS
Refractory Metals Electrofinishing Corp. ... RMEC
Refractory Period [*Medicine*] ... RP
Refractory Platinum Metal ... RPM
Refractory Reusable Surface Insulation (PDAA) ... RSI
Refractory Users Federation [*British*] (BI) ... RUF
Refrain (WGA) ... REF
Refresh [*Computer graphics*] ... RFRSH
Refresh [*Computer graphics*] ... RFSH
Refresh Memory (MCD) ... RM
Refresher (AABC) ... REF
Refresher Maintenance Lab ... RML
Refresher Training (NVT) ... REFTRA
Refresher Training [*Navy*] (NVT) ... RFT
Refrigerant [*Cooling*] [*Medicine British*] (ROG) ... REF
Refrigerant (MSA) ... RFGT
Refrigerant Transport Module [*Air-conditioning*] (PS) ... RTM
Refrigerant-Air Condition (DNAB) ... RAC
Refrigerate (KSC) ... REFR
Refrigerate (AAG) ... REFRG
Refrigerated [*Shipping*] (DS) ... R
Refrigerated (AAG) ... REFRD
Refrigerated Cargo Ship [*World War II*] ... AKF
Refrigerated Centrifuge ... RC
Refrigerated Covered Lighter [*Self-propelled*] [*Navy symbol*] ... YFR
Refrigerated Covered Lighter [*Non-self-propelled*] [*Navy symbol*] ... YFRN
Refrigerated Detector Unit (SAA) ... RDU
Refrigerated Fresh Water Medium [*Microbiology*] ... RFW
Refrigerated Seawater ... RSW
Refrigerated Service [*Shipping*] [*British*] ... REFRIG
Refrigerated Tank [*Liquid gas carriers*] ... R
Refrigerated Transmission Line ... RTL
Refrigerated Transportation Foundation (EA) ... RTF
Refrigerated Trap [*Biotechnology*] ... RT
Refrigerating [*or Refrigeration*] ... REFG
Refrigerating Engineers and Technicians Association (EA) ... RETA
Refrigerating Machinery ... REFMCHY
Refrigeration ... REFRIG
Refrigeration ... REFRIGN
Refrigeration [*Charges*] ... RFGN
Refrigeration and Air Conditioning Contractors Association - National [*Later, National Environmental Systems Contractors Association*] (EA) ... RACCA
Refrigeration, Compressor and Electrical Power, Airborne Pod Enclosure (DNAB) ... RCPP
Refrigeration, Compressor and Electrical Power, Trailer-Mounted (DNAB) ... RCPT
Refrigeration Compressor Rebuilders Association (EA) ... RCRA
Refrigeration Effect ... RE
Refrigeration Equipment Manufacturers Association [*Later, ARI*] (MCD) ... REMA

Refrigeration Installation Equipment (SAA) .... REIQ
Refrigeration Installation Equipment (SAA) .... RIE
[The] Refrigeration Research Foundation (EA) .... TRRF
Refrigeration Service Engineers Society (EA) .... RSES
Refrigeration System (MCD) .... RS
Refrigeration System [or Subsystem] [Skylab] [NASA] .... RSS
Refrigeration System Shield (MCD) .... RSS
Refrigeration Technician/Specialist (AAG) .... RT/S
Refrigeration Trade Association (NADA) .... RTA
Refrigeration Trade Association of America .... RTA
Refrigeration Unit (KSC) .... RU
Refrigerator .... R
Refrigerator (WGA) .... REF
Refrigerator .... REFGR
Refrigerator .... REFRIG
Refrigerator .... RFRG
Refrigerator Mechanical Household (MSA) .... RMH
Refrigerator, Refrigerated, or Cold Storage [Airplane, railway car, truck] .... REEFER
Refuel (AAG) .... RFL
Refueling .... REFUL
Refueling and Rearming [Air Force] .... R & R
Refueling Area Commander [Navy] (ANA) .... RAC
Refueling Mission [Air Force] .... RFM
Refueling Shutdown (IEEE) .... RSD
Refueling Water Storage Tank [Nuclear energy] (NRCH) .... RWST
Refueling Water Tank [Nuclear energy] (NRCH) .... RWT
Refueling Water Transfer and Storage [Nuclear energy] (NRCH) .... RTS
Refuelling (DA) .... RFLG
Refuel-On-The-Move [Army] (DOMA) .... ROM
Refuge from Flood (ADA) .... RFF
Refugee Agency [NATO] (NATG) .... RA
Refugee Cash Assistance [Office of Refugee Resettlement] [Department of Health and Human Services] (GFGA) .... RCA
Refugee Coordinator [Department of State] (GFGA) .... REF
Refugee Council of Australia .... RCOA
Refugee Documentation Centre [Information service or system] (IID) .... RDC
Refugee Policy Group (EA) .... RPG
Refugee Processing Center (MCD) .... RPC
Refugee Relief International (EA) .... RRI
Refugee Resettlement Program (MEDA) .... RRP
Refugee Resource Center [Defunct] .... RRC
Refugee Voices, a Ministry with Uprooted Peoples (EA) .... RV
Refugee Women in Development (EA) .... RefWID
Refugees International (EA) .... RI
Refugio, TX [FM radio station call letters] .... KZTX
Refugio, TX [Location identifier FAA] (FAAL) .... MNO
Refugio, TX [Location identifier FAA] (FAAL) .... RFG
Refugio, TX [Location identifier FAA] (FAAL) .... VDU
Refund [or Refunding] .... REF
Refund (AFM) .... REFD
Refund (WDAA) .... RFD
Refund Information File [IRS] .... REINF
Refund Information File [IRS] .... RFIF
Refund Information File [IRS] .... RIF
Refund Litigation Coordinator [IRS] .... RLC
Refund Statute Expiration Date [IRS] .... RSED
Refundable Income Tax Account .... RITA
Refundable Life Use Fee [Housing] (DICI) .... RLUF
Refunding .... RF
Refunding [Business term] .... RFG
Refunding Escrow Deposit [Finance] (DFIT) .... RED
Refurbish and Subassemblies Facilities [NASA] (NASA) .... RSF
Refurbish for Delivery (MCD) .... RFD
Refurbished .... REFURB
Refurbished Command Module [NASA] (KSC) .... RCM
Refurbishment (NASA) .... REF
Refurbishment and Modification .... R & M
Refurbishment Cost Study (KSC) .... RCS
Refurbishment Spare (NASA) .... RS
Refuse and Litter Advisory Committee [Australia] .... RALAC
Refuse Disposal [British Waterways Board sign] .... R
Refused .... R
Refused (ADA) .... REF
Refused, Not Reversible Error [Legal term] (DLA) .... Ref NRE
Refused, Not Reversible Error [Legal term] (ILCA) .... RNRE
Refused, Want of Merit [Legal term] (DLA) .... Ref WM
Refuse-Derived Fuel (ERG) .... RDF
Reg Resources Corp. [Vancouver Stock Exchange symbol] .... RRE
Regal Bahamas International Airlines [ICAO designator] (AD) .... RH
Regal Bahamas International Airways Ltd. [ICAO designator] (FAAC) .... RBH
Regal Beloit [AMEX symbol] .... RBC
Regal, Branch of EMI [Record label] [Spain] .... Reg
Regal Cinemas [NASDAQ symbol] (TTSB) .... REGL
Regal Cinemas, Inc. [Associated Press] (SAG) .... RegCin
Regal Cinemas, Inc. [NASDAQ symbol] (SAG) .... REGL
Regal Cinemas, Inc. [Associated Press] (SAG) .... RegICin
Regal Petroleum Ltd. [Vancouver Stock Exchange symbol] .... RGA
Regal-Beloit Corp. [AMEX symbol] (SPSG) .... RBC
Regal-Beloit Corp. [Associated Press] (SAG) .... RegalBel
Regal-Zonophone [Record label] [Great Britain] .... RZ
Regarding [JETDS nomenclature] .... H
Regarding .... RE
Regarding .... REG
Regardless of Destination Airport (FAAC) .... RODA

Regardless of Feature Size [Manufacturing term] .... RFS
Regency (VRA) .... Rgcy
Regency Airlines Ltd. [ICAO designator] (FAAC) .... RGY
Regency Health Services [NYSE symbol] (TTSB) .... RHS
Regency Health Services, Inc. [Associated Press] (SAG) .... RegHlt
Regency Health Services, Inc. [NYSE symbol] (SAG) .... RHS
Regency Realty [NYSE symbol] (SPSG) .... REG
Regency Realty Corp. [Associated Press] (SAG) .... RgcyRlt
Regency Resources [Vancouver Stock Exchange symbol] .... REG
Regenerable Affinity Chromatography Support .... RACS
Regenerable Carbon Dioxide and Humidity Control System (NASA) .... RCHCS
Regenerant Waste Treatment Subsystem [Nuclear energy] (NRCH) .... RWTS
Regenerate [Computer science] (WDMC) .... regen
Regenerate Address [Computer science] (MHDB) .... REGAD
Regenerated [Biology] .... R
Regenerated Cellulose Film [Organic chemistry] .... RCF
Regenerated Electrical Output .... REO
Regeneration (IAA) .... REG
Regeneration (AAG) .... REGEN
Regeneration Medium [Biology] .... RM
Regeneration Project [Later, CR] (EA) .... RP
Regeneration Thermoluminescence .... RTL
Regenerative Agriculture Association [Later, RI] (EA) .... RAA
Regenerative Carbon-Dioxide Removal System (MCD) .... RCRS
Regenerative Cyclic Reactor [Chemical engineering] .... RCR
Regenerative Fuel Cell .... RFC
Regenerative Fuel Cell Subsystem .... RFCS
Regenerative Generator [Electronics] (ECII) .... REGEN
Regenerative Heat Exchanger [Nuclear energy] (NRCH) .... RHX
Regenerative Injection Liquid Propellant Gun (MCD) .... RILPG
Regenerative Intercooled Turbine Engine (MCD) .... RITE
Regenerative Life Support System [NASA] (NASA) .... RLSS
Regenerative Liquid Propellant Gun (MCD) .... RLPG
Regenerative Thermal Oxidation [Metallurgy] .... RTO
Regenerative Turboprop Engines .... RTE
Regeneratively-Cooled Thrust Chamber .... RCTC
Regeneron Pharmaceuticals [NASDAQ symbol] (SPSG) .... REGN
Regeneron Pharmaceuticals, Inc. [Associated Press] (SAG) .... Regenrn
Re-Geniusing Project [Defunct] (EA) .... RP
Regensburger Neues Testament [A publication] (BJA) .... RNT
Regensburg-Oberhub [Germany ICAO location identifier] (ICLI) .... EDYR
Regent .... REG
Regent .... REGT
Regent [Record label] .... Rgt
Regent Air [Canada ICAO designator] (FAAC) .... RAH
Regent Assisted Living [NASDAQ symbol] (TTSB) .... RGNT
Regent Assisted Living, Inc. [Associated Press] (SAG) .... RegtAsst
Regent Assisted Living, Inc. [NASDAQ symbol] (SAG) .... RGNT
Regent Banchares Corp. [Associated Press] (SAG) .... RegntBc
Regent Bancshares [NASDAQ symbol] (TTSB) .... RBNKE
Regent Bancshares Corp. [NASDAQ symbol] (NQ) .... RBNK
Regent Bancshares Corp. [Associated Press] (SAG) .... RegBn
Regent Bancshares Corp. [Associated Press] (SAG) .... RegBnc
Regent Bancshares Corp. [Associated Press] (SAG) .... Regnt
Regent Bancshares Wrrt [NASDAQ symbol] (TTSB) .... RBNWE
Regent College Library [UTLAS symbol] .... RGT
Regent College, Vancouver, BC, Canada [Library symbol] [Library of Congress] (LCLS) .... CaBVaREC
Regent College, Vancouver, British Columbia [Library symbol National Library of Canada] (NLC) .... BVAREC
Regent's Canal Dock [British] .... RCD
Regents External Degree Examinations [New York] (EDAC) .... REDE
Regent's Line [Steamship] (MHDW) .... RL
Regeration [Computer science] (WDMC) .... regen
Reggan [Algeria] [ICAO location identifier] (ICLI) .... DAAN
Regge Field Theory [Particle Physics] .... RFT
Reggio Calabria [Italy ICAO location identifier] (ICLI) .... LICR
Reggio Calabria [Italy] [Seismograph station code, US Geological Survey] (SEIS) .... RCI
Reggio Calabria [Italy] [Airport symbol] (OAG) .... REG
Regia Anglorum [British] [An association] (DBA) .... RA
Regiae Societatis Sodalis [Fellow of the Royal Society] [Latin] .... RSS
Regie de l'Assurance Automobile du Quebec, Sillery, PQ, Canada [Library symbol Library of Congress] (LCLS) .... CaQQRAA
Regie de l'Assurance Automobile du Quebec, Sillery, Quebec [Library symbol National Library of Canada] (NLC) .... QQRAA
Regie de l'Assurance-Maladie du Quebec, Quebec, PQ, Canada [Library symbol Library of Congress] (LCLS) .... CaQQRAMQ
Regie de l'Assurance-Maladie du Quebec, Sillery, Quebec [Library symbol National Library of Canada] (NLC) .... QQRAMQ
Regie de l'Electricite et du Gaz, Montreal, PQ, Canada [Library symbol Library of Congress] (LCLS) .... CaQMREG
Regie de l'Electricite et du Gaz, Montreal, Quebec [Library symbol National Library of Canada] (NLC) .... QMREG
Regie des Rentes du Quebec, Quebec, PQ, Canada [Library symbol Library of Congress] (LCLS) .... CaQQRQ
Regie des Rentes du Quebec, Quebec, PQ, Canada [Library symbol Library of Congress] (LCLS) .... CaQQRRQ
Regie des Rentes du Quebec, Ste.-Foy, Quebec [Library symbol National Library of Canada] (NLC) .... QQRRQ
Regie des Services Publics, Ste.-Foy, PQ, Canada [Library symbol Library of Congress] (LCLS) .... CaQQRSP
Regie des Services Publics, Ste.-Foy, Quebec [Library symbol National Library of Canada] (NLC) .... QQRSP

Regie des Telegraphes et des Telephones [*Belgium Telecommunications service*] (TSSD) ... RTT
Regie des Ventes du Quebec, Quebec, PQ, Canada [*Library symbol Library of Congress Obsolete*] (LCLS) ... CaQQRV
Regie du Logement, Montreal, Quebec [*Library symbol National Library of Canada*] (NLC) ... QMRL
Regiere Mich Herr durch Deinen Heiligen Geist [*Rule Me, Lord, Through Thy Holy Spirit*] [*Motto of Ann, Margravine of Brandenburg (1575-1612)*] [*German*] ... RMHDDHG
Regiment ... R
Regiment ... REG
Regiment (AABC) ... REGT
Regiment ... RGT
Regiment Air Defense Center (NATG) ... RADC
Regiment de Marche d'Afrique [*African Marching Regiment*] [*French*] ... RMA
Regiment de Marche de la Legion Etrangere [*Foreign Legion Marching Regiment*] [*French*] ... RMLE
Regiment de Marche de Volontiers Etrangers [*Foreign Volunteers Marching Regiment*] [*French*] ... RMVE
Regiment de Zouaves ... RZ
Regiment Etranger de Cavalerie [*Foreign Cavalry Regiment*] [*French*] ... REC
Regiment Etranger d'Infanterie [*Foreign Infantry Regiment*] [*French*] ... REI
Regiment Etranger d'Infanterie (de Marche) [*Foreign Marching Infantry Regiment*] [*French*] ... REI(M)
Regiment Materiel Management Center [*Military*] (AABC) ... RMMC
Regiment of Cavalry [*British military*] (DMA) ... RC
Regiment South Western District [*British military*] (DMA) ... RSWD
Regiment Western Province [*British military*] (DMA) ... RWP
Regimental (ROG) ... REGIM
Regimental ... REGL
Regimental ... REGTL
Regimental Aid Post [*British*] ... RAP
Regimental Amalgamation Officer [*British military*] (DMA) ... RAO
Regimental Artillery Group [*OPFOR*] (GFGA) ... RAG
Regimental Aviation Squadron [*Army*] (ADDR) ... RAS
Regimental Beachhead [*Army*] ... RBH
Regimental Combat Team ... RCT
Regimental Command Post ... RCP
Regimental Corporal-Major [*British*] ... RCM
Regimental Court-Martial ... RCM
Regimental Headquarters ... RHQ
Regimental Inquiry Regulations [*British military*] (DMA) ... RIR
Regimental Institute [*British military*] (DMA) ... RI
Regimental Landing Group ... RLG
Regimental Landing Team [*Military*] ... RLT
Regimental Medical Officer (NATG) ... RMO
Regimental Munitions Officer [*Army*] ... RMO
Regimental Orders [*Army*] ... RO
Regimental Paymaster [*British military*] (DMA) ... RP
Regimental Police [*British*] ... RP
Regimental Quartermaster-Corporal [*British*] ... RQMC
Regimental Quartermaster-Sergeant [*British*] ... RQMS
Regimental Reserve Line ... RRL
Regimental Reserve Officer (ADA) ... RRO
Regimental Sergeant Major [*Army*] ... RSM
Regimental Stretcher-Bearer ... RSB
Regimental Supply Officer [*Army*] ... RSO
Regimental Training Line [*Army*] ... RTL
Regimented Inmate Discipline [*Mississippi State Penitentiary*] ... RID
Regimento de Artilharia Ligeira [*Light Artillery Regiment*] [*Portuguese*] ... RALI
Regina [*Queen*] [*Latin*] ... R
Regina [*Queen*] [*Latin*] ... REG
Regina [*French Guiana*] [*ICAO location identifier*] (ICLI) ... SOOR
Regina [*Canada*] [*Airport symbol*] (OAG) ... YQR
Regina Campus, Campion College, University of Saskatchewan, Saskatchewan [*Library symbol National Library of Canada*] (NLC) ... SRUC
Regina et Imperatrix [*Queen and Empress*] [*Latin*] ... R et I
Regina General Hospital, Regina, SK, Canada [*Library symbol Library of Congress*] (LCLS) ... CaSRG
Regina General Hospital, Saskatchewan [*Library symbol National Library of Canada*] (NLC) ... SRG
Regina Imperatrix [*Queen Empress*] [*Latin*] ... RI
Regina Public Library [*UTLAS symbol*] ... RGP
Regina Public Library, Regina, SK, Canada [*Library symbol Library of Congress*] (LCLS) ... CaSR
Regina Public Library, Saskatchewan [*Library symbol National Library of Canada*] (NLC) ... SR
Regina Resources [*Vancouver Stock Exchange symbol*] ... RNA
Regina, SK [*AM radio station call letters*] ... CBK
Regina, SK [*FM radio station call letters*] ... CBKF-FM
Regina, SK [*FM radio station call letters*] ... CBK-FM
Regina, SK [*Television station call letters*] ... CBKFT
Regina, SK [*Television station call letters*] ... CBKT
Regina, SK [*Television station call letters*] ... CFRE
Regina, SK [*FM radio station call letters*] (RBYB) ... CFWF-FM
Regina, SK [*FM radio station call letters*] ... CHMX
Regina, SK [*FM radio station call letters*] ... CIZL
Regina, SK [*AM radio station call letters*] ... CJME
Regina, SK [*AM radio station call letters*] ... CKCK
Regina, SK [*Television station call letters*] ... CKCK-TV
Regina, SK [*FM radio station call letters*] ... CKIT
Regina, SK [*AM radio station call letters*] ... CKRM
Regina, SK [*ICAO location identifier*] (ICLI) ... CYQR
Reginald P. Dawson Library, Town of Mount Royal, Quebec [*Library symbol National Library of Canada*] (NLC) ... QMRRD
Regio Decreto [*Royal Decree*] [*Latin*] (DLA) ... RD
Regio Umbilici [*Region of the Umbilicus*] [*Pharmacy*] ... Reg Umb
Region (AAG) ... REG
Region (DD) ... reg
Region (AFM) ... RGN
Region Air [*Seychelles*] [*ICAO designator*] (FAAC) ... RGA
Region Air, Inc. [*Canada ICAO designator*] (FAAC) ... RGR
Region Control Block [*Computer science*] (BUR) ... RCB
Region Control Task [*Computer science*] (BUR) ... RCT
Region Internal Computer Code [*Computer science*] ... RGICC
Region of Assured Mission Abort [*Military*] (CAAL) ... RAMA
Region of Influence ... ROI
Region of Interest [*Nuclear energy*] ... ROI
Region of Interest [*Nuclear energy*] (NRCH) ... ROI
Region One Cooperative Library Service Unit [*Library network*] ... ROC
Region Operations Control Center [*NORAD*] [*ICAO designator*] (FAAC) ... ROCC
Region Peaking Factor [*Nuclear energy*] (NRCH) ... RPF
Region, State, Area, County [*Code*] [*DoD*] ... RSAC
Region Wide [*Forestry*] ... RW
Regionair Ltd. [*British ICAO designator*] (FAAC) ... RGL
Regional (DD) ... regl
Regional ... REGL
Regional ... REGN
Regional ... RGNL
Regional Aboriginal Health Liaison Officer [*Australia*] ... RAHLO
Regional Acceleratory Phenomenon [*Physiology*] ... RAP
Regional Acceptance [*NASDAQ symbol*] (TTSB) ... REGA
Regional Acceptance Corp. [*NASDAQ symbol*] (SAG) ... REGA
Regional Acceptance Corp. [*Associated Press*] (SAG) ... RegAcp
Regional Accountable Depot [*Military*] ... RAD
Regional Accounting and Disbursing Center (DNAB) ... RAADC
Regional Accounting and Finance Test [*Military*] (AFM) ... RAFT
Regional Accounting Office [*Telecommunications*] (TEL) ... RAO
Regional Acid Deposition Model [*for acid rain*] [*Environmental Protection Agency*] ... RADM
Regional Acidification Information and Simulation [*International Institute for Applied Systems Analysis*] ... RAINS
Regional Acquisition Unit [*NASA*] (NASA) ... RAU
Regional Adjunct Language [*Computer science*] (PDAA) ... RAL
Regional Administrative Assistant (ADA) ... RAA
Regional Administrative Directors ... RAD
Regional Administrative Management Plan [*Department of Labor*] ... RAMP
Regional Administrative Office ... RAO
Regional Administrative Radio Conference (NITA) ... RARC
Regional Administrator ... RA
Regional Advisory Board [*American Hospital Association*] ... RAB
Regional Advisory Committee on Nuclear Energy ... RACNE
Regional Advisory Council (ACII) ... RAC
Regional Advisory Group [*Generic term*] (DHSM) ... RAG
Regional Advisory Service in Demographic Statistics [*United Nations*] (EY) ... RASDS
Regional Aeronautical Support Activity (AFIT) ... RASA
Regional African Satellite Communication System for the Development of Africa [*ITU*] [*United Nations*] (DUND) ... RASCOM
Regional African Satellite Communications System (ECON) ... RASCOM
Regional African Telecommunication Database [*International Telecommunication Union*] (DUND) ... RATDA
Regional Agricultural Credit Corp. ... RACC
Regional Agricultural Officer [*Ministry of Agriculture, Fisheries, and Food*] [*British*] ... RAO
Regional Air Defense Operations Center (NATG) ... RADOC
Regional Air Monitoring Station [*or System*] [*Environmental Protection Agency*] ... RAMS
Regional Air Navigation [*ICAO*] ... RAN
Regional Air Operations Center (NATG) ... RAOC
Regional Air Operations Plan (NATG) ... RAOP
Regional Air Pollution Study [*Environmental Protection Agency*] ... RAPS
Regional Air Priorities Control Office [*Army*] (AABC) ... RAPCO
Regional Air (Pty) Ltd. [*South Africa ICAO designator*] (FAAC) ... RAW
Regional Air Quality ... RAQ
Regional Air Traffic Control Center (NATG) ... RATCC
Regional Air Traffic Services School, Transport Canada [*Ecole Regionale des Services de la Circulation Aerienne, Transports Canada*], Richmond, British Columbia [*Library symbol National Library of Canada*] (NLC) ... BRTRA
Regional Airline Association (EA) ... RAA
Regional Airlines [*France ICAO designator*] (FAAC) ... RGI
Regional Allied Long-Lines Agency [*Formerly, RELLA*] (NATG) ... RALLA
Regional Analysis and Forecast System [*National Meteorological Center*] ... RAFS
Regional Analysis and Prediction [*Branch*] [*Marine science*] (OSRA) ... RAP
Regional and Domestic Air Route Area ... RDARA
Regional and Mesoscale Meteorology [*Branch*] [*Marine science*] (OSRA) ... RAMM
Regional and Mesoscale Meteorology [*Branch*] [*National Environmental Satellite, Data, and Information Service*] (USDC) ... RAMM
Regional and Urban Information Network [*Washington, DC*] ... RUIN
Regional and Urban Studies Information Center [*Department of Energy*] (IID) ... RUSTIC
Regional Area Forecast Center [*ICAO designator*] (FAAC) ... RAFC
Regional Arts Association [*British*] ... RAA
Regional Asbestos Coordinator (GNE) ... RAC
Regional Associations [*Marine science*] (MSC) ... RA
Regional ASW [*Antisubmarine Warfare*] **Command Center** [*Navy*] (DOMA) ... RACC
Regional Atmosphere Measurement and Analysis Network [*Marine science*] (OSRA) ... RAMAN
Regional Atmospheric Measurement and Analysis Network (USDC) ... RAMAN

Regional Atmospheric Modeling System (USDC) .... RAMS
Regional Atmospheric Modeling System [*Marine science*] (OSRA) .... RAMS
Regional Atmospheric Modeling System .... RAMS
Regional Atmospheric Transport Code for Hanford Emission Tracking [*Marine science*] (OSRA) .... RATCHET
Regional Atmospheric Transport Code for Hanford Emission Tracking (USDC) .... RATCHET
Regional Audit Manager .... RAM
Regional Authorities (Scotland) .... RS
Regional Automated Systems .... RAS
Regional Automatic Circuit Exchange (IAA) .... RACE
Regional Aviation Assistance Group [*FAA*] .... RAAG
Regional Aviation Supply Officer [*Navy*] (AFIT) .... RASO
Regional Battle Manager [*DoD*] .... RBM
Regional Bell Holding Co. (BYTE) .... RBHC
Regional Bell Holding Co. [*Computer science*] (TNIG) .... RHC
Regional Bell Operating Co. .... RBOC
Regional Blood Center [*Red Cross*] .... RBC
Regional Blood Flow [*Physiology*] .... RBF
Regional Bone Mass .... RBM
Regional Briefing Station .... RBS
Regional Bureau for Latin America and the Caribbean [*United Nations*] (ECON) .... RBLAC
Regional Bureau of the Middle East Committee for the Affairs of the Blind [*Saudi Arabia*] (EAIO) .... MECAB
Regional Bureau of the Middle East Committee for the Affairs of the Blind [*An association*] (EAIO) .... RBMECAB
Regional Business Unit .... RBU
Regional Case Development Officer [*Environmental Protection Agency*] (GFGA) .... RCDO
Regional Catering Officer [*British*] (DCTA) .... RCO
Regional Census Center [*Bureau of the Census*] (GFGA) .... RCC
Regional Center .... RC
Regional Center for Tropical Biology [*SEAMEO*] [*Indonesia*] [*Research center*] (IRC) .... BIOTROP
Regional Center for Tropical Meteorology [*National Hurricane Center*] .... RCTM
Regional Centers for Radiological Physics [*National Cancer Institute*] .... RCRP
Regional Centre for Drama and Music [*University of New England, Australia*] .... RCDM
Regional Centre for Seismology for South America (EAIO) .... RCSSA
Regional Centre for Services in Surveying, Mapping, and Remote Sensing [*West Africa*] .... RCSSMRS
Regional Centre for Training in Aerial Surveys (EAIO) .... RECTAS
Regional Cerebral Blood Flow [*Medicine*] .... rCBF
Regional Cerebral Blood Volume [*Medicine*] (MAE) .... RCBV
Regional Cerebral Metabolic Rate [*Brain research*] .... rCMR
Regional Check Processing Centers .... RCPC
Regional Civil and Defense Mobilization Boards .... RCDMB
Regional Civil Defense Coordination Boards [*DoD*] (AABC) .... RCDCB
Regional Civil Emergency Advisory Committee [*Formerly, JRCC*] [*Civil defense*] .... RCEAC
Regional Clean Air Incentive Market [*Environmental program*] (ECON) .... RECLAIM
Regional Climate Center [*Marine science*] (OSRA) .... RCC
Regional Climate Center (USDC) .... RCC
Regional Coastal Information Center [*National Marine Advisory Service*] (MSC) .... RCIC
Regional Colleges Principals' Association of Victoria [*Australia*] .... RCPA
Regional Commandant [*Air Force British*] .... RC
Regional Commission on Land and Water Use in the Near East (EA) .... RCLWUNE
Regional Commissioner [*Social Security Administration*] .... RC
Regional Committee for Community Medicine (DMAA) .... RCCM
Regional Communications Operations Center [*Military*] (MCD) .... RCOC
Regional Computerized Traffic Signal System .... RCTSS
Regional Conference for Latin America [*UN Food and Agriculture Organization*] .... LARC
Regional Conference for the Near East [*UN Food and Agriculture Organization*] .... NERC
Regional Conference on International Voluntary Service [*Commercial firm*] (EAIO) .... RCIVS
Regional Congress of Construction Employers (EA) .... RCCE
Regional Conservation Program .... RCP
Regional Contingency Construction Management (DOMA) .... RCCM
Regional Contract Property Officer .... RCPO
Regional Control Center [*Air Force*] (DOMA) .... RCC
Regional Control Station [*Military*] (MCD) .... RCS
Regional Cooperative Physics Group [*Educational institutions in Ohio, Michigan, Illinois and Pennsylvania*] (PDAA) .... RCPG
Regional Coordinating Unit [*Advisory Committee on Pollution of the Sea*] ...... RCU
Regional Coordination Committee [*Department of Health and Human Services*] .... RCC
Regional Council .... RC
Regional Council for International Education [*University of Pittsburgh*] .... RCIE
Regional Council on Human Rights in Asia (EAIO) .... RCHRA
Regional Dance America [*Defunct*] (EA) .... RDA
Regional Dance Association .... RDA
Regional Data Associates [*Information service or system*] (IID) .... RDA
Regional Data Center [*Marine science*] (MSC) .... RDC
Regional Defense Organization (DNAB) .... RDO
Regional Dental Activity (AABC) .... RDA
Regional Development Authority [*Victoria, Australia*] .... RDA
Regional Development Grant [*British*] (DCTA) .... RDG
Regional Development Incentives Act .... RDIA
Regional Development Laboratory [*Philadelphia, PA*] .... RDL
Regional Development Program [*Australia*] .... RDP

Regional Development Unit [*Manpower Services Commission*] (AIE) .... RDU
Regional Director .... RD
Regional Director of Motor Carriers [*FHWA*] (TAG) .... RDMC
Regional Disbursing Office .... RDO
Regional Dissemination Center [*NASA*] .... RDC
Regional Dissemination Centers [*NASA*] (PDAA) .... RDC
Regional Distribution Center [*TRW Automotive Aftermarket Group*] .... RDC
Regional Distributors and Carriers Conference (EA) .... RDCC
Regional Early Childhood Direction Centers (EDAC) .... RECDC
Regional Economic Area .... REA
Regional Economic Development Center [*Memphis State University*] [*Research center*] (RCD) .... REDC
Regional Economic Development Services Office [*USAID*] .... REDSO
Regional Economic Development Services Office for East and Southern Africa .... REDSO/ESA
Regional Economic Information System [*Department of Commerce*] [*Information service or system*] (IID) .... REIS
Regional Economic Planning Council [*British*] .... REPC
Regional Economic Projections Series [*NPA Data Services, Inc.*] [*Information service or system*] (CRD) .... REPS
Regional Education Board of the Christian Brothers (EA) .... REB
Regional Education Committee of the Christian Brothers [*Later, REB*] (EA) .... RECCB
Regional Education Laboratory .... REL
Regional Education Service Agency .... RESA
Regional Educational Advisory Council [*British*] .... REAC
Regional Educational Building Institute for Africa .... REBIA
Regional Educational Laboratory for the Carolinas and Virginia .... RELCV
Regional Educational Service Center .... RESC
Regional Educational Television Advisory Council .... RETAC
Regional Educators Annual Chemistry Teaching Symposium .... REACTS
Regional Ejection Fraction Image [*Medicine*] (DMAA) .... REFI
Regional Electricity Co. [*British*] (ECON) .... REC
Regional Electronics Centers [*British*] .... REC
Regional Emergency Transportation Center [*Military*] .... RETC
Regional Emergency Transportation Coordinator [*Military*] .... RETCO
Regional Emergency Transportation Representative .... RETREP
Regional Emissions Projection System [*Environmental Protection Agency*] .... REPS
Regional Employment Premium [*British*] .... REP
Regional Energy Education Network [*National Science Teachers Association*] .... REEN
Regional Energy Information System [*Minnesota State Department of Energy and Economic Development*] [*St. Paul*] [*Information service or system*] (IID) .... REIS
Regional Energy Resources Information Center [*Asian Institute of Technology*] [*British Information service or system*] (IID) .... RERIC
Regional Enforcement Activities Plan [*Environmental Protection Agency*] (ERG) .... REAP
Regional Enteritis [*Medicine*] .... RE
Regional Entry Test .... RET
Regional Environment Management Allocation Process (PDAA) .... REMAP
Regional Environmental Offices [*Air Force*] (DOMA) .... REO
Regional Environmental Study [*Australia*] .... RES
Regional Environmental Support Office (DNAB) .... RESO
Regional Environmental Training and Research Organization [*Retraining program for unemployed space-industry workers*] .... RETRO
Regional European Long Lines Agency (IAA) .... RELIA
Regional European Long-Lines Agency [*Later, RALLA*] (NATG) .... RELLA
Regional Evaluation Center (NVT) .... REC
Regional Examining Bodies [*British*] (DI) .... REB
Regional Executive Officer [*British*] .... REO
Regional Export Expansion Council [*Department of Commerce*] .... REEC
Regional Express Co. [*ICAO designator*] (FAAC) .... REC
Regional Field Officer [*Civil Defense*] .... RFO
Regional Field Specialist [*Civil Defense*] .... RFS
Regional Film Theatre [*British*] .... RFT
Regional Financial Associates Inc. .... RFA
Regional Financial Operating Plan .... RFOP
Regional Fishery Management Council [*National Oceanic and Atmospheric Administration*] (MSC) .... RFMC
Regional Forces [*ARVN*] .... RF
Regional Forces - Popular Forces [*Republic of Vietnam*] [*Army*] .... RF/PF
Regional Forward Scatter Branch [*Supreme Allied Commander, Europe*] (NATG) .... RFSB
Regional Freight Consolidation Center (AAGC) .... RFCC
Regional Frequency Supplies [*Telecommunications*] (TEL) .... RFS
Regional Fuel Tax Agreement [*FHWA*] (TAG) .... RFTA
Regional Further Education Adviser (AIE) .... RFEA
Regional Glucose Utilization [*Medicine*] (DMAA) .... RGU
Regional Government Technical Monitor [*Department of Housing and Urban Development*] (GFGA) .... RGTM
Regional Headquarters (NOAA) .... RH
Regional Headquarters (NITA) .... RHQ
Regional Health Authority [*British*] .... RHA
Regional Health Authority (Teaching) [*British*] .... RHA(T)
Regional Health Director [*HEW*] .... RHD
Regional Highway Traffic Model [*Database*] [*Obsolete*] .... RHTM
Regional Holding Co. .... RHC
Regional Hospital Boards [*British*] .... RHB
Regional Hospital Junior Staff Committee [*British*] (BABM) .... RHJSC
Regional Hospital Junior Staff Committee [*British*] (DAVI) .... RHJSC
Regional Hospitals Consultants' and Specialists' Association .... RHCSA
Regional Ileitis [*Medicine*] .... RI
Regional Industry Advisory Committee [*Civil Defense*] .... RIAC

Regional Information and Communications Exchange [*Rice University Library*] [*Houston, TX*] .... RICE
Regional Information Management System [*FHWA*] (TAG) .... RIMS
Regional Information Services Plan (NITA) .... RISP
Regional Information Sharing System [*Department of Justice*] .... RISS
Regional Information Technology Coordinators (NITA) .... RITC
Regional Initiative in Science Education .... RISE
Regional Initiatives in Science Education [*National Academy of Sciences*].... RISE
Regional Input-Output Modeling System .... RIMS II
Regional Institute of Higher Education and Development .... RIHED
Regional Institute of Social Welfare Research (EA) .... RISWR
Regional Interagency Coordinating Committee [*Department of Labor*] .... RICC
Regional Interagency Emergency Transportation Committee .... RIETCOM
Regional Islamic Da'Wah Council of Southeast Asia and the Pacific (EAIO) .... RISEAP
Regional Jet [*British Aerospace/Taiwan Aerospace Corp. joint venture*] (ECON) .... RJ
Regional Journal of Social Issues [*A publication*] .... Reg J Social Issues
Regional Justice Information Service [*St. Louis, MO*] .... REJIS
Regional Justice Information System .... RJIS
Regional Lagrangian Model of Air Pollution [*Marine science*] (OSRA) ..... RELMAP
Regional Lagrangian Model of Air Pollution (USDC) .... RELMAP
Regional Land Agent [*Ministry of Agriculture, Fisheries, and Food*] [*British*] ..... RLA
Regional Language Centre [*SEAMEO*] [*Singapore*] [*Research center*] (IRC) .... RELC
Regional Laser and Biotechnology Laboratories [*University of Pennsylvania*] [*Research center*] (RCD) .... RLBL
Regional Learning Resources Services [*Veterans Administration*] (GFGA).... RLRS
Regional Letter of Acceptance [*Department of Housing and Urban Development*] (GFGA) .... RLA
Regional Liaison Group (CINC) .... RLG
Regional Liaison Office [*Military*] (AFM) .... RLO
Regional Library, Canadian Coast Guard [*Bibliotheque Regionale, Garde CotiereCanadienne*] Dartmouth, Nova Scotia [*Library symbol National Library of Canada*] (NLC) .... NSHMT
Regional Library, Canadian Coast Guard [*Bibliotheque Regionale, Garde CotiereCanadienne*] North Vancouver, British Columbia [*Library symbol National Library of Canada*] (NLC) .... BVACG
Regional Library, Corner Brook, Newfoundland [*Library symbol National Library of Canada*] (NLC) .... NFCBR
Regional Library, Corner Brook, NF, Canada [*Library symbol Library of Congress*] (LCLS) .... CaNfCBr
Regional Library for the Blind and Physically Handicapped, Hartford, CT [*Library symbol Library of Congress*] (LCLS) .... Ct-BPH
Regional Library for the Blind and Physically Handicapped, Perkins School for the Blind, Watertown, MA [*Library symbol Library of Congress*] (LCLS) .... MWatP-BPH
Regional Library, Grand Falls, Newfoundland [*Library symbol National Library of Canada*] (NLC) .... NFGF
Regional Library, Lac Du Bonnet, Manitoba [*Library symbol National Library of Canada*] (NLC) .... MLDB
Regional Library, Lac Du Bonnet, MB, Canada [*Library symbol Library of Congress*] (LCLS) .... CaMLdB
Regional Library of Medicine [*Pan American Health Organization*] .... RLM
Regional Library, Transport Canada [*Bibliotheque Regionale de Transports Canada*] Edmonton, Alberta [*Library symbol National Library of Canada*] (NLC) .... AEMT
Regional Lime Technical Officer [*Ministry of Agriculture, Fisheries, and Food*] [*British*] .... RLTO
Regional Logistical Support Offices (DOMA) .... RLSO
Regional Lymph Node [*Medicine*] (CPH) .... RLN
Regional Lymph Node Cell [*Medicine*] (DMAA) .... RLNC
Regional Lymph Node Dissection [*Medicine*] .... RLND
Regional Maintenance Representative [*Military*] .... RMR
Regional Management Centre (AIE) .... RMC
Regional Management Officer [*Social Security Administration*] .... RMO
Regional Manager .... RM
Regional Manpower Administration .... RMA
Regional Marine Biological Centre [*UNESCO*] (MSC) .... RMBC
Regional Media Center .... RMC
Regional Medical Education Center [*Veterans Administration*] (GFGA) .... RMEC
Regional Medical Library .... RML
Regional Medical Library Program [*Department of Health and Human Services*] .... RMLP
Regional Medical Officer [*British*] .... RMO
Regional Medical Program .... RMP
Regional Medical Programs Service [*Health Services and Mental Health Administration, HEW*] .... RMPS
Regional Medical Training Center .... RMTC
Regional Meetings [*Quakers*] .... RM
Regional Mental Health Center of Oak Ridge, Oak Ridge, TN [*Library symbol Library of Congress*] (LCLS) .... TOMH
Regional Military Command Subcenter North [*Sweden ICAO location identifier*] (ICLI) .... ESPP
Regional Military Command Subcenter South [*Sweden ICAO location identifier*] (ICLI) .... ESDD
Regional Military Command Subcenter West [*Sweden ICAO location identifier*] (ICLI) .... ESII
Regional Military Government Officer [*World War II*] .... RMGO
Regional Ministers Conference on Cooperatives [*Australia*] .... RMCC
Regional Model Data Handling System [*Environmental Protection Agency*] (GFGA) .... RMDHS
Regional Motor Transport Officer [*British*] (DCTA) .... RMTO
Regional Municipality of Ottawa-Carleton, Ottawa, ON, Canada [*Library symbol Library of Congress*] (LCLS) .... CaOORM

Regional Municipality of Ottawa-Carleton, Transportation-Works Department, Ottawa, ON,Canada [*Library symbol*] [*Library of Congress*] (LCLS) .... CaoORMT
Regional Myocardial Blood Flow [*Cardiology*] (DAVI) .... RMBF
Regional Navy Youth Programs Officer (DNAB) .... RNYPO
Regional Neonatal Intensive-Care Unit (MEDA) .... RNICU
Regional Network for Agricultural Machinery [*Institute of Agricultural Engineering and Technology*] [*Philippines*] .... RNAM
Regional Network Measurement Center (MHDI) .... RNMC
Regional NOCN [*National Ocean Communications Network*] Node (USDC) ...... RNN
Regional NOCN [*National Ocean Communications Network*] Node [*Marine science*] (OSRA) .... RNN
Regional Notice [*FAA*] .... RENOT
Regional Nuclear Fuel Cycle Center [*National Science Foundation*] (NUCP) .... RNFCC
Regional Nuclear Fuel Cycle Centers .... RFNCC
Regional Nuclear Option (MCD) .... RNO
Regional Nuclear Power Authority .... RNPA
Regional Nuclear Power Co. .... RNPC
Regional Nursing Midwifery Committee [*National Health Service*] [*British*] (DI) .... RNMC
Regional Nursing Officer [*British*] .... RNO
Regional Occupation Center Program (OICC) .... ROCP
Regional Occupation Planning and Evaluation System (EDAC) .... ROPES
Regional Oceanographic Data Center [*Marine science*] (MSC) .... RODC
Regional Office [*or Officer*] .... RO
Regional Office, Alberta Agriculture, Airdrie, Alberta [*Library symbol National Library of Canada*] (NLC) .... AAAR
Regional Office, Alberta Agriculture, Barrhead, Alberta [*Library symbol National Library of Canada*] (NLC) .... ABAAR
Regional Office, Alberta Agriculture, Fairview, Alberta [*Library symbol National Library of Canada*] (NLC) .... AFAAR
Regional Office, Alberta Agriculture, Lethbridge, Alberta [*Library symbol National Library of Canada*] (NLC) .... ALAR
Regional Office, Alberta Agriculture, Red Deer, Alberta [*Library symbol National Library of Canada*] (NLC) .... ARDAR
Regional Office, Alberta Agriculture, Vermilion, Alberta [*Library symbol National Library of Canada*] (NLC) .... AVAR
Regional Office Building .... ROB
Regional Office for Central America and Panama .... ROCAP
Regional Office [*or Officer*] for Central American Programs [*Department of State*] .... ROCAP
Regional Office for Education, Asia and Pacific [*UNESCO*] (AIE) .... ROEAP
Regional Office for Education in Latin America and the Caribbean [*UNESCO*] [*Acronym is based on foreign phrase*] .... OREALC
Regional Office for Latin America and the Caribbean [*United Nations Environment Programme*] (EAIO) .... ROLAC
Regional Office for Science and Technology for Europe [*UNESCO*] [*Italy*] (EAIO) .... ROSTE
Regional Office for Science and Technology in Africa [*UNESCO*] [*See also BRUSTA*] [*Nairobi, Kenya*] (EAIO) .... ROSTA
Regional Office Monthly Personnel Status [*Department of Labor*] .... ROMPS
Regional Office Notice [*Aviation*] (FAAC) .... RENOT
Regional Office of Civilian Manpower Management .... ROCMM
Regional Office of Science and Technology [*UNESCO*] (MSC) .... ROST
Regional Office of Science and Technology for South and Central Asia [*UNESCO*] (IRC) .... ROSTSCA
Regional Office of Science and Technology for Southeast Asia [*UNESCO*] (IRC) .... ROSTSEA
Regional Office Systems [*Computer science*] .... RSA
Regional Officer in Charge [*CIA*] (VNW) .... ROIC
Regional Oil Combating Center [*United Nations Environment Programme*] (MSC) .... ROCC
Regional Operating Center [*NATO Integrated Communications System*] (NATG) .... ROC
Regional Operating Plan [*Department of Labor*] .... ROP
Regional Operations Control Center [*AT & T*] .... ROCC
Regional Operations Control Centre Information Display System [*NORAD*] .... RIDS
Regional Operators Program for Aircraft Reliability .... ROPAR
Regional Operators Program for Engine Reliability .... ROPER
Regional Organ Procurement Agency [*Medicine*] (DAVI) .... ROPA
Regional Organization for Airways Restudy .... ROAR
Regional Organization for the Protection of the Marine Environment [*Safat, Kuwait*] (EAIO) .... ROPME
Regional Organization of Liaison for Allocation of Circuit (NATG) .... ROLAC
Regional Oversight Policy [*Environmental Protection Agency*] (GFGA) .... ROP
Regional Oxidant Model [*Environmental Protection Agency*] (GFGA) .... ROM
Regional Paramedic Advisory Committee [*Emergency medicine*] (DAVI) ..... RPAC
Regional Parasite Research Laboratory [*US Department of Agriculture*] [*Research center*] (RCD) .... RPRL
Regional Particulate Model (USDC) .... RPM
Regional Particulate Model [*Marine science*] (OSRA) .... RPM
Regional Personnel Center .... RPC
Regional Personnel Officer [*Social Security Administration*] .... RPO
Regional Pests Officer [*Ministry of Agriculture, Fisheries, and Food*] [*British*] .... RPO
Regional Pharmaceutical Officer [*National Health Service*] [*British*] (DI) .... RPhO
Regional Plan Association (EA) .... RPA
Regional Plan Association, Inc., Library, New York, NY [*Library symbol Library of Congress*] (LCLS) .... NNreP
Regional Planning and Evaluation Agency [*California State Board of Education*] .... RPEA
Regional Planning Association (NADA) .... RPA
Regional Planning Commission .... RPC

Regional Planning Federation, Philadelphia, PA [*Library symbol Library of Congress Obsolete*] (LCLS) .... PPRPF
Regional Planning Group (NATG) .... RPG
Regional Planning Unit (OICC) .... RPU
Regional Plant Introduction Station (GNE) .... RPIS
Regional Pollution Studies in the Ligurian Sea [*Marine science*] (MSC) .... RAMOGE
Regional Ports Authority [*British*] .... RPA
Regional Postgraduate Medical Education Committee [*Medicine*] (DMAA) .... RPGMEC
Regional Poultry Research Laboratory [*East Lansing, MI*] [*Department of Agriculture*] (GRD) .... RPRL
Regional Preparedness Board [*Military*] (AABC) .... RPB
Regional Preparedness Committee [*Civil Defense*] .... RPC
Regional Pressure Setting (DA) .... RPS
Regional Primate Research Centers .... RPRC
Regional Printing Procurement Office [*Army*] .... RPPO
Regional Priority Program [*Army*] (AABC) .... RPP
Regional Processing Unit .... RPU
Regional Program [*or Project*] Officer (OICC) .... RPO
Regional Project for Tropical Medicine and Public Health [*SEAMEO*] [*Thailand*] [*Research center*] (IRC) .... TROPMED
Regional Project Research Program (EA) .... RRP
Regional Public Affairs Manager [*Nuclear energy*] (NRCH) .... RPAM
Regional Purchasing Office [*Defense Supply Agency*] .... RPO
Regional Rail [*TRB*] (TAG) .... RGR
Regional Railroad .... RR
Regional Realty Ltd., Ottawa, Ontario [*Library symbol National Library of Canada*] (BIB) .... OORR
Regional Recreation and Conservation Consultative Committee [*Thames Water Authority*] [*British*] .... RRCCC
Regional Relay Facility (DNAB) .... RRF
Regional Reporting Centers [*Navy*] (DOMA) .... RRC
Regional Representative of the Secretary of Transportation .... SECREP
Regional Research Institute for Human Services [*Portland State University*] [*Research center*] (RCD) .... RRIHS
Regional Resource Center .... RRC
Regional Resources Advisory Committee [*Army*] (AABC) .... RRAC
Regional Resources Ltd. [*Toronto Stock Exchange symbol Vancouver Stock Exchange symbol*] .... RGL
Regional Response Center [*Environmental Protection Agency*] (EG) .... RRC
Regional Response Team [*Environmental Protection Agency*] (EG) .... RRT
Regional Review Consultants [*American Occupational Therapy Association*] .... RRC
Regional Safety Coordinator [*Australia*] .... RSC
Regional Safety Inspector [*Ministry of Agriculture, Fisheries, and Food*] [*British*] .... RSI
Regional Safety Officer [*British*] (DCTA) .... RSO
Regional Sample Control Center (GNE) .... RSCC
Regional Science Association (EA) .... RSA
Regional Science Experience Center .... RSEC
Regional Seat of Government .... RSG
Regional Security Officer [*Foreign Service*] .... RSO
Regional Seismic Test Network [*Nuclear explosion detection*] .... RSTN
Regional Service Center [*Military*] (CINC) .... RSC
Regional Shipping Board (East) [*NATO*] .... RSB(E)
Regional Shipping Board (West) [*NATO*] .... RSB(W)
Regional Shipping Boards [*NATO*] (NATG) .... RSB
Regional Small Business Development Center [*Rutgers University*] [*Research center*] (RCD) .... RSBDC
Regional Solar Energy Center .... RSEC
Regional Specialized Meteorological Center [*Marine science*] (OSRA) .... RSMC
Regional Studies Association [*British*] (EAIO) .... RSA
Regional Study of the El Nino Phenomenon [*Peru-Chile-Columbia-Ecuador*] [*Marine science*] (OSRA) .... ERFEN
Regional Supplementary Procedures [*Aviation code*] .... SUPPS
Regional Teacher Resource Center [*NASA*] .... RTRC
Regional Team of Officers [*British*] .... RTO
Regional Technical Aid Center [*Agency for International Development*] .... RTAC
Regional Technical College (ACII) .... RTC
Regional Technical Report Centers [*Department of Commerce*] .... RTRC
Regional Technical Support [*Military*] .... RTS
Regional Telecommunications Hub [*Telecommunications*] (TEL) .... RTH
Regional Telecommunications Office [*DoD*] .... RTO
Regional Television News Australia .... RTNA
Regional Term Contract .... RTC
Regional Training Brigade [*Army*] (INF) .... RTB
Regional Training Liaison Officer [*Ministry of Agriculture, Fisheries, and Food*] [*British*] .... RTLO
Regional Training Officer (OICC) .... RTO
Regional Training Teams [*Army*] .... RTT
Regional Transit Authority [*Advanced vehicle*] .... CARTA
Regional Transport Commissioner .... RTC
Regional Transport Coordination Advisory Committee [*New South Wales, Australia*] .... RTCAC
Regional Transport Model [*Environmental Protection Agency*] (GFGA) .... RTM
Regional Transportation District, Technical Library, Denver, CO [*Library symbol Library of Congress*] (LCLS) .... CoDRT
Regional Treasurer [*British*] .... RT
Regional Underground Monolith Disposal [*Hazardous wastes*] .... RUMOD
Regional Urban Defense Intercept .... RUDI
Regional/Urban Development Assistance Team (DICI) .... R/UDAT
Regional User Group [*Computer science*] .... RUG
Regional Vascular Volume [*Hematology*] .... RVV
Regional Veterans Employment Representative [*Department of Labor*] .... RVER

Regional Veterinary Officer [*British*] .... RVO
Regional Wall Motion [*Medicine*] (DMAA) .... RWM
Regional War Labor Board .... RWLB
Regional Warning System .... RWS
Regional Water Authority [*British*] .... RWA
Regional Weather Service (NOAA) .... RWS
Regional Weekly News, Whippany, NJ [*Library symbol Library of Congress*] (LCLS) .... NjWhiR
Regional WIN [*Work Incentive*] Director [*Department of Health and Human Services*] (GFGA) .... RWD
Regional Works Officer [*British*] .... RWO
Regionalized Civilian Automated Pay System [*Air Force*] .... RECAPS
Regionalized Integrated Lake-Watershed Acidification Study [*Adirondack mountains*] .... RILWAS
Regionnair, Inc. [*Canada ICAO designator*] (FAAC) .... GIO
Regions Beyond Missionary Union [*Later, Regions Beyond Missionary Union International*] (EA) .... RBMU
Regions Financial [*NASDAQ symbol*] (TTSB) .... RGBK
Regions Financial Corp. [*Associated Press*] (SAG) .... RegnFn
Regions Financial Corp. [*NASDAQ symbol*] (SAG) .... RGBK
Regions of the World [*A publication*] .... RW
Regionsjukhuset, Medicinska Biblioteket [*Regional Hospital, Medical Library*], Orebro, Sweden [*Library symbol Library of Congress*] (LCLS) .... SwOrM
Regiopolis College, Kingston, ON, Canada [*Library symbol Library of Congress*] (LCLS) .... CaOKRC
Regiopolis - Notre Dame High School, Kingston, Ontario [*Library symbol National Library of Canada*] (NLC) .... OKRC
Regis College, Denver, CO [*Library symbol Library of Congress*] (LCLS) .... CoDR
Regis College, Denver, CO [*OCLC symbol*] (OCLC) .... COR
Regis College Lay Apostolate [*Defunct*] (EA) .... RCLA
Regis College Library, University of Toronto [*UTLAS symbol*] .... KRC
Regis College, Toronto, ON, Canada [*Library symbol Library of Congress*] (LCLS) .... CaOTREC
Regis College, Toronto, Ontario [*Library symbol National Library of Canada*] (NLC) .... OTREC
Regis College, Weston, MA [*Library symbol*] [*Library of Congress*] (LCLS) .... MWesR
Regis College, Weston, MA [*Library symbol Library of Congress*] (LCLS) .... MWestonR
Regis College, Weston, MA [*OCLC symbol*] (OCLC) .... REG
Regis Corp. [*Associated Press*] (SAG) .... Regis
Regis Corp. [*NASDAQ symbol*] (NQ) .... RGIS
Regis Development Corp. [*Vancouver Stock Exchange symbol*] .... RGD
REGIS [*Relational General Information System*] System Users' Group (EA) .... RSUP
[*A*] Register (IAA) .... AREG
Register [*Computer science*] .... R
Register (AAG) .... REG
Register .... REG
Register (AABC) .... REGIS
Register (ROG) .... REGR
Register (CET) .... RG
Register .... RGTR
Register, Address, Skip and Special Chip (IAA) .... RASS
Register Alias Table [*Computer science*] .... RAT
Register Allocator (IAA) .... RA
Register and Arithmetic/Logic Unit [*Computer science*] .... RALU
Register and Indexed Storage (MCD) .... RX
Register and Self-Test .... RST
Register and Storage (MCD) .... RS
Register, Berwick, Nova Scotia [*Library symbol National Library of Canada*] (NLC) .... NSBR
Register, Berwick, NS, Canada [*Library symbol*] [*Library of Congress*] (LCLS) .... CaNSBeR
Register Book [*A publication*] (DLA) .... Lib Reg
Register Book [*A publication*] (DLA) .... Reg Lib
Register Clock Pulse .... RCP
Register Containing (SAA) .... RC
Register Containing Word .... RCW
Register, Department of Justice and the Courts of the United States [*A publication*] .... RDJCT
Register Display Assembly .... RDA
Register Drive (MSA) .... RD
Register Enforced Automated Control Technique [*Cash register-computing system*] .... REACT
Register Field Address (IAA) .... RFA
Register File .... RF
Register Finder .... RF
Register Finder Grid (IAA) .... RFG
Register for International Service in Education [*Institute of International Education*] (IID) .... RISE
Register Holding Time (NITA) .... RHT
Register in Instruction [*Computer science*] (IAA) .... RIN
Register Indicator Panel .... RIP
Register Load and Read .... RLRD
Register Memory .... RM
Register Module .... REGM
Register (N) Stages (MCD) .... RG(N)
Register of Additional Locations [*Library of Congress*] .... RAL
Register of Apparel and Textile Designers [*British*] (DBA) .... RATD
Register of Business Opportunities in New South Wales [*Australia*] .... ROBIN
Register of Copyrights [*US*] .... RC
Register of Debates in Congress (Gales) [*1789-91*] [*A publication*] (DLA) .... Reg Deb (Gales)
Register of Environment Assessments and Statements (MCD) .... REAS

Register of Intelligence Publications (MCD) .... RIP
Register of Merit (WGA) .... ROM
Register of Plan Mobilization Producers .... RPMP
Register of Planned Emergency Procedures [*Military*] .... RPEP
Register of Private Agents [*Victoria, Australia*] .... RPA
Register of Rivers Discharging into the Oceans [*United Nations Environment Programme*] (MSC) .... RRDO
Register of Shipping of the USSR [*Ship classification society*] (DS) .... RS
Register of Solicitors Employing Trainees (ILCA) .... ROSET
Register of Veterinary Preparations and Animal Feeding Stuffs [*Australia*] .... RVPAFS
Register of Weather Stations [*Meteorological Office*] (PDAA) .... ROWS
Register of Writs [*A publication*] (DLA) .... Reg Writ
Register Output .... RO
Register Program Generator (HGAA) .... RPG
Register Select .... RS
Register Sender Inward [*Telecommunications*] (TEL) .... RSI
Register Sender Outward [*Telecommunications*] (TEL) .... RSO
Register Storage Unit .... RSU
Register to Register (MCD) .... RR
Register to Storage (NITA) .... RS
Register Ton .... RT
Register Traffic [*Telecommunications*] (TEL) .... RT
Register Transfer [*Computer science*] .... RT
Register Transfer Computer-Aided Design (MHDI) .... RTCAD
Register Transfer Language [*Computer science*] (CSR) .... RTL
Register Transfer Level .... RTL
Register Transfer Module [*Computer science*] (MDG) .... RTM
Register Translator [*Telecommunications*] (TEL) .... R/T
Registered .... R
Registered (ROG) .... RD
Registered [*Stock exchange term*] (SPSG) .... REG
Registered (EY) .... REGD
Registered .... REGD
Registered .... REGSTD
Registered Air Parcel Post .... RAPP
Registered Apartment Manager [*National Association of Home Builders*] [*Designation awarded by*] .... RAM
Registered Architect (IIA) .... RA
Registered Architect .... Reg Arch
Registered at the United States Patent Office (BARN) .... Reg US Pat Off
Registered Australian Mortgage Securities Trust .... RAMS
Registered Business Programmer [*Offered earlier by Data Processing Management Association, now discontinued*] (IEEE) .... RBP
Registered Cardiopulmonary Technologist [*Medicine*] (WGA) .... RCPT
Registered Cardiovascular Technologist [*Medicine*] (WGA) .... RCVT
Registered Care Technician [*Proposed by American Medical Association to alleviate nursing shortage*] .... RCT
Registered Check .... RC
Registered Clubs Association of New South Wales [*Australia*] .... RCANSW
Registered Communications Distribution Designer [*Building Industry Consul ting Service International*] [*Designation awarded by*] (TSSD) .... RCDD
Registered Competitive Market Maker [*Stock exchange term*] (SPSG) .... RCMM
Registered Connective Device (MHDB) .... RCD
Registered Criminologist .... RC
Registered Dairy Cattle Association of Australia .... RDCAA
Registered Dental Assistant (DMAA) .... RDA
Registered Dental Hygienist .... RDH
Registered Designs Appeal Tribunal (DLA) .... RDAT
Registered Diagnostic Medical Sonologist .... RDMS
Registered Dietitian .... RD
Registered Education Savings Plan [*Canada*] .... RESP
Registered Electroencephalographic Technician [*Medicine*] (AAMN) .... REEGT
Registered Engineering Technologist (DD) .... RET
Registered Environmental Assessor .... REA
Registered Environmental Manager .... REM
Registered Environmental Professional .... REP
Registered Environmental Property Assessor .... REPA
Registered Equipment Management [*Air Force*] (AFM) .... REM
Registered Equipment Management System [*Air Force*] .... REMS
Registered Expected Death .... RED
Registered Export Establishment .... REE
Registered Fever Nurse .... RFN
Registered Financial Planner [*International Association of Registered Fin ancial Planners*] [*Designation awarded by*] .... RFP
Registered Financial Planners Institute (EA) .... RFPI
Registered Fitness Appraiser [*Canadian Association of Sports Sciences*] .... RFA
Registered General Nurse .... RGN
Registered Hazardous Substances Professional [*Environmental science*] .... RHSP
Registered Health Underwriter [*NAHU*] .... RHU
Registered Health Visitor [*British*] .... RHV
Registered Home Ownership Savings Plan .... RHOSP
Registered Hypnotist .... L Hy
Registered Industrial and Cost Accountant .... RIA
Registered Industrial Social Worker [*Designation awarded by the American Association of Industrial Social Workers*] .... RISW
Registered Investment Adviser [*Securities*] .... RIA
Registered Laboratory Technician [*Medicine*] (WGA) .... RLT
Registered Laundry and Linen Director [*National Association of Institutio nal Linen Management*] [*Designation awarded by*] .... RLLD
Registered Magistrate (WDAA) .... RM
Registered Mail (WDAA) .... RM
Registered Mail Central Bureau [*Later, RMIA*] (EA) .... RMCB
Registered Mail Insurance Association (EA) .... RMIA
Registered Massage Therapist .... RMT
Registered Medical Assistants [*Later, ARMA*] (EA) .... RMA
Registered Medical Practitioner [*British*] (ROG) .... RMP
Registered Medical Technologist (American Society of Clinical Pathologists) .... MT(ASCP)
Registered Mental Nurse .... RMN
Registered Midwife [*British*] (DBQ) .... RM
Registered Music Teacher .... RMT
Registered Music Therapist .... RMT
Registered Nuclear Medicine Technologist (DAVI) .... RNMT
Registered Nurse .... RN
Registered Nurse Anesthetist .... RNA
Registered Nurse, Certified (MEDA) .... RNC
Registered Nurse, Certified in Nursing Administration, Advanced (MEDA) .... RN CNAA
Registered Nurse, Certified Specialist (MEDA) .... RN CS
Registered Nurse for Mental Defectives .... RNMD
Registered Nurse for the Mentally Handicapped [*British*] (DBQ) .... RNMH
Registered Nurse for the Mentally Subnormal [*British*] .... RNMS
Registered Nurse, Interim Permit (MEDA) .... RNIP
Registered Nurse Practitioner (AAMN) .... RNP
Registered Nurse Tutor [*British*] .... RNT
Registered Nurses Association of British Columbia, Kootenay District Nursing Archives, Blueberry Creek, BC, Canada [*Library symbol*] [*Library of Congress*] (LCLS) .... CaBBCRN
Registered Nurses Association of British Columbia, Vancouver, British Columbia [*Library symbol National Library of Canada*] (NLC) .... BVARN
Registered Nurses Association, Vancouver, BC, Canada [*Library symbol Library of Congress*] (LCLS) .... CaBVaRN
Registered Nursing Assistant .... RNA
Registered Nursing Home Association [*British*] (DBA) .... RNHA
Registered Occupational Therapist (DAVI) .... ROT
Registered Office (WDAA) .... RO
Registered Options Principal .... ROP
Registered Organization Data Bank .... RODATA
Registered Organization Development Consultant [*Organization Development Institute*] [*Designation awarded by*] .... RODC
Registered Pharmacist .... RG PH
Registered Pharmacist (DAVI) .... RP
Registered Pharmacist .... RPH
Registered Physical Therapist .... RPT
Registered Plumbers [*British*] .... RP
Registered Postal Packet .... RPP
Registered Professional Dietitian .... RPDt
Registered Professional Engineer (DD) .... PEng
Registered Professional Engineer (IEEE) .... RPE
Registered Professional Forester .... RPF
Registered Professional Nurse .... RPN
Registered Protective Circuit .... RPC
Registered Public Accountant .... RPA
Registered Publication Clerk [*or Custodian*] [*Navy*] .... RPC
Registered Publication Issuing Office [*Military*] .... RPIO
Registered Publication Mobile Issuing Office [*Military*] .... RPMIO
Registered Publication Shipment Memorandum .... RPSM
Registered Publication Unit .... RPU
Registered Publication Van Issuing Office [*Military*] (NVT) .... RPVIO
Registered Publications Manual [*Navy*] .... RPM
Registered Publications Memorandum .... RPM
Registered Publications Officer [*Navy*] (DNAB) .... RPO
Registered Publications Section - District Library [*Navy*] .... RPS-DL
Registered Publications Section - Personnel Library [*Navy*] .... RPS-PL
Registered Publications Subissuing Office [*Military*] (NVT) .... RPSIO
Registered Publications System .... RPS
Registered Real Estate Salespersons' Association [*Australia*] .... RRESA
Registered Record Administrator [*American Medical Record Association*] [*Medicine*] .... RRA
Registered Record Librarian [*Medicine*] .... RRL
Registered Recreation Therapist .... RRT
Registered Representative [*Wall Street stock salesman*] .... RR
Registered Respiratory Therapist .... RRT
Registered Retirement Investment Fund [*Canada*] .... RRIF
Registered Retirement Savings Plan [*Canada*] .... RRSP
Registered Sanitarian .... RS
Registered Schools Board [*Victoria, Australia*] .... RSB
Registered Ships' Plumbers [*British*] .... RP (Ships)
Registered Shoeing Smith [*Blacksmith*] [*Scotland*] .... RSS
Registered Sick Children's Nurse [*British*] .... RSCN
Registered Student Nurse Program [*Military*] (AABC) .... RSNP
Registered Student of the Institution of Body Engineers [*British*] (DBQ) .... RSBEI
Registered Technician [*American Registry of X-ray Technicians*] .... RT
Registered Technologist [*Radiology*] (DAVI) .... RT
Registered Technologist in Nuclear Medicine Technology (American Registry of Radiologic Technologists) (MAE) .... RTN(ARRT)
Registered Technologist in Radiation Therapy Technology (American Registry of Radiologic Technologists) (MAE) .... RTT(ARRT)
Registered Technologist in Radiography (American Registry of Radiologic Technologists) (MAE) .... RTR(ARRT)
Registered Technologist (Nuclear) (DAVI) .... TR(N)
Registered Technologist, Nuclear Medicine (MEDA) .... RTN
Registered Technologist, Radiography (MEDA) .... RTR
Registered Technologist (Radiology) (DAVI) .... RT(R)
Registered Technologist (Therapy) (DAVI) .... RT(T)
Registered Trade Name .... RTN
Registered Trademark (DAVI) .... R
Registered Trademark (BARN) .... Reg TM
Registered Trademark (CDAI) .... RT

Registered Trademark (DEN) ... RTM
Registered Transmitter (IAA) ... RT
Registered Vascular Technologist (DAVI) ... RVT
Registering (ROG) ... REGING
Register-to-Register Instruction (IAA) ... RR
Register-to-Register Operation (IAA) ... RR
Register-Transistor Logic [*Computer science*] ... RTL
Registrants Processing Manual [*Selective Service System*] ... RPM
Registrar (ROG) ... R
Registrar (ROG) ... REG
Registrar ... REGR
Registrar ... REGR
Registrar ... REGSTR
Registrar Data Group [*Information service or system*] (IID) ... RDG
Registrar of Aboriginal Corporations [*Australia*] ... RAC
Registrar of Births Deaths and Marriages [*Australia*] ... RBDM
Registrar of Cooperative Societies [*New South Wales, Australia*] ... RCS
Registrar of Finance Brokers [*Victoria, Australia*] ... RFB
Registrar's Book, Chancery [*A publication*] (DLA) ... Reg Lib
Registrar's Book, Keith's Court of Chancery [*Pennsylvania*] [*A publication*] (DLA) ... Keith Ch PA
Registration (ODBW) ... reg
Registration [*ICAO designator*] (FAAC) ... REG
Registration ... REGSTRTN
Registration Act ... RA
Registration/Admission, Disposition and Transfer [*Tri-Service Medical Information System*] (DNAB) ... R/ADT
Registration Appeals [*A publication*] (DLA) ... RA
Registration Appeals [*England*] [*A publication*] (DLA) ... Reg App
Registration Cases [*A publication*] (DLA) ... RC
Registration Cases [*A publication*] (DLA) ... Reg
Registration Cases [*England*] [*A publication*] (DLA) ... Reg Cas
Registration Division [*Environmental Protection Agency*] (EPA) ... RD
Registration of Interest ... ROI
Registration Offering Statistics System [*Securities and Exchange Commission*] (GFGA) ... ROS
Registration Services ... RS
Registration Type (NITA) ... RT
Registre International des Citoyens du Monde [*International Registry of World Citizens*] ... RICM
Registro de la Propiedad Industrial [*Spanish Patent Office*] [*Information service or system*] (IID) ... RPI
Registro Italiano [*Shipping*] (ROG) ... I
Registro Italiano [*Italian ship classification society*] (DS) ... RI
Registrum Omnium Brevium [*Register of Writs*] [*Latin A publication*] (DSA) .... Reg
Registrum Omnium Brevium [*Register of Writs*] [*Latin A publication*] (DLA) ... Reg Brev
Registrum Omnium Brevium [*Register of Writs*] [*Latin A publication*] (DLA) ... Reg Om Brev
Registrum Originale [*Latin A publication*] (DLA) ... Reg Orig
Registry ... REG
Registry (ROG) ... REGY
Registry ... RGSTY
Registry, Inc. (The) [*NASDAQ symbol*] (SAG) ... REGI
Registry, Inc. (The) [*Associated Press*] (SAG) ... Registry
Registry Number ... REGN
Registry Number ... RN
Registry Number/Chemical Abstracts Number [*American Chemical Society information file*] ... REG/CAN
Registry of Comparative Pathology (EA) ... RCP
Registry of Friendly Societies [*British*] ... FS
Registry of Friendly Societies [*British*] (ILCA) ... RFS
Registry of Interpreters for the Deaf (EA) ... RID
Registry of Italian Oddities (EA) ... RIO
Registry of Life Assurance Commission [*British*] ... ROLAC
Registry of Medical Technologists ... RMT
Registry of Tissue Reactions to Drugs [*Later, DETP*] (EA) ... TRD
Registry of Toxic Effects of Chemical Substances [*Department of Health and Human Services Information service or system A publication*] ... RTECS
Regius Professor [*The King's Professor*] [*British*] ... RegProf
Regius Professor [*The King's Professor*] [*British*] ... RP
Regius Professor of Divinity (ROG) ... RPD
Reglement [*Administrative Ordinance or Rule of Procedure*] [*French*] (ILCA)..... Regl
Reglement du Service International des Telecommunications de l'Aeronautique ... RSITA
Reglement International Concernant le Transport des Marchandises Dangereuses [*International Regulation Governing the Carriage of Dangerous Goods*] ... RID
Reglement Telegraphique [*Telegraph Regulations*] [*French*] ... RTG
Regna [*Queen*] [*Latin*] (DLA) ... R
Regnecentralen BASIC (NITA) ... RC BASIC
Regnecentralen COMAL (NITA) ... RC COMAL
Regnecentralen Computer (NITA) ... RC
Regolamento Internazionale Carrozze [*International Carriage and Van Union*] ... RIC
Regolamento Internazionale Veicoli [*Italian generic term meaning "International Regulation of Vehicles"*] [*Initialism also refers to International Wagon Union*] ... RIV
Regourd Aviation [*France ICAO designator*] (FAAC) ... REG
Regrade Unclassified Upon Receipt [*Air Force*] ... RUUR
Regressing Atypical Histiocytosis [*Medicine*] ... RAH
Regressing Friend Virus ... RFV
Regression Analysis [*Military*] (IAA) ... REG
Regression Analysis [*Military*] (IAA) ... REGRA
Regression Analysis Program [*Military*] ... RAP
Regression Coefficient [*Statistics*] (BARN) ... b
Regression Coefficient (AAMN) ... R
Regression Estimation of Event Probabilities (IEEE) ... REEP
Regression Expert [*Computer science*] ... REX
Regression Specification Error Test [*Statistics*] ... RESET
Regression Testing [*Computer science*] (IEEE) ... RT
Regression-Associated Protein [*Biochemistry*] ... RAP
Regressive Tax (MHDW) ... RT
Regroupement d'Artistes des Centres Alternatifs [*Association of National Non-Profit Artists' Centres ANNPAC*] [*Canada*] ... RACA
Regroupement des Auteurs-Editeurs Autonomes [*Canada*] ... RAEA
Regroupement des Guineens a l'Exterieur [*Rally of Guineans Abroad*] (PD) ... RGE
Regroupement des Independants et Paysans Camerounais [*Regrouping of Independents and Farmers of the Cameroons*] ... RIPC
Regroupement des Officiers Communistes [*Burkina Faso*] [*Political party*] (EY) ... ROC
Regroupement des Organisations Nationales Benevoles [*Also, National Voluntary Organizations*] (AC) ... ONBT
Regroupement des Partis de la Cote-D'Ivoire [*Regroupment of the Parties of the Ivory Coast*] ... RPCI
Regula Generalis [*General Rule or Order of Court*] [*Latin A publication*] (DLA) ... RG
Regula Placitandi [*Rule of Pleading*] [*Latin*] [*Legal term*] (BARN) ... Reg Pl
Regulae Generales [*A publication*] (DLA) ... Reg Gen
Regular (ADA) ... R
Regular (AAG) ... REG
Regular (ROG) ... REGUL
Regular (MSA) ... RGLR
Regular Air Force ... RAF
Regular Air Force ... REGAF
Regular Army ... RA
Regular Army and Militia [*British*] ... RAM
Regular Army Reserve ... RAR
Regular Army Reserve of Officers [*British*] ... RARO
Regular Army Special Reserve (ADA) ... RASR
Regular Associated Troupers (EA) ... RAT
Regular Best Asymptotically Normal (PDAA) ... RBAN
Regular Budget [*United Nations*] ... RB
Regular Care Technologist ... RCT
Regular Commissions Board [*British military*] (DMA) ... RCB
Regular Common Carrier Conference (EA) ... RCCC
Regular Defence Force Welfare Association [*Australia*] ... RDFWA
Regular Dialysis Treatment [*Medicine*] ... RDT
Regular Education Teachers and Principals Project (EDAC) ... RETAP
Regular Educator Expectancy Scale (EDAC) ... REES
Regular Eight [*Motion picture*] (VRA) ... REGE
Regular Expression (IAA) ... RE
Regular Expression [*Computer science*] (NHD) ... REGEXP
Regular Federal Funds [*Medicaid*] (GFGA) ... RFF
Regular Forces Employment Association [*British military*] (DMA) ... RFEA
Regular Geophysical Day ... RGD
Regular Inertial Navigator (MCD) ... RIN
Regular Insulin [*Pharmacology*] (DAVI) ... RI
Regular Member of the Third House [*Pseudonym used by Dr. Francis Bacon*] ... RMTH
Regular Military Compensation (AABC) ... RMC
Regular Nursery [*Neonatology*] (DAVI) ... reg nsy
Regular Officer Training Plan [*Canada*] ... ROTP
Regular Order ... R/O
Regular Overhaul [*Navy*] (NG) ... ROH
Regular Pending Transaction [*IRS*] ... PN
Regular Priority [*Wire service symbol*] (NTCM) ... R
Regular Production Option [*Automotive engineering*] ... RPO
Regular Public Transport (ADA) ... RPT
Regular Rate and Rhythm [*Cardiology*] (AAMN) ... RRR
Regular Reenlistment Bonus [*Military*] ... RRB
Regular Respirations [*Medicine*] (MEDA) ... RR
Regular Respirations [*Medicine*] (DAVI) ... RR
Regular Retail Price ... RRP
Regular Rhythm [*Cardiology*] (DAVI) ... RR
Regular Right Part Grammar (IAA) ... RRPG
Regular Route Carrier ... RRC
Regular Savings ... RS
Regular Sinus Rhythm [*Physiology*] ... RSR
Regular, Slotted, Corrugated [*Container*] ... RSC
Regular Spiking Activity [*Electrophysiology*] ... RSA
Regular Station [*Military*] ... RS
Regular Unleaded [*Shell Oil Co.*] ... RU
Regular Veterans Association (NADA) ... RVA
Regular Veterans Association of the United States (EA) ... RVA
Regular Way Delivery ... RWD
Regular World Day ... RWD
Regular World Interval ... RWI
Regularize Discriminant Analysis [*Mathematics*] ... RDA
Regularized Least-Squares [*Mathematics*] ... RLS
Regularly Scheduled [*Red Cross Volunteer*] ... RS
Regularly-Scheduled Training [*Military*] (ADDR) ... RST
Regulate (AAG) ... REG
Regulate (MSA) ... RGL
Regulated (MSA) ... RGLTD
Regulated Air Pressure System (MCD) ... RAPS
Regulated Business Operations Fund (AAGC) ... RBOF
Regulated Common Carrier [*Computer science*] (TNIG) ... RCC
Regulated Deficit Irrigation ... RDI

Regulated Electrical Supply Package .... RESP
Regulated Gallery [*Nuclear energy*] (NRCH) .... RG
Regulated Investment Company [*Business term*] .... RIC
Regulated Motor Carriers .... RMC
Regulated Output (FAAC) .... RO
Regulated Oxygen Supply (MCD) .... ROS
Regulated Oxygen System (NASA) .... ROS
Regulated Power Module .... RPM
Regulated Power Supply .... RPS
Regulated Substance [*Environmental Protection Agency*] .... RS
Regulated [*or Restricted*] **Takeoff Weight** (MCD) .... RTOW
Regulated-upon-Activation, Normal T Expressed and Secreted [*Immunology*] .... RANTES
Regulating .... R
Regulating [*Duties*] [*Navy British*] .... REG
Regulating (MSA) .... RGLT
Regulating Petty Officer [*British*] .... RPO
Regulating Petty Officer WREN [*Women's Royal Naval Service*] [*British military*] (DMA) .... REGPOWREN
Regulating Station [*Military*] .... RS
Regulating Station [*Army*] .... RSta
Regulating Valve Actuating Valve (KSC) .... RVAV
Regulation .... REG
Regulation (AAG) .... REGLN
Regulation (ROG) .... REGLON
Regulation .... REGULAT
Regulation and Information Management Division [*Environmental Protection Agency*] (EPA) .... RIMD
Regulation Appeals [*A publication*] (DLA) .... RA
Regulation Communication Center [*RSPA*] (TAG) .... RCC
Regulation Interpretation Memorandum [*Environmental Protection Agency*] .... RIM
Regulation Station [*Air Force*] .... RS
Regulations .... REGS
Regulations Governing the Meat Inspection [*of the USDA*] .... RGMI
Regulations of British Columbia [*Attorney General's Ministry*] [*No longer available online*] [*Information service or system*] (CRD) .... RBC
Regulations of Connecticut State Agencies [*A publication*] (DLA) .... Conn Agencies Reg
Regulations of Connecticut State Agencies (AAGC) .... Regs Conn State Agencies
Regulations of Office of the Secretary, Department of Transportation .... RSDT
Regulations of the Civil Aeronautics Board .... RCB
Regulations under the Federal Power Act .... RUFP
Regulations under the Natural Gas Act .... RNG
Regulator (DEN) .... REG
Regulator (AAG) .... REGR
Regulator .... REGT
Regulator (MSA) .... RGLTR
Regulator of Complement Activation [*Biochemistry*] .... RCA
Regulator of Mitotic Spindle Assembly [*Cytology*] .... RMS
Regulator of Mitotic Spindle Assembly (DMAA) .... RMSA
Regulator of Virion-Protein Expression [*Genetics*] .... REV
Regulators of G-Protein Signalling [*Biochemistry*] .... RGS
Regulatory [*Gene*] [*Genetics*] (DAVI) .... R
Regulatory .... RGLTRY
Regulatory Accounting Practices [*or Principles*] [*Business term*] .... RAP
Regulatory Activities Manpower System [*Nuclear energy*] (NRCH) .... RAMS
Regulatory Affairs Professionals Society (EA) .... RAPS
Regulatory Alternative [*Federal government*] (GFGA) .... RA
Regulatory Analysis [*Federal government*] (GFGA) .... RA
Regulatory Analysis Program [*Federal government*] .... RAP
Regulatory Analysis Review Group [*Comprising several federal agencies*] .... RARG
Regulatory Council [*FAA*] (MCD) .... RC
Regulatory Flexibility Act .... RFA
Regulatory Flexibility Analysis (AAGC) .... RFA
Regulatory Guide [*Nuclear energy*] (NRCH) .... RG
Regulatory Identifier Number [*Environmental Protection Agency*] .... RIN
Regulatory Impact Analysis [*or Assessment*] .... RIA
Regulatory Impact Statement .... RIS
Regulatory Information Distribution System [*Nuclear energy*] (NRCH) .... RIDS
Regulatory Information on Pesticide Products [*Database*] (IT) .... RIPP
Regulatory Information Service [*Congressional Information Service, Inc.*] [*Information service or system Defunct*] .... RIS
Regulatory Information Service Center [*Office of Management and Budget*] (GFGA) .... RISC
Regulatory Integration Division [*Environmental Protection Agency*] (GFGA) .... RID
Regulatory Light Chain [*Physiology*] .... RLC
Regulatory Manpower System [*Nuclear energy*] (NRCH) .... RMS
Regulatory Monitoring System (NRCH) .... RMS
Regulatory Negotiation .... REG-NEG
Regulatory Performance Summary [*Report*] [*Nuclear energy*] (NRCH) .... RPS
Regulatory Policy Division [*Environmental Protection Agency*] (EPA) .... RPD
Regulatory Reform Staff [*Environmental Protection Agency*] (EPA) .... RRS
Regulatory Requirements Review Committee [*Nuclear energy*] (NRCH) .... RRRC
Regulatory Technical Memorandum [*Nuclear energy*] (NRCH) .... RTM
Regulatory Volume Decrease [*Cytology*] .... RVD
Regulatory Volume Increase [*Cytology*] .... RVI
Regulatory-Catalytic Unit [*Physiology*] .... RC
Regulus Resources, Inc. [*Vancouver Stock Exchange symbol*] .... RGR
Regummed [*Philately*] .... RG
Regurgitate and Reingest [*Animal behavior*] .... R & R
Regurgitation [*Medicine*] (DAVI) .... regurg
RehabCare Corp. [*NASDAQ symbol*] (SPSG) .... RHBC
RehabCare Group [*NASDAQ symbol*] (TTSB) .... RHBC
RehabCare Group, Inc. [*Associated Press*] (SAG) .... RehabG
RehabCare Group, Inc. [*Associated Press*] (SAG) .... RehabGp
Rehabilicare, Inc. [*Associated Press*] (SAG) .... Rehabcre
Rehabilicare, Inc. [*NASDAQ symbol*] (SAG) .... REHB
Rehabilitate [*or Rehabilitation*] (AFM) .... REHAB
Rehabilitation .... REHAB
Rehabilitation .... REHABIL
Rehabilitation Act (OICC) .... RA
Rehabilitation and Chronic Disease Hospital Section [*American Hospital Association*] (EA) .... RCDHS
Rehabilitation and Research Center for Torture Victims (EAIO) .... RCT
Rehabilitation Artificial Limb, and Appliance Centre [*Australia*] .... RALAC
Rehabilitation Budgeting Program [*Telecommunications*] (TEL) .... REBUD
Rehabilitation Center .... RC
Rehabilitation Counselor .... RC
Rehabilitation Engineering Center for the Hearing Impaired [*Gallaudet College*] [*Research center*] (RCD) .... REC
Rehabilitation Engineering Centers [*Department of Health and Human Services*] .... REC
Rehabilitation Engineering Movement Advisory Panel (ACII) .... REMAP
Rehabilitation Engineering Program [*Research center*] (RCD) .... REP
Rehabilitation Evolution System [*Medicine*] .... RES
Rehabilitation in Australia [*A publication*] .... Rehab Aust
Rehabilitation Information Round Table (EA) .... RIR
Rehabilitation Information Round Table (EA) .... RIRT
Rehabilitation Institute of Chicago, Chicago, IL [*Library symbol*] [*Library of Congress*] (LCLS) .... ICRI
Rehabilitation Institute of Michigan .... RIM
Rehabilitation Institute of Montreal, Montreal, PQ, Canada [*Library symbol Library of Congress*] (LCLS) .... CaQMRI
Rehabilitation Institute of Montreal [*Institut de Rehabilitation de Montreal*] **Quebec** [*Library symbol National Library of Canada*] (NLC) .... QMRI
Rehabilitation International (EA) .... RI
Rehabilitation International USA .... RIUSA
Rehabilitation Medicine Service [*Veterans Administration*] .... RMS
Rehabilitation of Addicted Prisoners Trust [*British*] [*An association*] .... RAPT
Rehabilitation of Addicts by Relatives and Employers .... RARE
Rehabilitation of Offenders Act [*1974*] [*British*] (DCTA) .... ROA
Rehabilitation Record .... RR
Rehabilitation Record .... RREC
Rehabilitation Research and Development Program [*Veterans Administration*] (GFGA) .... RR & D
Rehabilitation Research and Training Center in Blindness and Low Vision [*Mississippi State University*] [*Research center*] (RCD) RTC-30
Rehabilitation Research and Training Centers [*Department of Health and Human Services*] .... RTC
Rehabilitation Research Foundation (EA) .... RRF
Rehabilitation Service Series .... RSS
Rehabilitation Services Administration [*Office of Special Education and Rehabilitive Services, Department of Education*] .... RSA
Rehabilitation Support Schedule (AFM) .... RSS
Rehabilitation Therapist [*or Therapy*] .... RT
Rehabilitative Engineering Research and Development Service [*Veterans Administration*] (GRD) .... RER & D
Rehabilitiation Institute, Detroit, MI [*Library symbol*] [*Library of Congress*] (LCLS) .... MiDRI
Rehearing [*Legal term*] (DLA) .... Reh'g
Rehearing Allowed [*Used in Shepard's Citations*] [*Legal term*] (DLA) .... Reh Allowed
Rehearing Denied [*Used in Shepard's Citations*] [*Legal term*] (DLA) .... Reh Den
Rehearing Denied by United States Supreme Court [*Legal term*] (DLA) .... US Reh Den
Rehearing Dismissed [*Used in Shepard's Citations*] [*Legal term*] (DLA) .... Reh Dis
Rehearing Dismissed by United States Supreme Court [*Legal term*] (DLA) .... US Reh Dis
Rehearsal Engineer (MCD) .... RE
Reheat (KSC) .... REHT
Reheater (AAG) .... RHR
Rehoboth [*Namibia*] [*ICAO location identifier*] (ICLI) .... FARH
Rehoboth Baster Association [*Namibia*] (PPW) .... RBA
Rehoboth Beach [*Delaware*] [*Airport symbol*] (AD) .... REH
Rehoboth Beach, DE [*Location identifier FAA*] (FAAL) .... REH
Rehoboth Beach, DE [*FM radio station call letters*] .... WGMD
Rehoboth Bevryde Demokratiese Party [*Rehoboth Free Democratic Party or Liberation Front*] [*Namibia*] [*Political party*] (EY) .... RBDP
Rehost Computer System [*Aviation*] (FAAC) .... RCS
Reich Ministry of Interior .... RMI
Reichelsheim [*Germany ICAO location identifier*] (ICLI) .... EDFB
Reichert Scientific Instruments, Buffalo, NY [*Library symbol*] [*Library of Congress*] (LCLS) .... NBuRSI
Reichhold Chemicals Ltd., Weston, Ontario [*Library symbol National Library of Canada*] (NLC) .... OTRCL
Reichhold Chemicals Ltd., Weston, Toronto, ON, Canada [*Library symbol Library of Congress*] (LCLS) .... CaOTRCL
Reichhold Ltd. [*Toronto Stock Exchange symbol*] .... RCL
Reichold [*Alabama*] [*Seismograph station code, US Geological Survey*] (SEIS) .... RHA
Reichsfinanzhof [*Reich Finance Court*] [*German*] (ILCA) .... RFH
Reichsgericht [*Reich Supreme Court*] [*German*] (ILCA) .... RG
Reichsleftfahrt Ministerium [*German Air Ministry*] [*World War II*] .... RLM
Reichsmark [*Later, DM*] [*Monetary unit*] [*German*] .... RM
Reichssicherheitshauptampt [*Central Security Office of the Reich*] [*NAZI Germany*] .... RSHA
Reid Crowther & Partners Ltd., Calgary, Alberta [*Library symbol National Library of Canada*] (BIB) .... ACRCP
Reid Vapor Pressure .... RVP
Reidland, KY [*FM radio station call letters*] .... WZZL

Reidovoe [*Former USSR Seismograph station code, US Geological Survey*] (SEIS) ... REI
Reid-Provident [*Commercial firm*] (DAVI) ... R-P
Reid-Rowell, Marietta, GA [*Library symbol*] [*Library of Congress*] (LCLS) ... GMarRR
Reid's Base Line [*Neuroanatomy*] ... RBL
Reid's Digest of Scotch Poor Law Cases [*A publication*] (DLA) ... Reid PL Dig
Reidsville, GA [*Location identifier FAA*] (FAAL) ... RVJ
Reidsville, GA [*FM radio station call letters*] ... WRBX
Reidsville, GA [*AM radio station call letters*] ... WTNL
Reidsville, NC [*Location identifier FAA*] (FAAL) ... OQA
Reidsville, NC [*Location identifier FAA*] (FAAL) ... SIF
Reidsville, NC [*FM radio station call letters*] ... WJMH
Reidsville, NC [*AM radio station call letters*] ... WREV
Reigate Resources (Canada) Ltd. [*Toronto Stock Exchange symbol*] ... RGC
Reigned ... R
Reilly's English Arbitration Cases [*A publication*] (DLA) ... Reilly
Reilly's European Arbitration. Lord Westbury's Decisions [*A publication*] (DLA) ... Reilly EA
Reimbursable Work Order [*Navy*] (NG) ... RWO
Reimburse (AABC) ... REIM
Reimburse (MSA) ... REIMB
Reimbursement Authorization (AFM) ... RA
Reimbursement in Accordance with Joint Travel Regulations ... REMBJTR
Reimbursement [*in Accordance with*] **Joint Travel Regulations** [*Military*] (DNAB) ... REIMBJTR
Reimbursement Refund Indicator [*Military*] (AFIT) ... RRI
Reimplantation [*Dentistry*] ... RI
Reims [*France ICAO location identifier*] (ICLI) ... LFEE
Reims [*France*] [*Airport symbol*] (OAG) ... RHE
Reims Aviation [*France ICAO aircraft manufacturer identifier*] (ICAO) ... RA
Reims/Champagne [*France ICAO location identifier*] (ICLI) ... LFSR
Reims/Prunay [*France ICAO location identifier*] (ICLI) ... LFQA
Reinbeck Courier, Reinbeck, IA [*Library symbol Library of Congress*] (LCLS) ... IaReiC
Reindeer Herders Association (EA) ... RHA
Reinforce ... REIN
Reinforce (AAG) ... REINF
Reinforced [*Technical drawings*] ... RE
Reinforced (AAG) ... REINFD
Reinforced (VRA) ... rnfd
Reinforced Alert (NATG) ... RA
Reinforced Brick Masonry ... R-B-M
Reinforced Carbon-Carbon (MCD) ... RCC
Reinforced Clostridial Medium [*Microbiology*] ... RCM
Reinforced Composite Joint ... RCJ
Reinforced Concrete [*Technical drawings*] ... RC
Reinforced Concrete [*Freight*] ... REFD CON
Reinforced Concrete Column [*Camutek*] [*Software package*] (NCC) ... RCCOL
Reinforced Concrete Culvert Pipe [*Technical drawings*] ... RCCP
Reinforced Concrete Detailing System (PDAA) ... RCDS
Reinforced Concrete Pavement ... RCP
Reinforced Concrete Pipe [*Technical drawings*] ... RCP
Reinforced Concrete Pressure Pipe ... RCPP
Reinforced Concrete Research Council (EA) ... RCRC
Reinforced Education Learning Laboratory (EA) ... RELL
Reinforced Metal [*Freight*] ... REFD MTL
Reinforced Oxide Throat Insert ... ROTI
Reinforced Plastic [*Packaging*] ... RP
Reinforced Plastics/Composites Institute [*Later, SPICI*] (EA) ... RP/CI
Reinforced Plywood [*Freight*] ... REFD PLYWD
Reinforced Porcelain System [*Dentistry*] ... RPS
Reinforced Pyrolytic Plastic (NASA) ... RPP
Reinforced Reaction Injection Molding [*Plastics technology*] ... RRIM
Reinforced Structural Plastic ... RSP
Reinforced Theatre Plan [*Military British*] ... RTP
Reinforced Thermoplastic ... RTP
Reinforced Thermoplastic Polyurethane [*Plastics*] ... RTPU
Reinforced Thermoplastics ... RTP
Reinforced Tile Lintel [*Technical drawings*] ... RTL
Reinforcement ... REFMT
Reinforcement (AAG) ... REINFM
Reinforcement ... RFT
Reinforcement and Resupply of Europe (MCD) ... RARE
Reinforcement Control Depot [*Air Force*] ... RCD
Reinforcement Designee [*Air Force*] (AFM) ... RD
Reinforcement/Resupply [*To Europe*] (DOMA) ... Re/Re
Reinforcement Support Category [*DoD*] ... RSC
Reinforcement Testing for System Training (SAA) ... RETEST
Reinforcement Training Unit [*Army*] (AABC) ... RTU
Reinforcement Unit [*British military*] (DMA) ... RU
Reinforcement Value [*Psychology*] ... RV
Reinforcements (DSUE) ... REO
Reinforcing (AAG) ... REINFG
Reinforcing Bar (AAG) ... REBAR
Reinforcing Steel [*Technical drawings*] ... RST
Reinforcing Stimulus ... RS
Reinhart, Boerner, Van Deuren, Norris and Rieselbach, Law Library, Milwaukee, WI [*Library symbol Library of Congress*] (LCLS) ... WMR
Reinitialize (MCD) ... REINIT
Reinitiate (SAA) ... RI
Reinsch Test [*For urine mercury and arsenic*] (DAVI) ... REINCH
Reinsertion of Direct Current (IAA) ... REDC
Reinstallation and Removal Record (KSC) ... RARR
Reinstate Card (IAA) ... RC
Reinstated [*Regulation or order reinstated*] [*Used in Shepard's Citations*] [*Legal term*] (DLA) ... Rein
Reinstatement and Replacement (ADA) ... R & R
Reinsurance ... REINSR
Reinsurance (ADA) ... RI
Reinsurance Association of America [*Washington, DC*] (EA) ... RAA
Reinsurance Australia Corp. [*Commercial firm*] ... ReAC
Reinsurance Group of Amer [*NYSE symbol*] (TTSB) ... RGA
Reinsurance Group of America [*Associated Press*] (SAG) ... ReinsGp
Reinsurance Group of America, Inc. [*NYSE symbol*] (SPSG) ... RGA
Reinsurance Offices Association [*British*] (AIA) ... ROA
Reinventing Government [*Nickname for National Performance Review*] ... ReGo
Reise und Industrieflug [*Airline*] [*Germany*] ... RFG
Reissue [*of a book or periodical*] [*Publishing*] ... RI
Reitan Evaluation of Hemispheric Abilities and Brain Improvement Training [*Neuropsychology test*] ... REHABIT
Reitan Indiana Aphasic Screening Test [*Speech and Language Therapy*] (DAVI) ... RIAST
Reitan Strength of Grip [*Medicine*] (DAVI) ... RSG
Reiter Protein Complement Fixation [*Obsolete test for syphilis*] ... RPCF
Reiter Protein Complement Fixation [*Obsolete test for syphilis*] (CPH) ... RPF
Reiter Protein Reagin [*Biochemistry*] (DAVI) ... RPR
Reiteration [*Printing*] (ROG) ... REIT
Reiteration [*Printers' term*] (DSUE) ... RET
Reiter's Disease [*Medicine*] (DMAA) ... RD
Reiter's Syndrome [*Medicine*] ... RS
Reitland-Franklin Unit (AAMN) ... RF
Reitman's (Canada) Ltd. [*Toronto Stock Exchange symbol*] ... RET
Reiz [*Stimulus*] [*German Psychology*] ... R
Reiz-Limen [*Stimulus threshold*] [*Psychology*] ... RL
Reject (IDOE) ... rej
Reject (MSA) ... REJ
Reject ... RJ
Reject Failure Rate ... RFR
Reject Processing and Control System (MHDB) ... RPCS
Reject Sequence Number [*Computer science*] ... RSN
Reject Suspense File [*Army*] ... RSF
Reject Unit [*IRS*] ... REJU
Rejectable Hazard Rate (IEEE) ... RHR
Rejectable Quality Level ... RQL
Rejected Takeoff [*Aviation*] (MCD) ... RTO
Rejected Takeoff Area Available [*Aviation*] (DA) ... RTOAA
Rejection (IDOE) ... rej
Rejection and Disposition Item ... RDI
Rejection Disposition Notice ... RDN
Rejection Disposition Report [*NASA*] (KSC) ... RDR
Rejection Notice (AAG) ... RN
Rejection Purchase Order (MCD) ... RPO
Rejection Slip (ADA) ... R/S
Rejection Tag (AAG) ... RT
Rejoin (AABC) ... REJN
Rejoined (WGA) ... REJD
Reko [*Solomon Islands*] [*Seismograph station code, US Geological Survey*] (SEIS) ... RKS
Rektorskommitten for de Nordiska Journalist Hogskolorna [*Committee for Nordic Universities of Journalism - CNUJ*] [*Defunct*] (EAIO) ... RNJ
Relais Musique [*Phonorecord series*] [*Canada*] ... RM
Relapse [*Medicine*] (DMAA) ... R
Relapse-Free Survival [*Oncology*] ... RFS
Related ... REL
Related ... RELAT
Related ... RELTD
Related ... RLTD
Related Antigen [*Immunology*] ... RAg
Related Experience (SAA) ... REX
Related Living Donor [*Medicine*] ... RLD
Related Payroll Expense ... RPE
Related Production Equipment (SAA) ... RPE
Related Returns Notification System [*IRS*] ... RRNS
Related Technical Instruction [*Bureau of Apprenticeship and Training*] [*Department of Labor*] ... RTI
Related Term [*Indexing*] ... RT
Related To (DAVI) ... R/T
Related-Party International Transaction ... RPIT
Relating To (AABC) ... RLT
Relation [*Computer science*] ... R
Relation ... REL
Relation (DD) ... rel
Relation (ROG) ... RELATN
Relation (MSA) ... RLTN
Relational Algebra Accelerator [*Computer board*] ... RAA
Relational Algebraic Interpreter ... RAIN
Relational Associative Processor (IEEE) ... RAP
Relational Data Base (PDAA) ... RDB
Relational Data Management System (MHDI) ... RDMS
Relational Database ... RDB
Relational Database Engine (PCM) ... RDE
Relational Database Management System [*Computer science*] (BYTE) ... RDBMS
Relational Database Systems Inc. (NITA) ... RDS
Relational General Information System ... REGIS
Relational Information Management [*Acronym is title of a book by Wayne Erickson*] (PCM) ... RIM
Relational Machine Language ... RML
Relational Query-by-Example [*Computer interface*] [*FoxPro*] (PCM) ... RQBE
Relational Structure Vertex Processor (PDAA) ... RSVP

Relational Technology, Inc. (MHDW)	RELY
Relational Technology Inc. (NITA)	RTI
Relations	REL
Relations	RELS
Relationship Anecdotes Paradigm Method [Psychology]	RAP
Relationship by Objective [Management technique]	RBO
Relationship Improvement Program (SAA)	RIP
Relative (IDOE)	rel
Relative	REL
Relative (AFM)	RLTV
Relative Abundance [Chemistry]	RA
Relative Accident Probability	RAP
Relative Accumulation Rate [Ecology]	RAR
Relative Accuracy Test (GFGA)	RAT
Relative Activity [Physiology]	RA
Relative Address	RA
Relative Address Programming Implementation Device [Computer science]	RAPID
Relative Aerobic Strain (PDAA)	RAS
Relative Air Density (OA)	RAD
Relative Antiair Defense Effectiveness Simulation [Military] (CAAL)	RAADES
Relative Basal Area of Conifer Species [Ecology]	RCBA
Relative Batch Monitor [Computer science] (MHDB)	RBM
Relative Bearing [Navigation]	RB
Relative Bearing [Aviation] (FAAC)	RLBG
Relative Bearing Indicator [Aviation] (DA)	RBI
Relative Binding Affinity [Chemistry]	RBA
Relative Biological Effectiveness [or Efficiency] [of stated types of radiation]	RBE
Relative Biological Value [Food science]	RBV
Relative Byte Address [Computer science] (MCD)	RBA
Relative Cardiac Dullness [Medicine]	RCD
Relative Casein Content [Food analysis]	RCC
Relative Centrifugal Force	RCF
Relative Citation Rate [Bibliography]	RCR
Relative Code (NITA)	RELCODE
Relative Competitive Preference [Marketing]	RCP
Relative Concentration [Symbol] (NRCH)	X/Q
Relative Conductor Volume	RCV
Relative Consumption Rate [Entomology]	RCR
Relative Corrected Death Rate [Medicine] (DMAA)	RCDR
Relative Corrector Program (IAA)	RCP
Relative [Force] Cost (MCD)	RC
Relative Covariance [Statistics]	RC
Relative Cumulative Frequency	RCF
Relative Density [Symbol] [IUPAC]	d
Relative Density	RD
Relative Detector Sensitivity [Robotics technology]	RDS
Relative Digestion Rate [Nutrition]	RDR
Relative Distinguished Name [Telecommunications] (OSI)	RDN
Relative Disturbance Gain [Control engineering]	RDG
Relative Effectiveness [or Efficiency] (MCD)	RE
Relative Electric Strength (MCD)	RES
Relative Element Address Designate (NITA)	READ
Relative Failure Frequency	RFF
Relative Flow [Rate]	RF
Relative Fluorescence [Analytical chemistry] (MAE)	RF
Relative Fluorescence Efficiency (DMAA)	RFF
Relative Fluorescent Intensity [Analytical chemistry]	RFI
Relative Force Capability (NATG)	RFC
Relative Frass Production [Ecology]	RFP
Relative Gain Array [Control engineering]	RGA
Relative Gas Expansion (AAMN)	RGE
Relative Gas Vacuolation [In algae]	RGV
Relative Growth Rate [Entomology]	RGR
Relative Hepatic Dullness [Medicine]	RHD
Relative Humidity	R
Relative Humidity (WDAA)	REL HUM
Relative Humidity	RH
Relative Humidity Control/Monitor (NASA)	RHCM
Relative Humidity Indicator (AAG)	RHI
Relative Humidity Monitor (GFGA)	RHM
Relative Ignition Temperature	RIT
Relative Impact Strength [Mechanical engineering]	RIS
Relative Importance Factor (NASA)	RIF
Relative Index of Combat Effectiveness [Military British]	RICE
Relative Index Register (NITA)	RIR
Relative Integral Square Error [Statistics] (IAA)	RISE
Relative Integrated Mean Square Error [Statistics]	RIMSE
Relative Intensity	RI
Relative Intensity Measures [of nursing care]	RIM
Relative Ionospheric Opacity Meter	RIOMETER
Relative Jostle Biological Effectiveness	RJBE
Relative Light Units [Analysis of light intensity]	RLU
Relative Luminous Efficiency (NATG)	RLE
Relative Matrix (MCD)	RELMAT
Relative Mean Square Error [Statistics]	RMSE
Relative Medullary Area [Medicine] (DMAA)	RMA
Relative Medullary Thickness [of kidney] [Medicine] (BABM)	RMT
Relative Medullary Thickness [of kidney] [Nephrology] (DAVI)	RMT
Relative Mobility [of ions] [Chemistry]	RM
Relative Molecular Mass (DOG)	Mr
Relative Motion Collision Avoidance Calculator (PDAA)	REMCALC
Relative Navigational Reference Beacon [Military] (CAAL)	RNRB
Relative Net Protein Ratio [Nutrition]	RNPR

Relative Nutritive Value [Nutrition]	RNV
Relative Operating Characteristics (MCD)	ROC
Relative Peak Area [Medicine]	RPA
Relative Performance Score [Telecommunications] (TEL)	RPS
Relative Plate Motion [Geophysics]	RPM
Relative Position Indication (NRCH)	RPI
Relative Position Velocity Technique	RPVT
Relative Potency (DAVI)	RP
Relative Power Density	RPD
Relative Pressure (KSC)	RP
Relative Price Effect	RPE
Relative Prime Transform	RPT
Relative Priority Test Circuit (MHDI)	RPTC
Relative Pronoun [Grammar] (WDAA)	REL PRON
Relative Pulse Height (OA)	RPH
Relative Quantum Efficiency (OA)	RQE
Relative Quantum Yield	RQY
Relative Rank	RR
Relative Record Data Set	RRDS
Relative Record Number [Computer science]	RRN
Relative Refractory Period [Medicine]	RRP
Relative Response	RR
Relative Retention Time	RRT
Relative Risk [Medicine]	RR
Relative Rod Position Indication [Nuclear energy] (NRCH)	RRPI
Relative Rumble Loudness Level (DICI)	RRLL
Relative Sea Level	RSL
Relative Sensitivity Factor [Analytical chemistry]	RSF
Relative Shunt Flow [Medicine] (DAVI)	Qsrel
Relative Signal Strength (IAA)	R
Relative Specific Activity	RSA
Relative Standard Accuracy [Testing methodology]	RSA
Relative Standard Deviation [Statistics]	RSD
Relative Standard Error [DOE] (TAG)	RSE
Relative Standard Mortality Rate (DMAA)	RSMR
Relative Stock Density [Pisciculture]	RSD
Relative Stopping Power [Nuclear energy] (NUCP)	RSP
Relative Substitution Frequency [of amino acids in proteins]	RSF
Relative Survival Rate [Statistics] (DAVI)	RSR
Relative Sweetness	RS
Relative System Capability	RSC
Relative System Sensitivity	RSS
Relative Threat Number [Military] (CAAL)	RTN
Relative Threat Priority [Military] (CAAL)	RTP
Relative Time Clock [Computer science] (MDG)	RTC
Relative to an Identified Distribution Transformation [Pharmacology]	RIDIT
Relative to the Solvent Front [Paper chromatography] [Analytical chemistry]	Rf
Relative Transcription Level [Genetics]	RTL
Relative Unit [Typography]	RU
Relative Universal Business Automation Code	RUBAC
Relative Value Index [Medicine] (MAE)	RVI
Relative Value Scale [or Schedule or Study] [Medicine]	RVS
Relative Value Unit	RVU
Relative Velocity Computer	RVC
Relative Vertebral Density	RVD
Relative Virtual Address [Computer science] (PCM)	RVA
Relative Voltage	VR
Relative Volt-Ampere	RVA
Relative Water Content	RWC
Relative Water Level	RWL
Relative Water-Level Recorder	RWLR
Relative Weight Response	RWR
Relative Worth (MCD)	RW
Relative Yield [Agriculture]	RY
Relative Yield Total [Agriculture]	RYT
Relative-Intensity Measure [Medicine] (DMAA)	RIM
Relatively Afferent Pupillary Defect [Ophthalmology]	RAPD
Relatively Easy to Test [Audiology]	RETT
Relative-Motion Control [Microcopy]	RMC
Relative-Motion Gauge	RMG
Relativistic and Spin-Orbit (PDAA)	RSO
Relativistic Electron Beam (MCD)	REB
Relativistic Electron Beam Accelerator	REBA
Relativistic Electron Coil Experiment (MCD)	RECE
Relativistic Electron Precipitation [Meteorology]	REP
Relativistic Heavy Ion Collider [Nuclear physics]	RHIC
Relativistic Kinematics (PDAA)	RELKIN
Relativistic Random-Phase Approximation [Electrodynamics]	RRPA
Relativity	REL
Relatore [Reporter] [Italian] (ILCA)	Rel
Relaxation (MSA)	RLXN
Relaxation Delay	RD
Relaxation Instruction [Psychology]	RI
Relaxation Map Analysis [Coatings]	RMA
Relaxation Oscillator Optically Tuned	ROOT
Relaxation Potential Model [Physics]	RPM
Relaxation Time	RT
Relaxation Time Index [Cardiology]	RTI
Relaxation Training [Psychology]	RT
Relaxation Volume (MAE)	RV
Relaxation-Sensitive Cell (PDAA)	RSC
Relaxed	R
Relaxed Pelvic Floor [Medicine]	RPF
Relaxed Skin Tension Line [Dermatology]	RSTL
Relaxed Static Stability [Aviation]	RSS

Relaxed Two-Color Stimulated Echo [*Spectroscopy*] R2CSE
Relaxed Vaginal Outlet [*Medicine*] .... RVO
Relaxin [*Biochemistry*] .... RLX
Relaxin [*Medicine*] (DAVI) .... URF
Relaxing Avalanche Mode (IAA) .... RAM
Relay (CET) .... K
Relay (DNAB) .... R
Relay (AAG) .... REL
Relay (AAG) .... RLY
Relay (DEN) .... RY
Relay Alarm (AAG) .... RYALM
Relay Antenna Subsystem [*NASA*] .... RAS
Relay Assemblies [*JETDS nomenclature*] [*Military*] (CET) .... RE
Relay Block (MSA) .... RB
Relay Computer (BUR) .... RC
Relay Control Unit (AAG) .... RCU
Relay Creek Resources Ltd. [*Vancouver Stock Exchange symbol*] .... RYK
Relay Drawer .... RD
Relay Driver .... RD
Relay Driver Module .... RDM
Relay Engineer (IAA) .... RE
Relay Equipment out of Operation (FAAC) .... RLANO
Relay Equipment Resumed Operation (FAAC) .... RLAOK
Relay Extractor Tool .... RET
Relay Junction Box (KSC) .... RJB
Relay Ladder Logic (ACII) .... RLL
Relay Logic .... RL
Relay Logic Unit (IAA) .... RLU
Relay Mirror Experiment .... RME
Relay Mode Control (IAA) .... RMC
Relay Panel .... RP
Relay Position Indicator .... RPI
Relay Power Supply (MCD) .... RPS
Relay Rack [*Telecommunications*] (TEL) .... RR
Relay Rack Panel .... RRP
Relay Radio Subsystem [*NASA*] .... RRS
Relay, Reporter, Responder [*Military*] (CAAL) .... R^3
Relay, Reporter, Responder (DWSG) .... RRR
Relay Selector (IAA) .... RS
Relay Services Association of Great Britain (BI) .... RSA
Relay Servicing Tool Kit .... RSTK
Relay Set [*Telecommunications*] (TEL) .... R/S
Relay Set Receiver [*Telecommunications*] (IAA) .... RSR
Relay Station (IAA) .... RSTN
Relay Storage Unit .... RSU
Relay Switch Group .... RSG
Relay Telemetry Subsystem [*NASA*] .... RTS
Relay Test and Verification System (MCD) .... RTVS
Relay Test System .... RTS
Relay Tester .... RT
Relay To [*ICAO*] (FAAC) .... RLA
Relay Transformer Header .... RTH
Relay Transmitter .... RT
Relay-Contact Network (PDAA) .... RCN
Relayed Correlation Spectroscopy (DMAA) .... RELAY
Relaynet International Message Exchange [*Information network*] [*Computer science*] (PCM) .... RIME
Relay-Operated Sampling Oscilloscope .... ROSO
Relay-Operated Voltage Divider .... ROVD
Releasable Asset Program [*Military*] (AFIT) .... RAM
Releasable Assets Program .... RAP
Releasable Assets Program - Transferable Assets Program [*Navy*] (NG) .... RAP-TAP
Release .... RE
Release (AAG) .... REL
Release (ROG) .... RELE
Release (MSA) .... RLSE
Release and Approval Center (MCD) .... RAC
Release and Material (MCD) .... R & M
Release Authorization .... RA
Release Card .... RC
Release Clause [*Real estate*] .... RC
Release Engine Mechanism (NASA) .... REM
Release Engine Module (MCD) .... REM
Release Engineering Change Proposal (MCD) .... RECP
Release Escape Mechanism (MCD) .... REM
Release Factor (NRCH) .... RF
Release for Experimental Flight Test (NG) .... REFT
Release for Issue (MCD) .... RFI
Release for Manufacture (DNAB) .... RFM
Release from Active Duty [*Army*] .... REFRAD
Release from Active Duty for Training [*Army*] (AABC) .... REFRACDUTRA
Release from Active Duty for Training [*Army*] (AABC) .... REFRADT
Release from Annual Active Duty for Training [*Army*] (AABC) .... REFRANACDUTRA
Release from Annual Training [*Army*] (AABC) .... REFRAT
Release Guard [*Telecommunications*] (TEL) .... RG
Release Guard [*Telecommunications*] (TEL) .... RLG
Release Guard Signal [*Telecommunications*] (EECA) .... RGS
Release Load .... RL
Release Note [*Shipping*] (DS) .... RN
Release of Excess Funds .... REF
Release of Genetically Engineered Microorganisms [*A conference*] .... REGEM
Release of Material for Issue .... RMI
Release Order Directive [*Later, ERO*] (NRCH) .... ROD
Release Paper Manufacturers Association [*British*] (DBA) .... RePMA
Release Point [*Ground traffic*] [*Military*] .... RP
Release Program Unit (DWSG) .... RPU
Release Schedule Code (SAA) .... RSC
Release Suspension for Issue and Use of Following Lots [*Military*] .... RSIUFL
Release Timer [*Telecommunications*] (TEL) .... RLST
Release Transmittal (MCD) .... RT
Release Unit [*Army*] (AABC) .... RU
Release Valve [*Nuclear energy*] (NRCH) .... RV
Release with Service (OICC) .... RWS
Released Data Index .... RDI
Released for Delivery (NG) .... RFD
Released from Active Duty [*Navy*] .... RAD
Released from Active Duty [*Navy*] (DNAB) .... RELACDU
Released from Active Duty Not Result of Demobilization [*Navy*] .... RFAD
Released on Own Recognizance [*Law*] .... ROR
Released Time .... RT
Released to Inactive Duty .... RID
Released Value [*Freight*] .... RV
Released-Action [*Pharmacy*] .... RA
Release-Engage [*or Engagement*] **Mechanism** (NASA) .... REM
Release-Inhibiting Factor [*Endocrinology*] (MAE) .... RI
Release-Inhibiting Factor [*Endocrinology*] .... RIF
Release-Quiesce [*Computer science*] .... RELQ
Releases Control Branch [*Edison, NJ*] [*Environmental Protection Agency*] (GRD) .... RCB
Releasing Factor [*Also, RH*] [*Endocrinology*] .... RF
Releasing Hormone [*Also, RF*] [*Endocrinology*] .... RH
Relevant [*Computer science*] [*Telecommunications*] .... R
Relevant Labor Force (DNAB) .... RLF
Relevant Market Area [*Automotive dealership territory*] .... RMA
Relevant, Original, Impact [*Advertising*] (WDMC) .... ROI
Relevent Industry Sales (PDAA) .... RIS
Reliability (MCD) .... R
Reliability .... REL
Reliability .... RELBL
Reliability [*or Reliable*] (AAG) .... RLB
Reliability Abstracts and Technical Reviews [*NASA*] .... RATR
Reliability Accelerated In-Service Echelon (MCD) .... RAISE
Reliability Action Center [*NASA*] (NASA) .... RAC
Reliability Action Report [*or Request*] .... RAR
Reliability Analysis (AAG) .... RA
Reliability Analysis Center [*Griffiss Air Force Base, NY*] [*DoD*] (GRD) .... RAC
Reliability Analysis of Microcircuit Failure in Avionic Systems (MCD) .... RAMFAS
Reliability and Aging Surveillance Program [*Air Force*] .... RASP
Reliability and Availability .... R & A
Reliability and Configuration Accountability System .... RECON
Reliability and Launch Operations (MCD) .... R & LO
Reliability and Maintainability [*Navy*] .... R & M
Reliability and Maintainability (IAA) .... RAM
Reliability and Maintainability Information System [*Air Force*] (GFGA) .... REMIS
Reliability and Maintainability Management Improvement Techniques [*Army*] .... RAMMIT
Reliability and Maintainability Program .... RAMP
Reliability and Maintainability Simulator .... RMS
Reliability and Maintainability Studies [*Army*] (RDA) .... RAMS
Reliability and Maintainability Technology Insertion Program [*DoD*] .... RAMTIP
Reliability and Maintenance Analysis (CAAL) .... RMA
Reliability and Marketing (WDAA) .... R & M
Reliability and Quality Assurance .... R & QA
Reliability and Quality Assurance Office [*NASA*] .... RQAO
Reliability and Quality Control (MCD) .... RQC
Reliability and System Test .... RAST
Reliability and Trend Indicator Reports (AAG) .... RTIR
Reliability Assessment (KSC) .... RA
Reliability Assessment for Management .... RAM
Reliability Assessment of Components (KSC) .... RAC
Reliability Assessment Prediction .... RAP
Reliability Assessment Prediction Model .... RAPM
Reliability Assessment Program .... RAP
Reliability Assessment Program with In-Plant Data .... RAPID
Reliability Assurance (MCD) .... RA
Reliability Assurance Instructions (KSC) .... RAI
Reliability Assurance Program (IAA) .... RAP
Reliability Assurance Test .... RAT
Reliability Assurance Warranty (MCD) .... RAW
Reliability Assurance Work Order (MCD) .... RAWO
Reliability, Availability, and Maintainability [*Army*] .... RAM
Reliability, Availability, and Maintainability Automated Data Collection System [*Army*] .... RAMADCS
Reliability, Availability, and Maintainability Demonstration .... RAMD
Reliability, Availability, and Maintenance Management Improvements Technique .... RAMMIT
Reliability, Availability, and Serviceability [*IBM Corp. slogan*] (MCD) .... RAS
Reliability, Availability, Maintainability, and Durability [*Army*] (AABC) .... RAM-D
Reliability, Availability, Maintainability, and Logistics (MCD) .... RAM/LOG
Reliability, Availability, Maintainability, Cost Effectiveness and Systems Effectiveness (MHDB) .... RAMCEASE
Reliability, Availability, Maintainability, Enhancement of Communications-Elect ronic Systems (AAGC) .... RAMECES
Reliability, Availability, Maintainability Program [*Army*] (IAA) .... RAMP
Reliability, Availability, Maintainability, Safety, and Human Factors [*Telecommunications*] (TEL) .... RAMSH
Reliability, Availability, Maintainability - Supportability (MCD) .... RAM-S
Reliability, Availability, Maintenance, Simulation [*Navy*] (DNAB) .... RAMSIM

Reliability, Availability, Security (IAA) ... RAS
Reliability, Availability, Service, Improvement (MHDI) ... RASI
Reliability, Availability, Serviceability and Improvability (NITA) ... RASI
Reliability, Availability, Serviceability, Integrity and Security (NITA) ... RASIS
Reliability, Availability, Serviceability, Useability, Installability (IAA) ... RASUI
Reliability Block Diagram (NITA) ... RBD
Reliability Centered Maintenance ... RCM
Reliability Centered Maintenance Strategy (MCD) ... RCMS
Reliability Central Data Management System [*Air Force*] (DIT) ... RCDMS
Reliability Committee [*NASA*] ... RELC
Reliability Component List (MCD) ... RCL
Reliability Control Engineering (AAG) ... RCE
Reliability Control Level (KSC) ... RCL
Reliability Control Specification ... RCS
Reliability Corporate Memory (IEEE) ... RCM
Reliability Critical Item List (AAG) ... RCIL
Reliability Critical Problem (AAG) ... RCP
Reliability Critical Ranking List (AAG) ... RCRL
Reliability Data Center (KSC) ... RDC
Reliability Data Control (IAA) ... RDC
Reliability Data Control Office (AAG) ... RDCO
Reliability Data Extractor (MCD) ... RDE
Reliability Demonstration Test ... RDT
Reliability Design Analysis (MCD) ... RDA
Reliability Design Analysis Report (AAG) ... RDAR
Reliability Design Index (DNAB) ... RDI
Reliability Design Review ... RDR
Reliability Design Support Document [*Nuclear energy*] (NRCH) ... RDSD
Reliability Design Test ... RDT
Reliability Design Verification Test ... RDVT
Reliability Development Growth Testing (RDA) ... RDGT
Reliability Development Testing (CAAL) ... RDT
Reliability Diagnostic Report (AAG) ... RDR
Reliability Engineering Analysis and Planning (PDAA) ... REAP
Reliability Engineering Analysis Report (IEEE) ... REAR
Reliability Engineering and Corrective Action Program ... RECAP
Reliability Engineering and Management Institute (EA) ... REMI
Reliability Engineering Model (KSC) ... REM
Reliability Evaluation and Control Technique ... REACT
Reliability Evaluation Continuous Analysis Program ... RECAP
Reliability Evaluation Program (IAA) ... REP
Reliability Evaluation Test ... RET
Reliability Evaluation Test Procedure ... RETP
Reliability Factor ... RF
Reliability Failure Diagnostic Team (AAG) ... RFDT
Reliability Failure Summary Support (SAA) ... RFSS
Reliability Field Unit ... RFU
Reliability Figure of Merit (IAA) ... RFM
Reliability Figure of Merit Analysis ... RFMA
Reliability Functional Block ... RFB
Reliability Growth/Development Test ... RGDT
Reliability Growth Management (MCD) ... RGM
Reliability Growth Program (PDAA) ... RGP
Reliability Human Engineering (AAG) ... RHE
Reliability Improvement Factor ... RIF
Reliability Improvement Program ... RIP
Reliability Improvement Selected Equipment (AABC) ... RISE
Reliability Improvement Warranty [*Navy*] ... RIW
Reliability, Inc. [*NASDAQ symbol*] (NQ) ... REAL
Reliability, Inc. [*Associated Press*] (SAG) ... Reliab
Reliability Index ... RI
Reliability Index Determination (MCD) ... RID
Reliability Information Retrieval System (MCD) ... RIRS
Reliability Information System ... RIS
Reliability Intensity Level (CAAL) ... RIL
Reliability Investigation Requests (KSC) ... RIR
Reliability Life Test ... RLT
Reliability, Maintainability, and Availability [*Standards*] ... RMA
Reliability, Maintainability, Cost Analysis (MCD) ... REMCA
Reliability, Maintainability, Supportability [*Automotive engineering*] ... RMS
Reliability Maturity Index [*Polaris*] ... RMI
Reliability Monitoring Index ... RMI
Reliability Monitoring of Subcontractors/Suppliers (MCD) ... REMOSS
Reliability Operating Characteristic ... ROC
Reliability Organization Instruction (AAG) ... ROI
Reliability Performance Measure [*QCR*] ... RPM
Reliability Planning and Management (MCD) ... RPM
Reliability Policy Committee (AAG) ... RPC
Reliability Program (IAA) ... RP
Reliability Program Plan (MCD) ... RPP
Reliability Project Engineer (NASA) ... RPE
Reliability Qualification Test (CAAL) ... RQT
Reliability Report (AAG) ... REL-R
Reliability Requirements Directive ... RRD
Reliability, Safety, and Quality Control ... RSQC
Reliability Safety Margin Test ... RSMT
Reliability Shakedown Test (PDAA) ... RST
Reliability Standard ... RS
Reliability Status Document (IAA) ... RSD
Reliability Summary (KSC) ... RS
Reliability, Surveillance, and Control (SAA) ... RS & C
Reliability Surveillance and Control (IAA) ... RSAC
Reliability Task Force (MCD) ... RTF
Reliability Technical Directive (AAG) ... RTD
Reliability Test Assembly ... RTA
Reliability Test Data Report ... RTDR
Reliability Test Evaluation (AAG) ... RTE
Reliability Test Outline (AAG) ... RTO
Reliability Test Plan (MCD) ... RTP
Reliability Test Requirements (AAG) ... RTR
Reliability Trouble and Failure Report ... RTFR
Reliability Variation Analysis ... RVA
Reliability Verification Tests ... RVT
Reliability Working Group (AAG) ... RWG
Reliability-Centered Maintenance [*DoD*] ... RCM
Reliable ... RELLI
Reliable Acoustic Path ... RAP
Reliable Acoustic Path SONAR (MCD) ... RAPS
Reliable Advanced Solid-State RADAR ... RASSR
Reliable Block Diagram (MCD) ... RBD
Reliable Corrective Action Summary (AAG) ... RCS
Reliable Detection Limit [*Analytical chemistry*] ... RDL
Reliable Flow Manager [*Computer science*] ... RFM
Reliable Life Ins [*NASDAQ symbol*] (TTSB) ... RLIFA
[*The*] **Reliable Life Insurance Co.** [*Associated Press*] (SAG) ... RelbLfe
[*The*] **Reliable Life Insurance Co.** [*NASDAQ symbol*] (NQ) ... RLIF
Reliable Operate RADAR Altimeter ... RORA
Reliable Test Analyzer [*Computer science*] ... RTA
Reliable Transaction Router [*Digital Equipment Corp.*] ... RTR
Reliable Transfer [*Telecommunications*] (OSI) ... RT
Reliable Transfer Server [*Telecommunications*] (OSI) ... RTS
Reliable Transfer Service Element [*Telecommunications*] (OSI) ... RTSE
Reliance Bancorp [*Associated Press*] (SAG) ... RelBcp
Reliance Bancorp [*NASDAQ symbol*] (SAG) ... RELY
Reliance Bancshares [*NASDAQ symbol*] (TTSB) ... RELI
Reliance Bancshares, Inc. [*NASDAQ symbol*] (SAG) ... RELI
Reliance Bancshares, Inc. [*Associated Press*] (SAG) ... ReliBsh
Reliance Group Hldgs [*NYSE symbol*] (TTSB) ... REL
Reliance Group Holdings, Inc. [*Formerly, Leasco Corp.*] [*NYSE symbol*] (SPSG) ... REL
Reliance Group Holdings, Inc. [*Formerly, Leasco Corp.*] [*Associated Press*] (SAG) ... RelGrp
Reliance, SD [*FM radio station call letters*] ... KPLO
Reliance, SD [*Television station call letters*] ... KPLO-TV
Reliance, SD [*FM radio station call letters*] ... KTSD
Reliance Steel & Aluminum [*NYSE symbol*] (TTSB) ... RS
Reliance Steel & Aluminum Co. [*Associated Press*] (SAG) ... RelStlAl
Reliance Steel & Aluminum Co. [*NYSE symbol*] (SAG) ... RS
Reliant Airlines, Inc [*ICAO designator*] (FAAC) ... RLT
Reliant Resources Ltd. [*Vancouver Stock Exchange symbol*] ... RRM
ReliaStar Fin I 8.20%'TOPrS' [*NYSE symbol*] (TTSB) ... RLRPrA
ReliaStar Financial [*NYSE symbol*] (TTSB) ... RLR
ReliaStar Financial Co. [*Associated Press*] (SAG) ... ReliaS
ReliaStar Financial Co. [*Associated Press*] (SAG) ... ReliaStar
ReliaStar Financial Co. [*NYSE symbol*] (SAG) ... RLR
ReliaStar Finl 10% Dep Pfd [*NYSE symbol*] (TTSB) ... RLRPr
Relic ... REL
Relie [*Bound*] [*Publishing*] [*French*] ... REL
Relief (AAG) ... REL
Relief (VRA) ... rel
Relief (AAG) ... RLF
Relief and Development Institute [*Formerly, International Disaster Institute*] [*Defunct*] (EA) ... RDI
Relief Claim ... RC
Relief Electronic Maintenance Technician ... REMT
Relief Electronics Specialist ... RES
Relief for Africans in Need (EA) ... RAIN
Relief from Face to Face [*Education*] ... RFF
Relief General Communications Vessel ... RAGC
Relief Landing Ground [*British military*] (DMA) ... RLG
Relief Medication Unit Index [*Medicine*] (DMAA) ... RMUI
Relief Pitcher [*Baseball*] ... RP
Relief Printing (DGA) ... R/P
Relief Radii (MSA) ... RR
Relief, Recovery, Reform [*Elements of the New Deal*] ... 3R's
Relief, Recovery, Reform [*Elements of the New Deal*] ... RRR
Relief Stamped (DGA) ... RS
Relief Transport Services Ltd. [*British ICAO designator*] (FAAC) ... RTS
Relief Valve ... RV
Relief Valve Augmented Bypass [*Nuclear energy*] (NRCH) ... REVAB
Relief Valve Discharge Piping [*Nuclear energy*] (NRCH) ... RVDP
Relief Valve Unit ... RVU
Relieve (AFM) ... RLV
Relieve of Booty [*Crime term*] ... ROB
Relieved (WGA) ... RELD
Relieved ... RLVD
Relieved from Assigned [*Military*] ... RFA
Relieved from Attached [*Army*] (AABC) ... RFAT
Relieved from Attached and Assigned [*Army*] ... RFAA
Relieving Officer (ROG) ... RO
Religieuses de la Sainte-Union des Sacres-Coeurs de Jesus et Marie [*Religious of the Holy Union of the Sacred Hearts*] [*Roman Catholic women's religious order*] ... SUSC
Religion ... REL
Religion [*or Religious*] ... RELIG
Religion (VRA) ... relig
Religion and Ethics Institute (EA) ... REI
Religion and Ethics Network (EA) ... REN
Religion and Family Life Section (EA) ... RFS
Religion and Labor Council of America [*Defunct*] (EA) ... RLCA

Religion and Labor Foundation .... RLF
Religion and Socialism Commission of the Democratic Socialists of America (EA) .... RSCDSA
Religion and the Public Order [*A publication*] (DLA) .... Rel & Pub Order
Religion in American Life (EA) .... RIAL
Religion in Communist Dominated Areas [*A publication*] .... RCDA
Religion in Literature and Life [*A publication*] .... RLL
Religion Index [*American Theological Library Association*] [*Information service or system*] .... RELI
Religion Index Database - Religion Index One; Religion Index Two; Research in Ministry [*American Theological Library Association*] [*Information service or system*] (CRD) .... RIO-RIT-RIM
Religion Newswriters Association (EA) .... RNA
Religion Publishing Group [*Defunct*] (EA) .... RPG
Religions, Ancient and Modern [*A publication*] .... RAM
Religiosae Adoratrices Pretiosissimo Sanguinis [*Sisters Adorers of the Precious Blood*] [*Roman Catholic religious order*] .... APB
Religious (DNAB) .... R
Religious [*A radio station format*] (WDMC) .... RL
Religious Action Center of Reform Judaism (EA) .... RAC/RJ
Religious Action Center of the Union of American Hebrew Congregations [*Later, RAC/RJ*] (EA) .... RACUAHC
Religious Activities Committee, National Safety Council (EA) .... RACNSC
Religious Altered State of Consciousness [*Psychology*] .... RASC
Religious and Mental Health Inventory .... RMHI
Religious and Military Order of Knights of the Holy Sepulchre (EA) .... RMOKHS
Religious Arts Guild [*Defunct*] (EA) .... RAG
Religious Book Publishing Division [*of Association of American Publishers*] [*RPG*] [*Superseded by*] .... RBPD
Religious Booksellers Association (EA) .... RBA
Religious Brothers of the Third Order Regular of St. Francis (TOCD) .... osf
Religious Coalition for Abortion Rights (EA) .... RCAR
Religious Committee for the ERA [*Equal Rights Amendment*] (EA) .... RCERA
Religious Communities for the Arts [*Defunct*] (EA) .... RCFA
Religious Conceptionist Missionaries [*Roman Catholic women's religious order*] .... RCM
Religious Conference Management Association (EA) .... RCMA
Religious Daughters of St. Joseph (TOCD) .... FSJ
Religious Drama Society of Great Britain (BI) .... RDS
Religious Education [*Secondary school course*] [*British*] .... RE
Religious Education [*A publication*] (BRI) .... Rel Ed
Religious Education Association (EA) .... REA
Religious Education Centre (AIE) .... REC
Religious Education Journal of Australia [*A publication*] (APTA) .... REJ
Religious Formation Conference (EA) .... RFC
Religious Freedom Restoration Act .... RFRA
Religious Heritage of America (EA) .... RHA
Religious Hospitallers of St. Joseph [*Roman Catholic women's religious order*] .... RHSJ
Religious Instruction (ADA) .... RI
Religious Instruction Association [*Later, PERSC*] .... RIA
Religious Leaders of America [*A publication*] .... RLA
Religious Liberty Association (NADA) .... RLA
Religious Liberty Foundation [*Defunct*] (EA) .... RLF
Religious Mercedarians of the Blessed Sacrament [*Roman Catholic women's religious order*] .... RMSS
Religious Missionaries of St. Dominic (Spanish Prov.) (TOCD) .... OP
Religious, Morale, Welfare, and Recreation [*Military*] (AFM) .... RMWR
Religious Network for Equality for Women (EA) .... RNEW
Religious News Service (EA) .... RNS
Religious Observance Index (BJA) .... ROI
Religious of Christian Education [*Roman Catholic women's religious order*] .... RCE
Religious of Christian Instruction [*Roman Catholic religious order*] .... RCI
Religious of Jesus-Mary [*Roman Catholic women's religious order*] .... RJM
Religious of Mary Immaculate [*Roman Catholic women's religious order*] .... RMI
Religious of St. Andrew [*Roman Catholic religious order*] .... RST
Religious of St. Joseph of Australia (TOCD) .... RSJ
Religious of the Apostolate of the Sacred Heart [*Roman Catholic women's religious order*] .... RA
Religious of the Assumption [*Roman Catholic women's religious order*] .... RA
Religious of the Blessed Virgin Mary (TOCD) .... RVM
Religious of the Eucharist [*Roman Catholic women's religious order*] .... RE
Religious of the Incarnate Word (TOCD) CVI
Religious of the Order of the Blessed Sacrament and Our Lady [*Sacramentine Nuns*] [*Roman Catholic religious order*] .... OSS
Religious of the Passion of Jesus Christ (TOCD) .... CP
Religious of the Sacred Heart of Mary [*Roman Catholic women's religious order*] .... RSHM
Religious Press Associations Postal Coalition (EA) .... RPAPC
Religious Program (NTCM) .... R
Religious Program Specialist [*Navy*] (DNAB) .... RP
Religious Program Specialist Seaman [*Navy rating*] (DNAB) .... RPSN
Religious Program Specialist Seaman Apprentice [*Navy rating*] (DNAB) .... RPSA
Religious Public Relations Council (EA) .... RPRC
Religious Requirements and Practices [*A publication*] .... RRP
Religious Research Association (EA) .... RRA
Religious Roundtable (EA) .... RR
Religious Science International (EA) .... RSI
Religious Sisters of Charity [*Roman Catholic religious order*] .... RSC
Religious Sisters of Mercy of Alma, Michigan (TOCD) .... RSM
Religious Sisters of the Apostolate of the Blessed Sacrament (TOCD) .... HMSS
Religious Society of Friends [*Quakers*], New York, NY [*Library symbol Library of Congress*] (LCLS) .... NNFL
Religious Speech Communication Association (EA) .... RSCA
Religious Studies [*A publication*] (BRI) .... Rel St
Religious Studies [*Secondary school course*] [*British*] .... RS
Religious Studies Library, McGill University, Montreal, Quebec [*Library symbol National Library of Canada*] (NLC) .... QMMD
Religious Studies Review [*A publication*] (BRI) .... Rel St Rev
Religious Task Force [*Defunct*] (EA) .... RTF
Religious Task Force on Central America (EA) .... RTFCA
Religious Task Force on El Salvador (EA) .... RTFES
Religious Teachers, Filippini [*Roman Catholic women's religious order*] .... MPF
Religious Tract Society [*British*] .... RTS
Religious Venerini Sisters (TOCD) .... MPV
Religious Zionists of America (EA) .... RZA
Reliquary (VRA) .... reliq
Reliquary and Illustrated Archaeologist [*A publication*] (ROG) .... REL
Reliquiae [*of Suetonius*] [*Classical studies*] (OCD) .... Rel
Reliquiae [*Remains*] [*Latin*] .... REL
Reliquiae [*Remains*] [*Latin*] .... RELIQ
Reliquum [*The Remainder*] [*Pharmacy*] .... RELIQ
Reliv' International [*AMEX symbol*] (TTSB) .... RLV
Reliv International, Inc. [*Associated Press*] (SAG) .... Reliv
Reliv International, Inc. [*NASDAQ symbol*] (SAG) .... RELV
Reliv' International, Inc. [*AMEX symbol*] (SPSG) .... RLV
Relizane [*Algeria*] [*ICAO location identifier*] (ICLI) .... DAAZ
Relizane [*Algeria*] [*Seismograph station code, US Geological Survey Closed*] (SEIS) .... REL
Reloadable Control Storage [*Computer science*] .... RCS
Relocatable [*Computer science*] .... REL
Relocatable Assembly Language Floating Point .... RALF
Relocatable Directory [*Computer science*] (IAA) .... RD
Relocatable Input/Output .... RIO
Relocatable Library [*Computer science*] .... RLIB
Relocatable Library Service Function [*Computer science*] (IAA) .... RSERV
Relocatable Output [*Computer science*] .... RO
Relocatable Over-The-Horizon [*Radar*] (DOMA) .... R-OTH
Relocatable Over-the-Horizon RADAR .... ROTHR
Relocatable Term [*Computer science*] (IAA) .... RT
Relocate (FAAC) .... RELCT
Relocate (AAG) .... RELOC
Relocate Out of Washington [*Navy*] (NG) .... ROW
Relocated .... RELCTD
Relocated .... RLCD
Relocating Linking Loader .... RLL
Relocation (IAA) .... RL
Relocation .... RLCTN
Relocation Address .... RA
Relocation Assistance [*HUD*] .... RA
Relocation Assistance Association of America [*Defunct*] (EA) .... RAAA
Relocation Dictionary .... RLD
Relocation Directory (NITA) .... RLD
Relocation Instruction Counter [*Computer science*] (OA) .... RIC
Relocation Library (HGAA) .... RL
Relocation List Directory .... RLD
Relocation Request [*Code*] [*Military*] (MCD) .... GEOREQ
Relocation Services Institute [*British*] (DBA) .... RSI
Relocation Site (NVT) .... RS
Relocation Time .... RT
Reluctance .... R
Reluctance (DEN) .... REL
Reluctance [*Symbol*] (DEN) .... S
Reluctivity (IDOE) V
REM [*Rapid Eye Movement*] **Behavior Disorder** [*Medicine*] .... RBD
REM [*Roentgen-Equivalent-Man*] **Equivalent Chemical** [*Irradiation unit*] .... REC
Remada [*Tunisia*] [*ICAO location identifier*] (ICLI) .... DTTD
Remain (ROG) .... REMN
Remain (FAAC) .... RMN
Remain Behind Equipment [*Navy*] (ANA) .... RBE
Remain in Effect after Discharge and Reenlistment [*Refers to orders*] [*Army*] .... READR
Remain in Place (MCD) .... RIP
Remain Intact Organization (EA) .... RIO
Remain Overnight Position [*Military*] (VNW) .... RON
Remain Well to Right of Course [*Aviation*] (FAAC) .... RWRC
Remainder (MSA) .... REM
Remainder .... REMR
Remainder (DLA) .... Rmdr
Remainderman [*Legal shorthand*] (LWAP) .... REMMAN
Remaining Cycles (MCD) .... RCY
Remaining Force Potential (MCD) .... RFP
Remaining Number of Operations .... ROPT
Remaining Oil in Place [*Petroleum industry*] .... ROIP
Remaining on Board .... ROB
Remaining Operating Time (NASA) .... ROT
Remaining [*or Rest*] **Overnight** [*Aviation*] .... RON
Remaining Overnight .... ROVNITE
Remaining Radiation Service (NATG) .... RRS
Remaining Useful Life Evaluation Rig [*Lubricant testing*] .... RULER
Remaining Velocity [*Ballistics*] .... RV
Remaining Work .... RWK
Remak's Ganglion [*Neurology*] .... RG
Remanded [*Legal term*] (DLA) .... Rem'd
Remanding [*Legal term*] (DLA) .... Rem'g
Remanso [*Brazil*] [*Airport symbol*] (AD) .... RSO
Remanufactured High Output .... RHO
Remark .... REM
Remark [*Aviation*] (FAAC) .... RM

Remark (AFM) ... RMK
Remark (FAAC) ... RMRK
Remarkable Criminal Trials [*A publication*] (DLA) ... Rem Cr Tr
Remarried Association of Long Island (EA) ... RALI
Remarried Parents, Inc. [*Defunct*] (EA) ... RPI
Remazolium Brilliant Blue [*Reactive dye composition*] ... RBB
REMEC Inc. [*NASDAQ symbol*] (TTSB) ... REMC
Remedia Amoris [*of Ovid*] [*Classical studies*] (OCD) ... Rem Am
Remedial ... RMDL
Remedial Action [*Navy*] ... RA
Remedial Action Program [*or Project, Plan*] (MCD) ... RAP
Remedial Action Program Information Center [*Department of Energy*] [*Also, an information service or system*] (IID) ... RAPIC
Remedial and Basic Skills Training (OICC) ... RBST
Remedial Design (EPA) ... RD
Remedial Design/Remedial Action [*Environmental Protection Agency*] (ERG) ... RD/RA
Remedial Education for Adults ... READ
Remedial Field Investigation (GNE) ... RFI
Remedial Gymnast [*British*] ... RG
Remedial Investigation [*Environmental Protection Agency*] (DOMA) ... RI
Remedial Investigation and Feasibility Study [*Environmental Protection Agency*] ... RI/FS
Remedial Maintenance (AFM) ... RM
Remedial Occupation Therapy ... ROT
Remedial Option [*Computer science*] ... ReOpt
Remedial Project Manager [*Navy*] ... RPM
Remedial Readin', Remedial Ritin', and Remedial Rithmetic [*Also, RRRRRR*] [*Humorous interpretation of the three R's*] ... 6R's
Remedial Readin', Remedial Ritin', and Remedial Rithmetic [*Also, 6R's*] [*Humorous interpretation of the three R's*] ... RRRRRR
Remedial Teachers' Association of Queensland [*Australia*] ... RTAQ
Remedium [*Remedy*] [*Pharmacy*] (ROG) ... REMED
Remedy Coordination Official (AAGC) ... RCO
Remedy Corp. [*Associated Press*] (SAG) ... Remdy
Remedy Corp. [*Associated Press*] (SAG) ... Remedy
Remedy Corp. [*NASDAQ symbol*] (SAG) ... RMDY
Remedy Temp, Inc. [*Associated Press*] (SAG) ... RemTp
RemedyTemp, Inc. [*NASDAQ symbol*] (SAG) ... REMX
Remember How You Treat Hazardous Materials [*E. I. Du Pont De Nemours & Co. program*] ... RHYTHM
Remember Pearl Harbor [*Group*] [*World War II*] ... RPH
Remember That Song (EA) ... RTS
Remembrance of the Holocaust Foundation (EA) ... RHF
Remer Elementary School, Remer, MN [*Library symbol*] [*Library of Congress*] (LCLS) ... MnRemE
Remigius [*Flourished, 841-908*] [*Authority cited in pre-1607 legal work*] (DSA) ... Rem
Remigius de Gonni [*Deceased, 1554*] [*Authority cited in pre-1607 legal work*] (DSA) ... Remigi
Reminder of Route Same (SAA) ... RRS
Reminder Shock ... RS
Remington [*Record label*] [*USA, Europe, etc.*] ... Rem
Remington and Ballinger's Code [*1910*] [*A publication*] (DLA) ... R & B
Remington and Ballinger's Code, Supplement [*1913*] [*A publication*] (DLA) ... R & B Supp
Remington Art Memorial Museum, Ogdensburg, NY [*Library symbol*] [*Library of Congress*] (LCLS) ... NOgRM
Remington Carpenter Township Public Library, Remington, IN [*Library symbol Library of Congress*] (LCLS) ... InRem
Remington Rand [*Commercial firm*] (NADA) ... RR
Remington Rand Corp. [*Later, a division of Sperry-Rand*] ... REM-RAND
Remington Rand Corp., Blue Bell, PA [*Library symbol Library of Congress*] (LCLS) ... ReR
Remington-Rand UNIVAC ... RRU
Remington's Code [*A publication*] (DLA) ... RC
Remington's Compiled Statutes [*1922*] [*A publication*] (DLA) ... RCS
Remington's Compiled Statutes, Supplement [*A publication*] (DLA) ... RCS Supp
Remington's Revised Statutes [*A publication*] (DLA) ... RRS
Remission [*Medicine*] ... Rm
Remission Inducing Drug, Au [*Chemical symbol for gold*], **Rheumatoid Arthritis** [*Gold-based drug manufactured by SmithKline Beckman Corp.*] ... RIDAURA
Remission Induction [*Oncology*] ... RI
Remission-Inducing Drug [*Medicine*] ... RID
Remit (AABC) ... REM
Remittance (DLA) ... Rem
Remittance (ROG) ... REMCE
Remittance (DSUE) ... REMIT
Remittance (DLA) ... Remitt
Remittance Advice (MCD) ... RA
Remittance Processing Systems [*IRS*] ... RPS
Remnant Hepatic Volume [*Hematology*] ... RHV
Remnant of Israel (EA) ... ROI
Remnant Tumor Index [*Surgery*] ... RTI
Remodeling ... REMOD
Remote [*Telecommunications*] (TEL) ... R
Remote [*Alaska*] [*Seismograph station code, US Geological Survey*] (SEIS) ... REM
Remote ... REMT
Remote (IAA) ... RM
Remote [*Telecommunications*] (MSA) ... RMT
Remote (AAG) ... RMTE
Remote [*Alaska*] [*Seismograph station code, US Geological Survey Closed*] (SEIS) ... RON
Remote Aboriginal Language Management Committee [*Australia*] ... RALMC
Remote Access [*Telecommunications*] (IAA) ... RA
Remote Access [*Telecommunications*] (IAA) ... RAC
Remote Access [*Computer science Telecommunications*] ... RAX
Remote Access Audio (NITA) ... RAA
Remote Access Audio Device [*Computer science*] (MHDB) ... RAA
Remote Access Computer Technique [*Computer science*] (IEEE) ... RACT
Remote Access Computing System (IAA) ... RAC
Remote Access Computing System [*Computer science*] ... RACS
Remote Access Editing System [*Computer science*] (IEEE) ... RAES
Remote Access Editing System [*Computer science*] (IAA) ... RES
Remote Access Interactive Debugger [*Computer science*] (IEEE) ... RAID
Remote Access Key ... RAK
Remote Access Line Monitor [*Cornet, Inc.*] ... REALM
Remote Access Maintenance Protocol [*Telecommunications*] ... RAMP
Remote Access Monitor (MCD) ... RAM
Remote Access Multi-User System (DNAB) ... RAMUS
Remote Access Planning for Institutional Development [*Computer science*] ... RAPID
Remote Access Point [*Telecommunications*] ... RAP
Remote Access Power Support (NITA) ... RAPS
Remote Access Procedure for Interactive Design [*General Motors Corp.*] ... RAPID
Remote Access Server [*Computer science*] (PCM) ... RAS
Remote Access Service [*Telecommunications*] ... RAS
Remote Access Services [*Microsoft Corp.*] [*Computer networking*] (PCM) ... RAS
Remote Access Switching and Patching ... RASP
Remote Acquisition Station [*Nuclear energy*] (NRCH) ... RAS
Remote Acquisition Unit [*NASA*] (NASA) ... RAU
Remote Acquisition Unit Interconnecting Station [*NASA*] (NASA) ... RAUIS
Remote Acquisiton and Command Unit [*NASA*] (NASA) ... RACU
Remote Activated Stores System (MCD) ... RASS
Remote Active Spectrometer ... RAS
Remote Afterload Brachytherapy [*Radiology*] (DAVI) ... RAB
Remote Air Battle Station ... RABS
Remote Airborne Television Display of Ground RADAR Coverage via TACAN (CET) ... RATAC
Remote Air-Ground Facility [*Aviation*] ... RAGF
Remote Alarm Transmission System ... RATS
Remote Amplifier and Adaption Box (NASA) ... RAAB
Remote Analog Submultiplexer (MCD) ... RASM
Remote Antiarmor Assault System (MCD) ... RAAAS
Remote Antiarmor Mine (RDA) ... RAAM
Remote Antiarmor Mine System [*Military*] (AABC) ... RAAMS
Remote Application and Advisory Box (MCD) ... RAAB
Remote Applications Protocol Suite (ACII) ... RAPS
Remote Area ... RA
Remote Area Conflict Information Center [*Battelle Memorial Institute*] ... RACIC
Remote Area Families Service [*Uniting Church*] [*Australia*] ... RAFS
Remote Area Instrument Landing Sensor [*Army*] ... RAILS
Remote Area Instrument Landing System [*Army*] ... RAILS
Remote Area Landing (NG) ... RAL
Remote Area Mobility Study (MCD) ... RAMS
Remote Area Monitoring (KSC) ... RAM
Remote Area Navigation [*FAA*] (TAG) ... RNAV
Remote Area Nurse ... RAN
Remote Area Power Supply ... RAPS
Remote Area Services Subsidy Scheme [*Australia*] ... RASS
Remote Area Support (MCD) ... RAS
Remote Area Tactical [*Location and Landing*] **System** ... RATS
Remote Area Teacher Education [*Australia*] ... RATE
Remote Area Teacher Education Program [*Australia*] ... RATEP
Remote Area Terminal ... RAT
Remote Area Terminal System ... RATS
Remote Area Weather Station (MCD) ... RAWS
Remote ARIA [*Apollo Range Instrumentation Aircraft*] **Control Center** [*NASA*] ... RACC
Remote Arm Reset (MCD) ... RAR
Remote Arm Set (MCD) ... RAS
Remote Arming Common Element System ... RACES
Remote Associates Test [*Psychology*] ... RAT
Remote Augmented Lift System (MCD) ... RALS
Remote Authentication Dial-In User Service [*Computer science*] (PCM) ... RADIUS
Remote Automated Issue, Document Entry, and Register System [*Army*] ... RAIDERS
Remote Automatic Calibration System (NASA) ... RACS
Remote Automatic Control System (KSC) ... RACS
Remote Automatic Detection Contingencies ... RADOC
Remote Automatic Meteorological Observing Station ... RAMOS
Remote Automatic Multipurpose Station ... RAMS
Remote Automatic Parts Input for Dealers (IAA) ... RAPID
Remote Automatic Telemetry Equipment ... RATE
Remote Automatic Weather Station ... RAWS
Remote Balance Control ... RBC
Remote Batch [*Computer science*] (IAA) ... RB
Remote Batch Access Method (IAA) ... RBAM
Remote Batch Entry (CMD) ... RBE
Remote Batch Facility ... RBF
Remote Batch Module ... RBM
Remote Batch Processing [*Computer science*] (IAA) ... RBP
Remote Batch System ... RBS
Remote Batch Terminal ... RBT
Remote Battle System ... RBS
Remote Black Concentrator [*Telecommunications*] (LAIN) ... RBC
Remote Bridge Management Software (HGAA) ... RBMS
Remote Buffer Unit (IAA) ... RBU

Remote Bulletin Board System [For IBM computers] [Telecommunications] ... RBBS
Remote Bus Isolator (SSD) ... RBI
Remote Call Forwarding [Bell System] ... RCF
Remote Center Air/Ground Facility [NASA] ... RCAG
Remote Center Compliance [Computer science] ... RCC
Remote Channel (NITA) ... RC
Remote Characterization System [Remote controlled vehicle] [Hazardous materials control] ... RCS
Remote Checkout Umbilical Array ... RCUA
Remote Circuit Breaker (MCD) ... RCB
Remote Cluster Executive (IAA) ... RCX
Remote Cluster Facility (IAA) ... RCF
Remote Combat Center (SAA) ... RCC
Remote Command and Control (MCD) ... RECO
Remote Communication Facility [FAA] (TAG) ... RCF
Remote Communication Message (IAA) ... RCOM
Remote Communication Outlet [ATCS] ... RCO
Remote Communication Processor (IAA) ... RCP
Remote Communications Air/Ground Facility [FAA] (TAG) ... RCAG
Remote Communications Central ... RCC
Remote Communications Complex ... RCC
Remote Communications Concentrator ... RCC
Remote Communications Console ... RCC
Remote Communicatios Central Set (SAA) ... RCCS
Remote Component ... RC
Remote Computer ... RC
Remote Computer Access Communications Service ... RCAC
Remote Computer Center (MCD) ... RCC
Remote Computer Communications Access Method [Computer science] (MHDB) ... RCCAM
Remote Computer Interface Subsystem (MHDB) ... RCIS
Remote Computer Interface Unit ... RCIU
Remote Computer Output Room (MCD) ... RCOR
Remote Computer-Controlled Hardware Monitor (MHDI) ... RCHM
Remote Computing Service ... RCS
Remote Concentrator ... RC
Remote Console [NASA computer] ... RECON
Remote Continual Verification [Telephonic monitoring system] ... RECOVER
Remote Control [Automotive engineering] ... R/CONT
Remote Control ... RC
Remote Control [Systems] (MCD) ... RCT
Remote Control [Of mines] (DOMA) ... RECO
Remote Control (KSC) ... RECON
Remote Control (IAA) ... RMC
Remote Control Amplifier (MCD) ... RCA
Remote Control and Status Equipment (MCD) ... RCSE
Remote Control Authority [FCC] (NTCM) ... RC
Remote Control Bandwidth ... RCB
Remote Control Center Development Facility (SSD) ... RCCDF
Remote Control Circuit Breaker (NASA) ... RCCB
Remote Control Complex (SAA) ... RCC
Remote Control Door Lock Receiver ... RCDLR
Remote Control Equipment (DIT) ... RCE
Remote Control Indicator (CAAL) ... RCI
Remote Control Interface ... RCI
Remote Control Interface Adapter (IAA) ... RCIA
Remote Control Location ... RCL
Remote Control Office ... RCO
Remote Control Operator ... RCO
Remote Control Oscillator ... RCO
Remote Control Panel ... RCP
Remote Control Rod Cluster Assembly (IAA) ... RCCA
Remote Control Set ... RCS
Remote Control Station (NITA) ... RCS
Remote Control (System) (DEN) ... RC(S)
Remote Control Terminal (MCD) ... RCT
Remote Control Tunnelling Machine ... RCTM
Remote Control Unit ... RCU
Remote Control Verification [Nuclear safeguards] ... RECOVER
Remote Control Video Switch (MCD) ... RCVS
Remote Control Water Sampler ... RCWS
Remote Controlled Target Vehicle [Military] (INF) ... RCTV
Remote Data [or Database] Access (NASA) ... RDA
Remote Data Acquisition Terminal (NRCH) ... RDAT
Remote Data Acquisition Unit ... RDAU
Remote Data Acquistion Subsystem [Computer science] (MHDB) ... REMAC
Remote Data Collection (MCD) ... RDC
Remote Data Concentrator ... RDC
Remote Data Entry (NITA) ... RDE
Remote Data Entry System (DMAA) ... RDES
Remote Data Input ... RDI
Remote Data Management ... RDM
Remote Data Objects [Computer science] ... RDO
Remote Data Objects [Computer science] ... RDO
Remote Data Processor ... RDP
Remote Data Service [Computer science] ... RDS
Remote Data Service [Computer science] ... RDS
Remote Data Transmitter ... RDT
Remote Data Uplink [SmartOffice] [Computer science] ... RDU
Remote Detonation Capability ... RDC
Remote Device Handler (IAA) ... RDH
Remote Device Interface Unit ... RDIU
Remote Digital Multiplexer (MCD) ... RDM
Remote Digital Readout ... RDR
Remote Digital Readout ... RDRD
Remote Digital Submultiplexer (KSC) ... RDSM
Remote Disc Operating System (NITA) ... REMDOS
Remote Display Control Panel (MCD) ... RDCP
Remote Display Link ... RDL
Remote Display Unit [American Solenoid Co.] [Somerset, NJ] ... RDU
Remote Distributed Terminal Controller (NITA) ... RDTC
Remote Docking Procedures Simulator (MCD) ... RDPS
Remote Electric Drive Turret ... RED-T
Remote Electrical Block Energization Clock Control Arrangement (IAA) ... REBECCA
Remote Electronic Alphanumeric Display [Computer science] (IEEE) ... READ
Remote Electronic Delivery of Information [Library science] ... REDI
Remote Electronic Microfilm in Storage Transmission and Retrieval [Computer science] (EECA) ... REMSTAR
Remote Electronic Microfilm Storage Transmission and Retrieval ... REMSTA
Remote Electronic Microfilm Storage Transmission and Retrieval (NITA) ... REMSTAR
Remote Emergency Salvage and Clean Up Equipment ... RESCUE
Remote Enable (IEEE) ... REN
Remote Energy Monitor Alarm System [Computer science] (MHDI) ... REMAS
Remote Entry Acquisition Package ... REAP
Remote Entry Flexible Security [Computer science] (MHDB) ... REFS
Remote Entry Services (MCD) ... RES
Remote Entry Subsystem (IAA) ... RES
Remote Event Module [Computer science] ... REM
Remote Exchange [Telecommunications] (TEL) ... RX
Remote Facility Inquiry [NASA] (KSC) ... RFI
Remote Fiber Fluorometer [Instrumentation] ... RFF
Remote Fiber Spectroscopy ... RFS
Remote File Access ... RFA
Remote File Inquiry [NASA] (NASA) ... RFI
Remote File Management System ... RFMS
Remote File Service [or System] [Computer science] (PCM) ... RFS
Remote File Sharing [Computer science] ... RFS
Remote Filter Niche [Nuclear energy] (NRCH) ... RFN
Remote Firing Unit (MCD) ... RFU
Remote Food Carriers [Army] (INF) ... RFC
Remote Frequency Display (MCD) ... RFD
Remote Function Activator ... RFA
Remote Gain Amplifier (IAA) ... RGA
Remote Gas Filter Correlation (KSC) ... RGFC
Remote Generalized Application Language [Computer science] (PDAA) ... REGAL
Remote Geophysical Monitor (MCD) ... RGM
Remote Global Computer Access Service (MHDB) ... RGCAS
Remote Graphics Instruction Set (HGAA) ... ReGIS
Remote Graphics Processor ... RGP
Remote Ground Switching ... RGS
Remote Hellfire Electronics [Army] ... RHE
Remote Image Confirming Sensor (MCD) ... RICS
Remote Image Processing System ... RIPS
Remote Image Protocol [Computer science] ... RIP
Remote Imagery Transceiver (DOMA) ... RIT
Remote Independently-Operated Transceiver ... RIOT
Remote Indicator Panel (CAAL) ... RIP
Remote Information Center ... RIC
Remote Information Exchange Terminal (MCD) ... RIXT
Remote Information Management System ... RIMS
Remote Information Query System [Information retrieval service] [Computer science] ... RIQS
Remote Information Retrieval and Management System [Computer science] (BUR) ... RIRMS
Remote Information System ... RIS
Remote Information Systems Center ... RISC
Remote Input Message Processor ... RIMP
Remote Input/Output (NITA) ... RIO
Remote Input/Output Controller [Computer science] (MHDB) ... RIOC
Remote Input/Output Terminal [Computer science] ... RIOT
Remote Input Terminal System [Computer science] (IAA) ... RITS
Remote Input-Output System [Computer science] (IAA) ... RIOS
Remote Instrument Package (PDAA) ... RIP
Remote Integrated Logistics Support Team [Military] (MCD) ... RILST
Remote Intelligence Acquisition ... RIA
Remote Interactive Communications [Xerox Corp.] ... RIC
Remote Intercomputer Communications Interface (MCD) ... RICC
Remote Interface Unit [NASA] (NASA) ... RIU
Remote Interrogation Information Exchange System (DNAB) ... RIIXS
Remote Job Entry [Computer science] (MHDI) ... REJEN
Remote Job Entry [Computer science] ... RJE
Remote Job Entry Protocol [Telecommunications] (OSI) ... RJEP
Remote Job Entry System (NITA) ... RES
Remote Job Entry Terminal System [Computer science] (MCD) ... RJETS
Remote Job Output [Computer science] ... RJO
Remote Job Processing [Computer science] ... RJP
Remote Job Processor (NITA) ... RJP
Remote Job System [Computer science] (MCD) ... RJS
Remote LAN [Linked Access Network] Node [DCA, Inc.] (PCM) ... RLN
Remote Launch Demonstration [Army] (DOMA) ... RLD
Remote Lift Fan [Aviation] ... RLF
Remote Line Adapter ... RLA
Remote Line Concentrator ... RLC
Remote Line Module [Telecommunications] ... RLM
Remote Line Printer (MCD) ... RLP
Remote Line Switch [Telecommunications] (TEL) ... RLS
Remote Line Tester (PDAA) ... RLT

Remote Line Unit [*Telecommunications*] ... RLU

Remote Load Controller [*NASA*] (MCD) ... RLC

Remote/Local (NASA) ... R/L

Remote Location (IAA) ... RL

Remote Lock Control [*Automotive engineering*] ... RLC

Remote Look Group Multiplexer (MCD) ... RLGM

Remote Look Group Multiplexer Cable Drive (MCD) ... RLGM-CD

Remote Loop Adapter [*Telecommunications*] ... RLA

Remote Magnetic Anomaly Detection ... REMAD

Remote Magnetic Indication ... RMI

Remote Maintenance, Administration, and Traffic System-1 [*Telecommunications*] (TEL) ... RMATS-1

Remote Maintenance Line [*Bell Laboratories*] ... RML

Remote Maintenance Monitor [*Computer science*] (MCD) ... RMM

Remote Maintenance Monitoring System [*FAA*] (TAG) ... RMMS

Remote Maintenance System ... RMS

Remote Maneuvering Unit [*NASA*] ... RMU

Remote Manipulation Subsystem Verification Plan [*NASA*] (MCD) ... RMSVP

Remote Manipulation Systems [*NASA*] ... ROMANS

Remote Manipulator [*NASA*] (NASA) ... RM

Remote Manipulator Arm [*NASA*] (MCD) ... RMA

Remote Manipulator Subsystem [*NASA*] (NASA) ... RMS

Remote Manipulator System [*NASA*] (IAA) ... RMS

Remote Manual (NRCH) ... RM

Remote Manual Control (NRCH) ... RMC

Remote Manual Switch [*Nuclear energy*] (NRCH) ... RMS

Remote Map Reader ... RMR

Remote Marshalling Base (MCD) ... REMAB

Remote Master Aircraft (MCD) ... RMAC

Remote Master Station (MCD) ... RMS

Remote Measurements Laboratory ... RML

Remote Memory Port Interface ... RMPI

Remote Message Concentrator (IAA) ... RMC

Remote Meter Reading ... RMR

Remote Meter Resetting System [*Postage meter*] ... RMRS

Remote Method Invocation [*Computer science*] ... RMI

Remote Method Invocation [*Computer science*] (DOM) ... RMI

Remote Minefield Identification and Deployment [*or Display*] **System** (MCD) ... REMIDS

Remote Missile Select ... RMS

Remote Monitor System ... RMS

Remote Monitoring [*Computer science*] ... RMON

Remote Monitoring and Control System [*Telecommunications*] ... RMCS

Remote Monitoring Sensor Unit (MCD) ... RMSU

Remote Monitoring Services Manager [*Telecommunications*] ... RSM

Remote Monitoring Unit [*Telecommunications*] ... RMU

Remote Motor/Safe and Arming Device ... RM/SAD

Remote Multimedia Mode [*Army*] ... RM^3

Remote Multiplexer [*Computer science*] (CAAL) ... RM

Remote Multiplexer (NITA) ... RMX

Remote Multiplexer Combiner (MCD) ... RMC

Remote Multiplexer/Demultiplexer Unit (SSD) ... RMDU

Remote Multiplexer System [*Computer science*] (IAA) ... RMS

Remote Multiplexer Unit [*Computer science*] (KSC) ... RMU

Remote Network (MHDB) ... RNET

Remote Network Access Controller ... RNAC

Remote Network Monitoring Management Information Base [*Telecommunications*] ... RMON MIB

Remote Network Processor ... RNP

Remote Ocean Surface Measuring System [*Navy*] (CAAL) ... ROMS

Remote Office Test Line [*Bell Laboratories*] ... ROTL

Remote On-Line Business Information Network [*Computer science*] (IEEE) ... ROBIN

Remote Online Print Executive System ... ROPES

Remote On-Line Subsystem [*Computer science*] (MHDI) ... ROLS

Remote Online System (NITA) ... ROLS

Remote Operated Door (MCD) ... ROD

Remote Operated Radiographic Inspection System ... RORIS

Remote Operated Valve (KSC) ... ROV

Remote Operating Location (MCD) ... ROL

Remote Operating System (IAA) ... ROS

Remote Operating System Conventional Operating Environment [*Computer science*] (IAA) ... ROSCOE

Remote Operational Control Center ... ROCC

Remote Operational Control Unit [*Military*] (CAAL) ... ROCU

Remote Operations [*Telecommunications*] (OSI) ... RO

Remote Operations and Maintenance Demonstration [*Nuclear energy*] ... ROMD

Remote Operations Protocol Machine [*Telecommunications*] (OSI) ... ROPM

Remote Operations Service [*Telecommunications*] (OSI) ... ROS

Remote Operations Service Element [*Computer science*] (TNIG) ... ROSE

Remote Operator Control Panel [*Electronics*] (IAA) ... ROCP

Remote Operator Facility [*Honeywell, Inc.*] ... ROF

Remote Operator Task Station [*Air Force*] ... ROTS

Remote Operator's Console ... ROC

Remote Optical Character Recognition [*Computer science*] ... ROCR

Remote Optical Sensing of Emissions [*Instrumentation*] ... ROSE

Remote Optical Sight [*Military*] (CAAL) ... ROS

Remote Optical System ... ROS

Remote Optical Viewing ... ROV

Remote Optical Viewing System ... ROVS

Remote Ordnance Neutralization Device (DWSG) ... ROND

Remote Parameter Control [*Automotive engineering*] ... RPC

Remote Payload Operations Center [*NASA*] (MCD) ... RPOC

Remote Payload Operations Control Center [*NASA*] (SSD) ... RPOCC

Remote Performance Monitoring (CET) ... RPM

Remote Performance Monitoring and Control ... RPMC

Remote Peripheral Equipment (IEEE) ... RPE

Remote Personnel Facility ... RPF

Remote Pickup [*FCC*] (NTCM) ... RE

Remote Pickup ... RP

Remote Pickup Unit ... RPU

Remote Plan Position Indicator (MCD) ... RPPI

Remote Plasma Chemical Vapor Deposition [*Coating technology*] [*Semiconductor technology*] ... RPCVD

Remote Position Control ... RPC

Remote Positioning Valve ... RPV

Remote Power Controller ... RPC

Remote Printer (BUR) ... RP

Remote Printing System ... RPS

Remote Procedure Call [*Computer science*] ... RPC

Remote Process Cell [*Nuclear energy*] (NRCH) ... RPC

Remote Process Crane Cave [*Nuclear energy*] (NRCH) ... RPCC

Remote Processing Facility (MCD) ... RPF

Remote Processing Service (BUR) ... RPS

Remote Processing System (IAA) ... RPS

Remote Processing Unit (KSC) ... RPU

Remote Processor (NITA) ... RP

Remote Processor Controller (NITA) ... RPC

Remote Program Load ... RPL

Remote Program Management ... RPM

Remote Programming System (MCD) ... RPS

Remote Query Update System [*Computer science*] ... RQUS

Remote RADAR Integration Station [*Military*] ... RRIS

Remote RADAR Operator (MCD) ... REMRO

Remote RADAR Tracking System (MHDI) ... RRTS

Remote Range Control Unit (MCD) ... RRCU

Remote Reading High Intensity Constant Monitoring Device (IAA) ... RRHICMD

Remote Readout Experiment ... REREX

Remote Readout Unit ... RROU

Remote Readout Unit ... RRU

Remote Reconnaissance Vehicle (NITA) ... RRV

Remote Record Address ... RRA

Remote Request Unit (CAAL) ... RRU

Remote Safe-and-Arm Device ... RSAD

Remote Safing Switch ... RSS

Remote Scanner-Encoder Unit [*Bell Laboratories*] ... RSEU

Remote Scanning Online Retrieval System (NITA) ... RESORS

Remote Secure Data Change (DNAB) ... RSDC

Remote Sensing Center [*Texas A & M University*] [*Research center*] (RCD) ... RSC

Remote Sensing Chemical Agent Alarm [*Army*] (INF) ... RSCAAL

Remote Sensing Device ... RSD

Remote Sensing Institute [*South Dakota State University*] [*Research center*] (RCD) ... RSI

Remote Sensing Laboratory [*University of Kansas, University of Minnesota*] [*Research center*] (MCD) ... RSL

Remote Sensing Oceanography [*Navy*] ... RSOC

Remote Sensing of Earth Resources ... RSER

Remote Sensing of Environment [*A publication*] (DNAB) ... RSE

Remote Sensing On-Line Retrieval System [*Canada Centre for Remote Sensing*] [*Department of Energy, Mines, and Resources Database*] [*Information service or system*] (IID) ... RESORS

Remote Sensing Research Program [*University of California*] ... RSRP

Remote Sensing Society [*Nottingham, England*] (EAIO) ... RSS

Remote Sensing Technology [*Automotive exhaust emissions*] ... RST

Remote Sensor Platoon ... RSP

Remote Service Facility (IAA) ... RSF

Remote Service Unit (NASA) ... RSU

Remote Session Access [*Telecommunications*] (OSI) ... RSA

Remote Session Access (NITA) ... RSA

Remote Shell [*Computer science*] (CDE) ... rsh

Remote Short Range Wind Sensor (MCD) ... RSRW

Remote Shutdown Panel (IEEE) ... RSDP

Remote Shutdown Panel [*Nuclear energy*] (NRCH) ... RSP

Remote Shutdown System (IEEE) ... RSS

Remote Site [*NASA*] (KSC) ... R/S

Remote Site (NITA) ... RS

Remote Slave Aircraft (MCD) ... RSAC

Remote Slave Station (MCD) ... RSS

Remote Spooling Communications Subsystem [*IBM Corp.*] [*Computer science*] (IBMDP) ... RSCS

Remote Spooling Control System [*Computer science*] (TNIG) ... RSCS

Remote Sprint Launching [*Military*] ... RSL

Remote Start Relay (IAA) ... RSR

Remote Start Unit Trainer (DWSG) ... RSUT

Remote Station ... RS

Remote Station [*Computer science*] ... RST

Remote Station Alarm ... RSA

Remote Station Communication Interface Equipment ... RSCIE

Remote Station Data Terminal ... RSDT

Remote Storage Activities ... RSA

Remote Store Controller ... RSC

Remote Subscriber Unit [*Telecommunications*] ... RSU

Remote Support Facility ... RSF

Remote Switching Partition (HGAA) ... RSP

Remote Switching System [*Telecommunications*] ... RSS

Remote Switching Unit [*Telecommunications*] ... RSU

Remote Synchronous Terminal Control Program (MHDI) ... RSTCP

Remote System Base (MHDI) ... RSB

Remote System Support Utility [*Telematics International, Inc.*] ... RSSU

Remote System Verification Program ... RSVP

Remote Tactical Airborne SIGINT [*Signals Intelligence*] **System** [*Air Force*]
(DOMA) .... RTASS
Remote Targeting System .... RTS
Remote Technical Assistance (NITA) .... RTA
Remote Technical Assistance and Information Network [*Computer science*] .... RETAIN
Remote Telecommunications Access Method [*Computer science*] .... RTAM
Remote Telemetry Unit .... RTU
Remote Telephone Interface .... RTI
Remote Telephone Subscribers' Association [*Australia*] .... RTSA
Remote Temperature Detector .... RTD
Remote Terminal [*Computer science*] .... RT
Remote Terminal Access Method [*Computer science*] (BUR) .... RTAM
Remote Terminal Controller .... RTC
Remote Terminal Emulator [*For teleprocessing validation*] .... RTE
Remote Terminal Input/Output .... RTIO
Remote Terminal Interactive Processor (MCD) .... RTIP
Remote Terminal Interface Package .... RTIP
Remote Terminal Network .... RTN
Remote Terminal Routine Package [*Computer science*] (IAA) .... RTRP
Remote Terminal Scanning System [*Computer science*] (IAA) .... RTS
Remote Terminal Site [*MTMC*] (TAG) .... RTS
Remote Terminal Supervisor (CMD) .... RTS
Remote Terminal System [*Computer science*] (IAA) .... RTS
Remote Terminal Unit .... RTU
Remote Test Access [*Telecommunications*] (TEL) .... RTA
Remote Test System [*Bell System*] .... RTS
Remote Testing System (NITA) .... RTS
Remote Timing and Data Distribution .... RTDD
Remote Tracking Network .... RTN
Remote Tracking Site [*Military*] .... RTS
Remote Tracking Station [*NASA*] .... RTS
Remote Transfer Point .... RTP
Remote Transmitter (FAAC) .... RTMTR
Remote Transmitter .... RTR
Remote Trunk Arrangement [*Telecommunications*] (TEL) .... RTA
Remote Tuning Technique .... RTT
Remote Underwater Detection Device [*Navy*] .... RUDD
Remote Underwater Fisheries Assessment System [*National Oceanic and Atmospheric Administration*] .... RUFAS
Remote Underwater Manipulator [*Oceanography*] .... RUM
Remote Underwater Marine Probe (SAA) .... RUMP
Remote Underwater Mine Countermeasure (PDAA) .... RUMIC
Remote Unit (NASA) .... RU
Remote Unit Monitor (MCD) .... RUM
Remote Unmanned Work System [*Navy*] .... RUWS
Remote User Access System [*Telecommunications*] .... RUAC
Remote User Service Station (MCD) .... RUSS
Remote User Shared Hardware [*Computer science*] .... RUSH
Remote User Terminal [*Computer science*] (CAAL) .... RUT
Remote Vehicle Checkout Facility [*NASA*] (NASA) .... RVCF
Remote View Airborne Night Classification System .... RVANCS
Remote Viewing System .... RVS
Remote Virtual Disk [*Computer science*] .... RVD
Remote Voltage Adjustment .... RVA
Remote Volume Control .... REVOCON
Remote Weight Indicator .... RWI
Remote Workcenter .... RWC
Remote-Access Immediate Response [*Computer science*] (MHDB) .... RAIR
Remote-Controlled Aerial Target (NATG) .... RCAT
Remote-Controlled Air-Ground Communication Site (MCD) .... RCAG
Remote-Controlled Vehicle (MCD) .... RCV
Remoted Targets System (MCD) .... RETS
Remote-Handled [*Waste*] [*Colorado*] (GAAI) .... RH
Remotely Accessible Management Systems [*Computer science*] .... RAMS
Remotely Activated Command and Control [*Military*] (CAAL) .... RACC
Remotely Augmented Vehicle [*Aircraft*] .... RAV
Remotely Employed Sensor [*Military*] (GFGA) .... REMS
Remotely Guided Autonomous Lightweight Torpedo (MCD) .... REGAL
Remotely Handled .... RH
Remotely Manned Vehicle .... RMV
Remotely Monitored Battlefield Area Sensor System (MCD) .... REMBASS
Remotely Operated Longwall Face (IEEE) .... ROLF
Remotely Operated Platform Electronic [*Submarine technology*] .... ROPE
Remotely Operated Platform for Ocean Science [*Marine science*] (OSRA) .... ROPOS
Remotely Operated Platform for Ocean Science (USDC) .... ROPOS
Remotely Operated Special Equipment [*Nuclear energy*] (SAA) .... ROSE
Remotely Operated Vehicle [*Underwater robot*] .... ROV
Remotely Piloted Aerial Observation Detection System (MCD) .... RPAODS
Remotely Piloted Craft [*Navy*] .... RPC
Remotely Piloted Helicopter .... RPH
Remotely Piloted Munitions [*Army*] .... RPM
Remotely Piloted Research Vehicle [*NASA*] .... RPRV
Remotely Piloted Vehicle [*Aircraft*] .... RPV
Remotely Piloted Vehicle - Institutional Trainer [*Military*] .... RPV-IT
Remotely Piloted Vehicle Investigation - Adjustment of Indirect Artillery Fire .... RPVI-AIAF
Remotely Piloted Vehicle Investigation - Emerging Sensors (MCD) .... RPVI-ES
Remotely Programmable Conference Arranger [*Telecommunications*] (TSSD) .... RPCA
Remotely Settable Fuze (MCD) .... RS
Remotely-Operated Mobile Manipulator (PDAA) .... ROMAN
Remotely-Operated Service Arm [*Nuclear energy*] (NUCP) .... ROSA
Remotely-Piloted Mini-Blimp (PDAA) .... RPMB

Remotely-Piloted Observation Aircraft Designator System (PDAA) .... RPOADS
Remote-Piloted Vehicle Experiment .... RPVX
Remote-Site Command Computer [*NASA*] .... RSCC
Remote-Site Computer Complex [*NASA*] .... RSCC
Remote-Site Data Processor [*NASA*] .... RSDP
Remote-Site Simulation Unit [*Navy*] (NVT) .... RSSU
Remote-Site Simulator Console [*NASA*] .... RSSC
Remote-Site Telemetry Computer [*NASA*] .... RSTC
Remote-Site Telemetry Processor [*NASA*] (KSC) .... RSTP
Remote-Voice Control .... RVC
Remotum [*Far Respiration*] [*Latin*] (MAE) .... R
Remount (WGA) .... RMT
Remount Purchasing Commission [*British military*] (DMA) .... RPC
Removable (AAG) .... RMVBL
Removable Instrument Assembly [*Nuclear energy*] (NRCH) .... RIA
Removable Media Memory Units .... RMMU
Removable Needle [*Medicine*] .... RN
Removable, Optical, Erasable Media [*Computer science*] (BTTJ) .... ROEM
Removable Overhead Structure (MCD) .... ROS
Removable Partial Denture (DAVI) .... RPD
Removable Patch Panel .... RPP
Removable Top Closure [*Nuclear energy*] (NRCH) .... RTC
Removal (ROG) .... REML
Removal (AAG) .... RMVL
Removal and Installation (NRCH) .... R & I
Removal and Installation (IAA) .... RAI
Removal Item - Ship's Record (MCD) .... RI-SR
Removal of [*Surgery*] (DAVI) X
Removal/Recertification .... R/RC
Removal-Replacement .... RR
Remove [*or Removal*] (AAG) .... REM
Remove [*Computer science*] [*Telecommunications*] .... rm
Remove (AAG) .... RMV
Remove and Replace (KSC) .... R & R
Remove and Replace (IAA) .... RAR
Remove Aquino from Malacanang before October [*Operation proposed by rebel military leader "Gringo" Honasan*] [*1987 Philippines*] .... RAMBO
Remove Audible Ring .... RAR
Remove Cloud From Title (MHDB) .... RCFT
Remove Directory [*Computer science*] .... RD
Remove Directory [*Computer science*] .... RMDIR
Remove Errors and Complete on Time (DNAB) .... REACOT
Remove Intoxicated Drivers [*An association*] .... RID
Remove Shutoff Valve (KSC) .... RSV
Removed (AAG) .... RMVD
Removing (AAG) .... RMVG
REMs [*Roentgen Equivalents, Man*] **per Hour** (DEN) .... r/h
Remsen Bell-Enterprise, Remsen, IA [*Library symbol Library of Congress*] (LCLS) .... IaRemBE
Remsen, NY [*AM radio station call letters*] .... WADR
Remsen, NY [*FM radio station call letters*] (RBYB) .... WRFM-FM
Remsen, NY [*FM radio station call letters*] .... WUUU
Remy's Reports [*145-162 Indiana*] [*15-33 Indiana Appellate*] [*A publication*] (DLA) .... Remy
Ren and Stimpy [*Cartoon characters*] .... R & S
Renabie Gold Trust [*Formerly, Barrick-Cullation Gold Trust*] [*Toronto Stock Exchange symbol*] .... RG
Renabie Mines (1981) Ltd. [*Toronto Stock Exchange symbol*] .... RBE
Renaissance .... REN
Renaissance [*Record label*] .... Ren
Renaissance (VRA) .... Renais
Renaissance and Reformation [*A publication*] (BRI) .... Ren & Ref
Renaissance Artists and Writers Association (EA) .... RAWA
Renaissance Business and Law Center, Inc. [*Detroit, MI*] (TSSD) .... RBLC
Renaissance Cap Growth & Inc Fd [*NASDAQ symbol*] (TTSB) .... RENN
Renaissance Capital Growth & Income Fund III [*Associated Press*] (SAG) .... RenaCap
Renaissance Capital Growth & Income Fund III [*NASDAQ symbol*] (SAG) .... RENN
Renaissance Commun [*NYSE symbol*] (TTSB) .... RRR
Renaissance Communications Corp. [*Associated Press*] (SAG) .... RenCm
Renaissance Communications Corp. [*NYSE symbol*] (SAG) .... RRR
Renaissance Educational Associates [*Defunct*] (EA) .... REA
Renaissance Energy Ltd. [*Toronto Stock Exchange symbol*] .... RES
Renaissance English Text Society (EA) .... RETS
Renaissance Entertainment [*NASDAQ symbol*] (TTSB) .... FAIR
Renaissance Entertainment Corp. [*NASDAQ symbol*] (SAG) .... FAIR
Renaissance Entertainment Corp. [*Associated Press*] (SAG) .... RenE
Renaissance Entertainment Corp. [*Associated Press*] (SAG) .... RenEnt
Renaissance Entmt Wrrt'A' [*NASDAQ symbol*] (TTSB) .... FAIRW
Renaissance Entmt Wrrt'B' [*NASDAQ symbol*] (TTSB) .... FAIRZ
Renaissance Golf Products [*NASDAQ symbol*] (TTSB) .... FGLF
Renaissance Hotel Group NV [*Associated Press*] (SAG) .... RenHtl
Renaissance Hotel Group NV [*NYSE symbol*] (SAG) .... RHG
Renaissance of Italian Youth (EA) .... RIY
Renaissance Quarterly [*A publication*] (BRI) .... Ren Q
Renaissance Society of America (EA) .... RSA
Renaissance Solutions [*NASDAQ symbol*] (TTSB) .... RENS
Renaissance Solutions, Inc. [*NASDAQ symbol*] (SAG) .... RENS
Renaissance Universal (EA) .... RU
RenaissanceRe Holdings [*NASDAQ symbol*] (TTSB) .... RNREF
RenaissanceRe Holdings Ltd. [*Associated Press*] (SAG) .... RenaissRe
RenaissanceRe Holdings Ltd. [*Associated Press*] (SAG) .... RenRe
RenaissanceRe Holdings Ltd. [*NYSE symbol*] (SAG) .... RNR
RenaissanceRe Holdings Ltd. [*NASDAQ symbol*] (SAG) .... RNREF

RenaissanceRe Solutions, Inc. [*Associated Press*] (SAG) .... RenSolu
Renal [*Medicine*] (MAE) .... ren
Renal Anastomosis [*Medicine*] .... REA
Renal Arterial Constriction [*Medicine*] .... RAC
Renal Artery [*Anatomy*] .... RA
Renal Artery Bypass [*Medicine*] .... RABP
Renal Artery Pressure [*Medicine*] .... RAP
Renal Artery Stenosis [*Medicine*] (MAE) .... RAS
Renal Blood Flow [*Medicine*] .... RBF
Renal Care Group [*NASDAQ symbol*] (TTSB) .... RCGI
Renal Cell Carcinoma [*Medicine*] .... RCC
Renal Cell Carcinoma, Papillary [*Medicine*] (DMAA) .... RCCP
Renal Cortical Tumor [*Oncology*] .... RCT
Renal Dialysis Treatment [*Nephrology*] .... RDT
Renal Dipeptidase [*An enzyme*] .... RDP
Renal Disease [*Medicine*] .... RD
Renal Erythropoietic Factor [*Medicine*] .... REF
Renal Excretion Rate [*Medicine*] (MAE) .... RER
Renal Failure [*Medicine*] .... RF
Renal Function Studies [*Medicine*] .... RFS
Renal Homotransplantation [*Medicine*] (DMAA) .... RHT
Renal Hypertensive Disease [*Medicine*] .... RHD
Renal Hypertensive Rat [*Medicine*] (DMAA) .... RHR
Renal Mesenchymal Tumor [*Oncology*] .... RMT
Renal Papillary Necrosis [*Nephrology*] (DAVI) .... RPN
Renal Physicians Association (EA) .... RPA
Renal Plasma Flow [*Medicine*] .... RPF
Renal Potassium Wasting (MAE) .... RKW
Renal Pressor Substance [*Medicine*] .... RPS
Renal Renin Activity [*Nephrology*] (DAVI) .... RRA
Renal Specialist [*Medicine*] .... RS
Renal Transplant [*Nephrology*] .... RT
Renal Transplant Unit [*National Health Service*] [*British*] (DI) .... RTU
Renal Treatment Center, Inc. [*NASDAQ symbol*] (SAG) .... RXTC
Renal Treatment Centers, Inc. [*Associated Press*] (SAG) .... RenalT
Renal Treatment Centers, Inc. [*Associated Press*] (SAG) .... RenalTrt
Renal Treatment Centers, Inc. [*NYSE symbol*] (SAG) .... RXT
Renal Treatment Ctrs [*NYSE symbol*] (TTSB) .... RXT
Renal Tubular Acidification Defect [*Medicine*] (DMAA) .... RTAD
Renal Tubular Defect [*Medicine*] (DMAA) .... RTD
Renal Tubule Acidosis [*Medicine*] .... RTA
Renal Tubule Necrosis [*Medicine*] .... RTN
Renal Vascular Resistance [*Medicine*] .... RVR
Renal Vein Plasma Renin Activity [*Medicine*] (DMAA) .... RVPRA
Renal Vein/Renal Activity [*Ratio*] [*Medicine*] .... RV/RA
Renal Vein Renin Concentration [*Medicine*] .... RVRC
Renal Vein Thrombosis [*Medicine*] .... RVT
Renal Venous Plasma [*Biochemistry*] (DAVI) .... RVP
Renal Venous Pressure (OA) .... RVP
Renal Venous Renin Assay [*Medicine*] (MAE) .... RVRA
Renal Vessel [*Medicine*] .... RV
Rename File [*Computer science*] .... REN
Renan Ltd. [*Moldova*] [*FAA designator*] (FAAC) .... RAN
Renastera Noastra [*Rumania*] [*A publication*] (BJA) .... RN
Renault Club of America [*Defunct*] (EA) .... RCA
Renault Owners Club of America (EA) .... ROCOA
Renault Truck Industries [*British subsidiary of Renault Vehicules Industriels*] .... RTI
Renault Vehicules Industriels [*Renault Industrial Vehicles*] [*Finland*] .... RVI
Renaut's Bodies [*Neurology*] .... RB
Rencon Mining Co. [*Vancouver Stock Exchange symbol*] .... REN
Rencontres Internationales des Assureurs Defense [*Genoa, Italy*] (EA) .... RIAD
Render (IAA) .... R
Render and Set [*Construction*] (IAA) .... RS
Render, Float, and Set [*Construction*] .... RFS
Render Safe Procedure [*Military*] .... RSP
Rendered (ROG) .... RD
Rendered (ADA) .... REND
Rendered (ROG) .... RENDD
Rendering (VRA) .... rndr
Rendezvous (AABC) .... RDVU
Rendezvous (KSC) .... RENDZ
Rendezvous (KSC) .... RNDZ
Rendezvous .... RV
Rendezvous and Docking [*Aerospace*] (MCD) .... RENDOCK
Rendezvous and Recovery (NASA) .... R & R
Rendezvous Compatible Orbit [*Aerospace*] .... RCO
Rendezvous Docking Simulator [*Aerospace*] .... RDS
Rendezvous Evaluation Pad [*NASA*] (KSC) .... REP
Rendezvous Exercise Pod (SAA) .... REP
Rendezvous Maneuver (MCD) .... RM
Rendezvous Mercury Capsule [*NASA*] (AAG) .... RMC
Rendezvous Orbit Insertion [*Aerospace*] .... ROI
Rendezvous Point Position [*Aerospace*] .... RPP
Rendezvous RADAR [*NASA*] (NASA) .... RENRAD
Rendezvous RADAR [*NASA*] .... RR
Rendezvous RADAR Electronics Assembly [*NASA*] (MCD) .... RREA
Rendezvous RADAR Electronics Unit [*NASA*] (MCD) .... RREU
Rendezvous RADAR Indicator [*NASA*] (NASA) .... RRI
Rendezvous RADAR System [*NASA*] (MCD) .... RRS
Rendezvous RADAR Transducer [*NASA*] (NASA) .... RRT
Rendezvous RADAR/Transponder [*NASA*] (KSC) .... RR/T
Rendezvous Retrieval, Docking, and Assembly [*of space vehicle or orbital station*] [*NASA*] (AAG) .... RRDA
Rendezvous Station Panel [*NASA*] (MCD) .... RSP
Rendezvous Vehicle [*NASA*] (KSC) .... RV
Rendsburg/Schachtholm [*Germany ICAO location identifier*] (ICLI) .... EDXR
Rendu-Osler-Weber Syndrome [*Medicine*] (DMAA) .... ROW
Rene Dubos Center for Human Environments (EA) .... RDCHE
Rene Guyon Society (EA) .... RGS
Renegotiate .... RNGT
Renegotiated-Rate Mortgage .... RRM
Renegotiation (AAGC) .... Reneg
Renegotiation Board [*Terminated, 1979*] [*Federal government*] .... RB
Renegotiation Board [*Terminated, 1979*] [*Federal government*] .... RNB
Renegotiation Board Regulation [*or Ruling*] .... RBR
Renegotiation Bulletins [*A publication*] (DLA) .... RB
Renegotiation Regional Office .... RRO
Renegotiation Regulations .... RR
Renegotiation Rulings (DLA) .... R RUL
Renewable .... REN
Renewable (MSA) .... RNWBL
Renewable Energy and Energy Efficiency Joint Ventures Advisory Committee [*Department of Energy*] (EGAO) .... REEEVAC
Renewable Energy Authority of Victoria [*Australia*] .... REAV
Renewable Energy Congressional Staff Group [*Defunct*] (EA) .... RECSG
Renewable Energy Info Center (EA) .... REIC
Renewable Energy Technologies Symposium and International Exposition [*Renewable Energy Institute*] (TSPED) .... RETSIE
Renewable Fuels Association (EA) .... RFA
Renewable Intensive Global Energy Scenario .... RIGES
Renewable Materials Institute [*College of Environmental Science and Forestry at Syracuse*] [*Research center*] (RCD) .... RMI
Renewable Natural Resources (DI) .... RNR
Renewable Natural Resources Foundation (EA) .... RNRF
Renewable Resources Library, Government of the Northwest Territories, Yellowknife, Northwest Territories [*Library symbol National Library of Canada*] (NLC) .... NWYRR
Renewable Resources Technical Information System [*Forest Service*] .... RRTIS
Renewable Term Insurance (MHDB) .... RTI
Renewable-Base Oxygenated Blend [*Automotive fuel*] .... RBOB
Renewal .... REN
Renewal (MSA) .... RNL
Renewal and Housing Assistance Report [*HUD*] .... RHA
Renewal and Housing Management [*HUD*] .... RHM
Renewal Assistance Administration [*HUD*] .... RAA
Renewal Not Required (AIA) .... RNR
Renewal Parts Data (MSA) .... RPD
Renewal Parts Leaflet (MSA) .... RPL
Renewal Projects Administration [*HUD*] .... RPA
Renewal Registration [*US Copyright Office class*] .... RE
Renewal-at-Birth [*A periodical subscription*] (WDMC) .... RAB
Renewed License [*FCC*] (NTCM) .... R
Renfrew, ON [*AM radio station call letters*] CHVR-1
Renfrew Public Library, Ontario [*Library symbol National Library of Canada*] (NLC) .... OR
Rengat [*Sumatra, Indonesia*] [*Airport symbol*] (AD) .... RGT
Rengat [*Indonesia*] [*Airport symbol*] (OAG) .... RGT
Rengat/Japura [*Indonesia*] [*ICAO location identifier*] (ICLI) .... WIPR
Renin [*An enzyme*] .... REN
Renin Activity (AAMN) .... RA
Renin Essential Hypertension [*Medicine*] (DMAA) .... REH
Renin Inhibitory Peptide [*Biochemistry*] .... RIP
Renin Release [*Endocrinology*] (MAE) .... RR
Renin Substrate [*Biochemistry*] .... RS
Renin-Angiotensin [*Medicine*] (DMAA) .... RA
Renin-Angiotensin System [*Endocrinology*] .... RAS
Renin-Angiotensin-Aldosterone [*Clinical nephrology*] .... RAA
Renin-Angiotensin-Aldosterone System [*Medicine*] (DMAA) .... RAAS
Renin-Release Rate [*Endocrinology*] (MAE) .... RRR
Renk [*Sudan*] [*ICAO location identifier*] (ICLI) .... HSRN
Renmark [*Australia Airport symbol*] (OAG) .... RMK
Renminbi [*Monetary unit*] [*China*] .... RMB
Rennell Island [*Solomon Islands*] [*Airport symbol*] (OAG) .... RNL
Renner's Gold Coast Colony Reports [*A publication*] (DLA) .... Ren
Renner's Gold Coast Colony Reports [*1868-1914*] [*Ghana*] [*A publication*] (DLA) .... RGCR
Renner's Reports, Notes of Cases, Gold Coast Colony and Colony of Nigeria [*1861-1914*] [*A publication*] (DLA) .... Renn
Rennes [*France*] [*Airport symbol*] (OAG) .... RNS
Rennes/Saint-Jacques [*France ICAO location identifier*] (ICLI) .... LFRN
Renninger & Graves, Inc., Philadelphia, PA [*Closed*] [*Library symbol*] [*Library of Congress*] (LCLS) .... ReGI
Reno [*Nevada*] [*Seismograph station code, US Geological Survey Closed*] (SEIS) .... REN
Reno [*Nevada*] [*Airport symbol*] (OAG) .... RNO
Reno Air [*NASDAQ symbol*] (TTSB) .... RENO
Reno Air Defense Sector [*ADC*] .... READS
Reno Air, Inc. [*NASDAQ symbol*] (SAG) .... RENO
Reno Air, Inc. [*Associated Press*] (SAG) .... RenoAir
Reno Air, Inc. [*ICAO designator*] (FAAC) .... ROA
Reno/International [*Nevada*] [*ICAO location identifier*] (ICLI) .... KRNO
Reno, NV [*Television station call letters*] .... KAME
Reno, NV [*AM radio station call letters*] .... KCBN
Reno, NV [*FM radio station call letters*] (RBYB) .... KDOT-FM
Reno, NV [*FM radio station call letters*] .... KHIT
Reno, NV [*AM radio station call letters*] (RBYB) .... KHIT-AM
Reno, NV [*AM radio station call letters*] (RBYB) .... KKOH
Reno, NV [*FM radio station call letters*] .... KNEV
Reno, NV [*Television station call letters*] .... KNPB
Reno, NV [*AM radio station call letters*] (RBYB) .... KNRC

Reno, NV [*Television station call letters*] ..... KOLO
Reno, NV [*AM radio station call letters*] ..... KOZZ
Reno, NV [*FM radio station call letters*] ..... KOZZ-FM
Reno, NV [*AM radio station call letters*] ..... KQLO
Reno, NV [*Television station call letters*] ..... KREN
Reno, NV [*FM radio station call letters*] ..... KRNO
Reno, NV [*Television station call letters*] ..... KRNV
Reno, NV [*FM radio station call letters*] (RBYB) ..... KRNV-FM
Reno, NV [*Television station call letters*] ..... KRXI
Reno, NV [*Television station call letters*] ..... KTVN
Reno, NV [*FM radio station call letters*] ..... KUNR
Reno, NV [*AM radio station call letters*] ..... KXEQ
Reno, NV [*AM radio station call letters*] ..... KXTO
Reno, NV [*FM radio station call letters*] ..... KZSR
Reno, NV [*Location identifier FAA*] (FAAL) ..... SPK
Renopericardial Canal [*Medicine*] ..... RPC
Renopericardial Canal, Kidney [*Medicine*] ..... RPCK
Renopericardial Canal, Pericardium [*Medicine*] ..... RPCP
Renovacion Espanola [*Spanish Renovation*] (PPE) ..... RE
Renovacion Nacional [*National Renovation*] [*Chile*] [*Political party*] (EY) ..... RN
Renovandus [*To Be Renewed*] [*Pharmacy*] (ROG) ..... RENOVAND
Renovascular Hypertension [*Medicine*] ..... RVH
Renovate (AABC) ..... RENV
Renovation and Storage [*Military*] (AFIT) ..... R & S
Renovation of Armament Manufacturing Program [*Army*] (MCD) ..... REARM
Renovetur [*Renew*] [*Pharmacy*] [*Latin*] (MAE) ..... ren
Renovetur Semel [*Renew Once*] [*Pharmacy*] ..... REN SEM
Renovo, PA [*FM radio station call letters*] (RBYB) ..... WXKW
Renown Aviation, Inc. [*ICAO designator*] (FAAC) ..... RGS
Renox Creek Resources [*Vancouver Stock Exchange symbol*] ..... RNX
Rensselaer, IN [*Location identifier FAA*] (FAAL) ..... RZL
Rensselaer, IN [*FM radio station call letters*] ..... WLQI
Rensselaer, IN [*FM radio station call letters*] ..... WPUM
Rensselaer, IN [*AM radio station call letters*] ..... WRIN
Rensselaer, NY [*AM radio station call letters*] ..... WQBK
Rensselaer, NY [*FM radio station call letters*] ..... WQBK-FM
Rensselaer Polytechnic Institute (GAGS) ..... RPI
Rensselaer Polytechnic Institute [*Troy, NY*] (MCD) ..... RPI
Rensselaer Polytechnic Institute/Center for Integrated Electronics [*Troy, NY*] ..... RPI/CIE
Rensselaer Polytechnic Institute/Microwave Acoustics Laboratory [*Troy, NY*] ..... RPI/MA
Rensselaer Polytechnic Institute Plasma Dynamics Laboratory [*Research center*] (RCD) ..... RPDL
Rensselaer Polytechnic Institute, Troy, NY [*Library symbol Library of Congress*] (LCLS) ..... NTR
Rensselaer Polytechnic Institute, Troy, NY [*OCLC symbol*] (OCLC) ..... YRM
Rent Advisory Board [*Cost of Living Council*] ..... RAB
Rent Charge ..... RC
Rent Control (MHDB) ..... RC
Rent Control System ..... RCS
Rent Free ..... RF
Rent Law Reports [*India*] [*A publication*] (DLA) ..... Rt Law Rep
Rent Officer [*British*] (ILCA) ..... RO
Rent Procedural Regulation (Office of Rent Stabilization) [*Economic Stabilization Agency*] [*A publication*] (DLA) ..... RPR
Rent Regulation (Office of Price Stabilization) [*Economic Stabilization Agency*] [*A publication*] (DLA) ..... RP
Rent Regulation (Office of Rent Stabilization) [*Economic Stabilization Agency*] [*A publication*] (DLA) ..... RR
Rent Way, Inc. [*Associated Press*] (SAG) ..... RntWay
Rent Way, Inc. [*NASDAQ symbol*] (SAG) ..... RWAY
Rental ..... RENT
Rental Agreement ..... RA
Rental Assistance Payment Program [*HUD*] ..... RAP
Rental Bond Board [*New South Wales, Australia*] ..... RBB
Rental Housing Assistance for Pensioners Program [*Australia*] ..... RHAPP
Rental Rehabilitation Grant [*Department of Housing and Urban Development*] (GFGA) ..... RRG
Rental Rehabilitation Program [*Department of Housing and Urban Development*] (GFGA) ..... RRP
Rental Service Association (EA) ..... RSA
Rental Service Corp. [*Associated Press*] (SAG) ..... RentlSrv
Rental Service Corp. [*NASDAQ symbol*] (SAG) ..... RSVC
Rentavion CA [*Venezuela*] [*ICAO designator*] (FAAC) ..... RNT
Rent-A-Wreck Amer Inc. [*NASDAQ symbol*] (TTSB) ..... RAWA
Rent-a-Wreck Industries Corp. [*Vancouver Stock Exchange symbol*] ..... RAW
Rent-a-Wreck of America, Inc. [*Los Angeles, CA*] [*NASDAQ symbol*] (NQ) ..... RAWA
Rent-a-Wreck of America, Inc. [*Associated Press*] (SAG) ..... RntWck
Rentech, Inc. [*Associated Press*] (SAG) ..... Rentch
Rentech, Inc. [*NASDAQ symbol*] (SAG) ..... RNTK
Renters Choice [*NASDAQ symbol*] (TTSB) ..... RCII
Renters Choice, Inc. [*NASDAQ symbol*] (SAG) ..... RCII
Renters Choice, Inc. [*Associated Press*] (SAG) ..... Renters
Renton Electrical Analog for Solution of Thermal Analogous Networks ..... REASTAN
Renton Public Library, Renton, WA [*Library symbol Library of Congress*] (LCLS) ..... WaRe
Renton, WA [*AM radio station call letters*] ..... KRIZ
Renton, WA [*Location identifier FAA*] (FAAL) ..... RNT
Rentrak Corp. [*NASDAQ symbol*] (NQ) ..... RENT
Rentrak Corp. [*Associated Press*] (SAG) ..... Rntrak
Rent-Way [*NASDAQ symbol*] (TTSB) ..... RWAY
Renumbered [*Existing article renumbered*] [*Used in Shepard's Citations*] [*Legal term*] (DLA) ..... Rn
Renunciation (ROG) ..... RENUNCN
Renville City Library, Renville, MN [*Library symbol*] [*Library of Congress*] (LCLS) ..... MnRen
Renwick Explorations Ltd. [*Vancouver Stock Exchange symbol*] ..... RWK
Renwick Public Library, Renwick, IA [*Library symbol Library of Congress*] (LCLS) ..... IaRen
Renzulli/Smith Learning Style Inventory (EDAC) ..... RSLSI
REO [*Rawson E. Olds*] **Club of America** (EA) ..... RCA
Reopened Claim [*Unemployment insurance*] (OICC) ..... RC
Reopening [*Investment term*] ..... REOP
Reorder Buffer [*Computer science*] ..... ROB
Reorder Cycle ..... RC
Reorder Lead Time [*Navy*] (NG) ..... RLT
Reorder Point [*Army*] ..... REOPT
Reorder Point [*Navy*] (NG) ..... ROP
Reorder Point [*Army*] ..... RP
Reorder Price ..... ROP
Reorder Tone Trunks [*Telecommunications*] (TEL) ..... ROTT
Reordering Level ..... ROL
Reordering Quality ..... ROQ
Reorganization Objectives, Army Division [*Military*] ..... ROAD
Reorganization Objectives, Army Division, Army and Corps [*Military*] (AABC) ..... RODAC
Reorganization of Combat Infantry Division [*Army*] (AABC) ..... ROCID
Reorganization of Engineer Active Forces (MCD) ..... REAF
Reorganization of the Interconnection Network (MHDI) ..... ROIN
Reorganize (EY) ..... REORG
Reorganized Church of Jesus Christ of Latter-Day Saints ..... RLDS
Reorganized Church of Jesus Christ of Latter-Day Saints, Independence, MO [*Library symbol Library of Congress*] (LCLS) ..... MoIRC
Repackaged Asset Vehicle ..... RAV
Repadre Resources Ltd. [*Vancouver Stock Exchange symbol*] ..... RPD
Repair (DNAB) ..... R
Repair (AAG) ..... REP
Repair (ROG) ..... REPR
Repair (MSA) ..... RPR
Repair ..... RPR
Repair Activity Accounting Number [*Navy*] ..... RAAN
Repair Activity Accounting Number [*Navy*] ..... RAN
Repair Activity Unit Identification Code (MCD) ..... RAUIC
Repair, Alignment, and Calibration (NVT) ..... RAC
Repair and Maintenance (IAA) ..... RAM
Repair and Maintenance Instruction [*Military*] ..... RMI
Repair and Maintenance Time Rate [*Automobile service*] ..... RMTR
Repair and Modification Directive (AAG) ..... RMD
Repair and Overhaul (MCD) ..... R/O
Repair and Overhaul Directive (AAG) ..... ROD
Repair and Rehabilitation of Paved Surfaces (MCD) ..... REREPS
Repair and Retrofix (IAA) ..... RAR
Repair and Return ..... R & R
Repair and Salvage Squadron [*Military*] ..... R & S SQ
Repair and Salvage Unit [*British military*] (DMA) ..... RSU
Repair and Storage Shelter (SAA) ..... RSS
Repair as Required (AAG) ..... RAR
Repair, Assemble, Maintain, Issue, and Supply (MUGU) ..... RAMIS
Repair, Assembly, and Maintenance Shop (IAA) ..... RAMS
Repair Assignment (AAG) ..... RA
Repair at Depot (MCD) ..... RAD
Repair at Intermediate (MCD) ..... RAI
Repair Cost Factor [*Navy*] ..... RCF
Repair Costs [*Technical drawings*] ..... RC
Repair Cycle ..... REPCY
Repair Cycle Float [*Military*] (AABC) ..... RCF
Repair Cycle Float Factor (MCD) ..... RCFF
Repair Cycle Level ..... RCL
Repair Cycle Monitor ..... RCM
Repair Cycle Support Unit ..... RCSU
Repair Cycle Time (MCD) ..... RCT
Repair Equipment [*Navy*] ..... RE
Repair Equipment for F-15 and Subsequent Programs [*Military*] (MCD) ..... RE
Repair, Evaluation, Maintenance, Rehabilitation ..... REMR
Repair Group Category [*Military*] (AFIT) ..... RGC
Repair Induction Code [*Module Maintenance Facility*] ..... RIC
Repair Lead Time ..... RLT
Repair Level Analysis [*Military*] (AFIT) ..... RLA
Repair Line Agreement (NASA) ..... RLA
Repair Manual ..... RM
Repair Manufacturer Codes ..... RMC
Repair of Repairables (MCD) ..... ROFR
Repair of Repairables (MCD) ..... ROR
Repair on Demand (DA) ..... ROD
Repair or Replacement ..... R/R
Repair Order ..... RO
Repair, Overhaul, Restoration (MCD) ..... ROR
Repair Parts and Special Tools List [*Army*] (AABC) ..... RPSTL
Repair Parts Catalog ..... RPC
Repair Parts Cost (MCD) ..... RPC
Repair Parts Decision List [*Military*] (CAAL) ..... RPDL
Repair Parts Directive Order ..... RPDO
Repair Parts Estimate (MCD) ..... RPE
Repair Parts Facility (MCD) ..... RPF
Repair Parts List [*Army*] (AABC) ..... RPL
Repair Parts Order [*Navy*] ..... RPO

Repair Parts Price List	RPPL
Repair Parts Program Management Plans	RPPMP
Repair Parts Program Plan [Army]	RPPP
Repair Parts Provisioning	RPP
Repair Parts Provisioning List	RPPL
Repair Parts Requisition	RPR
Repair Parts Selective List	RPSL
Repair Parts Support Material List	RPSML
Repair Parts Transporter (MCD)	RPT
Repair Period (NASA)	RP
Repair/Rebuild (MCD)	R/R
Repair Service Bureau [Telecommunications] (TEL)	RSB
Repair Sevice Attendant [Telecommunications] (TEL)	RSA
Repair Ship [Navy symbol]	AR
Repair Test Equipment [Aviation]	RTE
Repair Time	RT
Repair Time Ratio	RTR
Repairable Equipment Depot [British military] (DMA)	RED
Repairable Exchange	RX
Repairable Exchange Activity [Army]	RXA
Repairable Identification Code	RIC
Repairable Item Code	RIC
Repairable Item List (CAAL)	RIL
Repairable Provisioning Center (MCD)	RPC
Repairable Return Rate (DNAB)	RRR
Repairables Asset Management System [Military] (CAAL)	RAMS
Repair-at-Failure Maintenance (PDAA)	RAFM
Repaired in Works [British military] (DMA)	RIW
Repaired This Station (AFM)	RTS
Repair-Evacuator Group [Former USSR]	REG
Repairman (NATG)	REPM
Repairman (AABC)	RPMN
Repairman	RPRMN
Repairs and Maintenance	R & M
Repairs and Upkeep [Military]	R & U
Repairs and Utilities [Military]	R & U
Repairs and Utilities [Military] (IAA)	RAU
Repairs Completed [Military] (NVT)	RECOMP
Repairs, Heavy	RP/H
Repairs Liaison Officer [Landing craft and barges] [Navy]	RLO
Repairs, Light	RP/L
Repairs, Maintenance, and Improvements	RMI
Repairs to Other Vessels	ROV
Repairs-to-Extend [Marine science] (OSRA)	RTE
Repairs-to-Extend (USDC)	RTE
Repap Enterprises [NASDAQ symbol] (TTSB)	RPAPF
Repap Enterprises Corp., Inc. [Associated Press] (SAG)	Repap
Repap Enterprises Corp., Inc. [NASDAQ symbol] (NQ)	RPAP
Repap Enterprises Corp., Inc. [Toronto Stock Exchange symbol Vancouver Stock Exchange symbol]	RPP
Reparable Assets Control (AFM)	RAC
Reparable Item Movement Control [Military] (AFIT)	RIMC
Reparable Item Movement Control System [Military] (AFIT)	RIMCS
Reparable Processing Center (AFM)	RPC
Reparation Society of the Immaculate Heart of Mary (EA)	RSIHM
Reparations, Removal, and Demolition [Section] [Industry Branch, US Military Government, Germany]	RR & D
Reparatur-Technische Station [Repair and Technical Station] [German]	RTS
Reparto	REPTO
Repatriate (AABC)	REPAT
Repatriated American Military Personnel [World War II]	RAMPS
Repatriation Pension Decisions [Australia A publication]	RPD
Repayable to Either	RE
Repeal [Legal term] (DLA)	R
Repeal (ROG)	REP
Repeal [Legal shorthand] (LWAP)	RPL
Repeat (WDMC)	R
Repeat (WDMC)	rep
Repeat (AAG)	REP
Repeat (ADA)	REPT
Repeat [International telex abbreviation and wire-service jargon] (WDMC)	rpt
Repeat [International telex abbreviation and wire-service jargon] (WDMC)	RPT
Repeat (AAG)	RPT
Repeat Action [Medicine]	RA
Repeat Action Tablet [Pharmacology]	RAT
Repeat Attempt [Telecommunications] (TEL)	R/A
Repeat Cesarean Section [Obstetrics] (MAE)	R/CS
Repeat Cycle Timer	RCT
Repeat Discrepancy Report (MCD)	RDR
Repeat Expansion Detection [Genetics]	RED
Repeat Formation Tester [Well drilling]	RFT
Repeat Indication [Telecommunications] (TEL)	RI
Repeat Offenders Project	ROP
Repeat Squawk Sheet (MCD)	RSS
Repeat the Figures in Abbreviated Form [Aviation code]	ABV
Repeat Unit [Genetics]	RU
Repeatable Maintenance and Recall System (NASA)	RMRS
Repeated	RPTD
Repeated Attacks [Medicine]	RA
Repeated Measures Analysis of Variance [Statistics]	RMANOVA
Repeatedly Reactive	RR
Repeater (IAA)	R
Repeater	RP
Repeater (MSA)	RPTR
Repeater Amplitude Modulation (MCD)	RAM

Repeater Distribution Frame (NATG)	RDF
Repeater Media Interface Module [Telecommunications]	RMIM
Repeater Plan Position Indicator (NVT)	RPPI
Repeater Test Rack (DEN)	RTR
Repeat-Induced Point Mutation [Genetic engineering technique]	RIP
Repeating Antipersonnel Mine	RAM
Repeating Coil (MSA)	RPTC
Repeating Handheld Improved Non-Rifled Ordnance (PDAA)	RHINO
Repeating Slide Wire	RSW
Repeating Unit [Mathematics] (BARN)	repunit
Repellent (MSA)	RPLT
Repeller (MSA)	RPLR
Reperforated [Philately]	rpf
Reperforator [Telecommunications] (TEL)	REPERF
Reperforator/Transmitter [Teletypewriter] [Computer science]	R/T
Reperfusion in Acute Infarction, Rotterdam [Cardiology study]	REPAIR
Reperimento Documentazione Siderurgica [Iron and Steel Documentation Service] [Information service or system] (IID)	RDS
Repertoire (DLA)	Rep
Repertoire Bibliographique des Institutions Chretiennes [Bibliographical Repertory of Christian Institutions] [Centre de Recherche et de Documentation des Institutions Chretiennes] [France] [Information service or system] (CRD)	RIC
Repertoire de Jurisprudence Commerciale [Paris] [A publication] (DLA)	Rep de Jur Com
Repertoire de Notariae [Paris] [A publication] (DLA)	Rep de Not
Repertoire de Vedettes-Matiere [Laval Subject Authority Records] [UTLAS symbol]	RVM
Repertoire des Banques de Donnees en Conversationnel [Association Nationale de la Recherche Technique] [Information service or system]	REBK
Repertoire Pratique de Droit Belge [A publication] (ILCA)	RPDB
Repertorium Juridicum [Latin A publication] (DLA)	Rep Jur
Repertory (ADA)	REP
Repertory (WDMC)	rep
Repertory (ODBW)	rep
Repertory Dance Theatre [Salt Lake City, UT]	RDT
Repertory Theater (DSUE)	REP
Repertory Theatre (ODBW)	rep
Repetatur [Let It Be Repeated] [Pharmacy]	REP
Repetatur [Let It Be Repeated] [Pharmacy]	REPET
Repetatur [Let It Be Repeated] [Pharmacy]	REPT
Repetition (DSUE)	REP
Repetition (WDMC)	rep
Repetition (IAA)	REPET
Repetition (AAG)	RPTN
Repetition Maximum [Medicine]	RM
Repetition Rate	RR
Repetitive [Electronics]	R
Repetitive Activity Input/Output Plan (PDAA)	RAI/OP
Repetitive and Rapid Alternating Movements [Neurology] (DAVI)	RRAM
Repetitive Atrial Firing [Medicine] (DMAA)	RAF
Repetitive Bursts of Action Potential [Electrophysiology]	RBAP
Repetitive Counterelectrophoresis (PDAA)	RCE
Repetitive Electromagnetic Pulse Simulator [Army] (RDA)	REPS
Repetitive Element Column Analysis (PDAA)	RECA
Repetitive Excess Mixed Anhydride [Medicine] (DMAA)	REMA
Repetitive Explosive Device for Soil Displacement	REDSOD
Repetitive Extragenic Palindrome [or Palindromic] [Genetics]	REP
Repetitive Extrasystole [Cardiology]	RE
Repetitive Extrasystole Threshold [Cardiology]	RET
Repetitive Flight Plan [ICAO] (FAAC)	RPL
Repetitive Flight Plan Office [ICAO designator] (ICDA)	ZB
Repetitive LASER Desorption	RLD
Repetitive Monomorphic Ventricular Tachycardia [Cardiology]	RMVT
Repetitive Motion Injury	RMI
Repetitive Operation [Computer science] (MDG)	REP-OP
Repetitive Report Distribution Audit (AAG)	RRDA
Repetitive Square Wave Potential Signal [Electrochemistry]	RSWPS
Repetitive Strain Injury (PCM)	RSI
Repetitively Pulsed (MCD)	RP
Repetitively Pulsed Plasma Accelerator	REPPAC
Repetitively-Pulsed Plasma Accelerator (IAA)	RPPA
Rephael Society (EA)	RS
Replace (NVT)	REP
Replace (AAG)	REPL
Replace (FAAC)	RPLC
Replace Essential Supplies in Sufficient Time [Navy] (NVT)	RESIST
Replaceability (AAG)	R
Replaceable Display Light	RDL
Replaceable Item	RI
Replaceable Item Code	RIC
Replaceable Module	RM
Replaceable Pad (MCD)	RP
Replaceable Unit	RU
Replaced [Dentistry]	R
Replacement (DLA)	repl
Replacement (ECII)	REPL
Replacement (IAA)	RPL
Replacement Air Group	RAG
Replacement Algorithm	RA
Replacement Alpha Numeric Keyboard [Computer science] (DA)	RANK
Replacement and School Command [Military]	R & SC
Replacement and School Command [Military]	RSC
Replacement and Training School Command [Military]	RTSC
Replacement Battery Equipment	RBE

Replacement Battery Terminal Equipment .... RBTE
Replacement Carrier Air Group [*Military*] (AFIT) .... RCAG
Replacement Carrier Fighter Group [*V is Navy code for Fighter*] .... RCVG
Replacement Cost [*Insurance*] .... RC
Replacement Cost Accounting (ADA) .... RCA
Replacement Cost Valuation [*Insurance*] .... RCV
Replacement Culture Medium [*Microbiology*] .... RCM
Replacement Detachment [*Army*] .... RD
Replacement Factor [*Military*] .... RF
Replacement Flight Strip Printer [*Aviation*] (DA) .... RFSP
Replacement Forecasting System (IAA) .... REFORS
Replacement in Kind (NG) .... RIK
Replacement Inertial Measurement System .... RIMS
Replacement Ion Chromatography [*Spectrometry*] .... RIC
Replacement Naval Vessels .... RNV
Replacement of Photography Imagery Equipment (RDA) .... RPIE
Replacement Parts Co. .... REPCO
Replacement Pilot [*Navy*] .... RP
Replacement Price Accounting (ADA) .... RPA
Replacement Purchase Order .... RPO
Replacement Regulating Detachment [*Army*] .... RRD
Replacement Stream Input [*Military*] .... RSI
Replacement Task Distribution .... RTD
Replacement Training Center [*Military*] .... RTC
Replacement Training Detachment (MCD) .... RTD
Replacement Training Unit [*Military*] .... RTU
Replacement Unit .... RU
Replacement Unit Repair Level Analysis Model .... RURLAM
Replacement Weather Reconnaissance Aircraft (DNAB) .... RWRAT
Replacement-Cost-Adjusted Book Value (DICI) .... RCABV
Replenish (AABC) .... REPLN
Replenish (NVT) .... RPL
Replenishable Demand .... RD
Replenishing .... RPLNG
Replenishment .... RPNSM
Replenishment at Sea [*Navy*] .... RAS
Replenishment at Sea Corrective Action Program (MCD) .... RASCAP
Replenishment Demand Inventory System .... RDIS
Replenishment Oiler [*Navy ship symbol*] .... AOR
Replenishment Park [*British*] .... RP
Replenishment Spare Part .... RSP
Replica (VRA) .... repl
Replication [*Telecommunications*] (TEL) .... REP
Replication and Transfer [*Medicine*] (MAE) .... RTF
Replication Controller [*Computer science*] .... RC
Replication, Distribution, Installation, and Training [*Army*] (RDA) .... RDIT
Replication Fork Pause [*Genetics*] .... RFP
Replication Licensing Factor [*Genetics*] .... RLF
Replication Protein A [*Genetics*] .... RPA
Replication Synchronization Process [*Telecommunications*] (TEL) .... RSP
Replication-Terminator Protein [*Genetics*] .... RTP
Replicative Factor [*or Form*] [*Genetics*] .... RF
Replicative Intermediate [*Medicine*] (MAE) .... RI
Repligen Corp. [*Associated Press*] (SAG) .... Replgn
Repligen Corp. [*Cambridge, MA*] [*NASDAQ symbol*] (NQ) .... RGEN
Reply (ADA) .... R
Reply by Indorsement .... RBI
Reply by Mail (FAAC) .... REPML
Reply by Message (FAAC) .... REPMES
Reply Coupon [*Advertising*] .... RC
Reply Delay (MUGU) .... RD
Reply Delay Compensation (MUGU) .... RDC
Reply Finding [*Nuclear energy*] (NRCH) .... RF
Reply If Negative [*Military*] .... REPIN
Reply Paid .... RP
Reply Paid Postcard .... RPP
Reply Paid Telegram .... RPT
Reply Path Side Lobe Suppression (IAA) .... RSLS
Reply Postcard .... RPC
Reply Prepaid (IAA) .... RP
Reply Requested (NOAA) .... RYRQD
Repolarization [*Cardiology*] (DAVI) .... repol
Repolarization Opening [*Biochemistry*] .... RO
Repondez, s'Il Vous Plait [*The Favor of an Answer is Requested*] [*French*] .... RSVP
Repondez Vite, s'Il Vous Plait [*Please Reply at Once*] [*French*] .... RVSVP
Report (WDMC) .... rep
Report (AAG) .... REP
Report .... REPT
Report .... REPT
Report (AFM) .... RPRT
Report .... RPT
Report (WDMC) .... RPT
Report After Execution (AAGC) .... RAE
Report and Graph Designer Module [*Solomon Software*] [*Computer science*] (PCM) .... RGD
Report and Update Program Generator (IAA) .... RUG
Report Audit Summary (AAG) .... RAS
Report Authorization Record [*or Request*] (AAG) .... RAR
Report Back on Course [*Aviation*] (FAAC) .... RBOC
Report Back on Frequency [*Aviation*] (FAAC) .... RBOF
Report Bibliography .... RB
Report by Letter (NVT) .... REPLTR
Report by Message (DNAB) .... REPMSG
Report by the Scottish Land Court [*A publication*] (DLA) .... Sc La Rep
Report Change Notice (MCD) .... RCN
Report Collection Index [*Studsvik Energiteknik AB*] [*Database Nykoping, Sweden*] .... RECODEX
Report Control Number (MCD) .... RCN
Report Corrective Action Taken [*Military*] .... REPCAT
Report Definition Language [*Computer science*] (MHDB) .... RDL
Report Departing [*Aviation*] (DA) .... RD
Report Established in Block [*Aviation*] (FAAC) .... REIB
Report Evaluation Program (SAA) .... REP
Report/File Language (HGAA) .... RFI
Report for Duty [*Military*] .... REPDU
Report for Transportation .... REPTRANS
Report Format Generator .... RFG
Report Generator (CMD) .... RG
Report Generator Language [*Computer science*] (IEEE) .... RGL
Report Guide .... RG
Report Heading (BUR) .... RH
Report Identification Number [*Military*] (AABC) .... RIN
Report [*command indicated*] **If Present, Otherwise by Message** [*Navy*] .... RIPOM
Report Immediate Superior in Command [*Navy*] .... REPISIC
Report Immediately Upon Leaving [*Aviation*] (FAAC) .... RL
Report in Person or by Message to Command or Person Indicated .... REPERMSG
Report Landing Completed [*Aviation*] (FAAC) .... RLC
Report Leaving [*ICAO*] (FAAC) .... RL
Report Leaving Each Thousand Foot Level [*Aviation*] (FAAC) .... RLETFL
Report Level [*Aviation*] (FAAC) .... RLVL
Report. Meeting of the Australasian Association for the Advancement of Science [*A publication*] .... Rept Mtg AAAS
Report. Meeting of the Australian and New Zealand Association for the Advancement of Science [*A publication*] .... Rept Mtg ANZAAS
Report Missing Account Radio Failure [*Meteorology*] (FAAC) .... RADNO
Report My Arrival or Departure [*Aviation slang*] .... PX Me
Report Number (NITA) .... RN
Report of Accrued Obligations, Military Pay (AFM) .... RAOMP
Report of Assets in Long Supply .... RAILS
Report of Bellingham's Trial [*A publication*] (DLA) .... Bellingh Tr
Report of Commercial Cases [*1895-1941*] [*A publication*] (DLA) .... Rep Com Cas
Report of Contact [*Social Security Administration*] (OICC) .... RC
Report of Discrepancies .... ROD
Report of Federal Cash Transactions (OICC) .... RFCT
Report of Investigation .... RI
Report of Investigation [*Military*] (AFM) .... ROI
Report of Item Discrepancy [*Army*] (AABC) .... ROID
Report of Methodist Church Cases [*A publication*] (DLA) .... Meth Ch Ca
Report of Mining Cases Decided by the Railway and Canal Commission [*A publication*] (DLA) .... Bamber
Report of NAC/ENTAC (MCD) .... RON
Report of Obligation Military Pay (AFM) .... ROMP
Report of Observations/Samples Collected by Oceanographic Programs [*Intergovernmental Oceanographic Commission*] (MSC) .... ROSCOP
Report of Patients Evacuated [*Aeromedical evacuation*] .... RPE
Report of Student Answers [*Scoring sheet for the Scholastic Aptitude Test (SAT)*] (PAZ) .... ROSA
Report of Supply Activity (MCD) .... ROSA
Report of Survey [*Military*] .... RS
Report of the "Alexandra" Case, by Dudley [*A publication*] (DLA) .... Alex Cas
Report of the Attorney General of the State of Massachusetts [*A publication*] (DLA) .... Rep Mass Att'y Gen
Report of the Attorney General of the State of Nebraska [*A publication*] (DLA) .... Rep Neb Att'y Gen
Report of the Chesapeake Case, New Brunswick [*A publication*] (DLA) .... Ches Ca
Report of the Tichborne Trial [*London*] [*A publication*] (DLA) .... Tichb Tr
Report of Unsatisfactory or Defective Airborne Electronic Equipment [*Navy*] .... RUDAEE
Report of Unsatisfactory or Defective Aviation Ordnance Equipment [*Navy*] .... RUDAOE
Report of Unsatisfactory or Defective Instrumentation [*Navy*] .... RUDI
Report of Unsatisfactory or Defective Material [*Aircraft*] [*Navy*] .... RUDM
Report of Unsatisfactory or Defective Mine [*Navy*] (NG) .... RUDMIN
Report of Unsatisfactory or Defective Mine, Depth Charge, or Associated Equipment [*Navy*] (NG) .... RUDMINDE
Report of Unsatisfactory or Defective Torpedo Equipment [*Navy*] (NG) .... RUDTORPE
Report of Visit [*LIMRA*] .... ROV
Report of Visit of Foreign Nationals (AAG) .... RVFN
Report on Board [*Navy*] .... ROB
Report on Business (IT) .... ROB
Report on Course [*Aviation*] (DA) .... R-CRS
Report on Improved Manpower Management .... RIMM
Report on Individual Personnel (MCD) .... RIP
Report on Oceanographic Cruises and Data Stations (GNE) .... ROSCOP
Report on Reimbursable Transactions [*DoD*] .... RORT
Report on Syndicated Programs [*A.C. Nielsen Co.*] [*A publication*] (DOAD) .... ROSP
Report Originator System [*Military*] (CAAL) .... ROS
Report Over (DA) .... RO
Report Passing [*Aviation*] (FAAC) .... RPSG
Report Proceeding on Course [*Aviation*] (FAAC) .... RPOC
Report Processor Generator (MCD) .... RPG
Report Program Generator [*Programming language*] [*1962*] (IAA) .... RG
Report Program Generator [*Programming language*] [*1962*] .... RPG
Report Reaching [*ICAO*] (FAAC) .... RR
Report Review Committee [*National Academy of Sciences*] .... RRC
Report Serial Number [*Army*] .... RSN

Report Series Codes Dictionary [*A publication*] ..... RSCD
Report Starting Procedure Turn [*Aviation*] (DA) ..... RSPT
Report Test Number [*NASA*] ..... RTN
Report through Senior Naval Officer ..... REPSNO
Report Time Over (FAAC) ..... RTO
Report to Armed Forces ..... RTAF
Report to Commander [*Military*] ..... RPC
Report to Naval Reserve Center (DNAB) ..... REPNAVRESCEN
Report upon Arrival Thereat [*Army*] (AABC) ..... RUAT
Report When Established on Course [*Aviation*] (FAAC) ..... REOC
Report When Established Well to Right of Course [*Aviation*] (FAAC) ..... REWRC
Report Writer [*Computer science*] ..... R/W
Report Writer Control System [*COBOL*] [*Computer science*] ..... RWCS
Reportable Event (EPA) ..... RE
Reportable Item Control Code [*Army*] (AABC) ..... RICC
Reportable Item File [*Military*] (AFIT) ..... RIF
Reportable Item Master File [*Military*] (AFIT) ..... RIMF
Reportable Item Report [*NASA*] (NASA) ..... RIR
Reportable Items of Major Combinations [*Army*] (AABC) ..... RIMC
Reportable Occurrence [*Nuclear energy*] (NRCH) ..... RO
Reportable Quantity [*Hazardous substance emergency response*] ..... RQ
Reported ..... RPTD
Reported Altitude (IAA) ..... RALT
Reported Altitude Block Height (SAA) ..... RABH
Reported Altitude Change Indicator (IAA) ..... RACI
Reported for Active Duty [*Navy*] ..... RAD
Reported for Duty (FAAC) ..... RPFOD
Reported Frequency (NTCM) ..... RF
Reported Post Coastal (NATG) ..... RPC
Reported Visual Sensation [*Medicine*] (MAE) ..... RVS
Reporter (WDMC) ..... rep
Reporter ..... REP
[*The*] **Reporter** [*Boston, Los Angeles, New York, Washington*] [*A publication*] (DLA) ..... Reptr
Reporter ..... REPTR
Reporter, English Common Bench Reports [*A publication*] (DLA) ..... J Scott
Reporter, English Common Bench Reports [*A publication*] (DLA) ..... Scott J
Reporter of Debate [*US Senate*] ..... R of D
Reporter of Vol. 7, Modern Reports [*England*] [*A publication*] (DLA) ..... Benne
Reporter of Vols. 5 and 11, Heiskell's Tennessee Reports [*A publication*] (DLA) ..... Reese
Reporter on Scene (NTCM) ..... ROS
[*The*] **Reporter, Phi Alpha Delta** [*A publication*] (DLA) ..... The Rep
Reporter, Toms River, NJ [*Library symbol Library of Congress*] (LCLS) ..... NjTrR
Reporters Committee for Freedom of the Press (EA) ..... RCFP
Reporting Accounting Number (NG) ..... RAN
Reporting Activity (MCD) ..... RA
Reporting Activity Control Card [*Army*] (AABC) ..... RACC
Reporting and Requisitioning [*Air Force*] ..... R & R
Reporting and Routing Instructions [*Navy*] ..... RARI
Reporting File ..... RF
Reporting for Duty [*Air Force*] ..... RFD
Reporting Identification Symbol (IAA) ..... RIS
Reporting In and Out [*Military*] ..... RIO
Reporting Interface Record [*Computer science*] (IAA) ..... RIR
Reporting of Injuries, Diseases, and Dangerous Occurrences Regulations [*British*] ..... RIDDOR
Reporting Officer [*Navy*] ..... REPO
Reporting Officer (NATG) ..... REPTOF
Reporting Officer [*Army*] (AABC) ..... RO
Reporting Organizational File [*Military*] (AFM) ..... ROF
Reporting Point [*Aviation*] ..... REP
Reporting Post [*RADAR*] ..... RP
Reporting Post, Coastal Low [*RADAR*] ..... RP/CL
Reporting Post, Coastal Medium [*RADAR*] ..... RP/CM
Reporting Requirements Code (DNAB) ..... RRC
Reporting Research [*Queensland, Department of Education, Research Branch*] [*A publication*] ..... Rept Res
Reporting Responsibility [*DoD*] R2
Reporting System for Training [*Navy*] (NG) ..... REST
Reporting Time [*Filmmaking*] (WDMC) ..... RPT
Reporting Unit Code [*Computer science*] ..... RUC
[*The*] **Reports** [*1893-95*] [*England*] [*A publication*] (DLA) ..... Mews
Reports ..... R
Reports and Analysis ..... R & A
Reports and Analysis Letter (OICC) ..... RAL
Reports and Cases of Practice in Common Pleas Tempore Anne, George I, and Geor ge II, by Sir G. Coke [*Same as Cooke's Practice Reports*] [*1706-47 England*] [*A publication*] (DLA) ..... Co G
Reports and Information Retrieval Activity (NITA) ..... RIRA
Reports and Memorandum (MCD) ..... R & M
Reports and Statistics Branch [*US Military Government, Germany*] ..... R & S
[*The*] **Reports, Coke's English King's Bench** [*A publication*] (DLA) ..... R
[*The*] **Reports, Coke's English King's Bench** [*A publication*] (DLA) ..... The Rep
Reports Control Liaison Officer [*Army*] (AABC) ..... RCLO
Reports Control Officer [*Army*] (AABC) ..... RCO
Reports Control Symbol [*Military*] ..... RCS
Reports, Court of Chancery Tempore Finch [*1673-81*] [*A publication*] (DLA) ..... Rep T F
Reports, Court of Chancery Tempore Finch [*1673-81*] [*A publication*] (DLA) ..... Rep T Finch
Reports, Court of Chancery Tempore Finch [*1673-81*] [*England*] [*A publication*] (DLA) ..... Rep T Finch (Eng)
Reports Creation System ..... RCS
Reports Identification Symbol ..... RIS
Reports in Chancery [*1615-1712*] [*England*] [*A publication*] (DLA) ..... Ch R
Reports in Chancery [*A publication*] (DLA) ..... Ch Rep
Reports in Chancery [*A publication*] (DLA) ..... Ch Repts
Reports in Chancery [*21 English Reprint*] [*1615-1710*] [*A publication*] (DLA) ..... Chan Rep C
Reports in Chancery [*1615-1710*] [*England*] [*A publication*] (DLA) ..... Rep Ch
Reports in Chancery [*21 English Reprint*] [*A publication*] (DLA) ..... Rep in Can
Reports in Chancery [*21 English Reprint*] [*A publication*] (DLA) ..... Rep in Ch
Reports in Chancery [*21 English Reprint*] [*A publication*] (DLA) ..... Rep in Ch (Eng)
Reports in Courts of Appeal [*New Zealand*] [*A publication*] (DLA) ..... Rep in C of A
Reports Index Control (MCD) ..... RICS
Reports Management Liaison Officer [*Defense Supply Agency*] ..... RMLO
Reports Management Officer [*DoD*] ..... RMO
Reports Management System [*Office of Management and Budget*] [*Database*] ..... RMS
Reports of Bankruptcy and Companies Winding-Up Cases [*1918-41*] [*England*] [*A publication*] (DLA) ..... B & CR
Reports of Cases Concerning Settlements Tempore Holt [*England*] [*A publication*] (DLA) ..... RTH
Reports of Cases Decided in the Supreme Court of South Africa (Griqualand West Local Division), by Kitchin [*A publication*] (DLA) ..... GWL
Reports of Cases, Diwani Adalat, Madras [*A publication*] (DLA) ..... Rep Cas Madr
Reports of Cases in the Supreme Court of Natal [*A publication*] (DLA) ..... Phipson
Reports of Cases in Vice-Admiralty of Province of New York [*1715-88*] [*1925 Reprint*] [*A publication*] (DLA) ..... Hough V-Adm
Reports of Cases on Appeal [*Calcutta*] [*A publication*] (DLA) ..... Marshall
Reports of Cases Relating to Income Tax [*A publication*] (DLA) ..... Inc Tax Cas
Reports of Cases Relating to Income Tax [*1875*] [*A publication*] (DLA) ..... Rep Cas Inc Tax
Reports of Certain Judgments of the Supreme Court, Vice-Admiralty Court, and Full Court of Appeal, Lagos [*1884-92*] [*Nigeria*] [*A publication*] (DLA) ..... RCJ
Reports of Criminal Law Commissioners [*England*] [*A publication*] (DLA) ..... Rep Cr L Com
Reports of English Patent Cases [*1884*] [*A publication*] (DLA) ..... Cutler
Reports of English Patent Cases [*A publication*] (DLA) ..... RPC
Reports of English Railway Cases [*A publication*] (DLA) ..... Ry Cas
Reports of Inland Revenue Commissioners [*A publication*] (DLA) ..... IR Rep
Reports of Interest to Lawyers [*Merton Allen Associates*] [*Information service or system*] (CRD) ..... ROITL
Reports of International Arbitral Awards [*A publication*] (DLA) ..... Int'l Arb Awards
Reports of Irish Cases, by Sir John Davis [*1604-11*] [*A publication*] (DLA) ..... Dav
Reports of Irish Circuit Cases [*A publication*] (DLA) ..... Ir Cir Rep
Reports of Municipal Corporations [*A publication*] (DLA) ..... Rep MC
Reports of Patent Cases [*Legal*] [*British*] ..... RPC
Reports of Patent, Design, and Trade Mark Cases [*England, Scotland, Ireland*] [*A publication*] (DLA) ..... Pat Cas
Reports of Patent, Design, and Trade Mark Cases [*A publication*] (DLA) ..... R Pat Cas
Reports of Patent, Design, and Trade Mark Cases [*England*] [*A publication*] (DLA) ..... Rep Pat Cas
Reports of Patent, Design, and Trade Mark Cases [*A publication*] (DLA) ..... Rep Pat Des & Tr Cas
Reports of Patent, Design, and Trade Mark Cases [*A publication*] (DLA) ..... RPC
Reports of Patent Design and Trade Mark Cases [*United Kingdom*] [*A publication*] (DLA) ..... RPD & TM Cas
Reports of Patent, Design, and Trade Mark Cases [*Australia A publication*] ..... RPDTMC
Reports of Railway and Canal Traffic Cases [*1855-1950*] [*A publication*] (DLA) ..... Ry & Can
Reports of Railway and Canal Traffic Cases [*1855-1950*] [*A publication*] (DLA) ..... Ry & Can Tr Cas
Reports of Railway and Canal Traffic Cases [*1855-1950*] [*A publication*] (ILCA) ..... Ry & Can Traf Cas
Reports of Railway and Canal Traffic Cases [*1855-1950*] [*A publication*] ..... Ry Cas
Reports of Rating Cases [*Legal*] [*British*] ..... RRC
Reports of Restrictive Practices Cases [*A publication*] (DLA) ..... Restric Prac
Reports of Shipments [*Military*] ..... REPSHIPS
Reports of the Decisions of the Native Appeal Courts, Cape Province and the Orange Free State [*South Africa*] [*A publication*] (ILCA) ..... NAC (C & O)
Reports of the Decisions of the Native Appeal Courts (Transvaal and Natal) [*South Africa*] [*A publication*] (ILCA) ..... NAC (T & N)
Reports of the High Court of Griqualand [*1882-1910*] [*South Africa*] [*A publication*] (DLA) ..... G
Reports of the High Court of Griqualand [*1882-1910*] [*South Africa*] [*A publication*] (DLA) ..... Laur
Reports of the High Court of Griqualand West [*South Africa*] [*A publication*] (DLA) ..... HC
Reports of the High Court of South-West Africa [*A publication*] (DLA) ..... SA Law Reports SWA
Reports of the High Court of South-West Africa [*1920-46*] [*A publication*] (DLA) ..... SWA
Reports of the High Court of the Orange River Colony [*South Africa*] [*A publication*] (DLA) ..... ORC
Reports of the International Law Association [*A publication*] (DLA) ..... Int'l L Ass'n
Reports of the United States District Court of Hawaii [*A publication*] (DLA) ..... DCH
Reports of the Witwatersrand High Court [*Transvaal, South Africa*] [*A publication*] (DLA) ..... TH
Reports of the Witwatersrand High Court [*Transvaal, South Africa*] [*A publication*] (DLA) ..... TL
Reports on Chancery Practice [*England*] [*A publication*] (DLA) ..... Rep Ch Pr
Reports, Reviews, Meetings ..... RRM
Reports Tempore Chancellor King [*A publication*] (DLA) ..... KCR
Reports Tempore Finch, English Chancery [*A publication*] (DLA) ..... RTF

Reports Tempore Hardwicke [*England*] [*A publication*] (DLA) ... RTH
Reports Tempore Hardwicke, English King's Bench [*A publication*] (DLA) ... R T Hardw
Reports Tempore Holt, English Cases of Settlement [*A publication*] (DLA) ... Rep T Holt
Reports Tempore Holt, English King's Bench [*A publication*] (DLA) ... R T Holt
Reports Tempore Northington [*Eden. English Chancery Reports*] [*1757-67*] [*A publication*] (DLA) ... North
Reports Tempore Queen Anne [*11 Modern*] [*A publication*] (DLA) ... Rep QA
Reports Tempore Queen Anne [*11 Modern*] [*A publication*] (DLA) ... Rep T QA
Reports Tempore Queen Anne [*11 Modern*] [*England*] [*A publication*] (DLA) ... RTQA
Reports Tempore Saulsbury [*5-6 Delaware*] [*A publication*] (DLA) ... Sauls
Reports Tempore Talbot, English Chancery [*A publication*] (DLA) ... Rep T Talb
Repository for Germinal Choice [*A sperm bank*] ... RGC
Repository-Based Software Engineering ... RBSE
Repossess ... REPO
Repousse (VRA) ... repu
Represent (ROG) ... REPT
Representation (VRA) ... repres
Representation (ROG) ... REPRON
Representation Commissioner [*Canada*] ... REPC
Representation Dependent Accessing Language ... RDAL
Representation des Artistes Canadiens ... RAC
Representation Independent Language (NITA) ... RIL
Representation of Structure Diagrams Arranged Linearly [*Structure notation shorthand*] [*Chemistry*] ... ROSDAL
Representational Difference Analysis [*Genetic technique*] ... RDA
Representation-Independent Programming Language ... RIPL
Representation-Language Language [*Computer science*] ... RLL
Representative (WDMC) ... rep
Representative ... REP
Representative (ODBW) ... rep
Representative (AAG) ... REP
Representative ... REPR
Representative ... REPS
Representative (ROG) ... REPVE
Representative Assembly ... RA
Representative Calculating Operation ... RCO
Representative Church Body [*Ireland*] [*Church of England*] ... RCB
Representative Church Council [*Episcopalian*] ... RCC
Representative Conflict Situations [*Army*] ... RCS
Representative Elementary Volume [*Sampling for analysis*] ... REV
Representative for German Industry and Trade [*An association*] (EA) ... RGIT
Representative Fraction ... RF
Representative in Medical Council [*Royal College of Physicians*] [*British*] (ROG) ... RMC
Representative Observation Site [*Weather observing facility*] [*Air Force*] ... ROS
Representative of a Foreign Interest ... RFI
Representative of Commander Destroyers, Pacific Fleet ... REPCOMDESPAC
Representative of Maintenance Force ... REPFORMAINT
Representative of the Senate of the University of London (ROG) ... RUL
Representative Shuttle Environmental Control [*System*] [*NASA*] ... RSEC
Representative Shuttle Environmental Control System [*NASA*] (MCD) ... RECS
Representative Shuttle Environmental Control System [*NASA*] (MCD) ... RSECS
Representative to the Military Committee [*NATO*] ... REPMC
Representative Town Meeting ... RTM
Representative Volume Element ... RVE
Representatives for Experiment Review [*Nuclear energy*] (NRCH) ... RER
Representatives of Electronic Products Manufacturers [*Later, ERA*] ... REPM
Representatives of European Heating and Ventilating Associations ... REHVA
Representatives of Radio Parts Manufacturers (IAA) ... RRPM
Representing (DLA) ... Rep
Repressor [*Psychology*] (MAE) ... R
Repressor [*Genetics*] (DAVI) ... R
Repressor-Sensitizer Index [*Psychology*] ... RSI
Repressurization (MCD) ... REPR
Reprimand (DSUE) ... REP
Reprint ... R
Reprint (DLA) ... Rep
Reprint (WDMC) ... rep
Reprint (BJA) ... rept
Reprint ... RP
Reprint ... RPT
Reprint Expediting Service ... RES
Reprint of the Statutes of New Zealand [*A publication*] (DLA) ... NZ Repr Stat
Reprint of the Statutes of New Zealand [*A publication*] (DLA) ... Repr Stat NZ
Reprint under Consideration [*Publishing*] ... RPUC
Reprint with Corrections (DGA) ... RC
Reprinted ... REPR
Reprinted (WGA) ... RPTD
Reprinted Acts of Western Australia [*A publication*] (DLA) ... W Aust Repr Acts
Reprinting, No Date [*Publishing*] ... RPND
Reprocess (MCD) ... REPROC
Reprocessing Building Analytical Laboratory [*Nuclear energy*] (NRCH) ... RBAL
Reprocessing Building (Cable) Spreading Room [*Nuclear energy*] (NRCH) ... RBSR
Reprocessing Building Control Room [*Nuclear energy*] (NRCH) ... RBCR
Reproduce (KSC) ... REPRO
Reproducer (MSA) ... RPDR
Reproducers [*JETDS nomenclature*] [*Military*] (CET) ... RP
Reproducible (DNAB) ... R
Reproducible Ozalid (DNAB) ... RO
Reproducing [*JETDS nomenclature*] ... P
Reproducing Programs [*Computer science*] ... REP
Reproducing Punch [*Computer science*] (IAA) ... RP
Reproducing Unit ... RU
Reproduction (AFM) ... REPDN
Reproduction (VRA) ... reprd
Reproduction (ODBW) ... repro
Reproduction ... REPROD
Reproduction Assembly Sheet (MCD) ... RAS
Reproduction of Library Materials Section [*Resources and Technical Services Division of ALA*] ... RLMS
Reproduction Service Order (SAA) ... RSO
Reproduction Typing (DGA) ... REPRO TYP
Reproductive Effects Assessment Group [*Environmental Protection Agency*] (EPA) ... REAG
Reproductive Endocrinology Program [*University of Michigan*] [*Research center*] (RCD) ... REP
Reproductive Freedom Project [*ACLU*] [*Attempts to enforce the Supreme Court decisions guaranteeing a woman's right to choose abortion*] (EA) ... RFP
Reproductive Health Care Center ... RHCC
Reproductive Health Care Center/Planned Parenthood ... RHCC/PP
Reproductive Potential [*Genetics*] (DOG) ... r
Reproductive Rights National Network [*Defunct*] (EA) ... RRNN
Reproductive Success [*Genetics*] ... RS
Reproductive Toxicology Center [*Database*] [*Washington, DC*] ... REPROTOX
Reproductive Toxicology Center [*Database*] (IID) ... RTC
Reprogram Mode ... RPM
Reprogrammable Advanced Multimode Shipborne ECM System [*Canadian Navy*] ... RAMSES
Reprogrammable Microprocessor ... RMP
Reprogrammable Programmable Read-Only Memory [*Computer science*] (TEL) ... REPROM
Reprogrammable Read-Only Memory (NITA) ... REPROM
Reprogrammable Read-Only Memory [*Computer science*] (HGAA) ... RPROM
Repsol SA [*Associated Press*] (SAG) ... Repsol
Repsol SA ADS [*NYSE symbol*] (SPSG) ... REP
Repsol S.A. ADS [*NYSE symbol*] (TTSB) ... REP
Repton, AL [*FM radio station call letters*] (RBYB) ... WYNI-FM
Repton/Gamston [*British ICAO location identifier*] (ICLI) ... EGNE
Reptron Electronics [*NASDAQ symbol*] (TTSB) ... REPT
Reptron Electronics, Inc. [*NASDAQ symbol*] (SAG) ... REPT
Reptron Electronics, Inc. [*Associated Press*] (SAG) ... Reptrn
Repubblica Sociale Italiana [*Italian Socialist Republic*] [*Founded by Mussolini 1943-1945*] ... RSI
Republic ... R
Republic (EY) ... REP
Republic (MSA) ... REPB
Republic ... REPB
Republic [*ICAO designator*] (AD) ... RW
Republic at Romania (BARN) ... RR
Republic Automotive [*NASDAQ symbol*] (TTSB) ... RAUT
Republic Automotive Parts, Inc. [*NASDAQ symbol*] (NQ) ... RAUT
Republic Automotive Parts, Inc. [*Associated Press*] (SAG) ... RpAuto
Republic Bancorp [*NASDAQ symbol*] (TTSB) ... RBNC
Republic Bancorp, Inc. [*NASDAQ symbol*] (NQ) ... RBNC
Republic Bancorp, Inc. [*Associated Press*] (SAG) ... RepBcp
Republic Bancshares [*NASDAQ symbol*] (TTSB) ... REPB
Republic Bancshares, Inc. [*NASDAQ symbol*] (SAG) ... REPB
Republic Bancshares, Inc. [*Associated Press*] (SAG) ... RepubBsh
Republic Bank [*NASDAQ symbol*] (NQ) ... REPB
Republic Bank [*Associated Press*] (SAG) ... RepubBk
Republic Engineered Steels [*NASDAQ symbol*] (TTSB) ... REPS
Republic Engineered Steels, Inc. [*Associated Press*] (SAG) ... RepEStl
Republic Engineered Steels, Inc. [*NASDAQ symbol*] (SAG) ... REPS
Republic Environmental Systems [*NASDAQ symbol*] (TTSB) ... RESI
Republic Environmental Systems, Inc. [*Associated Press*] (SAG) ... RepEnv
Republic Environmental Systems, Inc. [*NASDAQ symbol*] (SAG) ... RESI
Republic Group [*Associated Press*] (SAG) ... RepGrp
Republic Group [*NYSE symbol*] (TTSB) ... RGC
Republic Gypsum Co. [*NYSE symbol*] (SPSG) ... RGC
Republic Industries [*NASDAQ symbol*] (TTSB) ... RWIN
Republic Industries, Inc. [*Associated Press*] (SAG) ... RepInd
Republic Industries, Inc. [*NASDAQ symbol*] (SAG) ... RWIN
Republic, MO [*FM radio station call letters*] ... KADI
Republic New York [*NYSE symbol*] (TTSB) ... RNB
Republic New York Corp. [*Associated Press*] (SAG) ... RepNY
Republic New York Corp. [*NYSE symbol*] (SPSG) ... RNB
Republic New York Corp. [*Associated Press*] (SAG) ... RNY
Republic NY $1.8125 cm Pfd [*NYSE symbol*] (TTSB) ... RNBPrE
Republic NY $1.9375 cm Pfd [*NYSE symbol*] (TTSB) ... RNBPrC
Republic NY Adj Rt Dep Pfd [*NYSE symbol*] (TTSB) ... RNBPrD
Republic of China (CDAI) ... RC
Republic of China ... ROC
Republic of China Air Force ... ROCAF
Republic of China Marine Corps ... ROCMC
Republic of China, Military Assistance Group, Vietnam ... ROCMAGV
Republic of China Navy ... ROCN
Republic of China Philatelic Exhibition ... ROCPEX
Republic of Korea [*ANSI three-letter standard code*] (CNC) ... KOR
Republic of Korea [*ANSI two-letter standard code*] (CNC) ... KR
Republic of Korea [*IYRU nationality code*] (IYR) ... RK
Republic of Korea ... ROK
Republic of Korea Air Force ... ROKAF
Republic of Korea Air Force Headquarters [*South Korea ICAO location identifier*] (ICLI) ... RKSF
Republic of Korea and US Combined Forces Command (MCD) ... ROKUSCFC
Republic of Korea Army ... ROKA

Republic of Korea Civic Action Program ... ROKAP
Republic of Korea Division Task Force ... ROKDTF
Republic of Korea Forces ... ROKF
Republic of Korea Forces in Vietnam ... ROKFV
Republic of Korea Government ... ROKG
Republic of Korea Indigenous Tank Program (MCD) ... ROKIT
Republic of Korea Marine Corps ... ROKMC
Republic of Korea Navy ... ROKN
Republic of Korea Presidential Unit Citation [*Military decoration*] ... ROKPUCE
Republic of Korea Presidential Unit Citation Badge [*Military decoration*] ... ROKPUC
Republic of New Africa (EA) ... RNA
Republic of Panama ... ROP
Republic of Panama ... RP
Republic of Portugal (BARN) ... RP
Republic of Singapore Air Force [*ICAO designator*] (ICDA) ... CE
Republic of Singapore Air Force (PDAA) ... RSAF
Republic of Singapore Air Force [*ICAO designator*] (FAAC) ... SAF
Republic of South Africa Research Reactor ... RSARR
Republic of the Marshall Islands ... RMI
Republic of the Philippines ... ROP
Republic of the Philippines ... RP
Republic of Vietnam ... RVN
Republic of Vietnam Air Force ... RVNAF
Republic of Vietnam Air Force (VNW) ... VNAF
Republic of Vietnam Armed Forces ... RVNAF
Republic of Vietnam Armed Forces Honor Medal, First Class [*Military decoration*] ... RVNAFHMFC
Republic of Vietnam Armed Forces Honor Medal, Second Class [*Military decoration*] ... RVNAFHMSC
Republic of Vietnam Campaign Medal [*Military decoration*] ... RVCM
Republic of Vietnam Campaign Medal [*Military decoration*] ... RVNCM
Republic of Vietnam Civil Actions Medal, First Class [*Military decoration*] ... RVNCAMFC
Republic of Vietnam Civil Actions Medal, Second Class [*Military decoration*] ... RVNCAMSC
Republic of Vietnam Civil Actions Medal, Unit Citation [*Military decoration*] (GFGA) ... RVNCAMUC
Republic of Vietnam Forces ... RVNF
Republic of Vietnam Gallantry Cross, Unit Citation [*Military decoration*] (GFGA) ... RVNGCUC
Republic of Vietnam Gallantry Cross Unit Citation with Palm [*Military decoration*] ... RVNGCUCW/P
Republic of Vietnam Marine Corps ... RVNMC
Republic of Vietnam Navy ... RVNN
Republic Sec Finl 7.5% Cv 'A' Pfd [*NASDAQ symbol*] (TTSB) ... RSFCP
Republic Sec Finl Cv'C'Pfd [*NASDAQ symbol*] (TTSB) ... RSFCO
Republic Security Financial [*Associated Press*] (SAG) ... RepSc
Republic Security Financial [*Associated Press*] (SAG) ... RepSec
Republic Security Financial Corp. [*NASDAQ symbol*] (NQ) ... RSFC
Republic Security Finl [*NASDAQ symbol*] (TTSB) ... RSFC
Republic Waste Industries, Inc. [*Associated Press*] (SAG) ... RepWst
Republic Waste Industries, Inc. [*NASDAQ symbol*] (SAG) ... RWIN
Republica Socialista Romania [*Socialist Republic of Romania*] (EY) ... RSR
Republicains Sociaux [*Social Republicans*] [*France Political party*] (PPE) ... RS
Republican ... R
Republican ... REP
Republican ... REPUB
Republican ... REPUB
Republican Citizens Committee of the United States (EA) ... RCCUS
Republican Communications Association (EA) ... RCA
Republican Congressional Leadership Council (EA) ... RCLC
Republican Governors Association (EA) ... RGA
Republican Law Students Association of New York (EA) ... RLSA
Republican Law Students Association of New York (EA) ... RLSA NY
Republican Liberty Caucus (EA) ... RLC
Republican Mainstream Committee (EA) ... RMC
Republican Majority Coalition [*Republican party faction*] ... RMC
Republican National Committee (EA) ... RNC
Republican National Hispanic Assembly of the United States (EA) ... RNHA
Republican Organizing Committee [*Political organization in opposition to the NPL of North Dakota*] ... ROC
Republican Party [*Iraq*] [*Political party*] (BJA) ... RP
Republican Party of Australia [*Political party*] ... RPA
Republican Party of India [*Political party*] (PPW) ... RPI
Republican People's Party [*Cumhuriyet Halk Partisi - CHP*] [*Turkey Political party*] (PPW) ... RPP
Republican Policy Committee ... RPC
Republican Postwar Policy Association [*Encouraged Republican Party to drop its isolationist viewpoint and take a stand for an American share in international collaboration after the war*] [*World War II*] ... RPPA
Republican Presidential Task Force (EA) ... RPTF
Republican Reliance Party [*Cumhuriyetci Guven Partisi - CGP*] [*Turkey Political party*] (PPW) ... RRP
Republican Senatorial Campaign Committee ... RSCC
Republican Turkish Party [*Cyprus*] [*Political party*] ... RTP
Republican Urban Professional [*Lifestyle classification*] ... Ruppie
Republican Women of Capitol Hill (EA) ... RWCH
Republicans Abroad (EA) ... RA
Republicans for Choice (EA) ... RFC
Republicans for Progress [*Defunct*] ... RFP
Republication [*NASA*] ... RE
Republic-Michigamme Public Library, Republic, MI [*Library symbol Library of Congress*] (LCLS) ... MiRep
Republiek van Suid-Afrika [*Republic of South Africa*] [*Afrikaans*] ... RSA
Republikeinse Party van Suidwesafrika [*Republican Party of South West Africa*] [*Namibia*] [*Political party*] (PPW) ... RP
Republique de la Cote d'Ivoire [*Republic of the Ivory Coast*] (BARN) ... RCI
Republique Francaise [*French Republic*] ... RF
Repudiate ... REPUD
Repulse Bay, NT [*ICAO location identifier*] (ICLI) ... CYUT
Repulsion ... REP
Repulsion (MSA) ... RPLSN
Repulsion Induction [*Motor*] ... RI
Repulsive Axon Guidance Signal [*Biochemistry*] ... RAGS
Repurchase Agreement [*Finance*] (DFIT) ... Repo
Repurchase Agreement [*Also, RP*] [*Investment term*] ... REPO
Repurchase Agreement [*Also, REPO*] [*Investment term*] ... RP
Reputation (DSUE) ... REP
Requalify ... REQUAL
Requena [*Peru*] [*ICAO location identifier*] (ICLI) ... SPQN
Request ... R
Request (AAG) ... REQ
Request (ROG) ... REQT
Request Advise as to Further Action [*Army*] (AABC) ... REQAFA
Request Altitude Changes En Route [*Aviation*] ... RACE
Request Answer By [*Date*] [*Military*] ... REQANS
Request Authority to Requisition [*Army*] (AFIT) ... REQAURQN
Request Block ... RB
Request Block Queue [*Computer science*] (IAA) ... RBQ
Request Clearance [*Aviation*] (FAAC) ... RQCL
Request Concurrent Travel of Dependents by Privately Owned Vehicle [*ALCAN Highway or Via Route Required*] [*Army*] (AABC) ... RCTDPOVALCAN
Request Consideration (SAA) ... REQON
Request Data and Respond [*Telecommunications*] (OSI) ... RDR
Request Diagnosis, Prognosis, Present Condition [*Army*] (AABC) ... DIPROG
Request Diagnosis, Prognosis, Present Condition, Probable Date and Mode of Disposition of Following Patient Reported in Your Hospital [*Military*] ... PROCON
Request Disconnect [*Telecommunications*] (OSI) ... RD
Request Disposition Instructions [*Army*] (AABC) ... REQDI
Request Flight Plan [*Aviation*] (DA) ... RQP
Request Following Information Be Forwarded This Office [*Army*] (AABC) ... REQFOLINFO
Request Follow-Up Action on Listed Requisitions Indicated Still Outstanding in Unit [*Army*] (AABC) ... RFALROU
Request for Accelerated Delivery (MCD) ... RFAD
Request for Action (KSC) ... RFA
Request for Additional Fire (MCD) ... RFAF
Request for Additional Information (NRCH) ... RAI
Request for Additional Work [*Navy*] (DNAB) ... RAW
Request for Alteration (AAG) ... RFA
Request for Analysis ... RFA
Request for Apollo Documents [*NASA*] (KSC) ... RAD
Request for Application ... RFA
Request for Approval of Contractual Support ... RACS
Request for Assistance (GFGA) ... RFA
Request for Authority to Complete (DOMA) ... RAC
Request for Authority to Contract [*Military*] ... RAC
Request for Authority to Develop a System or Change [*Military*] (AFIT) ... RADSOC
Request for Authority to Negotiate ... RAN
Request for Bid (AFM) ... RFB
Request for Change (KSC) ... RFC
Request for Change and/or Information (SAA) ... RC/I
Request for Checkage [*Navy*] ... R/C
Request for Comment [*Telecommunications*] (PCM) ... RFC
Request for Computer Program (NASA) ... RFCP
Request for Confirmation (MCD) ... RFC
Request for Connection [*Telecommunications*] (OSI) ... RFC
Request for Consultation Service (MCD) ... RCS
Request for Contract (GFGA) ... RFC
Request for Contract Clearance (AAGC) ... RCC
Request for Contract Investigation (MCD) ... RCI
Request for Contractual Procurement ... RCP
Request for Corrective Action (AAG) ... RCA
Request for Data Services ... RDS
Request for Delivery ... RFD
Request for Deviation ... RFD
Request for Deviation Approval (MCD) ... RDA
Request for Deviation Approval ... RFDA
Request for Discussion [*Electronic newsgroups*] ... RFD
Request for Document Change (NASA) ... RDC
Request for Effectivity (MCD) ... RFE
Request for Engineering Action (IAA) ... REA
Request for Engineering Authorization ... REA
Request for Engineering Change (MCD) ... REC
Request for Engineering Change Proposal [*NASA*] ... RECP
Request for Engineering Information (NG) ... REI
Request for Engineering Information (KSC) ... RFEI
Request for Engineering Investigation [*Nuclear energy*] (NRCH) ... REI
Request for Enhancement [*Computer science*] (NHD) ... RFE
Request for Equitable Adjustment [*Navy*] ... REA
Request for Estimate ... RE
Request for Estimate (KSC) ... RFE
Request for Expenditure ... RFE
Request for Factory Order (MCD) ... RFFO
Request for Factory Order (MCD) ... RFO
Request for Fire [*Military*] ... RFF
Request for Form ... RFF

Request for Grant Applications ... RFA
Request for Graphic Arts Service ... RGA
Request for Implementation Date ... RFID
Request for Information ... RFI
Request for Information (MCD) ... RI
Request for Information (MCD) ... RFI
Request for Inspection (IAA) ... RFI
Request for Instrumentation Clarification [*NASA*] (KSC) ... RIC
Request for Intelligence Information [*Military*] (INF) ... RII
Request for Interface Tool [*NASA*] (NASA) ... RIT
Request for Investigation ... RFI
Request for Issue ... RFI
Request for Manufacturing Development Authorization (AAG) ... RMDA
Request for Next Message ... RENM
Request for Orders [*Military*] ... RFO
Request for Part Approval (MCD) ... RFPA
Request for Parts Disposition (MCD) ... RFD
Request for Price Quotation ... RFP
Request for Price Quotation ... RPQ
Request for Procurement Action [*Authorization*] [*NASA*] (NASA) ... RPA
Request for Procurement Services ... RPS
Request for Programming [*Computer science*] ... RFP
Request for Proposal (MUGU) ... REP
Request for Proposal ... RFP
Request for Proposal Authorization [*NASA*] (NASA) ... RFPA
Request for Proposal Information [*Competitive bidding*] ... RFPI
Request for Proposal Preparation (SAA) ... RPP
Request for Proposal Supplement (DNAB) ... RFPS
Request for Purchase ... RFP
Request for Purchase Order Change Notice (AAG) ... RPOCN
Request for Qualifications (OICC) ... RFQ
Request for Quotation (AAG) ... R/Q
Request for Quotation ... RFQ
Request for Review of Tooling ... RRT
Request for Scientific Research (AAG) ... RSR
Request for Self Enhancement (IAA) ... RSE
Request for Services [*Social Security Administration*] ... RFS
Request for Services [*Social Security Administration*] ... RS
Request for Shipment (MCD) ... RFS
Request for Support (MCD) ... RS
Request for System Proposal (MHDI) ... RFSP
Request for Technical Action (MCD) ... RTA
Request for Technical Information [*Military*] ... RTI
Request for Technical Proposal ... RFTP
Request for Technical Proposal [*Military*] ... RTP
Request for Technical Samples (AAGC) ... RFTS
Request for Technology (DOM) ... RFT
Request for Tender (ADA) ... RFT
Request for Test or Inspection (MCD) ... RFTOI
Request for Waiver (MCD) ... RFW
Request Full Route Clearance [*FAA*] (TAG) ... FRC
Request if Desired (FAAC) ... REQID
Request Immediate Reply [*Business term*] (MHDB) ... RIR
Request in Trail Climb [*Aviation*] (FAAC) ... RITC
Request in Trail Descent [*Aviation*] (FAAC) ... RITD
Request Initialization Mode (IAA) ... RIM
Request Interim Reply By [*Date*] [*Military*] (AABC) ... REQINT
Request Item Be Placed on Back Order [*Army*] ... REQIBO
Request Level Change Enroute [*Aviation*] (DA) ... RLCE
Request Level Not Available [*Aviation*] (FAAC) ... RLNA
Request Liaison Engineering Order [*NASA*] (NASA) ... RLEO
Request Line Items Be Expedited for Vehicles [*or Equipment*] **Deadlined for Parts** [*Army*] (AABC) ... RLIEVDP
Request Loading Entry [*Computer science*] ... RLE
Request Monitor Entry [*Computer science*] ... RME
Request Next Character ... RNC
Request Nomination ... REQNOM
Request of Change (NASA) ... ROC
Request on File (FAAC) ... RQOF
Request Parameter List [*Computer science*] (BUR) ... RPL
Request Permission [*Navy*] (NVT) ... REQPER
Request Present Altitude [*Aviation*] (FAAC) ... RPA
Request Present Position [*Aviation*] (FAAC) ... RQPP
Request Programs Termination [*Computer science*] ... RPT
Request, Quandary and Deferment Plan ... RQDP
Request Recommendation (NVT) ... REQREC
Request/Response Unit [*Computer science*] ... RU
Request, Retrieve, and Report [*Computer science*] ... 3R
Request Select Entry [*Computer science*] ... RSE
Request Shipping Instructions [*Military*] ... REQSI
Request Supplementary Flight Plan Message [*Aviation code*] ... RQS
Request Supply Status and Expected Delivery Date [*Army*] (AABC) ... REQSSD
Request Supply Status of Following [*Army*] (AABC) ... REQSUPSTAFOL
Request the Pleasure of Your Company [*On invitations*] (DSUE) ... RPC
Request Time and Altitude Over [*Aviation*] (FAAC) ... RQTAO
Request to Expedite ... RTE
Request to Off-Load [*Shipping*] (DS) ... RTO
Request to Purchase ... RTP
Request to Send ... RS
Request to Send ... RTS
Request to Start Contract Definition ... RSCD
Request Tracer Be Initiated [*Military*] ... REQTRAC
Request Translator (SAA) ... RT
Request Travel Order (NOAA) ... RQTO
Request Unit of Issue Be Changed to Read [*Army*] (AABC) ... REQUCHRD
Request Your Recommendation (FAAC) ... REQRCM
Requesta Regni Hierosolymitani [*A publication*] (BJA) ... RH
Requested (FAAC) ... REQSTD
Requested Flight Level ... RFL
Requested for Information ... RFI
Requested Privilege Level [*Computer science*] ... RPL
Requester's Approval in Principle (NRCH) ... RAIP
Requesting Agency (MUGU) ... RA
Requesting Expeditor Unit (DNAB) ... REU
Request-Response Header [*Computer science*] (BUR) ... RH
Requests for Contractual Procurement (MUGU) ... RFCP
Requiescat [*He, or She Rests*] [*Latin*] ... R
Requiescat [*or Requiescant*] **in Pace** [*May He (She, or They) Rest in Peace*] [*Latin*] (GPO) ... RIP
Require (AAG) ... REQ
Require (ROG) ... REQRE
Require (IAA) ... REQU
Require (AAG) ... RQR
Require Identification ... RI
Required (AAG) ... REQD
Required ... RQRD
Required Availability Date [*Military*] ... RAD
Required Average Life (MCD) ... RAL
Required Beneficial Occupancy Data (SAA) ... RBOD
Required Carrier Return Character [*Computer science*] ... RCR
Required Cleanliness Level [*Automobile maintenance*] ... RCL
Required Date ... RD
Required Delivery Date (AABC) ... RDD
Required Delivery Date (ODBW) ... rdd
Required Execution Date (MCD) ... REQED
Required Freight Rate (DS) ... RFR
Required Functional Capability [*Navy*] ... RFC
Required Hangar Depth (MCD) ... RHD
Required Hangar Width (MCD) ... RHW
Required Inservice Manyears in Lieu of Controls [*Military*] ... REMILOC
Required Markup Declaration [*Computer science*] ... RMD
Required Myocardial Blood Flow [*Cardiology*] ... RMBF
Required Navigation Performance [*Aviation*] (FAAC) ... RNP
Required Navigation Performance Capability ... RNPC
Required Net Yield [*Business term*] (EMRF) ... RNY
Required Number of Days of Stock ... RDS
Required on Dock (KSC) ... ROD
Required Operational Capability [*Military*] (RDA) ... ROC
Required Operational Date ... ROD
Required Overseas Terminal Arrival Date (DNAB) ... ROTAD
Required Page-End Character [*Computer science*] ... RPE
Required Rate of Return [*Finance*] ... K
Required Rate of Return [*Finance*] ... RRR
Required Reserves ... RR
Required Resistance (IDOE) ... R_{req}
Required Response Spectrum (IEEE) ... RRS
Required Space Character [*Computer science*] ... RSP
Required Supply Rate [*Military*] (AABC) ... RSR
Required Technical Characteristic [*Military*] (CAAL) ... RTC
Required Time of Arrival (DA) ... RTA
Requirement (NVT) ... REQMNT
Requirement ... REQMT
Requirement (AAG) ... REQT
Requirement (AFM) ... RQMT
Requirement (IAA) ... RQR
Requirement ... RQRMNT
Requirement Action Number ... RAN
Requirement and Determination Execution System ... RDES
Requirement and Test Procedures ... RTP
Requirement Clearance Symbol [*Military*] (AFM) ... RCS
Requirement Objective Code ... ROBCO
Requirements (FAAC) ... RQMNTS
Requirements (KSC) ... RQTS
Requirements Action Directive (AFM) ... RAD
Requirements Advisory Group [*Air Force*] (MCD) ... RAG
Requirements Allocation Form ... RAF
Requirements Allocation Sheet ... RAS
Requirements Analysis ... RA
Requirements Analysis (MCD) ... REQANA
Requirements Analysis Form [*NASA*] (NASA) ... RAF
Requirements Analysis Material Sheet [*or Study*] (MCD) ... RAMS
Requirements Analysis Package [*Computer science*] ... RAP
Requirements Analysis Sheet [*NASA*] (KSC) ... RAS
Requirements and Capabilities Automated Planning System (MCD) ... REQCAPS
Requirements and Configuration ... R & C
Requirements and Design Branch (SAA) ... RDB
Requirements and Distribution (AFM) ... R & D
Requirements and Formulation Phase (MCD) ... RFP
Requirements and Objectives ... R & O
Requirements and Specification Documentation [*Computer science*] ... RASD
Requirements and Specifications Document [*NASA*] (NASA) ... RSD
Requirements Audit System ... RAS
Requirements Change Notice [*NASA*] (NASA) ... RCN
Requirements Change Proposal ... RCP
Requirements Contract ... RC
Requirements Contract Price List (AAGC) ... RCPL
Requirements Control Board (MCD) ... RCB
Requirements Control Symbol [*Military*] (MCD) ... RCS
Requirements Control System ... RCS
Requirements Correlation Matrix [*Air Force*] (DOMA) ... RCM
Requirements Data Bank [*Air Force*] (GFGA) ... RDB

Requirements Data Plan (NASA) ... RDP
Requirements Definition Document [*NASA*] (NASA) ... RDD
Requirements Determination and Exercise System [*Military*] (MCD) ... RD & ES
Requirements Development Plan [*NASA*] (NASA) ... RDP
Requirements Document [*NASA*] (KSC) ... RD
Requirements Document [*Army*] (RDA) ... ROC
Requirements Electronic Input System [*NASA*] (KSC) ... REINS
Requirements Engineering and Validation System ... REVS
Requirements Evaluated against Cargo Transportation (PDAA) ... REACT
Requirements for Close Air Support [*Army*] (MCD) ... RCAS
Requirements for Production [*Army*] (RDA) ... RFP
Requirements for Scheduled Test (MUGU) ... RST
Requirements for Total Mobilization Study ... RETMOB
Requirements for Work and Resources (MUGU) ... RFWAR
Requirements Formulation Document [*NASA*] (NASA) ... RFD
Requirements Inventory Analysis Report (AFM) ... RIAR
Requirements Inventory Management System (MCD) ... RIMS
Requirements Objective ... RO
Requirements Objectives Period ... ROP
Requirements Planning and Inventory Control System [*Computer science*] (IAA) ... RIS
Requirements Planning System [*Computer science*] ... RPS
Requirements Resources Review [*Board*] [*DoD*] (DOMA) ... R^3
Requirements Review [*NASA*] (NASA) ... RR
Requirements Review Board (SSD) ... RRB
Requirements Review Committee [*Navy*] ... RRC
Requirements Review Group [*Air Staff*] [*Air Force*] (MCD) ... RRG
Requirements Review Team ... RRT
Requirements Statement Analyzer ... RSA
Requirements Statement Language ... RSL
Requirements Status System [*NASA*] ... RSS
Requirements Tape Generator [*NASA*] ... RTG
Requirements Traceability Matrix ... RTM
Requirements Traceability Tool [*Computer science*] ... RTT
Requirements Type Contract [*Military*] (AABC) ... RTC
Requirements Validation Study (MCD) ... RVS
Requirements Verification (IEEE) ... REQVER
Requirements Verification Network [*NASA*] (NASA) ... RVN
Requirements Volatility ... RQTV
Requires ... REQS
Requires a Doctor [*Search and rescue symbol that can be stamped in sand or snow*] ... I
Requires an Engineer [*Search and rescue symbol that can be stamped in sand or snow*] ... W
Requires Food and Water [*Search and rescue symbol that can be stamped in sand or snow*] ... F
Requires Fuel and Oil [*Search and rescue symbol that can be stamped in sand or snow*] ... L
Requires Immediate Action (NOAA) ... RQIAC
Requires Medical Supplies [*Search and rescue symbol that can be stamped in sand or snow*] ... II
Requiring Activity Contract Administrator [*DoD*] ... RACA
Requisite Remedial Technology (EPA) ... RRT
Requisition ... REQ
Requisition (AAG) ... REQN
Requisition (AFM) ... RQN
Requisition Account Number ... RAN
Requisition Advice Care [*Military*] ... RAC
Requisition and Invoice Shipping Document ... RISD
Requisition Control Office ... RCO
Requisition Control Unit ... RCU
Requisition Distribution System ... RDS
Requisition Due Date (TEL) ... RDD
Requisition Exception Code [*Air Force*] (AFIT) ... REX
Requisition for Procurement [*DoD*] ... RFP
Requisition Held Up (DNAB) ... RHU
Requisition on Stores [*Nuclear energy*] (NRCH) ... ROS
Requisition on Warehouse [*Nuclear energy*] (NRCH) ... ROW
Requisition Priority Code Analysis System [*Army*] ... RPCAS
Requisition Processing Cycle (MCD) ... RPC
Requisition Processing Point [*Military*] ... RPP
Requisition Received Date [*Bell System*] (TEL) ... RRD
Requisition Restriction Code (DNAB) ... RR
Requisition Status File (DNAB) ... RSF
Requisitioning Objective [*Military*] (AABC) ... RO
Requisitions ... REQUONS
Requisitions/Objectives (CINC) ... R/O
Reradiation ... RERAD
Reroute [*Aviation*] (FAAC) ... RERTE
Reroute [*Telecommunications*] (TEL) ... RR
Reroute Inhibit [*Telecommunications*] (TEL) ... RRI
Rerum Naturalium Scriptores Graeci Minores [*A publication*] (OCD) ... Rer Nat Scr Graec Min
Rerum Politicarum Doctor [*Doctor of Political Science*] ... RPD
Rerun [*of a television show*] ... R
Rerun (AAG) ... RER
Res Care, Inc. [*Associated Press*] (SAG) ... ResCare
Res Care, Inc. [*NASDAQ symbol*] (SAG) ... RSCR
Res Ipsa Loquitur [*The Thing Speaks for Itself*] [*Latin*] (DLA) ... Res Ipsa
Res Ipsa Loquitur [*The Thing Speaks for Itself*] [*Latin*] ... RIL
Res Ipsa Loquitur [*Speaks for Itself*] [*Latin*] (LWAP) ... RIL
Res Judicatae [*A publication*] (DLA) ... Res Judic
Res Publica [*A publication*] (ILCA) ... Res Pub
Resale Price Maintenance ... RPM
Resawed (WGA) ... RES
Resazurin [*A pH indicator*] (DAVI) ... R
Resazurin Reduction Time [*Medicine*] (MAE) ... RRT
Rescind (AAG) ... RESC
Rescind [*Legal shorthand*] (LWAP) ... RESCD
Rescinded [*Legal term*] (DLA) ... R
Rescript of Gamma Eta Gamma [*A publication*] (DLA) ... Res Gamma Eta Gamma
Rescriptum [*Counterpart*] [*Latin*] ... RC
Rescue (WDAA) ... RES
Rescue (AFM) ... RESC
Rescue (AAG) ... RSQ
Rescue Ambulance [*Emergency medicine*] (DAVI) ... RA
Rescue and Assistance ... R & A
Rescue and Weather Reconnaissance Squadron [*Air Force*] ... RWRSq
Rescue and Weather Reconnaissance Wing [*Air Force*] ... RWRW
Rescue Boat ... RSQBT
Rescue Breathing Apparatus ... RBA
Rescue by Individuals Parachuted to Distressed Persons [*Air Force*] ... PARARESCUE
Rescue Combat Air Patrol [*Army*] ... RESCAP
Rescue Control Center ... RCC
Rescue Coordination Center [*Sweden ICAO location identifier*] (ICLI) ... ESOR
Rescue Coordination Center [*Coast Guard*] ... RCC
Rescue Coordination Center [*ICAO designator*] (ICDA) ... YC
Rescue Co-Ordination Center [*FAA designator*] (FAAC) ... YCY
Rescue Crew Commander (AFM) ... RCC
Rescue Equipment Locker (AAG) ... REL
Rescue, Inc. (EA) ... RI
Rescue Module [*NASA*] (NASA) ... RM
Rescue Motor Launch [*Air/sea rescue*] [*Navy*] ... RML
Rescue Ocean Tug [*Navy symbol*] ... ATR
Rescue Squadrons [*Navy symbol*] ... VH
Rescue Sub-Center [*ICAO*] (FAAC) ... RSC
Rescue Support Umbilical (MCD) ... RSU
Rescue Transport [*Navy symbol*] ... APR
Rescue Unit Home Port [*Navy*] (NVT) ... RUHP
Rescue Vessel ... RV
Rese Engineering Automatic Core Tester ... REACT
Research ... R
Research (AAG) ... RES
Research (IDOE) ... res
Research (AFM) ... RSCH
Research ... RSRCH
Research [*or Experimental*] [*Designation for all US military aircraft*] ... X
Research Activities Designators Management Information System ... RADMIS
Research Advisory Board (DAVI) ... RAB
Research Advisory Committee ... RAC
Research Advisory Council ... RAC
Research Advisory Institute, Inc. ... RAI
Research Aircraft for the Visual Environment [*Helicopters*] [*Army*] ... RAVE
Research Analysis Corp. [*Nonprofit contract agency*] [*Army*] ... RAC
Research Analysis Corporation Field Office, Europe [*Army*] (AABC) ... RACFOE
Research and Acquisition Communications Division [*Military*] ... RCD
Research and Advanced Development ... R & AD
Research and Advanced Development (MCD) ... RAD
Research and Advanced Technology ... R & AT
Research and Analysis ... R & A
Research and Analysis (IAA) ... RAA
Research and Applications Module [*NASA*] ... RAM
Research and Curriculum Unit [*Mississippi State University*] [*Research center*] (RCD) ... R/CU
Research and Demonstration [*Labor training*] ... R & D
Research and Demonstration Center for the Education of Handicapped Children and Youth [*Defunct*] (EA) ... RDCEHCY
Research and Development ... R & D
Research and Development (IAA) ... RAD
Research and Development (IAA) ... RAND
Research and Development (IDOE) ... R&D
Research and Development (DFIT) ... R&D
Research and Development [*Army*] ... RD
Research and Development Abstracts [*A publication*] ... RDA
Research and Development Acceptance Test ... RDAT
Research and Development Acquisition Committee [*Military*] ... RDAC
Research and Development, Army ... RDA
Research and Development Associates, Food and Container Institute (EA) ... RDAFCI
Research and Development Associates for Military Food and Packaging Systems (EA) ... R & DA
Research and Development Board [*Abolished, 1953, functions transferred to Department of Defense*] ... RDB
Research and Development Center for Teacher Education [*Department of Education*] (GRD) ... R & DCTE
Research and Development Center Library, Jackson, MS [*Library symbol Library of Congress*] (LCLS) ... MsJRD
Research and Development Center Library, SaskPower, Regina, Saskatchewan [*Library symbol National Library of Canada*] (NLC) ... SRPCRD
Research and Development Command (MCD) ... RADCOM
Research and Development Command [*Military*] ... RDC
Research and Development Contributions to Aviation Progress [*Air Force*] ... RADCAP
Research and Development Directorate [*Army*] ... RDD
Research and Development Division [*National Security Agency*] [*Obsolete*] ... RADE
Research and Development Electronic Security [*Military*] (AABC) ... R & DELSEC
Research and Development Establishment [*British*] ... RDE
Research and Development Field Unit [*Military*] ... RDFU

Research and Development Field Unit - Vietnam [Military] (MCD) .... RDFU-V
Research & Development, Gulf Canada Ltd., Mississauga, Ontario [Library symbol National Library of Canada] (NLC) .... OMGCR
Research and Development in Advanced Communication Technologies for Europe (NITA) .... RACE
Research and Development in Advanced Communications for Europe [European Community] (MHDB) .... RACE
Research and Development in Computer System (IAA) .... RADICS
Research and Development in Information and Library Science (NITA) .... RADIALS
Research and Development in the United States [Database] .... RADIUS
Research and Development Information Center (AFM) .... RADIC
Research and Development Information Exchange System [Navy] (DOMA) .... RDIXS
Research and Development Information System [Later, EPD/RDIS] [Electric Power Research Institute] [Information service or system] (IID) .... RDIS
Research and Development Institute, Inc. [Montana State University] [Research center] (RCD) .... RDI
Research and Development Institute of the United States [Research center] (RCD) .... RADIUS
Research and Development Kit .... RDK
Research and Development Laboratories, Public Works Canada [Laboratoires de Recherche et de Developpement, Travaux Publics Canada] Ottawa, Ontario [Library symbol Obsolete National Library of Canada] (NLC) .... OOPWR
Research and Development Library, Shaw Industries, Rexdale, Ontario [Library symbol National Library of Canada] (BIB) .... ORS
Research and Development Limited Partnership [Tax-shelter investment] .... RDLP
Research and Development Management Course [Army] .... RDMC
Research and Development Network [Formerly, ARPANET] .... R & DNET
Research and Development Objectives [Military] (AFM) .... RDO
Research and Development Objectives Document (MCD) .... RADOD
Research and Development of Instrumentation [Program] [Army] .... RDI
Research and Development Operational Needs (MCD) .... RADON
Research and Development Operations [Marshall Space Flight Center] [NASA] (NASA) .... R & DO
Research and Development Plan .... RDP
Research and Development Planning and Budgeting (AFIT) .... RDPB
Research and Development Planning Summary .... RDPS
Research and Development Program Planning [Database] [DTIC] .... R & DPP
Research and Development/Programming Budget Memorandum (MCD) .... RD/PBM
Research and Development Report .... RDR
Research and Development Service [FAA] (TAG) .... ARD
Research and Development Service [Army-Ordnance] .... RDS
Research and Development Society [British] (DBA) .... R & DSoc
Research and Development Survey .... RDS
Research and Economic Analysis Division [Office of Transportation] (GRD) .... READ
Research and Economic Programs [Department of the Treasury] (GRD) .... REP
Research and Education (MAE) .... R & E
Research and Education Association .... REA
Research and Education Center for Architectural Preservation [University of Florida] [Research center] (RCD) .... RECAP
Research and Education Community .... R&E
Research and Education Foundation for Chest Disease [Defunct] (EA) .... REFCD
Research and Educational Planning Center [University of Nevada - Reno] [Research center] (RCD) .... REPC
Research and Engineering .... R & E
Research and Engineering (IAA) .... RAE
Research and Engineering .... RE
Research and Engineering Apprenticeship Program [Army] (RDA) .... REAP
Research and Engineering Council (NADA) .... R&EC
Research and Engineering Council of the Graphic Arts Industry .... RECGA
Research and Engineering Council of the Graphic Arts Industry (EA) .... RECGAI
Research and Engineering Information Services [Exxon Research & Engineering Co.] (IID) .... REIS
Research and Engineering Policy Council [DoD] .... REPC
Research and Engineering Support Facility (MCD) .... RESF
Research and Engineers Professional Employees Association .... REPEA
Research and Evaluation Methods Program [University of Massachusetts] [Research center] (RCD) .... REMP
Research and Evaluation Section, Canada Council [Service de Recherche et d'Evaluation, Conseil des Arts du Canada], Ottawa, Ontario [Library symbol National Library of Canada] (BIB) .... OOCACR
Research and Experiments Department [Ministry of Home Security] [British World War II] .... RE
Research and Exploration [A publication] (BRI) .... Res & Exp
Research and Information Centre on Eritrea (EA) .... RICE
Research and Information Library, Canadian Life and Health Insurance Association, Toronto, Ontario [Library symbol National Library of Canada] (BIB) .... OTCLH
Research and Information Services for Education [Montgomery County Intermediate Unit] [King of Prussia, PA] .... RISE
Research and Information State Education Trust (AIE) .... RISE
Research and Instrumentation for National Bio-Science Operations (MUGU) .... RAINBO
Research and Laboratory Services Division [Health and Safety Executive] [British] (IRUK) .... RLSD
Research & Laser Technology, Inc. .... RLT
Research and Marketing Act [1946] .... RMA
Research and Microfilm Publications .... RMP
Research and No Development [Origin of name of RAND Corporation, a nonprofit national defense research organization] .... RAND

Research and Productivity Council [Canada] (IRC) .... RPC
Research and Program Management [NASA] .... RPM
Research and Reporting Committee [Interstate Conference of Employment Security Agencies] .... R & R
Research and Special Programs Administration [Department of Transportation] [Washington, DC] (GRD) .... RSPA
Research and Special Project Division [Bureau of National Affairs] [Information service or system] (IID) .... RSPD
Research and Statistics (IEEE) .... R & S
Research and Study .... R & S
Research and Technical Services [Military] .... RTS
Research and Technology .... R & T
Research and Technology .... RT
Research and Technology Advisory Council [Terminated, 1977] [NASA] (EGAO) .... RTAC
Research & Technology Centre, AMCA International Ltd., Kanata, Ontario [Library symbol National Library of Canada] (NLC) .... OKAI
[The] Research and Technology Coordinating Document [Army] (RDA) .... RTCOD
Research and Technology Division [Air Force] .... RTD
Research and Technology Laboratories [Army] (RDA) .... RTL
Research and Technology Objectives and Plans [NASA] (NASA) .... RTOP
Research and Technology Objectives and Plans Summary [NASA Information service or system] (CRD) .... RTOPS
Research and Technology Operating [or Operations] Plan [NASA] .... RTOP
Research and Technology Operations and Plans [NASA] (AAGC) .... RTOP
Research and Technology Work Unit Information System [Database] [Defense Technical Information Center] (CRD) .... R & T WUIS
Research and Technology Work Unit Summary .... R & TWUS
Research and Technology Work Unit Summary .... RATWUS
Research and Technology Work Unit Summary .... RTWUS
Research and Training Center on Independent Living (EA) .... RTCIL
Research Animal Alliance (EA) .... RAA
Research Animal Diagnostic and Investigative Laboratory [University of Missouri-Columbia] [Research center] (RCD) .... RADIL
Research Animal Holding Facility [NASA] (NASA) .... RAHF
Research Applications Policy Advisory Committee [National Science Foundation] (EGAO) .... RAPAC
Research Applied to National Needs [Formerly, IRRPOS] [National Science Foundation Obsolete] .... RANN
Research Assessment Exercise [Higher Education Funding Council] (AIE) .... RAE
Research Association for Petroleum Alternative Development .... RAPAD
Research Association for the Paper and Board, Printing and Packaging Industries [Research center] (IRC) .... PIRA
Research Association for the Paper and Board, Printing, and Packaging Industries [Research center British] (IRC) .... RAPBPPI
Research Association of Minority Professors (EA) .... RAMP
Research Aviation Coordinating Committee .... RACC
Research Aviation Facility [National Center for Atmospheric Research] .... RAF
Research Aviation Medicine [Navy program of research into aerospace medical techniques] .... RAM
Research Branch [Naval Technical Training Command] [Millington, TN] .... RBR
Research Branch, Ontario Ministry of Natural Resources, Toronto, Ontario [Library symbol National Library of Canada] (NLC) .... OTLR
Research Bulletin .... RB
Research Career Development Awards [Department of Health and Human Services] .... RCDA
Research Careers for Minority Scholars [National Science Foundation] .... RCMS
Research Center (IEEE) .... RC
Research Center for Advanced Study [University of Texas at Arlington] [Research center] (RCD) .... RCAS
Research Center for Group Dynamics [University of Michigan] [Research center] (RCD) .... RCGD
Research Center for Religion and Human Rights in Closed Societies (EA) .... RCRHRCS
Research Center for Urban and Environmental Planning [Princeton University] .... RCUEP
Research Center on Women (EA) .... RCW
Research Centers Directory [A publication] .... RCD
Research Centers in Minority Institutions Program [Bethesda, MD] [National Institutes of Health] (GRD) .... RCMI
Research Centre, Domtar Ltd., Senneville, Quebec [Library symbol National Library of Canada] (NLC) .... QSED
Research Centre for Canadian Ethnic Studies [University of Calgary] [Research center] (RCD) .... RCCES
Research Centre for Canadian Ethnic Studies, University of Calgary, Alberta [Library symbol National Library of Canada] (NLC) .... ACUCES
Research Centre for Islamic History, Art, and Culture [of the Organization of the Islamic Conference] (EAIO) .... IRCICA
Research Centre for Management of New Technology [Wilfrid Laurier University] [Canada Research center] (RCD) .... REMAT
Research Centre for the Education of the Visually Handicapped [University of Birmingham] [British] (CB) .... RCEVH
Research Centre for Women's Studies [University of Adelaide, Australia] .... RCWS
Research Centre Library, Du Pont Canada, Inc., Kingston, Ontario [Library symbol National Library of Canada] (NLC) .... OKD
Research Co., Atomic Energy of Canada Ltd. [Societe de Recherches, L'Energie Atomique du Canada Ltee] Ottawa, Ontario [Library symbol National Library of Canada] (NLC) .... OOAER
Research Computation Laboratory [University of Houston] [Research center] (RCD) .... RCL
Research Computing Center [University of New Hampshire] [Research center] (RCD) .... RCC
Research Conference on Instrumentation Science .... RCIS
Research Contract Support Office .... RCSO
Research Contracting Officer .... RCO

Research Coordinating Unit [Oklahoma State Department of Vocational and Technical Education] [Stillwater, OK] .... RCU
Research Council Employees' Association [Canada] .... RCEA
Research Council for Complementary Medicine [British] (IRUK) .... RCCM
Research Council of Makeup Artists (NTCM) .... RCMA
Research Council on Riveted and Bolted Structural Joints [Later, RCSC] (EA) .... RCRBSJ
Research Council on Structural Connections (EA) .... RCSC
Research Data Publication [Center] .... RDP
Research Defence Society [British] .... RDS
Research Department Explosive [Cyclonite] .... RDX
Research Department, J. E. Seagram & Sons Ltd., La Salle, Quebec [Library symbol National Library of Canada] (NLC) .... QLSS
Research, Design, and Standardization Organization [Indian Railways] [India] (PDAA) .... RDSO
Research, Development, and Acquisition [DoD] .... RD & A
Research, Development, and Acquisition (AAGC) .... RDA
Research Development and Acquisition Information Systems Activity [Army] (AAGC) .... RDAISA
Research, Development, and Acquisition Information Systems Agency [Army] (AABC) .... RDAISA
Research, Development, and Demonstration .... RD & D
Research, Development, and Engineering .... RD & E
Research, Development, and Engineering (RDA) .... RDE
Research, Development, and Engineering Center (RDA) .... RDEC
Research, Development, and Facilities (NOAA) .... RDF
Research, Development, and Operation [Military appropriation] .... RDO
Research, Development, and Production [NATO] (NATG) .... RD & P
Research, Development, and Standardization [Groups] [Army] (RDA) .... RDS
Research, Development, and Studies [Marine Corps] .... RD & S
Research, Development and Technology Investigation .... RDTI
Research, Development, and Test .... RDAT
Research, Development, and Testing .... RD & T
Research, Development, Diffusion [or Dissemination], and Evaluation ...... RDD & E
Research, Development, Engineering, and Acquisition (RDA) .... RDE & A
Research Development Exchange (OICC) .... RDE
Research Development Safety Management [Air Force] .... RDSM
Research, Development, Test, and Engineering (SSD) .... RDT & E
Research, Development, Test, and Evaluation (AAGC) .... RDT&E
Research, Development, Test, and Evaluation [DoD] .... RDTE
Research, Development, Test, and Evaluation, Army .... RDTEA
Research, Development, Test, and Evaluation, Navy .... RDT & EN
Research, Development, Test, Evaluation, and Engineering Program [DoD] (RDA) .... RDTE & E
Research Diagnostic Criteria [Medicine, psychiatry] .... RDC
Research Discussion Group (EA) .... RDG
Research Division Report .... RDR
Research Division Technical Report .... RDTR
Research Documentation Section [Public Health Service] [Information service or system] (IID) .... RDS
Research Documents Search [Information service or system] (IID) .... RDS
Research Earth Borer .... REB
Research, Education, and Assistance for Canadians with Herpes .... REACH
Research Effort Management Information Tabulation .... REMIT
Research EMP [Electromagnetic Pulse] Simulator I [Air Force] .... RES I
Research, Engineering, and Development .... RE & D
Research Engineering and Test (NASA) .... RE & T
Research Engineering Authorization (AAG) .... REA
Research, Engineering, Mathematics, and Physics Division [National Security Agency] [Obsolete] .... REMP
Research Engineering Standing Group [DoD] .... RESG
Research Engineers, Inc. [NASDAQ symbol] (SAG) .... RENG
Research Engineers, Inc. [Associated Press] (SAG) .... ResEngn
Research Enrichment in Research and Test Reactors Program [Department of Energy] .... RERTR
Research Ethics Board [Canada] .... REB
Research Ethics Committee .... REC
Research, Evaluation, and Experimental Program [Bureau of the Census] (GFGA) .... REX
Research, Evaluation, and Planning Assistance Staff [AID] .... REPAS
Research, Evaluation, and System Analysis [Navy] .... RESA
Research Expenditure Proposal .... REP
Research Experiences for Undergraduates [NSF grant program] .... REU
Research Facilities and Equipment Division [NASA] (MCD) .... RFED
Research Facilities Center [National Oceanic and Atmospheric Administration] (GRD) .... RFC
Research Fire Control (SAA) .... REFIC
Research Fiscal Office (SAA) .... RFO
Research Flight Facility [Air Force] .... RFF
Research for Better Schools, Inc. [Philadelphia, PA] [Department of Education] .... RBS
Research for Health Charities Group [British] .... RHCG
Research Foundation for Jewish Immigration (EA) .... RFJI
Research Foundation for the Study of Terrorism [British] .... RFST
Research Frigate [Navy symbol] (NVT) .... AGFF
Research Frontiers [NASDAQ symbol] (TTSB) .... REFR
Research Frontiers [Associated Press] (SAG) .... RschFrnt
Research Frontiers, Inc. [NASDAQ symbol] (SAG) .... REFR
Research Frontiers, Inc. [Associated Press] (SAG) .... RschFrt
Research Grants Staff [Environmental Protection Agency] (GFGA) .... RGS
Research Group for European Migration Problems .... REMP
Research Highlights [A publication] (DIT) .... RH
Research Hospital and Medical Center, Kansas City, MO [Library symbol Library of Congress] (LCLS) .... MoKRes

Research Improvement in Minority Institutions [Program] [National Science Foundation] .... RIMI
Research in Accrediting Efforts Project [Illinois] (EDAC) .... REA
Research in Advanced Communications in Europe [European Commission] .... RACE
Research in Automatic Photocomposition and Information Dissemination .... RAPID
Research in British Universities, Polytechnics, and Colleges [Formerly, SRBUC] [British Library] .... RBUPC
Research in Education [Monthly publication of ERIC] .... RIE
Research in International Economics of Disarmament and Arms Control [A program of Columbia University School of International Affairs] .... RIEDAC
Research in Laboratory Animal Medicine and Care .... RILAMAC
Research in Law and Economics [A publication] (DLA) .... Research L & Econ
Research in Parapsychology [A publication] .... RIP
Research in Progress (MCD) .... RIP
Research in Public Administration and Management [British] .... RPAM
Research in Science Education [National Science Foundation] (GRD) .... RISE
Research in Supersonic Environment .... RISE
Research in the Life Sciences Committee [National Academy of Sciences] .... RLS
Research in Undergraduate Institutions [A National Science Foundation program] .... RUI
Research, Inc. [Associated Press] (SAG) .... ReshInc
Research, Inc. [NASDAQ symbol] (NQ) .... RESR
Research Industries Corp. [NASDAQ symbol] (NQ) .... REIC
Research Industries Corp. [Associated Press] (SAG) .... ReshInd
Research Industry Office (MCD) .... RIO
Research Information Center and Advisory Service on Information Processing [National Bureau of Standards - National Science Foundation] .... RICASIP
Research Information Center and Library [Foster Wheeler Corp.] [Information service or system] (IID) .... RICAL
Research Information Center, DOFASCO, Inc., Hamilton, Ontario [Library symbol National Library of Canada] (NLC) .... OHDFR
Research Information Service [John Crerar Library] [Information service or system] (IID) .... RIS
Research Information Services [Georgia Institute of Technology] [Atlanta] [Information service or system] (IID) .... RIS
Research Information Services - Alexander Library .... RIS-ALEX
Research Information System [Rehabilitation Services Administration] (IID) .... RIS
Research Initiation and Support [National Science Foundation program] .... RIAS
Research Initiative into Silicon Hybrids [British] .... RISH
Research Institute [Fort Belvoir, VA] [United States Army Engineer Topographic Laboratories] (GRD) .... RI
Research Institute for Advanced Computer Science [University Space Research Association] [Research center] (RCD) .... RIACS
Research Institute for Advanced Studies [Martin Marietta Corp.] .... RIAS
Research Institute for Advanced Study, Baltimore, MD [Library symbol Library of Congress] (LCLS) .... MdBR
Research Institute for Asia and the Pacific [Australia] .... RIAP
Research Institute for Consumer Affairs [British] .... RICA
Research Institute for Diagnostic Engineering .... RIDE
Research Institute for Engineering Sciences [Wayne State University] [Research center] (RCD) .... RIES
Research Institute for Environmental Medicine [Army] (MCD) .... RIEM
Research Institute for Fragrance Materials (EA) .... RIFM
Research Institute for Information Science and Engineering, Inc. [Information service or system] (IID) .... RIISE
Research Institute for Innovative Technolgies for the Earth .... RITE
Research Institute for Iron, Steel, and Other Metals (MHDB) .... RIISOM
Research Institute for Management Executives [Washington, DC] .... RIME
Research Institute for Studies in Education [Iowa State University] [Research center] (RCD) .... RISE
Research Institute for Supersensonic Healing Energies .... RISHE
Research Institute for Telecommunications and Economics (NITA) .... RITE
Research Institute for the Behavioral and Social Sciences [Army] .... RIBSS
Research Institute for the Management of Technology [Southern California Technology Executives Network] [Research center] (RCD) .... RIMTech
Research Institute for the Natural Sciences .... RINS
Research Institute for the Study of Man [Army] (MCD) .... RISM
Research Institute of African and African Diaspora Arts (EA) .... RIAADA
Research Institute of America [New York, NY] [Information service or system] (IID) .... RIA
Research Institute of America Tax Coordinator [A publication] (DLA) .... RIA Tax
Research Institute of National Defense (NADA) .... RIND
Research Institute of Pharmaceutical Sciences [University of Mississippi] (PDAA) .... RIPS
Research Institute of Religious Jewry (EA) .... RIRJ
Research Institute of Scripps Clinic [Research center] (RCD) .... RISC
Research Institute of Temple University (KSC) .... RITU
Research Institute of the Study of Conflict and Terrorism [British] (DBA) .... RISCT
Research Institute on Care for the Elderly [British] (DBA) .... RICE
Research Institute on Immigration and Ethnic Studies [Smithsonian Institution] .... RIIES
Research Institute on International Change [Columbia University] .... RIIC
Research Institute on the Sino-Soviet Bloc (EA) .... RISSB
Research Institutes and Divisions [of National Institutes of Health] .... RID
Research Instrument Module (IAA) .... RIM
Research into Child Blindness [British] (DI) .... RICB
Research into Chronic Unemployment [British] .... RCU
Research into Drug Abuse Advisory Committee [Australia] .... RDAAC
Research into Lost Knowledge Organisation Trust (EAIO) .... RILKO
Research into One-Parent Families [British] .... ROPF
Research into Site Management (MHDB) .... RSM

Research Laboratories Technical Memorandum ... RLTM
Research Laboratory ... RESLAB
Research Laboratory ... RL
Research Laboratory for Archeology [*British*] ... RLA
Research Laboratory for Equine Infectious Diseases [*Cornell University*] [*Research center*] (RCD) ... EID
Research Laboratory for Mechanics of Materials (MCD) ... RLMM
Research Laboratory of Electronics [*MIT*] [*Research center*] ... RLE
Research Laboratory of Heat Transfer in Electronics [*MIT*] (MCD) ... RLHTE
Research Liaison Panel on Scientific Information Services (NITA) ... RELIPOSIS
Research Libraries Group [*An association Also, an information service or system*] (EA) ... RLG
Research Libraries Information Network [*Pronounced "arlen"*] [*Formerly, BALLOTS Research Libraries Group, Inc. Stanford, CA*] [*Library network*] [*Information service or system*] ... RLIN
Research Libraries Information Network, Stanford, CA [*Library symbol Library of Congress*] (LCLS) ... CStRLIN
Research Library, Algoma Steel Corp. Ltd., Sault Ste. Marie, Ontario [*Library symbol National Library of Canada*] (NLC) ... OSTMAS
Research Library, Duracell, Inc., Mississauga, Ontario [*Library symbol Obsolete National Library of Canada*] (NLC) ... OMDIR
Research Library for Edward Woodward (EA) ... RLEW
Research Library, Imperial Tobacco Co. of Canada Ltd., Montreal, Quebec [*Library symbol National Library of Canada*] (NLC) ... QMITR
Research Library, LRS Trimark Ltd., Ottawa, Ontario [*Library symbol National Library of Canada*] (BIB) ... OOLRS
Research Library, Yarmouth County Historical Society, Yarmouth, Nova Scotia [*Library symbol National Library of Canada*] (NLC) ... NSYHM
Research Machines (NITA) ... RM
Research Machines Ltd. (NITA) ... RML
Research Management Plan ... RMP
Research Materials [*National Institute of Standards and Technology*] ... RM
Research Materials Information Center [*ORNL*] ... RMIC
Research Medical [*NASDAQ symbol*] (TTSB) ... RMED
Research Medical, Inc. [*Associated Press*] (SAG) ... ReshMed
Research Medical, Inc. [*NASDAQ symbol*] (SAG) ... RMED
Research Member of the Technical Staff ... RMTS
Research Memorandum ... RM
Research Methods and Techniques ... RMT
Research Missile [*NATO*] ... XM
Research Natural Area [*National Science Foundation*] ... RNA
Research Note ... RN
Research Objective (MCD) ... RO
Research Officer [*British*] ... RO
Research on Automatic Computation Electronics ... RACE
Research on Computer Applications for the Printing and Publishing Industries ... ROCAPPI
Research on the Early Abilities of Children with Handicaps Project (EDAC) ... REACH
Research Online International, Inc. [*Information service or system*] (IID) ... ROI
Research Open Systems in Europe [*Computer science*] (BARN) ... ROSE
Research Operations Detachment (DNAB) ... RSCHOPSDET
Research Opportunity Announcement (AAGC) ... ROA
Research Optical Sensor (MCD) ... ROS
Research or Exploratory Development (PDAA) ... RXD
Research Paper ... RP
Research Participation for High School Teachers [*National Science Foundation*] ... RPHST
Research Planning Conference [*LIMRA*] ... RPC
Research Planning Diagram (PDAA) ... RPD
Research Planning Guide (MCD) ... RPG
Research Policy and Review Division [*of OEP*] ... RPRD
Research Price Index ... RPI
Research Program Development and Evaluation Staff [*Department of Agriculture*] ... RPDES
Research, Program, Planning, and Evaluation ... RPPE
Research Project Report [*A publication*] (EAAP) ... RPR
Research Publications ... RP
Research Publications, Inc., New Haven, CT [*Library symbol Library of Congress*] (LCLS) ... ResP
Research Publications International [*Database producer*] (IID) ... RPI
Research Queueing (MHDB) ... RESQ
[*The*] **Research Ranch** [*An association*] (EA) ... TRR
Research Reactor [*Nuclear energy*] (IAA) ... RR
Research Reactor, State College of Washington (NRCH) ... RSCW
Research Referral Service [*International Federation for Documentation*] [*Information service or system*] (IID) ... RRS
Research Report ... RR
Research Resources Center [*University of Illinois at Chicago*] [*Research center*] (RCD) ... RRC
Research Results Data Base [*Department of Agriculture*] [*Information service or system*] (IID) ... RRDB
Research Review Group (NRCH) ... RRG
Research Safety Vehicle [*Department of Transportation*] ... RSV
[*The*] **Research School of Pacific and Asian Studies** [*Australian National University*] (ECON) ... RSPAS
Research Scientist (ADA) ... RS
Research Security Administrators ... RSA
Research Selected Vote Profile [*Election poll*] ... RSVP
Research Services Department [*United Way of Greater Indianapolis*] [*Indiana*] [*Information service or system*] (IID) ... RSD
Research Services Directory [*A publication*] ... RSD
Research Services Ltd. [*Database producer*] [*Wembley, Middlesex, England*] ... RSL
Research Ship of Opportunity ... RSO
Research Society for Natural Therapeutics [*British*] (DBA) ... RSNT
Research Society for Victorian Periodicals (EA) ... RSVP
Research Society of America (IAA) ... RESA
Research Society on Alcoholism (EA) ... RSA
Research Sonobuoy Configuration (NG) ... RESOC
Research Space Surveillance Network ... RSSN
Research Station, Agriculture Canada [*Station de Recherches, Agriculture Canada*] **Agassiz, British Columbia** [*Library symbol National Library of Canada*] (NLC) ... BAGAG
Research Station, Agriculture Canada [*Station de Recherches, Agriculture Canada*] **Brandon, Manitoba** [*Library symbol National Library of Canada*] (NLC) ... MBAG
Research Station, Agriculture Canada [*Station de Recherches, Agriculture Canada*] **Charlottetown, Prince Edward Island** [*Library symbol National Library of Canada*] (NLC) ... PCAG
Research Station, Agriculture Canada [*Station de Recherches, Agriculture Canada*] **Delhi, Ontario** [*Library symbol National Library of Canada*] (NLC) ... ODEAG
Research Station, Agriculture Canada [*Station de Recherches, Agriculture Canada*] **Fredericton, New Brunswick** [*Library symbol National Library of Canada*] (NLC) ... NBFAG
Research Station, Agriculture Canada [*Station de Recherches, Agriculture Canada*] **Harrow, Ontario** [*Library symbol National Library of Canada*] (NLC) ... OHARAG
Research Station, Agriculture Canada [*Station de Recherches, Agriculture Canada*] **Kamloops, British Columbia** [*Library symbol National Library of Canada*] (NLC) ... BKAG
Research Station, Agriculture Canada [*Station de Recherches, Agriculture Canada*] **Kentville, Nova Scotia** [*Library symbol National Library of Canada*] (NLC) ... NSKR
Research Station, Agriculture Canada [*Station de Recherches, Agriculture Canada*] **Lacombe, Alberta** [*Library symbol National Library of Canada*] (NLC) ... ALAAG
Research Station, Agriculture Canada [*Station de Recherches, Agriculture Canada*] **Lennoxville, Quebec** [*Library symbol National Library of Canada*] (NLC) ... QLAG
Research Station, Agriculture Canada [*Station de Recherches, Agriculture Canada*], Melfort, Saskatchewan [*Library symbol National Library of Canada*] (BIB) ... SMEAG
Research Station, Agriculture Canada [*Station de Recherches, Agriculture Canada*] **Morden, Manitoba** [*Library symbol National Library of Canada*] (NLC) ... MMOAG
Research Station, Agriculture Canada [*Station de Recherches, Agriculture Canada*] **Ottawa, Ontario** [*Library symbol National Library of Canada*] (NLC) ... OOAGO
Research Station, Agriculture Canada [*Station de Recherches, Agriculture Canada*] **Regina, Saskatchewan** [*Library symbol National Library of Canada*] (NLC) ... SRAGR
Research Station, Agriculture Canada [*Station de Recherches, Agriculture Canada*] **St. John's, Newfoundland** [*Library symbol National Library of Canada*] (NLC) ... NFSAG
Research Station, Agriculture Canada [*Station de Recherches, Agriculture Canada*] **Saint-Jean, Quebec** [*Library symbol National Library of Canada*] (NLC) ... QSTJAG
Research Station, Agriculture Canada [*Station de Recherches, Agriculture Canada*] **Saskatoon, Saskatchewan** [*Library symbol National Library of Canada*] (NLC) ... SSAGR
Research Station, Agriculture Canada [*Station de Recherches, Agriculture Canada*] **Sidney, British Columbia** [*Library symbol National Library of Canada*] (NLC) ... BSAG
Research Station, Agriculture Canada. Station de Recherches, Agriculture Canada,Beaverlodge, Alberta [*Library symbol National Library of Canada*] (NLC) ... ABEAG
Research Station, Agriculture Canada [*Station de Recherches, Agriculture Canada*] **Ste-Foy, Quebec** [*Library symbol National Library of Canada*] (NLC) ... QSFAG
Research Station, Agriculture Canada [*Station de Recherches, Agriculture Canada*] **Summerland, British Columbia** [*Library symbol National Library of Canada*] (NLC) ... BSUAG
Research Station, Agriculture Canada [*Station de Recherches, Agriculture Canada*] **Swift Current, Saskatchewan** [*Library symbol National Library of Canada*] (NLC) ... SSCAG
Research Station, Agriculture Canada [*Station de Recherches, Agriculture Canada*] **Vineland Station, Ontario** [*Library symbol National Library of Canada*] (NLC) ... OVAGR
Research Station, Agriculture Canada [*Station de Recherches, Agriculture Canada*] **Winnipeg, Manitoba** [*Library symbol National Library of Canada*] (NLC) ... MWAG
Research Studies Institute ... RSI
Research Study Group (NATG) ... RSG
Research Study Requests ... RSR
Research Study Team ... RST
Research Summary ... RS
Research Surveillance Network ... RSN
Research Surveys of Great Britain Ltd. ... RSGB
Research Systems (MCD) ... RS
Research Systems Facility ... RSF
Research Target and Test Vehicle ... RTTV
Research Task Force for the Future of Reform Judaism [*Defunct*] (EA) ... RTFFRJ
Research Technical Information Centre, ESSO Petroleum Canada, Sarnia, Ontario [*Library symbol National Library of Canada*] (NLC) ... OSI
Research Technical Memorandum ... RTM
Research, Test, Development, and Evaluation (SSD) ... RTD & E
Research Test Site (AAG) ... RTS

Research Test Vehicle ..... RTV
Research Thrust Division [*Washington, DC DoD*] (GRD) ..... RTD
Research to Prevent Blindness (EA) ..... RPB
Research Torpedo Configuration (NG) ..... RETORC
Research Training and Development Branch [*Bethesda, MD*] [*National Heart, Lung, and Blood Institute*] (GRD) ..... RTDB
Research Training and Evaluation (OICC) ..... RTE
Research Triangle Institute, Technical Library, Durham, NC [*Library symbol Library of Congress*] (LCLS) ..... NcDurRT
Research Triangle Institutes [*Duke University, University of North Carolina at Chapel Hill, and North Carolina State University at Raleigh*] [*Research center*] ..... RTI
Research Triangle Park [*North Carolina*] ..... RTP
Research Underwater-Unmanned Weapons Sensor (DNAB) ..... RUUWS
Research Unit in Health and Behavioral Change [*University of Edinburgh*] [*Scotland*] (IRC) ..... RUHBC
Research Vehicle ..... RV
Research Vessel [*Marine science*] (OSRA) ..... R/V
Research Vessel ..... RV
Research Vessel Operators Council [*Defunct*] [*Marine science*] (OSRA) ..... RVOC
Research Vessel Operators Council [*Defunct*] (USDC) ..... RVOC
Research Vessel Service [*British*] (IRUK) ..... RVS
Research-Engineering Interaction (IEEE) ..... REI
Research-Extension Analytical Laboratory [*Ohio State University*] [*Research center*] (RCD) ..... REAL
Research-Octane-Number [*Fuel technology*] ..... RON
Research-Octane-Number-Barrels [*Fuel technology*] ..... RONB
Reseau Africain d'Institutions Scientifiques et Technologiques [*African Network of Scientific and Technological Institutions*] (EAIO) ..... RAIST
Reseau Canadian de Recherce sur les Bacterioses (AC) ..... RCRB
Reseau Canadien des Centres de Toxicologie (AC) ..... RCCT
Reseau Canadien d'Information sur le Patrimoine (AC) ..... RCIP
Reseau Canadien sur les Maladies Genetiques (AC) ..... RCMG
Reseau d'Action et d'Information pour les Femmes [*Canada*] ..... RAIF
Reseau d'Approvisionnement et de Debouches d'Affaires [*Business Opportunities Sourcing System - BOSS*] [*Canada*] ..... RADAR
Reseau de Radio Rurale des Pays en Developpement [*Developing Countries Farm Radio Network*] (EAIO) ..... RRRPD
Reseau des Amis de la Terre [*Network of Friends of the Earth*] [*France Political party*] (PPE) ..... RAT
Reseau des Bibliotheques Utilisant SIBIL [*Library Network of SIBIL Users*] [*University of Lausanne Switzerland*] [*Information service or system*] (IID) ..... REBUS
Reseau des Universites et de la Recherche [*Network of Universities and Research*] [*French*] [*Computer science*] (TNIG) ..... REUNIR
Reseau d'Innovations Educatives pour le Developpement en Afrique [*Network of Educational Innovation for Development in Africa*] (EAIO) ..... RIEDA
Reseau Documentaire en Sciences Humaines de la Sante [*Network for Documentation in the Human Sciences of Health*] [*Institut de l'Information Scientifique et Technique*] [*Information service or system*] (IID) ..... RESHUS
Reseau Europeen Integre d'Image et de Services [*European Integrated Network of Image and Services*] (EAIO) ..... REIS
Reseau Gouvernemental de Transmission par Paquets [*Government Packet Network - GPN*] [*Canada*] ..... RGTP
[*The*] **Reseau Interordinateur Scientifique Quebecois** [*Canada*] [*Computer science*] (TNIG) ..... RISQ
Reseaud'Information et de Communication Hospitalier (OSI) ..... RICHE
Reseaux Associes pour la Recherche Europeene [*Associated Networks for European Research*] ..... RARE
Resende [*Brazil ICAO location identifier*] (ICLI) ..... SBRS
Resent, Demand, Appreciate [*In Sidney Simon, Leland Howe, and Howard Kirschenbaum's book "Values Clarification"*] ..... RDA
Resentment [*Psychology*] ..... R
Reserv Glavnogo Komandovaniia [*Reserve of the High Command*] [*Former USSR*] ..... RGK
Reservation ..... reserva
Reservation (ROG) ..... RESERVON
Reservation (ROG) ..... RESVON
Reservation ..... RSVTN
Reservation, Information, Tourist Accommodation [*Computerized system for booking hotel rooms*] [*British*] ..... RITA
Reservatis Reservandis [*With All Reserve*] [*Latin*] ..... RR
Reserve ..... R
Reserve (EY) ..... RES
Reserve ..... RESRV
Reserve (ECII) ..... RSV
Reserve (MSA) ..... RSV
Reserve Active Status List (DOMA) ..... RASL
Reserve Adjustment Magnitude ..... RAM
Reserve Advisory Squadron ..... RAS
Reserve Affairs (DOMA) ..... RA
Reserve Air Force Officers [*Later, RAFRO*] [*British*] ..... RAFO
Reserve Air Maintenance Training (DNAB) ..... RAMTRA
Reserve Airborne Electronics Training Unit (DNAB) ..... RAETU
Reserve Airlift (NVT) ..... RESALIFT
Reserve and Guard Logistic Operations-Streamline [*Army*] (AABC) ..... REGLOS
Reserve and Process (NASA) ..... R & P
Reserve and Reserve Officers' Training Corps [*Army*] ..... R & ROTC
Reserve Antisubmarine Warfare Carrier Air Group [*Navy*] (DNAB) ..... RESANTISUBCARIARGRU
Reserve Antisubmarine Warfare Carrier Air Group [*Navy*] (DNAB) ..... RESASWCARAIREGRU
Reserve Antisubmarine Warfare Systems Analysis Mobilization Unit (DNAB) ..... RASAU
Reserve Antisubmarine Warfare Training Center [*Navy*] (DNAB) ..... RESASWTRACEN
Reserve Asset Ratio [*Banking*] (ADA) ..... RAR
Reserve Associate Manning Program [*Military*] ..... RAMP
Reserve Auxiliary Transformer (IEEE) ..... RAT
Reserve Bank (ADA) ..... RB
Reserve Bank of Australia ..... RBA
Reserve Bank of Australia. Bulletin [*A publication*] ..... Bull Reserve Bank Aust
Reserve Bank of India (ECON) ..... RBI
Reserve Bank of New Zealand ..... RBNZ
Reserve Blocked (IAA) ..... RB
Reserve Cargo-Handling Battalion [*Navy*] (DOMA) ..... RCHB
Reserve Center [*Navy*] (DNAB) ..... RESCEN
Reserve Combat Replacement Squadron (DNAB) ..... RCRS
Reserve Command Management Information System (DNAB) ..... RESCOMMIS
Reserve Component Assistance Coordinator (MCD) ..... RCAC
Reserve Component Automation System [*DoD*] ..... RCAS
Reserve Component Career Counselor [*Military*] (AABC) ..... RCCC
Reserve Component Common Personnel Data System [*Marine Corps*] (GFGA) ..... RCCPDS
Reserve Component Coordination Council (MCD) ..... RCCC
Reserve Component Equipment Readiness Improvement Program [*Military*] (AABC) ..... RCERIP
Reserve Component Infantry Officer Advance Course [*Military*] (INF) ..... RC-OAC
Reserve Component Issues Conference [*Military*] (MCD) ..... RCIC
Reserve Component Leader Development Action Plan [*Army*] (INF) ..... RC-LDAP
Reserve Component National Security Course [*National Defense University*] (INF) ..... RCNSC
Reserve Component National Security Seminar (MCD) ..... RCNSS
Reserve Component Officer Education System [*Army*] (INF) ..... RC-OES
Reserve Component Unit [*Army*] (AABC) ..... RCU
Reserve Component Virtual Training Program [*Army*] (RDA) ..... RCVTP
Reserve Component Virtual Training Program [*Army*] (INF) ..... RCVTP
Reserve Components [*Military*] ..... RC
Reserve Components Contingency Force [*Military*] ..... RCCF
Reserve Components, Individual Ready Reserve [*Military*] ..... RCIRR
Reserve Components Management Information System [*Army*] ..... RCMIS
Reserve Components Noncommissioned Officer Education System [*Army*] ..... RCNCOES
Reserve Components Personnel and Administration Center [*Army*] (AABC) ..... RCPAC
Reserve Components Personnel Directorate [*Office of Personnel Operations*] [*Army*] ..... RCPD
Reserve Components Program of the Army (AABC) ..... RCPA
Reserve Components Status Reporting [*Army*] (AABC) ..... RESTAT
Reserve Components Survivor Benefits Plan [*Military*] ..... RCSBP
Reserve Components Training Center [*Military*] ..... RCTC
Reserve Components Training Development Action Plan [*Army*] (DOMA) ..... RCTDAP
Reserve Components Transition to Modernization ..... RCTRANSMOD
Reserve Components Troop Basis [*Army*] (AABC) ..... RCTB
Reserve Components Troop Program [*Army*] ..... RCTP
Reserve Corps ..... RC
Reserve Cruise [*Navy*] (NVT) ..... RESCRU
Reserve Currency ..... RC
Reserve Decoration [*Navy British*] ..... RD
Reserve Defense Fleet [*Navy*] ..... RDF
Reserve Destroyer Division (DNAB) ..... RESDESDIV
Reserve Destroyer Squadron (DNAB) ..... RESDESRON
Reserve District ..... RESDIST
Reserve Duty Training [*Military*] ..... RDT
Reserve Enlisted Association [*Defunct*] (EA) ..... REA
Reserve Enlisted Program [*Military*] ..... REP
Reserve Enlistment Program 1963 (MCD) ..... REP 63
Reserve Entry Training Plan [*Canada*] ..... RETP
Reserve Equalization Committee [*Military*] ..... REC
Reserve Facility (DNAB) ..... RESFAC
Reserve Feed Water [*Technical drawings*] ..... RFW
Reserve Female Enlistment Program [*Military*] (DNAB) ..... RFEP
Reserve Flag Officer Policy Council [*Navy*] ..... RFPC
Reserve Fleet [*Navy*] ..... RESV
Reserve Flexibility [*Military*] (MCD) ..... REFLEX
Reserve Flight [*British military*] (DMA) ..... RF
Reserve Force ..... RF
Reserve Force Squadron (DNAB) ..... RESFORON
Reserve Forces Act ..... RFA
Reserve Forces Act of 1955, Six Months Trainee ..... RFASIX
Reserve Forces Act of 1955, Three Months Trainee ..... RFATHREE
Reserve Forces Benefit Association [*Later, REA*] (EA) ..... RFBA
Reserve Forces Duty [*Military*] (MCD) ..... RFD
Reserve Forces Modernization (MCD) ..... RFM
Reserve Forces Policy Board [*DoD*] ..... RFPB
Reserve Grade [*Military*] ..... RG
Reserve - In Commission [*Vessel status*] ..... RES/IC
Reserve - In Service [*Vessel status*] ..... RES/IS
Reserve Indication of Mobilization [*Army*] (AABC) ..... RIMOB
Reserve Intelligence Mobilization Readiness and Support Projects (MCD) ..... RIMRASP
Reserve, LA [*FM radio station call letters*] ..... WADU
Reserve Liaison Unit (DNAB) ..... RLU
Reserve List (ADA) ..... RL
Reserve Manpower Management and Pay System [*Marine Corps*] ..... REMMPS
Reserve Material [*Account*] **Navy** ..... RMN
Reserve Mechanical Transport [*British military*] (DMA) ..... RMT
Reserve Merchant Ship Defense System [*Navy*] (MCD) ..... RMSDS

Reserve Military Aviator .... RMA
Reserve Military Construction (DNAB) .... RESMILCON
Reserve Minority Report [*Army*] .... RMR
Reserve Mobile Construction Battalion .... RMCB
Reserve Naval Construction Battalion Center (DNAB) .... RNCBC
Reserve Naval Construction Battalion Center Detachment (DNAB) .... RNCBCDET
Reserve Naval Construction Battalion Maintenance Unit (DNAB) .... RNCBMU
Reserve Naval Construction Force [*Navy*] (PDAA) .... RNCF
Reserve Naval Construction Regiment (DNAB) .... RNCR
Reserve Naval Mobile Construction Battalion (DNAB) .... RNMCB
Reserve Naval Mobile Construction Battalion Detachment (DNAB) .... RNMCBDET
Reserve Naval Security Group (DNAB) .... RNSG
Reserve Naval Security Group Course (DNAB) .... RNSGC
Reserve of Officers [*British*] .... R of O
Reserve of Officers [*British*] .... RO
Reserve of Officers [*British*] .... ROO
Reserve of the Air Force .... RESAF
Reserve Officer Candidate .... ROC
Reserve Officer Performance Recording Activity .... ROPRA
Reserve Officer Personnel Act of 1954 .... ROPA
Reserve Officer Recording Activity .... RORA
Reserve Officers Association (NADA) .... ROA
Reserve Officers Association of the United States (EA) .... ROA
Reserve Officers Naval Architecture Group .... RONAG
Reserve Officers of the Naval Service [*Later, ROA*] .... RONS
Reserve Officers Personnel Management Act [*Proposed*] .... ROPMA
Reserve Officers Promotion Board [*Air Force*] .... ROPB
Reserve Officers Sanitary Corps .... ROSC
Reserve Officers' Training Corps [*Separate units for Army, Navy, Air Force*] .... ROTC
Reserve Officers' Training Corps Manual (AABC) .... ROTCM
Reserve Officers' Training Corps Region (AABC) .... ROTCR
Reserve Oil Tank (MSA) .... ROT
Reserve on Board .... ROB
Reserve on Extended Active Duty [*Military*] .... READ
Reserve Order .... RO
Reserve - Out of Commission [*Vessel status*] .... RES/OC
Reserve - Out of Service [*Vessel status*] .... RES/OS
Reserve Personnel [*Air Force*] (AFM) .... RP
Reserve Personnel and Administrative Center [*Army*] (DOMA) .... RCPAC
Reserve Personnel Appropriation .... RPA
Reserve Personnel, Army .... RPA
Reserve Personnel Management Information System [*Military*] .... REPMIS
Reserve Personnel, Marine Corps (MCD) .... RPMC
Reserve Personnel Master File [*Military*] .... RPMF
Reserve Personnel, Navy [*An appropriation*] .... RPN
Reserve Personnel Navy (DOMA) .... RPV
Reserve Purchase .... RP
Reserve Readiness and Mobility Squadron .... RRMS
Reserve Recognition Accounting [*Securities and Exchange Commission*] .... RRA
Reserve Regiment [*British military*] (DMA) .... RR
Reserve Reinforcement Processing Center [*Army*] (AABC) .... RRPC
Reserve Retired List [*Military*] .... RRL
Reserve Section [*Military*] .... RS
Reserve Service Control [*Navy*] .... RSC
Reserve Shutdown Hours (IAA) .... RH
Reserve Shutdown Planned Derated Hours [*Electronics*] (IEEE) .... RPDH
Reserve Shutdown Unit Derated Hours [*Electronics*] (IEEE) .... RUNDH
Reserve Shutdown Unplanned Derated Hours [*Electronics*] (IEEE) .... RUDH
Reserve Special Commendation Ribbon .... RSCR
Reserve Special Operations Group [*Army*] .... RSOG
Reserve Station Service Transformer [*Nuclear energy*] (NRCH) .... RSST
Reserve Stock (SAA) .... RS
Reserve Stock Point .... RSP
Reserve Storage Activity, Germersheim, West Germany [*Military*] .... RSAG
Reserve Storage Activity, Kaiserslautern, West Germany [*Military*] .... RSAK
Reserve Storage Activity, Luxembourg [*Military*] .... RSAL
Reserve Systems Analysis Division [*Military*] (DNAB) .... RSAND
Reserve Training [*USCG*] (TAG) .... RESERVE
Reserve Training .... RT
Reserve Training Center .... RESTRACEN
Reserve Training Center [*Army*] (DOMA) .... RTC
Reserve Training Corps .... RTC
Reserve Training Facility .... RESTRAFAC
Reserve Training Unit (MCD) .... RTU
Reserve Unit [*Equal to one US dollar*] [*International finance*] [*Former USSR*] .... RU
Reserve Unit Manpower Authorization System (MCD) .... RUMAS
Reserve Unit Personnel Performance Report .... RUPPERT
Reserve Veterinary Hospital [*British military*] (DMA) .... RVH
Reserve, WI [*FM radio station call letters*] .... WOJB
Reserved (ROG) .... RESVD
Reserved Air Freight .... RAF
Reserved Cases [*Ireland*] [*A publication*] (DLA) .... Res Cas
Reserved Cases [*1860-64*] [*A publication*] (DLA) .... Reserv Cas
Reserved Commodity List [*World War II*] .... RCL
Reserved for Hardware Use [*Computer science*] (IAA) .... RHU
Reserved for Software Use (IAA) .... RSU
Reserveoffizier-Bewerber [*Reserve officer applicant*] [*German military - World War II*] .... ROB
Reserves Available to Support Private, Noninterbank Deposits [*Federal Reserve System*] .... RPD
Reserves Embarked [*Navy*] (NVT) .... REEM
Reserves Embarked [*Navy*] (NVT) .... REM
Reserves to Loans Ratio .... RLR
Reservist Clothing Maintenance Allowance [*Military*] .... RCMA
Reservists on Active Duty [*Navy*] .... RAD
Reservoir (AAG) .... RES
Reservoir (AAG) .... RESVR
Reservoir [*Board on Geographic Names*] .... RSV
Reservoir (AAG) .... RSVR
Reservoir Level Sensor (MCD) .... RLS
Reset (MDG) .... R
Reset (MDG) .... RE
Reset .... RES
Reset .... RS
Reset [*Telecommunications*] (TEL) .... RST
Reset After Punch [*Computer science*] (IAA) .... RAP
Reset and Start (IAA) .... RAS
Reset Control Circuit .... RCC
Reset Data Available [*Computer science*] (MHDI) .... RDAV
Reset Flux Level .... RFL
Reset Gate .... RG
Reset In Proportion [*A printing instruction*] (WDMC) .... RIP
Reset Indicators Form Storage [*Computer science*] (IAA) .... RIS
Reset Indicators from Accumulator [*Computer science*] (IAA) .... RIA
Reset Indicators of the Left Half (IAA) .... RIL
Reset Indicators of the Right Half (IAA) .... RIR
Reset Inhibit Drive .... RID
Reset Inhibit Drum .... RID
Reset Steering .... RS
Reset Trigger .... RT
Reset-Set [*Computer science*] .... RS
Reset-Set Trigger .... RST
Resetting Half-Cycle .... RHC
Resettlement Grants [*British World War II*] .... RG
Reshaping the International Order [*Title of Club of Rome report*] .... RIO
Reshtigo, WI [*FM radio station call letters*] (RBYB) .... WSFQ-FM
Resid Fluid Catalytic Cracking [*Petroleum refining*] .... RFCC
Reside [*or Resident*] .... R
Residence .... RES
Residence .... RSDNC
Residence in Science and Technology .... REST
Residence Time [*Chemistry*] .... RT
Residence Time Distribution [*Chemical engineering*] .... RTD
Residencial .... RES
Residency .... resid
Residency Operations Group .... ROG
Residency Program in Social Medicine (DMAA) .... RPSM
Residency Review Committee [*Medicine*] .... RRC
Residency Review Committee for Emergency Medicine (EA) .... RRCEM
Resident .... RES
Resident .... RES
Resident .... RSDNT
Resident Access Methods (MCD) .... RAM
Resident Aerospace Medicine [*Physician in specialty training*] [*Military*] .... RAM
Resident Agent (AFM) .... RA
Resident Air Force Officer [*Australia*] .... RAFO
Resident Alien .... RA
Resident Apollo Project Office [*NASA*] (KSC) .... RAPO
Resident Apollo Spacecraft Program Office [*NASA*] (KSC) .... RASPO
Resident ARGMA [*Army Rocket and Guided Missile Agency*] **Zeus Project Engineer** (AAG) .... RAZPE
Resident Army Nike-X Project Engineer (AABC) .... RANXPE
Resident Army SENSCOM [*Sentinel Systems Command*] **Project Engineer** (AABC) .... RASPE
Resident Assembler Program .... RAP
Resident Assessment Protocol [*Occupational therapy*] .... RAP
Resident Assistant [*College housing*] .... RA
Resident Assistant .... RA
Resident Associate Program [*Smithsonian Institution*] .... RAP
Resident Auditor .... RA
Resident Care Aide .... RCA
Resident Careworker .... RCW
Resident Classification Index .... RCI
Resident Cost Inspector .... RCI
Resident Data Area (NASA) .... RDA
Resident Functional Atlas (DMAA) .... RFA
Resident Industrial Manager .... RIM
Resident Inspection Test Instruction .... RITI
Resident Inspector .... RINS
Resident Inspector of Naval Aircraft .... RINA
Resident Inspector of Naval Material .... RINM
Resident Inspector of Naval Material (MUGU) .... RINSMAT
Resident Inspector of Ordnance (AAG) .... RIO
Resident Inspector Office [*Coast Guard*] .... RIO
Resident Inspector-in-Charge .... RIC
Resident Integrated Logistics Support Activity [*Military*] (AFIT) .... RILSA
Resident Integrated Logistics Support Detachment [*Military*] (MCD) .... RILSD
Resident Loader (MHDI) .... RESLOAD
Resident Magistrate .... RM
Resident Maintenance Engineer (NATG) .... RME
Resident Management Corp. [*Public housing*] .... RMC
Resident Manufacturing Plan (SAA) .... RMP
Resident Medical Officer [*British*] .... RMO
Resident Monitor .... RMON
Resident Naval Inspector of Ordnance .... RINSORD
Resident Naval Inspector of Ordnance .... RNIO
Resident Naval Inspector of Powder .... RINSPOW
Resident Naval Officer [*Followed by place name*] (NATG) .... RNO
Resident Navy Inspector .... RNI

Resident Obstetric Officer [*British*] ..... ROO
Resident Officer-in-Charge [*Navy*] ..... RO in C
Resident Officer-in-Charge [*Military*] ..... ROIC
Resident Officer-in-Charge of Construction [*Military*] ..... ROICC
Resident Officer-in-Charge of Material [*Navy*] (DNAB) ..... ROICM
Resident Operating System ..... ROS
Resident Operational Support Equipment ..... ROSE
Resident Physician (WDAA) ..... RES PHYS
Resident Process Manager [*Computer science*] (PCM) ..... RPM
Resident Programmer Analyst [*Computer science*] ..... RPA
Resident Programming Language [*Computer science*] ..... RPL
Resident Provisioning Team [*NASA*] ..... RPT
Resident Pulmonary Lymphocyte [*Immunology*] ..... RPL
Resident Reactor Inspector [*Nuclear energy*] (NRCH) ..... RRI
Resident Representative (MUGU) ..... RESREP
Resident Research Associate ..... RRA
Resident School (MUGU) ..... RS
Resident Sector Management [*Computer science*] (IAA) ..... RSM
Resident Shop Control (SAA) ..... RSC
Resident Space Shuttle Project Office [*NASA*] (NASA) ..... RSSPO
Resident Study Group [*Army*] (MCD) ..... RSG
Resident Supervisor Call (BUR) ..... RSVC
Resident Supervisor of Shipbuilding Conversion and Repair (DNAB) ..... RESUPSHIP
Resident Supervisor of Shipping [*Navy*] (DNAB) ..... RSOS
Resident Surgical Officer [*British*] ..... RSO
Resident System Monitor ..... RSM
Resident Terminal Access Method [*Computer science*] ..... RTAM
Resident Training and Counseling Programs (OICC) ..... RTCP
Resident Training Detachment [*Army*] (INF) ..... RTD
Resident Training Equipment (MCD) ..... RTE
Resident Transient Area [*Computer science*] (IAA) ..... RTA
Resident United States Naval Officer ..... RUSNO
Residential Appraisal Report [*Real estate*] (EMRF) ..... RAR
Residential Building Technology Innovation Program (DICI) ..... RBTIP
Residential Care Alternatives ..... RCA
Residential Care Association [*British*] ..... RCA
Residential Children's Home (AIE) ..... RCH
Residential Colleges Committee (AIE) ..... RCC
Residential Communications Network [*Telecommunications service*] ..... RCN
Residential Conservation Service [*Offered by major electric and gas utilities*] ..... RCS
Residential Distillate Oil Combustion [*Industrial medicine*] ..... RDOC
Residential Energy Consumption Survey [*Department of Energy*] (GFGA) ..... RECS
Residential Health Care Facility [*Medicine*] (DHSM) ..... RHCF
Residential Hotels [*Public-performance tariff class*] [*British*] ..... RH
Residential Lease [*Real estate*] (ADA) ..... RL
Residential Manpower Center [*Job Corps*] ..... RMC
Residential Member [*American Institute of Real Estate Appraisers of the National Association of Realtors*] [*Designation awarded by*] ..... RM
Residential Model Conservation Standard [*Pacific Northwest Electric Power and Conservation Planning Council*] [*Portland, OR*] (EGAO) ..... MCS
Residential Rehabilitation Assistance Program [*Canada*] ..... RRAP
Residential Sales Council (EA) ..... RSC
Residential Social Worker (AIE) ..... RSW
Residential Space Planners International (EA) ..... RSPI
Residential Subsurface Transformer (IAA) ..... RST
Residential Support Center (OICC) ..... RSC
Residential Training College [*for disabled people*] [*British*] ..... RTC
Residential Transportation Energy Consumption [*DOE*] (TAG) ..... RTEC
Residential Transportation Energy Consumption Survey [*Department of Energy*] (GFGA) ..... RTECS
Residential Treatment Center [*Department of Health and Human Services*] (GFGA) ..... RTC
Residential Utility Consumer Action Group ..... RUCAG
Residential Wood Combustion ..... RWC
Resident's Admission Notes [*Medical records*] (DAVI) ..... RAN
Resident-Shared Page Index [*Computer science*] (OA) ..... RSPI
Residual (KSC) ..... RES
Residual (AAG) ..... RESID
Residual Air ..... RA
Residual Analysis Program [*Space Flight Operations Facility, NASA*] ..... RAP
Residual Capabilities Assessment (MCD) ..... RECA
Residual Current Circuit Breaker [*Electronics*] (EECA) ..... RCCB
Residual Current Device [*Electrical circuits*] ..... RCD
Residual Equivalent Return Loss ..... RERL
Residual Error Rate ..... RER
Residual Evaluation Center (MCD) ..... REC
Residual Field (AAG) ..... RESFLD
Residual Flux Density ..... RFD
Residual Functional Capacity [*Social Security Administration*] (OICC) ..... RFC
Residual Functional Capacity Assessment [*Social Security Administration*] (GFGA) ..... RFCA
Residual Gas Analyzer ..... RGA
Residual Hazards List [*NASA*] (NASA) ..... RHL
Residual Heat Removal [*Nuclear energy*] (NRCH) ..... RHR
Residual Heat Removal Pump [*Nuclear energy*] (NRCH) ..... RHRP
Residual Heat Removal Service Water [*Nuclear energy*] (NRCH) ..... RHRSW
Residual Heat Removal System [*Nuclear energy*] (NRCH) ..... RHRS
Residual Income ..... RI
Residual Item Selection List ..... RISL
Residual Lung Capacity [*Medicine*] ..... RLC
Residual Lymphatic Output [*Medicine*] (DMAA) ..... RLO
Residual Mantle Bouguer Anomaly [*Geology*] ..... RMBA
Residual Master File [*Computer science*] ..... RMF
Residual Oil Remover [*Lens cleaner*] [*V-Vax Products*] ..... ROR
Residual Oil Saturation [*Petroleum technology*] ..... ROS
Residual Organic Carbon [*Organic chemistry*] (DAVI) ..... ROC
Residual Particulate Organic Carbon [*Environmental science*] ..... RPOC
Residual Pressure Valve [*Automotive engineering*] ..... RPV
Residual Renal Function [*Medicine*] (DMAA) ..... RRF
Residual Resistance Ratio [*Metal purity*] ..... RRR
Residual Sum of Squares [*Statistics*] ..... RSS
Residual Support Force [*After main force redeployment*] [*Military*] ..... RSF
Residual Total Elongation [*Nuclear energy*] (NRCH) ..... RTE
Residual Vapor Detector (NATG) ..... RVD
Residual Variance ..... RV
Residual Volatile Matter [*Chemistry*] ..... RVM
Residual Volume [*Physiology*] ..... RV
Residual Volume per Total Lung Compliance [*Pulmonary function test*] (CPH) ..... RV/TLC
Residual Volume/Total Lung Capacity Ratio [*Physiology*] (MAE) ..... RV/TLC
Residual Yield [*Agriculture*] (OA) ..... RY
Residual-Area-Analysis Method [*Spectrometry*] ..... RAAM
Residuary (ROG) ..... RESY
Residue ..... RES
Residue Arithmetic Associative Processor [*Computer science*] (OA) ..... RAAP
Residue Manipulator (IAA) ..... RM
Residue Register (IAA) ..... RR
Residue Solvent Refining [*Lummus Crest, Inc. process*] ..... RSR
Residuum Desulfurization [*Petroleum technology*] ..... RDS
Residuum Fluid Cracking [*Petroleum refining*] ..... RFC
Residuum Hydrocracking Unit [*Petroleum refining*] ..... RHU
Residuum Oil Supercritical Extraction [*Petroleum refining*] ..... ROSE
Resignation (AFM) ..... RESIG
Resigned ..... RES
Resigned ..... RESD
Resigned ..... RESGD
Resigned ..... RESGND
Resigned ..... RSD
Resilient [*Technical drawings*] ..... RES
Resilient ..... RESIL
Resilient Floor Covering Institute (EA) ..... RFCI
Resilient Tile Institute [*Later, RFCI*] (EA) ..... RTI
Resin (VRA) ..... res
Resin Coated (MCD) ..... RC
Resin Hemoperfusion Column ..... RHC
Resin Infusion Under Flexible Tooling ..... RIFT
Resin Regeneration Subsystem [*Nuclear energy*] (NRCH) ..... RRS
Resin Skived Tape ..... RST
Resin Sluice Header (NRCH) ..... RSH
Resin T_3 Uptake [*Endocrinology*] ..... RT_3U
Resin T_4 Uptake [*Endocrinology*] ..... RT_4U
Resin Transfer Molding [*Plastics technology*] ..... RTM
Resin Uptake [*Endocrinology*] ..... RU
Resin Uptake Ratio [*Endocrinology*] ..... RUR
Resina [*Resin*] [*Pharmacy*] (ROG) ..... RESIN
Resin-Bonded Glass-Fiber (PDAA) ..... RBGF
Resin-Coated (VRA) ..... resco
Resin-Encapsulated Mica Capacitor ..... REMC
Resiniferatoxin [*Organic chemistry*] ..... RTX
Resin-in-Pulp [*Process for uranium ore treatment*] (IIA) ..... RIO
Resin-in-Pulp [*Ore processing*] ..... RIP
Resin-Modified Glass-Ionomer Cement [*Dental material*] ..... RMGIC
Resin-Treated Liner ..... RTL
Resist Inside the Army [*Peace-movement slang*] ..... RITA
Resist Pressure [*Industrial engineering*] ..... RP
Resistance [*Symbol*] [*IUPAC*] ..... R
Resistance [*or Resistor*] (AAG) ..... RES
Resistance (IDOE) ..... res
Resistance ..... RESIS
Resistance (AABC) ..... RST
Resistance Armee Tunisienne [*Tunisian Armed Resistance*] (PD) ..... RAT
Resistance Brazing ..... RB
Resistance Bulb Thermometer ..... RBT
Resistance Calibration (MCD) ..... R/CAL
Resistance, Capacitance & Inductive (NITA) ..... RCL
Resistance Coupled ..... RC
Resistance Decade Box ..... RDB
Resistance Determinant [*Medicine*] (MAE) ..... RD
Resistance Diode Logic (IAA) ..... RDL
Resistance Factor (DOG) ..... R factor
Resistance Factor ..... RF
Resistance Index ..... RI
Resistance Inducing Factor (ADA) ..... RIF
Resistance Inductance (IEEE) ..... RI
Resistance, Inductance, and Capacitance (NASA) ..... RIC
Resistance Inductance Capacitance (MSA) ..... RLC
Resistance International (EA) ..... RI
Resistance Management Plans [*To prevent insect adaptation to toxins*] ..... RMP
Resistance of the Airways on the Alveolar Side of the Point in the Airways whereIntraluminal Pressure Equals intrapleural Pressure [*Medicine*] (DAVI) ..... Rus
Resistance of the Airways on the Oral Side of the Point in the Airways Where Intraluminal Pressure Equals Intrapleural Pressure [*Medicine*] (DAVI) ..... Rds
Resistance Plate (AAG) ..... RP
Resistance Pressure Detector ..... RPD
Resistance Projection Welding [*Manufacturing term*] ..... RPW
Resistance Seam Welding ..... RSEW

Resistance Seam Welding - High Frequency .... RSEW-HF
Resistance Seam Welding - Induction .... RSEW-I
Resistance Soldering .... RS
Resistance Soldering Equipment .... RSE
Resistance Spot Welding .... RSW
Resistance Task Force [Defunct] (EA) .... RTF
Resistance Temperature Bridge (SAA) .... RTB
Resistance Temperature Bulb [NASA] .... RTB
Resistance Temperature Detector [Nuclear energy] .... RTD
Resistance Temperature Device [Nuclear energy] (NRCH) ..... RTD
Resistance Test (NASA) .... R-T
Resistance Thermometer [Electronics] (IAA) .... RT
Resistance Thermometer Device (IAA) .... RTD
Resistance to Bending Moment [Automotive engineering] .... RBM
Resistance to Venous Return [Medicine] (MAE) .... RVR
Resistance Transfer [Laboratory science] (DAVI) .... RT
Resistance Transfer Factor [of microorganisms to drugs] ...... RTF
Resistance Unit (MAE) .... RU
Resistance Welder Manufacturers Association (EA) .... RWMA
Resistance Welding (IEEE) .... RW
Resistance Welding Machine .... RWM
Resistance Zone .... RZ
Resistance-Capacitance .... RC
Resistance-Capacitance Coupled .... RCCPLD
Resistance-Capacitance Coupling (DNAB) .... RCC
Resistance-Capacitance Grounded Unity Gain Amplifier (IAA) ... RCGUGA
Resistance-Controlled Oscillator .... RCO
Resistance-Coupled Transistor Logic .... RCTL
Resistance-Inductance (IDOE) .... RL
Resistance-Nodulation-Division [Biochemistry] .... RND
Resistant .... RESIST
Resistant Plant Material [Soil science] .... RPM
Resistant Sporangia [Botany] .... RS
Resistence per Meter .... ohm/m
Resistencia [Argentina] [Airport symbol] (OAG) .... RES
Resistencia [Argentina ICAO location identifier] (ICLI) .... SARE
Resistencia [Argentina ICAO location identifier] (ICLI) .... SARR
Resistencia [Argentina ICAO location identifier] (ICLI) .... SARU
Resistencia (Ciudad) [Argentina ICAO location identifier] (ICLI) ... SARD
Resistencia da Guine-Bissau Movimento Bafata [Political party] (EY) ..... RGB-MB
Resistencia Nacional Mocambicana [Mozambique] .... RENAMO
Resistencia Nacional Mocambicana [Mozambican National Resistance]
   (PD) .... RNM
Resistencia Nicaraguense de Organizacion Civica [Political party] (EY) ..... RNOC
Resistive Divider Standard .... RDS
Resistive Exercise of Lower Extremities [Medicine] (DMAA) ... RELE
Resistive Exercises [orhtopedics] (DAVI) .... resist ex
Resistive Insulated-Gate Field Effect Transistor .... RIGFET
Resistive Null Voltage .... RNV
Resistive Read-Only Storage .... RROS
Resistive-Intermittent Positive Pressure [Medicine] (DMAA) ... RIPP
Resistively-Shunted Junction [Physics] .... RSJ
Resistor .... R
Resistor .... RES
Resistor .... res
Resistor (IDOE) .... RESIS
Resistor (IAA) .... RESIST
Resistor (WDAA) .... RS
Resistor (IAA) .... RSTR
Resistor .... RA
Resistor Assembly .... RA
Resistor Capacitor-Coupled Transistor Logic (IAA) .... RCC
Resistor Color Code (DEN) .... RD
Resistor Diode (IAA) .... RDL
Resistor Diode Logic .... RDL
Resistor Diode Transistor Logic (IEEE) .... RDTL
Resistor Diode Transistor Technique (IAA) .... RDT
Resistor Insulator Semiconductor (IAA) .... RIS
Resistor Logic (IEEE) .... RL
Resistor Qualification Program .... RQP
Resistor Qualification Test .... RQT
Resistor Qualification Test Program .... RQTP
Resistor Terminating Network .... RTN
Resistor Test Program .... RTP
Resistor Tolerance .... RT
Resistor Transistor .... RT
Resistor Tunnel Diode Transistor Logic (IAA) .... RTDTL
Resistor-Capacitor .... R-C
Resistor-Capacitor .... RESCAP
Resistor-Capacitor (IAA) .... RC
Resistor-Capacitor Circuit (IAA) .... RCT
Resistor-Capacitor Transistor (IAA) .... RCTL
Resistor-Capacitor Transistor Logic .... RCU
Resistor-Capacitor Unit (IAA) .... RCU
Resistor-in-the-Army [Peace movement slang during Vietnam War] (VNW) .... RITA
Resistor-Reactor Rectifier .... RRR
Resistor-Resistor Diode Transistor Logic (IAA) .... RRDTRL
Resistor-Resistor Transistor-Transistor Logic [Computer science] (IAA) .... RRTTL
Resistor-Transistor Logic [Computer science] (BUR) .... RTL
ResMed, Inc. [NASDAQ symbol] (SAG) .... RESM
ResMed, Inc. [Associated Press] (SAG) .... ResMed
RESNA [Rehabilitation Engineering Society of North America]: Association for
   the Advancement of Rehabilitation Technology [Association retains acronym
   from former name] (EA) .... RESNA
Resolu [Resolved, Decided] [French] (ILCA) .... Res
Resoluta [Music] (ROG) .... RESO

Resolute [Northwest Territories] [Seismograph station code, US Geological
   Survey] (SEIS) .... RES
Resolute [Canada] [Airport symbol] (OAG) .... YRB
Resolute Bay [Northwest Territories] [Geomagnetic observatory code] ..... RES
Resolute, NT [ICAO location identifier] (ICLI) .... CYRB
Resolute Resources [Vancouver Stock Exchange symbol] .... R
Resolution .... RES
Resolution .... res
Resolution (IDOE) .... RESOLN
Resolution (MSA) .... RE
Resolution Enhancement [Computer graphics] .... RET
Resolution Enhancement Technology [Printer feature] [Hewlett-Packard Co.]
   [Computer science] (PCM) .... RET
Resolution Funding Corp. [Established by the Financial Institutions Reform,
   Recovery, and Enforcement Act of 1989] .... REFCO
Resolution Funding Corp. [Established by the Financial Institutions Reform,
   Recovery, and Enforcement Act of 1989] .... RefCorp
Resolution Funding Corporation (USGC) .... REFCORP
Resolution Funding Corp. [Established by the Financial Institutions Reform,
   Recovery, and Enforcement Act of 1989] .... RFC
Resolution Multiplier (IAA) .... RM
Resolution of Initial Operational Techniques .... RIOT
Resolution Trust Corp. [Federal government instrumentality, established in
   1989] .... RTC
Re-Solv, the Society for the Prevention of Solvent and Volatile Substance
   Abuse [British] (EAIO) .... RS
Resolve (KSC) .... RESLV
Resolve (NASA) .... RSLV
Resolve, Inc. (EA) .... RI
Resolve through Sharing (EA) .... RTS
Resolved [Legal term] (DLA) .... R
Resolved [Legal term] (DLA) .... Res
Resolved (ROG) .... RESD
Resolver (IAA) .... RES
Resolver (MSA) .... RSLVR
Resolver (AAG) .... RSVR
Resolver Alignment Test Set .... RATS
Resolver Control .... RC
Resolver Control Transformer .... RCT
Resolver Differential (IAA) .... RD
Resolver Differential Generator .... RDG
Resolver Differential Transmitter (IAA) .... RDS
Resolver/Quantizer (IEEE) .... R/Q
Resolver Tracking Bridge .... RTB
Resolver Transformer [Computer science] (IAA) .... RT
Resolver-Transmitter .... RX
Resolving Gel [Biochemistry] .... RG
Resolving Power [of a lens] .... RP
Resonance Energy Transfer [Physical chemistry] .... RET
Resonance Enhanced Multiple Photon Ionisation [Physics] ..... REMPI
Resonance Escape Probability [Nuclear energy] (NRCH) .... REP
Resonance Integral [Nuclear energy] (NRCH) .... RI
Resonance Ionization Emission Spectroscopy .... RIES
Resonance Ionization Mass Spectrometry .... RIMS
Resonance Ionization Spectroscopy .... RIS
Resonance Light Scattering [Physics] .... RLS
Resonance Raman .... RR
Resonance Raman Scattering [Spectroscopy] .... RRS
Resonance Raman Spectroscopy .... RRS
Resonance Test Reactor .... RTR
Resonance-Enhanced X-Ray [Physics] .... REX
Resonant .... RESN
Resonant Backward Wave Oscillator (IAA) .... RBWO
Resonant Enhanced Multiphoton Ionization [Spectroscopy] .... REMPI
Resonant Fiber Optic Gyroscope .... RFOG
Resonant Frequency Tracking System .... REFTS
Resonant Frequency Vibration .... RFV
Resonant Gate Transistor [Computer science] .... RGT
Resonant Infrasonic Gauging System .... RIGS
Resonant Internal Reflection .... RIR
Resonant Multiphoton Ionization [Physics] .... REMPI
Resonant Nuclear Battery .... RNB
Resonant Nuclear Reaction [Physics] .... RNR
Resonant Nuclear Reaction Analysis [Physics] .... RNRA
Resonant Pulse Jet .... RESOJET
Resonant Reed Decoder .... RRD
Resonant Reed Filter .... RRF
Resonant Ring Filter [Computer science] (IAA) .... RRF
Resonant Transfer (IAA) .... RT
Resonant Tunneling Bipolar Transistor [Electronics] .... RTBT
Resonant Tunneling Transistor [Electronics] .... RTT
Resonantcavity Light-Emitting Diode [Electronics] .... RCLED
Resonant-Tunnelling Diode [Solid state physics] .... RTD
Resonate (KSC) .... RSN
Resonating Valence Bond [Physical chemistry] .... RVB
Resonating-Generalized Valence Bond [Physical chemistry] ... R-GVB
Resonator [Automotive engineering] .... RES
Resonator [Electronics] (IAA) .... RS
Resonator-Controlled Microwave Source (PDAA) .... RCMS
Resorcinol Diglycidyl Ether [Organic chemistry] .... RDGE
Resorcinol-Formaldehyde [Organic chemistry] .... RF
Resorcinol-Formaldehyde-Latex .... RFL
Resorcinol-Sulfur [Organic chemistry] (MAE) .... RS
Resorcylic Acid Lactone [Veterinary pharmacology] .... RAL
Resort .... RESRT

Resort .... RESRT
Resort .... Rsrt
Resort Airline, Inc. [*ICAO designator*] (FAAC) .... RST
Resort and Commercial Recreation Association (EA) .... RCRA
Resort Condominiums International (EA) .... RCI
Resort Income Investors, Inc. [*AMEX symbol*] (CTT) .... RII
Resort Income Investors, Inc. [*Associated Press*] (SAG) ...... RsrtIn
Resort Timesharing Council (EA) .... RTC
Resorts Leisure Exchange [*Commercial firm British*] .... RLE
Resorufin [*Organic chemistry*] .... RSR
Resound Corp. [*Associated Press*] (SAG) .... Resound
Resound Corp. [*NASDAQ symbol*] (SAG) .... RSND
Resource .... RESC
Resource .... RESRC
Resource Access Control Facility [*IBM Corp.*] .... RACF
Resource Access Projects [*Administration for Children, Youth and Families*]
   (EDAC) .... RAP
Resource Accounting and Cost Allocation (MHDI) .... RACA
Resource Accounting Project Tracking System (DNAB) .... RAPTS
Resource Allocation (MCD) .... RA
Resource Allocation and Control Technique [*Management*] .... REACT
Resource Allocation and Management Program (EDAC) .... RAMP
Resource Allocation and Mine Costing Model [*Department of Energy*]
   (GFGA) .... RAMC
Resource Allocation and Stress in Plants [*Research initiative*] [*bbscrc-
   Biotechnology and Biological Sciences Research Council*] [*British*] .... RASP
Resource Allocation and Validation Program .... RAVPRO
Resource Allocation Display [*Navy*] .... RAD
Resource Allocation for Transportation (DNAB) .... RAFT
Resource Allocation Formula .... RAF
Resource Allocation Process (AAGC) .... RAP
Resource Allocation Processor (CMD) .... RAP
Resource Allocation Recommendations [*Military*] .... RAR
Resource Allocation Working Party [*British*] .... RAWP
Resource America [*Commercial firm Associated Press*] (SAG) ...... RescAm
Resource America [*NASDAQ symbol*] (SAG) .... REXI
Resource America'A' [*NASDAQ symbol*] (TTSB) .... REXI
Resource Analysis and Planning System [*DoD*] (DOMA) ...... RAPS
Resource Analysis System (HGAA) .... RAS
Resource Analysts, Inc. .... RAI
Resource and Capabilities Model (KSC) .... RECAP
Resource and Land Investigation [*Program*] [*Department of the Interior*]
   (GRD) .... RALI
Resource and Mission Sponsor Plan [*Navy*] .... RMSP
Resource and Unit Monitoring (DOMA) .... RUM
Resource Application (ERG) .... RA
Resource Appraisal Group [*US Geological Survey*] .... RAG
Resource Appraisal Group Library, United States Geological Survey,
   Denver, CO [*OCLC symbol*] (OCLC) .... GIR
Resource Assessment and Conservation Engineering [*Environmental
   protection*] .... RACE
Resource Assistant (GNE) .... RA
Resource Availability Determination (MCD) .... RAD
Resource Bancshares Mortgage Group [*NASDAQ symbol*] (SAG) .... REMI
Resource Bancshares Mortgage Group [*Associated Press*] (SAG) .... RscBnc
Resource Bancshares Mtg Gp [*NASDAQ symbol*] (TTSB) .... REMI
Resource Bank [*NASDAQ symbol*] (TTSB) .... RBKV
Resource Based Learning (ADA) .... RBL
Resource Capital International Ltd. [*Toronto Stock Exchange symbol*] .... RC
Resource Category Code [*Military*] (CAAL) .... RCC
Resource Center, City of Edmonton Personnel Department, Alberta [*Library
   symbol National Library of Canada*] (NLC) .... AEPR
Resource Center for Consumers of Legal Services [*Later, NRCCLS*]
   (EA) .... RCCLS
Resource Center for Efficient Agricultural Production [*Macdonald College*]
   [*Research center*] (RCD) .... REAP
Resource Center for Nonviolence (EA) .... RCN
Resource Center for Nonviolence (EA) .... RCNV
Resource Center, Information Services, Indian and Northern Affairs
   Canada, British Columbia Region [*Centre de Ressources, Services
   d'Information, Affaires I ndiennes et du Nord Canadien, Bureau Regional de
   la CB*] Vancouver, British Columbia [*Library symbol National Library of
   Canada*] (NLC) .... BVAINA
Resource Centre, Algonquin College of Applied Arts and Technology
   [*Centre de Documentation, College Algonquin des Arts Appliques et de la
   Technologie*], Hawkesbury, Ontario [*Library symbol National Library of
   Canada*] (BIB) .... OHKAC
Resource Centre, City of Calgary Electric System, Alberta [*Library symbol
   National Library of Canada*] (NLC) .... ACES
Resource Centre, Department of Public Health, City of Toronto, Ontario
   [*Library symbol National Library of Canada*] (BIB) .... OTPHR
Resource Centre, Ecology Action Centre, Dalhousie University, Halifax,
   Nova Scotia [*Library symbol National Library of Canada*] (NLC) .... NSHDEA
Resource Centre, Ontario Women's Directorate [*Library symbol National
   Library of Canada*] (BIB) .... OTOW
Resource Centre, Ottawa Police Force, Ontario [*Library symbol National
   Library of Canada*] (BIB) .... OOPF
Resource Centre, Pacific Rim Institute for Tourism, Vancouver, British
   Columbia [*Library symbol National Library of Canada*] (BIB) .... BVAPR
Resource Centre, RCMP [*Royal Canadian Mounted Police*] Academy, Regina,
   Saskatchewan [*Library symbol National Library of Canada*] (NLC) .... SRRC
Resource Centre, St. Lawrence Campus, Champlain Regional College,
   Ste.-Foy, Quebec [*Library symbol National Library of Canada*] (NLC) ..... QSTFCR
Resource Centre, Saskatchewan Department of Social Services, Regina,
   Saskatchewan [*Library symbol National Library of Canada*] (NLC) .... SRSS

Resource Centre, School of Lanark County, Algonquin College of Applied
   Arts & Technology, Perth, Ontario [*Library symbol National Library of
   Canada*] (NLC) .... OPAC
Resource Centre, VIA Rail Canada, Inc. [*Centre de Documentation, VIA Rai l
   Canada, Inc.*] Montreal, Quebec [*Library symbol National Library of
   Canada*] (NLC) .... QMVR
Resource Code/Cost Category Input (SAA) .... RC/CCI
Resource Conservation and Development [*Department of Agriculture*] ..... RC & D
Resource Conservation and Recovery Act [*Pronounced "rickra"*] [*1976*] ...... RCRA
Resource Conservation and Recovery Information System (ERG) ...... RCRIS
Resource Constrained Procurement Objectives for Munitions Model
   [*Army*] .... RECPOM
Resource Consulting Teacher .... RCT
Resource Control Block [*Computer science*] (IBMDP) .... RCB
Resource Control Center [*Military*] (AFIT) .... RCC
Resource Cost Model (EDAC) .... RCM
Resource Data File (MCD) .... RDF
Resource Decision Network (PDAA) .... RDN
Resource Definition Table [*Computer science*] (IBMDP) ..... RDT
Resource Development .... RD
Resource Development Group Ltd. [*British*] .... RDG
Resource Development Services (EA) .... RDS
Resource Dispersion Hypothesis [*Animal ecology*] .... RDH
Resource Ecology and Fisheries Management [*Marine science*] (OSRA) ...... REFM
Resource Ecology and Fisheries Management (USDC) .... REFM
Resource Editor [*Computer science*] (DOM) .... ResEdit
Resource Engineering & Planning Co. .... REAP
Resource Evaluation Report (MCD) .... RER
Resource Executive (IAA) .... RESEX
Resource Holding Potential .... RHP
Resource Holding Power [*Fighting ability - animal defense*] .... RHP
Resource Identification Code [*Navy*] .... RIC
Resource Identification Table [*Computer science*] .... RSID
Resource Information Center System [*Search system*] .... RIC
Resource Information Systems, Inc. (IID) .... RISI
Resource Interchange File Format [*Computer science*] (PCM) .... RIFF
Resource Interchange File Format [*Computer science*] (CDE) .... RIFF
Resource Interface Module [*Datapoint*] .... RIM
Resource Library, Alberta Hospital Association, Edmonton, Alberta [*Library
   symbol National Library of Canada*] (NLC) .... AEAHA
Resource Library, Board of Education for the City of Etobicoke, Ontario
   [*Library symbol National Library of Canada*] (NLC) .... OTEBE
Resource Management Consultants [*Salem, NH*] [*Telecommunications*]
   (TSSD) .... RMC
Resource Management Corp. .... RMC
Resource Management Executive (MCD) .... RMX
Resource Management Expense Reporting System (MCD) ..... RMER
Resource Management Group [*Military*] .... RMG
Resource Management Information System [*Environmental Protection
   Agency*] .... RMIS
Resource Management Plan (GNE) .... RMP
Resource Management Review [*Military*] .... RMR
Resource Management Squadron [*Military*] .... RMS
Resource Management Study Group [*Military*] .... RMSG
Resource Management Support (NITA) .... RMS
Resource Management System (IAA) .... RMS
Resource Management System (IAA) .... RSM
Resource Management Team (MCD) .... RMT
Resource Management Wing [*Military*] .... RMW
Resource Manager .... RM
Resource Measurement Facility [*Computer science*] .... RMF
Resource Module (SSD) .... RM
Resource Mortgage Capital [*Formerly, RAC Mortgage Investment*] [*NYSE
   symbol*] (SPSG) .... RMR
Resource Mortgage Capital, Inc. [*Associated Press*] (SAG) .... RescM
Resource Mortgage Capital, Inc. [*NASDAQ symbol*] (SAG) .... RMRPO
Resource Mortgage Capital, Inc. [*Associated Press*] (SAG) .... RscM
Resource Mortgage Capital, Inc. [*Associated Press*] (SAG) .... RscMtg
Resource Mortgage Capital, Inc. [*Associated Press*] (SAG) .... RscMtge
Resource Mothers Development Project .... RMDP
Resource Mtg Cap 9.75% Cv 'A' Pfd [*NASDAQ symbol*] (TTSB) ...... RMRPP
Resource Mtg Cap cm Cv'B'Pfd [*NASDAQ symbol*] (TTSB) .... RMRPO
Resource Objectives, Inc. [*Ridgewood, NJ*] (TSSD) .... ROI
Resource Organizations and Meetings for Educators [*National Center for
   Research in Vocational Education*] [*Information service or system Defunct*]
   (CRD) .... ROME
Resource Planning and Evaluation [*Nuclear energy*] (NRCH) .... RPE
Resource Planning Associates, Cambridge, MA [*OCLC symbol*] (OCLC) ...... RPA
Resource Policy Center [*Dartmouth College*] [*Research center*] (RCD) ...... RPC
Resource Policy Institute (EA) .... RPI
Resource Processor [*Telecommunications*] (TSSD) .... RP
Resource Recycling Unit .... RRU
Resource Referral Program (WYGK) .... RRP
Resource Rent Royalty .... RRR
Resource Report .... RR
Resource Request Generator .... RRG
Resource Requirements Request [*Military*] (MCD) .... RRR
Resource Reservation Protocol [*Computer science*] .... RSVP
Resource Reservation Protocol [*Computer science*] .... RSVP
ReSource ReserVation Protocol [*Computer science*] .... RSVP
Resource Reservation Protocol [*Videoconferencing*] .... RSVP
Resource Self-Help/Affordability Planning Effort [*Program*] [*Federal
   government*] (RDA) .... RESHAPE
Resource Service Group Ltd. [*Toronto Stock Exchange symbol*] .... RSG
Resource Services Support Agreement (GNE) .... RSSA

Resource Sharing Alliance [*Library consortium*] (IT) ... RSA
Resource Sharing Executive (MHDI) ... RSEXEC
Resource Sharing Extention [*Computer science*] (CDE) ... RSX
Resource Sharing Protocol (IAA) ... RSP
Resource Sharing Time Sharing (NITA) ... RSTS
Resource Specialist Program ... RSP
Resource Status Monitor [*Systems Center, Inc.*] ... RSM
Resource Support List [*NASA*] (MCD) ... RSL
Resource Survey Satellite ... RSS
Resource System Time Sharing/Extended [*Computer science*] (BTTJ) ... RSTS/E
Resource Systems Management Division [*Environmental Protection Agency*] (GFGA) ... RSMD
Resource Teaching Program (OICC) ... RTP
Resource Tie Line [*An association*] ... RTL
Resource Unit Management ... RUM
Resource Utilization Factor ... RUF
Resource Utilization Group (DHSM) ... RUG
Resource Utilization Monitor ... RUM
Resource Utilization Time (NASA) ... RUT
Resource Vector Table [*Computer science*] (IBMDP) ... RVT
Resource-Adjacent Nation [*Ocean fishery management*] ... RAN
Resource-Based Industry (ODBW) ... RBI
Resource-Based Relative Value [*Health insurance*] ... RBRV
Resource-Based Relative Value Scale [*Medicare*] ... RBRVS
Resources [*Army*] ... Rcs
Resources ... RES
Resources ... Res
Resources (DD) ... RESR
Resources (AABC) ... RESRC
Resources ... RSCS
Resources Allocation and Multiproject Scheduling ... RAMPS
Resources Allocation Change Request ... RACR
Resources Analysis and Management ... RAM
Resources and Institutional Management Division [*NASA*] ... RIMD
Resources and Program Management [*NASA*] ... R & PM
Resources and Referral Services (OICC) ... RRS
Resources and Technical Services Division [*Later, ALCTS*] [*American Library Association*] (EA) ... RTSD
Resources Breakdown Structure [*Computer science*] (PCM) ... RBS
Resources, Community and Economic Development Division (AAGC) ... RCEDD
Resources Conservation (MCD) ... RECON
Resources Council (EA) ... RC
Resources, Entities Accounting Subsystem (MCD) ... REAS
Resources Evaluation and Management System [*Army*] ... REAMS
Resources Exchange Association Foundation [*Also known as REA Foundation*] (EA) ... REAF
Resources for Communication [*Information service or system*] (IID) ... RFC
Resources for Community Change [*Defunct*] (EA) ... RCC
Resources for Learning Development Unit (AIE) ... RLDU
Resources for the Future ... RFF
Resources Forecasting System ... RFS
Resources in Computer Education [*Northwest Regional Educational Laboratory Microcomputer Software and Information for Teachers*] [*No longer available online*] [*Information service or system*] ... RICE
Resources in Education [*Formerly, Research in Education*] [*National Institute of Education Database*] ... RIE
[*Series*] **Resources in Measurement & Control** (ACII) ... RMC
Resources in Vocational Education [*Database*] [*National Center for Research in Vocational Education*] [*Information service or system*] (CRD) ... RIVE
Resources Information Bank on Multicultural Education (AIE) ... RIBMESC
Resources Management and Administration Office [*Environmental Protection Agency*] (GFGA) ... RMAO
Resources Management Office [*NASA*] (KSC) ... RMO
Resources Management Online System (HGAA) ... REMOS
Resources Management Staff [*Environmental Protection Agency*] (GFGA) ... RMS
Resources Management System [*Army*] ... RMS
Resources on Educational Equity for the Disabled ... REED
Resources Planning and Mobilization Division [*of OEP*] ... RPMD
Resources Planning and Scheduling Method ... RPSM
Resources Protection Board ... RPB
Resources Section [*Resources and Technical Services Division*] [*American Library Association*] ... RS
Resources Status Report ... RSR
Resource-Sharing Executive (NITA) ... RSX
Resource-Sharing Time-Sharing System ... RSTS
Resourcing Enabling, Network for Evangelical Women ... RENEW
Respect voor Arbeid en Democratie [*Belgium Political party*] (EY) ... RAD
Respect voor Arbeid en Democratie/Union Democratique pour le Respect du Travail [*Respect for Labor and Democracy/Democratic Union for the Respect of Labor*] [*Belgium Political party*] (PPE) ... RAD-UDRT
Respectable Frere [*Worshipful Brother*] [*Freemasonry*] [*French*] (ROG) ... RF
Respectable Loge [*Worshipful Lodge*] [*Freemasonry*] [*French*] (ROG) ... RL
Respectfully [*Letter closing*] ... R
Respectfully (ROG) ... RESFLY
Respectfully (ROG) ... RESPY
Respectfully (ROG) ... RSPV
Respective (AABC) ... RESP
Respectively ... RESP
Respectively ... RESPLY
Respirable Dust Monitor (PDAA) ... RDM
Respirable Particulate [*Environmental science*] (GFGA) ... RP
Respirable Suspended Particulates ... RSP
Respiration ... R
Respiration (KSC) ... RESP
Respiration Ceased [*Medicine*] ... RC
Respirations [*on anesthesia chart*] (DAVI) ... O
Respirations [*Medicine*] (DAVI) ... respir
Respirations [*On anesthesia chart*] (DAVI) ... X
Respirations Have Ceased [*Medicine*] ... RHC
Respirator ... RESP
Respirator (MSA) ... RSPTR
Respirator Fit Test [*Environmental science*] (FFDE) ... RFT
Respiratory (CPH) ... Resp
Respiratory Aid Apparatus ... RAA
Respiratory Allergy [*Immunology*] ... RA
Respiratory and Enteric Orphan [*Virus*] (MAE) ... REO
Respiratory Arrest [*Medicine*] ... RA
Respiratory Battery, Acute [*Medicine*] (DAVI) ... RESP-A
Respiratory Bronchiole [*Medicine*] (MAE) ... RB
Respiratory Care [*Medicine*] ... RC
Respiratory Care Unit [*Medicine*] ... RCU
Respiratory Center [*Medicine*] ... RC
Respiratory Control Index [*Biochemistry*] ... RCI
Respiratory Control Ratio [*Medicine*] ... RCR
Respiratory Disease ... RD
Respiratory Distress [*Medicine*] (DAVI) ... RD
Respiratory Distress Syndrome [*Formerly, HMD*] [*Medicine*] ... RDS
Respiratory Energy Expenditure [*Physiology*] ... REE
Respiratory Exchange Rate ... RER
Respiratory Exchange Ratio [*Medicine*] (MAE) ... Re
Respiratory Exchange Ratio [*Medicine*] (DAVI) ... RER
Respiratory Failure [*Medicine*] ... RF
Respiratory Frequency [*Breaths per unit of time*] [*Medicine*] (DAVI) ... f
Respiratory Health Association (EA) ... RHA
Respiratory Illness [*Medicine*] ... RI
Respiratory Intensive Care System [*Medicine*] ... RICS
Respiratory Intensive Care Unit [*Medicine*] ... RICU
Respiratory Inversion Point [*Physiology*] ... RIP
Respiratory Minute Volume [*Physiology*] ... RMV
Respiratory Minute Volume [*Medicine*] (DAVI) ... V_E
Respiratory Movement ... RM
Respiratory Muscle Strength [*Physiology*] ... RMS
Respiratory Nursing Society (EA) ... RNS
Respiratory Protective Device [*Medicine*] ... RPD
Respiratory Quotient [*Also, RQ*] [*Physiology*] ... Q
Respiratory Quotient [*Also, Q*] [*Physiology*] ... RQ
Respiratory Rate [*Medicine*] ... RR
Respiratory Rate:Pulse Rate [*Index*] [*Medicine*] ... RP
Respiratory Resistance [*Medicine*] (DAVI) ... R_L
Respiratory Resistance Unit [*Medicine*] (DMAA) ... RRU
Respiratory Sinus Arrhythmia [*Medicine*] ... RSA
Respiratory/Surgical Intensive Therapy Unit [*of a hospital*] ... R/SITU
Respiratory Symptoms Complex [*Medicine*] ... RSC
Respiratory Syncytial [*Virus*] ... RS
Respiratory Syncytial Virus ... RSV
Respiratory Syncytial Virus [*Medicine*] ... RSV
Respiratory System [*Medicine*] ... RS
Respiratory Therapist (HCT) ... REST
Respiratory Therapy [*Medicine*] ... RT
Respiratory Therapy Technician (HCT) ... RESTT
Respiratory Tract Fluid [*Medicine*] ... RTF
Respiratory Tract Infection [*Medicine*] ... RTI
Respiratory Unit [*Medicine*] ... RU
Respiratory Volume [*Medicine*] (MAE) ... RV
Respiratory-Ordered Phase Encoding [*Medicine*] (DMAA) ... ROPE
Respiratory-Surgical Intensive Care Unit [*of a hospital*] (AAMN) ... R-SICU
Respironics, Inc. [*NASDAQ symbol*] (NQ) ... RESP
Respironics, Inc. [*Associated Press*] (SAG) ... Respirn
Respond [*or Response*] ... R
Respond (MSA) ... RSPD
Respondent ... RESP
Respondent ... RESPT
Responder [*Strain of mice*] ... R
Responder Beacon ... RSP
Respondere [*To Answer*] [*Pharmacy*] (ROG) ... RESPOND
Responding Officer [*Police term*] ... RO
Responding Superior in Command (MCD) ... RSIC
Response (AAG) ... RESP
Response (MSA) ... RSPS
Response Action Contractor [*Metallurgy*] ... RAC
Response Action Coordinator [*Environmental Protection Agency*] (ERG) ... RAC
Response Action Plan (GNE) ... RAP
Response Amplitude Operator (PDAA) ... RAO
Response Amplitude Probability Data ... RAPD
Response Analysis for Call Evaluation (IAA) ... RACE
Response Analysis Program [*Computer science*] (IBMDP) ... RAP
Response Analysis Tester [*NASA*] ... RATER
Response Byte [*Computer science*] ... RSP
Response, Conditioned [*Psychology*] (DAVI) ... Rc
Response Coordination Team [*Nuclear energy*] (NRCH) ... RCT
Response Data Word (MCD) ... RDW
Response Document Capability List Positive (IAA) ... RDCLP
Response Document Discard Positive [*Computer science*] (IAA) ... RDDP
Response Document End Positive [*Computer science*] (IAA) ... RDEP
Response Document General Reject (IAA) ... RDGR
Response Document Page Boundary Negative [*Computer science*] (IAA) ... RDPBN
Response Document Page Boundary Positive [*Computer science*] (IAA) ... RDPBP
Response Document Resynchronization Positive [*Computer science*] (IAA) ... RDRP
Response Errors [*Statistics*] ... R-A

Response Factor ... RF
Response Feedback System [*NASA*] ... RFS
Response Header (IAA) ... RH
Response/Lockout (MCD) ... R/LO
Response Memoranda [*Jimmy Carter administration*] ... RM
Response of Plants to Interacting Stress Program [*Electric Power Research Institute*] ... ROPIS
Response Oncology [*NASDAQ symbol*] (TTSB) ... ROIX
Response Oncology, Inc. [*Associated Press*] (SAG) ... RespOnc
Response Oncology, Inc. [*NASDAQ symbol*] (SAG) ... ROIXD
Response Profile Analysis [*National Demographics & Lifestyles, Inc.*] ... RPA
Response Rate (DAVI) ... RR
Response Regulator [*Biochemistry*] ... RR
Response Segmentation and Validation Program [*Donnelley Marketing InformationServices*] [*Information service or system*] (IID) ... RSVP
Response Session Abort Positive (IAA) ... RSAP
Response Session Change Control Positive (IAA) ... RSCCP
Response Session End Positive (IAA) ... RSEP
Response Surface Methodology ... RSM
Response System with Variable Prescriptions (EDAC) ... RSVP
Response Test Unit ... RTU
Response/Throughput Bias [*Computer science*] (BUR) ... RTB
Response Time [*Computer science*] ... RT
Response Time Module ... RTM
Response Time Reporting ... RTR
Response to Detail [*Rorschach*] [*Psychology*] ... D
Response to Human Being Movement [*Rorschach*] [*Psychology*] ... m
Response to Small Detail [*Rorschach*] [*Psychology*] ... d
Response to Stimulus [*Ratio*] [*Neurology*] (DAVI) ... RS
Response to Very Small Detail [*Rorschach*] [*Also written dd*] [*Psychology*] ... Dd
Response Type Road Roughness Meter [*FHWA*] (TAG) ... RTRRM
Response USA [*NASDAQ symbol*] (TTSB) ... RUOK
Response USA, Inc. [*Associated Press*] (SAG) ... Resp
Response USA, Inc. [*Associated Press*] (SAG) ... Respons
Response USA, Inc. [*NASDAQ symbol*] (SAG) ... RUOK
Response USA Wrrt'A' [*NASDAQ symbol*] (TTSB) ... RUOKW
Response USA Wrrt'B' [*NASDAQ symbol*] (TTSB) ... RUOKZ
Response Vacuum Reducer [*Mechanical engineering*] ... RVR
Response Word (NASA) ... RW
Response-per-Thousand [*Marketing*] ... RPM
Response-Produced Stimulation ... RPS
Response-Stimulus ... RS
Responsibility Analysis Chart (DNAB) ... RAC
Responsibility and Action ... R & A
Responsibility Assignment List [*NASA*] (NASA) ... RAL
Responsibility Assignment Matrix [*NASA*] (NASA) ... RAM
Responsibility Center [*Air Force*] (AFM) ... RC
Responsibility Center/Cost Center [*Military*] (AFIT) ... RC/CC
Responsibility for Student Achievement Scale (EDAC) ... RSA
Responsible ... RESP
Responsible (AFM) ... RESP
Responsible Educated Adolescents Can Help (EA) ... REACH
Responsible Engineer (NASA) ... RE
Responsible Engineering Activity ... REA
Responsible Engineering Office [*Military*] (AFIT) ... REO
Responsible Hospitality Institute (EA) ... RHI
Responsible Industry for a Sound Environment (EA) ... RISE
Responsible Local Agencies (OICC) ... RLA
Responsible National Oceanographic Data Center [*Marine science*] (MSC) ... RNODC
Responsible Office (AAGC) ... RO
Responsible Party (GNE) ... RP
Responsible Property Officer [*Army*] (AABC) ... RESPO
Responsible Property Officer [*Military*] (AFIT) ... RPO
Responsible Receiver ... RR
Responsible Reporting Office [*Telecommunications*] (TEL) ... RRO
Responsible System (NASA) ... RSYS
Responsible System Designer (NRCH) ... RSD
Responsible Task Leader (SSD) ... RTL
Responsible Test Engineer [*NASA*] (NASA) ... RTE
Responsible Test Organization [*NASA*] (MCD) ... RTO
Responsible Test Organization ... RTO
Responsible Training Center [*Air Training Command*] (MCD) ... RTC
Responsive Automated Materiel Management System [*Army*] (AABC) ... RAMMS
Responsive Environment Programmed Laboratory (IEEE) ... REPLAB
Responsive Multicultural Basic Skills Approach (EDAC) ... RMBS
Responsive Production Inventory ... RPI
Responsive Quantum Efficiency ... RQE
Responsorium [*Responsory*] ... R
Responsus [*To Answer*] [*Latin*] ... RS
Respublica [*Commonwealth*] [*Latin*] ... R
Respublica [*of Plato*] [*Classical studies*] (OCD) ... Resp
Ressources Phytogenetiques du Canada [*Plant Gene Resources of Canada - PGRC*] ... RPC
Rest [*in cell cycles*] [*Cytology*] (DAVI) ... R
Rest [*Commonly used*] (OPSA) ... REST
Rest ... RST
Rest ... RST
Rest and Convalescence (ADA) ... R & C
Rest and Exercise (DAVI) ... R & EW
Rest and Recreation ... R & R
Rest and Recuperation [*Military*] ... R & R
Rest and Rehabilitation [*Marine Corps*] ... R & R
Rest Camp ... RC
Rest Cure ... RC
Rest [*or Resting*] **Energy** [*Medicine*] ... RE
Rest, Ice, Compression, and Elevation, - Drugs, Incision, Exercise Therapy, and Surgery [*Treatment for knee injuries*] ... RICE-DIETS
Rest, Ice, Compression, Elevation [*Medicine*] ... RICE
Rest in Peace (TAG) ... RIP
Rest in Proportion [*Printing*] (WDMC) ... RIP
Rest of Canada [*English-speaking portion of Canada*] (ECON) ... ROC
Rest of Route Unchanged [*Aviation*] (FAAC) ... RORU
Rest of the United States [*Government's official term for its system of determining federal salaries*] ... RUS
Rest of World [*Newly industrialized countries of Asia*] ... ROW
Rest of You (IIA) ... ROY
Rest Overnight [*or Rest-of-Night*] [*Pronounced "ron" Chance for a candidate to catch some sleep during a traveling political campaign*] ... RON
Rest Pain [*Medicine*] (MAE) ... RP
Restabilization Reset Generator (SAA) ... RRG
Restart [*Computer science*] ... RESRT
Restart (NASA) ... RSTRT
Restart Capability (AAG) ... RSC
Restart Delay Relay (IAA) ... RDR
Restartable Cryogenic Propellant ... RCP
Restartable Cryogenic Vehicle ... RCV
Restartable Solid Variable Pulse [*Motor*] (MCD) ... RSVP
Restarting Computer and Symbol Generator (IAA) ... RCSG
Restauraciones Aeronauticas SA de CV [*Mexico ICAO designator*] (FAAC) ... RES
Restaurant (DSUE) ... RES
Restaurant (ROG) ... REST
Restaurant ... RESTO
Restaurant (WGA) ... RESTR
Restaurant (VRA) ... rstrau
Restaurant ... RSTRNT
Restaurant and Caterers' Association of New South Wales [*Australia*] ... RCANSW
Restaurant and Caterers' Association of Queensland [*Australia*] ... RCAQ
Restaurant and Caterers' Association of Victoria [*Australia*] ... RCAV
[*The*] **Restaurant/Hotel International Design Exposition** (ITD) ... RHIDEC
Restaurant Liquor [*License*] ... RL
Restaurant Wine [*License*] ... RW
Restaurants, Cafes, and Hotel Lounges [*Public-performance tariff class*] [*British*] ... H
Rested-State Contraction [*Obstetrics*] (MAE) ... RSC
Restiform Body [*Neuroanatomy*] ... RB
Restigouche Regional Museum, Dalhousie, NB, Canada [*Library symbol*] [*Library of Congress*] (LCLS) ... CaNBDRRM
Restigouche Regional Museum, Dalhousie, New Brunswick [*Library symbol National Library of Canada*] (NLC) ... NBDRRM
Resting Blood Pressure [*Cardiology*] (DAVI) ... RBP
Resting Energy Expenditure ... REE
Resting Expiratory Level [*Medicine*] (DMAA) ... REL
Resting Heart Rate [*Cardiology*] ... RHR
Resting Membrane Potential [*Neuroelectrochemistry*] ... RMP
Resting Membrane Potential [*Neurobiology*] ... RMP
Resting Metabolic Rate [*Physiology*] ... RMR
Resting Pressure [*Physiology*] (MAE) ... RP
Resting Pulse [*Physiology*] ... RP
Resting (Radio-)Nuclide Ejection Fraction [*Cardiology*] (DAVI) ... RNEF
Resting Radionuclide Ejection Fraction [*Medicine*] (DAVI) ... RREF
Resting Tension [*Biology*] ... RT
Resting Venous Pressure [*Medicine*] (DMAA) ... RVP
Restitution [*Legal shorthand*] (LWAP) ... REST
Restitution Incentive Program Operationalized as a Strategy Toward an Effective Learning Environment [*HEW*] ... RIPOSTE
Restitution of Conjugal Rights [*Legal*] [*British*] (ROG) ... RCR
Restless Legs Syndrome [*Medicine*] ... RLS
Reston and District Regional Library, Reston, Manitoba [*Library symbol National Library of Canada*] (NLC) ... MRP
Reston and District Regional Library, Reston, MB, Canada [*Library symbol Library of Congress*] (LCLS) ... CaMReP
Restor Industries [*NASDAQ symbol*] (TTSB) ... REST
Restor Industries, Inc. [*NASDAQ symbol*] (SAG) ... REST
Restor Industries, Inc. [*Associated Press*] (SAG) ... Restor
Restoration ... RESTOR
Restoration Control Point [*Telecommunications*] (TEL) ... RCP
Restoration of Aircraft to Combat Effectivity [*Army*] ... RACE
Restoration of Spontaneous Circulation ... ROSC
Restoration Priority (CET) ... RP
Restoration Priority [*Telecommunications*] (TEL) ... RSP
Restoration Survey ... RESTS
Restorative [*Pharmacology*] (DAVI) ... rest
Restore ... RES
Restore [*Computer science*] (ECII) ... RSR
Restore (MSA) ... RST
Restore a More Benevolent Order Coalition [*Later, NCAN*] (EA) ... RAMBO
Restore Our Alienated Rights [*Boston antibusing group*] ... ROAR
Restored (VRA) ... rest
Restored ... REST
Restored Oil Shales ... ROS
Restorer ... RESTR
Restrained Cursor (NITA) ... RC
Restraint and Life Support Assembly (MCD) ... RALSA
Restraint and Water Immersion Stress [*Medicine*] (DMAA) ... RWIS
Restraint of Trade (MHDW) ... RT
Restraint Release System (KSC) ... RRS
Restraint System Evaluation Program [*Department of Transportation*] ... RSEP
Restraints and Seclusion [*Psychiatry*] (DAVI) ... R & S

Restrict (AAG) .... REST
Restrict (AABC) .... RESTR
Restrict (MSA) .... RSTR
Restricted [Persons under eighteen (sixteen in some localities) not admitted
    unless accompanied by parent or adult guardian] [Movie rating] .... R
Restricted [Immunology] .... R
Restricted [Military document classification] .... R
Restricted [Security classification] [Military] .... RESTD
Restricted .... RSTD
Restricted .... RSTRD
Restricted Access Memory [Computer science] (MCD) .... RAM
Restricted Access Processor (SSD) .... RAP
Restricted Account [Banking] .... RA
Restricted Activity Day [Environmental medicine] .... RAD
Restricted Activity Days [Veterans Administration] (GFGA) ..... RAD
Restricted Area [Followed by identification] .... R
Restricted Articles [IATA] (DS) .... REART
Restricted Articles Regulation (DS) .... RAR
Restricted Articles Tariff .... RAT
Restricted Articles Terminal System [IATA] (DS) .... RATS
Restricted Availability (NG) .... RAV
Restricted Availability/Technical Availability (NVT) .... RA/TA
Restricted Bandwidth Techniques (NG) .... REBAT
Restricted Bulletin .... RB
Restricted Categorical Grammar .... RCG
Restricted Coulomb Energy .... RCE
Restricted Data [Security classification] .... RD
Restricted Data [Atomic Energy Act of 1954] .... RESDAT
Restricted Data Cover Folder (AAG) .... RDCF
Restricted Edge Emitting Diode [Electronics] (EECA) .... REED
Restricted Energy Loss .... REL
Restricted English Question-Answering (HGAA) .... REQUEST
Restricted Environmental Stimulation Technique .... REST
Restricted Express Lists/Physiological Activity Section [National Science
    Foundation] .... RELPAS
Restricted Hartree-Fock [Quantum mechanics] .... RHF
Restricted Landing Area [Aviation] .... RLA
Restricted Least Squares [Statistics] .... RLS
Restricted Line Officer .... RL
Restricted Line Officer (DNAB) .... RLO
Restricted Maximum Likelihood [Statistics] .... REML
Restricted Maximum Likelihood [Statistics] .... RML
Restricted Overhaul (MCD) .... ROV
Restricted RADAR Electronic Scan Technique (IAA) .... REST
Restricted Shipyard Availability Requiring Drydocking [Navy] (NVT) .... RAD
Restricted Stepsize [Statistics] .... RSS
Restricted Use Digital Instrument (OA) .... RUDI
Restricted Use Pesticide [Environmental Protection Agency] (GFGA) .... RUP
Restricted Users Group [Computer science] (ODBW) .... RUG
Restricted-Security Information (DNAB) .... R-SI
Restriction Endonuclease [An enzyme] .... RE
Restriction Endonuclease Fingerprinting [Analytical biochemistry] .... REF
Restriction Fragment Length Polymorphism [Genetics] .... RFLP
Restriction Fragment-Length Polymorphism (BARN) .... RIFLIP
Restriction of Extension (IAA) .... RE
Restriction of Privileges [British military] (DMA) .... RP
Restriction Orifice [Nuclear energy] (NRCH) .... RO
Restriction-Fragment Melting Polymorphism [Genetics] .... RFMP
Restrictive Cardiomyopathy [Cardiology] .... RC
Restrictive Covenant (MHDB) .... RC
Restrictive Fire Area [Military] (AABC) .... RFA
Restrictive Fire Line [Military] (AABC) .... RFL
Restrictive Fire Zone [Military] .... RFZ
Restrictive Practices Cases [1958-72] [England] [A publication] (DLA) ..... LRRPC
Restrictive Practices Court [Legal] [British] .... RPC
Restrictive Trade Practice .... RTP
Restrictive Trade Practices Commission .... RTPC
Restructured Air Assault Division (MCD) .... RAAD
Restructured Division Operations Manual (MCD) .... RDOM
Restructured Expanded Data (MCD) .... RED
Restructured Extended Executor [IBM command language] (PCM) ... REXX
Restructured General Support [Military] .... RGS
Restructured General Support Unit (MCD) .... RGSU
Restructured Infantry Battalion System (AABC) .... RIBS
Restructured Pork Chop [Food industry] .... RPC
Restructuring and Efficiency .... R & E
Restructuring the Undergraduate Learning Environment [National Science
    Foundation] .... RULE
Resublimed .... RESUB
Resubmission Turnaround Documents (MEDA) .... RTD
Result (IAA) .... RSLT
Resultant Physiological Acceleration .... RPA
Results .... RSLTS
Results Analysis, Computation, and Evaluation (MHDI) .... RACE
Results Analysis Plan (MCD) .... RAP
Results Not Observed (DNAB) .... RNO
Results of Marine Biological Investigations [Marine science] (MSC) .... ROMBI
Results to Follow (DAVI) .... RFOL
Resume (NASA) .... RSM
Resume Entry Device .... RED
Resume Normal Speed [Aviation] (FAAC) .... RNLS
Resume Sheet .... RS
Resume-Accelerate [Automotive engineering] .... RA
Resumed Operation [Aviation] (FAAC) .... RSOPN
Resupply (AABC) .... RESUP

Resupply Provisions [NASA] (KSC) .... RP
Resupply Provisions Module [NASA] (KSC) .... RPM
Resupply Vehicle [Military] .... RSV
Resurfacing, Restoration, and Rehabilitation [Also, RRR] [Later, 4R Federal
    Highway Administration] 3R
Resurfacing, Restoration, and Rehabilitation [US Federal Highway
    Administration] .... RRR
Resurfacing, Restoration, Rehabilitation, and Reconstruction [Formerly, 3R,
    RRR] [Federal Highway Administration] 4R
Resurgence Properties [Associated Press] (SAG) .... ResurP
Resurgence Properties [NASDAQ symbol] (SAG) .... RPIA
Resurrection (BJA) .... Res
Resurrection .... RESURR
Resuscitation [Medicine] (DAVI) .... RESC
Resuscitation .... RESUS
Resuscitation Research Center [University of Pittsburgh] [Research center]
    (RCD) .... RRC
Resuscitation Team .... RT
Resuscitation Therapy .... RT
Resynchronization Timer [Telecommunications] (OSI) .... RT
Resynchronizing (GAVI) .... RESYNCING
Resynchronizing State (IAA) .... RS
Retail .... RETL
Retail .... RTL
Retail Advertising Conference (EA) .... RAC
Retail Alarm for Display and Intruder (PDAA) .... RADI
Retail Associates Group, Inc. [Homesewing industry trade group] .... RAG
Retail Association for the Furnishing Trade [British] (BI) .... RAFT
Retail Bakers of America (EA) .... RBA
Retail, Book, Stationery, and Allied Trades Employees' Association [A
    union] [British] .... RBA
Retail Branch Stores Forum (EA) .... RBSF
Retail Clerks International Association [Later, UFCWIU] (EA) ... RCIA
Retail Computer Facilities .... RCF
Retail Confectioners International (EA) .... RCI
Retail Confectionery and Tobacconists' Association [British] (DI) .... RCTA
Retail Consortium [British] .... RC
Retail Credit Bureau (NADA) .... RCB
Retail Credit Co., Atlanta, GA [Library symbol Library of Congress]
    (LCLS) .... GARC
Retail Credit Group [British] .... RCG
Retail Credit Institute of America [Later, NFCC] .... RCIA
Retail Dental Delivery System [Dentistry] .... RDDS
Retail Development Management Services [British] .... RDMS
Retail Display Agreement (WDMC) .... RDA
Retail Distribution Station [Military] (AFM) .... RDS
Retail Distributors Association, Inc. [British] (BI) .... RDA
Retail Floorcovering Institute [Later, AFA] (EA) .... RFI
Retail Food Price-Reporting System .... RFPRS
Retail Fruit Trade Federation [British] (DBA) .... RFTF
Retail Grocery, Dairy, and Allied Trades Association [British] (BI) ...... RGDATA
Retail Industry Trade Action Coalition [Washington, DC] (EA) .. RITAC
Retail Information System (BUR) .... RIS
Retail Inventory Management/Stockage Policy [DoD] .... RIMSTOP
Retail Issue Outlets (NG) .... RIO
Retail Jewelers of America [Later, JA] (EA) .... RJA
Retail Liquor Dealer .... RLD
Retail Loss Prevention Association [New York, NY] (EA) .... RLPA
Retail Manager .... RM
Retail Merchants' Association of Canada .... RMA
Retail Office Furniture Forum (EA) .... ROFF
Retail Paint and Wallpaper Distributors of America [Later, NDPA] .... RPWDA
Retail Postal Outlet (DD) .... RPO
Retail Price Maintenance (DCTA) .... RPM
Retail Prices Index [British] .... RPI
Retail Prices Index Advisory Committee [Department of Employment]
    [British] .... RPIAC
Retail Sales Battery [Employment test] .... RSB
Retail, Service, and Repair .... RS & R
Retail Shops and Stores [Public-performance tariff class] [British] ...... RS
Retail Stockage Policy .... RSP
Retail Stockage Policy, Bulk Supplies (MCD) .... RSPB
Retail Stockage Policy, Evaluation (MCD) .... RSPE
Retail Stores Forum (EA) .... RSF
Retail Tobacco Dealers of America (EA) .... RTDA
Retail Traders' Association of Western Australia .... RTAWA
Retail Trading Standards Association (WDAA) .... RTSA
Retail Trading Zone (WDMC) .... RTZ
Retail, Wholesale, and Department Store Union (EA) .... RWDSU
Retail World [A publication] .... RW
Retailer .... RET
Retailers' Council of Australia .... RCA
Retailer's Uniform Agency .... RUA
Retain (AAG) .... RET
Retain (KSC) .... RTN
Retain on Board until Ultimate Assignment Received .... RETULSIGN
Retained .... RETD
Retained Accessory Power [Automotive engineering] .... RAP
Retained Earnings (TDOB) .... RE
Retained Foreign Body [Medicine] .... RFB
Retained Gastric Antrum Syndrome [Medicine] (DAVI) .... RGAS
Retained in Service [Military] (DNAB) .... RETSER
Retained Lund Fluid (DAVI) .... RLF
Retained Personnel [Military] .... RP
Retainer (ADA) .... RETNR

Retainer (ROG) ... RETR
Retainer (MSA) ... RTNR
Retaining ... RETG
Retaining (MSA) ... RTNG
Retaining Ring Kit ... RRK
Retalhuleu [*Guatemala*] [*ICAO location identifier*] (ICLI) ... MGRT
Retape ... RETP
Retard (AAG) ... RET
Retard (MSA) ... RTD
Retard [*Aviation*] (FAAC) ... RTRD
Retardation ... RTRDTN
Retardation Coil (MSA) ... RTDC
Retardation Factor ... RF
Retarded ... RETRD
Retarded (MAE) ... rtd
Retarded Bomb Fuze ... RBF
Retarded Citizens' Welfare Association of Tasmania [*Australia*] ... RCWAT
Retarded Infants Services [*Later, CFS*] (EA) ... RIS
Retarded Learner [*Education*] ... RL
Retarded Surface Wave ... RSW
Retarder [*Slow*] [*On clock-regulators*] [*French*] ... R
Retarding Field Analyzer [*Surface analysis*] ... RFA
Retarding Ion Mass Spectrometer [*Instrumentation*] ... RIMS
Retarding Potential Analyzer [*NASA*] ... RPA
Retarding Potential Analyzer Experiment [*NASA*] ... RPAE
Retarding Potential Difference (IEEE) ... RPD
Retendering Receipt Day (NRCH) ... RRD
Retention [*Insurance*] (MCD) ... RETEN
Retention [*Insurance*] ... RETNN
Retention and Disposal ... RD
Retention and Transfer Enhancement [*Military*] ... RATE
Retention Catheter [*Medicine*] ... RC
Retention Catheter [*Medicine*] (CPH) ... Ret Cath
Retention Control Point [*Military*] (INF) ... RCP
Retention Control Training [*Medicine*] ... RCT
Retention Curve [*U.S. EPA*] ... RETC
Retention File [*IRS*] ... RF
Retention Index ... RI
Retention Level of Supply [*Navy*] (NG) ... RLOS
Retention of Tears, Ectrodactyly, Ectodermal Dysplasia, and Strange Hair, Skin and Teeth Syndrome [*Medicine*] (DMAA) ... REEDS
Retention Pending Use [*Air Force*] ... RPU
Retention Register [*Computer science*] ... RETR
Retention Spermatemia Syndrome [*Medicine*] ... RSS
Retention Time [*Computer science*] ... RT
Retentive Substrate Shield [*i.e., saucer*] [*Slang*] ... RSS
Retest OK (MCD) ... RTOK
Rethel-Perthes [*France ICAO location identifier*] (ICLI) ... LFAP
Reticle [*Optics*] ... RTCL
Reticle Generator ... RG
Reticular [*Nucleus of thalamus*] [*Neuroanatomy*] ... R
Reticular Activating System [*Diffuse network of neurons in the brain*] ... RAS
Reticular Degeneration of the Pigment Epithelium [*Biochemistry*] (DAVI) ... RDPE
Reticular Erythematous Mucinosis [*Medicine*] (DMAA) ... REM
Reticular Formation [*Sleep*] ... RF
Reticular Lamina [*Ear anatomy*] ... RL
Reticularis Pontis Caudalis [*Brain anatomy*] ... RPC
Reticulated Grating (AAG) ... RG
Reticulated Siderocyte [*Cytology*] (AAMN) ... R-S
Reticulated Vitreous Carbon ... RVC
Reticulocyte [*Hematology*] (DAVI) ... RET
Reticulocyte [*Hematology*] ... RETIC
Reticulocyte Count [*Hematology*] (CPH) ... Retic Ct
Reticulocyte Production Index [*Hematology*] ... RPI
Reticulocyte Standard Buffer [*Medicine*] (DMAA) ... RSB
Reticuloendothelial [*or Reticuloendothelium*] [*Medicine*] ... RE
Reticuloendothelial Depressing Substance [*Medicine*] (AAMN) ... RDS
Reticuloendothelial Society (EA) ... RES
Reticuloendothelial System [*Medicine*] ... RES
Reticuloendotheliosis Virus ... REV
Reticulum [*Constellation*] ... Ret
Reticulum [*Constellation*] ... Reti
Reticulum Cell [*On Differential*] [*Hematology*] (DAVI) ... RE CEL
Reticulum Cell Sarcoma [*Medicine*] ... RCS
Reticulum Cell Sarcoma [*Pathology*] (DAVI) ... RSA
Reticulum Cells [*On differential*] [*Hematology*] (DAVI) ... RETUL
Reticulum-Cell Neoplasia [*Oncology*] ... RCN
Retina-Derived Growth Factor [*Biochemistry*] ... RDGF
Retinal Anlage [*Ophthalmology*] ... RA
Retinal Damage Threshold [*Ophthalmology*] ... RDT
Retinal Degeneration Slow [*Genetics*] ... RDS
Retinal Detachment [*Ophthalmology*] ... RD
Retinal Detachment, Oculus Dexter [*Right Eye*] [*Ophthalmology*] (DAVI) ... RDOD
Retinal Detachment, Oculus Sinister [*Left Eye*] [*Ophthalmology*] (DAVI) ... RDOS
Retinal Equivalent [*For Vitamin A*] ... RE
Retinal Ganglion Cell [*Neurochemistry*] ... RGC
Retinal Hemorrhage [*Medicine*] (DMAA) ... RH
Retinal Nerve Fiber Layer [*Anatomy*] ... RNFL
Retinal Pigment Epithelium ... RPE
Retinal Vein Occlusion [*Ophthalmology*] (DAVI) ... RVO
Retinal Visual Acuity Tester [*Ophthalmology*] ... RVAT
Retinitis Pigmentosa [*Eye disease*] [*Ophthalmology*] ... RP
Retinitis Proliferans [*Ophthalmology*] (DAVI) ... RP
Retinoblastoma [*Oncology*] ... Rb
Retinoblastoma Binding Protein (DMAA) ... RBBP
Retinohepatoendocrinologic [*Syndrome*] [*Medicine*] (DMAA) ... RHE
Retinoic Acid [*Biochemistry*] ... RA
Retinoic Acid Receptor [*Biochemistry*] ... RAR
Retinoic Acid Receptor Alpha (DMAA) ... RARA
Retinoic Acid Receptor Beta (DMAA) ... RARB
Retinoic Acid Responsive Element [*Biochemistry*] ... RARE
Retinoic Acid-Binding Protein [*Biochemistry*] (DAVI) ... RABP
Retinol-Binding Protein [*Biochemistry*] ... RBP
Retinopathy of Prematurity [*Medicine*] ... ROP
Retinoylphorbolacetate [*Biochemistry*] ... RPA
Retinyl Ester [*Organic chemistry*] ... RE
Retinyl Palmitate [*Organic chemistry*] ... RP
Retire to Staging Area [*Military*] ... RSA
Retired [*or Retiree*] ... R
Retired (AFM) ... RET
Retired (DD) ... ret
Retired (EY) ... RETD
Retired ... RTD
Retired ... RTRD
Retired Affairs Officers (EA) ... RAO
Retired after Finishing [*Yacht racing*] (IYR) ... RET
Retired and Pioneer Rural Carriers of United States (EA) ... RPRC
Retired Annuitant Pay Statement [*DoD*] ... RAPS
Retired Army Nurse Corps Association (EA) ... RANCA
Retired Army Personnel System ... RAPS
Retired Association for the Uniformed Services (NADA) ... RAUS
Retired Document File [*IRS*] ... RETF
[*The*] **Retired Enlisted Association** (EA) ... TREA
Retired Executives Action Clearing House [*British*] (DI) ... REACH
Retired Federal Employees Health Benefits Program (MCD) ... RFEHB
Retired Greyhounds as Pets (EA) ... RGP
Retired History File [*Army*] ... RHF
Retired in Place [*Telecommunications*] (TEL) ... RIP
Retired League Postmasters of the National League of Postmasters (EA) ... RLPNLP
Retired List ... RL
Retired Lives Reserve [*Insurance*] ... RLR
Retired Officer [*Military British*] ... RO
Retired Officers Association [*Military*] ... ROA
[*The*] **Retired Officers Association** (EA) ... TROA
Retired on Full Pay [*Military British*] ... RFP
Retired Pay Defense (NVT) ... RPD
Retired Pay Operations [*Army*] ... RPO
Retired Pay / Personnel System [*Military*] (DNAB) ... RPPS
Retired Personnel Data System [*Air Force*] ... RPDS
Retired Persons Services (EA) ... RPS
Retired Philosphers Association (EA) ... RPA
Retired Professionals Action Group [*Later, Gray Panthers*] ... RPAG
Retired Reserve [*Military*] ... RR
Retired Reserve Section ... RRS
Retired Senior Volunteer Program (EA) ... RSVP
Retired Senior Volunteer Program International (EA) ... RSVPI
Retired Servicemen's Family Protection Plan [*Military*] ... RSFPP
Retired Teachers Association (BARN) ... RTA
Retired Teamsters Fellowship Club (EA) ... RTFC
Retired Volunteer Coordinator ... RVC
Retiree Account Statement [*DoD*] ... RAS
Retiree Activity Days [*DoD*] ... RADS
Retiree Annuitant Pay System ... RAPS
Retiree Training for Extended Active Duty [*Military*] (MCD) ... RETREAD
Retirees to Eliminate State Income Source Tax [*An association*] ... RESIST
Retirement ... RTRMNT
Retirement Benefits Fund Board [*Australia*] ... RBFB
Retirement Benefits Fund Investment Trust [*Australia*] ... RBFIT
Retirement Care Assoc [*NYSE symbol*] (TTSB) ... RCA
Retirement Care Associates [*NYSE symbol*] (SAG) ... RCA
Retirement Care Associates, Inc. [*NASDAQ symbol*] (SAG) ... RCRE
Retirement Care Associates, Inc. [*Associated Press*] (SAG) ... RetrCre
Retirement Equity Act of 1984 (WYGK) ... REA
Retirement Exhibition [*British*] (ITD) ... RETIREX
Retirement Federation of Civil Service Employees of the United States Government [*Defunct*] (EA) ... RFCSEUSG
Retirement History Survey ... RHS
Retirement Improvement Program [*Air Force*] (AFM) ... RIP
Retirement Income ... RI
Retirement Income Credit ... RIC
Retirement Income Endowment [*Insurance*] ... RIE
Retirement Income Plan [*Insurance*] (MCD) ... RIP
Retirement Life Item ... RLI
Retirement Loss ... RL
Retirement Register File [*Computer science*] ... RRF
Retirement Service Officer [*DoD*] ... RSO
Retirement, Survivors, or Disability Insurance [*Social Security Administration*] (GFGA) ... RSDI
Retirement Systems Testing Section [*Social Security Administration*] ... RSTS
Retirement Village Association of New South Wales [*Australia*] ... RVANSW
Retirement Year Ending [*Army*] (AABC) ... RYE
Retirement-for-Cause [*Program*] [*Air Force*] ... RFC
Retires on Active Duty [*Military*] (MCD) ... ROAD
Retiro [*Bolivia*] [*ICAO location identifier*] (ICLI) ... SLRR
Retix [*NASDAQ symbol*] (SPSG) ... RETX
Retix, Inc. [*Associated Press*] (SAG) ... Retix
Retlaw Resources, Inc. [*Vancouver Stock Exchange symbol*] ... RER
Retorna Brevium [*The Return of Writs*] [*Latin Legal term*] (DLA) ... RET BREV
Retortable Barrier Container [*For food*] ... RBC

Retouch [*Graphic arts*] (DGA) .... R/T
Retouched (VRA) .... RETO
Retraced .... RETR
Retract .... RET
Retract (AAG) .... RETR
Retract Before Firing Contractor (NG) .... RBFC
Retractable Boom .... RB
Retractable Bow Propeller .... RBP
Retractationes [*of Augustine*] [*Classical studies*] (OCD) .... Retract
Retracting (WGA) .... RETRG
Retractor Bulb Motoneuron [*Neurology*] .... RBM
Retraining .... RETNG
Retraining .... RETRNG
Retraining (OICC) .... RT
Retraining and Reemployment Administration [*Terminated, 1947*] .... R & RA
Retraining and Reemployment Policy Board .... RRPB
Retraining Benefits [*Employment*] (OICC) .... RB
Retraining Group [*Air Force*] (AFM) .... RTGp
Retraining Objective Control Number [*Air Force*] (AFM) .... ROCN
Retransformation [*Medicine*] (DMAA) .... RT
Retransmission Identity Signal [*Telecommunications*] (TEL) .... RIS
Retransmission Request Signal [*Telecommunications*] (TEL) .... RRS
Retransmission Unit [*RADA*] [*Army*] (RDA) .... RU
Retransmit .... RETRANS
Retransmitted (AABC) .... REXMIT
Retread Manufacturers Association [*British*] (DBA) .... RMA
Retreat State Hospital, Hunlock Creek, PA [*OCLC symbol*] (OCLC) .... PHR
Retreatment Tumor, Nodes and Metastasis [*Staging of cancer*] (DAVI) .... rTNM
Retreats International (EA) .... RI
Retrievable Surface Storage Facility [*Nuclear energy*] .... RSSF
Retrieval Analysis and Presentation System [*Computer science*] .... RAPS
Retrieval and Acceleration of Promising Young Handicapped and Talented Program (EDAC) .... RAPYHT
Retrieval and Analysis of Navy Classified Information (DNAB) .... RANCIN
Retrieval and Composition (DIT) .... RECOMP
Retrieval and Processing Information for Display .... RAPID
Retrieval and Production for Integrated Data [*Computer science*] (MHDB) .... RAPID
Retrieval and Sort Processor [*Computer science*] .... RASP
Retrieval and Statistics Processing (NITA) .... RASP
Retrieval by Online Search [*Computer science*] .... ROSE
Retrieval by Title Words, Descriptors, and Classification (DIT) .... REWDAC
Retrieval Command Language [*Computer search language*] .... RECOL
Retrieval from the Literature on Electronics and Computer Sciences (PDAA) .... REFLECS
Retrieval Injury Threshold .... RIT
Retrieval of Enriched Textual Abstracts [*Information retrieval program*] .... RETA
Retrieval of Information by On-Line Terminal [*Atomic Energy Authority*] [*Computer science British*] .... RIOT
Retrieval of Special Portions from Nuclear Science Abstracts (DIT) .... RESPONSA
Retrieval System for Current Research in Agricultural Sciences [*Japan*] .... RECRAS
Retrieval through Automated Publication and Information Digest [*Computer science*] (DIT) .... RAPID
Retrieval Vessel (NASA) .... RV
Retrieve (KSC) .... RETR
Retrieve (MCD) .... RETRV
Retrieve (MSA) .... RTRV
Retrieve Resources Ltd. [*Vancouver Stock Exchange symbol*] .... RTV
Retro Table [*NASA*] .... RT
Retroactive (AAG) .... RETRO
Retroactive Continuity [*Computer science*] (NHD) .... RETCON
Retroactive Conversion (WDMC) .... RETROCON
Retroactive Family Allowance [*Military*] (DNAB) .... RETRO FA
Retroactive Inhibition [*Psychology*] .... RI
Retroactive Liability Insurance .... RIA
Retrobulbar [*Ophthalmology*] (DAVI) .... RB
Retrobulbar Neuritis [*Medicine*] .... RBN
Retrocorneal Pigmentation [*Medicine*] (DMAA) .... RCP
Retrodorsolateral Nucleus [*Neuroanatomy*] .... RDLN
Retrofire (KSC) .... RETRO
Retrofire (SAA) .... RETROF
Retrofire Officer .... RETRO
Retrofire Officer [*NASA*] (KSC) .... RFO
Retrofit .... RETRO
Retrofit Configuration Drawing (MCD) .... RCD
Retrofit Configuration Record [*NASA*] (NASA) .... RCR
Retrofit Configuration System (MCD) .... RCS
Retrofit Installation Data (MCD) .... RID
Retrofit Modification Kit .... RMK
Retrofit Order [*Navy*] (NG) .... RO
Retrograde .... RETRO
Retrograde (DAVI) .... RG
Retrograde Amnesia [*Medicine*] .... RA
Retrograde Conduction Time [*Medicine*] (DMAA) .... RCT
Retrograde Cystogram [*Medicine*] (MAE) .... RC
Retrograde Europe [*Army*] .... RETROEUR
Retrograde Femoral Catheter [*Medicine*] (DMAA) .... RFC
Retrograde Lipid Flow [*Hypothesis for biological cell movement*] .... RLF
Retrograde Processing Point (MCD) .... RPP
Retrograde Pyelogram [*Medicine*] .... REP
Retrograde Pyelogram [*Nephrology*] (DAVI) .... Retro pyelo
Retrograde Pyelogram [*Nephrology*] (DAVI) .... RGP
Retrograde Pyelogram [*Medicine*] .... RPG
Retrograde Pyelography [*Medicine*] .... RP
Retrograde River Crossing (MCD) .... RRC
Retrograde Rocket System .... RRS
Retrograde Ureterogram [*Medicine*] .... RUG
Retrograde Urogram [*Medicine*] (MAE) .... RU
Retrogressive .... RETROG
Retrolabyrinthine Vestibular Neurectomy [*Medicine*] .... RVN
Retrolental Fibroplasia [*Eye disease in premature babies*] .... RLF
Retromanubrial Dullness [*Medicine*] .... RMD
Retromolar Trigone [*Dentistry*] (MAE) .... RMT
Retromotor Simulator .... RMS
Retroperitoneal [*Medicine*] .... RP
Retroperitoneal Fibromatosis [*Oncology*] .... RF
Retroperitoneal Hemorrhage [*Medicine*] (DAVI) .... RPH
Retroperitoneal Lymph Node Dissection [*Medicine*] (CDI) .... RPLIND
Retroperitoneal Lymph Node Dissection [*Medicine*] (MEDA) .... RPLND
Retroperitoneal Lymph Nodes [*Medicine*] .... RPLN
Retroperitoneal Lymphadenectomy [*Oncology*] (DAVI) .... RPLND
Retroperitoneal Lymphoadenectomy [*Oncology*] (DAVI) .... RPLAD
Retroperitoneal Lymphoadenectomy [*Medicine*] (BABM) .... RPLAD
Retropharyngeal Soft Tissue Space [*Medicine*] (DMAA) .... RSTS
Retroplacental Gamma Globulin [*Immunology*] (DAVI) .... RPGG
Retropubic Cystourethropexy [*Urology*] (DAVI) .... RPCU
Retropubic Prostatectomy [*Medicine*] .... RPP
Retropubic Urethropexy [*Gynecology*] (DAVI) .... RPU
Retroreflector in Space [*Instrumentation*] .... RIS
Retro-Rocket (AAG) .... RETRO
Retro-Rocket [*Army*] (AABC) .... RR
Retro-Rocket UNIVAC (MUGU) .... RRU
Retrorocket-Assisted Parachute in Flight Delivery .... RAPID
Retrospective Bibliographies on Magnetic Tape (NASA) .... RBMT
Retrospective Bibliography, National Library of Canada [*Bibliographie Retrospective, Bibliotheque Nationale du Canada*] **Ottawa, Ontario** [*Library symbol National Library of Canada*] (NLC) .... OONLR
Retrospective Conversion (NITA) .... RECON
Retrospective Conversion of Bibliographic Records [*Library of Congress*] .... RECON
Retrospective Cost-Based Reimbursement [*Health insurance*] (GHCT) .... RCBR
Retrospective Data Management System .... RDMS
Retrospective Machine Readable Catalog [*Carrollton Press, Inc.*] [*Arlington, VA Bibliographic database Online version of the US Library of Congress Shelflist*] .... REMARC
Retrospective Method [*Insurance*] .... RM
Retrospective Search System (NITA) .... RETROSPEC
Retrospective Single Ion Monitoring [*Analytical chemistry*] .... RSIM
Retrospectively (DLA) .... Retrosp
Retroversion .... RV
Retroviral Transcript [*Genetics*] .... RT
Retrovirus .... RV
Retrovirus Epidemiology Donor Study [*Medicine*] .... REDS
Retrovirus Research Center [*Veterans Administration Medical Center*] [*Baltimore, MD*] .... RRC
Retry Pending (SSD) .... RPEN
Rettie, Crawford, and Melville's Session Cases, Fourth Series [*1873-98*] [*Scotland*] [*A publication*] (DLA) .... JC Rettie
Rettie, Crawford, and Melville's Session Cases, Fourth Series [*1873-98*] [*Scotland*] [*A publication*] (DLA) .... R (Ct of Sess)
Rettie, Crawford, and Melville's Session Cases, Fourth Series [*1873-98*] [*Scotland*] [*A publication*] (DLA) .... RC(J)
Rettie's Scotch Court of Session Cases, Fourth Series [*A publication*] (DLA) .... Rett
Rettie's Scotch Court of Session Cases, Fourth Series [*A publication*] (DLA) .... Rettie
Rettie's Scotch Court of Session Cases, Fourth Series [*House of Lords' Part*] [*A publication*] (DLA) .... RHL
Rettie's Scotch Court of Session Reports, Fourth Series [*A publication*] (DLA) .... R
Return [*or Returnable*] (AAG) .... RET
Return (ROG) .... RETN
Return (AAG) .... RTN
Return (ODBW) .... rtn
Return (FAAC) .... RTRN
Return Address .... RA
Return Address Register .... RAR
Return Address Stack (ECII) .... RAS
Return Air [*Technical drawings*] .... RA
Return America to Work [*Also translated as "Reaganomics Ain't Working"*] [*UAW bumper sticker slogan*] .... RAW
Return and Restore Status Register [*Computer science*] .... RTR
Return Battery Pack (KSC) .... RBP
Return Beam Camera .... RBC
Return Beam Vidicon [*Satellite camera*] .... RBV
Return Beam Vidicon Camera .... RBVC
Return Cargo [*Shipping*] (DS) .... r/c
Return Channel Control Orderwire [*Military*] (CAAL) .... RCCOW
Return Control Word .... RCW
Return Critical Control Circuit .... RCCC
Return Data Relay Measurement (SSD) .... RDRM
Return Data Word (MCD) .... RDW
Return Due Date [*IRS*] .... RDD
Return Free Tax System [*Internal Revenue Service*] (GFGA) .... RFTS
Return from Exception [*Computer science*] .... RTE
Return from Interrupt [*Computer science*] (NHD) .... RTI
Return from Overseas [*Military*] .... ROS
Return from Subroutine [*Computer science*] .... RTS

Return Head ... RHD
Return Jump [*Computer science*] (MHDI) ... RTJ
Return Line Tether [*NASA*] (MCD) ... RLT
Return Link (MCD) ... R/L
Return Loss ... RL
Return Material [*Navy*] (NG) ... RM
Return Material Credit Memo ... RMCM
Return of Activated Sludge (DICI) ... RAS
Return of Army Repairables (AABC) ... ROAR
Return of Forces to Germany [*Military*] ... REFORGER
Return of Post ... RP
Return of Repairables ... ROR
Return on Assets [*Business term*] ... ROA
Return on Assets Managed [*Finance*] ... ROAM
Return on Capital [*Finance*] ... ROC
Return on Capital Employed [*Accounting term*] ... ROCE
Return on Equity [*Finance*] ... ROE
Return on Investment [*Finance*] ... ROI
Return on Investment (WDMC) ... roi
Return on Managed Assets [*Business term*] ... ROMA
Return on Market Value [*Finance*] ... ROM
Return on Market Value [*Finance*] (WDAA) ... ROMV
Return on Net Assets ... RONA
Return on Original Investment [*Business term*] (MHDW) ... ROOI
Return on Receipt of Document [*Business term*] ... RORD
Return on Revenue ... ROR
Return on Sales ... ROS
Return Premium ... RP
Return Pressure Sensing (MCD) ... RPS
Return Rate (IEEE) ... RR
Return Register ... RR
Return Ticket ... RT
Return to Active Duty [*Military*] ... RAD
Return to Author [*Bookselling*] ... R/A
Return to Base [*Military*] ... RTB
Return to Bias ... RB
Return to Bias (IAA) ... RTB
Return to Clinic [*Nursing*] ... RTC
Return to Control ... RTC
Return to Duty [*Military*] (DNAB) ... RETNDU
Return to Duty [*Military*] ... RTD
Return to Earth [*NASA*] ... RTE
Return to Government Stores (SAA) ... RTGS
Return to Land and Management [*Agriculture*] ... RLM
Return to Launch Site [*NASA*] ... RTLS
Return to Military Control (AABC) ... RMC
Return to Neuter ... RTN
Return to Office (DAVI) ... RTO
Return to Port [*for Orders*] (DS) ... R/P
Return to Proper Station Upon Completion of Temporary Duty [*Military*] ... RPSCTDY
Return to Recovery Room [*Medicine*] (DAVI) ... RTRR
Return to Saturation ... RS
Return to Search ... RTS
Return to Sender ... RTS
Return to Service [*Aviation*] ... RTS
Return to Situation (SAA) ... RS
Return to Stock Memo ... RTSM
Return to Stores ... RTS
Return to Supplier (MCD) ... RTS
Return to Unit [*Military British*] ... RTU
Return to Work (DAVI) ... RTW
Return to Zero (IDOE) ... RZ
Return to Zero (Non-Polarized) (NITA) ... RZ(NP)
Return to Zero (Polarized) (NITA) ... RZ(P)
Return Trip Time ... RTT
Return Visit (DAVI) ... RV
Returned ... RETD
Returned [*Medicine*] (DHSM) ... RTD
Returned ... RTND
Returned Absentee (DNAB) ... RET-ABSTEE
Returned Absentees ... RTDA
Returned Ammunition Group (NATG) ... RAG
Returned by the Post Office (WDMC) ... RPO
Returned Customer Assignment Form (IAA) ... RCAF
Returned Development Workers Association (EAIO) ... RDWA
Returned Letter Office ... RLO
Returned on Hire ... ROH
Returned Peace Corps Volunteer ... RPCV
Returned Peace Corps Volunteers Committee on Central America [*Defunct*] (EA) ... RPCVCCA
Returned Sailors', Soldiers', Airmen's Imperial League of Australia [*British military*] (DMA) ... RSSAILA
Returned Servicemen's League [*British military*] (DMA) ... RSL
Returned Services Association (BARN) ... RSA
Returned to Produce [*Scrapping of automotive prototypes*] ... RTP
Returned to Vendor (AAG) ... RTV
Returned to Work ... R/W
Returned Volunteer Action [*British*] [*An association*] (DBA) ... RVA
Returnee [*Military*] ... RTNEE
Returning ... R
Returning Officer (ROG) ... RO
Returning to Ramp [*Aviation*] (FAAC) ... RTR
Returning to School Syndrome ... RTSS
Returns Compliance Program [*Internal Revenue Service*] ... RCP
Returns File Unit [*IRS*] ... RFU
Returns Program Manager [*IRS*] ... RPM
Return-to-Earth Digital [*NASA*] ... RTED
Return-to-Zero [*Recording scheme*] ... RTZ
Return-to-Zero Level ... RZL
Return-to-Zero Mark ... RZM
Return-to-Zero Recording [*Computer science*] ... RZ
Return-to-Zero Recording (Non-Polarized) [*Computer science*] (MHDB) ... RX(NP)
Retzius [*Neuron*] ... Rz
Reunification Democracy Party [*Political party South Korea*] ... RDP
Reunion [*MARC geographic area code Library of Congress*] (LCCP) ... i-re--
Reunion [*MARC country of publication code Library of Congress*] (LCCP) ... re
Reunion [*ANSI two-letter standard code*] (CNC) ... RE
Reunion [*ANSI three-letter standard code*] (CNC) ... REU
Reunion Air [*ICAO designator*] (AD) ... UU
Reunion Democratica para la Liberacion de Guinea Ecuatorial [*Democratic Movement for the Liberation of Equatorial Guinea*] [*Political party*] (PD) ... RDLGE
Reunion des Amateurs de Fox Terriers [*An association*] (EAIO) ... RAFT
Reunion Industries [*NASDAQ symbol*] (TTSB) ... RUNI
Reunion Internacional de Tecnicos de la Nutricion Animal [*International Meeting of Animal Nutrition Experts*] (EAIO) ... RITENA
Reunion Internationale des Laboratoires d'Essais et de Recherches sur les Materiaux et les Constructions [*International Union of Testing and Research Laboratories for Materials and Structures*] (EAIO) ... RILEM
Reunion Island [*Seismograph station code, US Geological Survey*] (SEIS) ... REU
Reunion Island [*Airport symbol*] (OAG) ... RUN
Reunion of Professional Entertainers (EA) ... ROPE
Reunion Resources [*Associated Press*] (SAG) ... ReunInd
Reunion Resources [*Commercial firm Associated Press*] (SAG) ... ReunRsc
Reunion Resources [*NASDAQ symbol*] (SAG) ... RUNI
Reunion Resources [*NASDAQ symbol*] (SAG) ... RUNR
Reunite, Inc. (EA) ... RI
Reus [*Spain ICAO location identifier*] (ICLI) ... LERS
Reus [*Spain*] [*Airport symbol*] (OAG) ... REU
Reusable Aerodynamic Space Vehicle ... RASV
Reusable Aerospace Passenger Transport (MCD) ... RAPT
Reusable Agena [*NASA*] (NASA) ... RAG
Reusable Carbon-Carbon (MCD) ... RCC
Reusable External Insulation [*of space shuttle*] [*NASA*] ... REI
Reusable Inflatable Salvage Equipment ... RISE
Reusable Interplanetary Transport Approach Vehicle ... RITA
Reusable Launch System [*Aerospace*] (IAA) ... RLS
Reusable Launch Vehicle [*Aerospace*] ... RLV
Reusable Launch Vehicle [*NASA*] ... RLV
Reusable Multipurpose Spacecraft [*Aerospace*] (IIA) ... RMS
Reusable Nuclear Shuttle [*NASA*] ... RNS
Reusable Nuclear Stage [*Aerospace*] ... RNS
Reusable Nuclear Vehicle [*Aerospace*] (KSC) ... RNV
Reusable One-Stage Orbital Space Truck [*Aerospace*] ... ROOST
Reusable Orbital Carrier [*Aerospace*] (MCD) ... ROC
Reusable Orbital Module Booster and Utility Shuttle [*Aerospace*] ... ROMBUS
Reusable Orbital Transport [*Aerospace*] ... ROT
Reusable Orbital Transport System [*Aerospace*] (IAA) ... ROTS
Reusable Orbital Transport Vehicle [*Aerospace*] ... ROTV
Reusable Software Implementation Program (SSD) ... RSIP
Reusable Solid Rocket Motor ... RSRM
Reusable Space Shuttle System [*Aerospace*] (KSC) ... RSSS
Reusable Surface Insulation [*NASA*] ... RSI
Reusable Surface Insulation Stresses [*NASA computer program*] ... RESIST
Reusable Training Grenade ... RTG
Reusable-Expendable-Reusable ... RER
Reusabler Engines, Partially Enternal Expendable Tankage (PDAA) ... REPEET
Reusing Junk as Something Else [*Conversion of junk into reusable items*] ... REJASE
Reusing Junk as Something Else (BARN) ... Rejasing
Reuters Hldgs ADS [*NASDAQ symbol*] (TTSB) ... RTRSY
Reuters Holdings Ltd. [*Associated Press*] (SAG) ... ReutrHd
Reuters Holdings Ltd. [*New York, NY NASDAQ symbol*] (NQ) ... RTRS
Reuters Money Network [*Reality Technologies*] (PCM) ... RMN
Reuters News Agency (WDMC) ... RN
Reutilization Expedite Assets Program [*DoD*] ... REAP
Reutilization Value Percentage [*DoD*] ... RVP
Rev. Peres Oblats, Winnipeg, Manitoba [*Library symbol National Library of Canada*] (NLC) ... MWO
Rev. Peres Oblats, Winnipeg, MB, Canada [*Library symbol Library of Congress*] (LCLS) ... CaMWO
Revco D.S. [*NYSE symbol*] (TTSB) ... RXR
Revco DS, Inc. [*Associated Press*] (SAG) ... Revco
Revco DS, Inc. [*NYSE symbol*] (SPSG) ... RXR
Revealed Preference Analysis [*Economics*] ... RP
Revelation [*New Testament book*] ... Rev
Revelation [*New Testament book*] ... Rv
Revel-Montgey [*France ICAO location identifier*] (ICLI) ... LFIR
Revelstoke, BC [*Television station call letters*] (RBYB) ... CHKL-3
Revelstoke, BC [*AM radio station call letters*] ... CKCR
Revelstoke Branch, Okanagan Regional Library, British Columbia [*Library symbol National Library of Canada*] (BIB) ... BRO
Revelstoke Companies Ltd. [*Toronto Stock Exchange symbol*] ... REV
Reventador [*Race of maize*] ... REV
Revenue ... REV
Revenue Account (WDAA) ... REV A/C
Revenue Act [*1962, 1964, 1971, 1976, 1978*] ... RA
Revenue Agent [*IRS*] ... RA
Revenue Agent's Report [*IRS*] ... RAR

Revenue Analysis from Parametric Usage Descriptions
[*Telecommunications*] (TEL) .... RAPUD
Revenue and Expenditure Control Act of 1968 .... RECA
Revenue and Retrieval (IAA) .... RAR
Revenue and Taxation Code [*A publication*] (DLA) .... Rev & TC
Revenue Anticipation Note .... RAN
Revenue Anticipation Notes .... RANS
Revenue Anticipation Warrant .... RAW
Revenue Bond [*Investment term*] .... RB
Revenue Canada .... RC
Revenue Canada, Customs and Excise .... RC-CE
Revenue Canada - Customs and Excise Institutions List [*Revenue Canada -
Customs and Excise*] [*Information service or system*] (CRD) .... INST
Revenue Canada, Montreal, PQ, Canada [*Library symbol Library of
Congress*] (LCLS) .... CaQMRE
Revenue Canada [*Revenu Canada*] Montreal, Quebec [*Library symbol
National Library of Canada*] (NLC) .... QMRE
Revenue Canada, Taxation .... RC-T
Revenue Canada Taxation Library [*UTLAS symbol*] .... RTX
Revenue Canada-Taxation, Centre for Career Development, Ottawa, ON,
Canada [*Library symbol Library of Congress*] (LCLS) .... CaOONRTC
Revenue Cases [*A publication*] (DLA) .... Rev Cas
Revenue, Civil, and Criminal Reporter [*Calcutta*] [*A publication*] (DLA)..... RC & CR
Revenue, Civil, and Criminal Reporter [*Calcutta*] [*A publication*]
(DLA) .... Rev C & C Rep
Revenue Cutter [*Coast Guard*] .... RC
Revenue Cutter [*Coast Guard symbol*] (DNAB) .... WYTM
Revenue Cutter Service [*Coast Guard*] .... RCS
Revenue Decisions, Supplement [*India*] [*A publication*] (DLA) .... RD Sup
Revenue, Judicial, and Police Journal [*Bengal*] [*A publication*]
(DLA) .... Rev J & PJ
Revenue, Judicial, and Police Journal [*A publication*] (DLA) ...... Rev Jud & Police J
Revenue, Judicial, and Police Journal [*Calcutta*] [*A publication*] (DLA) ..... RJ & PJ
Revenue Management System (ECON) .... RMS
Revenue Officer [*IRS*] .... RO
Revenue Passenger Kilometer (AIA) .... RPK
Revenue Passenger Mile .... RPM
Revenue per Mile .... RPM
Revenue Procedure [*Internal Revenue Service*] .... REV PROC
Revenue Properties Co. Ltd. [*Associated Press*] (SAG) .... ReyPrp
Revenue Properties Co. Ltd. [*NASDAQ symbol*] (SAG) .... RPCLF
Revenue Properties Ltd [*NASDAQ symbol*] (TTSB) .... RPCLF
Revenue Receipts Control Sheets [*IRS*] .... RRCS
Revenue Reconciliation Act of 1990 (WYGK) .... RRA
Revenue Release [*A publication*] (DLA) .... RR
Revenue Reports of Upper Provinces [*India*] [*A publication*] (DLA) .... Behari
Revenue Requirements Modeling System [*Department of Energy*]
(GFGA) .... RRMS
Revenue Ruling [*Internal Revenue Service*] .... REV RUL
Revenue Sharing .... RS
Revenue Sharing Advisory Service (EA) .... RSAS
Revenue Sharing Office [*Treasury*] (OICC) .... RSO
Revenue Steamer [*Coast Guard symbol*] (DNAB) .... WYTM
Revenue Support Grant (AIE) .... RSG
Revenue Tariff [*Australia Political party*] .... RevTar
Revenue Ton-Miles .... RTM
Reverberation [*Sound*] (WDMC) .... reverb
Reverberation (NTCM) .... REVERB
Reverberation Control of Gain .... RCG
Reverberation Elimination .... REVEL
Reverberation Index .... RI
Reverberation Strength .... RS
Reverberation Time (NTCM) .... RT
Reverberation Time .... RV
Reverberator [*Automotive engineering*] .... REVERB
Revere Public Library, Revere, MA [*Library symbol Library of Congress*]
(LCLS) .... MRev
Revere Resources [*Vancouver Stock Exchange symbol*] .... RVL
Reverend (DD) .... Rev
Reverend (ODBW) .... Rev
Reverend .... REV
Reverend (EY) .... REV
Reverend (ROG) .... REVD
[*The*] Reverend Doctor Jonathan Swift, Dean of Patrick's in Ireland
[*Pseudonym used by Jonathan Swift*] .... TRDJSDOPII
[*The*] Reverend Henry Ward Beecher [*American clergyman, 1813-1887*] ..... RHWB
Reverend Pere [*Reverend Father*] [*French*] .... RP
Reverends Peres [*Reverend Fathers*] [*French*] .... RRPP
Reverendus Admodum [*Very Reverend*] [*Latin*] .... RA
Reverendus Pater [*Reverend Father*] [*Latin*] .... RP
Reversal Film [*Cinematography*] (NTCM) .... REV
Reversal of Prior Entry [*Banking*] .... RE
Reversal Shift [*Psychometrics*] .... RS
Reversals per Inch (IAA) .... RPI
Reverse .... R
Reverse [*Giemsa method*] [*Chromosome stain*] .... R
Reverse (AAG) .... REV
Reverse (IDOE) .... rev
Reverse (VRA) .... rev
Reverse (MSA) .... RVS
Reverse (AABC) .... RVSE
Reverse Acronyms and Initialisms Dictionary [*Later, RAIAD*]
[*A publication*] .... RAID
Reverse Acronyms, Initialisms, and Abbreviations Dictionary [*Formerly,
RAID*] [*A publication*] .... RAIAD

Reverse Address Resolution Protocol [*Computer science*] (PCM) .... RARP
Reverse Annuity Mortgage .... RAM
Reverse Blocked .... RB
Reverse Blocking Diode Thyristor (IAA) .... RBDT
Reverse Circulation Drilling [*Mining technology*] .... RCD
Reverse Contactor (IAA) .... RCR
Reverse Course [*Aviation*] .... RC
Reverse Course and Advise [*Aviation*] (FAAC) .... RCADV
Reverse Current .... RC
Reverse Current (AAG) .... REVCUR
Reverse Current Device [*Electronics*] (MSA) .... RCD
Reverse Current/Overcurrent (KSC) .... RC/OC
Reverse Current Relay (IAA) .... RCR
Reverse Diels-Alder [*Organic chemistry*] .... RDA
Reverse Free .... RF
Reverse Garbage Truck (ADA) .... RGT
Reverse Gate .... RG
Reverse Geometry X-Ray (PS) .... RGX
Reverse Half-Line [*Feed*] .... RHL
Reverse Hemolytic Plaque Assay [*Clinical chemistry*] .... RHPA
Reverse Income Tax (MHDW) .... RIT
Reverse International Acronyms, Initialisms, and Abbreviations Dictionary
[*A publication*] .... RIAIAD
Reverse Interrupt [*Telecommunications*] (IAA) .... RVI
Reverse Interrupt Character [*Keyboard*] .... RVI
Reverse Isotope Dilution Assay [*Chemical analysis*] .... RIDA
Reverse Line Feed [*Telecommunications*] (OSI) .... RLF
Reverse Line Feed (NITA) .... RLF
Reverse Locking Relay (IAA) .... RLR
Reverse Osmosis - Deionization System [*Water purification*] .... RO-DI
Reverse Osmosis Water Purification Equipment (MCD) .... ROWPE
Reverse Osmosis Water Purification System (MCD) .... ROWPS
Reverse Osmosis Water Purification Unit [*Army*] (RDA) .... ROWPU
Reverse Passive Anaphylaxis [*Immunology*] .... RPCA
Reverse Passive Anaphylazis [*Medicine*] (DMAA) .... RPA
Reverse Passive Hemagglutination [*Clinical chemistry*] .... RPHA
Reverse Phase Ion-Pair Partition (DMAA) .... RPIPP
Reverse Phase Relay (IAA) .... RPR
Reverse Phase Thin-Layer Chromatography .... RPTLC
Reverse Polish Logic (NITA) .... RPL
Reverse Polish Notation [*Arithmetic evaluation*] [*Computer science*] (IEEE) .... RPN
Reverse Power Relay (IAA) .... RPR
Reverse Price Risk [*Finance*] (EMRF) .... RPR
Reverse Processing [*Chemical engineering*] .... RP
Reverse Pulse Polarography [*Analytical chemistry*] .... RPP
Reverse Radial Immunodiffusion (PDAA) .... RRID
Reverse Recovery [*Electronics*] .... RR
Reverse Reduction (DS) .... RR
Reverse Repurchase Agreement [*Investment term*] .... RRP
Reverse Self Check (AAG) .... RVSSC
Reverse Shot [*Filmmaking*] (WDMC) .... RevS
Reverse Shot [*Photography*] (WDMC) .... REVS
Reverse Shot [*Cinematography*] (NTCM) .... RS
Reverse Signal (IAA) .... RS
Reverse Sutured Eye [*Ophthalmology*] (DAVI) .... RSE
Reverse Switching Rectifier (IAA) .... RSR
Reverse Tie Point (KSC) .... RTP
Reverse Transcriptase [*An enzyme*] .... RT
Reverse Transcriptase Inhibitor [*Medicine*] .... RTI
Reverse Transcription-Polymerase Chain Reaction .... RT-PCR
Reverse Transfer Capacitance .... RTC
Reverse Triiodothyronine [*Endocrinology*] .... rT_3
Reverse Velocity Rotor .... RVR
Reverse Work (WGA) .... RW
Reverse Wound (MCD) .... RW
Reverse-Acting .... RACT
Reverseconducting Thyristor (IAA) .... RCT
Reversed (WDMC) .... rev
Reversed [*Legal term*] (DLA) .... Rev'd
Reversed Circular Vection [*Optics*] .... RCV
Reversed Field Experiment [*Nuclear energy*] (NRCH) .... RFX
Reversed Field Pinch [*Plasma physics*] (NRCH) .... RFP
Reversed [*or Reversing*] on Rehearing [*Used in Shepard's Citations*] [*Legal
term*] (DLA) .... Rev Reh
Reversed Passive Hemagglutination by Miniature Centrifugal Fast Analysis
[*Medicine*] (DMAA) .... RPHAMFCA
Reversed Phase [*Chromatography*] .... R-P
Reversed-Field Pinch Reactor [*Plasma physics*] (PDAA) .... RFPR
Reversed-Phase High-Performance Liquid Chromatography .... RP-HPLC
Reversed-Phase Liquid Chromatography .... RPLC
Reversed-Phase Series (PDAA) .... RPS
Reverse-Flow Diverter [*Engineering*] .... RFD
Reverse-Osmosis [*Physical chemistry*] .... RO
Reverse-Osmosis Desalination .... ROD
Reverse-Phase Chromatography .... RPC
Reverse-Phase Column .... RPC
Reversible (MSA) .... RVSBL
Reversible Counter .... RCT
Reversible Follow-Up System .... RFUS
Reversible Full Wave .... RFW
Reversible Full-Wave Alternating Current .... RFWAC
Reversible Full-Wave Direct Current .... RFWDC
Reversible Gelatin Matrix .... RGM
Reversible Gelatin Matrix System .... RGMS
Reversible Half-Wave .... RHW

Reversible Half-Wave Alternating Current ... RHWAC
Reversible Half-Wave Alternating Current - Direct Current ... RHWACDC
Reversible Half-Wave Direct Current ... RHWDC
Reversible Hydrogen Electrode ... RHE
Reversible Intravas Device ... RID
Reversible Ischemic Attack [*Medicine*] (DMAA) ... RIA
Reversible Ischemic Neurological Deficit [*or Disability*] [*Medicine*] ... RIND
Reversible Non-Linear Dimension Reduction ... RendeR
Reversible Obstructive Airway Disease (DAVI) ... ROAD
Reversible Sickled Cell [*Hematology*] ... RSC
Reversing [*Legal term*] (DLA) ... rev'g
Reversing Acidification in Norway ... RAIN
Reversing Gear Clutch (DS) ... RC
Reversion (ROG) ... REVN
Reversion ... REVON
Reversionary (ROG) ... REVERSY
Reversionary (ROG) ... REVY
Reversionary [*Legal shorthand*] (LWAP) ... RVSNY
Reversioner (ROG) ... REVR
Reverso [*Left-Hand Page of Open Book*] (ROG) ... VERSO
Revertive Pulsing ... RP
Revest-Shamir-Adelman [*Encryption Algorithm*] [*Theoretical mathematics*] (PCM) ... RSA
Review (AAMN) ... R
Review (AFM) ... REV
Review (WDMC) ... rev
Review (NVT) ... REVW
Review ... RW
Review and Analysis ... R & A
Review and Analysis of Companies in Holland [*Database*] (IID) ... REACH
Review and Analysis Process ... RAP
Review and Approval ... R & A
Review and Approval Document (MCD) ... RAD
Review and Command Assessment of Project [*Military*] ... RECAP
Review and Comment [*Aerospace*] ... R & C
Review and Concurrence Advisory Board ... RCAB
Review and Concurrence Authority ... RCA
Review, Approve or Disapprove, and Comment (MCD) ... RADC
Review Classification (NITA) ... RC
Review Conference ... REVCON
Review Copy (DGA) ... REV CPY
Review Cycle [*Military*] (AFIT) ... RC
Review, Evaluation, Disposition Board (AAG) ... RED
Review for Religious [*A publication*] (BRI) ... RR
Review. International Commission of Jurists [*A publication*] (DLA) ... Rev Int'l Comm Jur
Review Item Discrepancy (MCD) ... RID
Review Item Disposition [*NASA*] (NASA) ... RID
Review of Applied Entomology [*Database*] [*Commonwealth Institute of Entomology*] [*Information service or system*] (CRD) ... RAE
Review of Army Mobilization Planning (MCD) ... RAMP
Review of Contemporary Fiction [*A publication*] (BRI) ... RCF
Review of Contemporary Law [*A publication*] (DLA) ... Rev Contemp L
Review of Education and Training for Officers [*Military*] (RDA) ... RETO
Review of English Studies [*A publication*] (BRI) ... RES
Review of Environmental Effects of Pollutants [*Environmental Protection Agency*] (GFGA) ... REEP
Review of General Concepts of Separation Panel [*FAA*] (TAG) ... RGCSP
Review of Ghana Law [*A publication*] (DLA) ... Rev Ghana L
Review of Guard and Reserve Task Force (MCD) ... ROGAR
Review of Law and Social Change [*A publication*] (DLA) ... Rev L & Soc
Review of Law in Further Education (AIE) ... ROLFE
Review of Management Practices [*or Processes*] ... ROMP
Review of Medical and Veterinary Mycology [*Database*] [*Commonwealth Mycological Institute*] [*Information service or system*] (CRD) ... RMVM
Review of Metaphysics [*A publication*] (BRI) ... RM
Review of Plant Pathology [*Database*] [*Commonwealth Mycological Institute*] [*Information service or system*] (CRD) ... ROPP
Review of Polish Law [*A publication*] (DLA) ... Rev Pol L
Review of Polish Law and Economics [*Warsaw, Poland*] [*A publication*] (DLA) ... Rev of Polish Law and Econ
Review of Politics [*A publication*] (BRI) ... RP
Review of Reviews. Australian Edition [*A publication*] ... Rev Rev (A)
Review of Selected Code Legislation [*A publication*] (DLA) ... Rev Sel Code Leg
Review of Subjective Symptoms [*Medicine*] (DMAA) ... ROSS
Review of Symptoms [*Medical Records*] (DAVI) ... Rev of Sym
Review of Symptoms [*Medicine*] ... RS
Review of Systems [*Medical records*] (DAVI) ... Rev of Sys
Review of Systems [*Medicine*] ... ROS
Review of Systems [*Medical records*] (DAVI) ... RS
Review of Taxation of Individuals [*A publication*] (DLA) ... Rev Tax'n Indiv
Review of Vocational Qualifications (AIE) ... RVQ
Reviewed (WDMC) ... rev
[*To Be*] **Reviewed by Pathologist** [*Laboratory science*] (DAVI) ... REVL
Reviewer (AFM) ... REVR
Reviewer (DGA) ... REVWR
Reviewing Activity (MCD) ... RA
Reviewing Authority ... RA
Reviews in American History [*A publication*] (BRI) ... RAH
Reviews in Anthropology [*A publication*] (BRI) ... RA
Revisable Form Text [*Computer science*] (PCM) ... RFT
Revisable Form Text: Document Content Architecture [*IBM Corp.*] [*Computer science*] ... RFT:DCA
Revise (WDMC) ... rev
Revise [*or Revision*] (AAG) ... REV
Revise as Required (MCD) ... RAR
Revised (MCD) ... R
Revised [*Regulation or order revised*] [*Used in Shepard's Citations*] [*Legal term*] (DLA) ... Rv
Revised Accounting Procedures ... RAP
Revised and Expurgated Law Reports [*India*] [*A publication*] (DLA) ... RELR
Revised Appendix to Be Published (MCD) ... RATBP
Revised Behavior Problem Checklist [*Test*] ... RBPC
Revised Bogardus Social Distance Scale (EDAC) ... RBSDS
Revised Cases [*India*] [*A publication*] (DLA) ... Rev Cas (Ind)
Revised Civil Code [*A publication*] (DLA) ... Rev Civ Code
Revised Civil Statutes [*A publication*] (DLA) ... Rev Civ St
Revised Claim Valuation [*Insurance*] ... RCV
Revised Code ... RC
Revised Code of Civil Procedure [*A publication*] (DLA) ... Rev Code Civ Proc
Revised Code of Criminal Procedure [*A publication*] (DLA) ... Rev Code Cr Proc
Revised Code of Montana [*A publication*] ... RCM
Revised Code of Washington [*A publication*] (DLA) ... Wash Rev Code
Revised Code of Washington Annotated [*A publication*] (DLA) ... RCWA
Revised Collection of Selected Cases Issued by Chief Commissioner and Financial Commissioner of Oudh [*A publication*] (DLA) ... Oudh Rev Sel Cas
Revised Criminal Code [*A publication*] (DLA) ... Rev Cr Code
Revised Draft Presidential Memorandum ... RDPM
Revised Edition [*Publishing*] ... RE
Revised Edition (WDAA) ... REV ED
Revised Engine-Delivery Schedule (DNAB) ... REDS
Revised Engineer Active Force (MCD) ... REAF
Revised for Engineering Change Memorandum (SAA) ... RFECM
Revised General Regulation, General Accounting Office [*United States*] [*A publication*] (DLA) ... Rev Gen Reg
Revised Individual Allowance List [*Navy*] (NVT) ... RIAL
Revised Infant Temperament Questionnaire ... RITQ
Revised Interheater Mobility Study (DOMA) ... RIMS
Revised Laws [*A publication*] (DLA) ... RL
Revised Magnetic Standard ... RMS
Revised Management Procedure ... RMP
Revised Management Scheme [*International Whaling Commission*] ... RMS
Revised Master Allowance List [*Military*] (AFIT) ... RMAL
Revised Maximum Price Regulation [*World War II*] ... RMPR
Revised Occupant Simulation ... ROS
Revised Officer Military Occupational Speciality System (MCD) ... ROMOSS
Revised Ordinances [*A publication*] (DLA) ... Rev Ord
Revised Ordinances, Northwest Territories [*1888*] [*Canada*] [*A publication*] (DLA) ... Rev Ord NWT
Revised Ordinances, Northwest Territories [*Canada*] [*A publication*] (DLA) ... RONWT
Revised Penal Code [*A publication*] (DLA) ... Rev Pen Code
Revised Political Code [*A publication*] (DLA) ... Rev Pol Code
Revised Primary Drinking Water Regulations ... RPDWR
Revised Program and Budget Guidance [*Military*] ... RPBG
Revised Recommended Findings ... RRF
Revised Reports [*1759-1866*] [*England*] [*A publication*] (DLA) ... Rev R
Revised Reports [*England*] [*A publication*] (DLA) ... Rev Rep
Revised Reports [*England*] [*A publication*] (DLA) ... Revised Rep
Revised Reports [*Legal*] [*British*] ... RR
Revised Reports, Criminal Rulings [*1862-75*] [*India*] [*A publication*] (DLA) ... RR Cr R
Revised Ring Index [*A publication*] ... RRI
Revised Shapley Ames [*Catalogue of Bright Galaxies*] ... RSA
Revised Single Negotiating Text [*UN Law of the Sea Conference*] ... RSNT
Revised Standard Version [*of the Bible, 1952*] ... RSV
Revised Standard Version of the Bible [*A publication*] (BJA) ... RSV(RV)
Revised Statutes [*A publication*] (DLA) ... Rev St
Revised Statutes [*Various jurisdictions*] [*A publication*] (DLA) ... Rev Stat
Revised Statutes ... RS
Revised Statutes Annotated [*A publication*] (DLA) ... RSA
Revised Statutes of Alberta [*Canada*] [*A publication*] (DLA) ... RSA
Revised Statutes of British Columbia [*A publication*] (ILCA) ... RSBC
Revised Statutes of Canada [*A publication*] (DLA) ... Can Rev Stat
Revised Statutes of Canada [*Canada Department of Justice*] [*Information service or system*] (CRD) ... RSC
Revised Statutes of Manitoba [*Canada*] [*A publication*] (DLA) ... RSM
Revised Statutes of Nebraska [*A publication*] (DLA) ... Neb Rev Stat
Revised Statutes of Nebraska, Reissue ... RRS
Revised Statutes of New Brunswick [*Canada*] [*A publication*] (DLA) ... RSNB
Revised Statutes of Newfoundland [*Canada*] [*A publication*] (DLA) ... RSN
Revised Statutes of Nova Scotia [*Canada*] [*A publication*] (DLA) ... RSNS
Revised Statutes of Ontario [*Canada*] [*A publication*] (DLA) ... RSO
Revised Statutes of Prince Edward Island [*Canada*] ... RSPEI
Revised Statutes of Quebec [*Canada*] [*A publication*] (DLA) ... RSQ
Revised Statutes of Saskatchewan [*Canada A publication*] (DLA) ... RSS
Revised Supplementary Regulation ... RSR
Revised Token Test (EDAC) ... RTT
Revised Unified New Compiler with Its Basic Language Extended [*Computer science*] ... RUNCIBLE
Revised Uniform Limited Partnership Act (AAGC) ... RULPA
Revised Uniform Reciprocal Enforcement of Support Act (PAZ) ... RURESA
Revised Uniform Summary of Surveyed Weather Observations (MCD) ... RUSSWO
Revised Version (WDAA) ... REV VER
Revised Version [*of the Bible, 1881*] ... RV
Revised Version [*of the Bible*], Margin ... RVm
Revisers, Ink and Roller Makers' Auxiliaries [*A union*] [*British*] (DI) ... RIRMA
Revision [*Legal term*] (DLA) ... R
Revision (WDMC) ... rev

Revision [*Legal shorthand*] (LWAP) .... RVSN
Revision Block (MSA) .... RB
Revision Control System [*Computer science*] .... RCS
Revision Directive [*Drawings*] .... RD
Revision Message [*Aviation*] (DA) .... REV
Revision Notice (KSC) .... RN
Revision of Procurement Policy and Procedures .... ROP_3
Revision of Swift's Digest of Connecticut Laws [*A publication*] (DLA) .... Rev Sw Dig
Revision Proposal (NG) .... RP
Revision Record (MSA) .... RR
Revisionist History [*Taby, Sweden*] (EAIO) .... RH
Revista Biblica. Rafael Calzada [*Argentina*] [*A publication*] (BJA) .... RBiCalz
Revista Cubana de Derecho [*Havana, Cuba*] [*A publication*] (DLA) .... Rev Cubana de Derecho
Revista de Derecho. Colegio de Abogados de Puerto Rico [*A publication*] (DLA) .... Rev C Abo PR
Revista de Derecho Espanol y Americano [*Madrid, Spain*] [*A publication*] (DLA) .... Rev de Derecho Esp y Amer
Revista de Derecho, Jurisprudencia, y Ciencias Sociales y Gaceta de los Tribunales [*A publication*] (DLA) .... Rev de Derecho Jurispr y Cienc Soc
Revista. Faculdade de Direito. Universidade de Lisboa (Lisbon) [*A publication*] (DLA) .... Rev da Fac de Direito (Lisbon)
Revista. Faculdade de Direito. Universidade de Sao Paulo [*Sao Paulo, Brazil*] [*A publication*] (DLA) .... Rev de Fac de Direito (Sao Paulo)
Revista. Facultad de Derecho. Universidad Catolica Andres Bello (Caracas) [*A publication*] (DLA) .... Rev de la Fac de Derecho (Caracas)
Revista. Facultad de Derecho. Universidad de Caraboba [*Valencia, Venezuela*] [*A publication*] (DLA) .... Rev de la Fac de Derecho (Caraboba)
Revista. Facultad de Derecho y Ciencias Sociales [*Montevideo, Uruguay*] [*A publication*] (DLA) .... Rev de la Fac de Derecho y Cienc Soc
Revista General de Legislacion y Jurisprudencia [*Madrid, Spain*] [*A publication*] (DLA) .... Rev Gen de Legis y Jurispr
Revista. Instituto de Derecho Comparado [*Barcelona, Spain*] [*A publication*] (DLA) .... Rev del Inst de Derecho Comparado
Revista Internacional y Diplomatica. Publicacion Mensual [*Mexico*] [*A publication*] (DLA) .... Rev Internac y Diplom
Revista Juridica de Buenos Aires [*A publication*] (DLA) .... Rev Jur de Buenos Aires
Revista Trimestral de Jurisprudencia [*Rio De Janeiro, Brazil*] [*A publication*] (DLA) .... Rev Trimestr de Jurispr
[*The*] **Revitalization Corps** (EA) .... TRC
Revitalize Effective Utilization of Supply Excess [*Navy*] (NG) .... REUSE
Revival (VRA) .... rvl
Revival Centres of Australia .... RCA
Revival Fires (Christian Evangelizers Association) (EA) .... RFCEA
Revival Life Centre [*Australia*] .... RLC
Revloc, PA [*Location identifier FAA*] (FAAL) .... REC
Revlon Inc'A' [*NYSE symbol*] (TTSB) .... REV
Revlon, Inc. [*Research code symbol*] .... ZP
Revocable [*Business term*] .... REV
Revocation (ROG) .... REVOCN
Revocation .... REVOCON
Revoke (AABC) .... REVO
Revoked [*Legal term*] (DLA) .... R
Revoked Appointment and Returned to Civilian Status [*Navy*] .... RARC
Revoked Commission, Returned to Civilian Status [*Navy*] .... RCRC
Revoked or Rescinded in Part [*Existing regulation or order abrogated in part*] [*Used in Shepard's Citations*] [*Legal term*] (DLA) .... Rp
Revolucion Nacional [*Spain Political party*] (EY) .... RN
Revolute Joint (IAA) .... R
Revolution (AAG) .... REV
Revolution (WDMC) .... rev
Revolution (DSUE) .... REVO
Revolution (WGA) .... REVOL
Revolution Control Unit [*Automotive engineering*] .... RCU
Revolution Indicating System (MSA) .... RIS
Revolution per Orbit .... RPO
Revolutionaere Sozialisten (Oesterreichs) [*Revolutionary Socialists (Austria)*] [*Political party*] (PPE) .... RSO
Revolutionaire Socialistische Arbeiders Partij [*Revolutionary Socialist Workers' Party*] [*Netherlands Political party*] (PPE) .... RSAP
Revolutionaire Socialistische Partij [*Revolutionary Socialist Party*] [*Netherlands Political party*] (PPE) .... RSP
Revolutionary .... REVNRY
Revolutionary Action Movement .... RAM
Revolutionary Armed Forces of the Republic of Cuba .... RAFRC
Revolutionary Association of the Women of Afghanistan .... RAWA
Revolutionary Cells [*Revolutionary group*] [*West Germany*] .... RZ
Revolutionary Committee [*China*] .... REVCOM
Revolutionary Communist League of Britain [*Political party*] (PPW) .... RCLB
Revolutionary Communist Party (NADA) .... RCB
Revolutionary Communist Party of India [*Political party*] (PPW) .... RCP
Revolutionary Communist Party of India [*Political party*] (PPW) .... RCPI
Revolutionary Council of the Algerian People's Democratic Republic .... RCAPDR
Revolutionary Development [*South Vietnam*] .... RD
Revolutionary Development [*South Vietnam*] .... REV DEV
Revolutionary Development Cadre [*South Vietnam*] .... RDC
Revolutionary Development Hamlet Evaluation Report [*South Vietnam*] .... RDHER
Revolutionary Development Peoples Group [*South Vietnam*] [*Military*] (VNW) .... RDPG
Revolutionary Development Program [*South Vietnam*] .... RDP
Revolutionary Development Support [*South Vietnam*] .... RDS
Revolutionary Development Support Division [*South Vietnam*] .... RDSD
Revolutionary Development Support Plan [*or Program*] [*South Vietnam*] .... RDSP
Revolutionary Development Task Force [*South Vietnam*] .... RDTF
Revolutionary Government [*Vietnam*] .... RG
Revolutionary Justice Organization [*Lebanese terrorist group*] .... RJO
Revolutionary Mexican Historical Society (EA) .... RevMex
Revolutionary Military Council [*Grenada*] .... RMC
Revolutionary Movement of the Christian Left [*Ecuador*] [*Political party*] (PPW) .... MRIC
Revolutionary Socialist League (EA) .... RSL
Revolutionary Socialist Party [*Peru*] [*Political party*] (PD) .... PRC
Revolutionary Socialist Party [*India*] [*Political party*] (PPW) .... RSP
Revolutionary Trade Union Movement [*Czechoslovakia*] .... RTUM
Revolutionary United Front [*Sierra Leone*] [*Political party*] (EY) .... RUF
Revolutionary War Studies Forum (EA) .... RWSF
Revolutionary Workers League [*Canada*] .... RWL
Revolutionary Youth Movement [*Factions of Students for a Democratic Society. See RYM-I and RYM-II*] .... RYM
Revolutionary Youth Movement I [*Also known as "Weatherman"*] [*A faction of Students for a Democratic Society*] .... RYM-I
Revolutionary Youth Movement II [*A faction of Students for a Democratic Society*] .... RYM-II
Revolutions per Hour (DEN) .... R/H
Revolutions per Hour (MCD) .... RPH
Revolutions per Inch (IAA) .... RPI
Revolutions per Mile [*Automobile tires*] .... RPM
Revolutions per Minute .... R/M
Revolutions per Minute .... R/MIN
Revolutions per Minute [*e.g., in reference to phonograph records*] .... REV/MIN
Revolutions per Minute [*e.g., in reference to phonograph records*] .... RPM
Revolutions per Minute (IDOE) .... rpm
Revolutions per Minute/Second (DEN) .... RPM/S
Revolutions per Second .... R/S
Revolutions per Second .... REV/S
Revolutions per Second (AFM) .... RPS
Revolutions per Second (IDOE) .... rps
Revolutions-per-Minute Indicator .... RPMI
Revolutsiya, Nauka, Trud [*Revolution, Science, Labor*] [*Given name popular in Russia after the Bolshevik Revolution*] .... RENAT
Revolve (WDAA) .... REV
Revolve (MSA) .... RVLV
Revolver [*Military*] (AABC) .... RVLR
Revolving .... RVLG
Revolving Discussion Sequence .... RDS
Revolving Door Identification Model (EDAC) .... RDIM
Revolving Fund [*Finance*] .... RF
Revolving Fund for Natural Resources Exploration [*United Nations*] (EY) .... RFNRE
Revolving Radio Beacon [*ITU designation*] (CET) .... RT
Revolving Transmitter [*Telecommunications*] (IAA) .... RT
Revolving Underwriting Facility [*Finance*] .... RUF
Revue Administrative [*A publication*] (ILCA) .... RA
Revue. Barreau Canadien [*A publication*] (DLA) .... R du B Can
Revue Canadienne [*Quebec*] [*A publication*] (DLA) .... Rev Can
Revue Canadienne de Droit Communautaire [*A publication*] (DLA) .... Rev Can Dr Com
Revue Canadienne de Droit Familial [*A publication*] (DLA) .... Rev Can D Fam
Revue Canadienne de Theorie Politique et Sociale [*A publication*] .... RCTPS
Revue Critique de Legislation [*Paris*] [*A publication*] (DLA) .... Rev Crit de Leg
Revue Critique de Legislation et de Jurisprudence [*A publication*] (DLA) .... RCLJ
Revue Critique de Legislation et de Jurisprudence [*Montreal*] [*A publication*] (DLA) .... Rev Crit de Legis et Jur
Revue Critique de Legislation et de Jurisprudence de Canada [*A publication*] (DLA) .... RC
Revue Critique de Legislation et de Jurisprudence de Canada [*A publication*] (DLA) .... Rev Crit
Revue de Droit Administratif et de Droit Fiscal [*Lausanne, Switzerland*] [*A publication*] (DLA) .... RDAF
Revue de Droit Contemporain [*Brussels, Belgium*] [*A publication*] (DLA) .... Rev de Droit Contemp
Revue de Droit de McGill [*A publication*] (DLA) .... R de D McGill
Revue de Droit du Travail [*A publication*] (DLA) .... RDT
Revue de Droit Hongrois [*A publication*] (DLA) .... Rev de Droit Hong
Revue de Droit International pour le Moyen-Orient [*A publication*] (DLA) .... Rev Droit Int'l Moyen-Orient
Revue de Droit Penal Militaire et de Droit de la Guerre [*A publication*] (DLA) .... Rev de Droit Penal Mil et de Droit de la Guerre
Revue de Droit Penal Militaire et de Droit de la Guerre [*A publication*] (DLA) .... Rev Droit Penal Militaire et Dr de la Guerre
Revue de Droit Uniforme [*A publication*] (DLA) .... Rev de Droit Unif
Revue de Droit Uniforme [*A publication*] (DLA) .... Rev de Droit Uniforme
Revue de Droit. Universite de Sherbrooke [*A publication*] (DLA) .... Rev D US
Revue de Geomorphologie Dynamique [*A publication*] .... RGD
Revue de Jurisprudence [*Quebec*] [*A publication*] (DLA) .... R de J
Revue de Jurisprudence [*Quebec*] [*A publication*] (DLA) .... R de Jur
Revue de Jurisprudence [*Montreal*] [*A publication*] (DLA) .... Re de J
Revue de Jurisprudence [*Quebec*] [*A publication*] (DLA) .... Rev de Jur
Revue de Jurisprudence [*A publication*] (DLA) .... RJ
Revue de Jurisprudence et Legislation [*Montreal*] [*A publication*] (DLA) .... Re de L
Revue de Legislation [*Canada*] [*A publication*] (DLA) .... Rev de Legis
Revue de Legislation et de Jurisprudence [*Canada*] [*A publication*] (DLA) .... R de L
Revue de Legislation et de Jurisprudence [*A publication*] (DLA) .... R de L et de J
Revue de Legislation et de Jurisprudence [*Montreal*] [*A publication*] (DLA) .... Rev de Leg

Revue de Legislation et de Jurisprudence [*Quebec*] [*A publication*] (DLA) ... Rev Leg
Revue de l'Histoire des Religions [*A publication*] (OCD) ... Rev Hist Rel
Revue de Science Criminelle et de Droit Penal Compare [*Paris, France*] [*A publication*] (DLA) ... Rev de Sci Criminelle et de Droit Penal Compare
Revue de Theologie et des Questions Religieuses [*A publication*] (BJA) ... RThQr
Revue des Etudes Anciennes [*A publication*] (OCD) ... Rev Et Anc
Revue des Etudes Grecques [*A publication*] (OCD) ... Rev Et Grec
Revue des Etudes Latines [*A publication*] (OCD) ... Rev Et Lat
Revue du Droit [*A publication*] (DLA) ... R du D
Revue du Droit [*Quebec*] [*A publication*] (DLA) ... Rev du Dr
Revue du Marche Commun [*Review of the Common Market*] [*French*] ... RMC
Revue General Belge [*A publication*] (BJA) ... RGenBelge
Revue Generale de Droit [*A publication*] (DLA) ... Rev Gen
Revue Generale de Droit [*A publication*] (DLA) ... Rev Gen D
Revue Hittite et Asianique [*Paris*] [*A publication*] (BJA) ... RHittAs
Revue Internationale de Droit Compare [*A publication*] (DLA) ... Rev Int'l Droit Comp
Revue Internationale de Droit Penal [*A publication*] (DLA) ... Rev Int'l Dr Penal
Revue Internationale des Droits de l'Antiquite [*A publication*] (DLA) ... Rev Int'l des Droits de l'Antiquite
Revue Internationale du Droit d'Auteur [*A publication*] (DLA) ... Rev Int'l Dr Auteur
Revue Internationale Francaise du Droit des Gens [*A publication*] (DLA) ... Rev Internat Franc du Droit des Gens
Revue Ivoirienne de Droit [*A publication*] (DLA) ... Rev Ivoirienne de Droit
Revue Judiciaire, by Bruzard [*1843-44*] [*Mauritius*] [*A publication*] (DLA) ... RJ
Revue Juridique d'Alsace et de Lorraine [*A publication*] (DLA) ... Rev Jur d'Alsace et de Lorraine
Revue Juridique du Congo [*A publication*] (DLA) ... Rev Jur du Congo
Revue Legale [*Canada*] [*A publication*] (DLA) ... Rev Leg
Revue Legale [*A publication*] (DLA) ... Rev Legale
Revue Legale [*Canada*] [*A publication*] (DLA) ... RL
Revue Legale. New Series [*Canada*] [*A publication*] (DLA) ... Rev Leg NS
Revue Legale. New Series [*Canada*] [*A publication*] (DLA) ... RLNS
Revue Legale (Old Series) [*A publication*] (DLA) ... Rev Leg (OS)
Revue Legale (Old Series) [*Canada*] [*A publication*] (DLA) ... RLOS
Revue Legale Reports, Queen's Bench [*Canada*] [*A publication*] (DLA) ... RLQB
Revue Legale Reports, Supreme Court [*Canada*] [*A publication*] (DLA) ... RLSC
Revue Musicale [*A publication*] ... RMC
Revue Suisse du Droit International de la Concurrence [*Swiss Review of International Antitrust Law*] [*A publication*] (DLA) ... Rev Suisse Dr Int'l Concurrence
Revue Tunisienne de Droit [*Tunis, Tunisia*] [*A publication*] (DLA) ... Rev Tunisienne de Droit
Reward ... R
Reward (AFM) ... REW
Reward/Penalty ... R/P
Reward Resources Ltd. [*Vancouver Stock Exchange symbol*] ... RWR
Rewind ... R
Rewind (MDG) ... REW
Rewind ... RW
Rewind ... RWD
Rewind (MSA) ... RWND
Rewind and Unload ... RUN
Rework (MSA) ... REWK
Rework (AAG) ... RWK
Rework After Completion (SAA) ... RAC
Rework/Completion Tag [*Nuclear energy*] (NRCH) ... RCT
Rework Excellence Program [*Navy*] (DNAB) ... REP
Rework Inspection Team Report ... RITR
Rework Monitoring Test ... RMT
Rework Order (MCD) ... RO
Rework Print Image (IAA) ... RPI
Rework Removal Rate ... RRR
Rework/Scrap Tag (MCD) ... RST
Rework Support Conference [*Military*] (DNAB) ... RSC
Rewritable/Optical ... R/O
Rewritable Optical Disk [*Computer science*] (BARN) ... ROD
Rewritten [*FAR clauses*] (AAGC) ... R
Rex [*King*] [*Latin*] ... R
Rex Allen, Jr. Fan Club (EA) ... RAJFC
Rex Aviation (New Zealand) Ltd. [*ICAO designator*] (FAAC) ... TNZ
Rex et Imperator [*King and Emperor*] [*Latin*] ... R et I
Rex Francorum [*King of the Franks*] [*Latin*] ... RF
Rex Hospital Library, Raleigh, NC [*Library symbol*] [*Library of Congress*] (LCLS) ... NcRRH
Rex Putnam High School, Milwaukie, OR [*Library symbol Library of Congress*] (LCLS) ... OrMiPHS
Rex Silver Mines [*Vancouver Stock Exchange symbol*] ... REX
Rex Stores [*NYSE symbol*] (TTSB) ... RSC
Rex Stores Corp. [*Associated Press*] (SAG) ... RexStore
Rex Stores Corp. [*Formerly, Audio/Video Affiliates, Inc.*] [*NYSE symbol*] (SPSG) ... RSC
Rexall Sundown [*NASDAQ symbol*] (TTSB) ... RXSD
Rexall Sundown, Inc. [*Associated Press*] (SAG) ... RexlSun
Rexall Sundown, Inc. [*NASDAQ symbol*] (SAG) ... RXSD
Rexam PLC [*Associated Press*] (SAG) ... Rexam
Rexam PLC [*NASDAQ symbol*] (SAG) ... REXMY
Rexam Plc ADR [*NASDAQ symbol*] (TTSB) ... REXMY
Rexburg [*Idaho*] [*Seismograph station code, US Geological Survey*] (SEIS) ... REX
Rexburg, ID [*FM radio station call letters*] ... KADQ
Rexburg, ID [*FM radio station call letters*] ... KGTM
Rexburg, ID [*FM radio station call letters*] ... KRIC
Rexburg, ID [*AM radio station call letters*] ... KRXK
Rexburg, ID [*FM radio station call letters*] ... KWBH
Rexel, Inc. [*Associated Press*] (SAG) ... Rexel
Rexel, Inc. [*NYSE symbol*] (SAG) ... RXL
Rexene Corp. [*Associated Press*] (SAG) ... Rexene
Rexene Corp. [*NYSE symbol*] (SPSG) ... RXN
Rexfor, Ste.-Foy, Quebec [*Library symbol National Library of Canada*] (NLC) ... QSTFR
Rexford [*Montana*] [*Seismograph station code, US Geological Survey*] (SEIS) ... RXF
Rexford Minerals Ltd. [*Vancouver Stock Exchange symbol*] ... RXM
Rexhall Indus [*NASDAQ symbol*] (TTSB) ... REXL
Rexhall Industries [*Associated Press*] (SAG) ... Rexhall
Rexhall Industries, Inc. [*NASDAQ symbol*] (NQ) ... REXL
Rexon, Inc. [*NASDAQ symbol*] (NQ) ... REXN
Rexplore Resources International Ltd. [*Vancouver Stock Exchange symbol*] ... RXI
Rexworks, Inc. [*NASDAQ symbol*] (NQ) ... REXW
Rexworks, Inc. [*Associated Press*] (SAG) ... Rexwks
Rey Osterreigh and Recall [*Test*] [*Psychiatry*] (DAVI) ... RO 7 R
Reyes [*Bolivia*] [*Airport symbol*] (OAG) ... REY
Reyes [*Bolivia*] [*ICAO location identifier*] (ICLI) ... SLRY
Reye's Disease [*Medicine*] ... RD
Reye's Syndrome [*Medicine*] ... RS
Reye's Syndrome Society [*Later, NRSF*] (EA) ... RSS
Reykholar [*Iceland*] [*Airport symbol Obsolete*] (OAG) ... RHA
Reykjavik [*Iceland*] [*ICAO location identifier*] (ICLI) ... BICA
Reykjavik [*Iceland*] [*ICAO location identifier*] (ICLI) ... BICC
Reykjavik [*Iceland*] [*ICAO location identifier*] (ICLI) ... BIRD
Reykjavik [*Iceland*] [*ICAO location identifier*] (ICLI) ... BITA
Reykjavik [*Iceland*] [*Airport symbol*] (OAG) ... REK
Reykjavik [*Iceland*] [*Seismograph station code, US Geological Survey*] (SEIS) ... REY
Reykjavik Airport [*Iceland*] [*ICAO location identifier*] (ICLI) ... BIRK
Reykjavik [*Iceland*] **Keflavik Airport** [*Airport symbol*] (OAG) ... KEF
Reymann Memorial Farms [*West Virginia University*] [*Research center*] (RCD) ... RMF
Reynolds Alberta Museum, Wetaskiwin, Alberta [*Library symbol National Library of Canada*] (BIB) ... AWRAM
Reynold's Aluminum Co. of Canada Ltd. [*Toronto Stock Exchange symbol*] ... RAL
Reynolds Analogy Factor [*Physics*] ... RAF
Reynolds & Reynolds Co. [*NYSE symbol*] (SPSG) ... REY
Reynolds & Reynolds Co. [*Associated Press*] (SAG) ... ReyRey
Reynolds & Reynolds'A' [*NYSE symbol*] (TTSB) ... REY
Reynolds Electrical & Engineering Co. ... REECO
Reynolds Hydrodynamic Theory [*Physics*] ... RHT
Reynolds Industries, Corporate Library, Winston-Salem, NC [*Library symbol Library of Congress*] (LCLS) ... NcWsRI
Reynold's Life Insurance [*A publication*] (DLA) ... Reyn L Ins
Reynolds Metals [*NYSE symbol*] (TTSB) ... RLM
Reynolds Metals 7%'PRIDES' [*NYSE symbol*] (TTSB) ... RLMPrD
Reynolds Metals Co. [*Associated Press*] (SAG) ... ReyMt
Reynolds Metals Co. [*Associated Press*] (SAG) ... ReyMtl
Reynolds Metals Co. [*NYSE symbol*] (SPSG) ... RLM
Reynolds Metals Co., Executive Office Library, Richmond, VA [*Library symbol Library of Congress*] (LCLS) ... ViRR-E
Reynolds Metals Co., Packaging Research Division, Richmond, VA [*Library symbol Library of Congress*] (LCLS) ... ViRR-P
Reynolds Metals Co., Richmond, VA [*Library symbol Library of Congress*] (LCLS) ... ViRR
Reynolds Metals Co., Technical Information Services Library, Richmond, VA [*Library symbol Library of Congress*] (LCLS) ... ViRR-T
Reynolds Metals, Reduction Research Division, Sheffield, AL [*Library symbol Library of Congress*] (LCLS) ... ASheR
Reynold's Number [*Viscosity*] (MAE) ... NR
Reynolds Number [*Viscosity*] ... R
Reynolds Number [*Viscosity*] [*IUPAC*] ... Re
Reynolds Number [*Viscosity*] ... RN
Reynolds, Reports [*40-42 Mississippi*] [*A publication*] (DLA) ... Reyn
Reynolds, Reports [*40-42 Mississippi*] [*A publication*] (DLA) ... Reynolds
Reynolds' Spanish and Mexican Land Laws [*A publication*] (DLA) ... Reynolds' Land Laws
Reynolds Tobacco Co., Marketing Development Intelligence Center, Winston-Salem, NC [*Library symbol Library of Congress*] (LCLS) ... NcWsR-M
Reynolds Tobacco Co., Research and Development Technical Information Services, Winston-Salem, NC [*Library symbol Library of Congress*] (LCLS) ... NcWsR-R
Reynolds Tobacco Co., Winston-Salem, NC [*Library symbol*] [*Library of Congress*] (LCLS) ... NcWsR
Reynoldsville, PA [*FM radio station call letters*] ... WDSN
Reynosa [*Mexico*] [*Airport symbol*] (OAG) ... REX
Reynosa/General Lucio Blanco Internacional [*Mexico ICAO location identifier*] (ICLI) ... MMRX
Reza Shah Kibur University [*Iran*] ... RSKU
Rezayeh [*Iran*] [*Airport symbol*] (AD) ... RZY
RF Management [*NASDAQ symbol*] (TTSB) ... RFMC
RF Management Corp. [*Associated Press*] (SAG) ... RF M
RF Management Corp. [*Associated Press*] (SAG) ... RF Mgt
RF Management Corp. [*NASDAQ symbol*] (SAG) ... RFMC
R.F. Management Wrrt'A' [*NASDAQ symbol*] (TTSB) ... RFMCW
R.F. Management Wrrt'B' [*NASDAQ symbol*] (TTSB) ... RFMCZ
RF Monolithics [*NASDAQ symbol*] (TTSB) ... RFMI
RF Monolithics, Inc. [*Associated Press*] (SAG) ... RF Mono
RF Monolithics, Inc. [*NASDAQ symbol*] (SAG) ... RFMI
RF Power Products [*Associated Press*] (SAG) ... RF Pow
RF Power Products [*AMEX symbol*] (SAG) ... RFP

RFC Resource Finance Corp. [*Toronto Stock Exchange symbol*] ... RFC
RFC Resources Corp. [*Vancouver Stock Exchange symbol*] ... RFC
RFS Hotel Investors [*NASDAQ symbol*] (TTSB) ... RFSI
RFS Hotel Investors, Inc. [*NYSE symbol*] (SAG) ... RFS
RFS Hotel Investors, Inc. [*Associated Press*] (SAG) ... RFS Htl
RFS Hotel Investors, Inc. [*NASDAQ symbol*] (SAG) ... RFSI
RGB Computer & Video [*NASDAQ symbol*] (TTSB) ... EDIT
RGB Computer & Video [*Commercial firm Associated Press*] (SAG) ... RGB Cpt
RH [*or Rhesus*] **Immune Globulin** [*Immunology*] ... RHIG
Rhabdomyosarcoma [*Also, RMS*] [*Oncology*] ... RHM
Rhabdomyosarcoma [*Also, RHM*] [*Oncology*] ... RMS
Rhabdomyosarcoma, Alveolar [*Medicine*] (DMAA) ... RMSA
Rhabdomyosarcoma Chromosomal Region (DMAA) ... RMSCR
Rhaeto-Romance [*MARC language code Library of Congress*] (LCCP) ... roh
Rhame Elementary School, East Rockaway, NY [*Library symbol Library of Congress*] (LCLS) ... NErRE
Rhammus [*Pharmacology*] (ROG) ... RHAM
Rhapsody (WGA) ... RHAP
Rheims [*France*] [*Airport symbol*] (AD) ... RHE
Rhein [*Germany ICAO location identifier*] (ICLI) ... EDDU
Rheindahlen [*Germany ICAO location identifier*] (ICLI) ... EDUK
Rheine/Eschendorf [*Germany ICAO location identifier*] (ICLI) ... EDXE
Rheine-Bentlage [*Germany ICAO location identifier*] (ICLI) ... EDCE
Rheinflugzeugbau [*Germany ICAO aircraft manufacturer identifier*] (ICAO) ... RS
Rheingold-Rotary-Reciprocating [*Motor*] ... 3R
Rheinische Hypothekenbank AG [*Germany*] (EY) ... RHEINHYP
Rheinisches Museum fuer Philologie [*A publication*] (OCD) ... Rh Mus
Rheinisch-Westfaelisches Electrizitaetswerk AG [*Rheine-Westphalian Electricity Co.*] [*Germany*] ... RWE
Rheinland Air Service [*Germany ICAO designator*] (FAAC) ... RLD
Rhein-Main Air Base [*Germany ICAO location identifier*] (ICLI) ... EDAF
Rheintalflug-Rolf Seewald [*Austria ICAO designator*] (FAAC) ... RTL
Rhein-Westfalische Technische Hochschule, Aachen, Germany [*Library symbol Library of Congress*] (LCLS) ... GyAR
Rhein-Westfalische Technische Hochschule, Aachen, Germany [*Library symbol*] [*Library of Congress*] (LCLS) ... GyAR
RHEMA [*Restoring Hope through Educational and Medical Aid*] **International** (EA) ... RI
Rhenium [*Chemical element*] ... Re
Rheoencephalography [*Medicine*] ... REG
Rheological Boundary Layer [*Physics*] ... RBL
Rheology Research Center [*University of Wisconsin - Madison*] [*Research center*] (RCD) ... RRC
Rheometrics, Inc. [*Piscataway, NJ*] [*NASDAQ symbol*] (NQ) ... RHEM
Rheometrics, Inc. [*Associated Press*] (SAG) ... Rheomt
Rheometrics Mechanical Spectrometer ... RMS
Rheometrics Scientific [*NASDAQ symbol*] (TTSB) ... RHEM
Rheometrics Sound Analyzer ... RSA
Rheostat (IEEE) ... RH
Rheostat (AAG) ... RHEO
Rhesus [*Blood factor*] ... Rh
Rhesus [*of Euripides*] [*Classical studies*] (OCD) ... Rhes
Rhesus Diploid-Cell-Strain Rabies Vaccine ... RDRV
Rhesus Factor Negative [*Hematology*] (MAE) ... Rh Neg
Rhesus Factor Null [*Indicates all Rhesus factors are missing*] [*Hematology*] (DAVI) ... Rh_{null}
Rhesus Factor Positive [*Hematology*] (MAE) ... Rh Pos
Rhesus Monkey [*Medicine*] (DMAA) ... RhMk
Rhesus Monkey ... RM
Rhesus Monkey Kidney [*Medicine*] (DMAA) ... RhMK
Rhesus Monkey Kidney [*Medicine*] (DMAA) ... RhMkK
Rhesus Monkey Kidney [*Medicine*] ... RMK
Rhesus Rotavirus [*Medicine*] ... RRV
Rhetores Graeci [*A publication*] (OCD) ... Rhet
Rhetores Latini Minores [*A publication*] (OCD) ... Rhet Lat Min
Rhetoric ... RHET
Rhetoric Society of America (EA) ... RSA
Rhetorica [*of Aristotle*] [*Classical studies*] (OCD) ... Rh
Rhetorica ad Alexandrum [*of Aristotle*] [*Classical studies*] (OCD) ... Rh Al
Rhetorica ad Herennium [*First century BC*] [*Classical studies*] (OCD) ... Rhet Her
Rheumatic [*Medicine*] (MAE) ... rh
Rheumatic Fever [*Medicine*] ... RF
Rheumatic Fever (DAVI) ... rheu fev
Rheumatic Heart Disease [*Medicine*] ... RHD
Rheumatic Heart Disease (DAVI) ... rheu ht dis
Rheumatic Pain Modulation Disorder [*Medicine*] (DMAA) ... RPMD
Rheumatic Valvular Heart Disease [*Medicine*] (DMAA) ... RVHD
Rheumatism [*Medicine*] ... Rh
Rheumatism [*Medicine*] ... RHEUM
Rheumatoid Agglutinator [*Immunology*] ... Ragg
Rheumatoid Agglutinins [*Clinical chemistry*] ... RA
Rheumatoid Agglutinins [*Clinical chemistry*] (CPH) ... RH Agglut
Rheumatoid Arthritis [*Medicine*] ... RA
Rheumatoid Arthritis and Sjoegren Syndrome [*Medicine*] (DMAA) ... RASS
Rheumatoid Arthritis Diffuse Idiopathic Skeletal Hyperostosis (DAVI) ... RADISH
Rheumatoid Arthritis Factor [*Medicine*] (MAE) ... RAF
Rheumatoid Arthritis Nuclear Antigen [*Immunology*] ... RANA
Rheumatoid Arthritis Serum [*Factor*] [*Medicine*] ... RAS
Rheumatoid Factor [*Also known as IgM*] [*Immunology*] ... RF
Rheumatoid Factor-Like Activity [*Immunology*] (MAE) ... RFLA
Rheumatoid Factor-Like Substance [*Immunology*] (MAE) ... RFLS
Rheumatoid Spondylitis [*Medicine*] (DAVI) ... RS
Rheumatology (DAVI) ... RH
Rheumatology (DAVI) ... RHEU
Rheumatology [*Medical specialty*] (DHSM) ... RHU
Rhinal Fissure [*Anatomy*] ... RF
Rhine Air [*ICAO designator*] (AD) ... WU
Rhine Air AG [*Sweden ICAO designator*] (ICDA) ... KF
Rhine Evacuation and Control Command [*NATO*] (NATG) ... RECC
Rhine River and Basin [*MARC geographic area code Library of Congress*] (LCCP) ... er----
Rhine River Field Organization [*Post-World War II*] ... RRFO
Rhinelander [*Wisconsin*] [*Airport symbol*] (OAG) ... RHI
Rhinelander Public Library, Rhinelander, WI [*Library symbol Library of Congress*] (LCLS) ... WRh
Rhinelander Rabbit Club of America (EA) ... RRCA
Rhinelander, WI [*FM radio station call letters*] ... WHDG
Rhinelander, WI [*Television station call letters*] ... WJFW
Rhinelander, WI [*AM radio station call letters*] ... WOBT
Rhinelander, WI [*FM radio station call letters*] ... WRHN
Rhinelander, WI [*FM radio station call letters*] ... WXPR
Rhinitis [*Medicine*] ... R
Rhinitis [*Medicine*] ... RH
Rhino Resources [*Vancouver Stock Exchange symbol*] ... RNO
Rhinoceros (ROG) ... RH
Rhinoceros (DSUE) ... RHINO
Rhinology [*Medicine*] (DHSM) ... RHI
Rhinology [*Medicine*] ... Rhin
Rhinology [*Medicine*] ... RHINOL
Rhinoseptoplasty [*Otorhinolaryngology*] (DAVI) ... RSP
Rhipicephalus [*A genus of cattle tick*] (DAVI) ... Rh
Rhizobium [*A bacterium*] (DAVI) ... Rhiz
Rhizoctonia [*A fungus*] ... R
Rhizoctonia-Like Fungus ... RLF
Rhizome [*Botany*] ... Rz
Rhizomucor Meihei Lipase [*An enzyme*] ... RML
Rho (NUCP) ... R
Rho/Theta ... R/T
Rhoades Aviation, Inc. [*ICAO designator*] (FAAC) ... RDS
Rhodamine Isothiocyanate [*Biochemistry*] ... RhITC
Rhodamine Isothiocyanate [*Biochemistry*] ... RITC
Rhode Island [*MARC geographic area code Library of Congress*] (LCCP) ... n-us-ri
Rhode Island ... RHI
Rhode Island [*Postal code*] ... RI
Rhode Island [*MARC country of publication code Library of Congress*] (LCCP) ... riu
Rhode Island Agricultural Experiment Station [*University of Rhode Island*] [*Research center*] (RCD) ... RIAES
Rhode Island Atomic Energy Commission ... RIAEC
Rhode Island Board of Railroad Commission Reports [*A publication*] (DLA) ... RI Bd RC
Rhode Island Business Educators Association (EDAC) ... RIBEA
Rhode Island College (GAGS) ... Rhode Island C
Rhode Island College, Providence, RI [*OCLC symbol*] (OCLC) ... RCM
Rhode Island College, Providence, RI [*Library symbol Library of Congress*] (LCLS) ... RPRC
Rhode Island Compilation of Rules of State Agencies [*A publication*] (DLA) ... RI Comp of Rules of St Agencies
Rhode Island Constitution [*A publication*] (DLA) ... RI Const
Rhode Island Court Records [*A publication*] (DLA) ... RI Ct Rec
Rhode Island Decisions [*A publication*] (DLA) ... RI Dec
Rhode Island Department of State Library Services, Providence, RI [*OCLC symbol*] (OCLC) ... RDS
Rhode Island Department of State Library Services, Providence, RI [*Library symbol Library of Congress*] (LCLS) ... RPSL
Rhode Island Government Register [*A publication*] (AAGC) ... RIGR
Rhode Island Historical Society, George L. Shepley Collection, Providence, RI [*Library symbol Library of Congress*] (LCLS) ... RHi-Sh
Rhode Island Historical Society Library, Providence, RI [*OCLC symbol*] (OCLC) ... RHI
Rhode Island Historical Society, Providence, RI [*Library symbol Library of Congress*] (LCLS) ... RHi
Rhode Island Hospital, Peters House Medical Library, Providence, RI [*Library symbol Library of Congress*] (LCLS) ... RPH
Rhode Island Hospital, Providence, RI [*OCLC symbol*] (OCLC) ... RIH
Rhode Island Junior College [*Later, CCRI*] ... RIJC
Rhode Island Junior College, Knight Campus, Warwick, RI [*Library symbol Library of Congress*] (LCLS) ... RWarR
Rhode Island Library Film Cooperative [*Library network*] ... RILFC
Rhode Island Medical Society, Providence, RI [*Library symbol Library of Congress*] (LCLS) ... RPM
Rhode Island Open Pool Reactor ... RIOPR
Rhode Island Pupil Identification Scale [*Psychology*] ... RIPIS
Rhode Island Red [*Poultry*] ... RIR
Rhode Island Red Club of America (EA) ... RIRCA
Rhode Island Reports [*A publication*] (DLA) ... Rh I
Rhode Island Reports [*A publication*] (DLA) ... Rhode Island Rep
Rhode Island Reports [*A publication*] (DLA) ... RI Rep
Rhode Island School of Design (GAGS) ... Rhode Island Sch Design
Rhode Island School of Design ... RISD
Rhode Island School of Design, Providence, RI [*Library symbol Library of Congress*] (LCLS) ... RPD
Rhode Island State Archives, Providence, RI [*Library symbol Library of Congress*] (LCLS) ... R-Ar
Rhode Island State Law Library, Providence, RI [*Library symbol Library of Congress*] (LCLS) ... RPL
Rhode Island State Library, Providence, RI [*Library symbol Library of Congress*] (LCLS) ... R
Rhode Island Superior Court (DLA) ... Super Ct (RI)
Rhode Island Supreme Court Reports [*A publication*] (DLA) ... Rh I

Rhode Island Supreme Court Reports [*A publication*] (ILCA) ..... RI
Rhode Island Test of Language Structure ..... RITLS
Rhodes [*Greece*] [*Seismograph station code, US Geological Survey Closed*] (SEIS) ..... RHO
Rhodes 19 Class Association (EA) R-19/CA
Rhodes Bantam Class Association (EA) ..... RBCA
Rhodes, Inc. [*NYSE symbol*] (SPSG) ..... RHD
Rhodes, Inc. [*Associated Press*] (SAG) ..... Rhodes
Rhodes Island [*Greece*] [*Airport symbol*] (OAG) ..... RHO
Rhodes Scholar ..... RHSCH
Rhodesia [*Southern Rhodesia*] [*MARC geographic area code Library of Congress*] (LCCP) ..... f-rh--
Rhodesia [*Later, Zimbabwe*] (ROG) ..... R
Rhodesia [*Southern Rhodesia*] [*MARC country of publication code Library of Congress*] (LCCP) ..... rh
Rhodesia [*Later, Zimbabwe*] ..... RHO
Rhodesia ..... Rhod
Rhodesia & Nyasaland Airways ..... RANA
Rhodesia and Nyasaland Army Educational Corps [*British military*] (DMA) ..... RNAEC
Rhodesia and Nyasaland Court of Appeal Law Reports [*A publication*] (DLA) ..... RNCA
Rhodesia and Nyasaland Law Journal [*A publication*] (DLA) ..... RNLJ
Rhodesia and Nyasaland Law Reports [*1956*] [*A publication*] (DLA) ..... R & N
Rhodesia and Nyasaland Law Reports [*1956-64*] [*A publication*] (DLA) ..... R & NLR
Rhodesia Broadcasting Corp. ..... RBC
Rhodesia Railway Workers' Union ..... RRWU
Rhodesia Regiment [*British military*] (DMA) ..... RR
Rhodesian African Rifles [*Military unit*] ..... RAR
Rhodesian Air Askari Corps [*British military*] (DMA) ..... RAAC
Rhodesian Air Training Centre [*British military*] (DMA) ..... RATC
Rhodesian Air Training Group [*British military*] (DMA) ..... RATG
Rhodesian Court of Appeal Law Reports [*1939-46*] [*A publication*] (DLA) ..... Rh CA
Rhodesian Financial Gazette [*A publication*] ..... RFG
Rhodesian Front [*Later, Republican Front*] ..... RF
Rhodesian Government Party ..... RGP
Rhodesian Law Journal [*A publication*] (DLA) ..... Rh LJ
Rhodesian Law Journal [*A publication*] (DLA) ..... Rhodesian LJ
Rhodesian Law Journal [*A publication*] (DLA) ..... RLJ
Rhodesian Lawn Tennis Association ..... RLTA
Rhodesian Light Infantry [*Military unit*] ..... RLI
Rhodesian Ridgeback Club of the US (EA) ..... RRCUS
Rhodesian Television (AF) ..... RTV
Rhodian Law [*A publication*] (DLA) ..... Rho L
Rhodium [*Symbol is Rh*] [*Chemical element*] (ROG) ..... R
Rhodium [*Chemical element*] ..... Rh
Rhodium [*Chemistry*] ..... RHOD
Rhodium [*Correct symbol is Rh*] [*Chemical element*] ..... Ro
Rhodium Plate (MSA) ..... RH PL
Rhodium-Iron Resistance Thermometer ..... RIRT
Rhododendron Species Foundation (EA) ..... RSF
Rhodopseudomonas Virides [*A bacterium*] ..... rps
Rhodopsin [*Visual purple*] ..... R
Rhodopsin [*Visual Purple*] ..... Rh
Rhodopsin [*Optics*] [*Genetics*] (DOG) ..... RHO
Rhodopsin Kinase [*An enzyme*] ..... RK
Rhombic [*Antenna*] ..... RHO
Rhomboid [*Muscle*] [*Anatomy*] (DAVI) ..... rhom
Rhomboid [*Mathematics*] ..... RHOMB
Rhomboidal Air Controller (PDAA) ..... RAC
Rhonavia [*France ICAO designator*] (FAAC) ..... RHN
Rhonchi [*Rales*] [*Latin*] (MAE) ..... rh
Rhondda & Swansea Bay Railway [*Wales*] ..... RSB
Rhone Poulenc Overseas Ltd. [*Associated Press*] (SAG) ..... RhPOv
Rhone Poulence Overseas Ltd. [*Associated Press*] (SAG) ..... RhPOv
Rhone-Poul Overseas 8.125% Pref [*NYSE symbol*] (TTSB) ..... RPoPrA
Rhone-Poulenc [*France*] [*Research code symbol*] ..... AN
Rhone-Poulenc [*France*] [*Research code symbol*] ..... RP
Rhone-Poulenc ADR [*NYSE symbol*] (TTSB) ..... RP
Rhone-Poulenc Co. [*NYSE symbol*] (SAG) ..... RP
Rhone-Poulenc, Inc. [*Associated Press*] (SAG) ..... RhnPl
Rhone-Poulenc Overseas [*NYSE symbol*] (SPSG) ..... RPO
Rhone-Poulenc Pharma, Inc., Montreal, PQ, Canada [*Library symbol*] [*Library of Congress*] (LCLS) ..... CaQMRP
Rhone-Poulenc Pharma, Inc., Montreal, Quebec [*Library symbol National Library of Canada*] (NLC) ..... QMRP
Rhone-Poulenc Rorer [*NYSE symbol*] (SPSG) ..... RPR
Rhone-Poulenc SA (MHDW) ..... RHPOY
Rhone-Poulenc Systems (NITA) ..... RPS
Rhopalosiphum padi Virus ..... RPV
Rhoplex (VRA) ..... rplx
Rhumb Line ..... RL
Rhumbline Track [*Aviation*] (FAAC) ..... RLTK
Rhymney Railway [*Wales*] ..... RR
Rhyolite Resources [*Vancouver Stock Exchange symbol*] ..... RHY
RHYS Industries Ltd. [*Vancouver Stock Exchange symbol*] ..... RHV
Rhythm ..... R
Rhythm and Blues [*Music*] ..... R & B
Rhythm and Blues [*Music*] (BARN) ..... r'n'b
Rhythm and Blues Rock and Roll Society [*Later, RBRRSI*] (EA) ..... RBRRS
Rhythm and Blues Rock and Roll Society, Inc. (EA) ..... RBRRSI
Rhythm Strip [*Electrocardiogram*] (CPH) ..... RS
Rhythmic Motor Activity [*Physiology*] ..... RMA
Rhythmic Slow Activity [*Electroencephalography*] ..... RSA
Rhythmica [*of Aristoxenus*] [*Classical studies*] (OCD) ..... Rhythm
Ri Yue Tan [*China*] [*ICAO location identifier*] (ICLI) ..... RCSM
Rial [*Monetary unit*] [*Iran, Saudi Arabia, etc.*] ..... R
Rial [*Monetary unit*] [*Iran, Saudi Arabia, etc.*] ..... RL
Rib Cage [*Anatomy*] ..... RC
Rib Structure Station [*NASA*] (MCD) ..... RSS
Ribbed (AAG) ..... RIB
Ribbed Smoke Sheet [*Natural rubber*] ..... RSS
Ribbed Vault (VRA) ..... rib vlt
Ribbon (MSA) ..... RBN
Ribbon Bridge Erection Boat (MCD) ..... RBEB
Ribbon Bridge Transporter (MCD) ..... RBT
Ribbon-Frame Camera (MUGU) ..... RC
Ribbon-to-Ribbon (IAA) ..... RIR
Ribbon-to-Ribbon Regrowth [*of silicon for photovoltaic cells*] ..... RTR
Ribbonwork (VRA) ..... ribnwk
Ribeirao Preto [*Brazil*] [*Airport symbol*] (OAG) ..... RAO
Ribeirao Preto/Leite Lopes [*Brazil ICAO location identifier*] (ICLI) ..... SBRP
Riberac-Saint-Aulaye [*France ICAO location identifier*] (ICLI) ..... LFIK
Riberalta [*Bolivia*] [*Airport symbol*] (OAG) ..... RIB
Riberalta [*Bolivia*] [*Seismograph station code, US Geological Survey Closed*] (SEIS) ..... RTA
Riberalta [*Bolivia*] [*ICAO location identifier*] (ICLI) ..... SLRI
Ribgrass Mosaic Virus [*Plant pathology*] ..... RMV
Ribi ImmunoChem Res [*NASDAQ symbol*] (TTSB) ..... RIBI
Ribi Immunochem Research, Inc. [*NASDAQ symbol*] (NQ) ..... RIBI
Ribi Immunochem Research, Inc. [*Associated Press*] (SAG) ..... Ribilm
Ribitol [*or Ribityl*] [*Biochemistry*] ..... Rby
Riboflavin [*Pharmacology*] (DAVI) ..... B_2
Riboflavin [*Biochemistry*] ..... RF
Riboflavin Carrier Protein [*Immunology*] ..... RCP
Riboflavin-Binding Protein [*Biochemistry*] ..... RBP
Ribofuranosyltriazolecarboxamide [*Ribavirin*] [*Antiviral compound*] ..... RTCA
Ribonuclease [*An enzyme*] ..... RNase
Ribonuclease Inhibitor ..... RI
Ribonuclease Inhibitor [*Biochemistry*] ..... RNasin
Ribonuclease S [*An enzyme*] ..... RNS
Ribonuclease-P [*An enzyme*] ..... RNaseP
Ribonucleic Acid [*Biochemistry, genetics*] ..... RNA
Ribonucleic Acid [*A publication*] ..... RNA
Ribonucleic Acid, Chromosomal [*Biochemistry, genetics*] ..... cRNA
Ribonucleic Acid, Complementary [*Biochemistry, genetics*] ..... cRNA
Ribonucleic Acid, Diverse [*Biochemistry, genetics*] ..... dRNA
Ribonucleic Acid, H-Chain Messenger [*Biochemistry, genetics*] ..... H-mRNA
Ribonucleic Acid, Heavy Ribosomal [*Biochemistry, genetics*] ..... hrRNA
Ribonucleic Acid, Heterogeneous [*Biochemistry, genetics*] ..... hRNA
Ribonucleic Acid, Heterogeneous Nuclear [*Biochemistry, genetics*] ..... hnRNA
Ribonucleic Acid, Immune [*Biochemistry, genetics*] ..... I-RNA
Ribonucleic Acid, Light Ribosomal [*Biochemistry, genetics*] ..... lrRNA
Ribonucleic Acid, Messenger [*Biochemistry, genetics*] ..... mRNA
Ribonucleic Acid, Messenger - lac operon [*Biochemistry, genetics*] ..... lac-mRNA
Ribonucleic Acid, Messenger - Tryptophan Constitutive [*Biochemistry, genetics*] ..... Trp-mRNA
Ribonucleic Acid, Mini-Exon-Derived [*Biochemistry, genetics*] ..... medRNA
Ribonucleic Acid, Mitochondrial [*Biochemistry, genetics*] ..... mtRNA
Ribonucleic Acid, Nuclear [*Biochemistry, genetics*] ..... nRNA
Ribonucleic Acid Polymerase [*An enzyme*] ..... RNAP
Ribonucleic Acid Polymerase II [*An enzyme*] ..... RNAPII
Ribonucleic Acid, Polysomal [*Biochemistry, genetics*] ..... pRNA
Ribonucleic Acid, Ribosomal [*Biochemistry, genetics*] ..... rRNA
Ribonucleic Acid, Small Nuclear [*Biochemistry, genetics*] ..... snRNA
Ribonucleic Acid, Soluble [*Replaced by tRNA*] [*Biochemistry, genetics*] ..... sRNA
Ribonucleic Acid, Transfer [*Replaces sRNA*] [*Biochemistry, genetics*] ..... tRNA
Ribonucleic Acid, Transfer - Alanyl [*Biochemistry, genetics*] ..... Ala-tRNA
Ribonucleic Acid, Transfer - Aminoacyl [*or Aminoacylated*] [*Biochemistry, genetics*] ..... AA-tRNA
Ribonucleic Acid, Transfer - Formylmethionyl [*Biochemistry, genetics*] ..... fMet-tRNA
Ribonucleoprotein [*Biochemistry*] ..... RNP
Ribonucleoprotein, Heterogeneous [*Biochemistry*] ..... hnRNP
Ribonucleoprotein, Messenger [*Biochemistry*] ..... mRNP
RibonuCleoprotein Particle [*Biochemistry*] ..... RNB
Ribonucleoprotein, Small Cytoplasmic ..... scRNP
Ribonucleoprotein, Small Nuclear [*Biochemistry*] ..... snRNP
Ribonucleoside Diphosphate Reductase [*An enzyme*] ..... RDR
Ribonucleoside Triphosphate [*Biochemistry*] ..... rNTP
Ribonucleoside Triphosphate Reductase [*An enzyme*] ..... RTPR
Ribonucleotide Reductase [*An enzyme*] ..... RNR
Ribophosphate Pyrophosphokinase [*An enzyme*] ..... RPK
Ribos Phosphate [*Laboratory science*] (DAVI) ..... RP
Ribose [*One-letter symbol; see Rib*] ..... r
Ribose [*Also, r*] [*A sugar*] ..... Rib
Ribose Binding Protein [*Biochemistry*] ..... RBP
Ribose-5-Phosphate [*Biochemistry*] (MAE) R-5-P
Ribosephosphate Kinase (DMAA) ..... RPK
Ribosomal [*Protein*] [*Cytology*] ..... RI
Ribosomal DNA [*Deoxyribonucleic Acid*] [*Marine science*] (OSRA) ..... rDNA
Ribosomal DNA [*Deoxyribonucleic Acid*] (USDC) ..... rDNA
Ribosomal Gene Cluster [*Genetics*] ..... RGC
Ribosomal Protein [*Biochemistry*] ..... RP
Ribosome Binding Site [*Biochemistry*] ..... RBS
Ribosome Inactivating [*or Inhibiting*] **Protein** [*Biochemistry*] ..... RIP
Ribosome-Lamella Complex [*Physiology*] ..... RLC
Ribosome-Like Particle [*Cytology*] ..... RLP

Ribosome-Nascent Chain [*Biochemistry*] .... RNC
Ribothymidine [*One-letter symbol; see Thd*] .... T
Ribothymidine [*Also, T*] [*A nucleoside*] .... Thd
Ribozyme Pharmaceuticals [*NASDAQ symbol*] (TTSB) .... RZYM
Ribozyme Pharmaceuticals, Inc. [*Associated Press*] (SAG) .... Ribozym
Ribozyme Pharmaceuticals, Inc. [*NASDAQ symbol*] (SAG) .... RZYM
Ribs of Reinforced Shotcrete [*Engineering*] .... RRS
Ribulose [*Biochemistry*] .... Rbu
Ribulose Bisphosphate Carboxylase/Oxygenase (DOG) .... rbc
Ribulosebisphosphate [*Also, RDP*] [*Biochemistry*] .... RuBP
Ribulosebisphosphate Carboxylase [*Also, RUBISCO*] [*An enzyme*] .... RBPCase
Ribulosebisphosphate Carboxylase [*An enzyme*] .... RuBPCase
Ribulosebisphosphate Carboxylase/Oxygenase [*An enzyme*] .... RUBISCO
Ribulosebisphosphate Carboxylase/Oxygenase [*Also, RUBISCO*] [*An enzyme*] .... RuBPC/O
Ribulosediphosphate [*Also, RuBP*] [*Biochemistry*] .... RDP
Rib-Vertebra Angle [*Anatomy*] .... RVA
Rib-Vertebra Angle Difference [*Anatomy*] .... RVAD
RIC, Inc. [*ICAO designator*] (FAAC) .... SDD
Ricardus [*Authority cited in pre-1607 legal work*] (DSA) .... Ricar
Ricardus Anglicus [*Deceased, 1242*] [*Authority cited in pre-1607 legal work*] (DSA) .... R
Ricardus Anglicus [*Deceased, 1242*] [*Authority cited in pre-1607 legal work*] (DSA) .... Ri
Ricardus Malumbra [*Deceased, 1334*] [*Authority cited in pre-1607 legal work*] (DSA) .... Ric
Ricardus Petronius de Senis [*Deceased, 1314*] [*Authority cited in pre-1607 legal work*] (DSA) .... R de S
Ricardus Rufulus [*Authority cited in pre-1607 legal work*] (DSA) .... Ric Ruf
Rice, Applesauce, and Banana [*Diet*] (DAVI) .... RAB
Rice Association [*British*] (DBA) .... RA
Rice Black-Streaked Dwarf Virus [*Plant pathology*] .... RBSDV
Rice Blast Disease [*Fungal disease of crop plants*] .... RBD
Rice Council for Market Development (EA) .... RCMD
Rice Dwarf Virus [*Plant pathology*] .... RDV
Rice Elementary School, Rice, MN [*Library symbol*] [*Library of Congress*] (LCLS) .... MnRiE
Rice Export Association .... REA
Rice Flour (OA) .... RF
Rice Gall Dwarf Virus [*Plant pathology*] .... RGDV
Rice Genome Research Program [*Japan*] .... RGP
Rice Grassy Stunt Virus [*Plant pathology*] .... RGSTV
Rice Hoja Blanca Virus [*Plant pathology*] .... RHBV
Rice Husk Ash (PDAA) .... RHA
Rice Industry Coordination Committee [*New South Wales, Australia*] .... RICC
Rice Lake [*Wisconsin*] [*Airport symbol*] (OAG) .... RIE
Rice Lake Public Library, Rice Lake, WI [*Library symbol Library of Congress*] (LCLS) .... WRI
Rice Lake, WI [*AM radio station call letters*] .... WAQE
Rice Lake, WI [*FM radio station call letters*] .... WAQE-FM
Rice Lake, WI [*AM radio station call letters*] .... WJMC
Rice Lake, WI [*FM radio station call letters*] .... WJMC-FM
Rice Marketing Board of New South Wales [*Australia*] .... RMBNSW
Rice Marketing Board of Queensland [*Australia*] .... RMBQ
Rice Memorial Hospital, Willmar, MN [*Library symbol*] [*Library of Congress*] (LCLS) .... MnWilH
Rice Millers' Association (EA) .... RMA
Rice Necrosis Mosaic Virus [*Plant pathology*] .... RNMV
Rice Polishing Concentrate (OA) .... RPC
Rice Ragged Stunt Virus [*Plant pathology*] .... RRSV
Rice, Ramsperger, Kassel, Marcus [*Developers of a theorem in chemical kinetics, designated by the initial letters of their last names*] .... RRKM
Rice Research and Extension Center [*University of Arkansas*] [*Research center*] (RCD) .... RREC
Rice Stripe Virus [*Plant pathology*] .... RSTV
Rice Transitory Yellowing Virus [*Plant pathology*] .... RTYV
Rice Tungro Bacilliform Virus [*Plant pathology*] .... RTBV
Rice Tungro Isometric Virus [*Plant pathology*] .... RTIV
Rice Tungro Virus .... RTV
Rice University (GAGS) .... Rice U
Rice University, Fondren Library, Houston, TX [*OCLC symbol*] (OCLC) .... RCE
Rice University, Houston, TX [*Library symbol Library of Congress*] (LCLS) .... TxHR
Rice Yellow Mottle Virus [*Plant pathology*] .... RYMV
Ricegrowers' Association of Australia .... RAA
Ricegrowers' Cooperative Ltd. [*Australia*] .... RCL
Riceland Mosquito Management Plan [*Department of Agriculture*] .... RMMP
Rice's Code of Practice [*Colorado*] [*A publication*] (DLA) .... Rice's Code
Rice's Digest of Patent Office Decisions [*A publication*] (DLA) .... Rice Dig
Rice's Law of Evidence [*A publication*] (DLA) .... Rice Ev
Rice's South Carolina Equity Reports [*A publication*] (DLA) .... Rice Ch
Rice's South Carolina Equity Reports [*1838-39*] [*A publication*] (DLA) .... Rice Eq
Rice's South Carolina Law Reports [*1838-39*] [*A publication*] (DLA) .... Rice
Rice's South Carolina Law Reports [*A publication*] (DLA) .... Rice L (SC)
Riceville Record, Riceville, IA [*Library symbol Library of Congress*] (LCLS) .... IaRiR
Rich & Rare Canadian Whisky [*Gooderham's*] .... R & R
Rich Best Torque [*Automotive engineering*] .... RBT
Rich Bitch [*Slang*] .... RB
Rich Capital Corp. [*Vancouver Stock Exchange symbol*] .... RCQ
Rich Coast Res Ltd [*NASDAQ symbol*] (TTSB) .... KRHCF
Rich Coast Resouces [*NASDAQ symbol*] (SAG) .... KRHCF
Rich Coast Resources [*Associated Press*] (SAG) .... RichCst
Rich Coast Sulphur Ltd. [*Vancouver Stock Exchange symbol*] .... RCS
Rich Cut Virginia [*Tobacco*] (ROG) .... RCV
Rich International Airways, Inc. [*ICAO designator*] (FAAC) .... RIA
Rich International Airways, Inc. [*Air carrier designation symbol*] .... RIAX
Rich International White Trash [*Lifestyle classification*] .... Riwt
Rich Man, Poor Man [*Book title*] .... RMPM
Rich Resources Ltd. [*Vancouver Stock Exchange symbol*] .... RCH
Rich Text Format [*Computer science*] (BYTE) .... RTF
Rich Text Format [*Computer science*] .... rtf
Rich Urban Biker [*Lifestyle classification*] .... RUB
Rich Valley Public Library, Alberta [*Library symbol National Library of Canada*] (NLC) .... ARV
Richard Austen Butler [*1902-1982*] [*In book title "RAB: The Life of R. A. Butler"*] .... RAB
Richard D. Siegrest [*Alaska*] [*Seismograph station code, US Geological Survey*] (SEIS) .... RDS
Richard Eden Fan Club (EA) .... REFC
Richard Gimbel Foundation for Literary Research, Philadelphia, PA [*Library symbol Library of Congress Obsolete*] (LCLS) .... PPRGF
Richard H. Thornton Memorial Library, Oxford, NC [*Library symbol Library of Congress*] (LCLS) .... NcOG
Richard Hatch Fan Club (EA) .... RHFC
Richard Hatch Fan Fellowship [*Defunct*] (EAIO) .... RHFF
Richard II [*Shakespearean work*] R2
Richard III [*Shakespearean work*] R3
Richard J. Daley College, Chicago, IL [*Library symbol*] [*Library of Congress*] (LCLS) .... ICRD
Richard Jeffries Society (EAIO) .... RJS
Richard (King of England) (DLA) .... R
Richard (King of England) (DLA) .... Ric
Richard (King of England) (DLA) .... Rich
Richard Milhous Nixon [*US president, 1913-*] .... RMN
Richard Nixon [*In book title "RN - The Memoirs of Richard Nixon"*] .... RN
Richard of Cashel [*Pseudonym used by Richard Laurence*] .... RC
Richard Salter Storrs Library, Longmeadow, MA [*Library symbol Library of Congress*] (LCLS) .... MLon
Richard Stockton State College, Pomona, NJ [*Library symbol Library of Congress*] (LCLS) .... NjPoR
Richards Aviation, Inc. [*ICAO designator*] (FAAC) .... RVC
Richard's Bay [*South Africa*] [*ICAO location identifier*] (ICLI) .... FARB
Richards Bay [*South Africa*] [*Airport symbol*] (OAG) .... RCB
Richardson and Hook's Street Railway Decisions [*A publication*] (DLA) .... Rich & H
Richardson and Sayles' Select Cases of Procedure without Writ [*Selden Society Publication 60*] [*A publication*] (DLA) .... Rich & S
Richardson and Woodbury's Reports [*2 New Hampshire*] [*A publication*] (DLA) .... Rich & W
Richardson Boat Owners Association (EA) .... RBOA
Richardson Electr [*NASDAQ symbol*] (TTSB) .... RELL
Richardson Electronics Ltd. [*NASDAQ symbol*] (NQ) .... RELL
Richardson Electronics Ltd. [*Associated Press*] (SAG) .... RichEl
Richardson Emergency Psychodiagnostic Summary [*Psychology*] .... REP
Richardson Number [*Physics*] .... Ri
Richardson Public Library, Richardson, TX [*Library symbol Library of Congress*] (LCLS) .... TxRi
Richardson Securities of Canada, Winnipeg, Manitoba [*Library symbol National Library of Canada*] (NLC) .... MWRS
Richardson Securities of Canada, Winnipeg, MB, Canada [*Library symbol Library of Congress*] (LCLS) .... CaMWRS
Richardson-Merrell, Inc. [*Later, Richardson-Vicks, Inc.*] .... RMI
Richardson's Airway, Inc. [*ICAO designator*] (FAAC) .... RIC
Richardson's Attorney's Practice in the Court of King's Bench [*8th ed.*] [*1792*] [*A publication*] (DLA) .... Rich Pr KB
Richardson's Chancery Practice [*1838*] [*A publication*] (DLA) .... Rich Ch Pr
Richardson's Court of Claims Reports [*A publication*] (DLA) .... Rich Ct Cl
Richardson's Establishing a Law Practice [*A publication*] (DLA) .... Richardson Law Practice
Richardson's Law of Testaments and Last Wills [*A publication*] (DLA) .... Rich Wills
Richardson's New Dictionary of the English Language [*A publication*] (DLA) .... Rich Dict
Richardson's Practical Register of English Common Pleas [*A publication*] (DLA) .... Rich Pr Reg
Richardson's Practical Register of English Common Pleas [*A publication*] (DLA) .... Rich PRCP
Richardson's Practice Common Pleas [*England*] [*A publication*] (DLA) .... Rich CP
Richardson's Reports [*2-5 New Hampshire*] [*A publication*] (DLA) .... Rich
Richardson's Reports [*3-5 New Hampshire*] [*A publication*] (DLA) .... Rich NH
Richardson's Theological Word Book [*A publication*] (BJA) .... RTWB
Richardsons Westgarth [*Commercial firm British*] .... RW
Richard-Toll [*Senegal*] [*ICAO location identifier*] (ICLI) .... GOSR
Richard-Toll [*Senegal*] [*Airport symbol*] (OAG) .... RDT
Richey Electronics [*NASDAQ symbol*] (SAG) .... RCHY
Richey Electronics [*Associated Press*] (SAG) .... RichyEl
Richey Elementary School, Pasadena, TX [*Library symbol*] [*Library of Congress*] (LCLS) .... TxPRE
Richey's Irish Land Act [*A publication*] (DLA) .... Rich Land A
Richfield [*Utah*] [*Airport symbol*] (OAG) .... RIF
Richfield District Library, Richfield, ID [*Library symbol*] [*Library of Congress*] (LCLS) .... IdRi
Richfield, MN [*FM radio station call letters*] .... KDWB
Richfield, MN [*AM radio station call letters*] .... KEGE
Richfield Oil Corp., Economic Research Department, Los Angeles, CA [*Library symbol Library of Congress*] (LCLS) .... CLRO-E
Richfield Oil Corp., Research and Development Library, Anaheim, CA [*Library symbol Library of Congress*] (LCLS) .... CLRO-R
Richfield Oil Corp., Technical Library, Wilmington, CA [*Library symbol Library of Congress*] (LCLS) .... CLRO-T

Richfield Township Public Library, St. Helen, MI [*Library symbol Library of Congress*] (LCLS) .... MiSthe
Richfield, UT [*FM radio station call letters*] .... KKWZ
Richfield, UT [*AM radio station call letters*] .... KSVC
Richfield, UT [*Location identifier FAA*] (FAAL) .... RIF
Richfood Hldgs [*NASDAQ symbol*] (TTSB) .... RCHF
Richfood Holdings, Inc. [*NASDAQ symbol*] (NQ) .... RCHF
Richfood Holdings, Inc. [*Associated Press*] (SAG) .... Richfood
Richland [*Washington*] [*Airport symbol Obsolete*] (OAG) .... RLD
Richland Aviation [*ICAO designator*] (FAAC) .... RCA
Richland Center, WI [*AM radio station call letters*] .... WRCO
Richland Center, WI [*FM radio station call letters*] .... WRCO-FM
Richland College, Dallas, TX [*Library symbol Library of Congress*] (LCLS) .... TxDaR
Richland Community Library, Richland, MI [*Library symbol Library of Congress*] (LCLS) .... MiRicl
Richland County Library, Columbia, SC [*Library symbol Library of Congress*] (LCLS) .... ScCoR
Richland County Library, Columbia, SC [*OCLC symbol*] (OCLC) .... SRC
Richland Mine, Inc. [*Vancouver Stock Exchange symbol*] .... RHL
Richland, MS [*AM radio station call letters*] (RBYB) .... WWDF
Richland Operations Office [*Energy Research and Development Administration*] .... RL
Richland Operations Office [*Energy Research and Development Administration*] .... RLO
Richland Operations Office [*Energy Research and Development Administration*] .... ROO
Richland Parish Library, Rayville, LA [*Library symbol Library of Congress*] (LCLS) .... LRaR
Richland Plainsman, Richland, IA [*Library symbol Library of Congress*] (LCLS) .... IaRicP
Richland Press, Mellott, IN [*Library symbol Library of Congress*] (LCLS) .... InMelRP
Richland Public Library, Richland, WA [*Library symbol Library of Congress*] (LCLS) .... WaRi
Richland, WA [*AM radio station call letters*] .... KALE
Richland, WA [*FM radio station call letters*] .... KEGX
Richland, WA [*FM radio station call letters*] .... KFAE
Richland, WA [*FM radio station call letters*] .... KIOK
Richland, WA [*Television station call letters*] .... KNDU
Richland, WA [*FM radio station call letters*] .... KORD-FM
Richland, WA [*Television station call letters*] .... KTNW
Richland, WA [*Commercial waste site*] (GAAI) .... RICH
Richlands, VA [*AM radio station call letters*] (RBYB) .... WGTH
Richlands, VA [*FM radio station call letters*] .... WGTH-FM
Richlands, VA [*AM radio station call letters*] .... WRIC
Richlands, VA [*FM radio station call letters*] .... WRIC-FM
Richmark Resources Ltd. [*Vancouver Stock Exchange symbol*] .... RM
Richmond [*Australia ICAO location identifier*] (ICLI) .... ASRI
Richmond [*Branch in the Federal Reserve Regional banking system*] (BARN) .... E
Richmond [*Australia Airport symbol*] (OAG) .... RCM
Richmond [*Diocesan abbreviation*] [*Virginia*] (TOCD) .... RIC
Richmond [*Virginia*] [*Airport symbol*] .... RIC
Richmond [*Florida*] [*Seismograph station code, US Geological Survey Closed*] (SEIS) .... RIC
Richmond Academy of Medicine, Richmond, VA [*Library symbol Library of Congress*] (LCLS) .... ViRA
Richmond Academy of Medicine, Richmond, VA [*Library symbol*] [*Library of Congress*] (LCLS) .... ViRAM
Richmond Area Film Cooperative [*Library network*] .... RAFC
Richmond Area Library Directors [*Library network*] .... RALD
Richmond, BC [*AM radio station call letters*] .... CISL
Richmond - Cape Henry Environmental Laboratory [*NASA/USGS*] .... RICHEL
Richmond City Library, Richmond, UT [*Library symbol Library of Congress*] (LCLS) .... URi
Richmond City Library, Richmond, UT [*Library symbol*] [*Library of Congress*] (LCLS) .... URiL
Richmond College, Staten Island, NY [*Library symbol Library of Congress Obsolete*] (LCLS) .... NSiRC
Richmond Community School, Richmond, IN [*Library symbol Library of Congress*] (LCLS) .... InRCS
Richmond Community Schools, Richmond, IN [*OCLC symbol*] (OCLC) .... IRT
Richmond Contract Management District (SAA) .... RICMD
Richmond County Historical Society [*Societe d'Histoire du Comte de Richmond*] **Melbourne, Quebec** (NLC) .... QMRCH
Richmond County Law Library, Augusta, GA [*Library symbol Library of Congress*] (LCLS) .... GAuRC
Richmond Elementary School, Richmond, MN [*Library symbol*] [*Library of Congress*] (LCLS) .... MnRmE
Richmond Fellowship (EAIO) .... RF
Richmond Fellowship International [*British*] (EAIO) .... RFI
Richmond, Fredericksburg & Potomac Railroad Co. [*AAR code*] .... RFP
Richmond Guano Co., Richmond, VA [*Library symbol Library of Congress*] (LCLS) .... ViRG
Richmond Heights Memorial Library, Richmond Heights, MO [*Library symbol Library of Congress*] (LCLS) .... MoRih
Richmond Herald Ltd., Richmond, Surrey, United Kingdom [*Library symbol Library of Congress*] (LCLS) .... UkRiH
Richmond Hill, GA [*FM radio station call letters*] .... WRHQ
Richmond Hill, ON [*AM radio station call letters*] .... CHOG
Richmond Hill Public Library, Ontario [*Library symbol National Library of Canada*] (NLC) .... ORH
Richmond Hill Public Library, Richmond Hill, ON, Canada [*Library symbol Library of Congress*] (LCLS) .... CaORh
Richmond Hill School Company [*British military*] (DMA) .... RHSC
Richmond, IN [*Location identifier FAA*] (FAAL) .... RID
Richmond, IN [*FM radio station call letters*] .... WECI
Richmond, IN [*FM radio station call letters*] .... WFMG
Richmond, IN [*AM radio station call letters*] .... WKBV
Richmond, IN [*Television station call letters*] .... WKOI
Richmond, IN [*FM radio station call letters*] .... WQLK
Richmond, IN [*FM radio station call letters*] .... WVXR
Richmond International Raceway [*Auto racing*] .... RIR
Richmond, KY [*AM radio station call letters*] .... WCBR
Richmond, KY [*FM radio station call letters*] .... WEKU
Richmond, KY [*AM radio station call letters*] .... WEKY
Richmond, KY [*FM radio station call letters*] (RBYB) .... WLRO
Richmond Memorial Library, Batavia, NY [*Library symbol Library of Congress*] (LCLS) .... NBat
Richmond, MO [*FM radio station call letters*] .... KAYX
Richmond Museum and Archives, British Columbia [*Library symbol National Library of Canada*] (NLC) .... BRMA
Richmond Museum Association, Richmond, CA [*Library symbol*] [*Library of Congress*] (LCLS) .... CRicRM
Richmond National Battlefield Park .... RICH
Richmond Palladium-Item, Richmond, IN [*Library symbol Library of Congress*] (LCLS) .... InRPI
Richmond Professional Institute [*Virginia*] .... RPI
Richmond Public Library [*UTLAS symbol*] .... RPL
Richmond Public Library, British Columbia [*Library symbol National Library of Canada*] (NLC) .... BRI
Richmond Public Library, Richmond, BC, Canada [*Library symbol Library of Congress*] (LCLS) .... CaBRi
Richmond Public Library, Richmond, BC, Canada [*Library symbol*] [*Library of Congress*] (LCLS) .... CaBRi
Richmond Public Library, Richmond, CA [*Library symbol Library of Congress*] (LCLS) .... CRic
Richmond Public Library, Richmond, MI [*Library symbol Library of Congress*] (LCLS) .... MiRic
Richmond Public Library, Richmond, MN [*Library symbol*] [*Library of Congress*] (LCLS) .... MnRmP
Richmond Public Library, Richmond, VA [*Library symbol Library of Congress*] (LCLS) .... ViR
Richmond Public Library, Richmond, VA [*OCLC symbol*] (OCLC) .... VRP
Richmond Quartermaster Depot [*Virginia*] [*Merged with Defense General Supply Center*] .... RQMD
Richmond/Richard Evelyn Byrd International [*Virginia*] [*ICAO location identifier*] (ICLI) .... KRIC
Richmond Stock Exchange (IIA) .... RSE
Richmond Technical Institute, Hamlet, NC [*Library symbol Library of Congress*] (LCLS) .... NcHaR
Richmond Township Public Library, Palmer, MI [*Library symbol Library of Congress*] (LCLS) .... MiPal
Richmond, VA [*Location identifier FAA*] (FAAL) .... BNE
Richmond, VA [*Location identifier FAA*] (FAAL) .... RGJ
Richmond, VA [*FM radio station call letters*] .... WCVE
Richmond, VA [*Television station call letters*] .... WCVE-TV
Richmond, VA [*Television station call letters*] .... WCVW
Richmond, VA [*FM radio station call letters*] .... WDCE
Richmond, VA [*AM radio station call letters*] .... WFTH
Richmond, VA [*AM radio station call letters*] .... WLEE
Richmond, VA [*FM radio station call letters*] .... WMXB
Richmond, VA [*AM radio station call letters*] .... WREJ
Richmond, VA [*Television station call letters*] .... WRLH
Richmond, VA [*AM radio station call letters*] (RBYB) .... WRNL-AM
Richmond, VA [*AM radio station call letters*] .... WRVA
Richmond, VA [*AM radio station call letters*] .... WRVH
Richmond, VA [*FM radio station call letters*] .... WRVQ
Richmond, VA [*FM radio station call letters*] .... WRXL
Richmond, VA [*AM radio station call letters*] .... WTMM
Richmond, VA [*AM radio station call letters*] .... WTVR
Richmond, VA [*FM radio station call letters*] .... WTVR-FM
Richmond, VA [*Television station call letters*] .... WTVR-TV
Richmond, VA [*FM radio station call letters*] .... WVGO
Richmond, VA [*AM radio station call letters*] (RBYB) .... WVNZ-AM
Richmond, VA [*Television station call letters*] .... WWBT
Richmond, VA [*AM radio station call letters*] .... WXGI
Richport Resources Ltd. [*Vancouver Stock Exchange symbol*] .... RRO
Richtkreis [*Aiming Circle*] [*Gunnery term*] [*German military - World War II*] .... R
Richtlinien [*Instructions, Directions*] [*German*] (ILCA) .... RL
Richton International Corp. [*AMEX symbol*] (SPSG) .... RHT
Richton International Corp. [*Associated Press*] (SAG) .... Richton
Richton International Corp. (MHDW) .... RIHL
Richton Intl [*AMEX symbol*] (TTSB) .... RHT
Richton, MS [*FM radio station call letters*] .... WESV
Richton Park Library District, Richton Park, IL [*Library symbol Library of Congress*] (LCLS) .... IRp
Richview Township Public Library, Richview, IL [*Library symbol Library of Congress*] (LCLS) .... IRicv
Richwell Resources Ltd. [*Vancouver Stock Exchange symbol*] .... RWL
Richwood, LA [*FM radio station call letters*] .... KHLL
Richwood, OH [*FM radio station call letters*] (RBYB) .... WZJZ-FM
Richwood, WV [*AM radio station call letters*] .... WVAR
Ricinus communis Agglutinin [*Immunology*] .... RCA
Rick Lucus Helicopters Ltd. [*New Zealand*] [*FAA designator*] (FAAC) .... HPR
Rickards and Michael's English Locus Standi Reports [*A publication*] (DLA) .... Rick & M
Rickards and Saunders' English Locus Standi Reports [*1890-94*] [*A publication*] (DLA) .... Ric & S
Rickards and Saunders' English Locus Standi Reports [*A publication*] (DLA) .... Rick & S

Rickard's English Statutes [*A publication*] (DLA) .... Rick Eng St
Rickenbacker Air Force Base [*Ohio*] [*ICAO location identifier*] (ICLI) .... KLCK
Rickenbacker Air Force Base [*Formerly, Lockbourne Air Force Base*] [*Ohio*] .... RAFB
Rickenbacker Car Club of America (EA) .... RCCA
Rickettsia .... R
Rickettsial Battery [*Bacteriology*] (DAVI) .... RICK-A
Rickettsia-Like Bodies (CPH) .... RLB
Rickman Owners Club International (EA) .... ROCI
Ricks Cabaret International, Inc. [*NASDAQ symbol*] (SAG) .... RICK
Ricks Cabaret International, Inc. [*Associated Press*] (SAG) .... RickCab
Ricks Cabaret International, Inc. [*Associated Press*] (SAG) .... Ricks
Rick's Cabaret Intl [*NASDAQ symbol*] (TTSB) .... RICK
Rick's Cabaret Intl Wrrt [*NASDAQ symbol*] (TTSB) .... RICKW
Ricks College, David O. McKay Learning Resources Center, Rexburg, ID [*OCLC symbol*] (OCLC) .... RIC
Ricks College, Rexburg, ID [*Library symbol Library of Congress*] (LCLS) .... IdRR
Ricky and Vince Smith Fan Club (EA) .... RVSFC
Ricky Skaggs International Fan Club (EA) .... RSFC
Ricran [*Peru*] [*ICAO location identifier*] (ICLI) .... SPNR
Riddare af Wasa Order [*Knight of the Order of Vasa*] [*Sweden*] .... RWO
Riddell Sports [*NASDAQ symbol*] (TTSB) .... RIDL
Riddell Sports, Inc. [*Associated Press*] (SAG) .... Riddell
Riddell Sports, Inc. [*NASDAQ symbol*] (SPSG) .... RIDL
Ridden Standardbred Association (EA) .... RSA
Riddle's Lexicon [*A publication*] (DLA) .... Riddle's Lex
Riddle's Supplementary Proceedings [*New York*] [*A publication*] (DLA) .... Rid Sup Proc
Ride Inc. [*NASDAQ symbol*] (TTSB) .... RIDE
Ride, Inc. [*Associated Press*] (SAG) .... RideInc
Ride Quality Meter [*Automotive testing*] .... RQM
Ride Shared Vehicle Paratransit [*Transportation system*] .... RSVP
Ride Smoothing System [*Aviation*] .... RSS
Ride Snowboard Co. [*NASDAQ symbol*] (SAG) .... RIDE
Rideal-Walter Coefficient [*Pharmacy*] .... RW
Rideau Campus, Algonquin College of Applied Arts and Technology, Ottawa, On tario, [*Library symbol National Library of Canada*] (NLC) .... OOACR
Rideau Regional Centre, Ministry of Community and Social Services, Smiths Falls,Ontario [*Library symbol National Library of Canada*] (NLC) .... OSFCSR
Rideau Resources Corp. [*Vancouver Stock Exchange symbol*] .... RDU
Ride-Control Segment [*or System*] [*Aviation*] .... RCS
Ride-It-Out .... RIO
Rideout Pyrohydrolysis .... RPH
Rider Block Tagline System [*Military*] (CAAL) .... RBTS
Rider Club [*Commercial firm*] (EA) .... RC
Rider College (GAGS) .... Rider C
Rider College, Lawrenceville, NJ [*Library symbol Library of Congress*] (LCLS) .... NjLawR
Rider College Library, Lawrenceville, NJ [*OCLC symbol*] (OCLC) .... RID
Rider College, Trenton, NJ [*Library symbol Library of Congress*] (LCLS) .... NjTR
Rider Motorcycle Touring Club [*Later, RC*] [*Commercial firm*] (EA) .... RMTC
Riders Association [*Defunct*] .... RA
Riders of the Wind, the Field Events Player's Association (EA) .... ROW/FEPA
Ridexchange (EA) .... RIDEX
Ridge .... RDG
Ridge (MSA) .... RDG
Ridge [*Commonly used*] (OPSA) .... RDGE
Ridge [*Commonly used*] (OPSA) .... RIDGE
Ridge Elementary School, Bowling Green, OH [*Library symbol*] [*Library of Congress*] (LCLS) .... OBgRE
Ridge Farm Community Unit School District, Ridge Farm, IL [*Library symbol*] [*Library of Congress*] (LCLS) .... IRidSD
Ridge Instrument Development Laboratory [*Navy*] .... RIDL
Ridge Interdisciplinary Global Experiments [*NOAA, NSF, ONR, and USGS*] .... RIDGE
Ridge InterDisciplinary Global Experiments [*Program*] [*Marine science*] (OSRA) .... RIDGE
Ridge Regression [*Statistics*] .... RR
Ridge Transform Intersection [*Geology*] .... RTI
Ridge/Transform Intersection [*Geology*] .... RTI
Ridgebury, PA [*FM radio station call letters*] .... WMKB
Ridgecrest, CA [*AM radio station call letters*] .... KLOA
Ridgecrest, CA [*FM radio station call letters*] .... KLOA-FM
Ridgecrest, CA [*FM radio station call letters*] .... KZIQ
Ridgecrest, CA [*FM radio station call letters*] .... KZIQ-FM
Ridgecrest Resources [*Vancouver Stock Exchange symbol*] .... RCT
Ridgefield, CT [*AM radio station call letters*] .... WREF
Ridgefield Park Free Public Library, Ridgefield Park, NJ [*Library symbol Library of Congress*] (LCLS) .... NjRp
Ridgefield Public Library, Ridgefield, NJ [*Library symbol Library of Congress*] (LCLS) .... NjRf
Ridgeland, MS [*AM radio station call letters*] (RBYB) .... WIIN
Ridgeland, SC [*AM radio station call letters*] .... WNFO
Ridgeland, SC [*FM radio station call letters*] .... WSHG
Ridgeling [*Horse racing*] .... RIG
Ridges [*Postal Service standard*] (OPSA) .... RDGS
Ridges .... RDGS
Ridges [*Commonly used*] (OPSA) .... RIDGES
Ridgetown College of Agricultural Technology [*Canada*] (ARC) .... RCAT
Ridgetown College of Agricultural Technology, Ontario [*Library symbol National Library of Canada*] (NLC) .... ORRCAT
Ridgevalley School, Crooked Creek, Alberta [*Library symbol National Library of Canada*] (BIB) .... ACCRS
Ridgeview, Inc. [*NASDAQ symbol*] (SAG) .... RIDG

Ridgeview, Inc. [*Associated Press*] (SAG) .... Ridgevw
Ridgeville Public Library, Ridgeville, IN [*Library symbol Library of Congress*] (LCLS) .... InRid
Ridgeway, Lapp, and Schoales' Irish King's Bench Reports [*1793-95*] [*A publication*] (DLA) .... RL & S
Ridgeway, Lapp, and Schoales' Irish Term Reports [*A publication*] (DLA) .... Ridg L & S
Ridgeway, Lapp, and Schoales' Irish Term Reports [*A publication*] (DLA) .... Ridgew L & S (Ir)
Ridgeway, Lapp, and Schoales' Irish Term Reports [*A publication*] (ILCA) .... Ridgew L & S (Ire)
Ridgeway Tempore Hardwicke [*27 English Reprint*] [*A publication*] (DLA) .... Ridgew T Hardw (Eng)
Ridgeway's (Individual) Reports of State Trials in Ireland [*A publication*] (DLA) .... Ridg St Tr
Ridgeway's Irish Appeal (or Parliamentary) Cases [*A publication*] (DLA) .... Ridg Ap
Ridgeway's Irish Appeal (or Parliamentary) Cases [*A publication*] (DLA) .... Ridg App
Ridgeway's Irish Appeal (or Parliamentary) Cases [*A publication*] (DLA) .... Ridg PC
Ridgeway's Irish Appeal (or Parliamentary) Cases [*A publication*] (DLA) .... Ridg Pr Rep
Ridgeway's Irish Parliamentary Cases [*A publication*] (DLA) .... Ridgw Ir PC
Ridgeway's Irish Parliamentary Reports [*1784-96*] [*A publication*] (DLA) .... Ridg Parl Rep
Ridgeway's Irish Parliamentary Reports [*1784-96*] [*A publication*] (DLA) .... Ridgew Ir PC
Ridgeway's Reports of State Trials in Ireland [*A publication*] (DLA) .... Ridg Rep
Ridgeway's Reports Tempore Hardwicke, Chancery [*27 English Reprint*] [*1744-46*] [*A publication*] (DLA) .... Ridg T H
Ridgeway's Reports Tempore Hardwicke, Chancery [*27 English Reprint*] [*1744-46*] [*A publication*] (DLA) .... Ridg Temp H
Ridgeway's Reports Tempore Hardwicke, Chancery [*27 English Reprint*] [*1744-46*] [*A publication*] (DLA) .... Ridgew T Hardw
Ridgeway's Reports Tempore Hardwicke, Chancery and English King's Bench [*A publication*] (DLA) .... Ridg
Ridgeway's Reports Tempore Hardwicke, Chancery and English King's Bench [*A publication*] (DLA) .... Ridg & Hard
Ridgeway's Reports Tempore Hardwicke, Chancery and English King's Bench [*A publication*] (DLA) .... Ridg Cas
Ridgeway's Reports Tempore Hardwicke, Chancery and English King's Bench [*27 English Reprint*] [*A publication*] (DLA) .... Ridg T Hard
Ridgeway's Reports Tempore Hardwicke, Chancery and English King's Bench [*27 English Reprint*] [*A publication*] (DLA) .... Ridg T Hardw
Ridgeway's Reports Tempore Hardwicke, Chancery and English King's Bench [*A publication*] (DLA) .... Ridgew
Ridgeway's Reports Tempore Hardwicke, Chancery and English King's Bench [*A publication*] (DLA) .... RTH
Ridgewood Library, Ridgewood, NJ [*Library symbol Library of Congress*] (LCLS) .... NjRw
Ridgewood News, Ridgewood, NJ [*Library symbol Library of Congress*] (LCLS) .... NjRwN
Ridgewood Newspapers, Paramus, NJ [*Library symbol Library of Congress*] (LCLS) .... NjParR
Ridiculous Theatrical Company .... RTC
Ridihalgh, Eggers & Associates, Columbus, OH [*OCLC symbol*] (OCLC) .... REA
Riding for the Disabled Association (EAIO) .... RDA
Riding for the Disabled Association of Australia .... RDAA
Riding Master [*British*] .... RM
Riding Mountain National Park, Parks Canada [*Parc National Riding Mountain, Parcs Canada*] Wasagaming, Manitoba [*Library symbol National Library of Canada*] (NLC) .... MWPCR
Ridley Township Public Library, Folsom, PA [*Library symbol Library of Congress*] (LCLS) .... PFol
Ridley's Civil and Ecclesiastical Law [*A publication*] (DLA) .... Ridley Civil & Ecc Law
Riecam, SA [*Honduras*] [*FAA designator*] (FAAC) .... REM
Riedell's Reports [*68, 69 New Hampshire*] [*A publication*] (DLA) .... Ried
Rieger Syndrome [*Medicine*] (DMAA) .... RGS
Riemann, "Handbuch der Musikgeschichte" [*A publication*] .... RiHM
Riemann, "Musik Lexikon" [*A publication*] .... RiML
Riemann, "Musikgeschichte in Beispielen" [*A publication*] .... RiMB
Riemann Zeta Function [*Mathematics*] .... RZF
Riemann's Metrical Hypothesis [*Mathematics*] .... RMH
Rieti [*Italy ICAO location identifier*] (ICLI) .... LIQN
Rifampicin [*An antibacterial, antibiotic, and antituberculin*] (DAVI) .... RIF
Rifampicin [*An antibacterial, Antibiotic, and antituberculin*] (DAVI) .... RMP
Rifampin [*Also, RF, RIF, RMP*] [*Bactericide*] .... R/AMP
Rifampin [*Also, R/AMP, RIF, RMP*] [*Bactericide*] .... RF
Rifampin [*Also, R/AMP, RF, RMP*] [*Bactericide*] .... RIF
Rifampin [*Also, R/AMP, RF, RIF*] [*Bactericide*] .... RMP
Riffle .... R
Riffle Frequency .... RF
Rifle .... R
Rifle (DOMA) .... Rfl
Rifle .... RIF
Rifle and Pistol Team [*Navy*] .... R & PT
Rifle and Weapons Platoon [*Army Obsolete*] (AABC) .... RWP
Rifle Brigade .... RB
Rifle, CO [*AM radio station call letters*] .... KRGS
Rifle, CO [*FM radio station call letters*] .... KZKS
Rifle, CO [*Location identifier FAA*] (FAAL) .... RIL
Rifle Expert .... RE
Rifle Fine Grain [*British military*] (DMA) .... RFG
Rifle Large Grain [*British military*] (DMA) .... RLG

Rifle Marksman ..... RMM
Rifle Prize Money [*British military*] (DMA) ..... RPM
Rifle Public Library, Rifle, CO [*Library symbol Library of Congress*] (LCLS) ..... CoRi
Rifle Range ..... RR
Rifle Sharpshooter ..... RSS
Rifle Unqualified [*Military*] ..... RUQ
Rifle Volunteer Corps [*Military unit*] [*British*] ..... RVC
Rifle Volunteers ..... RV
Rifled Breech-Loading [*Gun*] ..... RBL
Rifled Muzzle-Loading [*Gun*] ..... RML
Rifleman (AABC) ..... RFLMN
Rifleman ..... RFN
Rifleman's Assault Weapon (MCD) ..... RAW
Rifleman's Breaching Munition Program [*Military*] (INF) ..... RBM
Rifleman's Gun Shield [*Military*] (INF) ..... RGS
Rifredo Mugello [*Italy ICAO location identifier*] (ICLI) ..... LIQM
Rift Valley [*MARC geographic area code Library of Congress*] (LCCP) ..... fr----
Rift Valley Fever ..... RVF
Rift Valley Fever Virus [*Medicine*] ..... RVFV
Rift Valley Research Mission in Ethiopia [*Anthropology*] ..... RVRME
Rift-Fracture-Fracture [*Geology*] ..... RFF
Rift-Rift-Fracture [*Geology*] ..... RRF
Riga [*Former USSR Airport symbol*] (OAG) ..... RIX
Riga Airclub (Latvian Professional Air Sport Center) [*FAA designator*] (FAAC) ..... RAK
Riga Airlines [*Latvia*] [*ICAO designator*] (FAAC) ..... RIG
Riga Skulte Airport [*Former USSR Airport symbol Obsolete*] (OAG) ..... RSC
Riga/Spilve [*Former USSR ICAO location identifier*] (ICLI) ..... UMRR
Rigby Public Library, Rigby, ID [*Library symbol*] [*Library of Congress*] (LCLS) ..... IdRig
Rigel Energy [*Associated Press*] (SAG) ..... Rigel
Rigel Energy [*Formerly, Total Canada Oil & Gas Ltd.*] [*AMEX symbol*] (SPSG) ..... RJL
Rigelyn Security [*Vancouver Stock Exchange symbol*] ..... RSY
Rigger [*British military*] (DMA) ..... R
Rigging (MSA) ..... RGNG
Rigging (ROG) ..... RIG
Rigging Fixtures (MCD) ..... RF
Rigging Template (MCD) ..... RGT
Rigging Tool (MCD) ..... RT
Riggins Resources [*Vancouver Stock Exchange symbol*] ..... RGN
Riggs National Corp. [*NASDAQ symbol*] (NQ) ..... RIGS
Riggs National Corp. [*Associated Press*] (SAG) ..... RigsNt
Riggs Natl Corp. [*NASDAQ symbol*] (TTSB) ..... RIGS
Right [*Direction*] ..... R
Right [*Politics*] ..... R
Right ..... RGT
Right [*Direction of Turn*] [*ICAO designator*] (FAAC) ..... RITE
Right (EY) ..... RT
Right (WDMC) ..... rt
Right (VRA) ..... rt
Right Accumulator (IAA) ..... RA
Right Acromio-Dorsoanterior [*A fetal position*] [*Obstetrics*] ..... RADA
Right Acromio-Dorsoposterior [*A fetal position*] [*Obstetrics*] ..... RADP
Right Add, Left Subtract [*Army field artillery technique*] (INF) ..... RALS
Right Aft (MCD) ..... RA
Right Aft Propulsion System [*Aerospace*] (GFGA) ..... RAPS
Right and Below (MEDA) ..... R & B
Right and Below (DAVI) ..... R & B
Right and Left ..... R/L
Right and Left Hands [*Work-factor system*] ..... R & LH
Right Angle (DEN) ..... RA
Right Angle ..... RTANG
Right Angle Adapter ..... RAA
Right Angle Bulkhead Receptacle ..... RABR
Right Angle Drive (PDAA) ..... RAD
Right Angle Panel Receptacle ..... RAPR
Right Angle Plug ..... RAP
Right Angle Pressure Cartridge ..... RAPC
Right Anterior Descending [*Medicine*] (DAVI) ..... RAD
Right Anterior Digestive [*Gland*] ..... RAD
Right Anterior Hemiblock [*Medicine*] (AAMN) ..... RAH
Right Anterior Oblique [*Medicine*] ..... RAO
Right Anterior Occipital [*Neurology*] (DAVI) ..... RAO
Right Anterior Thigh [*Anatomy*] ..... RAT
Right Arch [*Freemasonry*] ..... RA
Right Arithmetic Element ..... RAE
Right Arm [*Medicine*] ..... RA
Right Arm Recumbent [*Medicine*] (AAMN) ..... RAR
Right Ascension [*Navigation*] ..... RA
Right Ascension Angle ..... RAA
Right Ascension Encoder ..... RAE
Right Ascension Mean Sun [*Navigation*] ..... RAMS
Right Ascension of the Meridian [*Navigation*] ..... RAM
Right Atrial Appendage [*Medicine*] ..... RAA
Right Atrial Catheter [*Medicine*] (MEDA) ..... RAC
Right Atrial Catheter [*Cardiology*] (DAVI) ..... RAC
Right Atrial Enlargement [*Cardiology*] ..... RAE
Right Atrial Free Wall [*Medicine*] (DMAA) ..... RAFW
Right Atrial Hypertrophy [*Cardiology*] ..... RAH
Right Atrial Pressure [*Cardiology*] ..... RAP
Right Atrial Wall [*Medicine*] (DMAA) ..... RAW
Right Atrium [*Cardiology*] ..... RA
Right Attack Wing [*Women's lacrosse position*] ..... RAW
Right Auricle [*Anatomy*] ..... RA
Right Axilla (KSC) ..... RA
Right Axis Deviation [*Medicine*] ..... RAD
Right Bank ..... RBK
Right Base [*Aviation*] (FAAC) ..... RB
Right Border [*Genetics*] ..... RB
Right Border Cardiac Dullness [*Medicine*] (DMAA) ..... RBCD
Right Border of Dullness [*Cardiology*] ..... RBD
Right Brachial Artery [*Anatomy*] (DAVI) ..... RBA
Right Brachial Vein [*Anatomy*] (DAVI) ..... RBV
Right Breast Biopsy [*Gynecology*] (DAVI) ..... RBB
Right Breast Biopsy Examination [*Medicine*] (AAMN) ..... RBBX
Right Bronchus [*Anatomy*] (DAVI) ..... RB
Right Buccal Ganglion [*Dentistry*] ..... RBG
Right Bundle Branch [*Cardiology*] (AAMN) ..... RBB
Right Bundle-Branch Block [*Cardiology*] ..... RBBB
Right Bundle-Branch System Block [*Cardiology*] ..... RBBSB
Right Buttock [*Anatomy*] ..... RB
Right Buttock Line (MCD) ..... RBL
Right Caudate Nucleus [*Medicine*] (DMAA) ..... RCN
Right Center (WDMC) ..... CR
Right Center [*Position in soccer, hockey*] ..... RC
Right Center [*A stage direction*] ..... RC
Right Center Entrance (WDAA) ..... RCE
Right Center Entrance [*Theater*] (WDMC) ..... RCE
Right Cerebral Ganglion [*Anatomy*] ..... RCG
Right Chest [*Medicine*] ..... RC
Right Circular Polarization ..... RCP
Right Circularly Polarized Light ..... RCPL
Right Congestive Heart Failure [*Medicine*] (DMAA) ..... RCHF
Right Cornerback [*Football*] ..... RCB
Right Coronary Artery [*Anatomy*] ..... RCA
Right Coronary Sinus [*Cardiology*] (AAMN) ..... RCS
Right Costal Margin [*Medicine*] ..... RCM
Right Defense ..... RD
Right Defense Wing [*Women's lacrosse position*] ..... RDW
Right Deltoid [*Medicine*] ..... RD
Right Digestive Gland ..... RDG
Right Door [*Theater*] ..... RD
Right Dorso Anterior [*Medicine*] (MAE) ..... RD
Right Dorso Anterior [*Medicine*] (ROG) ..... RDA
Right Dorso Posterior [*Medicine*] (ROG) ..... RDP
Right Ear Advantage [*Medicine*] (DMAA) ..... REA
Right Ear, Warm Stimulus [*Medicine*] (MEDA) ..... RW
Right Edge [*Skating*] ..... R
Right Element Shift Right (SAA) ..... RSR
Right Eminent [*Freemasonry*] ..... RE
Right Eminent Grand Commander [*Freemasonry*] ..... REGC
Right End ..... RE
Right End-Expiratory Pressure [*Medicine*] (DMAA) ..... REEP
Right Esotropia [*Ophthalmology*] ..... RET
Right Excellent ..... RE
Right Exotropia [*Ophthalmology*] ..... RXT
Right External Carotid Artery [*Medicine*] (MEDA) ..... RECA
Right Eye [*Ophthalmology*] (DAVI) ..... R
Right Eye ..... RE
Right Femoral Artery [*Anatomy*] ..... RFA
Right Femoral Hernia [*Medicine*] (DMAA) ..... RFH
Right Femoral Vein [*Anatomy*] (DAVI) ..... RFV
Right Field [*or Fielder*] [*Baseball*] ..... RF
Right Foot ..... RF
Right Forearm [*Medicine*] (MEDA) ..... RFA
Right Forward [*Football*] ..... RF
Right Front ..... RF
Right Front Fluid Temperature [*Automotive engineering*] ..... RFFT
Right Front Lining Temperature [*Automotive engineering*] ..... RFLT
Right Frontoanterior [*A fetal position*] [*Obstetrics*] ..... RFA
Right Frontolateral [*Anatomy*] (AAMN) ..... RFL
Right Frontoposterior [*A fetal position*] [*Obstetrics*] ..... RFP
Right Frontotransverse [*A fetal position*] [*Obstetrics*] ..... RFT
Right Fullback [*Soccer*] ..... RB
Right Fullback [*Soccer*] ..... RF
Right Fullback [*Soccer*] ..... RFB
Right Gluteus [*Anatomy*] ..... RG
Right Gluteus Maziums [*Muscle*] [*Anatomy*] (DAVI) ..... RGM
Right Guard [*Football*] ..... RG
Right Gun ..... RG
Right Half Word ..... RHW
Right Halfback [*Soccer*] ..... RH
Right Halfback [*Soccer*] ..... RHB
Right Hand ..... RH
Right Hand Drive [*Automotive engineering*] ..... RHD
Right Hand Grip (DMAA) ..... RHG
Right Hand Man II [*Computer package*] [*Futurus, Inc.*] (PCM) ..... RHMII
Right Hand Panel (MCD) ..... RHP
Right Heart Bypass [*Medicine*] (MAE) ..... RHB
Right Heart Catheterization [*Medicine*] ..... RHC
Right Heart Failure [*Medicine*] ..... RHF
Right Hemisphere Lesion [*Cardiology*] (DAVI) ..... RHL
Right Hepatic Artery [*Medicine*] (DMAA) ..... RHA
Right Hepatic Lobe [*Anatomy*] ..... RHL
Right Hilar Lymph Node [*Anatomy*] (MAE) ..... RHLN
Right Homonymous Hemianopia [*Medicine*] (MEDA) ..... RHH
Right Honourable (EY) ..... RtHon

[*The*] **Right Honourable John G. Diefenbaker Centre, University of Saskatchewan, Saskatoon, Saskatchewan** [*Library symbol National Library of Canada*] (NLC) ... SSUJD
Right Hyperphoria [*Medicine*] ... RH
Right Hypertropia [*Ophthalmology*] ... RHT
Right Hypochondrium [*Medicine*] ... RHC
Right Iliac [*Crest*] [*Anatomy*] (DAVI) ... RI
Right Iliac Crest [*Anatomy*] (DAVI) ... RIC
Right Iliac Fossa [*Medicine*] ... RIF
Right Iliac Region [*Medicine*] (MAE) ... RIR
Right Inboard (MCD) ... RIB
Right Inboard Elevon [*Aviation*] (MCD) ... RIE
Right Inferior Oblique [*Projection*] [*Radiology*] (DAVI) ... RIO
Right Inferior Oblique [*Medicine*] (DMAA) ... RIO
Right Inferior Rectus [*Muscle*] [*Anatomy*] (DAVI) ... RIR
Right Inguinal Hernia [*Medicine*] ... RIH
Right Innominate Vein [*Anatomy*] (DAVI) ... RIV
Right Intercostal Margin [*Medicine*] ... RICM
Right Intercostal Space [*Anatomy*] (DAVI) ... RICS
Right Intermediate Bronchus [*Anatomy*] ... RIB
Right Internal Capsule [*Medicine*] (MEDA) ... RIC
Right Internal Carotid [*Artery*] [*Anatomy*] (DAVI) ... RIC
Right Internal Cartoid [*Medicine*] (MEDA) ... RIC
Right Internal Cartoid Artery (MEDA) ... RICA
Right Internal Fixation [*Orthopedics*] (DAVI) ... RIF
Right Internal Jugular [*Vein*] [*Anatomy*] ... RIJ
Right Internal Mammary Anastomosis [*Cardiology*] (DAVI) ... RIMA
Right Internal Mammary Artery [*Anatomy*] (AAMN) ... RIMA
Right Kidney ... RK
Right Kidney [*Urine Sample*] (DAVI) ... RKID
Right Knee Left [*Guitar playing*] ... RKL
Right Larval Retractor ... RLR
Right Lateral [*Medicine*] (MEDA) ... R LAT
Right Lateral (DAVI) ... RL
Right Lateral (DAVI) ... RT LAT
Right Lateral [*Medicine*] (MAE) ... rt lat
Right Lateral Femoral [*Site of injection*] [*Medicine*] ... RLF
Right Lateral Rectus [*Eye anatomy*] ... RLR
Right Lateral Rotation [*Medicine*] ... RLR
Right Lateral Thigh [*Medicine*] ... RLT
Right Left Bearing Indicator [*Navigation*] (IAA) ... RLBI
Right/Left Indicator (NVT) ... RLI
Right Leg ... RL
Right Line ... RL
Right Line Contactor (MCD) ... RLC
Right Line Contractor ... RLC
Right Linebacker (WGA) ... RLB
Right Long Leg Brace [*Medicine*] ... RLLB
Right Lower [*Medicine*] ... RL
Right Lower Border of Cardiac Dullness [*Cardiology*] ... RLBCD
Right Lower Extremity [*Medicine*] ... RLE
Right Lower Leg Brace [*Medicine*] ... RLLB
Right Lower Limb [*Medicine*] ... RLL
Right Lower Lobe [*Lungs*] ... RLL
Right Lower Medial [*Medicine*] (DMAA) ... RLM
Right Lower Quadrant [*Medicine*] (DMAA) ... RLQ
Right Lower Quadrant [*of abdomen*] [*Medicine*] ... RLQ
Right Lower Scapular Border [*Medicine*] (DMAA) ... RLSB
Right Lung ... RL
Right Main Gear (MCD) ... RMG
Right Mainstem Bronchus [*Medicine*] (DMAA) ... RMB
Right Man Coronary Artery [*Anatomy*] (DAVI) ... RMCA
Right Management Consultants, Inc. [*Associated Press*] (SAG) ... RghtMg
Right Management Consultants, Inc. [*Philadelphia, PA*] [*NASDAQ symbol*] (NQ) ... RMCI
Right Manubrial Dullness [*Anatomy*] (MAE) ... RMD
Right Medial Rectus [*Eye anatomy*] ... RMR
Right Mediolateral [*Episiotomy*] [*Obstetrics*] ... RML
Right Mediolateral Episiotomy [*Obstetrics*] (DAVI) ... RME
Right Mentoanterior [*A fetal position*] [*Obstetrics*] ... RMA
Right Mentolateral [*Episiotomy*] [*Obstetrics*] ... RML
Right Mentoposterior [*A fetal position*] [*Obstetrics*] ... RMP
Right Mentotransverse [*A fetal position*] [*Obstetrics*] ... RMT
Right Mgmt Consultants [*NASDAQ symbol*] (TTSB) ... RMCI
Right Mid ... RM
Right Midclavicular Line [*Anatomy*] (DAVI) ... RMCL
Right Middle Cerebral Artery [*Anatomy*] ... RMCA
Right Middle Cerebral Artery Thrombosis [*Cardiology*] (DAVI) ... RMCAT
Right Middle Ear Exploration [*otorhinolaryngology*] (DAVI) ... RMEE
Right Middle Finger (DMAA) ... RMF
Right Middle Lobe [*Lungs*] ... RML
Right Middle Lobe Syndrome [*Medicine*] (MEDA) ... RMLS
Right Midzone [*Medicine*] (DMAA) ... RMZ
Right Oblique Inguinal Hernia [*Medicine*] (DMAA) ... ROIH
Right Occipitoanterior [*A fetal position*] [*Obstetrics*] ... ROA
Right Occipitolateral [*Obstetrics*] ... ROL
Right Occipitolateral [*Position*] (DAVI) ... ROL
Right Occipitoposterior [*A fetal position*] [*Obstetrics*] ... ROP
Right Occipitotransverse [*A fetal position*] [*Obstetrics*] ... ROT
Right of Baseline (MCD) ... ROB
Right of Rescission [*Business term*] ... ROR
Right of Way ... R of W
Right of Way ... ROW
Right of Way ... RW
Right Opening (WDAA) ... RO
Right Orifice (WDAA) ... RO
Right Outboard (MCD) ... RO
Right Outboard (MCD) ... ROB
Right Outer Thigh [*Injection site*] ... ROT
Right Outside Position [*Dancing*] ... ROP
Right Panel Front [*Nuclear energy*] (NRCH) ... RPF
Right Pedal Ganglion ... RPG
Right Pedal Sinus ... RPS
Right Place at the Right Time [*A criterion for success*] ... RPRT
Right Posterior Oblique [*View*] [*Radiology*] (DAVI) ... RPO
Right Posterior Ventricular Preexcitation [*Medicine*] (DMAA) ... RPVP
Right Pulmonary Artery [*Medicine*] ... RPA
Right Pulmonary Vein [*Medicine*] ... RPV
Right Radical Neck Dissection [*Surgery*] (DAVI) ... RRND
Right Rear ... RR
Right Rear Fluid Temperature [*Automotive engineering*] ... RRFT
Right Rear Lining Temperature [*Automotive engineering*] ... RRLT
Right Reverend [*Of an abbot, bishop, or monsignor*] ... RR
Right Reverend [*Of an abbot, bishop, or monsignor*] ... RT RV
Right Reverend [*Of an abbot, bishop, or monsignor*] ... RTREV
Right Sacroanterior [*A fetal position*] [*Obstetrics*] ... RSA
Right Sacrolateral [*Position*] [*Obstetrics*] (DAVI) ... RSL
Right Sacroposterior [*A fetal position*] [*Obstetrics*] ... RSP
Right Sacrotransverse [*A fetal position*] [*Obstetrics*] ... RST
Right Sacrum [*Medicine*] (KSC) ... RS
Right Safety [*Sports*] ... RS
Right Salpingo-Oophorectomy [*Medicine*] ... RSO
Right Scapulo-Anterior [*A fetal position*] [*Obstetrics*] ... RScA
Right Scapuloposterior [*A fetal position*] [*Obstetrics*] ... RScP
Right Scapuloposterior Position [*of the fetus*] [*Obstetrics*] ... Sc DP
Right Short Leg Brace [*Medicine*] ... RSLB
Right Side ... RS
Right Side Up with Care ... RSWC
Right Stage Center [*A stage direction*] ... RSC
Right Start [*NASDAQ symbol*] (TTSB) ... RTST
Right Start, Inc. [*Associated Press*] (SAG) ... RgtStrt
Right Start, Inc. [*NASDAQ symbol*] (SPSG) ... RTST
Right Sternal Border [*Medicine*] ... RSB
Right Sternal Edge [*On Examination*] [*Cardiology*] (DAVI) ... RSE
Right Store (SAA) ... RST
Right Subclavian [*Medicine*] (DMAA) ... RSC
Right Subclavian Artery [*Anatomy*] (DAVI) ... RSA
Right Subclavian Vein [*Anatomy*] ... RSV
Right Substantia Nigra [*Medicine*] (DMAA) ... RSN
Right Superior Vena Cava [*Medicine*] (DMAA) ... RSVC
Right Tackle [*Football*] ... RT
Right Thigh [*Medicine*] (MAE) ... RT
Right Time of Departure/Arrival (DS) ... RT
Right to a Comprehensive Education (EAIO) ... RICE
Right to a Comprehensive Education [*British*] ... RtCE
Right to Choose Coalition [*Australia*] ... RCC
Right to Financial Privacy Act ... RFPA
Right to Know (EA) ... RK
Right to Know [*Laws*] ... RTK
Right to Know Committee of Correspondence [*Defunct*] (EA) ... RKCC
Right to Left ... RL
Right to Life League of Southern California (EA) ... RLLSC
Right to Use [*Telecommunications*] (TEL) ... RTU
Right to Work ... RTW
Right Trendelenburg [*Position*] [*Surgery*] (DAVI) ... R Tren
Right Triceps [*Anatomy*] (DAVI) ... TR
Right Turn, International (EA) ... RTI
Right Turn on Red [*i.e., on red traffic signal*] ... RTOR
Right Upper [*Medicine*] ... RU
Right Upper Arm [*Medicine*] ... RUA
Right Upper Entrance [*A stage direction*] ... RUE
Right Upper Extremity [*Medicine*] ... RUE
Right Upper Eyelid [*Medicine*] ... RUL
Right Upper Limb [*Medicine*] ... RUL
Right Upper Lobe [*of lung*] [*Medicine*] ... RUL
Right Upper Lung [*Medicine*] (MAE) ... RUL
Right Upper Outer [*Quadrant*] [*Anatomy*] (DAVI) ... RUO
Right Upper Outer Quadrant [*Site of injection*] [*Medicine*] ... RUOQ
Right Upper Pole [*Medicine*] (DMAA) ... RUP
Right Upper Quadrant [*of abdomen*] [*Medicine*] ... RUQ
Right Upper Sternal Border [*Anatomy*] (DMAA) ... RUSB
Right Upstage [*Theater*] (WDMC) ... RU
Right Ureteral Orifice [*Medicine*] ... RUO
Right Vastus Lateralis [*Muscle*] [*Anatomy*] (DAVI) ... RVL
Right Ventral Gluteal [*Injection site*] ... RVG
Right Ventricle [*of heart*] [*Cardiology*] ... RV
Right Ventricle End-Diastolic Volume [*Cardiology*] ... RVEDV
Right Ventricle Wall Thickness [*Medicine*] (DMAA) ... RVWT
Right Ventricular Assistance [*Cardiology*] ... RVA
Right Ventricular Cardiac Work Index [*Cardiology*] ... RCWI
Right Ventricular Diastolic Overload [*Cardiology*] (AAMN) ... RVDO
Right Ventricular Diastolic Volume [*Cardiology*] (DAVI) ... RVDV
Right Ventricular Dimension [*Cardiology*] ... RVD
Right Ventricular Dysfunction [*Medicine*] ... RVD
Right Ventricular Ejection Fraction [*Cardiology*] (DAVI) ... RVEF
Right Ventricular Ejection Time [*Cardiology*] (DAVI) ... RVET
Right Ventricular Ejection Time [*Medicine*] (MEDA) ... RVET
Right Ventricular End-Diastolic Compliance [*Cardiology*] ... RVED-CMP
Right Ventricular End-Diastolic Diameter [*Medicine*] (DMAA) ... RVEDD
Right Ventricular End-Diastolic Pressure [*Cardiology*] ... RVEDP

Right Ventricular End-Diastolic Pressure Index [*Cardiology*] ..... RVEDPI
Right Ventricular Endocardial [*Cardiology*] (DMAA) ..... RVECP
Right Ventricular End-Systolic Pressure [*Cardiology*] (DAVI) ..... RVESP
Right Ventricular End-Systolic Volume [*Cardiology*] ..... RVESV
Right Ventricular Enlargement [*Cardiology*] ..... RVE
Right Ventricular Filling Pressure [*Medicine*] (MEDA) ..... RVFP
Right Ventricular Hypertrophy [*Cardiology*] ..... RVH
Right Ventricular Initial Diastolic Pressure [*Medicine*] (MEDA) ..... RVIDP
Right Ventricular Internal Dimension [*Medicine*] (MEDA) ..... RVID
Right Ventricular Internal Dimension [*Cardiology*] (DAVI) ..... RVID
Right Ventricular Mean [*Medicine*] (DMAA) ..... RVM
Right Ventricular Outflow [*Medicine*] (MEDA) ..... RVO
Right Ventricular Outflow Tract [*Cardiology*] ..... RVOT
Right Ventricular Overactivity [*Medicine*] (MEDA) ..... RVO
Right Ventricular Overactivity [*Cardiology*] (DAVI) ..... RVO
Right Ventricular Overactivity [*Cardiology*] (DAVI) ..... RVOA
Right Ventricular Peak Filling Rate [*Medicine*] (DMAA) ..... RVPER
Right Ventricular Peak Filling Rate [*Medicine*] (DMAA) ..... RVPFR
Right Ventricular Pressure [*Medicine*] (DMAA) ..... RVP
Right Ventricular Stroke Work [*Cardiology*] ..... RVSW
Right Ventricular Stroke Work Index [*Cardiology*] ..... RVSWI
Right Ventricular Volume Overload [*Medicine*] (DMAA) ..... RVVO
Right Ventricular Weight [*Cardiology*] ..... RVW
Right Ventrolateral Gluteal [*Site of injection*] [*Medicine*] ..... RVLG
Right Visceral Ganglion [*Medicine*] ..... RVG
Right Visual Acuity [*Medicine*] ..... RVA
Right Visual Field [*Psychometrics*] ..... RVF
Right When Tested (NITA) ..... RWT
Right Wing ..... RW
Right Wing Down [*Aviation*] ..... RWD
Right Worshipful ..... RTW
Right Worshipful ..... RW
Right Worshipful Deputy Grand Master [*Freemasonry*] ..... RWDGM
Right Worshipful Grand Master [*Freemasonry*] ..... RWGM
Right Worshipful Master [*Freemasonry*] (ROG) ..... RWM
Right Worshipful Senior Grand Warden [*Freemasonry*] ..... RWSGW
Right Worthy ..... RW
Right Worthy Grand Representative [*Freemasonry*] ..... RWGR
Right Worthy Grand Secretary [*Freemasonry*] (ADA) ..... RWGS
Right Worthy Grand Templar [*Freemasonry*] ..... RWGT
Right Worthy Grand Treasurer [*Freemasonry*] ..... RWGT
Right Worthy Grand Warden [*Freemasonry*] ..... RWGW
Right Worthy Grand Worshipful [*Freemasonry*] (ROG) ..... RWGW
Right Worthy Junior Grand Warden [*Freemasonry*] ..... RWJGW
Right Wrong Omit (IAA) ..... RWO
Rightchoice Managed Care Co. [*Associated Press*] (SAG) ..... Rightch
Rightchoice Managed Care Co. [*NYSE symbol*] (SAG) ..... RIT
RightCHOICE Managed Care'A' [*NYSE symbol*] (TTSB) ..... RIT
Right-End-of-Tape ..... REOT
Right-Hand [*Music*] (DAS) ..... R
Right-Hand Circular [*NASA*] (KSC) ..... RHC
Right-Hand Circular Polarization [*NASA*] (IAA) ..... RCP
Right-Hand Circularly Polarized [*LASER waves*] ..... RHCP
Right-Hand Component (IAA) ..... RHC
Right-Hand Console ..... RHC
Right-Hand Control (IAA) ..... RHCTL
Right-Hand Equipment Bay [*Apollo*] [*NASA*] ..... RHEB
Right-Hand Forward Equipment Bay [*NASA*] (KSC) ..... RHFEB
Right-Hand Head ..... RHH
Right-Hand Page (WDMC) ..... RHP
Right-Hand Page [*Also, called Recto*] (WDMC) ..... rhp
Right-Hand Polarized Mode (IAA) ..... RHM
Right-Hand Side ..... RHS
Right-Hand Side Console [*NASA*] (KSC) ..... RHSC
Right-Handed (DAVI) ..... RtH
Right-Handed Pitcher [*Baseball*] ..... RHP
Right-Hand-Side by Centroid ..... RHSC
Rights [*Stock market term*] ..... RTS
Rights and Justice [*An association British*] (EAIO) ..... RJ
Rights in Data (OICC) ..... RD
Rights in Technical Data (AAGC) ..... RTD
Rights of Stockholders [*Investment term*] (MHDW) ..... ROS
Rights of Women [*British*] [*An association*] (DBA) ..... ROW
Rights Reserved ..... RR
Right-Sided Colon Cancer [*Medicine*] ..... RSC
Right-Sided Weakness [*Neurology*] (DAVI) ..... RSW
Right-to-Left Shunt Ratio [*Medicine*] (DAVI) ..... Qs/Qt
Right-to-Life (WDAA) ..... RTL
Rigid (MSA) ..... RGD
Rigid Airship [*Navy symbol*] ..... ZR
Rigid Boat ..... RB
Rigid Body ..... RB
Rigid Frame [*Revolver*] (DICI) ..... RF
Rigid Frame Selection Program ..... RFSP
Rigid Gas Permeable [*Contact lens*] ..... RGP
Rigid Intermediate Bulk Container ..... RIBC
Rigid Patrol Airship [*Navy symbol*] ..... ZRP
Rigid Plastic Foam ..... RPF
Rigid Proctosigmoidoscopy [*Proctoscopy*] ..... RPS
Rigid Raiding Craft [*British military*] (DMA) ..... RRC
Rigid Scouting Airship [*Navy symbol*] ..... ZRS
Rigid Seat Survival Kit (NG) ..... RSSK
Rigid Space Structure ..... RSS
Rigid Thermoplastic Polyurethane [*Organic chemistry*] ..... RTPU
Rigid Training Airship [*Navy symbol*] ..... ZRN
Rigid Urethane Foam ..... RUF
Rigid Waveguide ..... RWG
Rigid-Hull Inflatable [*US Coast Guard vessel*] ..... RHI
Rigid-Hull Inflatable Boat (DOMA) ..... RHIB
Rigid-Rotor [*Calculations*] ..... RR
Rigorous Approach to Industrial Software Engineering [*British*] ..... RAISE
Rigorous Imprisonment [*British military*] (DMA) ..... RI
Rigsdaler [*Numismatics*] ..... RGSDLR
Rijeka [*Former Yugoslavia*] [*ICAO location identifier*] (ICLI) ..... LYRI
Rijeka [*Former Yugoslavia*] [*Airport symbol*] (OAG) ..... RJK
Rijksinstituut voor Orlogsdocumentatie, Amsterdam, Netherlands [*Library symbol Library of Congress*] (LCLS) ..... NeAO
Rijksuniversitaire Centrum te Antwerpen [*State University Center of Antwerp*], Antwerpen, Belgium [*Library symbol Library of Congress*] (LCLS) ..... BeAR
Rijksuniversiteit Leiden, Leiden, Netherlands [*Library symbol Library of Congress*] (LCLS) ..... NeLR
Rijksuniversiteit te Utrecht, Utrecht, Netherlands [*Library symbol Library of Congress*] (LCLS) ..... NeUR
Rijnmond Air Services BV [*Netherlands ICAO designator*] (FAAC) ..... RAZ
Riker Laboratories, Inc. [*Research code symbol*] ..... R
Riker Laboratories, Inc., Northridge, CA [*Library symbol Library of Congress*] (LCLS) ..... CNoR
Riker Laboratories Ltd. [*Research code symbol*] [*British*] ..... WG
Rikitea [*Tuamotu Archipelago*] [*Seismograph station code, US Geological Survey*] (SEIS) ..... RKT
Rikkyo University Library [*UTLAS symbol*] ..... RUL
Riksforbundet Internationella Foereningen foer Invandrarkvinnor [*Sweden*] ..... RIFFI
Riley Aeronautics Corp. [*ICAO aircraft manufacturer identifier*] (ICAO) ..... RY
Riley Motor Club USA (EA) ..... RMCUSA
Riley's Datashare International Ltd. [*Toronto Stock Exchange symbol*] ..... RDI
Riley's Edition of Harper's South Carolina Reports [*A publication*] (DLA) ..... Ril Harp
Riley's Reports [*37-42 West Virginia*] [*A publication*] (DLA) ..... Riley
Riley's South Carolina Chancery Reports [*1836-37*] [*A publication*] (DLA) ..... Ril
Riley's South Carolina Chancery Reports [*A publication*] (DLA) ..... Riley
Riley's South Carolina Equity Reports [*A publication*] (DLA) ..... Ril
Riley's South Carolina Equity Reports [*A publication*] (DLA) ..... Riley Ch
Riley's South Carolina Equity Reports [*A publication*] (DLA) ..... Riley Eq
Riley's South Carolina Equity Reports [*A publication*] (DLA) ..... Riley Eq (SC)
Riley's South Carolina Law Reports [*A publication*] (DLA) ..... Riley
Riley's South Carolina Law Reports [*A publication*] (DLA) ..... Riley L (SC)
Rim [*Hawaii*] [*Seismograph station code, US Geological Survey*] (SEIS) ..... RIM
Rim Latch Set ..... RLS
Rim of Dorsal Lip ..... RDL
Rim of Lateral Lip ..... RLL
Rim of the Pacific [*Naval exercise; name refers to the four participating countries: Australia, Canada, New Zealand, and the United States*] ..... RIMPAC
Rim of the Pacific Evaluation (MCD) ..... ROPEVAL
Rim Vent Release [*Safety device for aerosol containers*] ..... RVR
Rima [*Oman*] [*ICAO location identifier*] (ICLI) ..... OORM
Rimacan Resources Ltd. [*Vancouver Stock Exchange symbol*] ..... RCN
Rimage Corp. [*Associated Press*] (SAG) ..... Rimage
Rimage Corp. [*NASDAQ symbol*] (SAG) ..... RIMG
Rimbey Public Library, Alberta [*Library symbol National Library of Canada*] (NLC) ..... ARI
Rimbo Bujang [*Indonesia*] [*ICAO location identifier*] (ICLI) ..... WIPC
Rimfire Adapter (MCD) ..... RFA
Rimini [*Italy ICAO location identifier*] (ICLI) ..... LIPR
Rimini [*Italy*] [*Airport symbol*] (AD) ..... RMI
Rimoil Corp. [*Toronto Stock Exchange symbol*] ..... RO
Rimouski [*Quebec*] [*Airport symbol*] (AD) ..... YRX
Rimouski [*Canada*] [*Airport symbol*] (OAG) ..... YXK
Rimouski, PQ [*Television station call letters*] ..... CFER
Rimouski, PQ [*AM radio station call letters*] ..... CFLP
Rimouski, PQ [*FM radio station call letters*] ..... CIKI
Rimouski, PQ [*Television station call letters*] ..... CIVB
Rimouski, PQ [*AM radio station call letters*] ..... CJBR
Rimouski, PQ [*FM radio station call letters*] ..... CJBR-FM
Rimouski, PQ [*Television station call letters*] ..... CJBRT
Rimouski-Mont Joli, PQ [*FM radio station call letters*] (RBYB) ..... CKMN-FM
Rimpa [*Afghanistan*] [*ICAO location identifier*] (ICLI) ..... OARP
Rimpac Industries [*Vancouver Stock Exchange symbol*] ..... RPI
Rimrock Airlines, Inc. [*ICAO designator*] (FAAC) ..... RIM
Rimrock Foundation Library, Billings, MT [*Library symbol*] [*Library of Congress*] (LCLS) ..... MtBilRF
Rimus (BJA) ..... R
Rinderpest Bovine Old Kabete [*A virus*] ..... RBOK
Rinderpest Virus ..... RPV
Riner's Reports [*2 Wyoming*] [*A publication*] (DLA) ..... Rin
Riner's Reports [*2 Wyoming*] [*A publication*] (DLA) ..... Riner
Rinforzando [*With Special Emphasis*] [*Music*] ..... RF
Rinforzando [*With Special Emphasis*] [*Music*] ..... RFZ
Rinforzando [*With Special Emphasis*] [*Music*] ..... RINF
Rinforzando [*With Special Emphasis*] [*Music*] ..... RINFZ
Ring [*Technical drawings*] ..... R
Ring Airfoil Grenade [*Army*] ..... RAG
Ring Airfoil Munition Projectile [*Army*] ..... RAMP
Ring and Pinion [*Automotive engineering*] ..... R & P
Ring Back [*Computer science*] (IAA) ..... RB
Ring Chromosome [*Medicine*] (MAE) ..... r
Ring Counter ..... RC
Ring Counter (MSA) ..... RCNTR
Ring Documentation (NITA) ..... RINGDOC

Ring Emitter Transistor ... RET
Ring Frame ... RF
Ring Guild of America [*Defunct*] (EA) ... RGA
Ring Index [*of chemical compounds*] [*A publication*] ... RI
Ring Index Pointer [*Computer science*] (OA) ... RIP
Ring Indicator [*MODEM*] (PCM) ... RI
Ring Interface Unit [*Telecommunications*] (OSI) ... RIU
Ring LASER Gyro [*Navy*] ... RLG
Ring LASER Gyro Navigation (MCD) ... RLGN
Ring LASER Technique ... RLT
Ring Lead [*Telecommunications*] (TEL) ... R
Ring Level (BUR) ... RL
Ring Micrometer ... RM
Ring Number Read [*Telecommunications*] (IAA) ... RNR
Ring Number Write [*Telecommunications*] (IAA) ... RNW
Ring Opening Metathesis Polymerization [*Organic chemistry*] ... ROMP
Ring Out and Stress Tester (PDAA) ... ROAST
Ring Road [*Traffic sign*] [*British*] ... R
Ring State Indicator [*Telecommunications*] (IAA) ... RSI
Ring System Descriptor (NITA) ... RSD
Ring Systems Handbook [*American Chemical Society*] [*A publication*] ... RSH
Ring Time [*Telecommunications*] (IAA) ... RT
Ring Tongue Terminal ... RTT
Ring Trip [*Telecommunications*] (TEL) ... RT
Ring-Around Programming (CAAL) ... RAP
Ringback Tone [*Telecommunications*] (TEL) ... RBT
Ring-Closed Circuit [*Computer science*] (IAA) ... RCC
Ringdown [*Telecommunications*] (TEL) ... RD
Ringer (WGA) ... RGR
Ringer ... RING
Ringer Corp. [*NASDAQ symbol*] (SAG) ... RING
Ringer Corp. [*Associated Press*] (SAG) ... Ringer
Ringer Equivalence Number [*Telephones*] ... REN
Ringer Lactated [*Medicine*] ... RL
Ringer's Lactate Solution [*Physiology*] ... RLS
Ringer's Solution [*Physiology*] ... RS
Ringgold County Historical Society, Mount Ayr, IA [*Library symbol Library of Congress*] (LCLS) ... IaMayrHi
Ringgold, GA [*FM radio station call letters*] (RBYB) ... WMPZ
Ringgold, GA [*FM radio station call letters*] ... WSGC
Ringi Cove [*Solomon Islands*] [*Airport symbol*] (OAG) ... RIN
Ringier Dokumentationszentrum [*Ringier Documentation Center*] [*Switzerland Information service or system*] (IID) ... RDZ
Ring-Infected Erythrocyte Surface Antigen [*Immunochemistry*] ... RESA
Ringing (MSA) ... RNGG
Ringing Circuit [*Telecommunications*] (IAA) ... RC
Ringing Generator [*Telecommunications*] (TEL) ... RG
Ringing Tone [*Telecommunications*] (TEL) ... RT
Ringing Tone No Reply (NITA) ... RTNR
Ringling Museum of the Circus, Sarasota, FL [*Library symbol Library of Congress*] (LCLS) ... FSRC
Ring-Ring Trip [*Telecommunications*] (TEL) ... RRT
Rings Present (NITA) ... RPR
Ringsted [*Denmark ICAO location identifier*] (ICLI) ... EKRS
Ringsted Dispatch, Ringsted, IA [*Library symbol Library of Congress*] (LCLS) ... IaRinD
Ringtone No Reply [*Telecommunications*] (TEL) ... RTNR
Ringwood's Principles of Bankruptcy [*18th ed.*] [*1947*] [*A publication*] (DLA) ... Ring Bank
Rinne [*Test*] [*Hearing Test*] (DAVI) ... R
Rinne's Test Negative [*Hearing test*] ... -R
Rinne's Test Positive [*Hearing test*] ... +R
Rinteln [*Germany ICAO location identifier*] (ICLI) ... EDVR
Rio [*River*] [*Spanish*] (ROG) ... R
Rio Air Express, SA [*Brazil*] [*FAA designator*] (FAAC) ... SKA
Rio Airways [*ICAO designator*] (AD) ... XO
Rio Airways, Inc. [*ICAO designator*] (FAAC) ... REO
Rio Algom Ltd. [*Associated Press*] (SAG) ... RioAl
Rio Algom Ltd. [*AMEX symbol Toronto Stock Exchange symbol*] (SPSG) ... ROM
Rio Algom Ltd., Toronto, ON, Canada [*Library symbol*] [*Library of Congress*] (LCLS) ... CaOTRAL
Rio Algom Ltd., Toronto, Ontario [*Library symbol National Library of Canada*] (NLC) ... OTRAL
Rio Alto Exploration Ltd. [*Toronto Stock Exchange symbol*] ... RAX
Rio Alzucar [*Panama*] [*Airport symbol*] (OAG) ... RIZ
Rio Blanco [*Colorado*] [*Seismograph station code, US Geological Survey Closed*] (SEIS) ... RBC
Rio Blanco County Traveling Library, Meeker, CO [*Library symbol Library of Congress Obsolete*] (LCLS) ... CoMeR
Rio Blanco Resources Ltd. [*Vancouver Stock Exchange symbol*] ... RBL
Rio Branco [*Brazil*] [*Airport symbol*] (OAG) ... RBR
Rio Branco/Presidente Medici [*Brazil ICAO location identifier*] (ICLI) ... SBRB
Rio Carpintero [*Cuba*] [*Seismograph station code, US Geological Survey*] (SEIS) ... RCC
Rio Colorado [*Argentina ICAO location identifier*] (ICLI) ... SAZQ
Rio Cuarto [*Argentina*] [*Airport symbol*] (OAG) ... RCU
Rio Cuarto/Area de Material [*Argentina ICAO location identifier*] (ICLI) ... SAOC
Rio De Janeiro [*Brazil*] [*Airport symbol*] (OAG) ... GIG
Rio De Janeiro [*Brazil*] [*Later, VSS*] [*Seismograph station code, US Geological Survey*] (SEIS) ... RDJ
Rio De Janeiro [*Brazil*] [*Airport symbol*] (OAG) ... RIO
Rio De Janeiro/Afonsos [*Brazil ICAO location identifier*] (ICLI) ... SBAF
Rio De Janeiro/Internacional Galeao [*Brazil ICAO location identifier*] (ICLI) ... SBGL
Rio De Janeiro/Jacarepagua [*Brazil ICAO location identifier*] (ICLI) ... SBJR
Rio De Janeiro/Santa Cruz [*Brazil ICAO location identifier*] (ICLI) ... SBSC
Rio De Janeiro/Santos Dumont [*Brazil ICAO location identifier*] (ICLI) ... SBRJ
Rio De Janeiro-Dumont [*Brazil*] [*Airport symbol*] (OAG) ... SDU
Rio Dell, CA [*FM radio station call letters*] (RBYB) ... KMGX
Rio Frio [*Costa Rica*] [*Airport symbol*] (OAG) ... RFR
Rio Frio O Progreso [*Costa Rica*] [*ICAO location identifier*] (ICLI) ... MRRF
Rio Gallegos [*Argentina*] [*Airport symbol*] (OAG) ... RGL
Rio Gallegos [*Argentina ICAO location identifier*] (ICLI) ... SAWG
Rio Grande [*Argentina*] [*Airport symbol*] (OAG) ... RGA
Rio Grande [*Brazil*] [*Airport symbol*] (AD) ... RGR
Rio Grande [*Brazil*] [*Airport symbol*] (OAG) ... RIG
Rio Grande (FAAC) ... RIOGD
Rio Grande [*Argentina ICAO location identifier*] (ICLI) ... SAWE
Rio Grande City, TX [*FM radio station call letters*] ... KCTM
Rio Grande College [*Ohio*] ... RGC
Rio Grande College, Rio Grande, OH [*Library symbol Library of Congress*] (LCLS) ... ORgC
Rio Grande College, Rio Grande, OH [*OCLC symbol*] (OCLC) ... RGC
Rio Grande do Sul [*Brazil*] [*Airport symbol*] (AD) ... RDS
Rio Grande Southern Railroad (IIA) ... RGS
Rio Grande Ventures Ltd. [*Vancouver Stock Exchange symbol*] ... RGV
Rio Grant [*Caja Del Rio*] [*New Mexico*] [*Seismograph station code, US Geological Survey*] [*Closed*] (SEIS) ... RIO
Rio Hacha, Guajira [*Colorado ICAO location identifier*] (ICLI) ... SKRH
Rio Hardy [*Mexico*] [*Seismograph station code, US Geological Survey*] (SEIS) ... RHM
Rio Hato [*Panama*] [*ICAO location identifier*] (ICLI) ... MPRH
Rio Hondo [*Argentina*] [*Airport symbol*] (AD) ... RHD
Rio Hondo Junior College Library, Whittier, CA [*OCLC symbol*] (OCLC) ... CRH
Rio Hondo Junior College, Whittier, CA [*Library symbol Library of Congress*] (LCLS) ... CWhR
Rio Hondo/Las Termas [*Argentina ICAO location identifier*] (ICLI) ... SANH
Rio Hotel & Casino [*NYSE symbol*] (TTSB) ... RHC
Rio Hotel & Casino [*Formerly, MarCor Resorts, Inc.*] [*NASDAQ symbol*] (SPSG) ... RIOH
Rio Hotel & Casino [*Associated Press*] (SAG) ... RioHtl
Rio Maranon [*Peru*] [*ICAO location identifier*] (ICLI) ... SPMA
Rio Mayo [*Argentina*] [*Airport symbol*] (AD) ... RFH
Rio Mayo [*Argentina*] [*Airport symbol*] (OAG) ... ROY
Rio Mayo [*Argentina ICAO location identifier*] (ICLI) ... SAWM
Rio Negro/Jose Maria Cordova [*Colorado ICAO location identifier*] (ICLI) ... SKRG
Rio Piedras, PR [*FM radio station call letters*] ... WFID
Rio Rancho, NM [*FM radio station call letters*] ... KZKL
Rio Saloya [*Ecuador*] [*ICAO location identifier*] (ICLI) ... SERS
Rio Seco [*Bolivia*] [*ICAO location identifier*] (ICLI) ... SLRS
Rio Sidra [*Panama*] [*Airport symbol*] (OAG) ... RSI
Rio Sierra Silver [*Vancouver Stock Exchange symbol*] ... RIO
Rio Sucio [*Colombia*] [*Airport symbol*] (AD) ... RSU
Rio Tigre [*Panama*] [*Airport symbol*] (OAG) ... RIT
Rio Tigre [*Peru*] [*ICAO location identifier*] (ICLI) ... SPRT
Rio Turbio [*Argentina*] [*Airport symbol*] (OAG) ... RYO
Rio Turbio [*Argentina ICAO location identifier*] (ICLI) ... SAWT
Rio Vista, CA [*FM radio station call letters*] ... KRVH
Rio Vista Mine [*California*] [*Seismograph station code, US Geological Survey*] (SEIS) ... RVM
Riobamba [*Ecuador*] [*ICAO location identifier*] (ICLI) ... SERB
Riohacha [*Colombia*] [*Airport symbol*] (OAG) ... RCH
Rioja [*Peru*] [*Airport symbol*] (OAG) ... RIJ
Rioja [*Peru*] [*ICAO location identifier*] (ICLI) ... SPJA
Rioja Wine Information Bureau (EA) ... RWIB
Riolos of Patras [*Greece*] [*Seismograph station code, US Geological Survey*] (SEIS) ... RLS
Rion-Des-Landes [*France ICAO location identifier*] (ICLI) ... LFIL
Riordan's Internet Privacy Enhanced Mail [*Computer science*] ... RIPEM
Rio-Sul [*ICAO designator*] (AD) ... SL
Rio-Sul, Servicos Aereos Regionais SA [*Brazil ICAO designator*] (ICDA) ... RI
Rio-Sul, Servicos Aereos Regionais SA [*Brazil*] [*ICAO designator*] (FAAC) ... RSL
Riot and Civil Commotion ... R & CC
Riot Control Agent (NVT) ... RCA
Riot Control Patrol Vehicle ... RCPV
Riot Control Vehicle ... RCV
Riot Exercise (DNAB) ... RIOTEX
Riot Relief Fund (EA) ... RRF
Riots, Civil Commotions, and Strikes [*Insurance*] ... RCC & S
Riots, Strikes, and Malicious Damage [*Insurance*] (ADA) ... RS & MD
Rip Out (DNAB) ... RO
Ripe Pulp Liquid [*A banana substrate*] ... RPL
Ripe Pulp Solid [*A banana substrate*] ... RPS
Ripe Skin Liquid [*A banana substrate*] ... RSL
Ripe Skin Solid [*A banana substrate*] ... RSS
Ripieno [*Additional*] [*Music*] ... RIP
Ripley Branch, Bruce County Public Library, Ontario [*Library symbol National Library of Canada*] (NLC) ... ORIP
Ripley County Historical Society, Versailles, IN [*Library symbol Library of Congress*] (LCLS) ... InVerRHi
Ripley, MS [*AM radio station call letters*] ... WCSA
Ripley, MS [*FM radio station call letters*] ... WKZU
Ripley, OH [*FM radio station call letters*] ... WAOL
Ripley, TN [*AM radio station call letters*] ... WTRB
Ripley, TN [*FM radio station call letters*] ... WTRB-FM
Ripley, WV [*FM radio station call letters*] ... WCEF
Ripley, WV [*FM radio station call letters*] ... WVRP
Ripling Electrochemical ... REC
Ripon College Library, Ripon, WI [*OCLC symbol*] (OCLC) ... WIP
Ripon College, Ripon, WI [*Library symbol Library of Congress*] (LCLS) ... WRipC

Ripon Society (EA) .... RS
Ripon, WI [*AM radio station call letters*] .... WCWC
Ripon, WI [*FM radio station call letters*] .... WRPN
Ripon, WI [*FM radio station call letters*] .... WTCX
Rip-Out Control Sheet (DNAB) .... RCS
Ripped [*Lumber*] (BARN) .... rip
Ripple .... RPL
Ripple Adder .... RA
Ripple Banking [*Electronics*] (ECII) .... RB
Ripple Factor .... RF
Ripple Mark Meter .... RMM
Ripple Resources Ltd. [*Vancouver Stock Exchange symbol*] .... RIP
Ripple-Blanking Input (IEEE) .... RBI
Ripple-Blanking Output (IEEE) .... RBO
Rippled Wall Amplifier .... RWA
Rippleside Elementary School, Rippleside Elementary IMC, Aitken, Mn [*Library symbol*] [*Library of Congress*] (LCLS) .... MnARE
Ripplesmere [*England*] .... RIPPLE
Ririe Public Library, Ririe, ID [*Library symbol*] [*Library of Congress*] (LCLS) .... IdRir
Risalpur [*Pakistan*] [*ICAO location identifier*] (ICLI) .... OPRS
RISC Single Chip [*IBM*] [*Computer science*] .... RSC
RISC [*Reduced-Instruction Set Computer*] **Technology** [*IBM Corp.*] .... RT
RISCORP Inc. 'A' [*NASDAQ symbol*] (TTSB) .... RISC
Rise [*Electronics*] .... R
Rise of Floor (DS) .... rf
[*The*] **Rise of Provincial Jewry** [*A publication*] (BJA) .... RPJ
Rise/Passive (MCD) .... R/P
Rise Resources, Inc. [*Vancouver Stock Exchange symbol*] .... RIS
Rise Time (DEN) .... RT
Rise Time (IDOE) .... t_r
Rise-Off-Disconnect (AAG) .... R-O-D
Rise-Off-Ground [*Model airplane*] (AAG) .... R-O-G
Riser [*Technical drawings*] .... R
Riser Foods Cl'A' [*AMEX symbol*] (TTSB) .... RSR
Riser Foods, Inc. [*Associated Press*] (SAG) .... Riser
Riser Foods, Inc. [*AMEX symbol*] (SPSG) .... RSR
Riser Valve [*NFPA pre-fire planning symbol*] (NFPA) .... RV
Rises .... R
Rise-Time Analyzer .... RTA
Rise-Time Indicator .... RTI
Rishiri [*Japan*] [*Airport symbol Obsolete*] (OAG) .... RIS
Rishiri Island [*Japan ICAO location identifier*] (ICLI) .... RJER
Rising Observational Sounding Equipment .... ROSE
Rising Sun Recorder, Rising Sun, IN [*Library symbol Library of Congress*] (LCLS) .... InRisR
Risk .... R
Risk Acceptance (NASA) .... RISKAC
Risk Analysis (MCD) .... RA
Risk and Insurance Management Society [*Database producer*] (EA) .... RIMS
Risk and Youth Smoking [*Project*] (AIE) .... RAYS
Risk Appraisal of Programs System .... RAPS
Risk Assessment (GFGA) .... RA
Risk Assessment Code (MCD) .... RAC
Risk Assessment Guidance for Superfund [*Environmental science*] .... RAGS
Risk Assessments Guidance for Superfund [*Environmental Protection Agency*] .... RAGS
Risk/Benefit Assessment of Drugs - Analysis and Response [*Post-marketing surveillance*] .... RAD-AR
Risk Capital [*Finance*] .... RC
Risk Capital Holdings [*NASDAQ symbol*] (TTSB) .... RCHI
Risk Capital Holdings, Inc. [*NASDAQ symbol*] (SAG) .... RCHI
Risk Capital Holdings, Inc. [*Associated Press*] (SAG) .... RiskCap
Risk Data Report [*Insurance*] .... RDR
Risk Evaluation [*Insurance*] .... RE
Risk Evaluation Force (DOMA) .... REF
Risk Exercise .... RE
Risk Management and the Prevention Plan [*Hazardous materials*] .... RMPP
Risk Management Plan [*Environmental Protection Agency*] .... RMP
Risk Management Plan .... RMP
Risk Management Program (MCD) .... RIMP
Risk Management Program [*Environmental Protection Agency*] .... RMP
Risk Management Program [*Environmental Protection Agency*] .... RMP
Risk of War .... ROW
Risk, Originality, and Virtuousity [*Scoring considerations in gymnastics competition*] .... ROV
Risk Ratio .... RR
Risk Reduction [*Branch*] [*Forecast Systems Laboratory*] (USDC) .... RR
Risk Reduction [*Branch*] [*Marine science*] (OSRA) .... RR
Risk Reduction Engineering Laboratory .... RREL
Risk Reference Dose (GNE) .... RRfd
Risk Studies Foundation (EA) .... RSF
Risk-Adjusted Multiple Hurdle Rates (ADA) .... RAMHR
Risk-Adjusted Profitability Measure [*Banking*] (ECON) .... RAPM
Risk-Adjusted Return on Capital [*Economics*] .... RAROC
Risk-Based Audit .... RBA
Risk-Driven Remediation .... RDR
Risk-Specific Dose [*Environmental science*] (FFDE) .... RSD
Risley Engineering and Materials Laboratory (PDAA) .... REML
Risley Family Association (EA) .... RFA
Risley Nuclear Establishment [*British*] (NUCP) .... RNE
Risley Nuclear Laboratories [*British*] (NUCP) .... RNL
Risley Nuclear Power Development Laboratories [*British*] (NUCP) .... RNPDL
Risoluto [*Resolutely*] [*Music*] (ROG) .... RISOL
Ristocetin Cofactor .... RCo
Ristocetin-Polymyxin [*Antibacterial mixture*] .... RP
Risvegliato [*Reanimated*] [*Music*] (ROG) .... RISVD
RIT Research Corp. .... RITRC
Rita Coyotepec [*Mexico*] [*Seismograph station code, US Geological Survey*] (SEIS) IIC
Ritardando [*Gradually Slower*] [*Music*] (ODBW) .... rit
Ritardando [*Gradually Slower*] [*Music*] .... RIT
Ritardando [*Gradually Slower*] [*Music*] .... RITAR
Ritardando [*Gradually Slower*] [*Music*] .... RITARD
Ritardando [*Gradually Slower*] [*Music*] (ROG) .... RITARO
Ritchie's Cases Decided by Francis Bacon [*1617-21*] [*A publication*] (DLA) .... Ritch
Ritchie's Equity [*Canada*] [*A publication*] (DLA) .... Ritchie
Ritchie's Equity Decisions [*Nova Scotia*] [*A publication*] (DLA) .... Ritch Eq Dec
Ritchie's Equity Decisions (Russell) [*Canada*] [*A publication*] (DLA) .... RED
Ritchie's Equity Reports [*1872-82*] [*Nova Scotia*] [*A publication*] (DLA) .... Ritch
Ritchie's Equity Reports [*Nova Scotia*] [*A publication*] (DLA) .... Ritch Eq Rep
Rite Aid [*NYSE symbol*] (TTSB) .... RAD
Rite Aid Corp. [*NYSE symbol*] (SPSG) .... RAD
Rite Aid Corp. [*Associated Press*] (SAG) .... RiteA
Rite Aid Corp. [*Associated Press*] (SAG) .... RiteAid
Rite Ecossais Ancien et Accepte [*Ancient and Accepted Scottish Rite*] [*Freemasonry*] [*French*] .... REA et A
Ritenuto [*Immediately Slower*] [*Music*] .... RIT
Ritenuto [*Immediately Slower*] [*Music*] .... RITEN
Ritenuto [*Immediately Slower*] [*Music*] (ROG) .... RITENO
Rites of Passage .... ROP
Ritidian Point, Guam Island [*Mariana Islands*] [*ICAO location identifier*] (ICLI) .... PGNW
Ritson's Jurisdiction of Courts-Leet [*A publication*] (DLA) .... Rits Cts Leet
Ritso's Introduction to the Science [*A publication*] (DLA) .... Rits Int
Rittenhouse Club, Philadelphia, PA [*Library symbol Library of Congress Obsolete*] (LCLS) .... PPRCI
Ritter-Oleson Technique [*Medicine*] (MAE) .... RO
Ritual (BJA) .... rit
Rituels Accadiens [*A publication*] (BJA) .... RACC
Rituels Accadiens [*A publication*] (BJA) .... RitAcc
Ritz Resources Ltd. [*Vancouver Stock Exchange symbol*] .... RTZ
Ritzaus Bureau [*Press agency*] [*Denmark*] .... RB
Ritzville Public Library, Ritzville, WA [*Library symbol Library of Congress*] (LCLS) .... WaRit
Rivadavia [*Argentina ICAO location identifier*] (ICLI) .... SASR
Rival Co. [*Associated Press*] (SAG) .... Rival
Rival Co. [*NASDAQ symbol*] (TTSB) .... RIVL
Rival Co. [*NASDAQ symbol*] (SAG) .... RIVL
Rival Manufacturing [*NASDAQ symbol*] (NQ) .... RIVL
Riva-Rocci Sphygmomanometer [*Medicine*] (DMAA) .... RR
Rive Droite [*Right Bank*] [*French*] .... RD
Rive'on Le-Khalkalah [*Tel Aviv*] (BJA) .... RL
River [*Maps and charts*] .... R
River .... RIV
River .... RIV
River [*Commonly used*] (OPSA) .... RIVER
River [*Commonly used*] (OPSA) .... RIVR
River [*Commonly used*] (OPSA) .... RVR
River and Flood Forecasting Service (NADA) .... RFFS
River and Harbor Aid to Navigation System [*Coast Guard*] .... RIHANS
River and Rainfall Station [*National Weather Service*] (NOAA) .... RRS
River Assault Craft [*Navy*] (ANA) .... RAC
River Assault Division [*Navy*] (VNW) .... RAD
River Assault Division [*Military*] .... RIVDIV
River Assault Flotilla [*Navy*] (VNW) .... RAF
River Assault Group [*Military*] .... RAG
River Assault Interdiction Division [*Navy*] (NVT) .... RAID
River Assault Squadron [*Navy*] (NVT) .... RAS
River Assault Squadron [*Navy*] (DNAB) .... RIVRON
River Assault Unit [*Navy*] .... RAU
River Bend Library System [*Library network*] .... RBLS
River Bend Library System, Coal Valley, IL [*Library symbol Library of Congress*] (LCLS) .... ICvR
River Bend Library System, Coal Valley, IL [*OCLC symbol*] (OCLC) .... IFK
River Bend Station [*Nuclear energy*] (NRCH) .... RBS
River Buoy Tender, Large or Small [*Coast Guard symbol*] (DNAB) .... WLR
River Cess [*Liberia*] [*Airport symbol*] (AD) .... RVC
River Conservation Fund [*Later, ARCC*] (EA) .... RCF
River District Office [*National Weather Service*] .... RDO
River Edge Free Public Library, River Edge, NJ [*Library symbol Library of Congress*] (LCLS) .... NjRive
River Falls, WI [*AM radio station call letters*] .... WEVR
River Falls, WI [*FM radio station call letters*] .... WEVR-FM
River Falls, WI [*FM radio station call letters*] .... WRFW
River Flotilla [*Military*] .... RIVFLOT
River Flotilla One [*Military*] .... RIVFLOTONE
River Forecast Center [*National Weather Service*] (NOAA) .... RFC
River Forest Bancorp [*NASDAQ symbol*] (NQ) .... RFBC
River Forest Bancorp [*Associated Press*] (SAG) .... RivFor
River Forest Public Library, River Forest, IL [*Library symbol Library of Congress*] (LCLS) .... IRivf
River Gauging Station .... RGS
River Grove, IL [*FM radio station call letters*] .... WRRG
River Grove Public Library, River Grove, IL [*Library symbol Library of Congress*] (LCLS) .... IRivg
River Gunboat [*Navy symbol*] .... PR
River Gunboat .... RGB

River Heights Elementary School, East Grand Forks, MN [*Library symbol*] [*Library of Congress*] (LCLS) ... MnEgfRE
River Ice Breaker (PDAA) ... RIB
[*The*] **River Jordan** [*A publication*] (BJA) ... RJ
River Lines, Inc. [*AAR code*] ... RL
River Management Tool ... RMT
River Monitor [*Navy symbol*] (DNAB) ... BMR
River Mouth [*Board on Geographic Names*] ... RMTH
River Name (BJA) ... RN
River Oaks Furniture [*NASDAQ symbol*] (TTSB) ... OAKS
River Oaks Furniture, Inc. [*NASDAQ symbol*] (SAG) ... OAKS
River Oaks Furniture, Inc. [*Associated Press*] (SAG) ... RvrOaks
River Patrol Craft [*Military*] (CINC) ... RPC
River Patrol Flotilla [*Navy*] (DNAB) ... RIVPATFLOT
River Patrol Force [*Navy*] (DNAB) ... RIVPATFOR
River Patrol Group [*Military*] (VNW) ... RPG
River Purification Board [*British*] (DCTA) ... RPB
River Quality Objective [*British*] (DCTA) ... RQO
River Quality Standard [*British*] (DCTA) ... RQS
River Road Environmental Technology Centre, Environment Canada [*Centre de Techologie Environnementale de River Road, Environnement Canada*] **Ottawa, Ontario** [*Library symbol National Library of Canada*] (NLC) ... OOEAPT
River Section (DNAB) ... RIVSEC
River Support Squadron [*Navy*] (DNAB) ... RIVSUPPRON
River Support Squadron [*Navy*] (VNW) ... RSS
[*The*] **River Terminal Railway Co.** [*AAR code*] ... RT
River Thames Society [*British*] ... RTS
River Torrens Improvement Standing Committee [*Australia*] ... RTISC
River Transport Escort Group (CINC) ... RTEG
River Transport Group [*South Vietnamese Navy*] (VNW) ... RTG
River Valley Bancorp [*NASDAQ symbol*] (SAG) ... RIVR
River Valley Bancorp [*Associated Press*] (SAG) ... RivrVlly
River Valley Community Library, Ontario [*Library symbol National Library of Canada*] (NLC) ... ORVC
River Water [*Nuclear energy*] (NRCH) ... RW
River Water Pumphouse [*Nuclear energy*] (NRCH) ... RWPH
River Water Supply System (IEEE) ... RWSS
River Water Treatment Area [*Nuclear energy*] (NRCH) ... RWTA
Rivera [*Uruguay*] [*Airport symbol*] (OAG) ... RVY
Rivera/Aeropuerto Deptal [*Uruguay*] [*ICAO location identifier*] (ICLI) ... SURV
Rivera and Tamayo Fault Exploration [*Marine science*] (MSC) ... RITA
Rivera Ocean Seismic Experiment ... ROSE
Riverband Acoustical Laboratory (KSC) ... RAL
Riverbank Army Ammunition Plant (AABC) ... RBAAP
Riverbank, CA [*AM radio station call letters*] ... KCBC
Rivercrest Christian School, Monticello, MN [*Library symbol*] [*Library of Congress*] (LCLS) ... MnMcR
Riverdahl Elementary School, Rockford, IL [*Library symbol*] [*Library of Congress*] (LCLS) ... IRoRvE
Riverdale Library District, Riverdale, IL [*Library symbol Library of Congress*] (LCLS) ... IRivd
Riverdale Publishing Co., Riverdale, NJ [*Library symbol Library of Congress*] (LCLS) ... NjRdR
Riverhead, NY [*Television station call letters*] ... WLIG
Riverhead, NY [*TV station call letters*] (RBYB) ... WLNY-TV
Riverhead, NY [*FM radio station call letters*] ... WRCN
Riverhead, NY [*AM radio station call letters*] ... WRHD
Riverhead, NY [*AM radio station call letters*] ... WRIV
Riverine Utility Craft [*Vehicle for transporting through shallow water and snow*] [*Navy symbol*] ... RUC
Rivers Pollution Prevention (ROG) ... RPP
Riversdale [*South Africa*] [*ICAO location identifier*] (ICLI) ... FARD
Riverside [*California*] [*Airport symbol*] (OAG) ... RAL
Riverside [*California*] [*Seismograph station code, US Geological Survey*] (SEIS) ... RVR
Riverside, CA [*Location identifier FAA*] (FAAL) ... JRD
Riverside, CA [*AM radio station call letters*] ... KDIF
Riverside, CA [*FM radio station call letters*] ... KGGI
Riverside, CA [*FM radio station call letters*] ... KOOJ
Riverside, CA [*AM radio station call letters*] ... KPRO
Riverside, CA [*Television station call letters*] ... KRCA
Riverside, CA [*FM radio station call letters*] ... KSGN
Riverside, CA [*FM radio station call letters*] ... KUCR
Riverside, CA [*FM radio station call letters*] ... KVAR
Riverside, CA [*Location identifier FAA*] (FAAL) ... MRX
Riverside, CA [*Location identifier FAA*] (FAAL) ... RAL
Riverside, CA [*Location identifier FAA*] (FAAL) ... RIV
Riverside City and County Public Library, Riverside, CA [*OCLC symbol*] (OCLC) ... CRP
Riverside City College [*California*] ... RCC
Riverside Elementary School, Brainerd, MN [*Library symbol*] [*Library of Congress*] (LCLS) ... MnBrRE
Riverside Elementary School, Grand Junction, CO [*Library symbol Library of Congress*] (LCLS) ... CoGjRE
Riverside Group, Inc. [*Jacksonville, FL*] [*NASDAQ symbol*] (NQ) ... RSGI
Riverside Group, Inc. [*Associated Press*] (SAG) ... RvrsGp
Riverside Hospital, Ottawa, ON, Canada [*Library symbol Library of Congress*] (LCLS) ... CaOORH
Riverside Hospital, Ottawa, Ontario [*Library symbol National Library of Canada*] (NLC) ... OORH
Riverside/March Air Force Base [*California*] [*ICAO location identifier*] (ICLI) ... KRIV
Riverside Methodist Hospital, Columbus, OH [*Library symbol Library of Congress*] (LCLS) ... OCoR
Riverside Methodist Hospital Library, Columbus, OH [*OCLC symbol*] (OCLC) ... RHC
Riverside Mountains [*California*] [*Seismograph station code, US Geological Survey*] (SEIS) ... RVS
Riverside National Bank [*Associated Press*] (SAG) ... RivrNtl
Riverside National Bank [*NASDAQ symbol*] (NQ) ... RNRC
Riverside, PA [*FM radio station call letters*] ... WLGL
Riverside Psychiatric Hospital, Portland, OR [*Library symbol Library of Congress*] (LCLS) ... OrPRP
Riverside Public Library and Riverside County Free Library, Riverside, CA [*Library symbol Library of Congress*] (LCLS) ... CRiv
Riverside Public Library, Riverside, IL [*Library symbol Library of Congress*] (LCLS) ... IRivs
Riverside Public Library, Riverside, NJ [*Library symbol Library of Congress*] (LCLS) ... NjRiv
Riverside Research Institute (MCD) ... RRI
Riverside/Rubidoux, CA [*Location identifier FAA*] (FAAL) ... RIR
Riverside School, Rockville Centre, NY [*Library symbol*] [*Library of Congress*] (LCLS) ... NRockRE
Riverside Secondary School, Windsor, ON, Canada [*Library symbol Library of Congress*] (LCLS) ... CaOWR
Riverside Secondary School, Windsor, Ontario [*Library symbol National Library of Canada*] (NLC) ... OWR
Riverton [*Wyoming*] [*Airport symbol*] (OAG) ... RIW
Riverton Resources Corp. [*Vancouver Stock Exchange symbol*] ... RRR
Riverton, WY [*FM radio station call letters*] ... KCWC
Riverton, WY [*Television station call letters*] ... KFNE
Riverton, WY [*FM radio station call letters*] ... KTAK
Riverton, WY [*FM radio station call letters*] ... KTRZ
Riverton, WY [*AM radio station call letters*] ... KVOW
Riverview [*South Africa*] [*ICAO location identifier*] (ICLI) ... FARV
Riverview [*Australia Seismograph station code, US Geological Survey*] (SEIS) ... RIV
Riverview Hospital, Port Coquitlam, BC, Canada [*Library symbol Library of Congress*] (LCLS) ... CaBPcRH
Riverview Hospital, Port Coquitlam, British Columbia [*Library symbol Library network*] (NLC) ... BEC
Riverview Savings Bank [*Associated Press*] (SAG) ... RivSvgs
Riverview Savings Bank [*NASDAQ symbol*] (SAG) ... RVSB
Riverview School, Grand Rapids, MN [*Library symbol*] [*Library of Congress*] (LCLS) ... MnGrRS
Riverview Svgs Bk FSB Camas [*NASDAQ symbol*] (TTSB) ... RVSB
Riverwood International Corp. [*Associated Press*] (SAG) ... RivwdInt
Riverwood International Corp. [*NYSE symbol*] (SPSG) ... RVW
Rivest Shamir Adleman ... RSA
Rivest-Shamir-Adelman [*Cryptography*] ... RSA
Rivet (AAG) ... RIV
Rivet (MSA) ... RVT
Rivet Fixture (AAG) ... RVFX
Rivet Joint [*RC-135 reconnaissance aircraft*] [*Air Force*] (DOMA) ... RJ
Rivet Pattern (AAG) ... RVPA
Rivet Setting Machine ... RSM
Riveted (DS) ... R
Riveted (MSA) ... RVTD
Riveted and Welded [*Shipping*] (DS) ... RW
Riveting Bar [*Tool*] (AAG) ... RVBR
Riveting Squeezer [*Tool*] (AAG) ... RVSZ
Riviana Foods [*NASDAQ symbol*] (TTSB) ... RVFD
Riviana Foods, Inc. [*Associated Press*] (SAG) ... Rivian
Riviana Foods, Inc. [*Associated Press*] (SAG) ... RivianaF
Riviana Foods, Inc. [*NASDAQ symbol*] (SAG) ... RVFD
Rivier College (GAGS) ... Rivier C
Rivier College, Nashua, NH [*Library symbol Library of Congress*] (LCLS) ... NhNaR
Riviera [*Record label*] [*France*] ... Riv
Riviera Beach, FL [*FM radio station call letters*] ... WOLL
Riviera Beach, FL [*AM radio station call letters*] ... WPOM
Riviera Explorations Ltd. [*Vancouver Stock Exchange symbol*] ... RE
Riviera Holding Corp. [*AMEX symbol*] (SAG) ... RIV
Riviera Holding Corp. [*Associated Press*] (SAG) ... Riviera
Riviera Holdings [*AMEX symbol*] (TTSB) ... RIV
Riviere au Renard, PQ [*FM radio station call letters*] ... CJRE
Riviere du Loup, PQ [*FM radio station call letters*] ... CIBM
Riviere du Loup, PQ [*Television station call letters*] ... CIMT
Riviere du Loup, PQ [*AM radio station call letters*] ... CJFP
Riviere du Loup, PQ [*Television station call letters*] ... CKRT
Riviere Du Loup, PQ [*ICAO location identifier*] (ICLI) ... CYRI
Riviere-Du-Loup [*Canada*] [*Airport symbol Obsolete*] (OAG) ... YRI
Rivington's Annual Register [*A publication*] (DLA) ... Riv Ann Reg
Rivista [*Review*] [*Italian*] (BJA) ... Riv
Rivista di Archeologia Cristiana [*A publication*] (OCD) ... Riv d Arch Crist
Rivista di Diritto Internazionale e Comparato del Lavoro [*Padua, Italy*] [*A publication*] (DLA) ... Riv di Diritto Internaz e Comparato del Lavoro
Rivista di Diritto Internazionale e Comparato del Lavoro [*Bologna, Italy*] [*A publication*] (DLA) ... Riv Dir Int e Comp del Lavoro
Rivista di Diritto Internazionale Privato e Processuale [*A publication*] (DLA) ... RDIPP
Rivista di Diritto Internazionale Privato e Processuale [*Padova, Italy*] [*A publication*] (DLA) ... Riv Dir Int'le Priv & Proc
Rivista di Storia e Letteratura Religiosa [*Florence*] [*A publication*] (BJA) ... RStorLettRel
Rivista Italiana per le Scienze Giuridiche [*A publication*] (OCD) ... Riv Ital per le Sc Giur
Rivolto [*Italy ICAO location identifier*] (ICLI) ... LIPI
Rivulet (ADA) ... RIVT
Rix-Dollar ... RD

Rix-Dollar [*British*] (ROG) ... RX
Riyadh [*Saudi Arabia*] [*ICAO location identifier*] (ICLI) ... OERY
Riyadh [*Saudi Arabia*] [*Airport symbol*] (OAG) ... RUH
Riyadh/King Khalid International [*Saudi Arabia*] [*ICAO location identifier*] (ICLI) ... OERK
Riyan [*People's Democratic Republic of Yemen*] [*ICAO location identifier*] (ICLI) ... ODAR
Riyan Mukalla [*South Arabia (Yemen)*] [*Airport symbol*] (AD) ... RIY
Rizzoli Corriere della Sera [*Publisher*] ... RCS
RJP Electronics [*Vancouver Stock Exchange symbol*] ... RJP
RJR Nabisco 10% 'TOPrS' [*NYSE symbol*] (TTSB) ... RNPrT
RJR Nabisco Holding Corp. [*Associated Press*] (SAG) ... RJR
RJR Nabisco Holding Corp. [*Associated Press*] (SAG) ... RJR Nab
RJR Nabisco Holdings [*NYSE symbol*] (SPSG) ... RN
RJR Nabisco Sr'B'Dep Pfd [*NYSE symbol*] (TTSB) ... RNPrB
RJR Nabisco Sr'C'PERCS [*NYSE symbol*] (TTSB) ... RNPrC
RL Microfilm Systems, Feasterville, PA [*Library symbol*] [*Library of Congress*] (LCLS) ... RmS
RLG [*Research Libraries Group, Inc.*] **Research-in-Progress Database** [*Information service or system*] (CRD) ... RIPD
RLI Corp. [*NYSE symbol*] (SPSG) ... RLI
RLI Corp. [*Associated Press*] (SAG) ... RLI Cp
RLIN [*Research Libraries Information Netword*] **code for the Library of Congress** ... DCLC
RMH Teleservices, Inc. [*Associated Press*] (SAG) ... RMH Tel
RMH Teleservices, Inc. [*NASDAQ symbol*] (SAG) ... RMHT
RMI Titanium [*NYSE symbol*] (SPSG) ... RTI
RMI Titanium Co. [*Associated Press*] (SAG) ... RMI Ti
RMP: Rural Marketing and Policy [*A publication*] ... RMP
RMS [*Remote Manipulator System*] **Planning System** (SSD) ... RPS
RN Aviation Ltd. [*British ICAO designator*] (FAAC) ... RMN
RNA [*Ribonucleic Acid*] **Amplification with In/Vitro Translation** [*Genetics*] ... RAWIT
RNA [*Ribonucleic Acid*] **Amplification with Transcript Sequencing** [*Genetics*] ... RAWTS
RNA [*Ribonucleic Acid*] **Binding Domain** [*Biochemistry*] ... RBD
RNA [*Ribonucleic Acid*] **Nuclear Protein** ... RNP
RNA [*Ribonucleic Acid*] **Recognition Motif** [*Genetics*] ... RRM
RNA [*Ribonucleic Acid*] **Virus Capsid** ... RVC
Ro [*Denmark ICAO location identifier*] (ICLI) ... EKRR
RO/RO [*Roll-On/Roll-Off*] **Discharge Facility** [*Army*] (RDA) ... RRDF
Roachdale Public Library, Roachdale, IN [*Library symbol Library of Congress*] (LCLS) ... InRo
Road ... R
Road [*Maps and charts*] (AAG) ... RD
Road (DD) ... Rd
Road ... RD
Road (ODBW) ... Rd
Road (WGA) ... RO
Road [*Commonly used*] (OPSA) ... ROAD
Road Accident Tabulation Language (PDAA) ... RATTLE
Road America [*Automotive raceway*] ... RA
Road/Automobile Communication System [*Automotive engineering*] ... RACS
Road Bend ... RB
Road Bitumen Association [*British*] (BI) ... RBA
Road Buffer (SAA) ... RB
Road Builders Training Association (EA) ... RBTA
Road Construction Unit (PDAA) ... RCU
Road Design and Road Costs [*British*] ... RDRC
Road Emulsion Association [*British*] (DBA) ... REAL
Road Environment Pollutant [*Automotive corrosion testing*] ... REP
Road Equivalent Tariff [*To finance ferries*] [*British*] (DI) ... RET
Road Haulage ... RH
Road Haulage Association [*British*] ... RHA
Road Haulage Cases [*1950-55*] [*England*] [*A publication*] (DLA) ... RHC
Road Haulage Vehicle (DCTA) ... RHV
Road Information Center [*Arab Contractors Co.*] (IID) ... RIC
[*The*] **Road Information Program** (EA) ... TRIP
Road Junction [*Maps and charts*] ... RJ
Road Load [*Automotive engineering*] ... RL
Road Load Horsepower [*Automotive engineering*] ... RLHP
Road Locomotive [*British*] ... RL
Road Markings Manufacturers and Contractors Association [*British*] (DBA) ... RMMCA
Road Mobile Intercontinental Ballistic Missile ... RMICBM
Road Octane Number [*Fuel technology*] ... RDON
Road Operators Safety Council [*British*] ... ROSC
Road Race Lincoln Register (EA) ... RRLR
Road Racing Drivers Club ... RRDC
Road Reconnaissance [*FAA*] (TAG) ... RC
Road Research Laboratory [*British*] ... RRL
Road Runners Club of America ... RRC
Road Runners Club of America (EA) ... RRCA
Road Safety and Motor Vehicle Regulation Branch, Transport Canada [*Direction de la Securite Routiere et de la Reglementation Automobile, Transports Canada*], Ottawa, Ontario [*Library symbol National Library of Canada*] (NLC) ... OOTRS
Road Safety Committee [*British police*] ... RSC
Road Safety Council [*Australia*] ... RSC
Road Safety Council of the Australian Capital Territory ... RSCACT
Road Safety Council of the Northern Territory [*Australia*] ... RSCNT
Road Sensing Suspension [*Automotive engineering*] ... RSS
Road Service ... R/S
Road Service Licence [*British*] (DCTA) ... RSL
Road Space [*Military*] ... RS
Road Surface Dressing Association [*British*] (DBA) ... RSDA
Road Tank Wagon (WDAA) ... RTW
Road Time Trials Council [*Bicycle racing competition*] [*British*] ... RTTC
Road Traffic ... RT
Road Traffic Accident [*British*] ... RTA
Road Traffic Act [*1962*] [*British A publication*] (DLA) ... RTA
Road Traffic Division [*British police*] ... RTD
Road Traffic Officer [*British police*] ... RTO
Road Traffic Regulation Act [*Town planning*] [*British*] ... RTRA
Road Traffic Reports [*A publication*] (DLA) ... RTR
Road Transport (NATG) ... RT
Road Transport Commission [*Australia*] ... RTC
Road Transport Industry Training Board [*British*] ... RITB
Road Transport Industry Training Board [*British*] (DCTA) ... RTITB
Road Truck [*Shipping*] (DCTA) ... RT
Road Vehicles Lighting Regulation (IAA) ... RVLR
Roadair Lines IC [*Canada ICAO designator*] (FAAC) ... RDL
Road-Holding [*In automobile name Rolls-Royce Bentley Turbo R*] ... R
Roadhouse Grill, Inc. [*NASDAQ symbol*] (SAG) ... GRLL
Roadhouse Grill, Inc. [*Associated Press*] (SAG) ... RdhseGr
Roadless Area Resource Evaluation ... RARE
Roadmaster Industries [*NYSE symbol*] (SAG) ... RDM
Roadmaster Industries [*Associated Press*] (SAG) ... Roadmst
Roadmasters and Maintenance of Way Association of America (EA) ... RMWAA
Roads [*Postal Service standard*] (OPSA) ... RDS
Roads ... RDS
Roads [*Commonly used*] (OPSA) ... ROADS
Roads and Landscape Planning [*British*] ... RLP
Roads and Transportation Association of Canada [*Ottawa, ON*] [*Formerly, Canadian Good Roads Association*] [*Research center*] ... RTAC
Roads and Transportation Association of Canada, Ottawa, ON, Canada [*Library symbol Library of Congress*] (LCLS) ... CaOORTA
Roads and Transportation Association of Canada [*Association des Routes et Transports du Canada*] **Ottawa, Ontario** [*Library symbol National Library of Canada*] (NLC) ... OORTA
Roads Corp. [*Victoria, Australia*] [*Commercial firm*] ... RC
Roadside Assistance Center [*Automotive Customer Service*] ... RAC
Roadside Business Association (EA) ... RBA
Roadside Delivery (ADA) ... RSD
Roadside Mailbox (ADA) ... RMB
Roadtown/Beef Island [*Virgin Islands*] [*ICAO location identifier*] (ICLI) ... TUPJ
Roadway ... RDWY
Roadway ... RDY
Roadway Analysis and Design System [*Computer science*] ... ROADS
Roadway Congestion Index [*BTS*] (TAG) ... RCI
Roadway Express [*NASDAQ symbol*] (TTSB) ... ROAD
Roadway Express, Inc. [*NASDAQ symbol*] (SAG) ... ROAD
Roadway Express, Inc. [*Associated Press*] (SAG) ... RoadwyEx
Roadway Powered Electric Vehicle ... RPEV
Roadway Powered Vehicle [*Automotive engineering*] ... RPV
Roadway Services, Inc. [*NASDAQ symbol*] (NQ) ... ROAD
Roadway Services, Inc. [*Associated Press*] (SAG) ... RoadSv
Roadway-Powered Transporter System [*Experimental vehicle*] ... RPTS
Roan [*Thoroughbred racing*] ... RO
Roan (Leather) [*Bookbinding*] (ROG) ... R
Roan (Leather) [*Bookbinding*] (ROG) ... RN
Roanne [*France*] [*Airport symbol*] (OAG) ... RNE
Roanne/Renaison [*France ICAO location identifier*] (ICLI) ... LFLO
Roanoke [*Virginia*] [*Airport symbol*] ... ROA
Roanoke, AL [*AM radio station call letters*] ... WELR
Roanoke, AL [*FM radio station call letters*] ... WELR-FM
Roanoke Bible College, Mary E. Griffith Memorial Library, Elizabeth City, NC [*Library symbol Library of Congress*] (LCLS) ... NcElcR
Roanoke College, Salem, VA [*Library symbol Library of Congress*] (LCLS) ... ViSaRC
Roanoke College, Salem, VA [*OCLC symbol*] (OCLC) ... VRO
Roanoke County Public Library, Roanoke, VA [*Library symbol*] [*Library of Congress*] (LCLS) ... ViRoC
Roanoke Electric Steel [*NASDAQ symbol*] (TTSB) ... RESC
Roanoke Electric Steel Corp. [*NASDAQ symbol*] (NQ) ... RESC
Roanoke Electric Steel Corp. [*Associated Press*] (SAG) ... Roan El
Roanoke Gas [*NASDAQ symbol*] (TTSB) ... RGCO
Roanoke Gas Co. [*NASDAQ symbol*] (SAG) ... RGCO
Roanoke Gas Co. [*Associated Press*] (SAG) ... RoanGas
Roanoke, IN [*FM radio station call letters*] ... WGL
Roanoke Memorial Hospital, Roanoke, VA [*Library symbol*] [*Library of Congress*] (LCLS) ... ViRoMH
Roanoke Public Library, Roanoke, IN [*Library symbol Library of Congress*] (LCLS) ... InRoa
Roanoke Public Library, Roanoke, VA [*Library symbol Library of Congress*] (LCLS) ... ViRo
Roanoke Rapids, NC [*Location identifier FAA*] (FAAL) ... RTK
Roanoke Rapids, NC [*Location identifier FAA*] (FAAL) ... RZZ
Roanoke Rapids, NC [*AM radio station call letters*] ... WCBT
Roanoke Rapids, NC [*FM radio station call letters*] ... WHGG
Roanoke Rapids, NC [*FM radio station call letters*] ... WPTM
Roanoke Rapids, NC [*Television station call letters*] ... WUNP
Roanoke Rapids, NC [*FM radio station call letters*] ... WZRU
Roanoke Rapids Public Library, Roanoke Rapids, NC [*Library symbol Library of Congress*] (LCLS) ... NcRr
Roanoke, VA [*Location identifier FAA*] (FAAL) ... CNQ
Roanoke, VA [*Location identifier FAA*] (FAAL) ... ODR
Roanoke, VA [*Location identifier FAA*] (FAAL) ... SZK
Roanoke, VA [*Location identifier FAA*] (FAAL) ... VIT
Roanoke, VA [*Television station call letters*] ... WBRA

Roanoke, VA [*Television station call letters*] .... WDBJ
Roanoke, VA [*Television station call letters*] .... WEFC
Roanoke, VA [*AM radio station call letters*] .... WFIR
Roanoke, VA [*Television station call letters*] .... WFXR
Roanoke, VA [*FM radio station call letters*] .... WPVR
Roanoke, VA [*FM radio station call letters*] .... WRDJ
Roanoke, VA [*AM radio station call letters*] .... WRIS
Roanoke, VA [*AM radio station call letters*] .... WROV
Roanoke, VA [*FM radio station call letters*] .... WRXT
Roanoke, VA [*AM radio station call letters*] .... WSLC
Roanoke, VA [*FM radio station call letters*] .... WSLQ
Roanoke, VA [*Television station call letters*] .... WSLS
Roanoke, VA [*FM radio station call letters*] .... WVTF
Roanoke, VA [*AM radio station call letters*] .... WWWR
Roanoke, VA [*FM radio station call letters*] .... WXLK
Roanoke Valley Library Association [*Library network*] .... RVLA
Roanoke-Chowan Technical Institute, Ahoskie, NC [*Library symbol Library of Congress*] (LCLS) .... NcAhRC
Roaring Spring, PA [*AM radio station call letters*] .... WKMC
Roast Beef [*Restaurant slang*] .... RB
Roasting (MSA) .... RSTG
Roatan [*Honduras*] [*Airport symbol*] (OAG) .... RTB
Roating Disk Electrode .... RDE
Rob and Bessie Welder Wildlife Foundation, Sinton, TX [*Library symbol Library of Congress*] (LCLS) .... TxSiW
Robards and Jackson's Reports [*26, 27 Texas*] [*A publication*] (DLA) .... Rob & J
Robards and Jackson's Reports [*26-27 Texas*] [*A publication*] (DLA) .... Robards & Jackson
Robards' Reports [*12, 13 Missouri*] [*A publication*] (DLA) .... Rob
Robards' Reports [*12, 13 Missouri*] [*A publication*] (DLA) .... Rob MO
Robards' Reports [*12, 13 Missouri*] [*A publication*] (DLA) .... Robards
Robards' Texas Conscript Cases [*1862-65*] [*A publication*] (DLA) .... Ro Rep
Robards' Texas Conscript Cases [*A publication*] (DLA) .... Rob
Robards' Texas Conscript Cases [*A publication*] (DLA) .... Rob Cons Cas (Tex)
Robards' Texas Conscript Cases [*A publication*] (DLA) .... Rob Consc Cas
Robards' Texas Conscript Cases [*1862-65*] [*A publication*] (DLA) .... Robards
Robarts School Library, London, Ontario [*Library symbol National Library of Canada*] (BIB) .... OLR
Robbery Armed .... RA
Robbery Armed - Unlawful Driving Away of an Automobile [*Police code*] .... RA-UDAA
Robbery Not Armed .... RNA
Robbins & Myers [*Associated Press*] (SAG) .... RobMyr
Robbins & Myers [*NASDAQ symbol*] (TTSB) .... ROBN
Robbins & Myers, Inc. [*NASDAQ symbol*] (NQ) .... ROBN
Robbins Elementary School, Syosset, NY [*Library symbol Library of Congress*] (LCLS) .... NSyoRE
Robbins Mills, Inc., Clarksville, VA [*Library symbol Library of Congress*] (LCLS) .... ViClR
Robbins' New Jersey Equity Reports [*67-70 New Jersey*] [*A publication*] (DLA) .... Robb
Robbins' New Jersey Equity Reports [*A publication*] (DLA) .... Robb (NJ)
Robbins Public Library, Arlington, MA [*Library symbol Library of Congress*] (LCLS) .... MAr
Robbins Public Library District, Robbins, IL [*Library symbol Library of Congress*] (LCLS) .... IRobb
Robbinsville, NC [*FM radio station call letters*] .... WCVP
Robbinsville, NJ [*Location identifier FAA*] (FAAL) .... RBV
Robb's United States Patent Cases [*A publication*] (DLA) .... Robb
Robb's United States Patent Cases [*A publication*] (DLA) .... Robb Pat Cas
Roberds, Inc. [*NASDAQ symbol*] (SAG) .... RBDS
Roberds, Inc. [*Associated Press*] (SAG) .... Roberds
Roberson, Fred, Louisville KY [*STAC*] .... RBF
Roberson Museum and Science Center, Binghamton, NY [*Library symbol*] [*Library of Congress*] (LCLS) .... NBiRM
Robersonville Public Library, Robersonville, NC [*Library symbol Library of Congress*] (LCLS) .... NcRov
Robert [*Phonetic alphabet*] [*Royal Navy World War I Pre-World War II*] (DSUE) .... R
Robert A. Taft Institute of Government [*Later, TTI*] (EA) .... RATIG
Robert A. Taft Sanitary Engineering Center (AABC) .... RATSEC
Robert & Carriere [*France*] [*Research code symbol*] .... RC
Robert B. Green Memorial Hospital, San Antonio, TX [*Library symbol Library of Congress*] (LCLS) .... TxSaGH
Robert E. Lee Memorial Association (EA) .... RELMA
Robert E. Lee Memorial Association, Stratford Hall, Stratford, VA [*Library symbol Library of Congress*] (LCLS) .... ViStrR
Robert F. Kennedy Memorial (EA) .... RFKM
Robert Francis Kennedy [*American politician, 1925-68*] .... RFK
Robert Gordon Institute of Technology [*Scotland*] .... RGIT
Robert Graham [*Designer's mark on US 1984 $1 Olympic commemorative coin*] .... RG
Robert Half International [*Associated Press*] (SAG) .... RbtHalf
Robert Half International [*Associated Press*] (SAG) .... RobtHalf
Robert Half International, Inc. [*NYSE symbol*] (SPSG) .... RHI
Robert Half Intl [*NYSE symbol*] (TTSB) .... RHI
Robert Jones [*Dressing*] [*Surgery*] (DAVI) .... RJ
Robert Louis Stevenson [*Nineteenth-century Scottish author*] .... RLS
Robert Lynd [*American author, 1892-1970*] [*Pseudonym*] .... YY
Robert Maynard Hutchins Center for the Study of Democratic Institutions (EA) .... RMHCSDI
Robert McLaughlin Gallery, Oshawa, ON, Canada [*Library symbol Library of Congress*] (LCLS) .... CaOOshR
Robert McLaughlin Gallery, Oshawa, Ontario [*Library symbol National Library of Canada*] (NLC) .... OOSHR
Robert Mines Ltd. [*Vancouver Stock Exchange symbol*] .... RRT
Robert Mondavi 'A' [*NASDAQ symbol*] (TTSB) .... MOND
Robert Morris Associates [*National Association of Bank Loan and Credit Officers*] [*Philadelphia, PA*] (EA) .... RMA
Robert Morris College, Coraopolis, PA [*Library symbol Library of Congress*] (LCLS) .... PCoR
Robert Morris College, Coraopolis, PA [*OCLC symbol*] (OCLC) .... ROB
Robert Moses Junior High School, North Babylon, NY [*Library symbol*] [*Library of Congress*] (LCLS) .... NNbMJ
Robert Mueller Municipal Airport [*FAA*] (TAG) .... AUS
Robert Owen Association (EA) .... ROA
Robert Plant International Fan Club (EA) .... RPIFC
Robert Redford Fan Club (EA) .... RRFC
Robert S. Kerr Environmental Research Laboratory [*Ada, OK*] [*Environmental Protection Agency*] (GRD) .... RSKERL
Robert Stigwood Orginazation [*Record label*] .... RSO
Robert Strange McNamara [*US Secretary of Defense, 1961-68*] .... RSM
Robert W. Carbonaro School, Valley Stream, NY [*Library symbol*] [*Library of Congress*] (LCLS) .... NVsCE
Robert Wood Johnson Foundation .... RWJF
Robert Wood Johnson Foundation Library, Princeton, NJ [*Library symbol Library of Congress*] (LCLS) .... NjPJ
Robert Wood Johnson Medical School [*New Jersey*] .... RWJ
Roberta Jo Society (EA) .... RJS
Robert's Arm Public Library, Newfoundland [*Library symbol National Library of Canada*] (BIB) .... NFRA
Robert's Digest [*Lower Canada*] [*A publication*] (DLA) .... Rob Dig
Robert's Digest of Vermont Reports [*A publication*] (DLA) .... Rob Dig
Roberts, IL [*Location identifier FAA*] (FAAL) .... RBS
Roberts Information Services, Inc. [*Information service or system*] (IID) .... ROBINS
Roberts, Leaming, and Wallis' County Court Reports [*1849-51*] [*A publication*] (DLA) .... RL & W
Roberts, Leaming, and Wallis' County Court Reports [*1849-51*] [*A publication*] (DLA) .... Rob L & W
Roberts on Admiralty and Prize [*A publication*] (DLA) .... Rob Adm & Pr
Roberts on Federal Liabilities of Carriers [*A publication*] (DLA) .... Roberts Emp Liab
Roberts on Frauds [*1805*] [*A publication*] (DLA) .... Rob Fr
Roberts on Fraudulent Conveyances [*A publication*] (DLA) .... Rob Fr Conv
Roberts on the Law of Personal Succession [*A publication*] (DLA) .... Rob Succ
Roberts Pharmaceutical [*NASDAQ symbol*] (TTSB) .... RPCX
Roberts Pharmaceutical Corp. [*Associated Press*] (SAG) .... RbtPhr
Roberts Pharmaceutical Corp. [*NASDAQ symbol*] (SAG) .... RPCX
Roberts' Principles of Equity [*A publication*] (DLA) .... Rob Eq
Roberts Public Library, Roberts, ID [*Library symbol*] [*Library of Congress*] (LCLS) .... IdRo
Roberts Radio Current Meter (NOAA) .... RRCM
Roberts' Reports [*29-31 Louisiana Annual*] [*A publication*] (DLA) .... Rob
Roberts' Reports [*29-31 Louisiana Annual*] [*A publication*] (DLA) .... Roberts
Roberts Syndrome [*Medicine*] (DMAA) .... RS
Roberts Wesleyan College [*Rochester, NY*] .... RWC
Roberts Wesleyan College, K. B. Keating Library, Rochester, NY [*OCLC symbol*] (OCLC) .... RVA
Roberts Wesleyan College, North Chili, NY [*Library symbol Library of Congress*] (LCLS) .... NNcR
Roberts. Wills and Codicils [*1826*] [*A publication*] (ILCA) .... Rob W
Robertsdale, AL [*AM radio station call letters*] .... WXWY
Robertsfield [*Liberia*] [*Airport symbol*] .... ROB
Robertson [*South Africa*] [*ICAO location identifier*] (ICLI) .... FARS
Robertson and Jacob's New York Marine Court Reports [*A publication*] (DLA) .... Rob Mar (NY)
Robertson Memorial Library, Higginsville, MO [*Library symbol*] [*Library of Congress*] (LCLS) .... MoHig
Robertson-Ceco Corp. [*Associated Press*] (SAG) .... RbtCeco
Robertson-Ceco Corp. [*NYSE symbol*] (SPSG) .... RHH
Robertson's English Ecclesiastical Reports [*A publication*] (DLA) .... Rob
Robertson's English Ecclesiastical Reports [*2 vols.*] [*1844-53*] [*A publication*] (DLA) .... Rob E
Robertson's English Ecclesiastical Reports [*2 vols.*] [*1844-53*] [*A publication*] (DLA) .... Rob Ecc
Robertson's English Ecclesiastical Reports [*2 vols.*] [*1844-53*] [*A publication*] (DLA) .... Rob Eccl
Robertson's English Ecclesiastical Reports [*A publication*] (DLA) .... Robertson
Robertson's English Ecclesiastical Reports [*163 English Reprint*] [*1844-53*] [*A publication*] (DLA) .... Robt Eccl
Robertson's English Ecclesiastical Reports [*163 English Reprint*] [*A publication*] (DLA) .... Robt Eccl (Eng)
Robertson's Handbook of Bankers' Law [*A publication*] (DLA) .... Rob Bank
Robertson's Handbook of Bankers' Law [*A publication*] (DLA) .... Robs Bankr
Robertson's History of the Reign of the Emperor Charles V [*A publication*] (DLA) .... Rob Car V
Robertson's Law of Personal Succession [*1836*] [*A publication*] (DLA) .... Rob Per Suc
Robertson's Law of Priority of Incumbrances [*A publication*] (DLA) .... Rob Prior
Robertson's Legitimation by Subsequent Marriage [*1829*] [*A publication*] (DLA) .... Rob Leg
Robertson's New York Superior Court Reports [*24-30*] [*A publication*] (DLA) .... Rob Sr Ct
Robertson's Reports [*24-30 New York Superior Court*] [*1863-68*] [*A publication*] (DLA) .... Rob
Robertson's Reports [*1 Hawaii*] [*A publication*] (DLA) .... Rob
Robertson's Reports [*24-30 New York Superior Court*] [*A publication*] (DLA) .... Rob (NY)
Robertson's Reports [*24-30 New York Superior Court*] [*A publication*] (DLA) .... Rob Super Ct
Robertson's Reports [*New York Marine Court*] [*A publication*] (DLA) .... Robertson

Robertson's Reports [*24-30 New York Superior Court*] [*A publication*] (DLA) ... Robertson
Robertson's Reports [*1 Hawaii*] [*A publication*] (DLA) ... Robertson
Robertson's Reports [*24-30 New York Superior Court*] [*A publication*] (DLA) ... Robertson's Rep
Robertson's Reports [*24-30 New York Superior Court*] [*A publication*] (DLA) ... Robt (NY)
Robertson's Sandwich Island Reports [*1 Hawaii*] [*A publication*] (DLA) ... Rob SI
Robertson's Scotch Appeal Cases [*1707-27*] [*A publication*] (DLA) ... Rob
Robertson's Scotch Appeal Cases [*1707-27*] [*A publication*] (DLA) ... Robert
Robertson's Scotch Appeal Cases [*1707-27*] [*A publication*] (DLA) ... Robertson
Robertson's Scotch Appeal Cases [*A publication*] (DLA) ... Robt Sc App Cas
Robertson's Scotch House of Lords Appeals [*A publication*] (DLA) ... Robert App
Robertson's Scotch House of Lords Appeals [*A publication*] (DLA) ... Robert App Cas
Robertsport/Cape Mount [*Liberia*] [*ICAO location identifier*] (ICLI) ... GLCM
Robertus [*Authority cited in pre-1607 legal work*] (DSA) ... R
Robertus [*Authority cited in pre-1607 legal work*] (DSA) ... Rober
Robertus Maranta [*Flourished, 16th century*] [*Authority cited in pre-1607 legal work*] (DSA) ... Rober Maran
Roberval [*Canada*] [*Airport symbol Obsolete*] (OAG) ... YRJ
[*The*] **Roberval & Saguenay Railway Co.** [*AAR code*] ... RS
Roberval, PQ [*AM radio station call letters*] ... CHRL
Roberval, PQ [*ICAO location identifier*] (ICLI) ... CYRJ
Robeson County Public Library, Lumberton, NC [*Library symbol Library of Congress*] (LCLS) ... NcLu
Robeson Technical Institute, Lumbarton, NC [*Library symbol Library of Congress*] (LCLS) ... NcLuR
Robeson Technical Institute, St. Pauls, NC [*Library symbol Library of Congress Obsolete*] (LCLS) ... NcStpR
Robin Avions [*Pierre Robin*] [*France ICAO aircraft manufacturer identifier*] (ICAO) ... DR
Robin Avions [*Pierre Robin*] [*France ICAO aircraft manufacturer identifier*] (ICAO) ... HR
Robin Avions [*Pierre Robin*] [*France ICAO aircraft manufacturer identifier*] (ICAO) ... R
Robin George Fan Club (EA) ... RGFC
Robin Hood Society [*British*] (DBA) ... RHS
Robin International, Inc. [*Toronto Stock Exchange symbol*] ... ROB
Robin Right Fan Club (EA) ... RRFC
Robinhood [*Queensland*] [*Airport symbol*] (AD) ... RFW
Robinhood [*Australia Airport symbol Obsolete*] (OAG) ... ROH
Robinia Mosaic Virus [*Plant pathology*] ... ROBMV
Robinson and Harrison's Digest [*Ontario*] [*A publication*] (DLA) ... R & H Dig
Robinson and Joseph's Digest [*Ontario*] [*A publication*] (DLA) ... R & J Dig
Robinson Community School District 2, Robinson, IL [*Library symbol Library of Congress*] (LCLS) ... IRobSD
Robinson Crusoe Island [*Juan Fernandez Archipelago*] [*Seismograph station code, US Geological Survey*] (SEIS) ... IJF
Robinson, IL [*Location identifier FAA*] (FAAL) ... PLX
Robinson, IL [*Location identifier FAA*] (FAAL) ... RSV
Robinson, IL [*AM radio station call letters*] ... WTAY
Robinson, IL [*FM radio station call letters*] (RBYB) ... WTYE
Robinson Jeffers Committee (EA) ... RJC
Robinson Jeffers Home [*Tor House*], Carmel, CA [*Library symbol Library of Congress*] (LCLS) ... CCarmJ
Robinson Little & Co. Ltd. [*Toronto Stock Exchange symbol*] ... RLC
Robinson Memorial Hospital, Ravenna, OH [*Library symbol*] [*Library of Congress*] (LCLS) ... ORaH
Robinson Nugent [*NASDAQ symbol*] (TTSB) ... RNIC
Robinson Nugent, Inc. [*NASDAQ symbol*] (NQ) ... RNIC
Robinson Nugent, Inc. [*Associated Press*] (SAG) ... RobNug
Robinson on Patents [*A publication*] (DLA) ... Rob Pat
Robinson Public Library, Robinson, IL [*Library symbol Library of Congress*] (LCLS) ... IRob
Robinson River [*Papua New Guinea*] [*Airport symbol*] (OAG) ... RNR
Robinson's Book of Entries [*A publication*] (DLA) ... Rob Ent
Robinson's Common Law of Kent, or Custom on Gavelkind [*5th ed.*] [*1897*] [*A publication*] (DLA) ... Rob Gav
Robinson's Elementary Law [*A publication*] (DLA) ... Rob El Law
Robinson's English Admiralty Reports [*1799-1808*] [*A publication*] (DLA) ... Ch Rob
Robinson's English Admiralty Reports [*1799-1809, 1838-1852*] [*A publication*] (DLA) ... Rob
Robinson's English Ecclesiastical Reports [*1844-53*] [*A publication*] (DLA) ... Rob
Robinson's English Ecclesiastical Reports [*1844-53*] [*A publication*] (DLA) ... Robinson
Robinson's Justice of the Peace [*1836*] [*A publication*] (DLA) ... Rob Jus
Robinson's Louisiana Reports [*1-4 Louisiana Annual*] [*1841-46*] [*A publication*] (DLA) ... Rob
Robinson's Louisiana Reports [*1-4 Louisiana Annual*] [*1841-46*] [*A publication*] (DLA) ... Rob LA
Robinson's Louisiana Reports [*1-4 Louisiana Annual*] [*A publication*] (DLA) ... Rob (LA Ann)
Robinson's Louisiana Reports [*1-12 Louisiana*] [*A publication*] (DLA) ... Rob Louis
Robinson's Louisiana Reports [*1-12 Louisiana*] [*A publication*] (DLA) ... Robinson
Robinson's Ontario Reports [*A publication*] (DLA) ... Robinson
Robinson's Practice [*A publication*] (DLA) ... Rob Pr
Robinson's Reports [*2-9, 17-23 Colorado Appeals*] [*A publication*] (DLA) ... Rob
Robinson's Reports [*38 California*] [*A publication*] (DLA) ... Rob
Robinson's Reports [*1-8 Ontario*] [*A publication*] (DLA) ... Rob
Robinson's Reports [*40, 41 Virginia*] [*A publication*] (DLA) ... Rob
Robinson's Reports [*1 Nevada*] [*A publication*] (DLA) ... Rob
Robinson's Reports [*38 California*] [*A publication*] (DLA) ... Rob Cal
Robinson's Reports [*2-9, 17-23 Colorado Appeals*] [*A publication*] (DLA) ... Rob Chr
Robinson's Reports [*2-9, 17-23 Colorado Appeals*] [*A publication*] (ILCA) ... Rob Colo
Robinson's Reports [*1 Hawaii*] [*A publication*] (DLA) ... Rob Hawaii
Robinson's Reports [*1 Nevada*] [*A publication*] (DLA) ... Rob Nev
Robinson's Reports [*1-8 Ontario*] [*A publication*] (DLA) ... Rob Ont
Robinson's Reports [*40, 41 Virginia*] [*A publication*] (DLA) ... Rob VA
Robinson's Reports [*38 California*] [*A publication*] (DLA) ... Robinson
Robinson's Reports [*1 Nevada*] [*A publication*] (DLA) ... Robinson
Robinson's Reports [*17-23 Colorado*] [*A publication*] (DLA) ... Robinson
Robinson's Reports [*40-41 Virginia*] [*A publication*] (DLA) ... Robinson
Robinson's Scotch Appeal Cases [*1840-41*] [*A publication*] (DLA) ... Rob
Robinson's Scotch Appeal Cases [*1840-41*] [*A publication*] (DLA) ... Rob App
Robinson's Scotch Appeal Cases [*1840-41*] [*A publication*] (DLA) ... Rob Cas
Robinson's Scotch Appeal Cases [*A publication*] (DLA) ... Rob Sc App
Robinson's Scotch Appeal Cases [*1840-41*] [*A publication*] (DLA) ... Robin Sc App
Robinson's Scotch Appeal Cases [*1840-41*] [*A publication*] (DLA) ... Robinson Sc App Cas
Robinson's Scotch House of Lords Appeals [*A publication*] (DLA) ... Robin App
Robinson's Scotch House of Lords Appeals [*A publication*] (DLA) ... Robinson
Robinson's Upper Canada Reports [*A publication*] (DLA) ... Rob
Robinson's Upper Canada Reports [*A publication*] (DLA) ... Rob UC
Robinson's Virginia Forms [*A publication*] (DLA) ... Rob Forms
Robinson-Sheppard, Montreal, Quebec [*Library symbol National Library of Canada*] (BIB) ... QMROS
Robinton Aereo CA [*Dominican Republic*] [*ICAO designator*] (FAAC) ... RBT
Robomatix Technologies [*NASDAQ symbol*] (SAG) ... RBMX
Robore [*Bolivia*] [*Airport symbol*] (AD) ... RBO
Robore [*Bolivia*] [*ICAO location identifier*] (ICLI) ... SLRB
Roborough [*England*] ... ROB
Robot Bomb [*Air Force*] ... ROBOMB
Robot Controller (IAA) ... RC
Robot Excavation [*Carnegie-Mellon Robotics Institute*] ... REX
Robot Institute of America (NADA) ... RIA
Robot Programming Language [*Computer science*] ... RPL
Robot Testing and Assessment Facility ... RTAF
Robot Vehicle Expressway ... RVX
Robotech Defense Force [*Defunct*] (EA) ... RDF
Robotic All-Terrain Lunar Exploration Rover [*NASA*] ... RATLER
Robotic Ammunition Landing System ... RALS
Robotic Assistant Labor Facilitator [*In the movie "Flight of the Navigator" (1986)*] ... RALF
Robotic Combat Vehicle [*Army*] (RDA) ... RCV
Robotic Command Center [*Army*] ... RCC
Robotic Deriveter System ... RDS
Robotic Industries Association (EA) ... RIA
Robotic Muscle Activator ... ROMAC
Robotic Obstacle-Breaching Assault Tank ... ROBAT
Robotic Operating Buddy [*Nintendo video game system accessory*] ... ROB
Robotic Sample Processor [*Automation*] ... RSP
Robotic Substrate Servicing System [*Space Automation and Robotics Center*] [*NASA*] ... RSSS
Robotic Tele-Excavation [*University of Southern California*] ... RTE
Robotic Telepresence ... RT
Robotic Vehicle (RDA) ... RV
Robotic Vision Sys [*NASDAQ symbol*] (TTSB) ... ROBV
Robotic Vision Systems, Inc. [*Associated Press*] (SAG) ... RobotVs
Robotic Vision Systems, Inc. [*NASDAQ symbol*] (NQ) ... ROBV
Robotics ... R
Robotics and Automation Applications Consulting Center [*Ford Motor Co.*] ... RAACC
Robotics & Automation Research Laboratory [*University of Toronto*] [*Research center*] (RCD) ... RAL
Robotics and Intelligent Systems Program [*Oak Ridge National Laboratory*] ... RISP
Robotics Information [*EIC/Intelligence, Inc.*] [*Information service or system*] (IID) ... RBOT
Robotics International Association of the Society of Manufacturing Engineers (BTTJ) ... RI
Robotics International of SME [*Society of Manufacturing Engineers*] (EA) ... RI/SME
Robotics Operating System ... ROS
Robotics Technology Development Program ... RTDP
Robotnicza Partia Polskich Socjalistow [*Workers Party of Polish Socialists*] [*Political party*] (PPE) ... RPPS
Robotnicza Partia Polskich Socjalistow - Lewica [*Workers Party of Polish Socialists - Left*] [*Political party*] (PPE) ... RPPS-Lewica
Robson on Law and Practice in Bankruptcy [*7th ed.*] [*1894*] [*A publication*] (DLA) ... Rob Bank
Robson on Law and Practice in Bankruptcy [*7th ed.*] [*1894*] [*A publication*] (DLA) ... Robs Bank
Robson on Law and Practice in Bankruptcy [*7 eds.*] [*1870-94*] [*A publication*] (DLA) ... Robson
Robson Petroleum Ltd. [*Toronto Stock Exchange symbol*] ... ROP
Robstown, TX [*AM radio station call letters*] ... KGLF
Robstown, TX [*FM radio station call letters*] ... KLUX
Robstown, TX [*FM radio station call letters*] ... KMIQ
Robstown, TX [*FM radio station call letters*] ... KSAB
Roburent [*Italy*] [*Seismograph station code, US Geological Survey*] (SEIS) ... ROB
Robust Detection Scheme [*Navigation*] (OA) ... RDS
Robust Expert Maintenance System [*US Army Tank-Automotive Command*] (RDA) ... REMS
Robust Sequential Probability Ratio Test [*Navy*] ... RSPRT
Robustrus Archistriatalis [*Bird brain anatomy*] ... RA

Robyn Hitchcock Fan Club (EA) ... RHFC
ROC Communities [*NYSE symbol*] (SPSG) ... RCI
ROC Communities [*Associated Press*] (SAG) ... ROC Cm
ROC Taiwan Fund [*Associated Press*] (SAG) ... ROC Fd
ROC Taiwan Fund SBI [*NYSE symbol*] (SPSG) ... ROC
Rocailles, Coquilles, et Cordeau [*Rocks, Shells, and String*] [*French*] ... ROCOCO
Rocca Di Papa [*Italy*] [*Seismograph station code, US Geological Survey*] (SEIS) ... RDP
Roccus. De Navibus et Naulo [*Maritime law*] [*A publication*] (DLA) ... Rocc
Roccus. De Navibus et Naulo [*Maritime law*] [*A publication*] (DLA) ... Rocc De Nav et Nau
Roccus on Insurance [*A publication*] (DLA) ... Roc Ins
Roccus on Insurance [*A publication*] (DLA) ... Roccus Ins
Rochdale Institute, New York, NY [*Library symbol Library of Congress*] (LCLS) ... NNRoI
Roche and Hazlitt's Bankruptcy Practice [*2nd ed.*] [*1873*] [*A publication*] (DLA) ... R & H Bank
Roche and Hazlitt's Bankruptcy Practice [*2nd ed.*] [*1873*] [*A publication*] (DLA) ... Roche & H Bank
Roche Associes Ltee., Centre de Documentation, Ste.-Foy, PQ, Canada [*Library symbol Library of Congress*] (LCLS) ... CaQSTFRA
Roche Associes Ltee., Group-Conseil, Ste.-Foy, Quebec [*Library symbol National Library of Canada*] (NLC) ... QQRA
Roche Associes Ltee., Groupe-Conseil, Ste.-Foy, PQ, Canada [*Library symbol Library of Congress*] (LCLS) ... CaQQRA
Roche, Dillon, and Kehoe's Irish Land Reports [*1881-82*] [*A publication*] (DLA) ... Roche D & K
Roche Harbor [*Washington*] [*Airport symbol*] (OAG) ... RCE
Roche Institute of Molecular Biology ... RIMB
Roche Memorial Library, Wyoming, IA [*Library symbol Library of Congress*] (LCLS) ... IaWyo
Roche Products Ltd. [*Great Britain*] [*Research code symbol*] ... TRK
Roche Psychiatric Service Institute ... RPSI
Rochefort/Saint-Agnant [*France ICAO location identifier*] (ICLI) ... LFDN
Rochefort/Soubise [*France ICAO location identifier*] (ICLI) ... LFXR
Rochelle, IL [*AM radio station call letters*] ... WRHL
Rochelle, IL [*FM radio station call letters*] ... WRHL-FM
Rochelle News, Rochelle, IL [*Library symbol*] [*Library of Congress*] (LCLS) ... IRocN
Rochelle Salt [*Potassium Sodium Tartrate*] [*Organic chemistry*] ... RS
Rochester [*British ICAO location identifier*] (ICLI) ... EGTO
Rochester [*England*] [*Airport symbol*] (AD) ... RCS
Rochester [*New York*] [*Airport symbol*] (OAG) ... ROC
Rochester [*Municipal borough in England*] (ROG) ... ROCH
Rochester [*Minnesota*] [*Airport symbol*] (OAG) ... RST
Rochester 3R's Union List of Serials, Rochester, NY [*OCLC symbol*] (OCLC) ... VRS
Rochester Commercial and Industrial [*Database*] ... RCI
Rochester Community College, Rochester, MN [*OCLC symbol*] (OCLC) ... RCC
[*The*] **Rochester Community Savings Bank** [*NASDAQ symbol*] (NQ) ... RCSB
Rochester Gas & El [*NYSE symbol*] (TTSB) ... RGS
Rochester Gas & Electric Corp. [*NYSE symbol*] (SPSG) ... RGS
Rochester Gas & Electric Corp. [*Associated Press*] (SAG) ... RochG
Rochester Gas & Electric Corp., Technical Information Center, Rochester, NY [*Library symbol Library of Congress*] (LCLS) ... NRGas
Rochester Gas & Electric Corp., TIC Library, Rochester, NY [*OCLC symbol*] (OCLC) ... RVB
Rochester General Hospital Library, Rochester, NY [*OCLC symbol*] (OCLC) ... RVC
Rochester Historical Society, Rochester, NY [*Library symbol Library of Congress*] (LCLS) ... NRHi
Rochester, IN [*Location identifier FAA*] (FAAL) ... RCR
Rochester, IN [*FM radio station call letters*] ... WROI
Rochester Institute of Technology (GAGS) ... RIT
Rochester Institute of Technology [*New York*] ... RIT
Rochester Institute of Technology Library [*UTLAS symbol*] ... RIT
Rochester Institute of Technology, Melbert B. Cary, Jr. Graphic Arts Collection,Rochester, NY [*Library symbol Library of Congress*] (LCLS) ... NRRI-C
Rochester Institute of Technology, Rochester, NY [*Library symbol Library of Congress*] (LCLS) ... NRRI
Rochester Institute of Technology, Wallace Memorial Library, Rochester, NY [*OCLC symbol*] (OCLC) ... RVE
Rochester Junior College [*Minnesota*] [*Later, Rochester Community College*] ... RJC
Rochester Medical [*NASDAQ symbol*] (TTSB) ... ROCM
Rochester Medical Corp. [*Associated Press*] (SAG) ... RochMed
Rochester Medical Corp. [*NASDAQ symbol*] (SAG) ... ROCM
Rochester Methodist Hospital, Rochester, MN [*Library symbol Library of Congress*] (LCLS) ... MnRMeH
Rochester Minerals [*Vancouver Stock Exchange symbol*] ... ROR
Rochester, MN [*FM radio station call letters*] ... KFSI
Rochester, MN [*FM radio station call letters*] ... KLSE
Rochester, MN [*FM radio station call letters*] ... KNXR
Rochester, MN [*AM radio station call letters*] ... KOLM
Rochester, MN [*FM radio station call letters*] ... KRCH
Rochester, MN [*AM radio station call letters*] ... KROC
Rochester, MN [*FM radio station call letters*] ... KROC-FM
Rochester, MN [*FM radio station call letters*] ... KRPR
Rochester, MN [*Television station call letters*] ... KTTC
Rochester, MN [*AM radio station call letters*] ... KWEB
Rochester, MN [*FM radio station call letters*] ... KWWK
Rochester, MN [*Television station call letters*] ... KXLT-TV
Rochester, MN [*FM radio station call letters*] ... KZSE
Rochester, MN [*Location identifier FAA*] (FAAL) ... MNK
Rochester Museum and Science Center, Rochester, NY [*Library symbol Library of Congress*] (LCLS) ... NRM
Rochester Museum and Science Center, Rochester, NY [*OCLC symbol*] (OCLC) ... VXR
Rochester, NH [*FM radio station call letters*] (RBYB) ... WSRI
Rochester, NH [*AM radio station call letters*] ... WZNN
Rochester, NY [*Location identifier FAA*] (FAAL) ... AVN
Rochester, NY [*Location identifier FAA*] (FAAL) ... MCU
Rochester, NY [*Location identifier FAA*] (FAAL) ... MWD
Rochester, NY [*AM radio station call letters*] ... WBBF
Rochester, NY [*FM radio station call letters*] ... WBEE
Rochester, NY [*FM radio station call letters*] ... WBER
Rochester, NY [*AM radio station call letters*] ... WCMF
Rochester, NY [*FM radio station call letters*] ... WCMF-FM
Rochester, NY [*FM radio station call letters*] ... WDKX
Rochester, NY [*AM radio station call letters*] ... WHAM
Rochester, NY [*Television station call letters*] ... WHEC
Rochester, NY [*AM radio station call letters*] ... WHTK
Rochester, NY [*FM radio station call letters*] ... WIRQ
Rochester, NY [*FM radio station call letters*] ... WJZR
Rochester, NY [*FM radio station call letters*] ... WKLX
Rochester, NY [*Television station call letters*] ... WOKR
Rochester, NY [*FM radio station call letters*] ... WPXY
Rochester, NY [*FM radio station call letters*] ... WRMM
Rochester, NY [*Television station call letters*] ... WROC
Rochester, NY [*FM radio station call letters*] ... WRUR
Rochester, NY [*Television station call letters*] ... WUHF
Rochester, NY [*FM radio station call letters*] ... WVOR
Rochester, NY [*AM radio station call letters*] ... WWWG
Rochester, NY [*AM radio station call letters*] ... WXXI
Rochester, NY [*FM radio station call letters*] ... WXXI-FM
Rochester, NY [*Television station call letters*] ... WXXI-TV
Rochester Psychiatric Center Library, Rochester, NY [*OCLC symbol*] (OCLC) ... RVF
Rochester Public Library, Alberta [*Library symbol National Library of Canada*] (NLC) ... AROC
Rochester Public Library, Rochester, AB, Canada [*Library symbol*] [*Library of Congress*] (LCLS) ... CaARoc
Rochester Public Library, Rochester, MN [*Library symbol Library of Congress*] (LCLS) ... MnR
Rochester Public Library, Rochester, MN [*OCLC symbol*] (OCLC) ... ROC
Rochester Public Library, Rochester, NY [*Library symbol Library of Congress*] (LCLS) ... NR
Rochester Public Library, Rochester, NY [*OCLC symbol*] (OCLC) ... YQR
Rochester Public Library, Rochester, VT [*Library symbol Library of Congress*] (LCLS) ... VtRoc
Rochester Public Schools, Library Processing Center, Rochester, MN [*OCLC symbol*] (OCLC) ... RPS
Rochester Public Schools, Rochester, MN [*Library symbol Library of Congress*] (LCLS) ... MnRPS
Rochester Reference Research and Resources Council, Rochester, NY [*Library symbol Library of Congress*] (LCLS) ... NRRR
Rochester Regional Library Council [*Information service or system*] (IID) ... RRLC
Rochester Regional Research Library Council [*Rochester, NY*] [*Library network*] ... RRRLC
Rochester Regional Research Library Council, Rochester, NY [*OCLC symbol*] (OCLC) ... VRR
Rochester/Rochester-Monroe County [*New York*] [*ICAO location identifier*] (ICLI) ... KROC
Rochester Sentinel, Rochester, IN [*Library symbol Library of Congress*] (LCLS) ... InRocS
Rochester State Junior College, Rochester, MN [*Library symbol Library of Congress*] (LCLS) ... MnRR
Rochester Subway Co. [*AAR code*] ... RSB
Rochester Volunteer Training Corps [*British military*] (DMA) ... RVTC
Rochester-Mercier [*New York*] [*Seismograph station code, US Geological Survey Closed*] (SEIS) ... RMO
Rochester-Odenbach [*New York*] [*Seismograph station code, US Geological Survey*] (SEIS) ... ROC
Rochus Curtius [*Flourished, 1470-1515*] [*Authority cited in pre-1607 legal work*] (DSA) ... Roc
Rochus Curtius [*Flourished, 1470-1515*] [*Authority cited in pre-1607 legal work*] (DSA) ... Roch
Rochus Curtius [*Flourished, 1470-1515*] [*Authority cited in pre-1607 legal work*] (DSA) ... Roch Curt
Rock [*Maps and charts*] ... R
Rock [*Maps and charts*] (MCD) ... RK
Rock [*Germany ICAO aircraft manufacturer identifier*] (ICAO) ... RO
Rock Analysis Storage System [*United States Geological Survey*] [*Information service or system*] (IID) ... RASS
Rock and Roll [*Music*] ... R & R
Rock and Roll [*Music*] (BARN) ... r'n'r
Rock and Roll Hall of Fame and Museum ... RnRHoF&M
Rock and Roll Hall of Fame Foundation (EA) ... RRHFF
Rock and Rye ... R & R
Rock Bass [*Ichthyology*] ... Rb
Rock Bottom Restaurants [*NASDAQ symbol*] (TTSB) ... BREW
Rock Bottom Restaurants, Inc. [*NASDAQ symbol*] (SAG) ... BREW
Rock Bottom Restaurants, Inc. [*Associated Press*] (SAG) ... RockBott
Rock Characterization Facility [*Nuclear waste storage*] ... RCF
Rock Chemical Database [*Ontario Geological Survey*] [*Canada Information service or system*] (CRD) ... PETROCH
Rock Coring Device ... RCD
Rock County Health Care Center, Janesville, WI [*Library symbol Library of Congress*] (LCLS) ... WJaRH

Rock Eagle [Georgia] [Seismograph station code, US Geological Survey] (SEIS) ..... REG
Rock Harbor, FL [FM radio station call letters] ..... WKLG
Rock Hill [South Carolina] [Airport symbol] (OAG) ..... RKH
Rock Hill, SC [Location identifier FAA] (FAAL) ..... RRP
Rock Hill, SC [AM radio station call letters] ..... WAVO
Rock Hill, SC [Television station call letters] ..... WFVT
Rock Hill, SC [FM radio station call letters] ..... WNSC
Rock Hill, SC [Television station call letters] ..... WNSC-TV
Rock Hill, SC [AM radio station call letters] ..... WRHI
Rock Information System [Carnegie Institution] [Databank] [National Science Foundation] (IID) ..... RKNFSYS
Rock Is Stoning Kids [Defunct] (EA) ..... RISK
Rock Island Arsenal [Illinois] [Army] ..... RIA
Rock Island Arsenal General Thomas J. Rodman Laboratory [Army] ..... RIA-R
Rock Island Arsenal Laboratories [Illinois] (MCD) ..... RIAL
Rock Island Arsenal/Science and Engineering Directorate [Illinois] ..... RIA/SE
Rock Island, IL [Television station call letters] ..... WHBF
Rock Island, IL [FM radio station call letters] (RBYB) ..... WHTS
Rock Island, IL [AM radio station call letters] ..... WKBF
Rock Island, IL [FM radio station call letters] ..... WVIK
Rock Island Lines [Railroad] ..... RI
Rock Island Public Library, Rock Island, IL [Library symbol Library of Congress] (LCLS) ..... IR
Rock Island Railroad Transportation and Employee Assistance Act [1980] ..... RITEA
Rock Island Southern Railroad (IIA) ..... RIS
Rock Island, WA [FM radio station call letters] ..... KXAA
Rock Mechanics Applied to Mine Planning (PDAA) ..... RAMPLAN
Rock Mechanics Laboratory [Pennsylvania State University] [Research center] (RCD) ..... RML
Rock Properties Information Center [Purdue University] [National Science Foundation] (IID) ..... RPIC
Rock Quality Designation [Mining technology] [Nuclear energy] (NRCH) ..... RQD
Rock Rapids, IA [Location identifier FAA] (FAAL) ..... RRQ
Rock River Elementary School, Rockford, IL [Library symbol] [Library of Congress] (LCLS) ..... IRoRrE
Rock Sound [Bahamas] [Airport symbol] (OAG) ..... RSD
Rock Sound/International, Eleuthera Island [Bahamas] [ICAO location identifier] (ICLI) ..... MYER
Rock Springs [Wyoming] [Airport symbol] (OAG) ..... RKS
Rock Springs, WY [Location identifier FAA] (FAAL) ..... AOP
Rock Springs, WY [Television station call letters] ..... KGWR
Rock Springs, WY [FM radio station call letters] ..... KQSW
Rock Springs, WY [AM radio station call letters] ..... KRKK
Rock Springs, WY [FM radio station call letters] ..... KSIT
Rock Springs, WY [FM radio station call letters] ..... KUWZ
Rock Springs, WY [FM radio station call letters] ..... KYCS
Rock Storage [Storage in excavated rock caverns] ..... ROCKSTORE
Rock Tenn Co. [NYSE symbol] (SAG) ..... RKT
Rock Tenn Co. [NASDAQ symbol] (SAG) ..... RKTN
Rock Tenn Co. [Associated Press] (SAG) ..... RockTen
Rock Valley Bee, Rock Valley, IA [Library symbol Library of Congress] (LCLS) ..... IaRvB
Rock Valley, IA [FM radio station call letters] ..... KQEP
Rockdale, NY [Location identifier FAA] (FAAL) ..... RKA
Rockdale, Sandow & Southern Railroad Co. [AAR code] ..... RSS
Rockdale, TX [FM radio station call letters] ..... KRXT
Rockdale, TX [Location identifier FAA] (FAAL) ..... RCK
Rockefeller Archive Center, Rockefeller University, North Tarrytown, NY [Library symbol] [Library of Congress] (LCLS) ..... NNttR
Rockefeller Center Cable ..... RCC
Rockefeller Center Properties [Associated Press] (SAG) ..... RockCtr
Rockefeller Center Properties, Inc. [NYSE symbol] (SPSG) ..... RCP
Rockefeller Ctr Prop [NYSE symbol] (TTSB) ..... RCP
Rockefeller Family & Associates, Inc., Office Library, New York, NY [Library symbol Library of Congress] (LCLS) ..... NNRocFA
Rockefeller Foundation ..... RF
Rockefeller Foundation, Library, New York, NY [OCLC symbol] (OCLC) ..... XRF
Rockefeller Foundation, New York, NY [Library symbol Library of Congress] (LCLS) ..... NNRocF
Rockefeller Institute for Medical Research ..... RIMR
Rockefeller Mountains [Antarctica] [Seismograph station code, US Geological Survey Closed] (SEIS) ..... RMA
[The] Rockefeller University (GAGS) ..... Rockefeller U
Rockefeller University, New York, NY [Library symbol Library of Congress] (LCLS) ..... NNRU
Rockefeller University, Population Council, Bio-Medical Library, New York, NY [Library symbol Library of Congress] (LCLS) ..... NNRU-P
Rockefeller University Press (DGA) ..... RUP
Rocker (AAG) ..... RKR
Rocker Arm [Mechanical engineering] ..... RKRA
Rocker Arm Oiling Time (PDAA) ..... RAOT
Rocket [Missile vehicle type symbol] ..... R
Rocket (AAG) ..... RKT
Rocket (MCD) ..... ROCK
Rocket and JATO [Jet-Assisted Takeoff] Section [Picatinny Arsenal] [Dover, NJ] ..... RJS
Rocket and Missile System [Army] ..... RAM
Rocket and Missile System [Army] ..... RAMS
Rocket Assist (RDA) ..... RA
Rocket Assisted Kinetic Energy [Army] (DOMA) ..... RAKE
Rocket Assisted Motor (WDAA) ..... RAM
Rocket Balloon [Navy] ..... ROCKOON
Rocket Balloon Instrument [Air Force] ..... ROBIN

Rocket Booster Development Program [Aerospace] (AAG) ..... RBDP
Rocket Booster Fuel Pod Pickup (MUGU) ..... RBFPP
Rocket Branch (AAG) ..... RB
Rocket Branch Panel (AAG) ..... RBP
Rocket Catapult ..... ROCAT
Rocket City Astronomical Association [Later, VBAS] (EA) ..... RCAA
Rocket Combustion Chamber (SAA) ..... RCC
Rocket Countermeasure Unit ..... RCU
Rocket Cruising Association (EA) ..... RCA
Rocket Cushioning Device (NG) ..... RCD
Rocket Development Laboratory [Air Force] ..... RDL
Rocket Development Section [Picatinny Arsenal] [Dover, NJ] ..... RDS
Rocket Engine Analyzer and Decision Instrumentation ..... READI
Rocket Engine and Motor Type Designation System ..... REMTDS
Rocket Engine Assembly ..... REA
Rocket Engine Band ..... REB
Rocket Engine Injector Valve ..... REIV
Rocket Engine Module (MCD) ..... REM
Rocket Engine/Nozzle Ejector ..... RENE
Rocket Engine Operations - Nuclear (IEEE) ..... REON
Rocket Engine Processor ..... REP
Rocket Engine Test Laboratory [Air Force] ..... RETL
Rocket Engine Thermal Strains with Cyclic Plasticity [Propellant] ..... RETSCP
Rocket Escape System with Cruise Using Electric Rotor (MCD) ..... RESCUER
Rocket Exercise [Military] (NVT) ..... ROCKEX
Rocket Exhaust Effects Facility (MCD) ..... REEF
Rocket Fuel Handler Clothing Outfit [Protective suit] ..... RFHCO
Rocket Guidance System (KSC) ..... RGS
Rocket Impacts on Stratospheric Ozone [Air Force] ..... RISO
Rocket Interferometer Tracking ..... RIT
Rocket Jet Plume ..... RJP
Rocket Launched Antisubmarine Torpedo (IAA) ..... RAT
Rocket Launcher ..... RL
Rocket Launcher Locator ..... RLL
Rocket Launching System ..... RLS
Rocket Lunar Attitude System ..... RLAS
Rocket Management (MCD) ..... RM
Rocket Management Office [Army] (RDA) ..... RMO
Rocket Management System (MCD) ..... RMS
Rocket Mission Evaluator (MCD) ..... RME
Rocket Motor ..... RM
Rocket Motor Case ..... RMC
Rocket Motor Igniter ..... RMI
Rocket Motor Plume ..... RMP
Rocket Motor Propellant (MUGU) ..... RMP
Rocket Motor Switching Unit (MCD) ..... RMSU
Rocket Motors Records Office Center [Navy] ..... RMROCK
Rocket/Nimbus Sounder Comparison [NASA] ..... RNSC
Rocket on Rotor ..... ROR
Rocket Orbital Bomber ..... ROBO
Rocket Projectile ..... RP
Rocket Propellant ..... RP
Rocket Propellant Information Agency (MCD) ..... RPIA
Rocket Propulsion Department [Royal Aircraft Establishment] [British] ..... RPD
Rocket Propulsion Establishment [British] (KSC) ..... RPE
Rocket Propulsion Laboratory [Air Force] ..... RPL
Rocket Propulsion Laboratory (NADA) ..... RPL
Rocket Propulsion Technician [Air Force] ..... RPT
Rocket, Radio, Longitudinal, Generator Powered (IAA) ..... RRLG
Rocket Research Corp. (MCD) ..... RRC
Rocket Research Institute ..... RRI
Rocket Research Laboratories (KSC) ..... RRL
Rocket Scoring Reliability (MCD) ..... RSR
Rocket Ship [Navy symbol] ..... LSMR
Rocket Signal, Green (IAA) ..... RSIGG
Rocket Signal, Red (IAA) ..... RSIGR
Rocket Stabilized Rod ..... RSR
Rocket Station ..... RKTSTA
Rocket Station (IAA) ..... RS
Rocket System (MCD) ..... RS
Rocket Target ..... RT
Rocket Technique Committee ..... RTC
Rocket Test Base ..... RTB
Rocket Test Facility ..... RTF
Rocket Test Vehicle (MCD) ..... RTV
Rocket Thrust Measuring System ..... RTMS
Rocket-Assisted Personnel Ejection Catapult ..... RAPEC
Rocket-Assisted Projectile (RDA) ..... RAP
Rocket-Assisted Takeoff [Aerospace] ..... RATO
Rocket-Assisted Takeoff Gear [Aviation] (IEEE) ..... RATOG
Rocket-Assisted Torpedo [Antisubmarine warfare] ..... RAT
Rocketborne Instrumentation (IAA) ..... RBI
Rocket-Borne Ozonesonde (SAA) ..... ROCOZ
Rocketborne Vacuum System ..... RVS
Rocketdyne Automatic Processing of Integrated Data [Computer science] ..... RAPID
Rocketdyne Digital Simulator [NASA] (NASA) ..... RDS
Rocketdyne Gun Propellant (MCD) ..... RGP
Rocketdyne Hybrid Simulator [NASA] (NASA) ..... RHS
Rocketdyne Mortar Propellant (MCD) ..... RMP
Rocketdyne - North American Aviation [Later, Rockwell International Corp.] (AAG) ..... R/NAA
Rocketeer ..... RKTR
Rocket-Ejection Seat Catapult Upward [Aviation] ..... RESCU
Rocket-Powered Target ..... RPT

Rocket-Propelled Grenade ... RPG
Rocket-Propelled Mines (NATG) ... RPM
Rocketsonde Observation (NOAA) ... ROCOB
Rockette Alumnae Association (EA) ... RAA
Rocket-Thrown Depth Charge (NG) ... RTDC
Rocket-Thrown Torpedo ... RTT
Rockford [*Diocesan abbreviation*] [*Illinois*] (TOCD) ... RCK
Rockford [*Illinois*] [*Airport symbol*] (OAG) ... RFD
Rockford [*England*] ... ROCKF
Rockford Area Vocational Center, Rockford, IL [*Library symbol*] [*Library of Congress*] (LCLS) ... IRoVC
Rockford College (GAGS) ... Rockford C
Rockford College, Rockford, IL [*OCLC symbol*] (OCLC) ... IBR
Rockford College, Rockford, IL [*Library symbol Library of Congress*] (LCLS) ... IRoC
Rockford Elementary School, Rockford, MN [*Library symbol*] [*Library of Congress*] (LCLS) ... MnRfE
Rockford High School, Rockford, MN [*Library symbol*] [*Library of Congress*] (LCLS) ... MnRfH
Rockford, IL [*FM radio station call letters*] ... WFEN
Rockford, IL [*FM radio station call letters*] ... WNIJ
Rockford, IL [*AM radio station call letters*] ... WNTA
Rockford, IL [*FM radio station call letters*] ... WQFL
Rockford, IL [*Television station call letters*] ... WQRF
Rockford, IL [*Television station call letters*] ... WREX
Rockford, IL [*AM radio station call letters*] ... WROK
Rockford, IL [*AM radio station call letters*] ... WRRR
Rockford, IL [*Television station call letters*] ... WTVO
Rockford, IL [*FM radio station call letters*] ... WZOK
Rockford Industries [*NASDAQ symbol*] (TTSB) ... ROCF
Rockford Industries, Inc. [*NASDAQ symbol*] (SAG) ... ROCF
Rockford Industries, Inc. [*Associated Press*] (SAG) ... Rockfrd
Rockford Infant Developmental Scales [*Child development test*] ... RIDES
Rockford Institute Center on Religion and Society (EA) ... RICRS
Rockford Memorial Hospital, Rockford, IL [*Library symbol Library of Congress*] (LCLS) ... IRoMH
Rockford, MI [*AM radio station call letters*] (RBYB) ... WISZ
Rockford, MI [*AM radio station call letters*] (RBYB) ... WMJH-AM
Rockford Middle School, Rockford, MN [*Library symbol*] [*Library of Congress*] (LCLS) ... MnRfM
Rockford Minerals, Inc. [*Toronto Stock Exchange symbol*] ... RFD
Rockford Newspapers, Inc., Rockford, IL [*Library symbol Library of Congress*] (LCLS) ... IRoR
Rockford Northern Illinois Library System, Rockford, IL [*Library symbol Library of Congress*] (LCLS) ... IRoNL
Rockford Public Library, Rockford, IL [*Library symbol Library of Congress*] (LCLS) ... IRo
Rockford Register, Rockford, IA [*Library symbol Library of Congress*] (LCLS) ... IaRcfR
Rockford, Rock Island & St. Louis Railroad ... RRI & StL
Rockhampton [*Australia ICAO location identifier*] (ICLI) ... ABRK
Rockhampton [*Australia Airport symbol*] (OAG) ... ROK
Rockhampton (ROG) ... ROKPTN
Rockhampton Aerial Services [*Australia*] ... RAS
Rockhurst College, Kansas City, MO [*Library symbol Library of Congress*] (LCLS) ... MoKR
Rockhurst High School, Kansas City, MO [*Library symbol Library of Congress*] (LCLS) ... MoKRh
Rockies (FAAC) ... RCKY
Rocking ... ROKG
Rockingham Community College, Wentworth, NC [*Library symbol Library of Congress*] (LCLS) ... NcWeR
Rockingham County Library, Leakesville, NC [*Library symbol Library of Congress*] (LCLS) ... NcLk
Rockingham County Public Library, Eden, NC [*Library symbol*] [*Library of Congress*] (LCLS) ... NcEdR
Rockingham County Public Library, Reidsville Branch Library, Reidsville, NC [*Library symbol Library of Congress*] (LCLS) ... NcEdR-R
Rockingham Free Public Library, Bellows Falls, VT [*Library symbol Library of Congress*] (LCLS) ... VtBef
Rockingham, NC [*Location identifier FAA*] (FAAL) ... RCZ
Rockingham, NC [*AM radio station call letters*] ... WAYN
Rockingham, NC [*AM radio station call letters*] ... WLWL
Rockingham, NC [*FM radio station call letters*] ... WRSH
Rockingham Public Library, Harrisonburg, VA [*Library symbol Library of Congress*] (LCLS) ... ViHar
Rockingham R. R. [*AAR code*] ... RKG
Rockingham Resources, Inc. [*Vancouver Stock Exchange symbol*] ... RKH
Rockingham-Richmond County Library, Rockingham, NC [*Library symbol Library of Congress*] (LCLS) ... NcRo
Rockland [*Maine*] [*Airport symbol*] (OAG) ... RKD
Rockland and Pollin [*Scale*] [*Psychology*] ... RP
Rockland Community College, Suffern, NY [*Library symbol Library of Congress*] (LCLS) ... NSufR
Rockland Community College, Suffern, NY [*OCLC symbol*] (OCLC) ... VVR
Rockland, MA [*FM radio station call letters*] ... WRPS
Rockland, ME [*Location identifier FAA*] (FAAL) ... SUH
Rockland, ME [*FM radio station call letters*] ... WMCM
Rockland, ME [*AM radio station call letters*] ... WRKD
Rockland Public Library, Ontario [*Library symbol National Library of Canada*] (NLC) ... ORO
Rockland School/Community Library, Rockland, ID [*Library symbol*] [*Library of Congress*] (LCLS) ... IdRoc
Rockland State Hospital, Medical Library, Orangeburg, NY [*Library symbol Library of Congress*] (LCLS) ... NOrbR
Rockledge, FL [*FM radio station call letters*] ... WHKR
Rockliffe Park Public Library, Ottawa, Ontario [*Library symbol National Library of Canada*] (BIB) ... OORP
Rocklin, CA [*AM radio station call letters*] ... KEBR
Rockmart, GA [*FM radio station call letters*] ... WTSH
Rockmart, GA [*AM radio station call letters*] ... WZOT
Rock-Mass Rating [*Mining technology*] ... RMR
Rockmaster Resources [*Vancouver Stock Exchange symbol*] ... RUN
Rock-Oldies-News-Commercials Operation [*Formula radio*] ... RONCO
Rockport Democrat, Rockport, IN [*Library symbol Library of Congress*] (LCLS) ... InRptD
Rockport Journal, Rockport, IN [*Library symbol Library of Congress*] (LCLS) ... InRptJ
Rockport Resources Ltd. [*Vancouver Stock Exchange symbol*] ... RPR
Rockport, TX [*FM radio station call letters*] ... KXCC
Rockport, TX [*Location identifier FAA*] (FAAL) ... RKP
Rockport-Ohio Township Public Library, Rockport, IN [*Library symbol Library of Congress*] (LCLS) ... InRpt
Rockridge Mining [*Vancouver Stock Exchange symbol*] ... RIM
Rocks & Minerals [*A publication*] (BRI) ... RocksMiner
Rockspan Resources [*Vancouver Stock Exchange symbol*] ... RKR
Rocksprings, TX [*Location identifier FAA*] (FAAL) ... RSG
Rock-Tenn 'A' [*NASDAQ symbol*] (TTSB) ... RKTN
Rockton & Rion Railway [*AAR code*] ... ROR
Rockton, IL [*FM radio station call letters*] ... WRWC
Rockville Centre [*Diocesan abbreviation*] [*New York*] (TOCD) ... RVC
Rockville Centre Public Library, Rockville Centre, NY [*Library symbol Library of Congress*] (LCLS) ... NRock
Rockville, IN [*FM radio station call letters*] ... WAXI
Rockville, MD [*AM radio station call letters*] ... WINX
Rockville Public Library, Rockville, IN [*Library symbol Library of Congress*] (LCLS) ... InRv
Rockwell City Advocate, Rockwell City, IA [*Library symbol Library of Congress*] (LCLS) ... IaRcA
Rockwell Hardness ... RH
Rockwell Hardness B-Scale (WDAA) ... R_B
Rockwell Hardness (C Scale) ... HRC
Rockwell Hardness C-Scale (WDAA) ... R_C
Rockwell International, Collins Canada Division, Toronto, ON, Canada [*Library symbol Library of Congress*] (LCLS) ... CaOTRIC
Rockwell International, Collins Radio Group, Technical Information Center, Dallas, TX [*Library symbol Library of Congress*] (LCLS) ... TxDaRI
Rockwell International Corp. [*ICAO aircraft manufacturer identifier*] (ICAO) ... AC
Rockwell International Corp. [*ICAO aircraft manufacturer identifier*] (ICAO) ... N
Rockwell International Corp. (MCD) ... RI
Rockwell International Corp. (NASA) ... RIC
Rockwell International Corp. [*Associated Press*] (SAG) ... RkInt
Rockwell International Corp. [*Associated Press*] (SAG) ... Rockwl
Rockwell International Corp. [*NYSE symbol Toronto Stock Exchange symbol*] (SPSG) ... ROK
Rockwell International Corp., Atomics International Division, Rocky Flats Plant,Golden, CO [*Library symbol Library of Congress*] (LCLS) ... CoGR
Rockwell International Corp., Pittsburgh, PA [*Library symbol Library of Congress*] (LCLS) ... PPiR
Rockwell International/Rocketdyne Division ... RI/RD
Rockwell International, Rocketdyne Division, Technical Information Center, Canoga Park, CA [*Library symbol Library of Congress*] (LCLS) ... CCpR
Rockwell International Science Center ... RISC
Rockwell International, Science Center, Thousand Oaks, CA [*Library symbol Library of Congress*] (LCLS) ... CToR
Rockwell International Suspension Systems Co. ... RISS
Rockwell Intl [*NYSE symbol*] (TTSB) ... ROK
Rockwell Intl $1.35 Cv PFd [*NYSE symbol*] (TTSB) ... ROKPrB
Rockwell Intl $4.75 Cv Pfd [*NYSE symbol*] (TTSB) ... ROKPr
Rockwell on Mines [*A publication*] (DLA) ... Rock Min
Rockwell Technical Information System [*Rockwell International Corp.*] [*Information service or system*] (IID) ... RTIS
Rockwell's Spanish and Mexican Law Relating to Mines [*A publication*] (DLA) ... Rock Sp Law
Rockwood Nat'l [*PC Symbol*] (TTSB) ... RNC
Rockwood, TN [*Location identifier FAA*] (FAAL) ... RKW
Rockwood, TN [*AM radio station call letters*] ... WOFE
Rockwood, TN [*FM radio station call letters*] ... WOFE-FM
Rocky ... RCKY
Rocky [*Quality of the bottom*] [*Nautical charts*] ... Rky
Rocky Band No. 1 Indian Band Library, Ontario [*Library symbol National Library of Canada*] (BIB) ... ORBI
Rocky Boy Tribal High School, Box Elder, MT [*Library symbol*] [*Library of Congress*] (LCLS) ... MtBeHS
Rocky Flats Area Office (SAA) ... RFA
Rocky Flats Area Office [*Energy Research and Development Administration*] ... RFAO
Rocky Flats Environmental Technology Site (DOGT) ... RFETS
Rocky Flats Environmental Technology Site ... RFETS
Rocky Flats Environmental Technology Site ... RFETS
Rocky Flats Environmental Technology Site [*Golden, CO*] (GAAI) ... RFETS
Rocky Flats/Nuclear Weapons Facilities Project [*Organization with goal of nuclear disarmament*] [*Defunct*] (EA) ... NWFP
Rocky Ford, CO [*FM radio station call letters*] ... KHUG
Rocky Ford Public Library, Rocky Ford, CO [*Library symbol Library of Congress*] (LCLS) ... CoRf
Rocky Harbour Public Library, Rocky Harbour, NF, Canada [*Library symbol Library of Congress*] (LCLS) ... CaNfRH
Rocky Harbour Public School, Newfoundland [*Library symbol National Library of Canada*] (NLC) ... NFRH

Rocky Hill Public Library, Rocky Hill, NJ [*Library symbol Library of Congress*] (LCLS) .... NjRh
Rocky Lane School, Fort Vermilion, Alberta [*Library symbol National Library of Canada*] (BIB) .... AFVRLS
Rocky Mount [*North Carolina*] [*Airport symbol*] (AD) .... RMT
Rocky Mount [*North Carolina*] [*Airport symbol*] (OAG) .... RWI
Rocky Mount, NC [*Location identifier FAA*] (FAAL) .... TYI
Rocky Mount, NC [*AM radio station call letters*] .... WEED
Rocky Mount, NC [*FM radio station call letters*] .... WESQ
Rocky Mount, NC [*AM radio station call letters*] .... WRMT
Rocky Mount, NC [*Television station call letters*] .... WRMY
Rocky Mount, NC [*FM radio station call letters*] (RBYB) .... WRQM-FM
Rocky Mount, NC [*FM radio station call letters*] .... WRSV
Rocky Mount, NC [*FM radio station call letters*] .... WSAY
Rocky Mount, NC [*FM radio station call letters*] .... WTRG
Rocky Mount, VA [*AM radio station call letters*] .... WFYN
Rocky Mount, VA [*AM radio station call letters*] .... WYTI
Rocky Mount, VA [*FM radio station call letters*] .... WZBB
Rocky Mountain [*Canada ICAO designator*] (FAAC) .... ROC
Rocky Mountain Airways [*ICAO designator*] (AD) .... JC
Rocky Mountain Airways, Inc. [*ICAO designator*] (FAAC) .... RMA
Rocky Mountain Arsenal [*Army*] (AABC) .... RMA
Rocky Mountain Association of Geologists (IAA) .... RMAG
Rocky Mountain Automated Clearing House Association .... RMACHA
Rocky Mountain Business Aircraft Association (IAA) .... RMBAA
Rocky Mountain Center for Occupational and Environmental Health [*University of Utah*] [*Research center*] (RCD) .... RMCOEH
Rocky Mountain Center on Environment (EPA) .... ROMCOE
Rocky Mountain Child Development Center [*University of Colorado*] [*Research center*] (RCD) .... RMCDC
Rocky Mountain Chocolate Factory [*Associated Press*] (SAG) .... RkMCh
Rocky Mountain Chocolate Factory [*Associated Press*] (SAG) .... RkMCn
Rocky Mountain Chocolate Factory, Inc. [*Durango, CO*] [*NASDAQ symbol*] (NQ) .... RMCF
Rocky Mountain Coal Mining Institute (EA) .... RMCMI
Rocky Mountain College [*Billings, MT*] .... RMC
Rocky Mountain College, Billings, MT [*Library symbol Library of Congress*] (LCLS) .... MtBilR
Rocky Mountain College Placement Association (AEBS) .... RMCPA
Rocky Mountain Educational Laboratory [*Closed*] .... RMEL
Rocky Mountain Elk Foundation (EA) .... RMEF
Rocky Mountain Energy [*Vancouver Stock Exchange symbol*] .... RME
Rocky Mountain Horse Association (EA) .... RMHA
Rocky Mountain House, AB [*ICAO location identifier*] (ICLI) .... CYRM
Rocky Mountain House Public Library, Alberta [*Library symbol National Library of Canada*] (NLC) .... ARMH
Rocky Mountain Institute (GNE) .... RMI
Rocky Mountain Internet, Inc. [*Associated Press*] (SAG) .... RkMInet
Rocky Mountain Internet, Inc. [*Associated Press*] (SAG) .... RkMInt
Rocky Mountain Internet, Inc. [*NASDAQ symbol*] (SAG) .... RMII
Rocky Mountain Laboratories [*National Institutes of Health*] .... RML
Rocky Mountain Lama Association (EA) .... RMLA
Rocky Mountain Mapping Center [*Colorado*] .... RMMC
Rocky Mountain Midget Racing Association [*Automobile competition organizer*] .... RMMRA
Rocky Mountain Mineral Law Foundation (EA) .... RMMLF
Rocky Mountain Mineral Law Review [*A publication*] (DLA) .... RMMLR
Rocky Mountain Mineral Law Review [*A publication*] (DLA) .... Rocky Mt Miner L Rev
Rocky Mountain Modern Language Association (EDAC) .... RMMLA
Rocky Mountain Motor Tariff Bureau, Inc. .... RMMTB
Rocky Mountain Motor Tariff Bureau, Inc., Denver CO [*STAC*] .... RMB
Rocky Mountain National Park .... ROMO
Rocky Mountain News, Denver, CO [*Library symbol*] [*Library of Congress*] (LCLS) .... CoDRN
Rocky Mountain Oil and Gas Association .... RMOGA
Rocky Mountain Poison Foundation .... RMPF
Rocky Mountain Psychological Association (MCD) .... RMPA
Rocky Mountain Region [*MARC geographic area code Library of Congress*] (LCCP) .... nr----
Rocky Mountain Regional Education Laboratory (AEBS) .... RMREL
Rocky Mountain Review of Language & Literature [*A publication*] (BRI) .... RMR
Rocky Mountain Special Education Instructional Materials Center, Greeley, CO [*Library symbol Library of Congress*] (LCLS) .... CoGrR
Rocky Mountain Spotted Fever .... RMSF
Rocky Mountains .... RM
Rocky Mtn Choc Factory [*NASDAQ symbol*] (TTSB) .... RMCF
Rocky Point Junior-Senior High School, Rocky Point, NY [*Library symbol Library of Congress*] (LCLS) .... NRkpJH
Rocky Shoes & Boots [*NASDAQ symbol*] (TTSB) .... RCKY
Rocky Shoes & Boots, Inc. [*NASDAQ symbol*] (SAG) .... RCKY
Rocky Shoes & Boots, Inc. [*Associated Press*] (SAG) .... RockySh
Rocky Slope Pipeline .... RSP
Rocky View School Division, Calgary, Alberta [*Library symbol National Library of Canada*] (NLC) .... ACRV
Rocky View School Division No. 41, Calgary, AB, Canada [*Library symbol*] [*Library of Congress*] (LCLS) .... CaACRV
Rockyford Municipal Library, Alberta [*Library symbol National Library of Canada*] (NLC) .... ARM
Rockyford Municipal Library, Rockyford, AB, Canada [*Library symbol Library of Congress*] (LCLS) .... CaARM
Rococco Resources Ltd. [*Vancouver Stock Exchange symbol*] .... RCO
Rococo Records [*Record label*] [*Canada, USA*] .... Roc
Rocori High School, Cold Spring, MN [*Library symbol*] [*Library of Congress*] (LCLS) .... MnClsR
Rod [*Measurement*] .... R
Rod .... RD
Rod and Custom [*A publication*] .... R & C
Rod Bank Coil Unit [*Nuclear energy*] (IAA) .... RBCH
Rod Cell Memory (IAA) .... RCM
Rod Cluster Control [*Nuclear energy*] (NRCH) .... RCC
Rod Cluster Control Assembly [*Nuclear energy*] (NRCH) .... RCCA
Rod Control .... RCONT
Rod Drive .... RDDR
Rod Drop Accident (IEEE) .... RDA
Rod Easterling and Jim Osburn [*Automobile named for designers*] .... REJO
Rod End Bearing [*Army helicopter*] .... REB
Rod Memory (IAA) .... RM
Rod Memory Computer [*NCR Corp.*] .... RMC
Rod Outer Segments [*of the retina*] .... ROS
Rod Position Indication System [*Nuclear energy*] (NRCH) .... RPIS
Rod Position Indicator [*Nuclear energy*] (NRCH) .... RPI
Rod Position Information System [*Nuclear energy*] (NRCH) .... RPIS
Rod Select Relay (IEEE) .... RSR
Rod Sequence Control System [*Nuclear energy*] (NRCH) .... RSCS
Rod Valgalliance [*Red Electoral Alliance*] [*Norway*] (PPE) .... RV
Rod Withdrawal Block [*Nuclear energy*] (NRCH) .... RWB
Rod Worth Minimizer [*Nuclear energy*] (NRCH) .... RWM
Rodale Intstitute (EA) .... RI
Rodale Research Center [*Horticulture*] .... RRC
Rodale's Organic Gardening [*A publication*] .... ROG
Rod-and-Frame Test (MAE) .... RFT
Rod-Block Monitor [*Nuclear energy*] (NRCH) .... RBM
Roddenbery Memorial Library, Cairo, GA [*Library symbol Library of Congress*] (LCLS) .... GCai
Rodders Against Street Racing .... RASR
Roddy Resources, Inc. [*Toronto Stock Exchange symbol*] .... ROD
Rodent and Primate Laboratory (SSD) .... RPL
Rodent Potency Dose .... RP
Rodeo Cowboys Association [*Later, PRCA*] (EA) .... RCA
Rodeo Foundation (EA) .... RF
Rodeo Historical Society (EA) .... RHS
Rodeo Information Commission (EA) .... RIC
Rodeo Information Foundation [*Later, Rodeo News Bureau*] .... RIF
Rodeo Media Association [*Defunct*] (EA) .... RMA
Rodeo Resources Ltd. [*Vancouver Stock Exchange symbol*] .... RDO
Rodericus Suarez [*Flourished, 15th century*] [*Authority cited in pre-1607 legal work*] (DSA) .... Rod
Rodez [*France*] [*Airport symbol*] (OAG) .... RDZ
Rodez/Marcillac [*France ICAO location identifier*] (ICLI) .... LFCR
Rodgers Antibodies [*Immunology*] (DAVI) .... Rg
Rodgers Antibodies [*Medicine*] (BABM) .... Rg
Rod-in-Tube .... RIT
Rodman & Renshaw Capital Group [*Associated Press*] (SAG) .... RodRen
Rodman & Renshaw Capital Group [*NYSE symbol*] (SPSG) .... RR
Rodman&Renshaw Cap [*NYSE symbol*] (TTSB) .... RR
Rodman's Reports [*78-82 Kentucky*] [*A publication*] (DLA) .... Rodm
Rodman's Reports [*78-82 Kentucky*] [*A publication*] (DLA) .... Rodman
Rodney Smith Tube [*Medicine*] (DAVI) .... RST
Rodoicus [*Authority cited in pre-1607 legal work*] (DSA) .... Ro
Rodoicus [*Authority cited in pre-1607 legal work*] (DSA) .... Rodo
Rodos/Maritsa [*Greece*] [*ICAO location identifier*] (ICLI) .... LGRD
Rodos/Paradisi [*Greece*] [*ICAO location identifier*] (ICLI) .... LGRP
Rodrigues Island [*Mauritius*] [*Airport symbol*] (OAG) .... RRG
Rodriguez de Mendoz/San Nicolas [*Peru*] [*ICAO location identifier*] (ICLI) .... SPLN
Rodriguez Island/Plaine Corail [*Mauritius*] [*ICAO location identifier*] (ICLI) .... FIMR
Roebling Wire Gauge .... RWG
Roederer Aviation [*ICAO designator*] (AD) .... EG
Roelker's Manual for Notaries and Bankers [*A publication*] (DLA) .... Roelk Man
Roemisch [*Roman*] [*German*] .... Rom
Roemische Adelsparteien und Adelsfamilien [*A publication*] (OCD) .... Rom Adelsparteien
Roemische Forschungen [*A publication*] (OCD) .... Rom Forsch
Roemische Religions-Geschichte [*A publication*] (OCD) .... Hist Rom Rel
Roemische Religions-Geschichte [*A publication*] (OCD) .... RR
Roemische Staatsverwaltung [*A publication*] (OCD) .... Staatsverw
Roemische Studien [*A publication*] (OCD) .... Rom Stud
Roemisches Staatsrecht [*A publication*] (OCD) .... Rom Staatsr
Roemisches Strafrecht [*A publication*] (OCD) .... Rom Strafr
Roentgen [*Also, RU*] [*Unit measuring X and gamma radiations*] .... r
Roentgen [*Ray*] [*Radiology*] (DAVI) x
Roentgen Administered Dose .... RAD
Roentgen Equivalent Man .... rem
Roentgen Equivalent Man (IDOE) .... rem
Roentgen Equivalent Physical (DOG) .... rep
Roentgen Kymography .... RKY
Roentgen per Hour at One Meter .... RHM
Roentgen per Minute (IAA) .... RMIN
Roentgen Ray [*Radiology*] (DAVI) .... XR
Roentgen Satellite [*Space research*] .... ROSAT
Roentgen Unit [*Also, r*] [*Measuring X and gamma radiations*] .... RU
Roentgen-Equivalent-Biological [*Irradiation unit*] .... REB
Roentgen-Equivalent-Mammal [*Irradiation unit*] .... REM
Roentgen-Equivalent-Man [*Later, Sv*] [*Irradiation unit*] .... REM
Roentgen-Equivalent-Man Period [*Irradiation Unit*] (MAE) .... REMP
Roentgen-Equivalent-Physical [*Irradiation unit*] .... REP
Roentgen-Isotope-Fluorescent Method of Analysis .... RIFMA
Roentgenology [*Radiology*] (DAVI) .... Rnt
Roentgenology [*Radiology*] .... Roent
Roentgens per Hour (DEN) .... r/h

Roentgens per Hour (AABC) ... r/hr
Roe's Manual for United States Commissioners [*A publication*] (DLA) ... Roe US Com
Roffensis [*Signature of Bishop of Rochester*] [*Latin*] (ROG) ... ROFFEN
Roffredus Beneventanus [*Flourished, 1215-43*] [*Authority cited in pre-1607 legal work*] (DSA) ... Ro
Roffredus Beneventanus [*Flourished, 1215-43*] [*Authority cited in pre-1607 legal work*] (DSA) ... Rof
Roffredus Beneventanus [*Flourished, 1215-43*] [*Authority cited in pre-1607 legal work*] (DSA) ... Rof Bn
Roffredus Beneventanus [*Flourished, 1215-43*] [*Authority cited in pre-1607 legal work*] (DSA) ... Roffe Be
Rofin-Sinar Technologies, Inc. [*Associated Press*] (SAG) ... RofnSinr
Rofin-Sinar Technologies, Inc. [*NASDAQ symbol*] (SAG) ... RSTI
Rog-Air Ltd. [*Canada ICAO designator*] (FAAC) ... FAD
Rogationist Fathers (TOCD) ... RCJ
Rogationist Fathers (TOCD) ... rcj
Rogel [*C.C. Sergio Gonzales*], Ing. [*Mexico ICAO designator*] (FAAC) ... ROG
Roger [*All right or OK*] [*Communications slang*] ... R
Roger [*Phonetic alphabet*] [*World War II*] (DSUE) ... R
Roger De Hoveden's Chronica [*A publication*] (DLA) ... Rog Hov
Roger Houghton Ltd. [*Publisher*] [*British*] ... RH
Roger Sessions Society (EA) ... RSS
Roger Williams College, Bristol, RI [*Library symbol Library of Congress*] (LCLS) ... RBrRW
Roger Williams College, Bristol, RI [*OCLC symbol*] (OCLC) ... RWB
Roger Williams College, Providence Campus, Providence, RI [*Library symbol Library of Congress*] (LCLS) ... RPR
Roger Wyburn-Mason and Jack M. Blount Foundation for the Eradication of Rheumatoid Disease (EA) ... RDF
Rogerius Beneventanus [*Flourished, 12th century*] [*Authority cited in pre-1607 legal work*] (DSA) ... Rog
Rogers, AR [*AM radio station call letters*] ... KAMO
Rogers, AR [*FM radio station call letters*] ... KAMO-FM
Rogers, AR [*Television station call letters*] ... KFAA
Rogers, AR [*AM radio station call letters*] ... KURM
Rogers, AR [*Location identifier FAA*] (FAAL) ... ROG
Rogers Aviation Ltd. [*British ICAO designator*] (FAAC) ... RAV
Rogers Cantel MobComm'B' [*NYSE symbol*] (TTSB) ... RCN
Rogers Cantel Mobile Communications [*NASDAQ symbol*] (SAG) ... RCMIF
Rogers Cantel Mobile Communications [*NYSE symbol*] (SAG) ... RCN
Rogers Cantel Mobile Communications [*Associated Press*] (SAG) ... RogCantl
Rogers' City Hall Recorder [*1816-22*] [*New York*] [*A publication*] (DLA) ... Rog CHR
Rogers City, MI [*Location identifier FAA*] (FAAL) ... PZQ
Rogers City, MI [*FM radio station call letters*] (RBYB) ... WELG
Rogers City, MI [*AM radio station call letters*] ... WHAK
Rogers City, MI [*FM radio station call letters*] ... WMLQ
Rogers City Public Library, Forest Grove, OR [*Library symbol Library of Congress*] (LCLS) ... OrF
Rogers Commun Cl 'A' [*TS, Symbol*] (TTSB) ... RCI.A
Rogers CommunCl'B' [*NYSE symbol*] (TTSB) ... RG
Rogers Communications, Inc. [*Toronto Stock Exchange symbol Vancouver Stock Exchange symbol*] ... RCI
Rogers Communications, Inc. [*NYSE symbol*] (SAG) ... RG
Rogers Communications, Inc. [*Associated Press*] (SAG) ... RogCm
Rogers Corp. [*AMEX symbol*] (SPSG) ... ROG
Rogers Corp. [*Associated Press*] (SAG) ... Rogers
Rogers Corp., Lurie Research and Development Center, Rogers, CT [*Library symbol Library of Congress*] (LCLS) ... CtRogR
Rogers Criminal Responsibility Assessment Scales [*Personality development test*] [*Psychology*] ... R-CRAS
Rogers' Ecclesiastical Law [*5th ed.*] [*1857*] [*A publication*] (DLA) ... Rog Ecc L
Rogers' Ecclesiastical Law [*A publication*] (DLA) ... Rog Ecc Law
Rogers Elementary School, Rogers, MN [*Library symbol*] [*Library of Congress*] (LCLS) ... MnRgE
Rogers Free Library, Bristol, RI [*Library symbol Library of Congress*] (LCLS) ... RBr
Rogers Group (EA) ... RG
Rogers Memorial Library, Southampton, NY [*Library symbol Library of Congress*] (LCLS) ... NSoa
Rogers. Mines, Minerals, and Quarries [*A publication*] (ILCA) ... Rog Min
Rogers' New City Hall Recorder [*A publication*] (DLA) ... Rog Rec
Rogers on Elections [*A publication*] (DLA) ... Rogers
Rogers on Elections and Registration [*A publication*] (DLA) ... Rog Elec
Rogers on Mines and Minerals [*A publication*] (DLA) ... Rog Min
Rogers on the Judicature Acts [*A publication*] (DLA) ... Rog Jud Acts
Rogers Pass Centre, Revelstoke, BC, Canada [*Library symbol*] [*Library of Congress*] (LCLS) ... CaBRRPC
Rogers Pass Centre, Revelstoke, British Columbia [*Library symbol National Library of Canada*] (NLC) ... BRRPC
Rogers' Reports [*47-51 Louisiana Annual*] [*A publication*] (DLA) ... Rogers
Rogers' Wrongs and Rights of a Traveller [*A publication*] (DLA) ... Rog Trav
Rogersville, AL [*FM radio station call letters*] ... WFIX
Rogersville, TN [*Location identifier FAA*] (FAAL) ... RVN
Rogersville, TN [*FM radio station call letters*] ... WJDT
Rogersville, TN [*AM radio station call letters*] ... WRGS
Roggianite [*A zeolite*] ... ROG
Rogosa SL Medium [*Microbiology*] (DAVI) ... RM
Rogue Community College, Grants Pass, OR [*Library symbol Library of Congress*] (LCLS) ... OrGR
Rogue Community College Library, Grants Pass, OR [*OCLC symbol*] (OCLC) ... ORR
Rogue River, OR [*FM radio station call letters*] ... KRRM
Rogue Valley Medical Center, Medford, OR [*Library symbol*] [*Library of Congress*] (LCLS) ... OrMeRM
Rogue Wave Software, Inc. [*Associated Press*] (SAG) ... RogWve
Rogue Wave Software, Inc. [*NASDAQ symbol*] (SAG) ... RWAV
Rogue's Gallery [*Defunct*] (EA) ... RG
Rohde Sentence Completions Test [*Psychology*] ... RSCT
Rohm & Haas [*NYSE symbol*] (TTSB) ... ROH
Rohm & Haas Co. [*NYSE symbol*] (SPSG) ... ROH
Rohm & Haas Co. [*Associated Press*] (SAG) ... RoHaas
Rohm & Haas Co., Bristol, PA [*Library symbol Library of Congress*] (LCLS) ... PBriR
Rohm & Haas Co., Research Library Services, Spring House, PA [*Library symbol Library of Congress*] (LCLS) ... PSphR
Rohm & Haas Co., Spring House, PA [*OCLC symbol*] (OCLC) ... RHA
Rohnert Park, CA [*FM radio station call letters*] ... KRPQ
Rohon-Beard (Cells) [*Neurology*] ... RB
Rohr, Inc. [*NYSE symbol*] (SPSG) ... RHR
Rohr Industries, Inc. [*Associated Press*] (SAG) ... Rohr
Rohtak [*India*] [*Seismograph station code, US Geological Survey Closed*] (SEIS) ... ROH
Roi Et [*Thailand*] [*ICAO location identifier*] (ICLI) ... VTUR
Rokeach Dogmatism Scale ... RDS
Rokeby [*Australia Airport symbol Obsolete*] (OAG) ... RKY
Rokitansky-Aschoff [*Sinus*] [*Gastroenterology*] ... RA
Rokitansky-Kuster-Hauser [*Syndrome*] [*Gynecology*] (DAVI) ... RKH
Rolampont [*France ICAO location identifier*] (ICLI) ... LFSU
Roland Air [*ICAO designator*] (AD) ... DU
Roland Air Defense System (MCD) ... ROLADES
Roland International Corp. Sound Space [*Electronic music*] ... RSS
Roland, OK [*FM radio station call letters*] (RBYB) ... KREU-FM
Roland, OK [*FM radio station call letters*] ... KYUC
Roland Simulation (MCD) ... ROLSIM
Rolandus Bandinelli [*Deceased, 1181*] [*Authority cited in pre-1607 legal work*] (DSA) ... Ro
Role Activity Performance Scale [*Mental health*] ... RAPS
Role Adaptable Weapons System [*Military*] ... RAWS
Role Category Questionnaire [*Psychology*] (EDAC) ... RCQ
Role Exchange/Education-Practice (MEDA) ... REEP
Role of Occupational Therapy with the Elderly [*Project*] ... ROTE
Role Perception Picture Inventory ... RPPI
Role Performance Scale [*Occupational therapy*] ... RPS
Role Taking Inventory ... RTI
Role-Playing Game [*Video game*] ... RPG
Role-Playing Game Association Network (EA) ... RPGAN
Role-Taking Task ... RTT
Rolf Institute (EA) ... RI
Rolf Jensen & Associates Ltd., Don Mills, Ontario [*Library symbol National Library of Canada*] (NLC) ... ODMRJ
Rolf Jensen & Associates Ltd., Vancouver, British Columbia [*Library symbol National Library of Canada*] (NLC) ... BVARJ
Rolfe Arrow, Rolfe, IA [*Library symbol Library of Congress*] (LCLS) ... IaRolA
Rolfe Public Library, Rolfe, IA [*Library symbol Library of Congress*] (LCLS) ... IaRol
Roll ... R
Roll ... RL
Roll ... RO
Roll Attitude Indicator [*NASA*] ... RAI
Roll Axis [*Aerospace*] (AAG) ... Z-Z
Roll Call Training ... RCT
Roll Center [*Automotive engineering*] ... RC
Roll Centering Pickoff (SAA) ... RCP
Roll Channel ... RC
Roll Drive and Brake Assembly ... RDBA
Roll Film [*Photography*] ... RF
Roll Follow-Up Amplifier ... RFA
Roll Follow-Up Amplifier ... RFUA
Roll Follow-Up Motor ... RFM
Roll Follow-Up Motor ... RFUM
Roll Follow-Up Operation ... RFO
Roll Follow-Up Operation ... RFUO
Roll Follow-Up System ... RFS
Roll Follow-Up System ... RFUS
Roll Forming Machine ... RFM
Roll in Only (NITA) ... RIO
Roll Integrated Flight Control Module (MCD) ... RIFCM
Roll Label Manufacturers Association (EA) ... RLMA
Roll Lift [*NASA*] (KSC) ... RL
Roll Limit Switch ... RLS
Roll Lock Actuator (MCD) ... RLA
Roll Manufacturers Institute (EA) ... RMI
Roll Microwave Sensor ... RMS
Roll Over Protective Structures [*NASA*] (KSC) ... ROPS
Roll Pad (MCD) ... RP
Roll, Pitch, and Yaw ... RPY
Roll Position Indicator (MCD) ... RPI
Roll Position Indicator Assembly ... RPIA
Roll Position Mechanism (MCD) ... RPM
Roll Radius (MCD) ... RR
Roll Rate Command/Attitude Hold (MCD) ... RRCAH
Roll Rate Sensor ... RRS
Roll Ratio Adjust Device (MCD) ... RRAD
Roll Ratio Controller (MCD) ... RRC
Roll Reference Gyro (AAG) ... RRG
Roll Roofing (AAG) ... RR
Roll Sheet Feeder ... RSF
Roll Stability Indicator [*NASA*] (KSC) ... RSI
Roll Stabilization ... RS

Roll Stabilization Platform ... RSP
Roll Vertical Pendulum (SAA) ... RVP
Roll Welding ... ROW
Roll Wrapping Machine ... RWM
Roll, Yaw, Pitch (MCD) ... R-Y-P
Roll Yoke ... RY
Rolla [*Missouri*] [*Seismograph station code, US Geological Survey*] (SEIS) ... ROL
Rolla, MO [*FM radio station call letters*] (RBYB) ... KDAA
Rolla, MO [*FM radio station call letters*] ... KMNR
Rolla, MO [*AM radio station call letters*] ... KMOZ
Rolla, MO [*AM radio station call letters*] ... KTTR
Rolla, MO [*FM radio station call letters*] ... KUMR
Rolla, MO [*FM radio station call letters*] ... KZNN
Rolla, ND [*Location identifier FAA*] (FAAL) ... RLL
Rolla/Vichy, MO [*Location identifier FAA*] (FAAL) ... VIH
Rolland, Inc. [*Toronto Stock Exchange symbol*] ... RL
Rolland Maintenance Institutional Trainer [*Army*] ... RMIT
Rolland Township Library, Blanchard, MI [*Library symbol Library of Congress*] (LCLS) ... MiBla
Rollback [*Telecommunications*] (TEL) ... RB
Rollback Disability Claims [*Social Security Administration*] (OICC) ... RB
Rollback Module [*Telecommunications*] (TEL) ... RM
Rollback Process [*Telecommunications*] (TEL) ... RP
Rolled (AAG) ... RLD
Rolled Alloyed Zinc ... RAZ
Rolled Alloyed Zinc Sheet ... RAZS
Rolled Gold ... RG
Rolled Gold Plate [*Metallurgy*] ... RGP
Rolled Hollow Section ... RHS
Rolled Homogeneous Armor [*Weaponry*] (INF) ... RHA
Rolled Zinc Manufacturers Association [*Defunct*] (EA) ... RZMA
Rolled Zinc Sheet ... RZS
Rolled-Steel Joist ... RSJ
Roller (MSA) ... RLR
Roller Bearing ... RB
Roller Bearing Corp. (MCD) ... RBC
Roller Bearing Engineers Committee (EA) ... RBEC
Roller Chock [*Shipfitting*] ... RC
Roller Coating ... RC
Roller Hockey Coaches Association (EA) ... RHCA
Roller Hockey Federation (EA) ... RHF
Roller Owners' Association [*British*] (BI) ... ROA
Roller Path Inclination [*Navy*] (DOMA) ... RPI
Roller Shutter ... RS
Roller Skating Business Magazine [*A publication*] (EAAP) ... RSB
Roller Skating Foundation of America [*Defunct*] (EA) ... RSFA
Roller Skating Rink Operators Association (EA) ... RSROA
Roller Skating Rink Operators Association (NADA) ... RSROAA
Roller Speed Skating Federation (EA) ... RSSF
Roller-Compacted Concrete ... RCC
Roller-Skating Rinks [*Public-performance tariff class*] [*British*] ... R
Rolle's Abridgment [*A publication*] (DLA) ... Ro
Rolle's Abridgment [*A publication*] (ILCA) ... Ro Abr
Rolle's Abridgment [*A publication*] (DLA) ... Rol
Rolle's Abridgment [*A publication*] (DLA) ... Rol Ab
Rolle's Abridgment [*A publication*] (DLA) ... Roll
Rolle's Abridgment [*A publication*] (DLA) ... Roll Abr
Rolle's Abridgment [*A publication*] (DLA) ... Rolle
Rolle's Abridgment of the Common Law [*A publication*] (DLA) ... Rolle Abr
Rolle's English King's Bench Reports [*A publication*] (DLA) ... Ro Rep
Rolle's English King's Bench Reports [*2 vols.*] [*A publication*] (DLA) ... Rol
Rolle's English King's Bench Reports [*2 vols.*] [*A publication*] (DLA) ... Roll
Rolle's English King's Bench Reports [*2 vols.*] [*1614-25*] [*A publication*] (DLA) ... Roll Rep
Rolle's English King's Bench Reports [*2 vols.*] [*1614-25*] [*A publication*] (DLA) ... Rolle
Rolle's English King's Bench Reports [*2 vols.*] [*1614-25*] [*A publication*] (DLA) ... Rolle R
Roll-Imitation Gold ... RIG
Rollin' Rock Club (EA) ... RRC
Rollin' Rock Club of Texas and Any Other State or Country of the World and OuterSpace ... RRCOTAAOSOCOTWAOS
Roll-In/Roll-Out [*Storage allocation*] [*Computer science*] ... RIRO
Rolling Airframe Missile ... RAM
Rolling Chassis [*Automotive engineering*] ... RC
Rolling Contour Optimization Theory [*Bridgestone Corp.*] ... RCOT
Rolling Green Elementary School, Rockford, IL [*Library symbol*] [*Library of Congress*] (LCLS) ... IRoRgE
Rolling Hills Elementary School, Commack, NY [*Library symbol*] [*Library of Congress*] (LCLS) ... NCoRE
Rolling Hills Public Library, Alberta [*Library symbol National Library of Canada*] (NLC) ... ARH
Rolling Hills Public Library, Rolling Hills, AB, Canada [*Library symbol*] [*Library of Congress*] (LCLS) ... CaARh
Rolling Hotel [*European bus-tour system*] ... ROTEL
Rolling Injection Planter (GNE) ... RIP
Rolling Liquid Transporter [*Army*] ... RLT
Rolling Mill Machinery and Equipment Association [*Defunct*] (EA) ... RMMEA
Rolling Moment [*Physics*] ... RM
Rolling on the Floor ... ROTF
Rolling on the Floor Laughing [*Internet language*] (PCM) ... ROFL
Rolling on the Floor Laughing [*Computer hacker terminology*] (NHD) ... ROTFL
Rolling Prairie Libraries, Decatur, IL [*Library symbol Library of Congress*] (LCLS) ... IDecR
Rolling Prairie Libraries, Decatur, IL [*OCLC symbol*] (OCLC) ... IHQ
Rolling Resistance [*Automotive engineering*] ... RR
Rolling Steel Door [*Technical drawings*] ... RSD
Rolling Stock (CINC) ... RST
Rolling Stones Fan Club (EA) ... RSFC
Rolling Thin Film Oven [*For testing asphaltic binders*] ... RTFO
Rolling Thunder Coordinating Committee [*Joint US Navy and Air Force group operating in Vietnam*] (VNW) ... RTCC
Rolling Vertical Landing (MCD) ... RVL
Rolling Vertical Takeoff and Landing [*Aviation*] (MCD) ... RVTOL
Rolling-Assisted Biaxially Textured Substrate [*Physics*] ... RABiTS
Rolling-Stock Jigsaws [*British*] ... RSJ
Rollingwood, TX [*AM radio station call letters*] ... KJCE
Rollins College (GAGS) ... Rollins C
Rollins College, Bush Science Library, Winter Park, FL [*Library symbol Library of Congress*] (LCLS) ... FWpR-S
Rollins College, Winter Park, FL [*Library symbol Library of Congress*] (LCLS) ... FWpR
Rollins Environ Sv [*NYSE symbol*] (TTSB) ... REN
Rollins Environmental Services, Inc. [*NYSE symbol*] (SPSG) ... REN
Rollins Environmental Services, Inc. [*Associated Press*] (SAG) ... RollinE
Rollins, Inc. [*NYSE symbol*] (SPSG) ... ROL
Rollins, Inc. [*Associated Press*] (SAG) ... Rollins
Rollins Truck Leasing [*NYSE symbol*] (SPSG) ... RLC
Rollins Truck Leasing [*Associated Press*] (SAG) ... RollLeas
Roll-Limiting Engine ... R Lim E
Roll-On [*Trailer ship*] (DICI) ... RO
Roll-On/Float-Off (DOMA) ... RO/FLO
Roll-On/Roll-Off [*Shipping*] (AFM) ... RO/RO
Roll-On, Roll-Off/Lift-On, Lift-Off [*Shipping*] (DS) ... Ro/Lo
Rollout (KSC) ... R
Rollout (MCD) ... R/O
Rollout (NASA) ... R-OUT
Rollover ... R/O
Roll-Over Protection Equipment (MCD) ... ROP
Roll-Over Protection System [*for tractors*] ... ROPS
Roll-Pitch Pickoff ... RPP
Roll-Pitch Resolver ... RPR
Roll-Pitch Resolver System ... RPRS
Rolls Court [*Legal*] [*British*] ... RC
Rolls' Court Reports [*A publication*] (DLA) ... Rolls Ct Rep
Rolls of the Assizes in Channel Islands [*A publication*] (DLA) ... Ch Is Rolls
Rolls of the Justices in Eyre for Gloucestershire, Worcestershire, and Staffordshire [*A publication*] (ILCA) ... Stenton G
Rolls of the Justices in Eyre in Yorkshire [*A publication*] (ILCA) ... Stenton Y
Rolls on Floor Laughing [*Internet language*] [*Computer science*] ... ROFL
Rolls Royce [*Automobile*] [*Slang*] (DSUE) ... RO-RO
Rolls Royce Ltd. [*British ICAO designator*] (FAAC) ... RRL
Rolls Royce Ltd. (Bristol Engine Division) [*British ICAO designator*] (FAAC) ... BTU
Rolls Royce Owners' Club of Australia ... RROCA
Rolls Series [*A publication*] (DLA) ... RS
Rolls-Japan 500 [*Type of Rolls-Royce engine*] ... RJ 500
Rolls-Royce [*Automobile*] ... RR
Rolls-Royce Enthusiasts (EA) ... RRE
Rolls-Royce of Canada Ltd., Montreal, PQ, Canada [*Library symbol Library of Congress*] (LCLS) ... CaQMRR
Rolls-Royce of Canada Ltd., Montreal, Quebec [*Library symbol National Library of Canada*] (NLC) ... QMRR
Rolls-Royce Owners' Club (EA) ... RROC
Rolm Corp. Library, Santa Clara, CA [*Library symbol Library of Congress*] (LCLS) ... CStclR
Rolodex Electronic Express ... REX
Rolpa [*Nepal*] [*Airport symbol*] (OAG) ... RPA
Rolpa [*Nepal*] [*ICAO location identifier*] (ICLI) ... VNRP
ROM [*Read-Only Memory*] **Address Gate** [*Computer science*] ... RAG
ROM [*Read-Only Memory*] **Address Register** ... RAR
ROM [*Read-Only Memory*] **BIOS** [*Pronounced "rye-ose"*] [*Computer science*] ... RIOS
ROM [*Rough Order of Magnitude*] **Control** ... RC
ROM [*Read-Only Memory*] **Instruction Register** ... RIR
ROM [*Read-Only Memory*] **Location Counter** ... RLC
ROM Memory Band (NITA) ... RMB
ROM Plus Input/Output (NITA) ... ROMIO
ROM Return Address Register ... RRAR
Rom Tech [*NASDAQ symbol*] (TTSB) ... ROMT
Rom Tech, Inc. [*NASDAQ symbol*] (SAG) ... ROMT
Rom Tech, Inc. [*Associated Press*] (SAG) ... RomTch
Roma [*Italy ICAO location identifier*] (ICLI) ... LIIB
Roma [*Italy ICAO location identifier*] (ICLI) ... LIII
Roma [*Italy ICAO location identifier*] (ICLI) ... LIJJ
Roma [*Italy ICAO location identifier*] (ICLI) ... LIRR
Roma [*Australia Airport symbol*] (OAG) ... RMA
Roma/Ciampino [*Italy ICAO location identifier*] (ICLI) ... LIRA
Roma/Fiumicino [*Italy ICAO location identifier*] (ICLI) ... LIRF
Roma, TX [*Location identifier FAA*] (FAAL) ... FAL
Roma, TX [*FM radio station call letters*] ... KBMI
Roma/Urbe [*Italy ICAO location identifier*] (ICLI) ... LIRU
Romac Industries, Inc. [*Associated Press*] (SAG) ... Romac
Romac Industries, Inc. [*NASDAQ symbol*] (SAG) ... ROMC
Romac Intl [*NASDAQ symbol*] (TTSB) ... ROMC
Romain de Tirtoff [*Also known as ERTE*] [*Couturier*] ... RT
Roman ... R
Roman [*Type*] [*Publishing*] ... ROM
Roman [*Type*] [*Publishing*] (ODBW) ... rom
Roman Catholic ... RC

Roman Catholic Archdiocesan Archivers, Halifax, NS, Canada [*Library symbol*] [*Library of Congress*] (LCLS) .... CaNSHRCA
Roman Catholic Archdiocesan Archives, Halifax, Nova Scotia [*Library symbol National Library of Canada*] (BIB) .... NSHRCA
Roman Catholic Archdiocese of Portland in Oregon, Chancery Office, Portland, OR [*Library symbol Library of Congress*] (LCLS) .... OrPCA
Roman Catholic Bishop of Fresno, Monterey-Fresno Diocesan Library, Fresno, CA [*Library symbol Library of Congress*] (LCLS) .... CFM
Roman Catholic Chancery Office, Winnipeg, Manitoba [*Library symbol National Library of Canada*] (NLC) .... MWRCC
Roman Catholic Chancery Office, Winnipeg, MB, Canada [*Library symbol*] [*Library of Congress*] (LCLS) .... CaMWRCC
Roman Catholic Chaplain [*Navy British*] .... RCCh
Roman Catholic Church .... RCC
Roman Catholic Church .... RCCH
Roman Catholic Church Curate (ROG) .... RCC
Roman Catholic Diocese of Boise, Boise, ID [*Library symbol*] [*Library of Congress*] (LCLS) .... IdBRC
Roman Catholic Priest (ROG) .... RCP
Roman Catholic School [*British*] .... R
Roman Corp. Ltd. [*Toronto Stock Exchange symbol*] .... RMN
Roman High Avoidance [*Behavior trait*] .... RHA
Roman Imperial Coinage [*A publication*] (OCD) .... RIC
[*The*] **Roman Inscriptions of Britain** [*A publication*] (OCD) .... RIB
Roman L. Hruska United States Meat Animal Research Center, Clay Center, NE [*OCLC symbol*] (OCLC) .... AGK
Roman Law (DLA) .... RL
Roman Martyrology .... RM
Roman Politics 220-150BC [*A publication*] (OCD) .... Rom Pol
[*The*] **Roman Revolution** [*1939*] [*A publication*] (OCD) .... Rom Rev
Roman Rule in Asia Minor [*A publication*] (OCD) .... Rom Rule Asia Min
Roman-British .... RB
Romance [*MARC language code Library of Congress*] (LCCP) .... roa
Romance .... ROM
Romance Is Treasured Always [*Annual award bestowed by Romance Writers of America. Acronym selected to honor cofounder, Rita Clay Estrada*] .... RITA
Romance of Empire Series [*A publication*] .... RES
Romance of Science Series [*A publication*] .... RSS
Romance Writers of America (EA) .... RWA
Romance Writers of America. Chapter Advisory Letter [*A publication*] (EAAP) .... CAL
Romance Writers Report [*A publication*] (EAAP) .... RWR
Romanche Sedimentary Sequence [*Geology*] .... RSS
Romanesque (VRA) .... Rmsq
Romani Imperii Semper Auctor [*Continual Increaser of the Roman Empire*] [*Latin*] .... RISA
Romania [*MARC geographic area code Library of Congress*] (LCCP) .... e-rm--
Romania [*License plate code assigned to foreign diplomats in the US*] .... ND
Romania .... R
Romania [*MARC country of publication code Library of Congress*] (LCCP) .... rm
Romania [*ANSI two-letter standard code*] (CNC) .... RO
Romania [*ANSI three-letter standard code*] (CNC) .... ROM
Romania (VRA) .... Rom
Romania [*International civil aircraft marking*] (ODBW) .... YR
Romanian [*MARC language code Library of Congress*] (LCCP) .... rum
Romanian Bank of Foreign Trade (IMH) .... RBFT
Romanian Baptist Association of United States and Canada [*Defunct*] (EA) .... RBAUSC
Romanian Catholic Exarchy in the United States of America (EA) .... RCEUSA
Romanian Communist Party [*Political party*] .... RCP
Romanian Communist Party (Bolshevik) [*Political party*] .... RCP(B)
Romanian Library, New York, NY [*Library symbol Library of Congress*] (LCLS) .... NNRom
Romanian Merchant Marine (AD) .... NAVROM
Romanian Missionary Society (EA) .... RMS
Romanian National Council (EA) .... RNC
Romanian Philatelic Club [*Defunct*] (EA) .... RPC
Romanian Studies Association of America (EA) .... RSAA
Romanian Workers' Party [*Political party*] .... RWP
Romanian-US Economic Council (EA) .... RUSEC
Romano Internacionalno Jekhethanibe [*International Romani Union*] (EA) .... RIJ
Romanovsky Dye [*Biological stain*] .... RD
Romans [*New Testament book*] (BJA) .... R
Romans [*New Testament book*] .... RM
Romans [*Old Testament book*] .... RO
Romans [*New Testament book*] .... Rom
Romans/Saint-Paul [*France ICAO location identifier*] (ICLI) .... LFHE
Romantic Novelists' Association [*British*] .... RNA
Romany [*MARC language code Library of Congress*] (LCCP) .... rom
Romany Records [*Record label*] .... Rom
Romavia [*Romania*] [*ICAO designator*] (FAAC) .... RMV
Rombauer [*Missouri*] [*Seismograph station code, US Geological Survey*] (SEIS) .... RMB
Romberg [*Medicine*] .... ROM
Romblon, Tablas Island [*Philippines*] [*ICAO location identifier*] (ICLI) .... RPMR
Rome [*Georgia*] [*Airport symbol Obsolete*] (OAG) .... RMG
Rome [*Georgia*] [*Seismograph station code, US Geological Survey*] (SEIS) .... RMG
Rome [*Monte Porzio Catone*] [*Italy*] [*Seismograph station code, US Geological Survey*] (SEIS) .... RMP
Rome [*Italy*] [*Airport symbol*] (OAG) .... ROM
Rome [*Italy*] [*Seismograph station code, US Geological Survey Closed*] (SEIS) .... ROM
Rome Air Development Center [*Griffiss Air Force Base, NY*] [*Air Force*] .... RADC
Rome Air Development Center Deputy for Electronic Technology [*ESD*] .... RADC/ETR
Rome Air Development Center, Griffiss AFB, NY [*OCLC symbol*] (OCLC) .... VYR
Rome Air Development Center, Rome, NY [*Library symbol Library of Congress*] (LCLS) .... NRomA
Rome Air Force Depot .... RAFD
Rome Air Materiel Area [*Deactivated*] [*Air Force*] .... RAMA
Rome Air Materiel Area [*Deactivated*] [*Air Force*] .... ROAMA
Rome Air Service Command [*Air Force*] .... RASC
Rome Air Technical Service Command [*Air Force*] .... RATSC
Rome Allied Area Command [*World War II*] .... RAAC
Rome and the Study of Scripture [*A publication*] (BJA) .... RSS
Rome [*Italy*] **Ciampino Airport** [*Airport symbol Obsolete*] (OAG) .... CIA
Rome Daily American [*An English-language newspaper in Italy*] [*A publication*] .... RDA
Rome, GA [*Location identifier FAA*] (FAAL) .... OYD
Rome, GA [*FM radio station call letters*] .... WKCX
Rome, GA [*AM radio station call letters*] .... WLAQ
Rome, GA [*FM radio station call letters*] .... WQTU
Rome, GA [*AM radio station call letters*] .... WRGA
Rome, GA [*AM radio station call letters*] .... WROM
Rome, GA [*Television station call letters*] .... WTLK-TV
Rome, GA [*AM radio station call letters*] .... WTSH
Rome/Griffiss Air Force Base [*New York*] [*ICAO location identifier*] (ICLI) .... KRME
Rome [*Italy*] **Leonardo Da Vinci (Fium) Airport** [*Airport symbol*] (OAG) .... FCO
Rome, NY [*Location identifier FAA*] (FAAL) .... FYQ
Rome, NY [*Location identifier FAA*] (FAAL) .... GSS
Rome, NY [*Location identifier FAA*] (FAAL) .... RME
Rome, NY [*AM radio station call letters*] .... WODZ
Rome, NY [*FM radio station call letters*] .... WODZ-FM
Rome, NY [*AM radio station call letters*] .... WRNY
Rome, NY [*FM radio station call letters*] (RBYB) .... WSKS
Rome, NY [*Location identifier FAA*] (FAAL) .... XVT
Rome, OR [*Location identifier FAA*] (FAAL) .... REO
Romeo [*Phonetic alphabet*] [*International*] (DSUE) .... R
Romeo and Juliet [*Shakespearean work*] .... R & J
Romeo and Juliet [*Shakespearean work*] .... Rom
Romeo and Juliet [*Shakespearean work*] (BARN) .... Rom & Jul
Romeo District Library, Romeo, MI [*Library symbol Library of Congress*] (LCLS) .... MiRom
Romeo Series L [*Alfa-Romeo*] [*Automotive model designation*] .... RL
Romeo Series L Normale [*Alfa-Romeo*] [*Automotive model designation*] .... RLN
Romeo Series L Sport [*Alfa-Romeo*] [*Automotive model designation*] .... RLS
Romeo Series L Super Sport [*Alfa-Romeo*] [*Automotive model designation*] .... RLSS
Romeo Series L Targa Florio [*Alfa-Romeo*] [*Automotive model designation*] .... RLTF
Romeo Series L Turismo [*Alfa-Romeo*] [*Automotive model designation*] .... RLT
Romeo Series M Unificto [*Alfa-Romeo*] [*Automotive model designation*] .... RMU
Romeoville, IL [*Location identifier FAA*] (FAAL) .... LOT
Rome-Utica [*New York*] [*Airport symbol*] (AD) .... UCA
Romex Resources, Inc. [*Vancouver Stock Exchange symbol*] .... RRI
Romford [*Postcode*] (ODBW) .... RM
Romilly's Notes of English Chancery Cases [*1767-87*] [*A publication*] (DLA) .... Rom
Romilly's Notes of English Chancery Cases [*1767-87*] [*A publication*] (DLA) .... Rom Cas
Romilly's Notes of English Chancery Cases [*A publication*] (DLA) .... Romilly NC (Eng)
Romilly's Observations on the Criminal Law [*3rd ed.*] [*1813*] [*A publication*] (DLA) .... Rom Cr Law
Romilly-Sur-Seine [*France ICAO location identifier*] (ICLI) .... LFQR
Romische Geschichte bis zum Beginn der Punischen Kriege [*A publication*] (OCD) .... Rom Gesch
Romney, WV [*FM radio station call letters*] .... WJGF
Romney, WV [*FM radio station call letters*] .... WJJB
Romorantin/Pruniers [*France ICAO location identifier*] (ICLI) .... LFYR
Romulus [*of Plutarch*] [*Classical studies*] (OCD) .... Rom
Romulus, NY [*Location identifier FAA*] (FAAL) .... RYK
Romulus, NY [*Location identifier FAA*] (FAAL) .... SSN
Ron Craddock Fan Club (EA) .... RCFC
Ron Pair .... RP
Ron Pair Enterprises [*Division of Wilson, Inc.*] .... RPE
Ronald Como, Inc. [*Perry Como's production firm; Ronald is his son*] .... RONCOM
Ronald Martin Groome [*Commercial firm British*] .... RMG
Ronald Reagan [*US president, 1911-*] .... RR
Ronald Reagan Home Preservation Foundation (EA) .... RRHPF
Ronald Reagan Philatelic Society (EA) .... RRPS
Ronald Wilson Reagan [*US president, 1911-*] .... RWR
Ronan City Library, Ronan, MT [*Library symbol*] [*Library of Congress*] (LCLS) .... MtRo
Ronan, MT [*FM radio station call letters*] .... KQRK
Ronceverte, WV [*AM radio station call letters*] .... WRON
Ronceverte, WV [*FM radio station call letters*] .... WRON-FM
Ronchi De'Legionari [*Italy ICAO location identifier*] (ICLI) .... LIPQ
Rondon [*Colombia*] [*Airport symbol Obsolete*] (OAG) .... RON
Rondonopolis [*Brazil*] [*Airport symbol*] (OAG) .... ROO
Rongelap [*Marshall Islands*] [*Airport symbol*] (OAG) .... RNP
Ronne [*Denmark ICAO location identifier*] (ICLI) .... EKRN
Ronne [*Denmark*] [*Airport symbol*] (OAG) .... RNN
Ronne Antarctic Research Expedition [*1947-48*] .... RARE
Ronneby [*Sweden ICAO location identifier*] (ICLI) .... ESDF
Ronneby [*Sweden*] [*Airport symbol*] (OAG) .... RNB
Ronnie McDowell Fan Club (EA) .... RMFC
Ronnie Milsap Fan Club (EA) .... RMFC
Ronnie Prophet International Fan Club (EA) .... RPIFC
Ronnie Smith Fan Club (EA) .... RSFC

Ronrico Explorations Ltd. [*Vancouver Stock Exchange symbol*] ... RRX
Ronson Corp. [*NASDAQ symbol*] (SAG) ... RONC
Ronson Corp. [*Associated Press*] (SAG) ... Ronson
Ronson Corp. 12% Cv Pfd [*NASDAQ symbol*] (TTSB) ... RONCP
Rontgen [*Measurement*] (EECA) ... R
Roo Rat Society (EA) ... RRS
Rood [*Unit of measurement*] ... R
Rood [*Unit of measurement*] ... RD
Rood [*Unit of measurement*] ... RO
Roodbar [*Iran*] [*ICAO location identifier*] (ICLI) ... OIGU
Roodhouse Public Library, Roodhouse, IL [*Library symbol Library of Congress*] (LCLS) ... IRoo
Roodsar [*Iran*] [*ICAO location identifier*] (ICLI) ... OIGR
Roof (VRA) ... rf
Roof (WGA) ... RF
Roof Coatings Manufacturers Association (EA) ... RCMA
Roof Consultants Institute (EA) ... RCI
Roof Diameter (IAA) ... RD
Roof Drain (AAG) ... RD
Roof Drainage Manufacturers Institute [*Defunct*] (EA) ... RDMI
Roof Fan (OA) ... RF
Roof Hatch [*Technical drawings*] ... RFH
Roof Leader (MSA) ... RL
Roof Research Center [*Oak Ridge, TN*] [*Oak Ridge National Laboratory*] [*Department of Energy*] (GRD) ... RRC
Roofer (WGA) ... RFR
Roofing (AAG) ... RFG
Roofing ... RFNG
Roofing ... ROOF
Roofing Industry Educational Institute (EA) ... RIEI
Rooikop [*South Africa*] [*ICAO location identifier*] (ICLI) ... FARK
Rook [*Chess*] ... R
Rookie of the Year ... ROY
Rookie Orientation Program [*Automobile racing*] ... ROP
Room (NFPA) ... R
Room (AAG) ... RM
Room (VRA) ... rm
Room (DD) ... Rm
Room ... RM
Room (ODBW) ... rm
Room (WDMC) ... rm
Room Air (DAVI) ... RA
Room Air (MEDA) ... RA
Room Air Blood Gases [*Medicine*] (DAVI) ... RABG
Room and Board ... R & B
Room and Pillar [*Coal mining*] ... RP
Room Cavity Ratio [*Lighting*] ... RCR
Room Humidifier (DMAA) ... RH
Room Index (PDAA) ... RI
Room Only ... RO
Room Plus, Inc. [*NASDAQ symbol*] (SAG) ... PLUS
Room Plus, Inc. [*Associated Press*] (SAG) ... RoomP
Room Plus, Inc. [*Associated Press*] (SAG) ... RoomPl
Room Sensible Heat Factor ... RSHF
Room, Tax, and Incidentals ... RTI
Room Temperature ... RT
Room Temperature Cure (NASA) ... RTC
Room Temperature Fluorescence [*Physics*] ... RTF
Room Temperature Gamma Detector ... RTGD
Room Temperature Vulcanizing (MCD) ... RTV
Room Usage Time ... RUT
Rooms Katholieke Partij Nederland [*Roman Catholic Party of the Netherlands*] [*Political party*] (PPE) ... RKPN
Rooms Katholieke Staatspartij [*Roman Catholic State Party*] [*Netherlands Political party*] (PPE) ... RKSP
Rooms Katholieke Volkspartij [*Roman Catholic People's Party*] [*Netherlands Political party*] (PPE) ... RKVP
Rooms Using Television [*Television ratings*] ... RUT
Room-Temperature Metallizing (SAA) ... RTM
Room-Temperature Phosphorimetry [*Spectrometry*] ... RTP
Roosevelt [*Washington*] [*Seismograph station code, US Geological Survey*] (SEIS) ... RPK
Roosevelt Center for American Policy Studies [*Defunct*] (EA) ... RCAPS
Roosevelt Community Library, Roosevelt, NY [*Library symbol Library of Congress*] (LCLS) ... NRoos
Roosevelt County Library, Wolf Point, MT [*Library symbol*] [*Library of Congress*] (LCLS) ... MtWp
Roosevelt Elementary School, St. Cloud, MN [*Library symbol*] [*Library of Congress*] (LCLS) ... MnStclR
Roosevelt Elementary School, Virginia, MN [*Library symbol*] [*Library of Congress*] (LCLS) ... MnVRE
Roosevelt Elementary School, Willmar, MN [*Library symbol*] [*Library of Congress*] (LCLS) ... MnWilRE
Roosevelt Financial Group, Inc. [*NASDAQ symbol*] (NQ) ... RFED
Roosevelt Financial Group, Inc. [*Associated Press*] (SAG) ... RsvltF
Roosevelt Financial Group, Inc. [*Associated Press*] (SAG) ... RsvltFn
Roosevelt Finl [*NASDAQ symbol*] (TTSB) ... RFED
Roosevelt Finl 6.5% Cv 'B' Pfd [*NASDAQ symbol*] (TTSB) ... RFEDP
Roosevelt Hospital, Medical Library, New York, NY [*Library symbol Library of Congress*] (LCLS) ... NNRH
Roosevelt Hospital, Medical Library, New York, NY [*OCLC symbol*] (OCLC) ... VVQ
Roosevelt Junior-Senior High School, Roosevelt, NY [*Library symbol*] [*Library of Congress*] (LCLS) ... NRoosJH
Roosevelt Roads [*Puerto Rico*] [*Seismograph station code, US Geological Survey*] (SEIS) ... RRD
Roosevelt Roads [*Puerto Rico*] [*Seismograph station code, US Geological Survey Closed*] (SEIS) ... RRP
Roosevelt Roads Naval Air Station [*Puerto Rico*] [*ICAO location identifier*] (ICLI) ... TJNR
Roosevelt Roads, PR [*Location identifier FAA*] (FAAL) ... NRR
Roosevelt University (GAGS) ... Roosevelt U
Roosevelt University, Chicago, IL [*OCLC symbol*] (OCLC) ... IAR
Roosevelt University, Chicago, IL [*Library symbol Library of Congress*] (LCLS) ... ICRC
Roosevelt University, North Campus, Arlington Heights, IL [*Library symbol Library of Congress*] (LCLS) ... ICRC-N
Roosevelt, UT [*FM radio station call letters*] ... KIFX
Roosevelt, UT [*AM radio station call letters*] ... KNEU
Roosevelt Warm Springs Foundation (EA) ... RWSF
Rooster Class Yacht Racing Association [*Defunct*] (EA) ... RCYRA
Root [*Mathematics*] (ROG) ... RT
Root Apex [*Botany*] ... RA
Root Beer Institute [*Defunct*] ... RBI
Root Canal [*Dentistry*] ... RC
Root Canal Anterior [*Dentistry*] ... RCA
Root Canal Bicuspid [*Dentistry*] ... RCB
Root Canal, Filing of [*Dentistry*] (DAVI) ... RF
Root Canal Molar [*Dentistry*] ... RCM
Root Canal Therapy [*Dentistry*] ... RCT
Root Canal Treatment [*Dentistry*] (DAVI) ... RCT
Root Cast [*Archaeology*] ... rc
Root Cause Analysis (MCD) ... RCA
Root Diameter (MSA) ... RD
Root Knot Nematode [*Plant pathology*] ... RKN
Root Locus (IAA) ... RTLOC
Root Mean Percentage Error [*Statistics*] ... RMPE
Root Mean Square [*Physics, statistics*] ... RMS
Root Mean Square (IDOE) ... rms
Root Mean Square Average [*Statistics*] (IAA) ... RS
Root Mean Square Deviation [*Statistics*] ... RMSD
Root Mean Square Error ... RMSE
Root Mean Square Value [*Statistics*] (IAA) ... RMSV
Root Mean Squared (DOM) ... rms
Root Primordia [*Botany*] ... RP
Root Rot [*Plant pathology*] ... RR
Root Stock [*Botany*] ... RS
Root Sum Square (DA) ... RSS
Root Tip Necrosis [*Plant pathology*] ... RN
Root Tolerance Index [*Botany*] ... RTI
Rooters Organized to Stimulate Interest and Enthusiasm [*Women baseball fans, Cincinnati*] ... ROSIE
Root's Connecticut Reports [*1774-89*] [*A publication*] (DLA) ... Root
Root's Connecticut Reports [*A publication*] (DLA) ... Root R
Root's Connecticut Reports [*A publication*] (DLA) ... Roots
Root's Connecticut Reports [*A publication*] (DLA) ... Root's Rep
Root's Connecticut Supreme Court Reports [*1789-98*] [*A publication*] (DLA) ... Root
Root's Digest of Law and Practice in Bankruptcy [*1818*] [*A publication*] (DLA) ... Root Bt Laws
Ropec Industries, Inc. [*Vancouver Stock Exchange symbol*] ... RBC
Roper Community Library and Resource Center, Inc., Roper, NC [*Library symbol*] [*Library of Congress*] (LCLS) ... NcRop
Roper Industries [*NASDAQ symbol*] (TTSB) ... ROPR
Roper Industries, Inc. [*Associated Press*] (SAG) ... Roper
Roper Industries, Inc. [*NASDAQ symbol*] (SAG) ... ROPR
Roper on Legacies [*4 eds.*] [*1799-1847*] [*A publication*] (DLA) ... Rop
Roper on Legacies [*A publication*] (DLA) ... Rop Leg
Roper on Revocation of Wills [*A publication*] (DLA) ... Rop Rev
Roper Organization (EA) ... RO
Roper's Law of Property between Husband and Wife [*2nd ed.*] [*1826*] [*A publication*] (DLA) ... Rop H & W
Roper's Law of Property between Husband and Wife [*A publication*] (DLA) ... Rop Husb & Wife
Roper's Law of Property between Husband and Wife [*2nd ed.*] [*1826*] [*A publication*] (DLA) ... Rop Prop
Ropes & Gray, Boston, MA [*Library symbol*] [*Library of Congress*] (LCLS) ... MBRG
Roquefort Association (EA) ... RA
Roraima Airways [*Guyana*] [*FAA designator*] (FAAC) ... ROR
Rorer on Inter-State Law [*A publication*] (DLA) ... Ror Int St L
Rorer on Railways [*A publication*] (DLA) ... Rorer RR
Rorer on Void Judicial Sales [*A publication*] (DLA) ... Ror Jud Sal
Rorer on Void Judicial Sales [*A publication*] (DLA) ... Rorer Jud Sales
Roros [*Norway ICAO location identifier*] (ICLI) ... ENRO
Roros [*Norway*] [*Airport symbol*] (OAG) ... RRS
Rorschach [*Test*] [*Psychology*] (DAVI) ... R
Rorschach [*Test*] ... ROR
Rorschach Content Test [*Psychology*] ... RCT
Rorschach Inkblot Test [*Psychiatry*] (DAVI) ... RIT
Rorvik [*Norway*] [*Airport symbol*] (AD) ... RVK
Rorvik/Ryum [*Norway ICAO location identifier*] (ICLI) ... ENRM
Rosa [*Zambia*] [*ICAO location identifier*] (ICLI) ... FLRO
Rosa [*Rose*] [*Pharmacology*] (ROG) ... ROS
Rosamond, CA [*FM radio station call letters*] ... KAVC
Rosamond, CA [*FM radio station call letters*] ... KLKX
Rosanky, TX [*Location identifier FAA*] (FAAL) ... RYU
Rosanne Cash Fan Club (EA) ... RCFC
Rosapata [*Bolivia*] [*ICAO location identifier*] (ICLI) ... SLRP

Rosario [*Argentina*] [*Airport symbol*] (OAG) ROS
Rosario [*Argentina ICAO location identifier*] (ICLI) SAAR
Rosario [*Paraguay*] [*ICAO location identifier*] (ICLI) SGRO
Rosary R
Rosary ROS
Rosary College (GAGS) Rosary C
Rosary College, River Forest, IL [*OCLC symbol*] (OCLC) IBE
Rosary College, River Forest, IL [*Library symbol Library of Congress*] (LCLS) IRivfR
Rosary Hill College [*New York*] RHC
Rosary Hill College, Buffalo, NY [*Library symbol Library of Congress Obsolete*] (LCLS) NBuRH
Rosary Novena for Life Committee (EA) RNLC
ROSAT [*Roentgen Satellite*] **All Sky Survey** RASS
Rosat International X-Ray Optical Survey [*Cosmology*] RIXOS
Roscoe on Actions [*1825*] [*A publication*] (DLA) Rosc Act
Roscoe on Real Actions [*A publication*] (DLA) Rose RA
Roscoe on Stamp Duties [*A publication*] (DLA) Rose St D
Roscoe Pound - American Trial Lawyers Foundation (EA) RP-ATLF
Roscoe Programming Facility (NITA) RPF
Roscoe, Snyder & Pacific Railway Co. [*AAR code*] RSP
ROSCOE User Group [*Princeton, NJ*] (CSR) RUG
Roscoe's Admiralty Jurisdiction and Practice [*A publication*] (DLA) Rosc Adm
Roscoe's Bills of Exchange [*2nd ed.*] [*1843*] [*A publication*] (DLA) Rosc Bills
Roscoe's Cape Of Good Hope [*A publication*] (DLA) R
Roscoe's Digest of Building Cases [*4th ed.*] [*1900*] [*A publication*] (DLA) Rosc Bdg Cas
Roscoe's Digest of Building Cases [*England*] [*A publication*] (DLA) Roscoe Bldg Cas
Roscoe's Digest of Building Cases [*England*] [*A publication*] (DLA) Roscoe's BC
Roscoe's Eastern District Reports [*Cape Of Good Hope*] [*A publication*] (DLA) EDR
Roscoe's English Prize Cases [*A publication*] (DLA) Eng Pr Cas
Roscoe's English Prize Cases [*A publication*] (DLA) EPC
Roscoe's English Prize Cases [*1745-1859*] [*A publication*] (DLA) Rosc PC
Roscoe's Jurist [*London*] [*A publication*] (DLA) Jur Ros
Roscoe's Jurist [*England*] [*A publication*] (DLA) Rosc Jur
Roscoe's Law of Evidence at Nisi Prius [*20 eds.*] [*1827-1934*] [*A publication*] (DLA) Rosc NP
Roscoe's Law of Evidence in Criminal Cases [*16 eds.*] [*1835-1952*] [*A publication*] (DLA) Rosc Cr
Roscoe's Law of Evidence in Criminal Cases [*16 eds.*] [*1835-1952*] [*A publication*] (DLA) Rosc Crim Ev
Roscoe's Law of Evidence in Criminal Cases [*16 eds.*] [*1835-1952*] [*A publication*] (DLA) Roscoe Cr Ev
Roscoe's Law of Light [*4th ed.*] [*1904*] [*A publication*] (DLA) Rosc Light
Roscoe's Nisi Prius Evidence [*20th ed.*] [*1934*] [*A publication*] (DLA) RNP
Roscoe's Nisi Prius Evidence [*20th ed.*] [*1934*] [*A publication*] (DLA) Rosc Ev
Roscoe's Outlines of Civil Procedure [*2nd ed.*] [*1880*] [*A publication*] (DLA) Rosc Civ Pr
Roscoe's Pleading [*1845*] [*A publication*] (DLA) Rosc Pl
Roscoe's Reports of the Supreme Court [*1861-78*] [*South Africa*] [*A publication*] (DLA) Rosc
Roscoe's Reports of the Supreme Court of Cape Of Good Hope [*South Africa*] [*A publication*] (DLA) Roscoe
Roscommon [*County in Ireland*] (WGA) Ros
Roscommon [*County in Ireland*] (ROG) ROSC
Roscommon [*County in Ireland*] ROSCOM
Roscommon, MI [*FM radio station call letters*] (RBYB) WQON
Rose (ROG) RO
Rose Bengal [*A dye*] RB
Rose Bengal Antigen (MAE) RBA
Rose Bengal Plate Test [*Agriculture*] (OA) RBPT
[*The*] **Rose + Croix Martinist Order** (EA) R + CMO
Rose Hall [*Guyana*] [*Airport symbol*] (AD) ROF
Rose Hill, NC [*FM radio station call letters*] WBSY
Rose Hill, NC [*AM radio station call letters*] WEGG
Rose Hybridizers Association (EA) RHA
Rose Knot Victor [*Gemini tracking ship*] RKV
Rose Library, Ogden, IL [*Library symbol Library of Congress*] (LCLS) IOgd
Rose Lookout Tower [*Oklahoma*] [*Seismograph station code, US Geological Survey*] (SEIS) RLO
Rose Polytechnic Institute [*Indiana*] RPI
Rose Polytechnic Institute, Terre Haute, IN [*Library symbol Library of Congress*] (LCLS) InTR
Rose Resources Corp. [*Vancouver Stock Exchange symbol*] ROS
Rose Technology Group Ltd., Toronto, Ontario [*Library symbol National Library of Canada*] (NLC) OTRT
Rose Trade Association [*British*] (DBA) RTA
Rose. Will Case [*New York*] [*A publication*] (DLA) Rose WC
Rosea Rubeae et Aureae Crucis [*The Order of the Rose of Ruby and the Cross of Gold*] RR et AC
Roseau [*Dominica*] [*ICAO location identifier*] (ICLI) TDPR
Roseau Elementary School, Roseau, MN [*Library symbol*] [*Library of Congress*] (LCLS) MnRosE
Roseau High School, Roseau, MN [*Library symbol*] [*Library of Congress*] (LCLS) MnRosH
Roseau, MN [*FM radio station call letters*] (RBYB) KANT
Roseau, MN [*AM radio station call letters*] KRWB
Roseau, MN [*FM radio station call letters*] (RBYB) KRWB-FM
Roseau, MN [*Location identifier FAA*] (FAAL) ROX
Roseau Public Library, Roseau, MN [*Library symbol*] [*Library of Congress*] (LCLS) MnRos
Roseberth [*Australia Airport symbol Obsolete*] (OAG) RSB
Roseberth [*Queensland*] [*Airport symbol*] (AD) RZB
Rosebud County Library, Forsyth, MT [*Library symbol*] [*Library of Congress*] (LCLS) MtFR
Roseburg [*Oregon*] [*Airport symbol*] (AD) RBG
Roseburg, OR [*Television station call letters*] KMTX-TV
Roseburg, OR [*Television station call letters*] KPIC
Roseburg, OR [*AM radio station call letters*] KQEN
Roseburg, OR [*AM radio station call letters*] KRNR
Roseburg, OR [*Television station call letters*] KROZ
Roseburg, OR [*FM radio station call letters*] KRSB
Roseburg, OR [*FM radio station call letters*] KSRS
Roseburg, OR [*AM radio station call letters*] KTBR
Roseburg, OR [*Location identifier FAA*] (FAAL) RBG
Rosedale Mennonite Missions (EA) RMM
Rosehaugh Stanhope Developments [*Commercial firm British*] RSD
Rose-Hulman Institute of Technology (GAGS) Rose-Hulman Inst Tech
Rose-Hulman Institute of Technology Library, Terre Haute, IN [*OCLC symbol*] (OCLC) IRQ
Roseires [*Sudan*] [*Airport symbol*] (OAG) RSS
Roseland Public Library, Roseland, NJ [*Library symbol Library of Congress*] (LCLS) NjRo
Roselend [*France*] [*Seismograph station code, US Geological Survey*] (SEIS) RSL
Rosella Plains [*Queensland*] [*Airport symbol*] (AD) RGO
Rosella Plains [*Australia Airport symbol Obsolete*] (OAG) RLP
Roselle Free Public Library, Roselle, NJ [*Library symbol Library of Congress*] (LCLS) NjRos
Rosemary Public Library, Alberta [*Library symbol National Library of Canada*] (NLC) ARO
Rosemary Public Library, Rosemary, AB, Canada [*Library symbol*] [*Library of Congress*] (LCLS) CaARo
Rosemead Graduate School of Psychology, Rosemead, CA [*Library symbol Library of Congress*] (LCLS) CRomR
Rosemere High School, Quebec [*Library symbol National Library of Canada*] (BIB) QRH
Rosemont College, Rosemont, PA [*Library symbol Library of Congress*] (LCLS) PRosC
Rosemont College, Rosemont, PA [*OCLC symbol*] (OCLC) RMC
Rosenbach Foundation, Philadelphia, PA [*Library symbol Library of Congress*] (LCLS) PPRF
Rosenbalm Aviation [*Air carrier designation symbol*] RAIX
Rosenberg, Avraham, and Gutnick [*Strain of bacteria named for its researchers: Eugene Rosenberg, Avraham Reisfield, and David Gutnick*] RAG-1
Rosenberg Library, Galveston, TX [*Library symbol Library of Congress*] (LCLS) TxGR
Rosenberg Self-Esteem Scale RSES
Rosenberg, TX [*FM radio station call letters*] (RBYB) KLTO
Rosenberger's Pocket Law Journal [*A publication*] (DLA) Rosenberger Pock LJ
Rosenberg-Richmond, TX [*AM radio station call letters*] KMPQ
Rosenburg, TX [*Television station call letters*] KXLN
Rosendale, NY [*FM radio station call letters*] WFNP
Roseneath [*New Zealand*] [*Seismograph station code, US Geological Survey Closed*] (SEIS) ROS
Rosenstiel School of Marine and Atmospheric Science [*University of Miami*] [*Research center*] (RCD) RSMAS
Rosenthal-Field Plossen [*Germany ICAO location identifier*] (ICLI) EDQP
Rose's Digest of Arkansas Reports [*A publication*] (DLA) Rose Dig
Rose's English Bankruptcy Reports [*A publication*] (DLA) Rose
Rose's English Bankruptcy Reports [*1810-16*] [*A publication*] (DLA) Rose Bankr
Rose's English Bankruptcy Reports [*A publication*] (DLA) Rose Bankr (Eng)
Rose's English Bankruptcy Reports [*A publication*] (DLA) Rose BC
Rose's Notes on United States Reports [*A publication*] (DLA) Rose Notes
Rose's Stores [*Associated Press*] (SAG) RoseStr
Rose's Stores [*NASDAQ symbol*] (SAG) RSTO
Rose's Stores Wrrt [*NASDAQ symbol*] (TTSB) RSTOW
Rosetown, SK [*AM radio station call letters*] CJYM
Rosette [*Cytology*] (DAVI) ROSE
Rosette Inhibition Titer [*Medicine*] (DMAA) RIT
Rosette Scan Seeker [*Army*] (DOMA) RSS
Rosette-Forming Cell [*Immunochemistry*] RFC
Roseville, CA [*AM radio station call letters*] KRCX
Roseville, CA [*FM radio station call letters*] KRXQ
Roseville Public Library, Roseville, CA [*Library symbol Library of Congress*] (LCLS) CRo
Roseville Public Library, Roseville, MI [*Library symbol Library of Congress*] (LCLS) MiRos
Rosewood (VRA) roswd
Rosewood Center, Owing Mills, MD [*Library symbol Library of Congress*] (LCLS) MdOmR
Rosewood, OH [*Location identifier FAA*] (FAAL) ROD
Rosh Hashanah [*New Year*] (BJA) RH
Rosh Hashanah [*New Year*] (BJA) RhSh
Rosh Pina/Mahanaim-I. Ben-Yaakov [*Israel*] [*ICAO location identifier*] (ICLI) LLIB
Rosh Pinah [*Namibia*] [*ICAO location identifier*] (ICLI) FARP
Rosh-Pina [*Israel*] [*Airport symbol*] (AD) MYH
Rosh-Pina [*Israel*] [*Airport symbol*] (OAG) RPN
Rosicrucian Fellowship (EA) RCF
Rosicrucian Fellowship (EA) RF
Rosicrucian Fraternity (EA) RF
Rosin [*Standard material for soldering*] R
Rosin Acid [*Organic chemistry*] RA
Rosin Activated [*Standard material for soldering*] RA
Rosin Amine-D-Acetate [*Medicine*] (DMAA) RADA
Rosin Core [*Foundry technology*] RC

Rosin Mildly Activated [*Standard material for soldering*] .... RMA
Roskilde [*Denmark*] [*Airport symbol*] (OAG) .... RKE
Roskilde Universitet [*Roskilde University*], Roskilde, Denmark [*Library symbol Library of Congress*] (LCLS) .... DnRoU
Roslyn High School, Roslyn Heights, NY [*Library symbol*] [*Library of Congress*] (LCLS) .... NRoslhHS
Roslyn High School, Roslyn, NY [*Library symbol Library of Congress*] (LCLS) .... NRoslHS
Roslyn Junior High School, Roslyn Heights, NY [*Library symbol*] [*Library of Congress*] (LCLS) .... NRoslhJH
Roslyn Junior High School, Roslyn, NY [*Library symbol Library of Congress*] (LCLS) .... NRoslJH
Roslyn, NY [*Location identifier FAA*] (FAAL) .... FWI
Rosmac Resources Ltd. [*Vancouver Stock Exchange symbol*] .... RCM
Rosmarinus [*Rosemary*] [*Pharmacology*] (ROG) .... ROSMAR
Rosner Television Systems, Inc. [*New York, NY*] [*Telecommunications*] (TSSD) .... RTS
Ross Air Training [*British ICAO designator*] (FAAC) .... RTY
Ross Aviation [*ICAO designator*] (AD) .... ZD
Ross Aviation, Inc. [*ICAO designator*] (FAAC) .... NRG
Ross Bay [*Newfoundland*] [*Airport symbol*] (AD) .... YRF
Ross Consumer Electronics [*British*] .... RCE
Ross Educational Philosophical Inventory (EDAC) .... REPI
Ross, Hardies, O'Keefe, Babcock, and Parsons, Chicago, IL [*Library symbol Library of Congress*] (LCLS) .... ICRHO
Ross Ice Shelf Geophysical and Glaciological Survey [*Ross Ice Shelf Project*] .... RIGGS
Ross Ice Shelf Project [*International cooperative research project*] .... RISP
Ross Laboratory Library, Columbus, OH [*OCLC symbol*] (OCLC) .... ORA
Ross' Leading Cases [*England*] [*A publication*] (DLA) .... Ross Lead Cas
Ross' Lectures on Conveyancing, Etc. [*Sc.*] [*A publication*] (DLA) .... Ross Conv
Ross Memorial Hospital, Medical Library, Lindsay, ON, Canada [*Library symbol*] [*Library of Congress*] (LCLS) .... CaOLiRM
Ross Memorial Library, St. Andrews, New Brunswick [*Library symbol National Library of Canada*] (BIB) .... NBSARM
Ross on Contracts [*A publication*] (DLA) .... Ross Cont
Ross on Vendors and Purchasers [*2nd ed.*] [*1826*] [*A publication*] (DLA) .... Ross V & P
Ross Sea Deep Water [*Marine science*] (MSC) .... RSDW
Ross Sea Shelf Water [*Ross Ice Shelf Project*] .... RSSW
Ross Sea Winter Water [*Marine science*] (MSC) .... RSWW
Ross Stores [*NASDAQ symbol*] (TTSB) .... ROST
Ross Stores, Inc. [*Associated Press*] (SAG) .... RossStr
Ross Stores, Inc. [*Newark, CA*] [*NASDAQ symbol*] (NQ) .... ROST
Ross Systems [*NASDAQ symbol*] (TTSB) .... ROSS
Ross Systems, Inc. [*NASDAQ symbol*] (SPSG) .... ROSS
Ross Systems, Inc. [*Associated Press*] (SAG) .... RossSy
Ross Technology [*NASDAQ symbol*] (TTSB) .... RTEC
Ross Technology, Inc. [*Associated Press*] (SAG) .... RossTch
Ross Technology, Inc. [*NASDAQ symbol*] (SAG) .... RTEC
Rossair [*ICAO designator*] (AD) .... RF
Rossair Pty Ltd. [*Australia ICAO designator*] (FAAC) .... RFS
Rossburn District Hospital, Rossburn, Manitoba [*Library symbol National Library of Canada*] (NLC) .... MRH
Rossburn District Hospital, Rossburn, MB, Canada [*Library symbol Library of Congress*] (LCLS) .... CaMRoH
Rossburn Regional Library, Manitoba [*Library symbol National Library of Canada*] (NLC) .... MRO
Rossburn Regional Library, Rossburn, MB, Canada [*Library symbol Library of Congress*] (LCLS) .... CaMRo
Rosseau Public Library, Ontario [*Library symbol National Library of Canada*] (NLC) .... OROS
Rossellini, Jr.; Godard, Pasolini, Gregoretti [*Title of episodic motion picture formed from surnames of its directors*] .... ROGOPAG
Rossendale Union of Boot, Shoe, and Slipper Operatives [*British*] (DCTA) .... RUBSSO
Rossendorfer Forschungs-Reaktor [*Rossendorf Research Reactor*] [*German*] .... RFS
Rossi X-ray Timing Explorer [*A satellite*] .... RXTE
Rossica Society of Russian Philately (EA) .... RSRP
Rossiiskaia Sotsial-Demokraticheskaia Rabochaya Partiia [*Russian Social Democratic Workers' Party*] [*Political party*] (PPE) .... RSDRP
Rossland Historical Museum, British Columbia [*Library symbol National Library of Canada*] (NLC) .... BRM
Rossland Historical Museum, Rossland, BC, Canada [*Library symbol Library of Congress*] (LCLS) .... CaBRM
Rossland Public Library, British Columbia [*Library symbol National Library of Canada*] (BIB) .... BR
Rosslyn Connecting Railroad Co. [*AAR code*] .... RC
Rossman Elementary School, Detroit Lakes, MN [*Library symbol*] [*Library of Congress*] (LCLS) .... MnDIRE
Rosso [*Mauritania*] [*ICAO location identifier*] (ICLI) .... GQNR
Ross's Leading Cases in the Law of Scotland (Land Rights) [*1638-1840*] [*A publication*] (DLA) .... Ross LC
Ross's Leading Cases in the Law of Scotland (Land Rights) [*A publication*] (DLA) .... Ross Ldg Cas
Ross's Leading Cases in the Law of Scotland (Land Rights) [*1638-1840*] [*A publication*] (DLA) .... Ross Lead Cas
Ross's Leading Cases on Commercial Law [*England*] [*A publication*] (DLA) .... Ross LC
Ross's Leading Cases on Commercial Law [*A publication*] (DLA) .... Ross Ldg Cas
Rossum's Universal Robots [*Acronym is title of play by Karel Capek*] .... RUR
Rossville, GA [*AM radio station call letters*] .... WCVT
Rossville, GA [*FM radio station call letters*] .... WLMX
Rost [*Norway ICAO location identifier*] (ICLI) .... ENRS
Rost [*Norway*] [*Airport symbol*] (OAG) .... RET
Rostaq [*Oman*] [*ICAO location identifier*] (ICLI) .... OORQ
Roster Chaplain - Ready Reserve [*Army*] .... RCRR
Roster of Employees Transferred [*Army*] .... RET
Roster of Exception [*Military*] (AABC) .... ROE
Roster of Required Events .... RRE
Rostov [*Former USSR Airport symbol*] (OAG) .... ROV
Rostov-Na-Donu [*Former USSR ICAO location identifier*] (ICLI) .... URRR
Rostral [*Anatomy*] .... R
Rostral Basilar Artery Syndrome [*Medicine*] (DMAA) .... RBAS
Rostral Interstitial Nucleus of Medial Longitudinal Fasciculus [*Neuroanatomy*] .... RIMLF
Rostral Length Index .... RLI
Rostral Migratory Stream [*Brain anatomy*] .... RMS
Rostrum Clubs of Australia .... RCA
Roswell [*New Mexico*] [*Airport symbol*] (OAG) .... ROW
Roswell Airlines, Inc. [*ICAO designator*] (FAAC) .... RAL
Roswell Carnegie Library, Roswell, NM [*Library symbol Library of Congress*] (LCLS) .... NmR
Roswell/Industrial Air Center [*New Mexico*] [*ICAO location identifier*] (ICLI) .... KROW
Roswell, NM [*FM radio station call letters*] .... KBCQ
Roswell, NM [*AM radio station call letters*] .... KBIM
Roswell, NM [*FM radio station call letters*] .... KBIM-FM
Roswell, NM [*Television station call letters*] .... KBIM-TV
Roswell, NM [*AM radio station call letters*] .... KCKN
Roswell, NM [*AM radio station call letters*] .... KCRX
Roswell, NM [*FM radio station call letters*] .... KEND
Roswell, NM [*FM radio station call letters*] .... KMOU
Roswell, NM [*Television station call letters*] .... KOBR
Roswell, NM [*AM radio station call letters*] .... KRDD
Roswell, NM [*Television station call letters*] .... KRPV
Roswell, NM [*AM radio station call letters*] .... KRSY
Roswell, NM [*FM radio station call letters*] .... KSFX
Roswell, NM [*FM radio station call letters*] .... KWFL
Roswell P. Flower Memorial Public Library, Watertown, NY [*Library symbol Library of Congress*] (LCLS) .... NWatt
Roswell Park Memorial Institute [*Research code symbol*] .... AB
Roswell Park Memorial Institute [*State University of New York at Buffalo*] [*Research center*] (RCD) .... RPMI
Roswell Park Memorial Institute [*Research code symbol*] .... TEM
Roswell Park Memorial Institute [*Research code symbol*] .... TEPA
Roswell Park Memorial Institute, Buffalo, NY [*OCLC symbol*] (OCLC) .... VZR
Roswell Public Library, Roswell, NM [*OCLC symbol*] (OCLC) .... ROS
Rosy Cross [*Freemasonry*] .... RSYCS
Rota [*Spain ICAO location identifier*] (ICLI) .... LERT
Rota [*Mariana Islands*] [*Airport symbol*] (OAG) .... ROP
Rota [*Nicaragua*] [*Seismograph station code, US Geological Survey*] (SEIS) .... RTN
Rota/International [*Mariana Islands*] [*ICAO location identifier*] (ICLI) .... PGRO
Rota Island, TT [*Location identifier FAA*] (FAAL) .... GRO
Rotable Pool Factor (MCD) .... RPF
Rotable Table .... ROTAB
Rotae Florentine [*Reports of the Supreme Court of Florence*] [*Latin A publication*] (DLA) .... Rot Flor
Rotary (AAG) .... ROT
Rotary .... RTRY
Rotary Analog Logic Unit (MCD) .... RALU
Rotary and Neostyle [*Duplicating machine*] [*Acronym is trademark*] .... RONEO
Rotary Assembly .... RA
Rotary Beam Antenna .... RBA
Rotary Carton Feed Unit .... RCFU
Rotary Clothes Hoist (ADA) .... RCH
Rotary Combustion [*Automobile*] .... RC
Rotary Combustion Engine (PDAA) .... RCE
Rotary Compression (IAA) .... RC
Rotary Converter (IAA) .... RC
Rotary [*or Rotating*] **Digital Audio Tape** .... RDAT
Rotary Disk Valve [*Automotive engineering*] .... RDV
Rotary Dispersion Colorimeter .... RDC
Rotary Drive Piston Motor .... RDPM
Rotary Dual Input for Analog Computation (SAA) .... ROD/AC
Rotary Dual Input for Analog Computation .... RODIAC
Rotary Engine [*Automotive engineering*] .... RE
Rotary Engine Air Pollution System [*Automotive engineering*] .... REAPS
Rotary Engine Antipollution System .... REAPS
Rotary Evaporator .... Rotavapor
Rotary Feed-Through .... RFT
Rotary Hydraulic Arresting Gear (PDAA) .... RHAG
Rotary Indexing Table .... RIT
Rotary International (EA) .... RI
Rotary Joint .... RJ
Rotary Joint Assembly .... RJA
Rotary Joint Reed .... RJR
Rotary Joint Reed Assembly .... RJRA
Rotary Limit Switch .... RLS
Rotary Linear Variable Differential Transformer .... RLVDT
Rotary Mirror Camera .... RMC
Rotary on Stamps Fellowship (EA) .... ROS
Rotary Oscillating Torque Actuators .... ROTAC
Rotary Out Trunk Switch [*Telecommunications*] (TEL) .... ROTS
Rotary Pellet Launcher [*Military*] (PDAA) .... RPL
Rotary Power International, Inc. [*Associated Press*] (SAG) .... RotaryPw
Rotary Power Internationl, Inc. [*NASDAQ symbol*] (SAG) .... RPII
Rotary Power Intl [*NASDAQ symbol*] (TTSB) .... RPII
Rotary Power Transformer .... RPT

Rotary Precision Switch .... RPS
Rotary Pressure Joint .... RPJ
Rotary Pulse Generator .... RPG
Rotary Pursuit [Test for motor skill] .... RP
Rotary Relative Position Indicator [Nuclear energy] (NRCH) .... RRPI
Rotary Seal Ring .... RSR
Rotary Selector (IAA) .... RS
Rotary Servo Actuator .... RSA
Rotary Shaft Indicator .... RSI
Rotary Shaft Seal .... RSS
Rotary Stepping Switch .... RSS
Rotary Stylus Electronics Recorder .... RSER
Rotary Switch (IAA) .... RS
Rotary Switch (MSA) .... RTRSW
Rotary Switch Art (IAA) .... RSA
Rotary Symbol Switch (MCD) .... RSS
Rotary System (IAA) .... RS
Rotary Takeoff and Landing [Aviation] (AIA) .... RTOL
Rotary Thumbwheel Switch .... RTS
Rotary to Digital (MCD) .... R/D
Rotary Transformer (IAA) .... RT
Rotary Ultrasonic Machining [Manufacturing term] .... RUM
Rotary Vacuum Pump .... RVP
Rotary Vane Air Cycle (MCD) .... ROVAC
Rotary Variable Differential Transducer [or Transformer] .... RVDT
Rotary Variable Inductive Transducer [Electronics] .... RVIT
Rotary Voice Coil [Computer technology] .... RVC
Rotary Wing [Aircraft designation] .... R
Rotary Wing [Aircraft designation] .... RW
Rotary Wing Aircraft .... RWA
Rotary Wing Turbine Hours [Aviation] (AIA) .... RWTH
Rotary-Wing Air-Sea-Rescue Aircraft [Navy symbol] (MUGU) .... HH
Rotatable Initial Susceptibility .... RIS
Rotatable Log Periodic Antenna (MCD) .... RLP
Rotatable Nozzle Assembly .... RNA
Rotatable Optical Cube .... ROC
Rotatable Pool Quantity .... RP
Rotatable Pool Rate (MCD) .... RPR
Rotatable Pool Unit (DNAB) .... RPU
Rotatable Porous-Prism Test Fixture .... RPPTF
Rotatable Porro-Mirror Test Fixture .... RPTF
Rotate (AAG) .... ROT
Rotate and Scale [Computer science] .... ROTSAL
Rotate and Slide (DNAB) .... ROTAS
Rotate Left [Computer science] .... ROL
Rotate Right [Computer science] .... ROR
Rotate through X Left [Computer science] .... ROXL
Rotate through X Right [Computer science] .... ROXR
Rotating Acoustic Stereo-Scanner [Telecommunications] (OA) .... RASS
Rotating Air Refueling Squadron (CINC) .... ROTE AREFS
Rotating Arm Basin .... RAB
Rotating Associative Relational Store (MHDI) .... RARES
Rotating Beam Ceilometer [Aviation] .... RBC
Rotating Biological Contractors [Processing equipment] .... RBC
Rotating Bomb Oxidation Test [Lubricant testing] [Automotive
    engineering] .... R-BOT
Rotating Bubble Membrane Radiator [Battelle Pacific Northwest
    Laboratories] .... RBMR
Rotating Catalytic Basket Reactor [Chemical engineering] .... RCBR
Rotating Coil Yoke .... RCY
Rotating Cylinder Flap .... RCF
Rotating Cylinder-Collector Electrode [Electrochemistry] .... RCCE
Rotating Diffusion Cell [Chemistry] .... RDC
Rotating Disc Electrode .... RDE
Rotating Disc Thin-Layer Chromatography .... RDTLC
Rotating Disk Contractor [Chemical engineering] .... RDC
Rotating Dome Valve [Military] (RDA) .... RDV
Rotating Electrical Machines Association [British] (DBA) .... REMA
Rotating Field Electrophoresis [Analytical biochemistry] .... RFE
Rotating Field Logic (IAA) .... RFL
Rotating Fighter Interceptor Squadron (CINC) .... ROT FIS
Rotating Fighter Interceptor Squadron Detachment (CINC) .... ROT FIS DET
Rotating Gel Electrophoresis .... RGE
Rotating Gold Ring-Disc Electrode (PDAA) .... RGRDE
Rotating Gravity Gradiometer .... RGG
Rotating Image Optical Scanner .... RIOS
Rotating Image Scanner .... RIS
Rotating Light [Navigation signal] .... ROT
Rotating Light or Beacon .... ROTLT/BCN
Rotating Lighthouse System (IAA) .... RLS
Rotating Linear Polarization .... RLP
Rotating Litter Chair [NASA] (KSC) .... RLC
Rotating Log Periodic Antenna .... RLPA
Rotating Machinery (IAA) .... RM
Rotating Magnetic Field [Spectrometry] .... RMF
Rotating Map, Cursor Centered [Automotive engineering] .... RMCC
Rotating Map, Cursor Moving [Automotive engineering] .... RMCM
Rotating Mirror LASER .... RML
Rotating Modulation Collimator .... RMC
Rotating Observation Platform (IAA) .... ROP
Rotating Optical Interferometer .... ROI
Rotating Optical Scanner .... ROS
Rotating Packed Disk Reactor [Chemical engineering] .... RPDR
Rotating Passing Scuttle .... RPS
Rotating Phase Array Antenna .... RPAA

Rotating Piston Machine (IAA) .... ROM
Rotating Platinum Electrode [Electrochemistry] .... RPE
Rotating Ring Disk Electrode .... RRDE
Rotating Service Structure [Kennedy Space Center] (MCD) .... RSS
Rotating Shadowband Radiometer (USDC) .... RSR
Rotating Shadowband Radiometer [Marine science] (OSRA) .... RSR
Rotating Shield Plug [Nuclear energy] (NRCH) .... RSP
Rotating Spherical Convection Facility (SSD) .... RSCF
Rotating Stratified Combustion [Automotive engineering] .... ROSCO
Rotating Surveillance Vehicle Platform [Military] (MCD) .... RSVP
Rotating Target Neutron Source [Nuclear physics] .... RTNS
Rotating Transformer .... ROT TX
Rotating Vertical Gradiometer .... RVG
Rotating Vertical Gravity Gradiometer .... RVGG
Rotating-Frame Overhauser Enchancement Spectroscopy [Organic
    chemistry] .... ROESY
Rotation (ROG) .... ROTN
Rotation Angiography [Medicine] (DMAA) .... RA
Rotation Axis Coordinate System (MCD) .... RACS
Rotation Combat Personnel .... RCP
Rotation Control (NASA) .... RC
Rotation Discrete Rate .... RT
Rotation in a Selected Plane .... RSP
Rotation Magnitude Ratio .... RMR
Rotation Planar Chromatography .... RPC
Rotation Project (DNAB) .... ROT PROJ
Rotation Remanent Magnetization (PDAA) .... RRM
Rotation/Translation Control Electronics (NASA) .... RTCE
Rotation Translation Hand Controller (NASA) .... RTHC
Rotational Air Weather Squadron (CINC) .... ROT AWS
Rotational Airborne Command and Control Center (CINC) .... ROT ABCCC
Rotational Autonomic Tester .... RAT
Rotational Base for Aviation Maintenance Personnel .... ROBAMP
Rotational Bomb Squadron (CINC) .... ROT BS
Rotational Direction Transmission .... RDT
Rotational Energy Transfer [Chemical physics] .... RET
Rotational Flight Simulator [Air Force] .... RFS
Rotational Hand Controller [NASA] .... RHC
Rotational Magnetic-Dipole Radiation [Astronomy] .... RMR
Rotational Position Sensing [Computer science] .... RPS
Rotational RADAR Calibration Squadron (CINC) .... ROT RCS
Rotational Tactical Assault Squadron (CINC) .... ROT TAS
Rotational Tactical Bomber Squadron (CINC) .... ROT TBS
Rotational Telemetry .... ROTEL
Rotational Test Facility [NASA] .... RTF
Rotational Troop Carrier Squadron (CINC) .... ROT TCS
Rotational Voltage Displacement Transmitter .... RVDT
Rotations per Minute .... RPM
Rotator [A type of muscle] (DAVI) .... ROT
Rotator [Electromagnetics] .... ROTR
Rote Armee Faktion [Red Army Faction (Baader-Meinhof Group)] [Terrorist
    group] [Germany] .... RAF
Rote/Lekunik [Indonesia] [ICAO location identifier] (ICLI) .... WRKR
Rotech Medical [NASDAQ symbol] (TTSB) .... ROTC
RoTech Medical Corp. [Orlando, FL] [NASDAQ symbol] (NQ) .... ROTC
Rotech Medical Corp. [Associated Press] (SAG) .... Rotech
Rotenburg/Wumme [Germany ICAO location identifier] (ICLI) .... EDCR
Roter Interactional Analysis System [Medicine] (DMAA) .... RIAS
Roterodamum [Rotterdam] (ROG) .... ROTERO
Rotex Turret Punch .... RTP
Roth [Germany ICAO location identifier] (ICLI) .... EDPR
Rothchild Gold [Vancouver Stock Exchange symbol] .... ROG
Rothenburg [Germany ICAO location identifier] (ICLI) .... EDFR
Rothesay [Scotland] [Airport symbol] (OAG) .... RAY
Rothmans Art Gallery, Stratford, ON, Canada [Library symbol Library of
    Congress] (LCLS) .... CaOStrAG
Rothmans Inc. [Formerly, Rothmans of Pall Mall Canada] [Toronto Stock
    Exchange symbol Vancouver Stock Exchange symbol] .... ROC
Rothmans of Pall Mall Ltd., Don Mills, Ontario [Library symbol National
    Library of Canada] (NLC) .... OTRPM
Rothsay Public School, Rothsay, MN [Library symbol] [Library of Congress]
    (LCLS) .... MnRothS
Rothschild Investment Trust .... RIT
Roti [Indonesia] [Airport symbol] (OAG) .... RTI
ROTI [Recording Optical Tracking Instrument] Tracker - Cocoa Beach
    [NASA] (KSC) .... RTCB
Roto Rooter, Inc. [Associated Press] (SAG) .... RotoRtr
Rotodrome .... RD
Rotogravure [Printing process] (NTCM) .... ROTO
Rotogravure Association .... RA
Rotometer .... ROTOMT
Rotonics Manufacturing [Formerly, Koala Technologies] [AMEX symbol]
    (SPSG) .... RMI
Rotonics Manufacturing [Associated Press] (SAG) .... Rotonic
Rotor .... R
Rotor (ADA) .... ROT
Rotor (MSA) .... RTR
Rotor Blade Antenna .... RBA
Rotor Blade Homing Antenna .... RBHA
Rotor Blade RADAR .... RBR
Rotor Burst Protection Program [NASA] .... RBPP
Rotor Current Meter .... RCM
Rotor Entry Vehicle [Aerospace] .... REV
Rotor Entry Vehicle System [Aerospace] .... REVS
Rotor Impulsive Noise [Helicopters] .... RIN

Rotor Power Output	RPO
Rotor Reentry Vehicle	RRV
Rotor Systems Research Aircraft [Army/NASA]	RSRA
Rotor Systems Research Vehicle	RSRV
Rotor Temperature Indicator and Control [Instrumentation]	RTIC
Rotor Test Apparatus (MCD)	RTA
Rotor Wing Agricultural Hours [Aviation] (AIA)	RWAH
Rotor Wing Hours [Aviation] (AIA)	RWH
Rotorace Inertial Navigation System (MCD)	RINS
Rotorcraft Helicopter [Pilot rating] (AIA)	ROTOR
Rotorcraft Master Plan [FAA] (TAG)	RMP
Rotorcraft Pilot's Associate [Army] (RDA)	RPA
Rotorcraft Simulator Motion Generator [Army] (RDA)	RSMG
Rotorcraft Systems Integration Simulator [Joint Army-NASA program] (RDA)	RSIS
Rotorcraft-Aircrew Systems Concepts Airborne Laboratory (RDA)	RASCAL
Roto-Rooter, Inc. [Cincinnati, OH] [NASDAQ symbol] (NQ)	ROTO
Rotors in Motion [Aviation] (AIA)	RIM
Rotors Not in Motion [Aviation] (AIA)	RNIM
Rotorua [New Zealand] [ICAO location identifier] (ICLI)	NZRO
Rotorua [New Zealand] [Seismograph station code, US Geological Survey Closed] (SEIS)	ROT
Rotorua [New Zealand] [Airport symbol] (OAG)	ROT
Rotorua Aero Club [New Zealand] [ICAO designator] (FAAC)	RAC
Rotten [Quality of the bottom] [Nautical charts]	rt
Rotter Incomplete Sentences Blank [Psychology]	RISB
Rotter Sentence Completion Test [Speech and language therapy] (DAVI)	RSCT
Rotterdam [Netherlands ICAO location identifier] (ICLI)	EHRD
Rotterdam (ROG)	ROTTER
Rotterdam [Netherlands] [Airport symbol] (OAG)	RTM
Rotterdam Energy Futures Exchange [Netherlands] (EY)	ROEFEX
Rotterdam, NY [FM radio station call letters] (RBYB)	WYSR
Rotterdam School of Management [Netherlands] (ECON)	RSM
Rotterdam-Rhine Pipeline [Oil]	RRP
Rottlund Co. [NASDAQ symbol] (SAG)	RHOM
Rottlund Co. [Associated Press] (SAG)	Rottlund
Rottnest Airbus [Airline code] [Australia]	WI
Rottnest Island [Australia Airport symbol] (OAG)	RTS
Rotulae Parliamentariae [Latin A publication] (DLA)	Rot Parl
Rotuli Clause [Close Roll] [Latin A publication] (DLA)	Rot Claus
Rotuli Curiae Regis [1194-99] [Latin A publication] (DLA)	Rot Cur Reg
Rotuli Curiae Regis [1194-99] [Latin A publication] (DLA)	Rotuli Curiae Reg
Rotuli Hundredorum [Latin A publication] (DLA)	RH
Rotuli Parliamentorum [1278-1533] [Latin A publication] (DLA)	RP
Rotuli Patenes [Latin A publication] (DLA)	Rot Pat
Rotuli Placitorum [Latin A publication] (DLA)	Rot Plac
Rotulus Chartarum [Charter Roll] [Latin A publication] (DLA)	Chart
Rotulus Chartarum [Charter Roll] [Latin A publication] (DLA)	Rot Chart
Rotulus Clausarum [Close Roll] [England] [A publication] (DLA)	Cl
Rotuma [Fiji] [ICAO location identifier] (ICLI)	NFNR
Rotuma [Fiji] [Airport symbol] (OAG)	RTA
Rotundus Nucleus (DAVI)	Rt
Rotz [Germany ICAO location identifier] (ICLI)	EDAQ
Rouen/Boos [France ICAO location identifier] (ICLI)	LFOP
Rouge Steel 'A' [NYSE symbol] (TTSB)	ROU
Rouge Steel Co. [NYSE symbol] (SAG)	ROU
Rouge Steel Co. [Associated Press] (SAG)	RougeStl
Rough [Appearance of bacterial colony]	R
Rough (AAG)	RGH
Rough	RO
Rough and Tumble Engineers' Historical Association (EA)	R & T
Rough Blanking Template (MCD)	RBT
Rough Cast (ADA)	RC
Rough Combustion Cutoff [NASA]	RCC
Rough Combustion Cutoff Assembly [NASA] (KSC)	RCCA
Rough Combustion Cutoff Replaceable Assembly [NASA] (KSC)	RCCP
Rough Cut Capacity Planning [Manufacturing management]	RCCP
Rough Cutting [Construction]	RC
Rough [Surfaced] Endoplasmic Reticulum [Cytology]	RER
Rough Field Landing	RFL
Rough Finish	RF
Rough Hard Sphere [Model of liquids]	RHS
Rough, Noncapsulated, Avirulent [With reference to bacteria]	RNA
Rough Opening [Technical drawings]	RO
Rough Order of Magnitude [Army] (AABC)	ROM
Rough Riders [The City of London Yeomanry] [Military unit] [British]	RR
Rough Riding Sergeant-Major [British military] (DMA)	RRSM
Rough Riding Staff Sergeant-Major [British military] (DMA)	RRSSM
Rough River Petroleum Corp. [Vancouver Stock Exchange symbol]	RRP
Rough Rock Public Library, Rough Rock, AZ [Library symbol Library of Congress] (LCLS)	AzRou
Rough Saw Template (MCD)	RST
Rough Sea [Navigation]	R
Rough Service, High Impact (DNAB)	RSHI
Rough Sunk Face [Construction]	RSF
Rough Template (AAG)	RGTP
Rough Terrain [Military] (AABC)	RT
Rough Terrain Container Handler (MCD)	RTCH
Rough Terrain Fork Lift	RTFL
Rough Terrain Forklift [Military]	RTFLFT
Rough Terrain Forklift Truck (MCD)	RTFLT
Rough Terrain Forklift Truck	RTFT
Rough Terrain Front Loader (MCD)	RTFL
Rough Terrain Vehicle	RTV
Rough-Air [or Turbulence] Speed [Aviation]	VRA

Roughness Height Rating (MSA)	RHR
Rough-Smooth Variation [Bacteriology] (DAVI)	R-S
Rougiers [France] [Seismograph station code, US Geological Survey Closed] (SEIS)	ROU
Rouleaux [Formation Differential] [Cytology] (DAVI)	ROUL
Rouletted (ROG)	ROUL
Roumania [IYRU nationality code] (IYR)	RM
Roumanian Jewish Federation of America [Defunct] (EA)	RJFA
Roumanian Pharmacopoeia [A publication]	Roum P
Round (AAG)	RD
Round	RND
Round	RND
Round Bobbin [A publication] (EAAP)	RB
Round Corners [Bookselling]	RC
Round Corners Silver Bevelled Deckle Edges [Bookbinding] (DGA)	RCSBDE
Round Corners Silver Bevelled Edges [Bookbinding] (DGA)	RCSBE
Round Corners Silver Edges [Bookbinding] (DGA)	RCSE
Round Die Bushing	RDB
Round Head	RDH
Round Head (IAA)	RDHD
Round Head	RH
Round Head Brass [Screw Head] (ECII)	RHB
Round Hill Field Station [MIT] (MCD)	RHFS
Round Hill Installation (SAA)	RHI
Round Hole [Looseleaf binding] (DGA)	RH
Round Hole Broach	RHB
Round House [Maps and charts]	RH
Round Lot [Unit of trading]	RL
Round Lot Orders [Unit of trading] (MHDW)	RLO
Round Maximum Pressure (NATG)	RMP
Round of Beam (DS)	ROB
Round Off (IAA)	RO
Round Off Error	ROE
Round Punch	RP
Round Pupil Intracapsular Cataract Extraction [Ophthalmology] (DAVI)	RPICCE
Round, Regular, and Equal [With reference to pupils of eyes]	RR & E
Round, Regular, and React Normally [Referring to the pupils of the eyes] (DAVI)	RRRN
Round Robin (IEEE)	RR
Round Robin [Aviation] (FAAC)	RRBN
Round Rock Public Library, Round Rock, TX [Library symbol] [Library of Congress] (LCLS)	TxRr
Round Rock, TX [FM radio station call letters]	KNLE
Round Table for the Management of Library Associations	RTMLA
Round Table International (EA)	RTI
Round Table of National Organizations for Better Education [Defunct] (EA)	RTNOBE
Round the Clock (DAVI)	RTC
Round the World	RTW
Round Trip	RT
Round Trips per Hour (MSA)	RTPH
Round Tube-Plate Fin [Heat exchanger]	RTPF
"Round Up" Administration Planning Staff [for the invasion of France] [World War II]	RAP
Rounders Association of Ireland (EAIO)	RAI
Roundheaded Screw (BARN)	rhs
Rounding	RDG
Rounding Control [Computer programming] (BYTE)	RC
Round-Nose Soft-Point Bullet	RNSP
Rounds [of ammunition] [Military]	RDS
Round's Law of Domicil [1861] [A publication] (DLA)	Round Dom
Round's Law of Lien [1863] [A publication] (DLA)	Round Lien
Rounds per Gun	RPG
Rounds per Gun per Minute	RGM
Rounds per Gun per Minute	RPGPM
Rounds per Minute [Military]	RDS/M
Rounds per Minute [Military] (INF)	RPM
Rounds per Mortar	RPMOR
Rounds per Mortar per Minute	RPMORPM
Round's Right of Light and Air [1868] [A publication] (DLA)	Round L & A
Roundtable [Bulletin board system] [Computer science] (PCM)	RT
Roundtable for Women Food-Beverage-Hospitality (EA)	RWFBH
Roundtable for Women in Foodservice [Later, RWFBH] (EA)	RWF
Round-Trip Light Time	RTLT
Roundup Central Elementary School Library, Roundup, MT [Library symbol] [Library of Congress] (LCLS)	MtRd-E
Roundup Magazine [A publication] (BRI)	Roundup M
Roundup, MT [Location identifier FAA] (FAAL)	RPX
Rourkela [India] [Airport symbol] (AD)	RRK
Rourkela [India] [ICAO location identifier] (ICLI)	VERK
Rous Conditioned Medium	RCM
Rous Sarcoma Virus [Same as ASV]	RSV
Rous Sarcoma Virus, Bryan [Strain]	RSV-Br
Rous Sarcoma Virus, Carr-Zilber Strain	CZ-RSV
Rous Sarcoma Virus, Prague Strain	PR-RSV
Rous Sarcoma Virus, Schmidt-Ruppin [Strain]	RSV-SR
Rous Sarcoma Virus, Schmidt-Ruppin Strain	SR-RSV
Rous-Associated Virus (MAE)	RAV
Rouse Capital 9.25%'QUIPS' [NYSE symbol] (TTSB)	RSEPrZ
Rouse Co. [Associated Press] (SAG)	Rouse
Rouse Co. [NYSE symbol] (SAG)	RSE
Rouse Co. Sr'A'Cv Pfd [NYSE symbol] (TTSB)	RSEPrA
Rouse's Copyhold Enfranchisement Manual [3rd ed.] [1866] [A publication] (DLA)	Rouse Cop

Rouse's Practical Conveyancer [*3rd ed.*] [*1867*] [*A publication*] (DLA) .... Rouse Conv
Rouse's Precedents and Conveyances of Mortgaged Property [*A publication*] (DLA) .... Rouse Pr Mort
Roush, W. F., Miami FL [*STAC*] .... RWF
Rousse [*Bulgaria*] [*ICAO location identifier*] (ICLI) .... LBRS
Roussel [*France*] [*Research code symbol*] .... R
Roussel [*France*] [*Research code symbol*] .... RU
Roussel Uclaf "Once-a-Month" Pill [*Contraceptive*] RU-486
Routair Aviation Services [*Nigeria*] [*FAA designator*] (FAAC) .... RUT
Route .... R
Route [*Commonly used*] (OPSA) .... ROUTE
Route .... RT
Route (AABC) .... RT
Route (AFM) .... RTE
Route .... RTE
Route (DD) .... rte
Route Accounting Subsystem [*Telecommunications*] (TEL) .... RAS
Route Capacity Control Airline (DS) .... RCCA
Route Contingency Reserve [*Aviation*] (DA) .... RCR
Route Control Digit [*Telecommunications*] (TEL) .... RCD
Route Digit Indicator [*Telecommunications*] (TEL) .... RDI
Route Forcast [*Aviation*] (FAAC) .... ROFOR
Route Guidance and Information System .... RGIS
Route Integration Instrumentation System (LAIN) .... RIIS
Route Monitoring Information [*Telecommunications*] (TEL) .... RMI
Route Opening Detachment (MCD) .... ROD
Route Order [*Military*] .... RO
Route Package (CINC) .... RP
Route Relief Requirements System [*Telecommunications*] (TEL) .... RRRS
Route/Route Destination [*Telecommunications*] (TEL) .... RRD
Route Selection Program (SAA) .... RSP
Route Selector .... RS
Route Signal (IAA) .... RS
Route Surveillance RADAR .... RSR
Route Switching [*Telecommunications*] (TEL) .... RS
Route Switching Subsystem (NITA) .... RSS
Route to Airlift Mobility through Partnership (MCD) .... RAMPART
Route Treatment [*Telecommunications*] (TEL) .... RT
Router Adapter .... RTAD
Router Cutter [*Tool*] (AAG) .... RTCU
Router Form .... RTFM
Router Guide .... RTGU
Router Header Word (NASA) .... RHW
Router Template .... RT
Router Template (AAG) .... RTTP
Routes Forestieres [*Forested Routes*] [*French*] (BARN) .... RF
Routine (KSC) .... R
Routine (AABC) .... ROUT
Routine .... RTN
Routine Admission Laboratory Tests [*Medicine*] .... RALT
Routine and Microscopic (DAVI) .... R & M
Routine Calls May Be Dispensed With .... ROCALDIS
Routine Coefficient of Variation [*Statistics*] .... RCV
Routine Coronary Care [*Orders*] [*Cardiology*] (DAVI) .... RCC
Routine Dialysis Therapy [*Medicine*] (DMAA) .... RDT
Routine Dynamic Display (MCD) .... RDD
Routine Economic Air Lift [*Army*] .... REAL
Routine Execution Selection Table [*Computer science*] (WDAA) .... REST
Routine for Executing Biological Unit Simulations [*Computer program*] .... REBUS
Routine for Executive Multi-Unit Simulation (PDAA) .... REMUS
Routine Interest Shipping (MCD) .... RIS
Routine Maintenance (AAG) .... RM
Routine Manual In / Manual Out [*Military*] (DNAB) .... RMI/MO
Routine Medical Care (DAVI) .... RTM
Routine Message Precedence [*Telecommunications*] (ADDR) .... RR
Routine Network-In-Dial (DNAB) .... RNID
Routine Network-In-Dial / Network-Out-Dial (DNAB) .... RNID/NOD
Routine Order .... RO
Routine Relay (KSC) .... RR
Routine Respiratory Care [*Medicine*] .... RRC
Routine Sequence Table .... RST
Routine Tag (SAA) .... RT
Routine Test (IAA) .... RT
Routine Test Dilution [*Analysis*] .... RTD
Routine Unsatisfactory Material Report (MCD) .... RUMR
Routine Unsatisfactory Material Report .... RVMR
Routine Urinalysis (DAVI) .... RUA
Routine Verification (SSD) .... RV
Routine Work Order (KSC) .... RWO
Routing .... RTG
Routing Accumulator (IAA) .... RGA
Routing and Clipping (MCD) .... R/C
Routing and Cost Estimate (IAA) .... RACE
Routing and Record Sheet [*Air Force*] .... R & R
Routing and Recording (IAA) .... RAR
Routing and Remote Access Service [*Microsoft Corp.*] .... RRAS
Routing and Remote Access Service [*Computer science*] .... RRAS
Routing and Switching System .... RSS
Routing and Work [*Military*] .... R & W
Routing Arbiter [*Telecommunications*] .... RA
Routing Automation Technique (PDAA) .... RAT
Routing Control Center (IAA) .... RCC
Routing Control Indicator [*Telecommunications*] (TEL) .... RCI
Routing Domain [*Computer science*] (TNIG) .... RD
Routing Domain [*Computer science*] (TNIG) .... RTG DOM
Routing Domain Identifier (TNIG) .... RDI
Routing Identification Code (NATG) .... RIC
Routing Identifier [*or Indicator*] (AFM) .... RI
Routing Information Process [*or Protocol*] [*Telecommunications*] (TEL) .... RIP
Routing Logic [*Radio Interface*] **Unit Diagnostic Program** [*Telecommunications*] .... RLUD
Routing Maintenance Protocol (BYTE) .... RTMP
Routing Manager .... RM
Routing Matrix (IAA) .... RM
Routing Office [*or Officer*] [*Navy*] .... RO
Routing Register (IAA) .... RGR
Routing Slip [*Military*] .... RS
Routing Table Maintenance Protocol [*Computer science*] .... RTMP
Routing Transit Number [*Telecommunications*] .... RTN
Routing Update Protocol [*Telecommunications*] (PCM) .... RTP
Routledge & Kegan Paul [*British publisher*] .... RKP
Roux Seguela Cayzac & Goudard [*Advertising agency*] (ECON) .... RSCG
Rouyn, PQ [*Television station call letters*] CFVS-1
Rouyn, PQ [*FM radio station call letters*] .... CHOA
Rouyn, PQ [*Television station call letters*] .... CIVA
Rouyn, PQ [*AM radio station call letters*] .... CKRN
Rouyn, PQ [*Television station call letters*] .... CKRN-TV
Rouyn, PQ [*ICAO location identifier*] (ICLI) .... CYUY
Rouyn Ressources Minieres, Inc. [*Toronto Stock Exchange symbol*] .... ROU
Rouyn-Noranda [*Canada*] [*Airport symbol*] (OAG) .... YUY
Rouyn-Noranda, PQ [*FM radio station call letters*] .... CJMM
Rovaniemi [*Finland ICAO location identifier*] (ICLI) .... EFPS
Rovaniemi [*Finland*] [*Airport symbol*] (OAG) .... RVN
Rovaniemi Airport [*Finland ICAO location identifier*] (ICLI) .... EFRO
Rover Airways International, Inc. [*ICAO designator*] (FAAC) .... ROV
Rover Flight Safety .... RFS
Rover Owners' Association of North America [*Defunct*] (EA) .... ROANA
Rover P4 Drivers Guild [*An association*] (EAIO) .... RDG
Rover Preflight Operations Procedures [*NASA*] (KSC) .... RPOP
Rover Sports Register [*An association*] (EAIO) .... RSR
Rover Tester Test Set .... RTTS
Roving Lunar Vehicle (AAG) .... RLV
Roving Vehicle [*NASA*] .... RV
Row [*Postal Service standard*] (OPSA) .... ROW
Row Address Select (IAA) .... RAS
Row Parity Check (IEEE) .... RPC
Row Select Read-Only Memory [*Computer science*] (IAA) .... RSROM
Row-Address Strobe (IEEE) .... RAS
Rowan Companies, Inc. [*NYSE symbol*] (SPSG) .... RDC
Rowan Companies, Inc. [*Associated Press*] (SAG) .... Rowan
Rowan Cos. [*NYSE symbol*] (TTSB) .... RDC
Rowan Memorial Hospital Area, Health Education Center, Salisbury, NC [*Library symbol Library of Congress*] (LCLS) .... NcSalRH
Rowan Public Library East Branch, Rockwell, NC [*Library symbol*] [*Library of Congress*] (LCLS) .... NcSal-E
Rowan Public Library, Salisbury, NC [*Library symbol Library of Congress*] (LCLS) .... NcSal
Rowan Public Library, South Rowan Branch, Landis, NC [*Library symbol Library of Congress*] (LCLS) .... NcSal-S
Rowan Technical Institute, Salisbury, NC [*Library symbol Library of Congress*] (LCLS) .... NcSalR
Rowa-Wagner KG [*Germany*] [*Research code symbol*] .... RW
Rowberrow [*England*] .... ROWB
Rowe Furniture [*NYSE symbol*] (TTSB) .... ROW
Rowe Furniture Corp. [*NYSE symbol*] (SPSG) .... ROW
Rowe Furniture Corp. [*Associated Press*] (SAG) .... RoweFrn
Rowed Over [*Rowing*] [*British*] (ROG) .... RO
Rowell's Contested Election Cases [*A publication*] (DLA) .... Rowell El Cas
Rowell's Reports [*45-52 Vermont*] [*A publication*] (DLA) .... Rowell
Rowe's Interesting Cases [*England and Ireland*] [*A publication*] (DLA) .... Int Cas
Rowe's Interesting Cases [*England and Ireland*] [*A publication*] (DLA) .... Int Case
Rowe's Interesting Cases [*England and Ireland*] [*1798-1823*] [*A publication*] (DLA) .... Rowe
Rowe's Interesting Parliamentary and Military Cases [*A publication*] (DLA) .... Rowe
Rowe's Irish Reports [*A publication*] (DLA) .... Rowe Rep
Rowe's Scintilla Juris [*A publication*] (DLA) .... Rowe Sci Jur
Rowesville [*South Carolina*] [*Seismograph station code, US Geological Survey*] (SEIS) .... ROW
Rowett Research Institute [*British*] (BI) .... RRI
Rowfant Club, Cleveland, OH [*Library symbol Library of Congress*] (LCLS) .... OCIRC
Rowland's Manual of the English Constitution [*1859*] [*A publication*] (DLA) .... Row Eng Const
Rowley Mile [*Horseracing*] [*British*] .... RM
Roxana Community Unit 1, Roxana, IL [*Library symbol Library of Congress*] (LCLS) .... IRoxCU
Roxana Farms [*Costa Rica*] [*ICAO location identifier*] (ICLI) .... MRRX
Roxana Public Library, Roxana, IL [*Library symbol Library of Congress*] (LCLS) .... IRox
Roxana Resources Ltd. [*Vancouver Stock Exchange symbol*] .... RXA
Roxanne Whipple Memorial Library, Winslow, AZ [*Library symbol Library of Congress*] (LCLS) .... AzWin
Roxas, Capiz [*Philippines*] [*ICAO location identifier*] (ICLI) .... RPVR
Roxas City [*Philippines*] [*Airport symbol*] (OAG) .... RXS
Roxas/Del Pilar, Palawan [*Philippines*] [*ICAO location identifier*] (ICLI) .... RPVL
Roxboro, NC [*FM radio station call letters*] .... WKRX
Roxboro, NC [*AM radio station call letters*] .... WRXO
Roxborough [*Queensland*] [*Airport symbol*] (AD) .... RFX

Roxburgh [*New Zealand*] [*Seismograph station code, US Geological Survey*] (SEIS) ... ROX
Roxburghe [*Style of bookbinding*] (ROG) ... ROXB
Roxburghshire [*County in Scotland*] ... ROXB
Roxbury Public Library, Succasunna, NJ [*Library symbol Library of Congress*] (LCLS) ... NjSu
Roxmark Mines Ltd. [*Toronto Stock Exchange symbol*] ... RMK
Roxwell Gold Mines [*Vancouver Stock Exchange symbol*] ... RXW
Roxy Petroleum Ltd. [*Toronto Stock Exchange symbol*] ... RXY
Roy Clark Fan Club (EA) ... RCFC
Roy Clayborne Fan Club (EA) ... RCFC
Roy Hill [*Western Australia*] [*Airport symbol*] (AD) ... RHL
Roy M. Huffington, Inc., Library, Houston, TX [*Library symbol Library of Congress*] (LCLS) ... TxHRH
Roy Rogers - Dale Evans Collectors Association (EA) ... RRDECA
Roy, UT [*AM radio station call letters*] ... KANN
Roy, UT [*FM radio station call letters*] ... KRGQ-FM
Roy, UT [*FM radio station call letters*] (RBYB) ... KRKR-FM
Roy, WA [*FM radio station call letters*] ... KWFJ
Royal ... R
Royal (ROG) ... RL
Royal ... ROY
Royal (ROG) ... RY
Royal [*Philately*] ... ryl
Royal ... RYL
Royal 1st Devon Imperial Yeomanry [*British military*] (DMA) ... R 1 DIY
Royal Academician [*or Academy*] [*British*] ... RA
Royal Academician (of Canada) (ROG) ... RAC
Royal Academy [*British*] (AIE) ... RA
Royal Academy Association [*British*] (NADA) ... RAA
Royal Academy of Arts [*British*] (ROG) ... RAA
Royal Academy of Arts in London [*British*] ... RA
Royal Academy of Dancing [*British*] (EAIO) ... RAD
Royal Academy of Dancing, United States Branch (EA) ... RAD
Royal Academy of Dramatic Art [*British*] ... RADA
Royal Academy of Music [*British*] ... RAM
Royal Academy Schools Certificate [*British*] ... Cert RAS
Royal Accounting System [*United States Geological Survey*] ... RAS
Royal Adelaide Show [*Australia*] ... RAS
Royal Aero Club [*British*] (BARN) ... R Ae C
Royal Aero Club [*British*] ... RAC
Royal Aeronautical Establishment [*British*] (IAA) ... RAE
Royal Aeronautical Society [*British*] (EAIO) ... RAeS
Royal Aeronautical Society [*British*] ... RAS
Royal African Society (EAIO) ... RAS
Royal Agricultural Benevolent Institution [*Church of England*] ... RABI
Royal Agricultural College [*British*] ... RAC
Royal Agricultural Society [*British*] (DAS) ... RAS
Royal Agricultural Society of England ... RASE
Royal Agricultural Society of the Commonwealth (EAIO) ... RASC
Royal Air [*ICAO designator*] (AD) ... TR
Royal Air Force [*British*] ... RAF
Royal Air Force [*Airline call sign*] [*British*] ... Rafair
Royal Air Force [*British ICAO designator*] (FAAC) ... RFR
Royal Air Force [*ICAO designator*] (AD) ... RR
Royal Air Force 1 Group [*British ICAO location identifier*] (ICLI) ... EGDH
Royal Air Force Air Station ... RAFSTN
Royal Air Force Base [*British*] ... RAFB
Royal Air Force Benevolent Fund [*British military*] (DMA) ... RAFBF
Royal Air Force Cinema Corp. [*British military*] (DMA) ... RAFCC
Royal Air Force Club [*British*] ... RAFC
Royal Air Force Coastal Command [*British*] ... RAFCC
Royal Air Force College [*British*] ... RAFC
Royal Air Force Educational Service [*British military*] (DMA) ... RAFES
Royal Air Force Establishments [*British*] ... AFE
Royal Air Force Fighter Command [*British*] ... RAFFC
Royal Air Force, Germany [*British military*] (DMA) ... RAFG
Royal Air Force Historical Society [*British*] (DBA) ... RAFHS
Royal Air Force Institute of Aviation Medicine [*British*] (IAA) ... RAFIAM
Royal Air Force Medical Service [*British*] ... RAFMS
Royal Air Force, Middle East [*British military*] (DMA) ... RAFME
Royal Air Force Nursing Service [*British military*] (DMA) ... RAFNS
Royal Air Force of Oman (Air Transport) [*ICAO designator*] (FAAC) ... MJN
Royal Air Force Regiment [*British*] ... RAFR
Royal Air Force Reserve of Officers [*Formerly, RAFO*] [*British*] ... RAFRO
Royal Air Force Sailing Association [*British*] (BI) ... RAFSA
Royal Air Force Service Police [*British military*] (DMA) ... RAFSP
Royal Air Force Small Arms Association [*British military*] (DMA) ... RAFSAA
Royal Air Force Staff College [*British*] ... RAFSC
Royal Air Force Station [*British*] (MCD) ... RAFS
Royal Air Force Supervisory Centre Communications [*British ICAO location identifier*] (ICLI) ... EGDD
Royal Air Force Support Command [*British*] ... RAFSC
Royal Air Force Volunteer Reserve [*British*] ... RAFVR
Royal Air Forces Association (EAIO) ... RAFA
Royal Air Forces Transport Command [*British*] ... RAFTC
Royal Air Inter-Compagnie d'Exploitation de Lignes Aer Interieures [*Morocco*] [*ICAO designator*] (FAAC) ... RAI
Royal Air International [*ICAO designator*] (AD) ... RN
Royal Air Maroc [*ICAO designator*] (AD) ... AT
Royal Air Maroc [*Morocco*] ... RAM
Royal Air Maroc - Compagnie Nationale de Transports Aeriens [*Morocco*] [*ICAO designator*] (FAAC) ... RAM
Royal Aircraft Establishment [*British Ministry of Defense*] [*Research center*] ... RAE
Royal Aircraft Establishment Sequence Calculator [*British*] (DEN) ... RASCAL
Royal Aircraft Factory [*World War I*] [*British*] ... RAF
Royal Albert Dock [*British*] ... RAD
Royal Albert Hall [*London, England*] ... RAH
Royal Albert Hall Orchestra ... RAHO
Royal Albert Institution [*British*] (DAS) ... RAI
Royal Alexandra Hospital, Edmonton, AB, Canada [*Library symbol Library of Congress*] (LCLS) ... CaAERA
Royal Alexandra Hospital, Edmonton, Alberta [*Library symbol National Library of Canada*] (NLC) ... AERA
Royal Alexandra Hospital, School of Nursing, Edmonton, AB, Canada [*Library symbol*] [*Library of Congress*] (LCLS) ... CaAERASN
Royal Alfred Merchant Seamen's Society [*British*] ... RAMSS
Royal Amateur Art Society [*British*] ... RAAS
Royal American [*ICAO designator*] (AD) ... JW
Royal American Airways, Inc. [*ICAO designator*] (FAAC) ... RLM
Royal and Ancient Golf Club [*Scotland*] ... RAGC
Royal and Ancient Golf Club of St. Andrews [*Recognized as the game's legislative authority in all countries except the US*] [*British*] ... R & A
Royal Antediluvian Order of Buffaloes ... RAOB
Royal Anthropological Institute [*British*] ... RAI
Royal Anthropological Institute News [*Later, Anthropology Today*] [*A publication*] ... RAIN
Royal Appliance Manufacturing [*NYSE symbol*] (SPSG) ... RAM
Royal Appliance Manufacturing [*Associated Press*] (SAG) ... RoylApl
Royal Appliance Mfg [*NYSE symbol*] (TTSB) ... RAM
Royal Arch [*Freemasonry*] ... RA
Royal Arch Chapter [*Freemasonry*] ... RAC
Royal Arch Knight Templar Priest [*Freemasonry*] ... RAKTP
Royal Arch Mason [*Freemasonry*] ... RAM
Royal Archaeological Institute [*British*] ... RAI
Royal Architectural Institute of Canada ... RAIC
Royal Ark Mariners ... RAM
Royal Armament Research and Development Establishment [*British*] ... RARDE
Royal Armament Research and Development Establishment, Enfield [*British military*] (DMA) ... RARDEN
Royal Armoured Corps [*British*] ... RAC
Royal Armoured Corps Centre [*British*] (MCD) ... RACC
Royal Armouries [*Tower of London*] ... RA
Royal Army Chaplains' Department [*British*] ... RACD
Royal Army Chaplains' Department [*British*] ... RAChD
Royal Army Clothing Department [*British*] ... RACD
Royal Army Dental Corps [*British*] ... RADC
Royal Army Educational Corps [*British*] ... RAEC
Royal Army Establishment [*British*] ... RAE
Royal Army Medical College [*British*] (MCD) ... RAMC
Royal Army Medical Corps [*Initialism also facetiously translated during World War I as "Rats after Moldy Cheese," "Rob All My Comrades," or "Run Away, Matron's Coming"*] [*British*] ... RAMC
Royal Army Medical Corps, Territorials [*British*] (ROG) ... RAMCT
Royal Army Ordnance Corps [*Formerly, AOC*] [*British*] ... RAOC
Royal Army Ordnance Corps (Engineering) [*British military*] (DMA) ... RAOC(E)
Royal Army Pay Corps [*Formerly, APC*] [*British*] ... RAPC
Royal Army Reserve [*British*] ... RAR
Royal Army Service Corps [*Formerly, ASC; later, RCT*] [*British*] ... RASC
Royal Army Service Corps/Royal Corps of Transport [*British*] ... RASC/RCT
Royal Army Veterinary Corps [*Formerly, AVC*] [*British*] ... RAVC
Royal Art ... RA
Royal Art Society of New South Wales [*Australia*] ... RASNSW
Royal Artillery [*British*] ... RA
Royal Artillery [*British*] ... RArt
Royal Artillery Association Benevolent Fund [*British military*] (DMA) ... RAABF
Royal Artillery Committee [*British military*] (DMA) ... RAC
Royal Artillery Flying Club [*British military*] (DMA) ... RAFC
Royal Artillery Institution [*British military*] (DMA) ... RAI
Royal Artist ... RA
Royal Asiatic Society [*British*] ... RAS
Royal Association for Disability and Rehabilitation [*British*] ... RADAR
Royal Association for the Longevity and Preservation of the Honeymooners (EA) ... RALPH
Royal Association in Aid of the Deaf and Dumb [*British*] (BI) ... RADD
Royal Association of British Dairy Farmers [*British*] (BI) ... RABDF
Royal Astronomical Society [*British*] ... RAS
Royal Astronomical Society of Canada ... RASC
Royal Astronomical Society, Toronto, ON, Canada [*Library symbol Library of Congress*] (LCLS) ... CaOTRA
Royal Astronomical Society [*Societe Royale d'Astronomie*] **Toronto, Ontario** [*Library symbol National Library of Canada*] (NLC) ... OTRA
Royal Australasian College of Physicians ... RACP
Royal Australasian College of Surgeons ... RACS
Royal Australian Air Force [*ICAO designator*] (FAAC) ... ASY
Royal Australian Air Force [*ICAO designator*] (FAAC) ... RAAF
Royal Australian Air Force Association ... RAAFA
Royal Australian Army Medical Corps (DAVI) ... RAAMC
Royal Australian Chemical Institute ... RACI
Royal Australian College of General Practitioners Family Medicine Program ... RACGPFMP
Royal Australian Historical Society. Journal and Proceedings [*A publication*] ... Royal Aust Hist Soc J Proc
Royal Australian Navy (DOMA) ... RAN
Royal Australian Navy (VNW) ... RAN
Royal Australian Navy Training Establishment ... RANTE
Royal Australian Planning Institute. Journal [*A publication*] ... R Aust Plan Inst J
Royal Australian Regiment (VNW) ... RAR
Royal Automobile Club [*Controlling body of motor racing in Britain*] ... RAC

Royal Automobile Club Motor Sports Council [*British*] (DI) ...... RACMSC
Royal Automobile Club of Canada .... RACC
Royal Automobile Club of Victoria .... RACV
Royal Auxiliary Air Force [*Formerly, AAF*] [*British*] .... R Aux AF
Royal Ballet School [*British*] (DI) .... RBS
Royal Bancshares of Pennsylvania [*NASDAQ symbol*] (SAG) ...... RBPA
Royal Bancshares of Pennsylvania [*Associated Press*] (SAG) ..... RyBPA
Royal Bancshares(PA)'A' [*NASDAQ symbol*] (TTSB) .... RBPAA
Royal Bank Canada [*MS Symbol*] (TTSB) .... RY
Royal Bank of Canada [*UTLAS symbol*] .... RBC
Royal Bank of Canada [*Toronto Stock Exchange symbol Vancouver Stock Exchange symbol*] .... RY
Royal Bank of Canada, Calgary, AB, Canada [*Library symbol*] [*Library of Congress*] (LCLS) .... CaACRB
Royal Bank of Canada, Calgary, Alberta [*Library symbol Obsolete National Library of Canada*] (NLC) .... ACRB
Royal Bank of Canada, Inc. [*Associated Press*] (SAG) .... RoyBk
Royal Bank of Canada, Inc. [*NYSE symbol*] (SAG) .... RY
Royal Bank of Canada, Information Resources, Toronto, ON, Canada [*Library symbol*] [*Library of Congress*] (LCLS) .... CaOTRBI
Royal Bank of Canada, Montreal, PQ, Canada [*Library symbol Library of Congress*] (LCLS) .... CaQMR
Royal Bank of Canada [*Banque Royale du Canada*] **Montreal, Quebec** [*Library symbol National Library of Canada*] (NLC) .... QMR
Royal Bank of Canada, Vancouver, BC, Canada [*Library symbol Library of Congress*] (LCLS) .... CaBVaRB
Royal Bank of Pennsylvania [*NASDAQ symbol*] (NQ) .... RBPA
Royal Bank of Scotland [*NYSE symbol*] (SPSG) .... RBS
Royal Bank of Scotland Group Ltd. [*Associated Press*] (SAG) ..... RBSc
Royal Bank of Scotland Group Ltd. [*Associated Press*] (SAG) ..... RBSct
Royal Bank of Scotland Group PLC [*Associated Press*] (SAG) ..... RBSc
Royal Belgian Air Force .... RBAF
Royal Berkshire Yeomanry Cavalry [*British*] (ROG) .... RBYC
Royal Bk Scotland Ex Cap Sec [*NYSE symbol*] (TTSB) .... RBSPrX
Royal Bk Scotland Pfd ADS [*NYSE symbol*] (TTSB) .... RBSPr
Royal Bk Scotland Pfd'B'ADS [*NYSE symbol*] (TTSB) .... RBSPrB
Royal Bk Scotland Pfd'C'ADS [*NYSE symbol*] (TTSB) .... RBSPrC
Royal Bk Scotland Pfd'D' ADS [*NYSE symbol*] (TTSB) .... RBSPrD
Royal Blind Homes [*Australia*] .... RBH
Royal Blind Society of New South Wales [*Australia*] .... RBSNSW
Royal Borough of Kensington and Chelsea [*England*] .... RBK & C
Royal Botanic Gardens and Domain Trust [*Australia*] .... RBGDT
Royal Botanic Gardens and National Herbarium [*Australia*] ...... RBGNH
Royal Botanic Gardens Sydney [*Australia*] .... RBGS
Royal Botanical Gardens, Hamilton, ON, Canada [*Library symbol Library of Congress*] (LCLS) .... CaOHRB
Royal Botanical Gardens, Hamilton, Ontario [*Library symbol National Library of Canada*] (NLC) .... OHRB
Royal British Colonial Society of Artists .... RBC
Royal British Legion [*British military*] (DMA) .... RBL
Royal British Legion of Scotland [*British*] (DBA) .... RBLS
Royal British Nurses' Association [*British*] (BI) .... RBNA
Royal British-Colonial Society of Artists, London [*1886*] (NGC) .. RBC
Royal Brunei Airlines [*ICAO designator*] (AD) .... BI
Royal Brunei Airlines [*ICAO designator*] (FAAC) .... RBA
Royal Brunei Armed Forces .... RBAF
Royal Bucks Hussars [*British military*] (DMA) .... RBH
Royal Bucks Yeomanry [*British military*] (DMA) .... RBY
Royal Burgh .... RB
Royal Caledonia Curling Club .... RCCC
Royal Caledonian Horticultural Society [*British*] (BI) .... RCHS
Royal Cambrian Academy [*British*] .... RCA
Royal Cambrian Academy of Art [*British*] .... RCA
Royal Canadian Academy .... RCA
Royal Canadian Academy of Arts .... RCA
Royal Canadian Air Force .... RCAF
Royal Canadian Air Force Association .... RCAFA
Royal Canadian Air Force Library, Montreal, PQ, Canada [*Library symbol Library of Congress*] (LCLS) .... CaQMRC
Royal Canadian Air Force [*Corps d'Aviation Royale du Canada*] **Montreal, Quebec** [*Library symbol National Library of Canada*] (NLC) ..... QMRC
Royal Canadian Air Force, Women's Division .... RCAF(WD)
Royal Canadian Armoured Corps .... RCAC
Royal Canadian Army (MCD) .... RCA
Royal Canadian Army Medical Corps .... RCAMC
Royal Canadian Army Museum, Canadian Forces Base, Shilo, Manitoba [*Library symbol National Library of Canada*] (NLC) .... MSCFAM
Royal Canadian Army Pay Corps .... RCAPC
Royal Canadian Army Service Corps .... RCASC
Royal Canadian Artillery .... RCA
Royal Canadian Corps of Signals .... RCCS
Royal Canadian Dental Corps .... RCDC
Royal Canadian Dragoons [*Military*] .... RCD
Royal Canadian Electrical and Mechanical Engineers .... RCEME
Royal Canadian Engineers .... RCE
Royal Canadian Field Artillery [*Military*] .... RCFA
Royal Canadian Fleet Reserve .... RCFR
Royal Canadian Garrison Artillery [*Military*] .... RCGA
Royal Canadian Horse Artillery .... RCHA
Royal Canadian Infantry Corps .... RCIC
Royal Canadian Institute (BARN) .... RCI
Royal Canadian Legion .... RCL
Royal Canadian Military Institute, Toronto, ON, Canada [*Library symbol Library of Congress*] (LCLS) .... CaOTMI

Royal Canadian Military Institute, Toronto, Ontario [*Library symbol National Library of Canada*] (NLC) .... OTMI
Royal Canadian Mint .... RCM
Royal Canadian Mounted Police [*Formerly, RNWMP*] .... RCMP
Royal Canadian Mounted Police Academy, Resource Centre, Regina, SK, Canada [*Library symbol Library of Congress*] (LCLS) .... CaSRRC
Royal Canadian Mounted Police, Crime Laboratory, Winnipeg, MB, Canada [*Library symbol Library of Congress*] (LCLS) .... CaMWRC
Royal Canadian Mounted Police Headquarters Reference Library, Ottawa, ON, Canada [*Library symbol Library of Congress*] (LCLS) ...... CaOOR
Royal Canadian Naval Air Station .... RCNAS
Royal Canadian Naval College [*1943-1948*] .... RCNC
Royal Canadian Naval Reserve .... RCNR
Royal Canadian Naval Volunteer Reserve [*1923-1945*] .... RCNVR
Royal Canadian Navy [*Obsolete*] .... RCN
Royal Canadian Navy Depot .... CANDEP
Royal Canadian Ordnance Corps .... RCOC
Royal Canadian Postal Corps [*Formerly, CPC*] .... RCPC
Royal Canadian Regiment [*Military*] .... RCR
Royal Canadian Rifles [*Military unit*] .... RCR
Royal Canadian Sea Cadets .... RCSC
Royal Canadian Sea Cadets Corps .... RCSCC
Royal Canberra Golf Club [*Australia*] .... RCGC
Royal Caribbean Cruise Line .... RCCL
Royal Caribbean Cruise Line [*NYSE symbol*] (SPSG) .... RCL
Royal Caribbean Cruises [*NYSE symbol*] (TTSB) .... RCL
Royal Caribbean Cruises [*Associated Press*] (SAG) .... RylCarb
Royal Carmarthen Fusiliers [*British military*] (DMA) .... RCF
Royal Center, IN [*FM radio station call letters*] .... WHZR
Royal Center Record, Royal Center, IN [*Library symbol Library of Congress*] (LCLS) .... InRoyR
Royal Central Asian Society [*British*] .... RCAS
Royal Channel Islands Yacht Club (BI) .... RCI
Royal Choral Association [*British*] (BI) .... RCA
Royal Choral Society [*British*] (EAIO) .... RCS
Royal City, WA [*FM radio station call letters*] .... KRCW
Royal Clan, Order of Scottish Clans [*Later, Independent Order of Foresters*] (EA) .... OSC
Royal Clinical Teacher [*British*] .... RCT
Royal College of Art [*British*] .... RCA
Royal College of Defence Studies [*British*] .... RCDS
Royal College of General Practitioners [*British*] .... RCGP
Royal College of Midwives [*British*] .... RCM
Royal College of Music [*British*] .... RCM
Royal College of Nursing [*British*] .... RCN
Royal College of Nursing, Australia .... RCNA
Royal College of Obstetricians and Gynaecologists [*British*] .... RCOG
Royal College of Organists [*British*] .... RCO
Royal College of Pathologists [*British*] .... RCP
Royal College of Pathologists [*British*] .... RCPath
Royal College of Physicians and Surgeons of Canada .... RCPS(C)
Royal College of Physicians and Surgeons of Glasgow .... RCPGlas
Royal College of Physicians and Surgeons of Glasgow .... RCPS
Royal College of Physicians and Surgeons of Glasgow (DBQ) .... RCPS(Glasg)
Royal College of Physicians and Surgeons (of United States of America) (EA) .... RCPS
Royal College of Physicians, Edinburgh .... RCPE
Royal College of Physicians, Edinburgh .... RCPEd
Royal College of Physicians, Edinburgh, United Kingdom [*Library symbol Library of Congress*] (LCLS) .... UkERCP
Royal College of Physicians, Ireland .... RCPI
Royal College of Physicians, London (ROG) .... RCPL
Royal College of Physicians, London, United Kingdom [*Library symbol Library of Congress*] (LCLS) .... UkLRCP
Royal College of Physicians of London [*British*] .... RCP
Royal College of Preceptors [*British*] (ROG) .... RCP
Royal College of Psychiatrists [*British*] (DAVI) .... RCP
Royal College of Psychiatrists [*British*] (DAVI) .... RCPsych
Royal College of Radiologists [*British*] .... RCR
Royal College of Science [*British*] .... RCS
Royal College of Surgeons [*British*] .... RCS
Royal College of Surgeons, Edinburgh .... RCSE
Royal College of Surgeons, Edinburgh (DAVI) .... RCSE
Royal College of Surgeons, Edinburgh .... RCSEd
Royal College of Surgeons, Edinburgh, United Kingdom [*Library symbol Library of Congress*] (LCLS) .... UkERCS
Royal College of Surgeons, England .... RCSEng
Royal College of Surgeons, Ireland .... RCSI
Royal College of Surgeons of England, London, United Kingdom [*Library symbol Library of Congress*] (LCLS) .... UkLRCS
Royal College of Veterinary Surgeons [*British*] .... RCVS
Royal Colonial Institute [*British*] .... RCI
Royal Columbian Hospital, New Westminster, BC, Canada [*Library symbol Library of Congress*] (LCLS) .... CaBNWRC
Royal Columbian Hospital, New Westminster, British Columbia [*Library symbol National Library of Canada*] (NLC) .... BNWRC
Royal Commission [*British*] .... RC
Royal Commission into Aboriginal Deaths in Custody [*Australia*] .... RCIADIC
Royal Commission on Corporate Concentration [*Canada*] .... RCCC
Royal Commission on Environmental Pollution [*British*] .... RCEP
Royal Commission on Historical Monuments [*British*] .... RCHM
Royal Commission on Local Government in Greater London [*British*] .... RCLGGL
Royal Commission on Social Policy [*Australia*] .... RCSP
Royal Commission on the Distribution of Income and Wealth [*British*] .... RCDIW

Royal Commission on the Future of the Toronto Waterfront, Toronto, Ontario [*Library symbol National Library of Canada*] (BIB) ... OTRCF
Royal Commission on the Press [*British*] ... RCP
Royal Commonwealth Military Forces (ADA) ... RCMF
Royal Commonwealth Society [*British*] ... RCS
Royal Commonwealth Society for the Blind [*British*] (DBA) ... RCSB
Royal Commonwealth Society of Queensland [*Australia*] ... RCSQ
Royal Co. of Archers [*British*] (DI) ... RCA
Royal Conservatory of Music [*Leipzig*] ... RCM
Royal Cornwall Agricultural Association [*British*] (DBA) ... RCAA
Royal Corps of Naval Constructors [*British*] ... RCNC
Royal Corps of Signals [*British*] (DMA) ... R SIGS
Royal Corps of Signals [*British*] ... RCS
Royal Corps of Transport [*Army British*] ... RCT
Royal Correspondence of the Assyrian Empire [*A publication*] (BJA) ... RCAE
Royal Cosmic Theology [*British*] ... RCT
Royal Courts of Justice [*British*] ... RCJ
Royal Crest [*British*] ... RC
Royal Crown [*Soft drink brand*] ... RC
Royal Crown Bottlers Association (EA) ... RCBA
Royal Crystal [*Vancouver Stock Exchange symbol*] ... RCY
Royal Curling Club of Canada ... RCCC
Royal Danish Air Force ... RDAF
Royal Danish Army (NATG) ... RDA
Royal Danish Ballet ... RDB
Royal Danish Navy (NATG) ... RDN
Royal Deccan Horse [*British military*] (DMA) ... RDH
Royal Defence Academy [*British*] ... RDA
Royal Defence Corps [*British*] ... RDC
Royal Dental Hospital, Melbourne [*Australia*] ... RDHM
Royal Designer for Industry [*British*] ... RDI
Royal Devon Yeomanry [*British military*] (DMA) ... RDY
Royal Devon Yeomanry Artillery [*British military*] (DMA) ... RDYA
Royal District Nursing Society of South Australia ... RDNSSA
Royal Docks Association [*British*] (BI) ... RDA
Royal Dockyard [*British*] ... RDY
Royal Dockyard Iron and Steel Shipbuilders' Society [*A union*] [*British*] ... RDISSS
Royal Dockyard Wood Caulkers' Association [*A union*] [*British*] ... RDWCA
Royal Dragoons [*British*] ... RD
Royal Drawing Society [*British*] ... RDS
Royal Dublin Fusiliers [*British*] ... RDF
Royal Dublin Society ... RDS
Royal Dublin Society, Ballsbridge, Dublin, Ireland [*Library symbol Library of Congress*] (LCLS) ... IreDR
Royal Durban Light Infantry [*British military*] (DMA) ... RDLI
Royal Dutch Petrol [*NYSE symbol*] (TTSB) ... RD
Royal Dutch Petroleum Co. [*NYSE symbol*] (SPSG) ... RD
Royal Dutch Petroleum Co. [*Associated Press*] (SAG) ... RoylD
Royal East African Navy [*British military*] (DMA) ... REAN
Royal East Kent Yeomanry [*Military unit*] [*British*] ... REKY
Royal Easter Show [*Australia*] ... RES
Royal Economic Society [*British*] ... R Econ S
Royal Economic Society [*British*] ... RES
Royal Electrical and Mechanical Engineers [*Military British*] ... REME
Royal Empire Society [*British*] ... RES
Royal Enfield Owners Club (EA) ... REOC
Royal Engineers [*Military British*] (ROG) ... R ENG
Royal Engineers [*Military British*] ... RE
Royal Engineers and Signal Corps [*Military British*] (IAA) ... RESC
Royal Engineers Balloon School [*British military*] (DMA) ... REBS
Royal Engineers Diving School [*British military*] (DMA) ... REDS
Royal Engineers Postal Section [*British military*] (DMA) ... REPS
Royal Engineers Reserve of Officers [*British*] ... RERO
Royal Entomological Society [*British*] ... RES
Royal Environmental Health Institute of Scotland [*British*] ... REHIS
Royal Exchange [*British*] ... RE
Royal Exhibition Buildings [*Melbourne, Australia*] ... REB
Royal Faculty of Physicians and Surgeons of Glasgow ... RFPS
Royal Faculty of Procurators in Glasgow, Glasgow, United Kingdom [*Library symbol Library of Congress*] (LCLS) ... UkGP
Royal Far West Children's Homes Scheme [*Australia*] ... RFWCHS
Royal Festival Hall [*London*] ... RFH
Royal Field Artillery [*Military British*] ... RFA
Royal Filling Factory [*British military*] (DMA) ... RFF
Royal Fine Art Commission [*British*] ... RFAC
Royal Fleet Auxiliary [*British*] ... RFA
Royal Fleet Reserve [*British*] ... RFR
Royal Flying Corps [*Later, RAF*] [*British*] ... RFC
Royal Flying Cross [*British*] (IIA) ... RFC
Royal Forestry Society of England [*British*] ... RFS
Royal Forth Yacht Club [*British*] (DBA) ... RFYC
Royal Free Hospital (ROG) ... RFH
Royal Fremantle Golf Club [*Australia*] ... RFGC
Royal Fusiliers [*Military unit*] [*British*] ... RF
Royal Garrison Artillery [*British*] ... RGA
Royal Garrison Regiment [*Military British*] (ROG) ... RGR
Royal General Theatrical Fund [*British*] (DI) ... RGTF
Royal Geographical Society [*British*] ... RGS
Royal Geographical Society of Australasia, South Australian Branch ... RGSSA
Royal Geographical Society. Proceedings [*A publication*] ... GSP
Royal Glasgow Institute of Fine Arts [*Scotland*] ... GI
Royal Glasgow Institute of Fine Arts [*Scotland*] ... RGI
Royal Glasgow Institute of Fine Arts [*Scotland*] ... RGIFA
Royal Gold Corp. [*Associated Press*] (SAG) ... RoyGld
Royal Gold Enterprises, Inc. [*Toronto Stock Exchange symbol*] ... RGS
Royal Gold, Inc. [*NASDAQ symbol*] (NQ) ... RGLD
Royal Green Jackets [*Military unit*] [*British*] ... RGJ
Royal Green Jackets, London [*Military unit*] [*British*] ... RGJLond
Royal Green Jackets Territorial and Army Volunteer Reserve [*Military unit*] [*British*] ... RGJTAVR
Royal Greenwich Conservatory [*British*] ... RGC
Royal Greenwich Observatory [*British*] ... RGO
Royal Grenadier Guards [*British*] ... RGG
Royal Grip [*NASDAQ symbol*] (TTSB) ... GRIP
Royal Grip, Inc. [*NASDAQ symbol*] (SAG) ... GRIP
Royal Grip, Inc. [*Associated Press*] (SAG) ... RoylGrip
Royal Guernsey Artillery [*British military*] (DMA) ... RGA
Royal Guide Dogs Association of Australia ... RGDAA
Royal Guide Dogs Association of Tasmania [*Australia*] ... RGDAT
Royal Gun Factory [*British military*] (DMA) ... RGF
Royal Gunpowder Factory [*British*] ... RGPF
Royal Gurkha Regiment [*British military*] (DMA) ... RGR
Royal Hamilton Light Infantry [*British military*] (DMA) ... RHLI
Royal Hawaiian Airways [*ICAO designator*] (AD) ... ZH
Royal Hellenic Air Force ... RHAF
Royal Hellenic Army (NATG) ... RHA
Royal Hellenic Navy [*Obsolete*] (NATG) ... RHN
Royal Hibernian Academy ... RHA
Royal Hibernian Military School [*Dublin*] ... RHMS
Royal Highland and Agricultural Society of Scotland [*British*] ... RHASS
Royal Highland Fusiliers [*Military unit*] [*British*] ... RHF
Royal Highland Regiment [*Military unit*] [*British*] ... RHR
Royal Highlanders [*Military unit*] [*British*] ... RH
Royal Highlanders of Canada [*Military unit*] [*World War I*] ... RHC
Royal Highness ... RH
Royal Historical Society [*British*] ... RHistS
Royal Historical Society [*British*] ... RHS
Royal Holloway College [*British*] (DI) ... RHC
Royal Horse Artillery [*British*] ... RHA
Royal Horse Guards [*British*] ... RHG
Royal Horse Guards and 1st Dragoons [*British military*] (DMA) ... RHG1D
Royal Horticultural Society [*British*] (ARC) ... RHS
Royal Horticultural Society of Ireland (PDAA) ... RHSI
Royal Horticultural Society of Victoria [*Australia*] ... RHSV
Royal Hospital [*Chelsea*] [*British military*] (DMA) ... RH
Royal Humane Society [*British*] ... RHS
Royal Humane Society of New South Wales ... RHSNSW
Royal Humane Society of South Australia [*Australia*] ... RHSSA
Royal Hussars [*Military unit*] [*British*] ... RH
Royal Incorporation of Architects in Scotland ... RIAS
Royal Indian Air Force ... RIAF
Royal Indian Army Service Corps [*British*] ... RIASC
Royal Indian Engineering College [*British*] ... RIEC
Royal Indian Marine ... RIM
Royal Indian Naval Reserve [*British military*] (DMA) ... RINR
Royal Indian Naval Volunteer Reserve [*British military*] (DMA) ... RINVR
Royal Indian Navy ... RIN
Royal Inniskilling Dragoon Guards [*Military unit*] [*British*] ... RIDG
Royal Inniskilling Dragoon Guards [*Military unit*] [*British*] ... VDG
Royal Inniskilling Fusiliers [*Military unit*] [*British*] ... RIF
Royal Institue of Geology [*British*] (NUCP) ... RIG
Royal Institute of British Architects (IID) ... RIBA
Royal Institute of British Architects, London [*1834*] (NGC) ... RIBA
Royal Institute of British Sculptors ... RIBS
Royal Institute of Chemistry [*Later, RSC*] [*British*] ... RIC
Royal Institute of Engineers [*British*] ... RIE
Royal Institute of International Affairs [*British*] ... RIIA
Royal Institute of Navigation (DS) ... RIN
Royal Institute of Oil Painters [*British*] ... ROI
Royal Institute of Oil Painters, London [*1883*] (NGC) ... ROI
Royal Institute of Painters in Water-Colours [*British*] ... RIPWC
Royal Institute of Painters in Water-Colours [*British*] (ROG) ... RIWC
Royal Institute of Painters in Water-Colours, London [*1831*] (NGC) ... RI
Royal Institute of Public Administration [*British*] ... RIPA
Royal Institute of Public Administration Australia [*Australia*] ... RIPAA
Royal Institute of Public Health and Hygiene [*British*] ... RIPH & H
Royal Institute of Technology Library (NITA) ... RITL
Royal Institute of the Architects of Ireland ... RIAI
Royal Institution [*British*] ... RI
Royal Institution of Chartered Surveyors [*British*] ... RICS
Royal Institution of Great Britain ... RIGB
Royal Institution of Naval Architects [*British*] ... RINA
Royal Institution of South Wales [*British*] ... RISW
Royal International Agricultural Show [*British*] (ITD) ... RAS
Royal International Horse Show [*British*] ... RIHS
Royal Iraqi Air Force ... RIAF
Royal Irish [*Military unit*] [*British*] ... RI
Royal Irish Academy ... RIA
Royal Irish Academy of Music ... RIAM
Royal Irish Automobile Club (EAIO) ... RIAC
Royal Irish Constabulary ... RIC
Royal Irish Dragoon Guards [*British military*] (DMA) ... RIDG
Royal Irish Dragoons [*British military*] (DMA) ... RID
Royal Irish Fusiliers [*Military unit*] [*British*] ... RIF
Royal Irish Fusiliers [*Military unit*] [*British*] (DMA) ... RIrF
Royal Irish Fusiliers Reserve Regiment [*Military unit*] [*British*] (DMA) ... FRR
Royal Irish Rifles [*British military*] (DMA) ... RIR
Royal Italian Opera ... RIO
Royal Jersey Artillery [*Military unit*] [*British*] ... RJA

Royal Jersey Light Infantry [*Military unit*] [*British*] .... RJLI
Royal Jersey Militia [*Military unit*] [*British*] .... RJM
Royal Jordanian [*ICAO designator*] (FAAC) .... RJA
Royal Jordanian Air Force .... RJAF
Royal Jordanian Air Force [*ICAO designator*] (FAAC) .... RJZ
Royal Jordanian Airlines (IMH) .... ALIA
Royal Jubilee Trust [*Provides financial aid to start new businesses*] [*British*] .... RJT
Royal Khmer Air Force [*Cambodia*] .... RKAF
Royal Khmer Government [*Cambodia*] .... RKG
Royal Knight [*British*] .... RK
Royal Lancashire Militia [*British military*] (DMA) .... RLM
Royal Lancers [*British military*] (DMA) .... RL
Royal Lao [*or Laotian*] **Army** [*Laos*] .... RLA
Royal Laotian Air Force .... RLAF
Royal Laotian Forces .... RLF
Royal Laotian Government .... RLG
Royal Lepage Ltd. [*Toronto Stock Exchange symbol Vancouver Stock Exchange symbol*] .... RLG
Royal Licence [*British*] .... RL
Royal Life High Income Trust [*British*] .... RLHIT
Royal Life Saving Society [*Studley, Warwickshire, England*] (EAIO) .... RLSS
Royal Literary Fund [*British*] .... RLF
Royal Liverpool Philharmonic Society [*British*] (DBA) .... RLPS
Royal London Militia .... RLM
Royal Mail [*British*] .... RM
Royal Mail Parcels Marketing [*British Post Office*] .... RMPM
Royal Mail Service [*British*] .... RMS
Royal Mail Special Delivery [*British Post Office facility*] (DCTA) .... RMSD
Royal Mail Steam Packet Co. .... RMSP
Royal Mail Steamship [*British*] .... RMS
Royal Malayan Navy Ship [*British military*] (DMA) .... RMNS
Royal Malayan Regiment [*British military*] (DMA) .... RMR
Royal Malaysian Air Force [*ICAO designator*] (FAAC) .... RMF
Royal Malaysian Navy .... RMALAN
Royal Malta Artillery [*Military unit*] [*British*] .... RMA
Royal Malta Fencible Artillery [*British military*] (DMA) .... RMFA
Royal Manchester College of Music [*British*] .... RMCM
Royal Marine Academy [*British*] .... RMA
Royal Marine Advisory Team [*British military*] (DMA) .... RMAT
Royal Marine Artillery [*Obsolete British*] .... RMA
Royal Marine Bands [*British military*] (DMA) .... RMB
Royal Marine Boom Patrol Detachment [*World War II*] .... RMBPD
Royal Marine Commando Brigade [*British*] .... RMCB
Royal Marine Commandos [*British*] .... RMC
Royal Marine Engineers [*British*] .... RME
Royal Marine Forces Volunteer Reserve [*Obsolete British*] .... RMFVR
Royal Marine Gunner [*British*] .... RMG
Royal Marine Labour Corps [*British military*] (DMA) .... RMLC
Royal Marine Light Infantry [*Obsolete British*] .... RMLI
Royal Marine Mobile Defended Base Organisation [*British military*] (DMA) .... RMMDBO
Royal Marine Observer [*British military*] (DMA) .... RM Obs
Royal Marine Office [*British*] .... RMO
Royal Marine Police [*British military*] (DMA) .... RMP
Royal Marine Routine Orders [*British military*] (DMA) .... RMRO
Royal Marine Signaller [*British military*] (DMA) .... RMS
Royal Marine Signalling Instructor [*British military*] (DMA) .... RMSI
Royal Marines [*British*] .... RM
Royal Marines Association [*British military*] (DMA) .... RMA
Royal Marines Auxiliary Brigade [*British military*] (DMA) .... RMAB
Royal Marines Badge [*British*] .... RMB
Royal Marines Reserve [*British*] .... RMR
Royal Marines Rifle Association [*British military*] (DMA) .... RMRA
Royal Marines School of Music [*British*] .... RMSchMus
Royal Martyr Church Union [*British*] (DBA) .... RMCU
Royal Masonic Institution for Girls [*British*] (BI) .... RMIG
Royal Medical and Chirurgical Society [*British*] (ROG) .... RMCS
Royal Medical Society [*British*] (DBA) .... RMS
Royal Medical Society, Edinburgh .... RMedSoc
Royal Medico-Psychological Association [*British*] .... RMPA
Royal Melbourne Hospital. Quarterly [*A publication*] .... R Melb Hosp Q
Royal Melbourne Philharmonic Society [*Australia*] .... RMPS
Royal Meteorological Society [*British*] .... R Met S
Royal Meteorological Society [*British*] .... RMS
Royal Microscopical Society [*British*] .... RMS
Royal Military Academy [*For cadets of Royal Engineers and Royal Artillery; frequently referred to as Woolwich*] [*British*] .... RMA
Royal Military Academy Sandhurst [*British*] .... RMAS
Royal Military Asylum [*British*] .... RMA
Royal Military College [*For army cadets; often referred to as Sandhurst*] [*British*] .... RMC
Royal Military College Certificate (Senior Department) [*British*] (ROG) .... MCC
Royal Military College, Kingston, ON, Canada [*Library symbol Library of Congress*] (LCLS) .... CaOKR
Royal Military College of Canada [*British military*] (DMA) .... RMCC
Royal Military College of Canada, Kingston, Ontario [*Library symbol National Library of Canada*] (NLC) .... OKR
Royal Military College of Canada, Science Engineering Library, Kingston, ON, Canada [*Library symbol*] [*Library of Congress*] (LCLS) .... CaOKRS
Royal Military College of Science [*British*] .... RMCS
Royal Military Police [*British*] .... RMP
Royal Military Police Training Centre [*British*] .... RMPTC
Royal Military School of Music [*British*] .... RMSM
Royal Mint [*British*] (DAS) .... RM
Royal Monmouthshire Royal Engineers (Militia) [*British military*] (DMA) .... R MON RE(M)
Royal Montreal Regiment [*Military unit*] .... RMR
Royal Moroccan Air Force .... RMAF
Royal Motor Yacht Club [*British*] (BI) .... RMYC
Royal Munster Fusiliers [*Military unit*] (DMA) .... MF
Royal Munster Fusiliers [*Military unit*] [*British*] .... RMF
Royal Museum of Scotland .... RMS
Royal Musical Association [*British*] .... RMA
Royal Name (BJA) .... RN
Royal National Agricultural and Industrial Association [*Australia*] .... RNAIA
Royal National Homing Union [*British*] (BI) .... RNHU
Royal National Institute for the Blind [*British*] .... RNIB
Royal National Institute for the Deaf [*British*] .... RNID
Royal National Life-Boat Institution [*British*] .... RNLBI
Royal National Life-Boat Institution [*British*] .... RNLI
Royal National Mission to Deep Sea Fishermen [*British*] .... RNMDSF
Royal National Rose Society [*British*] (EAIO) .... RNRS
Royal National Scottish Hospital .... RNSH
Royal Naval Air Force [*British*] .... RNAF
Royal Naval Air Service [*Precursor of Fleet Air Arm*] [*Initialism also facetiously translated during World War I as "Really Not a Sailor"*] [*British*] .... RNAS
Royal Naval Air Station [*British*] .... RNAS
Royal Naval Air Training Establishment [*British*] .... RNATE
Royal Naval Aircraft Maintenance Yard [*British*] .... RNAMY
Royal Naval Aircraft Workshop [*British*] .... RNAW
Royal Naval Aircraft Yard [*British*] .... RNAY
Royal Naval Armament Depot [*British*] .... RNAD
Royal Naval Artillery Volunteers [*British*] .... RNAV
Royal Naval Association [*British military*] (DMA) .... RNA
Royal Naval Auxiliary Hospital [*British military*] (DMA) .... RNAH
Royal Naval Auxiliary Service [*British*] .... RNXS
Royal Naval Auxiliary Sick Berth Reserve [*British military*] (DMA) .... RNASBR
Royal Naval Barracks [*British*] .... RNB
Royal Naval Beach Commando [*British*] .... RNBC
Royal Naval Benevolent Trust [*British*] .... RNBT
Royal Naval Bird Watching Society [*British*] .... RNBWS
Royal Naval Canadian Volunteer Reserve [*World War I*] .... RNCVR
Royal Naval College [*For future officers; often spoken of as Dartmouth*] [*British*] .... RNC
Royal Naval College, Greenwich [*British*] .... RNColl
Royal Naval College of Canada [*1911-1922*] .... RNCC
Royal Naval Detention Quarter [*British*] (DI) .... RNDQ
Royal Naval Division [*British*] .... RND
Royal Naval Endurance Triathlon Association [*British*] .... RNETA
Royal Naval Engineering College [*British*] .... RNEC
Royal Naval Engineering College [*British*] .... RNEColl
Royal Naval Engineering Service [*British*] .... RNES
Royal Naval Film Corp. [*British military*] (DMA) .... RNFC
Royal Naval Fund [*British*] (DAS) .... RNF
Royal Naval Hospital [*British*] .... RNH
Royal Naval Liaison Officer [*British*] .... RNLO
Royal Naval Minewatching Service [*British military*] (DMA) .... RNMS
Royal Naval Minewatching Service [*British*] (BI) .... RNMWS
Royal Naval Motor Boat Reserve [*British military*] (DMA) .... RNMBR
Royal Naval Officers Club [*Defunct*] (EA) .... RNOC
Royal Naval Patrol Service [*Obsolete British*] .... RNPS
Royal Naval Personnel Research Committee [*British*] .... RNP
Royal Naval Personnel Research Committee [*British*] (MCD) .... RNPRC
Royal Naval Physiological Laboratory [*Later, AMTE (PL)*] [*British*] .... RNPL
Royal Naval Reserve [*British*] .... RNR
Royal Naval Reserve Decoration [*British*] .... RD
Royal Naval Reserve (Trawlers) [*British military*] (DMA) .... RNR(T)
Royal Naval Rifle Association [*British military*] (DMA) .... RNRA
Royal Naval Sailing Association [*British*] .... RNSA
Royal Naval School [*British*] .... RNS
Royal Naval School of Music [*British military*] (DMA) .... RNS of M
Royal Naval Scientific Service [*British*] (DEN) .... RNSS
Royal Naval Sick Quarters [*British*] .... RNSQ
Royal Naval Special Reserve [*British military*] (DMA) .... RNSR
Royal Naval Staff College [*British*] .... RNSC
Royal Naval Stores Depot [*British*] .... RNSD
Royal Naval Supply and Transport Service [*British*] .... RNSTS
Royal Naval Training Establishment [*British military*] (DMA) .... RNTE
Royal Naval Training Unit [*British military*] (DMA) .... RNTU
Royal Naval Volunteer Postal Reserve [*British military*] (IAA) .... RNVPR
Royal Naval Volunteer (Reserve) [*British*] (ROG) .... RNV
Royal Naval (Volunteer) Reserve [*Obsolete World War II British*] .... RN(V)R
Royal Naval Volunteer Reserve (Air) [*British military*] (DMA) .... RNVR(A)
Royal Naval Volunteer Supplementary Reserve [*Obsolete World War II British*] .... RNVSR
Royal Naval Volunteer (Wireless) Reserve [*British military*] (DMA) .... RNV(W)R
Royal Naval Wireless Auxiliary Reserve [*British military*] (DMA) .... RNWAR
Royal Navy [*British ICAO designator*] (FAAC) .... NVY
Royal Navy [*British*] .... RN
Royal Navy Ballistic Missile [*British*] .... RNBM
Royal Navy Coast Volunteers [*British military*] (DMA) .... RNCV
Royal Navy Equipment Exhibition [*British*] .... RNEE
Royal Navy General Headquarters [*British*] .... RNGHQ
Royal Navy Polaris School [*British*] .... RNPS
Royal Neighbors of America (EA) .... RNA
Royal Nepal Airlines [*ICAO designator*] (AD) .... RA
Royal Nepal Airlines Corp. [*ICAO designator*] (FAAC) .... RNA
Royal Nepal Airlines Corp. .... RNAC
Royal Netherlands Air Force [*ICAO designator*] (FAAC) .... NAF

Royal Netherlands Air Force ... RNAF
Royal Netherlands Air Force ... RNLAF
Royal Netherlands Army ... RNA
Royal Netherlands Army ... RNLA
Royal Netherlands East Indies Air Force ... RNEIAF
Royal Netherlands East Indies Army ... RNEIA
Royal Netherlands East Indies Navy ... RNEIN
Royal Netherlands Institute of Engineers ... RNIE
Royal Netherlands Marine Corps ... RNMC
Royal Netherlands Naval Air Service ... RNNAS
Royal Netherlands Navy [*ICAO designator*] (FAAC) ... NRN
Royal Netherlands Navy (DOMA) ... RNLN
Royal Netherlands Navy ... RNN
Royal New Zealand ... RNZ
Royal New Zealand Air Force [*FAA designator*] (FAAC) ... KIW
Royal New Zealand Air Force ... RNZAF
Royal New Zealand Army (VNW) ... RNZA
Royal New Zealand Ballet ... NZB
Royal New Zealand Engineers ... RNZE
Royal New Zealand Infantry Regiment (VNW) ... RNZIR
Royal New Zealand Naval (Volunteer) Reserve ... RNZN(V)R
Royal New Zealand Navy ... RNZN
Royal North Australian Show Society ... RNASS
Royal North British Dragoons [*British military*] (DMA) ... RNBD
Royal North British Fusiliers [*British military*] (DMA) ... RNBF
Royal North Devon Hussars [*British military*] (DMA) ... RNDH
Royal North Devonshire Yeomanry Hussars [*British military*] (DMA) ... NDH
Royal North Gloucestershire Militia [*British military*] (DMA) ... NG
Royal North Gloucestershire Militia [*British military*] (DMA) ... RNGM
Royal North West Mounted Police [*Later, RCMP*] [*Canada*] ... RNWMP
Royal Northern Agricultural Society [*British*] (DBA) ... RNAS
Royal Northern and Clyde Yacht Club [*British*] (DBA) ... RNCYC
Royal Northern College of Music [*British*] ... RNCM
Royal Northumberland Fusiliers [*Military unit*] [*British*] ... NF
Royal Northumberland Fusiliers [*Military unit*] [*British*] ... RNF
Royal Norwegian Air Force [*ICAO designator*] (FAAC) ... NOW
Royal Norwegian Air Force ... RNAF
Royal Norwegian Air Force ... RNOAF
Royal Norwegian Army (MCD) ... RNA
Royal Norwegian Army (NATG) ... RNOA
Royal Norwegian Army ... RNORA
Royal Norwegian Army and Air Force ... RNAAF
Royal Norwegian Council for Scientific and Industrial Research (EAIO) ... RNCSIR
Royal Norwegian Navy ... RNN
Royal Norwegian Navy (NATG) ... RNON
Royal Norwegian Navy ... RNORN
Royal Norwegian Society of Sciences ... RNSS
Royal Nova Scotia Regiment [*Military unit*] ... RNSR
Royal Nova Scotia Yacht Squadron ... RNSYS
Royal Numismatic Society [*British*] ... RNS
Royal Oak Foundation (EA) ... ROF
Royal Oak, MI [*AM radio station call letters*] ... WEXL
Royal Oak Mines [*Associated Press*] (SAG) ... RoyalO
Royal Oak Mines [*AMEX symbol*] (SPSG) ... RYO
Royal Oak Public Library, Royal Oak, MI [*Library symbol Library of Congress*] (LCLS) ... MiRoy
Royal Oak Resources Ltd. [*Toronto Stock Exchange symbol*] ... ROL
Royal Observatory [*British*] ... RO
Royal Observatory, Edinburgh [*Scotland*] ... ROE
Royal Observer Corps [*British civilian aircraft observers*] [*World War II*] ... ROC
Royal Ocean Racing Club [*British*] ... RORC
Royal Octavo ... RO
Royal Oman Police [*ICAO designator*] (FAAC) ... ROP
Royal Ontario Museum [*Toronto, ON*] [*Research center*] ... ROM
Royal Ontario Museum, Canadiana Department, Toronto, ON, Canada [*Library symbol Library of Congress*] (LCLS) ... CaOTRMC
Royal Ontario Museum, Far Eastern Department, Toronto, ON, Canada [*Library symbol Library of Congress*] (LCLS) ... CaOTRMF
Royal Ontario Museum Library [*UTLAS symbol*] ... KRM
Royal Ontario Museum, Toronto, ON, Canada [*Library symbol Library of Congress*] (LCLS) ... CaOTRM
Royal Ontario Museum, Toronto, Ontario [*Library symbol National Library of Canada*] (NLC) ... OTRM
Royal Opera House [*Covent Garden, London*] ... ROH
Royal Optimizing Assembly Routine [*Computer science*] (IAA) ... ROAR
Royal Optimizing Assembly Routing [*Royal McBee Corp.*] [*Computer science*] ... ROAR
Royal Order of Jagie Ilo [*Later, SHOSJ*] (EA) ... ROJ
Royal Order of Piast (EA) ... ROP
Royal Order of Scotland (EA) ... ROS
Royal Order of Sputnik Chasers ... ROOSCH
Royal Ordnance Corps [*British*] ... ROC
Royal Ordnance Factory [*British*] ... RO
Royal Ordnance Factory [*British*] (NATG) ... ROF
Royal Ordnance Factory, Bishopton [*Scotland*] ... ROF-B
Royal Ottawa Hospital, Ontario [*Library symbol National Library of Canada*] (NLC) ... OORO
Royal Ottawa Hospital, Ottawa, ON, Canada [*Library symbol Library of Congress*] (LCLS) ... CaOORO
Royal Ottawa Regional Rehabilitation Centre, Royal Ottawa Hospital, Ontario [*Library symbol National Library of Canada*] (NLC) ... OORORR
Royal Ottawa Regional Rehabilitation Centre, Royal Ottawa Hospital, Ottawa, ON, Canada [*Library symbol Library of Congress*] (LCLS) ... CaOORORR
Royal Overseas League [*British*] (EAIO) ... ROL
Royal Overseas League [*British*] (DI) ... ROSL
Royal Pacific Sea Farms Ltd. [*Toronto Stock Exchange symbol Vancouver Stock Exchange symbol*] ... RPF
Royal Pakistan Army Service Corps [*British military*] (DMA) ... RPASC
Royal Pakistan Artillery [*British military*] (DMA) ... RPA
Royal Pakistan Engineers [*British military*] (DMA) ... RPE
Royal Pakistan Naval Volunteer Reserve [*British military*] (DMA) ... RPNVR
Royal Pakistan Navy [*British military*] (DMA) ... RPN
Royal Palm Beach, FL [*AM radio station call letters*] ... WLVJ
Royal Palm Beach, FL [*AM radio station call letters*] (RBYB) ... WPSP
Royal Palm Beach Ltd. [*Associated Press*] (SAG) ... RoyPlm
Royal Palm Beach Ltd. [*AMEX symbol*] (SPSG) ... RPB
Royal Panopticon (ROG) ... RP
Royal Parks Constabulary [*British*] ... RPC
Royal Perth Golf Club [*Australia*] ... RPGC
Royal Pharmaceutical Society of Great Britain (EAIO) ... RPSGB
Royal Philatelic Society of Canada ... RPSC
Royal Philharmonic Orchestra [*British*] ... RPO
Royal Philharmonic Society [*British*] (DI) ... RPhilS
Royal Philharmonic Society (EAIO) ... RPS
Royal Phoenix Airlines [*Nigeria*] [*ICAO designator*] (FAAC) ... DBO
Royal Photographic Society of Great Britain (DEN) ... RPS
Royal Photographic Society of Great Britain (EAIO) ... RPSGB
Royal Pigeon Racing Association [*British*] (DBA) ... RPRA
Royal Pioneer Corps [*British*] ... RPC
Royal Plastics Group [*NYSE symbol*] (TTSB) ... RYG
Royal Plastics Group Ltd. [*Associated Press*] (SAG) ... RoyPls
Royal Plastics Group Ltd. [*NYSE symbol*] (SAG) ... RYG
Royal Polytechnic Institute (ROG) ... RPI
Royal Postgraduate Medical School [*British*] ... RPMS
Royal Protection Branch [*of the London Metropolitan Police*] ... RPB
Royal Provincials [*British military*] (DMA) ... RP
Royal PTT Nederland ADS [*NYSE symbol*] (TTSB) ... KPN
Royal Queensland Bush Children's Health Scheme [*Australia*] ... RQBCHS
Royal Queensland Golf Club [*Australia*] ... RQGC
Royal Queensland Lawn Tennis Association [*Australia*] ... RQLTA
Royal RADAR Establishment [*British Research center*] ... RRE
Royal RADAR Establishment Automatic Computer (IAA) ... RREAC
Royal Red Cross [*British*] ... RRC
Royal Regiment of Artillery [*Military British*] ... RA
Royal Regiment of Fusiliers [*Military unit*] [*British*] ... RRF
Royal Regiment of Wales [*Military unit*] [*British*] ... RRW
Royal Research Ship [*British*] ... RRS
Royal Rhodesia Regiment [*British military*] (DMA) ... RRR
Royal Rhodesian Air Force ... RRAF
Royal Roads Military College [*Royal Roads, BC*] ... RRMC
Royal Roads Military College, Royal Roads, BC, Canada [*Library symbol Library of Congress*] (LCLS) ... CaBRC
Royal Roads Military College, Victoria, British Columbia [*Library symbol National Library of Canada*] (NLC) ... BRC
Royal Sanitary Association of Scotland ... RSAS
Royal Sanitary Institute [*Later, RSH*] [*British*] ... R San I
Royal Sanitary Institute (ROG) ... RSI
Royal Sappers and Miners [*British military*] (DMA) ... RS & M
Royal Saudi Air Force ... RSAF
Royal Saudi Arabian Navy Forces (MCD) ... RSNF
Royal School of Church Music [*British*] ... RSCHM
Royal School of Church Music [*British*] ... RSCM
Royal School of Military Engineering [*British military*] (DMA) ... RSME
Royal School of Mines [*British*] ... RSM
Royal School of Musketry [*Hythe*] [*Military British*] (ROG) ... RSM
Royal School of Needlework [*British*] ... RSN
Royal Scot Resources [*Vancouver Stock Exchange symbol*] ... RST
Royal Scots [*Military unit*] ... RS
Royal Scots Dragoon Guards [*British military*] (DMA) ... RSDG
Royal Scots Fusiliers [*Military unit*] ... RSF
Royal Scots Fusiliers [*Military unit*] (DMA) ... SF
Royal Scots Greys [*Military unit*] ... RSG
Royal Scottish Academician ... RSA
[*The*] **Royal Scottish Academy** ... RSA
Royal Scottish Academy, Edinburgh [*1826*] (NGC) ... RSA
Royal Scottish Academy of Music and Drama (AIE) ... RSAM
Royal Scottish Automobile Club (DBA) ... RSAC
Royal Scottish Country Dance Society (EAIO) ... RSCDS
Royal Scottish Forestry Society (EAIO) ... RSFS
Royal Scottish Geographical Society ... RSGS
Royal Scottish Pipe Band Association [*British*] (DBA) ... RSPBA
Royal Scottish Pipers' Society [*British*] (DBA) ... RSPS
Royal Scottish Society for Prevention of Cruelty to Children ... RSSPCC
Royal Scottish Society of Painters in Water Colours ... RSW
Royal Scottish Water-Colour Society (ROG) ... RSWS
Royal Shakespeare Company [*British*] ... RSC
Royal Shakespeare Society [*British*] (DI) ... RSS
Royal Signals and RADAR Establishment [*Computer chip designer*] [*England*] ... RSRE
Royal Signals Institution [*British*] (DEN) ... RSI
Royal Signals Research Establishment [*British*] ... RSRE
Royal Small Arms Factory [*British*] ... RSAF
Royal Society [*British*] ... RS
Royal Society, Dublin ... RSD
Royal Society for Asian Affairs [*British*] (DI) ... RSAA
Royal Society for Mentally Handicapped Children & Adults [*England*] ... MENCAP
Royal Society for Nature Conservation Wildlife Trusts Partnership (EAIO) ... RSNC

Royal Society for the Encouragement of Arts, Manufactures, and Commerce [British] (EAIO) .... RSA
Royal Society for the Prevention of Accidents [British] .... RoSPA
Royal Society for the Prevention of Accidents [British] (AIE) .... ROSPA
Royal Society for the Prevention of Accidents [British] .... RSPA
Royal Society for the Prevention of Cruelty to Animals [British] .... RSPCA
Royal Society for the Promotion of Health [British] (DAVI) .... RSPH
Royal Society for the Protection of Birds [British] .... RSPB
Royal Society, London [British] .... RSA
Royal Society of Antiquaries .... RSA
Royal Society of Antiquaries of Ireland .... RSAI
Royal Society of Arts, Manufacturing and Commerce [London] .... RSAMC
Royal Society of Australia (BARN) .... RSA
Royal Society of British Architects .... RBA
Royal Society of British Artists .... RBA
Royal Society of British Sculptors .... RBS
Royal Society of British Sculptors .... RBSc
Royal Society of Canada .... RSC
Royal Society of Chemistry [Chemical Society and Royal Institute of Chemistry] [Formed by a merger of] (EAIO) .... RSC
Royal Society of Edinburgh .... RSE
Royal Society of Health [Formerly, R San I] [British] .... RSH
Royal Society of Literature [British] .... RSL
Royal Society of Marine Artists [Formerly, SMA] [British] .... RSMA
Royal Society of Medicine [British] .... RSM
Royal Society of Medicine Foundation (EA) .... RSMF
Royal Society of Medicine, London, United Kingdom [Library symbol Library of Congress] (LCLS) .... UkLRSM
Royal Society of Miniature Painters, Sculptors, and Gravers [British] .... RMS
Royal Society of Musicians of Great Britain .... RSM
Royal Society of Musicians of Great Britain (EAIO) .... RSMGB
Royal Society of Northern Antiquaries (ROG) .... RSNA
Royal Society of Painter-Etchers and Engravers [British] .... RE
Royal Society of Painter-Etchers and Engravers, London [1880] (NGC) .... RE
Royal Society of Painters in Water-Colours [British] .... RSPWC
Royal Society of Painters in Water-Colours [British] (ROG) .... RSWC
Royal Society of Painters in Water-Colours [British] .... RWS
Royal Society of Painters in Water-Colours, London [1804] (NGC) .... RWS
Royal Society of Portrait Painters [British] .... RSPP
Royal Society of Tasmania [Australia] .... RST
Royal Society of Teachers [British] .... RST
Royal Society of the Arts [British] .... RSA
Royal Society of Tropical Medicine and Hygiene [British] (EAIO) .... RSTMH
Royal Society of Ulster Architects [British] (BI) .... RSUA
Royal South African Air Force .... RSAAF
Royal South Australian Bowling Association .... RSABA
Royal South Gloucestershire Light Infantry Militia [British military] (DMA) .... SG
Royal Statistical Society [British] (DI) .... RSS
Royal Statistical Society [British] .... SS
Royal Surgical Aid Society [British] (BI) .... RSAS
Royal Surrey Militia [British military] (DMA) .... RSM
Royal Sussex Regiment [Military unit] [British] .... RSR
Royal Swazi National Airways [ICAO designator] (AD) .... ZC
Royal Swazi National Airways Corp. [Swaziland] [ICAO designator] (FAAC) .... RSN
Royal Swedish Air Force .... RSAF
Royal Swedish Ballet .... RSB
Royal Swedish Library (Kungl. Biblioteket), Stockholm, Sweden [Library symbol Library of Congress] (LCLS) .... Sw
Royal Sydney Golf Club [Australia] .... RSGC
Royal Tank Corps [Military unit] [British] .... RTC
Royal Tank Regiment [Military unit] [British] .... RTR
Royal Television Society [British] .... RTS
Royal Thai Air Force .... RTAF
Royal Thai Air Force Base [Also, RTAFB] (VNW) .... RTAB
Royal Thai Air Force Base [Also, RTAB] (VNW) .... RTAFB
Royal Thai Air Force Contingent, Vietnam .... RTAFCONV
Royal Thai Armed Forces (CINC) .... RTARF
Royal Thai Army .... RTA
Royal Thai Army Rebuild Plant (MCD) .... RTARP
Royal Thai Army Volunteer Force (VNW) .... RTAVF
Royal Thai Government .... RTG
Royal Thai Marine Corps (CINC) .... RTMC
Royal Thai Military Assistance Group, Vietnam .... RTMAGV
Royal Thai Navy (CINC) .... RTN
Royal Thai Survey Department (CINC) .... RTSD
Royal Thames Yachting Club [British] .... RTYC
Royal Tongan Airlines [Tonga] [ICAO designator] (FAAC) .... HRH
Royal Town Planning Institute [British] .... RTPI
Royal Toxophilite Society [British] .... RTS
Royal Trust Co. Mortgage Corp. [Toronto Stock Exchange symbol] .... RTM
Royal Trust Energy Income Fund Trust Units [Toronto Stock Exchange symbol] .... RTE
Royal Trustco Ltd. [Toronto Stock Exchange symbol Vancouver Stock Exchange symbol] .... RYL
Royal Ulster Academy of Painting, Sculpture, and Architecture [Ireland] .... RUA
Royal Ulster Constabulary [British] .... RUC
Royal Ulster Rifles [Military unit] [British] .... RUR
Royal United Kingdom Benevolent Institution .... RUKBA
Royal United Service Museum [British military] (DMA) .... RUSM
Royal United Services Institute for Defence Studies [British] .... RUSI
Royal United Services Institute for Defence Studies [British] (DBA) .... RUSI
Royal University of Ireland .... RUI
Royal Veteran Battalion [British military] (DMA) .... RVB
Royal Veterinary College [British] .... RVC

Royal Veterinary College of Ireland .... RVCI
Royal Victoria Dock [British] (ROG) .... RVD
Royal Victoria Hospital Library, Montreal, PQ, Canada [Library symbol Library of Congress] .... CaQMRV
Royal Victoria Hospital, Montreal, Quebec [Library symbol National Library of Canada] (NLC) .... QMRV
Royal Victoria Hospital, Women's Pavillion, Montreal, PQ, Canada [Library symbol Library of Congress] (LCLS) .... CaQMRVW
Royal Victorian Chain .... RVC
Royal Victorian Institute of Architects. Journal [A publication] .... RVIAJ
Royal Victorian Motor Yacht Club [Australia] .... RVMYC
Royal Victorian Order .... RVO
Royal Victorian Yacht Club [Australia] .... RVYC
Royal Viking Line [Kloster Cruises of Norway] .... RVL
Royal Warrant [British] (ADA) .... RW
Royal Warrant for Pay and Promotion [British military] (DMA) .... PW
Royal Warwickshire Fusiliers [British military] (DMA) .... RWARF
Royal Warwickshire Regiment [Military unit] [British] (DMA) .... R War R
Royal Warwickshire Regiment [Military unit] [British] .... RW
Royal Watercolour Society [British] (EAIO) .... RWS
Royal Welch [or Welsh] Fusiliers [Military unit] [British] .... RWF
Royal Welsh Agricultural Society (BI) .... RWAS
Royal West [ICAO designator] (AD) .... TT
Royal West African Frontier Force [Military unit] [British] .... RWAFF
Royal West of England Academy .... RWA
Royal West of England Academy .... RWEA
Royal West of England Academy .... WEA
Royal West Surrey [Regiment] [Military unit] [British] .... RWS
Royal West Sussex [Regiment] [Military unit] [British] .... RWS
Royal Western Australian Bowling Association .... RWABA
Royal Western Australian Institute for the Blind [Australia] .... RWAIB
Royal Wiltshire Imperial Yeomanry [British military] (DMA) .... RWIY
Royal Wiltshire Yeomanry [Military unit] [British] .... RWY
Royal Windsor Foresters [British military] (DMA) .... RF
Royal Winnipeg Ballet .... RWB
Royal Winnipeg Ballet, Manitoba [Library symbol National Library of Canada] (NLC) .... MWR
Royal Winnipeg Ballet, Winnipeg, MB, Canada [Library symbol Library of Congress] (LCLS) .... CaMWR
Royal Yacht Squadron [British] .... RYS
Royal Yachting Association [British] (BI) .... RYA
Royal Yeomanry [Military unit] [British] .... RY
Royal Yeomanry Regiment [British military] (DMA) .... RYR
Royal Zoological Society [British] .... RZS
[The] Royal Zoological Society of Ireland (DI) .... RZSI
Royal Zoological Society of Scotland (EAIO) .... RZSS
Royale Airlines [ICAO designator] (AD) .... OQ
Royale & Allegro-Royale [Record label] .... Roy
Royale Energy [NASDAQ symbol] (TTSB) .... ROYL
Royale Energy Corp. [Associated Press] (SAG) .... RoyaleE
Royale Energy Corp. [NASDAQ symbol] (SAG) .... ROYL
Royale Investments, Inc. [NASDAQ symbol] (SAG) .... RLIN
Royale Investments, Inc. [Associated Press] (SAG) .... RoyIInv
Royale Invts Inc. [NASDAQ symbol] (TTSB) .... RLIN
Royall's Digest Virginia Reports [A publication] (DLA) .... Roy Dig
Royalon Petroleum [Vancouver Stock Exchange symbol] .... RYE
Royalstar Resources [Vancouver Stock Exchange symbol] .... RYQ
Royalton Public Library, Royalton, MN [Library symbol] [Library of Congress] (LCLS) .... MnRoy
Royalton School, Royalton, MN [Library symbol] [Library of Congress] (LCLS) .... MnRoyS
Royalton, VT [FM radio station call letters] (RBYB) .... WRJT
Royalty Monthly [A publication] .... R
Royalty Payment Mechanism .... RPM
Royalty Trust .... RT
Royan/Medis [France ICAO location identifier] (ICLI) .... LFCY
Royce Laboratories [NASDAQ symbol] (TTSB) .... RLAB
Royce Laboratories, Inc. [Miami, FL] [NASDAQ symbol] (NQ) .... RLAB
Royce Laboratories, Inc. [Associated Press] (SAG) .... RoycLab
Royce Micro-Cap Tr [NASDAQ symbol] (TTSB) .... OTCM
Royce OTC [Over the Counter] Micro Capital Fund [NASDAQ symbol] (SAG) .... OTCM
Royce OTC Micro Capital Fund [Associated Press] (SAG) .... RoyceMC
Royce Value Trust [NYSE symbol] (TTSB) .... RVT
Royce Value Trust, Inc. [Associated Press] (SAG) .... Royce
Royce Value Trust, Inc. [NYSE symbol] (SPSG) .... RVT
Royce Ventures Ltd. [Vancouver Stock Exchange symbol] .... RVE
Roycrofters-at-Large Association/Elbert Hubbard Foundation (EA) .... RALA-EHF
Royex Gold Mining Corp. [Toronto Stock Exchange symbol Vancouver Stock Exchange symbol] .... RGM
Roy-L Merchant Group, Inc. [Toronto Stock Exchange symbol] .... RLM
Royle on the Law of Stock Shares, Etc. [A publication] (DLA) .... Royle Stock Sh
Royscot Finance Group [Royal Bank of Scotland] .... RFG
Royston, GA [AM radio station call letters] .... WBIC
Royston, GA [FM radio station call letters] .... WPUP
RP [Retinitis Pigmentosa] Foundation Fighting Blindness (EA) .... RPFFB
RPC Energy Services, Inc. [NYSE symbol] (SPSG) .... RES
RPC Energy Services, Inc. [Associated Press] (SAG) .... RPC
RPC Inc. [NYSE symbol] (TTSB) .... RES
RPG System [International Business Machines Corp.] [Report Program Generator] (IAA) .... COFIRS
RPM, Inc. [Associated Press] (SAG) .... RPM
RPM, Inc. [NASDAQ symbol] (SAG) .... RPOW
RPS Realty Trust [NYSE symbol] (SPSG) .... RPS
R-Register [Computer science] .... R

rRNA[*Ribonucleic Acid*] **Transcription Unit** [*Genetics*] (DOG) .... rTU
RS Financial Corp. [*Formerly, Raleigh Federal Savings Bank*] [*NASDAQ symbol*] (NQ) .... RFBK
RS Financial Group [*Formerly, Raleigh Federal Savings Bank*] [*Associated Press*] (SAG) .... RS Fnl
RSI Retail Solutions, Inc. [*Vancouver Stock Exchange symbol*] .... RSL
RSI Systems [*NASDAQ symbol*] (TTSB) .... RSIS
RSI Systems, Inc. [*Associated Press*] (SAG) .... RSI Sys
RSI Systems, Inc. [*NASDAQ symbol*] (SAG) .... RSIS
RST Aviation, NV [*Belgium ICAO designator*] (FAAC) .... DMD
RSU [*Remote Subscriber Unit*] **Interface Module** [*Telecommunications*] .... RIM
RT Inds Inc. [*NASDAQ symbol*] (TTSB) .... RTIC
RT Industries, Inc. [*Associated Press*] (SAG) .... RT Ind
RT Industries, Inc. [*NASDAQ symbol*] (SAG) .... RTIC
RTI, Inc. [*Associated Press*] (SAG) .... RTI
RTI, Inc. [*NASDAQ symbol*] (NQ) .... RTII
RTSD [*Resources and Technical Services Division*] **Cataloging and Classification Section** .... RTSD CCS
RTSD [*Resources and Technical Services Division*] **Preservation of Library Materials Section** .... RTSD PLMS
RTSD [*Resources and Technical Services Division*] **Reproduction of Library Materials Section** .... RTSD RLMS
RTSD [*Resources and Technical Services Division*] **Resources Section** .... RTSD RS
RTSD [*Resources and Technical Services Division*] **Serials Section** .... RTSD SS
RTW, Inc. [*Associated Press*] (SAG) .... RTW
RTW, Inc. [*NASDAQ symbol*] (SAG) .... RTWI
RTZ Corp. [*NYSE symbol*] (SPSG) .... RTZ
RTZ Corp. ADR [*Associated Press*] (SAG) .... RTZ
RTZ Corp. plc ADS [*NYSE symbol*] (TTSB) .... RTZ
RTZ Services Ltd. [*British ICAO designator*] (ICDA) .... VD
Rub [*Medicine*] (MAE) .... R
Rubber .... R
Rubber .... RBR
Rubber .... RBR
Rubber (VRA) .... rbr
Rubber (AAG) .... RUB
Rubber Allocation Committee .... RAC
Rubber and Plastic Adhesive and Sealant Manufacturers Council [*Later, Adhesive and Sealant Council*] (EA) .... RPASMC
Rubber and Plastic Footwear Manufacturers' Association [*British*] (BI) .... RPFMA
Rubber and Plastics Industry (MCD) .... R & PI
Rubber and Plastics Research Association (NITA) .... RAPRA
Rubber Band (ADA) .... RB
Rubber Base [*Technical drawings*] .... RB
Rubber Base Impression [*Medicine*] (DMAA) .... Rb Imp
Rubber Bearing (DS) .... RB
Rubber Block (DNAB) .... RB
Rubber Block Drive [*Mechanical power transmission*] .... RBD
Rubber Continuous Liner (DS) .... RCL
Rubber Control Board .... RCB
Rubber Covered (IAA) .... RC
Rubber Covered Cable (MSA) .... RCC
Rubber Covered, Weatherproof (IAA) .... RCWP
Rubber Cushioned (WDAA) .... RC
Rubber Dam [*Medicine*] (DMAA) .... RD
Rubber Development Corp. [*Expired, 1947*] .... RDC
Rubber Export Association [*Defunct*] (EA) .... REA
Rubber Growers' Association [*Later, TGA*] (EAIO) .... RGA
Rubber Heel and Sole Institute [*Defunct*] (EA) .... RHSI
Rubber Hose Jacket (MSA) .... RHJ
Rubber Hydrocarbon .... RHC
Rubber Insulation [*Technical drawings*] .... RI
Rubber Insulation .... RINSUL
Rubber Insulation Material .... RIM
Rubber Manufacturers Association (EA) .... RMA
Rubber Manufacturers Association (NADA) .... RMA
Rubber Manufacturers' Association of Australia .... RMAA
Rubber Modified Silica Phenolie .... RMSP
Rubber Mold (MCD) .... RM
Rubber Non-Continuous Liner (DS) .... RN
Rubber Peptizing Agent .... RPA
Rubber Proofers' Association [*British*] (BI) .... RPA
Rubber Reclaimers Association [*Later, NARI*] (EA) .... RRA
Rubber Recyclers Association (EA) .... RRA
Rubber Research Institute (NADA) .... RRI
Rubber Reserve Board [*of the Reconstruction Finance Corp.*] .... RRB
Rubber Reserve Committee [*Navy*] .... RRC
Rubber Reserve Co. [*Dissolved, 1935, functions transferred to Reconstruction Finance Corporation*] .... RRC
Rubber Shippers Association [*Defunct*] .... RSA
Rubber Tile [*Technical drawings*] .... RBT
Rubber Trade Association [*British*] (DBA) .... RTA
Rubber Trade Association of New York (EA) .... RTA
Rubber Traders Society (NADA) .... RTS
Rubber-Air-Lead [*Tile*] .... RAL
Rubber-Capped .... R/C
Rubber-Covered Braided (IAA) .... RCB
Rubber-Covered, Braided, and Weatherproof (IAA) .... RCBWP
Rubber-Covered Double-Braided (IAA) .... RCDB
Rubber-Impregnated Chopped Strand (PDAA) .... RICS
Rubber-Insert Sound Isolation Coupling (DNAB) .... RISIC
Rubberized .... RBRIZED
Rubberized (AAG) .... RUBD
Rubberized Equipment Repair .... RER
Rubberized Inflatable Boat (DOMA) .... RIB

Rubbermaid, Inc. [*NYSE symbol*] (SPSG) .... RBD
Rubbermaid, Inc. [*Associated Press*] (SAG) .... Rubrmd
Rubber-Modified Asphalt Concrete .... RUMAC
Rubber-Tile Floor [*Technical drawings*] .... RTF
Rubber-Tired (SAA) .... RT
Rubber-Toughened Amorphous Nylon [*Organic chemistry*] .... RTAN
Rubber-Toughened Polymethyl Methacrylate [*Organic chemistry*] ... RTPMMA
Rubbery Wood Virus .... RWV
Rubbing (VRA) .... rub
Rubbing Keel [*of a ship*] (DS) .... RK
Rubbish .... RUBSH
Rubble Stone (AAG) .... RS
Rubblestone [*Technical drawings*] .... RBL
Rubefacient [*Producing Heat and Redness of the Skin*] [*Medicine*] (ROG) .... RUB
Rubella Vaccine (DAVI) .... RV
Rubella Vaccine-Like Virus (AAMN) .... RVV
Rubella Virus .... RV
Rubella Virus Vaccine [*Immunology*] (DAVI) .... RVV
Rubella Virus-Induced Mitotic Inhibitor .... RVIMI
Ruber [*Red*] [*Pharmacy*] .... RUB
Rubery Owen-Rockwell [*Automotive industry supplier*] .... ROR
Rubidazone [*An antibiotic*] .... RBZ
Rubidazone [*Zorubicin*]/**DIC** [*Dacarbazine*] [*Antineoplastic drug regimen*].... RUBIDIC
Rubidium [*Chemical element*] .... Rb
Rubidium Acid Phthalate [*Organic chemistry*] .... RAP
Rubidomycin [*See also D, Daunorubicin*] [*Antineoplastic drug*] .... R
Rubinstein on Conveyancing [*5th ed.*] [*1884*] [*A publication*] (DLA) ...... Rub Conv
Rubinstein-Taybi Parent Group (EA) .... RTPG
Rubinstein-Taybi Syndrome [*Medicine*] .... RTS
RUBISCO [*Ribulosebisphosphate Carboxylase/Oxygenase*] **Binding Protein** [*Biochemistry*] .... RBP
Ruble [*Monetary unit*] [*Former USSR*] .... R
Ruble [*Monetary unit*] [*Former USSR*] .... RB
Ruble [*Monetary unit*] [*Former USSR*] .... RBL
Ruble [*Monetary unit*] [*Former USSR*] .... RUB
Rubric (DLA) .... RUB
Rubricator [*MARC relator code*] [*Library of Congress*] (LCCP) .... rbr
Rubust Yellow Net Virus [*Plant pathology*] .... RYNV
Ruby (VRA) .... rby
Ruby [*Alaska*] [*Airport symbol*] (OAG) .... RBY
Ruby Crystal LASER .... RCL
Ruby, Emerald, Garnet, Amethyst, Ruby, Diamond [*Jewelry*] .... REGARD
Ruby Jewel Bearing .... RJB
Ruby LASER Pulse .... RLP
Ruby LASER Single Pulse .... RLSP
Ruby LASER System .... RLS
Ruby Mountain Mines [*Vancouver Stock Exchange symbol*] .... RUB
Ruby Resources Ltd. [*Vancouver Stock Exchange symbol*] .... RBY
Ruby Rod LASER .... RRL
Ruby Tuesday [*NYSE symbol*] (TTSB) .... RI
Ruby Tuesday, Inc. [*NYSE symbol*] (SAG) .... RI
Ruby Tuesday, Inc. [*Associated Press*] (SAG) .... RubyTu
Ruch Biblijny i Liturgiczny (BJA) .... RBL
Ruch Obywatelski-Akcja Demokratyczna [*Civil Movement for Democratic Action*] [*Poland*] [*Political party*] .... ROAD
Ruch Oporu Chlopskiego [*Movement of Peasant Resistance*] [*Poland Political party*] (PPE) .... ROCH
Ruchnoy Pulemyot Degtyaryov Light Machine Gun [*Soviet-made weaponry*] [*Also, RPDM, RPDM LMG*] (VNW) .... RPD LMG
Ruchnoy Pulemyot Degtyaryov Light Machine Gun [*Soviet-made weaponry*] [*Also, RPD LMG, RPDM LMG*] [*Military*] (VNW) .... RPDM
Ruchnoy Pulemyot Degtyaryov Light Machine Gun [*Soviet-made weaponry*] [*Also, RPD LMG, RPDM*] [*Military*] (VNW) .... RPDM LMG
Rucker-Gable Educational Programming Scale [*Psychology*] .... RGEPS
Rucker's Reports [*43-46 West Virginia*] [*A publication*] (DLA) .... Rucker
Ruckersville, VA [*FM radio station call letters*] .... WVSY
Rudder (NASA) .... RDR
Rudder (AAG) .... RUD
Rudder Angle Master Transmitter .... RAMT
Rudder Angle Order (MSA) .... RAO
Rudder Club (EA) .... RC
Rudder Lock-Out (MCD) .... RLO
Rudder Pedal Force Sensor (MCD) .... RPFS
Rudder Pedal Force Transducer (MCD) .... RPFT
Rudder Pedal Sensor Assembly (MCD) .... RPSA
Rudder Pedal Transducer (NASA) .... RPT
Rudder Pedal Transducer Assembly (NASA) .... RPTA
Rudder Reference Line [*NASA*] (NASA) .... RRL
Rudder Reference Plane [*NASA*] (NASA) .... RRP
Rudder Shaped Hull (PDAA) .... RUSH
Rudder Speed Brake [*Aviation*] (MCD) .... RD/SB
Rudder Speed Brake (MCD) .... RSB
Rudder Station (MCD) .... RS
Ruddick Corp. [*NYSE symbol*] (SPSG) .... RDK
Ruddick Corp. [*Associated Press*] (SAG) .... Ruddick
Rudge Enthusiasts Club (EA) .... REC
Rudimentary (ROG) .... RUDIM
Rudimentary Adaptive System for Computer-Aided Learning (PDAA) ..... RASCAL
Rudolf Nureyev Foundation .... RNF
Rudolph, WI [*FM radio station call letters*] .... WIZD
Rudyard School Public Library, Rudyard, MI [*Library symbol Library of Congress*] (LCLS) .... MiRud
Rudys Restaurant Group [*Associated Press*] (SAG) .... RdysRst
Rudys Restaurant Group [*NASDAQ symbol*] (SAG) .... RUDY
Rue [*Street*] [*French*] .... R

Rue [*Postal Service standard*] (OPSA) ... RUE
Rueckenfallschirm mit Zwangsausloesung [*Static-line, backpack parachute*] [*German military - World War II*] ... RZ
Rueckgang [*Return*] [*Music*] ... RG
Rueckwaertiges Armeegebiet [*Rear area of an army*] [*German military*] ... RA
Rueckwaertiges Heeresgebiet [*Rear area of a group of armies*] [*German military*] ... RH
Ruegg on Employer's Liability [*9th ed.*] [*1922*] [*A publication*] (DLA) ... Ruegg Emp L
Rufansa [*Zambia*] [*ICAO location identifier*] (ICLI) ... FLRU
Ruffed Grouse Society (EA) ... RGS
Ruffhead's Edition of the Statutes, by Serjeant Runnington [*1235-1785*] [*A publication*] (DLA) ... Ruff
Ruffhead's English Statutes [*A publication*] (DLA) ... Ruff St
Ruffhead's English Statutes [*A publication*] (DLA) ... Ruffh St
Ruffin and Hawks' Reports [*8 North Carolina*] [*A publication*] (DLA) ... Ruff
Ruffin and Hawks' Reports [*8 North Carolina*] [*A publication*] (DLA) ... Ruff & H
Ruffner-Carnegie Public Library, Manassas, VA [*Library symbol Library of Congress Obsolete*] (LCLS) ... ViMan
Rufinus [*Flourished, 1150-86*] [*Authority cited in pre-1607 legal work*] (DSA) ... Ru
Rufinus [*Flourished, 1150-86*] [*Authority cited in pre-1607 legal work*] (DSA) ... Ruf
Rufous-Sided Towhee [*Ornithology*] ... RT
Rugby Fives Association [*British*] (BI) ... RFA
Rugby Football Club ... RFC
Rugby Football League [*British*] (DBA) ... RFL
Rugby Football Schools Union [*British*] ... RFSU
Rugby Football Union [*British*] ... RFU
Rugby League [*British*] (DI) ... RL
Rugby, ND [*FM radio station call letters*] (RBYB) ... KVAG-FM
Rugby, ND [*AM radio station call letters*] (RBYB) ... KZZJ
Rugby, ND [*Location identifier FAA*] (FAAL) ... RUG
Rugby Union [*Controlling body of British rugby football*] ... RU
Rugby Union Football Club [*British*] (DAS) ... RUFC
Ruger Collectors Association (EA) ... RCA
Ruggedized Airborne Seeker Simulator (MCD) ... RASS
Ruggedized Airborne Video Recorder ... R-AVR
Ruhengeri [*Rwanda*] [*ICAO location identifier*] (ICLI) ... HRYU
Ruhr Regional Planning Authority [*Post-World War II*] ... RRPA
Ruhr-Universitat Bochum, Bochum, Germany [*Library symbol Library of Congress*] (LCLS) ... GyBochU
Rui Lopes Associates, Inc. [*Sunnyvale, CA*] [*Telecommunications*] (TSSD) ... RLA
Ruidoso [*New Mexico*] [*Airport symbol*] (OAG) ... RUI
Ruidoso Downs, NM [*AM radio station call letters*] ... KRUI
Ruidoso, NM [*AM radio station call letters*] ... KBUY
Ruidoso, NM [*FM radio station call letters*] ... KWES
Ruidoso, NM [*Location identifier FAA*] (FAAL) ... RUI
Ruidoso Public Library, Ruidoso, NM [*Library symbol Library of Congress*] (LCLS) ... NmRu
Ruin (ROG) ... RN
Ruinas De Copan [*Honduras*] [*ICAO location identifier*] (ICLI) ... MHRU
Ruinas de Copan [*Honduras*] [*Airport symbol*] (AD) ... RUY
Ruindi [*Zaire*] [*ICAO location identifier*] (ICLI) ... FZNR
Ruins ... Ru
Rukumkot (Chaurjhari) [*Nepal*] [*ICAO location identifier*] (ICLI) ... VNRK
Rule ... R
Rule for Court-Martial [*Military*] (INF) ... RCM
Rule In (DAVI) ... R/I
Rule Industries, Inc. [*NASDAQ symbol*] (NQ) ... RULE
Rule Industries, Inc. [*Associated Press*] (SAG) ... RuleInd
Rule Making [*Nuclear energy*] (NRCH) ... RM
Rule of Thumb ... ROT
Rule Oriented System for Implementing Expertise (MCD) ... ROSIE
Rule Out [*Medicine*] ... R/O
Rule Out Myocardial Infarction [*Medicine*] ... ROMI
Rule Resources Ltd. [*Vancouver Stock Exchange symbol*] ... RUL
Rule Then Example [*Computer science*] (BARN) ... RULEG
Rule-Based Expert System (LAIN) ... RBES
Ruled [*Followed by the dates of a monarch's reign*] ... R
Ruled ... RUL
Ruled Feint [*Paper*] (DGA) ... RF
Ruler ... r
Rulers of India [*A publication*] ... RI
Rules and Administration Committee [*US Senate*] ... R & A
Rules and Procedures (MSA) ... R & P
Rules and Regulations (IAA) ... RAR
Rules Committee [*House of Representatives*] (OICC) ... RC
Rules for Admission to Practice [*A publication*] (DLA) ... RAP
Rules for the Discipline of Attorneys [*A publication*] (DLA) ... RDA
Rules of Bankruptcy and Official Forms [*A publication*] (DLA) ... Bankr R
Rules of Bankruptcy and Official Forms [*A publication*] (DLA) ... Bankr Rule
Rules of Engagement [*Military*] (AABC) ... ROE
Rules of Engagement Exercise (DOMA) ... ROEX
Rules of Pleading, Practice, and Procedure [*A publication*] (DLA) ... RPPP
Rules of Practice in Patent Cases [*A publication*] (DLA) ... R Prac Patent Cases
Rules of Practice in Patent Cases [*A publication*] ... RPC
Rules of Practices and Procedure ... RPP
Rules of Procedure ... RP
Rules of the Air (AFM) ... ROA
Rules of the Air and Air Traffic Control [*ICAO Air Navigation Commission*] ... RAC
Rules of the American Stock Exchange [*A publication*] (DLA) ... Am Stock Exch Rules
Rules of the Supreme Court [*A publication*] (DLA) ... RSC
Rules of the Supreme Court [*A publication*] (DLA) ... Rules Sup Ct
Rules of the Supreme Court, Order [*Number*] (ILCA) ... RSCO
Rules on Appeal [*A publication*] (DLA) ... RA
Rules Peculiar to the Business of the Supreme Court [*A publication*] (DLA) ... RPBSC
Rules, Regulations, and By-Laws under New Zealand Statutes [*A publication*] (DLA) ... NZR Regs & B
Rules, Standards and Instruction (IAA) ... RSAI
Rules, Standards, and Instructions ... RS & I
Ruling Case Law ... RCL
Ruling Cases [*A publication*] (DLA) ... RC
Ruling Date [*IRS*] ... RD
Rulings Information System, Excise [*Revenue Canada - Customs and Excise*] [*Information service or system*] (CRD) ... RISE
Rulings of the Judicial Panel on Multidistrict Litigation [*A publication*] (DLA) ... Jud Pan Mult Lit
Rum (ROG) ... R
Rum River Vocational Center, Mora, MN [*Library symbol*] [*Library of Congress*] (LCLS) ... MnMrR
Rum, Romanism, and Rebellion [*Phrase coined during the Presidential campaign of 1884 to describe the Democratic party*] ... RRR
Rumangabo [*Zaire*] [*Seismograph station code, US Geological Survey*] (SEIS) ... RUM
Rumania ... RUM
Rumania (VRA) ... Rum
Rumanian National Committee [*Later, Romanian National Tourist Office*] (EA) ... RNC
Rumbek [*Sudan*] [*ICAO location identifier*] (ICLI) ... HSMK
Rumbo Tools for Visual Bask [*Computer science*] ... RTVB
Rumex Acetosa Polysaccharide [*Antineoplastic drug*] ... RA-P
Rumford, ME [*AM radio station call letters*] ... WRUM
Rumford, ME [*FM radio station call letters*] ... WWMR
Ruminant ... RUMIN
Rumjartar [*Nepal*] [*Airport symbol Obsolete*] (OAG) ... RUM
Rumjatar [*Nepal*] [*ICAO location identifier*] (ICLI) ... VNRT
Rumoi [*Japan*] [*Seismograph station code, US Geological Survey*] (SEIS) ... RMJ
Rumor Intelligence ... RUMINT
Rumrill-Hoyt Corp., Library, Rochester, NY [*OCLC symbol*] (OCLC) ... RVG
Rumsey Municipal Library, Alberta [*Library symbol National Library of Canada*] (NLC) ... ARUM
Rumsey Municipal Library, Rumsey, AB, Canada [*Library symbol Library of Congress*] (LCLS) ... CaARuM
Rumsford Sandy Loam [*Type of soil*] ... RSL
Run [*Distance sailed from noon to noon*] [*Navy British*] (ROG) ... R
Run [*Postal Service standard*] (OPSA) ... RUN
Run Back [*Typography*] ... RB
Run Cutting and Scheduling (DICI) ... Rucus
Run Down [*Typography*] ... RD
Run Executive [*Computer science*] ... REX
Run Identification [*Computer science*] ... RUNID
Run Length [*Computer science*] ... RL
Run Length/Amplitude [*Computer science*] ... RLA
Run Length Coding ... RLC
Run Length Discriminator (MCD) ... RLD
Run Like Hell [*Slang*] ... RLH
Run Occurrence Number (IAA) ... RON
Run of Book [*Advertising*] (WDMC) ... ROB
Run of Kiln ... RK
Run of Mine ... ROM
Run of Paper [*Business term*] ... ROP
Run of Press [*i.e., on an unspecified page or plate in web press set-up*] [*Printing*] ... ROP
Run of Publication (NTCM) ... ROP
Run of Reel [*Broadcasting*] (WDMC) ... ror
Run of Schedule [*Commercial announcement to be broadcast throughout the program schedule*] [*Advertising*] ... ROS
Run on Bank (MHDB) ... ROB
Run Round [*Typography*] (DGA) ... R/R
Run to Cladding Breach [*Nuclear energy*] (NRCH) ... RTCB
Run Unit (NITA) ... RU
Runaway Hotline (EA) ... RH
Runaway Inflation (MHDB) ... RI
Runaway Rotating Machine ... RRM
Runaway Shop (MHDB) ... RS
Runcible System Duplexer [*Telecommunications*] (IAA) ... RSD
Rundfunk im Amerikanischen Sektor Berlins [*Radio in American Sector*] [*Germany*] ... RIAS
Rundi [*MARC language code Library of Congress*] (LCCP) ... run
Rundu [*Namibia*] [*ICAO location identifier*] (ICLI) ... FARU
Rundu [*Namibia*] [*Airport symbol*] (OAG) ... NDU
Rung Sat Special Zone [*Vietnam*] ... RSSZ
Runge-Kutta Method [*Mathematics*] ... RKM
Runge-Kutta Second Order [*Mathematics*] ... RK II
Runge-Kutta-Nystroem [*Formula*] [*Mathematics*] ... RKN
Runic ... R
Runic [*Language, etc.*] (ROG) ... RU
Run-Length Encoding [*Computer science*] ... RLE
Run-Length-Limited [*Computer science*] ... RLL
Runnell's Reports [*38-56 Iowa*] [*A publication*] (DLA) ... Runn
Runnell's Reports [*38-56 Iowa*] [*A publication*] (DLA) ... Runnell
Runner (MSA) ... RNR
Runner Administration and Computerized Entry Routine [*Computer science*] (MHDI) ... RACER
Running ... RNG
Running Back [*Football*] ... RB
Running Days ... RD
Running Days (ODBW) ... rd
Running Forward ... RF

Running Head [*Printing*] (WDMC) ... RH
Running Light ... RNLT
Running Losses [*Automotive engineering*] ... RL
Running Object Table [*Computer science*] ... ROT
Running Process Word (IAA) ... RPW
Running Program Language [*Computer science*] ... RPL
Running Reverse ... RR
Running, Signal, and Anchor Lights ... RSALT
Running Telltale Light (MSA) ... RTTL
Running Time [*Movies*] (CDAI) ... RT
Running Time Meter (AAG) ... RTM
Running Title ... RT
Running Total (DAVI) ... RT
Running-Down Clause [*Business term*] ... RDC
Runnington on Ejectment [*2nd ed.*] [*1820*] [*A publication*] (DLA) ... Runn Eject
Runnington on Statutes [*A publication*] (DLA) ... Runn Stat
Runnymede Trust [*An association*] (EAIO) ... RT
Runoff Election ... RO
Run-of-Station [*Broadcasting*] (WDMC) ... ROS
Run-On [*Used in correcting manuscripts, etc.*] ... R-O
Runout (MSA) ... RO
Runover [*Publishing*] ... RO
Runs [*scored*] [*Baseball or cricket*] ... R
Runs Batted In [*Baseball*] ... RBI
Runs per Minute (IAA) ... RPM
Runstream [*Computer science*] ... RUN
Run-Time Debugger [*Computer science*] (PCM) ... RTD
Run-Time Debugging Aid (MHDB) ... RDA
Run-Time Debugging Unit (NITA) ... RDA
Run-Time Library [*Interdata*] ... RTL
Runtime Manager [*Computer science*] (PCM) ... RTM
Run-Time Reduction Ratio (MHDB) ... RRR
Runtime Type Information [*Computer science*] (PCM) ... RTTI
Runup and Taxi [*Air Force*] ... RT
Runway [*Aviation*] (DA) ... R
Runway (AABC) ... RNWY
Runway [*Aviation*] ... RW
Runway (AAG) ... RWY
Runway Alignment Indicator [*Aviation*] ... RAI
Runway Alignment Indicator Light [*or Lighting*] [*Aviation*] ... RAIL
Runway Alignment Indicator Light [*or Lighting*] **System** [*Aviation*] (MCD) ... RAILS
Runway Arresting Gear [*Aviation*] ... RAG
Runway Capacity to Serve the South East [*Airport planning group*] [*British*] (ECON) ... RUCATSE
Runway Center Line Lights [*ICAO designator*] (FAAC) ... RCLL
Runway Centerline [*Aviation*] ... RCL
Runway Centerline Light System [*FAA*] (TAG) ... RCLS
Runway Centerline Marking [*Aviation*] ... RCLM
Runway Condition Reading [*FAA*] (TAG) ... RCR
Runway Condition Reading [*Aviation*] (FAAC) ... RCR
Runway Delay Simulation Model [*FAA*] (TAG) ... RDSIM
Runway Duty Officer [*Aviation*] (MCD) ... RDO
Runway Edge Light [*ICAO designator*] (FAAC) ... REDL
Runway End Light [*Aviation*] (FAAC) ... RENL
Runway End Safety Area [*Aviation*] (DA) ... RESA
Runway Friction Measurement [*Aviation*] ... RFM
Runway Friction Measurement Test [*Aviation*] ... RFMT
Runway Guard Light [*Aviation*] (DA) ... RGL
Runway Identifiers and Approach Lighting [*Aviation*] (IAA) ... RIAL
Runway Identifiers with Glide Slope [*Aviation*] ... RIGS
Runway Lead-In Lighting System [*Aviation*] (FAAC) ... RLLS
Runway Light [*Aviation*] (DA) ... RL
Runway Lights [*Aviation*] (AIA) ... RNY
Runway Occupancy Time [*FAA*] (TAG) ... ROT
Runway Protection Zone [*FAA*] (TAG) ... RPZ
Runway Reference Point Downwind [*Aviation*] (FAAC) ... RRPD
Runway Reference Point Upwind [*Aviation*] (FAAC) ... RRPU
Runway Remaining Lights [*Aviation*] ... RRL
Runway Safety Area [*FAA*] (TAG) ... RSA
Runway Status Light System [*FAA*] (TAG) ... RSLS
Runway Supervisory [*MTMC*] (TAG) ... RSU
Runway Supervisory Officer [*Aviation*] (MCD) ... RSO
Runway Supervisory Unit [*Aviation*] (FAAC) ... RSU
Runway Surface Condition [*Aviation*] (MCD) ... RSC
Runway Surface Condition [*Aviation*] (FAAC) ... RSCD
Runway Threshold Light [*Aviation*] (FAAC) ... RTHL
Runway Touchdown Zone Light [*Aviation*] (FAAC) ... RTZL
Runway Visibility [*Aviation*] (AFM) ... RV
Runway Visibility Values [*Aviation*] ... RVV
Runway Vision Range System [*Aviation*] (DWSG) ... RVRS
Runway Visual Range [*Aviation*] ... RVR
Runway Visual Range Center [*Aviation*] (DA) ... RVRC
Runway Visual Range Midpoint [*Aviation*] ... RVRM
Runway Visual Range Not Available [*Aviation*] (FAAC) ... RVVNO
Runway Visual Range Rollout [*Aviation*] (FAAC) ... RVRR
Runway Visual Range Rollout Not Available [*Aviation*] (FAAC) ... RVRRNO
Runway Visual Range Touchdown [*Aviation*] (FAAC) ... RVRT
Runway Visual Range Touchdown Not Available [*Aviation*] (FAAC) ... RVRTNO
Runway-End Identification [*Aviation*] (NASA) ... REI
Runway-End Identification Lights [*Aviation*] ... REIL
Runway-End Lighting [*Aviation*] ... RUNEL
Ruoms [*France ICAO location identifier*] (ICLI) ... LFHF
Rupee [*Monetary unit*] [*Ceylon, India, and Pakistan*] ... R
Rupee [*Monetary unit*] [*Ceylon, India, and Pakistan*] ... RE
Rupees [*Monetary unit*] [*Ceylon, India, and Pakistan*] (ROG) ... RX
Rupees, Annas, Pies [*Monetary units*] [*India*] ... RAP
Rupert House [*Canada*] [*Airport symbol*] (OAG) ... YKQ
Rupert, ID [*AM radio station call letters*] ... KBBK
Rupert, ID [*FM radio station call letters*] ... KKMV
Rupert Journal [*A publication*] ... Rupert J
Rupert Newsletter [*A publication*] ... Rupert Newsl
Rupert, VT [*FM radio station call letters*] ... WMNV
Rupert, WV [*AM radio station call letters*] ... WYKM
Rupertsland Resources Co. Ltd. [*Toronto Stock Exchange symbol*] ... RUP
Rupiah [*Monetary unit*] [*Indonesia*] ... RP
Rupsi [*India*] [*Airport symbol*] (AD) ... RUP
Rupsi [*India*] [*ICAO location identifier*] (ICLI) ... VERU
Rupture (NASA) ... RUPT
Rupture Delivery Interval [*Obstetrics*] ... RDI
Rupture Disk (KSC) ... RD
Rupture of Membranes [*Medicine*] ... ROM
Rupture of the Bag of Waters [*Medicine*] (DMAA) ... RBOW
Ruptured ... RPTD
Ruptured Interventricular Septum [*Medicine*] (AAMN) ... RIVS
Ruptured Lumbar Disc [*Medicine*] ... RLD
Ruptured Membrane [*Medicine*] ... RM
Rural (MCD) ... R
Rural ... Ru
Rural ... RUR
Rural Abandoned Mine Program [*Department of Agriculture*] ... RAMP
Rural Adjustment and Finance Corp. of Western Australia [*Computer science*] ... RAFCWA
Rural Advancement Foundation International ... RAFI
Rural Advancement Fund International [*Later, RAFI-USA*] (EA) ... RAFI
Rural America, Inc. (EA) ... RAI
Rural American Women (EA) ... RAW
Rural and Industrial Development Authority (NADA) ... RIDA
Rural and Industries Bank of Western Australia ... R & IBWA
Rural and Industries Bank of Western Australia [*Commercial firm*] ... RIB
Rural and Remote Area ... RARA
Rural Area Redevelopment ... RAR
Rural Areas Development ... RAD
Rural Arts and Crafts Association [*Defunct*] (EA) ... RACA
Rural Assistance Authority [*New South Wales, Australia*] ... RAA
Rural Automatic Exchange (DEN) ... RAX
Rural Automatic Exchange [*Telecommunications*] (TEL) ... RURAX
Rural Bank (ADA) ... RB
Rural Cellular 'A' [*NASDAQ symbol*] (TTSB) ... RCCC
Rural Cellular Corp. [*NASDAQ symbol*] (SAG) ... RCCC
Rural Cellular Corp. [*Associated Press*] (SAG) ... RuralCel
Rural Civil Defense ... RCD
Rural Civil Defense Education Program ... RCDEP
Rural Clean Water Program [*Department of Agriculture*] ... RCWP
Rural Coalition (EA) ... RC
Rural Community Assistance Program (EA) ... RCAP
Rural Community Development Service [*Abolished, 1970*] [*Department of Agriculture*] ... RCDS
Rural Concentrated Employment Program [*Department of Labor*] ... RCEP
Rural Construction ... RC
Rural Construction Cadre [*Military*] ... RCC
Rural Cooperative and Recovery Act (OICC) ... RCRA
Rural Cooperative Housing ... RCH
Rural Cooperative Power Association ... RCPA
Rural Counselling Program [*Australia*] ... RCP
Rural Crafts Association [*British*] (DBA) ... RCA
Rural Deacon [*or Deaconry*] [*Church of England*] ... RD
Rural Dean [*Church of England*] ... RD
Rural Deanery [*Church of England*] ... RDN
Rural Delivery ... RD
Rural Development ... RD
Rural Development Abstracts [*Database*] [*Commonwealth Bureau of Agricultural Economics*] [*Information service or system*] (CRD) ... RDA
Rural Development Act [*1972*] (OICC) ... RDA
Rural Development Administration [*AEC*] ... RDA
Rural Development and Conservation [*Department of Agriculture*] ... RDC
Rural Development Board [*British*] ... RDB
Rural Development Centre [*University of New England, Australia*] ... RDC
Rural Development Insurance Fund [*Farmers Home Administration*] [*Department of Agriculture*] (GFGA) ... RDIF
Rural Development Service [*Department of Agriculture*] ... RDS
Rural Development Society (NADA) ... RDS
Rural District ... RD
Rural District Council [*British*] ... RDC
Rural District Council Executive Officer [*British*] ... RDCEO
Rural District Councils Association [*British*] ... RDCA
Rural District Memorial Library, Badgers Quay, Newfoundland [*Library symbol National Library of Canada*] (NLC) ... NFBQ
Rural District Memorial Library, Badgers Quay, NF, Canada [*Library symbol Library of Congress*] (LCLS) ... CaNfBQ
Rural Doctors' Association of Australia ... RDAA
Rural Economics Institute (OICC) ... REI
Rural Education and Small Schools [*Educational Resources Information Center (ERIC) Clearinghouse*] [*Appalachia University*] (PAZ) ... RC
Rural Education Association [*Later, NREA*] (EA) ... REA
Rural Educational and Development Association [*Canada*] ... REDA
Rural Electric Association (IAA) ... REA
Rural Electrification ... RE
Rural Electrification Administration [*Department of Agriculture*] ... REA
Rural Electrification Administration. Bulletin [*A publication*] (DLA) ... REA Bull

Rural Electrification and Telephone Revolving Fund [*Department of Agriculture*] .... RETRF
Rural Employment Action and Counseling Help [*Project*] .... REACH
Rural Enterprises Community Action Program .... RECAP
Rural Environment Planning Association [*Australia*] .... REPA
Rural Environmental Assistance Program [*Department of Agriculture*] .... REAP
Rural Environmental Conservation Program .... RECP
Rural Extension, Education and Training Abstracts [*Database*] [*Commonwealth Bureau of Agricultural Economics*] [*Information service or system*] (CRD) .... REETA
Rural Finance Council of Victoria [*Australia*] .... RFCV
Rural Financial Market .... RFM
Rural Fire Service [*Australia*] .... RFS
Rural Forestry Assistance [*Program*] [*Forest Service*] .... RFA
Rural Free Delivery [*of mail*] .... RFD
Rural Governments Coalition [*Defunct*] (EA) .... RGC
Rural Health Clinic [*Department of Health and Human Services*] (GFGA) .... RHC
Rural Health Initiative [*Medicine*] (DMAA) .... RHI
Rural Health Program [*Military*] (CINC) .... RHP
Rural Housing Alliance [*Later, RAI*] (EA) .... RHA
Rural Housing Assistance for Aborigines Program [*Australia*] .... RHAAP
Rural Housing Authority [*Western Australia*] .... RHA
Rural Housing Disaster .... RHD
Rural Housing Insurance Fund [*Department of Agriculture*] (GFGA) .... RHIF
Rural Industrial Technical Assistance [*Latin American building program*] ...... RITA
Rural Industrialization Program [*Department of Agriculture*] .... RIP
Rural Industries Bureau .... RIB
Rural Industry Council of Australia .... RICA
Rural Information Center [*Department of Agriculture Information service or system*] (IID) .... RIC
Rural Innovation Centre [*Western Australia*] .... RIC
Rural Institutions and Services Division [*FAO*] .... RISD
Rural Land Alliance (EA) .... RLA
Rural Land Protection Board [*Australia*] .... RLPB
Rural Letter Carriers' Association (NADA) .... RLCA
Rural Life, Kanawha, IA [*Library symbol Library of Congress*] (LCLS) .... IaKanRL
Rural Manpower Center [*Michigan State University*] .... RMC
Rural Manpower Development Program .... RMDP
Rural Manpower Services (OICC) .... RMS
Rural Marketing and Supply Association [*Australia*] .... RMSA
Rural Metro Corp. [*Associated Press*] (SAG) .... RuralMet
Rural Metro Corp. [*NASDAQ symbol*] (SAG) .... RURL
Rural Ministry Institute (EA) .... RMI
Rural Municipality (DLA) .... RM
Rural Municipality of Argyle Public Library, Baldur, Manitoba [*Library symbol National Library of Canada*] (NLC) .... MBA
Rural Municipality of Argyle Public Library, Baldur, MB, Canada [*Library symbol*] [*Library of Congress*] (LCLS) .... CaMBa
Rural Music Schools Association [*British*] .... RMSA
Rural Oxidants in the Southern Environment (USDC) .... ROSE
Rural Oxidants in the Southern Environment [*Marine science*] (OSRA) .... ROSE
Rural Pharmacists Association [*British*] (DBA) .... RPA
Rural Political Cadre [*Vietnam*] .... RPC
Rural Population File (MCD) .... RURPOP
Rural Practice Project [*An association Defunct*] (EA) .... RPP
Rural Preservation Association [*British*] .... RPA
Rural Press Club [*Queensland, Australia*] .... RPCQ
Rural Press Club of Victoria [*Australia*] .... RPCV
Rural Press Club of Western Australia .... RPCWA
Rural Primary Care Hospital .... RPCH
Rural Referral Center [*Health care*] .... RRC
Rural/Regional Education Association (AEE) .... R/REA
Rural Rehabilitation Technologies Database [*University of North Dakota*] [*Information service or system*] (IID) .... RRTD
Rural Rental Housing [*Loans*] [*Farmers Home Administration*] .... RRH
Rural Resident (OICC) .... RR
Rural Retreat, VA [*AM radio station call letters*] .... WCRR
Rural Retreat, VA [*FM radio station call letters*] .... WXBX
Rural Route .... RR
Rural Sanitary Authority [*British*] .... RSA
Rural Satellite Program [*US Agency for International Development*] [*Washington, DC*] [*Telecommunications*] (TSSD) .... RSP
Rural School Development Program [*Australia*] .... RSDP
Rural Service Center [*Agency for International Development*] .... RSC
Rural Sociological Society (EA) .... RSS
Rural Southern Voice for Peace [*An association*] (EA) .... RSVP
Rural Student Vocational Program [*Washington*] (EDAC) .... RSVP
Rural Suboffice [*British*] .... RSO
Rural Technical Assistance Program [*Department of Transportation*] .... RTAP
Rural Telephone Bank [*Department of Agriculture*] .... RTB
Rural Telephone System [*Telecommunications*] (OA) .... RTS
Rural Texas Domestic Violence Health Professionals Education Program (EDAC) .... RTDVHPEP
Rural Training Council of Australia .... RTCA
Rural Training Council of Victoria [*Australia*] .... RTCV
Rural Training Council of Western Australia .... RTCWA
Rural Uplook Service [*Ithaca, NY*] .... RUS
Rural Workers Accommodation Advisory Committee [*New South Wales, Australia*] .... RWAAC
Rural Youth Corps [*Defunct*] (EA) .... RYC
Rural Youth Movement of South Australia .... RYMSA
Rural Youth Organisation of New South Wales [*Australia*] .... RYONSW
Rural Youth Organisation of Queensland [*Australia*] .... RYOQ
Rural Youth Organisation of Tasmania [*Australia*] .... RYOT
Ruritan National (EA) .... RN

Rurrenabaque [*Bolivia*] [*Airport symbol*] (OAG) .... RBQ
Rurrenabaque [*Bolivia*] [*ICAO location identifier*] (ICLI) .... SLRQ
Rurutu [*French Polynesia*] [*ICAO location identifier*] (ICLI) .... NTAR
Rurutu Island [*French Polynesia*] [*Airport symbol*] (OAG) .... RUR
Rusaerolizing Airling [*Former USSR*] [*FAA designator*] (FAAC) .... KVM
Rusangu [*Zambia*] [*ICAO location identifier*] (ICLI) .... FLRG
Rusape [*Zimbabwe*] [*ICAO location identifier*] (ICLI) .... FVRU
Rush [*on teletype messages*] .... RX
Rush and Run (WDAA) .... RR
Rush & Tomkins [*Commercial firm British*] .... R & T
Rush City Elementary School, Rush City, MN [*Library symbol*] [*Library of Congress*] (LCLS) .... MnRcE
Rush City High School, Rush City, MN [*Library symbol*] [*Library of Congress*] (LCLS) .... MnRcH
Rush City Public Library, Rush City, MN [*Library symbol*] [*Library of Congress*] (LCLS) .... MnRc
Rush County Recorder's Office, Rushville, IN [*Library symbol Library of Congress*] (LCLS) .... InRusCR
Rush Enterprises, Inc. [*NASDAQ symbol*] (SAG) .... RUSH
Rush Enterprises, Inc. [*Associated Press*] (SAG) .... RushEnt
Rush Medical College, Chicago, IL [*Library symbol Library of Congress*] (LCLS) .... ICRM
Rush Medicine College (GAGS) .... Rush Med C
Rush Order Service .... ROS
Rush Release .... RR
Rush University, Chicago, IL [*OCLC symbol*] (OCLC) .... IDL
Rush Ventures, Inc. [*Vancouver Stock Exchange symbol*] .... REY
Rushford, MN [*FM radio station call letters*] .... KWNO
Rushlight Club (EA) .... RC
Rushmore Elementary School, Carle Place, NY [*Library symbol*] [*Library of Congress*] (LCLS) .... NCpRE
Rushmore Memorial Library, Highland Mills, NY [*Library symbol Library of Congress*] (LCLS) .... NHigm
Rushville, IL [*FM radio station call letters*] .... WKXQ
Rushville, IN [*FM radio station call letters*] .... WRCR
Rushville Republican, Rushville, IN [*Library symbol Library of Congress*] (LCLS) .... InRusR
Rushworth's Historical Collections [*A publication*] (DLA) .... Rushw
Rusk Manufacturers Association [*British*] (DBA) .... RMA
Rusk, TX [*AM radio station call letters*] .... KTLU
Rusk, TX [*FM radio station call letters*] .... KWRW
Ruskin Developments Ltd. [*Vancouver Stock Exchange symbol*] .... RKL
Russ Berrie & Co. [*NYSE symbol*] (SPSG) .... RUS
Russ Berrie & Co., Inc. [*Associated Press*] (SAG) .... RussBer
Russe [*Bulgaria*] [*Airport symbol*] (OAG) .... ROU
Russel Viper Serum Time [*Clinical chemistry*] .... RVST
Russell and Chesley's Nova Scotia Equity Cases [*A publication*] (DLA) .... Rus & C Eq Cas
Russell and Chesley's Nova Scotia Equity Cases [*A publication*] (DLA) .... Russ & C Eq Cas
Russell and Chesley's Nova Scotia Equity Reports [*A publication*] (DLA) .... R & C
Russell and Chesley's Nova Scotia Equity Reports [*A publication*] (DLA) .... Russ & Ches Eq
Russell and Chesley's Nova Scotia Equity Reports [*A publication*] (DLA) .... Russ & Eq
Russell and Chesley's Nova Scotia Reports [*A publication*] (DLA) .... NRR & C
Russell and Chesley's Nova Scotia Reports [*10-12 Nova Scotia Reports*] [*1875-79*] [*A publication*] (DLA) .... NSRR & C
Russell and Chesley's Nova Scotia Reports [*A publication*] (DLA) .... R & C
Russell and Chesley's Nova Scotia Reports [*A publication*] (DLA) ...... R & C N Sc
Russell and Chesley's Nova Scotia Reports [*10-12 Nova Scotia Reports*] [*1875-79*] [*A publication*] (DLA) .... Russ & C
Russell and Chesley's Nova Scotia Reports [*A publication*] (DLA) ...... Russ & Ches
Russell and District Regional Library, Russell, Manitoba [*Library symbol National Library of Canada*] (NLC) .... MRD
Russell and District Regional Library, Russell, MB, Canada [*Library symbol Library of Congress*] (LCLS) .... CaMRD
Russell & Dumoulin, Vancouver, British Columbia [*Library symbol National Library of Canada*] (NLC) .... BVARD
Russell and Geldert's Nova Scotia Reports [*A publication*] (DLA) .... NSRR & G
Russell and Geldert's Nova Scotia Reports [*A publication*] (DLA) .... R & G
Russell and Geldert's Nova Scotia Reports [*A publication*] (DLA) ...... R & G N Sc
Russell and Geldert's Nova Scotia Reports [*13-27 Nova Scotia Reports*] [*1879-95*] [*Canada*] [*A publication*] (DLA) .... Russ & G
Russell and Geldert's Nova Scotia Reports [*A publication*] (DLA) ...... Russ & Geld
Russell and Mylne's English Chancery Reports [*A publication*] (DLA) .... R & M
Russell and Mylne's English Chancery Reports [*A publication*] (DLA) ...... R & My
Russell and Mylne's English Chancery Reports [*1829-33*] [*A publication*] (DLA) .... Russ & M
Russell and Mylne's English Chancery Reports [*1829-33*] [*A publication*] (DLA) .... Russ & My
Russell and Ryan's English Crown Cases [*A publication*] (DLA) .... R & R
Russell and Ryan's English Crown Cases [*A publication*] (DLA) .... R & Ry CC
Russell and Ryan's English Crown Cases Reserved [*A publication*] (DLA) .... R & RCC
Russell and Ryan's English Crown Cases Reserved [*1799-1823*] [*A publication*] (DLA) .... Russ & R
Russell and Ryan's English Crown Cases Reserved [*A publication*] (DLA) .... Russ & R Cr Cas
Russell and Ryan's English Crown Cases Reserved [*168 English Reprint*] [*1799-1823*] [*A publication*] (DLA) .... Russ & RCC
Russell and Ryan's English Crown Cases Reserved [*1799-1823*] [*A publication*] (DLA) .... Russ & RCC (Eng)

Russell and Ryan's English Crown Cases Reserved [*A publication*] (DLA) ..... Russ & Ry
Russell Bodies [*Medicine*] ..... RB
Russell Branch, Russell Township Public Library, Ontario [*Library symbol National Library of Canada*] (BIB) ..... ORU
Russell Cave National Monument ..... RUCA
Russell Corp. [*NYSE symbol*] (SPSG) ..... RML
Russell Corp. [*Associated Press*] (SAG) ..... Russell
Russell, KS [*FM radio station call letters*] ..... KCAY
Russell, KS [*AM radio station call letters*] ..... KRSL
Russell, KS [*Location identifier FAA*] (FAAL) ..... RSL
Russell Memorial Library, Acuhnet, MA [*Library symbol*] [*Library of Congress*] (LCLS) ..... MAc
Russell Metals Cv'A' [*NASDAQ symbol*] (TTSB) ..... RUSAF
Russell Metals, Inc. [*NASDAQ symbol*] (SAG) ..... RUSAF
Russell Metals, Inc. [*Associated Press*] (SAG) ..... RussMtl
Russell on Arbitrators [*A publication*] (DLA) ..... Russ Arb
Russell on Crime [*12th ed.*] [*1964*] [*A publication*] (DLA) ..... Russ Crim
Russell on Crimes and Misdemeanors [*A publication*] (DLA) ..... Russ Cr
Russell on Crimes and Misdemeanors [*A publication*] (DLA) ..... Russ Crimes
Russell on Factors and Brokers [*A publication*] (DLA) ..... Russ Fact
Russell on Mercantile Agency [*A publication*] (DLA) ..... Russ Merc Ag
Russell, PA [*FM radio station call letters*] ..... WRLP
Russell Public Library, Middletown, CT [*Library symbol Library of Congress*] (LCLS) ..... CtM
Russell Public Schools, Russell, MN [*Library symbol*] [*Library of Congress*] (LCLS) ..... MnRusPS
Russell Research Center [*Department of Agriculture*] ..... RRC
Russell Sage College [*New York*] ..... RSC
Russell Sage College, Troy, NY [*Library symbol Library of Congress*] (LCLS) ..... NTRS
Russell Sage College, Troy, NY [*OCLC symbol*] (OCLC) ..... ZRS
Russell Sage Social Relations Test [*Psychology*] ..... RSSRT
Russell Senate Office Building [*Also, OSOB*] [*Washington, DC*] (DLA) ..... RSOB
Russell Springs, KY [*FM radio station call letters*] (RBYB) ..... WHVE
Russell Springs, KY [*AM radio station call letters*] (RBYB) ..... WIDS
Russell Township Public Library, Embrun Branch, Embrun, ON, Canada [*Library symbol*] [*Library of Congress*] (LCLS) ..... CaOERT
Russell Viper [*Time*] (MAE) ..... RV
Russell Viper Venom [*Medicine*] (DMAA) ..... RVV
Russell Viper Venom Time [*Medicine*] (DMAA) ..... RVVT
Russell's Contested Election Cases [*Massachusetts*] [*A publication*] (DLA) ..... Mass Election Cases
Russell's Contested Election Cases [*Massachusetts*] [*A publication*] (DLA) ..... Rus EC
Russell's Contested Election Cases [*Massachusetts*] [*A publication*] (DLA) ..... Russ
Russell's Contested Election Cases [*Massachusetts*] [*A publication*] (DLA) ..... Russ Con El (Mass)
Russell's Contested Election Cases [*Massachusetts*] [*A publication*] (DLA) ..... Russ Elect Cas
Russell's Election Cases [*1874*] [*Nova Scotia*] [*A publication*] (DLA) ..... Rus
Russell's Election Cases [*1874*] [*Nova Scotia*] [*A publication*] (DLA) ..... Rus Elec Rep
Russell's Election Cases [*1874*] [*Nova Scotia*] [*A publication*] (DLA) ..... Rus ER
Russell's Election Cases [*1874*] [*Nova Scotia*] [*A publication*] (DLA) ..... Russ
Russell's Election Cases [*1874*] [*Nova Scotia*] [*A publication*] (DLA) ..... Russ El Cas
Russell's Election Cases [*Nova Scotia*] [*A publication*] (DLA) ..... Russ Elect Cas
Russell's English Chancery Reports [*A publication*] (DLA) ..... Rus
Russell's English Chancery Reports [*A publication*] (DLA) ..... Russ
Russell's English Chancery Reports [*A publication*] (DLA) ..... Russ Ch
Russell's English Chancery Reports Tempore Elden [*A publication*] (DLA) ..... Russ T Eld
Russell's Irish Election Reports [*A publication*] (DLA) ..... Rus EC
Russell's Nova Scotia Equity Cases [*A publication*] (DLA) ..... Russ Eq
Russell's Nova Scotia Equity Cases [*A publication*] (DLA) ..... Russ Eq Cas
Russell's Nova Scotia Equity Cases [*A publication*] (DLA) ..... Russ N Sc
Russell's Nova Scotia Equity Decisions [*A publication*] (DLA) ..... Rus Eq Rep
Russell's Nova Scotia Equity Decisions [*A publication*] (DLA) ..... Russ Eq Rep
Russell's Nova Scotia Equity Decisions [*A publication*] (DLA) ..... Russell
Russell's Nova Scotia Equity Decisions [*A publication*] (DLA) ..... Russell NS
Russell's Owl Collectors Club (EA) ..... ROCC
Russell-Tyler-Ruthon High School, Tyler, MN [*Library symbol*] [*Library of Congress*] (LCLS) ..... MnTyHS
Russellville, AL [*AM radio station call letters*] ..... WJRD
Russellville, AL [*AM radio station call letters*] ..... WKAX
Russellville, AL [*FM radio station call letters*] ..... WSHK
Russellville, AR [*AM radio station call letters*] ..... KARV
Russellville, AR [*FM radio station call letters*] ..... KMTC
Russellville, AR [*FM radio station call letters*] ..... KXRJ
Russellville, AR [*Location identifier FAA*] (FAAL) ..... RUE
Russellville, KY [*FM radio station call letters*] ..... WJCE
Russellville, KY [*AM radio station call letters*] ..... WRUS
Russet ..... RUSS
Russet-Burbank Potato ..... RB
Russia ..... RUS
Russia (VRA) ..... Rus
Russia ..... RUSS
Russian [*MARC language code Library of Congress*] (LCCP) ..... rus
Russian Academy Of Sciences ..... RAS
Russian Air [*To distinguish call-signs and frequencies*] [*World War II British*] ..... RA
Russian American ..... RA
Russian and East European Institute [*Indiana University*] [*Research center*] (RCD) ..... REEI
Russian and East European Studies Area Program [*University of Pittsburgh*] [*Research center*] (RCD) ..... REES
Russian and Japanese Prize Cases [*London*] [*A publication*] (DLA) ..... Russ & Jap PC
Russian Aviation Trade [*House*] [*Russia; established in 1991*] (DOMA) ..... RATD
Russian Brotherhood Organization (NADA) ..... RBO
Russian Brotherhood Organization of the United States of America ..... RBO
Russian Brotherhood Organization of the USA (EA) ..... RBOUSA
Russian Children's Welfare Society - Outside of Russia (EA) ..... RCWS
Russian Commodity and Raw Materials Exchange [*Russian Federation*] (EY) ..... RCME
Russian Communist Party (Bolsheviks) [*Political party*] ..... RCP(b)
Russian Consolidated Mutual Aid Society of America (EA) ..... RCMASA
Russian Corps Combatants (EA) ..... RCC
Russian Dictionary [*A publication*] ..... RUSDIC
[*A*] **Russian digital computer** [*Moscow University*] ..... MINSK
Russian Foundation for Basic Research ..... RFBR
Russian Historical and Genealogical Society in America [*Later, RNAA*] (EA) ..... RHGSA
Russian Human Genome Project ..... RHGP
Russian Hydrometeorological Institute [*Marine science*] (OSRA) ..... RSHMI
Russian Immigrants' Representative Association In America ..... RIRAA
Russian Independent Mutual Aid Society (EA) ..... RIMAS
Russian Information and Communications Agency (IID) ..... RUSSICA
Russian Information Telegraph Agency [*Formerly, TASS*] ..... RITA
Russian Intelligence Service ..... RIS
Russian Mendeleev Chemical Society ..... RMCS
Russian Military [*World War II*] ..... RM
Russian Mission [*Alaska*] [*Airport symbol*] (OAG) ..... RSH
Russian Nobility Association in America (EA) ..... RNAA
Russian Numismatic Society (EA) ..... RNS
Russian Obuckhoff Rifle ..... RO
Russian Orchestra of the Americas ..... ROA
Russian Orthodox Catholic Mutual Aid Society of USA (EA) ..... ROCMAS
Russian Orthodox Catholic Women's Mutual Aid Society (EA) ..... ROCWMAS
Russian Orthodox Fraternity Lubov (EA) ..... ROFL
Russian Orthodox Theological Fund (EA) ..... ROTF
Russian People's Center (EA) ..... RPC
Russian Pharmacopoeia [*A publication*] ..... Rus P
Russian Privatization Center (ECON) ..... RPC
Russian Research Center [*Harvard University*] [*Research center*] (RCD) ..... RRC
Russian Review [*A publication*] (BRI) ..... Russ Rev
Russian SFSR [*MARC geographic area code Library of Congress*] (LCCP) ..... e-ur-ru
Russian SFSR [*MARC country of publication code Library of Congress*] (LCCP) ..... rur
Russian Social-Democratic Labor Party [*Political party*] ..... RSDLP
Russian Social-Democratic Labor Party (Bolsheviks) [*Political party*] ..... RSDLP(B)
Russian Social-Democratic Workers Party ..... RSDWP
Russian Soviet Federated Socialist Republic ..... RSFSR
Russian Space Agency ..... RSA
Russian Spring-Summer Encephalitis [*Medicine*] (MAH) ..... RSS
Russian Spring-Summer Encephalitis [*Medicine*] ..... RSSE
Russian Student Fund [*Defunct*] (EA) ..... RSF
Russian Television Network ..... RTN
Russian Text Analyzer ..... RUSTAN
Russian, Ukrainian, and Belorussian Newspapers [*A bibliographic publication*] ..... RUBN
Russian Underground Nuclear Test (MCD) ..... RUNT
Russian-American Institute for President Programs [*For technology transfer*] ..... RIPP
Russian-Spanish Dictionary [*A publication*] (SAA) ..... RUSPAND
Russkiy Obshche-Voyenskiy Soyuz [*Russian Armed Forces Union*] (LAIN) ..... ROVS
Russko-Jewrejsky Archiw [*A publication*] (BJA) ..... RJA
Rust and Oxidation (DNAB) ..... RO
Rust College, Holly Springs, MS [*Library symbol Library of Congress*] (LCLS) ..... MsHosR
Rust College, Holly Springs, MS [*OCLC symbol*] (OCLC) ..... RUS
Rust International Rust International, Birmingham, AL [*Library symbol*] [*Library of Congress*] (LCLS) ..... ABRI
Rust Preventative ..... RPVNTV
Rust Prevention Association [*Later, Crop Quality Council*] ..... RPA
Rust Preventive ..... RP
Rustad/Wickhem/Video, Inc. [*Madison, WI*] (TSSD) ..... RWV
Rustenburg [*South Africa*] [*ICAO location identifier*] (ICLI) ..... FARG
Rustication (VRA) ..... rustc
Ruston, LA [*FM radio station call letters*] (RBYB) ..... KAPI-FM
Ruston, LA [*FM radio station call letters*] ..... KLPI
Ruston, LA [*AM radio station call letters*] ..... KRUS
Ruston, LA [*FM radio station call letters*] ..... KXKZ
Ruston, LA [*Location identifier FAA*] (FAAL) ..... LPZ
Ruston, LA [*Location identifier FAA*] (FAAL) ..... RSN
Rustproof (MSA) ..... RSTPF
Ruta [*Rue*] [*Pharmacy*] (ROG) ..... RUT
Rutas Aereas, CA [*Venezuela*] [*FAA designator*] (FAAC) ..... RUC
Rutas Aereas Nacionales Sociedad Anonima [*Cargo airline*] [*Venezuela*] ..... RANSA
Ruteng [*Indonesia*] [*Airport symbol*] (OAG) ..... RTG
Ruteng/Satartacik [*Indonesia*] [*ICAO location identifier*] (ICLI) ..... WRKG
Rutgers Online Automated Retrieval Service [*Rutgers University*] (OLDSS) ..... ROARS
Rutgers Social Attribute Inventory [*Psychology*] ..... RSAI
Rutgers-[*The*] **State University** [*New Brunswick, NJ*] (PDAA) ..... RU

Rutgers-[*The*] **State University, College of South Jersey, Camden, NJ** [*Library symbol Library of Congress*] (LCLS) ... NjR-S
Rutgers-[*The*] **State University, Graduate School of Library and InformationScience, New Brunswick, NJ** [*OCLC symbol*] (OCLC) ... RUG
Rutgers-[*The*] **State University, Institute of Jazz Studies, Newark, NJ** [*OCLC symbol*] (OCLC) ... IJS
Rutgers-[*The*] **State University, New Brunswick, NJ** [*Library symbol Library of Congress*] (LCLS) ... NjR
Rutgers-[*The*] **State University, Rutgers-Camden School of Law, Camden, NJ** [*Library symbol Library of Congress*] (LCLS) ... NjR-L
Rutgers, The State University, Law School Library-Newark, Newark, NJ [*Library symbol*] [*Library of Congress*] (LCLS) ... NjR-NL
Rutgers University (GAGS) ... Rutgers U
Rutgers University. Law Review [*A publication*] (DLA) ... Rutgers UL Rev
Rutger-Waddington Case [*1784*] [*New York City*] [*A publication*] (DLA) ... Rutg Cas
Ruth [*Old Testament book*] ... RT
Ruth [*Old Testament book*] ... Ru
Ruth [*Nevada*] [*Seismograph station code, US Geological Survey Closed*] (SEIS) ... RUT
Ruth E. Dickinson Branch, Nepean Public Library, Ontario [*Library symbol National Library of Canada*] (BIB) ... ONRDB
Ruth Enlow Library of Garrett County, Oakland, MD [*Library symbol Library of Congress*] (LCLS) ... MdO
Ruth Jackson Society (EA) ... RJS
Ruth Rabbah (BJA) ... Rtr
Ruth Rabbah (BJA) ... RuthR
Ruth Suckhow Memorial Library, Earlville, IA [*Library symbol Library of Congress*] (LCLS) ... IaEarv
Ruthenium [*Chemical element*] ... Ru
Ruthenium Red [*Inorganic chemistry*] (OA) ... RR
Ruthenium Red Staining Layer [*Biology*] ... RRL
Rutherford [*Unit of strength of a radioactive source*] ... rd
Rutherford [*New Jersey*] [*Airport symbol*] (AD) ... RTF
Rutherford and Appleton Laboratory [*Observatory*] [*British*] ... RAL
Rutherford and George Island Township Public Library, Killarney, Ontario [*Library symbol National Library of Canada*] (NLC) ... OKRGI
Rutherford B. Hayes Library, Fremont, OH [*Library symbol Library of Congress*] (LCLS) ... OFH
Rutherford B. Hayes Presidential Center (EA) ... RBHPC
Rutherford Backscattering Spectroscopy ... RBS
Rutherford Birchard Hayes [*US president, 1822-1893*] ... RBH
Rutherford County Library, Inc., Rutherfordton, NC [*Library symbol Library of Congress*] (LCLS) ... NcRuR
Rutherford County Library, Inc., Spindale, NC [*Library symbol*] [*Library of Congress*] (LCLS) ... NcSpiR
Rutherford Free Public Library, Rutherford, NJ [*Library symbol Library of Congress*] (LCLS) ... NjRu
Rutherford High Energy Laboratory (MCD) ... RHEL
Rutherford Institute (EA) ... RI
Rutherford Ion Backscattering [*Medicine*] (DMAA) ... RIBS
Rutherfordium [*Proposed name for chemical element 104*] [*See also Ku*] ... Rf
Rutherford's Institutes of Natural Law [*A publication*] (DLA) ... Ruth Inst
Rutherfordton, NC [*Location identifier FAA*] (FAAL) ... RFE
Rutherfordton, NC [*AM radio station call letters*] ... WCAB
Ruthton Public Schools, Ruthton, MN [*Library symbol*] [*Library of Congress*] (LCLS) ... MnRuPS
Ruthven [*California*] [*Seismograph station code, US Geological Survey*] (SEIS) ... RUN
Ruthven Public Library, Ruthven, IA [*Library symbol Library of Congress*] (LCLS) ... IaRu
Ruthven Zipcode, Ruthven, IA [*Library symbol Library of Congress*] (LCLS) ... IaRuZ
Rutile [*CIPW classification*] [*Geology*] ... ru
Rutile-Paper-Slurry [*Grade of titanium dioxide*] ... RPS
Rutin [*Organic chemistry*] ... RU
Rutland [*Vermont*] [*Airport symbol*] (OAG) ... RUT
Rutland Biotech Ltd. [*Vancouver Stock Exchange symbol*] ... RBT
Rutland Community Library, Rutland, IL [*Library symbol Library of Congress*] (LCLS) ... IRut
Rutland Consolidated Community School District 230, Ottawa, IL [*Library symbol Library of Congress*] (LCLS) ... IOtRSD
Rutland Plains [*Australia Airport symbol Obsolete*] (OAG) ... RTP
Rutland Railway Corp. [*AAR code Terminated*] ... RUT
Rutland, VT [*Location identifier FAA*] (FAAL) ... DYO
Rutland, VT [*Location identifier FAA*] (FAAL) ... IRA
Rutland, VT [*FM radio station call letters*] ... WFTF
Rutland, VT [*FM radio station call letters*] ... WJEN
Rutland, VT [*FM radio station call letters*] ... WJJR
Rutland, VT [*FM radio station call letters*] ... WRVT
Rutland, VT [*AM radio station call letters*] ... WSYB
Rutland, VT [*Television station call letters*] ... WVER
Rutland, VT [*FM radio station call letters*] ... WZRT
Rutlandshire [*County in England*] (ROG) ... RUTD
Rutlandshire [*County in England*] ... RUTLDS
Rutledge College, Fayetteville, NC [*Library symbol Library of Congress*] (LCLS) ... NcFayR
Rutowski Optimization [*Computer program*] ... RUTOP
Rutshuru [*Zaire*] [*ICAO location identifier*] (ICLI) ... FZNC
Rutter Parent Questionnaire ... RPQ
Rutter Teacher Questionnaire ... RTQ
Ruvalcaba-Myhre-Smith Syndrome [*Medicine*] (DMAA) ... RMSS
RV-Aviation [*Finland ICAO designator*] (FAAC) ... RVI
RVNAF [*Republic of Vietnam Air Force*] **Improvement and Modernization Management System** ... RIMMS
Rwanda [*Aircraft nationality and registration mark*] (FAAC) ... 9XR
Rwanda [*MARC geographic area code Library of Congress*] (LCCP) ... f-rw--
Rwanda [*MARC country of publication code Library of Congress*] (LCCP) ... rw
Rwanda [*ANSI two-letter standard code*] (CNC) ... RW
Rwanda [*ANSI three-letter standard code*] (CNC) ... RWA
Rwandan Franc [*Monetary unit*] (IMH) ... RwF
Rwandan Patriotic Front [*Political party*] ... RPF
R-Wave Progression [*On Electrocardiograms*] [*Cardiology*] (DAVI) ... RWP
RX Medical Services [*AMEX symbol*] (TTSB) ... RXM
RX Medical Services [*AMEX symbol*] (SPSG) ... RXM
RX Medical Services Corp. [*Associated Press*] (SAG) ... RX Med
RY Financial Corp. [*Toronto Stock Exchange symbol*] ... XRY
RY II Financial Corp. [*Toronto Stock Exchange symbol*] ... XR
RY NT Financial Corp. [*Toronto Stock Exchange symbol*] ... XRN
Ryan Aeronautical Co., Lindbergh Field, San Diego, CA [*Library symbol Library of Congress*] (LCLS) ... CSdRA
Ryan Air (GAVI) ... XY
Ryan Air Service, Inc. [*FAA designator*] (FAAC) ... RCT
Ryan Air Services, Inc. [*ICAO designator*] (FAAC) ... RYA
Ryan and Moody [*1823-26*] [*A publication*] (DLA) ... Ry & Moo
Ryan and Moody's English Crown Cases [*A publication*] (DLA) ... RMCC
Ryan and Moody's English Crown Cases [*A publication*] (DLA) ... RMCCR
Ryan and Moody's English Crown Cases [*A publication*] (DLA) ... Ry MCC
Ryan and Moody's English Crown Cases Reserved [*A publication*] (DLA) ... R & MCC
Ryan and Moody's English Crown Cases Reserved [*A publication*] (DLA) ... Ry & MCC
Ryan and Moody's English Nisi Prius Reports [*A publication*] (DLA) ... R & M
Ryan and Moody's English Nisi Prius Reports [*A publication*] (DLA) ... R & MNP
Ryan and Moody's English Nisi Prius Reports [*A publication*] (DLA) ... Ry & M
Ryan and Moody's English Nisi Prius Reports [*A publication*] (DLA) ... Ry & MNP
Ryan and Moody's English Nisi Prius Reports [*171 English Reprint*] [*A publication*] (DLA) ... Ryan & M
Ryan and Moody's English Nisi Prius Reports [*171 English Reprint*] [*A publication*] (DLA) ... Ryan & M (Eng)
Ryan Automatic Plot Indicator Device ... RAPID
Ryan Aviation Corp. [*ICAO designator*] (FAAC) ... RYN
Ryan Beck & Co. [*NASDAQ symbol*] (TTSB) ... RBCO
Ryan, Beck & Co., Inc. [*West Orange, NJ*] [*NASDAQ symbol*] (NQ) ... RBCO
Ryan Beck Co., Inc. [*Associated Press*] (SAG) ... RyanBck
Ryan Foundation International [*India*] (EAIO) ... RYFO
Ryan Resources Ltd. [*Vancouver Stock Exchange symbol*] ... RYS
Ryan White National Fund (EA) ... RWNF
Ryanair [*Ireland*] [*ICAO designator*] (FAAC) ... RYR
Ryanodine Receptor [*Genetics*] ... RYR
Ryanodine Receptor Channel [*Biochemistry*] ... RyRC
Ryan's Family Steak Houses, Inc. [*NASDAQ symbol*] (NQ) ... RYAN
Ryans Family Steak Houses, Inc. [*Associated Press*] (SAG) ... RyanF
Ryan's Family Stk Hse [*NASDAQ symbol*] (TTSB) ... RYAN
Ryan's Hope [*Television program*] ... RH
Ryan's Medical Jurisprudence [*A publication*] (DLA) ... Ry Med Jur
Rybachye [*Former USSR Seismograph station code, US Geological Survey*] (SEIS) ... RYB
Rybnik [*Poland*] [*Seismograph station code, US Geological Survey*] (SEIS) ... RBN
Rycroft Municipal Library, Alberta [*Library symbol National Library of Canada*] (NLC) ... ARYM
Rycroft Municipal Library, Rycroft, AB, Canada [*Library symbol*] [*Library of Congress*] (LCLS) ... CaARyM
Rydberg [*Unit of energy*] [*Atomic physics Symbol*] ... ry
Rydberg Constant [*Spectroscopy*] [*Symbol*] (DEN) ... R
Rydberg Constant (IDOE) ... $R_{(00)}$
Ryde and Konstam's Reports of Rating Appeals [*1894-1904*] [*A publication*] (DLA) ... Ryde & K
Ryde and Konstam's Reports of Rating Appeals [*1894-1904*] [*A publication*] (DLA) ... Ryde & K Rat App
Ryde, Newport & Cowes Railway [*British*] ... RN & CR
Ryder System [*NYSE symbol*] (TTSB) ... R
Ryder System, Inc. [*NYSE symbol*] (SPSG) ... R
Ryder Systems, Inc. [*Associated Press*] (SAG) ... Ryder
Ryder Truck Rental ... RTR
Ryde's Rating Appeals [*1871-1904*] [*A publication*] (DLA) ... Ryde
Ryde's Rating Appeals [*1871-1904*] [*A publication*] (DLA) ... Ryde Rat App
Ryde's Rating Cases [*A publication*] (DLA) ... RRC
Rydge's Management Service [*A publication*] ... Rydges Mgmt Serv
Rye Free Reading Room, Rye, NY [*Library symbol Library of Congress*] (LCLS) ... NRy
Rye Historical Society, Rye, NY [*Library symbol Library of Congress*] (LCLS) ... NRyHi
Rye Terms ... RT
Ryegrass Cryptic Virus [*Plant pathology*] ... RCV
Ryegrass Mosaic Virus [*Plant pathology*] ... RGMV
Ryerson Institute, Toronto, ON, Canada [*Library symbol Library of Congress*] (LCLS) ... CaOTR
Ryerson International Development Centre [*Ryerson Polytechnical Institute*] [*Canada Research center*] (RCD) ... RIDC
Ryerson Polytechnical Institute, Toronto, Ontario [*Library symbol National Library of Canada*] (NLC) ... OTR
Ryerson Tull [*NYSE symbol*] (SAG) ... RT
Ryerson Tull [*Associated Press*] (SAG) ... RyerTull
Rygge [*Norway ICAO location identifier*] (ICLI) ... ENRY
Rykoff-Sexton, Inc. [*NYSE symbol*] (SPSG) ... RYK
Rykoff-Sexton, Inc. [*Associated Press*] (SAG) ... Rykoff
Ryland Group [*NYSE symbol*] (TTSB) ... RYL
Ryland Group, Inc. [*NYSE symbol*] (SPSG) ... RYL
Ryland Group, Inc. [*Associated Press*] (SAG) ... Ryland

Ryley Public Library, Alberta [*Library symbol National Library of Canada*] (NLC) .... ARY
Ryley Public Library, Ryley, AB, Canada [*Library symbol*] [*Library of Congress*] (LCLS) .... CaARy
Ryley's Placita Parliamentaria [*1290-1307*] [*England*] [*A publication*] (DLA) .... Ryl Plac Parl
RYMAC Mortgage Investment Corp. [*AMEX symbol*] (CTT) .... RM
Rymac Mortgage Investment Corp. [*Associated Press*] (SAG) .... Rymac
RYMAC Mtge Invest [*AMEX symbol*] (TTSB) .... RM
Ryman [*Office equipment and furniture store chain*] [*British*] .... R
Rymer Foods [*NYSE symbol*] (TTSB) .... RYR
Rymer Foods, Inc. [*Associated Press*] (SAG) .... Rymer
Rymer Foods, Inc. [*NYSE symbol*] (SPSG) .... RYR

Rymer's Foedera [*20 vols.*] [*1704-35*] [*A publication*] (DLA) .... Ry F
Rymer's Foedera [*20 vols.*] [*1704-35*] [*A publication*] (DLA) .... Rym F
Rynes Aviation, Inc. [*ICAO designator*] (FAAC) .... RAA
Ryom [*Catalog of music of Vivaldi*] (BARN) .... R
Ryom-Vivaldi [*Catalog of music of Vivaldi*] (BARN) .... RV
Rytmi [*Record label*] [*Finland*] .... Ryt
Ryukoku University [*UTLAS symbol*] .... RYU
Ryukyu Air Defense System .... RADS
Ryukyu Islands, Southern [*ja (Japan) used in records cataloged after January 1978*] [*MARC country of publication code Library of Congress*] (LCCP) .... ry
Ryukyu Philatelic Specialist Society (EA) .... RPSS
Rzeszow [*Poland*] [*Airport symbol*] (OAG) .... RZE
Rzeszow/Jasionka [*Poland ICAO location identifier*] (ICLI) .... EPRZ

S

By Meaning

S 2 Golf [*NASDAQ symbol*] (TTSB) ... GOLF
S. Allan Taylor Society (EA) ... SATS
S & K Famous Brands [*NASDAQ symbol*] (TTSB) ... SKFB
S & K Famous Brands, Inc. [*Associated Press*] (SAG) ... S K
S & K Famous Brands, Inc. [*NASDAQ symbol*] (NQ) ... SKFB
S & M Photolabels, Inc. [*Toronto Stock Exchange symbol*] ... SMF
S & T Bancorp [*Associated Press*] (SAG) ... S & T Bc
S & T Bancorp [*Associated Press*] (SAG) ... S & T Bcp
S & T Bancorp [*NASDAQ symbol*] (SAG) ... STBA
S. C. Johnson & Son, Inc., Racine, WI [*Library symbol Library of Congress*] (LCLS) ... WRacJ
S. Cornelia Young Memorial Library, Daytona Beach, FL [*Library symbol Library of Congress*] (LCLS) ... FDbY
S. D. Warren [*Paper manufacturer*] ... SDW
'S Gravenhage [*Netherlands ICAO location identifier*] (ICLI) ... EHGV
S I Technologies [*NASDAQ symbol*] (TTSB) ... SISI
S. L. Ross Environmental Research, Ottawa, Ontario [*Library symbol National Library of Canada*] (BIB) ... OOSLR
S Madill Ltd. [*Vancouver Stock Exchange symbol*] ... MDL
S Phase Fraction ... S-PF
S. S. Moyie Museum, Kaslo, British Columbia [*Library symbol National Library of Canada*] (NLC) ... BKSSM
S. S. White Co., Philadelphia, PA [*Library symbol Library of Congress Obsolete*] (LCLS) ... PPWD
S. Summerfield's Reports [*21 Nevada*] [*A publication*] (DLA) ... Summerfield S
S3, Inc. [*Associated Press*] (SAG) ... S3 Inc
S3, Inc. [*NASDAQ symbol*] (SAG) ... SIII
Sa Da Bandeira [*Angola*] [*Seismograph station code, US Geological Survey*] (SEIS) ... SDB
Sa da Bandiera [*Angola*] [*Airport symbol*] (AD) ... SDD
SA Ecuatoriana de Transportes Aereos [*Airline*] [*Ecuador*] ... SAETA
SA Exress Airways [*South Africa*] [*FAA designator*] (FAAC) ... EXY
Sa Grace [*His or Her Grace*] [*French*] ... SG
Sa Grandeur [*His or Her Highness*] [*French*] ... SG
Sa Hautesse [*His, or Her, Highness*] [*French*] ... SH
SA Holdings [*NASDAQ symbol*] (SAG) ... STEL
Sa Majeste Aulique [*His, or Her, Austrian Majesty*] [*French*] (ROG) ... SMA
Sa Majeste Britannique [*His or Her Britannic Majesty*] [*French*] ... SMB
Sa Majeste Catholique [*His or Her Catholic Majesty*] [*of Spain*] [*French*] ... SMC
Sa Majeste Imperiale [*His or Her Imperial Majesty*] [*French*] ... SMI
Sa Majeste Royale [*His, or Her, Royal Majesty*] [*French*] ... SMR
Sa Majeste Suedoise [*His, or Her, Swedish Majesty*] [*French*] (ROG) ... SMS
Sa Majeste Tres Chretienne [*His, or Her, Most Christian Majesty*] [*French*] ... SMTC
Sa Majeste Tres Fidele [*His, or Her, Most Faithful Majesty*] [*French*] ... SMTF
Sa Saintete [*His Holiness*] [*The Pope*] [*French*] ... SS
Sa Seigneurie [*His Lordship*] [*French*] ... SS
SA Telecommunications [*NASDAQ symbol*] (TTSB) ... STEL
SA Telecommunications, Inc. [*Associated Press*] (SAG) ... SA Telcm
SA Telecommunications, Inc. [*NASDAQ symbol*] (SAG) ... STEL
Saab Aircraft AB [*Sweden ICAO designator*] (FAAC) ... SCT
Saab Car Club of Australia ... SCCA
SAAB Club of North America [*SAAB Clubs of America*] [*Acronym is based on former name,*] (EA) ... SCA
Saab Direct Ignition [*Automotive engineering*] ... SDI
SAAB-Fairchild 340 [*Airplane code*] ... Sf3
Saabruecker Beitraege zur Altertumskunde [*Bonn*] [*A publication*] (BJA) ... SBA
SAAB-Scania AB [*Sweden ICAO aircraft manufacturer identifier*] (ICAO) ... MF
SAAB-Scania AB [*Sweden ICAO aircraft manufacturer identifier*] (ICAO) ... SB
Saada [*Yemen*] [*ICAO location identifier*] (ICLI) ... OYSH
Saahaqui [*Bolivia*] [*ICAO location identifier*] (ICLI) ... SLSQ
Saak [*Russian Federation*] [*ICAO designator*] (FAAC) ... SVL
Saanen [*Switzerland ICAO location identifier*] (ICLI) ... LSGK
Saanich Pioneer Society Museum, Saanichton, BC, Canada [*Library symbol*] [*Library of Congress*] (LCLS) ... CaBSPSM
Saanich Pioneer Society Museum, Saanichton, British Columbia [*Library symbol National Library of Canada*] (NLC) ... BSPSM
Saarbrucken [*Germany Airport symbol*] (OAG) ... SCN
Saarbruecken [*Germany ICAO location identifier*] (ICLI) ... EDRS
Saarland Airlines AG [*Germany ICAO designator*] (FAAC) ... SLL
Saarlandischer Rundfunk [*Radio network*] [*West Germany*] ... SR
Saarlouis/Dueren [*Germany ICAO location identifier*] (ICLI) ... EDRJ
Saat auf Hoffnung (BJA) ... SaH
Saatchi & Saatchi Advertising Worldwide (ECON) ... SSAW
Saba [*MARC geographic area code Library of Congress*] (LCCP) ... nwsd--
Saba [*Netherlands Antilles*] [*Airport symbol*] (OAG) ... SAB
Saba [*Netherlands Antilles*] [*Airport symbol*] (AD) ... SAM
Saba Petroleum [*AMEX symbol*] (TTSB) ... SAB
Saba Petroleum [*Associated Press*] (SAG) ... SabaPet
Saba Petroleum Co. [*AMEX symbol*] (SAG) ... SAB
Saba/Yrausquin [*Netherlands Antilles*] [*ICAO location identifier*] (ICLI) ... TNCS
Sabadell [*Spain ICAO location identifier*] (ICLI) ... LELL
Sabah [*Papua New Guinea*] [*Airport symbol*] (OAG) ... SBV
Sabah Air [*Malaysia*] [*ICAO designator*] (FAAC) ... SAX
Sabah Chinese Consolidated Party [*Malaysia*] [*Political party*] (FEA) ... SCCP
Sabah Chinese Party [*Malaysia*] [*Political party*] (FEA) ... PCS
Sabah United Party [*Malaysia*] [*Political party*] ... SUP
Sabana Grande, PR [*AM radio station call letters*] ... WYKO
Sabana, PR [*AM radio station call letters*] ... WJIT
Sabanettan, Tinian Island [*Mariana Islands*] [*ICAO location identifier*] (ICLI) ... PGNT
Sabang [*Indonesia*] [*ICAO location identifier*] (ICLI) ... WIAA
Sabang Merauke Raya Air Charter PT [*Indonesia*] [*ICAO designator*] (FAAC) ... SMC
Sabar [*Afghanistan*] [*ICAO location identifier*] (ICLI) ... OASR
Sabbath ... S
Sabbath ... SAB
SABENA [*Societe Anonyme Belge d'Exploitation de la Nav Aerienne*] [*Belgium ICAO designator*] (FAAC) ... SAB
Saber Aviation, Inc. [*ICAO designator*] (FAAC) ... SBR
Saber Enterprise Applications Manager [*Computer software*] [*Saber Software Corp.*] (PCM) ... SEAM
Sabhawala [*India*] [*Geomagnetic observatory code*] ... SAB
Sabin [*Unit of acoustic measurement*] (DEN) ... S
Sabina Public Library, Sabina, OH [*Library symbol Library of Congress*] (LCLS) ... OSa
Sabina Resources Ltd. [*Vancouver Stock Exchange symbol*] ... SBB
Sabine Parish Library, Many, LA [*Library symbol Library of Congress*] (LCLS) ... LManyS
Sabine Pass, TX [*Location identifier FAA*] (FAAL) ... SBI
Sabine River & Northern Railroad Co. [*AAR code*] ... SRN
Sabine Royalty Tr UBI [*NYSE symbol*] (TTSB) ... SBR
Sabine Royalty Trust [*Associated Press*] (SAG) ... SabnR
Sabine Royalty Trust [*NYSE symbol*] (SPSG) ... SBR
Sabinus [*Flourished, 5th or 6th century*] [*Authority cited in pre-1607 legal work*] (DSA) ... Sab
Sable [*Heraldry*] ... S
Sable [*Heraldry*] ... SA
Sable Gas Systems Ltd., Halifax, Nova Scotia [*Library symbol National Library of Canada*] (NLC) ... NSHSG
Sable Island, NS [*ICAO location identifier*] (ICLI) ... CYSA
Sable Resources Ltd. [*Vancouver Stock Exchange symbol*] ... SAE
Sabotage [*FBI standardized term*] ... SAB
Sabotage (AABC) ... SBTG
Saboted Light Armor Penetrator [*Weaponry*] (MCD) ... SLAP
Saboteurs for a Philistine America Redeemed from Kultur [*From book, "Bringing Down the House," by Richard P. Brickner*] ... SPARK
Sabot-Launched Electric Gun Kinetic Energy [*DoD*] ... SLEKE
Sabouraud Dextrose Agar [*Microbiology*] ... SAB
Sabouraud Dextrose Agar and Brain-Heart Infusion [*Microbiology*] ... SABHI
Sabra Computer (DNAB) ... SABRAC
Sabra Connection [*An association*] (EA) ... SC
Sabratek Corp. [*Associated Press*] (SAG) ... Sabratek
Sabratek Corp. [*NASDAQ symbol*] (SAG) ... SBTK
Sabre Airways Ltd. [*British*] [*FAA designator*] (FAAC) ... SBE
Sabre Foundation (EA) ... SF
Sabre Group Holdings, Inc. (The) [*Associated Press*] (SAG) ... SabreGr
Sabre Group Holdings, Inc. (The) [*NYSE symbol*] (SAG) ... TSG
Sabu/Tardanu [*Indonesia*] [*ICAO location identifier*] (ICLI) ... WRKS
Sabula Public Library, Sabula, IA [*Library symbol Library of Congress*] (LCLS) ... IaSab
Sabzevar [*Iran*] [*ICAO location identifier*] (ICLI) ... OIMS
SAC [*Strategic Air Command*] **Automated Command Control System - Data Processing System** (MCD) ... SACCS-DPS
SAC [*Strategic Air Command*] **Automated Total Information Network** (MCD) ... SATIN
SAC [*Strategic Air Command*] **Channel and Traffic Control Agency** (SAA) ... SCTCA
Sac City, IA [*Location identifier FAA*] (FAAL) ... SKI
SAC [*Strategic Air Command*] **Intelligence Data Processing System** (IAA) ... SIPS
SAC [*Strategic Air Command*] **Peacetime Airborne Reconnaissance** ... SPAR
Sac Sun, Sac City, IA [*Library symbol Library of Congress*] (LCLS) ... IaSacS

SAC [*Strategic Air Command*] **Telephone Net** ... STN
SAC Warning and Control System (MCD) ... SWCS
Saccharatae [*Sugar-Coated*] [*Pharmacy*] ... SACCH
Saccharin [*Sweetening agent*] ... SAC
Saccharin Sodium [*Sweetening agent*] ... SS
Saccharomyces Cerevisiae [*Bacterium*] ... SC
Sace [*South Africa*] [*ICAO location identifier*] (ICLI) ... FASU
Sacer Ordo Cisterciensis [*Order of Cistercians*] [*Roman Catholic men's religious order*] ... SO Cist
SACEUR [*Supreme Allied Commander, Europe*] **Command Alerting Reporting System** [*Army*] ... SCARS
SACEUR [*Supreme Allied Commander, Europe*] **Schedule Program** [*Army*] (AABC) ... SSP
SACEUR [*Supreme Allied Commander, Europe*] **Strategic Reserve** [*Army*] (NATG) ... SSR
Sachem Exploration [*Vancouver Stock Exchange symbol*] ... SAH
Sachem High School North, Holbrook, NY [*Library symbol Library of Congress*] (LCLS) ... NHolbHS
Sachem High School South, Lake Ronkonkoma, NY [*Library symbol Library of Congress*] (LCLS) ... NLakrHS
Sachem Public Library, Holbrook, NY [*Library symbol Library of Congress*] (LCLS) ... NHolb
Sachnoff Weaver & Rubenstein, Chicago, Il [*Library symbol*] [*Library of Congress*] (LCLS) ... ICSac
Sachon [*South Korea ICAO location identifier*] (ICLI) ... RKPS
Sachs/Freeman Associates, Inc. [*Telecommunications service*] (TSSD) ... SFA
Sachs Harbour [*Canada*] [*Airport symbol*] (OAG) ... YSY
Sachs Harbour, NT [*ICAO location identifier*] (ICLI) ... CYSY
Sachs, "History of Musical Instruments" [*A publication*] ... SaHMI
Sachse's Minutes, Norwich Mayoralty Court [*A publication*] (DLA) ... Sachse NM
Sachs-Georgi [*Test for syphilis*] [*Also, S-GT*] [*Obsolete*] ... SG
Sachs-Georgi Reaction [*On test for syphilis*] [*Infectious diseases*] (DAVI) ... SGR
Sachs-Georgi Test [*for syphilis*] [*Also, SG*] [*Obsolete*] ... S-GT
Sack ... SK
Sacks ... SX
Sacks Sentence Completion Test [*Psychology*] (DAVI) ... SSCT
Sackville, NB [*FM radio station call letters*] ... CHMA
SACLANT [*Supreme Allied Commander, Atlantic*] **Antisubmarine Warfare Research Center** (NATG) ... SASWREC
SACLANT [*Supreme Allied Commander, Atlantic*] **Approved NATO Common Infrastructure Program** (NATG) ... SANCIP
SACLANT [*Supreme Allied Commander, Atlantic*] **Authentification System** [*NATO*] (NATG) ... SACLAU
SACLANT [*Supreme Allied Commander, Atlantic*] **Distributing and Accounting Agency** (NATG) ... SLDAA
SACLANT Scheduled Program (MCD) ... SLSP
SACLANT [*Supreme Allied Commander, Atlantic*] **Staff Instruction Manual** (NATG) ... SIM
SACLANT [*Supreme Allied Commander, Atlantic*] **Staff Organization Manual** (NATG) ... SOM
SACLANT [*Supreme Allied Commander, Atlantic*] **Standing Exercise Orders** [*NATO*] (NATG) ... SACLEX
SACLANT [*Supreme Allied Commander, Atlantic*] **War Intelligence Organization** (NATG) ... SWIO
SAC-NORAD [*Strategic Air Command - North American Air Defense*] **OperationalWeapons Test Involving Military Electronics** ... SNOW TIME
Saco Defense Systems Division [*Maremont Corp.*] (RDA) ... SDSD
Saco, ME [*FM radio station call letters*] (RBYB) ... WRED
Saco Resources [*Vancouver Stock Exchange symbol*] ... SCQ
Sacra Caesarea Majestas [*Sacred Imperial Majesty*] [*Latin*] ... SCM
Sacra Congregatio [*Sacred Congregation*] [*Latin*] ... SC
Sacra Congregatio Concilii [*Sacred Congregation of the Council*] [*Latin*] ... SCC
Sacra Congregatio de Propaganda Fide [*Sacred Congregation for the Propagation of the Faith*] [*Latin*] ... SCPF
Sacra Congregatio Episcoporum et Regularium [*Sacred Congregation of Bishops and Regulars*] [*Latin*] ... SCEERR
Sacra Congregatio Indicis [*Sacred Congregation of the Index*] [*Latin*] ... SCI
Sacra Pagina [*Paris-Gembloux*] [*A publication*] (BJA) ... SP
Sacra Rituum Congregatio [*Sacred Congregation of Rites*] [*Latin*] ... SRC
Sacrae Theologiae Baccalaureus [*Bachelor of Sacred Theology*] [*Latin*] (GPO) ... STB
Sacrae Theologiae Baccalaureus [*Bachelor of Sacred Theology*] ... SThB
Sacrae Theologiae Doctor [*Doctor of Sacred Theology*] [*Latin*] ... STD
Sacrae Theologiae Doctor [*Doctor of Sacred Theology*] ... SThD
Sacrae Theologiae Lecentiatus [*Licentiate in Sacred Theology*] ... S ThL
Sacrae Theologiae Lector [*Reader in Sacred Theology*] [*Latin*] ... STL
Sacrae Theologiae Licentiatus [*Licentiate in Sacred Theology*] [*Latin*] ... STL
Sacrae Theologiae Magister [*Master of Sacred Theology*] ... STM
Sacrae [*or Sacrosanctae*] **Theologiae Professor** [*Professor of Sacred Theology*] ... STP
Sacral ... S
Sacral Nerve, First [*S2 is second sacral nerve, etc., through S5*] [*Anatomy*] [*Medicine*] (DAVI) ... S1
Sacral Vertebra, First [*S2 is second sacral vertabra, etc., through S5*] [*Anatomy*] (DAVI) ... S1
Sacrament (ROG) ... SACR
Sacramentine Nuns (TOCD) ... OSS
Sacramento [*California*] [*Airport symbol*] (AD) ... SAC
Sacramento [*California*] [*Airport symbol*] (OAG) ... SMF
Sacramento Air Logistics Center (NASA) ... SALC
Sacramento Air Logistics Center (MCD) ... SMALC
Sacramento Air Materiel Area ... SAMA
Sacramento Air Materiel Area (KSC) ... SMAMA
Sacramento Army Depot [*California*] (AABC) ... SAAD
Sacramento, CA [*Location identifier FAA*] (FAAL) ... FKZ
Sacramento, CA [*Location identifier FAA*] (FAAL) ... HUX
Sacramento, CA [*Television station call letters*] ... KCMY
Sacramento, CA [*Television station call letters*] ... KCRA
Sacramento, CA [*AM radio station call letters*] ... KCTC
Sacramento, CA [*FM radio station call letters*] ... KEDR
Sacramento, CA [*AM radio station call letters*] ... KFBK
Sacramento, CA [*FM radio station call letters*] ... KGBY
Sacramento, CA [*AM radio station call letters*] ... KHTK
Sacramento, CA [*AM radio station call letters*] ... KJAY
Sacramento, CA [*AM radio station call letters*] (RBYB) ... KMJI
Sacramento, CA [*FM radio station call letters*] ... KNCI
Sacramento, CA [*Television station call letters*] (RBYB) ... KPWB-TV
Sacramento, CA [*FM radio station call letters*] ... KQPT
Sacramento, CA [*FM radio station call letters*] ... KRAK-FM
Sacramento, CA [*FM radio station call letters*] ... KSEG
Sacramento, CA [*AM radio station call letters*] (RBYB) ... KSQR
Sacramento, CA [*Television station call letters*] ... KTXL
Sacramento, CA [*Television station call letters*] ... KVIE
Sacramento, CA [*FM radio station call letters*] ... KWOD
Sacramento, CA [*FM radio station call letters*] ... KXHV
Sacramento, CA [*FM radio station call letters*] ... KXJZ
Sacramento, CA [*AM radio station call letters*] ... KXOA
Sacramento, CA [*FM radio station call letters*] ... KXOA-FM
Sacramento, CA [*FM radio station call letters*] ... KXPR
Sacramento, CA [*Television station call letters*] ... KXTV
Sacramento, CA [*FM radio station call letters*] ... KYDS
Sacramento, CA [*FM radio station call letters*] ... KYMX
Sacramento, CA [*Location identifier FAA*] (FAAL) ... MCC
Sacramento, CA [*Location identifier FAA*] (FAAL) ... MHR
Sacramento, CA [*Location identifier FAA*] (FAAL) ... POK
Sacramento, CA [*Location identifier FAA*] (FAAL) ... RAF
Sacramento, CA [*Location identifier FAA*] (FAAL) ... SAC
Sacramento, CA [*Location identifier FAA*] (FAAL) ... SMF
Sacramento City College Library, Sacramento, CA [*OCLC symbol*] (OCLC) ... CSG
Sacramento City College, Sacramento, CA [*Library symbol Library of Congress*] (LCLS) ... CSSCiC
Sacramento City-County Library System, Sacramento, CA [*Library symbol Library of Congress*] (LCLS) ... CS
Sacramento County Law Library, Sacramento, CA [*Library symbol Library of Congress*] (LCLS) ... CSLL
Sacramento County Medical Society, Sacramento, CA [*Library symbol Library of Congress*] (LCLS) ... CSMed
Sacramento/Executive [*California*] [*ICAO location identifier*] (ICLI) ... KSAC
Sacramento/Mather Air Force Base [*California*] [*ICAO location identifier*] (ICLI) ... KMHR
Sacramento Municipal Utility District [*Photovoltaic energy systems*] ... SMUD
Sacramento Northern Railway [*AAR code*] ... SN
Sacramento Peak Observatory ... SPO
Sacramento/Sacramento Metropolitan [*California*] [*ICAO location identifier*] (ICLI) ... KSMF
Sacramento Test Center (MCD) ... STC
Sacramento Test Operations (MCD) ... SACTO
Sacred ... S
Sacred (ROG) ... SACR
Sacred Books of the East [*A publication*] (BJA) ... SBE
Sacred Books of the Old Testament [*The "Rainbow Bible"*] [*A publication*] (BJA) ... SBOT
Sacred Cat of Burma Fanciers (EA) ... SCBF
Sacred Dance Guild (EA) ... SDG
Sacred Earth Network [*An association*] (EA) ... SEN
Sacred Heart (ROG) ... SH
Sacred Heart College [*Cullman, AL*] ... SHC
Sacred Heart College, Cullman, AL [*Library symbol Library of Congress*] (LCLS) ... ACJ
Sacred Heart College, McCarthy Library, Belmont, NC [*Library symbol Library of Congress*] (LCLS) ... NcBeSH
Sacred Heart Dominican College [*Texas*] ... SHDC
Sacred Heart General Hospital, Eugene, OR [*Library symbol Library of Congress*] (LCLS) ... OrESH
Sacred Heart Hospital, Eau Claire, WI [*Library symbol Library of Congress*] (LCLS) ... WES
Sacred Heart Junior College [*North Carolina; Pennsylvania*] ... SHJC
Sacred Heart League (EA) ... SHL
Sacred Heart Medical Center, Spokane, WA [*Library symbol Library of Congress*] (LCLS) ... WaSpSH
Sacred Heart School, Freeport MN [*Library symbol*] [*Library of Congress*] (LCLS) ... MnFpS
Sacred Heart School of Theology, Hales Corners, WI [*Library symbol Library of Congress*] (LCLS) ... WHcS
Sacred Heart School, Sauk Rapids, MN [*Library symbol*] [*Library of Congress*] (LCLS) ... MnSrS
Sacred Heart School, Staples, MN [*Library symbol*] [*Library of Congress*] (LCLS) ... MnStS
Sacred Heart Seminary [*Detroit, MI*] ... SHS
Sacred Heart Seminary, Detroit, MI [*Library symbol Library of Congress*] (LCLS) ... MiDSH
Sacred Heart Seminary, Shelby, OH [*Library symbol Library of Congress*] (LCLS) ... OShelS
Sacred Heart University, Bridgeport, CT [*Library symbol Library of Congress*] (LCLS) ... CtBSH
Sacred Heart University, Library, Bridgeport, CT [*OCLC symbol*] (OCLC) ... SHU
Sacred Marriage Texts (BJA) ... SMT
Sacred Music Press (BJA) ... SMP
Sacred Scripture ... SS

Sacred to the Memory of -- [*Epitaphs*] (ROG) .... SM
Sacremento/McClellan Air Force Base [*California*] [*ICAO location identifier*] (ICLI) .... KMCC
Sacrifice [*Baseball*] .... S
Sacrifice [*Baseball*] .... SAC
Sacrifice (ROG) .... SACR
Sacrifice Fly [*Baseball*] .... SF
Sacrifice Hit [*Baseball*] .... SH
Sacrificial Anode Cathodic Protection (MCD) .... SACP
Sacrist (ROG) .... SACR
Sacristan .... SAC
Sacro Occipital Research Society International (EA) .... SORSI
Sacrococcygeal [*Anatomy*] .... SC
Sacrococcygeal Teratoma [*Oncology*] .... SCT
Sacrococcygeal to Inferior Pubic Point [*Anatomy*] (MAE) .... SCIPP
Sacrodextra Anterior [*A fetal position*] [*Obstetrics*] .... SDA
Sacrodextra Posterior [*A fetal position*] [*Obstetrics*] .... SDP
Sacrodextra Transversa [*A fetal position*] [*Obstetrics*] .... SDT
Sacroiliac [*Medicine*] .... SI
Sacroiliac Joint .... SIJ
Sacroiliac Joint [*Anatomy*] (DAVI) .... SIjt
Sacroiliac Orthosis [*Medicine*] .... SIO
Sacrolaeva Anterior [*A fetal position*] (AAMN) .... SLA
Sacrolaeva Posterior [*A fetal position*] (AAMN) .... SLP
Sacrolaeva Transversa [*A fetal position*] (AAMN) .... SLT
Sacropubic [*Anatomy*] (AAMN) .... Sp
Sacrosanctam Concilium [*Constitution on the Sacred Liturgy*] [*Vatican II document*] .... SC
Sacrum .... S
Sacrum Anterior [*A fetal position*] [*Obstetrics*] (DAVI) .... SA
Sacrum Palatium Apostolicum [*Sacred Apostolic Palace, Vatican, Quirinal*] [*Latin*] .... SPA
Sacrum Posterior [*A fetal position*] (DAVI) .... SP
Sacrum Romanum Imperium [*The Holy Roman Empire*] [*Latin*] .... SRI
Sacrum to Pubis [*Medicine*] (DMAA) .... SP
Sad Case [*An unpopular person*] [*Teen slang*] .... SC
Sad, Hostile, Anxious, Frustrating, Tenacious Patient Syndrome [*Medicine*] (DMAA) .... SHAFT
Sa'Dah [*Yemen Arab Republic*] [*Airport symbol*] (OAG) .... SYE
Saddle (AAG) .... SAD
Saddle (MSA) .... SDL
Saddle Back Butte [*California*] [*Seismograph station code, US Geological Survey*] (SEIS) .... SBB
Saddle Rock Elementary School, Great Neck, NY [*Library symbol Library of Congress*] (LCLS) .... NGrnSRE
Saddle Tank [*Trains*] [*British*] .... ST
Saddleback Community College District, Mission Viejo Campus, Mission Viejo, CA [*OCLC symbol*] (OCLC) .... SAD
Saddlery .... SAD
Saddlery Hardware Manufacturers Institute [*Defunct*] (EA) .... SHMI
S-Adenosylhomocysteine [*Biochemistry*] .... SAH
S-Adenosylhomocysteine [*Biochemistry*] .... SAHC
S-Adenosylmethionine [*Also, AdoMet, SAMe*] [*Biochemistry*] .... SAM
S-Adenosylmethionine [*Also, AdoMet, SAM*] [*Biochemistry*] .... SAMe
S-Adenosylmethionine Decarboxylase [*An enzyme*] .... SAM-DC
Sadism [*or Sadist*] (CDAI) .... S
Sadism and Masochism .... S & M
Sadler's Pennsylvania Cases [*A publication*] (DLA) .... Sad
Sadler's Pennsylvania Cases [*1885-88*] [*A publication*] (DLA) .... Sad PA Cas
Sadler's Pennsylvania Cases [*1885-88*] [*A publication*] (DLA) .... Sad PA Cs
Sadler's Pennsylvania Cases [*A publication*] (DLA) .... Sadler
Sadler's Pennsylvania Cases [*A publication*] (DLA) .... Sadler (PA)
Sadler's Wells Royal Ballet [*British*] .... SWRB
Sadler's Wells Theatre [*London*] .... SW
Sadlier [*William H.*], Inc. [*NASDAQ symbol*] (NQ) .... SADL
Sadlier [*William H.*], Inc. [*Associated Press*] (SAG) .... Sadlier
Sadlier (William H.) [*NASDAQ symbol*] (TTSB) .... SADL
Sado [*Japan ICAO location identifier*] (ICLI) .... RJSD
Sadr Diwani Adalat Cases, Madras [*India*] [*A publication*] (DLA) .... Chetty
Sadr Diwani Adalat Cases, Northwest Frontier [*Pakistan*] [*A publication*] (DLA) .... SADNWF
Sadr Diwani Adalat Reports [*Bombay, India*] [*A publication*] (DLA) .... SAD Bom
Sadr Diwani Adalat Reports [*India*] [*A publication*] (DLA) .... SDA
Sadr Foujdaree Adalat Reports [*India*] [*A publication*] (DLA) .... SFA
Sadr Nizamut Adalat Reports [*India*] [*A publication*] (DLA) .... SNA
Sadr Nizamut Adalat Reports [*India*] [*A publication*] (DLA) .... SNA Beng
Sadr Nizamut Adalat Reports, New Series [*1851-59*] [*Bengal, India*] [*A publication*] (DLA) .... SNA Beng (NS)
Saduccus [*Flourished, 13th century*] [*Authority cited in pre-1607 legal work*] (DSA) .... S
Saeculum .... SAEC
Saeculum [*Age, Century, Generation, Lifetime*] [*Latin*] (ROG) .... SAEC
Saegertown, PA [*FM radio station call letters*] .... WEOZ
SAES Getters SPA [*NASDAQ symbol*] (SAG) .... SAES
SAES Getters SPA [*Associated Press*] (SAG) .... SAESGet
SAES Getters S.p.A ADS [*NASDAQ symbol*] (TTSB) .... SAESY
SAF [*Society of American Florists*]- The Center for Commercial Floriculture (EA) .... SAF
Safair [*ICAO designator*] (AD) .... KP
Safair Freighters (Pty) Ltd. [*South Africa ICAO designator*] (FAAC) .... SFR
Safane [*Burkina Faso*] [*ICAO location identifier*] (ICLI) .... DHOF
Safari Club International (EA) .... SCI
Safari Club International Conservation Fund (EA) .... SCICF
Safari International Resources [*Vancouver Stock Exchange symbol*] .... SIR
Safe [*Task classification*] [*NASA*] (NASA) .... (S)

Safe (NASA) .... SF
[*A*] Safe [*Criminal slang*] V
Safe Access to Files of Estate [*Howrex Corp.*] [*Information service or system*] (IID) .... SAFE
Safe Air International, Inc. [*ICAO designator*] (FAAC) .... SDY
Safe Altitude Fuzing Option (SAA) .... SAFO
Safe Area Intelligence Brief (MCD) .... SAIB
Safe Area Intelligence Description (MCD) .... SAID
Safe Areas for Evasion (DOMA) .... SAFE
Safe Arm .... S/A
Safe, Arm, and Fuze .... SAF
Safe Arm Initiation from Electromagnetic Radiation .... SAIFER
Safe Arming Time .... SAT
Safe Arrival .... S/A
Safe Arrival (ODBW) .... sa
Safe Break Terminator (IAA) .... SBT
Safe Car Educational Institute .... SCEI
Safe Custody [*Banking*] .... SC
Safe Deposit [*Business term*] .... SD
Safe Deposit Box (MHDB) .... SDB
Safe Deposit Company (MHDW) .... SD CO
Safe Drinking Water Act [*1974*] .... SDWA
Safe Driver Attitude Test [*Educational test*] .... SDAT
Safe Emulsion Agar Gel [*Organic chemistry*] .... SEAgel
Safe Energy Communication Council (EA) .... SECC
Safe Engineering and Operations [*Program*] [*Marine Corps*] (DOMA) .... SEAOPS
Safe Eye Exposure Distance [*Air Force*] .... SEED
Safe Functional Requirements Document (MCD) .... SFRD
Safe High-Energy Explosive .... SHEE
Safe Hit [*Baseball*] .... Sh
Safe Integral Reactor [*Nuclear energy*] .... SIR
Safe Launch Angle Gate .... SLAG
Safe Leeward Position .... SLP
Safe Locker (AAG) .... SL
Safe Low-Power Critical Experiment [*Nuclear energy*] .... SLOWPOKE
Safe Manufacturers' Association .... SMA
Safe Manufacturers' National Association (EA) .... SMNA
Safe Military Infrared LASER Equipment .... SMILE
Safe Operating Area (IEEE) .... SOA
Safe Operating Area .... SOAR
Safe Operating Limit .... SOL
Safe Passage Path Map (SAA) .... SPPM
Safe Passage Route Creation Sheet (SAA) .... SPRCS
Safe Return Amnesty Committee (EA) .... SRAC
Safe Sector Altitude [*Aviation*] (DA) .... SSA
Safe Secure Railcar [*Army*] .... SSR
Safe Secure Trailer [*For transporting nuclear materials*] .... SST
Safe Separate/Timing (CINC) .... SST
Safe Separation Device .... SSD
Safe Shutdown [*Nuclear energy*] (NRCH) .... SS
Safe Shutdown Earthquake [*Nuclear energy*] (NRCH) .... SSE
Safe Shutdown Facility [*Nuclear energy*] (NRCH) .... SSF
Safe Shutdown Impoundment [*Nuclear energy*] (NRCH) .... SSI
Safe Tables Our Priority [*Protest organization compreised of parents and friends of E. coli victims*] (ECON) .... STOP
Safe Tables Our Priority .... STOP
Safe Teenage Rocketry .... STAR
Safe Tow Length .... STL
Safe Transport of Munitions (MCD) .... STOM
Safe Transport of Munitions Project (MCD) .... STORM
Safe Use Instructions [*General Motors Corp.*] .... SUI
Safe Water Coalition (EA) .... SWC
Safe Winter Driving League [*Defunct*] (EA) .... SWDL
Safe Women's Transport [*British*] .... SWT
Safe Working Load [*Shipping*] .... SWL
Safe Working Pressure .... SWP
SafeAir One-Federal Aviation Administration Administrator (FAAC) FAA-1
SafeAir Two-Federal Aviation Administration Deputy Administrator (FAAC) FAA-2
Safe-and-Arm (KSC) .... S & A
Safe-and-Arm Device .... SAD
Safebagar [*Nepal*] [*ICAO location identifier*] (ICLI) .... VNSR
SAFECO Corp. [*NASDAQ symbol*] (NQ) .... SAFC
Safeco Corp. [*Associated Press*] (SAG) .... Safeco
Safed [*Israel*] [*Seismograph station code, US Geological Survey Closed*] (SEIS) .... SAF
Safeguard (AABC) .... SFGD
Safeguard Antiballistic Missile System [*Military*] (WDAA) .... SABMS
Safeguard Army Depot (AABC) .... SGAD
Safeguard Central Training Facility [*Army*] (AABC) .... SAFCTF
Safeguard Command [*Army*] (AABC) .... SAFCMD
Safeguard Communications Agency [*Army*] .... SAFCA
Safeguard Communications Program Management Office [*Army*] (AABC) .... SAFCPMO
Safeguard Communications Program Manager [*Army*] (AABC) .... SAFCPM
Safeguard Data Processing Laboratory [*Army*] (AABC) .... SDPL
Safeguard Emergency Action Report [*Army*] (AABC) .... SEAR
Safeguard Health Enterpr [*NASDAQ symbol*] (TTSB) .... SFGD
Safeguard Health Enterprises, Inc. [*Associated Press*] (SAG) .... SafHlt
Safeguard Health Enterprises, Inc. [*NASDAQ symbol*] (NQ) .... SFGD
Safeguard Integrated Logistics Support Plan [*Army*] (AABC) .... SILSP
Safeguard Integrated Training Plan [*Army*] (AABC) .... SAFITP
Safeguard Inventory Control Center [*Army*] (AABC) .... SICC
Safeguard Logistics Command [*Army*] (AABC) .... SAFLOG

Safeguard Maintenance and Reporting Analysis System [*Army*]
(AABC) .... SMRAS
Safeguard Management Information System [*Army*] (AABC) .... SMIS
Safeguard Management Information System Operating Program [*Army*]
(AABC) .... SMISOP
Safeguard Material Balance Simulator .... SMBS
Safeguard Materiel Support Command [*Army*] (AABC) .... SAFMSC
Safeguard Project Office (MCD) .... SAFPO
Safeguard Public Affairs Coordinating Committee [*Army*] (AABC) .... SAFPACC
Safeguard Readiness Posture [*Army*] (AABC) .... SRP
Safeguard Scientifics [*NYSE symbol*] (TTSB) .... SFE
Safeguard Scientifics, Inc. [*NYSE symbol*] (SPSG) .... SFE
Safeguard Scientifics, Inc. [*Associated Press*] (SAG) .... SfgdSc
Safeguard Spartan System [*Aerospace*] (MCD) .... SSS
Safeguard System Command [*Obsolete Army*] .... SAFCOM
Safeguard System Command [*Obsolete Army*] (AABC) .... SAFSCOM
Safeguard System Command [*Obsolete Army*] (MCD) .... SSC
Safeguard System Command-RDT & E [*Research, Development, Test, and Evaluation*] Directorate [*Obsolete Army*] (MCD) .... SAFSC-D
Safeguard System Configuration Control Board [*Army*] (AABC) .... SSCCB
Safeguard System Design Release Schedule [*Army*] (AABC) .... SSDRS
Safeguard System Evaluation Agency [*Army*] (AABC) .... SAFSEA
Safeguard System Management Communications Network Program
[*Army*] (AABC) .... SSMCNP
Safeguard System Manager [*Army*] .... SAFSM
Safeguard System Master Plan [*Army*] (AABC) .... SSMP
Safeguard System Office [*Army*] (AABC) .... SAFSO
Safeguard System Simulation [*Missile system evaluation*] [*Army*] (RDA) .... SAFSIM
Safeguard Tactical Communications Plan [*Army*] (AABC) .... SAFTCP
Safeguard Tactical Communications System [*Army*] (AABC) .... SAFTCS
Safeguard Tactical Field Force [*Army*] (AABC) .... STFF
Safeguard Tactical Logistics Management .... STLM
Safeguard Test and Evaluation Program [*Army*] (AABC) .... STEP
Safeguard Transportation System [*Army*] (AABC) .... SAFTRANS
Safeguards Analysis for Effluents .... SAFE
Safeguards Analytical Laboratory Evaluation [*Nuclear energy*] .... SALE
Safeguards and Materials Management [*AEC*] .... SMM
Safeguards Area Ventilation System [*Nuclear energy*] (NRCH) .... SAVS
Safeguards Automated Facility Evaluation [*Nuclear energy*] (NRCH) .... SAFE
Safeguards Equipment Cabinet (IEEE) .... SEC
Safeguards Implementation Report [*Nuclear energy*] (NRCH) .... SIR
Safeguards Initiation Signal [*Nuclear energy*] (NRCH) .... SGIS
Safeguards Upgrade Rule Evaluation (PDAA) .... SURE
Safekeeping .... SK
Safekeeping .... Skg
Safeland Barrier (DNAB) .... SAFE-BAR
Safe-Practice Data Sheet (MSA) .... SPDS
Safe-Practice Procedure (MCD) .... SPP
Safer Sex .... SS
Safeskin Corp. [*Associated Press*] (SAG) .... Safeskin
Safeskin Corp. [*NASDAQ symbol*] (SAG) .... SFSK
Safe-to-Arm Signal .... STAS
Safe-to-Arm System (MUGU) .... STAS
Safety [*Football*] .... S
Safety (KSC) .... SAF
Safety .... SAFT
Safety (IAA) .... SF
Safety .... SFTY
Safety .... SFTY
Safety 1st, Inc. [*NASDAQ symbol*] (SAG) .... SAFT
Safety 1st, Inc. [*Associated Press*] (SAG) Sfty1st
Safety Activation Monitor (IEEE) .... SAM
Safety Advisory Board [*National Science Foundation*] (NUCP) .... SAB
Safety Advisory Committee (MCD) .... SAC
Safety Altitude [*Aviation*] (DA) .... SA
Safety Always Follows Everything You Do [*Sign*] .... SAFETY
Safety Analysis [*Nuclear energy*] (NRCH) .... SA
Safety Analysis [*or Assurance*] Diagram [*Nuclear energy*] (NRCH) .... SAD
Safety Analysis Input Data [*Nuclear energy*] (NRCH) .... SAID
Safety Analysis Report [*Nuclear energy*] .... SAR
Safety Analysis Report for Packaging [*NASA*] (NASA) .... SARP
Safety and Arming Detection Test Set (DWSG) .... SADTS
Safety and Arming Device .... S & A
Safety and Arming Device [*Military*] (AABC) .... SAD
Safety and Arming Test Aid (MCD) .... SATA
Safety & Environmental Protection Subcommittee [*Joint Army, Navy, NASA, Air Force*] .... S & EPS
Safety and Fitness Electronic Records System [*FHWA*] (TAG) .... SAFER
Safety and Flight Failure/Unsatisfactory Report .... SFFUR
Safety and Functional Evaluation [*Occupational therapy*] .... SAFE
Safety and Health Data Sheet [*Army*] .... SHDS
Safety and Health Management Division [*Department of Agriculture*]
(GFGA) .... SHMD
Safety and Health Regulations for Construction [*Bureau of Reclamation*].... SHRC
Safety and Health Standards Management Board (IAA) .... SHSMB
Safety and Operating Systems Office [*NASA*] .... SOSO
Safety and Reliability Directorate [*England*] (IID) .... SRD
Safety and Reliability Society [*British*] .... SaRS
Safety and Special Radio Services Bureau [*of FCC*] .... SSRSB
Safety, Arming, and Destruct (MCD) .... SAD
Safety Assessment .... SA
Safety Assessment Report (MCD) .... SAR
Safety Assurance Analysis (NASA) .... SAA
Safety Base Motion Picture (VRA) .... SBMP
Safety Based Negative (VRA) .... SFNG

Safety Bulletin .... SB
Safety Center (DNAB) .... SAFECEN
Safety Change Control Board (MCD) .... SCCB
Safety Compliance Certification Label [*Automotive engineering*] .... SCCL
Safety Components International, Inc. [*NASDAQ symbol*] (SAG) .... ABAG
Safety Components International, Inc. [*Associated Press*] (SAG) .... SftyCmp
Safety Components Intl. [*NASDAQ symbol*] (TTSB) .... ABAG
Safety Containment Isolation System (IEEE) .... SCIS
Safety Control Center (NASA) .... SCC
Safety Control Rod Axe Man [*Nuclear energy*] (IEEE) .... SCRAM
Safety Control Switch .... SCS
Safety Data and Analysis Unit [*British*] (DA) .... SDAU
Safety Data Sheet (KSC) .... SDS
Safety Destructor (NG) .... SD
Safety Education and Training .... SET
Safety Emissions Energy Economics [*Automotive research*] S3E
Safety Engineering Analysis (AFM) .... SEA
Safety Engineering Laboratory [*British*] (IRUK) .... SEL
Safety Engineering Program Plan [*Military*] (DNAB) .... SEPP
Safety Equipment [*British military*] (DMA) .... SE
Safety Equipment Distributors Association (EA) .... SEDA
Safety Equipment Institute (EA) .... SEI
Safety Equipment Manufacturers Agents Association (EA) .... SEMAA
Safety Equipment Requirements .... SEQUR
Safety Evaluation (NRCH) .... SE
Safety Evaluation Audit Report [*Nuclear energy*] (NRCH) .... SEAR
Safety Evaluation Report [*Nuclear energy*] (NRCH) .... SER
Safety Evaluation Supplement (IAA) .... SESUPP
Safety Extra Low Voltage (IAA) .... SELV
Safety Factor .... SF
Safety Features Actuation Signal [*Nuclear energy*] (NRCH) .... SFAS
Safety Fund [*NASDAQ symbol*] (TTSB) .... SFCO
Safety Glass [*Technical drawings*] .... SFGL
Safety Glazing Certification Council (EA) .... SGCC
Safety Guide (NRCH) .... SG
Safety Harbor, FL [*FM radio station call letters*] .... WYUU
Safety Hazard Analysis (MCD) .... SHA
Safety, Health and Environment (ACII) .... SHE
Safety, Health, and Environmental Resource Center International
(EA) .... SHERCI
Safety Helmet Council of America (EA) .... SHCA
Safety in Mines Research Establishment [*British*] .... SMRE
Safety in Mines Scattered Light Instrument (ADA) .... SIMSLIN
Safety Information Center [*National Safety Council*] (IID) .... SIC
Safety Information Letter (IEEE) .... SIL
Safety Information System [*Department of Transportation*] .... SIS
Safety Injection [*Nuclear energy*] (NRCH) .... SI
Safety Injection Actuation Signal [*Nuclear energy*] (NRCH) .... SIAS
Safety Injection and Refueling Water [*Nuclear energy*] (NRCH) .... SIRW
Safety Injection and Refueling Water Tank [*Nuclear energy*] (NRCH) .... SIRWT
Safety Injection Control System [*Nuclear energy*] (NRCH) .... SICS
Safety Injection Permissive Block (IEEE) .... SIPB
Safety Injection Pump (IEEE) .... SIP
Safety Injection Reserve Water Tank (IEEE) .... SIRWT
Safety Injection Signal [*Nuclear energy*] (IAA) .... SIS
Safety Injection System [*Nuclear energy*] (NRCH) .... SIS
Safety Injection Tank [*Nuclear energy*] (NRCH) .... SIT
Safety Injection Transmitter [*Nuclear energy*] (NRCH) .... SIT
Safety Inspection (IEEE) .... SI
Safety Instrumentation Package (MCD) .... SIP
Safety Instrumented System (ACII) .... SIS
Safety Integrity Level (ACII) .... SIL
Safety Investigation Regulations (IEEE) .... SIRA
Safety Level [*Army*] .... SL
Safety Limit [*Nuclear energy*] (NRCH) .... SL
Safety, Liquidity, Yield .... SLY
Safety Management Information Statistics [*FTA*] (TAG) .... SAMIS
Safety Management System [*NHTSA*] (TAG) .... SMS
Safety Manual Supplement .... SMS
Safety/NATOPS Frequency (MCD) .... SANAFREQ
Safety Notice (MCD) .... SN
Safety Observation Station .... SOS
Safety Observation Station Display Console .... SOSC
Safety of Flight [*NASA*] (NASA) .... SOF
Safety of Flight Requirements (AFM) .... SFR
Safety of Life at Sea .... SOLAS
Safety of Life at Sea [*An international agreement requiring operators of cruise ships to meet certain standards of construction and fire safety*] .... SOLAS
Safety of Life at Sea Conference [*Intergovernmental Maritime Consultative Organization*] (MSC) .... SOLAS
Safety of Life at Sea Convention (BARN) .... SOLAS
Safety on the Streets [*Project of National Safety Council*] .... SOS
Safety Operating Plan .... SOP
Safety Operating Procedure [*Kennedy Space Center*] [*NASA*] (NASA) .... SFOP
Safety Panel .... SP
Safety Parameter Display System [*Instrumentation*] .... SPDS
Safety Performance Analysis System [*FAA*] (TAG) .... SPAS
Safety, Pride, Efficiency, Compatibility, Knowledge (DNAB) .... SPECK
Safety Program Directive [*NASA*] .... SPD
Safety Quotient .... SQ
Safety Razor Collectors Guild (EA) .... SRCG
Safety Recall Order (MCD) .... SRO
Safety Recommendation (AAG) .... SR
Safety Recommendation Information System [*Database*] .... SRIS
Safety Release [*Army*] .... SR

Safety, Reliability, and Maintainability (SSD) ... SRM
Safety, Reliability, and Quality (NASA) ... SR & Q
Safety, Reliability, and Quality Assurance (NASA) ... SR & QA
Safety, Reliability, and Quality Assurance, and Protective Services [*Kennedy Space Center*] [*NASA*] (NASA) ... SF
Safety, Reliability, Maintainability, and Quality Assurance [*NASA*] (SSD) ... SRM & QA
Safety Relief Valve [*Nuclear energy*] (NRCH) ... S/R
Safety Relief Valve [*Nuclear energy*] (NRCH) ... SRV
Safety/Relief Valve Discharge Line [*Nuclear energy*] (NRCH) ... SRVDL
Safety Representative [*Insurance*] ... S/R
Safety Research Center [*Bureau of Mines*] ... SRC
Safety Research Experiment Facility [*Nuclear energy*] ... SAREF
Safety Research Information Service [*National Safety Council*] (IID) ... SRIS
Safety Review [*A publication*] ... SARE
Safety Review Board [*Nuclear energy*] (NRCH) ... SRB
Safety Rod [*Nuclear energy*] (NRCH) ... SR
Safety/Security Officer [*Military*] (AABC) ... SSO
Safety Sequence Unit (MCD) ... SSU
Safety Services [*Red Cross*] ... SS
Safety Services Field Representative [*Red Cross*] ... SSFR
Safety Services Representative [*Red Cross*] ... SSR
Safety Significant Operation [*Aerospace*] ... SSO
[*The*] **Safety Society** (EA) ... TSS
Safety Standards ... SAST
Safety Standdown/Safety Review (MCD) ... SS/SR
Safety Study Group (MCD) ... SSG
Safety Supervisor (MUGU) ... SS
Safety Supplements [*Air Force*] ... SS
Safety Switch ... SSW
Safety System Engineering (MCD) ... SSE
Safety Systems Laboratory [*Formerly, Office of Vehicle Systems Research*] [*Department of Transportation*] ... SSL
Safety Technology Applied to Rapid Transit [*Committee*] [*American Public Transit Association*] ... START
Safety Test Engineering Program [*AEC*] ... STEP
Safety Test Facility [*Nuclear energy*] ... STF
Safety Test Missile (MCD) ... STM
Safety Tool (MCD) ... ST
Safety Topic Discussion (AAG) ... STD
Safety Training for the Execution of Emergency Procedures [*NASA*] ... STEEP
Safety Valve (AAG) ... SV
Safety Weather Probability Study (MCD) ... SEWPS
Safety Weather Probability Study ... SWEPS
Safety-Critical Systems/Software [*British*] ... SCS
Safety-Kleen [*NYSE symbol*] (TTSB) ... SK
Safety-Kleen Corp. [*Associated Press*] (SAG) ... SaftKl
Safety-Kleen Corp. [*NYSE symbol*] (SPSG) ... SK
Safety-Related Control Air System [*Nuclear energy*] (NRCH) ... SRCAS
Safety-Related Controls and Instrumentation [*Nuclear energy*] (NRCH) ... SRCI
Safety-Related Display Instrumentation [*Nuclear energy*] (NRCH) ... SRDI
Safety-Related Operator Action [*Nuclear energy*] (NRCH) ... SROA
SafetyTek Corp. [*NASDAQ symbol*] (SPSG) ... SAFE
Safetytek Corp. [*Associated Press*] (SAG) ... Saftytk
Safeway, Inc. [*Associated Press*] (SAG) ... Safeway
Safeway, Inc. [*Associated Press*] (SAG) ... Safwy
Safeway, Inc. [*NYSE symbol*] (SPSG) ... SWY
Safeway Inc. Wrrts [*NYSE symbol*] (TTSB) ... SWY.WS
Safeway Stores, Inc. ... SSI
Saffery Champness International [*British accounting firm*] ... SC
Saffle [*Sweden ICAO location identifier*] (ICLI) ... ESGY
Safford [*Arizona*] [*Airport symbol*] (AD) ... SAD
Safford, AZ [*AM radio station call letters*] ... KATO
Safford, AZ [*FM radio station call letters*] ... KXKQ
Safford, AZ [*Location identifier FAA*] (FAAL) ... SAD
Safford City-Graham County Public Library, Safford, AZ [*Library symbol Library of Congress*] (LCLS) ... AzSaf
Saffron Walden [*Municipal borough in England*] ... SAFFWALD
Safi [*Morocco*] [*ICAO location identifier*] (ICLI) ... GMMS
Safia [*Papua*] [*Airport symbol*] (AD) ... SFK
Safia [*Papua New Guinea*] [*Airport symbol*] (OAG) ... SFU
Safing and Deservicing Facility [*NASA*] (NASA) ... SDF
Safing Area [*NASA*] (NASA) ... SA
Safing, Arming, and Fusing System [*Military*] (MCD) ... SAFS
Safing, Arming, Fusing, and Firing [*Military*] (MCD) ... SAFF
Safing, Cool Down, and Decontamination Area [*NASA*] (NASA) ... SCDA
Safiran Airlines [*Iran*] [*ICAO designator*] (FAAC) ... SFN
SAFSCOM [*Safeguard System Command*] **Document Quality Audit** (MCD) ... SDQA
Sag Harbor, NY [*AM radio station call letters*] ... WLNG
Sag Harbor, NY [*FM radio station call letters*] ... WLNG-FM
Sag Harbor Whaling and Historical Museum, Sag Harbor, NY [*Library symbol*] [*Library of Congress*] (LCLS) ... NShW
Saga [*Japan*] [*Seismograph station code, US Geological Survey*] (SEIS) ... SAG
Saga Communications [*AMEX symbol*] (SPSG) ... SGA
Saga Communications, Inc. [*Associated Press*] (SAG) ... SagaCm
Saga Communications'A' [*AMEX symbol*] (TTSB) ... SGA
Saga Petroleum ADS'A' [*NYSE symbol*] (TTSB) ... SPM.A
Saga Petroleum ADS'B' [*NYSE symbol*] (TTSB) ... SPM.B
Saga Petroleum AS [*Associated Press*] (SAG) ... SagaP
Saga Petroleum AS [*NYSE symbol*] (SAG) ... SPM
Saga Resources [*Vancouver Stock Exchange symbol*] ... SGA
Sagami Women's University [*UTLAS symbol*] ... SWU
Sagamore Children's Center, Melville, NY [*Library symbol Library of Congress*] (LCLS) ... NMelSC
Sagamore Hill National Historic Site ... SAHI
Sagarai [*Papua New Guinea*] [*Airport symbol*] (OAG) ... SGJ
Sag-Control Agent [*Automotive painting and finishing*] ... SCA
SAGE [*Semiautomatic Ground Environment*] **Air Traffic Integration** ... SATIN
SAGE [*Semiautomatic Ground Environment*] **Atabe Simulation System** (IAA) ... SASS
SAGE [*Semiautomatic Ground Environment*] **Back-Up** (IAA) ... SABU
SAGE [*Semiautomatic Ground Environment*] **Battery Routing Equipment** ... SABRE
SAGE [*Semiautomatic Ground Environment*] **BOMARC** [*Boring-Michigan Aeronautical Research Center*] (IAA) ... SABOC
SAGE [*Semiautomatic Ground Environment*] **Change Proposal** (IAA) ... SCP
Sage Colleges (GAGS) ... Sage C
SAGE [*Semiautomatic Ground Environment*] **Computer Program** ... SCP
SAGE [*Semiautomatic Ground Environment*] **Computer Programming Training** ... SCPT
SAGE [*Semiautomatic Ground Environment*] **Computer Project** [*Military*] (IAA) ... SCP
SAGE [*Semiautomatic Ground Environment*] **Computer Support Group** [*Military*] (IAA) ... SCSG
SAGE [*Semiautomatic Ground Environment*] **Control Center** ... SCC
SAGE [*Semiautomatic Ground Environment*] **Data Generator** (IAA) ... SADGE
SAGE [*Semiautomatic Ground Environment*] **Direction Center** [*Military*] (IAA) ... SDC
SAGE [*Semiautomatic Ground Environment*] **Division Commander** [*Military*] (IAA) ... SDC
SAGE [*Semiautomatic Ground Environment*] **Evaluation Exercise** [*Military*] (IAA) ... SEE
SAGE [*Semiautomatic Ground Environment*] **Evaluation Library Tape** ... SELT
SAGE [*Semiautomatic Ground Environment*] **Experimental Display Generator** [*Military*] (IAA) ... SEDGE
SAGE [*Semiautomatic Ground Environment*] **High Altitude Prototype Environment** [*Military*] (IAA) ... SHAPE
SAGE [*Semiautomatic Ground Environment*] **Improvement Program** (IAA) ... SIP
SAGE [*Semiautomatic Ground Environment*] **Intercept Target Simulation** ... SITS
SAGE [*Semiautomatic Ground Environment*] **Interceptor Simulator** ... SIS
Sage Laboratories, Inc. [*Associated Press*] (SAG) ... SageLb
Sage Laboratories, Inc. [*NASDAQ symbol*] (NQ) ... SLAB
Sage Labs [*NASDAQ symbol*] (TTSB) ... SLAB
Sage Library, Osage, IA [*Library symbol Library of Congress*] (LCLS) ... IaOsa
SAGE [*Semiautomatic Ground Environment*] **Maintenance Control** ... SMC
SAGE [*Semiautomatic Ground Environment*] **Maintenance Control Office** ... SMCO
Sage Resources Ltd. [*Vancouver Stock Exchange symbol*] ... SGS
SAGE [*Semiautomatic Ground Environment*] **Strobe Training Operator** (IAA) ... SASTRO
SAGE [*Semiautomatic Ground Environment*] **System Status Report** ... SSSR
SAGE [*Semiautomatic Ground Environment*] **System Training Mission** ... SSTM
SAGE [*Semiautomatic Ground Environment*] **System Training Program** ... STP
SAGE [*Semiautomatic Ground Environment*] **System Training Unit** ... SSTU
SAGE [*Semiautomatic Ground Environment*] **Tracking and Guidance Evaluation System** ... STRANGE
SAGE [*Semi-Automatic Ground Equipment*] **Training Requirements Section** (SAA) ... STRS
SAGE [*Semi-Automatic Ground Equipment*] **Training Specialist** (SAA) ... STS
Sagebrush Inc. [*NASDAQ symbol*] (TTSB) ... SAGE
Sageville, IA [*FM radio station call letters*] (RBYB) ... KIYX-FM
Saghez [*Iran*] [*ICAO location identifier*] (ICLI) ... OITS
Saginaw [*Michigan*] [*Airport symbol*] (OAG) ... MBS
Saginaw [*Diocesan abbreviation*] [*Michigan*] (TOCD) ... SAG
Saginaw Health Sciences Library, Saginaw, MI [*Library symbol Library of Congress*] (LCLS) ... MiSHS
Saginaw, MI [*Location identifier FAA*] (FAAL) ... MBS
Saginaw, MI [*Location identifier FAA*] (FAAL) ... TQR
Saginaw, MI [*Television station call letters*] ... WAQP
Saginaw, MI [*Television station call letters*] ... WEYI
Saginaw, MI [*FM radio station call letters*] ... WGER
Saginaw, MI [*FM radio station call letters*] ... WKCQ
Saginaw, MI [*FM radio station call letters*] (RBYB) ... WMJA
Saginaw, MI [*AM radio station call letters*] ... WSAM
Saginaw, MI [*AM radio station call letters*] ... WSGW
Saginaw, MI [*FM radio station call letters*] ... WTLZ
Saginaw Public Libraries, Butman-Fish Library, Saginaw, MI [*Library symbol Library of Congress*] (LCLS) ... MiS-B
Saginaw Public Libraries, Claytor Branch Library, Saginaw, MI [*Library symbol Library of Congress*] (LCLS) ... MiS-C
Saginaw Public Libraries, Saginaw, MI [*Library symbol Library of Congress*] (LCLS) ... MiS
Saginaw Public Libraries, South Jefferson Branch, Saginaw, MI [*Library symbol Library of Congress*] (LCLS) ... MiS-S
Saginaw Public Libraries, Zauel Memorial Library, Saginaw, MI [*Library symbol Library of Congress*] (LCLS) ... MiS-Z
Saginaw Valley College, University Center, MI [*Library symbol Library of Congress*] (LCLS) ... MiUcS
Saginaw Valley State College (GAGS) ... Sag Val St C
Saginaw Valley State College, University Center, MI [*OCLC symbol*] (OCLC) ... EZS
Sagitta [*Mathematics*] ... SAG
Sagitta [*Constellation*] ... Sge
Sagitta [*Constellation*] ... Sgte
Sagittal [*Anatomy*] (DAVI) ... sag
Sagittal Diameter [*Radiology*] (DAVI) ... Sag D
Sagittal Ray Trace ... SRT
Sagittal Sinus [*Anatomy*] ... SS
Sagittal Sinus Pressure [*Medicine*] ... SSP
Sagittarius [*Constellation*] ... SAG
Sagittarius [*Constellation*] ... Sgr

Sagittarius [*Constellation*] ... Sgtr
Sagittarius Dwarf Elliptical Galaxy [*Astrophysics*] ... SagDEG
Sagrada Biblia [*1944*] [*Eloino Nacar Fuster and Alberto Colunga*] (BJA) ... NC
Sagua La Grande [*Cuba ICAO location identifier*] (ICLI) ... MUSG
Saguache County Library, Center Branch, Center, CO [*Library symbol Library of Congress*] (LCLS) ... CoCenS
Saguache County Public Library, Saguache, CO [*Library symbol Library of Congress*] (LCLS) ... CoSag
Saguaro Cactus Virus ... SaV
Saguaro Cactus Virus [*Plant pathology*] ... SCV
Saguaro National Monument ... SAGU
Saguenay [*Canada*] [*Airport symbol*] (OAG) ... YBG
Sagwon, AK [*Location identifier FAA*] (FAAL) ... SAG
Sahali Resources, Inc. [*Vancouver Stock Exchange symbol*] ... SAC
Sahara ... Sah
Sahara Desert [*MARC geographic area code Library of Congress*] (LCCP) ... fd----
Sahara Gaming [*Associated Press*] (SAG) ... SahaG
Sahara Gaming [*Associated Press*] (SAG) ... SahGam
Sahara Gaming [*AMEX symbol*] (SPSG) ... SGM
Sahara Upwelling Experiment [*US, Spain*] (MSC) ... SUE
Saharan Air Layer [*Meteorology*] ... SAL
Saharan Air Outbreak [*Meteorology*] ... SAO
Saharan Arab Democratic Republic [*Morocco*] (PD) ... SADR
Saharan People's Support Committee (EA) ... SPSC
Saharanpur/Sarsawa [*India*] [*ICAO location identifier*] (ICLI) ... VISP
Sahel Aviation Service [*Mali*] [*ICAO designator*] (FAAC) ... SAO
Sahiwal [*Pakistan*] [*ICAO location identifier*] (ICLI) ... OPSW
Sahma [*Oman*] [*ICAO location identifier*] (ICLI) ... OOSM
Sahuarita, AZ [*AM radio station call letters*] ... KQTL
SAI Ambrosini SpA [*Italy ICAO aircraft manufacturer identifier*] (ICAO) ... SO
SAIC [*Science Applications International Corp.*] **Integrated Management Information System** (MCD) ... SIMIS
Said (ROG) ... SD
Said to Contain [*Cargo manifest description*] ... STC
Saidor [*Papua New Guinea*] [*Airport symbol*] (OAG) ... SDI
Saidpur [*Bangladesh*] [*Airport symbol*] (OAG) ... SPD
Saidpur [*Bangladesh*] [*ICAO location identifier*] (ICLI) ... VGSD
Saidu Sharif [*Pakistan*] [*ICAO location identifier*] (ICLI) ... OPSS
Saidu Sharif [*Pakistan*] [*Airport symbol*] (OAG) ... SDT
Saigo [*Japan*] [*Seismograph station code, US Geological Survey*] (SEIS) ... SAI
Saigon [*Vietnam*] ... SGN
Saigon [*South Vietnam*] [*Airport symbol*] (AD) ... SGN
Saigon Area Civilian Personnel Office [*Vietnam*] ... SACPO
Saigon Military Mission [*Vietnam*] ... SMM
Saigon Mission Association (EA) ... SMA
Saigon Officers Open Mess [*Vietnam*] ... SOOM
Saigon Special Zone [*Military*] ... SSZ
Saigon Transportation Terminal Command [*Republic of Vietnam Armed Forces*] ... STT
Sail Area ... SA
Sail Assist International Liaison Associates (EA) ... SAILA
SAIL [*Shuttle Avionics Integration Laboratory*] **Data Communications System** [*NASA*] (NASA) ... SDCS
Sail Dynamics Simulation Laboratory (MCD) ... SDSL
SAIL [*Shuttle Avionics Integration Laboratory*] **Interface System** [*NASA*] (NASA) ... SIS
Sail Only (CINC) ... SO
SAIL [*Shuttle Avionics Integration Laboratory*] **Test Implementation Requirements Document** [*NASA*] (NASA) ... STIRD
Sail Training Association (EA) ... STA
Sailed ... SD
Sailed ... SLD
Sailed as Per List (ODBW) ... sapl
Sailing (WGA) ... SLG
Sailing Date (DS) ... S/D
Sailing Directions [*British*] ... SD
Sailing Education Association ... SEA
Sailing Industry Association (EA) ... SIA
Sailing Order [*Navy*] (NVT) ... SAILORD
Sailing Plan Report ... SP
Sailing Report [*Navy*] (NVT) ... SAILEDREP
Sailing Report [*Navy*] ... SAILREP
Sailing Ship ... S
Sailing Vessel ... SV
Sailmaker [*Navy British*] ... SLMR
Sailmakers Institute (EA) ... SI
Sailors, Soldiers and Airmen's Mothers' Association of Australia ... SSAMA
Sailors' Union of the Pacific (EA) ... SUP
Sailplane Homebuilders Association (EA) ... SHA
Sainan-Gakuin-Daigaku (BJA) ... Sainan-G-D
Saint ... S
Saint ... SNT
Saint (EY) ... ST
Saint (ODBW) ... St
Saint ... ST
Saint (DD) ... St
Ste. Adele, PQ [*FM radio station call letters*] ... CIME
Ste. Agathe Des Monts, PQ [*ICAO location identifier*] (ICLI) ... CWOH
Saint Agnes Cathedral High School, Uniondale, NY [*Library symbol*] [*Library of Congress*] (LCLS) ... NUnStA
St. Agnes High School Library, Rochester, NY [*OCLC symbol*] (OCLC) ... RXI
Saint Agnes Hospital and Medical Center, Fresno, CA [*Library symbol Library of Congress*] (LCLS) ... CFSA
Saint Agnes Hospital, Baltimore, MD [*Library symbol Library of Congress*] (LCLS) ... MdBSt
Saint Agnes Hospital, Fond Du Lac, WI [*Library symbol Library of Congress*] (LCLS) ... WFonSA
St. Alban's Public Library, Newfoundland [*Library symbol National Library of Canada*] (NLC) ... NFSAL
St. Albans Public Library, St. Albans, NF, Canada [*Library symbol Library of Congress*] (LCLS) ... CaNfSal
St. Alban's Repertory Theater [*Washington, DC*] ... SART
St. Albans, VT [*FM radio station call letters*] ... WLFE
St. Albans, VT [*AM radio station call letters*] ... WWSR
St. Albans, WV [*AM radio station call letters*] ... WCOZ
St. Albans, WV [*FM radio station call letters*] ... WKLC
St. Albert, AB [*FM radio station call letters*] ... CFMG
St. Albert, AB [*AM radio station call letters*] ... CHMG
St. Albert Public Library, Alberta [*Library symbol National Library of Canada*] (NLC) ... ASA
St. Albert Public Library, St. Albert, AB, Canada [*Library symbol Library of Congress*] (LCLS) ... CaASA
St. Aloysious School, Olivia, MN [*Library symbol*] [*Library of Congress*] (LCLS) ... MnOlStA
Saint Aloysius Academy, Meridian, MS [*Library symbol Library of Congress*] (LCLS) ... MsMStA
Saint Alphonsus Regional Medical Center, Medical Library, Boise, ID [*Library symbol*] [*Library of Congress*] (LCLS) ... IdBSA
St. Amant Center, Winnipeg, Manitoba [*Library symbol National Library of Canada*] (NLC) ... MWSAC
Saint Amant Center, Winnipeg, MB, Canada [*Library symbol Library of Congress*] (LCLS) ... CaMWSAC
Saint Ambrose College [*Davenport, IA*] ... SAC
Saint Ambrose College, Davenport, IA [*Library symbol Library of Congress*] (LCLS) ... IaDaSA
St. Ambrose College, Davenport, IA [*OCLC symbol*] (OCLC) ... IOJ
St. Anastasis School, Hutchinson, MN [*Library symbol*] [*Library of Congress*] (LCLS) ... MnHuStA
St. Andrew Goldfields Ltd. [*Toronto Stock Exchange symbol*] ... SAS
St. Andrew Society [*Edinburgh, Scotland*] (EAIO) ... SAS
St. Andrews [*Washington*] [*Seismograph station code, US Geological Survey*] (SEIS) ... SAW
St. Andrews Airways [*ICAO designator*] (AD) ... CW
Saint Andrew's Ambulance Association [*British*] (DBA) ... StAAA
St. Andrews Branch, Stormount, Dundas, and Glengarry County Library, Ontario [*Library symbol National Library of Canada*] (BIB) ... OSTASDG
St. Andrews Campus, New Brunswick Community College [*Library symbol National Library of Canada*] (BIB) ... NBSTAC
St. Andrew's College, Saskatoon, Saskatchewan [*Library symbol National Library of Canada*] (NLC) ... SSSA
Saint Andrew's College, Saskatoon, SK, Canada [*Library symbol Library of Congress*] (LCLS) ... CaSSSA
St. Andrew's College, Winnipeg, Manitoba [*Library symbol National Library of Canada*] (NLC) ... MWSA
Saint Andrew's College, Winnipeg, MB, Canada [*Library symbol Library of Congress*] (LCLS) ... CaMWSA
St. Andrew's Cross ... X
Saint Andrews Golf Corp. [*NASDAQ symbol*] (SAG) ... SAGC
Saint Andrews Golf Corp. [*Associated Press*] (SAG) ... StAndr
Saint Andrews Golf Corp. [*Associated Press*] (SAG) ... StAndrew
Saint Andrews Golf Wrrt [*NASDAQ symbol*] (TTSB) ... SAGCW
St. Andrews Ltd. [*Canada ICAO designator*] (FAAC) ... SDA
St. Andrews, NF [*FM radio station call letters*] ... CFCV
Saint Andrews Presbyterian College, Laurinburg, NC [*Library symbol Library of Congress*] (LCLS) ... NcLS
St. Andrews Presbyterian College, Laurinburg, NC [*OCLC symbol*] (OCLC) ... NSP
St. Andrews, SC [*FM radio station call letters*] ... WMFX
St. Andrew's School, Elk River, MN [*Library symbol*] [*Library of Congress*] (LCLS) ... MnErSA
St. Andrew's School, High Prairie, Alberta [*Library symbol National Library of Canada*] (BIB) ... AHPSAS
St. Andrews School, St. Andrews, TN [*Library symbol Library of Congress*] (LCLS) ... TSS
St. Andrews Ukrainian Orthodox Society (EA) ... SAUOS
Ste. Anne Des Monts, PQ [*AM radio station call letters*] ... CBGN
Ste. Anne Des Monts, PQ [*AM radio station call letters*] ... CJMC
St. Anne School, Wabasso, MN [*Library symbol*] [*Library of Congress*] (LCLS) ... MnWaStA
Ste. Anne's Hospital, Ste.-Anne-De-Bellevue, PQ, Canada [*Library symbol Library of Congress*] (LCLS) ... CaQSTAH
Saint Anselm's Abbey, Washington, DC [*Library symbol Library of Congress*] (LCLS) ... DStAP
Saint Anselm's College [*Manchester, NH*] ... SAC
Saint Anselm's College, Manchester, NH [*Library symbol Library of Congress*] (LCLS) ... NhMSA
Saint Anselm's College, Manchester, NH [*OCLC symbol*] (OCLC) ... SAC
Saint Ansgar Enterprise, St. Ansgar, IA [*Library symbol Library of Congress*] (LCLS) ... IaStaE
St. Ansgar Hospital, Health Science Library, Moorhead, MN [*Library symbol*] [*Library of Congress*] (LCLS) ... MnMohSA
St. Ansgar's Scandinavian Catholic League (EA) ... SASCL
St. Anthony [*Zambia*] [*ICAO location identifier*] (ICLI) ... FLSA
Saint Anthony Friary, Marathon, WI [*Library symbol Library of Congress*] (LCLS) ... WMaraS
Saint Anthony Hospital, Memorial Medical Library, Denver, CO [*Library symbol Library of Congress*] (LCLS) ... CoDStA-M
Saint Anthony Hospital, Milwaukee, WI [*Library symbol Library of Congress*] (LCLS) ... WMSA

Saint Anthony Hospital, Pendleton, OR [*Library symbol Library of Congress*] (LCLS) ... OrPeSA
Saint Anthony Hospital, Rockford, IL [*Library symbol Library of Congress*] (LCLS) ... IRoStA
St. Anthony, ID [*AM radio station call letters*] ... KIGO
St. Anthony, NF [*Television station call letters*] ... CBNAT-4
St. Anthony, NF [*FM radio station call letters*] ... CFNN
St. Anthony, NF [*ICAO location identifier*] (ICLI) ... CYAY
St. Anthony Public Library, Newfoundland [*Library symbol National Library of Canada*] (NLC) ... NFSAN
St. Anthony Public Library, St. Anthony, ID [*Library symbol*] [*Library of Congress*] (LCLS) ... IdSa
St. Anthony Public Library, St. Anthony, NF, Canada [*Library symbol Library of Congress*] (LCLS) ... CaNfSan
St. Anthony School, St. Cloud, MN [*Library symbol*] [*Library of Congress*] (LCLS) ... MnStclSA
St. Anthony School, Watkins, MN [*Library symbol*] [*Library of Congress*] (LCLS) ... MnWatSA
Saint Anthony-On-Hudson Theological Seminary, Rensselaer, NY [*Library symbol Library of Congress*] (LCLS) ... NRenSA
Saint Anthony's Guild ... SAG
Saint Anthony's Guild, Franciscan Monastery, Paterson, NJ [*Library symbol Library of Congress*] (LCLS) ... NjPatSA
Saint Anthony's High School, Huntington Station, NY [*Library symbol*] [*Library of Congress*] (LCLS) ... NHsSAHS
Saint Anthony's Hospital, Medical Library, Alton, IL [*Library symbol Library of Congress*] (LCLS) ... IAlStA
St. Apollonia Guild (EA) ... SAG
St. Armand on the Legislative Power of England [*A publication*] (DLA) ... St Arm Leg Pow
St. Athan [*British ICAO location identifier*] (ICLI) ... EGDX
St. Athan MU [*British ICAO designator*] (FAAC) ... STN
St. Augustin [*Canada*] [*Airport symbol*] (OAG) ... YIF
St. Augustine [*Diocesan abbreviation*] [*Florida*] (TOCD) ... STA
St. Augustine Beach, FL [*FM radio station call letters*] (RBYB) ... WJQR
St. Augustine, FL [*Location identifier FAA*] (FAAL) ... SGJ
St. Augustine, FL [*AM radio station call letters*] ... WAOC
St. Augustine, FL [*FM radio station call letters*] ... WAYL
St. Augustine, FL [*FM radio station call letters*] ... WFCF
St. Augustine, FL [*AM radio station call letters*] ... WFOY
St. Augustine, FL [*FM radio station call letters*] (RBYB) ... WFSJ-FM
St. Augustine, FL [*FM radio station call letters*] ... WSOS
St. Augustine Historical Society, St. Augustine, FL [*Library symbol Library of Congress*] (LCLS) ... FSaHi
St. Augustine School, St. Cloud, MN [*Library symbol*] [*Library of Congress*] (LCLS) ... MnStclSt
Saint Augustine's College [*Raleigh, NC*] ... SAC
Saint Augustine's College, Raleigh, NC [*Library symbol Library of Congress*] (LCLS) ... NcRSA
St. Augustine's College, Raleigh, NC [*OCLC symbol*] (OCLC) ... NRA
St. Augustine's Seminary Library, University of Toronto [*UTLAS symbol*] ... KSA
Saint Augustine's Seminary, Toronto, ON, Canada [*Library symbol Library of Congress*] (LCLS) ... CaOTStA
St. Augustine's Seminary, Toronto, Ontario [*Library symbol National Library of Canada*] (NLC) ... OTSTA
Saint Barnabas Medical Center, Staff Library, Livingston, NJ [*Library symbol Library of Congress*] (LCLS) ... NjLivStB
St. Barnabas Medical Staff Library, Livingston, NJ [*OCLC symbol*] (OCLC) ... VYB
St. Barthelemy [*Leeward Islands, West Indies*] [*Airport symbol*] (AD) ... BTO
St. Barthelemy [*Leeward Islands*] [*Airport symbol*] (OAG) ... SBH
St. Bartholomew's Hospital [*London*] ... BARTS
Saint Basil's College [*Stamford, CT*] ... SBC
St. Basil's Seminary [*Collection transferred to OTSTM*] **Ontario** [*Library symbol National Library of Canada*] (NLC) ... OTSTB
Saint Bede Academy, Peru, IL [*Library symbol Library of Congress*] (LCLS) ... IPerStB
Saint Benedict College [*Indiana*] ... SBC
Saint Benedict's Abbey, Benet Library, Benet Lake, WI [*Library symbol Library of Congress*] (LCLS) ... WBelSB
Saint Benedict's Family Medical Center, Medical Library, Jerome, ID [*Library symbol*] [*Library of Congress*] (LCLS) ... IdJH
Saint Bernard Club of America (EA) ... SBCA
Saint Bernard College [*Alabama*] ... SBC
St. Bernard College, St. Bernard, AL [*Library symbol Library of Congress*] (LCLS) ... AStbC
Saint Bernard Parish Library, Chalmette, LA [*Library symbol Library of Congress*] (LCLS) ... LChSt
Saint Bernardine of Siena College [*New York*] ... SBSC
St. Bernard's School, Thief River Falls, MN [*Library symbol*] [*Library of Congress*] (LCLS) ... MnTSB
Saint Bernard's Seminary and College [*New York*] ... SBSC
St. Bernard's Seminary and College Library, Rochester, NY [*OCLC symbol*] (OCLC) ... RVH
Saint Bernard's Seminary and College, Rochester, NY [*Library symbol Library of Congress*] (LCLS) ... NRSB
St. Blazey [*British depot code*] ... STB
St. Bonaventure, NY [*FM radio station call letters*] ... WSBU
Saint Bonaventure University [*New York*] ... SBU
St. Bonaventure University (GAGS) ... St Bonaventure U
St. Bonaventure University, St. Bonaventure, NY [*Library symbol Library of Congress*] (LCLS) ... NStBU
St. Bonaventure University, St. Bonaventure, NY [*OCLC symbol*] (OCLC) ... VYS
St. Boniface Elementary School, Cold Spring, MN [*Library symbol*] [*Library of Congress*] (LCLS) ... MnClsS
Saint Boniface General Hospital Medical Library, Winnipeg, Manitoba [*Library symbol National Library of Canada*] (NLC) ... MWSBM
St. Boniface General Hospital, Medical Library, Winnipeg, MB, Canada [*Library symbol Library of Congress*] (LCLS) ... CaMWSBM
Saint Boniface General Hospital School of Nursing Library, Winnipeg, Manitoba [*Library symbol National Library of Canada*] (NLC) ... MWSBN
St. Boniface General Hospital, School of Nursing, Winnipeg, MB, Canada [*Library symbol Library of Congress*] (LCLS) ... CaMWSBN
St. Boniface, MB [*AM radio station call letters*] ... CKSB
St. Boniface, MB [*FM radio station call letters*] ... CKXL
Saint Boniface Public Library, Winnipeg, Manitoba [*Library symbol National Library of Canada*] (NLC) ... MWSB
St. Boniface Public Library, Winnipeg, MB, Canada [*Library symbol Library of Congress*] (LCLS) ... CaMWSB
St. Brendan Cup Committee in America [*Defunct*] (EA) ... SBCC
Saint Briavels [*England*] ... STBRIAV
St. Brieuc [*France*] [*Airport symbol*] (OAG) ... SBK
St. Brieux, SK [*Television station call letters*] ... CBKFT-4
Saint Cabrini Hospital Library, Seattle, WA [*Library symbol*] [*Library of Congress*] (LCLS) ... WaSSC
Saint Camillus Hospital, Wauwatosa, WI [*Library symbol Library of Congress*] (LCLS) ... WWaSC
Saint Catharine Junior College [*Kentucky*] ... SCJC
St. Catharines Historical Museum, Ontario [*Library symbol National Library of Canada*] (BIB) ... OSTCM
St. Catharines, ON [*FM radio station call letters*] (RBYB) ... CHTZ-FM
St. Catharines Public Library [*UTLAS symbol*] ... SCP
St. Catharines Public Library, Ontario [*Library symbol National Library of Canada*] (NLC) ... OSTC
St. Catharines Public Library, St. Catharines, ON, Canada [*Library symbol Library of Congress*] (LCLS) ... CaOStC
St. Catharines Teachers' College, Ontario [*Library symbol National Library of Canada*] (NLC) ... OSTCT
St. Catharines Teachers' College, Reference Library, St. Catharines, ON, Canad a [*Library symbol Library of Congress*] (LCLS) ... CaOStCTR
St. Catharines Teachers' College, St. Catharines, ON, Canada [*Library symbol Library of Congress*] (LCLS) ... CaOStCT
St. Catharines Teachers' Reference Library, Ontario [*Library symbol National Library of Canada*] (NLC) ... OSTCTR
St. Catherine/St. Catherine [*Egypt*] [*ICAO location identifier*] (ICLI) ... HESC
St. Catherine's Hospital, Kenosha, WI [*Library symbol Library of Congress*] (LCLS) ... WKenSC
St. Catherines, ON [*FM radio station call letters*] ... CHRE
St. Catherines, ON [*AM radio station call letters*] ... CHSC
St. Catherines, ON [*AM radio station call letters*] ... CKTB
Saint Charles Borromeo Seminary [*Pennsylvania*] ... SCBS
Saint Charles Borromeo Seminary, Overbrook, PA [*OCLC symbol*] (OCLC) ... RSC
Saint Charles Borromeo Seminary, Philadelphia, PA [*Library symbol Library of Congress*] (LCLS) ... PPStCh
St. Charles City-County Library, St. Charles, MO [*Library symbol Library of Congress*] (LCLS) ... MoStc
Saint Charles Hospital, Port Jefferson, NY [*Library symbol Library of Congress*] (LCLS) ... NPjSCH
Saint Charles Medical Center, Medical Library, Bend, OR [*Library symbol Library of Congress*] (LCLS) ... OrBeMC
St. Charles, MN [*FM radio station call letters*] (RBYB) ... KANP
St. Charles, MO [*FM radio station call letters*] ... KCLC
St. Charles, MO [*AM radio station call letters*] ... KIRL
Saint Charles Parish Library, Hahnville, LA [*Library symbol Library of Congress*] (LCLS) ... LHaSC
Saint Charles Public Library District, Saint Charles, IL [*Library symbol Library of Congress*] (LCLS) ... IStc
Saint Charles Public Library, Saint Charles, MI [*Library symbol Library of Congress*] (LCLS) ... MiStch
Saint Charles Seminary [*Later, SCBS*] [*Pennsylvania*] ... SCS
Saint Charles Seminary, Carthagena, OH [*Library symbol Library of Congress*] (LCLS) ... OCartSC
St. Christopher-Nevis [*ANSI two-letter standard code*] (CNC) ... KN
St. Christopher-Nevis [*ANSI three-letter standard code*] (CNC) ... KNA
St. Christopher-Nevis-Anguilla [*MARC geographic area code Library of Congress*] (LCCP) ... nwxi--
St. Christopher-Nevis-Anguilla [*MARC country of publication code Library of Congress*] (LCCP) ... xi
Saint Clair College, Windsor, ON, Canada [*Library symbol Library of Congress*] (LCLS) ... CaOWSC
St. Clair College, Windsor, Ontario [*Library symbol National Library of Canada*] (NLC) ... OWSC
St. Clair Community College, Port Huron, MI [*OCLC symbol*] (OCLC) ... EEC
Saint Clair Community College, Port Huron, MI [*Library symbol Library of Congress*] (LCLS) ... MiPhS
Saint Clair County Community Mental Health Services, Port Huron, MI [*Library symbol*] [*Library of Congress*] (LCLS) ... MiPhM
Saint Clair County Library, Osceola, MO [*Library symbol Library of Congress*] (LCLS) ... MoOs
St. Clair County Library System, Port Huron, MI [*OCLC symbol*] (OCLC) ... EYS
Saint Clair County Library System, Port Huron, MI [*Library symbol Library of Congress*] (LCLS) ... MiPh
Saint Clair County Mental Health Board, Belleville, IL [*Library symbol Library of Congress*] (LCLS) ... IBelSCM
St. Clair Paint & Wallpaper Corp. [*Toronto Stock Exchange symbol*] ... SCW
St. Clair Resources Ltd. [*Vancouver Stock Exchange symbol*] ... CS
Saint Clair Shores Public Library, Saint Clair Shores, MI [*Library symbol Library of Congress*] (LCLS) ... MiStc
St. Clare Capuchin Sisters (TOCD) ... CPC

Saint Clare Hospital, Monroe, WI [*Library symbol Library of Congress*] (LCLS) .... WMoS
Saint Clare's Hospital, Physicians' Library, Schenectady, NY [*Library symbol Library of Congress*] (LCLS) .... NSchStC
St. Clare's Mercy Hospital, St. John's, Newfoundland [*Library symbol National Library of Canada*] (NLC) .... NFSSC
Saint Clare's Mercy Hospital, St. John's, NF, Canada [*Library symbol Library of Congress*] (LCLS) .... CaNfSSC
Saint Clare's Mercy Hospital, School of Nursing, St. John's, NF, Canada [*Library symbol Library of Congress*] (LCLS) .... CaNfSSCN
St. Claude [*Guadeloupe*] [*Seismograph station code, US Geological Survey*] (SEIS) .... SCG
Saint Clement Hospital, Red Bud, IL [*Library symbol Library of Congress*] (LCLS) .... IRbSCH
St. Clement School, Grande Prairie, Alberta [*Library symbol National Library of Canada*] (BIB) .... AGPSCS
St. Clement's Church Case [*Philadelphia, PA*] [*A publication*] (DLA) .... St Clem
St. Cloud [*Diocesan abbreviation*] [*Minnesota*] (TOCD) .... SCL
St. Cloud Area Vo-Tech Institute, St. Cloud, MN [*Library symbol*] [*Library of Congress*] (LCLS) .... MnStclVT
St. Cloud Cathedral High School, St. Cloud, MN [*Library symbol*] [*Library of Congress*] (LCLS) .... MnStclCH
St. Cloud Hospital, Health Sciences Library, St. Cloud, MN [*Library symbol*] [*Library of Congress*] (LCLS) .... MnStclH
St. Cloud Media Services, St. Cloud, MN [*Library symbol*] [*Library of Congress*] (LCLS) .... MnStclMS
St. Cloud, MN [*Location identifier FAA*] (FAAL) .... JSK
St. Cloud, MN [*FM radio station call letters*] .... KCFB
St. Cloud, MN [*FM radio station call letters*] .... KCLD
St. Cloud, MN [*AM radio station call letters*] .... KNSI
St. Cloud, MN [*FM radio station call letters*] .... KVSC
St. Cloud, MN [*Television station call letters*] .... KXLI
St. Cloud, MN [*Location identifier FAA*] (FAAL) .... STC
St. Cloud, MN [*AM radio station call letters*] .... WJON
St. Cloud, MN [*FM radio station call letters*] .... WWJO
St. Cloud School of Nursing Library, St. Cloud, MN [*Library symbol*] [*Library of Congress*] (LCLS) .... MnStclN
St. Cloud South Elementary School, St. Cloud, MN [*Library symbol*] [*Library of Congress*] (LCLS) .... MnStclSE
St. Cloud State University .... SCSU
St. Cloud State University (GAGS) .... St Cloud St U
St. Cloud State University, St. Cloud, MN [*Library symbol Library of Congress*] (LCLS) .... MnStclS
St. Cloud State University, St. Cloud, MN [*OCLC symbol*] (OCLC) .... MST
Saint Columban's Seminary, Silver Creek, NY [*Library symbol Library of Congress Obsolete*] (LCLS) .... NSilStC
St. Croix [*Virgin Islands*] [*Seismograph station code, US Geological Survey*] (SEIS) .... SCV
St. Croix [*Virgin Islands*] [*Airport symbol*] .... STX
St. Croix/Alexander Hamilton [*Virgin Islands*] [*ICAO location identifier*] (ICLI) .... TISX
St. Croix Hotel and Tourism Association [*Virgin Islands*] (EAIO) .... SCHA
St. Croix Island (VRA) VI
St. Croix Public Library, St. Stephen, New Brunswick [*Library symbol National Library of Canada*] (NLC) .... NBSSSC
St. Croix [*Virgin Islands*] **Seaplane Base** [*Airport symbol*] (OAG) .... SSB
St. Croix, VI [*Location identifier FAA*] (FAAL) .... COY
St. David's Society of the State of New York (EA) .... SDS
Saint Dominic High School, Oyster Bay, NY [*Library symbol*] [*Library of Congress*] (LCLS) .... NOyStD
St. Edward, PE [*Television station call letters*] CKCW-2
St. Edward School, Minneota, MN [*Library symbol*] [*Library of Congress*] (LCLS) .... MnMinSE
Saint Edward's University [*Texas*] .... SEU
St. Edward's University (GAGS) .... St Edward's U
Saint Edward's University, Austin, TX [*Library symbol Library of Congress*] (LCLS) .... TxAuSE
St. Eleuthere, PQ [*AM radio station call letters*] .... CHRT
Saint Elizabeth Hospital, Appleton, WI [*Library symbol Library of Congress*] (LCLS) .... WASE
Saint Elizabeth Hospital, Baker, OR [*Library symbol Library of Congress*] (LCLS) .... OrBakSE
Saint Elizabeth Hospital, Danville, IL [*Library symbol*] [*Library of Congress*] (LCLS) .... IDanviSE
Saint Elizabeth Hospital, Danville, IL [*Library symbol Library of Congress*] (LCLS) .... IDanviStE
Saint Elizabeth Hospital, Dayton, OH [*Library symbol Library of Congress*] (LCLS) .... ODaStE
Saint Elizabeth Hospital, Health Science Library, Beaumont, TX [*Library symbol Library of Congress*] (LCLS) .... TxBeaSE
Saint Elizabeth Hospital, Health Sciences Library, Yakima, WA [*Library symbol Library of Congress*] (LCLS) .... WaYSE
St. Elizabeth Hospital Medical Center, Bannon Health Science Library, Lafayette, IN [*Library symbol*] [*Library of Congress*] (LCLS) .... InLSEH
Saint Elizabeth Medical Center, Covington, KY [*Library symbol Library of Congress*] (LCLS) .... KyCovStE
Saint Elizabeth's Hospital, Belleville, IL [*Library symbol Library of Congress*] (LCLS) .... IBelSH
Saint Elmo Community Unit, School District 202, Saint Elmo, IL [*Library symbol Library of Congress*] (LCLS) .... ISteSD
Saint Elmo Public Library, St. Elmo, IL [*Library symbol Library of Congress*] (LCLS) .... ISte
St. Etienne [*France*] [*Airport symbol*] (OAG) .... EBU
Saint Eustatius [*Antilles*] [*Airport symbol*] (OAG) .... EUX
Saint Fidelis College and Seminary [*Pennsylvania*] .... SFCS
Saint Francis Association for Catholic Evangelism [*Defunct*] (EA) .... FACE
St. Francis Capital [*NASDAQ symbol*] (TTSB) .... STFR
Saint Francis Capital Corp. [*NASDAQ symbol*] (SAG) .... STFR
Saint Francis Capital Corp. [*Associated Press*] (SAG) .... StFrancis
St. Francis Center (EA) .... SFC
Saint Francis College [*Indiana; Maine; New York; Pennsylvania; Wisconsin*] .... SFC
Saint Francis College, Brooklyn, NY [*Library symbol Library of Congress*] (LCLS) .... NBStF
St. Francis College, Brooklyn, NY [*OCLC symbol*] (OCLC) .... VZF
Saint Francis College, Burlington, WI [*Library symbol Library of Congress Obsolete*] (LCLS) .... WBurSFC
Saint Francis College, Fort Wayne, IN [*Library symbol Library of Congress*] (LCLS) .... InFwSF
St. Francis College (Indiana) (GAGS) .... St Francis C (Ind)
Saint Francis College, Loretto, PA [*Library symbol Library of Congress*] (LCLS) .... PLor
Saint Francis College, Loretto, PA [*OCLC symbol*] (OCLC) .... PSF
St. Francis College (Pennsylvania) (GAGS) .... St Francis C (Penn)
St. Francis Convent, Little Falls, MN [*Library symbol*] [*Library of Congress*] (LCLS) .... MnLfS
Saint Francis Hospital, Blue Island, IL [*Library symbol Library of Congress*] (LCLS) .... IBiS
Saint Francis Hospital, Health Science Library, Lynwood, CA [*Library symbol Library of Congress*] (LCLS) .... CLySF
Saint Francis Hospital, La Crosse, WI [*Library symbol Library of Congress*] (LCLS) .... WLacSF
Saint Francis Hospital, Medical Library, Memphis, TN [*Library symbol Library of Congress*] (LCLS) .... TMStF
Saint Francis Hospital, Milwaukee, WI [*Library symbol Library of Congress*] (LCLS) .... WMSFH
St. Francis Hospital of Buffalo, Buffalo, NY [*Library symbol*] [*Library of Congress*] (LCLS) .... NBuSFH
Saint Francis Hospital, Olean, NY [*Library symbol Library of Congress*] (LCLS) .... NOlSFH
Saint Francis Hospital, Peoria, IL [*Library symbol Library of Congress*] (LCLS) .... IPStF
Saint Francis Hospital, Roslyn, NY [*Library symbol Library of Congress*] (LCLS) .... NRoslH
Saint Francis Hospital, Wichita, KS [*Library symbol Library of Congress*] (LCLS) .... KWiSF
St. Francis, KS [*Location identifier FAA*] (FAAL) .... SYF
Saint Francis Medical Center, Health Science Library, Trenton, NJ [*Library symbol Library of Congress*] (LCLS) .... NjTStF
St. Francis Mission Community (TOCD) .... OSF
Saint Francis/Saint George Hospital, Cincinnati, OH [*Library symbol Library of Congress*] (LCLS) .... OCStFH
Saint Francis Seminary [*Wisconsin*] .... SFS
Saint Francis Seminary, Milwaukee, WI [*Library symbol Library of Congress*] (LCLS) .... WMSF
St. Francis Xavier School, Benson, MN [*Library symbol*] [*Library of Congress*] (LCLS) .... MnBenSF
St. Francis Xavier School, Buffalo, MN [*Library symbol*] [*Library of Congress*] (LCLS) .... MnBfSF
St. Francis Xavier School, Sartell, MN [*Library symbol*] [*Library of Congress*] (LCLS) .... MnSarS
St. Francis Xavier University, Antigonish, Nova Scotia [*Library symbol National Library of Canada*] (NLC) .... NSAS
Saint Francis Xavier University, Antigonish, NS, Canada [*Library symbol Library of Congress*] (LCLS) .... CaNSAS
Saint Francis Xavier University, Chemistry Department, Antigonish, NS, Canada [*Library symbol Library of Congress*] (LCLS) .... CaNSASC
St. Francis Xavier University Library [*UTLAS symbol*] .... SFX
St. Gabriel De Brandon, PQ [*FM radio station call letters*] .... CFNJ
St. Gabriel's Hall, Phoenixville, PA [*OCLC symbol*] (OCLC) .... PIH
St. Gabriel's Hospital, Little Falls, MN [*Library symbol*] [*Library of Congress*] (LCLS) .... MnLfSG
Saint Gaudens Montrejeau [*France ICAO location identifier*] (ICLI) .... LFIM
Ste. Genevieve, MO [*FM radio station call letters*] (RBYB) .... KPNT-FM
Saint Genevieve Resources Ltd. [*Toronto Stock Exchange symbol*] .... SGV
Saint George [*Australia Airport symbol*] (OAG) .... SGO
St. George [*South Carolina*] [*Seismograph station code, US Geological Survey*] (SEIS) .... SGS
Saint George [*Utah*] [*Airport symbol*] (OAG) .... SGU
St. George Association of the USA (EA) .... SGAUSA
Saint George Island [*Alaska*] [*Airport symbol*] (OAG) .... STG
Saint George Island, AK [*Location identifier FAA*] (FAAL) .... SGG
St. George Minerals [*Vancouver Stock Exchange symbol*] .... SGG
St. George, SC [*Location identifier FAA*] (FAAL) .... SZD
St. George, SC [*AM radio station call letters*] .... WQIZ
Saint George United Methodist Church, Philadelphia, PA [*Library symbol Library of Congress*] (LCLS) .... PPOS
St. George, UT [*AM radio station call letters*] .... KDXU
St. George, UT [*FM radio station call letters*] .... KRDC
St. George, UT [*AM radio station call letters*] .... KSGI
St. George, UT [*Television station call letters*] .... KUSG
St. George, UT [*FM radio station call letters*] .... KVYS
St. George, UT [*FM radio station call letters*] .... KZEZ
St. George, UT [*Location identifier FAA*] (FAAL) .... OZN
Saint George, UT [*Location identifier FAA*] (FAAL) .... SGU
St. Georges [*Grenada*] [*ICAO location identifier*] (ICLI) .... TGPG
St. Georges Branch, South Dumfries Public Library, Ontario [*Library symbol National Library of Canada*] (BIB) .... OSTG
St. George's Cathedral, Anglican Church of Canada, Kingston, Ontario [*Library symbol National Library of Canada*] (NLC) .... OKASG

St. George's College, Toronto, ON, Canada [Library symbol] [Library of Congress] (LCLS) .... CaOTSTG

St. George's College, Toronto, Ontario [Library symbol National Library of Canada] (NLC) .... OTSTG

St. Georges De Beauce, PQ [FM radio station call letters] .... CIRO

St. Georges de Beauce, PQ [AM radio station call letters] .... CKRB

St. Georges Public Library, Newfoundland [Library symbol National Library of Canada] (NLC) .... NFSGE

St. Georges Public Library, St. Georges, NF, Canada [Library symbol Library of Congress] (LCLS) .... CaNfSGe

St. George's Society of New York (EA) .... SGSNY

St. Gerard School, Grande Prairie, Alberta [Library symbol National Library of Canada] (BIB) .... AGPSGS

St. German's Doctor and Student [A publication] (DLA) .... St Ger D & S

Saint Gregory College [Oklahoma] .... SGC

Saint Gregory Seminary, Cincinnati, OH [Library symbol Library of Congress] (LCLS) .... OCStG

St. Helena [MARC geographic area code Library of Congress] (LCCP) .... lsxj--

St. Helena [ANSI two-letter standard code] (CNC) .... SH

St. Helena [ANSI three-letter standard code] (CNC) .... SHN

St. Helena [MARC country of publication code Library of Congress] (LCCP) .... xj

St. Helena and Dependencies Philatelic Society (EA) .... SHDPS

St. Helena, Ascension, and Tristan da Cunha Philatelic Society (EA) .... SHATCPS

Saint Helena, CA [FM radio station call letters] .... KVYN

Saint Helena Gold Mines [NASDAQ symbol] (SAG) .... SGOL

St. Helena Gold Mines ADR [NASDAQ symbol] (TTSB) .... SGOLY

St. Helena Gold Mines Ltd. [NASDAQ symbol] (NQ) .... SGOL

Saint Helena Gold Mines Ltd. [Associated Press] (SAG) .... StHlGd

St. Helena Public Library, St. Helena, CA [Library symbol Library of Congress] (LCLS) .... CSah

St. Helens [Tasmania] [Airport symbol] (AD) .... HLS

St. Helens, OR [AM radio station call letters] .... KOHI

St. Henry Catholic Church, School of Religion Library, Monticello, MN [Library symbol] [Library of Congress] (LCLS) .... MnMcSR

Saint Henry's Seminary, Belleville, IL [Library symbol Library of Congress] (LCLS) .... IBelS

St. Hilarion, PQ [FM radio station call letters] .... CIHO

Saint Hubert Society of America (EA) .... SHSA

Saint Hyacinth College and Seminary, Granby, MA [Library symbol Library of Congress] (LCLS) .... MGranbyS

St. Hyacinthe, PQ [FM radio station call letters] .... CFEI

St. Ignace, MI [AM radio station call letters] .... WIDG

St. Ignace, MI [FM radio station call letters] .... WMKC

St. Ignace Public Library, St. Ignace, MI [Library symbol Library of Congress] (LCLS) .... MiSti

St. Isidore Community Library [Bibliotheque de St-Isidore] Alberta [Library symbol National Library of Canada] (NLC) .... ASIC

Saint Isidore Community Library, Saint Isidore, AB, Canada [Library symbol] [Library of Congress] (LCLS) .... CaASiC

Saint Ives Laboratories, Inc. [Associated Press] (SAG) .... StIves

St. Ives Laboratories, Inc. [NASDAQ symbol] (NQ) .... SWIS

Saint James Hospital, Pontiac, IL [Library symbol Library of Congress] (LCLS) .... IPoH

St. James Lutheran School, Howard Lake, MN [Library symbol] [Library of Congress] (LCLS) .... MnHIS

St. James, MI [Location identifier FAA] (FAAL) .... SJX

St. James, MN [FM radio station call letters] .... KXAC

St. James, MN [FM radio station call letters] .... KXAX

St. James, MO [FM radio station call letters] .... KTTR

Saint James Parish Library, Lutcher, LA [Library symbol Library of Congress] (LCLS) .... LLu

St. James Press [Publisher] .... SJP

St. Jean Bosco Library, Matachewan, Ontario [Library symbol National Library of Canada] (BIB) .... OMSJB

St. Jean sur Richelieu, PQ [FM radio station call letters] .... CFZZ

Saint Jerome Hospital, Medical Library, Batavia, NY [Library symbol Library of Congress] (LCLS) .... NBatStJ

Saint Joan's International Alliance [See also AIJA] (EAIO) .... SJIA

Saint Joe Corp. [NYSE symbol] (SAG) .... SJP

Saint Joe Corp. [Associated Press] (SAG) .... StJoe

Saint Joe News, Saint Joe, IN [Library symbol Library of Congress] (LCLS) .... InStjN

St. Joe Paper [NYSE symbol] (TTSB) .... SJP

St. Joe Paper Co. [NYSE symbol] (SPSG) .... SJP

St. Joe Paper Co. [Associated Press] (SAG) .... StJoe

St. Johann, Tirol [Austria ICAO location identifier] (ICLI) .... LOIJ

Saint John [Virgin Islands] [Airport symbol] (OAG) .... SJF

St. John [Virgin Islands] [Seismograph station code, US Geological Survey] (SEIS) .... SJV

Saint John [Canada] [Airport symbol] (OAG) .... YSJ

St. John Ambulance (Nursing Cadets) [British] .... STJA(NC)

St. John Cantius Seminary, St. Louis, MO [Library symbol Library of Congress] (LCLS) .... MoSSJ

Saint John College of Cleveland [Ohio] .... SJCC

Saint John College of Cleveland, Cleveland, OH [Library symbol Library of Congress] (LCLS) .... OClstJ

Saint John Fisher College [Rochester, NY] .... SJFC

Saint John Fisher College, Rochester, NY [Library symbol Library of Congress] (LCLS) .... NRSJ

St. John Fisher College, Rochester, NY [OCLC symbol] (OCLC) .... VZJ

St. John Island (VRA) VI

St. John Knits [NYSE symbol] (TTSB) .... SJK

Saint John Knits, Inc. [NYSE symbol] (SAG) .... SJK

St. John Knits, Inc. [NYSE symbol] (SPSG) .... SJK

St. John Knits, Inc. [Associated Press] (SAG) .... StJohn

Saint John Knits, Inc. [Associated Press] (SAG) .... StJohn

Saint John, NB [AM radio station call letters] .... CBAT

St. John, NB [FM radio station call letters] .... CBD-FM

St. John, NB [AM radio station call letters] .... CFBC

St. John, NB [AM radio station call letters] .... CHSJ

St. John, NB [FM radio station call letters] .... CIOK

St. John, NB [FM radio station call letters] .... CJYC

St. John, NB [Television station call letters] .... CKLT

Saint John, NB [ICAO location identifier] (ICLI) .... CYSJ

St. John Nepomuk School, Lastrup, MN [Library symbol] [Library of Congress] (LCLS) .... MnLS

Saint John of Damascus Association of Orthodox Iconographers, Iconologists, and Architects (EA) .... SJDAOIIA

Saint John Parish Library, La Place, LA [Library symbol Library of Congress] (LCLS) .... LLap

Saint John Regional Library, New Brunswick [Library symbol National Library of Canada] (NLC) .... NBS

Saint John Regional Library, Saint John, NB, Canada [Library symbol Library of Congress] (LCLS) .... CaNBS

Saint John the Baptist, Clewer .... SJBC

Saint John Vianney Seminary, East Aurora, NY [Library symbol Library of Congress] (LCLS) .... NEAuS

Saint John Vocational School, New Brunswick [Library symbol National Library of Canada] (NLC) .... NBSVS

Saint John Vocational School, Saint John, NB, Canada [Library symbol Library of Congress] (LCLS) .... CaNBSVS

St. Johns [Antigua, Leeward Islands, West Indies] [Airport symbol] (AD) .... SJH

St. John's [Newfoundland] [Seismograph station code, US Geological Survey] (SEIS) .... STJ

St. Johns [Canada] [Airport symbol] (OAG) .... YYT

St. Johns, AZ [FM radio station call letters] .... KQZE

St. Johns, AZ [Location identifier FAA] (FAAL) .... SJN

Saint John's Church, Perth Amboy, NJ [Library symbol Library of Congress] (LCLS) .... NjPeraSt

St. John's College [Cambridge, England] (DAS) .... JOH

Saint John's College [California; Kansas; Maryland] .... SJC

Saint John's College, Annapolis, MD [Library symbol Library of Congress] (LCLS) .... MdAS

Saint John's College in Santa Fe, Santa Fe, NM [Library symbol Library of Congress] (LCLS) .... NmSStJ

St. John's College (Sante Fe) (GAGS) .... St John's C

Saint John's College, Winfield, KS [Library symbol Library of Congress] (LCLS) .... KWSJ

St. John's College, Winnipeg, Manitoba [Library symbol National Library of Canada] (NLC) .... MWSJ

Saint John's College, Winnipeg, MB, Canada [Library symbol Library of Congress] (LCLS) .... CaMWSJ

Saint John's Hospital, Fargo, ND [Library symbol Library of Congress] (LCLS) .... NdFStJ

St. John's Hospital, Longview, WA [Library symbol] [Library of Congress] (LCLS) .... WaLoSH

St. John's Hospital, St. Paul, MN [Library symbol Library of Congress] (LCLS) .... MnSSJ

Saint John's Hospital, Science Library, Springfield, IL [Library symbol] [Library of Congress] (LCLS) .... ISStH

St. John's Lutheran School, Atwater, MN [Library symbol] [Library of Congress] (LCLS) .... MnAtSJS

St. John's Lutheran School, Elk River, MN [Library symbol] [Library of Congress] (LCLS) .... MnErSJL

St. John's Lutheran School, Redwood Falls, MN [Library symbol] [Library of Congress] (LCLS) .... MnRwfSJL

St. John's Lutheran School, Winsted, MN [Library symbol] [Library of Congress] (LCLS) .... MnWnSJL

St. Johns, MI [FM radio station call letters] .... WWDX

St. Johns, MI [AM radio station call letters] .... WWSJ

St. John's, NF [AM radio station call letters] .... CBN

St. John's, NF [FM radio station call letters] .... CBN-FM

St. John's, NF [Television station call letters] .... CBNT

St. John's, NF [FM radio station call letters] .... CHMR

St. John's, NF [FM radio station call letters] .... CHOZ

St. John's, NF [Television station call letters] .... CJON

St. John's, NF [AM radio station call letters] (RBYB) .... CJYQ

St. John's, NF [FM radio station call letters] .... CKIX

St. John's, NF [ICAO location identifier] (ICLI) .... CYYT

St. John's, NF [AM radio station call letters] .... VOCM

St. John's, NF [FM radio station call letters] .... VOCM-FM

St. John's, NF [AM radio station call letters] .... VOWR

Saint John's Provincial Seminary [Plymouth, MI] .... SJPS

Saint John's Provincial Seminary, Plymouth, MI [Library symbol Library of Congress] (LCLS) .... MiPlySJ

Saint Johns Public Library, Saint Johns, AZ [Library symbol Library of Congress] (LCLS) .... AzSj

St. Johns River Terminal [AAR code] .... SJRT

St. John's School, Foley, MN [Library symbol] [Library of Congress] (LCLS) .... MnFoS

St. John's School, Wood Lake, MN [Library symbol] [Library of Congress] (LCLS) .... MnWISJ

Saint John's Seminary [Brighton, MA] .... SJS

Saint John's Seminary, Brighton, MA [OCLC symbol] (OCLC) .... BJO

Saint John's Seminary, Brighton, MA [Library symbol Library of Congress] (LCLS) .... MBtS

Saint John's Seminary, Camarillo, CA [Library symbol Library of Congress] (LCLS) .... CCamarSJ

Saint John's Seminary, Little Rock, AR [*Library symbol Library of Congress*] (LCLS) .... ArLSJ
Saint John's Seminary, San Antonio, TX [*Library symbol Library of Congress*] (LCLS) .... TxSaStJ
Saint John's Smithtown Hospital, Smithtown, NY [*Library symbol Library of Congress*] (LCLS) .... NSmSJH
St. Johns Tracking Station [*Newfoundland*] .... SJS
St. John's University [*Minnesota; New York*] .... SJU
St. John's University [*Minnesota; New York*] .... STJU
St. John's University, Collegeville, MN [*Library symbol Library of Congress*] (LCLS) .... MnCS
St. John's University, Collegeville, MN [*OCLC symbol*] (OCLC) .... MNJ
St. John's University, Division of Library and Information Science, Jamaica, NY [*OCLC symbol*] (OCLC) .... SJU
St. John's University, Jamaica, NY [*Library symbol Library of Congress*] (LCLS) .... NNStJ
St. John's University Library, Jamaica, NY [*OCLC symbol*] (OCLC) .... ZSJ
St. John's University (Minnesota) (GAGS) .... St John's U (Minn)
St. John's University (New York) (GAGS) .... St John's U (NY)
St. Johns/V. C. Bird [*Antigua Island*] [*ICAO location identifier*] (ICLI) .... TAPA
St. John-St. Andrew School, Melrose, MN [*Library symbol*] [*Library of Congress*] (LCLS) .... MnMeS
St. Johnsbury & Lamoille County R. R. [*AAR code*] .... SJLC
St. Johnsbury Atheneum, St. Johnsbury, VT [*Library symbol Library of Congress*] (LCLS) .... VtStjA
St. Johnsbury, VT [*FM radio station call letters*] (RBYB) .... WCKJ-FM
St. Johnsbury, VT [*FM radio station call letters*] .... WNKV
St. Johnsbury, VT [*AM radio station call letters*] .... WSTJ
St. Johnsbury, VT [*Television station call letters*] .... WVTB
St. Josaphat in Parma [*Diocesan abbrevation*] [*Ohio*] (TOCD) .... SJP
St. Joseph [*Missouri*] [*Airport symbol*] (AD) .... STJ
St. Joseph Belt Railway Co. [*AAR code*] .... SJB
Saint Joseph College [*West Hartford, CT*] .... SJC
Saint Joseph College (Connecticut) (GAGS) .... St Joseph C (Conn)
Saint Joseph College, West Hartford, CT [*Library symbol Library of Congress*] (LCLS) .... CtWeharS
Saint Joseph College, West Hartford, CT [*OCLC symbol*] (OCLC) .... STJ
Saint Joseph Community Hospital, Vancouver, WA [*Library symbol Library of Congress*] (LCLS) .... WaVStJ
St. Joseph Grain Exchange (EA) .... SJGE
Saint Joseph Hospital, Bellingham, WA [*Library symbol Library of Congress*] (LCLS) .... WaBeSJ
St. Joseph Hospital, Chicago, IL [*Library symbol*] [*Library of Congress*] (LCLS) .... ICStJ
Saint Joseph Hospital, Denver, CO [*Library symbol Library of Congress*] (LCLS) .... CoDStJ-M
Saint Joseph Hospital, Dickinson, ND [*Library symbol Library of Congress*] (LCLS) .... NdDiStJ
Saint Joseph Hospital, Medical and Nursing Library, Fort Worth, TX [*Library symbol Library of Congress*] (LCLS) .... TxFSJ
Saint Joseph Hospital, Memphis, TN [*Library symbol Library of Congress*] (LCLS) .... TMStJo
Saint Joseph Hospital, Orange, CA [*Library symbol Library of Congress*] (LCLS) .... COrSJH
Saint Joseph Hospital, Stockton, CA [*Library symbol Library of Congress*] (LCLS) .... CStoSJ
Saint Joseph Hospital, Tacoma, WA [*Library symbol Library of Congress*] (LCLS) .... WaTSJ
Saint Joseph Hospital, Wichita, KS [*Library symbol Library of Congress*] (LCLS) .... KWiSJ
Saint Joseph Intercommunity Hospital, Cheektowaga, NY [*Library symbol Library of Congress*] (LCLS) .... NCheH
St. Joseph Lab School, St. Joseph, MN [*Library symbol*] [*Library of Congress*] (LCLS) .... MnStjoL
Saint Joseph Light & Power [*NYSE symbol*] (SAG) .... SAJ
Saint Joseph Light & Power [*Associated Press*] (SAG) .... StJoLP
St. Joseph Light & Power Co. [*NYSE symbol*] (SPSG) .... SAJ
St. Joseph Light & Power Co. [*Associated Press*] (SAG) .... StJoLP
St. Joseph Lt & Pwr [*NYSE symbol*] (TTSB) .... SAJ
Saint Joseph Mercy Hospital, General Medical Library, Pontiac, MI [*Library symbol Library of Congress*] (LCLS) .... MiPonSJ
St. Joseph, MI [*FM radio station call letters*] .... WIRX
St. Joseph, MI [*AM radio station call letters*] .... WSJM
St. Joseph, Missouri, Public Utilities Commission Reports [*A publication*] (DLA) .... St J MO PUC
St. Joseph, MO [*Location identifier FAA*] (FAAL) .... AZN
St. Joseph, MO [*AM radio station call letters*] .... KFEQ
St. Joseph, MO [*AM radio station call letters*] .... KGNM
St. Joseph, MO [*FM radio station call letters*] .... KKJO
St. Joseph, MO [*Television station call letters*] .... KQTV
St. Joseph, MO [*AM radio station call letters*] .... KSFT
St. Joseph, MO [*Television station call letters*] .... KTAJ
St. Joseph, MO [*Location identifier FAA*] (FAAL) .... STJ
St. Joseph Public Library, St. Joseph, MO [*Library symbol Library of Congress*] (LCLS) .... MoStj
St. Joseph Railway .... StJ
St. Joseph School, Grande Prairie, Alberta [*Library symbol National Library of Canada*] (BIB) .... AGPSJS
St. Joseph School, Moorhead, MN [*Library symbol*] [*Library of Congress*] (LCLS) .... MnMohSJ
St. Joseph Seminary [*California*] [*Seismograph station code, US Geological Survey*] (SEIS) .... SJH
Saint Joseph Seminary, Teutopolis, IL [*Library symbol Library of Congress*] (LCLS) .... ITeuS
Saint Joseph Seminary, Washington, DC [*Library symbol Library of Congress*] (LCLS) .... DStJ
St. Joseph State Hospital, St. Joseph, MO [*Library symbol Library of Congress*] (LCLS) .... MoStjS
St. Joseph Terminal Railroad Co. [*AAR code*] .... SJT
St. Joseph, TN [*FM radio station call letters*] .... WJOR
Saint Joseph Township Library (Swearingen Memorial Library), St. Joseph, IL [*Library symbol Library of Congress*] (LCLS) .... IStjo
St. Joseph Township Public Library, Richards Landing, Ontario [*Library symbol National Library of Canada*] (NLC) .... ORLSTJ
Saint Joseph's Abbey, St. Benedict, LA [*Library symbol Library of Congress*] (LCLS) .... LStBA
Saint Joseph's Abbey, Spencer, MA [*Library symbol Library of Congress*] (LCLS) .... MSpeSJ
Saint Joseph's College [*California; Indiana; Maine; New Jersey; New York, Pennsylvania*] .... SJC
Saint Joseph's College, Academy of Food Marketing, Philadelphia, PA [*Library symbol Library of Congress*] (LCLS) .... PPSJ-AF
Saint Joseph's College, Brentwood, NY [*Library symbol Library of Congress*] (LCLS) .... NBrenSJ
Saint Joseph's College, Brooklyn, NY [*Library symbol Library of Congress*] (LCLS) .... NBStJC
St. Joseph's College, Brooklyn, NY [*OCLC symbol*] (OCLC) .... VZT
Saint Joseph's College for Women [*Later, SJC*] [*New York*] .... SJCW
St. Joseph's College Library, Suffolk Campus, Patchogue, NY [*OCLC symbol*] (OCLC) .... VZG
Saint Joseph's College, Mountain View, CA [*Library symbol Library of Congress*] (LCLS) .... CMvSJ
Saint Joseph's College, North Windham, ME [*Library symbol Library of Congress*] (LCLS) .... MeNwS
Saint Joseph's College, Patchogue, NY [*Library symbol Library of Congress*] (LCLS) .... NPatSJ
Saint Joseph's College, Philadelphia, PA [*Library symbol Library of Congress*] (LCLS) .... PPSJ
St. Joseph's College, Philadelphia, PA [*OCLC symbol*] (OCLC) .... SJD
Saint Joseph's College, Princeton, NJ [*Library symbol Library of Congress*] (LCLS) .... NjPStJ
Saint Joseph's College, Rensselaer, IN [*Library symbol Library of Congress*] (LCLS) .... InRenS
Saint Joseph's College, Rensselaer, IN [*OCLC symbol*] (OCLC) .... ISJ
St. Joseph's Elementary School, Pierz, MN [*Library symbol*] [*Library of Congress*] (LCLS) .... MnPiS
St. Joseph's Health Centre, George Pennal Library, Toronto, ON, Canada [*Library symbol*] [*Library of Congress*] (LCLS) .... CaOTSTJ
Saint Joseph's Hospital, Beaver Dam, WI [*Library symbol Library of Congress*] (LCLS) .... WBdSJ
Saint Joseph's Hospital, Bloomington, IL [*Library symbol Library of Congress*] (LCLS) .... IBloStJ
Saint Joseph's Hospital, Breese, IL [*Library symbol Library of Congress*] (LCLS) .... IBreSJH
Saint Joseph's Hospital, Chippewa Falls, WI [*Library symbol Library of Congress*] (LCLS) .... WCfSJ
Saint Joseph's Hospital, Health Center Library, Syracuse, NY [*OCLC symbol*] (OCLC) .... ZUN
Saint Joseph's Hospital, Kansas City, MO [*Library symbol Library of Congress*] (LCLS) .... MoKStJ
Saint Joseph's Hospital, London, ON, Canada [*Library symbol Library of Congress*] (LCLS) .... CaOLSJ
St. Joseph's Hospital, London, Ontario [*Library symbol National Library of Canada*] (NLC) .... OLSJ
Saint Joseph's Hospital, Marshfield, WI [*Library symbol Library of Congress*] (LCLS) .... WMarSJ
Saint Joseph's Hospital, Medical Information Services, Alton, IL [*Library symbol Library of Congress*] (LCLS) .... IAlStJ
Saint Joseph's Hospital, Medical Library, Lewiston, ID [*Library symbol*] [*Library of Congress*] (LCLS) .... IdLSJH
Saint Joseph's Hospital, Milwaukee, WI [*Library symbol Library of Congress*] (LCLS) .... WMSJ
St. Joseph's Hospital, St. Paul, MN [*Library symbol Library of Congress*] (LCLS) .... MnSSJos
St. Joseph's Hospital, Sarnia, Ontario [*Library symbol National Library of Canada*] (BIB) .... OSSJ
Saint Joseph's Hospital, School of Nursing and Medical Library, Syracuse, NY [*Library symbol Library of Congress*] (LCLS) .... NSySJ
Saint Joseph's Hospital, School of Nursing and Medical Library, Syracuse, NY [*Library symbol*] [*Library of Congress*] (LCLS) .... NSySJ
Saint Joseph's Infirmary, Atlanta, GA [*Library symbol Library of Congress*] (LCLS) .... GASJ
Saint Joseph's Priory, Somerset, OH [*Library symbol Library of Congress*] (LCLS) .... OSoSJ
St. Joseph's School, Waite Park, MN [*Library symbol*] [*Library of Congress*] (LCLS) .... MnWpS
Saint Joseph's Seminary [*Illinois; New York*] .... SJS
Saint Joseph's Seminary, Dunwoodie, Yonkers, NY [*Library symbol Library of Congress*] (LCLS) .... NYStJ
Saint Joseph's Seraphic Seminary [*New York*] .... SJSS
St. Joseph's Society of the Sacred Heart, Jospehite Fathers (TOCD) .... ssj
Saint Joseph's Teachers' College, Montreal, PQ, Canada [*Library symbol Library of Congress*] (LCLS) .... CaQMSJ
St. Joseph's Teachers' College, Montreal, Quebec [*Library symbol National Library of Canada*] (NLC) .... QMSJ
St. Joseph's University (Pennsylvania) (GAGS) .... St Joseph's U (Penn)
Saint Jude Children's Research Hospital, Memphis, TN [*Library symbol Library of Congress*] (LCLS) .... TMStJ
St. Jude Express [*An association*] (EA) .... SJE

St. Jude League *(EA)* .... SJL
St. Jude Medical *[NASDAQ symbol]* (TTSB) .... STJM
Saint Jude Medical, Inc. *[NYSE symbol]* (SAG) .... STJ
St. Jude Medical, Inc. *[NASDAQ symbol]* (NQ) .... STJM
Saint Jude Medical, Inc. *[Associated Press]* (SAG) ..... StJude
Saint Judes Central High School Public Library/Bay St. George South Public Library, St. Fintans, NF, Canada *[Library symbol Library of Congress]* (LCLS) .... CaNfSFJG
St. Judes Central High School Public Library/Bay St. George South Public LibraryLibrary, St. Fintans, Newfoundland *[Library symbol National Library of Canada]* (NLC) .... NFSFJG
St. Katherine's Dock *[Shipping]* *[British]* (ROG) ..... SKD
Saint Kitts *[Leeward Islands]* *[Airport symbol]* (OAG) .. SKB
St. Kitts *[St. Kitts]* *[Seismograph station code, US Geological Survey]* (SEIS) ..... SKI
St. Kitts and Nevis *[Aircraft nationality and registration mark]* (FAAC) V4
St. Kitts-Nevis Tourist Office *(EA)* .... SKNTO
Saint Landry Parish Library, Opelousas, LA *[Library symbol Library of Congress]* (LCLS) .... LOSL
St. Lawrence & Atlantic Railway .... StLAR
St. Lawrence Cement, Inc. *[Toronto Stock Exchange symbol]* .... ST
St. Lawrence College *[College Saint-Laurent]*, Brockville, Ontario *[Library symbol National Library of Canada]* (NLC) .... OBSL
Saint Lawrence College, Cornwall, ON, Canada *[Library symbol Library of Congress]* (LCLS) .... CaOCSL
St. Lawrence College *[College Saint-Laurent]*, Cornwall, Ontario *[Library symbol National Library of Canada]* (NLC) .... OCSL
Saint Lawrence College of Applied Arts and Technology, Brockville, ON, Canada *[Library symbol Library of Congress]* (LCLS) ...... CaOBSL
Saint Lawrence College of Applied Arts and Technology, Kingston, ON, Canada *[Library symbol Library of Congress]* (LCLS) ...... CaOKSL
St. Lawrence College of Applied Arts and Technology, Kingston, Ontario *[Library symbol National Library of Canada]* (NLC) .... OKSL
Saint Lawrence Hospital Medical Library, Lansing, MI *[Library symbol]* *[Library of Congress]* (LCLS) .... MiLStL
St. Lawrence Public Library, Newfoundland *[Library symbol National Library of Canada]* (NLC) .... NFSLA
St. Lawrence Public Library, St. Lawrence, NF, Canada *[Library symbol Library of Congress]* (LCLS) .... CaNfSLa
St. Lawrence Railroad *[Division of National Railway Utilization Corp.]* *[AAR code]* .... SLAW
St. Lawrence Seaway Authority *[See also AVMS]* *[Canada]* .... SLSA
Saint Lawrence Seaway Authority of Canada .... SLSAC
St. Lawrence Seaway Authority, Transport Canada *[Administration de la Voie Maritime du Saint-Laurent, Transports Canada]* Ottawa, Ontario *[Library symbol National Library of Canada]* (NLC) .... OOTSSA
Saint Lawrence Seaway Development Corp. *[Department of Transportation]* .... SLS
Saint Lawrence Seaway Development Corp. *[Department of Transportation]* .... SLSDC
Saint Lawrence Seminary *[Wisconsin]* .... SLS
Saint Lawrence State Hospital, Ogdensburg, NY *[Library symbol Library of Congress]* (LCLS) .... NOgSH
Saint Lawrence University *[Canton, NY]* .... SLU
St. Lawrence University *(GAGS)* .... St Lawrence U
Saint Lawrence University, Canton, NY *[Library symbol Library of Congress]* (LCLS) .... NCaS
St. Lawrence University, Canton, NY *[OCLC symbol]* (OCLC) ..... XLM
Saint Leo College, Saint Leo, FL *[Library symbol Library of Congress]* (LCLS) .... FSIC
Saint Leonard *[Canada]* *[Airport symbol]* (OAG) ..... YSL
Saint Leonard College, Dayton, OH *[Library symbol Library of Congress]* (LCLS) .... ODaStL
Saint Louis *[Senegal]* *[ICAO location identifier]* (ICLI) ..... GOSS
St. Louis *[Missouri]* *[Seismograph station code, US Geological Survey]* (SEIS) .... SLM
St. Louis *[Missouri]* *[Airport symbol]* .... STL
St. Louis *[Diocesan abbreviation]* *[Missouri]* (TOCD) .. STL
St. Louis *[Senegal]* *[Airport symbol]* (OAG) .... XLS
St. Louis & Ohio River Railroad .... StL & OR
St. Louis & South Western Railway .... StL & SW
St. Louis Area Support Center *[Military]* (MCD) ...... SLASC
St. Louis Army Ammunition Plant .... SLAAP
Saint Louis Art Museum, Richardson Memorial Library, St. Louis, MO *[Library symbol]* *[Library of Congress]* (LCLS) .... MoSR
St. Louis Art Museum, St. Louis, MO *[OCLC symbol]* (OCLC) ... MSR
St. Louis Blueliners *(EA)* .... SLB
St. Louis, Brownsville & Mexico *[AAR code]* .... SBM
St. Louis, Brownsville & Mexico *[Railway]* .... STLB & M
St. Louis College of Pharmacy, St. Louis, MO *[OCLC symbol]* (OCLC) .... MOP
St. Louis College of Pharmacy, St. Louis, MO *[Library symbol Library of Congress]* (LCLS) .... MoSCP
St. Louis Community College, Instructional Resource Technical Services, St. Louis, MO *[Library symbol Library of Congress]* (LCLS) ..... MoSCC
St. Louis County Helth Dept., Duluth, MN *[Library symbol]* *[Library of Congress]* (LCLS) .... MnDuSLH
St. Louis County Library, St. Louis, MO *[Library symbol Library of Congress]* (LCLS) .... MoSCo
Saint Louis De Montfort Hospital, Ottawa, ON, Canada *[Library symbol Library of Congress]* (LCLS) .... CaOOSLM
St. Louis Encephalitis *[Medicine]* .... SLE
St. Louis Encephalitis Virus .... SLEV
St. Louis Field Office, Eastern Area, Military Traffic Management and Terminal Service *[Army]* (AABC) .... SLFOEAMTMTS
Saint Louis Institute of Music .... SLIM
St. Louis, Iron Mountain & Southern Railway ...... StLIM & S

Saint Louis Junior College, Clayton, MO *[Library symbol Library of Congress Obsolete]* (LCLS) .... MoCIS
St. Louis/Lambert-St. Louis International *[Missouri]* *[ICAO location identifier]* (ICLI) .... KSTL
St. Louis Law Review *[A publication]* (DLA) ...... St Louis L Rev
St. Louis Medical Society, St. Louis, MO *[Library symbol Library of Congress]* (LCLS) .... MoSMed
St. Louis Mercantile Library Association, St. Louis, MO *[Library symbol Library of Congress]* (LCLS) .... MoSM
St. Louis, MI *[AM radio station call letters]* .... WMLM
St. Louis, MO *[Location identifier FAA]* (FAAL) ..... ABW
St. Louis, MO *[Location identifier FAA]* (FAAL) ..... BKY
St. Louis, MO *[Location identifier FAA]* (FAAL) ..... FZU
St. Louis, MO *[AM radio station call letters]* .... KATZ
St. Louis, MO *[FM radio station call letters]* .... KDHX
St. Louis, MO *[Television station call letters]* ...... KDNL
St. Louis, MO *[Television station call letters]* ...... KETC
St. Louis, MO *[FM radio station call letters]* .... KEZK
St. Louis, MO *[AM radio station call letters]* .... KIHT
St. Louis, MO *[FM radio station call letters]* .... KJSL
St. Louis, MO *[FM radio station call letters]* .... KLOU
St. Louis, MO *[Television station call letters]* ...... KMJM
St. Louis, MO *[Television station call letters]* ...... KMOV
St. Louis, MO *[AM radio station call letters]* .... KMOX
St. Louis, MO *[Television station call letters]* ...... KNLC
St. Louis, MO *[Television station call letters]* ...... KPLR
St. Louis, MO *[AM radio station call letters]* (RBYB) ... KRAM
St. Louis, MO *[FM radio station call letters]* .... KSD-FM
St. Louis, MO *[FM radio station call letters]* .... KSDK
St. Louis, MO *[FM radio station call letters]* (RBYB) ... KSIV-FM
St. Louis, MO *[AM radio station call letters]* .... KSTL
St. Louis, MO *[Television station call letters]* ...... KTVI
St. Louis, MO *[FM radio station call letters]* .... KWMU
St. Louis, MO *[FM radio station call letters]* .... KYKY
St. Louis, MO *[Location identifier FAA]* (FAAL) ..... LDZ
St. Louis, MO *[Location identifier FAA]* (FAAL) ..... LMR
St. Louis, MO *[Location identifier FAA]* (FAAL) ..... SJW
St. Louis, MO *[AM radio station call letters]* .... WEW
St. Louis, MO *[FM radio station call letters]* .... WIL
St. Louis, MO *[AM radio station call letters]* .... WKBQ
St. Louis, MO *[AM radio station call letters]* .... WRTH
Saint Louis Park Medical Center, Minneapolis, MN *[Library symbol Library of Congress]* (LCLS) .... MnMS
St. Louis Park, MN *[FM radio station call letters]* .. KDXL
St. Louis Park, MN *[AM radio station call letters]* .. KJJO
St. Louis Park, MN *[FM radio station call letters]* (RBYB) .. KMJZ-FM
St. Louis Park, MN *[AM radio station call letters]* (RBYB) .. KSGS-AM
St. Louis Post-Dispatch, St. Louis, MO *[Library symbol Library of Congress]* (LCLS) .... MoSPD
St. Louis Priory School, St. Louis, MO *[OCLC symbol]* (OCLC) ..... MOH
St. Louis Priory School, St. Louis, MO *[Library symbol Library of Congress]* (LCLS) .... MoSPS
Saint Louis Priory School, St. Louis, MO *[Library symbol]* *[Library of Congress]* (LCLS) .... MoSPSc
St. Louis Production Center .... SLPC
St. Louis Public Library *[Missouri]* .... SLPL
St. Louis Public Library, St. Louis, MO *[Library symbol Library of Congress]* (LCLS) .... MoS
St. Louis Public Library, St. Louis, MO *[OCLC symbol]* (OCLC) ... SVP
Saint Louis Roman Catholic Theological *[Kenrick]* Seminary, Webster Groves,MO *[Library symbol Library of Congress]* (LCLS) ..... MoWgK
St. Louis, San Francisco & Texas Railway Co. *[AAR code]* .... SLST
St. Louis, San Francisco & Texas Railway Co. ..... STL-SF & T
St. Louis Southwestern Railway Co. (IIA) .... SLSW
St. Louis Southwestern Railway Co. *[AAR code]* ... SSW
St. Louis Southwestern Railway Co. of Texas ...... STLSW of T
St. Louis *[Missouri]* Spirit of St. Louis Airport *[Airport symbol Obsolete]* (OAG) .... SUS
St. Louis University *[Missouri]* .... SLU
Saint Louis University *(GAGS)* .... St Louis U
St. Louis University *[Missouri]* .... STLU
St. Louis University. Intramural Law Review *[A publication]* (DLA) .... St LU Intra L Rev
St. Louis University, Law Library, St. Louis, MO *[OCLC symbol]* (OCLC) ...... SLU
St. Louis University, St. Louis, MO *[Library symbol Library of Congress]* (LCLS) .... MoSU
St. Louis University, School of Commerce and Finance, St. Louis, MO *[Library symbol Library of Congress]* (LCLS) .... MoSU-C
St. Louis University, School of Divinity, St. Louis, MO *[Library symbol Library of Congress]* (LCLS) .... MoSU-D
St. Louis University, School of Law, St. Louis, MO *[Library symbol Library of Congress]* (LCLS) .... MoSU-L
St. Louis University, School of Medicine, St. Louis, MO *[Library symbol Library of Congress]* (LCLS) .... MoSU-M
St. Louis University, School of Philosophy, St. Louis, MO *[Library symbol Library of Congress]* (LCLS) .... MoSU-P
St. Louis-San Francisco Railway Co. *[AAR code]* ... SLSF
St. Louis-San Francisco Railway Co. .... STL-SF
St. Lucia *[Aircraft nationality and registration mark]* (FAAC) J6
St. Lucia *[ANSI two-letter standard code]* (CNC) LC
St. Lucia *[ANSI three-letter standard code]* (CNC) .... LCA
St. Lucia *[MARC geographic area code Library of Congress]* (LCCP) ..... nwxk--
St. Lucia *[Seismograph station code, US Geological Survey Closed]* (SEIS) ..... SLI
St. Lucia *[West Indies]* *[Airport symbol]* (OAG) .... SLU
St. Lucia *[MARC country of publication code Library of Congress]* (LCCP) .... xk

St. Lucia [*West Indies*] **Hewanorra Airport** [*Airport symbol*] (OAG) .... UVF
St. Lucia Television Service .... SLTV
St. Lucia Tourist Board (EA) .... SLTB
St. Lucie Plant [*Nuclear energy*] (NRCH) .... SLP
Saint Lucie-Okeechobee Regional Library, Fort Pierce, FL [*Library symbol Library of Congress*] (LCLS) .... FFp
St. Luke's Gospel [*New Testament book*] (ROG) .... LU
Saint Luke's Hospital, Bellingham, WA [*Library symbol Library of Congress*] (LCLS) .... WaBeSL
St. Luke's Hospital, Bolling Medical Library, New York, NY [*OCLC symbol*] (OCLC) .... VVY
Saint Luke's Hospital, Duluth, MN [*Library symbol Library of Congress*] (LCLS) .... MnDuStL
Saint Luke's Hospital, Fargo, ND [*Library symbol Library of Congress*] (LCLS) .... NdFStL
Saint Luke's Hospital, Medical-Nursing Library, Denver, CO [*Library symbol Library of Congress*] (LCLS) .... CoDStL-M
Saint Luke's Hospital, Milwaukee, WI [*Library symbol Library of Congress*] (LCLS) .... WMSL
Saint Luke's Hospital of Kansas City, Kansas City, MO [*Library symbol Library of Congress*] (LCLS) .... MoKStL
Saint Luke's Hospital, Richard Walker Bolling Memorial Medical Library, New York, NY [*Library symbol Library of Congress*] (LCLS) .... NNStL
Saint Luke's Hospital, Spokane, WA [*Library symbol Library of Congress*] (LCLS) .... WaSpSL
Saint Luke's Hospital, Spokane, WA [*Library symbol*] [*Library of Congress*] (LCLS) .... WaSpStL
Saint Luke's Memorial Hospital Center, Medical Library, Utica, NY [*OCLC symbol*] (OCLC) .... ZUQ
Saint Luke's Memorial Hospital, School of Nursing, Racine, WI [*Library symbol Library of Congress*] (LCLS) .... WRacSL
Saint Luke's Regional Center Medical Library, Boise, ID [*Library symbol*] [*Library of Congress*] (LCLS) .... IdBSL
Saint Luke's School of Nursing, Fargo, ND [*Library symbol Library of Congress*] (LCLS) .... NdFStLN
St. Lunaire-Griquet Public Library, St. Lunaire, Newfoundland [*Library symbol National Library of Canada*] (NLC) .... NFSLG
Saint Lunaire-Griquet Public Library, St. Lunaire, NF, Canada [*Library symbol Library of Congress*] (LCLS) .... CaNfSLG
St. Maarten [*Netherlands Antilles*] [*Airport symbol*] (OAG) .... SFG
St. Maarten [*Netherlands Antilles*] [*Airport symbol*] .... SXM
St. Maarten Patriotic Alliance [*Netherlands Antilles*] [*Political party*] (EY) .... SPA
St. Maarten Tourist Office (EA) .... SMTO
Saint Margaret's House, Berkeley, CA [*Library symbol Library of Congress*] (LCLS) .... CBStM
Saint Marie [*Madagascar*] [*Airport symbol*] (OAG) .... SMS
Ste. Marie De Beauce, PQ [*AM radio station call letters*] .... CJVL
St. Maries, ID [*AM radio station call letters*] .... KOFE
St. Maries Public Library, St. Maries, ID [*Library symbol*] [*Library of Congress*] (LCLS) .... IdSm
St. Mark's Church Case [*Philadelphia, PA*] [*A publication*] (DLA) .... St Mark
St. Mark's Church, Niagara-On-The-Lake, ON, Canada [*Library symbol Library of Congress*] (LCLS) .... CaONSM
St. Martin Du Fouilloux [*France*] [*Seismograph station code, US Geological Survey*] (SEIS) .... MFF
St. Martin Hospitals Group [*British*] .... STM
St. Martin Parish Library, St. Martinville, LA [*Library symbol Library of Congress*] (LCLS) .... LStmSM
St. Martin (Sint Maarten) [*MARC geographic area code Library of Congress*] (LCCP) .... nwst--
Saint Martins Academy, Rapid City, SD [*Library symbol Library of Congress*] (LCLS) .... SdRS
Saint Martin's College [*Washington*] .... SMC
Saint Martin's College, Olympia, WA [*Library symbol Library of Congress*] (LCLS) .... WaOSM
St. Martin's Press .... SMP
St. Martin's School, Rogers, MN [*Library symbol*] [*Library of Congress*] (LCLS) .... MnRgS
St. Martinville, LA [*FM radio station call letters*] (RBYB) .... KAQE-FM
Saint Mary College, Leavenworth, KS [*Library symbol Library of Congress*] (LCLS) .... KLeS
Saint Mary College, Xavier, KS [*Library symbol Library of Congress*] (LCLS) .... KXSM
Saint Mary Corwin Hospital, Pueblo, CO [*Library symbol Library of Congress*] (LCLS) .... CoPStMH
St. Mary Help of Christians School, St. Cloud, MN [*Library symbol*] [*Library of Congress*] (LCLS) .... MnStclSM
Saint Mary Land & Exploration [*NASDAQ symbol*] (SAG) .... MARY
Saint Mary Land & Exploration [*Associated Press*] (SAG) .... StMary
St. Mary of Mt. Carmel, Long Prairie, MN [*Library symbol*] [*Library of Congress*] (LCLS) .... MnLpS
Saint Mary of the Lake Seminary [*Mundelein, IL*] .... SMLS
Saint Mary of the Lake Seminary, Mundelein, IL [*Library symbol Library of Congress*] (LCLS) .... IMunS
Saint Mary of the Plains College [*Dodge City, KS*] .... SMPC
St. Mary, PA [*AM radio station call letters*] .... WKBI
St. Mary, PA [*FM radio station call letters*] .... WKBI-FM
Saint Mary Parish Library, Franklin, LA [*Library symbol Library of Congress*] (LCLS) .... LFr
Saint Mary-Of-The-Woods College [*Indiana*] .... SMWC
St. Mary-Of-The-Woods College, Library, St. Mary-Of-The-Woods, IN [*OCLC symbol*] (OCLC) .... IMS
St. Mary-Of-The-Woods College, St. Mary-Of-The-Woods, IN [*Library symbol Library of Congress*] (LCLS) .... InStmaS
St. Mary's [*Zambia*] [*ICAO location identifier*] (ICLI) .... FLSM
Saint Mary's [*Alaska*] [*Airport symbol*] (OAG) .... KSM
Saint Mary's Academy, Portland, OR [*Library symbol Library of Congress*] (LCLS) .... OrPSMA
Saint Mary's, AK [*Location identifier FAA*] (FAAL) .... KSM
Saint Mary's Boys High School, Manhasset, NY [*Library symbol*] [*Library of Congress*] (LCLS) .... NManhSM
Saint Mary's College [*Indiana; Kansas; Michigan; Minnesota*] .... SMC
Saint Mary's College, Notre Dame, IN [*Library symbol Library of Congress*] (LCLS) .... InNdS
Saint Mary's College, Notre Dame, IN [*OCLC symbol*] (OCLC) .... ISN
Saint Mary's College of California .... SMCC
St. Mary's College of California, St. Mary's College, CA [*Library symbol Library of Congress*] (LCLS) .... CSmyS
St. Mary's College of Maryland, St. Mary's City, MD [*OCLC symbol*] (OCLC) .... MDS
St. Mary's College of Maryland, St. Mary's City, MD [*Library symbol Library of Congress*] (LCLS) .... MdStm
St. Mary's College of Minnesota (GAGS) .... St Mary's C
Saint Mary's College, Winona, MN [*Library symbol Library of Congress*] (LCLS) .... MnWinoSM
Saint Mary's College, Winona, MN [*OCLC symbol*] (OCLC) .... MNY
St. Mary's District Museum, St. Mary's, Ontario [*Library symbol National Library of Canada*] (BIB) .... OSTMYM
Saint Mary's Dominican College [*Louisiana*] .... SMDC
St. Mary's Dominican College, New Orleans, LA [*OCLC symbol*] (OCLC) .... LDO
Saint Mary's Dominican College, New Orleans, LA [*Library symbol Library of Congress*] (LCLS) .... LNSM
St. Mary's Elementary School, Melrose, MN [*Library symbol*] [*Library of Congress*] (LCLS) .... MnMeSM
St. Mary's, GA [*AM radio station call letters*] .... WECC
St. Mary's General Hospital, Kitchener, Ontario [*Library symbol National Library of Canada*] (NLC) .... OWTS
Saint Mary's General Hospital, Timmins, ON, Canada [*Library symbol*] [*Library of Congress*] (LCLS) .... CaOTiSMG
St. Mary's General Hospital, Timmins, Ontario [*Library symbol National Library of Canada*] (NLC) .... OTSMG
Saint Mary's General Hospital, Waterloo, ON, Canada [*Library symbol Library of Congress*] (LCLS) .... CaOWtS
Saint Mary's Hospital, Doctors' Library, Madison, WI [*Library symbol Library of Congress*] (LCLS) .... WMaSM
Saint Mary's Hospital, Duluth, MN [*Library symbol Library of Congress*] (LCLS) .... MnDuStM
Saint Mary's Hospital, East St. Louis, IL [*Library symbol Library of Congress*] (LCLS) .... IEsSMH
Saint Mary's Hospital, Green Bay, WI [*Library symbol Library of Congress*] (LCLS) .... WGrSM
Saint Mary's Hospital, Health Sciences Library, Richmond, VA [*Library symbol*] [*Library of Congress*] (LCLS) .... ViRStM
Saint Mary's Hospital, Henegen Medical Library, Streator, IL [*Library symbol Library of Congress*] (LCLS) .... IStrSMH
Saint Mary's Hospital, Kansas City, MO [*Library symbol Library of Congress*] (LCLS) .... MoKStM
Saint Mary's Hospital, Medical Library, Rochester, NY [*OCLC symbol*] (OCLC) .... RVI
Saint Mary's Hospital, Medical Staff and Nursing Library, Decatur, IL [*Library symbol Library of Congress*] (LCLS) .... IDecStM
Saint Mary's Hospital, Milwaukee, WI [*Library symbol Library of Congress*] (LCLS) .... WMSM
Saint Mary's Hospital, Minneapolis, MN [*Library symbol Library of Congress*] (LCLS) .... MnMSMH
Saint Mary's Hospital, Montreal, PQ, Canada [*Library symbol Library of Congress*] (LCLS) .... CaQMSMa
St. Mary's Hospital, Montreal, Quebec [*Library symbol National Library of Canada*] (NLC) .... QMSMA
Saint Mary's Hospital, Racine, WI [*Library symbol Library of Congress*] (LCLS) .... WRacSM
Saint Mary's Hospital, Rochester, MN [*Library symbol Library of Congress*] (LCLS) .... MnRStM
Saint Mary's Hospital, San Francisco, CA [*Library symbol Library of Congress*] (LCLS) .... CSfSM
Saint Mary's Hospital, School of Nursing, Madison, WI [*Library symbol Library of Congress*] (LCLS) .... WMaSM-N
Saint Mary's Hospital, Troy, NY [*Library symbol Library of Congress*] (LCLS) .... NTSM
Saint Mary's Junior College [*Minnesota; Missouri; North Carolina*] .... SMJC
Saint Mary's Junior College, Minneapolis, MN [*Library symbol Library of Congress*] (LCLS) .... MnMSMC
Saint Mary's Junior College, Raleigh, NC [*Library symbol Library of Congress*] (LCLS) .... NcRSM
St. Marys, KS [*FM radio station call letters*] .... KQTP
Saint Mary's Medical Center, Medical Library, Knoxville, TN [*Library symbol Library of Congress*] (LCLS) .... TKSMC
Saint Mary's Medical Center, Nursing School Library, Knoxville, TN [*Library symbol Library of Congress*] (LCLS) .... TKSMC-N
St. Mary's, OH [*FM radio station call letters*] (RBYB) .... WLVZ-FM
St. Mary's, PA [*Location identifier FAA*] (FAAL) .... OYM
St. Marys, PA [*FM radio station call letters*] .... WKVE
Saint Mary's Press [*Record label*] [*New York*] .... SMP
St. Mary's Public Library, Ontario [*Library symbol National Library of Canada*] (NLC) .... OSTMY
St. Marys Railroad Co. [*AAR code*] .... SM
St. Mary's School, Alexandria, MN [*Library symbol*] [*Library of Congress*] (LCLS) .... MnAleSM
St. Mary's School, Beaverlodge, Alberta [*Library symbol National Library of Canada*] (BIB) .... ABESS

St. Mary's School, Bird Island, MN [*Library symbol*] [*Library of Congress*] (LCLS) .... MnBiSM
Saint Mary's School for the Deaf, Buffalo, NY [*Library symbol Library of Congress*] (LCLS) .... NBuStM
St. Mary's School, Fort Vermilion, Alberta [*Library symbol National Library of Canada*] (BIB) .... AFVSMS
St. Mary's School, Little Falls, MN [*Library symbol*] [*Library of Congress*] (LCLS) .... MnLfSM
Saint Mary's School of Nursing, Milwaukee, WI [*Library symbol Library of Congress*] (LCLS) .... WMSMN
St. Mary's School, Pine City, MN [*Library symbol*] [*Library of Congress*] (LCLS) .... MnPcS
St. Mary's School, Tracy, MN [*Library symbol*] [*Library of Congress*] (LCLS) .... MnTrStM
St. Mary's School, Worthington, MN [*Library symbol*] [*Library of Congress*] (LCLS) .... MnWoSMS
Saint Mary's Seminary [*Connecticut; Missouri; Ohio; Vermont*] .... SMS
Saint Mary's Seminary and University, Baltimore, MD [*Library symbol Library of Congress*] (LCLS) .... MdBS
Saint Mary's Seminary and University, Philosophy Library, Baltimore, MD [*Library symbol Library of Congress*] (LCLS) .... MdBS-P
Saint Mary's Seminary, Cleveland, OH [*Library symbol Library of Congress*] (LCLS) .... OClStM
Saint Mary's Seminary, Ferndale, Norwalk, CT [*Library symbol Library of Congress*] (LCLS) .... CtNowaS
Saint Mary's Seminary, Perryville, MO [*Library symbol Library of Congress*] (LCLS) .... MoPeS
Saint Mary's Seminary, Randolph, VT [*Library symbol Library of Congress*] (LCLS) .... VtRaStM
St. Mary's University (GAGS) .... St Mary's U
St. Mary's University, Halifax, Nova Scotia [*Library symbol National Library of Canada*] (NLC) .... NSHS
Saint Mary's University, Halifax, NS, Canada [*Library symbol Library of Congress*] (LCLS) .... CaNSHS
Saint Mary's University, Law Library, San Antonio, TX [*Library symbol Library of Congress*] (LCLS) .... TxSaSM-L
St. Mary's University Library [*UTLAS symbol*] .... SMU
Saint Mary's University, Patrick Power Library, Community Tape Resource, Halifax, NS, Canada [*Library symbol*] [*Library of Congress*] (LCLS) .... CaNSHSPT
Saint Mary's University, San Antonio, TX [*OCLC symbol*] (OCLC) .... SNM
Saint Mary's University, San Antonio, TX [*Library symbol Library of Congress*] (LCLS) .... TxSaSM
St. Marys, WV [*FM radio station call letters*] .... WRRR
St. Marys, WV [*AM radio station call letters*] .... WVVW
St. Matthew High School, Gloucester, Ontario [*Library symbol National Library of Canada*] (BIB) .... OGSTM
Saint Matthew's Cathedral, Laramie, WY [*Library symbol Library of Congress*] (LCLS) .... WyLarSM
St. Matthews, KY [*FM radio station call letters*] .... WRKA
St. Matthews, SC [*AM radio station call letters*] .... WQKI
St. Mawgan [*British ICAO location identifier*] (ICLI) .... EGDG
St. Meinrad College and Seminary, St. Meinrad, IN [*Library symbol Library of Congress*] (LCLS) .... InStme
St. Meinrad College, St. Meinrad, IN [*OCLC symbol*] (OCLC) .... ISS
St. Michael [*Alaska*] [*Airport symbol*] (OAG) .... SMK
St. Michael, AK [*Location identifier FAA*] (FAAL) .... SMK
Saint Michael Hospital, Milwaukee, WI [*Library symbol Library of Congress*] (LCLS) .... WMSMi
St. Michael Parish School, St. Michael, MN [*Library symbol*] [*Library of Congress*] (LCLS) .... MnSmP
St. Michael School, Buckman, MN [*Library symbol*] [*Library of Congress*] (LCLS) .... MnBuS
St. Michael-Albertville High School, St. Michael, MN [*Library symbol*] [*Library of Congress*] (LCLS) .... MnSmH
St. Michael-Albertville Middle School, St. Michael, MN [*Library symbol*] [*Library of Congress*] (LCLS) .... MnSmM
St. Michaelisdonn [*Germany ICAO location identifier*] (ICLI) .... EDXM
Saint Michael's College [*Vermont*] .... SMC
St. Michael's College (GAGS) .... St Michael's C
St. Michael's College Library, University of Toronto [*UTLAS symbol*] .... KSM
Saint Michael's College, Library, Winooski, VT [*OCLC symbol*] (OCLC) .... SMD
Saint Michael's College, Winooski, VT [*Library symbol Library of Congress*] (LCLS) .... VtWinoS
St. Michael's Hospital and Convalescent and Nursing Center, Sauk Centre, MN [*Library symbol*] [*Library of Congress*] (LCLS) .... MnScSM
Saint Michael's Hospital, Stevens Point, WI [*Library symbol Library of Congress*] (LCLS) .... WSpS
St. Michael's Hospital, Toronto [*UTLAS symbol*] .... SMH
Saint Michael's Hospital, Toronto, ON, Canada [*Library symbol Library of Congress*] (LCLS) .... CaOTSM
St. Michael's Hospital, Toronto, Ontario [*Library symbol National Library of Canada*] (NLC) .... OTSM
Saint Michael's Institute, Spokane, WA [*Library symbol Library of Congress*] (LCLS) .... WaSpStM
Saint Michael's Passionist Monastery, Union City, NJ [*Library symbol Library of Congress*] (LCLS) .... NjUcSM
St. Moritz [*Switzerland ICAO location identifier*] (ICLI) .... LSXM
St. Moritz [*Switzerland*] [*Airport symbol*] (AD) .... TQV
Saint Nazaire [*France*] [*Airport symbol*] (OAG) .... SNR
Saint Nicholas Hospital, Sheboygan, WI [*Library symbol Library of Congress*] (LCLS) .... WSheSN
St. Nicholas in Chicago Ukrainian [*Diocesan abbreviation*] [*Illinois*] (TOCD) .... STN
St. Nicholas Society of the City of New York (EA) .... SNSCNY
Saint Norbert College [*Wisconsin*] .... SNC
Saint Norbert College, West De Pere, WI [*Library symbol Library of Congress*] (LCLS) .... WWdepSN
St. Olaf [*Record label*] .... StO
Saint Olaf College [*Northfield, MN*] .... SOC
Saint Olaf College, Kierkegaard Library, Northfield, MN [*Library symbol*] [*Library of Congress*] (LCLS) .... MnNS-K
Saint Olaf College, Northfield, MN [*Library symbol Library of Congress*] (LCLS) .... MnNS
Saint Olaf College, Northfield, MN [*OCLC symbol*] (OCLC) .... MNO
St. Patrick Community School, Grande Prairie, Alberta [*Library symbol National Library of Canada*] (BIB) .... AGPS
Saint Patrick Hospital, Missoula, MT [*Library symbol Library of Congress*] (LCLS) .... MtMisSP
St. Patrick's Missionary Society (TOCD) .... sps
St. Patrick's Missionary Society [*Roman Catholic men's religious order*] .... SPS
Saint Patrick's Seminary [*Menlo Park, CA*] .... SPS
Saint Patrick's Seminary, Menlo Park, CA [*Library symbol Library of Congress*] (LCLS) .... CMenSP
St. Patrick's Society for the Foreign Missions [*See also SSPME*] [*Kiltegan, County Wicklow, Republic of Ireland*] (EAIO) .... SPSFM
St. Paul [*Alaska*] [*Seismograph station code, US Geological Survey Closed*] (SEIS) .... SPP
St. Paul, AB [*AM radio station call letters*] .... CHLW
St. Paul & Duluth Railroad .... StP & D
St. Paul and Minneapolis [*Diocesan abbreviation*] [*Minnesota*] (TOCD) .... STP
St. Paul & Pacific Railroad .... StP & P
St. Paul & Sioux City Railroad .... StP & SC
St. Paul Bancorp [*NASDAQ symbol*] (TTSB) .... SPBC
St. Paul Bancorp, Inc. [*NASDAQ symbol*] (NQ) .... SPBC
Saint Paul Bancorp, Inc. [*Associated Press*] (SAG) .... StPaulBc
Saint Paul Bible College [*Saint Bonifacius, MN*] .... SPBC
Saint Paul Bible College, Saint Bonifacius, MN [*Library symbol Library of Congress*] (LCLS) .... MnStbSP
Saint Paul Capital LLC [*Associated Press*] (SAG) .... StPaulC
St. Paul Capital LLC [*Associated Press*] (SAG) .... StPaulC
St. Paul City Railway .... StPCyRy
Saint Paul Companies, Inc. [*NYSE symbol*] (SAG) .... SPC
[*The*] **St. Paul Companies, Inc.** [*Associated Press*] (SAG) .... StPaul
Saint Paul Companies, Inc. [*Associated Press*] (SAG) .... StPaul
St. Paul Cos. [*NYSE symbol*] (TTSB) .... SPC
St. Paul Cos. LLC 6%Cv'MIPS' [*NYSE symbol*] (TTSB) .... SPCPrM
Saint Paul Guild (EA) .... SPG
St. Paul Island [*Alaska*] [*ICAO location identifier*] (ICLI) .... PASN
St. Paul Island [*Alaska*] [*Airport symbol*] (OAG) .... SNP
St. Paul Island [*Alaska*] [*Seismograph station code, US Geological Survey Closed*] (SEIS) .... SPI
St. Paul Island, AK [*FM radio station call letters*] .... KUHB
St. Paul Island, AK [*Location identifier FAA*] (FAAL) .... SNP
Saint Paul Island, AK [*Location identifier FAA*] (FAAL) .... SPY
St. Paul, Minneapolis & Manitoba Railway .... StPM & M
St. Paul, MN [*Location identifier FAA*] (FAAL) .... HOF
St. Paul, MN [*FM radio station call letters*] .... KEEY
St. Paul, MN [*AM radio station call letters*] .... KLBB
St. Paul, MN [*FM radio station call letters*] .... KNOF
St. Paul, MN [*AM radio station call letters*] .... KSTP
St. Paul, MN [*FM radio station call letters*] .... KSTP-FM
St. Paul, MN [*Television station call letters*] .... KSTP-TV
St. Paul, MN [*Television station call letters*] .... KTCA
St. Paul, MN [*Television station call letters*] .... KTCI
St. Paul, MN [*Location identifier FAA*] (FAAL) .... STP
St. Paul, MN [*AM radio station call letters*] .... WDGY
St. Paul, MN [*FM radio station call letters*] .... WMCN
St. Paul Public Library, Alberta [*Library symbol National Library of Canada*] (NLC) .... ASTP
St. Paul Public Library, St. Paul, AB, Canada [*Library symbol*] [*Library of Congress*] (LCLS) .... CaASTP
St. Paul Public Library, St. Paul, MN [*Library symbol Library of Congress*] (LCLS) .... MnS
Saint Paul Public Library, St. Paul, MN [*Library symbol*] [*Library of Congress*] (LCLS) .... MnSP
St. Paul Public Library, St. Paul, MN [*OCLC symbol*] (OCLC) .... SPP
St. Paul Ramsey Hospital, St. Paul, MN [*Library symbol Library of Congress*] (LCLS) .... MnSSP
Saint Paul School of Theology, Kansas City, MO [*Library symbol Library of Congress*] (LCLS) .... MoKNT
St. Paul Seminary, St. Paul, MN [*Library symbol Library of Congress*] (LCLS) .... MnSS
Saint Paul Theological Seminary, Kansas City, MO [*Library symbol*] [*Library of Congress*] (LCLS) .... MoKStP
St. Paul Union Depot .... StPUD
St. Paul Union Depot Co. [*AAR code*] .... SPUD
St. Paul Union Stock Yards Co. .... StPUSY
Saint Paul University, Oblate Fathers Archives, Ottawa, ON, Canada [*Library symbol Library of Congress*] (LCLS) .... CaOOSUA
Saint Paul University, Ottawa, ON, Canada [*Library symbol Library of Congress*] (LCLS) .... CaOOSU
St. Paul University [*Universite St-Paul*] **Ottawa, Ontario** [*Library symbol National Library of Canada*] (NLC) .... OOSU
St. Paul, VA [*AM radio station call letters*] .... WXLZ
St. Paul-En-Foret [*France*] [*Seismograph station code, US Geological Survey*] (SEIS) .... SPF
St. Paul's Cathedral [*London, England*] .... SPC
Saint Paul's College [*Missouri; Virginia; Washington, DC*] .... SPC
Saint Paul's College, Concordia, MO [*Library symbol Library of Congress*] (LCLS) .... MoCStP

Saint Paul's College, Lawrenceville, VA [*OCLC symbol*] (OCLC) .... SPC
Saint Paul's College, Lawrenceville, VA [*Library symbol Library of Congress*] (LCLS) .... ViLawS
Saint Paul's College, Washington, DC [*Library symbol Library of Congress*] (LCLS) .... DStPC
St. Paul's College, Winnipeg, Manitoba [*Library symbol National Library of Canada*] (NLC) .... MWSP
Saint Paul's College, Winnipeg, MB, Canada [*Library symbol Library of Congress*] (LCLS) .... CaMWSP
Saint Paul's Hospital, Health Sciences Library, Vancouver, BC, Canada [*Library symbol Library of Congress*] (LCLS) .... CaBVaSPH
St. Paul's Lutheran School, Fulda, MN [*Library symbol*] [*Library of Congress*] (LCLS) .... MnFuStP
St. Pauls, NC [*AM radio station call letters*] .... WKKE
St. Pauls, NC [*FM radio station call letters*] .... WLRD
Saint Paul's School, Concord, NH [*Library symbol Library of Congress*] (LCLS) .... NhCSp
Saint Paul's School, Garden City, NY [*Library symbol*] [*Library of Congress*] (LCLS) .... NGcStP
St. Peter and St. Paul [*The Papal seal*] .... SPSP
Saint Peter College [*Maryland; New Jersey*] .... SPC
St. Peter, MN [*FM radio station call letters*] .... KGAC
St. Peter, MN [*FM radio station call letters*] .... KNGA
St. Peter, MN [*AM radio station call letters*] .... KRBI
St. Peter, MN [*FM radio station call letters*] .... KRBI-FM
St. Peter/Ording [*Germany ICAO location identifier*] (ICLI) .... EDXO
St. Peter's Abbey and College, Muenster, Saskatchewan [*Library symbol National Library of Canada*] (NLC) .... SMSP
Saint Peter's Abbey and College, Muenster, SK, Canada [*Library symbol Library of Congress*] (LCLS) .... CaSMuSP
Saint Peter's Academy, San Francisco, CA [*Library symbol Library of Congress*] (LCLS) .... CSfSPA
Saint Peter's College, Englewood Cliffs, NJ [*Library symbol Library of Congress*] (LCLS) .... NjEncStP
Saint Peter's College, Jersey City, NJ [*Library symbol Library of Congress*] (LCLS) .... NjJStP
Saint Peter's College, Jersey City, NJ [*OCLC symbol*] (OCLC) .... STP
Saint Peter's Community Hospital, Helena, MT [*Library symbol Library of Congress*] (LCLS) .... MtHSP
St. Peter's Dome Lookout [*New Mexico*] [*Seismograph station code, US Geological Survey*] (SEIS) .... SPD
Saint Peter's Hospital, Albany, NY [*Library symbol Library of Congress*] (LCLS) .... NAIS
Saint Peter's Hospital, Olympia, WA [*Library symbol Library of Congress*] (LCLS) .... WaOSP
St. Peter's Lutheran School, Balaton, MN [*Library symbol*] [*Library of Congress*] (LCLS) .... MnBaSPL
Saint Peter's Medical Center, New Brunswick, NJ [*Library symbol Library of Congress*] (LCLS) .... NjNbStP
St. Peter's School, Delano, MN [*Library symbol*] [*Library of Congress*] (LCLS) .... MnDeSP
Saint Peter's Seminary, London, ON, Canada [*Library symbol*] [*Library of Congress*] (LCLS) .... CaOLSP
St. Peter's Seminary, London, Ontario [*Library symbol National Library of Canada*] (NLC) .... OLSP
St. Petersburg [*Florida*] [*Airport symbol*] (OAG) .... PIE
St. Petersburg [*Diocesan abbreviation*] [*Florida*] (TOCD) .... SP
St. Petersburg/Albert Whitted [*Florida*] [*ICAO location identifier*] (ICLI) .... KSPG
St. Petersburg Beach, FL [*AM radio station call letters*] .... WRXB
St. Petersburg/Clearwater International [*Florida*] [*ICAO location identifier*] (ICLI) .... KPIE
St. Petersburg Commodity Exchange [*Russian Federation*] (EY) .... SCE
St. Petersburg, FL [*Location identifier FAA*] (FAAL) .... NOF
St. Petersburg, FL [*Location identifier FAA*] (FAAL) .... SPG
St. Petersburg, FL [*FM radio station call letters*] .... WCOF
St. Petersburg, FL [*FM radio station call letters*] .... WFTI
St. Petersburg, FL [*FM radio station call letters*] .... WKES
St. Petersburg, FL [*FM radio station call letters*] .... WQYK
St. Petersburg, FL [*AM radio station call letters*] .... WRBQ
St. Petersburg, FL [*AM radio station call letters*] .... WRMD
St. Petersburg, FL [*AM radio station call letters*] .... WSUN
St. Petersburg, FL [*Television station call letters*] .... WTOG
St. Petersburg, FL [*Television station call letters*] .... WTSP
St. Petersburg, FL [*Television station call letters*] .... WTTA
St. Petersburg Junior College [*Clearwater, FL*] .... SPJC
St. Petersburg Junior College, St. Petersburg, FL [*Library symbol Library of Congress*] (LCLS) .... FSpC
St. Petersburg [*Florida*] **Olympic Regatta Training** .... SPORT
St. Petersburg Public Library, St. Petersburg, FL [*Library symbol Library of Congress*] (LCLS) .... FSp
St. Philip's College, San Antonio, TX [*OCLC symbol*] (OCLC) .... SSP
St. Philip's College, San Antonio, TX [*Library symbol Library of Congress*] (LCLS) .... TxSaSP
St. Philips Marsh [*Bristol*] [*British depot code*] .... SPM
St. Philips Resources [*Vancouver Stock Exchange symbol*] .... SPP
St. Philips School, Bemidji, MN [*Library symbol*] [*Library of Congress*] (LCLS) .... MnBemSP
St. Philip's School, Litchfield, MN [*Library symbol*] [*Library of Congress*] (LCLS) .... MnLitSP
St. Photios Foundation (EA) .... SPF
St. Pierre [*Quebec*] [*Seismograph station code, US Geological Survey Closed*] (SEIS) .... SPR
Saint Pierre [*Canada*] [*Airport symbol*] (OAG) .... YPM
St. Pierre and Miquelon [*MARC geographic area code Library of Congress*] (LCCP) .... n-xl--
St. Pierre and Miquelon [*ANSI two-letter standard code*] (CNC) .... PM
St. Pierre and Miquelon [*ANSI three-letter standard code*] (CNC) .... SPM
St. Pierre and Miquelon [*MARC country of publication code Library of Congress*] (LCCP) xl
St. Pius V School, Albany, MN [*Library symbol*] [*Library of Congress*] (LCLS) .... MnAlSP
St.-Pius X High School, Ottawa, Ontario [*Library symbol National Library of Canada*] (BIB) .... OOSPX
Saint Procopius College [*Illinois*] .... SPC
St. Regis School, St. Regis, MT [*Library symbol*] [*Library of Congress*] (LCLS) .... MtStrS
St. Rita's Hospital, Sydney, Nova Scotia [*Library symbol National Library of Canada*] (NLC) .... NSSSRH
Saint Rita's Hospital, Sydney, NS, Canada [*Library symbol Library of Congress*] (LCLS) .... CaNSSSRH
St. Robert, MO [*FM radio station call letters*] (RBYB) .... KFLW
St. Rosalie Generating Station [*Nuclear energy*] (NRCH) .... SRGS
Saint Rose Academy, San Francisco, CA [*Library symbol Library of Congress*] (LCLS) .... CSfSRA
Ste. Rose Du Lac, MB [*Television station call letters*] CBWFT-4
Saint Saulge [*France*] [*Seismograph station code, US Geological Survey*] (SEIS) .... SSF
St. Sauveur Badole [*France*] [*Seismograph station code, US Geological Survey*] (SEIS) .... SSB
St. Sauveur De Carouges [*Seismograph station code, US Geological Survey*] (SEIS) .... SSC
St. Simons Island, GA [*FM radio station call letters*] (RBYB) .... WVVV
Saint Sophia Ukrainian Orthodox Seminary, South Bound Brook, NJ [*Library symbol Library of Congress*] (LCLS) .... NjSbbU
Saint Stanislaus Seminary, Cleveland, OH [*Library symbol Library of Congress*] (LCLS) .... OClSS
Saint Stanislaus Seminary, Florissant, MO [*Library symbol Library of Congress*] (LCLS) .... MoFloSS
St. Stephen, SC [*FM radio station call letters*] .... WTUA
Saint Stephen's College, Dover, MA [*Library symbol Library of Congress*] (LCLS) .... MDovS
Saint Tammany Parish Library, Covington, LA [*Library symbol Library of Congress*] (LCLS) .... LCovSt
St. Theresa [*Lesotho*] [*ICAO location identifier*] (ICLI) .... FXST
St. Theresa School, Wabasca, Alberta [*Library symbol National Library of Canada*] (BIB) .... AWASTS
Saint Theresa's Academy, Kansas City, MO [*Library symbol Library of Congress*] (LCLS) .... MoKStT
Saint Therese Point [*Canada*] [*Airport symbol*] (OAG) .... YST
St. Thomas [*Virgin Islands*] [*Airport symbol*] .... STT
St. Thomas [*Diocesan abbreviation*] [*Virgin Islands*] (TOCD) .... STV
St. Thomas [*Virgin Islands*] [*Seismograph station code, US Geological Survey*] (SEIS) .... VST
Saint Thomas Aquinas College, Sparkill, NY [*Library symbol Library of Congress*] (LCLS) .... NSpaT
St. Thomas Aquinas Foundation (EA) .... STAF
St. Thomas/Harry S. Truman [*Virgin Islands*] [*ICAO location identifier*] (ICLI) .... TIST
St. Thomas High School, Overland Park, KS [*Library symbol*] [*Library of Congress*] (LCLS) .... KovpST
Saint Thomas High School, Rockford, IL [*Library symbol Library of Congress*] (LCLS) .... IRoStT
Saint Thomas Hospital, Health Sciences Library, Nashville, TN [*Library symbol Library of Congress*] (LCLS) .... TNStT
St. Thomas Institute [*Research center*] (RCD) .... STI
Saint Thomas Institute, Cincinnati, OH [*Library symbol Library of Congress*] (LCLS) .... OCIS
St. Thomas Island (VRA) VI
St. Thomas More College, Saskatoon, Saskatchewan [*Library symbol National Library of Canada*] (NLC) .... SSM
Saint Thomas More College, Saskatoon, SK, Canada [*Library symbol Library of Congress*] (LCLS) .... CaSSM
St. Thomas More School, Fairview, Alberta [*Library symbol National Library of Canada*] (BIB) .... AFVSTS
St. Thomas More Society (EA) .... STMS
St. Thomas National Historic Site .... SATH
St. Thomas, ON [*FM radio station call letters*] .... CFHK
St. Thomas, PA [*Location identifier FAA*] (FAAL) .... THS
St. Thomas Psychiatric Hospital, Ontario [*Library symbol National Library of Canada*] (NLC) .... OSTTP
Saint Thomas Public Library, Charlotte Amalie, VI [*Library symbol Library of Congress*] (LCLS) .... VnSt
St. Thomas Public Library, Ontario [*Library symbol National Library of Canada*] (NLC) .... OSTT
St. Thomas Public Library, St. Thomas, ON, Canada [*Library symbol Library of Congress*] (LCLS) .... CaOStT
St. Thomas - St. John Hotel Association [*Virgin Islands*] (EAIO) .... STSJHA
St. Thomas [*Virgin Islands*] **Seaplane Base** [*Airport symbol*] (OAG) .... SPB
Saint Thomas Seminary [*Colorado; Connecticut; Kentucky*] .... STS
Saint Thomas Seminary, Bloomfield, CT [*Library symbol Library of Congress*] (LCLS) .... CtBlST
Saint Thomas Seminary, Denver, CO [*Library symbol Library of Congress*] (LCLS) .... CoDStT
Saint Thomas Seminary, Kenmore, WA [*Library symbol Library of Congress*] (LCLS) .... WaKenS
Saint Thomas University, Fredericton, NB, Canada [*Library symbol Library of Congress*] (LCLS) .... CaNBCS
St. Thomas University, Fredericton, New Brunswick [*Library symbol National Library of Canada*] (NLC) .... NBCS
St. Thomas, VI [*FM radio station call letters*] .... WIUJ

St. Timothy School, Maple Lake, MN [*Library symbol*] [*Library of Congress*] (LCLS) ... MnMIS
St. Vincent [*MARC geographic area code Library of Congress*] (LCCP) ... nwxm
St. Vincent [*Windward Islands*] [*Airport symbol*] (OAG) ... SVD
St. Vincent [*St. Vincent*] [*Seismograph station code, US Geological Survey Closed*] (SEIS) ... SVI
St. Vincent [*St. Vincent*] [*Seismograph station code, US Geological Survey*] (SEIS) ... SVT
St. Vincent [*MARC country of publication code Library of Congress*] (LCCP) ... xm
St. Vincent and the Grenadines [*Aircraft nationality and registration mark*] (FAAC) ... J8
St. Vincent and the Grenadines [*ANSI two-letter standard code*] (CNC) ... VC
St. Vincent and the Grenadines [*ANSI three-letter standard code*] (CNC) ... VCT
Saint Vincent College [*Latrobe, PA*] ... SVC
Saint Vincent College, Latrobe, PA [*Library symbol Library of Congress*] (LCLS) ... PLatS
Saint Vincent College, Latrobe, PA [*OCLC symbol*] (OCLC) ... PSV
Saint Vincent College of Nursing, Los Angeles, CA [*Library symbol Library of Congress*] (LCLS) ... CLStV
Saint Vincent de Paul (ADA) ... SVDP
Saint Vincent Hospital and Medical Center, Portland, OR [*Library symbol Library of Congress*] (LCLS) ... OrPStV
Saint Vincent Hospital, Green Bay, WI [*Library symbol Library of Congress*] (LCLS) ... WGrSV
Saint Vincent Hospital, Ottawa, ON, Canada [*Library symbol Library of Congress*] (LCLS) ... CaOOSV
St. Vincent Hospital [*Hopital St-Vincent*] **Ottawa, Ontario** [*Library symbol National Library of Canada*] (NLC) ... OOSV
St. Vincent National Movement [*Political party*] (PPW) ... SVNM
Saint Vincents Hospital, Billings, MT [*Library symbol Library of Congress*] (LCLS) ... MtBilSV
St. Vincent's Institute of Medical Research [*Australia*] ... SVIMR
Saint Vincent's Medical Center of Richmond, Staten Island, NY [*Library symbol Library of Congress*] (LCLS) ... NSiSV
St. Vital Public Library, Winnipeg, Manitoba [*Library symbol National Library of Canada*] (NLC) ... MWSV
Saint Vital Public Library, Winnipeg, MB, Canada [*Library symbol Library of Congress*] (LCLS) ... CaMWSV
Saint Xavier College [*Chicago, IL*] ... SXC
Saint Xavier College, Chicago, IL [*OCLC symbol*] (OCLC) ... ICS
Saint Xavier College, Chicago, IL [*Library symbol Library of Congress*] (LCLS) ... ICSX
St. Xavier University (GAGS) ... St Xavier U
Saint-Afrique-Belmont [*France ICAO location identifier*] (ICLI) ... LFIF
Saint-Andre-De L'Eure [*France ICAO location identifier*] (ICLI) ... LFFD
Saint-Barthelemy [*MARC geographic area code Library of Congress*] (LCCP) ... nwsb--
Saint-Barthelemy [*French Antilles*] [*ICAO location identifier*] (ICLI) ... TFFJ
Saint-Brieuc Armor [*France ICAO location identifier*] (ICLI) ... LFRT
Saint-Chamond/L'Horme [*France ICAO location identifier*] (ICLI) ... LFHG
Saint-Claude-Pratz [*France ICAO location identifier*] (ICLI) ... LFKZ
Saint-Cyre-L'Ecole [*France ICAO location identifier*] (ICLI) ... LFPZ
Saint-Denis/Gillot [*Reunion*] [*ICAO location identifier*] (ICLI) ... FMEE
Saint-Die/Remoneix [*France ICAO location identifier*] (ICLI) ... LFGY
Saint-Dizier/Robinson [*France ICAO location identifier*] (ICLI) ... LFSI
Sainte ... ST
Sainte [*French*] (EY) ... STE
Sainte Genevieve Archives, Sainte Genevieve County Court, Ste. Genevieve, MO [*Library symbol Library of Congress*] (LCLS) ... MoStgA
Sainte Rose Regional Library, Sainte Rose, MB, Canada [*Library symbol Library of Congress*] (LCLS) ... CaMStR
Sainte-Foy-La-Grande [*France ICAO location identifier*] (ICLI) ... LFDF
Sainte-Leocadie [*France ICAO location identifier*] (ICLI) ... LFYS
Sainte-Marie [*Madasgascar*] [*ICAO location identifier*] (ICLI) ... FMMS
Saintes/Thenac [*France ICAO location identifier*] (ICLI) ... LFXB
Saint-Etienne/Boutheon [*France ICAO location identifier*] (ICLI) ... LFMH
Saint-Etienne-En-Devoluy [*France ICAO location identifier*] (ICLI) ... LFNY
Saint-Florentin/Cheu [*France ICAO location identifier*] (ICLI) ... LFGP
Saint-Flour/Coltines [*France ICAO location identifier*] (ICLI) ... LFHQ
Saint-Francois [*French Antilles*] [*ICAO location identifier*] (ICLI) ... TFFC
Saint-Galmier [*France ICAO location identifier*] (ICLI) ... LFKM
Saint-Gaudens National Historic Site ... SAGA
Saint-Georges-De-L'Oyapock [*French Guiana*] [*ICAO location identifier*] (ICLI) ... SOOG
Saint-Girons/Antichan [*France ICAO location identifier*] (ICLI) ... LFCG
Saint-Gobain-Pont-A-Mousson [*French industrial giant*] ... SGPM
Saint-Hubert [*Belgium ICAO location identifier*] (ICLI) ... EBSH
Saint-Hubert [*Belgium ICAO location identifier*] (ICLI) ... EBSU
Saint-Hyacinthe Food Research Centre, Agriculture Canada [*Centre de Recherches Alimentaires de Saint-Hyacinthe, Agriculture Canada*] **Quebec** [*Library symbol National Library of Canada*] (NLC) ... QSHAG
Saint-Jean, PQ [*ICAO location identifier*] (ICLI) ... CYJN
Saint-Jean-D'Angely [*France ICAO location identifier*] (ICLI) ... LFIY
Saint-Jean-D'Avelanne [*France ICAO location identifier*] (ICLI) ... LFKH
Saint-Jean-En-Royans [*France ICAO location identifier*] (ICLI) ... LFKE
Saint-Junien [*France ICAO location identifier*] (ICLI) ... LFBJ
Saint-Laurent du Maroni [*French Guiana*] [*ICAO location identifier*] (ICLI) ... SOOM
Saint-Malo/Saint-Servan [*France ICAO location identifier*] (ICLI) ... LFEO
Saint-Martin/Grand'Case, Guadeloupe [*French Antilles*] [*ICAO location identifier*] (ICLI) ... TFFG
Saint-Martin-De-Londres [*France ICAO location identifier*] (ICLI) ... LFNL
Saint-Nazaire/Montoir [*France ICAO location identifier*] (ICLI) ... LFRZ
Saint-Omer/Wizernes [*France ICAO location identifier*] (ICLI) ... LFQN
Saintpaulia International (EA) ... SI
Saint-Pierre D'Oleron [*France ICAO location identifier*] (ICLI) ... LFDP
Saint-Pierre, Saint-Pierre-Et Miquelon [*France ICAO location identifier*] (ICLI) ... LFVP
Saint-Pierre-Pierrefonds [*Reunion*] [*ICAO location identifier*] (ICLI) ... FMEP
Saint-Quentin/Roupy [*France ICAO location identifier*] (ICLI) ... LFOW
Saint-Rambert-D'Albon [*France ICAO location identifier*] (ICLI) ... LFLR
Saints [*as in "SS Peter and Paul"*] ... SS
Saints (ODBW) ... Sts
Saints Alive in Jesus (EA) ... SAJ
Saint's Digest of Registration Cases [*England*] [*A publication*] (DLA) ... Saint
Saints Together [*Library cataloging*] (DGA) ... Sts Tog
Saint-Sacrement [*Blessed Sacrament*] [*French*] ... SS
Saint-Simon/Clastres [*France ICAO location identifier*] (ICLI) ... LFYT
Saint-Valery/Vittefleur [*France ICAO location identifier*] (ICLI) ... LFOS
Saint-Yan [*France ICAO location identifier*] (ICLI) ... LFLN
Saipan [*Mariana Islands*] [*Airport symbol*] (OAG) ... SPN
Saipan International Airport [*FAA*] (TAG) ... GSN
Saipan Island (Obyan)/International [*Mariana Islands*] [*ICAO location identifier*] (ICLI) ... PGSN
Saipan, MP [*AM radio station call letters*] ... KSAI
Saiq [*Oman*] [*ICAO location identifier*] (ICLI) ... OOSQ
Sair Aviation [*Canada ICAO designator*] (FAAC) ... SRA
SAIT [*Southern Alberta Institute of Technology*] **Library Technician Program** [*UTLAS symbol*] ... EUI
Sakai [*Japan*] [*Seismograph station code, US Geological Survey Closed*] (SEIS) ... SAA
Sakata [*Japan*] [*Seismograph station code, US Geological Survey*] (SEIS) ... SAK
Sakeji [*Zambia*] [*ICAO location identifier*] (ICLI) ... FLSJ
Sakhalinskie Aviatrassy [*Former USSR*] [*FAA designator*] (FAAC) ... SHU
Sakharov International Committee (EA) ... SIC
Sakhaviatrans [*Former USSR*] [*FAA designator*] (FAAC) ... SVT
Sako Collectors Association (EA) ... SCA
Sakon Nakhon [*Thailand*] [*ICAO location identifier*] (ICLI) ... VTUS
Sakon Nakhon/Bankhai [*Thailand*] [*ICAO location identifier*] (ICLI) ... VTUI
Sakon Nakhon/Nam Phung Dam (North) [*Thailand*] [*ICAO location identifier*] (ICLI) ... VTUE
Sakon Nakhon/Nam Phung Dam (South) [*Thailand*] [*ICAO location identifier*] (ICLI) ... VTUF
Saks Fifth Avenue [*Retail department store*] ... SFA
Saks Holdings [*NYSE symbol*] (TTSB) ... SKS
Sakura [*Japan*] [*Seismograph station code, US Geological Survey Closed*] (SEIS) ... SKU
Sal Island [*Cape Verde Islands*] [*Airport symbol*] (OAG) ... SID
Sal Luftverkehrs GmbH, Flughafen Leipzig-Halle [*Germany*] [*FAA designator*] (FAAC) ... SXN
Sal Oceanic Area Control Center [*Cape Verde*] [*ICAO location identifier*] (ICLI) ... GVSC
Sal Terrae. Revista Hispanoamericana de Cultura Ecclesiastica [*Santander, Spain*] [*A publication*] (BJA) ... SalTerz
Salad (WGA) ... SAL
Salad Manufacturers Association (EA) ... SMA
Salado [*Chile*] [*Seismograph station code, US Geological Survey Closed*] (SEIS) ... SDO
Salair, Inc. [*ICAO designator*] (FAAC) ... SIR
Salalah [*Oman*] [*ICAO location identifier*] (ICLI) ... OOSA
Salalah [*Oman*] [*Airport symbol*] (OAG) ... SLL
Salam [*Afghanistan*] [*ICAO location identifier*] (ICLI) ... OASL
Salamanca [*Spain ICAO location identifier*] (ICLI) ... LESA
Salamanca District Hospital, Salamanca, NY [*Library symbol Library of Congress*] (LCLS) ... NSalDH
Salamanca, NY [*AM radio station call letters*] ... WGGO
Salamanca, NY [*FM radio station call letters*] ... WQRT
Salaman's Liquidation and Composition with Creditors [*2nd ed.*] [*1882*] [*A publication*] (DLA) ... Sal Comp Cr
Salamaua Aerial Transport [*Australia*] ... SAT
Salamo [*Papua New Guinea*] [*Airport symbol*] (OAG) ... SAM
Salam-Weinberg-Glashow [*One unified field theory in physics*] ... SWG
Salang-I-Junubi [*Afghanistan*] [*ICAO location identifier*] (ICLI) ... OASS
Salang-I-Shamali [*Afghanistan*] [*ICAO location identifier*] (ICLI) ... OANS
Salant Corp. [*Associated Press*] (SAG) ... Salant
Salant Corp. [*Associated Press*] (SAG) ... Salnt
Salant Corp. [*AMEX symbol*] (SAG) ... SLT
Salant Corp. [*NYSE symbol*] (SPSG) ... SLT
Salant Corp. Wrrt [*AMEX symbol*] (TTSB) ... SLT.WS
Salaried Direct [*Ratio*] ... S/D
Salaried Legal Expense Voucher ... SLEV
Salaried Pharmacists' Association [*Australia*] ... SPA
Salaries and Allowances Tribunal [*Australia*] ... SAT
Salaries and Expenses ... S & E
Salaries, Wages, Overhead, and Benefits (NASA) ... SWOB
Salary (ADA) ... SAL
Salary (ROG) ... SALY
Salary Administration and Manpower Planning (PDAA) ... SAMP
Salary Band [*British*] (DCTA) ... SB
Salary Information Retrieval System (IEEE) ... SIRS
Salary Quotient at Lower Limits [*Business term*] ... SQUALL
Salary Reduction Plan [*Business term*] ... SRP
Salary Reduction Simplified Employee Pension ... SARSEP
Saldanha [*South Africa*] [*ICAO location identifier*] (ICLI) ... FASD
Sale [*Australia Airport symbol*] (OAG) ... SXE
Sale and Leaseback ... S & L
Sale and Lease-Back [*Business term*] (MHDB) ... S & LB
Sale and Leaseback (MHDW) ... SAL
Sale and Leaseback (DFIT) ... S&L
Sale at Valuation (WDAA) ... SAV
Sale by Reference ... SBR

Sale/Engineering/Development [*Honda*] [*Automotive engineering*] .... SED
Sale of Food and Drugs Act [*British*] .... SFDA
Sale or Return [*Business term*] (ADA) .... SOR
Sale Satisfaction Index [*Business term*] .... SSI
Salem [*Oregon*] [*Airport symbol*] (OAG) .... SLE
Salem, AR [*FM radio station call letters*] .... KSAR
Salem College, Salem, WV [*Library symbol Library of Congress*] (LCLS) ..... WvSaC
Salem College, Winston-Salem, NC [*Library symbol Library of Congress*] (LCLS) .... NcWsS
Salem College, Winston-Salem, NC [*OCLC symbol*] (OCLC) .... NSC
Salem Corp. [*Associated Press*] (SAG) .... Salem
Salem Corp. [*AMEX symbol*] (SPSG) .... SBS
Salem County Clerk, Salem, NJ [*Library symbol Library of Congress*] (LCLS) .... NjSalCoC
Salem County Historical Society, Salem, NJ [*Library symbol Library of Congress*] (LCLS) .... NjSalHi
Salem Generating Station [*Nuclear energy*] (GFGA) .... SGS
Salem Hospital, Salem, OR [*Library symbol Library of Congress*] (LCLS) ...... OrSaH
Salem, IL [*Location identifier FAA*] (FAAL) .... SLO
Salem, IL [*AM radio station call letters*] .... WJBD
Salem, IL [*FM radio station call letters*] .... WJBD-FM
Salem, IN [*Television station call letters*] .... WFTE
Salem, IN [*FM radio station call letters*] .... WKJK
Salem, IN [*AM radio station call letters*] .... WSLM
Salem, IN [*FM radio station call letters*] .... WSLM-FM
Salem Leader/Democrat, Salem, IN [*Library symbol Library of Congress*] (LCLS) .... InSaLD
Salem, MA [*AM radio station call letters*] .... WESX
Salem, MA [*FM radio station call letters*] .... WMWM
Salem Maritime National Historic Site .... SAMA
Salem, MI [*Location identifier FAA*] (FAAL) .... SVM
Salem, MO [*FM radio station call letters*] .... KMMC
Salem, MO [*AM radio station call letters*] .... KSMO
Salem, NH [*AM radio station call letters*] .... WNNW
Salem, NJ [*AM radio station call letters*] .... WJIC
Salem Nuclear Generating Station (NRCH) .... SNGS
Salem, OH [*FM radio station call letters*] .... WQXK
Salem, OH [*AM radio station call letters*] .... WSOM
Salem, OR [*Television station call letters*] .... KBSP
Salem, OR [*AM radio station call letters*] .... KBZY
Salem, OR [*AM radio station call letters*] .... KCCS
Salem, OR [*Television station call letters*] .... KEBN
Salem, OR [*FM radio station call letters*] (RBYB) .... KKRH
Salem, OR [*AM radio station call letters*] .... KSLM
Salem, OR [*Television station call letters*] (RBYB) .... KWBP
Salem, OR [*Location identifier FAA*] (FAAL) .... SLE
Salem Public Library, Salem, IN [*Library symbol Library of Congress*] (LCLS) .... InSa
Salem Public Library, Salem, MA [*Library symbol Library of Congress*] (LCLS) .... MSa
Salem Public Library, Salem, OH [*Library symbol Library of Congress*] (LCLS) .... OSal
Salem Public Library, Salem, OR [*Library symbol Library of Congress*] (LCLS) .... OrSa
Salem Public Library, Salem, OR [*OCLC symbol*] (OCLC) .... OSE
Salem Public Library, Salem, VA [*Library symbol Library of Congress*] (LCLS) .... ViSa
Salem, SD [*FM radio station call letters*] .... KIKN
Salem State College (GAGS) .... Salem St C
Salem State College, Salem, MA [*Library symbol Library of Congress*] (LCLS) .... MSaT
Salem Township, MI [*AM radio station call letters*] .... WSDS
Salem Township Public Library, Morrow, OH [*Library symbol Library of Congress*] (LCLS) .... OMorS
Salem, VA [*FM radio station call letters*] .... WJLM
Salem, VA [*FM radio station call letters*] .... WPIR
Salem, VA [*AM radio station call letters*] .... WTOY
Salem, WV [*FM radio station call letters*] .... WOBG
Salena Research Corp. [*Vancouver Stock Exchange symbol*] .... SLN
Salerno/Pontecagnano [*Italy ICAO location identifier*] (ICLI) .... LIRI
Sales .... SLS
Sales Activity Index [*Business*] (MHDB) .... SAI
Sales Aid (IAA) .... SA
Sales and Business Reservations Done Electronically .... SABRE
Sales and Marketing Executives International [*An association*] [*Cleveland, OH*] (WDMC) .... SMEI
Sales and Marketing Executives-International (EA) .... SME
Sales and Marketing Executives-International [*Cleveland, OH*] (EA) .... SME-I
Sales and Marketing Information Ltd. [*Database producer*] (IID) .... SAMI
Sales Areas Marketing, Inc. (DOAD) .... SAMI
Sales Associates Management Corp. [*Palm Springs, CA*] (EA) .... SAMCO
Sales Association of the Chemical Industry (EA) .... SACI
Sales Association of the Paper Industry [*New York, NY*] (EA) .... SAPI
Sales Authorization Request .... SAR
Sales Automation Association (EA) .... SAA
Sales Book .... SB
Sales Catalog Index Project Input On-Line [*Cleveland Museum of Art*] [*Information service or system*] (IID) .... SCIPIO
Sales Code .... S/C
Sales Contracting Officer [*Army*] .... SCO
Sales Costs .... SC
Sales Education Units .... SEU
Sales Engineer .... SE
Sales Environment Learning Laboratory [*Computer-based marketing game*] .... SELL
Sales Executives Club of New York (EA) .... SECNY
Sales Journal [*Accounting*] .... SJ
Sales Letter .... SL
Sales Letter Report .... SLR
Sales Management Organization Game .... SMOG
Sales Manager (WGA) .... SLSMGR
Sales Manager .... SM
Sales Manpower Foundation (EA) .... SMF
Sales Method Index [*LIMRA*] .... SMI
Sales Motivation Survey [*Test*] .... SMS
Sales of Products Other than Gasoline .... SPOG
Sales Office (MHDW) .... SO
Sales Operations Planning and Control [*Management*] .... SOPC
Sales Order .... SO
Sales Order Authority (AAG) .... SOA
Sales Order Processing [*Manufacturing management*] .... SOP
Sales Other than Gasoline [*Business term*] .... SOTG
Sales Processing Interactive Real-Time Inventory Technique [*NCR Corp. trademark*] .... SPIRIT
Sales Profitability and Contribution Evaluator [*Computer science*] .... SPACE
Sales Promotion Executives Association [*Later, MCEI*] (EA) .... SPEA
Sales, Purchases and Nominal Package (MHDB) .... SPANPAC
Sales Relations Survey [*Test*] .... SRS
Sales Release Order .... SRO
Sales Representatives and Commercial Travellers Guild [*Australia*] .... SRCTG
Sales Tax .... SLTX
Sales Tax .... ST
Sales Tax Branch, United States Internal Revenue Bureau (DLA) .... ST
Sales Tax Exemption Processing System [*Software*] .... STEP
Sales Tax Rulings [*Australia A publication*] .... ST Rulings
Sales Tax Rulings, United States Internal Revenue Bureau [*A publication*] (DLA) .... ST
Sales Transaction Audit [*Test*] .... STA
Sales Voucher [*Business term*] (DCTA) .... SV
Salesian Missionaries of Mary Immaculate [*See also SSMMI*] [*Gentilly, France*] (EAIO) .... SMMI
Salesian Youth Movement (EA) .... SYM
Salesianorum Congregatio [*Congregation of St. Francis of Sales*] [*Salesian Fathers*] [*Roman Catholic religious order*] .... SC
Salesians of Don Bosco [*Roman Catholic men's religious order*] .... SDB
Salesians of Don Bosco (TOCD) .... sdb
Salesman .... SLSMN
Salesman (WGA) .... SLSMN
Salesmen's Association of Paper and Allied Industries (EA) .... SAPAI
Salesmen's Association of the American Chemical Industry [*Later, SACI*] (EA) .... SAACI
Salesmen's Association of the Textile Dyeing and Printing Industry (EA) .... SATDPI
Sales-Point Information Computing Equipment [*Merchandising*] .... SPICE
Salford Information Technology Centre (NITA) .... SITC
Salford University Business Services [*British*] .... SUBS
Salford University Industrial Centre Ltd. [*British*] (IRUK) .... SUIC
Salic Law [*A publication*] (DLA) .... L Salic
Salicional [*Music*] .... SALIC
Salick Health Care, Inc. [*Associated Press*] (SAG) .... Salick
Salick Health Care, Inc. [*Beverly Hills, CA*] [*NASDAQ symbol*] (NQ) .... SHCI
Salick Health Care(New) [*NASDAQ symbol*] (TTSB) .... SHCID
Salicyl Acyl Glucuronide [*Organic chemistry*] .... SAG
Salicyl Phenolic Glucuronide [*Organic chemistry*] .... SPG
Salicylaldehyde Thiocarbohydrazone [*Organic chemistry*] .... SATCH
Salicylamide [*Analgesic compound*] .... SAM
Salicylamide, Phenacetin [*Acetophenetidin*], and Caffeine [*Pharmacy*] .... SPC
Salicylaslicylic Acid [*Later, salsalate*] (DAVI) .... SSA
Salicylate [*Medicine*] .... sal
Salicylate (BABM) .... salicyl
Salicylate [*Pharmacology*] (DAVI) .... salicyl
Salicylazosulfapyridine [*Antibacterial*] .... SAS
Salicylazosulfapyridine (DMAA) .... SASP
Salicylhydroxamic Acid [*Chelating agent*] .... SHAM
Salicylic Acid [*Organic chemistry*] .... SA
Salicylic Acid Binding Protein [*Biochemistry*] .... SABP
Salicylideniminobenzohydroxamic Acid [*Biochemistry*] .... SIBH
Salicylsalicylic Acid [*Organic chemistry*] (MAE) .... SSA
Salicyluric Acid [*Also, SUA*] [*Biochemistry*] .... SU
Salicyluric Acid [*Also, SU*] [*Biochemistry*] .... SUA
Salida, CO [*AM radio station call letters*] .... KVRH
Salida, CO [*FM radio station call letters*] .... KVRH-FM
Salida Public Library, Salida, CO [*Library symbol Library of Congress*] (LCLS) .... CoSa
Salima [*Malawi*] [*Airport symbol*] (AD) .... AIM
Salima [*Malawi*] [*ICAO location identifier*] (ICLI) .... FWSM
Salina [*Diocesan abbreviation*] [*Kansas*] (TOCD) .... SAL
Salina [*Utah*] [*Airport symbol*] (OAG) .... SBO
Salina [*Kansas*] [*Airport symbol*] (OAG) .... SLN
Salina Board of Trade (EA) .... SBT
Salina, KS [*Television station call letters*] .... KAAS
Salina, KS [*FM radio station call letters*] .... KCVS
Salina, KS [*AM radio station call letters*] .... KFRM
Salina, KS [*FM radio station call letters*] .... KHCD
Salina, KS [*AM radio station call letters*] .... KINA
Salina, KS [*AM radio station call letters*] .... KSAL
Salina, KS [*FM radio station call letters*] .... KSKG
Salina, KS [*FM radio station call letters*] .... KYEZ
Salina, KS [*FM radio station call letters*] .... KZBZ
Salina, KS [*Location identifier FAA*] (FAAL) .... SLN

Salina Public Library, Salina, KS [*Library symbol Library of Congress*] (LCLS) ... KSal
Salinas [*Ecuador*] [*ICAO location identifier*] (ICLI) ... SESA
Salinas [*Chile*] [*Seismograph station code, US Geological Survey*] (SEIS) ... SLN
Salinas [*Bolivia*] [*ICAO location identifier*] (ICLI) ... SLSJ
Salinas [*California*] [*Airport symbol*] (AD) ... SNS
Salinas, CA [*Television station call letters*] ... KCBA
Salinas, CA [*AM radio station call letters*] ... KCTY
Salinas, CA [*FM radio station call letters*] ... KDON
Salinas, CA [*AM radio station call letters*] (RBYB) ... KHTX
Salinas, CA [*FM radio station call letters*] ... KRAY
Salinas, CA [*Television station call letters*] ... KSBW
Salinas, CA [*AM radio station call letters*] ... KTGE
Salinas, CA [*AM radio station call letters*] ... KTOM
Salinas, CA [*FM radio station call letters*] ... KTOM-FM
Salinas, CA [*Location identifier FAA*] (FAAL) ... SNS
Salinas, CA [*Location identifier FAA*] (FAAL) ... UAD
Salinas, PR [*AM radio station call letters*] ... WHOY
Salinas Public Library, Salinas, CA [*Library symbol Library of Congress*] (LCLS) ... CSal
Salinas Public Library, Salinas, CA [*OCLC symbol*] (OCLC) ... SPU
Salinas Road [*California*] [*Seismograph station code, US Geological Survey*] (SEIS) ... SRC
Saline ... S
Saline [*Pharmacology*] (DAVI) ... S
Saline ... SAL
Saline Enema [*Medicine*] ... SE
Saline Infusion Sonohysterography [*Gynecological procedure*] ... SIS
Saline Injection [*Abortion technique*] ... SI
Saline, MI [*AM radio station call letters*] ... WAMX
Saline Public Library, Saline, MI [*Library symbol Library of Congress*] (LCLS) ... MiSal
Saline Retention Value ... SRV
Saline Soak ... SS
Saline Sodium Citrate [*Clinical chemistry*] ... SSC
Saline Solution [*Pharmacology*] (DAVI) ... SS
Saline Solution Enema [*Medicine*] ... SSE
Saline Water Conversion (MCD) ... SWC
Saline Water Conversion Program [*Department of the Interior*] ... SWCP
Salinger's Reports [*88-117 Iowa*] [*A publication*] (DLA) ... Sal
Salingyi [*Myanmar*] [*ICAO location identifier*] (ICLI) ... VBSL
Salinity Indicator ... SI
Salinity Management Plan [*Australia*] ... SMP
Salinity Pilot Program Advisory Council (EERA) ... SPPAC
Salinity Program Advisory Council (EERA) ... SPAC
Salinity, Temperature and Depth [*Probe*] [*Marine science*] (OSRA) ... STD
Salinity/Temperature/Density [*or Depth*] [*Oceanography*] ... STD
Salinity, Temperature, Sound-Velocity and Pressure-Sensing System (PDAA) ... STVP
Salinity-Conductivity-Temperature ... S-C-T
Salinometer (KSC) ... SAL
Salisbury [*England*] ... SALIS
Salisbury [*Zimbabwe*] [*Airport symbol Obsolete*] (OAG) ... SAY
Salisbury [*Maryland*] [*Airport symbol*] (OAG) ... SBY
Salisbury [*Postcode*] (ODBW) ... SP
Salisbury, CT [*FM radio station call letters*] ... WKZE
Salisbury Group (EAIO) ... SG
Salisbury, MD [*Location identifier FAA*] (FAAL) ... PQU
Salisbury, MD [*Location identifier FAA*] (FAAL) ... SBY
Salisbury, MD [*Television station call letters*] ... WBOC
Salisbury, MD [*Television station call letters*] ... WCPB
Salisbury, MD [*FM radio station call letters*] ... WDIH
Salisbury, MD [*AM radio station call letters*] ... WICO
Salisbury, MD [*FM radio station call letters*] ... WICO-FM
Salisbury, MD [*AM radio station call letters*] ... WJDY
Salisbury, MD [*FM radio station call letters*] ... WLVW
Salisbury, MD [*Television station call letters*] ... WMDT
Salisbury, MD [*FM radio station call letters*] ... WSBY
Salisbury, MD [*FM radio station call letters*] ... WSCL
Salisbury, MD [*AM radio station call letters*] ... WTGM
Salisbury, NC [*Location identifier FAA*] (FAAL) ... RUQ
Salisbury, NC [*Location identifier FAA*] (FAAL) ... SRW
Salisbury, NC [*FM radio station call letters*] (RBYB) ... WEND
Salisbury, NC [*FM radio station call letters*] ... WNDN
Salisbury, NC [*FM radio station call letters*] (RBYB) ... WOGR-FM
Salisbury, NC [*AM radio station call letters*] ... WSAT
Salisbury, NC [*AM radio station call letters*] ... WSTP
Salisbury Sound Association (EA) ... SSA
Salisbury State College, Salisbury, MD [*Library symbol Library of Congress*] (LCLS) ... MdSalS
Salisbury State College, Salisbury, MD [*OCLC symbol*] (OCLC) ... SSC
Salisbury State University (GAGS) ... Salisbury St U
Salisbury/Wicomico County [*Maryland*] [*ICAO location identifier*] (ICLI) ... KSBY
Salish Kootenai College Library, Pablo, MT [*Library symbol*] [*Library of Congress*] (LCLS) ... MtPaS
Salishan [*MARC language code Library of Congress*] (LCCP) ... sal
Saliva (MAE) ... sal
Saliva Diagnostic Sys Wrrt [*NASDAQ symbol*] (TTSB) ... SALVW
Saliva Diagnostic Systems [*Commercial firm Associated Press*] (SAG) ... Saliva
Saliva Diagnostic Systems [*NASDAQ symbol*] (SAG) ... SALV
Saliva Sample (MAE) ... SS
Salivary Caffeine Clearance [*Physiology*] ... SCC
Salivary Duct Carcinoma [*Oncology*] ... SDC
Salivary Gland Choristoma [*Medicine*] ... SGC
Salivary Gland Virus ... SGV
Salivary Peroxidase [*Medicine*] (DMAA) ... SAPX
Salivary Progesterone [*Medicine*] (DMAA) ... SP
Salivate (KSC) ... SLV
Salivation [*Treatment for syphilis*] [*Slang British*] (DSUE) ... SAL
Salivation, Lacrimation, Urination, Defecation [*Medicine*] (DMAA) ... SLUD
Salivation, Lacrimation, Urination, Defecation, Gastrointestinal Upset, Emesis [*Medicine*] (DMAA) ... SLUDGE
Salk Institute for Biological Studies ... SIBS
Salk Junior High School, Elk River, MN [*Library symbol*] [*Library of Congress*] (LCLS) ... MnErSJ
Salkeld's English King's Bench Reports [*91 English Reprint*] [*A publication*] (DLA) ... Salk
Salkeld's English King's Bench Reports [*91 English Reprint*] [*A publication*] (DLA) ... Salk (Eng)
Salkowski Positive Compound (OA) ... SPC
Salladasburg, PA [*FM radio station call letters*] (RBYB) ... WMYL-FM
Salladasburg, PA [*FM radio station call letters*] (RBYB) ... WRAK-FM
Sallanches-Mont-Blanc [*France ICAO location identifier*] (ICLI) ... LFHZ
Salle Palasz and Tri-Weapon Club (EA) ... SPTWC
Sallie H. Jenkins Memorial Public Library, Aulander, NC [*Library symbol*] [*Library of Congress*] (LCLS) ... NcAr
Sallie H. Jenkins Memorial Public Library, Aulander, NC [*Library symbol Library of Congress*] (LCLS) ... NcAu
Sallisaw, OK [*AM radio station call letters*] ... KKID
Sallisaw, OK [*FM radio station call letters*] ... KKUZ
Sallisaw, OK [*AM radio station call letters*] (RBYB) ... KKUZ-AM
Sallisaw, OK [*FM radio station call letters*] (RBYB) ... KMXJ-FM
Sallust [*Roman historian, 86-34BC*] [*Classical studies*] (ROG) ... SALL
Sally Field National Fan Club (EA) ... SFNFC
Salmagundi [*A publication*] (BRI) ... Salm
Salmagundi Club (EA) ... SC
Salmanassar (BJA) ... Salm
Salmanticensis [*Salmanca, Spain*] [*A publication*] (BJA) ... Salmant
Salmo Public Library, British Columbia [*Library symbol National Library of Canada*] (NLC) ... BSA
Salmon [*Philately*] ... sal
Salmon and Trout Association (DBA) ... S & TA
Salmon Arm, BC [*AM radio station call letters*] ... CKXR
Salmon Arm Museum and Heritage Association, British Columbia [*Library symbol National Library of Canada*] (NLC) ... BSAAM
Salmon Arm Museum and Heritage Association, Salmon Arm, BC, Canada [*Library symbol*] [*Library of Congress*] (LCLS) ... CaBSAAM
Salmon Calcitonin [*Endocrinology*] ... SCT
Salmon, ID [*AM radio station call letters*] ... KSRA
Salmon, ID [*FM radio station call letters*] ... KSRA-FM
Salmon, ID [*Location identifier FAA*] (FAAL) ... LKT
Salmon, ID [*Location identifier FAA*] (FAAL) ... SMN
Salmon Institute [*Formerly, CSI*] (EA) ... SI
Salmon P. Chase College of Law of Northern Kentucky State College (GAGS) ... Chase C Law
Salmon Poisoning Disease [*Medicine*] (AAMN) ... SPD
Salmon Protection Association of Western Newfoundland [*Canada*] (ASF) ... SPAWN
Salmon Public Library, Salmon, ID [*Library symbol*] [*Library of Congress*] (LCLS) ... IdSal
Salmon River Public Library, Riggins, ID [*Library symbol*] [*Library of Congress*] (LCLS) ... IdRg
Salmon Unlimited (EA) ... SU
Salmonella [*Bacteriology*] (MAE) ... S
Salmonella [*Bacteriology*] ... Sal
Salmonella Outbreak Detection Algorithm [*Medicine*] ... SODA
Salmonella-Shigella [*Microbiology*] ... SS
Salmonellosis-Resistance Factor ... SRF
Salmonid Enhancement Program [*Canada*] ... SEP
Salmon's Abridgment of State Trials [*A publication*] (DLA) ... Salm Abr
Salmon's Edition of the State Trials [*A publication*] (DLA) ... Salm St R
Salo [*Italy*] [*Seismograph station code, US Geological Survey*] (SEIS) ... SAL
Salomon Bros 2008 WW Dlr Gvt [*NYSE symbol*] (TTSB) ... SBG
Salomon Bros Fund [*NYSE symbol*] (TTSB) ... SBF
Salomon Bros High Income Fd [*NYSE symbol*] (TTSB) ... HIF
Salomon Bros W W Income Fd [*NYSE symbol*] (TTSB) ... SBW
Salomon Brothers 2008 World-Wide Direct Government Fund [*NYSE symbol*] (SPSG) ... SBG
Salomon Brothers 2008 Worldwide Dollar Government Term Trust [*Associated Press*] (SAG) ... Sal08Ww
Salomon Brothers Fund [*Associated Press*] (SAG) ... SalmSBF
Salomon Brothers Fund [*NYSE symbol*] (SPSG) ... SBF
Salomon Brothers High Income Fund [*NYSE symbol*] (SPSG) ... HIF
Salomon Brothers High Income Fund [*Associated Press*] (SAG) ... SalmHIF
Salomon Brothers Library, New York, NY [*OCLC symbol*] (OCLC) ... YSB
Salomon Brothers, New York, NY [*Library symbol Library of Congress*] (LCLS) ... NNSaB
Salomon Brothers Worldwide Income Fund [*Associated Press*] (SAG) ... SalWw
Salomon Brothers Worldwide Income Fund [*NYSE symbol*] (SPSG) ... SBW
Salomon Inc, 7.25% ORCL'ELKS' [*AMEX symbol*] (TTSB) ... OLK
Salomon, Inc. [*AMEX symbol*] (SPSG) ... AEK
Salomon, Inc. [*NYSE symbol*] (SAG) ... CXB
Salomon, Inc. [*AMEX symbol*] (SAG) ... DLK
Salomon, Inc. [*AMEX symbol*] (SAG) ... HLK
Salomon, Inc. [*AMEX symbol*] (SPSG) ... MEK
Salomon, Inc. [*AMEX symbol*] (SPSG) ... OLK
Salomon, Inc. [*AMEX symbol*] (SAG) ... OPY
Salomon, Inc. [*AMEX symbol*] (SAG) ... PLK
Salomon, Inc. [*Associated Press*] (SAG) ... SalAMGN
Salomon, Inc. [*Associated Press*] (SAG) ... SalDEC

Salomon, Inc. [*Associated Press*] (SAG) .... SalHWP
Salomon, Inc. [*Associated Press*] (SAG) .... Salmn
Salomon, Inc. [*Associated Press*] (SAG) .... SalMSFT
Salomon, Inc. [*Associated Press*] (SAG) .... Salomn
Salomon, Inc. [*Associated Press*] (SAG) .... SalORCL
Salomon, Inc. [*Associated Press*] (SAG) .... SalPRI
Salomon, Inc. [*Associated Press*] (SAG) .... SalSNPL
Salomon, Inc. [*NYSE symbol*] (SPSG) .... SB
Salomon, Inc. [*Associated Press*] (SAG) .... SBYen
Salomon, Inc. [*AMEX symbol*] (SAG) .... SEK
Salomon Inc. 5% MSFI'ELKA' [*AMEX symbol*] (TTSB) .... MEK
Salomon Inc. 5.25% HP'ELKS' [*AMEX symbol*] (TTSB) .... HLK
Salomon Inc. 6.50% AMGN'ELKS' [*AMEX symbol*] (TTSB) .... AEK
Salomon Inc. 6.75% DEC'ELKS' [*AMEX symbol*] (TTSB) .... DLK
Salomon Inc. 8.08% Dep Pfd [*NYSE symbol*] (TTSB) .... SBPrD
Salomon Inc. 8.40% Dep Pfd [*NYSE symbol*] (TTSB) .... SBPrE
Salomon Inc. 9.50% Dep Pfd [*NYSE symbol*] (TTSB) .... SBPrC
Salomon Inc. 6.125% PRI 'ELKS' [*AMEX symbol*] (TTSB) .... PLK
Salomon Inc. 7.625% SNPL'ELKS' [*AMEX symbol*] (TTSB) .... SEK
Salomon Page Group Ltd. [*Associated Press*] (SAG) .... SalPage
Salomon Page Group Ltd. [*Associated Press*] (SAG) .... SalPge
Salomon Page Group Ltd. [*NASDAQ symbol*] (SAG) .... SOLP
Salomon Phibro Oil Trust [*Associated Press*] (SAG) .... SalPhib
Salon [*France ICAO location identifier*] (ICLI) .... LFMY
Salon .... SLN
Salon/Eyguieres [*France ICAO location identifier*] (ICLI) .... LFNE
Salon International de la Machine Agricole .... SIMA
Salon International de l'Alimentation [*World Food Fair*] .... SIAL
Salon International de l'Informatique, de la Communication, et de l'Organisationdu Bureau [*Business equipment exhibition*] .... SICOB
Salon Litteraire, Artistique, et Diplomatique .... SLAD
Salon Resources Corp. [*Vancouver Stock Exchange symbol*] .... SAJ
Salonika [*Greece*] [*Airport symbol*] (AD) .... SKG
Saloon .... SLON
Salpa Aviation Co. Ltd. [*Sudan*] [*ICAO designator*] (FAAC) .... SLP
Salpingitis Isthmica Nodosum .... SIN
Salpingo-Oophorectomy [*Medicine*] .... SO
Salsalate [*Anti-inflammatory drug*] .... SSA
Salt (MAE) .... sal
Salt Acid .... SA
Salt Added .... SA
Salt Aggregation Test [*Clinical chemistry*] .... SAT
Salt and Pepa [*Rap recording group*] .... S-N-P
Salt and Pepper .... S & P
Salt Cay [*Turks and Caicos Islands*] [*ICAO location identifier*] (ICLI) .... MBSY
Salt Cay [*British West Indies*] [*Airport symbol*] (OAG) .... SLX
Salt Data Centre [*British*] .... SDC
Salt Depletion .... SD
Salt Distributors Association of America (EA) .... SDAA
Salt Dome Experimental Monitoring System (GFGA) .... SADEMS
SALT Education Fund [*Defunct*] (EA) .... SEF
Salt Flat, TX [*Location identifier FAA*] (FAAL) .... SFL
Salt Free [*Diet*] .... SF
Salt Gradient Solar Ponds [*Energy source*] .... SGSP
Salt Institute (EA) .... SI
Salt Lake City [*Utah*] [*ICAO location identifier*] (ICLI) .... KZLC
Salt Lake City [*Utah*] [*Seismograph station code, US Geological Survey*] (SEIS) .... SLC
Salt Lake City [*Utah*] [*Airport symbol*] (OAG) .... SLC
Salt Lake City/International [*Utah*] [*ICAO location identifier*] (ICLI) .... KSLC
Salt Lake City Public Library, Salt Lake City, UT [*Library symbol Library of Congress*] (LCLS) .... USI
Salt Lake City Public Library, Salt Lake City, UT [*OCLC symbol*] (OCLC) .... UUP
Salt Lake City, UT [*Location identifier FAA*] (FAAL) .... BNT
Salt Lake City, UT [*AM radio station call letters*] .... KALL
Salt Lake City, UT [*AM radio station call letters*] .... KAPN
Salt Lake City, UT [*FM radio station call letters*] (RBYB) .... KBEE
Salt Lake City, UT [*AM radio station call letters*] .... KCNR
Salt Lake City, UT [*FM radio station call letters*] .... KCPW
Salt Lake City, UT [*AM radio station call letters*] .... KDYL
Salt Lake City, UT [*AM radio station call letters*] .... KISN
Salt Lake City, UT [*FM radio station call letters*] .... KISN-FM
Salt Lake City, UT [*Television station call letters*] .... KJZZ-TV
Salt Lake City, UT [*FM radio station call letters*] .... KODJ
Salt Lake City, UT [*FM radio station call letters*] .... KRCL
Salt Lake City, UT [*FM radio station call letters*] .... KRSP
Salt Lake City, UT [*FM radio station call letters*] .... KSFI
Salt Lake City, UT [*AM radio station call letters*] .... KSL
Salt Lake City, UT [*Television station call letters*] .... KSL-TV
Salt Lake City, UT [*FM radio station call letters*] .... KSOP
Salt Lake City, UT [*Television station call letters*] .... KSTU
Salt Lake City, UT [*Television station call letters*] .... KTVX
Salt Lake City, UT [*FM radio station call letters*] (RBYB) .... KUBL
Salt Lake City, UT [*Television station call letters*] .... KUED
Salt Lake City, UT [*FM radio station call letters*] .... KUER
Salt Lake City, UT [*FM radio station call letters*] .... KUFR
Salt Lake City, UT [*Television station call letters*] .... KUTV
Salt Lake City, UT [*Location identifier FAA*] (FAAL) .... MOY
Salt Lake City, UT [*Location identifier FAA*] (FAAL) .... SLC
Salt Lake City, UT [*Location identifier FAA*] (FAAL) .... ZLC
Salt Lake County Library System, Midvale, UT [*Library symbol Library of Congress*] (LCLS) .... UM
Salt Lake County Library System, Salt Lake City, UT [*OCLC symbol*] (OCLC) .... UUC
Salt Lake, Garfield & Western Railway Co. [*AAR code*] .... SLGW

Salt Lake, UT [*AM radio station call letters*] (RBYB) .... KFNZ-AM
Salt Loading .... SL
Salt Manufacturing Association [*British*] .... SMA
Salt Producers Association [*Later, SI*] (EA) .... SPA
Salt Shaker Collectors Club [*Later, AAGSSCS*] (EA) .... SSCC
Salt Soluble Protein [*Food industry*] .... SSP
Salt Substitute (DAVI) .... SS
Salt Water .... SW
Salta [*Argentina ICAO location identifier*] (ICLI) .... SASA
Salta [*Argentina ICAO location identifier*] (ICLI) .... SASC
Salta [*Argentina*] [*Airport symbol*] (OAG) .... SLA
Salta [*Argentina*] [*Seismograph station code, US Geological Survey Closed*] (SEIS) .... SLT
Saltair [*Utah*] [*Seismograph station code, US Geological Survey*] (SEIS) .... SAU
Saltair Ltd. [*British ICAO designator*] (FAAC) .... SLT
Saltash [*England*] .... SALT
Salted .... SLTD
Salted Paper Print (VRA) .... SLPT
Saltfree Meal [*Airline notation*] .... WSML
Saltglaze (VRA) .... sltgz
Salt-Glazed Structural Facing Units [*Technical drawings*] .... SGSFU
Salt-Glazed Structural Unit Base [*Technical drawings*] .... SGSUB
Salt-Glazed Ware .... SGW
Saltillo [*Mexico ICAO location identifier*] (ICLI) .... MMIO
Saltillo [*Mexico*] [*Airport symbol*] (AD) .... SLW
Salto [*Uruguay*] [*Airport symbol*] (OAG) .... STY
Salto/Aeropuerto Deptal [*Uruguay*] [*ICAO location identifier*] (ICLI) .... SUSO
Salton City, CA [*Location identifier FAA*] (FAAL) .... SAS
Salton/Maxim Housewares [*NASDAQ symbol*] (SPSG) .... SALT
Salton Maxim Housewares, Inc. [*Associated Press*] (SAG) .... SaltMax
Salton's Magical Automatic Retriever of Texts [*Computer science*] .... SMART
Saltonstall-Kennedy [*Promote and Develop American Fisheries*] (USDC) .... S-K
Saltonstall-Kennedy Promote and Develop American Fisheries [*Marine science*] (OSRA) .... S-K
Saltpond [*Ghana*] [*ICAO location identifier*] (ICLI) .... DGAS
Salt-Poor Albumin [*Medicine*] .... SPA
Salt-Sensitive .... SS
Saltspring Island Public Library, Mary Hawkins Memorial Library, Ganges, BC, Canada [*Library symbol*] [*Library of Congress*] (LCLS) .... CaBGSI
Saltville, VA [*AM radio station call letters*] .... WXMY
Salt-Water Circulating Pump (MSA) .... SWCP
Salt-Water Cooling System [*Nuclear energy*] (NRCH) .... SWCS
Salt-Water Igniter .... SWI
Salt-Water Pump (MSA) .... SWP
Saluda Motor Lines [*AAR code*] .... SML
Saluda, SC [*FM radio station call letters*] .... WJRQ
Saluki Club of America (EA) .... SCA
Saluki Club of America (EA) .... SCOA
Salute America Committee (EA) .... SAC
Salutem Dicit [*Sends Greetings*] [*Latin*] .... SD
Salutem Plurimam Dicit [*He Wishes Much Health*] [*Latin*] .... SPD
Saluting (MSA) .... SAL
Salutis Gratia [*For the Sake of Safety*] [*Latin*] .... SG
Salva Ratificatione [*On Condition of Ratification*] [*Latin*] .... SR
Salvador [*Brazil*] (ROG) .... SALV
Salvador [*Brazil*] [*Airport symbol*] (OAG) .... SSA
Salvador/Dois de Julho [*Brazil ICAO location identifier*] (ICLI) .... SBSV
Salvador Society of Engineers .... SSE
Salvadoran Medical Relief Fund (EA) .... SMRF
Salvage [*Military*] (AFM) .... SALV
Salvage .... SLVG
Salvage and Rescue Ship [*Navy symbol*] .... ATS
Salvage Charges (ODBW) .... sc
Salvage Charges .... SC
Salvage Craft Tender [*Navy ship symbol*] .... ARST
Salvage Craft Tender [*Non-self-propelled*] [*Navy ship symbol*] .... YRST
Salvage Dive [*Military*] (MUGU) .... SALDV
Salvage Diver Badge [*Military decoration*] .... Salv Div Bad
Salvage Diver Badge [*Military decoration*] (GFGA) .... SALVDIVB
Salvage Dives [*Army*] .... SALVDV
Salvage Engineering Order (MCD) .... SEO
Salvage Exercise (MCD) .... SALVEX
Salvage Lift Craft, Heavy [*Non-self-propelled*] [*Navy ship symbol*] .... YHLC
Salvage Lift Craft, Light [*Self-propelled*] [*Navy ship symbol*] .... YLLC
Salvage Lift Craft, Medium [*Non-self-propelled*] [*Navy ship symbol*] .... YMLC
Salvage Lifting Ship [*Navy symbol*] .... ARSD
Salvage Loss .... SL
Salvage Mechanic [*Navy*] .... SM
Salvage Operational Control Center [*On submarine rescue ship during salvage operation*] .... SOCC
Salvage Operations [*Navy*] (NVT) .... SALVOPS
Salvage Sales Material Transfer .... SSMT
Salvage Ship [*Navy symbol*] .... ARS
Salvage Training [*Navy*] (NVT) .... SALVTNG
Salvage Tug [*Navy symbol*] (DNAB) .... ASL
Salvageable (AAG) .... S
Salvation .... SLVTN
Salvation and Laughter Together [*Defunct*] (EA) .... SALT
Salvation Army (EA) .... SA
Salvation Army Association of America (NADA) .... SAAA
Salvation Army Catherine Booth Bible College, Winnipeg, Manitoba [*Library symbol National Library of Canada*] (BIB) .... MWSACB
Salvation Army Grace Hospital, Windsor, Ontario [*Library symbol National Library of Canada*] (BIB) .... OWSAH

Salvation Army Guides and Guards, Brownies, and Sunbeams (EAIO) .... SAGGBS
Salvation Army Home League [*See also LF*] (EAIO) .... SAHL
Salvation Army League of Mercy [*British*] (EAIO) .... SALM
Salvation Army Library, Toronto, ON, Canada [*Library symbol Library of Congress*] (LCLS) .... CaOTSA
Salvation Army Medical Fellowship (EAIO) .... SAMF
Salvation Army Nurses' Fellowship (EAIO) .... SANF
Salvation Army Retired Officers Association .... SAROA
Salvation Army Shelter (DSUE) .... SAL
Salvation Army, Toronto, Ontario [*Library symbol National Library of Canada*] (NLC) .... OTSA
Salvation Army Youth Line [*Australia*] .... SYL
Salvation Army Youth Outreach Service [*Australia*] .... SAYOS
Salvex Resources Ltd. [*Vancouver Stock Exchange symbol*] .... SAL
Salvis Erroribus et Omissis [*Errors and Omissions Excepted*] [*Latin*] .... SEEO
Salvis Omissis [*Omissions Excepted*] [*Latin*] .... SO
Salvo Errore et Omission [*Errors or Omissions Excepted*] [*Latin*] .... SE & O
Salvo Honoris Titulo [*Latin*] .... SHT
Salvo in Flight [*Military*] (CAAL) .... SIF
Salvo Squeezebore (PDAA) .... SSB
Salyersville, KY [*AM radio station call letters*] .... WRLV
Salyersville, KY [*FM radio station call letters*] .... WRLV-FM
Salzburg [*Austria ICAO location identifier*] (ICLI) .... LOWS
Salzburg [*Austria*] [*Airport symbol*] (OAG) .... SZG
Salzburg Assembly: Impact of the New Technology .... SAINT
Salzburg Seminar in American Studies (EA) .... SSAS
Salzgitter/Drutte [*Germany ICAO location identifier*] (ICLI) .... EDVS
Sam & Libby, Inc. [*NASDAQ symbol*] (SPSG) .... SAML
Sam & Libby, Inc. [*Associated Press*] (SAG) .... SamLby
Sam Browne's Cavalry [*British military*] (DMA) .... SBC
SAM Colombia [*Airline flight code*] (ODBW) .... MM
Sam Davis Memorial Association (EA) .... SDMA
Sam Houston State University (GAGS) .... Sam Houston St U
Sam Houston State University, Huntsville, TX [*Library symbol Library of Congress*] (LCLS) .... TxHuT
SAM [*Surface-to-Air Missile*] **Intercept Missile** (DNAB) .... SIM
Sam Neua [*Laos*] [*Airport symbol*] (AD) .... KSN
Sam Neua [*Laos*] [*ICAO location identifier*] (ICLI) .... VLSN
Sam Rayburn Foundation .... SRF
Sam Rayburn High School, Pasadena, TX [*Library symbol*] [*Library of Congress*] (LCLS) .... TxPRH
SAMA [*Scientific Apparatus Makers Association*] **Group of Associations** (EA) .... SAMAGA
Samaero SA [*Romania*] [*ICAO designator*] (FAAC) .... RSB
Samaihuate [*Bolivia*] [*ICAO location identifier*] (ICLI) .... SLIH
Samaipata [*Bolivia*] [*Seismograph station code, US Geological Survey Closed*] (SEIS) .... SMB
Samajwadi Party [*Italy Political party*] (ECON) .... SP
Samangan [*Afghanistan*] [*ICAO location identifier*] (ICLI) .... OASM
Samantha Smith Foundation (EA) .... SSF
Samara [*Costa Rica*] [*ICAO location identifier*] (ICLI) .... MRSR
Samarbeidsnemden for Nordisk Skogforskning [*Nordic Forest Research Cooperation Committee - NFRCC*] [*Finland*] (EAIO) .... SNS
Samarbetsnamnden for de Nordiska Naturvetenskapliga Forskningraden [*Joint Committee of the Nordic Natural Science Research Councils - JCNNSRC*] (EA) .... NOS-N
Samarbetsorganisationen for Emballagefragor i Skandinavien [*Scandinavian Packaging Association*] [*Sweden*] (EA) .... SES
Samaria (BJA) .... Sam
Samaria [*Papua*] [*Airport symbol*] (AD) .... SIW
Samarinda [*Indonesia*] [*Airport symbol*] (OAG) .... SRI
Samarinda/Temindung [*Indonesia*] [*ICAO location identifier*] (ICLI) .... WRLS
Samaritan (BJA) .... Sam
Samaritan Air Service Ltd. [*Canada ICAO designator*] (FAAC) .... HLO
Samaritan Aramaic [*MARC language code Library of Congress*] (LCCP) .... sam
Samaritan Chronology (BJA) .... SamChron
Samaritan Free Hospital [*British*] (ROG) .... SH
Samaritan Health Services [*ICAO designator*] (FAAC) .... SMR
Samaritan Hospital, Troy, NY [*Library symbol Library of Congress*] (LCLS) .... NTS
Samaritan Keep Nursing Home, Medical Library, Watertown, NY [*Library symbol Library of Congress*] (LCLS) .... NWattKH
Samaritan Lay Missioners [*An association*] (EA) .... SLM
Samarium [*Obsolete form; see Sm*] [*Chemical element*] .... Sa
Samarium [*See Sa*] [*Chemical element*] .... Sm
Samarium Cobalt Magnet .... SCM
Samarkand [*Former USSR Seismograph station code, US Geological Survey*] (SEIS) .... SAM
Samarkand [*Former USSR Airport symbol*] (OAG) .... SKD
Samarkand [*Former USSR ICAO location identifier*] (ICLI) .... UTSS
Samarkano Resources [*Vancouver Stock Exchange symbol*] .... SAU
Sambailo [*Guinea*] [*ICAO location identifier*] (ICLI) .... GUSB
Samband Ungra Sjalfstaedismanna [*National Youth Organization of the Independence Party*] [*Iceland*] [*Political party*] (EAIO) .... SUS
Sambava [*Madagascar*] [*ICAO location identifier*] (ICLI) .... FMNS
Sambava [*Madagascar*] [*Airport symbol*] (OAG) .... SVB
Samborondon [*Ecuador*] [*ICAO location identifier*] (ICLI) .... SESM
Sambu [*Panama*] [*Airport symbol*] (OAG) .... SAX
Sambungan Komunikasi Data Packet [*Indonesia*] [*Telecommunications service*] (TSSD) .... SKDP
Samburg [*Tennessee*] [*Seismograph station code, US Geological Survey Closed*] (SEIS) DY4
Samburu [*Kenya*] [*ICAO location identifier*] (ICLI) .... HKSB
Same [*Tanzania*] [*ICAO location identifier*] (ICLI) .... HTSE
Same [*East Timor*] [*ICAO location identifier*] (ICLI) .... WPSM
Same as Above .... SAB
Same as Basic (KSC) .... SAB
Same as Basic Operations Directive (KSC) .... SABOD
Same as Basic Or (MUGU) .... SABOR
Same Case [*Same case as case cited*] [*Used in Shepard's Citations*] [*Legal term*] (DLA) .... S
Same Case [*Law*] .... SC
Same Coupling [*Music*] .... SC
Same Day .... SD
Same Day Surgery [*Medicine*] .... SDS
Same Direction Traffic (FAAC) .... SADT
Same Distribution Center Service Area [*US Postal Service*] .... SDC
Same Old Sludge [*Slang phrase used to describe television programming*] .... SOS
Same Old Stew [*Military slang*] [*Bowdlerized version*] .... SOS
Same Old Stuff [*Reference to the weather*] .... SOS
Same Old Thing [*Slang*] .... SOT
Same Only Softer [*Band leader's signal*] [*Slang*] .... SOS
Same Output Gate [*Computer science*] (AAG) .... SOG
Same Point (ILCA) .... SP
Same Principle (ILCA) .... SP
Same Sea and Country [*or Coast*] [*Shipping*] (DS) .... SS & C
Same Size [*Photography*] [*Printing*] (WDMC) .... S/S
Same Size [*Photography, publishing*] .... SS
Samedan [*Switzerland ICAO location identifier*] (ICLI) .... LSZS
Same-Day Funds Settlement [*Securities and Exchange Commission*] .... SDFS
Samenwerkende Elektriciteit Produktie Bedrijven [*Electric utility*] [*Netherlands*] .... SEP
Samenwerkingsverband voor Opleiding en Vorming op het Terrein van de Informatieverzorging via Netwerken [*Collective for Training and Education in Connection with Information Provision via Networks*] [*Ceased operation*] [*Netherlands Information service or system*] (IID) .... SOVIN
Samford University (GAGS) .... Samford U
Samford University, Birmingham, AL [*Library symbol Library of Congress*] (LCLS) .... ABH
Samford University, Cumberland School of Law, Cordell Hull Law Library, Birmingham, AL [*Library symbol Library of Congress*] (LCLS) .... ABH-L
Samfya [*Zambia*] [*ICAO location identifier*] (ICLI) .... FLYA
SAMI Online Operations (NITA) .... SOLO
SAMID [*Ship Antimissile Integrated Defense*] **System Operational Test** [*Navy*] (NVT) .... SAMSOT
Sammelbuch Griechischer Urkunden aus Aegypten [*A publication*] (BJA) .... SGU
Sammlung der Griechischen Dialektinschriften [*A publication*] (OCD) .... GDI
Sammons' Opuntia Virus [*Plant pathology*] .... SOV
SAMMS [*Standard Automated Materiel Management System*] **Automated Small Purchase System** .... SASPS
SAMMS [*Standard Automated Materiel Management System*] **Program Management Office** [*DoD*] .... SPMO
Samnordisk Planteforedling [*Internordic plant breeding*] [*An association Sweden*] (EAIO) .... SNP
Samoa (BARN) .... Sam
Samoa Air [*ICAO designator*] (AD) .... TS
Samoa Islands [*Aircraft nationality and registration mark*] (FAAC) 5W
Samoa Islands [*MARC geographic area code Library of Congress*] (LCCP) .... posh
Samoan [*ICAO designator*] (AD) .... OE
Samoan Pacific Law Journal [*A publication*] (DLA) .... Samoan PLJ
Samoa-Pago Pago [*Diocesan abbreviation*] (TOCD) .... SPP
Samodzielna Brygada Strzelcow Karpackich [*Poland*] .... SBSK
Samos [*Greece*] [*ICAO location identifier*] (ICLI) .... LGSM
Samos [*Greece*] [*Seismograph station code, US Geological Survey Closed*] (SEIS) .... SMS
Samos Island [*Greece*] [*Airport symbol*] (OAG) .... SMI
Samos Resources, Inc. [*Vancouver Stock Exchange symbol*] .... SSZ
Samostalna Demokratska Stranka [*Independent Democratic Party*] [*Former Yugoslavia*] [*Political party*] (PPE) .... SDS
Samoth Capital Corp. [*Toronto Stock Exchange symbol*] .... SCF
Samovar Hills, AK [*Location identifier FAA*] (FAAL) .... SMV
Samoyed Club of America (EA) .... SCA
Samozaryadnyi Karabin Simonova Carbine [*Soviet made semiautomatic rifle*] (VNW) .... SKS
Sampford [*England*] .... SAMPF
Sampit/H. Hasan [*Indonesia*] [*ICAO location identifier*] (ICLI) .... WRBS
Sample .... S
Sample (AAG) .... SAMP
Sample .... SMPL
Sample Acceptance Rate [*Statistics*] .... SAR
Sample Air Filter .... SAF
Sample and Analysis Management System [*Computer science*] .... SAM
Sample and Hold (IEEE) .... S/H
Sample and Hold (IAA) .... SAH
Sample and Hold Amplifier .... SHA
Sample Array .... SA
Sample Array System (KSC) .... SAS
Sample Assembly (MCD) .... SA
Sample Assignment Word .... SAW
Sample Cave Operating Area [*Nuclear energy*] (NRCH) .... SCOA
Sample Collection and Preparation Module [*X-ray spectrometry*] .... SCPM
Sample Collection Bag [*NASA*] .... SCB
Sample Control Tape [*Computer science*] .... SCT
Sample Data (NG) .... SD
Sample Data Collection .... SDC
Sample Data Collection Plan (MCD) .... SDCP
Sample Data Control System (MCD) .... SDCS
Sample Delay .... SD
Sample Display Service [*Department of Commerce*] .... SDS
Sample Gas .... SG

Sample Gas Cell [*Instrumentation*] ..... SGC
Sample Gas Flow ..... SGF
Sample Handling System [*Chemistry*] ..... SHS
Sample Inlet System [*Automotive exhaust emission testing*] ..... SIS
Sample Instruction Test Exercise (MCD) ..... SITE
Sample Interval ..... SI
Sample Item Portion ..... SIP
Sample Laboratory (MCD) ..... SL
Sample Lot Acceptance Testing ..... SLAT
Sample Management Facility ..... SMF
Sample Management System [*Laboratory science*] ..... SMS
Sample Method Survey [*for family housing requirements*] [*Military*] (AABC) ..... SAMS
Sample Mix Table [*Musical instrument digital interface*] ..... SMT
Sample Name ..... SN
Sample Noise Level ..... SNL
Sample Part ..... SP
Sample Polarity Coincidence Correlator (IAA) ..... SPCC
Sample Preparation Accessory [*Laboratory analysis*] ..... SPA
Sample Preparation and DNA [*Deoxyribonucleic Acid*] **Probe** ..... SPD
Sample Rate ..... SR
Sample Recovery Container [*NASA*] (KSC) ..... SRC
Sample Return Container [*NASA*] (NASA) ..... SRC
Sample Rock Container [*NASA*] ..... SRC
Sample Sink [*Nuclear energy*] (NRCH) ..... SS
Sample Size (EDAC) ..... SS
Sample Sound Technology [*Computer science*] ..... SST
Sample Station [*Nuclear energy*] (NRCH) ..... SS
Sample Tube ..... ST
Sample Valve Assembly ..... SVA
Sampled [*Tea trade*] (ROG) ..... SPD
Sampled Channel Filter ..... SCF
Sampled Data Channel Filter ..... SDCF
Sampled Data Simulator and Computer ..... SADSAC
Sampled Filter (IEEE) ..... SF
Sampled N-Path Filter (PDAA) ..... SNF
Sampled Servo [*Formatting scheme*] [*Computer science*] (PCM) ..... SS
Sampled-Data Nonlinearity Matrix (PDAA) ..... SDNM
Sampler (DEN) ..... SMP
Sampler Address Translator ..... SAT
Samples per Second (KSC) ..... S/S
Samples per Second ..... SPS
Sampling (MSA) ..... SMPLG
Sampling Aerospace Nuclear Debris ..... SAND
Sampling Analog Memory System ..... SAMS
Sampling and Analysis Plan ..... SAP
Sampling and Analytical Method ..... SAM
Sampling Close to the Injector ..... SCIP
Sampling Inspection Checklist ..... SICL
Sampling Inspection Procedures ..... SIP
Sampling Oscilloscope Recorder ..... SOR
Sampling Point (NRCH) ..... SP
Sampling System (NRCH) ..... SS
Sampling Visit (GNE) ..... SV
Sampling with Partial Replacement ..... SPR
Sampson Technical Institute, Clinton, NC [*Library symbol Library of Congress*] (LCLS) ..... NcCliS
Sampson-Clinton Public Library, Clinton, NC [*Library symbol Library of Congress*] (LCLS) ..... NcCli
Samradet for Nordisk Amatormusik [*Arhus, Denmark*] (EAIO) ..... SAMNAM
Samso [*Denmark ICAO location identifier*] (ICLI) ..... EKSS
Samson (BJA) ..... Sam
Samson Aviation Services [*British ICAO designator*] (FAAC) ..... SHL
Samson Data Systemen (NITA) ..... SDS
Samson Database Services (NITA) ..... SDBS
Samson Gold Corp. [*Vancouver Stock Exchange symbol*] ..... SSN
Samsonite Corp. [*NASDAQ symbol*] (SAG) ..... SAMC
Samsonite Corp. [*Associated Press*] (SAG) ..... Samsnte
Samsonov Density Meter [*Gravimetrics*] ..... SDM
Samsula, FL [*FM radio station call letters*] ..... WKTO
Samsun [*Turkey ICAO location identifier*] (ICLI) ..... LTAQ
Samsun [*Turkey*] [*Airport symbol*] (OAG) ..... SSX
Samsville [*Illinois*] [*Seismograph station code, US Geological Survey*] (SEIS) ..... SMV
Samsville, IL [*Location identifier FAA*] (FAAL) ..... SAM
Samuel [*Old Testament book*] (BJA) ..... S
Samuel [*Old Testament book*] ..... Sam
Samuel [*Old Testament Book*] (WGA) ..... Saml
Samuel [*Old Testament book*] ..... Sm
Samuel Butler Society [*Defunct*] (EA) ..... SBS
Samuel Feltman Ammunition Laboratory [*Army*] ..... SFAL
Samuel Gompers Stamp Club (EA) ..... SGSC
Samuel Johnson [*Initials used as pseudonym*] ..... SJ
Samuel Lutheran School, Marshall, MN [*Library symbol*] [*Library of Congress*] (LCLS) ..... MnMarLS
Samuel Lyman Atwood Marshall [*American general and author, 1900-1977*] ..... SLAM
Samuel Manu-Tech, Inc. [*Toronto Stock Exchange symbol*] ..... SMT
Samuel Taylor Coleridge [*Nineteenth-century British poet*] ..... STC
San [*Mali*] [*ICAO location identifier*] (ICLI) ..... GASN
San (VRA) ..... S
SAN [*Societe Aeronautique Normande*] [*France ICAO aircraft manufacturer identifier*] (ICAO) ..... SN
San Agustin [*Costa Rica*] [*ICAO location identifier*] (ICLI) ..... MRST
San Agustin [*Bolivia*] [*ICAO location identifier*] (ICLI) ..... SLZG
San Alberto [*Costa Rica*] [*ICAO location identifier*] (ICLI) ..... MRSA
San Andreas Fault ..... SAF
San Andreas Fault Experiment ..... SAFE
San Andreas Fault Zone [*Geology*] ..... SAFZ
San Andreas Geological Observatory [*California*] [*Seismograph station code, US Geological Survey*] (SEIS) ..... SAO
San Andreas Lake [*California*] [*Seismograph station code, US Geological Survey*] (SEIS) ..... SAC
San Andres [*Colombia*] [*Seismograph station code, US Geological Survey*] (SEIS) ..... SRD
San Andres Island [*Colombia*] [*Airport symbol*] (OAG) ..... ADZ
San Andres/Sesquicentenario, San Andres [*Colorado ICAO location identifier*] (ICLI) ..... SKSP
San Andros [*Bahamas*] [*Airport symbol*] (OAG) ..... SAQ
San Andros, Andros Island [*Bahamas*] [*ICAO location identifier*] (ICLI) ..... MYAN
San Angelo [*Diocesan abbreviation*] [*Texas*] (TOCD) ..... SAN
San Angelo [*Texas*] [*Airport symbol*] (OAG) ..... SJT
San Angelo/Mathis Field [*Texas*] [*ICAO location identifier*] (ICLI) ..... KSJT
San Angelo, TX [*Location identifier FAA*] (FAAL) ..... GOF
San Angelo, TX [*Television station call letters*] ..... KACB
San Angelo, TX [*AM radio station call letters*] ..... KCRN
San Angelo, TX [*FM radio station call letters*] ..... KCRN-FM
San Angelo, TX [*FM radio station call letters*] ..... KDCD
San Angelo, TX [*FM radio station call letters*] ..... KELI
San Angelo, TX [*AM radio station call letters*] ..... KGKL
San Angelo, TX [*FM radio station call letters*] ..... KGKL-FM
San Angelo, TX [*Television station call letters*] ..... KIDY
San Angelo, TX [*FM radio station call letters*] ..... KIXY
San Angelo, TX [*AM radio station call letters*] (RBYB) ..... KKSA
San Angelo, TX [*Television station call letters*] ..... KLST
San Angelo, TX [*FM radio station call letters*] ..... KSJT
San Angelo, TX [*FM radio station call letters*] (RBYB) ..... KUTX
San Angelo, TX [*FM radio station call letters*] (RBYB) ..... KWFR
San Angelo, TX [*FM radio station call letters*] ..... KYZZ
San Angelo, TX [*Location identifier FAA*] (FAAL) ..... SJT
San Anselmo Public Library, San Anselmo, CA [*Library symbol Library of Congress*] (LCLS) ..... CSa
San Antonio [*Texas*] [*Airport symbol*] ..... SAT
San Antonio [*Bolivia*] [*ICAO location identifier*] (ICLI) ..... SLST
San Antonio [*Venezuela*] [*Airport symbol*] (OAG) ..... SVZ
San Antonio Air Depot [*Air Force*] ..... SAAD
San Antonio Air Logistics Center [*Formerly, SAAMA*] [*Air Force*] (NASA) ..... SA-ALC
San Antonio Air Logistics Center, Directorate of Materiel Management [*Kelly Air Force Base, TX*] ..... SAALC/MM
San Antonio Air Materiel Area [*Later, SA-ALC*] [*Air Force*] ..... SAAMA
San Antonio Air Service Command [*Air Force*] ..... SAASC
San Antonio Air Technical Service Command [*Air Force*] ..... SAATSC
San Antonio College [*Texas*] ..... SAC
San Antonio College, San Antonio, TX [*OCLC symbol*] (OCLC) ..... SNC
San Antonio College, San Antonio, TX [*Library symbol Library of Congress*] (LCLS) ..... TxSaC
San Antonio Contracting Center [*Air Force*] ..... SACC
San Antonio Data Services Center [*Military*] ..... SADSC
San Antonio De Areco [*Argentina ICAO location identifier*] (ICLI) ..... SAAA
San Antonio De Los Banos [*Cuba ICAO location identifier*] (ICLI) ..... MUSA
San Antonio do Ica [*Brazil*] [*Airport symbol*] (AD) ..... SIC
San Antonio/International [*Texas*] [*ICAO location identifier*] (ICLI) ..... KSAT
San Antonio Joint Military Medical Command ..... SAJMMC
San Antonio/Kelly Air Force Base [*Texas*] [*ICAO location identifier*] (ICLI) ..... KSKF
San Antonio Oeste [*Argentina*] [*Airport symbol*] (OAG) ..... OES
San Antonio Oeste [*Argentina ICAO location identifier*] (ICLI) ..... SAVO
San Antonio On Line User Group (NITA) ..... SOLUG
San Antonio Procurement and Production Materiel Area [*Air Force*] ..... SAPPMA
San Antonio Public Library, San Antonio, TX [*OCLC symbol*] (OCLC) ..... SAP
San Antonio Public Library, San Antonio, TX [*Library symbol Library of Congress*] (LCLS) ..... TxSa
San Antonio/Randolf Air Force Base [*Texas*] [*ICAO location identifier*] (ICLI) ..... KRND
San Antonio Real Property Maintenance Agency [*Military*] ..... SARPMA
San Antonio Research and Development Procurement Office [*Air Force*] ..... SARDPO
San Antonio, Tachira [*Venezuela ICAO location identifier*] (ICLI) ..... SVSA
San Antonio, TX [*Location identifier FAA*] (FAAL) ..... AKY
San Antonio, TX [*Location identifier FAA*] (FAAL) ..... ANT
San Antonio, TX [*Location identifier FAA*] (FAAL) ..... IZR
San Antonio, TX [*Television station call letters*] ..... KABB
San Antonio, TX [*FM radio station call letters*] ..... KAJA
San Antonio, TX [*AM radio station call letters*] ..... KCHL
San Antonio, TX [*AM radio station call letters*] ..... KCOR
San Antonio, TX [*FM radio station call letters*] ..... KCYY
San Antonio, TX [*AM radio station call letters*] ..... KEDA
San Antonio, TX [*AM radio station call letters*] ..... KENS
San Antonio, TX [*Television station call letters*] ..... KENS-TV
San Antonio, TX [*Radio expansion station*] ..... KFIT EXP STN
San Antonio, TX [*Television station call letters*] ..... KHCE
San Antonio, TX [*FM radio station call letters*] ..... KISS
San Antonio, TX [*AM radio station call letters*] ..... KKYX
San Antonio, TX [*Television station call letters*] ..... KLRN
San Antonio, TX [*Television station call letters*] ..... KMOL
San Antonio, TX [*AM radio station call letters*] ..... KONO
San Antonio, TX [*FM radio station call letters*] ..... KPAC
San Antonio, TX [*FM radio station call letters*] ..... KQXT
San Antonio, TX [*FM radio station call letters*] ..... KROM
San Antonio, TX [*FM radio station call letters*] ..... KRTU

San Antonio, TX [*Television station call letters*] ..... KSAT
San Antonio, TX [*FM radio station call letters*] ..... KSJL
San Antonio, TX [*AM radio station call letters*] ..... KSLR
San Antonio, TX [*FM radio station call letters*] ..... KSTX
San Antonio, TX [*FM radio station call letters*] ..... KSYM
San Antonio, TX [*FM radio station call letters*] ..... KTFM
San Antonio, TX [*AM radio station call letters*] ..... KTKR
San Antonio, TX [*AM radio station call letters*] ..... KTSA
San Antonio, TX [*Television station call letters*] ..... KVDA
San Antonio, TX [*Television station call letters*] ..... KWEX
San Antonio, TX [*AM radio station call letters*] ..... KXTN
San Antonio, TX [*FM radio station call letters*] ..... KXTN-FM
San Antonio, TX [*FM radio station call letters*] ..... KYFS
San Antonio, TX [*AM radio station call letters*] (RBYB) ..... KZDC
San Antonio, TX [*FM radio station call letters*] ..... KZEP-FM
San Antonio, TX [*Location identifier FAA*] (FAAL) ..... MDA
San Antonio, TX [*Location identifier FAA*] (FAAL) ..... OSQ
San Antonio, TX [*Location identifier FAA*] (FAAL) ..... RND
San Antonio, TX [*Location identifier FAA*] (FAAL) ..... SKF
San Antonio, TX [*Location identifier FAA*] (FAAL) ..... SSF
San Antonio, TX [*Location identifier FAA*] (FAAL) ..... TRT
San Antonio, TX [*Location identifier FAA*] (FAAL) ..... UNY
San Antonio, TX [*Location identifier FAA*] (FAAL) ..... VQE
San Antonio, TX [*AM radio station call letters*] ..... WOAI
San Antonio, Uvalde & Gulf Railroad Co. ..... SAU & G
San Augustine, TX [*FM radio station call letters*] ..... KCOT
San Aurelio [*Bolivia*] [*ICAO location identifier*] (ICLI) ..... SLAU
San Benito [*California*] [*Seismograph station code, US Geological Survey*] (SEIS) ..... SBT
San Benito County Free Library, Hollister, CA [*Library symbol Library of Congress*] (LCLS) ..... CHoCL
San Bernadino [*Diocesan abbreviation*] [*California*] (TOCD) ..... SB
San Bernardino [*California*] [*Airport symbol*] (AD) ..... SBT
San Bernardino Air Materiel Area ..... SBAMA
San Bernardino, CA [*AM radio station call letters*] ..... KCKC
San Bernardino, CA [*FM radio station call letters*] ..... KFRG
San Bernardino, CA [*AM radio station call letters*] (RBYB) ..... KKLA
San Bernardino, CA [*AM radio station call letters*] ..... KMEN
San Bernardino, CA [*FM radio station call letters*] ..... KOLA
San Bernardino, CA [*Television station call letters*] ..... KSCI
San Bernardino, CA [*AM radio station call letters*] (RBYB) ..... KSZZ
San Bernardino, CA [*FM radio station call letters*] ..... KVCR
San Bernardino, CA [*Television station call letters*] ..... KVCR-TV
San Bernardino, CA [*Television station call letters*] ..... KZKI
San Bernardino, CA [*Location identifier FAA*] (FAAL) ..... SBD
San Bernardino, CA [*Location identifier FAA*] (FAAL) ..... SBT
San Bernardino County Free Library, San Bernardino, CA [*OCLC symbol*] (OCLC) ..... CBL
San Bernardino County Free Library, San Bernardino, CA [*Library symbol Library of Congress*] (LCLS) ..... CSbCL
San Bernardino/Norton Air Force Base [*California*] [*ICAO location identifier*] (ICLI) ..... KSBD
San Bernardino Public Library, San Bernardino, CA [*Library symbol Library of Congress*] (LCLS) ..... CSb
San Bernardino Public Library, San Bernardino, CA [*OCLC symbol*] (OCLC) ..... SBD
San Bernardino Valley College [*California*] ..... SBVC
San Bernardino-Inyo-Riverside Counties United Library Services [*Library network*] ..... SIRCULS
San Borja [*Bolivia*] [*ICAO location identifier*] (ICLI) ..... SLSB
San Borja [*Bolivia*] [*Airport symbol*] (OAG) ..... SRJ
San Bruno Free Public Library, San Bruno, CA [*Library symbol Library of Congress*] (LCLS) ..... CSbr
San Bruno Free Public Library, San Bruno, CA [*Library symbol*] [*Library of Congress*] (LCLS) ..... CSbrP
San Carlos [*Argentina ICAO location identifier*] (ICLI) ..... SAMS
San Carlos [*Ecuador*] [*ICAO location identifier*] (ICLI) ..... SESN
San Carlos, AZ [*FM radio station call letters*] ..... KCDX
San Carlos, CA [*Location identifier FAA*] (FAAL) ..... SQL
San Carlos, Cojedes [*Venezuela ICAO location identifier*] (ICLI) ..... SVCJ
San Carlos De Bariloche [*Argentina*] [*Airport symbol*] (OAG) ..... BRC
San Carlos De Bariloche [*Argentina ICAO location identifier*] (ICLI) ..... SAZS
San Carlos De Rio Negro, T. F. Amazonas [*Venezuela ICAO location identifier*] (ICLI) ..... SVSC
San Carlos Gutierrez [*Bolivia*] [*ICAO location identifier*] (ICLI) ..... SLSD
San Carlos Milling [*AMEX symbol*] (TTSB) ..... SAN
San Carlos Milling Co., Inc. [*AMEX symbol*] (SPSG) ..... SAN
San Carlos Milling Co., Inc. [*Associated Press*] (SAG) ..... SanCarlo
San Carlos/San Juan [*Nicaragua*] [*ICAO location identifier*] (ICLI) ..... MNSC
San Clemente 3-D Acoustic Range (MCD) ..... STAR
San Clemente, CA [*FM radio station call letters*] ..... KWVE
San Clemente Island [*California*] [*Seismograph station code, US Geological Survey*] (SEIS) ..... SCI
San Clemente Island, CA [*Location identifier FAA*] (FAAL) ..... NUC
San Clemente Naval Auxiliary Air Base [*California*] [*ICAO location identifier*] (ICLI) ..... KSCI
San Clemente Ocean Probing Experiment [*Marine science*] (OSRA) ..... SCOPE
San Clemente Ocean Probing Experiment (USDC) ..... SCOPE
San Cristobal [*Costa Rica*] [*ICAO location identifier*] (ICLI) ..... MRSB
San Cristobal [*Chile*] [*Seismograph station code, US Geological Survey Closed*] (SEIS) ..... SCR
San Cristobal (Galapagos) [*ICAO location identifier*] (ICLI) ..... SEST
San Cristobal/Paramillo, Tachira [*Venezuela ICAO location identifier*] (ICLI) ..... SVPM
San Diego [*California*] [*Airport symbol*] (OAG) ..... SAN
San Diego [*Diocesan abbreviation*] [*California*] (TOCD) ..... SD
San Diego [*California*] (GAAI) ..... SDG
San Diego & Arizona Eastern Railway Co. [*AAR code*] ..... SDAE
San Diego & Arizona Railway ..... SD & A
San Diego, CA [*Location identifier FAA*] (FAAL) ..... DCG
San Diego, CA [*FM radio station call letters*] ..... KBZT
San Diego, CA [*AM radio station call letters*] ..... KCBQ
San Diego, CA [*FM radio station call letters*] ..... KCBQ-FM
San Diego, CA [*AM radio station call letters*] (RBYB) ..... KDDZ-AM
San Diego, CA [*AM radio station call letters*] ..... KFMB
San Diego, CA [*FM radio station call letters*] ..... KFMB-FM
San Diego, CA [*Television station call letters*] ..... KFMB-TV
San Diego, CA [*FM radio station call letters*] ..... KFSD
San Diego, CA [*FM radio station call letters*] ..... KGB
San Diego, CA [*Television station call letters*] ..... KGTV
San Diego, CA [*FM radio station call letters*] ..... KIFM
San Diego, CA [*FM radio station call letters*] ..... KJQY
San Diego, CA [*FM radio station call letters*] (RBYB) ..... KKBH
San Diego, CA [*FM radio station call letters*] ..... KKLQ-FM
San Diego, CA [*FM radio station call letters*] (RBYB) ..... KMKX
San Diego, CA [*Television station call letters*] ..... KNSD
San Diego, CA [*AM radio station call letters*] ..... KOGO
San Diego, CA [*Television station call letters*] ..... KPBS
San Diego, CA [*FM radio station call letters*] ..... KPBS-FM
San Diego, CA [*AM radio station call letters*] ..... KPOP
San Diego, CA [*AM radio station call letters*] ..... KSDO
San Diego, CA [*FM radio station call letters*] ..... KSDS
San Diego, CA [*AM radio station call letters*] ..... KSON
San Diego, CA [*FM radio station call letters*] ..... KSON-FM
San Diego, CA [*TV station call letters*] (RBYB) ..... KSWB-TV
San Diego, CA [*Television station call letters*] ..... KTTY
San Diego, CA [*AM radio station call letters*] ..... KURS
San Diego, CA [*Television station call letters*] ..... KUSI
San Diego, CA [*FM radio station call letters*] ..... KYXY
San Diego, CA [*Location identifier FAA*] (FAAL) ..... MZB
San Diego, CA [*Location identifier FAA*] (FAAL) ..... NKX
San Diego, CA [*Location identifier FAA*] (FAAL) ..... NOR
San Diego, CA [*Location identifier FAA*] (FAAL) ..... NZY
San Diego, CA [*Location identifier FAA*] (FAAL) ..... PGY
San Diego, CA [*Location identifier FAA*] (FAAL) ..... SDM
San Diego City College, San Diego, CA [*Library symbol Library of Congress*] (LCLS) ..... CSdCiC
San Diego Coast Guard Air Base [*California*] [*ICAO location identifier*] (ICLI) ..... KDCG
San Diego - College [*California*] [*Seismograph station code, US Geological Survey*] (SEIS) ..... SND
San Diego College for Women [*California*] ..... SDCW
San Diego County Law Library, San Diego, CA [*OCLC symbol*] (OCLC) ..... CDL
San Diego County Library, San Diego, CA [*Library symbol Library of Congress*] (LCLS) ..... CSdCL
San Diego Field Test Operations [*Aerospace*] (AAG) ..... SFTO
San Diego G&E 5% Pfd [*AMEX symbol*] (TTSB) ..... SDOPrA
San Diego G&E 4.40% Pfd [*AMEX symbol*] (TTSB) ..... SDOPrC
San Diego G&E 4.50% Pfd [*AMEX symbol*] (TTSB) ..... SDOPrB
San Diego Gas & El $1.82 Pref [*AMEX symbol*] (TTSB) ..... SDOPrH
San Diego Gas & Electric Co. [*Associated Press*] (SAG) ..... SDgo
San Diego Gas & Electric Co. [*Associated Press*] (SAG) ..... SDieGs
San Diego Gas & Electric Co. [*AMEX symbol*] (SPSG) ..... SDO
San Diego Gas & Electric Co. [*NYSE symbol*] (SAG) ..... SDO
San Diego Historical Society, Junipero Serra Museum Library, San Diego, CA [*Library symbol Library of Congress*] (LCLS) ..... CSdHi
San Diego/International-Lindbergh Field [*California*] [*ICAO location identifier*] (ICLI) ..... KSAN
San Diego [*California*] **Montgomery Field** [*Airport symbol Obsolete*] (OAG) .... MYF
San Diego/North Island Naval Air Station [*California*] [*ICAO location identifier*] (ICLI) ..... KNZY
San Diego Oceanic Coordinating Committee ..... SANDOCC
San Diego Public Library, San Diego, CA [*Library symbol Library of Congress*] (LCLS) ..... CSd
San Diego Railroad Museum (EA) ..... SDRM
San Diego - Robinson [*California*] [*Seismograph station code, US Geological Survey Closed*] (SEIS) ..... SDC
San Diego/Santee, CA [*Location identifier FAA*] (FAAL) ..... SEE
San Diego Shrinkers Society (EA) ..... SDSS
San Diego Society of Natural History, Natural History Museum, Balboa Park, San Diego, CA [*Library symbol Library of Congress*] (LCLS) ..... CSdN
San Diego State College [*California*] ..... SDSC
San Diego State College, San Diego, CA [*OCLC symbol*] (OCLC) ..... CDS
San Diego State University (GAGS) ..... SDSU
San Diego State University [*California*] ..... SDSU
San Diego State University, Imperial Valley Campus, Imperial, CA [*Library symbol Library of Congress*] (LCLS) ..... CSdS-IV
San Diego Supercomputer Center [*California*] [*National Science Foundation*] ..... SDSC
San Diego Symposium for Biomedical Engineering ..... SDSBE
San Diego, TX [*FM radio station call letters*] ..... KUKA
San Diego Union-Tribune Publishing Co., San Diego, CA [*Library symbol Library of Congress*] (LCLS) ..... CSdUT
San Esteban [*Honduras*] [*Airport symbol*] (AD) ..... SET
San Felipe [*California*] [*Seismograph station code, US Geological Survey*] (SEIS) ..... SFL
San Felipe [*Mexico*] [*Seismograph station code, US Geological Survey*] (SEIS) ..... SFP
San Felipe [*Venezuela*] [*Airport symbol*] (AD) ..... SNF

San Felipe/Subteniente Nestor Arias, Yaracuy [*Venezuela ICAO location identifier*] (ICLI) .... SVSP
San Felix [*Venezuela*] [*Airport symbol*] (AD) .... SFX
San Fernando [*Argentina ICAO location identifier*] (ICLI) .... SADF
San Fernando [*Venezuela*] [*Airport symbol*] (OAG) .... SFD
San Fernando [*Spain*] [*Seismograph station code, US Geological Survey*] (SEIS) .... SFS
San Fernando, CA [*FM radio station call letters*] .... KYKF
San Fernando, CA [*Location identifier FAA*] (FAAL) .... SFR
San Fernando De Apure, Apure [*Venezuela ICAO location identifier*] (ICLI) .... SVSR
San Fernando De Atabapo, T. F. Amazonas [*Venezuela ICAO location identifier*] (ICLI) .... SVAT
San Fernando, La Union [*Philippines*] [*ICAO location identifier*] (ICLI) .... RPUS
San Fernando Observatory [*Research center*] (RCD) .... SFO
San Francisco [*California*] (ROG) .... FRISCO
San Francisco [*Branch in the Federal Reserve regional banking system*] (BARN) L
San Francisco [*California*] [*Mint mark, when appearing on US coins*] .... S
San Francisco [*California*] [*Navy*] .... S and FRAN
San Francisco [*California*] (BARN) .... San Fran
San Francisco [*California*] .... SF
San Francisco [*California*] [*Seismograph station code, US Geological Survey Closed*] (SEIS) .... SFB
San Francisco [*California*] [*Seismograph station code, US Geological Survey*] (SEIS) .... SFC
San Francisco [*Diocesan abbreviation*] [*California*] (TOCD) .... SFR
San Francisco AIDS Foundation (EA) .... SFAF
San Francisco Air Defense Sector [*ADC*] .... SFADS
San Francisco Art Institute (GAGS) .... San Fran Art Inst
San Francisco Ballet .... SFB
San Francisco Bay Area Rapid Transit District .... SFBARTD
San Francisco Bay Naval Shipyard .... SFBNS
San Francisco Bay Naval Shipyard (DNAB) .... SFBNSY
San Francisco, CA [*Location identifier FAA*] (FAAL) .... CSY
San Fernando, CA [*Location identifier FAA*] (FAAL) .... GWQ
San Francisco, CA [*FM radio station call letters*] .... KALW
San Francisco, CA [*FM radio station call letters*] (RBYB) .... KBGG
San Francisco, CA [*Television station call letters*] .... KBHK
San Francisco, CA [*AM radio station call letters*] .... KCBS
San Francisco, CA [*Television station call letters*] .... KCNS
San Francisco, CA [*FM radio station call letters*] .... KDFC
San Francisco, CA [*Television station call letters*] .... KDTV
San Francisco, CA [*FM radio station call letters*] .... KEAR
San Francisco, CA [*AM radio station call letters*] .... KEST
San Francisco, CA [*AM radio station call letters*] .... KFAX
San Francisco, CA [*FM radio station call letters*] .... KFOG
San Francisco, CA [*AM radio station call letters*] .... KFRC
San Francisco, CA [*FM radio station call letters*] .... KFRC-FM
San Francisco, CA [*AM radio station call letters*] .... KGO
San Francisco, CA [*Television station call letters*] .... KGO-TV
San Francisco, CA [*FM radio station call letters*] .... KIOI
San Francisco, CA [*AM radio station call letters*] .... KIQI
San Francisco, CA [*FM radio station call letters*] .... KITS
San Francisco, CA [*FM radio station call letters*] .... KKSF
San Francisco, CA [*FM radio station call letters*] (RBYB) .... KLLC-FM
San Francisco, CA [*FM radio station call letters*] .... KMEL
San Francisco, CA [*Television station call letters*] .... KMTP
San Francisco, CA [*AM radio station call letters*] .... KNBR
San Francisco, CA [*Television station call letters*] .... KOFY
San Francisco, CA [*AM radio station call letters*] .... KOIT
San Francisco, CA [*FM radio station call letters*] .... KOIT-FM
San Francisco, CA [*AM radio station call letters*] (RBYB) .... KPIX
San Francisco, CA [*FM radio station call letters*] (RBYB) .... KPIX-FM
San Francisco, CA [*Television station call letters*] .... KPIX-TV
San Francisco, CA [*FM radio station call letters*] .... KPOO
San Francisco, CA [*FM radio station call letters*] .... KQED
San Francisco, CA [*Television station call letters*] .... KQED-TV
San Francisco, CA [*Television station call letters*] .... KRON
San Francisco, CA [*FM radio station call letters*] .... KRQR
San Francisco, CA [*FM radio station call letters*] .... KSAN
San Francisco, CA [*AM radio station call letters*] .... KSFO
San Francisco, CA [*FM radio station call letters*] .... KSOL
San Francisco, CA [*Television station call letters*] .... KTSF
San Francisco, CA [*FM radio station call letters*] .... KUSF
San Francisco, CA [*FM radio station call letters*] .... KYCY
San Francisco, CA [*Location identifier FAA*] (FAAL) .... NMC
San Francisco, CA [*Location identifier FAA*] (FAAL) .... NOB
San Francisco, CA [*Location identifier FAA*] (FAAL) .... SIA
San Francisco Chamber of Commerce, Research Department Library, San Francisco, CA [*Library symbol Library of Congress*] (LCLS) .... CSfCC
San Francisco [*California*] **China Bas** [*Airport symbol*] (OAG) .... JCC
San Francisco Coast Guard Air Station [*California*] [*ICAO location identifier*] (ICLI) .... KSFS
San Francisco College for Women [*California*] .... SFCW
San Francisco College for Women, San Francisco, CA [*Library symbol Library of Congress*] (LCLS) .... CSfCW
San Francisco Conservatory of Music (GAGS) .... San Fran Conserv Music
San Francisco Energy Research Center [*Energy Research and Development Administration*] .... SFERC
San Francisco Grain Exchange [*Defunct*] (EA) .... SFGE
San Francisco Helicopter Airlines [*Air carrier designation symbol*] .... SAN
San Francisco Information Center [*Army Air Warning Service*] .... SFIC
San Francisco/International [*California*] [*ICAO location identifier*] (ICLI) .... KSFO
San Francisco - Josephine D. Randall Junior Museum [*California*] [*Seismograph station code, US Geological Survey*] (SEIS) .... SFM
San Francisco Laser Center [*Research center*] (RCD) .... SFLC
San Francisco Law Bulletin [*A publication*] (DLA) .... San Fr LB
San Francisco Law Bulletin [*A publication*] (DLA) .... San Fran Law Bull
San Francisco Law Bulletin [*A publication*] (ILCA) .... San Fran LB
San Francisco Law Journal [*A publication*] (DLA) .... San FLJ
San Francisco Law Journal [*A publication*] (DLA) .... San Fr LJ
San Francisco Law Journal [*A publication*] (DLA) .... San Fran LJ
San Francisco Law Journal [*A publication*] (DLA) .... SFLJ
San Francisco Law Library, San Francisco, CA [*Library symbol Library of Congress*] (LCLS) .... CSfL
San Francisco Maritime Museum, San Francisco, CA [*Library symbol Library of Congress*] (LCLS) .... CSfMM
San Francisco Men's Health Study [*Aids study*] .... SFMHS
San Francisco Movers Tariff Bureau, San Francisco CA [*STAC*] .... SFM
San Francisco (Moxos) [*Bolivia*] [*ICAO location identifier*] (ICLI) .... SLSF
San Francisco Museum of Art, San Francisco, CA [*Library symbol Library of Congress*] (LCLS) .... CSfMus
San Francisco Museum of Modern Art .... SFMOMA
San Francisco (Naciff) [*Bolivia*] [*ICAO location identifier*] (ICLI) .... SLZF
San Francisco Naval Shipyard .... SFN
San Francisco Naval Shipyard (DNAB) .... SFNS
San Francisco Naval Shipyard .... SFNSY
San Francisco [*California*] **Oakland** [*Airport symbol*] (OAG) .... OAK
San Francisco/Oakland [*California*] [*Airport symbol*] (OAG) .... SFO
San Francisco Operations Office [*Energy Research and Development Administration*] .... SAN
San Francisco Operations Office [*Energy Research and Development Administration*] .... SFOO
San Francisco Ordnance District [*Military*] .... SFOD
San Francisco Planning and Urban Research Association [*California*] [*Information service or system*] (IID) .... SPUR
San Francisco Port of Embarkation [*Military*] .... SFPE
San Francisco Port of Embarkation [*Military*] .... SFPOE
San Francisco Public Library [*California*] .... SFPL
San Francisco Public Library, San Francisco, CA [*Library symbol Library of Congress*] (LCLS) .... CSf
San Francisco Review [*A publication*] (BRI) .... SFR
San Francisco Review of Books [*A publication*] (BRI) .... SFRB
San Francisco - Rincon [*California*] [*Seismograph station code, US Geological Survey*] (SEIS) .... SFR
San Francisco, San Diego [*Proposed name for possible "super-city" formed by growth and mergers of other cities*] .... SANSAN
San Francisco Signal Corps Procurement District .... SFSCPD
San Francisco State College [*Later, California State University*] .... SFSC
San Francisco State University (GAGS) .... Cal St U (San Francisco)
San Francisco State University (GAGS) .... San Fran St U
San Francisco State University .... SFSU
San Francisco State University, San Francisco, CA [*OCLC symbol*] (OCLC) .... CSF
San Francisco State University, San Francisco, CA [*Library symbol Library of Congress*] (LCLS) .... CSfSt
San Francisco State University Videotex Cable Service [*Telecommunications service*] (TSSD) SFSU-35
San Francisco Stock Exchange .... SFSE
San Francisco Symphony Orchestra .... SFSO
San Francisco Theological Seminary [*San Anselmo, CA*] .... SFTS
San Francisco Theological Seminary, San Anselmo, CA [*Library symbol Library of Congress*] (LCLS) .... CSaT
San Francisco Vocational Competency Scale .... SFVCS
San Francisco Young Mens Health Study [*AIDS study*] .... SFYMHS
San Francisco-Oakland Bay Bridge .... SFOBB
San Gabriel, CA [*AM radio station call letters*] .... KALI
San German, PR [*FM radio station call letters*] .... WRPC
San German, PR [*AM radio station call letters*] .... WSOL
San German, PR [*FM radio station call letters*] (RBYB) .... WZGX-FM
San Gregorio [*Peru*] [*Seismograph station code, US Geological Survey Closed*] (SEIS) .... SGP
San Honorato [*Ecuador*] [*ICAO location identifier*] (ICLI) .... SESH
San Ignacio De Moxos [*Bolivia*] [*ICAO location identifier*] (ICLI) .... SLSM
San Ignacio de Moxos [*Bolivia*] [*Airport symbol*] (AD) .... SNM
San Ignacio De Velasco [*Bolivia*] [*ICAO location identifier*] (ICLI) .... SLSI
San Ignacio De Velasco [*Bolivia*] [*Airport symbol*] (OAG) .... SNG
San Isidro [*Dominican Republic*] [*ICAO location identifier*] (ICLI) .... MDSI
San Isidro De El General [*Costa Rica*] [*ICAO location identifier*] (ICLI) .... MRSI
San Jacinto Army Terminal .... SJART
San Jacinto, CA [*FM radio station call letters*] .... KWRP
San Jacinto, CA [*Location identifier FAA*] (FAAL) .... SJY
San Jacinto College, Pasadena, TX [*Library symbol Library of Congress*] (LCLS) .... TxPS
San Jacinto Fault Zone [*Geology*] .... SJFZ
San Jacinto Intermediate School, Pasadena, TX [*Library symbol*] [*Library of Congress*] (LCLS) .... TxPSjI
San Jacinto Museum of History Association, Deer Park, TX [*Library symbol Library of Congress*] (LCLS) .... TxHSJM
San Jacinto Museum of History Association, San Jacinto Monument, TX [*Library symbol Library of Congress*] (LCLS) .... TxSjM
San Jacinto Public Library, San Jacinto, CA [*Library symbol Library of Congress*] (LCLS) .... CSjac
San Javier [*Chile*] [*Seismograph station code, US Geological Survey Closed*] (SEIS) .... SJC
San Javier [*Bolivia*] [*Airport symbol*] (AD) .... SJV
San Javier [*Bolivia*] [*ICAO location identifier*] (ICLI) .... SLJV
San Joaquin [*Bolivia*] [*Airport symbol*] (AD) .... SJB

San Joaquin [*Bolivia*] [*ICAO location identifier*] (ICLI) ... SLJO
San Joaquin, CA (RBYB) ... KVPC
San Joaquin County General Hospital, Stockton, CA [*Library symbol Library of Congress*] (LCLS) ... CStoGH
San Joaquin County Historical Society, Stockton, CA [*Library symbol*] [*Library of Congress*] (LCLS) ... CStoHi
San Joaquin County Law Library, Stockton, CA [*Library symbol Library of Congress*] (LCLS) ... CStoSL
San Joaquin County Local Health District, Stockton, CA [*Library symbol Library of Congress*] (LCLS) ... CStoHD
San Joaquin County Teachers' Professional Library, Stockton, CA [*Library symbol Library of Congress*] (LCLS) ... CStoTP
San Joaquin de Abangares [*Costa Rica*] [*ICAO location identifier*] (ICLI) ... MRSS
San Joaquin Delta College, Stockton, CA [*Library symbol Library of Congress*] (LCLS) ... CStoSC
San Joaquin Delta College, Stockton, CA [*OCLC symbol*] (OCLC) ... CTO
San Joaquin Pioneer Museum and Haggin Art Galleries Library, Stockton, CA [*Library symbol Library of Congress*] (LCLS) ... CStoPM
San Joaquin Reservoir [*California*] [*Seismograph station code, US Geological Survey Closed*] (SEIS) ... SJQ
San Joaquin Valley Information Service, Fresno, CA [*Library symbol Library of Congress*] (LCLS) ... CFVI
San Joaquin Valley Library System [*Library network*] ... SJVLS
San Joaquin Valley Library System, Fresno, CA [*OCLC symbol*] (OCLC) ... SJL
San Joaquin Valley Wine Growers Association (EA) ... SJVWGA
San Jose [*Guatemala*] [*ICAO location identifier*] (ICLI) ... MGSJ
San Jose [*Costa Rica*] [*ICAO location identifier*] (ICLI) ... MRSJ
San Jose [*Ecuador*] [*ICAO location identifier*] (ICLI) ... SESJ
San Jose [*Diocesan abbreviation*] [*California*] (TOCD) ... SJ
San Jose [*California*] [*Airport symbol*] (OAG) ... SJC
San Jose [*Philippines*] [*Airport symbol*] (OAG) ... SJI
San Jose [*Costa Rica*] [*Airport symbol*] (OAG) ... SJO
San Jose [*Costa Rica*] [*Seismograph station code, US Geological Survey Closed*] (SEIS) ... SJR
San Jose [*Costa Rica*] [*Seismograph station code, US Geological Survey*] (SEIS) ... SJS
San Jose [*Bolivia*] [*Airport symbol*] (AD) ... SJS
San Jose [*Bolivia*] [*ICAO location identifier*] (ICLI) ... SLJE
San Jose, CA [*FM radio station call letters*] ... KBAY
San Jose, CA [*FM radio station call letters*] ... KEZR
San Jose, CA [*Television station call letters*] ... KICU
San Jose, CA [*AM radio station call letters*] ... KKSJ
San Jose, CA [*FM radio station call letters*] ... KLEL
San Jose, CA [*AM radio station call letters*] ... KLIV
San Jose, CA [*AM radio station call letters*] ... KLOK
San Jose, CA [*Television station call letters*] ... KLXV
San Jose, CA [*Television station call letters*] ... KNTV
San Jose, CA [*FM radio station call letters*] ... KOME
San Jose, CA [*FM radio station call letters*] ... KSJO
San Jose, CA [*FM radio station call letters*] ... KSJS
San Jose, CA [*AM radio station call letters*] ... KSJX
San Jose, CA [*Television station call letters*] ... KSTS
San Jose, CA [*Television station call letters*] ... KTEH
San Jose, CA [*Location identifier FAA*] (FAAL) ... RHV
San Jose, CA [*Location identifier FAA*] (FAAL) ... SJC
San Jose, CA [*Location identifier FAA*] (FAAL) ... SLV
San Jose City College [*California*] ... SJCC
San Jose City College, San Jose, CA [*Library symbol Library of Congress*] (LCLS) ... CSjCiC
San Jose De Buenavista/Antique [*Philippines*] [*ICAO location identifier*] (ICLI) ... RPVS
San Jose De Maipo [*Chile*] [*Seismograph station code, US Geological Survey Closed*] (SEIS) ... SJM
San Jose De Sisa [*Peru*] [*ICAO location identifier*] (ICLI) ... SPSJ
San Jose Del Cabo [*Mexico ICAO location identifier*] (ICLI) ... MMSD
San Jose Del Guaviare/S. J. Del Guaviore [*Colorado ICAO location identifier*] (ICLI) ... SKSJ
San Jose Del Guaviaro [*Colombia*] [*Airport symbol*] (OAG) ... SJE
San Jose Historical Society, San Jose, CA [*Library symbol*] [*Library of Congress*] (LCLS) ... CSjHi
San Jose/Juan Santamaria Internacional [*Costa Rica*] [*ICAO location identifier*] (ICLI) ... MROC
San Jose, MP [*FM radio station call letters*] ... KZMI
San Jose, Occidental Mindoro [*Philippines*] [*ICAO location identifier*] (ICLI) ... RPUH
San Jose, Philippines [*AM radio station call letters*] ... KCNM
San Jose Public Library, San Jose, CA [*Library symbol Library of Congress*] (LCLS) ... CSj
San Jose Public Library, San Jose, CA [*OCLC symbol*] (OCLC) ... SJP
San Jose State College [*California*] [*Later, San Jose State University*] ... SJSC
San Jose State University (GAGS) ... Cal St U (San Jose)
San Jose State University [*California*] ... SJSU
San Jose State University, San Jose, CA [*OCLC symbol*] (OCLC) ... CSJ
San Jose State University, San Jose, CA [*Library symbol Library of Congress*] (LCLS) ... CSjU
San Jose/Tobias Bolanos Internacional [*Costa Rica*] [*ICAO location identifier*] (ICLI) ... MRPV
San Juan [*Dominican Republic*] [*ICAO location identifier*] (ICLI) ... MDSJ
San Juan [*Argentina ICAO location identifier*] (ICLI) ... SANU
San Juan [*Puerto Rico*] ... SJ
San Juan [*Puerto Rico*] [*Seismograph station code, US Geological Survey*] (SEIS) ... SJG
San Juan [*Peru*] [*Seismograph station code, US Geological Survey Closed*] (SEIS) ... SJN
San Juan [*Diocesan abbreviation*] [*Puerto Rico*] (TOCD) ... SJN
San Juan [*Peru*] [*Airport symbol*] (AD) ... SJP
San Juan [*Puerto Rico*] [*Seismograph station code, US Geological Survey Closed*] (SEIS) ... SJP
San Juan [*Puerto Rico*] [*Airport symbol*] (OAG) ... SJU
San Juan [*Peru*] [*ICAO location identifier*] (ICLI) ... SPJN
San Juan [*Puerto Rico*] [*ICAO location identifier*] (ICLI) ... TJZS
San Juan [*Argentina*] [*Airport symbol*] (OAG) ... UAQ
San Juan 21 Class Association (EA) ... SJTCA
San Juan 24 North American Class Association (EA) ... SJ24NACA
San Juan Airlines [*ICAO designator*] (AD) ... YS
San Juan, AK [*Location identifier FAA*] (FAAL) ... WSJ
San Juan Aposento [*Peru*] [*ICAO location identifier*] (ICLI) ... SPAO
San Juan Basin Royalty Trust [*NYSE symbol*] (SPSG) ... SJT
San Juan Basin Royalty Trust [*Associated Press*] (SAG) ... SJuanB
San Juan Basin Rty Tr [*NYSE symbol*] (TTSB) ... SJT
San Juan Bautista City Library, San Juan Bautista, CA [*Library symbol Library of Congress*] (LCLS) ... CSjb
San Juan de Arama [*Colombia*] [*Airport symbol*] (AD) ... SJA
San Juan de Cesar [*Colombia*] [*Airport symbol*] (AD) ... SUM
San Juan De Fribal [*Bolivia*] [*ICAO location identifier*] (ICLI) ... SLJM
San Juan de Uraba [*Colombia*] [*Airport symbol*] (AD) ... SJR
San Juan Del Cesar [*Colombia*] [*Airport symbol*] (OAG) ... SJH
San Juan Del Sur [*Nicaragua*] [*Seismograph station code, US Geological Survey*] (SEIS) ... SSN
San Juan (Estancias) [*Bolivia*] [*ICAO location identifier*] (ICLI) ... SLJN
San Juan/Isla Grande [*Puerto Rico*] [*Airport symbol*] (OAG) ... SIG
San Juan/Isla Grande [*Puerto Rico*] [*ICAO location identifier*] (ICLI) ... TJIG
San Juan Island National Historic Park ... SAJH
San Juan Island Public Library, Friday Harbor, WA [*Library symbol*] [*Library of Congress*] (LCLS) ... WaFrh
San Juan Nepomuceno [*Paraguay*] [*ICAO location identifier*] (ICLI) ... SGJN
San Juan, PR [*Location identifier FAA*] (FAAL) ... CLA
San Juan, PR [*Location identifier FAA*] (FAAL) ... DDP
San Juan, PR [*Location identifier FAA*] (FAAL) ... NMR
San Juan, PR [*Location identifier FAA*] (FAAL) ... SIG
San Juan, PR [*AM radio station call letters*] ... WAPA
San Juan, PR [*Television station call letters*] ... WAPA-TV
San Juan, PR [*AM radio station call letters*] ... WBMJ
San Juan, PR [*AM radio station call letters*] (RBYB) ... WBOZ
San Juan, PR [*FM radio station call letters*] ... WCAD
San Juan, PR [*AM radio station call letters*] ... WIAC
San Juan, PR [*FM radio station call letters*] ... WIAC-FM
San Juan, PR [*FM radio station call letters*] ... WIOA
San Juan, PR [*AM radio station call letters*] ... WIPR
San Juan, PR [*FM radio station call letters*] ... WIPR-FM
San Juan, PR [*Television station call letters*] ... WIPR-TV
San Juan, PR [*AM radio station call letters*] ... WKAQ
San Juan, PR [*FM radio station call letters*] ... WKAQ-FM
San Juan, PR [*Television station call letters*] ... WKAQ-TV
San Juan, PR [*AM radio station call letters*] ... WKVM
San Juan, PR [*AM radio station call letters*] ... WOSO
San Juan, PR [*FM radio station call letters*] ... WPRM
San Juan, PR [*AM radio station call letters*] ... WQBS
San Juan, PR [*AM radio station call letters*] ... WQII
San Juan, PR [*FM radio station call letters*] ... WRTU
San Juan, PR [*Television station call letters*] ... WRWR
San Juan, PR [*Television station call letters*] ... WSJN
San Juan, PR [*Television station call letters*] ... WSJU
San Juan, PR [*AM radio station call letters*] ... WSKN
San Juan, PR [*AM radio station call letters*] ... WUNO
San Juan, PR [*FM radio station call letters*] ... WZNT
San Juan, PR [*Location identifier FAA*] (FAAL) ... ZSU
San Juan/Puerto Rico International [*Puerto Rico*] [*ICAO location identifier*] (ICLI) ... TJSJ
San Juan, TX [*AM radio station call letters*] ... KUBR
San Julian [*Argentina*] [*Airport symbol*] (OAG) ... ULA
San Julian/Cap. D. J. D. Vasquez [*Argentina ICAO location identifier*] (ICLI) ... SAWJ
San Julian (Escuela de Aviacion) [*Cuba ICAO location identifier*] (ICLI) ... MUSJ
San Justo/Aeroclub Argentino [*Argentina ICAO location identifier*] (ICLI) ... SADS
San Leandro Community Library Center, San Leandro, CA [*Library symbol Library of Congress*] (LCLS) ... CSl
San Lorenzo [*Ecuador*] [*ICAO location identifier*] (ICLI) ... SESL
San Lorenzo [*Argentina*] [*Seismograph station code, US Geological Survey*] (SEIS) ... SLA
San Lorenzo [*Cordillera*] [*ICAO location identifier*] (ICLI) ... SLLU
San Lorenzo [*Bolivia*] [*ICAO location identifier*] (ICLI) ... SLLZ
San Lucas [*Bolivia*] [*ICAO location identifier*] (ICLI) ... SLZK
San Luis [*Argentina*] [*Airport symbol*] (OAG) ... LUQ
San Luis [*Argentina ICAO location identifier*] (ICLI) ... SAOU
[*The*] **San Luis Central Railroad Co.** [*AAR code*] ... SLC
San Luis Dam [*California*] [*Seismograph station code, US Geological Survey*] (SEIS) ... SLD
San Luis Obispo [*California*] [*Airport symbol*] (OAG) ... SBP
San Luis Obispo [*Mexican state; city and county in California*] ... SL
San Luis Obispo, CA [*Location identifier FAA*] (FAAL) ... CSL
San Luis Obispo, CA [*Television station call letters*] ... KADE
San Luis Obispo, CA [*FM radio station call letters*] ... KCBX
San Luis Obispo, CA [*FM radio station call letters*] ... KCPR
San Luis Obispo, CA [*AM radio station call letters*] ... KGLW
San Luis Obispo, CA [*AM radio station call letters*] ... KJDJ
San Luis Obispo, CA [*FM radio station call letters*] ... KKJG
San Luis Obispo, CA [*AM radio station call letters*] (RBYB) ... KKJL
San Luis Obispo, CA [*FM radio station call letters*] (RBYB) ... KLFF
San Luis Obispo, CA [*Television station call letters*] ... KSBY

San Luis Obispo, CA [*FM radio station call letters*] ... KSLY
San Luis Obispo, CA [*AM radio station call letters*] ... KVEC
San Luis Obispo, CA [*FM radio station call letters*] (RBYB) ... KWQH-FM
San Luis Obispo, CA [*FM radio station call letters*] ... KZOZ
San Luis Obispo County Free Library, San Luis Obispo, CA [*Library symbol Library of Congress*] (LCLS) ... CSluCL
San Luis Obispo County Genealogical Society, Atascadero, CA [*Library symbol*] [*Library of Congress*] (LCLS) ... CAtaGS
San Luis Obispo Historical Society, San Luis Obispo, CA [*Library symbol*] [*Library of Congress*] (LCLS) ... CSluHi
San Luis Obispo Public Library, San Luis Obispo, CA [*Library symbol Library of Congress*] (LCLS) ... CSlu
San Luis Potosi [*Mexico ICAO location identifier*] (ICLI) ... MMSP
San Luis Potosi [*Mexico*] [*Airport symbol*] (AD) ... SLP
San Luis Rey College [*California*] ... SLRC
San Luis Valley Southern Railroad (IIA) ... SLVS
San Manuel Arizona Railroad Co. [*AAR code*] ... SMA
San Marco [*Satellite*] [*NASA/Italy*] ... SM
San Marcos [*Guatemala*] [*ICAO location identifier*] (ICLI) ... MGSM
San Marcos [*Colombia*] [*Airport symbol*] (AD) ... SRS
San Marcos, CA [*AM radio station call letters*] ... KPRZ
San Marcos, TX [*FM radio station call letters*] ... KEYI
San Marcos, TX [*FM radio station call letters*] ... KTSW
San Marcos, TX [*AM radio station call letters*] ... KUOL
San Marcos, TX [*Location identifier FAA*] (FAAL) ... RUM
San Marcos, TX [*Location identifier FAA*] (FAAL) ... SRZ
San Marino [*MARC geographic area code Library of Congress*] (LCCP) ... e-sm--
San Marino [*International vehicle registration*] (ODBW) ... RSM
San Marino [*ANSI two-letter standard code*] (CNC) ... SM
San Marino [*IYRU nationality code*] [*MARC country of publication code Library of Congress*] (LCCP) ... sm
San Marino [*ANSI three-letter standard code*] (CNC) ... SMR
San Marino [*International civil aircraft marking*] (ODBW) ... T7
San Marino Communist Party ... SMCP
San Marino Public Library, San Marino, CA [*Library symbol Library of Congress*] (LCLS) ... CSm
San Martin [*Argentina ICAO location identifier*] (ICLI) ... SAMI
San Martin, CA [*AM radio station call letters*] (RBYB) ... KZSJ
San Martin De Los Andes/Chapelco [*Argentina ICAO location identifier*] (ICLI) ... SAZY
San Mateo, CA [*FM radio station call letters*] ... KCSM
San Mateo, CA [*Television station call letters*] ... KCSM-TV
San Mateo, CA [*AM radio station call letters*] ... KOFY
San Mateo, CA [*FM radio station call letters*] ... KYLD
San Mateo County Free Library, Belmont, CA [*Library symbol Library of Congress*] (LCLS) ... CBelmS
San Mateo County Free Library, Belmont, CA [*OCLC symbol*] (OCLC) ... CZA
San Mateo County Historical Association, San Mateo, CA [*Library symbol Library of Congress*] (LCLS) ... CSmatHi
San Mateo Educational Resources Center [*San Mateo County Office of Education*] [*Information service or system*] (IID) ... SMERC
San Mateo Public Library, San Mateo, CA [*Library symbol Library of Congress*] (LCLS) ... CSmat
San Mateo Times, San Mateo, CA [*Library symbol Library of Congress*] (LCLS) ... CSmatT
San Matias [*Bolivia*] [*ICAO location identifier*] (ICLI) ... SLTI
San Miguel [*Panama*] [*Airport symbol*] (OAG) ... NMG
San Miguel [*Bolivia*] [*ICAO location identifier*] (ICLI) ... SLKQ
San Miguel [*Portugal*] [*Geomagnetic observatory code*] ... SMG
San Miguel Beer (DSUE) ... SAN MIG
San Miguel, CA [*Location identifier FAA*] (FAAL) ... SYL
San Miguel Island [*California*] [*Seismograph station code, US Geological Survey*] (SEIS) ... BSM
San Miguel Sea Lion Virus ... SMSV
San Nicolas De Bari [*Cuba ICAO location identifier*] (ICLI) ... MUNB
San Nicolas Island [*California*] [*Seismograph station code, US Geological Survey*] (SEIS) ... BSN
San Nicolas Island [*California*] [*Seismograph station code, US Geological Survey Closed*] (SEIS) ... SNC
San Nicolas Island ... SNI
San Nicolas Island, CA [*Location identifier FAA*] (FAAL) ... NSI
San Nicolas Island/San Nicolas Auxiliary Air Base [*California*] [*ICAO location identifier*] (ICLI) ... KNSI
San Onofre [*California*] [*Seismograph station code, US Geological Survey*] (SEIS) ... SNS
San Onofre Nuclear Generating Station (NRCH) ... SONGS
San Pedro [*Ivory Coast*] [*ICAO location identifier*] (ICLI) ... DISP
San Pedro [*Costa Rica*] [*ICAO location identifier*] (ICLI) ... MRSP
San Pedro [*Bolivia*] [*ICAO location identifier*] (ICLI) ... SLZB
San Pedro [*California*] ... SP
San Pedro [*California*] [*Airport symbol Obsolete*] (OAG) ... SPQ
San Pedro [*Belize*] [*Airport symbol*] (OAG) ... SPR
San Pedro [*Colombia*] [*Airport symbol*] (AD) ... SPX
San Pedro [*Ivory Coast*] [*Airport symbol*] (OAG) ... SPY
San Pedro de Jagua [*Colombia*] [*Airport symbol*] (AD) ... SPL
San Pedro De Macoris [*Dominican Republic*] [*ICAO location identifier*] (ICLI) ... MDSP
San Pedro De Poas [*Costa Rica*] [*Seismograph station code, US Geological Survey*] (SEIS) ... SPS
San Pedro Hill [*California*] [*Seismograph station code, US Geological Survey Closed*] (SEIS) ... SPH
San Pedro (Richard) [*Bolivia*] [*ICAO location identifier*] (ICLI) ... SLZJ
San Pedro (Salvatierra) [*Bolivia*] [*ICAO location identifier*] (ICLI) ... SLZX
San Pedro Sula [*Honduras*] [*ICAO location identifier*] (ICLI) ... MHSP
San Pedro Sula [*Honduras*] [*Airport symbol*] (OAG) ... SAP
San Pedro Sula [*Honduras*] [*Seismograph station code, US Geological Survey*] (SEIS) ... SSU
San Pedro Sula/La Mesa Internacional [*Honduras*] [*ICAO location identifier*] (ICLI) ... MHLM
San Quentin [*Prison*] ... Q
San Quentin [*California State Prison*] (AD) ... Quent
San Quentin Prison (AD) ... Q
San Quentin Quail [*A minor female*] [*Slang*] ... SQQ
San Quilmas (AD) ... Quilmas
San Rafael [*Argentina*] [*Airport symbol*] (OAG) ... AFA
San Rafael [*Argentina ICAO location identifier*] (ICLI) ... SAMR
San Rafael [*Ecuador*] [*ICAO location identifier*] (ICLI) ... SESR
San Rafael, CA [*AM radio station call letters*] ... KKHI
San Rafael, CA [*FM radio station call letters*] ... KKHI-FM
San Rafael, CA [*AM radio station call letters*] (RBYB) ... KNOB
San Rafael, CA [*FM radio station call letters*] ... KSRH
San Rafael, CA [*Location identifier FAA*] (FAAL) ... SRF
San Rafael (Isidoro) [*Bolivia*] [*ICAO location identifier*] (ICLI) ... SLZR
San Rafael Public Library, San Rafael, CA [*Library symbol Library of Congress*] (LCLS) ... CSr
San Ramon [*Bolivia*] [*ICAO location identifier*] (ICLI) ... SLRA
San Ramon [*Costa Rica*] [*Seismograph station code, US Geological Survey*] (SEIS) ... SRA
San Ramon/Capitan Alvarino [*Peru*] [*ICAO location identifier*] (ICLI) ... SPRM
San Ramon De Senac [*Bolivia*] [*ICAO location identifier*] (ICLI) ... SLSX
San Regis [*Peru*] [*ICAO location identifier*] (ICLI) ... SPRG
San Saba, TX [*AM radio station call letters*] ... KBAL
San Saba, TX [*FM radio station call letters*] (RBYB) ... KBAL-FM
San Salvador [*El Salvador*] [*Airport symbol*] (OAG) ... SAL
San Salvador [*El Salvador*] [*Seismograph station code, US Geological Survey*] (SEIS) ... SSS
San Salvador [*Bahamas*] [*Airport symbol*] (OAG) ... ZSA
San Salvador/El Salvador Internacional [*El Salvador*] [*ICAO location identifier*] (ICLI) ... MSLP
San Salvador/Ilopango Internacional [*El Salvador*] [*ICAO location identifier*] (ICLI) ... MSSS
San Sebastian [*Spain*] [*Airport symbol*] (OAG) ... EAS
San Sebastian [*Spain ICAO location identifier*] (ICLI) ... LESO
San Sebastian, PR [*Television station call letters*] ... WJWN
San Sebastian, PR [*AM radio station call letters*] ... WLRP
San Sebastian, PR [*AM radio station call letters*] ... WRSS
San Simon, AZ [*Location identifier FAA*] (FAAL) ... SSO
San Telmo (Cordillera) [*Bolivia*] [*ICAO location identifier*] (ICLI) ... SLTF
San Tome [*Venezuela*] [*Airport symbol*] (OAG) ... SOM
San Tome, Anzoategui [*Venezuela ICAO location identifier*] (ICLI) ... SVST
San Vicente Del Caguan [*Colorado ICAO location identifier*] (ICLI) ... SKSV
San Vincente Del Caguan [*Colombia*] [*Airport symbol*] (OAG) ... SVI
San Vito De Jaba [*Costa Rica*] [*ICAO location identifier*] (ICLI) ... MRSV
San Vittore [*Switzerland ICAO location identifier*] (ICLI) ... LSXV
San Xavier Mining Laboratory [*University of Arizona*] [*Research center*] (RCD) ... SXML
San Yo Yo [*Bolivia*] [*ICAO location identifier*] (ICLI) ... SLYY
Sanaa [*Yemen Arab Republic*] [*Airport symbol*] (OAG) ... SAH
Sanaa/International [*Yemen*] [*ICAO location identifier*] (ICLI) ... OYSN
Sanada [*Japan*] [*Seismograph station code, US Geological Survey*] (SEIS) ... SDJ
Sanae [*South Africa*] [*ICAO location identifier*] (ICLI) ... FASE
Sanae [*Antarctica*] [*Seismograph station code, US Geological Survey*] (SEIS) ... SNA
Sanair [*Ukraine*] [*FAA designator*] (FAAC) ... SAV
Sanana [*Indonesia*] [*Airport symbol*] (OAG) ... SQN
Sanana [*Indonesia*] [*ICAO location identifier*] (ICLI) ... WAPN
Sanandaj [*Iran*] [*Airport symbol*] (AD) ... KNT
Sanandaj [*Iran*] [*ICAO location identifier*] (ICLI) ... OICS
Sanandita [*Bolivia*] [*ICAO location identifier*] (ICLI) ... SLSN
Sanarelli-Schwartzman [*Reaction*] [*Medicine*] (DAVI) ... SS
Sanarelli-Shwartzman Phenomenon [*Medical research*] (DAVI) ... SSP
Sanatana Dharma Foundation [*Defunct*] (EA) ... SDF
Sanatorio Duran [*Costa Rica*] [*Seismograph station code, US Geological Survey*] (SEIS) ... SDS
Sanatorium ... SAN
Sanatorium ... SANAT
Sanborn and Berryman's Annotated Statutes [*Wisconsin*] [*A publication*] (DLA) ... Sanb & B Ann St
Sanborn, Inc. [*Associated Press*] (SAG) ... Sanb
Sanborn, Inc. [*NASDAQ symbol*] (SAG) ... SBRZ
Sanborn Pioneer, Sanborn, IA [*Library symbol Library of Congress*] (LCLS) ... IaSanP
Sanborn Public Library, Sanborn, IA [*Library symbol Library of Congress*] (LCLS) ... IaSan
Sanborn Public School, Sanborn, MN [*Library symbol*] [*Library of Congress*] (LCLS) ... MnSanPS
Sanborn-Pekin Free Library, Sanborn, NY [*Library symbol Library of Congress*] (LCLS) ... NSan
Sanco Consultants Ltd., Toronto, ON, Canada [*Library symbol*] [*Library of Congress*] (LCLS) ... CaOTSAC
Sanco Consultants Ltd., Toronto, Ontario [*Library symbol National Library of Canada*] (NLC) ... OTSAC
Sancta Mater Ecclesia [*Holy Mother Church*] [*Latin*] ... SME
Sancta Mater Maria [*Holy Mother Mary*] [*Latin*] ... SMM
Sancta Romana Ecclesia [*Most Holy Roman Church*] [*Latin*] ... SRE
Sancta Virgo [*Holy Virgin*] [*Latin*] ... SV
Sanctae Memoriae [*Of Holy Memory*] [*Latin*] ... SCM
Sanctae Memoriae [*Of Holy Memory*] [*Latin*] ... SM
Sanctae Romanae Ecclesiae [*Of the Most Holy Roman Church*] [*Latin*] ... SRE
Sancti [*Saints*] [*Latin*] ... SS

Sancti Patres [*Holy Fathers*] [*Latin*] ... SSPP
Sancti Spiritus [*Cuba ICAO location identifier*] (ICLI) ... MUSS
Sanctioned Ritual [*British Slang*] ... SR
Sanctissime Pater [*Most Holy Father*] [*Latin*] ... SP
Sanctissimus [*Most Holy*] [*Latin*] ... SS
Sanctissimus Dominus [*Most Holy Lord*] [*Latin*] ... SSD
Sanctissimus Dominus Noster [*Our Most Holy Lord, Jesus Christ*] [*Latin*] ... SSDN
Sanctitas Vestra [*Your Holiness*] [*Latin*] ... SV
Sanctuary [*Naval cadet's hiding place for smoking*] [*Slang British*] (DSUE) ... SANC
Sanctuary (VRA) ... sanct
Sanctuary Wood Multimedia [*Commercial firm Associated Press*] (SAG) ... SancWod
Sanctuary Wood Multimedia [*NASDAQ symbol*] (SAG) ... SWMC
Sanctuary Woods Multimedia [*NASDAQ symbol*] (TTSB) ... SWMCF
Sanctum Sanctorum [*Holy of Holies*] [*Freemasonry*] [*Latin*] ... SS
Sand [*Quality of the bottom*] [*Nautical charts*] ... S
Sand (WGA) ... SD
Sand and Ballast Merchants' Alliance [*British*] (BI) ... SBMA
Sand and Gravel Association of Great Britain ... SAGA
Sand and Gravel Association of Great Britain (BI) ... SAGAGB
Sand Bay [*Alaska*] [*Seismograph station code, US Geological Survey Closed*] (SEIS) ... SBY
Sand Collectors International (EAIO) ... SCI
Sand Creek [*Guyana*] [*Airport symbol*] (AD) ... SNL
Sand Lake Irish Gatherings Organization ... SLIGO
Sand Point [*Alaska*] [*Airport symbol*] (OAG) ... SDP
Sand Point, AK [*Location identifier FAA*] (FAAL) ... HBT
Sand Point, AK [*AM radio station call letters*] ... KSDP
Sand Point, AK [*Location identifier FAA*] (FAAL) ... SDP
Sand Scow [*Navy symbol*] (DNAB) ... YWN
Sand Springs, OK [*FM radio station call letters*] (RBYB) ... KTFX
Sand Springs, OK [*AM radio station call letters*] ... KTOW
Sand Springs, OK [*FM radio station call letters*] ... KTOW-FM
Sand Springs Railway Co. [*AAR code*] ... SS
Sand Technology Sys'A' [*NASDAQ symbol*] (TTSB) ... SNDCF
Sand Technology Systems International, Inc. [*Associated Press*] (SAG) ... SandTc
Sand Technology Systems International, Inc. [*NASDAQ symbol*] (NQ) ... SNDC
Sandakan [*Malaysia*] [*Airport symbol*] (OAG) ... SDK
Sandakan [*Malaysia*] [*ICAO location identifier*] (ICLI) ... WBKS
Sandale R. R. [*AAR code*] ... SNDL
Sandalwood (VRA) ... sndlwd
Sandane [*Norway*] [*Airport symbol*] (OAG) ... SDN
Sandane/Anda [*Norway ICAO location identifier*] (ICLI) ... ENSD
Sandars' Edition of Justinian's Institutes [*A publication*] (DLA) ... San Just
Sandars' Edition of Justinian's Institutes [*A publication*] (DLA) ... Sand Inst Just Introd
Sandars' Edition of Justinian's Institutes [*A publication*] (DLA) ... Sandars Just Inst
Sand-Asphalt-Sulfur [*Road paving material*] ... SAS
Sandata, Inc. [*NASDAQ symbol*] (NQ) ... SAND
Sandata, Inc. [*Associated Press*] (SAG) ... Sandata
Sandawe [*MARC language code Library of Congress*] (LCCP) ... sad
Sanday [*Scotland*] [*Airport symbol*] (OAG) ... NDY
Sanday [*Scotland*] [*Airport symbol*] (AD) ... SYC
Sandberg, CA [*Location identifier FAA*] (FAAL) ... SDB
Sandburst Branch, Lennox and Addington County Public Library, Bath, Ontario [*Library symbol National Library of Canada*] (BIB) ... OBLACS
Sandel On-Line Automated Reference [*Information service or system*] ... SOLAR
Sandels and Hill's Digest of Statutes [*Arkansas*] [*A publication*] (DLA) ... Sand & H Dig
Sandeman Public Library, Perth, United Kingdom [*Library symbol Library of Congress*] (LCLS) ... UkPe
Sanders Associates, Inc., Technical Library, Nashua, NH [*Library symbol Library of Congress*] (LCLS) ... NhNaS
Sanders Associates, Inc., Williamsville, NY [*Library symbol Library of Congress*] (LCLS) ... NWvS
Sanders Associates Video Input/Output Terminal Access Resource [*Computer science*] (IEEE) ... SAVITAR
Sanders Barotropic ... SANBAR
Sanders' Essays on Uses and Trusts [*5th ed.*] [*1844*] [*A publication*] (DLA) ... Sand Essays
Sanders' Essays on Uses and Trusts [*A publication*] (DLA) ... Sand Uses and Trusts
Sanders Intact Reentry Encapsulation (MCD) ... SIREN
Sanderson Farms [*NASDAQ symbol*] (TTSB) ... SAFM
Sanderson Farms, Inc. [*NASDAQ symbol*] (NQ) ... SAFM
Sanderson Farms, Inc. [*Associated Press*] (SAG) ... SandFm
Sanderson Tech, Inc. [*Vancouver Stock Exchange symbol*] ... SDT
Sandersville, GA [*Location identifier FAA*] (FAAL) ... OKZ
Sandersville, GA [*AM radio station call letters*] ... WSNT
Sandersville, GA [*FM radio station call letters*] ... WSNT-FM
Sandersville Railroad Co. [*AAR code*] ... SAN
Sandford's Heritable Succession in Scotland [*A publication*] (DLA) ... Sandf Suc
Sandford's New York Chancery Reports [*A publication*] (DLA) ... San Ch
Sandford's New York Chancery Reports [*A publication*] (DLA) ... Sand Ch
Sandford's New York Chancery Reports [*A publication*] (DLA) ... Sand Ch R
Sandford's New York Chancery Reports [*A publication*] (DLA) ... Sand Chy
Sandford's New York Chancery Reports [*A publication*] (DLA) ... Sandf Ch
Sandford's New York Chancery Reports [*A publication*] (DLA) ... Sandf Ch Rep
Sandford's New York Chancery Reports [*A publication*] (DLA) ... Sands Ch
Sandford's New York Chancery Reports [*A publication*] (DLA) ... Sanford's Ch R
Sandford's New York Superior Court Reports [*3-7 New York*] [*A publication*] (DLA) ... Sand
Sandford's New York Superior Court Reports [*A publication*] (DLA) ... Sand R
Sandford's New York Superior Court Reports [*A publication*] (DLA) ... Sand SC
Sandford's New York Superior Court Reports [*A publication*] (DLA) ... Sand SCR
Sandford's New York Superior Court Reports [*A publication*] (DLA) ... Sand Sup Ct Rep
Sandford's New York Superior Court Reports [*A publication*] (DLA) ... Sand Supr Ct R
Sandford's New York Superior Court Reports [*3-7 New York*] [*A publication*] (DLA) ... Sandf
Sandford's New York Superior Court Reports [*3-7 New York*] [*A publication*] (DLA) ... Sandf Ch (NY)
Sandford's New York Superior Court Reports [*3-7 New York*] [*A publication*] (ILCA) ... Sandf (NY)
Sandford's New York Superior Court Reports [*A publication*] (DLA) ... Sandf (NY) R
Sandford's New York Superior Court Reports [*A publication*] (DLA) ... Sandf R
Sandford's New York Superior Court Reports [*A publication*] (DLA) ... Sandf SC
Sandford's New York Superior Court Reports [*A publication*] (DLA) ... Sandf SCR
Sandford's New York Superior Court Reports [*A publication*] (DLA) ... Sandf Sup CR
Sandford's New York Superior Court Reports [*A publication*] (DLA) ... Sandf Sup Ct
Sandford's New York Superior Court Reports [*A publication*] (DLA) ... Sandf Superior Court R
Sandford's New York Superior Court Reports [*A publication*] (DLA) ... Sandford
Sandford's New York Superior Court Reports [*A publication*] (DLA) ... Sandford's SCR
Sandford's New York Superior Court Reports [*A publication*] (DLA) ... Sandford's Sup Ct R
Sandford's New York Superior Court Reports [*3-7 New York*] [*A publication*] (DLA) ... Sanf (NY)
Sandford's New York Superior Court Reports [*A publication*] (DLA) ... SSC
Sandhamn [*Sweden ICAO location identifier*] (ICLI) ... ESHS
Sandhill Decline [*Citrus blight*] ... SHD
Sandhills Agriculture Laboratory [*University of Nebraska - Lincoln*] [*Research center*] (RCD) ... SAL
Sandhills Community College, Southern Pines, NC [*Library symbol Library of Congress*] (LCLS) ... NcSpS
Sandhills Regional Library, Rockingham, NC [*Library symbol Library of Congress*] (LCLS) ... NcRoS
Sandhills Youth Center, McCain, NC [*Library symbol Library of Congress*] (LCLS) ... NcMccS
Sandia Air Force Material Study (MCD) ... SAMS
Sandia Airborne Computer ... SANDAC
Sandia Area Office [*Energy Research and Development Administration*] ... SAO
Sandia Corp. ... SC
Sandia Corp., Albuquerque, NM [*Library symbol Library of Congress*] (LCLS) ... NmAS
Sandia Corporation, Livermore Laboratory ... SCLL
Sandia Corporation, Sandia Laboratory (AABC) ... SCSL
Sandia Engineering Reactor [*Nuclear energy*] ... SER
Sandia Engineering Reactor Facility [*Nuclear energy*] ... SERF
Sandia Human Error Rate Bank [*NASA*] (NASA) ... SHERB
Sandia Interactive Graphics System ... SIGS
Sandia Laboratories, Albuquerque (AABC) ... SLA
Sandia Laboratories, Livermore (AABC) ... SLL
Sandia Laboratories, Livermore, CA [*Library symbol Library of Congress*] (LCLS) ... CLivS
Sandia National Laboratories [*Department of Energy*] [*Albuquerque, NM*] (GRD) ... SNL
Sandia National Laboratories/California (GAAI) ... SNL/CA
Sandia National Laboratories/New Mexico (GAAI) ... SNL/NM
Sandia National Laboratory (Albuquerque) ... SNLA
Sandia National Laboratory/California ... SNL/CA
Sandia National Laboratory/California (DOGT) ... SNL/CA
Sandia National Laboratory/New Mexico (DOGT) ... SNL/NM
Sandia National Laboratory/New Mexico ... SNL/NM
Sandia Nuclear Assembly for Reactor Experiments ... SNARE
Sandia Optical Disk Archival System [*Online map database*] [*Developed by Sandia National Laboratories for the USGS*] ... SODAS
Sandia Pulse Reactor ... SPO
Sandia Pulsed Reactor [*Nuclear energy*] ... SPR
Sandia Pulsed Reactor Facility [*Nuclear energy*] ... SPRF
Sandia Wind Balloon (MUGU) ... SWB
Sandia-Livermore Aeroheating Program ... SLAP
SanDisk Corp. [*Associated Press*] (SAG) ... SanDisk
SanDisk Corp. [*NASDAQ symbol*] (SAG) ... SNDK
Sandler's State Papers [*A publication*] (DLA) ... Sandl St Pap
Sand-Loaded [*Technical drawings*] ... SL
Sandnessjoen [*Norway*] [*Airport symbol*] (OAG) ... SSJ
Sandnessjoen/Stokka [*Norway ICAO location identifier*] (ICLI) ... ENST
Sandoa [*Zaire*] [*ICAO location identifier*] (ICLI) ... FZSD
Sandostain [*Antineoplastic drug*] (CDI) ... SSTN
Sandoval Community Unit School District 501, Sandoval, IL [*Library symbol Library of Congress*] (LCLS) ... ISandSD
Sandoway [*Myanmar*] [*Airport symbol*] (OAG) ... SNW
Sandoway [*Myanmar*] [*ICAO location identifier*] (ICLI) ... VBSY
Sandown (Isle Of Wight) [*British ICAO location identifier*] (ICLI) ... EGHN
Sandoz [*Italy*] [*Research code symbol*] ... DTHy
Sandoz [*Italy*] [*Research code symbol*] ... HM
Sandoz AG [*Switzerland*] [*Research code symbol*] ... BC
Sandoz AG [*Germany*] [*Research code symbol*] ... DRA
Sandoz AG [*Switzerland*] [*Research code symbol*] ... DW
Sandoz AG [*Switzerland*] [*Research code symbol*] ... PSC
Sandoz Canada, Inc., Dorval, PQ, Canada [*Library symbol*] [*Library of Congress*] (LCLS) ... CaQMSAC
Sandoz Canada, Inc., Dorval, Quebec [*Library symbol National Library of Canada*] (NLC) ... QMSAC

Sandoz Chemical, Charlotte, NC [*Library symbol*] [*Library of Congress*] (LCLS) .... NcCSC
Sandoz Clinical Assessment of Geriatrics [*Psychometrics*] .... SCAG
Sandoz Crop Protection Corp., Des Plaines, IL [*Library symbol*] [*Library of Congress*] (LCLS) .... IDesSC
Sandoz, Inc., Hanover, NJ [*Library symbol Library of Congress*] (LCLS) ...... NjHanS
Sandoz Pharmaceuticals [*Research code symbol*] .... CRA
Sandoz Pharmaceuticals [*Research code symbol*] .... HS
Sandoz Pharmaceuticals [*Research code symbol*] .... IBD
Sandoz Pharmaceuticals [*Research code symbol*] L
Sandoz Pharmaceuticals [*Research code symbol*] .... NC
Sandoz Pharmaceuticals [*Research code symbol*] .... SaH
Sandoz Pharmaceuticals [*Research code symbol*] .... TPN
Sandoz Pharmaceuticals [*Research code symbol*] .... TPO
Sandpiper Oil & Gas [*Vancouver Stock Exchange symbol*] .... SPQ
Sandpoint, ID [*FM radio station call letters*] .... KPND
Sandpoint, ID [*AM radio station call letters*] .... KSPT
Sandpoint, ID [*FM radio station call letters*] (RBYB) .... KSPT-FM
Sandpoint, ID [*Location identifier FAA*] (FAAL) .... SZT
Sandra [*Genotype of Phlox paniculata*] .... S
Sands Minerals [*Vancouver Stock Exchange symbol*] .... SDC
Sands Pharmaceutical Division, Jerram Pharmaceuticals Ltd., Toronto, Ontario [*Library symbol National Library of Canada*] (NLC) .... OTJPS
Sands Regent [*Associated Press*] (SAG) .... SandReg
[*The*] **Sands Regent** [*Reno, NV*] [*NASDAQ symbol*] (NQ) .... SNDS
Sandskeid [*Iceland*] [*ICAO location identifier*] (ICLI) .... BISS
Sandspit [*Canada*] [*Airport symbol*] (OAG) .... YZP
Sandspit, BC [*ICAO location identifier*] (ICLI) .... CYZP
Sandstone (VRA) .... sandst
Sandstone [*Lithology*] .... Sandst
Sandstone [*Lithology*] .... SS
Sandstone Area Hospital/Nursing Home, Sandstone, MN [*Library symbol*] [*Library of Congress*] (LCLS) .... MnSaH
Sandstone Elementary School, Sandstone, MN [*Library symbol*] [*Library of Congress*] (LCLS) .... MnSaE
Sandstone Junior/Senior High School, Sandstone, MN [*Library symbol*] [*Library of Congress*] (LCLS) .... MnSaJS
Sandstone Public Library, Sandstone, MN [*Library symbol*] [*Library of Congress*] (LCLS) .... MnSa
Sandstorm .... SA
Sandtoft [*British ICAO location identifier*] (ICLI) .... EGCF
Sandusky/Griffing [*Ohio*] [*ICAO location identifier*] (ICLI) .... KSKY
Sandusky Library Association, Sandusky, OH [*Library symbol Library of Congress*] (LCLS) .... OSand
Sandusky, MI [*AM radio station call letters*] .... WMIC
Sandusky, MI [*FM radio station call letters*] .... WNFR
Sandusky, MI [*FM radio station call letters*] .... WTGV
Sandusky, OH [*Location identifier FAA*] (FAAL) .... SKY
Sandusky, OH [*FM radio station call letters*] .... WCPZ
Sandusky, OH [*Television station call letters*] .... WGGN
Sandusky, OH [*AM radio station call letters*] .... WLEC
Sandusky, OH [*FM radio station call letters*] .... WVMS
Sandusky Public Library, Sandusky, MI [*Library symbol Library of Congress*] (LCLS) .... MiSan
Sandwell & Co., Vancouver, BC, Canada [*Library symbol Library of Congress*] (LCLS) .... CaBVaSC
Sandwell & Co., Vancouver, British Columbia [*Library symbol National Library of Canada*] (NLC) .... BVASC
Sandwell Swan Wooster, Inc. [*Toronto Stock Exchange symbol*] .... SLL
Sandwich (MSA) .... SAN
Sandwich .... SNDWCH
Sandwich Community High School, Sandwich, IL [*Library symbol Library of Congress*] (LCLS) .... ISanHS
Sandwich Community Hospital, Sandwich, IL [*Library symbol Library of Congress*] (LCLS) .... ISanCH
Sandwich Cooperative Bank [*Associated Press*] (SAG) .... SandCop
[*The*] **Sandwich Co-Operative Bank** [*Sandwich, MA*] [*NASDAQ symbol*] (NQ) .... SWCB
Sandwich Counterelectrophoresis [*Medicine*] (DMAA) .... SCEP
Sandwich Historical Society, Sandwich, MA [*Library symbol Library of Congress*] (LCLS) .... MSanHi
Sandwich, IL [*AM radio station call letters*] .... WAUR
Sandwich Islands .... S Isl
Sandwich Islands .... Sand Isls
Sandwich Islands .... SI
Sandwich Islands Reports [*Hawaii*] [*A publication*] (DLA) .... Sand I Rep
Sandwich Junior High School, Sandwich, IL [*Library symbol Library of Congress*] (LCLS) .... ISanJS
Sandwich, MA [*FM radio station call letters*] .... WSDH
Sandwich Plug (IAA) .... SNDPLG
Sandwich Township Public Library, Sandwich, IL [*Library symbol Library of Congress*] (LCLS) .... ISan
Sandwiched (IAA) .... SANDW
Sandwich-Wound (DEN) .... SW
Sandwip [*Bangladesh*] [*Airport symbol*] (AD) .... SDW
Sandy Corp. [*Associated Press*] (SAG) .... Sandy
Sandy Corp. [*AMEX symbol*] (SPSG) .... SDY
Sandy Creek-Pulaski, NY [*AM radio station call letters*] .... WSCP
Sandy Croft International Fan Club [*Defunct*] (EA) .... SCIFC
Sandy Hook Veterans Historical Society (EA) .... SHVHS
Sandy Lake Visitor Center, McGregor, MN [*Library symbol*] [*Library of Congress*] (LCLS) .... MnMcgrSL
Sandy Point [*Great Abaco Island, Bahamas*] [*Airport symbol*] (AD) .... SDT
Sandy Point, Abaco Island [*Bahamas*] [*ICAO location identifier*] (ICLI) .... MYAS

Sandy Public Library, Sandy, OR [*Library symbol Library of Congress*] (LCLS) .... OrSan
Sandy River, AK [*Location identifier FAA*] (FAAL) .... KSR
Sandy Spring Bancorp [*NASDAQ symbol*] (TTSB) .... SASR
Sandy Spring Bancorp, Inc. [*NASDAQ symbol*] (SAG) .... SASR
Sandy Spring Bancorp, Inc. [*Associated Press*] (SAG) .... SndySpr
Sandy Union High School, Sandy, OR [*Library symbol Library of Congress*] (LCLS) .... OrSanHS
Sandy, UT [*AM radio station call letters*] .... KTKK
Sanfebagar [*Nepal*] [*Airport symbol*] (OAG) .... FEB
Sanfilippo [*John B.*] **& Son** [*NASDAQ symbol*] (SPSG) .... JBSS
Sanfilippo [*John*] **& Son, Inc.** [*Associated Press*] (SAG) .... Sanfilp
Sanford & Eastern Railroad [*AAR code Terminated*] .... SE
Sanford Elementary School, Montevideo, MN [*Library symbol*] [*Library of Congress*] (LCLS) .... MnMovSE
Sanford, FL [*Location identifier FAA*] (FAAL) .... SFB
Sanford, FL [*Location identifier FAA*] (FAAL) .... SND
Sanford, FL [*AM radio station call letters*] .... WTRR
Sanford H. Calhoun High School, Merrick, NY [*Library symbol*] [*Library of Congress*] (LCLS) .... NMerkCH
Sanford, ME [*Location identifier FAA*] (FAAL) .... SFM
Sanford, ME [*FM radio station call letters*] .... WCDQ
Sanford, ME [*FM radio station call letters*] .... WSEW
Sanford, ME [*AM radio station call letters*] .... WSME
Sanford, NC [*FM radio station call letters*] .... WDCC
Sanford, NC [*FM radio station call letters*] .... WFJA
Sanford, NC [*AM radio station call letters*] .... WWGP
Sanford, NC [*AM radio station call letters*] .... WXKL
Sanford Public Library, Sanford, FL [*Library symbol Library of Congress*] (LCLS) .... FSan
Sanford Recreation Area .... SANF
Sanford's Reports [*59 Alabama*] [*A publication*] (DLA) .... San
Sanford's Reports [*59 Alabama*] [*A publication*] (DLA) .... Sanf
Sanfred Resources [*Vancouver Stock Exchange symbol*] .... SND
Sangamon County Medical Society, Springfield, IL [*Library symbol Library of Congress*] (LCLS) .... ISSM
Sangamon State University (PDAA) .... SSU
Sangamon State University, Springfield, IL [*OCLC symbol*] (OCLC) .... IAS
Sangamon State University, Springfield, IL [*Library symbol Library of Congress*] (LCLS) .... ISS
Sangamon Valley Academic Library Consortium [*Library network*] .... SVALC
Sangaredi [*Guinea*] [*ICAO location identifier*] (ICLI) .... GUSA
Sangata [*Indonesia*] [*ICAO location identifier*] (ICLI) .... WRLA
Sangay [*Ecuador*] [*ICAO location identifier*] (ICLI) .... SESG
Sanger, CA [*Television station call letters*] .... KMSG
Sangju [*South Korea ICAO location identifier*] (ICLI) .... RKTS
Sangkulirang [*Indonesia*] [*ICAO location identifier*] (ICLI) .... WRLU
Sangley Point Naval Station, Cavite [*Philippines*] [*ICAO location identifier*] (ICLI) .... RPMS
Sango [*MARC language code Library of Congress*] (LCCP) .... sag
SangStat Medical [*NASDAQ symbol*] (TTSB) .... SANG
SangStat Medical Corp. [*NASDAQ symbol*] (SAG) .... SANG
SangStat Medical Corp. [*Associated Press*] (SAG) .... Sangstat
Sang-Tuda [*Former USSR Seismograph station code, US Geological Survey Closed*] (SEIS) .... SAT
Sangudo Public and School Library, Alberta [*Library symbol National Library of Canada*] (NLC) .... ASANS
Sanguinarine [*Biochemistry*] .... Sa
Sanguinarine Extract [*Biochemistry*] .... SaE
Sanguine (VRA) .... sangu
Sanguineous [*Hematology*] (DAVI) .... sang
Sanhedrin (BJA) .... Sanh
Sanherib (BJA) .... Sanh
Sani Pass [*South Africa*] [*ICAO location identifier*] (ICLI) .... FASA
Sanibel, FL [*FM radio station call letters*] (RBYB) .... WDRR
Sanifill, Inc. [*NYSE symbol*] (SPSG) .... FIL
Sanifill, Inc. [*Associated Press*] (SAG) .... Sanifil
Sanikiluaq [*Canada*] [*Airport symbol*] (OAG) .... YSK
Sanikiluaq/Belcher Island, NT [*ICAO location identifier*] (ICLI) .... CYSK
Sanilac Township Library, Port Sanilac, MI [*Library symbol Library of Congress*] (LCLS) .... MiPs
Sanitaetskompanie [*Medical company*] [*German military - World War II*] .... SK
Sanitarium .... Sanit
Sanitary (AAG) .... SAN
Sanitary .... SANI
Sanitary .... Sanit
Sanitary .... Sn
Sanitary Authority [*British*] (ROG) .... SA
Sanitary Corps .... SC
Sanitary Corps [*Army*] .... SNC
Sanitary Drainage Fixture Unit (DAC) .... SDFU
Sanitary Engineer [*Academic degree*] .... San E
Sanitary Engineer [*Academic degree*] .... SE
Sanitary Engineering and Environmental Health Research Laboratory [*Research center*] (RCD) .... SEEHRL
Sanitary Engineering Center .... SEC
Sanitary Engineering Division [*MIT*] (MCD) .... SED
Sanitary Engineering Research Laboratory [*University of California*] (MCD) .... SERL
Sanitary Inspector [*British*] (ROG) .... SI
Sanitary Institute of America [*Later, IAWCM*] .... SIA
Sanitary Sewer Overflow [*Environmental Protection Agency*] .... SSO
Sanitary Sewer Overflow [*Environmental Protection Agency*] .... SSO
Sanitary Supply Wholesalers Association (EA) .... SSWA
Sanitary Towel [*British*] (DSUE) .... ST

Sanitation (WGA) .... SAN
Sanitation (DAVI) .... sanit
Sanitation .... SANITN
Sanitation Center [Food Service] [Army] .... SC
Sanitation Handbook of Consumer Protection Programs .... SHCPP
Sanitation Inspection Fish Establishment [National Marine Fisheries
    Service] (NOAA) .... SIFE
Sanitation Inspector [Military] (AABC) .... SANINSP
Sanitation Suppliers and Contractors Institute [Defunct] (EA) .... SSCI
Sanity on Sex [Group opposing sex education in schools] .... SOS
Sankt (VRA) .... S
Sanmina Corp. [NASDAQ symbol] (SAG) .... SANM
Sanmina Corp. [Associated Press] (SAG) .... Sanmina
Sanniquellie [Liberia] [ICAO location identifier] (ICLI) .... GLSK
Sano Corp. [NASDAQ symbol] (SAG) .... SANO
Sano Corp. [Associated Press] (SAG) .... SanoCo
Sanol Arzneimittel Dr. Schwarz [Germany] [Research code symbol] ... Diu
Sanol Arzneimittel Dr. Schwarz [Germany] [Research code symbol] ... V
Sans [Without] [Latin] (DAVI) .... ss
Sans Caffeine [Acronym used as brand name] .... SANKA
Sans Correction [Without correction] [Ophthalmology] (DAVI) ... s gl
Sans Correction [Without correction or without spectacles] [Ophthalmology]
    (DAVI) .... sc
Sans Domicile Fixe [No Fixed Address] [French] .... SDF
Sans Notre Garantie [Without Our Guarantee] [French Business term] .... SNG
Sans Serif [Typeface] [Printing] (NTCM) .... SS
Sans Souci [Canada] [Airport symbol] (OAG) .... YSI
Sans Souci, SC [AM radio station call letters] .... WHYZ
Sansanne-Mango [Togo] [ICAO location identifier] (ICLI) ...... DXMG
Sanscrit .... SANSC
Sanskrit [MARC language code Library of Congress] (LCCP) ... san
Sanskrit [Language, etc.] .... SANSK
Sanskrit [Language, etc.] .... SKR
Sanskrit [Language] (BARN) .... Skrt
Sanskrit [Afrikaans] .... SKT
Santa (VRA) .... S
Santa [Saint] [Italian] .... SN
Santa [Saint] [Italian] .... STA
Santa Ana [Bolivia] [Airport symbol Obsolete] (OAG) .... SBL
Santa Ana [Columbia] [Airport symbol] (AD) .... SLO
Santa Ana, CA [FM radio station call letters] (RBYB) .... KALI-FM
Santa Ana, CA [Television station call letters] .... KTBN
Santa Ana, CA [AM radio station call letters] .... KWIZ
Santa Ana, CA [FM radio station call letters] .... KWIZ-FM
Santa Ana, CA [FM radio station call letters] .... KYMS
Santa Ana, CA [Location identifier FAA] (FAAL) .... NZJ
Santa Ana, CA [Location identifier FAA] (FAAL) .... SNA
Santa Ana College [California] .... SAC
Santa Ana College, Santa Ana, CA [Library symbol Library of Congress]
    (LCLS) .... CStaC
Santa Ana De Huachi [Bolivia] [ICAO location identifier] (ICLI) ...... SLSH
Santa Ana De Yacuma [Bolivia] [ICAO location identifier] (ICLI) ...... SLSA
Santa Ana Public Library, Santa Ana, CA [Library symbol Library of
    Congress] (LCLS) .... CSta
Santa Anita Realty Enterprises, Inc. [Associated Press] (SAG) ... SAnitRt
Santa Anita Realty Enterprises, Inc. [NYSE symbol] (SPSG) ... SAR
Santa Anita Rlty(UNIT) [NYSE symbol] (TTSB) .... SAR
Santa Anna Di Valdieri [Italy] [Seismograph station code, US Geological
    Survey] (SEIS) .... STV
Santa Barbara [Honduras] [ICAO location identifier] (ICLI) .... MHSZ
Santa Barbara [Television program] .... SB
Santa Barbara [California] [Airport symbol] (OAG) .... SBA
Santa Barbara [California] [Seismograph station code, US Geological Survey]
    (SEIS) .... SBC
Santa Barbara [Monagas, Venezuela] [Airport symbol] (AD) ... SBR
Santa Barbara [Venezuela] [Airport symbol] (OAG) .... STB
Santa Barbara [Honduras] [Airport symbol] (AD) .... SZB
Santa Barbara Bancorp [NASDAQ symbol] (TTSB) .... SABB
Santa Barbara Bancorp [NASDAQ symbol] (SAG) .... SABB
Santa Barbara Bancorp [Associated Press] (SAG) .... SBarbBc
Santa Barbara, CA [FM radio station call letters] .... KCSB
Santa Barbara, CA [FM radio station call letters] .... KDB
Santa Barbara, CA [Television station call letters] .... KEYT
Santa Barbara, CA [FM radio station call letters] .... KFAC
Santa Barbara, CA [FM radio station call letters] .... KHTY
Santa Barbara, CA [AM radio station call letters] .... KIST
Santa Barbara, CA [AM radio station call letters] .... KQSB
Santa Barbara, CA [FM radio station call letters] .... KRUZ
Santa Barbara, CA [AM radio station call letters] .... KSPE
Santa Barbara, CA [AM radio station call letters] .... KTMS
Santa Barbara, CA [FM radio station call letters] .... KTYD
Santa Barbara, CA [FM radio station call letters] (RBYB) ... KZBN
Santa Barbara, CA [Location identifier FAA] (FAAL) .... SZN
Santa Barbara City College, Santa Barbara, CA [Library symbol Library of
    Congress] (LCLS) .... CStbCiC
Santa Barbara De Barinas, Barinas [Venezuela ICAO location identifier]
    (ICLI) .... SVSB
Santa Barbara De Parra [Bolivia] [ICAO location identifier] (ICLI) ... SLSO
Santa Barbara Del Zulia, Zulia [Venezuela ICAO location identifier] (ICLI) .... SVSZ
Santa Barbara Historical Society, Santa Barbara, CA [Library symbol]
    [Library of Congress] (LCLS) .... CStbHi
Santa Barbara Island (MUGU) .... SBI
Santa Barbara Museum of Natural History, Santa Barbara, CA [Library
    symbol Library of Congress] (LCLS) .... CStbM

Santa Barbara Public Library, Santa Barbara, CA [Library symbol Library of
    Congress] (LCLS) .... CStb
Santa Barbara Research Center [Hughes Aircraft Co.] .... SBRC
Santa Barbara (Versalles) [Bolivia] [ICAO location identifier] (ICLI) ... SLSW
Santa Barbara-Barinas [Venezuela] [Airport symbol] (AD) ..... SBB
Santa Catalina [Colombia] [Airport symbol] (AD) .... SCA
Santa Catalina, CA [Location identifier FAA] (FAAL) .... SXC
Santa Catalina Island [California] [Airport symbol] (AD) .... SXC
Santa Catalina Laboratory for Experimental Relativity by Astrometry
    [University of Arizona] [Research center] (RCD) .... SCLERA
Santa Cecilia [Ecuador] [ICAO location identifier] (ICLI) ..... SECE
Santa Clara [Cuba ICAO location identifier] (ICLI) .... MUSC
Santa Clara [Cuba] [Airport symbol] (AD) .... SNU
Santa Clara, CA [FM radio station call letters] .... KARA
Santa Clara, CA [AM radio station call letters] .... KNTA
Santa Clara, CA [FM radio station call letters] .... KSCU
Santa Clara County Free Library, San Jose, CA [Library symbol Library of
    Congress] (LCLS) .... CSjCL
Santa Clara County Historical and Genealogical Society, Santa Clara, CA
    [Library symbol] [Library of Congress] (LCLS) .... CStclHi
Santa Clara County Law Library, San Jose, CA [Library symbol] [Library of
    Congress] (LCLS) .... CSjL
Santa Clara De Guapiles [Costa Rica] [ICAO location identifier] (ICLI) ... MRSG
Santa Clara Law Review [A publication] (ILCA) .... Santa Clara LR
Santa Clara Law Review [A publication] (ILCA) .... SCLR
Santa Clara (Moxos) [Bolivia] [ICAO location identifier] (ICLI) ... SLSC
Santa Clara Public Library, Santa Clara, CA [Library symbol Library of
    Congress] (LCLS) .... CStcl
Santa Clara - Ricard [California] [Seismograph station code, US Geological
    Survey Closed] (SEIS) .... SCL
Santa Clara Systems, Inc. [San Jose, CA] [Telecommunications service]
    (TSSD) .... SCS
Santa Clara Valley Water District .... SCVWD
Santa Clarita Valley Historical Society, Newhall, CA [Library symbol] [Library
    of Congress] (LCLS) .... CNeHi
Santa Claus, IN [FM radio station call letters] (RBYB) ..... WAXL-FM
Santa Claus, IN [FM radio station call letters] (RBYB) .... WAZU
Santa Cruz [Portugal ICAO location identifier] (ICLI) .... LPSC
Santa Cruz [Costa Rica] [ICAO location identifier] (ICLI) .... MRSC
Santa Cruz [Argentina] [Airport symbol] (OAG) .... RZA
Santa Cruz [Argentina ICAO location identifier] (ICLI) .... SAWU
Santa Cruz [Argentina] [Seismograph station code, US Geological Survey
    Closed] (SEIS) .... SCA
Santa Cruz [California] [Seismograph station code, US Geological Survey
    Closed] (SEIS) .... SCC
Santa Cruz [Solomon Islands] [Airport symbol] (OAG) .... SCZ
Santa Cruz [Peru] [ICAO location identifier] (ICLI) .... SPNZ
Santa Cruz [Bolivia] [Airport symbol] (OAG) .... SRZ
Santa Cruz Acoustic Range Facility [Navy] .... SCARF
Santa Cruz Basin [California] (GAAI) .... SCB
Santa Cruz, CA [FM radio station call letters] .... KFER
Santa Cruz, CA [AM radio station call letters] .... KSCO
Santa Cruz, CA [FM radio station call letters] .... KUSP
Santa Cruz, CA [FM radio station call letters] .... KYLZ
Santa Cruz, CA [FM radio station call letters] (RBYB) ..... KZOL-FM
Santa Cruz, CA [FM radio station call letters] .... KZSC
Santa Cruz, CA [Location identifier FAA] (FAAL) .... SRU
Santa Cruz de Tenerife [Canary Islands] [Airport symbol] (AD) ... TCI
Santa Cruz/El Trompillo [Bolivia] [ICAO location identifier] (ICLI) ... SLCZ
Santa Cruz, Flores [Azores] [Airport symbol] (OAG) .... FLW
Santa Cruz Institute for Particle Physics [University of California, Santa Cruz]
    [Research center] (RCD) .... SCIPP
Santa Cruz Island [California] [Seismograph station code, US Geological
    Survey] (SEIS) .... BSC
Santa Cruz Island (MUGU) .... SCI
Santa Cruz Islands [MARC geographic area code Library of Congress]
    (LCCP) .... posc--
Santa Cruz La Palma [Canary Islands] [Airport symbol] (OAG) ... SPC
Santa Cruz Mountain Vintners (EA) .... SCMV
Santa Cruz Operation [Computer manufacturer] (PCM) .... SCO
Santa Cruz Operation [NASDAQ symbol] (TTSB) .... SCOC
Santa Cruz Operation, Inc. [Associated Press] (SAG) ...... SantCrz
Santa Cruz Operation, Inc. [NASDAQ symbol] (SAG) .... SCOC
Santa Cruz Public Library [Santa Cruz City and County Library], Santa Cruz,
    CA [Library symbol Library of Congress] (LCLS) .... CStcrCL
Santa Cruz Test Base (MCD) .... SCTB
Santa Cruz Test Facility (SAA) .... SCTF
Santa Elena [Costa Rica] [Seismograph station code, US Geological Survey]
    (SEIS) AR5
Santa Elena [Venezuela] [Airport symbol] (OAG) .... SNV
Santa Elena de Uairen, Bolivar [Venezuela ICAO location identifier] (ICLI) ... SVSE
Santa Elena, TX [Location identifier FAA] (FAAL) .... SNE
Santa Fe [New Mexico] [ICAO location identifier] (ICLI) ...... KSAF
Santa Fe [New Mexico] [Airport symbol] (OAG) .... SAF
Santa Fe [Argentina ICAO location identifier] (ICLI) .... SAFE
Santa Fe [Diocesan abbreviation] [New Mexico] (TOCD) ...... SFE
Santa Fe [Argentina] [Airport symbol] (OAG) .... SFN
Santa Fe City and County Public Library, Santa Fe, NM [Library symbol
    Library of Congress] (LCLS) .... NmS
Santa Fe Community College, Gainesville, FL [Library symbol Library of
    Congress] (LCLS) .... FGS
Santa Fe Ener Res 8.25%'DECS' [NYSE symbol] (TTSB) ... SFRPrA
Santa Fe Energy Res [NYSE symbol] (TTSB) .... SFR
Santa Fe Energy Res 7% Pfd [NYSE symbol] (TTSB) .... SFRPr
Santa Fe Energy Resources [Associated Press] (SAG) .... SFER

Santa Fe Energy Resources [*NYSE symbol*] (SPSG) ... SFR
Santa Fe Energy Tr 'SPERs' [*NYSE symbol*] (TTSB) ... SFF
Santa Fe Energy Trust [*Associated Press*] (SAG) ... SFeEnTr
Santa Fe Energy Trust Co. [*NYSE symbol*] (SAG) ... SFF
Santa Fe Financial [*NASDAQ symbol*] (TTSB) ... SFEF
Santa Fe Financial Corp. [*Associated Press*] (SAG) ... SanFeFn
Santa Fe Financial Corp. [*NASDAQ symbol*] (SAG) ... SFEF
Santa Fe Gaming [*AMEX symbol*] (TTSB) ... SGM
Santa Fe Gaming 8% Ex Pfd [*AMEX symbol*] (TTSB) ... SGMPr
Santa Fe Gaming Corp. [*Associated Press*] (SAG) ... SFeGam
Santa Fe Gaming Corp. [*AMEX symbol*] (SAG) ... SGM
Santa Fe, NM [*Television station call letters*] ... KASA
Santa Fe, NM [*Television station call letters*] ... KCHF
Santa Fe, NM [*Radio expansion station*] (RBYB) ... KKOB Exp Stn
Santa Fe, NM [*FM radio station call letters*] ... KKSS
Santa Fe, NM [*FM radio station call letters*] ... KLSK
Santa Fe, NM [*FM radio station call letters*] ... KNYN
Santa Fe, NM [*FM radio station call letters*] ... KOLT-FM
Santa Fe, NM [*FM radio station call letters*] (RBYB) ... KRZY-FM
Santa Fe, NM [*FM radio station call letters*] ... KSFR
Santa Fe, NM [*AM radio station call letters*] ... KSWV
Santa Fe, NM [*AM radio station call letters*] ... KTRC
Santa Fe, NM [*AM radio station call letters*] ... KVSF
Santa Fe, NM [*FM radio station call letters*] ... KZRQ
Santa Fe, NM [*FM radio station call letters*] ... KZXA
Santa Fe, NM [*Location identifier FAA*] (FAAL) ... SGB
Santa Fe Opera [*New Mexico*] ... SFO
Santa Fe Pac Pipeline [*NYSE symbol*] (TTSB) ... SFL
Santa Fe Pacific Gold Corp. [*NYSE symbol*] (SAG) ... GLD
Santa Fe Pacific Gold Corp. [*Associated Press*] (SAG) ... SFePGld
Santa Fe Pacific Pipeline Ltd. [*NYSE symbol*] (SPSG) ... SFL
Santa Fe Pacific Pipeline Partners Ltd. [*Associated Press*] (SAG) ... SFePP
Santa Fe Public Library, Santa Fe, NM [*OCLC symbol*] (OCLC) ... SFP
Santa Fe Regional Library [*Gainsville Public Library*] [*UTLAS symbol*] ... SFR
Santa Fe/Sauce Viejo [*Argentina ICAO location identifier*] (ICLI) ... SAAV
Santa Gertrudis Breeders International (EA) ... SGBI
Santa Helena [*Peru*] [*Seismograph station code, US Geological Survey Closed*] (SEIS) ... SHP
Santa Isabel [*Spanish Guinea*] [*Airport symbol*] (AD) ... SSG
Santa Isabel ADS [*NYSE symbol*] (TTSB) ... ISA
Santa Isabel Do Morro [*Brazil*] [*Airport symbol*] (OAG) ... IDO
Santa Isabel SA [*NYSE symbol*] (SAG) ... ISA
Santa Isabel SA [*Associated Press*] (SAG) ... SIsabel
Santa Juanita [*Bolivia*] [*ICAO location identifier*] (ICLI) ... SLJT
Santa Katarina [*Egypt*] [*Airport symbol*] (OAG) ... SKV
Santa Klaus (ROG) ... SK
Santa Lucia [*Mexico ICAO location identifier*] (ICLI) ... MMSM
Santa Lucia [*Cuba ICAO location identifier*] (ICLI) ... MUSL
Santa Lucia [*Chile*] [*Seismograph station code, US Geological Survey Closed*] (SEIS) ... STL
Santa Lucia (Cliza) [*Bolivia*] [*ICAO location identifier*] (ICLI) ... SLSL
Santa Margarita, CA [*FM radio station call letters*] ... KWSP
Santa Margherita [*Italy*] [*Airport symbol*] (AD) ... SMJ
Santa Maria [*Portugal ICAO location identifier*] (ICLI) ... LPPO
Santa Maria [*Brazil*] [*Airport symbol*] (OAG) ... RIA
Santa Maria [*Brazil ICAO location identifier*] (ICLI) ... SBSM
Santa Maria [*Azores*] [*Airport symbol*] (OAG) ... SMA
Santa Maria [*California*] [*Airport symbol*] (OAG) ... SMX
Santa Maria, CA [*Television station call letters*] ... KCOY
Santa Maria, CA [*AM radio station call letters*] ... KSBQ
Santa Maria, CA [*AM radio station call letters*] ... KSMA
Santa Maria, CA [*FM radio station call letters*] ... KSNI
Santa Maria, CA [*AM radio station call letters*] ... KTAP
Santa Maria, CA [*AM radio station call letters*] ... KUHL
Santa Maria, CA [*FM radio station call letters*] ... KXFM
Santa Maria, CA [*Location identifier FAA*] (FAAL) ... SMX
Santa Maria De Guacimo [*Costa Rica*] [*ICAO location identifier*] (ICLI) ... MRSO
Santa Maria Di Leuca [*Italy ICAO location identifier*] (ICLI) ... LIBY
Santa Maria Public Library, Santa Maria, CA [*Library symbol Library of Congress*] (LCLS) ... CStma
Santa Maria Resources Ltd. [*Toronto Stock Exchange symbol*] ... SMO
Santa Maria, Santa Maria Island [*Portugal ICAO location identifier*] (ICLI) ... LPAZ
Santa Maria Valley Railroad Co. [*AAR code*] ... SMV
Santa Marina Gold [*Vancouver Stock Exchange symbol*] ... SMJ
Santa Marta [*Costa Rica*] [*ICAO location identifier*] (ICLI) ... MRSM
Santa Marta [*Colombia*] [*Airport symbol*] (OAG) ... SMR
Santa Marta/Simon Bolivar [*Colorado ICAO location identifier*] (ICLI) ... SKSM
Santa Monica [*California*] [*Airport symbol*] (AD) ... SMO
Santa Monica Bank [*AMEX symbol*] (SAG) ... SMO
Santa Monica Bank [*Associated Press*] (SAG) ... SMonBk
Santa Monica, CA [*FM radio station call letters*] ... KACD
Santa Monica, CA [*AM radio station call letters*] ... KBLA
Santa Monica, CA [*FM radio station call letters*] ... KCRW
Santa Monica, CA [*Location identifier FAA*] (FAAL) ... SMO
Santa Monica City College [*California*] ... SMCC
Santa Monica City College, Santa Monica, CA [*Library symbol Library of Congress*] (LCLS) ... CStmoCiC
Santa Monica Public Library, Santa Monica, CA [*Library symbol Library of Congress*] (LCLS) ... CStmo
Santa Monica Public Library, Santa Monica, CA [*OCLC symbol*] (OCLC) ... SMP
Santa Paula, CA [*AM radio station call letters*] ... KKZZ
Santa Paula, CA [*FM radio station call letters*] ... KXBS
Santa Paula, CA [*Location identifier FAA*] (FAAL) ... SZP
Santa Rita [*Bolivia*] [*ICAO location identifier*] (ICLI) ... SLRT
Santa Rosa [*Argentina*] [*Airport symbol*] (OAG) ... RSA
Santa Rosa [*Argentina ICAO location identifier*] (ICLI) ... SAZR
Santa Rosa [*Ecuador*] [*ICAO location identifier*] (ICLI) ... SERO
Santa Rosa [*Diocesan abbreviation*] [*California*] (TOCD) ... SR
Santa Rosa [*California*] [*Airport symbol*] (OAG) ... STS
Santa Rosa, BC [*Television station call letters*] ... CISR
Santa Rosa Beach, FL [*FM radio station call letters*] ... WWAV
Santa Rosa, CA [*FM radio station call letters*] ... KBBF
Santa Rosa, CA [*Television station call letters*] ... KFTY
Santa Rosa, CA [*FM radio station call letters*] ... KLVR
Santa Rosa, CA [*AM radio station call letters*] ... KMXN
Santa Rosa, CA [*FM radio station call letters*] ... KRCB
Santa Rosa, CA [*AM radio station call letters*] ... KRRS
Santa Rosa, CA [*AM radio station call letters*] ... KSRO
Santa Rosa, CA [*FM radio station call letters*] ... KXFX
Santa Rosa, CA [*FM radio station call letters*] ... KZST
Santa Rosa De Abuna [*Bolivia*] [*ICAO location identifier*] (ICLI) ... SLWA
Santa Rosa De Copan [*Honduras*] [*ICAO location identifier*] (ICLI) ... MHSR
Santa Rosa De Yacuma [*Bolivia*] [*ICAO location identifier*] (ICLI) ... SLSR
Santa Rosa Junior College [*California*] ... SRJC
Santa Rosa Junior College, Santa Rosa, CA [*Library symbol Library of Congress*] (LCLS) ... CStrJC
Santa Rosa Junior College, Santa Rosa, CA [*OCLC symbol*] (OCLC) ... SAR
Santa Rosa, NM [*AM radio station call letters*] ... KSSR
Santa Rosalia [*Mexico*] [*Seismograph station code, US Geological Survey Closed*] (SEIS) ... SRL
Santa Rosa-Sonoma County Free Public Library, Santa Rosa, CA [*Library symbol Library of Congress*] (LCLS) ... CStr
Santa Sarita Mining [*Vancouver Stock Exchange symbol*] ... SRG
Santa Susana Field Laboratory [*NASA*] (NASA) ... SSFL
Santa Susana Propulsion Test Facility [*NASA*] (NASA) ... SSPTF
Santa Teresita [*Argentina ICAO location identifier*] (ICLI) ... SAZL
Santa Terezinha [*Brazil*] [*Airport symbol*] (OAG) ... STZ
Santa Vitoria [*Brazil*] [*Airport symbol*] (AD) ... CTQ
Santa Ynez, CA [*FM radio station call letters*] ... KAGA
Santa Ynez Peak [*California*] [*Seismograph station code, US Geological Survey*] (SEIS) ... SYP
Santacruz Electronics Export Processing Zone ... SEEPZ
Santagueda/Santagueda [*Colorado ICAO location identifier*] (ICLI) ... SKSG
Santana Petroleum [*Vancouver Stock Exchange symbol*] ... SNA
Santander [*Spain ICAO location identifier*] (ICLI) ... LEXJ
Santander [*Spain*] [*Airport symbol*] (OAG) ... SDR
Santander Fin Pref'A' [*NYSE symbol*] (TTSB) ... BSFPrA
Santander Fin Pref'B' [*NYSE symbol*] (TTSB) ... BSFPrB
Santander Fin Pref'C' [*NYSE symbol*] (TTSB) ... BSFPrC
Santander Finance Ltd. [*Associated Press*] (SAG) ... SantF
Santander Financial [*NYSE symbol*] (SPSG) ... BSF
Santander Overseas Bank [*NYSE symbol*] (SPSG) ... OPR
Santander Overseas Bank, Inc. [*Associated Press*] (SAG) ... SntO
Santander Overseas Bank, Inc. [*Associated Press*] (SAG) ... SntOv
Santander Overseas Bk 'B'Pfd [*NYSE symbol*] (TTSB) ... LPRPrB
Santander Overseas Bk 'D'Pfd [*NYSE symbol*] (TTSB) ... OPRPrD
Santander Overseas Bk'A' Pfd [*NYSE symbol*] (TTSB) ... LOPRPr
Santander Overseas Bk'C'Pfd [*NYSE symbol*] (TTSB) ... OPRPrC
Santaquin Canyon [*Utah*] [*Seismograph station code, US Geological Survey*] (SEIS) ... SUU
Santarem [*Brazil*] [*Airport symbol*] (OAG) ... STM
Santarem/Internacional [*Brazil ICAO location identifier*] (ICLI) ... SBSN
Sante Fe [*Panama*] [*Airport symbol*] (OAG) ... SFW
Sante Fe Pacific Gold [*NYSE symbol*] (TTSB) ... GLD
Santiago [*Spain ICAO location identifier*] (ICLI) ... LEST
Santiago [*Dominican Republic*] [*ICAO location identifier*] (ICLI) ... MDST
Santiago [*Panama*] [*ICAO location identifier*] (ICLI) ... MPSA
Santiago [*Chile*] [*Seismograph station code, US Geological Survey*] (SEIS) ... SAN
Santiago [*Chile*] [*ICAO location identifier*] (ICLI) ... SCEZ
Santiago [*Chile*] [*Airport symbol*] (OAG) ... SCL
Santiago [*Cuba*] [*Airport symbol*] (OAG) ... SCU
Santiago [*Bolivia*] [*ICAO location identifier*] (ICLI) ... SLTG
Santiago [*Brazil*] [*Airport symbol*] (AD) ... STG
Santiago [*Dominican Republic*] [*Airport symbol*] (OAG) ... STI
Santiago [*Spain*] [*Seismograph station code, US Geological Survey*] (SEIS) ... STS
Santiago/Arturo Merino Benitez (Edificio Direccion Meteorologica) [*Chile*] [*ICAO location identifier*] (ICLI) ... SCEM
Santiago Capital [*Vancouver Stock Exchange symbol*] ... SAA
Santiago, Chile, Tracking Station [*NASA*] (NASA) ... AGO
Santiago/Ciudad [*Chile*] [*ICAO location identifier*] (ICLI) ... SCSC
Santiago De Compostela [*Spain*] [*Airport symbol*] (OAG) ... SCQ
Santiago De Cuba/Antonio Maceo [*Cuba ICAO location identifier*] (ICLI) ... MUCU
Santiago De Maria [*El Salvador*] [*Seismograph station code, US Geological Survey*] (SEIS) ... SDM
Santiago Del Estero [*Argentina ICAO location identifier*] (ICLI) ... SANE
Santiago Del Estero [*Argentina*] [*Airport symbol*] (OAG) ... SDE
Santiago/Edificio Navegacion Aerea Arturo Merino Benitez [*Chile*] [*ICAO location identifier*] (ICLI) ... SCEN
Santiago/Eulogio Sanchez [*Chile*] [*ICAO location identifier*] (ICLI) ... SCTB
Santiago/Internacional Arturo Merino Benitez [*Chile*] [*ICAO location identifier*] (ICLI) ... SCEL
Santiago/Internacional Los Cerillos [*Chile*] [*ICAO location identifier*] (ICLI) ... SCTI
Santiago Library System [*Library network*] ... SLS
Santiago Library System, Orange, CA [*Library symbol Library of Congress*] (LCLS) ... COrS
Santiago Library System, Orange, CA [*OCLC symbol*] (OCLC) ... SLN
Santiago/Lo Prado [*Chile*] [*ICAO location identifier*] (ICLI) ... SCLP
Santiago/Los Leones [*Chile*] [*ICAO location identifier*] (ICLI) ... SCLE
Santiago/Mil el Bosque [*Chile*] [*ICAO location identifier*] (ICLI) ... SCBQ

Santiago/Ministerio de Defensa Nacional [*Chile*] [*ICAO location identifier*] (ICLI) ... SCMD
Santiago/Quinta Normal [*Chile*] [*ICAO location identifier*] (ICLI) ... SCON
Santo (VRA) ... S
Santo ... SN
Santo Angelo [*Brazil*] [*Airport symbol*] (OAG) ... GEL
Santo Angelo [*Brazil ICAO location identifier*] (ICLI) ... SBNM
Santo Antao [*Cape Verde Islands*] [*Airport symbol*] (OAG) ... NTO
Santo Antonio do Zaire [*Angola*] [*Airport symbol*] (AD) ... SZA
Santo Domingo [*Dominican Republic*] [*Airport symbol*] (OAG) ... HEX
Santo Domingo [*Dominican Republic*] [*ICAO location identifier*] (ICLI) ... MDCS
Santo Domingo [*Ciudad Trujillo*] [*Dominican Republic*] [*Seismograph station code, US Geological Survey*] (SEIS) ... SDD
Santo Domingo [*Dominican Republic*] [*Airport symbol*] (OAG) ... SDQ
Santo Domingo [*Venezuela*] [*Seismograph station code, US Geological Survey*] (SEIS) ... SDV
Santo Domingo [*Venezuela*] [*Airport symbol*] (AD) ... STD
Santo Domingo/De las Americas Internacional [*Dominican Republic*] [*ICAO location identifier*] (ICLI) ... MDSD
Santo Domingo De Los Colorados [*Ecuador*] [*ICAO location identifier*] (ICLI) ... SESD
Santo Domingo/Mayor Buenaventura Vivas A. B., Tachira [*Venezuela ICAO location identifier*] (ICLI) ... SVSO
Santo Domingo/Santo Domingo [*Chile*] [*ICAO location identifier*] (ICLI) ... SCSN
Santo/Pekoa [*Vanuatu*] [*ICAO location identifier*] (ICLI) ... NVSS
Santo Rosa [*Brazil*] [*Airport symbol*] (AD) ... SRA
Santorini [*Thira Islands*] [*Airport symbol*] (OAG) ... JTR
Santorini [*Greece*] [*ICAO location identifier*] (ICLI) ... LGSR
Santos [*Brazil ICAO location identifier*] (ICLI) ... SBST
Santos [*Brazil*] [*Airport symbol*] (AD) ... SSZ
Santos Dumont Experimental [*British military*] (DMA) ... SE
Santos Ltd. [*Associated Press*] (SAG) ... Santos
Santos Ltd. [*NASDAQ symbol*] (NQ) ... STOS
Santos Ltd ADR [*NASDAQ symbol*] (TTSB) ... STOSY
Santuario Madre del Buon Consiglio [*Pious Union of Our Mother of Good Counsel - PUMGC*] [*Genazzano, Italy*] (EAIO) ... SMBC
Sanyal's Criminal Cases between Natives and Europeans [*1796-1895*] [*India*] [*A publication*] (DLA) ... Sanyal
Sanyo Electric Co. Ltd. [*NASDAQ symbol*] (NQ) ... SANY
Sanyo Electric Co. Ltd. [*Associated Press*] (SAG) ... Sanyo
SANYO Electric Ltd ADS [*NASDAQ symbol*] (TTSB) ... SANYY
Sanza Pombo [*Angola*] [*ICAO location identifier*] (ICLI) ... FNPB
Sao Borja [*Brazil*] [*Airport symbol*] (AD) ... SBQ
Sao Carlos/Francisco Pereira Lopez [*Brazil ICAO location identifier*] (ICLI) ... SBSA
Sao Domingos [*Guinea-Bissau*] [*ICAO location identifier*] (ICLI) ... GGSD
Sao Domingos [*Brazil*] [*Airport symbol*] (AD) ... SDG
Sao Felipe, Fogo Island [*Cape Verde*] [*ICAO location identifier*] (ICLI) ... GVSF
Sao Filipe [*Cape Verde Islands*] [*Airport symbol*] (OAG) ... SFL
Sao Gabriel Da Cachoeira [*Brazil ICAO location identifier*] (ICLI) ... SBUA
Sao Hill [*Tanzania*] [*Airport symbol*] (AD) ... SIL
Sao Jorge Island [*Azores*] [*Airport symbol*] (OAG) ... SJZ
Sao Jorge, Sao Jorge Island [*Portugal ICAO location identifier*] (ICLI) ... LPSJ
Sao Jose Do Rio Preto [*Brazil ICAO location identifier*] (ICLI) ... SBSR
Sao Jose Do Rio Preto [*Brazil*] [*Airport symbol*] (OAG) ... SJP
Sao Jose Do Xingu [*Brazil*] [*Airport symbol*] (OAG) ... SXN
Sao Jose Dos Campos [*Brazil ICAO location identifier*] (ICLI) ... SBSJ
Sao Jose Dos Campos [*Brazil*] [*Airport symbol*] (OAG) ... SJK
Sao Luis/Marechal Cunha Machado [*Brazil ICAO location identifier*] (ICLI) ... SBSL
Sao Luiz [*Brazil*] [*Airport symbol*] (OAG) ... SLZ
Sao Madureira [*Brazil*] [*Airport symbol*] (AD) ... ZMD
Sao Miguel Do Araguaia [*Brazil*] [*Airport symbol*] (OAG) ... SQM
Sao Nicolau [*Cape Verde Islands*] [*Airport symbol*] (OAG) ... SNE
Sao Nicolau, Sao Nicolau Island [*Cape Verde*] [*ICAO location identifier*] (ICLI) ... GVSN
Sao Paulo [*Brazil*] [*Airport symbol*] (OAG) ... SAO
Sao Paulo (Campinas)/Viracopos [*Brazil ICAO location identifier*] (ICLI) ... SBKP
Sao Paulo/Congonhas [*Brazil ICAO location identifier*] (ICLI) ... SBSP
Sao Paulo [*Brazil*] **Congonhas Airport** [*Airport symbol*] (OAG) ... CGH
Sao Paulo de Olivenca [*Brazil*] [*Airport symbol*] (AD) ... SLV
Sao Paulo/Internacional Guarulhos [*Brazil ICAO location identifier*] (ICLI) ... SBGR
Sao Paulo/Marte [*Brazil ICAO location identifier*] (ICLI) ... SBMT
Sao Paulo [*Brazil*] **Viracopos Airport** [*Airport symbol*] (OAG) ... VCP
Sao Pedro Da Aldeia [*Brazil ICAO location identifier*] (ICLI) ... SBES
Sao Roque [*Brazil ICAO location identifier*] (ICLI) ... SBRQ
Sao Salvador [*Angola*] [*Airport symbol*] (AD) ... SSY
Sao Tome [*Sao Tome*] [*ICAO location identifier*] (ICLI) ... FPST
Sao Tome and Principe [*MARC geographic area code Library of Congress*] (LCCP) ... f-sf--
Sao Tome and Principe [*Aircraft nationality and registration mark*] (FAAC) ... S9
Sao Tome and Principe [*MARC country of publication code Library of Congress*] (LCCP) ... sf
Sao Tome and Principe [*ANSI two-letter standard code*] (CNC) ... ST
Sao Tome and Principe [*ANSI three-letter standard code*] (CNC) ... STP
Sao Tome Island [*Sao Tome Islands*] [*Airport symbol*] (OAG) ... TMS
Sao Vicente [*Cape Verde Islands*] [*Airport symbol*] (OAG) ... VXE
Sao Vicente, Sao Vicente Island [*Cape Verde*] [*ICAO location identifier*] (ICLI) ... GVSV
Saorstat Eireann [*Irish Free State*] ... SE
Sap No Defect ... SND
Sa-Pa [*Vietnam*] [*Seismograph station code, US Geological Survey*] (SEIS) ... SPV
Saperstein & Associates Ltd. [*Vancouver, BC*] [*Telecommunications*] (TSSD) ... SAL
Saphenopopliteal Junction [*Medicine*] (DMAA) ... SPJ
Saphenous Vein Bypass [*Cardiology*] (DMAA) ... SVB
Saphenous Vein Bypass Graft [*Cardiology*] (DAVI) ... SVBPG
Saphenous Vein Coronary Artery Bypass [*Cardiology*] ... SVCAB
Saphenous Vein Graft [*Cardiology*] ... SVG
Sapiens International Corp. [*Associated Press*] (SAG) ... Sapiens
Sapiens International Corp. [*NASDAQ symbol*] (SAG) ... SPNS
Sapiens Intl N.V. [*NASDAQ symbol*] (TTSB) ... SPNSF
Sapient Corp. [*NASDAQ symbol*] (TTSB) ... SAPE
Sapient Corp. [*NASDAQ symbol*] (SAG) ... SAPE
Sapient Corp. [*Associated Press*] (SAG) ... Sapient
Saponaria [*Soapwort*] [*Pharmacology*] (ROG) ... SAPON
Saponification [*or Saponify*] [*Analytical chemistry*] (AAMN) ... sap
Saponification [*Analytical chemistry*] ... SAPON
Saponification Equivalent [*Analytical chemistry*] ... SE
Saponification Number [*Analytical chemistry*] ... SN
Saponification Value [*Organic analytical chemistry*] ... SV
Saporamean Kampuchea News Agency [*Cambodia*] ... SPK
Saposoa [*Peru*] [*ICAO location identifier*] (ICLI) ... SPOA
Sapper [*Military*] ... SPR
Sapper Vehicle [*Military*] ... SV
Sappers and Miners [*British military*] (DMA) ... S & M
Sapphire [*Philately*] ... saph
Sapphire Vacuum Lens ... SVL
Sapphire Vacuum Lens Blank ... SVLB
Sapporo [*Japan ICAO location identifier*] (ICLI) ... RJCG
Sapporo [*Japan*] [*Seismograph station code, US Geological Survey*] (SEIS) ... SAP
Sapporo [*Japan*] [*Airport symbol*] (OAG) ... SPK
Sapporo/Chitose [*Japan*] [*Airport symbol*] (OAG) ... CTS
Sapporo/Chitose [*Japan ICAO location identifier*] (ICLI) ... RJCC
Sapporo/Okadama [*Japan*] [*Airport symbol*] (OAG) ... OKD
Sapporo/Okadama [*Japan ICAO location identifier*] (ICLI) ... RJCO
Sapporo Rat (Virus) ... SR-11
Sapulpa, OK [*AM radio station call letters*] ... KXOJ
Sapulpa, OK [*FM radio station call letters*] ... KXOJ-FM
Sapwood [*Forestry*] ... S
Sapwood [*Lumber*] (BARN) ... sap
Sapwood [*Botany*] ... SW
Saqani [*Fiji*] [*Airport symbol*] (OAG) ... AQS
Sara [*Vanuatu*] [*ICAO location identifier*] (ICLI) ... NVSH
Sara Bush Lincoln Health Center, Mattoon, IL [*Library symbol Library of Congress*] (LCLS) ... IMatL
Sara Lee Corp. [*Associated Press*] (SAG) ... SaraLee
Sara Lee Corp. [*NYSE symbol*] (SPSG) ... SLE
Sarab [*Iran*] [*ICAO location identifier*] (ICLI) ... OITA
Saraburi [*Thailand*] [*ICAO location identifier*] (ICLI) ... VTBE
Sarafotoxin [*Biochemistry*] ... SRT
Sarah Bernhardt [*French actress, 1844-1923*] ... SB
Sarah Hull Hallock Free Library, Milton, NY [*Library symbol Library of Congress*] (LCLS) ... NMilt
Sarah Lawrence College (GAGS) ... Sarah Lawrence C
Sarah Lawrence College [*Bronxville, NY*] ... SLC
Sarah Lawrence College, Bronxville, NY [*Library symbol Library of Congress*] (LCLS) ... NBronSL
Sarah Lawrence College, Bronxville, NY [*OCLC symbol*] (OCLC) ... VVS
Sarah Mellon Scaife Radiation Laboratory [*University of Pittsburgh*] (MCD) ... SMSRL
Sarajevo [*Former Yugoslavia*] [*ICAO location identifier*] (ICLI) ... LYSA
Sarajevo [*Yugoslavia*] [*Seismograph station code, US Geological Survey*] (SEIS) ... SAR
Sarajevo [*Former Yugoslavia*] [*Airport symbol*] (OAG) ... SJJ
Sarakhs [*Iran*] [*ICAO location identifier*] (ICLI) ... OIMC
Saralasin [*Antihypertensive*] ... SARA
Saran Yarn Co., Odenton, MD [*Library symbol Library of Congress Obsolete*] (LCLS) ... MdOdS
Saranac Lake [*New York*] [*Airport symbol*] (OAG) ... SLK
Saranac Lake Free Library, Saranac Lake, NY [*Library symbol Library of Congress*] (LCLS) ... NSl
Saranac Lake, NY [*Location identifier FAA*] (FAAL) ... SLK
Saranac Lake, NY [*AM radio station call letters*] ... WNBZ
Saranac Lake, NY [*FM radio station call letters*] ... WSLK
Saranac Lake, NY [*FM radio station call letters*] ... WSLL
Saranton Army Ammunition Plant (AABC) ... SAAP
Sarasota/Bradenton [*Florida*] [*Airport symbol*] ... SRQ
Sarasota, FL [*FM radio station call letters*] ... WAYG
Sarasota, FL [*FM radio station call letters*] ... WHPT
Sarasota, FL [*AM radio station call letters*] ... WKXY
Sarasota, FL [*FM radio station call letters*] ... WKZM
Sarasota, FL [*AM radio station call letters*] ... WQSA
Sarasota, FL [*AM radio station call letters*] ... WSPB
Sarasota, FL [*FM radio station call letters*] ... WSRZ
Sarasota, FL [*AM radio station call letters*] ... WTMY
Sarasota, FL [*Television station call letters*] ... WWSB
Sarasota Public Library, Sarasota, FL [*Library symbol Library of Congress*] (LCLS) ... FS
Saratoga & Encampment Valley Railroad (IIA) ... S & EV
Saratoga & Schuylerville Railroad (IIA) ... S & S
Saratoga Beverage Group [*Associated Press*] (SAG) ... SaratgBv
Saratoga Beverage Group [*NASDAQ symbol*] (SAG) ... TOGA
Saratoga Beverage Group'A' [*NASDAQ symbol*] (TTSB) ... TOGA
Saratoga Brands [*NASDAQ symbol*] (TTSB) ... STGA
Saratoga Brands, Inc. [*Associated Press*] (SAG) ... SaratgB
Saratoga Brands, Inc. [*Associated Press*] (SAG) ... SaratgBrd
Saratoga Brands, Inc. [*NASDAQ symbol*] (NQ) ... STGA
Saratoga Chancery Sentinel [*New York*] [*A publication*] (DLA) ... Sar Ch Sen
Saratoga Chancery Sentinel [*1841-47*] [*New York*] [*A publication*] (DLA) ... Sarat Ch Sent

Saratoga National Historical Park ... SARA
Saratoga Performing Arts Center [*Summer home of NYCB*] [*Saratoga Springs, NY*] ... SPAC
Saratoga Processing Co. Ltd. [*Vancouver Stock Exchange symbol*] ... SPC
Saratoga Springs, NY [*AM radio station call letters*] ... WCKM
Saratoga Springs, NY [*FM radio station call letters*] (RBYB) ... WKAJ-FM
Saratoga Springs, NY [*FM radio station call letters*] ... WSPN
Saratoga Trunk (DSUE) ... SARA
Saratoga, WY [*Location identifier FAA*] (FAAL) ... SAA
Saratov Aviation Division [*Former USSR*] [*FAA designator*] (FAAC) ... SOV
Saravan [*Iran*] [*ICAO location identifier*] (ICLI) ... OIZS
Saravane [*Laos*] [*ICAO location identifier*] (ICLI) ... VLSV
Saravena [*Colombia*] [*Airport symbol*] (OAG) ... RVE
Saravena [*Colombia*] [*Airport symbol*] (AD) ... SVN
Saravena/Saravena El Eden [*Colorado ICAO location identifier*] (ICLI) ... SKSA
Sarawak [*Malaysia*] (ROG) ... SARAW
Sarawak Communist Organization [*Malaya*] ... SCO
Sarawak Museum, Kuching, Malaysia [*Library symbol*] [*Library of Congress*] (LCLS) ... MlyKgM
Sarawak National Party [*Malaysia*] [*Political party*] (PPW) ... SNAP
Sarawak People's Organization [*Malaysia*] [*Political party*] (PPW) ... SAPO
Sarawak Supreme Court Reports [*A publication*] (DLA) ... SSC
Sarawak Trade Union Congress ... STUC
Sarawak United People's Party [*Malaysia*] [*Political party*] (PPW) ... SUPP
Sarayacu [*Ecuador*] [*ICAO location identifier*] (ICLI) ... SERY
Sarbah's Fanti Customary Laws [*Ghana*] [*A publication*] (DLA) ... FCL
Sarbah's Fanti Customary Laws [*Ghana*] [*A publication*] (DLA) ... Sar FCL
Sarbah's Fanti Customary Laws [*Ghana*] [*A publication*] (DLA) ... Sarbah FC
Sarbah's Fanti Law Cases [*1845-1903*] [*Ghana*] [*A publication*] (DLA) ... Sar FLR
Sarbah's Fanti Law Reports [*Gold Coast*] [*A publication*] (DLA) ... Sarbah
Sarbah's Fanti National Constitution [*Ghana*] [*A publication*] (DLA) ... Sar FNC
Sarbaz [*Iran*] [*ICAO location identifier*] (ICLI) ... OIZO
Sarcasm (DSUE) ... SARC
Sarcastics Anonymous (EA) ... SA
Sarcoidosis [*Medicine*] ... SAR
Sarcoidosis of Upper Respiratory Tract [*Medicine*] (CPH) ... SURT
Sarcoma [*Medicine*] ... SA
Sarcoma [*Medicine*] (MAE) ... sarc
Sarcoma ... SRC
Sarcoma Growth Factor ... SGF
Sarcoma Virus [*Medicine*] (MAE) ... SV
Sarcomeric Myosin Heavy Chain [*Muscle physiology*] ... SMHC
Sarcophagi (VRA) ... sarc
Sarcophagus (VRA) ... sarc
Sarcoplasmic Reticulum [*Anatomy*] ... SR
Sarcosine [*Biochemistry*] ... Sar
Sarcosyl [*Biochemistry*] ... Sar
Sardasht [*Iran*] [*ICAO location identifier*] (ICLI) ... OITC
Sarday [*Afghanistan*] [*ICAO location identifier*] (ICLI) ... OABS
Sardine-Anchovy Recruitment Project [*Marine science*] (OSRA) ... SARP
Sardinia [*Italy*] (ROG) ... SAR
Sardinia ... SARD
Sardinia (VRA) ... Sard
Sardonyx [*Gemstone*] (ROG) ... SARDX
Sare Pole Zahab [*Iran*] [*ICAO location identifier*] (ICLI) ... OICL
Sare Pul [*Afghanistan*] [*ICAO location identifier*] (ICLI) ... OASP
Sareskand [*Iran*] [*ICAO location identifier*] (ICLI) ... OITX
Sargent, NE [*FM radio station call letters*] ... KNJP
Sargodha [*Pakistan*] [*Airport symbol*] (AD) ... GDH
Sargodha [*Pakistan*] [*ICAO location identifier*] (ICLI) ... OPSR
Sargonic (BJA) ... Sarg
Sarh [*Chad*] [*ICAO location identifier*] (ICLI) ... FTTA
Sari [*Iran*] [*ICAO location identifier*] (ICLI) ... OINS
Sarin [*Nerve gas*] [*Army symbol*] ... GB
Sark International Airways Ltd. [*British ICAO designator*] (FAAC) ... JIM
Sarlat/Domme [*France ICAO location identifier*] (ICLI) ... LFDS
Sarmi [*Indonesia*] [*Airport symbol*] (OAG) ... ZRM
Sarmi/Orai [*Indonesia*] [*ICAO location identifier*] (ICLI) ... WAJI
Sarnia [*Canada*] [*Airport symbol*] (OAG) ... YZR
Sarnia Northern Collegiate, Ontario [*Library symbol National Library of Canada*] (NLC) ... OSNC
Sarnia Northern Collegiate, Sarnia, ON, Canada [*Library symbol Library of Congress*] (LCLS) ... CaOSNC
Sarnia Olefins and Aromatics Project [*Canadian ethylene project*] ... SOAP
Sarnia, ON [*FM radio station call letters*] ... CBEG
Sarnia, ON [*FM radio station call letters*] ... CFGX
Sarnia, ON [*AM radio station call letters*] ... CHOK
Sarnia, ON [*Television station call letters*] ... CKCO-3
Sarnia, ON [*AM radio station call letters*] ... CKTY
Sarnia, ON [*ICAO location identifier*] (ICLI) ... CYZR
Sarnia Public Library, Ontario [*Library symbol National Library of Canada*] (NLC) ... OS
Sarnia Public Library, Sarnia, ON, Canada [*Library symbol Library of Congress*] (LCLS) ... CaOS
Sarobi [*Afghanistan*] [*ICAO location identifier*] (ICLI) ... OASB
Sarospataki Reformatus Kollegium Nagykonyvtara, Sarospatak, Hungary [*Library symbol Library of Congress*] (LCLS) ... HuSpK
Sarrebourg/Buhl [*France ICAO location identifier*] (ICLI) ... LFGT
Sarreguemines/Neunkirch [*France ICAO location identifier*] (ICLI) ... LFGU
Sarre-Union [*France ICAO location identifier*] (ICLI) ... LFQU
Sarsat Center [*FAA designator*] (FAAC) ... ZSZ
Sarswati's Privy Council Judgments [*India*] [*A publication*] (DLA) ... Sar
Sartaneja [*Belize*] [*Airport symbol*] (OAG) ... SJX
Sartell High School, Sartell, MN [*Library symbol*] [*Library of Congress*] (LCLS) ... MnSarH
Sartell Middle School, Sartell, MN [*Library symbol*] [*Library of Congress*] (LCLS) ... MnSarM
Sartell, MN [*FM radio station call letters*] ... KKSR
Sartigan Granite [*Vancouver Stock Exchange symbol*] ... SGN
Sartre Society (EA) ... SS
Sarutani [*Japan*] [*Seismograph station code, US Geological Survey*] (SEIS) ... SRT
Sarzana/Luni [*Italy ICAO location identifier*] (ICLI) ... LIQW
SAS Census Access and Display System [*Information service or system*] (IID) ... SCADS
SAS Institute, Inc., Cary, NC [*Library symbol*] [*Library of Congress*] (LCLS) ... NcCyS
SAS [*Statistical Analysis System*] **Users Group International** (EA) ... SUGI
Sasasama [*Bolivia*] [*ICAO location identifier*] (ICLI) ... SLSS
Sash (WGA) ... SH
Sash Door ... SD
Sask Energy and Mines, Geological Laboratory, Regina, SK, Canada [*Library symbol*] [*Library of Congress*] (LCLS) ... CaSRSEMG
SASK TEL Corporate Library, Regina, Saskatchewan [*Library symbol National Library of Canada*] (NLC) ... SRST
Saskatchewan [*MARC geographic area code Library of Congress*] (LCCP) ... n-cn-sn
Saskatchewan [*Canadian province*] ... SASK
Saskatchewan [*Canada*] (DD) ... Sask
Saskatchewan [*Canadian province*] (ODBW) ... Sask
Saskatchewan [*Canadian province, postal code*] ... SK
Saskatchewan [*MARC country of publication code Library of Congress*] (LCCP) ... snc
Saskatchewan Accelerator Laboratory [*University of Saskatchewan*] [*Canada*] (IRC) ... SAL
Saskatchewan Archives Office, Saskatoon, Saskatchewan [*Library symbol National Library of Canada*] (NLC) ... SSA
Saskatchewan Archives, Regina, Saskatchewan [*Library symbol National Library of Canada*] (NLC) ... SRA
Saskatchewan Arts Board, Regina, Saskatchewan [*Library symbol National Library of Canada*] (NLC) ... SRSA
Saskatchewan Arts Board, Regina, SK, Canada [*Library symbol Library of Congress*] (LCLS) ... CaSRSA
Saskatchewan Association for the Retarded, John Dolan Resource Library, Saskatoon, SK, Canada [*Library symbol*] [*Library of Congress*] (LCLS) ... CaSSAMR
Saskatchewan Computer Utility Corp. [*SaskComp*], Regina, Saskatchewan [*Library symbol National Library of Canada*] (NLC) ... SRSCU
Saskatchewan Co-Operation and Co-Operative Development, Regina, Saskatchewan [*Library symbol National Library of Canada*] (NLC) ... SRSCCD
Saskatchewan Culture and Recreation, Regina, Saskatchewan [*Library symbol National Library of Canada*] (NLC) ... SRCR
Saskatchewan Culture and Recreation, Regina, SK, Canada [*Library symbol*] [*Library of Congress*] (LCLS) ... CaSRCR
Saskatchewan Department of Advanced Education and Manpower, Labour Market Plan, Regina, SK, Canada [*Library symbol*] [*Library of Congress*] (LCLS) ... CaSRAEL
Saskatchewan Department of Advanced Education and Manpower, Moose Jaw, Saskatchewan [*Library symbol National Library of Canada*] (NLC) ... SMJAEM
Saskatchewan Department of Advanced Education and Manpower, Moose Jaw, SK, Canada [*Library symbol*] [*Library of Congress*] (LCLS) ... CaSMJAEM
Saskatchewan Department of Advanced Education, Women's Services Branch, Regina, SK, Canada [*Library symbol*] [*Library of Congress*] (LCLS) ... CaSRAEW
Saskatchewan Department of Agriculture, Regina, Saskatchewan [*Library symbol National Library of Canada*] (NLC) ... SRAG
Saskatchewan Department of Agriculture, Regina, SK, Canada [*Library symbol Library of Congress*] (LCLS) ... CaSRAg
Saskatchewan Department of Consumer Affairs, Regina, Saskatchewan [*Library symbol National Library of Canada*] (NLC) ... SRCA
Saskatchewan Department of Consumer Affairs, Regina, SK, Canada [*Library symbol Library of Congress*] (LCLS) ... CaSRCA
Saskatchewan Department of Education, Regina, Saskatchewan [*Library symbol National Library of Canada*] (NLC) ... SRED
Saskatchewan Department of Education, Regina, SK, Canada [*Library symbol Library of Congress*] (LCLS) ... CaSREd
Saskatchewan Department of Energy and Mines, Regina, Saskatchewan [*Library symbol National Library of Canada*] (NLC) ... SRSEM
Saskatchewan Department of Health, Regina, Saskatchewan [*Library symbol National Library of Canada*] (NLC) ... SRPH
Saskatchewan Department of Health, Regina, SK, Canada [*Library symbol Library of Congress*] (LCLS) ... CaSRPH
Saskatchewan Department of Highways and Transportation, Regina, SK, Canada [*Library symbol Library of Congress*] (LCLS) ... CaSRHP
Saskatchewan Department of Justice, Communications Policy Branch, Regina, SK, Canada [*Library symbol*] [*Library of Congress*] (LCLS) ... CaSRJC
Saskatchewan Department of Labour, Regina, Saskatchewan [*Library symbol National Library of Canada*] (NLC) ... SRDL
Saskatchewan Department of Labour, Regina, SK, Canada [*Library symbol Library of Congress*] (LCLS) ... CaSRDL
Saskatchewan Department of Mineral Resources, Regina, Saskatchewan [*Library symbol National Library of Canada*] (NLC) ... SRMR
Saskatchewan Department of Mineral Resources, Regina, SK, Canada [*Library symbol Library of Congress*] (LCLS) ... CaSRMR
Saskatchewan Department of Municipal Affairs, Regina, SK, Canada [*Library symbol Library of Congress*] (LCLS) ... CaSRMA
Saskatchewan Department of Natural Resources, Forestry Branch, Prince Albert, SK, Canada [*Library symbol Library of Congress*] (LCLS) ... CaSPAF

Saskatchewan Department of Social Services, Personnel and Training Library, Regina, SK, Canada [*Library symbol Library of Congress*] (LCLS) .... CaSRSSPT

Saskatchewan Department of Social Services, Regina, SK, Canada [*Library symbol Library of Congress*] (LCLS) .... CaSRWP

Saskatchewan Department of Social Services, Resource Centre, Regina, SK, Canada [*Library symbol*] [*Library of Congress*] (LCLS) .... CaSRSSRC

Saskatchewan Department of the Environment, Regina, Saskatchewan [*Library symbol National Library of Canada*] (NLC) .... SRE

Saskatchewan Department of the Environment, Regina, SK, Canada [*Library symbol Library of Congress*] (LCLS) .... CaSRE

Saskatchewan Department of Tourism and Small Business, La Ronge, Saskatchewan [*Library symbol National Library of Canada*] (NLC) .... SLRTB

Saskatchewan Finance, Regina, Saskatchewan [*Library symbol National Library of Canada*] (NLC) .... SRSF

Saskatchewan Genealogical Society, Regina, Saskatchewan [*Library symbol National Library of Canada*] (NLC) .... SRGS

Saskatchewan Government Air Ambulance Service [*Canada*] [*FAA designator*] (FAAC) .... SLG

Saskatchewan Government Employees Association, Regina, Saskatchewan [*Library symbol National Library of Canada*] (NLC) .... SRGE

Saskatchewan Government Employees Association, Regina, SK, Canada [*Library symbol Library of Congress*] (LCLS) .... CaSRGE

Saskatchewan Government Insurance, Regina, Saskatchewan [*Library symbol National Library of Canada*] (NLC) .... SRGI

Saskatchewan Government Insurance, Regina, SK, Canada [*Library symbol Library of Congress*] (LCLS) .... CaSRGI

Saskatchewan Housing Corp., Regina, Saskatchewan [*Library symbol National Library of Canada*] (BIB) .... SRH

Saskatchewan Indian Cultural College, Saskatoon, Saskatchewan [*Library symbol National Library of Canada*] (NLC) .... SSIC

Saskatchewan Indian Cultural College, Saskatoon, SK, Canada [*Library symbol Library of Congress*] (LCLS) .... CaSSIC

Saskatchewan Indian Federated College [*University of Regina*] .... SIFC

Saskatchewan Indian Federated College, Regina, Saskatchewan [*Library symbol National Library of Canada*] (NLC) .... SRIFC

Saskatchewan Indian Federated College, Regina, SK, Canada [*Library symbol*] [*Library of Congress*] (LCLS) .... CaSRIFC

Saskatchewan Institute of Applied Arts, Saskatoon, Saskatchewan [*Library symbol National Library of Canada*] (NLC) .... SSAA

Saskatchewan Institute of Applied Arts, Saskatoon, SK, Canada [*Library symbol Library of Congress*] (LCLS) .... CaSSAA

Saskatchewan Institute of Pedology [*University of Saskatchewan*] [*Research center*] (RCD) .... SIP

Saskatchewan Intergovernmental Affairs, Regina, Saskatchewan [*Library symbol National Library of Canada*] (NLC) .... SRIA

Saskatchewan Intergovernmental Affairs, Regina, SK, Canada [*Library symbol Library of Congress*] (LCLS) .... CaSRIA

Saskatchewan International Labour Program [*Canada*] (CROSS) .... SILP

Saskatchewan Law [*A publication*] (DLA) .... Sask L

Saskatchewan Law Reports [*Canada*] [*A publication*] (DLA) .... Sask

Saskatchewan Law Reports [*Canada*] [*A publication*] (DLA) .... Sask LR

Saskatchewan Law Reports [*A publication*] (DLA) .... Sask R

Saskatchewan Law Reports [*A publication*] (DLA) .... SLR

Saskatchewan Libraries Retrospective Conversion [*UTLAS symbol*] .... LAS

Saskatchewan Library and Union Catalogue, Regina, Saskatchewan [*Library symbol National Library of Canada*] (NLC) .... SRP

Saskatchewan Mining Development Corp., Saskatoon, Saskatchewan [*Library symbol National Library of Canada*] (NLC) .... SSMD

Saskatchewan Mining Development Corp., Saskatoon, SK, Canada [*Library symbol Library of Congress*] (LCLS) .... CaSSMD

Saskatchewan Motion Pictures Association [*Canada*] (WWLA) .... SMPA

Saskatchewan Mounted Rifles (DMA) .... SMR

Saskatchewan Oil & Gas Corp. [*Toronto Stock Exchange symbol*] .... SKO

Saskatchewan Oil Co., Regina, Saskatchewan [*Library symbol National Library of Canada*] (NLC) .... SRO

Saskatchewan Oil Co., Regina, SK, Canada [*Library symbol*] [*Library of Congress*] (LCLS) .... CaSRO

Saskatchewan Parks and Renewable Resources, Regina, Saskatchewan [*Library symbol National Library of Canada*] (NLC) .... SRPR

Saskatchewan Power Corp., Regina, SK, Canada [*Library symbol Library of Congress*] (LCLS) .... CaSRPC

Saskatchewan Power Corp., Research and Development Center, Regina, SK, Canada [*Library symbol Library of Congress*] (LCLS) .... CaSRPCRD

Saskatchewan Property Management Corp., Regina, Saskatchewan [*Library symbol National Library of Canada*] (NLC) .... SRSPMC

Saskatchewan Provincial Library [*UTLAS symbol*] .... SRP

Saskatchewan Provincial Library and Union Catalogue, Regina, SK, Canada [*Library symbol Library of Congress*] (LCLS) .... CaSRP

Saskatchewan Public Service Commission, Regina, Saskatchewan [*Library symbol National Library of Canada*] (NLC) .... SRPS

Saskatchewan Public Service Commission, Regina, SK, Canada [*Library symbol Library of Congress*] (LCLS) .... CaSRPS

Saskatchewan Regional Libraries [*UTLAS symbol*] .... SKR

Saskatchewan Registered Nurses Association, Regina, Saskatchewan [*Library symbol National Library of Canada*] (NLC) .... SRN

Saskatchewan Registered Nurses Association, Regina, SK, Canada [*Library symbol Library of Congress*] (LCLS) .... CaSRN

Saskatchewan Research Council [*University of Saskatchewan*] [*Research center*] (RCD) .... SRC

Saskatchewan Research Council, Saskatoon, Saskatchewan [*Library symbol National Library of Canada*] (NLC) .... SSR

Saskatchewan Research Council, Saskatoon, SK, Canada [*Library symbol Library of Congress*] (LCLS) .... CaSSR

Saskatchewan Revised Statutes [*Canada*] [*A publication*] (DLA) ...... Sask Rev Stat

Saskatchewan Statutes [*Canada*] [*A publication*] (DLA) .... Sask Stat

Saskatchewan Teachers' Federation Saskatoon, Saskatchewan [*Library symbol National Library of Canada*] (NLC) .... SST

Saskatchewan Teachers' Federation, Saskatoon, SK, Canada [*Library symbol Library of Congress*] (LCLS) .... CaSST

Saskatchewan Technical Institute, Moose Jaw, Saskatchewan [*Library symbol National Library of Canada*] (NLC) .... SMJT

Saskatchewan Technical Institute, Moose Jaw, SK, Canada [*Library symbol Library of Congress*] (LCLS) .... CaSMJT

Saskatchewan Telecommunications [*Regina*] [*Information service or system*] (IID) .... SaskTel

Saskatchewan Tourism and Small Business, La Ronge, SK, Canada [*Library symbol*] [*Library of Congress*] (LCLS) .... CaSLrTB

Saskatchewan Trust Co. [*Toronto Stock Exchange symbol*] .... SKT

Saskatchewan Urban Affairs, Regina, Saskatchewan [*Library symbol National Library of Canada*] (NLC) .... SRUA

Saskatchewan Urban Affairs, Regina, SK, Canada [*Library symbol*] [*Library of Congress*] (LCLS) .... CaSRUA

Saskatchewan Water Resources Commission, Regina, Saskatchewan [*Library symbol National Library of Canada*] (NLC) .... SRWR

Saskatchewan Water Resources Commission, Regina, SK, Canada [*Library symbol Library of Congress*] (LCLS) .... CaSRWR

Saskatchewan Wheat Pool, Regina, Saskatchewan [*Library symbol National Library of Canada*] (NLC) .... SRW

Saskatchewan Wheat Pool, Research Library, Regina, SK, Canada [*Library symbol Library of Congress*] (LCLS) .... CaSRW

Saskatoon [*Saskatchewan*] [*Seismograph station code, US Geological Survey Closed*] (SEIS) .... SAS

Saskatoon [*Canada*] [*Airport symbol*] (OAG) .... YXE

Saskatoon Board of Education [*UTLAS symbol*] .... BES

Saskatoon Board of Education, Saskatchewan [*Library symbol National Library of Canada*] (NLC) .... SSBE

Saskatoon Board of Education, Saskatoon, SK, Canada [*Library symbol*] [*Library of Congress*] (LCLS) .... CaSSBE

Saskatoon Campus, Saskatchewan Indian Federated College, Saskatchewan [*Library symbol National Library of Canada*] (BIB) .... SSIFC

Saskatoon Collegiate Institute, Saskatchewan [*Library symbol National Library of Canada*] (NLC) .... SSCI

Saskatoon Collegiate Institute, Saskatoon, SK, Canada [*Library symbol Library of Congress*] (LCLS) .... CaSSCI

Saskatoon Gallery and Conservatory, Saskatchewan [*Library symbol National Library of Canada*] (NLC) .... SSGC

Saskatoon Gallery and Conservatory, Saskatoon, SK, Canada [*Library symbol Library of Congress*] (LCLS) .... CaSSGC

Saskatoon Public Library [*UTLAS symbol*] .... SPL

Saskatoon Public Library, Saskatchewan [*Library symbol National Library of Canada*] (NLC) .... SS

Saskatoon Public Library, Saskatoon, SK, Canada [*Library symbol Library of Congress*] (LCLS) .... CaSS

Saskatoon, SK [*AM radio station call letters*] CBKF-2

Saskatoon, SK [*FM radio station call letters*] .... CBKS

Saskatoon, SK [*Television station call letters*] .... CBKST

Saskatoon, SK [*FM radio station call letters*] (RBYB) .... CFCR-FM

Saskatoon, SK [*FM radio station call letters*] .... CFMC

Saskatoon, SK [*FM radio station call letters*] .... CFQC

Saskatoon, SK [*Television station call letters*] .... CFQC-TV

Saskatoon, SK [*Television station call letters*] .... CFSK

Saskatoon, SK [*FM radio station call letters*] .... CHSN

Saskatoon, SK [*AM radio station call letters*] .... CJWW

Saskatoon, SK [*AM radio station call letters*] .... CKOM

Saskatoon, SK [*ICAO location identifier*] (ICLI) .... CYXE

Saskatoon Technical Institute [*UTLAS symbol*] .... STI

Sasko Oil & Gas Ltd. [*Toronto Stock Exchange symbol Vancouver Stock Exchange symbol*] .... SOL

Saskoil, Regina, Saskatchewan [*Library symbol National Library of Canada*] (NLC) .... SRS

Saskoil, Regina, SK, Canada [*Library symbol Library of Congress*] (LCLS) .... CaSRS

SaskPower, Regina, Saskatchewan [*Library symbol National Library of Canada*] (NLC) .... SRPC

Sasol Ltd. [*NASDAQ symbol*] (NQ) .... SASO

Sasol Ltd. [*Associated Press*] (SAG) .... Sasol

Sasol Ltd ADR [*NASDAQ symbol*] (TTSB) .... SASOY

Sasquatch Investigations of Mid-America (EA) .... SIA

Sassafras Loamy Sand [*Type of soil*] .... SLS

Sassandra [*Ivory Coast*] [*ICAO location identifier*] (ICLI) .... DISS

Sassandra [*Ivory Coast*] [*Airport symbol*] (OAG) .... ZSS

Sasser, GA [*FM radio station call letters*] (RBYB) .... WEGC

Sasstown [*Liberia*] [*ICAO location identifier*] (ICLI) .... GLST

Sasstown [*Liberia*] [*Airport symbol*] (OAG) .... SAZ

SASTA [*South Australian Science Teachers Association*] Journal [*A publication*] .... SASTA JI

Sat-Air, Inc. [*ICAO designator*] (FAAC) .... FAE

Satan Worship .... SW

Satang [*Monetary unit in Thailand*] .... S

Satanic Ritual Abuse .... SRA

Satara [*India*] [*Seismograph station code, US Geological Survey Closed*] (SEIS) .... STA

Satchel Mouth [*Nickname of late trumpeter Louis Armstrong*] .... SATCHMO

SATCOM [*Satellite Communications*] Ground Terminal Interoperability .... SGTI

SATCOM [*Satellite Command*] Signal Analyser (DWSG) .... SSA

SATCOM Station Reports (MCD) .... SSR

SATCOM System Control Center (KSC) .... SSCC

SatCon Technology [*NASDAQ symbol*] (TTSB) .... SATC

Satcon Technology Corp. [*NASDAQ symbol*] (SAG) .... SATC

Satcon Technology Corp. [*Associated Press*] (SAG) ... Satcon
Satellite (IAA) ... S
Satellite [*Chromosomal*] [*Medicine*] (MAE) ... s
Satellite ... SAT
Satellite ... SAT
Satellite (IAA) ... SATEL
Satellite (AABC) ... SATL
Satellite ... STL
Satellite Access Nodes ... SAN
Satellite Active Archive [*Marine science*] (OSRA) ... SAA
Satellite Active Archive (USDC) ... SAA
Satellite Active Nullifier [*Antisatellite weapon*] ... SATAN
Satellite Aero, Inc. [*ICAO designator*] (FAAC) ... SXX
Satellite Aeromedical Research Vehicle ... SARV
Satellite Air, Surface, Subsurface Tactical Information Exchange System [*Navy*] (CAAL) ... SASSTIXS
Satellite Alert Force Employment ... SAFE
Satellite and Physicians Office Testing ... SPOT
Satellite and Production Services [*Tallahassee, FL*] [*Telecommunications*] (TSSD) ... SPS
Satellite Angular Radiometer (NOAA) ... SARA
Satellite Antenna (DWSG) ... SATANT
Satellite Antenna Test System [*NASA*] ... SATS
Satellite Array for International and National Telecommunications (MCD) ... SAINT
Satellite Assembly Building (MCD) ... SAB
Satellite Attack Sensor ... SAS
Satellite Attack Warning ... SAW
Satellite Attack Warning System ... SAWS
Satellite Attitude Acquisition ... SAA
Satellite Attitude Acquisition Technique ... SAAT
Satellite Attitude-Control Simulator [*NASA*] ... SACS
Satellite Automatic Monitoring System [*Programming language*] ... SAMS
Satellite Automatic Terminal Rendezvous and Coupling (MCD) ... SATRAC
Satellite Automatic Tracking Antenna (MCD) ... SATA
Satellite Automatic Tracking Antenna ... SATAN
Satellite Auto-Monitor System (NITA) ... SAMS
Satellite Balloon (IAA) ... SALON
Satellite Beach Public Library, Satellite Beach, FL [*Library symbol Library of Congress*] (LCLS) ... FSb
Satellite Broadcasters Association (EA) ... SBA
Satellite Broadcasting and Communications Association (EA) ... SBCA
Satellite Business Systems [*McLean, VA*] [*Telecommunications*] (MCD) ... SBS
Satellite Busy Box (SSD) ... SBB
Satellite Cable Audio Networks [*Cable-television service*] ... SCAN
Satellite Capture and Retrieval (AFM) ... SCAR
Satellite Carrier (IAA) ... SC
Satellite Charging at High Altitude (MCD) ... SCATHA
Satellite Cloud Photograph ... SCP
Satellite Collection Buoy Observations ... SCOBO
Satellite Collection of Meteorological Observations ... SCOMO
Satellite Command ... SATCOM
Satellite Committee Agency [*Army*] (MCD) ... SCA
Satellite Communication (NTCM) ... SATCOM
Satellite Communication Agency [*Army*] (IAA) ... SATCOM
Satellite Communication Concentrator ... SCC
Satellite Communication Control Facility ... SCCF
Satellite Communication Terminal [*Navy British*] (MCD) ... SCOT
Satellite Communication Terminal (MCD) ... SCT
Satellite Communications [*Military*] ... SATCOM
Satellite Communications [*Military*] ... SC
Satellite Communications Agency [*Army*] ... SATCOM AGEN
Satellite Communications Agency [*AEC/DCA*] ... SATCOMA
Satellite Communications Agency [*Army*] ... SCA
Satellite Communications Contingency Planning Group (NATG) ... SCCPG
Satellite Communications Control Centre [*British*] ... SCCC
Satellite Communications Control System (MCD) ... SCCS
Satellite Communications Controller ... SCC
Satellite Communications Network, Inc. [*Edison, NJ*] [*Telecommunications*] (TSSD) ... SCN
Satellite Communications Overseas Transmission ... SCOT
Satellite Communications Subsystem ... SCS
Satellite Communications System Control (NATG) ... SCSS
Satellite Communications Test Operations Center ... SCTOC
Satellite Communications Users Conference [*Convention*] (TSSD) ... SCUC
Satellite Communications Working Group [*NATO*] (NATG) ... SCWG
Satellite Computer ... SC
Satellite Computer-Operated Readiness Equipment [*SSD*] ... SCORE
Satellite Condition [*Military*] (AABC) ... SATCON
Satellite Configuration Control Element (MCD) ... SCCE
Satellite Control Center ... SCC
Satellite Control Department ... SCD
Satellite Control Engineering Office (IAA) ... SCEO
Satellite Control Facility [*Sunnyvale, CA*] [*NASA*] ... SCF
Satellite Control Network ... SCN
Satellite Control Officer [*Air Force*] ... SATLCONO
Satellite Control Satellite [*Telecommunications*] (TEL) ... SCS
Satellite Control Section (SSD) ... SCS
Satellite Control Squadron ... SACS
Satellite Control Squadron ... SCS
Satellite Data (MCD) ... SATDAT
Satellite Data Area (IAA) ... SDA
Satellite Data Broadcast Networks, Inc. [*New York, NY*] [*Telecommunications*] (TSSD) ... SATNET
Satellite Data Distribution System ... SDDS
Satellite Data Exchange ... SDX
Satellite Data for Fallout (MCD) ... SATFAL
Satellite Data Handling System ... SDHS
Satellite Data Link Standard (DOMA) ... SDLS
Satellite Data Network [*AgriData Resources, Inc.*] [*Telecommunications service Defunct*] (TSSD) ... SDN
Satellite Data Reduction [*Processor system*] ... SADAR
Satellite Data Services Division [*National Oceanic and Atmospheric Administration Information service or system*] (IID) ... SDSD
Satellite Data System [*Air Force*] ... SDS
Satellite Data System Spacecraft [*Air Force*] ... SDSS
Satellite Data System Study [*Air Force*] (SSD) ... SDSS
Satellite Data Transmission System (DIT) ... SDTS
Satellite Data Unit (DA) ... SDU
Satellite Databank [*European Space Agency*] [*Database*] ... SATELDATA
Satellite de Recherches et d'Environment Technique [*Satellite for Environmental and Technical Research*] [*France*] ... SRET
Satellite Delay Compensation Unit [*Telecommunications*] (LAIN) ... SDCU
Satellite Development Trust (NITA) ... SDT
Satellite Digital and Analog Display ... SDAD
Satellite Digital and Display System ... SDADS
Satellite Distribution Frame [*Telecommunications*] (TEL) ... SDF
Satellite Early Warning System ... SEWS
Satellite Earth Station ... SES
Satellite ECCM [*Electronics Counter Countermeasure*] **Communications Neural Network Syster** ... SECONNS
Satellite Educational and Informational Television ... SEIT
Satellite Electrostatic Triaxial Accelerometer ... SETA
Satellite Experiment Laboratory [*National Oceanic and Atmospheric Administration*] (GRD) ... SEL
Satellite Experimental Terminal (NATG) ... SET
Satellite Express [*Telecommunications*] ... SATX
Satellite Field Office [*Marine science*] (OSRA) ... SFO
Satellite Field Service Station [*Marine science*] (OSRA) ... SFSS
Satellite Field Services Stations [*National Weather Service*] ... SFSS
Satellite for Aerospace Research [*NASA*] ... SATAR
Satellite for Earth Observation ... SEO
Satellite for Orientation, Navigation, and Geodesy (IAA) ... SONG
Satellite Frost Forecast System [*Department of Agriculture*] ... SFFS
Satellite Grand Link System (NATG) ... SGLS
Satellite Graphic Job Processor [*Computer science*] ... SGJP
Satellite Ground Controlled Interception (NATG) ... SAT GCI
Satellite Ground Terminal ... SGT
Satellite Ground Terminal System ... SGTS
Satellite Image Mapping ... SIMAP
Satellite Imagery Dissemination System (MCD) ... SIDS
Satellite Imaging Spectrometer Experiment (USDC) ... SISEX
Satellite in Orbit (WDAA) ... SIO
Satellite Inertial Navigation Determination (MCD) ... SIND
Satellite Information Message Protocol ... SIMP
Satellite Information Processor ... SIP
Satellite Information Processor Operational Program (AFM) ... SIPOP
Satellite Infrared Experiment (MCD) ... SIRE
Satellite Infrared Spectrometer [*NASA*] ... SIRS
Satellite Infrared Spectrometer [*NASA*] ... SIS
Satellite Input to Numerical Analysis and Prediction [*National Weather Service*] ... SINAP
Satellite Inspection (IAA) ... SATIN
Satellite Inspection Technique (MCD) ... SAINT
Satellite Inspector and Satellite Interceptor [*Air Force spacecraft program*] ... SAINT
Satellite Inspector Program (AAG) ... SIP
Satellite Inspector System (AAG) ... SATIN
Satellite Inspector Target (MCD) ... SIT
Satellite Instructional Television Experiment [*NASA/Indian Space Research Organization, 1974*] ... SITE
Satellite Integrated Buoy ... SIB
Satellite Interceptor (KSC) ... SAINT
Satellite Interceptor Navigation System [*Navy*] (CAAL) ... SINS
Satellite Interceptor Program (IAA) ... SIP
Satellite Interceptor System [*Military*] (AFM) ... SIS
Satellite Interface Message Processor (IAA) ... SIMP
Satellite International Television Center [*Telecommunications*] (TEL) ... SITC
Satellite Ionospheric Beacons [*Military*] ... SIB
Satellite Kill ... SKILL
Satellite Laboratory (IAA) ... SATELLAB
Satellite Landing Ground [*British military*] (DMA) ... SLG
Satellite LASER Communication [*Military*] ... SLC
Satellite LASER Ranging [*for geodetic and geophysical measurements*] ... SLR
Satellite Laser Ranging ... SLR
Satellite LASER Ranging System ... SLRS
Satellite Launched from a Balloon (IAA) ... SALOON
Satellite Launching Ship [*Navy symbol Obsolete*] ... AGSL
Satellite Launching Vehicle [*Air Force*] ... SLV
Satellite Library Information Network ... SALINET
Satellite Low-Orbit Bombardment ... SLOB
Satellite Lucerne Transient Streak Virus ... sLTSV
Satellite Maintenance and Repair Techniques [*Air Force*] ... SMART
Satellite Master Antenna Television ... SMATV
Satellite Master Antenna Television Systems (NITA) ... SMATV
Satellite Materials Hardening (MCD) ... SMATH
Satellite Media Tour [*Journalism*] (WDMC) ... SMT
Satellite Monitoring and Remote Tracking ... SMART
Satellite Motion Simulator ... SMS
Satellite Multiservice System (NITA) ... SMS

Satellite Music Network (NTCM) ... SMN
Satellite Mutual Visibility ... SMV
Satellite Navigation (AABC) ... SATNAV
Satellite Navigation Alert Plotter (PDAA) ... SNAP
Satellite Navigation Map ... SNM
Satellite Networking Associates, Inc. [*New York, NY*] [*Telecommunications*] (TSSD) ... SNA
Satellite News Channel [*Cable-television system*] [*Went off the air October, 1983*] ... SNC
Satellite News Gathering [*Trademark*] (NTCM) ... SNG
Satellite News Vehicle (NTCM) ... SNV
Satellite Newsgathering Vehicle (WDMC) ... SNV
Satellite Nuclear Auxiliary Power [*Military*] (CAAL) ... SNAP
Satellite Nuclear Power Station (OA) ... SNPS
Satellite Object Number (MUGU) ... SONO
Satellite Observation (IAA) ... SATOBS
Satellite Observation System ... SOS
Satellite Observations (SAA) ... SATOBS
Satellite Observing System [*Marine science*] (OSRA) ... SOS
Satellite Ocean Analysis for Recruitment [*Marine science*] (OSRA) ... SOAR
Satellite Ocean Surveillance Evaluation Center ... SOSEC
Satellite Ocean Surveillance System ... SOSS
Satellite Oceanic Control Center ... SOCC
Satellite On-Board Attack Reporting System (MCD) ... SOARS
Satellite Operations Center [*Cape Kennedy*] ... SOC
Satellite Operations Complex ... SOC
Satellite Operations Control Center [*NASA*] (NASA) ... SOCC
Satellite Operations Control System ... SOCS
Satellite Operations Group [*Military*] ... SAOG
Satellite Operations Group [*Military*] ... SOG
Satellite Operators and Users Technical Committee [*Defunct*] (EA) ... SOUTC
Satellite Optical Surveillance Station (MCD) ... SOSS
Satellite Orbit Control ... SOC
Satellite Orbit Control Program (IAA) ... SOCP
Satellite Orbital Track and Intercept [*ARPA*] ... SORTI
Satellite Panicum Mosaic Virus ... SPMV
Satellite Paper Tape Transfer ... SATPATT
Satellite Parametric Reduction ... SPR
Satellite Personnel Activity [*Military*] ... SPA
Satellite Photo Electronic Analog Rectification System (IAA) ... SPEARS
Satellite Photoelectric Analog Rectification System ... SPEARS
Satellite Position Adjusting Rocket (SAA) ... SPAR
Satellite Position and Display System ... SPADS
Satellite Position Prediction and Display ... SPAD
Satellite Positioning and Tracking ... SPOT
Satellite Positioning Service ... SAPOS
Satellite Positive-Ion-Beam System [*Air Force*] (MCD) ... SPIBS
Satellite Power System (MCD) ... SPS
Satellite Precipitation and Cloud Experiment [*National Oceanic and Atmospheric Administration*] ... SPACE
Satellite Processing Center [*Military*] ... SPC
Satellite Processor [*Data transmission*] ... SP
Satellite Processor Access Method ... SPAM
Satellite Program Network (NITA) ... SPN
Satellite Programming Network [*Cable-television system*] ... SPN
Satellite Project for Adult and Continuing Education (AIE) ... SPACE
Satellite Protection for Area Defense [*ARPA*] ... SPAD
Satellite Racing Development [*British*] ... SRD
Satellite RADAR Altimetry [*Instrumentation*] ... SRA
Satellite RADAR Interferometry ... SRI
Satellite RADAR Station (NATG) ... SRS
Satellite Radiation Budget Climatology Project [*Marine science*] (OSRA) ... SRBCP
Satellite Radio Navigation (DNAB) ... SRN
Satellite Readout Station (MCD) ... SRS
Satellite Readout Station Upgrade (DWSG) ... SRSU
Satellite Receiving Antenna (NITA) ... Sat An
Satellite Receiving Station ... SRS
Satellite Reconnaissance Advance Notice (MCD) ... SATRAN
Satellite Reentry Vehicle ... SRV
Satellite Sequential Imaging ... SSI
Satellite Services, Inc. [*Houston, TX*] [*Telecommunications*] (TSSD) ... SSI
Satellite Servicing Technology (SSD) ... SST
Satellite Servicing Vehicle ... SSV
Satellite Simulation [*Military*] (CAAL) ... SATSIM
Satellite Simulation Observation and Research Balloon [*Military*] (DNAB) ... SATELLORB
Satellite Situation Center ... SSC
Satellite Situation Display Room ... SSDR
Satellite Situation Report (AAG) ... SSR
Satellite Solar Power Station [*or System*] [*NASA*] ... SSPS
Satellite Space System (IAA) ... SS
Satellite Stratospheric Monitor (NOAA) ... SSM
Satellite Supply Operations Officer [*Military*] (AFIT) ... SSOO
Satellite Surveillance Program [*Canada*] (MSC) ... SURSAT
Satellite Surveillance System (MCD) ... SSS
Satellite Switched Time Division Multiple Access ... SST-DMA
Satellite Switched Time Division Multiple Access (NITA) ... SSTDMA
Satellite Switchstream (NITA) ... SATSTREAM
Satellite Syndicated Systems [*Douglasville, GA*] [*Cable TV programming service*] [*Telecommunications*] ... SSS
Satellite System ... SS
Satellite System Development (IAA) ... SSD
Satellite System for Precise Navigation [*Air Force*] ... SSPN
Satellite System Monitoring Equipment ... SSME
Satellite Systems Corp. [*Virginia Beach, VA*] [*Telecommunications*] (TSSD) ... SSC
Satellite Systems Engineering, Inc. [*Bethesda, MD*] [*Information service or system*] (TSSD) ... SSE
Satellite Systems Monitoring Group [*INTELSAT*] ... SSMG
Satellite Systems Operations Guide [*INTELSAT*] ... SSOG
Satellite Systems Operations Plan [*INTELSAT*] ... SSOP
Satellite Technical and Operational Committee - Television (NTCM) ... STOC-TV
Satellite Technology Management [*NASDAQ symbol*] (SAG) ... STMI
Satellite Technology Management, Inc. [*Associated Press*] (SAG) ... SatTech
Satellite Technology Management, Inc. [*Torrance, CA*] [*Telecommunications*] (TSSD) ... STM
Satellite Telecommunications Analysis and Modeling Program ... STAMP
Satellite Telecommunications Automatic Routing ... STAR
Satellite Telecommunications Co. [*Japanese-American firm*] ... SATELCO
Satellite Telemetry Automatic Reduction System [*NASA*] ... STARS
Satellite Television [*Germany*] ... TV-SAT
Satellite Television Asia Region [*Hong Kong*] ... STAR
Satellite Television Corp. [*Washington, DC*] [*Telecommunications*] (TSSD) ... STC
Satellite Television Industry Association [*Formerly, SPACE*] (NTCM) ... STIA
Satellite Television Network [*Telecommunications Defunct*] (TSSD) ... STN
Satellite Terminal Guidance ... STG
Satellite Test Annex (SAA) ... STA
Satellite Test Center [*Air Force*] ... STC
Satellite Test Center Communications Subsystem (MCD) ... SCS
Satellite Test Vehicle (IAA) ... STV
Satellite Theater Network [*Falls Church, VA*] (TSSD) ... STN
Satellite Ticket Printer [*Travel industry*] ... STP
Satellite to Earth Missile (IAA) ... SEM
Satellite Tobacco Mosaic Virus [*Immunology*] ... STMV
Satellite Tobacco Necrosis Virus ... STNV
Satellite Tobacco Ringspot Virus ... STobRV
Satellite Tool Kit ... STK
Satellite Tracking (MCD) ... SATRACK
Satellite Tracking and Data Acquisition Department ... STADAD
Satellite Tracking and Data Acquisition Network [*Later, STDN*] ... STADAN
Satellite Tracking Annex (MUGU) ... STA
Satellite Tracking Center [*Sunnyvale, CA*] ... STC
Satellite Tracking Committee [*Military*] ... STC
Satellite Tracking Facility [*Air Force*] ... STF
Satellite Tracking Network (MCD) ... STN
Satellite Tracking of Balloons and Emergencies ... STROBE
Satellite Tracking Orbit Determination Program ... SATODP
Satellite Tracking Program [*of the Smithsonian Institution's Astrophysical Observatory*] ... STP
Satellite Tracking Station ... STS
Satellite Transmission and Reception Specialists [*Houston, TX*] [*Telecommunications*] (TSSD) ... STARS
Satellite Transmission Effects Simulation (MCD) ... STRESS
Satellite Transmission Experiment Linking Laboratories [*European Space Agency*] ... STELLA
Satellite Transmission Systems, Inc. [*Hauppauge, NY*] [*Telecommunications*] (TSSD) ... STS
Satellite Transponder Addressable Receiver ... STAR
Satellite under Test ... SUT
Satellite Undetected Duds ... SUDS
Satellite Unfurlable Antenna ... SUA
Satellite United Kingdom ... SatUK
Satellite Vehicle [*Instrument*] (EERA) ... SV
Satellite Video Exchange Society [*Canada*] (EAIO) ... SVES
Satellite Virus ... SV
Satellite Weather Information System [*National Oceanic and Atmospheric Administration*] ... SWIS
Satellite Weather Information System [*Marine science*] (OSRA) ... SWIS
Satellite Wildlife Research Project ... SWRP
Satellite X-Ray Test Facility ... SXTF
Satellite-Aided Search and Rescue System [*Telecommunications*] ... SASRS
Satellite-Based Advanced Air Traffic Management System [*Department of Transportation*] ... SAATMS
Satellite-Based Atomic Energy Detection System (IAA) ... SBAEDS
Satellite-Based Communication System ... SBCS
Satellite-Based Interceptor System (IAA) ... SBIS
Satellite-Based Maritime Search and Rescue System [*Telecommunications*] (TEL) ... SAMSARS
Satellite-Borne Instrumentation (SAA) ... SBI
Satellite-Controlled Clock ... SCC
Satellite-Interrogated Automatic Weather Station (NOAA) ... SIAWS
Satellite-Interrogated Environmental Buoy ... SIEB
Satellite-Like Virus ... SL
Satellite-Like Virus ... SLV
Satellite-Missile Observation Satellite [*or System*] ... SAMOS
Satellites, Balloons, and Rockets [*Air Force program*] ... SABAR
Satellites for Telecommunications, Applications, and Research [*Consortium*] ... STAR
Satellite-Switched ... SS
Satellite-to-Satellite (CET) ... STS
Satellite-to-Satellite Tracking ... SST
Satellite-to-Space Vehicle (SAA) ... STSV
Satellite-Tracked Submarine-Launched Antimissile (MCD) ... SATSLAM
Satena Servicios de Aeronavegacion A Territorios Nac [*Colombia*] [*ICAO designator*] (FAAC) ... NSE
Satenas [*Sweden ICAO location identifier*] (ICLI) ... ESIB
Saticon Mixed-Field [*Video technology*] ... SMF
Satiety Factor [*Physiology*] ... SF
Satin (VRA) ... sat
Satin Chrome Plated ... SCP

Satinwood (VRA) ... satwd
Satipo [*Peru*] [*ICAO location identifier*] (ICLI) ... SPIP
Satirae [*or Sermones*] [*of Horace*] [*Classical studies*] (OCD) ... Sat
Satisfaction [*Legal shorthand*] (LWAP) ... SATFN
Satisfaction (ROG) ... SATISFN
Satisfaction (ROG) ... SATON
Satisfaction ... STSFCTN
Satisfaction of Army Requirements through Space (MCD) ... SARTS
Satisfaction with Performance Scaled Questionnaire ... SPSQ
Satisfactory (AABC) ... SAT
Satisfactory (AFM) ... SATFY
Satisfactory (AAG) ... SATIS
Satisfactory (ROG) ... SATISFY
Satisfactory Evidence Received This Headquarters ... SERTH
Satisfactory/No Credit [*University grading system*] ... S/NC
Satisfactory Operation Factor [*Telecommunications*] (TEL) ... SOF
Satisfactory to Transfer (NOAA) ... SATTR
Satna [*India*] [*ICAO location identifier*] (ICLI) ... VIST
Satoko and Franz M. Joseph Foundation (EA) ... SFMJF
Satsuma Dwarf Virus [*Plant pathology*] ... SDV
Sattna [*Sweden ICAO location identifier*] (ICLI) ... ESNT
Satu Mare [*Romania*] [*ICAO location identifier*] (ICLI) ... LRSM
Satu Mare [*Romania*] [*Airport symbol*] (OAG) ... SUJ
Satun [*Thailand*] [*ICAO location identifier*] (ICLI) ... VTSA
Satura [*of Petronius*] [*Classical studies*] (OCD) ... Sat
Saturable Absorber Giant Pulsing (IAA) ... SAGP
Saturable Core (MSA) ... SC
Saturable Reactor ... SR
Saturable Reactor Coil ... SRC
Saturae Menippeae [*of Varro*] [*Classical studies*] (OCD) ... Sat Men
Saturate (AAG) ... SAT
Saturate (IDOE) ... sat
Saturate (AAG) ... SATUR
Saturated ... SATD
Saturated (IDOE) ... satd
Saturated (MAE) ... std
Saturated Calomel Electrode [*Electrochemistry*] ... SCE
Saturated Current Demand Logic ... SCDL
Saturated Discharge Temperature [*Refrigeration*] ... SDT
Saturated Fatty Acid [*Cardiology*] (DAVI) ... SFA
Saturated Hydrocarbon Weathering Ratio [*Ecology*] (DAVI) ... SHWR
Saturated Hydroxy-Terminated Polybutadiene ... SHTPB
Saturated Logic (IAA) ... SL
Saturated Optical Nonresonant Emission Spectroscopy ... SONRES
Saturated Solution [*Pharmacy*] (WGA) ... sat sol
Saturated Solution [*Pharmacy*] ... SS
Saturated Solution of Potassium Iodide [*Pharmacology*] (DAVI) ... KISS
Saturated Solution of Potassium Iodide [*Medicine*] ... SSKI
Saturated Suction Temperature [*Refrigeration*] ... SST
Saturated Vapor Pressure (IAA) ... SVP
Saturated-Drift Transistor-Diode Logic (IAA) ... SDTDL
Saturated-Unsaturated Transport [*Ground-water modeling*] ... SUTRA
Saturates, Aromatics, Resins, and Asphaltenes [*Crude oil analysis*] ... SARA
Saturating (WGA) ... SATG
Saturation (MAE) ... S
Saturation (IDOE) ... sat
Saturation ... SATN
Saturation Adiabatic Lapse Rate [*Meteorology*] (ADA) ... SALR
Saturation Alleviation Rules ... SAR
Saturation Arterial Oxygen [*Medicine*] (DAVI) ... SaO_2
Saturation Countermeasures Simulator ... SATSIM
Saturation Deficit ... SD
Saturation in the Blood Phase [*Medicine*] (DAVI) ... S
Saturation Index [*Chemistry*] ... SI
Saturation Isothermal Remanent Magnetization [*Paleomagnetics*] ... SIRM
Saturation Output Level [*Recording tapes*] ... SOL
Saturation Recovery [*NMR imaging*] ... SR
Saturation Sound Pressure Level ... SSPL
Saturation Transfer Electron Paramagnetic Resonance [*Physics*] ... STEPR
Saturatus [*Saturated*] [*Pharmacy*] ... SAT
Saturday ... S
Saturday ... SA
Saturday (EY) ... SAT
Saturday (ODBW) ... Sat
Saturday ... STDY
Saturday Evening Girls [*Decorators of Arts and Crafts pottery*] ... SEG
Saturday Evening Post [*A publication*] (BRI) ... SEP
Saturday Inspection [*Slang*] ... SI
Saturday Night [*A publication*] (BRI) ... SN
Saturday Night Live [*Television program*] ... SNL
Saturdays Only [*British railroad term*] ... SO
Saturn ... S
Saturn [*Rocket*] (KSC) ... SAT
Saturn [*Record label*] [*France*] ... Sat
Saturn ... SAT
Saturn Airways, Inc. [*Air carrier designation symbol*] ... SAAX
Saturn Airways, Inc. (MCD) ... STN
Saturn Apollo [*NASA*] (KSC) ... SA
Saturn Apollo Applications [*NASA*] (KSC) ... SAA
Saturn Apollo Applications Program [*NASA*] ... SAAP
Saturn Apollo Electrical Systems Integration Panel (IAA) ... SAESIP
Saturn Apollo Systems Utilization [*NASA*] ... SASU
Saturn Automatic Software System [*NASA*] ... SASS
Saturn Coupe [*An automobile*] (ECON) ... SC
Saturn Electrostatic Discharges [*Planetary science*] ... SED
Saturn Energy & Resources Ltd. [*Vancouver Stock Exchange symbol*] ... SGR
Saturn Engineering Liaison Request [*NASA*] (KSC) ... SELR
Saturn Instrumentation [*NASA*] ... SIU
Saturn Kilometer-Wave Radiation [*Planetary science*] ... SKR
Saturn Launch Computer Program (OA) ... SLCP
Saturn Launch Control Computer [*NASA*] (KSC) ... SLCC
Saturn Launch Facility [*NASA*] ... SLF
Saturn Launch Vehicle [*NASA*] (KSC) ... SLV
Saturn Launcher Computer Complex (IAA) ... SLCC
Saturn LM [*Lunar Module*] **Adapter** [*NASA*] ... SLA
Saturn Longitude System [*Planetary science*] ... SLS
Saturn Missile Test [*NASA*] ... SMT
Saturn Nuclear [*NASA*] (IAA) ... SN
Saturn Operational Display System [*NASA*] ... SODS
Saturn Operational Flight Control [*NASA*] ... SOFC
Saturn Orbiter [*NASA*] ... SO
Saturn Orbiter Probe [*NASA*] ... SOP
Saturn Orbiter Satellite Lander [*NASA*] ... SO/SL
Saturn Orbiter/Titan Probe (MCD) ... SOTP
Saturn Parts Sales [*NASA*] ... SPS
Saturn Program Office [*NASA*] (KSC) ... SPO
Saturn Project Office [*NASA*] (IAA) ... SPO
Saturn Propulsion System [*NASA*] ... SPS
Saturn Static Test Facility [*NASA*] ... SSTF
Saturn Systems Office [*NASA*] (SAA) ... SSO
Saturn Systems Test [*NASA*] ... SST
Saturn Test Oriented Language [*NASA*] ... STOL
Saturn Umbilical Maintenance [*NASA*] ... SUM
Saturn Workshop [*NASA*] ... SWS
Saturn Workshop Cockpit Simulation Trainer [*NASA*] ... SWCST
Saturnalia [*of Macrobius*] [*Classical studies*] (OCD) ... Sat
Saturn-Launched Meteoroid Satellite (IAA) ... SLMS
Saturted Surface Dry (DICI) ... SSD
Satz Rechen Zentrum [*Computer Composition Center*] [*Hartmann & Heenemann*] [*Information service or system*] (IID) ... SRZ
Sauble Beach Branch, Bruce County Public Library, Ontario [*Library symbol National Library of Canada*] (NLC) ... OSB
Sauces [*Bolivia*] [*ICAO location identifier*] (ICLI) ... SLSK
Saucier, MS [*FM radio station call letters*] (RBYB) ... WAOY
Saudarkrokur [*Iceland*] [*ICAO location identifier*] (ICLI) ... BIKR
Saudarkrokur [*Iceland*] [*Airport symbol*] (OAG) ... SAK
Saudi American Bank ... SAMBA
Saudi Arabia [*MARC geographic area code Library of Congress*] (LCCP) ... a-su--
Saudi Arabia [*International civil aircraft marking*] (ODBW) ... HZ
Saudi Arabia (VRA) ... S Arab
Saudi Arabia [*ANSI two-letter standard code*] (CNC) ... SA
Saudi Arabia [*ANSI three-letter standard code*] (CNC) ... SAU
Saudi Arabia [*MARC country of publication code Library of Congress*] (LCCP) ... su
Saudi Arabia - Kuwait - Iraq ... SAKI
Saudi Arabian ... SDI
Saudi Arabian Air Force ... SAAF
Saudi Arabian Airlines ... SDI
Saudi Arabian Airlines [*ICAO designator*] (AD) ... SV
Saudi Arabian Airlines [*ICAO designator*] (FAAC) ... SVA
Saudi Arabian Monetary Agency [*Riyadh*] ... SAMA
Saudi Arabian National Guard (RDA) ... SANG
Saudi Arabian National Liberation Front [*Political party*] (BJA) ... SANLF
Saudi Arabian Riyal [*Monetary unit*] (DS) ... SAR
Saudi International Bank ... SIB
Saudi Investment Banking Corp. ... SIBC
Saudi Naval Expansion Program (MCD) ... SNEP
Saudi Naval Expansion Program, Fleet Introduction Team (DNAB) ... SNEP FIT
Saudi Naval Expansion Program, Project Management Team (DNAB) ... SNEP PMT
Saudi Naval Expansion Program, Project Manager (DNAB) ... SNEP PROJMGR
Saudi Naval Expansion Program, Project Manager, Technical Assistance Field Team (DNAB) ... SNEP PROJMGRT AFT
Saudi Press Agency ... SPA
Saudi Riyal [*Monetary unit*] (BJA) ... SR
Saudia Arabia Airlines ... SAA
Saudia-Saudi Arabia Airlines [*Airline flight code*] (ODBW) ... SV
Saudi-British Bank ... SBB
Saudi-Oriented Guide Specifications (NITA) ... SOGS
Saudi-Sudanese Red Sea Joint Commission [*Commercial firm Jeddah, Saudi Arabia*] (EAIO) ... SSRSJC
Sauerbruch, Herrmannsdorfer, Gerson Diet [*Medicine*] (BABM) ... SHG
Sauerbruch, Herrmannsdorfer, Gerson Diet [*For tuberculosis*] (DAVI) ... SHG
Sauf Erreur ou Omission [*Errors and Omissions Excepted*] [*French*] ... SEOO
Saugatuck, MI [*FM radio station call letters*] ... WEVS
Saugeen Ontario Library Service [*UTLAS symbol*] ... SAU
Saugerties Public Library, Saugerties, NY [*Library symbol Library of Congress*] (LCLS) ... NSau
Saugus Ironworks National Historic Site ... SAIR
Sauk Centre, MN [*FM radio station call letters*] ... KMSR
Sauk Centre Public Library, Sauk Centre, MN [*Library symbol Library of Congress*] (LCLS) ... MnSc
Sauk Centre Public Schools, Sauk Centre, MN [*Library symbol*] [*Library of Congress*] (LCLS) ... MnScP
Sauk City, WI [*FM radio station call letters*] (RBYB) ... WMLI-FM
Sauk City, WI [*FM radio station call letters*] ... WMXF
Sauk County Historical Society, Baraboo, WI [*Library symbol Library of Congress*] (LCLS) ... WBaraHi
Sauk Rapids High School, Sauk Rapids, MN [*Library symbol*] [*Library of Congress*] (LCLS) ... MnSrH

Sauk Rapids, MN [*FM radio station call letters*] ... WHMH
Sauk Rapids, MN [*AM radio station call letters*] ... WVAL
Sauk Village Library District, Sauk Village, IL [*Library symbol Library of Congress*] (LCLS) ... ISv
Saul [*French Guiana*] [*ICAO location identifier*] (ICLI) ... SOOS
Saul A. Silverman Library, C. M. Hincks Treatment Centre, Toronto, Ontario [*Library symbol National Library of Canada*] (BIB) ... OTCMH
Saul Centers [*NYSE symbol*] (TTSB) ... BFS
Saul Centers [*Associated Press*] (SAG) ... SaulCntr
Saul [*B. F.*] **Real Estate Investment Trust** [*NYSE symbol*] (SPSG) ... BFS
Saulieu-Liernais [*France ICAO location identifier*] (ICLI) ... LFEW
Sault Area International Library Association [*Library network*] ... SAILA
Sault College of Applied Arts and Technology, Sault Ste. Marie, ON, Canada [*Library symbol Library of Congress*] (LCLS) ... CaOStMC
Sault College of Applied Arts and Technology, Sault Ste. Marie, Ontario [*Library symbol National Library of Canada*] (NLC) ... OSTMSC
Sault Meadows Energy [*Vancouver Stock Exchange symbol*] ... SOO
Sault Ste. Marie [*Michigan*] [*Airport symbol*] (OAG) ... CIU
Sault Ste. Marie [*Michigan*] [*Airport symbol*] (OAG) ... SSM
Sault Ste. Marie [*Canada*] [*Airport symbol*] (OAG) ... YAM
Sault Ste. Marie and 49th (SSM) Field Regiment RCA Historical Society, Ontario [*Library symbol National Library of Canada*] (NLC) ... OSTMH
Sault Ste. Marie and 49th (SSM) Field Regiment, RCA Historical Society, Sault Ste. Marie, ON, Canada [*Library symbol Library of Congress*] (LCLS) ... CaOStMH
Sault Ste. Marie Carnegie Public Library, Sault Ste. Marie, MI [*Library symbol Library of Congress*] (LCLS) ... MiSs
Sault Ste. Marie, MI [*FM radio station call letters*] ... WCMZ
Sault Ste. Marie, MI [*Television station call letters*] ... WGTQ
Sault Ste. Marie, MI [*AM radio station call letters*] ... WKNW
Sault Ste. Marie, MI [*FM radio station call letters*] ... WLSO
Sault Ste. Marie, MI [*AM radio station call letters*] ... WSOO
Sault Ste. Marie, MI [*FM radio station call letters*] ... WSUE
Sault Ste. Marie, MI [*Television station call letters*] ... WWUP
Sault Ste. Marie, MI [*FM radio station call letters*] ... WYSS
Sault Ste. Marie, ON [*FM radio station call letters*] ... CHAS
Sault Ste. Marie, ON [*Television station call letters*] ... CHBX
Sault Ste. Marie, ON [*Television station call letters*] ... CICO-20
Sault Ste. Marie, ON [*Television station call letters*] ... CJIC
Sault Ste. Marie, ON [*FM radio station call letters*] ... CJQM
Sault Ste. Marie, ON [*ICAO location identifier*] (ICLI) ... CYAM
Sault Ste. Marie Public Library, Ontario [*Library symbol National Library of Canada*] (NLC) ... OSTM
Sault Ste. Marie Public Library, Sault Ste. Marie, ON, Canada [*Library symbol Library of Congress*] (LCLS) ... CaOStM
Sault Ste. Marie/Sault Ste. Marie Municipal [*Michigan*] [*ICAO location identifier*] (ICLI) ... KSSM
Sault Sainte Marie Air Defense Sector (SAA) ... SMADS
Saumlaki [*Indonesia*] [*ICAO location identifier*] (ICLI) ... WAPI
Saumur/Saint-Florent [*France ICAO location identifier*] (ICLI) ... LFOD
Sauna Society of America (EA) ... SSA
Sauna - Swimming Pool - Storage Area [*Key fitting those locks in apartment complex*] ... SSS
Saunders Aircraft Corp. Ltd. [*Canada ICAO aircraft manufacturer identifier*] (ICAO) ... SA
Saunders and Austin's Locus Standi Reports [*1895-1904*] [*A publication*] (DLA) ... S & A
Saunders and Austin's Locus Standi Reports [*1895-1904*] [*A publication*] (DLA) ... Saund & A
Saunders and Austin's Locus Standi Reports [*A publication*] (DLA) ... Saund & Aust
Saunders and Bidder's Locus Standi Reports [*1905-19*] [*A publication*] (DLA) ... S & B
Saunders and Bidder's Locus Standi Reports [*England*] [*A publication*] (DLA) ... Saund & B
Saunders and Cole's English Bail Court Reports [*1846-48*] [*A publication*] (DLA) ... Bail Ct Rep
Saunders and Cole's English Bail Court Reports [*A publication*] (DLA) ... S & C
Saunders and Cole's English Bail Court Reports [*1846-48*] [*A publication*] (DLA) ... Saund & BC
Saunders and Cole's English Bail Court Reports [*1846-48*] [*A publication*] (DLA) ... Saund & C
Saunders and Cole's English Bail Court Reports [*82 RR*] [*1846-48*] [*A publication*] (DLA) ... Saund BC
Saunders and Macrae's English County Court Cases [*A publication*] (DLA) ... Saund & Mac
Saunders and Macrae's English County Courts and Insolvency Cases [*County Courts Cases and Appeals, II-III*] [*A publication*] (DLA) ... Saund & M
Saunders' King's Bench Reports [*1666-73*] [*A publication*] (DLA) ... Saund
Saunders' Magistrates' Courts Practice [*6th ed.*] [*1902*] [*A publication*] (DLA) ... Saund Mag Pr
Saunders' Militia Law [*4th ed.*] [*1855*] [*A publication*] (DLA) ... Saund Mil L
Saunders' Municipal Registration [*2nd ed.*] [*1873*] [*A publication*] (DLA) ... Saund Mun Reg
Saunders on Affiliation and Bastardy [*11th ed.*] [*1915*] [*A publication*] (DLA) ... Saund Bast
Saunders on Assault and Battery [*1842*] [*A publication*] (DLA) ... Saund Ass
Saunders on Negligence [*2nd ed.*] [*1878*] [*A publication*] (DLA) ... Saund Neg
Saunders on Warranties and Representations [*1874*] [*A publication*] (DLA) ... Saund War
Saunders' Pleading and Evidence [*A publication*] (DLA) ... Saund Pl & Ev
Saunders' Precedents of Indictments [*3rd ed.*] [*1904*] [*A publication*] (DLA) ... Saund Prec
Saurastra Law Reports [*India*] [*A publication*] (DLA) ... Sau LR
Saurimo [*Angola*] [*ICAO location identifier*] (ICLI) ... FNSA
Saurimo [*Angola*] [*Airport symbol*] (OAG) ... VHC
Sausage (DSUE) ... SAUS
Sausage Aerial [*Radio*] ... SA
Sausage and Meat Pie Manufacturers Association [*British*] (BI) ... SMPMA
Sausages, Potatoes, and Onions [*Meaning a cheap restaurant that specializes in these*] [*British slang*] ... SPO
Sausalito, CA [*Location identifier FAA*] (FAAL) ... JMC
Sausalito, CA [*Location identifier FAA*] (FAAL) ... SAU
Sausalito Free Public Library, Sausalito, CA [*Library symbol Library of Congress*] (LCLS) ... CSau
Sausse and Scully's Irish Rolls Court Reports [*1837-40*] [*A publication*] (DLA) ... S & S
Sausse and Scully's Irish Rolls Court Reports [*A publication*] (DLA) ... S & Sc
Sausse and Scully's Irish Rolls Court Reports [*1837-40*] [*A publication*] (DLA) ... Sau & Sc
Sausse and Scully's Irish Rolls Court Reports [*1837-40*] [*A publication*] (DLA) ... Sausse & Sc
Sauter Mean Diameter (KSC) ... SMD
Sauter Mean Droplet [*Diesel engine fuel injection*] ... SMD
Sauvagine [*A polypeptide*] ... SVG
Savage Information Services (IID) ... SIS
Savage's Cognitive Impairment Model ... SCIM
Savanair (Angola) Lda. [*FAA designator*] (FAAC) ... SVN
Savanna Army Depot [*Illinois*] (AABC) ... SVAD
Savanna Army Depot Activity (AABC) ... SVADA
Savanna Community Library, Silver Valley, Alberta [*Library symbol National Library of Canada*] (NLC) ... ASSC
Savanna Depot Activity [*Army*] ... SVDA
Savanna, IL [*Location identifier FAA*] (FAAL) ... SFY
Savanna, IL [*FM radio station call letters*] ... WCCI
Savanna Municipal Library, Silver Valley, AB, Canada [*Library symbol*] [*Library of Congress*] (LCLS) ... CaASvSC
Savanna Pastoral Neolithic [*Archeology*] ... SPN
Savanna Zone Soil [*Agriculture*] ... S
Savannah [*Tasmania*] [*Seismograph station code, US Geological Survey*] (SEIS) ... SAV
Savannah [*Georgia*] [*Airport symbol*] (OAG) ... SAV
Savannah & Atlanta Railway Co. [*AAR code*] ... SA
Savannah Area Vocational/Technical School, Savannah, GA [*Library symbol*] [*Library of Congress*] (LCLS) ... GSV
Savannah Bancorp [*NASDAQ symbol*] (TTSB) ... SAVB
Savannah Bancorp, Inc. [*NASDAQ symbol*] (SAG) ... SAVB
Savannah Bancorp, Inc. [*Associated Press*] (SAG) ... SavBcp
Savannah Bank of Nigeria ... SB
Savannah College of Art and Design [*Georgia*] ... SCAD
Savannah El & Pwr 6.64% Pfd [*NYSE symbol*] (TTSB) ... SAVPrB
Savannah Electric & Power Co. [*NYSE symbol*] (SPSG) ... SAV
Savannah Electric & Power Co. [*Associated Press*] (SAG) ... SavnEl
Savannah Foods & Ind [*NYSE symbol*] (TTSB) ... SFI
Savannah Foods & Industries, Inc. [*Associated Press*] (SAG) ... SavnFd
Savannah Foods & Industries, Inc. [*NYSE symbol*] (SPSG) ... SFI
Savannah, GA [*Location identifier FAA*] (FAAL) ... SVN
Savannah, GA [*FM radio station call letters*] ... WAEV
Savannah, GA [*AM radio station call letters*] ... WBMQ
Savannah, GA [*AM radio station call letters*] ... WCHY
Savannah, GA [*FM radio station call letters*] ... WCHY-FM
Savannah, GA [*AM radio station call letters*] ... WEAS
Savannah, GA [*FM radio station call letters*] ... WEAS-FM
Savannah, GA [*FM radio station call letters*] ... WHCJ
Savannah, GA [*FM radio station call letters*] ... WIXV
Savannah, GA [*AM radio station call letters*] ... WIZA
Savannah, GA [*FM radio station call letters*] ... WJCL
Savannah, GA [*Television station call letters*] ... WJCL-TV
Savannah, GA [*Television station call letters*] ... WSAV
Savannah, GA [*AM radio station call letters*] ... WSGA
Savannah, GA [*AM radio station call letters*] ... WSOK
Savannah, GA [*FM radio station call letters*] ... WSVH
Savannah, GA [*Television station call letters*] ... WTOC
Savannah, GA [*Television station call letters*] ... WVAN
Savannah, GA [*FM radio station call letters*] ... WYFS
Savannah, GA [*FM radio station call letters*] ... WZAT
Savannah, MO [*FM radio station call letters*] ... KSJQ
Savannah/Municipal [*Georgia*] [*ICAO location identifier*] (ICLI) ... KSAV
Savannah Public and Chatham-Effingham-Liberty Regional Library, Savannah, GA [*Library symbol Library of Congress*] (LCLS) ... GS
Savannah River Ecology Laboratory [*Department of Energy*] [*Aiken, SC*] ... SREL
Savannah River Laboratory [*Department of Energy*] [*Aiken, SC*] ... SRL
Savannah River Operation [*Office*] [*Energy Research and Development Administration*] ... SRO
Savannah River Operations Office (DOGT) ... SR
Savannah River Plant [*Department of Energy*] ... SRP
Savannah River Plant - Well DRB-10 [*South Carolina*] [*Seismograph station code, US Geological Survey*] (SEIS) ... SRPW
Savannah River Site (DOGT) ... SRS
Savannah River Site ... SRS
Savannah River Site [*Department of Energy*] [*Aiken, SC*] (GAAI) ... SRS
Savannah River Test Pile [*Nuclear energy*] (NRCH) ... SR
Savannah State College [*Georgia*] ... SSC
Savannah State College, Savannah, GA [*Library symbol Library of Congress*] (LCLS) ... GSSC
Savannah State Docks Railroad Co. [*AAR code*] ... SSDK
Savannah, TN [*Location identifier FAA*] (FAAL) ... HHY
Savannah, TN [*Location identifier FAA*] (FAAL) ... SNH
Savannah, TN [*FM radio station call letters*] ... WKWX
Savannah, TN [*AM radio station call letters*] ... WORM

Savannah, TN [*FM radio station call letters*] ... WORM-FM
Savannakhet [*Laos*] [*ICAO location identifier*] (ICLI) ... VLSK
Savannakhet [*Laos*] [*Airport symbol*] (AD) ... ZVK
Savant Lake Community Library, Ontario [*Library symbol National Library of Canada*] (NLC) ... OSALC
Savant Lake, ON [*FM radio station call letters*] ... CBQL
Save [*Benin*] [*ICAO location identifier*] (ICLI) ... DBBS
Save [*Computer science*] [*Telecommunications*] ... s
Save [*Benin*] [*Airport symbol*] (OAG) ... SVF
Save a Baby [*Later, LGM*] (EA) ... SB
Save a Cat League (EA) ... SCL
Save Address Register (IAA) ... SAR
Save America's Forests [*An association*] (EA) ... SAF
Save & Prosper [*Financial services group*] [*British*] ... S & P
Save Animals from Extinction [*Later, WPTI*] [*An association*] ... SAFE
Save Area Table [*Computer science*] (IBMDP) ... SAVT
Save as You Earn [*National Savings Plan*] [*British*] ... SAYE
Save British Science [*An association*] (AIE) ... SBS
Save British Science Society (DBA) ... SBS
Save Cash, Reduce Immediately Meat Prices [*Boston, MA, group protesting high cost of food, 1973*] ... SCRIMP
Save Data (IAA) ... SAVDAT
Save EPA [*Environmental Protection Agency*] **Working Group** (EA) ... SEPAWG
Save, Help Animals Man Exploits [*Connecticut organization*] ... SHAME
Save It [*Energy-saving campaign*] [*British*] ... SI
Save Lebanon (EA) ... SL
Save Life on Earth (EA) ... SLOE
Save Me, Oh God ... SMOG
Save Our American Resources [*Boy Scout project*] ... SOAR
Save Our Barns Committee (EA) ... SOBC
Save Our Constitution [*An association*] (EA) ... SOC
Save Our Schools (EA) ... SOS
Save Our Security (EA) ... SOS
Save Our Ship [*or Souls*] [*Popular explanation of Morse code letters used as a signal for extreme distress*] ... SOS
Save Our Shires [*British*] [*An association*] (DBA) ... SOS
Save Our Shores (EA) ... SOS
Save Our Snails [*An association*] ... SOS
Save Our Sons [*Cancer information service*] [*British*] ... SOS
Save Our Souls ... SOS
Save Our Strays (EA) ... SOS
Save Outdoor Sculpture [*Database producer*] (IID) ... SOS
Save Pound Animals from Research Experiments (EA) ... SPARE
Save the Battlefield Coalition (EA) ... SBC
Save the Bush Project [*Commonwealth*] (EERA) ... STB
Save the Children Alliance [*Gentofte, Denmark*] (EAIO) ... SCA
Save the Children Federation (EA) ... SCF
Save the Children Fund [*British*] (EAIO) ... SCF
Save the Children, Westport, CT [*Library symbol Library of Congress*] (LCLS) ... CtWepSC
Save the Flags of Fort Sumter [*Defunct*] (EA) ... SFFS
Save the Manatee Club (EA) ... SMC
Save the Manatee Club (EA) ... STM
Save the Oppressed People Committee [*Defunct*] (EA) ... STOP
Save the Strippers Wells (EA) ... SSW
Save the Tallgrass Prairie [*An association*] (EA) ... STP
Save the Theaters [*Defunct*] (EA) ... ST
Save the Theatres (EA) ... STT
Save the Whales (EA) ... STW
Save Uganda Movement ... SUM
Save Us from Formaldehyde Environmental Repercussions [*Later, CURE FormaldehydePoisoning Association*] (EA) ... SUFFER
Save Your Afterdeck [*Bowdlerized version*] ... SYA
Saved Registers Stack (ECII) ... SRS
Saveloy (DSUE) ... SAV
Saverne-Steinbourg [*France ICAO location identifier*] (ICLI) ... LFQY
Saves [*Baseball*] ... SV
Save-the-Redwoods League (EA) ... SRL
Savez Jevrejskih Opstina Jugoslavije (BJA) ... SJOJ
Savez Komunista - Pokret za Jugoslaviju [*League of Communists - Movement for Yugoslavia*] [*Political party*] ... SK-PJ
Savez Sindikata Jugoslavije [*Yugoslavia Federation of Trade Unions*] ... SSJ
Savez Socialisticke Omladine Jugoslavije [*League of Socialist Youth of Yugoslavia*] [*Political party*] (PPE) ... SSOJ
Savezna Komisija za Standardizacija [*Federal Commission for Standardization*] [*Yugoslavia*] ... SKS
Savigny on Possessions [*6th ed.*] [*1848*] [*A publication*] (DLA) ... Sav Pos
Savigny's Conflict of Laws [*2nd ed.*] [*1880*] [*A publication*] (DLA) ... Sav Conf Law
Savigny's History of the Roman Law [*A publication*] (DLA) ... Savigny Hist Rom Law
Savile's English Common Pleas Reports [*A publication*] (DLA) ... Sav
Savile's English Common Pleas Reports [*123 English Reprint*] [*1580-94*] [*A publication*] (DLA) ... Savile
Saville Advanced Remote Keying (MCD) ... SARK
Saville Systems [*Associated Press*] (SAG) ... Saville
Saville Systems [*NASDAQ symbol*] (SAG) ... SAVLY
Saville Systems ADS [*NASDAQ symbol*] (TTSB) ... SAVLY
Saving (WDAA) ... SVG
Saving and Preserving Arts and Cultural Environments (EA) ... SPACES
Savings [*Economics*] ... S
Savings (DLA) ... Sav
Savings ... SVGS
Savings ... SVNGS
Savings Account ... SA
Savings and Loan [*Association*] ... S & L
Savings and Loan (IAA) ... SAL
Savings and Loan (DFIT) ... S&L
Savings and Loan Foundation [*Later, FSI*] (EA) ... SLF
Savings and Retirement Plan ... SRP
Savings Association Insurance Fund [*Functions transferred from FSLIC, 1989*] [*Pronounced "safe"*] ... SAIF
Savings Associations Political Education Committee ... SAPEC
Savings Bank ... SB
Savings Bank Life Insurance ... SBLI
Savings Bank of the Finger Lakes FSB [*Associated Press*] (SAG) ... SB FingL
Savings Bank of the Finger Lakes FSB [*NASDAQ symbol*] (SAG) ... SBFL
Savings Bk of Finger Lakes [*NASDAQ symbol*] (TTSB) ... SBFL
Savings Bond [*Treasury Department security*] ... SB
Savings Bond Division [*Navy*] ... SBD
Savings Comparative Analysis [*Federal Home Loan Bank Board*] [*Database*] ... SCAN
Savings Deposit System [*Military*] (DNAB) ... SAV-DEP-SYS
Savings Depot [*Military*] (DNAB) ... SAVDEP
Savings Incentive Match Plan for Employees [*Business term*] ... SIMPLE
Savings Institutions Marketing Society of America ... SIMSA
Savings Transfer [*Banking*] ... SV
Savings Unit ... SU
Savio Club International [*Defunct*] (EA) ... SCI
Savio Club National Office (EA) ... SCNO
Savior ... SAV
Savonius Rotor Current Meter ... SRCM
Savonlinna [*Finland ICAO location identifier*] (ICLI) ... EFSA
Savonlinna [*Finland*] [*Airport symbol*] (OAG) ... SVL
Savoonga [*Alaska*] [*Airport symbol*] (OAG) ... SVA
Savoonga, AK [*Location identifier FAA*] (FAAL) ... SGA
Savoonga, AK [*Location identifier FAA*] (FAAL) ... ULL
Savoy Pictures Entertainment [*NASDAQ symbol*] (TTSB) ... SPEI
Savoy Pictures Entertainment, Inc. [*Associated Press*] (SAG) ... Savoy
Savoy Pictures Entertainment, Inc. [*NASDAQ symbol*] (SAG) ... SPEI
Savusavu [*Fiji*] [*ICAO location identifier*] (ICLI) ... NFNS
Savusavu [*Fiji*] [*Airport symbol*] (OAG) ... SVU
Savuti [*Botswana*] [*ICAO location identifier*] (ICLI) ... FBSV
Saw [*Myanmar*] [*ICAO location identifier*] (ICLI) ... VBSA
Saw Arbor [*Tool*] ... SAAR
Saw Diamond Abrasive (PDAA) ... SDA
Saw Fixture [*Tool*] (AAG) ... SAFX
Saw Fixture (MCD) ... SF
Saw Grinders' Trade Protective Society [*A union*] [*British*] ... SGTPS
Saw Jig [*Tool*] ... SAJI
Saw Machine Fixture (MCD) ... SMF
Saw Manufacturers' Association [*British*] (BI) ... SMA
Saw Mill Elementary School, North Bellmore, NY [*Library symbol Library of Congress*] (LCLS) ... NNbeSME
Saw Mill Junior High School, Commack, NY [*Library symbol*] [*Library of Congress*] (LCLS) ... NCoSJ
Sawako Corp. [*Associated Press*] (SAG) ... SawakoC
Sawako Corp. [*NASDAQ symbol*] (SAG) ... SWKO
Sawako Corp. ADR [*NASDAQ symbol*] (TTSB) ... SWKOY
Sawdust (VRA) ... sawdu
Sawin Society [*Defunct*] (EA) ... SS
Sawmakers' Association [*A union*] [*British*] ... SA
Sawmill [*Alaska*] [*Seismograph station code, US Geological Survey*] (SEIS) ... SML
Sawmill [*California*] [*Seismograph station code, US Geological Survey Closed*] (SEIS) ... SWM
Sawtek Inc. [*NASDAQ symbol*] (TTSB) ... SAWS
Sawtooth [*Architecture*] ... ST
Sawtooth Elementary School, Grand Marais, MN [*Library symbol*] [*Library of Congress*] (LCLS) ... MnGmSE
Sawtooth Generator ... SG
Sawtooth National Recreation Area [*Idaho*] ... SNRA
Sawtooth Timing Oscillator (DEN) ... STTO
Sawu [*Indonesia*] [*Airport symbol*] (OAG) ... SAU
Sawyer Brown Fan Club (EA) ... SBFC
Sawyer, Finn & Thatcher [*Advertising agency*] ... SF & T
Sawyer Rifle ... SR
Sawyers' General Representative Union [*British*] ... SGRU
Sawyer's United States Circuit Court Reports [*A publication*] (DLA) ... Saw
Sawyer's United States Circuit Court Reports [*A publication*] (DLA) ... Sawy
Sawyer's United States Circuit Court Reports [*A publication*] (DLA) ... Sawyer Circt
Sawyer's United States Circuit Court Reports [*A publication*] (DLA) ... Sawyer US Ct Rep
Saxa Vord [*British ICAO location identifier*] (ICLI) ... EGQR
Saxifrage Publications Group (EA) ... SPG
Saxitoxin [*A neurotoxin*] ... STX
Saxon ... S
Saxon ... SAX
Saxon Owners Registry (EA) ... SOR
Saxony ... Sax
Saxophone [*Music*] ... SAX
Saxophone (ODBW) ... sax
Saxton Industries [*Vancouver Stock Exchange symbol*] ... STI
Saxton Nuclear Engineering Corp. ... SNEC
Saxton's New Jersey Chancery Reports [*A publication*] (DLA) ... Sax
Saxton's New Jersey Chancery Reports [*A publication*] (DLA) ... Saxt
Saxton's New Jersey Chancery Reports [*A publication*] (DLA) ... Saxt Ch
Say Time Able [*Aviation*] (FAAC) ... SAYTA
Sayaboury [*Laos*] [*ICAO location identifier*] (ICLI) ... VLSB
Sayaboury [*Laos*] [*Airport symbol*] (AD) ... ZBY
Sayakhat [*Kazakhstan*] [*ICAO designator*] (FAAC) ... SAH

Saybolt Furol Seconds [*Oil viscosity*] .... SFs
Saybolt Furol Viscosity (BARN) .... SFV
Saybolt Second (IAA) .... S
Saybolt Seconds Furol [*Oil viscosity*] .... SSF
Saybolt Seconds Universal [*Oil viscosity*] .... SSU
Saybolt Universal Seconds [*Oil viscosity*] .... SUS
Saybolt Universal Viscosity (IAA) .... SUV
Sayer Head Sling [*Medicine*] .... SHS
Sayer's English King's Bench Reports [*96 English Reprint*] [*A publication*] (DLA) .... Say
Sayer's English King's Bench Reports [*96 English Reprint*] [*1751-56*] [*A publication*] (DLA) .... Sayer
Sayer's English King's Bench Reports [*96 English Reprint*] [*A publication*] (DLA) .... Sayer (Eng)
Sayett Group [*NASDAQ symbol*] (SAG) .... SAYT
Sayett Group, Inc. [*Associated Press*] (SAG) .... Sayett
Sayles' Annotated Civil Statutes [*Texas*] [*A publication*] (DLA) .... Sayles' Ann Civ St
Sayles' Revised Civil Statutes [*Texas*] [*A publication*] (DLA) .... Sayles' Civ St
Sayles' Revised Civil Statutes [*Texas*] [*A publication*] (DLA) .... Sayles' Rev Civ St
Sayles' Revised Civil Statutes [*Texas*] [*A publication*] (DLA) .... Sayles' St
Saynor Varah, Inc. [*Toronto Stock Exchange symbol*] .... SYV
Sayre Junior College [*Oklahoma*] .... SJC
Sayre, OK [*Location identifier FAA*] (FAAL) .... SYO
Sayre, PA [*AM radio station call letters*] .... WATS
Sayre's Cases on Admiralty [*A publication*] (DLA) .... Sayre Adm Cas
Sayun [*People's Democratic Republic of Yemen*] [*ICAO location identifier*] (ICLI) .... ODSY
Sayville Library, Sayville, NY [*Library symbol Library of Congress*] (LCLS) .... NSay
Sazemane Attalat Va Anmiyate Keshvar [*Iranian security and intelligence organization*] .... SAVAK
S-Band (KSC) .... SB
S-Band (NASA) .... S-BD
S-Band Acquisition Antenna [*Deep Space Instrumentation Facility, NASA*] ..... SAA
S-Band Antenna Switch (MCD) .... SBAS
S-Band Cassegrain Diplexer .... SCD
S-Band Cassegrain Monopulse .... SCM
S-Band Cassegrain Transmit .... SCT
S-Band Cassegrain Ultra .... SCU
S-Band Composite Feed .... SCF
S-Band Composite Feed System .... SCFS
S-Band Exciter [*System*] [*Also, SBES*] .... SBE
S-Band Exciter System [*Also, SBE*] .... SBES
S-Band Feed System .... SFS
S-Band Frequency Converter .... SFC
S-Band High Presicion Short Range Navigation (IAA) .... SHIRAN
S-Band High-Accuracy Ranging and Navigation .... SHIRAN
S-Band Megawatt Transmit .... SMT
S-Band Multifrequency .... SMF
S-Band Planetary RADAR .... SPR
S-Band Polar Ultra .... SPU
S-Band Polarization Diversity .... SPD
S-Band Power Amplifier .... SPA
S-Band RADAR Operational .... SRO
S-Band Radio Transmitter .... SRT
S-Band Receiver Filter .... SRF
S-Band Shuttle (SSD) .... SSH
S-Band Shuttle Forward (SSD) .... SSF
S-Band Shuttle Return (SSD) .... SSR
S-Band Simulator (SSD) .... S-SIM
S-Band Single Access (MCD) .... SSA
S-Band, Single Access Forward (SSD) .... SSAF
S-Band, Single Access Return (SSD) .... SSAR
S-Band Spread Spectrum Transponder (MCD) .... SSST
S-Band Telemetry Modification Kit (SAA) .... SBTM
S-Band Temperature Fahrenheit .... STF
S-Band Test Antenna .... STA
S-Band Tracking Processor System .... STPS
S-Band Transmit Filter .... STF
S-Band Transmitter System .... STS
S-Band Transponder .... SBX
S-Band Transponder Test Set (MCD) .... STTS
Sbarro, Inc. [*NYSE symbol*] (SAG) .... SBA
Sbarro, Inc. [*Associated Press*] (SAG) .... Sbarro
SBC [*Swiss Bank Corp.*] Australia .... SBCA
SBC Communications [*NYSE symbol*] (TTSB) .... SBC
SBC Communications, Inc. [*NYSE symbol*] (SAG) .... SBC
SBC Communications, Inc. [*Associated Press*] (SAG) .... SBC Com
SBE, Inc. [*Associated Press*] (SAG) .... SBE
SBE, Inc. [*NASDAQ symbol*] (NQ) .... SBEI
SBM Industries [*Formerly, Speed-O-Print Business Machines Corp.*] [*AMEX symbol*] (SPSG) .... SBM
SBM Industries [*Associated Press*] (SAG) .... SBM Ind
Sbornik Muzeia Antropologii i Etnografii [*A publication*] (BJA) .... SMAE
SBS Engineering, Inc. [*NASDAQ symbol*] (SAG) .... SBSE
SBS Technologies [*NASDAQ symbol*] (TTSB) .... SBSE
SBS Technologies, Inc. [*Associated Press*] (SAG) .... SBS Tech
SBS Technologies, Inc. [*NASDAQ symbol*] (SAG) .... SBSE
SC Bancorp [*Associated Press*] (SAG) .... SC Bcp
SC Bancorp [*AMEX symbol*] (SPSG) .... SCK
SC/EFC [*Spoiler Control/Elevator Feel Computer*] Control Panel (MCD) .... SC/EFC CP
SCA Chemical Services, Inc., Buffalo, NY [*Library symbol Library of Congress*] (LCLS) .... NBuSCA
Scaccaria [*Exchequer*] [*Latin*] (DLA) .... Sc
Scaccaria Curia [*Court of Exchequer*] [*Latin*] (DLA) .... Scac

Scaenicorum Romanorum Fragmenta [*A publication*] (OCD) .... Scaen Rom Frag
Scaffold Attachment Region [*Genetics*] .... SAR
Scaffold Industry Association (EA) .... SIA
Scaffolding and Shoring Institute [*Later, SSFI*] (EA) .... SSI
Scaffolding, Shoring, and Forming Institute (EA) .... SSFI
Scala [*Record label*] .... Sca
Scalable Architecture for Large Enterprises [*Computer software*] [*Symantec Corp.*] (PCM) .... SCALE
Scalable, Language-Independent, Ames Laboratory, One-Minute Measurement [*Computer technology*] .... SLALOM
Scalable Parallel Processor [*Computer science*] (CDE) .... SPP
Scalable Processing [*Northgate*] [*Computer science*] .... SP
Scalable Processing Architecture [*Computer hardware*] [*Northgate*] (PCM) .... SPA
Scalar [*Mathematics*] (ROG) .... S
Scalar Processor Architecture Reduced-Instruction-Set Computer (DOM) .... SPARC
Scalar Totalizer .... ST
Scalar Wave Equation .... SWE
Scalded Skin Syndrome [*Medicine*] (MAE) .... SSS
Scale .... SC
Scale (IDOE) .... sc
Scale (ECII) .... SCI
Scale .... SCL
Scale Factor .... SF
Scale Factor Error (KSC) .... SFE
Scale Factor Temperature Sensitivity .... SFTS
Scale for the Assessment of Negative Symptoms [*Medicine*] (DMAA) .... SANS
Scale for the Identification of School Phobia [*Test*] .... SIS
Scale Leaf [*Botany*] .... sl
Scale Manufacturers Association (EA) .... SMA
Scale Model .... SCMOD
Scale Model Engineering [*Initialism is brand name of tone arm*] .... SME
Scale of Beliefs in Extraordinary Phenomena [*Research test*] [*Psychology*] .... SOBEP
Scale of Institutional Differentiation (AEBS) .... SID
Scale of Socio-Egocentrism [*Psychology*] .... SSE
Scale of Teacher Attitudes toward Selective Behavior of Boy Pupils [*Satirical*] .... STATSBOBP
Scale plus Index plus Base .... SIB
Scaleable Coherent Interface [*Computer science*] .... SCI
Scaleable Processor Architecture [*Computer science*] .... SPARC
Scaled Depth of Burst (MCD) .... SDOB
Scaled Median Absolute Deviation [*Mathematics*] .... SMAD
Scaled Range Target System (MCD) .... SRTS
Scaled Skin Syndrome [*Dermatology*] (DAVI) .... SSS
Scaled Weapons Radius Squared (SAA) SWR2
Scaled-Particle Theory .... SPT
Scalene Node Biopsy [*Medicine*] .... SNB
Scales for Rating the Behavioral Characteristics of Superior Students [*Educational test*] .... SRBCSS
Scales of Attitudes toward Disabled Persons [*Occupational therapy*] .... SADP
Scales of Creativity and Learning Environment [*Educational test*] .... SCALE
Scales of Independent Behavior [*Occupational therapy*] .... SIB
Scale-up and Post Approval Changes [*FDA*] .... SUPAC
Scale-Up and Post Approval Changes [*Food and Drug Administration*] ...... SUPAC
Scaling Amplifier .... SA
Scaling and Display (NASA) .... SD
Scaling and Display Task (NASA) .... SDT
Scaling Erythema and Thickness [*Dermatology*] .... SET
Scalloped Tinned [*Configuration*] (MCD) .... ST
Scalp Vein [*Medicine*] .... SV
Scammon Bay [*Alaska*] [*Airport symbol*] (OAG) .... SCM
Scammon Bay, AK [*Location identifier FAA*] (FAAL) .... SCM
Scammon's Reports [*2-5 Illinois*] [*A publication*] (DLA) .... Sc
Scammon's Reports [*2-5 Illinois*] [*A publication*] (DLA) .... Scam
Scampton [*British ICAO location identifier*] (ICLI) .... EGXP
Scampton BAE [*British ICAO designator*] (FAAC) .... BBN
Scampton FTU [*British ICAO designator*] (FAAC) .... SAP
Scan (IAA) .... SCN
Scan Coherent Doppler Attachment .... SCODA
Scan Control Register (NITA) .... SCR
Scan Control Unit (IAA) .... SCU
Scan Conversion and Bright Display .... SCBD
Scan Conversion Equipment [*Television*] .... SCE
Scan Conversion Object Description Language [*Computer science*] (PCM) .... SCODL
Scan Conversion Tube .... SCT
Scan Converter and Display [*Systems*] .... SCAD
Scan Converter Display System (MCD) .... SCDS
Scan Converter Storage Tube .... SCST
Scan Converter [*or Counter*] System .... SCS
Scan Converter Yoke .... SCY
Scan Converting Video Tape Recorder (MCD) .... SCVTR
Scan Data (IAA) .... SD
Scan Data Out (IAA) .... SDO
Scan Display Generator .... SDG
Scan Gate Number .... SGN
Scan Graphics [*NASDAQ symbol*] (TTSB) .... SCNG
Scan on Receive Only (MCD) .... SORO
Scan Pattern Generator .... SPG
Scan Platform Inertial Thermal Simulator .... SPITS
Scan Platform Operations Program .... SPOP
Scan Programmer (DGA) .... SP
Scan Radius .... SR
Scan Rate .... SR

Scan Ratio (MCD) ..... SR
Scan True Bearing (NVT) ..... STB
SCANA Corp. [*Associated Press*] (SAG) ..... SCANA
SCANA Corp. [*NYSE symbol*] (SPSG) ..... SCG
Scanada Consultants Ltd., Ottawa, Ontario [*Library symbol National Library of Canada*] (NLC) ..... OOSCAC
Scanair Ltd. [*Denmark ICAO designator*] (FAAC) ..... VKG
Scancource Inc. Wrrt [*NASDAQ symbol*] (TTSB) ..... SCSCW
Scandalum Magnatum [*Defamation of Dignity*] [*Latin*] (ROG) ..... SCAN MAG
Scandia Controllability and Observability Analysis Program (NITA) ..... SCOAP
Scandinavia [*MARC geographic area code Library of Congress*] (LCCP) ..... ev----
Scandinavia ..... SCAND
Scandinavia Co. [*Formerly, Scandinavia Fund, Inc.*] [*AMEX symbol*] (SPSG) ..... SCF
Scandinavia Fund [*Associated Press*] (SAG) ..... ScandC
Scandinavian ..... SC
Scandinavian ..... SCAN
Scandinavian Agricultural Research Workers' Association ..... NJF
Scandinavian Airlines System [*Sweden ICAO designator*] (FAAC) ..... SAS
Scandinavian Airlines System [*Sweden*] [*ICAO designator*] (OAG) ..... SK
Scandinavian American Fraternity (EA) ..... SAF
Scandinavian Association for Thoracic and Cardiovascular Surgery (EA) ..... SATCS
Scandinavian Association of Directory Publishers (EAIO) ..... SADP
Scandinavian Association of Obstetricians and Gynaecologists (EA) ..... SSOG
Scandinavian Association of Paediatric Surgeons (EAIO) ..... SAPS
Scandinavian Association of Plastic Surgeons [*See also NPF*] (EAIO) ..... SAPS
Scandinavian Association of Urology (EA) ..... SAU
Scandinavian Association of Zone-Therapeutists [*Denmark*] (EAIO) ..... SFFF
Scandinavian Aviation Center AS [*Denmark ICAO designator*] (FAAC) ..... MEO
Scandinavian Broadcast System ..... SBS
Scandinavian Broadcasting [*NASDAQ symbol*] (SAG) ..... SBTV
Scandinavian Broadcasting [*Commercial firm Associated Press*] (SAG) ..... ScndBdc
Scandinavian Broadcstg Sys [*NASDAQ symbol*] (TTSB) ..... SBTVF
Scandinavian Collectors Club (EA) ..... SCC
Scandinavian Committee for Satellite Communications [*Telecommunications*] (TEL) ..... STSK
Scandinavian Council for Applied Research ..... SCAR
Scandinavian Countries Broadcast Satellite (MCD) ..... NORDSAT
Scandinavian Delegation [*British*] ..... SD
Scandinavian Dental Fair [*Danish Dental Association*] ..... SCANDEFA
Scandinavian Documentation Center [*Washington, DC*] ..... SCANDOC
Scandinavian Endodontic Association [*Sweden*] (EAIO) ..... SEA
Scandinavian Fraternity of America (EA) ..... SFA
Scandinavian Glioma Study Group [*Medicine*] (DMAA) ..... SGSG
Scandinavian Herpetological Society [*Denmark*] (EAIO) ..... SHS
Scandinavian Institute of Asian Studies [*See also CINA*] [*Later, NIAS*] (EAIO) ..... SIAS
Scandinavian Lead Zinc Association [*Stockholm, Sweden*] (EAIO) ..... SLZA
Scandinavian Migraine Society (EA) ..... SMS
Scandinavian Network (NITA) ..... SCANNET
Scandinavian Neurosurgical Society (EA) ..... SNS
Scandinavian Ornithological Union [*Lund, Sweden*] (EAIO) ..... SOU
Scandinavian Orthopaedic Association (EA) ..... SOA
Scandinavian Periodicals Index in Economics and Business [*Helsinki School of Economics Library*] [*Information service or system*] ..... SCANP
Scandinavian Pulp, Paper and Board Testing Committee [*Sweden*] (EAIO) ..... SCAN-Test
Scandinavian Radiological Society (EA) ..... SRS
Scandinavian Seminar (EA) ..... SS
Scandinavian Simvastatin Survival Study [*Cardiology*] 4S
Scandinavian Society of Anaesthesiologists (EA) ..... SSA
Scandinavian Society of Forensic Odontology (EA) ..... SSFO
Scandinavia Society of Forest Economics (EAIO) ..... SSFE
Scandinavian Sociological Association (EA) ..... SSA
Scandinavian Studies in Criminology [*1965*] [*A publication*] (DLA) ..... Sc St Crim
Scandinavian Studies in Criminology [*1965*] [*A publication*] (DLA) ..... Sc Stud Criminol
Scandinavian Studies in Criminology [*A publication*] (DLA) ..... Scand Stud Criminol
Scandinavian Studies in Law [*A publication*] (DLA) ..... Sc St L
Scandinavian Surgical Society (EAIO) ..... SSS
Scandinavian Tire and Rim Organization (EA) ..... STRO
Scandinavian Tourist Boards (EA) ..... STB
Scandinavian Travel Commission [*Later, Scandinavian National Travel Offices*] (EA) ..... STC
Scandinavian Twin Auroral RADAR Experiment [*Ionospheric science*] ..... STARE
Scandinavian Union for Non-Alcoholic Traffic (EA) ..... SUNAT
Scandinavian Yachting Association [*See also SKAN SF*] (EAIO) ..... SYA
Scandinavian-American Genealogical Society (EA) ..... SAGS
Scandium [*Chemical element*] ..... Sc
SC&T Intl [*NASDAQ symbol*] (TTSB) ..... SCTI
SC&T Intl Wrrt [*NASDAQ symbol*] (TTSB) ..... SCTIW
Scanfile [*Database*] [*Australia*] ..... SCAN
Scanforms, Inc. [*Associated Press*] (SAG) ..... Scanfrm
Scanforms, Inc. [*NASDAQ symbol*] (NQ) ..... SCFM
Scan-Graphics, Inc. [*Associated Press*] (SAG) ..... ScanGr
Scan-Graphics, Inc. [*NASDAQ symbol*] (NQ) ..... SCNG
Scania AB [*Associated Press*] (SAG) ..... ScaniaA
Scania AB [*Associated Press*] (SAG) ..... ScaniaB
Scania AB [*NYSE symbol*] (SAG) ..... SCV
Scania AB'A'ADS [*NYSE symbol*] (TTSB) ..... SCV.A
Scania AB'B'ADS [*NYSE symbol*] (TTSB) ..... SCV.B
Scanjet AB [*Sweden ICAO designator*] (FAAC) ..... SCJ
Scanned Optically Addressed Light Modulators (IAA) ..... SOALM
Scanned Probe Microscopy ..... SPM
Scanned Topographic Electroencephalograph ..... STEEG
Scanned-LASER Photoluminescence Microscope (PDAA) ..... SLPM
Scanner (IAA) ..... SC
Scanner [*Computer science*] ..... SCN
Scanner (MSA) ..... SCNR
Scanner Association of North America (EA) ..... SCAN
Scanner Control Power (MCD) ..... SCP
Scanner Control Unit ..... SCU
Scanner Input Language ..... SIL
Scanner Keyed Input Language ..... SKIL
SCANNET Service Centre (NITA) ..... SSC
Scanning ..... S
Scanning (IAA) ..... SCAN
Scanning (MSA) ..... SCNG
Scanning Acoustic Microscope ..... SAM
Scanning Analog-to-Digital Input Equipment [*National Institute of Standards and Technology*] ..... SADIE
Scanning and Measuring Projector ..... SMP
Scanning Auger Electron Spectroscopy ..... SAES
Scanning Auger Microprobe (IAA) ..... SAM
Scanning Auger Microscopy ..... SAM
Scanning Automated X-Ray Analysis Spectrometer (DICI) ..... SAXAS
Scanning Beam Instrument Landing System (KSC) ..... SBILS
Scanning Celestial Attitude Determination System ..... SCADS
Scanning Chemical Potential Microscope ..... SCPM
Scanning Control Register ..... SCR
Scanning Densitometer [*Instrumentation*] ..... SD
Scanning Electro-Acoustic Microscopy (MCD) ..... SEAM
Scanning Electrochemical Microscope ..... SECM
Scanning Electrochemical Microscope-Induced Desorption ..... SECMID
Scanning Electron Beam Excited Charge Collection (IAA) ..... SEBECC
Scanning Electron Micrograph ..... SEMG
Scanning Electron Microscope [*or Microscopy*] ..... SEM
Scanning Electron Microscope (DOG) ..... SEM
Scanning Electron Microscope and Particle Analyzer ..... SEMPA
Scanning Electron Microscopy [*Later, SMI*] [*An association*] (EA) ..... SEM
Scanning Electron Microscopy with Polarization Analysis ..... SEMPA
Scanning Electron Mirror Microscope (IAA) ..... SEMM
Scanning Electrostatic Analysis (NASA) ..... SEA
Scanning Encoding [*Computer science*] (MHDI) ..... SEN
Scanning for Information Parameters ..... SCIP
Scanning Force Microscope ..... SFM
Scanning Force Mode [*Microscopy*] ..... SFM
Scanning Gate ..... SG
Scanning Image Spectrometer ..... SIS
Scanning Interferometric Apertureless Microscope ..... SIAM
Scanning Interferometric Apertureless Microscope ..... SLAM
Scanning Ion Microscope ..... SIM
Scanning Ion-Conductance Microscope ..... SICM
Scanning Kinetic Spectroscopy ..... SKS
Scanning LASER Acoustic Microscope ..... SLAM
Scanning LASER Altimeter (SSD) ..... SLA
Scanning LASER Doppler System [*NASA*] ..... SLDS
Scanning LASER Doppler Vortex System [*NASA*] ..... SLDVS
Scanning LASER Mass Spectrometry ..... SLMS
Scanning LASER Ophthalmoscope ..... SLO
Scanning Laser Rangefinder ..... SLR
Scanning LASER System ..... SLS
Scanning Light Intensity Device ..... SLID
Scanning Line of Sight (KSC) ..... SLOS
Scanning Local Oscillator (NG) ..... SCALO
Scanning Low-Energy Electron Probe (IEEE) ..... SLEEP
Scanning Microscope Photometer (OA) ..... SMP
Scanning Microscopy International (EA) ..... SMI
Scanning Microwave Spectrometer ..... SCAMS
Scanning Multichannel Microwave ..... SMM
Scanning Multichannel [*or Multifrequency or Multispectral*] **Microwave Radiometer** ..... SMMR
Scanning Near-Field Optical Microscope (ECON) ..... SNOM
Scanning Near-Fried Optical Microscope ..... SNOM
Scanning Ocean Bottom SONAR ..... SOBS
Scanning Optical Microscope ..... SOM
Scanning Optical Vibration Analysis System (IAA) ..... SOVAS
Scanning Oscillator Technique (IAA) ..... SOT
Scanning Phased Array ..... SCP
Scanning Photoacoustic Microscopy ..... SPAM
Scanning Photoemission Microscope ..... SPM
Scanning Probe Microscopy ..... SPM
Scanning Pulse Immobilization ..... SPI
Scanning Radar Altimeter [*Marine science*] (OSRA) ..... SRA
Scanning Radar Altimeter (USDC) ..... SRA
Scanning Radiometer ..... SR
Scanning Reference Electrode (MCD) ..... SRE
Scanning Reference Electrode [*Corrosion testing*] ..... SRET
Scanning Reflection Electron Microscopy ..... SREM
Scanning Slit (MCD) ..... SL
Scanning Slit ..... SS
Scanning SQUID [*SuperConducting Quantum Interference Device*] **Microscope** [*Physics*] ..... SSM
Scanning Synthetic Aperture RADAR ..... SCANSAR
Scanning Telescope (KSC) ..... SCT
Scanning Transmission Electron Microscope ..... STEM
Scanning Transmission Electron Microscopy ..... STEM
Scanning Transmission Electron Microscopy - Transmission Electron Microscopy ..... STEM-TEM
Scanning Transmission Ion Microscopy ..... STIM

Scanning Transmission X-Ray Microscopy (MCD) ... STXM
Scanning Tunneling Microscope ... STM
Scanning Tunneling Spectroscopy ... STS
Scanning with Compensation ... SWC
Scanning X-Ray Microscopy (MCD) ... SXM
Scan-Optics [*NASDAQ symbol*] (TTSB) ... SOCR
Scan-Optics, Inc. [*Associated Press*] (SAG) ... ScanOp
Scan-Optics, Inc. [*NASDAQ symbol*] (NQ) ... SOCR
Scan-Pol Ltd. [*Poland ICAO designator*] (FAAC) ... SPL
SCANS [*Scheduling and Control by Automated Network Systems*] **ImplementationPlan** (SAA) ... SIP
Scans per Hour [*Photocopying, Microfilming*] ... SPH
ScanSource, Inc. [*Associated Press*] (SAG) ... ScanSrce
ScanSource, Inc. [*NASDAQ symbol*] (SAG) ... SCSC
Scan-to-Scan Correlation ... SSC
ScanVec Co. [*NASDAQ symbol*] (TTSB) ... SVECF
ScanVec Co. Ltd. [*Associated Press*] (SAG) ... ScanVec
ScanVec Co. Ltd. [*NASDAQ symbol*] (SAG) ... SVECF
Scan-with-Composition (MCD) ... SWC
Scapholunate Advanced Collapse [*Wrist*] [*Medicine*] (DMAA) ... SLAC
Scaphotrapeziotrapezoid [*Joint*] [*Anatomy*] (DAVI) ... STT
Scapula ... SC
Scapula (DMAA) ... SCAP
Scapulodextra Anterior [*A fetal position*] (AAMN) ... ScDA
Scapulodextra Posterior [*A fetal position*] (AAMN) ... ScDP
SCAR Team Report Analysis Program (MCD) ... STRAP
Scarboro Foreign Missions (TOCD) ... sfm
Scarboro Foreign Missions (TOCD) ... SFM
Scarboro Resources Ltd. [*Toronto Stock Exchange symbol*] ... SRO
Scarborough [*Ontario*] [*Seismograph station code, US Geological Survey Closed*] (SEIS) ... SCB
Scarborough Board of Education [*UTLAS symbol*] ... SBS
Scarborough Board of Education [*Professional Education Library*] [*UTLAS symbol*] ... SED
Scarborough Borough Board of Education, Toronto, ON, Canada [*Library symbol Library of Congress*] (LCLS) ... CaOTSED
Scarborough Borough Board of Education, Toronto, Ontario [*Library symbol National Library of Canada*] (NLC) ... OTSED
Scarborough Campus, University of Toronto [*UTLAS symbol*] ... SCC
Scarborough College, Ontario [*Library symbol National Library of Canada*] (NLC) ... OTSCC
Scarborough College, Scarborough, ON, Canada [*Library symbol Library of Congress*] (LCLS) ... CaOTSCC
Scarborough/Crown Point, Tobago [*Trinidad and Tobago*] [*ICAO location identifier*] (ICLI) ... TTCP
Scarborough, ME [*FM radio station call letters*] ... WPKM
Scarborough Public Library [*UTLAS symbol*] ... SCA
Scarborough Public Library, Albert Campbell Branch, Scarborough, ON, Canada [*Library symbol Library of Congress*] (LCLS) ... CaOTSPA
Scarborough Public Library, Cedarbrae Branch, Scarborough, ON, Canada [*Library symbol Library of Congress*] (LCLS) ... CaOTSPC
Scarborough Public Library, Ontario [*Library symbol National Library of Canada*] (NLC) ... OTSP
Scarborough Public Library, Scarborough, ON, Canada [*Library symbol Library of Congress*] (LCLS) ... CaOTSP
S-Carboxymethylcysteine [*An amino acid*] ... SCMC
Scarce [*Numismatics*] ... S
Scarce [*Bookselling*] (ROG) ... SC
Scarf Trailers Science Fiction Social Club [*Defunct*] (EA) ... STSFSC
Scarlet [*Philately*] ... scar
Scarlet (ROG) ... SCL
Scarlet Energy, Inc. [*Vancouver Stock Exchange symbol*] ... SRT
Scarlet Fever [*Medicine*] ... SF
Scarritt College for Christian Workers [*Tennessee*] ... SCCW
Scarsdale Public Library, Scarsdale, NY [*Library symbol Library of Congress*] (LCLS) ... NSca
SCATS [*Simulation, Checkout, and Training System*] **Main Distributing Frame** ... SMDF
Scatsta [*British ICAO location identifier*] (ICLI) ... EGPM
Scatter Detection and Ranging ... SCADAR
Scatter Factor Hepatocyte Growth Factor [*Biochemistry*] ... SF/HGF
Scatter Propagation Antenna ... SPA
Scatterable Minefield Warning [*Army*] (ADDR) ... SCATMINWARIN
Scattered ... SCT
Scattered ... SCTD
Scattered Clouds or Better (SAA) ... SCOB
Scattered X-Ray Internal Standard [*for surface analysis*] ... SXIS
Scattered-to-Heavy Clouds [*Meteorology*] (DNAB) ... SC-HC
Scattering Coefficient [*Photometry*] ... S
Scattering Matrix Method [*Materials research*] ... SMM
Scattering Structural Contour Map [*Surface analysis*] ... SSCM
Scattering With Aperture Limited Projection Electron Lithography [*AT&T development*] ... SCALPEL
Scatterometer ... SCAT
Scatterometer (USDC) ... SCATT
Scatula [*Package*] [*Pharmacy*] ... SCAT
Scatula Originalis [*Original Package*] [*Pharmacy*] ... SCAT ORIG
Scavenge (AAG) ... SC
Scavenge (AAG) ... SCAV
Scavenging, Oil Pump (MSA) ... SOP
Scavenging-Precipitation-Ion Exchange (IEEE) ... SPIE
SCB Computer Technology [*NASDAQ symbol*] (TTSB) ... SCBI
SCB Computer Technology, Inc. [*Associated Press*] (SAG) ... SCBCmp
SCB Computer Technology, Inc. [*NASDAQ symbol*] (SAG) ... SCBI
SCB [*Statistika Centralbyran*] **Regional Statistical Data Base** [*Sweden Information service or system*] (CRD) ... RSDB
SCB [*Statistika Centralbyran*] **Time Series Data Base** [*Sweden Information service or system*] (CRD) ... TSDB
Sccom Sud-Ouest [*France ICAO location identifier*] (ICLI) ... LFWB
SCEcorp [*NYSE symbol*] (SAG) ... SCE
SCEcorp [*Formerly, Southern California Edison Co.*] [*Associated Press*] (SAG) ... SCEcp
Scellino [*Shilling*] [*Monetary unit*] [*Italian*] ... scel
Scenario Development Language [*Military*] (CAAL) ... SDL
Scenario Oriented Corps Area Training System (MCD) ... SOCATS
Scenario-Oriented Recurring Evaluation (PDAA) ... SCORE
Scenario-Oriented Recurring Evaluation System [*Military*] ... SCORES
Scene ... SC
Scene [*Script notation*] (WDMC) ... sc
Scene Balance Algorithm [*Color-correction look-up tables for Photo CDs*] (PCM) ... SBA
Scene Matching Area Correlator [*Navy*] (MCD) ... SMAC
Scene of Crime ... SOC
Scene per Second (MCD) ... SPS
Scene Storage System (MCD) ... SSS
Scene-of-Action Commander [*Navy*] (NVT) ... SAC
Scenes-of-the-Crime Officer [*Scotland Yard*] ... SOCO
Scenic Airlines [*ICAO designator*] (AD) ... YR
Scenic Airlines, Inc. [*ICAO designator*] (FAAC) ... YRR
Scenic America (EA) ... SA
Scenic Elementary School, Grand Junction, CO [*Library symbol Library of Congress*] (LCLS) ... CoGjSE
Scenic Hudson (EA) ... SHI
Scenic Hudson Preservation Conference [*Later, SHI*] (EA) ... SHPC
Scented Cape [*Tea trade*] (ROG) ... SC
Scented Orange Pekoe [*Tea trade*] (ROG) ... SOP
Sceptre Investment Counsel Ltd. [*Toronto Stock Exchange symbol*] ... SZ
Sceptre Resources [*AMEX symbol*] (TTSB) ... SRL
Sceptre Resources Ltd. [*Associated Press*] (SAG) ... Sceptre
Sceptre Resources Ltd. [*AMEX symbol Toronto Stock Exchange symbol*] (SPSG) ... SRL
Schaffhausen [*Switzerland ICAO location identifier*] (ICLI) ... LSPF
Schaffner Ranch [*California*] [*Seismograph station code, US Geological Survey*] (SEIS) ... SNR
Schaie-Thurstone Adult Mental Abilities Test [*Intelligence test*] [*Psychology*] ... STAMAT
Schalk's Jamaica Reports [*A publication*] (DLA) ... Schalk
Schaller Herald, Schaller, IA [*Library symbol Library of Congress*] (LCLS) ... IaSchH
Schanis [*Switzerland ICAO location identifier*] (ICLI) ... LSZX
Schawk, Inc. [*Formerly, Filtertek Inc.*] [*Associated Press*] (SAG) ... Schawk
Schawk, Inc. [*Formerly, Filtertek Inc.*] [*NYSE symbol*] (SAG) ... SGK
Schawk Inc.'A' [*NYSE symbol*] (TTSB) ... SGK
Schedule ... S
Schedule (AABC) ... SCD
Schedule (IAA) ... SCED
Schedule (AAG) ... SCH
Schedule (ODBW) ... Sch
Schedule (ECII) ... SCHDL
Schedule (KSC) ... SCHED
Schedule (ROG) ... SCHEDE
Schedule (NG) ... SKED
Schedule Airlines Tour Office - Overseas ... SATO-OS
Schedule Allocation and Control (NASA) ... SAAC
Schedule Allocation Requirements (AAG) ... SAR
Schedule, Analysis, and Review Procedure [*NASA*] (KSC) ... SARP
Schedule and Allocations Working Group [*NASA*] (KSC) ... SAWG
Schedule and Cost-Control System (MHDB) ... SACCS
Schedule and Request (MCD) ... SAR
Schedule and Resources Procedure [*NASA*] (KSC) ... SARP
Schedule and Resources Status Report [*NASA*] (NASA) ... SRSR
Schedule Change Authorization [*NASA*] (NASA) ... SCA
Schedule Change Board [*NASA*] (NASA) ... SCB
Schedule Change Report ... SCR
Schedule Change Request [*NASA*] (NASA) ... SCR
Schedule Compliance-Evaluation [*Polaris*] ... SCE
Schedule Conference [*Military*] (NVT) ... SKEDCON
Schedule Control File ... SCF
Schedule Evaluation Model ... SEM
Schedule for Affective Disorders and Schizophrenia [*Psychological interview*] ... SADS
Schedule for Affective Disorders and Schizophrenia - Change Version [*Personality development test*] [*Psychology*] ... SADS-C
Schedule for Affective Disorders and Schizophrenia - Lifetime Version [*Personality development test*] [*Psychology*] ... SADS-L
Schedule for Classroom Activity Norms (EDAC) ... SCAN
Schedule for the Assessment of Negative Symptoms [*Psychometrics*] ... SANS
Schedule Generator ... SG
Schedule Interface Log ... SIL
Schedule of Implementation Procedures [*FAA*] (TAG) ... SIM
Schedule of Investment Projects ... SIP
Schedule of Organizational Change [*Air Force*] (AFM) ... SOC
Schedule of Recent Experience [*Psychometrics*] ... SRE
Schedule Order (MCD) ... SHO
Schedule Outlook Report (SAA) ... SOR
Schedule Performance Evaluation and Review Technique ... SPERT
Schedule Performance Index (MCD) ... SPI
Schedule Planning and Control System (MCD) ... SPCS
Schedule Program Evaluation and Review Technique (IAA) ... SPERT

Schedule Promulgated Separately [*Navy*] (NVT) .... SPS
Schedule Request Confirmation (SSD) .... SRC
Schedule Request Message (MCD) .... SRM
Schedule Shipment Record (MCD) .... SSR
Schedule Status Preprocessor (MCD) .... SSPP
Schedule Statusing and Performance Measurement (SSD) .... SSPM
Schedule, Technical, and Resources Report [*NASA*] (NASA) .... STARR
Schedule Variance (MCD) .... SV
Schedule Visibility System (AAG) .... SVS
Schedule-Cost Index (MCD) .... SCI
Schedule-Cost-Performance (IEEE) .... SCOPE
Scheduled/Actual (NASA) .... S/A
Scheduled Air Transport Rating .... SATR
Scheduled Airlines Ticket Office .... SATO
Scheduled Airlines Traffic Office [*Military*] .... SATO
Scheduled Cargo Service (IIA) .... SCS
Scheduled Depot Level Maintenance [*Navy*] .... SDLM
Scheduled Estimated Time of Departure [*Aviation*] (DA) .... SETD
Scheduled Input Control Method (MCD) .... SICM
Scheduled into Production .... SITP
Scheduled Issue Date [*Telecommunications*] (TEL) .... SID
Scheduled Issue Release System .... SIRS
Scheduled Maintenance (MCD) .... SM
Scheduled Maintenance Action .... SMA
Scheduled Maintenance and Reliability Team (MCD) .... SMART
Scheduled Maintenance Man-Hours (MCD) .... SMMH
Scheduled Maintenance Program (MCD) .... SMP
Scheduled Maintenance Replacement .... SMR
Scheduled Maintenance Replacement Time .... SMRT
Scheduled Maintenance Time [*Automotive engineering*] .... SMT
Scheduled Maintenance Time Ratio [*Automotive service*] .... SMTR
Scheduled Man-Hours (MCD) .... SMH
Scheduled Not Mission Capable Both [*Maintenance and supply*] (MCD)..... SNMCB
Scheduled Not Mission Capable Maintenance (MCD) .... SNMCM
Scheduled Oil Sampling [*Automotive engineering*] .... SOS
Scheduled Passenger Service (IIA) .... SPS
Scheduled Procurement of Essential Equipment Deliveries [*US Postal Service*] .... SPEED
Scheduled Program Printout (NATG) .... SPPO
Scheduled Release Date (MCD) .... SRD
Scheduled Removal Component (MCD) .... SRC
Scheduled Theater Airlift Route [*Air Force*] (DOMA) ...... STAR
Scheduled Time over Target (AFM) .... STOT
Scheduled Truck Service [*Army*] .... STS
Scheduled-Controlled Operant Behavior [*Environmental Protection Agency*] .... SCOB
Schedule-Induced Polydipsia [*Psychology*] .... SIP
Scheduler Work Area [*Computer science*] (IBMDP) .... SWA
Scheduler Work Area Data Set [*IBM Corp.*] (MCD) .... SWADS
Schedules and Status Summary [*NASA*] (KSC) .... SASS
Schedules Duty Officer (KSC) .... SDO
Schedules Planning and Analysis [*Aviation*] (DA) .... SPA
Scheduling .... SCHD
Scheduling Activity Control System [*PA Computers & Telecommunications Ltd.*] [*Software package*] (NCC) .... SACS
Scheduling Analysis Model for Mission Integrated Experiments [*NASA*] (KSC) .... SAMMIE
Scheduling and Control by Automated Network System .... SCANS
Scheduling and Reporting [*or Review*] Procedure [*NASA*] (KSC) .... SARP
Scheduling and Resource Management System [*Tymshare UK*] [*Software package*] (NCC) .... SRMS
Scheduling and Tracking System (MCD) .... SCATS
Scheduling Forecast .... SF
Scheduling Information Not Available (KSC) .... SINA
Scheduling Management Display .... SMD
Scheduling, Manpower Allocation, and Cost Control (MHDB) .... SMACC
Scheduling, Planning, Evaluation, and Cost Control [*Air Force*] .... SPECTROL
Scheer Energy Development Corp. [*Vancouver Stock Exchange symbol*] .... SYD
Schefferville [*Quebec*] [*Seismograph station code, US Geological Survey*] (SEIS) .... SCH
Schefferville [*Canada*] [*Airport symbol*] (OAG) .... YKL
Schefferville, PQ [*ICAO location identifier*] (ICLI) ..... CYKL
Scheffield Explorations [*Associated Press*] (SAG) .... SchfEx
Scheffield Explorations [*AMEX symbol*] (SAG) .... SHE
Scheib (Earl) [*AMEX symbol*] (TTSB) .... ESH
Scheib [*Earl*], Inc. [*AMEX symbol*] (SPSG) .... ESH
Scheib [*Earl*], Inc. [*Associated Press*] (SAG) .... Scheib
Scheibe-Flugzeugbau GmbH [*Germany ICAO aircraft manufacturer identifier*] (ICAO) .... SF
Scheiffer's Practice [*A publication*] (DLA) .... Scheif Pr
Schein (Henry) [*NASDAQ symbol*] (TTSB) .... HSIC
Schein [*Henry*], Inc. [*NASDAQ symbol*] (SAG) .... HSIC
Schellex Gold [*Vancouver Stock Exchange symbol*] .... SCE
Schema Representation Language (NITA) .... SRL
Schema Tuning, Evaluation, and Analytical Model (PDAA) .... STEAM
Schematic .... SCHEM
Schematic (AAG) .... SCHM
Schematic (VRA) .... schm
Schematic Block Diagram [*NASA*] (NASA) .... SBD
Schematic Change Notice .... SCN
Schematic Change Proposal .... SCP
Schematic Concept Formation .... SCF
Schematic Diagram .... SD
Scheme (ADA) .... SCH
Scheme (ROG) .... SCHE

Scheme Representation Language [*Artificial intelligence*] .... SRL
Schempp-Hirth KG [*Germany ICAO aircraft manufacturer identifier*] (ICAO) .... SS
Schenectady Army Depot (AABC) .... SCAD
Schenectady Chemicals, Inc., Schenectady, NY [*Library symbol Library of Congress*] (LCLS) .... NSchSC
Schenectady County Community College, Schenectady, NY [*Library symbol Library of Congress*] (LCLS) .... NSchC
Schenectady County Community College, Schenectady, NY [*OCLC symbol*] (OCLC) .... XJM
Schenectady County Public Library, Schenectady, NY [*Library symbol Library of Congress*] (LCLS) .... NSch
Schenectady Naval Reactors Office [*Energy Research and Development Administration*] .... SNR
Schenectady Naval Reactors Office [*Department of Energy*] [*Schenectady, NY*] (GAAI) .... SNRO
Schenectady, NY [*Location identifier FAA*] (FAAL) .... HEU
Schenectady, NY [*Location identifier FAA*] (FAAL) .... SCH
Schenectady, NY [*AM radio station call letters*] .... WGY
Schenectady, NY [*Television station call letters*] ...... WMHQ
Schenectady, NY [*FM radio station call letters*] .... WMHT
Schenectady, NY [*Television station call letters*] ...... WMHT-TV
Schenectady, NY [*Television station call letters*] ...... WRGB
Schenectady, NY [*FM radio station call letters*] .... WRUC
Schenectady, NY [*FM radio station call letters*] .... WRVE
Schenectady, NY [*AM radio station call letters*] .... WVKZ
Schenectady Operation [*Energy Research and Development Administration*] (MCD) .... SO
Schenectady Operations Office [*Energy Research and Development Administration*] .... SOO
Schenley Instant Market Reports .... SIMR
Scherenfernrohrstand [*Emplacement of battery commander's telescope*] [*German military - World War II*] .... SFST
Scherer [*R.P.*] Corp. [*Associated Press*] (SAG) .... Scherer
Scherer [*R.P.*] Corp. [*NYSE symbol*] (SPSG) .... SHR
Scherer Healthcare [*NASDAQ symbol*] (TTSB) .... SCHR
Scherer Healthcare, Inc. [*NASDAQ symbol*] (CTT) .... SCHR
Scherer Healthcare, Inc. [*Associated Press*] (SAG) ...... SchrHl
Scherer (R.P.) [*NYSE symbol*] (TTSB) .... SHR
Scherer's New York Miscellaneous Reports [*22-47*] [*A publication*] (DLA).... Scher
Schering [*Italy*] [*Research code symbol*] .... SCH
Schering AG [*Germany*] [*Research code symbol*] .... SH
Schering AG [*Germany*] [*Research code symbol*] .... ZK
Schering-Oriented Literature Analysis and Retrieval System [*Schering-Plough Corp.*] [*Information service or system*] (IID) .... SCHOLAR
Schering-Plough [*NYSE symbol*] (TTSB) .... SGP
Schering-Plough Corp. [*Research code symbol*] .... SCH
Schering-Plough Corp. [*Associated Press*] (SAG) .... SchrPl
Schering-Plough Corp. [*Commercial firm*] .... SP
Schering-Plough Corp. [*Research code symbol*] .... SRG
Scherzando [*Playful*] [*Music*] .... SCHERZ
Scheuthauer-Marie [*Syndrome*] (DAVI) .... SM
Schiapparelli [*Italy*] [*Research code symbol*] .... SAS
Schichtlade Kammer System [*Stratified Combustion Chamber System*] [*Automotive engineering German*] .... SKS
Schick Information Systems, Edmonton, AB, Canada [*Library symbol Library of Congress*] (LCLS) .... CaAESIS
Schick Information Systems, Edmonton, Alberta [*Library symbol Obsolete National Library of Canada*] (NLC) .... AESIS
Schick Shaving Experience [*Advertising slogan*] .... SSE
Schick's Schadel Hospital, Medical Library, Seattle, WA [*Library symbol Library of Congress*] (LCLS) .... WaSS
Schiedsgericht [*Arbitration Court*] [*German*] (ILCA) .... SchG
Schiff, Harden & Waite, Chicago, IL [*Library symbol*] [*Library of Congress*] (LCLS) .... ICSch
Schiff, Hardin & Waite, Chicago, IL [*OCLC symbol*] (OCLC) .... IBX
Schiffli Embroidery Manufacturers Promotion Board (EA) .... SEMPB
Schiffli Lace and Embroidery Manufacturers Association (EA) .... SLEMA
Schiffner Oilfield & Technology Corp. [*Vancouver Stock Exchange symbol*] .... SHF
Schiller [*German poet, 1759-1805*] (ROG) .... SCH
Schiller Park Public Library, Schiller Park, IL [*Library symbol Library of Congress*] (LCLS) .... ISp
Schilling [*Monetary unit*] [*Austria*] .... S
Schilling [*Monetary unit*] (ROG) .... SC
Schilling [*Monetary unit*] [*Austria*] .... SCH
Schilling Air Force Base (AAG) .... SCAFB
Schilling Body Coordination Test (EDAC) .... SBCT
Schilpp, Reed B., Los Angeles CA [*STAC*] .... SRB
Schindellegi [*Switzerland ICAO location identifier*] (ICLI) .... LSXS
Schipperke Club of America (EA) .... SCA
Schist [*Quality of the bottom*] [*Nautical charts*] ..... Sch
Schist (VRA) .... schst
Schistocytes [*Hematology*] (DAVI) .... HliS
Schistocytes [*Hematology*] (DAVI) .... SCHIS
Schistosoma [*A parasitic fluke*] (MAE) .... S
Schistosoma Bovis [*Parasitic fluke*] .... SB
Schistosoma Hematobium [*A parasitic fluke*] .... SH
Schistosoma Japonicum [*Parasitic fluke*] .... SJ
Schistosoma Mansoni [*A parasitic fluke*] .... SM
Schistosome-Derived Immunosuppressive Factor [*Immunology*] .... SDIF
Schizophrenia [*Medicine*] .... SCHIZ
Schizophrenia [*Psychology*] .... schizo
Schizophrenia [*Psychology*] .... sz
Schizophrenia: a National Emergency [*An association British*] .... SANE
Schizophrenia Association of Great Britain .... SAGB

Schizophrenia, Chronic Undifferentiated Type [*Psychiatry*] (DAVI) .... SCUT
Schizophrenia Fellowship of Victoria [*Australia*] .... SFV
Schizophrenia Spectrum [*Psychiatry*] (DAVI) .... SS
Schizophrenic Chronic Paranoid Type [*Medicine*] (DMAA) .... SCPT
Schizophrenics Anonymous (EA) .... SA
Schizophrenics Anonymous International [*Later, Canadian Schizophrenia Foundation*] (EA) .... SAI
Schizotypal Personality [*Medicine*] (DMAA) .... SP
Schlaraffia Nordamerika (EA) .... SNA
Schlarman High School, Danville, IL [*Library symbol*] [*Library of Congress*] (LCLS) .... IDanviHS
Schlegeis [*Austria*] [*Seismograph station code, US Geological Survey*] (SEIS) .... SCE
Schleicher & Schuell [*Filter-paper company*] .... S & S
Schleicher-Bruns [*Germany ICAO aircraft manufacturer identifier*] (ICAO) .... SE
Schleswig [*Germany ICAO location identifier*] (ICLI) .... EDCS
Schleswig Leader, Schleswig, IA [*Library symbol Library of Congress*] (LCLS) .... IaSchlL
Schlotzskys, Inc. [*NASDAQ symbol*] (SAG) .... BUNZ
Schlotzsky's Inc. [*NASDAQ symbol*] (TTSB) .... BUNZ
Schlotzskys, Inc. [*Associated Press*] (SAG) .... Schltzk
Schlumberger Ltd. [*Associated Press*] (SAG) .... Schlmb
Schlumberger Ltd. [*NYSE symbol*] (SPSG) .... SLB
Schlumberger Well Services, Houston, TX [*Library symbol Library of Congress*] (LCLS) .... TxHSW
Schlumberger-Doll Research Center, Ridgefield, CT [*OCLC symbol*] (OCLC) .... SDR
Schluszsatz [*Finale*] [*Music*] .... SCHLS
Schmele Instrument to Measure the Process of Nursing Care [*Medicine*] (DMAA) .... SIMP
Schmidt Number [*IUPAC*] .... Sc
Schmidt Rubin Rifle .... SCHRUB
Schmidt Telescope .... ST
Schmidt-Baker Camera (IIA) .... SBC
Schmidt-Cassegrain [*Telescope*] .... S/C
Schmidt-Ruppin Chick Embryo Fibroblast [*s*] .... SR-CEF
Schmidt-Ruppin Strain Rous Sarcoma Virus [*Oncology*] (DAVI) .... SRS-RSV
Schmidt's Civil Law of Spain and Mexico [*A publication*] (DLA) .... Schm Civil Law
Schmidt's Civil Law of Spain and Mexico [*A publication*] (DLA) .... Schmidt Civ Law
Schmidt's Law Journal [*New Orleans*] [*A publication*] (DLA) .... Schm LJ
Schmit Industries, Inc. [*NASDAQ symbol*] (SAG) .... SMIT
Schmitt Industries [*NASDAQ symbol*] (TTSB) .... SMIT
Schmitt Industries, Inc. [*Associated Press*] (SAG) .... Schmitt
Schmitt Industries, Inc. [*Vancouver Stock Exchange symbol*] .... SIW
Schmitt Trigger [*Electronics*] .... ST
Schmitthoff. Export Trade [*A publication*] (ILCA) .... Schm Exp
Schmulowitz Collection of Wit and Humor [*San Francisco Public Library*] .... SCOWAH
Schnecksville, PA [*FM radio station call letters*] .... WXLV
Schneider Corp. [*Toronto Stock Exchange symbol*] .... SCD
Schnellbahn [*High-Speed Railway*] [*German*] .... S-Bahn
Schnitzer Steel Ind'A' [*NASDAQ symbol*] (TTSB) .... SCHN
Schnitzer Steel Industries, Inc. [*NASDAQ symbol*] (SAG) .... SCHN
Schnitzer Steel Industries, Inc. [*Associated Press*] (SAG) .... Schnitzr
Schoales and Lefroy's Irish Chancery Reports [*1802-06*] [*A publication*] (DLA) .... S & L
Schoales and Lefroy's Irish Chancery Reports [*A publication*] (DLA) .... Sch & Lef
Schoales and Lefroy's Irish Chancery Reports [*A publication*] (DLA) .... Schoales & L
Schoenaur Rifle .... SCH
Schoenstatt Institute of Secular Priests (TOCD) .... ISSS
Schofield, WI [*AM radio station call letters*] .... WRIG
Schoharie County Historical Society, Schoharie, NY [*Library symbol Library of Congress*] (LCLS) .... NSchoCHi
Schoharie, NY [*FM radio station call letters*] .... WMYY
Scholar .... SCH
Scholar [*or Scholarship*] (ROG) .... SCHO
Scholar .... Schol
Scholar in Theology [*British*] .... S Th
Scholarly Book Center [*ACCORD*] [*UTLAS symbol*] .... SCB
Scholarly Communication: Online Publishing and Education (NITA) .... SCOPE
Scholarly Publishing & Academic Resources Coalition .... SPARC
Scholarly Resources, Incorporated, Wilmington, DE [*Library symbol Library of Congress*] (LCLS) .... SRI
Scholars Against the Escalating Danger of the Far Right (EA) .... SAEDFR
Scholars and Citizens for Freedom of Information (EA) .... SACFI
Scholars' Facsimiles & Reprints, Inc., Delmar, NY [*Library symbol Library of Congress*] (LCLS) .... SfR
Scholars for Teaching Excellence (DMAA) .... STE
Scholars Group Against the Invasion of Grenada (EA) .... SGAIG
Scholarship .... SCH
Scholarship .... SCHLSHP
Scholarship .... SCHOL
Scholarship Amount (NITA) .... SA
Scholarship, Education, and Defense Fund for Racial Equality .... SEDFRE
Scholarships, Fellowships, and Loans [*A publication*] .... SFL
Scholarships for Children of American Military Personnel (DNAB) .... SCAMP
Scholastic Aptitude Test [*Trademark of the College Entrance Examination Board*] .... SAT
Scholastic Aptitude Test - Mathematics [*College Entrance Examination Board*] .... SAT-M
Scholastic Aptitude Test - Verbal [*College Entrance Examination Board*] .... SAT-V
Scholastic Assessment Test [*Formerly, Scholastic Aptitude Test*] .... SAT
Scholastic Corp. [*NASDAQ symbol*] (SAG) .... SCHL
Scholastic Corp. [*Associated Press*] (SAG) .... ScholCp
Scholastic Proficiency Test - Higher Primary Level [*Educational test*] [*South Africa*] .... SPT-HP
Scholastic Rowing Association of America (EA) .... SRAA
Scholastic Science Fiction Federation [*Defunct*] (EA) .... SSFF
Scholia [*Classical studies*] (OCD) .... Schol
Scholia Bernensia ad Vergilii Bucolica et Georgica [*A publication*] (OCD) .... Schol Bern
Scholia Bobiensia [*Classical studies*] (OCD) .... Schol Bob
Scholia Cruquiana [*Classical studies*] (OCD) .... Schol Cruq
Scholia Florentina in Callimachum [*Classical studies*] (OCD) .... Schol Flor Callim
Scholiast [*Classical studies*] (OCD) .... Schol
Scholium [*Note*] [*Latin*] .... SCH
Scholium [*Note*] [*Latin*] (ROG) .... SCHOL
Schomberg's Treatise on the Maritime Laws of Rhodes [*A publication*] (DLA) .... Schomberg Mar Laws Rhodes
Schonlein-Henoch Purpura [*Medicine*] (DMAA) .... SH
Schonlein-Henoch Purpura [*Medicine*] (MEDA) .... SHP
School .... S
School (AFM) .... SCH
School (VRA) .... sch
School .... SCHL
School (WGA) .... SCHL
School (NVT) .... SCOL
School Ability Test [*Psychology*] .... SAT
School Achievement Record [*Australia*] .... SAR
School Administrator and Supervisor (GAGS) .... SAS
School Administrators and Supervisors Organizing Committee [*Later, AFSA*] (EA) .... SASOC
School Aid to Federally Impacted and Major Disaster Areas (OICC) .... SAFIMDA
School and College Ability [*Test*] [*of ETS*] .... SCA
School and College Ability Test [*of ETS*] .... SCAT
School and College Advisory Center [*Later, EGASCAC*] (EA) .... SCAC
School and College Conference on English .... SCCE
School and Group Travel Association (EAIO) .... SAGTA
School and Home Office Products Association (EA) .... SHOPA
School and Staffing Survey [*Department of Education*] (GFGA) .... SASS
School Apperception Method [*Psychology*] .... SAM
School Arts [*A publication*] (BRI) .... Sch Arts
School Assistance in Federally Affected Areas .... SAFA
School Attitude Measure [*Test*] [*Canadian Comprehensive Assessment Program*] .... SAM
School Band of America (AEBS) .... SBA
School Bookshop Association [*British*] (DI) .... SBA
[*The*] **School Brigade** [*Army*] (INF) .... TSB
School Broadcasting Council for the United Kingdom (BI) .... SBCUK
School Bus Manufacturers Institute (EA) .... SBMI
School Certificate .... SC
School Child Stress Scale [*Child development test*] [*Psychology*] .... SCSS
School, College, and University Partnerships Program [*Department of Education*] (GFGA) .... SCUP
School, College, Department of Education (AEE) .... SCDE
School Computer Use Plan (IEEE) .... SCUP
School Construction (OICC) .... SC
School Construction Systems Development [*Project*] [*of Educational Facilities Laboratories*] .... SCSD
School Curriculum Industry Partnership [*British*] (ECON) .... SCIP
School Dental Service .... SDS
School District 88, Skeena-Terrace, BC, Canada [*Library symbol Library of Congress*] (LCLS) .... CaBSS
School District 88, Skeena-Terrace, British Columbia [*Library symbol National Library of Canada*] (NLC) .... BSS
School District No. 51, Professional Library, Grand Junction, CO [*Library symbol Library of Congress*] (LCLS) .... CoGjSD-P
School District No. 51, Special Services Media Materials, Grand Junction, CO [*Library symbol Library of Congress*] (LCLS) .... CoGjSD
School District No. 51, Vocational Department, Grand Junction, CO [*Library symbol Library of Congress*] (LCLS) .... CoGjSD-V
School District No. 251, Menan, ID [*Library symbol*] [*Library of Congress*] (LCLS) .... IdMenSD
School Dropout Demonstration Assistance Act .... SDDAA
School Emergency Communication .... SECOM
School Facilities Council of Architecture, Education, and Industry [*Later, ASBO*] (EA) .... SFC
School Fees Insurance Agency Ltd. [*British*] .... SFIA
School Focused Secondment (AIE) .... SFS
School for Advanced Jewish Studies (BJA) .... SAJS
School for Advanced Military Studies [*Army*] .... SAMS
School for Girls (ADA) .... SG
School for International Training, Brattleboro, VT [*Library symbol Library of Congress*] (LCLS) .... VtBrtS
School for Latin America [*Military*] (AFM) .... SCHLA
School for Latin America [*Military*] .... SLM
School for Postgraduate Interdisciplinary Research on Interculturalism and Transnationality [*Aalborg University, Denmark*] .... SPIRIT
School for Resource and Environmental Studies [*Dalhousie University*] [*Canada*] (IRC) .... SRES
School Furniture Manufacturers' Association [*British*] (BI) .... SFMA
School Guarantee Program (DNAB) .... SGP
School Heads Advisory Committee [*National Association of Independent Schools*] (EDAC) .... SHAC
School Health Additional Referral Program [*Public Health Service*] .... SHARP
School Improvement Through Instructional Process [*Maryland*] (EDAC) .... SITIP
School in Agency Management [*LIMRA*] .... SAM
School in Basic Management [*LIMRA*] .... SBM
School in District Management [*LIMRA*] .... SDM

School in Sales Management [*LIMRA*] ... SSM
School Information and Research Service (EDAC) ... SIRS
School Interest Inventory [*Psychology*] ... SII
School Inventory [*Psychology*] ... SI
School Journal Association of London [*British*] (AIE) ... SJAL
School Kids with Income, Purchasing Power [*Lifestyle Classification*] ... Skippies
School Law Reporter. National Organization on Legal Problems in Education [*A publication*] (DLA) ... School L Rep (Nat'l Org on Legal Probs in Educ)
School Leavers [*Department of Employment*] [*British*] ... SL
School Leaving Age (AIE) ... SLA
School Lecturers' Association [*British*] ... SLA
School Librarian [*A publication*] (BRI) ... Sch Lib
School Libraries in Australia [*A publication*] ... School Libs Aust
School Library Association ... SLA
School Library Journal [*A publication*] (BRI) ... SLJ
School Library Manpower Project [*American Association of School Librarians*] (EA) ... SLMP
School Library Media Quarterly [*American Library Association*] ... SLMQ
School Lunch Program ... SLP
School Management Information Retrieval Service [*University of Oregon*] [*Eugene, OR*] ... SMIRS
School Management Study Group (EA) ... SMSG
School Mathematics Project [*British*] ... SMP
School Mathematics Study Group (IIA) ... SMSG
School Motivation Analysis Test [*Personality development test*] [*Psychology*] ... SMAT
School Natural Science Society [*British*] ... SNSS
School Nurse Practitioner ... SNP
School of Acquisition Management [*Army*] ... SACM
School of Advanced International Studies ... SAIS
School of Advanced International Studies [*Johns Hopkins University*] ... SAIS
School of Advanced International Studies, Johns Hopkins University, Washington, DC [*OCLC symbol*] (OCLC) ... JHS
School of Advanced International Studies. Review [*A publication*] (DLA) ... School of Advanced Studies Rev
School of Aerial Fighting [*British military*] (DMA) ... SAF
School of Aerospace Medicine [*Formerly, School of Aviation Medicine*] ... SAM
School of Aerospace Medicine, Brooks AFB, TX [*OCLC symbol*] (OCLC) ... TBM
School of Aerospace Medicine Color Threshold Test ... SAMCTT
School of Air Navigation [*British*] ... SAN
School of American Ballet [*New York*] ... SAB
School of American Research [*Research center*] (RCD) ... SAR
School of Applied Aerospace Sciences [*Air Force*] ... SAAS
School of Applied Health [*University of Texas*] ... SAH
School of Applied Tactics [*AAFSAT*] ... SAT
School of Architecture, University of Toronto, Ontario [*Library symbol National Library of Canada*] (NLC) ... OTUSA
School of Army Co-Operation [*Air Force British*] ... SAC
School of Artillery [*British military*] (DMA) ... S of A
School of Assets Management [*Later, School of Materiel Readiness*] [*Army*] ... SAM
School of Aviation Medicine [*Later, School of Aerospace Medicine*] (MCD) ... SCHAVMED
School of Aviation Medicine [*Later, School of Aerospace Medicine*] ... SCOLAVNMED
School of Aviation [*later, Aerospace*] **Medicine - Brooks** ... SAM-B
School of Chiropody Full Time [*British*] ... SF
School of Classical Ballet [*American Ballet Theater Foundation*] ... SCB
School of Combined Operations, Beach and Boat Section [*Military British*] ... SCOBBS
School of Community and Allied Health Resources ... SCAHR
School of Corresponding Studies [*Military*] (INF) ... SOCS
School of Electric Light [*British military*] (DMA) ... SEL
School of Engineering (MCD) ... SE
School of English Church Music [*Later, RSCM*] ... SECM
School of Field Studies [*Beverly, MA*] ... SFS
School of General Reconnaissance [*Air Force British*] ... SGR
School of Gunnery [*British military*] (DMA) ... S of G
School of Health Care Sciences, United States Air Force (AFM) ... SHCS USAF
School of Industrial Management [*MIT*] (MCD) ... SIM
School of Infantry [*British military*] (DMA) ... S of I
School of Journalism, University of King's College, Halifax, Nova Scotia [*Library symbol National Library of Canada*] (NLC) ... NSHKJ
School of Labor and Industrial Relations [*Michigan State University*] [*Research center*] (RCD) ... SLIR
School of Law. Review [*Canada*] [*A publication*] (DLA) ... SOL Rev
School of Law. Review. Toronto University [*Canada*] [*A publication*] (DLA) ... School of LR
School of Law. Review. Toronto University [*Canada*] [*A publication*] (DLA) ... U of T School of LR
School of Librarianship Automatic Cataloguing Experiment (NITA) ... SOLACE
School of Library and Information Science, University of Western Ontario [*EDUCATSS*] [*UTLAS symbol*] ... EUW
School of Library and Information Science, University of Western Ontario, London, Ontario [*Library symbol National Library of Canada*] (NLC) ... OLUS
School of Library, Archival, and Information Studies [*University of British Columbia, Vancouver*] [*Canada*] ... SLAIS
School of Library, Archival, and Information Studies, University of British Columbia, Vancouver, British Columbia [*Library symbol National Library of Canada*] (NLC) ... BVAULS
School of Library Service [*Columbia University*] [*Defunct*] ... SLS
School of Library Service, Dalhousie University [*EDUCATSS*] [*UTLAS symbol*] ... EUB
School of Library Service, Dalhousie University, Halifax, Nova Scotia [*Library symbol National Library of Canada*] (NLC) ... NSHDLS
School of Library Technology, Lakehead University [*EDUCATSS*] [*UTLAS symbol*] ... EUL
School of Library Technology, Lakehead University, Thunder Bay, Ontario [*Library symbol National Library of Canada*] (NLC) ... OTBLL
School of Living (EA) ... SOL
School of Logistics Science [*Army*] ... SLS
School of Management and Strategic Studies [*Founded 1982 by Richard Farson, offers a two-year management program through GTE Telenet*] ... SMSS
School of Management Information Systems [*Army*] ... SMIS
School of Maritime Operations [*British*] ... SMOPS
School of Materiel Readiness [*Formerly, SAM*] [*Army*] (RDA) ... SMR
School of Mathematical Sciences (EERA) ... SMS
School of Military Engineering ... SME
School of Military Government [*World War II*] ... SMG
School of Military Sciences Officer [*Air Force*] ... SCHMILSCIO
School of Musketry [*Military British*] (ROG) ... S of M
School of Naval Administration, Leland Stanford University ... SONA
School of Naval Co-Operation [*Air Force British*] ... SNC
School of Nursing (AAMN) ... SN
School of Nursing, Grace General Hospital, St. John's, Newfoundland [*Library symbol National Library of Canada*] (NLC) ... NFSGGHN
School of Nursing, Royal Alexandra Hospital, Edmonton, Alberta [*Library symbol National Library of Canada*] (NLC) ... AERASN
School of Nursing, St. Clare's Mercy Hospital, St. John's, Newfoundland [*Library symbol National Library of Canada*] (NLC) ... NFSSCN
School of Oriental and African Studies [*University of London*] ... SOAS
School of Physical and Health Education (Women), University of Toronto, Ontario [*Library symbol National Library of Canada*] (NLC) ... OTUSP
School of Physical Training [*British*] ... SPT
School of Practical Science ... SPS
School of Psychiatric Nursing, Selkirk, Manitoba [*Library symbol National Library of Canada*] (NLC) ... MSEPN
School of Psychiatric Nursing, Selkirk, MB, Canada [*Library symbol Library of Congress*] (LCLS) ... CaMSePN
School of Public and Urban Policy [*Pennsylvania University*] (PDAA) ... SPUP
School of Resource and Environmental Management (EERA) ... SREM
School of Resources and Environmental Studies, Dalhousie University, Halifax, Nova Scotia [*Library symbol National Library of Canada*] (NLC) ... NSHDIR
School of Social Studies [*British*] ... SSS
School of Social Work, University of Toronto, Ontario [*Library symbol National Library of Canada*] (NLC) ... OTUSW
School of Systems and Logistics [*Military*] ... SOSAL
School of Systems and Logistics [*Military*] ... SSL
School of Tank Technology [*British military*] (DMA) ... STT
School of Technical Training [*British military*] (DMA) ... STT
School of the Air [*Army*] (TSSD) ... SOA
[*The*] **School of the Art Institute of Chicago** (GAGS) ... Art Inst Chicago
School of the Art Institute of Chicago ... SAIC
School of the Art Institute of Chicago, Chicago, IL [*Library symbol Library of Congress*] (LCLS) ... ICA-S
School of the Art Institute of Chicago Library, Chicago, IL [*OCLC symbol*] (OCLC) ... ILO
School of the Ozarks, Point Lookout, MO [*OCLC symbol*] (OCLC) ... MOO
School of the Ozarks, Point Lookout, MO [*Library symbol Library of Congress*] (LCLS) ... MoPIS
School of the Salt Creek [*Ballet*] ... SSC
School of Theology at Claremont, Claremont, CA [*Library symbol Library of Congress*] (LCLS) ... CCSC
School of Theology at Claremont Library, Claremont, CA [*OCLC symbol*] (OCLC) ... CST
School of Visual Arts [*New York, NY*] ... SVA
School of Women Artists Network [*Australia*] ... SWAN
School Performance Information Regulations (AIE) ... SPIR
School Personnel Utilization ... SPU
School Practices Information File [*BRS Information Technologies*] [*Information service or system Defunct*] ... SPIF
School Practices Information Network [*Bibliographic Retrieval Services*] [*Information service or system*] (IID) ... SPIN
School Principal Job Functions Inventory [*Test*] ... SP-JFI
School Projectionist Club of America [*Defunct*] (EA) ... SPCA
School Psychology Certificate (PGP) ... SPC
School Psychology Specialist (PGP) ... SPS
School Quota Letter ... SQL
School Quota Number ... SQN
School Readiness Test [*Child development test*] ... SRT
School Readiness Tests for Blind Children ... STBC
School Related Resources Index [*Australia*] ... SRRI
School Response Team ... SRT
School Retrofit Design Analysis System (EDAC) ... SRDAS
School Science and Mathematics Association (EA) ... SSMA
School Science Curriculum Project ... SSCP
School Secretaries Association (DBA) ... SSA
School Ship [*Navy symbol*] (DNAB) ... YWN
School Sisters of Christ the King (TOCD) ... CK
School Sisters of Notre Dame (IIA) ... SSND
School Sisters of St. Francis (TOCD) ... OSF
School Sisters of St. Francis (TOCD) ... SSSF
School Sisters of the Third Order of St. Francis (Bethlehem, PA) (TOCD) ... OSF
School Sisters of the Third Order of St. Francis (Panhandle, TX) (TOCD) ... OSF
School Sisters of the Third Order of St. Francis (Pittsburgh, PA) (TOCD) ... OSF
School Squadron [*Air Force*] ... SCHS
School Student Transport Scheme [*Australia*] ... SSTS
School Superintendent Job Functions Inventory [*Test*] ... SS-JFI
School Television Service ... STS

School to Employment Program ... STEP
School Volunteer Services Program ... SVSP
School Year (AABC) ... SY
School-Aged Maternity (EDAC) ... SAM
School-Based Curriculum Development (ADA) ... SBCD
School-Based Decision Making (ADA) ... SBDM
Schoolboys Harness Aid for the Relief of the Elderly (AIE) ... SHARE
School-College Orientation Program of Pittsburgh ... SCOPP
Schooley's Mountain, NJ [*Location identifier FAA*] (FAAL) ... BWZ
Schoolhouse ... SH
Schoolhouse Energy Efficiency Demonstration Project (EDAC) ... SEED
School-Leavers' Training and Employment Preparation Scheme [*New Zealand Labor Department*] (BARN) ... STEPS
Schoolman-Schwartz Virus [*Medicine*] (DMAA) ... SSV
Schoolmaster [*Navy British*] ... Schm
Schoolmaster (ROG) ... SCHMR
Schoolmistresses' and Governesses' Benevolent Institution [*British*] (BI) ... SGBI
Schools and Colleges Online Accounting and Registration System (NITA) ... SCOLAR
Schools, Board of Education for the City of York, Toronto, Ontario [*Library symbol National Library of Canada*] (NLC) ... OTYBES
Schools Board of Tasmania [*Australia*] ... SBT
Schools' Campaign Against Racism [*British*] (DI) ... SCAR
Schools Computer Development Centre (AIE) ... SCDC
Schools Computers Administration and Management Project (AIE) ... SCAMP
Schools Council [*British*] ... SC
Schools Councils Classics Committee [*British*] ... SCC
Schools Cultural Studies Project (AIE) ... SCSP
Schools, Curriculum, Unusual, Geography, and Alumni [*University admisssion rating system*] ... SCUGA
Schools, Hamilton Board of Education, Ontario [*Library symbol National Library of Canada*] (NLC) ... OHBES
Schools History Project (AIE) ... SHP
Schools Industry Liaison Officer (AIE) ... SILO
Schools Information Centre on the Chemical Industry (AIE) ... SICCI
Schools Information Management System (AIE) ... SIMS
Schools In-Service Unit [*University of Birmingham*] [*British*] (AIE) ... SISU
Schools Music Association [*British*] (BI) ... SMA
Schools of Philosophy [*A publication*] ... SP
Schools of Theology in Dubuque [*Library network*] ... STD
Schools of Theology in Dubuque, Dubuque, IA [*Library symbol Library of Congress*] (LCLS) ... IaDuT
Schools of Theology in Dubuque, Dubuque, IA [*OCLC symbol*] (OCLC) ... IWT
Schools Sailing Association [*British*] ... SSA
Schoolship [*Navy*] (NVT) ... SCHLSHIP
Schoolship [*Navy*] (NVT) ... SCOLSHIP
School-to-School [*Red Cross Youth*] ... STS
Schooner (ROG) ... SC
Schooner ... SCH
Schooner ... SCHR
Schooner [*Shipping*] (ROG) ... SR
Schoool Leaving Certificate [*British*] (BARN) ... SLC
Schottenstein [*M. I.*] **Homes, Inc.** [*Associated Press*] (SAG) ... MISchott
Schottky Barrier Collector Transistor (IAA) ... SBCT
Schottky Barrier Diode [*Electronics*] ... SBD
Schottky Barrier Diode Transistor (IAA) ... SBDT
Schottky Barrier Diode Transistor-Transistor Logic (IAA) ... SBDTTL
Schottky Barrier Gate Field Effect Transistor (IAA) ... SBFET
Schottky Barrier Junction [*Electronics*] ... SBJ
Schottky Barrier Solar Cell [*Electronics*] (PDAA) ... SBSC
Schottky Barrier Transistor-Transistor Logic (IAA) ... SBTTL
Schottky Cell Array Technology ... SCAT
Schottky Clamped Transistor ... SCT
Schottky Clamped Transistor-Transistor Logic [*Electronics*] (IAA) ... STTL
Schottky Coupled Transistor Logic (IAA) ... SCTL
Schottky Diode (IAA) ... SD
Schottky Diode FET [*Field Effect Transistor*] **Logic** ... SDFL
Schottky Diode Field Effect Transistor Logic (MHDI) ... SDFT
Schottky Diode Transistor Logic (IAA) ... SDTL
Schottky Integrated Injection Logic (IAA) ... SIIL
Schottky Transistor Logic (IEEE) ... STL
Schottky Transistor Resistor Logic [*Electronics*] (IAA) ... STRL
Schottky Transistor-Transistor Logic ... S/TTL
Schottky Transistor-Transistor Logic (NITA) ... STTC
Schottky-Barrier Gate Gunn-Effect Digital Device [*Electronics*] (PDAA) ... SBG GEDD
Schouler on Bailments [*A publication*] (DLA) ... Sch Bailm
Schouler on Bailments [*A publication*] (DLA) ... Schouler Bailm
Schouler on Domestic Relations [*A publication*] (DLA) ... Sch Dom Rel
Schouler on Domestic Relations [*A publication*] (DLA) ... Schouler Dom Rel
Schouler on Husband and Wife [*A publication*] (DLA) ... Sch H & W
Schouler on the Law of Personal Property [*A publication*] (DLA) ... Sch Per Prop
Schouler on the Law of Personal Property [*A publication*] (DLA) ... Schouler Pers Prop
Schouler's History of the United States under the Constitution [*A publication*] (DLA) ... Schouler US Hist
Schreiber Public Library, Ontario [*Library symbol National Library of Canada*] (NLC) ... OSCH
Schreiber Publishing Co., Freehold, NJ [*Library symbol Library of Congress*] (LCLS) ... NjFrS
Schreiber Resources Ltd. [*Vancouver Stock Exchange symbol*] ... SCH
Schreiner Airways BV [*Netherlands ICAO designator*] (FAAC) ... SCH
Schreiner Institute, Kerrville, TX [*Library symbol Library of Congress*] (LCLS) ... TxKerS
Schroder Asian Growth [*Associated Press*] (SAG) ... SchroAsn
Schroder Asian Growth [*NYSE symbol*] (SAG) ... SHF
Schroder Asian Growth Fd [*NYSE symbol*] (TTSB) ... SHF
Schroeter, Goldmark & Bender, Seattle, WA [*Library symbol*] [*Library of Congress*] (LCLS) ... WaSSGB
Schuetzenmine [*Antipersonnel mine*] [*German military - World War II*] ... S-M
Schuler Homes [*NASDAQ symbol*] (TTSB) ... SHLR
Schuler Homes, Inc. [*Associated Press*] (SAG) ... Schuler
Schuler Homes, Inc. [*NASDAQ symbol*] (SAG) ... SHLR
Schuler Tuning ... ST
Schuller Corp. [*NYSE symbol*] (SAG) ... GLS
Schuller Corp. [*NYSE symbol*] (TTSB) ... GLS
Schuller Corp. [*Associated Press*] (SAG) ... Schuller
Schuller Corp. [*Associated Press*] (SAG) ... Schullr
Schulman (A.) [*NASDAQ symbol*] (TTSB) ... SHLM
Schulman [*A.*], Inc. [*Associated Press*] (SAG) ... Schulmn
Schulman [*A.*], Inc. [*NASDAQ symbol*] (NQ) ... SHLM
Schult Homes Corp. [*Associated Press*] (SAG) ... Schult
Schult Homes Corp. [*AMEX symbol*] (SPSG) ... SHC
Schult Homes Corp. (MHDW) ... SHCO
Schultes' Aquatic Rights [*1811*] [*A publication*] (DLA) ... Sch Aq R
Schultz Number ... Sch
Schultz Sav-O Stores [*NASDAQ symbol*] (TTSB) ... SAVO
Schultz Sav-O Stores, Inc. [*NASDAQ symbol*] (CTT) ... SAVO
Schultz Sav-O-Stores, Inc. [*Associated Press*] (SAG) ... Schultz
Schumacher Memorial Library, Ontario [*Library symbol National Library of Canada*] (BIB) ... OSM
Schumann Memorial Foundation [*Defunct*] (EA) ... SMF
Schumann Runge [*Spectral region*] ... SR
Schuster-Kubelka-Munk [*Optics*] ... SKM
Schutte Lanz [*World War I German aircraft designation*] ... SL
Schutzgemeinschaft Gegen Meinungsterror [*Guard Society Against Opinion Terror*] [*Germany*] ... SG
Schutzpolizist [*Policeman*] [*German*] ... Schupo
Schutzstaffel [*Elite Guard*] [*NAZI Germany*] ... SS
Schuylkill County Archives, Pottsville, PA [*Library symbol*] [*Library of Congress*] (LCLS) ... PPoAr
Schuylkill's Legal Register [*Pennsylvania*] [*A publication*] (ILCA) ... Schuyl Leg Reg
Schuylkill's Pennsylvania Legal Record [*A publication*] (DLA) ... Sch Leg Rec
Schuylkill's Pennsylvania Legal Record [*A publication*] (DLA) ... Sch LR
Schuylkill's Pennsylvania Legal Record [*A publication*] (DLA) ... Schuy Leg Rec (PA)
Schuylkill's Pennsylvania Legal Record [*A publication*] (DLA) ... Schuyl Leg Rec
Schuylkill's Pennsylvania Legal Record [*A publication*] (DLA) ... Schuyl Legal Rec
Schuylkill's Pennsylvania Register [*A publication*] (DLA) ... Sch Reg
Schuylkill's Pennsylvania Register [*A publication*] (DLA) ... Schuy Reg (PA)
Schwab [*Charles*] **Corp.** [*NYSE symbol*] (SPSG) ... SCH
Schwab [*Charles*] **Corp.** [*Associated Press*] (SAG) ... Schwab
Schwabach [*Germany ICAO location identifier*] (ICLI) ... EDIZ
Schwaebisch Gmuend [*Germany ICAO location identifier*] (ICLI) ... EDIX
Schwaebisch Hall/Hessental [*Germany ICAO location identifier*] (ICLI) ... EDOP
Schwaebisch Hall/Weckrieden [*Germany ICAO location identifier*] (ICLI) ... EDTX
Schwangerschaftsprotein [*Biochemistry*] (DAVI) ... SP
Schwangerschaftsprotein (BABM) ... SP
Schwann Cell [*Biology*] ... SC
Schwannoma-Derived Growth Factor [*Biochemistry*] ... SDGF
Schwartzman-Sanarelli Phenomenon [*Medicine*] (MAE) ... SSP
Schwartz-Slawsky-Herzfeld [*Theory*] [*Chemical kinetics*] ... SSH
Schwartz-Watson Test [*Medicine*] (MAE) ... SW
Schwarz Differential Medium (OA) ... SDM
Schwarz/Mann [*Supply company in biochemistry and chemistry*] ... SM
Schwarzenberger's Manual of International Law [*A publication*] (DLA) ... Schwarz Int L
Schwarzenberger's Manual of International Law [*A publication*] (ILCA) ... Schwarz Man Int L
Schwaz, Tirol [*Austria ICAO location identifier*] (ICLI) ... LOXS
Schweats, Inc., Trenton, NJ [*Library symbol Library of Congress*] (LCLS) ... NjTSch
Schweinfurt [*Germany ICAO location identifier*] (ICLI) ... EDOA
Schweinfurt-Sud [*Germany ICAO location identifier*] (ICLI) ... EDFS
Schweitzer Mauduit International Inc. [*Associated Press*] (SAG) ... SchMau
Schweitzer Mauduit International Inc. [*NYSE symbol*] (SAG) ... SWM
Schweitzer-Mauduit Intl [*NYSE symbol*] (TTSB) ... SWM
Schweizer Hilfswerk fuer Emigrationskinder (BJA) ... SHEK
Schweizer Reneke [*South Africa*] [*ICAO location identifier*] (ICLI) ... FASG
Schweizerische Afrika-Gesellschaft [*Swiss Society of African Studies*] (EAIO) ... SAG
Schweizerische Bundesbahnen [*Swiss Federal Railways*] ... SBB
Schweizerische Depeschenagentur AG [*Swiss News Agency*] (EY) ... SDA
Schweizerische Koordinationsstelle fuer Bildungsforschung [*Swiss Coordination Center for Research in Education*] [*Information service or system*] (IID) ... SKBF
Schweizerische Landesbibliothek [*Swiss National Library*], Bern, Switzerland [*Library symbol Library of Congress*] (LCLS) ... Sz
Schweizerische Partei der Behinderten und Sozialbenachteiligten [*Swiss Party of the Handicapped and Socially Disadvantaged*] [*Political party*] (PPW) ... SPBS
Schweizerische Theologische Zeitschrift [*Zurich*] [*A publication*] (BJA) ... STZ
Schweizerische Vereinigung fuer Parapsychologie ... SVPP
Schweizerische Volkspartei [*Swiss People's Party*] [*Political party*] ... SV
Schweizerische Zeitschrift fuer Strafrecht/Revue Penale Suisse [*Berne, Switzerland*] [*A publication*] (DLA) ... Schweiz Z f Strafrecht
Schweizerischer Gewerkschaftsbund [*Swiss Federation of Trade Unions*] ... SGB
Schweizerischer Katholischer Volksverein ... SKVV
Schweizerischer Verband Evangaelischer Arbeitnehmer [*A union*] [*Switzerland*] (DCTA) ... SVEA

Schweizerischer Verband Evangelischer Arbeiter und Angestellter [*Swiss Federation of Protestant Trade Unions*] .... SVEAA

Schweizerisches Institut fuer Hauswirtschaft .... SIH

Schweizerisches Jahrbuch fuer Internationales Recht/Annuaire Suisse de Droit In ternational [*Zurich, Switzerland*] [*A publication*] (DLA) .... Schweiz Jb f Internat Recht

Schwenkfelder Historical Library, Pennsburg, PA [*Library symbol Library of Congress*] (LCLS) .... PPeSchw

Schwenningen Am Nickar [*Germany ICAO location identifier*] (ICLI) .... EDTE

Schwitzer, Inc. [*Associated Press*] (SAG) .... Schwtz

Schwitzer, Inc. [*NYSE symbol*] (SPSG) .... SCZ

SCI Fin $3.125'TECONS' [*NYSE symbol*] (TTSB) .... SRVPrT

SCI Finance LLC, Inc. [*Associated Press*] (SAG) .... SCI Fn

SCI Satellite Conferencing International Corp. [*Formerly, Valclair Resources, Ltd.*] [*Vancouver Stock Exchange symbol*] .... SCI

SCI Systems [*NASDAQ symbol*] (TTSB) .... SCIS

SCI Systems, Inc. [*Associated Press*] (SAG) .... SCI Sys

SCI Systems, Inc. [*NASDAQ symbol*] (NQ) .... SCIS

Sciacca [*Italy ICAO location identifier*] (ICLI) .... LICS

Sciatic [*Nerve*] [*Anatomy*] (DAVI) .... SC

Scibe Airlift [*Zaire*] [*ICAO designator*] (FAAC) .... SBZ

SciClone Pharmaceuticals [*NASDAQ symbol*] (TTSB) .... SCLN

SciClone Pharmaceuticals, Inc. [*Associated Press*] (SAG) .... SciClone

SciClone Pharmaceuticals, Inc. [*NASDAQ symbol*] (SAG) .... SCLN

Science (WGA) .... S

Science .... SC

Science (IDOE) .... sc

Science .... SCI

Science [*A publication*] (BRI) .... Sci

Science (AFM) .... SCI

Science Achievement Awards for Students .... SAAS

Science Activities for the Visually Impaired (AIE) .... SAVI

Science Advisors [*Army*] (RDA) .... SA

Science Advisory Board [*Environmental Protection Agency*] .... SAB

Science Analysis and Mission Planning Directorate [*NASA*] .... SAMPD

Science and Advanced Technology Laboratory [*Army*] (RDA) .... SATL

Science and Application (NASA) .... S & A

Science and Application Space Platform (MCD) .... SASP

Science and Applications [*NASA*] (SSD) .... SAA

Science and Applications Advocacy Group .... SAAG

Science and Applications Directorate [*NASA*] .... S & AD

Science and Applications Information System (SSD) .... SAIS

Science and Education Administration [*Department of Agriculture*] .... SEA

Science and Education Management Staff [*Department of Agriculture*] (GFGA) .... SEMS

Science and Engineering Academy of South Africa .... SEASA

Science and Engineering Committee for a Secure World (EA) .... SECSW

Science and Engineering Committee on Advisory to NOAA [*National Oceanic and Atmospheric Administration*] [*Defunct*] (USDC) .... SECAN

Science and Engineering Committee on Advisory to NOAA [*National Oceanic and Atmospheric Administration*] [*Marine science*] (OSRA) .... SECAN

Science & Engineering Consultants [*Reston, VA*] (TSSD) .... S & EC

Science and Engineering Information Center Co. (IID) .... SEICO

Science and Engineering Policy Studies Unit (AIE) .... SEPSU

Science and Engineering Research Council [*British Defunct*] .... SERC

Science and Engineering Research Council Network [*Later, SERCNET*] .... SRCNET

Science and Engineering Technician Education Program [*National Science Foundation*] .... SETEP

Science and Environmental Health Policy Project .... SEHPP

Science and Freedom [*A publication*] .... Sci Freedom

Science and Geography Education [*Database*] .... SAGE

Science and Mathematics Analysis Center [*ERIC*] .... SMAC

Science and Medicine Library, University of Toronto, Ontario [*Library symbol National Library of Canada*] (NLC) .... OTUH

Science and Public Affairs [*A publication*] .... SPA

Science and Public Policy Studies Group [*Newsletter*] .... SSPSG

Science & Society [*A publication*] (BRI) .... S&S

Science and Technology (NATG) .... S & T

Science and Technology (EERA) .... S&T

Science and Technology (WDAA) .... SC & T

Science and Technology Advisory Committee [*NASA*] (MCD) .... STAC

Science and Technology Advisory Panel .... STAP

Science and Technology Aerospace Reports (NITA) .... STAR

Science and Technology Agency (STA) .... STA

Science and Technology Agency [*of Japan*] (EERA) .... STA

Science and Technology Agency of Japan (EERA) .... STAJ

Science and Technology Agent (SDI) .... STA

Science and Technology Center [*National Science Foundation*] .... STC

Science and Technology Center, Far East Office [*Army*] (AABC) .... STCFEO

Science and Technology Center for Superconductivity [*National Science Foundation*] .... STCS

Science and Technology Corp. (RDA) .... STC

Science and Technology Desk Reference [*A publication*] .... STDR

Science and Technology Employment [*Longman Cartermill Ltd.*] [*Scotland*] [*Information service or system*] (CRD) .... STEM

Science and Technology Evaluation and Prioritization System [*Program*] (RDA) .... STEPS

Science and Technology for Environmental Protection Program [*Australia*] .... STEP

Science and Technology for Regional Innovation and Development in Europe [*EC*] (ECED) .... STRIDE

Science and Technology in Society (AIE) .... SATIS

Science and Technology Information Institute [*Information service or system*] (IID) .... STII

Science and Technology Information Service for Parliament [*British*] (IAA) .... STISP

Science and Technology Information System [*National Science Foundation*] .... STIS

Science and Technology Objectives (MCD) .... STO

Science and Technology Objectives Guide (MCD) .... STOG

Science and Technology Policies Information Exchange Programme [*SPINES*] [*UNESCO*] [*Superseded by*] [*Information service or system*] (IID) .... PIPS

Science and Technology Policies Information Exchange System [*UNESCO*] [*Bibliographic database*] (IID) .... SPINES

Science and Technology Policy [*Marine science*] (OSRA) .... STP

Science and Technology Policy (USDC) .... STP

Science and Technology Policy Implementation [*Project*] .... STPI

Science and Technology Policy Office [*Supersedes OST*] [*National Science Foundation*] .... STPO

Science and Technology Political Action Committee (EA) .... SCITEC-PAC

Science and Technology Regional Organizations [*British*] .... SATROS

Science and Technology Research Abstracts [*A publication*] .... SATRA

Science and Technology Research Center [*North Carolina*] (MCD) .... STRC

Science and Technology Section [*Association of College and Research Libraries*] .... STS

Science Applications, Inc. (NRCH) .... SAI

Science Applications, Inc. Global Computer Network (MCD) .... SAINET

Science Applications Incorporated Plan Monitoring System .... SAIPMS

Science Applications, Inc. - Software Design and Documentation Language (MCD) .... SAI-SDDL

Science Applications International Corp. .... SAIC

Science Applications International Corporation [*Marine science*] (OSRA) .... SAIC

Science, Applications, Technology Transfer, and Training [*System*] [*National Institutes of Health*] .... SATT

Science Associates/International [*Publisher*] (EA) .... SAI

Science Books & Films [*A publication*] (BRI) .... SB

Science Career Facilitation Project [*National Science Foundation*] .... SCFP

Science Citation Index Search [*Institute for Scientific Information*] [*Philadelphia, PA Bibliographic database*] .... SCISEARCH

Science Classroom Behavior Q-Sort (EDAC) .... SCBQ

Science Clubs of America (EA) .... SCA

Science College Ability Test (EDAC) .... SCAT

Science Communication Division [*George Washington University Medical Center*] [*Information service or system*] (IID) .... SCD

Science Council of Canada .... SCC

Science Council of Canada, Ottawa, ON, Canada [*Library symbol Library of Congress*] (LCLS) .... CaOOSCC

Science Council of Canada [*Conseil des Sciences du Canada*] Ottawa, Ontario [*Library symbol National Library of Canada*] (NLC) .... OOSCC

Science Council of Japan (MCD) .... SCJ

Science Court and Research Institute (EA) .... SCRI

Science Curriculum Improvement [*Study*] [*Education*] .... SCI

Science Curriculum Improvement Study [*Education*] .... SCIS

Science Data Conditioning System .... SDCS

Science Data Processing Facility (SSD) .... SDPF

Science Data System Support Equipment .... SDSSE

Science Data Team .... SDT

Science Dynamics [*NASDAQ symbol*] (TTSB) .... SIDY

Science Dynamics Corp. [*Associated Press*] (SAG) .... SciDyn

Science Dynamics Corp. [*NASDAQ symbol*] (NQ) .... SIDY

Science Education Development and Research Division [*National Science Foundation*] (GRD) .... SEDR

Science Education for Public Understanding Project [*Australia*] .... SEPUP

Science Education Information Analysis Center [*ERIC*] .... SEIAC

Science End-to-End Test [*Space*] .... SEET

Science, Engineering, and Related Career Hints [*Scientific Manpower Commi ssion*] [*A publication*] .... SEARCH

Science Engineering Library, Royal Military College of Canada, Kingston, Ontario [*Library symbol National Library of Canada*] (BIB) .... OKRS

Science Engineering News [*National Oceanic and Atmospheric Administration*] .... SEN

Science Ethic Society (EA) .... SES

Science Experiment Test Laboratory [*NASA*] .... SETL

Science Experiments Integration Laboratories .... SEIL

Science Fiction [*Also, SF*] .... SCI-FI

Science Fiction [*Also, SCI-FI*] .... SF

Science Fiction (WDMC) .... sf

Science Fiction and Fantasy [*Literary genre*] .... SF/F

Science Fiction and Fantasy RoundTable [*GE Information Services*] [*Information service or system*] (CRD) .... SFRT

Science Fiction and Fantasy Workshop (EA) .... SF & FW

Science Fiction Book Review Index 1923-1973 [*A publication*] .... SFBRI

Science Fiction Chronicle [*A publication*] (BRI) .... SF Chr

Science Fiction Foundation (EA) .... SFF

Science Fiction Pen Pal Club (EA) .... SFPPC

Science Fiction Poetry Association (EA) .... SFPA

Science Fiction Research Association (EA) .... SFRA

Science Fiction Writers of America (EA) .... SFWA

Science Foods, Inc. [*AMEX symbol*] (SAG) .... PDK

Science Foods, Inc. [*Associated Press*] (SAG) .... SciF

Science for the People (EA) .... SFTP

Science Frontiers [*An association*] (EA) .... SF

Science in General Management [*British*] (DI) .... SIGMA

Science in Social Context .... SISCON

Science, Industry, and Business Library [*New York, NY*] .... SIBL

Science Information Association .... SIA

Science Information Council [*National Science Foundation*] .... SIC

Science Information Exchange [*Later, SSIE*] [*Smithsonian Institution*] .... SIE

Science Information Facility [*FDA*] .... SIF
Science Information Resource Center [*Harper & Row*] [*Information service or system*] .... SIRC
Science Information Service (EA) .... SIS
Science Information Services [*Franklin Institute*] .... SIS
Science Information Services Organization [*Franklin Institute*] (IID) .... SISO
Science Innovation Program [*Australia*] .... SIPS
Science Management Corp. [*AMEX symbol*] (SPSG) .... SMG
Science Management Office [*Marine science*] (OSRA) .... SMO
Science Management Office (USDC) .... SMO
Science Masters Association (IAA) .... SMA
Science, Mathematics, and Engineering (RDA) .... SME
Science, Mathematics, and Environmental Education [*Educational Resources Information Center (ERIC) Clearinghouse*] [*Ohio State University*] (PAZ) .... SE
Science, Mathematics, and Environmental Education Information Analysis Center .... SMEAC
Science, Mathematics, and Related Technologies .... SMART
Science Mathematics Engineering and Technology .... SMET
Science, Mathematics, Foreign Languages .... SMFL
Science Museum, London, United Kingdom [*Library symbol Library of Congress*] (LCLS) .... UkLS
Science Museum of Minnesota, Louis S. Headley Memorial Library, St. Paul, MN [*Library symbol*] [*Library of Congress*] (LCLS) .... MnSSM
Science Museum of Victoria [*State*] (EERA) .... SMV
Science of Creative Intelligence [*Transcendental meditation*] .... SCI
Science of Survival .... SOS
Science of To-Day Series [*A publication*] .... STS
Science on 4 [*Radio program*] [*British*] SO4
Science Operations Ground System [*Space telescope software*] .... SOGS
Science Operations Planning Team .... SOPT
Science Operations Support Equipment .... SOSE
Science Organization Development Board [*National Academy of Sciences*] .... SODB
Science Pilot .... SP
Science Policy Foundation [*Later, ISPF*] [*British*] .... SPF
Science Policy Research Division [*of Congressional Research Service, Library of Congress*] .... SPRD
Science Policy Research Unit [*Research center British*] (IRC) .... SPRU
Science Press [*Information service or system*] (IID) .... SP
Science Process Competency Test (EDAC) .... SPCT
Science Procurement Information Network [*Canada*] .... SPIN
Science Recommendation Team .... SRT
Science Reference and Information Service (IID) .... SRIS
Science Reference Library (NITA) .... SRL
Science Requirements Strategy [*Viking lander mission*] [*NASA*] .... SRS
Science, Research, and Technology .... SRT
Science Research Associates (AEBS) .... SRA
Science Research Associates Primary Mental Abilities [*Psychology*] (AEBS) .... SRAPMA
Science Research Council [*Later, SERC*] [*British*] .... SRC
Science Research Temperament Scale [*Psychology*] .... SRTS
Science Resources Planning Office [*National Science Foundation*] .... SRPO
Science Service .... SS
Science Steering Group [*NASA*] .... SSG
Science Studies' Perception Questionnaire (AIE) .... SSPQ
Science Talent Search (EA) .... STS
[*The*] **Science Teacher** [*A publication*] .... TST
Science Teacher Inventory of Need (EDAC) .... STIN
Science Teachers' Authoring Facility (AIE) .... STAF
Science Teaching Achievement Recognition .... STAR
Science Team Analysis Facility [*NASA*] .... STAF
Science, Technology, and Economic Development .... STED
Science Technology and Education Division [*British Council*] (AIE) .... STED
Science Technology and Innovation Advisory Council [*Ireland*] .... STIAC
Science, Technology and Mathematics [*Adult Literacy Project*] [*Australia*] .... STEM
Science, Technology, and Society .... STS
Science, Technology, Engineering, Medicine Public Relations Association [*Great Britain*] .... STEMPRA
Science Train .... ST
Science Working Group (EERA) .... SWG
Science Working Panel [*NASA*] .... SWP
Science-by-Mail (EA) .... SBM
Science-Fiction Studies [*A publication*] (BRI) .... SFS
Sciences - A Process Approach [*National Science Foundation*] .... SAPA
[*UK Liaison Committee for*] **Sciences Allied to Medicine and Biology** (ACII) .... SAMB
Sciences and Humanities Research Institute [*Iowa State University*] [*Research center*] (RCD) .... SHRI
Sciences Library, Natural Sciences Centre, University of Western Ontario, London, Ontario [*Library symbol National Library of Canada*] (NLC) .... OLUM
Scientiae Baccalaureus [*Bachelor of Science*] [*Latin*] .... Sc B
Scientiae Doctor [*Doctor of Science*] [*Latin*] .... Sc D
Scientiae Doctor [*Doctor of Science*] (ADA) .... SD
Scientific .... SCIENT
Scientific .... SCNTFC
Scientific/Academic Computing Center [*State University of New York Health Science Center at Brooklyn*] [*Research center*] (RCD) .... S/ACC
Scientific Adviser to the Army Council [*World War II*] .... SA/AC
Scientific Advisory Board [*Air Force*] .... SAB
Scientific Advisory Committee [*Presidential*] [*Terminated*] .... SAC
Scientific Advisory Committee, Defence Services Panel [*British World War II*] .... SAC(DP)
Scientific Advisory Committee on Kangaroos [*Australia*] .... SACK
Scientific Advisory Council [*Ministry of Supply*] [*British World War II*] .... SAC
Scientific Advisory Group on Effects [*DoD Washington, DC*] (EGAO) .... SAGE
Scientific Advisory Panel [*Arlington, VA*] [*Environmental Protection Agency*] (EGAO) .... SAP
Scientific Advisory Team [*Navy*] (MCD) .... SAT
Scientific Aid to Indochina [*Task force established 1973 by Scientists' Institute for Public Information*] .... SAI
Scientific Airlock (MCD) .... SAL
Scientific American [*A publication*] (BRI) .... SA
Scientific American Medicine - Compact Disc [*Electronic publication*] .... SAM-CD
Scientific and Commercial Interpreter and Program Translator (IAA) .... SCRIPT
Scientific and Commercial Subroutine Interpreter and Program Translator .... SCRIPT
Scientific and Commercial Subroutine Interpreter and Program Translator (IAA) .... SCROPT
Scientific and Engineering .... S & E
Scientific and Engineering Computation .... SEC
Scientific and Engineering Computer Network (MCD) .... SENET
Scientific and Engineering Computing Council (MCD) .... SECC
Scientific and Engineering Data Processing Center .... SEDPC
Scientific and Engineering Personnel [*Military*] .... SEP
Scientific and Management Advisory Committee [*Terminated, 1973*] [*Army Computer Systems Command*] .... SAMAC
Scientific & Medical Publications of France, Inc. .... SMPF
Scientific and Optical Instruments .... SOI
Scientific and Technical (MCD) .... SAT
Scientific and Technical Aerospace Reports Administrator (AAGC) .... STARA
Scientific and Technical Analysis and Programs Directorate .... STAP
Scientific and Technical Application Forecasts .... STAF
Scientific and Technical Assessment of Environmental Pollutants [*Marine science*] (MSC) .... STAEP
Scientific and Technical Association of the People's Republic of China .... STAPRC
Scientific and Technical Communication .... SATCOM
Scientific and Technical Exploitation Program (AFM) .... STEP
Scientific and Technical Information [*Facility*] [*NASA*] .... STI
Scientific and Technical Information [*System*] [*Canada*] .... STI
Scientific and Technical Information and Communication (SAA) .... STINCOM
Scientific and Technical Information Centre, Laboratory and Scientific Services Division, Revenue Canada Customs and Excise [*Centre d'Information Scientifique et Technique, Division du Laboratoire et des Services Scientifiques, Revenu Canada Douanes et Accise*] **Ottawa, Ontario** [*Library symbol National Library of Canada*] (NLC) .... OOSTI
Scientific and Technical Information Dissemination [*NASA*] .... STID
Scientific and Technical Information Division [*NASA*] (IEEE) .... STID
Scientific and Technical Information Facility [*NASA*] .... SATIF
Scientific and Technical Information Facility [*NASA*] .... STIF
Scientific and Technical Information Modular System [*NASA*] (MCD) .... STIMS
Scientific and Technical Information Network [*Internet*] (AAGC) .... STINET
Scientific and Technical Information Network .... STN
Scientific and Technical Information Office [*Army*] .... STINFO
Scientific and Technical Information Office [*NASA*] .... STIO
Scientific and Technical Information Officers (NITA) .... STINFO
Scientific and Technical Information Program (MCD) .... STIP
Scientific and Technical Information Reviewed and Exploited [*A publication*] (RDA) .... SATIRE
Scientific and Technical Information Service (NITA) .... SATIS
Scientific & Technical Information Services, Inc. [*Information service or system*] (IID) .... STIS
Scientific and Technical Information System and Service (PDAA) .... STI/SS
Scientific and Technical Information Team [*Army*] (GFGA) .... STIT
Scientific and Technical Information Team, Continental United States [*Army*] (AABC) .... STIT-CONUS
Scientific and Technical Information Team, Europe [*Army*] (AABC) .... STIT-EUR
Scientific and Technical Information Team, Far East [*Army*] (AABC) .... STIT-FE
Scientific and Technical Intelligence [*Military*] (RDA) .... S & TI
Scientific and Technical Intelligence Center [*DoD*] .... STIC
Scientific and Technical Intelligence Liaison Officer (MCD) .... STILO
Scientific and Technical Intelligence Register (AFM) .... STIR
Scientific and Technical Liaison Office [*AFSC*] .... STLO
Scientific and Technical Modular System .... STMS
Scientific and Technical Organizations and Agencies Directory [*A publication*] .... STOAD
Scientific and Technical Personnel Data System [*National Science Foundation*] (GFGA) .... STPDS
Scientific and Technical Research Council of Turkey [*Ankara*] [*Information service or system*] (IID) .... TUBITAK
Scientific and Technological Library Literature [*Conference*] .... SATELLITE
Scientific and Technological Research (DEN) .... STR
Scientific Apparatus Makers Association [*Later, SAMAGA*] (EA) .... SAMA
Scientific Applications of Nuclear Explosions (SAA) .... SANE
Scientific Apprehension of God's Awesome Nature .... SAGAN
Scientific Arithmetic Unit .... SAU
Scientific Assistant [*Ministry of Agriculture, Fisheries, and Food*] [*British*] .... SA
Scientific Assistant Land Agent [*Ministry of Agriculture, Fisheries, and Food*] [*British*] .... SALA
Scientific Associates, Inc. (AAG) .... SAI
Scientific Balloon Facility .... SBF
Scientific Bureau of Investigation [*In radio series "Armstrong of the SBI"*] .... SBI
Scientific Business Systems (NITA) .... SBS
Scientific Calculator Machine (NITA) .... SCM
Scientific Certification Systems (EA) .... SCS
Scientific Civil Service [*British*] .... SCS
Scientific Clearinghouse and Documentation Services Division [*National Science and Technology Authority*] [*Information service or system*] (IID) .... SCDSD

Scientific Committee [*NATO*] (NATG) .... SCOM
Scientific Committee for Food [*European union*] .... SCF
Scientific Committee of National Representatives [*NATO*] .... SCNR
Scientific Committee on Antarctic Research [*ICSU*] [*Cambridge, England*] (EAIO) .... SCAR
Scientific Committee on Oceanic Research [*ICSU*] [*Halifax, NS*] (EAIO) .... SCOR
Scientific Committee on Problems of the Environment [*ICSU*] (EA) .... SCOPE
Scientific Committee on Solar Terrestrial Physics (EA) .... SCOSTEP
Scientific Committee on the Effects of Atomic Radiation .... SCEAR
Scientific Communication and Technology Transfer [*System*] [*University of Pennsylvania*] .... SCATT
Scientific Computation of Optimal Programs (IEEE) .... SCOOP
Scientific Computation of Optimum Procurement [*Air Force*] .... SCOOP
Scientific Computer Division [*Army Tank-Automotive Command*] .... SCD
Scientific Computers, Inc. (MCD) .... SCI
Scientific Computing and Automation .... SCA
Scientific Computing Facility .... SCF
Scientific Computing Feature (NITA) .... SCF
Scientific Computing Group [*University of Toronto*] [*Research center*] (RCD) .... SCG
Scientific Computing Laboratory Work Request (IAA) .... SCLWR
Scientific Continuous Simulation Language (IAA) .... SCSL
Scientific Control Systems (DIT) .... SCS
Scientific Co-Operation Bureau for the European and North American Region [*United Nations*] (EA) .... SC/BSE
Scientific Cooperative Operational Research Expedition [*National Oceanic and Atmospheric Administration*] (MSC) .... SCORE
Scientific Data Automation System (IEEE) .... SDAS
Scientific Data Center (MCD) .... SDC
Scientific Data Collection Exercise .... SDCE
Scientific Data Recorder .... SDR
Scientific Data System [*Later, XDS*] .... SDS
Scientific Data Systems Corporation (NITA) .... SDS
Scientific DataLink [*Comtex Scientific Corp.*] [*Information service or system*] (IID) .... SDL
Scientific Design [*Group*] .... SD
Scientific Discoveries and Discoverers [*A publication*] .... SDD
Scientific Distribution Technique .... SDT
Scientific Document Delivery System .... SDDS
Scientific Documentation Center Ltd. [*Dunfermline, Fife, Scotland*] .... SDC
Scientific Ecology Group Inc. (GAAI) .... SEG
Scientific Elementary Basic Language [*1963*] [*Computer science*] (CSR) .... SCELBAL
Scientific Engineering Information Center (KSC) .... SCENIC
Scientific Equipment (KSC) .... SEQ
Scientific Equipment Bay [*NASA*] (KSC) .... SEB
Scientific Estimates Committee [*Military*] (AABC) .... SEC
Scientific Evaluation and Research of Charismatic Healing [*An association*] (EA) .... SEARCH
Scientific Event Alert Network [*Smithsonian Institution*] [*Washington, DC*] (MCD) .... SEAN
Scientific Exchange Agreement .... SEA
Scientific Exploration of the Atlantic Shelf Committee .... SEASC
Scientific Exploration Society (EA) .... SES
Scientific Film Association (IAA) .... SFA
Scientific Games Hldgs [*NASDAQ symbol*] (TTSB) .... SGIH
Scientific Games Holding Corp. [*Associated Press*] (SAG) .... SciGm
Scientific Games Holding Corp. [*NASDAQ symbol*] (SAG) .... SGIH
Scientific Glass Apparatus Co., Inc. .... SGA
Scientific Group on Methodologies for the Safety Evaluation of Chemicals [*International Council of Scientific Unions*] .... SGOMSEC
Scientific Information and Documentation Division [*Later, ESIC*] .... SIDD
Scientific Information and Education Council of Physicians (EA) .... SIECOP
Scientific Information Center .... SIC
Scientific Information Centre, Defence and Civil Institute of Environmental Medicine, Canada Department of National Defence [*Centre d'Information Scientifique, Institut Militaire et Civil de Medecine de l'Environnement, Ministere de la Defense Nationale*] **Downsview, Ontario** [*Library symbol National Library of Canada*] (NLC) .... OTDR
Scientific Information [*or Instruction*] **Processor** [*Honeywell, Inc.*] .... SIP
Scientific Information Program on Eutrophication [*University of Wisconsin*] .... SIPE
Scientific Information Retrieval (NITA) .... SIR
Scientific Information Retrieval, Inc. [*Database management system*] [*Information service or system*] (IID) .... SIR
Scientific Information Systems Department [*Information service or system*] (IID) .... SISD
Scientific Instruction Set .... SIS
Scientific Instrument (NASA) .... SI
Scientific Instrument Computer and Data Handling (SSD) .... SIC & DH
Scientific Instrument Makers Trade Society [*A union*] [*British*] .... SIMTS
Scientific Instrument Manufacturers' Association [*British*] .... SIMA
Scientific Instrument Manufacturers' Association of Japan .... SIMAJ
Scientific Instrument Module [*NASA*] .... SIM
Scientific Instrument Package [*NASA*] (KSC) .... SIP
Scientific Instrument Research Association [*British*] .... SIRA
Scientific Instrument Society (EA) .... SIS
Scientific Instrumentation & Research Division (ACII) .... SIRCH
Scientific Instrumentation Information Network and Curricula [*National Science Foundation*] .... SIINC
Scientific Instrumentation Module Bay [*NASA*] (KSC) .... SIMBAY
Scientific Inventory Control Technique (IAA) .... SICT
Scientific Inventory Management and Control .... SIMCON
Scientific Laboratory Facility .... SLF

Scientific Library and Documentation Division [*National Science and Technology Authority*] [*Philippines*] [*Information service or system*] (IID) .... SLDD
Scientific Machine Automation Corp. .... SMAC
Scientific Manpower Commission (EA) .... SMC
Scientific Marriage Foundation (EA) .... SMF
Scientific Memorandum .... SM
Scientific Microsystems Inc. (NITA) .... SMS
Scientific Mission Support .... SMS
Scientific Note .... SN
Scientific Numeric Database Service [*National Research Council of Canada*] [*Information service or system*] (IID) .... CAN/SND
Scientific Officer [*Also, SO*] [*Ministry of Agriculture, Fisheries, and Food*] [*British*] .... ScO
Scientific Officer [*Ministry of Agriculture, Fisheries, and Food*] [*Also, ScO*] [*British*] .... SO
Scientific Opportunities Offered by a Nuclear Submarine [*A publication*] .... SOONS
Scientific Paper .... SP
Scientific Parameters for Health and the Environment, Retrieval and Estimation [*Database*] [*Environmental Protection Agency Washington, DC*] .... SPHERE
Scientific Passenger Pod (MCD) .... SPD
Scientific Passenger Pod [*NASA*] .... SPP
Scientific Pollution and Environmental Control Society .... SPEC
Scientific Power Switching .... SPS
Scientific Process & Research, Inc. [*Information service or system*] (IID) .... SPR
Scientific Processor (BUR) .... SP
Scientific Products .... S/P
Scientific Programs Unit [*Commonwealth*] (EERA) .... SPU
Scientific Reference Service [*HEW*] .... SRS
Scientific Report .... SR
Scientific Research .... SR
Scientific Research and Development Branch [*Home Office*] [*British*] (IRUK) .... SRDB
Scientific Research Committee [*Australia*] .... SRC
Scientific Research in British Universities and Colleges [*Later, RBUPC*] [*British Library*] .... SRBUC
Scientific Research Institute for Atomic Energy Reactors [*Former USSR*] .... SRIAER
Scientific Research Laboratory (AAG) .... SRL
Scientific Research Project Support [*National Science Foundation*] .... SRPS
Scientific Research Proposal (AAG) .... SRP
Scientific Research Society of America (EA) .... RESA
Scientific Research Society of America [*Later, Sigma XI, The Scientific Research Society of America*] (AAG) .... SRS
Scientific Research Society of America [*Later, Sigma XI, The Scientific Research Society of America*] .... SRSA
Scientific Research Tax Credit [*Canada*] .... SRTC
Scientific Review Board [*Intergovernmental Oceanographic Commission*] (GFGA) .... SRB
Scientific Services Program [*Army Research Office*] (RDA) .... SSP
Scientific Software Group .... SSG
Scientific Software Group .... SSG
Scientific Software Products, Inc. [*Information service or system*] (IID) .... SSP
Scientific Steering Group [*Marine science*] (OSRA) .... SSG
Scientific Steering Group [*Tropical Ocean-Global Atmosphere*] (USDC) .... SSG
Scientific Subroutine Library .... SSL
Scientific Subroutine Package [*Computer science*] .... SSP
Scientific Subroutine System [*Computer science*] (BUR) .... SSS
Scientific Support Coordinator (FFDE) .... SSC
Scientific Support Division [*National Severe Storms Laboratory*] (USDC) .... SSD
Scientific Support Division [*Marine science*] (OSRA) .... SSD
Scientific Support Laboratory [*CDEC*] (MCD) .... SSL
Scientific Survey Module (IAA) .... SSM
Scientific Systems, Inc. .... SSI
Scientific, Technical, and Medical .... STM
Scientific, Technical, and Research Commission (EY) .... STRC
Scientific Technical and Societal Information (NITA) .... STSI
Scientific/Technical Careers Advisory Committee [*Environmental Protection Agency*] (GFGA) .... S/TCAC
Scientific/Technical Information (AAGC) .... STINFO
Scientific, Technical, Intelligence, and Program Information System [*HEW*] .... STIPIS
Scientific Technical Report .... STR
Scientific, Technological, and International Affairs Directorate [*National Science Foundation*] .... STIA
Scientific Technologies [*NASDAQ symbol*] (TTSB) .... STIZ
Scientific Technology, Inc. [*Associated Press*] (SAG) .... SciTch
Scientific Technology, Inc. [*NASDAQ symbol*] (NQ) .... STIZ
Scientific Terminal System (IAA) .... STS
Scientific Time Sharing Corp. [*Host*] [*Information service or system*] (IID) .... STSC
Scientific Visualization (CDE) .... SV
Scientific Wild Aim Guess [*Bowdlerized version*] .... SWAG
Scientific Wild-Aim Guess System [*Bowdlerized version*] (MCD) .... SWAGS
Scientific Word Processor [*Computer science*] .... SWP
Scientific Working Group [*EXAMETNET*] .... SWG
Scientifically Treated Petroleum [*A motor fuel oil additive*] [*Initials reported, by extension of meaning, also to stand for a hallucinogenic drug, DOM*] .... STP
Scientifically Treated Petroleum [*Trade-name for a gasoline additive*] (BARN) .... STP
Scientific-Atlanta [*NYSE symbol*] (TTSB) .... SFA
Scientific-Atlanta, Inc. [*Associated Press*] (SAG) .... SciAtl
Scientific-Atlanta, Inc. [*NYSE symbol*] (SPSG) .... SFA
Scientist .... SCNTST
Scientist-Man Year .... SMY

Scientist-Pilot [*NASA*] (KSC) .... SPT
Scientists Against Nuclear Arms [*British*] [*An association*] (DBA) .... SANA
Scientists and Engineers (RDA) .... S & E
Scientists and Engineers Emigrant Fund .... SEEF
Scientists and Engineers Field Experience with Soldiers (RDA) .... SEFEWS
Scientists and Engineers for National Development [*Scholarship program*] .... SEND
Scientists and Engineers for Secure Energy (EA) SE2
Scientists and Engineers for Social and Political Action [*Later, SFTP*] (EA) .... SESPA
Scientists and Engineers in Economic Development [*National Science Foundation*] .... SEED
Scientists and Professional Engineers Employment Registry [*Career Technologies Corp. - CTC*] [*Andover, MA*] [*Information service or system*] (IID) .... SPEER
Scientists' Center for Animal Welfare (EA) .... SCAW
Scientists' Committee for Public Information [*Defunct*] .... SCPI
Scientists' Committee for Radiation Information (EA) .... SCRI
Scientists, Engineers, Technicians .... SET
Scientists for Life (EA) .... SFL
Scientists for Life [*An association Defunct*] (EA) .... SL
Scientists for Sakharov, Orlov, and Shcharansky (EA) .... SOS
Scientists' Group for Reform of Animal Experimentation (EA) .... SGRAE
Scientists in the Sea Program [*National Oceanic and Atmospheric Administration*] (MSC) .... SITS
Scientists' Institute for Public Information (EA) .... SIPI
SciGenetics, Inc. [*NASDAQ symbol*] (SAG) .... SCGN
SciGenetics, Inc. [*Associated Press*] (SAG) .... SciGen
SCI-International Voluntary Service (EA) .... SCI-IVS
Scilicet [*Namely*] [*Latin*] (DLA) .... S
Scilicet [*Namely*] [*Legal term Latin*] .... SC
Scilicet [*Scire Licet*] [*It is permitted to know*] [*Latin*] (WDMC) .... sc
Scilicet [*Namely*] [*Legal term Latin*] .... SCIL
Scilicet [*Namely*] [*Legal term Latin*] .... SS
Scilly Isles/St. Mary's [*British ICAO location identifier*] (ICLI) .... EGHE
Scinde Horse [*British military*] (DMA) .... SH
Scinde Irregular Horse [*British military*] (DMA) .... SIH
Scintillating Fiber Telescope for Energetic Radiation [*Proposed, 1996*] .... SIFTER
Scintillation Counter [*Instrumentation*] .... SC
Scintillation Detector (IEEE) .... ScD
Scintillation Proximity Assay [*Analytical biochemistry*] .... SPA
Scintillator [*Nucleonics*] .... SCINT
Scintilore Explorations Ltd. [*Toronto Stock Exchange symbol*] .... SLP
Scintiscan [*Medicine*] .... SCAN
Scintiscanning [*Medicine*] .... SS
Scintrex Ltd. [*Toronto Stock Exchange symbol*] .... SCT
Scios, Inc. [*NASDAQ symbol*] (SAG) .... SCIO
Scios Inc. [*NASDAQ symbol*] (TTSB) .... SCIO
Scios, Inc. [*Associated Press*] (SAG) .... Scios
Scios Inc. Wrrt'D' [*NASDAQ symbol*] (TTSB) .... SCIOZ
Scios Nova, Inc. [*NASDAQ symbol*] (SPSG) .... SCIO
Scios Nova, Inc. [*Associated Press*] (SAG) .... Scios
Scios Nova, Inc. [*Associated Press*] (SAG) .... SciosNov
Scioto Technical College, Lucasville, OH [*Library symbol Library of Congress Obsolete*] (LCLS) .... OLuS
Scioto Village High School, Powell, OH [*Library symbol Library of Congress*] (LCLS) .... OPowS
Scipio Society of Naval and Military History (EA) .... SSNMH
Scire Facias [*Please make known*] [*A writ to enforce, annul, or vacate a judgment, patent, charter or other matter of record*] [*Legal term*] [*Latin*] .... SCI FA
Scire Facias [*Make Him Know*] [*Latin*] (LWAP) .... SCI FA
Scire Facias ad Disprobandum Debitum [*Latin*] (DLA) .... Sci Fa ad Dis Deb
Scissor, Shear, and Manicure Implement Manufacturers Association [*Later, National Association of Scissors and Shears Manufacturers*] (EA) .... SSMIMA
Scissor Workboard Hands' Society [*A union*] [*British*] .... SWHS
Scissors Bridge (DWSG) .... SB
SciTech Book News [*A publication*] (BRI) .... SciTech
Scitex Corp. Ltd. [*Associated Press*] (SAG) .... Scitex
Scitex Corp. Ltd. [*NASDAQ symbol*] (NQ) .... SCIX
Scitex Corp. Ord [*NASDAQ symbol*] (TTSB) .... SCIXF
Scitex Graphic Arts Users Association (EA) .... SGAUA
Scitex Graphic Arts Users Group [*Later, SGAUA*] (EA) .... SGAUG
Scituate Historical Society, Scituate, MA [*Library symbol Library of Congress*] (LCLS) .... MScitHi
Sclavonic [*Language, etc.*] (ROG) .... SCLAV
Scleral Buckling [*Ophthalmalogy*] (CPH) .... SB
Scleral Buckling Procedure [*Medicine*] (MAE) .... SBP
Scleral Cautery [*Ophthalmology*] (CPH) .... SC
Sclerite-Inducing Membrane [*Entomology*] .... SIM
Sclerocorneal Junction [*Ophthalmology*] (DAVI) .... SCJ
Sclerocorneall [*Ophthalmology*] (DAVI) .... SC
Scleroderma [*Medicine*] (DAVI) .... SCL
Scleroderma [*Medicine*] .... SCLERO
Scleroderma [*Medicine*] (DAVI) .... SD
Scleroderma Association (EA) .... SA
Scleroderma Federation (EA) .... SF
Scleroderma International Foundation (EA) .... SIF
Scleroderma Renal Crisis [*Medicine*] .... SRC
Scleroderma Research Foundation (EA) .... SRF
Scleroderma Support Group (EA) .... SSG
Scleroscope .... SCLER
Scleroscope Hardness .... SH
Sclerosing Hyaline Necrosis [*Medicine*] .... SHN
Sclerosing Leukoencephalopathy [*Medicine*] (DMAA) .... SL
Sclerosing Papillomatous Pattern [*Medicine*] .... SPP
Sclerosing Sweat Duct Carcinoma [*Oncology*] .... SSDC
Sclerosis [*Medicine*] .... SCLER
Sclerotherapy [*Medicine*] .... ST
Sclerotinia minor [*A fungus*] .... Sm
Sclerotinia sclerlatiorum (Causative Agent of Peanut Blight) .... SS
SCN [*Stock Control Number*] **Index and Log** .... SIL
Scobey, MT [*FM radio station call letters*] .... KCGM
Scobey, MT [*Location identifier FAA*] (FAAL) .... SCO
Scolasticat de l'Immaculee-Conception, Montreal, PQ, Canada [*Library symbol Library of Congress*] (LCLS) .... CaQMSI
Scolasticat de l'Immaculee-Conception, Montreal, Quebec [*Library symbol National Library of Canada*] (NLC) .... QMSI
Scolia Anonyma [*Classical studies*] (OCD) .... Scol Anon
Scolia Attica [*Classical studies*] (OCD) .... Scol Att
Scoliosis Association (EA) .... SA
Scoliosis Association of the United Kingdom (EAIO) .... SAUK
Scoliosis Research Society (EA) .... SRSO
Scone [*Australia Airport symbol*] (OAG) .... NSO
Scooter (AAG) .... SCTR
Scoot-Tours Touring Scooter Riders Association (EA) .... STTSRA
Scope Change (MCD) .... SC
Scope Indus [*AMEX symbol*] (TTSB) .... SCP
Scope Industries [*Associated Press*] (SAG) .... Scope
Scope Industries [*AMEX symbol*] (SPSG) .... SCP
Scope Octal Debugging Tape .... SODT
Scope of Word Addendum (MCD) .... SWA
Scope of Work (MCD) .... SOW
Scope Plot (IAA) .... SCOPLT
Scoping Emergency Cooling Heat Transfer [*Nuclear energy*] (KSC) .... SECHT
Scopolamine [*Anticholinergic compound*] .... SCOP
Scopus Technology [*NASDAQ symbol*] (TTSB) .... SCOP
Scopus Technology, Inc. [*NASDAQ symbol*] (SAG) .... SCOP
Scopus Technology, Inc. [*Associated Press*] (SAG) .... Scopus
SCOR US Corp. [*Associated Press*] (SAG) .... SCOR U
SCOR US Corp. [*NYSE symbol*] (SPSG) .... SUR
Scorable Unit .... SU
Scorched Aluminum Powder .... SAP
Scorcorp Industries, Inc. [*Vancouver Stock Exchange symbol*] .... SRJ
Score (AABC) .... SC
Score (ROG) .... SCR
Score Board [*NASDAQ symbol*] (TTSB) .... BSBL
[*The*] **Score Board, Inc.** [*NASDAQ symbol*] (NQ) .... BSBL
Score Board, Inc. [*Associated Press*] (SAG) .... ScoreBd
Score Resources [*Vancouver Stock Exchange symbol*] .... SCO
Score, Teach, and Record [*Teaching machine*] .... STAR
Scorer and Analyzer [*Computerized educational testing*] .... SCORAN
Scoresbysund [*Greenland*] [*ICAO location identifier*] (ICLI) .... BGSC
Scoresbysund [*Greenland*] [*Seismograph station code, US Geological Survey Closed*] (SEIS) .... SCO
Scoriae [*Quality of the bottom*] [*Nautical charts*] .... Sc
Scoring (ADA) .... SCG
Scoring Booklet (MCD) .... SB
Scoring Criteria (MCD) .... SC
Scoring Reliability (MCD) .... SR
Scorpion Resources [*Vancouver Stock Exchange symbol*] .... SCB
Scorpion Toxin [*Immunology*] .... SCT
Scorpius [*Constellation*] .... Sco
Scorpius [*Constellation*] .... Scor
Scot .... S
Scotch and Divorce Appeals [*1866-75*] [*A publication*] (DLA) .... LR Sc & Div
Scotch and Divorce Appeals [*English Law Reports*] [*A publication*] (DLA) .... Sc & Div App
Scotch Court of Session Cases [*A publication*] (DLA) .... Sc Sess Cas
Scotch Court of Session Cases [*A publication*] (DLA) .... Sess Ca
Scotch Court of Session Cases [*A publication*] (DLA) .... Sess Cas
Scotch Court of Session Cases [*A publication*] (DLA) .... Sess Cas Sc
Scotch Court of Session Cases Decided by the English Judges [*1655-61*] [*A publication*] (DLA) .... Eng Judg
Scotch Court of Session Cases, Fifth Series, by Fraser [*A publication*] (DLA) .... Fraser (Scot)
Scotch Court of Session Cases, First Series [*A publication*] (DLA) .... Ct Sess Ist Ser
Scotch Gaelic [*Language*] (BARN) .... Sc Gael
Scotch Malt Whisky Society (DBA) .... SMWS
Scotch Munitions Appeals Reports [*Edinburgh and Glasgow*] [*A publication*] (DLA) .... Sc Mun App Rep
Scotch Plains Public Library, Scotch Plains, NJ [*Library symbol Library of Congress*] (LCLS) .... NjScp
Scotch Quality Beef and Lamb Association [*British*] (DBA) .... SQBLA
Scotch Revised Reports [*A publication*] (DLA) .... Sc RR
Scotch Roman [*Typography*] (DGA) .... SC ROM
Scotch Session Cases [*A publication*] (DLA) .... SSC
Scotch Whisky Association [*British*] (DBA) .... SWA
Scotch-Irish Foundation (EA) .... SIF
Scotch-Irish Society of the United States of America (EA) .... SIS
Scotch-Irish Society of the United States of America (EA) .... SISUSA
Scotia Sun, Port Hawkesbury, Nova Scotia [*Library symbol National Library of Canada*] (NLC) .... NSPSS
Scotia-Fundy Regional Library, Fisheries and Oceans Canada [*Bibliotheque de la Region Scotia-Fundy, Peches et Oceans Canada*], Halifax, Nova Scotia [*Library symbol National Library of Canada*] (NLC) .... NSHF
Scotland [*MARC geographic area code Library of Congress*] (LCCP) .... e-uk-st
Scotland (VRA) .... Scot
Scotland [*or Scottish*] (EY) .... SCOT
Scotland (ROG) .... SCOTL

Scotland [*MARC country of publication code Library of Congress*] (LCCP) .... stk
Scotland Bancorp [*AMEX symbol*] (TTSB) .... SSB
Scotland Bancorp, Inc. [*Associated Press*] (SAG) .... ScotBcp
Scotland Bancorp, Inc. [*AMEX symbol*] (SAG) .... SSB
Scotland County Memorial Library, Laurinburg, NC [*Library symbol Library of Congress*] (LCLS) .... NcL
Scotland Iceland (IAA) .... SCOTICE
Scotland Neck Memorial Library, Scotland Neck, NC [*Library symbol Library of Congress*] (LCLS) .... NcScn
Scotland Neck, NC [*FM radio station call letters*] .... WWRT
Scotland Neck, NC [*AM radio station call letters*] .... WYAL
Scotland School for Veterans' Children, Scotland, PA [*OCLC symbol*] (OCLC) .... PIV
Scotland [*or*] **Scottish** (ODBW) .... Scot
Scotland to Iceland Submarine Cable System [*Telecommunications*] (TEL) .... SCOTICE
Scotland Yard .... SYD
Scotopic Critical Flicker Frequency [*Magnetic environment*] .... SCFF
Scots .... SC
Scots Ancestry Research Society [*British*] (DBA) .... SARS
Scots Guards [*Military unit*] [*British*] .... SG
Scots Language Society [*British*] (DBA) .... SLS
Scots Law Times [*A publication*] (DLA) .... Sc LT
Scots Law Times [*A publication*] (DLA) .... Scot LT
Scots Law Times (Lyon Court Reports) [*A publication*] (DLA) .... SLT (Lyon Ct)
Scots Law Times (Notes of Recent Decisions) [*A publication*] (DLA) .... SLT (Notes)
Scots Law Times Reports [*A publication*] (DLA) .... Scots LTR
Scots Law Times Sheriff Court Reports [*A publication*] (DLA) .... SLT (Sh Ct)
Scots Revised Reports [*A publication*] (DLA) .... Sc Rev Rept
Scots Revised Reports [*1707-1873*] [*A publication*] (DLA) .... Scots RR
Scots Revised Reports [*A publication*] (DLA) .... SRR
Scots Styles Book [*A publication*] (ILCA) .... SSB
Scotsman Industries [*NYSE symbol*] (TTSB) .... SCT
Scotsman Industries, Inc. [*Associated Press*] (SAG) .... Scotmn
Scotsman Industries, Inc. [*NYSE symbol*] (SPSG) .... SCT
Scott Air Force Base [*Illinois*] .... SAFB
Scott Air Force Base Library, Scott AFB, IL [*OCLC symbol*] (OCLC) .... BLV
Scott and Jarnigan on the Law of Telegraphs [*A publication*] (DLA) .... Sco & J Tel
Scott & Stringfellow Financial [*Associated Press*] (SAG) .... ScotStrng
Scott & Stringfellow Financial, Inc. [*Richmond, VA*] [*NASDAQ symbol*] (NQ) .... SCOT
Scott & Stringfellow Financial, Inc. [*Associated Press*] (SAG) .... ScotSt
Scott and White Memorial Hospital, Temple, TX [*Library symbol Library of Congress*] (LCLS) .... TxTemH
Scott Aviation, Lancaster, NY [*Library symbol*] [*Library of Congress*] (LCLS) .... NLanS
Scott Base [*Antarctica*] [*Seismograph station code, US Geological Survey*] (SEIS) .... SBA
Scott City, KS [*AM radio station call letters*] .... KFLA
Scott City, KS [*FM radio station call letters*] .... KSKL
Scott County Courthouse, Davenport, IA [*Library symbol Library of Congress*] (LCLS) .... IaDaCoC
Scott County Historical Society, Benton, MO [*Library symbol*] [*Library of Congress*] (LCLS) .... MoBeHi
Scott County Library, Eldridge, IA [*Library symbol Library of Congress*] (LCLS) .... IaEldr
Scott County Library, Gate City, VA [*Library symbol Library of Congress*] (LCLS) .... ViGcS
Scott County Library, Shakopee, MN [*Library symbol Library of Congress*] (LCLS) .... MnShS
Scott County Public Library, Scottsburg, IN [*Library symbol Library of Congress*] (LCLS) .... InSc
Scott, Foresman Achievement Test (EDAC) .... SFAT
Scott Industrial Foam .... SIF
Scott Joplin Commemorative Committee (EA) .... SJCC
Scott Joplin Ragtime Festival (EA) .... SJRF
Scott Library [*A publication*] .... SLA
Scott Paper Co. [*NYSE symbol*] (SPSG) .... SPP
Scott Paper Ltd. [*Associated Press*] (SAG) .... ScottP
Scott Paper Ltd. [*Toronto Stock Exchange symbol Vancouver Stock Exchange symbol*] .... SPL
Scott Polar Research Institute [*Cambridge, England*] .... SPRI
Scott/Stringfellow Finl [*NASDAQ symbol*] (TTSB) .... SCOT
Scottdale, PA [*FM radio station call letters*] .... WLSW
Scottie Gold Mines Ltd. [*Vancouver Stock Exchange symbol*] .... SDL
Scottish (ROG) .... SCO
Scottish [*or Scotsman*] (ROG) .... SCOT
Scottish Academic Live Television Interconnect and Research Environment (AIE) .... SALTIRE
Scottish Adult Basic Education Unit (AIE) .... SABEU
Scottish Adult Basic Education Unit .... SCADEU
Scottish Adult Literacy Resource Agency .... SCALRA
Scottish Advisory Committee on Computers in the Health Service .... SACCHS
Scottish Aeromodellers Association (DBA) .... SAA
Scottish Agricultural Industries [*Commercial firm*] .... SAI
Scottish Agricultural Organisation Society (DBA) .... SAOS
Scottish Agricultural Statistics Service [*University of Edinburgh*] (IRC) .... SAAS
Scottish Air Traffic Control Centre [*British ICAO location identifier*] (ICLI) .... EGPX
Scottish Airways Flyers Ltd. [*ICAO designator*] (FAAC) .... SKO
Scottish Amateur Athletic Association .... SAAA
Scottish Amateur Boxing Association [*British*] (DBA) .... SABA
Scottish Amateur Gymnastics Association (DBA) .... SAGA
Scottish Amateur Music Association (DBA) .... SAMA
Scottish Amateur Rowing Association (DBA) .... SARA
Scottish Amateur Swimming Association (DBA) .... SASA
Scottish Amateur Wrestling Association (DBA) .... SAWA
Scottish Amicable Investment Managers [*Finance*] .... SAIM
Scottish and Divorce Appeals [*1866-75*] [*A publication*] (DLA) .... LR Sc & D App
Scottish and Divorce Cases before the House of Lords [*A publication*] (DLA) .... LR Sc & D App
Scottish & Newcastle Breweries [*Commercial firm British*] .... S & N
Scottish and Universal Investments .... SUITS
Scottish & York Holdings Ltd. [*Toronto Stock Exchange symbol*] .... SYH
Scottish Anglers National Association (DBA) .... SANA
Scottish Anti-Vivisection Society (DI) .... SAVS
Scottish Appeal Reports [*A publication*] (DLA) .... Scot App Rep
Scottish Archery Association (DBA) .... SAA
Scottish Arts Council (EAIO) .... SAC
Scottish Assessors' Association (DBA) .... SAA
Scottish Association for Educational Management and Administration (AIE) .... SAEMA
Scottish Association for Marine Science .... SAMS
Scottish Association for Mental Health [*British*] .... SAMH
Scottish Association for National Certificates and Diplomas .... SANCAD
Scottish Association for the Deaf (DBA) .... SAD
Scottish Association for the Teaching of English as a Foreign Language (AIE) .... SATEFL
Scottish Association of Advisers in Physical Education (DBA) .... SAAPE
Scottish Association of Care and Resettlement Offenders (DBA) .... SACRO
Scottish Association of Children's Panels (DBA) .... SACP
Scottish Association of Family Conciliation Services (DBA) .... SAFCOS
Scottish Association of Geography Teachers [*British*] .... SAGT
Scottish Association of Local Government to Educational Psychologists [*British*] .... SALGEP
Scottish Association of Local Sports Councils (DBA) .... SALSC
Scottish Association of Master Bakers (DBA) .... SAMB
Scottish Association of Metals (DBA) .... SAM
Scottish Association of Milk Product Manufacturers (DBA) .... SAMPM
Scottish Association of Operative Coachmakers [*A union*] .... SAOC
Scottish Association of Opticians (DAS) .... SAO
Scottish Association of Plane Makers [*A union*] .... SAPM
Scottish Association of Public Transport (DBA) .... SAPT
Scottish Association of University Teachers [*A union*] .... SAUT
Scottish Association of Writers [*British*] .... SAW
Scottish Association of Young Farmers' Clubs (EAIO) .... SAYFC
Scottish Australian Heritage Council .... SAHC
Scottish Australian Horse Council .... SAHC
Scottish Auto-Cycle Union (DBA) .... SACU
Scottish Automobile Club (DI) .... SAC
Scottish Aviation Ltd. [*ICAO aircraft manufacturer identifier*] (ICAO) .... BT
Scottish Aviation Ltd. [*ICAO aircraft manufacturer identifier*] (ICAO) .... SC
Scottish Badminton Union (EAIO) .... SBU
Scottish Basketball Association (DBA) .... SBA
Scottish Blackface Sheep Breeders Association (EA) .... SBSBA
Scottish Book Marketing Group .... SBMG
Scottish Building and Public Works Exhibition [*Scottish Exhibitions Ltd.*] (TSPED) .... SCOTBUILD
Scottish Building Contractors Association (DBA) .... SBCA
Scottish Bus Group Ltd. (DCTA) .... SBG
Scottish Business Education Council (DCTA) .... SCOTBEC
Scottish Campaign to Resist the Atomic Menace .... SCRAM
Scottish Canoe Association (DBA) .... SCA
Scottish Carpet Manufacturers Association (DBA) .... SCMA
Scottish Cashmere Association (DBA) .... SCA
Scottish Cashmere Producers Association (DBA) .... SCPA
Scottish Cement Merchants Association (DBA) .... SCMA
Scottish Center for Agricultural Engineering .... SCAE
Scottish Central Committee on Modern Languages (AIE) .... SCCML
Scottish Central Library (PDAA) .... SCL
Scottish Central Library, Edinburgh, United Kingdom [*Library symbol Library of Congress*] (LCLS) .... UkES
Scottish Centre for Education Overseas (AIE) .... SCEO
Scottish Centre for the Tuition of the Disabled [*Queen Margaret College*] (CB) .... SCTD
Scottish Centre of Agricultural Engineering [*British*] (IRUK) .... SCAE
Scottish Certificate in Office Studies .... SCOS
Scottish Certificate of Education .... SCE
Scottish Certificate of Education Examination Board .... SCEEB
Scottish Chess Association (DBA) .... SCA
Scottish Child and Family Alliance (DBA) .... SCAFA
Scottish Church History Society (EAIO) .... SCHS
Scottish Church Union .... SCU
Scottish Churches Action for World Development (EAIO) .... SCAWD
Scottish Clay Pigeon Association (DBA) .... SCPA
Scottish Colleges In-Service Education of Teachers (AIE) .... SCINSET
Scottish Combined Societies [*Australia*] .... SCS
Scottish Commercial Travellers Association (DBA) .... SCTA
Scottish Committee Action on Smoking and Health (EAIO) .... SCASH
Scottish Committee on Open Learning (AIE) .... SCOL
Scottish Community Education Council (EAIO) .... SCEC
Scottish Computers in Schools Project (AIE) .... SCMP
Scottish Confederation of Tourism (DBA) .... SCOT
Scottish Conservative Party [*Political party*] .... SCP
Scottish Constitution (ADA) .... SC
Scottish Convention of Women (DI) .... SCOW
Scottish Cooperative Development Committee .... SCDC
Scottish Co-Operative Wholesale Society .... SCWS
Scottish Corn Trade Association (DBA) .... SCTA
Scottish Council for Civil Liberties (DI) .... SCCL

Scottish Council for Community Education .... SCCE
Scottish Council for Educational Technology (IID) .... SCET
Scottish Council for Research in Education .... SCRE
Scottish Council for Single Homeless (DBA) .... SCSH
Scottish Council for Single Parents (DBA) .... SCSP
Scottish Council for Voluntary Organisations (DBA) .... SCVO
Scottish Council of Civil Liberties (DBA) .... SCCL
Scottish Council of Dance (DBA) .... SCD
Scottish Council of Development and Industry (DI) .... SCDI
Scottish Council of Social Service (DI) .... SCSS
Scottish Council of Textile Trade Unions (DCTA) .... SCTTU
Scottish Countryside Activities Council (DBA) .... SCAC
Scottish Countryside Rangers Association (DBA) .... SCRA
Scottish Court of Session Cases, New Series [A publication] (DLA) ...... SC (Scot)
Scottish Courts Administration (ILCA) .... SCA
Scottish Credit Accumulation and Transfer (AIE) .... SCOTCAT
Scottish Cricket Union (DBA) .... SCU
Scottish Criminal Records Office [Office of Population Census and Surveys]
    [British] .... SCRO
Scottish Crofters Union (DBA) .... SCU
Scottish Crop Research Institute .... SCRI
Scottish Crop Research Institute [Research center] (IRC) .... SCRI
Scottish Croquet Association (DBA) .... SCA
Scottish Cross Country Union (DBA) .... SCCU
Scottish Cyclists Union (DBA) .... SCU
Scottish Daily Newspaper Society (DBA) .... SDNS
Scottish Dairy Trade Federation (DBA) .... SDTF
Scottish Dance Teacher's Alliance [Glasgow, Scotland] (EAIO) ..... SDTA
Scottish Dancing Association of Australia .... SDAA
Scottish Darts Association (DBA) .... SDA
Scottish Decorators Federation (EAIO) .... SDF
Scottish Deerhound Club of America (EA) .... SDCA
Scottish Development Agency (DS) .... SDA
Scottish Development Department (DCTA) .... SDD
Scottish Diploma in Agriculture .... SDA
Scottish Diploma in Dairying .... SDD
Scottish Diploma in Horticulture .... SDH
Scottish Diploma in Poultry Husbandry .... SDP
Scottish District [Council] .... SD
Scottish Economic Planning Department [British] .... SEPD
Scottish Economic Society [British] .... SES
Scottish Education and Action for Development (EAIO) .... SEAD
Scottish Education Department .... SED
Scottish Egg Trade Association (DBA) .... SETA
Scottish Electrical Training Scheme Ltd. [British] .... SETS
Scottish Electro-Static Discharge Association (EAIO) .... SESDA
Scottish Engineering Exhibition for Design, Production, and Automation
    [Scottish Exhibitions Ltd.] (TSPED) .... SCOTENG
Scottish, English, and European Textiles [Commercial firm] ..... SEET
Scottish Episcopal Youth Fellowship .... SEYF
Scottish European Airways [ICAO designator] (AD) .... WW
Scottish European Airways Ltd. [British ICAO designator] (FAAC) ...... SEU
Scottish Evangelistic Council (DBA) .... SEC
Scottish Examining Board (DCTA) .... SEB
Scottish Federation of Fishermen's Co-Operatives (DBA) .... SFFC
Scottish Federation of Housing Associations (DBA) .... SFHA
Scottish Federation of Meat Traders Associations (DBA) .... SFMTA
Scottish Federation of Merchant Tailors (DBA) .... SFMT
Scottish Federation of Sea Anglers (DBA) .... SFSA
Scottish Field Studies Association [British] .... SFSA
Scottish Film Council .... SFC
Scottish Fish Merchants Federation (DBA) .... SFMF
Scottish Football Association (DI) .... SFA
Scottish Football League (DBA) .... SFL
Scottish Forces [World War II] .... SCOFOR
Scottish Furniture Manufacturers Association (DBA) .... SFMA
Scottish Further and Higher Education Association (DBA) ...... SFHEA
Scottish Further Education Association [British] .... SFEA
Scottish Gaelic Texts Society (DBA) .... SGTS
Scottish Games Association (EAIO) .... SGA
Scottish Glass Association (DBA) .... SGA
Scottish Gliding Union (DBA) .... SGU
Scottish Golf Union (DBA) .... SGU
Scottish Grand Lodge of Freemasons .... SGLF
Scottish Guild of Servers [Episcopalian] .... SGS
Scottish Hang Gliding Federation (DBA) .... SHGF
Scottish Harp Society of America (EA) .... SHSA
Scottish Health Education Group (DI) .... SHEG
Scottish Health Visitors Association (DBA) .... SHVA
Scottish Heritable Trust .... SHT
Scottish Heritage USA (EA) .... SHUSA
Scottish Higher National Certificate .... SHNC
Scottish Higher National Diploma .... SHND
Scottish Historic and Research Society of Delaware Valley (EA) ...... SHRSDV
Scottish History from Contemporary Writers [A publication] ..... SHCW
Scottish History Society (EA) .... SHS
Scottish Hockey Association (DBA) .... SHA
Scottish Home and Health Department (ILCA) .... SHHD
Scottish Home Department (ILCA) .... SHD
Scottish Homosexual Rights Group (DBA) .... SHRG
Scottish Horse [British military] (DMA) .... SH
Scottish Hotel, Catering, and Licensed Trade Exhibition [Scottish Exhibitions
    Ltd.] (TSPED) .... SCOTHOT
Scottish Indoor Bowling Association (DBA) .... SIBA
Scottish Industrial Heritage Scoeity (DBA) .... SIHS

Scottish Industry and Commerce Trade Fair (ITD) .... SI & CTF
Scottish Inland Waterways Association (DBA) .... SIWA
Scottish Institute of Adult and Continuing Education (DBA) ..... SIACE
Scottish Institute of Adult Education (DI) .... SIAE
Scottish Institute of Agricultural Engineering [Research center] (IRC) ...... SIAE
Scottish Island Area [Council] .... SIA
Scottish Journal of Theology [A publication] (BJA) .... SJTh
Scottish Jurist [1829-73] [A publication] (DLA) .... J
[The] Scottish Jurist [Edinburgh] [A publication] (DLA) .... Jur (Sc)
Scottish Jurist [A publication] (DLA) .... Sc Jur
Scottish Jurist [A publication] (DLA) .... Scot Jur
Scottish Jurist [1829-73] [A publication] (DLA) .... SJ
Scottish Keep Fit Association (DBA) .... SKFA
Scottish Kennel Club (BARN) .... SKC
Scottish Knitwear Association (DBA) .... SKA
Scottish Labour Party [Political party] (PPW) .... SLP
Scottish Ladies Golfing Association (DBA) .... SLGA
Scottish Land Court Reports [A publication] (DLA) LC
Scottish Land Court Reports [Supplement to Scottish Law Review]
    [A publication] (DLA) .... Sc La R
Scottish Land Court Reports [A publication] (DLA) .... SLC
Scottish Land Court Reports [A publication] (DLA) .... SLCR
Scottish Land Court Reports [A publication] (DLA) .... SLR
Scottish Landowners Federation (DBA) .... SLF
Scottish Law Journal [Glasgow] [A publication] (DLA) ...... Scot Law J
Scottish Law Journal [Edinburgh] [A publication] (DLA) .... SLJ
Scottish Law Journal and Sheriff Court Record [A publication] (DLA) .... Sc LJ
Scottish Law Journal and Sheriff Court Record [A publication] (DLA) ..... Scot LJ
Scottish Law Magazine [Edinburgh, Scotland] [A publication] (DLA) ...... Scot L Mag
Scottish Law Magazine and Sheriff Court Reporter [A publication]
    (DLA) .... SC LM
Scottish Law Magazine and Sheriff Court Reporter [A publication]
    (DLA) .... Scot LM
Scottish Law Reporter [Edinburgh] [A publication] (DLA) ...... Sc L Rep
Scottish Law Reporter [A publication] (DLA) .... Sc LR
Scottish Law Reporter [A publication] (DLA) .... Scot L Rep
Scottish Law Reporter [A publication] (DLA) .... Scot LR
Scottish Law Reporter [Edinburgh] [A publication] (DLA) .... SLR
Scottish Law Review and Sheriff Court Reports [A publication] (DLA) .... Sc LR
Scottish Law Review and Sheriff Court Reports [A publication] (DLA) .... SL Rev
Scottish Law Review and Sheriff Court Reports [1885-1963] [A publication]
    (DLA) .... SLR
Scottish Lawn Tennis Association (DBA) .... SLTA
Scottish Leaving Certificate .... SLC
Scottish Legal Action Group (ILCA) .... SLAG
Scottish Legal Action Group. Bulletin [A publication] (DLA) ...... SCOLAG Bull
Scottish Liberal Party [Political party] .... SLP
Scottish Libraries Cooperative Automation Project .... SCOLCAP
Scottish Library Association .... SLA
Scottish Licensed Trade Association (DBA) .... SLTA
Scottish Liturgy [Episcopalian] .... SL
Scottish Malt Distillers [British] .... SMD
Scottish Marine Biological Association [British] (IRUK) .... SMBA
Scottish Marine Industries Association (DBA) .... ScoMIA
Scottish Master Plasterers Association (DBA) .... SMPA
Scottish Master Wrights and Builders Association (DBA) ..... SMWBA
Scottish Metropolitan [Property developer] .... SCOTMET
Scottish Microelectronics Development Programme (NITA) ..... SMDP
Scottish Milk Marketing Board (DI) .... SMMB
Scottish Milk Records Association (DBA) .... SMRA
Scottish Mothers' Union [Episcopalian] .... SMU
Scottish Motor Racing Club (DBA) .... SMRC
Scottish Motor Trade Association (DBA) .... SMTA
Scottish Mountain Leadership Certificate (DI) .... SMLC
Scottish Mountaineering Club (BARN) .... SMC
Scottish National Antarctic Expedition [1902-04] .... ScotNAE
Scottish National Camps Association (DBA) .... SNCA
Scottish National Certificate .... SNC
Scottish National Dancing Association [Australia] .... SNDA
Scottish National Dictionary [A publication] .... SND
Scottish National Dictionary Association .... SNDA
Scottish National Diploma .... SND
Scottish National Farmers' Union .... SNFU
Scottish National Orchestra Society .... SNOS
Scottish National Party [Political party] (PPW) .... SNP
Scottish National Town Planning Council (DAS) .... SNTPC
Scottish Nationalists .... SCOTNATS
Scottish Netball Association (DBA) .... SNA
Scottish Neuroscience Group (DBA) .... SNG
Scottish Newspaper Publishers' Association (DBA) .... SNPA
Scottish Nursery Nurses Examination Board (DI) .... SNNEB
Scottish [Communion] Office [Episcopalian] .... SO
Scottish Office Education Department (AIE) .... SOED
Scottish Offshore Training Association (DBA) .... SCOTA
Scottish Open Tech Training Support Unit (AIE) .... SCOTTSU
Scottish Operative Coach Makers' Association [A union] ..... SOCMA
Scottish Ornithologists' Club [British] .... SOC
Scottish Paraplegic (Spinal Injury) Association [British] .... SPA
Scottish Passenger Agents Associaiton (DBA) .... SPAA
Scottish Peat and Land Development Association (DBA) ...... SPALDA
Scottish Peer (ROG) .... SP
Scottish Pelagic Fishermen's Association (DBA) .... SPFA
Scottish Pharmaceutical Federation [British] .... SPF
Scottish Physical Education Association [British] .... SPEA
Scottish Pistol Association (DBA) .... SPA

Scottish Plant Owners Association (DBA) .... SPOA
Scottish Poetry Library Association (DBA) .... SPLA
Scottish Prayer Book [*Episcopalian*] .... SPB
Scottish Pre-School Play Association (DBA) .... SPPA
Scottish Primary Mathematics Group (AIE) .... SPMG
Scottish Professional Golfers Association (BARN) .... SPGA
Scottish Provident Institution [*Commercial firm*] .... SPI
Scottish Provision Trade Association (DBA) .... SPTA
Scottish Publishers Association (DBA) .... SPA
Scottish Railway Preservation Society (DBA) .... SRPS
Scottish Reactor Research Centre (DEN) .... SRRC
Scottish Record Office .... SRO
Scottish Record Society [*Glasgow*] (EA) .... SRS
Scottish Records Association (DBA) .... SRA
Scottish Recreational Land Association (DBA) .... SRLA
Scottish Reformation Society (DBA) .... SRS
Scottish Regional [*Council*] .... SR
Scottish Rifle Association (DI) .... SRA
Scottish Rifles [*Military unit*] [*British*] .... SR
Scottish Rite of Freemasonry Library, Chicago, IL [*Library symbol Library of Congress*] (LCLS) .... ICSR
Scottish Rite of Freemasonry, Northern Jurisdiction USA, Supreme Council Library, Lexington, MA [*Library symbol Library of Congress*] (LCLS) .... MLexSC
Scottish Rite of Freemasonry, Southern Jurisdiction USA, Supreme Council Library, Washington, DC [*Library symbol Library of Congress*] (LCLS) .... DSC
Scottish River Purification Board .... SRPB
Scottish River Purification Boards Association .... SRPBA
Scottish Rock Garden Club (DBA) .... SRGS
Scottish Rugby Union (DAS) .... SRU
Scottish Salmon Growers' Association .... SSGA
Scottish Salmon Smokers Association (DBA) .... SSSA
Scottish School of Non-Destructive Testing [*Research center*] (IRUK) .... SSNDT
Scottish Schoolmasters Association [*British*] .... SSA
Scottish Schools Rugby Union (AIE) .... SSRU
Scottish Schools Science Equipment Research Centre (CB) .... SSSERC
Scottish Sea Fishers' Union .... SSFU
Scottish Secondary Teachers' Association (DI) .... SSTA
Scottish Ship Chandlers Association (DBA) .... SSCA
Scottish Shipmasters' Association [*A union*] .... SSA
Scottish Ski Club (DBA) .... SSC
Scottish Society for Industrial Archaeology (EA) .... SSIA
Scottish Society for Northern Studies .... SSNS
Scottish Society for the Mentally Handicapped (EAIO) .... SSMH
Scottish Society of Autistic Children (DBA) .... SSAC
Scottish Society of Boilermakers [*A union*] .... SSB
Scottish Society of Crop Research .... SSCR
Scottish Society of History Medicine (DBA) .... SSHM
Scottish Society of Mentally Handicapped (DBA) .... SSMH
Scottish Society of Prevention of Cruelty to Animals (DBA) .... SSPCA
Scottish Society of Prevention of Vivisection (DBA) .... SSPV
Scottish Society of Women Artists (DBA) .... SSWA
Scottish Solar Energy Group (DBA) .... SSEG
Scottish Speed Skating Union (DBA) .... SSSU
Scottish Spina Bifida Association (DBA) .... SSBA
Scottish Spinal Cord Injury Association (DBA) .... SSCIA
Scottish Sporting Car Club (DBA) .... SSCC
Scottish Spring Fair (ITD) .... SSF
Scottish Squash Rackets Association (EAIO) .... SSRA
Scottish Standing Conference of Voluntary Youth Organisations (AIE) .... SSCVYO
Scottish Stone Cutters' Association [*A union*] .... SSCA
Scottish Sub-Aqua Club (DBA) .... SSAC
Scottish Surfing Federation (DBA) .... SSF
Scottish Table Tennis Association (DBA) .... STTA
Scottish Tartans Society (EA) .... STS
Scottish Teachers Nursing Association (DBA) .... STNA
Scottish Teachers Salaries Committee [*British*] .... STSC
Scottish Technical Education Council [*British*] .... SCOTEC
Scottish Technician and Vocational Educational Council (ACII) .... SCOTVEC
Scottish Television (DI) .... STV
Scottish Terrier Club of America (EA) .... STCA
Scottish Textile and Technical Centre Ltd. [*British*] (IRUK) .... STTC
Scottish Thoracic Society .... STHS
Scottish Timber Trade Association (DBA) .... STTA
Scottish Tourist Board (DCTA) .... ScTB
Scottish Tourist Board (EAIO) .... STB
Scottish Tourist Guides Association (DBA) .... STGA
Scottish Trades Union Congress .... STUC
Scottish Trampoline Association (DBA) .... STA
Scottish Tramway and Transport Society (DBA) .... STTS
Scottish Tramway Museum Society (DCTA) .... STMS
Scottish Union of Fishermen .... SUF
Scottish Union of Power Loom Overlookers .... SUPLO
Scottish Union of Students (AEBS) .... SUS
Scottish United Services Museum [*British military*] (DMA) .... SUSM
Scottish Universities Accommodation Consortium (AIE) .... SUAC
Scottish Universities Research and Reactor Centre [*Research center*] (IRC) .... SURRC
Scottish Universities Sports Federation (AIE) .... SUSF
Scottish Variety Orchestra (DI) .... SVO
Scottish Vocational Education Council (ODBW) .... SCOTVEC
Scottish Vocational Qualification (AIE) .... SVQ
Scottish Volleyball Association (DBA) .... SVA
Scottish War Veterans of America (EA) .... SWVA
Scottish Water Ski Associaton (DBA) .... SWSA
Scottish White Fish Producers Association (DBA) .... SWFPA
Scottish Wholesale Druggist Association (DBA) .... SWDA
Scottish Wild Land Group (DBA) .... SWLG
Scottish Wildlife Trust [*British*] .... SWT
Scottish Wirework Manufacturers Association (DBA) .... SWMA
Scottish Women's Amateur Athletic Association (DBA) .... SWAAA
Scottish Women's Hospital [*British military*] (DMA) .... SWH
Scottish Women's Indoor Bowling Association (DBA) .... SWIBA
Scottish Women's Rural Institutes (DI) .... SWRI
Scottish Woollen Industry .... SWI
Scottish Woollen Trade Mark Association (DBA) .... SWTMA
Scottish Youth Hostels Association .... SYHA
Scott's ABC Guide to Costs [*2nd ed.*] [*1910*] [*A publication*] (DLA) .... Sc Costs
Scotts Bluff and Agate Fossil Beds National Monuments .... SCBL
Scotts Co. [*Associated Press*] (SAG) .... Scotts
Scotts Co. [*NASDAQ symbol*] (SAG) .... SCTT
Scotts Co.'A' [*NYSE symbol*] (TTSB) .... SMG
Scott's Costs in the High Court [*4th ed.*] [*1880*] [*A publication*] (DLA) .... Sco Costs
Scott's English Common Pleas Reports [*A publication*] (DLA) .... Sc
Scott's English Common Pleas Reports [*A publication*] (DLA) .... Sco
Scott's English Common Pleas Reports [*A publication*] (DLA) .... Scott
Scott's English Common Pleas Reports [*A publication*] (DLA) .... Scott (Eng)
Scott's Hospitality, Inc. [*Toronto Stock Exchange symbol*] .... SRC
Scott's Intestate Laws [*A publication*] (DLA) .... Sco Int
Scott's Liquid Gold [*NYSE symbol*] (TTSB) .... SGD
Scotts Liquid Gold Co. [*Associated Press*] (SAG) .... ScotLiq
Scotts Liquid Gold Co. [*NYSE symbol*] (SAG) .... SGD
Scott's Monthly Stamp Journal [*A publication*] .... SMSJ
Scott's New English Common Pleas Reports [*A publication*] (DLA) .... Sc NR
Scott's New English Common Pleas Reports [*A publication*] (DLA) .... Sco NR
Scott's New English Common Pleas Reports [*A publication*] (DLA) .... Scott NR
Scotts Peak [*Tasmania*] [*Seismograph station code, US Geological Survey*] (SEIS) .... SPK
Scott's Reports [*25, 26 New York Civil Procedure*] [*A publication*] (DLA) .... Scott
Scott's Standard Postage Stamp Catalogue [*A publication*] .... S
Scottsbluff [*Nebraska*] [*Airport symbol*] (OAG) .... BFF
Scottsbluff, NE [*Location identifier FAA*] (FAAL) .... GIG
Scottsbluff, NE [*Television station call letters*] .... KDUH
Scottsbluff, NE [*FM radio station call letters*] .... KMOR
Scottsbluff, NE [*AM radio station call letters*] .... KNEB
Scottsbluff, NE [*FM radio station call letters*] .... KNEB-FM
Scottsbluff, NE [*AM radio station call letters*] .... KOLT
Scottsbluff, NE [*Television station call letters*] .... KSTF
Scottsbluff Public Library, Scottsbluff, NE [*Library symbol Library of Congress*] (LCLS) .... NbS
Scottsboro, AL [*FM radio station call letters*] .... WKEA
Scottsboro, AL [*AM radio station call letters*] .... WWIC
Scottsboro, AL [*AM radio station call letters*] .... WZCT
Scottsburg, IN [*FM radio station call letters*] .... WMPI
Scottsdale, AZ [*AM radio station call letters*] .... KOPA
Scottsdale, AZ [*FM radio station call letters*] .... KSLX
Scottsdale, AZ [*Location identifier FAA*] (FAAL) .... SDL
Scottsdale Charter, Inc. [*ICAO designator*] (FAAC) .... SNW
Scottsdale Public Library, Scottsdale, AZ [*OCLC symbol*] (OCLC) .... AZD
Scottsdale Public Library, Scottsdale, AZ [*Library symbol Library of Congress*] (LCLS) .... AzS
Scottsville, KY [*AM radio station call letters*] .... WLCK
Scottsville, KY [*FM radio station call letters*] .... WVLE
Scottville, MI [*FM radio station call letters*] .... WKZC
Scotty Lake [*Alaska*] [*Seismograph station code, US Geological Survey*] (SEIS) .... SCT
Scourer [*s*] [*or Scouring Freight*] .... SCR
Scout [*or Scouting*] (DNAB) .... SCO
Scout (AABC) .... SCT
Scout and Guide Graduate Association [*British*] (BI) .... SAGGA
Scout/Antitank Mission [*Army*] (INF) .... SCAT
Scout Association (EAIO) .... SA
Scout Association of Australia .... SAA
Scout Car, Half Track [*Army*] .... SctCHt
Scout Crew Qualification Course [*Army*] .... SCQC
Scout Cruiser [*Navy symbol Obsolete*] .... CS
Scout Evaluation Vehicle .... SEV
Scout Helicopter Special Task Force (MCD) .... SHSTF
Scout Leader (WDAA) .... SL
Scout Observation Plane [*Navy symbol*] .... VSO
Scout Observation Service Unit [*Navy*] .... SOSU
Scout Weapons Team [*Army*] (DOMA) .... SWT
Scout-Attack [*Helicopter*] (MCD) .... SCAT
Scout-Bombing Plane [*Navy symbol*] .... VSB
Scouting [*Naval aircraft designation*] .... S
Scouting and Amphibian Plane [*Coast Guard*] .... SAP
Scouting Experimental [*British*] (DMA) .... SE
Scouting Force [*Navy*] .... SCOFOR
Scouting Force [*Navy*] .... SF
Scouting Landplane .... SLP
Scouting, Observation, and Sniping [*British military*] (DMA) .... SO & S
Scouting Seaplane .... SSP
Scouting Squadron .... SCORON
Scouting Training Center [*Navy*] .... SCOTRACEN
Scouting-Bombing Plane [*When prefixed to Navy aircraft designation*] .... SB
Scouting-Observation Plane [*When prefixed to Navy aircraft designation*] .... SO
Scouts' Esperanto League (EA) .... SEL
Scouts on Stamps Society International (EA) .... SOSSI

Scout-Training Plane [*Navy symbol*] ... VSN
Scoville Memorial Library, Salisbury, CT [*Library symbol*] [*Library of Congress*] (LCLS) ... CtSal
SCP Pool [*NASDAQ symbol*] (TTSB) ... POOL
SCP Pool Corp. [*NASDAQ symbol*] (SAG) ... POOL
SCP Pool Corp. [*Associated Press*] (SAG) ... SCPPool
Scrabble Crossword Game Players [*Later, NSA*] (EA) ... SCGP
Scram Discharge [*Nuclear energy*] (NRCH) ... SD
Scram Discharge Volume [*Nuclear energy*] (NRCH) ... SDV
Scramble and Recovery Procedure (SAA) ... SARP
Scramble Status and Weather (SAA) ... SSW
Scramble-on-Warning ... SOW
Scranton [*Diocesan abbreviation*] [*Pennsylvania*] (TOCD) ... SCR
Scranton Law Times [*Pennsylvania*] [*A publication*] (DLA) ... Scr LT
Scranton, PA [*AM radio station call letters*] ... WARM
Scranton, PA [*AM radio station call letters*] ... WEJL
Scranton, PA [*FM radio station call letters*] ... WEZX
Scranton, PA [*AM radio station call letters*] ... WGBI
Scranton, PA [*FM radio station call letters*] ... WGGY
Scranton, PA [*AM radio station call letters*] ... WICK
Scranton, PA [*Television station call letters*] ... WNEP
Scranton, PA [*Television station call letters*] ... WOLF
Scranton, PA [*Television station call letters*] ... WSWB
Scranton, PA [*AM radio station call letters*] (RBYB) ... WTSS
Scranton, PA [*FM radio station call letters*] ... WUSR
Scranton, PA [*FM radio station call letters*] ... WVIA
Scranton, PA [*Television station call letters*] ... WVIA-TV
Scranton, PA [*FM radio station call letters*] ... WVMW
Scranton, PA [*FM radio station call letters*] ... WWDL
Scranton, PA [*Television station call letters*] ... WYOU
Scranton Public Library, Scranton, PA [*Library symbol Library of Congress*] (LCLS) ... PSc
Scranton Public Library, Scranton, PA [*Library symbol*] [*Library of Congress*] (LCLS) ... PScL
Scranton Public Library, Scranton, PA [*OCLC symbol*] (OCLC) ... SCR
Scranton, SC [*FM radio station call letters*] ... WSQN
Scranton State General Hospital, Scranton, PA [*OCLC symbol*] (OCLC) ... PHG
Scranton-Wilkes-Barre [*Pennsylvania*] [*Airport symbol*] (AD) ... AVP
Scrap Carriage [*British military*] (DMA) ... SC
Scrap Classification List [*DoD*] ... SCL
Scrap Rubber and Plastics Institute (EA) ... SRPI
Scrap Salvage Division [*Navy*] ... SSD
Scraped-Surface Heat Exchanger [*Process engineering*] ... SSHE
Scraper ... SRPR
Scrapie [*Animal pathology*] ... Scr
Scrapie-Associated Fibrils [*Neuroanatomy*] ... SAF
Scraping ... SRPG
Scratch ... SCR
Scratch Hardness [*Aerospace*] ... SH
Scratch Pad [*Computer science*] ... SCPD
Scratch Pad [*Computer science*] ... SP
Scratch Pad Control Register [*Computer science*] (IAA) ... SPCR
Scratch Pad Line [*NASA*] (MCD) ... SPL
Scratch Pad Memory (IAA) ... SCM
Scratch Pad Memory [*Computer science*] ... SPAD
Scratch Pad Memory [*Computer science*] (BUR) ... SPM
Scratch Pad Memory Address [*Computer science*] (IAA) ... SPAM
Scratch Pad Memory Address Register [*Computer science*] (MHDI) ... SPMAR
Scratch Pad Module [*Computer science*] (IAA) ... SPM
Scratched Surface Recording (IAA) ... SSR
Scratchley and Brabook's Building Societies [*2nd ed.*] [*1882*] [*A publication*] (DLA) ... Scrat & Bra
Scratchley's Building Societies [*5th ed.*] [*1883*] [*A publication*] (DLA) ... Scrat Bdg Soc
Scratchley's Life Assurance [*13th ed.*] [*1887*] [*A publication*] (DLA) ... Scrat Life Ass
Screaming Eagle Replacement Training School [*Vietnam*] [*Army*] (VNW) ... SERTS
Screaming Eagles Users Group [*Defunct*] (EA) ... SEUG
Screen (IAA) ... S
Screen (IDOE) ... s
Screen [*Technical drawings*] ... SCN
Screen (WGA) ... SCR
Screen [*Laboratory science*] (DAVI) ... SCREN
Screen ... SCRN
Screen (VRA) ... scrn
Screen [*s*] [*or Screening Freight*] ... SCRN
Screen (DAVI) ... SR
Screen Activated Machine [*Parimutuel wagering*] ... SAM
Screen Actors Guild (EA) ... SAG
Screen Advertising Association Ltd. [*British*] (BI) ... SAA
Screen Advertising World Association [*British*] (EAIO) ... SAWA
Screen Capture Test [*Computer science*] ... SCT
Screen Cartoonists Guild [*Defunct*] (EA) ... SCG
Screen Composers Association (NADA) ... SCA
Screen Composers of America (EA) ... SCA
Screen Coordinator [*Military*] (CAAL) ... SC
Screen Definition Facility [*Computer science*] ... SDF
Screen Design Aid [*Computer science*] (HGAA) ... SDA
Screen Directors' Guild of America [*Later, DGA*] ... SDG
Screen Directors International Guild [*Absorbed by Directors Guild of America*] (EA) ... SDIG
Screen Door ... SCD
Screen Extras Guild (EA) ... SEG
Screen Filtration Pressure [*Clinical chemistry*] (AAMN) ... SFP
Screen Filtration Resistance [*Clinical chemistry*] (AAMN) ... SFR
Screen Flag [*Navy British*] ... SC
Screen for Aeronautical Material - Not in Stock (DNAB) ... SAM-NIS
Screen Format Generator (IAA) ... SFG
Screen Grid [*Electrode or vacuum tube*] ... SG
Screen Grid Current ... SGC
Screen Grid Input ... SI
Screen Grid Modulation ... SGM
Screen Grid Voltage (IAA) ... SGV
Screen Image Buffer [*Computer science*] ... SIB
Screen Management System [*Computer technology*] ... SMS
Screen Manufacturers Association (EA) ... SMA
Screen Oriented Disk Utility [*Computer science*] ... SODU
Screen Pattern Analyzer and Rescreening Key [*Printing process*] ... SPARK
Screen Print (AAG) ... SNPR
Screen Printing and Display News [*A publication*] (DGA) ... SPDN
Screen Printing Association International (EA) ... SPAI
Screen Printing Technical Foundation (EA) ... SPTF
Screen Process Printing Association [*Later, SPAI*] (EA) ... SPPA
Screen Producers' Association [*Australia*] ... SPA
Screen Producers Guild [*Later, PGA*] (EA) ... SPG
Screen Resistance (IDOE) ... R_s
Screen Voltage (IDOE) ... E_s
Screen Writers Guild (WDMC) ... SWG
Screen-Based Electronic Typewriter (WDMC) ... SBET
Screen-Based Equipment ... SBE
ScreenCam Movie [*Computer software*] (CDE) ... SCM
Screened Granulated Aluminate [*Inorganic chemistry*] ... SGA
Screened Resistor Evaporated Transistor Logic (IAA) ... SRETL
Screened through Matching [*Parapsychology*] ... STM
Screener Proficiency Evaluation and Report System [*FAA*] (TAG) ... SPEARS
Screen-Grid N-Channel Metal Oxide Semiconductor ... SGNMOS
Screening and Costing Staff [*NATO*] (NATG) ... SCS
Screening Breath Tester [*Drunken driving*] ... SBT
Screening Country Requirements Against Plus Excess [*DoD*] ... SCRAPE
Screening Exercise [*Military*] (NVT) ... SCREENEX
Screening Information Data Set [*Environmental science*] ... SIDS
Screening Inspection for Electronic Parts [*NASA*] ... SIEP
Screening/Inspection System (DNAB) ... SIS
Screening Kit of Language Development [*Child development test*] ... SKOLD
Screening Smoke [*Mixture*] ... HC
Screening Speech Articulation Test [*Educational test*] ... SSAT
Screening Test for Auditory Perception ... STAP
Screening Test for Identifying Central Auditory Disorders ... SCAN
Screening Test of Academic Readiness [*Child development test*] ... STAR
Screening Test of Adolescent Language [*Educational test*] ... STAL
Screening Test of Spanish Grammar (EDAC) ... STSG
Screening Tests for Young Children and Retardates (MAH) ... STYCAR
Screening Tracking and Retrieval ... STAR
Screenprint (VRA) ... scrnpr
Screenwriting Coalition for Industry Professionals and Teachers (EDAC) ... SCRIPT
Screw ... SC
Screw (AAG) ... SCR
Screw Dislocation Line [*Crystullography*] ... SDL
Screw Displacement Axis ... SDA
Screw Down ... SCRDN
Screw Down Non-Return Valve (DS) ... SDNR
Screw Focusing Adjustment [*Optical*] (ROG) ... SFA
Screw Integrated Control System - Pontoon Air Cushion Kit [*Army*] (RDA) ... SICS-PACK
Screw Machine Feeder ... SMF
Screw Machine Metal Part ... SMMP
Screw Motorship (IAA) ... SM
Screw, Nut, Bolt, and Rivet Trade Union [*British*] ... SNBRTU
Screw Research Association (EA) ... SRA
Screw Steamer ... SS
Screw Terminal ... SCRTERM
Screw Terminal ... ST
Screw Thread Insert ... STI
Screw Thread Tool Manufacturers Association [*British*] (DBA) ... STTMA
Screw Worm Fly ... SWF
Screwdriver (MSA) ... SCDR
Screwed (MDG) ... SCD
Screwed and Coupled ... S/C
Screwed Bonnet ... SCRDB
Screwworm Adult Suppression System [*Medicine*] ... SWASS
Screwworm Research Laboratory [*Department of Agriculture*] (GRD) ... SRL
Scribe ... S
Scribe [*MARC relator code*] [*Library of Congress*] (LCCP) ... scr
Scribe Ezra [*Freemasonry*] ... SCE
Scribe Nehemiah [*Freemasonry*] ... SCN
Scribner, NE [*Location identifier FAA*] (FAAL) ... SCB
Scribner on the Law of Dower [*A publication*] (DLA) ... Scrib Dow
Scrieve Board ... SB
Scrim-Reinforced Material [*Nonwoven sheets*] ... SRM
Scrip (ROG) ... SCP
Scrip (ADA) ... SCR
Scrip Department (MHDB) ... SD
Scripophila Helvetica (EA) ... SH
Scripps [*E. W.*] **Co.** [*Associated Press*] (SAG) ... Scripps
Scripps Cooperative Oceanic Productivity Expedition [*1956*] ... SCOPE
Scripps Coronary Radiation to Inhibit Proliferation Post-Stenting ... SCRIPPS
Scripps EW [*NYSE symbol*] (SAG) ... SSP
Scripps Institution of Oceanography [*La Jolla, CA*] [*Research center*] ... SIO

Scripps Tuna Oceanographic Research ... STOR
Scripps Visibility Laboratory ... SVL
Scripps-Booth Register [*An association*] (EA) ... SBR
Scripps(E.W.)'A' [*NYSE symbol*] (TTSB) ... SSP
Scripps-Howard News Service [*Washington, DC*] (WDMC) ... SHN
Script [*Films, television, etc.*] ... SC
Script [*Films, television, etc.*] ... SCP
Script Applier Mechanism [*Programming language*] [*1975*] (CSR) ... SAM
Script Mathematical Formula Formatter [*IBM Corp.*] ... SMFF
Scripta Hierosolymitana (BJA) ... SH
Scripta Pontificii Instituti Biblici [*A publication*] (BJA) ... SPIB
Scripta Universitatis atque Bibliotecae Hierosolymitanarum Jerusalem [*A publication*] (BJA) ... SUBH
Scripta Universitatis atque Bibliotecae Hierosolymitanarum Jerusalem [*A publication*] (BJA) ... SUnBH
Scriptomatic Addressing Computer (HGAA) ... SAC
Scriptores Ecclesiastici [*Ecclesiastical Authors*] [*Latin*] (ROG) ... ECCL
Scriptores Historiae Augustae [*Classical studies*] (OCD) ... SHA
Scriptum [*Something Written*] [*Latin*] (ROG) ... SCRIP
Scripture (BJA) ... Scr
Scripture ... SCRIP
Scripture ... SCRIPT
Scripture (VRA) ... script
Scripture Gift Mission/USA (EA) ... SGM/USA
Scripture Press Ministries (EA) ... SPM
Scripture Reader (ROG) ... SR
Scripture Union [*British*] ... SU
Scriptwriters' Association International [*Defunct*] (EA) ... SAI
Scriven on the Law of Copyholds [*7th ed.*] [*1896*] [*A publication*] (DLA) ... Scriv Cop
Scriven on the Law of Copyholds [*A publication*] (DLA) ... Scriven
Scroll (VRA) ... scl
Scroll Symbolic Tracer (IAA) ... SST
[*The*] **Scrolls and the New Testament** [*K. Stendahl*] [*A publication*] (BJA) ... SNT
Scrolls from the Wilderness of the Dead Sea. Smithsonian Institution Exhibit Catalogue [*Washington, DC*] (BJA) ... SWDS
Scrophularia Mottle Virus [*Plant pathology*] ... SCRMV
Scrum Half [*Rugby*] (WGA) ... SH
Scruple [*Medicine*] (DMAA) ... S
Scruple ... SC
Scruple ... SCR
Scruple [*Pharmacology*] (DAVI) ... SCR
Scruple Apothecaries ... SAP
Scrupulus [*Scruple*] [*Latin*] [*Pharmacy*] (DAVI) ... SC
Scruse Air [*ICAO designator*] (AD) ... SF
Scrutton on Charter-Parties [*18th ed.*] [*1974*] [*A publication*] (DLA) ... Scrut Charter
Scrutton on Charter-Parties [*16 eds.*] [*1886-1955*] [*A publication*] (DLA) ... Scrutton
SCS/Compute, Inc. [*NASDAQ symbol*] (SAG) ... SCOMC
SCS Compute, Inc. [*Associated Press*] (SAG) ... SCSCmp
SCSI Accessed Fault-Tolerant Enclosures [*Computer science*] ... SAF-TE
SCSI [*Small Computer System Interface*] **Configuration Auto Magically** [*Computer science*] (PCM) ... SCAM
SCTA Air St. Martin [*ICAO designator*] (FAAC) ... ASM
Scuba Diver Badge [*Military decoration*] (GFGA) ... SCUBADIV
Scuba Retailers Association (EA) ... SRA
Scudder New Asia Fd [*NYSE symbol*] (TTSB) ... SAF
Scudder New Asia Fund [*NYSE symbol*] (SPSG) ... SAF
Scudder New Asia Fund [*Associated Press*] (SAG) ... ScudNA
Scudder New Europe Fund [*NYSE symbol*] (SPSG) ... NEF
Scudder New Europe Fund [*Associated Press*] (SAG) ... ScdNE
Scudder World Income Opportunities Ltd. [*Associated Press*] (SAG) ... ScudWld
Scudder World Income Opportunities Ltd. [*NYSE symbol*] (SAG) ... SWI
Scudder World Inc. Oppt Fd [*NYSE symbol*] (TTSB) ... SWI
Scugog Public Library, Ontario [*Library symbol National Library of Canada*] (NLC) ... OSC
Scugog Public Library, Scugog, ON, Canada [*Library symbol Library of Congress*] (LCLS) ... CaOSc
Scullery (MSA) ... SCLY
Scully, Scott, Murphy, and Presser, Garden City, NY [*Library symbol Library of Congress*] (LCLS) ... NGcSS
Sculpsit [*He, or She, Engraved It*] [*Latin*] ... SC
Sculpsit [*He, or She, Engraved It*] [*Latin*] ... SCULP
Sculpsit [*He, or She, Engraved It*] [*Latin*] ... SCULPS
Sculptor ... SC
Sculptor [*Constellation*] ... Scl
Sculptor [*Constellation*] ... Scul
Sculptor ... SCULP
Sculptor [*or Sculpture*] ... SCULPT
Sculptors Guild (EA) ... SG
Sculptors' Society [*Australia*] ... SS
Sculptors Society of Canada ... SSC
Sculpture (ROG) ... SCULP
Sculpture (VRA) ... sculp
Sculpture Center (EA) ... SC
Sculpture in the Environment [*In Best by SITE, Inc.*] ... SITE
Sculpture of the Hellenistic Age [*A publication*] (OCD) ... Sculpt Hellenist Age
Sculpture Review [*A publication*] (BRI) ... Sculpt R
Sculptured Flexible Circuit [*Electronics*] ... SFC
Sculthorpe [*British ICAO location identifier*] (ICLI) ... EGUP
Scunner [*Missile*] ... SCUD
Scuola de Sviluppo Economico [*Italy*] ... SSE
Scupper ... SCUP
Scurry Area Canyon Reef Operators Committee ... SACROC
Scurry County Library, Snyder, TX [*Library symbol Library of Congress*] (LCLS) ... TxSn
Scurry, TX [*Location identifier FAA*] (FAAL) ... SCY
Scurry-Rainbow Oil Ltd. [*Toronto Stock Exchange symbol*] ... SCR
Scusciuban [*Somalia*] [*ICAO location identifier*] (ICLI) ... HCMS
Scuttle ... S
Scutum [*of Hesiod*] [*Classical studies*] (OCD) ... Sc
Scutum [*Constellation*] ... Sct
Scutum [*Constellation*] ... Scut
Scutum [*of Hesiod*] [*Classical studies*] (OCD) ... Scut
Scythe Makers' Association [*A union*] [*British*] ... SMA
Scythia (VRA) ... Scyt
Scythian [*Geology*] ... S
SDA [*Software Design Associates*] **Users' Groups** [*Later, IUG*] (EA) ... SDAUG
SDC Sydney Development Corp. [*Toronto Stock Exchange symbol Vancouver Stock Exchange symbol*] ... SSD
SDI [*Strategic Defense Initiative*] **Network Interface Processor Engine** (SDI) ... SNIPE
SDL, Inc. [*Associated Press*] (SAG) ... SDL Inc
SDL, Inc. [*NASDAQ symbol*] (SAG) ... SDLI
SDNB Financial [*Associated Press*] (SAG) ... SDNB
SDNB Financial [*NASDAQ symbol*] (TTSB) ... SDNB
SDNB Financial Corp. [*NASDAQ symbol*] (NQ) ... SDNB
SDPC [*Shuttle Data Processing Complex*] **Configuration/Isolation Unit** [*NASA*] ... SCIU
Se Ruega Contestacion [*The Favor of a Reply Is Requested*] [*Spanish*] ... SRC
Sea (ADA) ... S
Sea [*Maps and charts*] ... SE
Sea Acceptance Trial ... SAT
Sea Activated Parachute Automatic Crew Release (MCD) ... SEAPAC
Sea, Air, and Land ... SEAL
Sea, Air, and Land Team [*Refers to Navy personnel trained in unconventional warfare*] ... SEAL
Sea/Air Chemical Exchange [*Marine science*] (MSC) ... SEAREX
Sea, Air, Land, and Underwater Targets [*Navy*] ... SALUT
Sea Air Mariner ... SAM
Sea/Air Search Exercise [*NATO*] (NATG) ... SEARCHEX
Sea and Foreign Service Duty [*A Navy pay status*] ... S & FSD
Sea and Foreign Service Duty (Aviation) [*A Navy pay status*] ... S & FSD(A)
Sea and Foreign Service Duty (Submarine) [*A Navy pay status*] ... S & FSD(S)
Sea and Foreign Service Office (DNAB) ... SANDFSO
Sea and Weather Observations [*Navy*] (NVT) ... SEAWEA
Sea Automated Data Systems Activity [*Navy*] ... SEAADSA
Sea Barge Carrying Ships [*MARAD*] [*MTMC*] (TAG) ... SEABEE
Sea Base (MCD) ... SB
Sea Blue Histiocytosis [*Medicine*] ... SBH
Sea Cadet Association (EAIO) ... SCA
Sea Cadet Corps [*Navy British*] ... SCC
Sea Cadet Cruise [*Navy*] (NVT) ... SEACAD
Sea Cliff Elementary School, North Shore, NY [*Library symbol*] [*Library of Congress*] (LCLS) ... NNosCE
Sea Cliff Elementary School, Sea Cliff, NY [*Library symbol*] [*Library of Congress*] (LCLS) ... NSeacES
Sea Cont Ltd. $4 cm Cv Pfd [*NYSE symbol*] (TTSB) ... SCRPrE
Sea Cont Ltd. $4.125cm Cv Pfd [*NYSE symbol*] (TTSB) ... SCRPrD
Sea Cont Ltd. $2.10'82 Pfd [*NYSE symbol*] (TTSB) ... SCRPrC
Sea Cont Ltd $1.46 1/4cmPfd [*NYSE symbol*] (TTSB) ... SCRPr
Sea Containers Inc. [*Steamship*] (MHDW) ... SCI
Sea Containers Ltd. [*NYSE symbol*] (SPSG) ... SCR
Sea Containers Ltd. [*Associated Press*] (SAG) ... SeaC
Sea Containers Ltd. [*Associated Press*] (SAG) ... SeaCont
Sea Containers Ltd. [*Associated Press*] (SAG) ... SeaCt
Sea Containers Ltd. [*Associated Press*] (SAG) ... SeaCt
Sea Containers Ltd Cl'A' [*NYSE symbol*] (TTSB) ... SCRA
Sea Containers Ltd Cl'B' [*NYSE symbol*] (TTSB) ... SCR B
Sea Control Ship [*Navy*] (NVT) ... SCS
Sea Control Ship (Lead Ship) [*Navy*] (MCD) ... SCS(LS)
Sea Counterinfiltration Patrol (CINC) ... SCIP
Sea Damaged ... SD
Sea Depth Transducer ... SDT
Sea Duty ... SEADU
Sea Duty Pay [*Navy*] ... SDP
Sea Echelon Area [*Navy*] (NVT) ... SEA
Sea Education Association (EA) ... SEA
Sea Energy Absorber/Bumper Barge (SAA) ... SEA/B
Sea Fish Industry Authority [*British*] ... SFIA
Sea Flood ... SF
Sea Frontier ... SEAFRON
Sea Frontier Force [*Navy*] ... SFF
Sea Frontiers [*A publication*] (BRI) ... SeaFront
Sea Gallantry Medal [*Navy British*] ... SGM
Sea Gold Oil Corp. [*Vancouver Stock Exchange symbol*] ... SGO
Sea Grant ... SG
Sea Grant Association (EA) ... SGA
Sea Grant Institute [*University of Wisconsin*] [*Research center*] (RCD) ... SGI
Sea Grant Law and Policy Journal [*A publication*] (DLA) ... Sea Grant L & Pol'y J
Sea Grant Law Journal [*A publication*] (DLA) ... Sea Grant LJ
Sea Grant Network [*National Oceanic and Atmospheric Administration Information service or system*] (IID) ... SGNET
Sea Heritage Foundation (EA) ... SHF
Sea History [*A publication*] (BRI) ... Sea H
Sea Ice Mechanics Initiative [*Marine science*] (OSRA) ... SIMI
Sea Ice Microbial Colony ... SIMCO
Sea Ice Observation Code [*Marine science*] (MSC) ... ICEOB
Sea Ice Penetrometer (PDAA) ... SIP

Sea Island Air Ltd. [Canada ICAO designator] (FAAC) ..... SIL
Sea Isle, NJ [Location identifier FAA] (FAAL) ..... SIE
Sea King Replacement [Naval aircraft] [British] ..... SKR
Sea Laboratory ..... SEALAB
Sea, Lake, and Overland Surge Hurricane ..... SLOSH
Sea Lake and Overland Surges from Hurricanes [Model] (USDC) ..... SLOSH
Sea Lamprey Control Centre, Fisheries and Oceans Canada [Centre de Controle des Lamproies de Mer, Peches et Oceans Canada] Sault Ste. Marie, Ontario [Library symbol National Library of Canada] (NLC) ..... OSTMEF
Sea Landing Division [NATO] ..... SLD
Sea [or Submarine or Surface]-Launched Ballistic Missile [Navy] (CAAL) ..... SLBM
Sea Level ..... SL
Sea Level and Overland Surge from Hurricanes [National Oceanic and Atmospheric Administration] ..... SLOSH
Sea Level, Standard Day ..... SLS
Sea Lines of Communication [NATO] (NATG) ..... SLOC
Sea Lite Beam Director [Navy] (DOMA) ..... SLBD
Sea Loading Pipe Line [Technical drawings] ..... SLPL
Sea Mammal Research Unit [British] (ARC) ..... SMRU
Sea Mapping and Remote Characterization I [Oceanography] ..... SeaMARCI
Sea of Japan ..... JS
Sea of Japan (NVT) ..... SOJ
Sea of Peace (IAA) ..... SOP
Sea Photo Analysis [Navy] ..... SPA
Sea Photo Diffraction Analysis (PDAA) ..... SPDA
Sea Planning Automated Data System ..... SEAPADS
Sea Platform (MCD) ..... SP
Sea Port of Export [MTMC] (TAG) ..... SPOE
Sea Post Office ..... SPO
Sea Rangers' Association [British] (DI) ..... SRA
Sea Rehabilitation [Navy] (NVT) ..... SEHAB
Sea Reinforcement and Resupply of Europe (MCD) ..... SEA RARE
Sea Requirement [Canadian Navy] ..... SEAREQ
Sea Satellite [NASA] ..... SEASAT
Sea School [Marine Corps] ..... SEAS
Sea Scout - Nonrigid Airship [Royal Naval Air Service] [British] ..... SS
Sea Scout Zero - Nonrigid Airship [Royal Naval Air Service] [British] ..... SSZ
Sea Search Attack Development Unit ..... SADU
Sea Service [British military] (DMA) ..... SS
Sea Shepherd Conservation Society (EA) ..... SSCS
Sea Skimming Test Vehicles ..... SSTV
Sea State ..... SS
Sea Surface Chlorophyll Concentration ..... SSCC
Sea Surface Height [Oceanography] ..... SSH
Sea Surface Salinity ..... SSS
Sea Surface Temperature [Oceanography] ..... SST
Sea Surface Temperature Imaging Radiometer ..... SSTIR
Sea Surveillance and Coordination [Navy] (DOMA) ..... SSC
Sea Synthetic Aperture RADAR ..... SEASAR
Sea Systems Calibration Management Information System (DNAB) ..... SEACALMIS
Sea Systems Command [Also, NSSC] [Navy] ..... SSC
Sea Systems Modification and Modernization by Modularity [Program] (DNAB) ..... SEAMOD
Sea Test and Evaluation Capability [Navy] (CAAL) ..... SEATEC
Sea Test Phase [Navy] (CAAL) ..... STP
Sea Test Range (MUGU) ..... STR
Sea Training Staff [Canadian Navy] ..... STS
Sea Transport Department [British military] (DMA) ..... STD
Sea Transport Officer ..... STO
Sea Trials [Navy] (NVT) ..... STRL
Sea Turtle Rescue Fund (EA) ..... STRF
Sea Warfare Interim Model (CINC) ..... SWIM
Sea World Research Institute [Marine science] (GNE) ..... SWRI
Sea-1 Aquafarms Ltd. [Vancouver Stock Exchange symbol] ..... SNQ
Sea-Air Interaction Laboratory [Oceanography] ..... SAIL
Sea-Air Rescue ..... SAR
Sea-Air Temperature Difference Correction ..... S
Sea-Animal Locomotion (SAA) ..... SAL
Sea-Based Air Master Plan (MCD) ..... SBAMP
Sea-Based Antiballistic Missile (IAA) ..... SABMIS
Sea-Based Mobile Logistics Supply [Navy] (CAAL) ..... SMLS
Sea-Based Weapons and Advance Tactics School (DOMA) ..... SWATS
Seabed Working Group [Nuclear energy] (NUCP) ..... SWG
SEABEE [Construction Battalion] [Navy] (MCD) ..... CB
Seabee Club International (EA) ..... SCI
SEABEE Support and Equipment Office [Navy] ..... SSEO
SEABEE Tactical Equipment Management [Navy] ..... STEM
SEABEE Tactically Installed, Navy Generated, Engineer Resources [System] [Navy] (NVT) ..... STINGER
SEABEE Team [Navy] (NVT) ..... SEABT
SEABEE Technical Assistance Team [Navy] ..... STAT
SEABEE Training Advisory Team [Navy] ..... STAT
SEABEE Veterans of America (EA) ..... SVA
SeaBird Conductivity and Temperature Recorder [Marine science] (OSRA) ..... SEACAT
SeaBird Conductivity and Temperature Recorder (USDC) ..... SEACAT
Seabird Group (EAIO) ..... SG
Seaboard Air Line Railroad [Later, SCL] [AAR code] ..... SAL
Seaboard Bancorp [Associated Press] (SAG) ..... SbdBcp
Seaboard Bancorp [NASDAQ symbol] (NQ) ..... SEAB
Seaboard Coast Line Railroad Co. [Subsidiary of Seaboard Coast Line Industries] [Later, CSX Corp.] [AAR code] ..... SCL
Seaboard Corp. [Associated Press] (SAG) ..... SbdCp
Seaboard Corp. [AMEX symbol] (SPSG) ..... SEB

Seaboard Oil [NASDAQ symbol] (TTSB) ..... SBRD
Seaboard Oil Co. [NASDAQ symbol] (SAG) ..... SBRD
Seaboard Oil Co. [Associated Press] (SAG) ..... SeabdOil
Seaboard World Airlines (MHDW) ..... SWA
Seaboard World Airlines, Inc. [ICAO designator] ..... SB
Seaboard World Airlines, Inc. [Air carrier designation symbol] ..... SBWX
Seaboard World Airlines, Inc. (MCD) ..... SEA
Seaboard World Airlines, Inc. ..... SW
Seaboard World Airways (MHDB) ..... SEABOARD
Seaborne Aircraft Platform (ADA) ..... SAP
Seaborne [or Ship-Launched] Antiballistic Missile Intercept System [Navy] ..... SABMIS
Seaborne Army Maintenance Facilities ..... SAMF
Seaborne Environmental Reporting System ..... SERS
Seaborne on Vendors and Purchasers [9th ed.] [1926] [A publication] (DLA) ..... Sea Vend
Seaborne on Vendors and Purchasers [9th ed.] [1926] [A publication] (DLA) ..... Seab Vend
Seaborne Powered Target [Navy] (NVT) ..... SEPTAR
Seaborne Supply of the Northeast Command (DNAB) ..... SUNEC
Seaborne Tracking and Ranging Station ..... STARS
Seabright Explorations, Inc. [Toronto Stock Exchange symbol] ..... SBX
Seabright Resources, Inc. [Toronto Stock Exchange symbol] ..... SBT
Seabrook Nuclear Station (NRCH) ..... SNS
Seabrook Sea Island Cotton ..... SBSI
Seabrook, TX [FM radio station call letters] ..... KRTS
Seabury Divinity School, Faribault, MN [Library symbol Library of Congress] (LCLS) ..... MnFS
Seaclutter Visibility [Navy] (CAAL) ..... SCV
Seacoast ..... SEAC
Seacoast Anti-Pollution League (EA) ..... SAPL
Seacoast Banking Corp. Florida [Associated Press] (SAG) ..... SeacBk
Seacoast Banking Corp. of Florida [Stuart, FL] [NASDAQ symbol] (NQ) ..... SBCF
Seacoast Banking FL'A' [NASDAQ symbol] (TTSB) ..... SBCFA
Seacoast Newspapers, Brick Town, NJ [Library symbol Library of Congress] (LCLS) ..... NjBrS
Seacor Holdings [NYSE symbol] (SAG) ..... CKH
Seacor Holdings [NASDAQ symbol] (SAG) ..... CKOR
Seacor Holdings [Associated Press] (SAG) ..... Seacor
Seadrome ..... S/D
Seadrome [Aviation] (FAAC) ..... SEADRM
Seafarers and International House (EA) ..... SIH
Seafarers Education Service [British] ..... SES
Seafarers' International Union of North America [AFL-CIO] ..... SIU
Seafarers' International Union of North America (EA) ..... SIUNA
Seafarers' International Union of North America [AFL-CIO] (EA) ..... SUNA
Seafarers' International Union of North America [AFL-CIO]; Atlantic, Gulf, Lakes, and Inland Waters District ..... SIU-AGLI
Seafarers' International Union of North America [AFL-CIO]; Atlantic, Gulf, Lakes, and Inland Waters District ..... SIU-AGLIW
Seafarers' International Union of North America [AFL-CIO]; Inlandboatmen's Union of the Pacific ..... SIU-IUP
Seafarers' International Union of North America [AFL-CIO]; International Union of Petroleum Workers ..... SIU-IUPW
Seafarers' International Union of North America [AFL-CIO]; Marine Cooks and Stewards' Union ..... SIU-MCS
Seafarers' International Union of North America [AFL-CIO]; Pacific Coast Marine Firemen, Oilers, Watertenders, and Wipers Association ..... SIU-MFOW
Seafarers' International Union of North America [AFL-CIO]; Sailors' Union of the Pacific ..... SIU-SUP
Seafarers' International Union of North America [AFL-CIO]; Transporation Services and Allied Workers ..... SIU-TSAW
Seafield Capital Corp. [Associated Press] (SAG) ..... Seafld
Seafield Capital Corp. [NASDAQ symbol] (SPSG) ..... SFLD
Seafloor Construction Experiment [Navy] ..... SEACON
Seafloor Geosciences Division (EA) ..... SGD
Seafood ..... SEAFD
Seafood Products Research Center [Public Health Service] (GRD) ..... SPRC
Seaford, DE [Television station call letters] ..... WDPB
Seaford, DE [AM radio station call letters] ..... WJPY
Seaford, DE [FM radio station call letters] ..... WSUX
Seaford Harbor Elementary School, Seaford, NY [Library symbol] [Library of Congress] (LCLS) ..... NSeaHE
Seaford Manor Elementary School, Seaford, NY [Library symbol] [Library of Congress] (LCLS) ..... NSeaME
Seaford Middle School, Seaford, NY [Library symbol] [Library of Congress] (LCLS) ..... NSeaMS
Seaford Public Library, Seaford, NY [Library symbol Library of Congress] (LCLS) ..... NSea
Seaford Senior High School, Seaford, NY [Library symbol] [Library of Congress] (LCLS) ..... NSeaSH
Seagate Technology [NYSE symbol] (TTSB) ..... SEG
Seagate Technology, Inc. [Associated Press] (SAG) ..... Seagate
Seagate Technology, Inc. [NYSE symbol] (SAG) ..... SEG
Seager on Parliamentary Registration [A publication] (DLA) ..... Seag Parl Reg
Seagoing Assembly-Integration-Launch System ..... SAILS
Seagoing Buoy Tender [Coast Guard] (NVT) ..... WLB
Seagoing Buoy Tender Replacement Vessel [USCG] (TAG) ..... WLBR
Seagoing Dredge [Navy symbol] ..... AGD
Seagoing Platform for Acoustic Research [NOL] ..... SPAR
[The] Seagram Co. Ltd. [Associated Press] (SAG) ..... Seagram
[The] Seagram Co. Ltd. [NYSE symbol Toronto Stock Exchange symbol Vancouver Stock Exchange symbol] ..... VO
Seagram Museum, Waterloo, Ontario [Library symbol National Library of Canada] (BIB) ..... OWSM

Seagram's Gin and Tonic .... SGT
Seagrass Ecosystem Study [*Marine science*] (MSC) .... SES
Seagrass Ecosystems Component Study [*Marine science*] (MSC) .... SECS
Seagreen Air Transport [*Antigua and Barbuda*] [*ICAO designator*] (FAAC) .... ESA
Seagull Energy [*NYSE symbol*] (TTSB) .... SGO
Seagull Energy Corp. [*Associated Press*] (SAG) .... SeagullE
Seagull Energy Corp. [*NYSE symbol*] (SPSG) .... SGO
Seahead Pressure Simulator .... SHPS
Seakeeping Data Analysis Center [*Navy*] .... SEADAC
Seal (NASA) .... SL
Seal and Label Institute .... SLI
SEAL [*Subsea Equipment Associates Ltd.*] **Atmospheric System** .... SAS
Seal Bay [*Alaska*] [*Airport symbol*] (OAG) .... SYB
Seal Cove Public Library, Newfoundland [*Library symbol National Library of Canada*] (NLC) .... NFSC
Seal Cove Public Library, Seal Cove, NF, Canada [*Library symbol Library of Congress*] (LCLS) .... CaNfSC
[*The*] **Seal Cylinders of Western Asia** [*A publication*] (BJA) .... SC
Seal In (IAA) .... SI
Seal Pressure Ratio .... SPR
Seal Rescue Fund (EA) .... SRF
Seal Research and Fisheries Unit [*British*] .... SRFU
Seal Steam Regulator [*Nuclear energy*] (NRCH) .... SSR
SEAL [*Sea, Air, Land*] **Tactical Insertion Craft** [*Navy*] (DOMA) .... STIC
SEAL [*Sea, Air, Land*] **Tactical Training** (DOMA) .... STT
SEAL [*Sea, Air, and Land*] **Team Assault Boat** [*Navy*] (VNW) .... STAB
Seal to Parents [*Genealogy*] (PCM) .... STP
Sealable Coherent Interface [*Computer science*] .... SCI
Sea-Land Service, Inc. [*AAR code*] .... SLS
Sealant [*Technical drawings*] .... SNT
Sealant and Waterproofers Institute (EA) .... SWI
Sealant Manufacturers Conference [*Federation of British Rubber and Allied Manufacturers*] (BI) .... SMC
Sea-Launched Air Missile (NVT) .... SLAM
Sea-Launched Ballistic Missile Detection and Warning .... SLBMD & W
Sea-Launched Cruise Missile [*Pronounced "slick-em"*] (AABC) .... SLCM
Sea-Launched Intercontinental Ballistic Missile (MUGU) .... SLICB
Sea-Launched Intercontinental Ballistic Missile (SAA) .... SLICBM
Sea-Launched Intermediate-Range Ballistic Missile (MUGU) .... SLIRBM
Sea-Launched Missile .... SLM
Sealectro Small Reliable Miniature (IAA) .... SSRM
Sealed .... SLD
Sealed Air [*NYSE symbol*] (TTSB) .... SEE
Sealed Air Corp. [*Associated Press*] (SAG) .... SealdAir
Sealed Air Corp. [*NYSE symbol*] (SPSG) .... SEE
Sealed and Delivery (MHDI) .... SAD
Sealed Argon Bubbling [*Steelmaking*] .... SAB
Sealed Authentication System [*Military*] .... SAS
Sealed Beam Lamp .... SBL
Sealed Cathode Ray Tube .... SCRT
Sealed Head Access Area [*Nuclear energy*] (NRCH) .... SHAA
Sealed Housing for Evaporative Determinations [*EPA engine test*] .... SHED
Sealed Insulating Glass Manufacturers Association (EA) .... SIGMA
Sealed Knot [*An association*] (EAIO) .... SK
Sealed Lead Acid [*Battery*] [*Automotive engineering*] .... SLA
Sealed Package Quality Assurance (IEEE) .... SPAQUA
Sealed with a Kiss [*Correspondence*] .... SWAK
Sealed with a Lick 'Cause a Kiss Won't Stick [*Correspondence*] (DSUE) .... SWALCAKWS
Sealed with a Loving Kiss [*Correspondence*] .... SWALK
Sealed with a Nice Kiss [*Correspondence*] .... SWANK
Sealer .... SLR
Sea-Level Canal Study (IID) .... SLC
Sea-Level Indicator (KSC) .... SLI
Sea-Level Pressure .... SLP
Sea-Level Rise [*Climatology*] .... SLR
Sea-Level Static .... SLS
Sea-Level Takeoff .... SLTO
Sealift Express [*Military*] .... SEA-EX
Sealift Obligation Report [*Army*] .... SEALOB
Sealift Procurement and National Security [*Study*] .... SPANS
Sealift Readiness Program [*Military*] .... SRP
Seal-In Device (MSA) .... SID
Sealing .... SEG
Sealink Ticket and Reservation System [*Sealink UK Ltd.*] [*Information service or system*] (IID) .... STARS
Sealright Co. [*NASDAQ symbol*] (TTSB) .... SRCO
Sealright Co., Inc. [*Associated Press*] (SAG) .... Sealrgt
Sealright Co., Inc. [*Kansas City, MO*] [*NASDAQ symbol*] (NQ) .... SRCO
Seam Welding System .... SWS
Seaman [*Navy*] E3
Seaman [*Navy*] .... S
Seaman [*Military British*] .... SMN
Seaman .... SMN
Seaman [*Navy rating*] .... SN
Seaman Apprentice [*Navy*] E2
Seaman Apprentice [*Navy rating*] .... SA
Seaman Apprentice, Boatswain's Mate, Striker [*Navy rating*] .... BMSA
Seaman Apprentice, Commissaryman, Striker [*Navy rating*] .... CSSA
Seaman Apprentice, Communications Technician, Striker [*Navy rating*] .... CTSA
Seaman Apprentice, Data Processing Technician, Striker [*Navy rating*] .... DPSA
Seaman Apprentice, Disbursing Clerk, Striker [*Navy rating*] .... DKSA
Seaman Apprentice, Electronics Technician, Striker [*Navy rating*] .... ETSA
Seaman Apprentice, Fire Control Technician, Striker [*Navy rating*] .... FTSA
Seaman Apprentice, Gunner's Mate, Striker [*Navy rating*] .... GMSA
Seaman Apprentice, Instrumentman, Striker [*Navy rating*] .... IMSA
Seaman Apprentice, Journalist, Striker [*Navy rating*] .... JOSA
Seaman Apprentice, Lithographer, Striker [*Navy rating*] .... LISA
Seaman Apprentice, Mineman, Striker [*Navy rating*] .... MNSA
Seaman Apprentice, Missile Technician, Striker [*Navy rating*] .... MTSA
Seaman Apprentice, Musician, Striker [*Navy rating*] .... MUSA
Seaman Apprentice, Nuclear Submarine Engineering Technician [*Navy rating*] (DNAB) .... SANSET
Seaman Apprentice, Opticalman, Striker [*Navy rating*] .... OMSA
Seaman Apprentice, Personnelman, Striker [*Navy rating*] .... PNSA
Seaman Apprentice, Polaris Field Electronics [*Navy rating*] (DNAB) .... SAPFE
Seaman Apprentice, Polaris Field Launcher [*Navy rating*] (DNAB) .... SAPFL
Seaman Apprentice, Postal Clerk, Striker [*Navy rating*] .... PCSA
Seaman Apprentice, Quartermaster, Striker [*Navy rating*] .... QMSA
Seaman Apprentice, RADARman Striker [*Navy rating*] .... RDSA
Seaman Apprentice, Radioman, Striker [*Navy rating*] .... RMSA
Seaman Apprentice, Ship's Serviceman, Striker [*Navy rating*] .... SHSA
Seaman Apprentice, Signalman, Striker [*Navy rating*] .... SMSA
Seaman Apprentice, SONAR Technician, Striker [*Navy rating*] .... STSA
Seaman Apprentice, Storekeeper, Striker [*Navy rating*] .... SKSA
Seaman Apprentice, Yeoman, Striker [*Navy rating*] .... YNSA
Seaman, Boatswain's Mate, Striker [*Navy rating*] .... BMSN
Seaman, Commissaryman, Striker [*Navy rating*] .... CSSN
Seaman, Communications Technician, Striker [*Navy rating*] .... CTSN
Seaman, Data Processing Technician, Striker [*Navy rating*] .... DPSN
Seaman, Data Systems Technician, Striker [*Navy rating*] .... DSSN
Seaman, Disbursing Clerk, Striker [*Navy rating*] .... DKSN
Seaman (Electronics Field) [*Navy rating*] (DNAB) .... SN(EF)
Seaman, Electronics Technician, Striker [*Navy rating*] .... ETSN
Seaman, Fire Control Technician, Striker [*Navy rating*] .... FTSN
Seaman, First Class [*Navy*] S1C
Seaman Furniture [*NASDAQ symbol*] (TTSB) .... SEAM
Seaman Furniture Co., Inc. [*Uniondale, NY*] [*NASDAQ symbol*] (NQ) .... SEAM
Seaman Furniture Co., Inc. [*Associated Press*] (SAG) .... SeamanF
Seaman Gunner [*British Obsolete*] .... SG
Seaman, Gunner's Mate, Striker [*Navy rating*] .... GMSN
Seaman, Instrumentman, Striker [*Navy rating*] .... IMSN
Seaman, Journalist, Striker [*Navy rating*] .... JOSN
Seaman (Junior College) [*Navy rating*] (DNAB) .... SN(JC)
Seaman (Junior College Nuclear Field Electronics) [*Navy rating*] (DNAB) .... SN(JCNE)
Seaman (Junior College Nuclear Submarine Engineering Technician) [*Navy rating*] (DNAB) .... SN(JCNSET)
Seaman (Junior College Polaris Field Electronics) [*Navy rating*] (DNAB) .... SN(JCPE)
Seaman (Junior College Polaris Field Launcher) [*Navy rating*] (DNAB) .... SN(JCPL)
Seaman (Junior College Technical) [*Navy rating*] (DNAB) .... SN(JCT)
Seaman (Junior College Technical Electrician) [*Navy rating*] (DNAB) .... SN(JCE)
Seaman, Lithographer, Striker [*Navy rating*] .... LISN
Seaman, Mineman, Striker [*Navy rating*] .... MNSN
Seaman, Missile Technician, Striker [*Navy rating*] .... MTSN
Seaman, Musician, Striker [*Navy rating*] .... MUSN
Seaman Neck Elementary School, Levittown, NY [*Library symbol*] [*Library of Congress*] (LCLS) .... NLevSNE
Seaman (Operator) [*British military*] (DMA) .... S(O)
Seaman, Opticalman, Striker [*Navy rating*] .... OMSN
Seaman, Personnelman, Striker [*Navy rating*] .... PNSN
Seaman (Polaris Field Electronics) [*Navy rating*] (DNAB) .... SN(PFE)
Seaman (Polaris Field Launcher) [*Navy rating*] (DNAB) .... SN(PFL)
Seaman, Postal Clerk, Striker [*Navy rating*] .... PCSN
Seaman, Quartermaster, Striker [*Navy rating*] .... QMSN
Seaman, RADARman, Striker [*Navy rating*] .... RDSN
Seaman, Radioman, Striker [*Navy rating*] .... RMSN
Seaman Recruit [*Navy*] E1
Seaman Recruit [*Navy*] .... SR
Seaman Recruit (Electronics Field) [*Navy rating*] (DNAB) .... SR(EF)
Seaman Recruit (High School) [*Navy rating*] (DNAB) .... SR(HS)
Seaman Recruit (Nuclear Field Electronics) [*Navy rating*] (DNAB) .... SR(NFE)
Seaman Recruit (Nuclear Submarine Engineering Technician) [*Navy rating*] (DNAB) .... SR(NSET)
Seaman Recruit (Polaris Field Electronics) [*Navy rating*] (DNAB) .... SR(PFE)
Seaman Recruit (Polaris Field Launcher) [*Navy rating*] (DNAB) .... SR(PFL)
Seaman, Ship's Serviceman, Striker [*Navy rating*] .... SHSN
Seaman, Signalman, Striker [*Navy rating*] .... SMSN
Seaman, SONAR Technician, Striker [*Navy rating*] .... STSN
Seaman, Storekeeper, Striker [*Navy rating*] .... SKSN
Seaman Torpedoman [*Obsolete Navy*] .... ST
Seaman, Yeoman, Striker [*Navy rating*] .... YNSN
Seamanship Exercise (NVT) .... SEAMEX
Seamen [*British military*] (DMA) .... SM
Seamen's and Firemen's Society [*A union*] [*British*] .... SFS
Seamen's Center [*Later, Seamen and International House*] (EA) .... SC
Seamen's Church Institute of New York/New Jersey (EA) .... SCI
Seamen's Church Institute, Philadelphia, PA [*Library symbol Library of Congress Obsolete*] (LCLS) .... PPSCI
Seamen's Loyal Standard Association [*A union*] [*British*] .... SLSA
Seamen's Protection Society [*A union*] [*British*] .... SPS
Seamen's Union [*British*] .... SU
Seamen's United Protection Society [*A union*] [*British*] .... SUPS
SEAMEO [*Southeast Asia Ministers of Education Organization*] **Regional Center for Graduate Study and Research in Agriculture** [*Philippines*] [*Research center*] (IRC) .... SEARCA
Seamless (DAC) .... S
Seamless (AAG) .... SMLS

Seamless Garment Network (EA) .... SGN
Seamless Steel Tubing .... SSTU
Seamstress (WGA) .... SMSTRS
Seaplane [Russian symbol] .... KOR
Seaplane [Navy] .... S
Seaplane .... S/P
Seaplane Base .... SPB
Seaplane Bomber [Russian symbol] .... MTB
Seaplane Carrier [Navy symbol Obsolete] .... CVS
Seaplane Depot Ship .... SPD
Seaplane Pilots Association (EA) .... SPA
Seaplane Reconnaissance Aircraft .... SR
Seaplane Reconnaissance Unit .... SRU
Seaplane Repair Base .... SRB
Seaplane Shuttle Transport [New York-Philadelphia air-link] .... SST
Seaplane Tender [Navy symbol] .... AV
Seaplane Tender, Destroyer [Navy symbol Obsolete] .... AVD
Seaplane Wrecking Derrick [Self-propelled] [Navy symbol] .... YSD
Seaport .... SEAPT
Seaport .... SPT
Seaport Navigation Co. [Later, SNCO] [AAR code] .... SENA
Seaport Navigation Co. [AAR code] .... SNCO
Seaports of Debarkation (MCD) .... SPOD
Seaports of Embarkation (MCD) .... SPOE
SEAQ Automated Execution Facility [Software package] .... SAEF
Sear-Brown Associates Information Center Library, Rochester, NY [OCLC symbol] (OCLC) .... RVJ
Sear-Brown Associates, PC, Rochester, NY [Library symbol Library of Congress] (LCLS) .... NRSe
Search .... S
Search (MCD) .... SCH
Search (AAG) .... SRCH
Search and Automatic Track Array RADAR .... SEATAR
Search and Automatic Track Fixed Array RADAR .... SEAFAR
Search and Clear [Military] .... S & C
Search and Destroy [Army] (AABC) .... S & D
Search and Destroy (MCD) .... SAD
Search and Destroy Armor Munition (MCD) .... SADARM
Search and Range Homing .... SARAH
Search and Range RADAR .... SRR
Search and Reconnaissance [Air Force] .... SR
Search and Recovery [Military] .... SR
Search and Release (AAG) .... SAR
Search and Replace Automatically [Computer science] (DGA) .... SARA
Search and Rescue (FAAC) .... SAR
Search and Rescue [Marine science] (OSRA) .... SAR
Search and Rescue .... SR
Search & Rescue 22 [British ICAO designator] (FAAC) .... SRD
Search & Rescue 202 [British ICAO designator] (FAAC) .... SRG
Search and Rescue Aid .... SARA
Search and Rescue and Homing .... SARAH
Search and Rescue, Atlantic [Coast Guard] .... SARLANT
Search and Rescue Capability Upgrade Project [Canadian Navy] .... SARCUP
Search and Rescue Center (CINC) .... SARC
Search and Rescue Central [Navy] .... SARCEN
Search and Rescue - Civil Air Patrol (MCD) .... SARCAP
Search and Rescue Combat Air Patrol (IAA) .... SARCAP
Search and Rescue Communicator [Navy] .... SARCOM
Search and Rescue Coordination Center [Air Force] .... SARCC
Search and Rescue Detachment [Navy] (NG) .... SARDET
Search and Rescue Exercise (MCD) .... SAREX
Search and Rescue Exercise [Navy] (DOMA) .... SAREX
Search & Rescue HQ [British ICAO designator] (FAAC) .... SRW
Search and Rescue Management Information System [BTS] (TAG) .... SARMIS
Search and Rescue Mission Coordinator [Australia] .... SARMC
Search and Rescue, Pacific [Coast Guard] (DNAB) .... SARPAC
Search and Rescue Program [Military] .... SAR
Search and Rescue Radio Beacon .... SRRB
Search and Rescue Satellite [Navy] .... SARSAT
Search and Rescue Satellite System [Navy] (MCD) .... SARSS
Search and Rescue Satellite-Aided Tracking [NASA] .... SARSAT
Search and Rescue Ship (KSC) .... SRS
Search and Rescue Simulation [Coast Guard] .... SARSIM
Search and Rescue Task Force [Military] (VNW) .... SARTAF
Search and Rescue, Telephone [Coast Guard] .... SARTEL
Search and Rescue Using Satellites [Air Force] .... SARUS
Search and Rescue-Beacon Equipment (MCD) .... SARBE
Search and Seizure Bulletin [A publication] (DLA) .... Search & Seizure Bull
Search and Track RADAR .... STR
Search AntiRADAR Tactical Aircraft, K-Band .... SARTACK
Search Attack Unit .... SAU
Search Control (IEEE) .... SC
Search Control Number (MCD) .... SCN
Search Date (NITA) .... SD
Search Decision Rule [Computer science] .... SDR
Search Depth [Navy] (NVT) .... SD
Search, Detection and Recognition [Military] .... SDR
Search for Common Ground (EA) .... SCG
Search for Critical Weakness [Aerospace] (AAG) .... SFCW
Search for Education, Elevation, and Knowledge [Program] .... SEEK
Search for Excellence in Science and Mathematics Education [Graduate program at University of California at Berkeley] .... SESAME
Search for Excellence in Science Education [National Science Teacher Association] (EDAC) .... SESE
Search for Extraterrestrial Intelligence .... SETI

Search for Extraterrestrial Radio Emission from Nearby Developed Intelligent Populations .... SERENDIP
Search for Random Success [Aerospace] (AAG) .... SFRS
[The] Search for Signs of Intelligent Life in the Universe [Lily Tomlin one-woman show written by Jane Wagner] .... TSFSOILITU
Search for Simulated Submarine Casualty Exercise [Navy] (NVT) .... SMASHEX
Search for the Odd Shape [Neuropsychology test] .... SOSH
Search for Tomorrow Fan Club [Defunct] (EA) .... SFTFC
Search Group, Inc. [An association] (EA) .... SGI
Search Information Tape Equipment .... SITE
Search, Inspection, and Recovery (NVT) .... SIR
Search Jam System .... SJS
Search, Locate, Communications, or Kill (MCD) .... SEALOCK
Search Mode Acquisition [Telecommunications] (LAIN) .... SMA
Search Mode Logic .... SML
Search Month (NITA) .... SM
Search of Enemy Air Defense (MCD) .... SEACS
Search of the Library Information Collection [Search system] .... SLIC
Search Optical Augmentation LASER (MCD) .... SOAL
Search Pattern Assessment Model [Military] (CAAL) .... SPAM
Search Plane [Navy symbol] .... VS
Search Program for Infrared Spectra [Canada Institute for Scientific and Technical Information] [Information service or system] .... SPIR
Search RADAR .... SR
Search RADAR Alignment Test [Military] (CAAL) .... SRAT
Search RADAR Designation Alignment (MCD) .... SRDA
Search RADAR Element (IAA) .... SRE
Search RADAR Input Device (MCD) .... SRID
Search RADAR Satellite Simulation [Military] (CAAL) .... SR SATSIM
Search RADAR Simulation Group [Military] (CAAL) .... SRSG
Search RADAR Terminal .... SRT
Search RADAR Terrain Clearance (NG) .... SRTC
Search Radar Terrain Clearance (DOMA) .... SRTC
Search/Rescue [When the first letter of a pair] [Designation for all US military aircraft] .... H
Search Signal Generator .... SSG
Search/Track .... S/T
Search Track Intermediate Frequency [Military] .... STIF
Search Unit Tracing and Recording System .... SUTARS
Search Year (NITA) .... SY
Searchable Physics Information Notes (NITA) .... SPIN
Searchable Physics Information Notices [American Institute of Physics] [New York, NY Bibliographic database] .... SPIN
Search-a-Word [Neuropsychology test] .... SAW
Searched, Silenced, Safeguarded, Segregated, and Sped Out of the Area [US POW hadling practice] (VNW) .... SSSSS
Search-Height Integration Program (SAA) .... SHIP
Searching Together Educational Ministries (EA) .... STEM
Searchless Self-Adjusting System .... SSAS
Searchlight (MSA) .... SCHLT
Searchlight .... SL
Searchlight .... SLT
Searchlight and Sound Locator [Navy] .... SLT & SDL
Searchlight Battery [Army] .... SLBtry
Searchlight Carrier [British] .... SC
Searchlight Control [JETDS nomenclature] L
Searchlight Control [Military] .... SLC
Searchlight Illumination Exercise [Also, LITEX] [Military] (NVT) .... LIGHTEX
Searchlight Illumination Exercise [Also, LIGHTEX] [Military] (NVT) .... LITEX
Searchlight Militia Depot (Royal Artillery) [British military] (DMA) .... SLMD(RA)
Searchlight Operator [British military] (DMA) .... SLO
Searchlight RADAR .... SLRD
Search-while-Track (CAAL) .... SWT
Searcy, AR [AM radio station call letters] .... KWCK
Searcy, AR [FM radio station call letters] .... KWCK-FM
Searcy, AR [Location identifier FAA] (FAAL) .... SRC
Searington Elementary School, Albertson, NY [Library symbol] [Library of Congress] (LCLS) .... NAlbSE
Searle [G. D.] & Co. [Research code symbol] .... SC
Searle and Smith's English Probate and Divorce Reports [1859-60] [A publication] (DLA) .... S & S
Searle and Smith's English Probate and Divorce Reports [A publication] (DLA) .... S & Sm
Searle and Smith's English Probate and Divorce Reports [A publication] (DLA) .... Sea & Sm
Searle and Smith's English Probate and Divorce Reports [1859-60] [A publication] (DLA) .... Searle & Sm
Searle and Smith's English Probate and Divorce Reports [A publication] (DLA) .... Searle Sm
Searle's Cape Of Good Hope Reports [South Africa] [A publication] (DLA) .... S
Searle's Cases in the Supreme Court [1850-67] [South Africa] [A publication] (DLA) .... S
Searle's Minnesota Digest [A publication] (DLA) .... Searle Dig
Searle's Supreme Court Reports [1850-67] [Cape Colony] [A publication] (DLA) .... Searle
Sears Canada [TS Symbol] (TTSB) .... SCC
Sears Canada, Inc. [Toronto Stock Exchange symbol] .... SCC
Sears Point [California] [Seismograph station code, US Geological Survey] (SEIS) .... SNT
Sears Point International Raceway [California] .... SPIR
Sears, Roebuck 8.88% Dep Pfd [NYSE symbol] (TTSB) .... SPrA
Sears Roebuck Acceptance Corp. .... SRAC
Sears, Roebuck & Co. [NYSE symbol] (SPSG) .... S
Sears, Roebuck & Co. [Associated Press] (SAG) .... Sears

Sears, Roebuck & Co., Chicago, IL [*Library symbol Library of Congress*] (LCLS) .... ICSears
Searsport, ME [*FM radio station call letters*] .... WBYA
Sears,Roebuck [*NYSE symbol*] (TTSB) .... S
Sea-Salt Aerosol Water [*Oceanography*] .... SSAW
SEASAT [*Sea Satellite*]- A Scatterometer System [*NASA*] .... SASS
SEASAT Users Group of Europe (MSC) .... SURGE
Sea-Service Temperature Anomaly [*Marine science*] (OSRA) .... SSTA
Seashore Environmental Alliance .... SEA
Seaside, CA [*FM radio station call letters*] (RBYB) .... KISE-FM
Seaside, CA [*FM radio station call letters*] (RBYB) .... KJMY
Seaside, CA [*FM radio station call letters*] .... KLMY
Seaside, CA [*FM radio station call letters*] .... KVRG
Seaside, OR [*AM radio station call letters*] (RBYB) .... KSWB
Seaside Support League - POW/MIA [*Prisoner of War/Missing in Action*] (EA) .... SSL-POW/MIA
Season .... SN
Season and Sunspot Number (DNAB) .... SSN
Seasonal [*Business term*] (OICC) .... S
Seasonal Affective Disorder [*Type of depression caused by long nights, short days*] .... SAD
Seasonal Affective Disorder Syndrome [*Psychiatry*] (DAVI) .... SADS
Seasonal Agricultural Service .... SAS
Seasonal Agricultural Worker .... SAW
Seasonal Derated Hours (IEEE) .... SDH
Seasonal Derating (IEEE) .... SD
Seasonal Derating Factor (IEEE) .... SDF
Seasonal Employee [*Business term*] (MHDB) .... SE
Seasonal Employees in Agriculture .... SEA
Seasonal Energy Efficiency Rating (AAGC) .... SEER
Seasonal Energy Syndrome [*Psychology*] (DAVI) .... SES
Seasonal Energy-Efficiency Ratio [*of heat pumps, air conditioners, etc.*] .... SEER
Seasonal Equatorial Atlantic Experiment .... SEQUAL
Seasonal Fluctuation (MHDB) .... SF
Seasonal Food [*Department of Employment*] [*British*] .... SF
Seasonal High Water Level (GNE) .... SHWL
Seasonal Industry (MHDW) .... SI
Seasonal Net Outgassing [*Oceanography*] .... SNO
Seasonal Unemployment (MHDW) .... SU
Seasonally Adjusted (WGA) .... SA
Seasonally Adjusted Annual Retail [*Automotive sales*] .... SAAR
Seasonal-to-Interannual Climate Prediction Program (USDC) .... SCPP
Seasonal-to-Interannual Climate Prediction Program [*Marine science*] (OSRA) .... SCPP
Seasoned (WGA) .... SD
Seasoning Manufacturers Association [*British*] (DBA) .... SMA
Seastar Resource Corp. [*Vancouver Stock Exchange symbol*] .... SRR
Sea-State Correction [*Doppler navigation*] (DEN) .... SSC
Seat (WGA) .... S
Seat .... ST
Seat Back Assembly [*Aerospace*] (MCD) .... SBA
Seat Belt Control Apparatus .... SBCA
Seat Bucket Read (NG) .... SBR
Seat Cabs .... SC
Seat Index Point [*Automotive design*] .... SIP
Seat Lock Pin Handle .... SLPH
Seat Mile .... SM
Seat Miles per Gallon [*BTS*] (TAG) .... SMPG
Seat of Government [*Washington, DC*] .... SOG
Seat of the Pants .... SOP
Seat Reference Point .... SRP
Seat Reservation System (IAA) .... SRS
Sea-Tangle [*Nautical charts*] .... Stg
Seatbelt Retractor Module [*Automotive engineering*] .... SRM
Seated (WGA) .... STD
Seater .... STER
Seater (ADA) .... STR
Seating [*Technical drawings*] .... STG
Seating Reference Point [*49CFR571*] (TAG) .... SGRP
SEATO [*Southeast Asia Treaty Organization*] **Administrative Publication** ...... SEAP
SEATO [*Southeast Asia Treaty Organization*] **Central Distribution Agency** (NATG) .... SCDA
SEATO [*Southeast Asia Treaty Organization*] **Military Planning Office** (CINC) .... SMPO
Seaton's Forms in Chancery [*A publication*] (DLA) .... Seat F Ch
Sea-to-Shore Rotation Survey (DNAB) .... SEAVEY
Seatoun [*New Zealand*] [*Seismograph station code, US Geological Survey Closed*] (SEIS) .... STN
Seatrain Lines, Inc. [*AAR code*] .... STL
Seattle [*Washington*] [*ICAO location identifier*] (ICLI) .... KRSE
Seattle [*Washington*] [*Seismograph station code, US Geological Survey Closed*] (SEIS) .... SEA
Seattle Army Terminal .... SART
Seattle Army Terminal Detachment (AABC) .... SATD
Seattle Art Museum, Seattle, WA [*Library symbol Library of Congress*] (LCLS) .... WaSA
Seattle, Auburn [*Washington*] [*ICAO location identifier*] (ICLI) .... KZSE
Seattle Boeing Field/King Country International [*Washington*] [*ICAO location identifier*] (ICLI) .... KBFI
Seattle Central Community College, District Technical Services, Seattle, WA [*Library symbol*] [*Library of Congress*] (LCLS) .... WaSC-D
Seattle Central Community College, Seattle, WA [*Library symbol Library of Congress*] (LCLS) .... WaSC
Seattle Film Works [*Associated Press*] (SAG) .... SeattleF
Seattle Film Works, Inc. [*Associated Press*] (SAG) .... SeatlF

Seattle FilmWorks [*NASDAQ symbol*] (SAG) .... FOTO
Seattle First National Bank, Seattle, WA [*OCLC symbol*] (OCLC) .... SFN
Seattle Genealogical Society, Seattle, WA [*Library symbol Library of Congress*] (LCLS) .... WaSG
Seattle Historical Society, Seattle, WA [*Library symbol Library of Congress*] (LCLS) .... WaSHi
Seattle - Marshall [*Washington*] [*Seismograph station code, US Geological Survey Closed*] (SEIS) .... STT
Seattle Midwifery School, Seattle, WA [*Library symbol*] [*Library of Congress*] (LCLS) .... WaSSM
Seattle National Fisheries Research Center [*Seattle, WA*] [*Department of the Interior*] (GRD) .... SNFRC
Seattle Ocean Services Unit [*National Oceanic and Atmospheric Administration*] (GFGA) .... SOSU
Seattle Pacific College [*Washington*] .... SPC
Seattle Pacific College, Seattle, WA [*Library symbol Library of Congress*] (LCLS) .... WaSPC
Seattle Pacific University (GAGS) .... Seattle Pac U
Seattle Port of Embarkation .... SEPE
Seattle Public Library, Seattle, WA [*Library symbol Library of Congress*] (LCLS) .... WaS
Seattle Public Schools, Library Technical Service, Seattle, WA [*Library symbol Library of Congress*] (LCLS) .... WaSPS
Seattle/Seattle-Tacoma International [*Washington*] [*ICAO location identifier*] (ICLI) .... KSEA
Seattle/Tacoma [*Washington*] [*Airport symbol*] (OAG) .... SEA
Seattle/Tacoma International Airport (GAVI) .... SEA/TAC
Seattle University (GAGS) .... Seattle U
Seattle University, Seattle, WA [*Library symbol Library of Congress*] (LCLS) .... WaSU
Seattle, WA [*Location identifier FAA*] (FAAL) .... BFI
Seattle, WA [*AM radio station call letters*] .... KBLE
Seattle, WA [*FM radio station call letters*] .... KCMU
Seattle, WA [*Television station call letters*] .... KCTS
Seattle, WA [*AM radio station call letters*] .... KEZX
Seattle, WA [*Television station call letters*] .... KHCV
Seattle, WA [*FM radio station call letters*] .... KING-FM
Seattle, WA [*Television station call letters*] .... KING-TV
Seattle, WA [*AM radio station call letters*] .... KIRO
Seattle, WA [*FM radio station call letters*] .... KIRO-FM
Seattle, WA [*Television station call letters*] .... KIRO-TV
Seattle, WA [*Television station call letters*] .... KISW
Seattle, WA [*AM radio station call letters*] .... KJR
Seattle, WA [*FM radio station call letters*] .... KJR-FM
Seattle, WA [*AM radio station call letters*] .... KKDZ
Seattle, WA [*AM radio station call letters*] (RBYB) .... KLFE
Seattle, WA [*AM radio station call letters*] .... KMPS
Seattle, WA [*FM radio station call letters*] .... KMPS-FM
Seattle, WA [*FM radio station call letters*] .... KNDD
Seattle, WA [*FM radio station call letters*] .... KNHC
Seattle, WA [*AM radio station call letters*] (RBYB) .... KNWX
Seattle, WA [*AM radio station call letters*] .... KOMO
Seattle, WA [*Television station call letters*] .... KOMO-TV
Seattle, WA [*AM radio station call letters*] .... KPLZ
Seattle, WA [*AM radio station call letters*] (RBYB) .... KRPM-AM
Seattle, WA [*Television station call letters*] .... KTZZ
Seattle, WA [*FM radio station call letters*] .... KUBE
Seattle, WA [*FM radio station call letters*] .... KUOW
Seattle, WA [*AM radio station call letters*] .... KVI
Seattle, WA [*FM radio station call letters*] (RBYB) .... KWJZ
Seattle, WA [*FM radio station call letters*] .... KYCW
Seattle, WA [*FM radio station call letters*] .... KZOK
Seattle, WA [*Location identifier FAA*] (FAAL) .... NEJ
Seattle, WA [*Location identifier FAA*] (FAAL) .... SSL
Seattle, WA [*Location identifier FAA*] (FAAL) .... SZI
Seattle, WA [*Location identifier FAA*] (FAAL) .... ZSE
Seavan Management Information System .... SEAMIST
Sea-Viewing Wide Field-of-View Sensor [*Marine science*] (OSRA) .... SeaWiFS
Sea-Viewing Wide-Field Sensor [*Oceanography*] (ECON) .... SeaWiFS
Seaward Defence Boat [*British military*] (DMA) .... SDB
Seaward Defense Craft (NATG) .... SDC
Seaward Defense Exercise [*NATO*] (NATG) .... SEADEX
Seaward Extension Simulator (SAA) .... SES
Seawater .... SW
Sea-Water Acetic Acid Test (PDAA) .... SWAAT
Seawater Activated Release System [*Navy*] (CAAL) .... SEAWARS
Seawater Conversion Laboratory (KSC) .... SWCL
Seawater Feed .... SWF
Seaway Food Town [*NASDAQ symbol*] (TTSB) .... SEWY
Seaway Food Town, Inc. [*Associated Press*] (SAG) .... SeawFd
Seaway Food Town, Inc. [*NASDAQ symbol*] (NQ) .... SEWY
Seaway Multi-Corp Ltd. [*Toronto Stock Exchange symbol*] .... SWH
Seaway Port Authority of Duluth .... SPAD
Seaway Valley Libraries [*Formerly, Stormont, Dundas, and Glengarry Counties Publi c Library*], Cornwall, ON, Canada [*Library symbol Library of Congress*] (LCLS) .... CaOCSDG
Seaweed [*Quality of the bottom*] [*Nautical charts*] .... Wd
SeaWiFS [*Sea-Viewing Wide Field-of-View Sensor*] **Data Analysis System** (USDC) .... SeaDas
Seawind Resources, Inc. [*Vancouver Stock Exchange symbol*] .... SWI
Seaworthiness Impairment (NVT) .... SWI
Seaworthy (ADA) .... S/W
Seba Beach Public Library, Alberta [*Library symbol National Library of Canada*] (NLC) .... ASB
Sebastian on Trade-Marks [*5th ed.*] [*1911*] [*A publication*] (DLA) .... Seb Tr M

Sebastian on Trade-Marks [*A publication*] (DLA) .... Seb Trade-Marks
Sebastianus Medices [*Flourished, 16th century*] [*Authority cited in pre-1607 legal work*] (DSA) .... Sebast Med
Sebastianus Sapia [*Deceased, 1523*] [*Authority cited in pre-1607 legal work*] (DSA) .... Seb Sapi
Sebastianus Sapia [*Deceased, 1523*] [*Authority cited in pre-1607 legal work*] (DSA) .... Sebast Sap
Sebastianus Vantius [*Flourished, 16th century*] [*Authority cited in pre-1607 legal work*] (DSA) .... Seb Vant
Sebastianus Vantius [*Flourished, 16th century*] [*Authority cited in pre-1607 legal work*] (DSA) .... Sebast Vant
Sebastopol, CA [*FM radio station call letters*] (RBYB) .... KJZY
Sebastopol Public Library, Sebastopol, CA [*Library symbol Library of Congress*] (LCLS) .... CSeb
Sebba [*Burkina Faso*] [*ICAO location identifier*] (ICLI) .... DHES
Sebba [*Burkina Faso*] [*Airport symbol*] (OAG) .... XSE
Sebeka School, Sebeka, MN [*Library symbol*] [*Library of Congress*] (LCLS) .... MnSebS
Sebenico [*Yugoslavia*] [*Seismograph station code, US Geological Survey Closed*] (SEIS) .... SEB
Sebewaing Township Library, Sebewaing, MI [*Library symbol Library of Congress*] (LCLS) .... MiSe
Sebha [*Libya*] [*ICAO location identifier*] (ICLI) .... HLLS
Sebha [*Libya*] [*Airport symbol*] (OAG) .... SEB
Sebir [*or Sebirin*] (BJA) .... Seb
Sebright Club of America (EA) .... SCA
Sebring, FL [*Location identifier FAA*] (FAAL) .... AUE
Sebring, FL [*Location identifier FAA*] (FAAL) .... SEF
Sebring, FL [*AM radio station call letters*] .... WITS
Sebring, FL [*AM radio station call letters*] .... WJCM
Sebring, FL [*FM radio station call letters*] (RBYB) .... WYMR
Sebum Excretion Rate (OA) .... SER
SEC Practice Section (TDOB) .... SECPS
Secadal [*Educador*] [*ICAO location identifier*] (ICLI) .... SESE
Secant .... SEC
Secant (IDOE) .... sec
Secant, Hyperbolic .... SECH
Secaucus Free Public Library, Secaucus, NJ [*Library symbol Library of Congress*] (LCLS) .... NjSe
Secaucus Home News, Secaucus, NJ [*Library symbol Library of Congress*] (LCLS) .... NjSeH
Secaucus, NJ [*Television station call letters*] .... WWOR
Sec-Butyl Percarbonate [*Organic chemistry*] .... SBP
Secchi Disk .... SD
Sechelt, BC [*FM radio station call letters*] .... CISE
Sechelt Public Library, British Columbia [*Library symbol National Library of Canada*] (NLC) .... BSE
SECNAV [*Secretary of the Navy*] **Advisory Board on Education and Training** [*Pensacola, FL*] (EGAO) .... SABET
SECNAV [*Secretary of the Navy*] **Advisory Board on Educational Requirements** (NG) .... SABER
SECNAV [*Secretary of the Navy*] **Advisory Board on Scientific Education** (DNAB) .... SABOSE
SECNAV [*Secretary of the Navy*] **Advisory Commission on Manpower** (NG) .... SACOM
SECNAV [*Secretary of the Navy*] **Advisory Commission on Youth** (NG) .... SACAY
Seco-Cemp Ltd. [*Toronto Stock Exchange symbol*] .... SC
Secom General [*NASDAQ symbol*] (TTSB) .... SECM
Secom General Corp. [*NASDAQ symbol*] (NQ) .... SECM
Secom General Corp. [*Associated Press*] (SAG) .... Secom
SECOMO [*Software Engineering Cost Model*] **Non-COCOMO Factor** [*Constructive Cost Model*] .... SNCF
Second [*Symbol*] [*SI unit of time*] .... s
Second [*or Secondary*] .... S
Second (AFM) .... SEC
Second (IDOE) .... sec
Second (ODBW) .... sec
Second Air Division Association (EA) 2ADA
Second Allied Tactical Air Force Central Europe .... TWOATAF
Second Amendment Foundation (EA) .... SAF
Second Attack [*Men's lacrosse position*] .... SA
Second Audio Program .... SAP
Second Bancorp [*NASDAQ symbol*] (TTSB) .... SECD
Second Bancorp, Inc. [*Associated Press*] (SAG) .... SecBn
Second Bancorp, Inc. [*NASDAQ symbol*] (SPSG) .... SECD
Second Bancorp, Inc. [*Associated Press*] (SAG) .... SecndB
Second Base [*or Baseman*] [*Baseball*] 2B
Second Bncp $1.50 Cv Pfd'A' [*NASDAQ symbol*] (TTSB) .... SECDP
Second Bombardment Association (EA) .... SBA
[*A*] **Second Book of Danish Verse** [*A publication*] .... BoDS
Second Book of Judgments (Huxley) [*England*] [*A publication*] (DLA) .... Sec Bk Judg
[*A*] **Second Book of Russian Verse** [*A publication*] .... BoRS
Second Chance Opportunities and Education for Women (AIE) .... SCOPE
Second Check Character Flip-Flop [*Computer science*] (MHDB) .... SCCFF
Second City Television [*Television program, the title of which was later changed to its initialism*] .... SCTV
Second Class Diver Badge [*Military decoration*] .... SC Div Bad
Second Class Open [*Train ticket*] (DCTA) .... SO
Second Class Passengers [*Shipping*] [*British*] .... SND
Second Coast Guard District [*St. Louis, MO*] [*USCG*] (TAG) D2
Second Computer Inquiry (TSSD) CI2
Second Consortium of Local Authorities .... SCOLA
Second Corinthians [*New Testament book*] .... 2 CO
Second Cover [*Periodicals*] (WDMC) 2C
Second Defense [*Men's lacrosse position*] .... SD
Second Destination Transportation (MCD) .... SDT
Second Development Decade [*United Nations*] .... SDD
Second Difference [*Statistics*] (OA) .... SD
Second Division of Executive Officers [*A union*] [*British*] .... SDEO
Second Dynamic Response and Kinematics Experiment [*Marine science*] (MSC) .... S DRAKE
Second Edition List of Australian Subject Headings [*A publication*] .... SLASH
Second Entrance [*Theatrical slang*] .... SE
Second Fleet [*Atlantic*] [*Navy*] .... SECFLT
Second Focal Distance [*Symbol*] [*Optics*] (ROG) .... F''
Second Folio Edition [*1632*] [*Shakespearean work*] F2
Second Foot (IAA) .... SECFT
Second Generation Data Processing System (MCD) .... SGDPS
Second Generation Non-English-Speaking Background NESB2
Second Genration Tank Sight [*Army*] .... SGTS
Second Harmonic (PDAA) .... SH
Second Harmonic AC [*Alternating Current*] **Voltammetry** [*Instrumentation*] .... SHACV
Second Harmonic Distortion (IAA) .... SHD
Second Harvest, the National Food Bank Network (EA) .... SH
Second Home All-Inclusive First Trust [*Real estate*] .... SHAFT
Second Husbands Alliance for Fair Treatment .... SHAFFT
Second in Command 2IC
Second Independence Movement [*Ecuador*] [*Political party*] (PPW) .... MSI
Second International BIOMASS Experiment .... SIBEX
Second International Mathematics Study .... SIMS
Second International Science Study [*International Association for the Evaluation of Educational Achievement*] .... SISS
Second Language Acquisition .... SLA
Second Language Learning in the Primary Classroom (AIE) .... SLIPP
Second Large ESRO [*European Space Research Organization*] **Project** .... SLEP
Second Law of Thermodynamics .... SLT
Second Layer of Soil Next Below the Surface Layer (BARN) .... B
Second Level Interrupt Handler (CMD) .... SLIH
Second Lieutenant [*Army*] 2LT
Second Lieutenant [*Air Force, Army, Marine Corps*] O1
Second Lieutenant [*Army*] .... SECLT
Second Lieutenant .... SL
Second Main Watch .... SMW
Second Malignant Neoplasm [*Medicine*] (DMAA) .... SMN
Second Marine Aircraft Wing .... SMAW
Second Marine Division Association (EA) .... SMDA
Second Mortgage [*Banking*] .... SM
Second Multiyear Contract [*Military*] (RDA) .... MY II
Second Nicaraguan Campaign Medal .... SNCM
Second Officer [*British military*] (DMA) 2/O
Second Opinion [*An association Defunct*] (EA) .... SO
Second Opinion (DAVI) .... SO
Second Opinion Program [*Later, NSOP*] (EA) .... SOP
Second Order Attitude Reference Set (MCD) .... SOARS
Second Order Coherent Multiple Access (PDAA) .... SOCMA
Second Order Logic .... SOL
Second Overtone Band .... SOB
Second Pilot [*Aviation*] (AIA) P2
Second Preferred Stock [*Investment term*] .... SPS
Second Presbyterian Church Library, Chattanooga, TN [*Library symbol Library of Congress*] (LCLS) .... TCSPr
Second Readiness State (AAG) .... SRS
Second Regional Assistance Command [*US advisory command*] [*Vietnam*] (VNW) .... SRAC
Second Republic of Korea Army .... SROKA
Second Rib [*Anatomy*] (DMAA) .... C_2
Second Routing (MCD) .... SR
Second Search Character [*Computer science*] (IAA) .... SSC
Second Stage .... SS
Second Statute of Westminster [*A publication*] (DSA) W2
Second Statute of Westminster [*A publication*] (DSA) .... West II
Second Surface Mirror .... SSM
Second Surgical Opinion [*Insurance*] (WYGK) .... SSO
Second Surgical Opinion Program (DAVI) .... SSOP
Second Surgical Opinion Program (MEDA) .... SSOP
Second Task Fleet .... SECTASKFLT
Second Telecommunications Carrier Selection Team [*Australia*] .... STCST
Second Time Around Echo .... STAE
Second Time Around Racers [*Car racing*] .... STAR
Second Transcript [*Genetics*] T2
Second User Systems Ltd. (NITA) .... SUS
Second Wives Association of North America (EA) .... SWAN
Second Wives Coalition (EA) .... SWC
Second Wives of America Demanding Equality .... SWADE
Second World Climate Conference (EERA) .... SWCC
Secondary [*Preferred form is sec*] [*Chemistry*] .... s
Secondary [*Chemistry*] .... Sec
Secondary .... SEC
Secondary (IDOE) .... sec
Secondary (AABC) .... SECD
Secondary .... SECDY
Secondary [*ICAO designator*] (FAAC) .... SRY
Secondary Accountability Center (AAG) .... SAC
Secondary Address Code .... SAC
Secondary Address Code Indicator .... SACI
Secondary Address Vector Table [*Computer science*] (IBMDP) .... SAVT
Secondary Air Anti-Backfire Valve [*Automotive engineering*] .... SABFV
Secondary Air Bypass Valve [*Automotive engineering*] .... SABV

Secondary Air Force Specialty ... SAFS
Secondary Air Injection [*Automotive engineering*] ... SAI
Secondary Air Pulse Valve [*Automotive engineering*] ... SAPV
Secondary Air Switching Valve [*Automotive engineering*] ... SASV
Secondary Aircraft Maintenance Base ... SAMB
Secondary Alarm Station [*Nuclear energy*] (NRCH) ... SAS
Secondary Alerting System (IAA) ... SAS
Secondary Alkane Sulfonate [*Surfactant*] [*Organic chemistry*] ... SAS
Secondary Amenorrhea [*Medicine*] (MAE) ... SA
Secondary Anemia [*Medicine*] (MAE) ... SA
Secondary Anticoagulation System [*Medicine*] (DMAA) ... SACS
Secondary Assistance Scheme [*Australia*] ... SAS
Secondary Audio Program ... SAP
Secondary Audio Program Services [*Television*] (BARN) ... SAPS
Secondary Auxiliary Nuclear Power ... SANP
Secondary Battery [*Military*] ... SB
Secondary Boycott [*Legal shorthand*] (LWAP) ... S/BOY
Secondary Buffer [*Chemistry*] ... SB
Secondary Building Unit [*Physical chemistry*] ... SBU
Secondary Butyl Alcohol [*Organic chemistry*] ... SBA
Secondary Carpet Backing ... SCB
Secondary Category Code (NITA) ... SCC
Secondary Certified Reference Material [*Nuclear energy*] (NRCH) ... SCRM
Secondary Checkpoint File ... SCF
Secondary Chemical Control System [*Nuclear energy*] (NRCH) ... SCCS
Secondary Chemical Equilibria [*Chromatography*] ... SCE
Secondary Code ... SC
Secondary Colleges Staff Association [*Tasmania, Australia*] ... SCSA
Secondary Combustion Chamber [*Furnace technology*] ... SCC
Secondary Communications Authorization (IEEE) ... SCA
Secondary Confinement [*or Containment*] [*Nuclear energy*] (IEEE) ... SC
Secondary Container Transfer Area [*Nuclear energy*] (NRCH) ... SCTA
Secondary Containment Cooling (IEEE) ... SCC
Secondary Containment Purge and Pressure Control System [*Nuclear energy*] (NRCH) ... SCPPS
Secondary Control Assembly [*Nuclear energy*] (NRCH) ... SCA
Secondary Control Point ... SCP
Secondary Control Rod Drive Mechanism [*Nuclear energy*] (NRCH) ... SCRDM
Secondary Control Rod Driveline [*Nuclear energy*] (NRCH) ... SCRD
Secondary Control Rod System [*Nuclear energy*] (NRCH) ... SCRS
Secondary Control Ship [*Navy*] (NVT) ... SCS
Secondary Control System (MCD) ... SCS
Secondary Control Unit [*Aerospace*] (AAG) ... SCU
Secondary Coolant Line [*or Loop*] [*NASA*] (NASA) ... SCL
Secondary Coolant System [*Nuclear energy*] (NRCH) ... SCS
Secondary Cross-Connection Point (NITA) ... SCP
Secondary Current Distribution [*Electroplating*] ... SCD
Secondary Curriculum Study Center [*of NASSP*] ... SCSC
Secondary Data Display System (MCD) ... SDDS
Secondary Distribution [*Investment term*] ... SD
Secondary Distribution Center (AAG) ... SDC
Secondary Education (AIE) ... SE
Secondary Education [*A publication*] ... Second Ed
Secondary Education Board ... SEB
Secondary Education Text-Books [*A publication*] ... SETB
Secondary Electric Power System (IAA) ... SEPS
Secondary Electron (MCD) ... SE
Secondary Electron Conduction [*Television camera system*] ... SEC
Secondary Electron Conduction [*Television camera system*] ... SECON
Secondary Electron Emission ... SEE
Secondary Electron Multiplier (IAA) ... SE
Secondary Electron Multiplier [*Detector*] ... SEM
Secondary Electron Scattering ... SES
Secondary Electron Yield ... SEY
Secondary Electron Yield Measurement ... SEYM
Secondary Electron Yield Measurement System ... SEYMS
Secondary Electron Yield System ... SEYS
Secondary Electron-Mixed Radiation Dosimeter (IEEE) ... SEMIRAD
Secondary Emission (IAA) ... SE
Secondary Emission Conductivity ... SEC
Secondary Emission Material (IAA) ... SEM
Secondary Emission Microscope ... SEM
Secondary Emission Monitor ... SEM
Secondary Enrichment Medium [*Microbiology*] ... SEM
Secondary Failure [*NASA*] (KSC) ... SF
Secondary Feedback Element (IAA) ... SFE
Secondary Flow Control System [*Nuclear energy*] (NRCH) ... SFCS
Secondary Freon Loop (NASA) ... SFL
Secondary Grammar School (ADA) ... SGS
Secondary Grid Emission ... SGE
Secondary Gun Pointer [*Navy*] ... SGP
Secondary Heads Association [*British*] (DBA) ... SHA
Secondary Hypertrophic Osteoarthropathy [*Medicine*] ... SHO
Secondary Imagery Dissemination System (DOMA) ... SIDS
Secondary Impedance (IAA) ... SECIMP
Secondary Index Field [*Computer science*] (MHDI) ... XDFLD
Secondary Influent Treatment System ... SITS
Secondary Infrared Calibration System ... SICS
Secondary Injection ... SI
Secondary Injection Control/Jet Interaction Control ... SIC/JIC
Secondary Injection/Jet Interaction ... SI/JI
Secondary Injection System ... SIS
Secondary Injection Thrust Vector Control ... SITVC
Secondary Inventory Control Activity (MCD) ... SICA
Secondary Ion Acclerator Mass Spectrometry ... SIAMS
Secondary Ion Mass Spectrometry [*or Spectroscopy*] ... SIMS
Secondary Item [*Army*] ... SI
Secondary Item Control Center ... SICC
Secondary Item Materiel Excess [*DoD*] ... SIMEX
Secondary Item Procurement Appropriation [*Army*] ... SIPA
Secondary Landing Site [*NASA*] (NASA) ... SLS
Secondary Lead Smelters Association (EA) ... SLSA
Secondary Level English Proficiency Test ... SLEP
Secondary Life Support System [*NASA*] ... SLSS
Secondary Line of Sight [*Sextants*] ... SLOS
Secondary Liquid Waste Management System [*Nuclear energy*] (NRCH) ... SLWMS
Secondary Logic Unit ... SLU
Secondary Market [*Investment term*] ... SM
Secondary Market Operation ... SMO
Secondary Maximum Contaminant Level (EG) ... SMCL
Secondary Memory [*Computer science*] (BUR) ... SM
Secondary Mesenchyme Cell [*Cytology*] ... SMC
Secondary Metal Institute (EA) ... SMI
Secondary Military Occupational Specialty ... SMOS
Secondary Military Occupational Specialty Code (AABC) ... SMOSC
Secondary Modern School [*British*] ... S
Secondary Mortgage Market (ADA) ... SMM
Secondary Multiplexing Unit ... SMU
Secondary National Ambient Air Quality Standards [*Environmental Protection Agency*] (GFGA) ... SNAAQS
Secondary Navy Enlisted Classification (DNAB) ... SNEC
Secondary Neutrals Mass Spectrometry ... SNMS
Secondary Next of Kin [*Army*] (AABC) ... SNOK
Secondary Operand Unit (IAA) ... SEOP
Secondary Operation ... SOP
Secondary Oxygen Pack [*NASA*] ... SOP
Secondary Particulate Emissions [*Environmental Protection Agency*] (GFGA) ... SPE
Secondary Plant Joint Test Group (DNAB) ... SPJTG
Secondary Plant System [*Nuclear energy*] (NRCH) ... SPS
Secondary Power Integration Test (MCD) ... SPIT
Secondary Power Source ... SPS
Secondary Power System [*or Subsystem*] (MCD) ... SPS
Secondary Power-Generating Subsystem (IAA) ... SPGS
Secondary Propulsion System [*NASA*] (KSC) ... SECPS
Secondary Propulsion System [*NASA*] ... SPS
Secondary Protocol Identifier (TNIG) ... SPI
Secondary Pulmonary Hemosiderosis [*Medicine*] (MAE) ... SPH
Secondary RADAR (IEEE) ... SECAR
Secondary RADAR [*RADAR beacon*] ... SECRA
Secondary RADAR (IAA) ... SR
Secondary RADAR System ... SRS
Secondary Recovery Ships [*NASA*] (KSC) ... SRS
Secondary Refrigerant Freezing (PDAA) ... SRF
Secondary Replaceable Unit ... SRU
Secondary Resistance (IDOE) ... R_s
Secondary Resistance (IDOE) ... R_{sec}
Secondary Sampling System [*Nuclear energy*] (NRCH) ... SSS
Secondary School ... SS
Secondary School Admission Test Board (EA) ... SSAT
Secondary School Admission Test Board (EA) ... SSATB
Secondary School Admissions Center [*Defunct*] (EA) ... SSAC
Secondary School Examinations Council [*British*] (BI) ... SSEC
Secondary School Mathematics Curriculum Improvement Study [*National Science Foundation*] ... SSMCIS
Secondary School Science Project [*Princeton University*] (AEE) ... SSSP
Secondary School Theatre Association [*Defunct*] (EA) ... SSTA
Secondary School Theatre Conference [*Later, SSTA*] (EA) ... SSTC
Secondary Schools, Metropolitan Toronto School Board, Ontario [*Library symbol National Library of Canada*] (NLC) ... OTMTSS
Secondary Social Security Number ... SSSN
Secondary Sources ... SS
Secondary Standard Dosimetry Laboratory ... SSDL
Secondary Stock Point (DNAB) ... SSP
Secondary Surge Tank [*Nuclear energy*] (NRCH) ... SST
Secondary Surveillance ... SS
Secondary Surveillance RADAR ... SSR
Secondary Surveillance RADAR Digitizer (IAA) ... SSRD
Secondary Target [*Military*] ... STGT
Secondary Target Line [*Army*] ... STL
Secondary Teacher [*A publication*] ... Second Teach
Secondary, Technical, and University Teachers' Insurance Society [*British*] (BI) ... STUTIS
Secondary Training for Alaskan Rural Students (EDAC) ... STARS
Secondary Type Battery [*JETDS nomenclature*] [*Military*] (CET) ... BB
Secondary Valve ... SV
Secondary Waste Treatment System [*Nuclear energy*] (NRCH) ... SWTS
Secondary [*or Shake*] **Wave** [*Earthquakes*] ... S
Secondary Waveform Generator [*Telecommunications*] (TEL) ... SWFG
Secondary Winding (IAA) ... S
Secondary Winding (IAA) ... SECWND
Secondary Yield Measurement ... SYM
Secondary Yield Measurement System ... SYMS
Secondary Zone ... SZ
Secondary-Image-Registration [*Photography*] ... SIR
Second-Class Mail Publications [*Later, ASCMP*] (EA) ... SCMP
Second-Class Post Office ... SCPO
Second-Degree Stochastic Dominance [*Statistics*] ... SSD
Second-Foot (WDAA) ... S-FT

Secondhand (ADA) ... SH
Second-Harmonic Band ... SHB
Second-Harmonic Discrimination System (MCD) ... SHDS
Second-Harmonic Generation [*LASER*] ... SHG
Second-Harmonic Resonance (MCD) ... SR
Second-Order Gradient ... SOG
Second-Order Transition Temperature ... SOTT
Seconds per Revolution [*or Rotation*] (NVT) ... SPR
Seconds Saybolt Furol [*Oil viscosity*] (IAA) ... SSF
Second-Stage Conduit ... SSC
Second-Stage Conduit Container ... SSCC
Second-Stage Engine Cutoff ... SSECO
Second-Stage Hydraulics ... SSH
Second-Stage Ignition ... SSI
Second-Stage Motor ... SSM
Second-Stage Motor Container ... SSMC
Second-Stage Rocket Motor ... SSRM
Second-Stage Separation Device ... SSSD
Second-Stage Tail Off (IAA) ... SSTO
Second-Tier Securities Market [*Investment term*] ... SSM
Second-Time-Around-Beacon-Echo (PDAA) ... STABE
Secours International de Caritas Catholica [*Belgium*] (EAIO) ... SICC
Secret [*Security classification*] ... S
Secret (AFM) ... SEC
Secret and Confidential Files [*Navy*] ... S-C
Secret Army for the Liberation of Armenia ... SALA
Secret Army for the Liberation of Corsica ... SALC
Secret Army Organization [*English initialism for OAS, terrorist group in Algeria and metropolitan France*] ... SAO
Secret Control Station [*NASA*] (KSC) ... SCS
Secret Cover Sheet (AAG) ... SCS
Secret Delivery Station (SAA) ... SDS
Secret Document Number ... SDN
Secret Formerly Restricted ... SFRD
Secret Intelligence Service [*British*] ... SIS
Secret - Limited Distribution - Not Releasable to Foreigners [*Security classification*] ... SNFLD
Secret Marriage Rite (BJA) ... SMR
Secret - No Foreigners [*Security classification*] ... SNF
Secret Paper Reconstitution Mechanism [*Device to reclaim documents that have been inadvertently shredded*] ... SPERM
Secret Pass Mine [*Vancouver Stock Exchange symbol*] ... SQP
Secret - Restricted Data [*Security classification*] ... SRD
Secret Service ... SS
Secret - Special Access Required [*Security classification*] (MCD) ... S-SAR
Secret Work in Process (MCD) ... SWIP
Secret Writing [*Espionage*] ... SW
Secretaria de Agricultura y Ganaderia [*Mexico*] ... SAG
Secretaria de Comercio y Fomento Industrial [*Secretariat of Trade and IndustrialPromotion*] [*Mexico*] (CROSS) ... SECOFI
Secretaria de Estado de Recursos Hidricos [*Argentina*] ... SERH
Secretaria de Integracion Turistica Centroamericana ... SITCA
Secretaria de Recursos Hidraulicos [*Mexico*] ... SRH
Secretaria Ejecutiva Permanente del Convenio Andres Bello [*Permanent Executive Secretariat of the Andres Bello Convention*] (EAIO) ... SECAB
Secretaria Nacional de Transportes [*Brazil*] (EY) ... SNT
Secretaria Permanente del Acuerdo Sudamericano de Estupefacientes y Psicotropicos [*Permanent Secretariat of the South American Agreement on Narcotic Drugs and Psychotropic Substances - PSSAANDPS*] [*Argentina*] (EAIO) ... SPASEP
Secretariado da Propaganda Nacional [*Portugal*] ... SPN
Secretariado Latinoamericano de Trotskismo Orthodoxo [*Peru*] ... SLATO
Secretariado Latinoamericano de la Compania de Jesus [*Latin American Bureau of Society of Jesus*] (EAIO) ... SELACJ
Secretarial (WGA) ... secl
Secretarial ... SECL
Secretarial ... SECRL
Secretarial ... SECTL
Secretarial Automated Data Index ... SADI
Secretarial Information System (EPA) ... SIS
Secretarial Language Certificate [*British*] (DI) ... SLC
Secretarial Language Diploma [*British*] (DI) ... SLD
Secretarial Panel For the Evaluation of Epidemiologic Research Activities for the Department of Energy (EGAO) ... SPEERA
Secretarial Performance Review [*DoD*] (DOMA) ... SPR
Secretarial Studies Certificate (AIE) ... SSC
Secretarial, Word Processing, and/or Medical Office Assistant Programs [*Association of Independent Colleges and Schools specialization code*] ... SE
Secretariat ... SEC
Secretariat ... SECR
Secretariat ... SECT
Secretariat a la Jeunesse, Conseil Executif, Quebec, Quebec [*Library symbol National Library of Canada*] (NLC) ... QQSAJ
Secretariat des Conferences Intergouvernementales Canadiennes ... SCIC
Secretariat Europeen des Fabricants d'Emballages Metalliques Legers [*European Secretariat of Manufacturers of Light Metal Packages*] (EA) ... SEFEL
Secretariat Europeen des Professions Liberales, Independantes et Sociales [*European Secretariat of the Liberal, Independant and Social Professions*] [*EC*] (ECED) ... SEPLIS
Secretariat for Catholic-Jewish Relations (EA) ... CJR
Secretariat for Electronic Test Equipment [*DoD*] ... SETE
Secretariat for Hispanic Affairs (National Conference of Catholic Bishops) (EA) ... SHA
Secretariat for the Nordic Energy Information Libraries (IID) ... SNEIL
Secretariat General de l'Aviation Civile et Commerciale [*France*] ... SGACC
Secretariat General for Civil Aviation [*French*] ... SGAC
Secretariat International de l'Enseignement Universitaire des Sciences de l'Education ... SIEUSE
Secretariat International des Artistes Catholiques ... SIAC
Secretariat International des Enseignants Secondaires Catholiques [*International Secretariat of Catholic Secondary School Teachers*] [*Acronym used in association name, SIESC Pax Romana Nijmegen, Netherlands*] (EAIO) ... SIESC
Secretariat International des Groupements Professionnels des Industries Chimiques des Pays de la CEE ... SIIC
Secretariat International des Ingenieurs, des Agronomes, et des Cadres Economiques Catholiques [*International Secretariat of Catholic Technologists, Agriculturists, and Economists*] [*Paris, France*] (EAIO) ... SIIAEC
Secretariat International des Juristes pour l'Amnistie en Uruguay [*France*] ... SIJAU
Secretariat Linguistiques Nordiques [*Nordic Language Secretariat - NLS*] [*Oslo, Norway*] (EAIO) ... SLN
Secretariat of Fisheries [*Mexico*] [*Marine science*] (OSRA) ... SEPESCA
Secretariat of Fisheries [*Mexico*] (USDC) ... SEPESCA
Secretariat of National Aboriginal and Islander Child Care [*Australia*] ... SNAICC
Secretariat of the Council for Scientific Policy [*British*] ... SCSP
Secretariat of the United Nations ... SEC(UN)
Secretariat Professionnel International de l'Enseignement [*International Federation of Free Teachers' Unions - IFFTU*] [*Amsterdam, Netherlands*] (EAIO) ... SPIE
Secretariat State-Defense Military Information Control Committee ... SSDMIC
Secretariats Professionnels Internationaux ... SPI
Secretaries and Managers' Association of Australia ... SMAA
Secretaries' Association of Australia ... SAA
Secretary ... S
Secretary (BARN) ... scty
Secretary (ODBW) ... Sec
Secretary (DD) ... sec
Secretary (EY) ... SEC
Secretary ... SECTY
Secretary ... SECY
Secretary ... SECY
Secretary for Logistics Planning [*Air Force*] ... SLP
Secretary for Scotland ... SS
Secretary General (WDAA) ... SEC GEN
Secretary Joint Chiefs of Staff (MCD) ... SJCS
Secretary, Joint Staff [*Military*] (CINC) ... SJS
Secretary of Defense ... SD
Secretary of Defense [*DoD*] (VNW) ... SecDef
Secretary of Defense ... SECDEF
Secretary of Defense [*DoD*] (VNW) ... SOD
Secretary of Defense Decision Memorandum ... SDDM
Secretary of Energy Advisory Board [*Department of Energy*] (EGAO) ... SEAB
Secretary of Labor (OICC) ... SOL
Secretary of Navy Decision Memorandum ... SNDM
Secretary of State ... S of S
Secretary of State ... SOS
Secretary of State ... SS
Secretary of State Department [*Canada*] ... SS
Secretary of State for Air [*British*] ... SSA
Secretary of State for Defence [*British*] (RDA) ... S of S
Secretary of State for War [*British*] ... SSW
Secretary of State Library at National Defence [*Bibliotheque du Secretariat d'Etat a la Defense Nationale*], Ottawa, Ontario [*Library symbol National Library of Canada*] (NLC) ... OONDT
Secretary of the Air Force ... SAF
Secretary of the Air Force, Administrative Assistant ... SAFAA
Secretary of the Air Force Correction Board ... SAFCB
Secretary of the Air Force, Financial Management ... SAFFM
Secretary of the Air Force for Research and Development (IAA) ... SAFRD
Secretary of the Air Force General Counsel ... SAFGC
Secretary of the Air Force (Installations and Logistics) ... SAFIL
Secretary of the Air Force, Manpower and Reserve Affairs ... SAFMR
Secretary of the Air Force, Missile and Satellite Systems (SAA) ... SAFMS
Secretary of the Air Force, Office of Information ... SAFOI
Secretary of the Air Force, Office of Information Services ... SAFIS
Secretary of the Air Force, Office of Legislative Liaison ... SAFLL
Secretary of the Air Force Order (AFM) ... SAFO
Secretary of the Air Force Personnel Council ... SAFPC
Secretary of the Air Force Program Review (MCD) ... SPR
Secretary of the Air Force, Requirements Review ... SAFRR
Secretary of the Air Force Space Liaison (MCD) ... SAFSL
Secretary of the Air Force, Special Assistant for Installations ... SAFIE
Secretary of the Air Force, Special Assistant for Intelligence ... SAFIN
Secretary of the Air Force, Special Projects ... SAFSP
Secretary of the Army ... SA
Secretary of the Army ... SECARMY
Secretary of the Army Decision Memorandum [*Army*] (RDA) ... SADM
Secretary of the Army, Office of the Assistant Secretary ... SAOAS
Secretary of the Army Research and Study [*Fellowship*] ... SARS
Secretary of the Army's Mobility, Opportunity, and Development Program (MCD) ... SAMOD
Secretary of the General Staff [*Army*] ... SGS
Secretary of the Interior (DLA) ... Sec Int
Secretary of the Navy (NOAA) ... SECNA
Secretary of the Navy ... SECNAV
Secretary of the Navy ... SN
Secretary of the Navy Instruction ... SECNAVINST
Secretary of Transportation (DOMA) ... SECTRANS
Secretary of Transportation (NATG) ... SOT

Secretary of War [*Obsolete*] .... SECWAR
Secretary of War [*Obsolete*] .... SW
Secretary/Treasurer [*or Secretary and Treasurer*] .... ST
[*The*] **Secretary, United States Delegation United Nations Military Staff Committee** .... USSECMILCOMUN
Secretary-General [*United Nations*] .... SG
Secretary-General (NATG) .... SYG
Secretary-General of the United Nations .... S-G(UN)
Secretary's Commission on Achieving Necessary Skills [*Department of Labor*] .... SCANS
Secretary's Commission on Nursing [*Department of Health and Human Services*] .... SCN
Secretary's Committee on Mental Retardation [*Department of Health and Human Services*] .... SCMR
Secretary's Committee on Research on Reorganization [*Navy*] .... SCOROR
Secretary's Memorandum [*Military*] .... SM
Secretary's Office [*Navy*] .... SO
Secretary's Office, Management Engineer [*Navy*] .... SOME
Secretary's Office, Navy Department .... SOND
Secretary's Office, Office of Research and Development [*Navy*] .... SONRD
Secretary's Office, Records Administration [*Navy*] .... SORA
Secretary's Office, Shore Establishments Division [*Incorporated into SECP, 1944*] [*Navy*] .... SOSED
Secretary's Office, Transportation Branch [*Navy*] .... SOTB
Secretary's Open Forum (EA) .... SOF
Secretary's Order .... SO
Secretary's Pesticide Advisory Committee [*HEW*] .... SPAC
Secretary's Records Correspondence Unit [*Department of Labor*] .... SRCU
Secretary-Treasurer (DNAB) .... SEC-TREAS
Secretary-Treasurer (DD) .... sec-treas
Secreted Alkaline Phosphatase [*Biochemistry*] .... SEAP
Secreted Protein Acidic and Rich in Cysteine [*Biochemistry*] .... SPARC
Secretin [*Endocrinology*] .... S
Secretin [*Biochemistry*] .... SEC
Secretin Receptor [*Medicine*] (DMAA) .... SCTR
Secretin-Stimulated Acid Output [*Clinical chemistry*] .... SAO
Secretion Rate [*Endocrinology*] .... SR
Secretory Carcinoma of Endometrium .... SCE
Secretory Coil [*Medicine*] (MEDA) .... SC
Secretory Component [*Supersedes SP, TP*] [*Immunology*] .... SC
Secretory Immunoglobin [*Immunology*] .... SIg
Secretory Immunoglobulin A [*Immunology*] .... S-IgA
Secretory Leukoprotease Inhibitor [*Biochemistry*] .... SLPI
Secretory Otitis Media [*Medicine*] (MAE) .... SOM
Secretory Piece [*Superseded by SC, Secretory Component*] [*Immunology*] .... SP
Secretory Protein [*Endocrinology*] .... SP
Secretory Rate Maximum [*Physiology*] .... SRM
Secretory Substance [*Botany*] .... S
Secteur Art et Architecture, Universite Laval, Quebec, Quebec [*Library symbol National Library of Canada*] (NLC) .... QQLAAA
Section .... S
Section (WDMC) .... s
Section (IDOE) .... sec
Section (AAGC) .... Sec
Section .... SEC
Section (ROG) .... SECN
Section (KSC) .... SECT
Section .... SECT
Section (VRA) .... sect
Section (MDG) .... SXN
Section 8(a) of the Small Business Act [*Pertaining to minority and other disadvantaged business*] (AAGC) 8A
Section Base [*Military*] .... SB
Section Base [*Navy*] (DNAB) .... SECBASE
Section Base [*Navy*] .... SECTBASE
Section Carry Look Ahead (MHDB) .... SCLA
Section Chief, Display Control Unit [*Army*] .... SCDCU
Section Code (NITA) .... SC
Section Control Station [*RADAR*] .... SCS
Section Cross Reference (MCD) .... SCR
Section d'Eclaireurs-Skieurs [*of Chasseurs Alpins, French Army*] .... SES
Section Definition (IAA) .... SD
Section Department Authority .... SDA
Section d'Oceanographie d'Universite de Quebec a Rimouski [*Canada*] (MSC) .... SOUQAR
Section for Metropolitan Hospitals (EA) .... SMH
Section for Rehabilitation Hospitals and Programs [*American Hospital Association*] (EA) .... SRHP
Section for Women in Public Administration (EA) .... SWPA
Section Francaise de l'Internationale Ouvriere [*French Section of the Workers International*] .... SFID
Section Francaise de l'Internationale Ouvriere [*French Socialist Party*] .... SFIO
Section Gunnery Trainer [*Army*] .... SGT
Section Heading (NITA) .... SH
Section Heading Code [*Online database field identifier*] .... SH
Section Leader [*Nuclear energy*] (NRCH) .... SL
Section List (MCD) .... SL
Section List Number (MCD) .... SLN
Section of Criminal Justice [*American Bar Association*] (EA) .... SCJ
Section of Independent Political Entity [*Board on Geographic Names*] .... PCLX
Section of International Law and Practice (EA) .... SILP
Section of Medical Information Science (IAA) .... SMIS
Section of Populated Place [*Board on Geographic Names*] .... PPLX
Section Office .... SECOFF
Section Officer [*British military*] (DMA) .... SO
Section on Gay and Lesbian Legal Issues [*Association of American Law Schools*] (EA) .... SGLLI
Section on Individual Rights and Responsibilities (EA) .... SIRR
Section on Women and Psychology [*Canadian Psychology Association*] .... SWAP
Section Patrol [*Navy*] .... SP
Section Properties [*Camutek*] [*Software package*] (NCC) .... SPROPS
Section Report .... SR
Section Technical Manual [*Jet Propulsion Laboratory, NASA*] .... STM
Sectional .... SECTL
Sectional Aeronautical Chart (NOAA) .... SAC
Sectional Aeronautical Chart .... SECAC
Sectional Center (EECA) .... SC
Sectional Center Facility [*Air Force*] (AFM) .... SCF
Sectional Center Facility [*First three digits of the ZIP code*] [*US Postal Service*] .... SCF
Sectional Chamber Association [*British*] (DBA) .... SCA
Sectional Classification Code (NITA) .... SCC
Sectional Linear Programming [*Computer science*] .... SLP
Sectionalized .... SECTLZD
Sectionalized Carrier and Multipurpose Vehicle [*Military*] .... SCAMP
Sectionalized Vertical Antenna .... SVA
Sectionalized Work Requirements Package (MCD) .... SWRP
Sections (ADA) .... SS
Sections Administratives Specialisees [*French Army*] .... SAS
Sector (IAA) .... S
Sector (MSA) .... SCTR
Sector .... SEC
Sector Aid Defense Commander (NATG) .... SADC
Sector Airlines [*Canada ICAO designator*] (FAAC) .... XTR
Sector Antiair Warfare Coordinator [*Center*] (NVT) .... SAAWC
Sector Command Headquarters (SAA) .... SCH
Sector Command Post [*Military*] .... SCP
Sector Design and Analysis Tool [*FAA*] (TAG) .... SDAT
Sector Direction Center Operating Instruction (SAA) .... SDCOI
Sector Frequency Only [*Military*] (CAAL) .... SFO
Sector List Drop Interval [*FAA*] (TAG) .... SLDI
Sector Management and Direct Support Logistics Center [*Navy*] (DNAB) .... SM & DSL
Sector Number (MUGU) .... SN
Sector Operations Center [*Air Force*] .... SOC
Sector Operations Control Center [*NORAD*] (FAAC) .... SOCC
Sector Scan Engagement [*Military*] (CAAL) .... SSE
Sector Scan Indicator .... SSI
Sector Scan Receive Only [*Military*] (LAIN) .... SSRO
Sector/Subsector .... S/SS
Sector Switching Center [*Telecommunications*] (TEL) .... SSC
Sector System Training Leader (SAA) .... SSTL
Sector TACAN [*Tactical Air Navigation*] **System** .... SETAC
Sector Working Party [*British*] (DCTA) .... SWP
Sectoraal Verband Landbouwwetenschappen [*Committee on International Education in Agricultural Sciences*] [*Netherlands*] (EAIO) .... SVLW
Sectoral Adjustment Loan [*World Bank*] .... SECAL
Sectored File Channel (NITA) .... SFC
Sectored File Controller .... SFC
Sectorial Association Transportation Equipment & Machinery Manufacturing (AC) .... SATEMM
Sectors per Track .... SPT
Secular .... SEC
Secular College .... SC
Secular Franciscan Order [*Formerly, TOSF*] [*Roman Catholic religious order*] .... SFO
Secular Institute of Pius X (EA) .... ISPX
Secular Institute of Schoenstatt Sisters of Mary (TOCD) .... ISSM
Secular Order of Discalced Carmelites [*Rome, Italy*] (EAIO) .... OCDS
Secular Organizations for Sobriety (EA) .... SOS
Secular Periodic Perturbation .... SPP
Secular Society of America [*Defunct*] .... SS of A
Secular Unemployment [*Business term*] (MHDW) .... SU
Secular Variation [*Geophysics*] .... SV
Secunda [*South Africa*] [*ICAO location identifier*] (ICLI) .... FASC
Secundum [*According To*] [*Latin*] .... SEC
Secundum Artem [*According to the Art*] [*Latin*] .... SA
Secundum Artem [*According to the Art*] [*Latin*] .... SEC ART
Secundum Artis Leges [*According to the Rules of the Art*] [*Latin*] (ADA) .... SAL
Secundum Legem [*According to Law*] [*Latin*] .... SEC LEG
Secundum Legem [*According to Law*] [*Latin*] .... SL
Secundum Naturam [*According to Nature*] [*Latin*] .... SEC NAT
Secundum Naturam [*According to Nature*] [*Latin*] .... SN
Secundum Regulam [*According to Rule*] [*Latin*] .... SEC REG
Secure (KSC) .... SEC
Secure Access Unit (HGAA) .... SAU
Secure Acoustic Data Relay (NVT) .... SADR
Secure Acoustic Data Relay Terminal (MCD) .... SADRT
Secure Airborne RADAR Bombing Equipment (IAA) .... SABRE
Secure Airborne RADAR Control .... SARC
Secure Airborne RADAR Equipment .... SABRE
Secure (Anchor Type) [*Navy symbol*] .... CQR
Secure Authentication System (IIA) .... SAS
Secure Automated Fabrication [*Line*] [*Nuclear energy*] .... SAF
Secure Automatic Communications Network .... SACNET
Secure Automatic Data Information Exchange [*System*] .... SADIE
Secure Base of Operation (WDAA) .... SBO
Secure Communications Equipment Program [*Air Force*] (CET) .... SCEP
Secure Communications Processor (NITA) .... SCOMP
Secure Communications System [*Military*] (CAAL) .... SCS

Secure Computing [*NASDAQ symbol*] (TTSB) ... SCUR
Secure Computing Corp. [*NASDAQ symbol*] (SAG) ... SCUR
Secure Computing Corp. [*Associated Press*] (SAG) ... SecComp
Secure Conferencing Project ... SCP
Secure Data Cartridge (BYTE) ... SDC
Secure Data Network System [*Computer science*] ... SDNS
Secure Digital Net Radio Interface Unit [*Army*] (RDA) ... SDNRIU
Secure Echo-Sounding Equipment [*SONAR*] [*Navy*] ... SESE
Secure Electronic Payments Protocol [*Telecommunications*] ... SEPP
Secure Electronic Transactions [*Computer science*] ... SET
Secure Electronic Transactions (PCM) ... SET
Secure Encryption of Tactical Analog Data ... SETAD
Secure Encryption Payment Protocol [*Computer science*] ... SEPP
Secure Exchange Technology ... SET
Secure Facility (MCD) ... SF
Secure Fast Packet Switching [*Telecommunications*] ... SFPS
Secure File Manager [*Telecommunications*] (OSI) ... SFM
Secure File System [*Telecommunications*] (OSI) ... SFS
Secure Hypertext Transport Protocol [*Computer science*] ... S-HTTP
Secure Identification Feature ... SIF
Secure Identification Operating Procedure ... SIOP
Secure Imagery Transmission System [*Military*] (CAAL) ... SITS
Secure Key-Issuing Authority [*Computer science*] ... SKIA
Secure Local-Area Network [*Computer science*] ... SELANE
Secure Mobile, Anti-Jam, Reliable Tactical Trainer [*Army*] ... SMART-T
Secure Operations (MCD) ... SO
Secure Prioritized ATM [*Asynchronous Transfer Mode*] **Network** [*Telecommunications*] ... Spanet
Secure Range Safety [*NASA*] (KSC) ... SRS
Secure Record and Playback System (MCD) ... SRPS
Secure Reserve Forces [*Military*] (MCD) ... SRF
Secure Resource Force Target List (MCD) ... SRFTL
Secure Sockets Layer [*Computer science*] (PCM) ... SSL
Secure Submarine Communications (KSC) ... SCSCO
Secure Submarine Communications ... SESCO
Secure Systems Corp. [*Manassas, VA*] [*Telecommunications Defunct*] (TSSD) ... SSC
Secure Task Group, Common (MCD) ... STGC
Secure Telephone Unit [*Computer science*] ... STU
Secure Terminal Unit-II Militarized ... STU-IIM
Secure Transaction Technology ... STT
Secure Transaction Technology [*Telecommunications*] ... STT
Secure Transfer Protocol [*Computer science*] (DOM) ... STP
Secure Transmission of Acoustic Data (NVT) ... SETAD
Secure Voice Access Console [*Army*] (AABC) ... SEVAC
Secure Voice Access Systems [*Army*] (AABC) ... SEVAS
Secure Voice and Graphic Conferencing (MCD) ... SVGC
Secure Voice Communications (AFM) ... SEVOCOM
Secure Voice Cord Board [*Telecommunications*] (TEL) ... SECORD
Secure Voice Equipment (NATG) ... SVE
Secure Voice Improvement Program [*DoD*] ... SVIP
Secure Voice Kit (DWSG) ... SVK
Secure Voice Switch ... SVS
Secure Voice System [*Telecommunications*] ... SVS
Secure Voice Terminal (MCD) ... SVT
Secure Wire Access Terminal (MCD) ... SWAT
Secured (ROG) ... SECD
Secured Returns Code [*IRS*] ... SRC
Securing ... SECRG
Securing Bands ... SB
Securities [*or Security*] (AAG) ... SEC
Securities and Exchange Board of India (ECON) ... SEBI
Securities and Exchange Commission ... SEC
Securities and Exchange Commission (DLA) ... Sec & Ex C
Securities and Exchange Commission ... SECO
Securities and Exchange Commission Compliance (Prentice-Hall, Inc.) [*A publication*] (DLA) ... SEC Compl (P-H)
Securities and Exchange Commission Decisions and Reports [*A publication*] (DLA) ... SEC
Securities and Exchange Commission Docket [*A publication*] (DLA) ... SEC Docket
Securities and Exchange Commission Judicial Decisions [*A publication*] (DLA) ... SEC Jud Dec
Securities and Exchange Commission News Digest [*A publication*] ... SEND
Securities and Exchange Commission Organization ... SECO
Securities and Exchange Commission, Washington, DC [*OCLC symbol*] (OCLC) ... SEC
Securities and Futures Authority [*Finance British*] (ECON) ... SFA
Securities and Futures Commission [*Hong Kong*] ... SFC
Securities and Investments Board [*British*] ... SIB
Securities and Investments Board and the Marketing of Investments Board Organisation Commission [*British*] ... SIB-MIBOC
[*The*] **Securities Association** [*British*] ... TSA
Securities Communications Network, Inc. [*Englewood, CO*] (TSSD) ... SCN
Securities Data Base System [*Information service or system*] (IID) ... SDB
Securities Exchange Act [*1934*] ... SEA
Securities Exchange of Thailand ... SET
Securities Hazards Expert [*In film title*] ... SHE
Securities Industry Association (EA) ... SIA
Securities Industry Automation Corp. [*NYSE/ASE*] [*New York, NY*] ... SIAC
Securities Industry Committee on Arbitration (DFIT) ... SICA
Securities Industry Communication [*Western Union Corp.*] [*Information service or system*] ... SICOM
Securities Investor Protection Act [*1970*] ... SIPA
Securities Investor Protection Corp. ... SIP
Securities Investor Protection Corp. [*Government insurance agency for brokerage accounts*] [*Pronounced "sipic"*] ... SIPC
Securities Lending Service [*Australian Stock Exchange*] ... SLS
Securities Order Matching [*Computer science*] ... SOM
Securities Regulation Guide [*Prentice-Hall, Inc.*] [*A publication*] (DLA) ... Sec Reg Guide
Securities Research Co. ... SRC
Securities Shipped as Instructed ... SHP
Securities Transaction [*Banking*] ... SE
Securities Transfer Association (EA) ... STA
Securities-Investment Trust Enterprise ... SITE
Security (IAA) ... S
Security ... SCRTY
Security (AFM) ... SCTY
Security ... SEC
Security ... SECY
Security ... SY
Security Access Control [*Computer science*] ... SAC
Security, Accuracy, Propriety, and Policy ... SAPP
Security Administrator Tool for Analyzing Networks ... SATAN
Security Agency Study [*Nuclear energy*] (NRCH) ... SAS
Security Alarm Technician Program [*Association of Independent Colleges and Schools specialization code*] ... SA
Security Alert Team [*Military*] (AFM) ... SAT
Security Analysis Tool for Auditing Networks [*Computer science*] (CDE) ... SATAN
Security and Facilities [*DoD*] ... S & F
Security and Freedom through Encryption [*Proposed legislative bill*] ... SAFE
Security and Intelligence Foundation [*Later, CIS*] (EA) ... SIF
Security and Intelligence Service [*Army*] ... SID
Security and Operational Inspection [*Army*] ... SOI
Security and Safety Equipment (IMH) ... SSE
Security and Vulnerability Analysis (MCD) ... SVA
Security Appeals Tribunal [*Australia*] ... SAT
Security, Aptitude, Fitness Evaluation [*Test*] ... SAFE
Security Archives Holdings [*Data storage company*] [*British*] ... SAH
Security Assistance (MCD) ... SA
Security Assistance Accounting Center [*Military*] (AFIT) ... SAAC
Security Assistance and Sales [*DoD*] ... SAS
Security Assistance - General Operational Requirement [*Military*] (AFIT) ... SA-GOR
Security Assistance Management Information System (MCD) ... SAMIS
Security Assistance Management Manual [*A publication*] (AAGC) ... SAMM
Security Assistance Management Squadron ... SAMS
Security Assistance Manpower Accounting System (MCD) ... SAMAS
Security Assistance Master Planning and Phasing ... SAMPAP
Security Assistance Master Planning and Phasing (MCD) ... SAMPSP
Security Assistance Office ... SAO
Security Assistance Organizations (DOMA) ... SAO
Security Assistance Policy Coordinating Office [*Military*] ... SAPCO
Security Assistance Program (MCD) ... SAP
Security Assistance Program Review Commission ... SAPRC
Security Assistance Steering Group [*Military*] ... SASG
Security Assistance Team [*Military*] (AABC) ... SAT
Security Assistance Training Management Office [*Army*] ... SATMO
Security Assistance Training Program [*Military*] ... SATP
Security Audit and Field Evaluation (IAA) ... SAFE
Security Bancorp [*Associated Press*] (SAG) ... SecBcp
Security Bancorp [*Formerly, Security Federal Savings Bank*] [*NASDAQ symbol*] (NQ) ... SFBM
Security Bank Corp. [*NASDAQ symbol*] (SAG) ... SBCM
Security Bank Corp. [*Associated Press*] (SAG) ... SecuBk
Security Bank Holding Co. [*NASDAQ symbol*] (SAG) ... SBHC
Security Bank Holding Co. [*Associated Press*] (SAG) ... SecBHld
Security Call [*Economics*] ... SC
Security Cap Ind Tr 7% Cv Pfd [*NYSE symbol*] (TTSB) ... SCNPrB
Security Cap Ind Tr 9.40% Pfd [*NYSE symbol*] (TTSB) ... SCNPrA
Security Cap Pac Cv'A'Pfd [*NYSE symbol*] (TTSB) ... PTRPrA
Security Cap Pac Tr Sr'B'Pfd [*NYSE symbol*] (TTSB) ... PTRPrB
Security Cap Pacific Tr [*NYSE symbol*] (TTSB) ... PTR
Security Capital [*NASDAQ symbol*] (TTSB) ... SECP
Security Capital Atlantic, Inc. [*NYSE symbol*] (SAG) ... SCA
Security Capital Atlantic, Inc. [*Associated Press*] (SAG) ... SecCapA
Security Capital Corp. [*Associated Press*] (SAG) ... SecCap
Security Capital Corp. [*NASDAQ symbol*] (SAG) ... SECP
Security Capital Ind Tr [*NYSE symbol*] (TTSB) ... SCN
Security Capital Industrial Trust [*Associated Press*] (SAG) ... ScCap
Security Capital Industrial Trust Co. [*NYSE symbol*] (SAG) ... SCN
Security Capital Industrial Trust Co. [*Associated Press*] (SAG) ... SecCapTr
Security Capital Pacific Trust [*NYSE symbol*] (SAG) ... PTR
Security Capital Pacific Trust [*Associated Press*] (SAG) ... ScCPT
Security Capital Pacific Trust [*Associated Press*] (SAG) ... SecCaPT
Security Change Request [*Military*] (GFGA) ... SCR
Security Classification Code (MCD) ... SSC
Security Classification Control Officer [*Military*] ... SCCO
Security Classification Guide (AFM) ... SCG
Security Classification Procedure [*Military*] ... SCP
Security Clearance Case Files [*Military*] (AABC) ... SCCF
Security, CO [*FM radio station call letters*] ... KHII
Security, CO [*FM radio station call letters*] (RBYB) ... KSKX-FM
Security Coding Device (NATG) ... SCD
Security Committee ... SECOM
Security Commodity Code (AAG) ... SCC
Security Connecticut Corp. [*Associated Press*] (SAG) ... SecurCT
Security Connecticut Corp. [*NYSE symbol*] (SAG) ... SRC

Security Consultants International .... SECOIN
Security Container Institute [*Defunct*] (EA) .... SCI
Security Container System [*Army*] (AABC) .... SCS
Security Control Center [*NASA*] (KSC) .... SCC
Security Control of Air Traffic [*FAA*] .... SCAT
Security Control of Air Traffic and Air Navigation Aids [*FAA*] .... SCATANA
Security Control of Air Traffic and Electromagnetic Radiations [*During an air defense emergency*] [*FAA*] .... SCATER
Security Control Point [*Military*] (MUGU) .... SCPT
Security Control System (IAA) .... SCS
Security Coordination Committee (NATG) .... SCC
Security Council (NADA) .... SC
Security Council of the United Nations .... SC
Security Council of the United Nations .... SC(UN)
Security Devices Laboratory (SAA) .... SDL
Security Disconnect [*Computer science*] (ECII) .... SD
Security Dynamics Technologies [*NASDAQ symbol*] (TTSB) .... SDTI
Security Dynamics Technologies, Inc. [*NASDAQ symbol*] (SAG) .... SDTI
Security Dynamics Technologies, Inc. [*Associated Press*] (SAG) .... SecDyn
Security Environmental Systems, Inc. [*Vancouver Stock Exchange symbol*] .... SEM
Security Equipment Building .... SEB
Security Equipment Industry Association (EA) .... SEIA
Security Equipment Integration Working Group .... SEIWG
Security Escort Team [*Military*] .... SET
Security Executive, Control at Ports [*British World War II*] .... SE(P)
Security Filter Processor .... SFP
Security First Corp. [*Associated Press*] (SAG) .... SecurFst
Security First Corp. [*NASDAQ symbol*] (NQ) .... SFSL
Security First Network Bank [*Associated Press*] (SAG) .... SecFstNt
Security First Network Bank [*NASDAQ symbol*] (SAG) .... SFNB
Security First Network Bank [*NASDAQ symbol*] (TTSB) .... SFNB
Security Forces [*Japanese army*] .... SF
Security Forecast [*Control Risks Information Services - CRIS*] [*British Information service or system*] (IID) .... SF
Security Group [*Military*] .... SCTYG
Security Group [*Military*] (DNAB) .... SG
Security Group Headquarters .... SECGRUHQ
Security Guard (SAA) .... SG
Security Guard Window (AAG) .... SGW
Security Home Mortgage Investment Corp. [*Toronto Stock Exchange symbol*] .... SHM
Security Identification Zone .... SIZ
Security Identity .... SI
Security Information Network .... SIN
Security Inspection [*Military*] (NVT) .... SECINSP
Security Institute of New South Wales [*Australia*] .... SINSW
Security Intelligence Centre [*British World War II*] .... SIC
Security Intelligence Corps .... SIC
Security Intelligence Liaison Office [*Central Mediterranean Forces*] [*Navy*] .... SILO
Security Intelligence, Middle East [*Navy*] .... SIME
Security List (WDAA) .... SL
Security Lock Association [*British*] (DBA) .... SLA
Security Log [*Telecommunications*] (TEL) .... SCLOG
Security Management System [*Computer science*] .... SMS
Security Manual (AAG) .... SM
Security Market Line .... SML
Security Military Space Program (MUGU) .... SMSP
Security Monitor (AAG) .... SM
Security National Financial Corp. [*Associated Press*] (SAG) .... SecNtl
Security National Financial Corp. [*NASDAQ symbol*] (SAG) .... SNFC
Security Natl Finl 'A' [*NASDAQ symbol*] (TTSB) .... SNFCA
Security of the First World [*Rap music group*] S1W
Security Office .... SO
Security Pacific [*Bank*] (ECON) .... SecPac
Security Pacific Asian Bank .... SPAB
Security Pacific Bank [*Hong Kong*] .... SecPac
Security Pacific National Bank (NITA) .... SPNB
Security Pacific National Bank, Los Angeles, CA [*Library symbol Library of Congress*] (LCLS) .... CLSF
Security Police [*Air Force*] (AFM) .... SP
Security Police Automated System [*Air Force*] (GFGA) .... SPAS
Security Police Flight [*Air Force*] .... SPF
Security Police Group [*Air Force*] .... SPG
Security Police Squadron [*Air Force*] .... SCTYPOLICESq
Security Police Squadron [*Air Force*] .... SPS
Security Procedure (NRCH) .... SP
Security Program Manager [*Military*] (GFGA) .... SPM
Security Public Library, Security, CO [*Library symbol Library of Congress*] (LCLS) .... CoSe
Security Publication [*Navy*] .... SP
Security Requirements Check List (MCD) .... SRCL
Security Response Team [*Military*] .... SRT
Security Rules and Regulations .... SRR
Security Screening Board [*Army*] .... SSB
Security Service .... SS
Security Service Guide (SAA) .... SSG
Security Service School [*Air Force*] .... SCTYSERSCH
Security Services [*Vancouver Stock Exchange symbol*] .... SSR
Security Squadron [*Air Force*] .... SCTYSq
Security Support Activity .... SSA
Security Support Detachment (MCD) .... SSD
Security Support Squadron .... SSPTS
Security Supporting Assistance [*US government program for promoting economic and political stability in areas of strategic interest*] .... SSA
Security Survey Report [*Nuclear energy*] .... SSR
Security System Organization .... SSO
Security Systems, Inc. [*In TV series "Max Headroom"*] .... SS
Security Systems, Inc. [*In TV series "Max Headroom"*] .... SSI
Security Systems Inspectorate [*Established in 1987*] [*British*] .... SSI
Security Termination Statement [*Military*] (AFM) .... STS
Security Test and Evaluation [*Military*] (GFGA) .... ST & E
Security Threat Intelligence Cell (LAIN) .... STIC
Security Time Control .... STC
Security Traders Association (EA) .... STA
Security Traders Association of New York .... STANY
Security Traders Automated Quotation [*System*] .... STAQ
Security Trading of Office Property .... STOP
Security Training Center .... STC
Security Vehicle Patrol [*Air Force*] (AFM) .... SVP
Security Violation (AAG) .... SV
Security Watch .... SW
Security Window Screen and Guard .... SWSG
Security-Insecurity Inventory [*Psychology*] .... SII
Secus [*Otherwise*] [*Latin*] (ILCA) .... Sec
SED Systems Ltd., Aerospace Products Division, Saskatoon, SK, Canada [*Library symbol Library of Congress*] (LCLS) .... CaSSEDA
Seda Speciality Packaging [*Commercial firm Associated Press*] (SAG) .... SedaSpc
Seda Speciality Packaging [*NASDAQ symbol*] (SAG) .... SSPC
Sedalia [*Missouri*] [*Airport symbol Obsolete*] (OAG) .... DMO
Sedalia, MO [*AM radio station call letters*] .... KDRO
Sedalia, MO [*Television station call letters*] .... KMOS
Sedalia, MO [*FM radio station call letters*] .... KSDL
Sedalia, MO [*AM radio station call letters*] .... KSIS
Sedalia Public Library, Sedalia, MO [*Library symbol Library of Congress*] (LCLS) .... MoSe
Sedalia Public Library, Sedalia, MO [*Library symbol*] [*Library of Congress*] (LCLS) .... MoSed
Sedalia-Marshall-Booville Stage Line, Inc. [*ICAO designator*] (FAAC) .... STG
Sedan .... SD
Sedan (AAG) .... SED
Sedan/Douzy [*France ICAO location identifier*] (ICLI) .... LFSJ
Sedative [*Medicine*] (ROG) .... SED
Sedative Urinary Antibiotic (DAVI) .... SUA
Seddin [*German Democratic Republic*] [*Later, NGK*] [*Geomagnetic observatory code*] .... SED
Sedentary [*Biology*] .... S
Seder Eliyahu Rabbah (BJA) .... SER
Seder of Triennial Cycle (BJA) .... S
Seder 'Olam (BJA) .... SO
Seder 'Olam Rabbah (BJA) .... SOR
Seder 'Olam Zuta (BJA) .... SOZ
Sedes [*Greece*] [*ICAO location identifier*] (ICLI) .... LGSD
Sedes [*A Stool*] [*Medicine*] .... Sed
Sedgewick Public Library, Alberta [*Library symbol National Library of Canada*] (NLC) .... ASE
Sedgwick and Wait on the Trial of Title to Land [*A publication*] (DLA) .... Sedg & W Tit
Sedgwick and Wait on the Trial of Title to Land [*A publication*] (DLA) .... Sedg & W Tr Title Land
Sedgwick on Statutory and Constitutional Law [*A publication*] (DLA) .... Sedg St & Const Law
Sedgwick on Statutory and Constitutional Law [*A publication*] (DLA) .... Sedg Stat Law
Sedgwick on the Measure of Damage [*A publication*] (DLA) .... Sedg Dam
Sedgwick Public Library, Sedgwick, CO [*Library symbol Library of Congress*] (LCLS) .... CoSed
Sedgwick's Leading Cases on Damages [*A publication*] (DLA) .... Sedg L Cas
Sedgwick's Leading Cases on Real Property [*A publication*] (DLA) .... Sedg L Cas
Sediment [*or Sedimentation*] .... SED
Sediment Community Oxygen Consumption [*Marine biology*] .... SCOC
Sediment Oxygen Demand [*of water bodies*] .... SOD
Sedimentary Chlorophyll Degradation Product [*Paleontology*] .... SCDP
Sedimentary Organic Carbon [*Marine science*] .... SOC
Sedimentary Phosphate Method .... SPM
Sedimentation Coefficient [*Physical chemistry*] .... s
Sedimentation Field Flow Fractionation [*For separation of colloids*] .... SFFF
Sedimentation Rate [*Hematology*] (DAVI) .... sed rt
Sedimentation Rate .... SR
Sedimentation Rate Test .... SRT
Sedimentation Time .... ST
Sedimented Red Cell [*Hematology*] (MAE) .... SRC
Sedition [*FBI standardized term*] .... SED
Seditious Libeler .... SL
Sedna Information Management System [*Sedna Corp.*] [*Information service or system*] (IID) .... SIMS
Sedona [*Arizona*] [*Airport symbol*] (OAG) .... SDX
Sedona Air Center, Inc. [*ICAO designator*] (FAAC) .... SED
Sedona, AZ [*AM radio station call letters*] .... KAZM
Sedona, AZ [*FM radio station call letters*] .... KQST
Sedona, AZ [*FM radio station call letters*] .... KSED
Sedona, AZ [*Location identifier FAA*] (FAAL) .... SEZ
Sedona Industries Ltd. [*Toronto Stock Exchange symbol*] .... SPD
Sedona Public Library, Sedona, AZ [*Library symbol Library of Congress*] (LCLS) .... AzSe
See .... S
See a Solicitor [*British*] .... SS
See Also [*Indexing code*] .... SA
See Before Setting [*Typography*] (DGA) .... SBS
See Comments [*Routing slip*] .... SC

See Copy ... SC
See Facts [*BBC "dial-a-page" news broadcast*] [*British*] ... CEEFAX
See Footnote (ROG) ... SFN
See, I Told You So [*Rush Limbaugh's mantra and book title*] (ECON) ... SITYS
See Me Please ... SMP
See Note (ROG) ... SN
See Order Blank [*Laboratory science*] (DAVI) ... SOB
See Our Message ... SOM
See Our Message [*Aviation*] (FAAC) ... SOMSG
See Safe [*Bookselling*] (DGA) ... S/S
See Separate Bacteriology Report (DAVI) ... SSBR
See You Home [*Teen slang*] ... SYH
See You Later [*Telegrapher's slang*] ... CUL
See You Later [*Computer science*] (DOM) ... CUL8R
See Your Service (FAAC) ... SYS
SEEA-Southeast European Airlines [*Greece*] [*ICAO designator*] (FAAC) ... GRE
Seeburg Industries, Inc. [*NASDAQ symbol*] ... SEEB
Seed (WGA) ... SD
Seed Certification Committee [*Queensland, Australia*] ... SCC
Seed Coat [*Botany*] ... SC
Seed Industry Association of Australia ... SIAA
Seed Industry Development Program [*UN Food and Agriculture Organization*] ... SIDP
Seed Mass [*Botany*] ... SM
Seed, Oil, Cake, and General Produce Association [*British*] (BI) ... SOCGPA
Seed Pea Group [*Defunct*] (EA) ... SPG
Seed Production [*Agriculture*] ... SP
Seed Savers Exchange (EA) ... SSE
Seedling (WGA) ... SDL
Seeing Essential English [*Sign language system for the hearing impaired*] ... SEE
Seeing Eye [*An association*] (EA) ... SE
Seeing Problems [*Research test*] [*Psychology*] ... SP
Seeing through Arithmetic Tests (AEBS) ... STAT
Seeing-Eye Elephant Network [*A computer-assisted instruction program*] (EDAC) ... SEEN
Seek and Destroy RADAR-Assisted Mission (MCD) ... SADRAM
Seek Command (IAA) ... SK
Seek Out New Suppliers ... SONS
Seek Time per Track ... STT
Seeker ... SKR
Seeker Azimuth Orientation [*Air Force*] ... SAZO
Seeker Evaluation Test System [*Military*] ... SETS
Seeker Head Position ... SHP
Seeker Head Position Display [*Military*] (CAAL) ... SHPD
Seeker Test Unit (MCD) ... STU
Seeker-Killer-Utility Lasers (DOMA) ... SKUL
Seeking, Asking, and Written [*Questionnaire*] (PDAA) ... SAW
Seeking, Locating, Annihilating, Monitoring [*Army project, Vietnam*] ... SLAM
Seeking of Noetic Goals Test [*Personality development test*] [*Psychology*] ... SONG
Seek-Storm RADAR ... SSR
Seelenlaenge [*Barrel length*] [*German military - World War II*] ... S
Seeley's Bay Branch, Rideau Lakes Union Library, Ontario [*Library symbol National Library of Canada*] (BIB) ... OSBR
Seeley's Illustrated Pocket Library [*A publication*] ... SIPL
Seelyville, IN [*FM radio station call letters*] ... WTHC
Seeman Composite Resin Infusion Molding Process ... SCRIMP
Seemingly Unrelated Regression [*Statistics*] ... SUR
SEEQ Technology [*NASDAQ symbol*] (TTSB) ... SEEQ
SEEQ Technology, Inc. [*NASDAQ symbol*] (NQ) ... SEEQ
Seer (WGA) ... SR
Seer Tech [*NASDAQ symbol*] (TTSB) ... SEER
Seer Technologies, Inc. [*NASDAQ symbol*] (SAG) ... SEER
Seer Technologies, Inc. [*Associated Press*] (SAG) ... SeerTc
Sefer ha-Shanah (BJA) ... SH
Sefer Torah. Post-Talmudic Tractate (BJA) ... SefT
Sefer Torah. Tefillin. Mezuzah ... STaM
Sefer Yezirah (BJA) ... SY
Seffner, FL [*AM radio station call letters*] ... WQYK
Sefid-Roud [*Iran*] [*Seismograph station code, US Geological Survey*] (SEIS) ... SRI
Sefire Inscriptions (BJA) ... Sf
Sefwi-Bekwai [*Ghana*] [*ICAO location identifier*] (ICLI) ... DGSB
Segamat [*Malaysia*] [*ICAO location identifier*] (ICLI) ... WMAZ
Sege [*Solomon Islands*] [*Airport symbol*] (OAG) ... EGM
Segment (AAG) ... SEG
Segment ... SEGM
Segment (IAA) ... SG
Segment Address Field ... SAF
Segment Address Register [*Telecommunications*] ... SAR
Segment Arrival Storage Area (KSC) ... SAS
Segment Base Register (BUR) ... SBR
Segment Control (SSD) ... SC
Segment Control BIT [*Binary Digit*] ... SCB
Segment Control Module (IAA) ... SCM
Segment Descriptor Block ... SDB
Segment Descriptor Word ... SDW
Segment End of Pulse ... SEOP
Segment End Pulse ... SEP
Segment Entry Save Register [*Computer science*] (MHDI) ... SESR
Segment Frequency Algorithm ... SFA
Segment Identification Register ... SIR
Segment Limits End (NITA) ... SLE
Segment Limits Origin ... SLO
Segment Long-Spacing Collagen Fiber ... SLS
Segment Map Table Entry (IAA) ... SMTE
Segment Mark (IAA) ... SM
Segment Ready Storage ... SRS
Segment Root (IAA) ... SR
Segment Search Argument [*Computer science*] (BUR) ... SSA
Segment Stack Number ... SSN
Segment Table [*Computer science*] (IBMDP) ... SGT
Segment Table [*Computer science*] (OA) ... ST
Segment Table Address [*Computer science*] (IAA) ... STA
Segment Table Address Register [*Computer science*] (IAA) ... STAR
Segment Table Base [*Computer science*] (IAA) ... STB
Segment Table Entry [*Computer science*] (MDG) ... STE
Segment Table Origin ... STO
Segment Table Origin Register [*Computer science*] (BUR) ... STOR
Segment Table Origin Register (ECII) ... STOR
Segment Table Register ... STR
Segment Tag BITS [*Binary Digits*] ... STB
Segmental Limb Systolic Pressure [*Medicine*] (DMAA) ... SLP
Segmental Necrotizing Glomerulonephritis [*Medicine*] ... SNGN
Segmental Sequential Irradiation (AAMN) ... SSI
Segmental Wall Motion [*Medicine*] (DMAA) ... SWM
Segmentation System (IAA) ... SEGSYS
Segmentation Violation [*Computer science*] (NHD) ... SEGV
Segmented Aperture-Synthetic Aperture RADAR ... SASAR
Segmented Continuous Flow Analysis [*Analytical chemistry*] ... SCFA
Segmented Expanding Die (MCD) ... SED
Segmented Filamentous Bacteria ... SFB
Segmented Flow Analysis ... SFA
Segmented Gamma Scanner [*Nuclear energy*] (NRCH) ... SGS
Segmented Level Programming [*Computer science*] (IEEE) ... SLP
Segmented Maintenance Cask [*Nuclear energy*] (NRCH) ... SMC
Segmented Mirror Telescope [*Astronomy*] ... SMT
Segmented Neutrophils [*Also, polymorphonuclear leukocytes and segmented white cells*] [*Immunochemistry*] (DAVI) ... segs
Segmented Virtual Display File ... SVDF
Segner's Fortified Edd Meat [*Growth medium for phage*] ... SFEM
Segno [*Sign*] [*Music*] ... SEG
Segou [*Mali*] [*ICAO location identifier*] (ICLI) ... GASG
Segou [*Mali*] [*Airport symbol*] (AD) ... SZU
Segregated Ballast Tank [*Shipping construction*] ... SBT
Segregated Continuous Stirred Tank Reactor [*Chemical engineering*] ... SCSTR
Segregation Distorter [*Genetics*] ... SD
Segregation Distortion (DOG) ... SD
Segregator, Facer, Canceller Machine ... SEFACAN
Segue [*Follows*] [*Music*] ... SEG
Segue Software [*NASDAQ symbol*] (TTSB) ... SEGU
Segue Software, Inc. [*NASDAQ symbol*] (SAG) ... SEGU
Segue Software, Inc. [*Associated Press*] (SAG) ... SegueS
Seguela [*Ivory Coast*] [*ICAO location identifier*] (ICLI) ... DISG
Seguela [*Ivory Coast*] [*Airport symbol*] (OAG) ... SEO
Seguenega [*Burkina Faso*] [*ICAO location identifier*] (ICLI) ... DHCS
Seguente [*And Following*] [*Italian*] (ILCA) ... S
Seguin, TX [*FM radio station call letters*] ... KSMG
Seguin, TX [*AM radio station call letters*] ... KWED
Seguin, TX [*Location identifier FAA*] (FAAL) ... SEQ
Segundo Corral/Segundo Corral Alto [*Chile*] [*ICAO location identifier*] (ICLI) ... SCSR
Seguro Resources [*Vancouver Stock Exchange symbol*] ... SSP
Sehlabathebe [*Lesotho*] [*ICAO location identifier*] (ICLI) ... FXSE
Sehonghong [*Lesotho*] [*ICAO location identifier*] (ICLI) ... FXSH
Sehonghong [*Lesotho*] [*Airport symbol*] (OAG) ... SHK
Sehore [*India*] [*Seismograph station code, US Geological Survey*] (SEIS) ... SEH
Sehr Dringend [*Very urgent, used preceding German coded messages*] ... SD
Sehulea [*Papua New Guinea*] [*Airport symbol*] (OAG) ... SXH
SEI Corp. [*NASDAQ symbol*] (NQ) ... SEIC
SEI Corp. [*Associated Press*] (SAG) ... SEICorp
SEI Investments Co. [*Associated Press*] (SAG) ... SEI Inv
SEI Investments Co. [*NASDAQ symbol*] (SAG) ... SEIC
Seibels Bruce Group [*NASDAQ symbol*] (TTSB) ... SBIGE
[*The*] **Seibels Bruce Group, Inc.** [*NASDAQ symbol*] (NQ) ... SBIG
Seibels [*Bruce*] **Group, Inc.** [*Associated Press*] (SAG) ... Seibel
Seiler ALGOL Digitally Simulated Analog Computer ... SADSAC
Seiler Laboratory ALGOL Simulated Hybrid [*Computer science*] ... SLASH
Seiler Pollution Ctl Sys [*NASDAQ symbol*] (TTSB) ... SEPC
Seiler Research Laboratory [*Air Force*] (MCD) ... SRL
Seine Island [*Island off the coast of France*] (ROG) ... SI
Seiners Association [*Later, PSVOA*] ... SA
Seingalt Society (EA) ... SS
Seis De Agosto [*Bolivia*] [*ICAO location identifier*] (ICLI) ... SLWD
Seismic/Acoustic Feature Extraction (MCD) ... S/AFE
Seismic Air Gun ... SAG
Seismic Array Analysis Center [*IBM Corp.*] ... SAAC
Seismic Array Data Analyzer (IEEE) ... SADA
Seismic Computerized Alert Network [*For warning of an earthquake*] ... SCAN
Seismic Data Analysis ... SDA
Seismic Data Analysis Center ... SDAC
Seismic Data Laboratory [*Teledyne Geotech*] ... SDL
Seismic Detection and Ranging ... SDR
Seismic Detector (MCD) ... SD
Seismic Electric Signal ... SES
Seismic Feature Extraction (MCD) ... SFE
Seismic Group Recorder [*Geophysics*] ... SGR
Seismic Intrusion Detector [*or Device*] [*Army*] ... SID
Seismic Personnel Intrusion Detector (PDAA) ... SPID
Seismic Qualification Review Team [*Nuclear energy*] (NRCH) ... SQRT
Seismic Recording System ... SRS

Seismic Reflection Profile [*Marine science*] (MSC) .... SRP
Seismic Safety Margins Research Program [*Nuclear Regulatory Commission*] .... SSMRP
Seismic Sea-Wave Warning System .... SSWWS
Seismic Section Profiler .... SSP
Seismic Spectral Amplitude Measurement .... SSAM
Seismic Survival Indicator [*Earthquake analysis program*] [*Computer science*] .... SSI
Seismic Tunnel Detector [*DoD*] (VNW) .... STD
Seismic Underwater Explorer .... SUE
Seismic Velocity Discontinuity [*Geology*] .... SVD
Seismocardiogram .... SMG
Seismocardiography [*Medicine*] .... SCG
Seismograph Service Ltd. [*British*] .... SSL
Seismographic .... SEISMOG
Seismologic .... SEISMOL
Seismological Data Center [*Environmental Science Services Administration*] .... SDC
Seismological Research Observatory [*Australia*] .... SRO
Seismological Society of America (EA) .... SSA
Seite [*Page*] [*German*] .... S
Seitel, Inc. [*NYSE symbol*] (SPSG) .... SEI
Seitel, Inc. [*Associated Press*] (SAG) .... Seitel
Seize Detector .... SD
Seize Detector Control .... SDC
Seize Signal Detector .... SSD
Seized Boat [*Coast Guard symbol*] (DNAB) .... WYTM
Seizure [*Telecommunications*] (TEL) .... SZ
Seizure [*Medicine*] .... sz
Seizure Resistant [*Neurology*] (DAVI) .... SR
Seizure Sensitive [*Neurology*] (DAVI) .... SS
Seizure-Brain Damage [*Medicine*] (DMAA) .... S-BD
Seizures per Circuit per Hour [*Telecommunications*] (TEL) .... SCH
Sek Kong [*Hong Kong*] [*ICAO location identifier*] (ICLI) .... VHSK
Sekake [*Lesotho*] [*ICAO location identifier*] (ICLI) .... FXSK
Sekakes [*Lesotho*] [*Airport symbol*] (OAG) .... SKQ
Sekber Golongan Karya [*Joint Secretariat of Functional Groups*] [*Indonesia*] [*Political party*] (PPW) .... GOLKAR
Sekcja Pracy Spolecznej [*A publication*] (BJA) .... SPS
Sekira Hodshit [*Tel Aviv*] (BJA) .... SH
Sekretno-Politicheskoye Upravleniye [*Secret Political Directorate*] [*Former USSR*] (LAIN) .... SPU
Sektion fuer Systementwicklung [*GID*] [*Information retrieval*] .... SFS
SEL [*Space Environmental Laboratory*] **Data Acquisition and Display System** (USDC) .... SELDADS
SEL [*Space Environmental Laboratory*] **Research and Analysis System** (USDC) .... SELRAS
Selah, WA [*AM radio station call letters*] (RBYB) .... KCHT-AM
Selah, WA [*AM radio station call letters*] .... KUTI
Selah, WA [*AM radio station call letters*] .... KYXE
Selanpaa [*Finland ICAO location identifier*] (ICLI) .... EFSE
Selaru [*Indonesia*] [*ICAO location identifier*] (ICLI) .... WAPS
Selas Corp. of Amer [*AMEX symbol*] (TTSB) .... SLS
Selas Corp. of America [*Associated Press*] (SAG) .... Selas
Selas Corp. of America [*AMEX symbol*] (SPSG) .... SLS
Selawik [*Alaska*] [*Airport symbol*] (OAG) .... WLK
Selawik, AK [*Location identifier FAA*] (FAAL) .... WLK
Selbyville, DE [*FM radio station call letters*] .... WSBL
Selco Mining Corp., Red Lake, Ontario [*Library symbol National Library of Canada*] (NLC) .... ORLS
Selco Mining Corp., Toronto, ON, Canada [*Library symbol*] [*Library of Congress*] (LCLS) .... CaOTSML
Selco Mining Corp., Toronto, Ontario [*Library symbol National Library of Canada*] (NLC) .... OTSML
Selden Society (DLA) .... Seld Soc
Selden Society (EA) .... SS
Selden Society Yearbook [*United States*] [*A publication*] (DLA) .... Seld Soc Yrbk
Selden's Dissertatio ad Fletam [*A publication*] (ILCA) .... Seld Fl
Selden's Jani Anglorum [*A publication*] (ILCA) .... Seld J
Selden's Judicature in Parliaments [*1681*] [*A publication*] (DLA) .... Seld JP
Selden's Mare Clausum [*A publication*] (ILCA) .... Seld Mar Cl
Selden's Mare Clausum [*A publication*] (DLA) .... Seld Mare Claus
Selden's New York Court of Appeals Notes [*A publication*] (DLA) .... Seld Notes
Selden's New York Court of Appeals Notes of Cases [*1st ed.*] [*1853*] [*A publication*] (DLA) .... Selden Notes
Selden's New York Court of Appeals Reports [*A publication*] (DLA) .... Seld R
Selden's New York Court of Appeals Reports [*A publication*] (DLA) .... Selden
Selden's New York Reports [*5-10 New York*] [*A publication*] (DLA) .... Seld
Selden's Office of Lord Chancellor [*1671*] [*A publication*] (DLA) .... Sel Off Ch
Selden's Office of Lord Chancellor [*1671*] [*A publication*] (DLA) .... Seld Off Ch
Selden's Titles of Honor [*A publication*] (DLA) .... Seld Tit Hon
Seldom Reaches Destination .... SRD
Seldovia [*Alaska*] [*Seismograph station code, US Geological Survey*] (SEIS) .... SLV
Seldovia, AK [*Location identifier FAA*] (FAAL) .... SOV
Seldovia Public Library, Seldovia, AK [*Library symbol Library of Congress*] (LCLS) .... AkSeld
Selebi-Phikwe [*Botswana*] [*ICAO location identifier*] (ICLI) .... FBSP
Selebi-Phikwe [*Botswana*] [*Airport symbol*] (OAG) .... PKW
Selebi-Pikwe [*Botswana*] [*Later, PKW*] [*Airport symbol*] (OAG) .... SBE
Select [*or Selection*] (AAG) .... SEL
Select (ROG) .... SELEC
Select ADC [*Analog-to-Digital Converter*] **Register** [*Computer science*] (MDG) .... SLAR
Select Address .... SA
Select Address and Contract Operate .... SACO
Select Address and Operate .... SAO
Select Address [*and Provide*] **Output Signal** .... SAOS
Select Appointments Holdings [*NASDAQ symbol*] (SAG) .... SELA
Select Appointments Holdings [*Associated Press*] (SAG) .... SlctApp
Select Bills in Eyre [*Selden Society Publication No. 30*] [*England*] [*A publication*] (DLA) .... Bolland
Select Cases [*Oudh, India*] [*A publication*] (DLA) .... SC
Select Cases [*37-39 Alabama*] [*A publication*] (DLA) .... Shep
Select Cases, Central Provinces [*India*] [*A publication*] (DLA) .... Sel Cas
Select Cases in Chancery [*1724-33*] [*England*] [*A publication*] (DLA) .... Cas Ch
Select Cases in Chancery [*England*] [*A publication*] (DLA) .... Cas in C
Select Cases in Chancery [*England*] [*A publication*] (DLA) .... Cases in Ch
Select Cases in Chancery [*Legal*] [*British*] .... SCC
Select Cases in Chancery [*England*] [*A publication*] (DLA) .... Sel Cas Ch
Select Cases in Chancery Tempore King [*1724-33*] [*England*] [*A publication*] (DLA) .... King Cas Temp
Select Cases in Chancery Tempore King [*25 English Reprint*] [*1724-33*] [*A publication*] (DLA) .... SCL
Select Cases in Chancery Tempore King [*25 English Reprint*] [*1724-33*] [*A publication*] (DLA) .... Sel Ca T King
Select Cases in Chancery Tempore King [*25 English Reprint*] [*1724-33*] [*A publication*] (DLA) .... Sel Cas Ch (T King)
Select Cases in Chancery Tempore King [*England*] [*A publication*] (DLA) .... Sel Cas T King
Select Cases in Chancery Tempore King, Edited by Macnaghten [*1724-33*] [*England*] [*A publication*] (DLA) .... Cas T K
Select Cases in Chancery Tempore King, Edited by Macnaghten [*1724-33*] [*England*] [*A publication*] (DLA) .... Cas T King
Select Cases in Chancery Tempore King, Edited by Macnaghten [*1724-33*] [*England*] [*A publication*] (DLA) .... King
Select Cases in Chancery Tempore King, Edited by Macnaghten [*1724-33*] [*A publication*] (DLA) .... Macn Sel Cas
Select Cases in Chancery Tempore King, Edited by Macnaghten [*England*] [*A publication*] (DLA) .... SCC
Select Cases in Chancery Tempore King, Edited by Macnaghten [*England*] [*A publication*] (DLA) .... Sel Ch Cas
Select Cases in Evidence (Strange) [*England*] [*A publication*] (DLA) .... Sel Cas Ev
Select Cases in King's Bench under Edward I (Sayles) [*England*] [*A publication*] (DLA) .... Sel Cas KB Edw I
Select Cases in the Court of Requests, Edited by I. S. Leadam [*Selden Society Publications, Vol. 12*] [*A publication*] (DLA) .... Leadam Req
Select Cases, Newfoundland [*A publication*] (DLA) .... Sel Cas NF
Select Cases, Northwest Provinces [*India*] [*A publication*] (DLA) .... Sel Cas NWP
Select Cases Relating to Evidence (Strange) [*A publication*] (DLA) .... SCE
Select Cases, Sadr Diwani [*Bengal*] [*A publication*] (DLA) .... SAD Beng
Select Cases, Sadr Diwani Adalat [*India*] [*A publication*] (DLA) .... Sel Cas DA
Select Cases, Sadr Diwani Adalat [*Bengal, Bombay, India*] [*A publication*] (DLA) .... Sel Cas SDA
Select Cases, Sadr Diwani Adalat [*Bombay, India*] [*A publication*] (DLA) .... Sel Dec Bomb
Select Cases Tempore Napier [*Ireland*] [*A publication*] (DLA) .... Sel Cas T Nap
Select Cases with Opinions by a Solicitor [*A publication*] (DLA) .... Sel Cas with Opin
Select Collection of Cases [*England*] [*A publication*] (DLA) .... Sel Col Cas
Select Commission on Immigration and Refugee Policy (NADA) .... SCRIP
Select Committee .... SC
Select Committee [*Army Materiel Command*] .... SELCOM
Select Committee on Nationalised Industries [*British*] .... SCNI
Select Committee on Ocean Policy [*Interagency Committee on Marine Science and Engineering*] (USDC) .... SOPS
Select Committee on Ocean Policy Study [*Federal Council for Science and Technology*] .... SCOPS
Select Committee to Arrange a New Deal to Avoid Litigation [*Toledo, OH, group formed in 1973 to humorously protest results of the Michigan-Toledo "War of 18 35"*] .... SCANDAL
Select Committee to Conduct a Study and Investigation of All Matters Relating tothe Need for Adequate Supplies of Newsprint, Printing and Wrapping Paper, Paper Products, Paper, Pulp and Plywood [*US Congress*] [*World War II*] .... SCCSIAMRNASNPWPPPPPP
Select Concrete Objectives for Research Emphasis (PDAA) .... SCORE
Select Decking [*Lumber*] .... SEL DECK
Select Decrees, Sadr Adalat [*Madras, India*] [*A publication*] (DLA) .... Sel Dec Madr
Select Drive System [*Automotive engineering*] .... SDS
Select Frequency .... SF
Select Information Exchange [*Information service or system*] (IID) .... SIE
Select Law Cases [*England*] [*A publication*] (DLA) .... Sel L Cas
Select Manual Entry Switch .... SLME
Select Merchantable [*Lumber*] .... SEL MERC
Select Order (IAA) .... SO
Select Pleas, Starrs, and Other Records from the Rolls of the Exchequer of the Jews, Edited by J. M. Riggs [*Selden Society Publications, Vol. 15*] [*A publication*] (DLA) .... Rigg
Select Read Numerically .... SLRN
Select Software Tools [*NASDAQ symbol*] (SAG) .... SLCT
Select Software Tools [*Associated Press*] (SAG) .... Slct ADR
Select Standby .... SS
Select Structural [*Lumber*] .... SEL STR
Select Technical Requirements Information Program .... STRIP
Select Time (WDAA) .... ST
Selecta Vision [*RCA brand name for tape cartridges of TV programs*] .... SV
Selectable Two-Area Nozzle (MCD) .... STAN
Selectable Unit (BUR) .... SU
Selectair Ltd. [*British ICAO designator*] (FAAC) .... SEL
Selected Abstract Test Suite [*Telecommunications*] (OSI) .... SATS
Selected Abstracts: Library, Information [*Australia A publication*] .... SALI

Selected Acquisition Report [*Military*] ... SAR
Selected Acquisitions Information and Management System (PDAA) ... SAIMA
Selected Acquisitions, Information, and Management System ... SAIMS
Selected Alternate Processing Separation (MCD) ... SAPS
Selected Altitude Layer [*Decoder*] ... SAL
Selected Ammunition (RDA) ... SA
Selected and Amplified Binding [*Sequence or site*] [*Genetics*] ... SAAB
Selected and Retained Graduate (DNAB) ... SERGRAD
Selected Angle of Attack (MCD) ... AOAS
Selected Appeals, Sadr Diwani Adalat [*Bengal, India*] [*A publication*] (DLA) ... Sel App Beng
Selected Applicant Service (NITA) ... SAS
Selected Area Channelling Pattern (MCD) ... SACP
Selected Area [*Electron*] **Diffraction** [*Also, SAED*] [*Analysis of solids*] ... SAD
Selected Area Electron Diffraction [*Also, SAD*] [*Surface analysis*] ... SAED
Selected Area Electron Diffraction Pattern [*Analysis of solids*] ... SADP
Selected Areas for Evasion [*Military*] (MCD) ... SAFE
Selected Armor Defeating Artillery Munitions (MCD) ... SADARM
Selected Attack Option (MCD) ... SAO
Selected Calibration and Alignment Test (MCD) ... SCAT
Selected Calling System [*Military*] (AFM) ... SECAL
Selected Cancers Study [*Centers for Disease Control*] ... SCS
Selected Categories in Microfiche [*National Technical Information Service*] ... SCIM
Selected Classification Service (NITA) ... SCS
Selected Command Unit Review (MCD) ... SCUR
Selected Configuration Item List (MCD) ... SCIL
Selected Configured Item (MCD) ... SCI
Selected Contents of Periodicals for Educators (AEBS) ... SCOPE
Selected Current Aerospace Notices [*NASA*] ... SCAN
Selected Decisions by Umpire for Northern Ireland, Respecting Claims to Benefit [*A publication*] (DLA) ... UID
Selected Decisions of the Board of Revenue, Bihar and Orissa [*A publication*] (DLA) ... B & O Bd of Rev
Selected Decisions of the Native Appeal Court (Central Division) [*1948-51*] [*South Africa*] [*A publication*] (DLA) ... NAC (C)
Selected Decisions of the Native Appeal Court (Southern Division) [*South Africa*] [*A publication*] (ILCA) ... NAC (S)
Selected Decisions of the Native Appeal Court, Transvaal and Natal [*A publication*] (DLA) ... NA T & N
Selected Descriptive Item ... SDI
Selected Dissemination of Documents ... SDD
Selected Dissemination of Information - Key Word Out of Context (DNAB) ... SDI-KWOC
Selected Dissemination of MARC (NITA) ... SELDOM
Selected Effects Armament Subsystem [*Army*] (RDA) ... SEAS
Selected Enlisted Personnel for Overseas Service [*Military*] (AABC) ... SEPOS
Selected Equipment List (NVT) ... SEL
Selected Equipment Status Report [*Navy*] (NG) ... SESR
Selected Essential Stockage Availability Method ... SESAME
Selected Financial Assistance [*British*] (DCTA) ... SFA
Selected History Update and Reporting (MCD) ... SHUR
Selected Honor Guards (MCD) ... SHG
Selected Inertial Equipment ... SIE
Selected Inventor Service (NITA) ... SIS
Selected Inventory Management [*Military*] (CAAL) ... SIM
Selected Ion Current Profile [*Spectrometry*] ... SICP
Selected Ion Monitoring [*Chromatography*] ... SIM
Selected Ion Storage [*For spectometry*] ... SIS
Selected Item (MCD) ... SI
Selected Item Configuration Log ... SICL
Selected Item Configuration Record (MCD) ... SICR
Selected Item Drawing (MCD) ... SID
Selected Item Exchange (MCD) ... SIE
Selected Item List ... SIL
Selected Item Management ... SIM
Selected Item Management System [*Military*] (AABC) ... SIMS
Selected Item Reporting ... SIR
Selected Item Review (MCD) ... SIR
Selected Items Management System - Expanded (MCD) ... SIMS-X
Selected Items Status Report [*Army*] (AABC) ... SISR
Selected Job Queue (IAA) ... SJQ
Selected Judgments, Lower Burma [*A publication*] (DLA) ... SJLB
Selected Judgments of the Divisional Courts [*Ghana*] [*A publication*] (DLA) ... D Ct
Selected Judgments of the Divisional Courts [*Ghana*] [*A publication*] (DLA) ... GC Div C
Selected Judgments of the Federal Supreme Court [*1956-61*] [*Nigeria*] [*A publication*] (DLA) ... FSC
Selected Judgments of the Full Court [*1923-25*] [*Ghana*] [*A publication*] (DLA) ... FC '23-25
Selected Judgments of the Full Court [*1926-29*] [*Ghana*] [*A publication*] (DLA) ... FC '26-29
Selected Judgments of the Full Court, Accra and Gold Coast [*A publication*] (DLA) ... FC
Selected Judgments of the Supreme Court of Israel [*A publication*] (DLA) ... SC Is
Selected Judgments, Zambia [*A publication*] (DLA) ... SJZ
Selected Legally Protected Animals [*Marine science*] (MSC) ... SLPA
Selected Letter and Abbreviated Name Guide [*Environmental Protection Agency A publication*] (GFGA) ... SLANG
Selected List of Published Material [*Her Majesty's Stationery Office*] [*British*] ... SLPM
Selected Listing in Combination (NITA) ... SLIC
Selected Major Exploratory Advanced Development Objective (MCD) ... SMEADO
Selected Management Data Report [*DoD*] ... SMDR
Selected Marine Corps Reserve ... SMCR
Selected Material Handling Equipment [*Army*] (RDA) ... SMHE
Selected Methods for Attracting the Right Targets [*Bombing system*] (AFM) ... SMART
Selected Metropolitan Statistical Area [*FHWA*] (TAG) ... SMSA
Selected Mucosal Biopsy [*Medicine*] (DMAA) ... SMB
Selected Natural Diamond ... SND
Selected Natural Diamond - Metal Bond ... SND-MB
Selected Nodes List [*Telecommunications*] (TEL) ... SNL
Selected Non-Communist Countries ... SNCC
Selected Non-Communist Countries Defense Intelligence Projection for Planning (MCD) ... SNCCDIPP
Selected Nonpriority List Item [*Military*] ... SNPRI
Selected Numeric Service (NITA) ... SNS
Selected Objects for Living Actively [*Commercial firm specializing in home furnishings for the elderly*] ... SOLA
Selected Outpatient Psychiatric Clinic [*Health insurance*] (GHCT) ... SOPC
Selected Period Investment [*Finance*] (WDAA) ... SPI
Selected Product Quality Review [*DoD*] ... SPQR
Selected Quantile Output Device [*Electronics*] ... SQUOD
Selected Reagent Ion Chemical Ionization [*Spectroscopy*] ... SCRICI
Selected Reference Point (GAVI) ... SRP
Selected References on Environmental Quality as It Relates to Health [*A publication*] ... SROEQ
Selected Refresher Training [*Navy*] (NVT) ... SELREFTRA
Selected Refresher Training [*Navy*] (NVT) ... SELRFT
Selected Regardless of Race, Color, Creed, or National Orgin (SAA) ... SRCO
Selected Reserve [*Military*] ... SELRES
Selected Reserve Augmentee (DOMA) ... SRA
Selected Reserve Force [*Units*] [*of Army National Guard Discontinued, 1969*] ... SRF
Selected Reserve Incentive Program [*Army*] ... SRIP
Selected Source List (AAG) ... SSL
Selected Special Weather Report [*Aviation*] (FAAC) ... SPECI
Selected Television [*Commercial firm British*] ... SELCTV
Selected Television Video Disc System (NITA) ... SELECTAVISION
Selected Test Optimization Program (MCD) ... STOP
Selected Water Resources Abstracts [*US Geological Survey*] [*Information service or system*] (CRD) ... SWRA
Selected Words in Full Title (NITA) ... SWIFT
Selected-Ion Flow Tube [*Instrumentation*] ... SIFT
Selected-Reaction Monitoring [*Spectrometry*] ... SRM
Selection [*Literature*] ... sel
Selection (AAG) ... SELN
Selection Acknowledge [*Computer science*] (MHDB) ... SACK
Selection and Training [*Military*] (LAIN) ... S & T
Selection Board [*Military*] ... SB
Selection Classification Age Maturity Program [*Medical screening procedure for athletes*] ... SCAM
Selection Coefficient (DOG) ... s
Selection Control Board [*NASA*] (NASA) ... SCB
Selection Control Element ... SCE
Selection Copy and Reporting (IEEE) ... SCORE
Selection Filter (MCD) ... SF
Selection Filter Control (MCD) ... SFC
Selection Interview Blueprint [*LIMRA*] ... SIB
Selection of Cases Decided in the Native Appeal and Divorce Court, Cape and Orange Free State [*A publication*] (DLA) ... NA & D C & O
Selection of Exempt Organization Returns for Examination [*IRS*] ... SERFE
Selection, Referral, and Followup ... SR & F
Selection to Activate Random Testing [*Module*] [*NASA*] ... START
Selection Work Sheets/Summary Parts ... SWS/SUM PTS
Selective (IAA) ... SEL
Selective Access to Tactical Information (PDAA) ... SATI
Selective Aortic Arch Perfusion [*Medicine*] (DMAA) ... SAAP
Selective Arterial Secretin Injection Test [*Medicine*] (DMAA) ... SAST
Selective Automatic Computational Matching and Positioning (MCD) ... SACMAP
Selective Automatic Computational Matching and Positioning System ... SACMAPS
Selective Automatic Decade Turnover, Absolute Control (IAA) ... SADTAC
Selective Automatic Monitoring ... SAM
Selective Automonitoring Tracing Routine (IAA) ... SAM
Selective Availability ... SA
Selective Bibliography (MCD) ... SB
Selective Calling [*Radio*] ... SELCAL
Selective Catalytic [*or Catalyst*] **Reduction** ... SCR
Selective Catalytic Reduction ... SCR
Selective Chopper Radiometer ... SCR
Selective Combat Range Artillery Missile ... SCRAM
Selective Complement Accumulator ... SCM
Selective Compliance Assembly Robot Arm [*IBM Corp.*] ... SCARA
Selective Conscientious Objection ... SCO
Selective Control Valve [*Hydraulics*] ... SCV
Selective Conversion and Retention [*Navy*] ... SCORE
Selective Cooperative Indexing of Management Periodicals [*Database*] [*European Business School Librarians Group*] [*Information service or system*] (CRD) ... SCIMP
Selective Coronary Angiogram (DAVI) ... SCA
Selective Curtailment of Reports and Paperwork [*Navy*] ... SCRAP
Selective Data Management System (MHDI) ... SELDAM
Selective Data Processing (IAA) ... SDP
Selective Dissemination of Documentation (NITA) ... SDD

Selective Dissemination of Information [*System*] [*Computer science*] .... SDI
Selective Dissemination of Information Online [*National Library of Medicine*] [*Bethesda, MD Bibliographic database*] .... SDILINE
Selective Dissemination of Microfiche .... SDM
Selective Dissemination of Technical Information [*Computer science*] .... SDTI
Selective Early Annuity [*Army*] .... SEA
Selective Early Retirement [*Army*] .... SER
Selective Early Retirement Board [*Army*] (INF) .... SERB
Selective Electron-Capture Sensitization [*Analytical chemistry*] .... SECS
Selective Electronic Training [*Navy*] (NG) .... SET
Selective Elution Solvent Chromatography .... SESC
Selective Employment Payments [*British*] .... SEP
Selective Employment Plan .... SEP
Selective Employment Tax [*British*] .... SET
Selective Enforcement Audit [*Automotive engineering*] .... SEA
Selective Enlistment Bonus [*Navy*] (NVT) .... SEB
Selective Epitaxial Growth [*Semiconductor technology*] .... SEG
Selective Estrogen Receptor Modulators .... SERMS
Selective Estrogen-Receptor Modulator [*Medicine*] .... SERM
Selective Excitation of Probe Ion Luminescence [*Analytical chemistry*] .... SEPIL
Selective File Retrieval .... SFR
Selective Fisheries Information Service (IID) .... ISFIS
Selective Fisheries Information Service (IID) .... SFIS
Selective Gastric Vagotomy [*Medicine*] (DMAA) .... SGV
Selective Gastric Vagotomy and Pyloroplasty [*Medicine*] (CPH) .... SGV & P
Selective High-Frequency Antenna Coupler System [*Military*] (CAAL) .... SACS
Selective Identification .... SI
Selective Identification Feature [*Military decoder modification*] .... SIF
Selective Identification Feature/Identification Friend or Foe [*Military*] (AFM) .... SIF/IFF
Selective Inactivation Photodynamic Unit .... SIPU
Selective Information Dissemination and Retrieval [*Computer science*] (DIT) .... SIDAR
Selective Information Retrieval [*Computer science*] .... SIR
Selective Insurance Gr [*NASDAQ symbol*] (TTSB) .... SIGI
Selective Insurance Group [*Associated Press*] (SAG) .... SelctIn
Selective Insurance Group, Inc. [*Branchville, NJ*] [*NASDAQ symbol*] (NQ) .... SIGI
Selective Interference Modulation Spectrometer .... SIMS
Selective Interrogation Feature (MCD) .... SIF
Selective Intracoronary Thrombolysis [*Cardiology*] (DAVI) .... SICT
Selective Inventory Management of Secondary Items [*Navy*] .... SIMSI
Selective Ion Recording [*Spectrometry*] .... SIR
Selective LASER [*Light Amplification by Stimulated Emission of Radiation*] **Sintering** [*Desktop manufacturing*] .... SLS
Selective Letters [*or Listing*] **in Combination** .... SLIC
Selective Line Printing (IAA) .... SLP
Selective Market Coverage [*Advertising*] (WDMC) .... SMC
Selective Message Transaction (NASA) .... SMT
Selective Moving Target Indicator (IEEE) .... SMTI
Selective Multiple Addresses Radio and Television Service [*A program delivery service introduced by RCA*] .... SMARTS
Selective Myocardial Cell Necrosis [*Cardiology*] .... SMCN
Selective Niobium Anodization Process [*Semiconductor technology*] .... SNAP
Selective Nitrogen Oxide Reduction [*Combustion technology*] .... SNR
Selective Noncatalytic Reduction [*Combustion technology*] .... SNCR
Selective Noncatalytic Reduction [*Combustion technology*] .... SNR
Selective Notification of Information .... SNI
Selective Nuclear Transfer .... SNT
Selective Optical Lock-On [*Sighting device*] .... SOLO
Selective Oxidation Process (PDAA) .... SOP
Selective Paging Communications System .... SPCS
Selective Parallel Running (NITA) .... SPR
Selective Paramagnetic Relaxation Reagent [*Chemistry*] .... SPRR
Selective Parenteral and Enteral Anti-Sepsis Regimen [*Medicine*] (DMAA) .... SPEAR
Selective Permutation Indexing [*Library of Congress*] .... SPINDEX
Selective Population Inversion [*Physics*] .... SPI
Selective Population Transfer [*Physics*] .... SPT
Selective Prepositioning of Materiel Configured to Unit Sets [*Army*] (AABC) .... SPOMCUS
Selective Printing [*Computer science*] .... SPRINT
Selective Printing of Items from Tape [*Computer science*] .... SPIT
Selective Proximal Vagotomy [*Medicine*] (DMAA) .... SPV
Selective Purchases .... SP
Selective Radiation Detector .... SRD
Selective Record Service (NITA) .... SRS
Selective Reenlistment Bonus [*Military*] (AABC) .... SRB
Selective Reenlistment Program [*Air Force*] .... SRP
Selective Reject [*Computer science*] (MHDI) .... SREJ
Selective Reserve Unit [*Navy*] (NVT) .... SRU
Selective Restricted Availability (MCD) .... SRA
Selective Retention Indicators (NVT) .... SRI
Selective Ride Control [*Suspension systems*] [*Automotive engineering*] .... SRC
Selective Ringing .... SR
Selective Sequence Electronic Calculator [*Computer science*] .... SSEC
Selective Serotonin Re-ceptake Indicator [*Medicine*] .... SSR
Selective Serotonin Re-uptake Inhibitor [*Antidepressant*] .... SSRI
Selective Service .... SELS
Selective Service .... SS
Selective Service [*Military*] .... SSVC
Selective Service Act .... SSA
Selective Service Board .... SSB
Selective Service Class [*for Registrant Available for Military Service*] 1-A
Selective Service Class [*for a Conscientious Objector Available for Noncombatant Military Service Only*] 1-A-O
Selective Service Class [*for a Member of Armed Forces of the US, the National Oceanic and Atmospheric Administration, or the Public Health Service*] 1-C
Selective Service Class [*for Qualified Member of Reserve Component, or Student Taking Military Training, Including ROTC and Accepted Aviation Cadet Applicant*] 1-D
Selective Service Class [*for Registrant Not Currently Subject to Processing for Induction*] 1-H
Selective Service Class [*for Conscientious Objector Available for Alternate Service Contributing to Maintenance of National Health, Safety, or Interest*] 1-O
Selective Service Class [*for Conscientious Objector Performing Alternate Service Contributing to Maintenance of National Health, Safety, or Interest*] 1-W
Selective Service Class [*for Registrant Deferred Because of Civilian Occupation, Other than Agriculture, or Non-Degree Study*] 2-A
Selective Service Class [*for Man Physically Disqualified for Military Service but Engaged in Work in the National Health, Safety, or Interest*] [*Obsolete*] 2-A-F
Selective Service Class [*for Man Deferred or Deferrable from Military Service Because of His Necessity to War Production*] [*Obsolete*] 2-B
Selective Service Class [*for Man Physically Disqualified for Military Service but Necessary to War Production*] [*Obsolete*] 2-B-F
Selective Service Class [*for Registrant Deferred from Military Service Because of Agricultural Occupation*] 2-C
Selective Service Class [*for Registrant Deferred Because of Study for the Ministry*] 2-D
Selective Service Class [*for Registrant Deferred Because of Activity in Study*] 2-S
Selective Service Class [*for Registrant Deferred by Reason of Extreme Hardship to Dependents; or Registrant with Child or Children*] 3-A
Selective Service Class [*for Man Deferred from Military Service Because Induction Would Cause Extreme Hardship and Privation to a Wife, Child, or Parent*] [*Obsolete*] 3-D
Selective Service Class [*for Registrant with Sufficient Prior Active Service to Satisfy Requirements of Law (Veteran)*] 4-A
Selective Service Class [*for Public Officials Deferred by Law*] 4-B
Selective Service Class [*for Aliens Not Currently Liable for Military Service*] 4-C
Selective Service Class [*for a Minister of Religion*] 4-D
Selective Service Class [*for a Conscientious Objector Available for, Assigned to, or Released from Work of National Importance*] [*Obsolete*] 4-E
Selective Service Class [*Unqualified for military service for physical reasons*] 4-F
Selective Service Class [*for Registrant Exempt from Service During Peace (Surviving Son or Brother)*] 4-G
Selective Service Class [*for Conscientious Objector Who Has Completed Alternate Service Contributing to National Health, Safety, or Interest*] 4-W
Selective Service classification suggested by comedian Bob Hope for himself during World War II [*Y stood for "yellow"*] 4Y
Selective Service College Qualifying Test .... SSCQT
Selective Service Law Reporter [*A publication*] (DLA) .... Sel Serv L Rep
Selective Service Law Reporter [*A publication*] (DLA) .... Sel Serv L Rptr
Selective Service Regulations .... SSRG
Selective Service System .... SSS
Selective Service System (USGC) .... SSS
Selective Service Youth Advisory Committee [*Military*] (VNW) .... SSYAC
Selective Signaling .... SS
Selective Tape Listing [*Computer science*] (IAA) .... STL
Selective Tape Print .... STP
Selective Top-to-Bottom Algorithm (DIT) .... STBA
Selective Traffic Enforcement Program [*Department of Transportation*] .... STEP
Selective Training and Retention [*Navy*] .... STAR
Selective Tubal Occlusion Procedure [*Medicine*] .... S/TOP
Selective Venous Catheterization [*Cardiology*] .... SVC
Selective Visceral Angiography [*Medicine*] (AAMN) .... SVA
Selective Volunteer [*Navy*] .... SV
Selective Yield Delayed Coking [*Foster Wheeler USA Corp. process*] .... SYDEC
Selectively Aimable Warhead (MCD) .... SAW
Selectively Conductive Molding Device .... SCMD
Selectively Cross Linked .... SCL
Selectively Doped Heterojunction Transistor (NITA) .... SDHT
Selectively Doped Heterostructure Transistor .... SDHT
Selectively-Induced X-Ray Emission Spectroscopy .... SIXES
Selectivity Clear Accumulator .... SCA
Select-Operate-Sense .... SEOPSN
Selector (IAA) .... SEL
Selector (AAG) .... SELR
Selector (NITA) .... SLC
Selector Channel .... SC
Selector Channel .... SELCH
Selector Channel .... SLC
Selector Channel Emulation Unit .... SCEU
Selector Channel Emulator Unit (NITA) .... SCEU
Selector Checkout Unit .... SCU
Selector Control Box [*Aerospace*] (MCD) .... SCB
Selector Control Interface Unit (MCD) .... SCIU
Selector File Channel .... SFC
Selector Group Matrix [*Telecommunications*] (TEL) .... SGX
Selector Input/Output Processor [*Computer science*] (IEEE) .... SIOP
Selector Subchannels .... SSC
Selector Switch (MCD) .... SELSW
Selector Switch (IEEE) .... SS
Selena Research [*Vancouver Stock Exchange symbol*] .... SLN
Selenaheptadecanoic Acid [*Organic chemistry*] .... SHDA
Selenite Brilliant Green (MAE) .... SBG
Selenite Cystine Broth (OA) .... SCB
Selenium [*Chemical element*] .... SE

Selenium [*Chemical element*] (DOG) ... Se
Selenium Control Rectifier [*Nuclear energy*] (NRCH) ... SCR
Selenium Diode ... SD
Selenium Diode Matrix Alloy Logic (IAA) ... SMALL
Selenium Rectifier (IAA) ... SELRECT
Selenium Rectifier [*Electronics*] ... SR
Selenium Rectifier Stack ... SRS
Selenium Stack Rectifier ... SSR
Selenium-Tellurium Development Association (EA) ... S-TDA
Selenoid Driver (IAA) ... SD
Selenoid Valve (MCD) ... SV
Selenological and Engineering Explorer ... SELENE
Seletar [*Singapore*] [*ICAO location identifier*] (ICLI) ... WSSL
Seleucid Era (BJA) ... SE
Seleucid Era (BJA) ... Sel
Self (DAVI) ... SE
Self Addressing Memory (IAA) ... SAM
Self Blood Glucose Monitoring [*Endocrinology*] (DAVI) ... SBGM
Self Breast Examination [*for cancer*] ... SBE
Self Changing Gear (DCTA) ... SCG
Self Compatible ... SC
Self Determination for DC [*District of Columbia*] (EA) ... SDDC
Self Dual (IAA) ... SD
Self Electrooptic Effect Device [*Optical analog of a transistor*] ... SEED
Self Employment [*Social Security Administration*] (OICC) ... SE
Self Employment Income [*Social Security Administration*] (OICC) ... SEI
Self Extracting [*Computer science*] ... exe
Self Focusing [*Optics*] (EECA) ... SELFOC
Self Help Association for Stammerers [*British*] (DI) ... SHAS
Self Help Foundation (EA) ... SHF
Self Incompatible ... SI
Self Inflicted (MAE) ... SI
Self Inking (DGA) ... si
Self Leisure Interest Profile ... SLIP
Self Leveling Unit for Removing Pollution [*Marine science*] (MSC) ... SLURP
Self Potential [*Log*] ... SP
Self Profile Q-Sort [*Child development test*] ... SPQS
Self Protection System (MCD) ... SPS
Self Publishing Association [*British*] (DBA) ... SPA
Self Raising (WDAA) ... SR
Self Serve Laundry [*Military*] (INF) ... SSL
Self Shank (WDAA) ... S/S
Self Simulation ... SS
Self Storage Association of Australia ... SSAA
Self Valuation Test [*Psychology*] ... SVT
Self Verification ... SV
Self Winding Clock Association (EA) ... SWICA
Self-Accelerating Decomposition Temperature ... SADT
Self-Acceptance, Faulty Information, Effectiveness Counselling or Training [*Sex therapy*] ... SAFE
Self-Actualization Inventory [*Test*] ... SAI
Self-Adapting Report Generator [*Computer science*] (MHDI) ... SARG
Self-Adaptive Flexible Format Retrieval and Storage System [*Computer science*] (IID) ... SAFRAS
Self-Adaptive System ... SAS
Self-Addressed Envelope ... SAE
Self-Addressed Stamped Envelope ... SASE
Self-Addressed Stamped Envelope (ODBW) ... sase
Self-Adhesive Foreign Object (PDAA) ... SAFO
Self-Adjusting Ball-Up [*A state of confusion which may, or may not, clear up of itself*] [*Military slang*] ... SABU
Self-Adjusting Clutch ... SAC
Self-Adjusting Electric Brake ... SAEB
Self-Adjusting Military Foul-Up [*Slang*] ... SAMFU
Self-Adjusting System of Scientific Information Flow ... SASSIF
Self-Administered [*Drugs*] ... SA
Self-Administered Alcoholism Screening Test ... SAAST
Self-Administered Alcoholism Screening Test [*Medicine*] (DMAA) ... SAST
Self-Administered Medication (DAVI) ... SAM
Self-Administered Medication [*Medicine*] (MEDA) ... SAM
Self-Administration of Psychotropic Drugs (AAMN) ... SAPD
Self-Agglomerator (PDAA) ... SAG
Self-Aligned Emitter (IAA) ... SAE
Self-Aligned Gate (IAA) ... SAG
Self-Aligned Strip Buried Heterostructure (NITA) ... SSBH
Self-Aligned Superintegration Logic (IAA) ... SSL
Self-Aligning Boost and Reentry [*Air Force*] ... SABRE
Self-Aligning Gate Metal Oxide Semiconductor (IEEE) ... SAGMOS
Self-Aligning Hydraulic Cylinder ... SAHC
Self-Aligning Implantation of N-Layer Technology (MCD) ... SAINT
Self-Aligning Swivel Joint ... SASJ
Self-Aligning Swivel Joint ... SSJ
Self-Aligning Thick Oxide [*Process*] ... SATO
Self-Analysis [*Psychology*] (DAVI) ... SA
Self-Analysis Inventory [*Psychology*] ... SAI
Self-Articulating Femoral [*Medicine*] ... SAF
Self-Assembled Monolayer [*Physical chemistry*] ... SAM
Self-Assessment Depression Scale (AAMN) ... SAD
Self-Assigned Descriptors from Self and Cited Titles [*Automatic indexing*] ... SADSACT
Self-Balancing Bridge ... SBB
Self-Balancing Electronics Recorder ... SBER
Self-Calibrating Omnirange ... SCOR
Self-Canceling Installment Note ... SCIN
Self-Care [*Medicine*] ... SC
Selfcare, Inc. [*Associated Press*] (SAG) ... Selfcare
Selfcare, Inc. [*AMEX symbol*] (SAG) ... SLF
Self-Centered-Altruism Fad ... SCAF
Self-Check (AAG) ... SC
Self-Checking Automatic Testing Equipment ... SCATE
Self-Checking Number ... SCN
Self-Cleaning [*Engineering*] ... SLFCLN
Self-Cleaning Air Cleaner ... SCAC
Self-Closing ... SC
Self-Compensating Network [*Telecommunications*] (TEL) ... SCN
Self-Concept and Motivation Inventory (DMAA) ... SCAMIN
Self-Conducted Tender Availability [*Navy*] (NVT) ... SELFTAV
Self-Consistent Field [*Quantum mechanics*] ... SCF
Self-Consistent Field Molecular Orbital (OA) ... SCFMO
Self-Consistent Local Orbital [*Method*] [*Mathematics*] ... SCLO
Self-Consistent Perturbation Theory [*Physics*] ... SCPT
Self-Consistent Phonon ... SCP
Self-Consistent Renormalization Theory [*Quantum mechanics*] ... SCR
Self-Contained [*Housing*] [*British*] ... S/C
Self-Contained ... SC
Self-Contained ... SCNTN
Self-Contained Adverse-Weather Night Attack ... SCANA
Self-Contained Adverse-Weather Night Attack (MCD) ... SCAWNA
Self-Contained Airborne Multipurpose Pod (MCD) ... SCAMP
Self-Contained All-Weather Landing and Taxiing (MCD) ... SALT
Self-Contained Ancillary Modular Platform [*Woods Hole Oceanographic Institution*] ... SCAMP
Self-Contained Atmospheric Personnel [*or Protective*] **Ensemble** [*Suit*] [*Aerospace*] ... SCAPE
Self-Contained Automated Robotic Factory ... SCARF
Self-Contained Automatic Tactical Air Navigation (IAA) ... SATAN
Self-Contained Automatic Test System ... SCATS
Self-Contained Automatic Transmitter (MCD) ... SCAT
Self-Contained Breathing Apparatus ... SCBA
Self-Contained Canister (MCD) ... SCC
Self-Contained Guidance Package (AAG) ... SCGP
Self-Contained Imaging Micro-Profiler [*Instrumentation*] ... SCIMP
Self-Contained Inertial Navigation System (DOMA) ... SCINS
Self-Contained Instrument Package (KSC) ... SCIP
Self-Contained Munitions ... SCM
Self-Contained Navigation [*NASA*] ... SCN
Self-Contained Navigation System [*NASA*] ... SCNS
Self-Contained Navigation System ... SCNS
Self-Contained Night Attack (MCD) ... SCNA
Self-Contained Perspective Approach Rotor Blade RADAR (IAA) ... SPARR
Self-Contained Self-Rescuer [*Breathing device*] ... SCSR
Self-Contained Starting System [*NASA*] ... SCSS
Self-Contained, Toxic Environment, Protective Outfit [*Army*] (INF) ... STEPO
Self-Contained Training Capability (DNAB) ... SCTC
Self-Contained Underwater Breathing Apparatus ... SCUBA
Self-Contained Underwater Breathing Apparatus (ODBW) ... scuba
Self-Contained Underwater Pinger Unit [*SONAR*] ... SCUPU
Self-Containing Automatic Navigation (IAA) ... SCAN
Self-Control Rating Scale ... SCRS
Self-Controlled Analgesia [*Medicine*] (CDI) ... SCA
Self-Corrected Remedial Aid and Media [*Teaching method*] ... SCRAM
Self-Correcting Automatic Navigator ... SCAN
Self-Coupled Optical Pickup (NITA) ... SCOOP
Self-Decoding Readout ... SDR
Self-Defence Agency [*Japan*] (ECON) ... SDA
Self-Defense Corps [*Vietnam*] ... SDC
Self-Defense Force [*Japan*] ... SDF
Self-Defense Force [*Vietnam*] (VNW) ... SDF
Self-Defense Suite [*Air Force*] (DOMA) ... SDS
Self-Defense Test Ship ... SDTS
Self-Deploying Space Station ... SDSS
Self-Description Inventory [*Vocational guidance test*] ... SDI
Self-Description Questionnaire ... SDQ
Self-Destroying [*Projectile*] ... SD
Self-Destruct ... SD
Self-Destruct Circuit (SAA) ... SDC
Self-Destruct Unit ... SDU
Self-Development Test [*Military*] (INF) ... SDT
Self-Directed Learning (ADA) ... SDL
Self-Directed Search ... SDS
Self-Directed-Learning Readiness Scale (MEDA) ... SDLRS
Self-Disinfecting Elastomer ... SDE
Self-Eject Launch Facility [*NASA*] (MCD) ... SELF
Self-Eject Launch Technique [*NASA*] (KSC) ... SELT
Self-Electro-Optic Effect [*Computer imaging*] ... SEED
Self-Elevating Platform ... SEP
Self-Employed Pension [*British*] ... SEP
Self-Employed Retirement Plan [*Keogh plan*] ... SERP
Self-Employed Women's Association [*India*] ... SEWA
Self-Employment Contributions Act of 1954 [*under which self-employed persons contribute to OASDI coverage for themselves*] ... SECA
Self-Employment Tax [*IRS*] ... SET
Self-Emptying Blind Loop [*Gastroenterology*] ... SEBL
Self-Erecting Marine Platform (PDAA) ... SEMP
Self-Erecting Space Laboratory (AAG) ... SESL
Self-Esteem Inventory [*Coopersmith*] (EDAC) ... SEI
Self-Esteem Questionnaire [*Personality development test*] [*Psychology*] ... SEQ
Self-Evacuating Multilayer Insulation [*System*] ... SEMI
Self-Evident Meteorological Code (NATG) ... SEMET
Self-Evident Statement [*Used in correcting manuscripts, etc.*] ... SE

Self-Extending Translator (IEEE) ... SET
Self-Extinguishing (IAA) ... SE
Self-Extinguishing Fiber [*Monsanto Co. trademark*] ... SEF
Self-Extracting Archive [*Computer science*] (DOM) ... SEA
Self-Feeling Awareness Scale [*Psychology*] (EDAC) ... SFAS
Self-Ferrying Trans-Ocean Rotary-Wing Crane [*Helicopter*] ... STORC
Self-Filling Blind Loop (DMAA) ... SFBI
Self-Filling Blind Loop [*Gastroenterology*] ... SFBL
Self-floating Integrated Deck (PDAA) ... SFID
Self-Forging Fragment [*Warhead*] (MCD) ... SFF
Self-Gating and Shipboard, General Use, Armored (IAA) ... SGA
Self-Generated Noise [*Oceanography*] ... SGN
Self-Generating ... SLFGEN
Self-Generating Dictionary ... SGD
Self-Generating Master [*Information management system*] [*Computer science*] ... SELGEM
Self-Generation Reactor [*Nuclear energy*] (NRCH) ... SGR
Self-Guided Vehicle ... SGV
Self-Heating Group Ration [*Military*] (INF) ... SHGR
Self-Heating Individual Meal [*Military*] (INF) ... SHIM
Self-Heating Individual Meal Module [*Army*] (RDA) ... SHIMM
Self-Heating Individual Ration [*Army*] (RDA) ... SHIR
Self-Heating Meal, Ordered Ready-to-Eat [*Army*] (RDA) ... SMORE
Self-Help Crafts [*An association*] (EA) ... SHC
Self-Help Enterprises (EA) ... SHE
Self-Help for Hard of Hearing People (EA) ... SHHH
Self-Help Improvement Program ... SHIP
Self-Help is Necessary Everywhere [*Navy*] (DNAB) ... SHINE
Self-Help Issue Point [*Army*] ... SHIP
Selfhelp of Emigres from Central Europe (EA) ... SECE
Self-Help Opportunity Center [*Department of Labor*] [*Washington, DC*] (AEBS) ... SHOC
Self-Ignition Temperature ... SIT
Self-Indicating ... SLFIND
Self-Indication Ratio ... SIR
Self-Induced Transparency (IAA) ... SIT
Self-Induced Water Intoxication and Psychosis [*Medicine*] (DMAA) ... SIWIP
Self-Inductance [*Symbol*] [*IUPAC*] ... L
Self-Induction (IAA) ... SI
Self-Inflating Surface Target ... SIST
Self-Inflicted Injury [*Medicine*] (DMAA) ... SII
Self-Inflicted Wound [*Military*] ... SIW
Self-Initiating Antiaircraft Munition [*ARPA*] ... SIAM
Self-Injurious Behavior [*Abnormal psychology*] ... SIB
Self-Injurious Behavior Inhibiting System [*Psychology*] ... SIBIS
Self-Insurance Group (WYGK) ... SIG
Self-Insurance Institute of America (EA) ... SIIA
Self-Insured Benefits Plan [*Human resources*] (WYGK) ... SIBP
Self-Insured Retention [*Insurance*] ... SIR
Self-Insurers Association ... SIA
Self-Interstitial Atom ... SIA
Self-Interview Checklist [*Navy*] (NVT) ... SICL
Self-Interview Inventory [*Psychology*] ... SII
Selfix, Inc. [*Associated Press*] (SAG) ... Selfix
Selfix, Inc. [*NASDAQ symbol*] (CTT) ... SLFX
Self-Launching Glider ... SLG
Self-Launching Motor Glider [*Aviation*] (DA) ... SLMG
Self-Learning Audio Visual Education [*National Foundation for the Prevention of Oral Disease*] ... SAVE
Self-Loading Disk Dump and Reload (IAA) ... SDDRL
Self-Loading Memory Print (IAA) ... SLMP
Self-Loading Random Access Edit (IAA) ... SLRE
Self-Loading Rifle (MCD) ... SLR
Self-Loading Tape (AFM) ... SLT
Self-Loading Tape Edit (IAA) ... SLTE
Self-Locking [*Engineering*] ... SLFLKG
Self-Lubricating Bearing ... SLB
Self-Lubricating Exterior (IAA) ... SLX
Self-Maintenance Period [*British military*] (DMA) ... SMP
Self-Managed Account (WYGK) ... SMA
Self-Management Program (DAVI) ... SMP
Self-Maneuvering Unit [*Air Force*] ... SMU
Self-Metering Instrumentation ... SMI
Self-Modulating Derivative Optical Spectrometer (IAA) ... SMODOS
Self-Monitoring (DAVI) ... SM
Self-Monitoring, Analysis and Reporting Technology [*Computer science*] ... SMART
Self-Monitoring Negative Checklist (EDAC) ... SMNC
Self-Monitoring of Blood Glucose [*Medicine*] ... SMBG
Self-Mutilators Support Group (EA) ... SMSG
Self-Noise Reduction ... SNORE
Self-Observation and Report Technique ... SORT
Self-Obtained Smear [*Medicine*] (DMAA) ... SOS
Self-Opening Sack [*Paper bag*] ... SOS
Self-Optimizing and Adaptive ... SOA
Self-Optimizing Automatic Pilot ... SOAP
Self-Organized Criticality [*Physics*] ... SOC
Self-Organizing Binary Logical Network [*OTS*] ... SOBLIN
Self-Organizing Control ... SOC
Self-Organizing Flight Control System ... SOFCS
Self-Organizing Large Information Dissemination System (IEEE) ... SOLID
Self-Organizing Machine ... SOM
Self-Organizing Map [*Computer science*] (CDE) ... SOM
Self-Organizing Multiple-Access Discrete Address [*Computer science*] (IEEE) ... SOMADA
Self-Organizing System ... SOS
Self-Orthogonal Convolutional Code (PDAA) ... SOCC
Self-Paced Instruction (IEEE) ... SPI
Self-Paced Instruction for Competency Education (EDAC) ... SPICE
Self-Perception Inventory [*Personality development test*] [*Psychology*] ... SPI
Self-Phasing Array ... SPA
Self-Polishing Copolymer [*Anti-fouling paint*] (DS) ... SPC
Self-Pollinated [*Botany*] ... S
Self-Power Density Spectrum (IAA) ... SPDS
Self-Powered [*Gun*] (MCD) ... SP
Self-Powered Gamma Detector [*Nuclear energy*] (NRCH) ... SPGD
Self-Powered Neutron Detector ... SND
Self-Powered Neutron Detector [*Nuclear energy*] (NRCH) ... SPND
Self-Powered Reference Junction ... SPRJ
Self-Powered Thermocouple Reference Junction ... SPTRJ
Self-Powered Thermocouple Reference Junction ... STRJ
Self-Programmed Electronic Equation Delineator ... SPEED
Self-Programmed Individualized Education (IEEE) ... SPIE
Self-Programming Automatic Circuit Evaluator ... SPACE
Self-Programming Compiler [*Software*] [*Computer science*] ... SPC
Self-Propagating High-Temperature Synthesis [*Ceramic technolgy*] ... SHS
Self-Propagating-Star Formation [*Galactic science*] ... SPSF
Self-Propelled [*Military*] ... SP
Self-Propelled Air-to-Surface Missile (MCD) ... SPASM
Self-Propelled Anthropomorphic Manipulator [*Moon machine*] ... SAM
Self-Propelled Anti-Aircraft Gun [*Former Soviet Union*] ... SPAAG
Self-Propelled Antitank Gun (MCD) ... SPAT
Self-Propelled Barracks Ship [*Navy symbol*] ... APB
Self-Propelled Crane for Aircraft Maintenance and Positioning (MCD) ... SCAMP
Self-Propelled Elevated Maintenance Stand (MCD) ... SPEMS
Self-Propelled Gun [*British military*] (DMA) ... SPG
Self-Propelled Howitzer (MCD) ... SPH
Self-Propelled Hyperbaric Lifeboat (DS) ... SPHL
Self-Propelled Immersible Drive-Off Trolley [*British*] (DI) ... SPIDOT
Self-Propelled Launcher [*British military*] (DMA) ... SPL
Self-Propelled Launcher Loader (MCD) ... SPLL
Self-Propelled Mount [*Military*] ... SPM
Self-Propelled Recoilless Rifle [*British military*] (DMA) ... SPRR
Self-Propelled Robot Craft (IEEE) ... SPRC
Self-Propelled Underwater Missile (IAA) ... SPU
Self-Propelled Underwater Research Vehicle ... SPURV
Self-Protected Air-to-Air Missile Concept Evaluation Program [*Army*] ... SAMCEP
Self-Protection Weapon ... SPW
Self-Protection Weapon System ... SPWS
Self-Pumped Phase Conjugator [*Optics*] ... SPPC
Self-Quenching Control ... SQC
Self-Quenching Detector ... SQD
Self-Rating Depression Scale [*Psychology*] ... SDS
Self-Rating Psychiatric Inventory List [*Personality development test*] [*Psychology*] ... SPIL
Self-Rating Scale [*Psychology*] ... SRS
Self-Reading Dosimeter (IEEE) ... SRD
Self-Realization Fellowship (EA) ... SRF
Self-Recording Penetrometer ... SRP
Self-Recording Unit (IAA) ... SRU
Self-Rectifying ... SR
Self-Referenced Fringe (MCD) ... SRF
Self-Regulating Error-Correct Coder-Decoder ... SECO
Self-Regulatory Agency [*Securities*] [*British*] ... SRA
Self-Regulatory Organisation [*Financial Services Act of 1986*] [*British*] ... SRO
Selfreliance Association of American Ukrainians (EA) ... SAAU
Self-Renewal Occupational Field ... SROF
Self-Repair Technique ... SRT
Self-Repairing Flight Control System ... SRFCS
Self-Report Assertiveness Test for Boys ... SRAT-B
Self-Reported Delinquency (EDAC) ... SRD
Self-Reporting Questionnaire [*Medicine*] (DMAA) ... SRQ
Self-Representing Unit (GFGA) ... SRU
Self-Resonant Frequency ... SRF
Self-Restraining Pipe Joint ... SRPJ
Self-Restraint Joint ... SRJ
Self-Retaining Bolt ... SRB
Selfridge Army/Air National Guard Base (MCD) ... SANGB
Selfridge's Trial [*A publication*] (DLA) ... Self Tr
Self-Righteousness Questionnaire [*Psychology*] (EDAC) ... SRQ
Self-Rising Flour and Corn Meal Program [*Later, HBA*] (EA) ... SFCMP
Self-Rising Flour Institute [*Later, HBA*] ... SRFI
Self-Scaling Variable Metric [*Algorithms*] [*Computer science*] ... SSVM
Self-Scoring Answer Sheet (DNAB) ... SSAS
Self-Screening Jammer (MCD) ... SSJ
Self-Screening Noise Jammer (MCD) ... SSNJ
Self-Sealing [*Engineering*] ... SLFSE
Self-Sealing Aerospace Vehicle (IAA) ... SSAV
Self-Sealing Fuel Tank ... SSFT
Self-Service Financial Terminal [*Computer science*] (MHDI) ... SSFT
Self-Service Storage Association [*Later, SSA*] (EA) ... SSSA
Self-Service Store ... SSS
Self-Service Supply Center [*Military*] (AFIT) ... SSSC
Self-Service Unit ... SSU
Self-Shifting Synchronizing (PDAA) ... SSS
Self-Steering Array Repeater (IAA) ... STAR
Self-Sterilizing-Material [*Pharmacology*] ... SSM
Self-Storing Tubular Extensionable Member (IAA) ... STEM
Self-Sufficiency Ratio [*Business term*] ... SSR
Self-Sustained Emission ... SSE

Self-Synchronizing [*or Synchronous*] (IAA) .... SELSYN
Self-Synchronous [*Trade name*] [*Motor*] .... SELSYN
Self-Tapping [*Screw*] [*Design engineering*] .... SLFTPG
Self-Teaching Exportable Package .... STEP
Self-Test .... ST
Self-Test Antenna Radiation [*Military*] (CAAL) .... STAR
Self-Test Automatic Readout .... STAR
Self-Test Input [*Electronics*] .... STI
Self-Test Logic [*Navy Navigation Satellite System*] (DNAB) .... STL
Self-Test Mode .... STM
Self-Test Output [*Automotive engineering*] .... STO
Self-Test Program (MCD) .... STP
Self-Test Select .... STS
Self-Testing and Repairing [*Computer self-repair*] .... STAR
Self-Toning [*Paper*] [*Photography*] (ROG) .... ST
Self-Tracking Automatic Lock-On Circuit (PDAA) .... STALOC
Self-Training and Assessment of Readiness .... STAR
Self-Training Interpretive Retrieval System .... STIRS
Self-Trapped Exciton [*Physical chemistry*] .... STE
Self-Tuning Vibration Absorber [*Navy*] (CAAL) .... STVA
Self-Ventilated (MSA) .... SV
Self-Wiring Data [*Telecommunications*] (TEL) .... SWD
Selibabi [*Mauritania*] [*ICAO location identifier*] (ICLI) .... GQNS
Selibaby [*Mauritania*] [*Airport symbol*] (OAG) .... SEY
Seligman, AZ [*FM radio station call letters*] (RBYB) .... KJJJ-FM
Seligman, AZ [*FM radio station call letters*] (RBYB) .... KZKE
Seligman, MO [*FM radio station call letters*] (RBYB) .... KJEM
Seligman Quality Muni Fd [*NYSE symbol*] (TTSB) .... SQF
Seligman Quality Municipal Fund [*Associated Press*] (SAG) .... SeligQual
Seligman Quality Municipal Fund [*NYSE symbol*] (SPSG) .... SQF
Seligman Select Muni Fund [*NYSE symbol*] (TTSB) .... SEL
Seligman Select Municipal Fund [*NYSE symbol*] (SPSG) .... SEL
Seligman Select Municipal Fund [*Associated Press*] (SAG) .... SeligSel
Seligmann's Buffered Salt Solution [*Medicine*] (DMAA) .... SBSS
Selinsgrove, PA [*Location identifier FAA*] (FAAL) .... SEG
Selinsgrove, PA [*FM radio station call letters*] .... WQSU
Selinsgrove, PA [*AM radio station call letters*] .... WYGL
Seljacko-Demokratska Koalicija [*Peasant-Democratic Coalition*] [*Former Yugoslavia*] [*Political party*] (PPE) .... SDK
Selkirk College, Castlegar, BC, Canada [*Library symbol Library of Congress*] (LCLS) .... CaBCS
Selkirk College, Castlegar, British Columbia [*Library symbol National Library of Canada*] (NLC) .... BCS
Selkirk College Library [*UTLAS symbol*] .... SEL
Selkirk College, Vocational Division, Nelson, BC, Canada [*Library symbol Library of Congress*] (LCLS) .... CaBNSV
Selkirk Communications Ltd. [*Toronto Stock Exchange symbol*] .... SKH
Selkirk Community Library, Manitoba [*Library symbol National Library of Canada*] (NLC) .... MSEL
Selkirk Community Library, Selkirk, MB, Canada [*Library symbol Library of Congress*] (LCLS) .... CaMSEC
Selkirk, MB [*FM radio station call letters*] .... CFQX
Selkirk Mental Health Centre, Manitoba [*Library symbol National Library of Canada*] (NLC) .... MSEMH
Selkirk Mental Health Centre, Selkirk, MB, Canada [*Library symbol Library of Congress*] (LCLS) .... CaMSeMH
Selkirk Remote Sensing Ltd. [*Canada ICAO designator*] (FAAC) .... SRS
Selkirkshire [*County in Scotland*] .... SELK
Selkup [*MARC language code Library of Congress*] (LCCP) .... sel
Sell Overseas America, the Association of American Export [*Redondo Beach, CA*] (EA) .... SOSA
Sell Under the Guise of Market Research [*Marketing*] [*British*] .... SUG
Sella, Nasion, A [*Anthropometric landmark*] .... SNA
Sella, Nasion, B [*Anthropometric landmark*] .... SNB
Sella Turcica-Nasion [*Plane that passes through these points*] [*Cephalometrics*] .... S-N (Plane)
Sel-Leb Marketing [*NASDAQ symbol*] (TTSB) .... SELB
Sel-Leb Marketing, Inc. [*NASDAQ symbol*] (SAG) .... SELB
Sel-Leb Marketing, Inc. [*Associated Press*] (SAG) .... Sel-Leb
Sel-Leb Marketing Wrrt [*NASDAQ symbol*] (TTSB) .... SELBW
Sellectek Industries, Inc. [*Vancouver Stock Exchange symbol*] .... SLT
Seller Critical Design Review [*NASA*] (NASA) .... SCDR
Seller Data Requirements List (MCD) .... SDRL
Seller Pollution Control [*Associated Press*] (SAG) .... SellrPol
Seller Pollution Control [*NASDAQ symbol*] (SAG) .... SEPC
Seller-Furnished Equipment (MCD) .... SFE
Seller's Approved Configuration Baseline Document [*NASA*] (NASA) .... SCBD
Seller's Delivery in Seven Days [*Stock exchange term*] S7
Seller's Engineering Memo [*NASA*] (NASA) .... SEM
Seller's Guide to Government Purchasing [*A publication*] .... SGGP
Seller's Option [*Stock exchange term*] .... SO
Seller's Option (ODBW) .... so
Seller's Option to Double [*Stock exchange term*] .... SOD
Sellersburg Star, Sellersburg, IN [*Library symbol Library of Congress*] (LCLS) .... InSelS
Sellersville, PA [*FM radio station call letters*] .... WBYO
Sellin Center for Studies in Criminology and Criminal Law (EA) .... SCSCCL
Selling [*Exchange rate marking*] [*British*] .... SG
Selling Areas-Marketing, Inc. [*Originator and database*] [*New York, NY Information service or system*] (IID) .... SAMI
Selling Expense (AAGC) .... SE
Selling, General, and Administrative Expenses .... SG & A
Selling Price .... SP
Selling Short [*or Short Sale*] [*Investment term*] .... SS
Selling-Areas Distribution Index (WDMC) .... SADI
Sell-Off (AAG) .... SO
Sell-Off Date (AAG) .... SOD
Sell-Off Impact Prognosticator [*Aerospace*] (AAG) .... SOIP
Sellon's Practice [*A publication*] (DLA) .... Sel Pr
Sellon's Practice in the King's Bench [*A publication*] (DLA) .... Sell Pr
Sellon's Practice in the King's Bench [*A publication*] (DLA) .... Sell Prac
Selma [*Alabama*] [*Airport symbol*] (AD) .... SES
Selma, AL [*Location identifier FAA*] (FAAL) .... CAQ
Selma, AL [*Location identifier FAA*] (FAAL) .... POJ
Selma, AL [*Location identifier FAA*] (FAAL) .... SEM
Selma, AL [*Television station call letters*] .... WAKA
Selma, AL [*FM radio station call letters*] .... WALX
Selma, AL [*FM radio station call letters*] (RBYB) .... WAPR-FM
Selma, AL [*FM radio station call letters*] .... WDXX
Selma, AL [*AM radio station call letters*] .... WHBB
Selma, AL [*AM radio station call letters*] .... WMRK
Selma, AL [*AM radio station call letters*] .... WTQX
Selma/Craig Air Force Base [*Alabama*] [*ICAO location identifier*] (ICLI) .... KSEM
Selma [*Alabama*] **Interreligious Project** (EA) .... SIP
Selma, NC [*AM radio station call letters*] .... WBZB
Selma Project Education Alternatives Center [*Alabama*] (EA) .... SPEAC
Selma Public Library, Selma, NC [*Library symbol*] [*Library of Congress*] (LCLS) .... NcSe
Selma/Selfield [*Alabama*] [*ICAO location identifier*] (ICLI) .... KSES
Selmaville Community Consolidated District 10, Salem, IL [*Library symbol Library of Congress*] (LCLS) .... ISalCD
Selmer, TN [*Location identifier FAA*] (FAAL) .... SZY
Selmer, TN [*AM radio station call letters*] .... WDTM
Selmer, TN [*FM radio station call letters*] .... WSIB
Selmer, TN [*FM radio station call letters*] .... WXOQ
Selous Foundation (EA) .... SF
SELSYN [*Military*] (BARN) .... sels
Selvac Corp. [*Associated Press*] (SAG) .... Selvac
Selvac Corp. [*NASDAQ symbol*] (NQ) .... SLVC
Selve-Kornbegel-Dornheim [*Name of a German small arms ammunition factory*] [*World War II*] .... SKD
Selvi [*Italy*] [*Research code symbol*] .... S
Selwyn College [*Cambridge*] [*British*] (ROG) .... SELW
Selwyn's Law of Nisi Prius [*A publication*] (DLA) .... Sel NP
Selwyn's Law of Nisi Prius [*England*] [*A publication*] (DLA) .... Selw
Selwyn's Law of Nisi Prius [*England*] [*A publication*] (DLA) .... Selw NP
SEMA [*Specialty Equipment Manufacturers Association*] **Action Team** .... SAT
Semahot (BJA) .... Sm
Semahoth (BJA) .... Sem
Semantic Analyzing Machine .... SAM
Semantic Correlation [*Machine-aided indexing*] .... SEMCOR
Semantic Differential .... SD
Semantic Feature Analysis (EDAC) .... SFA
Semantic Information Retrieval [*Massachusetts Institute of Technology*] [*Computer science*] (DIT) .... SIR
Semantic Networks for Conceptual Analysis (NITA) .... SENECA
Semantic Reaction .... SR
Semantically Oriented Lexical Archive .... SOLAR
Semantic-Meta-Language .... SML
Semantics-Oriented Language [*Computer science*] (PDAA) .... SEMANOL
Semaphore .... SEM
Semarang [*Indonesia*] [*Airport symbol*] (OAG) .... SRG
Semarang/Achmad Yani [*Indonesia*] [*ICAO location identifier*] (ICLI) .... WIIS
Sematan [*Sarawak, Malaysia*] [*Airport symbol*] (AD) .... BSE
Sematan [*Indonesia*] [*ICAO location identifier*] (ICLI) .... WBGN
Sembach [*Germany ICAO location identifier*] (ICLI) .... EDAS
Sembawang [*Singapore*] [*ICAO location identifier*] (ICLI) .... WSAG
Semble [*It Seems*] .... SEM
Semel [*Once*] .... SEM
Semel in Die [*Once a Day*] [*Pharmacy*] .... SEMEL in D
Semel in Die [*Once a Day*] [*Pharmacy*] .... sid
Semen (WGA) .... SEM
Semen Analysis .... SA
Semendua [*Zaire*] [*ICAO location identifier*] (ICLI) .... FZBS
Semenogelin (DMAA) .... SEMG
Semeru [*Java*] [*Seismograph station code, US Geological Survey Closed*] (SEIS) .... SMR
Semester .... SEM
Semester Hour .... SH
Semi .... S
Semi [*One-Half*] [*Pharmacy*] .... SEM
Semi Knocked Down [*Shipping*] (DS) .... SKD
Semi Process Inc. (NITA) .... SPI
Semiactive Gravity-Gradient System [*NASA*] .... SAGS
Semiactive Guidance [*Military*] (IIA) .... SAG
Semiactive Homer [*Missiles*] .... SAH
Semi-Active Homing RADAR [*Military*] (RDA) .... SAHR
Semiactive LASER [*Military*] (CAAL) .... SAL
Semiactive LASER/Infrared (DWSG) .... SAL/IR
Semiactive LASER-Guided Projectile (MCD) .... SAL-GP
Semiactive on Target .... SAOT
Semiactive RADAR (MCD) .... SAR
Semiactive RADAR Alternate Head .... SARAH
Semiactive RADAR Antiair Guidance System .... SRAG
Semiactive RADAR Missile .... SEARAM
Semi-Active RADAR Simulator [*Military*] .... SARS
Semi-Actuator Ejector (MCD) .... SAE
Semi-Airspace (NITA) .... SAS
Semiannual (WDMC) .... SA
Semiannual .... SA

Semiannual Density Variation [*Geophysics*] ... SADV
Semiannual Inventory Report [*Military*] (AFM) ... SAIR
Semiannual Inventory Report [*Navy*] (NVT) ... SIR
Semiannual Oscillation [*Astronomy*] ... SAO
Semiannual Progress Report ... SAPR
Semiannual RADWASTE [*Radioactive Waste*] **Effluent Release** (GFGA) ... SERR
Semiannual Report ... SAR
Semi-Annual Service Program [*Army*] (INF) ... SSP
Semi-Annual Status Report (MHDI) ... SASR
Semiannual Technical Progress Report ... STPR
Semiannually ... S
Semi-Arid Grain Research and Development (GNE) ... SAFGAR
Semi-Arid Tropical Crops Information Service (IID) ... SATCRIS
Semiarid Tropics [*Geography*] ... SAT
Semi-Armor-Piercing [*Projectile*] [*Nickname: Sex-Appeal Pete*] [*Military*] ... SAP
Semi-Armor-Piercing High Explosive [*Projectile*] (MCD) ... SAPHE
Semi-Armor-Piercing Incendiary [*Projectile*] (NATG) ... SAPI
Semi-Ascending Order Arrangement (PDAA) ... SAOA
Semiautogenous Grinding System [*Ore-crushing process*] ... SAG
Semi-Automated Artwork Generator System (PDAA) ... SAAGS
Semiautomated Business Research Environment [*Computerized reservation network*] [*American Airlines*] ... SABRE
Semi-Automated Computer-Oriented Text (PDAA) ... SCOT
Semi-Automated Forces [*Army*] (RDA) ... SAFOR
Semiautomated Mechanical Transmission [*Automotive engineering*] ... SAMT
Semiautomated Reconstruction Facility [*Military*] (CAAL) ... SARF
Semiautomated Reconstruction System [*Military*] (CAAL) ... SARS
Semiautomatic ... SA
Semiautomatic (IAA) ... SEMIAUT
Semiautomatic Active Memory (SAA) ... SAM
Semiautomatic Air Traffic Control (IAA) ... SATCO
Semiautomatic Analog Setting (IEEE) ... SATANAS
Semi-Automatic Back-Up [*Military*] (IAA) ... SABU
Semiautomatic Bibliographic Information Retrieval ... SABIR
Semiautomatic Bibliographic Information Retrieval System (DIT) ... SABIRS
Semiautomatic Bleeder Valve ... SBV
Semiautomatic BOMARC Local Environment (MCD) ... SABLE
Semiautomatic Checkout Equipment [*DoD*] ... SACE
Semiautomatic Circuit Performance Monitor [*Navy*] (MCD) ... SCPM
Semiautomatic Coding ... SAC
Semiautomatic Command to Line of Sight [*Military*] ... SACLOS
Semiautomatic Controller (CAAL) ... SAC
Semiautomatic Coordinate Reader (DNAB) ... SACR
Semiautomatic Decentralized Intercept Environment [*Air Force*] ... SADIE
Semiautomatic Defense System (NG) ... SADS
Semiautomatic Detection Device ... SADD
Semi-Automatic Document Feed (NITA) ... SADF
Semi-Automatic Document Feeder (HGAA) ... SADF
Semiautomatic Encoding of Chemistry for Information Retrieval (DIT) ... SECIR
Semiautomatic Facility for Terminal Area Control ... SAFTAC
Semiautomatic Failure Anticipation Recording Instrumentation ... SAFARI
Semiautomatic Film Mounter (SAA) ... SAM
Semiautomatic Flight Inspection [*FAA*] ... SAFI
Semiautomatic Flight Inspection Aircraft (FAAC) ... SAFI
Semiautomatic Flight Operations Center ... SAFOC
Semiautomatic Ground Control of Interceptors [*Military*] (IAA) ... SAGCI
Semiautomatic Ground Environment [*Military*] ... SAGE
Semiautomatic Height Finder ... SAHF
Semiautomatic Imagery Screening Subsystem (MCD) ... SIS
Semiautomatic Inserting Machine (SAA) ... SAIM
Semiautomatic Integrated Documentation ... SAID
Semiautomatic Line Test Equipment (NG) ... SALTE
Semiautomatic Low-Data-Rate Input (SAA) ... SALDRI
Semiautomatic Mathematics (IEEE) ... SAM
Semiautomatic Meteorological Station (SAA) ... SAMS
Semiautomatic Mounter [*3M Co.*] ... SAM
Semiautomatic Population Analysis System (MCD) ... SAPAS
Semiautomatic Program Checkout (IAA) ... SAPCH
Semiautomatic Program Checkout Equipment (AAG) ... SAPCHE
Semiautomatic RADAR Identification Equipment (MCD) ... SARIE
Semiautomatic Range Azimuth and Height [*Subsystem*] ... SARAH
Semiautomatic Rifle [*Army*] ... SAR
Semiautomatic Shop Test Equipment (NG) ... SASTE
Semi-Automatic Speaker Identification System (PDAA) ... SASIS
Semiautomatic Stock Control ... SASC
Semiautomatic Tactical Control and Airspace Management System (MCD) ... SATCAMS
Semiautomatic Technical Control ... SATEC
Semiautomatic Technical Information Retrieval ... SATIRE
Semiautomatic Telegraph Exchange (WDAA) ... SATEX
Semiautomatic Test Equipment [*NASA*] ... SAT
Semiautomatic Test Equipment [*NASA*] ... SATE
Semiautomatic Transistor Tester [*NASA*] ... SATT
Semiautomatic Weapons ... SAW
Semiautonomous Acoustic/Magnetic [*Vehicle*] (DOMA) ... SAM
Semiautonomous Underwater Vehicle (DOMA) ... SAUV
Semi-Balance [*Model*] (USDC) ... SB
Semi-Balance [*Model*] [*Marine science*] (OSRA) ... SB
Semicactus [*Horticulture*] ... SC
Semicarbazide-Sensitive Amine Oxidase [*Biochemistry*] ... SSAO
Semicircular (MAE) ... SC
Semiclosed [*Anatomy*] ... SC
Semiclosed Circle Absorber (DAVI) ... SCCA
Semicolon (WDMC) ... sem
Semicolon ... SEM
Semicolon (AABC) ... SMCLN
Semiconducting Quantum Interference Device (MCD) ... SQUID
Semiconductor ... SC
Semiconductor ... SCR
Semiconductor (IAA) ... SEMICON
Semiconductor ... SEMICOND
Semiconductor (IAA) ... SIC
Semiconductor Active Memory [*Computer science*] (IAA) ... SAM
Semiconductor Advanced Memory [*Computer science*] (IAA) ... SAM
Semiconductor Anticoincidence Detection System ... SADS
Semiconductor Anticoincidence Detector ... SAD
Semiconductor Bilateral Switch (MSA) ... SBS
Semiconductor Bridge ... SCB
Semiconductor Chip Protection Act of 1984 ... SCPA
Semiconductor Complex, Ltd. [*Commercial firm*] [*India*] ... SCL
Semiconductor Controlled Switch (MSA) ... SCS
Semiconductor Curve Tracer ... SCT
Semiconductor Device (IAA) ... SCD
Semiconductor Device (IAA) ... SD
Semiconductor Devices Council [*Joint Electronic Device Engineering Council*] (MCD) ... SDC
Semiconductor Diode LASER [*Also, TDL*] ... SDL
Semiconductor Disk Memory ... SDM
Semiconductor Electronic Memory (IAA) ... SEM
Semiconductor Equipment and Materials Institute (EA) ... SEMI
Semiconductor Equipment Communications Standard (NITA) ... SECS
Semiconductor Functional Block (IEEE) ... SFB
Semiconductor Industry & Business Survey [*Database*] [*HTE Management Resources*] [*Information service or system*] (CRD) ... SIBS
Semiconductor Industry Association (EA) ... SIA
Semiconductor Infrared Photography (PDAA) ... SCIRP
Semiconductor Injector LASER ... SIL
Semiconductor Integrated Circuit ... SCIC
Semiconductor Integrated Circuit ... SIC
Semiconductor LASER Amplifier ... SEMLAM
Semiconductor LASER Array Techniques ... SEMLAT
Semiconductor Laser International Corp. [*Associated Press*] (SAG) ... SemiLas
Semiconductor Laser International Corp. [*NASDAQ symbol*] (SAG) ... SLIC
Semiconductor Laser Intl [*NASDAQ symbol*] (TTSB) ... SLIC
Semiconductor Laser Wrrt [*NASDAQ symbol*] (TTSB) ... SLICW
Semiconductor/Liquid Junction ... S/LJ
Semiconductor Magnetic Field Detector (IAA) ... SMD
Semiconductor Manufacturing Equipment [*Sumitomo Metals*] ... SME
Semiconductor Manufacturing Technology (DOMA) ... SEMATECH
Semiconductor Manufacturing Technology Consortium ... SEMATECH
Semiconductor Memory ... SM
Semiconductor Memory Integrated Device (MCD) ... SMID
Semiconductor Memory Module ... SMM
Semiconductor Network (IEEE) ... SN
Semiconductor Neutron Dosimeter ... SND
Semiconductor on Thermoplastic on Dielectric [*Technology*] (IAA) ... STD
Semiconductor Packaging Materials [*AMEX symbol*] (SAG) ... SEM
Semiconductor Packaging Materials [*Associated Press*] (SAG) ... SemPck
Semiconductor Parameter Retrieval [*Information Handling Services*] [*Database*] ... SCPR
Semiconductor Pkg Materials [*NASDAQ symbol*] (TTSB) ... SEMX
Semiconductor Productivity Network (NITA) ... SPN
Semiconductor Products (IAA) ... SCP
Semiconductor Research and Development Laboratory (IAA) ... SRDL
Semiconductor Research Cooperative ... SRC
Semiconductor Safety Association (EA) ... SSA
Semiconductor Silicon Detector ... SSD
Semiconductor Specialists, Inc. (IAA) ... SSI
Semiconductor Storage Model (NITA) ... SSM
Semiconductor Storage Module ... SSM
Semiconductor Storage Unit [*Computer science*] ... SSU
Semiconductor Trade Agreement [*US and Japan*] (ECON) ... STA
Semiconductor Transistor (IAA) ... SLAM
Semiconductor Unilateral Switch (MSA) ... SUS
Semiconductor-Controlled Rectifier ... SCR
Semiconductor-Insulator-Semiconductor ... SIS
Semiconductor-Insulator-Semiconductor System ... SISS
Semiconductor-Metal-Semiconductor ... SMS
Semicontinuous Activated Sludge [*Test*] [*Environmental Protection Agency*] (FFDE) ... SCAS
Semi-Darkness (DNAB) ... SD
Semidehydroascorbate [*Biochemistry*] ... SDA
Semidetached (ADA) ... SD
Semidiameter ... SD
Semidrachma [*Half a Drachm*] [*Latin Pharmacy*] (MAE) ... semid
Semidrachma [*Half a Drachma*] [*Pharmacy*] ... SEMIDR
Semi-Effective List [*British military*] (DMA) ... SEL
Semiempirical Absorption Loss Formula [*Radio*] ... SEALF
Semi-Empirical Design of Impellers [*Hydraulics*] [*Computer-aided design*] ... SEDI
Semiempirical Natural Orbital [*Physical chemistry*] ... SNO
Semienclosed ... SEN
Semi-Engineered Prototype [*Automotive engineering*] ... SEP
Semienriched Minimal [*Agar*] ... SEM
Semiequilibrium Dialysis [*Physical chemistry*] ... SED
Semifinal Splice [*Telecommunications*] (TEL) ... SS
Semifinished [*Steel or other material*] ... SF
Semi-Finished [*Automotive engineering*] ... S-FIN
Semifireproof (MSA) ... SFPRF
Semi-Fire-Resistive Construction ... SFR
Semifixed [*Ammunition*] (NATG) ... SF

Semifixed ... SFXD
Semi-Floating [*Automotive engineering*] ... SF
Semiflush ... SFLS
Semi-Fowler's [*Position*] [*Surgery*] (DAVI) ... SF
Semihomogeneous Experiment [*Nuclear energy*] ... SHE
Semi-Homogeneous Fuel Reactor (IAA) ... SHR
Semihora [*Half an Hour*] [*Pharmacy*] ... SEMIH
Semihorizontal Heart Position (MAE) ... SHHP
Semi-Implicit Pressure-Linked Equation [*Algorithm*] ... SIMPLE
Semi-Insulating ... SI
Semi-Insulating Polycrystalline Silicon [*Photovoltaic energy systems*] ... SIPOS
Semi-Interpenetrating Polymer Network [*Organic chemistry*] ... SIPN
Semi-Interquartile Range [*Medicine*] (DMAA) ... SIQR
Semi-Interquartile Range or Quartile Deviation [*Statistics*] ... Q
Semi-Lagrangian and Semi-Geostrophic Finite Element [*Model*] [*Marine science*] (OSRA) ... SSF
Semi-Lagrangian and Semi-Geostrophic Finite Element [*Model*] (USDC) ... SSF
Semilente [*Insulin*] [*Pharmacology*] (DAVI) ... S
Semilinang/Peranap [*Indonesia*] [*ICAO location identifier*] (ICLI) ... WIBP
Semilinear Erection System (SAA) ... SLES
Semi-Major Axis [*of a comet*] [*In astronomical units*] ... A
Semimajor Axis ... SMA
Semimat (IAA) ... SM
Semimembranous [*Anatomy*] (DAVI) ... SM
Semi-Micro Xerography ... SMX
Semimobile (WGA) ... SEM
Semimobile ... SMBL
Semimobile Intercontinental Ballistic Missile ... SMICBM
Semimonthly ... SM
Semimonthly Progress Reports [*Navy*] ... S-MPR
Seminaire de Joliette, Joliette, PQ, Canada [*Library symbol Library of Congress*] (LCLS) ... CaQJJ
Seminaire de Joliette, Quebec [*Library symbol National Library of Canada*] (NLC) ... QJJ
Seminaire de Nicolet, Nicolet, PQ, Canada [*Library symbol Library of Congress*] (LCLS) ... CaQNicS
Seminaire de Nicolet, Quebec [*Library symbol National Library of Canada*] (NLC) ... QNICS
Seminaire de Quebec, Quebec [*Library symbol National Library of Canada*] (NLC) ... QQS
Seminaire de Quebec, Quebec, PQ, Canada [*Library symbol Library of Congress*] (LCLS) ... CaQQS
Seminaire de St.-Hyacinthe, St.-Hyacinthe, PQ, Canada [*Library symbol Library of Congress*] (LCLS) ... CaQStHS
Seminaire de Saint-Jean, Saint-Jean, PQ, Canada [*Library symbol Library of Congress Obsolete*] (LCLS) ... CaQStJS
Seminaire de Sherbrooke, Quebec [*Library symbol National Library of Canada*] (NLC) ... QSHERS
Seminaire de Sherbrooke, Sherbrooke, PQ, Canada [*Library symbol Library of Congress*] (LCLS) ... CaQSherS
Seminaire de Sherbrooke, Sherbrooke, PQ, Canada [*Library symbol Library of Congress Obsolete*] (LCLS) ... CaQSherSS
Seminaire de St-Hyacinthe, Quebec [*Library symbol National Library of Canada*] (NLC) ... QSTHS
Seminaire de Trois-Rivieres, Quebec [*Library symbol National Library of Canada*] (NLC) ... QTS
Seminaire des Trois-Rivieres, Trois-Rivieres, PQ, Canada [*Library symbol Library of Congress*] (LCLS) ... CaQTS
Seminaire Saint Augustine, Cap Rouge, PQ, Canada [*Library symbol Library of Congress*] (LCLS) ... CaQCRS
Seminaire Ste.-Marie, Shawinigan, PQ, Canada [*Library symbol Library of Congress*] (LCLS) ... CaQSHS
Seminaire St. Martial [*Haiti*] [*Seismograph station code, US Geological Survey Closed*] (SEIS) ... SSM
Seminaire St-Augustin, Cap-Rouge, Quebec [*Library symbol National Library of Canada*] (NLC) ... QCRS
Seminaire Ste-Marie, Shawinigan, Quebec [*Library symbol National Library of Canada*] (NLC) ... QSHS
Seminal (WGA) ... SEM
Seminal Acid Phosphatase [*An enzyme*] ... SAP
Seminal Fluid [*Medicine*] ... SF
Seminal Groove ... SGR
Seminal Vesicle [*Anatomy*] (WGA) ... sem ves
Seminal Vesicle [*Anatomy*] ... SV
Seminal Vesicle Epithelium [*Anatomy*] ... SVE
Seminal Vesicle Mesenchyme [*Anatomy*] ... SVM
Seminal Vesicle Microsome [*Anatomy*] ... SVM
Seminal Vesicle Protein [*Biochemistry*] ... SVP
Seminar Clearinghouse International, Inc. [*Information service or system*] (IID) ... SCI
Seminar Information Service Database [*Seminar Information Service, Inc.*] [*Information service or system*] (CRD) ... SIS
Seminar on the Acquisition of Latin American Library Materials (EA) ... SALALM
Seminar Press ... SP
Seminare/Konferenzen [*Seminars/Conferences*] [*Society for Business Information*] [*Information service or system*] [*Defunct*] (IID) ... SEMIKON
Seminarians for Ministerial Renewal [*Later, NFCS*] (EA) ... SMR
Seminario Internacional de Administracao Universitaria ... SIAU
Seminars Directory [*A publication*] ... SD
Seminars on Aeroanxiety Relief ... SOAR
Seminars on Practical Applications of Research Knowledge [*Advertising Research Foundation*] ... SPARK
Seminary ... SEM
Seminary ... SEMY
Seminary ... SMNRY
Seminary ... SMRY
Seminary College of Jewish Studies (BJA) ... SCJS
Seminary in Exile [*Liberal-oriented Lutheran seminary*] ... SEMINEX
Seminary of Saint Pius X, Erlanger, KY [*Library symbol Library of Congress*] (LCLS) ... KyErP
Seminex [*Concordia Seminary in Exile*] **Library, St. Louis, MO** [*OCLC symbol*] (OCLC) ... STS
Seminiferous Growth Factor [*Biochemistry*] ... SGP
Seminole Community College, Sanford, FL [*Library symbol Library of Congress*] (LCLS) ... FSanS
Seminole Community College, Sanford, FL [*OCLC symbol*] (OCLC) ... FSS
Seminole County Public Library System, Casselberry, FL [*Library symbol Library of Congress*] (LCLS) ... FCas
Seminole, OK [*FM radio station call letters*] ... KIRC
Seminole, OK [*Location identifier FAA*] (FAAL) ... SRE
Seminole Resources, Inc. [*Vancouver Stock Exchange symbol*] ... SNL
Seminole, TX [*Location identifier FAA*] (FAAL) ... GNC
Seminole, TX [*AM radio station call letters*] ... KIKZ
Seminole, TX [*FM radio station call letters*] ... KSEM
Semioccupied Molecular Orbital [*Physical chemistry*] ... SOMO
Semiopen Position [*Dancing*] ... SOP
Semiorganic Polymer ... SOP
Semiotic Abstracts [*A publication*] ... SEMA
Semiotic Society of America (EA) ... SSA
Semipalatinsk [*Former USSR Seismograph station code, US Geological Survey*] (SEIS) ... SEM
Semipermanent Repellent (ADA) ... SPR
Semipermanently Associated [*Telecommunications*] (TEL) ... SPA
Semi-Permanet Release Agent ... SPRA
Semipermeable Dressing [*Medicine*] ... SPD
Semipermeable Membrane ... SPM
Semipostal ... SP
Semipost-Pay, Pay-Station [*Telecommunications*] (TEL) ... SPPAY
Semipost-Pay, Pay-Station [*Telecommunications*] (TEL) ... SPPS
Semiprivate [*Room*] ... S/P
Semipublic [*Telecommunications*] (TEL) ... SP
Semiquantitative Fibrinogen [*Hematology*] ... SQF
Semirandom Access Memory ... SRAM
Semi-Recessed Oxide (PDAA) ... SEMIROX
Semi-Registered Tank [*Liquid gas carriers*] ... S
Semireinforcing Furnace [*Carbon black manufacture*] ... SRF
Semirom [*Iran*] [*ICAO location identifier*] (ICLI) ... OIFI
Semis [*One-Half*] [*Pharmacy*] ... S
Semis [*One-Half*] [*Latin Pharmacy*] (MAE) ... semi
Semis [*One-Half*] [*Pharmacy*] ... SS
Semisolid Material [*Metallurgy*] ... SSM
Semisopochnoi Island [*Alaska*] [*Seismograph station code, US Geological Survey Closed*] (SEIS) ... SSI
Semispectral Primitive Equation Model [*Marine science*] (OSRA) ... SPEM
Semispectral Primitive Equation Model (USDC) ... SPEM
Semisteel ... SS
Semi-Submarine Ice-Breaking Tanker (PDAA) ... SSIT
Semi-Submerged Trimaran [*Tri-hull ship design invented by Calvin Gongwer*] ... SST
Semisubmersible [*Drilling unit*] ... SS
Semisubmersible Crane Vessel ... SSCV
Semi-Tech Corp. [*NASDAQ symbol*] (SAG) ... SEMC
Semi-Tech Corp. [*Associated Press*] (SAG) ... SemiTch
Semi-Tech Corp. 'A' [*NASDAQ symbol*] (TTSB) ... SEMCF
Semi-Tech Microelectronics, Inc. [*Toronto Stock Exchange symbol*] ... SWP
Semitendinosus [*Muscle*] ... ST
Semitendinosus Tendon [*Anatomy*] ... STT
Semitic [*Language, etc.*] ... SEM
Semitic [*MARC language code Library of Congress*] (LCCP) ... sem
Semitic Study Series [*A publication*] (BJA) ... SSS
Semitool Europe Ltd. [*British ICAO designator*] (FAAC) ... STE
Semitool, Inc. [*Associated Press*] (SAG) ... Semitool
Semitool, Inc. [*NASDAQ symbol*] (SAG) ... SMTL
Semitrailer [*Truck and trailer rigs*] (DAVI) ... semi
Semitrailer ... STLR
Semitrailer Petroleum Van (DWSG) ... STPV
Semitrailer Van Mount ... STVM
Semitrailer Van Mount ... SVM
Semitrailer-Mounted Fabric Tank [*for water distribution*] [*Army*] ... SMFT
Semivital ... SVTL
Semi-Wadcutter [*Ammunition*] ... SWC
Semiweekly ... SW
Semliki Forest Virus ... SFV
Semlyachik [*Former USSR Seismograph station code, US Geological Survey*] (SEIS) ... SEL
Semmerzake [*Belgium ICAO location identifier*] (ICLI) ... EBSZ
Semmes-Murphey Clinic, Memphis, TN [*Library symbol Library of Congress*] (LCLS) ... TMSMC
SEMMS [*Solar Electric Multiple-Mission Spacecraft*] **Coordinating Group** [*NASA*] ... SCG
Semnan [*Iran*] [*ICAO location identifier*] (ICLI) ... OIIS
Semo Aviation [*ICAO designator*] (AD) ... VV
Semongkong [*Lesotho*] [*ICAO location identifier*] (ICLI) ... FXSM
Semongkong [*Lesotho*] [*Airport symbol Obsolete*] (OAG) ... SOK
Semonides [*Seventh century BC*] [*Classical studies*] (OCD) ... Semon
Semora, NC [*FM radio station call letters*] (RBYB) ... WPXX
Sempati Air PT [*Indonesia*] [*ICAO designator*] (FAAC) ... SSR
Sempati Air Transport PT [*Indonesia*] [*ICAO designator*] (FAAC) ... SMP
Semper Paratus [*Always Ready*] [*Coast Guard motto*] ... SPAR

Semper Paratus [US Coast Guard Women's Auxiliary; name taken from Coast Guard motto] .... SPARS
Sempervivium Society [Burgess Hill, West Sussex, England] (EAIO) .... SS
Sempervivum Fanciers Association (EA) .... SFA
Semplak/Atang Senjaya [Indonesia] [ICAO location identifier] (ICLI) .... WIAJ
Semporna [Malaysia] [Airport symbol] (OAG) .... SMM
Semporna [Malaysia] [ICAO location identifier] (ICLI) .... WBKA
Sempre [Throughout] [Music] .... SEM
Sempre [Throughout] [Music] .... SEMP
Semtech Corp. [Associated Press] (SAG) .... Semtch
Semtech Corp. [AMEX symbol] (SPSG) .... SMH
Semtech Corp. [NASDAQ symbol] (SAG) .... SMTC
Semur-En-Auxois [France ICAO location identifier] (ICLI) .... LFGQ
Semyenovka [Former USSR ICAO location identifier] (ICLI) .... UKKS
Sen [Monetary unit in Japan] .... S
Sena Maduereira [Brazil] [Airport symbol] (AD) .... MAQ
Senair Charter Ltd. [British ICAO designator] (FAAC) .... SEN
Senanga [Zambia] [ICAO location identifier] (ICLI) .... FLSN
Senanga [Zambia] [Airport symbol] (OAG) .... SXG
Senate .... S
Senate .... SEN
Senate Aeronautical and Space Sciences Committee (AAG) .... SASSC
Senate Appropriations Committee (NVT) .... SAC
Senate Appropriations Defense Subcommittee .... SADS
Senate Armed Services Committee .... SASC
Senate Bill [with number] (GPO) .... S
Senate Bill [in state legislatures] .... SB
Senate Bonding and Currency Committee (OICC) .... SBCC
Senate Budget Committee .... SBC
Senate Children's Caucus (EA) .... SCC
Senate Committee Report (AFIT) .... SREPT
Senate Comprehensive Integrated Automated Printing System .... SCIAPS
Senate Concurrent Resolution (DLA) .... SC Res
Senate Concurrent Resolution (AFIT) .... SCONRES
Senate Concurrent Resolution (CDAI) .... SCR
Senate Copper Caucus (EA) .... SCC
Senate Document (DLA) .... S Doc
Senate Document .... SD
Senate Document (DLA) .... Sen Doc
Senate Executive Document [A publication] (DLA) .... S Exec Doc
Senate Executive Report [A publication] (DLA) .... S Exec Rep
Senate File (OICC) .... SF
Senate Historical Office .... SHO
Senate Interstate and Foreign Commerce Committee .... SIFCC
Senate Joint Resolution .... SJR
Senate Joint Resolution (AFIT) .... SJRES
Senate Journal [A publication] (DLA) .... Sen J
Senate Journal [A publication] (DLA) .... Sen Jo
Senate Military Affairs Committee [British] (DAS) .... SMAC
Senate Office Building .... SOB
Senate Operating Agency (MCD) .... SOA
Senate Permanent Investigating Subcommittee (AAG) .... SPIS
Senate Post Office .... SPO
Senate Press Secretaries Association (EA) .... SPSA
Senate Radio-Television Correspondents Association (NTCM) .... SRTCA
Senate Rail Caucus (EA) .... SRC
Senate Recedes .... SR
Senate Recording Studio .... SRS
Senate Report [A publication] (DLA) .... Sen Rep
Senate Report .... SR
Senate Reports [A publication] (DLA) .... S Rep
Senate Resolution (AAGC) .... S Res
Senate Resolution .... SR
Senate Resolution (AFIT) .... SRES
Senate Select Committee on Agricultural and Veterinary Chemicals [Australia] .... SSCAVC
Senate Select Committee on Intelligence (MCD) .... SSCI
Senate Special Committee on National Defence [Canada] .... SSCND
Senate Staff Club (EA) .... SSC
Senate Standing Committee on Foreign Affairs, Defence, and Trade [Australia] .... SSCFADT
Senate Standing Committee on Industry, Science, and Technology [Australia] .... SSCIST
Senate Standing Committee on the Environment, Recreation, and the Arts [Australia] .... SSCERA
Senate Standing Committee on Trade and Commerce [Australia] .... SSCTC
Senate Steel Caucus (EA) .... SSC
Senate Tourism Caucus (EA) .... STC
Senate Treaty Documents [A publication] (DLA) .... S Treaty Doc
Senate Veterans Affairs Committee .... SVAC
Senate Wine Caucus (EA) .... SWC
Senate-House Joint Reports [A publication] (DLA) .... SHJR
Senatobia, MS [FM radio station call letters] .... WKNA
Senatobia, MS [AM radio station call letters] .... WSAO
Senator .... SEN
Senator (ODBW) .... Sen
Senator (DFIT) .... Sen
Senator .... SEN
Senator Aviation Charter GmbH, Koln [Germany] [FAA designator] (FAAC) .... SNA
Senator Joseph R. McCarthy Foundation (EA) .... SJRMF
Senatus Consulto [By the Decree of the Senate] [Latin] .... SC
Senatus Consultum [Classical studies] (OCD) .... SC
Senatus Decreto [By Decree of the Senate] [Latin] .... SD
Senatus Populusque Romanus [The Senate and People of Rome] [Latin] .... SPQR

Send a Block Message [Computer science] (ECII) .... SBM
Send and Receive .... SR
Send by Airmail (NOAA) .... SDAML
Send Common [Computer science] (MHDI) .... SC
Send Data [Computer science] .... SD
Send Digits [Telecommunications] (TEL) .... SD
Send Hub [Telegraphy] (TEL) .... SH
Send Leg [Telegraphy] (TEL) .... SL
Send Only .... SO
Send Out Succor .... SOS
Send Priority and Route Digit [Telecommunications] (TEL) .... SPR
Send Processor .... SP
Send Receive (NITA) .... SR
Send Receive Bomb (IAA) .... SRB
Send Receive Switch [Telecommunications] (IAA) .... SRS
Send Reference Equivalent, Search RADAR [Telecommunications] (TEL) .... SRE
Send Register Control [Computer science] .... SRC
Send Test Message (AAG) .... STM
Sendai [Japan ICAO location identifier] (ICLI) .... RJSS
Sendai [Japan] [Airport symbol] (OAG) .... SDJ
Sendai [Mukaiyama] [Japan] [Seismograph station code, US Geological Survey] (SEIS) .... SEN
Send-a-Message (MCD) .... SAM
Sender (KSC) .... SDR
Sender Freies Berlin [Radio network] [West Germany] .... SFB
Sendero Luminoso [Shining Path] [Peru] (PD) .... SL
Sender's Composition Message [Cable] .... SCM
Sending (MSA) .... SNDG
Sending [Electronics] (ECII) .... SNG
Sending Complete [Telecommunications] (TEL) .... SC
Sending Reference Equivalent (NITA) .... SRE
Send-Only-Multipoint (DNAB) .... SOM
Send-Receive (IDOE) .... S-R
Send-Receive Logic (ECII) .... SRL
Seneca [the Younger] [First century AD] [Classical studies] (OCD) .... Sen
Seneca [the Elder] [First century BC] [Classical studies] (OCD) .... Sen
Seneca Army Depot [New York] (AABC) .... SEAD
Seneca College, Willowdale, ON, Canada [Library symbol Library of Congress] (LCLS) .... CaOTSC
Seneca College, Willowdale, Ontario [Library symbol National Library of Canada] (NLC) .... OTSC
Seneca Falls, NY [AM radio station call letters] .... WSFW
Seneca Falls, NY [FM radio station call letters] .... WSFW-FM
Seneca Foods Cl'A' [NASDAQ symbol] (TTSB) .... SENEA
Seneca Foods Cl'B' [NASDAQ symbol] (TTSB) .... SENEB
Seneca Foods Corp. [NASDAQ symbol] (NQ) .... SENE
Seneca Foods Corp. [Associated Press] (SAG) .... Seneca
Seneca, IL [FM radio station call letters] (RBYB) .... WAIZ
Seneca Junior High School, Holbrook, NY [Library symbol Library of Congress] (LCLS) .... NHolbSJ
Seneca, KS [FM radio station call letters] .... KMZA
Seneca Nation of Indians .... SNI
Seneca Nation of Indians (DOGT) .... SNI
Seneca Public Library, Seneca, IL [Library symbol Library of Congress] (LCLS) .... ISen
Seneca, SC [FM radio station call letters] (RBYB) .... WPEK
Seneca, SC [AM radio station call letters] .... WSNW
Seneca Underwater Test and Evaluation Center .... SUTEC
Senegal [Aircraft nationality and registration mark] (FAAC) 6V
Senegal [Aircraft nationality and registration mark] (FAAC) 6W
Senegal [MARC geographic area code Library of Congress] (LCCP) .... f-sg--
Senegal [IYRU nationality code] (IYR) .... SE
Senegal [ANSI three-letter standard code] (CNC) .... SEN
Senegal .... Seneg
Senegal [MARC country of publication code Library of Congress] (LCCP) .... sg
Senegal [ANSI two-letter standard code] (CNC) .... SN
Senegal (VRA) .... sngl
Senegal and Gambia .... SENEGAMBIA
Senegalair [Senegal] [ICAO designator] (FAAC) .... SGL
Senekal [South Africa] [ICAO location identifier] (ICLI) .... FASN
Senes Consultants Ltd., Willowdale, Ontario [Library symbol National Library of Canada] (NLC) .... OWSCL
Senescence-Associated Gene [Biochemistry] .... SAG
Senescent-Soybean-Pod Agar [Microbiology] .... SSPA
Senetek Ltd. [NASDAQ symbol] (NQ) .... SNTK
Senetek Ltd. [NASDAQ symbol] (SAG) .... SNTW
Senetek Ltd. [NASDAQ symbol] (SAG) .... SNTZ
Senetek PLC [Associated Press] (SAG) .... Senetek
Senetek PLC [Associated Press] (SAG) .... Sntk
Senetek Plc ADS [NASDAQ symbol] (TTSB) .... SNTKY
Senetek Plc Wrrt'A' [NASDAQ symbol] (TTSB) .... SNTWF
Senetek Plc Wrrt'B' [NASDAQ symbol] (TTSB) .... SNTZF
Senggeh [Indonesia] [ICAO location identifier] (ICLI) .... WAJS
Senggo [Indonesia] [Airport symbol] (OAG) .... ZEG
Sengstaken-Blakemore [Tube] [Gastroenterology] (DAVI) .... SB
Sengstaken-Blakemore [Tube] [Medicine] (MEDA) .... SB
Sengwarden [Germany ICAO location identifier] (ICLI) .... EDZE
Senhor Do Bonfim [Brazil] [Airport symbol] (OAG) .... SEI
Senile Brain Disease [Medicine] (DMAA) .... SBD
Senile Cognitive Decline [Medicine] .... SCD
Senile Dementia [Medicine] .... SD
Senile Dementia of the Alzheimer Type [Medicine] .... SDAT
Senile Keratosis [Dermatology] (DAVI) .... SK
Senile Macular Degeneration [Medicine] .... SMD
Senile Parkinsonism [Medicine] (DMAA) .... sP

Senile Plaque [*Neurology*] ... SP
Senior (EY) ... SEN
Senior (ODBW) ... Sen
Senior ... SENR
Senior ... SNR
Senior (ODBW) ... Snr
Senior (ODBW) ... Sr
Senior ... SR
Senior (DFIT) ... Sr
Senior (DD) ... sr
Senior ... SR
Senior Acting Field Officer [*Military British*] (ROG) ... SAFO
Senior Action in a Gay Environment (EA) ... SAGE
Senior Administrative Medical Officer (DMAA) ... SAMO
Senior Administrative Officer [*British military*] (DMA) ... SAO
Senior ADP Policy Officer (AAGC) ... SADPO
Senior Advisor [*Military*] ... SA
Senior Advisory Group [*Policymakers who advised President Johnson, especially regarding Vietnam*] (VNW) ... SAG
Senior Advisory Group [*Nuclear Regulatory Commission*] (GFGA) ... SAG
Senior Advisory Group on Biotechnology [*British*] ... SAGB
Senior Advocates International [*Defunct*] (EA) ... SAI
Senior Air Force Instructor ... SAFI
Senior Air Force Officer [*Present*] (AFM) ... SAFO
Senior Air Force Representative (AFM) ... SAFR
Senior Air Staff Officer [*British*] ... SASO
Senior Air Traffic Control Officer (NATG) ... SATCO
Senior Aircraft Communicator (IAA) ... SACOM
Senior Aircraft Crewman Badge [*Military decoration*] (GFGA) ... SRACCMB
Senior Aircraft Crewman Badge [*Military decoration*] (AABC) ... SrAcftCrmnBad
Senior Aircraftman [*British military*] (DMA) ... SAC
Senior Aircraftwoman [*British military*] (DMA) ... SACW
Senior Airman ... SrA
Senior Apperception Technique [*Personality development test*] [*Psychology*] ... SAT
Senior Appointments Selection Committee [*British*] ... SASC
Senior Aptitude Tests [*Educational test*] ... SAT
Senior Arms Control Group [*National Security Council*] ... SACG
Senior Arms Control Planning Group [*Pronounced "sack pig"*] [*DoD*] ... SACPG
Senior Army Advisor ... SAA
Senior Army Advisor (AABC) ... SRAA
Senior Army Advisor, Army National Guard (AABC) ... SAAARNG
Senior Army Advisor, Army National Guard (AABC) ... SRAAG
Senior Army Advisor, Army Reserve (AABC) ... SRAAR
Senior Army Advisor, United States Army Reserve (AABC) ... SAAUSAR
Senior Army Aviator (AABC) ... SRARAV
Senior Army Aviator Badge [*Military decoration*] (GFGA) ... SRARAVB
Senior Army Aviator Badge [*Military decoration*] ... SrArAvBad
Senior Army Instructor ... SAI
Senior Army Materiel Command Orientation Seminar ... SAMCOS
Senior Army Representative ... SAR
Senior Army Reserve Commanders Association ... SARCA
Senior Assistant Editor [*Publishing*] ... SAE
Senior Assistant Secretary ... SAS
Senior Associate of the Australian Institute of Bankers ... AAIB(Snr)
Senior Beadle [*Ancient Order of Foresters*] ... SB
Senior Bond (MHDW) ... SB
Senior British Naval Officer ... SBNO
Senior British Naval Officer, Western Atlantic ... SBNOWA
Senior Cameraman ... SC
Senior Canadian Naval Officer [*British military*] (DMA) ... SCNO
Senior Chaplain [*Navy British*] ... SenCh
Senior Chaplain to the Forces [*British*] ... SCF
Senior Chief Aircrew Survival Equipmentman [*Formerly, Senior Chief Parachute R igger*] [*Navy rating*] ... PRCS
Senior Chief Aviation Machinist's Mate [*Navy rating*] ... ADCS
Senior Chief Builder [*Navy rating*] ... BUCS
Senior Chief Commissaryman [*Later, MSCS*] [*Navy rating*] ... CSCS
Senior Chief Damage Controlman [*Navy rating*] ... DCCS
Senior Chief Data Processing Technician [*Formerly, MACS*] [*Navy rating*] ... DPCS
Senior Chief Executive Officer [*Civil Service*] [*British*] ... SCEO
Senior Chief Gunner's Mate, Technician [*Navy rating*] ... GMTCS
Senior Chief Hull Maintenance Technician [*Formerly, SFCS*] [*Navy rating*] ... HTCS
Senior Chief Illustrator Draftsman [*Navy rating*] ... DMCS
Senior Chief Instrumentman [*Navy rating*] ... IMCS
Senior Chief Interior Communications Electrician [*Navy rating*] ... ICCS
Senior Chief Journalist [*Navy rating*] ... JOCS
Senior Chief Lithographer [*Navy rating*] ... LICS
Senior Chief Machine Accountant [*Later, DPCS*] [*Navy rating*] ... MACS
Senior Chief Mess Management Specialist [*Formerly, CSCS, SDCS*] [*Navy rating*] ... MSCS
Senior Chief Officer [*British military*] (DMA) ... SCO
Senior Chief Officer, Shore Signal Service (IAA) ... SCOSS
Senior Chief Officer, Shore Wireless Service (IAA) ... SCOSWS
Senior Chief Opticalman [*Navy rating*] ... OMCS
Senior Chief Patternmaker [*Navy rating*] ... PMCS
Senior Chief Personnelman [*Navy rating*] ... PNCS
Senior Chief Petty Officer [*Navy*] ... E8
Senior Chief Petty Officer [*Navy rating*] ... SCPO
Senior Chief Photographer's Mate [*Navy rating*] ... PHCS
Senior Chief Photographic Intelligenceman [*Navy rating*] ... PTCS
Senior Chief Postal Clerk [*Navy rating*] ... PCCS
Senior Chief Quartermaster [*Navy rating*] ... QMCS
Senior Chief RADARman [*Navy rating*] ... RDCS
Senior Chief Radioman [*Navy rating*] ... RMCS
Senior Chief Shipfitter [*Later, HTCS*] [*Navy rating*] ... SFCS
Senior Chief Ship's Serviceman [*Navy rating*] ... SHCS
Senior Chief Signalman [*Navy rating*] ... SMCS
Senior Chief SONAR Technician [*Navy rating*] ... STCS
Senior Chief SONARman [*Navy rating*] ... SOCS
Senior Chief Steelworker [*Navy rating*] ... SWCS
Senior Chief Steward [*Later, MSCS*] [*Navy rating*] ... SDCS
Senior Chief Storekeeper [*Navy rating*] ... SKCS
Senior Chief Torpedoman's Mate [*Navy rating*] ... TMCS
Senior Chief TRADEVMAN [*Training Devices Man*] [*Navy rating*] ... TDCS
Senior Citizen Discount ... SCD
Senior Citizen Ski Touring Committee (EA) ... SCSTC
Senior Citizens League [*Defunct*] (EA) ... SCL
Senior Citizens of America [*Defunct*] (EA) ... SCA
Senior Citizens' Opportunities for Personal Enrichment [*Federal antipoverty program*] ... SCOPE
Senior Citizen's Services [*A publication*] ... SCS
Senior Civil Affairs Office, Police [*British*] ... SCAO(P)
Senior Civil Affairs Officer ... SCAO
Senior Civil Emergency Planning Committee [*NATO*] (NATG) ... SCEPC
Senior Civilian Representative, Attorney General [*Department of Justice civil disturbance unit*] ... SCRAG
Senior Clerical Medical Officer (DMAA) ... SCMO
Senior Clinical Medical Officer [*British*] ... SCMO
Senior Command Course [*British military*] (DMA) ... SCC
Senior Commanders Orientation Course (MCD) ... SCOC
Senior Commercial Pilot's Licence [*British*] (DBQ) ... SCPL
Senior Commercial Pilot's Licence/Helicopters [*British*] (AIA) ... SCPL/H
Senior Common Room [*in British colleges and public schools*] ... SCR
Senior Community Service Employment Program (EA) ... SCSEP
Senior Companion Program (EA) ... SCP
Senior Conformation Judges Association (EA) ... SCJA
Senior Conformation Judges Association Education Fund (EA) ... SCJAEF
Senior Contractor Representative ... SCR
Senior Control Center [*Air Force*] ... SRCC
Senior Cook General Mess [*British military*] (DMA) ... SCGM
Senior Counsel [*Ireland*] ... SC
Senior Deacon [*Freemasonry*] ... SD
Senior Dental Officer [*Navy*] (DNAB) ... SENDENTALO
Senior Direction Station (SAA) ... SDS
Senior Director Technician (SAA) ... SDT
Senior Duty Officer [*Air Force British*] ... SDO
Senior Editor [*Publishing*] ... SE
Senior Electronic Engineer (IAA) ... SEE
Senior Electronic Technician [*National Weather Service*] ... SET
Senior Engineer Officer [*Navy*] ... SEO
Senior Enlisted Academy [*Navy*] ... SEA
Senior Enlisted Advisor [*AFSC*] ... CMS
Senior Enlisted Advisor [*Navy*] ... SEA
Senior Enlisted Advisor, Communications/Operations [*Navy*] (DNAB) ... SEACO
Senior Enlisted Advisor, Navy (DNAB) ... SEAN
Senior Enlisted Bachelor Quarters [*Army*] (AABC) ... SEBQ
Senior Enlisted Evaluation Reports [*Military*] (INF) ... SEERS
Senior Environmental Employment ... SEE
Senior Environmental Employment Program [*Environmental Protection Agency*] ... SEE
Senior Equipment Staff Officer [*Air Force British*] ... SESO
Senior Evaluator (MCD) ... SEVAL
Senior Executive Leadership Program [*Australia*] ... SELP
Senior Executive/Management Development Plan (DNAB) ... SEMDP
Senior Executive Officer [*Civil Service*] [*British*] ... SEO
Senior Executive Service [*Civil Service*] ... SES
Senior Executive Staff (AAGC) ... SES
Senior Executives Association (EA) ... SEA
Senior Experimental Officer [*Also, SExO, SXO*] [*Ministry of Agriculture, Fisheries, and Food*] [*British*] ... SEO
Senior Experimental Officer [*Also, SEO, SXO*] [*Ministry of Agriculture, Fisheries, and Food*] [*British*] ... SExO
Senior Experimental Officer [*Also, SEO, SExO*] [*Ministry of Agriculture, Fisheries, and Food*] [*British*] ... SXO
Senior Explosive Ordnance Disposal Badge [*Military decoration*] (GFGA) ... SREODB
Senior Fellow ... SF
Senior Fellow of the Institute of Energy [*British*] (DBQ) ... SFInstE
Senior Fellow of the Institute of Fuel [*British*] (DI) ... SFInstF
Senior Fellow, Trinity College, Dublin (ROG) ... SFTCD
Senior Field Service Representative [*DoD*] ... SFSR
Senior Firefighter [*Australia*] ... SFF
Senior Flag Officer [*British military*] (DMA) ... SFO
Senior Flight Surgeon [*Army*] (AABC) ... SFS
Senior Flight Surgeon Badge [*Military decoration*] (GFGA) ... SRFLSBAD
Senior Flight Surgeon Badge [*Military decoration*] (AABC) ... SrFltSurgBad
Senior Functional Policy Official (AAGC) ... SFPO
Senior Gleaners (EA) ... SG
Senior Grade ... SG
Senior Grand Deacon [*Freemasonry*] ... SGD
Senior Grand Warden [*Freemasonry*] ... SGW
Senior Health Insurance Information Program ... SHIIP
Senior High Assessment of Reading Performance [*Educational test*] ... SHARP
Senior High Income Portfolio [*NYSE symbol*] (SPSG) ... ARK
Senior High Income Portfolio [*Associated Press*] (SAG) ... SenHgh
Senior High Income Portfolio II [*NYSE symbol*] (SPSG) ... SAL
Senior High Income Portfolio II [*Associated Press*] (SAG) ... SenHgh2

Senior High School .... SHS
Senior Hospital Medical Officer [*British*] .... SHMO
Senior House Officer [*British*] .... SHO
Senior Hunter [*Purebred canine award*] .... SH
Senior Independent Pioneer [*Lifestyle classification*] .... Sippy
Senior Industrial Development Field Adviser [*United Nations*] .... SIDFA
Senior Information Officer (DCTA) .... SIO
Senior Information Technology Officer .... SITO
Senior Instructor Operator [*Military*] (INF) .... SIO
Senior Intelligence Committee (DOMA) .... SIC
Senior Intelligence Officer (MCD) .... SIO
Senior Intelligence Service [*CIA personnel*] .... SIS
Senior Intensified Program [*Education*] .... SIP
Senior Interagency Group [*Federal government*] .... SIG
Senior Interagency Group (Space) .... SIGSPACE
Senior Interdepartmental Group [*Department of State*] .... SIG
Senior Interdepartmental Group / Interdepartmental Regional Group (DNAB) .... SIG/IRG
Senior International Joint Intelligence Course (MCD) .... SIJIC
Senior Interservice Control Board (DNAB) .... SICB
Senior Level Management .... SLM
Senior Life Saving [*Red Cross*] .... Sr LS
Senior Logistics Aviation Representative (MCD) .... SLAR
Senior Logistics Readiness Review Board [*Fort Lewis*] (MCD) .... SLRRB
Senior Magistrate .... SM
Senior Maintenance Rating [*British military*] (DMA) .... SMR
Senior Management Committee (AIE) .... SMC
Senior Management Forum [*Information Industry Association*] .... SMF
Senior Management Team (AIE) .... SMT
Senior Manager .... SM
Senior Marine Advisor .... SMA
Senior Marketing Officers Research Group [*LIMRA*] .... SMORG
Senior Marketing Officers Seminar [*LIMRA*] .... SMOS
Senior Master Sergeant [*Air Force*] E8
Senior Master Sergeant (MCD) .... SMG
Senior Master Sergeant .... SMSGT
Senior Mechanical Transport Officer [*British military*] (DMA) .... SMTO
Senior Medical Consultant .... SMC
Senior Medical Investigator .... SMI
Senior Medical Officer [*Military*] (DNAB) .... SENMEDO
Senior Medical Officer [*Military*] .... SMO
Senior Medical Officer of Health [*British*] (DAVI) .... SMOH
Senior Medical Resident (DAVI) .... SMR
Senior Medical Student (DAVI) .... SMS
Senior Medical Technician .... SMT
Senior Member (DNAB) .... SENMEM
Senior Member (DNAB) .... SRMBR
Senior Member of Institute of Electrical and Electronic Engineers .... SMIEEE
Senior Member of the Institution of Radio Engineers .... SMIRE
Senior Military Attache .... SMA
Senior Military Government Officer [*World War II*] .... SMGO
Senior Military Liaison Officer .... SMLO
Senior Mission Controller (MCD) .... SMC
Senior National Representatives SONAR [*Four Power Army*] (MCD) .... SNR
Senior NATO Logistician Conference (NATG) .... SNLC
Senior Naval Aviator (NVT) .... SENAV
Senior Naval Aviator .... SENAVAV
Senior Naval Aviator Present .... SNAP
Senior Naval Member .... SNM
Senior Naval Officer .... SNO
Senior Naval Officer Adriatic [*British*] .... SNOAD
Senior Naval Officer, Landings [*British*] .... SNOL
Senior Naval Officer, Military Airlift Command (MCD) .... SENAVOMAC
Senior Naval Officer on Board .... SNOB
Senior Naval Officer, Persian Gulf [*British military*] (DMA) .... SNOPG
Senior Naval Officer Present .... SNOP
Senior Naval Officer, West Indies [*British*] .... SNOWI
Senior Navigation Officer [*Air Force British*] .... SNO
Senior Navigator [*Air Force*] .... SN
Senior Noncommissioned Officer .... SNCO
Senior Noncommissioned Officer Course .... SNCOC
Senior Nursing Officer [*British*] .... SNO
Senior Nursing Sister [*Navy British*] .... SNS
Senior Officer [*Military, police*] .... SO
Senior Officer Afloat [*Navy Canada*] .... CANCOMFLT
Senior Officer Afloat Atlantic [*Navy Canada*] .... CANCOMFLTLANT
Senior Officer Afloat Pacific [*Navy Canada*] .... CANCOMFLTPAC
Senior Officer Assault Ships and Craft (India) [*British*] .... SOASC(I)
Senior Officer [*or Officer in Charge*] **at ____** [*Navy Canada*] .... CANAVCHARGE
Senior Officer Escort [*British military*] (DMA) .... SOE
Senior Officer Executive Management Course [*Naval War College*] .... SOEMC
Senior Officer Legal Orientation (MCD) .... SOLO
Senior Officer Logistics Management Course [*Military*] (INF) .... SOLMC
Senior Officer Management Office [*Army*] (INF) .... SOMO
Senior Officer, Minesweepers [*British military*] (DMA) .... SOMS
Senior Officer Present .... SOP
Senior Officer Present Afloat [*Navy*] .... SOPA
Senior Officer Present (Ashore) [*Navy*] .... SOP(A)
Senior Officer Present, United States Navy .... SOPUS
Senior Officer Present, United States Navy (SAA) .... SOPUSN
Senior Officer Preventive Logistics Course (MCD) .... SOPLC
Senior Officer Refresher Training .... SORT
Senior Officer Reserve Fleet East Coast [*Navy Canada*] .... CANRESLANT
Senior Officer Reserve Fleet West Coast [*Navy Canada*] .... CANRESPAC
Senior Officer, Royal Naval Establishment (India) [*British World War II*] .... SORNE(I)
Senior Officer Service .... SOS
Senior Officer Structure .... SOS
Senior Officers Materiel Review Board [*Army*] (AABC) .... SOMRB
Senior Officers' Quarters .... SOQ
Senior Officers' War Course [*British*] .... SOWC
Senior Officials Group on IT [*Information Technologies*] **Standardisation** [*British*] .... SOGITS
Senior Officials Group on Telecommunications (OSI) .... SOG
Senior Operator License [*Nuclear energy*] (NRCH) .... SOL
Senior Opportunities and Services [*OEO*] .... SOS
Senior Ordnance Mechanical Engineer [*British military*] (DMA) .... SOME
Senior Parachutist Badge [*Military decoration*] (GFGA) .... SPRCHTB
Senior Parachutist Badge [*Military decoration*] .... SRPARABAD
Senior Parachutist Badge [*Military decoration*] .... SrPrchtBad
Senior Partner .... SP
Senior Patrol Inspection [*Immigration and Naturalization Service*] .... SPI
Senior Performance Review Board (MHDB) .... SPRB
Senior Personnel Staff Officer [*Air Force British*] .... SPSO
Senior Physical Training Instructor [*British military*] (DMA) .... SPTI
Senior Pilot [*Air Force*] .... SP
Senior Plan Network [*Information service or system*] (HCT) .... SPN
Senior Policy Group for Canadian Production Sharing .... SPGCPS
Senior Principal Medical Officer [*British*] (DI) .... SPMO
Senior Principal Scientific Officer [*Ministry of Agriculture, Fisheries, and Food*] [*British*] .... SPSO
Senior Private Secretary .... SPS
Senior Project Engineer .... SPE
Senior Project Manager .... SPM
Senior Puisne Judge [*British*] (ILCA) .... SPJ
Senior Quarters Officer [*British military*] (DMA) .... SQO
Senior Radio Installation and Manufacture Officer (IAA) .... SRIMO
Senior Range Officer .... SRO
Senior Ranking Officer [*Army*] (ADDR) .... SRO
Senior Rater Potential Evaluation [*Army*] .... SRPE
Senior Reactor Operator [*Nuclear energy*] (NRCH) .... SRO
Senior Real Estate Analyst [*Society of Real Estate Appraisers*] [*Designation awarded by*] .... SREA
Senior Real Property Appraiser [*Society of Real Estate Appraisers*] [*Designation awarded by*] .... SRPA
Senior Registered Options Principal [*Investment term*] .... SROP
Senior Registrar .... SR
Senior Research Officer [*Ministry of Agriculture, Fisheries, and Food*] [*British*] .... SRO
Senior Reserve Officers' Training Corps [*Military*] (AABC) .... SROTC
Senior Resident Inspector [*Nuclear energy*] (NRCH) .... SRI
Senior Residential Appraiser [*Society of Real Estate Appraisers*] [*Designation awarded by*] .... SRA
Senior Review Board .... SRB
Senior Reviewer .... SR
Senior Royal Air Force Officer [*British military*] (DMA) .... SRAFO
Senior Royal Canadian Air Force Liaison Officer, St. Johns, Newfoundland, Canada .... CANAIRNEW
Senior Safety Officer [*Navy*] (CAAL) .... SSO
Senior Savers Guide Publishing, Inc. [*Vancouver Stock Exchange symbol*] .... SSG
Senior Scholars (EA) .... SS
Senior Scientific Assistant [*Ministry of Agriculture, Fisheries, and Food*] [*British*] .... SSA
Senior Scientific Officer [*Ministry of Agriculture, Fisheries, and Food*] [*British*] .... SSO
Senior Scientist on Board [*Navy*] .... SSOB
Senior Secondary Headmasters' Association [*British*] .... SSHMA
Senior Security [*Investment term*] .... SS
Senior Security Network (EA) .... SSN
Senior Service College [*Army*] (AABC) .... SSC
Senior Service College Fellowship Program [*Army*] (RDA) .... SSCFP
Senior Service School [*Military*] (AFM) .... SSS
Senior Social Worker (ADA) .... SSW
Senior South African Individual Scale [*Intelligence test*] .... SSAIS
Senior Staff Officer [*Military British*] .... SSO
Senior Staff Officer for Civil Affairs [*British World War II*] .... SSOCA
Senior Staff Technical Representative (MCD) .... SSTR
Senior Strategic Income Fund [*Associated Press*] (SAG) .... SenrStrat
Senior Strategic Income Fund [*NYSE symbol*] (SAG) .... SSN
Senior Supply Officer [*Military British*] .... SSO
Senior Teacher (ADA) .... ST
Senior Technical Officer (WDAA) .... STO
Senior Technical Representative .... STR
Senior Technical Staff Officer [*British*] .... STSO
Senior Technician of the Welding Institute [*British*] (DBQ) .... SenTechWeldI
Senior Test Laboratory Engineer (IAA) .... STLE
Senior Tour Players Dev Wrrt [*NASDAQ symbol*] (TTSB) .... SRTRW
Senior Tour Players Development [*Associated Press*] (SAG) .... SeniorTP
Senior Tour Players Development [*Associated Press*] (SAG) .... SenTP
Senior Tour Players Development [*NASDAQ symbol*] (SAG) .... SRTR
Senior Tour Players Dvlmt [*NASDAQ symbol*] (TTSB) .... SRTR
Senior Training Corps [*British*] .... STC
Senior Training Officer .... STO
Senior Under-Officer [*Royal Military Academy*] [*British*] (ROG) .... SUO
Senior United Kingdom Liaison Officer [*Later, BJSM*] [*British*] .... SUKLO
Senior United States Liaison Officer [*National Security Agency*] .... SUSLO
Senior United States Military Observer Palestine .... SUSMOP
Senior United States Naval Officer .... SUSNO

Senior United States Naval Officer, Commander Allied Naval Forces, Baltic Approaches (DNAB) ... SENUSNAVOFFNAVBALTAP
Senior United States Representative to Defense Production Board [*NATO*] (NATG) ... SUSREP
Senior Veterinary Officer [*British military*] (DMA) ... SVO
Senior Vice President ... SVP
Senior Warden [*Freemasonry*] ... SW
Senior Warrant Officer [*British*] (DI) ... SenWO
Senior Watch Officer [*Navy*] (NVT) ... SWO
Senior Weapon Director [*Air Force*] ... SWD
Senior Wolf [*An accomplished philanderer*] [*Slang*] ... SW
Senior Woodward [*Ancient Order of Foresters*] ... SW
Senior Year Electro-optical Reconnaissance System [*Air Force*] (DOMA) ... SYERS
Senior-Reliability Engineer (IAA) ... SRE
Seniors Cooperative Alert Network [*An association*] (EA) ... SCAN
Senlac Resources, Inc. [*Toronto Stock Exchange symbol*] ... SEN
Senn d'Or [*Vancouver Stock Exchange symbol*] ... SDJ
Sennacieca Asocio Tutmonda [*Nationless Worldwide Association*] (EAIO) ... SAT
Sennae [*Of Senna*] [*Pharmacy*] (ROG) ... SEN
Sennaherib (BJA) ... Senn
Sennar [*Sudan*] [*ICAO location identifier*] (ICLI) ... HSNR
Senneterre, PQ [*FM radio station call letters*] ... CIBO
Seno [*Laos*] [*Airport symbol*] (AD) ... SND
Senor [*Mister*] [*Spanish*] ... S
Senor [*Mister*] [*Spanish*] ... SNR
Senor [*Mister*] [*Spanish*] ... SR
Senora [*Mrs.*] [*Spanish*] ... SNRA
Senores [*Sirs, Gentlemen*] [*Spanish*] ... SRES
Senorita [*Miss*] [*Spanish*] ... Srita
Senorita [*Miss*] [*Spanish*] ... SRTA
Sensat Technologies Ltd. [*Vancouver Stock Exchange symbol*] ... SSA
, Sensation [*or Musculatory*] [*or Sensory Orthopedics and physical therapy*] (DAVI) ... CMS
Sensation [*Psychology*] ... S
Sensation [*Unit*] (DAVI) ... SA
Sensation Level [*Audiometry*] ... SL
Sensation of Transcendence ... SOT
Sensation Units ... SU
Sensation-Intuition [*Jungian psychology*] ... S-I
Sense (IAA) ... SEN
Sense Amplifier ... SA
Sense Amplifier (NITA) ... SAMP
Sense Amplifier Blocking Oscillator ... SABO
Sense and Destroy Armor [*Army*] (RDA) ... SADARM
Sense [*or Search*] **and Destroy Armor Munition** ... SADARM
Sense and Sensibility [*Novel by Jane Austen*] ... S & S
Sense Byte [*Computer science*] (IAA) ... SB
Sense Device Status Word ... SDSW
Sense Indicator (IAA) ... SI
Sense Light Test (SAA) ... SLT
Sense Lights On (SAA) ... SLN
Sense Line Register ... SLR
Sense of Humor Failure [*British Slang*] ... SOHF
Sense Printer ... SPR
Sense Printer Test (SAA) ... SPT
Sense Punch [*Computer science*] (IAA) ... SPU
Sense Switch [*Military*] (AFIT) ... SSW
Sensibility Reciprocal (WGA) ... SR
Sensible Atmosphere (SAA) ... SA
Sensible Heat Factor (IAA) ... SHF
Sensible Policy in Information Resources and Information Technology [*Defunct*] (EA) ... SPIRIT
Sensing, Identifying, Predicting, Deciding, and Executing ... SIPDE
Sensing, Identifying, Deciding, Predicting, and Executing ... SIDPE
Sensing with Active Microwave ... SAM
Sensitive ... SEN
Sensitive (MSA) ... SENS
Sensitive Acoustic Detection Equipment (PDAA) ... SADE
Sensitive Activity Vulnerability Estimate ... SAVE
Sensitive Command Network ... SCN
Sensitive Command Network/Sensitive Information Network (CET) ... SCN/SIN
Sensitive Compartmented Information [*Military*] ... SCI
Sensitive High Mass Resolution Ion Microprobe ... SHRIMP
Sensitive Information (MCD) ... SI
Sensitive Information Network ... SIN
Sensitive New Age Guy ... SNAG
Sensitive New-Age Guy ... SNAG
Sensitive Nuclear Material (NUCP) ... SNM
Sensitive Projects and Installation List (MCD) ... SPIL
Sensitive Thrust Stand System ... STSS
Sensitive Wildlife Information System [*Army*] (IID) ... SWIS
Sensitive-Membrane-Antigen-Rapid-Test ... SMART
Sensitivity (DEN) ... S
Sensitivity (IAA) ... SENS
Sensitivity Prediction from the Acoustic Reflex [*Audiometry*] ... SPAR
Sensitivity Ratio ... SR
Sensitivity Response [*Cell*] [*Radiology*] ... SR
Sensitivity Temperature Error Program (MCD) ... STEP
Sensitivity Training ... ST
Sensitivity Training Impact Model ... STIM
Sensitivity-of-Method [*FDA*] ... SOM
Sensitivity-Time Control [*RADAR*] ... STC
Sensitization Response ... SR
Sensitization Test ... STT
Sensitized (MSA) ... SNTZD
Sensitized Activated ... SA
Sensitized Human Cell (PDAA) ... SHC
Sensitized Material Print (MSA) ... SMP
Sensitized Room Temperature Phosphorescence ... SRTP
Sensitized Stainless Steel (NRCH) ... SSS
Sensitized-Erythrocyte-Lysis (PDAA) ... SEL
Sensitizing (MSA) ... SNTZG
Sensomatic Elect [*NYSE symbol*] (TTSB) ... SRM
Sensor (AAG) ... SEN
Sensor [*Automotive engineering*] ... SENS
Sensor (AAG) ... SNSR
Sensor [*Genetics*] ... SS
Sensor Accuracy Check Site (MCD) ... SACS
Sensor Analog Relay System ... SARS
Sensor and Effector (SSD) ... S & E
Sensor and Engagement Controller [*Army*] ... SEC
Sensor and Source ... SAS
Sensor Based System (BUR) ... SBS
Sensor Board Control Unit (NITA) ... SBCU
Sensor Communication and Display System (MCD) ... SCDS
Sensor Control and Management Platoon [*Marine Corps*] ... SCAMP
Sensor Control Anti-Anti-Radiation Missile RADAR Evaluation (PDAA) ... SCARE
Sensor Control/Data Display Set (MCD) ... SC/DDS
Sensor Control Unit (MCD) ... SCU
Sensor Controller (MCD) ... S/C
Sensor Controller Alert Network ... SCAN
Sensor Data Processing Facility (MCD) ... SDPF
Sensor Data Processing Laboratory (MCD) ... SDPL
Sensor Data Record [*For spacecraft*] ... SDR
Sensor Equivalent Visibility ... SEV
Sensor Evolutionary Development (MCD) ... SED
Sensor Experimental Evaluation and Review [*Strategic Defense Initiative*] ... SEER
Sensor for Airborne Terrain Analysis ... SATAN
Sensor Fuzed Weapon ... SFW
Sensor Image Simulator (MCD) ... SIS
Sensor Integration and Display Sharing [*Military*] (CAAL) ... SIADS
Sensor Integration System (DWSG) ... SIS
Sensor Interface Assembly ... SIA
Sensor Interface Data System [*Military*] (CAAL) ... SIDS
Sensor Interface Electronics Assembly (MCD) ... SIEA
Sensor Monitoring Set (MCD) ... SMS
Sensor of Tail Region Emitters (MCD) ... SENTRE
Sensor Operation Room (AFM) ... SOR
Sensor Operator (MCD) ... SENSO
Sensor Payload Vehicle ... SPV
Sensor Processing Subsystem (GAVI) ... SPS
Sensor Processor (BUR) ... SP
Sensor Readout Unit (MCD) ... SRU
Sensor Referenced and Computer Controlled [*For remote manipulators*] ... SRCC
Sensor Reporting Post ... SRP
Sensor Response Model ... SRM
Sensor Return [*Automotive engineering*] ... SRTN
Sensor Select Panel (MCD) ... SSP
Sensor Signal Conditioner ... SSC
Sensor Simulator Unit ... SSU
Sensor Supervisor [*Military*] (CAAL) ... SS
Sensor System Microwave/Imager ... SSM/I
Sensor System Microwave/Temperature ... SSM/T
Sensor System Simulation ... SENSIM
Sensor, Tank, Off-Route Mine (MCD) ... STORM
Sensor Technology as Applied to the Marine Corps ... STEAM
Sensor Upgrade and Refurbishment Effort [*Marine Corps*] (MCD) ... SURE
Sensor Weapons Control and Command ... SEWACO
Sensor-Based Control Adapter ... SBCA
Sensor-Based Control Unit [*Computer science*] ... SBCU
Sensorimotor Rhythm [*Neurophysiology*] ... SMR
Sensorineural Acuity Level [*Medicine*] ... SAL
Sensorineural Hearing Loss [*Medicine*] ... SHL
Sensorineural Hearing Loss [*Medicine*] (MAE) ... SNHL
Sensorium [*Neurology*] (DAVI) ... SENS
Sensormatic Canada Ltd. [*Toronto Stock Exchange symbol*] ... SEC
Sensormatic Electronics Corp. [*Associated Press*] (SAG) ... Sensormt
Sensor-Pointing Platform (SSD) ... SPP
Sensor-Referenced Positioning System ... SRPS
Sensors and Control Systems Institute [*Beltsville, MD*] [*Department of Agriculture*] (GRD) ... SCSI
Sensorstat System [*Vancouver Stock Exchange symbol*] ... SNS
Sensory ... SENS
Sensory ... SNSRY
Sensory Aids Evaluation and Development Center [*MIT*] ... SAEDE
Sensory Communication Research Laboratory [*Gallaudet College*] [*Research center*] (RCD) ... SCRL
Sensory Deprivation Syndrome [*Medicine*] ... SDS
Sensory Detection Method [*for measuring blood pressure*] ... SDM
Sensory Distal Latency [*Medicine*] ... SDL
Sensory Evaluation Test [*Army*] ... SET
Sensory Evoked Potential [*Neurophysiology*] ... SEP
Sensory Evoked Response [*Medicine*] (DMAA) ... SER
Sensory Integration ... SI
Sensory Integration and Praxis Test [*Occupational therapy*] ... SIPT
Sensory Integration Special Interest Section [*American Occupational Therapy Association*] ... SISS
Sensory Integration Training ... SIT

Sensory Isolation Experiment (SAA) ... SIE
Sensory Mother Cell [*Genetics*] ... SMC
Sensory Nerve Action Potential [*Neurophysiology*] ... SNAP
Sensory Nerve Conduction Velocity [*Neurology*] (DAVI) ... SNCV
Sensory Neuron [*Anatomy*] (DAVI) ... SN
Sensory Organ [*Anatomy*] ... SO
Sensory Organ Mother Cell [*Genetics*] ... SMC
Sensory Organ Precursor [*Cytology*] ... SOP
Sensory Organ Precursor [*Biochemistry*] ... SOP
Sensory Rhodopsin [*Biochemistry*] ... SR
Sensory Urgency [*Neurology*] (DAVI) ... SU
Sensory-Afferent/Motor-Efferent [*Neurology*] ... SAME
Sensory-to-Motor [*Ratio*] ... S/M
Sensu Lato [*In a Wide Sense*] [*Latin*] ... s lat
Sensu Lato [*In a Broad Sense*] [*Latin*] ... SL
Sensu Stricto [*In a Narrow Sense*] [*Latin*] (MAE) ... s str
Sensu Stricto [*In a Narrow Sense*] [*Latin*] ... SS
Sent to Printer [*Publishing*] ... STP
Sent to Typesetter [*Publishing*] ... STT
Sent Wrong [*i.e., misdirected*] ... SW
SENTEL Corp. [*FAA designator*] (FAAC) ... SEL
Sentence [*Linguistics*] ... S
Sentence (AABC) ... SENT
Sentence Appraiser and Diagrammer ... SAD
Sentence Combining Exercise [*Education*] (EDAC) ... SCE
Sentence Completion Technique [*or Test*] ... SCT
Sentence Imitation Screening Test [*Speech and language test*] ... SIST
Sentence Modifier [*Linguistics*] ... SM
Sentence Suspended ... SS
Sentence Synthesizing Program ... SSP
Sentence to be Confined [*Navy*] (DNAB) ... SENT CONF
Sentence to Lose Pay [*Navy*] (DNAB) ... SENT LP
Sentenced (WGA) ... SENTD
[*The*] **Sentencing Project** (EA) ... TSP
Sentenza [*Decision, Judgment*] [*Italian*] (ILCA) ... Sent
Sentenza della Corte d'Assise [*Decision of the Assize Court*] [*Italian*] (ILCA) ... C Ass
Sentenza della Corte di Appello [*Decision of the Court of Appeal*] [*Italian*] (ILCA) ... C App
Sentenza della Corte Suprema di Cassazione [*Decision or Judgment of the Supreme Court of Appeals*] [*Italian*] (ILCA) ... Cass
Sentenza della Sezione Civile della Corte di Cassazione [*Decision of the Court of Appeal, Civil Division*] [*Italian*] (ILCA) ... Cass Civ
Sentenza della Sezione Penale della Corte di Cassazione [*Decision of the Court of Appeal, Criminal Division*] [*Italian*] (ILCA) ... Cass Pen
Senterpartiet [*Center Party*] [*Norway Political party*] (PPE) ... Sp
Sentex Sensing Technologies [*NASDAQ symbol*] (TTSB) ... SENS
Sentex Sensing Technologies [*Associated Press*] (SAG) ... Sentex
Sentex Sensing Technology, Inc. [*Ridgefield, NJ*] [*NASDAQ symbol*] (NQ) ... SENS
Sentinel Event Notification System for Occupational Risks [*Medicine*] ... SENSOR
Sentinel Ledger, Ocean City, NJ [*Library symbol Library of Congress*] (LCLS) ... NjOcS
Sentinel Logistics Command ... SENLOG
Sentinel on Station ... SOS
Sentinel Operating System (IEEE) ... SENTOS
Sentinel Project Office [*Army*] (MCD) ... SENPO
Sentinel Publishing Co., East Brunswick, NJ [*Library symbol Library of Congress*] (LCLS) ... NjEbS
Sentinel System Evaluation Agency [*DoD*] ... SENSEA
Sentinel System Evaluation Agency [*DoD*] ... SSEA
Sentinel Systems Command [*Army*] (MCD) ... SENSCOM
Sentinel Systems Office [*Military*] ... SENSO
Sentinel-Spartan System (MCD) ... SSS
Sento Technical Innovations Corp. [*Associated Press*] (SAG) ... SentoTch
Sento Technical Innovations Corp. [*NASDAQ symbol*] (SAG) ... SNTO
Sentral Organisasi Buruh Pantjasila [*Central Organization of Pantjasila Labor*] [*Indonesia*] ... SOBP
Sentral Organisasi Karyawan Sosialis Indonesia [*Central Organization of Indonesian Socialist Workers*] ... SOKSI
Sentry Dog Patrol (AFM) ... SDP
SENTRY [*Survey Entry*] **Hazard Control** ... SHC
Sentry Interceptor Subsystem Contractor [*DoD*] ... SISC
SENTRY [*Survey Entry*] **Interceptor System Simulator** ... SIS-S
SENTRY [*Survey Entry*] **Project Office** ... SPO
Sentry Resources Corp. [*Formerly, Sentry Oil & Gas*] [*Vancouver Stock Exchange symbol*] ... SOX
Senza [*Without*] [*Music*] ... S
Senza [*Without*] [*Music*] ... SEN
Senza Interruzione [*Without Interruption or Pause*] [*Music*] ... S INT
Senza Interruzione [*Without Interruption or Pause*] [*Music*] (ROG) ... S INTER
Senza Pedale [*Without Pedals*] [*Music*] ... SP
Senza Sordini [*Without Mutes*] [*Music*] ... S SORD
Senza Sordini [*Without Mutes*] [*Music*] ... SS
Senza Tempo [*Without Regard to Time*] [*Music*] ... ST
Senzan [*Japan*] [*Seismograph station code, US Geological Survey*] (SEIS) ... SNZ
Seo De Urgel [*Spain ICAO location identifier*] (ICLI) ... LESU
Seo De Urgel [*Spain*] [*Airport symbol*] (OAG) ... LEU
Seosan [*South Korea ICAO location identifier*] (ICLI) ... RKTM
Seoul [*South Korea*] [*Airport symbol*] (OAG) ... SEL
Seoul [*Keizyo*] [*South Korea*] [*Seismograph station code, US Geological Survey*] (SEIS) ... SEO
Seoul City [*South Korea ICAO location identifier*] (ICLI) ... RKSL
Seoul East [*Sinchonri*] [*South Korea ICAO location identifier*] (ICLI) ... RKSM
Seoul/Kimpo International [*South Korea ICAO location identifier*] (ICLI) ... RKSS
Seoul Law Journal [*A publication*] (DLA) ... Seoul LJ
Seoul National University [*Korea*] ... SNU
Seoul National University, Seoul, Korea [*Library symbol Library of Congress*] (LCLS) ... KoSNU
Seoul/Yungsan [*South Korea ICAO location identifier*] (ICLI) ... RKSY
Sepal [*Botany*] (WGA) ... SEP
Separable Costs-Remaining Benefits (PDAA) ... SC-RB
Separat-Abdruck (BJA) ... SA
Separate (AFM) ... SEP
Separate (WDMC) ... sep
Separate (ROG) ... SEPE
Separate ... SEPT
Separate Absorption and Multiplication Region Avalanche Photodiode ... SAM-APD
Separate Absorption, Grading, and Multiplication Layers [*Semiconductor technology*] ... SAGM
Separate Access Landing System [*Aviation*] (DA) ... SALS
Separate Administrative Unit [*Work Incentive Program*] ... SAU
Separate Audio Program [*Television broadcasting*] ... SAP
Separate Battery [*Army*] ... SEP Btry
Separate Bias, Common Control ... SBCC
Separate Bias, Single Control ... SBSC
Separate Channel Signalling (NITA) ... SCS
Separate Correspondence (MCD) ... SEPCOR
Separate Cover ... SC
Separate Effects and Systems Effects Tests [*Nuclear energy*] (NRCH) ... SEASET
Separate Element Pricing (IAA) ... SP
Separate Engineering Control Air Limits [*Environmental science*] ... SECAL
Separate Index Access Method [*Computer science*] (BUR) ... SIAM
Separate Infantry Brigade Light (INF) ... SIBL
Separate Ion Formation and Drift ... SIFAD
Separate Lead [*Cables*] ... SL
Separate Magnetic (NTCM) ... SEPMAG
Separate Operating Agency [*Air Force*] (AFM) ... SOA
Separate Partition Option ... SPO
Separate Parts List (MSA) ... SPL
Separate Rations [*Military*] ... SR
Separate Reporting Activities [*Army*] ... SRA
Separate Sampling and Excitation Analysis [*Spectroscopy*] ... SSEA
Separate Superheater Reactor [*Nuclear energy*] ... SSR
Separate Telegram ... SEPTEL
Separate Track and Illumination RADAR [*Military*] (CAAL) ... STIR
Separate Trading of Registered Interest and Principal of Securities [*Investment term*] ... STRIPS
Separate Trading of Registered Interest and Principal of Securities (TDOB) ... STRIPS
Separate Transporter and Mobile Launcher ... STML
Separated ... SEPD
Separated ... SEPTD
Separated Associated Fluid Interaction Model [*Chemical engineering*] ... SAFIM
Separated Atom [*Atomic physics*] ... SA
Separated Career Employee ... SCE
Separated Orbit Cyclotron (IEEE) ... SOC
Separated Statistical Ensemble [*Physical chemistry*] ... SSE
Separated, Widowed, or Divorced [*New York City association*] ... SWORD
Separately Binned ... SB
Separating ... SEPG
Separating ... SEPTG
Separation ... S
Separation (IAA) ... SEP
Separation (WDMC) ... sep
Separation (ROG) ... SEPARON
Separation (AAG) ... SEPN
Separation and Control of Aircraft Using Nonsynchronous Techniques [*Collision avoidance*] [*RCA*] ... SECANT
Separation by Implantation of Oxygen [*Semiconductor technology*] ... SIMOX
Separation Center [*Navy*] ... SEPCEN
Separation Designation Number ... SDN
Separation Factor [*Chemical analysis*] ... SF
Separation Instrument Package [*NASA*] (MCD) ... SIP
Separation Mechanism Subsystem [*NASA*] (NASA) ... SMS
Separation Monitor and Control System [*NASA*] (MCD) ... SMCS
Separation Monitoring Control Unit [*NASA*] (MCD) ... SMCU
Separation Parameter ... SEP
Separation Processing [*Military*] ... SEPROS
Separation Program Designator [*Military*] (AABC) ... SPD
Separation Program Number [*DoD*] (VNW) ... SPIN
Separation Program Number [*Military*] ... SPN
Separation, Quality Analysis of RADAR Data (SAA) ... SQORD
Separation Questionnaire [*Military*] (DNAB) ... SEPQUES
Separation Systems Division [*Energy Research and Development Administration*] ... SSD
Separation Test Vehicle ... STV
Separation Transfer Point [*Army*] (ADDR) ... STP
Separation Ullage ... SU
Separation-Initiated Timer ... SIT
Separative Work Unit [*Measure of uranium enrichment capability*] ... SWU
Separator ... SEPTR
Separator Assembly Fuel-Vacuum [*Automotive engineering*] ... SAFV
Separator for Heavy Ion Reaction Products ... SHIP
Separator-Key Generator-Recombiner (MCD) ... SKR
Separatum [*Separately*] [*Latin*] (MAE) ... separ
Sephardic [*Jews from Spain, Portugal, North Africa, and the Mediterranean*] (BJA) ... Seph

Sephardic House [An association] (EA) .... SH
Sephardic Jewish Brotherhood of America (EA) .... SJBA
Sepia [Stamp collecting] (ROG) .... SEP
Sepia (VRA) .... sep
Sepracor, Inc. [NASDAQ symbol] (SPSG) .... SEPR
Sepracor, Inc. [Associated Press] (SAG) .... Sepracr
Sepragen Cop. [NASDAQ symbol] (SAG) .... SPGNA
Sepragen Corp. [Associated Press] (SAG) .... Sepragn
Sepragen Corp. [Associated Press] (SAG) .... Sprgn
Sepragen Corp. 'A' [NASDAQ symbol] (TTSB) .... SPGNA
Sepragen Corp. Unit [NASDAQ symbol] (TTSB) .... SPGNU
Sepragen Corp. Wrrt'A' [NASDAQ symbol] (TTSB) .... SPGNW
Sepragen Corp. Wrrt'B' [NASDAQ symbol] (TTSB) .... SPGNZ
Septal Defect [Medicine] .... SD
Septem [Seven] [Latin] (MAE) .... sept
Septem Contra Thebas [of Aeschylus] [Classical studies] (OCD) .... Sept
September .... S
September (ADA) .... SE
September (AFM) .... SEP
September (EY) .... SEPT
September (ROG) .... SEPTR
September (CDAI) .... Spt
September and March [Denotes semiannual payments of interest or dividends in these months] [Business term] .... S & M
September Days Club (EA) .... SDC
September, December, March, and June [Denotes quarterly payments of interest or dividends in these months] [Business term] .... SDMJ
September Resources Ltd. [Vancouver Stock Exchange symbol] .... STB
Septic [Classified advertising] (ADA) .... SPT
Septic .... SPTC
Septic Inflammation [Medicine] .... SI
Septic Tank-Subsurface Absorption System .... ST-SAS
Septic Workup [Bacteriology] (DAVI) .... SWU
Sept-Iles [Quebec] [Seismograph station code, US Geological Survey] (SEIS) .... SIC
Sept-Iles [Canada] [Airport symbol] (OAG) .... YZV
Sept-Iles, PQ [FM radio station call letters] .... CBSI
Sept-Iles, PQ [Television station call letters] .... CBST
Sept-Iles, PQ [Television station call letters] .... CIVG
Sept-Iles, PQ [AM radio station call letters] .... CKCN
Sept-Iles, PQ [ICAO location identifier] (ICLI) .... CYZV
Septo-Optic Dysplasia [Medicine] (DMAA) .... SOD
Septuagint [Version of the Bible] LXX
Septuagint [Version of the Bible] .... SEP
Septuagint [Version of the Bible] (BJA) .... Sept
Septuagint and Cognate Studies (BJA) .... SCS
Septum [Anatomy] (DAVI) .... S
Septum [Medicine] (CPH) .... sept
Septum Pellucidum [Brain anatomy] .... SP
Septum-Equipped Programmable Injector [Gas chromatography] .... SPI
Septuple (MSA) .... SPT
Sepulchrum [Sepulchre] [Latin] .... S
Sepulot [Malaysia] [Airport symbol] (AD) .... SPE
Sepultus [Buried] [Latin] .... S
Sepultus [Buried] [Latin] (ROG) .... SEP
Sepultus [Buried] [Latin] .... SEPULT
Sequa $5cm Cv Pfd [NYSE symbol] (TTSB) .... SQAPr
Sequa Corp. [Associated Press] (SAG) .... Sequa
Sequa Corp. [Associated Press] (SAG) .... SequaA
Sequa Corp. [Associated Press] (SAG) .... SequaB
Sequa Corp. [NYSE symbol] (SPSG) .... SQA
Sequa Corp. 'B' [NYSE symbol] (TTSB) .... SQA.B
Sequa Corp. Cl'A' [NYSE symbol] (TTSB) .... SQA.A
Sequana Therapeutics [NASDAQ symbol] (TTSB) .... SQNA
Sequana Therapeutics, Inc. [Associated Press] (SAG) .... SequTh
Sequana Therapeutics, Inc. [NASDAQ symbol] (SAG) .... SQNA
Sequel .... SEQ
Sequel (WDMC) .... seq
Sequence (WDMC) .... seq
Sequence and Monitor (IAA) .... SAM
Sequence Chart Analyzer (IAA) .... SCA
Sequence Charts (AAG) .... SC
Sequence Checking Routine .... SCR
Sequence Checking Tape .... SCT
Sequence Coding and Search System .... SCSS
Sequence Coding System (IAA) .... SCS
Sequence Control Area [NASA] (KSC) .... SCA
Sequence Control Chart .... SCC
Sequence Control Number Register [Computer science] .... SCNR
Sequence Control System (KSC) .... SCS
Sequence Control Unit [Aerospace] (KSC) .... SCU
Sequence Controlled Calculator (IAA) .... SCC
Sequence Controller .... SC
Sequence Counter .... SC
Sequence Electronique Couleur avec Memoire [Color Sequence with Memory] [French color television system] .... SECAM
Sequence Event Diagram (DNAB) .... SED
Sequence Flash Lights [FAA] .... SFL
Sequence Flow [Tracing technique] .... SEFLO
Sequence for Opportunities and Negatives [Rand Corp.] .... SOON
Sequence History .... SH
Sequence Information Data .... SID
Sequence Initiate Update .... SIU
Sequence Line Number [Army] .... SLN
Sequence Milestone System .... SMS

Sequence Monitor .... SM
Sequence Number .... S/N
Sequence Number Indicator .... SNI
Sequence of Controls .... SOC
Sequence of Coverage and Speed (SAA) .... SCASP
Sequence of Events .... SE
Sequence of Events .... SOE
Sequence of Events Generator .... SEG
Sequence of Pulse Intervals .... SPI
Sequence Operated Lock (IAA) .... SOL
Sequence Parameter Checking (SAA) .... SPC
Sequence Programmer [Computer science] (AAG) .... SP
Sequence Recall [Neuropsychology test] .... SEQREC
Sequence Relay (KSC) .... SQR
Sequence Switch Driver .... SSD
Sequence Thin-Layer Chromatography .... STLC
Sequence Timer .... ST
Sequence-Control Register [Computer science] (EECA) .... SCR
Sequenced Flashing Lights .... SFR
Sequenced Flashing Lights [Aviation] (DA) .... SSAL
Sequenced Inventory of Communication Development (EDAC) .... SICD
Sequenced Inventory of Communicative Development [Speech and language therapy] (DAVI) .... SICD
Sequenced Packet Exchange [Telecommunications] (PCM) .... SPX
Sequenced Packet Protocol [Computer science] (PCM) .... SPP
Sequence-Independent Single Primer Amplification [Genetics] .... SISPA
Sequencer (IAA) .... SEQ
Sequencer (AAG) .... SEQR
Sequencer and Monitor (KSC) .... S & M
Sequencer Chassis .... SCH
Sequencer Control Assembly .... SCA
Sequencer-Iteration Control [Computer science] (MHDI) .... SEQ-IC
Sequence-Specific Oligonucleotide [Probe] [Medicine] (DMAA) .... SSO
Sequence-Tagged Connector [Genetics] .... STC
Sequence-Tagged Site [Genetics] .... STS
Sequencing and Command Systems Specialist [NASA] .... SCS
Sequencing Batch Reactor [Chemical engineering] .... SBR
Sequencing by Hybridization [Genetics] .... SBH
Sequency-Division Multiplexing (IEEE) .... SDM
Sequens [Sequence] [Latin] (AABC) .... SEQ
Sequens [Following] [Latin] .... SEQ
Sequent Computer Sys [NASDAQ symbol] (TTSB) .... SQNT
Sequent Computer Systems, Inc. [Associated Press] (SAG) .... Sequnt
Sequent Computer Systems, Inc. [NASDAQ symbol] (NQ) .... SQNT
Sequente [And in What Follows] [Latin] .... SEQ
Sequentes [or Sequentia] [The Following Plural form] [Latin] .... SEQQ
Sequenti Luce [The Following Day] [Latin] (ADA) .... SEQ LUCE
Sequentia [What Follows] [Latin] (ROG) .... SS
Sequential (IAA) .... SEQL
Sequential Access (IAA) .... SA
Sequential Access Memory [Computer science] (IEEE) .... SAM
Sequential Access Method [IBM Corp.] [Computer science] .... SAM
Sequential Action Flow Routine [Military British] .... SAFER
Sequential Analog-Digital Computer (DIT) .... SADC
Sequential Analysis for Force Development (MCD) .... SAFE
Sequential Analysis of Chemistry Constituents (DAVI) .... SAL
Sequential and Iterative Operation Unit X (IEEE) .... SIOUX
Sequential Assessment of Mathematics Inventory .... SAMI
Sequential Atrioventricular [Pacing] [Medicine] (DMAA) .... SAV
Sequential Automated .... SA
Sequential Automatic Recorder and Annunciator .... SARA
Sequential Boolean Analyzer (PDAA) .... SBA
Sequential Central Port Injection .... SCPI
Sequential Coding .... SECO
Sequential Collation [or Collection] of Ranges [Army] .... SECOR
Sequential Color and Memory (IAA) .... SECAM
Sequential Comparison Index [Measures effect of chemical pollution in lakes and streams] .... SCI
Sequential Compatibility Firing [Aerospace] .... SCF
Sequential Component Automatic Testing (MSA) .... SCAT
Sequential Control [Teletype] [Computer science] .... SECO
Sequential Control Counter [Computer science] (BUR) .... SCC
Sequential Control Guidance (KSC) .... SCG
Sequential Control Logic .... SCL
Sequential Controlled Automatic Transistor Start (NITA) .... SCATS
Sequential Correlation .... SQ
Sequential Correlation of Range (IAA) .... SECOR
Sequential Cosine Ranging [System] (MUGU) .... SECOR
Sequential Customer Order Processing Electronically .... SCOPE
Sequential Decision Making Device (IAA) .... SDMD
Sequential Degradation Analysis .... SDA
Sequential Detection of Emerging Competitive Target .... SDEC
Sequential Developmental Exercises [Occupational therapy] (DAVI) .... SEQ DEV EX
Sequential Deviation .... SDEV
Sequential Disk (IAA) .... SD
Sequential Electric Fuel Injection [Automotive engineering] .... SEFI
Sequential Elution Solvent Chromatography .... SESC
Sequential Emitter Coupled Logic (IAA) .... SECL
Sequential Encoder-Decoder (IAA) .... SECO
Sequential Environmental Stress .... SES
Sequential Events Control System [NASA] (KSC) .... SECS
Sequential Events Controller [NASA] (NASA) .... SEC
Sequential Events Recorder .... SER
Sequential Excitation Fluorescence [Aviation Navy] .... SEF
Sequential Explicit Stochastic Linear Programming [Computer science] .... SESLP

Sequential Filter Regeneration [*Automotive engineering*] .... SFR
Sequential Fuel Injection [*Automotive engineering*] .... SFI
Sequential Function Chart (ACII) .... SFC
Sequential Functional Analysis (IAA) .... SFA
Sequential Generalized Nonlinear Least Squares [*Statistics*] .... SGNLS
Sequential Headturn Test .... SHTT
Sequential Hemibody [*Irradiation*] [*Medicine*] (DMAA) .... SHB
Sequential Impaction Cascade Sieve Volumetric Air (MAE) .... SICSVA
Sequential Inference Machine [*Computer science*] .... SIM
Sequential Interval Timer .... SIT
Sequential Launch Adapter [*Missiles*] (RDA) .... SLA
Sequential Machine Controller [*Programming language*] [*1977-78*] (CSR) .... SMC
Sequential Mechanism for Automatic Recording and Testing .... SMART
Sequential Multiobjective Problem Solving .... SEMOPS
Sequential Multiple Analysis [*or Analyzer*] [*Clinical chemistry*] .... SMA
Sequential Multiple Analysis Plus Computer (PDAA) .... SMAC
Sequential Multiple Analyzer Computerized [*Laboratory science*] (DAVI) .... SMAC
Sequential Multipoint Injection [*Automotive engineering*] .... SMPI
Sequential Optimization (MCD) .... SEQOPT
Sequential Oral Contraceptive (HGAA) .... SOC
Sequential Partition System (IAA) .... SPS
Sequential Payload Delivery System (MCD) .... SPDS
Sequential Polling and Review of Interacting Teams of Experts (PDAA) .... SPRITE
Sequential Position and Covariance Estimation (IEEE) .... SPACE
Sequential Prime Implicant Form .... SPIF
Sequential Probability Ratio [*Statistics*] .... SPR
Sequential Probability Ratio Test [*Statistics*] .... SPRT
Sequential Processing Machine (DIT) .... SPM
Sequential Processor .... SP
Sequential Programmed Automatic Recording Transistor Analyzer .... SPARTA
Sequential Pulse [*Medicine*] (DAVI) .... SP
Sequential Pulse Counting [*Spectrometry*] .... SEQ
Sequential Quadrature Inband [*Television system*] (DEN) .... SEQUIN
Sequential Quadrature Inband [*Television system*] (IAA) .... SQIN
Sequential Range Policy (PDAA) .... SRP
Sequential Rough Handling (MCD) .... SRH
Sequential Scheduling System (IAA) .... SSS
Sequential Similarity Detection Algorithm .... SSDA
Sequential Single Frequency Code System [*Telecommunications*] (TEL) .... SSFC
Sequential Spectrometer Accessory [*Instrumentation*] .... SSA
Sequential Spot Jamming [*Military*] (CAAL) .... SSJ
Sequential Subsystem Controllers (MCD) .... SSC
Sequential Switch .... SS
Sequential Table Lookup .... STL
Sequential Test of Educational Programs (DMAA) .... STEP
Sequential Test of Educational Progress-Writing Test (EDAC) .... STEP-W
Sequential Test Plan Generator (PDAA) .... STPG
Sequential Tests of Educational Progress [*of ETS; given in 10th and 12th grades*] .... STEP
Sequential Thermal Anhysteric Magnetization [*Helical scan videotape duplicating system*] (NTCM) .... STAM
Sequential Ultrafiltration [*Nephrology*] (DAVI) .... SUF
Sequential Unconstrained Minimization Technique .... SUMT
Sequential Unmanned Scanning and Indicating Equipment (IAA) .... SUSIE
Sequential Variance .... SVAR
Sequential Weight Increasing Factor Technique (IAA) .... SWIFT
Sequentially Controlled Automatic Transmitter Start .... SCATS
Sequentially Operated Teletypewriter Universal Selector .... SOTUS
Sequentially Sampling Sediment Trap [*Marine science*] (OSRA) S3T
Sequentially Sampling Sediment Trap (USDC) S3T
Sequentially Timed Events Plotting [*In publication title, "Investigating Accidents with STEP"*] [*Marcel Decker, Inc.*] .... STEP
Sequentially Timed Events Process [*Engineering*] .... STEP
Sequential-Phase (CET) .... S-P
Sequentibus [*In the Following Places*] [*Latin*] (ADA) .... SEQQ
Sequentibus [*In the Following Places*] [*Latin*] .... SQQ
Sequestration [*Orthopedics*] (DAVI) .... seq
Sequestrum [*Medicine*] .... SEQ
Sequitur [*It Follows*] [*Latin*] .... SEQ
Sequitur [*It Follows*] [*Latin*] (WGA) .... sequ
Sequoia and Kings Canyon National Parks .... SEQU
Sequoia Resources Ltd. [*Vancouver Stock Exchange symbol*] .... SQR
Sequoia Systems [*NASDAQ symbol*] (TTSB) .... SEQS
Sequoia Systems, Inc. [*NASDAQ symbol*] (SAG) .... SEQS
Sequoia Systems, Inc. [*Associated Press*] (SAG) .... Sequoi
Sequoyah Nuclear Power Plant (NRCH) .... SNPP
Sequoyah Regional Library, Canton, GA [*Library symbol Library of Congress*] (LCLS) .... GCanS
SEQUUS Pharmaceuticals [*NASDAQ symbol*] (TTSB) .... SEQU
Sequus Pharmaceuticals, Inc. [*NASDAQ symbol*] (SAG) .... SEQU
Sequus Pharmaceuticals, Inc. [*Associated Press*] (SAG) .... Sequus
Seragen, Inc. [*Associated Press*] (SAG) .... Seragen
Seragen, Inc. [*NASDAQ symbol*] (SAG) .... SRGN
Seraph (VRA) .... srph
Seraphic Society for Vocations [*Defunct*] (EA) .... SSV
Serb Democratic Party [*Croatia*] [*Political party*] (EY) .... SDP
Serb National Federation (EA) .... SNF
Serber-Wilson Method [*Nuclear energy*] (NRCH) .... SWM
Serbia .... SERB
Serbian Democratic Party [*Bosnia-Herzegovina*] [*Political party*] (EY) .... SDP
Serbian National Defense Council (EA) .... SNDC
Serbian Radical Party [*Political party*] .... SRP
Serbian Renaissance Movement [*Political party*] (EY) .... SRM
Serbian Socialist Party [*Political party*] .... SSP
Serbian-American Bar Association (EA) .... SABA
Serbo-Croatian (Cyrillic) [*MARC language code Library of Congress*] (LCCP) .... scc
Serbo-Croatian (Roman) [*MARC language code Library of Congress*] (LCCP) .... scr
SERC Network (NITA) .... SERCNET
Serena Consolidated High School District 390, Serena, IL [*Library symbol Library of Congress*] (LCLS) .... ISerSD
Serendipitous Survey Catalog [*Infrared Astronomical Satellite*] [*Astronomy*] .... SSC
Serendipity Association (EA) .... SA
Serendipity Association for Research and Implementation of Holistic Health and World Peace (EA) .... SARIHHWP
Serenity, Tranquility, Peace [*Experimental hallucinogen developed by DOW Chemical Co.*] (IIA) .... STP
Serenje [*Zambia*] [*ICAO location identifier*] (ICLI) .... FLSE
Serenpet, Inc. [*Associated Press*] (SAG) .... Serenpet
Serenpet, Inc. [*Associated Press*] (SAG) .... Serenpt
Serenpet, Inc. [*AMEX symbol*] (SPSG) .... SRI
Serer [*MARC language code Library of Congress*] (LCCP) .... srr
Serge and Natalie Koussevitzky [*Acronym was name of summer home of Boston Symphony Orchestra conductor and his first wife*] .... SERANAK
Sergeant [*Air Force*] E4
Sergeant [*Army, Marine Corps*] E5
Sergeant .... SERG
Sergeant .... SERGT
Sergeant (WGA) .... SG
Sergeant (AABC) .... SGT
Sergeant .... SGT
Sergeant (ODBW) .... Sgt
Sergeant and Rawle's Pennsylvania Reports [*1824-28*] [*A publication*] (DLA) .... S & R
Sergeant and Rawle's Pennsylvania Reports [*A publication*] (DLA) .... Serg & R
Sergeant and Rawle's Pennsylvania Reports [*A publication*] (DLA) .... Serg & Raw
Sergeant and Rawle's Pennsylvania Supreme Court Reports [*1814-28*] [*A publication*] (DLA) .... Serg & Rawl
Sergeant First Class .... SFC
Sergeant Instructor [*Military British*] .... SI
Sergeant Instructor of Musketry .... SIM
Sergeant Major [*Marine Corps*] E9
Sergeant Major (AABC) .... SGM
Sergeant Major .... SGTMAJ
Sergeant Major .... SM
Sergeant Major .... SMAJ
Sergeant Major Academy [*Army*] .... SMA
Sergeant Major of the Army E9
Sergeant Major of the Army (AABC) .... SMA
Sergeant Navigator [*British*] .... SN
Sergeant on Attachment [*A publication*] (DLA) .... Serg Att
Sergeant on Mechanics' Lien Law [*A publication*] (DLA) .... Serg Mech L
Sergeant on the Land Laws of Pennsylvania [*A publication*] (DLA) .... Serg Land Laws PA
Sergeant Production Automatic Test Equipment .... SPATE
Sergeant Wilson's English King's Bench Reports [*1724-74*] [*A publication*] (DLA) .... Wils KB
Sergeant-at-Law .... SL
Sergeant-Major Instructor [*British military*] (DMA) .... SMI
Sergeant-Major Instructor of Gunnery [*British military*] (DMA) .... SMIG
Sergeant's Constitutional Law [*A publication*] (DLA) .... Serg Const L
Sergeant's Land Laws of Pennsylvania [*A publication*] (DLA) .... Serg LL
Serial .... S
Serial (AFM) .... SER
Serial .... SER
Serial (WDMC) .... ser
Serial Access Memory [*Computer science*] .... SAM
Serial Accountability Transmittal .... SAT
Serial Addressable Multiplexer (IAA) .... SAMUX
Serial Analysis Delay [*Computer science*] (ECII) .... SAD
Serial Analysis of Gene Expression [*Genetics*] .... SAGE
Serial ASCII Instrument Loop [*Computer science*] (OSI) .... SAIL
Serial Binary (CET) .... SB
Serial BIT [*Binary Digit*] **Error Detector** .... SBED
Serial Block (MSA) .... SB
Serial Carry Enable Input (IAA) .... SCEI
Serial Character Printer (OA) .... SCP
Serial Communication Interface [*Computer science*] .... SCI
Serial Communication Unit for Long Links .... SCULL
Serial Communications Controller .... SCC
Serial Copy Management System [*for digital audio tape recording machines*] .... SCMS
Serial Copy Master System (DOM) .... SCMS
Serial Cryptographic Device (MHDB) .... SCD
Serial Data Interface [*Computer science*] (CDE) .... SDI
Serial Data Transmission .... SDT
Serial Data Transmitter/Receiver [*Telecommunications*] (TEL) .... SDTR
Serial Digit Input/Output [*Computer science*] .... SDIO
Serial Dilution Indicator [*Clinical chemistry*] .... SDI
Serial Endosymbiotic Theory [*Evolution*] .... SET
Serial Engineering Order (MCD) .... SEO
Serial Entry Printer .... SEP
Serial Event Timer and Recorder .... SETAR
Serial Flechette Rifle (PDAA) .... SFR
Serial Focal Seizures [*Medicine*] .... SFS
Serial Frame Camera (CAAL) .... SFC
Serial Infrared Communications Interface [*Hewlett Packard Co.*] (PCM) .... SIR
Serial Infrared Specification [*Computer science*] (PCM) .... SIR

Serial Input [Computer science] (EECA) .... SI
Serial Input Adapter .... SIA
Serial Input Data [Computer science] .... SID
Serial Input/Output (MCD) .... SIO
Serial Input/Output Channel .... SIOC
Serial Input System (MCD) .... SIS
Serial Interface Board .... SIB
Serial Interface Chip .... SIC
Serial Line Interface Protocol (DMAA) .... SLIP
Serial Line Intermit Protocol .... SLIP
Serial Line Internet Protocol [Telecommunications] (PCM) .... SLIP
Serial Line Unit .... SLU
Serial/Lot Item Tracking (DNAB) .... SLIT
Serial Memory (NITA) .... SMEM
Serial Memory Address Counter [Computer] .... SMAC
Serial Motor Seizures [Medicine] .... SMS
Serial Multiplexer Interface Adapter (NASA) .... SMIA
Serial Network Interface (PDAA) .... SNI
Serial Number .... SERNO
Serial Number .... SN
Serial Number (MDG) .... SNO
Serial Number Configuration List (MCD) .... SNCL
Serial Number Conversion List .... SNCL
Serial Number Tracking .... SNT
Serial Output .... SO
Serial Output Adapter .... SOA
Serial Output Data [Computer science] .... SOD
Serial Output Special (MCD) .... SOS
Serial Parallel Multiplier (IAA) .... SPM
Serial Parallel Pipeline Multiplier (IAA) .... SPPM
Serial Parallel Serial (NITA) .... SPS
Serial Peripheral Interface [Electronics] .... SPI
Serial Poll Active State (IAA) .... SPAS
Serial Poll Disable (IAA) .... SPD
Serial Poll Enable (IAA) .... SPE
Serial Poll Idle State (IAA) .... SPIS
Serial Poll Mode State (IAA) .... SPMS
Serial Printer (IAA) .... SPR
Serial Probe Recognition [Psychometrics] .... SPR
Serial Publications of Foreign Governments [A bibliographical publication] ...... SFG
Serial Reaction Time Task [Physiology] .... SRTT
Serial Reference Number .... SRN
Serial Sections (BABM) .... ser sect
Serial Sections [Pathology] (DAVI) .... ser sect
Serial Shift Counter [Computer science] .... SSC
Serial Signalling Scheme (PDAA) .... SSS
Serial Storage Architecture [Computer science] (CDE) .... SSA
Serial Tasking [Computer science] (IAA) .... ST
Serial Thrombin Time [Medicine] (MAE) .... STT
Serial to Parallel (KSC) .... S/P
Serial Tunneling [Computer science] .... Stun
Serial-In, Parallel-Out [Telecommunications] (TEL) .... SIPO
Serialized Assembly Breakdown List (SAA) .... SABL
Serialized Control and Record [or Reporting] System (NASA) .... SCARS
Serialized Job Processor .... SJP
Serialized Missile Accounting and Control System .... SMACS
Serialized On-Line Automatic Recording [Computer science] (IEEE) .... SOLAR
Serialized Parts List [NASA] (MCD) .... SPL
Serialized Weapons Information Management System [Navy] .... SWIMS
Serializer/Deserializer .... SD
Serializer/Deserializer .... SERDES
Serializer-Deserializer Cyclic Redundancy Check (PDAA) .... SERDES CRC
Serially Balanced Sequence [Statistics] .... SBS
Serially Reusable Resource [Computer science] .... SRR
Serial-Parallel-Serial Structure (IAA) .... SPS
Serials in Swaziland University Libraries [A publication] .... SISUL
Serials Industry Systems Advisory Committee [Book Industry Study Group] [Information service or system] (IID) .... SISAC
Serials Master List .... SML
Serials On-Line [National Library of Medicine] [Bethesda, MD Database] .... SERLINE
Serials Record, National Library of Canada [Enregistrement des Publications en Serie, Bibliotheque Nationale du Canada] Ottawa, Ontario [Library symbol National Library of Canada] (NLC) .... OONLP
Serials Review [A publication] (BRI) .... Ser R
Serials Round Table [Later, RTSD] [American Library Association] .... SRT
Serials Section [Resources and Technical Services Division] [American Library Association] .... SS
Serials Titles Automated Records [US National Agricultural Library] [Beltsville, MD] [A publication] .... STAR
Serial-Section Electron Microscopy .... SSEM
Serib Wings [Italy ICAO designator] (FAAC) .... ISW
Series .... S
Series .... SE
Series (AAG) .... SER
Series (IDOE) .... ser
Series [Deltiology] .... SRS
Series "A" Bonds or Debentures [Investment term] .... A
Series "B" Bonds or Debentures [Investment term] .... B
Series Book Collectors' Society (EA) .... SBCS
Series "C" Bonds or Debentures [Investment term] C
Series Computation of Reliability and Probability [Computer science] ...... SCRAP
Series Control Relay .... SCR
Series Hybrid Vehicle .... SHV
Series Mode Rejection .... SMR

Series Mode Rejection Factor (IAA) .... SMRF
Series Number [Online database field identifier] ....
Series of Standard Additions .... SSA
Series Parallel Network (IAA) .... SPN
Series Relay [Electronics] (IAA) .... SR
Series Relay [Electronics] .... SRE
Series Relay (IEEE) .... SRLY
Series Resistance (IDOE) .... R$_s$
Series Separate .... SS
Series Statement [Online database field identifier] .... SE
Series Tee Junction .... STJ
Series Winding [Wiring] (DNAB) .... SW
Series-Parallel [Computer science] (IAA) .... SP
Series-Parallel Interface [Computer science] .... SPI
Series-Parallel-Serial Configuration [Electronics] (MDG) .... SPS
Series-Tuned Parallel-Stabilized [Computer science] (IAA) .... STPS
Series-Tuned Series-Stabilized [Computer science] (IAA) .... STSS
Serigraph (VRA) .... seri
Serikat Buruh Angkutan Udara [Airways' Union] [Indonesia] .... SERBAUD
Serikat Buruh Batik [Batik Workers' Union] [Indonesia] .... SBB
Serikat Buruh Beras dan Seluruh Indonesia [Rice and Tapioca Workers' Union of Indonesia] .... SEBBETSI
Serikat Buruh Daehrah Autonoom [Civil Servants' Union] [Indonesia] .... SEBDA
Serikat Buruh Djawantan Pekerdjaan Umun [Public Works' Union] [Indonesia] .... SBDPU
Serikat Buruh Djawatan Perindustrian [Department of Industry Workers' Union] [Indonesia] .... SBDP
Serikat Buruh Garam dan Soda Negeri [Salt Workers' Association] [Indonesia] .... SBGSN
Serikat Buruh Gelas Indonesia [Glass Workers' Union of Indonesia] .... SBGI
Serikat Buruh Gula Proklamasi [Sugar Workers' Union] [Indonesia] .... SBGP
Serikat Buruh Harian Indonesia [Newspaper Employees' Union of Indonesia] .... SERBUHI
Serikat Buruh Hotel, Rumah-Makan dan Toko [Hotel, Restaurant and Shops' Workers' Union] [Indonesia] .... SBHRT
Serikat Buruh Industri [Industrial Workers' Union] [Indonesia] .... SBI
Serikat Buruh Industri dan Umum [Industrial and General Workers' Union] [Indonesia] .... SERBIUM
Serikat Buruh Maclaine, Watson [Maclaine Watson Co. Workers' Union] [Indones ia] .... SBMW
Serikat Buruh Makanan dan Minuman [Food Workers' Union] [Indonesia] .... SERBUMAMI
Serikat Buruh Minjak dan Tambang [Oil and Minerals Workers' Union] [Indonesia] .... SERBUMIT
Serikat Buruh Minjak Kelapa Seluruh [Coconut Oil Workers' Union] [Indonesia] .... SERBUMIKSI
Serikat Buruh Minjak Shell Indonesia [Union of Oil Workers for Shell of Indonesia] .... SBMSI
Serikat Buruh Minjak, Stanvac [Oil Workers' Union, Stanvac] [Indonesia] .... SEBUMI
Serikat Buruh Muslimin Indonesia [Moslem Workers' Union of Indonesia] .... SERBUMUSI
Serikat Buruh Obat Seluruh Indonesia [All Indonesian Medicinal Factory Workers' Union] .... SBOSI
Serikat Buruh Pegadaian [Pawnshop Workers' Union] [Indonesia] .... SBP
Serikat Buruh Pegawai Negeri dan Daeran Otonom [Civil Servants Workers' Union] [Indonesia] .... SESPENDO
Serikat Buruh Pekerdjaan Umum [Public Workers' Ministry Union] [Indonesia] .... SBPU
Serikat Buruh Pelabuhan dan Pelajaran [Dockworkers' Union] [Indonesia].... SBPP
Serikat Buruh Pelabuhan Indonesia [Dockworkers' Union of Indonesia] .... SBPI
Serikat Buruh Pendidikan, Pengadjaran dan Kebudjaan [Department of Education Workers' Union] [Indonesia] .... SBPPK
Serikat Buruh Pendjahit Indonesia [Tailors' Union of Indonesia] .... SBPI
Serikat Buruh Penerbangan [Airways' Unions] [Indonesia] .... SBP
Serikat Buruh Perhubungan dan Transport [Communications and Transportation Workers' Union] [Indonesia] .... SBPT
Serikat Buruh Perkebunan Indonesia [Plantation Workers' Union of Indonesia] .... SERBUPI
Serikat Buruh Persuahaan Kaju and Bangunan [Building, Road and Irrigation Workers' Union] [Indonesia] .... SBPKB
Serikat Buruh Pertambangan Indonesia [Mining Workers' Union of Indonesia] .... SERBUPRI
Serikat Buruh Pertambangan Timah [Tin Mine Labor Union] [Indonesia] .... SBPT
Serikat Buruh Pertjetakan Indonesia [Printing Workers' Union of Indonesia] .... SPBI
Serikat Buruh Perusahaan Gula [Sugar Workers' Union] [Indonesia] .... SBPG
Serikat Buruh Qantas [Qantas Labor Union] [Indonesia] .... SBQ
Serikat Buruh Radio Republik Indonesia [Broadcasting Workers' Association of Indonesia] .... SBRRI
Serikat Buruh Rokok Indonesia [Cigarette Workers' Union of Indonesia] ..... SABRI
Serikat Buruh Rokok Indonesia [Cigarette Workers' Union of Indonesia] .... SBRI
Serikat Buruh Seluruh Indonesia [All Indonesian Laborers' Union] .... SBSI
Serikat Buruh Sepatu Keradjinan Kulit Karet [Shoe Workers' Union] [Indonesia] .... SBSKK
Serikat Buruh Tambang [Mine Workers' Union] [Indonesia] .... SBT
Serikat Buruh Tambang Timah [Tin Mine Laborers' Union] [Indonesia] .... SBTT
Serikat Buruh Teknik [Technicians' Union] [Indonesia] .... SBT
Serikat Buruh Teknik dan Pelabuhan [Technical and Harbour Workers' Union] [Indonesia] .... SBTP
Serikat Buruh Teknik Umum [Indonesia] .... SBTU
Serikat Buruh Textil [Textile Workers' Union] [Indonesia] .... SBT
Serikat Buruh Umum [General Workers' Union] [Indonesia] .... SERBU
Serikat Buruh Unilever Indonesia [Unilever Employees' Union of Indonesia] .... SERBUNI

Serikat Nelajan Indonesia [*Sailors' Union of Indonesia*] ..... SARNI
Serikat Pamong Desa Indonesia [*Village Officials' Union of Indonesia*] ..... SARIPADI
Serikat Pelajaran Seluruh Indonesia [*Sailors' Union of Indonesia*] ..... SPSI
Serikat Sekerdja Balai Penelitian Tekstil [*Textile Research Institute Workers' Union*] [*Indonesia*] ..... SSBPT
Serikat Sekerdja Bank Koporasi, Tani dan Nelajan Disingkat [*Cooperative, Farmers and Fishers Bank Employees' Union*] [*Indonesia*] ..... SSBKTN
Serikat Sekerdja Bank Pembangunan Indonesia [*Indonesian Development Bank Employees' Union*] ..... SSBPI
Serikat Sekerdja Biro/Dinas Pembangunan Usaha Tani [*Agricultural Development Service Workers' Union*] [*Indonesia*] ..... SSB/DPUT
Serikat Sekerdja/Buruh Ketapradja Djakarta Raja [*General Union of Government Officials of Greater Djakarta*] [*Indonesia*] ..... SSBKD
Serikat Sekerdja Departemen Agama [*Brotherhood of Employees of Department of Religious Affairs*] [*Indonesia*] ..... SESDA
Serikat Sekerdja Kementerian Dalam Negeri [*Union of Workers in the Department of Interior*] [*Indonesia*] ..... SSKDN
Serikat Sekerdja Kementerian Pertaganan [*Ministry of Defense Workers' Unions*] [*Indonesia*] ..... SSKP
Serikat Sekerdja Pabrik Sendjata dan Mesiu [*Armaments' Union*] [*Indonesia*] ..... SSPSM
Serikat Sekerdja Pamong Pradja [*Public Officials' Union*] [*Indonesia*] ..... SSPP
Serikat Sekerdja Pos, Telegrap dan Telepon [*National Postal, Telegraph and Telephone Employees' Union*] [*Indonesia*] ..... SSPTT
Serikat Sekerdja Topografi Indonesia [*Indonesian Topography Employees' Union*] ..... SSTI
Serine [*One-letter symbol; see Ser*] ..... S
Serine [*Also, S*] [*An amino acid*] ..... Ser
Serine [*An amino acid*] (DOG) ..... ser
Serine Dehydrase [*An enzyme*] (MAE) ..... SDH
Serine Dehydratase [*An enzyme*] ..... SD
Serine Glycerophosphatide [*Biochemistry*] (MAE) ..... SGP
Serine Proteinase Inhibitor [*Biochemistry*] ..... SERPIN
Serine-Rich Entamoeba Histolytica Protein [*Biochemistry*] ..... SREHP
Serine-Threonine Kinase [*An enzyme*] ..... STK
Serious Chemical Distribution Incident ..... SCDI
Serious Fraud Office [*Proposed*] [*British government*] ..... SFO
Serious Habitual Offender [*Criminology*] ..... SHO
Serious Incident Report [*Military*] (AFM) ..... SIR
Serious Injury Frequency Rate ..... SIFR
Serious List [*Hospital administration*] (DAVI) ..... SL
Serious Literary, Artistic, Political, or Scientific Value [*Obscenity law*] (NTCM) ..... SLAPS
Serious Music [*Canadian Broadcasting Corp. record series prefix*] ..... SM
Serious Offenders Review Council [*New South Wales, Australia*] ..... SORC
Seriously [*or Severely*] **Emotionally Disturbed** ..... SED
Seriously Ill [*Military*] (AABC) ..... SI
Seriously Ill List [*Military*] ..... SIL
Seriously Wounded (DAVI) ..... SW
Seriously Wounded in Action [*Military*] ..... SWA
Serjeant [*Military British*] (ROG) ..... SERJ
Serjeant [*Military British*] (DMA) ..... Serjt
Serjeant [*Military British*] (DMA) ..... Sjt
Serjeant-Major [*Military British*] (ROG) ..... SERJT-MAJ
Serka [*Afghanistan*] [*ICAO location identifier*] (ICLI) ..... OASK
Sermiligaq [*Greenland*] [*ICAO location identifier*] (ICLI) ..... BGSG
Sermon ..... S
Sermon ..... SER
Sermon (ROG) ..... SERM
Serologic Blocking Factor [*Cardiology*] ..... SBF
Serological [*Examination*] [*Immunology*] (DAVI) ..... sero
Serological Test for Syphilis [*Medicine*] ..... STS
Serological Test for Syphilis-Quantitation [*Medicine*] (DAVI) ..... STS-QN
Serologically Defined [*Immunology*] ..... SD
Serologically Determined [*Medicine*] ..... SD
Serologicals Corp. [*NASDAQ symbol*] (SAG) ..... SERO
Serologicals Corp. [*Associated Press*] (SAG) ..... Serolog
Serologicals Inc. [*NASDAQ symbol*] (TTSB) ..... SERO
Serondela [*Botswana*] [*ICAO location identifier*] (ICLI) ..... FBSD
Serondela [*Botswana*] [*Airport symbol*] (AD) ..... SDS
Seronegative Inflammatory Polyarthritis [*Medicine*] (DMAA) ..... SNIPA
Seronera [*Tanzania*] [*ICAO location identifier*] (ICLI) ..... HTSN
Seronera [*Tanzania*] [*Airport symbol*] (AD) ..... SEU
Serosa to Lumen [*Anatomy*] (DAVI) ..... S-L
Serotin Reuptake Inhibitor [*Pharmacology*] ..... SRI
Serotonin N-Acetyltransferase [*An enzyme*] ..... SNAT
Serous Otitis Media [*Ear inflammation*] ..... SOM
Serous Retinal Detachment [*Ophthalmology*] ..... SRD
Serowe [*Botswana*] [*ICAO location identifier*] (ICLI) ..... FBSR
Serpa [*Portugal*] [*Airport symbol*] (AD) ..... SPP
Serpens [*Constellation*] ..... Ser
Serpens [*Constellation*] ..... Serp
Serpent River Band Public Library, Cutler, Ontario [*Library symbol National Library of Canada*] (NLC) ..... OCSR
Serpentine Superlattice [*Physics*] ..... SSL
Serra ..... SA
Serra Cooperative Library System [*Library network*] ..... SCLS
Serra Cooperative Library System, San Diego, CA [*Library symbol Library of Congress*] (LCLS) ..... CSdSer
Serra Cooperative Library System, San Diego, CA [*OCLC symbol*] (OCLC) ..... SLS
Serra International (EA) ..... SI
Serra Norte [*Brazil*] [*Airport symbol*] (OAG) ..... RRN
Serrate (MSA) ..... SERR
Serrated Black Letters [*Tire design*] [*Automotive engineering*] ..... SBL
Serratia Marcescens [*Bacterium*] ..... SM
Sert [*Libya*] [*Airport symbol Obsolete*] (OAG) ..... SRX
SERTEL [*Servicios Telereservacios SA de CV*] [*ICAO designator*] (FAAC) ..... LOM
Sertoli-Cell Androgenic Inhibitory Factor [*Endocrinology*] ..... SCAIF
Sertoli-Cell Culture Medium [*Clinical chemistry*] ..... SCCM
Sertoli-Cell Protein [*Immunology*] ..... SCP
Sertoma International (EA) ..... SI
Sertorius [*of Plutarch*] [*Classical studies*] (OCD) ..... Sert
Serui [*Indonesia*] [*Airport symbol*] (OAG) ..... ZRI
Serui/Sujarwo Condronegoro [*Indonesia*] [*ICAO location identifier*] (ICLI) ..... WABO
Serum ..... S
Serum Agar Measuring Aid ..... SAMA
Serum Agglutination Test (OA) ..... SAT
Serum Alanine Aminotransferase [*An enzyme*] ..... SALT
Serum Albumin [*Serology*] ..... SA
Serum Alkaline Phosphatase [*Clinical chemistry*] ..... SAP
Serum Amylase [*Medicine*] (DMAA) ..... S-AMY
Serum Amyloid A [*Clinical chemistry*] ..... SAA
Serum Amyloid P [*Clinical chemistry*] ..... SAP
Serum Angiotensin Converting Enzyme [*Activity*] [*Serology*] ..... SACE
Serum Aspartate Aminotransferase [*An enzyme*] ..... SAST
Serum Aspartate Aminotransferase [*Medicine*] (DMAA) ..... SAST
Serum Bactericidal Titer [*Clinical chemistry*] ..... SBT
Serum Beta-Glucuronidase Activity [*Serology*] ..... SBGA
Serum Bile Acid [*Medicine*] (DMAA) ..... SBA
Serum Bilirubin [*Clinical chemistry*] ..... SB
Serum Calcium [*Biochemistry*] (DAVI) ..... S_{ca}
Serum Cancer-Suppressive Peptide [*Oncology*] ..... SCSP
Serum Chemistry Graft (MAE) ..... SCG
Serum Cholesterol Level [*Clinical chemistry*] (OA) ..... SCL
Serum Cholesterol-Binding Reserve [*Medicine*] ..... SCBR
Serum Cholinesterase [*An enzyme*] ..... SChE
Serum Complement [*Medicine*] (DMAA) ..... SC
Serum Copper Level [*Clinical chemistry*] (AAMN) ..... SCL
Serum Creatine Kinase [*An enzyme*] ..... SCK
Serum Creatine Phosphokinase [*An enzyme*] (AAMN) ..... SCPK
Serum Creatinine [*Hematology*] ..... SCr
Serum Defect [*Medicine*] (MAE) ..... SD
Serum Digoxin Concentration [*Clinical chemistry*] ..... SDC
Serum Digoxin Level [*Cardiology*] (DAVI) ..... SDL
Serum Dilution Test [*Clinical chemistry*] ..... SDT
Serum Fibrinogen [*Medicine*] (MAE) ..... SF
Serum Free Fatty Acid [*Medicine*] (DMAA) ..... SFFA
Serum Free Medium ..... SFM
Serum Free Thyroxine Fraction [*Endocrinology*] (DAVI) ..... FT_4F
Serum From a Pregnant Woman (DAVI) ..... PS
Serum Globulin [*Medicine*] (MAE) ..... SG
Serum Glucose [*Medicine*] (DAVI) ..... SG
Serum Glutamic Oxaloacetic Transaminase [*An enzyme*] ..... SGOT
Serum Glutamic-Pyruvic Transaminase [*An enzyme*] ..... SGPT
Serum Growth Hormone [*Endocrinology*] ..... SGH
Serum Hepatitis [*Medicine*] ..... SH
Serum Hepatitis Associated Antibody [*Hematology*] ..... SHA-Ab
Serum Hepatitis Associated Antigen [*Hematology*] ..... SHAA
Serum Hepatitis Associated Antigen-Antibody [*Hematology*] ..... SHAA-Ab
Serum Hydroxybutyrate Dehydrogenase [*An enzyme*] ..... SHBD
Serum Immune Globulin [*Immunochemistry*] ..... SIG
Serum Immunoractive Human Parathormone [*Immunology*] (DAVI) ..... SIhPTH
Serum Immunoreactive Parathyroid Hormone [*Endocrinology*] ..... SIPTH
Serum Immunoreative Erythropoietin [*Immunochemistry*] ..... SIE
Serum Inducible Repeat [*Genetics*] ..... SIR
Serum Inhibitory Titer [*Clinical chemistry*] ..... SIT
Serum Insulin Concentration [*Medicine*] (DMAA) ..... SIC
Serum Iron [*Serology*] ..... SI
Serum Isocitric Dehydrogenase (MAE) ..... SICD
Serum Lactate Dehydrogenase [*Also, SLDH*] [*An enzyme*] ..... SLD
Serum Lactate Dehydrogenase [*Also, SLD*] [*An enzyme*] ..... SLDH
Serum Leucine Aminopeptidase [*An enzyme*] (MAE) ..... SLAP
Serum Lipophosphoprotein [*Serology*] ..... SLPP
Serum Malic Dehydrogenase [*An enzyme*] ..... SMD
Serum Methyl Alcohol Level [*Medicine*] (DMAA) ..... SMAL
Serum Neutralization Test ..... SN
Serum Normal Agglutinator [*Hematology*] ..... SNagg
Serum Ornithine Carbamyltransferase [*Medicine*] (DMAA) ..... S-OCT
Serum Parvovirus-Like Virus [*Medicine*] (DMAA) ..... SPLV
Serum Precipitable Iodine [*Serology*] ..... SPI
Serum Prostatic Acid Phosphatase [*An enzyme*] ..... SPAP
Serum Protein Electrolytes [*Biochemistry*] (DAVI) ..... SPE
Serum Protein Electrophoresis ..... SPE
Serum Protein Electrophoresis [*Clinical chemistry*] ..... SPEP
Serum Protein Electrophoretogram [*Clinical chemistry*] ..... SPEG
Serum Protein-Bound Iodine [*Clinical chemistry*] (AAMN) ..... SPBI
Serum Prothrombin Conversion Accelerator [*Factor VII*] [*Also, PPCA Hematology*] ..... SPCA
Serum Reserve Cholesterol Binding Capacity [*Medicine*] (DMAA) ..... SRCBC
Serum Resin Triiodothyronine [*Uptake*] [*Endocrinology*] (DAVI) ..... RT_3
Serum Response Element [*Biochemistry*] ..... SRE
Serum Response Element [*Genetics*] ..... SRE
Serum Response Factor [*Biochemistry*] ..... SRF
Serum Samples from Infertile Women [*Immunochemistry*] ..... SIW
Serum Serologic [*Immunochemistry*] ..... Ss
Serum Sickness [*Medicine*] ..... SS
Serum Sickness-Like Illness [*Medicine*] ..... SSLI
Serum Sodium [*Organic chemistry*] (DAVI) ..... S_{Na}
Serum Theophylline Concentration [*Clinical chemistry*] ..... STC

Serum Thrombotic Accelerator [*Serology*] ..... STA
Serum Thymic-Like Activity [*Biochemistry*] ..... STA
Serum Thyroxine [*Measured by column chromatographic technique*] [*Endocrinology*] (DAVI) ..... $T_4(c)$
Serum Thyroxine [*Measured by displacement analysis*] [*Endocrinology*] (DAVI) ..... $T_4(D)$
Serum Thyroxine Radioisotope Assay [*Endocrinology*] (DAVI) ..... $T_4(RIA)$
Serum Triiodothyronine Radioimmunoassay [*Endocrinology*] (DAVI) ..... $T_3(RIA)$
Serum Trypsin Inhibitor [*Serology*] ..... STI
Serum Urea Nitrogen [*Clinical medicine*] ..... SUN
Serum Uric Acid [*Clinical chemistry*] ..... SUA
Serum Wassermann Reaction [*Clinical chemistry*] ..... SWR
Serum Xanthine Oxidase [*Clinical chemistry*] (AAMN) ..... SeXO
Serum-Inhibition Factor [*Medicine*] (DMAA) ..... SIF
Serum-Killing Level [*Pharmacology*] (DAVI) ..... SKL
Serum-Response Enhancer [*Genetics*] ..... SRE
Serum-Supplemented Medium [*Microbiology*] ..... SSM
Serum-Treated Red Blood Cell [*Clinical chemistry*] ..... SRBC
Serum-Treated Zymosan [*Clinical chemistry*] ..... STZ
Serva [*Preserve*] [*Latin*] (WGA) ..... SERV
Servant [*Legal shorthand*] (LWAP) ..... S
Servant ..... SER
Servant ..... SERV
Servant ..... SERVT
Servant Allowance [*British military*] (DMA) ..... SA
Servantes de l'Agneu Divin [*Sisters of the Lamb of God*] [*Roman Catholic religious order*] ..... AD
Servants in Faith and Technology (EA) ..... SIFAT
Servants of Charity [*Roman Catholic men's religious order*] ..... SC
Servants of Charity (TOCD) ..... sc
Servants of Jesus (TOCD) ..... SJ
Servants of Mary (TOCD) ..... OSM
Servants of Our Lady of the Most Holy Trinity (TOCD) ..... slt
Servants of Our Lady Queen of the Clergy [*Roman Catholic women's religious order*] ..... SRC
Servants of St. Joseph (TOCD) ..... SSJ
Servants of the Blessed Sacrament (TOCD) ..... SJS
Servants of the Blessed Sacrament (TOCD) ..... SSS
Servants of the Holy Heart of Mary [*Roman Catholic women's religious order*] ..... SSCM
Servants of the Holy Infancy of Jesus (TOCD) ..... OSF
Servants of the Holy Paraclete [*Roman Catholic men's religious order*] ..... SP
Servants of the Paraclete (TOCD) ..... sp
Servants of the Paraclete (TOCD) ..... sP
Servants of the Sacred Heart of Jesus and of the Poor [*Roman Catholic women's religious order*] ..... SSHJP
Servants' United Effort [*Lemonade*] [*Slang British*] (DSUE) ..... SUE
Servas International (EA) ..... SI
Serve and Enrich Retirement by Volunteer Experience [*Staten Island, NY, project*] ..... SERVE
Server Macro Expansion [*Computer science*] ..... SMX
Server Macro Expansion [*Computer science*] ..... SMX
Server Message Blocks (PCM) ..... SMB
Server Requester Programming Interface [*Computer science*] (CDE) ..... SRPI
Server Requewst Manager [*Computer science*] ..... SRM
Server Technology, Inc. [*Information service or system*] (IID) ..... STI
Serveur Universitaire National de l'Information Scientifique et Technique [*Online service*] ..... SUNIST
Servian (ROG) ..... SERV
Service [*Military document classification*] (INF) ..... S
Service (NATG) ..... SER
Service (AAG) ..... SERV
Service (ROG) ..... SERVE
Service (IAA) ..... SRCS
Service ..... Srvc
Service ..... Srve
Service ..... SV
Service (AFM) ..... SVC
Service ..... SVC
Service ..... SVCE
Service Acceptance Trials (NVT) ..... SAT
Service Access Point ..... SAP
Service Access Point Identifier [*Telecommunications*] (OSI) ..... SAPI
Service Acquisition Executive [*DoD*] ..... SAE
Service Action (AAG) ..... S/A
Service Action Analysis (AAG) ..... SAA
Service Action Change Analysis (AAG) ..... SACA
Service Action Drawing (AAG) ..... SAD
Service Action Log (AAG) ..... SAL
Service Action Parts List (AAG) ..... SAPL
Service Activities of Voluntary Engineers ..... SAVE
Service Activity System ..... SAS
Service Administratif Canadien aux Organismes (AC) ..... SACO
Service Administratif Canadien Outre-Mer [*Canadian Executive Service Overseas - CESO*] ..... SACO
Service Advertising Protocol [*Computer science*] (PCM) ..... SAP
Service Adviser [*or Attache*] [*British*] ..... SA
Service Advisory Group (NATG) ..... SAG
Service Aerien Francais [*France ICAO designator*] (FAAC) ..... SHP
Service Aerien Gouvernmental Ministere des Transports Gouvernment du Quebec [*Canada ICAO designator*] (FAAC) ..... BOM
Service Aggregated Module ..... SAM
Service Agreement (MCD) ..... SA
Service Aid (IAA) ..... SA
Service Air [*Nuclear energy*] (NRCH) ..... SA
Service Air System (NRCH) ..... SAS
Service Aircraft Instrumentation Package (MCD) ..... SAIP
Service Analysis Report [*Telecommunications*] (TEL) ..... SAR
Service Analysis Request [*Telecommunications*] (TEL) ..... SAR
Service and Compliance Administration [*US wage/price controls agency*] ..... SCA
Service and Cooling Umbilical [*Aerospace*] (MCD) ..... SCU
Service and Hardware Difficulty Reports (MCD) ..... SHDR
Service and Health Record (DAVI) ..... SERVHEL
Service and Methods Demonstration [*Program*] [*TRB*] (TAG) ..... SMD
Service and Overhaul Change (MSA) ..... SOC
Service and Regulatory Announcement, Department of Agriculture [*A publication*] (DLA) ..... SRA
Service and Repair Identification Tag (MCD) ..... SRIT
Service Announcements in Science and Technology [*National Technical Information Service*] (EA) ..... SAST
Service Annual Survey [*Bureau of the Census*] (GFGA) ..... SAS
Service Application [*Military*] (AFIT) ..... S/A
Service Application Code [*Navy*] ..... SAC
Service Approved Status List [*Navy*] (DNAB) ..... SASL
Service Aptitude Rating [*Military*] (NVT) ..... SAR
Service Area (IAA) ..... SA
Service Area Computer (IAA) ..... SAC
Service Arm (KSC) ..... SA
Service Assigned Requests (MCD) ..... SAR
Service Assistant [*Telecommunications*] (TEL) ..... SA
Service at Military Installations [*Red Cross*] ..... SMI
Service at Veterans Administration Offices [*Red Cross*] ..... SVAO
Service Attitude Measurement [*Bell System*] ..... SAM
Service Audiovisual Management Office [*Army*] ..... SAVMO
Service Availability [*AT & T*] ..... SAV
Service Available During Scheduled Operations [*ICAO*] (FAAC) ..... HS
Service Available to Meet Operational Requirements [*ICAO*] (FAAC) ..... HO
Service Benefit Plan [*Military*] (AABC) ..... SBP
Service Billing Record ..... SBR
Service Brake Activator [*Automotive engineering*] ..... SBA
Service Bulletin ..... SB
Service Bureau (IAA) ..... SB
Service Bureau Corp. ..... SBC
Service Business Marketing Association (EA) ..... SBMA
Service Canadien pour les Etudiants et les Stagiaires d'Outre-Mer ..... SCESOM
Service Ceiling ..... S/C
Service Ceiling ..... SCEIL
Service Ceiling [*Aerospace engineering*] ..... SRVCLG
Service Center [*IRS*] ..... SC
Service Center Advantage Network [*Federal-Mogul Corp.*] ..... SCAN
Service Center Audit Program [*IRS*] ..... SCAP
Service Center Control File [*IRS*] ..... SCCF
Service Center for Aging Information [*Department of Health and Human Services*] [*Information service or system*] (IID) ..... SCAN
Service Center for Teachers of History (EA) ..... SCTH
Service Center Internal Computer Code [*Computer science*] ..... SCICC
Service Center Math Error [*IRS*] ..... SCME
Service Center of Private Enterprise ..... SCOPE
Service Center Replacement System [*Computer science*] ..... SCRS
Service Center Taxpayer Notice [*IRS*] ..... SCTN
Service Center Unpostable [*IRS*] ..... SCUP
Service Central de la Lutte Anti-terroriste [*Central Anti-Terrorist Service*] [*France*] (ECON) ..... SCLAT
Service Central des Approvisionements et Materiels Americains [*Central Office of American Supplies and Equipment*] [*World War II*] ..... SCAMA
Service Central des Enquetes et Etudes Statistiques [*Central Service for Statistical Inquiries and Studies*] [*Ministry of Agriculture Paris, France*] ..... SCEES
Service Certificate [*Military British*] ..... SC
Service Change ..... SC
Service Change Committee [*Military*] ..... SCC
Service Change Information (MCD) ..... SCI
Service Change Release and Manufacture (MCD) ..... SCRAM
Service Charge [*Banking*] ..... SC
Service Checkout Equipment (IAA) ..... SCE
Service Children's Education Authority [*Ministry of Defence*] [*British*] ..... SCEA
Service Cinematographique des Armees [*France*] ..... SCA
Service City, AK [*Location identifier FAA*] (FAAL) ..... SEV
Service Civil International [*Australia*] ..... SCI
Service Civil International [*International Voluntary Service*] [*India*] ..... SCI
Service Civil International - United States of America (EA) ..... SCI-USA
Service Club [*Military enlisted men's club*] ..... SC
Service Code [*Telecommunications*] (TEL) ..... SC
Service Code Automatic Tester [*Automotive engineering*] ..... SCAT
Service Coding and Data Collection (AAG) ..... SCDC
Service Command [*Marine Corps*] ..... SC
Service Command [*Army*] ..... ServC
Service Command [*Army*] ..... SVC
Service Command Air Transportation ..... SCAT
Service Command, Fleet Marine Force, Pacific ..... SERVCOMFMFPAC
Service Command Module [*Aerospace*] (MCD) ..... SCM
Service Command Unit ..... SCU
Service Computation Date [*Military*] (AFM) ..... SCD
Service Connected [*Medicine*] ..... SC
Service Connected Disability [*Medicine*] (AAMN) ..... SCD
Service Contract Act [*1965*] ..... SCA
Service Contract Act Wage Determination (AAGC) ..... SCAWD
Service Control Drawing ..... SCD
Service Control Layer [*Computer science*] ..... SCL
Service Control Manager [*Computer science*] ..... SCM
Service Control Point [*DoD*] (AFIT) ..... SCP

Service Corporation [*Medicine*] (HCT) .... SC
Service Corp. International [*NYSE symbol*] (SPSG) .... SRV
Service Corp. International [*Associated Press*] (SAG) .... SvceCp
Service Corp. Intl [*NYSE symbol*] (TTSB) .... SRV
Service Corps of Retired Executives (NADA) .... SCORE
Service Corps of Retired Executives Association [*Washington, DC*] (EA) .... SCORE
Service Counter Terminal [*Banking*] .... SCT
Service Craft Modernization Program [*Navy*] (CAAL) .... SCMP
Service Cryptologic Agencies [*Military*] .... SCA
Service Cryptologic Elements [*Army*] .... SCE
Service Cryptologic Organizations (MCD) .... SCO
Service d'Aide aux Forces Alliees [*World War II*] .... SAFA
Service Data Unit (TNIG) .... SDU
Service Dated (ROG) .... SD
Service de Bibliographie sur l'Informatique [*Paris Gestion Informatique*] [*France Information service or system*] (CRD) .... SB-I
Service de Documentation et de Bibliotheque, Complexe Scientifique, Ste.-Foy, Quebec [*Library symbol National Library of Canada*] (NLC) .... QQCS
Service de Documentation et de Bibliotheque, Quebec, PQ, Canada [*Library symbol Library of Congress*] (LCLS) .... CaQQCS
Service de Documentation et de Reference, Confederation des Caisses Populaires et d'Economie Desjardins du Quebec, Levis, Quebec [*Library symbol National Library of Canada*] (NLC) .... QLCCP
Service de Documentation et d'Information Techniques de l'Aeronautique .... SDIT
Service de Documentation Exterieure et de Contre-Espionnage [*Pronounced "suh-deck"*] [*Intelligence organization France Later, DGSE*] .... SDECE
Service de Documentation Interministerielle [*Interministerial Documentation Service*] [*National Telecommunications Research Center*] [*Information service or system*] (IID) .... SDI
Service de la Bibliotheque de Ville de Laval, Chomedey, Quebec [*Library symbol National Library of Canada*] (BIB) .... QCS
Service de la Documentation et de l'Audiovisuel, Conservatoire de Musique de Quebec, Quebec [*Library symbol National Library of Canada*] (NLC) .... QQCMQ
Service de la Documentation, Ministere de la Sante et des Services Sociaux du Q uebec, Quebec, Quebec [*Library symbol National Library of Canada*] (NLC) .... QQIAS
Service de la Documentation, Ministere de la Sante et des Services Sociaux du Quebec, Montreal, Quebec [*Library symbol National Library of Canada*] (NLC) .... QMSA
Service de Presse Baptiste Europeen [*European Baptist Press Service - EBPS*] (EAIO) .... SPBE
Service de Presse de l'Eglise du Silence [*Belgium*] .... EGLISI
Service de Previsions Ionospherique Militaire .... SPIM
Service de Reference, Conseil de la Sante et des Services Sociaux de la Region de Montreal Metropolitain, Montreal, Quebec [*Library symbol National Library of Canada*] (NLC) .... QMCSSS
Service Dealer's Newsletter [*Lynott Associates*] [*A publication*] (IID) .... SDN
Service Delivery Area [*Job Training and Partnership Act*] (OICC) .... SDA
Service Deputy/Director (MUGU) .... SD/D
Service des Archives de l'Universite de Montreal, Montreal, PQ, Canada [*Library symbol Library of Congress*] (LCLS) .... CaQMUA
Service des Archives de l'Universite de Montreal, Quebec [*Library symbol National Library of Canada*] (NLC) .... QMUA
Service des Archives de l'Universite du Quebec a Montreal [*Library symbol National Library of Canada*] (BIB) .... QMUQA
Service des Archives de l'Universite du Quebec a Montreal, Montreal, PQ, Canada [*Library symbol*] [*Library of Congress*] (LCLS) .... CaQMUQA
Service des Etudes Ecologiques Regionales [*Canada*] .... SEER
Service des Etudes et Inventaires Bio-Physiques [*Quebec*] .... SEIB
Service des Organisations Aeronautiques Internationales [*France*] .... SOAI
Service Difficulty Report (MCD) .... SDR
Service Disabled Veterans Insurance .... SDVI
Service Division [*Navy*] .... SERVDIV
Service Dress .... SD
Service du Traitement de l'Information, Ministere des Finances, Duberger, Quebec [*Library symbol National Library of Canada*] (NLC) .... QQFTI
Service du Traitement Industriel des Residus Urbains [*France*] .... TIRU
Service du Travail Obligatoire [*French labor force*] [*World War II*] .... STO
Service Educational Activities [*Military*] (AABC) .... SEA
Service Element (TNIG) .... SE
Service Employees International Union (EA) .... SEIU
Service Employers Association (EA) .... SEA
Service, Employment, Redevelopment [*Operation for Mexican-Americans*] [*Later, SER - Jobs for Progress*] .... SER
Service Employment Redevelopment Operation (OICC) .... SERO
Service Engine Soon [*Automotive engineering*] .... SES
Service Engineer .... SE
Service Engineering Department Report .... SEDR
Service Engineering Man-Hours .... SEMH
Service Entrance (IAA) .... SE
Service Environment Power System (IAA) .... SEPS
Service Equipment (AAG) .... SE
Service Evaluation System [*Telecommunications*] (TEL) .... SES
Service Evaluation Telemetry (AAG) .... SET
Service Factor (MSA) .... SF
Service Flying Training School [*British*] .... SFTS
Service for Admission to College and University [*Canada*] (AEBS) .... SACU
Service Force [*Navy*] .... SERVFOR
Service Force, Atlantic Fleet .... SERVLANT
Service Force, Atlantic Fleet, Subordinate Command .... SERVLANTSUBORDCOMD
Service Force, Pacific Fleet .... SERVPAC
Service Force, South Pacific, Subordinate Command .... SERFORSOPACSUBCOM
Service Force, Southwest Pacific Fleet .... SERVSOWESPAC
Service Forces, Atlantic [*Navy*] .... SERLANT
Service Forces, Pacific [*Navy*] .... SERPAC
Service Fuel Oil .... SFO
Service General des Moyens d'Enseignement, Ministere de l'Education du Quebec, Montreal, Quebec [*Library symbol National Library of Canada*] (NLC) .... QMSGME
Service Generale des Moyens de l'Enseignement [*Canada*] .... SGME
Service Geologique National [*National Geological Survey*] [*Bureau of Geological and Mining Research*] [*Information service or system*] (IID) .... SGN
Service Goods Movement System (IAA) .... SEGMOS
Service Government Life Insurance (DOMA) .... SGLI
Service Group (MUGU) .... SG
Service Hours [*Electronics*] (IEEE) .... SH
Service in Information and Analysis [*Host*] [*British*] (BUR) .... SIA
Service in Military and Veterans Hospitals [*Red Cross*] .... SMVH
Service in Random Order (IAA) .... SIRO
Service, Inc., Omaha NE [*STAC*] .... SIC
Service Incroyance et Foi [*Canadian Catholic Conference*] .... SIF
Service Indicator [*Telecommunications*] (TEL) .... SI
Service Indicator Associated Field [*Telecommunications*] (TEL) .... SIAF
Service Industries USA [*A publication*] .... SUSA
Service Industry Accounting [*Sybiz International, Inc.*] [*Computer program*] (PCM) .... SIA
Service Information Letter .... SIL
Service Information-Diffusion [*Information Dissemination Office*] [*National Institute for Research in Informatics and Automation*] [*Information service or system*] (IID) .... SEDIS
Service Instruction .... SI
Service Instructions Message [*Telecommunications*] (TEL) .... SIM
Service Interception [*Telecommunications*] (TEL) .... SVI
Service International de Microfilm, Paris, France [*Library symbol Library of Congress*] (LCLS) .... SIM
Service International de Recherches [*International Tracing Service*] [*Red Cross*] .... SIR
Service International de Recherches (du Comite International de la Croix-Rouge) [*International Tracing Service of the International Committee of the Red Cross*] .... SIR(CICR)
Service Interruption .... SI
Service Inventory Control Center [*DoD*] .... SICC
Service Job Analysis [*A publication*] .... SJA
Service Junior .... SJ
Service Junior - Oil-Resistant .... SJO
Service Junior - Thermoplastic .... SJT
Service Kit .... SK
Service Letter (MCD) .... SL
Service Level Reporter [*IBM Corp.*] .... SLR
Service Life Assessment Program [*Military*] .... SLAP
Service Life Evaluation .... SLE
Service Life Extension Program [*Military*] (MCD) .... SLEP
Service Life Not Completed (DNAB) .... SLNC
Service Life Test Report (AAG) .... SLTR
Service Link Network [*Bell Laboratories*] .... SLN
Service Location Protocol [*Computer science*] .... SLP
Service/Maintenance (NASA) .... S/M
Service Man (NVT) .... SVCMN
Service Management System [*Telecommunications*] .... SMS
Service Manipulator System (SSD) .... SMS
Service Manual .... SM
Service Mark [*Trademarks*] .... SM
Service Mart .... SERVMART
Service Member [*Military*] (AABC) .... SM
Service Members Occupational Conversions and Training Acts .... SMOCTA
Service Men's Center [*World War II*] .... SMC
Service Merchandise [*NYSE symbol*] (TTSB) .... SME
Service Merchandise Co., Inc. [*NYSE symbol*] (SPSG) .... SME
Service Merchandise Co., Inc. [*Associated Press*] (SAG) .... SvcMer
Service Merchandisers of America [*Later, NASM*] (EA) .... SMA
Service Message [*Aviation code*] .... SVC
Service Message Protocol Data Unit [*Telecommunications*] (OSI) .... SMPDU
Service Module [*NASA*] .... SM
Service Module Deluge Purge System [*NASA*] (KSC) .... SMDPS
Service Module Electrical Power System [*NASA*] (KSC) .... SEPS
Service Module Jettison Controller [*NASA*] (MCD) .... SMJC
Service Module Oxidizer [*NASA*] .... SMO
Service Module Reaction Control System [*NASA*] (KSC) .... SMRCS
Service Module Sequence Controller [*NASA*] .... SMSC
Service Module Simulator (IAA) .... SMS
Service Module Technician [*NASA*] (KSC) .... SMT
Service Monitoring [*Telecommunications*] (TEL) .... SM
Service National des Liberations Conditionnelles [*Canada*] .... SNLC
Service National des Sauveteurs [*Canada*] .... SNS
Service Not Required .... SNR
Service Note (MSA) .... SN
Service Number [*Military*] .... SERNO
Service Number [*Navy*] .... SERVNO
Service Number [*Military*] .... SN
Service Object Pair Instance (DMAA) .... SOPI
Service Observance Bureau [*A telephone-monitoring section of the Bell System*] .... SOB
Service of Supply [*Later, ASF*] [*Army*] .... SOS
Service of Supply, South Pacific Area [*Navy World War II*] .... SOSSPA
Service off the Shelf (IAA) .... SOS
Service Office .... SERVO

Service, Office, and Retail Workers Union of Canada .... SORWUC
Service on Sight [*Computer warranty program offered by Hyundai Electronics*] (PCM) .... SOS
Service Operational Requirement .... SOR
Service Order .... SO
Service Order, Customer Records, and Terminal Entry System .... SOCRATES
Service Order Mechanization [*or Mechanized*] System [*AT & T*] .... SOMS
Service Order System [*Telecommunications*] (TEL) .... SOS
Service Package (OA) .... SP
Service Panel .... SP
Service Part Number .... SPN
Service Parts Information Notice .... SPIN
Service/Parts Sales Work Order (MCD) .... S/PSWO
Service Pay and Allowances [*Military British*] .... SPA
Service Pedalogique Interafricain .... SPI
Service Phase (MCD) .... SP
Service Police [*British military*] (DMA) .... SP
Service Priority List (BUR) .... SPL
Service Processor (IEEE) .... SP
Service Processor (BUR) .... SVP
Service Profile Identifier [*Computer science*] .... SPID
Service Project Drawing .... SPD
Service Propulation Engine (IAA) .... SPE
Service Propulsion System [*or Subsystem*] [*NASA*] (KSC) .... SERPS
Service Propulsion System [*or Subsystem*] [*NASA*] .... SPS
Service Propulsion Unit .... SPU
Service Protection Network (NITA) .... SPN
Service Provider ID (PCM) .... SPID
Service Provider Interface [*Computer science*] .... SPI
Service Provider's Network Management Center .... SNMC
Service Publication Form (AAG) .... SPF
Service Publication Instruction (AAG) .... SPI
Service Publications (AAG) .... SP
Service Record .... SERVREC
Service Record [*Military*] .... SR
Service Record and Allied Papers [*Military*] .... SRAP
Service Record and Health Record [*Military*] .... SERVHEL
Service Record and Pay Record [*Military*] .... SERVPA
Service Record Book [*Military*] .... SRB
Service Record, Health Record, Pay Account, and Personal Effects [*Military*] .... SERANDA
Service Record, Pay Record, and Health Record [*Military*] .... SERVPAHEL
Service Recording and Data Analysis System (IEEE) .... SRDAS
Service Repair Manual .... SRM
Service Report .... SR
Service Representative Report (MCD) .... SRR
Service Request .... SRQ
Service Request Acknowledgment [*Air Force*] (CET) .... SR-ACK
Service Request Block [*Computer science*] (BUR) .... SRB
Service Request Not Honored (IAA) .... SRNH
Service Request State (IAA) .... SRQS
Service Revealed Deficiency [*or Difficulty*] .... SRD
Service Rifle [*British military*] (DMA) .... SR
Service Rights Layer [*Computer science*] .... SRL
Service Rum Diluted [*British military*] (DMA) .... SRD
Service School [*Military*] .... SVS
Service School Command [*Navy*] .... SERVSCOLCOM
Service Schools Command (MCD) .... SSC
Service Schools Command Detachment [*Navy*] (DNAB) .... SERVSCOLCOMDET
Service Security Layer [*Computer science*] .... SSL
Service Shop Requirement Notice .... SSRN
Service Sink (MSA) .... SS
Service Sink [*Technical drawings*] .... SSK
Service Social International [*International Social Service - ISS*] [*Geneva, Switzerland*] (EAIO) .... SSI
Service, Sort and Merge [*Computer science*] .... SESAME
Service, Sort, and Merge [*Computer science*] (IEEE) .... SESOME
Service Squadron [*Navy*] .... SERON
Service Squadron [*Navy*] .... SERRON
Service Squadron [*Navy*] .... SERVON
Service Squadron (AAG) .... SS
Service Stars [*Military decoration*] .... SvcStrs
Service Station & Garage Management [*Canada A publication*] .... SSGM
Service Station Dealers of America (EA) .... SSDA
Service Storage Facility [*Military*] .... SSF
Service Structure (KSC) .... SS
Service, Supply, and Procurement [*Military*] .... SS & P
Service Support Arrangement .... SSA
Service Support Force [*Military*] .... SSF
Service Tabulating (AAG) .... ST
Service Tabulating Form (AAG) .... STF
Service Technician Advancement, Recruitment, and Training .... START
Service Technician Education Program .... STEP
Service Technique Externe (IAA) .... STE
Service Technique Militaire [*Switzerland*] .... STM
Service Technology Corp. [*of Ling-Temco-Vought, Inc.*] .... STC
Service Test [*Military*] .... ST
Service Test and Evaluation Program [*FAA*] (TAG) .... STEP
Service Test and Evaluation Program .... STEP
Service Test Model (NG) .... STM
Service Test Review .... STR
Service to Chapters [*Red Cross*] .... STC
Service to Claimants [*Unemployment Insurance Service*] [*Department of Labor*] .... STC

Service to Mankind [*Meaning of name of Sertoma International Organization*] .... SERTOMA
Service to Military Families [*Red Cross*] .... SMF
Service to Military Families Representative [*Red Cross*] .... SMFR
Service to the Armed Forces .... SAF
Service to the Fleet [*A publication*] (DNAB) .... STTF
Service Tools (AAG) .... STTF
Service Tools Institute [*Later, HTI*] (EA) .... STI
Service Trials Unit .... STU
Service Trouble Report .... STR
Service Unit [*Military*] .... SU
Service Universitaire Canadien Outre-Mer [*Canadian University Service Overseas - CUSO*] .... SUCO
Service Vehicle .... SV
Service Volontaire Mennonite [*Mennonite Voluntary Service*] .... SVM
Service Water [*Nuclear energy*] (NRCH) .... SW
Service Water Booster Pump [*Nuclear energy*] (IEEE) .... SWBP
Service Water Pressurization Pump [*Nuclear energy*] (IEEE) .... SWPP
Service Water Pump [*Nuclear energy*] (NRCH) .... SWP
Service Water Reservoir [*Nuclear energy*] (NRCH) .... SWR
Service Water Storage Tank [*Nuclear energy*] (IEEE) .... SWST
Service Water System [*Nuclear energy*] (NRCH) .... SWS
Service Weapons Acceptability Tests .... SWAT
Service Weapons Operational Procedures (MCD) .... SWOP
Service Weapons Test (NVT) .... SWPT
Service Women in Non-Traditional Environmental Roles [*Canadian armed forces*] .... SWINTER
Service Zone Indication [*Computer science*] (IAA) .... SZI
Serviceability Objective .... SO
Serviceability Self-Test (MCD) .... SST
Serviceable .... SVCBL
Service-Craft and Boats Machine Accounting Report [*Navy*] (NG) .... SABMAR
Service-Craft and Boats Machine Accounting System [*Navy*] (DNAB) ...... SAMAS
Serviced [*Automotive advertising*] .... SRVCD
Serviced Apartment .... SA
Service-Factor Amperes (MSA) .... SFA
Serviceman's Opportunity for College Associate Degree [*Military*] (MCD) .... SOCAD
ServiceMaster Ltd. [*Associated Press*] (SAG) .... Svcmstr
ServiceMaster Ltd. [*NYSE symbol*] (SPSG) .... SVM
Servicemaster Ltd. Partnership [*Associated Press*] (SAG) .... Svcmst
ServiceMaster L.P. [*NYSE symbol*] (TTSB) .... SVM
Servicemen's Dependents Allowance Act .... SDAA
Servicemen's Group Life Insurance [*Military*] .... SGLI
Servicemen's Mutual Aid and Savings Fund [*South Vietnam*] .... SMASF
Servicemen's Opportunity College [*DoD*] .... SOC
Servicemen's Readjustment Act .... SRA
Services Aeronautiques Roannais [*France ICAO designator*] (FAAC) .... RNS
Services After-Care Scheme [*British*] .... SACS
Services and Equipment .... S & E
Services and Techniques for Advanced Real-Time Systems [*Computer science*] (IAA) .... STARS
Services by Satellite, Inc. [*Defunct*] .... SATSERV
Services de Formation et de Consultation aux Bandes [*Department of Indian and Inuit Affairs*] [*Canada*] .... SFCB
Services Electronic Research Establishment [*British*] (DEN) .... SERE
Services Electronic Research Laboratory [*British*] .... SERL
Services Engineering Computer-Aided Design [*Pierce Management Services*] [*Software package*] (NCC) .... SECAD
Services Flight [*Military*] .... SVF
Services for Crippled Children .... SCC
Services Industrial Professional Technical Union [*Ireland*] (EAIO) .... SIPTU
Services Information Management System [*DoD*] (GFGA) .... SIMS
Services Kinema Corp. [*British military*] (DMA) .... SKC
Services Missionnaires des Jeunes [*Canada*] .... SMJ
Services No Longer Required .... SNLR
Services Public Relations Officer [*British military*] (DMA) .... SPRO
Services Sound and Video Corp. [*British*] .... SSVC
Services Squadron .... SVS
Services Techniques des Construction et Armes Navales / France Outre Mer [*French river patrol boat used in Vietnam*] (VNW) .... STCAN/FOM
Services to Ongoing Mature Aging [*Counseling group*] .... SOMA
Services to User Populations Section [*Disbanded by the Board at the Midwinter meeting*] .... SUPS
Services Valve Life Test Establishment [*British*] (MCD) .... SVLTE
Services Valve Test Laboratory [*British*] (NATG) .... SVTL
Services Vegetable Production [*British military*] (DMA) .... SVP
Service-Specific Practice Cost Percentage [*Medicine*] (DMAA) .... SSPCP
Service-Wide Supply .... SWS
Servicing (AAG) .... S
Servicing .... SVCG
Servicing (IAA) .... SVG
Servicing Control Unit [*Telecommunications*] (TEL) .... SCU
Servicing Diagram .... SD
Servicing Flight [*British military*] (DMA) .... SF
Servicing Hotels and the Caribbean Community .... SHACC
Servicing Log [*Telecommunications*] (TEL) .... SVLOG
Servicing Support Center (SSD) .... SSC
Servicio Aereo de Honduras SA [*ICAO designator*] (FAAC) .... SHA
Servicio Aereo de Honduras Sociedad Anonima .... SAHSA
Servicio Autonomo Nacional de Acueductos y Alcantarillados [*Honduras*] .... SANAA
Servicio Cooperativo Interamericano de Educacion .... SCIDE
Servicio de Aeronavegacion a Territorios Nacionales [*Colombian airline*] .... SATENA

Servicio de Consulta a Bancos de Informacion [*Database Consultation Service*] [*Information service or system Mexico*] (IID) .... SECOBI
Servicio de Helicopteros SL [*Spain ICAO designator*] (FAAC) .... SDH
Servicio de Vigilancia Aerea del Ministerio de Seguridad Publica [*Costa Rica*] [*ICAO designator*] (FAAC) .... MSP
Servicio, Desarrollo y Paz [*Service, Development, and Peace*] [*An association Mexico*] (CROSS) .... SEDEPAC
Servicio Especializado de Carga Aerea [*Columbia*] [*FAA designator*] (FAAC) .... SEZ
Servicio Europeo de Universitarios Latinoamericanos [*Belgium*] .... SEUL
Servicio Geodesico Interamericano [*Inter-American Geodetic Survey - IAGS*] [*United States*] .... SGI
Servicio Informativo Continental [*Press agency*] [*Argentina*] .... SIC
Servicio Intelligencia Militar [*Military Intelligence Service*] [*Dominican Republic*] .... SIM
Servicio Latinoamericano y Asiatico de Vivienda Popular [*Latin American and Asian low Income Housing Service*] [*Chile*] (EAIO) .... SELAVIP
Servicio Leo Lopez SA de CV [*Mexico ICAO designator*] (FAAC) .... LLA
Servicio Oficial de Difusion Radio Electrica [*Radio and television network*] [*Uruguay*] .... SODRE
Servicio Universitario Mundial [*World University Service*] .... SUM
Servicios a la Navegacion en el Espacio Aereo Mexicano [*Mexico ICAO designator*] (FAAC) .... SENEAM
Servicios a la Navegacion en el Espacio Aereo Mexicano [*Mexico ICAO designator*] (FAAC) .... XMX
Servicios a la Navegacion en el Espacio Aereo Mexicano (SENEAM) [*Mexico ICAO designator*] (ICDA) .... XM
Servicios Aereolineas Mexicanas SA de CV [*Mexico ICAO designator*] (FAAC) .... SMS
Servicios Aereos Amazonicos [*Peru*] [*FAA designator*] (FAAC) .... AZN
Servicios Aereos Barsa SA de CV [*Mexico ICAO designator*] (FAAC) .... SBS
Servicios Aereos Cruzeiro do Sul SA [*Brazil*] [*ICAO designator*] (FAAC) .... CRZ
Servicios Aereos de La Capital [*Colombia*] [*ICAO designator*] (FAAC) .... SAD
Servicios Aereos de Los Angeles SA de CV [*Mexico ICAO designator*] (FAAC) .... AGE
Servicios Aereos de Pilotos Ejecutivos [*Colombia*] [*ICAO designator*] (FAAC) .... SAR
Servicios Aereos del Nazas SA de CV [*Mexico ICAO designator*] (FAAC) .... NAZ
Servicios Aereos del Sol SA de CV [*Mexico ICAO designator*] (FAAC) .... AOS
Servicios Aereos del Vaupes Ltd. [*Colombia*] [*ICAO designator*] (FAAC) .... SDV
Servicios Aereos do Vale Amazonico SA [*Brazil*] [*ICAO designator*] (FAAC) .... TNS
Servicios Aereos Especiales de Jalisco SA de CV [*Mexico ICAO designator*] (FAAC) .... SJA
Servicios Aereos Especializados en Transportes Petroleros [*Colombia*] [*ICAO designator*] (FAAC) .... KSP
Servicios Aereos Gadel SA de CV [*Mexico ICAO designator*] (FAAC) .... GDE
Servicios Aereos Gana SA de CV [*Mexico*] [*FAA designator*] (FAAC) .... GNA
Servicios Aereos Nacionales [*Ecuador*] [*ICAO designator*] (FAAC) .... SAN
Servicios Aereos Norte Sur SA de CV [*Mexico ICAO designator*] (FAAC) .... SNE
Servicios Aereos Poblanos, SA de CV [*Mexico*] [*FAA designator*] (FAAC) .... POB
Servicios Aereos Rutas Oriente SA de CV [*Mexico ICAO designator*] (FAAC) .... SRO
Servicios Aereos Sunset, SA de CV [*Mexico*] [*FAA designator*] (FAAC) .... SSE
Servicios Aereos y Fotograficos, SA de CV [*Mexico*] [*FAA designator*] (FAAC) .... FTG
Servicios Aeroes Litoral SA de CV [*Mexico ICAO designator*] (FAAC) .... SLI
Servicios Aeronauticos Latina America .... SALA
Servicios Aeros de Chihuahua Aerochisa SA de CV [*Mexico ICAO designator*] (FAAC) .... AHI
Servicios Auxiliares de Transportes [*ICAO designator*] (FAAC) .... SATA
Servicios Auxiliares de Transportes Aereos [*Brazil*] [*ICAO designator*] (FAAC) .... STS
Servicios de Carga Aerea [*National Airlines*] [*Costa Rica*] (EY) .... SERCA
Servicios de Transporte Aereo, SA de CV [*Mexico*] [*FAA designator*] (FAAC) .... SVI
Servicios do Aerotaxisa e Abastecimento do Vale Amazonica [*Airline*] [*Brazil*] .... SAVA
Servicios Electricos del Gran Buenos Aires, SA [*Electrical utility*] [*Argentina*] .... SEGBA
Servicios Informativos Procesados [*Processed Information Services*] [*Mexico*] (CROSS) .... SIPRO
Servicios Politecnicos Aereos SA [*Spain ICAO designator*] (FAAC) .... SPASA
Servicios Telereservacios SA de CV [*ICAO designator*] (FAAC) .... SERTEL
Servicious de Alquiler Aereo SA de CV [*Mexico ICAO designator*] (FAAC) .... SQL
Servico Acoriana de Transportes Aereos [*Portugal ICAO designator*] (FAAC) .... SAT
Servico de Alimentacao da Providencia Social [*Brazil*] .... SAPS
Servico de Inspecao de Produtos de Origem Animal [*Brazil*] .... SIPOA
Servico de Inspecao dos Produtos Agropecuarios e Materiais Agricolas [*Brazil*] .... SIPAMA
Servico de Propaganda e Educacao Sanitaria [*Brazil*] .... SPES
Servico des Transportes Aereos [*Portuguese West Africa*] .... STA
Servico, Inc. [*AMEX symbol*] (SPSG) .... SER
Servico Inc. [*AMEX symbol*] (TTSB) .... SER
Servico, Inc. [*Associated Press*] (SAG) .... Servico
Servicos Aereos Cruzeiro do Sul SA [*Brazilian airline*] .... CRUZEIRO
Servicos Auxiliares de Transportes Aereos (SATA) [*Brazil ICAO designator*] (ICDA) .... XT
Servier [*France*] [*Research code symbol*] .... S
Serving (MSA) .... SERG
Serving (FAAC) .... SVG
Serving Area Concept [*Bell System*] .... SAC
Serving Brother [*Church of England*] .... SB
Serving Brother, Order of St. John of Jerusalem [*British*] .... SBStJ
Serving Point [*Telecommunications*] .... SP
Serving Sister, Order of St. John of Jerusalem [*British*] .... SSStJ
Serving Test Center [*Bell System*] .... STC
Serving the Indigent Sick .... SIS
Servisair Ltd. [*British ICAO designator*] (FAAC) .... SGH
Servite Fathers (TOCD) .... osm
Servite Missionary Sisters of the Sorrowful Mother (TOCD) .... MMD
Servites (TOCD) .... OSM
Servizio Informazioni Difesa [*Defense Intelligence Service*] [*Italy*] .... SID
Servizio Informazioni Esercito [*Italy*] [*Forces Intelligence Service*] .... SIE
Servizio Informazioni Militare [*Military Intelligence Service*] [*Italy*] .... SIM
Servo (KSC) .... SVO
Servo Adapter Coupler .... SAC
Servo Amplifier .... SA
Servo Amplifier (IAA) .... SRVAMPL
Servo Chart Drive .... SCD
Servo Control Cabinet [*Military*] (CAAL) .... SCC
Servo Drive System .... SDS
Servo Gear Train Assembly .... SGTA
Servo Inlet (IAA) .... SRVIN
Servo Meter Panel (AAG) .... SMP
Servo Nozzle Control (MCD) .... SNC
Servo Parameter Shift .... SPS
Servo Power Amplifier (NASA) .... SPA
Servo Power Assembly (MCD) .... SPA
Servo Preamplifier .... SPA
Servo Pressure Control Console .... SPCC
Servo Repeater Indicator .... SRI
Servo Repeater Unit .... SRU
Servo Return (IAA) .... SRVRET
Servo Summing Junction .... SSJ
Servo Tape Display .... STD
Servo Test System .... STS
Servo Test Unit .... STU
Servo Tester With Automatic Data Acquisition and Reduction (IAA) .... STADAR
Servo-Actuated Assembly .... SAA
Servo-Controlled Positioner .... SCP
Servo-Controlled Positioning System .... SCPS
Servocylinder Test Set (MCD) .... STS
Servomechanism .... SERVO
Servomechanisms and Data Processing Laboratory [*Massachusetts Institute of Technology*] (MCD) .... SDPL
Servomechanisms Laboratory [*MIT*] (MCD) .... SL
Servomotor (IAA) .... SM
Servomotor [*Control systems*] .... SVMTR
Servomotor Rate Generator .... SRG
Servotronics, Inc. [*Associated Press*] (SAG) .... Servotr
Servotronics, Inc. [*AMEX symbol*] (SPSG) .... SVT
Servovalve .... S/V
Serv-Tech, Inc. [*Associated Press*] (SAG) .... SrvTch
Serv-Tech, Inc. [*NASDAQ symbol*] (NQ) .... STEC
Servus Dei [*Servant of God*] [*Latin*] .... SD
Ses Altesses Imperiales [*Their Imperial Highnesses*] [*French*] (ROG) .... SSAAII
SES [*Shuttle Engineering System*] **Cockpit Interface** [*NASA*] (SSD) .... SCI
Sesheke [*Zambia*] [*ICAO location identifier*] (ICLI) .... FLSS
Sesheke [*Zambia*] [*Airport symbol*] (AD) .... SJQ
Seshote [*Lesotho*] [*ICAO location identifier*] (ICLI) .... FXSS
Seshute's [*Lesotho*] [*Airport symbol*] (OAG) .... SHZ
Sesone [*Herbicide*] [*Trademark of Union Carbide Corp.*] .... SES
Sesquihora [*An Hour and a Half*] [*Pharmacy*] (ROG) .... SESQUIH
Sesquihora [*An Hour and a Half*] [*Pharmacy*] .... SESQUIHOR
Sesquiplane [*Navy*] .... S
Sesquiterpenoid Stress Metabolite [*Plant physiology*] .... SSM
Session .... SESS
Session Cases [*Legal term British*] .... SC
Session Cases, High Court of Justiciary Section [*1906-16*] [*Scotland*] [*A publication*] (DLA) .... Sess Cas
Session Control [*Computer science*] (IBMDP) .... SC
Session Control Block [*Computer science*] (BUR) .... SCB
Session Control Properties [*Computer science*] .... SCP
Session Handler .... SH
Session Laws (DLA) .... SL
Session Laws of Colorado [*A publication*] (DLA) .... Colo Sess Laws
Session Laws of Hawaii [*A publication*] (DLA) .... Haw Sess Laws
Session Laws of Hawaii [*A publication*] (DLA) .... Hawaii Sess Laws
Session Laws of Idaho [*A publication*] (DLA) .... Idaho Sess Laws
Session Laws of Kansas [*A publication*] (DLA) .... Kan Sess Laws
Session Laws of North Carolina [*A publication*] (DLA) .... NC Sess Laws
Session Laws. Wyoming [*A publication*] (DLA) .... Wyo Sess Laws
Session Notes [*Scotland*] [*A publication*] (DLA) .... Sess N
Session Notes [*Scotland*] [*A publication*] (DLA) .... SN
Session of Peace [*Legal*] [*British*] (ROG) .... SP
Session Protocol Data Unit [*Telecommunications*] (OSI) .... SPDU
Session Protocol Machine [*Telecommunications*] (OSI) .... SPM
Session Service [*Telecommunications*] (OSI) .... SS
Session Service Data Unit [*Telecommunications*] (OSI) .... SSDU
Sessions .... SS
Sessions Cases (House of Lords) [*Legal*] [*British*] .... SC(HL)
Sessions Cases (Judiciary Reports) [*Legal*] [*British*] .... SC(J)
Sessions Cases, King's Bench [*1710-48*] [*England*] [*A publication*] (DLA) .... Sess Ca
Sessions Cases, King's Bench [*England*] [*A publication*] (DLA) .... Sess Cas
Sessions Settlement Cases, King's Bench [*England*] [*A publication*] (DLA) .... Sess Cas KB
Sesuncia [*An Ounce and a Half*] [*Pharmacy*] (ROG) .... SESUNC

Sesura [*North Korea ICAO location identifier*] (ICLI) ... ZKSR
Set ... S
Set ... SE
Set Asychronous Response Mode Extended [*Telecommunications*] (OSI) ... SARME
Set Asynchronous Balanced Mode ... SABM
Set Asynchronous Balanced Mode Extended [*Telecommunications*] (OSI) ... SABME
Set Asynchronous Response Mode ... SARM
Set Back Front Axle [*Automotive engineering*] ... SBFA
Set Ballistic Gain Table ... SETBGT
Set Carry ... STC
Set/Clear [*Flip-flop*] [*Computer science*] ... SC
Set Clock ... SC
Set Clock (IAA) ... SCK
Set Complete Radio ... SCR
Set Conditionally [*Computer science*] ... SCC
Set Course [*Navigation*] ... S/C
Set Driver (SAA) ... STD
Set Equation Transformation System [*1970*] [*Computer science*] (CSR) ... SETS
Set Format Identifier ... SFID
Set Gate ... SG
Set Graphics Rendition [*Computer science*] (PCM) ... SGR
Set Identification ... SETID
Set Indicators of the Left Half (SAA) ... SIL
Set Indicators of the Right Half (SAA) ... SIR
Set Interrupt Mask [*Computer science*] ... SIM
Set Location Counter (CMD) ... SLC
Set Meals [*School meals*] [*British*] ... S
Set Mode (BUR) ... SM
Set Normal Response Mode [*Telecommunications*] (OSI) ... SNRM
Set Normal Response Mode Extended [*Telecommunications*] (OSI) ... SNRME
Set Overrides Clear (IEEE) ... SOC
Set Pattern (IAA) ... SP
Set Point ... SP
Set Point Control [*Computer science*] (ECII) ... SPC
Set Point Controller ... SPC
Set Point Station ... SPS
Set Priority Level [*Computer science*] (NHD) ... SPL
Set Reset Trigger [*Flipflop*] [*Computer science*] (IAA) ... SRT
Set Screw [*Technical drawings*] ... SS
Set Screw ... SSCR
Set Sign Minus (SAA) ... SSM
Set Sign Plus (SAA) ... SSP
Set Steering ... SS
Set Strobe Time [*Computer science*] (OA) ... SST
Set System Mask (HGAA) ... SSM
Set the Date Now [*Association supporting the end of US military involvement in Indochina*] [*Defunct*] (EA) ... STDN
Set Theoretic Data Structure (IAA) ... STDS
Set Theoretic Language [*1971*] [*Computer science*] (CSR) ... SETL
Set Theoretic Language - BALM [*1973*] [*Computer science*] (CSR) ... SETB
Set Theory Analysis and Measure of Information Characteristics ... STAMIC
Set Trigger ... ST
Set Up [*Freight*] ... SU
Set Up in Carloads [*Freight*] ... SUCL
Set Up in Less than Carloads [*Freight*] ... SULCL
Set Value ... SV
Set Vertical Format (IAA) ... SVF
Set-and-Test-Sequence-Number [*Computer science*] (IBMDP) ... STSN
Setback Axle [*Truck engineering*] ... SBA
Set-Down Pool [*Nuclear energy*] (NRCH) ... SDP
Seth G. Huntington [*Designer's mark on US bicentennial half dollar*] ... SGH
Setif [*Algeria*] [*Seismograph station code, US Geological Survey*] (SEIS) ... SET
Setif [*Algeria*] [*Airport symbol*] (AD) ... STF
Setif/Ain-Arnat [*Algeria*] [*ICAO location identifier*] (ICLI) ... DAAS
Seton Hall University (GAGS) ... Seton Hall U
Seton Hall University [*South Orange, NJ*] ... SHU
Seton Hall University, Law Library, Newark, NJ [*Library symbol Library of Congress*] (LCLS) ... NjSooS-L
Seton Hall University, South Orange, NJ [*Library symbol Library of Congress*] (LCLS) ... NjSooS
Seton Hall University, South Orange, NJ [*OCLC symbol*] (OCLC) ... STH
Seton Hill College [*Greensburg, PA*] ... SHC
Seton Hill College, Greensburg, PA [*Library symbol Library of Congress*] (LCLS) ... PGbSH
Seton Psychiatric Institute, Baltimore, MD [*Library symbol Library of Congress*] (LCLS) ... MdBSet
Seton Shrine Center (EA) ... SSC
Seton Sisters of Our Lady of Guadalupe, Tucson (TOCD) ... SSLOG
Seton's Forms of Decrees, Judgments, and Orders in Equity [*7 eds.*] [*1830-1912*] [*A publication*] (DLA) ... Seton
Seton's Forms of Decrees, Judgments, and Orders in Equity [*7th ed.*] [*1912*] [*A publication*] (DLA) ... Seton Dec
Set-Oriented Retrieval Module ... SORM
Setpoint Digital Control (IAA) ... SDC
Setpoint Precision Infrared Angular Scanner (PDAA) ... SPIRAS
Set-Reset [*Flip-Flop*] [*Computer science*] ... S-R
Set-Reset Clocked Data [*Computer science*] ... SRCD
Set-Reset Flip-Flop [*Computer science*] ... SRFF
Sets in Use [*Television rating*] (WDMC) ... SIU
Sets, Kits, and Outfits (MCD) ... SKO
Sets My Teeth on Edge ... SMTOE
Sets Tabular Material [*Phototypesetting computer*] ... SETAB
Sette Cama [*Gabon*] [*Airport symbol*] (AD) ... ZKM
Sette-Cama [*Gabon*] [*ICAO location identifier*] (ICLI) ... FOOS
Setter (MSA) ... SETR
Set-Theoretic Approach to Relations (PDAA) ... STAR
Setting (MSA) ... SET
Settlement (ROG) ... SET
Settlement (ROG) ... SETTLET
Settlement (ROG) ... SETTT
Settlement and Accelerated Funds Exchange [*Chicago, IL*] ... SAFE
Settlement and Removal Cases in English King's Bench [*A publication*] (DLA) ... Sett & Rem
Settlement and Removal Cases in English King's Bench [*A publication*] (DLA) ... Sett Cas
Settlement Cases [*A publication*] (DLA) ... Sett
Settlement Date [*Business*] (MHDB) ... SD
Settlement Houses Employment Development [*Large group of settlement houses*] ... SHED
Settlement Information Strategy [*Australia*] ... SIS
Settlement, Payment, Accounting, Credit Extension (MHDB) ... SPACE
Settlement Problem-Oriented Language [*Computer science*] (IEEE) ... SEPOL
Settlement Register [*Computer science*] ... SR
Settlement with Conditions [*Environmental Protection Agency*] (GFGA) ... SWC
Settler [*Genealogy*] ... SETTL
Settling ... SET
Settling (MSA) ... SETLG
Set-Up [*Control*] **Module** [*Telecommunications*] (TEL) ... SUM
Set-Up Sheet (AAG) ... SUSH
Set-Up Time ... SUT
Set-Valued Logic [*Computer science*] ... SVL
Seumayam [*Indonesia*] [*ICAO location identifier*] (ICLI) ... WITS
Seva Foundation (EA) ... SF
Sevastopol [*Former USSR Seismograph station code, US Geological Survey Closed*] (SEIS) ... SEV
Seveh [*Iran*] [*ICAO location identifier*] (ICLI) ... OIIV
Seven (ROG) ... S
Seven ... SEV
Seven Bar Flying Service, Inc. [*ICAO designator*] (FAAC) ... SBF
Seven Falls [*Quebec*] [*Seismograph station code, US Geological Survey Closed*] (SEIS) ... SFA
Seven Hills Financial Corp. [*Associated Press*] (SAG) ... SevnHil
Seven Hills Financial Corp. [*NASDAQ symbol*] (SAG) ... SHFC
Seven Hills Finl [*NASDAQ symbol*] (TTSB) ... SHFC
Seven Mile High Resources, Inc. [*Vancouver Stock Exchange symbol*] ... SVH
Seven Nights [*A week*] (ROG) ... SE'NNIGHT
Seven Oaks General Hospital, Education Services, Winnipeg, MB, Canada [*Library symbol Library of Congress*] (LCLS) ... CaMWSOGH
Seven Rivers Library Cooperative, Iowa City, IA [*Library symbol Library of Congress*] (LCLS) ... IaIaS
Seven Seas Cruising Association (EA) ... SSCA
Seven Springs Center [*An association*] (EA) ... SSC
[*The*] **Seven Tablets of Creation** [*L. W. King*] [*A publication*] (BJA) ... STC
Seven-Conductor [*Wire or cable*] (MSA) ... 7/C
Sevenhill [*Australia Seismograph station code, US Geological Survey Closed*] (SEIS) ... SNL
Sevenson Enviro Svcs [*NASDAQ symbol*] (TTSB) ... SEVN
Sevenson Environmental Services, Inc. [*Associated Press*] (SAG) ... SevEnv
Sevenson Environmental Services, Inc. [*NASDAQ symbol*] (NQ) ... SEVN
Seventeenth Coast Guard District [*Juneau, AK*] [*USCG*] (TAG) ... D17
Seventeenth-Century News [*A publication*] (BRI) ... Sev Cent N
Seventh Avenue [*New York City*] ... SA
Seventh Coast Guard District [*Miami, FL*] [*USCG*] (TAG) ... D7
Seventh Day Adventist Kinship International (EA) ... SDAKI
Seventh Day Adventist School, Holland, MN [*Library symbol*] [*Library of Congress*] (LCLS) ... MnHldSDS
Seventh Day Adventists Junior Academy, Portage, MI [*Library symbol*] [*Library of Congress*] (LCLS) ... MiPorS
Seventh Day Baptist General Conference (EA) ... SDBGC
Seventh Day Baptist Historical Society (EA) ... SDBHS
Seventh Day Baptist Historical Society Library, Janesville, WI [*Library symbol*] [*Library of Congress*] (LCLS) ... WJaSDHi
Seventh Day Baptist Historical Society, Plainfield, NJ [*Library symbol Library of Congress*] (LCLS) ... NjPlaSDB
Seventh Day Baptist Missionary Society (EA) ... SDBMS
Seventh Day Baptist World Federation (EA) ... SDBWF
Seventh Fleet [*Navy*] ... SEVENTHFLT
Seventh Fleet [*Pacific*] [*Navy*] ... SEVFLT
Seventh Fleet Intelligence Center [*Navy*] ... SEFIC
Seventh Generation [*NASDAQ symbol*] (TTSB) ... SVNG
Seventh Generation Fund for Indian Development (EA) ... SGFID
Seventh Level, Inc. [*Associated Press*] (SAG) ... 7th Level
Seventh Level, Inc. [*NASDAQ symbol*] (SAG) ... SEVL
Seventh United States Army ... SUSA
Seventh-Day Adventist ... SDA
Seventh-Day Adventist Church Musicians Guild [*Defunct*] (EA) ... SDACMG
Seventh-Day Adventist Dietetic Association (EA) ... SDADA
Seventh-Day Adventist Kinship Canada [*Defunct*] (EAIO) ... SDAKC
Seventh-Day Adventist World Service [*ADRA*] [*Superseded by*] (EA) ... SAWS
Seventy (ROG) ... S
Seventy Plus Ski Club (EA) ... SPSC
Severable Government Equipment ... SGE
Several ... SEV
Several (ROG) ... SEVL
Several Compilers Reworked and Modified ... SCRAM
Several Dancers Core [*Houston, TX and Atlanta, GA*] ... SDC
Several Dates ... SD
Severance Pay [*Military*] ... SEVP

Severance Tax (MHDB) ... ST
Severe [*Used to qualify weather phenomena*] ... SEV
Severe (MAE) ... SV
Severe Accident Research Plan [*Nuclear energy*] (NRCH) ... SARP
Severe Accident Risk Reduction Program [*Nuclear energy*] (NRCH) ... SARRP
Severe Accident Sequence Analysis [*Nuclear energy*] (NRCH) ... SASA
Severe Acoustic Noise ... SAN
Severe Acoustic Noise Environment ... SANE
Severe Aplastic Anemia [*Hematology*] ... SAA
Severe Aster Yellows [*Plant pathology*] ... SAY
Severe Childhood Autosomal Recessive Muscular Dystrophy [*Medicine*] ... SCARMD
Severe Combined Anaemia and Thrombocytopenia (ECON) ... SCAT
Severe Combined Immune Deficiency [*Immunology*] ... SCID
Severe Core Damage Analysis Package [*Nuclear energy*] (NRCH) ... SCDAP
Severe Duty [*Truck*] ... SD
Severe Environment Memory Series [*or System*] [*Computer science*] ... SEMS
Severe Environment Power System (IEEE) ... SEPS
Severe Environmental Air Launch Study (KSC) ... SEALS
Severe Environmental Storms and Mesoscale Experiment [*National Science Foundation/National Oceanic and Atmospheric Administration*] ... SESAME
Severe Fuel Damage (GAAI) ... SFD
Severe Impairment Battery [*Neuropsychological test*] ... SIB
Severe Learning Difficulties (AIE) ... SLD
Severe Local Storm [*National Weather Service*] ... SELS
Severe Myoclonic Epilepsy of Infancy [*Medicine*] (DMAA) ... SMEI
Severe Noise Environment ... SNE
Severe Parental Punishment ... SPP
Severe Renal Insufficiency [*Medicine*] ... SRI
Severe, Right-Moving [*Thunderstorm*] ... SR
Severe Storm Forecast Center [*U.S. Weather Service*] (BARN) ... SSFC
Severe Weather Avoidance Nationwide [*National Oceanic and Atmospheric Administration*] ... SWAN
Severe Weather Avoidance Plan (FAAC) ... SWAP
Severe Weather Avoidance Program (GAVI) ... SWAP
Severe Weather Forecast [*National Weather Service*] (FAAC) ... WW
Severe Weather Warning (KSC) ... SWW
Severed ... SEV
Severely and Profoundly Handicapped ... SPH
Severely and Profoundly Impaired ... SPI
Severely Diabetic ... SD
Severely Handicapped ... SH
Severely Handicapped ... SVH
Severely Impaired Renal Function [*Medicine*] (DMAA) ... SIRF
Severely Mentally Ill (GFGA) ... SMI
Severely Mentally Retarded ... SMR
Severely, Profoundly Handicapped (OICC) ... SP
Severely Subnormal ... SSN
Severest Critic [*Initialism used by E. B. White to describe his wife*] ... SC
Severide Resources, Inc. [*Vancouver Stock Exchange symbol*] ... SVE
Severity ... S
Severity Adjusted Death Rate [*Medicine*] (DHSM) ... SADR
Severity of Alcohol Dependence Questionnaire ... SADQ
Severity of Illness [*Medicine*] (DMAA) ... SOI
Severity of Illness Index [*Health insurance*] (GHCT) ... SII
Severity of Ozone Cracking (PDAA) ... SOC
Severn and Potomac Reserve District [*Marine Corps*] ... S & P RES DIS
Severn House [*Publisher*] [*British*] ... SH
Severn River Naval Command ... SRNC
Severn Tunnel Junction [*British depot code*] ... STJ
Severo-Kurilsk [*Former USSR Seismograph station code, US Geological Survey*] (SEIS) ... SKR
Severouralsk [*Former USSR ICAO location identifier*] (ICLI) ... USSE
Severus [*of Scriptores Historiae Augustae*] [*Classical studies*] (OCD) ... Sev
Sevestre and Marshall's Bengal Reports [*A publication*] (DLA) ... App Cas Beng
Sevestre's Bengal High Court Appeal Cases [*1864-68*] [*India*] [*A publication*] (DLA) ... Sev App Cas
Sevestre's Bengal High Court Reports [*India*] [*A publication*] (DLA) ... Sev HC
Sevestre's Sadr Diwani Adalat Reports [*Bengal, India*] [*A publication*] (DLA) ... Sev SDA
Sevierville, TN [*FM radio station call letters*] ... WMYU
Sevierville, TN [*AM radio station call letters*] ... WSEV
Sevilla [*Spain ICAO location identifier*] (ICLI) ... LECS
Sevilla [*Spain ICAO location identifier*] (ICLI) ... LEZL
Sevilla/Moron [*Spain ICAO location identifier*] (ICLI) ... LEMO
Sevilla/Tablada [*Spain ICAO location identifier*] (ICLI) ... LETA
Sevilla-El Copero Base [*Spain ICAO location identifier*] (ICLI) ... LEEC
Seville [*Spain*] [*Airport symbol*] (OAG) ... SVQ
Seville Touring Sedan [*General Motors Corp.*] ... STS
Seville Township Library, Riverdale, MI [*Library symbol Library of Congress*] (LCLS) ... MiRd
Sevres [*China*] (ROG) ... SEV
Sewage [*or Sewer*] (AAG) ... SEW
Sewage Disposal [*British Waterways Board sign*] ... S
Sewage Microparticulates [*Oceanography*] ... SM
Sewage Plant Manufacturers' Association [*British*] (BI) ... SPMA
Sewage Treatment Plant ... STP
Sewage Treatment System [*Navy*] (CAAL) ... STS
Sewage Treatment Works ... STW
Sewall Early Education Developmental Profiles ... SEED
Sewanee Review [*A publication*] (BRI) ... Sew R
Sewanee, TN [*Location identifier FAA*] (FAAL) ... UOS
Sewanee, TN [*FM radio station call letters*] ... WUTS
Sewanhaka High School, Floral Park, NY [*Library symbol*] [*Library of Congress*] (LCLS) ... NFlpSH
Seward [*Alaska*] [*Seismograph station code, US Geological Survey*] (SEIS) ... SEW
Seward, AK [*AM radio station call letters*] ... KSWD
Seward, AK [*Location identifier FAA*] (FAAL) ... SWD
Seward Community Library, Seward, AK [*Library symbol*] [*Library of Congress*] (LCLS) ... AkSew
Seward Community Library, Seward, AK [*Library symbol Library of Congress*] (LCLS) ... AkSew
Seward House, Auburn, NY [*Library symbol Library of Congress*] (LCLS) ... NAuS
Seward, NE [*FM radio station call letters*] ... KZKX
Seward, NE [*Location identifier FAA*] (FAAL) ... SWT
Seward Park [*Washington*] [*Seismograph station code, US Geological Survey*] (SEIS) ... SPW
Seward Public Library, Seward, NE [*Library symbol Library of Congress*] (LCLS) ... NbSe
Sewed ... SD
Sewed ... SWD
Sewell on Coroners [*1843*] [*A publication*] (DLA) ... Sew Cor
Sewell on the Law of Sheriffs [*1842*] [*A publication*] (DLA) ... Sew Sh
Sewell on the Law of Sheriffs [*A publication*] (DLA) ... Sewell Sheriffs
Sewer ... SWR
Sewer Drain ... SD
Sewer Pipe [*Telecommunications*] (TEL) ... SP
Sewer Vent Pipe ... SVP
Sewerage and Sewage Disposal (DCTA) ... S & SD
Sewing ... SEW
Sewing (WGA) ... SEWG
Sewing Machine ... SM
Sewing Machine Dealers Association Ltd. [*British*] (BI) ... SMDA
Sewing Machine Repair Program [*Association of Independent Colleges and Schools specialization code*] ... SW
Sewing Machine Trade Association (EA) ... SMTA
Sex Addicts Anonymous (EA) ... SAA
Sex and Love Addicts Anonymous (EA) ... SLAA
Sex and Shopping [*Themes of Judith Krantz's novels*] ... S & S
Sex Appeal [*Slang*] ... SA
Sex Arousal Mechanism [*Medicine*] ... SAM
Sex Attitudes Survey [*Psychology*] ... SAS
Sex Change [*Biology*] ... SC
Sex Chromatin (MAE) ... SC
Sex Chromatin Test (MAE) ... SCT
Sex Chromosome Abnormality ... SCA
Sex Cord Tumor with Annular Tubules [*Medicine*] (DMAA) ... SCTAT
Sex Discrimination Act [*1975*] [*British*] (DCTA) ... SDA
Sex Equity in Education Program (EA) ... SEEP
Sex Equity in Educational Leadership Project [*Oregon*] (EDAC) ... SEEL
Sex Hormone (MAE) ... SH
Sex Information and Education Council of Canada ... SIECCAN
Sex Information and Education Council of the United States ... SECUS
Sex Information and Education Council of the US (EA) ... SIECUS
Sex Information Council of America [*Later, CSIE*] (EA) ... SICAM
Sex Inventory [*Psychology*] ... SI
Sex Knowledge and Aptitude [*Test*] ... SKAT
Sex Knowledge Inventory [*Premarital and marital relations test*] ... SKI
Sex Offender ... SO
Sex Problems Court Digest [*A publication*] (DLA) ... Sex Prob Ct Dig
Sex Ratio [*Biology*] ... SEXRAT
Sex Ratio [*Biology*] ... SR
Sex Ratio at Birth [*Demographics*] ... SRB
Sex, Silk, Swords, and Swash [*Elements of historical romances*] ... 4S's
Sex Steroid Binding Globulin [*Endocrinology*] ... SSBG
Sexagesimo-quarto [*Book up to 7-1/2 centimeters in height*] [*Bibliography*] ... SF
Sexaholics Anonymous (EA) ... SA
Sexaholics Anonymous (PAZ) ... SA
Sex-Hormone-Binding Globulin [*Endocrinology*] ... SHBG
Sexless [*Connector*] ... SXL
Sex-Limited Protein [*Immunology*] ... SLP
Sex-Limited Protein [*Genetics*] (DOG) ... Slp
Sex-Ratio Organism [*Entomology*] ... SRO
Sextans [*Constellation*] ... Sex
Sextans [*Constellation*] ... Sext
Sextant (WDAA) ... SEXT
Sextant (NASA) ... SXT
Sextant (MSA) ... SXTN
Sexton and Malone [*Comic book*] [*CBC TV series*] ... S & M
Sexton Summit, OR [*Location identifier FAA*] (FAAL) ... SXT
Sextuple (MSA) ... SXT
Sextus Empiricus [*Third century AD*] [*Classical studies*] (OCD) ... Sext Emp
Sextus Pomponius [*Flourished, 2nd century*] [*Authority cited in pre-1607 legal work*] (DSA) ... S Pomp
Sextus Pomponius [*Flourished, 2nd century*] [*Authority cited in pre-1607 legal work*] (DSA) ... Sex Pomp
Sexual (DAVI) ... sex
Sexual Abuse ... SA
Sexual Abuse Anonymous (EA) ... SAA
Sexual Abuse Victims Anonymous [*Canada*] ... SAVA
Sexual and Personal Relationships of the Disabled (AIE) ... SPOD
Sexual Assault Research Association (EA) ... SARA
Sexual Attitude Reassessment [*Medicine*] ... SAR
Sexual Communications Inventory [*Marital relations test*] [*Psychology*] ... SCI
Sexual Concerns Checklist [*Premarital and marital relations test*] ... SCC
Sexual Differentiation Scale [*Psychometrics*] ... SDS
Sexual Freedom League (EA) ... SFL
Sexual Function Index [*Medicine*] (DMAA) ... SFI
Sexual Function of Women [*Medicine*] (DMAA) ... SFW
Sexual Harassment ... SH

Sexual Harassment Guidelines ... SHG
Sexual Intercourse (ADA) ... SI
Sexual Knowledge Questionnaire ... SKQ
Sexual Law Reform Society [*British*] ... SLRS
Sexual Law Reporter [*A publication*] (DLA) ... Sex L Rep
Sexual Law Reporter [*A publication*] (DLA) ... Sex LR
Sexual Medicine Today [*A publication*] ... SMT
Sexual Myths [*Scale*] ... SM
Sexual Over-Seriousness [*Attitude disorder*] ... SOC
Sexual Self-Efficacy Scale [*Medicine*] (DMAA) ... SSES
Sexuality Preference Profile ... SPP
Sexually Dimorphic Nucleus [*Brain anatomy*] ... SDN
Sexually Transmitted Disease [*Medicine*] ... STD
Sexually-Acquired Reactive Arthritis [*Medicine*] (PDAA) ... SARA
Sexually-Transmitted Infection [*Medicine*] (DI) ... STI
Seybold Report on Office Systems (HGAA) ... SROS
Seychelles [*MARC geographic area code Library of Congress*] (LCCP) ... i-se--
Seychelles [*Aircraft nationality and registration mark*] (FAAC) ... S7
Seychelles [*ANSI two-letter standard code*] (CNC) ... SC
Seychelles [*bi (British Indian Ocean Territory) used in records cataloged before January 1978*] [*MARC country of publication code Library of Congress*] (LCCP) ... se
Seychelles ... SY
Seychelles [*ANSI three-letter standard code*] (CNC) ... SYC
Seychelles Agence de Presse [*News agency*] (EY) ... SAP
Seychelles Democratic Party ... SDP
Seychelles International Safari Air Ltd. [*ICAO designator*] (FAAC) ... SIS
Seychelles Law Reports [*A publication*] (DLA) ... Seych LR
Seychelles Law Reports [*1921-23*] [*A publication*] (DLA) ... SLR
Seychelles People's Progressive Front (PPW) ... SPPF
Seychelles People's United Party [*Political party*] (PPW) ... SPUP
Seychelles Popular Anti-Marxist Front [*Political party*] (PD) ... SPAMF
Seyfarth, Shaw, Fairweather & Geraldson, Chicago, IL [*Library symbol Library of Congress*] (LCLS) ... ICSey
Seymchan [*Former USSR Seismograph station code, US Geological Survey*] (SEIS) ... SEY
Seymour Daily Tribune, Seymour, IN [*Library symbol Library of Congress*] (LCLS) ... InSeyT
Seymour Herald, Seymour, IA [*Library symbol Library of Congress*] (LCLS) ... IaSeyH
Seymour, IN [*Location identifier FAA*] (FAAL) ... EQZ
Seymour, IN [*Location identifier FAA*] (FAAL) ... SER
Seymour, IN [*FM radio station call letters*] (RBYB) ... WKLO
Seymour, IN [*AM radio station call letters*] ... WQKC
Seymour, IN [*AM radio station call letters*] ... WZZB
Seymour Library, Auburn, NY [*Library symbol Library of Congress*] (LCLS) ... NAu
Seymour Public Library, Seymour, IN [*Library symbol Library of Congress*] (LCLS) ... InSey
Seymour Resources [*Vancouver Stock Exchange symbol*] ... SYM
Seymour, TN [*FM radio station call letters*] ... WJBZ
Seymour, TX [*AM radio station call letters*] ... KSEY
Seymour, TX [*FM radio station call letters*] ... KSEY-FM
Seymour, WI [*FM radio station call letters*] ... WECB
Seymour-Moss International Ltd. [*Vancouver Stock Exchange symbol*] ... XMI
Seymour's Merchant Shipping Acts [*2nd ed.*] [*1857*] [*A publication*] (DLA) ... Sey Merch Sh
Sezanne-Saint-Remy [*France ICAO location identifier*] (ICLI) ... LFFZ
Sezary Cell [*Medicine*] (DMAA) ... SC
Sezary Syndrome [*Dermatology*] ... SS
Sezegnin [*Switzerland ICAO location identifier*] (ICLI) ... LSHS
Sezione [*Division*] [*Italian*] (ILCA) ... Sez
Sfax [*Tunisia*] [*Airport symbol*] (OAG) ... SFA
Sfax/El Maou [*Tunisia*] [*ICAO location identifier*] (ICLI) ... DTTX
Sferics Correlation Detection System ... SCORDES
Sferics, Position [*or Pulse*], Azimuth, Rate, and Spectrum Analyzer ... SPARSA
SFFed Corp. [*Formerly, San Francisco Federal Savings & Loan Association*] [*NASDAQ symbol*] (SPSG) ... SFFD
SFFED Corp. [*Associated Press*] (SAG) ... SFFed
SFI Foundation (EA) ... SFI
SFM Corp. [*Later, EXX, Inc.*] [*AMEX symbol*] (SPSG) ... SFM
SFO [*San Francisco and Oakland*] **Helicopter Airlines, Inc.** [*ICAO designator*] (OAG) ... OH
SFO [*San Francisco and Oakland*] **Helicopter Airlines, Inc.** [*Air carrier designation symbol*] ... SFO
SFOF [*Space Flight Operations Facility*] **Communications Terminal Subsystem** [*NASA*] ... SCTS
Sforzando [*With Additional Accent*] [*Music*] ... Sf
Sforzando [*With Additional Accent*] [*Music*] ... Sforz
Sforzando [*With Additional Accent*] [*Music*] ... Sfz
Sforzato Piano [*Sudden change from forte to piano*] [*Music*] (ROG) ... SFP
SFS Bancorp [*NASDAQ symbol*] (TTSB) ... SFED
SFS Bancorp, Inc. [*NASDAQ symbol*] (SAG) ... SED
SFS Bancorp, Inc. [*Associated Press*] (SAG) ... SFS Bcp
SFT-Sudanese Flight [*ICAO designator*] (FAAC) ... STF
Sfumato (VRA) ... sfm
SFX Broadcasting, Inc. [*Associated Press*] (SAG) ... SFX Brd
SFX Broadcasting, Inc. [*NASDAQ symbol*] (SAG) ... SFXB
SFX Broadcasting'A' [*NASDAQ symbol*] (TTSB) ... SFXBA
SGOT [*Surface Serum Glutamic-Oxaloacetic*] (DAVI) ... S
Sgraffito (VRA) ... sgrf
SGS Thomson Microelectronics, NV [*Associated Press*] (SAG) ... SGS TM
SGS Thomson Microelectronics, NV [*NYSE symbol*] (SAG) ... STM
SGS-THOMSON N.V. [*NYSE symbol*] (TTSB) ... STM
Sgt. Pepper's Lonely Hearts Club [*Defunct*] (EA) ... SPLHC
SGV Bancorp [*NASDAQ symbol*] (TTSB) ... SGVB
SGV Bancorp, Inc. [*Associated Press*] (SAG) ... SGV BC
SGV Bancorp, Inc. [*NASDAQ symbol*] (SAG) ... SGVB
Sha Na Na [*An association Defunct*] (EA) ... SNN
Sha'arei Zedek (BJA) ... SZ
Shabair [*Zaire*] [*ICAO designator*] (FAAC) ... SHB
Shabbath (BJA) ... Shab
Shabunda [*Zaire*] [*ICAO location identifier*] (ICLI) ... FZMW
Shackamaxon Society (EA) ... SS
Shackle (AAG) ... SH
Shade ... SHD
Shade ... SHD
Shade Tobacco Growers Agricultural Association (EA) ... STGAA
Shadow Box Optical Landing System ... SBOLS
Shadow Communications Agency [*British Labour Party*] ... SCA
Shadow Mountain National Recreation Area ... SHMO
Shadow Open Market Committee ... SOMC
Shadyside, OH [*FM radio station call letters*] ... WEEL
Shaft (MSA) ... SFT
Shaft Alignment and Vibration (DNAB) ... SHAVIB
Shaft Angle [*Technical drawings*] ... SA
Shaft Angle Encoder (KSC) ... SAE
Shaft Center (MSA) ... SC
Shaft Cutting Machine [*Mining technology*] ... SCM
Shaft Drive Axis [*Aerospace*] (KSC) ... SDA
Shaft Driver, Left ... SDL
Shaft Driver, Right ... SDR
Shaft Gear ... SHFTGR
Shaft Horsepower ... S
Shaft Horsepower ... SHP
Shaft Main Engine ... S
Shaft Optimum Alignment Procedure (DNAB) ... SOAP
Shaft Position Encoder ... SPE
Shaft Position Transducer ... SPT
Shaft Rate (NVT) ... SR
Shaft Revolutions per Minute (DNAB) ... SRPM
Shaft Speed Indicator ... SSI
Shaft-Driven Compressor (DOMA) ... SDC
Shaft-Driven Counter ... SDC
Shafter, CA [*FM radio station call letters*] (RBYB) ... KGZO-FM
Shafter, CA [*FM radio station call letters*] ... KLOD
Shafter, CA [*FM radio station call letters*] (RBYB) ... KLYD
Shafter, CA [*FM radio station call letters*] (RBYB) ... KRME-FM
Shafter, CA [*FM radio station call letters*] ... KXHA
Shafter, CA [*FM radio station call letters*] ... KZBA
Shafter, CA [*Location identifier FAA*] (FAAL) ... MIT
Shafter Historical Society, Shafter, CA [*Library symbol*] [*Library of Congress*] (LCLS) ... CShaHi
Shafting [*Freight*] ... SHFTG
Shaftless Expander-Compressor ... SEC
Shaftsbury [*England*] ... SHAFT
Shaft-to-Bore Misalignment ... STBM
Shageluk [*Alaska*] (OAG) ... SHX
Shageluk, AK [*Location identifier FAA*] (FAAL) ... SHX
Shags Rocks Passage [*Oceanography*] ... SRP
Shahdad [*Iran*] [*ICAO location identifier*] (ICLI) ... OIKS
Shaheen Air International [*Pakistan*] [*ICAO designator*] (FAAC) ... SAI
Shaheen Airport Services [*Pakistan*] [*ICAO designator*] (FAAC) ... SHN
Shahr Abad [*Iran*] [*ICAO location identifier*] (ICLI) ... OIMX
Shahre Babak [*Iran*] [*ICAO location identifier*] (ICLI) ... OIKA
Shahrekord [*Iran*] [*ICAO location identifier*] (ICLI) ... OIFS
Shahrud [*Iran*] [*Seismograph station code, US Geological Survey*] (SEIS) ... SHD
Shahzand [*Iran*] [*ICAO location identifier*] (ICLI) ... OIHD
Shakaichosa-Kenkyusho Consumer Index Summary Report [*Marketing Intelligence Corp.*] [*Japan Information service or system*] (CRD) ... SCI/SR
Shakawe [*Botswana*] [*ICAO location identifier*] (ICLI) ... FBSW
Shakedown [*Nuclear energy*] (NRCH) ... SD
Shakedown (AABC) ... SHKDN
Shakedown [*Navy*] (NVT) ... SKDN
Shakedown Cruise [*Navy*] (ANA) ... SHKDNCRU
Shakedown Cruise [*Navy*] ... SKDNC
Shakedown Cruise [*Navy*] (NVT) ... SKDNCRU
Shaken and Circulatory Oxidation Test (PDAA) ... SCOT
Shaken Baby Syndrome (CPH) ... SBS
Shaken Child Syndrome (CPH) ... SCS
Shakeproof (MSA) ... SHPRF
Shaker Heights City School District, Shaker Heights, OH [*Library symbol Library of Congress*] (LCLS) ... OShS
Shaker Heights City School District, Shaker Heights, OH [*OCLC symbol*] (OCLC) ... SKR
Shaker Heights, OH [*Television station call letters*] ... WOIO
Shaker Heights Public Library, Shaker Heights, OH [*Library symbol Library of Congress*] (LCLS) ... OSh
Shaker Heights Public Library, Shaker Heights, OH [*Library symbol*] [*Library of Congress*] (LCLS) ... OShL
Shaker Heights Public Library, Shaker Heights, OH [*OCLC symbol*] (OCLC) ... SHP
Shaker Museum Foundation (EA) ... SMF
Shaker Museum Foundation, Inc., Old Catham, NY [*Library symbol Library of Congress*] (LCLS) ... NOcaS
Shakespeare ... SHAK
Shakespeare (BARN) ... Shaks
Shakespeare Association of America (EA) ... SAA
Shakespeare Birthplace Trust (EA) ... SBT
Shakespeare Data Bank, Inc. [*Information service or system*] (IID) ... SDB
Shakespeare for Students [*A publication*] ... SFS

Shakespeare Oxford Society (EA) .... SOS
Shakespeare Quarterly [*A publication*] (BRI) .... Shakes Q
Shakespeare Reading Society [*British*] (DBA) .... SRS
Shakespeare Recording Society [*Commercial firm*] (EA) .... SRS
Shakespeare Society of America (EA) .... SSA
Shakespearean Authorship Society [*Later, SAT*] (EA) .... SAS
Shakespearean Authorship Trust [*England*] (EAIO) .... SAT
Shakespearean Criticism [*A publication*] .... SC
Shakey's Franchised Dealers Association (EA) .... SFDA
Shakopee, MN [*AM radio station call letters*] .... KKCM
Shaktoolik [*Alaska*] [*Airport symbol*] (OAG) .... SKK
Shaktoolik, AK [*Location identifier FAA*] (FAAL) .... SKK
Shakwak Exploration Co. [*Vancouver Stock Exchange symbol*] .... SHA
Shale [*Lithology*] .... SH
Shall .... SH
Shallot Latent Virus [*Plant pathology*] .... SLV
Shallotte, NC [*FM radio station call letters*] .... WCCA
Shallotte, NC [*FM radio station call letters*] .... WLTT
Shallotte, NC [*AM radio station call letters*] .... WVCB
Shallow .... Sh
Shallow Bed Liquid Chromatography .... SBLC
Shallow Cathode Barrier (IAA) .... SCB
Shallow Draft Barge (MCD) .... SDB
Shallow Draft Board (NASA) .... SDB
Shallow Habitat Air Dive [*Navy*] .... SHAD
Shallow Resources, Inc. [*Vancouver Stock Exchange symbol*] .... SWO
Shallow Spherical Sandwich Shell .... SSSS
Shallow Underwater Missile .... SUM
Shallow Underwater Mobile (IAA) .... SUM
Shallow Water (DOMA) .... SW
Shallow Water Acoustic Tracking System [*Navy*] (CAAL) .... SWATS
Shallow Water Acoustics .... SWA
Shallow Water Antitraffic Mine [*Military*] .... SWATM
Shallow Water Attack Craft [*Navy symbol*] .... SW
Shallow Water Attack Craft, Light (MCD) .... SWAC
Shallow Water Attack Craft, Light [*Navy symbol*] (NVT) .... SWAL
Shallow Water Attack Craft, Medium [*Navy symbol*] (NVT) .... SWAM
Shallow Water Diver [*British military*] (DMA) .... SW
Shallow Water Oceanographic Research Data [*System*] [*Naval Ordnance Laboratory and Naval Oceanographic Office*] .... SWORD
Shallow Water SONAR .... SWS
Shallow-Water Mine Countermeasures (DOMA) .... SWMCM
Shalmaneser (BJA) .... Shalm
Shalom Network (EA) .... SN
Sham Feeding [*Medicine*] (DMAA) .... SF
Sham Ovariectomized [*Endocrinology*] .... SOVX
Sham Ovariectomy [*Endocrinology*] .... SOV
Shaman Pharmaceuticals [*NASDAQ symbol*] (TTSB) .... SHMN
Shaman Pharmaceuticals, Inc. [*Associated Press*] (SAG) .... Shaman
Shaman Pharmaceuticals, Inc. [*NASDAQ symbol*] (SAG) .... SHMN
Shamokin, PA [*AM radio station call letters*] .... WISL
Shamokin, PA [*FM radio station call letters*] .... WISL-FM
Shamrock Airlines [*Air carrier designation symbol*] .... SALX
Shamrock Resources, Inc. [*Vancouver Stock Exchange symbol*] .... SHJ
Shamshernagar [*Bangladesh*] [*ICAO location identifier*] (ICLI) .... VGSH
Shamshernagar [*Bangladesh*] [*Airport symbol*] (AD) .... ZHM
Shan [*MARC language code Library of Congress*] (LCCP) .... shn
Shan State Army [*Myanmar*] [*Political party*] (EY) .... SSA
Shan State Nationalities Liberation Organization [*Myanmar*] (PD) .... SSNLO
Shan State Progressive Party [*Myanmar*] [*Political party*] (EY) .... SSPP
Shan United Revolutionary Army [*Myanmar*] (PD) .... SURA
Shandon Resources, Inc. [*Vancouver Stock Exchange symbol*] .... SHN
Shandong Airlines [*China*] [*FAA designator*] (FAAC) .... CDG
Shandong Huaneng Power Development ADR [*NYSE symbol*] (SAG) .... SH
Shandong Huaneng Power Development ADR [*Associated Press*] (SAG) .... ShanHua
Shandong Huaneng Pwr ADS [*NYSE symbol*] (TTSB) .... SH
Shand's Practice, Scotch Court of Sessions [*A publication*] (DLA) .... Shand Pr
Shand's Reports [*11-41 South Carolina*] [*A publication*] (DLA) .... Sh
Shand's Reports [*11-41 South Carolina*] [*A publication*] (DLA) .... Shand
Shane Resources [*Vancouver Stock Exchange symbol*] .... SEI
Shanell International Energy Corp. [*Vancouver Stock Exchange symbol*] .... SIE
Shanghai .... SH
Shanghai [*China*] [*Airport symbol*] (OAG) .... SHA
Shanghai [*China*] [*ICAO location identifier*] (ICLI) .... ZSHA
Shanghai Airlines [*China*] [*ICAO designator*] (FAAC) .... CSH
Shanghai Book Traders .... SBT
Shanghai City [*China*] [*ICAO location identifier*] (ICLI) .... ZSSA
Shanghai/Hongqiao [*China*] [*ICAO location identifier*] (ICLI) .... ZSSS
Shanghai/Longhua [*China*] [*ICAO location identifier*] (ICLI) .... ZSSL
Shanghai Municipality [*China, Mainland*] [*MARC geographic area code Library of Congress*] (LCCP) .... a-cc-sm
Shanghai Petrochemical [*NYSE symbol*] (SPSG) .... SHI
Shanghai Petrochemical ADS [*NYSE symbol*] (TTSB) .... SHI
Shanghai Petrochemical Co. [*Associated Press*] (SAG) .... ShangPt
Shanghai Petrochemical Co. [*Commercial firm*] [*China*] .... SPC
Shank (AAG) .... SHK
Shankland's Tennessee Public Statutes [*A publication*] (DLA) .... Shankland's St
Shannock Corp. [*Vancouver Stock Exchange symbol*] .... SNK
Shannon [*Ireland*] [*ICAO location identifier*] (ICLI) .... EINN
Shannon [*Ireland*] [*ICAO location identifier*] (ICLI) .... EISL
Shannon [*Ireland*] [*ICAO location identifier*] (ICLI) .... EISU
Shannon [*Ireland*] [*Airport symbol*] (OAG) .... SNN
Shannon & Wilson, Inc., Seattle, WA [*Library symbol Library of Congress*] (LCLS) .... WaSSW
Shannon/Ballygirreen [*Ireland*] [*ICAO location identifier*] (ICLI) .... EIAA
Shannon Executive Aviation Ireland Ltd. [*ICAO designator*] (FAAC) .... SXA
Shannon Free Airport Development Company (ACII) .... SFADCO
Shannon Municipal Library, Sexsmith, AB, Canada [*Library symbol*] [*Library of Congress*] (LCLS) .... CaASeSM
Shannon Municipal Library, Sexsmith, Alberta [*Library symbol National Library of Canada*] (NLC) .... ASSM
Shannon Park Marine Center [*West Washington University*] [*Anacortes, WA*] .... SPMC
Shannon's Tennessee Annotated Code [*A publication*] (DLA) .... Shannon's Code
Shannon's Tennessee Cases [*A publication*] (DLA) .... Shan Cas
Shannon's Tennessee Cases [*A publication*] (DLA) .... Ten Cas
Shannon's Unreported Tennessee Cases [*A publication*] (DLA) .... Shan
Shannon's Unreported Tennessee Cases [*A publication*] (DLA) .... Shannon Cas (Tenn)
Shannon's Unreported Tennessee Cases [*1847-1894*] [*A publication*] (DLA) .... Tenn Cas
Shansi Province [*China, Mainland*] [*MARC geographic area code Library of Congress*] (LCCP) .... a-cc-sh
Shante [*Myanmar*] [*ICAO location identifier*] (ICLI) .... VBST
Shanti Bahini [*Peace Force*] [*Bangladesh*] [*Political party*] .... SB
Shanti Project (EA) .... SP
Shantou [*China*] [*Airport symbol*] (OAG) .... SWA
Shantou [*China*] [*ICAO location identifier*] (ICLI) .... ZGOW
Shantung [*Province in China*] (ROG) .... SHANT
Shantung Province [*China, Mainland*] [*MARC geographic area code Library of Congress*] (LCCP) .... a-cc-sp
Shanwick [*British ICAO location identifier*] (ICLI) .... EGGX
Shanxi Airlines [*China*] [*FAA designator*] (FAAC) CXI
Shape (MSA) .... SHP
SHAPE [*Supreme Headquarters Allied Powers Europe*] **Air Defense Technology Center** [*Later, STC*] [*NATO*] .... SADTC
Shape and Hamiltonian Consistent [*Physics*] .... SHC
SHAPE [*Supreme Headquarters Allied Powers Europe*] **Annual Command Exercise** [*NATO*] (NATG) .... SHAPEX
SHAPE [*Supreme Headquarters Allied Powers Europe*] **Centralized Training Facility** [*NATO*] (NATG) .... SCTF
SHAPE [*Supreme Headquarters Allied Powers Europe*] **Communications Electronics Board** [*NATO*] (NATG) .... SCEB
Shape Descriptor [*A-frame, for example. The shape resembles the letter for which it is named*] .... A
Shape Descriptor [*C-clamp, for example. The shape resembles the letter for which it is named*] C
Shape Descriptor [*Dining el, for example. The shape resembles the letter for which it is named*] L
Shape Descriptor [*S-curve, for example. The shape resembles the letter for which it is named*] .... S
Shape Descriptor [*T-bar and T-square, for example. The shape resembles the letter for which it is named*] .... T
Shape Descriptor [*U-turn, for example. The shape resembles the letter for which it is named*] .... U
Shape Descriptor [*V-sign, for example. The shape resembles the letter for which it is named.*] V
SHAPE [*Supreme Headquarters Allied Powers Europe*] **Emergency Operating Procedures** [*NATO*] (NATG) .... SEOP
Shape Factor of a Structure [*Heat transmission symbol*] .... S
Shape Memory [*Metallurgy*] .... SM
Shape Memory Alloy (RDA) .... SMA
Shape Memory Effect [*Metal alloy property*] .... SME
Shape of Base of Leaf [*Botany*] .... BSHAP
SHAPE [*Supreme Headquarters Allied Powers Europe*] **Operations Center** [*NATO*] (NATG) .... SHOC
Shape Selective Cracking (PDAA) .... SSC
SHAPE [*Supreme Headquarters Allied Powers Europe*] **Technical Center** [*Formerly, SADTC*] [*NATO*] (NATG) .... SHATC
SHAPE [*Supreme Headquarters Allied Powers Europe*] **Technical Center** [*Formerly, SADTC*] [*The Hague, Netherlands*] [*NATO*] .... STC
Shaped Beam Antenna .... SBA
Shaped Charge [*of explosive*] .... SC
Shaped Charge Jet (MCD) .... SCJ
Shaped Charge Liner .... SCL
Shaped Substrata Meanderline (MCD) .... SSML
Shaped Tube Electrolytic Machining [*GE*] .... STEM
Shaper Block (MCD) .... SB
Shaping Circuit [*Electronics*] (OA) .... SC
Shaping Network (MCD) .... SN
Shaping Network Assembly (SSD) .... SNA
Shapiro, Barney, Newark NJ [*STAC*] .... SBY
Sharable and Read Only [*Computer science*] (PCM) .... SRO
SHARAF Name Authority [*UTLAS symbol*] .... SHNA
Sharbot Lake Branch, Frontenac County Library, Ontario [*Library symbol National Library of Canada*] (BIB) .... OSLFC
Shard Hospital Online Real-Time Time-Sharing (PDAA) .... SHORT
Share .... SH
Share [*Stock exchange term*] .... SHR
Share (ODBW) .... shr
Share Assembly Program [*Computer science*] .... SAP
Share Compiler-Assembler, Translator .... SCAT
Share Distribution (ECII) .... SD
Share European Association (HGAA) .... SEAS
SHARE Foundation (EA) .... SHARE
Share Happily and Reap Endlessly [*Hollywood women's charity organization*] .... SHARE
Share Holder Action Group [*Australia*] .... SHAG
Share Information Service [*British*] (DCTA) .... SIS

Share Internal FORTRAN Translator [*Computer science*] (IEEE) .... SIFT
Share Library User Report [*Computer science*] (OA) .... SLUR
Share News on Automatic Coding Systems [*Computer science*] .... SNACS
Share of Market (NITA) .... SM
Share of Market [*Advertising*] .... SOM
Share of Market [*Lundberg Survey, Inc.*] [*Information service or system*] (CRD) .... SOM
Share of Voice [*Advertising*] .... SOV
Share Operating System [*Computer science*] .... SOS
Share Our Strength (EA) .... SOS
Share Price Index (ADA) .... SPI
Share Registration and Dividend Warrants (MHDB) .... SHREAD
Share the Work Coalition [*Defunct*] (EA) .... SWC
Share Valuation Division [*Inland Revenue*] [*British*] .... SVD
Share Your Birthday Foundation [*Defunct*] (EA) .... SYBF
Share-a-Ride International (EA) .... SARI
Sharebuilder Investment Plan [*Banking*] .... SIP
Shared Acquisitions and Retention System .... SHARES
Shared Aperture Medium-Range Tracker (MCD) .... SAMRT
Shared Appreciation Mortgage [*Banking*] .... SAM
Shared Area Resources Exchange [*Library network*] .... SHARE
Shared Batch Area [*Computer science*] (IBMDP) .... SBA
Shared Bibliographic Input .... SBI
Shared Bibliographic Input Experiment [*Special Libraries Association*] .... SBIE
Shared Catalog Accessed Through Terminals [*Data processing system*] .... SCATT
Shared Contingency Computer Center (MHDI) .... SCCC
Shared Currency Option Under Tender (ODBW) .... SCOUT
Shared Data Set (OA) .... SDS
Shared Data Set Integrity .... SDSI
Shared Demand Assignment Signaling (MCD) .... SDAS
Shared Direct Memory Access [*Sperry UNIVAC*] .... SDMA
Shared Direct Memory Access Contoller [*Computer science*] (MHDI) .... SDMAC
Shared Energy Savings .... SES
Shared Enqueue (MHDI) .... SNQ
Shared Equipment Need Date (NASA) .... SEND
Shared Equity Mortgage .... SEM
Shared File System [*Telecommunications*] .... SFS
Shared Graphics Work Space .... SGWS
Shared Hospital Accounting System [*Computer science*] .... SHAS
Shared Housing Resource Center [*Later, NSHRC*] (EA) .... SHRC
Shared Information (PCM) .... SI
Shared Information Elicitation Facility [*Computer science*] .... SHIEF
Shared Information Service (CMD) .... SIS
Shared Laboratory Information System .... SLIS
Shared Library Services, South Huron Hospital, Exeter, Ontario [*Library symbol National Library of Canada*] (BIB) .... OESH
Shared Line Adapter .... SLA
Shared Main Memory (NITA) .... SMM
Shared Mass Storage .... SMS
Shared Medical Sys [*NASDAQ symbol*] (TTSB) .... SMED
Shared Medical Systems Corp. [*Associated Press*] (SAG) .... ShrMed
Shared Medical Systems Corp. [*NASDAQ symbol*] (NQ) .... SMED
Shared Memory [*Computer science*] (BUR) .... SM
Shared Mobile Radio [*Telecommunications*] .... SMR
Shared Multiport Memory .... SMM
Shared Nearest Neighbor (NASA) .... SNN
Shared On-Line Airline Reservations (IAA) .... SOLAR
Shared Page Table [*Computer science*] (OA) .... SPT
Shared Peripheral Area (NASA) .... SPA
Shared Peripheral Interface .... SPI
Shared Processing Network [*Marine science*] (OSRA) .... SPN
Shared Processing Network (USDC) .... SPN
Shared Registry System [*Computer science*] .... SRS
Shared Research Equipment Collaborative Research Program [*Oak Ridge, TN*] [*Oak Ridge National Laboratory*] [*Department of Energy*] (GRD) .... SHaRE
Shared Resource Management [*Computer science*] .... SRM
Shared Resources Programmming (NITA) .... SRP
Shared Services, Agriculture Canada [*Services en Commun, Agriculture Canada*], Regina, Saskatchewan [*Library symbol National Library of Canada*] (NLC) .... SRAGE
Shared Tape Allocation Manager .... STAM
Shared Tech Cellular [*NASDAQ symbol*] (TTSB) .... STCL
Shared Tech Fairchild [*NASDAQ symbol*] (TTSB) .... STCH
Shared Technologies Cellular, Inc. [*Associated Press*] (SAG) .... ShrdTch
Shared Technologies Cellular, Inc. [*NASDAQ symbol*] (SAG) .... STCL
Shared Technologies, Inc. [*Associated Press*] (SAG) .... ShdTech
Shared Technologies, Inc. [*NASDAQ symbol*] (NQ) .... STCH
Shared Tenant Services [*Telecommunications*] (TSSD) .... STS
Shared Virtual Area [*Computer science*] .... SVA
Shared Whois Project .... SWIP
Shared-Time Repair of Big Electronic Systems [*Computer science*] ...... STROBES
Shareholder Credit Accounting .... SCA
Shareholder Valuation Analysis .... SVA
Shareholders' Equity [*Business term*] .... SE
Share-Purchase Tax Credit [*Canada*] .... SPTC
Shares [*Stock exchange term*] .... SHS
Shares of Beneficial Interest [*Stock exchange term*] .... SBI
Shares Time With [*Broadcasting term*] .... ST
Sharing Joint Venture .... SJV
Sharing of Missionaries Abroad [*Church of England*] .... SOMA
Sharing Time (NTCM) .... S
Sharjah [*United Arab Emirates*] [*Airport symbol*] (OAG) .... SHJ
Sharjah/International [*United Arab Emirates*] [*ICAO location identifier*] (ICLI) .... OMSJ
Sharjah Ruler's Flight [*United Arab Emirates*] [*ICAO designator*] (FAAC) .... SHJ

Shark Attack File (DNAB) .... SAF
Shark Bay [*Western Australia*] [*Airport symbol*] (AD) .... SHB
Shark Liver Oil .... SLO
Shark Research Panel [*Navy*] (DNAB) .... SRP
Sharkey's Practice of Election Committees [*2nd ed.*] [*1866*] [*A publication*] (DLA) .... Shark Elec
Sharlott Hall Museum, Prescott Historical Society, Prescott, AZ [*Library symbol Library of Congress*] (LCLS) .... AzPrSH
Sharm E Sheikh [*Israel*] [*Airport symbol*] (OAG) .... SSH
Sharm es-Sheikh [*Israel*] [*Airport symbol*] (AD) .... SFS
Sharnbrook [*England*] .... SHARNB
Sharon, CT [*AM radio station call letters*] .... WKZE
Sharon, CT [*FM radio station call letters*] .... WQQQ
Sharon Energy Ltd. [*Vancouver Stock Exchange symbol*] .... SHY
Sharon Gless Fan Club (EA) .... SGFC
Sharon, PA [*AM radio station call letters*] .... WPIC
Sharon, PA [*FM radio station call letters*] .... WYFM
Sharon Public Library, Sharon, MA [*Library symbol Library of Congress*] (LCLS) .... MSha
Sharon Smith International Fan Club (EA) .... SSIFC
Sharon Temple, Sharon, ON, Canada [*Library symbol*] [*Library of Congress*] (LCLS) .... CaOShT
Sharon Temple, Sharon, Ontario [*Library symbol National Library of Canada*] (NLC) .... OSHT
Sharp .... S
Sharp Cash [*Prompt payment*] .... SC
Sharp [*I. P.*] Communications Network [*I.P. Sharp Associates Ltd.*] [*Toronto, ON*] (TSSD) .... IPSANET
Sharp National Account Program [*Sharp Electronics Corp.*] .... SNAP
Sharp Numeric Assembler Program [*Sharp Electronics Corp.*] (IAA) .... SNAP
Sharp on Congregational Courts [*A publication*] (DLA) .... Sharp Cong Ct
Sharpe Army Depot [*California*] .... SHAD
Sharpe Army Depot Library, Lathrop, CA [*Library symbol Library of Congress*] (LCLS) .... CLatA
Sharpe Energy and Resources Ltd. [*Vancouver Stock Exchange symbol*] ...... SHG
Sharpened Romberg [*Equilibrium*] .... SR
Sharpener (MSA) .... SHRP
Sharper Image [*NASDAQ symbol*] (TTSB) .... SHRP
Sharper Image Corp. [*NASDAQ symbol*] (NQ) .... SHRP
Sharper Image Corp. [*Associated Press*] (SAG) .... ShrpIm
Sharper-than-the-Average-Gook [*American POW slang*] (VNW) .... STAG
Sharpshooter [*Army*] .... s
Sharpshooter [*Military decoration*] (AABC) .... SpS
Sharpshooter [*Marine Corps*] .... SS
Sharpshooter Qualification Badge [*Military decoration*] (AABC) .... SpsQualBad
Sharpshooters Yeomanry [*British military*] (DMA) .... SSY
Sharpstein's Insurance Digest [*A publication*] (DLA) .... Sharp Ins Dig
Sharpsville, PA [*FM radio station call letters*] (RBYB) .... WWSY-FM
Sharswood and Budd's Leading Cases on Real Property [*A publication*] (DLA) .... Am LCRP
Sharswood and Budd's Leading Cases on Real Property [*A publication*] (DLA) .... Shars & B Lead Cas Real Prop
Sharswood's Commercial Law [*A publication*] (DLA) .... Shars Comm L
Sharswood's Edition of Blackstone's Commentaries [*A publication*] (DLA) .... Shars Bl Comm
Sharswood's Edition of Blackstone's Commentaries [*A publication*] (DLA) .... Shars Black
Sharswood's Lectures on the Profession of the Law [*A publication*] (DLA) .... Shars Law Lec
Sharswood's Legal Ethics [*A publication*] (DLA) .... Shars Leg Eth
Sharswood's Table of Cases, Connecticut [*A publication*] (DLA) .... Shars Tab Ca
Sharurah [*Saudi Arabia*] [*ICAO location identifier*] (ICLI) .... OESH
Sharurah [*Saudi Arabia*] [*Airport symbol*] (OAG) .... SHW
Shashi [*China*] [*Airport symbol*] (OAG) .... SHS
Shasper Industries Ltd. [*Toronto Stock Exchange symbol*] .... SHQ
Shasta County Free Library, Redding, CA [*Library symbol Library of Congress*] (LCLS) .... CRedCL
Shasta County Office of Education, Redding, CA [*Library symbol*] [*Library of Congress*] (LCLS) .... CRedE
Shasta Dam [*California*] [*Seismograph station code, US Geological Survey Closed*] (SEIS) .... SHS
Shaunavon, SK [*Television station call letters*] CBCP-1
Shaunavon, SK [*AM radio station call letters*] .... CJSN
Shauri (BJA) .... Sh
Shavano Air [*ICAO designator*] (AD) .... ZK
Shavano Air, Inc. [*ICAO designator*] (FAAC) .... SHV
Shaving [*Freight*] .... SHVG
Shaw Air Force Base [*South Carolina*] .... SAFB
Shaw and Dunlop's Scotch Court of Session Reports, First Series [*A publication*] (DLA) .... Sh & Dunl
Shaw and Dunlop's Scotch Court of Session Reports, First Series [*A publication*] (DLA) .... Shaw & D
Shaw and Dunlop's Scotch Court of Session Reports, First Series [*A publication*] (DLA) .... Shaw & Dunl
Shaw and Maclean's House of Lords Cases [*A publication*] (DLA) .... S & M
Shaw and Maclean's Scotch Appeal Cases [*A publication*] (DLA) .... Sh & Macl
Shaw and Maclean's Scotch Appeal Cases [*A publication*] (DLA) .... Shaw & M
Shaw and Maclean's Scotch Appeal Cases [*1835-38*] [*A publication*] (DLA) .... Shaw & M Sc App Cas
Shaw and Maclean's Scotch Appeal Cases [*A publication*] (DLA) .... Shaw & Macl
Shaw Avenue Elementary School, Valley Stream, NY [*Library symbol*] [*Library of Congress*] (LCLS) .... NVsSAE
Shaw Cablesystems Ltd. [*Toronto Stock Exchange symbol*] .... SCL
Shaw, Dunlop, and Bell's Scotch Court of Session Cases, First Series [*1821-38*] [*A publication*] (DLA) .... Shaw Dunl & B

Shaw, Dunlop, and Bell's Scotch Court of Session Reports, First Series [*A publication*] (DLA) ... S
Shaw, Dunlop, and Bell's Scotch Court of Session Reports, First Series [*1821-38*] [*A publication*] (DLA) ... S & D
Shaw, Dunlop, and Bell's Scotch Court of Session Reports, First Series [*1821-38*] [*A publication*] (DLA) ... SD & B
Shaw, Dunlop, and Bell's Scotch Court of Session Reports, First Series [*A publication*] (DLA) ... Shaw D & B
Shaw, Dunlop, and Bell's Supplement, Containing House of Lords Decisions [*A publication*] (DLA) ... SD & B Sup
Shaw, Dunlop, and Bell's Supplement, Containing House of Lords Decisions [*Scotland*] [*A publication*] (DLA) ... SD & B Supp
Shaw, Dunlop, and Bell's Supplement, Containing House of Lords Decisions [*Scotland*] [*A publication*] (DLA) ... Shaw D & B Supp
Shaw Group [*NASDAQ symbol*] (NQ) ... SHAW
Shaw Group [*Associated Press*] (SAG) ... ShawGp
Shaw Indus [*NYSE symbol*] (TTSB) ... SHX
Shaw Industries, Inc. [*Associated Press*] (SAG) ... Shaw
Shaw Industries, Inc. [*NYSE symbol*] (SPSG) ... SHX
Shaw Industries Ltd. [*Toronto Stock Exchange symbol*] ... SHL
Shaw Society of America [*Defunct*] (EA) ... SSA
Shaw University, Raleigh, NC [*Library symbol Library of Congress*] (LCLS) ... NcRSh
Shaw, Wilson, and Courtenay's Scotch Appeals Reports [*Wilson and Shaw's Reports*] [*A publication*] (DLA) ... Sh W & C
Shaw, Wilson, and Courtenay's Scotch Appeals Reports, House of Lords [*A publication*] (DLA) ... Shaw W & C
Shawano, WI [*FM radio station call letters*] ... WOWN
Shawano, WI [*AM radio station call letters*] ... WTCH
Shawbury [*British ICAO location identifier*] (ICLI) ... EGOS
Shawbury FTU [*British ICAO designator*] (FAAC) ... SYS
Shawinigan Engineering Co. Ltd., Montreal, PQ, Canada [*Library symbol Library of Congress*] (LCLS) ... CaQMSWP
Shawinigan Engineering Ltd. Co., Montreal, Quebec [*Library symbol National Library of Canada*] (NLC) ... QMSWP
Shawinigan Falls [*Quebec*] [*Seismograph station code, US Geological Survey Closed*] (SEIS) ... SHF
Shawinigan Lake Historical Society, British Columbia [*Library symbol National Library of Canada*] (NLC) ... BSLHS
Shawinigan Lake Historical Society, Shawinigan, BC, Canada [*Library symbol*] [*Library of Congress*] (LCLS) ... CaBSLHS
Shawinigan, PQ [*AM radio station call letters*] ... CKSM
Shawmut National Corp. [*Associated Press*] (SAG) ... ShawN
Shawmut National Corp. [*Associated Press*] (SAG) ... ShawNt
Shawmut National Corp. [*NYSE symbol*] (SPSG) ... SNC
Shawnee Correctional Center, Vienna, IL [*Library symbol*] [*Library of Congress*] (LCLS) ... IViS
Shawnee Library System [*Library network*] ... SHLS
Shawnee Library System, Carterville, IL [*Library symbol Library of Congress*] (LCLS) ... ICtvS
Shawnee Library System, Carterville, IL [*OCLC symbol*] (OCLC) ... IUI
Shawnee Medical Center Medical Library, Shawnee Mission, KS [*OCLC symbol*] (OCLC) ... KSM
Shawnee Mission Medical Center, Merriam, KS [*Library symbol Library of Congress*] (LCLS) ... KMrS
Shawnee, OK [*FM radio station call letters*] ... KABH
Shawnee, OK [*TV station call letters*] (RBYB) ... KAQS
Shawnee, OK [*AM radio station call letters*] ... KGFF
Shawnee, OK [*Location identifier FAA*] (FAAL) ... SNL
Shawnee State College, Portsmouth, OH [*Library symbol Library of Congress*] (LCLS) ... OPosmS
Shawnee State Community College, Portsmouth, OH [*OCLC symbol*] (OCLC) ... OSS
Shaw's Criminal Cases, Scotch Justiciary Court [*A publication*] (DLA) ... Shaw Crim Cas
Shaw's Decisions in Scotch Court of Sessions, First Series [*A publication*] (DLA) ... Shaw Dec
Shaw's Digest of Decisions [*Scotland*] [*A publication*] (DLA) ... Sh Dig
Shaw's Digest of Decisions [*Scotland*] [*A publication*] (DLA) ... Shaw Dig
Shaw's Justiciary Court, Criminal Cases [*Scotland*] [*A publication*] (DLA) ... Sh Crim Cas
Shaw's Parish Law [*A publication*] (DLA) ... Shaw PL
Shaw's Scotch Appeal Cases [*A publication*] (DLA) ... Sh
Shaw's Scotch Appeal Cases [*A publication*] (DLA) ... Shaw
Shaw's Scotch Appeal Cases, English House of Lords [*A publication*] (DLA) ... Shaw App
Shaw's Scotch Appeal Cases, House of Lords [*A publication*] (DLA) ... S
Shaw's Scotch Appeal Cases, House of Lords [*1821-24*] [*A publication*] (DLA) ... S App
Shaw's Scotch Appeal Cases, House of Lords [*A publication*] (DLA) ... Sh App
Shaw's Scotch Appeal Cases, House of Lords [*A publication*] (DLA) ... Sh Sc App
Shaw's Scotch Appeal Cases, House of Lords [*1821-24*] [*A publication*] (DLA) ... Shaw HL
Shaw's Scotch Appeal Cases, House of Lords [*1821-24*] [*A publication*] (DLA) ... Shaw Sc App Cas
Shaw's Scotch Court of Session Cases [*A publication*] (DLA) ... S
Shaw's Scotch Court of Session Cases [*A publication*] (DLA) ... Sh Ct of Sess
Shaw's Scotch Court of Session Cases, First Series [*A publication*] (DLA) ... Shaw
Shaw's Scotch Justiciary Cases [*A publication*] (DLA) ... S Just
Shaw's Scotch Justiciary Cases [*A publication*] (DLA) ... Sh
Shaw's Scotch Justiciary Cases [*A publication*] (DLA) ... Sh Jus
Shaw's Scotch Justiciary Cases [*A publication*] (DLA) ... Shaw
Shaw's Scotch Session Cases [*A publication*] (DLA) ... Sh
Shaw's Scotch Teind [*Tithe*] **Cases** [*A publication*] (DLA) ... S Teind
Shaw's Scotch Teind [*Tithe*] **Cases** [*1821-31*] [*A publication*] (DLA) ... Shaw TC
Shaw's Scotch Teind [*Tithe*] **Court Decisions** [*A publication*] (DLA) ... Sh Teind Ct
Shaw's Scotch Teind [*Tithe*] **Court Decisions** [*1821-31*] [*A publication*] (DLA) ... Shaw Teind
Shaw's Scotch Teind [*Tithe*] **Court Reports** [*A publication*] (DLA) ... Sh
Shaw's Scotch Teind [*Tithe*] **Court Reports** [*A publication*] (DLA) ... Shaw
Shaw's Scotch Teind [*Tithe*] **Court Reports** [*A publication*] (DLA) ... Shaw T Cas
Shayna International Industry [*Vancouver Stock Exchange symbol*] ... SWA
Sheaf Catalogue [*Library term*] (DGA) ... Sh/Cat
Shear [*Type of seismic wave*] ... S
Shear ... SHR
Shear Area Transition Temperature (PDAA) ... SATT
Shear Horizontal Acoustic Plate Model [*Instrumentation*] ... SHAPM
Shear Layer [*or Load*] ... SL
Shear Modulus [*Symbol*] [*IUPAC*] ... G
Shear Plate [*Technical drawings*] ... SP
Shear Strength (AAG) ... SS
Shear Thinning Index (PDAA) ... STI
Shearing (MSA) ... SHRNG
Shearing, Piling, and Disking [*Forest management*] ... SPD
Shearman and Redfield on the Law of Negligence [*A publication*] (DLA) ... S & R Neg
Shearman and Redfield on the Law of Negligence [*A publication*] (DLA) ... S & R on Neg
Shearman and Redfield on the Law of Negligence [*A publication*] (DLA) ... Sh & R Neg
Shearman and Redfield on the Law of Negligence [*A publication*] (DLA) ... Shear & R Neg
Shearman and Redfield on the Law of Negligence [*A publication*] (DLA) ... Shearm & Red Neg
Shearman & Sterling Library, New York, NY [*Library symbol*] [*Library of Congress*] (LCLS) ... NNSS
Shearon Harris Nuclear Power Plant (GFGA) ... SHNPP
Shearon Harris Plant [*Nuclear energy*] (NRCH) ... SHP
Shear-Stress Responsive Element [*Biochemistry*] ... SSRE
Shearwood on Contract [*1897*] [*A publication*] (DLA) ... Shear Cont
Shearwood on Personal Property [*1882*] [*A publication*] (DLA) ... Shear Pers Pr
Shearwood on Real Property [*3rd ed.*] [*1885*] [*A publication*] (DLA) ... Shear R Pr
Shearwood's Bar Examinations [*A publication*] (DLA) ... Shear Bar Ex
Sheath (IAA) ... SHTH
Sheath of Skeletal Axis ... SSA
Sheathing [*Technical drawings*] ... SH
Sheathing (MSA) ... SHTHG
Sheave (MSA) ... SHV
Sheba Aviation [*Yemen*] [*FAA designator*] (FAAC) ... SYE
Sheba Copper Mines [*Vancouver Stock Exchange symbol*] ... SHE
Shebandowan Resources [*Vancouver Stock Exchange symbol*] ... SBW
Shebear [*England*] ... SHEB
Sheberghan [*Afghanistan*] [*ICAO location identifier*] (ICLI) ... OASG
Shebi'it (BJA) ... Sheb
Shebi'it (BJA) ... Shebi
Sheboygan [*Wisconsin*] [*Airport symbol*] (OAG) ... SBM
Sheboygan County Federated Library System, Mead Public Library, Sheboygan, WI [*OCLC symbol*] (OCLC) ... WSD
Sheboygan Falls, WI [*FM radio station call letters*] (RBYB) ... WBFM-FM
Sheboygan Memorial Hospital, Sheboygan, WI [*Library symbol Library of Congress*] (LCLS) ... WSheM
Sheboygan, WI [*Location identifier FAA*] (FAAL) ... FAH
Sheboygan, WI [*Location identifier FAA*] (FAAL) ... SBM
Sheboygan, WI [*AM radio station call letters*] ... WCNZ
Sheboygan, WI [*AM radio station call letters*] ... WHBL
Sheboygan, WI [*FM radio station call letters*] ... WSHS
Sheboygan, WI [*FM radio station call letters*] ... WWJR
Shebu'oth (BJA) ... Shebu
Shedden Public Library, Spanish, Ontario [*Library symbol National Library of Canada*] (NLC) ... OSNS
Sheehan Memorial Emergency Hospital, Buffalo, NY [*Library symbol Library of Congress*] (LCLS) ... NBuSMH
Sheep (ROG) ... S
Sheep (ROG) ... SH
Sheep Anti-Guinea Pig Gamma Globulin (OA) ... SAGPGG
Sheep Canyon [*Utah*] [*Seismograph station code, US Geological Survey Closed*] (SEIS) ... SCU
Sheep Cell Agglutination Test ... SCAT
Sheep Choroid Plexus ... SCP
Sheep Creek Mountain [*Alaska*] [*Seismograph station code, US Geological Survey*] (SEIS) ... SCM
Sheep Erythrocyte Agglutination [*Test*] ... SEA
Sheep Erythrocyte Agglutination Test [*Medicine*] (DMAA) ... SEAT
Sheep Erythrocyte Antibody [*Medicine*] (DMAA) ... SLEA
Sheep Hemolyzate Supernatant ... SHS
Sheep Industry Development Program (EA) ... SIDP
Sheep Industry Liaison Committee [*New South Wales, Australia*] ... SILC
Sheep Mountain, AK [*Location identifier FAA*] (FAAL) ... SMU
Sheep Pulmonary Adenomatosis [*Medicine*] (DMAA) ... SPA
Sheep Red Blood Cell [*s*] [*Also, SRC*] ... SRBC
Sheep Red Cell [*s*] [*Also, SRBC*] ... SRC
Sheep Red Cell Rosette Forming Cells (AAMN) ... SRFC
Sheep River Community Library, Black Diamond, AB, Canada [*Library symbol*] [*Library of Congress*] (LCLS) ... CaABdSRC
Sheep River Community Library, Black Diamond, Alberta [*Library symbol National Library of Canada*] (NLC) ... ABDSRC
Sheep Seminal Vesicle ... SSV
Sheep Skin [*Bookbinding*] (ROG) ... SH
Sheepmeat Council of Australia ... SCA

Sheepskin Export Packers' Association of Australia ... SEPAA
Sheet [*Genetics*] ... S
Sheet (AAG) ... SH
Sheet (AAG) ... SHT
Sheet (VRA) ... sht
Sheet ... SHT
Sheet, Bar, Tubing (IAA) ... SBT
Sheet Explosive Loading Technique ... SELT
Sheet Harbour, NS [*Television station call letters*] ... CBHT-4
Sheet Iron ... SHI
Sheet Iron [*Freight*] ... SHT IRN
Sheet Iron and Light Plate Workers' Society [*A union*] [*British*] ... SILPWS
Sheet Iron or Steel [*Freight*] ... SHT IRN STL
Sheet Metal [*Freight*] ... SHT MTL
Sheet Metal ... SM
Sheet Metal and Air Conditioning Contractors' National Association (EA) ... SMACNA
Sheet Metal Assembler Riveter (MCD) ... SMAR
Sheet Metal Enclosure ... SME
Sheet Metal Industries Association [*British*] (BI) ... SMIA
Sheet Metal Industry Promotion Plan (EA) ... SMIPP
Sheet Metal Insert Process ... SIP
Sheet Metal Occupational Health Institute (EA) ... SMOHI
Sheet Metal Workers' International Association (EA) ... SMW
Sheet Metal Workers' International Association (EA) ... SMWIA
Sheet Molding Compound [*Plastics technology*] ... SMC
Sheet Molding Compound Automotive Alliance [*An association*] ... SMCAA
Sheet Steel (IAA) ... SHS
Sheet Steel Ware [*Freight*] ... SHT STL WRE
Sheeting [*Freight*] ... SHTG
Sheet-Metal Screw (DAC) ... SMS
Sheets per Hour (WDMC) ... SPH
Sheffield [*Tasmania*] [*Seismograph station code, US Geological Survey*] (SEIS) ... SFF
Sheffield [*England*] (BARN) ... Shef
Sheffield [*England*] ... SHEFD
Sheffield, AL [*FM radio station call letters*] (RBYB) ... WAKD
Sheffield, AL [*AM radio station call letters*] ... WBTG
Sheffield, AL [*FM radio station call letters*] ... WBTG-FM
Sheffield and Midland Railway [*British*] (ROG) ... SMR
Sheffield Centre for Environmental Research [*British*] (CB) ... SCER
Sheffield City Libraries, Central Library, Sheffield, United Kingdom [*Library symbol Library of Congress*] (LCLS) ... UkSh
Sheffield District Railway (ROG) ... SDR
Sheffield Exploration [*ECM Symbol*] (TTSB) ... SHE EC
Sheffield, IL [*Commercial waste site*] (GAAI) ... SHEF
Sheffield Interchange Organization (NITA) ... SINTO
Sheffield Lighter Trades Employers' Association [*British*] (DCTA) ... SLTEA
Sheffield, MA [*FM radio station call letters*] ... WBSL
Sheffield Medical Technologies [*Associated Press*] (SAG) ... ShefldMd
Sheffield Medical Technologies, Inc. [*AMEX symbol*] (SPSG) ... SHM
Sheffield Medl Tech [*AMEX symbol*] (TTSB) ... SHM
Sheffield Package Analysis and Identification of Data [*Commercial & Industrial Development Bureau*] [*Software package*] (NCC) ... SPAID
Sheffield People's Resource for Information Technology [*British*] (AIE) ... SPRITE
Sheffield Press, Sheffield, IA [*Library symbol Library of Congress*] (LCLS) ... IaShefP
Sheffield Sawmakers' Protection Society [*A union*] [*British*] (DCTA) ... SSPS
Sheffield University Metals Advisory Centre [*British*] (IRUK) ... SUMAC
Sheffield Urban and Regional Instructional Simulation System [*British*] ... SURISS
Sheffield Wool Shear Workers' Trade Union [*British*] (DCTA) ... SWSWTU
Shefford [*England*] ... SHEFF
Sheftall Record Book [*A publication*] (BJA) ... SRB
Sheghnan [*Afghanistan*] [*ICAO location identifier*] (ICLI) ... OASN
Sheik Hussein [*Ethiopia*] [*ICAO location identifier*] (ICLI) ... HASH
Sheild ... SHLD
Sheil's Sketches of the Irish Bar [*A publication*] (DLA) ... Sheil Ir Bar
Shekalim (BJA) ... Shek
Shekel (ODBW) ... NIS
Shekhupura [*Pakistan*] [*ICAO location identifier*] (ICLI) ... OPSP
Shelburne County Museum, Nova Scotia [*Library symbol National Library of Canada*] (NLC) ... NSSCM
Shelburne County Museum, Shelburne, NS, Canada [*Library symbol*] [*Library of Congress*] (LCLS) ... CaNSShCM
Shelburne Museum, Inc., Research Library, Shelburne, VT [*Library symbol Library of Congress*] (LCLS) ... VtShelM
Shelburne, NS [*FM radio station call letters*] ... CJLS-1
Shelburne, NS [*FM radio station call letters*] ... CKBW-2
Shelburne Public Library, Ontario [*Library symbol National Library of Canada*] (NLC) ... OSH
Shelburne Public Library, Shelburne, ON, Canada [*Library symbol*] [*Library of Congress*] (LCLS) ... CaOSH
Shelby American Automobile Club (EA) ... SAAC
Shelby Can-Am [*Racing car*] ... SCA
Shelby County Court House, Memphis, TN [*Library symbol*] [*Library of Congress*] (LCLS) ... TMSCC
Shelby County Memorial Hospital, Shelbyville, IL [*Library symbol Library of Congress*] (LCLS) ... IShCoH
Shelby County Museum, Harlan, IA [*Library symbol Library of Congress*] (LCLS) ... IaHarS
Shelby County Recorder's Office, Shelbyville, IN [*Library symbol Library of Congress*] (LCLS) ... InSheCR
Shelby Dodge Automobile Club [*Defunct*] (EA) ... SDAC
Shelby Memorial Library, Columbia, MS [*Library symbol Library of Congress*] (LCLS) ... MsCba
Shelby, MT [*AM radio station call letters*] ... KSEN
Shelby, MT [*FM radio station call letters*] ... KZIN
Shelby, MT [*Location identifier FAA*] (FAAL) ... SBX
Shelby, NC [*Location identifier FAA*] (FAAL) ... EHO
Shelby, NC [*Location identifier FAA*] (FAAL) ... SLP
Shelby, NC [*AM radio station call letters*] ... WADA
Shelby, NC [*AM radio station call letters*] ... WOHS
Shelby, NC [*FM radio station call letters*] ... WWMG
Shelby, OH [*FM radio station call letters*] ... WSWR
Shelby Owners of America (EA) ... SOA
Shelby Public Library, Shelby, MI [*Library symbol Library of Congress*] (LCLS) ... MiSh
Shelby State Community College, Memphis, TN [*Library symbol Library of Congress*] (LCLS) ... TMSS
Shelby Township Library, Utica, MI [*Library symbol Library of Congress*] (LCLS) ... MiUtS
Shelby Williams Ind [*NYSE symbol*] (TTSB) ... SY
Shelby Williams Industries, Inc. [*Associated Press*] (SAG) ... Shelby
Shelby Williams Industries, Inc. [*NYSE symbol*] (SPSG) ... SY
Shelby's Rabbit Eater [*In model name Omni SRE, proposed for Dodge car designed by Carroll Shelby*] ... SRE
Shelbyville [*Tennessee*] [*Airport symbol*] (AD) ... SYI
Shelbyville, IL [*Location identifier FAA*] (FAAL) ... SYZ
Shelbyville, IL [*FM radio station call letters*] ... WEJT
Shelbyville, IL [*AM radio station call letters*] ... WSHY
Shelbyville, IN [*Location identifier FAA*] (FAAL) ... SHB
Shelbyville, IN [*FM radio station call letters*] ... WENS
Shelbyville, IN [*AM radio station call letters*] ... WOOO
Shelbyville, KY [*AM radio station call letters*] ... WCND
Shelbyville, KY [*FM radio station call letters*] ... WTHQ
Shelbyville News, Shelbyville, IN [*Library symbol Library of Congress*] (LCLS) ... InSheN
Shelbyville, TN [*Location identifier FAA*] (FAAL) ... SYI
Shelbyville, TN [*AM radio station call letters*] ... WHAL
Shelbyville, TN [*AM radio station call letters*] ... WLIJ
Shelbyville, TN [*FM radio station call letters*] ... WYCQ
Shelbyville, TN [*FM radio station call letters*] (RBYB) ... WZPC-FM
Shelbyville-Shelby County Public Library, Shelbyville, IN [*Library symbol Library of Congress*] (LCLS) ... InShe
Sheldahl Co. [*Associated Press*] (SAG) ... Sheldl
Sheldahl, Inc. [*NASDAQ symbol*] (NQ) ... SHEL
Sheldon Art Museum, Middlebury, VT [*Library symbol Library of Congress*] (LCLS) ... VtMiS
Sheldon County Historical Society, Sheldon, IA [*Library symbol Library of Congress*] (LCLS) ... IaSheHi
Sheldon, IA [*AM radio station call letters*] ... KIWA
Sheldon, IA [*FM radio station call letters*] ... KIWA-FM
Sheldon, IA [*Location identifier FAA*] (FAAL) ... SHL
Sheldon Jackson College, Sitka, AK [*Library symbol Library of Congress*] (LCLS) ... AkSJ
Sheldon Jackson Junior College [*Sitka, AK*] [*Later, Sheldon Jackson College*] ... SJJC
Sheldon Mail, Sheldon, IA [*Library symbol Library of Congress*] (LCLS) ... IaSheM
Sheldon on Subrogation [*A publication*] (DLA) ... Sheld Subr
Sheldon Point [*Alaska*] [*Airport symbol*] (OAG) ... SXP
Sheldon Public Library, Sheldon, IA [*Library symbol Library of Congress*] (LCLS) ... IaShe
Sheldon Sun, Sheldon, IA [*Library symbol Library of Congress*] (LCLS) ... IaSheS
Sheldon Township Public Library, Sheldon, IL [*Library symbol Library of Congress*] (LCLS) ... IShe
Sheldon's Real Property Statutes [*9th ed.*] [*1893*] [*A publication*] (DLA) ... Shel R Pr St
Sheldon's Superior Court Reports [*Buffalo, New York*] [*A publication*] (DLA) ... Buff Super Ct
Sheldon's Superior Court Reports [*Buffalo, New York*] [*A publication*] (DLA) ... Buff Super Ct (NY)
Sheldon's Superior Court Reports [*Buffalo, New York*] [*A publication*] (DLA) ... Sh
Sheldon's Superior Court Reports [*Buffalo, New York*] [*A publication*] (DLA) ... Sheld
Sheldon's Superior Court Reports [*Buffalo, New York*] [*A publication*] (DLA) ... Sheldon
Shelf [*Technical drawings*] ... SH
Shelf Dynamics Program [*CUE*] (MSC) ... SDP
Shelf Edge Exchange Processes [*Oceanography*] (NOAA) ... SEEP
Shelf Life (NASA) ... SL
Shelf Life Code (MCD) ... SLC
Shelf Life Data [*Army*] ... SLD
Shelf Life Item [*Military*] (AABC) ... SLI
Shelf Life Limit (MCD) ... SLL
Shelf List [*A card catalog arranged in call number order*] ... SL
Shelf Stock ... SS
Shelford on Highways [*4th ed.*] [*1869*] [*A publication*] (DLA) ... Shel High
Shelford on Joint Stock Companies [*2nd ed.*] [*1870*] [*A publication*] (DLA) ... Shel J St Com
Shelford on Joint-Stock Companies [*A publication*] (DLA) ... Shelf J St Cos
Shelford on Lunacy [*2nd ed.*] [*1847*] [*A publication*] (DLA) ... Shel Lun
Shelford on Lunacy [*A publication*] (DLA) ... Shelf Lun
Shelford on Marriage and Divorce [*1841*] [*A publication*] (DLA) ... Shel M & D
Shelford on Marriage and Divorce [*A publication*] (DLA) ... Shelf Mar & Div
Shelford on Mortmain and Charitable Uses [*1836*] [*A publication*] (DLA) ... Shel Mort
Shelford on Probate, Legacy, Etc. [*2nd ed.*] [*1861*] [*A publication*] (DLA) ... Shel Prob

Shelford on Railways [*4th ed.*] [*1869*] [*A publication*] (DLA) .... Shel Ry
Shelford on Wills [*1838*] [*A publication*] (DLA) .... Shel Will
Shelford on Wills [*A publication*] (DLA) .... Shel Wills
Shelford's Bankrupt and Insolvency Law [*3rd ed.*] [*1862*] [*A publication*] (DLA) .... Shel Bank
Shell .... S
Shell [*Computer science*] (CDE) .... sh
Shell .... SHL
Shell (VRA) .... shl
Shell (AAG) .... SHL
Shell Aircraft Ltd. [*British ICAO designator*] (FAAC) .... SHE
Shell Analysis .... SA
Shell Canada Ltd. [*Toronto Stock Exchange symbol Vancouver Stock Exchange symbol*] .... SHC
Shell Canada Ltd. [*UTLAS symbol*] .... SHL
Shell Canada Ltd., Calgary, AB, Canada [*Library symbol Library of Congress*] (LCLS) .... CaACSC
Shell Canada Ltd., Research Center Library, Calgary, AB, Canada [*Library symbol*] [*Library of Congress*] (LCLS) .... CaACSCL
Shell Canada Ltd., Toronto, ON, Canada [*Library symbol Library of Congress*] (LCLS) .... CaOTSCL
Shell Canada Ltd., Toronto, Ontario [*Library symbol National Library of Canada*] (NLC) .... OTSCL
Shell Canada'A'vtg [*TS Symbol*] (TTSB) .... SHC
Shell Chemical Co., Deer Park, TX [*Library symbol Library of Congress*] (LCLS) .... TxDpSC
Shell Chemical Co., Denver, CO [*Library symbol Library of Congress*] (LCLS) .... CoDSC
Shell Chemical Co., Information Services Library, San Ramon, CA [*Library symbol Library of Congress*] (LCLS) .... CSraS
Shell Chemical Co., Torrance, CA [*Library symbol Library of Congress Obsolete*] (LCLS) .... CTS
Shell Claus Offgas Treating [*Chemical engineering*] .... SCOT
Shell Development Co. [*Research code symbol*] .... OS
Shell Development Co. [*Research code symbol*] .... SH
Shell Development Co., Bellaire Research Center, Houston, TX [*Library symbol Library of Congress*] (LCLS) .... TxHSD
Shell Development Co., Emeryville, CA [*Library symbol Library of Congress Obsolete*] (LCLS) .... CEvS
Shell Development Co., Modesto, CA [*Library symbol Library of Congress*] (LCLS) .... CMSh
Shell Flue Gas Desulfurization [*Air pollution control*] .... SFGD
Shell Fragment (MAE) .... SF
Shell Fragment Wound [*Medicine*] .... SFW
Shell Gland .... SG
Shell Gun .... SG
Shell Higher Olefin Process [*Petrochemistry*] .... SHOP
Shell Lake, WI [*Location identifier FAA*] (FAAL) .... SSQ
Shell Lake, WI [*AM radio station call letters*] .... WCSW
Shell Lake, WI [*FM radio station call letters*] .... WGMO
Shell Metal Extractant .... SME
Shell Model .... SM
Shell Oil Co. [*Toronto Stock Exchange symbol*] (SPSG) .... SUO
Shell Oil Co., Deer Park, TX [*Library symbol Library of Congress*] (LCLS) .... TxDpS
Shell Oil Co., Denver, CO [*Library symbol Library of Congress*] (LCLS) .... CoDSO
Shell Oil Co., Information and Computing Services Center Library, Houston, TX [*Library symbol Library of Congress*] (LCLS) .... TxHSOIC
Shell Oil Co., Information and Library Services Library, Houston, TX [*Library symbol Library of Congress*] (LCLS) .... TxHSOF
Shell Oil Co., New Orleans, LA [*Library symbol Library of Congress*] (LCLS) .... LNSO
Shell Oil Co. of Canada, Montreal, PQ, Canada [*Library symbol Library of Congress*] (LCLS) .... CaQMSO
Shell Oil Co. of Canada, Montreal, Quebec [*Library symbol National Library of Canada*] (NLC) .... QMSO
Shell Oil Development Co., Westhollow Research Center Library, Houston, TX [*Library symbol Library of Congress*] (LCLS) .... TxHSDW
Shell Pipe Line Corp., R and D Library, Houston, TX [*Library symbol Library of Congress Obsolete*] (LCLS) .... TxHSP
Shell Research Centre, Oakville, Ontario [*Library symbol National Library of Canada*] (NLC) .... OOAKS
Shell Rock News, Shell Rock, IA [*Library symbol*] [*Library of Congress*] (LCLS) .... IaShrN
Shell Rock Public Library, Shell Rock, IA [*Library symbol Library of Congress*] (LCLS) .... IaShr
Shell Shock .... SS
Shell Technology Enterprise Programme [*British*] .... STEP
Shell Theory Automated for Rotational Structures .... STARS
Shell Theory Automated for Rotational Structures - II (MCD) .... STARS II
Shell Transient Asymmetric Response .... STAR
Shell Transp/Trad ADR [*NYSE symbol*] (TTSB) .... SC
Shell Transport & Trading Co. Ltd. [*NYSE symbol*] (SPSG) .... SC
Shell Transport & Trading Co. Ltd. [*Associated Press*] (SAG) .... ShellTr
Shell Western E & P Inc., Woodcreek Library, Houston, TX [*Library symbol*] [*Library of Congress*] (LCLS) .... TxHSWE
Shellac (MSA) .... SHL
Shell-Destroying [*Device*] .... SD
Shell-Destroying Tracer [*Ammunition*] .... SDT
Shelledy Elementary School, Fruita, CO [*Library symbol Library of Congress*] (LCLS) .... CoFruSE
Shellee Morris Fan Club (EA) .... SMFC
Sheller-Globe Corp. .... SG
Shelley Public Library, Shelley, ID [*Library symbol*] [*Library of Congress*] (LCLS) .... IdS
Shelley's Cases in Vol. 1 of Coke's Reports [*A publication*] (DLA) .... Shel Ca
Shellfish Institute of North America [*Also known as Oyster Growers and Dealers Association of North America*] (EA) .... SINA
Shelling Report [*Military*] (NATG) .... SHELLREP
Shelling Report [*Military*] .... SHELREP
Shelling Report [*Military*] (MUGU) .... SHELREPT
Shells [*Quality of the bottom*] [*Nautical charts*] .... sh
Shells Seafood Rest Wrrt [*NASDAQ symbol*] (TTSB) .... SHLLW
Shells Seafood Restaurants [*NASDAQ symbol*] (TTSB) .... SHLL
Shells Seafood Restaurants, Inc. [*NASDAQ symbol*] (SAG) .... SHLL
Shells Seafood Restaurants, Inc. [*Associated Press*] (SAG) .... ShllsS
Shells Seafood Restaurants, Inc. [*Associated Press*] (SAG) .... ShllsSea
Shell-Supported Ring Frame .... SSRF
Shelly School, Shelly, MN [*Library symbol*] [*Library of Congress*] (LCLS) .... MnSheS
Shelter [*Bureau of the Census*] .... S
Shelter (WGA) .... SHLTR
Shelter Advertising Association [*Minneapolis, MN*] (EA) .... SAA
Shelter Analysis for New Designs (DNAB) .... SAND
Shelter Available for Emergency .... SAFE
Shelter Complex Headquarters [*Civil Defense*] .... SCH
Shelter Components Corp. [*Associated Press*] (SAG) .... SheltCm
Shelter Components Corp. [*AMEX symbol*] (SPSG) .... SST
Shelter Deck (DNAB) .... SD
Shelter Deck .... SDK
Shelter Decontamination Unit .... SDU
Shelter Equipment .... SE
Shelter Equipment Vault .... SEV
Shelter Housed Automatic Digital Random Access [*Computer science*] .... SHADRAC
Shelter Island Public Library Society, Shelter Island, NY [*Library symbol Library of Congress*] (LCLS) .... NShei
Shelter Management [*Civil Defense*] .... SM
Shelter Management Instructor [*Civil Defense*] .... SMI
Shelter Management Training [*Civil Defense*] .... SMT
Shelter Neighborhood Action Project .... SNAP
Shelter Oil & Gas Ltd. [*Toronto Stock Exchange symbol*] .... SIA
Shelter Rock Elementary School, Manhasset, NY [*Library symbol*] [*Library of Congress*] (LCLS) .... NManhSE
Shelter Rock Public Library, Albertson, NY [*Library symbol Library of Congress*] (LCLS) .... NAlb
Shelter Taxi [*NASA*] (KSC) .... S/T
Shelter Warden [*British Home Defence*] [*World War II*] .... SW
Shelter-Afrique (EAIO) .... SH-AF
Sheltered [*Takeoff area for seaplanes*] [*For chart use only*] .... S
Sheltered Employment Procurement and Consultancy Service (AIE) .... SEPACS
Sheltered Placement Scheme (AIE) .... SPS
Shelters [*JETDS nomenclature*] [*Military*] (CET) .... S
Shelton, CT [*FM radio station call letters*] .... WRXC
Shelton Public Library, Shelton, WA [*Library symbol Library of Congress*] (LCLS) .... WaSh
Shelton State Community College, Tuscalossa, AL [*Library symbol*] [*Library of Congress*] (LCLS) .... ATuSC
Shelton, WA [*AM radio station call letters*] .... KMAS
Shelton, WA [*Location identifier FAA*] (FAAL) .... MNC
Shelton, WA [*Location identifier FAA*] (FAAL) .... SHN
Shelving Manufacturers Association (EA) .... SMA
Shemkha [*Former USSR Seismograph station code, US Geological Survey*] (SEIS) .... SHE
Shemya [*Alaska*] [*Seismograph station code, US Geological Survey*] (SEIS) .... SMY
Shemya Air Force Base [*Alaska*] [*ICAO location identifier*] (ICLI) .... PASY
Shemya Island [*Alaska*] [*Airport symbol*] (OAG) .... SYA
Shemya WWII Veterans Association (EA) .... SWVA
Shenandoah [*A publication*] (BRI) .... Shen
Shenandoah College and Conservatory of Music, Winchester, VA [*Library symbol Library of Congress*] (LCLS) .... ViWnS
Shenandoah, IA [*AM radio station call letters*] .... KMA
Shenandoah, IA [*AM radio station call letters*] .... KYFR
Shenandoah, IA [*Location identifier FAA*] (FAAL) .... SDA
Shenandoah National Park .... SHEN
Shenandoah Natural History Association (EA) .... SNHA
Shenandoah, PA [*AM radio station call letters*] .... WMBT
Shenandoah Public Library, Shenandoah, IA [*Library symbol Library of Congress*] (LCLS) .... IaSh
Shenandoah Resources Ltd. [*Vancouver Stock Exchange symbol*] .... SHH
Shenandoah Valley Independent College Library Cooperative [*Library network*] .... SVICLC
Shendi [*Sudan*] [*ICAO location identifier*] (ICLI) .... HSND
Shensi Province [*China, Mainland*] [*MARC geographic area code Library of Congress*] (LCCP) .... a-cc-ss
Shenyang [*China*] [*Airport symbol*] (OAG) .... SHE
Shenyang [*China*] [*ICAO location identifier*] (ICLI) .... ZYSH
Shenyang/Dongta [*China*] [*ICAO location identifier*] (ICLI) .... ZYYY
Shenyang Regional Administration of CAA of China [*ICAO designator*] (FAAC) .... CBF
Shenzhen Airlines [*China*] [*FAA designator*] (FAAC) .... CSZ
Shepard Insurance Group [*Vancouver Stock Exchange symbol*] .... SHR
Shepard-Pruden Memorial Library, Edenton, NC [*Library symbol Library of Congress*] (LCLS) .... NcEdt
Shepard's Causes of Action [*A publication*] .... COA
Shepard's Citations [*A publication*] (AAGC) .... Shep
Shepard's Preparing for Settlement and Trial [*A publication*] .... PST
Shepherd Bay, NT [*ICAO location identifier*] (ICLI) .... CYUS
Shepherd College, Shepherdstown, WV [*Library symbol Library of Congress*] (LCLS) .... WvShS
Shepherd, MI [*AM radio station call letters*] .... WMMI

Shepherd Products Ltd. [*Toronto Stock Exchange symbol*] ... SEP
Shepherd's Alabama Reports [*A publication*] (DLA) ... Sh
Shepherd's Alabama Reports [*A publication*] (DLA) ... Shep
Shepherd's Center of America ... SCA
Shepherds Fold Ministries (EA) ... SFM
Shepherd's Reports [*19-21, 24-41, 60, 63, 64 Alabama*] [*A publication*] (DLA) ... Shepherd
Shepherd's Select Cases [*Alabama*] [*A publication*] (DLA) ... Shep Sel Cas
Shepherd's Select Cases [*Alabama*] [*A publication*] (DLA) ... Sheph Sel Cas
Shepherdstown Public Library, Shepherdstown, WV [*Library symbol Library of Congress*] (LCLS) ... WvSh
Shepherdstown, WV [*FM radio station call letters*] ... WSHC
Shepherdsville, KY [*AM radio station call letters*] ... WBUL
Shepherdsville, KY [*FM radio station call letters*] ... WEHR
Shepley's Reports [*13-18, 21-30 Maine*] [*A publication*] (DLA) ... Sh
Shepley's Reports [*13-18, 21-30 Maine*] [*A publication*] (DLA) ... Shep
Shepley's Reports [*13-18, 21-30 Maine*] [*A publication*] (DLA) ... Shepley
Sheppard Air Force Base [*Texas*] (AAG) ... SAFB
Sheppard Air Force Base [*Texas*] (AAG) ... SHAFB
Sheppard Memorial Library, Greenville, NC [*Library symbol Library of Congress*] (LCLS) ... NcGrS
Sheppard Technical Training Center (AFM) ... STTC
Sheppard-Pratt Hospital, Baltimore, MD [*Library symbol Library of Congress*] (LCLS) ... MdBSP
Sheppard's Abridgment [*A publication*] (DLA) ... Shep Abr
Sheppard's Action on the Case [*A publication*] (DLA) ... Shep Act
Sheppard's Cases of Slander, Etc. [*A publication*] (DLA) ... Shep Cas
Sheppard's Precedent of Precedents [*9th ed.*] [*1825*] [*A publication*] (DLA) ... Shep Prec
Sheppard's Touchstone [*A publication*] (DLA) ... Touch
Sheppard's Touchstone by Preston [*A publication*] (DLA) ... Prest Shep T
Sheppard-Turpin-England [*Machine carbine codesigned by Sheppard and Turpin*] ... STEN
Sheraton Executive Traveler [*Sheraton Corp.*] ... SET
Sherborne [*Urban district in England*] ... SHERB
Sherbourne County Historical Society, Becker, MN [*Library symbol*] [*Library of Congress*] (LCLS) ... MnBHi
Sherbrooke Daily Record, Quebec [*Library symbol National Library of Canada*] (NLC) ... QSHERD
Sherbrooke Daily Record, Sherbrooke, PQ, Canada [*Library symbol Library of Congress*] (LCLS) ... CaQSherD
Sherbrooke Forest Park [*Victoria, Australia*] [*Airport symbol*] (AD) ... SFP
Sherbrooke Library, Sherbrooke, PQ, Canada [*Library symbol Library of Congress*] (LCLS) ... CaQSherL
Sherbrooke, PQ [*Television station call letters*] ... CFKS
Sherbrooke, PQ [*FM radio station call letters*] ... CFLX
Sherbrooke, PQ [*AM radio station call letters*] ... CHLT
Sherbrooke, PQ [*Television station call letters*] ... CHLT-TV
Sherbrooke, PQ [*FM radio station call letters*] ... CITE-1
Sherbrooke, PQ [*Television station call letters*] ... CIVS
Sherbrooke, PQ [*Television station call letters*] ... CKSH
Sherbrooke, PQ [*AM radio station call letters*] ... CKTS
Sherbrooke, PQ [*ICAO location identifier*] (ICLI) ... CYSC
Sherbrooke University Institut de Recherche et d'Enseignement pour les Cooperatives [*Canada Research center*] (RCD) ... IRECUS
Sherburne Public Library, Sherburne, NY [*Library symbol Library of Congress*] (LCLS) ... NSherb
Sherburn-In-Elmet [*British ICAO location identifier*] (ICLI) ... EGCJ
Shergottite Parent Body [*Planetary science*] ... SPB
Sheridan [*Wyoming*] [*Airport symbol*] (OAG) ... SHR
Sheridan, AR [*FM radio station call letters*] ... KEZQ
Sheridan, AR [*AM radio station call letters*] ... KGHT
Sheridan, AR [*FM radio station call letters*] (RBYB) ... KVLO-FM
Sheridan Broadcasting Network ... SBN
Sheridan College, Oakville, ON, Canada [*Library symbol Library of Congress*] (LCLS) ... CaOOakSC
Sheridan College, Oakville, Ontario [*Library symbol National Library of Canada*] (NLC) ... OOAKSC
Sheridan College, Sheridan, WY [*Library symbol Library of Congress*] (LCLS) ... WyShS
Sheridan County Free Library, Plentywood, MT [*Library symbol*] [*Library of Congress*] (LCLS) ... MtPw
Sheridan County Fulmer Public Library, Sheridan, WY [*Library symbol Library of Congress*] (LCLS) ... WyShF
Sheridan Elementary School District 272, Sheridan, IL [*Library symbol Library of Congress*] (LCLS) ... ISherESD
Sheridan Healthcare [*NASDAQ symbol*] (TTSB) ... SHCR
Sheridan Healthcare, Inc. [*NASDAQ symbol*] (SAG) ... SHCR
Sheridan Healthcare, Inc. [*Associated Press*] (SAG) ... Sheridan
Sheridan News, Sheridan, IN [*Library symbol Library of Congress*] (LCLS) ... InSherN
Sheridan Park Hospital, Inc., Tonawanda, NY [*Library symbol Library of Congress*] (LCLS) ... NTonS
Sheridan Park Research Community, Cominco Ltd., Mississauga, Ontario [*Library symbol National Library of Canada*] (NLC) ... OMCS
Sheridan Public Library, Sheridan, OR [*Library symbol Library of Congress*] (LCLS) ... OrShe
Sheridan, WY [*Location identifier FAA*] (FAAL) ... BNS
Sheridan, WY [*AM radio station call letters*] ... KROE
Sheridan, WY [*FM radio station call letters*] ... KROE-FM
Sheridan, WY [*Television station call letters*] ... KSGW
Sheridan, WY [*AM radio station call letters*] ... KWYO
Sheridan, WY [*FM radio station call letters*] ... KWYO-FM
Sheridan, WY [*Location identifier FAA*] (FAAL) ... SHR
Sheridan's Practice, King's Bench [*A publication*] (DLA) ... Sher Pr
Sheridian Healtcare, Inc. [*NASDAQ symbol*] (SAG) ... SHCR
Sheriff (DLA) ... Sh
Sheriff ... SHER
Sheriff Court [*Legal*] [*British*] ... SHCT
Sheriff Court Reports [*Scotland*] [*A publication*] (DLA) ... Sh Ct Rep
Sheriff Court Reports [*Scotland*] [*A publication*] (DLA) ... Sher Ct Rep
Sheriff Guards International [*Nigeria*] (EAIO) ... SGI
Sheriff's Office [*or Officer*] (ROG) ... SO
Shering Corp., Bloomfield, NJ [*Library symbol Library of Congress*] (LCLS) ... NjBIS
Sherman [*Texas*] [*Airport symbol*] (OAG) ... SWI
Sherman Anti-Trust Act (MHDB) ... SAA
Sherman Anti-Trust Act (MHDB) ... SATA
Sherman Army Airfield [*Fort Leavenworth, KS*] ... SAAF
Sherman College of Straight Chiropractic, Spartanburg, SC [*Library symbol*] [*Library of Congress*] (LCLS) ... ScSpS
Sherman Crater - Mount Baker [*Washington*] [*Seismograph station code, US Geological Survey Closed*] (SEIS) ... SCW
Sherman Fairchild Technology Center (MCD) ... SFTC
Sherman Library and Gardens, Corona Del Mar, CA [*Library symbol*] [*Library of Congress*] (LCLS) ... CCdmS
Sherman Mental Impairment Test [*Psychology*] ... SMIT
Sherman Public Library, Sherman, TX [*Library symbol*] [*Library of Congress*] (LCLS) ... TxSh
Sherman Tanks Converted into Tractors by Vickers Armstrong ... SHERVICK
Sherman, TX [*FM radio station call letters*] ... KIKM
Sherman, TX [*AM radio station call letters*] ... KJIM
Sherman, TX [*FM radio station call letters*] ... KWSM
Sherman, TX [*AM radio station call letters*] ... KXEB
Sherman, TX [*Television station call letters*] ... KXII
Sherman-Denison, TX [*Location identifier FAA*] (FAAL) ... DNI
Sherman's Marine Insurance [*A publication*] (DLA) ... Sher Mar Ins
Sherratt & Hughes [*Commercial firm British*] ... S & H
Shergold, Inc. [*Toronto Stock Exchange symbol*] ... SG
Sherritt Gordon Mines Ltd. [*Toronto Stock Exchange symbol*] ... SE
Sherritt Gordon Mines Ltd., Fort Saskatchewan, AB, Canada [*Library symbol Library of Congress*] (LCLS) ... CaAFsSG
Sherritt Gordon Mines Ltd., Fort Saskatchewan, Alberta [*Library symbol National Library of Canada*] (NLC) ... AFSSG
Sherweeod, AR [*FM radio station call letters*] ... KLPQ
Sherwin Williams Chemicals, Chicago, IL [*Library symbol Library of Congress*] (LCLS) ... ICSW
Sherwin-Williams [*NYSE symbol*] (TTSB) ... SHW
Sherwin-Williams Co. [*Associated Press*] (SAG) ... Sherwin
Sherwin-Williams Co. [*NYSE symbol*] (SPSG) ... SHW
Sherwin-Williams Co. of Canada Ltd., Montreal, Quebec [*Library symbol National Library of Canada*] (NLC) ... QMSW
Sherwin-Williams Co. of Canada, Montreal, PQ, Canada [*Library symbol Library of Congress*] (LCLS) ... CaQMSW
Sherwood Anderson Society (EA) ... SAS
Sherwood, AR [*AM radio station call letters*] ... KMTL
Sherwood Foresters [*Military unit*] [*British*] ... SF
Sherwood Group [*NYSE symbol*] (SAG) ... SHD
Sherwood Group [*Associated Press*] (SAG) ... ShwdGp
Sherwood Hall, Laramie, WY [*Library symbol Library of Congress*] (LCLS) ... WyLarSh
Sherwood Number ... Sh
Sherwood Public Library, Sherwood, OR [*Library symbol Library of Congress*] (LCLS) ... OrSh
Sherwood Rangers Imperial Yeomanry [*British military*] (DMA) ... SRIY
Sherwood Rangers Yeomanry [*Military unit*] [*British*] ... SRY
Sherwood Yeomanry and Light Infantry [*British military*] (DMA) ... SY & LI
Sheshegwaning Band Public Library, Ontario [*Library symbol National Library of Canada*] (NLC) ... OSHB
Shetland (WGA) ... Shet
Shetland Isles ... SI
Shetland Knitwear Trades Association [*British*] (DBA) ... SKTA
Shetland Oil Terminal Environmental Advisory Group ... SOTEAG
Shetland Pony Identification Bureau ... SPIB
Shetland Pony Study Book Society [*British*] (DBA) ... SPSBS
Shevchenko Scientific Society (EA) ... SSS
Shevi'it (BJA) ... Shev
Shevu'ot (BJA) ... Shevu
Shiatsu Education Center of America [*Later, Ohashi Institute - OI*] (EA) ... SECA
Shichikawa [*Japan*] [*Seismograph station code, US Geological Survey*] (SEIS) ... SKW
Shield (MSA) ... SH
Shield (AAG) ... SHLD
Shield and Seismic Support [*Nuclear energy*] (NRCH) ... SSS
Shield Building Vent [*Nuclear energy*] (IAA) ... SBV
Shield Building Ventilation System [*Nuclear energy*] (NRCH) ... SBVS
Shield Design Code [*Nuclear energy*] (NRCH) ... SDC
Shield Development [*Vancouver Stock Exchange symbol*] ... SHD
Shield Mock-Up Reactor ... SMR
Shield of David (BJA) ... SD
Shield Plug Storage Station [*Nuclear energy*] (NRCH) ... SPSS
Shield Plug/Support Cylinder [*Nuclear energy*] (NRCH) ... SP/SC
Shield Test Air Reactor [*Nuclear energy*] ... STAR
Shield Test and Irradiation Reactor [*Nuclear energy*] ... STIR
Shield Test Experiment [*Nuclear energy*] (NRCH) ... STE
Shield Test Facility [*Nuclear energy*] (GFGA) ... STF
Shield Test Pool Facility [*Nuclear energy*] ... STPF
Shield, Union City, NJ [*Library symbol Library of Congress*] (LCLS) ... NjUcS
Shielded Diatomic Orbitals [*Atomic physics*] ... SDO
Shielded Hot-Air-Drum Evaporator [*Concentrator for hazardous wastes*] ... SHADE

Shielded Inert Gas Metal Arc (IAA) .... SIGMA
Shielded Metal Arc [*Nickel and alloy welding*] .... SMA
Shielded Metal Arc Cutting [*Welding*] .... SMAC
Shielded Metal Arc Welding .... SMAW
Shielded Mild Detonating Cord .... SMDC
Shielded Neutron Assay Probe [*Nuclear energy*] (NRCH) .... SNAP
Shielded Tunable Magnetron .... STM
Shielded Twisted-Pair [*Computer science*] (PCM) .... STP
Shielded Voltage Tunable Magnetron .... SVTM
Shielding Analysis Form [*Civil Defense*] .... SAF
Shielding Effectiveness (IEEE) .... SE
Shielding Effectiveness Factor .... SEF
Shielding Experiment Facility Reactor [*Nuclear energy*] .... SEFR
Shielding Standard Design Method (MCD) .... SSDM
Shielding Technologies Inc. .... STI
Shields Class Association (EA) .... SCA
Shiel's Cape Colony Reports [*A publication*] (DLA) .... Shiel
Shiel's Cape Times Law Reports [*South Africa*] [*A publication*] (DLA) .... Sh
Shift .... SFT
Shift (MSA) .... SHF
Shift .... SHFT
Shift Accumulator Left, Including Sign (IAA) .... SAS
Shift Advance Driver .... SA
Shift and Select [*Computer science*] (MDG) .... SSL
Shift Control [*Computer science*] (IAA) .... SC
Shift Control Counter [*Computer science*] (MDG) .... SC
Shift Count Register .... SCR
Shift Engineer (NRCH) .... SE
Shift Forward .... SF
Shift In [*Transistor*] (IAA) .... SI
Shift In, Shift Out (IEEE) .... SISO
Shift Indicator Light [*Automotive engineering*] .... SIL
Shift Left .... SL
Shift Left and Count Instructions [*Computer science*] (MDG) .... SLC
Shift Left Double [*Computer science*] (PCM) .... SHLD
Shift Left Out/Shift Right In .... SLO/SRI
Shift Operations Maintenance Manager (SSD) .... SOMM
Shift Operations Manager (NRCH) .... SOM
Shift Pattern Generator [*Automotive engineering*] .... SPG
Shift Pulses .... SP
Shift Register (NITA) .... SHFTR
Shift Register [*Computer science*] (IAA) .... SHR
Shift Register .... SR
Shift Register Available .... SRA
Shift Register Drive .... SRD
Shift Register Generator [*Computer science*] (IAA) .... SRG
Shift Register Label (NITA) .... SRL
Shift Register Memory .... SRM
Shift Register Partition (IAA) .... SRP
Shift Register Recognizer (IEEE) .... SRR
Shift Reverse .... SR
Shift Right .... SR
Shift Right Double [*Computer science*] (PCM) .... SHRD
Shift, Rotate, Check, Control (IAA) .... SRCC
Shift Ship Superintendent [*Navy*] (DNAB) .... SSS
Shift Supervisor (IEEE) .... SS
Shift Technical Adviser [*Nuclear energy*] (NRCH) .... STA
Shift Technical Engineer [*Nuclear energy*] (NRCH) .... STE
Shift Word, Extracting .... SWE
Shift Word, Substituting .... SWS
Shift-In Character [*Keyboard*] [*Computer science*] .... SI
Shift-Out [*Computer science*] (IAA) .... SO
Shift-Out Character [*Keyboard*] [*Computer science*] .... SO
Shiftout Modular Redundancy (MHDI) .... SMR
Shift-Register Transfer [*Computer science*] .... SRT
Shiga-Like Toxin [*Biochemistry*] .... SLT
Shigella [*Bacteriology*] (AAMN) .... Sh
Shigella [*Bacteriology*] .... Shig
Shigella Mutant [*A bacterium*] (DAVI) .... SM
Shigella Sonnei [*A bacterium*] (DAVI) .... SS
Shikimate Dehydrogenase [*An enzyme*] .... SKDH
Shikimic Acid [*Biochemistry*] .... Shk
Shikotan [*Former USSR Seismograph station code, US Geological Survey*] (SEIS) .... SHO
Shillelagh [*Army surface-to-surface missile*] (AABC) .... SHIL
Shilling [*Monetary unit in Tanzania*] .... EASH
Shilling [*Monetary unit in Britain*] [*Obsolete*] .... S
Shilling [*Monetary unit in Britain*] [*Obsolete*] .... SH
Shilling [*Monetary unit in Uganda*] .... U SH
Shillman's Workmen's Compensation Cases [*Ireland*] [*A publication*] (DLA) .... Shill WC
Shillong [*India*] [*Seismograph station code, US Geological Survey*] (SEIS) .... SHL
Shilo Canadian Forces Base, MB [*ICAO location identifier*] (ICLI) .... CYLO
Shiloh Community Unit School District, Hume, IL [*Library symbol*] [*Library of Congress*] (LCLS) .... IHumSD
Shiloh Industries [*NASDAQ symbol*] (TTSB) .... SHLO
Shiloh Industries, Inc. [*Associated Press*] (SAG) .... Shiloh
Shiloh Industries, Inc. [*NASDAQ symbol*] (SAG) .... SHLO
Shiloh Military Trail Library, Memphis, TN [*Library symbol Library of Congress*] (LCLS) .... TMSM
Shiloh National Military Park .... SHIL
Shiloh Resources Ltd. [*Vancouver Stock Exchange symbol*] .... SIU
Shima Resources [*Vancouver Stock Exchange symbol*] .... SIM
Shimizu [*Japan*] [*Seismograph station code, US Geological Survey*] (SEIS) .... SHM
Shimmy Showing [*From one girl to another, in reference to dress disarrangement*] .... SS
Shimofusa [*Japan ICAO location identifier*] (ICLI) .... RJTL
Shimojishima [*Ryukyu Islands*] [*ICAO location identifier*] (ICLI) .... RORS
Shimojishima [*Japan*] [*Airport symbol*] (OAG) .... SHI
Shimonoseki [*Japan*] [*Seismograph station code, US Geological Survey*] (SEIS) .... SHN
Shinbweyang [*Myanmar*] [*ICAO location identifier*] (ICLI) .... VBSW
Shindand [*Afghanistan*] [*ICAO location identifier*] (ICLI) .... OASD
Shingle .... SHNG
Shingle [*Quality of the bottom*] [*Nautical charts*] .... Sn
Shingle Lap Extendable Exit Cone (MCD) .... SLEEC
[*The*] **Shingle. Philadelphia Bar Association** [*A publication*] (DLA) .... Shingle
Shingle Point, YT [*ICAO location identifier*] (ICLI) .... CYUA
Shingle Springs, CA [*FM radio station call letters*] .... KSSJ
Shingletown, CA [*FM radio station call letters*] (RBYB) .... KHZL
Shinkiari [*Pakistan*] [*Seismograph station code, US Geological Survey*] (SEIS) .... SIP
Shinn's Treatise on American Law of Replevin [*A publication*] (DLA) .... Shinn Repl
Shinowara-Jones-Reinhard Unit [*Medicine*] (MAE) .... SJR
Shinshu-Shinmachi [*Japan*] [*Seismograph station code, US Geological Survey*] (SEIS) .... SSJ
Shinyanga [*Tanzania*] [*ICAO location identifier*] (ICLI) .... HTSY
Shinyanga [*Tanzania*] [*Airport symbol*] (OAG) .... SHY
Shionomisaki [*Japan*] [*Seismograph station code, US Geological Survey*] (SEIS) .... SHJ
Ship [*Missile launch environment symbol*] .... R
Ship .... S
Ship .... SH
Ship Abstracts [*Helsinki University of Technology*] [*Bibliographic database*] .... SA
Ship Acceptance Test [*Navy*] (CAAL) .... SAT
Ship Account Number [*Navy*] .... SAN
Ship Acoustics Department [*David W. Taylor Naval Ship Research and Development Center*] .... SAD
Ship Acquisition and Improvement Council [*Navy*] (ANA) .... SAIC
Ship Acquisition and Improvement Council-Working Group [*Navy*] (ANA) .... SAIC-WG
Ship Acquisition and Improvement Panel [*Navy*] (CAAL) .... SAIP
Ship Acquisition Contract Administration Manual (MCD) .... SACAM
Ship Acquisition Plan [*Navy*] .... SAP
Ship Acquisition Plan [*Navy*] (CAAL) .... SHAP
Ship Acquisition Project Manager [*Navy*] (DOMA) .... SHAMP
Ship Acquisition Project Manager [*Navy*] .... SHAPM
Ship Acquisition Study [*Navy*] .... SHIPACS
Ship Activation, Maintenance, and Repair .... SAM & R
Ship Activation, Maintenance, and Repair .... SAMAR
Ship Active Item Listing (DNAB) .... SAIL
Ship Aircraft Inertial Alignment System (NG) .... SAIAS
Ship Aircraft Locating Equipment .... SALES
Ship Alteration (MCD) .... S/A
Ship Alteration [*Navy*] .... SHIPALT
Ship Alteration and Repair Package [*Navy*] (CAAL) .... SARP
Ship Alteration Completion System .... SACS
Ship Alteration Cost Variance Account Report .... SACVAR
Ship Alteration Management Information System [*Discontinued*] [*Navy*] .... SAMIS
Ship Alteration Material Management System .... SAMMS
Ship Alteration Material Survey (DNAB) .... SAMS
Ship Alteration Package [*Navy*] (DNAB) .... SAP
Ship Alteration Suite [*Navy*] (CAAL) .... SAS
Ship and Goods [*British*] (ROG) .... SG
Ship and Marine Requirements Technology Board [*British*] (ODBW) .... SMRTB
Ship and Marine Technology Requirements Board [*British*] .... SMTRB
Ship and Shore Installation (MCD) .... SSI
Ship Angle and Range (SAA) .... SARA
Ship Antimissile Integrated Defense [*Program*] [*Navy*] .... SAMID
Ship Antimissile System Engagement Model [*Navy*] (CAAL) .... SAMSEM
Ship ASW [*Antisubmarine Warfare*] **Readiness Effectiveness Measuring Program** .... SHAREM
Ship Attitude Record System .... SARS
Ship Authorized Leave (NG) .... SAL
Ship Authorized Level (MCD) .... SAL
Ship Automatic Torpedo Countermeasures (MCD) .... SATC
Ship Casualty Library [*Maritime Data Network, Inc.*] [*Information service or system*] (CRD) .... SC
Ship Characteristics Board .... SCB
Ship Characteristics Improvement Board [*Navy*] (DOMA) .... SCIB
Ship Class .... SHPCL
Ship Command-Launch Control Subsystem [*Navy*] (CAAL) .... SCLCS
Ship Configuration Detail List [*Navy*] .... SCDL
Ship Configuration List [*Navy*] (CAAL) .... SCL
Ship Construction Subsidy Regulations [*Canada*] .... SCSR
Ship Construction Test Plan [*Navy*] (CAAL) .... SCTP
Ship Constructive and Shipwrights' Association [*A union*] [*British*] .... SCSA
Ship Constructive Association [*A union*] [*British*] .... SCA
Ship Control .... SCONT
Ship Control Center .... SCC
Ship Control Station [*Navy*] (CAAL) .... SCS
Ship Controlled Intercept [*RADAR*] [*Navy*] .... SCI
Ship Cost Adjustment [*Navy*] .... SCA
Ship Course .... SCOU
Ship Defense System .... SDS
Ship Description File (DNAB) .... SDF
Ship Descriptions (NITA) .... SHIPDES
Ship Design File (OA) .... SDF

Ship Design Manager ... SDM
Ship Destination Room (NATG) ... SDR
Ship Destination Test [*Intelligence test*] ... SD
Ship Development Objective [*Navy*] ... SDO
Ship Development Plan [*Navy*] ... SDP
Ship Discharge Package [*Military*] (INF) ... SDP
Ship Distance ... SDIS
Ship Diversion Room (NATG) ... SDR
Ship Doppler (IAA) ... SDOP
Ship Draft Indicating System (MSA) ... SDIS
Ship Draft Indicator Transmitter (MSA) ... SDIT
Ship Earth Station [*INMARSAT*] ... SES
Ship Electronic Module Assembly Test (DNAB) ... SEMAT
Ship Electronics System Evaluation Facility [*Navy*] (CAAL) ... SESEF
Ship Emitter Location Report [*Navy*] (CAAL) ... SELOR
Ship Equipment Accounting System (MCD) ... SEACS
Ship/Equipment/Alterations [*Navy*] (NG) ... SEA
Ship/Equipment/Alterations Summary [*Navy*] (NG) ... SEAS
Ship Equipment Configuration Accounting System (NVT) ... SECAS
Ship Equipment Configuration List (MCD) ... SECL
Ship Exercise Vehicle ... SEV
Ship Fire Control (AAG) ... SFC
Ship Form Online Design System [*British Ship Research Association*] [*Software package*] (NCC) ... SFOLDS
Ship Gyrocompass Equipment [*Navy*] (CAAL) ... SGCE
Ship Heading Marker [*Navigation*] ... SHM
Ship/Helicopter Acoustic Range-Prediction System [*Navy*] (NVT) ... SHARPS
Ship Helicopter Extended Delivery System [*Navy*] (NVT) ... SHEDS
Ship History and Inventory Record [*Navy*] (NG) ... SHIR
Ship Immediately [*Military*] ... SHIPIM
Ship Improvement Guide ... SIG
Ship Improvement Program ... SIP
Ship in Production ... SIP
Ship Inertial Navigational System ... SINS
Ship Information Booklet [*Navy*] ... SIB
Ship Installed RADIAC [*Radiation Detection, Indication, and Computation*] **System** (NATG) ... SIRS
Ship Instrumentation Manager (KSC) ... SIM
Ship Integrated Communications System [*Canadian Navy*] ... SHINCOM
Ship Integrated Electronic System ... SIES
Ship Integrated Electronic Warfare System ... SINEWS
Ship Intelligence Officer/Enlisted Intel Assistant (DOMA) ... SIO/EIA
Ship Item (MCD) ... SI
Ship Launched Missile (IAA) ... SLM
Ship Letter Telegram ... SLT
Ship Liaison Officer [*Navy*] (CAAL) ... SLO
Ship Library [*Maritime Data Network, Inc.*] [*Information service or system*] (CRD) ... SL
Ship Life-Cycle Management ... SLCM
Ship Life-Cycle Reference Matrix [*Navy*] ... SLCRM
Ship, Machinery, Marine Technology International Exhibition ... SMM
Ship Magnetic Submarine Detector ... SMSD
Ship Maintenance Planning Data (MCD) ... SMPD
Ship Maintenance Test ... SMT
Ship Management Information System (MCD) ... SMIS
Ship Manning Document [*Navy*] ... SMD
Ship Mean Time (IAA) ... SMT
Ship Missile Interface ... SMI
Ship Motion Simulator ... SMS
Ship Movement Library [*Maritime Data Network, Inc.*] [*Information service or system*] (CRD) ... SM
Ship of Opportunity Program [*National Oceanic and Atmospheric Administration*] (GFGA) ... SOOP
Ship on Depot Transfer Order [*Military*] ... SHIPDTO
Ship Operating Automation ... SOA
Ship Operational Characteristics Study (DOMA) ... SOCS
Ship Operational Support Inventory [*Navy*] (DNAB) ... SHIPOSI
Ship Operations Manager [*NASA*] (KSC) ... SOM
Ship Our Ships Program [*Navy*] (DNAB) ... SOS
Ship Overhaul Assistance Program (MCD) ... SOAP
Ship Overhaul Improvement Program [*Navy*] ... SOIP
Ship Overhaul Schedule Milestone [*Navy*] ... SOSM
Ship Overhaul Test Program ... SOTP
Ship Passive Integrated Navigation System (DNAB) ... SPINS
Ship Performance Department [*David W. Taylor Naval Ship Research and Development Center*] ... SPD
Ship Planning Document (DNAB) ... SPD
Ship Planning System ... SPS
Ship Portable Electrical/Electronic Test Equipment Requirement List [*Navy*] (CAAL) ... SPETERL
Ship Position and Altitude Measurement System (MCD) ... SPAMS
Ship Position and Attitude Measurement (IEEE) ... SPAM
Ship Position Interpolation Computer ... SPIC
Ship Position Interpolation Unit ... SPIU
Ship Position Transmitter ... SPT
Ship Production Control System (PDAA) ... SPCS
Ship Program Life Cycle [*Navy*] ... SPLC
Ship Program Schedule ... SPS
Ship Project Directive [*Navy*] ... SPD
Ship Qualification Test [*or Trial*] [*Navy*] ... SQT
Ship Qualification Trial Team [*Navy*] (NG) ... SQTT
Ship Qualification Trials in Port [*Navy*] (NVT) ... SQTIPT
Ship Radio Authorization [*Army*] (AABC) ... SRA
Ship Readiness Improvement Plan [*Navy*] (NG) ... SRIP
Ship Regular Freight [*Military*] (AABC) ... SHRF
Ship Repair Agreement [*MARAD*] (TAG) ... SRA
Ship Repair and Maintenance [*National Shipping Authority*] ... SRM
Ship Repair Facility [*Navy*] (NVT) ... SRF
Ship Repair Ratings ... SR
Ship Repair Technician [*Navy*] (DNAB) ... SHIPREPTECH
Ship Repair Training Unit ... SRTU
Ship Repair Unit ... SRU
Ship Repair Yard (CINC) ... SRY
Ship Replaceable Assembly (MCD) ... SRA
Ship Safety Officer ... SSO
Ship Self Defense System ... SSDS
Ship Service ... SS
Ship Service Diesel Generator [*Navy*] (CAAL) ... SSDG
Ship Service Gas Turbine [*Navy*] (CAAL) ... SSGT
Ship Service Turbo Generator (MSA) ... SSTG
Ship Shortage Log (AAG) ... SSL
Ship Signals Exploitation Space [*Navy*] (CAAL) ... SSES
Ship Simulation Model [*Navy*] ... SSM
Ship Speed ... SSP
Ship Stamp Society [*British*] (DBA) ... SSS
Ship Station [*ITU designation*] (CET) ... MS
Ship Station ... SS
Ship Status ... SHSTS
Ship Store Office [*Navy*] (DNAB) ... SHIPSTO
Ship Structure Committee (EA) ... SSC
Ship, Submersible (Nuclear-Powered) ... SSN
Ship Suppliers' Organization of the European Community [*Hague, Netherlands*] (EAIO) ... SSOEC
Ship Support Improvement Program [*DoD*] ... SSIP
Ship System ... SS
Ship System Engineering Group [*British*] ... SSEG
Ship System Life Cycle [*Navy*] ... SSLC
Ship System Test Contractor (MCD) ... SSTC
Ship Systems Command [*Navy*] ... SHIPSYSCOM
Ship Systems Command [*Navy*] ... SSC
Ship Systems Equipment Acquisition Manual (MCD) ... SSEAM
Ship Systems Integration Data (MCD) ... SSID
Ship Systems Operational Requirements ... SSOR
Ship Test Management Plan [*Navy*] (CAAL) ... STMP
Ship Test Organization (DNAB) ... STO
Ship Tethered Aerial Platform (PDAA) ... STAPL
Ship to Aircraft (DEN) ... SA
Ship to Apply on Requisition [*Military*] ... SHIPREQ
Ship to Arrive By ___ [*Military*] ... SHPTARBY
Ship to Component Record [*Navy*] ... SCR
Ship Tracking and Retrieval System [*MARAD*] (TAG) ... STARS
Ship Training Detachment ... STD
Ship Trial (MCD) ... ST
Ship Turn Transmitter ... STT
Ship Type Electronics Plan [*Navy*] (NG) ... STEP
Ship Upkeep Information System [*Ministry of Defense*] [*British*] (PDAA) ... SUIS
Ship Vulnerability Model (MCD) ... SVM
Ship Waste Off-Loading Barge [*Navy*] (CAAL) ... SWOB
Ship Weapon Coordinator (NVT) ... SWC
Ship Weapons Installation Manual (MCD) ... SWIM
Ship Weapons System Integration Requirements [*Navy*] ... SWSIR
Ship Work Breakdown Structure [*Navy*] (CAAL) ... SWBS
Ship Workload and Priority Systems [*Navy*] ... SWAPS
Ship-Based Long-Range Missile System (DNAB) ... SLMS
Shipboard (MSA) ... SHPBD
Shipboard Acoustic Processor [*Navy*] (CAAL) ... SAP
Shipboard Acoustic Warfare Integrated Defense (NVT) ... SAWID
Shipboard Air-Launched Weapons Installation System (NG) ... SALWIS
Shipboard Allowance List (MSA) ... SAL
Shipboard Antenna Pedestal ... SAP
Shipboard Antisubmarine Attack Teacher [*Navy*] ... SASAT
Shipboard Automated Decoy Integration System [*Navy*] ... SADIS
Shipboard Cable, Heat and Oil Resistant, Flexible (IAA) ... SHOF
Shipboard Census Report [*FHWA*] (TAG) ... SCR
Shipboard Chaff Decoy System [*Navy*] ... SCDS
Shipboard Command and Launch Subsystem (MCD) ... SCLS
Shipboard Communication Area Network (DWSG) ... SCAN
Shipboard Communications Terminal ... SSCT
Shipboard Data Multiplex System (MCD) ... SDMS
Shipboard Data Terminal (MCD) ... SDT
Shipboard Decoy (DWSG) ... SBD
Shipboard Distribution Only [*Navy*] (CAAL) ... SDO
Shipboard Electromagnetic Capability Improvement Program [*Navy*] (NVT) ... SEMCIP
Shipboard Electromagnetic Computability Analysis (DNAB) ... SEMCA
Shipboard Electromagnetic Interference [*Navy*] (CAAL) ... SEMI
Shipboard Electronic Readiness Team [*Navy*] (CAAL) ... SERT
Shipboard Electronic Repair Team [*Navy*] (DOMA) ... SERT
Shipboard Electronics Warfare [*Navy*] ... SEW
Shipboard Environmental Checkout Facility (DNAB) ... SECOF
Shipboard Environmental Data Acquisition System [*National Oceanic and Atmospheric Administration*] (MSC) ... SEAS
Shipboard Equipments Environmental Design Study (PDAA) ... SEEDS
Shipboard Expendable Bathythermograph [*System*] [*Naval Oceanographic Office*] ... SXBT
Shipboard Fire Detection System (DWSG) ... SFDS
Shipboard Gauge Calibration Program (DNAB) ... SGCP
Shipboard Gravity Measuring System ... SGMS
Shipboard Hazards Appraisal and Defense (CINC) ... SHAD
Shipboard Identification Demolition Model [*Navy*] ... SIDM

Shipboard Impact Locator System .... SILS
Shipboard Information System Development Group [*Maritime Transportation ResearchBoard*] (PDAA) .... SISDG
Shipboard Information, Training, and Education [*System*] [*Navy*] (NVT) .... SITE
Shipboard Infrared Electronic Warfare System .... SIREWS
Shipboard Integrated Maintenance Program [*Navy*] (NG) .... SIMP
Shipboard Integrated Man-Machine System (SAA) .... SHIMMS
Shipboard Integrated Processing Display System [*Military*] .... SHIN PADS
Shipboard Intelligence (DOMA) .... SHBD INT
Shipboard Intercept Receiver [*Navy*] .... SIR
Shipboard Intermediate Range Combat System [*Navy*] .... SIRCS
Shipboard Joint Uniform Military Pay System [*Navy*] (DNAB) .... SJUMPS
Shipboard Landing Assist Device .... SLAD
Shipboard Long-Range Input .... SLRI
Shipboard Maintenance Action Form (DNAB) .... SMAF
Shipboard Maintenance Manpower Analysis System [*Navy*] (DNAB) .... SMMAS
Shipboard Marriage Test .... SMT
Shipboard Meteorological Satellite Readout Station .... SMSRS
Shipboard Microfilm Program [*Navy*] (DNAB) .... SMP
Shipboard Mobile Very Low Frequency [*Navy*] (DNAB) .... SMVLF
Shipboard Nontactical ADP [*Automatic Data Processing*] **Program** [*Navy*] (CAAL) .... SNAP
Shipboard Nuclear Weapon Security [*Navy*] (CAAL) .... SNWS
Shipboard Oceanographic Survey System .... SOSS
Shipboard Operational Readiness System [*Navy*] (CAAL) .... SORS
Ship(board) Operations [*Navy*] (DNAB) .... SHIPOPS
Shipboard Ordnance Infrared Decoy (MCD) .... SOID
Shipboard Ordnance Requirement Computer System [*Navy*] .... SORCS
Shipboard Organizational Troubleshooting System (MCD) .... SORTS
Shipboard Passive Surveillance and Detection System (PDAA) .... SPSD
Shipboard Platforms for Landing and Servicing Helicopters .... SPLASH
Shipboard Pollution Abatement System [*Navy*] (CAAL) .... SPAS
Shipboard RADAR System .... SRS
Shipboard Safety Watch [*Navy*] (DNAB) .... SSW
Shipboard Satellite Communications System .... SSCS
Shipboard Signal Exploration System (MCD) .... SSES
Shipboard Signal Processing Control Program [*Navy*] (CAAL) .... SSPCP
Shipboard Simulators [*Navy*] (DOMA) .... SBS
Shipboard SONAR Bouy Interface Kit (DWSG) .... SSIK
Shipboard [*Weapon*] **Suitability Test** [*Navy*] (NG) .... SST
Shipboard Surveillance RADAR System (MCD) .... SSURADS
Shipboard Tactical Airborne Remote Piloted Vehicle [*Navy*] (CAAL) .... STAR
Shipboard Tactical Electronic Warfare System [*Navy*] .... STEWS
Shipboard Tactical Satellite Communications (DNAB) .... STSC
Shipboard Target Tracking System .... STTS
Shipboard Test [*Navy*] (DNAB) .... SBT
Shipboard Toxicological Operational Protective System [*Navy*] .... STOPS
Shipboard Transmitting Antenna .... STA
Shipboard Uniform Automatic Data Processing System [*Navy*] .... SUADPS
Shipboard Very Low Frequency [*Navy*] (NG) .... SVLF
Shipboard Voice-Enhanced Navigation System [*for blind sailors*] .... SVEN
Shipboard Wave Meter .... SWM
Shipborne Containerized Air Defense System .... SCADS
Shipborne Electronic Deflection Array RADAR (MCD) .... SEDAR
Shipborne Fighter Control [*Navy*] (CAAL) .... SFC
Shipborne Integrated Machinery Control System [*Canadian Navy*] .... SHINMACS
Shipborne SATCOM Terminal [*British*] .... SCOT
Shipbuilder (MSA) .... SHBLDR
Shipbuilders and Repairers' National Association [*British*] (BI) .... SRNA
Shipbuilders', Boiler, and Gasometer Makers' Society [*A union*] [*British*] .... SBGMS
Shipbuilders Council of America (EA) .... SCA
Shipbuilding [*Navy*] .... SB
Shipbuilding .... SHIPBLDG
Shipbuilding Advisory Council [*British*] .... SAC
Shipbuilding and Conversion, Navy .... SCN
Shipbuilding and Drydock Company .... SBDC
Shipbuilding and Marine Engineering [*Department of Employment*] [*British*] .... SME
Shipbuilding and Ship Repair [*Department of Employment*] [*British*] .... SSR
Shipbuilding Company .... SBCO
Shipbuilding Corp. .... SBCORP
Shipbuilding Exports Association [*British*] (BI) .... SEA
Shipbuilding Industrial Training Board [*British*] .... SITB
Shipbuilding Industries Pension Scheme [*British*] .... SIPS
Shipbuilding Industry Board [*British*] .... SIB
Shipbuilding Material Management Systems [*Navy*] (NG) .... SMMS
Shipbuilding, Ship Repairing, and Engineering Industrial Union [*British*] .... SSREIU
Shipbuilding Stabilization Committee [*World War II*] .... SSC
Shipbuilding Temporary Assistance Program .... STAP
Shipcraft Guild (EA) .... SCG
Shipcraft Guild (EA) .... SG
Ship-Design Engineering-Aided by Interactive Remote Display (PDAA) .... SEABIRD
Shipdham [*British ICAO location identifier*] (ICLI) .... EGSA
Shipfitter [*Navy symbol*] .... FP
Shipfitter [*Navy*] .... SF
Shipfitter (AAG) .... SFTR
Shipfitter, Construction Battalion [*Navy*] .... SFCB
Shipfitter, Construction Battalion, Blacksmith [*Navy*] .... SFCBB
Shipfitter, Construction Battalion, Mechanical Draftsman [*Navy*] .... SFCBM
Shipfitter, Construction Battalion, Pipe Fitter and Plumber [*Navy*] .... SFCBP
Shipfitter, Construction Battalion, Rigger [*Navy*] .... SFCBR
Shipfitter, Construction Battalion, Steelworker [*Navy*] .... SFCBS
Shipfitter, Construction Battalion, Welder [*Navy*] .... SFCBW
Shipfitter, First Class [*Navy*] SF1
Shipfitter, Metalsmith [*Navy*] .... SFM
Shipfitter, Pipefitter [*Navy*] .... SFP
Shipfitter, Second Class [*Navy*] SF2
Shipfitter, Ship Repair [*Navy*] .... SFSR
Shipfitter, Ship Repair, Chipper-Caulker [*Navy*] .... SFSRC
Shipfitter, Ship Repair, Diver [*Navy*] .... SFSRD
Shipfitter, Ship Repair, Driller-Reamer [*Navy*] .... SFSRL
Shipfitter, Ship Repair, Pipe Fitter-Plumber [*Navy*] .... SFSRP
Shipfitter, Ship Repair, Riveter [*Navy*] .... SFSRR
Shipfitter, Ship Repair, Shipfitter [*Navy*] .... SFSRS
Shipfitter, Ship Repair, Steelworker-Anglesmith [*Navy*] .... SFSRF
Shipfitter, Ship Repair, Welder [*Navy*] .... SFSRW
Shipfitter, Third Class [*Navy*] SF3
Shiplap (DAC) .... S/L
Shiplap (DAC) .... S/LAP
Shiplap (WGA) .... SHLP
Ship-Launched Air Targeting (MCD) .... SLAT
Ship-Launched ASW [*Antisubmarine Warfare*] **Two-Way Expendable** [*Buoy*] [*Navy*] (CAAL) .... SLATE
Ship-Launched Missile System (IAA) .... SLMS
Shipley Personal Inventory [*Medicine*] (DMAA) .... SPI
Shipley-Hartford Scale [*Psychology*] (DAVI) .... SHS
Shipley-Institute of Living Scale for Measuring Intellectual Impairment [*Psychology*] .... SILS
Shiplovers' Society [*Australia*] .... SS
Shipmasters' Society [*A union*] [*British*] .... SS
Shipment .... SHIP
Shipment (DNAB) .... SHIPMT
Shipment .... SHIPT
Shipment (AABC) .... SHPMT
Shipment (AAG) .... SHPT
Shipment (ODBW) .... shpt
Shipment Control System [*Military*] .... SCONS
Shipment Detail Card [*Military*] .... SDC
Shipment Document Release [*Military*] (AFIT) .... SDR
Shipment Document Release and Control [*Military*] (AFIT) .... SDR & C
Shipment Exception Code [*Military*] (AFIT) .... SEX
Shipment Memorandum [*Navy*] .... SM
Shipment of Household Goods (NOAA) .... SHPHG
Shipment [*or Shipping*] **Order** .... SO
Shipment/Performance Notification [*DoD*] .... SPN
Shipment Planning and Movement [*Army*] .... SPAM
Shipment Planning System [*Military*] .... SHIPS
Shipment Planning Worksheet .... SPW
Shipment Planning Worksheet (MCD) .... SPWS
Shipment [*or Shipping*] **Request** .... SR
Shipment Status Correlation .... SSC
Shipment Status System [*Military*] (AABC) .... STATEM
Shipment Unit [*Army*] .... SU
Ship-of-Opportunity Program [*Marine science*] (OSRA) .... SOP
Ship-of-the-Line .... SL
Ship-of-the-Line .... S-of-L
Shipowners Association of the Pacific Coast [*Defunct*] (EA) .... SAPC
Shipowners Claims Bureau [*New York, NY*] (EA) .... SCB
Shipowner's Liability [*Business term*] .... SL
Shipowner's Liability [*Business term*] .... SOL
Shipowners Refrigerated Cargo Research Association [*Research center British*] (IRUK) .... SRCRA
Shipped Assembled .... S/A
Shipped Not Credited [*Military*] (AFIT) .... SNC
Shipped on Board a Specified Vessel (DS) .... SOB
Shipped Unassembled (MHDW) .... SUA
Shippensburg, PA [*AM radio station call letters*] .... WSHP
Shippensburg, PA [*FM radio station call letters*] .... WSYC
Shippensburg State College, Shippensburg, PA [*Library symbol Library of Congress*] (LCLS) .... PShS
Shippensburg State College, Shippensburg, PA [*OCLC symbol*] (OCLC) .... SQP
Shippensburg University of Pennsylvania (GAGS) .... Shippensburg U
Shipper .... SHPR
Shipper and Carrier [*Business term*] .... S & C
Shipper Pays Taxes .... SPT
Shipper/Receiver [*Difference*] .... S/R
Shipper Service Control Office [*Military*] (AABC) .... SSCO
Shipper-Receiver Difference (NRCH) .... S-RD
Shipper's Export Declaration [*Customs Service*] .... SED
Shipper's Export Document [*FHWA*] (TAG) .... SED
Shippers for Competitive Ocean Transportation [*Washington, DC*] (EA) .... SCOT
Shippers Forecasts [*Symbol*] [*National Weather Service*] .... FM
Shipper's Load and Count [*Bills of lading*] .... SL & C
Shipper's Load and Tally [*Bills of lading*] .... SL & T
Shippers National Freight Claim Council [*Later, TCPC*] (EA) .... SNFCC
Shippers of Recycled Textiles [*An association*] (EA) .... SORT
Shippers Oil Field Traffic Association (EA) .... SOFTA
Shipper's Weights [*Bills of lading*] .... SW
Shipping (WGA) .... SHG
Shipping .... SHIPG
Shipping (ODBW) .... shpg
Shipping .... SHPG
Shipping .... SHPNG
Shipping Accumulation Numbers (AAG) .... SAN
Shipping Advisory Committee [*NATO*] .... SHADCOM
Shipping and Air Cargo Commodity Statistics [*Australia*] .... SACCS
Shipping and Forwarding Agent .... S & FA

Shipping and Handling (WDMC) ... S and H
Shipping and Packing Cost (NASA) ... SPC
Shipping and Storage ... S & S
Shipping and Storage Container Ballistic Missile (IAA) ... SSCBM
Shipping Annual Data [*Department of Commerce*] (GFGA) ... SA
Shipping Authority ... SA
Shipping Board ... SB
Shipping Container ... SC
Shipping Container ... SHCR
Shipping Container Institute ... SCI
Shipping Contract (MCD) ... SC
Shipping Control [*NATO*] (NATG) ... SHIPCON
Shipping Control Administrator Japan ... SCAJAP
Shipping Control Authority (NVT) ... SCA
Shipping Control Authority, Japan (DNAB) ... SCAJAP
Shipping Control Exercise [*NATO exercises*] (NATG) ... NCSX
Shipping Control Office, Forward Area [*Navy*] ... SCOFA
Shipping Control Office, Marianas [*Navy*] ... SCOMA
Shipping Control War Plan [*Navy*] ... WPSC
Shipping Coordinating Committee [*Coast Guard*] ... SHC
Shipping Corp. of India Ltd. ... SCI
Shipping Corp. of New Zealand (CDA) [*Toronto Stock Exchange symbol*] ... SNZ
Shipping Data [*Military*] ... SHIPDA
Shipping Data Follows ... SHIPDAFOL
Shipping Date ... SHIPDAT
Shipping Defence Advisory Committee [*General Council of British Shipping*] (DS) ... SDAC
Shipping Fever [*An influenza serotype*] ... SF-4
Shipping Fever Virus [*Medicine*] (DMAA) ... SFV
Shipping Gazette [*London*] [*A publication*] (DLA) ... Ship Gaz
Shipping/Handling (WGA) ... S/H
Shipping Instruction Sheet ... SIS
Shipping Instructions (AFM) ... SI
Shipping Monthly Data [*Department of Commerce*] (GFGA) ... SM
Shipping Note [*Business term*] ... SN
Shipping Number ... S/N
Shipping Operations Information System (OA) ... SOIS
Shipping Order [*Military*] ... SHIPGO
Shipping Order (WGA) ... SO
Shipping Order (ODBW) ... so
Shipping Port ... SP
Shipping/Production Scheduling ... SPS
Shipping Receipt [*Business term*] ... SR
Shipping Request/Packing Sheet (MCD) ... SR/PS
Shipping Situation [*British*] ... SS
Shipping Summary ... SHIPSUM
Shipping Ticket [*Military*] ... ST
Shippingport Atomic Power Station (NRCH) ... SAPS
Shipp's Reports [*66-67 North Carolina*] [*A publication*] (DLA) ... Sh
Shipp's Reports [*66-67 North Carolina*] [*A publication*] (DLA) ... Shipp
Shiprepairers and Shipbuilders Independent Association [*British*] (DS) ... SSIA
Ship's 3-M Improvement Plan [*Navy*] (NVT) ... SMIP
Ship's Advanced Communications (IAA) ... SACOM
Ship's Advanced Electronic Warfare (MCD) ... SAEW
Ship's Advanced Electronic Warfare System (NVT) ... SAEWS
Ships Air Coordinator (MCD) ... SAC
Ship's Air Maintenance Facility [*Navy*] (NVT) ... SAMF
Ship's Aircraft Inertial System Alignment Console ... SAISAC
Ship's Alteration Management System [*Navy*] ... SAMS
Ships Analysis and Retrieval Program [*Navy*] ... SHARP
Ships and Air Systems Integration [*Navy*] ... SASI
Ships and Aircraft Supplemental Data Tables [*Navy*] ... SASDT
Ships and Analysis and Retrieval Project (NITA) ... SHARP
Ships and Facilities, Navy (NG) ... SFN
Ships Angle Tracking and Doppler System (IAA) ... SADOPS
Ships Anti-Missile Integrated Defense System (PDAA) ... SAMIDS
Ship's Apparent Time [*Navigation*] ... SAT
Ship's Armament Inventory List [*Navy*] ... SAIL
Ships Authorized Data List ... SADL
Ship's Capability Impaired [*Navy*] ... SCI
Ship's Capability Impaired for Lack of Parts [*Navy*] ... SCIP
Ship's Center Display [*Navy*] (NVT) ... SCD
Ships Characteristics Board ... SCB
Ship's Clerk ... SCLK
Ships' Clerk Trade Association [*A union*] [*British*] ... SCTA
Ship's Construction Item List (MCD) ... SCIL
Ships Construction, Navy [*Funding*] ... SCN
Ship's Cook [*Navy*] ... SC
Ship's Cook, Butcher [*Navy*] ... SCB
Ship's Destination Authority (NVT) ... SDA
Ship's Diver [*Navy British*] ... SHD
Ship's Drawing Index (DNAB) ... SDI
Ships Editorial Association [*Navy*] ... SEA
Ship's Electrical and Electronic Data System (DNAB) ... SEEDS
Ship's Electronics Allowance List [*Navy*] ... SEAL
Ships Emergency Automatic Buoyancy and Stability System [*Seabass Ltd.*] ... SEABASS
Ships' Essential Equipment Requisition Expediting Program [*Navy*] (NVT) ... SEEREP
Ships Force Overhaul Management Systems [*Navy*] ... SFOMS
Ship's Force Work Item (DNAB) ... SFWI
Ship's Force Worklist Instruction ... SFWLI
Ship's Head [*Heading*] [*Navigation*] ... SH
Ship's Heading Servo ... SHS
Ship's Inertial Marine Navigational System (IAA) ... SINS
Ship's Inertial Navigation System ... SINS
Ship's Information Officer [*Navy*] ... SIO
Ship's Installation [*Navy*] ... SI
Ships Integrated Communications System (MCD) ... SICS
Ships Integrated Defense System ... SIDS
Ships Intermediate Maintenance Activity (DOMA) ... SIMA
Ship's Keyboard Display Unit ... SKDU
Ship's Loading Characteristics Pamphlet [*Navy*] (NVT) ... SLCP
Ship's Manifest (ADA) ... SM
Ship's Master Index Listing of Equipment (MCD) ... SMILE
Ship's Material Account ... SMA
Ships Material Office, Atlantic ... SMOA
Ships Material Office, Atlantic (MCD) ... SMOLANT
Ships Material Office, Pacific ... SMOP
Ships Material Office, Pacific (MCD) ... SMOPAC
Ship's Mean Time [*Navigation*] ... SMT
Ship's Missile System (MCD) ... SMS
Ship's Mission Profile [*Navy*] (CAAL) ... SMP
Ship's Navigation and Aircraft Inertial Alignment System [*Navy*] (NG) ... SNAIAS
Ships on Stamps Unit (EA) ... SOSU
Ship's Operational Program [*Navy*] (NVT) ... SOP
Ship's Operational Readiness Test ... SORT
Ships Operational Safety [*A publication*] ... SOS
Ship's Option ... SO
Ships Ordnance Summary ... SOS
Ships Organization Manual (DOMA) ... SORM
Ship's Parts Control Center ... SPCC
Ship's Parts Integration List ... SPIL
Ship's Passive Surveillance and Detection System [*Navy*] (CAAL) ... SPSDS
Ship's Plan Index ... SPI
Ship's Plan of the Day [*Navy*] (DNAB) ... SPOD
Ship's Plotting Board ... SPB
Ships Precise Identification Emitter (MCD) ... SPIE
Ship's Qualification Assistance Team [*Navy*] ... SQAT
Ships Records (MCD) ... SR
Ships Records Management System (MCD) ... SRMS
Ships Recreational Library, Canadian Forces Base Halifax [*Bibliotheque Recreative, Base des Forces Canadiennes Halifax*], Nova Scotia [*Library symbol National Library of Canada*] (BIB) ... NSHNS
Ships Repair Facility, Atlantic (DNAB) ... SRFLANT
Ships Repair Facility, Pacific (DNAB) ... SRFPAC
Ship's Repair Party [*Navy British*] ... SRP
Ship's Restricted Availability Date [*Navy*] (DNAB) ... SRAD
Ship's Self-Contained Navigation System ... SSCNS
Ship's Service Force [*Navy*] ... SSF
Ship's Service Gas Turbine Generator [*Navy*] (NVT) ... SSGTG
Ships Service Generator (DOMA) ... SSG
Ship's Service Motor Generator [*Navy*] (NVT) ... SSMG
Ship's Service Power Unit [*Navy*] (CAAL) ... SSPU
Ship's Service Stores ... SSS
Ships Service Turbine (MCD) ... SST
Ship's Serviceman [*Navy rating*] ... SH
Ship's Serviceman, Barber [*Navy rating*] ... SSMB
Ship's Serviceman, Cobbler [*Navy rating*] ... SSMC
Ship's Serviceman, First Class [*Navy rating*] ... SH1
Ship's Serviceman, Laundryman [*Navy rating*] ... SSML
Ship's Serviceman, Second Class [*Navy rating*] ... SH2
Ship's Serviceman, Tailor [*Navy rating*] ... SSMT
Ship's Serviceman, Third Class [*Navy rating*] ... SH3
Ship's Speed Converter (MCD) ... SSC
Ship's Stores and Commissary Stores [*Navy*] ... SS & CS
Ship's Stores and Profit, Navy ... SSPN
Ship's Stores Ashore [*Navy*] ... SSA
Ship's Stores Profit [*Navy*] ... SSP
Ships Submersible Ballistic Nuclear [*British military*] (DMA) ... SSBN
Ship's Systems Operational Readiness Test (MCD) ... SSORT
Ships Systems Operational Requirements ... SSORT
Ships Tactical Environmental Control Receiver ... STECR
Ships Taken Up from Trade ... STUFT
Ships Technical Data Management Information System [*Navy*] ... STEDMIS
Ships Technical Publication System [*Navy*] ... STEPS
Ship's Test and Inspection Department [*Navy*] (DNAB) ... STID
Ship's Test and Readiness Evaluation Procedure ... STREP
Ships Towed Acoustic Project (DWSG) ... STAP
Ship's Toxicological Protective System ... STOP
Ship's Transducer Location System (DNAB) ... STLS
Ship's Value Manual (DNAB) ... SVM
Ship's Warrant [*Marine Corps*] ... SW
Shipside (AABC) ... SHPSD
Shipside ... SS
Ships-in-Bottles Association of America (EA) ... SBAA
Ships-on-Order Library [*Maritime Data Network, Inc.*] [*Information service or system*] (CRD) ... SO
Ship-Tended Acoustic Relay [*Military*] ... STAR
Ship-to-Shore (MUGU) ... S/S
Ship-to-Shore ... STS
Ship-to-Shore RADAR [*or Radio*] (DEN) ... SR
Ship-to-Surface Vessel ... SSV
Ship-Towed Acoustic Deception Device (MCD) ... STADD
Shipwrecked Fishermen and Mariners Royal Benevolent Society [*British*] (BI) ... SFMS
Shipwright ... SH
Shipwright Lieutenant [*British military*] (DMA) ... Sh L
Shipwrights' and Shipwrights Iron Workers' Association [*A union*] [*British*] ... SSIWA

Shipyard ... SY
Shipyard ... SYD
Shipyard Accuracy Checksite (MCD) ... SACS
Shipyard Agreement [*MARAD*] (TAG) ... SA
Shipyard Checkout Spare ... SYCOSPARE
Shipyard Checkout Test ... SYCOT
Shipyard Installation Test Procedure [*or Program*] ... SITP
Shipyard Labour Supply Officer [*British*] ... SLSO
Shipyard Overhaul Availability ... SOA
Shipyard Overhaul Test Program ... SOTP
Shipyard Restricted Availability [*Navy*] (CAAL) ... SRA
Shirakawa [*Japan*] [*Seismograph station code, US Geological Survey*] (SEIS) ... SHR
Shiraki [*Japan*] [*Seismograph station code, US Geological Survey*] (SEIS) ... SHK
Shiraz [*Iran*] [*ICAO location identifier*] (ICLI) ... OIST
Shiraz [*Iran*] [*Seismograph station code, US Geological Survey*] (SEIS) ... SHI
Shiraz [*Iran*] [*Airport symbol*] (OAG) ... SYZ
Shiraz/International [*Iran*] [*ICAO location identifier*] (ICLI) ... OISS
Shire (ADA) ... S
Shire ... Sh
Shire Horse Society [*British*] (DI) ... SHS
Shire Indaselassie [*Ethiopia*] [*Airport symbol*] (OAG) ... SHC
Shiremanstown, PA [*AM radio station call letters*] ... WWII
Shires Association of New South Wales [*Australia*] ... SANSW
Shirl J. Winter [*Designer's mark when appearing on US coins*] ... SW
Shirley, NY [*Location identifier FAA*] (FAAL) ... HKC
Shirley on Magisterial Law [*2nd ed.*] [*1896*] [*A publication*] (DLA) ... Shir Mag L
Shirley's Dartmouth College Case [*A publication*] (DLA) ... Shir DC Ca
Shirley's Leading Crown Cases [*England*] [*A publication*] (DLA) ... Shirl LC
Shirley's Reports [*49-55 New Hampshire*] [*A publication*] (DLA) ... Sh
Shirley's Reports [*49-55 New Hampshire*] [*A publication*] (DLA) ... Shirl
Shirley's Reports [*49-55 New Hampshire*] [*A publication*] (DLA) ... Shirley
Shirley's Sketch of the Criminal Law [*2nd ed.*] [*1889*] [*A publication*] (DLA) ... Shir Cr L
Shiroles [*Costa Rica*] [*ICAO location identifier*] (ICLI) ... MRSH
Shiroyama [*Japan*] [*Seismograph station code, US Geological Survey*] (SEIS) ... SRY
Shirtsleeve Garment Assembly [*NASA*] ... SGA
Shirttail Gulch [*California*] [*Seismograph station code, US Geological Survey*] (SEIS) ... SHG
Shirvan [*Iran*] [*ICAO location identifier*] (ICLI) ... OIMW
Shirwell [*England*] ... SHIRW
Shishah Sedarim (BJA) ... SHaS
Shishmaref [*Alaska*] [*Airport symbol*] (OAG) ... SHH
Shishmaref, AK [*Location identifier FAA*] (FAAL) ... SHH
Shiva Corp. [*Associated Press*] (SAG) ... Shiva
Shiva Corp. [*NASDAQ symbol*] (SAG) ... SHVA
Shiwan'Gandu [*Zambia*] [*ICAO location identifier*] (ICLI) ... FLSH
Shiyan Automotive Transmission Factory [*China*] ... SATF
Shizuoka [*Japan*] [*Seismograph station code, US Geological Survey*] (SEIS) ... SHZ
SHL Systemhouse, Inc. [*Toronto Stock Exchange symbol*] ... SHK
Shnat Sherut Scheme (BJA) ... SSS
Shne Luhot Ha-Berit (BJA) ... ShLH
Shoal (ROG) ... SH
Shoal ... SHL
Shoal ... SHL
Shoal [*Commonly used*] (OPSA) ... SHOAL
Shoal Petroleum [*Vancouver Stock Exchange symbol*] ... SHP
Shoals (MCD) ... SHLS
Shoals ... SHLS
Shoals [*Commonly used*] (OPSA) ... SHOALS
Shoals News, Shoals, IN [*Library symbol Library of Congress*] (LCLS) ... InShoN
Shoals Public Library, Shoals, IN [*Library symbol Library of Congress*] (LCLS) ... InSho
Shobdon [*British ICAO location identifier*] (ICLI) ... EGBS
Shock (WGA) ... SH
Shock (MSA) ... SHK
Shock Absorber [*Automotive engineering*] ... S/ABS
Shock Absorber ... SHABS
Shock and Vibration ... S & V
Shock and Vibration Information Center [*Terminated Navy*] (MCD) ... SVIC
Shock Attenuating Cellular Concrete [*Army*] ... SACON
Shock Attenuation (AAG) ... SA
Shock Excited Filter (IAA) ... SEF
Shock Front (SAA) ... SF
Shock Hydrodynamic Elastic Plastic (MCD) ... SHEP
Shock Isolator Air Compressor (DWSG) ... SIAC
Shock Landing Analysis (MCD) ... SLAN
Shock Mount ... SM
Shock Position Ratio ... SPR
Shock Related ... SR
Shock Remanent Magnetization (OA) ... SRM
Shock Resistance ... SR
Shock Thermodynamics Applied Research [*Department of Energy*] ... STAR
Shock Time-of-Arrival [*Marine science*] (OSRA) ... STOA
Shock Time-of-Arrival (USDC) ... STOA
Shock Trauma Unit [*Emergency medicine*] (DAVI) ... STU
Shock Troops [*Military*] (WDAA) ... ST
Shock Tube ... ST
Shock Tube Test ... STT
Shock Tunnel ... ST
Shock Two-Dimensional Eulerian Elastic Plastic [*Computer code*] ... STEEP
Shock Wave (IAA) ... SW
Shock Wave Control ... SWC
Shock Wave Data Center [*Lawrence Radiation Laboratory*] ... SWDC
Shock Wave Generator ... SWG
Shock Wave Interaction ... SWI
Shock Wave Profile ... SWP
Shock Wave Sensor (RDA) ... SWS
Shock-Absorbing Concretes (RDA) ... SACON
Shock-Induced Thermal Fragmentation [*Astrophysics*] ... STF
Shock-Isolation Support ... SIS
Shock-Isolation System ... SIS
Shock-on-Shock ... SOS
Shock-to-Detonation Transition (MCD) ... SDT
Shodair Children's Hospital, Helena, MT [*Library symbol Library of Congress*] (LCLS) ... MtHS
Shodair Hospital, Helena, MT [*Library symbol*] [*Library of Congress*] (LCLS) ... MtHSH
Shode ... SHD
Shoe and Allied Trades Research Association [*Later, Footwear Technology Centre*] [*British*] (EA) ... SATRA
Shoe Carnival [*NASDAQ symbol*] (TTSB) ... SCVL
Shoe Carnival, Inc. [*NASDAQ symbol*] (SAG) ... SCVL
Shoe Carnival, Inc. [*Associated Press*] (SAG) ... ShoeCarn
Shoe Cove Satellite Receiving Station [*Canada*] ... SCSRS
Shoe Lace Manufacturers Association [*Defunct*] (EA) ... SLMA
Shoe Pattern Manufacturers Association [*Defunct*] (EA) ... SPMA
Shoe Service Institute of America (EA) ... SSIA
Shoe Suppliers Association of America (EA) ... SSAA
Shoe Width Grater than D (BARN) ... E
Shoe Width Greater than A and Less than C (BARN) ... B
Shoe Width Greater than B and Less than D (BARN) ... C
Shoe Width Greater than C and Less than E (BARN) ... D
Shoe Width Less than A (BARN) ... AA
Shoe width Less than AA (BARN) ... AAA
Shoe Width Less than AAA (BARN) ... AAAA
Shoe Width Less than B (BARN) ... A
Shoemaker (MSA) ... SHMKR
Shoemaker-Levy 9 [*Comet or asteroid that crashed into Jupiter in 1994*] ... S-L 9
Shoes Fan Club (EA) ... SFC
Shogun Developments Corp. [*Vancouver Stock Exchange symbol*] ... SGD
Sholapur [*India*] [*ICAO location identifier*] (ICLI) ... VASL
Sholem Aleichem Folk Institute (EA) ... SAFI
Sholia Resources Ltd. [*Vancouver Stock Exchange symbol*] ... SHT
Sholodge, Inc. [*NASDAQ symbol*] (SAG) ... LODG
Sholodge, Inc. [*Associated Press*] (SAG) ... SholodgE
Sho-Me Financial [*NASDAQ symbol*] (TTSB) ... SMFC
Sho-Me Financial Corp. [*Associated Press*] (SAG) ... Sho-Me
Sho-Me Financial Corp. [*NASDAQ symbol*] (SAG) ... SMFC
Shomer Shabbat (BJA) ... ShSh
Shome's Law Reporter [*India*] [*A publication*] (DLA) ... Shome LR
Shomrei Mitzvot Yotzei Russia (BJA) ... SHAMYR
Shomrim Society (EA) ... SS
Shona [*MARC language code Library of Congress*] (LCCP) ... sho
Shoney's, Inc. [*NYSE symbol*] (SPSG) ... SHN
Shoney's, Inc. [*Associated Press*] (SAG) ... Shoney
Shongamba [*Zaire*] [*ICAO location identifier*] (ICLI) ... FZVH
Shoot Apical Meristem [*Botany*] ... SAM
Shoot Bud [*Botany*] ... SB
Shoot Down Test (SAA) ... SDT
Shoot Emergence [*Botany*] ... SE
Shoot Them, Shovel Them, Shut Up [*Ranchers way of dealing with predatory animals*] ... 3S
Shoot Tip [*Botany*] ... ST
Shoot Tip Abscission Scar [*Botany*] ... SS
Shooter Air Courier Corp. [*Canada ICAO designator*] (FAAC) ... SHR
Shooters Club of America [*Defunct*] ... SCA
Shooters' Rights Association [*British*] (DBA) ... SRA
Shoot-Fail-Shoot [*Military*] ... SFS
Shooting [*FBI standardized term*] ... SH
Shooting, Hunting, Outdoor Trade Show ... SHOT
Shop (WGA) ... SH
Shop Accessory [*Drawing*] (NG) ... SA
Shop and Display Equipment Association [*British*] (EAIO) ... SDEA
Shop at Home [*NASDAQ symbol*] (TTSB) ... SATH
Shop at Home, Inc. [*NASDAQ symbol*] (SAG) ... SATH
Shop at Home, Inc. [*Associated Press*] (SAG) ... ShopHm
Shop Call (MCD) ... SC
Shop Carpenter ... SC
Shop Control Number (DNAB) ... SCN
Shop Distribution Standards (KSC) ... SDS
Shop, Distributive and Allied Employees' Association [*Australia*] ... SDAEA
Shop Drawing (AAG) ... SD
Shop/Lab Configuration Layout [*NASA*] (MCD) ... SLCL
Shop Manual [*Air Force*] (AAG) ... SM
Shop Mechanic's Test ... SMT
Shop Missile Assembly and Maintenance ... SMSA
Shop Operations Load Analysis Reporting ... SOLAR
Shop Order ... SO
Shop Order Control ... SOC
Shop Order Control Board ... SOCB
Shop Order Load Analysis and Reporting [*IBM Corp.*] ... SL & R
Shop Order Shop (SAA) ... SOS
Shop Out of Stock (SAA) ... SOS
Shop Overload Parts (AAG) ... SOP
Shop Portable Aircraft Maintenance [*Army*] ... SPAM
Shop Procedure Bulletin [*A publication*] (EAAP) ... SBP
Shop Process Card [*Navy*] (DNAB) ... SPC
Shop Readiness Objective ... SRO

Shop Repair Data Sheets ... SRDS
Shop Repair Order ... SRO
Shop Resident Control (SAA) ... SRC
Shop Steward ... SS
Shop Stock Items Bin (MCD) ... SSIB
Shop Stock List (MCD) ... SSL
Shop Support Request [*NASA*] (NASA) ... SSR
Shop Telegraph (IAA) ... ST
Shop Television Network [*Vancouver Stock Exchange symbol*] ... SHS
Shop Visit Rate (DOMA) ... SVR
Shopco Laurel Centre Ltd. [*AMEX symbol*] (SPSG) ... LSC
Shopco Laurel Centre Ltd. [*Associated Press*] (SAG) ... Shopco
Shopco Laurel Centre L.P. [*AMEX symbol*] (TTSB) ... LSC
Shope Fibroma Growth Factor [*Biochemistry*] ... SFGF
Shope Fibroma Virus [*Medicine*] (DMAA) ... SFV
Shope Papilloma Virus ... SPV
Shopfitting Research and Development Council [*British*] (BI) ... SRDC
Shop-Fixed Interface (DNAB) ... SFI
Shopko Stores [*Associated Press*] (SAG) ... Shopko
Shopko Stores [*NYSE symbol*] (SPSG) ... SKO
Shoplifters Anonymous International (EA) ... SAI
Shoplifters Take Everybody's Money ... STEM
Shoppe ... SHP
Shopper-News Beacon, Fair Lawn, NJ [*Library symbol Library of Congress*] (LCLS) ... NjFNB
Shoppers Association for Value Economy (EA) ... SAVE
Shoppers Guide, Cherry Hill, NJ [*Library symbol Library of Congress*] (LCLS) ... NjChSG
Shopping by Television [*British Telecom*] ... ShopTV
Shopping Center (MHDW) ... SC
Shopping Concourses [*Public-performance tariff class*] [*British*] ... SC
Shopping Hours Reform Council [*British*] (DBA) ... SHRC
Shop-Replaceable Assembly [*NASA*] ... SRA
Shop-Replaceable Unit [*NASA*] (NASA) ... SRU
Shoprite Group Ltd. [*British ICAO designator*] (FAAC) ... SHG
Shops Act [*1950*] [*British*] (ILCA) ... SA
Shops and Labs [*NASA*] (NASA) ... S/L
SHORAD [*Short Range Air Defense*] **Data Link** [*Army*] ... SDL
Shore ... HR
Shore ... SHO
Shore [*Commonly used*] (OPSA) ... SHOAR
Shore ... SHOR
Shore [*Commonly used*] (OPSA) ... SHORE
Shore (MCD) ... SHR
Shore Activity Load List ... SALL
Shore Activity Management Support [*Navy*] (NVT) ... SAMS
Shore Activity Manpower Planning System (DNAB) ... SAMPS
Shore Alteration ... SHOREALT
Shore ASW [*Antisubmarine Warfare*] **Command Center** (DOMA) ... SACC
Shore Based [*Navy symbol*] ... VP
Shore Bombardment [*Navy*] (NVT) ... SHOBOM
Shore Bombardment Training [*Navy*] (NVT) ... SHOBOMTNG
Shore Connection (IAA) ... SHCON
Shore Duty [*Navy*] ... SHORDU
Shore Duty Beyond the Seas Is Required by the Public Interest [*Navy*] ... SHOROUTPUBINST
Shore Duty Commencemnt Date [*Navy*] (DNAB) ... SHDCD
Shore Duty Is Required by the Public Interest [*Navy*] ... SHORPUBINT
Shore Duty Survey ... SHORVEY
Shore Electronic Engineering Activity, Pacific ... SEEAPAC
Shore Electronic Engineering Office [*Navy*] ... SEEO
Shore Electronics Reconnaissance System ... SELREC
Shore ELINT [*Electromagnetic Intelligence*] **System** [*Navy*] (NG) ... SHEL
Shore Establishment Realignment [*Navy*] (NVT) ... SER
Shore Establishments Division [*Navy*] ... SED
Shore Facilities Planning and Programming System [*Navy*] ... SFPPS
Shore Fire Control Party [*Military*] ... SFCP
Shore Fire Control Party Training [*Navy*] (NVT) ... SFCPTNG
Shore Installations and Facilities Planning and Programming System [*Navy*] (MCD) ... SIFPPS
Shore Intermediate Maintenance Activity [*Navy*] (NVT) ... SIMA
Shore Labourers Society [*A union*] [*British*] ... SLS
Shore Manning Document [*Navy*] (NVT) ... SHMD
Shore Mode Data Transmitter (MCD) ... SMDT
Shore Party [*Navy*] ... SP
Shore Patrol [*Navy*] (NVT) ... SHOPAT
Shore Patrol [*Navy*] ... SP
Shore Patrol Headquarters ... SPHQ
Shore Patrol Officer [*Navy*] ... SPO
Shore Plant Electronic Equipment List (MUGU) ... SPEEL
Shore Police [*Navy*] ... SP
Shore Protection Manual [*Army*] ... SPM
Shore Publishers, Inc., Oakhurst, NJ [*Library symbol Library of Congress*] (LCLS) ... NjOaS
Shore Requirements, Standards, and Manpower Planning System [*Navy*] ... SHORSTAMPS
Shore Requirements Strength and Manpower Planning System [*Navy*] (ANA) ... SHORSTRAMPS
Shore Road Elementary School, Bellmore, NY [*Library symbol*] [*Library of Congress*] (LCLS) ... NBellmSE
Shore Signal Service [*British Royal Navy*] ... SSS
Shore Station Development Board ... SSDB
Shore Survey Team (DNAB) ... SST
Shore Targeting Terminal [*Navy*] (CAAL) ... STT
Shore Terminal Box (MSA) ... STB
Shore Wireless Service [*British military*] (DMA) ... SWS
Shore-Based (CINC) ... SHOB
Shore-Based Acceptance Checkout Equipment ... SACE
Shore-Based Air Force, Forward Area, Central Pacific ... AIRFORWARD
Shore-Based Correlation Subsystem [*Navy*] (CAAL) ... SBCS
Shore-Based Interfare Requirement Date ... SIRD
Shore-Based Landing Aids (MCD) ... SBLA
Shore-Based Message Service System (DNAB) ... SBMSS
Shore-Based Prototype [*Nuclear energy*] (OA) ... SBP
Shore-Based Search Squadron [*Navy symbol*] ... VS
Shore-Based Tracking System ... SBTS
Shore-Based Transmitting Antenna ... STA
Shore-Establishment Planning Analysis and Review Cooperation [*or Coordination*] [*Navy*] (NG) ... SPARC
Shoreham [*British ICAO location identifier*] (ICLI) ... EGKA
Shoreham Nuclear Power Station (NRCH) ... SNPS
Shoreham-By-Sea [*England*] [*Airport symbol*] (OAG) ... ESH
Shoreham-Wading River High School, Shoreham, NY [*Library symbol Library of Congress*] (LCLS) ... NShorHS
Shoreham-Wading River Public Library, Shoreham, NY [*Library symbol Library of Congress*] (LCLS) ... NShor
Shorekote/Rafiqui [*Pakistan*] [*ICAO location identifier*] (ICLI) ... OPRQ
Shoreline (MSA) ... SHLN
Shoreline Community College, Seattle, WA [*Library symbol Library of Congress Obsolete*] (LCLS) ... WaSC-Sh
Shoreline Community College, Seattle, WA [*Library symbol Library of Congress*] (LCLS) ... WaSSh
Shoreline Erosion Advisory Service [*Bureau of Flood Protection*] ... SEAS
Shoreline Financial [*Associated Press*] (SAG) ... ShorlnFn
Shoreline Financial [*NASDAQ symbol*] (TTSB) ... SLFC
Shoreline Financial Corp. [*NASDAQ symbol*] (NQ) ... SLFC
Shoreline Modeling System [*US Army Corps of Engineers*] ... SMS
Shoreline Protection [*Type of water project*] ... SP
Shore-Required Operational Capability [*Navy*] ... SHOROC
Shore-Required Operational Capability [*Navy*] (DNAB) ... SHROC
Shores [*Commonly used*] (OPSA) ... SHOARS
Shores [*Commonly used*] (OPSA) ... SHORES
Shores ... SHRS
Shores (MCD) ... SHRS
Shorewood Packaging [*NASDAQ symbol*] (TTSB) ... SHOR
Shorewood Packaging Corp. [*NASDAQ symbol*] (NQ) ... SHOR
Shorewood Packaging Corp. [*Associated Press*] (SAG) ... Shorwd
Shorouk Air [*Egypt*] [*ICAO designator*] (FAAC) ... SHK
Shorr Imagery Test [*Personality development test*] [*Psychology*] ... SIT
Short (ROG) ... SH
Short (MSA) ... SHT
Short Address Form (NITA) ... SAF
Short Airfield for Tactical Support [*Marine Corps*] ... SATS
Short and Long Arm [*Automotive engineering*] ... SLA
Short Approach Light [*Aviation*] ... SAL
Short Approach Light System [*Aviation*] ... SALS
Short Approach Light System with Sequenced Flashers [*Aviation*] ... SALSF
Short Arc Quads [*Medicine*] ... SAQ
Short Arm Cast [*Medicine*] (MEDA) ... SAC
Short Arm Posterior Molded Splint [*Medicine*] (MEDA) ... SAPMS
Short Axis [*Medicine*] (DMAA) ... SAX
Short Backfire [*Antenna*] ... SBF
Short Baseline SONAR (PDAA) ... SBS
Short Basic Battery Test (NVT) ... SBBT
Short Beam Shear ... SBS
Short Bed/Continuous Development [*Chamber for thin-layer chromatography*] [*Analytical biochemistry*] ... SB/CD
Short Bill ... SB
Short Brothers & Harland Ltd. [*ICAO aircraft manufacturer identifier*] (ICAO) ... SH
Short Brothers PLC [*British ICAO designator*] (FAAC) ... SBL
Short Chain Acyl-Coenzyme A Dehydrogenase (DMAA) ... SCAD
Short Channel Effect (IAA) ... SCE
Short Children's Depression Inventory [*Psychology*] ... SCDI
Short Circuit ... S
Short Circuit ... SC
Short Circuit ... SCI
Short Circuit (AAG) ... SHCRT
Short Circuit Ampere (IAA) ... SCA
Short Circuit Conductance Matrix (PDAA) ... SCCM
Short Code Address (NITA) ... SCA
Short Consensus Repeat [*Biochemistry*] ... SCR
Short Course [*of instruction*] ... SC
Short Course Off-Road Event [*Off-road vehicle racing*] ... SCORE
Short Current Abstracts and Notes (DIT) ... SCAN
Short Day [*Botany*] ... SD
Short Delay ... SD
Short Delivery ... SD
Short Delivery (ODBW) ... sd
Short Distance Swimmer ... SDS
Short Double Upright Brace [*Orthopedics*] (DAVI) ... SDU
Short Double Upright Brace [*Medicine*] (DMAA) ... SDUB
Short Duration ... SD
Short Expeditious Landing Field (CINC) ... SELF
Short Field Aircraft ... SFA
Short Flashing Light [*Navigation signal*] ... SFL
Short Food Drape [*Dietetics*] (DAVI) ... SFD
Short Form Catalog (IAA) ... SFC
Short Form Provisioning Parts List [*NASA*] (NASA) ... SFPPL
Short Form Research Contract (AAGC) ... SFRC
Short Form Test of Academic Aptitude (EDAC) ... SFTAA

Short Format ... SF
Short Growth Rate (OA) ... SGR
Short Imaginal Process Inventory [*Personality development test*] [*Psychology*] ... SIPI
Short Increment Sensitivity Index [*Medicine*] ... SISI
Short Interest [*Brokerage*] ... SI
Short Interspaced Repeated Segments [*Of DNA*] [*Medicine*] (BABM) ... SINES
Short Interspaced Repeated Segments [*of Deoxyribonucleic Acid*] [*Genetics*] (DAVI) ... SINES
Short Interspersed Nucleotide Element [*Genetics*] ... SINE
Short Interval Identification ... SII
Short Interval Plan [*Management principles*] ... SIP
Short Interval Scheduling [*Quality control*] ... SIS
Short Irregular Pulses ... SIP
Short Landed [*Tea trade*] (ROG) ... SL
Short Latency Response [*Neurology*] ... SLR
Short Latent Evoked Potential [*Medicine*] (DMAA) ... SLEP
Short Lead Time Material (DNAB) ... SLTM
Short Leaf Yellow Pine [*Lumber*] ... SLYP
Short Leg Brace [*Medicine*] ... SLB
Short Leg Cast [*Medicine*] (MEDA) ... SLC
Short Leg Posterior Molded Splint [*Medicine*] (MEDA) ... SLPMS
Short Leg Walking Cast [*Medicine*] (MEDA) ... SLWC
Short Length Record (IAA) ... SLRC
Short Length Super HIPPO [*High Internal Pressure Producing Orifice*] (MCD) ... SLSH
Short Lengths [*Construction*] ... SL
Short Letter (DCTA) ... SL
Short Little Ugly Feller [*Nickname for A-7 aircraft*] (MCD) ... SLUF
Short LOFAR [*Low-Frequency Acquisition and Ranging*] **Alerting Message** (NVT) ... SLAM
Short Luteal Phase [*Medicine*] (DMAA) ... SLP
Short Magazine Lee-Enfield Rifle ... SMLE
Short Market Value [*Investment term*] ... SMV
Short Message Service ... SMS
Short Meter [*Music*] ... SM
Short Meter Double [*Music*] ... SMD
Short Michigan Alcoholism Screening Test (EDAC) ... SMAST
Short Module [*NASA*] (NASA) ... SM
Short Nickel Line Accumulating Register Calculator (PDAA) ... SNARC
Short Notice Annual Practice [*Military*] ... SNAP
Short No-Voltage Tester [*Ground surveillance RADAR system*] (MCD) ... SNVT
Short Octal Load (IAA) ... SOL
Short of Exchange [*Economics*] ... SOE
Short of Luck (DSUE) ... SOL
Short Open Reading [*Frame*] [*Genetics*] (DAVI) ... sor
Short Page ... SP
Short Particular Metre [*Music*] ... SPM
Short Path Infrared (MCD) ... SHOPAIR
Short Path Infrared Tester (KSC) ... SPIRT
Short Perforation [*Philately*] ... SP
Short Period ... SP
Short Period Oscillation ... SPO
Short Persistence ... SP
Short Planning Analysis and Review Cooperation ... SPARC
Short Planning Identification File ... SPIDE
Short Portable Mental Status Questionnaire (EDAC) ... SPMSQ
Short Position [*Investment term*] ... SP
Short Procedure Unit [*Medicine*] (CPH) ... SPU
Short Product Life Cycle [*Business term*] (MHDB) ... SPLC
Short Psychiatric Evaluation Scale (CPH) ... SPES
Short Pulse ... SP
Short Pulse Experimental RADAR Techniques (MCD) ... SPERT
Short Pulse Generator ... SPG
Short Pulse RADAR (IAA) ... SPR
Short Ragweed [*Immunology*] ... SRW
Short Ragweed Pollen [*Immunology*] ... SRP
Short Range ... SR
Short Range Aids [*USCG*] (TAG) ... SRA
Short Range Construction Program [*Military*] ... SRCP
Short Range Thermal Imaging Equipment (PDAA) ... SHORTIE
Short Rate ... SR
Short Reflex Arc ... SRA
Short Residence Time [*Chemical engineering*] ... SRT
Short Rib-Polydactyly Syndrome [*Medicine*] (DMAA) ... SRPS
Short Rotary Furnace [*Metallurgy*] ... SRF
Short Run [*Economics*] ... SR
Short Run Average Costs ... SRAC
Short Run Job (MCD) ... SRJ
Short Run Marginal Cost (MHDB) ... SRMC
Short Segmented Cask [*Nuclear energy*] (NRCH) ... SSC
Short Sequence Deinking [*Recycling*] ... SSD
Short Service Commissions [*Army British*] ... SSC
Short Side ... SHTSD
Short Sight (ADA) ... SS
Short Sleeves ... SS
Short Spike Burst [*Medicine*] (DMAA) ... SSB
Short Stature, Hyperextensibility of Joints or Hernia or Both, Ocular Depression, Rieger Anomaly, Teething Delayed [*Medicine*] (DMAA) ... SHORT
Short Stay (DAVI) ... SS
Short Story Criticism [*A publication*] ... SSC
Short, Straight Hollow Hosel [*Golf clubs*] ... S2H2
Short System Ground Check ... SSGC
Short Takeoff (MCD) ... STO
Short Takeoff and Landing [*Aviation*] ... STOL
Short Takeoff and Landing Airport [*London, England*] ... Stolport
Short Take-Off and Landing and Maneuvering Technology Demonstrator [*Air Force*] ... SMTD
Short Takeoff and Vertical Landing (MCD) ... STOVL
Short Takeoff Arrested Landing (MCD) ... STOAL
Short Takeoff Gross Weight [*Aviation*] ... STOGW
Short Tandem Repeat Polymorphisms [*Genetics*] ... STRP
Short Tau Inversion Recovery [*Medicine*] (DMAA) ... STIR
Short Term Analysis Services [*Scientific Services Program*] [*Army*] (RDA) ... STAS
Short Term Conflict Alert System [*Aviation*] (DA) ... STCA
Short Term Enrichment Program [*of US Information Agency*] ... STEP
Short Term Leaflet. Ministry of Agriculture, Fisheries, and Food [*A publication*] ... STL
Short Term Projections [*Townsend, Greenspan & Co., Inc.*] [*No longer available online*] [*Information service or system*] ... STP
Short Term Reinitialization [*Army*] ... STR
Short Tests of Clerical Ability ... STCA
Short Time (IAA) ... ST
Short Time Constant (MSA) ... SHTC
Short Time Constant ... STC
Short Time Duty (IAA) ... STD
Short Time Test (IAA) ... STT
Short Title Catalog [*A publication*] ... STC
Short Title File (NITA) ... STF
Short Ton [*2000 lbs.*] ... SHTN
Short Ton [*2000 lbs.*] ... ST
Short Ton [*2000 lbs.*] (AABC) ... STON
Short Ton Unit ... STU
Short Tons Raw Value ... STRV
Short Tour [*Military*] ... ST
Short Tour Return Date [*Military*] ... STRD
Short Tour Return Date [*Military*] ... TDR
Short Track Auto Racing Series [*Car racing*] ... STARS
Short Track Auto Racing Stars [*An association*] ... STARS
Short Training Courses (AIE) ... STC
Short Vehicle Integrated Management System ... SVIMS
Short Vertical Lower Left ... SVLL
Short Vertical Lower Right ... SVLR
Short/Vertical Takeoff and Landing [*Aviation*] (NATG) ... S/VTOL
Short Vertical Upper Left ... SVUL
Short Vertical Upper Right ... SVUR
Short Wave (IAA) ... SHW
Short Wavelength LASER ... SWL
Short Wavelength Limit ... SWL
Short Wavelength Prime [*Camera for spectra*] ... SWP
Short Wavelength Radiation (KSC) ... SWR
Short Weight ... SW
Short Wheelbase ... SWB
Short Wing Piper Club (EA) ... SWPC
Shortage (AABC) ... SHRTG
Shortage (AFM) ... SHTG
Shortage Specialty Pay [*Navy*] (NVT) ... SSP
Shortages and Valuable Excesses [*Navy*] (NG) ... SAVE
Short-Alcohol Dependence Data [*Medicine*] (DMAA) ... SADD
Short-Arc Geodetic Adjustment [*Geophysics*] ... SAGA
Short-Arc Reduction of RADAR Altimetry ... SARRA
Short-Arc Xenon Lamp ... SAXL
Short-Arc Xenon Lamp ... SXL
Short-Arm Cast [*Orthopedics*] (DAVI) ... SAC
Short-Arm Navicular Cast [*Orthopedics*] (DAVI) ... SANC
Short-Arm Splint [*Orthopedics*] (DAVI) ... SAS
Short-Chain Fatty Acids [*Biochemistry*] ... SCFA
Short-Circuit Current ... SCC
Short-Circuit Output Current ... SCOC
Short-Circuit Protection ... SCP
Short-Circuit Ratio ... SCR
Short-Circuited Terminating Line (IAA) ... SCTL
Short-Circuited Transmission Line ... SCTL
Short-Circuit-Stable ... SCS
Short-Contact-Time Fluidized Reactors [*Chemical engineering*] ... SCTFR
Short-Course Chemotherapy [*Medicine*] ... SCC
Short-Day Plant [*Botany*] ... SDP
Short-Delay Monostable [*Circuitry*] ... SDM
Shorted Emitter Switch (IAA) ... SES
Shortened (ROG) ... SHORTD
Shortened Disjuctive Normal Form (PDAA) ... SDNF
Shortened Electrochemical Systole [*Cardiology*] (DAVI) ... QS_2I
Shortening Allowance [*Carpentry*] ... SA
Shortening Fraction [*Cardiology*] ... SF
Shorter College, Rome, GA [*Library symbol Library of Congress*] (LCLS) ... GRS
Shorter Interval Scheduling [*Quality control*] (IAA) ... SIS
Shorter Oxford Dictionary [*A publication*] ... SOD
Shorter Oxford English Dictionary [*A publication*] ... SOED
Shorter Range Intermediate-Range Nuclear Forces (DOMA) ... SRINF
Shorter Range Scheduling ... SRS
Shorter Workweek [*Business term*] (MHDB) ... SW
Shortest Access Time First ... SATF
Shortest Activity from Shortest Project ... SASP
Shortest Connected Network ... SCN
Shortest Job First [*Computer science*] ... SJF
Shortest Latency Time First ... SLTF
Shortest Operation First ... SOF
Shortest Path ... SP
Shortest Path First (TNIG) ... SPF
Shortest Possible Route (MCD) ... SPR

Shortest Processing Time First [Computer science] (MHDI) .... SPTF
Shortest Programming Time First (NITA) .... SPTF
Shortest Remaining First Time (HGAA) .... SRFT
Shortest Remaining Processing Time (PDAA) .... SRPT
Shortest Remaining Time First [Computer science] .... SRTF
Shortest Seek Time First .... SSTF
Shorthair Guinea Pig [Medicine] (DMAA) .... SR
Shorthand .... S/H
Shorthand Coding .... SHACO
Shorthand Note .... SHN
Shorthand Programming Language in COBOL [Common Business-Oriented Language] Environment [Computer science] (MHDI) .... SPLICE
Shorthand Typist (Higher Grade) [British military] (DMA) .... SHG
Shorthand Typist (Lower Grade) [British military] (DMA) .... SLG
Shorthand Writer [British military] (DMA) .... ST
Short-Handed Goal [Hockey] .... SHG
Shorthaul Customer Modem (NITA) .... SCM
Short-Intrusion Fuze (RDA) .... SIF
Short-Leg Cast [Orthopedics] (DAVI) .... SLC
Short-Leg Nonwalking Cast [Medicine] (DMAA) .... SLNWC
Short-Leg Splint [Orthopedics] (DAVI) .... SLS
Short-Leg Walking Cast [Orthopedics] (DAVI) .... SLWC
Short-Leg Walking Cast [Medicine] (DMAA) .... SLWC
Short-Length, Nonbuoyant Torpedo System .... SNTS
Short-Lived Large Energy Fluctuation [Physics] .... SLEF
Short-Long [as of a signal light's flash cycle] .... S-L
Short-Long Flashing Light [Navigation signal] .... S-LFL
Shortness of Breath [Cardiology] .... SB
Shortness of Breath [Cardiology] .... SOB
Shortness of Breath on Exertion [Cardiology] .... SBE
Short-Period Tremors [Volcanology] .... SPT
Short-Pulse LASER .... SPL
Short-Range Acquisition (MCD) .... SRA
Short-Range Aid to Navigation (IAA) .... SHORAN
Short-Range Aids to Navigation [Navy] .... SRAN
Short-Range Air Defense [Army] (NATG) .... SHORAD
Short-Range Air Defense .... SHORD
Short-Range Air Defense Command and Control .... SHORAD C²
Short-Range Air Defense System [Army] (RDA) .... SHORADS
Short-Range Air-to-Air Missile (MCD) .... SRAAM
Short-Range Air-to-Surface Missile .... SHRAM
Short-Range Air-to-Surface Missile (MCD) .... SRASM
Short-Range Antiradiation Missile .... SRARM
Short-Range Antitank Weapon .... SRAW
Short-Range Applied Technology .... SRAT
Short-Range Attack Missile .... SCRAM
Short-Range Attack Missile [Military] .... SRAM
Short-Range Attack Missile System (IAA) .... SRAMS
Short-Range Attack Missile (Tactical) [Military] .... SRAM(T)
Short-Range Ballistic Missile .... SRBM
Short-Range Bomber Defense Missile .... SRBDM
Short-Range Doppler .... SHODOP
Short-Range Guided Rocket .... SRGR
Short-Range Impact Point (MUGU) .... SRIP
Short-Range Intercept Missile (MCD) .... SRIM
Short-Range Man-Portable Antitank Weapons Technology .... SMAWT
Short-Range Missile [Projected; not to be confused with SRAM] .... SRM
Short-Range Missile Launcher .... SRML
Short-Range MODEM .... SRM
Short-Range Navigation .... SHORAN
Short-Range Navigation System (FAAC) .... SHORN
Short-Range Navigation Vehicle [System] [Air Force] .... SHANICLE
Short-Range Nuclear Forces .... SNF
Short-Range Omnidirectional Beacon [Aerospace] .... SROB
Short-Range Order [Solid state physics] .... SRO
Short-Range RADAR .... SRR
Short-Range Recovery (IEEE) .... SRR
Short-Range Search (MCD) .... SRS
Short-Range Station Keeping (NG) .... SRSK
Short-Range Surface-to-Air Guided Weapon (IAA) .... SRSAGM
Short-Range Surveillance and Target Acquisition System (PDAA) ...... SHORSTAS
Short-Range Tactical Ballistic Missile .... SRTBM
Short-Range Task Force .... SRTF
Short-Range Thermal Sight [Army] (INF) .... SRTS
Short-Range Track via Missile [Military] (CAAL) .... SRTVM
Short-Range Training Round [Army] (INF) .... SRTR
Short-Range Transport [Aircraft] (NATG) .... SRT
Short-Range Vehicle to Roadside Communication [FHWA] (TAG) .... SVRC
Short-Range Viewer .... SRV
Short-Range Wideband Radio (MCD) .... SRWBR
Short-Run Average Total Cost [Economics] .... SRATC
Short-Run Average Variable Cost [Economics] .... SRAVC
Short-Run Incremental Cost (ADA) .... SRIC
Short-Run Manufacturing Facility (MCD) .... SRMF
Short-Run Marginal Cost Curve [Economics] .... SMC
Shorts 330 [Airplane code] Sh3
Shorts 360 [Airplane code] Sh6
Shortstop .... SS
Shortt on Informations, Criminal, Quo Warranto, Mandamus, and Prohibition [1887] [A publication] (DLA) .... Shortt Inf
Shortt on Informations, Criminal, Quo Warranto, Mandamus, and Prohibition [A publication] (DLA) .... Shortt Inform
Shortt on Literature and Art [2nd ed.] [1884] [A publication] (DLA) .... Shortt Lit
Shortt on Works of Literature [2nd ed.] [1884] [A publication] (DLA) .... Sh Lit
Shortt on Works of Literature [2nd ed.] [1884] [A publication] (DLA) .... Sh Litt

Short-Term Anti-Jam (MCD) .... STAJ
Short-Term Anxiety-Provoking Psychotherapy (PDAA) .... STAPP
Short-Term Arrangements [Department of State] .... STA
Short-Term Auction-Rate Stock [Investment term] .... STARS
Short-Term Auditory Retrieval and Storage Test .... STARS
Short-Term Averaging (CAAL) .... STA
Short-Term Coal Analysis System [Department of Energy] (GFGA) .... SCOAL
Short-Term Cost Plan [NASA] (NASA) .... STCP
Short-Term Debt (MHDW) .... STD
Short-Term Disability .... STD
Short-Term Dynamic Psychotherapy .... STDP
Short-Term Emergency Assistance .... STEA
Short-Term Energy Monitoring [Colorado State University] .... STEM
Short-Term Exposure Limit [Environmental chemistry] .... STEL
Short-Term Goal (DAVI) .... STG
Short-Term Holiday (MHDB) .... STH
Short-Term Inhalation Limits [of air pollutants] .... STIL
Short-Term Integrated Forecasting System [Department of Energy] (GFGA) .... STIFS
Short-Term Integration (CAAL) .... STI
Short-Term Irradiation Facility [Nuclear energy] (NRCH) .... STIF
Short-Term Lethal Concentration [of air pollutants] .... STLC
Short-Term Loan (ADA) .... STL
Short-Term Memory .... STM
Short-Term Monetary Support [Finance] .... STMS
Short-Term Money Market .... STMM
Short-Term Note-Issuance Facility [Banking] .... SNIF
Short-Term Nuclear Annual Power Production Simulation Model [Department of Energy] (GFGA) .... SNAPPS
Short-Term Objective .... STO
Short-Term Potentiation [Neurology] .... STP
Short-Term Program [Nuclear energy] (NRCH) .... STP
Short-Term Public Exposure Limit (MCD) .... STPL
Short-Term Reconaissance and Target Acquisition Team [US Special Forces] (VNW) .... STRATA
Short-Term Returns .... STR
Short-Term Stay [in hospital] [British] .... ST
Short-Term Test [Toxicology] .... STT
Short-Term Vehicle Park (DS) .... STVP
Short-Term Visual Storage [or Store] [Psychophysiology] .... STVS
Short-Term Waviness [Surface finish] .... STW
Short-Terms Abroad .... STA
Short-Time Fourier Transform (DMAA) .... STFT
Short-to-Medium-Range Air Defense System [Army] (RDA) .... SHOMADS
Short-Tube Vertical [Evaporator] .... STV
Shortwave (FAAC) .... SHRTWV
Shortwave [Electronics] .... SW
Shortwave Converter .... SWC
Short-Wave Diathermy [Medicine] .... SWD
Shortwave Fadeouts .... SWF
Shortwave Infrared .... SWIR
Short-Wave Interference [Telecommunications] (IAA) .... SWI
Shortwave Listener [Radio] .... SWL
Shortwave Ratio (DEN) .... SWR
Short-Wave Sleep (OA) .... SWS
Shortwave Transmitter .... SWT
Shoshone Peak [Nevada] [Seismograph station code, US Geological Survey] (SEIS) .... SSP
Shoshone Public Library, Shoshone, ID [Library symbol] [Library of Congress] (LCLS) .... IdSh
Shoshone-Bannock Library, Fort Hall, ID [Library symbol] [Library of Congress] (LCLS) .... IdFh
Shoshoni Gold [Vancouver Stock Exchange symbol] .... SOI
Shosin Society (EA) .... SS
Shot .... SO
Shot Noise Optical Optimization Communication System with Stops [NASA] .... SOPS
Shot Peening Fixture (MCD) .... SPNF
Shot through Obscuration MILES [Multiple Integrated LASER Engagement System] [Army] .... STOM
Shotgun Red Fan Club (EA) .... SRFC
Shotgun Wedding [Forced marriage] [Slang] .... SW
Shots per Gun per Minute [Military] (NVT) .... SPGPM
Shots per Minute [Military] (RDA) .... SPM
Should (ROG) .... SHD
Should Be .... S/B
Should Cost (MCD) .... SC
Should Cost Analysis (MCD) .... SCA
Shoulder (AAG) .... sh
Shoulder (MSA) .... SHLD
Shoulder (MSA) .... SHLDR
Shoulder Disarticulation [Medicine] (MAE) .... SD
Shoulder Disarticulation [Medicine] .... SDA
Shoulder Dislocation .... SD
Shoulder Extension [Sports medicine] .... SEXT
Shoulder External Rotation [Sports medicine] .... SEXR
Shoulder Flexion [Sports medicine] .... SFLX
Shoulder Horizontal Flexion [Sports medicine] .... SHFL
Shoulder Internal Rotation [Sports medicine] .... SINR
Shoulder Pitch (MCD) .... SP
Shoulder Season [Airline fare code] .... O
Shoulder Sleeve Insignia [Military] (AABC) .... SSI
Shoulder Yaw (MCD) .... SY
Shoulder-Elbow Orthosis [Medicine] .... SEO
Shoulder-Elbow-Wrist Orthosis [Medicine] .... SEWO

Shoulder-Elbow-Wrist-Hand Orthosis [*Medicine*] .... SEWHO
Shoulder-Launched Antitank Missile [*Army*] .... SLAM
Shoulder-Launched Multipurpose Assault Weapon (MCD) .... SMAW
Shoulder-Mounted Assault Weapon (DWSG) .... SMAW
Show (WGA) .... SH
Show [*Automotive advertising*] .... SHO
Show and Breed Secretaries' Association [*British*] (BI) .... SBSA
Show Business Association [*New York, NY*] (EA) .... SBA
Show Cause [*Legal shorthand*] (LWAP) .... S/C
Show Cause Notice .... SCN
Show Cause Order [*Legal shorthand*] (LWAP) .... SCO
Show Folks of America (EA) .... SFA
Show Jumper [*or Jumping*] [*Horsemanship*] [*British*] (DI) .... SJ
Show Low [*Arizona*] [*Airport symbol Obsolete*] (OAG) .... SOW
Show Low, AZ [*FM radio station call letters*] .... KRFM
Show Low, AZ [*AM radio station call letters*] .... KVSL
Show Low, AZ [*AM radio station call letters*] .... KVWM
Show Low, AZ [*FM radio station call letters*] .... KVWM-FM
Show Low Public Library, Show Low, AZ [*Library symbol Library of Congress*] (LCLS) .... AzSh
Show Nothing Unless Bad .... SNUB
Show of Equipment and Supplies for the Graphic Arts (DGA) .... SESGA
ShowBiz Pizza Time [*NASDAQ symbol*] (TTSB) .... SHBZ
ShowBiz Pizza Time, Inc. [*NASDAQ symbol*] (CTT) .... SHBZ
ShowBiz Pizza Time, Inc. [*Associated Press*] (SAG) .... Showbiz
Showboat, Inc. [*NYSE symbol*] (SPSG) .... SBO
Showboat, Inc. [*Associated Press*] (SAG) .... Showbt
Showcase .... SHWCS
Shower .... SHR
Shower and Toilet (AAG) .... SH & T
Shower Drain (AAG) .... SD
Shower over Tub [*Real estate*] .... SOT
Showers (AAG) .... SH
Shower's English King's Bench Reports [*A publication*] (DLA) .... Sh
Shower's English King's Bench Reports [*A publication*] (DLA) .... Show
Shower's English King's Bench Reports [*A publication*] (DLA) .... Show KB
Shower's English King's Bench Reports [*89 English Reprint*] [*1678-95*] [*A publication*] (DLA) .... Shower KB
Shower's English King's Bench Reports [*89 English Reprint*] [*A publication*] (DLA) .... Shower KB (Eng)
Shower's English Parliamentary Cases [*A publication*] (DLA) .... Sh
Shower's English Parliamentary Cases [*A publication*] (DLA) .... Show
Shower's English Parliamentary Cases [*1 English Reprint*] [*A publication*] (DLA) .... Show Parl Cas
Shower's English Parliamentary Cases [*1 English Reprint*] [*A publication*] (DLA) .... Show PC
Shower's English Parliamentary Cases [*1 English Reprint*] [*A publication*] (DLA) .... Shower PC (Eng)
Showing [*Technical drawings*] .... SHO
SHOWME [*VERALEX, Inc.*] [*Information service or system*] (CRD) .... SME
Showmen's Guild of Australia .... SGA
Showmen's League of America (EA) .... SLA
Shown (AAG) .... SHN
Showroom [*Automotive advertising*] .... SHWRM
Showroom Stock [*Automotive classification*] .... SS
Showscan Entertainment [*NASDAQ symbol*] (TTSB) .... SHOW
Showscan Entertainment, Inc. [*NASDAQ symbol*] (SAG) .... SHOW
Showscan Entrtainment, Inc. [*Associated Press*] (SAG) .... Shwscn
Showtime [*Cable television channel*] .... SHOW
Showy [*Horticulture*] .... shwy
Shrady on Suicide and Intemperance in Life Insurance [*A publication*] (DLA) .... Shr Sui
Shrapnel .... SHRAP
Shrapnel Fragment (MAE) .... SF
Shrapnel Fragment Wound (MAE) .... SFW
Shredded [*Freight*] .... SHRD
Shredder (MSA) .... SHRDR
Shreemati Nathibai Domodar Thackersey Women's University [*India*] .... SNDT
Shreve Memorial and Caddo Parish Extension Library, Shreveport, LA [*Library symbol Library of Congress*] (LCLS) .... LSh
Shreveport [*Diocesan abbreviation*] [*Louisiana*] (TOCD) .... SHP
Shreveport [*Louisiana*] [*Airport symbol*] (OAG) .... SHV
Shreveport/Barksdale Air Force Base [*Louisiana*] [*ICAO location identifier*] (ICLI) .... KBAD
Shreveport, LA [*Location identifier FAA*] (FAAL) .... BAD
Shreveport, LA [*Location identifier FAA*] (FAAL) .... DTN
Shreveport, LA [*Location identifier FAA*] (FAAL) .... EMG
Shreveport, LA [*Location identifier FAA*] (FAAL) .... FOG
Shreveport, LA [*Location identifier FAA*] (FAAL) .... JKC
Shreveport, LA [*AM radio station call letters*] .... KBCL
Shreveport, LA [*FM radio station call letters*] .... KDAQ
Shreveport, LA [*AM radio station call letters*] .... KEEL
Shreveport, LA [*AM radio station call letters*] .... KFLO
Shreveport, LA [*AM radio station call letters*] .... KIOU
Shreveport, LA [*FM radio station call letters*] .... KITT
Shreveport, LA [*Television station call letters*] .... KLTS
Shreveport, LA [*FM radio station call letters*] .... KMJJ
Shreveport, LA [*Television station call letters*] .... KMSS
Shreveport, LA [*AM radio station call letters*] .... KOKA
Shreveport, LA [*AM radio station call letters*] .... KRMD
Shreveport, LA [*FM radio station call letters*] .... KRMD-FM
Shreveport, LA [*FM radio station call letters*] (RBYB) .... KRUF-FM
Shreveport, LA [*FM radio station call letters*] .... KSCL
Shreveport, LA [*Television station call letters*] (RBYB) .... KSHV
Shreveport, LA [*Television station call letters*] .... KSLA
Shreveport, LA [*Television station call letters*] .... KTBS
Shreveport, LA [*FM radio station call letters*] .... KVKI
Shreveport, LA [*AM radio station call letters*] .... KWKH
Shreveport, LA [*FM radio station call letters*] .... KWKH-FM
Shreveport, LA [*Location identifier FAA*] (FAAL) .... SHV
Shreveport/Regional Airport [*Louisiana*] [*ICAO location identifier*] (ICLI) .... KSHV
Shrewsbury [*British depot code*] .... SALOP
Shrike Improved Display System [*Military*] (NVT) .... SIDS
Shrimp Association of the Americas (EA) .... SAOTA
Shrimp Harvesters Coalition of the Gulf and South Atlantic States (EA) .... SHCGSAS
Shrine Directors Association of North America (EA) .... SDANA
Shrine Recorders Association of North America (EA) .... SRANA
Shriners Burn Institute .... SBI
Shriners Hospitals for Crippled Children (EA) .... SHFCC
Shrink Mock-Up Template (MSA) .... SMUT
Shrink Template .... ST
Shrinking Stock [*Corporate investment*] .... SS
Shrivenham [*England*] .... SHRIV
Shrobarova [*Czechoslovakia*] [*Seismograph station code, US Geological Survey*] (SEIS) .... SRO
Shropshire [*County in England*] .... SALOP
Shropshire [*County in England*] .... SHROPS
Shropshire Imperial Yeomanry [*British military*] (DMA) .... SIY
Shropshire Light Infantry [*British military*] (DMA) .... SLI
Shropshire Sheep Breeders Association and Flock Book Society [*British*] (DBA) .... SSBA
Shropshire Yeomanry [*British military*] (DMA) .... SY
Shroud (AAG) .... SHD
Shroud [*Engineering*] .... SHRD
Shroud Fin [*Engineering*] .... SHRDF
Shroud of Turin Research Project (EA) .... STURP
Shrub [*Botany*] .... S
Shrub and Tree Growers of Australia .... STGA
Shrugard Storage Centers [*Associated Press*] (SAG) .... Shurgard
Shrunk Back-to-Back [*Packaging of volumes*] [*Publishing*] .... SB
Shrunken-2 Gene [*In sweet corn*] .... sh_2
Shuangyang General Aviation Co. [*China*] [*FAA designator*] (FAAC) .... CSY
Shubert Archive, New York, NY [*Library symbol*] [*Library of Congress*] (LCLS) .... NNShA
Shubert Elementary School, Baldwin, NY [*Library symbol Library of Congress*] (LCLS) .... NBaldSE
Shubert Entertainment and Arts Ticketing System [*National computerized theatre-ticket selling system*] .... SEATS
Shuffle Master [*NASDAQ symbol*] (TTSB) .... SHFL
Shuffle Master, Inc. [*NASDAQ symbol*] (SAG) .... SHFL
Shuffle Master, Inc. [*Associated Press*] (SAG) .... ShufMst
Shugart Associates Systems Interface .... SASI
Shulhan 'Arukh (BJA) .... ShA
Shulhan 'Arukh (BJA) .... ShAr
Shumaker and Longsdorf's Cyclopedic Dictionary [*A publication*] (DLA) .... Cyclop Dict
Shungnak [*Alaska*] [*Airport symbol*] (OAG) .... SHG
Shungnak, AK [*Location identifier FAA*] (FAAL) .... SHG
Shungwayah Freedom Party [*Kenya*] .... SFP
Shunt [*Electricity*] .... SH
Shunt Ahead [*Railroad signal arm*] [*British*] .... S
Shunt Capacitor (IAA) .... SC
Shunt Feedback Schottky Clamped [*Electronics*] .... SFSCL
Shunt Mounted Chip (IAA) .... SMC
Shunt Procedure [*Medicine*] (MAE) .... SP
Shunt Reactor [*Electricity*] (IAA) .... SR
Shur Tepa [*Afghanistan*] [*ICAO location identifier*] (ICLI) .... OAST
Shurgard Storage Centers [*NYSE symbol*] (SAG) .... SHU
Shuswap Flight Centre Ltd. [*Canada ICAO designator*] (FAAC) .... SFC
Shut Down .... S/D
Shut Down Amplifier (IAA) .... SDA
Shutdown (NASA) .... SHDN
Shutdown (NASA) .... SHUTDN
Shutdown Cooling [*Nuclear energy*] (NRCH) .... SDC
Shutdown Cooling System [*Nuclear energy*] (NRCH) .... SCS
Shutdown Cooling System [*Nuclear energy*] (NRCH) .... SDCS
Shutdown Cooling System Heat Exchange [*Nuclear energy*] (NRCH) .... SCSHX
Shutdown Heat Removal System [*Nuclear energy*] (NRCH) .... SHRS
Shutdown Logic Diagram [*Nuclear energy*] (NRCH) .... SLD
Shutdown Margin [*Nuclear energy*] (NRCH) .... SDM
Shutdown Mode (IEEE) .... SDM
Shutdown Reactor Cooling [*Nuclear energy*] (NRCH) .... SRC
Shutdown Reactor Head Cooling [*Nuclear energy*] (NRCH) .... SRHC
Shutdown Request [*NASA*] (KSC) .... SR
Shute Harbour [*Australia Airport symbol*] .... JHQ
Shute Harbour [*Queensland*] [*Airport symbol*] (AD) .... SHU
Shut-in Casing Pressure [*Well drilling technology*] .... SICP
Shut-In Society .... SIS
Shut-Off (AAG) .... S-O
Shut-Off Lights (SAA) .... SOL
Shut-Off Valve .... SOV
Shutout [*Sports*] .... SHO
Shutout [*Sports*] .... SO
Shutter (AAG) .... SHTR
Shutter Value [*Photography*] .... SV
Shuttle (MCD) .... SH
Shuttle (MSA) .... SHTL
Shuttle (SSD) .... SHUT
Shuttle Activation Task Force [*NASA*] (NASA) .... SATAF

Shuttle Active-Microwave Experiments (MCD) ... SAMEX
Shuttle Aerosurface Actuator Simulator [NASA] (MCD) ... SAAS
Shuttle Amateur Radio Experiment [NASA] ... SAREX
Shuttle Astronaut Recruitment Program [NASA] (MCD) ... SARP
Shuttle Attached Teleoperator [NASA] (NASA) ... SATO
Shuttle Attachment Manipulator [NASA] ... SAM
Shuttle Attachment Manipulator System [NASA] ... SAMS
Shuttle Authorized Document [NASA] (NASA) ... SAD
Shuttle Automated Management System (SSD) ... SAMS
Shuttle Automated Mass Properties [NASA] (MCD) ... SAMP
Shuttle Avionics Breadboard [NASA] (NASA) ... SAB
Shuttle Avionics Integration Division [NASA] (SSD) ... SAID
Shuttle Avionics Integration Laboratory [NASA] ... SAIL
Shuttle Avionics Laboratory [NASA] (NASA) ... SAL
Shuttle Avionics Test System [NASA] (NASA) ... SATS
Shuttle Avionics Verification and Evaluation [NASA] (NASA) ... SAVER
Shuttle Carrier Aircraft [NASA] (NASA) ... SCA
Shuttle Command and Voice Multiplexer (MCD) ... SCVM
Shuttle Critical Design Review [NASA] (NASA) ... SCDR
Shuttle Data Management [NASA] (MCD) ... SDM
Shuttle Data Processing Complex [NASA] (MCD) ... SDPC
Shuttle Data Processor (MCD) ... SDP
Shuttle Data Tape (NASA) ... SDT
Shuttle Derived Vehicle (MCD) ... SDV
Shuttle Design Directive [NASA] (NASA) ... SDD
Shuttle Dynamic Simulation [NASA] (NASA) ... SDS
Shuttle Electrical Power Analysis Program [NASA] ... SEPAP
Shuttle Electrical Power Analysis Report [NASA] (NASA) ... SEPAR
Shuttle Electronic Hardware [NASA] ... SEH
Shuttle Engineering Approach/Rollout Control Hybrid Simulation (NASA) ... SEARCHS
Shuttle Engineering Review Board [NASA] (NASA) ... SERB
Shuttle Engineering Simulation [NASA] (NASA) ... SES
Shuttle Engineering System [NASA] (SSD) ... SES
Shuttle Entry Air Data Sensor [NASA] (MCD) ... SEADS
Shuttle Entry Air Data System [or Subsystem] (NASA) ... SEADS
Shuttle Equipment Record System [NASA] (NASA) ... SERS
Shuttle Events Control Subsystem [NASA] (NASA) ... SECS
Shuttle Events Sequential Control (MCD) ... SESC
Shuttle Experiment Support Equipment ... SESE
Shuttle Flight Operations Manual [NASA] (MCD) ... SFOM
Shuttle Flight Status [NASA] (MCD) ... SFS
Shuttle Ground Operations Simulator [NASA] (NASA) ... SGOS
Shuttle High-Energy Astrophysics Laboratory [NASA] (SSD) ... SHEAL
Shuttle Imaging Microwave System [NASA] (NASA) ... SIMS
Shuttle Imaging RADAR [of earth's surface] [NASA] ... SIR
Shuttle Imaging Spectrometer Experiment [NASA] ... SISEX
Shuttle, Inc. [ICAO designator] (FAAC) ... USS
Shuttle Induced Atmosphere (NASA) ... SIA
Shuttle Information Management Accountability System [NASA] (NASA) ... SIMAS
Shuttle Information System [NASA] (MCD) ... SIS
Shuttle Infrared Leeside Temperature Sensing [NASA] (NASA) ... SILTS
Shuttle Integrated Test [NASA] (NASA) ... SIT
Shuttle Integration Device [NASA] (NASA) ... SID
Shuttle Interface Equipment [NASA] (NASA) ... SIE
Shuttle Interface Simulator [NASA] (NASA) ... SIS
Shuttle Interface Test [NASA] (NASA) ... SIT
Shuttle Interface Verification Equipment [NASA] (NASA) ... SIVE
Shuttle Inventory Management System [NASA] (NASA) ... SIMS
Shuttle Landing Facility [NASA] (MCD) ... SLF
Shuttle Launch Center [Vandenberg Air Force Base, CA] [NASA] ... SLC
Shuttle Launch Support System (MCD) ... SLSS
Shuttle Launched Research Vehicle [NASA] (NASA) ... SLRV
Shuttle Logistics Support Aircraft (MCD) ... SLSA
Shuttle Loop Transit [NASA] ... SLT
Shuttle Main Propulsion Test (SSD) ... SMPT
Shuttle Main Propulsion Test Requirement Board [NASA] (MCD) ... SMPTRB
Shuttle Management [Kennedy Space Center] [NASA] (NASA) ... SM
Shuttle Master Verification Plan [NASA] (NASA) ... SMVP
Shuttle Master Verification Requirements Document [NASA] (NASA) ... SMVRD
Shuttle Meeting Action - Item Review Tracking [NASA] (NASA) ... SMART
Shuttle Mission Control Center [NASA] (NASA) ... SMCC
Shuttle Mission Engineering Simulator [NASA] (NASA) ... SMES
Shuttle Mission Evaluation Simulation [NASA] (NASA) ... SMES
Shuttle Mission Simulator [NASA] (NASA) ... SMS
Shuttle Mission Simulator Computer Complex [NASA] (MCD) ... SMSCC
Shuttle Model Test and Analysis System [NASA] (NASA) ... SMTAS
Shuttle Multispectral Infrared Radiometer [NASA] (GFGA) ... SMIR
Shuttle Multispectral Infrared Radiometer [NASA] ... SMIRR
Shuttle Operational Capability Assessment Report [NASA] (MCD) ... SOCAR
Shuttle Operational Data (MCD) ... SOD
Shuttle [or Spacecraft] Operational Data Book [NASA] ... SODB
Shuttle Operational Data System [NASA] (MCD) ... SODS
Shuttle Operations and Planning Center [NASA] (MCD) ... SOPC
Shuttle Operations Automated Reporting System [NASA] (NASA) ... SOARS
Shuttle Operations Planning Complex ... SOPC
Shuttle Orbital Application [NASA] ... SOA
Shuttle Orbital Applications and Requirements [NASA] ... SOAR
Shuttle Orbiter Medical System (MCD) ... SOMS
Shuttle Orbit-Injection Propulsion System Analysis [NASA] ... SOPSA
Shuttle Pallet Satellite [NASA] ... SPAS
Shuttle Payload Accommodation Document [NASA] (MCD) ... SPAD
Shuttle/Payload Contamination Evaluation Program (MCD) ... SPACE
Shuttle/Payload Integration Activities Plan (NASA) ... SPIAP

Shuttle Payload Integration and Development Program Office [NASA] ... SPIDO
Shuttle Payload Integration and Development Program Office [Johnson Space Center] (NASA) ... SPIDPO
Shuttle Payload Integration Facility [NASA] (MCD) ... SPIF
Shuttle Payload Operations Contractor (NASA) ... SPOC
Shuttle Payload Opportunity Carrier ... SPOC
Shuttle Payload Vertical Processing Facility [NASA] (MCD) ... SPVPF
Shuttle Pin Clutch ... SPC
Shuttle Portable Onboard Computer [NASA] ... SPOC
Shuttle Preferred Pyrotechnic Items List [NASA] (NASA) ... SPPIL
Shuttle Problem Action [or Analysis] Data System [NASA] (NASA) ... SPADS
Shuttle Procedures Simulator [NASA] (NASA) ... SPS
Shuttle Processing Contractor [NASA] ... SPC
Shuttle Program Data Management System [NASA] (SSD) ... SPDMS
Shuttle Program Implementation Instruction [NASA] (NASA) ... SPII
Shuttle Program Information Management System [NASA] ... SPIMS
Shuttle Project Notice [Kennedy Space Center] [NASA] (NASA) ... SPN
Shuttle Project Office [NASA] (KSC) ... SPO
Shuttle Projects - Air Force Liaison Office [Kennedy Space Center] [NASA] (NASA) ... SP-AF
Shuttle Projects - Flight and Ground Systems Office [Kennedy Space Center] [NASA] (NASA) ... SP-FGS
Shuttle Projects - Integrated Logistics Support [Kennedy Space Center] [NASA] (NASA) ... SP-ILS
Shuttle Projects - Logistics Management Office [NASA] (GFGA) ... SP-LMO
Shuttle Projects - Management Planning and Control Office [Kennedy Space Center] [NASA] (NASA) ... SP-MPC
Shuttle Projects Office [Kennedy Space Center] [NASA] (NASA) ... SP
Shuttle Projects - Off-Site Offices [NASA] (GFGA) ... SP-OSO
Shuttle Projects - Operations Planning and Integration [NASA] (GFGA) ... SP-OPI
Shuttle Projects - Operations Planning Office [Kennedy Space Center] [NASA] (NASA) ... SP-OPN
Shuttle Projects - Payload Integration Office [Kennedy Space Center] [NASA] (NASA) ... SP-PAY
Shuttle Projects - Performance Management Systems Office [NASA] (GFGA) ... SP-PMS
Shuttle Projects - Program Control Office [NASA] (GFGA) ... SP-PCO
Shuttle Projects - Project Assessment and Integration Staff [NASA] (GFGA) ... SP-PAI
Shuttle Projects - Site Management Office [NASA] (GFGA) ... SP-SMO
Shuttle Radar Topography Mission [NASA] ... SRTM
Shuttle Range Safety System [NASA] (NASA) ... SRSS
Shuttle Refurbish Facility [NASA] (NASA) ... SRF
Shuttle Remote Manipulator System (SSD) ... SRMS
Shuttle Requirements Definition [NASA] (NASA) ... SRD
Shuttle Requirements Document [NASA] (NASA) ... SRD
Shuttle Requirements Review [NASA] (MCD) ... SRR
Shuttle Requirements Traceability [NASA] (MCD) ... SRT
Shuttle SBUV [Solar Backscatter Ultraviolet] (USDC) ... SSBUV
Shuttle SBUV [Solar Backscatter Ultraviolet] [Marine science] (OSRA) ... SSBUV
Shuttle Service and Access Tower [NASA] (NASA) ... SSAT
Shuttle Simulation Aircraft [NASA] (NASA) ... SSA
Shuttle Solar Backscatter Ultraviolet Instrument (MCD) ... SSBUV
Shuttle Stowage Installation Drawing (NASA) ... SSID
Shuttle Student Involvement Project [NASA] ... SSIP
Shuttle Support Group (MCD) ... SSG
Shuttle System [NASA] (MCD) ... SS
Shuttle System Commodity List [NASA] ... SSCL
Shuttle System Commonality List [NASA] (NASA) ... SSCL
Shuttle System Contractor [NASA] (NASA) ... SSC
Shuttle System Integrated Test Plan [NASA] (NASA) ... SSITP
Shuttle System Interface Block Diagram [NASA] (NASA) ... SSIBD
Shuttle System Payload Data [NASA] (NASA) ... SSPD
Shuttle System Payload Definition Study [NASA] (NASA) ... SSPD
Shuttle System Payload Description [NASA] (NASA) ... SSPD
Shuttle Technology Panel [NASA] ... STP
Shuttle Test Director [NASA] (MCD) ... STD
Shuttle Test Group [NASA] (NASA) ... STSG
Shuttle Test Station (NASA) ... STS
Shuttle Training Aircraft [NASA] ... STA
Shuttle Transportation System (MCD) ... STS
Shuttle Transportation Systems Operations Program Office [Johnson Space Center] (NASA) ... STSOPO
Shuttle Turnaround Analysis Group [NASA] (NASA) ... STAG
Shuttle Turnaround Analysis Report [NASA] (NASA) ... STAR
Shuttle Unique Equipment (MCD) ... SUE
Shuttle Uplink Text and Graphics Scanner (NASA) ... SUTAGS
Shuttle Upper-Atmosphere Mass Spectrometer [NASA] (MCD) ... SUMS
Shuttle Upper-Stage System (SSD) ... SUSS
Shuttle Users Review and Evaluation [NASA] (NASA) ... SURE
Shuttle Vehicle [NASA] (NASA) ... SV
Shuttle Vehicle Assembly and Checkout [NASA] (GFGA) ... SVAC
Shuttle Vehicle Assembly Building [NASA] (NASA) ... SVAB
Shuttle Vehicle Booster [NASA] (NASA) ... SVB
Shuttle Versus Current Expendable Launch Vehicle [NASA] (KSC) ... SHVSCE
Shuttle Versus New Expendable Launch Vehicle [NASA] (KSC) ... SHVSNE
Shuttle Working Group [NASA] (NASA) ... SWG
Shuttle-Derived Launch Vehicle [NASA] (SSD) ... SDLV
Shuttle-Pointed Autonomous Research Tool for Astronomy [NASA] ... SPARTAN
Shuyak Island [Alaska] [Seismograph station code, US Geological Survey] (SEIS) ... SHU
Si De Ka Quarterly [Ann Arbor, MI] [A publication] (DLA) ... SDK
SI Diamond Technology [Commercial firm Associated Press] (SAG) ... SI Diam
SI Diamond Technology [Commercial firm NASDAQ symbol] (SAG) ... SIDT

S.I. Handling Sys [*NASDAQ symbol*] (TTSB) .... SIHS
SI Handling Systems [*Associated Press*] (SAG) .... SI Hand
SI Handling Systems, Inc. [*NASDAQ symbol*] (NQ) .... SIHS
Si Non Valeat [*If It Is Not Effective*] [*Pharmacy*] (ROG) .... SI N VAL
Si Non Valeat [*If It Is Not Effective*] [*Pharmacy*] .... Si Non Val
Si Opus Sit [*If Needed*] [*Pharmacy*] .... S Op S
Si Opus Sit [*If There Be Occasion*] [*Pharmacy*] (ROG) .... SI OP SIT
Si Opus Sit [*If Needed*] [*Pharmacy*] .... SOS
SI Technologies, Inc. [*Associated Press*] (SAG) .... SI Tech
SI Technologies, Inc. [*NASDAQ symbol*] (SAG) .... SISI
Si Vales, Bene Est; Ego Quoque Valeo [*I Hope You're Well; I Am*] [*Latin*] .... SVBEEQV
Si Vires Permittant [*If the Strength Will Bear It*] [*Pharmacy*] (ROG) .... SI VIR PERM
Si Vires Permittant [*If the Strength Will Bear It*] [*Pharmacy*] (ROG) .... VIR
SIA [*Semiconductor Industry Association*] **Statistical Review** [*A publication*] (EAAP) .... SSR
SIAI-Marchetti SpA [*Italy ICAO aircraft manufacturer identifier*] (ICAO) .... SM
Sialagogue [*Promoting Flow of Saliva*] [*Medicine*] (ROG) .... SIAL
Sialic Acid [*Biochemistry*] .... SIA
Sialodacryoadenitis [*Virology*] .... SDAV
Sialyltransferase Activity [*Medicine*] .... STA
Siam .... SM
Siam, Gulf of [*MARC geographic area code Library of Congress*] (LCCP) .... af----
SIAM [*Society for Industrial and Applied Mathematics*] **Institute for Mathematics and Society** .... SIMS
SIAM Review [*A publication*] (BRI) .... SIAM Rev
SIAMA [*Society for Interest of Active Missionaries Abroad*] **USA, Inc.** [*Defunct*] (EA) .... SUSAI
Siamese Breeders of America [*Later, GSCC*] (EA) .... SBA
Siamese Cat Society of America (EA) .... SCSA
Sian [*Republic of China*] [*Seismograph station code, US Geological Survey Closed*] (SEIS) .... SIA
Sian [*China*] [*Airport symbol*] (AD) .... SIA
Sian [*Republic of China*] [*Seismograph station code, US Geological Survey*] (SEIS) .... SPE
Siassi [*Papua New Guinea*] [*Airport symbol*] (OAG) .... SSS
Siata/Fiat 8V Register (EA) .... SFER
Sibambe [*Ecuador*] [*ICAO location identifier*] (ICLI) .... SESB
Sibasa [*South Africa*] [*Airport symbol*] (OAG) .... SBC
Siberia [*MARC geographic area code Library of Congress*] (LCCP) .... e-urs-
Siberia (VRA) .... Sib
Siberia .... SIB
Siberia Commodity Exchange [*Russian Federation*] (EY) .... SCE
Siberian Flood Basalt Province [*Geology*] .... SFBP
Siberian Husky Club of America (EA) .... SHCA
Siberian Husky Eye Anomaly Research Committee (EA) .... SearcH
Sibi [*Pakistan*] [*ICAO location identifier*] (ICLI) .... OPSB
SIBIA Neurosciences [*NASDAQ symbol*] (TTSB) .... SIBI
SIBIA Neurosciences, Inc. [*NASDAQ symbol*] (SAG) .... SIBI
SIBIA Neurosciences, Inc. [*Associated Press*] (SAG) .... SIBIA
Sibiti [*Congo*] [*ICAO location identifier*] (ICLI) .... FCBS
Sibiti [*Congo*] [*Airport symbol*] (OAG) .... SIB
Sibiu [*Romania*] [*Airport symbol*] (OAG) .... SBZ
Sibiu/Turnisor [*Romania*] [*ICAO location identifier*] (ICLI) .... LRSB
Sibley Gazette and Tribune, Sibley, IA [*Library symbol*] [*Library of Congress*] (LCLS) .... IaSibG
Sibley, IA [*FM radio station call letters*] (RBYB) .... KAJQ
Sibley-Lehninger [*Unit*] (MAE) .... SL
Sibling .... Sib
Sibling (DOG) .... sib
Sibling Relationship (DAVI) .... sib-ship
Siblings (DAVI) .... SS
Siblings for Significant Change (EA) .... SSC
Siblings Helping Persons with Autism through Resources and Energy (MEDA) .... SHARE
Siblings of Disabled Children (EA) .... SODC
Siblings of Sudden Infant Death Syndrome Victims [*Medicine*] .... SSIDS
Sibola Mines Ltd. [*Vancouver Stock Exchange symbol*] .... SIB
Sibolga/Pinang Sori [*Indonesia*] [*ICAO location identifier*] (ICLI) .... WIMS
Sibu [*Malaysia*] [*Airport symbol*] (OAG) .... SBW
Sibu [*Malaysia*] [*ICAO location identifier*] (ICLI) .... WBGS
Sibylline Oracles (BJA) .... SibOr
Sibylline Oracles (Pseudepigrapha) (BJA) .... OrSibyll
Sibyllines (BJA) .... Sib
Sic Porro [*So Forth*] [*Latin*] .... SP
Sicanna Industries Ltd. [*Vancouver Stock Exchange symbol*] .... SA
Sicardus Fabri de Vauro [*Deceased, 1323*] [*Authority cited in pre-1607 legal work*] (DSA) .... S de V
Sicasica [*Bolivia*] [*Seismograph station code, US Geological Survey Closed*] (SEIS) .... SCS
Siccus [*Dry*] [*Latin*] (ADA) .... SIC
Si-Chang Flying Service Co. Ltd. [*Thailand*] [*ICAO designator*] (FAAC) .... SCR
Sicherheitsdienst [*Police Duty*] [*NAZI Germany*] .... SD
Sicherheitspolizei [*Security Police*] [*NAZI*] (BJA) .... SIPO
Sichuan Airlines [*China*] [*ICAO designator*] (FAAC) .... CSC
Sicily (VRA) .... Sic
Sicily .... SIC
Sick .... S
Sick .... SK
Sick Bay .... SB
Sick Bay Attendant [*Navy*] .... SBA
Sick Bay Chief Petty Officer [*British military*] (DMA) .... SBCPO
Sick Building Syndrome [*Medicine*] .... SBS
Sick Call [*Medicine*] (DMAA) .... SC
Sick in Hospital .... SH
Sick in Quarters .... SIQ
Sick Kids Need Involved People (EA) .... SKIP
Sick Leave (AFM) .... SL
Sick Officer Quarters .... SOQ
Sick Quarters [*Navy British*] .... SQ
Sick Sinus Syndrome [*Medicine*] .... SSS
Sickels' Opinions of the New York Attorneys-General [*A publication*] (DLA) .... Sick Op
Sickels' Reports [*46-85 New York*] [*A publication*] (DLA) .... Sick
Sickels' United States Mining Laws and Decisions [*A publication*] (DLA) .... Sick Min Dec
Sickle Cell [*Medicine*] .... SC
Sickle Cell Anemia [*Medicine*] .... SCA
Sickle Cell Anemia Test [*Medicine*] (AAMN) .... SCAT
Sickle Cell Disease [*Medicine*] .... SCD
Sickle Cell Disease Association of America [*Formerly the National Association for Sickle Cell Disease (NASCD)*] (PAZ) .... SCDAA
Sickle Cell Disease Foundation of Greater New York (EA) .... SCDFGNY
Sickle Cell Hemoglobin D [*Disease*] [*Medicine*] .... S-D
Sickle Cell Trait (AAMN) .... SCT
Sickle Cells [*Hematology*] (DAVI) .... SICK
Sickle Forgers' Trade Society [*A union*] [*British*] .... SFTS
Sickle Grinders' Association [*A union*] [*British*] .... SGA
Sickle Hemoglobin [*Screen*] [*Hematology*] (DAVI) .... SHb
Sickle Red Blood Cells [*Hematology*] (DAVI) .... SRBC
Sickle-Cell Chronic Lung Disease [*Medicine*] (DMAA) .... SCLD
Sickle-Cell Crisis [*Hematology*] (DAVI) .... SCC
Sickle-Cell Hemoglobin C [*Disease*] (DAVI) .... S-C
Sickle-Cell Thalassemia [*Hematology*] (DAVI) .... S-T
Sickness and Accident [*Insurance*] .... S & A
Sickness due to Misconduct [*Military*] (DNAB) .... SKMC
Sickness Impact Profile [*National Institutes of Health*] .... SIP
Sico, Inc. [*Toronto Stock Exchange symbol*] .... SIC
Sicula Oceanicas SA [*Shipping line*] [*Italy*] .... SIOSA
Sida [*Iceland*] [*Seismograph station code, US Geological Survey*] (SEIS) .... SID
Sidamo [*MARC language code Library of Congress*] (LCCP) .... sid
Sidbec-Dosco Ltd./Ltee., Montreal, Quebec [*Library symbol National Library of Canada*] (NLC) .... QMSDL
Sidbec-Dosco Ltd., Montreal, PQ, Canada [*Library symbol Library of Congress*] (LCLS) .... CaQMSDL
Side .... S
Side and Back Rack System (PDAA) .... SBRS
Side and Face Milling [*Cutter*] (IAA) .... SAF
Side Buoyancy Tank .... SBT
Side by Side (AAG) .... SS
Side Cabin .... SC
Side Car [*Army*] .... Sc
Side Compartment [*Automotive engineering*] .... S/COMPT
Side Contact [*Valves*] (DEN) .... SC
Side Control Valves .... SCV
Side Cutting Edge Angle (IAA) .... SCEA
Side Deck .... SD
Side Detection System [*Delco*] (RDA) .... SDS
Side Discharge Loader [*Mining*] .... SDL
Side Door .... SD
Side Door Trim [*Automotive engineering*] .... SDT
Side Drum .... SD
Side Effect [*Medicine*] .... SE
Side Effects Questionnaire [*Medicine*] (DMAA) .... SEQ
Side Entry Goniometer .... SEG
Side Frequency (DEN) .... SF
Side Impact Protection [*Automotive safety system*] (PS) .... SIP
Side Judge [*Football*] .... SJ
Side Lay [*Printing machine*] (DGA) .... S/L
Side Line Indexing Method [*Spectrometry*] .... SLIM
Side Load (AAG) .... SL
Side Load Arresting Mechanism (KSC) .... SLAM
Side Loadable Warping Tug [*Navy*] (CAAL) .... SLWT
Side Lobe [*Entomology*] .... SIDLOB
Side Looking Modular Multi-Mission RADAR (PDAA) .... SLAMMR
Side Note .... SN
Side Panel [*Automotive engineering*] .... S/PNL
Side Rails [*On a bed*] [*Medicine*] .... SR
Side Rails Up [*On a bed*] (DAVI) .... SRU
Side Scatter .... SS
Side Seam .... SS
Side Seams Closed [*Freight*] .... SD SMS CLSD
Side Seams Not Closed [*Freight*] .... S SMS N CLSD
Side Shield [*Automotive engineering*] .... S/SHLD
Side Signal (IAA) .... S
Side Slip (MCD) .... SS
Side Tank [*on a ship*] (DS) .... SDT
Side Tank [*on a ship*] (DS) .... ST
Side to Side .... SS
Side Transfer Optimum Warehousing .... STOW
Side Upset Jaw (MSA) .... SUJ
Side Valve [*Automotive engineering*] .... SV
Side View (MSA) .... SV
Side Water Depth .... SWD
Side Wheel (DS) .... SDW
Side Wheel .... SW
Side-Angle-Side (Rule) [*Geometry*] .... SAS
Side-Arm Controller [*Aviation*] .... SAC
Sideband [*Radio frequency*] (AAG) .... SB
Sideband Address (PCM) .... SBA

Sideband Intermediate Frequency Communications System (AAG) ... SIFCS
Sidebands Only (IAA) ... SBO
Sidebrazed Ceramic DIP [*Dual In-line Package*] (CDE) ... CDIP
Side-Chain Liquid Crystalline Polymer [*Organic chemistry*] ... SCLCP
Side-Effects Expectancy Questionnaire [*Psychology*] ... SEEQ
Side-Impact Dummy [*Collision testing device*] ... SID
Side-Impact Finite Element Model [*Automotive safety*] [*Computer-assisted design*] ... SIFEM
Side-Impact Protection System [*Automotive safety*] ... SIPS
Sidelever [*Rifles*] (DICI) ... S/L
Sidell District Library, Sidell, IL [*Library symbol Library of Congress*] (LCLS) ... ISid
Sidelobe (CAAL) ... SL
Side-Lobe Blanking [*RADAR*] ... SLB
Sidelobe Blanking Indicator ... SLBI
Side-Lobe Cancellation [*RADAR*] ... SLC
Side-Lobe Clutter ... SLC
Sidelobe Pulse Rejection [*Military*] (CAAL) ... SLPR
Side-Lobe Suppression RADAR ... SLS
Side-Looking Aerial [*or Airborne*] **RADAR** [*Military*] ... SLAR
Side-Looking Airborne Radar [*Marine science*] (OSRA) ... SLAR
Side-Looking Air-to-Ground [*RADAR*] ... SLAG
Side-Looking Coherent All-Range Focused ... SCARF
Side-Looking LASER Altimeter (RDA) ... SLA
Side-Looking Mapping RADAR ... SMR
Side-Looking RADAR (AFM) ... SLR
Side-Looking RADAR System ... SRS
Side-Looking SONAR ... SLS
Sidepull [*Bicycle*] (DICI) ... SP
Sideradougou [*Burkina Faso*] [*ICAO location identifier*] (ICLI) ... DHOS
Sidereal Hour Angle ... SHA
Sidereal Polar Axis Celestial Equipment ... SPACE
Siderfin's King's Bench Reports [*82 English Reprint*] [*A publication*] (DLA) ... Sid
Siderfin's King's Bench Reports [*82 English Reprint*] [*A publication*] (DLA) ... Sid (Eng)
Sideroblast [*Hematology*] (AAMN) ... SB
Sideroblastic Anemia [*Hematology*] ... SA
Siderocyte [*Hematology*] (AAMN) ... S
Siderocytes [*In Differential*] [*Hematology*] (DAVI) ... SIDER
Siderphile Superheavy Element [*Physics*] ... SHE
Siderurgica del Orinoco [*Government steel company*] [*Venezuela*] ... SIDOR
Side-Saddle Association [*British*] (DBA) ... SSA
Side-Stick Control System ... SSCS
Side-Stick Controller ... SSC
Sidestream Smoke [*from cigarettes*] ... SS
Side-Support Jack ... SSJ
Sidetone [*Telecommunications*] (TEL) ... ST
Sidetone Objective Loudness Rating [*of telephone connections*] (IEEE) ... SOLR
Sidetone Path Loss [*Telecommunications*] (TEL) ... STPL
Sidetone Reduction [*Telecommunications*] (TEL) ... STR
Side-to-Side [*Anastomosis*] [*Cardiology*] (DAVI) ... SS
Side-to-Side Anastamosis [*Medicine*] (CPH) ... SSA
Side-to-Side Portacaval Shunt [*Medicine*] (DMAA) ... SSPS
Sidewall Indentation [*Tire manufacturing*] ... SWI
Sideward (WGA) ... SWD
Sideway Force Coefficient Routine Investigating Machine [*Department of Transport*] [*British*] ... SCRIM
Sideways-Looking Airborne Multi-Mode Radar (DOMA) ... SLAMMR
Sideways-Spinning Tube [*Spectrometry*] ... SST
Sidewinder [*Naval ordnance*] ... SIWDR
Sidewinder ... SW
Sidewinder Acquisition Track (IEEE) ... SWAT
Sidewinder Angle Tracking [*Missiles*] (NG) ... SWAT
Sidewinder Control System (DWSG) ... SCS
Sidewinder Expanded Acquisition Mode (MCD) ... SEAM
Sidewinder Generator Unit (NG) ... SGU
Sidfin Air Ltd. [*Zambia*] [*ICAO designator*] (FAAC) ... SID
Sidi Bel Abbes [*Algeria*] [*ICAO location identifier*] (ICLI) ... DAOS
Sidi Hakoma Tuff [*Geology*] ... SHT
Sidi Ifni [*Morocco*] [*ICAO location identifier*] (ICLI) ... GMMF
Sidi Ifni [*Morocco*] [*Airport symbol*] (AD) ... SII
Sidi Slimane [*Morocco*] [*ICAO location identifier*] (ICLI) ... GMSL
Sidi-Bou-Said [*Tunisia*] [*Seismograph station code, US Geological Survey*] (SEIS) ... SBS
Siding (AAG) ... SDG
Siding ... SIDE
Sidley & Austin, Chicago, IL [*OCLC symbol*] (OCLC) ... IFI
Sidley and Austin Library, Chicago, IL [*Library symbol Library of Congress*] (LCLS) ... ICSA
Sidley & Austin, Washington, DC [*Library symbol*] [*Library of Congress*] (LCLS) ... DSA
Sidney [*Montana*] [*Airport symbol*] (OAG) ... SDY
Sidney [*Nebraska*] [*Airport symbol*] (OAG) ... SNY
Sidney [*New York*] [*Airport symbol*] (OAG) ... SXY
Sidney Argus-Herald, Sidney, IA [*Library symbol*] [*Library of Congress*] (LCLS) ... IaSidAH
Sidney Community Library, Sidney, IL [*Library symbol Library of Congress*] (LCLS) ... ISidn
Sidney, MT [*FM radio station call letters*] (RBYB) ... KTHC
Sidney, MT [*Location identifier FAA*] (FAAL) ... SDY
Sidney, NE [*AM radio station call letters*] ... KSID
Sidney, NE [*FM radio station call letters*] ... KSID-FM
Sidney New York Historical Society, Sidney, NY [*Library symbol*] [*Library of Congress*] (LCLS) ... NSidHi
Sidney, NY [*AM radio station call letters*] ... WCDO
Sidney, NY [*FM radio station call letters*] ... WCDO-FM
Sidney, OH [*AM radio station call letters*] ... WMVR
Sidney, OH [*FM radio station call letters*] ... WMVR-FM
Sidney on Government [*A publication*] (DLA) ... Sid Gov
Sidney Public Library, Sidney, MT [*Library symbol*] [*Library of Congress*] (LCLS) ... MtSid
Sidney Public Library, Sidney, NE [*Library symbol Library of Congress*] (LCLS) ... NbSi
Sidney Township Public Library, Batawa, Ontario [*Library symbol National Library of Canada*] (BIB) ... OBS
Sido, Robert F., Edwardsville IL [*STAC*] ... SRF
Sidoktaya [*Myanmar*] [*ICAO location identifier*] (ICLI) ... VBSO
Sidonius Apollinaris [*Fifth century AD*] [*Classical studies*] (OCD) ... Sid Apoll
SIDPERS [*Standard Installation/Division Personnel System*] **Authorized Strength File** [*Military*] (AABC) ... SASF
SIDPERS [*Standard Installation/Division Personnel System*] **Interface Branch** [*Military*] (INF) ... SIB
SIDPERS [*Standard Installation/Division Personnel System*] **Organization Master File** [*Military*] (AABC) ... SOMF
SIDPERS [*Standard Installation/Division Personnel System*] **Personnel File** [*Military*] (AABC) ... SPF
Sidrah (BJA) ... S
Siebel Systems, Inc. [*NASDAQ symbol*] (SAG) ... SEBL
Siebel Systems, Inc. [*Associated Press*] (SAG) ... SiebelS
Siebelwerke ATG GmbH [*Germany ICAO aircraft manufacturer identifier*] (ICAO) ... LF
Siebelwerke ATG GmbH [*Germany ICAO aircraft manufacturer identifier*] (ICAO) ... SG
Siebert Financial Corp. [*NASDAQ symbol*] (SAG) ... SIEB
Siebert Financial Corp. [*Associated Press*] (SAG) ... Siebert
Siebert Telecommunications Consulting, Inc. [*Cincinnati, OH*] [*Telecommunications*] (TSSD) ... STCI
Siecle [*Century*] [*French*] ... S
Siecor Corp., Technical Information Center, Hickory, NC [*Library symbol Library of Congress*] (LCLS) ... NcHyS
Siecor Electro-Optic Products [*Research Triangle Park, NC*] (TSSD) ... SEOP
Siegel Scale of Support for Innovation (DMAA) ... SSSI
Siegenberg [*Germany ICAO location identifier*] (ICLI) ... EDAV
Siegerland [*Germany ICAO location identifier*] (ICLI) ... EDKS
Siegfried AG [*Switzerland*] [*Research code symbol*] ... Ba
Siegfried AG [*Switzerland*] [*Research code symbol*] ... D
Siegfried AG [*Switzerland*] [*Research code symbol*] ... SA
Siegfried AG [*Switzerland*] [*Research code symbol*] ... SD
Siem Reap [*Cambodia*] [*Airport symbol*] (AD) ... REP
Siemens [*Symbol*] [*SI unit of electric conductance*] ... S
Siemens [*Unit of electric conductance*] ... Sie
Siemens Agronaut Reactor [*Germany*] ... SAR
Siemens Computer (NITA) ... SICOMP
Siemens Metal Oxide Varistor (IAA) ... SIOV
Siemens per Meter ... S/M
Siemens Unit ... SU
Siemens-Schuckert Werke [*Germany*] ... SSW
Siemont Resources, Inc. [*Vancouver Stock Exchange symbol*] ... SET
Siem-Reap [*Cambodia*] [*ICAO location identifier*] (ICLI) ... VDSR
Siena [*Italy ICAO location identifier*] (ICLI) ... LIQS
Siena [*Italy*] [*Seismograph station code, US Geological Survey*] (SEIS) ... SIE
Siena College, Loudonville, NY [*Library symbol Library of Congress*] (LCLS) ... NLouvS
Siena College, Memphis, TN [*Library symbol Library of Congress*] (LCLS) ... TMS
Siena Heights College [*Adrian, MI*] ... SHC
Siena Heights College (GAGS) ... Siena Heights C
Siena Heights College, Adrian, MI [*OCLC symbol*] (OCLC) ... EEH
Siena Heights College, Adrian, MI [*Library symbol Library of Congress*] (LCLS) ... MiAdS
Sienna [*Philately*] ... sien
Sienna Resources Ltd. [*Toronto Stock Exchange symbol*] ... SNN
Sierra [*Phonetic alphabet*] [*International*] (DSUE) ... S
Sierra ... SA
Sierra Army Depot [*California*] (AABC) ... SIAD
Sierra Carriers and Mountaineering Group (EA) ... SCMG
Sierra Club (EA) ... SC
Sierra Club and Friends of the Earth [*Marine science*] (MSC) ... SC & FE
Sierra Club Legal Defense Fund (EA) ... SCLDF
Sierra Club Radioactive Waste Campaign [*Later, RWC*] (EA) ... SCRWC
Sierra Club, San Francisco, CA [*Library symbol Library of Congress*] (LCLS) ... CSfSC
Sierra College, Rocklin, CA [*Library symbol Library of Congress*] (LCLS) ... CRocS
Sierra Conservation Center, Jamestown, CA [*Library symbol Library of Congress*] (LCLS) ... CJaS
Sierra Cooperative Pilot Project [*Department of the Interior*] ... SCPP
Sierra County Free Library, Downieville, CA [*Library symbol Library of Congress*] (LCLS) ... CDv
Sierra Express, Inc. [*ICAO designator*] (FAAC) ... SIE
Sierra Foothill Winery Association (EA) ... SFWA
Sierra Grande [*Argentina ICAO location identifier*] (ICLI) ... SAVS
Sierra Grande [*Argentina*] [*Airport symbol*] (OAG) ... SGV
Sierra Health Services [*NYSE symbol*] (TTSB) ... SIE
Sierra Health Services, Inc. [*NYSE symbol*] (SAG) ... SIE
Sierra Health Services, Inc. [*Associated Press*] (SAG) ... SierHS
Sierra Home Services [*NASDAQ symbol*] (SAG) ... SHSC
Sierra Home Services [*Commercial firm Associated Press*] (SAG) ... SieraHm
Sierra Home Services [*Commercial firm Associated Press*] (SAG) ... SierH
Sierra Home Svc Cos. [*NASDAQ symbol*] (TTSB) ... SHSC
Sierra Leone [*Aircraft nationality and registration mark*] (FAAC) ... 9L
Sierra Leone [*MARC geographic area code Library of Congress*] (LCCP) ... f-sl--

Sierra Leone [*MARC country of publication code Library of Congress*] (LCCP) ... sl
Sierra Leone [*ANSI two-letter standard code*] (CNC) ... SL
Sierra Leone [*ANSI three-letter standard code*] (CNC) ... SLE
Sierra Leone [*International vehicle registration*] (ODBW) ... WAL
Sierra Leone Airlines ... SLA
Sierra Leone Airways [*ICAO designator*] (AD) ... LJ
Sierra Leone Alliance Movement (PD) ... SLAM
Sierra Leone Broadcasting Service ... SLBS
Sierra Leone Council of Labour ... SLCL
Sierra Leone Democratic Party [*Political party*] (EY) ... SLDP
Sierra Leone Full Court Reports [*A publication*] (DLA) ... SLFC
Sierra Leone Law Recorder [*A publication*] (DLA) ... SLLR
Sierra Leone Organization Society ... SLOS
Sierra Leone People's Party [*Political party*] (PD) ... SLPP
Sierra Leone Railway (MHDB) ... SLR
Sierra Leone Royal Artillery [*British military*] (DMA) ... SLRA
Sierra Leone Students Union of the Americas (EA) ... SaLSUA
Sierra Madre Free Public Library, Sierra Madre, CA [*Library symbol Library of Congress*] (LCLS) ... CSie
Sierra Madre Resources [*Vancouver Stock Exchange symbol*] ... SQC
Sierra National Airlines [*Sierra Leone*] [*ICAO designator*] (FAAC) ... SLA
[*The*] **Sierra Network** [*Computer science*] ... TSN
Sierra Nevada (FAAC) ... SIERNEV
Sierra Nevada Batholith [*Geology*] ... SNB
Sierra Nevada Fault [*Geology*] ... SNF
Sierra Nevada Gold [*Vancouver Stock Exchange symbol*] ... SDD
Sierra On-Line [*NASDAQ symbol*] (TTSB) ... SIER
Sierra On-Line, Inc. [*NASDAQ symbol*] (CTT) ... SIER
Sierra On-Line, Inc. [*Associated Press*] (SAG) ... SierOn
Sierra Pac Pw [*Associated Press*] (SAG) ... SierraP
Sierra Pac Pw [*NYSE symbol*] (SAG) ... SRP
Sierra Pacific Airlines [*ICAO designator*] (FAAC) ... SPA
Sierra Pacific Resources [*Associated Press*] (SAG) ... SierPac
Sierra Pacific Resources [*NYSE symbol*] (SPSG) ... SRP
Sierra Railroad Co. [*AAR code*] ... SERA
Sierra Railroad Co. (IIA) ... SR
Sierra Research Corp., Buffalo, NY [*Library symbol Library of Congress*] (LCLS) ... NBuSR
Sierra Semiconductor [*NASDAQ symbol*] (SPSG) ... SERA
Sierra Semiconductor Corp. [*Associated Press*] (SAG) ... SierraSem
Sierra Semiconductor Corp. [*Associated Press*] (SAG) ... SierSm
Sierra Tahoe Bancorp [*Associated Press*] (SAG) ... SierTah
Sierra Tahoe Bancorp [*NASDAQ symbol*] (SAG) ... STBS
Sierra Vista, AZ [*FM radio station call letters*] ... KKYZ
Sierra Vista, AZ [*AM radio station call letters*] (RBYB) ... KLTW-AM
Sierra Vista, AZ [*AM radio station call letters*] ... KNXN
Sierra Vista, AZ [*AM radio station call letters*] ... KTAN
Sierra Vista, AZ [*FM radio station call letters*] ... KZMK
Sierra Vista Public Library, Sierra Vista, AZ [*Library symbol*] [*Library of Congress*] (LCLS) ... AzSv
SierraWest Bancorp [*Associated Press*] (SAG) ... SierWst
SierraWest Bancorp [*NASDAQ symbol*] (SAG) ... SWBS
Sieve (NASA) ... SIV
Sieve ... SV
Sieve Pore [*Botany*] ... SP
Sievert [*SI unit for radioactive dose equivalent*] ... Sv
Sieving Coefficient [*Laboratory science*] (DAVI) ... SC
Sieving Coefficient for Sodium [*Organic chemistry*] (DAVI) ... SC_{Na}
SIFCO Indus [*AMEX symbol*] (TTSB) ... SIF
SIFCO Industries, Inc. [*AMEX symbol*] (SPSG) ... SIF
SIFCO Industries, Inc. [*Associated Press*] (SAG) ... Sifco
Sifra on Leviticus [*A publication*] (BJA) ... SLv
Sifre on Deuteronomy [*A publication*] (BJA) ... SDt
Sifre on Numbers (BJA) ... SNu
Sifre Zuta on Numbers (BJA) ... SZutNu
Sifrei Deuteronomy (BJA) ... SifDeut
Sifrei Numbers (BJA) ... SifNum
Sifrei Zuta (BJA) ... SifZut
Sifting of Information for Technology of Reactors [*MIT-AEC study*] ... SIFTOR
SIGCORP, Inc. [*NYSE symbol*] (TTSB) ... SIG
Sight and Sound [*A publication*] (BRI) ... Si & So
Sight Current Generator ... SCG
Sight Draft [*Business term*] ... SD
Sight Draft Bill of Lading Attached [*Business term*] ... SDBL
Sight Draft Documents Against Payment [*Business term*] ... SDDP
Sight Dullness [*on Auscultation*] [*Medicine*] (DAVI) ... M_1
Sight Enhancement, Education, and Technology ... SEETEC
Sight Erection Support ... SES
Sight Feed Valve ... SFV
Sight Fire Control ... SFC
Sight Resource [*NASDAQ symbol*] (TTSB) ... VISN
Sight Resource Wrrt [*NASDAQ symbol*] (TTSB) ... VISNZ
Sight Resources Corp. [*Associated Press*] (SAG) ... SightRes
Sight Resources Corp. [*Associated Press*] (SAG) ... StRes
Sight Resources Corp. [*NASDAQ symbol*] (SAG) ... VISN
Sight Restoration Society (EA) ... SRS
Sight, Sound, and Touch [*Ways to identify proper belt tension*] [*Automotive engineering*] ... SST
Sight Survey Unit ... SSU
Sight Switch Technology System (PDAA) ... SSTS
Sight System Passive Infrared [*Sensor*] [*Army*] ... SSPI
Sight Unit Infantry Trilux [*British*] ... SUIT
Sight Unit Small Arms Trilux [*British*] ... SUSAT
Sigi Air [*Bulgaria*] [*ICAO designator*] (FAAC) ... BGR
Sigillo Locus [*Place for the Seal*] [*Latin*] (ROG) ... SL
Sigillum [*Seal*] [*Latin*] (WGA) ... SIGILL
SIGINT/Electronic Warfare Coordination Element (MCD) ... SEWC
SIGINT Equipment Operator Simulator [*Military*] ... SEOS
SIGINT/EW [*Signal Intelligence/Electronic Warfare*] **Maintenance Trainer** [*Army*] ... SEMT
SIGINT [*Signal Intelligence*] **Operational Tasking Authority** [*Military*] ... SOTA
SIGINT [*Signal Intelligence*] **Operations Readiness Review** [*Military*] (AABC) ... SORR
SIGINT [*Signal Intelligence*] **Requirements Validation and Evaluation Subcommittee** ... SIRVES
SIGINT/SIGSEC Facilities Data Reporting System (MCD) ... SSDR
SIGINT Support Element (MCD) ... SSE
SIGINT [*Signal Intelligence*] **Support Element/Electronic Warfare Element** [*Military*] (AABC) ... SSE/EWE
SIGINT Support Plan (MCD) ... SSP
SIGINT Surveillance and Reporting System (MCD) ... SSRS
Siglufjordur [*Iceland*] [*ICAO location identifier*] (ICLI) ... BISI
Siglufjordur [*Iceland*] [*Airport symbol*] (OAG) ... SIJ
Siglum for Tablets in the Frau Professor Hilprecht Collection of Babylonian Antiquities [*Jena*] (BJA) ... HS
Sigma (NUCP) ... S
Sigma Alpha Iota [*International professional music fraternity for women*] (EA) ... SAI
Sigma Center Information Storage and Retrieval System ... SCISRS
Sigma Circuits [*NASDAQ symbol*] (TTSB) ... SIGA
Sigma Circuits, Inc. [*NASDAQ symbol*] (SAG) ... SIGA
Sigma Circuits, Inc. [*Associated Press*] (SAG) ... SigmaC
Sigma Delta Chi [*Fraternity*] (NTCM) ... SDX
Sigma Delta Epsilon, Graduate Women in Science (EA) ... SDE/GWIS
Sigma Delta Kappa [*Fraternity*] ... SDK
Sigma Designs [*NASDAQ symbol*] (TTSB) ... SIGM
Sigma Designs, Inc. [*Fremont, CA*] [*NASDAQ symbol*] (NQ) ... SIGM
Sigma Designs, Inc. [*Associated Press*] (SAG) ... SigmDg
Sigma Gamma Epsilon [*Society*] ... SGE
Sigma Immunoassay [*Test for rubella*] ... SIA
Sigma Mines (Quebec) Ltd. [*Toronto Stock Exchange symbol*] ... S
Sigma Nu [*A national fraternity*] ... SN
Sigma Phi Delta (EA) ... SPD
Sigma Reaction ... SR
Sigma Science [*Vancouver Stock Exchange symbol*] ... SCG
Sigma Security, Inc. [*Vancouver Stock Exchange symbol*] ... SGA
Sigma Tau [*Later, Tau Beta Pi Association*] ... ST
Sigma Theta Tau International Nursing Library, Indianapolis, IN [*Library symbol*] [*Library of Congress*] (LCLS) ... InISIN
Sigma Units ... SU
Sigma Xi [*Society*] ... SX
Sigma Xi Society ... SXS
Sigma-Aldrich [*NASDAQ symbol*] (TTSB) ... SIAL
Sigma-Aldrich Corp. [*NASDAQ symbol*] (NQ) ... SIAL
Sigma-Aldrich Corp. [*Associated Press*] (SAG) ... SigmAl
Sigmacom Systems [*Vancouver Stock Exchange symbol*] ... SCS
Sigmatron International [*NASDAQ symbol*] (SAG) ... SGMA
Sigmatron International [*Associated Press*] (SAG) ... Sigmatr
Sigmoid Volvulus [*Gastroenterology*] (DAVI) ... SV
Sigmoidoscope [*or Sigmoidoscopy*] [*Medicine*] (AAMN) ... SIG
Sigmoidoscopy [*Medicine*] ... sigmo
Sigmoidoscopy [*Medicine*] (DAVI) ... sigmoid
Sigmund Freud Archives (EA) ... SFA
Sign [*or Signed*] ... S
Sign (MAE) ... SG
Sign (BUR) ... SN
Sign and Display Trades Union [*British*] (BI) ... SDTU
Sign Code (IAA) ... SI
Sign Error Root Modulus Error ... SERME
Sign Extend [*Computer science*] (NHD) ... SEX
Sign Extended (IAA) ... SE
Sign Off ... S/O
Sign Off [*Computer science*] (MDG) ... S/OFF
Sign Off Brother, I've Got Mine [*Remark used by seamen who avoided risky assignments during World War II*] [*Also used as hoax by National Maritime Union for name of organization issuing pamphlet about low state of merchant marine service*] ... SOBIGM
Sign On [*Computer science*] (MDG) ... S/ON
Sign on Table (IAA) ... SNT
Sign Post ... SP
Sign Signature (AAG) ... S/S
Sign Status Matrix (GAVI) ... SSM
Signa [*Write*] [*Pharmacy*] ... S
Signa [*Write*] [*Pharmacy*] ... SIG
Signa [*Label*] [*Pharmacy*] (ROG) ... SIGN
Signa Nomine Proprio [*Label with the Proper Name*] [*Pharmacy*] ... Sig N Pro
Signa Nomine Proprio [*Label with the Proper Name*] [*Latin*] [*Pharmacy*] (DAVI) ... SIG N PRO
Signal [*Telecommunications*] (TEL) ... S
Signal ... SGL
Signal ... SIG
Signal (WDMC) ... sig
Signal (IAA) ... SIGN
Signal Access ... SA
Signal Acquisition Unit (NASA) ... SAU
Signal Actuated Gate ... SAG
Signal Agency (IAA) ... SIGAGCY
Signal Air Defense Engineering Agency (IAA) ... SIGAIRDEFENGRAGCY
Signal Air Warning (IAA) ... SAW
Signal Aircraft Warning ... SAW

Signal Airways Service ... SAS
Signal Algorithmic Processing System [*Navy*] ... SAPS
Signal Amplitude Sampler and Totalizing Unit (IEEE) ... SASTU
Signal Analysis ... SA
Signal Analysis Course [*Navy*] (DNAB) ... SAC
Signal Analysis System [*Electronics*] ... SAS
Signal Analyzer ... SA
Signal Analyzing Monitor (KSC) ... SAM
Signal and Conditioning (KSC) ... S & C
Signal and Homing Light (IAA) ... SALT
Signal Apparel [*NYSE symbol*] (TTSB) ... SIA
Signal Apparel Co., Inc. [*Associated Press*] (SAG) ... SgnlApl
Signal Apparel Co., Inc. [*NYSE symbol*] (SPSG) ... SIA
Signal Appliance Association [*Later, RSS*] ... SAA
Signal Attenuation (AAG) ... SA
Signal Automatic Air Traffic Control System ... SATCO
Signal Automatic RADAR Processing ... SARP
Signal Averaged Eectrocardiography [*Medicine*] ... SAECG
Signal Aviation Branch ... SAB
Signal Aviation Company (IAA) ... SIGAVNCO
Signal Aviation Test and Support Activity ... SATSA
Signal Band ... SB
Signal Band (Energy) in Mainlobe Count [*Military*] ... SBMLCNT
Signal Band Indication ... SBI
Signal Band Mainlobe ... SBML
Signal Battalion [*Army*] ... SB
Signal Battalion [*Army*] ... SIGBAT
Signal Battalion (IAA) ... SIGBN
Signal Board Computer (HGAA) ... SBC
Signal Boatswain ... SB
Signal Canceling Device ... SCD
Signal Center [*Military*] (AABC) ... SIGCEN
Signal Center and School [*Army*] (MCD) ... SCS
Signal Circuits Design Section ... SCDS
Signal Collection and Jamming ... SC & J
Signal Command Management System [*Military*] (AABC) ... SCMS
Signal Communication (IAA) ... SIGCOM
Signal Communication Agency (IAA) ... SIGCOMMAGCY
Signal Communication by Orbiting Relay Equipment [*Radio*] ... SCORE
Signal Communication Security Agency (IAA) ... SIGCOMMSECAGCY
Signal Communications System [*Air Force*] ... SCS
Signal Company [*Military*] (IAA) ... SCO
Signal Company (IAA) ... SIGCO
Signal Company (IAA) ... SIGCOY
Signal Company Aircraft Warning Hawaii - Signal Aircraft Warning Regiment HawaiiAssociation (EA) ... SCAWH-SAWRH
Signal Company, Airline (IAA) ... SIGCOA
Signal Company, Cable (IAA) ... SIGCOC
Signal Company, Wing (IAA) ... SIGCOWG
Signal Company, Wireless (IAA) ... SIGCOW
Signal Comparator ... SC
Signal Conditioner ... SC
Signal Conditioner (IAA) ... SCR
Signal Conditioner (MCD) ... SIGCONDR
Signal Conditioner Assembly Request (MCD) ... SCAR
Signal Conditioner Assembly Review (MCD) ... SCAR
Signal Conditioning Amplifier ... SCAMP
Signal Conditioning and Detection Electronics (MCD) ... SCADE
Signal Conditioning and Display Unit [*NASA*] (NASA) ... SCDU
Signal Conditioning Assembly [*NASA*] (KSC) ... SCA
Signal Conditioning Electronics Assembly ... SCEA
Signal Conditioning Equipment ... SCE
Signal Conditioning Index (ECII) ... SCIX
Signal Conditioning Module ... SCM
Signal Conditioning Network (IAA) ... SIGCONDNET
Signal Conditioning Rack ... SCR
Signal Conditioning Subsystem Group (MCD) ... SCSG
Signal Conditioning System (KSC) ... SCS
Signal Conditioning Unit (NASA) ... SCU
Signal Construction Battalion (IAA) ... SIGCONSBN
Signal Control (DEN) ... SICO
Signal Control Unit (NASA) ... SCU
Signal Conversion Equipment [*Telecommunications*] ... SCE
Signal Conversion Equivalent (NITA) ... SCE
Signal Conversion Relay [*Telecommunications*] (TEL) ... SCR
Signal Corps [*Later, Communications and Electronics Command*] [*Army*] ... SC
Signal Corps [*Later, Communications and Electronics Command*] [*Army*] ... SIGC
Signal Corps [*Later, Communications and Electronics Command*] [*Army*] ... SIGCOR
Signal Corps Administrative Network [*Obsolete Army*] ... SCAN
Signal Corps Aircraft Signal Service [*Obsolete Army*] ... SCASS
Signal Corps Aviation School [*Obsolete Army*] ... SCAS
Signal Corps Aviation Test and Support Detachment [*Military*] (IAA) ... SCATSD
Signal Corps Base Depot [*Military*] (IAA) ... SCBD
Signal Corps Engineering Laboratories [*Obsolete Army*] ... SCEL
Signal Corps Engineering Laboratories [*Fort Monmouth, NJ*] ... SIGC
Signal Corps General Development Laboratory [*Obsolete Army*] ... SCGDL
Signal Corps General Research Laboratory [*Military*] (IAA) ... SCGRL
Signal Corps Ground Signal Agency [*Military*] (IAA) ... SCGSA
Signal Corps Ground Signal Service [*Obsolete Army*] ... SCGSS
Signal Corps Intelligence Agency [*Obsolete Army*] ... SCIA
Signal Corps Intermediate Supply Deport [*Army*] (IAA) ... SCISD
Signal Corps Item [*Obsolete Army*] (NATG) ... SCI
Signal Corps Laboratory [*Obsolete Army*] ... SCL
Signal Corps Letter (MCD) ... SCL
Signal Corps Logistics Evaluation Committee [*Obsolete Army*] (KSC) ... SCLEC
Signal Corps Mobile Television System [*Military*] (IAA) ... SCMTVS
Signal Corps Photographic Laboratory [*Obsolete Army*] ... SCPL
Signal Corps Pictorial Center [*Obsolete Army*] ... SCPC
Signal Corps RADAR Laboratory [*Obsolete Army*] ... SCRL
Signal Corps Radio [*Followed by model number*] [*Obsolete Army*] ... SCR
Signal Corps Radio Laboratory [*Army*] (IAA) ... SCRL
Signal Corps Random-Access Memory (DNAB) ... SCRAM
Signal Corps Replacement Training Center [*Obsolete Army*] ... SCRTC
Signal Corps Reserve [*Military*] (IAA) ... SIGRES
Signal Corps Technical Requirements (MCD) ... SCTR
Signal Corps Training [*Military*] (IAA) ... SCT
Signal Corps Training Center [*Military*] (IAA) ... SCTC
Signal Corps Unit Training Group [*Military*] (IAA) ... SCUTG
Signal/Data (MHDI) ... SIG/DAT
Signal Data Converter ... SDC
Signal Data Demodulator ... SDD
Signal Data Demodulator Set [*or System*] ... SDDS
Signal Data Processing System ... SDPS
Signal Data Processor ... SDP
Signal Data Recorder [*or Reproducer*] (MCD) ... SDR
Signal Data Recording Set (MCD) ... SDRS
Signal De Mont [*France*] [*Seismograph station code, US Geological Survey*] (SEIS) ... SMF
Signal Density Model (MCD) ... SDM
Signal Depot (IAA) ... SIGDEP
Signal Depot Company [*Military*] (IAA) ... SIGDEPCO
Signal Detection Theory ... SDT
Signal Digit (IAA) ... SD
Signal Dispatch Point [*Telecommunications*] (TEL) ... SDP
Signal Distributing Office [*British military*] (IAA) ... SDO
Signal Distribution Officer [*British military*] (DMA) ... SDO
Signal Distribution Room [*NASA*] (KSC) ... SDR
Signal Distribution System ... SDS
Signal Distribution Unit (AAG) ... SDU
Signal Division [*SHAPE*] (NATG) ... SIGDIV
Signal Engineering Agency (IAA) ... SIGENGRAGCY
Signal Engineering Laboratories (AAG) ... SEL
Signal Enhancement Seismograph ... SES
Signal Equipment (IAA) ... SIGEQUIP
Signal Equipment Depot (IAA) ... SED
Signal Equipment Support Agency ... SESA
Signal Evaluation Airborne Laboratory [*FAA*] ... SEAL
Signal Excess (NVT) ... SE
Signal Exercise (NATG) ... SIGEX
Signal Flow Diagram (MCD) ... SFD
Signal Flow Graph ... SFG
Signal Flow Matrix (IAA) ... SFM
Signal [*System*] **for Assessment and Modification** [*of behavior*] [*Patented*] ... SAM
Signal Format Development Team [*France*] ... SFDT
Signal Framing Bits [*Telecommunications*] (ACRL) ... Fs
Signal Frequency ... SF
Signal Frequency Generator [*Telecommunications*] (OA) ... SFG
Signal Frequency Receiver [*Telecommunications*] (OA) ... SFR
Signal Generating Station (CET) ... SGS
Signal Generator ... SG
Signal Generator (IEEE) ... SIGGEN
Signal Ground (BUR) ... SG
Signal Ground (AAG) ... SGRD
Signal Ground (IAA) ... SIGGND
Signal Handling Equipment (AAG) ... SHE
Signal Heavy Construction Battalion (IAA) ... SIGHVCONSTBN
Signal Hill Energy Corp. [*Vancouver Stock Exchange symbol*] ... SGH
Signal Hill Public Library, Signal Hill, CA [*Library symbol Library of Congress*] (LCLS) ... CSh
Signal Identification (NITA) ... SID
Signal Information and Monitoring Service [*American radio monitoring service*] ... SIAM
Signal Intelligence (MCD) ... SI
Signal Intelligence [*Military*] (AABC) ... SIGINT
Signal Intelligence [*US surveillance satellite*] ... SIGLINT
Signal Intelligence Agency (IAA) ... SIGINTELAGCY
Signal Intelligence/Electronic Warfare (MCD) ... SIGINT/EW
Signal Intelligence/Electronic Warfare Coordination Center (NVT) ... S/EWCC
Signal Intelligence Service [*Later, Army Security Agency*] ... SIS
Signal Interface ... SI
Signal Interface Unit (MCD) ... SIU
Signal Level ... SL
Signal Level Converter (DWSG) ... SLC
Signal Level Meter (NTCM) ... SLM
Signal Lieutenant [*British military*] (DMA) ... Sig L
Signal Light Bare (MSA) ... SLB
Signal Line Isolator ... SLI
Signal Lines Pair Combination (IAA) ... SLPC
Signal Long Lines ... SLL
Signal Master (IAA) ... SIGMR
Signal Master (IAA) ... SMR
Signal Master (IAA) ... SMSTR
Signal Material Support (DNAB) ... SIGMS
Signal Measurement and Analysis System ... SIGMAS
Signal Memory Recorder (NITA) ... SMR
Signal Message Center (IAA) ... SIGMSGCEN
Signal Messenger Service (NATG) ... SMS
Signal Missile Support [*Air Force*] (MUGU) ... SMS
Signal Missile Support Agency (IAA) ... SIGMSLSPTAGCY

Signal Missile Support Agency [*Air Force*] (AAG) .... SMSA
Signal Mountain, TN [*FM radio station call letters*] .... WZST
Signal Network .... SIGNET
Signal Node .... SN
Signal Officer (IAA) .... SIGNO
Signal Officer .... SIGO
Signal Officer (IAA) .... SIGOFFR
Signal Officer .... SO
Signal Officer (IAA) .... SOC
Signal Officer (IAA) .... SOF
Signal Officer-in-Chief [*British military*] (DMA) .... SO-in-C
Signal Officers' Reserve Corps .... SORC
Signal Operating Procedure (IAA) .... SOP
Signal Operation Battalion (IAA) .... SIGOPNBN
Signal Operation [*or Operating*] Instructions .... SOI
Signal Optimization Program [*Federal Highway Administration*] .... SIGOP
Signal Oscillator (OA) .... SO
Signal Output (MHDI) .... SIGOUT
Signal Plus Noise and Distortion .... SINAD
Signal Plus Noise-to-Noise (IAA) .... SNN
Signal Point Ground (NASA) .... SPG
Signal Point Identification (IAA) .... SPI
Signal Pre-emption System .... SPS
Signal Presence Indicator (CAAL) .... SPI
Signal Processing and Display Equipment .... SPADE
Signal Processing and Spectral Control .... SPSC
Signal Processing [*or Processor*] Arithmetic Unit [*Navy*] .... SPAU
Signal Processing Element [*Navy*] .... SPE
Signal Processing, Evaluation, Alert, and Report [*Navy*] (NVT) .... SPEAR
Signal Processing in Evacuated Electronic Devices .... SPEED
Signal Processing in the Element (MCD) .... SPRITE
Signal Processing Language [*Computer science*] (CSR) .... SPL
Signal Processing Peripheral .... SPP
Signal Processing Program [*BV Engineering*] [*Computer science*] .... SPP
Signal Processing System (KSC) .... SPS
Signal Processing Test Facility .... SPTF
Signal Processing Unit .... SPU
Signal Processor (NASA) .... S/P
Signal Processor Assembly [*NASA*] .... SPA
Signal Processor Checkout (CAAL) .... SIPCO
Signal Processor Group .... SPG
Signal Processor Group Test Assembly .... SPGTA
Signal Processor Techniques Department .... SPTD
Signal Procurement Office (IAA) .... SIGPROCOFC
Signal Programmer and Conditioner [*Air Force Eastern Test Range*] .... SPAC
Signal Property Office [*Military*] .... SPO
Signal Publication [*British*] .... SP
Signal Quality Detector .... SQD
Signal Quality Error [*Computer science*] (PCM) .... SQE
Signal RADAR Maintenance Unit (IAA) .... SRMU
Signal Recognition Particle [*Biochemistry*] .... SRP
Signal Recognition Particle Receptor (DMAA) .... SRPR
Signal Regulation (IAA) .... SR
Signal Repair Company [*Military*] (IAA) .... SIGREPCO
Signal Replacement Training Center (IAA) .... SRTC
Signal Research Center, Inc., Des Plaines, IL [*Library symbol*] [*Library of Congress*] (LCLS) .... IDesS
Signal Reserve Corps .... SRC
Signal Responder Unit (AAG) .... SRU
Signal Return [*Electronics*] .... SIGRTN
Signal Routing and Interface (MCD) .... SRI
Signal School (IAA) .... SIGSCH
Signal Section (IAA) .... SIGSEC
Signal Security [*Military*] (AABC) .... SIGSEC
Signal Security Agency [*Later, Army Security Agency*] .... SSA
Signal Security Assessment System [*Military*] (CAAL) .... SSAS
Signal Security Element [*Military*] (AABC) .... SSE
Signal Seeking Device .... SSD
Signal Selection Switchboard (CAAL) S3
Signal Selector (DNAB) .... SIG SEL
Signal Selector (DEN) .... SS
Signal Selectro Logic (ECII) .... SSL
Signal Service Battalion [*Military*] (IAA) .... SIGSVCBN
Signal Service Company [*Military*] (IAA) .... SIGSERVCO
Signal Sight Back (SAA) .... SSB
Signal Source Distribution Center (AAG) .... SSDC
Signal Station [*Nautical charts*] .... Sig Sta
Signal Station [*Navigation*] .... SIGSTN
Signal Strength [*Broadcasting*] .... S
Signal Strength (IAA) .... SIGSTR
Signal Strength [*Broadcasting*] (KSC) .... SS
Signal Strength, Center Frequency [*Broadcasting*] .... SS/CF
Signal Strength Monitor [*Broadcasting*] .... SSM
Signal Strength Radio Frequency (IAA) .... SRF
Signal Structure Parametric Filter [*Telecommunications*] (OA) .... SSPF
Signal Summing Unit [*Aviation*] .... SSU
Signal Supply Agency (IAA) .... SIGSUPAGNCY
Signal Supply Agency .... SSA
Signal Supply Battalion [*Military*] (IAA) .... SIGSUPBN
Signal Support Battalion [*Military*] (IAA) .... SIGSPTBN
Signal Susceptibility and Vulnerability Assessment [*Military*] (CAAL) .... SSVA
Signal Switching System .... SSS
Signal Technical Intelligence Team [*Army*] (AABC) .... STIT
Signal Technology [*AMEX symbol*] (TTSB) .... STZ
Signal Technology Corp. [*Associated Press*] (SAG) .... SgnlTech

Signal Technology Corp. [*AMEX symbol*] (SAG) .... STZ
Signal Termination Module [*NASA*] (NASA) .... STM
Signal to Background .... SB
Signal to Background Ratio [*Instrumentation*] .... SBR
Signal to Distortion Ratio (NITA) .... SDR
Signal to Interference plus Noise Ratio (MCD) .... SINR
Signal to Noise Ratio [*Unweighted*] (CMD) .... S/N
Signal Tracing Tester .... STT
Signal Track and Illuminating RADAR [*Canadian Navy*] .... STIR
Signal Tracking Filter .... STF
Signal Training (IAA) .... SIGTNG
Signal Training, All Arms (IAA) .... STAA
Signal Training Brigade (MCD) .... STB
Signal Training Center (IAA) .... SIGTC
Signal Training Center (IAA) .... SIGTNGCEN
Signal Training Centre [*British military*] (DMA) .... STC
Signal Training Detachment (IAA) .... SIGTNGDET
Signal Transducer and Activator of Transcription [*Biochemistry*] .... STAT
Signal Transducers and Activators of Transcription [*Biochemistry*] .... STAT
Signal Transducing Factor [*Biochemistry*] .... STF
Signal Transfer Point [*Telecommunications*] (TEL) .... STP
Signal Transfer Unit .... STU
Signal Transmission Reception and Distribution (IEEE) .... STRAD
Signal Underwater Exploding [*British military*] (DMA) .... SUE
Signal Underwater Sound .... SUS
Signal Wireless Officer (IAA) .... SWO
Signal Word Index of Field and Title - Literature Abstract Specialized Search (DIT) .... SWIFT LASS
Signal Word Index of Field and Title - Scientific Information Retrieval (DIT) .... SWIFT SIR
Signaling (MSA) .... SNLG
Signaling and Supervision Techniques Study .... SSTS
Signaling and Supervisory Control .... SSC
Signaling Connection Control Part [*Telecommunications*] .... SCCP
Signaling Conversion Circuit [*Telecommunications*] (TEL) .... SCC
Signaling Ground [*Telecommunications*] (TEL) .... SGD
Signaling Information Field [*Telecommunications*] (TEL) .... SIF
Signaling Information Receiver/Transmitter (MCD) .... SIRT
Signaling Interworking Subsystem [*Telecommunications*] (TEL) .... SIS
Signaling Link Selection [*Telecommunications*] (TEL) .... SLS
Signaling Link Termination [*Telecommunications*] .... SLT
Signaling Module [*Telecommunications*] (TEL) .... SM
Signaling Not a Number [*Computer programming*] (BYTE) .... SNaN
Signaling Projector [*British*] .... SP
Signaling Range Extender [*Telecommunications*] (TEL) .... SRE
Signaling System [*Telecommunications*] (TEL) .... SS
Signaling Unit .... SU
Signalled (ROG) .... SGNLD
Signaller [*British military*] (DMA) .... S
Signalling and Switching Processor (NITA) .... SSP
Signalling Preprocessing Program (PDAA) .... SPRP
Signalling System Alternating Current (NITA) .... SSAC
Signalling System Multi-Frequency (NITA) .... SSMF
Signalling System-Direct Current (NITA) .... SSDC
Signalling Terminal Equipment [*Telecommunications*] (OSI) .... STE
Signalman [*Military British*] .... SGMN
Signalman [*Navy rating British*] .... SIG
Signalman .... SIGMN
Signalman [*Navy rating*] .... SM
Signalman, First Class [*Navy rating*] SM1
Signalman, Second Class [*Navy rating*] SM2
Signalman, Third Class [*Navy rating*] SM3
Signalmen's United and Sick Society [*A union*] [*British*] .... SUSS
Signals and Electronic Warfare Research and Development Act .... SERDA
Signals Dispatch Service (IAA) .... SDS
Signals Division [*British military*] (DMA) .... SD
Signals Experimental Establishment [*British military*] (DMA) .... SEE
Signals Exploitation Space (MCD) .... SES
Signals Fading Badly .... ZFB
Signals Flying Unit [*British*] .... SFU
Signals Information Processing System [*Navy*] (DOMA) .... SIGIPS
Signals Intelligence Analysis System (MCD) .... SIAS
Signals Operator (ADA) .... SIGSOP
Signals Research and Development Establishment [*British*] .... SRDE
Signals Research and Development Laboratory [*Army British*] .... SRDL
Signals Warfare Center [*Warrenton, VA*] [*Army*] .... SWC
Signals Warfare Laboratory [*Army*] (RDA) .... SWL
Signal-Sequence Receptor [*Biochemistry*] .... SSR
Signal-to-Clutter .... S/C
Signal-to-Distortion (IAA) .... SD
Signal-to-Interference .... S/I
Signal-to-Interference Ratio .... SIR
Signal-to-Intermodulation [*Ratio*] .... SI
Signal-to-Intermodulation Ratio (IDOE) .... S/I
Signal-to-Jamming - plus Noise Ratio .... S/J + N
Signal-to-Noise Improvement [*Data transmission*] (IEEE) .... SNI
Signal-to-Noise Improvement Factor (IAA) .... SNIF
Signal-to-Noise Merit .... SNM
Signal-to-Noise plus Interference Ratio .... S/N + I
Signal-to-Noise Plus Interference Ratio .... SNIR
Signal-to-Noise Ratio [*Radio*] (WDMC) .... S/R
Signal-to-Noise Ratio .... SNR
Signal-to-Noise Ratio and Distortion (IAA) .... SINAD
Signal-to-Noise Ratio Due to Channel Noise (IAA) .... SNRCN
Signal-to-Noise Ratio Estimator .... SNORE

Signal-to-Noise, Weighted ... S/Nw
Signature ... S
Signature (WDMC) ... s
Signature (AABC) ... SGNR
Signature (AFM) ... SIG
Signature (WDMC) ... sig
Signature (DAVI) ... sign
Signature ... SIGNE
Signature (ROG) ... SIGNRE
Signature Analysis ... SA
Signature Analysis Methods for Mission Identification ... SAMMI
Signature and Propagation Laboratory [*Army*] (RDA) ... SPL
Signature Authorization Card [*or Chart*] (AAG) ... SAC
Signature Book (ROG) ... SB
Signature Card [*Banking*] (MHDW) ... Sig CD
Signature Characterization Facility (MCD) ... SCF
Signature Inns, Inc. [*NASDAQ symbol*] (SAG) ... SGNS
Signature Inns, Inc. [*Associated Press*] (SAG) ... SignInns
Signature Library Intelligence Catalogue ... SLIC
Signature Missing ... Sig Mis
Signature of Fragmented Tanks ... SOFT
Signature Overlap Range Prediction ... SORAP
Signature Overlay Range Prediction (MCD) ... SORP
Signature Resorts, Inc. [*NASDAQ symbol*] (SAG) ... SIGR
Signature Resorts, Inc. [*Associated Press*] (SAG) ... SigRsrts
Signature Security Service [*DoD*] ... SSS
Signature Unknown ... Sig Unk
Signatures (WGA) ... SGG
Signatures (WGA) ... SIGG
Signature-Tagged Transposon Method [*Genetics*] ... STM
Sign-Digit Subtractor ... SDS
Signed [*Before signature on typed copy of a document, original of which was signed*] ... /S/
Signed (DFIT) ... S
Signed (WGA) ... SD
Signed (WGA) ... SG
Signed ... SGD
Signed (WDMC) ... sgd
Signed (ODBW) ... sgd
Signed & Dated (VRA) ... s&d
Signed and Limited Edition [*Publishing*] ... S & L
Signed and On Chart [*Hospital administration*] (DAVI) ... S & OC
Signed and Sealed ... SS
Signed Digit (IAA) ... SD
Signed, Directed Graph [*Mathematics*] ... SDG
Signed Division [*Computer science*] ... DIVS
Signed Exact English ... SEE
Signed Integer [*Computer science*] ... SI
Signed Judgments of the Military Courts in the Administered Territories [*Israel*] (BJA) ... SJMC
Signed Multiplication [*Computer science*] ... MULS
Signed Out Against Advice [*Medicine*] ... SOAA
Signed Out Against Medical Advice ... SOMA
Signed Photograph ... SP
Signed Short Integer [*Computer science*] ... SSI
Signed-Off Sick ... SOS
Signer [*MARC relator code*] [*Library of Congress*] (LCCP) ... sgn
Signet Banking [*NYSE symbol*] (TTSB) ... SBK
Signet Banking Corp. [*NYSE symbol*] (SPSG) ... SBK
Signet Banking Corp. [*Associated Press*] (SAG) ... SignetB
Signet Group [*NASDAQ symbol*] (SPSG) ... SIGGY
Signet Group [*Associated Press*] (SAG) ... SignetGp
Signet Group [*Associated Press*] (SAG) ... SigntG
Signet Group ADR [*NASDAQ symbol*] (TTSB) ... SIGGY
Signet Grp $1.06 Cv Pfd [*NASDAQ symbol*] (TTSB) ... SIGGZ
Signet Resources, Inc. [*Vancouver Stock Exchange symbol*] ... SGZ
Signetur [*Let It Be Entitled*] [*Pharmacy*] (ROG) ... S
Signetur [*Let It Be Labelled*] [*Pharmacy*] ... SIG
Signetur Nomine Proprio [*Let It Be Written Upon with the Proper Name*] [*Pharmacy*] (ROG) ... SIGN N P
Sign-Filled Half-Word Designator [*Computer science*] ... XH
Significance (ROG) ... SIGNCE
Significance Level ... SL
Significant (FAAC) ... SGFNT
Significant ... sig
Significant Action Report [*Military*] (MCD) ... SAR
Significant Activities of Daily Living (WYGK) ... SADL
Significant Activity of Daily Living [*Insurance*] ... SADL
Significant Air Gap ... SAG
Significant Asymptomatic Bacteriuria [*Medicine*] (MAE) ... SAB
Significant Business Issue (MCD) ... SBI
Significant Characteristics (MCD) ... SC
Significant Combat Equipment [*Army*] ... SCE
Significant Construction Deficiency [*Nuclear energy*] (NRCH) ... SCD
Significant Counterintelligence Briefs (AFM) ... SCIB
Significant Criminal Enforcement Project [*Bureau of Alcohol, Tobacco, and Firearms*] ... SCEP
Significant Data Selection ... SIDASE
Significant Deficiency Report [*Nuclear energy*] (IEEE) ... SDR
Significant Digit [*Mathematics*] ... SD
Significant Digit Arithmetic ... SDA
Significant Digit Scanner (IAA) ... SDS
Significant Emotional Events ... SEE
Significant Event Report (IEEE) ... SER
Significant Events Evaluation and Information Network ... SEE-IN
Significant Figure (IAA) ... SF
Significant Figures [*Mathematics*] (BARN) ... sig fig
Significant Glandular Enlargement [*Endocrinology*] (DAVI) ... SGE
Significant Indications Summary ... SIS
Significant Industrial Use ... SIU
Significant Meteorological Information (GAVI) ... SIGMET
Significant Meteorological Information [*FAA*] (TAG) ... SIGMET
Significant Milestone Integration Lateral Evaluation [*Computer science*] ... SMILE
Significant New Alternatives Policy [*Environmental science*] ... SNAP
Significant New Use Notice [*Government emissions regulations*] ... SNUN
Significant New Use Rule [*Government emissions regulations*] ... SNUR
Significant New Use Rules [*Environmental Protection Agency*] ... SNUR
Significant Noncompliance Action Program [*Environmental Protection Agency*] (GFGA) ... SNAP
Significant Noncomplier [*Environmental Protection Agency*] (GFGA) ... SNC
Significant Operating Event Report (IEEE) ... SOER
Significant Operating Experience (IEEE) ... SOE
Significant Other [*Term for members of unmarried couples*] ... SO
Significant Probability Mapping ... SPM
Significant Regulatory Action [*Office of Management and Budget*] (GFGA) ... SRA
Significant Structural Item (NASA) ... SSI
Significant Technical Milestone (SDI) ... STM
Significant Testing (IAA) ... SIG
Significant Wave Height [*Oceanography*] ... SWH
Significant Weather [*Aviation*] (FAAC) ... SIGWX
Significant Word in the Full Title [*Computer science*] (DIT) ... SWIFT
Significantly Underutilized Employee Program [*DoD*] ... SUE
Signify (ROG) ... SIGNF
Signifying (ROG) ... SIG
Signing Exact English [*Sign language system for the hearing impaired*] ... SEE
Signor [*Mister*] [*Italian*] ... S
Signor [*Mister*] [*Italian*] ... SR
Signora [*Madam*] [*Italian*] ... Siga
Signora [*Madam*] [*Italian*] (ROG) ... SIGNA
Signore [*or Signora*] (EY) ... SIG
Signorina [*Miss*] [*Italian*] ... Signa
Signorolus de Homodeis de Mediolano [*Flourished, 14th-15th century*] [*Authority cited in pre-1607 legal work*] (DSA) ... Signor de Homod
Signorolus de Homodeis de Mediolano [*Flourished, 14th-15th century*] [*Authority cited in pre-1607 legal work*] (DSA) ... Sigo
Signs (DAVI) ... Sx
Signs and Symptoms [*Medicine*] ... S & S
Signs: Journal of Women in Culture and Society [*A publication*] (BRI) ... Signs
Signtech, Inc. [*Toronto Stock Exchange symbol*] ... SNH
Sigonella [*Italy ICAO location identifier*] (ICLI) ... LICZ
Sigourney News-Review, Sigourney, IA [*Library symbol*] [*Library of Congress*] (LCLS) ... IaSigNR
SIGPLAN Technical Committee on APL [*A Programming Language*] [*Association for Computing Machinery*] (CSR) ... STAPL
SIGSEC Resources and Equipment Needs (MCD) ... SIREN
Siguanea, Isla De La Juventud [*Cuba ICAO location identifier*] (ICLI) ... MUSN
Siguiri [*Guinea*] [*Airport symbol*] (AD) ... GII
Siguiri [*Guinea*] [*ICAO location identifier*] (ICLI) ... GUSI
Sihanouk [*Cambodia*] [*ICAO location identifier*] (ICLI) ... VDSV
Sihora [*India*] [*ICAO location identifier*] (ICLI) ... VASA
SII [*Systems Integrators, Incorporated*] **Eastern Regional Users Group** [*Defunct*] (EA) ... SERUG
Siimes Aviation AB [*Finland ICAO designator*] (FAAC) ... SII
Sikaman Gold Resources Ltd. [*Toronto Stock Exchange symbol*] ... SKG
Sikandrabad [*India*] [*ICAO location identifier*] (ICLI) ... VISB
Sikasso [*Mali*] [*ICAO location identifier*] (ICLI) ... GASK
Sikeston, MO [*FM radio station call letters*] (RBYB) ... KBXB-FM
Sikeston, MO [*AM radio station call letters*] ... KMPL
Sikeston, MO [*AM radio station call letters*] ... KSIM
Sikeston, MO [*FM radio station call letters*] ... KSTG
Sikeston, MO [*Location identifier FAA*] (FAAL) ... SIK
Sikh Council of North America [*Defunct*] (EA) ... SCNA
Sikh Local Infantry [*British military*] (DMA) ... SLI
Sikiang River and Basin [*China, Mainland*] [*MARC geographic area code Library of Congress*] (LCCP) ... a-ccs-
Sikka [*Former USSR Seismograph station code, US Geological Survey Closed*] (SEIS) ... SKK
Sikkim [*MARC geographic area code Library of Congress*] (LCCP) ... a-sk--
Sikkim [*ii (India) used in records cataloged after January 1978*] [*MARC country of publication code Library of Congress*] (LCCP) ... sk
Sikkim Parishad [*India*] [*Political party*] (PPW) ... SP
Sikorsky Aircraft Division [*United Aircraft Corp.*] [*ICAO aircraft manufacturer identifier*] (ICAO) ... SK
Sikorsky Engineering Report ... SER
Sikorsky Program Operations Tracking System (MCD) ... SPOTS
Sikouras Pictures Unit [*NASDAQ symbol*] (TTSB) ... SKRSU
S'il Vous Plait [*If You Please*] [*French*] ... SVP
Silane to Molten Silane [*Photovoltaic energy systems*] ... SMS
Silas Bronson Public Library, Waterbury, CT [*Library symbol Library of Congress*] (LCLS) ... CtWB
Silaswood Elementary School, Huntington Station, NY [*Library symbol*] [*Library of Congress*] (LCLS) ... NHsSE
Silchar [*India*] [*Airport symbol*] (OAG) ... IXS
Silchar/Kumbhirgram [*India*] [*ICAO location identifier*] (ICLI) ... VEKU
Silcon-Computing Instrument Patch-Programmed (SAA) ... SCIPP
Silcorp Ltd. [*Toronto Stock Exchange symbol*] ... SIL
Silence [*Navigation*] ... SI
Silence (MSA) ... SIL
Silenced Reconnaissance Weapon (MCD) ... SRW
Silencing (MSA) ... SILG

Silent [Dance terminology] ... S
Silent (NTCM) ... SIL
Silent [Films, television, etc.] ... ST
Silent Attack Warning System (MCD) ... SAWS
Silent Canyon Resources Ltd. [Vancouver Stock Exchange symbol] ... SCN
Silent Communication Alarm Network [NASA] ... SCAN
Silent Compact Auxiliary Power ... SCAP
Silent Energy Sources for Tactical Applications (MCD) ... SIESTA
Silent, Lightweight, Electric Energy Plant (RDA) ... SLEEP
Silent Liquid Integral Cooler (MHDI) ... SLIC
Silent Mating Loci [Genetics] ... SML
Silent Propulsion System (MCD) ... SPS
Silent Running Society (EA) ... SRS
Silent Tactical Attack Reconnaissance System ... STARS
Silent Treatment [Psychology] (DAVI) ... SITr
Silent Videotape Recording (DOAD) ... SILVTR
Silent Witness [Vancouver Stock Exchange symbol] ... SWT
Siler City, NC [AM radio station call letters] ... WNCA
Silfi [Saudi Arabia] [Airport symbol] (AD) ... ZUL
Silgarhi Doti [Nepal] [Airport symbol] (OAG) ... SIH
Silhouette Harness Board (MCD) ... SHB
Silhouette Model [Military] (INF) ... SILMOD
Silhouette Print (VRA) ... SILPT
Silhouetting Underwater Detecting System ... SUDS
Silica and Moulding Sands Association [British] (BI) ... SAMSA
Silica Gel [Analytical chemistry] ... SG
Silica RADOME Technique ... SRT
Silica-Forsterite-Anorthite-Diopside [Lunar geology] ... Si-Fo-An-Di
Silica-Forsterite-Diopside [Lunar geology] ... Si-Fo-Di
Silicart, Inc., Montreal, Quebec [Library symbol National Library of Canada] (NLC) ... QMSIL
... S
Silicate ... SIL
Silicate ... SIL
Silicate-Oxy-Apatite (PDAA) ... SOAP
Silicia Fume [Inorganic chemistry] ... SF
Silicoaluminophosphate [Inorganic chemistry] ... SAPO
Silico-Manganese Steel ... SMS
Silicon [Chemical element] ... Si
Silicon (IDOE) ... Si
Silicon Alloy Diffused (IAA) ... SAD
Silicon, Aluminum, Oxygen, and Nitrogen [A ceramic] ... SIALON
Silicon and Aluminum Metal-Oxide Semiconductor (ADA) ... SAMOS
Silicon Annular Transistor ... SAT
Silicon Architectures Research Initiative [British] ... SARI
Silicon Avalanche Light Emitter ... SALE
Silicon Avalanche Suppressor [Telecommunications] ... SAS
Silicon Bidirectional Switch (IAA) ... SBS
Silicon Bilateral Switch ... SBS
Silicon Borne Bond (IAA) ... SBB
Silicon Capacitance Absolute Pressure Sensor ... SCAP
Silicon Carbide (IDOE) ... SiC
Silicon Cell Bridge ... SCB
Silicon Circuit Board ... SCB
Silicon Coated (IAA) ... SIC
Silicon Coating by Inverted Meniscus (PDAA) ... SCIM
Silicon Computing Instrument, Patch Programmed (IAA) ... SCIPP
Silicon Controlled Avalanche Transistor [Electronics] (BARN) ... SCAT
Silicon Controlled Rectifier Regulated Direct Current (PDAA) ... SCRDC
Silicon Diode Pellet ... SDP
Silicon Diode Target Tube ... SDTT
Silicon Disk Drive [Computer science] ... SDD
Silicon Elastimeter Ablator [NASA] ... SEA
Silicon Epitaxial Planar Transistor (IAA) ... SEPT
Silicon Epitaxial Wafer ... SEW
Silicon Gate Field Effect Transistor (IAA) ... SIGFET
Silicon Gate Transistor (IAA) ... SGT
Silicon Gate-Controlled Switch ... SGCS
Silicon Germanium ... SIGE
Silicon Germanium [Computer science] ... SiGe
Silicon Graphics [NYSE symbol] (SPSG) ... SGI
Silicon Graphics (MHDW) ... SGIC
Silicon Graphics [Associated Press] (SAG) ... SilcnGph
Silicon Graphics Incorporated [Computer science] ... SGI
Silicon Grown Diffused (IAA) ... SGD
Silicon Imaging Device (IEEE) ... SID
Silicon Integrated Circuit ... SIC
Silicon Integrated Device Technology (IAA) ... SIDT
Silicon Integrated Monolithic Circuit ... SIMC
Silicon Intensified Target (NITA) ... SIT
Silicon Intensifier Target ... SIT
Silicon Intensifier Tube ... SIT
Silicon Junction Diode (IDOE) ... SL
Silicon Lacquer ... SLIC
Silicon Language for Integrated Circuit (NITA) ... SLP
Silicon Light Pulser ... SLPA
Silicon Light Pulser Array ... SLPM
Silicon Light Pulser Matrix ... SLS
Silicon Light Source ... SILC
Silicon Ltd. [NASDAQ symbol] (SAG) ... SilcLtd
Silicon Ltd. [Associated Press] (SAG) ... SilLtd
Silicon Ltd. [Associated Press] (SAG) ... SILZ
Silicon Ltd. [NASDAQ symbol] (SAG) ... SilCLV
Silicon Liquid Crystal Light Valve [NASA] ... SILCF
Silicon Ltd [NASDAQ symbol] (TTSB) ... SILZF
Silicon Ltd Wrrt [NASDAQ symbol] (TTSB)

Silicon Monolithic Circuit ... SMC
Silicon Multiplier Detector ... SMD
Silicon Needle Transducer ... SNT
Silicon Nitrate ... SN
Silicon Nitride Film ... SNF
Silicon Nitride Oxide Silicon (IAA) ... SNOS
Silicon Nitride-Masked Thermally-Oxidized Post-Diffused Mesa Process (PDAA) ... SIMTOP
Silicon of Insulating Substrate (MCD) ... SIS
Silicon on Ceramic [Technique for producing solar cells] ... SOC
Silicon on Insulating Substrate (PDAA) ... SOIS
Silicon Overlay Epitaxial (IAA) ... SOE
Silicon Photodiode ... Sc-PD
Silicon Photodiode ... SPD
Silicon Planar Controlled Rectifier (IAA) ... SPCR
Silicon Planar Epitaxial (IAA) ... SPE
Silicon Planar Multiple Diode (IAA) ... SPMD
Silicon Planar Transistor ... SPT
Silicon Point-Contact (IDOE) ... spc
Silicon Power Rectifier ... SPR
Silicon Precision Alloy Transistor ... SPAT
Silicon Pulser Array ... SPA
Silicon Readout Cell ... SRC
Silicon Rectifier ... SR
Silicon Rectifier Column ... SRC
Silicon Rubber ... SR
Silicon Rubber Insulation ... SRI
Silicon Single Diffused (IAA) ... SSD
Silicon Storage Tech [NASDAQ symbol] (TTSB) ... SSTI
Silicon Storage Technology (PCM) ... SST
Silicon Storage Technology, Inc. [Associated Press] (SAG) ... SiliconS
Silicon Storage Technology, Inc. [NASDAQ symbol] (SAG) ... SSTI
Silicon Stud-Mounted Diode ... SSMD
Silicon Target Image Sensor ... STIS
Silicon Target Intensifier ... STI
Silicon Target Intensifier Vidicon ... STIV
Silicon Transistor Corp. (IAA) ... STC
Silicon Triple Diffused (IAA) ... STD
Silicon Tube ... ST
Silicon Unidirectional Switch (IAA) ... SUS
Silicon Unilateral Diffused Transistor ... SUDT
Silicon Unilateral Switch ... SUS
Silicon Valley Bancshares [Associated Press] (SAG) ... SilicVly
Silicon Valley Bancshares [NASDAQ symbol] (NQ) ... SIVB
Silicon Valley Bancshrs [NASDAQ symbol] (TTSB) ... SIVB
Silicon Valley Group [NASDAQ symbol] (TTSB) ... SVGI
Silicon Valley Group, Inc. [Associated Press] (SAG) ... SilicnVl
Silicon Valley Group, Inc. [NASDAQ symbol] (NQ) ... SVGI
Silicon Valley Group Lithography (ECON) ... SVGL
Silicon Valley Information Center [Database producer] (IID) ... SVIC
Silicon Valley Information Center, San Jose, CA [Library symbol] [Library of Congress] (LCLS) ... CSjSV
Silicon Valley Research [NASDAQ symbol] (TTSB) ... SVRI
Silicon Valley Research, Inc. [Associated Press] (SAG) ... SiliValR
Silicon Valley Research, Inc. [NASDAQ symbol] (SAG) ... SVRI
Silicon Videcon [TV system] ... SIV
Silicon Video Memory ... SVM
Silicon Vidicon Target ... SVT
Silicon Voltage Reference Diode ... SVRD
Silicon Zener Voltage Regulator ... SZVR
Silicon-Aluminum Oxynitride ... SIAON
Silicon-Borne Bonds (IAA) ... SBB
Silicon-Borne Oxygen System (SAA) ... SBOS
Silicon-Controlled Rectifier [Electronics] ... SCR
Silicon-Controlled Rectifier [Dimmer] [Television] (WDMC) ... SCR dimmer
Silicon-Controlled Rectifier Indicator Driver (IAA) ... SCRID
Silicon-Controlled Switch ... SCS
Silicone [Organic chemistry] ... SI
Silicone Brake Fluid (MCD) ... SBF
Silicone Carbide Whisker ... SCW
Silicone Coated ... SC
Silicone Quadrant Detector (MCD) ... SQD
Silicone Rubber-Insulated Fixture Wire, Flexible Stranding (IAA) ... SFF
Silicone Varnish ... SV
Silicone-Based Brake Fluid [Automotive engineering] ... SBBF
Silicones Health Council (EA) ... SHC
Silicon-Insulated Gate ... SIG
Silicon-Insulating Compound ... SIC
Siliconix, Inc. [NASDAQ symbol] (NQ) ... SILI
Siliconix, Inc. [Associated Press] (SAG) ... Silicnx
Siliconized Silicon Carbide (SAA) ... Si-SIC
Silicon-Modified Polyether [Organic chemistry] ... SMP
Silicon-on-Insulator ... SOI
Silicon-on-Insulator and Polysilicon (PDAA) ... SIP
Silicon-on-Sapphire [Integrated circuit] ... SOS
Silicon-on-Sapphire Complementary Metal Oxide Semiconductor (IAA) ... SOSCMOS
Silicon-on-Sapphire Field Effect Transistor (IAA) ... SOSFET
Silicon-on-Sapphire Random Access Memory (IAA) ... SOSRAM
Silicon-on-Something-Else [Telecommunications] (TEL) ... SOSE
Silicon-on-Spinel (IAA) ... SOS
Silicon-Powered Transistor ... SPT
Silicon-Rich Silicon Oxide [Inorganic Chemistry] ... SRSO
Silicon-Symmetrical Switch (CET) ... SSS
Silicotungstate [Inorganic chemistry] ... ST

Silistra [*Bulgaria*] [*Airport symbol*] (OAG) ..... SLS
Silius Italicus [*First century AD*] [*Classical studies*] (OCD) ..... Sil
Siljansnas [*Sweden ICAO location identifier*] (ICLI) ..... ESVS
Silk (AAG) ..... S
Silk (VRA) ..... slk
Silk and Man-Made Fibre Users' Association [*British*] (BI) ..... SMFUA
Silk and Rayon Manufacturers Association [*Defunct*] (EA) ..... SRMA
Silk and Rayon Print Institute [*Defunct*] (EA) ..... SRPI
Silk and Rayon Printers and Dyers Association of America (EA) ..... SRPDAA
Silk Association of Great Britain (EAIO) ..... SAB
Silk Commission Manufacturers Association [*Defunct*] (EA) ..... SCMA
Silk Covered (IAA) ..... SC
Silk Screen (ADA) ..... S/S
Silkair (Singapore) Pte Ltd. [*ICAO designator*] (FAAC) ..... SLK
Silk-Covered Wire (IAA) ..... SCW
Silknit Ltd. [*Toronto Stock Exchange symbol*] ..... SIK
Silkridge Resources [*Vancouver Stock Exchange symbol*] ..... SIS
Silkscreen (VRA) ..... slksc
Silkscreen (MSA) ..... SSCRN
Silkworm Cytoplasmic Polyhedrosis Virus (PDAA) ..... SCPV
Silky Terrier Club of America (EA) ..... STCA
Sill on Composition in Bankruptcy [*A publication*] (DLA) ..... Sill Comp
Sillimanite [*Mineralogy*] ..... SIL
Silly Little Job (DSUE) ..... SLJ
Silly Old Bugger [*Officer over the age of 39*] [*British*] (DSUE) ..... SOB
Silly Old Grandmother with Pictures in Purse ..... SOGWPIP
Silo Hardsite Defense ..... SHD
Silo Installation Refurbish (SAA) ..... SIR
Silo Launched [*Missile launch environment symbol*] L
Silo Stored [*Missile launch environment symbol*] ..... H
Silo Subassembly (SAA) ..... SSA
Silo Support Plan (SAA) ..... SSP
Siloam Springs, AK [*Location identifier FAA*] (FAAL) ..... SLG
Siloam Springs, AR [*FM radio station call letters*] ..... KLRC
Siloam Springs, AR [*FM radio station call letters*] ..... KMCK
Siloam Springs, AR [*AM radio station call letters*] ..... KUOA
Silok [*Ecuador*] [*ICAO location identifier*] (ICLI) ..... SESK
Silo-Launch Test Facility ..... SLTF
Silsbee, TX [*AM radio station call letters*] ..... KKAS
Silsbee, TX [*FM radio station call letters*] ..... KWDX
Siltronics Ltd. [*Toronto Stock Exchange symbol*] ..... SLX
Siltronics Ltd., Kanata, Ontario [*Library symbol National Library of Canada*] (NLC) ..... OKFI
Siltstone [*Lithology*] ..... STS
Silty Soil [*Agronomy*] ..... Si
Silurian [*Geology*] (DOG) ..... S
Silurian [*Period, era, or system*] [*Geology*] ..... SIL
Silva Mind Control [*Psychic system*] ..... SMC
Silvae [*of Statius*] [*Classical studies*] (OCD) ..... Silv
Silvair, Inc. [*ICAO designator*] (FAAC) ..... IJS
Silvaire [*ICAO aircraft manufacturer identifier*] (ICAO) ..... SL
Silver [*Chemical element*] (DOG) ..... Ag
Silver ..... S
Silver (VRA) ..... si
Silver (AAG) ..... SIL
Silver (ROG) ..... SILV
Silver [*Automotive advertising*] ..... SLVR
Silver ..... SLVR
Silver Acorn Developments [*Vancouver Stock Exchange symbol*] ..... SAR
Silver & Gold Senior Citizens Library, Eden, ID [*Library symbol*] [*Library of Congress*] (LCLS) ..... IdEdS
Silver and Pewter Collectors Society [*Defunct*] (EA) ..... S & PCS
Silver Bay Public Library, Silver Bay, MN [*Library symbol*] [*Library of Congress*] (LCLS) ..... MnSib
Silver Bevelled Deckle Edges [*Bookbinding*] (DGA) ..... SBDE
Silver Bevelled Edges [*Bookbinding*] (DGA) ..... SBE
Silver Box Resources [*Vancouver Stock Exchange symbol*] ..... SBO
Silver Braze (MSA) ..... SB
Silver Brazing Union (MSA) ..... SBU
Silver Cadmium Battery ..... SCB
Silver Certificate ..... SC
Silver City [*New Mexico*] [*Airport symbol*] (OAG) ..... SVC
Silver City [*New Mexico*] [*Seismograph station code, US Geological Survey*] (SEIS) ..... SVM
Silver City Airways Ltd. ..... SCAL
Silver City, NM [*Television station call letters*] ..... KOVT
Silver City, NM [*FM radio station call letters*] ..... KSCQ
Silver City Public Library, Silver City, NM [*Library symbol Library of Congress*] (LCLS) ..... NmSc
Silver Cloud Mines [*Vancouver Stock Exchange symbol*] ..... SIV
Silver Creek [*California*] [*Seismograph station code, US Geological Survey*] (SEIS) ..... SVC
Silver Crown [*Class of racing cars*] ..... SC
Silver Cup Resources Ltd. [*Vancouver Stock Exchange symbol*] ..... SCP
Silver Diethyldithiocarbamate [*Organic chemistry*] ..... SDDC
Silver Diner Dvlpmt [*NASDAQ symbol*] (TTSB) ..... SLVR
Silver Drake Resources [*Vancouver Stock Exchange symbol*] ..... SRD
Silver Eagle Resources [*Vancouver Stock Exchange symbol*] ..... SER
Silver Edge [*Bookbinding*] (DGA) ..... SE
Silver Falls Resources [*Vancouver Stock Exchange symbol*] ..... SFL
Silver Gate [*Montana*] [*Seismograph station code, US Geological Survey*] (SEIS) ..... SGM
Silver Gelatin Print (VRA) ..... SGPT
Silver Hart Mines Ltd. [*Vancouver Stock Exchange symbol*] ..... SVM
Silver Hill Mines [*Vancouver Stock Exchange symbol*] ..... SLI
Silver Institute (EA) ..... SI
Silver Iodide [*Pharmacology*] (DAVI) ..... AgI
Silver Iodine Generator ..... SID
Silver King Communic [*NASDAQ symbol*] (TTSB) ..... SKTV
Silver King Communications [*NASDAQ symbol*] (SAG) ..... SKTV
Silver King Communications [*Associated Press*] (SAG) ..... SlvKing
Silver Lady Resources [*Vancouver Stock Exchange symbol*] ..... SLV
Silver Lake, KS [*FM radio station call letters*] (RBYB) ..... KCVT-FM
Silver Lake Resources, Inc. [*Toronto Stock Exchange symbol*] ..... SVL
Silver Library [*A publication*] ..... SL
Silver Life-Saving Medal [*Military decoration*] (GFGA) ..... SLM
Silver Life-Saving Medal [*Military decoration*] ..... SLSM
Silver Marten Rabbit Club (EA) ..... SMRC
Silver Medalist ..... SM
Silver Methenamine [*Biological stain*] ..... SM
Silver Mica [*Capacitor*] ..... SM
Silver Nitrate [*Pharmacology*] (DAVI) ..... $AgNO_3$
Silver Oxide [*Chemistry*] (DAVI) ..... Ag_2O
Silver Oxide Electrode ..... SOE
Silver Plains [*Queensland*] [*Airport symbol*] (AD) ..... VPA
Silver Plate ..... SP
Silver Princess Resources [*Vancouver Stock Exchange symbol*] ..... SVP
Silver Protein [*An antiseptic*] ..... SP
Silver Recovery Unit ..... SRU
Silver Ridge Resources, Inc. [*Vancouver Stock Exchange symbol*] ..... SIG
Silver Sceptre Resources [*Vancouver Stock Exchange symbol*] ..... SST
Silver/Silver Chloride Electrode ..... SSCE
Silver Solder ..... SILS
Silver/Somatostatin Positive Structure [*Anatomy*] ..... SSPS
Silver Spring, MD [*AM radio station call letters*] ..... WKDL
Silver Spring Metro Complex (USDC) ..... SSMC
Silver Spring Metropolitan Complex [*Marine science*] (OSRA) ..... SSMC
Silver Spring Mining [*Vancouver Stock Exchange symbol*] ..... SPG
Silver Springs, FL [*FM radio station call letters*] (RBYB) ..... WNDD
Silver Spur Resources [*Vancouver Stock Exchange symbol*] ..... SS
Silver Standard [*Vancouver Stock Exchange symbol*] ..... SS
Silver Star [*Military decoration*] ..... SS
Silver Star Citation [*Military award*] ..... SSC
Silver Star Medal [*Military decoration*] ..... SSM
Silver State [*ICAO designator*] (AD) ..... ZG
Silver Strike Resources [*Vancouver Stock Exchange symbol*] ..... SSY
Silver Sulfadiazine [*An anti-infective used in burn therapy*] (DAVI) ..... SSD
Silver Talon Mines Ltd. [*Vancouver Stock Exchange symbol*] ..... SVD
Silver Tax Division (Internal Revenue Bulletin) [*A publication*] (DLA) ..... Sil
Silver Tusk Mines [*Vancouver Stock Exchange symbol*] ..... SPK
Silver Users Association (EA) ..... SUA
Silver Wings Fraternity (EA) ..... SWF
Silver Wyandotte Club of America (EA) ..... SWCA
Silverado Foods [*AMEX symbol*] (TTSB) ..... SLV
Silverado Foods, Inc. [*Associated Press*] (SAG) ..... SilverFds
Silverado Foods, Inc. [*AMEX symbol*] (SAG) ..... SLV
Silverado Mines [*NASDAQ symbol*] (TTSB) ..... GOLDF
Silverado Mines Ltd. [*Vancouver Stock Exchange symbol*] ..... SAD
Silverado Mines Ltd. [*Associated Press*] (SAG) ..... SlvMin
Silver-Band Frequency Modulation (IEEE) ..... SBFM
Silvercraft SpA [*Italy ICAO aircraft manufacturer identifier*] (ICAO) ..... SV
Silverdale, WA [*AM radio station call letters*] ..... KITZ
Silver-Dye-Bleach (PDAA) ..... SDB
Silvered Copper [*Wire*] (IEEE) ..... SC
Silvered Optics ..... SO
Silverhawk Resources [*Vancouver Stock Exchange symbol*] ..... SVW
Silver-Intensified Gold [*Biological stain*] ..... SIG
Silverleaf Resources Ltd. [*Vancouver Stock Exchange symbol*] ..... SVF
Silverman Needle Biopsy [*Pathology*] (DAVI) ..... SNB
Silvermaque Mining Ltd. [*Toronto Stock Exchange symbol*] ..... SMQ
Silvermine [*South Africa*] [*ICAO location identifier*] (ICLI) ..... FASV
Silvermine Guild Arts Center (EA) ..... SGAC
Silvermine Guild Center for the Arts [*Later, SGAC*] (EA) ..... SGCA
Silvernail's New York Citations [*A publication*] (DLA) ..... Silv Cit
Silvernail's New York Court of Appeals Reports [*A publication*] (DLA) ..... Sil (Ct of Ap)
Silvernail's New York Court of Appeals Reports [*A publication*] (DLA) ..... Silv A
Silvernail's New York Court of Appeals Reports [*A publication*] (DLA) ..... Silv App
Silvernail's New York Court of Appeals Reports [*A publication*] (DLA) ..... Silv Ct App
Silvernail's New York Court of Appeals Reports [*A publication*] (DLA) ..... Silv Ct App (NY)
Silvernail's New York Court of Appeals Reports [*A publication*] (DLA) ..... Silvernail's NY Rep
Silvernail's New York Criminal Reports [*9-14 New York*] [*A publication*] (DLA) ..... Silv
Silvernail's New York Reports [*1886-92*] [*A publication*] (DLA) ..... Silv
Silvernail's New York Supreme Court Reports [*A publication*] (DLA) ..... Sil (Sup Ct)
Silvernail's New York Supreme Court Reports [*1889-90*] [*A publication*] (DLA) ..... Silv
Silvernail's New York Supreme Court Reports [*A publication*] (DLA) ..... Silv Sup
Silvernail's New York Supreme Court Reports [*A publication*] (DLA) ..... Silv (Sup Ct)
Silvernail's New York Supreme Court Reports [*A publication*] (DLA) ..... SS
Silvernail's New York Unreported Cases [*A publication*] (DLA) ..... Silv Unrep
Silver-Plated Bronze ..... SPB
Silver-Plated Copper ..... SPC
Silver-Plated Copper (IDOE) ..... spc
Silver-Plated Copperweld Conductor (IAA) ..... SPCN
Silverplating ..... SiLPTG

SilverPlatter Information, Inc. [*Commercial firm*] .... SP
Silver-Platter Information Retrieval System [*Computer science*] .... SPIRS
Silverpoint (VRA) .... sipt
Silverquest Resources [*Vancouver Stock Exchange symbol*] .... SQT
Silver-Russell Syndrome [*Medicine*] .... SRS
Silverside Resources, Inc. [*Toronto Stock Exchange symbol*] .... SVS
Silversmith .... S
Silver-Staining Nucleolar Organizer Region [*Biochemistry*] (DAVI) .... AgNOR
Silversword Corp. [*Vancouver Stock Exchange symbol*] .... SLW
Silverton, CO [*FM radio station call letters*] .... KTRN
Silverton Public Library, Silverton, CO [*Library symbol Library of Congress*] (LCLS) .... CoSi
Silverton Public Library, Silverton, OR [*Library symbol Library of Congress*] (LCLS) .... OrSil
Silverton Resources Ltd. [*Toronto Stock Exchange symbol*] .... SVT
Silverware .... SILWR
Silvery Slocan Historical Museum, New Denver, British Columbia [*Library symbol National Library of Canada*] (NLC) .... BNDS
Silver-Zinc Battery .... SZB
Silver-Zinc Cell .... SZC
Silver-Zinc Electrochemical Cell .... SZEC
Silver-Zinc Electrochemical Cell .... SZECC
Silver-Zinc Secondary [*or Storage*] **Battery** .... SZSB
Silvester Godinho [*Deceased, 1244*] [*Authority cited in pre-1607 legal work*] (DSA) .... Sil
Silvester Godinho [*Deceased, 1244*] [*Authority cited in pre-1607 legal work*] (DSA) .... Silve
Silvester Godinho [*Deceased, 1244*] [*Authority cited in pre-1607 legal work*] (DSA) .... Silvr
Silviculture .... SILVIC
Silwood Centre for Pest Management [*Imperial College*] [*British*] (CB) .... SCPM
Sim [*Papua New Guinea*] [*Airport symbol*] (OAG) .... SMJ
SIM International Resource Center, Charlotte, NC [*Library symbol*] [*Library of Congress*] (LCLS) .... NcCSI
Simanggang [*Malaysia*] [*Airport symbol*] (AD) .... SGG
Simanggang [*Malaysia*] [*ICAO location identifier*] (ICLI) .... WBGY
Simao [*China*] [*Airport symbol*] (OAG) .... SYM
Simara [*Nepal*] [*ICAO location identifier*] (ICLI) .... VNSI
Simba Resources, Inc. [*Vancouver Stock Exchange symbol*] .... SMB
Simbai [*Papua New Guinea*] [*Airport symbol*] (OAG) .... SIM
Simcoe County Archives, Minesing, ON, Canada [*Library symbol Library of Congress*] (LCLS) .... CaOMinSA
Simcoe County Archives, Minesing, Ontario [*Library symbol National Library of Canada*] (NLC) .... OMSA
Simcoe County Co-op, Barrie, ON, Canada [*Library symbol Library of Congress*] (LCLS) .... CaOBaS
Simcoe County Co-Op, Barrie, Ontario [*Library symbol National Library of Canada*] (NLC) .... OBAS
Simcoe Erie Investors Ltd. [*Toronto Stock Exchange symbol*] .... SEV
Simcoe, ON [*AM radio station call letters*] .... CHNR
Simcoe, ON [*ICAO location identifier*] (ICLI) .... CWMK
Simcoe Public Library, Ontario [*Library symbol National Library of Canada*] (NLC) .... OSIP
Simcoe Public Library, Simcoe, ON, Canada [*Library symbol Library of Congress*] (LCLS) .... CaOSiP
Simenti [*Senegal*] [*ICAO location identifier*] (ICLI) .... GOTS
Simenti [*Senegal*] [*Airport symbol*] (OAG) .... SMY
Simeon on Elections [*A publication*] (DLA) .... Sim Elect
Simes [*Italy*] [*Research code symbol*] .... S
Simes [*Italy*] [*Research code symbol*] X
Simes and Smith on the Law of Future Interests [*A publication*] (DLA) .... Simes & S Future Interests
Simferopol [*Former USSR Seismograph station code, US Geological Survey*] (SEIS) .... SIM
Simferopol [*Former USSR Airport symbol*] (OAG) .... SIP
Simferopol [*Former USSR ICAO location identifier*] (ICLI) .... UKFF
Simhat Torah (BJA) .... ST
Simi Valley, CA [*AM radio station call letters*] .... KWNK
Simian Acquired Immunodeficiency Syndrome [*Animal pathology*] .... SAIDS
Simian Foam-Virus [*Medicine*] (DMAA) .... SF
Simian Foamy Virus .... SFV
Simian Haemorrhagic Fever Virus .... SHFV
Simian Hemorrhagic Fever [*Medicine*] (DMAA) .... SHF
Simian Immunodeficiency Virus .... SIV
Simian Rotavirus [*Pathology*] .... SR
Simian Sarcoma Associated Virus .... SSAV
Simian Sarcoma Virus [*Oncology*] .... SIS
Simian Sarcoma Virus [*Also, SSV*] .... SiSV
Simian Sarcoma Virus [*Also, SiSV*] .... SSV
Simian Sarcoma Virus-Simian Sarcoma Associated Virus [*Complex*] .... SSV-SSAV
Simian Society of America (EA) .... SSA
Simian T-Cell Lymphotropic Virus .... STLV
Simian Virus .... SV
Simian Virus 40 [*A DNA virus in non-human primates*] (DOG) .... SV 40
Simikot [*Nepal*] [*Airport symbol*] (OAG) .... IMK
Simikot [*Nepal*] [*ICAO location identifier*] (ICLI) .... VNST
Similar (AAG) .... SIM
Similar (AAG) .... SIML
Similar (ROG) .... SIMLR
Similarity Graft Clustering Analysis [*Plant phylogeny*] .... SIMGCA
Similarity Index .... S
Similarity Index .... SI
Simile [*In a Similar Manner*] [*Music*] .... SIM
Simile (WDMC) .... sim
Similkameen Valley Museum, Keremeos, BC, Canada [*Library symbol*] [*Library of Congress*] (LCLS) .... CaBKESVM
Similkameen Valley Museum, Keremeos, British Columbia [*Library symbol National Library of Canada*] (NLC) .... BKESVM
Simla [*India*] [*Airport symbol*] (AD) .... SBJ
Simla [*India*] [*Seismograph station code, US Geological Survey Closed*] (SEIS) .... SMI
Simla [*India*] [*ICAO location identifier*] (ICLI) .... VISM
Simla Rifles [*British military*] (DMA) .... SR
Simmons [*ICAO designator*] (AD) .... FP
Simmons Airlines [*ICAO designator*] (AD) .... MQ
Simmons and Conover's Reports [*99-100 Wisconsin*] [*A publication*] (DLA) .... Sim & C
Simmons College (GAGS) .... Simmons C
Simmons College, Boston, MA [*Library symbol Library of Congress*] (LCLS) .... MBSi
Simmons College, Boston, MA [*OCLC symbol*] (OCLC) .... SCL
Simmons First National Corp. [*Pine Bluff, AK*] [*NASDAQ symbol*] (NQ) .... SFNC
Simmons First National Corp. [*Associated Press*] (SAG) .... SimnFt
Simmons First Natl [*NASDAQ symbol*] (TTSB) .... SFNCA
Simmons Major Market Research, Inc. [*New York, NY Information service or system*] (IID) .... SMMR
Simmons Market Research Bureau, Inc. [*Database producer*] [*New York, NY*] .... SMRB
Simmons on Courts-Martial [*A publication*] (DLA) .... Sim Ct M
Simmons Outdoor Corp. [*Chicago, IL NASDAQ symbol*] (NQ) .... SIMM
Simmons Outdoor Corp. [*Associated Press*] (SAG) .... SimnOut
Simmons' Reports [*95-97, 99 Wisconsin*] [*A publication*] (DLA) .... Sim
Simmons Teen-Age Research Study [*Simmons Market Research Bureau, Inc.*] [*Information service or system*] (CRD) .... STARS
Simmons' Wisconsin Digest [*A publication*] (DLA) .... Sim Dig
Simmons-Boardman Publishing Corp., New York, NY [*Library symbol Library of Congress Obsolete*] (LCLS) .... NNSB
Simon & Schuster [*Publisher*] .... S & S
Simon de Bisignano [*Flourished, 1174-79*] [*Authority cited in pre-1607 legal work*] (DSA) .... S
Simon de Bisignano [*Flourished, 1174-79*] [*Authority cited in pre-1607 legal work*] (DSA) .... Si
Simon de Paris [*Deceased, 1273*] [*Authority cited in pre-1607 legal work*] (DSA) .... S
Simon de Southwell [*Flourished, 1184-1209*] [*Authority cited in pre-1607 legal work*] (DSA) .... S de S
Simon DeBartolo Group, Inc. [*Associated Press*] (SAG) .... SimnD
Simon DeBartolo Group, Inc. [*Associated Press*] (SAG) .... SimonDeB
Simon DeBartolo Group, Inc. [*NYSE symbol*] (SAG) .... SPG
Simon Fraser Gallery, Simon Fraser University, Burnaby, British Columbia [*Library symbol National Library of Canada*] (NLC) .... BVASG
Simon Fraser Resources [*Vancouver Stock Exchange symbol*] .... SFR
Simon Fraser University [*Canada*] .... SFU
Simon Fraser University, Burnaby, British Columbia [*Library symbol National Library of Canada*] (NLC) .... BVAS
Simon Fraser University Library [*UTLAS symbol*] .... SFU
Simon Fraser University, Map Library, Vancouver, BC, Canada [*Library symbol Library of Congress*] (LCLS) .... CaBVaSM
Simon Fraser University, Simon Fraser Gallery, Burnaby, BC, Canada [*Library symbol Library of Congress*] (LCLS) .... CaBVaSG
Simon Fraser University, Vancouver, BC, Canada [*Library symbol Library of Congress*] (LCLS) .... CaBVaS
Simon Property [*Associated Press*] (SAG) .... SimonPr
Simon Property Group [*NYSE symbol*] (SPSG) .... SPG
Simon Reyes [*Cuba ICAO location identifier*] (ICLI) .... MUSR
Simon Transportation Services, Inc. [*NASDAQ symbol*] (SAG) .... SIMN
Simon Transportation Services, Inc. [*Associated Press*] (SAG) .... SimonT
Simon Transportation Svcs'A' [*NASDAQ symbol*] (TTSB) .... SIMN
Simon Wiesenthal Center (EA) .... SWC
Simon-Carves of Canada Ltd., Willowdale, Ontario [*Library symbol National Library of Canada*] (NLC) .... OWSCC
Simonds' Digest of Patent Office Decisions [*United States*] [*A publication*] (DLA) .... Sim Dig Pat Dec
Simonds' Law of Design Patents [*A publication*] (DLA) .... Sim Des Pat
Simond's Patent Law [*A publication*] (DLA) .... Sim Pat L
Simonides [*Fifth century BC*] [*Classical studies*] (OCD) .... Simon
Simons and Stuart's English Chancery Reports [*57 English Reprint*] [*A publication*] (DLA) .... Sim & S
Simons and Stuart's English Chancery Reports [*57 English Reprint*] [*A publication*] (DLA) .... Sim & St
Simons and Stuart's English Chancery Reports [*57 English Reprint*] [*A publication*] (DLA) .... Sim & Stu (Eng)
Simons and Stuart's English Vice-Chancellors' Reports [*1822-26*] [*A publication*] (DLA) .... S & S
Simons and Stuart's English Vice-Chancery Reports [*57 English Reprint*] [*A publication*] (DLA) .... Sim & Stu
Simons' English Chancery Reports [*57-60 English Reprint*] [*1826-50*] [*A publication*] (DLA) .... Sim
Simons' English Chancery Reports [*57-60 English Reprint*] [*A publication*] (DLA) .... Sim (Eng)
Simons' English Vice-Chancery Reports, New Series [*61 English Reprint*] [*A publication*] (DLA) .... Sim NS
Simons' English Vice-Chancery Reports, New Series [*61 English Reprint*] [*A publication*] (DLA) .... Sim NS (Eng)
Simons' Law of Interpleader [*A publication*] (DLA) .... Sim Int
Simon's Law Relating to Railway Accidents [*1862*] [*A publication*] (DLA) .... Sim Ry Acc
Simon's Tax Cases [*United Kingdom*] [*A publication*] (DLA) .... Simon's TC
Simosato [*Japan*] [*Later, HTY*] [*Geomagnetic observatory code*] .... SSO

Simpang [Malaysia] [ICAO location identifier] (ICLI) ... WMKF
Simpatico Wines [Vancouver Stock Exchange symbol] ... SMW
Simple (DAVI) ... simp
Simple [or Simplified] Abbreviated Visual Approach Slope Indicator [FAA] ... SAVASI
Simple Alert (NATG) ... SA
Simple Algebraic Language for Engineers [Computer science] ... SALE
Simple Analytical Interactive Language [Computer science] ... SAIL
Simple Antenna (MCD) ... AT
Simple Approach Lighting System [Aviation] (FAAC) ... SALS
Simple Architecture Microprocessor ... SAM
Simple Arithmetic Expression ... SAE
Simple Assembly Plan ... SAP
Simple, Average, or Difficult (AAG) ... SAD
Simple Bin Assignment Problem ... SBAP
Simple Boolean Expression [Mathematics] ... SBE
Simple Checkout-Oriented Program Language ... SCOPE
Simple Communications Programming Environment [Computer science] ... SCOPE
Simple Complex Reaction-Time Apparatus ... SCRAP
Simple Cost-Effective Microprocessor (MHDI) ... SCMP
Simple Design ... SD
Simple Designational Expression ... SDE
Simple Detection Response ... SDR
Simple Doublet Antenna ... SDA
Simple Electronic Computer [Birkbeck College] [London, England] (DEN) ... SEC
Simple Environment Factor ... SEF
Simple Exponentially-Weighted Moving-Average (PDAA) ... SEWMA
Simple Formattable Document [Telecommunications] (OSI) ... SFD
Simple Harmonic Motion ... SHM
Simple Harmonic Motion (IAA) ... SMH
Simple Hypocalcemic Tetany [Medicine] ... SHT
Simple Image-Processing Package (BYTE) ... SIMPP
Simple Interest [Banking] ... SI
Simple Internet Protocol (TNIG) ... SIP
Simple Least Recently Used Stack Model (MHDI) ... SLRUM
Simple Left to Right [Computer science] ... SLR
Simple Line Source Model [Environmental Protection Agency] (GFGA) ... SLSM
Simple Linear Regression [Statistics] ... SLR
Simple Mail Interface [Computer science] (CDE) ... SMI
Simple Mail Transfer Protocol [Computer science] (PCM) ... SMTP
Simple Maintenance ... SM
Simple Management Protocol [Computer science] (DOM) ... SMP
Simple Mastectomy [Medicine] ... SM
Simple [or Small] Matter of Programming (NHD) ... SMOP
Simple Modeling and Planning [SIMPLAN Users Group] [New York, NY] (CSR) ... SIMPLAN
Simple Modelling of Class Analogy [Data analysis] [Computer science] ... SIMCA
Simple Motor Unit Action Potential [Medicine] ... SMUAP
Simple Network Interacting Program Executive (PDAA) ... SNIPE
Simple Network Management Protocol [Computer science] ... SNMP
Simple Output Format Translator (IEEE) ... SOFT
Simple Phrase Grammar ... SPG
Simple Phrase Language [Computer science] ... SPL
Simple Phrase System ... SPS
Simple Printing ... SP
Simple Programming Language [Computer science] ... SPL
Simple Prose Coefficient [Publishing] ... SPC
Simple, Quick & Affordable [Office furniture] ... SQA
Simple Random Sample [Statistics] ... SRS
Simple Reaction Time [Psychometry] ... SRT
Simple Sequence Repeat [Genetics] ... SSR
Simple Sequence Repeats [Genetics] ... SSR
Simple Serial (MHDI) ... SIMSER
Simple Shift Register Generator ... SSRG
Simple Sinusoidal Quantity ... SSQ
Simple Spike ... SS
[A] Simple Systematic Integration of Statistical Techniques (BUR) ... ASSIST
Simple Test Approach for Readability [General Electric] ... STAR
Simple Transition to Economical Processing (IEEE) ... STEP
Simple Transition to Electronic Processing ... STEP
Simple User Interface Toolkit [University of Virginia] ... SUIT
Simple Vector Format [Proposed Standard] (EERA) ... SVF
Simple Vertex Delivery [Medicine] ... SVD
Simple Wear ... SW
Simple-Adjoint [Method] (USDC) ... SA
Simple-Minded Approach to Squeezed Hollerith Text (SAA) ... SMASHT
Simple-Minded Artificial Intelligence (PDAA) ... SMARTIE
Simple-Minded Artificial Intelligence (IAA) ... SMARTII
Simple-Minded Learning Machine (IEEE) ... SMLM
Simpler Spelling Association [Later, PSC] (EA) ... SSA
Simple-Sequence Length Polymorphism [Genetics] ... SSLP
Simpleton (DSUE) ... SIMP
Simplex ... S
Simplex ... SIM
Simplex (MAE) ... simp
Simplex [Mathematics] ... SPLX
Simplex [Transmission direction] (CET) ... SX
Simplex Circuit ... SPX
Simplex Data Distribution Unit ... SDDU
Simplex Drop Out (IAA) ... SD
Simplex Instrument [Telegraphy] ... SPX
Simplex Remote Communications Central ... SRCC
Simplex Signaling (IAA) ... SX
Simplex TELEX over Radio ... SITOR
Simplex Working [Telecommunications] (ADDR) ... WX
Simplicity, Efficiency, Lower Rates, and Fairness Tax Plan ... SELF
Simplicity Is Greatness [See also GIS] ... SIG
Simplicity, Useability, Reliability, Economy ... SURE
Simplification, Clarification, Unification, Decimalization, Standardization ... SCUDS
Simplification of International Trade Procedures [Committee or Board] [British] ... SITPRO
Simplification, Standardization, Specialization [Economics] ... 3S
Simplification Task (MCD) ... ST
Simplified Account - Numbering System ... SANS
Simplified Accountancy Language (PDAA) ... SIMAL
Simplified Acquisition of Base Engineering Requirements [Air Force] ... SABER
Simplified Acquisition Procedure (AAGC) ... SAP
Simplified Acquisition Threshold (AAGC) ... SAT
Simplified Acute Physiology Score [Medicine] ... SAPS
Simplified Aid for EVA Rescue [NASA] ... SAFER
Simplified Aircraft Instrument Landing System (PDAA) ... SAILA
Simplified Aircraft Instrument Landing System ... SAILS
Simplified and Regularized Writing System ... SRWS
Simplified Automatic Data Plotter ... SADAP
Simplified Bank Loan Participation Plan [Small Business Administration] ... SBLP
Simplified Boiling Water Reactor [Developed by General Electric Co.] [Nuclear energy] ... SBWR
Simplified Chemical Protective Equipment [Army] (DOMA) ... SCPE
Simplified Clearance Procedure [Customs] (DS) ... SCP
Simplified Collective Protection Equipment [Military] (RDA) ... SCPE
Simplified Colorimetric Analysis (MCD) ... SCAN
Simplified Combustion Form Function (MCD) ... SCOFF
Simplified Computer Code ... SCC
Simplified Control ... SIMCON
Simplified Directional Approach System [Aviation] ... SDAS
Simplified Directional Facility [Aviation] ... SDF
Simplified Drive Train [Navistar International Corp.] [Truck engineering] ... SDT
Simplified Early Maturities Participation Plan [Small Business Administration] ... SEMP
Simplified Electronic Tracking (IAA) ... SETA
Simplified Electronic Tracking Apparatus [Air Force] ... SETA
Simplified Employee Pension ... SEP
Simplified Employee Pension Plan (DFIT) ... SEP
Simplified Employee Pension Plan ... SEPP
Simplified Engineering Technique ... SET
Simplified Fault Isolation Test (MCD) ... SFIT
Simplified Federal Urban Driving Schedule [Electric vehicle testing] ... SFUDS
Simplified Firing System ... SFS
Simplified High-Accuracy Guidance [NASA] (NASA) ... SHAG
Simplified Hourly Absence Reporting (MCD) ... SHAR
Simplified Inertial Guidance ... SIG
Simplified Inertial Guidance System (MCD) ... SIGS
Simplified Inertial Guidance-Demonstration [Army] (RDA) ... SIG-D
Simplified Input for TIROS Operational Satellite System (IAA) ... SIFT
Simplified Input for Toss [Computer science] ... SIFT
Simplified Interpretive COBOL Operating System (PDAA) ... SICLOPS
Simplified Labor and Performance (MCD) ... SLAP
Simplified Language for Abstract Mathematical Structures [Computer science] (IEEE) ... SLAMS
Simplified Logic Diagram (IAA) ... SLD
Simplified Logistics and Improved Maintenance (MCD) ... SLIM
Simplified Mainframe Administration System (MCD) ... SMFAS
Simplified Message Processing Simulation (IEEE) ... SMPS
Simplified Method to Achieve Regulated Training ... SMART
Simplified Model Predictive Control [Chemical engineering] [Computer science] ... SMPC
Simplified Modeling and Planning [Programming language] [1973] (CSR) ... SIMPLAN
Simplified Modular Frame Assignment System [Telecommunications] (TEL) ... SMFA
Simplified Modular Frame Assignment System [Bell System] ... SMFAS
Simplified Molecular Input Line Editor [or Entry] System [Computer science] ... SMILES
Simplified Needs Assessment Profile System [Developed by Texas Instruments, Inc.] ... SNAP
Simplified Neutron Transport Computer Code ... SNTCC
Simplified Numerical Automatic Programmer [Computer science] ... SNAP
Simplified Perturbed Hard Chain Theory [Equation of state] ... SPHCT
Simplified Practice Recommendation ... SPR
Simplified Predetermined Motion Time System (MHDB) ... SPMTS
Simplified Procedures for Analysis of Data (OA) ... SPAD
Simplified Processing Station (MCD) ... SPS
Simplified Procurement in a Competitive Environment (AAGC) ... SPICE
Simplified Program Evaluation and Review Technique [Trademark] ... SPERT
Simplified Programming for Acquisition and Control (IEEE) ... SIMPAC
Simplified Programming Language for Artists [1978] [Computer science] (CSR) ... SPLAT
Simplified Real-Time Monitor [Computer science] (MHDI) ... SRTM
Simplified Short ALS [Approach Light System] with Runway Alignment Indicator Lights [Aviation] ... SSALR
Simplified Short ALS [Approach Light System] with Sequenced Flashers [Aviation] ... SSALF
Simplified Short Approach Light [Aviation] ... SSAL
Simplified Short Approach Light System [Aviation] ... SSALS
Simplified Short Approach Light System with Rail [FAA] (TAG) ... SSALR
Simplified Short Approach Light System with Runway Alignment Indicator Lights [Aviation] ... SSALSR
Simplified Spelling ... SS

Simplified Spelling Society (EA) .... SSS
Simplified Storage Management [*Computer science*] .... SSM
Simplified Tactical Approach and Terminal Equipment .... STATE
Simplified Tactical Approach and Terminal Equipment System .... STATES
[*The*] Simplified Test Equipment [*Army*] (INF) .... STE
Simplified Test Equipment for Internal Combustion Engine Powered Material (MCD) .... STE/ICEPM
Simplified Test Equipment for Internal Combustion Engines (RDA) .... STE/ICE
Simplified Test Equipment - Transitional [*Army*] .... STE-T
Simplified Test Equipment-Expandable [*Army*] (RDA) .... STE-X
Simplified Three Axes Reference System (IAA) .... STARS
Simplified Transient Radiation Analysis Program (MCD) .... STRAP
Simplified Unit Invoice Accounting Plan .... SUIAP
Simplified User Logistics [*Military*] (AABC) .... SUL
Simplified Vapor Detector .... SVD
Simplify Obscure ALGOL [*Algorithmic Language*] Programs (MCD) .... SOAP
Simplon Resources Ltd. [*Vancouver Stock Exchange symbol*] .... SMP
Simply Extended and Modified Batch Environmental Graphical System (MHDI) .... SEMBEGS
Simply Interactive PC (PCM) .... SIPC
Simply Simon - The Official Simon MacCorkindale Fan Club (EA) .... SSOSMFC
Simply Transformed Manufacture .... STM
Simposio Internacional de Macromoleculas [*International Symposium on Macromolecules*] .... SIM
Simpson Air Ltd. [*Canada ICAO designator*] (FAAC) .... NCS
Simpson Bible College [*Later, Simpson College*] [*California*] .... SBC
Simpson College, Indianola, IA [*Library symbol Library of Congress*] (LCLS) .... IaIndianS
Simpson College, Indianola, IA [*Library symbol*] [*Library of Congress*] (LCLS) .... IaIndS
Simpson College, Indianola, IA [*OCLC symbol*] (OCLC) .... IOK
Simpson Dysmorphia Syndrome [*Medicine*] (DMAA) .... SDYS
Simpson Indus [*NASDAQ symbol*] (TTSB) .... SMPS
Simpson Industries, Inc. [*Associated Press*] (SAG) .... SimpInd
Simpson Industries, Inc. [*NASDAQ symbol*] (NQ) .... SMPS
Simpson Manufacturing [*NASDAQ symbol*] (TTSB) .... SMCO
Simpson Manufacturing Co., Inc. [*Associated Press*] (SAG) .... SimpsnMf
Simpson Manufacturing Company, Inc. [*NASDAQ symbol*] (SAG) .... SMCO
Simpson on Infants [*4th ed.*] [*1926*] [*A publication*] (DLA) .... Simp Inf
Simpson Quadrature Used Adaptively - Noise Killed (PDAA) .... SQUANK
Simpson, Thacher & Bartlett, Law Library, New York, NY [*Library symbol*] [*Library of Congress*] (LCLS) .... NNSTB
Simpson's Multipliers [*Naval architecture*] .... SM
Simra [*Nepal*] [*Airport symbol*] (OAG) .... SIF
SIMS Communications [*NASDAQ symbol*] (TTSB) .... SIMS
Sims Communications, Inc. [*NASDAQ symbol*] (SAG) .... SIMS
Sims Communications, Inc. [*Associated Press*] (SAG) .... SimsC
Sims Communications, Inc. [*Associated Press*] (SAG) .... SimsCm
SIMS Communications Unit [*NASDAQ symbol*] (TTSB) .... SIMSU
Sims Communications Wrrt'A' [*NASDAQ symbol*] (TTSB) .... SIMSW
Sims Communications Wrrt'B' [*NASDAQ symbol*] (TTSB) .... SIMSZ
Simula, Inc. [*Associated Press*] (SAG) .... Simula
Simula, Inc. [*AMEX symbol*] (SPSG) .... SMU
Simulataneous-Lobe Comparison [*RADAR*] (IAA) .... SLC
Simulate [*or Simulation*] (WDAA) .... SML
Simulate Antiaircraft Weapons (SAA) .... SAW
Simulated [*or Simulation*] (AABC) .... SIM
Simulated (VRA) .... sim
Simulated A/C Maintenance Training System (MCD) .... SAMTS
Simulated Ab Initio Molecular Orbitals [*Atomic physics*] .... SAMO
Simulated Accelerometer Assembly .... SAA
Simulated Acid Rain .... SAR
Simulated Activities of Daily Living (DMAA) .... SADL
Simulated Aerial Combat Maneuver .... SACM
Simulated Air Defense System [*RADAR*] .... SADS
Simulated Air Launch Environment (MCD) .... SALE
Simulated Air Training Bundle (MCD) .... SATB
Simulated Airborne RADAR System (MCD) .... SARS
Simulated Airborne Transpondent System (MCD) .... SATS
Simulated Aircraft Maintenance Trainer (MCD) .... SAMT
Simulated Aircraft RADAR Data .... SARD
Simulated All-Purpose Language (PDAA) .... SIMAL
Simulated Annealing [*Physics*] .... SA
Simulated Approach [*Aviation*] (FAAC) .... SIM
Simulated Area Weapons Effects .... SAWE
Simulated Area Weapons Effects - Indirect Fire .... SAWE-IF
Simulated Area Weapons Effects - Nuclear, Biological, Chemical - Casualty Assesment System [*Army*] .... SAWE-NBC-CAS
Simulated Assignment Model .... SAM
Simulated BOMARC [*Boeing-Michigan Aeronautical Research Center*] Program (IAA) .... SBP
Simulated Boolean-Oriented Language (IAA) .... SIMBOL
Simulated Canadian Society [*Simulation game*] .... SIMCANSOC
Simulated Catalyst Activity Test [*Analytical chemistry*] .... SCAT
Simulated Combat Operations Range Equipment (MCD) .... Score
Simulated Command Module (IAA) .... SCM
Simulated Communications Deception [*Army*] (INF) .... SCD
Simulated Core Assembly [*Nuclear energy*] (NRCH) .... SCA
Simulated Core Mock-Up [*or Model*] [*Nuclear energy*] (NRCH) .... SCM
Simulated Countercurrent Moving-Bed Chromatographic Reactor [*Chemical engineering*] .... SCMBCR
Simulated Countercurrent Moving-Bed Chromatographic Reactor [*Chemical engineering*] .... SCMCR
Simulated Data Generation (IAA) .... SDG
Simulated Data Generator .... SDG
Simulated Data Reduction Program .... SDRP
Simulated Data Tape .... SDT
Simulated Distillation Gas Chromatography .... SDGC
Simulated Dynamic Missile [*Military*] (CAAL) .... SDM
Simulated Dynamic Target [*Military*] (CAAL) .... SDT
Simulated Ejector Ready Panel .... SERP
Simulated Electronic Warfare Training [*Army*] .... SEWT
Simulated Emergency Test .... SET
Simulated EMP [*Electromagnetic Pulse*] Ground Environment [*Air Force*] .... SIEGE
Simulated Engine Failure (ADA) .... SEF
Simulated Fire .... SIMFIRE
Simulated Flame Out [*Aviation*] .... SFO
Simulated Flight - Automatic .... SFA
Simulated Flight Hour (MCD) .... SFH
Simulated Flight - Manual .... SFM
Simulated Flight Tests .... SFT
Simulated Flight Training Ltd. [*British ICAO designator*] (FAAC) .... SIM
Simulated Flow Method .... SFM
Simulated Frequency Analysis and Recording (MCD) .... SIMFAR
Simulated Generation Control .... SGC
Simulated Greenwich Mean Time (MCD) .... SGMT
Simulated Ground Plane [*Automotive engineering*] .... SGP
Simulated Ground Water [*Analytical chemistry*] .... SGW
Simulated High-Level Waste [*Nuclear engineering*] .... SHLW
Simulated Hospital Administration and Planning Exercise .... SHAPE
Simulated Inertial Measurement Unit (NASA) .... SIMU
Simulated Input Preparation System (IEEE) .... SIPS
Simulated Input Processor [*Computer science*] .... SIP
Simulated Installation Fixture (AAG) .... SIFX
Simulated Instrument Flight Rules (AAG) .... SIFR
Simulated Interface Calibration .... SIC
Simulated Intermediate Automatic Test Equipment-Maintenance Training System [*Air Force*] .... SIATE-MTS
Simulated Interpersonal Problem Situation (EDAC) .... SIPS
Simulated Laboratory Module .... SLM
Simulated LASER Target .... SLT
Simulated Launch Demonstration [*NASA*] (KSC) .... SLD
Simulated Launch Test [*NASA*] (KSC) .... SLT
Simulated Launch Vehicle (MCD) .... SLV
Simulated Linguistic Computer .... SLC
Simulated Machine Analysis (IAA) .... SMA
Simulated Maintenance Training System [*Air Force*] .... SMTS
Simulated Mechanical Impact Test Equipment (MCD) .... SMITE
Simulated Message Analysis and Conversion Subsystem .... SMACS
Simulated Midcourse Interaction Test [*NASA*] .... SMIT
Simulated Missile (AAG) .... SM
Simulated Mission Endurance Test (MCD) .... SMET
Simulated Mission Firing .... SIMFIRE
Simulated Moving Bed [*Chemical engineering*] .... SMB
Simulated Navigation Systems .... SIMNS
Simulated Network Analysis Program (SAA) .... SNAP
Simulated Network Simulations (KSC) .... SNS
Simulated Night Vertical Pinpoint .... SNVPP
Simulated Occupant [*People Machine*] [*Office of Civil Defense*] .... SIMOC
Simulated Off-the-Pad Ejection [*NASA*] .... SOPE
Simulated Operational Computer (KSC) .... SOC
Simulated Operational Training [*Navy*] (DNAB) .... SOT
Simulated Operational Vehicle (MCD) .... SOV
Simulated Optical Range Target (MCD) .... SORT
Simulated Output Program [*Computer science*] .... SOP
Simulated Parts Sketch (MCD) .... SPS
Simulated Pave Penny Omnidirectional Target (MCD) .... SPOT
Simulated Planetary Landing Capsule (DNAB) .... SPLC
Simulated Problem Input Evaluation .... SPIE
Simulated Procedure for Obtaining Common Knowledge .... SPOCK
Simulated Program for Investigation of Nuclear Effects .... SPINE
Simulated Raman Scattering .... SRS
Simulated Reentry Vehicle .... SRV
Simulated Remote Sites [*NASA*] (KSC) .... SRS
Simulated Remote Sites Subsystem [*NASA*] (KSC) .... SRSS
Simulated Remote Station [*NASA*] .... SRS
Simulated Remote Station Control Center .... SRSCC
Simulated Remote Station Control Console [*NASA*] (IAA) .... SRSCC
Simulated Robot (NITA) .... SIR
Simulated Social Skills Training (AIE) .... SSST
Simulated Society .... SIMSOC
Simulated Spacecraft [*NASA*] .... SSC
Simulated Spinal Fluid [*Medicine*] .... SSF
Simulated Strapdown Inertial Navigation (MCD) .... SIMSIN
Simulated Strike (SAA) .... SS
Simulated Structural Test (KSC) .... SST
Simulated System (CAAL) .... SIMSYS
Simulated Tactical Operations Systems [*Army*] (RDA) .... SIMTOS
Simulated Tank and Antiarmor Gunnery System (INF) .... STAGS
Simulated Tank Antiarmor Gunnery System - Dragon [*Army*] (INF) .... STAGS-D
Simulated Tape Load .... STL
Simulated Tax and Transfer System [*Social Security Administration*] (GFGA) .... STATS
Simulated Test Markets [*Market research*] (WDMC) .... STM
Simulated Time in Turn (SAA) .... STIT
Simulated Total Atomic Global Exchange [*DoD*] .... STAGE
Simulated Tracking Evaluation Program (SAA) .... STEP
Simulated Trajectories Error Analysis Program [*NASA*] .... STEAP
Simulated Video (MCD) .... SV
Simulated Water Entry Test [*Nuclear energy*] .... SWET

Simulated Work Experience .... SWE
Simulates, Analyzes, Visualizes, Activated Circuitry (DNAB) .... SAVAC
Simulating Digital Systems .... SDS
Simulating Large Explosive Detonable Gas Experiments .... SLEDGE
Simulating Oriented Language .... SOI
Simulating Part (AAG) .... SIPT
Simulation (IAA) .... SIM
Simulation Analysis and Modeling .... SAAM
Simulation and Assignment of Traffic to Urban Road Networks [*Kins Developments Ltd.*] [*Software package*] (NCC) .... SATURN
Simulation and Checkout Equipment [*NASA*] (KSC) .... SIMCHE
Simulation and Computer [*Computer science*] .... SIMCOM
Simulation and Control Rack .... SCR
Simulation and Control Systems Division [*General Electric Co.*] (MCD) .... SCSD
Simulation and Evaluation of Chemical Synthesis [*Computer science*] .... SECS
Simulation and Gaming Method for Analysis of Logistics [*Army*] .... SIGMALOG
Simulation and Training .... S & T
Simulation and Training Advanced Research System [*Air Force*] .... STARS
Simulation and Training Device [*Army*] .... SATD
Simulation and Training Laboratory (SSD) .... SATLAB
Simulation as a Basis for Social Agents' Decisions [*Computer science*] .... SIMBAD
Simulation by Incremental Stochastic Transition Matrices (MCD) .... SISTM
Simulation Center [*Deep Space Network, NASA*] .... SIMCEN
Simulation, Checkout, and Training System .... SCATS
Simulation Communications Electronics [*Group of computer programs*] [*Army*] .... SIMCE
Simulation Complex (NASA) .... SIMCOM
Simulation Control and Training System (NASA) .... SCATS
Simulation Control Area [*NASA*] (MCD) .... SCA
Simulation Control Center [*NASA*] (KSC) .... SCC
Simulation Control Data Package [*NASA*] (NASA) .... SCDP
Simulation Control Program [*Military*] (CAAL) .... SCP
Simulation Control Subsystem (KSC) .... SCS
Simulation Controller .... SIMCON
Simulation Conversion Assembly [*Deep Space Instrumentation Facility, NASA*] .... SCA
Simulation Coordinator .... SC
Simulation, Corps Automated Procedures (MCD) .... SIMCAP
Simulation Council (IAA) .... SC
Simulation Councils, Inc. .... SCI
Simulation Data Conversion Center [*Space Flight Operations Facility, NASA*] .... SDCC
Simulation Data Conversion System [*Space Flight Operations Facility, NASA*] .... SDCS
Simulation Data Language .... SDL
Simulation Data Subsystem (KSC) .... SDS
Simulation Development Program [*DASA*] .... SIMDEP
Simulation Facility [*NASA*] .... SIMFAC
Simulation for Tank/Antitank Evaluation (NATG) .... STATE
Simulation Generating System (MHDI) .... SIMGEN
Simulation Hardware Load Boxes (NASA) .... SHLB
Simulation Hardware System [*NASA*] (MCD) .... SHS
Simulation High-Level Programming Language [*Computer science*] (BARN) .... SIMSCRIPT
Simulation Implementation Machine Programming Languages (KSC) .... SIMPL
Simulation in the Service of Society S3
Simulation Input Tape .... SIT
Simulation Interface Buffer (SSD) .... SIB
Simulation Interface Subsystem (KSC) .... SIS
Simulation Kinetics [*Analysis*] [*Toxicology*] (DAVI) .... Simkin
Simulation Language [*Computer science*] (MHDI) .... SIML
Simulation Language [*1964*] [*Computer science*] .... SIMULA
Simulation Language [*Computer science*] (BUR) .... SL
Simulation Language Based on Programming Language, Version One SIMPL/1
Simulation Language for Alternative Modeling [*Computer science*] (CSR) .... SLAM
Simulation Linear Integrated Circuit [*Electronics*] (OA) .... SLIC
Simulation Management Plan .... SMP
Simulation, Manual and Computerized .... SMAC
Simulation Mission Operation Computer [*NASA*] (MCD) .... SMOC
Simulation Model Object Working Group .... SMOWOG
Simulation Model of Automobile Collisions (IAA) .... SMAC
Simulation Model of Interceptor Terminal Effectiveness .... SMITE
Simulation Modeling System [*FAA*] (TAG) .... SMS
Simulation Monitor and Control Console (KSC) .... SMCC
Simulation Monitor and Control System (CAAL) .... SMCS
Simulation Monitor-Recorder (SAA) .... SIM M-R
Simulation Net Executor (NITA) .... SIMNEX
Simulation Network .... SIMNET
Simulation Object Domain Working Group .... SODW
Simulation of Airlift Resources [*Air Force*] .... SOAR
Simulation of Analog and Hybrid Computers .... SAHYB
Simulation of Analog Methods [*Computer science*] .... SAM
Simulation of Analogical Network (IAA) .... SIMANNE
Simulation of Apollo Reliability [*NASA*] (KSC) .... SOAR
Simulation of Closure and Rendezvous Approach Techniques for Early Spacecraft (IAA) .... SOCRATES
Simulation of Combined Analog Digital Systems [*Computer science*] (IEEE) .... SCADS
Simulation of Industrial Management Problems [*Program*] [*1958*] [*Computer science*] (CSR) .... SIMPLE
Simulation of Life Insurance Decisions [*Game*] .... SOLID
Simulation of Logic Design .... SOLD
Simulation of Machine Indexing .... SMI
Simulation of Personnel Operations [*Army Research Institute for the Behavioral and Social Sciences*] (RDA) .... SIMPO
Simulation of Propulsion Engine Cycle [*NASA*] .... SPEC
Simulation of Reentry Target Interceptor Endgame (MCD) .... SORTIE
Simulation of Research and Development .... SIMRAND
Simulation of Solar Electric Propulsion [*NASA*] .... SIMSEP
Simulation of Tactical Alternative Responses (MCD) .... STAR
Simulation of the Columbia University Libraries [*Data processing research*] .... SCUL
Simulation of the Underlying Processes in Decisions (MCD) .... STUPID
Simulation of Turbofan Engine [*Air Force*] .... SMOTE
Simulation of Utilization, Resources, Cost, and Efficiency .... SOURCE
Simulation Operation Computer (IAA) .... SOC
Simulation Operations Center [*NASA*] (KSC) .... SOC
Simulation Operations Plan [*NASA*] (KSC) .... SOP
Simulation Oriented Language [*Computer science*] .... SOL
Simulation Package [*Computer science*] .... SIMPAC
Simulation Package for University Research and Teaching (PDAA) .... SPURT
Simulation Planning Panel [*NASA*] (NASA) .... SPP
Simulation Process Control Unit (MCD) .... SPCU
[*A*] **Simulation Process Oriented Language** [*1972*] [*Computer science*] (CSR) .... ASPOL
Simulation Processor and Formatter (MCD) .... SPAF
Simulation Program (IAA) .... SIMP
Simulation Program for Sequential System (PDAA) .... SPROSS
Simulation Program with Integrated Circuit Emphasis (MCD) .... SPICE
Simulation Programming Language [*Computer science*] .... SPL
Simulation Punch .... SIMPU
Simulation Reconfiguration Data Collection Subsystem (SSD) .... SRDCS
Simulation Reference Number .... SRN
Simulation Report .... SR
Simulation Routine (IAA) .... SI
Simulation Scheduled Order (SSD) .... SIMSHO
Simulation Study Series (KSC) .... SSS
Simulation Supervisor .... SIMSUP
Simulation Supervisor (SAA) .... SS
Simulation Support Module .... SSM
Simulation Support Processor .... SSP
Simulation Tables - Environment and Dynamic (SAA) .... STEADY
Simulation Tape Alarm Indicator (SAA) .... STAI
Simulation Tape Conversion .... STC
Simulation Tape Print Program .... STAPP
Simulation/Test Acceptance Facility [*Army*] (RDA) .... STAF
Simulation Test Environment to Evaluate Team Load (SAA) .... STEEL
Simulation, Training, and Instrumentation Command [*Army*] (RDA) .... STRICOM
Simulation-Aided Fault Evaluation (MCD) .... SAFE
Simulative Electronic Deception [*Army*] (ADDR) .... SED
Simulative Procedure Oriented Language (MCD) .... SIMUPOL
Simulator [*Computer science*] .... SIM
Simulator (AAG) .... SIMR
Simulator Certification .... SIMCERT
Simulator Compiler [*Computer*] .... SIMCOM
Simulator Control (MCD) .... SC
Simulator Control Panel [*NASA*] .... SCP
Simulator Equipment Requirements for Accelerating Procedural Evolution .... SERAPE
Simulator for Air-to-Air Combat [*Air Force*] .... SAAC
Simulator for Antitank Tactical Training [*Army*] (INF) .... SWATT
Simulator for Electronic Warfare Training .... SEWT
Simulator for Transportation Analysis and Planning (DNAB) .... SITAP
Simulator Initiation (MCD) .... SI
Simulator Interface Device (MCD) .... SID
Simulator Landing Attachment for Night Landing Training .... SLANT
Simulator Load .... SML
Simulator Missile Airborne and Ground (MCD) .... SMAG
Simulator of Immediate Memory in Learning Experiments .... SIMILE
Simulator Operating System (IAA) .... SOS
Simulator Operation and Maintenance Program (MCD) .... SOM
Simulator or Creative Reasoning Applied to Education Systems (IAA) .... SOCRATES
Simulator Panel Set (MCD) .... SPS
Simulator, Projectile, Airburst, Liquid [*Chemical defense device*] [*Military*] (RDA) .... SPAL
Simulator Test Set (CAAL) .... STS
Simulator Trainer Command and Control .... SIMTRACC
Simulator Training .... ST
Simulator Universal Radio Variability Library .... SURVAL
Simulators [*JETDS nomenclature*] [*Military*] (CET) .... SM
Simultaneous (AABC) .... SIMUL
Simultaneous Analysis of Variance .... SANOVA
Simultaneous Baseband Transmission [*of information*] .... SBT
Simultaneous Binaural Midplane Localization [*Audiometry*] .... SBMPL
Simultaneous Broadcast .... SB
Simultaneous Buying and Selling Arrangement .... SBS
Simultaneous Chest Compression and Ventilation [*Medicine*] .... SCV
Simultaneous Color System (IAA) .... SCS
Simultaneous Compass Locator at Middle Marker [*Aviation*] (FAAC) .... SLMM
Simultaneous Compass Locator at Outer Marker [*Aviation*] (FAAC) .... SLOM
Simultaneous Converging Instrument Approaches [*FAA*] (TAG) .... SCIA
Simultaneous Distillation-Extraction [*Chemical engineering*] .... SDE
Simultaneous Double Fire [*Automotive engineering*] .... SDF
Simultaneous Dual Field of View .... SDFOV
Simultaneous Engineering .... SE
Simultaneous Equation Solver [*Computer program*] .... SEQS

Simultaneous Evoked [*Cortical*] **Response** [*Neurophysiology*] ... SER
Simultaneous Foveal Perception [*Ophthalmology*] ... SFP
Simultaneous Impact Rate (AFM) ... SIR
Simultaneous Interface Operation [*Printer technology*] [*Computer science*] (PCM) ... SIO
Simultaneous Interpenetrating Networks [*Organic chemistry*] ... SIN
Simultaneous Laryngoscopy and Abdominal Thrusts [*Medicine*] (DMAA) ... SLAT
Simultaneous Line Over-Relaxation [*Nuclear energy*] ... SLOR
Simultaneous Macular Perception [*Ophthalmology*] ... SMP
Simultaneous Membership Program [*Military*] ... SMP
Simultaneous Multichannel Autoanalyzer [*Laboratory science*] (DAVI) ... SMA
Simultaneous Multicomponent Rank Annihilation [*Mathematics*] ... SMRA
Simultaneous Multiphasic Analysis [*Medicine*] ... SMA
Simultaneous Multiple Angle Reconstruction Technique [*Medicine*] (DMAA) ... SMART
Simultaneous Multiple Image Correlation ... SIMICOR
Simultaneous Multiple Peptide Synthesis [*Biochemistry*] ... SMPS
Simultaneous Observations [*RADAR and optical*] ... SIMOBS
Simultaneous Operation ... SIMOP
Simultaneous Operation Limited Ordinal Modular Network (NITA) ... SOLOMON
Simultaneous Operation Linked Ordinal Modular Network ... SOLOMON
Simultaneous Operations on Intersecting Runways [*FAA*] (TAG) ... SOIR
Simultaneous Operations on Intersecting Wet Runways [*FAA*] (TAG) ... SOIWR
Simultaneous Oral Spelling [*Gillingham method*] [*Education*] ... SOS
Simultaneous Oxidation-Reduction Catalyst [*Automotive engineering*] ... SORC
Simultaneous Parallel Array Grammers (MHDI) ... SIMPARAG
Simultaneous Peripheral Operation Online [*Computer science*] (MCD) ... SPOOL
Simultaneous Prism and Cover (Test) [*Ophthalmology*] ... SPC
Simultaneous Processing of Off-Line Item ... SPOOL
Simultaneous Processing Operation System [*Control Data Corp.*] [*Computer science*] ... SIPROS
Simultaneous Production Operation Online ... SPOOL
Simultaneous Purging Extraction [*Chemistry*] ... SPE
Simultaneous Range Adcock Antenna [*Military RADAR*] ... SRA
Simultaneous Rotating and Reciprocating Technique (DNAB) ... SRRT
Simultaneous Saccharification and Fermentation [*Chemical engineering*] ... SSF
Simultaneous Saccharification and Fermentation [*Biochemistry*] ... SSF
Simultaneous Single Frequency Outlet ... SSFO
Simultaneous Tape Read and Write ... STRAW
Simultaneous Temperature Alarm Readout ... STAR
Simultaneous Test Procedure [*Statistics*] ... STP
Simultaneous Track Processor ... STP
Simultaneous Transmission and Reception RADAR [*DoD*] (ECON) ... STAR
Simultaneous Transmission and Recovery of Alternating Pictures [*TV system*] ... STRAP
Simultaneous Transmission of Range Signals and Voice ... S
Simultaneous Unlimited Rigorous Block Analytical Triangulation [*Apollo program*] [*NASA*] ... SURBAT
Simultaneous Voice/Data ... SVD
Simultaneous Wide Area Telecommunications Service (TSSD) ... SWAT
Simultaneously (NASA) ... SIMO
Simushir [*Former USSR Seismograph station code, US Geological Survey*] (SEIS) ... SIU
Simware, Inc. [*NASDAQ symbol*] (SAG) ... SIMWF
Simware, Inc. [*Associated Press*] (SAG) ... Smware
Sin Ano [*Without Year*] [*Publishing*] [*Spanish*] ... sa
Sin Errores y Omisiones [*Errors and Omissions Excepted*] [*Business term Spanish*] ... SEO
Sinabang/Lasikin [*Indonesia*] [*ICAO location identifier*] (ICLI) ... WITG
Sinagawa [*Japan*] [*Seismograph station code, US Geological Survey Closed*] (SEIS) ... SIN
Sinai (BJA) ... SI
Sinai Field Mission [*US government*] ... SFM
Sinai Hospital, Detroit, MI [*Library symbol Library of Congress*] (LCLS) ... MiDSn
Sinai Hospital, Staff Library, Baltimore, MD [*Library symbol Library of Congress*] (LCLS) ... MdBSH
Sinair [*France ICAO designator*] (FAAC) ... SIN
Sinaota [*Bolivia*] [*ICAO location identifier*] (ICLI) ... SLOT
Sinapis [*Mustard*] [*Pharmacology*] (ROG) ... SINAP
Sinatra Music Society (EAIO) ... SMS
Sinatra Society of America (EA) ... SSA
Sinatra Society of Japan [*Tokyo*] (EAIO) ... SSJ
Since Major Overhaul (DA) ... SMOH
Sinclair Broadcast Group, Inc. [*NASDAQ symbol*] (SAG) ... SBGI
Sinclair Broadcast Group, Inc. [*Associated Press*] (SAG) ... Sinclair
Sinclair Broadcast Group'A' [*NASDAQ symbol*] (TTSB) ... SBGI
Sinclair Community College, Dayton, OH [*Library symbol Library of Congress*] (LCLS) ... ODaSC
Sinclair Community College, Dayton, OH [*OCLC symbol*] (OCLC) ... SIN
Sinclair Lewis Foundation, Sauk Centre, MN [*Library symbol Library of Congress*] (LCLS) ... MnScL
Sinclair, WY [*Location identifier FAA*] (FAAL) ... SIR
Sinclair-Koppers Co. [*Later, Arco Polymers, Inc.*] ... SK
Sinclair's Manuscript Decisions, Scotch Session Cases [*A publication*] (DLA) ... Sinclair
Sind Law Reporter [*India*] [*A publication*] (DLA) ... SLR
Sind Sadr Court Reports [*India*] [*A publication*] (DLA) ... SSCR
Sindacato Autonomo Unificato Ferrovieri Italiani [*Autonomous Union of Italian Railroad Workers*] ... SAUFI
Sindacato Ferrovieri Italiani [*Union of Italian Railroad Workers*] ... SFI
Sindacato Italiano Artisti Belle Arti [*Italian Union of Fine Arts*] ... SIABA
Sindacato Italiano Lavoratori Appalti Ferroviari [*Italian Union of Railroad Contract Workers*] ... SILAF
Sindacato Italiano Lavoratori Cappellai ed Affini [*Italian Federation of Hat and Allied Workers*] ... SILCA
Sindacato Italiano Lavoratori del Petrolio [*Italian Union of Oil Workers*] ... SILP
Sindacato Italiano Lavoratori Postelegrafonici [*Italian Union of Postal and Telegraph Workers*] ... SILP
Sindacato Italiano Odonototecnici Diplomati [*Italian Union of Odontotechnicians*] ... SIOD
Sindacato Italiano Ostetriche [*Italian Union of Midwives*] ... SIO
Sindacato Italiano Pescatori [*Italian Union of Fishermen*] ... SIP
Sindacato Lavoratori Amministrativi e Technichi [*Union of Administration and Technical Workers*] [*Somalia*] ... SLAT
Sindacato Lavoratori della Somalia [*Workers Union of Somalia*] ... SLS
Sindacato Nazionale Attrazionisti Viaggianti [*National Union of Traveling Entertainers*] [*Italy*] ... SNAV
Sindacato Nazionale Dipendenti Amministrazioni Finanziarie [*National Union of Financial Administration Employees*] [*Italy*] ... SINDAF
Sindacato Nazionale Dipendenti Corte dei Conti e Magistrature Amministrative [*National Union of General Accounting Office Employees*] [*Italy*] ... SINACMA
Sindacato Nazionale Dipendenti Marina Mercantile [*National Union of Merchant Marine Workers*] [*Italy*] ... SINAMN
Sindacato Nazionale Dipendenti Ministero Agricoltura e Foreste [*National Union of Ministry of Agriculture and Forestry Employees*] [*Italy*] ... SINAF
Sindacato Nazionale Dipendenti Ministero del Lavori Pubblici [*National Union of Employees in the Ministry of Public Welfare*] [*Italy*] ... SILAP
Sindacato Nazionale Dipendenti Ministero del Lavoro e Previdenza Sociale [*National Union of Ministry of Labor and Social Security Employees*] [*Italy*] ... SINAMIL
Sindacato Nazionale Dipendenti Ministero Difesa [*National Union of Ministry of Defense Employees*] [*Italy*] ... SINADIMID
Sindacato Nazionale Dipendenti Ministero Grazia e Giustizia [*National Union of Ministry of Justice Employees*] [*Italy*] ... SNADIGC
Sindacato Nazionale Dipendenti Ministero Industria e Commercio Estero [*National Union of Ministry of Industry and Foreign Commerce Employees*] [*Italy*] ... SINCOE
Sindacato Nazionale e Dipendenti Ministero Africa Italiana [*National Union of Former Italian Employees of African Ministry*] [*Italy*] ... SINAMAI
Sindacato Nazionale Esperti Laureati Propagandisti Industrie Farmaceutiche [*National Union of University Graduated Experts for Propaganda in Pharmaceutical Industries*] [*Italy*] ... SNELPIF
Sindacato Nazionale Insegnanti Elementari [*National Union of Elementary Teachers*] [*Italy*] ... SNIE
Sindacato Nazionale Lavoratori Italcable [*National Union of Cable Workers*] [*Italy*] ... SILI
Sindacato Nazionale Lavoratori Vetro e Ceramica [*National Union of Glass and Ceramics' Workers*] [*Italy*] ... SLAVCA
Sindacato Nazionale Ministero Pubblica Istruzione [*National Union of Ministry of Public Instructors*] [*Italy*] ... SINAPI
Sindacato Nazionale Scuola Elementare [*National Union of Elementary School Teachers*] [*Italy*] ... SINASCEL
Sindacato Nazionale Scuola Media [*National Union of Intermediate School Teachers*] [*Italy*] ... SNSM
Sindacato Nazionale Tabacchine [*National Union of Women Tobacco Workers*] [*Italy*] ... SNT
Sindacato Petrolieri e Methanieri [*Union of Oil and Methane Gas Workers*] [*Italy*] ... SPEM
Sindacato Scuola non Statale [*Union of Private Schools' Employees*] [*Italy*] ... SINS
Sindal [*Denmark ICAO location identifier*] (ICLI) ... EKSN
Sindbis Core Protein [*Virology*] ... SCP
Sindhi [*MARC language code Library of Congress*] (LCCP) ... snd
Sindicato de Escritores y Artistas [*Ecuador*] ... SEA
Sindicato de Trabajadores Mineros de Llallagua ... STML
Sindicato Nacional dos Empregados do Comercio e da Industria da Provincia de Mocambique [*National Union of Commercial and Industrial Workers of Mozambique*] ... SNECI
Sindicato Unificado de Trabajadores de la Standard Fruit Co. [*Honduras*] ... SUTRASFCO
Sinding Larsen [*disease*] [*or Larsen's disease, or Larsen-Johansson disease*] [*An association known as Larsen's Disease, or Larsen-Johansson Disease*] [*Orthopedics*] (DAVI) ... SL
Sine [*Without*] [*Latin*] ... S
Sine [*Mathematics*] ... SIN
Sine [*Without*] [*Latin*] ... SIN
Sine (IDOE) ... sin
Sine [*Without*] [*Latin*] ... SN
Sine Acido Thymonucleico [*Without Thymonucleic Acid*] ... SAT
Sine Anno [*Without Date of Publication*] [*Latin*] ... SA
Sine Correction [*Without lenses*] [*Ophthalmology*] ... SC
Sine Cosine Multiplier (IAA) ... SCM
Sine Dato [*Undated book*] [*Latin*] ... SD
Sine Die [*Without Day*] [*Latin*] ... SD
Sine Expressione [*Without Expressing*] [*Latin*] (MAE) ... s expr
Sine Fraude Sua [*Without Fraud on His Part*] [*Latin*] (DLA) ... SFS
Sine, Hyperbolic ... SINH
Sine Legitima Prole [*Without Lawful Issue*] [*Latin*] ... SLP
Sine Loco [*Without Place*] [*Latin*] ... SL
Sine Loco, Anno, vel Nomine [*Without Place, Year, or Name*] [*Latin*] ... SLAN
Sine Loco et Anno [*Without Place and Year*] [*Latin*] ... SL & A
Sine Loco et Anno [*Without Place and Year*] [*Latin*] (DGA) ... sleta
Sine Loco Nec Data [*Without Place or Date of Printing*] [*Latin*] ... SLND
Sine Mascula Prole [*Without Male Issue*] [*Latin*] ... SMP
Sine Nobilitate [*Without Nobility*] [*Notation used at Oxford University to indicate that a student was untitled*] [*Latin*] ... S Nob
Sine Nomine [*Without Name*] [*Latin*] (WGA) ... sn
Sine Numero [*Without Number*] [*Latin*] ... sn
Sine of the Amplitude (IEEE) ... SN

Sine Prole [*Died Without Issue*] [*Latin*] ... SP
Sine Prole Legitima [*Without Legitimate Issue*] [*Latin*] ... SPL
Sine Prole Mascula [*Without Male Issue*] [*Latin*] ... SPM
Sine Prole Mascula Superstite [*Without Surviving Male Issue*] [*Latin*] (ADA) ... SPMS
Sine Prole Superstite [*Without Surviving Issue*] [*Latin*] ... SPS
Sine Tempore [*At the Time Announced*] [*Latin*] ... st
Sine Vibration Control ... SVC
Sine Wave Amplitude Modulation ... SWAM
Sine Wave Generator ... SWG
Sine Wave Inverter ... SWI
Sine Wave Response ... SWR
Sine Wave Response Filter [*Program*] ... SWRF
Sine-Cosine ... SC
Sine-Cosine (IDOE) ... sc
Sinecure (ROG) ... SIN
Sine-Kosine Multiplier ... SKM
Sinemurian [*Geology*] ... Sin
Sine-Random Generator ... SRG
Sine-Random Vibration Control ... SRVC
Sines [*Portugal ICAO location identifier*] (ICLI) ... LPSI
Sinfonia [*Symphony*] [*Music*] ... SINF
Sing with the Earth John Denver Fan Club (EA) ... SWEJDFC
Singapore [*Aircraft nationality and registration mark*] (FAAC) ... 9V
Singapore [*MARC geographic area code Library of Congress*] (LCCP) ... a-si--
Singapore [*IYRU nationality code*] (IYR) ... KS
Singapore [*ANSI two-letter standard code*] (CNC) ... SG
Singapore [*ANSI three-letter standard code*] (CNC) ... SGP
Singapore [*MARC country of publication code Library of Congress*] (LCCP) ... si
Singapore [*Airport symbol*] (OAG) ... SIN
Singapore ... SING
Singapore (WDAA) ... SNG
Singapore [*Singapore*] [*ICAO location identifier*] (ICLI) ... WSAR
Singapore [*Singapore*] [*ICAO location identifier*] (ICLI) ... WSJC
Singapore Admiralty Local Staff Union ... SALSU
Singapore Airlines ... SIA
Singapore Airlines [*ICAO designator*] (AD) ... SQ
Singapore Airlines [*Airline flight code*] (ODBW) ... SQ
Singapore Airlines Ltd. [*ICAO designator*] (FAAC) ... SIA
Singapore Association of Trade Unions ... SATU
Singapore Badminton Association (EAIO) ... SBA
Singapore Bank Employees' Union ... SBEU
Singapore Broadcast Authority ... SBA
Singapore Bus Workers' Union ... SBWU
Singapore Business Houses Employees' Union ... SBHEU
Singapore Changi [*Singapore*] [*ICAO location identifier*] (ICLI) ... WSSS
Singapore Clerical and Administrative Workers' Union ... SCAWU
Singapore Democratic Party [*Political party*] (PPW) ... SDP
Singapore Electronic and Engineering, Ltd. (IAA) ... SEEL
Singapore Federation of Services' Unions ... SFSU
Singapore Federation of Unions of Government Employees ... SFUGE
Singapore Fund [*NYSE symbol*] (SPSG) ... SGF
Singapore Fund [*Associated Press*] (SAG) ... Singap
Singapore General Employees' Union ... SGEU
Singapore Government Administrative and Clerical Services' Union ... GACSU
Singapore Institute of Standards and Industrial Research ... SISIR
Singapore Interbank Offered Rate ... SIBOR
Singapore International Building Exhibition ... SIBEX
Singapore International Monetary Exchange ... SMEX
Singapore Justice Party [*Political party*] (PPW) ... SJP
Singapore Law Reports [*1946-49, 1953-56*] [*A publication*] (DLA) ... SLR
Singapore Malays National Organization [*Pertubohan Kebangsaan Melayu Singapore*] [*Political party*] (PPW) ... SMNO
Singapore Monetary Exchange (ECON) ... SIMEX
Singapore National Institute of Chemistry ... SNIC
Singapore National Union of Journalists ... SNUJ
Singapore People's Alliance ... SPA
Singapore Press Holdings (ECON) ... SPH
Singapore Royal Engineers (Volunteers) [*British military*] (DMA) ... SRE(V)
Singapore Sawmill Workers' Union ... SSWU
Singapore Stock Exchange (ODBW) ... SES
Singapore Trade Union Congress ... STUC
Singapore Volunteer Artillery [*British military*] (DMA) ... SVA
Singapore Volunteer Artillery Corps [*British military*] (DMA) ... SVAC
Singapore Volunteer Corps [*British military*] (DMA) ... SVC
Singapore Volunteer Infantry [*British military*] (DMA) ... SVI
Singapore Volunteer Rifles [*British military*] (DMA) ... SVR
Singapore Wood Workers' Union ... SWWU
Singapore-Seletar [*Singapore*] [*Airport symbol*] (OAG) ... XSP
Singer [*Music*] ... SGR
Singer Co., Link Division, Binghamton, NY [*Library symbol Library of Congress*] (LCLS) ... NBiSL
Singer Co. NV [*NYSE symbol*] (SPSG) ... SEW
Singer Co. NV [*Associated Press*] (SAG) ... Singer
Singer Information Services Co. (IAA) ... SISCO
Singer Owners Club (EA) ... SOC
Singer's Probate Cases [*Pennsylvania*] [*A publication*] (DLA) ... Singer Prob Cas (PA)
Singer's Probate Court [*Pennsylvania*] [*A publication*] (DLA) ... Singers
Singh & Choudry [*Publisher*] [*British*] ... S & C
Singh's Mosquito [*Tissue culture medium*] [*Microbiology*] (DAVI) ... SM-1
Singh's Mosquito [*Tissue culture medium*] (BABM) ... SM-L
Singida [*Tanzania*] [*ICAO location identifier*] (ICLI) ... HTSD
Singing ... SG
Singing Machine Company, Inc. [*NASDAQ symbol*] (SAG) ... SING
Singing Machine Co., Inc. [*Associated Press*] (SAG) ... Singing
Singing Machine Co., Inc. [*Associated Press*] (SAG) ... SingM
Singing Point [*Telecommunications*] (TEL) ... SP
Singing Return Loss [*Telecommunications*] (TEL) ... SRL
Singing Tree Press [*Publisher's imprint*] ... STP
Singkawang II [*Indonesia*] [*ICAO location identifier*] (ICLI) ... WIOI
Singkep/Dabo [*Indonesia*] [*ICAO location identifier*] (ICLI) ... WIKS
Singkep Island [*Indonesia*] [*Airport symbol*] (AD) ... SIQ
Single [*One way fare*] [*British*] ... S
Single ... S
Single (MSA) ... SGL
Single (AAG) ... SGLE
Single ... SNGL
Single (IDOE) ... uni-
Single Access (MCD) ... SA
Single Acetate (AAG) ... L
Single Acetate Single Cotton [*Wire insulation*] (AAG) ... L/C
Single Acting Cylinder ... SAC
Single Action [*Firearm*] ... SA
Single Action [*Maintenance*] **Form** (NVT) ... SAF
Single Action Maintenance Instruction (NG) ... SAMI
Single Address Assembly Machine Language [*Computer science*] (MCD) ... SAAL
Single Address Code (AAG) ... SAC
Single Administrative Document [*European trade contract*] [*1986*] (DCTA) ... SAD
Single Advanced Signal Processor [*Military*] (CAAL) ... SASP
Single Aircraft Tracking Program (IAA) ... SATP
Single Airlift Organization (CINC) ... SAO
Single Allocation and Reservation Study (MCD) ... SARS
Single Ammunition Logistics System - Korea (MCD) ... SALS-K
Single Amplitude (IAA) ... SA
Single Anchor Leg Mooring [*Oil platform*] ... SALM
Single Anchor Leg Storage (PDAA) ... SALS
Single and Double [*Reduction gears*] ... S & D
Single and Double Simultaneous Stimulation [*Neuropsychology test*] ... SDSS
Single and Double Simultaneous Stimulation Test [*Neuropsychology test*] ... SDSST
Single Angle Scattering ... SAS
Single Anomalous Scattering [*Crystallography*] ... SAS
Single Application Data Sheet ... SADS
Single Application Method [*College admissions*] ... SAM
Single Armor [*Telecommunications*] (TEL) ... SA
Single Army Battlefield Requirements Evaluator [*Army*] ... SABRE
Single Array Test System (MCD) ... SATS
Single Article Announcement [*American Chemical Society publication*] ... SAA
Single Asphalt Surface Treatment ... SAST
Single Assignment Mathematical Programming Language [*1971*] [*Computer science*] (CSR) ... SAMPLE
Single Association Control Function [*Telecommunications*] (OSI) ... SACF
Single Association Object [*Telecommunications*] (OSI) ... SAO
Single Attached Stations [*Computer science*] (TNIG) ... SAS
Single Attack Integrated System ... SAINTS
Single Attack Option ... SAO
Single Audio System (CAAL) ... SAS
Single Barrier Failure (SSD) ... SBF
Single Base Solid Propellant (MSA) ... SBSP
Single Bayonet [*Lamp base*] (NTCM) ... SB
Single Binocular Vision ... SBV
Single Black Female [*Classified advertising*] (CDAI) ... SBF
Single Black Male [*Classified advertising*] ... SBM
Single Blind [*Experimental condition*] ... SB
Single Board Computer ... SBC
Single Board Computer ... SBC
Single Braid (CET) ... SB
Single Breath ... SB
Single Breath Diffusing Capacity of the Lungs for Carbon Monoxide [*Medicine*] (DAVI) ... D_{LCOSB}
Single Breath Nitrogen [*Test*] [*Medicine*] ... SBN_2
Single Bridgewire Apollo Standard Initiator [*Explosive*] ... SBASI
Single Burst Correcting ... SBC
Single Burst Probability of Hit [*Military*] (AABC) ... SBPH
Single Byte Command Code Set Mapping [*Computer science*] ... SBCCS
Single Byte Interleaved ... SBI
Single Camshaft Type A [*Cosworth racing engines*] [*Automotive engineering*] ... SCA
Single Cantilevered Axle ... SAXLE
Single Carburetor [*Automotive engineering*] ... SC
Single Card Reader [*Computer science*] (IAA) ... SCR
Single Carrier Initiated Single Carrier Multiplication (MCD) ... SCISCM
Single Case ... SC
Single Catastrophic Failure (AAG) ... SCF
Single Cell ... SC
Single Cell Cytotoxicity Assay [*Clinical chemistry*] ... SCCA
Single Chain Antibody Fragment [*Botany*] (ECON) ... SCAB
Single Chamber Controllable Motor (MCD) ... SCCM
Single Change of Station (IAA) ... SCS
Single Channel Amplitude Monopulse Processing ... SCAMP
Single Channel Analyzer ... SCA
Single Channel Communications Controller (NITA) ... SCCC
Single Channel Control Unit ... SCCU
Single Channel Monitoring (NITA) ... SCL
Single Channel Objective Tactical Terminal [*Army*] (RDA) ... SCOTT
Single Channel Per Carrier Multiple Access Demand Assignment Equipment (NITA) ... SPADE
Single Channel Radio Access Subsystem (MCD) ... SCRA
Single Channel Simplex ... SCS

Single Channel Tactical Radio Communications [*Army*] (RDA) .... SINCTRAC
Single Channel Transponder (MCD) .... SCT
Single Channel Transponder (DWSG) .... SCTR
Single Channel Voice Frequency [*Telecommunications*] (OSI) .... SCVF
Single Channel Voice Frequency (NITA) .... SCVF
Single Character Recognition .... SCR
Single Chemical (MAE) .... SC
Single Chip Module [*Electronics*] (CDE) .... SCM
Single Circuit [*Electricity*] .... SC
Single Column .... SC
Single Column Inch (ADA) .... SCI
Single Column Model (USDC) .... SCM
Single Column Model [*Marine science*] (OSRA) .... SCM
Single Comb .... SC
Single Commutation Direct Current (IAA) .... SCDC
Single Component Peak [*Spectra*] .... SCP
Single Composition Lathe-Cut [*Dental alloy*] .... SCL
Single Composition Spherical [*Dental alloy*] .... SCS
Single Conditioning Unit .... SCU
Single Conductor [*Wire or cable*] 1/C
Single Conductor Cable (MSA) .... SCC
Single Conductor Cable [*JETDS nomenclature*] [*Military*] (CET) .... WS
Single Conductor, Degaussing, Armored (IAA) .... SDGA
Single Conductor, Heat and Flame Resistant, Armor [*Cable*] .... SHFA
Single Conductor, Shipboard General Use, Armored (IAA) .... SSGA
Single Contact [*Switch*] .... SC
Single Contact Midge Flange .... SCMF
Single Control Support (BUR) .... SCS
Single Copy Complexity [*Genetics*] .... SCC
Single Copy Order Plan [*Later, STOP*] [*Bookselling*] .... SCOP
Single Coronary Artery Bypass [*Cardiology*] (DMAA) .... SCABG
Single Coronary Artery Bypass Graft [*Cardiology*] .... SCABG
Single Cost Factor .... SCF
Single Cotton Covered (IDOE) .... scc
Single Cotton Enameled (IDOE) .... sce
Single Cotton Varnish [*Wire insulation*] (AAG) CV
Single Cotton-Covered [*Wire insulation*] .... SCC
Single Cotton-Covered Enameled [*Wire insulation*] (DEN) .... SCE
Single Counter .... SC
Single Crochet .... SC
Single Crystal .... SC
Single Crystal (IDOE) .... sc
Single Crystal Automatic Neutron Diffractometer .... SCAND
Single Crystal Filament .... SCF
Single Crystal LASER Fusion [*For dating of geological material*] .... SCLF
Single Crystal Meteorite .... SCM
Single Crystal Needle .... SCN
Single Crystal Orthoferrites .... SCO
Single Current (IAA) .... SC
Single Cycle Execute .... SCE
Single Dad's Hotline [*Defunct*] (EA) .... SDH
Single Deck [*Navigation*] .... SD
Single Degaussing Cable .... SDGA
Single Degree of Freedom [*Also, SDOF*] [*Acoustics*] .... SDF
Single Degree of Freedom [*Also, SDF*] [*Acoustics*] .... SDOF
Single Density [*Computer science*] (IAA) .... SD
Single Department Purchasing [*Agency*] [*Military*] .... SDP
Single Determination .... SD
Single Diaphragm [*Automotive engineering*] .... SD
Single Diaphragm Distributor [*Automotive engineering*] .... SDD
Single Differential Cross Section .... SDCS
Single Disk Storage Device [*Computer science*] (BUR) .... SDSD
Single Distilled .... SD
Single Document Interface [*Computer science*] (CDE) .... SDI
Single Domain [*Grains in rocks*] [*Geophysics*] .... SD
Single Drift Correction .... SDC
Single Driver's License [*Law*] .... SDL
Single Drug Resistance .... SDR
Single Dry Plate (IAA) .... SDP
Single Echelon Multi-Base Resource Allocation Technique (PDAA) .... SEMBRAT
Single Edge Notched .... SEN
Single Edge Notched Beam [*Materials science and technology*] .... SENB
Single Electron MOS [*Metal Oxide Semiconductor*] **Memory** .... SEMM
Single Electron Response [*Electronics*] (OA) .... SER
Single Electron Transistor [*Physics*] .... SET
Single Employer Pension Plan Amendments Act of 1986 (WYGK) .... SEPPA
Single End .... SE
Single End Strip Adhesion (PDAA) .... SESA
Single Engine .... SE
Single Engine .... SENG
Single Engine Control System Application (MCD) .... SECSA
Single Engine Flight Training .... SEFT
Single Engine Land [*Pilot rating*] (AIA) .... SEL
Single Engine Sea [*Pilot rating*] (AIA) .... SES
Single Entry [*Bookkeeping*] .... SE
Single Entry/Single Exit .... SE/SE
Single Equivalent Formant (IAA) .... SEF
Single Error Correcting .... SEC
Single Error Correcting and Partial Double Error Detecting [*Computer science*] (MHDI) .... SECPDED
Single Escape Peak Efficiency [*Nuclear science*] (OA) .... SEPE
Single Escape Tower .... SET
Single European Act [*EEC*] .... SEA
Single European Banking Licence .... SEBL
Single European Market .... SEM
Single Event Upset (SSD) .... SEU
Single Exhaust [*Automotive engineering*] .... S/EXH
Single Face .... S/F
Single Face .... SIF
Single Failure Analysis [*Nuclear energy*] (NRCH) .... SFA
Single Failure Point [*NASA*] (MCD) .... SFP
Single Failure Point Analysis [*NASA*] (KSC) .... SFPA
Single Failure Point Summary [*NASA*] (NASA) .... SFPS
Single Family Detached [*Real estate terminology*] (EMRF) .... SFD
Single Family Dwelling [*Economics*] .... SFD
Single Feeder .... SF
Single Fiber Electromyography [*Neurophysiology*] .... SFEMG
Single Fiber Tensile Kinetic [*Method for studying permanent hair waving*] .... SFTK
Single Floating-Gate Amplifier [*Electronics*] (PDAA) .... SFGA
Single Flow (NASA) .... S/F
Single Flux Quantum [*Pulse*] [*Physics*] .... SFQ
Single Frequency [*Telecommunications*] .... SF
Single Frequency Approach [*FAA*] (TAG) .... SFA
Single Frequency Signaling Unit .... SFSU
Single Fronted Weatherboard (ADA) .... SFWB
Single Geometric Model [*Computer-assisted design*] .... SGM
Single Gimbal Control Moment Gyro [*Navigation*] .... SGCMG
Single Gourmet (EA) .... SG
Single Green Silk-Covered [*Wire insulation*] .... SGS
Single Groove [*Insulators*] .... SG
Single Groove, Single Petticoat [*Insulators*] .... SGSP
Single Ground Point [*NASA*] (MCD) .... SGP
Single Gun Unit [*British military*] (DMA) .... SGU
Single Heterostructure (MCD) .... SH
Single Highest Peak [*Aerospace*] .... SHP
Single High-Resolution File [*Computer science*] .... SHR
Single Identifying Number .... SIN
Single Imaging RADAR .... SIR
Single in Line [*Electronics*] (EECA) .... SIL
Single Income, Couple of Kids [*Lifestyle classification*] .... Sick
Single Income, Kids [*Lifestyle classification*] .... Sik
Single Income, Lots of Kids .... SILK
Single Income, Money Problems [*Lifestyle classification*] .... Simp
Single Income, No Kids [*Lifestyle classification*] .... Sink
Single In-Line Memory Module [*Computer science*] .... SIMM
Single In-Line Module [*Computer science*] .... SILM
Single In-Line Package [*Computer science*] .... SIP
Single In-Line PIN [*Computer science*] (PCM) .... SIP
Single In-Line Plastic (IAA) .... SIP
Single Input Multiple Data Stream (IAA) .... SIMD
Single Instruction .... SI
Single Instruction Execute .... SIE
Single Instruction, Multiple Data (IEEE) .... SIMD
Single Instruction Multiple Data Stream (NITA) .... SIMD
Single Instruction Multiple Data Stream (IAA) .... SIMDS
Single Instruction, Single Data (IEEE) .... SISD
Single Instruction Single Data Stream (IAA) .... SISD
Single Instruction Single Data Stream (NITA) .... SISDATA
Single Instruction Stream, Multiple Data Stream [*Computer science*] (MHDI) .... SIS-MDS
Single Instruction Stream, Single Data Stream [*Computer science*] (MHDI) .... SIS-SDS
Single Integrated Attack Team .... SIAT
Single Integrated Damage Anaysis Capability (MCD) .... SIDAC
Single Integrated Development Test Cycle .... SIDTC
Single Integrated Development Test Cycle (MCD) .... SIDTEC
Single Integrated Development Test System .... SIDTS
Single Integrated Operational [*or Operations*] **Plan** [*Military*] (AFM) .... SIOP
Single Integrated Operational Plan - Extremely Sensitive Information [*Security level above Top Secret*] .... SIOP-ESI
Single Integrated Test Cycle [*Army*] .... SITC
Single, Intelligent, and Educated and Growing Old [*Lifestyle classification*] .... Siego
Single Internal Mammary Artery [*Medicine*] (DMAA) .... SIMA
Single Isolated Whell Load [*ICAO*] (FAAC) .... SIWL
Single Isomorphous Replacement [*Crystallography*] .... SIR
Single Isomorphous Replacement, Anomalous Scattering [*Crystallography*] .... SIRAS
Single Item, Multisource (IEEE) .... SIMS
Single Item Release .... SIR
Single Item Removal [*Maintenance*] .... SIR
Single Item, Single Source (IEEE) .... SISS
Single Item Squawk Sheet .... SIS
Single Jewish [*Classified advertising*] .... SJ
Single Jewish Female [*Classified advertising*] .... SJF
Single Jewish Male [*Classified advertising*] .... SJM
Single Jewish Woman [*Classified advertising*] .... SJW
Single Junction Latching Circulator .... SJLC
Single Langmuir Probe (IAA) .... SLP
Single Language Dedicated Time-Sharing System .... SLDTSS
Single Large Expensive Disk [*Computer science*] (PCM) .... SLED
Single Launch Contractor (KSC) .... SLC
Single Layer Metallization (IAA) .... SLAM
Single Layer Polysilicon (IAA) .... SLP
Single Lead [*Cables*] (IAA) .... SL
Single Lead Covered (IAA) .... SLC
Single Ledger [*Accounting*] .... SL
Single Level Power Management System .... SLPMS
Single Line .... SL
Single Line Control (BUR) .... SLC

Single Line Internet Protocol [*Telecommunications*] (DOM) .... SLIP
Single Line Synchronous Adapter (MCD) .... SSA
Single Line to Ground (IAA) .... SLG
Single Line Working [*Railway engineering term*] (DCTA) .... SLW
Single Linear Polarization .... SLP
Single Link Procedures (TNIG) .... SLP
Single Longitudinal Mode .... SLM
Single Loop Operation [*Nuclear energy*] (NRCH) .... SLO
Single Loop Programmable Indicating Controller (NITA) .... SLPC
Single, Lots of Income, No Kids [*Lifestyle classification*] .... Slink
Single Macro Language [*Computer science*] .... SML
Single Manager [*Military*] .... SM
Single Manager Approach .... SMA
Single Manager for Ammunition [*DoD*] (MCD) .... SMA
Single Manager for Ammunition, Conventional [*DoD*] .... SMAC
Single Manager for Conventional Ammunition [*DoD*] .... SMCA
Single, Married, Widowed, Divorced, Separated .... SMWDSEP
Single Message Rate Timing .... SMRT
Single Minute Exchange of Die [*Manufacturing*] .... SMED
Single Mission Air Medal (DNAB) .... SMAM
Single Mode .... SM
Single Mode Alignment (CAAL) .... SMAL
Single Module Engine Control [*Automotive engineering*] .... SMEC
Single Molecule Detection [*Analytical chemistry*] .... SMD
Single Molecule Spectroscopy .... SMS
Single Mothers by Choice (EA) .... SMC
Single Motor Unit .... SMU
Single Negotiating Text [*UN Law of the Sea Conference*] .... SNT
Single Nephron Glomerular Filtration Rate .... SNGFR
Single Net Information and Position [*Reporting procedures*] [*Navy*] (NVT) .... SNIP
Single Net Integrated Procedure [*Military*] (CAAL) .... SNIP
Single Noise Exposure Level .... SENEL
Single Nuclear Attack Case Study [*DoD*] .... SNACS
Single Nucleotide Polymorphism [*Genetics*] .... SNP
Single Nucleotide Polymorphism [*Genetics*] .... SNP
Single Number Access Plan [*Telecommunications*] (TEL) .... SNAP
Single Nylon Enamelled (IAA) .... SNE
Single Object Tracking RADAR (MCD) .... SOTR
Single Operation Responsibility (IAA) .... SOR
Single Orbit Computation .... SOC
Single Order Release (MCD) .... SOR
Single Organ System Failure [*Medicine*] (DMAA) .... SOSF
Single Oriental Female [*Classified advertising*] .... SOF
Single Oriental Male [*Classified advertising*] .... SOM
Single Overhead Camshaft [*Automotive engineering*] .... SOHC
Single Palmar Crease [*Medicine*] (DMAA) .... SPC
Single Paper [*Wire insulation*] (AAG) .... P
Single Paper Covered [*Wire insulation*] (IAA) .... SPC
Single Paper Double Cotton [*Wire insulation*] (AAG) .... PDC
Single Paper Single Cotton [*Wire insulation*] (AAG) .... PC
Single Parameter Analysis .... SPA
Single Parent of the Year .... SPOTY
Single Particle .... SP
Single Pass Fit Program (MCD) .... SPFP
Single Passenger Reservation System [*DoD*] .... SPRS
Single Path Doppler [*RADAR*] (AAG) .... SPD
Single Path Error Correcting Teleprinter over Radio [*Telecommunications*] (IAA) .... SPECTOR
Single Payer Across the Nation [*Health insurance*] .... SPAN
Single Payment (ILCA) .... SP
Single Pedestrians League Against Taxes and Traffic [*British*] (DI) .... SPLATT
Single Persons for Tax Equality Association (EAIO) .... SPTEA
Single Pet Lover .... SPL
Single Photon Absorptiometry [*Analytical chemistry*] .... SPA
Single Photon Emission Computed Tomography .... SPECT
Single Photon Emission Tomography .... SPET
Single Pickle Ordinary [*Metal industry*] .... SPO
Single Pilot Instrument Flight Rules [*Program*] .... SPIFR
Single Pilot Instrument Rating [*Aviation*] (DA) .... SPIR
Single Ply Roofing Institute (EA) .... SPRI
Single Point Buoy Mooring [*Oil platform*] .... SPBM
Single Point Failure (NASA) .... SPF
Single Point Injection [*Automotive engineering*] .... SPI
Single Point of Contact (GFGA) .... SPOC
Single Position Automatic [*Tester*] .... SPA
Single Potential Analysis of Cavernous Electrical Activity [*Medicine*] (DMAA) .... SPACE
Single Precision (NASA) .... SP
Single Precision Orbit Determination Program [*NASA*] .... SPODP
Single Precision Unpacked Rounded [*floating-point package*] [*Computer program system Sperry Rand Corp.*] .... SPUR
Single Premium Immediate Annuities [*Insurance*] .... SPIA
Single Premium Variable Life Investment [*Insurance*] .... SPVLI
Single Premium Whole Life Insurance Policy .... SPWL
Single Prime Contractor [*Weapon system procurement*] [*Air Force*] (AAG) .... SPC
Single Prime Contractor Policy [*Air Force*] (AAG) .... SPCP
Single Processor Interface .... SPI
Single Product Cost Leadership (MHDB) .... SPCL
Single Program Element Funding [*Military*] (AABC) .... SPEF
Single Program Initiated [*Computer science*] (IAA) .... SPI
Single Program Initiation [*Computer science*] .... SPI
Single Program Initiator [*Computer science*] (ECII) .... SPI
Single Program Manager [*Air Force*] .... SPM
Single Programmer .... SP
Single Project Funding (MCD) .... SPF
Single Propellant Loading (AFM) .... SPL
Single Pulse Selection System .... SPSS
Single Purpose .... SP
Single Quantum Well [*Physics*] .... SQW
Single Radial Diffusion [*or Immunodiffusion*] [*Analytical biochemistry*] .... SRD
Single Radial Diffusion Test [*Medicine*] (DMAA) .... SRDT
Single Radial Hemolysis [*Immunochemistry*] .... SRH
Single Radial Immunodiffusion [*Medicine*] (DMAA) .... SRID
Single Radical Hemolysis [*Hematology*] (DAVI) .... SRH
Single Readiness Information System [*NORRS*] .... SIRIN
Single Reduction .... SR
Single Region Execution .... SRE
Single Register Machine .... SRM
Single Relaxation Time Approximation [*Physics*] .... SRTA
Single Requesting Terminal [*Computer science*] (IBMDP) .... SRT
Single Requirements Determination System .... SRDS
Single Reversal Permanent Magnet (IAA) .... SRPM
Single Role Mine-Hunter [*Military*] (PDAA) .... SRMH
Single Rotating Directional Transmission [*Military*] (CAAL) .... SRDT
Single Rotating Knife .... SRKN
Single Rotation Engine (IAA) .... SRE
Single Rotation Machine (IAA) .... SIM
Single Round Container [*for toxic chemicals*] [*Army*] .... SRC
Single Round Effectiveness (NATG) .... SRE
Single Run Time (IAA) .... SRT
Single Rural Eligible [*Classified advertising*] .... SRE
Single Scale Integration (IAA) .... SSI
Single Scan .... SS
Single Scattering [*Photonics*] .... SS
Single Screw .... SISC
Single Screw Ship .... SSS
Single Seat Attack Weapon System [*Military*] .... SSAWS
Single Seat Night Attack Program (MCD) .... SSNAP
Single Seated .... SS
Single, Separated, Widowed, or Divorced .... SSWD
Single Service Institute [*Later, FPI*] (EA) .... SSI
Single Service Logistics Support Manager (MCD) .... SSLSM
Single Service Training Manager (MCD) .... SSTM
Single Ship Deep Sweep (DOMA) .... SSDS
Single Shot .... SS
Single Shot Engagement Kill Probability (MCD) .... SSEKP
Single Shot Kill Probability (MCD) .... SSRP
Single Shot Probability of Kill [*Military*] .... SSPK
Single Shoulder Contrast Arthrography [*Radiology*] (DAVI) .... SSCA
Single Sideband .... SS
Single Sideband .... SSB
Single Sideband Amateur Radio Association (IAA) .... SSBARA
Single Sideband Amplitude Modulation (KSC) .... SSBAM
Single Sideband Amplitude Modulation [*Telecommunications*] (IAA) .... SSBM
Single Sideband Angle Modulation [*Telecommunications*] (IAA) .... SSBM
Single Sideband Communications System .... SSCS
Single Sideband Doppler Very-High-Frequency Omnidirectional Range [*FAA*] .... SSDVOR
Single Sideband Exciter .... SSE
Single Sideband Filter .... SSBF
Single Sideband Filter .... SSF
Single Sideband Frequency Modulation (IEEE) .... SSBFM
Single Sideband Frequency Modulation .... SSFM
Single Sideband Generator .... SSBG
Single Sideband Generator .... SSG
Single Sideband Modulation .... SSBM
Single Sideband Modulation .... SSM
Single Sideband Phase Modulation [*Telecommunications*] (IAA) .... SSPM
Single Sideband Reduced Carrier [*Telecommunications*] (IAA) .... SSRC
Single Sideband Signal Multiplier [*Telecommunications*] .... SSM
Single Sideband Suppressed Carrier [*Telecommunications*] .... SSBSC
Single Sideband Suppressed Carrier .... SSSC
Single Sideband Suppressed Carrier Amplitude Modulation (NITA) .... SSB-SC/AM
Single Sideband Suppressed Carrier Optical Modulator .... SSBSCOM
Single Sideband Transmission [*Telecommunications*] (TEL) .... SST
Single Sideband with Carrier [*Telecommunications*] (IAA) .... SSBWC
Single Sideband with Suppressed Carrier, Amplitude Modulated [*Telecommunications*] (IAA) .... SSBSCAM
Single Sided Frame [*Telecommunications*] (TEL) .... SSF
Single Signal .... SS
Single Signal (IEEE) .... SSIG
Single Signal Receiver [*Telecommunications*] (IAA) .... SSR
Single Signal Superhet (IAA) .... SSS
Single Signal Supersonic [*Heterodyne*] (DEN) .... SSS
Single Signaling Unit [*Telecommunications*] (TEL) .... SSU
Single Silk [*Wire insulation*] .... S
Single Silk [*Wire insulation*] (AAG) .... SI
Single Silk [*Wire insulation*] (IAA) .... SS
Single Silk Covered (IDOE) .... ssc
Single Silk Covering over Enamel Insulation [*Telecommunications*] (TEL) .... SSE
Single Silk Enameled (IDOE) .... ssc
Single Silk Varnish [*Wire insulation*] (AAG) .... SV
Single Silk-Covered [*Wire insulation*] .... SSC
Single Silk-Covered Wire [*Insulation*] (IAA) .... SSCW
Single Solar Flare .... SSF
Single Source of Supply (MCD) .... SSOS
Single Source Processor-SIGINT [*Signal Intelligence*] .... SSP-S
Single Speed [*Automotive engineering*] .... S/SPD
Single Stage to Orbit [*NASA*] .... SSTO
Single Station Doppler (IAA) .... SSD

Single Station Unit Fielding Training [*Air Force*] [*Navy*] (DOMA) .... SSUFT
Single Step (IAA) ...... SSF
Single Stock Fund [*DoD*] ...... SSF
Single Stock Point [*Military*] (AFIT) ...... SSP
Single Stout [*Beer*] (ROG) ...... SS
Single Strength [*Citrus juices*] ...... SSGJ
Single Strength Grapefruit Juice ...... SSGJ
Single Strength Orange Juice ...... SSOJ
Single String (MCD) ...... SS
Single Strip Engine System ...... SSES
Single Strokes per Minute (MSA) ...... SSPM
Single Subscriber Terminal [*Army*] (RDA) ...... SST
Single Subsonic Jet ...... SSJ
Single Subsonic Jet ...... SSSJ
Single Supply Support Control Point (MCD) ...... SSSCP
Single Sweep Operation ...... SSO
Single Swing Blocking Oscillator (MSA) ...... SSBO
Single Switched Suppressed Carrier [*Telecommunications*] (IAA) ...... SSBSC
Single System Image ...... SSI
Single System Operator (WDMC) ...... SSO
Single Systems Trainer [*NASA*] (MCD) ...... SST
Single Tape Armored (IAA) ...... STA
Single Target Attack ...... STA
Single Target Track [*Navy*] (NG) ...... STT
Single Target Track on Target [*Navy*] ...... STTOT
Single Thread System ...... STS
Single Threshold Element [*Computer science*] (IAA) ...... STE
Single Throw [*Switch*] ...... ST
Single Tire ...... ST
Single Title Order Plan [*Formerly, SCOP*] [*ABA*] ...... STOP
Single Token Ring [*Telecommunications*] (OSI) ...... STR
Single Tone Keying ...... STK
Single Tooth Indexer ...... STI
Single Track Master Operational Recording Tape Processing (IAA) .... STMP
Single Transferable Vote ...... STV
Single Transition Time (IAA) ...... STT
Single Transmission Time (NITA) ...... STT
Single Turn (MSA) ...... ST
Single Umbilical Artery [*Medicine*] (MAE) ...... SUA
Single Underwater Sound (MCD) ...... SUS
Single, Unemployed, No Kids [*Lifestyle classification*] ...... Sunk
Single Unit Pack [*for vehicles*] ...... SUP
Single Unit Package [*Pharmacy*] ...... SUP
Single Unit Parameter ...... SUP
Single Unit Retrieval Format ...... SURF
Single Uptake [*Boilers*] ...... SU
Single User [*The military activity that has the sole interest in an item of supply*] [*DoD*] ...... SU
Single User Drive Module [*Computer science*] (MHDI) ...... SUDM
Single Value ...... SV
Single Valve [*Automobile model, Stutz Motors*] ...... SV
Single Variable Control ...... SVC
Single Vehicle Accident [*Automotive safety*] ...... SVA
Single Vendor Integrity (MCD) ...... SVI
Single Ventricle [*Cardiology*] (DAVI) ...... SV
Single Vibrational Level [*Physics*] ...... SVL
Single Vibrations [*Half cycles*] ...... SV
Single Vibrations [*Half cycles*] ...... VS
Single Virtual Storage [*IBM Corp.*] [*Computer science*] ...... SVS
Single Wafer Etching (NITA) ...... SWE
Single Wall (AAG) ...... SW
Single Wall [*Carbon*] Nanotube ...... SWNT
Single Weight ...... SW
Single Weight Baryta [*Photography*] (OA) ...... SWB
Single Well Oil Production Ship [*British*] ...... SWOPS
Single Wheel [*Landing gear*] [*Aviation*] (DA) ...... SW
Single White Female [*Classified advertising*] ...... SWF
Single White Male [*Classified advertising*] ...... SWM
Single White Silk-Covered [*Wire insulation*] ...... SWS
Single Width, Single Inlet (OA) ...... SWSI
Single Wire Armored [*Cables*] ...... SWA
Single Wire Connector ...... SWC
Single Wire Junction ...... SWJ
Single Wire Multiplex Network [*Automotive engineering*] ...... SMN
Single with Bath [*Hotel room*] ...... SWB
Single Woman and No Kids [*Lifestyle classification*] ...... Swank
Single Woman Earning Lots in London [*Lifestyle classification*] ...... Swell
Single Word Dump ...... SWD
Single-Actuated Voice Recorder ...... SAVOR
Single-Asset Property Company [*British*] ...... SAPCO
Single-Award Schedule (AAGC) ...... SAS
Single-Axis Acoustic Levitator ...... SAAL
Single-Axis Inertial Drift Erection Test ...... SAIDET
Single-Axis Platform ...... SAP
Single-Axis Reference ...... SAR
Single-Axis Reference System ...... SARS
Single-Band Beaconry [*RADAR*] ...... SBB
Single-Beam Klystron (MSA) ...... SBK
Single-BIT [*Binary Digit*] Alternation Recording ...... SAR
Single-BIT [*Binary Digit*] Error Correction and Double-BIT Error Detection [*Binary Digit*] ...... SECDED
Single-Board Engine Controller [*Automotive engineering*] ...... SBEC
Single-Braided Rubber-Covered (IAA) ...... SBRC
Single-Breasted ...... SB

Single-Breath Diffusing Capacity of the Lung for Carbon Monoxide [*Medicine*] (MEDA) ...... DLCO-SB
Single-Breath Nitrogen [*Test*] (DAVI) ...... SBN
Single-Breath Nitrogen Test [*Physiology*] ...... SBNT
Single-Breath Test (MAE) ...... SBT
Single-Bubble Sonoluminescence [*Physics*] ...... SBSL
Single-Buoy Mooring [*Oil tanker*] ...... SBM
Single-Business Service ...... SBS
Single-Carrier Space-Charge-Limited Current ...... SCSCLC
Single-Cause Mortality Tape [*National Center for Health Statistics databank*] ...... SCMT
Single-Cell Biosensor [*Analytical biochemistry*] ...... SCB
Single-Cell Protein ...... SCP
Single-Cell Test (MCD) ...... SCT
Single-Chain Ribosome-Inactivating Protein [*Biochemistry*] ...... SCRIP
Single-Chain Urokinase-Like Plasminogen Activator [*Anticlotting agent*] .... SCUPA
Single-Channel Ground and Airborne Radio System [*or Subsystem*] (MCD) ...... SINCGARS
Single-Channel Ground and Airborne Radio System, Very High Frequency ...... SINCGARS-V
Single-Channel Interface [*Computer science*] ...... SCI
Single-Channel MODEM [*Telecommunications*] (TEL) ...... SCM
Single-Channel Reception (DEN) ...... SCR
Single-Channel-per-Carrier [*Telecommunications*] ...... SCPC
Single-Channel-per-Carrier, Pulse-Code-Modulation, Multiple-Access, Demand-Assignment Equipment [*Telecommunications*] ...... SPADE
Single-Charge Exchange [*Physics*] (OA) ...... SCE
Single-Charge Exchange ...... SCX
Single-Column Ion Chromatography ...... SCIC
Single-Comb White Leghorn [*Poultry*] ...... ScWL
Single-Concept User-Adaptable Microcomputer-Based Instructional Technique (EDAC) ...... SUMIT
Single-Cylinder ...... SCYL
Single-Degree-of-Freedom Gyroscope (SAA) ...... SDFG
Single-Dimensional Deflection System (IAA) ...... SDDS
Single-Drift Region (IEEE) ...... SDR
Single-Edge Contact (PCM) ...... SEC
Single-Electron Capacitance Spectroscopy ...... SECS
Single-Electron Rise Time [*Scintillation counting*] (IEEE) ...... SERT
Single-Electron Tunneling [*Physics*] ...... SET
Single-Electron-Transfer [*Organic chemistry*] ...... SET
Single-Employer Pension Plan Amendments Act [*1986*] (GFGA) ...... SEPPAA
Single-Ended Boiler (DS) ...... SB
Single-Ended Boiler (DS) ...... SEB
Single-Ended Boiler Survey (DS) ...... SEBS
Single-Ended, Cylindrical Boiler [*Navy*] ...... SE
Single-Engine Control Speed (DNAB) ...... SECS
Single-Engined Aircraft (IAA) ...... SEAC
Single-Engined Helicopter (MCD) ...... SEH
Single-Feeder ...... SFDR
Single-Fiber Action Potential (DMAA) ...... SFAP
Single-Frequency Amplifier [*Electronics*] (ECII) ...... SFA
Single-Frequency Oscillator (IDOE) ...... SFO
Single-Frequency Outlet ...... SFO
Single-Fronted (ADA) ...... SF
Single-Hoist Ordnance Loading System [*Navy*] (DNAB) ...... SHOLS
Single-Hung (DAC) ...... SH
Single-Input, Single-Output [*Process engineering*] ...... SISO
Single-Lens Reflex [*Camera*] ...... SLR
Single-Level Data Link Control (IAA) ...... SDLC
Single-Level Dynamic Scan [*Radiology*] (DAVI) ...... SLDS
Single-Line Approach ...... SLA
Single-Line Color Bar (IEEE) ...... SLCB
Single-Line Missile Assembly Building ...... SLMAB
Single-Locus [*Light flashes*] ...... SL
Single-Loop Controller (ACII) ...... SLC
Single-Manager Operating Agency [*Military*] ...... SMOA
Single-Mode Fiber [*Optics*] (CDE) ...... SMF
Single-Monitor Graphic Adaptor [*Computer graphics*] ...... SGA
Single-Nephron Glomerular Filtration Rate [*Medicine*] (MAE) ...... SGFR
Single-Occupancy Vehicle (ECON) ...... SOV
Single-Peaked (IAA) ...... SP
Single-Pedestal Flat-Top [*Desk*] ...... SPFT
Single-Pedestal Typewriter [*Desk*] ...... SPTW
Single-Phase 1PH
Single-Phase ...... SP
Single-Phase ...... S-Ph
Single-Phase Full Wave ...... SPFW
Single-Phase Full-Wave Bridge (DWSG) ...... SPFWBR
Single-Phase Half Wave ...... SPHW
Single-Photon Infrared Emission Spectroscopy ...... SPIRES
Single-Ply Roofing ...... SPR
Single-Point Articulated Loading Tower [*Engineering*] ...... SPALT
Single-Point Emergency Equipment Divestment ...... SPEED
Single-Point Failure Analysis (KSC) ...... SPFA
Single-Point Failure Potential (KSC) ...... SPFP
Single-Point Ground (MCD) ...... SPG
Single-Point Management ...... SPM
Single-Point Mooring [*Oil platform*] ...... SPM
Single-Point Mooring Buoy [*Navy*] ...... SBM
Single-Point Orbit Calculator ...... SPOC
Single-Point Refueling (MCD) ...... SPR
Single-Pole [*Switch*] ...... SP
Single-Pole (IDOE) ...... sp
Single-Pole Circuit Breaker (IAA) ...... SPCB

Single-Pole, Double-Throw [Switch] .... SPDT
Single-Pole, Double-Throw, Double-Break [Switch] .... SPDTDB
Single-Pole, Double-Throw, Normally-Closed, Double-Break [Switch] .... SPDTNCDB
Single-Pole, Double-Throw, Normally-Open [Switch] .... SPDTNO
Single-Pole, Double-Throw, Normally-Open, Double-Break [Switch] .... SPDTNODB
Single-Pole, Double-Throw Switch .... SPDTSW
Single-Pole, Quadruple-Throw [Switch] (IEEE) SP4T
Single-Pole, Single-Throw [Switch] .... SPST
Single-Pole, Single-Throw, Normally-Closed [Switch] .... SPSTNC
Single-Pole, Single-Throw, Normally-Open [Switch] .... SPSTNO
Single-Pole, Single-Throw, Normally-Open, Double-Make [Switch] ..... SPSTNODM
Single-Pole, Single-Throw Switch .... SPSTSW
Single-Pole Snap Switch (IAA) .... SPSS
Single-Pole Switch .... SPS
Single-Pole Switch .... SPSW
Single-Pole, Triple-Throw [Switch] (IEEE) SP3T
Single-Pole, Triple-Throw [Switch] (CET) .... SPTT
Single-Precision Floating Point [Computer science] .... SPFP
Single-Premium Deferred Annuity [Insurance] .... SPDA
Single-Premium Life [Insurance] .... SPL
Single-Premium Life Insurance (MHDW) .... SPLI
Single-Premium Whole Life [Insurance] .... SPL
Single-Rod Burst Test [Nuclear energy] (NRCH) .... SRBT
Single-Room Occupancy [Housing] .... SRO
Singles and Doubles Configuration Interaction [Quantum chemistry] (MCD) .... SDCI
Singles in Agriculture [An association] (EA) .... SIA
Singles in Service (EA) .... SIS
Singles Press Association (EA) .... SPA
Single-Seated Fighter .... SSF
Single-Shot Hit Probability .... SSHP
Single-Shot Kill Probability .... SSKP
Single-Shot Multivibrator .... SSMV
Single-Shot Probability [Military] .... SSP
Single-Sideband Transmitted Carrier (IEEE) .... SSTC
Single-Sideboard (IEEE) .... SSBD
Single-Sided Double Density (NITA) .... SDDD
Single-Sided, Double-Density Disk [Magnetic disk] [Computer science] .... SSDD
Single-Sided Pulse Width Modulation [Telecommunications] .... SPWM
Single-Sided, Single-Density Disk [Magnetic disk] [Computer science] .... SSSD
Single-Sided Wideband Analog Modulation [Telecommunications] (IAA) .... SSWAM
Single-Silo Hardsite Defense .... SSHD
Single-Site Catalyst [Chemistry] .... SSC
Single-Stage Command (NASA) .... SSC
Single-Stage Earth-Orbital Reusable Vehicle (MCD) .... SERV
Single-Stage Fan .... SSF
Single-Stage Hydrocracker [Chemical engineering] .... SSHC
Single-Station DOVAP [Doppler, Velocity, and Position] .... SSD
Single-Step Acidulation Granulation [Fertilizer technology] .... SSAG
Single-Strand Annealing [Genetics] .... SSA
Single-Strand Break [Genetics] .... SSB
Single-Strand Conformation Polymorphism [Genetics] .... SSCP
Single-Strand Conformational Analysis [Analytical biochemistry] .... SSCA
Single-Strand Conformational Polymorphism Electrophoresis [Analytical biochemistry] .... SSCPE
Single-Stranded [or ss] [Genetics] .... SS
Single-Stranded DNA [Deoxyribonucleic Acid] Binding Protein [Biochemistry] .... SSB
Singlet Delta Oxygen .... SDO
Single-Thread All-Purpose Program .... STAPP
Single-Throw (IDOE) .... st
Singleton [Australia Airport symbol] (OAG) .... SIX
Singleton Materials Engineering Laboratories [Tennessee Valley Authority] (GRD) .... SME
Single-Trip Container .... STC
Single-Use Diagnostic System [Trademark of the Murex Corp.] .... SUDS
Single-Valve First-Actuation [Nuclear energy] (NRCH) .... SVA
Single-Variable Bypass Program [DoD] .... SVBP
Single-Voyage Permit .... SVP
Single-Wall Nanotube [Materials science] .... SWNT
Single-Warhead Intercontinental Ballistic Missile (MCD) .... SICBM
Single-Weight [Paper] .... SWT
Single-Well Tracer Test [Petroleum technology] .... SWTT
Single-Wheel Dynamometer .... SWDYN
Single-Wheel Loading [Aviation] .... SWL
Singly Resonant Oscillator (IEEE) .... SRO
Singly-Occupied Molecular Orbital [Physical chemistry] .... OMO
Singora [Thailand] [Airport symbol] (AD) .... SGZ
Singular .... S
Singular (BJA) .... Sg
Singular (WDMC) .... SING
Singular .... sing
Singular .... SINGR
Singular Multinomial Distribution [Statistics] .... SMD
Singular Value Decomposition [Mathematics] .... SVD
Singularity Analyzer [Computer science] .... SINGAN
Singularity Expansion Method .... SEM
Singular-Spectrum Analysis [Meteorology] .... SSA
Singular-Value Analysis [Industrial control] .... SVA
Singulorum [Of Each] [Pharmacy] .... SING
Sinhalese [Language] (BARN) .... Sinh
Sinhalese [MARC language code Library of Congress] (LCCP) .... snh

Sining [Republic of China] [Seismograph station code, US Geological Survey] (SEIS) .... SNN
Sinister [Left] [Latin] .... S
Sinister [Counterclockwise configuration] [Biochemistry] .... (S)
Sinister [Left] [Latin] .... SINIST
Sinistra [Left Hand] [Music] .... S
Sinistra [Left Hand] [Music] .... SIN
Sinistra Mano [Left Hand] .... SM
Sinistral Sig (EA) .... SS
Sinj [Yugoslavia] [Seismograph station code, US Geological Survey Closed] (SEIS) .... SNJ
Sink .... S
Sink (AAG) .... SK
Sink Beater (ADA) .... SB
Sink Resistant Plastic (PDAA) .... SRP
Sink to Source Relation .... SSR
Sinkaling Khamti [Myanmar] [ICAO location identifier] (ICLI) .... VBSK
Sinkiang Uighur Autonomous Region [China, Mainland] [MARC geographic area code Library of Congress] (LCCP) .... a-cc-su
Sinking Fund [Finance] .... SF
Sinking Fund Return [Finance] (MHDW) .... SFR
Sinn Fein [Political front of the Irish Republican Army] .... SF
Sinnamary [French Guiana] [ICAO location identifier] (ICLI) .... SOOY
Sinner Saved [Pseudonym used by William Huntington] .... SS
Sinnspruche, Aphorismen, und Lebensweisheiten [Mottos, Aphorisms, and Witticisms] [Society for Business Information] [Information service or system] (IID) .... BONMOT
Sino American Cooperative Organization (EA) .... SACO
Sino Business Machine [Vancouver Stock Exchange symbol] .... SBN
Sino-American Amity Fund (EA) .... SAAF
Sino-American Cultural and Economic Association .... SACEA
Sino-American Cultural Society (EA) .... SACS
Sino-American Medical Rehabilitation Association .... SAMRA
Sino-American Pharmaceutical Association .... SAPA
Sino-American Technical Cooperation Association .... SATCA
Sinoaortic Deafferentation [Medicine] .... SAD
Sinoaortic Denervation [Physiology] .... SAD
Sinoatrial [Medicine] .... SA
Sinoatrial Conduction Time [Cardiology] .... SACT
Sinoatrial Node [Medicine] .... SAN
Sinoatrial Node [Medicine] .... SN
Sinoatrial Node Weakness Syndrome [Medicine] (DMAA) .... SANWS
Sinoauricular [Medicine] .... SA
Sinoauricular Node [Medicine] (DMAA) .... SAN
Sino-British Trade Council (DS) .... SBTC
Sinoe [Liberia] [Airport symbol] (OAG) .... SNI
Sinopia (VRA) .... snpa
Sino-Soviet Bloc .... SSB
Sino-Tibetan [MARC language code Library of Congress] (LCCP) .... sit
SINS [Ship Inertial Navigational System] Bedplate Mirror Assembly .... SBMA
Sinsinawa Dominican Apostolic Volunteer Program (EA) .... SDAVP
Sint Eustatius [MARC geographic area code Library of Congress] (LCCP) ... nweu--
Sint Maarten [Netherlands Antilles] [Airport symbol] (AD) .... SXM
Sintang/Susilo [Indonesia] [ICAO location identifier] (ICLI) .... WIOS
Sinter [Record label] [Brazil] .... Sin
Sinter [Metallurgy] .... SNTR
Sinter Metals 'A' [NYSE symbol] (TTSB) .... SNM
Sinter Metals Co. [Associated Press] (SAG) .... SinterMtl
Sinter Metals Co. [NYSE symbol] (SAG) .... SNM
Sintered Aluminium Product [Nuclear energy] (NUCP) .... SAP
Sintered Aluminum Powder .... SAP
Sintered Aluminum Powder-Clad Uranium Carbide .... SAPUC
Sintered Ferrous Part .... SFP
Sintered Iron Rotating Band .... SIRB
Sintered Lead Bronze .... SLB
Sintered Metal Powder Process (MCD) .... SMPP
Sintered Silicon Carbide (MCD) .... SSC
Sintered Zinc Battery .... SZB
Sintered Zinc Oxide Resistor .... SZOR
Sintered Zinc Resistor .... SZR
Sinton, TX [AM radio station call letters] .... KDAE
Sinton, TX [FM radio station call letters] .... KNCN
Sinton, TX [FM radio station call letters] .... KOUL
Sintra [Portugal ICAO location identifier] (ICLI) .... LPST
Sint-Truiden [Belgium ICAO location identifier] (ICLI) .... EBST
Sinus Aestuum [Bay of Billows] [Lunar area] .... SA
Sinus Area of Leaf [Botany] .... SAREA
Sinus Arrhythmia [Cardiology] (MAE) .... SA
Sinus Bradycardia [Cardiology] .... SB
Sinus Cycle Length [Cardiology] .... SCL
Sinus Histiocytes with Massive Lymphadenopathy [Clinical chemistry] ...... SAML
Sinus Histiocytosis [Medicine] .... SH
Sinus Iridum [Bay of Rainbows] [Lunar area] .... SI
Sinus Medii [Central Bay] [Lunar area] .... SM
Sinus [or Sinoatrial] Nerve [Anatomy] (DAVI) .... SN
Sinus Node Disease [Cardiology] (CPH) .... SND
Sinus [or Sinoatrial] Node Dysfunction [Cardiology] (DAVI) .... SND
Sinus Node Electrogram [Medicine] (DMAA) .... SNE
Sinus Node Recovery Time [Cardiology] .... SNRT
Sinus Node Recovery Time [Medicine] (DMAA) .... SRT
Sinus Node Recovery Time Corrected [Cardiology] .... SNRTC
Sinus Node Recovery Time, Indirect Measuring [Medicine] (DMAA) .... SNRTi
Sinus Rhythm [Medicine] .... SR
Sinus Rhythm, No Ectopy [Medicine] (MEDA) .... SR/NE
Sinus Rhythm, No Ectopy [Cardiology] (DAVI) .... SR/NE

Sinus Roris [*Bay of Dew*] [*Lunar area*] ... SR
Sinus Tachycardia [*Cardiology*] ... ST
Sinus Venosus [*Anatomy*] ... SV
Sinuses, Nose, and Throat [*Anatomy*] (DAVI) ... SNT
Sinusoidal [*Otorhinolaryngology*] (DAVI) ... sine
Sinusoidal Amplitude Modulation [*Physics*] ... SAM
Sinusoidal Collagen [*Anatomy*] ... SC
Sinusoidal Frequency Modulation [*Physics*] ... SFM
Sinusoidal Hydrodynamic Modulation [*Electrochemistry*] ... SHM
Sinusoidal Input Describing Function [*Computer science*] ... SIDF
Sinusoidal Membrane Vesicle [*Anatomy*] ... SMV
Sinusoidal Pressure Generator ... SPG
Sion [*Switzerland ICAO location identifier*] (ICLI) ... LSGS
Sion [*Switzerland*] [*Airport symbol*] ... SIR
Sion [*Switzerland*] [*Seismograph station code, US Geological Survey Closed*] (SEIS) ... SIS
SIOP [*Single Integrated Operations Plan*] **Force Application Review Group** (CINC) ... SFARG
SIOP [*Single Integrated Operations Plan*] **Integrated Data Base** (MCD) ... SIDA
SIOP Reconnaissance Plan (MCD) ... SRP
Siouan [*MARC language code Library of Congress*] (LCCP) ... sio
Sioux Army Depot ... SXAD
Sioux Center, IA [*FM radio station call letters*] ... KDCR
Sioux Center, IA [*AM radio station call letters*] (RBYB) ... KSOU-AM
Sioux Center, IA [*FM radio station call letters*] (RBYB) ... KSOU-FM
Sioux Center, IA [*FM radio station call letters*] ... KTSB
Sioux Center, IA [*AM radio station call letters*] ... KVDB
Sioux Center, IA [*Location identifier FAA*] (FAAL) ... SOY
Sioux Center Public Library, Sioux Center, IA [*Library symbol Library of Congress*] (LCLS) ... IaSce
Sioux City [*Iowa*] [*ICAO location identifier*] (ICLI) ... KSUX
Sioux City [*Diocesan abbreviation*] [*Iowa*] (TOCD) ... SC
Sioux City [*Iowa*] [*Airport symbol*] (OAG) ... SUX
Sioux City Air Defense Sector [*ADC*] ... SCADS
Sioux City & New Orleans Barge Line [*AAR code*] ... SNBL
Sioux City Grain Exchange (EA) ... SCGE
Sioux City, IA [*Television station call letters*] ... KCAU
Sioux City, IA [*FM radio station call letters*] ... KGLI
Sioux City, IA [*Television station call letters*] ... KMEG
Sioux City, IA [*AM radio station call letters*] ... KMNS
Sioux City, IA [*FM radio station call letters*] ... KMSC
Sioux City, IA [*AM radio station call letters*] ... KSCJ
Sioux City, IA [*FM radio station call letters*] ... KSEZ
Sioux City, IA [*Television station call letters*] ... KSIN
Sioux City, IA [*FM radio station call letters*] ... KTFC
Sioux City, IA [*Television station call letters*] ... KTIV
Sioux City, IA [*FM radio station call letters*] ... KWIT
Sioux City, IA [*AM radio station call letters*] (RBYB) ... KWSL
Sioux City, IA [*Location identifier FAA*] (FAAL) ... OIQ
Sioux City Public Library, Sioux City, IA [*Library symbol Library of Congress*] (LCLS) ... IaSc
Sioux City Public Library, Sioux City, IA [*OCLC symbol*] (OCLC) ... IWP
Sioux City Terminal Railway [*AAR code*] ... SCT
Sioux County Capital, Orange City, IA [*Library symbol Library of Congress*] (LCLS) ... IaOcSC
Sioux County Index, Hull, IA [*Library symbol Library of Congress*] (LCLS) ... IaHul
Sioux County Index-Reporter, Hull, IA [*Library symbol Library of Congress*] (LCLS) ... IaHuIR
Sioux Falls [*South Dakota*] [*Airport symbol*] (OAG) ... FSD
Sioux Falls [*Diocesan abbreviation*] [*South Dakota*] (TOCD) ... SFS
Sioux Falls Carnegie Free Public Library, Sioux Falls, SD [*Library symbol Library of Congress*] (LCLS) ... SdSif
Sioux Falls College [*South Dakota*] ... SFC
Sioux Falls College, Sioux Falls, SD [*OCLC symbol*] (OCLC) ... SDF
Sioux Falls College, Sioux Falls, SD [*Library symbol Library of Congress*] (LCLS) ... SdSifC
Sioux Falls Public Library, Sioux Falls, SD [*OCLC symbol*] (OCLC) ... SDD
Sioux Falls, SD [*Location identifier FAA*] (FAAL) ... FSD
Sioux Falls, SD [*Location identifier FAA*] (FAAL) ... JOU
Sioux Falls, SD [*FM radio station call letters*] ... KAUR
Sioux Falls, SD [*FM radio station call letters*] ... KCFS
Sioux Falls, SD [*AM radio station call letters*] ... KCGN
Sioux Falls, SD [*FM radio station call letters*] ... KCSD
Sioux Falls, SD [*Television station call letters*] (RBYB) ... KCSD-TV
Sioux Falls, SD [*AM radio station call letters*] ... KELO
Sioux Falls, SD [*FM radio station call letters*] ... KELO-FM
Sioux Falls, SD [*Television station call letters*] ... KELO-TV
Sioux Falls, SD [*FM radio station call letters*] ... KKLS-FM
Sioux Falls, SD [*FM radio station call letters*] ... KMXC
Sioux Falls, SD [*AM radio station call letters*] ... KNWC
Sioux Falls, SD [*FM radio station call letters*] ... KNWC-FM
Sioux Falls, SD [*FM radio station call letters*] ... KRRO
Sioux Falls, SD [*FM radio station call letters*] ... KRSD
Sioux Falls, SD [*Television station call letters*] ... KSFY
Sioux Falls, SD [*AM radio station call letters*] ... KSOO
Sioux Falls, SD [*Television station call letters*] ... KTTW
Sioux Falls, SD [*FM radio station call letters*] ... KTWB
Sioux Falls, SD [*AM radio station call letters*] ... KWSN
Sioux Falls, SD [*AM radio station call letters*] ... KXRB
Sioux Lookout [*Canada*] [*Airport symbol*] (OAG) ... YXL
Sioux Lookout, ON [*ICAO location identifier*] (ICLI) ... CYXL
Sioux Lookout Public Library, Ontario [*Library symbol National Library of Canada*] (NLC) ... OSL
Sioux Lookout Public Library, Sioux Lookout, ON, Canada [*Library symbol Library of Congress*] (LCLS) ... CaOSI
Sioux Narrows, ON [*FM radio station call letters*] ... CBQS
Sioux Narrows Public Library, Ontario [*Library symbol National Library of Canada*] (NLC) ... OSN
Sioux Rapids, IA [*FM radio station call letters*] ... KTFG
Sioux Valley-Round Lake-Brewster Public School, Round Lake, MN [*Library symbol*] [*Library of Congress*] (LCLS) ... MnRIPS
Siouxland Health Sciences Consortium [*Library network*] ... SHSLC
Siouxland Libraries Cooperative, Sioux City, IA [*Library symbol Library of Congress*] (LCLS) ... IaScS
Sipald Resources [*Vancouver Stock Exchange symbol*] ... SIP
Sipaliwini [*Surinam*] [*ICAO location identifier*] (ICLI) ... SMSI
Sipay Word Analysis Test [*Educational test*] ... SWAT
Sipex Corp. [*Associated Press*] (SAG) ... SipexCp
Sipex Corp. [*NASDAQ symbol*] (SAG) ... SIPX
SIPEX Corp. [*NASDAQ symbol*] (TTSB) ... SIPX
Siphon (MSA) ... SPHN
Siphon Withdrawal Response ... SWR
Sipora/Rokot [*Indonesia*] [*ICAO location identifier*] (ICLI) ... WIBR
Sipuati [*Bolivia*] [*ICAO location identifier*] (ICLI) ... SLSG
Sir ... SR
Sir Albert Sakzewski Virus Research Centre [*Australia*] ... SASVRC
Sir Albert Sakzewski Virus Research Centre [*Austria*] ... SASVRC
Sir Arthur Sullivan Society [*British*] (DBA) ... SASS
Sir Douglas Quintet Fan Club (EA) ... SDQFC
Sir Francis Bacon ... SFB
Sir George Williams Campus, Concordia University, Montreal, Quebec [*Library symbol National Library of Canada*] (NLC) ... QMG
Sir Hugh Young's Working Party for Estimation of Civilian Relief Requirements [*World War II*] ... YWP
Sir Lowry's Pass [*South Africa*] [*ICAO location identifier*] (ICLI) ... FASP
Sir Robert Borden High School, Nepean, Ontario [*Library symbol National Library of Canada*] (BIB) ... ONSR
Sir Sandford Fleming College, Frost Campus, Lindsay, ON, Canada [*Library symbol*] [*Library of Congress*] (LCLS) ... CaOLiSF
Sir Sandford Fleming College of Applied Arts and Technology, Peterborough, ON, Canada [*Library symbol Library of Congress*] (LCLS) ... CaOPeTSF
Sir T. Raymond's English King's Bench Reports [*A publication*] (DLA) ... Sir T Ray
Sir Thomas Beecham Society (EA) ... TBS
Sir Thomas Roddick Hospital, Medical Library, Stephenville, NF, Canada [*Library symbol*] [*Library of Congress*] (LCLS) ... CaNFSTR
Sir Wilfred Grenfell College, Memorial University, Corner Brook, Newfoundland [*Library symbol National Library of Canada*] (NLC) ... NFCBM
Sir Wilfrid Laurier High School Library, Carleton Board of Education, Ottawa, Ontario [*Library symbol National Library of Canada*] (BIB) ... OOWLS
Sirach [*Ecclesiasticus*] [*Old Testament book*] ... SI
Sirach [*Old Testament book*] [*Roman Catholic canon*] ... Sir
Sirajgang [*Bangladesh*] [*Airport symbol*] (AD) ... SAJ
Sirco International Corp. [*NASDAQ symbol*] (NQ) ... SIRC
Sirco International Corp. [*Associated Press*] (SAG) ... Sirco
Sirco Intl [*NASDAQ symbol*] (TTSB) ... SIRC
Sirco-France, Paris, France [*Library symbol Library of Congress*] (LCLS) ... FrPS
Sire ... S
Siren ... SN
Siren, WI [*Location identifier FAA*] (FAAL) ... BXR
Sirena [*Costa Rica*] [*ICAO location identifier*] (ICLI) ... MRSN
[*The*] **Sirena Apparel Group** [*Associated Press*] (SAG) ... SirenaA
[*The*] **Sirena Apparel Group** [*NASDAQ symbol*] (SAG) ... SIRN
Sirey. Jurisprudence [*France*] [*A publication*] (DLA) ... S Jur
Siri Island [*Iran*] [*ICAO location identifier*] (ICLI) ... OIBS
Siria [*Venezuela*] [*Seismograph station code, US Geological Survey*] (SEIS) ... SIR
Sirius [*Record label*] [*Sweden*] ... Sir
Sirius Resources [*Vancouver Stock Exchange symbol*] ... SRV
Sirjan [*Iran*] [*ICAO location identifier*] (ICLI) ... OIKY
Sirop [*Syrup*] [*Pharmacy*] ... syr
Sirotherm Demineralization Process ... SDP
Sirrom Capital [*NASDAQ symbol*] (TTSB) ... SROM
Sirrom Capital Corp. [*Associated Press*] (SAG) ... Sirrom
Sirrom Capital Corp. [*NASDAQ symbol*] (SAG) ... SROM
Sirsenk/Bamarni [*Iraq*] [*ICAO location identifier*] (ICLI) ... ORBB
SIS Bancorp, Inc. [*Associated Press*] (SAG) ... SIS Bncp
SIS Bancorp, Inc. [*NASDAQ symbol*] (SAG) ... SISB
Sis Fan Club [*Later, RFC*] (EA) ... SFC
SIS [*Superconductivity Information System*] **Published Information Database** [*Office of Scientific and Technical Information*] [*Department of Energy*] ... SPID
Siscoe Callahan [*Vancouver Stock Exchange symbol*] ... SCM
Sishen [*South Africa*] [*ICAO location identifier*] (ICLI) ... FASS
Sishen [*South Africa*] [*Airport symbol*] (OAG) ... SIS
Siskiyou County Public Library, Yreka, CA [*OCLC symbol*] (OCLC) ... CIY
Siskiyou County Public Library, Yreka, CA [*Library symbol Library of Congress*] (LCLS) ... CYrS
Siskon Gold 'A' [*NASDAQ symbol*] (TTSB) ... SISK
Siskon Gold Corp. [*NASDAQ symbol*] (SAG) ... SISK
Siskon Gold Corp. [*Associated Press*] (SAG) ... Siskon
Sisseton Library, Sisseton, SD [*Library symbol Library of Congress*] (LCLS) ... SdSi
Sisseton, SD [*FM radio station call letters*] ... KBWS
Sisseton, SD [*FM radio station call letters*] ... KSWS
Siste, Viator [*Stop, Traveller*] [*Latin*] (ROG) ... SV
Sistema de Documentacion sobre Poblacion en America Latina [*Latin American Population Documentation System*] [*Economic Commission for Latin America and the Caribbean*] [*United Nations*] [*Information service or system*] (IID) ... DOCPAL

Sistema de Informacion Bursatil [*Stock Exchange Information System*] [*Madrid Stock Exchange*] [*Information service or system*] (IID) ... SIB
Sistema de Vigilancia de Amazonia [*Amazon Surveillance System*] [*Brazil*] ... SIVAN
Sistema Nacional de Informacion [*National Information System*] [*Colorado*] (IID) ... SNI
Sistema Nacional de Informacion Documental en Educacion [*National System of Documentary Information on Education*] [*Information service or system*] (IID) ... SINIE
Sister ... S
Sister ... SIS
Sister ... SIS
Sister ... SIST
Sister ... SR
Sister Chromatic Exchange Analysis (DAVI) ... SCE
Sister Chromatid Exchange [*Cytology*] ... SCE
Sister Cities International (EA) ... SCI
Sister Elizabeth Kenny Foundation [*Later, SKI*] ... SEKF
Sister Kenny Institute (EA) ... SKI
Sister of Arts ... Ar S
Sister of Arts ... AS
Sister of Arts ... SA
Sister Servants of Christ the King [*Roman Catholic religious order*] ... SSCK
Sister Servants of Mary Immaculate [*Roman Catholic religious order*] ... SSMI
Sister Servants of the Holy Ghost and Mary Immaculate [*Roman Catholic religious order*] ... SHG
Sister Servants of the Holy Spirit of Perpetual Adoration (TOCD) ... SSpSdeAP
Sister Servants of the Poor (TOCD) ... SdeP
Sisterhood Is Powerful Institute (EA) ... SIPI
Sisterhood of Black Single Mothers (EA) ... SBSM
Sisterhood of the Holy Nativity [*Episcopalian religious order*] ... SHN
Sisteron-Theze [*France ICAO location identifier*] (ICLI) ... LFNS
Sisters All Learning Together [*Feminist group*] ... SALT
Sisters Auxiliaries of the Apostolate [*Roman Catholic religious order*] ... AA
Sisters Auxiliaries of the Apostolate (TOCD) ... SAA
Sisters for a Christian Community ... SFCC
Sisters, Home Visitors of Mary [*Roman Catholic religious order*] ... HVM
Sisters in Crime [*An association*] ... SinC
Sisters Island, AK [*Location identifier FAA*] (FAAL) ... EEF
Sisters Island, AK [*Location identifier FAA*] (FAAL) ... SSR
Sisters Minor of the Mary Immaculate (TOCD) ... SMMI
Sisters Oblates to Divine Love [*Roman Catholic religious order*] ... RODA
Sisters Oblates to the Blessed Trinity (TOCD) ... OBT
Sisters of Bethany [*Roman Catholic religious order*] ... CVD
Sisters of Bon Secours [*Roman Catholic religious order*] ... CBS
Sisters of Charity [*Anglican religious community*] ... SC
Sisters of Charity Hospital, Buffalo, NY [*Library symbol Library of Congress*] (LCLS) ... NBuSCH
Sisters of Charity of Blessed Virgin Mary (TOCD) ... BVM
Sisters of Charity of Cincinnati, Ohio (TOCD) ... SC
Sisters of Charity of Incarnate Word, Houston, TX (TOCD) ... CCVI
Sisters of Charity of Jesus and Mary [*See also ZLJM*] [*Belgium*] (EAIO) ... SCJM
Sisters of Charity (of Leavenworth) [*Roman Catholic religious order*] ... SCL
Sisters of Charity of Montreal (Grey Nuns) (TOCD) ... SGM
Sisters of Charity (of Nazareth) [*Roman Catholic religious order*] ... SCN
Sisters of Charity of Ottawa [*Grey Nuns of the Cross*] [*Roman Catholic religious order*] ... SCO
Sisters of Charity of Our Lady, Mother of Mercy [*Roman Catholic religious order*] ... SCMM
Sisters of Charity of Our Lady, Mother of the Church [*Roman Catholic religious order*] ... SCMC
Sisters of Charity of Our Lady of Mercy [*Roman Catholic religious order*] ... OLM
Sisters of Charity of Providence [*Religious order*] ... FCSP
Sisters of Charity of Quebec [*Grey Nuns*] [*Roman Catholic religious order*] ... SCQ
Sisters of Charity of Quebec (Grey Nuns) (TOCD) ... SCO
Sisters of Charity of Rolling Meadows (TOCD) ... SCRH
Sisters of Charity (of St. Augustine) [*Roman Catholic religious order*] ... CSA
Sisters of Charity of St. Charles Borromeo [*See also LCB*] (EAIO) ... SCSCB
Sisters of Charity of St. Hyacinthe [*Grey Nuns*] [*Roman Catholic religious order*] ... SCSH
Sisters of Charity of St. Jeanne Antide Thouret [*Italy*] (EAIO) ... SCSJAT
Sisters of Charity of St. Joan Antida (TOCD) ... SCSJA
Sisters of Charity of St. Louis [*Roman Catholic religious order*] ... SCSL
Sisters of Charity of St. Vincent de Paul [*Roman Catholic religious order*] ... CSVP
Sisters of Charity of Saint Vincent de Paul (EA) ... SC
Sisters of Charity of St. Vincent de Paul [*Roman Catholic religious order*] ... SVZ
Sisters of Charity of St. Vincent de Paul (TOCD) ... VZ
Sisters of Charity of St. Vincent de Paul, Halifax [*Roman Catholic religious order*] ... SCH
Sisters of Charity of Seton Hill, Greensburg, PA (TOCD) ... SC
Sisters of Charity of the Blessed Virgin Mary [*Roman Catholic religious order*] ... BVM
Sisters of Charity of the Immaculate Conception of Ivrea (TOCD) ... SCIC
Sisters of Charity of the Infant Mary (TOCD) ... IM
Sisters of Christ the King [*Roman Catholic religious order*] ... SCK
Sisters of Christian Charity (TOCD) ... SCC
Sisters of Divine Compassion [*Roman Catholic religious order*] ... RDC
Sisters of Divine Providence (TOCD) ... CDP
Sisters of Divine Providence of Kentucky (TOCD) ... CDP
Sisters of Divine Providence of San Antonio, TX (TOCD) ... CDP
Sisters of Emanuel (TOCD) ... SE
Sisters of Guadalupe [*Roman Catholic religious order*] ... OLG
Sisters of Holy Cross (TOCD) ... CSC
Sisters of Holy Redeemer (TOCD) ... CSR
Sisters of Holy Spirit (TOCD) ... CSSp
Sisters of Loretto at the Foot of the Cross [*Roman Catholic religious order*] ... SL
Sisters of Mary Immaculate (TOCD) ... SMI
Sisters of Mary, Mother of God (TOCD) ... SMMG
Sisters of Mercy (TOCD) ... RSM
Sisters of Mercy [*Roman Catholic religious order*] ... RSM
Sisters of Mercy [*Roman Catholic religious order*] ... SM
Sisters of Mercy (Ballyahannon, Ireland) (TOCD) ... RSM
Sisters of Mercy (Cork and Ross) (TOCD) ... SM
Sisters of Mercy, Daughters of Christian Charity of St. Vincent de Paul [*Roman Catholic religious order*] ... SMDC
Sisters of Mercy (Mayo, Ireland) (TOCD) ... RSM
Sisters of Mercy of Ardagh & Clonmacnois (TOCD) ... RSM
Sisters of Mercy of Christian Charity of St. Vincent de Paul of Hungary (TOCD) ... SMDC
Sisters of Mercy of Portland (TOCD) ... RSM
Sisters of Mercy of the Americas (TOCD) ... RSM
Sisters of Mercy of the Blessed Sacrament (TOCD) ... HMSS
Sisters of Mercy of Tralee (TOCD) ... SM
Sisters of Mercy (Sligo) (TOCD) ... RSM
Sisters of Notre Dame [*Roman Catholic religious order*] ... SND
Sisters of Notre Dame de Namur [*Roman Catholic religious order*] ... SND
Sisters of Notre Dame de Namur (TOCD) ... SNDdeN
Sisters of Notre Dame de Namur [*Roman Catholic religious order Rome, Italy*] (EAIO) ... SNDN
Sisters of Our Lady [*Roman Catholic religious order*] ... SOL
Sisters of Our Lady of Charity (TOCD) ... OLC
Sisters of Our Lady of Charity of Refuge [*Roman Catholic religious order*] ... OLCR
Sisters of Our Lady of Charity of the Good Shepherd [*Roman Catholic religious order*] ... RGS
Sisters of Our Lady of Charity of the Good Shepherd [*Roman Catholic religious order Rome, Italy*] (EAIO) ... SOLCGS
Sisters of Our Lady of Christian Doctrine [*Roman Catholic religious order*] ... RCD
Sisters of Our Lady of Mercy [*Mercedarians*] [*Roman Catholic religious order*] ... SOLM
Sisters of Our Lady of Perpetual Help (TOCD) ... SOLPH
Sisters of Our Lady of Providence [*Roman Catholic religious order*] ... OLP
Sisters of Our Lady of Refuge (TOCD) ... RFR
Sisters of Our Lady of Sorrows [*Roman Catholic religious order*] ... OLS
Sisters of Our Lady of the Garden [*Roman Catholic religious order*] ... OLG
Sisters of Perpetual Adoration (TOCD) ... APG
Sisters of Providence [*Roman Catholic religious order*] ... SP
Sisters of Providence and of the Immaculate Conception [*Roman Catholic religious order*] ... SPIC
Sisters of Providence of Saint Mary-of-the-Woods, IN (TOCD) ... SP
Sisters of Reparation of the Congregation of Mary [*Roman Catholic religious order*] ... SRCM
Sisters of Reparation of the Sacred Wounds of Jesus (TOCD) ... SR
Sisters of St. Ann (TOCD) ... SSA
Sisters of St. Ann of Providence [*Roman Catholic religious order*] ... SSA
Sisters of St. Anne (TOCD) ... SSA
Sisters of St. Anne Bangalone (TOCD) ... SAB
Sisters of St. Augustine (TOCD) ... OSA
Sisters of St. Benedict, Convent and Academy of the Immaculate Conception, Ferdinand, IN [*Library symbol*] [*Library of Congress*] (LCLS) ... InFerC
Sisters of St. Casimir [*Roman Catholic religious order*] ... SSC
Sisters of Ste. Chretienne [*Roman Catholic religious order*] ... SSCH
Sisters of St. Clare (TOCD) ... OSC
Sisters of St. Elizabeth [*Roman Catholic religious order*] ... SSE
Sisters of St. Elizabeth, Convent Station (TOCD) ... SC
Sisters of St. Francis (TOCD) ... OSF
Sisters of Saint Francis, Clinton, Iowa (TOCD) ... OSF
Sisters of St. Francis of Christ the King (TOCD) ... OSF
Sisters of St. Francis of Dillingen [*See also SFD*] [*Rome, Italy*] (EAIO) ... SSFD
Sisters of Saint Francis of Milvale, Pennsylvania (TOCD) ... OSF
Sisters of St. Francis of Penance and Christian Charity (TOCD) ... OSF
Sisters of St. Francis of Perpetual Adoration (TOCD) ... OSF
Sisters of St. Francis of Savannah, MO (TOCD) ... OSF
Sisters of St. Francis of the Congregation of Our Lady of Lourdes, Sylvania, Ohio (TOCD) ... OSF
Sisters of St. Francis of the Holy Cross (TOCD) ... OSF
Sisters of St. Francis of the Holy Eucharist (TOCD) ... OSF
Sisters of St. Francis of the Holy Family (TOCD) ... OSF
Sisters of St. Francis of the Immaculate Conception (TOCD) ... OSF
Sisters of St. Francis of the Immaculate Heart of Mary (Hankinson, North Dakota) (TOCD) ... OSF
Sisters of St. Francis of the Martyr St. George (TOCD) ... OSF
Sisters of Saint Francis of the Providence of God (TOCD) ... OSF
Sisters of St. Francis of the Third Order Regular (Williamsville, New York) (TOCD) ... OSF
Sisters of Ste. Jeanne D'Arc (TOCD) ... SJA
Sisters of St. John Bosco (Taylor, TX) (TOCD) ... SJB
Sisters of St. John of God [*Wexford, Republic of Ireland*] (EAIO) ... SSJG
Sisters of St. John the Baptist (TOCD) ... CSJB
Sisters of St. John the Baptist [*See also SSGB*] [*Roman Catholic religious order Rome, Italy*] (EAIO) ... SSJB
Sisters of St. Joseph [*Roman Catholic religious order*] ... SSJ
Sisters of St. Joseph Benedict Cottolengo (TOCD) ... SSJC
Sisters of St. Joseph (Boston, Brighton) (TOCD) ... CSJ
Sisters of St. Joseph (Buffalo) (TOCD) ... SSJ
Sisters of St. Joseph (Burlington) (TOCD) ... SSJ
Sisters of St. Joseph (Chicago, Lagrange Park) (TOCD) ... CSJ
Sisters of St. Joseph (Cleveland) (TOCD) ... CSJ
Sisters of St. Joseph (Erie) (TOCD) ... SSJ

Sisters of St. Joseph (Kalamazoo, Nazareth) (TOCD) ... SSJ
Sisters of St. Joseph (Lafayette, IN) (TOCD) ... CSJ
Sisters of St. Joseph (Lyons, France) (TOCD) ... CSJ
Sisters of St. Joseph of Carondelet (TOCD) ... CSJ
Sisters of St. Joseph of Chambery (TOCD) ... CSJ
Sisters of Saint Joseph of Chestnut Hill, Philadelphia (TOCD) ... SSJ
Sisters of St. Joseph of Cluny (TOCD) ... SJC
Sisters of St. Joseph of Medaille (TOCD) ... CSJ
Sisters of St. Joseph of Peace (TOCD) ... CSJP
Sisters of St. Joseph of St. Augustine, Florida (TOCD) ... SSJ
Sisters of St. Joseph of St. Mark (TOCD) ... SJSM
Sisters of St. Joseph of St. Mark [*Roman Catholic religious order*] ... SSJSM
Sisters of St. Joseph of the Third Order of St. Francis [*Roman Catholic religious order*] ... SSJ
Sisters of St. Joseph of the Third Order of St. Francis (TOCD) ... SSJ-TOSF
Sisters of St. Joseph (Ogdensburg) (TOCD) ... SSJ
Sisters of St. Joseph (Orange) (TOCD) ... CSJ
Sisters of St. Joseph (Pittsburgh, Baden) (TOCD) ... CSJ
Sisters of St. Joseph (Rochester) (TOCD) ... SSJ
Sisters of St. Joseph (Rockville Centre, Brentwood) (TOCD) ... CSJ
Sisters of St. Joseph (Salina, Concordia) (TOCD) ... CSJ
Sisters of St. Joseph (Springfield, MA) (TOCD) ... SSJ
Sisters of St. Joseph the Worker (TOCD) ... SJW
Sisters of St. Joseph (Wheeling) (TOCD) ... SSJ
Sisters of St. Joseph (Wichita) (TOCD) ... CSJ
Sisters of St. Martha of Antigonish N.S. (TOCD) ... CSM
Sisters of St. Martha of Prince Edward Island [*Roman Catholic religious order*] ... CSM
Sisters of St. Mary of Namur [*Roman Catholic religious order*] ... SSMN
Sisters of St. Mary of Oregon [*Roman Catholic religious order*] ... SSMO
Sisters of St. Mary of the Presentation [*Roman Catholic religious order*] ... SMP
Sisters of St. Mary of the Third Order of St. Francis [*Roman Catholic religious order*] ... SSM
Sisters of St. Paul of Chartres (TOCD) ... SPC
Sisters of St. Philip Neri Missionary Teachers [*Roman Catholic religious order*] ... RF
Sisters of St. Rita (TOCD) ... OSA
Sisters of Sainte Marthe [*of St. Hyacinthe*] [*Roman Catholic religious order*] ... SMSH
Sisters of Saints Cyril and Methodius [*Roman Catholic religious order*] ... SSCM
Sisters of Service [*Roman Catholic religious order*] ... SOS
Sisters of Social Service [*Roman Catholic religious order*] ... SSS
Sisters of Social Service of Los Angeles, Inc. (TOCD) ... SSS
Sisters of the Assumption (TOCD) ... SASV
Sisters of the Assumption of the Blessed Virgin [*Roman Catholic religious order*] ... SASV
Sisters of the Blessed Sacrament [*Roman Catholic religious order*] ... SBS
[*The*] **Sisters of the Blessed Sacrament for Indians and Colored People** (TOCD) ... SBS
Sisters of the Catholic Apostolate (Pallottine) (TOCD) ... CSAC
Sisters of the Child Jesus [*Roman Catholic religious order*] ... SCJ
Sisters of the Congregation of Notre Dame [*Roman Catholic religious order*] ... CND
Sisters of the Congregation of St. Agnes [*Roman Catholic religious order*] ... CSA
Sisters of the Cross and Passion [*Roman Catholic women's religious order*] ... CP
Sisters of the Cross of the Sacred Heart of Jesus (Mexico) (TOCD) ... RCSCJ
Sisters of the Divine Redeemer [*Roman Catholic religious order*] ... SDR
Sisters of the Divine Saviour [*Roman Catholic religious order*] ... SDS
Sisters of the Eucharistic Covenant (TOCD) ... SEC
Sisters of the Good Samaritan (ADA) ... SGS
[*The*] **Sisters of the Good Shepherd** (TOCD) ... RGS
Sisters of the Holy Faith [*Roman Catholic religious order*] ... SHF
Sisters of the Holy Family [*Roman Catholic religious order*] ... SHF
Sisters of the Holy Ghost [*Roman Catholic religious order*] ... CHG
Sisters of the Holy Guardian Angels [*Roman Catholic religious order*] ... SAC
Sisters of the Holy Humility of Mary [*Roman Catholic religious order*] ... HHM
Sisters of the Holy Infant Jesus [*Roman Catholic religious order*] ... HIJ
Sisters of the Holy Infant Jesus [*Roman Catholic religious order*] ... IJ
Sisters of the Holy Names of Jesus and Mary [*Roman Catholic religious order*] ... SNJM
Sisters of the Holy Redeemer [*Roman Catholic religious order*] ... SHR
Sisters of the Holy Rosary of Fatima (Mexico) (TOCD) ... HRF
Sisters of the Holy Spirit (TOCD) ... SHS
Sisters of the Holy Spirit and Mary Immaculate (TOCD) ... SHSp
Sisters of the Holy Union (TOCD) ... SUSC
Sisters of the Humility of Mary [*Roman Catholic religious order*] ... HM
Sisters of the Immaculate Conception [*Roman Catholic religious order*] ... CIC
Sisters of the Immaculate Conception (TOCD) ... RCM
Sisters of the Immaculate Heart of Mary [*Roman Catholic religious order*] ... CMF
Sisters of the Immaculate Heart of Mary [*California Institute of the Most Holy and Immaculate Heart of the BVM*] [*Roman Catholic religious order*] ... IHM
Sisters of the Infant Jesus [*Nursing Sisters of the Sick Poor*] [*Roman Catholic religious order*] ... CIJ
Sisters of the Infant Jesus (TOCD) ... IJ
Sisters of the Lamb of God (TOCD) ... AD
Sisters of the Living Word [*Roman Catholic religious order*] ... SLW
Sisters of the Love of God (TOCD) ... RAD
Sisters of the Most Holy and Immaculate Heart of Blessed Virgin Mary (Wichita Foundation) (TOCD) ... IHM
Sisters of the Most Holy Sacrament [*Roman Catholic religious order*] ... MHS
Sisters of the Most Holy Trinity (TOCD) ... OSST
Sisters of the Most Precious Blood (O'Fallon, MO) (TOCD) ... CPPS
Sisters of the Order of St. Basil the Great (TOCD) ... OSBM
Sisters of the Pious Schools (TOCD) ... SchP
Sisters of the Poor Child Jesus [*Roman Catholic religious order*] ... PCJ
Sisters of the Precious Blood (Dayton, Ohio) (TOCD) ... CPPS
Sisters of the Presentation of Mary [*Roman Catholic religious order*] ... PM
Sisters of the Presentation of Mary [*Roman Catholic religious order*] ... SP
Sisters of the Presentation of the B.V.M. (TOCD) ... PBVM
Sisters of the Resurrection (TOCD) ... CR
Sisters of the Sacred Heart of Jesus of Saint Jacut (TOCD) ... SSCJ
Sisters of the Sacred Hearts of Jesus and Mary (TOCD) ... SHJM
Sisters of the Sacred Hearts of Jesus and Mary [*Roman Catholic religious order*] ... SHJM
Sisters of the Sacred Hearts of Jesus and Mary [*Roman Catholic religious order*] ... SSHJM
Sisters of the Sorrowful Mother [*Third Order of St. Francis*] [*Roman Catholic religious order*] ... SSM
Sisters of the Third Franciscan Order (TOCD) ... OSF
Sisters of the Third Order of St. Francis of Penance and Charity (TOCD) ... OSF
Sisters of the Third Order of St. Francis of the Perpetual Adoration [*Roman Catholic religious order*] ... FSPA
Sisters of the Third Order of St. Francis (Peoria, IL) (TOCD) ... OSF
Sisters of the Third Order Regular of St. Francis of the Congregation of Our Lady of Lourdes (TOCD) ... OSF
Sisters of the Visitation of the Congregation of the Immaculate Heart of Mary [*Roman Catholic religious order*] ... SVM
Sisters, OR [*FM radio station call letters*] ... KPXA
Sisters Poor Servants of the Mother of God [*Roman Catholic religious order*] ... SMG
Sisters Public Library, Sisters, OR [*Library symbol Library of Congress*] (LCLS) ... OrSi
Sisters Servants of Mary [*Roman Catholic religious order*] ... S de M
Sisters Servants of Mary (TOCD) ... SM
Sisters Servants of the Blessed Sacrament [*Roman Catholic religious order*] ... SSBS
Sisters, Servants of the Immaculate Heart of Mary [*Roman Catholic religious order*] ... IHM
Sisters Servants of the Most Sacred Heart (TOCD) ... SSH
Sit and Dangle [*Orthopedics*] (DAVI) ... S/D
Sit Tibi Terra Levis [*May the Earth Lie Light on Thee*] [*Letters found on Roman tombs*] [*Latin*] ... STTL
Sit Venia Verbo [*Forgive the Expression*] [*Latin*] ... SVV
Site [*Archaeology*] ... S
Site Acceptance Evaluation [*Army*] (AABC) ... SAE
Site Acceptance Review [*Military*] ... SAR
Site Acceptance Test [*Military*] (AABC) ... SAT
Site Activation [*NASA*] (MCD) ... SA
Site Activation and Support Plan (MCD) ... SASP
Site Activation Board [*NASA*] (KSC) ... SAB
Site Activation Commander [*Army*] (AABC) ... SACMDR
Site Activation Need Date [*NASA*] (NASA) ... SAND
Site Activation Phase ... SAP
Site Activation/Phased Support Plan [*Military*] (MCD) ... SA/PSP
Site Activation Task Force [*Military*] ... SATAF
Site Activation Task Force (BARN) ... SATF
Site Activity [*or Alternation*] **Task Force** [*NASA*] (KSC) ... SATAF
Site Alteration Tests ... SAT
Site Approval and Market Analysis [*FHA*] ... SAMA
Site Assessment and Mitigation ... SA/M
Site Assignment Time ... SAT
Site Characterization and Analysis Penterometer System [*Army*] (RDA) ... SCAPS
Site Concurrence Letter (AFM) ... SCL
Site Configuration Control Board [*NASA*] (NASA) ... SCCB
Site Configuration Message [*NASA*] ... SCM
Site Contingency [*Nuclear energy*] (NRCH) ... SC
Site Control Block [*Computer science*] (OA) ... SCB
Site Cutover Manager [*Telecommunications*] (TEL) ... SCOM
Site Data Processor ... SDP
Site Defense [*Military*] (AABC) ... SD
Site Defense of Minuteman [*Missiles*] (MCD) ... SDM
Site Defense Project Office [*Military*] (AABC) ... SDPO
Site Defense RADAR ... SDR
Site Development and Facilities Utilization Plan [*Oak Ridge National Laboratory*] ... SDP
Site Document Order Section (SAA) ... SIDOS
Site Emergency Plan [*Nuclear energy*] (NRCH) ... SEP
Site Enforcement Tracking System [*Environmental Protection Agency*] (GFGA) ... SETS
Site Engineer (NITA) ... SE
Site Evaluation Report (MCD) ... SER
Site Field Force [*Army*] (AABC) ... SFF
Site Format Dump Tape (MCD) ... SFDT
Site Holdings, Inc. [*NASDAQ symbol*] (SAG) ... SITE
Site Holdings, Inc. [*Associated Press*] (SAG) ... SiteHld
Site, Inc. (EA) ... SI
Site Information Generation and Material Accountability Plan [*Army*] (AABC) ... SIGMA
Site Inspection and Test Procedure [*Nuclear energy*] (NRCH) ... SITP
Site Installation Requirements List (AAG) ... SIRL
Site Integrated Stabilization Plan ... SISMP
Site Investigation ... SI
Site Ion Exchange Effluent Plant [*Nuclear energy*] ... SIXEP
Site Maintenance Area (AAG) ... SMA
Site Modification Facility ... SMF
Site Number Assignment List (SAA) ... SNAL
Site of Special Scientific Interest [*Great Britain*] ... SSI
Site of Special Scientific Interest [*British*] ... SSSI
Site Peculiar Facility Change (AAG) ... SPFC

Site Peculiar Interference (AAG) .... SPI
Site Population Factor [*Nuclear energy*] (NRCH) .... SPF
Site Population Index [*Nuclear energy*] (NRCH) .... SPI
Site Production and Reduction System .... SPARS
Site Programmer Course .... SPC
Site Readiness Review [*NASA*] (NASA) .... SRR
Site Resident Engineer [*Telecommunications*] (TEL) .... SRE
Site Safety [*Nuclear energy*] (NRCH) .... SS
Site Safety Analysis Report [*Nuclear energy*] (NRCH) .... SSAR
Site Safety Evaluation Report [*Nuclear energy*] (NRCH) .... SSER
Site Security Maintenance Team .... SSMT
Site Security Supervisor (AFM) .... SSS
Site Selection Criteria (AAG) .... SSC
Site Server [*Microsoft Corp.*] [*Computer science*] .... SSE
Site Space Surveillance Monitor (AFM) .... SSSM
Site Suitability [*Nuclear energy*] (NRCH) .... SS
Site Suitability Report [*Nuclear energy*] (NRCH) .... SSR
Site Suitability Source Term [*Nuclear energy*] (NRCH) .... SSST
Site Survey Payload (MCD) .... SSP
Site Tactical Optimized Range Air Defense System .... STORADS
Site Team Leader [*Nuclear energy*] (NRCH) .... STL
Site Treatment Plan (DOGT) .... STP
Site-Directed Mutagenesis [*Biochemistry*] .... SDM
Site-Directed Spin Labeling [*Physical chemistry*] .... SDSL
Siteki [*Swaziland*] [*ICAO location identifier*] (ICLI) .... FDST
Sitel Corp. [*Associated Press*] (SAG) .... Sitel
Sitel Corp. [*NASDAQ symbol*] (SAG) .... SITL
Site-Specific Natural Isotope Fractionation [*Analytical chemistry*] .... SNIF
Sithe Energies, Inc. [*Associated Press*] (SAG) .... Sithe
Sithe Energies USA, Inc. [*NYSE symbol*] (SPSG) .... SYT
Sitia [*Greece*] [*ICAO location identifier*] (ICLI) .... LGST
Sitiawan [*Malaysia*] [*ICAO location identifier*] (ICLI) .... WMBA
Sitka [*Alaska*] [*ICAO location identifier*] (ICLI) .... PASI
Sitka [*Alaska*] [*Airport symbol*] (OAG) .... SIT
Sitka, AK [*Location identifier FAA*] (FAAL) .... BKA
Sitka, AK [*Location identifier FAA*] (FAAL) .... JPI
Sitka, AK [*FM radio station call letters*] .... KCAW
Sitka, AK [*AM radio station call letters*] .... KIFW
Sitka, AK [*FM radio station call letters*] .... KSBZ
Sitka, AK [*Television station call letters*] .... KTNL
Sitka, AK [*Location identifier FAA*] (FAAL) .... NOU
Sitka, AK [*Location identifier FAA*] (FAAL) .... SIT
Sitka Council on Alcohism and Other Drug Abuse, Sitka, AK [*Library symbol*] [*Library of Congress*] (LCLS) .... AkSC
Sitka National Monument .... SITK
Sitka School District, Sitka, AK [*Library symbol*] [*Library of Congress*] (LCLS) .... AkSSD
Sitkalidak Island [*Alaska*] [*Seismograph station code, US Geological Survey*] (SEIS) .... SKD
Sitkinak Island [*Alaska*] [*Seismograph station code, US Geological Survey*] (SEIS) .... SII
Sitkinak Island, AK [*Location identifier FAA*] (FAAL) .... SKJ
Sitogluside [*Organic chemistry*] (DAVI) .... BSSG
Sitra Cargo Systems [*Peru*] [*ICAO designator*] (FAAC) .... SCG
SITS [*SAGE Intercept Target Simulation*] **Probability of Detection and Conversion** (MCD) .... SPODAC
Sitterdorf [*Switzerland ICAO location identifier*] (ICLI) .... LSZV
Sitting Atop [*Molecular configuration*] .... SAT
Sittings for Middlesex at Nisi Prius [*A publication*] (DLA) .... Middx Sit
Sittwe [*Myanmar*] [*ICAO location identifier*] (ICLI) .... VBRA
Situate (ROG) .... SITE
Situated Atop an Extendable Mast (SAA) .... STEM
Situation (AFM) .... SIT
Situation (ROG) .... SITN
Situation Analysis and Vulnerability Estimate (MCD) .... SAVE
Situation Attention Display .... SAD
Situation Audit (MCD) .... SA
Situation Center [*NATO*] (NATG) .... SITCEN
Situation Comedy [*Television*] .... SITCOM
Situation Commercial [*Advertisement imitating a TV sitcom*] .... Sit-Comm
Situation Console (IAA) .... SC
Situation Display .... SD
Situation Display .... SID
Situation Display Console (DOMA) .... SDC
Situation Display Converter .... SDC
Situation Display Generator .... SDG
Situation Display Generator Element .... SDGE
Situation Display Indicator [*Aviation*] (OA) .... SDI
Situation Display Matrix (IAA) .... SDM
Situation Information Display .... SID
Situation Intelligence Brief (DNAB) .... SIB
Situation Map (MCD) .... SITMAP
Situation Normal, All Fouled Up [*Military slang*] [*Bowdlerized version*] .... SNAFU
Situation Normal - Everything Fouled Up [*Bowdlerized version Obsolete*] (DSUE) .... SNEFU
Situation Normal, Really All Fouled Up [*Military slang*] [*Bowdlerized version*] .... SNRAFU
Situation Projected Display .... SPD
Situation Questionnaire .... SQ
Situation Report .... SITREP
Situation Summary [*Military*] (NVT) .... SITSUM
Situation Track Display .... STK
Situation Unchanged, Still Fouled Up [*Military slang*] [*Bowdlerized version*] .... SUSFU
Situational Attitude Scale-Women (EDAC) .... SASW
Situational Awareness [*Navy*] (DOMA) .... SA
Situational Control of Daily Activities .... SCDA
Situational Training Exercise [*Army*] (INF) .... STX
Situationally Caused Error .... SCE
Situs [*Placed*] [*Latin*] .... S
Situs Ambiguus with Polysplenia [*Medicine*] (DMAA) .... SAP
Sitzungsbericht [*Transaction*] [*German*] .... SB
Sitzungsbericht [*Transaction*] [*German*] (BJA) .... Sber
Sitzungsberichte [*Proceedings*] [*German*] (OCD) .... Sitz
Sitzungsberichte der Akademie der Wissenschaften in Wien [*A publication*] (OCD) .... Sitz Wien
Sitzungsberichte der Oesterreichischen Akademie der Wissenschaften in Wien [*A publication*] (BJA) .... SBAkWissWien
Siuna [*Nicaragua*] [*ICAO location identifier*] (ICLI) .... MNSI
Sivas [*Turkey ICAO location identifier*] (ICLI) .... LTAR
Sivas [*Turkey*] [*Airport symbol*] (OAG) .... VAS
Sivrihisar [*Turkey ICAO location identifier*] (ICLI) .... LTAV
Six [*Roman numeral*] (DAVI) VI
Six Axis Motion System (PDAA) .... SAMS
Six BIT [*Binary Digit*] **Transcode** (CMD) .... SBT
Six Hundred Megacycle Air Defense RADAR .... SADR
Six Nations Public Library, Ohsweken, ON, Canada [*Library symbol*] [*Library of Congress*] (LCLS) .... CaOOhSN
Six Nations Public Library, Ohsweken, Ontario [*Library symbol National Library of Canada*] (BIB) .... OOSN
Six Node Averaging Program [*Computer science*] .... SNAP
Six Point Mooring [*Oil platform*] .... SPM
Sixaola [*Costa Rica*] [*ICAO location identifier*] (ICLI) .... MRSX
Six-Axis Manipulator (PDAA) .... SAM
Six-BIT [*Binary Digit*] **Universal Random Character Set** [*Computer science*] .... SBURCS
Six-Day War [*Arab-Israeli War, 1967*] (BJA) .... SDW
Six-Factor Automated Vocational Assessment System [*Vocational guidance test*] .... SAVAS
Sixpenny [*England*] .... SIXP
Sixteen Personality Factors Test [*Psychology*] (DAVI) .... SPFT
Sixteenmo [*Book from 15 to 17-1/2 centimeters in height*] .... S
Sixteenth [*Stock and commodity price quotes*] .... Steenth
Sixteenth Century Journal [*A publication*] (BRI) .... Six Ct J
Sixth Allied Tactical Air Force, Southeastern Europe [*NATO*] (NATG) .... SIXATAF
Sixth Fleet [*Atlantic*] [*Navy*] .... SIXFLT
Sixth Fleet [*Atlantic*] [*Navy*] .... SIXTHFLT
Sixth Fleet Escort Evaluation Program [*Navy*] .... SEEP
Sixth Marine Division Association [*Later, 6th MAR DIV*] (EA) .... SMDA
Sixth Word Designator [*Computer science*] .... S
Sixth-Plate (VRA) .... SIXT
Sixth-Year Specialist Program [*Library science*] .... SYSP
Sixx Hldgs [*NASDAQ symbol*] (TTSB) .... SIXX
Sixx Holdings, Inc. [*Associated Press*] (SAG) .... Sixx
Sixx Holdings, Inc. [*NASDAQ symbol*] (SAG) .... SIXX
Six-Year Defense Plan [*Used briefly from the late 1980s to 1991*] (DOMA) .... SYDP
Size (VRA) .... sz
Size (IAA) .... SZ
Size, Activity, Location, Type Report [*Military*] (INF) .... SALT
Size, Activity, Location, Unit, Time, Equipment (MCD) .... SALUTE
Size Exclusion [*Analytical chemistry*] .... SEX
Size Exclusion Chromatography .... SEC
Size Exclusion-High Performance Liquid Chromatography .... SE-HPLC
Size of Sample [*Statistics*] (DAVI) .... N
Size of Spawning Stock [*Fishery management*] .... SSB
Size Selective Inlet [*Environmental Protection Agency*] (GFGA) .... SSI
Size, Temperature, Application, Material, Pressure, Ends, and Delivery [*To aid selection of industrial hose*] .... STAMPED
Size Up, Interview, Rate [*Mnemonic used by Responsible Beverage Service in its bartender training program*] .... SIR
Sized (NTCM) .... S
Sized and Calendered [*Paper*] .... S & C
Sized and Calendered [*Paper*] .... SC
Sized and Supercalendered [*Paper*] .... S & SC
Sizeler Property Inv operty Inv [*NYSE symbol*] (TTSB) .... SIZ
Sizeler Property Investors, Inc. [*NYSE symbol*] (SPSG) .... SIZ
Sizeler Property Investors, Inc. [*Associated Press*] (SAG) .... SizelerP
Size-Press Coated [*Publishing*] .... SPC
Size-Selective Precipitation [*Physics*] .... SSP
Sizing Aerospace Vehicle Structures [*NASA*] .... SAVES
Sizing Float Level .... SFL
Sizzler International [*NYSE symbol*] (SPSG) .... SZ
Sizzler International, Inc. [*Associated Press*] (SAG) .... Sizzler
SJ Huvudkontor [*Swedish State Railways*] (DCTA) .... SJ
SJNB Financial Corp. [*Associated Press*] (SAG) .... SJNB
SJNB Financial Corp. [*NASDAQ symbol*] (NQ) .... SJNB
SJNB Finl [*NASDAQ symbol*] (TTSB) .... SJNB
Sjobo [*Sweden ICAO location identifier*] (ICLI) .... ESFJ
Sjoegren's Syndrome [*Medicine*] .... SS
Sjogren Syndrome [*Medicine*] (DMAA) .... SjS
Sjogren-Larsson [*Syndrome*] [*Medicine*] (DAVI) .... SL
Sjogren's Syndrome A [*Medicine*] .... SS-A
Sjogren's Syndrome Antibody [*Immunology*] (DAVI) .... SS-Ab
Sjogren's Syndrome B [*Medicine*] .... SS-B
Sjogren's Syndrome Foundation (EA) .... SSF
SJS Bancorp [*NASDAQ symbol*] (TTSB) .... SJSB
SJS Bancorp, Inc. [*Associated Press*] (SAG) .... SJS Bcp
SJS Bancorp, Inc. [*NASDAQ symbol*] (SAG) .... SJSB
SJW Corp. [*AMEX symbol*] (SPSG) .... SJW

Skadden, Arps, Slate, Meagher & Flom, New York, NY [*Library symbol Library of Congress*] (LCLS) .... NNSAS
Skaggs Telecommunications Service [*Salt Lake City, UT*] [*Telecommunications*] (TSSD) .... STS
Skagit/Hanford Nuclear Project (NRCH) .... S/HNP
Skagit Nuclear Project (NRCH) .... SNP
Skagit River Railroad (IIA) .... SR
Skagit Valley College, Mount Vernon, WA [*Library symbol Library of Congress*] (LCLS) .... WaMtvS
Skagit Valley Hospital, Mount Vernon, WA [*Library symbol*] [*Library of Congress*] (LCLS) .... WaMtvH
Skagway [*Alaska*] [*Airport symbol*] (OAG) .... SGY
Skagway Air Service, Inc. [*ICAO designator*] (FAAC) .... SGY
Skagway, AK [*Location identifier FAA*] (FAAL) .... SGY
Skagway Public Library, Skagway, AK [*Library symbol Library of Congress*] (LCLS) .... AkSk
Skalnate-Pleso [*Czechoslovakia*] [*Seismograph station code, US Geological Survey*] (SEIS) .... SPC
Skalstugan [*Sweden*] [*Seismograph station code, US Geological Survey*] (SEIS) .... SKA
Skandinavisk Jodisk Ungdomsforbund (BJA) .... SJUF
Skandinavisk Migraeneselskab [*Scandinavian Migraine Society*] (EAIO) .... SMS
Skandinaviska Enskilda Banken [*Scandinavian Private Bank*] [*Sweden*] .... S-E
Skandinaviska Enskilda Banken [*Sweden*] .... SEB
Skandinaviska Lackteknikers Forbund [*Federation of Scandinavian Paint and Varnish Technologists*] [*Sweden*] (EAIO) .... SLF
Skandinaviska Seglarforbundet [*Scandinavian Yachting Association - SYA*] (EAIO) .... SKAND SF
Skandinaviska Simuleringssaellskapet [*Scandinavian Simulation Society*] [*Also, SSS*] (EA) .... SIMS
Skaneateles [*New York*] [*Seismograph station code, US Geological Survey*] (SEIS) .... SKN
Skaneateles Short Line Railroad Corp. [*Later, SSL*] [*AAR code*] .... SKSL
Skaneateles Short Line Railroad Corp. [*AAR code*] .... SSL
Skardu [*Pakistan*] [*Airport symbol*] (AD) .... KDU
Skardu [*Pakistan*] [*ICAO location identifier*] (ICLI) .... OPSD
Skargardsflyg, AB, Finland [*FAA designator*] (FAAC) .... LND
Skarpsville, PA [*FM radio station call letters*] .... WRKU
Skate Sailing Association of America (EA) .... SSAA
Skead Branch, Nickel Centre Public Library, Ontario [*Library symbol National Library of Canada*] (NLC) .... OSKNC
Skeena Resources Ltd. [*Vancouver Stock Exchange symbol*] .... SKE
Skegair [*British ICAO designator*] (FAAC) .... SKA
Skegness/Ingoldmells [*British ICAO location identifier*] (ICLI) .... EGNI
Skein .... SK
Skein (ROG) .... SKN
Skein Dyers Association of America [*Later, SRPDAA*] (EA) .... SDAA
Skeletal [*Orthopedics*] (DAVI) .... sk
Skeletal (AAG) .... SKEL
Skeletal Axis of Basal Piece .... SABP
Skeletal Axis of Branchial Filament .... SABRF
Skeletal Axis of Palp .... SAPP
Skeletal Axis of Pinnule .... SAP
Skeletal Growth Factor [*Genetics*] .... SGF
Skeletal Muscle Relaxant [*Drug*] .... SMR
Skeletal Muscle Ventricle [*Medicine*] .... SMV
Skeletal Repair System [*Medicine*] .... SRS
Skeletal Rod of Palp .... SRPP
Skeletal Traction [*Orthopedics*] (DAVI) .... sk tr
Skeletal Traction [*Orthopedics*] (DAVI) .... sk tx
Skeletal Troponin C [*Biochemistry*] .... STnC
Skeletals (DCTA) .... SK
Skeleton Flight Plan .... SFP
Skeleton Key (DSUE) .... SKET
Skeleton Records [*Army*] .... SR
Skelleftea [*Sweden ICAO location identifier*] (ICLI) .... ESNS
Skelleftea [*Sweden*] [*Airport symbol*] (OAG) .... SFT
Skelly Resources Ltd. [*Vancouver Stock Exchange symbol*] .... SLY
Skene's, Urethral, and Bartholin's [*Glands*] [*Anatomy*] (DAVI) .... SUB
Sketch (VRA) .... sk
Sketch (AAG) .... SK
Sketch Pad Layout (MCD) .... SKPL
Sketch-in-Depth [*Parthorn*] [*Software package*] (NCC) .... SID
Skew Buffer .... SKB
Skewbald [*Color of a horse*] (BARN) .... sk
Skewed Circular Arc Method of Analysis .... SCAMA
Skewing the Pitch Angle .... SKV
Skewness (WGA) .... Sk
SKF AB [*Associated Press*] (SAG) .... SKF
SKF AB [*Goteborg, Sweden*] [*NASDAQ symbol*] (NQ) .... SKFR
SKF AB ADR [*NASDAQ symbol*] (TTSB) .... SKFRY
Ski Area Suppliers Association (EA) .... SASA
Ski Club of Great Britain (DI) .... SCGB
Ski Council of America [*Defunct*] (EA) .... SCA
Ski Industries America (EA) .... SIA
SKI Ltd. [*Associated Press*] (SAG) .... SKI
S-K-I Ltd. [*Killington, VT*] [*NASDAQ symbol*] (NQ) .... SKII
S-K-I Ltd [*NASDAQ symbol*] (TTSB) .... SKII
Ski Resort Marketing Association [*Defunct*] (EA) .... SRMA
Ski Retailers Council [*Inactive*] (EA) .... SRC
Ski Retailers International (EA) .... SRI
Ski Touring Council [*Defunct*] (EA) .... STC
Skiathos [*Greece*] [*Airport symbol*] (OAG) .... JSI
Skiathos [*Greece*] [*ICAO location identifier*] (ICLI) .... LGSK
Skibob Association of Great Britain (DBA) .... SAGB

Skid (AAG) .... S
Skid .... SD
Skid .... SKD
Skid Jacket Water Cooling Pump [*Nuclear energy*] (NRCH) .... SJWCP
Skid Strip (KSC) .... SS
Skidmore College, Saratoga Springs, NY [*Library symbol Library of Congress*] (LCLS) .... NSsS
Skidmore College, Saratoga Springs, NY [*OCLC symbol*] (OCLC) .... VZS
Skidmore, Owings & Merrill [*Architectural firm*] .... SOM
Skidmore's Mining Statutes [*A publication*] (DLA) .... Skid Min
Skidrow Joe Fan Club (EA) .... SJFC
Skid-to-Turn .... STT
Skidway Institute of Oceanography [*Georgia*] (NOAA) .... SIO
Skien [*Norway*] [*Airport symbol*] (OAG) .... SKE
Skien/Geiteryggen [*Norway ICAO location identifier*] (ICLI) .... ENSN
Skiff, Ice [*Coast Guard*] (DNAB) .... SKI
Skiff, Light [*Coast Guard*] (DNAB) .... SKL
Skiff, Medium [*Coast Guard*] (DNAB) .... SKM
Ski-Free Marine [*Vancouver Stock Exchange symbol*] .... SFM
Skikda [*Algeria*] [*ICAO location identifier*] (ICLI) .... DABP
Skilak [*Cooper Landing*] [*Alaska*] [*Seismograph station code, US Geological Survey*] (SEIS) .... SKL
Skilda [*Algeria*] [*Airport symbol*] (AD) .... SKI
Skill .... SKLL
[The] Skill Alignment Module [*Army*] (INF) .... TSAM
Skill Centre Manager (AIE) .... SCM
Skill Component .... SC
Skill Components Research Laboratory [*Air Force*] (MCD) .... SCRL
Skill Development Base [*Army*] (AABC) .... SDB
Skill Development Program [*Australia*] .... SDP
Skill Escalation Employment Development (EA) .... SEED
Skill Identifier [*Career development*] [*Army*] (RDA) .... SI
Skill Improvement Program [*Bureau of Apprenticeship and Training*] [*Department of Labor*] .... SIP
Skill in Personnel through On-Site Training [*Department of Labor*] .... SPOT
Skill, Knowledge, and Ability [*or Attitude*] [*Employment*] .... SKA
Skill/Knowledge Improvement Program [*Navy*] (DNAB) .... SKIP
Skill Knowledge Tests .... SKT
Skill Level .... SKL
Skill Level .... SL
Skill Performance Aid [*Army*] (RDA) .... SPA
Skill Performance Aids .... SPAS
Skill Qualification Identifier [*Army*] (INF) .... SQI
Skill Qualification Score [*Military*] (AABC) .... SQS
Skill Qualification Test [*Army*] .... SQT
Skill Qualification Test Requirements Alert Message .... SRAM
Skill Qualification Test Requirements Alert Notice .... SRAN
Skill Qualification Test (Written Component) [*Army*] (INF) .... SQT(WC)
Skill Speciality Identifier (MCD) .... SSI
Skill Specialty Code (MCD) .... SSC
Skill Specialty Evaluation Code [*Army*] .... SS EVAL
Skill Technical (INF) .... ST
Skill Training Improvement Program [*Department of Labor*] .... STIP
Skilled (MSA) .... SKD
Skilled and Unskilled Workers' Union - Somali Republic .... SUWU
Skilled Labor (MHDW) .... SL
Skilled Nursing and Related Long Term Care Services (EA) .... SNRLTCS
Skilled Nursing Care .... SNC
Skilled Nursing Extended Care Facility (DAVI) .... SNEF
Skilled Nursing Facility .... SNF
Skilled Nursing Home .... SNH
Skillman's New York Police Reports [*A publication*] (DLA) .... Burlesque Reps
Skillman's New York Police Reports [*A publication*] (DLA) .... Skill Pol Rep
Skills and Knowledges .... S & K
Skills for Working in a Multicultural Society [*Australia*] .... SWIMS
Skills Inventory Coordinator .... SIC
Skills Inventory Retrieval System (MCD) .... SIRS
Skills, Knowledge, Abilities, and Personnel [*Attributes*] (MCD) .... SKAP
Skills, Knowledges, Aptitudes, Temperaments, Interests (OICC) .... SKATI
Skills Level Improvement Program .... SLIP
Skills Support System [*Education*] .... SSS
Skills Training Adjustment Group [*Educational project sponsored by The Hartford*] .... STAG
Skills Training Agency [*British*] .... STA
Skills Training Program .... STP
Skillshare National Information Processing System [*Australia*] .... SNIPS
Skim Milk (MAE) .... SM
Skimmed .... SK
Skimmed Milk Powder (ADA) .... SMP
Skin (DAVI) .... SK
Skin (DAVI) .... SKI
Skin and Cancer Foundation of Australia .... SCFA
Skin and Facial Stapler [*Surgery*] (DAVI) .... SFS
Skin Cancer Foundation (EA) .... SCF
Skin Care Association of America (EA) .... SCAA
Skin Condition Data Form [*Medicine*] (DMAA) .... SCDF
Skin Conductance .... SC
Skin Conductance Level [*Physiology*] .... SCL
Skin Conductance Reading [*on Biofeedback*] [*Psychiatry*] (DAVI) .... SCR
Skin Conductance Response .... SCR
Skin Destruction [*Medicine*] .... SD
Skin Diver Contact Air Lenses .... SCAL
Skin Dose .... SD
Skin Electric Tracing (IAA) .... SECT
Skin Endpoint Titration [*Medicine*] (MEDA) .... SET

Skin Erythema Dose [*Medicine*] ... SED
Skin Fibroblast [*Clinical chemistry*] ... SF
Skin Graft [*Medicine*] ... SG
Skin, Head, Eyes, Ears, Nose, and Throat [*Medicine*] (DMAA) ... SHEENT
Skin, Hide, and Leather Traders Association [*British*] (EAIO) ... SHLTA
Skin, Hide, and Leather Trades Association [*British*] (DBA) ... SHALTA
Skin Impedance [*Neurology*] (DAVI) ... Sz
Skin Inserted Detonator (MCD) ... SID
Skin Painting [*Method of administering experimental chemicals*] ... SP
Skin Perfusin Pressure [*Medicine*] (DMAA) ... SPP
Skin Potential (MAE) ... SP
Skin Potential Level ... SPL
Skin Potential Response [*Physiology*] ... SPR
Skin Prick [*Immunology*] ... SP
Skin Prick Test [*Immunology*] ... SPT
Skin Protection Factor [*Medicine*] ... SPF
Skin Reactive Factor [*Immunochemistry*] ... SRF
Skin Resistance [*Physiology*] (MAE) ... SR
Skin Resistance Level [*Physiology*] ... SRL
Skin Resistance Response [*Physiology*] ... SRR
Skin Respiratory Factor [*Physiology*] ... SRF
Skin Self Examination [*Medicine*] ... SSE
Skin Sensitizing Antibody (AAMN) ... SSA
Skin Surface Lipid [*Physiology*] ... SSL
Skin Sympathetic Activity [*Medicine*] (DMAA) ... SSA
Skin Temperature (OA) ... ST
Skin Temperature [*Medicine*] ... Ts
Skin Temperature Recovery Time [*Medicine*] (DMAA) ... STRT
Skin Temperature Test [*Physiology*] ... STT
Skin Test ... ST
Skin Test Dose ... STD
Skin Test for Delayed Hypersensitivity [*Medicine*] (DMAA) ... STDH
Skin Test Index [*Chemical medicine*] ... STI
Skin Test Unit ... STU
Skin Thickness [*Medicine*] (DMAA) ... ST
Skin to Tumor Distance [*Medicine*] (MAE) ... STD
Skin Track (MUGU) ... ST
Skin Unit Dose [*Medicine*] (DMAA) ... SUD
Skin-Associated Lymphoid Tissue [*Dermatology*] ... SALT
Skin-Film Distance [*Medicine*] (MAE) ... SFD
Skinfold Thickness [*Medicine*] ... SFT
Skinker's Reports [*65-79 Missouri*] [*A publication*] (DLA) ... Skinker
Skinned (MSA) ... SK
Skinner Investigation Platform ... SKIP
Skinner's English King's Bench Reports [*A publication*] (DLA) ... Skin
Skinner's English King's Bench Reports [*90 English Reprint*] [*1681-98*] [*A publication*] (DLA) ... Skinner
Skinner's English King's Bench Reports [*90 English Reprint*] [*A publication*] (DLA) ... Skinner (Eng)
Skinner's School Officers Training Corps [*British military*] (DMA) ... SSOTC
Skinners' Society [*A union*] [*British*] ... SS
Skip ... SK
Skip (BUR) ... SKP
Skip Flag [*Computer science*] (MDG) ... SF
Skip Line Printer [*Computer science*] (ECII) ... SKP
Skipper [*Navy British*] ... Skr
Skiptrace (LAIN) ... SKT
Skirt (MSA) ... SKT
Skirt Buildup (SAA) ... SBU
Skirted ... SKD
Skive [*Denmark ICAO location identifier*] (ICLI) ... EKSV
Skiver [*Leather bookbinding*] (DGA) ... Sk
Sklar Aphasia Scale [*Psychology*] ... SAS
Skoda Air [*Czechoslovakia*] [*ICAO designator*] (FAAC) ... SOA
Skogar [*Iceland*] [*Airport symbol*] (AD) ... SKR
Skokie, IL [*FM radio station call letters*] ... WTMX
Skokie Public Library, Skokie, IL [*OCLC symbol*] (OCLC) ... IHG
Skokie Public Library, Skokie, IL [*Library symbol Library of Congress*] (LCLS) ... ISk
Skolta Esperanto-Ligo [*Scouts' Esperanto League*] (EAIO) ... SEL
Skopje [*Former Yugoslavia*] [*ICAO location identifier*] (ICLI) ... LYSK
Skopje [*Yugoslavia*] [*Seismograph station code, US Geological Survey*] (SEIS) ... SKO
Skopje [*Former Yugoslavia*] [*Airport symbol*] (OAG) ... SKP
Skorpion Air [*Bulgaria*] [*ICAO designator*] (FAAC) ... SPN
Skot [*Unit of luminance*] ... sk
Skovde [*Sweden ICAO location identifier*] (ICLI) ... ESGQ
Skovde/Hospital [*Sweden ICAO location identifier*] (ICLI) ... ESHO
Skowhegan Free Public Library, Skowhegan, ME [*Library symbol Library of Congress*] (LCLS) ... MeSk
Skowhegan, ME [*FM radio station call letters*] ... WHQO
Skowhegan, ME [*AM radio station call letters*] ... WSKW
Skowhegan, ME [*FM radio station call letters*] ... WTOS
Skrydstrup [*Denmark ICAO location identifier*] (ICLI) ... EKSP
Skrydstrup [*Denmark*] [*Airport symbol*] (OAG) ... SKS
Skukum Gold [*Vancouver Stock Exchange symbol*] ... SKV
Skukuza [*South Africa*] [*ICAO location identifier*] (ICLI) ... FASZ
Skukuza [*South Africa*] [*Airport symbol*] (OAG) ... SZK
Skull Fracture [*Medicine*] ... SkFx
Skull Occipital Mandibular Immobilization [*Orthosis*] [*Dentistry*] (DAVI) ... SOMI
Skull Series [*Radiology*] (DAVI) ... SS
Skwentna [*Alaska*] [*Seismograph station code, US Geological Survey*] (SEIS) ... SKT
Skwentna, AK [*Location identifier FAA*] (FAAL) ... SKW
Sky Air Cargo Services (UK) Ltd. [*British ICAO designator*] (FAAC) ... NJA
Sky & Telescope [*A publication*] (BRI) ... S&T
Sky Care Ltd. [*New Zealand*] [*ICAO designator*] (FAAC) ... SCE
Sky Cavalry ... SKYCAV
Sky Clear [*ICAO*] (FAAC) ... SKC
Sky Condition [*Aviation*] (FAAC) ... SK
Sky Freighters NV [*Belgium ICAO designator*] (FAAC) ... SFI
Sky Games International Ltd. [*NASDAQ symbol*] (SAG) ... SKYFC
Sky Games International Ltd. [*NASDAQ symbol*] (SAG) ... SKYG
Sky Games International, Ltd. [*Associated Press*] (SAG) ... SkyGms
Sky Games Intl [*NASDAQ symbol*] (TTSB) ... SKYGF
Sky Harbor Air Service, Inc. [*ICAO designator*] (FAAC) ... SHC
Sky Line for Air Services Ltd. [*Sudan*] [*ICAO designator*] (FAAC) ... SLY
Sky Liners Air Services Ltd. [*Suriname*] [*ICAO designator*] (FAAC) ... LNR
Sky One Express Airlines, Inc. [*ICAO designator*] (FAAC) ... SYF
Sky Ranch for Boys (EA) ... SRB
Sky Scientific [*NASDAQ symbol*] (TTSB) ... SKYS
Sky Service [*Belgium ICAO designator*] (FAAC) ... SKS
Sky Survey Instrument ... SSI
Sky Tours, Inc. [*ICAO designator*] (FAAC) ... SKE
Sky View Center Elementary School, Rockford, IL [*Library symbol*] [*Library of Congress*] (LCLS) ... IRoSvE
Sky Wave Observation Timer (IAA) ... SOT
Sky West [*ICAO designator*] (AD) ... YT
Sky West, Inc. [*ICAO designator*] (FAAC) ... SKW
Skybridge International, Inc. [*Vancouver Stock Exchange symbol*] ... SKB
Skybus, Inc. [*ICAO designator*] (FAAC) ... FLH
Skycare Management Services Ltd. [*British ICAO designator*] (FAAC) ... SKC
Skycharter (Malton) Ltd. [*Canada ICAO designator*] (FAAC) ... SKL
Skycraft Air Transport, Inc. [*Canada ICAO designator*] (FAAC) ... SKG
Skycraft, Inc. [*ICAO designator*] (FAAC) ... SKF
Skycy Freighters International Ltd. [*Kenya*] [*ICAO designator*] (FAAC) ... SIF
Skydoor Media & Entmt [*NASDAQ symbol*] (TTSB) ... SKDR
Skye Terrier Club of America (EA) ... STCA
Skyfreight, Inc. [*ICAO designator*] (FAAC) ... SFT
Skyfreighters [*ICAO designator*] (AD) ... BZ
Skyfreighters Corp. [*ICAO designator*] (FAAC) ... SKB
Skygold Resources [*Vancouver Stock Exchange symbol*] ... SYO
Skyguard Ltd. [*British ICAO designator*] (FAAC) ... SKD
Skyhawk Resources, Inc. [*Vancouver Stock Exchange symbol*] ... SYK
Skyhigh Resources Ltd. [*Vancouver Stock Exchange symbol*] ... SHU
Skyjet, Inc. [*Antigua and Barbuda*] [*ICAO designator*] (FAAC) ... SKJ
Skylab [*NASA*] (KSC) ... SL
Skylab Advisory Group for Experiments [*NASA*] ... SAGE
Skylab Best Estimate of Trajectory [*NASA*] ... SKYBET
Skylab Communication Terminal [*NASA*] (KSC) ... SCT
Skylab Communications Engineer [*NASA*] ... SKYCOM
Skylab Data Task [*NASA*] ... SDT
Skylab End-to-End Test System [*NASA*] ... SETS
Skylab Extravehicular Visor Assembly [*NASA*] ... SEVA
Skylab Ground Support Network [*NASA*] ... SGSN
Skylab Launch Data System [*NASA*] (KSC) ... SLDS
Skylab Medical Experiments Altitude Test [*NASA*] ... SMEAT
Skylab Mission Evaluation Report [*NASA*] (MCD) ... SMER
Skylab Mobile Laboratory [*NASA*] (KSC) ... SML
Skylab Operational Environment [*NASA*] ... SOE
Skylab Operations Handbook [*NASA*] (MCD) ... SLOH
Skylab Operations Handbook [*NASA*] ... SOH
Skylab Orbital Workshop [*NASA*] ... SOW
Skylab Orbit-Deorbit System [*NASA*] (MCD) ... SODS
Skylab Process Control Unit [*NASA*] ... SPCU
Skylab Program Directive [*NASA*] (KSC) ... SLPD
Skylab Program Directive [*NASA*] (KSC) ... SPD
Skylab Program Office [*NASA*] (KSC) ... SLPO
Skylab Rescue [*NASA*] (KSC) ... SLR
Skylab Simulation, Checkout, and Training System [*NASA*] ... SSCATS
Skylab Simulator [*NASA*] (KSC) ... SLS
Skylab Student Project [*NASA*] ... SSP
Skylab Systems Integration Equipment [*NASA*] (MCD) ... SSIE
Skylab Terminal System [*NASA*] ... STS
Skylab Upwelling Experiment [*Marine science*] (MSC) ... SUE
Skylab Video Documentation Project [*NASA*] (KSC) ... SVDP
Skylands Cmnty Bk NJ [*NASDAQ symbol*] (TTSB) ... SKCB
Skylands Community Bank [*NASDAQ symbol*] (SAG) ... SKCB
Skylands Community Bank [*Associated Press*] (SAG) ... SkylCBk
Skylands Park Management [*Associated Press*] (SAG) ... SkylandP
Skylands Park Management [*Associated Press*] (SAG) ... Skylnd
Skylands Park Management [*NASDAQ symbol*] (SAG) ... SKYP
Skylands Park Mgmt [*NASDAQ symbol*] (TTSB) ... SKYP
Skylands Pk Mgmt Wrrt [*NASDAQ symbol*] (TTSB) ... SKYPW
Skylane Air Charter [*British ICAO designator*] (FAAC) ... SKK
Skylark Resources Ltd. [*Vancouver Stock Exchange symbol*] ... SKR
Skylight [*Technical drawings*] ... SKL
Skylight (AAG) ... SLT
Skyline [*Norway ICAO designator*] (FAAC) ... SEG
Skyline Aviation Services, Inc. [*ICAO designator*] (FAAC) ... SKN
Skyline Chili [*NASDAQ symbol*] (TTSB) ... SKCH
Skyline Chili, Inc. [*Cincinnati, OH*] [*NASDAQ symbol*] (NQ) ... SKCH
Skyline Chili, Inc. [*Associated Press*] (SAG) ... SkyChili
Skyline College Library, San Bruno, CA [*OCLC symbol*] (OCLC) ... CSY
Skyline College, San Bruno, CA [*Library symbol Library of Congress*] (LCLS) ... CSbrS
Skyline Corp. [*NYSE symbol*] (SPSG) ... SKY
Skyline Corp. [*Associated Press*] (SAG) ... Skyline
Skyline Explorations Ltd. [*Vancouver Stock Exchange symbol Toronto Stock Exchange symbol*] ... SKX

Skyline Hikers of the Canadian Rockies (EA) .... SHCR
Skyline Multimedia Entertainment [*NASDAQ symbol*] (SAG) .... SKYL
Skyline Multimedia Entertainment [*Associated Press*] (SAG) .... SkyM
Skyline Multimedia Entertainment [*Associated Press*] (SAG) .... SkyMl
Skyline Multimedia Entertainment [*Associated Press*] (SAG) .... SkyMult
Skyline Multimedia Entmt [*NASDAQ symbol*] (TTSB) .... SKYL
Skyline Multimedia Entmt Wrrt'B' [*NASDAQ symbol*] (TTSB) .... SKYLZ
Skyline Multimeida Entmt Wrrt'A' [*NASDAQ symbol*] (TTSB) .... SKYLW
Skyline Network Service [*Satellite Business Systems*] [*McLean, VA*]
  [*Telecommunications*] (TSSD) .... SNS
Skylink Airlines [*Canada ICAO designator*] (FAAC) .... SKI
SkyMall, Inc. [*NASDAQ symbol*] (SAG) .... SKYM
SkyMall, Inc. [*Associated Press*] (SAG) .... SkyMall
Skyplan Services Ltd. [*Canada ICAO designator*] (FAAC) .... XXS
Skyport [*Airport symbol*] .... TL
Skyrocket Exploration [*Vancouver Stock Exchange symbol*] .... SKY
Skyros [*Greece*] [*ICAO location identifier*] (ICLI) .... LGSY
Skyrover Ltd. [*British ICAO designator*] (FAAC) .... SKR
Skysat Commun Network'A' [*NASDAQ symbol*] (TTSB) .... SKATA
Skysat Communications Network Corp. [*NASDAQ symbol*] (SAG) .... SKAT
Skysat Communications Network Corp. [*Associated Press*] (SAG) .... Skysat
Skysat Communications Network Corp. [*Associated Press*] (SAG) .... SkysatC
Skysat Communications Network Corp. [*Associated Press*] (SAG) .... Skyst
Skysat Communicns Ntwk Wrrt'A' [*NASDAQ symbol*] (TTSB) .... SKATW
Skysat Communicns Ntwk Wrrt'B' [*NASDAQ symbol*] (TTSB) .... SKATZ
Skyscraper (VRA) .... skyscr
Skyservice FBO, Inc. [*Canada*] [*FAA designator*] (FAAC) .... SSV
Skystar International [*ICAO designator*] (FAAC) .... SSK
Skystream Airlines [*ICAO designator*] (AD) .... DN
Skytrak Aeronautical Systems Ltd. [*British*] [*FAA designator*] (FAAC) .... STD
Skyward Aviation Ltd. [*Canada ICAO designator*] (FAAC) .... SGK
Skywatch Ltd. [*British ICAO designator*] (FAAC) .... SKH
Skywave Correction [*Aircraft navigation*] .... SWC
Skywave Synchronization (DEN) .... SR
Skywave Synchronized Long-Range Aid to Navigation .... SSLORAN
Skyway .... SKWY
Skyway [*Postal Service standard*] (OPSA) .... SKWY
Skyway [*Commonly used*] (OPSA) .... SKYWAY
Skyway Business Travel Ltd. [*British ICAO designator*] (FAAC) .... SWY
Skyway Resources Ltd. [*Vancouver Stock Exchange symbol*] .... SYW
Skyways AB [*Sweden ICAO designator*] (FAAC) .... SKX
Skyways Africa Ltd. [*Kenya*] [*ICAO designator*] (FAAC) .... SAE
SkyWest, Inc. [*St. George, UT*] [*NASDAQ symbol*] (NQ) .... SKYW
SkyWest, Inc. [*Associated Press*] (SAG) .... SkyWest
Skywings AB [*Sweden ICAO designator*] (FAAC) .... SCF
Skywork SA [*Switzerland ICAO designator*] (FAAC) .... SRK
Skyworld Airlines, Inc. [*ICAO designator*] (FAAC) .... SPC
Skyworld Resources & Development Ltd. [*Vancouver Stock Exchange
  symbol*] .... SKD
SL Industries [*NYSE symbol*] (TTSB) .... SL
SL Industries, Inc. [*NYSE symbol*] (SPSG) .... SL
SL Industries, Inc. [*Associated Press*] (SAG) .... SL Ind
Slab Construction .... SLABCON
Slab Penetration and Reflection Calculation .... SPARC
SLAC Positron-Electron Asymmetric Ring .... SPEAR
Slack and Penalty .... SLKPEN
Slack Frame Program .... SFP
Slacked Unconstrained Minimization Technique (PDAA) .... SLUMT
Slade's Compilation of the Statutes of Vermont [*A publication*] (DLA) .... Sl St
Slade's Reports [*15 Vermont*] [*A publication*] (DLA) .... Slade
Slag Employers Association [*British*] (DBA) .... SEA
Slain (ROG) .... SL
Slander [*or Slanderous*] [*FBI standardized term*] .... SLAN
Slandsville [*South Carolina*] [*Seismograph station code, US Geological
  Survey*] (SEIS) .... SVS
Slant Hole Distance [*Nuclear energy*] (OA) .... SHD
Slant Range .... SLAR
Slant Range .... SR
Slant Range Fuze (NG) .... SLARF
Slant Visual Range .... SVR
Slargando [*Slackening*] [*Music*] (ROG) .... SLAR
Slargando [*Slackening*] [*Music*] .... SLARG
Slate (KSC) .... S
Slate (AAG) .... SL
Slate (VRA) .... sla
Slate (MSA) .... SLT
Slate Creek, AK [*Location identifier FAA*] (FAAL) .... SLX
Slate Falls Airways Ltd. [*Canada ICAO designator*] (FAAC) .... SYJ
Slate Island, ON [*ICAO location identifier*] (ICLI) .... CYSS
Slate Mountain [*Nevada*] [*Seismograph station code, US Geological Survey
  Closed*] (SEIS) .... STM
Slate Run, PA [*Location identifier FAA*] (FAAL) .... SLT
Slater Hall Information Products [*Database producer*] (IID) .... SHIP
Slater Industries, Inc. [*Toronto Stock Exchange symbol*] .... SSI
Slater Orbital Exponents [*Atomic physics*] .... SOE
Slater Public Library, Slater, IA [*Library symbol Library of Congress*]
  (LCLS) .... IaSla
Slater Steels Corp. [*Formerly, Slater Steel Industries*] [*Toronto Stock Exchange
  symbol*] .... SSI
Slaters' Society [*A union*] [*British*] .... SS
Slater-Type Orbital [*Atomic structure*] .... STO
Slate-Shingle Roof [*Technical drawings*] .... SSR
Slaton, TX [*FM radio station call letters*] .... KJAK
Slats and Flaps Control System [*Aerospace technology*] (EECA) .... SFCS
Slaughter [*England*] .... SLAUGH

Slave [*LORAN stations*] .... S
Slave Clock (IAA) .... SC
Slave Emulator Control Unit .... SECU
Slave Gyro Assembly .... SGA
Slave Gyro Control System .... SGCS
Slave Gyro Leveling Integrator .... SGLI
Slave Lake, AB [*Television station call letters*] CFRN-9
Slave Lake, AB [*AM radio station call letters*] .... CKWA
Slave Lake, AB [*ICAO location identifier*] (ICLI) .... CYZH
Slave Lake Municipal Library, Alberta [*Library symbol National Library of
  Canada*] (NLC) .... ASLM
Slave Lake Municipal Library, Slave Lake, AB, Canada [*Library symbol*]
  [*Library of Congress*] (LCLS) .... CaSlM
Slave Manipulator Arm [*Astronautics*] .... SMA
Slave Processing Unit .... SPU
Slave Programmable Read-Only Memory .... S-P/ROM
Slave Programmable ROM (NITA) .... SPROM
Slave Register Set .... SRS
Slave Service Area [*Telecommunications*] (IAA) .... SSA
Slaved Gyro (MCD) .... S/G
Slaved Illuminator [*Military*] (CAAL) .... SI
Slaved Illuminator Data Converter [*Military*] (CAAL) .... SIDC
Slavic [*MARC language code Library of Congress*] (LCCP) .... sla
Slavic American National Association (EA) .... SANA
Slavic and East European Section [*Association of College and Research
  Libraries*] .... SEES
Slavic Book of Enoch (BJA) .... SlavEnoch
Slavic Gospel Association (EA) .... SGA
Slavic Review [*A publication*] (BRI) .... Slav R
Slaving Pick-Off .... SPO
Slaving Signal Amplifier .... SSA
Slaving Torquer Amplifier .... STA
Slavonic [*Language, etc.*] .... SLAV
Slavonic Benevolent Order of the State of Texas [*Temple, TX*] (EA) .... SBOST
Slayton Elementary School, Slayton, MN [*Library symbol*] [*Library of
  Congress*] (LCLS) .... MnSlyES
Slayton Junior-Senior High School, Slayton, MN [*Library symbol*] [*Library of
  Congress*] (LCLS) .... MnSlyJSH
Slayton, MN [*FM radio station call letters*] (RBYB) .... KJOE
Slayton Public Library, Slayton, MN [*Library symbol*] [*Library of Congress*]
  (LCLS) .... MnSly
SLCM [*Sea-Launched Cruise Missile*] Survivability Steering Group [*Navy*]
  (CAAL) .... SSSG
Sled Dogs Co. [*Associated Press*] (SAG) .... SledDogs
Sled Dogs Co. [*NASDAQ symbol*] (SAG) .... SNOW
Sled Towed Array (MCD) .... STAR
Sledborne Event Time Digitizer .... SETD
Sledborne Time Digitizer .... STD
Sleep .... SLP
Sleep Analyzing Hybrid Computer (PDAA) .... SAHC
Sleep Apnea [*Medicine*] (DMAA) .... SA
Sleep Apnea Syndrome [*Medicine*] .... SAS
Sleep Apnea-Hypersomnolence Syndrome [*Medicine*] (DMAA) .... SAHS
Sleep Apnoeia Research Association [*Australia*] .... SARA
Sleep Deprivation (PDAA) .... SD
Sleep Disturbance with Anxiety and Depression [*Combat behavior disorder*]
  [*Military*] (INF) .... S-A-D
Sleep Research Society (EA) .... SRS
Sleep Stage Change Frequency [*Medicine*] (DMAA) .... SSCF
Sleep with Rapid Eye Movement .... S-REM
Sleep-Disordered Breathing [*Medicine*] (DMAA) .... SDB
Sleeper Public Library, Ubly, MI [*Library symbol Library of Congress*]
  (LCLS) .... MiUb
Sleep-Induction/Rapid Reawakening System [*Military*] (RDA) .... SIRRA
Sleeping [*Medicine*] .... S
Sleeping Car Porters Union (MHDB) .... SCP
Sleeping Gold Ltd. [*Vancouver Stock Exchange symbol*] .... SGL
Sleeping Mountain [*Nevada*] [*Seismograph station code, US Geological
  Survey Closed*] (SEIS) .... SMN
Sleeping Time .... ST
Sleeping-Out Pass [*British armed forces*] .... SOP
Sleep-Learning Association (EA) .... SLA
Sleep-Onset REM [*Rapid Eye Movement*] .... SOREM
Sleepout (ADA) .... SO
Sleep-Related Breathing Disorder [*Medicine*] (DMAA) .... SRBD
Sleepy Eye, MN [*FM radio station call letters*] .... KNUJ
Sleepy Hollow Restorations, Tarrytown, NY [*Library symbol Library of
  Congress*] (LCLS) .... NTaS
Sleet [*Meteorology*] .... E
Sleet [*Meteorology*] (BARN) .... rs
Sleet Shower [*Meteorology*] (BARN) .... EW
Sleetmute [*Alaska*] [*Airport symbol*] (OAG) .... SLQ
Sleetmute, AK [*Location identifier FAA*] (FAAL) .... SLQ
Sleeve [*Technical drawings*] .... SL
Sleeve (AAG) .... SLV
Sleeve Bearing (KSC) .... SB
Sleeve Dipole Antenna .... SDA
Sleeve Stub Antenna .... SSA
Sleeving [*Electricity*] .... SLVG
Sleighton School, Darling, PA [*OCLC symbol*] (OCLC) .... PII
Slentando [*Slackening*] [*Music*] (ROG) .... SLENT
Slept All Night [*Medicine*] (DMAA) .... SAN
Slesvigske Parti [*Schleswig Party*] [*Denmark Political party*] (PPE) .... SL
Slew Rate .... SR
Slewable Electro-Optical Sensor System .... SEOSS

Slewed [*Antenna*] ... S
Slewed-Launch Interceptor Missile ... SLIM
Slew-Induced Distortion ... SID
Sliac [*Former Czechoslovakia*] [*ICAO location identifier*] (ICLI) ... LKSL
Sliac [*Former Czechoslovakia*] [*Airport symbol*] (OAG) ... SLD
Slice (MSA) ... SLC
Slice Control Central (SAA) ... SCC
Slice Successive Overrelaxation ... SSOR
Slicer (IAA) ... SLC
Slick (MCD) ... SLK
Slick Airways, Inc. ... SLI
Slide (AAG) ... SL
Slide ... SLD
Slide Agglutination (PDAA) ... SA
Slide and Tape ... ST
Slide Fastener Association [*Defunct*] (EA) ... SFA
Slide Latex Agglutination [*Clinical chemistry*] (AAMN) ... SLA
Slide Lobe Indicator ... SLI
Slide, Script, and Tape ... SST
Slide Valve ... SV
Slide-In Unit [*Telecommunications*] (TEL) ... SIU
Slidel, LA [*Location identifier FAA*] (FAAL) ... SIL
Slidell Computer Complex [*Slidell, LA*] [*NASA*] ... SCC
Slidell, LA [*FM radio station call letters*] ... WLTS
Slidell, LA [*AM radio station call letters*] ... WSLA
Slidell, LA [*Television station call letters*] (RBYB) ... WUPL
Slides (WDMC) ... s
Sliding ... SLDG
Sliding Door ... SD
Sliding Door (AAG) ... SLD
Sliding Electron Gun ... SEG
Sliding Expansion Joint [*Technical drawings*] ... SEJ
Sliding Filter (NASA) ... SF
Sliding Glass Door (ADA) ... SGD
Sliding Padeye (MCD) ... SPE
Sliding Roof [*Automotive advertising*] ... SRF
Sliding Scale (AAG) ... SS
Sliding Watertight Door ... SWD
Sliding-Coil Gauge (RDA) ... SCG
Slight (DAVI) ... SLT
Slight (DAVI) ... St
Slight Trace (CPH) ... Sl Tr
Slight Trace ... ST
Slightly ... SL
Slightly (WDMC) ... sl
Slightly Active (MAE) ... SA
Slightly Soluble ... SLS
Slightly Staining ... SLST
Slightly-Grounded Lightplane (PDAA) ... SGL
Sligo [*County in Ireland*] (ROG) ... SLO
Slim and Steve: the Bogart and Bacall Fan Club (EA) ... BBFC
Slim Line Diffuser (OA) ... SLD
Slim Whitman Appreciation Society of Great Britain (EAIO) ... SWASGB
Slim Whitman Appreciation Society of Scotland (EAIO) ... SWASS
Slim Whitman Appreciation Society of the United States (EA) ... SWAS
Slime Mold [*Biochemistry*] (DAVI) ... SM
Sling Ring ... SR
Slinger ... SLGR
Slip ... S
Slip [*Knitting*] ... SL
Slip (ADA) ... SLP
Slip Coupling (DS) ... SC
Slip End (OA) ... SE
Slip Factor ... SF
Slip Fit (MSA) ... SF
Slip Full Load (IAA) ... SFL
Slip Joint [*Technical drawings*] ... SJ
Slip Made Out (MAE) ... SMO
Slip on Show [*Indicates a woman's slip is showing*] (DSUE) ... SOS
Slip One, Knit One, Pass Slipped Stitch Over [*Knitting*] (BARN) ... skpo
Slip One, Knit One, Pass Slipped Stitch Over [*Knitting*] (BARN) ... skpsso
Slip Opinion (AAGC) ... Slip op
Slip Ring [*Electricity*] ... SR
Slip Sent [*Laboratory science*] (DAVI) ... SS
Slip, Slip, Knit [*Knitting*] (BARN) ... SSK
Slip Stitch [*Knitting*] ... SLST
Slip-Cast-Fused Silica (RDA) ... SCFS
Slipped Capital Femoral Epiphysis [*Orthopedics*] (DAVI) ... SCFE
Slipped Femoral Epiphysis [*Medicine*] (DMAA) ... SFE
Slipped Mutagenic Intermediate [*Biochemistry*] ... SMI
Slipped Up [*Horse racing*] ... S
Slippery Rock, PA [*FM radio station call letters*] ... WRSK
Slippery Rock State College [*Pennsylvania*] ... SRSC
Slippery Rock State College, Slippery Rock, PA [*Library symbol Library of Congress*] (LCLS) ... PSrS
Slippery Rock State College, Slippery Rock, PA [*OCLC symbol*] (OCLC) ... SRS
Slippery Rock University of Pennsylvania (GAGS) ... Slippery Rock U
Slipsheeting (DGA) ... S/Shtg
Slit ... SLT
Slit Lamp [*Instrumentation*] ... SL
Slit Lamp Examination [*Medicine*] (DMAA) ... SLE
Sloan Digital Sky Survey [*Astronomy*] ... SDSS
Sloan on Landlord and Tenant [*New York*] [*A publication*] (DLA) ... Sloan L & T
Sloane Aviation Ltd. [*British ICAO designator*] (FAAC) ... SLN
Sloane, Donald R., New York NY [*STAC*] ... SDR
Sloane Physics Laboratory [*Yale*] (MCD) ... SPL
Sloane Ranger [*Member of a British social set satirized in "The Official Sloane Ranger Handbook, The First Guide to What Really Matters in Life"*] [*Name is derived from Sloane Square in Chelsea*] ... SR
Sloan-Kettering [*Cancer-treatment compound*] (MAE) ... SK
Sloan-Kettering Institute for Cancer Research ... SKI
Sloan-Kettering Institute for Cancer Research, Rye, NY [*Library symbol Library of Congress*] (LCLS) ... NRyS
Sloan's New York Legal Register [*A publication*] (DLA) ... Sloan Leg Reg
Sloan's Supermarkets [*AMEX symbol*] (TTSB) ... SLO
Sloans Supermarkets [*Associated Press*] (SAG) ... SloanSup
Sloan's Supermarkets, Inc. [*Formerly, Designcraft Industries, Inc.*] [*AMEX symbol*] (SPSG) ... SLO
Slocan Development [*Vancouver Stock Exchange symbol*] ... SLO
Slocan Forest Products Ltd. [*Toronto Stock Exchange symbol Vancouver Stock Exchange symbol*] ... SFF
Slocum Society (EA) ... SS
S-Locus-Specific Glycoprotein [*Botany*] ... SLSG
Sloga Fraternal Life Insurance Society [*Milwaukee, WI*] (EA) ... SFLIS
Sloop ... SLP
Sloop (ROG) ... SP
Sloop-of-War ... SLPW
Slop Sink ... SS
Slope [*Technical drawings*] ... S
Slope (MSA) ... SLP
Slope Difference [*Statistics*] ... SD
Slope Occurrence ... SO
Slope Quantized Pulse Code Modulation [*Telecommunications*] (IAA) ... SQPCM
Slope Range ... SL RNG
Slope-Clearing Events [*Geology*] ... SCE
Sloppy [*Horse racing*] ... SLY
Sloppy [*Track condition*] [*Thoroughbred racing*] ... SY
Sloppy Joe [*Sandwich*] ... SJ
Slosson Articulation, Language Test with Phonology [*Child development test*] ... SALT-P
Slosson Drawing Coordination Test ... SDCT
Slosson Intelligence Test ... SIT
Slosson Oral Reading Tests ... SORT
Slosson Post-Observational Testing Screen [*Educational test*] ... SPOTS
Slosson Pre-Observational Record Screen [*Educational test*] ... SPORS
Slot Allocation Procedure [*Aviation*] (DA) ... SLAP
Slot Array Antenna ... SAA
Slot Cell Inserter ... SCI
Slot Dipole Ranging Test (OA) ... SDRT
Slot Format [*Microfiltration*] ... SF
Slot Reference Point (DA) ... SRP
Slotted (IAA) ... SLOT
Slotted (MSA) ... SLTD
Slotted Array X-Band Antenna ... SAXA
Slotted Envelope Network (MHDI) ... SENET
Slotted Metal Window ... SMW
Slotted Waveguide ... SWG
Slotting Saw ... SLSA
Slough [*Postcode*] (ODBW) ... SL
Slough [*British depot code*] ... SLO
Slough [*Maps and charts*] ... Slu
Slough Observer Ltd., Slough, United Kingdom [*Library symbol Library of Congress*] (LCLS) ... UkSlO
Slov-Air [*Slovakia*] [*ICAO designator*] (FAAC) ... OIR
Slovak [*MARC language code Library of Congress*] (LCCP) ... slo
Slovak Air Force [*FAA designator*] (FAAC) ... SQF
Slovak Catholic Federation (EA) ... SCF
Slovak Catholic Federation of America [*Later, SCF*] (EA) ... SCFA
Slovak Catholic Sokol [*An association*] (EA) ... SCS
Slovak Government Flying Service [*FAA designator*] (FAAC) ... SSG
Slovak Gymnastic Union Sokol of the USA (EA) ... SGUS
Slovak League of America (EA) ... SLA
Slovak League of America Heritage Foundation (EA) ... SLAHF
Slovak National Party [*Former Czechoslovakia*] [*Political party*] (EY) ... SNP
Slovak National Party [*Political party*] (ECON) ... SNS
Slovak Relief Fund (EA) ... SRF
Slovak Studies Association (EA) ... SSA
Slovak World Congress (EAIO) ... SWC
Slovak Writers and Artists Association (EA) ... SWAA
Slovak-American Cultural Center (EA) ... SACC
Slovak-American National Council (EA) ... SANC
Slovene Franciscan Fathers (EA) ... SFF
Slovene National Benefit Society (EA) ... SNBS
Slovene National Benefit Society (EA) ... SNPJ
Slovenia [*International civil aircraft marking*] (ODBW) ... SL
Slovenia ... Slov
Slovenian [*MARC language code Library of Congress*] (LCCP) ... slv
Slovenian Association [*Australia*] ... SA
Slovenian Christian Democrats [*Political party*] ... SCD
Slovenian Democratic Union - National Democratic Party [*Political party*] (EY) ... SDU-NDP
Slovenian Farmers' Association - People's Party (EY) ... SFA-PP
Slovenian Mutual Benefit Association [*Later, AMLA*] (EA) ... SMBA
Slovenian Research Center of America (EA) ... SRCA
Slovenian Women's Union (EA) ... SWU
Slovenly Suburb ... SLURB
Slovenska Ljudska Stranka [*Slovene People's Party*] [*Former Yugoslavia*] [*Political party*] (PPE) ... SLS
Slovenska L'Udova Strana [*Slovak People's Party*] [*Also, HSL'S*] [*Political party*] (PPE) ... SL'S

Slovo o Knige [*A publication*] ..... SOK
Slow ..... S
Slow [*Track condition*] [*Thoroughbred racing*] ..... SL
Slow [*Aviation*] (DA) ..... SLO
Slow ..... SLW
Slow Access Charge-Coupled Memory [*Computer science*] (PDAA) ..... SACCM
Slow Blowing (IAA) ..... SB
Slow Burning ..... SB
Slow Call (WDAA) ..... SC
Slow Code Scanner ..... SCS
Slow Component ..... SC
Slow Component Axonal Particulate [*Neurology*] ..... SCAP
Slow Continuous Ultrafiltration [*Medicine*] (DMAA) ..... SCUF
Slow Curing [*Asphalt grade*] ..... SC
Slow Cyclotron Wave (IAA) ..... SCW
Slow Death Factor [*Medicine*] ..... SDF
Slow Electrical Process [*Human brain*] ..... SEP
Slow Extension Motoneuron [*Neurology*] ..... SEMN
Slow Filling Period [*Cardiology*] ..... SFP
Slow Fire [*Military*] ..... SF
Slow Flexor Motoneuron [*Neurology*] ..... SFMN
Slow Flying Aircraft ..... SFA
Slow Frequency Hopping (MCD) ..... SFH
Slow Glass Etch (IAA) ..... SGE
Slow Inhibitory Potential [*Electrophysiology*] ..... SIP
Slow Initial Function (AAMN) ..... SF
Slow Lift-Off (MCD) ..... SLO
Slow Motion (NTCM) ..... SLO MO
Slow Moving ..... SM
Slow Moving Vehicle [*Emblem to prevent rear-end collisions*] ..... SMV
Slow Muscle [*Skeletal muscle pharmacology*] ..... S
Slow Negative Wave [*Medicine*] (DMAA) ..... SNW
Slow Neutron Reactor [*Nuclear energy*] (NRCH) ..... SNR
Slow Operate [*Relay*] ..... SO
Slow Operate Relay (IAA) ..... SOR
Slow Oxidative [*Fibers*] [*Neuroanatomy*] ..... SO
Slow Paroxysmal Atrial Tachycardia [*Medicine*] (DMAA) ..... SPAT
Slow Release [*Electronics*] ..... SR
Slow Release Matrix Device [*US Army Corps of Engineers*] ..... SRMD
Slow Release Relay [*Electronics*] (IAA) ..... SR
Slow Releasing Factor of Anaphylaxis [*Immunology*] (DAVI) ..... SRF-A
Slow Response Action Potentials [*Neurophysiology*] ..... SRAP
Slow Rotation Room [*NASA*] ..... SRR
Slow Running (IAA) ..... SR
Slow Setting [*Asphalt grade*] ..... SS
Slow Space Charge Wave (IAA) ..... SSCW
Slow Speed ..... SLSP
Slow Spinal Cord Compression Syndrome [*Medicine*] (DMAA) ..... SSCCS
Slow Strain Rate [*Tensile test*] ..... SSR
Slow Strain Rate Technique [*Nuclear energy*] (NUCP) ..... SSRT
Slow Synchronization (IAA) ..... SLOSYN
Slow Takeoff and Landing (IAA) ..... STOL
Slow Thyroxine-Binding Globulin [*Endocrinology*] ..... sTBG
Slow Time Constant (MCD) ..... STC
Slow Vital Capacity [*Medicine*] (MAE) ..... SVC
Slow Wave [*Electroencephalograph*] ..... SW
Slow (Wave) Sleep [*Neurology*] (DAVI) ..... SS
Slow Wave Structure [*Satellite delay tube*] (NTCM) ..... SWS
Slow Write, Fast Read [*Computer science*] (IEEE) ..... SWFR
Slow-Acting [*Pharmacy*] ..... SA
Slow-Acting Antirheumatic Drug [*Pharmacy*] ..... SAARD
Slow-Acting Antirheumatic Drugs [*Medicine*] ..... SAARD's
Slow-Acting Relay (IAA) ..... SA
Slowdown ..... SD
Slowdown (AAG) ..... SLD
Slowdown Area ..... SDA
Slowdown Density ..... SDD
Slowdown Length ..... SDL
Slowdown Model ..... SDM
Slowdown Power ..... SDP
Slowdown Strike (MHDB) ..... SS
Slowed-Down Video [*RADAR*] ..... SDV
Slowed-Down Video [*RADAR*] (CET) ..... SV
Slowest Processing Time ..... SPT
Slowing Down Spectrometer (PDAA) ..... SDS
Slowly Moving Object [*Astronomy*] ..... SMO
Slowly Varying Envelope Approximation [*Computer science*] (IAA) ..... SVEA
Slow-Moving Protease ..... SMP
Slow-Phase Velocity [*Ophthalmology*] ..... SPV
Slow-Reacting Factor of Anaphylaxis [*Medicine*] (MEDA) ..... SRF-A
Slow-Reacting Substance [*of anaphylaxis*] [*Leukotriene C Immunology*] ..... SRS
Slow-Reacting Substance of Anaphylaxis [*Immunology*] ..... SRS-A
Slow-Recovery Capsules [*Pharmacy*] ..... SRC
Slow-Run-Through Trials [*Navy*] (NG) ..... SRT
Slow-Scan Television ..... SSTV
Slow-Scan Video Simulator ..... SSVS
SLow-Wave Activity [*Medicine*] (DMAA) ..... SWA
Slow-Wave Encephalography [*Neurology*] (DAVI) ..... SWE
Slow-Wave Sleep ..... SWS
Sludge (MSA) ..... SLG
Sludge Removal Barge [*Navy*] ..... YBR
Sludge Removal Barge [*Non-self-propelled*] [*Navy symbol*] ..... YSR
Sludge Retention Time [*Wastewater treatment*] ..... SRT
Sludge to Oil Reactor System [*Battelle Memorial Institute*] ..... STORS
Sludge Tracking Acoustical Experiment [*Marine science*] (MSC) ..... STAX
Sludge Volume Index [*Wastewater treatment*] ..... SVI
Slug Discharge Control Plan [*Pollution prevention*] ..... SDCP
Slug Ejector Punch ..... SEP
Slugger [*Percentage*] [*Baseball*] ..... SLG
Slugging Average [*Baseball*] ..... SA
Slugging Percentage [*Baseball*] ..... SP
Sluice [*or Stop*] **Valve** ..... SV
Slum on a Shingle [*Army breakfast dish*] [*Bowdlerized version*] ..... SOS
Slumber Lodge Development Corp. Ltd. [*Vancouver Stock Exchange symbol*] ..... SLD
Slupsk [*Poland*] [*Airport symbol*] (OAG) ..... OSP
Slurry Reactor Experiment ..... SLURREX
Slurry Response Number [*Well drilling technology*] ..... SRN
Slurry Technology Association [*Later, CSTA*] (EA) ..... STA
Slurry-Fed Ceramic Matter [*Nuclear energy*] (NUCP) ..... SFCM
Slurry-Infiltrated Fiber-Concrete (BARN) ..... SIFCON
Slush on Runway [*NWS*] (FAAC) ..... SLR
Slutsk [*Later, LNN*] [*Former USSR Geomagnetic observatory code*] ..... SLU
SM Exports Ltd. [*British ICAO designator*] (FAAC) ..... SME
Smack (ROG) ..... SK
Smack [*Ship*] ..... SMK
Smalandsstenar [*Sweden ICAO location identifier*] (ICLI) ..... ESMY
Smale and Giffard's English Vice-Chancellors' Reports [*A publication*] (DLA) ..... Sma & Giff
Smale and Giffard's English Vice-Chancellors' Reports [*A publication*] (DLA) ..... Smale & G
Smale and Giffard's English Vice-Chancery Reports [*A publication*] (DLA) ..... S & G
Smale and Giffard's English Vice-Chancery Reports [*A publication*] (DLA) ..... Sm & G
Small [*Size designation for clothing, etc.*] ..... S
Small (WDMC) ..... s
Small ..... SM
Small (VRA) ..... sm
Small (AAG) ..... SM
Small, Able Battlefield Aircraft [*Military British*] ..... SABA
Small Acoustic Device Simulating Aircraft Carrier (NVT) ..... SADSAC
Small Advertisement (DGA) ..... S/AD
Small Aerial Surveillance and Target Acquisition (PDAA) ..... STSTA
Small Aerostat Surveillance System [*Army*] (DOMA) ..... SASS
Small Affluent Variable [*Moko disease of banana*] [*Plant pathology*] ..... SAV
Small Agile Battlefield Aircraft [*British Aerospace Ltd.*] ..... SABA
Small Airbreathing System Synthesis (MCD) ..... SASS
Small Aircraft Carrier [*Navy symbol*] CVL
Small Airport Runway Indicator (IAA) ..... SARI
Small Airship Surveillance System, Low Intensity Target Exploitation [*Army*] ..... SASS LITE
Small Airway Disease [*Medicine*] (DAVI) ..... SAD
Small Airway Obstruction [*Medicine*] (DMAA) ..... SAO
Small Ammunition Ship [*Navy symbol*] (DNAB) ..... AEL
Small Amount (CPH) ..... Sm Amt
Small and Disadvantaged Business Utilization [*Department of Commerce*] ..... SADBU
Small and Disadvantaged Business Utilization Office [*Army*] (RDA) ..... SADBUO
Small and Disadvantaged Business Utilization Specialist [*Federal government*] (GFGA) ..... SADBUS
Small and Medium-Size Enterprises ..... SME
Small and Medium-Sized Businesses ..... SMB
Small and Medium-Sized Libraries Section [*Public Library Association*] ..... SMLS
Small and Specialists Publishers Exhibition ..... SPEX
Small Angle Separator System [*Superheavy element research*] ..... SASSY
Small Angle Tagger (MCD) ..... SAT
Small Animal (DAVI) ..... sm an
Small Animal Care Hospital [*Medicine*] (DMAA) ..... SACH
Small Applications Satellite (KSC) ..... SAS
Small Applications Technology Satellite (MCD) ..... SATS
Small Area Direct Path [*Military*] (CAAL) ..... SADP
Small Area Plotting Sheet ..... SAPS
Small Arms [*All firearms other than cannon*] ..... SA
Small Arms (NATG) ..... SMA
Small Arms Alignment Fixture [*Weaponry*] (INF) ..... SAAF
Small Arms Ammunition ..... SAA
Small Arms Ammunition Depot ..... SAAD
Small Arms and Machine Gun School [*British military*] (DMA) ..... SA & MGS
Small Arms Common Module Fire Control System [*Army*] ..... SACMFCS
Small Arms Expert Marksmanship Ribbon [*Military decoration*] (AFM) ..... SAEMR
Small Arms Fire [*Military*] (VNW) ..... SAF
Small Arms Flash, Noise Gunfire Simulator [*Army*] ..... SAFNGS
Small Arms for Air Defense (MCD) ..... SAFAD
Small Arms Interpost Competition [*Military*] ..... SAIC
Small Arms Master Plan [*Military document*] (INF) ..... SAMP
Small Arms Post Competition ..... SAPC
Small Arms Projected Line Charge [*Military*] (INF) ..... SAPLIC
Small Arms Readiness Training Section [*National Guard*] ..... SARTS
Small Arms Remote Target System (MCD) ..... SARTS
Small Arms Research and Development Center [*Army*] ..... SARDC
Small Arms School [*British military*] (DMA) ..... SAS
Small Arms School Corps [*Military British*] ..... SASC
Small Arms Suppression Evaluation (MCD) ..... SASE
Small Arms Systems Agency [*Army*] (RDA) ..... SASA
Small Arms Target Practice [*Navy*] ..... SATP
Small Arms Target System [*British military*] (DMA) ..... SATS
Small Arms Transmitter [*Army*] (INF) ..... SAT
Small Arms Weapon ..... SAW
Small Arms Weapon Study [*Army*] ..... SAWS

Small Arms Weapons Effects Simulator [Military] (PDAA) ...... SAWES
Small Arms Weapons System (NATG) ...... SAWS
Small Astronomy Satellite ...... SAS
Small Austere Air Field (MCD) ...... SAAF
Small Automatic Exchange [Telecommunications] (TEL) ...... SAX
Small Autonomous Research Package ...... SARP
Small Auxiliary Floating Drydock, Non-Self-Propelled [Navy symbol]
  (DNAB) ...... ARDL
Small Auxin Up RNA [Ribonucleic Acid] [Botany] ...... SAUR
Small Ballistic Reentry Vehicle ...... SBRV
Small Base Unit [Telecommunications] ...... SBU
Small Battle Unit [Navy] (NVT) ...... SBU
Small Bayonet Cap ...... SBC
Small Block [Automotive engineering] ...... SB
Small Boat ...... SB
Small Boat Unit (DOMA) ...... SBU
Small Bonds ...... SB
Small Bore (ADA) ...... SB
Small Bowel ...... SB
Small Bowel Follow-Through [Medicine] (MAE) ...... SBFT
Small Bowel Follow-Through [Medicine] ...... SMBFT
Small Bowel Obstruction [Medicine] (MAE) ...... SBO
Small Bowel Transit Time [Medicine] (DMAA) ...... SBTT
Small Bowel Transit Time [Gastroenterology] ...... SMTT
Small Box-Respirator [British military] (DMA) ...... SBR
Small Business ...... SB
Small Business Administration ...... SBA
Small Business and Economic Utilization Advisor [Army] (AABC) ...... SBEUA
Small Business and Labor Surplus Advisor (AABC) ...... SBLSA
Small Business Assistance Center [Worcester, MA] (EA) ...... SBAC
Small Business Assistance Program ...... SBAP
Small Business Association of Apparel Manufacturers (EA) ...... SBAAM
Small Business Association of Australia ...... SBAA
Small Business Centre [British] ...... SBC
Small Business Combined Association [Australia] ...... SBCA
Small Business Competitiveness Demonstration Program (AAGC) ...... SBCDP
Small Business Computer (BUR) ...... SBC
Small Business Corp. of South Australia [Commercial firm] ...... SBCSA
Small Business Council (NADA) ...... SBC
Small Business Council of America (EA) ...... SBCA
Small Business Development Center [Lehigh University, University of
  Alabama in Birmingham] [Research center] ...... SBDC
Small Business Development Corp. ...... SBDC
Small Business Edition [Microsoft Corp.] [Computer software] (PCM) ...... SBE
Small Business Export Trade Corp. ...... SBETC
Small Business Exporters Association (EA) ...... SBEA
Small Business Financial Manager [Microsoft] [Computer science] ...... SBFM
Small Business Foundation of America [Boston, MA] (EA) ...... SBFA
Small Business Funding ...... SBF
Small Business Innovation Development Act [1982] ...... SBIA
Small Business Innovation Development Act [1982] ...... SMIDA
Small Business Innovation Research (AAGC) ...... SBIR
Small Business Innovation Research Program [Small Business
  Administration] ...... SBIR
Small Business Innovation Research/Small Business Technology Transfer
  [Army] (RDA) ...... SBIR/STTR
Small Business Innovative Research [Marine science] (OSRA) ...... SBIR
Small Business Innovative Research [Program] ...... SBIR
Small Business Innovative Research (USDC) ...... SBIR
Small Business Institute [Small Business Administration] ...... SBI
Small Business Investment Company [Generic term] ...... SBIC
Small Business Investment Company [Generic term] ...... SBICo
Small Business Investment Corporation (AAGC) ...... SBIC
Small Business Investment Corp. (DFIT) ...... SBIC
Small Business Legislative Council [Washington, DC] (EA) ...... SBLC
Small Business Loans Act [Canada] ...... SBLA
Small Business Network [Baltimore, MD] (EA) ...... SBN
Small Business Office ...... SBO
Small Business Ombudsman [Federal government] (GFGA) ...... SBO
Small Business Reports [A publication] (BRI) ...... Sm Bus Rep
Small Business Server [Microsoft Corp.] ...... SBS
Small Business Service Bureau [Worcester, MA] (EA) ...... SBSB
Small Business / Small Disadvantaged Business (SSD) ...... SB/SDB
Small Business Sourcebook [A publication] ...... SBS
Small Business Specialist [DoD] ...... SBS
Small Business Start-Up Index [A publication] ...... SBSI
Small Business Support Center Association [Houston, TX] (EA) ...... SBSCA
Small Business System (ADA) ...... SBS
Small Business Systems Group [Westford, MA] [Telecommunications]
  (TSSD) ...... SBSG
Small Business Technical Adviser (AAGC) ...... SBTA
Small Business Technology Transfer (AAGC) ...... SBTT
Small Business Technology Transfer Resources (GAVI) ...... STTR
Small Business United [Later, NSBU] (EA) ...... SBU
Small Businesses' Association [British] (DCTA) ...... SBA
Small Caliber Smart Munition [Army] (RDA) ...... SCSM
Small Caliber Weapon Systems Laboratory (MCD) ...... SCWSL
Small Cap (WDAA) ...... SC
Small Capacity Memory [Computer science] (IAA) ...... SCM
Small Capital Letters (WDMC) ...... s caps
Small Capitals [Typography] ...... SC
Small Capitals [Typography] ...... SCAPS
Small Capitals [Typography] (WGA) ...... sm cap
Small Capitals [Typography] (BARN) ...... smc
Small Car Automatic Transit [System] ...... SCAT

Small Card Automated Layout Program (IAA) ...... SCALP
Small Card Design Automation (IAA) ...... SCDA
Small Card Final Test System (SAA) ...... SCFTS
Small Card Release Processing [Computer science] (IAA) ...... SCRP
Small Cardioactive Peptide [Biochemistry] ...... SCP
Small Cell (Anaplastic) Carcinoma of the Lung [Oncology] ...... SCCL
Small Cell Cancer [Oncology] ...... SCC
Small Center Contact ...... SCC
Small Chemical Businesses [American Chemical Society] ...... SChB
Small Claims Board of Contract Appeals ...... SCBCA
Small Claims Court [Northern Territory, Australia] ...... SCC
Small Cleaved Cell [Medicine] (DMAA) ...... SCC
Small Coastal Transport [Navy symbol Obsolete] ...... APC
Small College Goals Inventory [Test] ...... SCGI
Small Column Insulated Delays (MCD) ...... SCID
Small Communications Augmentation Package (MCD) ...... SCAP
Small Communications Ship [Navy symbol] (DNAB) ...... AGCL
Small Compact [Car size] ...... SC
Small Company Fund [Phillips and Drew Fund Management] [British] ...... SCF
Small Company Online Data [Computer science] (PDAA) ...... SCOLD
Small Component Handling System [Nuclear energy] (NRCH) ...... SCHS
Small Components Evaluation Loop [Nuclear energy] (NRCH) ...... SCEL
Small Components Structural ...... SCS
Small Components Test Loop [Nuclear energy] ...... SCTL
Small Compressor Colorimeter (MCD) ...... SCC
Small Computer Algorithmic Language (DNAB) ...... SMAGOL
Small Computer Algorithmic Language ...... SMALGOL
Small Computer Analytical and Mathematical Programming System
  (IEEE) ...... SCAMPS
Small Computer and Office Systems [Honeywell, Inc.] ...... SCOS
Small Computer Program [Army] (RDA) ...... SCP
Small Computer Program Index [No longer published] [ALLM Books] (IID) ...... SCPI
Small Computer System ...... SCS
Small Computer System Interface [Pronounced "scuzzy"] ...... SCSI
Small Computers in the Arts Network [Defunct] (EA) ...... SCAN
Small Container Intermodal Distribution System (PDAA) ...... SCIDS
Small Craft ...... SC
Small Craft Assets, Training, and Turnover of Resources (DNAB) ...... SCATTOR
Small Craft Instruction and Training School [Navy] ...... SCIATS
Small Craft Instructor [Red Cross] ...... SCI
Small Craft Instructor Trainer [Red Cross] ...... SCIT
Small Craft Repair Facility [Navy] (NVT) ...... SCRF
Small Craft Training Center ...... SCTC
Small Craft Training Center [Navy] (DNAB) ...... SMACRATRACEN
Small Craft Training Center [Navy] (DNAB) ...... SMACTRACEN
Small Current Amplifying Device ...... SCAD
Small Current Element ...... SCE
Small Cycle Observation Recording ...... SCOR
Small Cytoplasmic RNA [Ribanucleic Acid] (BARN) ...... scRNA
Small Damage (DS) ...... s/d
Small Database Project (NITA) ...... SDBP
Small Defense Industries Association [Later, Strategic Industries
  Association] ...... SDIA
Small Defense Plants Administration [Terminated, 1953] ...... SDPA
Small Development Requirement [Military] ...... SDR
Small Digital Switch (NITA) ...... SDS
Small Disadvantaged Business [Department of Commerce] ...... SDB
Small Disadvantaged Business Concerns ...... SDBC
Small Disadvantaged Business Utilization Program (DOMA) ...... SDBUP
Small Distribution Phenomena ...... SDP
Small Earlywood Vessel [Tree-ring property] ...... SEV
Small Earth-Approacher [Asteroid] ...... SEA
Small Edison Screw ...... SES
Small Electrical Appliance Marketing Association [British] (DBA) ...... SEAMA
Small Emplacement Excavations [or Excavator] [Army] ...... SEE
Small End (OA) ...... SE
Small End-Expiratory Pressure [Medicine] (DAVI) ...... SEEP
Small End-Up (IAA) ...... SEU
Small Engine Fuel Injection System ...... SEFIS
Small Engine Servicing Dealers Association (EA) ...... SESDA
Small Enterprise Association of Australia and New Zealand ...... SEANZ
Small Expendable Air-Dropped Remote Ocean Platform [Marine science]
  (MSC) ...... SEADROP
Small Extension Node [Telecommunications] (LAIN) ...... SEN
Small Farmers Association [British] (DBA) ...... SFA
Small Faults [Philately] ...... SmFlts
Small Firms Employment Subsidy (MHDB) ...... SFES
Small Firms Merit Award for Research and Technology [British] ...... SMART
Small Firms Service [British] ...... SFS
Small Firms Technical Enquiry Service [British] ...... SMTES
Small Flow Indicator ...... SFI
Small Fluidal Round Colonies [Moko disease of Banana] [Plant pathology] ...... SFR
Small for Gestational Age [Pediatrics] ...... SGA
Small Formation Flyer (SSD) ...... SFF
Small Gas Turbine ...... SGT
Small Gene Fragment [Genetics] ...... SGF
Small Granular Vesicle [Cytology] ...... SGV
Small Group Instructor [or Instruction] [Army] (INF) ...... SGI
Small Group Therapy ...... SGT
Small Group Trial ...... SGT
Small Guided Missile Motorboat [Navy symbol] (DNAB) ...... PTG
Small Harbor Tug [Self-propelled] [Navy symbol] ...... YTL
Small Heat-Transfer Loop [Nuclear energy] (NRCH) ...... SHTL
Small Heavy Seeds [Botany] ...... SH

Small Homes Council-Building Research Council [*University of Illinois*] [*Research center*] (RCD)	SHC-BRC
Small Hydro Society [*Defunct*] (EA)	SHS
Small Hydrofoil Aircraft Carrier (DNAB)	SHAC
Small Inclusions [*Diamond clarity grade*]	SI
Small Independent Action Force [*Military*]	SIAF
Small Independent Brewers' Association [*British*] (ECON)	SIBA
Small Independent Radio Stations [*An association British*]	SIRS
Small Independent Record Manufacturers Association [*Stanford, CT*] (EA)	SIRMA
Small Industry Development Network [*Georgia Institute of Technology*]	SIDN
Small Instrument Pointing System (MCD)	SIPS
Small Integral Rocket/Ramjet (MCD)	SIRR
Small Intensely Fluorescent [*Cytology*]	SIF
Small Interactive Image Processing System [*NASA*]	SMIPS
Small Intercontinental Ballistic Missile (MCD)	SICBM
Small Intercontinental Ballistic Missile (MCD)	SICM
Small Interplanetary Probe Experiment (DNAB)	SMIPE
Small Interplanetary Probes (SAA)	SIP
Small Intestine [*Anatomy*]	SI
Small Intestine Metaplasia [*Medicine*]	SIM
Small Intestine Rinse [*Physiology*]	SIR
Small, Irregular, Agglutinated Rooms [*Architecture*]	SIAR
Small Landlord's Association [*British*] (DBA)	SLA
Small Lattice Experiment	SLE
Small Launch Vehicle [*Air Force*] (DOMA)	SLV
Small Library Computing, Inc. [*Information service or system*] (IID)	SLC
Small Light Antisubmarine Helicopter	SLASH
Small Light Seeds [*Botany*]	SL
Small, Lightweight Altitude-Transmission Equipment [*FAA*]	SLATE
Small Lightweight GPS [*Global Positioning System*] **Receivers** [*Army*] (RDA)	SLGR
Small Local Exchange [*Telecommunications*] (TEL)	SLE
Small Lot Optimum Procurement (PDAA)	SLOP
Small Luxury Hotel Association (EA)	SLHA
Small Lymphocyte Cell Lymphoma [*Oncology*]	SLCL
Small Lymphocytes [*Hematology*]	SL
Small Lymphocytic Lymphoma [*Medicine*] (DMAA)	SLL
Small Lymphoma [*Oncology*]	SL
Small Machine Organizer (IAA)	SMO
Small Magazine Publishers Group (EA)	SMPG
Small Magellanic Cloud [*Astronomy*]	SMC
Small Magnetospheric Observatory [*Satellite*] [*NASA*]	SMO
Small Magnetospheric Satellite [*NASA*]	SMS
Small Main-Belt Asteroid Spectroscopic Survey	SMASS
Small Manned Anti-Submarine Helicopter (SAA)	SMASH
Small Mass Store (IAA)	SMS
Small Materials Recovery Facility [*for recycling of glass, plastics, etc.*]	SMRF
Small Minesweeper [*Navy symbol*]	ML
Small Missile Range (MCD)	SMR
Small Missile Telecamera	SMT
Small Missions to Asteroids/Comets [*NASA, proposed*]	SMACS
Small Modular Recovery Vehicle System [*Nuclear energy*]	SMRVS
Small Molecule Gel Permeation Chromatography	SMGPC
Small Motor Manufacturers Association [*Libertyville, IL*] (EA)	SMMA
Small Navigation Buoy (DNAB)	SNB
Small Network Management Packet [*Marine science*] (OSRA)	SNMP
Small Network Management Packet (USDC)	SNMP
Small Nonoverlapping Offset [*Oceanography*]	SNOO
Small Nuclear	sn
Small Nuclear Adapted Power Source	SNAP
Small Nuclear Auxiliary Power	SNAP
Small Nuclear Ribonucleoprotein Particle [*Genetics*]	SNURP
Small Nuclear Rocket Engine	SNRE
Small Nuclear Stage (KSC)	SNS
Small Object Detector	SOD
Small Office, Home Office (PCM)	SOHO
Small Office Microfilm	SOM
Small Office Microfilm Systems (NITA)	SOM
Small Oiler [*Navy symbol*] (DNAB)	AOL
Small Oocyte	SO
Small Orbiting Earth Resources Observatory (IEEE)	SOERO
Small Order Execution System [*Business term*]	SOES
Small Oriented Diode (IAA)	SOD
Small Outline (NITA)	SO
Small Outline Gullwing [*Electronics*] (CDE)	SOG
Small Outline Integrated Circuit [*Computer science*]	SOIC
Small Outline J Leaded (NITA)	SOJ
Small Packet	SP
Small Paper [*Printing*]	SP
Small Parcels and Rolls [*Postal Service*]	SPR's
Small Passive Navigation System (DNAB)	SPANS
Small Payload Ejection and Recovery for the Space Shuttle [*NASA*] (MCD)	SPEAR
Small Peripheral Controller	SPC
Small Peripheral Unit (IAA)	SPU
Small Permanent Communications and Display Segment (MCD)	SPCDS
Small Perturbation Theory	SPT
Small Pica	SM
Small Pica	SP
Small Pig Keepers' Council [*British*] (BI)	SPKC
Small Plaque	SP
Small Portable Analysis and Diagnostic Equipment [*Aircraft maintenance*]	SPADE
Small Portable Operational Terminal (LAIN)	SPOT
Small Portable RADAR Torch	SPRAT
Small Power System Program (IAA)	SPSP
Small Premises [*Hairdressers, doctors, dentists, etc.*] [*Public-performance tariff class*] [*British*]	SP
Small Press [*A publication*] (BRI)	Sm Pr
Small Press Review [*A publication*] (BRI)	Sm Pr R
Small Press Writers and Artists Organization (EA)	SPWAO
Small Pressurized Water Reactor	SPWR
Small Primate Unrestrained Test	SPURT
Small Processing Element [*Computer science*]	SPE
Small Profits, Quick Returns	SPQR
Small Quantity Burner Exemption [*Environmental Protection Agency*] (EPA)	SQBE
Small Quantity Generator [*Automotive engineering Environmental Protection Agency*]	SQG
Small RADAR Homing Interceptor	SRHL
Small RADAR-Homing Interceptor Technology	SRHIT
Small Repair Parts Transporter	SRPT
Small, Replaceable Assembly (RDA)	SRA
Small Research Satellite (KSC)	SRS
Small Retailers Association of South Australia	SRASA
Small Rigid Dome	SRD
Small Ring	SR
Small Ring Sparger [*Engineering*]	SRS
Small River Monitor [*Navy symbol*] (DNAB)	BMRL
Small Rocket Lift Device	SRLD
Small Rotating Plug [*Nuclear energy*] (NRCH)	SRP
Small Round-Structured Virus [*Medicine*]	SRSV
Small Sample Assay System [*Nuclear energy*] (NRCH)	SSAS
Small Saver Certificate [*Banking*]	SSC
Small Scientific Computer (IAA)	SSC
Small Scientific Satellite [*NASA*]	S^3
Small Scientific Satellite [*NASA*]	SSS
Small Seaplane Tender [*Navy symbol Obsolete*]	AVP
Small Search Area (SAA)	SSA
Small Seismic Intrusion Detector (PDAA)	MICROSID
Small Self-Administered Scheme [*Pensions*] [*British*]	SSAS
Small Self-Contained Payload (NASA)	SSCP
Small Semiconductor Memory	SSM
Small, Shelly Fauna [*Paleontology*]	SSF
Small Ship Combat Data System	SSCDS
Small Ship Data System (MUGU)	SSDS
Small Ship Tactical Data System [*Navy*] (CAAL)	SSTDS
Small Ship Teletype Information Exchange System [*or Subsystem*] (MCD)	SSTIXS
Small Ship Typhoon Air Defense System (MCD)	SSTADS
Small Ships Accounting System (DNAB)	SSHACS
Small Signal	SS
Small Signal Gain (IEEE)	SSG
Small Solar Satellite [*NASA*]	SSS
Small Solar-Power System [*Energy source*]	SSPS
Small Sortie Payload [*NASA*] (NASA)	SSP
Small Starlight Scope [*Light-intensifying device*]	SSS
Small Structures Survey [*Civil Defense*]	SSS
Small Subcompact [*Car size*]	SS
Small Subunit [*Genetics*]	SSU
Small Synaptic Vesicle [*Neurobiology*]	SSV
Small Systems Executive (IAA)	SSX
Small Tactical Aerial Mobility Platform [*Proposed*] [*Marine Corps*]	STAMP
Small Tactical Airlifter [*Military British*]	STA
Small Tactical Terminal (USDC)	STT
Small Tactical Terminal [*Marine science*] (OSRA)	STT
Small Terminal Evasive Missile System (MCD)	STEMS
Small Terminal-Oriented Computer System (IAA)	STOCS
Small Test Vessel [*Nuclear energy*] (NRCH)	STV
Small Tight Aspect Ratio Tokamak [*Plasma physics*]	START
Small Towns Institute (EA)	STI
Small Transmitter Coated with Paraffin	ST-P
Small Transmitter Coated with Silicon Rubber	ST-SR
Small Transport Aircraft Technology (MCD)	STAT
Small Transportable Communications Stations	STRACS
Small Transportable Communications Terminal	STCT
Small Transportable Link Terminal	STLT
Small Tug [*Army*]	ST
Small Ultimate Size [*Telecommunications*] (TEL)	SUS
Small Unified Reactor Facility Systems for Isotopes, Desalting, and Electricity [*Nuclear energy*]	SURFSIDE
Small Unilamellar Vesicle [*Pharmacy Biochemistry*]	SUV
Small Unilamellar Vessel [*Medicine*] (DMAA)	SUV
Small Unit Action [*Military*] (CINC)	SUA
Small Unit Delivery System (MCD)	SUDS
Small Unit Evaluation and Training (MCD)	SUET
Small Unit Fire Support Weapon (MCD)	SUFSW
Small Unit Navigation System	SUNS
Small Unit Radio [*Military*] (INF)	SUR
Small Unit Support Vehicle [*Military*] (RDA)	SUSV
Small Unit Training Team [*Military*]	SUTT
Small Unit Transceiver [*Military*] (INF)	SUT
Small University Libraries	SUL
Small Vehicles, Program Manager	SVPM
Small Volume Infusion [*Pharmacology*] (DAVI)	SMI
Small Volume Nebulizer [*Pharmacology*] (DAVI)	SVN
Small Volume Parenteral [*Pharmacy*]	SVP
Small Warhead and Reentry Multiple System	SWARMS
Small Wars Operational Research Division [*Military*] (INF)	SWORD

Small Waterplane Air Cushion Ship .... Swaacs
Small Waterplane Area Single Hull Ship .... Swash
Small Waterplane Area Twin Hull .... SWATH
Small Waterplane Area Twin Hull [*Ship*] [*Navy*] .... SWATH
Small Wind Energy Conversion Systems .... SWECS
Small Winemakers' Forum [*Australia*] .... SWF
Small, Yellow, Constipated [*Stool*] [*Gastroenterology*] (DAVI) .... SYC
Small-Angle Light Scattering .... SALS
Small-Angle Neutron Scattering .... SANS
Small-Angle Scattering (OA) .... SAS
Small-Angle X-ray [*Instrumentation*] .... SAX
Small-Angle X-Ray Diffraction .... SAXD
Small-Angle X-Ray Scattering .... SAXS
Small-Angle X-Ray Scattering .... SAXS
Small-Animal Anesthesia Machine [*Instrumentation*] .... SAAM
Small-Bowel Syndrome (DAVI) .... SBS
Small-Break Loss of Coolant Accident [*Nuclear energy*] (NRCH) .... SBLOCA
Small-Caliber Ammunition (MSA) .... SCA
Small-Caliber Ammunition Modernization Program [*Army*] (RDA) .... SCAMP
Small-Cell Bronchogenic Carcinoma [*Oncology*] (DAVI) .... SCBC
Small-Cell Carcinoma of the Bronchus [*Medicine*] (DMAA) .... SCCB
Small-Cell Lung Cancer [*Oncology*] .... SCLC
Small-Core Memory [*Computer science*] .... SCM
Small-Diameter Component Cask [*Nuclear energy*] (NRCH) .... SDCC
Small-End Forward [*of command module*] .... SEF
Smaller Business Association of New England [*Waltham, MA*] (EA) .... SBANE
Smaller Business of America [*Defunct*] (EA) .... SB of A
Smaller Communities Program [*Department of Labor*] .... SCP
Smaller Communities Services Program [*Department of Labor*] .... SCSP
Smaller Companies International Trust [*British*] .... SCIT
Smaller Companies Market [*Business term*] .... SCM
Smaller Manufacturers Medical Device Association [*Inactive*] (EA) .... SMMDA
Smaller Profit Margin .... SPM
Smaller War Plants Corp. [*World War II*] .... SWPC
Smaller Word .... SWD
Smallest Addressable Unit .... SAU
Smallest Publishable Unit .... SPU
Smallest Replaceable Defective Element .... SRDE
Smallest Replaceable Unit (MCD) .... SRU
Smallest Serving Factor (PDAA) .... SSF
Smallest Set of Smallest Rings [*Organic chemistry*] .... SSSR
Smallest Subunit [*Genetics*] .... SS
Small-for-Dates [*Medicine*] (MEDA) .... SFD
Small-Inventory Top-Tier Site [*Industrial hazard designation*] [*British*] .... SITTS
Small-Medium Local Exchange [*Telecommunications*] (TEL) .... SMLE
Small-Mouth Bass [*Ichthyology*] .... Sb
Small-Order Automatic Execution Facility [*London Stock Exchange*] [*British*] .... SAEF
Small-Particle Aerosol .... SPA
Small-Particle Aerosol Generator (DAVI) .... SPAG
Small-Particle Heat-Exchange Receiver [*Solar energy technology*] .... SPHER
Small-Probe Atmospheric Structure [*NASA*] .... SAS
Small-Probe Nephelometer [*NASA*] .... SN
Small-Probe Net Flux Radiometer [*NASA*] .... SNFR
Smalls Oilfield Services [*NASDAQ symbol*] (SAG) .... FISH
Smalls Oilfield Services [*Associated Press*] (SAG) .... SmlOil
Smalls Oilfield Services [*Associated Press*] (SAG) .... SmOi
Small-Scale Disturbance Field .... SD
Small-Scale Gap Test [*Explosive*] .... SSGT
Small-Scale Hydroelectric Project .... SSH
Small-Scale Integrated Circuit .... SSIC
Small-Scale Integration .... SSI
Small-Scale Raiding Force [*Military*] .... SSRF
Small-Size Nuclear Power Plant .... SSNPP
Small-Size Pressurized Water Reactor [*Nuclear energy*] .... SSPWR
Smalltalk on a RISC (NITA) .... SOAR
Small-Time Operator [*Slang*] .... STO
Small-to-Medium Enterprise .... SME
Small-Turbine Advanced Gas Generator .... STAGG
Smallworldwide PLC [*Associated Press*] (SAG) .... Smallww
Smallworldwide PLC [*NASDAQ symbol*] (SAG) .... SWLD
Smara [*Morocco*] [*Airport symbol*] (OAG) .... SMW
Smart & Biggar, Ottawa, Ontario [*Library symbol National Library of Canada*] (BIB) .... OOSB
Smart & Final, Inc. [*NYSE symbol*] (SPSG) .... SMF
Smart & Final, Inc. [*Associated Press*] (SAG) .... SmrtFn
Smart Armor System [*Army*] .... SAS
Smart Battery Data .... SBD
Smart Business Supersite [*Internet resource*] [*Computer science*] .... SBS
Smart Card Industry Association (EA) .... SCIA
Smart Contract Preparation Environment [*Computer science*] (RDA) .... SCOPE
Smart Distributed Systems (ACII) .... SDS
Smart End-Effector [*Robotics*] (ECON) .... SMARTee
Smart Energy System [*IBM Corp.*] [*Computer science*] (PCM) .... SES
Smart Front End .... SFE
Smart Howitzer Automated Management System [*US Army Human Engineering Laboratory*] (RDA) .... SHAMS
Smart Integral Linearizer [*Instrumentation*] .... SIL
SMART Modular Tech [*NASDAQ symbol*] (TTSB) .... SMOD
SMART Modular Technologies, Inc. [*NASDAQ symbol*] (SAG) .... SMOD
SMART Modular Technologies, Inc. [*Associated Press*] (SAG) .... SmtMod
Smart Noise Equipment [*RADAR jammer*] [*Air Force*] .... SNOE
Smart Set International [*Program to discourage drug abuse*] [*Defunct*] (EA) .... SSI
Smart Target-Activated Fire and Forget [*Antitank weapon system*] (RDA) .... STAFF
Smart Weapons Operability Enhancement (RDA) .... SWOE
Smart Weapons Systems [*Army*] (RDA) .... SWS
SmarTalk TeleServices, Inc. [*Associated Press*] (SAG) .... SmarTlk
SmarTalk TeleServices, Inc. [*NASDAQ symbol*] (SAG) .... SMTK
Smartel Communications [*NASDAQ symbol*] (TTSB) .... STCCF
Smartel Communications Corp. [*Associated Press*] (SAG) .... Smartel
Smartel Communications Corp. [*NASDAQ symbol*] (SAG) .... STCCF
Smartflex Systems [*NASDAQ symbol*] (SAG) .... SFLX
Smartflex Systems [*Associated Press*] (SAG) .... Smrtflx
Smartmac User Group (EA) .... SUG
SMART's Own Concordance Constructor, Extremely Rapid [*Cornell University*] [*Computer science*] .... SOCCER
SmartServ Online [*NASDAQ symbol*] (TTSB) .... SSOL
SmartServ Online, Inc. [*Associated Press*] (SAG) .... SmrtSr
SmartServ Online, Inc. [*Associated Press*] (SAG) .... SmrtSrv
SmartServ Online, Inc. [*NASDAQ symbol*] (SAG) .... SSOL
SmartServ Online Wrrt [*NASDAQ symbol*] (TTSB) .... SSOLW
SMC Corp. [*Associated Press*] (SAG) .... SMC Cp
SMC Corp. [*NASDAQ symbol*] (SAG) .... SMCC
Smectic Phase [*Physical chemistry*] .... SM
Smectite [*Agronomy*] .... Sm
Smectite-Illite [*Clay mineral*] .... S/I
Smedes and Marshall's Mississippi Chancery Reports [*A publication*] (DLA) .... S & M
Smedes and Marshall's Mississippi Chancery Reports [*A publication*] (DLA) .... S & M Ch
Smedes and Marshall's Mississippi Chancery Reports [*A publication*] (DLA) .... S & M Ch R
Smedes and Marshall's Mississippi Chancery Reports [*A publication*] (DLA) .... S & M Ch Rep
Smedes and Marshall's Mississippi Chancery Reports [*A publication*] (DLA) .... S & M Chy
Smedes and Marshall's Mississippi Chancery Reports [*A publication*] (DLA) .... S & Mar Ch
Smedes and Marshall's Mississippi Chancery Reports [*A publication*] (DLA) .... Smed & M Ch
Smedes and Marshall's Mississippi Chancery Reports [*A publication*] (DLA) .... Smedes & M Ch
Smedes and Marshall's Mississippi Chancery Reports [*A publication*] (DLA) .... Smedes and Marshall's Chy Repts
Smedes and Marshall's Mississippi Reports [*9-22 Mississippi*] [*1843-50*] [*A publication*] (DLA) .... S & M
Smedes and Marshall's Mississippi Reports [*9-22 Mississippi*] [*A publication*] (DLA) .... S & Mar
Smedes and Marshall's Mississippi Reports [*9-22 Mississippi*] [*A publication*] (DLA) .... Sm & M
Smedes and Marshall's Mississippi Reports [*9-22 Mississippi*] [*A publication*] (DLA) .... Sm & M Ch
Smedes and Marshall's Mississippi Reports [*A publication*] (DLA) .... Smed & M
Smedes and Marshall's Mississippi Reports [*A publication*] (DLA) .... Smedes & M (Miss)
Smedvig Asa [*Associated Press*] (SAG) .... SmedvA
Smedvig Asa [*Associated Press*] (SAG) .... SmedvB
Smedvig Asa [*NYSE symbol*] (SAG) .... SMV
Smelting .... SMELT
Smert' Shpionam [*Death to the Spies*] [*Former Soviet Union state security organization, often referred to in the popular James Bond espionage stories*] .... SMERSH
Smethport, PA [*FM radio station call letters*] .... WQRM
Smethurst on Locus Standi [*1867*] [*A publication*] (DLA) .... Smeth LS
Smiling Sons of the Friendly Shillelaghs .... SSOFS
Smith Air (1976) Ltd. [*Canada ICAO designator*] (FAAC) .... SML
Smith Air, Inc. [*ICAO designator*] (FAAC) .... SMH
Smith and Bates' American Railway Cases [*A publication*] (DLA) .... Sm & BRR Cas
Smith and Bates' American Railway Cases [*A publication*] (DLA) .... Smith & B
Smith and Bates' American Railway Cases [*A publication*] (DLA) .... Smith & BRRC
Smith and Batty's Irish King's Bench Reports [*1824-25*] [*A publication*] (DLA) .... S & B
Smith and Batty's Irish King's Bench Reports [*A publication*] (DLA) .... Sm & Bat
Smith and Batty's Irish King's Bench Reports [*A publication*] (DLA) .... Smi & Bat
Smith and Batty's Irish King's Bench Reports [*A publication*] (DLA) .... Smith & B
Smith and Batty's Irish King's Bench Reports [*A publication*] (DLA) .... Smith & Bat
Smith and Guthrie's Missouri Appeal Reports [*81-101 Missouri*] [*A publication*] (DLA) .... Sm & G
Smith and Guthrie's Missouri Appeal Reports [*81-101 Missouri*] [*A publication*] (DLA) .... Smith & G
Smith and Heiskell [*Tennessee*] [*A publication*] (DLA) .... Smith & H
Smith & Nephew Pharmaceuticals Ltd. [*Great Britain*] [*Research code symbol*] .... HP
Smith and Sager's Drainage Cases [*Canada*] [*A publication*] (DLA) .... Sm & S
Smith and Soden on Landlord and Tenant [*2nd ed.*] [*1878*] [*A publication*] (DLA) .... Sm & Sod L & T
Smith and Wesson (MCD) .... S & W
Smith Antigen [*Immunology*] .... Sm
Smith (A.O.) Cl'A' [*AMEX symbol*] (TTSB) .... SMC.A
Smith AO Corp. [*NYSE symbol*] (SAG) .... AOS
Smith AO Corp. [*Associated Press*] (SAG) .... SmithAO
Smith AO Corp. [*Associated Press*] (SAG) .... SmthAOA
Smith Barney High Income Opportunity Fund [*NYSE symbol*] (SPSG) .... HIO
Smith Barney Holdings [*Associated Press*] (SAG) SBrSP01
Smith Barney Holdings [*NYSE symbol*] (SAG) .... XSB
Smith Barney Inter Muni Fd [*AMEX symbol*] (TTSB) .... SBI
Smith Barney Intermediate Quality Municipal Fund [*AMEX symbol*] (SAG) .... SBI
Smith Barney Intermediate Quality Municipal Fund [*Associated Press*] (SAG) .... SmtBln

Smith Barney Muni Fund [*AMEX symbol*] (TTSB) ... SBT
Smith Barney Municipal Fund [*AMEX symbol*] (SPSG) ... SBT
Smith Barney Municipal Fund [*Associated Press*] (SAG) ... SmtBrnM
Smith Benevolent Sick and Burial Society [*British*] ... SBSBS
Smith Collection. British Museum [*London*] (BJA) ... Sm
Smith College (GAGS) ... Smith C
Smith College, Northampton, MA [*Library symbol Library of Congress*] (LCLS) ... MNS
Smith College, Northampton, MA [*OCLC symbol*] (OCLC) ... SNN
Smith College, Sophia Smith Collection, Northampton, MA [*Library symbol Library of Congress*] (LCLS) ... MNS-S
Smith Corona Corp. [*NYSE symbol*] (SPSG) ... SCO
Smith [*A.O.*] **Corp.** [*NYSE symbol*] (SAG) ... ACS
Smith [*A. O.*] **Corp.** [*AMEX symbol*] (SPSG) ... SMC
Smith [*A.O.*] **Corp.** [*Associated Press*] (SAG) ... Smth
Smith [*A.O.*] **Corp.** [*Associated Press*] (SAG) ... SmthAO
Smith County High School Library, Carthage, TN [*Library symbol Library of Congress*] (LCLS) ... TCaS
Smith County Memorial Hospital, Carthage, TN [*Library symbol Library of Congress*] (LCLS) ... TCaMH
Smith Elementary School, Uniondale, NY [*Library symbol Library of Congress*] (LCLS) ... NUnSE
Smith Environmental Tech [*NASDAQ symbol*] (TTSB) ... SMTH
Smith Environmental Technologies Corp. [*Associated Press*] (SAG) ... SmithEnv
Smith Environmental Technologies Corp. [*NASDAQ symbol*] (SAG) ... SMTH
Smith Falls Public Library, Ontario [*Library symbol National Library of Canada*] (NLC) ... OSMF
Smith Falls Public Library, Smith Falls, ON, Canada [*Library symbol Library of Congress*] (LCLS) ... CaOSmf
Smith/Greenland [*Advertising agency*] ... S/G
Smith International, Inc. [*NYSE symbol*] (SPSG) ... SII
Smith International, Inc. [*Associated Press*] (SAG) ... SmithIn
Smith Intl [*NYSE symbol*] (TTSB) ... SII
Smith, Kline & French Canada Ltd., Mississauga, Ontario [*Library symbol National Library of Canada*] (NLC) ... OMSK
Smith, Kline & French Canada Ltd., Niagara Falls, ON, Canada [*Library symbol Library of Congress*] (LCLS) ... CaOMSK
Smith, Kline & French Co. [*Later, SmithKline Corp.*], Montreal, PQ, Canada [*Library symbol Library of Congress*] (LCLS) ... CaQMSK
Smith, Kline & French Co. [*Later, SmithKline Corp.*], Swedeland, PA [*Library symbol Library of Congress*] (LCLS) ... PSwS
Smith, Kline & French Laboratories [*Canada*] (IIA) ... SKL
Smith Kline Diagnostics (DAVI) ... SK
Smith Kline Diagnostics (DAVI) ... SKD
Smith, Leland C., Oakland CA [*STAC*] ... SLE
Smith Micro Software [*NASDAQ symbol*] (TTSB) ... SMSI
Smith Micro Software, Inc. [*Associated Press*] (SAG) ... SmithMic
Smith Micro Software, Inc. [*NASDAQ symbol*] (SAG) ... SMSI
Smith, Miller, and Patch [*Commercial firm*] (DAVI) ... SMP
Smith on Constitutional and Statutory Construction [*A publication*] (DLA) ... Sm Const Cons
Smith on Contracts [*8th ed.*] [*1885*] [*A publication*] (DLA) ... Sm Con
Smith on Contracts [*A publication*] (DLA) ... Smith Cont
Smith on Conveyancing [*A publication*] (DLA) ... Sm Conv
Smith on Ecclesiastical Courts [*7th ed.*] [*1920*] [*A publication*] (DLA) ... Sm Ecc Cts
Smith on English Registration [*A publication*] (DLA) ... Smith
Smith on Executory Interest [*A publication*] (DLA) ... Sm Ex Int
Smith on Executory Interest [*A publication*] (DLA) ... Smith Ext Int
Smith on Forensic Medicine [*10th ed.*] [*1955*] [*A publication*] (DLA) ... Sm For Med
Smith on Joint-Stock Companies [*A publication*] (DLA) ... Sm J St Comp
Smith on Master and Servant [*8th ed.*] [*1931*] [*A publication*] (DLA) ... Sm M & S
Smith on Mercantile Law [*13th ed.*] [*1931*] [*A publication*] (DLA) ... Sm Merc L
Smith on Mercantile Law [*A publication*] (DLA) ... Smith Merc Law
Smith on Negligence [*2nd ed.*] [*1884*] [*A publication*] (DLA) ... Sm Neg
Smith on Patents [*2nd ed.*] [*1854*] [*A publication*] (DLA) ... Sm Pat
Smith on the Law of Real and Personal Property [*A publication*] (DLA) ... Sm R & P Prop
Smith Point, TX [*Location identifier FAA*] (FAAL) ... MHF
Smith Predictor [*Process control*] ... SP
Smith, R. H., Minneapolis MN [*STAC*] ... SRH
Smith, Reporter (7, 12 Heiskell's Tennessee Reports) [*A publication*] (DLA) ... Smith
Smith [*Charles E.*] **Residential Realty, Inc.** [*Associated Press*] (SAG) ... SmithRR
Smith [*Charles E.*] **Residential Realty, Inc.** [*NYSE symbol*] (SAG) ... SRW
Smith River Library, Smith River, CA [*Library symbol Library of Congress*] (LCLS) ... CSmi
Smith Surface Antigen [*Medicine*] (DMAA) ... SSA
Smith Township Public Library, Bridgenorth, Ontario [*Library symbol National Library of Canada*] (BIB) ... OBRIS
Smith(A.O.) [*NYSE symbol*] (TTSB) ... AOS
Smith(Charles E.)Res Rlty [*NYSE symbol*] (TTSB) ... SRW
Smith-Corona Laboratory, Cortland, NY [*Library symbol Library of Congress*] (LCLS) ... NCortSC
Smithers [*Canada*] [*Airport symbol*] (OAG) ... YYD
Smithers, BC [*AM radio station call letters*] ... CFBV
Smithers, BC [*ICAO location identifier*] (ICLI) ... CYYD
Smithers Public Library, British Columbia [*Library symbol National Library of Canada*] (NLC) ... BS
Smithers Public Library, Smithers, BC, Canada [*Library symbol*] [*Library of Congress*] (LCLS) ... CaBS
Smithfield Companies [*NASDAQ symbol*] (SAG) ... HAMS
Smithfield Co., Inc. [*Associated Press*] (SAG) ... Smthfld
Smithfield Cos. [*NASDAQ symbol*] (TTSB) ... HAMS
Smithfield Foods [*NASDAQ symbol*] (TTSB) ... SFDS
Smithfield Foods, Inc. [*NASDAQ symbol*] (NQ) ... SFDS
Smithfield Foods, Inc. [*Associated Press*] (SAG) ... SmthF
Smithfield, NC [*Location identifier FAA*] (FAAL) ... EUU
Smithfield, NC [*AM radio station call letters*] ... WMPM
Smithfield, RI [*FM radio station call letters*] ... WJMF
Smithfield, UT [*FM radio station call letters*] ... KNUC
Smithfield, VA [*AM radio station call letters*] ... WKGM
Smith-Houghton Infrared Temperature Sounder (NOAA) ... SHIRTS
Smith-Hughes Act (MHDW) ... SHA
Smith-Hurd Illinois Annotated Statutes [*A publication*] (AAGC) ... Ill Ann Stat
Smith-Hurd's Illinois Annotated Statutes [*A publication*] (DLA) ... Ill Ann Stat
Smith-Hurd's Illinois Annotated Statutes [*A publication*] (DLA) ... SHA
Smith-Hurd's Illinois Annotated Statutes [*A publication*] (DLA) ... Smith-Hurd
Smith-Hurd's Illinois Annotated Statutes [*A publication*] (DLA) ... Smith-Hurd Ann St
Smithkline Beecham Clincal Labs [*ICAO designator*] (FAAC) ... SBQ
SmithKline Beecham ADS [*NYSE symbol*] (TTSB) ... SBH
SmithKline Beecham Clinical Laboratories ... SBCL
Smithkline Beecham Ltd. [*NYSE symbol*] (SAG) ... SBE
Smithkline Beecham Ltd. [*Associated Press*] (SAG) ... SmtBc
SmithKline Beecham Ltd. [*Associated Press*] (SAG) ... SmthBc
SmithKline Beecham Ltd. ADS [*NYSE symbol*] (SPSG) ... SBH
SmithKline Corp. [*Formerly, Smith, Kline & French Co.*] [*Research code symbol*] ... SKF
SmithKline Corp., Philadelphia, PA [*Library symbol Library of Congress*] (LCLS) ... PPSKF
Smith-Magenis Chromosome Region [*Medicine*] (DMAA) ... SMCR
Smith-Midland [*NASDAQ symbol*] (TTSB) ... SMID
Smith-Midland Corp. [*NASDAQ symbol*] (SAG) ... SMID
Smith-Midland Corp. [*Associated Press*] (SAG) ... SmithM
Smith-Midland Corp. [*Associated Press*] (SAG) ... SmithMid
Smith-Midland Wrrt [*NASDAQ symbol*] (TTSB) ... SMIDW
Smithosonian Jazz Masterworks Orchestra ... SJMO
Smith's Action at Law [*12th ed.*] [*1876*] [*A publication*] (DLA) ... Sm Act
Smith's Actions at Law [*A publication*] (DLA) ... Smith Act
Smith's Admiralty Practice [*4th ed.*] [*1892*] [*A publication*] (DLA) ... Sm Adm Pr
Smith's Chancery Practice [*7th ed.*] [*1862*] [*A publication*] (DLA) ... Sm Ch Pr
Smith's Chancery Practice [*A publication*] (DLA) ... Smith Ch Pr
Smith's Chancery Rules [*A publication*] (DLA) ... Smith Rules
Smith's Circuit Courts-Martial Reports [*Maine*] [*A publication*] (DLA) ... Sm CCM
Smith's Circuit Courts-Martial Reports [*Maine*] [*A publication*] (DLA) ... Smith CCM
Smith's Condensed Alabama Reports [*A publication*] (DLA) ... Sm Cond Ala
Smith's Condensed Alabama Reports [*A publication*] (DLA) ... Smith Cond
Smith's Condensed Alabama Reports [*A publication*] (DLA) ... Smith Cond Rep
Smith's Court of Appeals Reports [*15-27, 147-162 New York*] [*A publication*] (DLA) ... Smith NY
Smith's Dictionary of Greek and Roman Antiquities [*A publication*] (DLA) ... Smith Dict Antiq
Smith's Education for the English Bar [*A publication*] (DLA) ... Sm Ed
Smith's Election Cases [*United States*] [*A publication*] (DLA) ... Smith Cong Election Cases
Smith's Elements of Law [*A publication*] (DLA) ... Sm El
Smith's English King's Bench Reports [*A publication*] (DLA) ... Sm Eng
Smith's English King's Bench Reports [*A publication*] (DLA) ... Sm KB
Smith's English King's Bench Reports [*A publication*] (DLA) ... Smith KB
Smiths Falls, ON [*FM radio station call letters*] ... CFMO
Smiths Falls, ON [*AM radio station call letters*] ... CJET
Smith's Flight System [*Aviation*] (AIA) ... SFS
Smith's Food & Drug Centers [*NYSE symbol*] (SPSG) ... SFD
Smith's Food & Drug Centers, Inc. [*Associated Press*] (SAG) ... SmtFD
Smith's Food & Drug'B' [*NYSE symbol*] (TTSB) ... SFD
Smith's Forms of Procedure [*A publication*] (DLA) ... Sm Forms
Smiths Grove, KY [*FM radio station call letters*] ... WBLG
Smith's Indiana Reports [*A publication*] (DLA) ... Smith
Smith's Indiana Reports [*A publication*] (DLA) ... Smith Ind
Smith's Indiana Reports [*A publication*] (DLA) ... Smith's (Ind) R
Smith's Indiana Reports [*A publication*] (DLA) ... Smith's R
Smith's Inquiry into the Nature and Causes of the Wealth of Nations [*A publication*] (DLA) ... Smith Wealth Nat
Smith's Landlord and Tenant [*A publication*] (DLA) ... Sm L & T
Smith's Law Journal [*London*] [*A publication*] (DLA) ... LJ Sm
Smith's Law Journal [*A publication*] (DLA) ... Smith LJ
Smith's Law of Receivers [*A publication*] (DLA) ... Smith Rec
Smith's Law of Reparation [*A publication*] (DLA) ... Smith Repar
Smith's Laws of Pennsylvania [*A publication*] (DLA) ... Smith Laws PA
Smith's Laws of Pennsylvania [*A publication*] (DLA) ... Smith's Laws
Smith's Lawyer and His Profession [*A publication*] (DLA) ... Sm Lawy
Smith's Leading Cases [*A publication*] (DLA) ... SLC
Smith's Leading Cases [*A publication*] (DLA) ... Sm LC
Smith's Leading Cases [*A publication*] (DLA) ... Smith LC
Smith's Leading Cases [*A publication*] (DLA) ... Smith Lead Cas
Smith's Leading Cases [*A publication*] (DLA) ... Smith's Lead Cas
Smith's Leading Cases on Commercial Law [*A publication*] (DLA) ... Sm L Cas Com L
Smith's Manual of Common Law [*12th ed.*] [*1905*] [*A publication*] (DLA) ... Sm Com L
Smith's Manual of Common Law [*A publication*] (DLA) ... Smith Com Law
Smith's Manual of Equity Jurisprudence [*A publication*] (DLA) ... Smith Man Eq Jur
Smith's New Hampshire Reports [*A publication*] (DLA) ... Cheshire
Smith's New Hampshire Reports [*A publication*] (DLA) ... Grafton
Smith's New Hampshire Reports [*A publication*] (DLA) ... Merrimack
Smith's New Hampshire Reports [*A publication*] (DLA) ... Rock
Smith's New Hampshire Reports [*A publication*] (DLA) ... Rockingham
Smith's New Hampshire Reports [*A publication*] (DLA) ... Smith
Smith's New Hampshire Reports [*A publication*] (DLA) ... Smith NH

Smith's New Hampshire Reports [*A publication*] (DLA) ... Strafford
Smith's New Hampshire Reports [*A publication*] (DLA) ... Sullivan
Smith's Principles of Equity [*A publication*] (DLA) ... Sm Eq
Smith's Principles of Equity [*A publication*] (DLA) ... Sm Pr Eq
Smith's Probate Law and Practice [*A publication*] (DLA) ... Sm Prob L
Smith's Reports [*1-4 Indiana*] [*A publication*] (DLA) ... Sm Ind
Smith's Reports [*61-84 Maine*] [*A publication*] (DLA) ... Sm ME
Smith's Reports [*81-83 Missouri Appeals*] [*A publication*] (DLA) ... Smith
Smith's Reports [*2-4 South Dakota*] [*A publication*] (DLA) ... Smith
Smith's Reports [*1-11 Wisconsin*] [*A publication*] (DLA) ... Smith
Smith's Reports [*54-62 California*] [*A publication*] (DLA) ... Smith
Smith's Reports [*61-84 Maine*] [*A publication*] (DLA) ... Smith
Smith's Reports [*61-84 Maine*] [*A publication*] (DLA) ... Smith ME
Smith's Reports [*1-11 Wisconsin*] [*A publication*] (DLA) ... Smith Wis
Smith's Scotch Poor Law [*A publication*] (DLA) ... Sm Poor L
Smith's Statute Law [*A publication*] (DLA) ... Sm Stat Law
Smith's Weekly [*A publication*] ... SW
Smithsonian [*A publication*] (BRI) ... Smith
Smithsonian Air and Space Museum ... SASM
Smithsonian Archaeometric Research Collection and Records [*Facility*] ... SARCAR
Smithsonian Associates [*Later, Smithsonian Resident Associate Program*] ... SA
Smithsonian Astrophysical Observatory [*Cambridge, MA*] ... SAO
Smithsonian Center for Short-Lived Phenomena ... SCSLP
Smithsonian Earth Physics Satellite ... SEPS
Smithsonian Environmental Research Center ... SERC
Smithsonian Institution ... SI
Smithsonian Institution (BARN) ... Smith Inst
Smithsonian Institution, Archives of American Art, Washington, DC [*Library symbol Library of Congress*] (LCLS) ... DSI-AAA
Smithsonian Institution/Astrophysical Observatory (KSC) ... SI/AO
Smithsonian Institution, Astrophysical Observatory, Cambridge, MA [*Library symbol Library of Congress*] (LCLS) ... MCSA
Smithsonian Institution Bibliographic Information System ... SIBIS
Smithsonian Institution, Cooper-Hewitt Museum of Decorative Arts and Design, NewYork, NY [*Library symbol*] [*Library of Congress*] (LCLS) ... NNSC
Smithsonian Institution, Hirshhorn Museum and Sculpture Garden, Washington, DC [*Library symbol Library of Congress*] (LCLS) ... DSI-HMS
Smithsonian Institution Information Leaflets ... SIL
Smithsonian Institution Information Retrieval System (DIT) ... SIIRS
Smithsonian Institution Libraries ... SIL
Smithsonian Institution, Museum of African Art, Washington, DC [*Library symbol Library of Congress*] (LCLS) ... DSI-MAA
Smithsonian Institution, Museum Reference Center, Washington, DC [*Library symbol Library of Congress*] (LCLS) ... DSI-Mus
Smithsonian Institution, National Collection of Fine Arts, Washington, DC [*Library symbol Library of Congress*] (LCLS) ... DSI-NCF
Smithsonian Institution, National Museum of History and Technology, Washington, DC [*Library symbol Library of Congress*] (LCLS) ... DSI-MHT
Smithsonian Institution, National Museum of Natural History, Office of Anthropology, Washington, DC [*Library symbol Library of Congress*] (LCLS) ... DSI-SOA
Smithsonian Institution, National Portrait Gallery, Washington, DC [*Library symbol Library of Congress*] (LCLS) ... DSI-NPG
Smithsonian Institution, National Space and Air Museum, Washington, DC [*Library symbol Library of Congress*] (LCLS) ... DSI-NAS
Smithsonian Institution Press [*Publisher*] ... SIP
Smithsonian Institution Traveling Exhibition Service ... SITES
Smithsonian Institution, Washington, DC [*Library symbol Library of Congress*] (LCLS) ... DSI
Smithsonian Institution, Washington, DC [*OCLC symbol*] (OCLC) ... SMI
Smithsonian Institution's Marine Station ... SMS
Smithsonian Marine Station at Link Port ... SMSLP
Smithsonian Oceanographic Sorting Center ... SOSC
Smithsonian Office of Anthropology ... SOA
Smithsonian Package for Algebra and Symbolic Mathematics (MCD) ... SPASM
Smithsonian Precision Optical Tracking ... SPOT
Smithsonian Research Foundation (BARN) ... SRF
Smithsonian Resident Associate Program (EA) ... RAP
Smithsonian Science Information Exchange [*National Technical Information Service*] [*Later, FEDRIP*] ... SSIE
Smithsonian Tropical Research Institute [*Miami, FL*] ... STRI
Smithton [*Australia Airport symbol*] (OAG) ... SIO
Smithton Community Consolidated School District 130, Smithton, IL [*Library symbol Library of Congress*] (LCLS) ... ISmSD
Smithtown [*Tasmania*] [*Airport symbol*] (AD) ... SIO
Smithtown General Hospital, Smithtown, NY [*Library symbol Library of Congress*] (LCLS) ... NSmGH
Smithtown High School East. Smithtown, NY [*Library symbol*] [*Library of Congress*] (LCLS) ... NSmHSE
Smithtown High School West, Smithtown, NY [*Library symbol*] [*Library of Congress*] (LCLS) ... NSmHSW
Smithtown, NY [*FM radio station call letters*] ... WFRS
Smithtown, NY [*Television station call letters*] ... WHSI
Smithtown, NY [*FM radio station call letters*] ... WMJC
Smithtown Public Library, Smithtown, NY [*Library symbol Library of Congress*] (LCLS) ... NSm
Smithville, GA [*FM radio station call letters*] ... WZIQ
Smithville, TN [*Location identifier FAA*] (FAAL) ... SKN
Smithville, TN [*AM radio station call letters*] ... WJLE
Smithville, TN [*FM radio station call letters*] ... WJLE-FM
Smithway Motor Xpress Corp. [*Associated Press*] (SAG) ... SmithMo
Smithway Motor Xpress Corp. [*NASDAQ symbol*] (SAG) ... SMXC
Smith-Winnick-Abrams-Prausnitz [*Vapor pressure correlation equation*] ... SWAP
SMM Enterprises Ltd. [*Vancouver Stock Exchange symbol*] ... SM
Smocking Arts Guild of America (EA) ... SAGA
Smoke [*Weather charts*] ... K
Smoke (NFPA) ... S
Smoke (AAG) ... SMK
Smoke ... SMO
Smoke/Aerosol Steering Group [*DARCOM*] (RDA) ... SASG
Smoke and Fog ... SMOG
Smoke, Cloud, and Radiation in Brazil ... SCAR-B
Smoke Control and Pressurization Panel [*NFPA pre-fire planning symbol*] (NFPA) ... SP
Smoke Control Association [*Defunct*] (EA) ... SCA
Smoke Curtain Installation [*British military*] (DMA) ... SCI
Smoke Destruction System ... SDS
Smoke Detector (NASA) ... SD
Smoke Detector/Fire Suppression (GFGA) ... SD/FS
Smoke Dispersion Pod ... SDP
Smoke Effectiveness Manual Model (MCD) ... SEMM
Smoke Extract ... SE
Smoke Generating Fuel (IAA) ... SGF
Smoke Generator ... SG
Smoke Layer Aloft [*Meteorology*] (FAAC) ... KLYR
Smoke Layer Estimated (Feet) Deep [*Meteorology*] (FAAC) ... KDEP
Smoke Number [*Emissions measurement*] (EG) ... SN
Smoke Point Improvement [*Petroleum refining*] ... SPI
Smoke Puff Limiter [*Automotive engineering*] ... SPL
Smoke Removal tube [*Used in laser therapy*] [*Gynecology*] (DAVI) ... SRT
Smoke Screen Generative Device ... SSGD
Smoke Stand (MSA) ... SS
Smoked (WGA) ... SMKD
Smoke-Emitting Diode [*Computer hacker terminology*] (NHD) ... SED
Smokeless (AAG) ... SMKLS
Smokeless Powder ... SP
Smokeless Powder, Diphenylamine (DNAB) ... SPD
Smokeless Powder, Diphenylamine, Flashless (DNAB) ... SPDF
Smokeless Powder, Diphenylamine, Nonvolatile (DNAB) ... SPDN
Smokeless Powder, Diphenylamine, Reworked (DNAB) ... SPDW
Smokeless Propellant (NATG) ... SP
Smokeless Propellant in Demonstration Experimental Rocket (KSC) ... SPIDER
Smokeless Rocket Motor (MCD) ... SRM
Smokeless Tobacco Council (EA) ... STC
Smoker (DAVI) ... SM
Smoker's Rights Alliance (EA) ... SRA
Smokestack [*s*] [*Freight*] ... SMKSTK
Smoki People [*An association*] (EA) ... SP
Smoking Policy Institute (EA) ... SPI
Smoking-Attributable Chronic Obstructive Pulmonary Disease ... SACOPD
Smoky Lake Public Library, Alberta [*Library symbol National Library of Canada*] (NLC) ... ASL
Smoky Lake Public Library, Smoky Lake, AB, Canada [*Library symbol*] [*Library of Congress*] (LCLS) ... CaASl
Smoky Mountain R. R. [*AAR code*] ... SMTN
Smoldering Multiple Myeloma [*Medicine*] (DMAA) ... SMM
Smoloskyp, Ukrainian Information Service (EA) ... SUIS
Smooth [*Appearance of bacterial colony*] ... S
Smooth (MSA) ... SM
Smooth [*NWS*] (FAAC) ... SMTH
Smooth Approach Orifice [*Mechanical engineering*] ... SAO
Smooth Bore [*Ballistics*] ... SB
Smooth Bore Muzzle Loading [*British military*] (DMA) ... SBML
Smooth, Capsulated, Virulent [*Bacteriology*] ... SCV
Smooth Contour [*Technical drawings*] ... SC
Smooth Curve - Smooth Earth ... SCSE
Smooth [*Surfaced*] **Endoplasmic Reticulum** [*Cytology*] ... SER
Smooth Muscle [*Medicine*] (DMAA) ... SM
Smooth Muscle Activating Factor ... SMAF
Smooth Muscle Antibody (AAMN) ... SMA
Smooth Muscle Cell [*Cytology*] ... SMC
Smooth Muscle Cell-Chemotactic Factor [*Oncology*] ... SMC-CF
Smooth Muscle Form of Myosin Light Chain Kinase [*An enzyme*] ... SM MLCK
Smooth Muscle Myosin Heavy Chain [*Biochemistry*] ... SMMHC
Smooth Muscle-Derived Elastogenic Factor [*Biochemistry*] ... SMEF
Smooth Neck ... SMNK
Smooth Particle Hydrodynamic ... SPH
Smooth Rock Falls Public Library, Ontario [*Library symbol National Library of Canada*] (NLC) ... OSRF
Smooth Rock Falls Public Library, Smooth Rock Falls, ON, Canada [*Library symbol*] [*Library of Congress*] (LCLS) ... CaOSrf
Smooth Sea [*Navigation*] ... S
Smoothed-Particle Hydrodynamics [*Statistical mechanics*] ... SPH
Smooth-Face Structural Clay Tile [*Technical drawings*] ... SFSCT
Smoothing by Spectral Dispersion [*LASER technology*] ... SSD
Smoothing Heading Spot (SAA) ... SHS
Smooth-Muscle Myosin [*Biology*] ... SMM
Smooth-Rough Variation [*Medicine*] (MAE) ... S-R
Smooth-Surface Built-Up Roof [*Technical drawings*] ... SSBR
Smorzando [*Slower and Softer*] [*Music*] ... SMORZ
Smouldering Leukemia [*Medicine*] (DMAA) ... SML
SMT Health Services [*Associated Press*] (SAG) ... SMT
SMT Health Services, Inc. [*NASDAQ symbol*] (SAG) ... SHED
SMT Health Services, Inc. [*Associated Press*] (SAG) ... SMT Hlt
SMT Health Svcs [*NASDAQ symbol*] (TTSB) ... SHED
SMT Health Svcs Wrrt [*NASDAQ symbol*] (TTSB) ... SHEDW
Smucker [*J. M.*] **Co.** [*NYSE symbol*] (SPSG) ... SJM
Smucker [*J.M.*] **Co.** [*Associated Press*] (SAG) ... Smckr
Smucker (J.M.) Cl'A' [*NYSE symbol*] (TTSB) ... SJM.A

Smucker (J.M.) Cl'B' [*NYSE symbol*] (TTSB) .... SJM.B
Smudge Cell [*hematology*] (DAVI) .... SMUD
Smudge Pot .... SMP
Smuggling [*FBI standardized term*] .... SMUG
Smurf Collectors' Club International (EA) .... SCCI
Smyrna [*Washington*] [*Seismograph station code, US Geological Survey*] (SEIS) .... SYR
Smyrna, DE [*FM radio station call letters*] .... WSRV
Smyrna, GA [*AM radio station call letters*] .... WAZX
Smyrna, GA [*FM radio station call letters*] .... WSTR
Smyrna Public Library, Smyrna, DE [*OCLC symbol*] (OCLC) .... SMY
Smyrna/Sewart Air Force Base [*Tennessee*] [*ICAO location identifier*] (ICLI) .... KSYM
Smyrna, TN [*Location identifier FAA*] (FAAL) .... MQY
Smyrna, TN [*Location identifier FAA*] (FAAL) .... SWZ
Smyrna, TN [*FM radio station call letters*] .... WRLG
Smyrna, TN [*AM radio station call letters*] .... WZRS
Smyth on the Law of Homestead and Exemptions [*A publication*] (DLA) .... Smy Home
Smyth on the Law of Homesteads and Exemptions [*A publication*] (DLA) .... Sm Homest
Smythe and Bourke's Irish Marriage Cases [*1842*] [*A publication*] (DLA) .... Smy & B
Smythe's Irish Common Pleas Reports [*1839-40*] [*A publication*] (DLA) .... Smy
Smythe's Irish Common Pleas Reports [*1839-40*] [*A publication*] (DLA) .... Smythe
Snack (CDAI) .... S
Snack Food Association (EA) .... SFA
Snack, Nut, and Crisp Manufacturers' Association [*British*] .... SNACMA
Snake Approach Scale [*Psychology*] .... SAS
Snake Bay [*Australia Airport symbol*] (OAG) .... SNB
Snake in the Box (IAA) .... SIB
Snake Ranch Flats [*New Mexico*] [*Seismograph station code, US Geological Survey Closed*] (SEIS) .... SRF
Snake River Conservation Research Center [*University of Idaho*] [*Research center*] (RCD) .... SRCRC
Snake River School and Community Library, Blackfoot, ID [*Library symbol*] [*Library of Congress*] (LCLS) .... IdBfS
Snake Torpedo Destruction System .... STDS
Snake Venom [*Medicine*] .... SV
Snake Venom Phosphodiesterase [*Also, SVPD, SVPDE*] [*An enzyme*] .... SVP
Snake Venom Phosphodiesterase [*Also, SVP, SVPDE*] [*An enzyme*] .... SVPD
Snake Venom Phosphodiesterase [*Also, SVP, SVPD*] [*An enzyme*] .... SVPDE
Snake-Shark (SAA) .... SNARK
Snakeye Free-Fall [*Navy*] (DNAB) .... SEFF
Snakeye Low-Drag [*Navy*] (DNAB) .... SELD
Snakeye Retarded [*Navy*] (DNAB) .... SERET
SNAM SpA [*Italy ICAO designator*] (FAAC) .... SNM
Snap Action .... SA
Snap Action Bimetal [*Automotive engineering*] .... SAB
Snap Action Spool Valve .... SASV
Snap Action Switch .... SAS
Snap Action Thermostat .... SAT
SNAP [*Systems for Nuclear Auxiliary Power*] **Critical Facility** (NRCH) .... SCF
SNAP [*Systems for Nuclear Auxiliary Power*] **Development Reactor** .... SDR
SNAP [*Systems for Nuclear Auxiliary Power*] **Experimental Reactor** .... SER
SNAP [*Systems for Nuclear Auxiliary Power*] **Experimental Test Facility** .... SETF
SNAP [*Systems for Nuclear Auxiliary Power*] **Generalized Critical Facility** .... SGCF
Snap Lock Environmental [*Electrical engineering*] .... SLE
Snap Lock Limit Switch .... SLLS
SNAP [*Soluble NAF Attachment Protein*] **Receptor** [*Medicine*] .... SNARE
Snap Shield Test Facility Reactor [*Nuclear energy*] (IAA) .... STF
SNAP [*Systems for Nuclear Auxiliary Power*] **Shield Test Irradiation Reactor** .... STIR
Snapdragon [*Horticulture*] .... snap
Snap-On Tools Corp. [*NYSE symbol*] (SPSG) .... SNA
Snap-On Tools Corp. [*Associated Press*] (SAG) .... SnapOn
Snatch [*Block*] [*Design engineering*] .... SNH
SNC Group, Inc. [*Toronto Stock Exchange symbol*] .... SNU
SNC, Inc., Montreal, Quebec [*Library symbol National Library of Canada*] (NLC) .... QMSNC
Snci-Tours Benin Inter Regional [*ICAO designator*] (FAAC) .... STB
Snead Junior College [*Boaz, AL*] .... SJC
Sneak Attack Defense Coordinator [*Military*] (CAAL) .... SADC
Sneak Circuit Analysis [*NASA*] (NASA) .... SCA
Sneak Circuit Analysis Report Summary [*NASA*] (GFGA) .... SCARS
Sneak Circuit Report [*NASA*] (NASA) .... SCR
Sneak Circuit/Worst Case Analysis (MCD) .... SC/WCA
Sneed's Kentucky Decisions [*2 Kentucky*] [*A publication*] (DLA) .... KY Dec
Sneed's Kentucky Decisions [*2 Kentucky*] [*A publication*] (DLA) .... Sneed
Sneed's Kentucky Decisions [*2 Kentucky*] [*A publication*] (DLA) .... Sneed Dec
Sneed's Tennessee Reports [*33-37 Tennessee*] [*A publication*] (DLA) .... Sneed
Sneed's Tennessee Reports [*A publication*] (DLA) .... Sneed Tenn
Sneed's Tennessee Reports [*A publication*] (DLA) .... Sneed (Tenn) Rep
Sneedville, TN [*Television station call letters*] .... WSJK
Snell & Wilmer, Phoenix, AZ [*Library symbol*] [*Library of Congress*] (LCLS) .... AzPhSW
Snell Memorial Foundation, Inc. .... SMF
Snell Motorcycle .... SM
Snellen [*Test types*] [*Ophthalmology*] .... SN
Snellen Chart [*Ophthalmology*] .... SC
Snell's Principles in Equity [*A publication*] (DLA) .... Snell Eq
Sniff, Paw, Urinate, and Defecate [*Ungulate territorial marking procedure*] .... SPUD
Sniffer [*Exhaust trail indicator*] **Exercise** [*Military*] (NVT) .... SNIFFEX
Snijders-Oomen Non-Verbal Intelligence Scale (AEBS) .... SON
Snipe Class International Racing Association (EA) .... SCIRA
Sniper [*British military*] (DMA) .... S
Sniper Weapon Sight (INF) .... SWS
Sniper Weapon System (INF) .... SWS
Sniper Weapon System [*Army*] .... SWS
Sniper's Post [*British military*] (DMA) .... SP
Sniping, Observation, and Scouting [*Course*] [*World War I*] [*Military British*] .... SOS
S-Nitroso-N-Acetylcysteine [*Biochemistry*] .... SNAC
S-Nitroso-N-Acetylpenicilamine [*Biochemistry*] .... SNAP
SNOBOL Implementation Language Reimplemented [*1974*] [*Computer science*] (CSR) .... SIL
Sno-Isle Regional Library, Marysville, WA [*Library symbol Library of Congress*] (LCLS) .... WaMaS
Snorkel (MSA) .... SNKL
Snorkel Detection Exercise [*Military*] (NVT) .... SNORKEX
Snout Length [*Pisciculture*] .... SNL
Snout-to-Vent Length [*Biometry*] .... SVL
Snow [*Meteorology*] .... S
Snow [*Ship's rigging*] (ROG) .... SW
Snow and Ice Distributed Active Archive Center (USDC) .... SIDAAC
Snow and Ice Distributed Active Archive Center [*Marine science*] (OSRA) .... SIDAAC
Snow and Ice on Runway [*NWS*] (FAAC) .... SIR
Snow and Ice Traversing Equipment [*Army*] .... SITE
Snow and Winstanley's Chancery Practice [*A publication*] (DLA) .... Sn & W Ch
Snow Biz [*An association*] (EA) .... SB
Snow College, Ephraim, UT [*Library symbol Library of Congress*] (LCLS) .... UES
Snow Cover [*Meteorology*] .... SC
Snow Depth Increase in Past Hour [*NWS*] (FAAC) .... SNOINCR
Snow Grains [*ICAO*] (FAAC) .... SG
Snow Hill, MD [*Location identifier FAA*] (FAAL) .... SWL
Snow Hill, NC [*FM radio station call letters*] (RBYB) .... WAGO-FM
Snow, Ice, and Permafrost Research Establishment .... SIPRE
Snow Lake Community Library, Manitoba [*Library symbol National Library of Canada*] (NLC) .... MSL
Snow Lake Community Library, Snow Lake, MB, Canada [*Library symbol Library of Congress*] (LCLS) .... CaMSL
Snow Lake Mines Ltd. [*Vancouver Stock Exchange symbol*] .... SLM
Snow Monitoring Tire [*Automotive engineering*] .... SMT
Snow Pellets [*ICAO*] (FAAC) .... GS
Snow Shower [*Meteorology*] (BARN) .... SW
Snow Showers [*ICAO*] (FAAC) .... SHSN
Snow Showers [*Meteorology*] .... SNSH
Snow Survey Telemetry Network [*Department of Agriculture*] .... SNOTEL
Snowbank [*NWS*] (FAAC) .... SNBNK
Snowbird Community Library, Robbinsville, NC [*Library symbol Library of Congress*] (LCLS) .... NcRobS
Snowbird, TN [*Location identifier FAA*] (FAAL) .... SOT
Snowfall [*NWS*] (FAAC) .... SNWFL
Snowflake [*NWS*] (FAAC) .... SNFLK
Snowmass Village, CO [*FM radio station call letters*] .... KSNO
Snowmelt-Runoff Model [*Hydrology*] .... SRM
Snow's Reports [*3 Utah*] [*A publication*] (DLA) .... Snow
Snowshoe Hare .... SSH
Snowwater Resources Ltd. [*Vancouver Stock Exchange symbol*] .... SNW
Snowy Mountains Scheme [*Australia*] .... SMS
Snubber [*Mechanical engineering*] .... SNBR
Snunit Aviation [*Israel*] [*ICAO designator*] (FAAC) .... SNU
Snyder [*Texas*] [*Airport symbol*] (AD) .... SNK
Snyder Communications .... SNC
Snyder Communications, Inc. [*NYSE symbol*] (SAG) .... SNC
Snyder Communications, Inc. [*Associated Press*] (SAG) .... SnyderC
Snyder Oil cm Dep Ex Pfd [*NYSE symbol*] (TTSB) .... SNYPrA
Snyder Oil Corp. [*NYSE symbol*] (SPSG) .... SNY
Snyder Oil Corp. [*Associated Press*] (SAG) .... Snyder
Snyder Oil Corp. [*Associated Press*] (SAG) .... SnyderOil
Snyder Oil Corp. [*Associated Press*] (SAG) .... Snydr
Snyder on Mines and Mining [*A publication*] (DLA) .... Snyder Mines
Snyder on Religious Corporations [*A publication*] (DLA) .... Sny Rel Corp
Snyder Research Co. [*Information service or system*] (IID) .... SRC
Snyder, TX [*TV station call letters*] (RBYB) .... KPCB-TV
Snyder, TX [*AM radio station call letters*] .... KSNY
Snyder, TX [*FM radio station call letters*] .... KSNY-FM
Snyder, TX [*Location identifier FAA*] (FAAL) .... SDR
Snyder, TX [*Location identifier FAA*] (FAAL) .... SNK
Snyder's Notaries' and Commissioners' Manual [*A publication*] (DLA) .... Sny Not Man
Snyder-Thielen Feline Sarcoma Virus [*Veterinary medicine*] (MEDA) .... ST-FeSv
So Cal Edison 8.375%'QUIDS' [*AMEX symbol*] (TTSB) .... SCE.Q
So Handicapped All Read Easily .... SHARE
So Much Of .... SMO
So Much of Paragraph .... SMOP
SO Resources [*Vancouver Stock Exchange symbol*] .... SOY
So Union Financing 9.48%'TOPrS' [*NYSE symbol*] (TTSB) .... SUGPrA
So West Gas Cap 1 9.125%'TOPrS' [*NYSE symbol*] (TTSB) .... SWXPrA
Soalala [*Madagascar*] [*Airport symbol*] (OAG) .... DWB
Soalala [*Madagascar*] [*ICAO location identifier*] (ICLI) .... FMNO
Soap and Detergent Association (EA) .... SDA
Soap and Detergent Industry Association [*British*] (DBA) .... SDIA
Soap and Water [*Enema*] [*Medicine*] .... S & W
Soap Perfumery and Cosmetics [*A publication*] .... SPC
Soap Solution .... SS
Soap Suds Enema [*Medicine*] .... SSE
Soapstone (VRA) .... soapst
Soapsuds .... SS

Soaring Association of Canada .... SAC
Soaring Society of America (EA) .... SSA
Soave-Redlich-Kwong [*Equation of state*] .... SRK
Sobek's International Explorer's Society [*Commercial firm*] (EA) .... SIES
SOBELAIR [*Societe Belge de Transport Aeriens*] [*Belgium ICAO designator*] (FAAC) .... SLR
Sobeys Stores Ltd. [*Toronto Stock Exchange symbol*] .... SYS
Sobieski Bancorp [*NASDAQ symbol*] (TTSB) .... SOBI
Sobieski Bancorp, Inc. [*NASDAQ symbol*] (SAG) .... SOBI
Sobieski Bancorp, Inc. [*Associated Press*] (SAG) .... Sobieski
Sobral [*Brazil*] [*Airport symbol*] (AD) .... SOB
Soc Trang [*South Vietnam*] [*Airport symbol*] (AD) .... SOA
So-Called .... SC
Socanav, Inc. [*Toronto Stock Exchange symbol*] .... SVX
So.Carolina E&G 5% cmPfd [*NYSE symbol*] (TTSB) .... SACPr
Socastee, SC [*FM radio station call letters*] .... WMYB
Soccer Association for Youth (EA) .... SAY
Soccer Association of the United States (EA) .... SAUS
Soccer Federation of Western Australia .... SFWA
Soccer Industry Council of America (EA) .... SICA
Sochi [*Former USSR Seismograph station code, US Geological Survey*] (SEIS) .... SOC
Sochi [*Former USSR ICAO location identifier*] (ICLI) .... URSS
Sociaal-Democratische Arbeiders Partij [*Social Democratic Workers' Party*] [*Netherlands Political party*] (PPE) .... SDAP
Sociaal-Democratische Bond [*Social Democratic League*] [*Netherlands Political party*] (PPE) .... SDB
Sociaal-Wetenschappelijk Informatie- en Documentatiecentrum [*Social Science Information and Documentation Center*] [*Netherlands Information service or system*] (IID) .... SWIDOC
Social .... SCL
Social .... SOC
Social .... SOCL
Social Action and the Law [*A publication*] (DLA) .... Soc Action & L
Social Action Party [*Thailand*] [*Political party*] (FEA) .... SAP
Social Actions Office [*or Officer*] [*Air Force*] (AFM) .... SAO
Social Activist Professors Defense Foundation [*Defunct*] (EA) .... SAPDF
Social Adequacy Index .... SAI
Social Administration Association [*British*] .... SAA
Social Affairs Recreation and Sports Association .... SARSA
Social Affairs Unit [*British*] .... SAU
Social Alternatives [*A publication*] .... Soc Alt
Social and Athletic Club .... SAC
Social & Community Planning Research [*British*] .... SCPR
Social and Demographic Research Institute [*University of Massachusetts*] [*Research center*] (RCD) .... SADRI
Social and Economic Archive Centre [*British*] .... SEAC
Social and Economic Development Strategy .... SEDS
Social and Economic Statistics Administration [*Terminated, 1975*] [*Department of Commerce*] .... SESA
Social and Emotional Behavior .... SEB
Social and Human Sciences Documentation Centre [*UNESCO*] (DUND) .... SHS/DC
Social and Labour Bulletin [*A publication*] (ILCA) .... Soc Lab Bull
Social and Labour Bulletin [*A publication*] .... Soc Labour Bull
Social and Liberal Democrats [*British Political party*] (ECON) .... SLD
Social and Prevocational Information Battery .... SPIB
Social and Rehabilitation Service [*Abolished, 1977*] [*HEW*] .... SRS
[*A*] **Social and Religious History of the Jews** [*S. W. Baron*] [*A publication*] (BJA) .... SRH
[*A*] **Social and Religious History of the Jews** [*S. W. Baron*] [*A publication*] (BJA) .... SRHJ
Social and Technical Sciences .... SATS
Social Assessment of Fisheries Resources .... SAFR
Social Assessment of Technology (PDAA) .... SAT
Social Avoidance and Distress Scale [*Psychology*] .... SADS
Social Avoidance Distress [*Scale*] .... SAD
Social Behavior Assessment [*Social skills test*] .... SBA
Social Behavior Rating Scale .... SBRS
Social Behavior Standards .... SBS
Social Biology Films [*National Science Foundation project*] .... SB
Social Care Association [*British*] (DBA) .... SCA
Social Change Media [*Australia*] .... SCM
Social Competence Intervention Package for Preschool Youngsters (EDAC) .... SCIPPY
Social Competence Inventory for Adults [*Psychology*] .... SCIA
Social Competence Inventory for Older Persons [*Psychology*] .... SCIOP
Social Competence Scale .... SCS
Social Credit Group [*British*] (DAS) .... SCG
Social Credit Party [*British*] .... SC
Social Credit Party (NADA) .... SCP
Social Credit Party [*British*] .... SOCRED
Social Credit Party of Canada [*Parti Credit Social du Canada*] (PPW) .... SCP
Social Data Exchange Association [*Council for Community Services*] [*Information service or system*] (IID) .... SODEX
Social Democracy Popularist Party [*Turkey Political party*] .... SDPP
Social Democrat Party and Liberal [*British*] .... SODPAL
Social Democratic Alliance [*British*] .... SDA
Social Democratic Alliance of Macedonia [*Political party*] (EY) .... SDAM
Social Democratic and Labour Party [*Northern Ireland*] [*Political party*] (PPW) .... SDLP
Social Democratic and Liberal Party [*British Political party*] .... SDLP
Social Democratic Federation [*Later, SDP*] [*Early British political party, members of which were sometimes referred to as "Silly Damn Fools"*] .... SDF
Social Democratic Federation [*Japan Political party*] (PPW) .... SDF
Social Democratic Federation [*Iceland*] [*Political party*] (PPW) .... SDF
Social Democratic Front [*Ghana*] [*Political party*] (PPW) .... SDF
Social Democratic Front [*Cameroon*] [*Political party*] (EY) .... SDF
Social Democratic Party [*Germany*] .... SD
Social Democratic Party [*Hungary*] [*Political party*] .... SDP
Social Democratic Party [*Nigeria*] [*Political party*] .... SDP
Social Democratic Party [*Albania*] [*Political party*] (EY) .... SDP
Social Democratic Party [*Philippines*] [*Political party*] (PPW) .... SDP
Social Democratic Party [*Thailand*] [*Political party*] (PPW) .... SDP
Social Democratic Party [*Germany Political party*] .... SDP
Social Democratic Party [*Trinidad and Tobago*] [*Political party*] (PPW) .... SDP
Social Democratic Party [*British Political party*] .... SDP
Social Democratic Party [*Australia Political party*] .... SDP
Social Democratic Party [*Iceland*] [*Political party*] (PPW) .... SDP
Social Democratic Party [*Turkey Political party*] (PPW) .... Sodep
Social Democratic Party [*Germany*] [*Political party*] .... SPD
Social Democratic Party of Canada .... SDPC
Social Democratic Party of Croatia [*Political party*] .... SDPC
Social Democratic Party of Hungary [*Political party*] (EAIO) .... SDPH
Social Democratic Party of Japan [*Political party*] (EAIO) .... SDPJ
Social Democratic Party of Slovenia [*Political party*] (EY) .... SDPS
Social Democratic Party - Party of Democratic Reform [*Croatia*] [*Political party*] .... SDP-PDR
Social Democrats, USA (EA) .... SDUSA
Social Desirability Scale (EDAC) .... SDS
Social Development Division Library, Social Planning Department, City of Halifax, Nova Scotia [*Library symbol National Library of Canada*] (NLC) .... NSHSP
Social Development Program for Poor Areas [*UNICEF*] (ECON) .... SPPA
Social Economic and Political Studies of the Middle East [*A publication*] (BJA) .... SEPSME
Social Economic Council [*Sociaal Economische Raad*] [*Netherlands*] .... SEC
Social Economisch Wetgeving. Tijdschrift voor Europees en Economisch Recht [*A publication*] (DLA) .... Soc Econ Wetgeving
Social Education [*A publication*] (BRI) .... SE
Social Education Centre (AIE) .... SEC
Social Emotional .... SE
Social England Series [*A publication*] .... SENS
Social Forces [*A publication*] (BRI) .... SF
Social Function Index [*Medicine*] (DMAA) .... SFI
Social/Health Maintenance Organization [*Department of Health and Human Services*] .... SHMO
Social History .... SH
Social History (DAVI) .... SHx
Social History Curators Group [*British*] (DBA) .... SHCG
Social History Society of the United Kingdom .... SHS
Social Implications of Computers (IAA) .... SIC
Social Independiente [*Netherlands Antilles*] [*Political party*] (EY) .... SI
Social Information System [*Medicine*] (DMAA) .... SIS
Social Insurance Number [*Canada*] .... SIN
Social Intelligence Quotient [*In book title*] .... SIQ
Social Intelligence Test [*Psychology*] .... SIT
Social Interaction and Creativity in Communication System [*Educational test*] .... SICCS
Social Interaction Code .... SIC
Social Investment Forum (EA) .... SIF
Social Issues Research Associates (EA) .... SIRA
Social Issues Resources Series [*A publication*] .... SIRS
Social Justice Consultative Council [*Victoria, Australia*] .... SJCC
Social Law Library, Boston, MA [*Library symbol Library of Congress*] (LCLS) .... MBS
Social Legislation Information Service (EA) .... SLIS
Social Mapping Matrix Assessment (EDAC) .... SMMA
Social Marginal Productivity .... SMP
Social Marketing International Association [*Queretaro, Mexico*] [*Defunct*] (EAIO) .... SMIA
Social Maturity Age .... SMA
Social Maturity Quotient .... SMQ
Social Meaning of Legal Concepts [*A publication*] (ILCA) .... Soc Mean Leg Con
Social, Military, Ethnic, Religious, and Fraternal Groups [*Market segment*] .... SMERF
Social Organisation Limited .... SOL
Social Planning and Research Council of British Columbia, Vancouver [*Library symbol National Library of Canada*] (BIB) .... BVASP
Social Planning Around Neighbourhoods [*Australia*] .... SPAN
Social Planning Council of Winnipeg, Manitoba [*Library symbol National Library of Canada*] (NLC) .... MWSPC
Social Planning Council of Winnipeg, Winnipeg, MB, Canada [*Library symbol Library of Congress*] (LCLS) .... CaMWSPC
Social Planning, Policy & Development Abstracts [*Sociological Abstracts, Inc.*] [*Database*] .... SOPODA
Social Policy and Administration Network [*A publication*] .... SPAN
Social Policy Research Group, Inc. [*Information service or system*] (IID) .... SPRG
Social Problems Research Institute [*University of South Carolina at Columbia*] [*Research center*] (RCD) .... SPRI
Social Problems Series [*A publication*] .... SPS
Social Problem-Solving Test (EDAC) .... SPST
Social Process Research Institute [*Research center*] (RCD) .... SPRI
Social Progress Trust Fund [*Inter-American Development Bank*] .... SPTF
Social Psychiatry Research Institute (EA) .... SPRI
Social Questions of Today [*A publication*] .... SQD
Social Quotient [*Psychology*] .... SQ
Social Readjustment Rating Scale [*Psychometrics*] .... SRRS
Social Register .... SR
Social Rehabilitation Center [*Psychology*] (DAVI) .... SRC

Social Rehabilitation Clinic (EA) .... SRC
Social Relations Test [Psychology] .... SRT
Social Research and Applications [Research center] (RCD) .... SRA
Social Research Association [British] .... SRA
Social Research Group [George Washington University] [Research center] (RCD) .... SRG
Social Research Institute [University of Utah] [Research center] (RCD) .... SRI
Social Responsibilities Round Table [American Library Association] (EA) .... SRRT
Social Responsibility Auditing (ADA) .... SRA
Social Revolutionary Anarchist Federation (EA) .... SRAF
Social Science (DD) .... SocSc
Social Science .... SS
Social Science Citation Index Search [Database] .... SOCIAL SCISEARCH
Social Science Computer Research Institute [University of Pittsburgh] [Pennsylvania] [Information service or system] (IID) .... SSCRI
Social Science Computer Review [A publication] (BRI) .... SocSciComR
Social Science Computing Laboratory [University of Western Ontario] [Information service or system] (IID) .... SSCL
Social Science Data Archive [University of Iowa] [Iowa City] [Information service or system] (IID) .... SSDA
Social Science Data Archive [Carleton University] [Canada Information service or system] (IID) .... SSDA
Social Science Data Center [University of Connecticut] [Research center] (IID) .... SSDC
Social Science Data Center [University of Pennsylvania] [Philadelphia] [Information service or system] (IID) .... SSDC
Social Science Data Library [University of North Carolina] [Chapel Hill] [Information service or system] (IID) .... SSDL
Social Science Documentation Centre [UNESCO] (IID) .... SSDC
Social Science Documentation Centre [Indian Council of Social Science Research] [Information service or system] (IID) .... SSDC
Social Science Education Consortium (EA) .... SSEC
Social Science Federation of Canada [Research center] (IRC) .... SSFC
Social Science Institute [Washington University] [Research center] (RCD) .... SSI
Social Science Quarterly [A publication] (BRI) .... SSQ
Social Science Research Center [Mississippi State University] [Research center] (RCD) .... SSRC
Social Science Research Council (EA) .... SSRC
Social Science Research Facilities Center [University of Minnesota] [Research center] (RCD) .... SSRFC
Social Science Research Institute [University of Maine at Orono] [Research center] (RCD) .... SSRI
Social Science Research Institute [of CRESS] [University of Hawaii at Manoa] [Research center] (RDA) .... SSRI
Social Science Series [A publication] .... SSS
Social Sciences and Humanities Research Council of Canada [UTLAS symbol] .... SSH
Social Sciences and Humanities Research Council of Canada .... SSHRC
Social Sciences and Humanities Research Council of Canada [Pronounced "sherk"] [See also CRSHC] .... SSHRCC
Social Sciences and Humanities Research Council of Canada [Conseil de Recherches en Sciences Humaines du Canada] Ottawa, Ontario [Library symbol National Library of Canada] (NLC) .... OOSSHRC
Social Sciences Center [University of Nevada] [Research center] (RCD) .... SSC
Social Sciences Information Utilization Laboratory .... SSIUL
Social Sciences Research Council of Canada [See also CCRSS] [Later, SSHRCC] .... SSRCC
Social Sciences Services and Resources (EA) .... SSSR
Social Scientists Against Nuclear War (EA) .... SSNW
Social Security (DAVI) .... SocSec
Social Security .... SS
Social Security Account Number .... SSAN
Social Security Acquisition Regulation [A publication] (AAGC) .... SSAR
Social Security Act [1935] [Also, SSACT] .... SSA
Social Security Act [1935] [Also, SSA] .... SSACT
Social Security Acts Amendments [A publication] (DLA) .... SSAA
Social Security Administration [Department of Health and Human Services] .... SSA
Social Security Administration Data Acquisition and Response System .... SSADARS
Social Security Administration Library, Baltimore, MD [OCLC symbol] (OCLC) .... SSL
Social Security Advisory Committee [British] .... SSAC
Social Security Advisory Council [Australia] .... SSAC
Social Security Bank [Ghana] (EY) .... SSB
Social Security Benefit Protection Service (EA) .... SSBPS
Social Security Board [Abolished, 1946] .... SSB
Social Security Disability .... SSD
Social Security Disability Income (DAVI) .... SSDI
Social Security Disability Insurance .... SSDI
Social Security Income (DAVI) .... SSI
Social Security Information .... SSI
Social Security Information System [ILO] [United Nations] (DUND) .... SSIS
Social Security Journal [A publication] .... Soc Sec J
Social Security Number [Followed by numerals] (DAVI) .... SS
Social Security Number (AABC) .... SSN
Social Security Number Check .... SSNCHK
Social Security Number Key Index File [IRS] .... SKIF
Social Security Pensions Act [1975] [British] (DCTA) .... SSPA
Social Security Quarterly [A publication] .... Soc Sec Q
Social Security Tax Ruling [Internal Revenue Bulletin] [A publication] (DLA) .... SST
Social Security Taxes (Prentice-Hall, Inc.) [A publication] (DLA) .... P-H Soc Sec Taxes
Social Self-Defense Committee [Also, SSDC] [Poland] (PD) .... KOR
Social Service .... SS

Social Service Commission of the American Ethical Union (EA) .... SSCAEU
Social Service Department, Prince Albert, Saskatchewan [Library symbol National Library of Canada] (NLC) .... SPAS
Social Service Department, Prince Albert, SK, Canada [Library symbol Library of Congress] (LCLS) .... CaSPAS
Social Service Handbooks [A publication] .... SSH
Social Service Reporting Requirements [HEW] .... SSRR
Social Service Review [A publication] (BRI) .... Soc Ser R
Social Services Block Grant [Department of Health and Human Services] .... SSBG
Social Services Review [A publication] .... Soc Services Rev
Social Shopper .... SS
Social Status Study [Psychology] .... SSS
Social Studies [A publication] (BRI) .... SS
Social Studies Priorities, Practices, and Needs (EDAC) .... SPAN
Social Studies/Social Science Education [Educational Resources Information Center (ERIC) Clearinghouse] [Indiana University] (PAZ) .... SO
Social Surveys .... SS
Social Systems and Human Resources [National Science Foundation] (MCD) .... SSHR
Social Systems Research Center [California State University, Dominguez Hills] [Research center] (RCD) .... SSRC
Social Systems Research Institute [University of Wisconsin - Madison] [Research center] (RCD) .... SSRI
Social Welfare History Archives Center [University of Minnesota] [Research center] (RCD) .... SWHA
Social Welfare History Group [Western Michigan University] [Kalamazoo] (EA) .... SWHG
Social Work [A publication] (BRI) .... Soc W
Social Work [or Worker] .... SW
Social Work Case Manager (DMAA) .... SWCM
Social Work Vocational Bureau (EA) .... SWVB
Social Workers for Nuclear Disarmament (EA) .... SWND
Social World Service (DAVI) .... SWS
Social-Breakdown Syndrome (MAE) .... SBS
Social-Democrat Party [Zambia] [Political party] (EY) .... SDP
Social-Democratic Association [Political party] (EAIO) .... SDA
Social-Democratic Party of Finland .... SDPF
Socialdemokratiet i Danmark [Social Democratic Party of Denmark] [Political party] (PPE) .... SD
Social-Emotional Dimension Scale [Behavior problems test] .... SEDS
Socialism: Theory and Practice [A publication] .... STP
Socialist .... S
Socialist (EY) .... SOC
Socialist (ODBW) .... Soc
Socialist Action [An association] (EA) .... SA
Socialist Alliance of the Working People [Serbia] [Political party] .... SAWP
Socialist Alliance of the Working People of Yugoslavia [Political party] (EY) .... SAWPY
Socialist Alliance - Socialist Party of Macedonia [Political party] (EY) .... SA-SPM
Socialist and Democratic People's Union [Mauritania] [Political party] (EY) .... SDPU
Socialist and Revolutionary Labour Party [Gambia] [Political party] (PD) .... SRLP
Socialist Democratic Party [South Korea Political party] (EY) .... SDP
Socialist Educational Association [British] .... SEA
Socialist Electoral League [Norway] (PPW) .... SEL
Socialist Federal Republic of Yugoslavia .... SFRY
Socialist Group [EC] (ECED) .... S
Socialist Group in the European Parliament [See also GSPE] (EAIO) .... SGEP
Socialist Health Association [British] (DBA) .... SHA
Socialist International [Political party] (EAIO) .... SI
Socialist International Research Council [British] .... SIRC
Socialist International Women (EA) .... SIW
Socialist Janata Party [India] [Political party] (ECON) .... SJP
Socialist Labor Party [Egypt] [Political party] (PPW) .... SLP
Socialist Labor Party of America [Political party] (EA) .... SLP
Socialist Labor Party of Turkey [Turkiye Sosyalist Isci Partisi] [Political party] (PPW) .... SLPT
Socialist Labour Party of Canada .... SLPC
Socialist Medical Association [British] .... SMA
Socialist Movement for the United States of Europe .... SMUSE
Socialist Objectives Committee [Australian Labor Party] .... SOC
Socialist Party .... SP
Socialist Party of Albania [Political party] (EY) .... SPA
Socialist Party of Australia [Political party] .... SPA
Socialist Party of Canada [Political party] .... SPC
Socialist Party of Chile [Political party] .... SPC
Socialist Party of Croatia [Political party] (EY) .... SPC
Socialist Party of Cyprus [Political party] (EAIO) .... SPC
Socialist Party of Great Britain (PPW) .... SPGB
Socialist Party of Japan [Nikon Shakaito] [Political party] (PPW) .... SPJ
Socialist Party of Kurdistan [Iraq] [Political party] (MENA) .... SPK
Socialist Party of New Zealand [Political party] (PPW) .... SPNZ
Socialist Party of San Marino [Political party] (EAIO) .... SPSM
Socialist Party of Slovenia [Political party] (EY) .... SPS
Socialist Party of Sri Lanka .... SPSL
Socialist Party of Thailand [Political party] (FEA) .... SPT
Socialist Party of the United States of America (EA) .... SP-USA
Socialist Party - Social Democratic Federation [Later, Socialist Party of the United States of America] (EA) .... SP-SDF
Socialist People's Libyan Arab Jamahiriya [Gathering of the masses] [Muammar Qaddafi's name for his country] .... Splaj
Socialist Republic of Romania .... SRR
Socialist Republic of Vietnam .... SRV
Socialist Revolution Party [Turkey Political party] (PPW) .... SRP
Socialist Revolutionary [Former USSR] .... SR

Socialist Revolutionary Party [India] [Political party] (PPW) .... SRP
Socialist Revolutionary Party [Former USSR Political party] .... SRP
Socialist Scholars Conference (EA) .... SSC
Socialist Union of Central and Eastern Europe (PD) .... SUCEE
Socialist Unionist Movement [Al Haraka at Tawhidiyya al Ishtirakiyya] [Syria]
[Political party] (PPW) .... SUM
Socialist Unity Center of India [Political party] (PPW) .... SUCI
Socialist Unity Front [Romania] [Political party] (PPW) .... SUF
Socialist Unity Party of New Zealand .... SUPNZ
Socialist Unity Party of West Berlin [Germany] .... SUPWB
Socialist Workers' Party [British Political party] (PPW) .... SWP
Socialisticka Radnicka Partija Jugoslavije [Socialist Workers' Party of
Yugoslavia] [Political party] (PPE) .... SRP
Socialistische Arbeiderspartij [Socialist Workers' Party] [Netherlands Political
party] (PPW) .... SAP
Socialistische Partij [Socialist Party] [Belgium Political party] (PPW) .... SP
Socialistische Partij Suriname [Surinam Socialist Party] [Political party]
(PPW) .... SPS
Socialization and Handling [Pet-adoption terminolgy] .... S/H
Socially Acceptable Monitoring Instrument (BABM) .... SAMI
Socially Acceptable Monitoring Instruments [Medicine] .... SAMI
Socially and Ecologically Responsible Geographers [Defunct] (EA) .... SERGE
Socially Concerned Upwardly Mobile Professional [Lifestyle
classification] .... SCRUMPie
Socially Housed [Experimental animals] .... SH
Socially Maladjusted .... SM
Socially-Appropriate Technology (PDAA) .... SAT
Socially-Oriented Comprehensive Memory-Assist Computer (IIA) .... SOCMAC
Social-Services Department [British] .... SSD
Socicated Unilamellar Vesicles .... SUV
Sociedad Aerea del Caqueta [Airline] [Colorado] .... SADELCA
Sociedad Aerea del Caqueta Ltd. [Colombia] [ICAO designator] (FAAC) .... SDK
Sociedad Aeronautica de Medellin [Colombia] [ICAO designator] (FAAC) .... SAM
Sociedad Aeronautica de Medellin Consolidada [Colorado] .... SAM
Sociedad Aeronautica Medellin [ICAO designator] (AD) .... MM
Sociedad Anglo-Chilena [Anglo-Chilean Society] (EAIO) .... SAC
Sociedad Astronomica de Espana y America [Hispano-American
Astronomical Society] (EAIO) .... SADEYA
Sociedad Centroamericana de Farmacologia [Central American Society of
Pharmacology - CASP] (EAIO) .... SCF
Sociedad Chilena de Quimca .... SCQ
Sociedad Colombiana de Transporte Ferroviario SA [Public rail services]
(EY) .... STF
Sociedad de Amistad Mexico Albania [Mexico-Albania Friendship Society]
(EAIO) .... SAMA
Sociedad Ecuatoriana de Transportes Aereos Ltda. [Ecuador] [ICAO
designator] (FAAC) .... SET
Sociedad en Comandita [Limited partnership company] [Spanish] .... S en C
Sociedad Espanol de Automoviles de Turismo [Spanish automobile
manufacturer; acronym used as name of its cars] .... SEAT
Sociedad Espanola de Documentacion e Informacion Cientifica [Spanish
Society for Documentation and Information Sciences] [Information service or
system] (IID) .... SEDIC
Sociedad Espanola de Radiodifusion [Broadcasting organization] .... SER
Sociedad Hispano-Francesa de Energia Nuclear SA [Nuclear energy
Spanish] (NRCH) .... HIFRENSA
Sociedad Honoraria Hispanica (EA) .... SHH
Sociedad Iberoamericana de Biologia Celular [Ibero-American Society for
Cell Biology - IASCB] (EAIO) .... SIABC
Sociedad Iberoamericana de Filosofia [Spain] (EAIO) .... SIF
Sociedad Interamericana de Desarrollo de Financiamiento Cooperativo
[Inter-American Society for the Development of Cooperative Financing]
[Buenos Aires, Argentina] (EAIO) .... SIDEFCOOP
Sociedad Interamericana de Planeficacion [Inter-American Planning Society]
[Mexico] .... SIAP
Sociedad Interamericana de Prensa [Inter-American Press Association] .... SIP
Sociedad Interamericana de Psicologia [Interamerican Society of
Psychology] (EAIO) .... SIP
Sociedad Internacional de Ingenieros Forestales Tropicales [International
Society of Tropical Foresters] (EAIO) .... SIIFT
Sociedad Latinoamericana de Estudios sobre America Latina y el Caribe
[Mexico] (EAIO) .... SOLAR
Sociedad Mexicana de Computacion Electronica [Mexico] .... SMCE
Sociedad Mixta Siderurgia Argentina [Steel producer in Argentina] .... SOMISA
Sociedad Panamericana de Quimioterapia de la Tuberculosis [Pan
American Society for Chemotherapy of Tuberculosis - PASCT] (EA) .... SAQT
Sociedad Quimica [Associated Press] (SAG) .... SocQuim
Sociedad Quimica y Minera [NYSE symbol] (SPSG) .... SQM
Sociedad Quimica Y Minera ADS [NYSE symbol] (TTSB) .... SQM
Sociedade Acoriana de Transportes Aereos Ltda. [Airline] [Portugal] .... SATA
Sociedade Brasileira de Discos Historicos J. Leon [Record label]
[Brazil] .... SBDH
Sociedade Brasileira de Turismo (ROTATUR) [Brazil] [ICAO designator]
(FAAC) .... RTR
Sociedade Internacional de Trilogia Analitica [International Society of
Analytical Trilogy - ISAT] [Sao Paulo, Brazil] (EAIO) .... SITA
Sociedade Latinoamericana de Hepatologia [Latin American Society of
Hepatology - LASH] (EAIO) .... SLH
Sociedade Portuguesa de Helicopteros Lda. [Portugal] [FAA designator]
(FAAC) .... SPH
Sociedades Biblicas Unidas [United Bible Societies] [British] (EAIO) .... SBU
Societa' Adriatica [Italy ICAO designator] (FAAC) .... ADH
Societa Aero Trasporti Italiani SpA [Italy ICAO designator] (ICDA) .... BM
Societa' Aerotaxi SUD [Italy ICAO designator] (FAAC) .... SGT
Societa Agricola Italo-Somala [Italo-Somali Agricultural Society] .... SAIS

Societa Altair [Italy ICAO designator] (ICDA) .... SM
Societa Anonima [Stock company] [Italian] .... S/A
Societa Anonima Italiana [Stock company] [Italian] .... SAI
Societa Anonima Navigazione Aerea [Italy] .... SANA
Societa Anonima Transadriatica [Italy] .... SAT
Societa' Besit SRL [Italy] [FAA designator] (FAAC) .... BST
Societa Ceirano Automobili Torino [Early Italian auto manufacturer] .... SCAT
Societa Dante Alighieri, Universite Laval, Quebec, Quebec [Library symbol
National Library of Canada] (NLC) .... QQLAI
Societa di Intermediazione Mobiliare [Finance Italy] (ECON) .... SIM
Societa di San Patrizio per le Missioni Estere [St. Patrick's Society for the
Foreign Missions - SPSFM] [Kiltegan, County Wicklow, Republic of
Ireland] (EAIO) .... SSPME
Societa Editrice Internazionale [Italy] [Publisher] .... SEI
Societa in Accomandita per Azioni [Limited Partnership with Shares]
[Italian] (IMH) .... SapA
Societa Incremento Turismo Aereo [Italy] .... SITAR
Societa Internazionale de Psicologia della Scrittura [International Society of
Psychology of Handwriting - ISPH] (EAIO) .... SIPS
Societa Internazionale Scotista [International Scotist Society - ISS] (EAIO) .... SIS
Societa Italiana della Union Chimique Belge [Italy] .... SIUCB
Societa Italiana di Agopuntura [Italy] .... SIA
Societa Italiana di Farmacia Ospedaliera [Italy] .... SIFO
Societa Italiana di Medicina Psicosomatica [Italy] .... SIMP
Societa Italiana di Metapsichica [Italy] .... SIM
Societa Italiana per l'Esercizio Telefonico [Italian Society for Telephone Use]
[Information service or system] (IID) .... SIP
Societa Italiana Pubblicita Per Azioni [Italian radio and television advertising
company] .... SIPRA
Societa Italiana Resine [Italy] .... SIR
Societa' Italjet [Italy ICAO designator] (FAAC) .... ITJ
Societa Nazionale di Informatica delle Camere di Commerces Italiane
[National Information Company of Italian Chambers of Commerce]
[Information service or system] (IID) .... CERVED
Societa Prodotti Antibiotici [Italy] [Research code symbol] .... SPA-S
Societa Ricerche Impianti Nucleari [Italy] .... SORIN
Societa Servizi Trasporti [Italy] [FAA designator] (FAAC) .... STI
Societa' Siba Aviation [Italy ICAO designator] (FAAC) .... SIB
Societa' Tea Italia [Italy ICAO designator] (FAAC) .... TEI
Societal Institute of the Mathematical Sciences [Research center] (RCD) .... SIMS
Societas [Society] [Latin] .... S
Societas Adunationis [Franciscan Friars or Sisters of the Atonement] [Roman
Catholic religious order] .... SA
Societas Docta (EA) .... SD
Societas Ergophthalmologica Internationalis [International
Ergophthalmological Society] [Stockholm, Sweden] (EAIO) .... SEI
Societas Fratrum Sacris Cordis [Brothers of the Sacred Heart] [Roman
Catholic religious order] .... SC
Societas Internationalis Limnologiae Theoreticae et Applicae [International
Association of Theoretical and Applied Limnology] .... SIL
Societas Internationalis Medicinae Generalis [International Society of General
Practice] [Klagenfurt, Austria] (EAIO) .... SIMG
Societas Jesu [Society of Jesus] [Jesuits] [Roman Catholic men's religious
order] .... SJ
Societas Linguistica Europaea [Linguistic Society of Europe] [Austria]
(EAIO) .... SLE
Societas Liturgica (EA) .... SL
Societas Mariae [Congregation of Mary] [Marists] [Roman Catholic religious
order] .... SM
Societas Mariae Montfortana [Missionaries of the Company of Mary] [Montfort
Fathers] [Roman Catholic religious order] .... SMM
Societas Parisiensis Missionum ad Exteros [Paris Foreign Missions Society]
[Roman Catholic men's religious order] .... MEP
Societas Patrum Misericordiae [Fathers of Mercy] [Roman Catholic religious
order] .... SPM
Societas Rosicruciana [Freemasonry] .... SOC ROS
Societas Sanctae Crucis [Society of the Holy Cross] [Latin] .... SSC
Societas Sancti Joseph Sanctissimi Cordis [St. Joseph's Society of the
Sacred Heart] [Josephites] [Roman Catholic men's religious order] .... SSJ
Societas Sanctissimi Sacramenti [Congregation of the Blessed Sacrament]
[Roman Catholic men's religious order] .... SSS
Societas Verbi Divini [Society of the Divine Word] [Roman Catholic men's
religious order] .... SVD
Societatis Antiquariorum Socius [Fellow of the Society of Antiquaries]
[British] .... SAS
Societatis Historiae Socius [Fellow of the Historical Society] [Latin] .... SHS
Societatis Philosophicae Americanae Socius [Member of the American
Philosophical Society] [Latin] .... SPAS
Societatis Regiae Socius [or Sodalis] [Fellow of the Royal Society] [Latin]
(GPO) .... SRS
Societe [Company] [French Business term] .... Ste
Societe 3S Aviation (Aerope) [France ICAO designator] (FAAC) .... OPE
Societe a Responsabilite Limitee [Private Limited Company] [French] .... SARL
Societe Aerienne de Transport Guyane Antilles [French Guiana Air
Transport] .... SATGA
Societe Aeronautique Jurassienne [ICAO designator] (AD) .... YX
Societe Africaine de Culture [Society of African Culture] .... SAC
Societe Air Bretagne Service [France ICAO designator] .... ABH
Societe Americaine pour l'Etude de la Numismatique Francaise (EA) .... SAPENF
Societe Anonyme [French] (WDMC) .... SA
Societe Anonyme Belge d'Exploitation de la Navigation Aerienne [Sabena
Belgian World Airlines] .... SAB
Societe Anonyme Belge d'Exploitation de la Navigation Aerienne [Belgian
World Airlines] [Facetious translation: Such a Bad Experience, Never
Again] .... SABENA

Societe Anonyme de Transports Aeriens Air-Guadeloupe [*France ICAO designator*] (FAAC) ...... AGU
Societe Auxiliare et Miniere du Pacifique [*France*] (PDAA) ...... SAMIPAC
Societe Belge de Transports Pan Air [*Airline*] [*Belgium*] ...... SOBELAIR
Societe Beneluxienne de Phlebologie [*Benelux Phlebology Society - BPS*] (EA) ...... SBP
Societe Beninoise pour la Promotion du Tourisme (EY) ...... SBPT
Societe Bibliographique du Canada (AC) ...... SBC
Societe Burundaise de Financement [*Development bank*] (EY) ...... SBF
Societe Camerounaise de Tourisme (EY) ...... SOCATOUR
Societe Canadienne d'Astronomie ...... SCA
Societe Canadienne de Cardiologie [*Canadian Cardiovascular Society*] (EAIO) ...... SCC
Societe Canadienne de Criminologie ...... SCC
Societe Canadienne de Droit Canonique (AC) ...... SCDC
Societe Canadienne de Genie Civil ...... SCGC
Societe Canadienne de Genie Electrique ...... SCGE
Societe Canadienne de Genie Electrique et Informatique [*Canadian Society for Electrical and Computer Engineering*] [*Canada*] (EAIO) ...... SCGEI
Societe Canadienne de Genie Mecanique ...... SCGM
Societe Canadienne de Genie Medical et Biologique ...... SCGMB
Societe Canadienne de Geotechnique [*Canadian Geotechnical Society*] (EAIO) ...... SCG
Societe Canadienne de la Population [*Canadian Population Society - CPS*] .... SCP
Societe Canadienne de la Recherche Operationnelle ...... SCRO
Societe Canadienne de la Surete Industrielle ...... SCSI
Societe Canadienne de l'Heritage Industriel (AC) ...... SCIH
Societe Canadienne de l'Histoire de l'Eglise [*Canadian Society of Church History - CSCH*] ...... SCHE
Societe Canadienne de l'Histoire de l'Eglise Catholique [*Canadian Catholic History Association - CCHA*] ...... SCHEC
Societe Canadienne de l'Histoire Juive [*Canadian Jewish Historical Association - CJHS*] ...... SCHJ
Societe Canadienne de Meteorologie et d'Oceanographie [*Canadian Meteorological and Oceanographic Society - CMOS*] ...... SCMO
Societe Canadienne de Musique Folklorique ...... SCMF
Societe Canadienne de Pedatrie [*Canadian Paediatric Society*] (EAIO) ...... SCP
Societe Canadienne de Peintres en Aquarelle (AC) ...... SCPA
Societe Canadienne de Physiologie de l'Exercice [*Formerly, Canadian Association of Sport Sciences*] (AC) ...... SCPE
Societe Canadienne de Physiologie Vegetale (AC) ...... SCPV
Societe Canadienne de Recherche en Geriatrie ...... SCRG
Societe Canadienne de Theologie [*Canadian Theological Society - CTS*] ...... SCT
Societe Canadienne d'Economie Rurale et Gestion Agricole [*Canadian Agricultural Economics and Farm Management Society - CAEFMS*] ...... SCERGA
Societe Canadienne d'Education Comparee et Internationale (EAIO) ...... SCECI
Societe Canadienne d'Education par l'Art (AC) ...... SCEA
Societe Canadienne d'Enseignement Postscolaire ...... SCEP
Societe Canadienne des Anesthesistes [*Canadian Anaesthetists' Society*] (EAIO) ...... SCA
Societe Canadienne des Brevets et d'Exploitation ...... SCBE
Societe Canadienne des Directeurs d'Association [*Formerly, Institute of Canadian Trade Association Executives*] (AC) ...... SCDA
Societe Canadienne des Eleveurs de Chevres ...... SCEC
Societe Canadienne des Etudes Bibliques [*Canadian Society of Biblical Studies - CSBS*] ...... SCEB
Societe Canadienne des Etudes Classiques [*Classical Association of Canada - CAC*] ...... SCEC
Societe Canadienne des Infirmieres en Sante Respiratoire (AC) ...... SCISR
Societe Canadienne des Microbiologistes [*Canadian Society of Microbiologists*] (EAIO) ...... SCM
Societe Canadienne des Pharmaciens d'Hopitaux [*Canadian Society of Hospital Pharmacists*] (EAIO) ...... SCPH
Societe Canadienne des Relations Publiques ...... SCRP
Societe Canadienne des Technologistes de Laboratoire [*Canadian Society of Laboratory Technologists*] (EAIO) ...... SCTL
Societe Canadienne des Technologistes en Orthopedie [*Canadian Society of Orthopaedic Technologists*] (EAIO) ...... SCTO
[*La*] Societe Canadienne des Therapeutes Respiratoires (AC) ...... SCTR
Societe Canadienne d'Esthetique [*Canadian Society for Aesthetics - CSAC*] ...... SCE
Societe Canadienne d'Etude du Dix-Huitieme Siecle (AC) ...... SCEDS
Societe Canadienne d'Etudes de la Renaissance [*Canadian Society for Renaissance Studies - CSRS*] ...... SCER
Societe Canadienne d'Etudes Ethniques (AC) ...... SCEE
Societe Canadienne d'Hermeneutique [*Canadian Society for Hermeneutics - CSH*] ...... SCH
Societe Canadienne d'Histoire de la Medecine [*Canadian Society for the History of Medicine - CSHM*] ...... SCHM
Societe Canadienne d'Histoire de la Rhetorique [*See also CSHR*] [*Canada*] ...... SCHR
Societe Canadienne d'Histoire et de Philosophie des Mathematiques [*Canadian Society for the History and Philosophy of Mathematics - CSHPM*] ...... SCHPM
Societe Canadienne d'Histoire et de Philosophie des Sciences [*Canadian Society for the History and Philosophy of Science - CSHPS*] ...... SCHPS
Societe Canadienne d'Histoire Orale [*Canadian Oral History Association - COHA*] ...... SCHO
Societe Canadienne d'Hypotheques et de Logement [*Central Mortgage and Housing Corp. - CMHC*] ...... SCHL
Societe Canadienne d'Ingenierie Hospitaliere ...... SCIH
Societe Canadienne d'Onomastique (AC) ...... SCO
Societe Canadienne d'Orientation et de Consultation ...... SCOC
Societe Canadienne du Genie Chimique ...... SCGCh
Societe Canadienne du Genie Rural ...... SCGR

Societe Canadienne du Sida (AC) ...... SCS
Societe Canadienne du Sommeil (AC) ...... SCS
Societe Canadienne pour Etudes d'Intelligence par Ordinateur (EY) ...... SCEIO
Societe Canadienne pour la Couleur dans les Arts, l'Industrie et la Science (EAIO) ...... SCCAIC
Societe Canadienne pour la Prevention de Cruaute aux Enfants ...... SCPCE
Societe Canadienne pour l'Analyse de Documents [*Indexing and Abstracting Society of Canada*] ...... SCAD
Societe Canadienne pour les Etudes Italiennes [*Canadian Society for Italian Studies - CSIS*] ...... SCEI
Societe Canadienne pour l'Etude Comparee des Civilisations [*Canadian Society for the Comparative Study of Civilizations - CSCSC*] ...... SCECC
Societe Canadienne pour l'Etude de la Religion [*Canadian Society for the Study of Religion - CSSR*] ...... SCER
Societe Canadienne pour l'Etude de l'Education [*Canadian Society for the Study of Education - CSSE*] ...... SCEE
Societe Canadienne pour l'Etude de l'Enseignement Superieur [*Canadian Society for the Study of Higher Education - CSSHE*] ...... SCEES
Societe Canadienne pour l'Etude des Noms [*Canadian Society for the Study of Names - CSSN*] ...... SCEN
Societe Centrafricaine de Transport Aerien [*Central African Republic*] [*ICAO designator*] (FAAC) ...... SNS
Societe Central de l'Uranium et des Minerals et Metaux Radioactifs [*France*] ...... SCUMRA
Societe Chaleng Air [*France ICAO designator*] (FAAC) ...... CLG
Societe Chimique des Charbonnages [*France*] ...... SCC
Societe Collective de Retransmission du Canada (AC) ...... SCR
Societe Commerciale de Banque Credit Lyonnais-Cameroun (EY) ...... SCBCL-C
Societe Cooperative Oecumenique de Developpement [*Ecumenical Development Cooperative Society - EDCS*] [*Netherlands*] (EAIO) ...... SCOD
Societe Culinaire Philanthropique [*New York, NY*] (EA) ...... SCP
Societe d'Aide Technique et de Cooperation [*An independent French company*] ...... SATEC
Societe d'Amenagement de l'Outaouais, Hull, PQ, Canada [*Library symbol Library of Congress*] (LCLS) ...... CaQHSA
Societe d'Amenagement de l'Outaouais, Hull, Quebec [*Library symbol National Library of Canada*] (NLC) ...... QHSA
Societe d'Animation du Jardin et de l'Institut Botaniques [*Canada*] ...... SAJIB
Societe d'Applications Generals d'Electricite et de Mecanique [*France*] ...... SAGEM
Societe d'Applications Industrielle de la Physique ...... SAIP
Societe de Banque Occidentale [*France*] (EY) ...... SDBO
Societe de Biologie Experimentale [*Society for Experimental Biology*] (EAIO) ...... SBE
Societe de Chimie Industrielle (EA) ...... SCI
Societe de Construction des Musees du Canada ...... SCMC
Societe de Controle et d'Exploitation de Transports Auxiliaires [*France*] ...... SCETA
Societe de Cooperation pour le Developpement International, Ste.-Foy, Quebec [*Library symbol National Library of Canada*] (BIB) ...... QSFCD
Societe de Developpement de la Baie James, Montreal, PQ, Canada [*Library symbol Library of Congress*] (LCLS) ...... CaQMSDB
Societe de Developpement de la Baie James, Montreal, Quebec [*Library symbol National Library of Canada*] (NLC) ...... QMSDB
Societe de Developpement de l'Industrie Cinematographique Canadienne [*Canadian Film Development Corp. - CFDC*] ...... SDICC
Societe de Developpement de l'Industrie Touristique en Algerie (EY) ...... SODITAL
Societe de Developpement du Livre et du Periodique [*Society for the Development of Books and Periodicals*] [*Canada*] ...... SDLP
Societe de Developpement International Desjardins, Levis, Quebec [*Library symbol National Library of Canada*] (BIB) ...... QLSD
Societe de Droits d'Execution du Canada [*Performing Rights Organization of Canada - PROC*] ...... SDE
Societe de Fluoration de l'Uranium [*An international nuclear fuel company*] .... SFU
Societe de Genealogie des Cantons de l'Est, Sherbrooke, Quebec [*Library symbol National Library of Canada*] (NLC) ...... QSHERSG
Societe de Geologie Appliquee aux Gites Mineraux [*Society for Geology Applied to Mineral Deposits*] [*ICSU*] (EAIO) ...... SGA
Societe de Gestion de l'Aeroport de Libreville [*Airline*] [*Gabon*] (EY) ...... ADL
Societe de Gestion et d'Exploitation de l'Aeroport de Conakry [*Guinea*] (EY) ...... SOGEAC
Societe de Jesus, Marie et Joseph [*Society of Jesus, Mary and Joseph*] [*Netherlands*] (EAIO) ...... SJMJ
Societe de la Bourse de Valeurs Mobilieres de Bruxelles [*Stock exchange*] [*Belgium*] (EY) ...... SBVM
Societe de la Psychologie Medicale de Langue Francaise [*French-Language Society of Medical Psychology - FLSMP*] (EA) ...... SPMLF
Societe de Marie Reine d'Ecosse [*Mary Queen of Scots Society*] (EAIO) ...... SMRE
Societe de Microelectronique Industrielle de Sherbrooke, Inc. [*University of Sherbrooke*] [*Canada Research center*] (RCD) ...... SMIS INC
Societe de Micro-informatique et de Telecommunications (NITA) ...... SMT
Societe de Musique des Universites Canadiennes [*Canadian University Music Society - CUMS*] ...... SMUC
Societe de Neuro-Chirurgie de Langue Francaise [*Society of French-Speaking Neurosurgeons - SFSN*] (EAIO) ...... SNCLF
Societe de Nutrition et de Dietetique de Langue Francaise [*French-Language Society of Nutrition and Dietetics - FLSND*] [*France*] (EAIO) .... SNDLF
Societe de Perception de Droit d'Auteur du Canada (AC) ...... SPDAC
Societe de Physiotherapie Cardiorespiratoire du Canada (AC) ...... SCRPC
Societe de Protection des Infirmieres et Infirmiers du Canada (AC) ...... SPIIC
Societe de Radiodiffusion de la France d'Outre-Mer [*Society for Radio Broadcasting of Overseas France*] ...... SORAFOM
Societe de Radio-Television du Quebec, Montreal, Quebec [*Library symbol National Library of Canada*] (NLC) ...... QMRQ

Societe de Raffinage d'Uranium [*France*] .... SRU
Societe de Recherche en Orientation Humaine [*Canada*] .... SROH
Societe de Stockage et de Commercialisation des Produits Vivriers [*Development organization*] [*Burundi*] (EY) .... SOBECOV
Societe de Transports et de Tourisme [*Mali*] [*ICAO designator*] (FAAC) .... STC
Societe d'Eco-Amenagement [*Commercial firm France*] (ECON) .... SECA
Societe d'Edition et de Publications en Exlusivite .... SEPE
Societe d'Editions Medico-Pharmaceutiques [*Medical-Pharmaceutical Publishing Co.*] [*France*] [*Information service or system*] (IID) .... SEMP
Societe d'Electronique et d'Automatique [*Became part of Compagnie Internationale d'Informatique*] .... SEA
Societe Demographique Nordique [*Nordic Demographic Society - NDS*] (EAIO) .... SDN
Societe d'Energie de la Baie James, Centre de Documentation, Montreal, PQ, Canada [*Library symbol Library of Congress*] (LCLS) .... CaQMSEBJ
Societe d'Energie de la Baie James, Montreal, PQ, Canada [*Library symbol Library of Congress*] (LCLS) .... CaQMSEB
Societe d'Energie Nucleaire Franco-Belge des Ardennes [*Belgian-French power consortium*] .... SENA
Societe des Americanistes .... SAM
Societe des Amis d'Alexandre Dumas (EA) .... SAAD
Societe des Amis de l'Institut Metapsychique International [*Society of Friends of the International Metaphysical Institute*] (EAIO) .... SAIMI
Societe des Amis d'Eugene Delacroix (EAIO) .... SAED
Societe des Artistes en Arts Visuels du Quebec [*1980, founded 1966 as SAPQ, CPQ from 1978, CAPQ from 1982*] [*Canada*] (NGC) .... SAAVQ
Societe des Artistes Francais, Paris [*1880*] [*French*] (NGC) .... SAF
Societe des Artistes Professionels du Quebec, Montreal, PQ, Canada [*Library symbol Library of Congress*] (LCLS) .... CaQMSAP
Societe des Artistes Professionnels du Quebec [*1966, CPQ from 1978, SAAVQ from 1980, CAPQ from 1982*] [*Canada*] (NGC) .... SAPQ
Societe des Artistes Professionnels du Quebec, Montreal, Quebec [*Library symbol National Library of Canada*] (NLC) .... QMSAP
Societe des Arts Plastiques de la Province de Quebec, Quebec City [*1955*] [*Canada*] (NGC) .... SAP
Societe des Auteurs et Compositeurs Dramatiques [*Society of Dramatic Authors and Composers*] [*Paris, France*] (EAIO) .... SACD
Societe des Auteurs, Recherchistes, Documentalistes, et Compositeurs [*Canada*] .... SARDEC
Societe des Bains de Mer [*Monte Carlo*] .... SBM
Societe des Comptables de Direction au Canada [*Society of Management Accountants of Canada - SMAC*] .... SCDC
Societe des Comptables en Administration Industrielle du Canada .... SCAI
Societe des Ecrivains Canadiens [*Society of Canadian Writers*] .... SEC
Societe des Ecrivains Luxembourgeois de Langue Francaise .... SELF
Societe des Eleveurs de Bovins Canadiens (AC) .... SEBC
Societe des Etudes Bloyennes [*France*] (EAIO) .... SEB
Societe des Etudes Socialistes [*Society for Socialist Studies - SSS*] .... SES
Societe des Ingenieurs Civils de France .... SICF
Societe des Ingenieurs do Telecommunication [*Belgium*] .... SITEL
Societe des Missionnaires d'Afrique [*Society of Missionaries of Africa*] (EA) .... SMA
Societe des Nations [*League of Nations*] .... SDN
Societe des Participations Gardinier [*French fertilizer firm*] .... SOPAG
Societe des Petroles d'Afrique Equatoriale Francaise [*French Equatorial African Petroleum Co.*] .... SPAEF
Societe des Professeurs Francais et Francophones en Amerique (EA) .... SPFA
Societe d'Ethologie Veterinaire [*Society for Veterinary Ethology - SVE*] [*Edinburgh, Scotland*] (EAIO) .... SEV
Societe d'Etudes de Marche et d'Informatique [*Society for the Study of Marketing and Informatics*] [*Information service or system Defunct*] (IID) .... SEMI
Societe d'Etudes de Mathematiques Appliquees [*France*] .... SEMA
Societe d'Etudes et d'Expansion [*Studies and Expansion Society - SES*] [*Later, Et Ex*] (EAIO) .... SEE
Societe d'Etudes Nucleaires et de Techniques Avancees [*France*] .... SENTA
Societe d'Etudes pour le Developpement Economique et Social [*Society for the Study of Economic and Social Development*] [*Information service or system France*] (IID) .... SEDES
Societe d'Etudes pour l'Equipement Miniere, Agricole, et Industrial du Gabon [*Gabon Society for Study of Mining, Agricultural, and Industrial Equipment*] .... SEPEMIAG
Societe d'Exploitation Aeropostale [*France ICAO designator*] (FAAC) .... ARP
Societe d'Histoire de la Riviere Saint Jean, Fredericton, New Brunswick [*Library symbol National Library of Canada*] (BIB) .... NBFS
Societe d'Histoire Regionale de St.-Hyacinthe, St.-Hyacinthe, PQ, Canada [*Library symbol Library of Congress*] (LCLS) .... CaQStHHR
Societe d'Histoire Regionale de St-Hyacinthe, Quebec [*Library symbol National Library of Canada*] (NLC) .... QSTHHR
Societe du Caoutchouc Butyl [*France*] .... SOCABU
Societe en Commandite Simple [*Simple Partnership*] [*Belgium*] .... SCS
Societe et Federation Internationale de Cardiologie [*International Society and Federation of Cardiology*] [*Switzerland*] (EAIO) .... SFIC
Societe Europeene de Fabrication de Combustibles a Base d'Eranium pour Reacteursa Eau Legere [*France*] (PDAA) .... EUROFUEL
Societe Europeene de Psychiatrie de l'Enfant et de l'Adolescent [*European Society of Child and Adolescent Psychiatry - ESCAP*] (EAIO) .... SEPEA
Societe Europeene de Radiobiologie [*European Society for Radiation Biology - ESRB*] (EAIO) .... SERB
Societe Europeenne de Culture [*European Society of Culture - ESC*] (EAIO) .... SEC
Societe Europeenne de la Science et de la Technologie des Membranes [*European Society of Membrane Science and Technology - ESMST*] (EA) .... SESTM
Societe Europeenne de Materials Mobiles [*France*] (PDAA) .... SEMM
Societe Europeenne de Neuro+radiologie [*European Neuroradiological Association*] [*France*] (EAIO) .... SEN
Societe Europeenne de Neuroscience [*European Neuroscience Association - ENA*] (EA) .... SEN
Societe Europeenne de Sociologie Rurale [*European Society for Rural Sociology*] .... SESR
Societe Europeenne de Teleguidage [*Five European firms organized in 1958 under French law to act as European prime contractor for production of HAWK missiles*] [*NATO*] .... SETEL
Societe Europeenne d'Energie Atomique .... SEEA
Societe Europeenne des Jeunes de la Croix-Bleue [*European Society for Blue Cross Youth - ESBCY*] (EAIO) .... SEJCR
Societe Europeenne d'Etudes et d'Essais d'Environnement [*France*] (PDAA) .... SEEEE
Societe Europeenne d'Hematologie .... SEH
Societe Europeenne pour la Formation des Ingenieurs [*European Society for Engineering Education*] (EA) .... SEFI
Societe Europeenne pour le Traitement de l'Information [*European Society for the Processing of Information*] .... SETI
Societe Europeenne pour l'Etude et l'Integration des Systemes Spatiaux .... SETIS
Societe Europenne pour la Formation des Ingenieurs (ACII) .... SEFE
Societe Financiere Europeenne .... SFE
Societe Financiere Internationale [*International Finance Society*] .... SFI
Societe Francaise d'Acoustique [*French Society of Acoustics - FSA*] (EAIO) .... SFA
Societe Francaise de Chimie [*French Chemical Society - FCS*] (EAIO) .... SFC
Societe Francaise d'Enquetes par Sondages [*French opinion-polling organization*] .... SOFRES
Societe Francaise d'Equipements pour la Navigation Aerienne (MCD) .... SFENA
Societe Franco-Americaine de Constructions Atomiques (NRCH) .... FRAMATOME
Societe Francophone de Primatologie [*Francophone Primatological Society - FPS*] [*France*] (EAIO) .... SFDP
Societe Frederic Chopin [*International Frederic Chopin Foundation*] (EAIO) .... SFC
Societe Generale Australia .... SGA
Societe Generale de Banque [*Bank Society*] [*Information service or system*] (IID) .... SGB
Societe Generale de Banque aux Antilles [*Guadeloupe*] (EY) .... SGBA
Societe Generale pour l'Industrie, Geneve, Switzerland [*Library symbol Library of Congress*] (LCLS) .... SzGSI
Societe Generale-Komercni Banka [*Former Czechoslovakia*] (EY) .... SGKB
Societe Helitrans France [*ICAO designator*] (FAAC) .... HTF
Societe Heraldique du Canada [*Heraldry Society of Canada*] (EAIO) .... SHC
Societe Historique Acadienne [*Acadian Historical Society*] (EA) .... SHA
Societe Historique de Montreal, Montreal, PQ, Canada [*Library symbol Library of Congress*] (LCLS) .... CaQMSH
Societe Historique de Montreal, Quebec [*Library symbol National Library of Canada*] (NLC) .... QMSH
Societe Historique des Cantons de l'Est, Sherbrooke, PQ, Canada [*Library symbol Library of Congress*] (LCLS) .... CaQSherSH
Societe Historique du Canada [*Canadian Historical Association - CHA*] .... SHC
Societe Historique du Comte de Shefford, Granby, Quebec [*Library symbol National Library of Canada*] (NLC) .... QGSH
Societe Historique du Saguenay, Chicoutimi, PQ, Canada [*Library symbol Library of Congress*] (LCLS) .... CaQCSH
Societe Historique du Saguenay, Chicoutimi, Quebec [*Library symbol National Library of Canada*] (NLC) .... QCSH
Societe Historique et Folklorique Francaise [*Defunct*] (EA) .... SHFF
Societe Industrielle de Mecanique et de Carrosserie Automobile [*French automobile manufacturer; acronym used as name of its cars*] .... SIMCA
Societe Industrielle et Agriculturelle du Niari [*Industrial and Agricultural Society of Niari*] .... SIAN
Societe Intercontinental d'Assurances pour le Commerce et l'Industrie [*Intercontinental Assurance Company of Commerce and Industry*] [*France*] .... SIACI
Societe International de Telecommunications Aeronautiques [*Belgium ICAO designator*] (FAAC) .... SIT
Societe Internationale Arthurienne, [*International Arthurian Society*] **North American Branch** (EA) .... SIA
Societe Internationale d'Acupuncture [*International Society of Acupuncture*] .... SIA
Societe Internationale d'Audiologie .... AUDI
Societe Internationale de Biologie Clinique [*World Association of Anatomic and Clinical Pathology Societies*] .... SIBC
Societe Internationale de Biologie Mathematique [*International Society of Mathematical Biology*] (EAIO) .... SIBM
Societe Internationale de Biometeorologie [*International Society of Biometeorology*] (EAIO) .... SIB
Societe Internationale de Cardiologie [*International Society of Cardiology*] .... SIC
Societe Internationale de Chirurgie [*International Society of Surgery - ISS*] [*Basel, Switzerland*] (EA) .... SIC
Societe Internationale de Chirurgie Orthopedique et de Traumatologie [*International Society of Orthopaedic Surgery and Traumatology*] [*Brussels, Belgium*] (EAIO) .... SICOT
Societe Internationale de Criminologie [*International Society of Criminology*] (EA) .... SIC
Societe Internationale de Defense Sociale [*International Society for Social Defence - ISSD*] [*Paris, France*] (EAIO) .... SIDS
Societe Internationale de Droit Sociale .... SIDS
Societe Internationale de Gastro-Enterologie .... SIGE
Societe Internationale de la Lepre [*International Leprosy Association*] .... SIL
Societe Internationale de la Moselle [*International Moselle Co.*] .... SIM
Societe Internationale de la Science du Sol .... SISS
Societe Internationale de la Science Horticole [*International Society for Horticultural Science - ISHS*] (EAIO) .... SISH

Societe Internationale de Linguistique Fonctionelle [*International Society of Functional Linguistics*] (EAIO) .... SILF
Societe Internationale de Mecanique des Roches [*International Society for Rock Mechanics - ISRM*] (EAIO) .... SIMR
Societe Internationale de Mecanique des Sols et de Travaux de Fondations [*International Society for Soil Mechanics and Foundation Engineering - ISSMFE*] .... SIMSTF
Societe Internationale de Medecine Cybernetique [*International Society of Cybernetic Medicine*] .... SIMC
Societe Internationale de Medecine de Catastrophe [*International Society for Disaster Medicine - ISDM*] [*Switzerland*] (EA) .... SIMC
Societe Internationale de Musicologie [*International Musicological Society*].... SIM
Societe Internationale de Mycologie Humaine et Animale [*International Society for Human and Animal Mycology - ISHAM*] [*British*] (EA) .... SIMHA
Societe Internationale de Pathologie Geographique [*International Society of Geographical Pathology*] [*Australia*] (EAIO) .... SIPG
Societe Internationale de Psychologie des Sports [*International Society of Sports Psychology*] (EAIO) .... SIPS
Societe Internationale de Psychopathologie de l'Expression [*International Society of Art and Psychopathology*] .... SIPE
Societe Internationale de Recherche en Litterature d'Enfance et de Jeunesse [*International Research Society for Children's Literature - IRSCL*] (EA) .... SIRLEJ
Societe Internationale de Telecommunications Aeronautiques, Societe Cooperative (SITA) [*ICAO designator*] (ICDA) .... XS
Societe Internationale de Transfusion Sanguine [*International Society of Blood Transfusion - ISBT*] [*Paris, France*] (EA) .... SITS
Societe Internationale d'Education Continue en Dentisterie [*International Society of Continuing Education in Dentistry - ISCED*] [*Brussels, Belgium*] (EAIO) .... SIECD
Societe Internationale d'Electrochimie [*International Society of Electrochemistry*] .... SIE
Societe Internationale des Artistes Chretiens [*International Society for Christian Artists*] [*Lydiate, Merseyside, England*] (EAIO) .... SIAC
Societe Internationale des Bibliotheques et Musees des Arts du Spectacle [*International Association of Libraries and Museums of the Performing Arts*] (EAIO) .... SIBMAS
Societe Internationale des Techniques d'Imagerie Mentals [*International Society for Mental Imagery Techniques in Psychotherapy and Psychology*] [*Paris, France*] (EAIO) .... SITIM
Societe Internationale des Telecommunications Aeronautiques [*International Society of Aeronautical Telecommunications*] [*London, England*] .... SITA
Societe Internationale d'Ethnographie et de Folklore [*International Society for Ethnology and Folklore*] .... SIEF
Societe Internationale d'Etude du Dix-Huitieme Siecle [*International Society for Eighteenth-Century Studies - ISECS*] (EAIO) .... SIEDS
Societe Internationale d'Hematologie [*International Society of Hematology - ISH*] [*Buenos Aires, Argentina*] (EA) .... SIH
Societe Internationale d'Oncologie Pediatrique [*International Society of Pediatric Oncology*] [*Leeds, England*] (EAIO) .... SIOP
Societe Internationale d'Ophtalmologie Geographique [*International Society of Geographic Opthalmology*] (EAIO) .... SIOG
Societe Internationale d'Urologie [*International Society of Urology - ISU*] [*Paris, France*] (EAIO) .... SIU
Societe Internationale Fernand de Vischer pour l'Histoire des Droits de l'Antiquite (EA) .... SIDA
Societe Internationale pour la Musique Contemporaine [*International Society for Contemporary Music*] .... SIMC
Societe Internationale pour la Readaptation des Invalides .... SIRI
Societe Internationale pour la Recherche sur les Maladies de Civilisation et l'Environment [*International Society for Research on Civilization Diseases and Environment*] [*Brussels, Belgium*] (EAIO) .... SIRMCE
Societe Internationale pour le Developpement des Organisations [*International Society for the Development of Organizations*] (EAIO) .... SIDO
Societe Internationale pour l'Enseignement Commercial [*International Society for Business Education*] [*Lausanne, Switzerland*] (EAIO) .... SIEC
Societe Internationale pour l'Etude de la Philosophie Medievale [*International Society for the Study of Medieval Philosophy*] (EAIO) .... SIEPM
Societe Interprofessionnelle pour la Compensation des Valeurs Mobilieres [*French depository body*] .... SICOVAM
Societe Ivoirenne de Navigation Maritime [*Ivory Coast*] (EY) .... SIVOMAR
Societe Ivoirenne de Transport Maritime [*The Ivorian national shipping industry*] .... SITRAM
Societe Ivoirienne des Chemins de Fer [*Railway system*] [*The Ivory Coast*] (EY) .... SICF
Societe Jean-Jacques Rousseau [*Switzerland*] (EAIO) .... SJJR
Societe Jules Verne [*France*] (EAIO) .... SJV
Societe Lao Import-Export (EY) .... SOLIMPEX
Societe Malienne d'Importation et d'Exportation [*Malian Import Export Co.*] .... SOMIEX
Societe Medicale Internationale d'Endoscopie et de Radiocinematographie [*International Medical Society for Endoscopy and Radiocinematography*] .... SMIER
Societe Mediterraneenne de Chimiotherapie [*Mediterranean Society of Chemotherapy - MSC*] [*Italy*] (EAIO) .... SMC
Societe Miniere Louvem, Inc. [*Toronto Stock Exchange symbol*] .... LOV
Societe National ELF Aquitaine [*National ELF Aquitaine Co.*] [*Associated Press*] (SAG) .... ElfAquit
Societe Nationale de Transport et de Commercialisation des Hydrocarbures .... SONATRACH
Societe Nationale d'Electricite .... SNEL
Societe Nationale des Beaux-Arts, Paris [*1890*] [*French*] (NGC) .... SNBA
Societe Nationale des Chemins de Fer Algeriens [*Algerian Railways*] .... SNCFA
Societe Nationale des Chemins de Fer Belges [*Belgian National Railways*] .... SCNB
Societe Nationale des Chemins de Fer Francais [*French National Railways*] .... SNCF
Societe Nigerienne de Banque (EY) .... SONIBANQUE
Societe Nigerienne de Transports Aeriens [*Niger*] [*ICAO designator*] (FAAC) .... SNI
Societe Nigerienne de Transports Aeriens [*Niger*] [*ICAO designator*] (FAAC) .... SONITA
Societe Nouvelle d'Editions pour l'Industrie [*Industrial News Publishing Company*] (IID) .... SNEI
Societe Nouvelle d'Exploitation Air Provence [*France ICAO designator*] (FAAC) .... APR
Societe Novajet [*France ICAO designator*] (FAAC) .... NJT
Societe Planetaire pour l'Assainissement de l'Energie [*Planetary Association for Clean Energy*] (EAIO) .... SPAE
Societe pour Aviation et ses Derives [*France*] [*World War I airplane*] .... SPAD
Societe pour la Protection de la Nature en Israel [*Society for the Protection of Nature in Israel*] [*Tel Aviv*] (EAIO) .... SPNI
Societe pour le Credit et le Developpement en Oceanie [*Commercial bank*] [*French Polynesia*] (EY) .... SOCREDO
Societe pour le Developpement et l'Exploitation du Palmier a Huile [*Ivory Coast*] .... SODEPALM
Societe pour le Patrimoine Musical Canadien (AC) .... SPMG
Societe pour l'Informatique [*Company for Informatics*] [*Information service or system Defunct*] (IID) .... SPI
Societe pour une Confederation au Moyen-Orient [*Society for Middle East Confederation - SMEC*] [*Israel*] (EAIO) .... SCMO
Societe pour Vaincre la Pollution [*Canada*] .... SVP
Societe Protectrice des Animaux en Afrique du Nord [*Society for the Protection of Animals in North Africa - SPANA*] (EAIO) .... SPAAN
Societe Quebecoise d'Exploration Miniere [*Quebec Mining Exploration Co.*] .... SOQUEM
Societe Quebecoise d'Information Juridique [*Quebec Society for Legal Information*] [*Information service or system*] (IID) .... SOQUIJ
Societe Quebecoise d'Initiatives Petrolieres, Ste.-Foy, Quebec [*Library symbol National Library of Canada*] (NLC) .... QQSIP
Societe Quebecoise d'Initiatives Petrolieres, Ste-Foy, PQ, Canada [*Library symbol Library of Congress*] (LCLS) .... CaQQSIP
Societe Rorschach Internationale [*International Rorschach Society*] [*Originally, Societe Internationale du Test de Rorschach et Autres Methodes Projectives*] .... SIR
Societe Royale d'Astronomie du Canada .... SRAC
Societe Royale du Canada [*Royal Society of Canada - RSC*] .... SRC
Societe Scandinave de Simulation [*Scandinavian Simulation Society*] [*Finland*] (EAIO) .... SSS
Societe Seca [*France ICAO designator*] (FAAC) .... CEK
Societe Suisse de Microelectronique et d'Horlogerie [*Commercial firm*] (ECON) .... SMH
Societe Suisse de Radiodiffusion et Television [*Radio and television network*] [*Switzerland*] .... SSR
Societe Theosophique [*Theosophical Society*] .... ST
Societe Tunisienne de l'Air [*Tunisia*] [*ICAO designator*] .... TU
Societe Tunisienne de l'Air [*Airline*] [*Tunisia*] .... TUNISAIR
Societe Universitaire Europeenne de Recherches Financieres (EAIO) .... SUERF
Societie pour l'Expansion des Exportations [*Export Development Corp.*] [*Canada*] .... SEE
Society .... SCTY
Society (ROG) .... SO
Society .... SOC
Society (ODBW) .... Soc
Society [*A publication*] (BRI) .... Soc
Society (ROG) .... SOCY
Society Against Elephant Exploitation (EA) .... SOCELEX
Society Against Have a Nice Day (NADA) .... SAHAND
Society Against Vivisection (EA) .... SAV
Society American Gastrointestinal Endoscopic Surgeons (EA) .... SAGES
Society and Commerce Publications .... SOCOM
Society Devoted to the Sacred Heart [*Roman Catholic women's religious order*] .... SDSH
Society Farsarotul (EA) .... SF
Society for a World Service Federation [*Defunct*] (EA) .... SWSF
Society for Academic Achievement (EA) .... SAA
Society for Academic Freedom and Scholarship [*Canada*] .... SAFS
Society for Academic Gaming and Simulation in Education and Training .... SAGSET
Society for Adolescent Medicine (EA) .... SAM
Society for Adolescent Psychiatry (EA) .... SAP
Society for Advanced Medical Systems [*Later, AMIA*] .... SAMS
Society for Advancement in Nursing (EA) .... SAIN
Society for Advancement of Chicanos and Native Americans in Science (EA) .... SACNAS
Society for Advancement of Management [*Cincinnati, OH*] (EA) .... SAM
Society for Aerospace Engineers (AAGC) .... SAE
Society for Agricultural Training through Integrated Voluntary Activities (EA) .... SATIVA
Society for Aid and Rehabilitation of Drug Addicts [*Hong Kong*] .... SARDA
Society for Airline Meteorologists (IAA) .... SALE
Society for American Archaeology (EA) .... SAA
Society for American Baseball Research (EA) .... SABR
Society for American Cuisine [*Later, SCA*] (EA) .... SAC
Society for American Indian Studies (EA) .... SAIS
Society for American Indian Studies and Research [*Formerly, SAIS*] (EA) .... SAISR
Society for American Philosophy [*Defunct*] (EA) .... SAP

Society for Analytical Chemistry [*British*] .... SAC
Society for Analytical Cytology (EA) .... SAC
Society for Ancient Greek Philosophy (EA) .... SAGP
Society for Ancient Numismatics (EA) .... SAN
Society for Anglo-Chinese Understanding [*British*] (EAIO) .... SACU
Society for Animal Protective Legislation (EA) .... SAPL
Society for Animal Rights [*Later, ISAR*] (EA) .... SAR
Society for Animal Welfare in Israel (EAIO) .... SAWI
Society for Anthropology in Community Colleges (EA) .... SACC
Society for Application Research [*British*] (DBA) .... SAR
Society for Applied Anthropology (AEBS) .... SAA
Society for Applied Anthropology (EA) .... SFAA
Society for Applied Bacteriology (EA) .... SAB
Society for Applied Learning Technology (EA) .... SALT
Society for Applied Sociology (EA) .... SAS
Society for Applied Spectroscopy (EA) .... SAS
Society for Armenian Studies (EA) .... SAS
Society for Arts and Crafts New South Wales [*Australia*] .... SACNSW
Society for Asian and Comparative Philosophy (EA) .... SACP
Society for Asian Art (EA) .... SAA
Society for Asian Music (EA) .... SAM
Society for Assisted Reproductive Technology (EA) .... SART
Society for Austrian and Habsburg History (EA) .... SAHH
Society for Automating Better Education (IAA) .... SABE
Society for Automation in Business Education [*Later, SDE*] (EA) .... SABE
Society for Automation in English and the Humanities [*Later, SDE*] .... SAEH
Society for Automation in Professional Education [*Later, SDE*] .... SAPE
Society for Automation in the Fine Arts [*Later, SDE*] .... SAFA
Society for Automation in the Sciences and Mathematics .... SASM
Society for Automation in the Social Sciences [*Later, SDE*] .... SASS
Society for Back Pain Research [*British*] .... SBPR
Society for Behavioral Kinesiology .... SBK
Society for Behaviorial Pediatrics (EA) .... SBP
Society for Biological Rhythm .... SBR
Society for Biomaterials (EA) .... SB
Society for Biomedical Engineering Technicians (DMAA) .... SBET
Society for Biomolecular Screening .... SBS
Society for Business Ethics [*Santa Clara, CA*] (EA) .... SBE
Society for Calligraphy (EA) .... SfC
Society for Calligraphy and Handwriting (EA) .... SCH
Society for Cardiac Angiography and Interventions (EA) .... SCA & I
Society for Caribbean Linguistics [*St. Augustine, Trinidad*] (EAIO) .... SCL
Society for Carribean Studies (EAIO) .... SCS
Society for Checking the Abuses of Public Advertising [*British*] .... SCAPA
Society for Children with Craniosynostosis (EA) .... SCC
Society for Ch'ing Studies (EA) .... SCS
Society for Cinema Studies (EA) .... SCS
Society for Citizen Education in World Affairs [*Later, CEA*] .... SCEWA
Society for Clinical and Experimental Hypnosis (EA) .... SCEH
Society for Clinical Ecology [*Later, AAEM*] (EA) .... SCE
Society for Clinical Trials (EA) .... SCT
Society for College and University Planning (EA) .... SCUP
Society for Collegiate Journalists (EA) .... SCJ
Society for Colonial History [*Defunct*] (EA) .... SCH
Society for Comic Art Research and Preservation .... SCARP
Society for Commercial Archeology (EA) .... SCA
Society for Companion Animal Studies (EAIO) .... SCAS
Society for Completely Removing All Parking Meters .... SCRAP
Society for Computer Applications in Engineering, Planning, and Architecture (EA) .... CEPA
Society for Computer Applications in Engineering, Planning, and Architecture [*Later, CEPA*] (EA) .... SCAEPA
Society for Computer Medicine [*Later, AMIA*] (EA) .... SCM
Society for Computer Science in Biology and Medicine .... SCSBM
Society for Computer Simulation [*Later, SCSI*] (EA) .... SCS
Society for Computer Simulation International (EA) .... SCSI
Society for Computer-Aided Engineering (EA) .... SCAE
Society for Computers and Law [*Abingdon, Oxfordshire, England*] (EAIO) .... SCL
Society for Conceptual and Content Analysis by Computer (EA) .... SCCAC
Society for Conservation Biology (EA) .... SCB
Society for Conservative Studies [*Later, YAF*] (EA) .... SCS
Society for Coptic Archaeology (EA) .... SCA
Society for Creative Anachronism (EA) .... SCA
Society for Creative Ethics [*Later, SPC*] (EA) .... SCE
Society for Crippled Children and Adults, Winnipeg, MB, Canada [*Library symbol Library of Congress*] (LCLS) .... CaMWSC
Society for Cross-Cultural Research (EA) .... SCCR
Society for Cryobiology (EA) .... SC
Society for Cultural Anthropology (EA) .... SCA
Society for Cultural Relations between the Peoples of the British Commonwealth and the USSR .... SCR
Society for Cutting Up Men .... SCUM
Society for Czechoslovak Philately (EA) .... SCP
Society for Developmental Biology (EA) .... SDB
Society for Drug Research (EAIO) .... SDR
Society for Ear, Nose, and Throat Advances in Children (EA) .... SENTAC
Society for Earthquake and Civil Engineering Dynamics [*British*] .... SECED
Society for Ecological Restoration (EA) .... SER
Society for Economic Botany (EA) .... SEB
Society for Economic, Social, Cultural Study and Expansion in Central Africa .... SEAC
Society for Education in Film and Television [*British*] .... SEFT
Society for Education through Art [*British*] .... SEA
Society for Educational Data Systems [*Later, SDE*] .... SEDS
Society for Educational Reconstruction (EA) .... SER
Society for Educational Visits and Exchanges in Canada [*Societe Educative de Visites et d'Echanges au Canada*] .... SEVEC
Society for Educative Communication (EA) .... SEC
Society for Electro-Acoustic Music in the United States (EA) .... SEAMUS
Society for Electroanalytical Chemistry .... SEAC
Society for Emotional Development in Children [*Canada*] .... SEDC
Society for Ending Needless and Silly Expenditure [*British*] (DI) .... SENSE
Society for Engineering in Agriculture [*Australia*] .... SEA
Society for Entrepreneurship Research and Application [*Defunct*] (EA) .... SERA
Society for Environmental Geochemistry and Health (EA) .... SEGH
Society for Environmental Stabilization [*Defunct*] (EA) .... SES
Society for Environmental Stress Analysis (IAA) .... SESA
Society for Environmental Therapy [*British*] .... SET
Society for Environmental Truth (EA) .... SET
Society for Epidemiologic Research (EA) .... SER
Society for Ethnic Missions [*Australia*] .... SEM
Society for Ethnomusicology (EA) .... SEM
Society for Exact Philosophy (EA) .... SEP
Society for Experimental and Descriptive Malacology (EA) .... SEDM
Society for Experimental Biology (EAIO) .... SEB
Society for Experimental Biology and Medicine (EA) .... SEBM
Society for Experimental Mechanics (EA) .... SEM
Society for Experimental Stress Analysis [*Later, SEM*] (EA) .... SESA
Society for Film History Research [*British*] (BI) .... SFHR
Society for Folk Arts Preservation (EA) .... SFAP
Society for Foodservice Management (EA) .... SFM
Society for Foodservice Systems (EA) .... SFS
Society for Freedom in Science .... SFS
Society for French American Cultural Services and Educational Aid (EA) .... FACSEA
Society for French Historical Studies (EA) .... SFHS
Society for French Studies [*British*] .... SFS
Society for French-American Affairs [*Defunct*] (EA) .... SFAA
Society for General Microbiology [*British*] .... SGM
Society for General Music (EA) .... SGM
Society for General Systems Research (EA) .... SGSR
Society for German-American Studies (EA) .... SGAS
Society for Glass Science and Practices (EA) .... SGSP
Society for Gynecologic Investigation (EA) .... SGI
Society for Health and Human Values (EA) .... SHHV
Society for HematoPathology (EA) .... SH
Society for Historians of American Foreign Relations (EA) .... SHAFR
Society for Historians of the Early American Republic (EA) .... SHEAR
Society for Historical Archaeology (EA) .... SHA
Society for Historical Research (EA) .... SHR
Society for History Education (EA) .... SHE
Society for History in the Federal Government (EA) .... SHFG
Society for History, Research, and Preservation (EA) .... SHRP
Society for Hospital Epidemiology of America .... SHEA
Society for Hospital Planning and Marketing of the American Hospital Association (EA) .... SHPM
Society for Hospital Planning of the American Hospital Association [*Later, SHPM*] (EA) .... SHP
Society for Hospital Social Work Directors (EA) .... SHSWD
Society for Human Ecology (EA) .... SHE
Society for Human Resource Management (EA) .... SHRM
Society for Humane Abortion (EA) .... SHA
Society for Humanistic Anthropology (EA) .... SHA
Society for Humanistic Judaism (EA) .... SHJ
Society for Humanity and Social Reform [*British*] .... SHSR
Society for Hungarian Philately (EA) .... SHP
Society for Hybrid Microelectronics (IAA) .... SHM
Society for Iberian and Latin American Thought (EA) .... SILAT
Society for Indecency to Naked Animals [*A hoax association*] .... SINA
Society for Individual Liberty (EA) .... SIL
Society for Individual Responsibility [*Defunct*] (EA) .... SIR
Society for Industrial and Applied Mathematics (EA) .... SIAM
Society for Industrial Archeology (EA) .... SIA
Society for Industrial Microbiology (EA) .... SIM
Society for Information Display (EA) .... SID
Society for Information Management [*Chicago, IL*] (EA) .... SIM
Society for Integrative Graphology [*Defunct*] (EA) .... SIG
Society for Interests of Active Missionaries in Asia, Africa, and America (EAIO) .... SIAMA
Society for International Development (EA) .... SID
Society for International Numismatics (EA) .... SIN
Society for Invertebrate Pathology (EA) .... SIP
Society for Investigative Dermatology (EA) .... SID
Society for Iranian Studies (EA) .... SIS
Society for Italian Historical Studies (EA) .... SIHS
Society for Italian Studies (AIE) .... SIS
Society for Italian-American Scientists and Physicians (EA) .... SIASP
Society for Italic Handwriting (EA) .... SIH
Society for Italic Handwriting (EA) .... SIHW
Society for Italic Handwriting, Western American Branch [*Later, WASIH*] (EA) .... WABSIH
Society for Japanese Irises (EA) .... SJI
Society for Latin American Anthropology (EA) .... SLAA
Society for Latin American Studies [*British*] .... SLAS
Society for Libertarian Life [*Defunct*] (EA) .... SLL
Society for Libyan Studies (EAIO) .... SLS
Society for Life History Research (EA) .... SLHR
Society for Life History Research in Psychopathology [*Later, SLHR*] (EA) .... SLHRP
Society for Light Treatment and Biological Rhythms .... SLTBR

Society for Linguistic Anthropology (EA) ... SLA
Society for Literature and Science ... SLS
Society for Louisiana Irises (EA) ... SLI
Society for Low Temperature Biology (EA) ... SLTB
Society for Machine Intelligence [*Defunct*] (EA) ... SMI
Society for Magnetic Resonance Imaging (EA) ... SMRI
Society for Management Information Systems (EA) ... SMIS
Society for Manitobans with Disabilities, Inc., Winnipeg, Manitoba [*Library symbol National Library of Canada*] (NLC) ... MWSC
Society for Marketing Professional Services [*Alexandria, VA*] (EA) ... SMPS
Society for Medical Anthropology (EA) ... SMA
Society for Medieval and Renaissance Philosophy (EA) ... SMRP
Society for Medieval Archaeology (EA) ... SMA
Society for Menstrual Cycle Research (EA) ... SMCR
Society for Microcomputers in Life and Education (EDAC) ... SMILE
Society for Mining, Metallurgy, and Exploration [*In association name, SMME, Inc.*] (EA) ... SMME
Society for Mining, Metallurgy, and Exploration, Inc. [*In association name, SME , Inc.*] (EA) ... SME
Society for Mucopolysaccharide Diseases (EA) ... MPS
Society for Music in the Liberal Arts College (AEBS) ... SMILAC
Society for Music Teacher Education (EA) ... SMTE
Society for Musteline Arts and Literature (EA) ... SMAL
Society for Natural Philosophy (EA) ... SNP
Society for Nautical Research [*British*] (EAIO) ... SNR
Society for Neuroscience (EA) ... SN
Society for New Language Study (EA) ... SNLS
Society for New Testament Study [*Exeter, Devonshire, England*] (EA) ... SNTS
Society for Nondestructive Testing [*Later, ASNT*] (KSC) ... SNDT
Society for Nondestructive Testing [*Later, ASNT*] (EA) ... SNT
Society for Nonprofit Organizations (EA) ... SNPO
Society for North American Union (EA) ... SNAU
Society for Northwestern Vertebrate Biology (EA) ... SNVB
Society for Nursing History [*Defunct*] (EA) ... SNH
Society for Nutrition Education (EA) ... SNE
Society for Obstetric Anesthesia and Perinatology (EA) ... SOAP
Society for Occlusal Studies (EA) ... SOS
Society for Occupational and Environmental Health (EA) ... SOEH
Society for Office-Based Surgery [*Later, ASOS*] (EA) ... SOBS
Society for Optical and Quantum Electronics ... SOQE
Society for Pacific Coast Native Irises (EA) ... SPCNI
Society for Participatory Research in Asia [*India*] (EAIO) ... PRIA
Society for Pediatric Dermatology (EA) ... SPD
Society for Pediatric Psychology (EA) ... SPP
Society for Pediatric Radiology (EA) ... SPR
Society for Pediatric Research (EA) ... SPR
Society for Pediatric Urology (EA) ... SPU
Society for Pentecostal Studies (EA) ... SPS
Society for Personality Assessment (EA) ... SPA
Society for Personnel Administration [*Later, IPMA*] (EA) ... SPA
Society for Phenomenology and Existential Philosophy (EA) ... SPEP
Society for Philosophy and Public Affairs (EA) ... SPPA
Society for Philosophy and Technology (EA) ... SPT
Society for Philosophy of Creativity (EA) ... SPC
Society for Philosophy of Religion (EA) ... SPR
Society for Photographic Education (EA) ... SPE
Society for Physical Research [*British*] (BI) ... SPR
Society for Policy Modeling (EA) ... SPM
Society for Post-Medieval Archaeology [*British*] ... SPMA
Society for Prevention of Rock and Roll and Corruption of American Youth [*Organization in 1956 movie "Shake, Rattle and Roll"*] ... SPRACAY
Society for Prevention of Unwholesome Diet [*National Potato Council*] ... SPUD
Society for Private and Commercial Earth Stations [*Telecommunications Information service or system*] (EA) ... SPACE
Society for Proclaiming Britain in Israel ... SPBI
Society for Projective Techniques and Personality Assessment [*Later, SPA*] ... SPT & PA
Society for Promoting and Encouraging the Arts and Knowledge of the Church (EA) ... SPEAK
Society for Promoting Christian Knowledge [*Publisher*] [*British*] ... SPCK
Society for Promotion of Educational Reform through Teacher Training [*British*] ... SPERTTT
Society for Provincial Notaries General [*British*] ... SPNG
Society for Psychical Research [*British*] ... SPR
Society for Psychological Anthropology (EA) ... SPA
Society for Psychophysiological Research (EA) ... SPR
Society for Psychosomatic Research (EAIO) ... SPR
Society for Public Administration ... SPA
Society for Public Health Education (EA) ... SOPHE
Society for Pure English ... SPE
Society for Quality Assurance ... SQA
Society for Radiation Oncology Administrators (EA) ... SROA
Society for Radiological Protection [*British*] (DEN) ... SRP
Society for Range Management (EA) ... SRM
Society for Rational Individualism [*Later, SIL*] (EA) ... SRI
Society for Reformation Research (EA) ... SRR
Society for Religion in Higher Education [*Later, SVHE*] (EA) ... SRHE
Society for Reproductive Surgeons (EA) ... SRE
Society for Research in Child Development (EA) ... SRCD
Society for Research in the Psychology of Music and Music Education [*British*] ... SRPMME
Society for Research into Higher Education [*Guildford, Surrey, England*] (EAIO) ... SRHE
Society for Research into Hydrocephalus and Spina Bifida (EA) ... SRHB
Society for Research into Hydrocephalus and Spina Bifida (EA) ... SRHSB
Society for Research on Rapport and Telekinesis [*Defunct*] (EA) ... SORRAT
Society for Risk Analysis (EA) ... SRA
Society for Romanian Studies (EA) ... SRS
Society for Scholarly Publishing (EA) ... SSP
Society for Scientific Exploration (EA) ... SSE
Society for Sedimentary Geology [*Formerly, Society of Economic Paleontologists a nd Mineralogists*] (EA) ... SEPM
Society for Sex Therapy and Research (EA) ... SSTAR
Society for Siberian Irises (EA) ... SSI
Society for Slovene Studies (EA) ... SSS
Society for Social Responsibility in Engineering (EERA) ... SSRE
Society for Social Responsibility in Science (EA) ... SSRS
Society for Social Studies of Science (EA) ... 4S
Society for Socialist Studies [*See also SES*] [*Canada*] ... SSS
Society for Software Quality (EA) ... SSQ
Society for South Asian Studies (EAIO) ... SSAS
Society for South India Studies (EA) ... SSIS
Society for Spanish and Portuguese Historical Studies (EA) ... SSPHS
Society for Spreading the Knowledge of True Prayer [*British*] (BI) ... SSKTP
Society for Strategic and Long Range Planning [*Later, Strategic Planning Society - SP*] (EAIO) ... SLRP
Society for Strings (EA) ... SS
Society for Surgery of the Alimentary Tract (EA) ... SSAT
Society for Technical Communication (EA) ... STC
Society for Techno-Innovation of Agriculture, Forestry and Fisheries [*Japan*] ... STAFF
Society for Test Anxiety Research (EA) ... STAR
Society for Textual Scholarship (EA) ... STS
Society for Thai Philately (EA) ... STP
Society for the Advancement of Agricultural Studies [*British*] ... SAAS
Society for the Advancement of Ambulatory Care [*Defunct*] (EA) ... SAAC
Society for the Advancement of American Philosophy (EA) ... SAAP
Society for the Advancement of Anaesthesia in Dentistry (EAIO) ... SAAD
Society for the Advancement of Behavior Analysis (EA) ... SABA
Society for the Advancement of Continuing Education for Ministry (EA) ... SACEM
Society for the Advancement of Economic Theory (EA) ... SAET
Society for the Advancement of Education (EA) ... SAE
Society for the Advancement of Fission Energy [*Defunct*] (EA) ... SAFE
Society for the Advancement of Food Service Research (EA) ... SAFSR
Society for the Advancement of Games and Simulation in Education and Training [*British*] (DBA) ... SAGSET
Society for the Advancement of Good English [*Defunct*] (EA) ... SAGE
Society for the Advancement of Judaism (EA) ... SAJ
Society for the Advancement of Material and Process Engineering (EA) ... SAMPE
Society for the Advancement of Research into Anorexia [*British*] (DBA) ... SARA
Society for the Advancement of Scandinavian Study (EA) ... SASS
Society for the Advancement of Social Psychology (EA) ... SASP
Society for the Advancement of Space Travel [*Defunct*] (MCD) ... SAST
Society for the Advancement of the Field Theory (EA) ... SAFT
Society for the Advancement of the George Economy [*Defunct*] (EA) ... SAGE
Society for the Advancement of the Tourism Industry ... SATI
Society for the Advancement of Travel for the Handicapped (EA) ... SATH
Society for the Anthropology of Europe (EA) ... SAE
Society for the Anthropology of Visual Communication (EA) ... SAVC
Society for the Anthropology of Visual Communication ... SAVICOM
Society for the Application of Free Energy (EA) ... SAFE
Society for the Area of Biological and Chemical Overlap ... SABCO
Society for the Arts, Religion, and Contemporary Culture (EA) ... ARC
Society for the Assistance of Ladies in Reduced Circumstances [*British*] (DI) ... SALRC
Society for the Bibliography of Natural History (EA) ... SBNH
Society for the Christian Commonwealth ... SCC
Society for the Collection of Brand-Name Pencils [*Inactive*] (EA) ... SCBNP
Society for the Comparative Study of Society and History (EA) ... CSSH
Society for the Conservation of Bighorn Sheep (EA) ... SCBS
Society for the Development of Techniques in Industrial Marketing [*British*] ... SDTIM
Society for the Diffusion of Useful Knowledge ... SDUK
Society for the Elimination of Acronyms ... SEA
Society for the Emancipation of the American Male ... SEAM
Society for the Encouragement of Research and Invention [*Defunct*] (EA) ... SERI
Society for the Eradication of Television (EA) ... SET
Society for the Exploration of Psychotherapy Integration (EA) ... SEPI
Society for the Family of Man (EA) ... SFM
Society for the Furtherance and Study of Fantasy and Science Fiction (EA) ... SF3
Society for the Health Education [*British*] ... SHE
Society for the History of Alchemy and Chemistry (EA) ... SHAC
Society for the History of Authorship, Reading and Publishing (EA) ... SHARP
Society for the History of Czechoslovak Jews (EA) ... SHCJ
Society for the History of Discoveries (EA) ... SHD
Society for the History of Natural History [*British*] (EAIO) ... SHNH
Society for the History of Technology (EA) ... SHOT
Society for the History of Technology (EA) ... SHT
Society for the History of the Germans in Maryland (EA) ... SHGM
Society for the Humanities (EA) ... SH
Society for the Investigation of Recurring Events (EA) ... SIRE
Society for the Investigation of the Unexplained (EA) ... SITU
Society for the Maintenance of the Apostolic See (DICI) ... SMAS
Society for the Maintenance of the Faith [*British*] ... SMF
Society for the Ministry of Women in the Church [*British*] (BI) ... SMWC

Society for the Parents of Fugitive Children [*Fictional organization in film "Taking Off"*] ... SPFC
Society for the Philosophical Study of Dialectical Materialism (EA) ... SPSDM
Society for the Philosophical Study of Marxism (EA) ... SPSM
Society for the Philosophy of Sex and Love (EA) ... SPSL
Society for the Preservation and Advancement of the Harmonica (EA) ... SPAH
Society for the Preservation and Appreciation of Antique Motor Fire Apparatus inAmerica (EA) ... SPAAMFAA
Society for the Preservation and Appreciation of Antique Motor Fire Apparatus inAmerica ... SPAAMFAA
Society for the Preservation and Encouragement of Barber Shop Quartet Singing inAmerica (EA) ... SPEBSQSA
Society for the Preservation and Enhancement of the Recognition of Millard Fillmore, Last of the Whigs (EA) ... SPERMFLOW
Society for the Preservation and Enjoyment of Carriages in America [*Defunct*] (EA) ... SPECA
Society for the Preservation of American Business History (EA) ... SPABH
Society for the Preservation of Beers from the Wood [*British*] (EAIO) ... SPBW
Society for the Preservation of Birds of Prey (EA) ... SPBP
Society for the Preservation of English Language and Literature (EA) ... SPELL
Society for the Preservation of Film Music (EA) ... SPFM
Society for the Preservation of Long Island Antiquities, Setauket, NY [*Library symbol Library of Congress*] (LCLS) ... NSetSP
Society for the Preservation of Natural History Collections (EA) ... SPNHC
Society for the Preservation of New England Antiquities (EA) ... SPNEA
Society for the Preservation of New England Antiquities, Boston, MA [*Library symbol Library of Congress*] (LCLS) ... MBSpnea
Society for the Preservation of Old Mills (EA) ... SPOCM
Society for the Preservation of Old Mills (EA) ... SPOOM
Society for the Preservation of Poultry Antiquities (EA) ... SPPA
Society for the Preservation of Rural Industries and Village Enterprises [*British*] (ODBW) ... STRIVE
Society for the Preservation of the Greek Heritage (EA) ... SPGH
Society for the Preservation of Variety Arts (EA) ... SPVA
Society for the Prevention of Asbestosis and Industrial Diseases [*British*] (DI) ... SPAID
Society for the Prevention of Crime [*Defunct*] (EA) ... SPC
Society for the Prevention of Cruelty to Animals ... SPCA
Society for the Prevention of Cruelty to Children ... SPCC
Society for the Prevention of Cruelty to Young Singers ... SPCTYS
Society for the Prevention of Disparaging Remarks about Brooklyn ... SPDRAB
Society for the Prevention of Drug Addiction ... SPODA
Society for the Prevention of Married Men Posing as Bachelors ... SFPOMMPAB
Society for the Prevention of World War III [*Defunct*] ... SPWWIII
Society for the Promotion of African, Asian, and Latin American Literature [*See also GFLAAL*] [*Germany*] (EAIO) ... SPAALAL
Society for the Promotion of Engineering Education [*Later, ASEE*] ... SPEE
Society for the Promotion of Hellenic Studies (EA) ... SPHS
Society for the Promotion of Mohammedan Missions [*Defunct*] (EA) ... SPMM
Society for the Promotion of Nature Reserves [*British*] (BI) ... SPNR
Society for the Promotion of New Music [*British*] ... SPNM
Society for the Promotion of Otherwise Overlooked Football Scores ... SPOOFS
Society for the Promotion of Roman Studies (EAIO) ... SPRS
Society for the Promotion of Science and Scholarship (EA) ... SPOSS
Society for the Promotion of Scientific Industry [*British*] ... SPSI
Society for the Propagation of the Faith (EA) ... SPF
Society for the Propagation of the Gospel [*Later, USPG*] [*British*] ... SPG
Society for the Propagation of the Gospel among the Jews [*British*] ... SPGJ
Society for the Propagation of the Gospel in Foreign Parts [*British*] (DAS) ... SPGFP
Society for the Protection of Ancient Buildings (EA) ... SPAB
Society for the Protection of Animals Abroad [*British*] (EAIO) ... SPANA
Society for the Protection of Animals in North Africa [*See also SPAAN*] (EAIO) ... SPANA
Society for the Protection of East Asians' Human Rights/USA (EA) ... SPEAHR
Society for the Protection of Old Fishes (EA) ... SPOOF
Society for the Protection of Science and Learning [*British*] ... SPSL
Society for the Protection of the Unborn through Nutrition (EA) ... SPUN
Society for the Protection of Unborn Children (EA) ... SPUC
Society for the Psychological Study of Lesbian and Gay Issues (EA) ... SPSLGI
Society for the Psychological Study of Social Issues (EA) ... SPSSI
Society for the Publication of American Music [*Record label*] ... SPAM
Society for the Punishment of War Criminals (EA) ... SPWC
Society for the Registration of Estate Agents and Mortgage Brokers (MHDB) ... SCREAM
Society for the Rehabilitation of the Facially Disfigured [*Later, National Foundation for Facial Reconstruction*] (EA) ... SRFD
Society for the Relief of Distress [*British*] ... SRD
Society for the Right to Die (EA) ... SRD
Society for the Scientific Study of Religion (EA) ... SSSR
Society for the Scientific Study of Sex (EA) ... SSSS
Society for the Second Self (EA) ... SSS
Society for the Social History of Medicine [*Oxford, England*] (EAIO) ... SSHM
Society for the Study of Addiction to Alcohol and Other Drugs (EAIO) ... SSA
Society for the Study of Alchemy and Early Chemistry [*British*] ... SSAEC
Society for the Study of Amphibians and Reptiles (EA) ... SSAR
Society for the Study of Architecture in Canada [*Established 1974*] ... SSAC
Society for the Study of Artificial Intelligence and the Simulation of the Brain (MHDI) ... AISB
Society for the Study of Blood (EA) ... SSB
Society for the Study of Breast Disease (EA) ... SSBD
Society for the Study of Caucasia (EA) ... SSC
Society for the Study of Development and Growth [*Later, SDB*] (EA) ... SSDG
Society for the Study of Dictionaries and Lexicography [*Later, DSNA*] (EA) ... SSDL
Society for the Study of Early China (EA) ... SSEC
Society for the Study of Evolution (EA) ... SSE
Society for the Study of Fertility [*British*] ... SSF
Society for the Study of Human Biology (EA) ... SSHB
Society for the Study of Inborn Errors of Metabolism [*Middleway, England*] (EAIO) ... SSIEM
Society for the Study of Indigenous Languages of the Americas (EA) ... SSILA
Society for the Study of Internationalism (EA) ... SSI
Society for the Study of Labour History [*Sheffield, England*] (EA) ... SSLH
Society for the Study of Male Psychology and Physiology (EA) ... SSMPP
Society for the Study of Medical Ethics [*British*] ... SSME
Society for the Study of Medieval Languages and Literature [*British*] ... SSMLL
Society for the Study of Midwestern Literature (EA) ... SSML
Society for the Study of Multi-Ethnic Literature of the United States (BARN) ... MELUS
Society for the Study of Myth and Tradition (EA) ... SSMT
Society for the Study of Process Philosophies (EA) ... SSPP
Society for the Study of Religion and Communism (EA) ... SSRC
Society for the Study of Reproduction (EA) ... SSR
Society for the Study of Social Biology (EA) ... SSSB
Society for the Study of Social Problems (EA) ... SSSP
Society for the Study of Southern Literature (EA) ... SSSL
Society for the Study of Symbolic Interaction (EA) ... SSSI
Society for the Study of Theology [*British*] ... SST
Society for the Study of Women in Legal History (EA) ... SSWLH
Society for the Study of Women in Legal History (EA) ... WLH
Society for the Suppression of Speculative Stamps [*Defunct*] ... SSS
Society for the Systematic Documentation of Paranormal Experiments (EA) ... SSDPE
Society for Theatre Research (EA) ... STR
Society for Theological Discussion [*Defunct*] (EA) ... STD
Society for Theriogenology (EA) ... ST
Society for thr Aid of Psychological Minorities (NADA) ... SAPM
Society for Traditional Music (EA) ... STM
Society for Traumatic Stress Studies (EA) ... STSS
Society for Treatment of Autism, Calgary, AB, Canada [*Library symbol*] [*Library of Congress*] (LCLS) ... CaACSTA
Society for Treatment of Autism, Calgary, Alberta [*Library symbol National Library of Canada*] (NLC) ... ACSTA
Society for Understanding Cats, Kangaroos, Elks, and Reptiles [*Slang*] ... SUCKER
Society for Underwater Technology (EA) ... SUT
Society for Urban Anthropology (EA) ... SUA
Society for Utopian Studies (EA) ... SUS
Society for Values in Higher Education (EA) ... SVHE
Society for Vascular Surgery (EA) ... SVS
Society for Vector Ecology (EA) ... SVE
Society for Veterinary Ethology [*See also SEV*] [*Edinburgh, Scotland*] (EAIO) ... SVE
Society for Visiting Scientists Ltd. [*British*] (BI) ... SVS
Society for Visual Anthropology (EA) ... SVA
Society for Visual Education, Inc. (AEBS) ... SVE
Society for Wang Applications and Programs (CSR) ... SWAP
Society for Women in Philosophy (EA) ... SWIP
Society for Women in Philosophy, Midwest Division (EA) ... SWIPMD
Society for Women in Philosophy, Pacific Division (EA) ... SWPPD
Society for Women in Philosophy, Southwest Division (EA) ... SWPSD
Society for Women in Philosophy, Southwestern Division (EA) ... SW-SWIP
Society for Women in Plastics (EA) ... SWP
Society for Worldwide Interbank Financial Telecommunication [*Banking netw ork*] [*Belgium*] ... SWIFT
Society for Worldwide Interbank Financial Transactions (NITA) ... SWIFT
Society for Young Victims [*Later, SYV/MCC*] (EA) ... SYV
Society for Young Victims, Missing Children Center (EA) ... SYV/MCC
Society in Aid of Children Inoperable in their Motherland [*Australia*] ... SACIM
Society in Opposition to Human-Animal Hybridization ... SOHAH
Society Islands (BARN) ... Soc Is
Society Islands ... Soc Isl
Society of Acoustic Technology (IAA) ... SAT
Society of Actuaries ... SA
Society of Actuaries (EA) ... SOA
Society of Administrative Mental Health Offices [*British*] (BI) ... SAMHO
Society of Advanced Motorists Sydney [*Australia*] ... SAMS
Society of Advertising Musicians, Producers, Arrangers, and Composers ... SAMPAC
Society of Aeronautical Historians [*Netherlands*] (EAIO) ... SAH
Society of Aeronautical Weight Engineers (IAA) ... SAWE
Society of Aerospace Material and Process Engineers (AEBS) ... SAMPE
Society of Aerospace Medicine (NADA) ... SAM
Society of African and Afro-American Students ... SAAS
Society of African Culture [*France*] (EAIO) ... SAC
Society of African Missions [*Roman Catholic men's religious order*] ... SMA
Society of African Missions (TOCD) ... sma
Society of Air Force Anesthesiologists [*Later, DMEF*] (EA) ... SAFA
Society of Air Force Physicians (EA) ... SAFP
Society of Air Line Meteorologists ... SALM
Society of Air Safety Investigators [*Later, ISASI*] ... SASI
Society of Airway Pioneers (EA) ... SOAP
Society of Alexandria [*Defunct*] (EA) ... SA
Society of All Cargo Correspondents [*British*] [*An association*] (DBA) ... SACC
Society of Allied Weight Engineers (EA) ... SAWE
Society of American Archivists (EA) ... SAA
Society of American Bacteriologists [*Later, ASM*] ... SAB
Society of American Business Editors and Writers [*Columbia, MO*] (EA) ... SABEW

Society of American Business Writers [*Later, SABEW*] ..... SABW
Society of American Etchers (NADA) ..... SAE
Society of American Fight Directors (EA) ..... SAFD
Society of American Florists (EA) ..... SAF
Society of American Florists and Ornamental Horticulturists [*Later, SAF*] ..... SAFOH
Society of American Foresters (EA) ..... SAF
Society of American Graphic Artists (EA) ..... SAGA
Society of American Historians [*Defunct*] (EA) ..... SAH
Society of American Historical Artists (EA) ..... SAHA
Society of American Inventors (EA) ..... SAI
Society of American Law Teachers (EA) ..... SALT
Society of American Legion Founders [*Defunct*] (EA) ..... SALF
Society of American Magicians (EA) ..... SAM
Society of American Military Engineers (EA) ..... SAME
Society of American Registered Architects (EA) ..... ARA
Society of American Registered Architects (EA) ..... SARA
Society of American Silversmiths (EA) ..... SAS
Society of American Travel Writers (EA) ..... SATW
Society of American Value Engineers (EA) ..... SAVE
Society of American Ventriloquists [*Defunct*] (EA) ..... SAV
Society of American Vintage-Radio Enthusiasts ..... SAVE
Society of American Wars (EA) ..... SAW
Society of American Wood Preservers [*Defunct*] (EA) ..... SAWP
Society of Americanists [*Paris, France*] (EA) ..... SAM
Society of Americans for Firearms Elimination (EA) ..... SAFFE
Society of Americans for Vashchenko Emigration (EA) ..... SAVE
Society of Americans of Colonial Descent [*Defunct*] (EA) ..... SACD
Society of Anaesthetists of West Africa [*Nigeria*] (EAIO) ..... SAWA
Society of Analytical Psychology (AIE) ..... SAP
Society of Animal Artists (EA) ..... SAA
Society of Antiquaries [*British*] ..... SA
Society of Antiquaries of Scotland (EAIO) ..... SAS
Society of Antique Label Collectors (EA) ..... SLC
Society of Antique Modelers (EA) ..... SAM
Society of Archer-Antiquaries (EA) ..... SAA
Society of Architects and Allied Technicians (NADA) ..... SATT
Society of Architects and Associated Technicians [*British*] (BI) ..... SAAT
Society of Architectural Administrators (EA) ..... SAA
Society of Architectural Historians (EA) ..... SAH
Society of Architectural Historians (of Great Britain) ..... SAH(GB)
Society of Archivists [*British*] ..... SA
Society of Army Historical Research [*British*] (BI) ..... SAHR
Society of Arthritic Gardeners ..... SAG
Society of Arts [*British*] ..... SA
Society of Assistants Training in Preparatory Schools [*British*] ..... SATIPS
Society of Associated Financial Executives ..... SAFE
Society of Association Executives [*British*] (EAIO) ..... SAE
Society of Australasian Specialists [*Later, SASO*] ..... SAS
Society of Australasian Specialists/Oceania (EA) ..... SASO
Society of Authors (DGA) ..... SA
Society of Authors [*British*] (EAIO) ..... SOA
Society of Authors, Composers, and Editors of Music (NADA) ..... SACEM
Society of Authors' Representatives (EA) ..... SAR
Society of Automotive Analysts (EA) ..... SAA
Society of Automotive Engineers [*Acronym is now organization's official name*] (EA) ..... SAE
Society of Automotive Engineers abstracts (NITA) ..... SAE abstracts
Society of Automotive Engineers, Inc. (AAGC) ..... MAM
Society of Automotive Engineers, Inc. (AAGC) ..... SAE
Society of Automotive Engineers, New York, NY [*Library symbol Library of Congress*] (LCLS) ..... NNSAE
Society of Automotive Historians (EA) ..... SAH
Society of Automotive-Electrical Technicians [*British*] (DBA) ..... SAET
Society of Basque Studies in America (EA) ..... SBSA
Society of Batik Artists [*Defunct*] (EA) ..... SBA
Society of Bead Researchers (EA) ..... SBR
Society of Beer and Sordid Sex Professional Invitational Fishing Tournament and Gastronomical Extravaganza ..... SOBASSPIFTAGE
Society of Behavioral Medicine (EA) ..... SBM
Society of Biblical Literature (EA) ..... SBL
Society of Biblical Literature and Exegesis [*Later, SBL*] (EA) ..... SBLE
Society of Biological Psychiatry (EA) ..... SBP
Society of Biomedical Equipment Technicians (EA) ..... SBET
Society of Bookmen (DGA) ..... SOB
Society of British Aerospace Companies (MCD) ..... SBAC
Society of British Aircraft Constructors ..... SBAC
Society of British Fight Directors (DBA) ..... SBFD
Society of British Gas Industries (BI) ..... SBGI
Society of British Neurological Surgeons ..... SBNS
Society of British Printing Ink Manufacturers (BI) ..... SBPIM
Society of British Snuff Blenders (EAIO) ..... SBSB
Society of British Theatre Designers (DBA) ..... SBTD
Society of Broadcast Engineers (EA) ..... SBE
Society of Business Advisory Professions (EA) ..... SBAP
Society of Business Economists (EAIO) ..... SBE
Society of Business Folk [*Defunct*] (EA) ..... SBF
Society of Business Magazine Editors [*Later, ASBPE*] ..... SBME
Society of Business Publication Designers [*Later, SPD*] (EA) ..... SBPD
Society of Cable Television Engineers (EA) ..... SCTE
Society of California Pioneers (EA) ..... SCP
Society of California Pioneers, San Francisco, CA [*Library symbol Library of Congress*] (LCLS) ..... CSfCP
Society of Canadian Artists [*Formerly, Society of Co-Operative Artists*] ..... SCA
Society of Canadian Artists, Montreal [*1868-72*] (NGC) ..... SCA
Society of Canadian Cine Amateurs ..... SCCA
Society of Canadian Painter-Etchers and Engravers [*1916-76*] (NGC) ..... CPE
Society of Carbide and Tool Engineers (EA) ..... SCTE
Society of Carbide Engineers [*Later, SCTE*] (EA) ..... SCE
Society of Cardiological Technicians [*British*] ..... SCT
Society of Cardiovascular and Interventional Radiology (EA) ..... SCIR
Society of Cardiovascular and Interventional Radiology (EA) ..... SCVIR
Society of Cardiovascular Anesthesiologists (EA) ..... SCA
Society of Cardiovascular Radiology [*Later, SCVIR*] (EA) ..... SCR
Society of Carnival Glass Collectors ..... SCGC
Society of Casual Safety Engineers ..... SCSE
Society of Catering and Hotel Management Consultants [*British*] (DBA) ..... SCHMC
Society of Catholic College Teachers of Sacred Doctrine [*Later, CTS*] (EA) ..... SCCTSD
Society of Catholic Medical Missionaries, Inc. [*Medical Mission Sisters*] [*Roman Catholic religious order*] ..... SCMM
Society of Certified Consumer Credit Executives (EA) ..... SCCCE
Society of Certified Credit Executives [*St. Louis, MO*] (EA) ..... SCCE
Society of Certified Data Processors [*AICCP*] [*Superseded by*] (EA) ..... SCDP
Society of Certified Insurance Counselors [*Austin, TX*] (EA) CIC
Society of Certified Kitchen Designers (EA) ..... SCKD
Society of Chain Link Fencing Manufacturers [*British*] (DBA) ..... SCLFM
Society of Chartered Property and Casualty Underwriters [*Malvern, PA*] (EA) ..... CPCU
Society of Chartered Property and Casualty Underwriters (EA) ..... SCPCU
Society of Cheese Connoisseurs [*British*] (DBA) ..... SCC
Society of Chemical Industries (NADA) ..... SCI
Society of Chemical Industry (EA) ..... SCI
Society of Chemical Industry, American Section (EA) ..... SCIAS
Society of Chief Architects of Local Authorities [*British*] ..... SCALA
Society of Chief Building Regulation Officers [*British*] (DBA) ..... SOCBRO
Society of Chief Inspectors and Advisers [*British*] (AIE) ..... SCIA
Society of Chief Personnel Officers [*British*] ..... SOCPO
Society of Children's Book Writers (EA) ..... SCBW
Society of Christ [*Roman Catholic men's religious order*] ..... SCh
Society of Christ (TOCD) ..... sch
Society of Christian Engineers (EA) ..... SCE
Society of Christian Ethics (EA) ..... SCE
Society of Christian Philosophers (EA) ..... SCP
Society of Cinema Collectors and Historians (EA) ..... SCCH
Society of Cinematologists [*Later, SCS*] (EA) ..... SOC
Society of Civil and Public Servants [*A union*] [*British*] (DCTA) ..... SCPS
Society of Civil Engineering Technicians [*British*] (DBA) ..... SCET
Society of Civil Servants [*British*] ..... SCS
Society of Classical Homeopathy [*Australia*] ..... SCH
Society of Cleaning Technicians (EA) ..... SCT
Society of Clerks of Valuation Panels [*British*] (DBA) ..... SCVP
Society of Clinical and Medical Electrologists (EA) ..... SCME
Society of Clinical Masseurs [*Australia*] ..... SCM
Society of Clinical Surgery [*Defunct*] (EA) ..... SCS
Society of Collision Repair Specialists (EA) ..... SCRS
Society of Colonial Wars ..... SCW
Society of Commercial Seed Technologists (EA) ..... SCST
Society of Commercial Teachers (EAIO) ..... SCT
Society of Commissioned Officers (EA) ..... SCO
Society of Communications Engineers and Analysts ..... SCEA
Society of Community Medicine [*Later, SPH*] (EAIO) ..... SCM
Society of Company and Commercial Accountants [*Edgbaston, Birmingham, England*] (EAIO) ..... SCCA
Society of Company Meeting Planners (EA) ..... SCMP
Society of Competitor Intelligence Professionals (EA) ..... SCIP
Society of Composers (EA) ..... SCI
Society of Composers, Authors and Music Publishers of Canada [*Canada*] (WWLA) ..... SOCAN
Society of Computed Body Tomography (EA) ..... SCBT
Society of Computer Intelligence (IAA) ..... SCI
Society of Connoisseurs in Murder (EA) ..... SOCIM
Society of Construction Law [*British*] (DBA) ..... SCL
Society of Construction Superintendents (EA) ..... SCS
Society of Consumer Affairs (NADA) ..... SCA
Society of Consumer Affairs Professionals in Business [*Alexandria, VA*] (EA) ..... SOCAP
Society of Cosmetic Chemists (EA) ..... SCC
Society of Cosmetic Scientists (EAIO) ..... SCS
Society of Cost Estimating and Analysis (EA) ..... SCEA
Society of Costa Rica Collectors (EA) ..... SOCORICO
Society of County Librarians [*British*] ..... SCL
Society of County Secretaries [*British*] ..... SCS
Society of County Secretaries [*British*] (DBA) ..... SOCS
Society of County Treasurers [*British*] ..... SCT
Society of Craft Designers (EA) ..... SCD
Society of Craftsmen Bakers [*British*] (BI) ..... SCB
Society of Critical Care Medicine (EA) ..... SCCM
Society of Critical Care Nurses of Canada ..... SCCNC
Society of Daily Communicants [*Defunct*] (EA) ..... SDC
Society of Dairy Technology [*British*] ..... SDT
Society of Dance History Scholars (EA) ..... SDHS
Society of Dance Research [*British*] (DBA) ..... SDR
Society of Data Educators (EA) ..... SDE
Society of Daughters of Holland Dames (EA) ..... SDHD
Society of Descendants of Colonial Hispanics (EA) ..... SDCH
Society of Designer-Craftsmen [*British*] (EAIO) ..... SD-C
Society of Designers in Ireland (EAIO) ..... SDI
Society of Diagnostic Medical Sonographers (EA) ..... SDMS

Society of Die Casting Engineers (EA) .... SDCE
Society of Dirty Old Men [Defunct] (EA) .... SDOM
Society of Dismas (EA) .... SOD
Society of Divine Vocations [Vocationist Fathers] [Roman Catholic religious order] .... SDV
Society of Dyers and Colourists (EAIO) .... SDC
Society of Early Recorded Music (EA) .... SERM
Society of Earthbound Extraterrestrials (EA) .... SEE
Society of Economic Geologists (EA) .... SEG
Society of Editors (DGA) .... SOE
Society of Education Officers [British] .... SEO
Society of Educational Programmers and Systems Analysts [Later, SDE] .... SEPSA
Society of Educators and Scholars (EA) .... SES
Society of Electronic and Radio Technicians (IAA) .... SERT
Society of Electronics and Automation (IAA) .... SEA
Society of Electronics Engineers .... SEE
Society of Electroscience [British] (DBA) .... SElec
Society of Engineering Associates [Australia] .... SEA
Society of Engineering Illustrators (EA) .... SEI
Society of Engineering Office Workers (EA) .... SEOW
Society of Engineering Psychologists [Later, DAEEP] (EA) .... SEP
Society of Engineering Science (EA) .... SES
Society of Engineers .... SE
Society of Engineers and Machinists [A union] [British] .... SEM
Society of English and American Lawyers [British] (DBA) .... SEAL
Society of Environmental Engineers [Later, Institute of Environmental Sciences] .... SEE
Society of Environmental Graphics Designers (EA) .... SEGD
Society of Environmental Improvement [British] (DBA) .... SEI
Society of Environmental Toxicology and Chemistry (EA) .... SETAC
Society of Equestrian Artists [British] (DBA) .... SEA
Society of Ethnic and Special Studies (EA) .... SESS
Society of Ethnobiology (EA) .... SE
Society of European Stage Authors and Composers .... SESAC
Society of European Stage Authors and Composers [Nashville, TN] (WDMC) .... SESAC Inc.
Society of Evangelical Agnostics [Defunct] (EA) .... SEA
Society of Exchange Counselors (EA) .... SEC
Society of Experimental Psychologists (EA) .... SEP
Society of Experimental Social Psychology [Defunct] (EA) .... SESP
Society of Experimental Test Pilots (EA) .... SETP
Society of Exploration Geophysicists (EA) .... SEG
Society of Explosives Engineers (EA) .... SEE
Society of Eye Surgeons (EA) .... SES
Society of Family Practitioner Committees [British] (DBA) .... SFPC
Society of Federal Artists and Designers [Later, FDC] (EA) .... SFAD
Society of Federal Labor Relations Professionals (EA) .... SFLRP
Society of Federal Linguists (EA) .... SFL
Society of Filipino Accountants (EA) .... SFA
Society of Film and Television Arts Ltd. [British] (BI) .... SFTA
Society of Film Distributors [British] .... SFD
Society of Financial Examiners (EA) .... SFE
Society of Financial Examiners (EA) .... SOFE
Society of Fine Art Auctioneers [British] (DBA) .... SOFAA
Society of Fire Engineers .... SFE
Society of Fire Protection Engineers (EA) .... SFPE
Society of Fire Protection Technicians (EA) .... SFPT
Society of Flavor Chemists (EA) .... SFC
Society of Flight Test Engineers (EA) .... SFTE
Society of Floristry [British] (DBA) .... SoF
Society of Floristry Diploma [British] (DI) .... SFDip
Society of Folk Harpers and Craftsmen (EA) .... SFHC
Society of Forensic Toxicologists (EA) .... SOFT
Society of Former Special Agents of the Federal Bureau of Investigation (EA) .... SFSAFBI
Society of Franciscan Servants of Jesus and Mary [Anglican religious community] .... FSJM
Society of Freight Car Historians (EA) .... SFCH
Society of French-Speaking Neurosurgeons (EA) .... SFSN
Society of Friendly Boilermakers [A union] [British] .... SFB
Society of Friends Community Relations Committee [British] .... SRC
Society of Friends of Icons [Germany] (EAIO) .... SFI
Society of Friends of Puerto Rico (EA) .... FOPR
Society of Friends of the Touro Synagogue (EA) .... SFTS
Society of Furnace Builders [British] (BI) .... SFB
Society of Gas Lighting (EA) .... SGL
Society of Gastroenterology Nurses and Associates (EA) .... SGNA
Society of Gastrointestinal Assistants [Later, SGNA] (EA) .... SGA
Society of Genealogists (EA) .... SG
Society of General Internal Medicine (EA) .... SGIM
Society of General Physiologists (EA) .... SGP
Society of Geniuses of Distinction [Defunct] (EA) .... SGD
Society of Geriatric Ophthalmology (EA) .... SGO
Society of Ghana Philatelists [Defunct] (EA) .... SGP
Society of Gilders (EA) .... SG
Society of Glass and Ceramic Decorators (EA) .... SGCD
Society of Glass Decorators [Later, SGCD] (EA) .... SGD
Society of Glass Technology (EAIO) .... SGT
Society of Goldsmiths, Jewellers, and Kindred Trades [A union] [British] .... SGJKT
Society of Government Economists (EA) .... SGE
Society of Government Meeting Planners (EA) .... SGMP
Society of Governmental Appraisers [Later, Association of Governmental Appraisers] (EA) .... SGA

Society of Grain Elevator Superintendents [Later, GEAPS] .... SGES
Society of Graphic Art [British] .... SGA
Society of Graphic Art, Toronto [1912, founded c.1903 as GAC, CSGA from 1923] [Canada] (NGC) .... SGA
Society of Graphic Designers of Canada (EAIO) .... GDC
Society of Graphic Fine Art [British] (DBA) .... SGFA
Society of Graphical and Allied Trades [British] .... SOGAT
Society of Gynecologic Oncologists (EA) .... SGO
Society of Head and Neck Surgeons (EA) .... SHNS
Society of Headmasters of Independent Schools [British] .... SHMIS
Society of Health and Beauty Therapists [British] (DBA) .... SHBTh
Society of Hearing Aid Audiologists [Later, NHAS] (EA) .... SHAA
Society of Helpers (TOCD) .... HHS
Society of Helpers of the Holy Souls [Roman Catholic women's religious order] .... HHS
Society of Hispanic Professional Engineers (EA) .... SHPE
Society of Hospital Laundry Managers [British] (BI) .... SHLM
Society of Illustrators (EA) .... SI
Society of Incentive Travel Executives [New York, NY] (EA) .... SITE
Society of Independent and Private School Data Education [Later, SDE] (EA) .... SIPSDE
Society of Independent Financial Advisors [Englewood, CO] (EA) .... SIFA
Society of Independent Gasoline Marketers of America [Washington, DC] (EA) .... SIGMA
Society of Independent Motion Picture Producers .... SIMPP
Society of Independent Producers (NTCM) .... SIP
Society of Independent Professional Earth Scientists (EA) .... SIPES
Society of Indexers (EAIO) .... SI
Society of Indiana Pioneers (EA) .... SIP
Society of Indochina Philatelists (EA) .... SICP
Society of Industrial Accountants of Canada .... SIA
Society of Industrial and Cost Accountants of Canada .... SICA
Society of Industrial and Office Realtors (EA) .... SIOR
Society of Industrial Artists and Designers [British] (DI) .... SIAD
Society of Industrial Civil Defence Officers [British] (BI) .... SICDO
Society of Industrial Emergency Services Officers [British] (DBA) .... SIESO
Society of Industrial Engineers [Later, SAM] .... SIE
Society of Industrial Realtors [Association name and designation awarded by this group] [Washington, DC] (EA) .... SIR
Society of Industrial Tutors [British] .... SIT
Society of Inkwell Collectors (EA) .... SIC
Society of In-Plant Graphics Management Associations .... SIGMA
Society of Instrument and Control Engineers of Japan (IAA) .... SICEJ
Society of Instrument Technology [British] .... SIT
Society of Insurance Accountants [Crozet, VA] (EA) .... SIA
Society of Insurance Research [Appleton, WI] (EA) .... SIR
Society of Insurance Trainers and Educators (EA) .... SITE
Society of Inter-Celtic Arts and Culture (EA) .... ICS
Society of Inter-Celtic Arts and Culture (EA) .... SICAC
Society of International Friendship (EA) .... SIF
Society of International Gas Tanker and Terminal Operators (EAIO) .... SIGTTO
Society of International Secretaries .... SIS
Society of International Treasurers (EAIO) .... SIT
Society of Interpretation of Britain's Heritage (DBA) .... SIBH
Society of Inventors of Games and Mathematical Attractions [British] .... SIGMA
Society of Israel Philatelists (EA) .... SIP
Society of Jewish Bibliophiles (EA) .... SJB
Society of Jewish Composers, Publishers, and Songwriters [Defunct] (EA) .... SJCPS
Society of Jewish Science (EA) .... SJS
Society of Jews and Christians .... SJC
Society of Journeymen Brushmakers [A union] [British] .... SJB
Society of Kastorians "Omonoia" (EA) .... SKO
Society of King Charles the Martyr (EA) .... SKCM
Society of Land Economists [Australia] .... SLE
Society of Landscape Studies [British] (DBA) .... SLS
Society of Laundry Engineers and Allied Trades (IAA) .... SLEAT
Society of Leather Technologists and Chemists [British] .... SLTC
Society of Licensed Aircraft Engineers and Technologists (EAIO) .... SLAET
Society of Licensed Aircraft Engineers and Technologists (DA) .... SLEAT
Society of Limerents (EA) .... SL
Society of Lithographic Artists, Designers, and Engineers [British] .... SLADE
Society of Local Authority Chief Executives [British] (DBA) .... SOLACE
Society of Local Council Clerks [British] .... SLCC
Society of Local Government Barristers [British] (DLA) .... SLGB
Society of Logistics Engineers (MCD) .... SLE
Society of Logistics Engineers (EA) .... SOLE
Society of Loose Actors Revolving [SOLAR Theater, Inc.] .... SOLAR
Society of Loyalist Descendants (EA) .... SLD
Society of Magazine Writers [Later, ASJA] (EA) .... SMW
Society of Make-up Artists (NTCM) .... SMA
Society of Malawi. Journal [A publication] .... SMJ
Society of Males Who Appreciate Cute Knees [Group opposing below-the-knee fashions introduced in 1970] .... SMACK
Society of Management Accountants .... SMA
Society of Management Accountants of Canada .... SMAC
Society of Management Accountants of Ontario [Canada] (DD) .... SMAO
Society of Management Information Technology [British] .... MIT
Society of Manufacturer's Agents [Later, SMR] (EA) .... SMA
Society of Manufacturers' Representatives (EA) .... SMR
Society of Manufacturing Engineers (EA) .... SME
Society of Manufacturing Engineers, Dearborn, MI [Library symbol] [Library of Congress] (LCLS) .... MiDbME
Society of Marine Architects and Marine Engineers (EA) .... SMAME
Society of Marine Artists [British] .... SMA

Society of Marine Consultants (EA) .... SMC
Society of Marine Port Engineers (EA) .... SMPE
Society of Maritime Arbitrators (EA) .... SMA
Society of Mary (Marianists) (TOCD) .... SM
Society of Mary Missionary Sisters (TOCD) .... SMMS
Society of Mary Reparatrix [*Roman Catholic women's religious order*] .... SMR
Society of Master Printers Scotland (DBA) .... SMPS
Society of Master Shoe Repairers [*British*] (DBA) .... SMSR
Society of Medalists .... SM
Society of Medalists [*Defunct*] (EA) .... SOM
Society of Medical Administrators (EA) .... SMA
Society of Medical Consultants to the Armed Forces (EA) .... SMCAF
Society of Medical Friends of Wine (EA) .... SMFW
Society of Medical Jurisprudence (EA) .... SMJ
Society of Medical Officers of Health [*British*] .... SMOH
Society of Medical-Dental Management Consultants (EA) .... SMD
Society of Medical-Dental Management Consultants (EA) .... SMDMC
Society of Memorial Cancer Center .... SMCC
Society of Mental Welfare Officers [*British*] (BI) .... SMWO
Society of Metaphysicians (EA) .... S of M
Society of Metaphysicians [*British*] (DBA) .... SOM
Society of Metropolitan Treasurers [*British*] .... SMT
Society of Military Engineers (KSC) .... SME
Society of Military Ophthalmologists (EA) .... SMO
Society of Military Orthopaedic Surgeons (EA) .... SMOS
Society of Military Orthopedics Surgeons (DAVI) .... SOMOS
Society of Military Otolaryngologists [*Later, SMO-HNS*] (EA) .... SMO
Society of Military Otolaryngologists - Head and Neck Surgeons (EA) .... SMO-HNS
Society of Military Widows (EA) .... SMW
Society of Mineral Analysts (EA) .... SMA
Society of Miniature Painters [*British*] (ROG) .... SMP
Society of Miniature Rifle Clubs [*British*] (ROG) .... SMRC
Society of Miniaturists (EA) .... SM
Society of Mining Engineers of American Institute of Mining, Metallurgical, and Petroleum Engineers [*Later, SME, Inc.*] (EA) .... SME of AIME
Society of Missionaries of Africa (EAIO) .... MAfr
Society of Model Aeronautical Engineers [*British*] .... SMAE
Society of Model and Experimental Engineers [*British*] (BI) .... SMEE
Society of Motion Picture and Television Art Directors (EA) .... SMPTAD
Society of Motion Picture and Television Engineers (EA) .... SMPTE
Society of Motion Picture Art Directors [*Later, SMPTAD*] (EA) .... SMPAD
Society of Motion Picture Engineers [*Later, SMPTE*] (NTCM) .... SMPE
Society of Motor Manufacturers and Traders [*Defunct*] (EA) .... SMMT
Society of Multivariate Experimental Psychology (EA) .... SMEP
Society of Municipal Arborists (EA) .... SMA
Society of Museum Archaeologists [*British*] (DBA) .... SMA
Society of National Association Publications (EA) .... SNAP
Society of Naval Architects and Marine Engineers (EA) .... SNAME
Society of Nematologists (EA) .... SON
Society of Neurological Surgeons (EA) .... SNS
Society of Neurosurgical Anesthesia and Critical Care (EA) .... SNACC
Society of Neurosurgical Anesthesia and Neurological Supportive Care [*Later, SNACC*] (EA) .... SNANSC
Society of Newspaper Design (EA) .... SND
Society of Non-Invasive Vascular Technology (EA) .... SNIVT
Society of Non-Smokers (EA) .... SONS
Society of North American Goldsmiths (EA) .... SNAG
Society of Norwegian American Engineers (IAA) .... SNAE
Society of Nuclear Medical Technologists [*Defunct*] (EA) .... SNMT
Society of Nuclear Medicine (EA) .... SNM
Society of Nuclear Medicine - Technology Section (DAVI) .... SNM-TS
Society of Nuclear Scientists and Engineers [*Defunct*] .... SNSE
Society of Occupational Medicine [*British*] .... SOM
Society of Office Automation Professionals [*Later, AMS*] [*Telecommunications service Willow Grove, PA*] (TSSD) .... SOAP
Society of Old Testament Study [*British*] (DBA) .... SOTS
Society of Operative Stonemasons [*A union*] [*British*] .... SOS
Society of Oral Physiology and Occlusion .... SOPO
Society of Ornamental Turners (EA) .... SOT
Society of Orthodox Youth Organizations (EA) .... SOYO
Society of Our Lady of the Most Holy Trinity (TOCD) .... SOLT
Society of Our Lady of the Most Holy Trinity (TOCD) .... solt
Society of Our Lady of the Way (EA) .... SOLW
Society of Our Mother of Peace (TOCD) .... smp
Society of Our Mother of Peace (TOCD) .... SMP
Society of Packaging and Handling Engineers [*Later, IoPP*] (EA) .... SPHE
Society of Painters in Tempera (EA) .... SPT
Society of Paper Money Collectors (EA) .... SPMC
Society of Park and Recreation Educators (EA) .... SPRE
Society of Parrot Breeders and Exhibitors (EA) .... SPBE
Society of Participating Artists [*Record label*] .... SPA
Society of Patient Representatives [*Later, NSPR*] (EA) .... SPR
Society of Pelvic Surgeons (EA) .... SPS
Society of Perinatal Obstetricians (EA) .... SPO
Society of Peripheral Vascular Nursing (EA) .... SPVN
Society of Petroleum Engineers (EA) .... SPE
Society of Petroleum Engineers of American Institute of Mining, Metallurgical, and Petroleum Engineers (EA) .... SPE of AIME
Society of Petroleum Engineers Production Operations Symposium and Exhibition (ITD) .... SPEPOS
Society of Petroleum Evaluation Engineers (IAA) .... SPEE
Society of Phantom Friends (EA) .... SPF
Society of Philatelic Americans [*Defunct*] (EA) .... SPA
Society of Philatelists and Numismatists (EA) .... SPAN
Society of Philaticians [*Defunct*] (EA) .... SP
Society of Philippine Surgeons in America (EA) .... SPSA
Society of Philosophers in America (EA) .... SPA
Society of Photographers and Artist Representatives (EA) .... SPAR
Society of Photographic Illustrators (EA) .... SPI
Society of Photographic Scientists and Engineers (EA) .... SPSE
Society of Photo-Optical Instrumentation Engineers [*International Society for Optical Engineering*] .... SPIE
Society of Photo-Technologists (EA) .... SPT
Society of Physics Students (EA) .... SPS
Society of Picture Researchers and Editors [*British*] (DBA) .... SPREd
Society of Planning Officials .... SPO
Society of Plastics Engineers (EA) .... SPE
Society of Polish-American Travel Agents (EA) .... SPATA
Society of Political Item Enthusiasts (EA) .... SPIE
Society of Portrait Sculptors [*British*] (BI) .... SPS
Society of Post Office Engineers [*Pronounced "spowee"*] [*British*] (DCTA) .... SPOE
Society of Post Office Managers [*A union*] [*British*] .... SPOM
Society of Power Industry Biologists (EA) .... SPIB
Society of Pragmatic Mysticism (EA) .... SPM
Society of Prayer for World Peace (EAIO) .... SPWP
Society of Priests for a Free Ministry (EA) .... SPFM
Society of Private and Pioneer Numismatics (EA) .... SPPN
Society of Private Printers [*Middlesex, England*] .... SPP
Society of Professional Archeologists (EA) .... SOPA
Society of Professional Assessors [*Address unknown*] .... SPA
Society of Professional Audio Recording Services (EA) .... SPARS
Society of Professional Benefit Administrators [*Washington, DC*] (EA) .... SPBA
Society of Professional Business Consultants [*Chicago, IL*] (EA) .... SPBC
Society of Professional Data Processors (IAA) .... SPDP
Society of Professional Drivers (EA) .... SPD
Society of Professional Engineering Checkers .... SPEC
Society of Professional Investigators (EA) .... SPI
Society of Professional Journalists [*Also, SDX*] (NTCM) .... SPJ
Society of Professional Journalists, Sigma Delta Chi (EA) .... SPJ SDX
Society of Professional Management Consultants [*Association name and designation awarded by this group*] [*Englewood, NJ*] (EA) .... SPMC
Society of Professional Pilots (EA) .... SPP
Society of Professional Well Log Analysts (EA) .... SPWLA
Society of Professionals in Dispute Resolution (EA) .... SPIDR
Society of Professors of Child and Adolescent Psychiatry (EA) .... SPCAP
Society of Professors of Child Psychiatry [*Later, SPCAP*] (EA) .... SPCP
Society of Professors of Education (EA) .... SPE
Society of Projective Techniques [*Later, SPA*] (EA) .... SPT
Society of Prospective Medicine (EA) .... SPM
Society of Protozoologists (EA) .... SP
Society of Psychologists in Addictive Behaviors [*Later, PAB*] (EA) .... SPAB
Society of Public Health (EAIO) .... SPH
Society of Public Health Educators (DAVI) .... SPHE
Society of Public Relations Counsellors .... SPRC
Society of Public Teachers of Law [*British*] (DLA) .... SPTL
Society of Publication Designers (EA) .... SPD
Society of Radio Operators .... SRO
Society of Radiographers (EAIO) .... SR
Society of Ration Token Collectors (EA) .... SRTC
Society of Real Estate Appraisers [*Later, AI*] (EA) .... SREA
Society of Record Dealers of America .... SORD
Society of Recorder Players [*British*] (DBA) .... SRP
Society of Recreation Executives (EA) .... SRE
Society of Registration Officers - Births, Deaths, and Marriages [*British*] (DBA) .... SRO
Society of Relay Engineers [*British*] .... SRE
Society of Reliability Engineers (EA) .... SRE
Society of Remedial Gymnasts (EA) .... SRG
Society of Reproduction Engineers [*Later, IAVCM*] (EA) .... SRE
Society of Reproductive Endocrinologists (EA) .... SRE
Society of Research Administrators (EA) .... SRA
Society of Residential Appraisers [*Later, AI*] .... SRA
Society of Retired Catholic Persons (EA) .... SRCP
Society of Rheology (EA) .... SOR
Society of Rheology [*Later, SoR*] (EA) .... SR
Society of Richmond County Descendants (EA) .... SRCD
Society of Risk Management Consultants [*Baton Rouge, LA*] (EA) .... SRMC
Society of Roadcraft [*British*] (DBA) .... SoR
Society of Roller Skating Teachers of America (EA) .... SRSTA
Society of Romance Linguistics [*Nancy, France*] (EAIO) .... SRL
Society of Romanian Air Transports [*ICAO designator*] (FAAC) .... SRT
Society of Romanian Air Transports [*ICAO designator*] (FAAC) .... STAR
Society of Rosicrucians (EA) .... SR
Society of Rural Financial Officers [*British*] (BI) .... SORFO
Society of Rural Financial Officers [*British*] (BI) .... SRFO
Society of Russian Veterans of the World War (EA) .... SRV
Society of St. Columban (TOCD) .... SSC
Society of St. Columban, St. Columban's Foreign Mission Society (TOCD) .... ssc
Society of Saint Edmund (TOCD) .... sse
Society of St. Edmund [*Roman Catholic men's religious order*] .... SSE
Society of St. Francis [*Anglican religious community*] .... SSF
Society of St. Francis Xavier for the Foreign Missions [*Also known as Xaverian Missionaries*] (EAIO) .... SX
Society of Saint Gregory [*British*] (DBA) .... SSG
Society of St. Gregory of America [*Later, CMAA*] (EA) .... SSGA
Society of St. John the Divine [*Anglican religious community*] .... SSJD
Society of St. John the Evangelist [*Anglican religious community*] .... SSJE
Society of St. Margaret [*Anglican religious community*] .... SSM

Society of St. Monica (EA) ... SSM
Society of St. Paul for the Apostolate of Communications [*Pauline Fathers*] [*Roman Catholic religious order*] ... SSP
Society of St. Peter Apostle (EA) ... SSPA
Society of St. Peter the Apostle for Native Clergy [*Later, SSPA*] (EA) ... SSPANC
Society of St. Stephen (EA) ... SSS
Society of St. Sulpice [*Sulpicians*] [*Roman Catholic men's religious order*] ... SS
Society of St. Teresa of Jesus (TOCD) ... STJ
Society of St. Ursula (TOCD) ... SU
Society of St. Vincent De Paul [*Paris, France*] (EAIO) ... SSVP
Society of St. Vincent de Paul ... SVP
Society of Sales Professionals [*Automotive sales certification program*] ... SASP
Society of Satellite Professionals [*Later, SSPI*] (EA) ... SSP
Society of Satellite Professionals International (TSSD) ... SSPI
Society of Saunterers, International (EA) ... SOS Intl
Society of Saunterers, International (EA) ... SSI
Society of Savings and Loan Controllers [*Later, Financial Managers Society*] (EA) ... SSLC
Society of Scale Beam and Weighing Machinists [*A union*] [*British*] ... SSBWM
Society of School Librarians International (EA) ... SSLI
Society of Scottish Artists (DBA) ... SSA
Society of Scribes (EA) ... SOS
Society of Scribes and Illuminators (EA) ... SSI
Society of Security Analysts ... SSA
Society of Senior Aerospace Executives (EA) ... SSAE
Society of Separationists (EA) ... SOS
Society of Separationists (EA) ... SS
Society of Shipping Executives [*British*] (BI) ... SSE
Society of Shuttlemakers [*A union*] [*British*] ... SOS
Society of Shuttlemakers [*A union*] [*British*] ... SS
Society of Signalmen (EA) ... SOS
Society of Signalmen (EA) ... SS
Society of Silver Collectors (EA) ... SSC
Society of Small Craft Designers (EA) ... SSCD
Society of Soft Drink Technologists (EA) ... SSDT
Society of Spanish and Spanish-American Studies (EA) ... SSSAS
Society of Spanish Engineers, Planners, and Architects (EA) ... SSEPA
Society of Sponsors of the United States Navy (EA) ... SSUSN
Society of Stage Directors and Choreographers (EA) ... SSDC
Society of Stage Directors and Choreographers (EA) ... SSTDC
Society of State Directors of Health, Physical Education, and Recreation (EA) ... SSDHPER
Society of Strip Illustration [*British*] (DBA) ... SSI
Society of Study Addiction [*British*] (DBA) ... SSA
Society of Surgical Oncology (EA) ... SSO
Society of Surveying Technicians (EAIO) ... SST
Society of Systematic Zoology (EA) ... SSZ
Society of Teachers in Business Education [*British*] (EAIO) ... STBE
Society of Teachers in Education of Professional Photography (EA) ... STEPP
Society of Teachers of Emergency Medicine (EA) ... STEM
Society of Teachers of Family Medicine (EA) ... STFM
Society of Teachers of Professional Photography [*Later, STEPP*] (EA) ... STOPP
Society of Teachers of Speech and Drama [*British*] ... STSD
Society of Teachers of the Alexander Technique (EAIO) ... STAT
Society of Teachers Opposed to Physical Punishment ... STOPP
Society of Technical Civil Servants [*British*] (BI) ... STCS
Society of Technical Writers and Editors [*Later, STWP, STC*] ... STWE
Society of Technical Writers and Publishers [*Formerly, STWE*] [*Later, STC*] (EA) ... STWP
Society of Telecom Executives [*Trade union*] [*British*] ... STE
Society of Telecommunications Consultants (EA) ... STC
Society of Telecommunications Executives (NITA) ... STE
Society of Telecommunications Professionals (TSSD) ... STP
Society of Telegraphic Engineers [*British*] ... STEL
Society of Television Pioneers (EA) ... STP
Society of Test Engineers [*British*] (DBA) ... STE
Society of the Ark and the Dove (EA) ... SAD
Society of the Bible in the Hands of Its Creators [*Defunct*] (EA) ... SBHC
Society of the Brothers of Charity (TOCD) ... sfc
Society of the Catholic Apostolate [*Pallottines*] [*Roman Catholic men's religious order*] ... SAC
Society of the Catholic Apostolate, Pallottine Fathers (TOCD) ... sac
Society of the Chemical Industry (NADA) ... SCI
Society of the Cincinnati (EA) ... SC
Society of the Cincinnati, Washington, DC [*Library symbol*] [*Library of Congress*] (LCLS) ... DSoC
Society of the Classic Guitar (EA) ... SCG
Society of the Companions of the Holy Cross (EA) ... SCHC
Society of the Compassionate Friends [*Later, TCF*] (EA) ... SCF
Society of the Descendants of the Colonial Clergy (EA) ... SDCC
Society of the Descendants of the Schwenkfeldian Exiles (EA) ... SDSE
Society of the Descendants of Washington's Army at Valley Forge (EA) ... DVF
Society of the Devotees of Jerusalem (EA) ... SDJ
Society of the Divine Compassion [*Anglican religious community*] ... SDC
Society of the Divine Savior (TOCD) ... sds
Society of the Divine Savior (TOCD) ... SDS
Society of the Divine Word (TOCD) ... SVD
Society of the Divine Word (TOCD) ... svd
Society of the Founders and Friends of Norwich, Connecticut (EA) ... SFFNC
Society of the Founders of Norwich, Connecticut (EA) ... SFNC
Society of the Friends of Ancient and Historical Dubrovnik [*Croatia*] (EAIO) ... SFAHD
Society of the Friends of the Holy Father ... SFHF
Society of the Golden Section [*Defunct*] (EA) ... SGS
Society of the Good Shepherd [*Anglican religious community*] ... SGS
Society of the Holy Child Jesus [*Roman Catholic women's religious order*] ... SHCJ
Society of the Incarnation of the Eternal Son [*Anglican religious community*] ... SIES
Society of the Little Flower (EA) ... SLF
Society of the Most Holy Trinity [*Anglican religious community*] ... SHT
Society of the Plastics Industry (EA) ... SPI
Society of the Plastics Industry of Canada ... SPIC
Society of the Precious Blood (TOCD) ... CPPS
Society of the Precious Blood (TOCD) ... cpps
Society of the Precious Blood [*Anglican religious community*] ... SPB
Society of the President Street Fellows (EA) ... SPSF
Society of the Priest of Saint Sulpice, Sulpician Fathers (TOCD) ... ss
Society of the Priests of St. Sulpice [*See also CPSS*] [*Paris, France*] (EAIO) ... SPSS
Society of the Sacred Cross [*Anglican religious community*] ... SSC
Society of the Sacred Heart [*Roman Catholic women's religious order*] ... RSCJ
Society of the Sacred Mission [*Anglican religious community*] ... SSM
Society of the Servants of Mary [*Anglican religious community*] ... SSM
Society of the Silurians (EA) ... SS
Society of the Sisters, Faithful Companions of Jesus [*Roman Catholic religious order*] ... FCJ
Society of the Sisters of St. Ursula of the Blessed Virgin [*Roman Catholic religious order*] ... SU
Society of the Sisters of the Church (TOCD) ... SSC
Society of the War of 1812 in the Commonwealth of Pennsylvania (EA) ... SWCP
Society of Theatrical Carpenters [*A union*] [*British*] ... STC
Society of Thoracic and Cardiovascular Surgeons [*British*] (DBA) ... STCVS
Society of Thoracic Radiology (EA) ... STR
Society of Thoracic Surgeons (EA) ... STS
Society of Town Clerks [*British*] (BI) ... STC
Society of Town Planning Technicians [*British*] ... STPT
Society of Toxicologic Pathologists (EA) ... STP
Society of Toxicology (EA) ... SOT
Society of Tractor Engineers [*Later, SAE*] ... STE
Society of Traditional Roman Catholics (EA) ... STRC
Society of Translators of Quebec [*Canada*] ... STQ
Society of Trauma Nurses ... STN
Society of Travel and Tourism Educators (EA) ... STTE
Society of Tribologists and Lubrication Engineers (EAIO) ... STLE
Society of Turkish Architects, Engineers, and Scientists in America (EA) ... STAESA
Society of Tympanuchus Cupido Pinnatus (EA) ... STCP
Society of Typographic Arts [*Later, ACD*] (EA) ... STA
Society of Typographic Designers [*British*] (EAIO) ... STD
Society of Typographic Designers of Canada (DGA) ... STDC
Society of United States Air Force Flight Surgeons ... SUSAFFS
Society of United States Air Force Flight Surgeons (EA) ... USAF/EDA
Society of United States Air Force Flight Surgeons (EA) ... USAFSAM/ED
Society of University Cartographers [*British*] ... SUC
Society of University Otolaryngologists [*Later, SOU-HNS*] (EA) ... SUO
Society of University Otolaryngologists - Head and Neck Surgeons (EA) ... SUO-HNS
Society of University Patent Administrators (EA) ... SUPA
Society of University Surgeons (EA) ... SUS
Society of University Urologists (EA) ... SUU
Society of Vacuum Coaters (EA) ... SVC
Society of Vertebrate Paleontology (EA) ... SVP
Society of Vietnamese Rangers (EA) ... SVR
Society of Voluntary Associates [*British*] (DBA) ... SOVA
Society of Wedding Photographers [*British*] (DBA) ... SWP
Society of West End Theatre [*British*] (DBA) ... SWET
Society of Wildlife Art Nations [*British*] (DBA) ... SWAN
Society of Wine Educators (EA) ... SWE
Society of Wireless Pioneers (EA) ... SOWP
Society of Wireless Pioneers ... SWP
Society of Woman Geographers (EA) ... SWG
Society of Women Artists [*British*] (DBA) ... SWA
Society of Women Engineers (EA) ... SWE
Society of Women in Military Aviation (EA) ... SWMA
Society of Women Journalists (DGA) ... SWJ
Society of Women Musicians, Inc. [*British*] (BI) ... SWM
Society of Women Writers (DGA) ... SWW
Society of Women Writers and Journalists (DGA) ... SWWJ
Society of Wood Science and Technology (EA) ... SWST
Society of World War One Aero Historians [*Defunct*] (EA) ... SWWOAH
Society of Young Publishers (DGA) ... SYP
Society Promoting Training Women [*British*] (DBA) ... SPTW
Society that Opposes Pornography ... STOP
Society to Advance Foreclosure Education [*Defunct*] (EA) ... SAFE
Society to Conquer Mental Illness [*Defunct*] (EA) ... SCMI
Society to Curtail Ridiculous, Outrageous, and Ostentatious Gift Exchange (EA) ... SCROOGE
Society to Encourage Miniskirts [*New York group opposing below-the-knee fashions introduced in 1970*] ... STEMS
Society to Exterminate Neo-Communist Harbingers ... STENCH
Society to Help Avoid Redundant Effort [*in data processing*] ... SHARE
Society to Humiliate, Aggravate, Mortify, and Embarrass Smokers ... SHAME
Society to Preserve and Encourage Radio Drama, Variety, and Comedy (EA) ... SPERDVAC
Society to Preserve the Engrossing Enjoyment of DXing (EA) ... SPEEDX
Society to Support Home Confinement [*British*] (DBA) ... SSHC
Society's League Against Molestation (EA) ... SLAM

Socijaldemokratski Savez Makedonije [Social Democratic Alliance of Macedonia] [Political party] (EY) .... SDSM
Socijalisticka Partija Jugoslavije [Socialist Party of Yugoslavia] [Political party] (PPE) .... SPJ
Socijalisticka Partija Srbije [Socialist Party of Serbia] [Political party] (EY) ... SPS
Socijalisticka Savez Radnog Naroda Jugoslavije [Socialist Alliance of Working People of Yugoslavia - SAWPY] [Political party] (PPE) .... SSRNJ
Socijalisticka Stranka Jugoslavije [Yugoslav Socialist Party] [Political party] (EAIO) .... SSJ
Socioeconomic .... SE
Socio-Economic Benefit .... SEB
Socio-Economic Demographic Information System [Lawrence Berkeley Laboratory] [Database] .... SEEDIS
Socio-Economic Grade (ODBW) .... SEG
Socio-Economic Information Management System (NITA) .... SIMS
Socioeconomic Military Program (CINC) .... SEMP
Socio-Economic Model of the Planet Earth (PDAA) .... SEMPE
Socioeconomic Monitoring Survey (DAVI) .... SMS
Socio-Economic Research Division, Parks Canada Program, Environment Canada [Division de la Recherche Socio-Economique, Programme Parcs Canada, Environnement Canada] Ottawa, Ontario [Library symbol National Library of Canada] (NLC) .... OOEPSE
Socioeconomic Status [or Strata] .... SES
Socio-Economic-Status-Indicator (WDMC) .... SESI
Sociolinguistics Program (EA) .... SP
Sociological Practice Association (EA) .... SPA
Sociological Research Association (EA) .... SRA
Sociological Resources for Secondary Schools (AEBS) .... SRSS
Sociological Resources for Social Studies [Project of American Sociological Association] .... SRSS
Sociological Review [A publication] (BRI) .... Socio R
Sociologists for Women in Society (EA) .... SWS
Sociologists in Business (EA) .... SB
Sociology .... SOC
Sociology (DD) .... Soc
Sociology .... SOCIOL
Sociology .... SOCLGY
Sociology (ROG) .... SOCY
Sociology and Economic Aspects of Medicine [American Medical Association Information service or system] (CRD) .... SEAM
Sociology of Education Association (EA) .... SEA
Sociomoral Reflection Maturity Score (EDAC) .... SRMS
Sociomoral Reflection Measures (EDAC) .... SRM
Sociomoral Reflection Objective Measure (EDAC) .... SROM
Sociopathic Personality Disorder [Psychiatry] (DAVI) .... SPD
Socio-Sexual Knowledge and Attitudes Test [Psychology] .... SSKAT
Sociosystem Laboratory .... SSL
Socio-Technical Systems [Management technique] .... STS
Socio-Technological-Economic-Military [DoD] .... STEM
Socity of Mary, Marianists (TOCD) .... sm
Socius [or Sodalis] [Fellow] .... S
Socjaldemokracja Rzeczypospolitej Polskiej [Social Democracy of the Republic of Poland] [Political party] (EY) .... SDRP
Sockellafette [Pedestal mount] [German military - World War II] .... SL
Socket (DEN) .... SK
Socket (MSA) .... SKT
Socket (IAA) .... SO
Socket (AAG) .... SOC
Socket Communications [NASDAQ symbol] (TTSB) .... SCKT
Socket Communications, Inc. [NASDAQ symbol] (SAG) .... SCKT
Socket Communications, Inc. [Associated Press] (SAG) .... Socket
Socket Communications, Inc. [Associated Press] (SAG) .... SocketC
Socket Communications Wrrt [NASDAQ symbol] (TTSB) .... SCKTW
Socket Head (AAG) .... SCH
Socket Screw Products Bureau [Defunct] (EA) .... SSPB
Socket Service [Computer science] (PCM) .... SS
Socket Weld .... SW
Socket Welding .... SWLDG
Socket Wrench Joint .... SWJ
Socony Mobil Automatic Real Time (DIT) .... SMART
Socorro [New Mexico] [Seismograph station code, US Geological Survey] (SEIS) .... SNM
Socorro - La Joya [New Mexico] [Seismograph station code, US Geological Survey Closed] (SEIS) .... SRM
Socorro, NM [Location identifier FAA] (FAAL) .... FIA
Socorro, NM [FM radio station call letters] .... KMXQ
Socorro, NM [Location identifier FAA] (FAAL) .... ONM
Socorro Public Library, Socorro, NM [Library symbol Library of Congress] (LCLS) .... NmSo
Socotra [People's Democratic Republic of Yemen] [ICAO location identifier] (ICLI) .... ODAS
Socotra Island [MARC geographic area code Library of Congress] (LCCP) .... i-xo--
Socrates [Greek philosopher, 470-399BC] (ROG) .... SOC
Socttish Amateur Football Association (DBA) .... SAFA
Sod Growers Association of Mid-America (EA) .... SGA of M-A
Sod House, NV [Location identifier FAA] (FAAL) .... SDO
Sod House Society (EA) .... SHS
Sod House Society of Nebraska [Later, SHS] (EA) .... SHSN
Soda Fountain .... SDFTN
Soda Fountain Manufacturers Association .... SFMA
Soda Lime Glass .... SLG
Soda Pulp Manufacturers Association [Defunct] (EA) .... SPMA
Soda Springs, ID [AM radio station call letters] .... KBRV
Soda Springs, ID [FM radio station call letters] .... KFIS

Soda Springs Public Library, Soda Springs, ID [Library symbol] [Library of Congress] (LCLS) .... IdSs
Sodak Gaming [NASDAQ symbol] (TTSB) .... SODK
Sodak Gaming, Inc. [Associated Press] (SAG) .... Sodak
Sodak Gaming, Inc. [NASDAQ symbol] (SAG) .... SODK
Sodalite [A zeolite] .... SOD
Sodankyla [Finland ICAO location identifier] (ICLI) .... EFSO
Sodankyla [Finland] [Seismograph station code, US Geological Survey] (SEIS) .... SOD
Sodbury [England] .... SODB
Soddu [Ethiopia] [Airport symbol] (AD) .... SXU
Soddy-Daisy, TN [FM radio station call letters] .... WFXS
Soddy-Daisy, TN [AM radio station call letters] .... WSDT
Soddy-Daisy, TN [AM radio station call letters] .... WTYR
Soderhamn [Sweden ICAO location identifier] (ICLI) .... ESCL
Sodisco, Inc. [Toronto Stock Exchange symbol] .... SDN
Sodium [Chemical element] (AAMN) .... Na
Sodium (DHSM) .... SOD
Sodium Acid Phosphatase [or Sodium Biphosphate] [Pharmacology] (DAVI) .... sod acid phos
Sodium Acid Pyrophosphate [Also, SAPP] [Leavening agent, meat additive] .... SAP
Sodium Acid Pyrophosphate [Also, SAP] [Leavening agent, meat additive] .... SAPP
Sodium Advanced Fast Reactor .... SAFR
Sodium Alkane Sulfonate [Detergent intermediate] .... SAS
Sodium Aluminum Phosphate [Inorganic chemistry] .... SALP
Sodium Aluminum Sulfate [Organic chemistry] .... SAS
Sodium and Potassium [Urine test] [Biochemistry] (DAVI) .... Na & K
Sodium and Potassium Spot [Urine Test] (DAVI) .... Na & KSP
Sodium Aurothiomalate [Organometallic chemistry] .... SATM
Sodium Azide, Fecal [Medium] [Microbiology] (DAVI) .... SF
Sodium Barbital-Sucrose EDTA Buffer .... BSE
Sodium Bicarbonate [Inorganic chemistry] .... SB
Sodium Bicarbonate [Inorganic chemistry] (MAE) .... sod bicarb
Sodium Bis(methoxyethoxy)aluminum Hydride [Organic chemistry] .... SBAH
Sodium Bisulfite [Inorganic chemistry] .... SB
Sodium Bitartrate [Inorganic chemistry] .... SBT
Sodium Borate [Inorganic chemistry] .... SB
Sodium Borohydride [Inorganic chemistry] .... SBH
Sodium Bromide [Pharmacology] (DAVI) .... NaBr
Sodium Carbonate [CIPW classification] [Geology] .... nc
Sodium Cellulose Phosphate [Kidney-stone drug] .... SCP
Sodium Cellulose Sulfate [Organic chemistry] .... SCS
Sodium Characterization System [Nuclear energy] (NRCH) .... SCS
Sodium Chemical Technology Facility [Nuclear energy] (NRCH) .... SCTF
Sodium Chemistry Control System [Westinghouse Corp.] (IEEE) .... SCCS
Sodium Chloride [Salt] [Chemistry] (DAVI) .... NaCl
Sodium Chloride Calomel Electrode .... SSCE
Sodium Chloride-Sodium Citrate [Analytical chemistry] .... SSC
Sodium Cleaning Facility [Nuclear energy] (NRCH) .... SCF
Sodium Components Test Installation [Nuclear energy] .... SCTI
Sodium Cromoglycate [Pharmacology] .... SCG
Sodium Deoxycholate [Organic chemistry] .... SDC
Sodium Deuterium Reactor .... SDR
Sodium Didecylsulfate-Poly-Acrylamide Gel Electrophoresis [Medicine] (DMAA) .... SDS/PAGE
Sodium Dihydrobis(methoxyethoxy)aluminate [Organic chemistry] .... SDMA
Sodium Dimethyldithiocarbamate [Also, SDDC] [Organic chemistry] .... SDD
Sodium Dimethyldithiocarbamate [Also, SDD] [Organic chemistry] .... SDDC
Sodium Dodecyl Sulfate [Also, SLS] [Organic chemistry] .... SDS
Sodium Dodecylbenzene Sulfonate [Organic chemistry] .... SDBS
Sodium Ethyl Xanthate [Organic chemistry] .... SEX
Sodium Excretion [Rate] [Medicine] (DAVI) .... U_{NaV}
Sodium [Na] Experimental Reactor of Zero Power [British] (DEN) .... NERO
Sodium Fluoride [Chemistry] (DAVI) .... NaF
Sodium Formaldehyde Sulfoxylate [Organic chemistry] .... SFS
Sodium Glycodihydrofusidate [Hemolytic] .... SGDHF
Sodium Graphite Reactor [Nuclear energy] .... SGR
Sodium Graphite Reactor Critical Assembly (IEEE) .... SGRCA
Sodium Heat Engine .... SHE
Sodium Hexadecyl Sulfate [Organic chemistry] .... SHS
Sodium Hexametaphosphate [Inorganic chemistry] .... SHMP
Sodium Hydrogen Phosphate-Tryptone-Yeast Extract [Growth medium] [Microbiology] .... NaTY
Sodium Hydroxide .... NaOH
Sodium Hydroxide (AD) .... NaOH
Sodium Hydroxide Addition [Nuclear energy] (NRCH) .... SHA
Sodium Hydroxide Purge System (IEEE) .... SHPS
Sodium Hydroxybutyrate [Organic chemistry] .... SHB
Sodium Hypochlorite [Inorganic chemistry] .... SHC
Sodium Iodide [Pharmacology] (DAVI) .... nal
Sodium Ionization Detector [Nuclear energy] (NRCH) .... SID
Sodium Iron Pyrophosphate .... SIP
Sodium Iron Pyrophosphate .... SIPP
Sodium Lactate (MAE) .... SL
Sodium Lauryl Sulfate [Also, SDS] [Organic chemistry] .... SLS
Sodium Loop Safety Facility [Nuclear energy] .... SLSF
Sodium Mechanisms Test Installation [Nuclear energy] (NRCH) .... SMTI
Sodium Mercaptopyruvate [Organic chemistry] .... SMP
Sodium Metasilicate [CIPW classification] [Geology] .... ns
Sodium Methyldithiocarbamate [Fungicide] .... SMDC
Sodium Monochloroacetate [Organic chemistry] .... SMCA
Sodium Naphthalene Acetate (IIA) .... SNA
Sodium N-Glycoloylarsanilic [or N-Glycolylarsanilic] Acid [Pharmacology] .... SNGA

Sodium Nitrilotriacetate .... SNTA
Sodium Nitrobenzene Sulfonate [*Organic chemistry*] .... SNBS
Sodium Nitroprusside [*Pharmacology*] (DAVI) .... NITRO
Sodium Nitroprusside [*An antihypertensive and reagent*] [*Pharmacology*] (DAVI) .... NTP
Sodium Nitroprusside [*A vasodilator*] .... SNP
Sodium Nonanoyloxybenzene Sulfonate [*Detergent formulation*] .... SNOBS
Sodium Ortho-Phenylphenoxide [*Organic chemistry*] .... SOPP
Sodium Pentachlorophenoxide [*Insecticide*] .... SPP
Sodium Pentathol [*Nickname*] .... SO-PE
Sodium Pentothal [*Thiopental Sodium*] [*A brand name*] [*Pharmacology*] (DAVI) .... Na Pent
Sodium Polyacrylate [*Organic chemistry*] .... SPA
Sodium Polyanetholesulfonate [*Analytical biochemistry*] .... SPS
Sodium Polystyrene Sulfonate [*Organic chemistry*] .... SPS
Sodium Pregnanediol Glucuronide [*Medicine*] (DMAA) .... NaPG
Sodium Pump Test Facility [*Energy Research and Development Administration*] .... SPTF
Sodium Purification and Characterization System [*Nuclear energy*] (NRCH) .... SPACS
Sodium Purity In-Line Analytical Module [*Nuclear energy*] (NRCH) .... SPIAM
Sodium Pyridinethione [*Organic chemistry*] .... SPT
Sodium Pyrophosphate Buffer [*Analytical chemistry*] .... SPPB
Sodium Reabsorption Rate [*Biochemistry*] (DAVI) .... Na_{reab}
Sodium Reactor Experiment [*Nuclear energy*] .... SRE
Sodium Removal Development Apparatus [*Nuclear energy*] (NRCH) .... SRDA
Sodium Removal Station [*Nuclear energy*] (NRCH) .... SRS
Sodium Restricted Diet [*Medicine*] (DMAA) .... SRD
Sodium Salicylate [*Organic chemistry*] (OA) .... SS
Sodium Sampling Package [*Nuclear energy*] (NRCH) .... SSP
Sodium Silicofluoride [*Inorganic chemistry*] .... SSF
Sodium Spot [*Urine Test*] [*Biochemistry*] (DAVI) .... Na-Spt
Sodium Stearoyl Lactylate .... SSL
Sodium Styrenesulfonate [*Organic chemistry*] .... SSS
Sodium Sulfite [*Inorganic chemistry*] .... SS
Sodium Taurodihydrofusidate [*Organic chemistry*] .... STDF
Sodium Tetradecyl Sulfate [*Pharmacology*] (DAVI) .... STD
Sodium Tetradecyl Sulfate [*Organic chemistry*] .... STS
Sodium Thermionic Detector (SAA) .... STD
Sodium Thiopental [*A general anesthetic*] (DAVI) .... STP
Sodium Thiosulfate [*Inorganic chemistry, biochemistry*] .... STS
Sodium Trichloroacetate [*Organic chemistry*] .... STCA
Sodium Triphosphate [*or Sodium Tripolyphosphate*] [*Also, STPP Inorganic chemistry*] .... STP
Sodium Tripolyphosphate [*Also, STP*] [*Inorganic chemistry*] .... STPP
Sodium Vapor .... SV
Sodium-Adsorption-Ratio .... SAR
Sodium(carboxymethyl)cellulose [*Organic chemistry*] .... SCMC
Sodium-Cooled Graphite Assembly [*Nuclear energy*] .... SCGA
Sodium-Cooled Reactor [*Nuclear energy*] .... SCR
Sodium-Cooled Research Reactor [*Nuclear energy*] (NUCP) .... SORA
Sodium-Dependent High-Affinity Choline Uptake [*Biochemistry*] .... SDHACU
Sodium-Water Reaction [*Nuclear energy*] (NRCH) .... SWR
Sodium-Water Reaction Pressure Relief Subsystem [*Nuclear energy*] (NRCH) .... SWRPRS
Sodium-Water Reaction Test [*Nuclear energy*] (NUCP) .... SWAT
Sodo [*Ethiopia*] [*ICAO location identifier*] (ICLI) .... HASD
Sodomy [*FBI standardized term*] .... SOD
Sodus, NY [*FM radio station call letters*] .... WNNR
Sodus Township Library, Sodus, MI [*Library symbol Library of Congress*] (LCLS) .... MiSod
Soengei Langka [*Sumatra*] [*Seismograph station code, US Geological Survey Closed*] (SEIS) .... SLS
Soest [*Germany ICAO location identifier*] (ICLI) .... EDUS
Soesterberg [*Netherlands ICAO location identifier*] (ICLI) .... EHSB
Soeurs de Bon Sauveur [*France*] (EAIO) .... SBS
Soeurs de la Charite de Besancon [*Sisters of Charity*] [*France*] (EAIO) .... SCB
Soeurs de la Croix de Chavanod [*Sisters of the Cross of Chavanod*] [*France*] (EAIO) .... SCC
Soeurs de la Providence de Portieux (EAIO) .... SPP
Soeurs de l'Assomption, Nicolet, PQ, Canada [*Library symbol Library of Congress*] (LCLS) .... CaQNicA
Soeurs de L'Assomption, Nicolet, Quebec [*Library symbol National Library of Canada*] (NLC) .... QNICA
Soeurs de Notre-Dame du Saint-Rosaire, Rimouski, Quebec [*Library symbol National Library of Canada*] (NLC) .... QRN
Soeurs de Saint Louis [*Sisters of Saint Louis*] (EAIO) .... SSL
Soeurs Grises de Montreal [*Sisters of Charity, Grey Nuns of Montreal*] [*Roman Catholic religious order*] .... SGM
Soeurs Missionnaires de la Societe de Marie [*Missionary Sisters of the Society of Mary*] (EAIO) .... SMSM
Soeurs Missionnaires du Coeur Immacule de Marie [*Missionary Sisters of the Immaculate Heart of Mary*] [*Italy*] (EAIO) .... ICM
Soeurs Salesiennes Missionnaires de Marie Immaculee [*Salesian Missionaries of Mary Immaculate - SMMI*] [*Gentilly, France*] (EAIO) .... SSMMI
Sofamar Danek Group [*NYSE symbol*] (SPSG) .... SDG
Sofamor Danek Group [*Associated Press*] (SAG) .... Sofamor
Sofati Container Line [*Shipping line*] .... SCL
Soferim (BJA) .... Sof
Soffeh [*Iran*] [*ICAO location identifier*] (ICLI) .... OIFF
Soffit (VRA) .... sft
Sofia [*Bulgaria*] [*ICAO location identifier*] (ICLI) .... LBSF
Sofia [*Bulgaria*] [*Airport symbol*] (OAG) .... SOF
Sofia [*Bulgaria*] [*Seismograph station code, US Geological Survey*] (SEIS) .... SOF
Soft .... S
Soft [*Horse racing*] .... SF
Soft [*Quality of the bottom*] [*Nautical charts*] .... sft
Soft and Hard Acid and Base (PDAA) .... SHAB
Soft Carrier Turn Off (HGAA) .... SCTO
Soft Cast Iron .... SCI
Soft Consumable Item List .... SCIL
Soft Contact Lens .... SCL
Soft Drawn .... SD
Soft Drink and Beer Bottlers Association [*British*] (DBA) .... SD & BBA
Soft Drug [*One that is metabolized to an inactive compound*] .... SD
Soft Ejection Murmur [*Cardiology*] (DAVI) .... SEM
Soft Elastic Capsule [*Pharmacy*] .... SEC
Soft Elastic Gelatin [*Medicine*] (DMAA) .... SEG
Soft Enhancement of Percutaneous Absorption [*Pharmacy*] .... SEPA
Soft Fibre Manufacturers' Institute [*Defunct*] (EA) .... SFMI
Soft Focus [*Cinematography*] (NTCM) .... SF
Soft Gamma-Ray Repeater [*Astrophysics*] .... SGR
Soft Gelatin [*Pharmacy*] .... SG
Soft Independent Modeling of Class Analogy [*Analytical chemistry technique*] .... SIMCA
Soft Lander Probe [*Aerospace*] .... SLP
Soft Landing (MCD) .... SL
Soft Landing Vehicle [*NASA*] .... SLV
Soft LASER .... SL
Soft Launch Control Center (IAA) .... SLCC
Soft Lunar Landing and Return (SAA) .... SOLLAR
Soft Manual (NASA) .... SM
Soft Mock-Up [*NASA*] (MCD) .... SMU
Soft Pad [*Missile launch environment symbol*] .... P
Soft Particle Spectrometer [*Geophysics*] .... SPS
Soft Radiation (IAA) .... SR
Soft Sarcoma [*Oncology*] .... SS
Soft Service Building (SAA) .... SSB
Soft Sized [*Paper*] (DGA) .... SS
Soft Target of Opportunity [*Terrorism*] (DI) .... STO
Soft Tissue Calcification [*Medicine*] .... STC
Soft tissue Hematoma [*Hematology*] (DAVI) .... STH
Soft Tissue Sarcoma [*Oncology*] .... STS
Soft Top [*Automotive advertising*] .... SFT
Soft Valve .... SV
Soft White Winter [*Wheat*] (OA) .... SWW
Soft Wired Control (IAA) .... SWC
Soft Wired Integrated Numerical Controller (IAA) .... SWINC
Soft X-Ray Appearance Potential (IAA) .... SXAP
Soft X-Ray Appearance Potential Spectrometer [*or Spectroscopy*] .... SXAPS
Soft X-Ray Background [*Astronomy*] .... SXRB
Soft X-Ray Experiment [*Also, SXX*] .... SXE
Soft X-Ray Experiment [*Also, SXE*] .... SXX
Soft X-Ray LASER .... SXL
Soft X-Ray Projection Lithography .... SXPL
Soft X-Ray Region .... SXR
Soft X-Ray Telescope (SSD) .... SXRT
Soft X-Ray Telescope [*Astronomy*] (PS) .... SXT
Softdesk, Inc. [*NASDAQ symbol*] (SAG) .... SDSK
Softdesk, Inc. [*Associated Press*] (SAG) .... Softdesk
SofTec, Inc. [*Associated Press*] (SAG) .... Softech
SofTech, Inc. [*NASDAQ symbol*] (NQ) .... SOFT
Softening Point (MCD) .... SP
Softening Temperature of Ash .... STA
Softkey International [*NASDAQ symbol*] (TTSB) .... SKEY
Softkey International, Inc. [*NASDAQ symbol*] (SAG) .... SKEY
Softkey International, Inc. [*Associated Press*] (SAG) .... Softkey
Softkey Intl Wrrt [*NASDAQ symbol*] (TTSB) .... SKEYW
Softkey Software Products, Inc. [*Toronto Stock Exchange symbol*] .... SSK
Soft-Load Closed Transition Transfer Switch .... SLCTTS
Softnet Systems [*Formerly, Vader Group, Inc.*] [*AMEX symbol*] (SPSG) .... SOF
Softnet Systems [*Associated Press*] (SAG) .... Softnet
SoftQuad International, Inc. [*Associated Press*] (SAG) .... SftQuad
SoftQuad International, Inc. [*NASDAQ symbol*] (SAG) .... SWEB
SoftQuad Intl [*NASDAQ symbol*] (TTSB) .... SWEBF
SoftSearch, Inc. [*Information service or system*] (IID) .... SS
Soft-Serv Dairy Products Association [*Later, NSSFFA*] (EA) .... SSDPA
Soft-Sized Super-Calendered [*Paper*] .... SSSC
Soft-Tissue Swelling [*Radiology*] (DAVI) .... STS
Soft-Tissue View [*Radiology*] (DAVI) .... STV
Software [*Computer science*] .... S
Software (EERA) .... S/W
Software [*Computer science*] (RDA) .... SFT
Software (NASA) .... SFTWE
Software [*Computer science*] (MCD) .... SFTWR
Software .... SFTWR
Software (NASA) .... SFW
Software [*Computer science*] .... SOFT
Software [*Computer science*] .... SW
Software 2000 [*NASDAQ symbol*] (TTSB) .... SFWR
Software 2000, Inc. [*NASDAQ symbol*] (SAG) .... SFWR
Software 2000, Inc. [*Associated Press*] (SAG) .... Software
Software Abstracts for Engineers [*CITIS Ltd.*] [*Ireland*] [*Information service or system*] (CRD) .... SAFE
Software Acceptance Review .... SAR
Software Acceptance Test .... SAT
Software Acceptance Test Procedures .... SATP
Software Access International, Inc. [*Information service or system*] (IID) .... SAI
Software Acquisition Manager (AAGC) .... SAM

Software and Interoperability Test Facility [*Fort Huachuca, AZ*] [*United States Army Electronic Proving Ground*] (GRD) .... SCITEF
Software Applications .... SA
Software Artistry [*Associated Press*] (SAG) .... SftArt
Software Artistry [*NASDAQ symbol*] (SAG) .... SWRT
Software Avionics Command Support (NASA) .... SACS
Software Block Update [*Army*] .... SBU
Software Capability Evaluation (RDA) .... SCE
Software Career Link [*Database producer*] [*Burlington, MA*] .... SCL
Software Change Notice (DOMA) .... SCN
Software Change Order (MCD) .... SCO
Software Change Proposal (MCD) .... SCP
Software Change Request [*NASA*] .... SCR
Software Checkout Console [*Army*] .... SCC
Software Communications Service .... SCS
Software Conceptual Design [*Computer science*] .... SCD
Software Conference [*Trademark*] .... SOFTCON
Software Configuration Accounting and Reporting System .... SCARS
Software Configuration Control Board (KSC) .... SCCB
Software Configuration Item [*Computer science*] .... SCI
Software Configuration Management (IEEE) .... SCM
Software Configuration Management (MCD) .... SW/CM
Software Configuration Management Plan [*Computer science*] .... SCMP
Software Configuration Management Plan (DOMA) .... SCMP
Software Configuration Review Board (CAAL) .... SCRB
Software Contractor [*NASA*] (NASA) .... S/C
Software Control Authorization [*NASA*] (KSC) .... SCA
Software Control Board [*Apollo*] [*NASA*] .... SCB
Software Controlled Communication Services (MCD) .... SCCS
Software Correction Report (CAAL) .... SCR
Software Cost Reduction [*Computer science*] .... SCR
Software Critical Design Review [*NASA*] (NASA) .... SCDR
Software Data Base Document [*Computer science*] (MHDI) .... SDBD
Software Defined Network [*Telecommunications*] .... SDN
Software Description Document [*NASA*] (NASA) .... SDD
Software Design Description [*Computer science*] (IEEE) .... SDD
Software Design Document [*NASA*] (NASA) .... SDD
Software Design Language .... SDL
Software Design Requirement [*NASA*] (NASA) .... SDR
Software Design Review [*NASA*] (MCD) .... SDR
Software Design Review Board [*NASA*] (NASA) .... SDRB
Software Design Specification [*NASA*] (NASA) .... SDS
Software Detailed Design Document [*Army*] .... SDDD
Software Developers [*NASDAQ symbol*] (TTSB) .... SDEV
Software Developers [*Commercial firm Associated Press*] (SAG) .... SoftwrDv
[*The*] Software Developer's Co., Inc. [*NASDAQ symbol*] (NQ) .... SDEV
Software Developer's Kit [*Computer science*] (BYTE) .... SDK
Software Development and Integration Facility [*NASA*] (NASA) .... SDIF
Software Development and Maintenance Suppport System [*Computer science*] (MHDI) .... SDMSS
Software Development and Verification Facilities [*NASA*] (NASA) .... SDVF
Software Development and Verification System [*NASA*] .... SWDVS
Software Development Board [*Computer science*] (MHDI) .... SDB
Software Development Computer [*NASA*] (NASA) .... SDC
Software Development Computer Facility .... SDCF
Software Development Environment [*NCR Corp.*] .... SDE
Software Development Facility [*Military*] (CAAL) .... SDF
Software Development File .... SDF
Software Development Folder (MCD) .... SDF
Software Development Framework (RDA) .... SDF
Software Development Handbook [*NASA*] (NASA) .... SDH
Software Development Kit [*Computer science*] (PCM) .... SDK
Software Development Laboratory [*NASA*] (NASA) .... SDL
Software Development Language [*Burroughs Corp.*] .... SDL
Software Development Library .... SDL
Software Development Methodology (IAA) .... SDM
Software Development Note [*NASA*] (NASA) .... SDN
Software Development Plan [*NASA*] (NASA) .... SDP
Software Development Processor (NITA) .... SDP
Software Development Specification (IAA) .... SDS
Software Development System .... SDS
Software Development System (MCD) .... SWDS
Software Distribution Operation (IAA) .... SDO
Software Dynamics [*Buena Park, CA*] (TSSD) .... SD
Software Encapsulation Methodologies .... SEM
Software Encapsulation Template .... SET
Software End Product [*Army*] .... SEP
Software Engineering (MCD) .... SE
Software Engineering and Management .... SEAM
Software Engineering Bibliographic Data Base [*Data and Analysis Center for Software*] [*Information service or system*] .... SEBD
Software Engineering Bibliographic Database [*Air Force Systems Command*] [*Information service or system*] (CRD) .... SEB
Software Engineering Change Proposal (MCD) .... SECP
Software [*or System*] Engineering Cost Model .... SECOMO
Software Engineering Data [*Data and Analysis Center for Software*] [*Information service or system*] .... SED
Software Engineering Demonstrator Initiative [*British*] .... SEDI
Software Engineering Design [*Army*] .... SED
Software Engineering Directorate [*Army*] (RDA) .... SED
Software Engineering Facility .... SEF
Software Engineering Institute [*DoD*] .... SEI
Software Engineering Laboratory [*NASA*] (MCD) .... SEL
Software Engineering Practice .... SEP
Software Engineering Requirement [*Army*] .... SER

Software Engineering Research Projects [*Data and Analysis Center for Software*] [*Database*] .... SERP
Software Engineering Technology .... SET
Software Engineering Terminology [*Computer science*] (IEEE) .... SET
Software Enhancement and Maintenance [*Contract*] .... SEAM
Software Enhancement Proposal .... SEP
Software Error Effects Analysis .... SEEA
Software Error Notification [*Computer science*] .... SEN
Software Exchange [*Computer science*] (NHD) .... SEX
Software Extraordinaire, Inc. [*Telecommunications service*] (TSSD) .... SXI
Software Facilities and Standards [*Computer science*] (TEL) .... SFS
Software/Firmware Development Plan .... SFDP
Software Fix [*NASA*] .... SOFIX
Software Flight Article Configuration Inspection [*NASA*] (NASA) .... SFACI
Software Functional Description [*Computer science*] (MHDI) .... SFD
Software Generation Center (MCD) .... SGC
Software Generation System .... SGS
Software/Hardware [*Cost*] .... S/H
Software/Hardware Operational Control .... SHOC
Software Hazard Analysis [*Military*] .... SHA
Software Help in Applications, Research and Education [*International program to develop meteorological analysis and display software for developing countries*] (USDC) .... SHARE
Software Help in Applications, Research and Education [*International program to develop meteorological analysis and display software for developing countries*] [*Marine science*] (OSRA) .... SHARE
Software Houses Association (IAA) .... SHA
Software Impact Assessment [*NASA*] (NASA) .... SIA
Software Implementation .... SI
Software Implementation Monitor [*Computer science*] (MHDI) .... SIMON
Software Implementation Specifications [*NASA*] (NASA) .... SIS
Software Implemented Fault Tolerance [*NASA*] .... SIFT
Software Implemented Friden Translator [*Computer science*] .... SWIFT
Software in Print [*Technique Learning*] [*Information service or system*] (IID) .... SIP
Software Incident Report (MCD) .... SIR
Software Industry Association (IAA) .... SIA
Software Information (IAA) .... SOFI
Software Initiated Restart (NASA) .... SIR
Software Institute of America [*Andover, MA*] [*Telecommunications*] (TSSD) .... SIA
Software Instrumentation Package [*Sperry UNIVAC*] [*Computer science*] .... SIP
Software Integrated Schedule [*NASA*] (NASA) .... SIS
Software integrated Test [*NASA*] (KSC) .... SIT
Software Integration Readiness Review [*NASA*] (NASA) .... SIRR
Software Integration Test (IAA) .... SIT
Software Interface Document (MCD) .... SID
Software Interrupt [*Computer science*] .... SWI
Software Life Cycle Management .... SLCM
Software Life Cycle Management Plan (DNAB) .... SLCMP
[*The*] Software Link, Inc. [*Software manufacturer*] .... TSL
Software Loadable System [*Computer science*] (PCM) .... SLS
Software Maintenance Association (EA) .... SMA
Software Maintenance Function [*Computer science*] (TEL) .... SMF
Software Management Plan [*NASA*] (MCD) .... SMP
Software Management System/360 Problem Program Efficiency SMS/360PPE
Software Manufacturing Industry in Australia [*Database*] .... SMIAL
Software Marketing (IAA) .... SOFTMARK
Software Master Library [*Computer science*] (TEL) .... SML
Software Message Generator [*Computer science*] (TEL) .... SMG
Software Metering and Resource Tracking [*Computer science*] .... SMART
Software Migration Kit [*Microsoft, Inc.*] [*Computer science*] (PCM) .... SMK
Software Notification Service (NITA) .... SNS
Software Optimization for the Retrieval of Data [*Computer science*] (MHDI) .... SWORD
Software Package for Unique Reports (GFGA) .... SPUR
Software Parts List [*Computer science*] (TEL) .... SPL
Software Preliminary Design Review [*NASA*] (NASA) .... SPDR
Software Problem Report [*NASA*] (NASA) .... SPR
Software Process Improvement Plan (AAGC) .... SPIP
Software Procurement Specification .... SPS
Software Producers' Association (NITA) .... SPA
Software Product Assurance (SSD) .... SPA
Software Product Description [*Computer science*] (MHDI) .... SPD
Software Product Specification .... SPS
Software Production Facility [*NASA*] (NASA) .... SPF
Software Productivity Consortium (MCD) .... SPC
Software Products Scheme [*Computer science*] (DCTA) .... SPS
Software Professionals [*NASDAQ symbol*] (TTSB) .... SFTW
Software Professionals, Inc. [*Associated Press*] (SAG) .... SftProf
Software Professionals, Inc. [*NASDAQ symbol*] (SAG) .... SFTW
Software Programmer's Manual .... SPM
Software Programming Language [*Computer science*] (IEEE) .... SPL
Software Publishers Association (EA) .... SPA
Software Publishing [*NASDAQ symbol*] (TTSB) .... SPCO
Software Publishing Corp. [*Associated Press*] (SAG) .... SftwPb
Software Publishing Corp. .... SPC
Software Publishing Corp. [*Mountain View, CA*] [*NASDAQ symbol*] (NQ) .... SPCO
Software Quality Assurance [*Computer science*] (IEEE) .... SQA
Software Quality Assurance Plan [*Computer science*] (IAA) .... SQUP
Software Quality Assurance Program Plan [*Computer science*] .... SQAPP
Software Quality Assurance Program Plan .... SQUAPP
Software Quality Evaluation (MCD) .... SQE
Software [*Firmware*] Quality Evaluation Plan .... SQEP
Software Quality Program Plan .... SQPP
Software Quality Standards and Procedures Manual .... SQSPM
Software Recording Facility .... SRF

Software Recovery Facility [*Computer science*] (IBMDP) .... SRF
Software Release Notice [*NASA*] (NASA) .... SRN
Software Renewal Program [*Food and Nutrition Service*] [*Department of Agriculture*] (GFGA) .... SRP
Software Requirements Analysis .... SRA
Software Requirements Change Board [*NASA*] (NASA) .... SRCB
Software Requirements Change Board Directive [*NASA*] (NASA) .... SRCBD
Software Requirements Control Board [*NASA*] (NASA) .... SRCB
Software Requirements Control Board Directive [*NASA*] (NASA) .... SRCBD
Software Requirements Document [*Computer science*] .... SRD
Software Requirements Engineering Methodology .... SREM
Software Requirements Review [*NASA*] (NASA) .... SRR
Software Requirements Specification [*NASA*] (NASA) .... SRS
Software Research and Development Group [*University of Calgary*] [*Research center*] (RCD) .... SRDG
Software Review Working Group [*Computer science*] (MHDI) .... SRWG
Software Sciences Institute (NITA) .... SSI
Software Sciences Ltd. [*British*] .... SSL
Software Sciences Teleordering (NITA) .... SST
Software/Segment Specification .... SSS
Software Service System [*Anti-piracy device invented by Ryoichi Mori of the Japan Electronics Industry Development Association*] (BYTE) .... SSS
Software Slave Library [*Computer science*] (TEL) .... SSL
Software Specification Language .... SSL
Software Specification Review .... SSR
Software Specification Sheet [*Computer science*] (IAA) .... SSS
Software Spectrum [*NASDAQ symbol*] (TTSB) .... SSPE
Software Spectrum, Inc. [*Associated Press*] (SAG) .... SoftSpc
Software Spectrum, Inc. [*NASDAQ symbol*] (SPSG) .... SSPE
Software Staging Section [*Social Security Administration*] .... SSS
Software Standards and Procedures Manual (SSD) .... SSPM
Software Steering Committee (LAIN) .... SSC
Software Support Activity (SSD) .... SSA
Software Support Center [*Army*] (RDA) .... SSC
Software Support Environment (SSD) .... SSE
Software Support Environment Development Facility (SSD) .... SSEDF
Software Support Environment Integration Facility (SSD) .... SSEIF
Software Support Environment Operation Facility (SSD) .... SSEOF
Software Support Environment Production Facility (SSD) .... SSEPF
Software Support Environment Software Production Facility (SSD) .. SSESPF
Software Support Facility (MCD) .... SSF
Software Support Group (NITA) .... SSG
Software Support Production Facility (SSD) .... SSPF
Software Support Production Integration Facility (SSD) .... SSPIF
Software Support Transition Plan [*Army*] .... SSTP
Software System Change (MCD) .... SSC
Software System Design [*Computer science*] .... SSD
Software System Design Document (MCD) .... SSDD
Software Systems .... SS
Software T & E Panel (RDA) .... STEP
Software Technology and Engineering Center Staff [*Social Security Administration*] .... STECS
Software Technology for Adaptable, Reliable Systems [*Military*] .. STARS
Software Test and Evaluation Process [*DoD*] .... STEP
Software Test and Integration Laboratory [*NASA*] (NASA) .... STIL
Software Test Description [*DoD*] .... STD
Software Test Facility [*NASA*] (MCD) .... STF
Software Test Plan [*DoD*] .... STP
Software Test Procedure .... STPR
Software Test Report .... STR
Software Theft Opposition Project [*Project STOP*] [*Information service or system*] (CRD) .... STOP
Software Timing and Control .... STAC
Software Tool for Evaluating System Designs [*Computer science*] (MHDI) .... STESD
Software Tool Information Database [*Air Force Systems Command*] [*Information service or system*] (CRD) .... STI
Software Tools for Application to Real Time Systems [*British*] ... STARTS
Software Top Level Design Document [*Army*] .... STLDD
Software Trouble Note [*NASA*] (NASA) .... STN
Software Trouble Report (MCD) .... STR
Software Trouble Reporting Service (NITA) .... STR
Software Update Distribution System [*Computer software*] [*Frye Computer Systems, Inc.*] (PCM) .... SUDS
Software Users Guide to Available Resources [*Australia A publication*] .... SUGAR
Software User's Manual [*Army*] .... SUM
Software Utility Package (NITA) .... SOUP
Software Validation and Control System (MCD) .... SOVAC
Software Verification Plan [*Computer science*] (IAA) .... SVP
Software Verification Readiness Review [*NASA*] (NASA) .... SVRR
Software Verification Report [*Computer science*] (IAA) ...... SVR
Software Work Breakdown Structure (MCD) .... SWBS
Software Work Breakdown Structure (MCD) .... SWWBDS
Software Work Breakdown Structure .... SWWBS
Software Working Group [*NASA*] (NASA) .... SWG
Software-Aided Multiform Input [*Software*] [*Computer science*] .. SWAMI
Software-Controlled Electronic-Processing Traffic-Recording Equipment (PDAA) .... SCEPTRE
Software-Defined Broadbank Network (CDE) .... SDBN
Softwood (WGA) .... SFTWD
Softwood .... SW
Softwood .... SWD
Softwood Bleached Kraft [*Pulp and paper technology*] .... SBK
Sogdian [*MARC language code Library of Congress*] (LCCP) .... sog
Sogenannt [*So-Called*] [*German*] .... SOG

Sogepet Ltd. [*Toronto Stock Exchange symbol*] .... SPT
Sogervair/Transoceanic Aviation [*France ICAO designator*] (FAAC) ... OAT
Sogndal [*Norway*] [*Airport symbol*] (OAG) .... SOG
Sogndal/Haukasen [*Norway ICAO location identifier*] (ICLI) .. ENSG
Sohar [*Oman*] [*ICAO location identifier*] (ICLI) .... OOSH
Sohio Engineered Materials Co., Research and Development Library, Niagara Falls, NY [*Library symbol*] [*Library of Congress*] (LCLS) ... NNiaSE
SOI Industries, Inc. [*AMEX symbol*] (SPSG) .... SOI
SOI Industries, Inc. [*Associated Press*] (SAG) .... SOI Ind
S.O.I Industries(New) [*AMEX symbol*] (TTSB) .... SOI
Soil and Health Foundation [*Later, RI*] (EA) .... SHF
Soil and Health Society [*Later, RI*] (EA) .... SHS
Soil and Moisture Conservation .... SMC
Soil and Terrain Database [*USA*] (EERA) .... SOTER
Soil and Water Conservation Association of Australia (EERA) ... SWCAA
Soil and Water Conservation Districts Foundation, Davis Conservation Library, League City, TX [*Library symbol Library of Congress*] (LCLS) .... TxLcD
Soil and Water Conservation Research Division [*of ARS, Department of Agriculture*] .... SWC
Soil and Water Management Association (NADA) .... SAWA
Soil and Water Management Association [*British*] .... SAWMA
Soil and Water Resources Conservation Act [*1977*] .... RCA
Soil Association [*Bristol, England*] (EAIO) .... SA
Soil Association of South Australia .... SASA
Soil Brightness Index .... SBI
Soil Characteristics .... SC
Soil Classification and Mapping Branch [*Department of Agriculture*] (IID) ... SCAM
Soil Conservation Council [*South Australia*] .... SCC
Soil Conservation District [*Agriculture*] .... SCD
Soil Conservation Service [*Department of Agriculture*] .. SCS
Soil Conservation Society of America (EA) .... SCSA
Soil Data Storage and Retrieval Unit [*Department of Agriculture*] (IID) .... SDS & RU
Soil Engineering Problem-Oriented Language [*Computer science*] ... SEPOL
Soil Erosion Service [*Became Soil Conservation Service, 1935*] ... SES
Soil Extract .... SE
Soil Management Program [*of Tasmania*] [*State*] (EERA) .. SMP
Soil Mechanics .... SM
Soil Mechanics Experiment [*NASA*] .... SME
Soil Mechanics Information Analysis Center [*Army Corps of Engineers*] (IID) .... SMIAC
Soil Moisture Deficit (PDAA) .... SMD
Soil Moisture Strength Prediction [*Army*] .... SMSP
Soil Nutrient Availability .... SNA
Soil Organic Carbon .... SOC
Soil Organic Matter .... SOM
Soil Pipe .... SP
Soil Pit .... SP
Soil Psychrometer .... SP
Soil Research Institute, Agriculture Canada [*Institut de Recherches sur les Sols, Agriculture Canada*] Ottawa, Ontario [*Library symbol National Library of Canada*] (NLC) .... OOAGSR
Soil Sampler Control Unit .... SSCU
Soil Science Society of America (EA) .... SSSA
Soil Stack .... SSK
Soil Survey Investigations Report .... SSIR
Soil Test Ordnance Multipurpose Exploration Rocket (SAA) ... STOMPER
Soil Vacuum Extraction [*Computer science*] .... SVE
Soil Vapor Extraction [*Environmental science*] .... SVE
Soil Vapor Survey [*Environmental chemistry*] .... SVS
Soil Vegetation Atmosphere Transfer (EERA) .... SVAT
Soil Water Deficit [*Soil science*] .... SWD
Soil, Water, Estuarine Monitoring [*Environmental Protection Agency*] (GFGA) .... SWEMS
Soil Water Information Processing System .... SWIPS
Soilborne Wheat Mosaic Virus .... SBWMV
Soil-Derived Fulvic Acid .... SFA
Soiled [*Deltiology*] .... S
Soil-Plant-Atmosphere [*Computer simulation model*] .... SPAM
Soil-Plant-Atmosphere-Research [*Agriculture*] .... SPAR
Soil-Pore Liquid Monitoring Device (GNE) .... SPLMD
Soils Information Retrieval Systems [*Database*] [*Army Corps of Engineers*] .... SIRS
Soils, Trees, and Grass Program (EERA) .... STAG
Soil-Test Water Probe .... SWP
Soil-Water Infiltration & Movement .... SWIM
Soil-Wheel Interaction Performance .... SWIP
Sointula Museum, British Columbia [*Library symbol National Library of Canada*] (NLC) .... BSOM
Sointula Museum, Sointula, BC, Canada [*Library symbol*] [*Library of Congress*] (LCLS) .... CaBSOM
Soissons/Cuffies [*France ICAO location identifier*] (ICLI) ... LFAH
Soiuz Trudovogo Krest'ianstva [*Union of Working Peasantry*] [*Russian*] ... STK
Sojourner Truth Organization (EA) .... STO
Soka Gakkai International [*An association*] .... SGI
Sokcho [*South Korea ICAO location identifier*] (ICLI) ... RKND
Sokode [*Togo*] [*ICAO location identifier*] (ICLI) ... DXSK
Sokol USA, East Orange, NJ [*Library symbol Library of Congress*] (LCLS) .... NjEoS
Sokoto [*Nigeria*] [*ICAO location identifier*] (ICLI) ... DNSO
Sokoto [*Nigeria*] [*Airport symbol*] (OAG) .... SKO
Sol [*Monetary unit in Peru*] .... S
Sola [*Vanuatu*] [*ICAO location identifier*] (ICLI) ... NVSC
Sola [*Vanuatu*] [*Airport symbol*] (OAG) .... SLH
Sola International [*NYSE symbol*] (TTSB) .... SOL

Sola International, Inc. [*NYSE symbol*] (SAG) ... SCL
Sola International, Inc. [*Associated Press*] (SAG) ... Sola
Solana, FL [*FM radio station call letters*] (RBYB) ... WCVU
Solanaceae Enthusiasts [*Defunct*] (EA) ... SE
Solania [*Costa Rica*] [*Seismograph station code, US Geological Survey*] (SEIS) ... AR4
Solano College, Fairfield, CA [*Library symbol*] [*Library of Congress*] (LCLS) ... CFaS
Solano County Genealogical Society, Vacaville, CA [*Library symbol*] [*Library of Congress*] (LCLS) ... CVaSGS
Solano County Library, Fairfield, CA [*Library symbol Library of Congress*] (LCLS) ... CFa
Solanum Apical Leaf-Curling Virus ... SALCV
Solanum Nodiflorum Mottle Virus [*Plant pathology*] ... SNMV
Solanum Yellows Virus [*Plant pathology*] ... SYV
Solar (ADA) ... S
Solar (AAG) ... SLR
Solar ... SLR
Solar (AAG) ... SOL
Solar Absorption Index (CET) ... K
Solar Activity Monitoring Satellite (MCD) ... SAMSAT
Solar Alignment Bay (OA) ... SAB
Solar Altitude Control System ... SACS
Solar and Backscatter Ultraviolet Spectrometer (MCD) ... SBUV
Solar and Backscattered Ultraviolet and Total Ozone Mapping System ... SBUV/TOMS
Solar and Earth Radiation Monitor (NOAA) ... SERM
Solar and Electric Racing Association ... SERA
Solar and Energy Research Facility [*University of Arizona*] [*Research center*] (RCD) ... SERF
Solar and Heliospheric Observatory [*European Space Agency*] ... SOHO
Solar and Interplanetary Programme [*International Council of Scientific Unions*] ... SIP
Solar and Interplanetary Variability [*Meteorology*] ... SIV
Solar and Wind Energy Research Program Information Centre, Alberta Research Council, Edmonton, Alberta [*Library symbol Obsolete National Library of Canada*] (NLC) ... AERSWE
Solar Anomalous and Magnetospheric Particle Explorer ... SAMPEX
Solar, Anomalous, and Magnetospheric Particle Explorer Satellite ... SAM-PEX
Solar Arc Lamp ... SAL
Solar Arc Lamp Assembly ... SALA
Solar Array (KSC) ... SA
Solar Array Batteries ... SAB
Solar Array Drive Electronics (LAIN) ... SADE
Solar Array Drive Motor ... SADM
Solar Array Drive System ... SADS
Solar Array Experiment (SSD) ... SAE
Solar Array Failure Analysis ... SAFA
Solar Array Flight Experiment (MCD) ... SAFE
Solar Array Leaf ... SAL
Solar Array Manufacturing Industry Costing Standards ... SAMICS
Solar Array Manufacturing Industry Simulation ... SAMIS
Solar Array Release and Deployment (MCD) ... SARD
Solar Array Reorientation System ... SARS
Solar Array Structure ... SAS
Solar Array System (MCD) ... SAS
Solar Array Wing (MCD) ... SAW
Solar Array Wing Simulator (MCD) ... SAWS
Solar Aspect Sensor ... SAS
Solar Atmospheric Tide (IAA) ... SAT
Solar Aureole Almucantar Radiance (PDAA) ... SAAR
Solar Backscatter Ultraviolet [*Ozone measurement*] ... SBUV
Solar BAckscatter Ultraviolet (USDC) ... SBUV
Solar Backscatter Ultraviolet Experiment (IAA) ... SBUV
Solar Beam Experiment ... SBE
Solar Box Cookers International [*An association*] (EA) ... SBCI
Solar Cell ... SC
Solar Cell Electric Power System (RDA) ... SCEPS
Solar Cell Module ... SCM
Solar Cell Panel ... SCP
Solar Cell Panel Assembly ... SCPA
Solar Central Receiver Reformer (PDAA) ... SCRR
Solar Coil (IAA) ... SC
Solar Collector Subassembly (MCD) ... SCS
Solar Communications ... SOCOM
Solar Connections to Transient Interplanetary Processes [*Program*] (USDC) ... SOLTIP
Solar Connections to Transient Interplanetary Processes [*Program*] [*Marine science*] (OSRA) ... SOLTIP
Solar Constant (IAA) ... SC
Solar Constant Variations ... SCV
Solar Corona Diagnostic Mission [*NASA*] (SSD) ... SCDM
Solar Corona Explorer [*Project*] [*NASA*] ... SCE
Solar Coronal X-Ray ... SCX
Solar Corpuscular Radiation (IAA) ... SCR
Solar Cosmic Radiation [*or Ray*] ... SCR
Solar Cosmic Ray Early Warning System (MUGU) ... SCREWS
Solar Daily Variation ... SDV
Solar Desalination Plant ... SDP
Solar Disk Simulator ... SDS
Solar Domestic Hot Water ... SDHW
Solar Dynamic (SSD) ... SD
Solar Eclipse Atmospheric and Ionospheric Measurements Project (IEEE) ... SEAIMP
Solar Eclipse Sensor (MCD) ... SES
Solar Ecliptic ... SE
Solar Electric Communication Satellite ... SECS
Solar Electric Generating System ... SEGS
Solar Electric Multiple-Mission (MCD) ... SEMM
Solar Electric Multiple-Mission Spacecraft ... SEMMS
Solar Electric Power [*or Propulsion*] ... SEP
Solar Electric Propulsion Integration Technology (PDAA) ... SEPSIT
Solar Electric Propulsion System [*NASA*] ... SEPS
Solar Electric Propulsion System Technology ... SEPST
Solar Electric Test Satellite ... SETS
Solar Electromagnetic Radiation Flux [*Model*] (USDC) ... SERE
Solar Electromagnetic Radiation Flux [*Model*] [*Marine science*] (OSRA) ... SERF
Solar Electromagnetic Radiation Study for Solar Cycle 22 [*Marine science*] (OSRA) ... SOLERS22
Solar Electromagnetic Radiation Study for Solar Cycle 22 (USDC) ... SOLERS22
Solar Electro-Optical Network (MCD) ... SEON
Solar Electro-Optical Observing Network (USDC) ... SEON
Solar Electro-Optical Observing Network [*Marine science*] (OSRA) ... SEON
Solar Energetic Particle ... SEP
Solar Energy and Energy Conservation Act of 1980 ... SEECA
Solar Energy and Energy Conversion Laboratory [*University of Florida*] [*Research center*] (RCD) ... SEECL
Solar Energy Applications Laboratory [*Colorado State University*] [*Research center*] (RCD) ... SEAL
Solar Energy Assisted Heat Pump System ... SAHPS
Solar Energy Collector ... SEC
Solar Energy Concentrator ... SEC
Solar Energy Conservation Program [*Department of Energy*] ... SECP
Solar Energy Construction Association [*Defunct*] (EA) ... SECA
Solar Energy Density ... SED
Solar Energy Flux ... SEF
Solar Energy Flux Density ... SEFD
Solar Energy Generating System (IAA) ... SEGS
Solar Energy Industries Association (EA) ... SEIA
Solar Energy Information Center ... SEIC
Solar Energy Information Data Bank [*Department of Energy*] ... SEIDB
Solar Energy Information Services (IID) ... SEIS
Solar Energy Institute of America [*Later, SEINAM*] (MCD) ... SEIA
Solar Energy Institute of North America [*Defunct*] (EA) ... SEINAM
Solar Energy Intelligence Report [*Business Publishers Inc.*] [*No longer available online*] [*Information service or system*] (CRD) ... SEIR
Solar Energy Monitor in Space [*NASA*] (MCD) ... SEMIS
Solar Energy Research Institute [*Golden, CO*] [*Department of Energy*] ... SERI
Solar Energy Research Institute, Golden, CO [*Library symbol Library of Congress*] (LCLS) ... CoGSE
Solar Energy Society [*Later, International Solar Energy Society*] (EA) ... SES
Solar Energy Society of America (EA) ... SESA
Solar Energy Society of Canada, Inc. [*Societe d'Energie Solaire du Canada*] ... SESCI
Solar Energy Society of Ireland [*International Solar Energy Society*] ... SESI
Solar Energy System Economic Feasibility Program [*Army*] (RDA) ... SOLFEAS
Solar Energy Thermionic [*Program*] [*NASA*] ... SET
Solar Energy Thermionic Conversion System [*NASA*] ... SETS
Solar Energy Update [*A publication*] ... SEU
Solar Environment Monitor ... SEM
Solar Environment Simulator ... SES
Solar Environmental Laboratory [*National Oceanic and Atmospheric Administration*] ... SEL
Solar Equivalent Hours ... SEH
Solar Explorer [*NASA*] ... SE
Solar Extreme Ultraviolet Telescope and Spectrograph (MCD) ... SERTS
Solar Facility Design Integration (MCD) ... SFDI
Solar Flare [*Astronomy*] ... SF
Solar Flare Effect [*Physics*] ... SFE
Solar Flare Proton ... SFP
Solar Flare Radiation ... SFR
Solar Flare X-Ray Polarimeter (NASA) ... SFEX
Solar Flux Density ... SFD
Solar Forecast [*Air Force*] (IAA) ... SFC
Solar Forecast Center [*Air Force*] (IEEE) ... SFC
Solar Forecast Facility [*Air Force*] (MCD) ... SFF
Solar Generator (IAA) ... SG
Solar Greenhouse Association (EA) ... SGA
Solar Heat Exchanger Drive (IAA) ... SHED
Solar Heat Reflecting (KSC) ... SHR
Solar Heating and Air Conditioning ... SHAC
Solar Heating and Cooling of Buildings [*Energy Research and Development Administration*] ... SHACOB
Solar Heliospheric Observatory ... SOHO
Solar High-Energy Particles ... SHEP
Solar Hydrogen Rocket Engine ... SOHR
Solar Inertial (MCD) ... SI
Solar Inertial Attitude (NASA) ... SIA
Solar Instrument Probe (MUGU) ... SIP
Solar Internal Dynamics Mission (SSD) ... SIDM
Solar Interplanetary Model ... SIM
Solar Keratosis [*Dermatology*] (DAVI) ... SK
Solar Lobby [*An association*] (EA) ... SL
Solar Magnetic [*System*] [*NASA*] ... SM
Solar Magnetic Field ... SMF
Solar Magnetospheric ... SM
Solar Maximum Analysis [*Meteorology*] ... SMA
Solar Maximum Mission [*NASA*] (MCD) ... SMM
Solar Maximum Mission Satellite ... SOLAR MAX
Solar Maximum Repair Mission [*NASA*] (NASA) ... SMRM

Solar Maximum Satellite [*NASA*] (MCD) ... SMS
Solar Maximum Year [*August, 1979-February, 1981*] ... SMY
Solar Mesosphere Explorer (MCD) ... SME
Solar Microwave Interferometer Imaging System ... SMIIS
Solar Monitor Constant (SSD) ... SMC
Solar Neutrino Unit [*Astrophysics*] ... SNU
Solar Observing and Forecasting Network [*Air Force*] ... SOFNET
Solar Observing Optical Network [*Air Force*] ... SOON
Solar Optical Communications System (IAA) ... SOCOM
Solar Optical Telescope ... SOT
Solar Optical Universal Polarimeter ... SOUP
Solar Oscillations Imager [*Instrumentation*] ... SOI
Solar Panel ... SP
Solar Panel Substrate ... SPS
Solar Panel Technology (SSD) ... SPT
Solar Particle Alert Network [*National Oceanic and Atmospheric Administration*] ... SPAN
Solar Particle Beams ... SPB
Solar Particle Intensity Composition Experiment [*NASA*] ... SPICE
Solar Particle Monitoring System [*NASA*] (KSC) ... SPMS
Solar Particles and Radiations Monitoring Organization ... SPARMO
Solar Perturbation and Atmospheric Density Measurement Satellite ... SPADES
Solar Photometry Probe (AAG) ... SPP
Solar Photovoltaic Energy Advisory Committee [*Terminated, 1986*] (EGAO) ... SPEAC
Solar Physics (NASA) ... SP
Solar Physics Payload [*NASA*] (MCD) ... SPP
Solar Pointing Aerobee Rocket Control System ... SPARCS
Solar Pointing Control ... SPC
Solar Polar Mission (MCD) ... SPM
Solar Power Array ... SPA
Solar Power Module ... SPM
Solar Power Satellite [*NASA*] ... SPS
Solar Power System (MCD) ... SPS
Solar Power Unit Demonstrator ... SPUD
Solar Probe Spacecraft [*Pioneer satellite*] ... SPS
Solar Proton Albedo Neutron Decay ... SPAND
Solar Proton Alert Network ... SPAN
Solar Proton Alpha Spectrometer ... SPAS
Solar Proton Event [*Geophysics*] ... SPE
Solar Proton Monitor ... SPM
Solar Proton Stream [*Geophysics*] (SAA) ... SPS
Solar Proton-Monitoring Experiment (PDAA) ... SPME
Solar Pumped LASER (SSD) ... SPL
Solar Pumped Plasma (SSD) ... SPP
Solar Radiation [*Satellite system*] [*Navy*] ... SOLRAD
Solar Radiation ... SR
Solar Radiation (NOAA) ... SRAD
Solar Radiation and Thermospheric Structure [*Japanese satellite*] ... SRATS
Solar Radiation Flux ... SRF
Solar Radiation - High-Altitude [*Satellite system*] [*Navy*] ... SOLRAD-HI
Solar Radiation Pressure ... SRP
Solar Radiation Research Branch [*Air Resources Laboratory*] (USDC) ... SRRB
Solar Radiation Research Branch [*Marine science*] (OSRA) ... SRRB
Solar Radiation Satellite (IAA) ... SRS
Solar Radiation Simulator ... SRS
Solar Radiation Simulator System ... SRSS
Solar Radiation Test ... SRT
Solar Radio Astronomy Experiment ... SRAE
Solar Radio Observatory ... SRO
Solar Radio Telescope ... SRT
Solar Radio Telescope Network ... SRTN
Solar Rating and Certification Corp. (EA) ... SRCC
Solar Reference ... SR
Solar Reflectory Beacon ... SRB
Solar Satellite Power Station ... SSPS
Solar Scientific Airlock ... SOL-SAL
Solar Scientific Airlock (MCD) ... S-SAL
Solar Sea Power Plant [*NASA*] ... SSPP
Solar Simulation Module ... SSM
Solar Simulator (MCD) ... SS
Solar Spectrum and Transmittance [*Solar energy research*] ... SOLTRAN
Solar Stabilization Computer ... SSC
Solar Stereoscopic Mission [*NASA*] ... SSM
Solar System (IAA) ... SS
Solar System Barycenter [*Astronomy*] ... SSBC
Solar System Data Processing System ... SSDPS
Solar System Exploration Committee [*NASA*] ... SSEC
Solar Technical Information Program [*Solar Energy Research Institute*] [*Information service or system*] (IID) ... STIP
Solar Telescope Network ... STN
Solar Terrestrial Observatory (SSD) ... STO
Solar Thermal [*Energy source*] ... ST
Solar Thermal Advanced Research Center [*University of Houston*] [*Research center*] (RCD) ... STARC
Solar Thermal Central Receiver ... STCR
Solar Thermal Central Receiver System ... STCRS
Solar Thermal Commission (PDAA) ... STC
Solar Thermal Electric Conversation (MCD) ... STEC
Solar Thermal Energy System ... STES
Solar Thermal Power System ... STPS
Solar Thermal Vacuum ... STV
Solar Thermionic Electrical Power System ... STEPS
Solar Thermionic Electrical Propulsion System (IAA) ... STEPS
Solar Total Energy Test Facility [*Energy Research and Development Administration*] ... STETF
Solar Tracking System ... STS
Solar Trade Association [*British*] (DBA) ... STA
Solar Transition Region [*Solar physics*] ... STR
Solar Turboelectric Drive (IAA) ... STED
Solar Ultraviolet Measurements of Emitted Radiation [*Instrumentation*] ... SUMER
Solar Ultraviolet Monitor (MCD) ... SUM
Solar Ultraviolet Spectral Irradiance Monitor (MCD) ... SUSIM
Solar Vacuum Head [*Astronomy*] (OA) ... SVH
Solar Vacuum Telescope ... SVT
Solar Vane Actuators ... SVA
Solar Water Heating ... SWH
Solar Wind [*Astronomy*] ... SW
Solar Wind Compensator [*or Composition*] [*Apollo 11*] [*NASA*] ... SWC
Solar Wind Composition Detector (PDAA) ... SWCD
Solar Wind Composition Experiment (PDAA) ... SWCE
Solar Wind Experiment [*NASA*] (KSC) ... SWE
Solar Wind Ion Composition Spectrometer (MCD) ... SWICS
Solar Wind Spectrometer ... SWS
Solar Wing (MCD) ... SW
Solar X-Ray Imager [*Marine science*] (OSRA) ... SXI
Solar X-Ray Imager (USDC) ... SXI
Solar Zenith Angle [*Geophysics*] ... SZA
Solar-Assisted Gas Energy [*Water heating*] [*NASA*] ... SAGE
Solar-Assisted Heat Pump (PDAA) ... SAHP
Solar-Based Solar Power Satellite ... SSPS
Solar-Chemical [*Energy conversion process*] ... SOLCHEM
Solarized Advanced Gas Turbine (MCD) ... SAGT
Solar-Mates [*NASDAQ symbol*] (TTSB) ... SOLR
Solar-Mates, Inc. [*Associated Press*] (SAG) ... SolarMt
Solar-Mates, Inc. [*NASDAQ symbol*] (SAG) ... SOLR
Solar-Mates, Inc. [*Associated Press*] (SAG) ... SolrMt
Solar-Mates Inc. Unit [*NASDAQ symbol*] (TTSB) ... SOLRU
Solar-Mates Wrrt [*NASDAQ symbol*] (TTSB) ... SOLRW
Solar-Orbital Communications (IAA) ... SOCOM
Solar-Oriented Experimental Package [*NASA*] ... SOEP
Solar-Terrestrial Energy Program ... STEP
Solar-Terrestrial Energy Transfer Studies [*Meteorology*] ... STETS
Solar-Terrestrial Environment Model [*to predict the terrestrial effects of solar events*] ... STEM
Solar-Terrestrial Physics (IID) ... STP
Solar-Terrestrial Physics - Meteorology ... STP-M
Solar-Terrestrial Physics - Meteorology [*International Council of Scientific Unions*] ... STP-MET
Solar-Terrestrial Probe [*NASA*] ... STP
Solartron Electronic Group (IAA) ... SEG
Solatron Automatic Keyboard Instructor ... SAKI
Solberg, NJ [*Location identifier FAA*] (FAAL) ... SBJ
Solco Basel AG [*Switzerland*] [*Research code symbol*] ... S
Sold ... SL
Sold ... SLD
Sold as Is [*Philately*] ... SAI
Sold, Not Yet Paid Out ... SNYPO
Sold Out (ADA) ... SO
Solder ... SLD
Solder (MSA) ... SLDR
Solder ... SOL
Solder Circuit Etch ... SCE
Solder End Ball Valve ... SEBV
Solder Makers' Association [*British*] (BI) ... SMA
Solder Mask Over Bare Copper [*Electronics*] ... SMOBC
Soldering ... S
Soldering ... SOLD
Soldier [*Slang, probably from Government Issue*] ... GI
Soldier ... SLDR
Soldier ... sol
Soldier as a System [*Symposium*] (RDA) ... SAAS
Soldier Capabilities ... SC
Soldier Crew Tent [*Army*] (INF) ... SCT
Soldier Data Tag ... SDT
Soldier Enhancement Program [*Army*] (INF) ... SEP
Soldier Housing and Retirement Equity ... SHARE
Soldier Modernization Plan [*Army*] (INF) ... SMP
Soldier Operator Maintainer Testing (MCD) ... SOMT
Soldier Orientation and Development (MCD) ... SOD
Soldier out of Luck [*Military slang*] ... SOL
Soldier Physical Fitness School [*Army*] (INF) ... SPFS
Soldier Portable On-System Repair Tool [*Military*] ... SPORT
Soldier Qualification Test (MCD) ... SQT
Soldier/Robot Interface Program Vehicle [*Military*] (RDA) ... SRIP
Soldier, Sailor, Airman, Marine [*A publication*] ... SAM
Soldier Support Center ... SSC
Soldier Support Center - National Capitol Region [*Army*] ... SSC-NCR
Soldier Support Division [*US Army Training and Doctrine Command*] (INF) ... SSD
Soldier Systems Command [*Army*] (INF) ... SSCOM
Soldier Training Publications [*Military*] (INF) ... STP
Soldier-Information Interface (RDA) ... SII
Soldier-Integrated Protective Ensemble [*Army*] (INF) ... SIPE
Soldier-Machine Interface [*Army*] (RDA) ... SMI
Soldier-Operator-Maintainer-Tester-Evaluator [*Military*] (PDAA) ... SOMTE
Soldiers' and Sailors' Civil Relief Act [*1940*] ... SSCRA
Soldiers Christian Association [*British military*] (DMA) ... SCA
Soldiers for Peace (EA) ... SP

Soldiers' Home [*Later, US Soldiers' and Airmen's Home*] [*Government agency*] ... SH
Soldier's Mail, Rush Like Hell [*On correspondence*] ... SMRLH
Soldier's Manual ... SM
Soldier's Manual of Common Tasks [*A publication*] (ADDR) ... SMCT
Soldier's Medal [*Military decoration*] ... SM
Soldier's Medal [*Military decoration*] ... SOLM
Soldiers Memorial Hospital, Middleton, Nova Scotia [*Library symbol National Library of Canada*] (NLC) ... NSMS
Soldiers of Freedom (EA) ... SF
Soldiers Radio and Television [*Information service or system Military*] ... SRTV
Soldier's, Sailor's, and Airmen's Deposit Program (DNAB) ... SSADP
Soldiers, Sailors, and Airmen's Family Association [*British*] ... SSAFA
Soldiers, Sailors, Marines, and Airmen's Club [*Washington, DC*] ... SSMA
Soldiers Service Dress [*British military*] (DMA) ... SSD
Soldiers Total Abstinence Association [*British military*] (DMA) ... STAA
Soldotna, AK [*FM radio station call letters*] ... KKIS
Soldotna, AK [*FM radio station call letters*] ... KPEN-FM
Soldotna, AK [*AM radio station call letters*] ... KSLD
Soldotna, AK [*AM radio station call letters*] ... KSRM
Soldotna, AK [*Location identifier FAA*] (FAAL) ... SXQ
Soldotna Public Library (Joyce Carver Memorial Library), Soldotna, AK [*Library symbol Library of Congress*] (LCLS) ... AkSol
Sole Charge [*Ecclesiastical*] [*British*] (ROG) ... SC
Sole Community Hospital ... SCH
Sole Parent's Pension ... SPP
Sole Proprietor (MHDW) ... SP
Sole Source (SAA) ... SS
Sole Source Review Board (MCD) ... SSRB
Sole Supporting Parent ... SSP
Solectron Corp. [*NYSE symbol*] (SPSG) ... SLR
Solectron Corp. [*Associated Press*] (SAG) ... Solectron
Soledad, CA [*FM radio station call letters*] ... KLUE
Soledad, CA [*AM radio station call letters*] (RBYB) ... KVRG
Soleil-Babinet Compensator [*Optics*] ... SBC
Solenoid (AAG) ... SOL
Solenoid Array Pattern Evaluator ... SAPE
Solenoid Detector Collaboration [*Physics*] ... SDC
Solenoid Driver (IAA) ... SD
Solenoid Hydraulic Valve ... SHV
Solenoid Valve [*Mechanical engineering*] ... SOLV
Solenoid Valve (KSC) ... SV
Solenoid Valve-Carburetor Bowl Vent [*Automotive engineering*] ... SVCBV
Solenoid Vent Valve [*Automotive engineering*] ... SVV
Solenoidal Detector Collaboration [*Particle detection*] ... SDC
Solenoid-Operated Air Valve (IAA) ... SOAV
Solenoid-Operated Valve ... SOV
Solent Container Service [*British*] (DS) ... SCS
Solenzara, Corse [*France ICAO location identifier*] (ICLI) ... LFKS
Sole-Source Aquifer (GNE) ... SSA
Soleus Muscle [*Anatomy*] ... SOL
Sol-Gel [*Materials science*] ... SG
Soli Deo Gloria [*Glory to God Alone*] [*Latin*] ... SDG
Solicitation ... SOLIC
Solicitation Document ... SD
Solicitation for Offers [*A publication*] (AAGC) ... SFO
Solicitation Mailing List (AAGC) ... SML
Solicitation Preparation ... SOLIC PREP
Solicitation Review Panel [*Air Force*] ... SRP
Solicited Volunteer [*In drug studies*] ... SV
Soliciting [*FBI standardized term*] ... SOL
Solicitor ... SOL
Solicitor ... SOLCR
Solicitor ... SOLCR
Solicitor ... SOLR
Solicitor General ... SG
Solicitor General [*Legal term*] (DLA) ... Sol G
Solicitor General [*Legal term*] (DLA) ... Sol Gen
Solicitor General Canada ... SGC
Solicitor General, Prairies [*UTLAS symbol*] ... SGP
Solicitor of Labor [*Department of Labor*] ... SOL
Solicitor Quarterly [*1962-65*] [*A publication*] (DLA) ... Sol Q
Solicitor, Supreme Court ... SSC
Solicitor-at-Law ... SL
Solicitor-General's Office [*Australia*] ... SGO
Solicitors' Board [*Queensland, Australia*] ... SB
Solicitors' Clerks' Gazette [*1921-40*] [*A publication*] (DLA) ... Sol Cl Gaz
Solicitors' Financial Services [*British*] ... SFS
Solicitors' Journal [*A publication A publication*] (DLA) ... SJ
Solicitors' Journal and Reporter [*A publication*] (DLA) ... Sol J & R
Solicitor's Law Opinion, United States Internal Revenue Bureau [*A publication*] (DLA) ... LO
Solicitor's Managing Clerks' Gazette [*1941-62*] [*A publication*] (DLA) ... Sol Man Cl Gaz
Solicitor's Memorandum [*IRS*] (AAGC) ... SM
Solicitor's Memorandum, United States Internal Revenue Bureau [*A publication*] (DLA) ... SM
Solicitor's Opinion [*A publication*] (DLA) ... O
Solicitor's Opinion [*A publication*] (DLA) ... S
Solicitor's Opinion [*Legal term*] (DLA) ... SO
Solicitor's Opinion [*Especially of Internal Revenue Bureau*] [*United States*] (DLA) ... Sol Op
Solicitor's Recommendation [*Internal Revenue Bureau*] [*United States*] [*A publication*] (DLA) ... SR
Solicitor's Undertaking (DCTA) ... SOL U/T
Solid [*Chemistry*] ... (s)
Solid ... S
Solid ... SLD
Solid (MSA) ... SOL
Solid Amine Water Desorbed (NASA) ... SAWD
Solid Angles ... SOLAN
Solid Ankle Cushion Heel [*Foot prosthesis*] ... SACH
Solid Assembly Building ... SAB
Solid Base Bullet ... SB
Solid Blank Delay Line ... SBDL
Solid Bleached Sulphate [*Fiber for paperboard packaging*] ... SBS
Solid Body [*Technical drawings*] ... SB
Solid Bowl Centrifuge ... SBC
Solid Carbide Tool Institute (EA) ... SCTI
Solid Cast Iron Propeller (DS) ... SCIP
Solid Cast Steel Propeller (DS) ... SCSP
Solid Catalysts (KSC) ... SCAT
Solid Combustion Synthesis [*Physics*] ... SCS
Solid Core [*Technical drawings*] ... SC
Solid Dielectric Cable ... SDC
Solid Discharge Data System [*Environmental Protection Agency*] (GFGA) ... SDDS
Solid Drawn ... SD
Solid Ducted Rocket (MCD) ... SDR
Solid Electrolyte Capacitor ... SEC
Solid Electrolyte Fuel Cell [*Chemistry*] ... SOFC
Solid Electrolyte Interphase [*Battery technology*] ... SEI
Solid Electrolyte Potentiometry ... SEP
Solid Electrolyte Tantalum Capacitor ... SETC
Solid Extract [*Pharmacy*] ... SE
Solid Fat Content [*Food analysis*] ... SFC
Solid Fat Index [*Food analysis*] ... SFI
Solid Fiberboard ... SFB
Solid Freeform Fabrication [*Metallurgy*] ... SFF
Solid Fuel (ADA) ... SF
Solid Fuel Administration for War [*Terminated, 1947*] [*World War II*] ... SFAW
Solid Fuel Advisory Council [*British*] (DI) ... SFAC
Solid Fuel Advisory Council of America [*Defunct*] (EA) ... SFACA
Solid Fuel Engine ... SFE
Solid Fuel Ramjet ... SFRJ
Solid Fuels Administration [*Terminated, 1954*] ... SFA
Solid Homogeneous Assembly [*Nuclear energy*] ... SHA
Solid Homogeneous Critical Assembly [*Nuclear reactor*] [*Japan*] ... SHCA
Solid Immersion Lens [*Computer science*] (PCM) ... SIL
Solid Ink Density (DGA) ... SID
Solid Leather Case and Bag Makers' Association [*A union*] [*British*] ... SLCBMA
Solid Logic (IAA) ... SL
Solid Logic Dense (BUR) ... SLD
Solid Logic Design Automation (IAA) ... SLDA
Solid Logic Process Automation (IAA) ... SLPA
Solid Logic Technique [*Computer science*] (IEEE) ... SLT
Solid Logic Technology ... SLT
Solid Measure (ROG) ... SM
Solid Moderated Reactor [*Nuclear energy*] ... SMR
Solid Motor Assembly Building [*for Missiles*] ... SMAB
Solid Motor Processing and Storage Car ... SMPSA
Solid Motor Processing Area [*NASA*] (KSC) ... SMPA
Solid Neutral ... SN
Solid Organs Not Palpable [*Medicine*] ... SONP
Solid Oxide Fuel Cell [*Energy source*] ... SOFC
Solid Oxygen ... SOX
Solid Phase Alloy Nucleation (PDAA) ... SPAN
Solid Phase Epitaxy ... SPE
Solid Phase Microextraction [*Chemistry*] ... SPME
Solid Phase Organic Chemistry ... SPOC
Solid Phase Receptacle [*Laboratory testing*] ... SPR
Solid Phase Synthesis [*Chemistry*] ... SPS
Solid Pipeline Research and Development Association (HGAA) ... SPRDA
Solid Polymer Electrolyte ... SPE
Solid Polymer Fuel Cell [*Energy source*] ... SPFC
Solid Propellant ... SP
Solid Propellant Advanced Ramjet Kinetic Energy (MCD) ... SPARK
Solid Propellant Information ... SPI
Solid Propellant Information Agency [*Air Force*] ... SPIA
Solid Propellant Intercontinental Ballistic Missile (IAA) ... SPICBM
Solid Radioactive Waste System [*Nuclear energy*] (NRCH) ... SRWS
Solid RADWASTE [*Radioactive Waste*] **System** [*Nuclear energy*] (NRCH) ... SRS
Solid Rocket ... SR
Solid Rocket Motor Upgrade [*Air Force*] ... SRMU
Solid Shield (MCD) ... SS
Solid Smokeless Fuels Federation [*British*] (BI) ... SSFF
Solid Solution (OA) ... SS
Solid State ... SS
Solid State Amplifier (NTCM) ... SSA
Solid State Circuit (IAA) ... SSCT
Solid State Component Control System [*Nuclear energy*] (NRCH) ... SSCCS
Solid State Devices (IAA) ... SSD
Solid State Extended Memory (MCD) ... SSEM
Solid State Floppy Disk Card (PCM) ... SSF-DC
Solid State Frequency Changer [*Military*] (CAAL) ... SSFC
Solid State Frequency Converter (DA) ... SSC
Solid State Instrument Landing System (MCD) ... SSILS
Solid State Lamp (MCD) ... SSL
Solid State Phased Array (MCD) ... SSPA
Solid State Power Amplifier (DA) ... SSPA
Solid State RADAR Beacon Decoder (DWSG) ... SSRBD

Solid State Relay (IEEE)	SSR
Solid State Track Detector [Instrumentation]	SSTD
Solid State Track Link [TOW] (MCD)	SSTL
Solid State Transfer Switch	SSTS
Solid Statement Library (HGAA)	SSL
Solid Strand Burning Rate (KSC)	SSBR
Solid Substrate Fermentation	SSF
Solid Substrate Room Temperature Phosphorescence	SSRTP
Solid Surface Burning Facility (SSD)	SSBF
Solid Surface Interaction Experiment	SSIE
Solid Tantalum Capacitor (PDAA)	STC
Solid Uncured Propellant (MCD)	SOUP
Solid Waste	SW
Solid Waste and Emergency Response [Environmental Protection Agency] (GFGA)	SWERD
Solid Waste Assessment Test	SWAT
Solid Waste Barrel Storage [Nuclear energy] (NRCH)	SWBS
Solid Waste Council of the Paper Industry [Defunct] (EA)	SWCPI
Solid Waste Disposal Act [1965]	SWDA
Solid Waste Engineering Transfer System	SWETS
Solid Waste Information Management System (GAAI)	SWIMS
Solid Waste Information Retrieval System [Environmental Protection Agency]	SWIRS
Solid Waste Litter	SWL
Solid Waste Management Association	SWMA
Solid Waste Management Office [Later, Office of Solid Waste Management Programs] [Environmental Protection Agency]	SWMO
Solid Waste Management Planning Software	SWPlan
Solid Waste Management System [Nuclear energy] (NRCH)	SWMS
Solid Waste Management Unit [Environmental science]	SWMU
Solid Waste Management Unit (GNE)	SWMU
Solid Waste Office [Later, Office of Solid Waste Management Programs] [Environmental Protection Agency]	SWO
Solid Waste Packaging [Nuclear energy] (NRCH)	SWP
Solid Waste Processing [Nuclear energy] (NRCH)	SWP
Solid Waste Processing System [Nuclear energy] (NRCH)	SWP(S)
Solid Waste Shipping Room [Nuclear energy] (NRCH)	SWSR
Solid Waste System [Nuclear energy] (NRCH)	SWS
Solid Wastes Cask [Nuclear energy] (NRCH)	SWC
Solidaridad de Trabajadores Cristianos [Nicaragua] [Political party] (EY)	STC
Solidaridad de Trabajadores Vascos [Solidarity of Basque Workers] [In exile Spain]	STV
Solidaridad Espanola [Spanish Solidarity] [Political party] (PPW)	SE
Solidariteits Komitee Argentiniee [Netherlands]	SKAN
Solidarites Agricoles et Alimentaires [France] (EERA)	SOLAGRAL
Solidaritet med Israel	SMIL
Solidarity: A Socialist-Feminist Network [Defunct] (EA)	SSFN
Solidarity International (EA)	SI
Solidarity with Aboriginal Australians Group	SWAAG
Solidarity with Solidarity [See also SzS] [Defunct] (EAIO)	SwS
Solidarnosc z Solidarnoscia [Solidarity with Solidarity - SwS] [Defunct] (EAIO)	SzS
Solid-Core Nuclear Rocket [NASA]	SCNR
Solidification (BARN)	solidif
Solidified Carbon Dioxide [Freight]	SLD CARB DI
Solidified High Waste Level [Nuclear energy] (NUCP)	SHWL
Solidified Liquid (MAE)	SL
Solidified Nitroglycerol [or Nitroglycerin] [Explosive]	SNG
Solid-Liquid Fluidized Bed [Chemical engineering]	SLFB
Solid-Liquid Interdiffusion (IAA)	SLID
Solid-Liquid Phase-Transfer Catalysis	SLPTC
Solid-Liquid-Gas [Phase diagram line]	SLG
Solidor Resources, Inc. [Vancouver Stock Exchange symbol]	SLZ
Solid-Particle Filter Dye [Color film technology]	SPFD
Solid-Phase Extraction	SPE
Solid-Phase Fluorescent Immunoassay [Oncology] (DAVI)	SPFI
Solid-Phase Immunoabsorption [Medicine] (DMAA)	SPIA
Solid-Phase Microextraction [Chemistry]	SPME
Solid-Phase Peptide Synthesis [Biochemistry]	SPPS
Solid-Phase Pressure Forming [Shell Chemical Co.]	SPPF
Solid-Phase Radioimmunoassay [or Radioimmunoprecipitation Assay] [Clinical medicine]	SPRIA
Solid-Phase Reactor	SPR
Solid-Propellant Augmented Rocket Motor [Navy]	SPARM
Solid-Propellant Combustion	SPC
Solid-Propellant Conference	SPC
Solid-Propellant Electric Thruster [Aerospace]	SPET
Solid-Propellant Exhaust Effects (MCD)	SPREE
Solid-Propellant Gas Generator (AAG)	SPGG
Solid-Propellant Intermediate Range Ballistic Missile (AAG)	SPIRBM
Solid-Propellant Rocket	SPR
Solid-Propellant Rocket Engine	SPRE
Solid-Propellant Rocket Ignition Test and Evaluation (KSC)	SPRITE
Solid-Propellant Rocket Intercept Missile [ARPA/AMC]	SPRINT
Solid-Propellant Rocket Static Test Panel [Military]	SPSTP
Solid-Propellant Surveillance Panel [Military]	SPSP
Solid-Propulsion Optimization Code (MCD)	SPOC
Solid-Rocket Booster [NASA]	SRB
Solid-Rocket Booster Assembly Building [NASA] (NASA)	SRBAB
Solid-Rocket Booster Disassembly Facility [NASA] (NASA)	SDAF
Solid-Rocket Booster Disassembly Facility [NASA] (NASA)	SRBDF
Solid-Rocket Booster Processing Facility [NASA] (NASA)	SRBPF
Solid-Rocket Motor	SRM
Solids Handling and Processing Association (EAIO)	SHAPA
Solids Moisture Gauge	SMG
Solids Not Fat	SNF
Solids Retention Time [Water pollution]	SRT
Solid-Solution CERMET [NASA] (NASA)	SSC
Solid-State Abstracts	SSA
Solid-State Acoustoelectric Light Scanner	SALS
Solid-State Air Data Computer (MCD)	SSADC
Solid-State Amorphization [Metallurgy]	SSA
Solid-State Analog-to-Digital Computer	SADIC
Solid-State and Molecular Theory Group [MIT] (MCD)	SMTG
Solid-State and Molecular Theory Group [MIT] (MCD)	SSMTG
Solid-State Audio Clock (DWSG)	SSAC
Solid-State Audio Oscillator	SSAO
Solid-State Celestial Tracker	SSCT
Solid-State Circuit (MCD)	SC
Solid-State Circuit	SSC
Solid-State Circuits Council [IEEE] (EA)	SSCC
Solid-State Computer	SSC
Solid-State Control Transformer	SSCT
Solid-State Control Transformer	SSCX
Solid-State Culture [Biology]	SSC
Solid-State Detector	SSD
Solid-State Disk [Computer science]	SSD
Solid-State Dosimeter	SSD
Solid-State Electric Logic (NG)	SOSTEL
Solid-State Electrolyte (IAA)	SSE
Solid-State Electronic Chronograph	SSEC
Solid-State Electronics	SSE
Solid-State Electronics Laboratory [Stanford University] (MCD)	SSEL
Solid-State Electro-Optic Filter	SSEF
Solid-State Fermentation	SSF
Solid-State Flight Data Recorder (GAVI)	SSFDR
Solid-State Functional Block (IAA)	SFB
Solid-State Gamma Switch	SSGS
Solid-State Image Intensifier	SSII
Solid-State Imaging [Physics]	SSI
Solid-State Imaging Spectrometer	SIS
Solid-State Inverter	SSI
Solid-State Jammer	SSJ
Solid-State Klystron	SOLISTRON
Solid-State Klystron Power Supply	SSKPS
Solid-State LASER	SSL
Solid-State LASER Light Source	SLLS
Solid-State LASER System	SSLS
Solid-State Local Oscillator	SSLO
Solid-State Logic Protection System [Nuclear energy] (NRCH)	SSLPS
Solid-State Logic Timer	SSLT
Solid-State Mass Spectrometer	SSMS
Solid-State Materials (CET)	SSM
Solid-State Microwave Amplifier	SSMA
Solid-State Neutral Dosimeter	SSND
Solid-State Nuclear Track Detection (PDAA)	SSNTD
Solid-State Optical Detector	SSOD
Solid-State Optical MASER	SSOM
Solid-State Oscillator	SSO
Solid-State, Parallel, Expandable, Differential Analyzer Computer	SPEDAC
Solid-State Photodiode	SSP
Solid-State Pneumatic	SSP
Solid-State Pneumatic Logic	SSPL
Solid-State Power Controller [NASA]	SSPC
Solid-State Preamplifier	SSP
Solid-State Products [Electronics] (IAA)	SSP
Solid-State Protection System [Nuclear energy] (IEEE)	SSPS
Solid-State Sciences Committee [National Research Council] [Physics]	SSSC
Solid-State Scientific (IAA)	SSS
Solid-State Silicon Target	SSST
Solid-State Solenoid Driver	SSSD
Solid-State Spectrometer	SSS
Solid-State Storage Device [Computer science]	SSD
Solid-State Switching (NG)	SSS
Solid-State System	SSS
Solid-State Target Monoscope (PDAA)	SSTM
Solid-State Technology (IAA)	SST
Solid-State Timer-Controller	SSTC
Solid-State Track Recorder (PDAA)	SSTR
Solid-State Transducer Intercompartmental Catheter [Instrumentation]	STIC
Solid-State Transmitter (MCD)	SST
Solid-State Welding	SSW
Solid-Supported Liquid Membrane [Chemical engineering]	SSLM
Solid-Surface, Room-Temperature Phosphorescence [Physics]	SS-RTP
Solidus [Shilling] [Latin]	S
Soligen Technologies [ECM Symbol] (TTSB)	SGT EC
Soligen Technologies, Inc. [AMEX symbol] (SAG)	SGT
Soligen Technologies, Inc. [Associated Press] (SAG)	Soligen
Soliloquy [Theater term]	SOL
SOLINET [Southeastern Library Network] Center, Atlanta, GA [OCLC symbol] (OCLC)	QYM
Solitaire [Jewelry] (ROG)	SOL
Solitary [Biology]	S
Solitary Autonomous Nodule [Medicine] (DMAA)	SAN
Solitary Pulmonary Nodule [Medicine] (DAVI)	SPN
Solitary Rectal Ulcer [Medicine] (DMAA)	SRU
Solitary Tract Nucleus [Also, NST] [Anatomy]	STN
Solitary Ulcer of Rectum Syndrome [Medicine] (DMAA)	SURS
Solitary Ulcer Syndrome [Medicine] (DMAA)	SUS
Solleftea [Sweden ICAO location identifier] (ICLI)	ESNB

Sollieres-Sardieres [*France ICAO location identifier*] (ICLI) ... LFKD
Sollingen [*Germany ICAO location identifier*] (ICLI) ... EDAL
Solo [*Music*] ... S
Solo [*Indonesia*] [*Airport symbol*] (OAG) ... SOC
Solo/Adi Sumarmo Wiryokusumo [*Indonesia*] [*ICAO location identifier*] (ICLI) ... WRSQ
Solo Events Board [*Auto racing*] ... SEB
Solo International Resources Ltd. [*Vancouver Stock Exchange symbol*] ... SOZ
Solo Serve Corp. [*NASDAQ symbol*] (SAG) ... SOLOQ
Solo Wargamers Association (EAIO) ... SWA
Soloman's Court of Request Appeals [*Ceylon*] [*A publication*] (DLA) ... Sol
Solomon [*Biblical king*] (ROG) ... SOL
Solomon Airlines Ltd. [*Solomon Islands*] [*ICAO designator*] (FAAC) ... SOL
Solomon, AK [*Location identifier FAA*] (FAAL) ... SOL
Solomon Islands [*Aircraft nationality and registration mark*] (FAAC) ... H4
Solomon Islands [*MARC geographic area code Library of Congress*] (LCCP) ... posn--
Solomon Islands [*ANSI two-letter standard code*] (CNC) ... SB
Solomon Islands (BARN) ... SI
Solomon Islands [*ANSI three-letter standard code*] (CNC) ... SLB
Solomon Islands ... Sol Is
Solomon Islands Airways [*ICAO designator*] (AD) ... IE
Solomon Islands Airways Ltd. (FEA) ... SOLAIR
Solomon Islands Cultural Traditional Leaders Movement ... SICTLM
Solomon Islands Liberal Party [*Political party*] (EY) ... SILP
Solomon Islands United Party [*Political party*] (PPW) ... SIUPA
Solomon Page Group Ltd. [*Associated Press*] (SAG) ... SalPge
Solomon Page Group Ltd. [*NASDAQ symbol*] (SAG) ... SOLP
Solomon Page Group Ltd. [*Associated Press*] (SAG) ... SolPage
Solomon R. Guggenheim Museum, New York, NY [*Library symbol Library of Congress*] (LCLS) ... NNGu
Solomon Schecter Day School Association (EA) ... SSDSA
Solomon-Bloembergen-Morgan Equation [*Medicine*] (DMAA) ... SBM
Solomon-Page Grp Wrrt [*NASDAQ symbol*] (TTSB) ... SOLPW
Solomons Ano Sagufenua [*Solomon Islands*] [*Political party*] (FEA) ... SAS
Solon [*of Plutarch*] [*Classical studies*] (OCD) ... Sol
Solon Economist, Solon, IA [*Library symbol*] [*Library of Congress*] (LCLS) ... IaSolE
Soloway, Wright & Houston Law Firm, Ottawa, Ontario [*Library symbol National Library of Canada*] (BIB) ... OOSWH
Solubilis [*Soluble*] [*Pharmacy*] ... SOL
Solubility ... S
Solubility ... SOLY
Solubility Index [*Water*] ... SI
Solubilization by Incipient Development (OA) ... SID
Soluble (MSA) ... SLBL
Soluble ... SOL
Soluble (IDOE) ... sol
Soluble Adhesion Molecule [*Biochemistry*] ... SAM
Soluble Antigen [*Immunochemistry*] ... SAg
Soluble Antigen Fluorescent-Antibody [*Immunology*] ... SAFA
Soluble Cytotoxic Mediator [*Immunology*] ... SCM
Soluble Egg Antigen [*Medicine*] (DMAA) ... SEA
Soluble Factor (DAVI) ... SF
Soluble Fibrin-Fibrinogen Complex [*Hematology*] ... SFC
Soluble Gelatin ... SG
Soluble Glycoprotein [*Medicine*] (MAE) ... SGP
Soluble Immune Response Suppressor [*Immunology*] ... SIRS
Soluble in Alkaline Solution ... SA
Soluble Insulin ... SI
Soluble Leishmania Antigen [*Immuno chemistry*] ... SLA
Soluble Lytic Transglycosylase [*An enzyme*] ... SLT
Soluble Methane Monooxygenase [*Biochemistry*] ... SMMO
Soluble N-Ethylmaleimide-Sensitive Fusion Attachment Proteins [*Biochemistry*] ... SNAP
Soluble Nonreactive Phosphorus [*Marine science*] ... SNP
Soluble NSF [*N-Ethylmaleimide-Sensitive Fusion Protein*] **Receptors** [*Biochemistry*] ... SNARE
Soluble Nucleoprotein ... SNP
Soluble Organic Fraction [*Environmental chemistry*] ... SOF
Soluble Organic Fractions ... SOF
Soluble Polysaccharide of Soybean [*Food technology*] ... SPS
Soluble Powder (GNE) ... SP
Soluble Protein Preparation [*Biochemistry*] ... SPP
Soluble Reactive Phosphorus (USDC) ... SRP
Soluble Reactive Phosphorus [*Marine science*] (OSRA) ... SRP
Soluble, Repository [*With reference to penicillin*] ... SR
Soluble, Repository, Plus Dihydrostreptomycin [*Referring to penicillin*] [*Pharmacology*] (DAVI) ... SRD
Soluble Solids [*Chemistry*] ... SS
Soluble Solids Content [*Analytical chemistry*] ... SSC
Soluble Suppressor Factor [*Immunology*] ... SSF
Soluble Threshold Limit Concentration [*Environmental chemistry*] ... STLC
So-Luminaire Systems [*Vancouver Stock Exchange symbol*] ... SLS
Solus Outdoor Advertising Association [*British*] (BI) ... SOOA
Solute (DAVI) ... S
Solute (AAMN) ... SOLU
South Rawdon Museum, Nova Scotia [*Library symbol National Library of Canada*] (NLC) ... NSSRM
Solutio [*Solution*] [*Pharmacy*] ... SOL
Solution ... SLN
Solution ... SLTN
Solution (IDOE) ... sol
Solution ... SOL
Solution ... SOLN
Solution Annealed (MCD) ... SA
Solution Crystal Facility (SSD) ... SCF
Solution Crystal Growth ... SCG
Solution Development Record ... SDR
Solution [*or Solvent*] **Free Energy** [*Physical chemistry*] ... SFE
Solution Gas Drive [*Petroleum engineering*] ... SGS
Solution Gas-Oil Ratio ... SGOR
Solution Mining Research Institute (EA) ... SMRI
Solution of Glucose (OA) ... SG
Solution of Ions [*Office of Naval Research*] ... SOLION
Solution of Linearized Equations of Motion ... SLEM
Solution of Ordinary Differential Equations Routine (IAA) ... SOLDIER
Solution Output Processor (PDAA) ... SOP
Solution Provider [*Microsoft workgroup*] (PCM) ... SP
Solution Space ... SS
Solution to Customer Aircraft Troubles (MCD) ... SCAT
Solution to Environmental and Economic Problems ... STEEP
Solution Treat and Age [*Metals*] ... STA
Solution-Based Styrene-Butadiene Rubber [*Materials science*] ... SSBR
Solution-Dyed Nylon ... SDN
Solution-Gelatin (SDI) ... Sol-Gel
Solution-Liquid-Solid [*Chemistry*] ... SLS
Solutions Generation Environment [*Computer science*] (BTTJ) ... SGE
Solutions to Employment Problems [*A program of National Association of Manufacturers*] ... STEP
Solution-Sol-Gel [*Materials science*] ... SSG
Solutrean (VRA) ... Soltr
Solutus [*Dissolved*] [*Pharmacy*] (ROG) ... SOLUT
Solvang, CA [*FM radio station call letters*] ... KSYV
Solvated Metal Atom Dispersion [*Chemistry*] ... SMAD
Solvated Metal Atom Impregnation [*Chemistry*] ... SMAI
Solve [*or Solutus*] [*Dissolve or Dissolved*] [*Pharmacy*] (ROG) ... SOL
Solve [*Dissolve*] [*Pharmacy*] ... SOLV
Solve Cum Calore [*Dissolve by Heating*] [*Pharmacy*] ... SOLVE C CAL
Solvent (WGA) ... SLV
Solvent (MSA) ... SLVT
Solvent ... SOLV
Solvent Abuse Foundation for Education (EA) ... SAFE
Solvent Deasphalting ... SDA
Solvent Detergent Treated Frozen Plasma ... SD-FP
Solvent Extraction (DEN) ... SX
Solvent Extraction and Electrowinning [*Metallurgy*] ... SXEW
Solvent Extraction Feed [*Nuclear energy*] (NRCH) ... SXF
Solvent Extraction Milling (BARN) ... SEM
Solvent Service Unit ... SSU
Solvent-Induced Force [*Physical chemistry*] ... SIF
Solvent-Refined Coal ... SRC
Solvents Industry Association [*British*] (DBA) ... SIA
Solvent-Separated Ion-Pair [*Physical chemistry*] ... SSIP
Solver for Implicit Equations [*Computer language*] ... SIMPLE
Solv-Ex Corp. [*NASDAQ symbol*] (NQ) ... SOLV
Solv-Ex Corp. [*Associated Press*] (SAG) ... SolvEx
Solving Community Obstacles and Restoring Employment [*Occupational therapy*] ... SCORE
Solving Problems of Access to Careers in Engineering and Science (EDAC) ... SPACES
Solway Elementary School, Bemidji, MN [*Library symbol*] [*Library of Congress*] (LCLS) ... MnBemSE
Solwezi [*Zambia*] [*ICAO location identifier*] (ICLI) ... FLSW
Soma Dendrite Membrane ... SDM
Somali [*MARC geographic area code Library of Congress*] (LCCP) ... f-so--
Somali Abo Liberation Front [*Ethiopia*] [*Political party*] (PD) ... SALF
Somali Airlines [*ICAO designator*] (AD) ... HH
Somali Airlines [*Somalia*] [*ICAO designator*] (FAAC) ... SOM
Somali Cat Club of America ... SCCA
Somali Current Monitoring System [*Marine science*] (MSC) ... SCMS
Somali Democratic Alliance [*Political party*] (EY) ... SDA
Somali Democratic Movement [*Political party*] (EY) ... SDM
Somali Eastern and Central Front [*Political party*] (EY) ... SECF
Somali Islamic Movement [*Political party*] ... SIM
Somali National Front [*Political party*] (EY) ... SNF
Somali National League ... SNL
Somali National Movement [*Political party*] (PD) ... SNM
Somali National News Agency ... SONNA
Somali National Union ... SNU
Somali Patriotic Front [*Political party*] (EY) ... SPF
Somali Patriotic Movement [*Political party*] (EY) ... SPM
Somali Salvation Front (PD) ... SSF
Somali Shilling [*Monetary unit*] ... SO SH
Somali Socialist Revolutionary Party ... SSRP
Somali, Tigray, and Ormo Resistance Monitor [*British*] ... STORM
Somali Youth League [*Political party*] (AF) ... SYL
Somalia [*Aircraft nationality and registration mark*] (FAAC) ... 6O
Somalia [*ANSI two-letter standard code*] (CNC) ... SO
Somalia [*MARC country of publication code Library of Congress*] (LCCP) ... so
Somalia [*MARC language code Library of Congress*] (LCCP) ... som
Somalia [*ANSI three-letter standard code*] (CNC) ... SOM
Somalia Law Reports [*A publication*] (DLA) ... Som LR
Somalia National Alliance ... SNA
Somaliland Scouts [*Military unit*] [*British*] ... S
Soman [*Nerve gas*] [*Army symbol*] ... GD
Somanetics Corp. [*NASDAQ symbol*] (SAG) ... SMTS
Somanetics Corp. [*Associated Press*] (SAG) ... Soma
Somanetics Corp. [*Associated Press*] (SAG) ... Somanetc
Somanetics Corp. Wrrt'B' [*NASDAQ symbol*] (TTSB) ... SMTSZ

Somascan Fathers (TOCD) .... CRS
Somascan Fathers, Order of St. Jerome Aemilian (TOCD) .... crs
Somatic [*Pertaining to the body or the body wall*] (DAVI) .... somat
Somatic Cell Concentration (OA) .... SCC
Somatic Crossing-Over [*Medicine*] (DMAA) .... SCO
Somatic Inkblot Series [*Personality development test*] [*Psychology*] .... SIS
Somatic Nervous System .... SNS
Somatically Evoked Field [*Neurophysiology*] .... SEF
Somatically Evoked Potential [*Neurophysiology*] .... SEP
Somatics Society [*Commercial firm*] (EA) .... SS
Somatix Therapy [*NASDAQ symbol*] (TTSB) .... SOMA
Somatix Therapy Corp. [*NASDAQ symbol*] (SAG) .... SOMA
Somatix Therapy Corp. [*Associated Press*] (SAG) .... Somtix
Somatogen, Inc. [*NASDAQ symbol*] (SPSG) .... SMTG
Somatogen, Inc. [*Associated Press*] (SAG) .... Somatgn
Somatolactin [*Biochemistry*] .... SL
Somatomedin [*Biochemistry*] .... SM
Somatomedin A [*Biochemistry*] .... SMA
Somatomedin C [*Biochemistry*] .... SMC
Somatosensory Brain Stem Evoked Potential [*Neurology*] (DAVI) .... SBEP
Somatosensory Evoked Potential [*Neurology*] (DAVI) .... SEM
Somatosensory Evoked Potential [*Neurology*] (DAVI) .... SEP
Somatosensory Evoked Potential [*Neurophysiology*] .... SSEP
Somatosensory Evoked Response [*Neurophysiology*] .... SER
Somatosensory Evoked Response [*Neurophysiology*] .... SSER
Somatostatin [*Biochemistry*] .... SOM
Somatostatin [*Biochemistry*] .... SRIH
Somatostatin [*Also, GH-RIF, GH-RIH, GRIF, SRIF*] [*Endocrinology*] .... SS
Somatostatin-Like Immunoreactivity .... SLI
Somatostatin-Like Immunoreactivity .... SOM-LI
Somatotrophic [*Growth*] **Hormone** [*Also, GH, STH*] [*Endocrinology*] .... SH
Somatotrophic [*Growth*] **Hormone** [*Also, GH, SH*] [*Endocrinology*] .... STH
Somatotrophin [*Endocrinology*] .... SOM
Somatotrophin-Releasing Factor [*Endocrinology*] .... SRF
Somatotrophin-Releasing Inhibiting Factor [*Also, GH-RIF, GH-RIH, GRIF, SS*] [*Endocrinology*] .... SRIF
Somatotropin Release Inhibiting Hormone [*Biochemistry*] .... SRIH
Somatotropin-Releasing Hormone [*Endocrinology*] (MAE) .... SRH
Sombra Township Museum, Ontario [*Library symbol National Library of Canada*] (BIB) .... OSOTM
Sombrero [*Chile*] [*Seismograph station code, US Geological Survey*] (SEIS) .... SOM
Some American Artists [*An association*] (EA) .... SAA
Some Essential Learner Outcomes [*Minnesota*] (EDAC) .... SELO
Some Remarks on Abstract Machines [*Computer science*] .... SRAM
Some Tools for Evaluating Parallel Programs [*Computer science*] (MHDI) .... STEPPS
Somers, CT [*FM radio station call letters*] .... WDJW
Somers Historical Society, Somers, NY [*Library symbol Library of Congress*] (LCLS) .... NSoHi
Somers Library, Somers, NY [*Library symbol Library of Congress*] (LCLS) .... NSo
Somerset [*Colorado*] [*Seismograph station code, US Geological Survey*] (SEIS) .... SMC
Somerset [*County in England*] .... SOM
Somerset and Cornwall Light Infantry [*British military*] (DMA) .... SCLI
Somerset & Dorset Joint Railway [*British*] .... S & DJR
Somerset & Dorset Joint Railway [*British*] (ROG) .... S & DR
Somerset Community College, Somerset, KY [*OCLC symbol*] (OCLC) .... KTC
Somerset Community College, Somerset, KY [*Library symbol Library of Congress*] (LCLS) .... KySoC
Somerset County [*England*] (BARN) .... Soms
Somerset County Clerk, Somerville, NJ [*Library symbol Library of Congress*] (LCLS) .... NjSoCoC
Somerset County College, Somerville, NJ [*Library symbol Library of Congress*] (LCLS) .... NjSoS
Somerset County College, Somerville, NJ [*OCLC symbol*] (OCLC) .... SOC
Somerset County Historical and Genealogical Society, Somerset, PA [*Library symbol Library of Congress*] (LCLS) .... PSomHi
Somerset County Library, Bridgewater, NJ [*OCLC symbol*] (OCLC) .... SOM
Somerset County Library, Somerville, NJ [*Library symbol Library of Congress*] (LCLS) .... NjSoCo
Somerset County Vocational and Technical School, Bridgewater, NJ [*OCLC symbol*] (OCLC) .... SOV
Somerset East [*South Africa*] [*ICAO location identifier*] (ICLI) .... FAST
Somerset Group [*NASDAQ symbol*] (TTSB) .... SOMR
[*The*] **Somerset Group, Inc.** [*Indianapolis, IN*] [*NASDAQ symbol*] (NQ) .... SOMR
Somerset Group, Inc. [*Associated Press*] (SAG) .... SomrGp
Somerset Hospital, Somerville, NJ [*Library symbol Library of Congress*] (LCLS) .... NjSoH
Somerset, KY [*Location identifier FAA*] (FAAL) .... CDX
Somerset, KY [*Location identifier FAA*] (FAAL) .... SME
Somerset, KY [*FM radio station call letters*] .... WDCL
Somerset, KY [*Television station call letters*] .... WKSO
Somerset, KY [*FM radio station call letters*] .... WLLK
Somerset, KY [*FM radio station call letters*] .... WSEK
Somerset, KY [*AM radio station call letters*] .... WSFC
Somerset, KY [*FM radio station call letters*] .... WTHL
Somerset, KY [*AM radio station call letters*] .... WTLO
Somerset Legal Journal [*Pennsylvania*] [*A publication*] (DLA) .... Som
Somerset Legal Journal [*Pennsylvania*] [*A publication*] (DLA) .... Som Leg J (PA)
Somerset Legal Journal [*Pennsylvania*] [*A publication*] (DLA) .... Som LJ
Somerset Legal Journal [*A publication*] (DLA) .... Somerset LJ
Somerset Library [*Bibliotheque Somerset*], **Manitoba** [*Library symbol National Library of Canada*] (BIB) .... MS
Somerset Light Infantry [*Military unit*] [*British*] .... SLI
Somerset Messenger-Gazette, Somerville, NJ [*Library symbol Library of Congress*] (LCLS) .... NjSoM
Somerset, PA [*Location identifier FAA*] (FAAL) .... SOZ
Somerset, PA [*Location identifier FAA*] (FAAL) .... SYS
Somerset, PA [*AM radio station call letters*] .... WADJ
Somerset, PA [*AM radio station call letters*] .... WVSC
Somerset, PA [*FM radio station call letters*] .... WVSC-FM
Somerset Public Library, Somerset, MA [*Library symbol*] [*Library of Congress*] (LCLS) .... MSom
Somerset Savings Bank [*Associated Press*] (SAG) .... SomstSv
Somerset Savings Bank [*NASDAQ symbol*] (SAG) .... SOSA
Somerset Spectator, Somerset, NJ [*Library symbol Library of Congress*] (LCLS) .... NjSosS
Somerset State Hospital, Somerset, PA [*OCLC symbol*] (OCLC) .... PHS
Somerset, TX [*AM radio station call letters*] .... KCHG
Somersetshire [*County in England*] .... SOM
Somersetshire [*County in England*] (ROG) .... SOMST
Somersetshire Pleas (Civil and Criminal), Edited by Chadwyck-Healey and Landon [*Somerset Record Society Publications, Vols. 11, 36, 41, 44*] [*A publication*] (DLA) .... Sm Pl
Somersetshire Pleas (Civil and Criminal), Edited by Chadwyck-Healey and Landon [*Somerset Record Society Publications, Vols. 11, 36, 41, 44*] [*A publication*] (DLA) .... Som Pl
Somersworth, NH [*FM radio station call letters*] (RBYB) .... WBYY-FM
Somersworth, NH [*FM radio station call letters*] .... WRGW
Somerton Public Library, Somerton, AZ [*Library symbol Library of Congress*] (LCLS) .... AzSo
Somerville Belkin Industries Ltd. [*Toronto Stock Exchange symbol*] .... SBI
Somerville Free Public Library, Somerville, NJ [*Library symbol Library of Congress*] (LCLS) .... NjSo
Somerville, TN [*AM radio station call letters*] (RBYB) .... WSTN-AM
Something About Myself Inventory (EDAC) .... SAM
Something about the Author [*A publication*] .... SATA
Something about the Author Autobiography Series [*A publication*] .... SAAS
Something Is Better than Nothing .... SIBTN
Something to Advantage [*Advertising*] [*Legal term*] .... SOMEG to ADV
Something to Help Everyone Reduce Load on Computers [*Army*] .... SHERLOC
Sometimes .... SOMET
Somewhat (DNAB) .... SMWHT
Sommelier Society of America (EA) .... SSA
Sommers' Equivocation Network for Significant Expressions (SAA) .... SENSE
Somner on Gavelkind [*A publication*] (DLA) .... Somn on Gav
Somnolent [*A metabolic test*] (DAVI) .... SOM
Somnolent Metabolic Rate [*Medicine*] .... SMR
Somnus [*Sleep*] [*Latin*] (ROG) .... SOM
Somogyi Unit [*of amylase*] [*Clinical chemistry*] .... SU
Somonauk Community Unit, School District 432, Somonauk, IL [*Library symbol Library of Congress*] (LCLS) .... ISomSD
Somonauk Public Library, Somonauk, IL [*Library symbol Library of Congress*] (LCLS) .... ISom
Somplago [*Italy*] [*Seismograph station code, US Geological Survey Closed*] (SEIS) .... SMP
Son .... S
Son Altesse [*His or Her Highness*] [*French*] .... SA
Son Altesse Electorale [*His Highness the Elector*] [*French*] (ROG) .... SAE
Son Altesse Imperiale [*His or Her Imperial Highness*] [*French*] .... SAI
Son Altesse Royale [*His or Her Royal Highness*] [*French*] .... SAR
Son Altesse Serenissime [*His or Her Serene Highness*] [*French*] .... SAS
Son and Coheir [*Genealogy*] .... S and COH
Son and Heir [*Genealogy*] .... S and H
So'n Cal Ed 4.32% cm Pfd [*AMEX symbol*] (TTSB) .... SCEPrD
Son Compte [*His, or Her, Account*] [*French*] .... S/C
Son Of [*Genealogy*] .... S/O
Son of a Bitch .... SOB
Son of a Witch (EA) .... SW
Son of Temperance [*A heavy drinker*] [*Slang*] .... SOT
Son San Juan Air Force Base [*Spain ICAO location identifier*] (ICLI) .... LESJ
Sona Systems Ltd. (Canada) [*Vancouver Stock Exchange symbol*] .... SSF
Sonar [*JETDS nomenclature*] .... Q
SONAR [*Sonic Azimuth and Ranging*] [*British military*] (DMA) .... S
SONAR .... SNR
SONAR Accuracy Check Site (NVT) .... SACS
SONAR Acoustique Remorque [*Acoustic imaging system*] [*French*] .... SAR
SONAR Array [*Sounding system*] [*Navy*] .... SONARRAY
SONAR Automatic Controller (IAA) .... SNAC
SONAR Breakout Cable .... SBC
SONAR Calibration and Alignment Steering Group .... SCASG
SONAR Calibration Set .... SCS
SONAR Certification Test .... SCT
SONAR Channel [*Navy*] (CAAL) .... SC
Sonar Class Association (EA) .... SCA
SONAR Communications Set .... SCS
SONAR Commutator Assemblies [*JETDS nomenclature*] [*Military*] (CET) .... CA
SONAR Control Room .... SCR
SONAR Control Room (MSA) .... SONCR
SONAR Control Room .... SRCR
SONAR Countermeasures and Deception [*Military*] .... SONCM
SONAR Data Computer [*Navy*] (CAAL) .... SDC
SONAR Data Recorder .... SDR
SONAR Detection Opportunity [*Navy*] (CAAL) .... SDO
SONAR Dome Flow Noise .... SDFN
SONAR Dome Rubber Window (NVT) .... SDRW
SONAR Early Warning .... SEW
SONAR Echo Simulator .... SES
SONAR Evaluation and Assistance [*Teams*] .... SEA

SONAR Frequency [Military] (CAAL) .... SF
SONAR Information Center (NVT) .... SIC
SONAR In-Situ Mode Assessment System (MSC) .... SIMAS
SONAR Instrumentation Probe (IAA) .... SIP
SONAR Locator, Altimeter, and Depthometer .... SLAD
SONAR Nacelle [Sonacelle] .... SONAC
SONAR Phase Shifter .... SPS
SONAR Schoolship [Navy] (NVT) .... SOSS
SONAR Signal Processor .... SSP
SONAR Signal Simulator .... SSS
SONAR Signaling (NVT) .... SST
SONAR Surveillance System [Military] .... SOSUS
SONAR Systems Project Management Office .... SSPMO
SONAR Technician [Navy rating] .... ST
SONAR Technician, First Class [Navy rating] ST1
SONAR Technician, Ground [Navy rating] (DNAB) .... STG
SONAR Technician, Ground, Seaman [Navy rating] (DNAB) .... STGSN
SONAR Technician, Ground, Seaman Apprentice [Navy rating] (DNAB) .... STGSA
SONAR Technician, Second Class [Navy rating] ST2
SONAR Technician, Submarine [Navy rating] (DNAB) .... STS
SONAR Technician, Submarine, Seaman [Navy rating] (DNAB) .... STSSN
SONAR Technician, Submarine, Seaman Apprentice [Navy rating] (DNAB) .... STSSA
SONAR Technician, Third Class [Navy rating] ST3
SONAR Test System .... STS
SONAR Test Tower Facility .... STTF
SONAR Transducer Test and Evaluation Center, Naval Electronics Laboratory [San Diego, CA] [Navy] .... TRANSDEC
SONARman [Navy] .... SO
SONARman [Navy] .... SOM
SONARman First Class [Navy] SO1
SONARman Harbor Defense [Navy] (IAA) .... SOH
SONARman Harbor Defense [Navy] .... SOMH
SONARman Second Class [Navy] SO2
SONARman Third Class [Navy] SO3
Sonat, Inc. [NYSE symbol] (SPSG) .... SNT
Sonat, Inc. [Associated Press] (SAG) .... Sonat
Sonat Offshore Drilling [NYSE symbol] (TTSB) .... RIG
Sonat Offshore Drilling, Inc. [NYSE symbol] (SPSG) .... RIG
Sonat Offshore Drilling, Inc. [Associated Press] (SAG) .... SonatOff
Sonata [Music] (WGA) .... SON
Sonchus Virus [Plant pathology] .... SONV
Sonchus Yellow Net Virus [Plant pathology] .... SYNV
Soncino (BJA) .... Sonc
Soncino Books of the Bible [London] [A publication] (BJA) .... SBB
[The] Soncino Books of the Bible (Bornemouth) [A publication] (BJA) .... SoncinoB
Soncino Chumash [A publication] (BJA) .... SC
Sonderabdruck (BJA) .... SA
Sonderborg [Denmark ICAO location identifier] (ICLI) .... EKSB
Sonderborg [Denmark] [Airport symbol] (OAG) .... SGD
Sondre Stromfjord [Greenland] [ICAO location identifier] (ICLI) .... BGSF
Sondre Stromfjord [Greenland] [Airport symbol] (OAG) .... SFJ
Sondrestrom [Greenland] [ICAO location identifier] (ICLI) .... BGGL
Sonepat [India] [Seismograph station code, US Geological Survey Closed] (SEIS) .... SNP
Sonesta International Hotels Corp. [NASDAQ symbol] (NQ) .... SNST
Sonesta International Hotels Corp. [Associated Press] (SAG) .... Sonesta
Sonesta Intl Hotels [NASDAQ symbol] (TTSB) .... SNSTA
Sonet Transmission Manager [Adaptive Corp.] .... STM
Song (ROG) .... S
Song and Dance Act [Slang] .... S & D
Song of Moses (BJA) .... SM
Song of Solomon [Old Testament book] .... S of S
Song of Solomon [Old Testament book] (ROG) .... S of Sol
Song of Solomon [Old Testament book] .... Song Sol
Song of Songs [Old Testament book] [Roman Catholic canon] (BJA) .... Sg
Song of Songs [Old Testament book] [Roman Catholic canon] .... SGS
Song of Songs [Old Testament book] [Roman Catholic canon] .... Song
Song of Songs [Old Testament book] [Roman Catholic canon] (BJA) .... SoS
Song of Songs Rabbah (BJA) .... SongR
Song of the Three Children [Old Testament book] [Apocrypha] .... Song 3 Childr
Song of the Three Children [Old Testament book] [Apocrypha] (BJA) .... SongCh
[The] Song of the Three Holy Children [Apocrypha] .... Song of Three Childr
Song Position Pointer [Computer science] (PCM) .... SPP
Song San-Ri [South Korea ICAO location identifier] (ICLI) .... RKSX
Song Sparrow [Ornithology] .... SS
Songa [Zaire] [ICAO location identifier] (ICLI) .... FZSC
Songadh [India] [ICAO location identifier] (ICLI) .... VASG
Songea [Tanzania] [ICAO location identifier] (ICLI) .... HTSO
Songea [Tanzania] [Airport symbol] (OAG) .... SGX
Songhai [MARC language code Library of Congress] (LCCP) .... son
Songhor [Iran] [ICAO location identifier] (ICLI) .... OICO
Songkhla [Thailand] [Seismograph station code, US Geological Survey] (SEIS) .... SNG
Songkhla [Thailand] [ICAO location identifier] (ICLI) .... VTSH
Songkhla/Hat Yai [Thailand] [ICAO location identifier] (ICLI) .... VTSS
Songo [Mozambique] [ICAO location identifier] (ICLI) .... FQSG
Songo [Mozambique] [Airport symbol] (OAG) .... SOO
Songsmith Society (EA) .... SS
Songwriters and Lyricists Club (EA) .... SLC
Songwriters Club [Later, SLC] (EA) .... SC
Songwriters Guild of America (EA) .... SGA
Songwriters Guild of Great Britain .... SWG
Songwriters Protective Association [Later, AGAC] .... SPA
Songwriters Resources and Services [Later, NAS] (EA) .... SRS

Sonic Arts Network [An association British] (EAIO) .... SAN
Sonic Azimuth and Ranging [British military] (DMA) .... SONAR
Sonic Azimuth Detector (MCD) .... SONAD
Sonic Boom [Computer program] [NASA] .... SBOOM
Sonic Boom Panel [Aerospace] (MCD) .... SBP
Sonic Boom Research Program .... SBRP
Sonic Corp. [NASDAQ symbol] (SPSG) .... SONC
Sonic Corp. [Associated Press] (SAG) .... Sonic
Sonic Delay Line .... SDL
Sonic Depth Finder .... SDF
Sonic End Fire for Azimuth and Range .... SEFAR
Sonic Environmental Systems, Inc. [NASDAQ symbol] (SAG) .... SONA
Sonic Environmental Systems, Inc. [Associated Press] (SAG) .... Sonic
Sonic Environmental Systems, Inc. [Associated Press] (SAG) .... SonicEnv
Sonic Extract [Cytology] .... SE
Sonic Fatigue Test Laboratory (AAG) .... SFTL
Sonic Frequency System .... SFS
Sonic High-Accuracy Ranging and Positioning System .... SHARPS
Sonic Instrument Measurement and Control (AAG) .... SIMAC
Sonic Key (MCD) .... SK
Sonic Layer Depth (NVT) .... SLD
Sonic Log .... SL
Sonic Noise Analyzer .... SONOAN
Sonic Observation of the Trajectory and Impact of Missiles .... SOTIM
Sonic Pulse-Echo Instrument Designed for Extreme Resolution (IEEE) .... SPIDER
Sonic Ranging and Detection (KSC) .... SORAD
Sonic Solutions [NASDAQ symbol] (SAG) .... SNIC
Sonic Solutions Co. [Associated Press] (SAG) .... SonicSol
Sonic Telegraphy .... S/T
Sonic Telex System [Sonicair] [Phoenix, AZ] [Telecommunications] (TSSD) .... STS
Sonic True Airspeed and Mach Number Indicator .... STAMNI
Sonic Underwater Navigation System (WDAA) .... SUNS
Sonically-Induced Narrowing [Physics] .... SK
Sonicraft, Inc., Chicago, IL [Library symbol Library of Congress] (LCLS) .... ICSon
Sonics & Materials [NASDAQ symbol] (TTSB) .... SIMA
Sonics & Materials, Inc. [NASDAQ symbol] (SAG) .... SIMA
Sonics & Materials, Inc. [AMEX symbol] (SAG) .... SMS
Sonics & Materials, Inc. [Associated Press] (SAG) .... SonicM
Sonics & Materials Wrrt [NASDAQ symbol] (TTSB) .... SIMAW
Sonics and Ultrasonics (MCD) .... SU
Sonkajarvi-Jyrkka [Finland ICAO location identifier] (ICLI) .... EFSJ
Sonmez Airlines [Turkey] [ICAO designator] (FAAC) .... SMZ
Sonneberg [Federal Republic of Germany] [Seismograph station code, US Geological Survey Closed] (SEIS) .... SON
Sonneck Society (EA) .... SS
Sonnenschein, Carlin, Nath & Rosenthal, Chicago, IL [Library symbol] [Library of Congress] (LCLS) .... ICSCN
Sonnenschein, Carlin, Nath & Rosenthal, Chicago, IL [OCLC symbol] (OCLC) ILV
Sonnets [Shakespearean work] .... Son
Sonning [England] .... SONN
Sonny James and Friends [An association Defunct] (EA) .... SJF
Sonoangiography [Medicine] (DMAA) .... SAG
Sonobuoy (NVT) .... SB
Sonobuoy .... SONB
Sonobuoy .... SONO
Sonobuoy Acoustic Operator [Navy] (CAAL) .... SAO
Sonobuoy Control Panel .... SCP
Sonobuoy Interface Unit [Navy] (CAAL) .... SIU
Sonobuoy Launch Container (NVT) .... SLC
Sonobuoy Launch Tube [Navy] (CAAL) .... SLT
Sonobuoy Launcher Pneumatic System .... SLPS
Sonobuoy Localization System (NVT) .... SLS
Sonobuoy Missile Impact Location System [Navy] (CAAL) .... SMILS
Sonobuoy Placement Assortment Model (MCD) .... SPAM
Sonobuoy Qualification Facility [Navy] (CAAL) .... SQUAF
Sonobuoy Receiver Logic [Navy] (CAAL) .... SRL
Sonobuoy Reference System [Navy] (CAAL) .... SRS
Sonobuoy Referenced Position [Navy] (NG) .... SRP
Sonobuoy Thinned Random Array Program [Navy] (CAAL) .... STRAP
Sonoco Prd $2.25 Sr'A'Cv Pfd [NYSE symbol] (TTSB) .... SONPrA
Sonoco Products [NYSE symbol] (TTSB) .... SON
Sonoco Products Corp. [NYSE symbol] (SAG) .... SCN
Sonoco Products Corp. [NYSE symbol] (SAG) .... SON
Sonoco Products Corp. [Associated Press] (SAG) .... Sonoco
Sonoco Products Corp. [Associated Press] (SAG) .... SonocoP
Sonoencephalogram (AAMN) .... SEG
Sonogram [Medicine] (DHSM) .... SONO
Sonoluminescence [Physics] .... SL
Sonoma County Grape Growers Association (EA) .... SCGGA
Sonoma County Wineries Association [Sonoma County Wine Growers Associatio n] [Acronym is based on former name,] (EA) .... SCWGA
Sonoma Public Library, Sonoma, CA [Library symbol Library of Congress] (LCLS) .... CSom
Sonoma Public Library, Sonoma, CA [Library symbol] [Library of Congress] (LCLS) .... CSomL
Sonoma State College, Rohnert Park, CA [OCLC symbol] (OCLC) .... CSO
Sonoma State University (GAGS) .... Cal St U (Sonoma)
Sonor Investments Ltd. [Toronto Stock Exchange symbol] .... SNI
Sonor Petroleum Corp. [Toronto Stock Exchange symbol] .... SOR
Sonora [Record label] [Sweden] .... SON
Sonora, CA [FM radio station call letters] .... KTUO
Sonora, CA [AM radio station call letters] .... KVML
Sonora, CA [FM radio station call letters] .... KZSQ

Sonora Gold Corp. [*Toronto Stock Exchange symbol Vancouver Stock Exchange symbol*] ... SON
Sonora Gold Corp. (MHDW) ... SONNF
Sonora Public Library, Sonora, CA [*Library symbol Library of Congress*] (LCLS) ... CSo
Sonora, TX [*AM radio station call letters*] ... KHOS
Sonora, TX [*FM radio station call letters*] ... KHOS-FM
Sonora, TX [*Location identifier FAA*] (FAAL) ... SOA
Sonoswitch ... SONOSW
Sons and Daughters in Touch [*An association*] ... SDIT
Sons and Daughters of Malta (EA) ... SDM
Sons and Daughters of Oregon Pioneers (EA) ... SDOP
Sons and Daughters of Pioneer Rivermen (EA) ... SDPR
Sons and Daughters of the First Settlers of Newbury, Massachusetts (EA) ... SDFSNM
Sons and Daughters of the Soddies (EA) ... SDS
Sons of Bosses International [*Later, NFBC*] [*An association*] (EA) ... SOB's
Sons of Charity [*France*] (EAIO) ... SC
Sons of Confederate Veterans (EA) ... SCV
Sons of David (BJA) ... SofD
Sons of Divine Providence (TOCD) ... FDP
Sons of Divine Providence (TOCD) ... fdp
Sons of Italy Supreme Lodge (EA) ... SISL
Sons of Jewish War Veterans of the United States of America (EA)... SJWVUSA
Sons of Liberty (EA) ... SL
Sons of Light [*An association*] ... SOL
Sons of Malta ... SM
Sons of Mary Missionary Society (TOCD) ... FMSI
Sons of Mary Missionary Society (TOCD) ... fmsi
Sons of Norway (EA) ... S/N
Sons of Phoenix [*Freemasonry*] (ROG) ... S of P
Sons of Scotland Benevolent Association (EA) ... SSBA
Sons of Sherman's March to the Sea (EA) ... SSMS
Sons of Spanish American War Veterans (EA) ... SSAWV
Sons of Temperance ... S of T
Sons of Temperance ... ST
Sons of Temperance of North America [*Defunct*] (EA) ... STNA
Sons of the American Legion (EA) ... SAL
Sons of the American Revolution ... SAR
Sons of the American Revolution, Empire State Society Library, New York, NY [*Library symbol Library of Congress*] (LCLS) ... NNSAR
Sons of the American Revolution, National Society Library, Washington, DC [*Library symbol Library of Congress*] (LCLS) ... DNSAR
Sons of the Desert (EA) ... SOD
Sons of the Holy Family [*Roman Catholic men's religious order*] ... SF
Sons of the Holy Family (TOCD) ... sf
Sons of the Revolution in the State of New York, New York, NY [*Library symbol Library of Congress*] (LCLS) ... NNSR
Sons of the Whiskey Rebellion (EA) ... SWR
Sons of Union Veterans of the Civil War (EA) ... SUVCW
Sons of Veterans ... SV
Sonsonate/Acajutla [*El Salvador*] [*ICAO location identifier*] (ICLI) ... MSAC
SONUS Pharmaceuticals [*NASDAQ symbol*] (TTSB) ... SNUS
Sonus Pharmaceuticals, Inc. [*NASDAQ symbol*] (SAG) ... SNUS
Sonus Pharmaceuticals, Inc. [*Associated Press*] (SAG) ... SonusP
Sony Corp. ADR [*NYSE symbol*] (TTSB) ... SNE
Sony Corp. America [*NYSE symbol Toronto Stock Exchange symbol Vancouver Stock Exchange symbol*] (SPSG) ... SNE
Sony Corp. America [*Associated Press*] (SAG) ... SonyCp
Sony Dynamic Digital Sound [*Surround-sound technology*] (PS) ... SDDS
Sony Music Entertainment (ECON) ... SME
Sony Pictures Entertainment [*Commercial firm*] (ECON) ... SPE
Soo Line Corp. [*NYSE symbol and AAR code*] (SPSG) ... SOO
Sooke Region Museum, Sooke, British Columbia [*Library symbol National Library of Canada*] (NLC) ... BSORM
Soon as Possible ... SAP
Soon to be Pushing Up Daisies [*Lifestyle classification*] (ECON) ... SPUD
Soonair Lines, Inc. [*ICAO designator*] (FAAC) ... SNL
Sooner Energy Corp. [*Vancouver Stock Exchange symbol*] ... SGY
Sooner Exchange for Educational Knowledge [*Oklahoma*] (EDAC) ... SEEK
SOON's [*Solar Observing Optical Network*] **Solar Patrol on Tape** [*Marine science*] (OSRA) ... SOONSPOT
SOON's [*Solar Observing Optical Network*] **Solar Patrol on Tape** (USDC) ... SOONSPOT
Soot Blower (AAG) ... SB
Soot Trap and Regeneration System [*Diesel engine exhaust emission controls*] ... STARS
Sooty Mangabey Monkey ... SMM
SOPA [*Senior Officer Present Afloat*] **Administrative Duties** [*Military*] (NVT) ... SOPAD
Soperton, GA [*FM radio station call letters*] ... WKTM
Sopherim (BJA) ... Soph
Sophia University [*UTLAS symbol*] ... SUL
Sophicated Optimized Fuel Injection System ... SOFIS
Sophista [*of Plato*] [*A publication*] (OCD) ... Soph
Sophister [*British*] (ROG) ... SOPH
Sophisticated Automatic RADAR Processing (PDAA) ... SARP
Sophisticated Data Research, Inc. [*Information service or system*] (IID) ... SDR
Sophisticated Operating System [*Apple III microcomputer*] [*Computer science*] ... SOS
Sophisticated Optimized Fuel Injection System [*Automotive engineering*] ... SOFIS
Sophisticated String Editor (IEEE) ... SEDIT
Sophisticated Training Program ... SOTAP
Sophisticated Vocabulary (AAG) ... SV
Sophistici Elenchi [*of Aristotle*] [*Classical studies*] (OCD) ... Soph El
Sophocles [*Greek poet, 496-406BC*] [*Classical studies*] (ROG) ... SOPH
Sophomore ... SOPH
Sophonias [*Old Testament book*] [*Douay version*] ... Soph
Soprano ... S
Soprano ... SOP
Soprano, Alto ... SA
Soprano, Alto, Bass ... SAB
Soprano, Alto, Tenor, Bass ... SATB
Soprano Saxophone ... SS
Soprano, Tenor, Bass ... STB
Sopron [*Hungary*] [*Seismograph station code, US Geological Survey*] (SEIS) ... SOP
Soqotri (BJA) ... Soq
Soquel, CA [*AM radio station call letters*] ... KOQI
SOQUEM [*Societe Quebecoise d'Exploration Miniere*] **Documentation, Ste.-Foy,Quebec** [*Library symbol National Library of Canada*] (NLC) ... QSFS
SOQUEM [*Societe Quebecoise d'Exploration Miniere*], Ste.-Foy, PQ, Canada [*Library symbol Library of Congress*] (LCLS) ... CaQSFS
Sorata Development, Inc. [*Vancouver Stock Exchange symbol*] ... SOA
Sorbitol Dehydrogenase [*Also, Sorb D*] [*An enzyme*] ... SDH
Sorbitol Dehydrogenase (DMAA) ... SODH
Sorbitol Dehydrogenase [*Also, SDH*] [*An enzyme*] ... Sorb D
Sorel, PQ [*FM radio station call letters*] ... CJSO
Soren Kierkegaard Society [*Copenhagen, Denmark*] (EA) ... SKS
Sorenson Lighted Controls, Inc. ... SOLICO
Sorgento Rapido [*Reactor*] (NRCH) ... SORA
Sorghum and Millets Information Center [*ICRISAT*] [*India*] ... SMIC
Sorghum Soy Pellet (OA) ... SSP
Soria [*Record label*] ... Sor
Soritol [*Biochemistry*] (DAVI) ... Sorb
Sorkjosen [*Norway ICAO location identifier*] (ICLI) ... ENSR
Sorkjosen [*Norway*] [*Airport symbol*] (OAG) ... SOJ
Soroa [*Cuba*] [*Seismograph station code, US Geological Survey*] (SEIS) ... SOR
Soroako [*Indonesia*] [*Airport symbol*] (OAG) ... SQR
Soroako [*Indonesia*] [*ICAO location identifier*] (ICLI) ... WAAS
Sorong [*Indonesia*] [*Airport symbol*] (OAG) ... SOQ
Sorong/Jefman [*Indonesia*] [*ICAO location identifier*] (ICLI) ... WASS
Soroptimist Federation of the Americas [*Later, Soroptimist International of theAmericas*] (EA) ... SFA
Soroptimist International [*Cambridge, England*] (EAIO) ... SI
Soroptimist International d'Europe [*Soroptimist International of Europe*] (EAIO) ... SIE
Soroptimist International of Great Britain and Ireland (EAIO) ... SIGBI
Soroptimist International of the Americas (EA) ... SIA
Soroptimist International of the South West Pacific [*Sydney, NSW, Australia*] (EAIO) ... SISWP
Soror [*Sister*] ... SR
Sorores a Caritate Sanctae Crucis [*Sisters of Mercy of the Holy Cross*] [*Roman Catholic religious order*] ... SCSC
Sorores a Sacro Corde Jesus [*Sisters of the Sacred Heart of Jesus*] [*Roman Catholic religious order*] ... SSCJ
Sorores Carmelitae a Caritate [*Carmelite Sisters of Charity*] [*Roman Catholic religious order*] ... CaCh
Sorores Franciscanae Beatae Mariae Virginis Angelorum [*Franciscan Sisters of Our Lady of the Holy Angels*] [*Roman Catholic religious order*] ... BMVA
Soroti [*Uganda*] [*ICAO location identifier*] (ICLI) ... HUSO
Soroti [*Uganda*] [*Airport symbol*] (OAG) ... SRT
Soroti [*Uganda*] [*Airport symbol*] (AD) ... SZI
Sorptive Minerals Institute (EA) ... SMI
Sorreisa [*Norway*] [*Airport symbol*] (AD) ... SRR
Sorrel Resources Ltd. [*Toronto Stock Exchange symbol*] ... SO
Sorry [*Communications operator's procedural remark*] ... SRI
Sorsogon, Sorsogon [*Philippines*] [*ICAO location identifier*] (ICLI) ... RPXU
Sort and Merge ... SAM
Sort File Description [*Computer science*] ... SD
Sort Generator (BUR) ... SG
Sort Key Edit [*Library of Congress*] ... SKED
Sort Merge and Reduction Tapes (CAAL) ... SMART
Sort Merge Generator (IAA) ... SMG
Sort/Message (NITA) ... S/M
Sort Program [*Computer science*] (IAA) ... SP
Sort Program Generator [*Computer science*] (BUR) ... SPG
Sort Program, Sort Routine [*Computer science*] (IAA) ... SORO
Sort Re-Entrant Access Method [*Computer science*] (MHDI) ... SRAM
Sorted (MCD) ... SRTD
Sorter Reader ... SR
Sorter Reader Buffer ... SRB
Sorter Reader Buffered (NITA) ... SRB
Sorter Reader Flow ... SRF
Sortie Effectiveness Model [*NASA*] (MCD) ... SEM
Sortie Lab [*NASA*] ... SL
Sortie Lab Simulator [*NASA*] (NASA) ... SLS
Sortie Rate (MCD) ... SR
Sortie Support System (MCD) ... SSS
Sortie Turn Around Maintenance Operations Simulation [*NASA*] (KSC) ... STAMOS
Sorties per Day [*Air Force*] (AFIT) ... SD
Sorties per Inspection Cycle [*Air Force*] (AFIT) ... SIC
Sorting and Assembly of New Data ... SAND
Sorting Code Number (DCTA) ... SCN
Sorting It Out [*An association Defunct*] (EA) ... SIO
Sorting Office [*British*] (ROG) ... SO
Sorting, Updating, Report Generating, Etc. [*IBM Corp.*] [*Computer science*] ... SURGE

SOS: Human Rights for Guyana (EA) ... SOS:HRG
SOS Sahel International (EAIO) ... SOSSI
SOS Staffing Services, Inc. [*Associated Press*] (SAG) ... SOS Stf
SOS Staffing Services, Inc. [*NASDAQ symbol*] (SAG) ... SOSS
SOS Staffing Svcs [*NASDAQ symbol*] (TTSB) ... SOSS
Sosialistikon Ergatikon Komma tis Elladas [*Socialist Labor Party of Greece*] [*Forerunner of Greek Communist Party (KKE)*] (PPE) ... SEKE
Sosialistisk Folkepartiet [*Socialist People's Party*] [*Norway Political party*] (PPE) ... SF
Sosialistisk Ungdom [*Norway*] ... SU
Sosialistisk Valgforbund [*Socialist Electoral Alliance*] [*Norway Political party*] (PPE) ... SV
Sosialistisk Venstreparti [*Socialist Left Party*] [*Norway Political party*] (PPE) ... SV
Sostenuto [*Sustained*] [*Music*] ... SOS
Sostenuto [*Sustained*] [*Music*] ... SOST
Sostenuto [*Sustained*] [*Music*] ... SOSTEN
SOSUS Estimated Position (NVT) ... SEP
SOSUS Probability Area (NVT) ... SPA
Sosyal Demokrasi Halkci Partisi [*Social Democratic Populist Party*] [*Turkey Political party*] (MENA) ... SDHP
Sosyal Demokrasi Halkci Partisi [*Social Democratic Populist Party*] [*Turkey Political party*] (EAIO) ... SHP
Sosyal Demokrat Partisi [*Social Democratic Party*] [*Turkish Cyprus*] [*Political party*] (EY) ... SDP
Sosyalist Birlik Partisi [*Socialist Unity Party*] [*Turkey Political party*] (EY) ... SBP
Sosyalist Parti [*Socialist Party*] [*Turkey Political party*] (EY) ... SP
Sotah (BJA) ... Sot
Sotheby Parke Bernet [*Formerly, PB*] [*Manhattan art auction house*] ... SPB
Sotheby's Hldgs Cl'A' [*NYSE symbol*] (TTSB) ... BID
Sotheby's Holdings, Inc. [*Associated Press*] (SAG) ... Sothbys
Sotheby's Holdings, Inc. Class A [*NYSE symbol*] (SPSG) ... BID
Sotos Syndrome Support Association (EA) ... SSSA
Sotsyalistisher Kinder Farband (BJA) ... SKIF
Sotto Protesto [*Under Protest*] [*Italian*] ... S/P
Sotto Protesto per Mettere in Conto [*Under Protest to Place to Account*] [*Italian*] ... S/P/C
Sotto Voce [*In an Undertone*] [*Music*] ... SV
Sotziki [*Peru*] [*ICAO location identifier*] (ICLI) ... SPZK
Sou [*Monetary unit in France*] ... S
Souanke [*Congo*] [*ICAO location identifier*] (ICLI) ... FCOS
Souanke [*Congo*] [*Airport symbol*] (OAG) ... SOE
Souchong [*Tea trade*] (ROG) ... S'HONG
Souchong [*Tea trade*] (ROG) ... SOU
Sough (AAG) ... S
Soul and Calypso [*Music*] ... SOCA
Soul Assurance Prayer Plan (EA) ... SAPP
Soul Asylum [*Rock-music group*] ... SA
Soulac-Sur-Mer [*France ICAO location identifier*] (ICLI) ... LFDK
Soule's Dictionary of English Synonymes [*A publication*] (DLA) ... Soule Syn
Souls on Board (BARN) ... SOB
SouMOBc [*NASDAQ symbol*] (SAG) ... SMBC
SouMOBc Co. [*Associated Press*] (SAG) ... SouMoBc
Sound [*Audiology*] ... S
Sound [*Board on Geographic Names*] ... SD
Sound [*Films, television, etc.*] ... SD
Sound (WDMC) ... sd
Sound ... SND
Sound (AAG) ... SND
Sound Absorption Material [*Aviation*] ... SAM
Sound Advice [*NASDAQ symbol*] (TTSB) ... SUND
Sound Advice, Inc. [*Associated Press*] (SAG) ... SoundA
Sound Advice, Inc. [*NASDAQ symbol*] (NQ) ... SUND
Sound Amplification System ... SAS
Sound and Communications Industries Federation [*British*] (DBA) ... SCIF
Sound and Flash (IAA) ... SAF
Sound and Flash [*Military*] ... SF
Sound Bearing Station (IAA) ... SBSTA
Sound Blaster [*Computer science*] (DOM) ... SB
Sound Blaster Instrument [*PC sound format*] ... SBI
Sound Bytes Developer's Kit [*Computer science*] ... SBDK
Sound Channel [*Navy*] (CAAL) ... SC
Sound Data Acquisition System [*Automotive engineering*] ... SDAS
Sound Detecting and Ranging ... SODAR
Sound Effect (NTCM) ... SE
Sound Effects [*Script code*] ... SFX
Sound Effects Amplifier (IIA) ... SEA
Sound Energy Density ... SED
Sound Energy Flux ... SEF
Sound Exchange [*A sound conversion program*] (PCM) ... SOX
Sound Fixing and Ranging ... SFAR
Sound Fixing and Ranging [*Navy underground sound system*] ... SOFAR
Sound Fixing and Ranging/Bomb Fuze [*Navy underground sound system*] (SAA) ... SOFAR/BF
Sound Fusing and Ranging ... SOFAR
Sound Generation (MCD) ... SG
Sound Ideas, Inc. [*Vancouver Stock Exchange symbol*] ... SID
Sound in Air [*JETDS nomenclature*] ... N
Sound in Sync (IAA) ... SIS
Sound Intensity Diagram (MCD) ... SIGRAM
Sound Intensity Level ... SIL
Sound Interface Device [*Computer chip*] ... SID
Sound Interference Device ... SID
Sound Interference Level [*NASA*] (NASA) ... SIL
Sound Intermediate Frequency ... SIF
Sound Investment (MHDW) ... SI
Sound Isolation Room ... SIR
Sound Learning Society [*British*] ... SLS
Sound Level (NASA) ... SL
Sound Level Indicator ... SLI
Sound Level Measuring Set ... SLMS
Sound Level Meter ... SLM
Sound Level Plot [*Military*] (CAAL) ... SLP
Sound Level Recorder ... SLR
Sound Locator [*Military*] ... SL
Sound Management [*Radio Advertising Bureau*] [*A publication*] ... SM
Sound Motion Picture Operator [*Navy*] ... SMPO
Sound Motion Picture Technician [*Navy*] ... SMP
Sound Movie Projector Technician [*Navy*] (DNAB) ... SMPT
Sound Navigation and Ranging ... SONAR
Sound Negative (IAA) ... SN
[*The*] **Sound of London** [*Record label*] ... TSOL
Sound of Music [*Dolls by Alexander*] [*Doll collecting*] ... SOM
[*The*] **Sound of Philadelphia** [*Song*] ... TSOP
Sound Off ... S/O
Sound on Film ... SOF
Sound on Sound (NTCM) ... SOS
Sound on Sync (IAA) ... SOS
Sound on Tape [*Videotape*] ... SOT
Sound on Vision (IAA) ... SOV
Sound Operator [*Navy*] ... SDOPR
Sound Positive (IAA) ... SP
Sound Power Level [*Acoustics*] ... SPL
Sound Powered (CAAL) ... SP
Sound Powered Phone (IAA) ... SPP
Sound Pressure Level [*Acoustics*] ... SPL
Sound Production Sample [*Medicine*] (DMAA) ... SPS
Sound Protective Helmet [*Military*] ... SPH
Sound Ranging (MUGU) ... SDRNG
Sound Ranging ... SORNG
Sound Ranging ... SR
Sound Ranging ... SRG
Sound Ranging Battery (IAA) ... SRBTRY
Sound Ranging Central (IAA) ... SRC
Sound Ranging Control ... SORC
Sound Ranging Control ... SRC
Sound Ranging Evaluation Model (MCD) ... SREM
Sound Ranging Group (IAA) ... SRGR
Sound Ranging Section (IAA) ... SRS
Sound Ranging Set ... SRS
Sound Rating (IEEE) ... SR
Sound Receiving/Transmitting Equipment ... SRTE
Sound Recorder-Reproducer (MSA) ... SRR
Sound Recording Co. [*Record label*] ... SRC
Sound Recordings [*US Copyright Office class*] ... SR
Sound Recordings Specialists [*Record label*] ... SRS
Sound Reference Laboratory [*Orlando, FL*] [*Navy*] ... SRL
Sound Reinforcement (NTCM) ... SR
Sound Report ... SR
Sound Reproduction Equipment (DEN) ... SRE
Sound Research Laboratories Ltd. [*Research center British*] (IRUK) ... SRL
Sound Retrieval System [*Hughes Aircraft Co.*] ... SRS
Sound Search Station ... SOSS
Sound, Sense, Today, Tomorrow, Thereafter [*Teacher's Guide, published by Department of Transportation, for promoting supersonic travel*] ... SST-T-T
Sound Source Interactive, Inc. [*Associated Press*] (SAG) ... SndSrce
Sound Source Interactive, Inc. [*NASDAQ symbol*] (SAG) ... SSII
Sound Suppression System (NASA) ... SSS
Sound Surveillance Evaluation Center [*Navy*] (NVT) ... SSEC
Sound Surveillance System [*Navy*] ... SOSSUS
Sound Surveillance System (MSA) ... SOSUS
Sound Surveillance System ... SOSVS
Sound Surveillance System Control Center (MCD) ... SSCC
Sound Surveillance Undersea (MCD) ... SOSUS
Sound Surveillance Underwater System [*Navy*] ... SOSUS
Sound System ... SS
Sound Tape [*Films, television, etc.*] ... S
Sound Telegraphy [*Telecommunications*] (IAA) ... ST
Sound Transmission Class [*Followed by number, indicates FHA rating of sound insulating quality of a partition construction*] ... STC
Sound Trap (OA) ... ST
Sound Underwater Signal Source (MCD) ... SUSS
Sound Underwater Source [*Navy*] (CAAL) ... SUS
Sound Velocity Indicator ... SVI
Sound Velocity Profile ... SVP
Sound Velocity Structure ... SVS
Sound, Velocity, Temperature, Pressure ... SVTP
Sound/Video Unlimited ... S/VU
Sound Whistle [*British railroad term*] ... SW
Sound-Activated Mobile (PDAA) ... SAM
Sound-Apperception Test [*Psychology*] ... SAT
Sound-Deadened Steel (PDAA) ... SDS
Sounder (MSA) ... SDR
Sounding (MSA) ... SNDG
Sounding Doubtful [*Nautical charts*] ... SD
Sounding Equipment (IAA) ... SE
Sounding Machine [*Engineering*] ... SMACH
Sounding Rocket System ... SRS
Sounding Tube ... ST
Soundman (IAA) ... SOM
Soundness of Approach (MCD) ... SOA

Sound-on-Disk (DEN) .... SOD
Sound-Operated Noise Attenuation Device (IAA) .... SONAD
Sound-Powered Microphone .... SPM
Sound-Powered Telephone .... SPT
Soundproof (MSA) .... SNDPRF
Soundproof [*Technical drawings*] .... SP
Sounds of Our Times, Cook Studio [*Record label*] .... SOT
Soup and Gravy Manufacturers Association [*British*] (DBA) .... SGMA
Sour, Imported Heavy Gas Oil [*Petroleum chemistry*] .... SIHGO
Source .... S
Source (MSA) .... SCE
Source [*Online database field identifier*] .... SO
Source .... SRC
Source .... SRC
Source Acquisitions File (MCD) .... SAF
Source Address .... SA
Source Address Register [*Telecommunications*] .... SAR
Source and Application Inspection Equipment .... SAFE
Source and Application Inspection Equipment .... SAIE
Source and Fissionable [*Material*] [*Obsolete; see SS*] [*Nuclear energy*] .... SF
Source and Special [*Material*] [*Nuclear energy*] .... SS
Source and Time Frame (NITA) .... ST
Source Application of Funds Report (MCD) .... SAFR
Source Assessment Sampling System [*Environmental Protection Agency*] .... SASS
Source Capacitance (IDOE) .... C_S
Source Capital [*NYSE symbol*] (TTSB) .... SOR
Source Capital $2.40 Pfd [*NYSE symbol*] (TTSB) .... SORPr
Source Capital Corp. [*Associated Press*] (SAG) .... SrceCap
Source Capital, Inc. [*NYSE symbol*] (SPSG) .... SOR
Source Capital, Inc. [*Associated Press*] (SAG) .... SourcC
Source Capital, Inc. [*Associated Press*] (SAG) .... SrcCp
Source Classification Code [*Environmental Protection Agency*] .... SCC
Source Code .... SC
Source Code (NITA) .... SOCO
Source Code Control System [*Computer science*] .... SCCS
Source Code Indicator (MCD) .... SCI
Source Codes (MCD) .... SOCDS
Source Coding and Data Collection .... SCDC
Source Coding Team (SAA) .... SCT
Source Co. [*NASDAQ symbol*] (TTSB) .... SORC
Source Control Document (NASA) .... SCD
Source Control Document (MCD) .... SOCD
Source Control Drawing .... SCD
Source Control Drawing .... SOCD
Source Control Number .... SOCN
Source Coupled FET Logic (NITA) .... SCFL
Source Data Acquisition (BUR) .... SDA
Source Data Automated Fitness Report System [*Military*] (DNAB) .... SDAFRS
Source Data Automation [*Military*] .... SDA
Source Data Automation Equipment .... SDAE
Source Data Automation System [*Military*] (AABC) .... SDAS
Source Data Collection .... SODAC
Source Data Communication Retrieval .... SDCR
Source Data Entry .... SDE
Source Data Entry Package [*Computer science*] (MHDI) .... SDEP
Source Data Information .... SDI
Source Data Operating System (IAA) .... SDOS
Source Data Operation (MDG) .... SDO
Source Data Processing .... SDP
Source Data Utility .... SDU
Source/Destination [*Inspection/Acceptance Point*] (MCD) .... SD
Source Development Fund [*Supply and Services Canada*] .... SDF
Source Distribution Technique .... SDT
Source Document [*Computer science*] .... SD
Source Document Folders [*IRS*] .... SDF
Source Entry Utility .... SEU
Source Evaluation Board [*NASA*] .... SEB
Source Evaluation Committee [*NASA*] (NASA) .... SEC
Source Evaluation Panel [*NASA*] (NASA) .... SEP
Source Evaluation Team [*Army*] .... SET
Source Factor [*Nuclear energy*] (NRCH) .... SF
Source Handshake .... SH
Source Identification and Ordering Authorization [*DoD*] .... SIOATH
Source Image Distortion .... SID
Source Image Format (DOM) .... SIF
Source Impedance .... SI
Source Information Control System (NITA) .... SICS
Source Input Data Edit System .... SIDES
Source Input Format [*Computer science*] .... SIF
Source Inventory and Emission Factor Analysis [*Environmental Protection Agency*] .... SIEFA
Source Jamming .... SJ
Source Label Indicating and Coding Equipment .... SLICE
Source Language [*Computer science*] (BUR) .... SL
Source Language Debug [*Computer science*] (IEEE) .... SLD
Source Language Input Program .... SLIPR
Source Language Processor [*Computer science*] (BUR) .... SLP
Source Level .... SL
Source Library (IAA) .... SL
Source Library [*Computer science*] .... SLIB
Source Library Image Delivery Expeditor [*Computer science*] (MHDI) .... SLIDE
Source Library System [*Computer science*] .... SLS
Source Library Update [*Computer science*] .... SLU
Source Lines of Code (SSD) .... SLOC
Source Mail [*Electronic mail*] .... SMAIL
Source, Maintenance, and Recoverability (MCD) .... SMR
Source Management of Resources and Time (DNAB) .... SMART
Source Media [*NASDAQ symbol*] (TTSB) .... SRCM
Source Media, Inc. [*Associated Press*] (SAG) .... SrceMed
Source Media, Inc. [*NASDAQ symbol*] (SAG) .... SRCM
Source Name (NITA) .... SN
Source/Object Library (NITA) .... SOL
Source of Assignment (MCD) .... SOA
Source of Repair (MCD) .... SOR
Source of Supply .... SOS
Source of Supply (AFM) .... SS
Source of Supply Code .... SOSC
Source of Supply Modifier .... SOSM
Source One Mortgage Services [*NYSE symbol*] (SAG) .... SMQ
Source One Mortgage Services [*NYSE symbol*] (SAG) .... SOM
Source One Mortgage Services [*Associated Press*] (SAG) SrceOne25
Source One Mortgage Services [*Associated Press*] (SAG) .... SrcOne
Source One Mtg 8.42%'A'Pfd [*NYSE symbol*] (TTSB) .... SOMPrA
Source One Mtg 9.375%'QUICS' [*NYSE symbol*] (TTSB) .... SMQ
Source Oriented Data Acquisition .... SODA
Source Performance Evaluation and Reporting .... SPEAR
Source Power Gain .... SPG
Source Program [*Computer science*] (IAA) .... SP
Source Program Editor (MHDB) .... SEDIT
Source Program Library .... SPL
Source Program Maintenance [*IBM Corp.*] .... SPM
Source Program Maintenance Online .... SPMOL
Source Program Utility Routine .... SPUR
Source Range [*Nuclear energy*] (NRCH) .... SR
Source Range Channel (IEEE) .... SRC
Source Range Flux Monitoring [*Nuclear energy*] (NRCH) .... SRFM
Source Range Monitor [*Nuclear energy*] (NRCH) .... SRM
Source Range Neutron Flux Channel (IEEE) .... SRNFC
Source Range Neutron Flux Monitor (IAA) .... SANFM
Source Record Punch .... SRP
Source Reduction Review Program [*Environmental science*] .... SRRP
Source Region Electromagnetic Pulse .... SREMP
Source Resistance (IDOE) .... R_S
Source Resources Ltd. [*Vancouver Stock Exchange symbol*] .... SSU
Source Routing Transparent [*Telecommunications*] .... SRT
Source Selection (MCD) .... SS
Source Selection Activity [*or Authority*] [*Military*] .... SSA
Source Selection Advisory Board [*Marine science*] (OSRA) .... SSAB
Source Selection Advisory Board (USDC) .... SSAB
Source Selection Advisory Council [*Military*] (AFM) .... SSAC
Source Selection Board [*NASA*] .... SSB
Source Selection Board/General Procurement (MCD) .... SSB/GP
Source Selection Evaluation Board [*Military*] (AFM) .... SSEB
Source Selection Evaluation Plan .... SSEP
Source Selection Evaluation Team (AAGC) .... SSET
Source Selection Evaluation Test .... SSET
Source Selection Official (NASA) .... SSO
Source Selection Plan .... SSP
Source Selection Team (AAGC) .... SST
Source Service Access Point .... SSAP
Source Services Corp. [*Associated Press*] (SAG) .... SrceSrv
Source Services Corp. [*NASDAQ symbol*] (SAG) .... SRSV
Source/Sink [*Computer science*] (IBMDP) .... S/S
Source/Source [*Inspection/Acceptance point*] (MCD) .... SS
Source Spot Noise Figure .... SSNF
Source Statement Library [*Computer science*] .... SSL
Source Storage and Retrieval System [*Computer science*] (MHDI) .... SSRS
Source Telecomputing Corp. [*McLean, VA*] [*Telecommunications*] (TSSD) .... STC
Source Test Data System [*Environmental Protection Agency*] .... SOTDAT
Source Translation and Optimization [*Computer science*] .... STO
Sourcebook in Applied Mathematics [*National Science Foundation project*] .... SAM
Source-Coder's Cost Analysis Model (PDAA) .... SCAM
Source-Level Debugger [*Motorola, Inc.*] .... SLD
Source-Receptor Relation [*Environmental chemistry*] .... SRR
Source-Route Bridge [*Computer science*] (PCM) .... SRB
Sources de Financement des Entreprises [*CCMC Informatique de Gestion*] [*Database*] .... SOFIE
Sources of Ambient MicroSeismic Oceanic Noise Experiment [*Office of Naval Research*] .... SAMSON
Sources of Information on Social Security [*British*] .... SISS
Sources Public Library [*UTLAS symbol*] .... SOU
Sources Public Library, Roxboro, PQ, Canada [*Library symbol Library of Congress*] (LCLS) .... CaQRo
Sources Public Library [*Bibliotheque Municipale des Sources*] **Roxboro, Quebec** [*Library symbol National Library of Canada*] (NLC) .... QR
Sources to Upgrade the Career Counseling and Employment of Special Students [*Florida*] (EDAC) .... SUCCESS
Source-Term Control Loop [*Nuclear energy*] (NRCH) .... STCL
Source-to-Axis Distance (MAE) .... SAD
Source-to-Film Distance [*Radiology*] .... SFD
Source-to-Skin [*or -Surface*] **Distance** [*Radiology*] .... SSD
Source-Tuned X-Ray Fluorescence [*Spectroscopy*] .... STXRF
Souris Valley Regional Care Center, Weyburn, Saskatchewan [*Library symbol National Library of Canada*] (NLC) .... SWSVC
Sous-Commission des Cartes Tectoniques [*Subcommittee for Tectonic Maps of the Commission for the Geological Map of the World - STMCGMW*] (EAIO) .... SCT
South [*or Southern*] .... S

South (VRA) .... S
South [*or Southern*] .... SO
South (ROG) .... SOU
South .... STH
South Africa [*Formerly, FY*] [*License plate code assigned to foreign diplomats in the US*] .... BL
South Africa [*MARC geographic area code Library of Congress*] (LCCP) .... f-sa--
South Africa [*Later, BL*] [*License plate code assigned to foreign diplomats in the US*] .... FY
South Africa (VRA) .... S Afr
South Africa .... S Afr
South Africa [*IYRU nationality code*] .... SA
South Africa [*MARC country of publication code Library of Congress*] (LCCP) .... sa
South Africa (EY) .... SAF
South Africa .... So Afr
South Africa [*ANSI two-letter standard code*] (CNC) .... ZA
South Africa [*ANSI three-letter standard code*] (CNC) .... ZAF
South Africa - Britain Trade Association (DBA) .... SABRITA
South Africa Club of North America [*Defunct*] (EA) .... SACNA
South Africa Department of Posts and Telecommunications (TSSD) .... SAPT
South Africa Foundation (EA) .... SAF
South Africa Law Reports, Appellate Division [*A publication*] (DLA) .... App D
South Africa Law Reports, Griqualand West Local Division [*A publication*] (DLA) .... GWLD
South Africa National Union for Mineworkers .... SANUM
South African Administrative Pay and Clerical Corps [*British military*] (DMA) .... SAAPCC
South African Air Force .... SAAF
South African Air Force Headquarters [*ICAO location identifier*] (ICLI) .... FAAH
South African Air Force Tactical Support Command [*ICAO location identifier*] (ICLI) .... FATS
South African Airways [*ICAO designator*] .... SA
South African Airways [*ICAO designator*] (FAAC) .... SAA
South African Alliance (PPW) .... SAA
South African Archaeological Bulletin [*A publication*] .... SAAB
South African Associated Newspapers .... SAAN
South African Astronomical Observatory .... SAAO
South African Astronomical Observatory .... SANO
South African Atomic Energy Board .... SAAEB
South African Bankers' Journal [*Cape Town, South Africa*] [*A publication*] (DLA) .... S Afr Bankers J
South African Bibliographical and Information Network (NITA) .... SABINET
South African Black Alliance [*Political party*] (PPW) .... SABA
South African Breweries .... SAB
South African Breweries [*Commercial firm*] .... SAB
South African Broadcasting Corp. .... SABC
South African Bureau of Standards [*National standards organization*] .... SABS
South African Colored People's Organization .... SACPO
South African Communist Party .... SACP
South African Confederation of Labour .... SACL
South African Congress of Democrats .... SACOD
South African Congress of Trade Unions .... SACTU
South African Corps of Military Police [*British military*] (DMA) .... SACMP
South African Council for Scientific and Industrial Research .... SACSIR
South African Council for Scientific and Industrial Research, Pretoria, South Africa [*Library symbol Library of Congress*] (LCLS) .... SaPS
South African Council of Transport Workers .... SACTW
South African Customs Union .... SACU
South African Defence Forces .... SADF
South African Development Coordination Committee [*Australia*] .... SADCC
South African Education Program [*New York, NY*] .... SAEP
South African Federation of Trade Unions .... SAFTU
South African Foreign Trade Organisation .... SAFTO
South African Fundamental Atomic Reactor Installation .... SAFARI
South African General Electric Co. .... SAGE
South African Geographical Journal [*A publication*] .... SAGJ
South African Indian Congress (PD) .... SAIC
South African Individual Scale for the Blind [*Intelligence test*] .... SAISB
South African Institute for Medical Research .... SAIMR
South African Institute of Civil Engineering Technicians and Technologists (EAIO) .... SAICETT
South African Institute of Racial Relations .... SAIRR
South African Iron & Steel Corp. .... ISCOR
South African Journal of African Affairs [*A publication*] .... SAJAA
South African Journal of Science [*A publication*] .... SAJS
South African Labour Party .... SALP
South African Law Reports, Appellate [*A publication*] (DLA) .... S Afr LR App
South African Law Reports, Cape Provincial Division [*South Africa*] [*A publication*] (DLA) .... CPD
South African Law Reports, Cape Provincial Division [*1910-46*] [*A publication*] (DLA) .... SA Law Reports CP
South African Law Reports, Cape Provincial Division [*1910-46*] [*A publication*] (DLA) .... SA Law Reports CPD
South African Law Reports, Cape Provincial Division [*1910-46*] [*A publication*] (DLA) .... SALRCP
South African Law Reports, Eastern Districts Local Division [*South Africa*] [*A publication*] (DLA) .... EDL
South African Law Reports, Griqualand West Local Division [*A publication*] (DLA) .... GWD
South African Law Reports, Natal Province Division [*1910-46*] [*A publication*] (DLA) .... N
South African Law Reports, Natal Province Division [*1910-46*] [*A publication*] (DLA) .... NLR
South African Law Reports, Natal Province Division [*A publication*] (DLA) .... NPD
South African Law Reports, Natal Province Division [*1910-46*] [*A publication*] (DLA) .... SA Law Reports NPD
South African Law Reports, Orange Free State Provincial Division [*1910-46*] [*A publication*] (DLA) .... O
South African Law Reports, Orange Free State Provincial Division [*1910-46*] [*A publication*] (DLA) .... SAL Reports OPD
South African Law Reports, South West African Reports [*A publication*] (DLA) .... SALR SWA
South African Law Reports, Transvaal Provincial Division [*South Africa*] [*A publication*] (DLA) .... TPD
South African Law Reports, Witwatersrand Local Division [*A publication*] (DLA) .... WLD
South African Law Review [*A publication*] (DLA) .... S Afr L Rev
South African Law Times [*A publication*] (DLA) .... S Afr LT
South African Law Times [*A publication*] (DLA) .... SALT
South African Law Times [*A publication*] (DLA) .... So Afr LT
South African Medical Corps .... SAMC
South African Medical Literature [*South African Research Council*] [*Information service or system*] (CRD) .... SAMED
South African Military Refugee Aid Fund [*Defunct*] (EA) .... SAMRAF
South African National Antarctic Expedition .... SANAE
South African National Bibliography .... SANB
South African Naval Forces .... SANF
South African Naval Service .... SANS
South African Non-Racial Olympic Committee (EAIO) .... SANROC
South African Online User Group (NITA) .... SAOUG
South African Party [*Political party*] (PPW) .... SAP
South African Picture Analysis Test [*Psychology*] .... SAPAT
South African Police (ECON) .... SAP
South African Police Union (ECON) .... SAPU
South African Press Association .... SAPA
South African Prize Cases (Juta) [*A publication*] (DLA) .... So Afr Prize Cas
South African Railways .... SAR
South African Rates and Data [*A publication*] (IMH) .... SARAD
South African Regional Committee for Conservation and Utilization of Soil .... SARCCUS
South African Republic .... SAR
South African Republic High Court Reports [*A publication*] (DLA) .... SAR
South African Republic High Court Reports [*A publication*] (DLA) .... Sth Afr Rep
South African Retrospective Information System (NITA) .... SARIS
South African Rock Lobster Association [*Defunct*] .... SARLA
South African Students' Organization (PD) .... SASO
South African Supreme Court Appellate Division Reports [*A publication*] (DLA) .... AD
South African Tax Cases [*A publication*] (DLA) .... S Afr Tax
South African Tax Cases [*A publication*] (DLA) .... S Afr Tax Cas
South African Tax Cases [*A publication*] (DLA) .... SA Tax Cas
South African Tax Cases [*A publication*] (DLA) .... SATC
South African Tourism Board .... SATB
South African Tourism Board (EA) .... SATOUR
South African Typographical Union .... SATU
South African Water Information Centre [*Information service or system*] (IID) .... SAWIC
South African Women's Auxiliary Naval Service [*British military*] (DMA) .... SAWANS
South African Women's Auxiliary Services .... SAWAS
South African Written Language Test [*Educational test*] .... SAWLT
South Alabama Bancorp [*NASDAQ symbol*] (SAG) .... SABC
South Alabama Bancorp [*Associated Press*] (SAG) .... SouAla
South Alberta Light Horse (DMA) .... SALH
South Albuquerque Works [*AEC*] .... SAW
South Amboy Public Library, South Amboy, NJ [*Library symbol Library of Congress*] (LCLS) .... NjSoa
South Amboy Publishing Co., South Amboy, NJ [*Library symbol Library of Congress*] (LCLS) .... NjSoaP
South America [*MARC geographic area code Library of Congress*] (LCCP) .... s-----
South America (VRA) .... S Am
South America .... S Amer
South America .... SA
South America and Far East .... SAFE
South America Indian Mission [*Later, SAM*] (EA) .... SAIM
South America Mission (EA) .... SAM
South America/South Atlantic Region [*DoD*] .... SAM/SAR
South America/South Atlantic Region [*Aviation*] .... SAM/SAT
South American .... SAM
South American Airlines [*Peru*] [*ICAO designator*] (FAAC) .... SCN
South American Athletic Confederation (EAIO) .... SAAC
South American Datum .... SAD
South American Explorers Club (EA) .... SAEC
South American Indian [*MARC language code Library of Congress*] (LCCP) .... sai
South American Land Mammal Age [*Geological epoch*] .... SALMA
South American Liaison Group (CINC) .... SALG
South American Missionary Society of the Episcopal Church (EA) .... SAMS-USA
South American Program Library (IAA) .... SAL
South American Region [*USTTA*] (TAG) .... SAM
South American Series [*A publication*] .... SAS
South American Travel Organization .... SATO
South and Central American Indian Information Center (EA) .... SAIIC
South and Western Australia Judgements Bulletin [*A publication*] .... SWAJB
South Andros [*Bahamas*] [*Airport symbol*] (OAG) .... TZN
South Arabian (BJA) .... SA
South Asia Nuclear Weapons-Free Zone .... SANWFZ
South Asian Association for Regional Cooperation .... SAARC
South Asian Cooperative Environment Programme (GNE) .... SACEP

South Asian Microform Project, South Asian Microform and Library Committee, Association for Asian Studies, Center for Research Libraries, Chicago, IL [*Library symbol Library of Congress*] (LCLS) ... ICRL(SAMP)
South Asian Seas ... SAS
South Asian Studies Association of Australia and New Zealand ... SASA
South Atlantic ... SA
South Atlantic ... SAT
South Atlantic ... SATL
South Atlantic Anomaly [*NASA*] (KSC) ... SAA
South Atlantic Anomaly Probe [*NASA-CNAE*] ... SAAP
South Atlantic Bight [*A region off the southeastern coast of the United States*] [*Geography*] ... SAB
South Atlantic Bight Recruitment Experiment (USDC) ... SABRE
South Atlantic Bight Recruitment Experiment [*Marine science*] (OSRA) ... SABRE
South Atlantic Coast ... SAC
South Atlantic Convergence Zone [*Marine science*] (OSRA) ... SCAZ
South Atlantic Cooperative Investigation Phase [*Marine science*] (MSC) ... TRIDENT
South Atlantic Cooperative Investigations [*Military*] ... SACI
South Atlantic Division [*Army Corps of Engineers*] ... SAD
South Atlantic Force [*Later, Command*] [*Navy World War II*] ... SOLANT
South Atlantic Force [*Later, Command*] [*Navy World War II*] ... SOLANTFOR
South Atlantic Intercollegiate Sailing Association ... SAISA
South Atlantic League [*Nickname: Sally*] [*Baseball*] ... SAL
South Atlantic Ltd. [*Vancouver Stock Exchange symbol*] ... SCV
South Atlantic Ocean [*MARC geographic area code Library of Congress*] (LCCP) ... ls----
South Atlantic Quarterly [*A publication*] (BRI) ... SAQ
South Atlantic Ventilation Experiment [*Marine science*] (OSRA) ... SAVE
South Atlantic Ventilation Experiment (USDC) ... SAVE
South Australia (BARN) ... S AUS
South Australia ... S Aust
South Australia [*State in Australia*] (BARN) ... SA
South Australia [*MARC geographic area code Library of Congress*] (LCCP) ... u-at-sa
South Australia Acts [*1866-1936*] [*A publication*] (DLA) ... S Austl Acts
South Australia Brewing Co. [*Commercial firm*] ... SABC
South Australia Industrial Reports [*A publication*] (DLA) ... S Aust Indus R
South Australia. Parliamentary Debates [*A publication*] ... SAPD
South Australian Aboriginal Child Care Agency ... SAACCA
South Australian Aboriginal Sports and Recreation Association ... SAASRA
South Australian Adoption Panel ... SAAP
South Australian Amateur Water Polo Association ... SAAWPA
South Australian Apple and Pear Shippers' Association ... SAAPSA
South Australian Artillery [*British military*] (DMA) ... SAA
South Australian Association for Gifted and Talented Children ... SAAGTC
South Australian Association for the Teaching of English ... SAATE
South Australian Association of Permanent Building Societies ... SAAPBS
South Australian Athletic League ... SAAL
South Australian Badminton Association ... SABA
South Australian Birth Defects Registry ... SABDR
South Australian Bookmakers' League ... SABL
South Australian Bowling Association ... SABA
South Australian Brake Specialist Association ... SABSA
South Australian Brewing Holdings [*Commercial firm*] ... SABH
South Australian Canning Fruitgrowers' Association ... SACFA
South Australian Cat Breeders' Association ... SACBA
South Australian Centre for Human Development ... SACHD
South Australian Centre for Manufacturing ... SACM
South Australian Chamber of Fruit and Vegetable Industries ... SACFVI
South Australian Chamber of Mines and Energy ... SACME
South Australian Chicken Meat Council ... SACMC
South Australian Children's Ballet Company ... SACBC
South Australian Club ... SAC
South Australian Committee on Access and Mobility ... SACAM
South Australian Conference of the Seventh-Day Adventist Church ... SACSDAC
South Australian Council of Social Service ... SACSS
South Australian Council on the Ageing ... SACA
South Australian Country Fire Service ... SACFS
South Australian Cycling Federation ... SACF
South Australian Dairy Products Manufacturers' Association ... SADPMA
South Australian Darts Association ... SADA
South Australian Deaf Sports and Social Club ... SADSSC
South Australian Debating Association ... SADA
South Australian Deer Breeders' Association ... SADBA
South Australian Dog Racing Control Board ... SADRCB
South Australian Drag Racers' Association ... SADRA
South Australian Electricity Trust ... SAET
South Australian Equestrian Centre ... SAEC
South Australian Exporters Association ... SAEA
South Australian Film Investment Advisory Committee ... SAFIAC
South Australian Fishing Industry Council ... SAFIC
South Australian Fishing Industry Training Council ... SAFITC
South Australian Flower Growers' Association ... SAFGA
South Australian Food and Beverage Industry Training Council ... SAFBITC
South Australian Football Association ... SAFA
South Australian Gas Co. [*Commercial firm*] ... SAG
South Australian Government Gazette [*A publication*] ... SAGG
South Australian Government Railways ... SAR
South Australian Grape Growers' Association ... SAGGA
South Australian Greyhound Racing Control Board ... SAGRCB
South Australian Group of Chief Executives of Tertiary Institutions ... SAGE
South Australian Gymnastic Association ... SAGA
South Australian Hard Court Tennis League ... SAHCTL
South Australian Harness Racing Club ... SAHRC
South Australian Herd Recorders' Association ... SAHRA
South Australian High School Principals' Association ... SAHSPA
South Australian Housing Trust ... SAHT
South Australian Huntingtons Disease Association ... SAHDA
South Australian Independent Schools' Board ... SAISB
South Australian Industrial Court and Industrial Commission ... SAICIC
South Australian Institute of Educational Research ... SAIER
South Australian Law Librarians Bulletin [*A publication*] ... SALLB
South Australian Law Reports [*A publication*] (ILCA) ... S Austrl LR
South Australian Livestock Exporters' Association ... SALEA
South Australian Local Government Grants Commission ... SALGGC
South Australian Maritime Museum ... SAMM
South Australian Master Builder [*A publication*] ... SA Mast Build
South Australian Meat Exporters' Association ... SAMEA
South Australian Methodist Historical Society. Journal [*A publication*] (ADA) ... SAMHSJ
South Australian Metropolitan Fire Service ... SAMFS
South Australian Multicultural and Ethnic Affairs Commission ... SAMEAC
South Australian Occupational Health and Safety Commission ... SAOHSC
South Australian Olympic Council ... SAOC
South Australian Parliamentary Papers [*A publication*] ... SAPP
South Australian Philatelic Council ... SAPC
South Australian Planning Commission ... SAPC
South Australian Plastics and Rubber Industry Training Committee ... SAPRITC
South Australian Professional Shark Fishermen's Association ... SAPSFA
South Australian Psychological Board ... SAPB
South Australian Recreation Institute ... SARI
South Australian Restaurant Association ... SARA
South Australian Retail Industry Training Council ... SARITC
South Australian Rowing Association ... SARA
South Australian Rugby Union ... SARU
South Australian Rural Advisory Council ... SARAC
South Australian Salaried Lawyers' Association ... SASLA
South Australian Sawmillers' Association ... SASA
South Australian Shark Fishermen's Association ... SASFA
South Australian Sports Medicine Centre ... SASMC
South Australian State Emergency Services ... SASES
South Australian Statutes [*1837-1975*] [*A publication*] (DLA) ... S Austl Stat
South Australian Stock Medicines Board ... SASMB
South Australian Stock Salesmen's Association ... SASSA
South Australian Stud Merino Sheepbreeders' Association ... SASMSA
South Australian Superannuation Board ... SASB
South Australian Superannuation Board Fund Investment Trust ... SASBFIT
South Australian Table Tennis Association ... SATTA
South Australian Teachers' Journal [*A publication*] ... S Aust Teach J
South Australian Tennis Association ... SATA
South Australian Timber Corp. [*Commercial firm*] ... SATC
South Australian Timber Industry Training Council ... SATITC
South Australian Totalisator Board ... SATAB
South Australian Trailer Boat Club ... SATBC
South Australian Uranium Advisory Committee ... SAUAC
South Australian Urban Land Trust ... SAULT
South Australian Waste Management Commission ... SAWMC
South Australian Water Resources Council ... SAWRC
South Australian Wheatgrower [*A publication*] ... S Aust Wheatgr
South Australian Woods and Forests Department ... SAWFD
South Australian Writers' Centre ... SAWC
South Bannock District Library, Downey Branch, Downey, ID [*Library symbol*] [*Library of Congress*] (LCLS) ... IdD
South Bannock District Library, Lava Hot Springs Branch, Lava Hot Springs, ID [*Library symbol*] [*Library of Congress*] (LCLS) ... IdD-L
South Bay Cooperative Library System [*Library network*] ... SBCLS
South Beloit, IL [*AM radio station call letters*] ... WBEL
South Bend [*Indiana*] [*Airport symbol*] (OAG) ... SBN
South Bend, IN [*Location identifier FAA*] (FAAL) ... UXW
South Bend, IN [*FM radio station call letters*] ... WETL
South Bend, IN [*AM radio station call letters*] ... WHLY
South Bend, IN [*FM radio station call letters*] ... WHME
South Bend, IN [*Television station call letters*] ... WHME-TV
South Bend, IN [*AM radio station call letters*] ... WNDU
South Bend, IN [*FM radio station call letters*] ... WNDU-FM
South Bend, IN [*Television station call letters*] ... WNDU-TV
South Bend, IN [*Television station call letters*] ... WNIT
South Bend, IN [*FM radio station call letters*] ... WNSN
South Bend, IN [*FM radio station call letters*] ... WRBR
South Bend, IN [*AM radio station call letters*] ... WSBT
South Bend, IN [*Television station call letters*] ... WSBT-TV
South Bend, IN [*FM radio station call letters*] ... WUBS
South Bend, IN [*FM radio station call letters*] ... WUBU
South Bend Public Library, South Bend, IN [*Library symbol Library of Congress*] (LCLS) ... InS
South Bend Public Library, South Bend, IN [*Library symbol*] [*Library of Congress*] (LCLS) ... InSL
South Bend Public Library, South Bend, IN [*OCLC symbol*] (OCLC) ... ISO
South Bend Tribune, South Bend, IN [*Library symbol Library of Congress*] (LCLS) ... InST
South Bend, WA [*FM radio station call letters*] (RBYB) ... KFMY-FM
South Benton Star Press, Blairstown, IA [*Library symbol Library of Congress*] (LCLS) ... IaBlaSP
South Boston, VA [*Location identifier FAA*] (FAAL) ... SBV
South Boston, VA [*AM radio station call letters*] ... WHLF
South Boston, VA [*FM radio station call letters*] ... WJLC
South Boston, VA [*FM radio station call letters*] ... WQOK
South Boston, VA [*AM radio station call letters*] ... WSBV

South Bristol Township, NY [*FM radio station call letters*] (RBYB) .... WNVE
South Britain [*England and Wales*] .... SB
South Brooklyn Railway Co. [*AAR code*] .... SBK
South Brunswick Free Public Library, Monmouth Junction, NJ [*Library symbol Library of Congress*] (LCLS) .... NjMj
South Buffalo Railway Co. [*AAR code*] .... SB
South Burlington, VT [*FM radio station call letters*] .... WXXX
South by East .... SbE
South by South East (EERA) .... SSE
South by South West (EERA) .... SSW
South by West .... SbW
South Caicos [*Turks and Caicos Islands*] [*ICAO location identifier*] (ICLI) .... MBSC
South Caicos [*British West Indies*] [*Airport symbol*] (OAG) .... XSC
South Canterbury Mounted Rifles [*British military*] (DMA) .... SCMR
South Carleton High School, Richmond, Ontario [*Library symbol National Library of Canada*] (NLC) .... ORIS
South Carolina [*MARC geographic area code Library of Congress*] (LCCP) .... n-us-sc
South Carolina [*Postal code*] .... SC
South Carolina [*MARC country of publication code Library of Congress*] (LCCP) .... scu
South Carolina Aeronautics Commission [*FAA designator*] (FAAC) .... PLT
South Carolina Association of Biology Teachers (EDAC) .... SCABT
South Carolina Bar Association Reports [*A publication*] (DLA) .... So Car BA Rep
South Carolina Cmnty Banc [*NASDAQ symbol*] (TTSB) .... SCCB
South Carolina Community Bancshare [*NASDAQ symbol*] (SAG) .... SCCB
South Carolina Community Bancshares, Inc. [*Associated Press*] (SAG) .... SCCBcsh
South Carolina Constitutional Court Reports [*A publication*] (DLA) .... Rep Const Ct
South Carolina Constitutional Reports (Treadway, Mill, or Harper) [*A publication*] (DLA) .... So Car Const
South Carolina Department of Archives and History, Columbia, SC [*Library symbol Library of Congress*] (LCLS) .... ScCoAH
South Carolina Department of Health and Environmental Control (DOGT) .... SCDHEC
South Carolina Department of Health and Environmental Control .... SCDHEC
South Carolina Department of Health and Environmental Control, Columbia, SC [*Library symbol*] [*Library of Congress*] (LCLS) .... ScCoHE
South Carolina Educational Television [*Columbia*] [*Telecommunications*] (TSSD) .... SCETV
South Carolina Electric & Gas Co. [*NYSE symbol*] (SPSG) .... SAC
South Carolina Electric & Gas Co. [*Associated Press*] (SAG) .... SCrE
South Carolina Equity Reports [*A publication*] (DLA) .... SC Eq
South Carolina Handicapped Services Information System (EDAC) .... SCHSIS
South Carolina Historical Society, Charleston, SC [*Library symbol Library of Congress*] (LCLS) .... ScHi
South Carolina Law Journal [*A publication*] (DLA) .... SCLJ
South Carolina Law Journal [*Columbia*] [*A publication*] (DLA) .... So Car LJ
South Carolina Law Reports [*A publication*] (DLA) .... S Car R
South Carolina Law Reports [*Pre-1868*] [*A publication*] (DLA) .... SCL
South Carolina Law Reports [*A publication*] (DLA) .... So Car R
South Carolina Public Service Commission Reports [*A publication*] (DLA) .... SCPSC
South Carolina Reports [*A publication*] (DLA) .... S Ca
South Carolina Reports [*A publication*] (DLA) .... S Car
South Carolina Reports [*A publication*] (DLA) .... SC
South Carolina Reports [*A publication*] (DLA) .... SCR
South Carolina Reports [*A publication*] (DLA) .... So C
South Carolina Reports [*A publication*] (DLA) .... So Car
South Carolina Reports [*A publication*] (DLA) .... South Car
South Carolina Review [*A publication*] (BRI) .... South CR
South Carolina State College .... SCSC
South Carolina State College, Orangeburg, SC [*Library symbol Library of Congress*] (LCLS) .... ScOrS
South Carolina State College, Orangeburg, SC [*OCLC symbol*] (OCLC) .... SGW
South Carolina State Library, Columbia, SC [*OCLC symbol*] (OCLC) .... DSC
South Carolina State Library, Columbia, SC [*Library symbol Library of Congress*] (LCLS) .... Sc
South Carolina State Register [*A publication*] (AAGC) .... SC Regs
South Carolina State University (GAGS) .... So Car St U
South Carolina Supreme Court, Columbia, SC [*Library symbol Library of Congress*] (LCLS) .... Sc-SC
South Carolina Unemployment Compensation Commission Decisions [*A publication*] (DLA) .... SCUCC Dec
South Carolina Unemployment Compensation Commission Reports of Hearings [*A publication*] (DLA) .... SCUCCR
South Carolina Waterfowl Association .... SCWA
South Carolina Wing, Civil Air Patrol [*FAA designator*] (FAAC) .... BKR
South Central .... SCEN
South Central [*ICAO designator*] (AD) .... XE
South Central Air, Inc. [*ICAO designator*] (FAAC) .... SCA
South Central Kansas Library System [*Library network*] .... SCKLS
South Central Library System [*Library network*] .... SCLS
South Central Minnesota Interlibrary Exchange [*Library network*] .... SMILE
South Central Regional Library, Hamilton, ON, Canada [*Library symbol Library of Congress*] (LCLS) .... CaOHSC
South Central Regional Library, Morden, Manitoba [*Library symbol National Library of Canada*] (NLC) .... MMOW
South Central Regional Library System [*UTLAS symbol*] .... SCL
South Central Regional Medical Library Program [*Library network*] .... TALON
South Central Research Library Council [*Library network*] (IID) .... SCRLC
South Central Research Library Council, Ithaca, NY [*Library symbol Library of Congress*] (LCLS) .... NISCR
South Central Research Library Council, Ithaca, NY [*OCLC symbol*] (OCLC) .... YSC
South Central Reservoir Investigation [*Department of the Interior*] (GRD) .... SCRI
South Charleston, WV [*FM radio station call letters*] .... WJYP
South Charleston, WV [*AM radio station call letters*] .... WSCW
South China Force [*World War II*] .... SOCHINAFOR
South China Patrol [*Navy World War II*] .... SOPAT
South China Sea and Area [*MARC geographic area code Library of Congress*] (LCCP) .... ao----
South China Sea Fisheries Development and Coordinating Program [*Marine science*] (OSRA) .... SCSP
South Coast Airlines [*ICAO designator*] (AD) .... SS
South Coast One Design [*Cruising boat*] .... SCOD
South Coast Recycled Auto Project [*Air pollution controls credits from mobile sources for stationary sources*] .... SCRAP
South Congaree, SC [*FM radio station call letters*] .... WFMV
South County Public Library District of Calhoun County, Brussels, IL [*Library symbol Library of Congress*] (LCLS) .... IBrus
South Dakota [*MARC geographic area code Library of Congress*] (LCCP) .... n-us-sd
South Dakota .... S DAK
South Dakota [*Postal code*] .... SD
South Dakota [*MARC country of publication code Library of Congress*] (LCCP) .... sdu
South Dakota Bar Journal [*A publication*] (DLA) .... SDB Jo
South Dakota Bar Journal [*A publication*] (DLA) .... So Dak B Jo
South Dakota Board of Railroad Commissioners Opinions [*A publication*] (DLA) .... SDRC Ops
South Dakota Codified Laws [*A publication*] (DLA) .... SD Codified Laws
South Dakota Codified Laws [*A publication*] .... SDCL
South Dakota Codified Laws Annotated [*A publication*] (AAGC) .... SD Codified Laws
South Dakota Codified Laws, Annotated [*A publication*] (DLA) .... SD Codified Laws Ann
South Dakota Compiled Laws, Annotated [*A publication*] (DLA) .... SD
South Dakota Compiled Laws, Annotated [*A publication*] (DLA) .... SD Comp Laws Ann
South Dakota Compiled Laws, Annotated [*A publication*] (DLA) .... SD Compiled Laws Ann
South Dakota Department of Cultural Affairs, Historical Resources Center, Pierre, SD [*Library symbol Library of Congress*] (LCLS) .... SdHi
South Dakota Department of Education and Cultural Affairs, Historical Resources Center, Pierre, SD [*Library symbol Library of Congress*] (LCLS) .... SdPEC
South Dakota Historical Resource Center, Pierre, SD [*OCLC symbol*] (OCLC) .... SDH
South Dakota Medical Information Exchange [*University of South Dakota*] [*Sioux Falls*] [*Telecommunications*] (TSSD) .... SDMIX
South Dakota Register [*A publication*] (DLA) .... SD Admin Reg
South Dakota Register [*A publication*] (AAGC) .... SDR
South Dakota Reports [*A publication*] (DLA) .... S Dak
South Dakota Reports [*A publication*] (DLA) .... SD
South Dakota School of Mines and Technology (GAGS) .... So Dak Sch M&T
South Dakota School of Mines and Technology, Rapid City, SD [*Library symbol Library of Congress*] (LCLS) .... SdRM
South Dakota School of Mines and Technology, Rapid City, SD [*OCLC symbol*] (OCLC) .... SMT
South Dakota Session Laws [*A publication*] (DLA) .... SD Sess Laws
South Dakota State Bar Journal [*A publication*] (DLA) .... SD St BJ
South Dakota State Library Commission, Pierre, SD [*Library symbol Library of Congress*] (LCLS) .... Sd
South Dakota State Library Commission, Pierre, SD [*OCLC symbol*] (OCLC) .... SDS
South Dakota State Library for the Handicapped, Pierre, SD [*Library symbol Library of Congress*] (LCLS) .... Sd-BPH
South Dakota State University [*Brookings, SD*] .... SDSU
South Dakota State University (GAGS) .... So Dak St U
South Dakota State University, Brookings, SD [*Library symbol Library of Congress*] (LCLS) .... SdB
South Dakota State University, Minuteman Graduate Center Library, Ellsworth AFB,Rapid City, SD [*Library symbol Library of Congress*] (LCLS) .... SdB-M
South Dakota Supreme Court Library, Pierre, SD [*Library symbol Library of Congress*] (LCLS) .... Sd-SC
South Dakota Uniform Probate Code [*A publication*] (DLA) .... SD Uniform Prob Code
South Daytona, FL [*AM radio station call letters*] .... WPUL
South Devon Herd Book Society [*British*] (DBA) .... SDHBS
South Devon Railway (ROG) .... SDR
South Division (ROG) .... SD
South Dumfries Township Public Library, Glen Morris Branch, Glen Morris, ON, Canada [*Library symbol*] [*Library of Congress*] (LCLS) .... CaOGmSD
South Dunfries Public Library, St. George Branch, St. George, ON, Canada [*Library symbol*] [*Library of Congress*] (LCLS) .... CaOStG
South East Air [*British ICAO designator*] (FAAC) .... SEE
South East Asia International Exhibition of Packaging Machinery and Materials and Food Processing Machinery .... ASIAPACK
South East Asia Iron and Steel Institute (EA) .... SEAISI
South East Asia Microform Project, Center for Research Libraries, Chicago, IL [*Library symbol*] [*Library of Congress*] (LCLS) .... ICRL-SEA
South East Asia Universal Realtime Information Cataloging and Administration System .... SEA-URICA
South East Asian Fisheries Development Centre (EAIO) .... SEAFDC
South East Asian Fisheries Development Centre .... SEAFDEC
South East Asian International Automated Manufacturing Technology and Robotics Show and Conference .... AUTOMASIA
South East Asian Ministers of Education Secretariat [*Australia*] .... SEAMES

South East Asian Personal Computer Hardware and Software Show ..... PERCOMPASIA
South East Asian Region Network for Geosciences [*International Council of Scientific Unions*] ..... SEARNG
South East Asia's International Exhibition of Textile and Garment Machinery and Fabrics Trade ..... ASIATEX
South East College of Air Training [*British ICAO designator*] (FAAC) ..... SEC
South East Cultural Trust [*South Australia*] ..... SECT
South East Economic Development Council [*Australian Capital Territory*] ..... SEEDC
South East England Tourist Board (DCTA) ..... SEETB
South East London College [*London, England*] ..... SELC
South East London Technical College [*British*] (DI) ..... SELTEC
South East Professional Fishermen's Association [*Australia*] ..... SEPFA
South East Regional Forum for Adult and Continuing Education [*British*] (DI) ..... SERFACE
South East Trawl Fishing Industry Association [*Australia*] ..... SETFIA
South East Wales Access Consortium (AIE) ..... SEWAC
South Eastern Alaska/Washington/Oregon Minimum Earned Premium Scale [*Aviation*] (AIA) ..... SEA/W/O MEPS
South Eastern Discotheque Association [*British*] (DBA) ..... SEDA
South Eastern Intercollegiate Sailing Association ..... SEISA
South Eastern New York Library Resources Council, Poughkeepsie, NY [*Library symbol*] [*Library of Congress*] (LCLS) ..... NPSNL
South Eastern Reporter [*A publication*] (DLA) ..... Southeastern Rep
South Eastern Reporter, Second Series [*West*] [*A publication*] (AAGC) SE2d
South Eastern State College [*Oklahoma*] ..... SESC
South Equatorial Belt [*Planet Jupiter*] ..... SEB
South Equatorial Countercurrent [*Oceanography*] (MSC) ..... SECC
South Equatorial Current [*Oceanography*] (MSC) ..... SEC
South European Pipeline [*Oil*] ..... SEPL
South Florida Oil Spill Research Center [*Marine science*] (OSRA) ..... SFOSRC
South Florida Oil Spill Research Center (USDC) ..... SFOSRC
South Following [*Astronomy*] ..... SF
South Galactic Pole ..... SGP
South Galway [*Queensland*] [*Airport symbol*] (AD) ..... ZGL
South Gastonia, NC [*AM radio station call letters*] ..... WGAS
South Georgia [*United Kingdom*] [*Geomagnetic observatory code*] ..... SGG
South Georgia College [*Douglas*] ..... SGC
South Georgia College, Douglas, GA [*Library symbol Library of Congress*] (LCLS) ..... GDoS
South Georgia Railway Co. [*AAR code Terminated*] ..... SG
South Gillies Library, Ontario [*Library symbol National Library of Canada*] (BIB) ..... OSG
South Glamorgan [*County in Wales*] ..... S GLAM
South Glens Falls, NY [*AM radio station call letters*] ..... WSTL
South Grove Elementary School, Syosset, NY [*Library symbol Library of Congress*] (LCLS) ..... NSyoSGE
South Hadley, MA [*FM radio station call letters*] ..... WMHC
South Hamilton Record-News, Jewell, IA [*Library symbol Library of Congress*] (LCLS) ..... IaJewR
South Hardin Signal-Review, Hubbard, IA [*Library symbol Library of Congress*] (LCLS) ..... IaHubS
South Haven, MI [*AM radio station call letters*] ..... WCSY
South Haven, MI [*FM radio station call letters*] ..... WCSY-FM
South High School, Commack, NY [*Library symbol*] [*Library of Congress*] (LCLS) ..... NCoHS-S
South Hill, VA [*AM radio station call letters*] ..... WJWS
South Hill, VA [*FM radio station call letters*] ..... WSHV
South Hills Library Association, Pittsburgh, PA [*OCLC symbol*] (OCLC) ..... PSL
South Hillsboro City Schools, Hillsboro, OH [*Library symbol Library of Congress*] (LCLS) ..... OHilS
South Holland Public Library, South Holland, IL [*Library symbol Library of Congress*] (LCLS) ..... ISho
South Houston Elementary School, South Houston, TX [*Library symbol*] [*Library of Congress*] (LCLS) ..... TxShoShE
South Houston High School, South Houston, TX [*Library symbol*] [*Library of Congress*] (LCLS) ..... TxShoHH
South Houston Intermediate School, South Houston, TX [*Library symbol*] [*Library of Congress*] (LCLS) ..... TxShoHI
South Huntington Public Library, Huntington Station, NY [*Library symbol Library of Congress*] (LCLS) ..... NHsS
South India Teachers' Union ..... SITU
South Ingalls [*Colorado*] [*Seismograph station code, US Geological Survey Closed*] (SEIS) ..... SIG
South Interlake Regional Library, Stonewall, Manitoba [*Library symbol National Library of Canada*] (NLC) ..... MSTOS
South Interlake Regional Library, Stonewall, MB, Canada [*Library symbol Library of Congress*] (LCLS) ..... CaMStoS
South Irish Horse [*British military*] (DMA) ..... SIH
South Island [*New Zealand*] (BARN) ..... SI
South Jacksonville, IL [*FM radio station call letters*] ..... WJVO
South Jersey Ad-Visor, Cologne, NJ [*Library symbol Library of Congress*] (LCLS) ..... NjColS
South Jersey Indus [*NYSE symbol*] (TTSB) ..... SJL
South Jersey Industries, Inc. [*NYSE symbol*] (SPSG) ..... SJI
South Jersey Industries, Inc. [*Associated Press*] (SAG) ..... SoJerIn
South Jersey Law School Dictum [*A publication*] (DLA) ..... So Jersey LS Dictum
South Kanaga [*Alaska*] [*Seismograph station code, US Geological Survey*] (SEIS) AD6
South Karori [*New Zealand*] [*Seismograph station code, US Geological Survey*] (SEIS) ..... SNZO
South Kauai, HI [*Location identifier FAA*] (FAAL) ..... SOK
South Kensington [*District of London*] (ROG) ..... SK
South Kent, CT [*FM radio station call letters*] ..... WGSK
South Korea ..... SK
South Korea Conventional Air Target List (MCD) ..... SKCATL
South Korea Republic ..... SKR
South Korean Central Intelligence Agency [*Later, Agency for National Security Planning*] (PD) ..... KCIA
South Lake Tahoe, CA [*FM radio station call letters*] ..... KGLE
South Lake Tahoe, CA [*AM radio station call letters*] ..... KOWL
South Lake Tahoe, CA [*FM radio station call letters*] ..... KRLT
South Lake Tahoe, CA [*AM radio station call letters*] ..... KTHO
South Lake Tahoe, CA [*FM radio station call letters*] (RBYB) ..... KZZF-FM
South Lake Tahoe, CA [*Location identifier FAA*] (FAAL) ..... LTA
South Lancashire Regiment [*British*] ..... SLR
South Latitude ..... SL
South Latitude ..... SLAT
South Lebanon Army ..... SLA
South London College [*London, England*] ..... SLC
South London Regiment of Volunteers [*British military*] (DMA) ..... SLRV
South London (Volunteers) Medical Staff Corps [*British military*] (DMA) ..... SLMSC
South Luzon Force [*Army World War II*] ..... SLF
South Lyon Public Library, South Lyon, MI [*Library symbol Library of Congress*] (LCLS) ..... MiSl
South Main Elementary School, Bowling Green, OH [*Library symbol*] [*Library of Congress*] (LCLS) ..... OBgSME
South Marysburgh Township Public Library, Milford, Ontario [*Library symbol National Library of Canada*] (BIB) ..... OMSMT
South Miami, FL [*AM radio station call letters*] ..... WAXY
South Middlesex Rifle Volunteers [*British military*] (DMA) ..... SMRV
South Molle Island [*Australia Airport symbol*] (OAG) ..... SOI
South Molle Islands [*Queensland*] [*Airport symbol*] (AD) ..... QSM
South Mountain [*Washington*] [*Seismograph station code, US Geological Survey*] (SEIS) ..... SMW
South Mountain Restoration Center, South Mountain, PA [*OCLC symbol*] (OCLC) ..... PIM
South Naknek [*Alaska*] [*Airport symbol*] (OAG) ..... WSN
South Naknek, AK [*Location identifier FAA*] (FAAL) ..... WSN
South Nassau Communities Hospital, Oceanside, NY [*Library symbol Library of Congress*] (LCLS) ..... NOcH
South Natick Historical, Natural History, and Library Society, South Natick, MA [*Library symbol Library of Congress*] (LCLS) ..... MSonHi
South Nottinghamshire Hussars [*British military*] (DMA) ..... SNH
South Nottinghamshire Yeomanry Cavalry [*British military*] (DMA) ..... SNYC
South Oaks Hospital, Amityville, NY [*Library symbol Library of Congress*] (LCLS) ..... NAmiSH
South Of [*In outdoor advertising*] (WDMC) ..... S/O
South of Broad Street [*Reference is to residents of the historic and aristocratic section of Charleston, South Carolina*] ..... SOB's
South of Houston Street [*See also NoHo, SoSo, TriBeCa*] [*Artists' colony in New York City*] ..... SoHo
South of Ireland Yeomanry [*British military*] (DMA) ..... SIY
South of Market [*District of San Francisco*] ..... SoMa
South of Scotland Electricity Board (ECON) ..... SSEB
South of SoHo [*See also NoHo, SoHo, TriBeCa*] [*Artists' colony in New York City*] ..... SoSo
South Omaha Terminal Railway Co. [*AAR code*] ..... SOT
South Orange, NJ [*FM radio station call letters*] ..... WSOU
South Orange Public Library, South Orange, NJ [*Library symbol Library of Congress*] (LCLS) ..... NjSoo
South Oroville, CA [*FM radio station call letters*] (RBYB) ..... KYIX
South Pacific [*MARC geographic area code Library of Congress*] (LCCP) ..... ps----
South Pacific ..... SP
South Pacific Action Committee for Human Ecology and Environment (EERA) ..... SPACHEE
South Pacific Action Network ..... SPAN
South Pacific Air Transportation Service [*Navy*] ..... SPATS
South Pacific Airline SA [*Chile*] [*ICAO designator*] (FAAC) ..... SPF
South Pacific Airlines of New Zealand (AD) ..... PQ
South Pacific Applied Geoscience Commission (EERA) ..... SOPAC
South Pacific Area [*World War II*] ..... SPA
South Pacific Association for Commonwealth Literature and Language Studies (EAIO) ..... SPACLALS
South Pacific Association for Teacher Education [*Later, ATEA*] (EA) ..... SPATE
South Pacific Association of Environmental Institutions ..... SPAEI
South Pacific Base Command [*Navy World War II*] ..... SOPACBACOM
South Pacific Base Command [*Navy World War II*] ..... SPBC
South Pacific Bureau for Economic Cooperation (EERA) ..... SPEC
South Pacific Bureau for Economic Cooperation in Developing Uniform Maritime Standards for the Pacific Area [*Suva, Fiji*] (EAIO) ..... SPBEC
South Pacific Combat Air Transport [*World War II*] ..... SCAT
South Pacific Command [*Navy*] ..... SOPAC
South Pacific Commission [*See also CPS*] (EAIO) ..... SPC
South Pacific Communications [*Navy*] ..... SOPACCOMS
South Pacific Convergence Zone (MCD) ..... SPCZ
South Pacific Countries (EERA) ..... SOPAC
South Pacific Deep Water ..... SPDW
South Pacific Division [*Army World War II*] ..... SPD
South Pacific Environment Protection Convention (EERA) ..... SPREP
South Pacific Forum [*Australia*] ..... SPF
South Pacific Forum Fisheries Agency [*Honiara, Solomon Islands*] (EAIO) ..... SPFFA
South Pacific Gold [*Vancouver Stock Exchange symbol*] ..... SFG
South Pacific Information Network System [*Australia*] ..... SPINS
South Pacific Island Airways [*ICAO designator*] (AD) ..... HK
South Pacific Island Airways, Inc. [*ICAO designator*] (FAAC) ..... SPI
South Pacific Islands Fisheries Development Agency [*Noumea, New Caledonia*] (EAIO) ..... SPIFDA

South Pacific Nuclear Free Treaty ... SPNFT
South Pacific Nuclear Free Zone (EERA) ... SPNFZ
South Pacific Nuclear Free Zone Treaty ... SPNFZT
South Pacific Organizations Coordinating Committee (EERA) ... SPOCC
South Pacific Regional Environment Program (EERA) ... SPREP
South Pacific Regional Environment Programme [*of the South Pacific Commission*] [*New Caledonia*] ... SPREP
South Pacific Trade Commission [*Australia*] ... SPTC
South Pacific Trade Commissioner Service [*Australia*] ... SPTCS
South Pacific Trade Union Forum [*14-nation group opposed to nuclear testing and dumping in the Pacific*] ... SPTUF
South Padre Island, TX [*FM radio station call letters*] ... KJIB
South Padre Island, TX [*FM radio station call letters*] ... KZSP
South Paris, ME [*AM radio station call letters*] ... WKTQ
South Pasadena Public Library, South Pasadena, CA [*Library symbol Library of Congress*] (LCLS) ... CSp
South Pierce Railroad [*AAR code*] ... SOPR
South Pittsburg Municipal Hospital, South Pittsburg, TN [*Library symbol Library of Congress*] (LCLS) ... TSpMH
South Pittsburg, TN [*AM radio station call letters*] ... WEPG
South Pittsburg, TN [*FM radio station call letters*] ... WKXJ
South Place Ethical Society [*British*] ... SPES
South Plainfield Free Public Library, South Plainfield, NJ [*Library symbol Library of Congress*] (LCLS) ... NjSop
South Plains (FAAC) ... SPLNS
South Plains Association of Governments ... SPAG
South Plains College, Levelland, TX [*Library symbol Library of Congress*] (LCLS) ... TxLeS
South Point [*Hawaii*] [*Seismograph station code, US Geological Survey*] (SEIS) ... SPT
South Pointe Enterprises [*Associated Press*] (SAG) ... SouPoint
South Pointe Enterprises [*NASDAQ symbol*] (SAG) ... STPN
South Polar Cap [*A filamentary mark on Mars*] ... SPC
South Polar Distance ... SPD
South Polar Region ... SPR
South Pole [*Also, SP*] ... PS
South Pole [*Also, PS*] ... SP
South Pole [*Antarctica*] [*Seismograph station code, US Geological Survey*] (SEIS) ... SPA
South Pole Air Shower Experiment [*Astronomy*] ... SPASE
South Pole Infrared Explorer [*University of Chicago*] [*Research center*] (RCD) ... SPIREX
South Pole Station [*National Weather Service*] ... SPS
South Portland, ME [*Location identifier FAA*] (FAAL) ... CZU
South Proceeding [*Astronomy*] ... SP
South Puget Sound Community College Library, Olympia, WA [*Library symbol*] [*Library of Congress*] (LCLS) ... WaOSPS
South Queensland Airways [*Australia*] ... SQA
South Rawdon Museum, South Rawdon, NS, Canada [*Library symbol*] [*Library of Congress*] (LCLS) ... CaNSSrM
South Repeater [*NASA*] (MCD) ... SORPTR
South River-Machar Union Public Library, South River, Ontario [*Library symbol National Library of Canada*] (NLC) ... OSRM
South Salem Elementary School, Port Washington, NY [*Library symbol Library of Congress*] (LCLS) ... NPtwSSE
South Salem Library, South Salem, NY [*Library symbol Library of Congress*] (LCLS) ... NSos
South Salt Lake, UT [*AM radio station call letters*] ... KKDS
South Salt Lake, UT [*AM radio station call letters*] ... KSOP
South San Francisco, CA [*Location identifier FAA*] (FAAL) ... SFS
South San Francisco Free Public Library, South San Francisco, CA [*Library symbol Library of Congress*] (LCLS) ... CSsf
South Saskatchewan Committee for World Development, Regina, Saskatchewan [*Library symbol National Library of Canada*] (NLC) ... SRWD
South Saxon (ROG) ... SS
South Seattle Community College, Seattle, WA [*Library symbol Library of Congress*] (LCLS) ... WaSC-S
South Senior High School, Valley Stream, NY [*Library symbol Library of Congress*] (LCLS) ... NVsSSH
South Shaver Elementary School, Pasadena, TX [*Library symbol*] [*Library of Congress*] (LCLS) ... TxPSSE
South Shore [*AAR code*] ... SSH
South Shore News, Bridgewater, Nova Scotia [*Library symbol National Library of Canada*] (NLC) ... NSBSSN
South Shore News, Bridgewater, NS, Canada [*Library symbol*] [*Library of Congress*] (LCLS) ... CaNSBSSN
South Shore Regional Library, Bridgewater, Nova Scotia [*Library symbol National Library of Canada*] (NLC) ... NSBS
South Shore Regional Library, Bridgewater, NS, Canada [*Library symbol Library of Congress*] (LCLS) ... CaNSBS
South Side [*In outdoor advertising*] (WDMC) ... S/S
South Side Middle School, Rockville Centre, NY [*Library symbol*] [*Library of Congress*] (LCLS) ... NRockSMS
South Side Senior High School, Rockville Centre, NY [*Library symbol*] [*Library of Congress*] (LCLS) ... NRockSSH
South Simpson, AK [*Location identifier FAA*] (FAAL) ... SSP
South Sioux City, NE [*FM radio station call letters*] (RBYB) ... KSFT-FM
South Slavic Benevolent Union Sloga [*Later, Sloga Fraternal Life Insurance Society*] (EA) ... SSBUS
South Slavonian Socialist Labor Federation [*Defunct*] (EA) ... SSSLF
South Somerset Yeomanry [*British military*] (DMA) ... SSY
South Staffordshire Regiment [*Military unit*] [*British*] ... SSR
South State Cooperative Library System, Los Angeles, CA [*OCLC symbol*] (OCLC) ... SGL
South Stickney District Library, Burbank, IL [*Library symbol Library of Congress*] (LCLS) ... IBur
South Street Financial Center [*NASDAQ symbol*] (SAG) ... SSFC
South Street Financial Center [*Associated Press*] (SAG) ... SthStrF
South Street Seaport Museum (EA) ... SSSM
South Street Seaport Museum, New York, NY [*Library symbol*] [*Library of Congress*] (LCLS) ... NNSSS
South Suburban Genealogical and Historical Society, South Holland, IL [*Library symbol Library of Congress*] (LCLS) ... IShoShi
South Sydney Greens [*Political party Australia*] ... SSG
South Tanaga [*Alaska*] [*Seismograph station code, US Geological Survey*] (SEIS) ... AK2
South Tanaga [*Alaska*] [*Seismograph station code, US Geological Survey Closed*] (SEIS) ... AT2
South Temperate Zone ... STeZ
South Terrace Elementary School, Carlton, MN [*Library symbol*] [*Library of Congress*] (LCLS) ... MnCtE
South Texas College of Law (GAGS) ... So Tex C Law
South Texas College of Law, Houston, TX [*Library symbol Library of Congress*] (LCLS) ... TxHSTL
South Texas Junior College, Houston, TX [*Library symbol Library of Congress*] (LCLS) ... TxHSTC
South Texas Library System [*Library network*] ... STLS
South Texas Outer Continental Shelf ... STOCS
South Texas Project [*Nuclear energy*] (NRCH) ... STP
South Thames College [*London, England*] ... STC
South Tibetan Detachment [*Geology*] ... STD
South Tibetan Detachment System [*Geology*] ... STDS
South Tropical Disturbance [*of the planet Jupiter*] (BARN) ... STD
South Tropical Zone [*Planet Jupiter*] ... STrZ
South Tucson, AZ [*AM radio station call letters*] ... KMRR
South Tucson, AZ [*AM radio station call letters*] ... KXEW
South Universal Commodity Exchange [*Ukraine*] (EY) ... SUCE
South Vandenberg Air Force Base [*California*] (NASA) ... SVAFB
South Vietnam (CINC) ... SVN
South Vietnamese ... SVNESE
South Vietnamese Air Force (VNW) ... SVNAF
South Vietnamese Armed Forces (VNW) ... SVAF
South Vietnamese Liberation Army (VNW) ... SVNLA
South Vietnamese Marine Corps (VNW) ... SVNMC
South Vietnamese National Police Force (VNW) ... SVNNP
South Vietnamese Navy (VNW) ... SVNN
South Vietnamese Special Forces (VNW) ... SVNSF
South Wales ... SW
South Wales Borderers [*Military unit*] [*British*] ... SWB
South Wales Miners' Federation (DAS) ... SWMF
South West Academic Libraries Cooperative Automation Project (NITA) ... SWALCAP
South West Africa [*Namibia*] [*MARC geographic area code Library of Congress*] (LCCP) ... f-sx--
South West Africa [*Namibia*] [*MARC country of publication code Library of Congress*] (LCCP) ... sx
South West Africa Air Force Headquarters [*Namibia*] [*ICAO location identifier*] (ICLI) ... FASW
South West Africa National Union [*Namibia*] [*Political party*] (PPW) ... SWANU
South West Africa People's Organization [*Namibia*] (PD) ... SWAPO
South West African People's Organisation (EERA) ... SWAPO
South West Air Ltd. [*Canada ICAO designator*] (FAAC) ... SWC
South West Bay [*Vanuatu*] [*ICAO location identifier*] (ICLI) ... NVSX
South West Business and Industry Exhibition [*British*] (ITD) ... SWB & IE
South West City, MO [*AM radio station call letters*] ... KLTK
South West Development Authority [*Western Australia*] ... SWDA
South West London College [*London, England*] ... SWLC
South West Prop Tr [*NYSE symbol*] (TTSB) ... SWP
South West Queensland Initiative (EERA) ... SWQI
South Westchester BOCES [*Boards of Cooperative Educational Services*] [*UTLAS symbol*] ... SWB
South Western Examinations Board [*Education*] (AIE) ... SWExB
South Western Industrial Research Ltd. [*British*] (ARC) ... SWIRL
South Western Reporter [*A publication*] (DLA) ... So West Rep
South Western Reporter [*National Reporter System*] [*A publication*] (DLA) ... SW
South Western Reporter [*A publication*] (DLA) ... SW Rep
South Western Reporter [*A publication*] (DLA) ... SW Repr
South Western Reporter [*A publication*] (DLA) ... SWR
South Western Reporter, Second Series [*A publication*] (DLA) ... SW 2d
South Western Reporter, Second Series [*West*] [*A publication*] (AAGC) ... SW2d
South Weymouth, MA [*Location identifier FAA*] (FAAL) ... NDK
South Weymouth, MA [*Location identifier FAA*] (FAAL) ... NZW
South Weymouth/South Weymouth Naval Air Station [*Massachusetts*] [*ICAO location identifier*] (ICLI) ... KNZW
South Whitley Cleveland Township Public Library, South Whitley, IN [*Library symbol Library of Congress*] (LCLS) ... InSow
South Whitley, IN [*FM radio station call letters*] ... WLZQ
South Whitley Tribune-News, South Whitley, IN [*Library symbol Library of Congress*] (LCLS) ... InSowTN
South Williamsport, PA [*AM radio station call letters*] ... WFXX
South Williamsport, PA [*FM radio station call letters*] ... WZXR
South Woods Junior High School, Syosset, NY [*Library symbol*] [*Library of Congress*] (LCLS) ... NSyoSwJ
South Yamouth, MA [*FM radio station call letters*] ... WOCN
South Yemen Dinar (BJA) ... SYD
South Yorkshire Railway [*British*] (ROG) ... SYR
South-African Constabulary [*Military British Defunct*] (ROG) ... SAC
South-African Garrisons Institutes [*Military British*] (ROG) ... SAGI
Southall [*British depot code*] ... SHL

Southall [*Postcode*] (ODBW) .... UB
Southam, Inc. [*Toronto Stock Exchange symbol Vancouver Stock Exchange symbol*] .... STM
Southampton [*British ICAO location identifier*] (ICLI) .... EGHI
Southampton [*British ICAO location identifier*] (ICLI) .... EGRI
Southampton [*City in England*] (ROG) .... SOHAM
Southampton [*England*] [*Airport symbol*] (OAG) .... SOU
Southampton [*City in England*] (ROG) .... SOUTHN
Southampton [*England*] .... STHMPN
Southampton Branch, Bruce County Public Library, Ontario [*Library symbol National Library of Canada*] (NLC) .... OSO
Southampton Center of Long Island University, Southampton, NY [*OCLC symbol*] (OCLC) .... XSC
Southampton Court Leet Records [*A publication*] (DLA) .... Hearnshaw
Southampton Hospital, Southampton, NY [*Library symbol Library of Congress*] (LCLS) .... NSoaH
Southampton, NY [*FM radio station call letters*] .... WHFM
Southampton, NY [*FM radio station call letters*] .... WPBX
Southampton, NY [*FM radio station call letters*] .... WRLI
Southampton Oceanography Centre [*British*] .... SOC
Southampton University Man-Powered Aircraft [*British*] .... SUMPAC
Southampton University Yacht Research Group [*British*] .... SUYR
Southard's New Jersey Law Reports [*4-5 New Jersey*] [*A publication*] (DLA) .... Southard
Southaven, MS [*AM radio station call letters*] .... WAVN
Southbank Aviation [*Australia*] .... SA
Southbound .... SB
Southbound (WGA) .... SOBND
Southbridge, MA [*AM radio station call letters*] .... WESO
Southbridge, MA [*FM radio station call letters*] .... WQVR
Southdale-Hennepin Area Library, Edina, MN [*Library symbol Library of Congress*] (LCLS) .... MnEdS
Southdown $2.875cm Cv'D' Pfd [*NYSE symbol*] (TTSB) .... SDWPrD
Southdown Elementary School, Huntington, NY [*Library symbol*] [*Library of Congress*] (LCLS) .... NhuSE
Southdown, Inc. [*NYSE symbol*] (SPSG) .... SDW
Southdown, Inc. [*Associated Press*] (SAG) .... Soudw
Southdown, Inc. [*Associated Press*] (SAG) .... Soudwn
Southdowns [*Zambia*] [*ICAO location identifier*] (ICLI) .... FLSO
Southeast .... SE
Southeast .... STHEST
Southeast Air, Inc. [*ICAO designator*] (FAAC) .... SEA
Southeast Airlines, Inc. [*ICAO designator Obsolete*] (OAG) .... SL
Southeast Airmotive Corp. [*ICAO designator*] (FAAC) .... SPU
Southeast Alabama Multitype System, Montgomery, AL [*Library symbol*] [*Library of Congress*] (LCLS) .... AMSoE
Southeast Archeological Center [*US Department of the Interior*] [*Research center*] (RCD) .... SEAC
South-East Area Libraries (NITA) .... SEAL
Southeast Area Monitoring and Assessment Program (USDC) .... SEAMAP
Southeast Area Monitoring and Assessment Program [*Marine science*] (OSRA) .... SEAMAP
Southeast Arkansas Regional Library, Monticello, AR [*Library symbol Library of Congress*] (LCLS) .... ArMonD
Southeast Asia .... SEA
Southeast Asia (NG) .... SEASIA
Southeast Asia Airlift System [*Vietnam*] [*Also, SEAAS*] [*Air Force*] (VNW) .... SEAIR
Southeast Asia Airlift System [*Vietnam*] [*Also, SEAIR*] [*Air Force*] (VNW) .... SEASS
South-East Asia Association of Science Editors (PDAA) .... EDITEAST
Southeast Asia Association on Seismology and Earthquake Engineering .... SEASEE
Southeast Asia Buildup (CINC) .... SEABU
Southeast Asia Center (EA) .... SEAC
Southeast Asia Collective Defense Treaty (AABC) .... SEACDT
Southeast Asia Command .... SEAC
Southeast Asia Commonwealth .... SEACOM
South-East Asia Commonwealth Cable (NITA) .... SEACOM
Southeast Asia Communications (MCD) .... SEACOM
Southeast Asia Communications Research (MCD) .... SEACORE
Southeast Asia Coordination Council [*Military*] .... SEACOORD
Southeast Asia DataBase (MCD) .... SEADAB
Southeast Asia Development Advisory Group [*Department of State*] .... SEADAG
South-East Asia Development Division [*Overseas Development Administration*] [*British*] (DS) .... SEADD
Southeast Asia Information Center (NG) .... SEAIC
Southeast Asia Information Group (AFM) .... SEAIG
Southeast Asia Integrated Tactical Air Control System (CINC) .... SEAITACS
Southeast Asia Land Forces [*British*] .... SEALF
Southeast Asia Logistic Requirement (AFM) .... SEALR
Southeast Asia Management Information Center [*Navy*] .... SEAMIC
Southeast Asia Microfilm Project [*Library network*] .... SEAM
Southeast Asia Military Air Reservation Facility (CINC) .... SEAMARF
Southeast Asia Mohawk Revision Program [*Army aviation*] .... SEAMORE
Southeast Asia Multisensor Armed Surveillance Helicopter .... SMASH
Southeast Asia Night Operations [*Army*] .... SEANITEOPS
Southeast Asia NOTAM [*Notice to Airmen*] **Center** [*Military*] .... SEANC
Southeast Asia Operational Requirements (MCD) .... SEAOR
Southeast Asia Operational Sensor System (MCD) .... SEAOPSS
Southeast Asia Petroleum Exploration Society .... SEAPEX
Southeast Asia Program [*Cornell University*] [*Research center*] (RCD) .... SEAP
Southeast Asia Programs Directorate .... SEAPRO
Southeast Asia Regional Computer Confederation (EA) .... SEARCC
Southeast Asia Regional Council .... SEARC
Southeast Asia Rescue Foundation (EA) .... SARF
Southeast Asia Resource Center (EA) .... SRC
Southeast Asia Science Cooperation Office .... SEASCO
Southeast Asia Tactical Information Communications Center (DNAB) .... SEATICC
Southeast Asia Telecommunications System [*Military*] (AABC) .... SEATELCOM
Southeast Asia Tin Research and Development Center [*Malaysia*] (IRC) .... SEATRAD
Southeast Asia Translation and Interrogation Center [*Navy*] .... SEATIC
Southeast Asia Treaty Organization [*International organization formed to combat the spread of Communism*] (VNW) .... SEATO
Southeast Asia Treaty Organization Standardization Agreement .... SEASTAG
Southeast Asia Wideband System [*Military*] .... SEAWBS
Southeast Asian Agency for Regional Transport and Communications Development (EAIO) .... SEATAC
Southeast Asian Art and Culture [*Foundation*] .... SEAAC
South-East Asian Fisheries Information System [*Marine science*] (OSRA) .... SEAFIS
Southeast Asian Geotechnical Society (EAIO) .... SEAGS
Southeast Asian Learners (MEDA) .... SEAL
Southeast Asian Mathematical Society [*Singapore, Singapore*] .... SEAMS
Southeast Asian Ministers of Education Organization .... SEAMO
Southeast Asian Nuclear Weapons Free Zone .... SEANWFZ
Southeast Asian Program for Potato Research and Development (GNE) .... SAPPRAD
Southeast Asian Refugees (MEDA) .... SEAR
Southeast Asian Regional Branch of the International Council on Archives (EAIO) .... SARBICA
Southeast Asian Regional Center for Education in Science and Mathematics [*Malaysia*] .... RECSAM
Southeast Asian Science and Mathematics Experiment [*RECSAM*] .... SEASAME
Southeast Aviation Group, Inc. [*ICAO designator*] (FAAC) .... SBD
Southeast Bering Sea Carrying Capacity [*Study*] [*Marine science*] (OSRA) .... SEBSCC
Southeast by East .... SEbE
Southeast by South .... SEbS
Southeast Community College, Fairbury, NE [*Library symbol Library of Congress*] (LCLS) .... NbFbC
Southeast Community College, Lincoln, NE [*Library symbol Library of Congress*] (LCLS) .... NbLSc
Southeast Community College, Milford, NE [*Library symbol Library of Congress*] (LCLS) .... NbMiS
Southeast Correct Craft, Inc. [*ICAO designator*] (FAAC) .... SOT
Southeast Division Naval Facilities Engineering Command .... DIRSOEASTDOCKS
Southeast Dubois County, School Corp. Library, Ferdinand, IN [*OCLC symbol*] (OCLC) .... XSD
Southeast/East Asian English Publications in Print [*Japan Publications Guide Service*] [*Japan Information service or system*] (CRD) .... AEPP
Southeast European Airlines [*Greece*] [*ICAO designator*] (FAAC) .... SEEA
Southeast Fisheries Center [*Miami, FL*] [*National Marine Fisheries Service*] (MSC) .... SEFC
Southeast Fisheries Science Center [*Marine science*] (OSRA) .... SFSC
Southeast Florida and Caribbean Recruitment [*Marine science*] (OSRA) .... SEFCAR
Southeast Florida and Caribbean Recruitment (USDC) .... SEFCAR
Southeast Florida Outfalls Experiment (USDC) .... SEAFLOE
Southeast Florida Outfalls Experiment [*Marine science*] (OSRA) .... SEAFLOE
Southeast Indian Ridge [*Antarctica*] [*Geology*] .... SEIR
Southeast Institute for Group and Family Therapy (EA) .... SI
Southeast Iowa Academic Libraries [*Library network*] .... SIAL
Southeast Island School District, Ketchikan, AK [*Library symbol*] [*Library of Congress*] (LCLS) .... AkKSISD
Southeast Kansas Library System [*Library network*] .... SEKLS
Southeast Kansas Library System, Iola, KS [*Library symbol Library of Congress*] (LCLS) .... KIoS
Southeast Library Service Area [*Library network*] .... SELSA
Southeast Louisiana Library Network Cooperative [*Library network*] .... SEALLINC
Southeast Louisiana Library Network Cooperative (SEALLING), New Orleans, LA [*Library symbol Library of Congress*] (LCLS) .... LNSL
Southeast Mediterranean Area [*NATO*] (NATG) .... MEDSOUEAST
Southeast Metropolitan Board of Cooperative Services, Processing Center, Littleton, CO [*OCLC symbol*] (OCLC) .... COQ
Southeast Metropolitan Board of Cooperative Services, Professional Information Center, Denver, CO [*Library symbol Library of Congress*] (LCLS) .... CoDSP
Southeast Michigan Council of Governments [*Detroit, MI*] .... SEMCOG
Southeast Missouri State University (GAGS) .... Southeast Mo St U
Southeast Missouri State University, Cape Girardeau, MO [*Library symbol Library of Congress*] (LCLS) .... MoCgS
Southeast Missouri State University, Cape Girardeau, MO [*OCLC symbol*] (OCLC) .... SEM
Southeast Monsoon .... SEM
Southeast Pacific Area .... SEPA
Southeast Pacific Command [*Navy*] .... SOEASTPAC
Southeast Pacific Force [*later, Command*] [*Navy*] .... SEPACFOR
Southeast Poultry Research Laboratory [*University of Georgia*] [*Research center*] (RCD) .... SEPRL
Southeast Regional Library, Weyburn, Saskatchewan [*Library symbol National Library of Canada*] (NLC) .... SWSE
Southeast Regional Library, Weyburn, SK, Canada [*Library symbol Library of Congress*] (LCLS) .... CaSWSE
Southeast Singles Association .... SESA
Southeast Skyways [*ICAO designator*] (AD) .... SE
Southeast Texas Information Network Association .... SETINA
Southeast Water Laboratory [*Environmental Protection Agency*] .... SEWL
Southeastbound [*ICAO designator*] (FAAC) .... SEB

Southeastern ..... STHESTN
Southeastern Adult Education Association (AEBS) ..... SAEA
Southeastern Airways Corp. [*ICAO designator*] (FAAC) ..... PTM
Southeastern & Chatham Railway [*Nickname: Seldom Ever Caught Running*] ..... SE & CR
Southeastern Association for Research in Astronomy [*University of Georgia*] [*Research center*] (RCD) ..... SARA
Southeastern Association of Fish and Wildlife Agencies (EA) ..... SAFWA
Southeastern Association of Game and Fish Commissioners [*Later, SAFWA*] (EA) ..... SAGFC
Southeastern Association of School Business Officials (AEBS) ..... SASBO
Southeastern Baptist Theological Seminary, Wake Forest, NC [*Library symbol Library of Congress*] (LCLS) ..... NcWfSB
Southeastern Baptist Theological Seminary, Wake Forest, NC [*OCLC symbol*] (OCLC) ..... NVS
Southeastern Bible College [*Lakeland, FL*] ..... SBC
South-Eastern Bible College [*Florida*] ..... SEBC
Southeastern Center for Contemporary Art [*North Carolina*] ..... SECCA
Southeastern Center for Electrical Engineering Education [*Air Force*] ..... SCEEE
Southeastern Christian College, Winchester, KY [*Library symbol Library of Congress*] (LCLS) ..... KyWnS
Southeastern College of the Assemblies of God, Lakeland, FL [*Library symbol*] [*Library of Congress*] (LCLS) ..... FLISC
Southeastern Command ..... SEC
Southeastern Community College, Whiteville, NC [*Library symbol Library of Congress*] (LCLS) ..... NcWhS
Southeastern Community Development Association [*Defunct*] (EA) ..... SECDA
Southeastern Commuter Airlines [*ICAO designator*] (AD) ..... WH
Southeastern Composers' League (EA) ..... SCL
Southeastern Conference (EA) ..... SEC
Southeastern Conference on Latin American Studies [*United States*] ..... SECOLAS
Southeastern Conference on Linguistics ..... SECOL
Southeastern Connecticut Library Association [*Library network*] ..... SECLA
Southeastern Consortium of University Transportation Centers [*MTMC*] (TAG) ..... SECUTC
Southeastern Cooperative Wildlife Disease Study [*University of Georgia*] [*Research center*] (RCD) ..... SCWDS
Southeastern Cottonseed Crushers Association (EA) ..... SCCA
Southeastern Educational Improvement Laboratory [*Research Triangle Park, NC*] [*Department of Education*] (GRD) ..... SEIL
Southeastern Educational Laboratory ..... SEL
Southeastern Electric Exchange ..... SEE
Southeastern Electric Reliability Council [*Regional power council*] ..... SERC
Southeastern Fabric Association (EA) ..... SFA
Southeastern Field Research Laboratory [*Pennsylvania State University*] ..... SEFRL
Southeastern Fish Control Station [*Department of the Interior*] (GRD) ..... SEFCL
Southeastern Fisheries Association (EA) ..... SFA
Southeastern Forest Experiment Station [*Asheville, NC*] [*Department of Agriculture*] (GRD) ..... SEFES
Southeastern General Hospital, Medical Library, Lumberton, NC [*Library symbol Library of Congress*] (LCLS) ..... NcLuH
Southeastern Intercollegiate Athletic Association (MCD) ..... SIAC
Southeastern Jurisdictional Conference [*United Methodist Church*] ..... SEJ
Southeastern Kentucky Regional Library Cooperative [*Library network*] ..... SEKRLC
Southeastern Libraries Cooperating [*SELCO*], Rochester Public Library, Rochester, MN [*Library symbol Library of Congress*] (LCLS) ..... MnRS
Southeastern Library Association (AEBS) ..... SELA
Southeastern Library Association (AEBS) ..... SLA
Southeastern Library Network [*Library network*] ..... SLN
Southeastern Library Network [*Atlanta, GA*] [*Library network*] ..... SOLINET
South-Eastern Library Network (NITA) ..... SOLINET
Southeastern Library Network [*SOLINET*], Atlanta, GA [*Library symbol*] [*Library of Congress*] (LCLS) ..... GASL
Southeastern Library Network, Atlanta, GA [*OCLC symbol*] (OCLC) ..... TQU
Southeastern Library Network, Atlanta, GA [*OCLC symbol*] (OCLC) ..... TQV
Southeastern Louisiana University (GAGS) ..... Southeastern La U
Southeastern Louisiana University, Hammond, LA [*Library symbol Library of Congress*] (LCLS) ..... LHS
Southeastern Louisiana University, Hammond, LA [*OCLC symbol*] (OCLC) ..... LSH
Southeastern Lumber Manufacturers Association (EA) ..... SLMA
Southeastern Manufactured Housing Institute [*Later, Manufactured Housing Institute*] (EA) ..... SEMHI
Southeastern Marine Trades Exhibit and Conference [*National Marine Manufacturers Association*] (TSPED) ..... SEMTEC
Southeastern Massachusetts Cooperating Libraries [*Library network*] ..... SMCL
Southeastern Massachusetts Health Sciences Libraries Consortium [*Library network*] ..... SEMCC
Southeastern Massachusetts Technological Institute [*Later, Southeastern Massachusetts University*] ..... SMTI
Southeastern Massachusetts University [*North Dartmouth*] ..... SMU
Southeastern Massachusetts University, North Dartmouth, MA [*Library symbol Library of Congress*] (LCLS) ..... MNodS
Southeastern Massachusetts University, North Dartmouth, MA [*OCLC symbol*] (OCLC) ..... SMU
Southeastern Mich Gas Ent [*NASDAQ symbol*] (TTSB) ..... SMGS
Southeastern Michigan Gas Enterprises, Inc. [*Associated Press*] (SAG) ..... SMchG
Southeastern Michigan Gas Enterprises, Inc. [*NASDAQ symbol*] (NQ) ..... SMGS
Southeastern Missouri State College ..... SMSC
Southeastern New York Library Resources Council [*Highland, NY*] [*Library network*] ..... SENYLRC
Southeastern Ohio Library Organization [*Library network*] ..... SOLO
Southeastern Oklahoma State University (GAGS) ..... Southeastern Okla St U
Southeastern Peanut Association (EA) ..... SPA
Southeastern Pecan Growers Association (EA) ..... SEPGA
Southeastern Pecan Growers Association ..... SPGA
Southeastern Pennsylvania Development Corp. ..... SPEDCO
Southeastern Pennsylvania Theological Library Association [*Library network*] ..... SEPTLA
Southeastern Pennsylvania Transportation Authority ..... SEPTA
Southeastern Plant Environment Laboratories [*Duke University and North Carolina State University*] ..... SEPEL
Southeastern Poultry and Egg Association (EA) ..... SPEA
Southeastern Power Administration [*Department of Energy*] ..... SEPA
Southeastern Psychological Association (MCD) ..... SEPA
Southeastern Radiological Health Laboratory (SAA) ..... SERHL
South-Eastern Railway [*British*] ..... SER
Southeastern Regional Arts Council ..... SERAC
Southeastern Regional Biomedical Information System (AEBS) ..... SERBIS
Southeastern Regional Library Center, Lovington, NM [*Library symbol Library of Congress*] (LCLS) ..... NmLovS
Southeastern Regional Medical Library Program [*Emory University*] [*Library network*] (IID) ..... SERMLP
Southeastern Reporter [*National Reporter System*] [*A publication*] (DLA) ..... SE
Southeastern Reporter [*A publication*] (DLA) ..... So East Rep
Southeastern Reporter, Second Series [*A publication*] (DLA) ..... SE 2d
Southeastern Reservoir Investigation [*Department of the Interior*] (GRD) ..... SRI
Southeastern Resource Policy Association (EA) ..... SERPA
Southeastern Simulation Council ..... SSC
Southeastern State College [*Later, Southeastern Oklahoma State University*] ..... SSC
Southeastern State College, Durant, OK [*Library symbol Library of Congress*] (LCLS) ..... OkDurS
Southeastern Stock Exchange ..... SSE
Southeastern Test and Training Area [*Military*] (MCD) ..... SETTA
Southeastern Theatre Conference (EA) ..... SETC
Southeastern Thrift and Bank Fund [*Associated Press*] (SAG) ..... SestThr
Southeastern Thrift & Bank Fund [*NASDAQ symbol*] (SAG) ..... STBF
Southeastern United States ..... SEUS
Southeastern United States Seismic Network (NRCH) ..... SEUSSN
Southeastern Universities Research Association, CEBAF Library, Newport News, VA [*Library symbol*] [*Library of Congress*] (LCLS) ..... ViNeA
[*The*] **Southeastern Universities Research Association Network** (TNIG) ..... SURAnet
Southeastern University [*Washington, DC*] ..... SEU
Southeastern Wisconsin Health Systems Agency, Health Science Library, Milwaukee,WI [*Library symbol Library of Congress*] (LCLS) ..... WMSWH
Southeastern Yiddish (BJA) ..... SEY
Southend [*British ICAO location identifier*] (ICLI) ..... EGMC
Southend [*Scotland*] [*Airport symbol*] (AD) ..... SEN
Southend [*County borough in England*] ..... SEND
Southend Jet Centre Ltd. [*British ICAO designator*] (FAAC) ..... SJC
Souther Gold Resources [*Vancouver Stock Exchange symbol*] ..... STG
Southerland, J. C., Dearborn, MI [*STAC*] ..... SJC
Southerly ..... SLY
Southerly [*A publication*] ..... STHLY
Southern (VRA) ..... S
Southern (WGA) ..... SON
Southern ..... SRN
Southern ..... STHN
Southern ..... STHRN
Southern Adirondack Library System [*Library network*] ..... SALS
Southern Adirondack Library System, Saratoga Springs, NY [*Library symbol Library of Congress*] (LCLS) ..... NSsSA
Southern Adirondack Library System, Saratoga Springs, NY [*OCLC symbol*] (OCLC) ..... VVA
Southern Africa Association [*British*] (EAIO) ..... SAA
Southern Africa Committee (EA) ..... SAC
Southern Africa Fund [*NYSE symbol*] (SAG) ..... SOA
Southern Africa Fund [*Associated Press*] (SAG) ..... SouAfrica
Southern Africa Institute of Fundraising (NFD) ..... SAIF
Southern Africa Media Center (EA) ..... SAMC
Southern Africa Regional Tourism Council (EAIO) ..... SARTOC
Southern Africa Road Federation [*See also SAPF*] (EAIO) ..... SARF
Southern Africa Society of Aquatic Scientists (EAIO) ..... SASAS
Southern Africa - The Imprisoned Society [*An association British*] ..... SATIS
Southern African Catholic Bishops' Conference (EAIO) ..... SACBC
Southern African Catholic Bishops' Conference - Justice and Peace Commission (EAIO) ..... SACBC-JPC
Southern African Center for Ivory Marketing ..... SACIM
Southern African Centre for Co-Operation in Agricultural Research (EY) ..... SACCAR
Southern African Development Community (ECON) ..... SADC
Southern African Literature Society [*Botswana*] (EAIO) ..... SALS
Southern African Society for Quaternary Research (EAIO) ..... SASQUA
Southern African Society of University Teachers of Accounting (EAIO) ..... SASUTA
Southern African Solidarity Congress [*Zimbabwe*] [*Political party*] (PPW) ..... SASCON
Southern African Territories ..... SAT
Southern African Trade Union Coordination Council [*Gaborone, Botswana*] (EAIO) ..... SATUCC
Southern African Treaty Organization (NADA) ..... SATO
Southern African Wildlife Management Association [*See also NVSA*] (EAIO) ..... SAWMA
Southern Agricultural Energy Center ..... SAEC
Southern Air Command [*South Africa*] [*ICAO location identifier*] (ICLI) ..... FASF
Southern Air Ltd. [*British ICAO designator*] (FAAC) ..... HSN
Southern Air Materiel Area, Europe ..... SAMAE

Southern Air Materiel Area, Pacific [*Army*] (AFIT) .... SAMAP
Southern Air Procurement District .... SOAPD
Southern Air Traffic Control Centre [*British*] .... SATCC
Southern Air Transport, Inc. .... SAT
Southern Air Transport, Inc. [*ICAO designator*] (FAAC) .... SJM
Southern Air Transport, Inc. [*Air carrier designation symbol*] .... SRAX
Southern Air Transport, Inc. .... SRN
Southern Airlines [*Australia*] .... SAL
Southern Airlines and Freighters [*Australia*] .... SA & F
Southern Airlines Ltd. [*British ICAO designator*] (FAAC) .... STH
Southern Airways [*ICAO designator*] .... SO
Southern Airways (MCD) .... SOA
Southern Airways [*Air carrier designation symbol*] .... SOU
Southern Alberta Institute of Technology [*UTLAS symbol*] .... SAI
Southern Alberta Institute of Technology [*Calgary, AB*] .... SAIT
Southern Alberta Institute of Technology, Calgary, AB, Canada [*Library symbol Library of Congress*] (LCLS) .... CaACSA
Southern Alberta Institute of Technology, Calgary, Alberta [*Library symbol National Library of Canada*] (NLC) .... ACSA
Southern Anthropological Society .... SAS
Southern Appalachian Coal Operators Association (EA) .... SACOA
Southern Appalachian Dulcimer Association (EA) .... SADA
Southern Appalachian Migrant [*Cincinnati slang*] .... SAM
Southern Appalachian Regional Seismic Network [*Geology*] .... SARSN
Southern Appalachian Studies [*Defunct*] (EA) .... SAS
Southern Area Command [*Military*] (AABC) .... SACOM
Southern Arkansas University, Magnolia, AR [*OCLC symbol*] (OCLC) .... ASA
Southern Army Worm [*Agronomy*] .... SAW
Southern Arts Association [*British*] (DBA) .... SAA
Southern Ash Association [*Defunct*] (EA) .... SAA
Southern Association [*Baseball league*] .... SA
Southern Association for Institutional Research (EDAC) .... SAIR
Southern Association of Agricultural Scientists (EA) .... SAAS
Southern Association of College and University Business Officers (AEBS) .... SACUBO
Southern Association of Colleges and Schools (EA) .... SACS
Southern Association of Junior Colleges (AEBS) .... SAJC
Southern Association of Science and Industry (EA) .... SASI
Southern Association on Children under Six (EA) .... SACUS
Southern Atlantic Modern Language Association .... SAMLA
Southern Atlantic Satellite Communication .... SASCOM
Southern Attack Force [*Navy*] .... SAF
Southern Aviation Ltd. [*Ghana*] [*ICAO designator*] (FAAC) .... STV
Southern Banc Co., Inc. [*AMEX symbol*] (SAG) .... SRN
Southern Banc Co., Inc. [*Associated Press*] (SAG) .... SthnBnc
Southern Banc(AL) [*AMEX symbol*] (TTSB) .... SRN
Southern Baptist College [*Walnut Ridge, AR*] .... SBC
Southern Baptist Convention .... SBC
Southern Baptist Convention Flyers [*Defunct*] (EA) .... SBCF
Southern Baptist Convention Foreign Mission Board, Richmond, VA [*Library symbol*] [*Library of Congress*] (LCLS) .... ViRSBF
Southern Baptist Convention Historical Commission, Nashville, TN [*Library symbol Library of Congress*] (LCLS) .... TNSB
Southern Baptist Foundation (EA) .... SBF
Southern Baptist Press Association (EA) .... SBPA
Southern Baptist Theological Seminary, Louisville, KY [*OCLC symbol*] (OCLC) .... KTS
Southern Baptist Theological Seminary, Louisville, KY [*Library symbol Library of Congress*] (LCLS) .... KyLoS
Southern Baptist Women in Ministry/Folio (EA) .... SBWM/F
Southern Base Section [*England*] .... SBS
Southern Bean Mosaic Virus .... SBMV
Southern Bean Mosaic Virus - Cowpea Strain .... SBMV-C
Southern Bean Mosaic Virus - Strain B .... SBMV-B
Southern Bell Telephone & Telegraph Co. (KSC) .... SBTT
Southern Bible College, Houston, TX [*Library symbol Library of Congress*] (LCLS) .... TxHSB
Southern Blot Hybridization [*Biochemistry*] .... SBH
Southern Bluefin Tuna [*Fish*] .... SBT
Southern Branch Library, Alberta Research Council, Calgary, Alberta [*Library symbol National Library of Canada*] (NLC) .... ACRS
Southern Building Code Congress, International .... SBCC
Southern Building Code Congress, International (EA) .... SBCCI
Southern Business Group [*Commercial firm*] [*British*] .... SBG
Southern Cal Water [*NYSE symbol*] (TTSB) .... SCW
Southern California .... SC
Southern California [*Military*] (NVT) .... SOCAL
Southern California Answering Network [*Los Angeles Public Library*] [*Information service or system*] .... SCAN
Southern California Association of Governments .... SCAG
Southern California Coastal Water Research Project (NOAA) .... SCCWRP
Southern California College, Costa Mesa, CA [*Library symbol Library of Congress*] (LCLS) .... CCmS
Southern California College, Costa Mesa, CA [*OCLC symbol*] (OCLC) .... CSM
Southern California College of Optometry (GAGS) .... So Cal C Optometry
Southern California College of Optometry, Fullerton, CA [*Library symbol Library of Congress*] (LCLS) .... CFlCO
Southern California Earthquake Center .... SCEC
Southern California Edison Co. [*AMEX symbol*] (SAG) .... SCE
Southern California Edison Co. [*Associated Press*] (SAG) .... SCEd
Southern California Edison Co. [*Associated Press*] (SAG) SCEd44
Southern California Edison Co., Los Angeles, CA [*Library symbol Library of Congress*] (LCLS) .... CLSCE
Southern California Figure-Ground Visual Perception Test .... SCFGVPT
Southern California Film Circuit [*Library network*] .... SCFC
Southern California Genealogical Society, Burbank, CA [*Library symbol*] [*Library of Congress*] (LCLS) .... CBbGS
Southern California Industry-Education Council (SAA) .... SCIEC
Southern California Interlibrary Loan Project [*Library network*] .... SCILL
Southern California Kinesthesia and Tactile Perception Tests .... SCKTPT
Southern California Motor Accuracy Test .... SCMAT
Southern California Off-Road Event [*An association*] .... SCORE
Southern California Online User Group (NITA) .... SCOUG
Southern California Perceptual Motor Tests .... SCPMT
Southern California Postrotary Nystagmus Test .... SCPNT
Southern California Rapid Transit District, Los Angeles, CA [*OCLC symbol*] (OCLC) .... CRD
Southern California Regional Information Study [*Bureau of Census*] .... SCRIS
Southern California Sector, Western Sea Frontier .... SOCALSEC
Southern California Seismic Network .... SCSN
Southern California Sensory Integration Test [*Ayres*] [*Education*] .... SCSIT
Southern California Timing Association (EA) .... SCTA
Southern California Water Co. [*Associated Press*] (SAG) .... SCalWat
Southern California Water Co. [*NYSE symbol*] (SAG) .... SCW
Southern Canada Power Co. Library, Montreal, PQ, Canada [*Library symbol Library of Congress*] (LCLS) .... CaQMSC
Southern Canada Power Co., Montreal, Quebec [*Library symbol National Library of Canada*] (NLC) .... QMSC
Southern Center for Research and Innovation, Inc. [*University of Southern Mississippi*] [*Research center*] (RCD) .... SCRI
Southern Central Kansas Environmental Education Center (EDAC) .... SKEEC
Southern Christian Leadership Conference (EA) .... SCLC
Southern Classification .... SC
Southern Coal Producers Association [*Defunct*] (EA) .... SCPA
Southern Coalition for Educational Equity (EA) .... SCEE
Southern Coastal Plains Expedition [*National Oceanic and Atmospheric Administration*] (MSC) .... SCOPE
Southern College of Optometry [*Tennessee*] .... SCO
Southern College of Optometry (GAGS) .... So C Optometry
Southern College of Optometry, Memphis, TN [*Library symbol Library of Congress*] (LCLS) .... TMSO
Southern College Personnel Association (AEBS) .... SCPA
Southern College University Union .... SCUU
Southern Colorado State College, Pueblo, CO [*Library symbol Library of Congress*] (LCLS) .... CoPS
Southern Command [*British military*] (DMA) .... SC
Southern Command (MCD) .... SOCOM
Southern Command [*Military*] (AFM) .... SOUTHCOM
Southern Command Network [*Military*] (GFGA) .... SCN
Southern Communications Area [*Military*] .... SCA
Southern Community Bancshares, Inc. [*NASDAQ symbol*] (SAG) .... SCBS
Southern Community Bancshares, Inc. [*Associated Press*] (SAG) .... SthCoB
Southern Co. [*NYSE symbol*] (SPSG) .... SO
Southern Co. [*Associated Press*] (SAG) .... SouthnCo
Southern Conference (EA) .... SC
Southern Conference Educational Fund (EA) .... SCEF
Southern Conference on Language Teaching, Inc. (EDAC) .... SCOLT
Southern Connecticut State College [*New Haven*] .... SCSC
Southern Connecticut State College, Division of Library Science, New Haven, CT [*OCLC symbol*] (OCLC) .... SCC
Southern Connecticut State College, New Haven, CT [*Library symbol Library of Congress*] (LCLS) .... CtNhN
Southern Connecticut State University (GAGS) .... So Conn St U
Southern Cooperative Development Program [*Sponsored by Southern Consumers Education Foundation*] .... SCDP
Southern Copper Ltd. [*Commercial firm Australia*] .... SCL
Southern Corn Leaf Blight (OA) .... SCLB
Southern Cotton Association (EA) .... SCA
Southern Cotton Ginners Association (EA) .... SCGA
Southern Cross [*Australia Airport symbol*] (OAG) .... SQC
Southern Cultures [*A publication*] (BRI) .... South Cul
Southern Cypress Manufacturers Association (EA) .... SCMA
Southern Defense Command [*Army*] .... SDC
Southern Development Foundation (EA) .... SDF
Southern District (DLA) .... SD
Southern Economic Association (EA) .... SEA
Southern Education and Library Board [*Northern Ireland*] (AIE) .... SELB
Southern Education Foundation (EA) .... SEF
Southern Education Program [*Defunct*] (EA) .... SEP
Southern Education Reporting Service .... SERS
Southern Educational Communications Authority [*Television network*] [*Obsolete*] .... SECA
Southern Electronics [*NASDAQ symbol*] (TTSB) .... SECX
Southern Electronics Corp. (IAA) .... SEC
Southern Electronics Corp. [*Tucker, GA*] [*NASDAQ symbol*] (NQ) .... SECX
Southern Electronics Corp. [*Associated Press*] (SAG) .... SoElec
Southern Energy Homes [*NASDAQ symbol*] (TTSB) .... SEHI
Southern Energy Homes, Inc. [*NASDAQ symbol*] (SAG) .... SEHI
Southern Energy Homes, Inc. [*Associated Press*] (SAG) .... SthnEH
Southern Energy Homes, Inc. [*Associated Press*] (SAG) .... SthnEnH
Southern Europe (NATG) .... SE
Southern Europe - ACTISUD [*Authority for the Coordination of Inland Transport in Southern Europe*] [*NATO*] (NATG) .... SE/ACT
Southern Europe - Inland Waterways Transport [*NATO*] (NATG) .... SE/IWT
Southern Europe - Ports and Beaches [*NATO*] (NATG) .... SE/PB
Southern Europe - Railroad Transport [*NATO*] (NATG) .... SE/RRT
Southern Europe - Road Transport [*NATO*] (NATG) .... SE/RT
Southern Europe Shipping Group [*NATO*] (NATG) .... SESG
Southern European Atomic Task Force [*Military*] .... SEATAF
Southern European Broadcasting Service [*DoD*] (GFGA) .... SEB

Southern European Network (DNAB) .... SEN
Southern European Task Force [NATO] .... SETAF
Southern European Western Mediterranean Regional Planning Group
 [NATO] (NATG) .... SEWMRPG
Southern Examining Accreditation Council (AIE) .... SEAC
Southern Farm Equipment Manufacturers (EA) .... SFEM
Southern Federation of Temple Youth .... SOFTY
Southern Financial Bancorp [NASDAQ symbol] (SAG) .... SFFB
Southern Financial Bancorp [Associated Press] .... SouFncl
Southern Financial Federal Savings Bank [NASDAQ symbol] (SAG) .... SFFB
Southern Financial Federal Savings Bank [Associated Press] (SAG) .... SouFncl
Southern Finl Bancorp [NASDAQ symbol] (TTSB) .... SFFB
Southern Fleece Washers Association [British] (DBA) .... SFWA
Southern Forest Institute [Defunct] (EA) .... SFI
Southern Forest Products Association .... SF
Southern Forest Products Association (EA) .... SFPA
Southern Forestry Information Network [Forest Service] (IID) .... SOUTHFORNET
Southern Freight Association .... SFA
Southern Freight Inspection Bureau .... SFIB
Southern Freight Tariff Bureau .... SFTB
Southern Frontier Air Transport Ltd. [Canada ICAO designator] (FAAC) .... SFS
Southern Furniture Manufacturers Association [Later, AFMA] (EA) .... SFMA
Southern Galactic Pole .... SGP
Southern Gas Basin [British] .... SGB
Southern Governors Conference .... SGC
Southern Great Plains (USDC) .... SGP
Southern Great Plains [Marine science] (OSRA) .... SGP
Southern Group of Forces [Former USSR] (NATG) .... SGF
Southern Growth Policies Board .... SGPB
Southern Harbour Public Library, Newfoundland [Library symbol National Library of Canada] (NLC) .... NFSH
Southern Harbour Public Library, Southern Harbour, NF, Canada [Library symbol] [Library of Congress] (LCLS) .... CaNfSH
Southern Hardwood Lumber Manufacturers Association [Later, HMA] (EA) .... SHLMA
Southern Hardwood Producers [Later, HMA] (EA) .... SHP
Southern Hardwood Square Association (EA) .... SHSA
Southern Hemisphere .... SH
Southern Hemisphere Balloon Experiment (SAA) .... SHBE
Southern Hemisphere Cap [on Triton] .... SHC
Southern Hemisphere Nuclear Free Zone [Australia] .... SHNFZ
Southern Hemisphere VLBI [Very-Long-Baseline Interferometry] Experiment [For observing intergalactic radio components] .... SHEVE
Southern Historical Association (EA) .... SHA
Southern Historical Press, Easley, SC [Library symbol Library of Congress] (LCLS) .... ShP
Southern Hockey League .... SHL
Southern Humanities Conference (EA) .... SHC
Southern Humanities Review [A publication] (BRI) .... South HR
Southern Idaho College of Education, Albion, ID [Library symbol Library of Congress Obsolete] (LCLS) .... IdAIS
Southern Illinois University .... SIU
Southern Illinois University (GAGS) .... So III U
Southern Illinois University at Carbondale, Carbondale, IL [OCLC symbol] (OCLC) .... SOI
Southern Illinois University at Carbondale Center for Electron Microscopy [Research center] (RCD) .... SEM
Southern Illinois University at Edwardsville (GAGS) .... So III U (Edwardsville)
Southern Illinois University, Carbondale .... SIUC
Southern Illinois University, Carbondale, IL [Library symbol Library of Congress] (LCLS) .... ICarbS
Southern Illinois University, Edwardsville Campus, Edwardsville, IL [OCLC symbol] (OCLC) .... IAT
Southern Illinois University, Edwardsville Campus, Edwardsville, IL [Library symbol Library of Congress] (LCLS) .... IEdS
Southern Illinois University Press .... SIUP
Southern Illinois University, School of Dental Medicine, Biomedical Library, Edwardsville, IL [Library symbol Library of Congress] (LCLS) .... IEdS-D
Southern Illinois University, School of Law Library, Carbondale, IL [OCLC symbol] (OCLC) .... SOL
Southern Illinois University, School of Medicine, Springfield, IL [OCLC symbol] (OCLC) .... IAV
Southern Illinois University, School of Medicine, Springfield, IL [Library symbol Library of Congress] (LCLS) .... ISUM
Southern Indiana Gas & Electric Co. [NYSE symbol] (SPSG) .... SIG
Southern Indiana Gas & Electric Co. [Associated Press] (SAG) .... SoIndGs
Southern Indiana Railway, Inc. [AAR code] .... SIND
Southern Indiana Railway, Inc. [Later, SIND] [AAR code] .... SOI
Southern Industrial Railroad, Inc. [AAR code] .... SIRR
Southern Interstate Nuclear Board .... SINB
Southern Iowa Library Cooperative, Ottumwa, IA [Library symbol Library of Congress] (LCLS) .... IaOtS
Southern Jersey Airways, Inc. [ICAO designator] (FAAC) .... ALC
Southern Korean Interim Legislative Assembly .... SKILA
Southern Labor Union .... SLU
Southern Launch Vehicle [Australia] .... SLV
Southern Law Journal [Tuscaloosa, AL] [A publication] (DLA) .... South Law J
Southern Law Journal [A publication] (DLA) .... South LJ
Southern Law Journal and Reporter [A publication] (DLA) .... So LJ
Southern Law Journal and Reporter [A publication] (DLA) .... South Law J & Rep
Southern Law Journal and Reporter [A publication] (DLA) .... South LJ & Rep
Southern Law Quarterly [A publication] (DLA) .... So LQ
Southern Law Review [St. Louis, MO] [A publication] (DLA) .... So L Rev
Southern Law Review [A publication] (DLA) .... So L Rev
Southern Law Review [Nashville, TN] [A publication] (DLA) .... So LR

Southern Law Review [A publication] (DLA) .... South L Rev
Southern Law Review [A publication] (DLA) .... South Law Rev
Southern Law Review, New Series [St. Louis, MO] [A publication] (DLA) .... So L Rev NS
Southern Law Review, New Series [St. Louis, MO] [A publication] (DLA) .... So LRNS
Southern Law Review, New Series [A publication] (DLA) .... South L Rev NS
Southern Law Review, New Series [A publication] (DLA) .... South Law Rev NS
Southern Law Times [A publication] (DLA) .... So Law T
Southern Law Times [A publication] (DLA) .... So LT
Southern Lawyer [A publication] (DLA) .... So Law
Southern Lights [Vancouver Stock Exchange symbol] .... SLG
Southern Line of Communications [World War II] .... SOLOC
Southern Living [A publication] (BRI) .... S Liv
Southern Maine Library District, Portland, ME [OCLC symbol] (OCLC) .... SML
Southern Manufacturing Technology Show and Conference (ITD) .... SMTS
Southern Maritime Zone (DNAB) .... SMZ
Southern Maryland Regional Library Resource Center [Library network] .... SMRLA
Southern Materials Resource Centre, Alberta Education, Calgary, Alberta [Library symbol National Library of Canada] (NLC) .... ACEM
Southern Methodist College, Orangeburg, SC [Library symbol] [Library of Congress] (LCLS) .... ScOrSM
Southern Methodist University [Texas] .... SMU
Southern Methodist University (GAGS) .... So Meth U
Southern Methodist University, Bridwell Library, Dallas, TX [OCLC symbol] (OCLC) .... ISB
Southern Methodist University, Business Information Center, Dallas, TX [Library symbol] [Library of Congress] (LCLS) .... TxDaM-B
Southern Methodist University, Central Library, Dallas, TX [OCLC symbol] (OCLC) .... ISM
Southern Methodist University, Dallas, TX [Library symbol Library of Congress] (LCLS) .... TxDaM
Southern Methodist University, Law Library, Dallas, TX [OCLC symbol] (OCLC) .... IUF
Southern Methodist University, Law Library, Dallas, TX [Library symbol Library of Congress] (LCLS) .... TxDaM-L
Southern Methodist University, Perkins School of Theology, Dallas, TX [Library symbol Library of Congress] (LCLS) .... TxDaM-P
Southern Methodist University, Science/Engineering Library, Dallas, TX [Library symbol Library of Congress] (LCLS) .... TxDaM-SE
Southern Microfilm Corporation, Houston, TX [Library symbol Library of Congress] (LCLS) .... SmC
Southern Mineral [NASDAQ symbol] (TTSB) .... SMIN
Southern Mineral Corp. [NASDAQ symbol] (NQ) .... SMIN
Southern Mineral Corp. [Associated Press] (SAG) .... SoMinrl
Southern Minnesota Railroad .... SM
Southern Missionary College [Tennessee] .... SMC
Southern Missionary College, Collegedale, TN [Library symbol Library of Congress] (LCLS) .... TCollSM
Southern Missionary College, Collegedale, TN [OCLC symbol] (OCLC) .... TMS
Southern Missouri Bancorp [NASDAQ symbol] (TTSB) .... SMBC
Southern Motor Carriers Rate Conference .... SMCRC
Southern Motor Carriers Rate Conference, Atlanta GA [STAC] .... SMC
Southern Mutual Help Association (EA) .... SMHA
Southern National [NYSE symbol] (TTSB) .... SNB
Southern National Corp. [NYSE symbol] (SAG) .... SNB
Southern National Corp. [Associated Press] (SAG) .... SoNat
Southern National Corp. [Associated Press] (SAG) .... SoNatCp
Southern Nazarene University (GAGS) .... So Nazarene U
Southern Nevada [ICAO designator] (AD) .... FO
Southern New Eng Telecom [NYSE symbol] (TTSB) .... SNG
Southern New England Marine Sciences Association .... SNEMSA
Southern New England Telecommunications Corp. [New Haven, CT] (TSSD) .... SNET
Southern New England Telecommunications Corp. [Associated Press] (SAG) .... SNETel
Southern New England Telecommunications Corp. [NYSE symbol] (SPSG) .... SNG
Southern New York Railway [AAR code] .... SNY
Southern Newspaper Publishers Association .... SNPA
Southern Ocean Cloud Experiment (EERA) .... SOCEX
Southern Ocean Float Experiment [Marine science] (MSC) .... SOFEX
Southern Ocean Racing Conference .... SORC
Southern Ocean Waves Experiment (USDC) .... SOWEX
Southern Ocean Waves Experiment [Marine science] (OSRA) .... SOWEX
Southern Ohio Aviation Sales Co. [ICAO designator] (FAAC) .... SOH
Southern Ohio Correctional Facility, Lucasville, OH [Library symbol Library of Congress] (LCLS) .... OLuCF
Southern Oregon College .... SOC
Southern Oregon College, Ashland, OR [Library symbol Library of Congress] (LCLS) .... OrAshS
Southern Oregon Library Federation [Library network] .... SOLF
Southern Oregon State College (GAGS) .... So Ore St C
Southern Oscillation [Meteorology] .... SO
Southern Oscillation Index .... SOI
Southern Oxidant Study (USDC) .... SOS
Southern Oxidant Study [Marine science] (OSRA) .... SOS
Southern Pac Petrol NL [NASDAQ symbol] (TTSB) .... SPPTY
Southern Pacific Communications (NITA) .... SPC
Southern Pacific Communications Corp. .... SPC
Southern Pacific Communications Corp. .... SPCC
Southern Pacific Communications' Switched Long Distance Service [Telecommunications] (TEL) .... SPRINT
Southern Pacific Co. .... SPCO

Southern Pacific Co., San Francisco, CA [Library symbol Library of Congress] (LCLS) .... CSfSP
Southern Pacific Funding Corp. [NYSE symbol] (SAG) .... SFC
Southern Pacific Funding Corp. [Associated Press] (SAG) .... SPacFd
Southern Pacific Funding Corp. [Associated Press] (SAG) .... SPacFdg
Southern Pacific International Fan Club (EA) .... SPIFC
Southern Pacific Petroleum [Associated Press] (SAG) .... SoPacPet
Southern Pacific Petroleum [Associated Press] (SAG) .... SoPcPt
Southern Pacific Petroleum NL [NASDAQ symbol] (NQ) .... SPPT
Southern Pacific Pipelines and International Tank Terminals [Two companies jointly building deepwater port to accommodate outsize oil carriers] .... SPPLITT
Southern Pacific Rail [NYSE symbol] (TTSB) .... RSP
Southern Pacific Rail Corp. [Associated Press] (SAG) .... SouPacR
Southern Pacific Railroad Co. [NYSE symbol] (SPSG) .... RSP
Southern Pacific Railroad Co. .... SOPAC
Southern Pacific Transportation Co. [AAR code] .... SP
Southern Paper Trade Association [Defunct] (EA) .... SPTA
Southern Peaks Public Library, Alamosa, CO [Library symbol] [Library of Congress] (LCLS) .... CoAlS
Southern Peanut Warehousemen's Association (EA) .... SPWA
Southern Peru Copper [NYSE symbol] (TTSB) .... PCU
Southern Peru Copper Corp. [NYSE symbol] (SAG) .... PCU
Southern Peru Copper Corp. [Associated Press] (SAG) .... SPeruC
Southern Petroleum Corp. [Vancouver Stock Exchange symbol] .... SOU
Southern Philippines Federation of Labor .... SPFL
Southern Pine [Utility pole] [Telecommunications] (TEL) .... SP
Southern Pine Association [Later, SFPA] (EA) .... SPA
Southern Pine Inspection Bureau (EA) .... SPIB
Southern Pines [North Carolina] [Airport symbol] (AD) .... SOP
Southern Pines, NC [Location identifier FAA] (FAAL) .... SDZ
Southern Pines, NC [Location identifier FAA] (FAAL) .... SOP
Southern Pines, NC [AM radio station call letters] .... WEEB
Southern Pines, NC [FM radio station call letters] .... WIOZ
Southern Pines, NC [FM radio station call letters] (RBYB) .... WKQB
Southern Pines Public Library, Southern Pines, NC [Library symbol Library of Congress] (LCLS) .... NcSp
Southern Plains Range Research Station [Oklahoma State University] [Research center] (RCD) .... SPRRS
Southern Plastics Co. .... SOPLASCO
Southern Ports Foreign Committee, Chicago IL [STAC] .... SPC
Southern Ports Foreign Freight Committee .... SPFFC
Southern Poverty Law Center (EA) .... SPLC
Southern Prairie Library System, Altus, OK [Library symbol Library of Congress] (LCLS) .... OkAlS
Southern Prairie Library System, Altus, OK [OCLC symbol] (OCLC) .... OKP
Southern Pressure Treaters Association (EA) .... SPTA
Southern Procurement Division [Navy] .... SPD
Southern Production Program, Inc. .... SPPI
Southern Provinces Mounted Rifles [British military] (DMA) .... SPMR
Southern Public Administration Education Foundation (EA) .... SPAEF
Southern Pulpwood Conservation Association [Later, SFI] (EA) .... SPCA
Southern Railway Employees' Sangh [India] .... SRES
Southern Railway System [AAR code] .... SOU
Southern Railway System (MCD) .... SRS
Southern Regional Council (EA) .... SRC
Southern Regional Educational Board .... SREB
Southern Regional Examinations Board [Education] (AIE) .... SREB
Southern Regional Plant Introduction Station [University of Georgia] [Research center] (RCD) .... SRPIS
Southern Regional Research Center [Department of Agriculture] [New Orleans, LA] (GRD) .... SRRC
Southern Reporter [A publication] (DLA) .... S
Southern Reporter [A publication] (DLA) .... S Rep
Southern Reporter [National Reporter System] [A publication] (DLA) .... So
Southern Reporter [A publication] (DLA) .... So Rep
Southern Reporter [A publication] (DLA) .... So Repr
Southern Reporter [National Reporter System] [A publication] (DLA) .... South
Southern Reporter [A publication] (DLA) .... Southern
Southern Reporter [A publication] (DLA) .... Southern Rep
Southern Reporter, Second Series [West] [A publication] (AAGC) S2d
Southern Reporter, Second Series [West] [A publication] (AAGC) .... So 2d
Southern Reporter, Second Series [A publication] (DLA) .... So 2d
Southern Research Institute (AAG) .... SORI
Southern Research Institute .... SRI
Southern Research Institute, Birmingham, AL [Library symbol Library of Congress] (LCLS) .... ABSR
Southern Review [A publication] (BRI) .... South R
Southern Rhodesia [ANSI two-letter standard code Obsolete] (CNC) .... RH
Southern Rhodesia [ANSI three-letter standard code Obsolete] (CNC) .... RHO
Southern Rhodesia [Later, Zimbabwe] .... SR
Southern Rhodesia African National Congress .... SRANC
Southern Rhodesia Armoured Car Regiment [British military] (DMA) .... SRACR
Southern Rhodesia Artillery [British military] (DMA) .... SRA
Southern Rhodesia Corps of Military Police [British military] (DMA) .... SRCMP
Southern Rhodesia General Service Corps [British military] (DMA) .... SRGSC
Southern Rhodesia High Court Reports [A publication] (DLA) .... SR
Southern Rhodesia High Court Reports [1911-55] [A publication] (DLA) .... SR HCR
Southern Rhodesia Native Appeal Court Reports [A publication] (DLA) .... NA So Rhod
Southern Rhodesia Reports [A publication] (DLA) .... Burns-Begg
Southern Rhodesia Transport Corps [British military] (DMA) .... SRTC
Southern Rhodesian African Trade Union Congress .... SRATUC
Southern Rhodesian Trade Unions Congress .... SRTUC

Southern Rice Export Corp. (EA) .... SREC
Southern Riverina Advisory Service [Australia] .... SRAS
Southern Rock Lobster Zone [Australia] .... SRLZ
Southern Rock Lobster Zone (EERA) .... SRLZ
Southern Rock Mountain Trench [Geology] .... SRMT
Southern Rural Action, Inc. .... SRA
Southern San Luis Valley Railroad Co. [AAR code] .... SSLV
Southern Satellite Systems, Inc. [Tulsa, OK] [Telecommunications] (TSSD) .... SSS
Southern School of Pharmacy, Mercer University, Atlanta, GA [Library symbol Library of Congress] (LCLS) .... GAPh
Southern Seaplane, Inc. [ICAO designator] (FAAC) .... SSC
Southern Sec Life Ins [NASDAQ symbol] (TTSB) .... SSLI
Southern Security Life Insurance Co. [Associated Press] (SAG) .... SoScLfe
Southern Security Life Insurance Co. [NASDAQ symbol] (NQ) .... SSLI
Southern Seminary and Junior College [Virginia] .... SSJC
Southern Shark Fishery [Australia] .... SSF
Southern Shark Fishery Management Advisory Committee (EERA) .... SSFMAC
Southern Shark Fishery Management Plan [Australia] .... SSFMP
Southern Signal Corps School .... SSCS
Southern Society of Genealogists (EA) .... SSG
Southern Sotho [MARC language code Library of Congress] (LCCP) .... sso
Southern Speech Communication Association (EA) .... SSCA
Southern Star Resources Ltd. [Vancouver Stock Exchange symbol] .... SSL
Southern State College [Arkansas; South Dakota] .... SSC
Southern State College, Magnolia, AR [Library symbol Library of Congress] (LCLS) .... ArMagS
Southern State Community College, Sardinia, OH [Library symbol Library of Congress] (LCLS) .... OSarS
Southern State Community College, Wilmington, OH [OCLC symbol] (OCLC) .... OSC
Southern State Community College, Wilmington, OH [Library symbol Library of Congress] (LCLS) .... OWilmS
Southern States [MARC geographic area code Library of Congress] (LCCP) .... n-usu-
Southern States Industrial Council [Later, USIC] (EA) .... SSIC
Southern Student Organizing Committee [Defunct] .... SSOC
Southern Subtropical Indian Ocean .... SSIO
Southern Sudan Liberation Front (BJA) .... SSLF
Southern Sudanese Political Association [Sudan] [Political party] (MENA) .... SSPA
Southern Tablelands [New South Wales] [Region] (EERA) .... ST
Southern Technical Institute, Marietta, GA [OCLC symbol] (OCLC) .... GAS
Southern Technical Institute, Marietta, GA [Library symbol Library of Congress] (LCLS) .... GMarS
Southern Technology Applications Center [University of Florida] [Gainesville] [NASA] [Information service or system] (IID) .... STAC
Southern Television [British] (DI) .... STV
Southern Texas Law Journal [A publication] (DLA) .... So Tex LJ
Southern Textile Association (EA) .... STA
Southern Thoracic Surgical Association (EA) .... STSA
Southern Tier Library System [Library network] .... STLS
Southern Tier Library System, Corning, NY [Library symbol Library of Congress] (LCLS) .... NCorniS
Southern Tier Library System, Corning, NY [OCLC symbol] (OCLC) .... ZSA
Southern Tourist Board [British] (DCTA) .... STB
Southern Traffic League .... STL
Southern Transgressive Zone [Geology] .... STZ
Southern Transportation League (EA) .... STL
Southern Travel Directors Council .... STDC
Southern Troops and Landing Force .... STLF
Southern Union [NYSE symbol] (TTSB) .... SUG
Southern Union College [Wadley, AL] .... SUC
Southern Union Co. [Associated Press] (SAG) .... SoUCo
Southern Union Co. [Associated Press] (SAG) .... SoUnCo
Southern Union Co. [Associated Press] (SAG) .... SouUnCo
Southern Union Co. [NYSE symbol] (SAG) .... SUG
Southern Union Financing [Associated Press] (SAG) .... SoUnF
Southern Union Financing [NYSE symbol] (SAG) .... SUG
Southern Union Resources [Vancouver Stock Exchange symbol] .... SIO
Southern Universities Joint Board [for school examinations] [British] (DCTA) .... SUJB
Southern Universities' Management Services (AIE) .... SUMS
Southern Universities Nuclear Institute .... SUNI
Southern University (GAGS) .... So Univ
Southern University and Agricultural and Mechanical College (GAGS) .... So U & A&M C
Southern University at New Orleans, New Orleans, LA [Library symbol Library of Congress] (LCLS) .... LScS-N
Southern University at New Orleans, New Orleans, LA [OCLC symbol] (OCLC) .... LSU
Southern University in New Orleans .... SUNO
Southern University, Law Library, Baton Rouge, LA [OCLC symbol] (OCLC) .... LSC
Southern University, Library, Baton Rouge, LA [OCLC symbol] (OCLC) .... LSB
Southern University Press (DGA) .... SUP
Southern University Press Marketing Group [Acronym is pronounced "soupmug"] .... SUPMG
Southern University, Scotlandville, Baton Rouge, LA [Library symbol Library of Congress] (LCLS) .... LScS
Southern Utah State College, Cedar City, UT [Library symbol Library of Congress] (LCLS) .... UCS
Southern Utah State College, Cedar City, UT [OCLC symbol] (OCLC) .... UUA
Southern Victoria Historical Society, Perth-Andover, NB, Canada [Library symbol] [Library of Congress] (LCLS) .... CaNBPaSV

Southern Victoria Historical Society, Perth-Andover, New Brunswick [*Library symbol National Library of Canada*] (NLC) ... NBPASV
Southern Waste Information Exchange (GNE) ... SWIE
Southern Water Authority [*British*] (DCTA) ... SWA
Southern Water Resources Scientific Information Center [*Raleigh, NC*] ... SWRSIC
Southern Westchester BOCES School, Elmsford, NY [*Library symbol*] [*Library of Congress*] (LCLS) ... NElmsSW
Southern Wholesalers Association [*Atlanta, GA*] (EA) ... SWA
Southern Wisconsin Colony and Training School, Medical Library, Union Grove, WI [*Library symbol Library of Congress*] (LCLS) ... WUgSC
Southern Wood Seasoning Association ... SWSA
Southern Woodwork Association [*Defunct*] (EA) ... SWA
Southern Yellow Pine ... SYP
Southern Yemen (Aden) [*MARC geographic area code Library of Congress*] (LCCP) ... a-ys--
Southern Yemen (Aden) [*MARC country of publication code Library of Congress*] (LCCP) ... ys
Southern Yiddish (BJA) ... SY
Southernera Resources Ltd. [*Toronto Stock Exchange symbol*] ... SUF
Southern's Computer-Assisted Retrieval Service [*University of Southern Mississippi*] (OLDSS) ... SCARS
Southfield, MI [*FM radio station call letters*] ... WSHJ
Southfield Public Library, Southfield, MI [*Library symbol Library of Congress*] (LCLS) ... MiSf
SouthFirst Bancshares [*AMEX symbol*] (TTSB) ... SZB
Southfirst Bancshares, Inc. [*Associated Press*] (SAG) ... Sthfst
Southfirst Bancshares, Inc. [*Associated Press*] (SAG) ... SthfstB
Southfirst Bancshares, Inc. [*AMEX symbol*] (SAG) ... SZB
Southflight Aviation Ltd. [*New Zealand*] [*ICAO designator*] (FAAC) ... SFL
Southhold, NY [*FM radio station call letters*] ... WBAZ
Southington, CT [*AM radio station call letters*] ... WNTY
Southland Corp. [*NASDAQ symbol*] (TTSB) ... SLCM
[*The*] **Southland Corp.** [*NASDAQ symbol*] (NQ) ... SLCM
Southland Corp. [*Associated Press*] (SAG) ... SouthldCp
Southland Hussars [*British military*] (DMA) ... SH
Southlands Mining [*Vancouver Stock Exchange symbol*] ... SSM
Southmore Elementary School, Pasadena, TX [*Library symbol*] [*Library of Congress*] (LCLS) ... TxPSI
South'n Cal Ed 4.08% Pfd [*AMEX symbol*] (TTSB) ... SCEPrB
South'n Cal Ed 4.24% Pfd [*AMEX symbol*] (TTSB) ... SCEPrC
South'n Cal Ed 4.78% Pfd [*AMEX symbol*] (TTSB) ... SCEPrE
South'n Cal Ed 5.80% Pfd [*AMEX symbol*] (TTSB) ... SCEPrG
South'n Cal Ed 7.36% Pfd [*AMEX symbol*] (TTSB) ... SCEPrP
South'n Cal Gas cm6%PfdA vtg [*PC symbol*] (TTSB) ... SOUPr
Southold Free Library, Southold, NY [*Library symbol Library of Congress*] (LCLS) ... NSoo
Southpaw's International [*Defunct*] (EA) ... SI
Southport Aerospace Centre [*Canada*] [*FAA designator*] (FAAC) ... XPG
Southport, NC [*Location identifier FAA*] (FAAL) ... SUT
Southport, NC [*FM radio station call letters*] ... WSFM
Southport, NY [*FM radio station call letters*] ... WOKN
Southport-Brunswick County Library, Leland Branch Library, Leland, NC [*Library symbol Library of Congress*] (LCLS) ... NcSopS-L
Southport-Brunswick County Library, West Brunswick Branch Library, Shallotte, NC [*Library symbol Library of Congress*] (LCLS) ... NcSopS-W
Southshore Corp. [*NASDAQ symbol*] (SAG) ... SHSO
Southshore Corp. [*Associated Press*] (SAG) ... SouthCp
Southside ... STHSD
Southside Bancshares [*NASDAQ symbol*] (SAG) ... SBCO
Southside Bancshares [*Associated Press*] (SAG) ... SouBnc
Southside Hospital, Bay Shore, NY [*Library symbol Library of Congress*] (LCLS) ... NBsSH
Southside Virginia Community College, Christanna Campus, Alberta, VA [*Library symbol Library of Congress*] (LCLS) ... ViAlbS
Southside Virginia Community College, John H. Daniel Campus, Keysville, VA [*Library symbol Library of Congress*] (LCLS) ... ViKeS
South-Southeast ... SSE
South-Southwest ... SSW
SouthTrust Corp. [*NASDAQ symbol*] (NQ) ... SOTR
Southtrust Corp. [*Associated Press*] (SAG) ... Southtrst
Southview Elementary School, Braham, MN [*Library symbol*] [*Library of Congress*] (LCLS) ... MnBhSE
Southwall Technologies [*NASDAQ symbol*] (TTSB) ... SWTX
Southwall Technologies, Inc. [*Associated Press*] (SAG) ... Souwal
Southwall Technologies, Inc. [*NASDAQ symbol*] (NQ) ... SWTX
Southwark [*Borough of London*] (ROG) ... SWARK
Southwark [*England*] ... SWK
Southwark College [*London, England*] ... SC
Southwell [*City in England*] (ROG) ... SOUTHW
Southwest ... STHWST
Southwest ... SW
Southwest Academic Library Consortium [*Library network*] (IID) ... SWALC
Southwest Africa (MCD) ... SW
South-West Africa ... SW Af
Southwest Africa ... SWA
Southwest Airlines [*NYSE symbol*] (TTSB) ... LUV
Southwest Airlines [*ICAO designator*] (AD) ... NU
Southwest Airlines [*ICAO designator*] (AD) ... WN
Southwest Airlines Co. [*NYSE symbol*] (SPSG) ... LUV
Southwest Airlines Co. [*ICAO designator*] (FAAC) ... SWA
Southwest Airlines Co. [*Air carrier designation symbol*] ... SWAX
Southwest Airlines Co. [*Associated Press*] (SAG) ... SwstAirl
Southwest Alliance for Latin America [*Defunct*] (EA) ... SALA
Southwest Approach (DNAB) ... SWA
Southwest Area Monsoon Project (USDC) ... SWAMP
Southwest Arkansas Regional Library, Hope, AR [*Library symbol*] [*Library of Congress*] (LCLS) ... ArHo
Southwest Asia ... SWA
Southwest Asia Petroleum Distribution Operation Project [*Army*] ... SWAPDOP
Southwest Association of Indian Arts (BARN) ... SWIA
Southwest Athletic Conference (EA) ... SAC
Southwest Atlantic Fisheries Advisory Commission [*FAO*] ... SWAFAC
Southwest Atomic Energy Associates ... SAEA
Southwest Bancorp [*NASDAQ symbol*] (SAG) ... OKSB
Southwest Bancorp [*Associated Press*] (SAG) ... SwstBc
Southwest Bancorp [*Associated Press*] (SAG) ... SwstBcp
Southwest Bancshares [*NASDAQ symbol*] (TTSB) ... SWBI
Southwest Bancshares, Inc. [*Associated Press*] (SAG) ... SwBcsh
Southwest Bancshares, Inc. [*NASDAQ symbol*] (SAG) ... SWBI
Southwest Banks [*NASDAQ symbol*] (TTSB) ... SWBA
Southwest Banks, Inc. [*Associated Press*] (SAG) ... SthwestB
Southwest Banks, Inc. [*NASDAQ symbol*] (SAG) ... SWBA
Southwest Baptist College, Bolivar, MO [*OCLC symbol*] (OCLC) ... MOB
Southwest Baptist College, Bolivar, MO [*Library symbol Library of Congress*] (LCLS) ... MoBolS
Southwest Bcp 9.2% cm 'A'Pfd [*NASDAQ symbol*] (TTSB) ... OKSBP
Southwest Biomedical Research Institute [*Arizona State University*] [*Research center*] (RCD) ... SBRI
Southwest Border Regional Commission [*Department of Commerce*] ... SBRC
Southwest by South ... SWbS
Southwest by West ... SWbW
Southwest Center for Advanced Studies [*Later, University of Texas at Dallas*] ... SCAS
Southwest Center for Manufacturing Technology [*University of New Mexico*] [*Research center*] (RCD) ... SIMTC
Southwest City, MO [*FM radio station call letters*] ... KWMQ
Southwest Conference [*College sports*] ... SWC
Southwest Council of La Raza [*Mexican-American organization*] (EA) ... SWCLR
Southwest Division, Bureau of Yards and Docks [*Navy*] (MUGU) ... SOWESTDIVDOCKS
Southwest Division Naval Facilities Engineering Command ... DIRSOWESTDOCKS
Southwest Educational Development Laboratory (EA) ... SEDL
Southwest Educational Development Laboratory ... SWEDL
Southwest Electronic Exhibit ... SWEE
Southwest Experimental Fast Oxide Reactor [*Nuclear energy*] ... SEFOR
Southwest Fisheries Center [*La Jolla, CA*] [*Department of Commerce*] ... SWFC
Southwest Fisheries Science Center [*San Diego, CA*] ... SWFSC
Southwest Florida International Airport [*FAA*] (TAG) ... RSW
Southwest Foundation for Research and Education, San Antonio, TX [*Library symbol Library of Congress*] (LCLS) ... TxSaSFRE
Southwest Gas [*NYSE symbol*] (TTSB) ... SWX
Southwest Gas Capital I [*Associated Press*] (SAG) ... SwGas
Southwest Gas Corp. [*Associated Press*] (SAG) ... SwtGas
Southwest Gas Corp. [*NYSE symbol*] (SPSG) ... SWX
Southwest Georgia Financial Corp. [*AMEX symbol*] (SAG) ... SGB
Southwest Georgia Financial Corp. [*Associated Press*] (SAG) ... SwGAFn
Southwest Georgia Regional Library, Bainbridge, GA [*Library symbol Library of Congress*] (LCLS) ... GBaS
South-West Gold Corp. [*Vancouver Stock Exchange symbol*] ... SWG
Southwest Idaho Regional Library System [*Library network*] ... SIRLS
Southwest Institute for Research on Women [*University of Arizona*] [*Research center*] (RCD) ... SIROW
Southwest Michigan Library Cooperative [*Library network*] ... SMLC
Southwest Microfilm, Inc., El Paso, TX [*Library symbol Library of Congress*] (LCLS) ... SwM
Southwest Minnesota State College, Marshall, MN [*Library symbol Library of Congress*] (LCLS) ... MnMarS
Southwest Missouri State College, Springfield, MO [*Library symbol Library of Congress*] (LCLS) ... MoSpS
Southwest Missouri State University (PDAA) ... SMSU
Southwest Missouri State University (GAGS) ... Southwest Mo St U
Southwest Missouri State University, Springfield, MO [*OCLC symbol*] (OCLC) ... MOU
Southwest Museum, Braum Research Library, Los Angeles, CA [*Library symbol*] [*Library of Congress*] (LCLS) ... CLSM-B
Southwest Museum, Los Angeles, CA [*Library symbol Library of Congress*] (LCLS) ... CLSM
Southwest National [*NASDAQ symbol*] (TTSB) ... SWPA
Southwest National Corp. [*Greensburg, PA*] [*NASDAQ symbol*] (NQ) ... SWPA
Southwest National Corp. [*Associated Press*] (SAG) ... SwstNat
Southwest New Jersey Consortium for Health Information Service, Voorhees, NJ [*OCLC symbol*] (OCLC) ... NCI
Southwest New Jersey Consortium for Health Information Services [*Library network*] ... SWNJ
Southwest Ohio Regional Data Center [*University of Cincinnati*] [*Research center*] (RCD) ... SORDC
Southwest Pacific ... SWP
Southwest Pacific Area [*World War II*] ... SWPA
Southwest Pacific Command [*Navy*] ... SOWESPAC
Southwest Pacific Command [*Navy*] (DNAB) ... SOWESTPACCOM
Southwest Pacific Command [*Navy*] ... SWPC
Southwest Pacific Force [*Later, Southwest Pacific Command*] [*Navy*] ... SWPF
Southwest Pacific Island Arc [*Oceanography*] ... SWPIA
Southwest Parks and Monuments Association (EA) ... SPMA
Southwest Placement Association (AEBS) ... SPA
Southwest Placement Association (AEBS) ... SWPA
Southwest Power Pool [*Regional power council*] ... SPP
Southwest Power Pool [*Regional power council*] (NRCH) ... SWPP
Southwest RADAR Balloon [*for illegal drug interdiction*] ... SOWRBALL

Southwest Radio Church [*An association*] ... SRC
Southwest Realty Ltd. [*Later, Southwestern Property Trade*] **AM** (SPSG) ... SWL
Southwest Regional Educational Laboratory (AEBS) ... SREL
Southwest Regional Laboratory [*Research center*] (RCD) ... SWRL
Southwest Regional Laboratory for Educational Research and Development ... SWRL
Southwest Regional Laboratory for Educational Research and Development, Los Alamitos, CA [*Library symbol Library of Congress*] (LCLS) ... CLoaS
Southwest Regional Library Service System [*Library network*] ... SWRLSS
Southwest Regional Library Service System, Durango, CO [*OCLC symbol*] (OCLC) ... CDA
Southwest Regional Library System [*Library network*] ... SWIRLS
Southwest Regional Office for Spanish Speaking (EA) ... SWROSS
Southwest Research and Information Center (EA) ... SRIC
Southwest Research Corp. ... SRC
Southwest Research Institute ... SRI
Southwest Research Institute, San Antonio, TX [*Library symbol Library of Congress*] (LCLS) ... TxSaSR
Southwest Review [*A publication*] (BRI) ... SWR
Southwest School, Grand Rapids, MN [*Library symbol*] [*Library of Congress*] (LCLS) ... MnGrSS
Southwest Sea Frontier [*Navy*] ... SOWESSEAFRON
Southwest Securities Group [*NASDAQ symbol*] (SPSG) ... SWST
Southwest Securities Group [*Associated Press*] (SAG) ... SwstSec
Southwest Securities Grp [*NASDAQ symbol*] (TTSB) ... SWST
Southwest Semiconductor and Electronics Exposition (TSPED) ... SSE
Southwest Spanish Mustang Association (EA) ... SSMA
Southwest State University, Marshall, MN [*OCLC symbol*] (OCLC) ... MNV
Southwest Tech [*Vancouver Stock Exchange symbol*] ... STW
Southwest Technical College, Granite Falls, MN [*Library symbol*] [*Library of Congress*] (LCLS) ... MnGfTC
Southwest Technical College, Pipestone, MN [*Library symbol*] [*Library of Congress*] (LCLS) ... MnPpTC
Southwest Texas Junior College, Uvalde, TX [*Library symbol Library of Congress*] (LCLS) ... TxUvS
Southwest Texas State University (GAGS) ... Southwest Tex St U
Southwest Texas State University, San Marcos, TX [*OCLC symbol*] (OCLC) ... TXI
Southwest Texas State University, San Marcos, TX [*Library symbol Library of Congress*] (LCLS) ... TxSmS
Southwest (United States) [*MARC geographic area code Library of Congress*] (LCCP) ... n-ust-
Southwest United States ... SWUS
Southwest Universities Computer Network (NITA) ... SWUCNET
Southwest University Libraries Systems Cooperative Project (NITA) ... SWULSCP
Southwest Voter Registration Education Project (EA) ... SVREP
Southwest Voter Research Institute [*San Antonio, TX*] (CROSS) ... SVRI
South-West Water Authority [*British*] (DCTA) ... SWWA
Southwest Water Co. [*Associated Press*] (SAG) ... SwWatr
Southwest Water Co. [*La Puente, CA*] [*NASDAQ symbol*] (NQ) ... SWWC
Southwest Wisconsin Library System, Fennimore, WI [*OCLC symbol*] (OCLC) ... WSW
Southwestbound [*ICAO designator*] (FAAC) ... SWB
Southwestern ... STHWSTN
Southwestern American Indian Society [*Later, SAISR*] (EA) ... SAIS
Southwestern and Rocky Mountain Division [*AAAS division*] ... SWARM
Southwestern Assemblies of God College, Waxahachie, TX [*Library symbol Library of Congress*] (LCLS) ... TxWaS
Southwestern at Memphis, Memphis, TN [*Library symbol Library of Congress*] (LCLS) ... TMSC
Southwestern at Memphis, Memphis, TN [*OCLC symbol*] (OCLC) ... TWS
Southwestern Automated Clearing House Association ... SWACHA
Southwestern Baptist Theological Seminary, Fort Worth, TX [*OCLC symbol*] (OCLC) ... TSW
Southwestern Baptist Theological Seminary, Fort Worth, TX [*Library symbol Library of Congress*] (LCLS) ... TxFS
Southwestern Christian College, Terrell, TX [*Library symbol Library of Congress*] (LCLS) ... TxTerS
Southwestern College, Winfield, KS [*OCLC symbol*] (OCLC) ... KKX
Southwestern College, Winfield, KS [*Library symbol Library of Congress*] (LCLS) ... KWS
Southwestern Community Unit, School District 9, Piasa, IL [*Library symbol Library of Congress*] (LCLS) ... IPiaSD
Southwestern Connecticut Library Council [*Library network*] ... SWLC
Southwestern Connecticut Library Council, Bridgeport, CT [*OCLC symbol*] (OCLC) ... SWC
Southwestern Cooperative Educational Laboratory ... SWCEL
Southwestern Division [*Army Corps of Engineers*] ... SWD
South-Western Educational Publishing [*International Thomson Publishing Co.*] ... S-W
Southwestern Energy [*NYSE symbol*] (TTSB) ... SWN
Southwestern Energy Co. [*NYSE symbol*] (SPSG) ... SWN
Southwestern Energy Co. [*Associated Press*] (SAG) ... SwnEnrg
Southwestern Federation of Geological Societies ... SFGS
Southwestern Freight Bureau ... SWFB
Southwestern Freight Bureau, St. Louis MO [*STAC*] ... SFB
Southwestern Indian Polytechnic Institute [*New Mexico*] ... SIPI
Southwestern Industrial Traffic League (EA) ... SITL
Southwestern Industrial Traffic League (EA) ... SWITL
Southwestern Irrigated Cotton Growers Association ... SWIG
Southwestern Law Journal and Reporter [*A publication*] (DLA) ... Southw LJ
Southwestern Law Review [*A publication*] (DLA) ... SWL Rev
Southwestern Legal Foundation (DLA) ... SLF
Southwestern Legal Foundation (EA) ... SWLF
Southwestern Library Association (AEBS) ... SLA
Southwestern Library Association ... SWLA
Southwestern Library Interstate Cooperative Endeavor ... SLICE
Southwestern Life Corp. [*Formerly, ICH Corp.*] [*AMEX symbol*] (SAG) ... SLC
Southwestern Life Corp. [*Formerly, ICH Corp.*] [*Associated Press*] (SAG) ... SwnLfe
Southwestern Life Corp. [*Formerly, ICH Corp.*] [*Associated Press*] (SAG) ... SwnLife
Southwestern Livestock and Forage Research Station [*Oklahoma State University*] [*Research center*] (RCD) ... SLAFRS
Southwestern Manitoba Regional Library, Melita, Manitoba [*Library symbol National Library of Canada*] (NLC) ... MMES
Southwestern Manitoba Regional Library, Melita, MB, Canada [*Library symbol Library of Congress*] (LCLS) ... CaMMeS
Southwestern Monuments Association [*Later, SPMA*] (EA) ... SWMA
Southwestern Motor Freight Bureau ... SWMFB
Southwestern Motor Freight Bureau, Dallas TX [*STAC*] ... SWB
Southwestern Ohio Rural Libraries [*Library network*] ... SWORL
Southwestern Ohio Rural Library, Wilmington, OH [*Library symbol Library of Congress*] (LCLS) ... OWilm-O
Southwestern Oklahoma State University (GAGS) ... Southwestern Okla St U
Southwestern Oklahoma State University ... SWOSU
Southwestern Order Retrieval and Distribution [*Southwest Bell Telephone Co.*] ... SORD
Southwestern Oregon Community College, Coos Bay, OR [*Library symbol Library of Congress*] (LCLS) ... OrCbS
Southwestern Oregon Community College, Coos Bay, OR [*OCLC symbol*] (OCLC) ... SWO
Southwestern Peanut Growers Association (EA) ... SPGA
Southwestern Peanut Shellers Association (EA) ... SWPSA
Southwestern Political Science Quarterly [*A publication*] (DLA) ... SW Pol Sci Q
Southwestern Power Administration [*Department of Energy*] ... SPA
Southwestern Power Administration [*Department of Energy*] ... SWPA
Southwestern Property Trust, Inc. [*Later, South West Property Trust*] [*NYSE symbol*] (SPSG) ... SWP
Southwestern Property Trust, Inc. [*Associated Press*] (SAG) ... SwPropT
Southwestern Psychological Association (IAA) ... SPA
Southwestern Psychological Association (MCD) ... SWPA
Southwestern Public Service Co. [*NYSE symbol*] (SPSG) ... SPS
Southwestern Public Service Co. [*Associated Press*] (SAG) ... SwtPS
Southwestern Public Service Co., Amarillo, TX [*Library symbol Library of Congress*] (LCLS) ... TxAmSP
Southwestern PubSv [*NYSE symbol*] (TTSB) ... SPS
Southwestern Radiological Health Laboratory [*HEW*] ... SRHL
Southwestern Radiological Health Laboratory [*HEW*] ... SWRHL
Southwestern Railway [*British*] (ROG) ... SWR
Southwestern Regional Library, Silver City, NM [*Library symbol Library of Congress*] (LCLS) ... NmScSW
Southwestern Regional Library, Windsor, ON, Canada [*Library symbol Library of Congress*] (LCLS) ... CaOWS
Southwestern Regional Library, Windsor, Ontario [*Library symbol Obsolete National Library of Canada*] (NLC) ... OWS
Southwestern Regional Manpower Advisory Committee [*Terminated, 1974*] [*Department of Labor*] (EGAO) ... SWRMPAC
Southwestern Research Institute [*San Antonio, TX*] [*Research center*] ... SWRI
Southwestern Research Institute, Houston, TX [*Library symbol Library of Congress*] (LCLS) ... TxHSR
Southwestern State College, Weatherford, OK [*Library symbol Library of Congress*] (LCLS) ... OkWeaT
Southwestern Technical Institute, Sylva, NC [*Library symbol Library of Congress*] (LCLS) ... NcSyS
Southwestern Townships [*South Africa*] ... SOWETO
Southwestern Union College, Keene, TX [*Library symbol Library of Congress*] (LCLS) ... TxKeeS
Southwestern Union for the Study of Great Religions (EA) ... SUSGR
Southwestern University, Georgetown, TX [*Library symbol Library of Congress*] (LCLS) ... TxGeoS
Southwestern University, Georgetown, TX [*OCLC symbol*] (OCLC) ... TXX
Southwestern University School of Law (GAGS) ... Southwestern U Law
Southwestern University School of Law (DLA) ... SWUSL
Southwestern University, School of Law, Los Angeles, CA [*Library symbol Library of Congress*] (LCLS) ... CLSL
Southwest-West Central Educational Cooperative Service Unit, Montevideo, MN [*Library symbol*] [*Library of Congress*] (LCLS) ... MnMovSEC
Southwire Co., Carrollton, GA [*Library symbol Library of Congress*] (LCLS) ... GCarrS
Southwood College, Salemburg, NC [*Library symbol Library of Congress*] (LCLS) ... NcSbP
Souvenir ... SUV
Souvenir and Novelty Trade Association (EA) ... SANTA
Souvenir Card Collectors Society (EA) ... SCCS
Souvenir China Collectors Society (EA) ... SCCS
Souvenir Sheet [*Philately*] ... SS
Sovdeborg [*Sweden ICAO location identifier*] (ICLI) ... ESMI
Sovereign ... SOV
Sovereign Bancorp [*NASDAQ symbol*] (TTSB) ... SVRN
Sovereign Bancorp 6.25% Cv Pfd [*NASDAQ symbol*] (TTSB) ... SVRNP
Sovereign Bancorp, Inc. [*Associated Press*] (SAG) ... SovBcp
Sovereign Bancorp, Inc. [*NASDAQ symbol*] (NQ) ... SVRN
Sovereign Base Area (DNAB) ... SBA
Sovereign Grand Inspector-General [*Freemasonry*] (ROG) ... SGIG
Sovereign Hospitaller Order of Saint John (EA) ... HOSJ
Sovereign Hospitaller Order of St. John (EA) ... SHOSJ
Sovereign Military Order [*British*] ... SMO

Sovereign Military Order of Malta (EA) .... SMOM
Sovereign Order of Saint John of Jerusalem (EA) .... OSJ
Sovereigns [Monetary unit] [Obsolete British] .... SOVS
Sovetski Zhelezno-Dorozhni [Soviet railways] [Former USSR] .... SZD
Sovetsky [Former USSR ICAO location identifier] (ICLI) .... USTW
Sovetsky Rudnik [Former USSR ICAO location identifier] (ICLI) .... UNKO
Sovetskyaya Kolonia [Soviet Colony] .... SK
Soviet .... SOV
Soviet Academy of Sciences .... SAS
Soviet Air Defense .... SAD
Soviet Air Defense Aviation (MCD) .... APVO
Soviet Air Demonstration .... SAD
Soviet Air Force .... SoAF
Soviet Air Forces (DOMA) .... SAF
Soviet Amphibious Armored Reconnaissance Vehicle (MCD) .... BRDM
Soviet Antarctic Expedition .... SAE
Soviet Antarctic Expedition [1955-] .... SovAE
Soviet Breeder Reactor .... SBR
Soviet Bureau of Information .... SBI
Soviet Central Asia [MARC geographic area code Library of Congress] (LCCP) .... e-uro-
Soviet Cost Analysis Model [CIA] .... SCAM
Soviet Extended Planning Annex (MCD) .... SEPA
Soviet Far East (FEA) .... SFE
Soviet Government Purchasing Commission [World War II] .... SGPC
Soviet Hydrometeorological Service .... SHS
Soviet Independent Business Directory [A publication] .... SIBD
Soviet Intelligence Services .... SIS
Soviet Jewry Law Review [A publication] (DLA) .... Soviet Jewry L Rev
Soviet Jewry Legal Advocacy Center (EA) .... SJLAC
Soviet Jewry Research Bureau (EA) .... SJRB
Soviet Jewry Solidarity Day (BJA) .... SJSD
Soviet Long-Range Air (MCD) .... SLRA
Soviet Mediterranean Squadron [NATO] (NATG) .... SOVMEDRON
Soviet Military Administration .... SMA
Soviet Military Liaison Mission [Army] .... SMLM
Soviet Military Power [A publication 1981-1991; changed in 1992 to Forces in Transition] (DOMA) .... SMP
Soviet Missile Range Instrumented Ship (CINC) .... SMRIS
Soviet Mission to the United Nations (LAIN) .... SMUN
Soviet Mission to the United States (WDAA) .... SMUS
Soviet Narodnykh Komissarov [Council of People's Commissars] [Former USSR] (LAIN) .... SNK
Soviet Narodnykh Komissarov [Council of People's Commissars] [Former USSR] (LAIN) .... SOVNARKOM
Soviet Naval Air Force .... SNAF
Soviet Naval Aviation .... SNA
Soviet Naval Infantry (DOMA) .... SNI
Soviet Naval Interdiction Possibilities, Europe .... SNIPE
Soviet News Bureau .... SNB
Soviet Nuclear Artillery Projectile (MCD) .... SNAP
Soviet Occupied Zone (NATG) .... SOZ
Soviet Ocean Surveillance System (MCD) .... SOSS
Soviet Oceanographic Surveillance (MCD) .... SOS
Soviet Order of Battle (DOMA) .... SOB
Soviet Orientation Team (MCD) .... SOT
Soviet Science and Technology [IFI/Plenum Data Corp.] [Information service or system] (IID) .... SST
Soviet Sciences in the News [A publication] .... SSN
Soviet Ship Vulnerability Program .... SSVP
Soviet Socialist Republic .... SSR
Soviet Space Event Support Ships (CINC) .... SSESS
Soviet Statutes and Decisions [A publication] (DLA) .... Soviet Stat & Dec
Soviet Tactical Nuclear Study (MCD) .... STANS
Soviet Union [The USSR] .... SU
Soviet Union Airborne Early Warning and Interceptor Control System (MCD) .... SUAEWICS
Soviet Union Airborne Warning and Control System (MCD) .... SUAWACS
Soviet Year-Book of International Law [A publication] (DLA) .... Soviet YB Int'l L
Soviet Zone Germany (NATG) .... SZG
Soviet Zone of Occupation of Germany (NATG) .... SZOG
Soviet-American Committee on Health Cooperation .... SACHC
Soviet-American Gallium Experiment [Particle physics] .... SAGE
Soviet-American Gas and Aerosol [Experiment] (USDC) .... SAGA
Soviet-American Trade Association .... SATRA
Sovran Bank Corp. Library, Norfolk, VA [Library symbol] [Library of Congress] (LCLS) .... ViNSo
Sovran Self Storage [NYSE symbol] (TTSB) .... SSS
Sovran Self Storage, Inc. [Associated Press] (SAG) .... SovranSS
Sovran Self Storage, Inc. [Associated Press] (SAG) .... SoVrnSS
Sovran Self Storage, Inc. [NYSE symbol] (SAG) .... SSS
Sowbane Mosaic Virus .... SoMV
Sowind Air Ltd. [Canada ICAO designator] (FAAC) .... SOW
Sowjetische Aktiengesellschaften [Soviet Corporations] [Germany] .... SAG
Sowjetische Besatzungszone [Soviet Occupation Zone] [East Germany] .... SBZ
Sowjetische Kontrollkommission .... SKK
Sowjetische Militaeradministration .... SMAD
Sowthistle Yellow Vein Virus .... SYVV
Soy Base Formula [Nutrition] .... SBF
Soy Protein Council (EA) .... SPC
Soy Protein Flour [Food technology] .... SPF
Soy Protein Hydrolyzate .... SPH
Soy Protein Isolate [Food technology] .... SPI
Soya Food Research Council .... SFRC
Soybean [Medicine] (DMAA) .... SB

Soybean Agglutinin [Immunology] .... SBA
Soybean Corn Silage (OA) .... SCS
Soybean Council of America [Defunct] .... SBCA
Soybean Council of America [Defunct] (EA) .... SCA
Soybean Cyst Nematode [Botany] .... SCN
Soybean Dwarf Virus [Plant pathology] .... SDV
Soybean Dwarf Virus [Plant pathology] .... SOYDV
Soybean Growers of America (EA) .... SGA
Soybean Insect Research Information Center [University of Illinois] [Champaign, IL] .... SIRIC
Soybean Integrated Crop Management Model .... SICM
Soybean Lecithin [Biochemistry] .... SBL
Soybean Mosaic Virus [Plant pathology] .... SMV
Soybean Mosaic Virus [Plant pathology] .... SOYMV
Soybean Oil .... SBO
Soybean Oil Meal .... SBOM
Soybean Research Advisory Institute [Terminated, 1984] (EGAO) .... SRAI
Soybean Trypsin Inhibition [Biochemistry] .... STI
Soybean (Trypsin) Inhibitor [Biochemistry] .... SBI
Soybean Trypsin Inhibitor .... SBTI
Soycrafters Association of North America (EA) .... SANA
Soyfoods Association of North America (EA) .... SANA
Soyo [Angola] [ICAO location identifier] (ICLI) .... FNSO
Soyo [Angola] [Airport symbol] (OAG) .... SZA
Soysal Adelet Partisi [Social Justice Party] [Turkish Cyprus] [Political party] (PPE) .... SAP
Soyuz Sovetskikh Sotsialisticheskikh Respublik [Union of Soviet Socialist Republics] .... SSSR
Sozial Demokratesch Partei [Social Democratic Party] [Luxembourg] [Political party] (PPE) .... SDP
Sozialdemokratische Partei der Schweiz [Social Democratic Party of Switzerland] [Political party] (PPE) .... SPS
Sozialdemokratische Partei Deutschlands [Social Democratic Party of Germany] [West Germany] .... SPD
Sozialdemokratische Partei Oesterreichs [Social Democratic Party of Austria] [Political party] .... SPO
Sozialdemokratische Partei Suedtirols [Social Democratic Party of South Tirol] [Political party] (PPE) .... SPS
Soziale Buergerpartei [Social Citizen's Party] [Germany Political party] (PPW) .... SBP
Soziale Demokratische Union [Social Democratic Union] [Germany Political party] (PPW) .... SDU
Sozialgericht [Social Security Court] [German] (ILCA) .... SG
Sozialistische Volksorganisation [Socialist National Community] [Lithuania] [Political party] (PPE) .... SOVOG
Sozialistische Einheitspartei Deutschlands [Socialist Unity Party of Germany] [Political party] (PPW) .... SED
Sozialistische Einheitspartei Westberlins [Socialist Unity Party of West Berlin] [Germany Political party] (PPW) .... SEW
Sozialistische Partei Oesterreichs [Socialist Party of Austria] .... SPOE
Sozialistische Reichspartei [Socialist Reich Party] [Germany Political party] (PPE) .... SRP
Sozialistischer Deutscher Studentenbund [Student political organization] [Germany] .... SDS
Sozialwissenschaftliche Dokumentation [Social Sciences Documentation Center] [Vienna Chamber of Labor] [Information service or system] (IID) .... SOWIDOK
Sozialwissenschaftliche Experten und Gutachter [Social Science Experts] [NOMOS Datapool Database] (IID) .... SPEX
Sozialwissenschaftliches LiteraturInformationssystem [Database] [Informationszentrum Sozialwissenschaften Social Sciences Literature Information System] [German] [Information service or system] (CRD) .... SOLIS
Soziolistische Linheitspartei Deutschlands [Socialist Unity Party] [German] (BARN) .... SED
Spa/La Sauveniere [Belgium ICAO location identifier] (ICLI) .... EBSP
Space (IAA) .... S
Space [Crocheting] .... sp
Space .... SP
Space (ECII) .... SP
Space .... SPC
Space Activity Suit .... SAS
Space Adaptation Syndrome [NASA] .... SAS
Space Adaptation Syndrome Experiment [Pronounced "Sassy"] [Space shuttle experiment developed in Canada] .... SASE
Space Aeronautics [A publication] .... SA
Space Age Microcircuits (IAA) .... SAM
Space Age News (AAG) .... SAN
Space Agency Forum on International Space Year .... SAFISY
Space Air Relay Communications (MCD) .... SPARC
Space Air Vehicle (IAA) .... SAV
Space Allocation and Reservation Program (MCD) .... SARP
Space Allocation Requirement Procedures (MCD) .... SARP
Space Analyst Intervention Display System (MCD) .... SAIDS
Space and Astronautics Orientation Course (NG) .... SAOC
Space and Ballistic Missile System Training Equipment (SAA) .... SBMSTE
Space and Communications Group [of General Motors Corp.] .... SCG
Space and Component Log .... SACL
Space and Data Tracking Network (SSD) .... SDTN
Space and Earth Science Advisory Committee [NASA] .... SESAC
Space and Electronic Warfare (DOMA) .... SEW
Space and Flight Equipment Association (IAA) .... SFEA
Space and Flight Equipment Association (IAA) .... SAFEA
Space and Information System .... SIS
Space and Information Systems Division [NASA] .... SID
Space and Missile Systems Center [Air Force] (AAGC) .... SMC

Space and Missile Systems Office [*Air Force*] ... SAMSO
Space and Missile Systems Organization [*Merger of Ballistic Systems Division and Space Systems Division*] [*Air Force*] ... SAMSO
Space and Missile Systems Organization Regulation [*Later, SDR*] [*Air Force*] (NASA) ... SAMSOR
Space and Missile Test and Evaluation Center [*Air Force*] (DOMA) ... SAMTEC
Space and Missile Test Center [*Air Force*] ... SAMTEC
Space and Missile Test Center Detachment 1 [*Patrick Air Force Base, FL*] ... SAMTEC/DET 1
Space and Missile Test Center Manual [*Air Force*] (MCD) ... SAMTECM
Space and Missile Test Organization [*Vandenberg Air Force Base, CA*] [*Air Force*] ... SAMTO
Space and Naval Warfare Systems Command [*Washington, DC Navy*] (GRD) ... SPAWAR
Space and Power ... SP
Space and Range RADAR [*NASA*] ... SPANDAR
Space and Reentry System (IAA) ... SRS
Space and Strategic Defense Command [*Army*] (RDA) ... SSDC
Space and Tactical System Corp. (MCD) ... SPACETAC
Space and Unexplained Celestial Events Research Society [*Defunct*] (EA) ... SAUCERS
Space and Upper Atmospheric Research Committee [*Pakistan*] ... SUPARCO
Space Antennae Diversity [*Telecommunications*] (TEL) ... SAD
Space Applications Advisory Committee ... SAAC
Space Applications Board [*National Academy of Engineering*] ... SAB
Space Assemble and Maintenance (SSD) ... SAM
Space Assembly, Maintenance, and Servicing (SSD) ... SAMS
Space Astronomy Laboratory [*University of Florida*] [*Research center*] (RCD) ... SAL
Space Automation and Robotics Center [*University of Michigan*] [*Research center*] (RCD) ... SpARC
Space Available (ADA) ... S/A
Space Available Mail [*Military*] (AABC) ... SAM
Space Available Travel ... SAT
Space Bandwidth Product (IAA) ... SBW
Space Base [*NASA*] (KSC) ... SB
Space Biomedical Research Institute [*Houston, TX*] [*NASA*] ... SBRI
Space Biospheres Venture [*Commercial firm*] (ECON) ... SBV
Space Booster (SAA) ... SB
Space Borne Data-Conditioning System (IAA) ... SDCS
Space Branch (IAA) ... SB
Space Business Development Operation (AAG) ... SBDO
Space Cabin Environment [*Skylab*] [*NASA*] ... SCE
Space Cabin Simulator (IEEE) ... SCS
Space Capsule (IAA) ... SC
Space Capsule Regulator and Monitor ... SCRAM
Space Cargo Handler and Manipulator for Orbital Operations ... SCHMOO
Space Chamber Analyzer - Thermal Environment [*NASA*] ... SCATE
Space Chamber Complex (MCD) ... SCC
Space Character [*Keyboard*] (AAG) ... SP
Space Charge Atomizing Precipitaters (KSC) ... SCAP
Space Charge Grid ... SCG
Space Charge Limited ... SCL
Space Charge Limited Diode (IAA) ... SCLD
Space Charge Limited Thin Film Triode (DICI) ... SCLTFT
Space Charge Recombination (IAA) ... SCR
Space Charge Wave (PDAA) ... SCW
Space Checkout and Launch Equipment ... SCALE
Space Combat Tactics (SAA) ... SCT
Space Combat Weapon System (IAA) ... SCWS
Space Command [*Military*] ... SPACECOM
Space Command and Control System ... SPACCS
Space Command Station (AAG) ... SCS
Space Communication System (IAA) ... SCS
Space Communications ... SPACECOM
Space Communications and Tracking ... SCAT
Space Communications Corp. [*Japan*] (ECON) ... SSC
Space Communications Division [*Military*] ... SPCD
Space Communications for Orbiting Relay Equipment (MCD) ... SCORE
Space Communications Network ... SPAN
Space Communications Station Operation ... SCSO
Space Component Lifetime (SSD) ... SCL
Space Construction Automated Fabrication Experiment Definition Study (MCD) ... SCAFEDS
Space Control ... SPACON
Space Control Center (DOMA) ... SPACC
Space Control Document [*NASA*] (KSC) ... SCD
Space Control Station ... SCC
Space Council [*National Aeronautics and Space Administration*] (USDC) ... SC
Space Council [*NASA*] [*Marine science*] (OSRA) ... SC
Space Data Corp. ... SDC
Space Defense Center [*Military*] (MCD) ... SDC
Space Defense Command and Control System (MCD) ... SPADCCS
Space Defense Corp. (MCD) ... SDC
Space Defense Operations Center [*DoD*] ... SPADOC
Space Defense Project Office [*AMC*] ... SDPO
Space Defense System (AAG) ... SDS
Space Defense Systems Program (DNAB) ... SDSP
Space Detection and Tracking (IAA) ... SDT
Space Detection and Tracking System [*Military*] ... SPADATS
Space Detection and Tracking System Center [*Air Force*] ... SPADATSC
Space Detection and Tracking System Improved [*Air Force*] (IAA) ... SPADATSIMP
Space Detection and Tracking System Sensors [*Air Force*] ... SPADATSS
Space Detection Network [*Military*] ... SPADETS
Space Development Conference ... SPC
Space Development Corp. ... SDC
Space Disturbance Forecast Center [*Environmental Science Services Administration*] (IEEE) ... SDFC
Space Disturbances Laboratory [*Boulder, CO*] ... SDL
Space Division [*Los Angeles, CA*] [*Air Force*] ... SD
Space Division Evaluator [*NASA*] (NASA) ... SDE
Space Division Multiple Access ... SDMA
Space Division Multiple Access/Spacecraft Switched-Time Division Multiple Access (PDAA) ... SDMA/SS-TDMA
Space Division Multiplexing [*Physics*] ... SDM
Space Division Regulation [*NASA*] (NASA) ... SDR
Space Division Shuttle Simulator [*NASA*] (NASA) ... SDSS
Space Division Switching [*Telecommunications*] ... SDS
Space Documentation Service [*NASA/ESRO*] (DIT) ... SDS
Space Dynamics Laboratories [*Utah State University*] [*Research center*] (RCD) ... SDL
Space Education Foundation [*Later, AEF*] ... SEF
Space Electric Power Office [*AEC*] ... SEPO
Space Electric Ramjet [*Air Force*] ... SERJ
Space Electric [*or Electronic*] **Rocket** (DNAB) ... SER
Space Electric [*or Electronic*] **Rocket Test** ... SERT
Space Electronic Package ... SEP
Space Electronic Security Division [*Military*] ... SESD
Space Electronics and Telemetry (MCD) ... SET
Space Electronics Detection System (KSC) ... SEDS
Space Electronics Support Equipment (MCD) ... SESE
Space Emergency Reentry Vehicle [*NASA*] ... SERV
Space Energy Association (EA) ... SEA
Space Engagement Node ... SEN
Space Engineering Document [*NASA*] (IAA) ... SED
Space Environment Center [*Marine science*] (OSRA) ... SEC
Space Environment Center ... SEC
Space Environment Division [*NASA*] ... SED
Space Environment Laboratory [*Boulder, CO*] [*Department of Commerce National Oceanic and Atmospheric Administration*] ... SEL
Space Environment Laboratory Data Acquisition and Display System [*National Oceanic and Atmospheric Administration*] ... SELDADS
Space Environment Laboratory Simulation [*NASA*] ... SELS
Space Environment Monitor [*NASA*] ... SEM
Space Environment Monitor System [*NASA*] (NASA) ... SEMS
Space Environment Services Center [*Boulder, CO*] [*National Oceanic and Atmospheric Administration*] (KSC) ... SESC
Space Environment Simulation Laboratory [*NASA*] ... SESL
Space Environment Simulator [*NASA*] ... SES
Space Environment Test Division [*NASA*] ... SETD
Space Environmental Chamber (AAG) ... SEC
Space Environmental Control System (AAG) ... SECS
Space Environmental Experiment [*NASA*] (IAA) ... SEE
Space Environmental Facility (SAA) ... SEF
Space Environmental Research Facility ... SERF
Space Environmental Support System ... SESS
Space Equivalent (IAA) ... SE
Space Erectable Structure ... SES
Space Experiment on Relativistic Theories of Gravitation (PDAA) ... SERTOG
Space Experiment Support Program (MCD) ... SESP
Space Experimental Satellite Program [*NASA*] (SSD) ... SESP
Space Experiments with Particle Accelerators [*Spacelab mission*] ... SEPAC
Space Exploration (AAG) ... SE
Space Exploration Initiative [*NASA*] ... SEI
Space Exploration Program Council [*NASA*] ... SEPC
Space Exposed Experiment Developed for Students ... SEEDS
Space Filler [*Philately*] ... SF
Space Flight [*A publication*] ... SF
Space Flight Acceleration Profile Simulator [*NASA*] ... SFAPS
Space Flight Center [*NASA*] ... SFC
Space Flight Ground Environment Panel [*NASA*] (KSC) ... SFGEP
Space Flight Instrumentation (AAG) ... SFI
Space Flight Operations [*NASA*] ... SFO
Space Flight Operations Complex [*NASA*] ... SFOC
Space Flight Operations Director [*NASA*] ... SFOD
Space Flight Operations Facility [*NASA*] ... SFOF
Space Flight Operations Memorandum [*NASA*] ... SFOM
Space Flight Operations Plan [*NASA*] ... SFOP
Space Flight Systems (SAA) ... SFS
Space Flight Test System (MCD) ... SFTS
Space Flight Tracking and Data Network [*Formerly, STADAN*] [*NASA*] ... STDN
Space Flyer Unit (SSD) ... SFU
Space Forecast Center [*Air Force*] (GFGA) ... SFC
Space Frame and Unit Integrating System ... SF/UIS
Space Frame RADOME ... SFR
Space Frequency Equivalence (MCD) ... SFE
Space Full Time Equivalent (AIE) ... SFTE
Space Futures Society (EA) ... SFS
Space General Corp. (MCD) ... SGC
Space Geodesy Altimetry Study [*Raytheon Co.*] ... SGAS
Space Ground Support Operations [*NASA*] (KSC) ... SGSO
Space Hammer ... SPAMMER
Space Hand Tool [*NASA*] ... SHT
Space Heater (KSC) ... SPH
Space Imbalanced Military Occupational Specialty ... SIMOS
Space Impact Hand Tool [*NASA*] ... SIHT
Space Impact Tool [*NASA*] ... SIT
Space Industries, Inc. ... SII

Space Influences on the Terrestrial Environment [*Marine science*] (OSRA) ... SITE
Space Influences on the Terrestrial Environment [*Space Enviromental Laboratory*] (USDC) ... SITE
Space Informatics Network Experiment [*European Space Agency*] ... SPINE
Space [*formerly, Shuttle*] **Infrared Telescope Facility** [*NASA*] ... SIRTF
Space Inspection ... SPIN
Space Institute [*University of Tennessee*] [*Research center*] (RCD) ... SI
Space Integrated Controls Experiment (DOMA) ... SPICE
Space Intelligence [*Parapsychology*] ... SI
Space Intercept (SAA) ... SPIN
Space Interceptor Missile (MCD) ... SIM
Space Intruder Detector [*Burglar alarm*] ... SID
Space Invariant Point Spread Function (PDAA) ... SIPSF
Space Investigations Documentation System [*NASA*] ... SIDS
Space Laboratory (KSC) ... S/L
Space Laboratory Module (IAA) ... SLM
Space Laboratory Operations ... SLO
Space Laboratory Simulator [*NASA*] ... SLS
Space LASER (SSD) ... SLASER
Space Launch Complex [*NASA*] ... SLC
Space Launch System ... SLS
Space Launch Vehicle [*NASA*] ... SLV
Space Logistics Maintenance and Repair (IAA) ... SLOMAR
Space Logistics, Maintenance, and Rescue ... SLOMAR
Space Maintenance Analysis Center (IAA) ... SMAC
Space Maintenance and Repair Techniques ... SMART
Space Management and Retail Tracking System [*Information Resources, Inc.*] ... SMART
Space Manufacturing Facility ... SMF
Space Medicine (SAA) ... SM
Space Medicine Advisory Group (MCD) ... SPAMAG
Space Meteorology Branch [*NASA*] ... SMB
Space Migration, Intelligence Increase, Life Extension [*Idea advanced by Timothy Leary, 1960's counterculture figure*] ... SMI^2LE
Space Mission Survivability Implementation Plan ... SMSIP
Space Missions Group [*Ford Aerospace & Communications Corp.*] [*Detroit, MI*] [*Telecommunications service*] (TSSD) ... SMG
Space Navigation ... SPAN
Space Navigation Network (IAA) ... SPANNET
Space Navigation System (OA) ... SNS
Space Nuclear Auxiliary Power ... SNAP
Space Nuclear Electric Propulsion Test ... SNEPT
Space Nuclear Propulsion ... SNP
Space Nuclear Propulsion Office [*Later, Division of Space Nuclear Systems, of Energy Research and Development Administration*] [*AEC-NASA*] ... SNPO
Space Nuclear Propulsion Office, Albuquerque [*See SNPO*] ... SNPOA
Space Nuclear Propulsion Office, Cleveland [*See SNPO*] ... SNPOC
Space Nuclear Propulsion Office, Nevada [*See SNPO*] ... SNPON
Space Nuclear System ... SNS
Space Nuclear Systems Office [*AEC/NASA*] ... SNSO
Space Object Identification (AFM) ... SOI
Space Object Identification Central Analysis System ... SOICAS
Space Object Identification Summary (MCD) ... SOISCUM
Space Object Identification System ... SOIS
Space Operation Command System [*NASA*] (IAA) ... SOCS
Space Operation Directorate (SSD) ... SOD
Space Operations and Flight Techniques [*NASA*] (NASA) ... SOFT
Space Operations Center ... SOC
Space Operations Controller ... SOC
Space Operations Management System (PDAA) ... SOMS
Space Operations Support (NVT) ... SPAOPSUP
Space Orbital Bomber (AAG) ... SOB
Space Ordnance Systems, Inc. (MCD) ... SOS
Space Parts Control Center (MUGU) ... SPCC
Space Parts Working Group ... SPWG
Space Patrol (AAG) ... SP
Space Patrol Active Defense ... SPAD
Space Patrol for Air Defense ... SPAD
Space Philatelists International Society (EA) ... SPIS
Space Physics Aeronautics Network (USDC) ... SPAN
Space Physics Analysis Network [*Database*] ... SPAN
Space Physics Laboratory [*Aerospace corporation*] ... SPL
Space Physics Research Laboratory [*University of Michigan*] [*Research center*] (RCD) ... SPRL
Space Planning System [*Applied Research of Cambridge Ltd.*] [*Software package*] (NCC) ... SPS
Space Plasma Analysis Network [*NASA*] ... SPAN
Space Plasma Experiment [*NASA*] (SSD) ... SPEX
Space Plasma High-Voltage Interaction Experiment [*Spacecraft*] [*NASA*] ... SPHINX
Space Plasma Physics Payload Group [*NASA*] (SSD) ... SPPG
Space Platform (SSD) ... SP
Space Plus Capsule (WDAA) ... SPANSULE
Space Polymer Chemistry (SSD) ... SPC
Space Position Value [*Outdoor advertising*] (NTCM) ... SPV
Space Power and Electric Propulsion Division [*Formerly, Nuclear Systems and Space Power Division*] [*NASA*] ... SPEPD
Space Power Facility ... SPF
Space Power Internal Combustion Engine (MCD) ... SPICE
Space Power System (CET) ... SPS
Space Power Systems Conference ... SPSC
Space Power Systems Division [*NASA*] ... SPSD
Space Power Tool ... SPT
Space Power Unit Reactor [*Air Force*] ... SPUR
Space Precision Altitude Reference System (MCD) ... SPAR
Space Precision Altitude [*or Attitude*] **Reference System** ... SPARS
Space Principles, Applications, and Doctrine [*Air Force Systems Command*] ... SPAD
Space Probe (IAA) ... SP
Space Probe Optical Recording Telescope [*Army*] ... SPORT
Space Probe RADAR Altimeter (KSC) ... SPRA
Space Processing Applications [*Program*] [*NASA*] ... SPA
Space Processing Applications Rocket [*NASA*] ... SPAR
Space Processing Equipment [*Astronautics*] ... SPE
Space Program Advisory Council [*Terminated, 1977*] [*NASA*] ... SPAC
Space Program American Citizens' Effort ... SPACE
Space Program Analysis and Review Council [*Air Force*] ... SPARC
Space Program Language Implementation Tool (KSC) ... SPLIT
Space Programming Language [*Computer science*] ... SPL
Space Programming Language Machine ... SPLM
Space Programs Laboratory [*Fort Belvoir, VA*] [*United States Army Engineer Topographic Laboratories*] (GRD) ... SPL
Space Projects Center [*NASA*] ... SPC
Space Propulsion and Power Division [*NASA*] ... SPPD
Space Propulsion Automated Synthesis Modeling [*Program*] ... SPASM
Space Propulsion Research Facility (AAG) ... SPRF
Space Qualified Booster ... SQB
Space Qualified Booster Charger ... SQBC
Space Qualified LASER ... SQL
Space Radar Laboratory [*NASA*] ... SRL
Space Radiation Analysis Group [*NASA*] ... SPAG
Space Radiation Analysis Group [*NASA*] (NASA) ... SRAG
Space Radiation Effects Laboratory [*Langley, VA*] [*NASA*] ... SREL
Space Radiation Evaluation System [*NASA*] (KSC) ... SPARES
Space Recovery Systems (KSC) ... SRS
Space Recovery [*or Rescue*] **Vehicle** ... SRV
Space Remote Sensing Center ... SRSC
Space Replaceable Unit (MCD) ... SRU
Space Requirement Forms (AAG) ... SRF
Space Requirement Program (MCD) ... SRP
Space Research and Technology [*Report*] [*NASA*] (KSC) ... SPART
Space Research Capsule [*or Conic*] [*NASA*] ... SPARC
Space Research Corp., Mansonville, Quebec [*Library symbol National Library of Canada*] (NLC) ... QMASRC
Space Research Corp., Masonville, PQ, Canada [*Library symbol Library of Congress*] (LCLS) ... CaQMaSRC
Space Research Council [*British*] ... SRC
Space Research Facilities Branch [*National Research Council of Canada*] ... SRFB
Space Research Institute [*Defunct*] (EA) ... SRI
Space Research Organization Netherlands ... SRON
Space Science Advisory Committee [*European Space Agency*] ... SSAC
Space Science Analysis and Command [*Team*] [*NASA*] ... SSAC
Space Science Analysis Area [*Space Flight Operations Facility, NASA*] ... SSAA
Space Science and Engineering Center [*University of Wisconsin - Madison*] [*Research center*] (RCD) ... SSEC
Space Science and Engineering Laboratory [*Pennsylvania State University*] ... SSEL
Space Science Board [*National Research Council*] ... SSB
Space Science Committee [*Formerly, Provisional Space Science Advisory Board for Europe*] [*of the European Science Foundation*] (EA) ... SSC
Space Science Data Center [*NASA*] (MCD) ... SSDC
Space Science Development Facility (SAA) ... SSDF
Space Science Development Facility-North American Aviation (SAA) ... SSDF-NAA
Space Science Steering Committee ... SSSC
Space Sciences (IAA) ... SS
Space Sciences Division [*Jet Propulsion Laboratory*] ... SSD
Space Sciences Laboratory [*University of California, Berkeley*] [*Research center NASA*] (MCD) ... SSL
Space Sciences Office (IAA) ... SSO
Space Segment (SSD) ... SS
Space Selector Terminal (SAA) ... SST
Space Settlement Studies Program (EA) ... SSSP
Space Settlers' Society [*Defunct*] (EAIO) ... SSS
Space Ship Experimental ... SSX
Space Shuttle [*NASA*] (KSC) ... SS
Space Shuttle Access Tower [*NASA*] (MCD) ... SSAT
Space Shuttle Cargo Handling System [*NASA*] (NASA) ... SSCHS
Space Shuttle Crew Safety Panel [*NASA*] (NASA) ... SSCSP
Space Shuttle Display [*NASA*] ... SSD
Space Shuttle Display and Simulation [*NASA*] ... SSDS
Space Shuttle Engineering and Operations Support [*NASA*] (MCD) ... SSEOS
Space Shuttle Engines [*NASA*] (MCD) ... SSE
Space Shuttle Flight and Ground System Specification [*NASA*] (NASA) ... SSFGSS
Space Shuttle Functional Simulator [*NASA*] (KSC) ... SSFS
Space Shuttle Furnace Facility [*NASA*] (SSD) ... SSFF
Space Shuttle Main Engine [*NASA*] ... SSME
Space Shuttle Main Engine Controller [*NASA*] (MCD) ... SSMEC
Space Shuttle Main Engine Controller Assembly [*NASA*] (NASA) ... SSMECA
Space Shuttle Maintenance Baseline [*NASA*] (MCD) ... SSMB
Space Shuttle Mission Control Center [*NASA*] (SSD) ... SSMCC
[*The*] **Space Shuttle Operator's Manual** ... SSOM
Space Shuttle Orbiter [*NASA*] (RDA) ... SSO
Space Shuttle Payload Data Activity [*NASA*] (NASA) ... SSPDA
Space Shuttle Payload Data Study [*NASA*] (NASA) ... SSPDS
Space Shuttle Payload Planning Steering Group [*NASA*] (NASA) ... SSPPSG
Space Shuttle Program [*NASA*] (NASA) ... SSP
Space Shuttle Program Ground Support Equipment [*NASA*] (GFGA) ... SSPGSE

Space Shuttle Program Manager [*NASA*] (NASA) .... SSPM
Space Shuttle Program Office [*NASA*] (KSC) .... SSPO
Space Shuttle Program Resident Office [*NASA*] (NASA) .... SSPRO
Space Shuttle Program Schedule [*NASA*] (NASA) .... SSPS
Space Shuttle Simulation [*NASA*] .... SSS
Space Shuttle Simulation Display [*NASA*] .... SSSD
Space Shuttle Structures and Materials Working Group [*NASA*]
  (PDAA) .... SMWG
Space Shuttle Synthesis Program [*National Academy of Sciences*] .... SSSP
Space Shuttle System [*NASA*] (KSC) .... SSS
Space Shuttle System Segment (MCD) .... SSSS
Space Shuttle System Specification [*NASA*] (NASA) .... SSSS
Space Shuttle Task Force [*NASA*] .... SSTF
Space Shuttle Task Group [*NASA*] (KSC) .... SSTG
Space Shuttle Test Conductor [*NASA*] (NASA) .... SSTC
Space Shuttle Vehicle [*NASA*] .... SSV
Space Shuttle Vehicle/Guidance, Control, and Navigation [*NASA*] ..... SSV/GC & N
Space Simulation Facility (AAG) .... SSF
Space Simulation Laboratory .... SSL
Space Simulation Test Facility (AAG) .... SSTF
Space Simulator (IEEE) .... SS
Space Station (AAG) .... SS
Space Station Approved EEE [*Electrical, Electronic, and
  Electromechanical*] Parts List (SSD) .... SSAEPL
Space Station Assembly Technology (SSD) .... SSAT
Space Station Change Request (SSD) .... SSCR
Space Station Communication and Tracking System (SSD) .... SSCTS
Space Station Communication System (SSD) .... SSCS
Space Station Control Board (SSD) .... SSCB
Space Station Control Board Directive (SSD) .... SSCBD
Space Station Data Management System [*NASA*] (SSD) .... SSDMS
Space Station Data System (NASA) .... SSDS
Space Station Environmental Control System .... SSECS
Space Station Hazardous Processing Facility (SSD) .... SSHPF
Space Station Information System (NASA) .... SSIS
Space Station Master Verification Plan [*NASA*] (SSD) .... SSMVP
Space Station Master Verification Requirement [*NASA*] (SSD) .... SSMVR
Space Station Mathematical Model .... SSMM
Space Station Module [*NASA*] (KSC) .... SSM
Space Station Office [*NASA*] (SSD) .... SSO
Space Station Operations and Control Center [*NASA*] (SSD) .... SSOCC
Space Station Operations Center [*NASA*] (SSD) .... SSOC
Space Station Operations Language [*NASA*] (SSD) .... SSOL
Space Station Processing Facility [*NASA*] (SSD) .... SSPF
Space Station Program [*NASA*] (SSD) .... SSP
Space Station Program Element [*NASA*] (SSD) .... SSPE
Space Station Program Participant [*NASA*] (SSD) .... SSPP
Space Station Remote Manipulator System [*NASA*] (SSD) .... SSRMS
Space Station Rendezvous and Proximity Operations Simulator [*NASA*]
  (SSD) .... SSRPOS
Space Station Simulator .... SSS
Space Station Simulator Trainee [*or Trainer*] [*NASA*] (SSD) .... SSST
Space Station Support Center (SSD) .... SSSC
Space Station Systems Analysis Study [*NASA*] (SSD) .... SSSAS
Space Station Task Force [*NASA*] .... SSTF
Space Station Training Facility [*NASA*] (SSD) .... SSTF
Space Station User Information System [*NASA*] (SSD) .... SSUIS
Space Station Work Package [*NASA*] (SSD) .... SSWP
Space Structure Assembly (SSD) .... SSA
Space Studies Institute (EA) .... SSI
Space Subsystem Control Facility (NATG) .... SSCF
Space Suit Assembly (KSC) .... SSA
Space Suit Communications System (MCD) .... SSCS
Space Suit Communicator [*Apollo*] [*NASA*] .... SSC
Space Support Wing [*Military*] .... SSW
Space Surveillance and Tracking System [*Military*] .... SSTS
Space Surveillance Control Center .... SSCC
Space Surveillance Network .... SSN
Space Surveillance Operations Center (SAA) .... SSOC
Space Surveillance System [*Navy*] .... SPASUR
Space Surveillance System [*Navy*] (MCD) .... SSS
Space Surveillance Technology .... SST
Space Switch [*Telecommunications*] (TEL) .... SS
Space Switch [*Telecommunications*] (TEL) .... SSW
Space System (IAA) .... SS
Space System Effectiveness Model .... SSEM
Space Systems and Applications [*NASA*] (NASA) .... SS & A
Space Systems Center .... SSC
Space Systems Division [*Air Force*] .... SSD
Space Systems Operating Procedures [*NASA*] (MCD) .... SSOP
Space Systems Operational Design Criteria Manual [*NASA*] .... SSODCM
Space Systems Support Squadron .... SSSS
Space Task Group [*Later, Manned Spacecraft Center*] [*NASA*] .... STG
Space Technical Information Control (MCD) .... STIC
Space Technology Analysis and Mission Planning (MCD) .... STAMP
Space Technology and Advanced Research .... STAR
Space Technology and Research Center [*Research center*] (RCD) .... STAR
Space Technology Applications .... STA
Space Technology Applications and Research Laboratory [*NASA*] .... STARLAB
Space Technology Applied to Rural Papago Advanced Health Care
  (SSD) .... STARPAHC
Space Technology Program Center .... STC
Space Technology Data Report .... STDR
Space Technology Experiments Platform .... STEP
Space Technology, Inc. (MCD) .... STI

Space Technology Laboratories [*of TRW Group*] .... STL
Space Technology Operations and Research Laboratory (IEEE) .... STORLAB
Space Technology Payload [*NASA*] (MCD) .... STP
Space Technology Products [*NASA*] (IAA) .... STP
Space Technology Requirements Engineering Test of Component
  Hardware [*NASA*] (KSC) .... STRETCH
Space Technology Satellite (IAA) .... STS
Space, Telecommunications, and Radioscience Laboratory [*Stanford
  University*] [*Research center*] (RCD) .... STARLab
Space Telescope [*NASA*] .... ST
Space Telescope Data Capture Facility [*NASA*] (SSD) .... STDCF
Space Telescope Guidance [*NASA*] .... STG
Space Telescope Imaging Spectrograph .... STIS
Space Telescope Operations Control Center [*NASA*] (NASA) .... STOCC
Space Telescope Science Institute [*Johns Hopkins University*] [*Research
  center*] (RCD) .... ST SCI
Space Telescope Science Institute .... STScI
Space Telescope Science Institute [*NASA*] .... STSI
Space Telescope Science Institute, Baltimore, MD [*Library symbol*] [*Library
  of Congress*] (LCLS) .... MdBSTS
Space Telescope Task Team [*NASA*] .... STTT
Space Terminal Auxiliary Reactor (IAA) .... STAR
Space Terminal Evaluation Program .... STEP
Space Test and Reentry Technology .... START
Space Test and Transportation Program (DOMA) .... STTP
Space Test Center [*Air Force*] .... STC
Space Test Group [*Military*] .... STESTG
Space Test Operations Section .... STOS
Space Test Program [*Air Force*] .... STP
Space Test Vehicle [*NASA*] (KSC) .... STV
Space Thermal Vacuum Chamber (SAA) .... STVC
Space Thermionic Auxiliary Reactor [*Nuclear energy*] .... STAR
Space Thermoelectric Power (IAA) .... STEP
Space Thrust Evolution and Disposal Investigation [*Air Force*] .... STEDI
Space, Time, and Beyond [*Dance work choreographed by Marie
  Chouinard*] .... STAB
Space Tool for Extravehicular Emergencies .... STEVE
Space Topics Study Group (EA) .... STSG
Space Toy Information Center [*Defunct*] (EA) .... STIC
Space Track Facility .... STF
Space Track Interim Fire Control .... STIFC
Space Track Sensor Computer (IAA) .... SPASEC
Space Tracking and Acquisition Data Network .... STADN
Space Tracking and Data Acquisition Network .... STADAN
Space Tracking and Data Acquisition Network (IAA) .... STANDAN
Space Tracking System [*Air Force*] (MCD) .... SPACETRACK
Space Trajectory Radiation Exposure Procedure .... STREP
Space Transport and Reentry Tests .... START
Space Transportation Air-Breathing Technology Evaluation [*DoD*] .... STATE
Space Transportation Architecture Study [*1985*] .... STAS
Space Transportation Association (EA) .... STA
Space Transportation Booster Engine .... STBE
Space Transportation Main Engine .... STME
Space Transportation System .... STS
Space Transportation System Cost Model [*NASA*] (KSC) .... STSCM
Space Transportation System Operations Contact [*NASA*] (SSD) .... STSOC
Space Transportation System Spacelab Processing Facility [*NASA*]
  (SSD) .... STSSPF
Space Ultrareliable Modular Computer .... SUMC
Space Ultravacuum Research Facility (LAIN) .... SURF
Space Ultraviolet Radiation Environment (MCD) .... SURE
Space Unit (EA) .... SU
Space Vehicle .... SV
Space Vehicle Booster [*NASA*] (MCD) .... SVB
Space Vehicle Booster Test (AAG) .... SVBT
Space Vehicle Code .... SVC
Space Vehicle Dynamic Simulator [*NASA*] (NASA) .... SVDS
Space Vehicle Electronics (SAA) .... SVE
Space Vehicle Mission Analysis .... SVMA
Space Vehicle Number [*Aviation*] (FAAC) .... SVN
Space Vehicle Operations (MCD) .... SVO
Space Vehicle Sectoring Code .... SVSC
Space Vehicle Simulator (AAG) .... SVS
Space Vehicle System (IAA) .... SVS
Space Vehicle Test .... SVT
Space Vehicle Test (Supervisor) .... SVT(S)
Space Vehicles Division [*NASA*] (MCD) .... SVD
Space Velocity [*Chemical engineering*] .... SV
Space Visualization [*Visual perception*] .... SV
Space Visualization Contralateral Use [*Occupational therapy*] .... SVCU
Space Visualization Test .... SVT
Space Warning and Control System [*NORAD*] .... SWACS
Space Warning and Control System [*NORAD*] (IAA) .... SWCS
Space Weapon Systems [*Air Force*] .... SWS
Space Weather and Terrestrial Hazards [*Proposed satellite*] .... SWATH
Space, Weight, and Power .... SWP
Space Wing [*Military*] .... SWG
Space-Based Antimissile .... SBAM
Space-Based Hypervelocity Rail Gun [*Military*] (SDI) .... SBHRG
Space-Based Infrared System [*Military*] .... SBIRS
Space-Based Interceptor [*Military*] (SDI) .... SBI
Space-Based Kinetic Energy Weapon [*Military*] (MCD) .... SBKEW
Space-Based Kinetic Kill Vehicle [*Military*] .... SBKKV
Space-Based LASER [*Military*] .... SBL
Space-Based LASER Weapon (MCD) .... SLW

Space-Based Neutral Particle Beam [*Military*] (SDI) .... SBNPB
Space-Based Particle Beam [*Military*] (SDI) .... SBPB
Space-Based RADAR (MCD) .... SBR
Space-Based Space Surveillance (MCD) .... SBSS
Space-Based Tug [*NASA*] .... SBT
Space-Based Wide-Area Surveillance [*Air Force*] (DOMA) ...... SBWAS
Spaceborne (KSC) .... SBN
Spaceborne Computer .... SBC
Spaceborne Computer Engineering Conference (MCD) .... SCEC
Spaceborne Earth Applications Ranging System (MCD) .... SPEAR
Spaceborne Earth Applications Ranging System [*NASA*] .... SPEARS
Spaceborne Imaging RADAR .... SIR
Spaceborne Infrared Tracker .... SIT
Spaceborne Intensified Radiometer for Imaging Vetroviolet Spectroscopy
  (MCD) .... SIRIVS
Spaceborne LASER Ranging .... SBLS
Spaceborne Programmer .... SBP
Spaceborne Programming Language [*Computer science*] (IAA) .... SPL
Spaceborne Reconnaissance System .... SRS
Spaceborne Software Systems Study (DNAB) .... SSSS
Space-Charge-Limited Current .... SCLC
Space-Charge-Limited Insulated-Gate Field Effect Transistor
  (PDAA) .... SCLIGFET
Space-Controlled Army Measurements Probe .... SCAMP
Spacecraft (MCD) .... SC
Spacecraft Acceptance Review (MCD) .... SAR
Spacecraft Adapter [*NASA*] .... SA
Spacecraft Adapter [*NASA*] (KSC) .... SCA
Spacecraft Adapter Simulator (IAA) .... SCAS
Spacecraft Analysis (KSC) .... SPAN
Spacecraft Antenna System .... SAS
Spacecraft Array for Michelson Spectral Inferometry .... SAMSI
Spacecraft Assembly and Encapsulation Facility [*NASA*] (NASA) .... SAEF
Spacecraft Assembly Building [*NASA*] (MCD) .... SAB
Spacecraft Assembly Facility [*NASA*] .... SAF
Spacecraft Assessment Report [*NASA*] (KSC) .... SCAR
Spacecraft Attitude Display (MCD) .... SAD
Spacecraft/Capsule .... S/C
Spacecraft Central Timing Equipment [*NASA*] .... SCTE
Spacecraft Charging at High Altitudes [*Satellite*] .... SCATHA
Spacecraft Checkout Facility .... SCF
Spacecraft Command Control Unit (KSC) .... SCCU
Spacecraft Command Encoder (MCD) .... SCE
Spacecraft Communicator (IAA) .... SC
Spacecraft Communicator .... SCOM
Spacecraft Components (NITA) .... SPACECOMPS
Spacecraft Control Center [*NASA*] (KSC) .... SCC
Spacecraft Control Facility [*NASA*] (MCD) .... SCF
Spacecraft Control Laboratory Experiment (MCD) .... SCOLE
Spacecraft Control System (NASA) .... SCS
Spacecraft Data Analysis Team [*NASA*] .... SDAT
Spacecraft Data Handling Equipment .... SDHE
Spacecraft Data Simulator [*NASA*] (KSC) .... SDC
Spacecraft Design Book .... SDB
Spacecraft Design Specification .... SDS
Spacecraft Elapsed Time .... SET
Spacecraft Event Time .... SCET
Spacecraft Ground Controlled Approach (IAA) .... SGCA
Spacecraft Ground Elapsed Time .... SGET
Spacecraft Ground Operational Support System Interface Test System
  (IAA) .... SGITS
Spacecraft Information Viewing Device .... SIVD
Spacecraft Instrumentation Test Equipment .... SITE
Spacecraft Integration Project Office .... SIPO
Spacecraft Interface Specification (MCD) .... SCIS
Spacecraft Interface Unit (NASA) .... SCIU
Spacecraft Landing Strut .... SLS
Spacecraft LM [*Lunar Module*] Adapter [*NASA*] .... SLA
Spacecraft Magnetic Test Facility [*Goddard Space Flight Center*] [*NASA*] ..... SMTF
Spacecraft Maneuver Engine Transients [*Apollo program*] [*NASA*] .... SMET
Spacecraft Material [*NASA*] (SSD) .... SCM
Spacecraft Meteorology Group (KSC) .... SMG
Spacecraft Observer (KSC) .... S/CO
Spacecraft Oceanography Project [*Navy*] .... SPOC
Spacecraft Operations [*NASA*] (KSC) .... SCO
Spacecraft Operations and Checkout Facility (AAG) .... SOCF
Spacecraft Operations Control Center .... SOCC
Spacecraft Operations Manual .... SOM
Spacecraft Operations Planning Section .... SOPS
Spacecraft Oscillograph Recording System .... SORS
Spacecraft Payload Adapter (MCD) .... SCPA
Spacecraft Performance Analysis and Command [*NASA*] .... SPAC
Spacecraft Performance Analysis Area .... SPAA
Spacecraft Performance and Flight Path Analysis Directorate [*NASA*] .... SPFPAD
Spacecraft Platform [*NASA*] .... SCP
Spacecraft Prelaunch Automatic Checkout Equipment [*NASA*] ...... SPACE
Spacecraft Propulsion System (AAG) .... SPS
Spacecraft Protective Landing Area for the Advancement of Science and
  Humanities [*Landing zone for flying saucers near Mt. Rainier, WA*] .... SPLAASH
Spacecraft Received Time .... SCR
Spacecraft Research Foundation [*Defunct*] (EA) .... SRF
Spacecraft Software Division [*NASA*] (NASA) .... SSD
Spacecraft Support Planning Section .... SSPS
Spacecraft Support Unit .... SSU

Spacecraft Switched Time Division Multiple Access
  [*Telecommunications*] .... SSTDMA
Spacecraft System [*NASA*] (KSC) .... SCS
Spacecraft System Console .... SSC
Spacecraft System Integration .... SSI
Spacecraft System Integration Support .... SSIS
Spacecraft System Integration Support Service .... SSISS
Spacecraft System Support .... SSS
Spacecraft System Test [*NASA*] .... SST
Spacecraft System Test Console [*NASA*] .... SSTC
Spacecraft Systems Controller Unit [*NASA*] (KSC) .... SSCU
Spacecraft Systems Monitor (IAA) .... SCSM
Spacecraft Systems Monitor [*NASA*] (MCD) .... SSM
Spacecraft Systems Officer (SAA) .... SSO
Spacecraft Technical Control Center (MDG) .... STCC
Spacecraft Technology and Advanced Reentry Tests [*Air Force*] .... START
Spacecraft Technology Division [*NASA*] (KSC) .... STD
Spacecraft Telecommunications System .... STS
Spacecraft Telemetry Command Data Handling System .... STCDHS
Spacecraft Telemetry Regenerator (MCD) .... STR
Spacecraft Television - Ground Data Handling System [*NASA*] .... SCTV-GDHS
Spacecraft Television Video Data .... STVD
Spacecraft Terminal Thrust .... STT
Spacecraft Test Conductor (SAA) .... SC/TC
Spacecraft Test Conductor [*NASA*] (KSC) .... STC
Spacecraft Test Engineering [*NASA*] (KSC) .... STE
Spacecraft Test Facility .... STF
Spacecraft Tracking and Data Network (NITA) .... STDN
Spacecraft Tracking Station [*NASA*] (KSC) .... STS
Spacecraft Vicinity Equipment (IAA) .... SCVE
Spacecraft-Orientation-Control [*NASA*] (IAA) .... SOC
Spacecraft-Orientation-Control System .... SOCS
Spaced Antenna (USDC) .... SA
Spaced Antenna [*Marine science*] (OSRA) .... SA
Spaced Antenna Imaging Doppler Interferometer [*Marine science*]
  (OSRA) .... SAIDA
Spaced Antenna Imaging Doppler Interferometer (USDC) .... SAIDI
Spaced Doublet (IAA) .... SD
Spaced Triplet (SAA) .... ST
Spaceflight Meteorology Group [*NASA*] (NASA) .... SMG
Space-Ground Link (MCD) .... SGL
Space-Ground Link Station [*NASA*] (NASA) .... SGLS
Space-Ground Link System (IAA) .... SGLS
SPACEHAB Inc. [*NASDAQ symbol*] (TTSB) .... SPAB
Spacelab [*NASA*] (NASA) .... SL
Spacelab Data Processing Facility (MCD) .... SLDPF
Spacelab Disposition Record [*NASA*] (NASA) .... SDR
Spacelab Engineering [*European Research National Organization*] (MCD) .... SLE
Spacelab Engineering Model Unit [*NASA*] (MCD) .... SLEMU
Spacelab Integration (MCD) .... SLI
Spacelab Late Access Kit [*NASA*] (NASA) .... SLAK
Spacelab Mission Development [*NASA*] (MCD) .... SMD
Spacelab Opportunity Payload [*NASA*] (MCD) .... SOP
Spacelab Orbiter Common Hardware [*NASA*] (MCD) .... SOCH
Spacelab/Orbiter Interface Simulator [*NASA*] (NASA) .... SOIS
Spacelab Payload Accommodations Handbook [*NASA*] (MCD) ...... SPAH
Spacelab Payload Integration and Coordination in Europe [*NASA*]
  (NASA) .... SPICE
Spacelab Payload Project Office [*NASA*] .... SPPO
Spacelab Payload Standard Modular Electronics (MCD) .... SPSME
Spacelab Payloads Processing Project (NASA) .... SPPP
Spacelab Processing Facility [*NASA*] (NASA) .... SPF
Spacelab Program Board [*NASA*] (NASA) .... SLPB
Spacelab Program Office [*European Research National Organization*]
  (MCD) .... SLP
Spacelab Program Office [*NASA*] .... SPO
Spacelab Stored Program Command [*NASA*] (MCD) .... SSPC
Spacelab Subsystem [*NASA*] (NASA) .... SL-SS
Spacelab Subsystem Segment [*NASA*] (NASA) .... SL-SSS
Spacelab Support Module Simulator [*NASA*] (MCD) .... SLSMS
Spacelab Technology [*NASA*] (NASA) .... ST
Spacelab Transfer Tunnel (NASA) .... STT
Spacelab Ultraviolet Telescope .... SUOT
Spacelab Window Adapter Assembly (NASA) .... SWAA
SpaceLabs Medical [*NASDAQ symbol*] (TTSB) .... SLMD
SpaceLabs Medical, Inc. [*NASDAQ symbol*] (SAG) .... SLMD
SpaceLabs Medical, Inc. [*Associated Press*] (SAG) .... SpaceLb
Space-Launched Air Missile (MCD) .... SLAM
Space-Launched Ballistic Missile (IAA) .... SLBM
Space-Like Vector .... SLV
Space-Occupying Lesion [*Medicine*] .... SOL
Spacer .... S
Spacer [*Technical drawings*] .... SPC
Spacer .... SPCR
Spacer (AAG) .... SPR
Spacers [*Electron transfer*] .... Sp
Spacesaver Material Accounting Resource Terminal [*Spacesaver
  Corp.*] .... SMART
Space-Syncromesh .... SPASYN
Spacetec IMC [*NASDAQ symbol*] (TTSB) .... SIMC
Spacetec IMC Corp. [*NASDAQ symbol*] (SAG) .... SIMC
Spacetec IMC Corp. [*Associated Press*] (SAG) .... Spacetec
Space-Time .... ST
Space-Time Autoregressive [*Statistics*] .... STAR
Space-Time Autoregressive Integrated Moving Average [*Statistics*] .... STARIMAR

Space-Time Continuum .... STC
Space-Time Moving Average [*Statistics*] .... STMA
Space-Time Unit [*Computer*] .... STU
Space-Time Yield [*Chemical engineering*] .... STY
Space-Time-Space [*Digital switching structure*] [*Telecommunications*] (TEL) .... STS
Space-to-Ground Link Subsystem [*NASA*] .... SGLS
Space-Vehicle-to-Space-Vehicle (SAA) .... SVTSV
Spache Diagnostic Test [*Psychiatry*] (DAVI) .... SDT
Spache's Diagnostic Reading Scales (EDAC) .... SDRS
Spacial Factor .... SF
Spacious (ADA) .... SPAC
Spadafore Diagnostic Reading Test [*Educational test*] .... SDRT
Spade (ADA) .... S
Spade [*Freight*] .... SPA
Spade and Shovel Makers' Trade Society [*A union*] [*British*] .... SSMTS
Spade Tongue Terminal .... STT
Spaero JSP [*Ukraine*] [*FAA designator*] (FAAC) .... SPF
Spaghetti (DSUE) .... SPAG
Spaghetti Warehouse [*NYSE symbol*] (TTSB) .... SWH
Spaghetti Warehouse, Inc. [*Associated Press*] (SAG) .... SpgWre
Spaghetti Warehouse, Inc. [*NYSE symbol*] (SPSG) .... SWH
Spain [*IYRU nationality code*] (IYR) .... E
Spain [*ANSI two-letter standard code*] (CNC) .... ES
Spain [*ANSI three-letter standard code*] (CNC) .... ESP
Spain .... SP
Spain [*MARC country of publication code Library of Congress*] (LCCP) .... sp
Spain (VRA) .... Spa
Spain Fund [*NYSE symbol*] (SPSG) .... SNF
Spain Fund [*Associated Press*] (SAG) .... Spain
Spainair [*Spain ICAO designator*] (FAAC) .... SPP
Spain-Morocco Network [*Armed Forces Radio-Television*] (DNAB) .... SMN
Spair [*Russian Federation*] [*ICAO designator*] (FAAC) .... PAR
Spalding College (GAGS) .... Spalding C
Spalding College, Louisville, KY [*Library symbol Library of Congress*] (LCLS) .... KyLoN
Spalding on Copyright [*A publication*] (DLA) .... Spald Cop
Spallation Neutron Source .... SNS
Spalling Resistance Index (IEEE) .... SRI
SPALT [*Special Projects Alterations*] **Evaluation Area** .... SEA
SPALT [*Special Projects Alterations*] **Improvement Program** .... SIP
SPALT [*Special Projects Alterations*] **Information Shut** .... SIS
SPALT [*Special Projects Alterations*] **Information System** .... SIS
SPALT [*Special Projects Alterations*] **Planning and Authorization Report** .... SPAR
SPALTRA [*Special Projects Alterations, Training*] **Control Activity** .... SCA
Spam Exterminator [*Unisyn*] [*Computer science*] .... SpamEx
Span Analysis (NITA) .... SPAN
Span East Airlines, Inc. [*Air carrier designation symbol*] .... SEAX
SPAN [*Spacecraft Analysis*] **Mission Evaluation Action Request** [*NASA*] (GFGA) .... SMEAR
SPAN [*Space Physics Analysis Network*] **Ocean Network Information Center** [*Database*] .... SONIC
Span Terminating Equipment [*Telecommunications*] (TEL) .... STE
Span-America Med Sys [*NASDAQ symbol*] (TTSB) .... SPAN
Span-America Medical Systems, Inc. [*NASDAQ symbol*] (NQ) .... SPAN
Span-America Medical Systems, Inc. [*Associated Press*] (SAG) .... SpanAm
Spangdahlem [*Germany ICAO location identifier*] (ICLI) .... EDAD
Spangler, PA [*FM radio station call letters*] (RBYB) .... WXLJ-FM
Spangler, PA [*FM radio station call letters*] .... WXVE
Spaniard (ROG) .... SPAN
Spaniards Bay Public Library, Newfoundland [*Library symbol National Library of Canada*] (NLC) .... NFSB
Spaniards Bay Public Library, Spaniards Bay, NF, Canada [*Library symbol Library of Congress*] (LCLS) .... CaNfSB
Spaniel Breeders Society (EA) .... SBS
Spanish [*Language in tables*] (BARN) .... E
Spanish (ROG) .... SP
Spanish .... SPA
Spanish [*MARC language code Library of Congress*] (LCCP) .... spa
Spanish .... SPAN
Spanish Air Force .... SAF
Spanish Air Materiel Area .... SPAMA
Spanish and English .... SPANGLISH
Spanish Association for Medical Education [*British*] (EAIO) .... SAME
Spanish Base Construction Program .... SBCP
Spanish Benevolent Society "La Nacional" (EA) .... SBS
Spanish Broadcasting System .... SBS
Spanish Campaign Medal .... SPCM
Spanish Catalonian Battalion (PD) .... PRE
Spanish Chamber of Commerce [*Taiwan*] (EAIO) .... SCOC
Spanish Colonial Research Center [*University of New Mexico*] [*Research center*] (RCD) .... SCRC
Spanish Colonial Style [*Cigars*] .... SCS
Spanish Columbia, San Sebastian [*Record label*] [*Spain*] .... SpC
Spanish Communication Region [*Air Force*] (MCD) .... SCR
Spanish Communist Party .... SCP
Spanish Decca, San Sebastian [*Record label*] [*Spain*] .... SpD
Spanish/English Language Performance Screening (EDAC) .... S/ELPS
Spanish/English Reading and Vocabulary Screening Test .... SERVS
Spanish Evangelical Publishers Association (EA) .... SEPA
Spanish Festival [*Record label*] .... SpFest
Spanish Fork, UT [*FM radio station call letters*] (RBYB) .... KBKK
Spanish Fork, UT [*AM radio station call letters*] .... KHQN
Spanish Heritage (EA) .... SH
[*The*] **Spanish Information Network** [*Later, Spanish International Network*] [*Cable- television system*] (WDMC) .... SIN
Spanish International Network [*Cable-television system*] .... SIN
Spanish Literature Committee (EA) .... SLC
Spanish Market Selection [*Cigars*] .... SMS
Spanish Moss .... SM
Spanish Music Center [*Commercial firm*] (EA) .... SMC
Spanish Mustang Registry (EA) .... SMR
Spanish Navy .... SNY
Spanish Odeon, Barcelona [*Record label*] [*Spain*] .... SpOd
Spanish Open Pool Reactor .... SOPR
Spanish Oral Reading Text (EDAC) .... SORT
Spanish Paprika Institute (EA) .... SPI
Spanish Philatelic Society Spanish Civil War Study Group [*Defunct*] (EA) .... SPS-SCWG
Spanish RCA Victor [*Record label*] .... SpV
Spanish Refugee Aid (EA) .... SRA
Spanish River Reserve Band Public Library, Ontario [*Library symbol National Library of Canada*] (NLC) .... OSRR
Spanish Sahara [*Western Sahara*] [*MARC geographic area code Library of Congress*] (LCCP) .... f-ss--
Spanish Sahara [*Western Sahara*] [*MARC country of publication code Library of Congress*] (LCCP) .... ss
Spanish Speaking Mental Health Research Center [*Public Health Service*] [*Research center*] (RCD) .... SSMHRC
Spanish Telefunken [*Record label*] .... SpT
Spanish Territories in Northern Morocco [*Spanish North Africa*] (LCCP) .... f-sh--
Spanish Territories in Northern Morocco [*Spanish North Africa*] [*MARC country of publication code Library of Congress*] (LCCP) .... sh
Spanish Texas Microfilm Center, Goliad, TX [*Library symbol Library of Congress*] (LCLS) .... TxGoS
Spanish Universal Network [*Cable-television system*] .... SUN
Spanish War Service Medal .... SPWSM
Spanish Wells [*Bahamas*] [*Airport symbol*] (AD) .... SWL
Spanish World Gospel Mission (EA) .... SWGM
Spanish-American (DAVI) .... SA
Spanish-Barb Breeders Association (EA) .... SBBA
Spanish-Surnamed American .... SSA
Spanlink Communications [*NASDAQ symbol*] (TTSB) .... SPLK
Spanlink Communications, Inc. [*Associated Press*] (SAG) .... Spanlink
Spanlink Communications, Inc. [*NASDAQ symbol*] (SAG) .... SPLK
Spanner (AAG) .... SPNR
Spanning Tree Algorithm [*Computer science*] (PCM) .... STA
Spansule [*Pharmacology*] (DAVI) .... Span
Spansules [*Pharmacology*] (CPH) .... spans
Spar [*Buoy*] .... S
Spar Aerospace Ltd. [*Toronto Stock Exchange symbol*] .... SPZ
Spar Aerospace Ltd., Weston, ON, Canada [*Library symbol Library of Congress*] (LCLS) .... CaOWSA
Spar Aerospace Ltd., Weston, Ontario [*Library symbol National Library of Canada*] (NLC) .... OWSA
Spar Aerospace Products, Toronto, ON, Canada [*Library symbol Library of Congress*] (LCLS) .... CaOTSAP
Spar Aerospace Products, Toronto, Ontario [*Library symbol National Library of Canada*] (NLC) .... OTSAP
Spar Material Factor [*Yacht racing regulation*] .... SMF
Spar Technology Ltd., Ste.-Anne-De-Bellevue, PQ, Canada [*Library symbol Library of Congress*] (LCLS) .... CaQSTAS
Spar Technology Ltd., Ste-Anne-De-Bellevue, Quebec [*Library symbol National Library of Canada*] (NLC) .... QSTAS
S-Parameter Acquisition and Manipulation [*Computer software program*] [*General Motors Corp.*] .... SPAM
Spare (AAG) .... SP
Spare [*Telecommunications*] (TEL) .... SPR
Spare Band Surveillance System (MCD) .... SBSS
Spare Disposition (MCD) .... SD
Spare Guidance System .... SPGS
Spare Module Replacement Analysis .... SMRA
Spare Operation Support .... SOS
Spare Part .... SP
Spare Parts Analysis, Documentation, and Evaluation .... SPADE
Spare Parts Application Data List .... SPADL
Spare Parts Catalog .... SPC
Spare Parts Change Request .... SPCR
Spare Parts Distributing Center [*Navy*] .... SPDC
Spare Parts Inventory Control (MHDB) .... SPIC
Spare Parts Kit .... SPK
Spare Parts List .... SPL
Spare Parts List for Codification .... SPLC
Spare Parts Order [*NASA*] (NASA) .... SPO
Spare Parts Provisioning .... SPP
Spare Parts Provisioning Card .... SPPC
Spare Parts Provisioning for Combat .... SPARC
Spare Parts Provisioning List [*NASA*] (NASA) .... SPPL
Spare Parts Review Initiatives [*Army*] (RDA) .... SPRINT
Spare Parts Sales Work Order .... SPSWO
Spare Parts Selection List .... SPSL
Spare Parts Support Package .... SPSP
Spare Parts Support Package for Aerospace Ground Equipment (MCD) .... SPSP-AGE
Spare Parts Transfer .... SPT
Spare Parts Withdrawal (MCD) .... SPW
Sparebanken Rogaland [*Rogaland Savings Bank*] [*Norway*] .... SR
Spares .... S
Spares Accounting Replenishment System [*NASA*] (KSC) .... SARS
Spares Acquisition Incorporated with Production List (MCD) .... SAIPL
Spares Acquisition Integrated with Production .... SAIP

Spares and Repair Parts [*Navy*] ... S & RP
Spares and Repair Parts Support [*Navy*] (NG) ... SPARPS
Spares Application Data List ... SADL
Spares Calculation Model ... SCM
Spares Change Advance Notice (MCD) ... SCAN
Spares Components Reidentification and Modification [*Program*] [*DoD*] ... SCRAM
Spares Control, Release, and Monitoring ... SCRAM
Spares Coordination Record (SAA) ... SCR
Spares Determination Method [*Bell System*] ... SDM
Spares Disposition Code [*NASA*] (NASA) ... SDC
Spares Handling Expense ... SHE
Spares Integrated Data System (MCD) ... SIDS
Spares Integrated Reporting and Control [*System*] ... SIRC
Spares Item Inventory Record (MCD) ... SIIR
Spares Level Activity Model (MCD) ... SLAM
Spares Management Improvement Program (DOMA) ... SMIP
Spares Management System ... SMS
Spares Master Data Log (IAA) ... SMDL
Spares Multiple Item Order (AAG) ... SMIO
Spares Optimization Model [*NASA*] (NASA) ... SOM
Spares Order Processing (MCD) ... SOP
Spares Planning (AAG) ... SP
Spares Provisioning and Requirements Effectiveness Model (PDAA) ... SPAREM
Spares Receiving Checklist (NRCH) ... SRC
Spares Recommendation List (MCD) ... SRL
Spares Recommendation Sheet (MCD) ... SRS
Spares Requirement ... SR
Spares Requirement Order ... SRO
Spares Requirement Schedule (MCD) ... SRS
Spares Shipping Order ... SSO
Spares Status Inquiry (AAG) ... SSI
Spare-Time Production for Gain [*FAO*] ... STPG
Sparing Fitting [*Cargo battens*] [*Shipping*] (DS) ... SF
Sparingly Soluble ... SS
Spark (AAG) ... SP
Spark (MSA) ... SPK
Spark Analysis for Traces [*Spectrometry*] ... SAFT
Spark Chamber Automatic Scanning System (DNAB) ... SASS
Spark Control [*Automotive engineering*] ... SC
Spark Control Computer [*Automotive engineering*] ... SCC
Spark Delay Device [*Automotive engineering*] ... SDD
Spark Delay Valve [*Automotive engineering*] ... SDV
Spark Gap (DEN) ... SG
Spark Gap Modulation ... SGM
Spark Ignition ... SI
Spark Ignition System ... SIS
Spark Plug (IAA) ... SP
Spark Plug ... SPPL
Spark Plug Collectors of America (EA) ... SPCA
Spark Plug Collectors of America (EA) ... SPCOA
Spark Port Vacuum [*Automotive engineering*] ... SPV
Spark Proof (IAA) ... SPKPRF
Spark Source Mass Spectroscopy ... SSM
Spark Source Mass Spectroscopy ... SSMS
Spark Thrust Augmentor (SAA) ... STA
Sparkman Centre for International Public Health Education (AIE) ... SCIPHE
Sparks Elementary School, Pasadena, TX [*Library symbol*] [*Library of Congress*] (LCLS) ... TxPSpE
Sparks International Official Fan Club (EAIO) ... SIFC
Sparks International Official Fan Club (EA) ... SIOFC
Sparks Memorial Library, Berrien Springs, MI [*Library symbol Library of Congress*] (LCLS) ... MiBs
Sparks, NV [*AM radio station call letters*] ... KPLY
Sparks, NV [*FM radio station call letters*] (RBYB) ... KQNV
Sparks, NV [*FM radio station call letters*] ... KSRN
Sparks' Rangoon Decisions [*British Burma*] [*A publication*] (DLA) ... Rang Dec
Sparks' Reports [*British Burma*] [*A publication*] (DLA) ... Sparks
Sparks-Goosen-Drake Engine [*Auto racing*] ... SGD
Sparrevohn [*Alaska*] [*Seismograph station code, US Geological Survey*] (SEIS) ... SVW
Sparrevohn Air Force Station [*Alaska*] [*ICAO location identifier*] (ICLI) ... PASV
Sparrevohn, AK [*Location identifier FAA*] (FAAL) ... CRN
Sparrevohn, AK [*Location identifier FAA*] (FAAL) ... SQA
Sparrevohn, AK [*Location identifier FAA*] (FAAL) ... SVW
Sparrow Antiradiation Missile (MCD) ... SPARM
Sparrow (E.W.) Hospital Library, Lansing, MI [*Library symbol*] [*Library of Congress*] (LCLS) ... MiLS
Sparse Distributed Memory [*Computer science*] ... SDM
Sparta [*Greece*] [*Airport symbol Obsolete*] (OAG) ... SPJ
Sparta Acquisition Digital Equipment (MCD) ... SPADE
Sparta Foods [*Commercial firm Associated Press*] (SAG) ... SpartaFd
Sparta Foods [*Commercial firm NASDAQ symbol*] (SAG) ... SPFO
Sparta Free Library, Sparta, WI [*Library symbol Library of Congress*] (LCLS) ... WSpa
Sparta, GA [*FM radio station call letters*] ... WMGZ
Sparta, IL [*Location identifier FAA*] (FAAL) ... SAR
Sparta, IL [*AM radio station call letters*] ... WHCO
Sparta, MO [*FM radio station call letters*] ... KLTQ
Sparta, NC [*AM radio station call letters*] ... WCOK
Sparta, NJ [*Location identifier FAA*] (FAAL) ... SAX
Sparta Pharmaceutical, Inc. [*Associated Press*] (SAG) ... SpartaPh
Sparta Pharmaceutical, Inc. [*Associated Press*] (SAG) ... SprtaP
Sparta Pharmaceutical, Inc. [*Associated Press*] (SAG) ... SprtP
Sparta Pharmaceutical, Inc. [*NASDAQ symbol*] (SAG) ... SPTA
Sparta Pharmaceutical, Inc. [*Associated Press*] (SAG) ... SptaP
Sparta Pharmaceuticals [*NASDAQ symbol*] (TTSB) ... SPTA
Sparta Pharmaceuticals Wrrt'A' [*NASDAQ symbol*] (TTSB) ... SPTAW
Sparta Pharmaceuticals Wrrt'B' [*NASDAQ symbol*] (TTSB) ... SPTAZ
Sparta Surgical [*NASDAQ symbol*] (TTSB) ... SPSG
Sparta Surgical Corp. [*Associated Press*] (SAG) ... SprtaSur
Sparta Surgical Corp. [*Associated Press*] (SAG) ... SprtS
Sparta Surgical Corp. [*Associated Press*] (SAG) ... SprtS96
Sparta Surgical Corp. [*NASDAQ symbol*] (SAG) ... SPSG
Sparta Surgical Corp. [*Associated Press*] (SAG) ... SptSu
Sparta Surgical Unit [*NASDAQ symbol*] (TTSB) ... SPSGU
Sparta Surgical Wrrt [*NASDAQ symbol*] (TTSB) ... SPSGW
Sparta, TN [*Location identifier FAA*] (FAAL) ... HEM
Sparta, TN [*Location identifier FAA*] (FAAL) ... SRB
Sparta, TN [*AM radio station call letters*] ... WSMT
Sparta, TN [*FM radio station call letters*] ... WSMT-FM
Sparta, TN [*AM radio station call letters*] ... WTZX
Sparta, WI [*Location identifier FAA*] (FAAL) ... CMY
Sparta, WI [*FM radio station call letters*] ... WCOW
Sparta, WI [*AM radio station call letters*] ... WKLJ
Spartacist League (EA) ... SL
Spartacus Youth League (EA) ... SYL
Spartan ... Spar
Spartan Guidance Computer [*Missiles*] (AABC) ... SGC
Spartan Hardware Inspection Discrepancy [*Missiles*] (MCD) ... SHID
Spartan Homing Sensor [*Missiles*] ... SHS
Spartan Improved Performance Study [*Missiles*] (AABC) ... SIPS
Spartan Management Action Board [*Missiles*] (MCD) ... SMAB
Spartan Material Availability Control [*Army*] ... SMAC
Spartan Material List [*Missiles*] (MCD) ... SML
Spartan Missile Equipment [*Missiles*] (MCD) ... SME
Spartan Motors [*NASDAQ symbol*] (TTSB) ... SPAR
Spartan Motors, Inc. [*Charlotte, MI*] [*NASDAQ symbol*] (NQ) ... SPAR
Spartan Motors, Inc. [*Associated Press*] (SAG) ... SpartMot
Spartan of Canada Ltd., London, Ontario [*Library symbol National Library of Canada*] (NLC) ... OLS
Spartan Potential Production Problem Analysis [*Missiles*] (MCD) ... SPPPA
Spartan Production Program Producibility Analysis [*Missiles*] (MCD) ... SPPPA
Spartan Program [*Missiles*] (MCD) ... SP
Spartan Safety Hazard Report [*Missiles*] (MCD) ... SSHR
SPARTAN Santa Monica Checkout [*NASA*] ... SSMCO
Spartan Simulation [*Missile system evaluation*] (RDA) ... SPARSIM
Spartan Tactical Equipment Verification Site [*Missiles*] (MCD) ... STEVS
Spartan-Approved Parts List [*Missiles*] (MCD) ... SAPL
Spartanburg County Public Library, Spartanburg, SC [*Library symbol Library of Congress*] (LCLS) ... ScSp
Spartanburg County Public Library, Spartanburg, SC [*OCLC symbol*] (OCLC) ... SPL
Spartanburg Methodist College, Spartanburg, SC [*Library symbol*] [*Library of Congress*] (LCLS) ... ScSpSM
Spartanburg, SC [*Location identifier FAA*] (FAAL) ... FRT
Spartanburg, SC [*Location identifier FAA*] (FAAL) ... SPA
Spartanburg, SC [*AM radio station call letters*] ... WASC
Spartanburg, SC [*AM radio station call letters*] ... WMMZ
Spartanburg, SC [*AM radio station call letters*] ... WORD
Spartanburg, SC [*Television station call letters*] ... WRET
Spartanburg, SC [*AM radio station call letters*] ... WSPA
Spartanburg, SC [*FM radio station call letters*] ... WSPA-FM
Spartanburg, SC [*Television station call letters*] ... WSPA-TV
Spartanburg Technical College, Spartanburg, SC [*Library symbol*] [*Library of Congress*] (LCLS) ... ScSpTC
Spartan-Furnished Property [*Missiles*] (MCD) ... SFP
Spartan-Furnished Property Request List [*Missiles*] (MCD) ... SFPRL
Spartech Corp. [*NYSE symbol*] (SAG) ... SEH
Spartech Corp. [*Associated Press*] (SAG) ... Spartch
Sparti [*Greece*] [*ICAO location identifier*] (ICLI) ... LGSP
Sparton Corp. [*NYSE symbol*] (SPSG) ... SPA
Sparton Corp. [*Associated Press*] (SAG) ... Sparton
Sparton of Canada Ltd., London, ON, Canada [*Library symbol*] [*Library of Congress*] (LCLS) ... CaOLS
Sparton Resources, Inc. [*Toronto Stock Exchange symbol*] ... SPN
Sparwood Public Library, British Columbia [*Library symbol National Library of Canada*] (NLC) ... BSPA
SPASA Servicios Politecnicos Aereos SA [*Spain ICAO designator*] (FAAC) ... SPS
Spasmodic Torticollis [*Medicine*] ... ST
Spasmolytic Polypeptide [*Biochemistry*] ... SP
Spastic Centre of New South Wales [*Australia*] ... SCNSW
Spastic Centres of South Australia ... SCOSA
Spastic Centres of South Australia ... SCSA
Spastic Paraplegia, X-Linked [*Medicine*] (DMAA) ... SPGX
Spastic Society of Victoria [*Australia*] ... SSV
Spatial Ability [*Psychology*] ... S
Spatial Antimissile Research Test in Australia (IAA) ... SPARTA
Spatial Average, Temporal Average [*Medicine*] (DMAA) ... SATA
Spatial Average Temporal Peak [*Medicine*] (DMAA) ... SATP
Spatial Computer ... SPAC
Spatial Data Management System (MCD) ... SDMS
Spatial Data Option ... SDO
Spatial Data Transfer Standard [*Computer science*] ... SDTS
Spatial Database Engine ... SDE
Spatial Delayed-Response [*Ophthalmology*] ... SDR
Spatial Disorientation Trainer [*Military*] ... SDT
Spatial Distribution Functions [*Of molecules*] ... SDF
Spatial Emotional (Stimuli) ... SE

Spatial Equalization ... SEq
Spatial Frequency Analyzer ... SFA
Spatial, High-Accuracy Position Encoding Sensor (SSD) ... SHAPES
Spatial Inertial Reference Equipment ... SPIRE
Spatial Information Management ... SIM
Spatial Light Modulator [*Computer imaging*] ... SLM
Spatial Light Modulator [*Optical computing*] ... SLM
Spatial Modulation of Magnetization [*Medicine*] (DMAA) ... SPAMM
Spatial Nonemotional (Stimuli) ... SNE
Spatial Operational Sequence Diagram ... SOSD
Spatial Orientation Trainer [*Air Force*] ... SOT
Spatial Paradigm for Information Retrieval and Exploration [*Computer science*] ... SPIRE
Spatial Property Analyzer ... SPAYZ
Spatial Reference System [*Mapping*] (EERA) ... SRS
Spatial Sound Around [*Acoustics*] ... SSA
Spatial Spectrum Center Shifting (PDAA) ... SSCS
Spatial Technology, Inc. [*Associated Press*] (SAG) ... SpatialT
Spatial Technology, Inc. [*AMEX symbol*] (SAG) ... STY
Spatial Transformation of Sound Fields ... STSF
Spatial Vectorcardiogram [*Cardiology*] ... SVCG
Spatial Visual Evoked Response (OA) ... SVER
Spatialight, Inc. [*NASDAQ symbol*] (SAG) ... SLHT
Spatialight, Inc. [*Associated Press*] (SAG) ... Spatialght
Spatializer Audio Labs [*NASDAQ symbol*] (TTSB) ... SPAZ
Spatializer Audio Labs, Inc. [*Associated Press*] (SAG) ... Spatlzr
Spatializer Audio Labs, Inc. [*NASDAQ symbol*] (SAG) ... SPAZ
Spatially Orientated Referencing Systems Association (EERA) ... SORSA
Spatiotemporal Chaos [*Physics*] ... STC
Spaulding Teacher Activity Rating Schedule (EDAC) ... STARS
Spaulding's Reports [*71-73 Maine*] [*A publication*] (DLA) ... Spaulding
Spawning Mark ... SM
Speak ... S
Speak Easy International Foundation (EA) ... SEIF
Speaker (AAG) ... SPKR
Speaker (IDOE) ... spkr
Speaker Amplifier ... SA
Speaker Authentication Technique ... SAT
Speaker Independent Recognition (IAA) ... SIR
Speaker Intercom ... SI
Speaker Intercom Assembly [*NASA*] ... SIA
Speaker Intercom System (KSC) ... SIS
Speaker of the House of Keys [*British*] (ROG) ... SHK
Speaking to American Youth (AEBS) ... SAY
Spearfish [*South Dakota*] [*Airport symbol*] (AD) ... SPF
Spearfish, SD [*FM radio station call letters*] ... KBHU
Spearfish, SD [*FM radio station call letters*] (RBYB) ... KDDX
Spearfish, SD [*FM radio station call letters*] ... KSLT
Spearfish, SD [*Location identifier FAA*] (FAAL) ... SPF
Spearman on Highways [*1881*] [*A publication*] (DLA) ... Spear High
Spearman, TX [*FM radio station call letters*] ... KRDF
Spear's Law of Extradition [*A publication*] (DLA) ... Spear Ext
Spears' South Carolina Chancery Reports [*A publication*] (DLA) ... Sp Ch
Spears' South Carolina Chancery Reports [*A publication*] (DLA) ... Spear Ch
Spears' South Carolina Equity Reports [*A publication*] (DLA) ... Sp Eq
Spears' South Carolina Equity Reports [*A publication*] (DLA) ... Spear Eq
Spears' South Carolina Equity Reports [*1842-44*] [*A publication*] (DLA) ... Spears
Spears' South Carolina Equity Reports [*A publication*] (DLA) ... Spears Eq
Spears' South Carolina Law Reports [*1842-44*] [*A publication*] (DLA) ... Sp
Spears' South Carolina Law Reports [*1842-44*] [*A publication*] (DLA) ... Spear
Spears' South Carolina Law Reports [*A publication*] (DLA) ... Spears
Spec Racer [*Automotive classification*] ... SR
Specia [*France*] [*Research code symbol*] ... RP
Special ... S
Special (AFM) ... SP
Special (IDOE) ... sp
Special (MSA) ... SPCL
Special [*or Specialist*] (KSC) ... SPEC
Special ... SPEC
Special (ROG) ... SPECL
Special (AAG) ... SPL
Special Abilities of an Individual [*Symbol*] [*Psychology*] ... s
Special Acceptance Inspection Equipment ... SAIE
Special Acceptance Test Equipment (MCD) ... SATE
Special Access ... SA
Special Access, Compartmented (MCD) ... SC
Special Access Only (MCD) ... SAO
Special Access Program (DOMA) ... SAP
Special Access Required ... SAR
Special Access Space (CAAL) ... SAS
Special Accident Insurance (MCD) ... SAI
Special Accounting Class [*Navy*] (DNAB) ... SAC
Special Accounts Property Disposal Officer [*Military*] ... SAPDO
Special Action [*Military*] (AFM) ... SA
Special Action Force [*Military*] ... SAF
Special Action Office [*Phased out, 1975*] [*Department of Justice*] ... SAO
Special Action Office for Drug Abuse Prevention [*Terminated, 1975*] [*FDA*] ... SAODAP
Special Action Office for Mexico [*Drug Enforcement Administration*] ... SAO/MEX
Special Active Duty for Training [*Military*] (AABC) ... SADT
Special Activities [*Air Force*] ... S/A
Special Activities Group [*Air Force*] ... SAG
Special Activities Office [*Air Force*] (AFM) ... SAO
Special Activities Squadron [*Air Force*] ... SAS
Special Activity Wing (MUGU) ... SPAWG
Special Adapter Device (IAA) ... SAD
Special Administrative Region [*Hong Kong*] ... SAR
Special Adult Learning Programmes Association (AIE) ... SALPA
Special Adviser to the President on Foreign Trade [*New Deal*] ... SAPFT
Special Advisory Committee [*Navy*] (DNAB) ... SAC
Special Advisory Committee on Telecommunications (NTCM) ... SACT
Special Advisory Committee on Telecommunications ... SCAT
Special Advisory Message ... SAM
Special Advisory Working Group (NATG) ... SAWG
Special Aeronautical Material [*Navy*] (NG) ... SPAM
Special Aeronautical Requirement [*Navy*] (NG) ... SAR
Special Agent (AFM) ... SA
Special Agent in Charge [*FBI*] ... SAC
Special Agent in Charge [*Department of the Treasury*] ... SAIC
Special Agents Mutual Benefit Association [*FBI standardized term*] ... SAMBA
Special Agricultural Worker ... SAW
Special Air Force Airlift Mission (NASA) ... SAAM
Special Air Mission [*Aircraft*] [*Military*] ... SAM
Special Air Mission Squadron [*Vietnam Air Force*] (AFM) ... SAMSq
Special Air Operations ... SAO
Special Air Route Designators (CINC) ... SARDS
Special Air Service [*British commando unit*] ... SAS
Special Air Services [*Australia*] (VNW) ... SAS
Special Air Task Force [*Navy*] ... SATFOR
Special Air Warfare (AFM) ... SAW
Special Air Warfare Center ... SAWC
Special Air Warfare Forces (AFM) ... SAWF
Special Airborne Medical Care Unit (MCD) ... SAMCU
Special Airborne Weapon Subsystem (MCD) ... SAWS
Special Aircraft Project Office (AAG) ... SAPO
Special Aircraft Service Shop (NG) ... SASS
Special Airfield Pavement Program (NATG) ... SAPP
Special Airlift Assignment Missions [*Military*] ... SAAMS
Special Airlift Requirement Directive [*Air Force*] (AFM) ... SARD
Special Airlift Requirement Document [*Army*] ... SARD
Special Airlift Summary [*MTMC*] (TAG) ... SAS
Special Air-Report [*Aviation code*] ... ARS
Special Airspace Management System/Military Airspace Management System [*FAA*] (TAG) ... SAMS/MAMS
Special Allied Airborne Reconnaissance Force [*Teams parachuted into POW areas to take supplies to prisoners or to help them get out*] [*World War II*] ... SAARF
Special Ammunition and Analysis Section [*Picatinny Arsenal*] [*Dover, NJ*] ... SAAS
Special Ammunition Load [*Army*] (AABC) ... SAL
Special Ammunition Logistical Element ... SALE
Special Ammunition Section [*Picatinny Arsenal*] [*Army*] ... SAS
Special Ammunition Site [*Army*] ... SAS
Special Ammunition Stockage [*Army*] (AABC) ... SAS
Special Ammunition Storage (RDA) ... SAS
Special Ammunition Supply Activity (MCD) ... SASA
Special Ammunition Supply Point [*Army*] ... SASP
Special Ammunition Support Command [*Army*] (AABC) ... SASCOM
Special Analysis Center [*Marine science*] (OSRA) ... SAC
Special Analysis of Net Radio [*Study*] ... SPANNER
Special Analysis Office ... SAO
Special and Administrative Provisions [*of the Tariff Act of 1930*] ... SAP
Special and Selected Law Cases [*1648*] [*England*] [*A publication*] (DLA) ... Sp & Sel Cas
Special Antarctic Blend [*Fuel*] ... SAB
Special Antimissile Research Tests in Australia ... SPARTA
Special Appaaratus Rack (IAA) ... SAR
Special Application [*Lift truck*] ... SA
Special Application Alarm Monitoring System ... SAAMS
Special Application of Finite Element Representation [*Marine science*] (OSRA) ... SAFER
Special Applications Routine (IAA) ... SARO
Special Approaches to Juvenile Assistance [*Defunct*] (EA) ... SAJA
Special Arbitrage Account ... SAA
Special Arc Light Operation Area (DNAB) ... SALOA
Special Area [*RADAR*] ... SA
Special Area Code [*Bell System*] ... SAC
Special Army Evaluation Board (AABC) ... SAEB
Special Army Review Team (MCD) ... SART
Special Army Signal Service (IAA) ... SASS
Special Army Squadron [*British*] (DI) ... SAS
Special Artificer [*Navy*] ... SA
Special Artificer, Instruments, Typewriter, and Office Equipment Repairman [*Navy*] ... SAITR
Special Artificer, Instruments, Watch Repairman [*Navy*] ... SAIWR
Special Artificer, Optical [*Navy*] ... SAO
Special Artificer, Special Devices, Machine Gun Trainer [*Navy*] ... SADMG
Special Artificer, Special Synthetic Training Devices [*Navy*] ... SAD
Special Asian Warfare Training and Orientation Center [*Located on the Hawaiian island of Oahu*] (VNW) ... SAWTOC
Special Assembly for Fast Installations [*Telecommunications*] (TEL) ... SAFFI
Special Assessment Bond ... SAB
Special Assignment [*Navy*] ... SA
Special Assignment [*Military*] (NVT) ... SPCLASGN
Special Assignment Air Mission [*Navy*] (NVT) ... SAAM
Special Assignment Airlift [*Air Force*] (AFM) ... SAA
Special Assignment Airlift & Mission [*MTMC*] (TAG) ... SAAM
Special Assignment Airlift Movement [*Army*] (AABC) ... SAAM
Special Assistance Team [*Navy*] (NG) ... SAT
Special Assistant (GFGA) ... SA

Special Assistant [*Navy*] ..... SPAST
Special Assistant for Arms Control [*Military*] ..... SAAC
Special Assistant for Civilian Personnel [*Navy*] (DNAB) ..... SACP
Special Assistant for Civilian Personnel / Equal Employment Opportunity [*Navy*] (DNAB) ..... SACP/EEO
Special Assistant for Consumer Affairs [*White House*] [*Obsolete*] ..... SACA
Special Assistant for Contracting Integrity (AAGC) ..... SACI
Special Assistant for Counterinsurgency and Special Activities [*Military*] (AFM) ..... SACSA
Special Assistant for Environmental Services [*Military*] ..... SAES
Special Assistant for Growing Enterprises [*Division of National American Wholesale Grocer's Association*] ..... SAGE
Special Assistant for Material Readiness [*Army*] ..... SAMR
Special Assistant for Military Assistance Affairs [*Army*] (AABC) ..... SAMAA
Special Assistant for Strategic Mobility [*Military*] (AFM) ..... SASM
Special Assistant for Surface Missile System ..... SASMS
Special Assistant to the Chief of Staff for Special Warfare [*Army*] ..... SAC/SSW
Special Assistant to the President for Science and Technology ..... SAPST
Special Assistant to the Secretary of the Navy ..... SASN
Special Assistant to the Secretary of the Navy (DNAB) ..... SPECASTSECNAV
Special Associated Logistics Course (MCD) ..... SALC
Special Astrophysics Observatory ..... SAO
Special Atomic Demolition Munitions [*Military*] (AABC) ..... SADM
Special Attention Personnel [*US VIP troops*] (VNW) ..... SAP
Special Audit Division (AAGC) ..... OAD
Special Automated Distribution List (AFIT) ..... SADL
Special Aviation Fire and Explosion Reduction (EGAO) ..... SAFER
Special Back Care [*Medicine*] ..... SBC
Special Background Investigation (NVT) ..... SBI
Special Bibliography ..... SB
Special Billing [*Telecommunications*] (TEL) ..... SB
Special Block Purchase ..... SBP
Special Block Sale ..... SBS
Special Board for Public Works [*New Deal*] ..... SBPW
Special Boat Section [*British military*] (DMA) ..... SBS
Special Boat Squadron [*British commando unit*] (DMA) ..... SB Sqn
Special Boat Squadron [*British commando unit*] ..... SBS
Special Boiling Point (IAA) ..... SBP
Special Branch [*British police*] ..... SB
Special Branch [*Navy British*] ..... Sp
Special Bridge Replacement Program 1970 [*MTMC*] (TAG) ..... SBRP
Special Bulletin. New York Department of Labor [*A publication*] (DLA) ..... SB
Special Business and Contract Directories [*A publication*] ..... SBCD
Special Business Directories [*A publication*] ..... SBD
Special Business Unit ..... SBU
Special Businessowners Policy [*Insurance*] ..... SBP
Special Buyer Credit Limit (MHDW) ..... SBCL
Special Care [*Medicine*] ..... SC
Special Care Baby Unit [*Medicine*] ..... SCBU
Special Care Nursery ..... SCN
Special Care Unit ..... SCU
Special Cargo Airlines [*Russian Federation*] [*ICAO designator*] (FAAC) ..... SCI
Special Category (MSA) ..... SPCAT
Special Category (AABC) ..... SPECAT
Special Category Army with Air Force ..... SCARWAF
Special Category Navy with Air Force ..... SCNAWAF
Special Category Patient [*Aeromedical evacuation*] ..... SCP
Special Center of Research [*HEW*] ..... SCOR
Special Certification Roster ..... SCR
Special Change Notice (KSC) ..... SCN
Special Characters Table [*Computer science*] (IBMDP) ..... SCT
Special Checkout Equipment [*NASA*] (NASA) ..... SCOE
Special Circuit ..... SC
Special Circular ..... SC
Special Claim on Residual Equity ..... SCORE
Special Cleaning ..... SPCLN
Special Code ..... SPC
Special Collections Division, University of British Columbia, Vancouver, BritishColumbia [*Library symbol National Library of Canada*] (NLC) ..... BVAUS
Special Command ..... SPECOM
Special Commission on Weather Modification ..... SCWC
Special Commissioner (DLA) ..... Sp C
Special Commissions of Income Tax [*British*] ..... SCIT
Special Committee for the International Biological Program [*National Research Council*] ..... SCIBP
Special Committee for the International Geophysical Year ..... SCIGY
Special Committee for United States Exports [*Washington, DC*] (EA) ..... SCUSE
Special Committee for Workplace Product Liability Reform (EA) ..... SCWPLR
Special Committee on Antarctic Research [*Marine science*] (OSRA) ..... SCEP
Special Committee on Antarctic Research [*International Council of Scientific Unions*] (USDC) ..... SCEP
Special Committee on Atlantic Research ..... SCAR
Special Committee on Atomic Research [*Pugwash Conference*] ..... SCAR
Special Committee on Compromising Emanations [*Military*] (AABC) ..... SCOCE
Special Committee on Environmental Information [*Special Libraries Association*] ..... SCEI
Special Committee on Latin American Coordination ..... SLAC
Special Committee on Migration and Resettlement [*Department of State*] [*World War II*] ..... SCMR
Special Committee on Oceanographic Research ..... SCOR
Special Committee on Paperless Entries [*California interbank group*] ..... SCOPE
Special Committee on Problems of the Environment [*of International Council of Scientific Unions*] ..... SCOPE
Special Committee on Space Technology (KSC) ..... SCOST
Special Committee on the Adequacy of Range Facilities (MUGU) ..... SCARF
Special Committee on Trade ..... SCT
Special Committee on Water Research [*International Council of Scientific Unions*] ..... SCOWR
Special Committee Opposing Resurgent Nazism ..... SCORN
Special Common [*Projectile*] ..... SPC
Special Commonwealth African Assistance Plan ..... SCAAP
Special Communications Alteration ..... SPECOMALT
Special Communications Division [*Navy*] (DNAB) ..... SPECOMDIV
Special Communications System (MCD) ..... SCS
Special Compartmented Intelligence [*DoD*] (MCD) ..... SCI
Special Compartmented Intelligence Facility [*DoD*] ..... SCIF
Special Competition Advocate (AAGC) ..... SCA
Special Computer Service (IAA) ..... SCS
Special COMSEC Advisory Group [*US Army Communications Command*] (MCD) ..... SCAG
Special Conditioning Equipment ..... SCE
Special Conditions (MCD) ..... S/C
Special Constable ..... SC
Special Constituency Section for Mental Health and Psychiatric Services (EA) ..... SCSMHPS
Special Consultative Committee on Security [*OAS*] ..... SCCS
Special Consultative Group [*NATO*] ..... SCG
Special Contingency Stockpile [*Military*] (AABC) ..... SCS
Special Control Item [*Code*] ..... SCI
Special Control Item Code ..... SCIC
Special Coordinating Committee [*National Security Council*] [*Terminated, 1981*] ..... SCC
Special Coordination Committee (Intelligence) (MCD) ..... SCC(I)
Special Court Regional Railroad Reorganization Act [*A publication*] (DLA) ..... Regional Rail Reorg Ct
Special Court Regional Railroad Reorganization Act [*A publication*] (DLA) ..... Sp Ct RRRA
Special Court-Martial ..... SCM
Special Court-Martial ..... SPCM
Special Court-Martial, Air Force [*United States*] (DLA) ..... ACMS
Special Court-Martial, Coast Guard [*United States*] (DLA) ..... CGCMS
Special Court-Martial Order ..... SPCMO
Special Court-Martial without a Military Judge (AFM) ..... SPCMWOMJ
Special Crew Time (DNAB) ..... SCT
Special Criminal Court (DLA) ..... Sp Cr Ct
Special Crisis Intervention Program (OICC) ..... SCIP
Special Criteria for Retrograde of Army Materiel (AABC) ..... SCRAM
Special Cryptologic Control Number (DNAB) ..... SCC NR
Special Customer-Oriented Language ..... SPECOL
Special Customs Invoice ..... SCI
Special Day Class [*Education*] ..... SDC
Special Defence Intelligence Notice (MCD) ..... SDIN
Special Defense Acquisition Fund [*Military*] ..... SDAF
Special Defense Intelligence Estimate (MCD) ..... SDIE
Special Defense Projects Department ..... SDPD
Special Defense Property Disposal Account [*DoD*] ..... SDPDA
Special Delivery ..... SD
Special Delivery (WDAA) ..... SP DEL
Special Denatured Formula [*Applied to alcohol*] ..... SDF
Special Depot Level Maintenance ..... SDLM
Special Development Assistance Fund ..... SDAF
Special Development Groups [*Navy*] ..... SDG
Special Devices [*NASDAQ symbol*] (TTSB) ..... SDII
Special Devices Center [*Navy*] ..... SDC
Special Devices Center [*Navy*] ..... SPECDEVCEN
Special Devices, Inc. [*NASDAQ symbol*] (SPSG) ..... SDII
Special Devices, Inc. [*Associated Press*] (SAG) ..... SpclDv
Special Diary Transcript [*Military*] ..... SPEDIAT
Special Disbursing Agent, Bureau of Indian Affairs [*United States*] (DLA) ..... SDA
Special Discriminant (CAAL) ..... SPDI
Special Dispatch Rider ..... SDR
Special Distress Signal (DEN) ..... SDS
Special District Bond ..... SDB
Special Docking Simulator [*NASA*] (KSC) ..... SDS
Special Doctrine Equipment Group [*Army*] ..... SDEG
Special Document ..... SD
Special Domestically Available Documents [*NASA*] (KSC) ..... SDAD
Special Drawing Rights [*International Monetary Fund*] ..... SDR
Special Drawing Rights (TDOB) ..... SDR
Special Drawing Rights [*Investment term*] (DFIT) ..... SDR
Special Drill [*Tool*] (AAG) ..... SPDR
Special Duty [*Military*] ..... SD
Special Duty Assignment (AFM) ..... SDA
Special Duty Assignment Pay [*Army*] (INF) ..... SDAP
Special Duty Assignment Proficiency Pay [*Air Force*] ..... SDAPP
Special Duty Officer (MCD) ..... SDO
Special Duty Only [*Military*] ..... SDO
Special Economic Acquisition Provision [*Procurement*] ..... SEAP
Special Economic Zone ..... SEZ
Special Edition [*Car model designation*] ..... SE
Special Eduation Local Planning Agency (EDAC) ..... SELPA
Special Education (DAVI) ..... Spec Ed
Special Education ..... SPED
Special Education Administration Task Simulation Game ..... SEATS
Special Education Director ..... SPED
Special Education in the Regular Classroom Project [*U.S. Office of Special Educ ation and Rehabilitation Services*] (EDAC) ..... SERC
Special Education Instructional Materials Centers [*Office of Education*] [*Database producer*] (IID) ..... SEIMC
Special Education Programs [*Department of Education*] [*Formerly, BEH*] ..... SEP

Special Education Resource Teacher ... SERT
Special Education Review Team ... SERT
Special Education Specialist (PGP) ... Sp Ed S
Special Education Specialist (GAGS) ... SpES
Special Education Specialist (PGP) ... SPS
Special Educational Needs (AIE) ... SEN
Special Educational Needs Joint Initiative for Training (AIE) ... SENJIT
Special Effect Generator [*Video technology*] ... SEG
Special Effects (NTCM) ... EFX
Special Effects [*Filmmaking*] ... SPFX
Special Effects Warhead (MCD) ... SEW
Special Electric Motors [*Manufacturing company*] [*British*] ... SEM
Special Electrical Devices (AABC) ... SED
Special Electromagnetic Interference (MCD) ... SEMI
Special Electron Tube Section ... SETS
Special Electronic Mission Aircraft (RDA) ... SEMA
Special Electronics Air Mobility System [*Army*] ... SEAMS
Special Elementary Education for the Disadvantaged ... SEED
Special Elite Forces Society (EA) ... SEFS
Special Emergency Campaign [*Red Cross fund-raising*] ... SEC
Special Emergency Programme for the Horn of Africa [*World Food Programme*] [*United Nations*] ... SEPHA
Special Emergency Reaction Team ... SERT
Special Emergency Reaction Team Facility ... SERF
Special Emphasis Program [*DoD*] ... SEP
Special Emphasis Reliability Area (MCD) ... SERA
Special Emphasis Study (NASA) ... SES
Special Engineering Investigation (MCD) ... SEI
Special Engineering Order [*NASA*] (NASA) ... SEO
Special Engineering Review of Events Nobody Envisioned ... SERENE
Special Engineering Test (IAA) ... SET
Special English Language Materials for Overseas University Students ... SELMOUS
Special Enlistment Bonus (MCD) ... SEB
Special Enrollment Period [*Department of Health and Human Services*] (GFGA) ... SEP
Special Entry Flying List [*Navy British*] ... SEF
Special Environment Powder Diffractometer ... SEPD
Special Environmental Radiometallurgy Facility [*Nuclear energy*] (NRCH) ... SERF
Special Environmental Sample Container [*NASA*] (PDAA) ... SESC
Special Environmental Storage Requirements (MCD) ... SESR
Special Equipment ... SE
Special Equipment (AAG) ... SPEQ
Special Equipment Authorization (AAG) ... SEA
Special Equipment Item (MCD) ... SEI
Special Equipment Option [*Automotive assembly*] ... SEO
Special Equipment Parts and Assemblies Section (AAG) ... SEP & A
Special Equipment Vehicle [*Military*] ... SEV
Special Essential Elements of Information (MCD) ... SEEI
Special Event Charter Flight [*Aviation*] (DA) ... SEC
Special Event Search and Master Analysis (GAVI) ... SESMA
Special Exchange Service [*Telecommunications*] (TEL) ... SES
Special Executive for Counterintelligence, Terrorism, Revenge, and Extortion [*Fictitious organization whose agents were characters in the late Ian Fleming's "James Bond" mysteries*] ... SPECTRE
Special Exercise [*Navy*] (NVT) ... SPEX
Special Expanded Display (IAA) ... SED
Special Experience Identifier [*Military*] ... SEI
Special Experimental Display Generation (IAA) ... SEDGE
Special Experimental Display Generation Program (SAA) ... SEDGE
Special Exploitation Service [*South Vietnamese studies and observations group*] [*Military*] (VNW) ... SES
Special Explosive Ordnance Disposal Supplies and Equipment [*Army*] (AABC) ... SEODSE
Special Extensive Routine Functions (NITA) ... SERF
Special Extra Deep Drawing (MCD) ... SEDD
Special Facilities ... SF
Special Features (NITA) ... SF
Special Federal Aviation Regulation [*FAA*] ... SFAR
Special Federal Aviation Regulation 38 [*FAA*] (TAG) ... SFAR-38
Special Federal Project Funds [*Medicaid Program*] (GFGA) ... SFPF
Special Federal Responsibilities (OICC) ... SFR
Special Film Project ... SFP
Special Filter Wheel [*Military*] (CAAL) ... SFW
Special Fixtures (MCD) ... SF
Special Flight Area Rule [*Aviation*] ... SFAR
Special Flight Charts [*Air Force*] ... SFC
Special Flight Test ... SFT
Special Flight Test Instrumentation (MCD) ... SFTI
Special Flight Test Instrumentation Pool (NG) ... SFTIP
Special Flood Hazard Area [*Information service or system*] (EMRF) ... SFHA
Special Forces [*Military*] ... SF
Special Forces Assessment and Selection [*Military*] (INF) ... SFAS
Special Forces Association (EA) ... SFA
Special Forces Association [*Fraternal group of discharged military personnel who returned to live in Saigon*] (VNW) ... SFAS
Special Forces Auxiliary [*Military*] ... SFA
Special Forces Burst Communications Systems [*Army*] (RDA) ... SFBCS
Special Forces Command [*Navy*] (DNAB) ... SPECFORCOM
Special Forces Co. [*Military*] (CINC) ... SFCO
Special Forces Direct Action [*Army*] ... SFDA
Special Forces Group [*Military*] ... SFG
Special Forces Operational Base [*Army*] ... SFOB
Special Forces Operational Detachment [*Army*] (AABC) ... SFOD
Special Forces Qualification Course [*Military*] (INF) ... SFQC
Special Forces Reconnaissance [*Army*] ... SFR
Special Forces Tab [*Military*] (GFGA) ... SFTab
Special Foreign Activities [*Military*] (AABC) ... SFA
Special Foreign Currency [*US counterpart funds*] ... SFC
Special Foreign Currency Program [*National Institute of Standards and Technology*] ... SFCP
Special Foreign Currency Science Information [*Program*] [*National Science Foundation*] ... SFCSI
Special Foreign Currency Science Information Program [*National Science Foundation*] ... SFCSIP
Special Fraction [*Typography*] (WDMC) ... SF
Special Friends of Dottie West (EA) ... SFDW
Special Function Key [*Calculators*] ... SFK
Special Function Unit ... SFU
Special Fund for Youth [*UNESCO*] (EAIO) ... SFY
Special Furnish Off Machine [*Paper*] (DGA) ... SFOM
Special Furnished Equipment (MCD) ... SFE
Special Furnished Property (MCD) ... SFP
Special Gas Taper [*Thread*] ... SGT
Special Government Design (DNAB) ... SGD
Special Grade (DNAB) ... SG
Special Group [*NATO*] ... SG
Special Group Inclusive Tour [*Airline fare*] ... SGIT
Special Handling (MCD) ... SPECHNDLG
Special Handling Area (EECA) ... SHA
Special Handling Code ... SHC
Special Handling Designator (MCD) ... SHD
Special Handling Equipment ... SHE
Special Handling Inventory Procedure (MCD) ... SHIP
Special Handling Service for Aircraft [*ICAO designator*] (ICDA) ... XH
Special Handling Service for Aircraft [*FAA designator*] (FAAC) ... XHA
Special Hard-Target Assault Weapon LAW (RDA) ... SHAWL
Special Hazards ... SH
Special Health Authority [*Government body*] [*British*] ... SHA
Special High Grade [*Zinc metal*] ... SHG
Special Honor ... SH
Special Impact Program (OICC) ... SIP
Special Industrial Radio Service Association (EA) ... SIRSA
Special Industrial Services [*United Nations Industrial Development Organization*] ... SIS
Special Information Center (MCD) ... SIC
Special Information Retrieval ... SIR
Special Information System (MCD) ... SIS
Special Information Tones [*Telecommunications*] ... SIT
Special Initial Clothing Monetary Allowance [*Military*] (DNAB) ... SICMA
Special Initial Clothing Monetary Allowance - Civilian [*Military*] (DNAB) ... SICMA-CIV
Special Initial Clothing Monetary Allowance - Naval Aviation Cadet [*Navy*] (DNAB) ... SICMA-NAVCAD
Special Initial Clothing Monetary Allowance - Naval Aviation Officer Candidate [*Navy*] (DNAB) ... SICMA-NAOC
Special In-Process Review (MCD) ... SIPR
Special Inquiry [*Classification system used by doctors on Ellis Island to detain, re-examine, and possibly deny entry to certain immigrants*] ... SI
Special Inquiry [*FBI term*] ... SPIN
Special Inquiry Officer ... SIO
Special Inspection (MCD) ... SI
Special Inspection, Army Nuclear Matters (MCD) ... SIANM
Special Inspection Equipment ... SIE
Special Inspection Requirement ... SIR
Special Institution for Scientific and Technological Education and Research [*In proposal stage, 1964, in Great Britain*] ... SISTER
Special Instruction ... SI
Special Instruction (DOMA) ... SPINS
Special Instruction Indicator (AAGC) ... SII
Special Intelligence [*Army*] (AABC) ... SI
Special Intelligence (MCD) ... SPINT
Special Intelligence Brief (MCD) ... SIB
Special Intelligence Communications (MCD) ... SI COMMS
Special Intelligence Communications [*Later, DIN/DSSCS*] ... SPINTCOM
Special Intelligence Communications [*Later, DIN/DSSCS*] (CET) ... SPINTCOMM
Special Intelligence Detachment [*Military*] (CINC) ... SID
Special Intelligence/Electronic Warfare (MCD) ... SI/EW
Special Intelligence Officer [*Military*] (NVT) ... SIO
Special Intelligence Service ... SIS
Special Intelligence/Special Activities Office (MCD) ... SI/SAO
Special Intercept Priorities Group [*Armed Forces Security Agency*] ... SIPG
Special Inter-Departmental Selection Committee [*UN Food and Agriculture Organization*] ... SISCO
Special Interest Aircraft (NVT) ... SPINTAC
Special Interest Auto Club [*Defunct*] (EA) ... SIAC
Special Interest Automobiles [*A publication*] ... SIA
Special Interest Committee ... SIC
Special Interest Committee on Program Documentation [*Association for Computing Machinery*] ... SICDOC
Special Interest Group ... SIG
Special Interest Group/Arts and Humanities [*of the American Society for Information Science*] ... SIG/AH
Special Interest Group/Automated Language Processing [*American Society for Information Science*] ... SIG/ALP
Special Interest Group/Behavioral and Social Sciences [*of the American Society for Information Science*] ... SIG/BSS
Special Interest Group/Biological and Chemical Information Systems [*of the American Society for Information Science*] ... SIG/BC

Special Interest Group/Classification Research [*of the American Society for Information Science*] .... SIG/CR

Special Interest Group/Costs, Budgeting, and Economics [*of the American Society for Information Science*] .... SIG/CBE

Special Interest Group/Education for Information Science [*of the American Society for Information Science*] .... SIG/ES

Special Interest Group for Architecture of Computer Systems (EA) ..... SIGARCH

Special Interest Group for Business Data Processing and Management (EA) .... SIGBDP

Special Interest Group for Computer Personnel Research (EA) ...... SIGCPR

Special Interest Group for Computer Science Education (EA) .... SIG CSE

Special Interest Group for Computer Uses in Education (EA) .... SIGCUE

Special Interest Group for Computers and Society (EA) .... SIGCAS

Special Interest Group for Computers and Society [*Association for Computing Machinery*] (EA) .... SIGCS

Special Interest Group for Computers and the Physically Handicapped (EA) .... SIGCAPH

Special Interest Group for Design Automation (EA) .... SIGDA

Special Interest Group for Mathematical Programming [*Defunct*] (EA)..... SIGMAP

Special Interest Group for Symbolic and Algebraic Manipulation (EA) .... SIGSAM

Special Interest Group for Systems Documentation (EA) .... SIGDOC

Special Interest Group for University and College Computing Services (EA) .... SIGUCCS

Special Interest Group/Foundations of Information Science [*of the American Society for Information Science*] .... SIG/FIS

Special Interest Group/Information Analysis Centers [*of the American Society for Information Science*] .... SIG/IAC

Special Interest Group/Information Services to Education [*of the American Society for Information Science*] .... SIG/ISE

Special Interest Group/Library Automation and Networks [*of the American Society for Information Science*] .... SIG/LA

Special Interest Group/Nonprint Media [*of the American Society for Information Science*] .... SIG/NPM

Special Interest Group on Ada (EA) .... SIGADA

Special Interest Group on APL Programming Language (EA) .... SIGAPL

Special Interest Group on Artificial Intelligence (EA) .... SIGART

Special Interest Group on Automata and Computability Theory (EA) ..... SIGACT

Special Interest Group on Biomedical Computing (EA) .... SIGBIO

Special Interest Group on CD-ROM Applications and Technology (AAGC) .... SIGCAT

Special Interest Group on Computer and Human Interaction (EA) .... SIGCHI

Special Interest Group on Computer Graphics (EA) .... SIGGRAPH

Special Interest Group on Computer Systems, Installation Management [*Association for Computing Machinery*] .... SIGCOSIM

Special Interest Group on Data Communication (EA) .... SIGCOMM

Special Interest Group on Electronic Funds Transfer (MHDI) .... SIGEFT

Special Interest Group on File Description and Translation [*Association for Computing Machinery*] [*Later, Special Interest Group on the Management of Data*] .... SIGFIDET

Special Interest Group on Graphics (NITA) .... SIGGRAPH

Special Interest Group on Information Retrieval (EA) .... SIGIR

Special Interest Group on Language Analysis and Studies in the Humanities [*Association for Computing Machinery*] .... SIGLASH

Special Interest Group on Lexicography [*National Security Agency*] .... SIGLEX

Special Interest Group on Management of Data (EA) .... SIGMOD

Special Interest Group on Measurement and Evaluation (EA) .... SIGMETRICS

Special Interest Group on Microprogramming and Microarchitecture (EA) .... SIGMICRO

Special Interest Group on Minicomputers [*Later, SIGSMALL*] [*Association for Computing Machinery*] (CSR) .... SIGMINI

Special Interest Group on Numerical Control [*Military*] .... SIGNUM

Special Interest Group on Numerical Mathematics (EA) .... SIGNUM

Special Interest Group on Office Automation [*Later, SIGOIS*] .... SIGOA

Special Interest Group on Office Information Systems (EA) .... SIGOIS

Special Interest Group on Operating Systems (EA) .... SIGOPS

Special Interest Group on Personal Computing [*Association for Computing Machinery*] .... SIGPC

Special Interest Group on Phobias and Related Anxiety Disorders (EA) .... SIGPRAD

Special Interest Group on Programming Languages (EA) .... SIGPLAN

Special Interest Group on Real Time Processing [*Association for Computing Machinery*] .... SIGREAL

Special Interest Group on Security, Audit, and Control (EA) .... SIGSAC

Special Interest Group on Simulation (EA) .... SIGSIM

[*A*] Special Interest Group on Small and Personal Computing Systems and Applications [*An association for Computing Machinery*] (HGAA).... SIGSMALL/PC

Special Interest Group on Small and Personal Computing Systems Applications (EA) .... SIGSPCSA

Special Interest Group on Small Computing Systems and Applications [*Later, SIGSMALL*] [*Association for Computing Machinery*] (EA) .... SIGSCSA

Special Interest Group on Small Computing Systems and Applications [*Formerly, SIGSCSA*] [*Association for Computing Machinery*] (EA) .... SIGSMALL

Special Interest Group on Social and Behavioral Science Computing [*Association for Computing Machinery*] .... SIGSOC

Special Interest Group on Software Engineering (EA) .... SIGSOFT

Special Interest Group on the WWW .... SIG-WEB

Special Interest Group on Translation [*National Security Agency*] .... SIGTRAN

Special Interest Group on University Computing Centers (IAA) .... SIGUCC

Special Interest Group on Urban Data Systems, Planning, Architecture, and Civil Engineering [*Association for Computing Machinery*] .... SIGSPAC

[*A*] Special Interest Group on User Online Interaction [*An association for Computing Machinery*] (HGAA) .... SIG/UOI

Special Interest Group on Voice [*National Security Agency*] .... SIGVOICE

Special Interest Group on Zero-Based Budgeting and Automated Data Processing (MHDI) .... SIG/ZBB/ADP

Special Interest Group/Reprographic Technology [*of the American Society for Information Science*] .... SIG/RT

Special Interest Group/Selective Dissemination of Information [*American Society for Information Science*] .... SIG/SDI

Special Interest Item Code [*Military*] (AABC) .... SIIC

Special Interest Items (MCD) .... SII

Special Interest Launch [*Military*] (AFIT) .... SIL

Special Interest Sections Steering Committee [*American Occupational Therapy Association*] .... SISSC

Special Interest Sessions .... SIS

Special Interest Vessel [*Navy*] .... SIV

Special International Committee on Antarctic Research .... SCAR

Special Intervention [*Medicine*] .... SI

Special Investigation Branch [*Army British*] .... SIB

Special Investigation Wing (MUGU) .... SPINVESWG

Special Investigations District [*Air Force*] .... SPECINVESDIST

Special Investigative Group [*DoD*] .... SIG

Special Investigative Requirement (AFM) .... SIR

Special Investor Account [*Stock purchasing*] .... SIA

Special Isotope Separation [*Physics*] .... SIS

Special Issue of Equipment .... SIOE

Special Issue Rating System [*Veterans Administration*] .... SIRS

Special Item Number (AAGC) .... SIN

Special Items Management Office .... SIMO

Special Job Procedure [*Navy*] (NG) .... SJP

Special Joint Meeting .... SJM

Special Landing Forces [*Marine Corps*] .... SLF

Special Language Interpreting Matrix (IAA) .... SLIM

Special LASER Technology Development Program .... SLTDP

Special [*or Specific*] Launch Trajectory (AFM) .... SLT

Special Launch Vehicle Group [*NASA*] (KSC) .... SLVG

Special Layout (MCD) .... SL

Special Leave Refused .... SLR

Special Leave Without Pay .... SLWOP

Special Leave Without Pay .... SWOP

Special Lectures. Law Society of Upper Canada [*A publication*] (DLA) .... Lect LSUC

Special Liaison Unit [*Military intelligence*] [*World War II*] .... SLU

Special Libraries [*A publication*] (BRI) .... SL

Special Libraries Association (EA) .... SLA

Special Libraries Cataloguing, Inc. [*Information service or system*] (IID) .... SLC

Special Libraries Cataloguing, Inc. [*UTLAS symbol*] .... VSL

Special Libraries Cataloguing, Inc., North Vancouver, BC, Canada [*Library symbol*] [*Library of Congress*] (LCLS) .... CaBNvSL

Special Libraries Cataloguing, Inc., North Vancouver, British Columbia [*Library symbol National Library of Canada*] (NLC) .... BNVSL

Special Libraries in Queensland [*Australia A publication*] .... SLIQ

Special Light Rifle (NATG) .... SLR

Special Line Unit (NITA) .... SLU

Special Linear [*Group theory, mathematics*] .... SL

Special Liquids Tanker [*Navy*] (MCD) .... AOS

Special List of Equipment [*Air Force*] .... SLOE

Special Litigation Division [*Environmental Protection Agency*] (GFGA) .... SLD

Special Logistics Actions, South Vietnam (CINC) .... SLAV

Special Logistics Actions, Thailand (AABC) .... SLAT

Special Low-Dispersion [*Optics*] .... SLD

Special Machine [*Tool*] (AAG) .... SPMC

Special Machine Tool Standard (IAA) .... SMTS

Special Maintenance Project [*FAA*] .... SMP

Special Maintenance Support Facility (MCD) .... SMSF

Special Manufacturing Instruction .... SMI

Special Manufacturing Procedure .... SMP

Special Market Area (NTCM) .... SMA

Special Marketing Program [*Business*] .... SMP

Special Material Identification Code .... SMIC

Special Materials Services, Manitoba Department of Education, Winnipeg, Manitoba [*Library symbol National Library of Canada*] (NLC) .... MWESM

Special Meal [*Diabetic, low-cholesterol, low-calorie, hypoglycemic, or gluten-free*] [*Airline notation*] (ADA) .... SPML

Special Measuring Device (NASA) .... SMD

Special Medical Advisory Group (DMAA) .... SMAG

Special Memorandum .... SM

Special Messenger [*Army*] .... Sp Msgr

Special Metals Corp., Library, New Hartford, NY [*OCLC symbol*] (OCLC) ...... ZUY

Special Metals Corp., New Hartford, NY [*Library symbol Library of Congress*] (LCLS) .... NNhS

Special Microwave Devices Operation [*Raytheon Co.*] .... SMDO

Special Middle East Sealift Agreement (DOMA) .... SMESA

Special Military Construction Study Group (AABC) .... SMCSG

Special Military Intelligence Activities Team (CINC) .... SMIAT

Special Military Operation .... SMO

Special Minesweeper [*Navy symbol*] .... MSS

Special Mint Set [*Numismatics*] .... SMS

Special Miscellaneous Account .... SMA

Special Mission Aircraft (DOMA) .... SMA

Special Mission Aircraft Flights (NATG) .... SMAF

Special Mission Alteration .... SMA

Special Mission Attack Computer .... SMAC

Special Mission Support Force [*Navy*] (DOMA) .... SMSF

Special Mission Utility Transport [*Aviation*] .... SMUT

Special Missions Operational Test and Evaluation Center [*Hurlburt Field, FL*] .... SMOTEC

Special Mobile Provost Section [*British military*] (DMA) .... SMPS

Special Mobility Vehicle ... SMV
Special Modifying Factor (DEN) ... SMF
Special Money Requisition [*Military*] ... SMR
Special Monitor Output Generator (IEEE) ... SMOG
Special Monthly Compensation (MAE) ... SMC
Special Monthly Pension (DAVI) ... SMP
Special Mouth Care [*Medicine*] ... SMC
Special Multiperil [*Insurance*] ... SMP
Special Multiperil Insurance ... SMI
Special National Intelligence Estimates [*Summaries of foreign policy information and advice prepared for the president*] [*Known informally as "sneeze"*] ... SNIE's
Special Naval Observer ... SPENAVO
Special Naval Operations (NVT) ... SNO
Special Navy Control Program (MCD) ... SNCP
Special Navy Distribution List (DOMA) ... SNDL
Special Navy Task Force (MUGU) ... SNTF
Special Navy Task Force Commander ... SNTFC
Special Navy Task Force for Surface Missile Systems (MUGU) ... SNTF(SMS)
Special Needs Action Programme [*Education*] (AIE) ... SNAP
Special Needs in the Ordinary School (AIE) ... SNIOS
Special Needs Support Team [*Education*] (AIE) ... SNST
Special NGO [*Nongovernmental Organization*] **Committee on Disarmament** (EA) ... SNGOD
Special Night Answer Position [*Telecommunications*] ... SNAP
Special Night Squads [*Palestine*] (BJA) ... SNS
Special Notification Anticipating Receipt of Direction ... SNARD
Special Nuclear [*Material*] ... SN
Special Nuclear Effects Laboratory ... SNEL
Special Nuclear Material ... SNM
Special Nuclear Material ... SNUM
Special Observer [*US Army group in London*] [*World War II*] ... SPOBS
Special Ocean Wave Model ... SOWM
Special Offering [*Stocks*] (MHDW) ... SP OFF
Special Officer Personnel Requirements [*Military*] ... SOPR
Special Old Oil Price ... SOOP
Special Olympics [*Later, SOI*] (EA) ... SO
Special Olympics Australia ... SOA
Special Olympics International (EA) ... SOI
Special Olympics Ireland (EAIO) ... SOI
Special Open Allotment [*Military*] (AABC) ... SOA
Special Operating Agency [*Military*] (AABC) ... SOA
Special Operating Forces, Pacific [*Military*] ... SOFPAC
Special Operating Procedure (IEEE) ... SOP
Special Operation Radio Antenna Kit [*Military*] (RDA) ... SORAK
Special Operational Contract Requirements (AAG) ... SOCR
Special Operational Forces Taiwan (CINC) ... SOFT
Special Operations ... SO
Special Operations [*Navy*] (NVT) ... SPECOPS
Special Operations ... SPOPS
Special Operations ADP [*Automatic Data Processing*] **System** (DOMA) ... SOAS
Special Operations Aircraft ... SOA
Special Operations and Research Division [*Air Resources Laboratory*] (USDC) ... SORD
Special Operations and Research Division [*Marine science*] (OSRA) ... SORD
Special Operations Aviation Combat Mission Simulator [*Military*] ... SOACMS
Special Operations Aviation Regiment [*Military*] ... SOAR
Special Operations Capability [*Marine Corps*] (DOMA) ... SOC
Special Operations Capable Exercise (DOMA) ... SOCEX
Special Operations Center, Pacific Command (CINC) ... SOCPAC
Special Operations Combat Control Team (DOMA) ... SOCCT
Special Operations Command [*Military*] (AABC) ... SOC
Special Operations Command [*Military*] ... SOCOM
Special Operations Command and Control Element ... SOCCE
Special Operations Command, Central Command [*Military*] ... SOCCENT
Special Operations Command, Europe [*Military*] (DOMA) ... SOCEUR
Special Operations Command Research, Analysis, and Threat Evaluation System (DOMA) ... SOCRATES
Special Operations Communications Elements [*Military*] (GFGA) ... SOCSE
Special Operations Coordination [*DoD*] ... SOCOORD
Special Operations Detachment [*Military*] (AABC) ... SOD
Special Operations Division [*Office of Preparedness, General Services Administration*] ... SOD
Special Operations Evaluation System (DNAB) ... SOES
Special Operations Executive [*British research unit corresponding to OSS*] [*World War II*] ... SOE
Special Operations Executive, Special Operations [*British World War II*] ... SOE/SO
Special Operations Force [*Military*] ... SOF
Special Operations Force Aircrew Training System [*Military*] ... SOF ATS
Special Operations Force LASER Marker [*Military*] (RDA) ... SOFLAM
Special Operations Group [*Navy*] ... SOG
Special Operations Group [*Air Force*] (AFM) ... SOGp
Special Operations Improved Crypto System [*Military*] (RDA) ... SOICS
Special Operations Industry Group [*Army*] ... SOIG
Special Operations/Low Intensity Conflict [*Army*] ... SOLIC
Special Operations, Low Level (MCD) ... SOLL
Special Operations Photo Processing Cell (MCD) ... SOPPC
Special Operations Power Source [*Military*] (RDA) ... SOPS
Special Operations Research, Development, and Acquisition Center [*Military*] ... SORDAC
Special Operations Research Office ... SORO
Special Operations Response Team [*Prison management*] ... SORT
Special Operations Signal Battalion (DOMA) ... SOSB
Special Operations Squadron [*Air Force*] ... SOS
Special Operations Squadron ... SOSQ
Special Operations Squadron [*Air Force*] ... SPECOPNSSq
Special Operations Support Battalion (DOMA) ... SOSB
Special Operations Support Element [*Military*] (GFGA) ... SOSE
Special Operations Task Force [*Military*] (GFGA) ... SOTF
Special Operations Task Force, Europe [*Military*] ... SOTFE
Special Operations Team (ADA) ... SOT
Special Operations Training Group [*Marine Corps*] (DOMA) ... SOTG
Special Operations Wing [*Military*] (MCD) ... SOW
Special Operations Wing [*Air Force*] (AFM) ... SOWg
Special Operator Service Traffic [*Telecommunications*] (TEL) ... SOST
Special Opportunities Counties and Cities Program [*Tennessee Valley Authority*] ... SOCC
Special Optical Tracking System [*NASA*] ... SPEOPT
Special Order Discharge ... SOD
Special Order of the Commandant of the Marine Corps ... SOCMC
Special Order Perfect Price [*for undamaged merchandise*] ... SOPP
Special Order Price ... SOP
Special Orders [*Military*] ... SO
Special Ordnance Depot Tool Identification, Classification, Inventory, and Obsolescence Analysis Program [*Popularly called "Soda Cap"*] ... SODTICIOAP
Special Organizational Services [*An association*] (EA) ... SOS
Special Package Auto Policy [*Insurance*] ... SPAP
Special Paper ... SP
Special Pathogens Branch [*Centers for Disease Control*] ... SPB
Special Patrol Group [*of the London Metropolitan Police, providing protection for public figures*] ... SPG
Special Patrol Insertion/Extraction (MCD) ... SPIE
Special Pay for Duty Subject to Hostile Fire [*Military*] ... SPDHF
Special Pay for Hostile Duty [*Military*] (AFM) ... SPHD
Special Peacetime Program Requirements [*DoD*] ... SPPR
Special Performance ... SP
Special Performance Group [*In automobile name SAAB 900 Turbo SPG*] ... SPG
Special Perishable Tool (MCD) ... SPT
Special Personal Attack Message [*Internet-delivered direct mail*] [*Computer science*] ... SPAM
Special Placement Officer (ADA) ... SPO
Special Planning (AAG) ... SP
Special Planning Group [*Special Operations Force*] (DOMA) ... SPG
Special Plans and Operation [*Military*] ... SP & O
Special Police Radio Inquiry Network [*New York City*] ... SPRINT
Special Political Agricultural Community Education [*Milk cooperative trust fund*] ... SPACE
Special Political Committee [*Australia*] ... SPC
Special Position Identification ... SPI
Special Position Identification Pulse (CET) ... SPIP
Special Power Excursion Reactor Test [*US reactor facilities*] ... SPERT
Special Power Unit (NTCM) ... SPU
Special Prefix Code [*Northern Telecom*] [*Telecommunications*] ... SPRE
Special Prelaunch Analysis Request [*NASA*] (KSC) ... SPAR
Special Premiers Conference (EERA) ... SPC
Special Preparations Necessary for Test [*Laboratory science*] (DAVI) ... S
Special Procedures for Expediting Equipment Development (MCD) ... SPEED
Special Processes and Sequencing (NASA) ... SP & S
Special Product (MCD) ... SP
Special Product Quotation (IAA) ... SPQ
Special Production Fund [*Australian Film Commission*] ... SPF
Special Products and Program Support ... SPPS
Special Proficiency [*British military*] (DMA) ... SP
Special Proficiency at Rugged Training and Nation Building [*Training program for Green Berets*] [*Army*] ... SPARTAN
Special Proficiency Pay [*British military*] (DMA) ... SPP
Special Program ... SP
Special Program/Analysis Guidance [*DoD*] ... SPAG
Special Program Code [*Navy*] ... SPC
Special Program Number (MUGU) ... SPN
Special Program Requirement (AFM) ... SPR
Special Program Review [*Army*] (RDA) ... SPR
Special Program to List Amplitudes of Surges from Hurricanes ... SPLASH
Special Programs and Analysis Division [*Environmental Protection Agency*] (GFGA) ... SPAD
Special Programs and Rehabilitation under Unemployment Compensation [*Department of Labor*] ... SPRUCE
Special Programs Incorporating Custom Elective ... SPICE
Special Programs Increasing Counseling Effectiveness [*Pennsylvania State Department of Public Instruction*] ... SPICE
Special Progress [*Program*] [*Education*] ... SP
Special Progressive Aircraft Rework ... SPAR
Special Project Activities (MCD) ... SPA
Special Project Code [*IRS*] ... SPC
Special Project Control File [*IRS*] ... SPCF
Special Project Evaluation and Anti-War Warfare Research (DOMA) ... SPEAR
Special Project Group [*DoD*] ... SPG
Special Project Report ... SPR
Special Projects ... SP
Special Projects Alterations [*Navy*] ... SPALT
Special Projects Alterations, Training [*Navy*] ... SPALTRA
Special Projects Data Facility ... SPDF
Special Projects in Science Education ... SPISE
Special Projects Liaison Offices, United Kingdom [*Navy*] (DNAB) ... SPECPROJOUK
Special Projects of Regional and National Significance [*HHS*] ... SPRANS
Special Projects Office [*Navy*] ... SPO
Special Projects Officer, Technical Representative [*Navy*] (DNAB) ... SPOTR

Special Projects Operations Center [*Allied Force Headquarters*] [*World War II*] .... SPOC
Special Projects Program Order (AAG) .... SPPO
Special Projects School for Air .... SPSA
Special Projects, United Kingdom .... SPUK
Special Propellants .... SP
Special Provisions (AAGC) .... SP
Special Psychiatric Hospital [*Former USSR*] .... SPH
Special Public Assistance .... SPA
Special Publication .... SP
Special Purchase (ADA) .... SP
Special Purchase Allowance (DOAD) .... SPA
Special Purchase Office [*DoD*] .... SPUR
Special Purpose [*JETDS nomenclature*] .... Q
Special Purpose .... SP
Special Purpose Alteration (MCD) .... SPA
Special Purpose Chaff [*Navy*] (CAAL) .... SPC
Special Purpose Computer .... SPC
Special Purpose Dexterous Manipulator .... SPDM
Special Purpose Electronic Area Correlator (MHDI) .... SPEAC
Special Purpose Electronic Test Equipment [*Military*] (CAAL) .... SPETE
Special Purpose Electronics (MCD) .... SPE
Special Purpose End Effector (MCD) .... SEE
Special Purpose End Effector (MCD) .... SPEE
Special Purpose Force (MCD) .... SPF
Special Purpose Grant .... SPG
Special Purpose Jammer [*Military*] (CAAL) .... SPJ
Special Purpose Marine Air Ground Task Force (DOMA) .... SPMAGTF
Special Purpose Nursing Home [*Australia*] .... SPNH
Special Purpose Operational Computing Kernel [*Pilot training device developed at Georgia Institute of Technology*] .... SPOCK
Special Purpose Processor .... SPP
Special Purpose Support Equipment .... SPSE
Special Purpose Test [*Nuclear energy*] (NRCH) .... SPT
Special Purpose Test Equipment (MCD) .... SPTE
Special Purpose Unilateral Repetitive Modulation (IEEE) .... SPURM
Special Qualifications Identifiers [*Army*] (AABC) .... SQI
Special Qualifications/Special Designation (NVT) .... SQ/SD
Special Quick Disconnect Coupling .... SQDC
Special Radiation Experiment [*Marine science*] (OSRA) .... SPECTRE
Special Rate Order [*Business term*] .... SRO
Special Rated Thrust [*Aerospace*] (MCD) .... SRT
Special Real-Time Command (MCD) .... SRT
Special Real-Time Command (KSC) .... SRTC
Special Real-Time Operating System (PDAA) .... SRTOS
Special Reamer [*Tool*] (AAG) .... SPRM
Special Reconnaissance [*Special Operations Force*] (DOMA) .... SR
Special Recreation, Inc. (EA) .... SRI
Special Re-Education .... SRE
Special Refractories Association [*Defunct*] (EA) .... SRA
Special Regional Operations (NATG) .... SRO
Special Register .... SR
Special Regular Commissions [*Army British*] .... SRC
Special Regulations [*Military*] .... SR
Special Reimbursement Rate (AFM) .... SRR
Special Release Card (IAA) .... SRC
[*The*] Special Relief League [*Defunct*] (EA) .... TSRL
Special Repair Activity (MCD) .... SRA
Special Report .... SR
Special Report Writer [*NASA*] .... SRR
Special Reporting Facility [*Department of State*] .... SRF
Special Representative for Trade Negotiations [*Later, USTR*] [*Executive Office of the President*] .... SRTN
Special Representatives of the Secretary General [*United Nations*] .... SRSG
Special Requisition Priority Number .... SRPN
Special Research Bureau [*Department of External Affairs*] [*Canada*] .... SRB
Special Research Contract (AAGC) .... SRC
Special Research Detachment [*Army*] .... SRD
Special Research Study Memorandum .... SRSM
Special Reserve .... SR
Special Reserve Components Program [*Military*] .... SRCP
Special Revenue Sharing (OICC) .... SRS
Special Reverse Charge (IAA) .... SRCS
Special Review Board [*Military*] (INF) .... SRB
Special Review Team [*Nuclear energy*] (NRCH) .... SRT
Special Risk Insurance Fund [*Federal Housing Administration*] .... SRIF
Special Rules Area .... SRA
Special Rules Zone .... SRZ
Special Run Operations Sheet (IAA) .... SROS
Special Safeguarding Measures [*Telecommunications*] (TEL) .... SSM
Special Safeguards Study [*Nuclear energy*] (NRCH) .... SSS
Special Safety Safeguards (NRCH) .... SSS
Special Save Register [*Computer science*] (IAA) .... SSAR
Special Scientific Report .... SSR
Special Scientific Report - Fisheries .... SSR-F
Special Screw .... SPSCR
Special Secretariat for Informatics (NITA) .... SSI
Special Security Facility .... SSF
Special Security Force (DOMA) .... SSF
Special Security Group (MCD) .... SSG
Special Security Investigation Requirement (AFM) .... SSIR
Special Security Office [*or Officer*] [*Military*] (CINC) .... SSO
Special Security Office, Defense Intelligence Agency (CINC) .... SSODIA
Special Security Squadron .... SSS
Special Sense Organ [*Medicine*] (DMAA) .... SSO

Special Senses [*Medicine*] (DAVI) .... SS
Special Sensor Microwave/Imager (USDC) .... SSM/I
Special Sensor Microwave Imager [*Marine science*] (OSRA) .... SSMI
Special Sensor Microwave/Imager [*Marine science*] (OSRA) .... SSMI/I
Special Sensor-Lightning .... SSL
Special Separation Benefit [*DoD*] .... SSB
Special Series .... SS
Special Service [*Vessel load line mark*] .... SS
Special Service Agreement [*UN Food and Agriculture Organization*] .... SSA
Special Service Authorization [*FCC*] (NTCM) .... SSA
Special Service Battalion [*British military*] (DMA) .... SSB
Special Service Center [*Bell System*] .... SSC
Special Service Clergyman [*Church of England*] .... SSC
Special Service Division [*Army Services Forces*] [*World War II*] .... SSD
Special Service Force [*Canadian and US troops under combined command*] [*World War II*] .... SSF
Special Service Officer [*Military*] .... SSO
Special Service Training Group [*World War II*] .... SSTG
Special Service Unit [*Military*] .... SSU
Special Service Unit Training Center [*World War II*] .... SSUTC
Special Service Work Order [*Telecommunications*] (TEL) .... SSWO
Special Services [*Military*] .... SPS
Special Services [*Military*] (DAVI) .... SS
Special Services Forecasting System [*Telecommunications*] (TEL) .... SSFS
Special Services Management Bureau [*Telecommunications*] (TEL) .... SSMB
Special Services Protection [*Telecommunications*] (TEL) .... SSP
Special Services Request [*Travel industry*] .... SSR
Special Session .... SS
Special Session of Oyer and Terminer [*Legal*] [*British*] (ROG) .... SSOT
Special Session of Peace [*Legal*] [*British*] (ROG) .... SSP
Special Session on Disarmament [*A special session of the UN General Assembly held from May 23 to June 28, 1978*] .... SSOD
Special Settlement [*Business term*] .... SS
Special Shaped .... SPSHP
Special Signal Analysis System [*Electronic countermeasures system*] .... SSAS
Special Signal Conditioning Unit .... SSCU
Special Signal Exploitation Spaces (NVT) .... SSES
Special Source Materials [*Nuclear energy*] (NRCH) .... SS
Special Source Survey (AAGC) .... SSS
Special Spectrum Study Committee .... SSSC
Special Staff .... SS
Special Staff, United States Army .... SSUSA
Special State Defense Study Group [*Military*] .... SSDSG
Special Steel Summary Invoice [*International Trade Administration*] .... SSSI
Special Stockpile Engineering Investigation Program (MCD) .... SSEIP
Special Strike (NATG) .... SS
Special Strike Teletype (NATG) .... SST
Special Student Access to Vocational Education Project (EDAC) .... SSAVE
Special Studies Branch [*Supreme Headquarters Allied Powers Europe*] (NATG) .... SSB
Special Studies Group [*Joint Chiefs of Staff*] [*Military*] .... SSG
Special Studies Program [*Australia*] .... SSP
Special Study .... SS
Special Subject for Inspection [*DoD*] .... SSI
Special Subject Operational Evaluation .... SSOE
Special Subjects .... SS
Special Supplementary Clothing Monetary Allowance [*Military*] .... SSCMA
Special Support Activity [*National Security Agency*] (DOMA) .... SSA
Special Support Equipment .... SSE
Special Support Group [*FBI*] (CINC) .... SSG
Special Support Services .... SSS
Special Surveillance Inspection (MCD) .... SSI
Special Surveillance Vehicle [*Navy*] (DNAB) .... SSV
Special Survey [*Lloyd's Register of Shipping*] (DS) .... SS
Special Survey Automated Controls [*Lloyd's Register of Shipping*] (DS) .... SSA
Special Survey of Inert Gas System [*Lloyd's Register of Shipping*] (DS) .... SSIGS
Special Survey of Refrigerated Machinery [*Lloyd's Register of Shipping*] (DS) .... SSR
Special Survey of the Hull [*Lloyd's Register of Shipping*] (DS) .... SSH
Special Survey of the Machinery [*Lloyd's Register of Shipping*] (DS) .... SSM
Special Surveys and Analysis Branch [*National Center for Education Statistics*] [*Department of Education*] (GFGA) .... SSAB
Special Tactical Air Surveillance System (IAA) .... STASS
Special Tank Task Force (MCD) .... STTF
Special Task Air Group .... STAG
Special Task Force [*Army*] .... STF
Special Task Group/Special Task Force [*Army*] (MCD) .... STG/STF
Special Task Stores [*Military British*] .... STS
Special Tax Bond .... STB
Special Tax Ruling [*Internal Revenue Service*] [*United States*] [*A publication*] (DLA) .... Sp Tax Rul
Special Technical and Economic Mission .... STEM
Special Technical Assistance Program (EA) .... STAP
Special Technical Factors (MCD) .... STF
Special Technical Publication (MCD) .... STP
Special Techniques Repair Analysis Aircraft Damage [*Navy*] (NVT) .... STRAAD
Special Technology Group [*National Technical Information Service*] (MCD) .... STG
Special Telemetry Equipped Missile .... STEM
Special Temporary Allowance .... STA
Special Temporary Authorization [*FCC*] .... STA
Special Temporary Employment Programme (AIE) .... STEP
Special Temporary Enlistment [*Coast Guard*] .... STE
Special Term [*Legal term*] (DLA) .... SP T
Special Test .... ST
Special Test and Maintenance Unit .... STMU

Special Test Army Reserve Limited Objective	STARLO
Special Test Equipment	STE
Special Test Equipment Order (MCD)	STEO
Special Test Equipment Repair Facility	STERF
Special Test Instructions (SAA)	STI
Special Test Missile	STM
Special Test, Permanent [Aircraft classification letter]	N
Special Test System [Air Force] (AFM)	STS
Special Test, Temporary [Aircraft classification letter]	J
Special Test Unit (CET)	STU
Special Test Vehicle	STV
Special Text [Military]	ST
Special Theory of Relativity	STR
Special Therapeutic and Rehabilitation Activities Fund [Department of Veterans Affairs]	STRAF
Special Tool List	STL
Special Tool Production	STP
Special Tooling (GFGA)	ST
Special Tooling / Special Test Equipment [Navy] (DNAB)	ST/STE
Special Tools and Handling Equipment	STHE
Special Tools and Test Equipment	STTE
Special Tracker [Military] (CAAL)	SPLTRK
Special Trade Passenger Ship (PDAA)	STP
Special Trade Representative	STR
Special Traffic Notice [British] (DCTA)	STN
Special Training Devices Program (AFM)	STDP
Special Training Enlistment Program	STEP
Special Training Equipment Program Document (AFIT)	STEP
Special Training Group [Military]	STG
Special Training Standard [Air Force] (AFM)	STS
Special Training Unit	STU
Special Translation	ST
Special Travel Industry Council on Energy Conservation	STICEC
Special Treatment and Rehabilitative Training [Prisons project]	START
Special Treatment and Review [Navy] (NG)	STAR
Special Treatment Room [Medicine] (DAVI)	STR
Special Treatment Steel	STS
Special Trial Judge [US Tax Court]	STJ
Special Triple-Electron Nuclear Double Resonance [Spectroscopy]	ST-ENDOR
Special Troops [Army]	Sp Trs
Special Tube Analyzing Recorder	STAR
Special Tube Feeding [Medicine]	STF
Special Types [JETDS nomenclature]	S
Special Unitary [Algebra]	SU
Special United Nations Fund for Economic Development	SUNFED
Special Urban Survey 1987 [Bureau of the Census] (GFGA)	SUS
Special Use Airspace (GAVI)	SUA
Special Use Airspace [FAA] (TAG)	SUA
Special Utility Program [NASA] (KSC)	SUP
Special Vehicle Engineering [Ford Motor Co.]	SVE
Special Vehicle Management [Automotive engineering]	SVM
Special Vehicle Operation [Ford Motor Co.]	SVO
Special Vehicle Option [Automobile production]	SVO
Special Vehicle Team [Automotive engineering]	SVT
Special Verification Commission (DOMA)	SVC
Special Virus Cancer Program [National Cancer Institute]	SVCP
Special Virus Leukemia Program [National Cancer Institute]	SVLP
Special Visitors Program [Australia]	SVP
Special Visual Flight Rules [Aviation]	SVFR
Special Warfare (DOMA)	SPECWAR
Special Warfare (NVT)	SPW
Special Warfare	SPWAR
Special Warfare	SW
Special Warfare Armored Transporter [A vehicle]	SWAT
Special Warfare Aviation Detachment [Army]	SWAD
Special Warfare Center [Later, J. F. Kennedy Center for Special Warfare] [Army]	SWC
Special Warfare Craft [Navy] (CAAL)	SWC
Special Warfare Craft, Light [Navy symbol]	SWCL
Special Warfare Craft, Medium [Navy symbol]	SWCM
Special Warfare Mission (AABC)	SWM
Special Warhead Arming Control (AFM)	SWAC
Special Warning Function (MCD)	SWF
Special Warning Receiver (MCD)	SWR
Special Wash Up [Printing] (DGA)	SWU
Special Watch Zone [Navy] (NVT)	SWZ
Special Water Dispenser [British military] (DMA)	SWD
Special Weapon	SW
Special Weapon Equipment Test (SAA)	SWET
Special Weapon Systems [Military]	SWS
Special Weapon Technical Command [Navy] (MCD)	SWTC
Special Weapons and Tactics [Police]	SWAT
Special Weapons Center [or Command]	SWC
Special Weapons Development Board	SWDB
Special Weapons Emergency Separation System (AFM)	SWESS
Special Weapons Equipment List	SWEL
Special Weapons Equipment List Single Theater Requisitioning Agency	SWELSTRA
Special Weapons Experimental Tactical Test Unit	SWETTU
Special Weapons Facility [Navy]	SWF
Special Weapons Ferry Control Office [or Officer]	SWEFCO
Special Weapons Inspection Report	SWIR
Special Weapons Integration Subcommittee (SAA)	SWIS
Special Weapons Loading (SAA)	SWL
Special Weapons Operation Center [Army] (AABC)	SWOC

Special Weapons Ordnance Devices	SWOD
Special Weapons Ordnance Publication [Navy] (NVT)	SWOP
Special Weapons Overflight Guide (AFM)	SWOG
Special Weapons Project [Military]	SWP
Special Weapons Project Analysis (SAA)	SWPAN
Special Weapons Supply Depot	SWSD
Special Weapons Supply Memorandum [Army] (AABC)	SWSM
Special Weapons Technical Instructions [Army] (AABC)	SWTI
Special Weapons Test	SWT
Special Weapons Test and Tactical Evaluation Unit	SWTTEU
Special Weapons Training Allowance	SWTA
Special Weapons Unit, Atlantic [Navy] (DNAB)	SWULANT
Special Weapons Unit, Pacific [Navy] (DNAB)	SWUPAC
Special Weather Intelligence (MCD)	SWI
Special Weather Report [Aviation] (DA)	SPECI
Special Wire Assembly Planning System (MCD)	SWAPS
Special Wireless Group [World War II British]	SWG
[A] Special Wish Foundation (EA)	ASWF
Special Word Indexed Full Text Alpha Numeric Storage with Easy Retrieval [Software]	SWIFT-ANSWER
Special Working Group	SWG
Special Working Party [Military]	SWP
Special World Intervals	SWI
Special Wrenches and Techniques [Automotive repair]	SWAT
Speciale Prototipo [Special Prototype] [Italy]	SP
Special-Effects Generator [Filmmaking] (WDMC)	SEG
Special-Environment Powder Diffractometer [Crystallography]	SEPD
Specialised Banking Furniture International [Manufacturer] [British]	SBFI
Specialised Oceanographic Centre (EERA)	SOC
Specialised Organics Information Service [British] (DBA)	SORIS
Specialist [Ecology]	S
Specialist (ADA)	SP
Specialist (WDMC)	sp
Specialist	SPCLST
Specialist	SPECLST
Specialist 4 [Army]	E4
Specialist 4 [Army]	SP4
Specialist 5 [Obsolete Army]	E5
Specialist 5 [Obsolete Army]	SP5
Specialist 6 [Obsolete Army]	E6
Specialist 6 [Obsolete Army]	SP6
Specialist 7 [Obsolete Army]	E7
Specialist 7 [Army]	SP7
Specialist 8 [Obsolete Army]	E8
Specialist 8 [Obsolete Army]	SP8
Specialist 9 [Obsolete Army]	E9
Specialist 9 [Obsolete Army]	SP9
Specialist, Air Stations Operations Desk - Time Shack [Navy rating]	SPXTS
Specialist, Archivist [Navy rating]	SPXAC
Specialist, Armed Forces Radio Service and Special Naval Radio Units [Navy rating]	SPXRS
Specialist, Artist [Navy rating]	SPXAR
Specialist, Ballistics [Navy rating]	SPXBL
Specialist Blood Banking (DAVI)	SBB
Specialist, Cable Censor [Navy rating]	SPXCC
Specialist, Cartographer [Navy rating]	SPXCT
Specialist Certificate in Gerontology (GAGS)	SCG
Specialist, Chaplain's Assistant [Navy rating]	SPW
Specialist, Chemical Warfare [Navy rating]	SPCW
Specialist Claims Control Unit [British]	SCCU
Specialist, Classification Interviewer [Navy rating]	SPC
Specialist, Communications Specialist, Cryptographer [Navy rating]	SPQCR
Specialist, Communications Specialist, Radio Intelligence [Navy rating]	SPQIN
Specialist, Communications Specialist, Registered Publication Clerk [Navy rating]	SPQRP
Specialist, Communications Specialist, Technician [Navy rating]	SPQTE
Specialist Component Producer	SCP
Specialist Computer Centres (NITA)	SCC
Specialist, Crystal Grinder [Navy rating]	SPXCG
Specialist Degree (PGP)	SD
Specialist Degree (PGP)	SP
Specialist Degree (PGP)	Spt
Specialist, Discharge Interviewer [Navy rating]	SPXDI
Specialist Duty Only [Navy personnel designation]	SDO
Specialist, Engineering Draftsman [Navy rating]	SPXED
Specialist, Engineering Inspector [Navy rating]	SPOEN
Specialist, Fingerprint Expert [Navy rating]	SPXFP
Specialist, Firefighter [Navy rating]	SPF
Specialist, Gauge Specialist [Navy rating]	SPXGU
Specialist, Gunnery [Navy rating]	SPG
Specialist, Gunnery, Antiaircraft Gunnery Instructor [Navy rating]	SPGN
Specialist, Gunnery, Aviation Free Gunnery Instructor [Navy rating]	SPGM
Specialist in Applied Biology (GAGS)	SpAppBiol
Specialist in Art (GAGS)	SpA
Specialist in Blood Bank Technical (DAVI)	SBB
Specialist in Blood Bank Technology (HCT)	SBBT
Specialist in Community College Teaching (GAGS)	SCCT
Specialist in Counseling (PGP)	Sp C
Specialist in Education (GAGS)	EdS
Specialist in Education (GAGS)	SEd
Specialist in Education [Academic degree]	Sp Ed
Specialist in Guidance and Counseling (GAGS)	SGC
Specialist in Library Science (PGP)	SLS
Specialist in Optical Science (GAGS)	OpS
Specialist in Psychological Services (PGP)	S Psy S

Specialist in Psychology (PGP) .... Psy S
Specialist in Public Administration (GAGS) .... SPA
Specialist in School Administration (GAGS) .... SSA
Specialist in School Psychology (GAGS) .... SSP
Specialist in Science (GAGS) .... ScS
Specialist in Science (GAGS) .... SpS
Specialist in Speech Pathology and Audiology (GAGS) .... SSPA
Specialist Insectivore .... SI
Specialist, Inspector of Aviation Material [Navy rating] .... SPOAV
Specialist, Inspector of Naval Material [Navy rating] .... SPO
Specialist, Intelligence Duties [Navy rating] .... SPXID
Specialist, Interpreter [Navy rating] .... SPXIR
Specialist, Journalist [Navy rating] .... SPXJO
Specialist, Key Punch Operator and Supervisor [Navy rating] .... SPXKP
Specialist Knowledge Services [British organization for occult research] .... SKS
Specialist, Link Trainer Instructor [Navy rating] .... SPLT
Specialist, Mail Clerk [Navy rating] .... SPM
Specialist, Motion Picture Production [Navy rating] .... SPPMP
Specialist, Motion Picture Service - Booker [Navy rating] .... SPEPS
Specialist, Naval Correspondent [Navy rating] .... SPXNC
Specialist, Operations - Plotting and Chart Work [Navy rating] .... SPXQM
Specialist, Ordnance Inspector [Navy rating] .... SPOOR
Specialist Personal GPS Receiver .... SPGR
Specialist, Personnel Supervisor [Women's Reserve] [Navy rating] .... SPS
Specialist, Personnel Supervisor, V-10 [Navy rating] .... SPSPS
Specialist, Petroleum Technician [Navy rating] .... SPOPE
Specialist, Photogrammetry [Navy rating] .... SPPPG
Specialist, Photographer, Laboratory [Navy rating] .... SPPLB
Specialist, Photographic Specialist [Navy rating] .... SPP
Specialist, Physical Training Instructor [Navy rating] .... SPA
Specialist, Pigeon Trainer [Navy rating] .... SPXPI
Specialist, Plastic Expert [Navy rating] .... SPXPL
Specialist, Port Security [Coast Guard] .... SPPS
Specialist, Position Classifier [Navy rating] .... SPXPC
Specialist, Public Information [Navy rating] .... SPXPR
Specialist, Public Relations [Coast Guard] .... SPPR
Specialist, Punched Card Accounting Machine Operator [Navy rating] .... SPI
Specialist Qualifications [British military] (DMA) .... SQ
Specialist, Recreation and Welfare Assistant [Navy rating] .... SPERW
Specialist, Recruiter [Navy rating] .... SPR
Specialist, Research Laboratory [Navy rating] .... SPXRL
Specialist, Shore Patrol and Security [Navy rating] .... SPS
Specialist, Special Project [Navy rating] .... SPXOP
Specialist, Strategic Services [Navy rating] .... SPXST
Specialist, Teacher [Navy rating] .... SPT
Specialist Teams Royal Engineers [Military British] .... STRE
Specialist, Telephone Switchboard Operator and Supervisor [Navy rating] .... SPXSB
Specialist, Third Class (GFGA) Sp3c
Specialist, Topographic Draftsman [Navy rating] .... SPXTD
Specialist Training [Navy] (NVT) .... SPECTNG
Specialist, Transport Airman [Navy rating] .... SPV
Specialist (Transportation) [Coast Guard] .... SP(TR)
Specialist, Utility [Women's Reserve] [Navy rating] .... SPU
Specialist, Visual Training Aids [Navy rating] .... SPXVA
Specialist, V-Mail [Navy rating] .... SPPVM
Specialists Training Center .... STC
Speciality Equipment [Associated Press] (SAG) .... SpclEqp
Speciality Equipment [NASDAQ symbol] (SAG) .... SPEQ
Speciality Paperboard, Inc. [NASDAQ symbol] (SAG) .... SPBI
Speciality Paperboard, Inc. [Associated Press] (SAG) .... SpclPap
Speciality Shopping Centre [British] .... SSC
Specialize .... SPECL
Specialized Acid-Soluble Spore Protein [Bacteriology] .... SASP
Specialized Aircraft Maintenance - Strategic Air Command (AAG) .... SAM-SAC
Specialized Armoured Development Establishment [British military] (DMA) .... SADE
Specialized Armoured Establishment [British military] (DMA) .... SAE
Specialized Carriers and Rigging Association (EA) .... SC & RA
Specialized Carriers & Rigging Association .... SCRA
Specialized Center of Research in Atherosclerosis [University of Chicago] [Research center] (RCD) .... SCOR
Specialized Center of Research in Ischemic Heart Disease [University of Alabama at Birmingham] [Research center] (RCD) .... SCOR
Specialized Common Carrier [Telecommunications] (NRCH) .... SCC
Specialized Customer Premises Equipment [for the handicapped] .... SCPE
Specialized Employability Assistance to Claimants (OICC) .... SEAC
Specialized Exhibition (IMH) .... SE
Specialized Health Prods Intl [NASDAQ symbol] (TTSB) .... SHPI
Specialized Health Products International, Inc. [NASDAQ symbol] (SAG) .... SHPI
Specialized Health Products International, Inc. [Associated Press] (SAG) .... SpecHlth
Specialized Information Retrieval and Library Services (IID) .... SIRLS
Specialized Mobile Radio .... SMR
Specialized Mobile Radio System .... SMRS
Specialized Oceanographic Center [National Oceanic and Atmospheric Administration] (MSC) .... SOC
Specialized Operating System (DNAB) .... SIROS
Specialized Repair Activity .... SRA
Specialized Safety and Flight Operations .... SS & FO
Specialized Satellite Service Operators [British] .... SSSO
Specialized Small Business Investment Company .... SSBIC
Specialized Storage Depot .... SSD
Specialized Support Department [Air Force] (AFM) .... SSD
Specialized Support Depot [Army] (AABC) .... SSD

Specialized Surplus Sales Office [Military] .... SSSO
Specialized System Test Contractor .... SSTC
Specialized Systems Test Teams (SAA) .... SSTT
Specialized Technique for Efficient Typesetting .... STET
Specialized Textile Information Service .... STIS
Specialized Trade Mission [Department of Commerce] .... STM
Specialized Training and Reassignment [Military] .... STAR
Specialized Training and Reassignment (Student) [Military] .... STAR(S)
Specialized Training for Army Readiness [Army Reserve] .... STAR
Specialized Treatment Facility [Medicine] (MEDA) .... STF
Specialized Undergraduate Pilot Training [Air Force] .... SUPT
Specialized Unit Maintenance Support (MCD) .... SUMS
Specialized Youth Units [Canada] .... SYUS
Specially Constructed Vehicle [Automotive engineering] .... SPCN
Specially Denatured .... SD
Specially Denatured Alcohol .... SDA
Specially Designated Distributor [Liquor] .... SDD
Specially Designated Merchant [Liquor sales] .... SDM
Specially Designated Vehicle .... SDV
Specially Equipped Traffic Accident Car [British police] .... SETAC
Specially Important Brothers and Sisters (of Our Patients) [Medicine] .... SIBS
Specially Meritorious Medal .... SMM
Specially Prepared Individuals for Key Events [Paramilitary training] (ECON) .... SPIKE
Specially Prepared Tape Program (SAA) .... SPRTAP
Specially Promoted Programme [British] .... SPP
Specially Protected Area [Australia] .... SPA
Specially Protected Area (EERA) .... SPA
Specially Reserved Area [Australia] .... SRA
Specially-Oriented Advertisements [Consumer Protection Packet - US Post Office] .... SOA
Special-Purpose Aircraft [Drone vehicle] [Military] .... SPA
Special-Purpose Cable Assembly .... SPCA
Special-Purpose Engineering Analysis Language (MCD) .... SPEAL
Special-Purpose Equipment .... SPE
Special-Purpose Individual Weapon [A rifle that fires flechettes or darts] [Pronounced "spew"] .... SPIW
Special-Purpose Language [Computer science] .... SPL
Special-Purpose Lead Azide (MCD) .... SPLA
Special-Purpose Manipulator System [NASA] (NASA) .... SPMS
Special-Purpose Materials (MCD) .... SPM
Special-Purpose Monitoring Station [Environmental Protection Agency] .... SPMS
Special-Purpose Multiprocessor [Computer science] .... SPMP
Special-Purpose RADAR .... SPR
Special-Purpose RADAR Set .... SPRS
Special-Purpose Receiving Facility .... SPRF
Special-Purpose Reconnaissance Aircraft [Navy] .... SPRA
Special-Purpose Requirements [Army] .... SPR
Special-Purpose SONAR (MCD) .... SPS
Special-Purpose Test Program (MCD) .... SPTP
Special-Purpose Vehicle [Military] .... SPV
Specialty .... SPCLTY
Specialty (WGA) .... SPLTY
Specialty Advertising Association [Later, SAAI] .... SAA
Specialty Advertising Association International [Irving, TX] (EA) .... SAAI
Specialty Advertising Business [A publication] (EAAP) .... SA
Specialty Advertising Guild International [Later, SAA] (EA) .... SAGI
Specialty Advertising National Association [Later, SAA] (EA) .... SANA
Specialty Aromatic Compound [Organic chemistry] .... SAC
Specialty Automotive Manufacturers Association [Newport Beach, CA] (EA) .... SAMA
Specialty Bakery Owners of America (EA) .... SBOA
Specialty Catalog Corp. [NASDAQ symbol] (SAG) .... CTLG
Specialty Catalog Corp. [Associated Press] (SAG) .... SpecCata
Specialty Chemical Res [AMEX symbol] (TTSB) .... CHM
Specialty Chemical Resources [AMEX symbol] (SAG) .... CHM
Specialty Chemical Resources, Inc. [Associated Press] (SAG) .... SpcChm
Specialty Code .... SC
Specialty Coffee Association of America (EA) .... SCAA
Specialty Electronics Development Corp. .... SEDCOR
Specialty Equipment [Commercial firm Associated Press] (SAG) .... SpclEqp
Specialty Equipment [NASDAQ symbol] (SAG) .... SPEQ
Specialty Equipment Manufacturers Association .... SEMA
Specialty Equipment Market Association [Later, SFI] (EA) .... SEMA
Specialty Glass Products, Inc. .... SGP
Specialty Knowledge Test [Military] (AFM) .... SKT
Specialty Medical Group (DMAA) .... SMG
Specialty Occupational Outlook [A publication] .... SOO
Specialty Paper and Board Affiliates [Later, API] (EA) .... SPBA
Specialty Paperboard [NASDAQ symbol] (TTSB) .... SPBI
Specialty Paperboard, Inc. [NASDAQ symbol] (SAG) .... SPBI
Specialty Paperboard, Inc. [Associated Press] (SAG) .... SpclPap
Specialty Retail Group [Commercial firm Associated Press] (SAG) .... SpecRetl
Specialty Retail Group [NASDAQ symbol] (SAG) .... SRGC
Specialty Review Group [Medicine] (DMAA) .... SRG
Specialty Skill Identifier [Military] (AABC) .... SSI
Specialty Steel Industry of the United States (EA) .... SSIUS
Specialty Telecnstrctrs Wrrt [NASDAQ symbol] (TTSB) .... SCTRW
Specialty Teleconstructioners [NASDAQ symbol] (SAG) .... SCTR
Specialty Teleconstructioners [Associated Press] (SAG) .... SpecTelec
Specialty Teleconstructioners [Associated Press] (SAG) .... SpTelc
Specialty Teleconstructors [NASDAQ symbol] (TTSB) .... SCTR
Specialty Tools and Fasteners Distributors Association (EA) .... STAFDA
Specialty Training System .... STS
Specialty Vehicles Institute of America (EA) .... SVIA

Specialty Wire Association [*Later, AWPA*] .... SWA
Special-Type Ellipsometer .... STE
Species .... S
Species [*Also, sp*] .... SP
Species (EERA) .... Sp
Species (WGA) .... SPEC
Species [*Plural form*] [*Also, spp*] .... SPP
Species Conservation Monitoring Unit (GNE) .... SCMU
Species Indeterminata [*Species Indeterminate*] [*Latin*] (MAE) .... sp indet
Species Inquirendae [*Species of Doubtful Status*] [*Latin*] (MAE) .... sp inquir
Species Iris Group of North America (EA) .... SIGNA
Species Nova [*New Species*] [*Biology*] .... sp nov
Species Novum [*New Species*] [*Also, sp nov*] [*Biology*] (DAVI) .... sp n
Species Plantarum Project (EERA) .... SPP
Species Services Unit [*of the Bureau of Meteorology*] (EERA) .... SSU
Species Specific Defense Reaction .... SSDR
Species Survival Commission (EERA) .... SSC
Species Survival Plans [*Program sponsored by the American Association of Zoological Parks and Aquariums to protect certain endangered species*] .... SSP
Species-Area [*Ecology*] .... SA
Specifiable Coordinating Positioning Equipment (PDAA) .... SCOPE
Specific (AAG) .... SP
Specific .... SPEC
Specific (WGA) .... SPECIF
Specific Absorption Rate .... SAR
Specific Acoustic Capacitance .... SAC
Specific Acoustic Impedance .... SAI
Specific Acoustic Resistance .... SAR
Specific Activity .... SA
Specific Activity Report .... SAR
Specific Adaptation to Improved Demands [*Sports medicine*] .... SAID
Specific Adaptive Strategy (EDAC) .... SAB
Specific Air Range [*Military*] (LAIN) .... SAR
Specific Airway Conductance .... sGAW
Specific Antigen [*Immunology*] .... SA
Specific Application Service Element [*Telecommunications*] (OSI) .... SASE
Specific Aptitude Test .... SAT
Specific Aptitude Test Battery .... SATB
Specific Behavioral Objectives [*Aviation*] .... SBO
Specific Candlepower (NASA) .... SCP
Specific Chemical Oxygen Demand Value [*for Complete Oxidation*] .... SCOD
Specific Clauses and Conditions (NATG) .... SCC
Specific Cleavage Product [*Biochemistry*] .... SCP
Specific Collection Area [*Environmental science*] (FFDE) .... SCA
Specific Combining Ability .... SCA
Specific Commodity Rates (DS) .... SCR
Specific Compliance [*Laboratory terminology*] (DAVI) .... C/V_L
Specific Conductance [*Expressed per liter of lung volume at which G is measured*] [*Medicine*] (DAVI) .... GAW/V_1
Specific Control Number .... SCN
Specific Cueing .... SC
Specific Damping Capacity [*Metals*] .... SDC
Specific Desensitizing Vaccine [*Medicine*] (ADA) .... SDV
Specific Diagnosis Service [*Medicine*] (DMAA) .... SDS
Specific Direct Operating Costs .... SDOC
Specific Dynamic Action [*of foods*] [*Physiology*] .... SDA
Specific Dynamic Effect [*Medicine*] .... SDE
Specific Energy Absorption .... SEA
Specific Energy Consumption [*Automotive engineering*] .... SEC
Specific Excess Power (MCD) .... SEP
Specific Factor .... S
Specific Financial Transactions .... SFT
Specific Force Integrating Receiver [*Air Force*] .... SFIR
Specific Fuel Consumption .... SFC
Specific Granule Deficiency [*Physiology*] .... SGD
Specific Gravity [*Also, SPG, SPGR*] .... SG
Specific Gravity (IDOE) .... sp gr
Specific Gravity [*Also, SP, SPGR, SPG*] (DAVI) .... SP GRV
Specific Gravity (DAVI) .... spec grav
Specific Gravity [*Also, SP, SPGR*] .... SPG
Specific Gravity [*Also, SG, SPG*] .... SPGR
Specific Gravity Indicator .... SGI
Specific Heat .... SP/HT
Specific Heat at Constant Volume [*Chemistry*] (DAVI) Cv
Specific Heat Capacity [*Symbol*] [*IUPAC*] c
Specific Immune Response Enhancing Factor [*Medicine*] (DMAA) .... SIREF
Specific Impulse (MCD) .... ISP
Specific Impulse (IAA) .... SI
Specific Impulse (MSA) .... SIMP
Specific Individual Licence [*Importing*] [*British*] (DS) .... SIL
Specific Inductive Capacitance .... SIC
Specific Inductive Capacity (IDOE) .... SIC
Specific Information Requirement [*Military*] (INF) .... SIR
Specific Infrared Detector .... SID
Specific Insulation Resistance .... SIR
Specific Intelligence Collection Requirements [*Military*] (AFM) .... SICR
Specific Inventory (OA) .... SI
Specific Language [*or Learning*] **Disability** [*Education*] .... SLD
Specific Language Impairment .... SLI
Specific Leaf Area [*Botany*] .... SLA
Specific Leaf Weight [*Botany*] .... SLW
Specific Learning Disability (ADA) .... SPELD
Specific Line of Precipitin [*Immunology*] .... SLP
Specific Linear Optimal Control Program [*Hydrofoil*] [*Grumman Aerospace Corp.*] .... SLOCOP
Specific Living Space (AAG) .... SLS
Specific Lung Resistance .... SLR
Specific Macrophage Arming Factor [*Hematology*] .... SMAF
Specific Management Functional Area [*Telecommunications*] (OSI) .... SMFA
Specific Management Information Protocol [*Telecommunications*] (OSI) .... SMIP
Specific Management Information Service [*Telecommunications*] (OSI) .... SMIS
Specific, Measurable, Agreed-To, Reachable, Time-Specific [*Management technique*] .... SMART
Specific Mobilization Material Requirement [*Military*] (AFIT) .... SMMR
Specific Mobilization Reserve Stock [*Military*] (AFIT) .... SMRS
Specific Operating Instruction (AFM) .... SOI
Specific Operational Requirement [*Military*] .... SOR
Specific Optimal Control .... SOC
Specific Optimal Estimation (PDAA) .... SOE
Specific Oxygen Uptake Rate [*In wastewater*] .... SOUR
Specific Pavement Studies [*FHWA*] (TAG) .... SPS
Specific Performance [*Legal shorthand*] (LWAP) .... SP
Specific Power .... SP
Specific Price Reduction .... SPR
Specific Productivity Index (IEEE) .... SPI
Specific Propellant Consumption .... SPC
Specific Purpose Payment .... SPP
Specific Range .... SR
Specific Reactant Consumption [*Engine*] .... SRC
Specific Reactivity [*Exhaust emissions*] [*Automotive engineering*] .... SR
Specific Reactivity - Maximum Incremental Reactivity [*Exhaust emissions*] [*Automotive engineering*] .... SR-MIR
Specific Red Cell Adherence [*Test*] [*Clinical chemistry*] .... SRCA
Specific Repair Methods [*Boeing*] .... SRM
Specific Resistance (IAA) .... SPR
Specific Resistance (IAA) .... SR
Specific Resistance, Airway [*Medicine*] .... SRaw
Specific Searching Image [*Tendency of birds to select prey of the color to which they have been accustomed*] .... SSI
Specific Serotonin Reuptake Inhibitor [*Antidepressant*] .... SSRI
Specific, Sincere, Immediate, Private, and Personal [*Management technique*] .... SSIP
Specific Soluble Substance [*Polysaccharide hapten*] .... SSS
Specific Surface .... S
Specific Surface (WDAA) .... SP SURF
Specific Surface Diameter .... SSD
Specific Taste Changes .... STC
Specific Temperature Excursion .... STE
Specific Tensile Strength .... STS
Specific Thalamic Projection System [*Medicine*] (DMAA) .... STPS
Specific Thermal Capacity .... STC
Specific Vocational Preparation [*US Employment Service*] [*Department of Labor*] .... SVP
Specific Volume (DEN) .... SPVOL
Specific Volume [*Symbol*] [*IUPAC*] v
Specific Weight .... SW
Specificaiton Technology Evaluation Program (MHDI) .... STEP
Specifically Authorized Representative [*Air Force*] .... SAR
Specifically Designated Intelligence Position (AFM) .... SDIP
Specifically Designated Special Air Mission [*Aircraft*] [*Air Force*] .... SDSAM
Specification .... S
Specification .... SPC
Specification .... SPCFCTN
Specification (IDOE) .... spec
Specification (AAGC) .... Spec
Specification (AFM) .... SPEC
Specification (DAVI) .... specif
Specification (ROG) .... SPECIFN
Specification and Description Language [*Telecommunications*] (TEL) .... SDL
Specification Approval Form (MCD) .... SAF
Specification Approval Record (MCD) .... SAR
Specification Change .... SC
Specification Change Log [*NASA*] (NASA) .... SCL
Specification Change Memorandum .... SCM
Specification Change Notice [*NASA*] .... SCN
Specification Clarification Request (MCD) .... SCR
Specification Compliance Agreement (MCD) .... SCA
Specification Compliance Concept Agreements (MCD) .... SCCA
Specification Control (IAA) .... SC
Specification Control Board [*NASA*] (NASA) .... SCB
Specification Control Document [*or Drawing*] [*NASA*] (NASA) .... SCD
Specification Control Drawing (MCD) .... SPCD
Specification Control Group (IAA) .... SCG
Specification Control Group Directive (KSC) .... SCGD
Specification Data Base .... SPECD
Specification Document [*NASA*] (NASA) .... SD
Specification for Contract Change (DNAB) .... SCC
Specification for Design .... SD
Specification for Structure .... SS
Specification Information Retrieval System [*Computer science*] (MCD) .... SIR
Specification Information System .... SIS
Specification, Instrumentation, and Range Safety .... SIRS
Specification Interpretation Documentation (MCD) .... SID
Specification Interpretation Documents (MCD) .... SIDS
Specification Language [*Computer science*] (MHDI) .... SPECLE
Specification Memo (AAG) .... SM
Specification of Profits with Interaction under Trial and Error Response .... SPRINTER
Specification of Wiring (IAA) .... SW
Specification Performance Validation [*Military*] (CAAL) .... SPV

Specification Preparing Activity (AAGC) ... SPA
Specification Release Order [*Nuclear energy*] (NRCH) ... SRO
Specification Requirement ... SR
Specification Requirement Sheet (RDA) ... SRS
Specification Requirements Manual [*NASA*] (NASA) ... SRM
Specification Requirements Manual (MCD) ... SRMC
Specification Requirements Table [*NASA*] (NASA) ... SRT
Specification Review and Improvement Program [*Navy*] (NG) ... SRIP
Specification Review Board [*Navy*] (DNAB) ... SRB
Specification Revision Notice (MCD) ... SRN
Specification Revision Sheet [*NASA*] (NASA) ... SRS
Specification Serial Number [*Military*] ... SSN
Specification Serial of Individual Assigned ... SSIA
Specification Status Report [*Nuclear Regulatory Commission*] (GFGA) ... SSR
Specification Technical Review and Improvement Program [*Navy*] (NG) ... STRIP
Specification Test Material (MCD) ... STM
Specification Transmittal Notice (MCD) ... STN
Specification Verification [*Computer science*] (IEEE) ... SPECVER
Specification Verification Open Item Report ... SVOIR
Specification Writers Association of Canada ... SWAC
Specifications (IDOE) ... specs
Specifications (WDMC) ... spex
Specifications and Data Management Office [*Military*] ... SDMO
Specifications Drawing Baseline Index (DNAB) ... SDBI
Specifications Drawing Index (DNAB) ... SDI
Specifications for Non-Heat-Set Advertising Printing ... SNAP
Specifications for Web Offset Publications [*Printing technology*] ... SWOP
Specifications Subject to Change without Notice ... SSTCWN
Specifications Technology, Inc. ... STI
Specificity (DMAA) ... SPEC
Specific-Line Capacitance [*or Capacity*] (IAA) ... SLC
Specific-Pathogen Free [*Medicine*] ... SPF
Specified (ROG) ... SPECIFD
Specified Acceptable Fuel Design Limit [*Nuclear energy*] (NRCH) ... SAFDL
Specified Actions Table [*Military*] ... SAT
Specified Bovine Offal [*Animal feed regulation*] ... SBO
Specified Command Middle East [*Military*] ... SPECOMME
Specified Hours ... SH
Specified Minimum Yield Strength ... SMYS
Specified Organ Transplant [*Health insurance*] (GHCT) ... SOT
Specified Period of Time Contract ... SPTC
Specified Strike Zone [*Army*] (AABC) ... SSZ
Specified Value (MCD) ... SV
Specify Task Asynchronous Exit [*Computer science*] ... STAE
Specifying Queries as Relational Expressions [*Programming language*] [*1973*] [*Computer science*] (CSR) ... SQUARE
Specimen ... SP
Specimen (AAG) ... SPEC
Specimen (DSUE) ... SPECI
Specimen (WGA) ... SPN
Specimen Coordinate Automated Measuring Machine [*Defunct*] ... SCAMM
Specimen Input to Digital Automatic Computer ... SPIDAC
Specimen Lost by Reference Laboratory (DAVI) ... REFL
Specimen Mass Measurement Device [*NASA*] (KSC) ... SMMD
Specimen Not Available [*Medicine*] (DMAA) ... SNA
Specimen Research Centrifuge (SSD) ... SRC
Specimen Return Container (SAA) ... SRC
Specimen Return Control (SAA) ... SRC
Specimen Unobtainable [*Laboratory science*] (DAVI) ... NSPE
Speck (WGA) ... SP
Speck-Fehraltorf [*Switzerland ICAO location identifier*] (ICLI) ... LSZK
Speckled [*Quality of the bottom*] [*Nautical charts*] ... spk
Spec's Music [*NASDAQ symbol*] (TTSB) ... SPEK
Spec's Music, Inc. [*Associated Press*] (SAG) ... SpecMu
Spec's Music, Inc. [*Miami, FL*] [*NASDAQ symbol*] (NQ) ... SPEK
Spectacle [*or Spectacular*] (WGA) ... Spec
Spectacle Dispenser [*Navy technician*] ... SD
Spectacle Makers Co. (Dispenser) [*British*] (DI) ... SMC(Disp)
Spectacles (ROG) ... SPECS
Spectacula [*of Martial*] [*Classical studies*] (OCD) ... Spect
Spectair Industry [*Vancouver Stock Exchange symbol*] ... SPA
Spectator [*A publication*] (BRI) ... Spec
Spectinomycin Resistance ... Spcr
Spectra Calculation from Activated Nuclide Sets (PDAA) ... SCANS
Spectra Mode of Operation through Hardware (IAA) ... SMOOTH
Spectra Ventures Ltd. [*Vancouver Stock Exchange symbol*] ... SAV
Spectra Vision, Inc. [*Formerly, SPI Holdings, Inc.*] [*Associated Press*] (SAG) ... SpectV
Spectra Vision, Inc. [*Formerly, SPI Holdings, Inc.*] [*Associated Press*] (SAG) ... SpectVis
Spectra Vision, Inc. [*Formerly, SPI Holdings, Inc.*] [*AMEX symbol*] (SAG) ... SVN
Spectral Analysis ... SPECAN
Spectral Analysis and Recognition Computer [*NASA*] ... SPARC
Spectral Application of Finite Element Representation (USDC) ... SAFER
Spectral Bandwidth ... SBW
Spectral Combinations for Reconnaissance Exploitation [*Photography*] ... SCORE
Spectral Comparative Pattern Recognizer ... SCEPTRON
Spectral Control Technique ... SCT
Spectral Correlation RADAR (MCD) ... SPECOR
Spectral Density Function ... SDF
Spectral Dependence Photocurrent ... SDP
Spectral Diagnostics [*NASDAQ symbol*] (TTSB) ... DIAGF
Spectral Diagnostics, Inc. [*NASDAQ symbol*] (SAG) ... DIAG
Spectral Diagnostics, Inc. [*Associated Press*] (SAG) ... Spectral
Spectral Distribution ... SD
Spectral Distribution Analyzer ... SDA
Spectral Edge [*Cardiology*] ... SE
Spectral Energy Distribution ... SED
Spectral Imaging Sensor ... SIS
Spectral Index of Sample [*Experimentation*] ... SIS
Spectral Line Width ... SLW
Spectral Map Analysis ... SMA
Spectral Mapping ... SPECMAP
Spectral Matrix Method (KSC) ... SMM
Spectral Multilayer Filter ... SMF
Spectral Pattern-Oblique Transillumination (RDA) ... SPOT
Spectral Pitch [*Neurophysiology*] ... SP
Spectral Power Density [*Electronics*] ... SPD
Spectral Power Distribution (MCD) ... SPD
Spectral Processing Analysis System (PDAA) ... SPANS
Spectral Radiation Experiment (USDC) ... SPECTRE
Spectral Recording [*Trademark of Dolby Laboratories Licensing Corp.*] ... SR
Spectral Recording-Digital [*Sound Technology*] (PS) ... SR-D
Spectral Redistribution Function (IAA) ... SRF
Spectral Shift Control Reactor [*Nuclear energy*] ... SSCR
Spectral Technology and Applied Research ... STAR
Spectral Theory of Diffraction (IAA) ... STD
Spectral Transfer Coefficient ... STC
Spectral Transmission Interference Filter ... STIF
SpectraLink Corp. [*NASDAQ symbol*] (SAG) ... SLNK
SpectraLink Corp. [*NASDAQ symbol*] (TTSB) ... SLNK
SpectraLink Corp. [*Associated Press*] (SAG) ... SpecLink
Spectrametrics, Inc. ... SMI
SpecTran Corp. [*Associated Press*] (SAG) ... Spctran
SpecTran Corp. [*NASDAQ symbol*] (NQ) ... SPTR
[*The*] **Spectranetics Corp.** [*Associated Press*] (SAG) ... Spectra
[*The*] **Spectranetics Corp.** [*NASDAQ symbol*] (SPSG) ... SPNC
SpectraScience, Inc. [*Associated Press*] (SAG) ... SpecSci
SpectraScience, Inc. [*NASDAQ symbol*] (SAG) ... SPSI
SpectraScience Inc. [*NASDAQ symbol*] (TTSB) ... SPSI
Spectravac Power Conversion Systems, Inc., Mississauga, Ontario [*Library symbol National Library of Canada*] (NLC) ... OMS
SpectraVision Inc. 'B' [*AMEX symbol*] (TTSB) ... SVN
Spectrian Corp. [*NASDAQ symbol*] (SAG) ... SPCT
Spectrian Corp. [*Associated Press*] (SAG) ... Spectrian
Spectrin Alpha (DMAA) ... SPTA
Spectrin Alpha, Nonerythroid (DMAA) ... SPTAN
Spectro-Angular Density Method of Forecasting Ocean Waves [*Marine science*] (MSC) ... DSA
Spectrochemical [*or Spectrographic, Spectrometric, or Spectroscopic*] **Oil Analysis Program** [*Air Force*] ... SOAP
Spectroelectrochemistry ... SEC
Spectrograph ... SPECT
Spectrograph Assembly (KSC) ... SA
Spectrographic Telescope ... SCT
Spectrometer (NASA) ... SPECT
Spectrometer Digital System ... SDS
Spectrometer with Interference Selective Amplitude Modulation [*Physics*] ... SISAM
Spectrometric Gas Analysis ... SGA
Spectrometric Oil Analysis Device ... SOAD
Spectronics Micro Sytems [*Computer science*] ... SMS
Spectronix Automatic Fire Extinguishing [*System*] [*For armored vehicles*] ... SAFE
Spectrophosphorimeter ... SPM
Spectrophotofluorometer ... SFM
Spectrophotofluorometer ... SPF
Spectrophotometer Input-Output System ... SIOS
Spectrophotometric Process Ink (DGA) ... SPI
Spectrophotometric Transient Analysis Method for Multiple Positions and Species ... STAMPS
Spectroradiometer Visible System ... SVS
Spectroscopic Phase-Modulated Ellipsometry ... SPME
Spectroscopic Survey Telescope [*Proposed*] [*Joint project of the University of Texas and Pennsylvania State University*] ... SSST
Spectroscopic Survey Telescope [*Proposed*] [*Joint project of the University of Texas and Pennsylvania State University*] ... SST
Spectroscopy [*Medicine*] (DMAA) ... SY
Spectroscopy Society of Canada [*Societe de Spectroscopie du Canada*] ... SSC
Spectrothermal Emission Aerosol Particle Analyzer ... SEAPA
Spectrum ... SPEC
Spectrum (IDOE) ... spec
Spectrum ... SPECT
Spectrum Air Service, Inc. [*ICAO designator*] (FAAC) ... XSA
Spectrum Analysis ... SA
Spectrum Analysis Unit ... SAU
Spectrum Analyzer ... SPA
Spectrum Analyzer (IDOE) ... spec an
Spectrum Analyzer Component (MCD) ... SAC
Spectrum Characteristics Analysis and Measurement [*FAA*] ... SCAM
Spectrum Clear Except Known Signals (MUGU) ... SCEKS
Spectrum Clear of Unknown Signals (MUGU) ... SCOUS
Spectrum Communications & Electronics Corp. [*Telecommunications service*] (TSSD) ... SCE
Spectrum Control [*NASDAQ symbol*] (TTSB) ... SPEC
Spectrum Control, Inc. [*NASDAQ symbol*] (NQ) ... SPEC
Spectrum Controls, Inc. [*Associated Press*] (SAG) ... SpecCtl
Spectrum Display Unit ... SDU
Spectrum Efficient Network Unit (MCD) ... SENU
Spectrum HoloByte [*NASDAQ symbol*] (TTSB) ... SBYT

Spectrum HoloByte, Inc. [*NASDAQ symbol*] (SAG) .... SBYT
Spectrum HoloByte, Inc. [*Associated Press*] (SAG) .... SpecHol
Spectrum Identification Voltage [*Military*] (CAAL) .... SIV
Spectrum Index .... SI
Spectrum Industrial Resources [*Vancouver Stock Exchange symbol*] .... SPM
Spectrum Management (NTCM) .... SM
Spectrum Management Licence [*Telecommunications British*] .... SML
Spectrum Management Task Force [*Electromagnetic spectrum regulation*] (NTCM) .... SMTF
Spectrum Monitoring Unit .... SMU
Spectrum of Time Project [*Astronomy*] .... STP
Spectrum Planning Subcommittee [*FCC*] .... SPS
Spectrum Resolver Integrator .... SRI
Spectrum Resources, Inc. [*St. Charles, MO*] [*Telecommunications*] (TSSD) .... SRI
Spectrum Roentgen-Gamma [*Proposed international space observatory*] .... SRG
Spectrum Signal Processing [*Commercial firm Associated Press*] (SAG) .... SpctSig
Spectrum Signal Processing [*NASDAQ symbol*] (SAG) .... SSPI
Spectrum Signal Processing [*NASDAQ symbol*] (TTSB) .... SSPIF
Spectrum Signature (NG) .... S/S
Specular Reflectance Accessory [*Spectrophotometry*] .... SRA
Specular Reflection Computer Program (MCD) .... SPREC
Speculation (WGA) .... SPEC
Speculative [*Standard & Poor's bond rating*] [*Investment term*] .... B
Speculative Elements [*Moody's bond rating*] [*Investment term*] .... Ba
Speculative Gains Tax .... SGT
Speculative Masonry [*Freemasonry*] .... SM
Speculative - Often in Default [*Moody's bond rating*] .... Ca
Speculative Resource [*Minerals*] .... SR
Speculator [*Guillelmus Durandi*] [*Deceased, 1296*] [*Authority cited in pre-1607 legal work*] (DSA) .... Spec
Speculator [*Guillelmus Durandi*] [*Deceased, 1296*] [*Authority cited in pre-1607 legal work*] (DSA) .... Specu
Speculator [*Guillelmus Durandi*] [*Deceased, 1296*] [*Authority cited in pre-1607 legal work*] (DSA) .... Specula
Speculum [*Obstetrics*] (DAVI) .... spec
Speculum [*A publication*] (BRI) .... Specu
Speech .... S
Speech (WGA) .... SP
Speech .... SPCH
Speech Adaptor Box (NITA) .... SAB
Speech Amplifier (IAA) .... SA
Speech Analog Compression and Editing [*Loop*] (IAA) .... SPACE
Speech and Drama Teachers Association of Queensland [*Australia*] .... SDTAQ
Speech and Hearing [*Medicine*] .... S & H
Speech and Hearing Language Research Centre [*Macquarie University, Australia*] .... SHLRC
Speech and Language Technology [*British*] .... SALT
Speech and Reading Enrichment Program .... SAREP
Speech Application Programming Interface (PCM) .... SAPI
Speech Application Programming Interface [*Microsoft Corp.*] .... SAPI
Speech Association of America [*Later, SCA*] (EA) .... SAA
Speech Auto-Instructional Device .... SAID
Speech Command Auditory Display System (MCD) .... SCADS
Speech Communication (IAA) .... SC
Speech Communication Association (EA) .... SCA
Speech Communications Index Meter .... SCIM
Speech Detection Threshold [*Otorhinolaryngology*] (DAVI) .... SDT
Speech Foundation of America (EA) .... SFA
Speech Identification System (IAA) .... SIDS
Speech Input Device (IAA) .... SID
Speech Intelligibility (RDA) .... SI
Speech Interference Level .... SIL
Speech Interpolation [*Telecommunications*] (TEL) .... SI
Speech Language Pathologist .... SLP
Speech Language Therapist .... SLT
Speech/Noise [*Ratio*] [*Electronics*] .... S/N
Speech Parameter Extraction Experimental Comparison System (IAA) .... SPEECS
Speech Pathologist .... SP
Speech Pathology (DAVI) .... Sp Path
Speech Plus Duplex (IAA) .... SD
Speech Predictive Encoded Communications [*Telephone channels*] .... SPEC
Speech Predictive Encoding System [*Telephone channels*] (IAA) .... SPEC
Speech Processing Chip (NITA) .... SPC
Speech Processing Device .... SPD
Speech Reception Test [*Audiometry*] (MAE) .... SRT
Speech Reception Thresholds [*Audiometry*] .... SRT
Speech Recognition .... SR
Speech Recognition API [*All-Purpose Interface*] (PCM) .... SRAPI
Speech Recognition Application Programming Interface Committee [*Microsoft Corp.*] .... SRAPI
Speech Recognition Computer .... SRC
Speech Recognition Technology [*Computer science*] (CDE) .... SRT
Speech Rehabilitation Institute (EA) .... SRI
Speech Reinforcement System .... SRS
Speech Research Branch [*Navy*] (DNAB) .... SPEEREBRA
Speech Sounds Perception Test (EDAC) .... SSPT
Speech Therapist .... ST
Speech Therapy (DAVI) .... ST
Speech Threshold [*Speech and language therapy*] (DAVI) .... ST
Speech Transmission Index .... STI
Speech Transmission Index Device [*Using*] **Artificial Signals** .... STIDAS
Speech Understanding Research .... SUR
Speech Understanding System .... SUS
Speech with Alternating Masking Index [*Discrimination test*] .... SWAMI
Speech with Duplex Telegraph .... S + DX
Speech-Compatible Tactile Communicant (MCD) .... SCOTAC
Speech-Controlled Respirometer for Ambulation Measurement [*Medicine*] (DMAA) .... SCRAM
Speech-Operated Noise Adjusting Device [*Telecommunications*] (TEL) .... SONAD
Speeck Awareness Threshold [*Otorhinolaryngology*] (DAVI) .... SAT
Speed .... S
Speed (MSA) .... SP
Speed (AABC) .... SPD
Speed .... SPD
Speed and Heading [*Navy Navigation and Satellite System*] (DNAB) .... SPHG
Speed and Throtte Automatic Network (PDAA) .... SATAN
Speed Brake (MCD) .... SB
Speed Brake (NASA) .... SPBK
Speed Brake (MCD) .... SPBR
Speed Brake (MCD) .... SPDBK
Speed Brake Command (NASA) .... SBC
Speed Brake Hand Control (NASA) .... SBHC
Speed Change Rate .... SCR
Speed Class Sequencing .... SCS
Speed Coaches Association (EA) .... SCA
Speed Command Attitude/Target [*FAA*] .... SCAT
Speed Command of Attitude/Thrust (IAA) .... SCAT
Speed Control Approach/Takeoff .... SCAT
Speed Control Circuit (DNAB) .... SCC
Speed Control System (PDAA) .... SCS
Speed Control Valve .... SCV
Speed Controller [*Nuclear energy*] (NRCH) .... SC
Speed Converter .... SPCONV
Speed Density .... SD
Speed Disk [*Computer program*] (PCM) .... SD
Speed Indicator (IAA) .... SI
Speed Limiting Point [*Aviation*] (FAAC) .... SLP
Speed Lock [*Computer science*] (PCM) .... SL
Speed Made Good [*Navy*] (NVT) .... SMG
Speed Made Good Over the Ground (NATG) .... SOG
Speed Made Good Through the Water (NATG) .... STW
Speed Measuring Device (PDAA) .... SMD
Speed Navigation (MCD) .... SPD NAV
Speed of Advance [*Military*] .... SOA
Speed of Approach .... SOA
Speed of Approach Measurement Indicator (PDAA) .... SAMI
Speed of Light in Vacuum [*Symbol*] c
Speed of Relative Movement .... SRM
Speed of Service [*Telecommunications*] (TEL) .... SOS
Speed of Sound .... SOS
Speed Phase Lock .... SPL
Speed Position and Track (MCD) .... SPOT
Speed Power Product (IAA) .... SPP
Speed, Power, Quietness, and Reliability [*Automotive engineering*] .... SPQR
Speed Reading Self-Taught [*Learning International*] .... SRST
Speed Recorder (IEEE) .... SR
Speed Regulator .... SPREG
Speed Regulator .... SR
Speed Sensor (NRCH) .... SS
Speed Switch (IEEE) .... SPS
Speed through Aerial Resupply [*Air Force*] .... STAR
Speed Tolerant Recording [*Electronic Processors, Inc.*] .... STR
Speed Transmitter (NRCH) .... ST
Speedball Up-Range Launch Facility [*Army*] (AABC) .... SULF
Speedbrake Thrust Control [*Aerospace*] (MCD) .... SBTC
Speed-Controlled Spark [*Automotive engineering*] .... SCS
Speed-Controlled Volume .... SCV
Speed-Dependent Damping [*Automotive engineering*] .... SDD
Speed-Dependent Damping Control [*Automotive engineering*] .... SDDC
Speeded Reading of Word List [*Neuropsychology test*] .... SRWL
SPEEDEX [*Systemwide Project for Electronic Equipment at Depots Extended*] **Automatic Scheduling System** [*Military*] .... SASS
SPEEDEX [*Systemwide Project for Electronic Equipment at Depots Extended*] **Operating Instructions** .... SOI
SpeedFam International, Inc. [*NASDAQ symbol*] (SAG) .... SFAM
SpeedFam International, Inc. [*Associated Press*] (SAG) .... SpdFam
Speedfam Intl [*NASDAQ symbol*] (TTSB) .... SFAM
Speed-Gate-Pull-Off (PDAA) .... SGPO
Speedletter .... S/L
Speedletter .... SPDLTR
Speed-Modulated Augmented Thrust System (NG) .... SMATS
Speedometer .... SPDMTR
Speedometer (MSA) .... SPDOM
Speedometer [*Automotive engineering*] .... SPEEDO
Speed-Sensitive Steering [*Automotive engineering*] .... SSS
Speedway .... SPDWY
Speedway Motorsports [*NYSE symbol*] (TTSB) .... TRK
Speedway Motorsports, Inc. [*Associated Press*] (SAG) .... SpeedM
Speedway Motorsports, Inc. [*NYSE symbol*] (SAG) .... TRK
Speedway Public Library, Speedway, IN [*Library symbol Library of Congress*] (LCLS) .... InSp
Speedway Riders Association [*British*] (DBA) .... SRA
Speed-Welding Wire Feeder .... SWWF
Speedwings SA [*Switzerland ICAO designator*] (FAAC) .... SPW
Speedy .... SPDY
Speedy Drill Template (MCD) .... SDT
Speers' [*or Spears'*] **South Carolina Equity Reports** [*A publication*] (DLA) .... Speers Eq

Speers' [*or Spears'*] **South Carolina Equity Reports** [*A publication*] (DLA) ... Speers Eq (SC)
Speers' [*or Spears'*] **South Carolina Law Reports** [*A publication*] (DLA) ... Speers
Speers' [*or Spears'*] **South Carolina Law Reports** [*A publication*] (DLA) ... Speers L (SC)
Speilberger's Trait-Anxiety Inventory (EDAC) ... STAI
Speizman Ind [*NASDAQ symbol*] (TTSB) ... SPZN
Speizman Industries, Inc. [*Associated Press*] (SAG) ... Speizmn
Speizman Industries, Inc. [*NASDAQ symbol*] (SAG) ... SPZN
Speleological ... SPELEOL
Speleological Union of Ireland (EAIO) ... SUI
Spell Out [*Proofreading*] (WDMC) ... sp
Spelling (WDMC) ... sp
Spelling ... SP
Spelling and Reading Tests ... SPAR
Spelling Entertainment Group [*Formerly, Charter Co.*] [*NYSE symbol*] (SPSG) ... SP
Spelling Entertainment Grp [*NYSE symbol*] (TTSB) ... SP
Spelling Entertainment, Inc. [*Associated Press*] (SAG) ... SpellEnt
Spelling on Extraordinary Relief in Equity and in Law [*A publication*] (DLA) ... Spell Extr Rel
Spelling Patterns ... SPELPAT
Spelling Reform (ADA) ... SR
Spelling's Treatise on Injunctions and Other Extraordinary Remedies [*A publication*] (DLA) ... Spell Extr Rem
Spelman on Feuds [*A publication*] (DLA) ... Spel Feuds
Spelman's Glossarium Archaiologicum [*A publication*] (DLA) ... Sp Glos
Spelman's Glossarium Archaiologicum [*A publication*] (DLA) ... Spel Gl
Spelman's Glossarium Archaiologicum [*3 eds.*] [*1626-87*] [*A publication*] (DLA) ... Spelm
Spelman's Glossarium Archaiologicum [*3 eds.*] [*1626-87*] [*A publication*] (DLA) ... Spelman
Spelman's Law Tracts [*A publication*] (DLA) ... Spel LT
Spelman's Reports, Manuscript, English King's Bench [*A publication*] (DLA) ... Spel Rep
Spencar Explorations Ltd. [*Vancouver Stock Exchange symbol*] ... SXE
Spence Bay [*Canada*] [*Airport symbol*] (OAG) ... YYH
Spence Bay, NT [*ICAO location identifier*] (ICLI) ... CYYH
Spence on Copyright of Designs [*A publication*] (DLA) ... Spence Cop
Spence on Patentable Inventions [*1851*] [*A publication*] (DLA) ... Spence Pat Inv
Spencer [*Iowa*] [*Airport symbol*] (OAG) ... SPW
Spencer Evening World, Spencer, IN [*Library symbol Library of Congress*] (LCLS) ... InSpeW
Spencer Gulf Prawn Fishery [*Australia*] ... SGPF
Spencer, IA [*AM radio station call letters*] ... KICD
Spencer, IA [*FM radio station call letters*] ... KICD-FM
Spencer, IA [*FM radio station call letters*] ... KIGL
Spencer, IA [*Location identifier FAA*] (FAAL) ... LTU
Spencer, IN [*FM radio station call letters*] ... WSKT
Spencer Information Storage and Retrieval System (DIT) ... SPINSTRE
Spencer Kellogg Division, Textron, Inc., Buffalo, NY [*Library symbol Library of Congress*] (LCLS) ... NBuSK
Spencer, NY [*FM radio station call letters*] ... WCII
Spencer, OK [*FM radio station call letters*] ... KROU
Spencer Public-Owen County Contractual Library, Spencer, IN [*Library symbol Library of Congress*] (LCLS) ... InSpe
Spencer, TN [*FM radio station call letters*] ... WWEE
Spencer, WI [*FM radio station call letters*] ... WOSQ
Spencer, WV [*AM radio station call letters*] ... WVRC
Spencer, WV [*FM radio station call letters*] ... WVRC-FM
Spencer-Mead [*Commercial firm*] (DAVI) ... Spencer-M
Spencer's Law Reports [*20 New Jersey*] [*A publication*] (DLA) ... Spen (NJ)
Spencer's Law Reports [*20 New Jersey*] [*A publication*] (DLA) ... Spenc
Spencer's Law Reports [*20 New Jersey*] [*A publication*] (DLA) ... Spencer
Spencer's Reports [*10-20 Minnesota*] [*A publication*] (DLA) ... Spenc
Spencer's Reports [*10-20 Minnesota*] [*A publication*] (DLA) ... Spencer
Spencerville & Elgin Railroad Co. [*AAR code*] ... SPEG
Spencerville, OH [*FM radio station call letters*] (RBYB) ... WBCJ-FM
Spence's Equitable Jurisdiction of the Court of Chancery [*A publication*] (DLA) ... Spence Ch
Spence's Equitable Jurisdiction of the Court of Chancery [*A publication*] (DLA) ... Spence Eq Jur
Spence's Origin of Laws [*A publication*] (DLA) ... Spence Or L
Spend Today and Retire Tomorrow [*Consumer pension plan*] ... START
SpenderMenders [*An association*] (EA) ... SM
SpenderMenders International [*Defunct*] (EA) ... SMI
Spens' Select Cases [*Bombay, India*] [*A publication*] (DLA) ... Spens Sel Cas
Spenser Society (EA) ... SS
Spent Fuel [*Nuclear energy*] (NRCH) ... SF
Spent Fuel Building Isolation [*Nuclear energy*] (NRCH) ... SFBI
Spent Fuel Cooling System [*Nuclear energy*] (NRCH) ... SFCS
Spent Fuel Pit [*Nuclear energy*] (NRCH) ... SFP
Spent Fuel Pool [*Nuclear energy*] (NRCH) ... SFP
Spent Fuel Pool Area Ventilation System [*Nuclear energy*] (NRCH) ... SFPAVS
Spent Fuel Pool Cooling and Cleanup System [*Nuclear energy*] (NRCH) ... SFPCCS
Spent Fuel Pool Cooling System [*Nuclear energy*] (NRCH) ... SFPCS
Spent Fuel Storage Pool [*Nuclear energy*] (NRCH) ... SFSP
Spent Fuel Storage Pool [*Nuclear energy*] (NUCP) ... SPSF
Spent Fuel Transfer Tubes [*Nuclear energy*] (NRCH) ... SFTT
Spent Fuel Transportation Accident [*Nuclear energy*] (NRCH) ... SFTA
Spent Nuclear Fuel ... SNF
Spent Nuclear Material (IEEE) ... SNM
Spent Nuclear Material Pool (IEEE) ... SNMP
Spent Pot Lining Insolubilisation Technology [*Metallurgy*] ... SPLIT
Spent Resin Storage Tank [*Nuclear energy*] (IAA) ... SPST
Spent Resin Tank [*Nuclear energy*] (NRCH) ... SRT
Spent Stage Experimental Support Module (KSC) ... SSESM
Spent Sulfite Liquor [*Papermaking*] ... SSL
Sperm Aster [*Cytology*] ... SA
Sperm Cervical Mucus Penetration Test [*Clinical chemistry*] ... SCMPT
Sperm Entry Point [*into egg*] ... SEP
Sperm Immobilization Test [*Clinical chemistry*] ... SIT
Sperm [*or Spore*] **Mother-Cell** ... S-M-C
Sperm Outer Defense Fiber [*Medicine*] (DMAA) ... SODF
Sperm Reservoir Length Index ... SPRI
Sperm Wassermann Reaction [*Urology*] (DAVI) ... SWR
Sperm Whale ... SW
Spermatocyte ... SC
Spermatophore Length ... SPL
Spermatophore Length Index ... SPLI
Spermatozoa (DOG) ... sperm
Spermatozoa (DAVI) ... SPRM
Spermatozoan (DOG) ... sperm
Sperm-Coating Antigen ... SCA
Spermicide-Germicide Compound [*Medicine*] (DMAA) ... SGC
Spermidine [*Biochemistry*] ... Spd
Spermiogenesis Growth Factor [*Biochemistry*] ... SGF
Sperm-Release Pheromone [*Biology*] ... SRF
Sperm-Washing Insemination Method ... SWIM
Speronara [*Ship's rigging*] (ROG) ... SA
Sperry Air Arm Division ... SAAD
Sperry Air Data Equipment ... SPADE
Sperry Airborne Data Acquistion System (IAA) ... SADAS
Sperry & Hutchinson Co. ... S & H
Sperry Canada Automatic Tester ... SCAT
Sperry Computer-Aided Message Processor [*British*] ... SCAMP
Sperry Continuity and Resistance Tester ... SCART
Sperry Gyroscope Division [*Sperry Rand Corp.*] (MCD) ... SGD
Sperry Heading and Attitude Reference Platform (SAA) ... SHARP
Sperry Inertial RADAR Altimeter ... SPIRAL
Sperry Kalman Optical Reset [*Ship's Inertial Navigation System*] [*Navy*] (DNAB) ... SKOR
Sperry Program for Advancing Careers through Education ... SPACE
Sperry Quick Updating of Internal Documentation (IEEE) ... SQUID
Sperry Rand Corp., Sperry Gyroscope Division, Great Neck, NY [*Library symbol Library of Congress*] (LCLS) ... NGrnS
Sperry Rand Research Center (MCD) ... SRRC
Sperry Rand Research Center, Sudbury, MA [*Library symbol Library of Congress*] (LCLS) ... MSuSR
Sperry UNIVAC Information Center, Blue Bell, PA [*OCLC symbol*] (OCLC) ... SPE
Sperry UNIVAC Material System ... SUMS
Sperry UNIVAC Minicomputer Management of Interactive Terminals ... SUMMIT
Sperry UNIVAC, St. Paul, MN [*Library symbol Library of Congress*] (LCLS) ... MnSSpU
Sperry Utah Engineering Laboratory (MCD) ... SUEL
Spertus College of Judaica [*Chicago, IL*] (BJA) ... SCJ
Spertus College of Judaica, Chicago, IL [*Library symbol Library of Congress*] (LCLS) ... ICJS
Speyer [*Germany ICAO location identifier*] (ICLI) ... EDRY
Sphenoethmoidal [*Suture*] [*Medicine*] ... SE
Spheno-Occipital [*Synchondrosis*] [*Medicine*] ... SO
Sphenopalatine Ganglion [*Neurology*] (DAVI) ... SPAG
Sphere [*or Spherical*] ... S
Sphere Drake Holdings [*NYSE symbol*] (SPSG) ... SD
Sphere Drake Holdings [*Associated Press*] (SAG) ... SphrDrk
Sphere of Influence ... SOI
Sphere of Influence People ... SOIP
Sphere of Positon (SAA) ... SOP
Spherical [*Buoy*] ... SP
Spherical (ROG) ... SPH
Spherical ... SPHER
Spherical Angles from Points (MCD) ... SANGFPT
Spherical Attitude Indicator (MCD) ... SAI
Spherical Candlepower ... SCP
Spherical Cartridge ... SPCTG
Spherical Cavity Flow ... SCF
Spherical Electrostatic Analyzer ... SEA
Spherical Equivalent ... SE
Spherical Error Precision [*or Probability*] ... SEP
Spherical Eyeball [*Aviation*] (OA) ... SE
Spherical Gear Coupling ... SGC
Spherical Harmonic Analysis [*Geophysics*] ... SHA
Spherical Harmonic Coefficient [*Geophysics*] ... SHC
Spherical Harmonic Series (SAA) ... SHS
Spherical Joint (IAA) ... S
Spherical Lens [*Ophthalmology*] (DAVI) ... S
Spherical Lens [*Ophthalmology*] ... SPH
Spherical Micro Integrated Lens ... SMILE
Spherical Polar ... SP
Spherical Probable Error ... SPE
Spherical Radiation Absorber (MCD) ... SRA
Spherical Retarding Potential Analyzer (MCD) ... SRPA
Spherical Roller Bearing ... SRB
Spherical Symmetry ... SS
Spherical Tank [*Liquid gas carriers*] ... sp
Spherical Torus Experiment [*Oak Ridge National Laboratory*] ... STX
Spherical Wave Expansion [*Telecommunications*] (TEL) ... SWE
Spherocytes [*Also, SPHER*] [*Hematology*] (DAVI) ... SPHE
Spherocytes [*Also, SPHE*] [*Hematology*] (DAVI) ... SPHER

Spheroidal Graphite [*Metallurgy*] ... SG
Spheroidal Graphite [*Ductile iron*] ... SG
Spheroidal Oral Drug Absorption System [*Medicine*] (DMAA) ... SODAS
Sphincter Tone [*Medicine*] (MAE) ... ST
Sphingolipid Activator Protein [*Biochemistry*] ... SAP
Sphingomyelin [*Also, Sph*] [*Biochemistry*] ... SM
Sphingomyelin [*Also, SM, Sph*] [*Biochemistry*] (DAVI) ... SP
Sphingomyelin [*Also, SM, SP*] [*Biochemistry*] (DAVI) ... Sph
Sphingosine [*Also, SM*] [*Biochemistry*] ... Sph
Sphinx Mining Inc. [*Vancouver Stock Exchange symbol*] ... SXM
SPI [*Society of the Plastics Industry*] **Composites Institute** (EA) ... SPICI
SPI Holdings, Inc. [*Later, SpectraVision, Inc.*] [*AMEX symbol*] (SPSG) ... SPI
Spice Entertainment Companies, Inc. [*Associated Press*] (SAG) ... SpiceEnt
Spice Entertainment Companies, Inc. [*NASDAQ symbol*] (SAG) ... SPZE
Spice Trade Association [*British*] (DBA) ... STA
Spiced Ham [*Hormel (George A.) & Co.*] ... SPAM
Spicer Elementary School, Spicer, MN [*Library symbol*] [*Library of Congress*] (LCLS) ... MnSpES
Spicer Public Library, Spicer, MN [*Library symbol*] [*Library of Congress*] (LCLS) ... MnSpP
Spicules [*Quality of the bottom*] [*Nautical charts*] ... Spi
Spider [*Engineering acoustics*] ... SPDR
SPIE - the International Society for Optical Engineering (EA) ... SPIE
Spiece Associates, Winnipeg, Manitoba [*Library symbol National Library of Canada*] (NLC) ... MWSPA
Spiece Associates, Winnipeg, MB, Canada [*Library symbol*] [*Library of Congress*] (LCLS) ... CaMWSPA
Spiegel Cl'A' [*NASDAQ symbol*] (TTSB) ... SPGLA
Spiegel, Inc. [*NASDAQ symbol*] (NQ) ... SPGL
Spiegel, Inc. [*Associated Press*] (SAG) ... Spiegel
Spieker Prop 9.45%'B' Pfd [*NYSE symbol*] (TTSB) ... SPKPrB
Spieker Properties [*Associated Press*] (SAG) ... SpiekerP
Spieker Properties [*Associated Press*] (SAG) ... Spiekr
Spieker Properties [*NYSE symbol*] (SPSG) ... SPK
Spies Public Library, Menominee, MI [*Library symbol Library of Congress*] (LCLS) ... MiMe
Spigot and Socket ... S & S
Spike (MSA) ... SPK
Spike Jones International Fan Club (EA) ... SJIFC
Spike on Master and Servant [*3rd ed.*] [*1872*] [*A publication*] (DLA) ... Spike M & S
Spike Wave [*Medicine*] (DMAA) ... SW
Spikenard (AD) ... nard
Spikes Plant [*Wheat*] ... S/P
Spike-Wave Stupor [*Medicine*] (DMAA) ... SWS
Spiking Activity [*Medicine*] (DMAA) ... SA
Spill Control Association of America (EA) ... SCAA
Spill Control Recovery Valve (PDAA) ... SCRV
Spill Planning Exercise and Response System [*USCG*] (TAG) ... SPEARS
Spill Prevention Control and Countermeasure [*Petroleum industry*] ... SPCC
Spilled Oil Research Team [*National Oceanic and Atmospheric Administration*] (MSC) ... SOR
Spilled Oil Response Team [*Marine science*] (MSC) ... SORT
Spillover Factor ... SOF
Spills, Accidents, and Mixtures [*of Exxon Corp.'s "Stop SAM" safety program*] ... SAM
Spin Armed Fuze ... SAF
Spin Axis (AAG) ... SA
Spin Axis Declination [*Aerospace*] (MCD) ... SADEC
Spin Block (MSA) ... SB
Spin Density-Weighted (DMAA) ... SDW
Spin Dependent Resonance [*Physics*] ... SDR
Spin Device ... SD
Spin Echo Double Resonance [*Physics*] ... SEDOR
Spin Flip Raman [*LASER*] ... SFR
Spin Lattice Relaxation ... SLR
Spin Motor Interruption Technique ... SMIT
Spin Motor Rate Detector (IAA) ... SMRD
Spin Motor Rotation [*or Running*] **Detector** (MCD) ... SMRD
Spin Motor Run Discrete (NASA) ... SMRD
Spin Motor Supply ... SMS
Spin Muon Collaboration [*Nuclear research*] ... SMC
Spin On Glass [*Microlithography*] ... SOG
Spin on Straight Rail ... SOSR
Spin Polarization Induced Nuclear Overhauser Effect [*Physics*] ... SPINOE
Spin Polarization-Induced Nuclear Overhauser Effect [*Physics*] ... SPINOE
Spin Polarized [*Physics*] ... SP
Spin Quantum Number [*Atomic physics*] (DEN) ... s
Spin Quantum Number [*Atomic physics*] ... SQN
Spin Recovery Parachute ... SRP
Spin Reference Axis (KSC) ... SRA
Spin Stabilized Guided Projectile (MCD) ... SSGP
Spin Stretch Factor [*Textile technology*] ... SSF
Spin Synchronous Clock ... SSC
Spin Test Facility [*NASA*] ... STF
Spin Transition [*Physics*] ... ST
Spin Tuned Magnetron ... STM
Spina Bifida [*Medicine*] ... SB
Spina Bifida and Anencephaly [*Medicine*] ... SBA
Spina Bifida Aperta [*Medicine*] (DMAA) ... SBA
Spina Bifida Association of America (EA) ... SBAA
Spina Bifida Association of South Australia ... SBASA
Spina Bifida Association of Tasmania [*Australia*] ... SBAT
Spina Bifida Association of Victoria [*Australia*] ... SBAV
Spina Bifida Association of Western Australia ... SBAWA
Spinach Carbonic Anhydrase [*An enzyme*] ... SCA
Spinach Latent Virus [*Plant pathology*] ... SPLV
Spinach Temperate Virus [*Plant pathology*] ... STEV
Spinal Analysis Machine ... SAM
Spinal and Bulbar Muscular Atrophy [*Medicine*] ... SBMA
Spinal Cord [*Medicine*] (MAE) ... sp cd
Spinal Cord Blood Flow ... SCBF
Spinal Cord Disease [*Neurology*] (DAVI) ... SCD
Spinal Cord Evoked Potential [*Medicine*] (DMAA) ... SCEP
Spinal Cord Injury [*Medicine*] ... SCI
Spinal Cord Injury Care System [*University of Alabama in Birmingham*] [*Research center*] (RCD) ... SCICS
Spinal Cord Injury Research Center [*Ohio State University*] [*Research center*] (RCD) ... SCIRC
Spinal Cord Injury Service [*Medicine*] ... SCIS
Spinal Cord Society (EA) ... SCS
Spinal Cord-Insured (MCD) ... SCI
Spinal Dorsal Horn [*Anatomy*] ... SDH
Spinal Dural Arteriovenous Fistula [*Medicine*] (DMAA) ... SDAVF
Spinal Fluid [*Medicine*] ... SF
Spinal Fluid [*Medicine*] (MAE) ... sp fl
Spinal Fluid Count [*Medicine*] ... SFC
Spinal Fluid Pressure [*Medicine*] ... SFP
Spinal Injuries Association [*British*] ... SIA
Spinal Instrumentation and Fusion [*Neurology*] (DAVI) ... SI & F
Spinal Kinematic Instrument [*Medicine*] ... SKI
Spinal Muscular Atrophy [*Aran-Duchenne type*] (PAZ) ... adult progressive SMA
Spinal Muscular Atrophy [*Kugelberg-Welander disease*] (PAZ) ... juvenile SMA
Spinal Muscular Atrophy [*Medicine*] ... SMA
Spinal Nucleus of the Bulbocavernosus [*Neuroanatomy*] ... SNB
Spinal Progressive Amyotrophy [*Medicine*] (DMAA) ... SPA
Spinal Progressive Muscular Atrophy [*Medicine*] (AAMN) ... SPMA
Spindale, NC [*AM radio station call letters*] ... WGMA
Spindale, NC [*FM radio station call letters*] ... WNCW
Spindale Public Library, Spindale, NC [*Library symbol Library of Congress*] (LCLS) ... NcSpi
Spin-Density Wave [*Physics*] ... SDW
Spin-Dependent Delocalization [*Physical chemistry*] ... SDD
Spin-Dependent Luminescence [*Physics*] ... SPDL
SPINDEX Users' Network (NITA) ... SUN
Spin-Dipolar [*Physics*] ... SD
Spindle (MSA) ... SPDL
Spindle Pole Body [*Cell biology*] ... SPB
Spindle Speed Override (IAA) ... SSO
Spine [*or Spinal*] ... SP
Spine Point Bullet ... SP
Spin-Echo Correlated Spectroscopy ... SECSY
Spin-Echo Fourier Transform [*Physics*] ... SEFT
Spin-Echo Scan [*Roentgenology*] ... SE
Spinel [*CIPW classification*] [*Geology*] ... sp
Spine-Tech, Inc. [*Associated Press*] (SAG) ... SpineT
Spine-Tech, Inc. [*Associated Press*] (SAG) ... SpineTch
Spine-Tech, Inc. [*NASDAQ symbol*] (SAG) ... SPYN
Spin-Flip Raman LASER (PDAA) ... SFRL
Spinivasan's Reports of Income Tax Cases [*India*] [*A publication*] (DLA) ... ITC
Spinks' Ecclesiastical and Admiralty [*Upper Canada*] [*A publication*] (DLA) ... Eccl & Adm
Spinks' English Admiralty Prize Cases [*164 English Reprint*] [*1854-56*] [*A publication*] (DLA) ... Sp
Spinks' English Admiralty Prize Cases [*1854-56*] [*A publication*] (DLA) ... Sp Pr Cas
Spinks' English Admiralty Prize Cases [*A publication*] (DLA) ... Spinks PC
Spinks' English Admiralty Prize Cases [*164 English Reprint*] [*A publication*] (DLA) ... Spinks Prize Cas
Spinks' English Admiralty Prize Cases [*164 English Reprint*] [*A publication*] (DLA) ... Spinks Prize Cas (Eng)
Spinks' English Ecclesiastical and Admiralty Reports [*A publication*] (DLA) ... E & A
Spinks' English Ecclesiastical and Admiralty Reports [*1853-55*] [*A publication*] (DLA) ... Ecc & Ad
Spinks' English Ecclesiastical and Admiralty Reports [*A publication*] (DLA) ... Eccl & Ad
Spinks' English Ecclesiastical and Admiralty Reports [*A publication*] (DLA) ... Sp
Spinks' English Ecclesiastical and Admiralty Reports [*164 English Reprint*] [*1853-55*] [*A publication*] (DLA) ... Sp Ecc & Ad
Spinks' English Ecclesiastical and Admiralty Reports [*164 English Reprint*] [*A publication*] (DLA) ... Spinks
Spinks' English Ecclesiastical and Admiralty Reports [*164 English Reprint*] [*A publication*] (DLA) ... Spinks Eccl & Adm (Eng)
Spinnable Cotton Waste Equalization Program ... SCWEP
Spinnaker Inds [*NASDAQ symbol*] (SAG) ... SPNI
Spinnaker Industries [*Associated Press*] (SAG) ... Spinakr
Spinnaker Industries [*NASDAQ symbol*] (TTSB) ... SPNI
Spinnbarkheit [*With reference to cervical mucus*] [*Medicine*] ... SPK
Spinners and Weavers Association of Korea [*Defunct*] (EA) ... SWAK
Spinning Continuous Filament ... SCF
Spinning Crucible Furnace ... SCF
Spinning Form (MCD) ... SPF
Spinning Form [*Tool*] (AAG) ... SPFM
Spinning Form Block (MCD) ... SFB
Spinning Satellite for Electric Rocket Test ... SERT
Spinning Satellite for Electric Rocket Test (IAA) ... SFERT
Spinning Solid Upper Stage (RDA) ... SSUS
Spinning Solid Upper Stage - Atlas Class Spacecraft (MCD) ... SSUS-A
Spinning Solid Upper Stage - Delta Class Spacecraft (MCD) ... SSUS-D
Spinning Solid Upper Stage Project (MCD) ... SSUSP

Spinning Space Station ..... SSS
Spinning Star [*Astronomy*] ..... SPINAR
Spinning Tubular Projectile (MCD) ..... STUP
Spinning Unguided Rocket Trajectory ..... SPURT
Spinning Vehicle Simulator ..... SVS
Spino-Bulbar Muscular Atrophy [*Medicine*] ..... SBMA
Spinocerebellar Ataxia [*Genetics*] ..... SCA
Spinocerebellar Degeneration-Slow Eye Movements Syndrome [*Medicine*] (DMAA) ..... SDSEM
Spin-Orbit Coupling [*Physical chemistry*] ..... SOC
Spin-Orbital (IAA) ..... SO
Spinothalamic Tract [*Brain anatomy*] ..... STT
Spin-Polarized Hartree-Fock [*Atomic wave-function*] ..... SPHF
Spin-Polarized Inverse Photoemission [*Physics*] ..... SPIPE
Spin-Polarized Inverse Photoemission Spectroscopy ..... SPIPES
Spin-Polarized Low-Energy Electron Microscopy ..... SPLEEM
Spin-Polarized Photoelectron Diffraction [*Physics*] ..... SPPD
Spin-Polarized Photoemission Spectroscopy ..... SPPES
Spin-Rotation [*Physics*] ..... SR
Spin-Scan Cloud Camera [*NASA*] ..... SSCC
Spin-Stabilized [*Rockets*] ..... SS
Spin-Stabilized Aircraft Rocket ..... SSAR
Spin-Stabilized Impulsively Controlled Missile (MCD) ..... SSICM
Spin-Stabilized Rockets ..... SSR
Spin-Stabilized Spacecraft ..... SSS
Spin-Stabilized Upper Stage [*NASA*] (NASA) ..... SSUS
Spinster ..... S
Spinster (ADA) ..... SPIN
Spinster ..... SPR
Spiny Lobster Undersea Research Project ..... SLURP
Spiracular Organ [*Fish anatomy*] ..... SO
Spiral ..... SPIR
Spiral (MSA) ..... SPL
Spiral Aftereffect [*Aerospace*] ..... SAE
Spiral Aftereffect Test [*Psychology*] (AEBS) ..... SAET
Spiral Aftereffect Test [*Psychology*] ..... SAT
Spiral Fin Tubing ..... SFT
Spiral Having Nuclear Regions Less Conspicuous than Sa Class and Greater than Scwith Arms Wider Open than Sa Class [*Astronomy*] (BARN) ..... Sb
Spiral Having the Least Conspicuous Nuclear Regions and with Arms Very Loosely Coiled [*Astronomy*] (BARN) ..... Sc
Spiral Optics [*Vancouver Stock Exchange symbol*] ..... SEU
Spiral Point Drill Geometry ..... SPDG
Spiral to Spiral ..... SS
Spiral Wound [*Medicine*] (MAE) ..... SW
Spiral Wrap Tubing ..... SWT
Spiral X-Ray Computed Tomography [*Medicine*] (DMAA) ..... SXCT
Spiral-Defect Chaos [*Physics*] ..... SDC
Spiral-Ecological Approach to Supervision (EDAC) ..... SEAS
Spire Corp. [*NASDAQ symbol*] (NQ) ..... SPIR
Spire Corp. [*Associated Press*] (SAG) ..... Spire
Spirex [*Wire binding*] (DGA) ..... Spx
Spiridon Lake [*Alaska*] [*Seismograph station code, US Geological Survey*] (SEIS) ..... SPL
Spiriformis Medialis Nucleus [*Brain anatomy*] ..... SpM
Spirillum [*Bacteriology*] (MAE) ..... S
Spirillum (MAE) ..... Sp
Spirit ..... SP
Spirit ..... SPT
Spirit Airlines, Inc. [*FAA designator*] (FAAC) ..... SWG
Spirit and Breath Association (EA) ..... SBA
Spirit, John Denver Fan Club (EA) ..... SJDFC
Spirit Lake Beacon, Spirit Lake, IA [*Library symbol*] [*Library of Congress*] (LCLS) ..... IaSplB
Spirit Lake, IA [*FM radio station call letters*] ..... KUOO
Spirit Lake, IA [*Location identifier FAA*] (FAAL) ..... SRK
Spirit of Adventure (EA) ..... SOA
Spirit of the Future Creative Institute [*Commercial firm*] (EA) ..... SFCI
Spirit of the Laws (Montesquieu) [*A publication*] (DLA) ..... Sp Laws
Spirit Petroleum [*Vancouver Stock Exchange symbol*] ..... SPX
Spirit River Municipal Library, Alberta [*Library symbol National Library of Canada*] (NLC) ..... ASRm
Spirit River Municipal Library, Spirit River, AB, Canada [*Library symbol*] [*Library of Congress*] (LCLS) ..... CaASrM
Spirit Varnish Resistance Ink (DGA) ..... SVR
Spiritoso [*With Animation*] [*Music*] ..... SPIR
Spiritoso [*With Animation*] [*Music*] ..... SPIRIT
Spirits ..... SPTS
Spiritual (DAVI) ..... SPIR
Spiritual Advisory Council (EA) ..... SAC
Spiritual Counterfeits Project (EA) ..... SCP
Spiritual Frontiers Fellowship [*Later, SFFI*] (EA) ..... SFF
Spiritual Frontiers Fellowship International (EA) ..... SFFI
Spiritual Life Institute of America (EA) ..... SLIA
Spiritual Ministry for Adults (EA) ..... SMA
Spiritual Regeneration Movement [*Foundation of America*] (EA) ..... SRM
Spiritual Unity of Nations [*An association*] ..... SUN
Spiritualist Association of Great Britain (BI) ..... SA
Spiritualist Association of Great Britain ..... SAGB
Spiritualist Yoga Fellowship (EAIO) ..... SYF
Spiritualists National Union [*British*] (DBA) ..... SNU
Spiritus [*Spirit*] [*Latin*] [*Pharmacy*] (DAVI) ..... SP
Spiritus [*Spirit*] [*Pharmacy*] ..... SPIR
Spiritus [*Spirit*] [*Latin*] (ROG) ..... SPIRIT
Spiritus [*Spirit*] [*Latin Pharmacy*] (MAE) ..... spt
Spiritus Frumenti [*Whisky*] [*Pharmacy*] (ROG) ..... SF
Spiritus in Deo [*Spirit Rests in God*] [*Latin*] ..... SID
Spiritus Vini [*Alcoholic Spirit*] [*Latin*] ..... sv
Spiritus Vini Gallici [*Brandy*] [*Pharmacy*] (ROG) ..... SVG
Spiritus Vini Industrialis [*Industrial Alcohol*] [*Pharmacy*] ..... SVI
Spiritus Vini Methylatus [*Methylated Spirit*] [*Pharmacy*] ..... SVM
Spiritus Vini Rectificatus [*Rectified Spirit of Wine*] [*Pharmacy*] ..... SVR
Spiritus Vini Tenuis [*Proof Spirit of Wine*] [*Pharmacy*] ..... SVT
Spiritus Vinosus [*Ardent Spirit*] [*Pharmacy*] (ROG) ..... SV
Spiro Agnew Fans and Rooters, Inc. ..... SAFARI
Spiroglycol [*Organic chemistry*] ..... SPG
Spirohydantoin Aziridine [*Biochemistry*] ..... SHAZ
Spirometry ..... SP
Spiroplasmavirus citri [*Bacteriology*] ..... SC
Spiroplasmavirus citri [*Bacteriology*] ..... SVC
Spissus [*Dried*] [*Pharmacy*] ..... SPISS
Spitze [*Point*] [*Music*] ..... SP
Spjald [*Denmark ICAO location identifier*] (ICLI) ..... EKSD
Splanchnic Artery Occlusion [*Medicine*] ..... SAO
Splanchnic Blood Flow [*Physiology*] ..... SBF
Splash Block ..... SB
Splash Detection RADAR [*Military*] ..... SDR
Splash Detection RADAR System (MCD) ..... SDRS
Splash Detection System ..... SDS
Splash Plate ..... SP
Splash Shield [*Automotive engineering*] ..... SP/SHLD
Splash Technology Holdings, Inc. [*Associated Press*] (SAG) ..... SplashT
Splash Technology Holdings, Inc. [*NASDAQ symbol*] (SAG) ..... SPLH
Splash Zone ..... SZ
Splashproof (MSA) ..... SP
Splat Cooled (OA) ..... SC
Spleen Antigen [*Complement Fixation*] **Test** [*Immunology*] ..... SPAT
Spleen Concanavalin A Medium [*Immunoassay*] ..... SCM
Spleen Focus Formation Virus ..... SFFV
Spleen Necrosis Virus ..... SNV
Spleen Repopulating Activity [*Medicine*] (DMAA) ..... SRA
Splenic Collateral [*Gastroenterology*] (DAVI) ..... SC
Splenic Localization Index [*Medicine*] (MAE) ..... SLI
Splenic Mononuclear Cell [*Cytology*] ..... SMNC
Splenium of the Corpus Callosum [*Anatomy*] ..... SCC
Splenorenal Shunt [*Medicine*] ..... SRS
Splice [*Telecommunications*] (TEL) ..... SPL
Splice ..... SPLC
Splice Acceptor [*Genetics*] ..... SA
Splice Donor [*Genetics*] ..... SD
Splice Junction Mutation [*Genetics*] ..... SPL
Splice Plug Assembly ..... SPA
Splicing Factor [*Genetics*] ..... SF
Splicing of Cross Correlation Function (IAA) ..... SPOC
Spline [*Engineering*] ..... SPLN
Splinting [*Dentistry*] ..... SP
Split [*Former Yugoslavia*] [*ICAO location identifier*] (ICLI) ..... LYSP
Split [*In stock listings of newspapers*] ..... S
Split (MSA) ..... SPT
Split [*Former Yugoslavia*] [*Airport symbol*] (OAG) ..... SPU
Split Anterior Tibial Tendon [*Medicine*] (DMAA) ..... SPLATT
Split Anterior Tibial Transfer [*Orthopedics*] (DAVI) ..... SPLATT
Split Anterior Tibial Transfer, Tendo Achillis Lengthening, and Toe Flexor Release [*Orthopedics*] (DAVI) ..... SPLATT TALTFR
Split Armature Receiver Capsule (PDAA) ..... SARC
Split Cycle and Offset Optimization Technique [*FHWA*] (TAG) ..... SCOOT
Split End [*Football*] ..... SE
Split End Vector [*System for plant cell transformation*] ..... SEV
Split Field Motor (IAA) ..... SFM
Split Function Study (MAE) ..... SFS
Split Group Aperture ..... SGA
Split Hand/Foot Deformity [*Medicine*] (DMAA) ..... SHFD
Split Investment Company [*Generic term*] ..... SIC
Split Level [*Home*] [*Classified advertising*] ..... SL
Split Phase [*Electronics*] (IAA) ..... SPPH
Split Phase Motor ..... SPM
Split Product of Fibrin (MAE) ..... SPF
Split Renal Function [*Medicine*] (MAE) ..... SRF
Split Renal Function Study [*Medicine*] (MAE) ..... SRFS
Split Ring [*Technical drawings*] ..... SR
Split Rock Elementary School, Syosset, NY [*Library symbol Library of Congress*] (LCLS) ..... NSyoSRE
Split Second Timing ..... SST
Split Stage Demonstrator (MCD) ..... SSD
Split Thickness [*Skin Graft*] [*Plastic surgery*] (DAVI) ..... ST
Split Thickness Autogenous Graft [*Plastic surgery*] (DAVI) ..... STAG
Split Thickness Graft [*Medicine*] ..... STG
Split Thickness Skin Graft ..... STSG
Split Wing Ramjet ..... SWRJ
Split-Channel Reservation Multiple Access (PDAA) ..... SRMA
Split-Level Charge-Recovery Logic [*Computer science*] ..... SCRL
Split-Level Ranch [*House*] ..... SPLANCH
Split-Product Vaccine [*Immunology*] ..... SPV
Split-Screen Display ..... SSD
Splitter ..... SPLTR
Splitter/Combiner (NASA) ..... S/C
Splitter Damper (OA) ..... SD
Split-Thickness Skin Excision [*Medicine*] (DMAA) ..... STSE
Splitting [*Electronics*] ..... SP

Splitting Amplifier (AFM)	SA
Spofa Ltd. [Czechoslovakia] [Research code symbol]	IZ
Spofa Ltd. [Czechoslovakia] [Research code symbol]	MF
Spofford, TX [Location identifier FAA] (FAAL)	PFO
Spogli Elettronici dell'Italiano delle Origini e del Duecento [A lexical, morphological, and syntactical inventory of Old Italian texts]	SEIOD
Spoiled Kids of the Eighties [Offspring of the Yuppies] [Lifestyle classification]	Skoteys
Spoiler Assisted Ground Effect (MCD)	SAGE
Spoiler Control/Elevator Feel Computer (MCD)	SC/EFC
Spoiler Control Elevator Feel System (MCD)	SCEFS
Spoilers in Nozzle	S
Spokane [Washington] [Airport symbol] (OAG)	GEG
Spokane [Diocesan abbreviation] [Washington] (TOCD)	SPK
Spokane [Washington] [Seismograph station code, US Geological Survey Closed] (SEIS)	SPO
Spokane Community College, Spokane, WA [Library symbol Library of Congress] (LCLS)	WaSpS
Spokane Community College, Spokane, WA [Library symbol] [Library of Congress] (LCLS)	WaSpSC
Spokane County Law Library, Spokane, WA [Library symbol Library of Congress] (LCLS)	WaSpSL
Spokane County Library, Spokane, WA [Library symbol Library of Congress] (LCLS)	WaSpCo
Spokane County Library, Spokane, WA [Inactive] [OCLC symbol] (OCLC)	WSN
Spokane County Medical Library, Spokane, WA [Library symbol Library of Congress] (LCLS)	WaSpM
Spokane/Fairchild Air Force Base [Washington] [ICAO location identifier] (ICLI)	KSKA
Spokane Falls Community College, Spokane, WA [Library symbol Library of Congress] (LCLS)	WaSpSF
Spokane/Felts [Washington] [ICAO location identifier] (ICLI)	KSFF
Spokane/International [Washington] [ICAO location identifier] (ICLI)	KGEG
Spokane International Railroad Co. [AAR code]	SI
Spokane, Portland & Seattle Railway System [AAR code]	SPS
Spokane Public Library, Spokane, WA [Library symbol Library of Congress] (LCLS)	WaSp
Spokane Public Schools, Curriculum Library, Spokane, WA [Library symbol Library of Congress] (LCLS)	WaSpPS
Spokane Stock Exchange [Washington]	SSE
Spokane, WA [Location identifier FAA] (FAAL)	AVT
Spokane, WA [Location identifier FAA] (FAAL)	FRC
Spokane, WA [FM radio station call letters] (RBYB)	KAEP
Spokane, WA [FM radio station call letters]	KAGU
Spokane, WA [AM radio station call letters]	KAQQ
Spokane, WA [Television station call letters]	KAYU
Spokane, WA [FM radio station call letters]	KDRK
Spokane, WA [FM radio station call letters]	KEEH
Spokane, WA [FM radio station call letters] (RBYB)	KEZE-FM
Spokane, WA [AM radio station call letters]	KGA
Spokane, WA [Television station call letters]	KHQ
Spokane, WA [FM radio station call letters]	KISC
Spokane, WA [AM radio station call letters]	KJRB
Spokane, WA [FM radio station call letters]	KKZX
Spokane, WA [AM radio station call letters]	KMBI
Spokane, WA [FM radio station call letters]	KMBI-FM
Spokane, WA [FM radio station call letters]	KNJY
Spokane, WA [FM radio station call letters]	KPBX
Spokane, WA [Television station call letters]	KREM
Spokane, WA [AM radio station call letters]	KSBN
Spokane, WA [FM radio station call letters]	KSFC
Spokane, WA [Television station call letters]	KSKN
Spokane, WA [FM radio station call letters]	KSPO
Spokane, WA [Television station call letters]	KSPS
Spokane, WA [AM radio station call letters]	KTRW
Spokane, WA [AM radio station call letters]	KUDY
Spokane, WA [FM radio station call letters]	KWRS
Spokane, WA [AM radio station call letters]	KXLY
Spokane, WA [FM radio station call letters]	KXLY-FM
Spokane, WA [Television station call letters]	KXLY-TV
Spokane, WA [FM radio station call letters]	KZZU
Spokane, WA [Location identifier FAA] (FAAL)	MZS
Spokane, WA [Location identifier FAA] (FAAL)	OLJ
Spokane, WA [Location identifier FAA] (FAAL)	SFF
Spokane, WA [Location identifier FAA] (FAAL)	SKA
Spoken English for Industry and Commerce (AIE)	SEFIC
Spoken Language Services, Inc.	SLS
Spoken Voice (MEDA)	SV
Spoken Voice (DAVI)	SV
Spondylitic Caudal Myelopathy [Medicine] (DMAA)	SCM
Spondylitic Caudal Radiculopathy [Medicine] (DMAA)	SCR
Spondyloarthropathy [Medicine] (MEDA)	SPA
Spondyloepimetaphyseal Dysplasia [Medicine] (DMAA)	SEMD
Spondylo-Epimetaphyseal Dysplasia with Joint Laxity [Medicine] (DMAA)	SEMDJL
Spondyloepiphyseal Dysplasia, Late [Medicine] (DMAA)	SEDL
Spondyloepiphyseal Dysplasia Tarda [Medicine] (DMAA)	SEDT
Spondyloepiphysial Dysplasia [Medicine]	SED
Spondylometaphyseal Dysplasias [Medicine]	SMD
Sponge (WGA)	SP
Sponge [Quality of the bottom] [Nautical charts]	Spg
Sponge	SPNG
Sponge and Chamois Institute (EA)	SCI
Spongiform Encephalopathy Advisory Committee [British]	SEAC
Sponsor (NITA)	SP

Sponsor	SPON
Sponsor (AFM)	SPON
Sponsor	SPR
Sponsor Code (NITA)	SC
Sponsor Identification [Television]	SI
Sponsor Identification Index [Advertising] (NTCM)	SII
Sponsor Program Number [Military]	SPN
Sponsor Program Proposal (MCD)	SPP
Sponsored	S
Sponsored [or Sponsoring] Agency (MCD)	SA
Sponsoring	SPONG
Sponsoring Agency [Online database field identifier]	SN
Sponsoring Organization (NITA)	SPO
Sponsoring Organization Zip Code (NITA)	SZ
Sponsoring Program (NITA)	SP
Sponsors of Open Housing Investment [Later, Fund for an Open Society] (EA)	SOHI
Sponsor's Profit and Risk Allowance [Department of Housing and Urban Development] (GFGA)	SPRA
Sponsor's Program Review [Navy] (DOMA)	SPR
Sponsors' Standards Advisory Committee [American National Standards Institute]	SSAC
Spontaneous	S
Spontaneous	Sp
Spontaneous (WGA)	SPON
Spontaneous	SPONT
Spontaneous Abortion (DAVI)	SAB
Spontaneous Abortion [Medicine] (DMAA)	SAb
Spontaneous Abortion [Medicine] (MAE)	Spont Ab
Spontaneous Acute Bacterial Peritonitis [Medicine]	SABP
Spontaneous Assisted Vaginal Delivery [Medicine] (DMAA)	SAVD
Spontaneous Bacterial Peritonitis [Medicine]	SBP
Spontaneous Blastogenesis [Medicine] (DMAA)	SB
Spontaneous Cell-Mediated Cytotoxicity [Medicine] (DMAA)	SCMC
Spontaneous Cycle Length	SCL
Spontaneous Delivery [Obstetrics]	SD
Spontaneous Discharge Rate [Audiology]	SR
Spontaneous Divergent Academic [Test] [Education]	SDA
Spontaneous Electrical Activity [Physiology] (AAMN)	SEA
Spontaneous Excitatory Postsynaptic Current [Neurophysiology]	SEPSC
Spontaneous Fission [Radioactivity]	SF
Spontaneous Hemorrhagic Necrosis [Medicine]	SHN
Spontaneous Hole Filling [Spectrometry]	SPHF
Spontaneous Human Combustion	SHC
Spontaneous Ignition Temperature	SIT
Spontaneous Inhibitory Postsynaptic Current [Neurophysiology]	sIPSC
Spontaneous Interictal Spike [Medicine] (DMAA)	SIS
Spontaneous Killer [Cells] [Immunology] (DAVI)	SK
Spontaneous Lesion [Medicine] (MAE)	SPL
Spontaneous Lymphocyte Transportation (PDAA)	SLT
Spontaneous Motor Activity [Neurophysiology]	SMA
Spontaneous Osteonecrosis of the Knee [Orthopedics] (DAVI)	SONK
Spontaneous Paroxysmal Atrial Fibrillation [Medicine] (DMAA)	SPAF
Spontaneous Peripheral Operations Online Spooling [Computer science] (IAA)	SPOOL
Spontaneous Potential [Log]	SP
Spontaneous Premature Rupture of Membrane [Medicine] (DMAA)	SPROM
Spontaneous Reporting System [Food and Drug Administration]	SRS
Spontaneous Rupture of Bag of Water [Obstetrics] (DAVI)	SRBOW
Spontaneous Rupture of Bag of Waters [Medicine] (MEDA)	SRBOW
Spontaneous Rupture of Membrane [Medicine] (DMAA)	SROM
Spontaneous Rupture of Membranes [Obstetrics] (DAVI)	SPROM
Spontaneous Rupture of Membranes, Not In Labor [Obstetrics] (DAVI)	SPROM NIL
Spontaneous Suppressor Cell Activity [Medicine] (DMAA)	SSCA
Spontaneous Swallows [Gastroenterology]	SW
Spontaneous Symmetry Breaking [Physics]	SSB
Spontaneous Synaptic Current [Neuroscience]	SSC
Spontaneous Transient Outward Current [Physiology]	STOC
Spontaneous Vaginal Delivery [Gynecology]	SVD
Spontaneous Ventilation [Medicine] (MEDA)	SV
Spontaneous Vetex Delivery [Obstetrics] (DAVI)	SVD
Spontaneously Emitted Light	SEL
Spontaneously Hypertensive	SH
Spontaneously Hypertensive Rats	SHR
Spontaneously Hypertensive Stroke-Prone Rat [Medicine] (DMAA)	SHSP
Spontaneously Responding Hyperthyroidism [Endocrinology]	SRH
Spool	S
Spool	SL
Spool (MSA)	SP
Spool Multileaving [Computer science] (IBMDP)	SML
Spool Piece Head [Nuclear energy] (NRCH)	SP/Hd
Spool Selector Valve	SSV
Spooling (MSA)	SPG
Spoon (WGA)	SP
Spoon and Fork	SPORK
Spoon River College, Canton, IL [Library symbol Library of Congress] (LCLS)	ICanS
Spoon River College, Canton, IL [OCLC symbol] (OCLC)	IDS
Spooner Mines & Oils Ltd. [Toronto Stock Exchange symbol]	SPO
Spooner's Reports [12-15 Wisconsin] [A publication] (DLA)	Spoon
Spooner's Reports [12-15 Wisconsin] [A publication] (DLA)	Spooner
Spoons (ROG)	SPNS
Sporadic Bovine Encephalomyelitis [Veterinary medicine]	SBE
Sporadic Burkitt's Lymphoma [Medicine]	SBL

Sporadic Cerebral Amyloid Angiopathy [*Medicine*] (DMAA) .... SCAA
Sporadic Depression [*Medicine*] (DMAA) .... SD
Sporadic Depressive Disease [*Medicine*] (DMAA) .... SDD
Sporadic Olivopontocerebellar Ataxia [*Medicine*] (DMAA) .... SOPCA
Sporadic Testicular Agenesis Syndrome [*Medicine*] (DMAA) .... STAS
Sporadic Ulcerating and Mutilating Acropathy [*Medicine*] (DMAA) .... SUMA
Spore Newsletter [*A publication*] .... SNL
Spore Plasma [*Botany*] .... SP
Spore Surface [*Immunology*] .... SS
Spore Tip Mucilage [*Mycology*] .... STM
Spore Wall [*Botany*] .... SW
Spores Injected into Wounded Kernels [*Plant pathology*] .... SW
Sporotrichosis [*A fungal infection*] (DAVI) .... SPORO
Sporozoite Surface Protein [*Biochemistry*] .... SSP
Sport [*In automobile model name "Honda Civic S"*] .... S
Sport .... SP
Sport .... SPRT
Sport and Recreation Association of RMIT [*Royal Melbourne Institute of Techn ology*] Union .... SARMIT
Sport Balloon Society of the United States of America (EA) .... SBSUSA
Sport Chalet [*NASDAQ symbol*] (TTSB) .... SPCH
Sport Chalet, Inc. [*NASDAQ symbol*] (SAG) .... SPCH
Sport Chalet, Inc. [*Associated Press*] (SAG) .... SptChalt
Sport Fishery Research Foundation [*Later, SFRP*] (EA) .... SFRF
Sport Fishery Research Program (EA) .... SFRP
Sport Fishing Institute (EA) .... SFI
Sport for All Clearinghouse [*Belgium*] (EAIO) .... SAC
Sport Haley, Inc. [*NASDAQ symbol*] (SAG) .... SPOR
Sport Haley, Inc. [*Associated Press*] (SAG) .... SprtHaley
Sport Information Resource Centre [*Coaching Association of Canada*] [*Database*] (IID) .... SIRC
Sport Information Resource Centre [*Centre de Documentation de Reference pour le Sport*] Ottawa, Ontario [*Library symbol National Library of Canada*] (NLC) .... OOFS
Sport Leicht [*Sports Lightweight (Car)*] [*German*] .... SL
Sport Leicht Coupe [*Sports Lightweight Coupe*] [*German*] .... SLC
Sport Leicht Renn [*Sports Lightweight Racing (Car)*] [*German*] .... SLR
Sport Luxury Edition [*Automobile classification*] .... SLE
Sport Management Art and Science Society [*Defunct*] (EA) .... SMARTS
Sport Medicine Council of Canada .... SMCC
Sport of Kings Society (EA) .... SOKS
Sport Supply Group [*AMEX symbol*] (SAG) .... GYM
Sport Supply Group [*NYSE symbol*] (SPSG) .... GYM
Sport Supply Group [*Associated Press*] (SAG) .... SportSup
Sport Supply Group [*Associated Press*] (SAG) .... SptSup
Sport Supply Grp Wrrt [*AMEX symbol*] (TTSB) .... GYM.WS
Sport, Travel, Art, and Recreation .... STAR
Sport und Sportwissenschaftliche Informationssystem [*Sport and Sports-Scientific Information System*] [*West Germany*] (IID) .... SUSIS
Sportavia Puetzer GmbH & Co. KG [*Germany ICAO aircraft manufacturer identifier*] (ICAO) .... SP
Sportbike Enthusiast Club of America (EA) .... SECA
Sport-Haley [*NASDAQ symbol*] (TTSB) .... SPOR
Sporting .... SPORT
Sporting (ROG) .... SPORT
Sporting (WDAA) .... SPTG
Sporting Arms and Ammunition Manufacturers Institute (EA) .... SAAMI
Sporting Goods Agents Association (EA) .... SGAA
Sporting Goods Jobbers Association [*Later, NASGW*] .... SGJA
Sporting Goods Manufacturers Agents Association [*Later, SGRA*] .... SGMAA
Sporting Goods Manufacturers Association [*North Palm Beach, FL*] (EA) .... SGMA
Sporting Goods Manufacturers' Credit Interchange [*Defunct*] (EA) .... SGMCI
Sporting Goods Representatives Association [*of SIRA*] [*Later, SGAA*] (EA) .... SGRA
Sporting Owner Drivers' Club Ltd. [*British*] (BI) .... SODC
Sporting Traditions [*A publication*] .... Spor Tr
Sportliteratur [*Bundesinstitut fuer Sportwissenschaft*] [*Germany Information service or system*] (CRD) .... SPOLIT
Sport-Luxury Vehicle .... SLV
Sportmart, Inc. [*NASDAQ symbol*] (SAG) .... SPMT
Sportmart, Inc. [*Associated Press*] (SAG) .... Sprtmrt
Sportmart Inc.'A' [*NASDAQ symbol*] (TTSB) .... SPMTA
Sports Air Travel, Inc. [*ICAO designator*] (FAAC) .... WCC
Sports Ambassadors (EA) .... SA
Sports & Recreation, Inc. [*Associated Press*] (SAG) .... SportRec
Sports & Recreation, Inc. [*NYSE symbol*] (SAG) .... WON
Sports Authority [*NYSE symbol*] (TTSB) .... TSA
[*The*] Sports Authority, Inc. [*Associated Press*] (SAG) .... SptAuth
[*The*] Sports Authority, Inc. [*NYSE symbol*] (SAG) .... TSA
Sports Bribery [*FBI standardized term*] .... SB
Sports Car Club of America (EA) .... SCCA
Sports Car Collectors Society of America [*Defunct*] (EA) .... SCCSA
Sports Car Collectors Society of America [*Later, SCCSA*] (EA) .... SCSA
Sports Club [*AMEX symbol*] (SAG) .... SCY
Sports Club Co., Inc. [*AMEX symbol*] (SAG) .... SCY
Sports Club Company, Inc. [*Associated Press*] (SAG) .... SportsClb
Sports Council [*British*] (EAIO) .... SC
Sports Development Program [*Australia*] .... SDP
Sports Emotion Test [*Research test*] [*Psychology*] .... SET
Sports Exchange Network [*Cable TV programming service*] .... SEN
Sports Fans Connection [*A publication*] .... SFC
Sports Federation of Canada (EAIO) .... SFC
Sports Federation of Victoria [*Australia*] .... SFV
Sports Fishing Initiative [*Marine science*] (OSRA) .... SFI

Sports Fishing Initiative (USDC) .... SFI
Sports for the People [*Defunct*] (EA) .... SP
Sports Foundation (EA) .... SF
Sports Hall of Shame [*Defunct*] (EA) .... SHS
Sports Industries Commission [*New South Wales, Australia*] .... SIC
Sports Industries Representatives Association (EA) .... SIRA
Sports Information Director .... SID
Sports Injury Nurses Association [*Australia*] .... SINA
Sports Lawyers Association (EA) .... SLA
Sports Media [*NASDAQ symbol*] (TTSB) .... SPTS
Sports Media, Inc. [*Associated Press*] (SAG) .... SportM
Sports Media, Inc. [*Associated Press*] (SAG) .... SptM
Sports Media, Inc. [*NASDAQ symbol*] (SAG) .... SPTS
Sports Media Wrrt'B' [*NASDAQ symbol*] (TTSB) .... SPTSZ
Sports Media Wrrt'C' [*NASDAQ symbol*] (TTSB) .... SPTSL
[*The*] Sports Network [*Cable-television system*] [*Information service or system*] (IID) .... TSN
Sports Network, Inc. [*Later, HSN*] .... SNI
Sports Philatelists International (EA) .... SPI
Sports Program (NTCM) .... S
Sports Racer [*Automotive classification*] .... SR
Sports Science and Sports Medicine Centre [*Australia*] .... SSSMC
Sports Sciences [*NASDAQ symbol*] (TTSB) .... SSCI
Sports Sciences, Inc. [*Associated Press*] (SAG) .... SprtS
Sports Sciences, Inc. [*Associated Press*] (SAG) .... SprtSci
Sports Sciences, Inc. [*NASDAQ symbol*] (SAG) .... SSCI
Sports Sciences Wrrt [*NASDAQ symbol*] (TTSB) .... SSCIW
Sports Technique and Reaction Trainer [*Computerized training program for baseball and tennis*] .... START
Sports Trainers Digest [*A publication*] .... STD
Sports Turf Managers Association [*Defunct*] (EA) .... STMA
Sports Turf Research Institute [*British*] (IRUK) .... STRI
Sports Writers' Association [*British*] (BI) .... SWA
Sportscar Vintage Racing Association (EA) .... SVRA
Sportscar World Championship [*Auto racing*] .... SWC
Sportsman Pilots Association .... SPA
Sportsplex Owners and Directors of America .... SODA
Sportswear .... SPORTSWR
Sportswear Salesmen's Association (EA) .... SSA
Sport-Utility Vehicle [*Type of truck*] .... SUV
Sportwissenschaftliche Forschungsprojekte [*Bundesinstitut fuer Sportwissenschaft*] [*Germany Information service or system*] (CRD) .... SPOFOR
Sporulation Capacity [*of fungi*] .... SC
Sporulation per Lesion [*Plant pathology*] .... SPL
Spot Accumulation and Melting of Snow (PDAA) .... SAMOS
Spot Authorization Plan [*WPB*] [*Obsolete*] .... SAP
Spot Check (AAG) .... SC
Spot Face .... SF
Spot Face Other Side [*Technical drawings*] (MSA) .... SFO
Spot Inspection [*Military*] (AFM) .... SI
Spot Intelligence Report [*Air Force*] .... SPIREP
Spot Inventory .... SI
Spot Noise Figure .... SNF
Spot Price [*Investment term*] .... SP
Spot Product Prices [*Database*] [*Petroleum Intelligence Weekly*] [*Information service or system*] (CRD) .... SPP
Spot Radio Report (WDMC) .... SRR
Spot Report [*Military*] (NVT) .... SPOTREP
Spot Wind [*Meteorology*] (DA) .... SPOT
Spotlight (MSA) .... SLT
Spotlight [*Record label*] [*Australia*] .... Spot
Spotlight Magazine, Asbury Park, NJ [*Library symbol Library of Congress*] (LCLS) .... NjAsS
Spotsylvania, VA [*FM radio station call letters*] .... WYSK
Spotted Swine Record [*Later, National Spotted Swine Record*] (EA) .... SSR
Spotter Reconnaissance [*Air Force British*] .... S/R
Spottiswoode's English Equity Reports [*A publication*] (DLA) .... Spott Eq Rep
Spottiswoode's Equity [*Scotland*] [*A publication*] (DLA) .... Spott
Spottiswoode's Equity [*Scotland*] [*A publication*] (DLA) .... Spottis Eq
Spottiswoode's Equity [*Scotland*] [*A publication*] (DLA) .... Spottisw
Spottiswoode's Equity [*Scotland*] [*A publication*] (DLA) .... Spottisw Eq
Spottiswoode's Practices [*Scotland*] [*A publication*] (DLA) .... Spottis Pr
Spottiswoode's Styles [*Scotland*] [*A publication*] (DLA) .... Spottis St
Spotweld [*Technical drawings*] .... SW
Spotweld Accessory [*Tool*] (AAG) .... SWAC
Spotweld Fixture [*Tool*] .... SWFX
Spotweld Machine [*Tool*] .... SWM
Spotweld Pattern [*Tool*] (AAG) .... SWPA
Spotweld Template (MCD) .... SWT
Spousal Remainder Trust [*Banking*] .... SRT
Spouse .... SP
Spouse [*Citizens band radio slang*] .... XY
Spouse Observation Checklist .... SOC
Spouse's Allowance [*Canada*] .... SA
Spouses of Gays Association [*Defunct*] (EA) .... SGA
Spouses of Gays Association (EA) .... SOGA
Sprague Electric Co. [*ICAO designator*] (FAAC) .... SPE
Sprague on International Law [*A publication*] (DLA) .... Spr Int L
Sprague Voltage-Sensitive Switch .... SVSS
Sprague-Dawley [*Rat variety*] .... SP
Sprague-Dawley-Ivanovas Rat [*Medicine*] (DMAA) .... SIV
Sprague's United States District Court (Admiralty) Decisions [*A publication*] (DLA) .... Spr
Sprague's United States District Court (Admiralty) Decisions [*A publication*] (DLA) .... Sprague

Spratley Island [*MARC geographic area code Library of Congress*] (LCCP) ... aoxp--
Spratly Islands [*ANSI two-letter standard code*] (CNC) ... SI
Spratly Islands [*ANSI three-letter standard code*] (CNC) ... SPR
Spratly Islands [*MARC country of publication code Library of Congress*] (LCCP) ... xp
Spray [*ICAO*] (FAAC) ... PY
Spray (VRA) ... spy
Spray Aeration Vacuum Extraction System [*Navy*] ... SAVE
Spray Arrester Gear (MCD) ... SPRAG
Spray Calciner [*Nuclear energy*] (NUCP) ... SC
Spray Equipment Manufacturers' Association [*British*] (BI) ... SEMA
Spray Pressure [*Agriculture*] ... SP
Spray Public Library, Spray, NC [*Library symbol*] [*Library of Congress*] (LCLS) ... NcSpr
Spray System Compressed Air [*Nuclear energy*] (NRCH) ... SSCA
Spray Volume - Spray Pressure ... SV-SP
Sprayed (WGA) ... SPD
Sprayed Acoustical Ceiling [*Technical drawings*] ... SAC
Sprayed Concrete Association [*British*] (EAIO) ... SCA
Sprayed Mineral Fiber Manufacturers Association (EA) ... SMFMA
Sprayer (MSA) ... SPYR
Spray-On Foam Insulation (NASA) ... SOFI
Spraytight ... SPT
Spread Correlation ... SC
Spread Spectrum (CET) ... SS
Spread Spectrum Modulation (NATG) ... SSM
Spread Spectrum Modulation Equipment [*NATO*] (MCD) ... SSME
Spread Spectrum Random Access System [*Telecommunications*] (TEL) ... SSRA
Spread Spectrum/Time Division Multiple Access (MCD) ... SS/TDMA
Spreader (MSA) ... SPRDR
Spreading [*Freight*] ... SPRDNG
Spreading Activation Processor for Information Encoded in Network Structure [*Department of Education*] ... SAPIENS
Spreading Coefficient ... SC
Spreading Cortical Depression ... SCD
Spreading Depression [*Medicine*] (DMAA) ... SD
Spreading Ocean Floor ... SOF
Spreadsheet Anthropometric Scaling System [*Army*] (RDA) ... SASS
Spread-Spectrum Multiple Access [*Satellite communications*] ... SSMA
Spread-Spectrum Multiplexing [*Telecommunications*] (IAA) ... SSMUX
Spreckels Industries [*NASDAQ symbol*] (TTSB) ... YALE
Spreckels Industries, Inc. [*NASDAQ symbol*] (SAG) ... SPKL
Spreckels Industries, Inc. [*Associated Press*] (SAG) ... Spreckel
Spreen-Benton Sentence Repetition Test [*Speech and language therapy*] (DAVI) ... SBSRT
Spring ... SPG
Spring (AAG) ... SPG
Spring [*Commonly used*] (OPSA) ... SPNG
Spring (MSA) ... SPR
Spring ... SPRG
Spring [*Commonly used*] (OPSA) ... SPRING
Spring [*Commonly used*] (OPSA) ... SPRNG
Spring Apply, Hydraulic Release [*Truck brakes*] ... SAHR
Spring Arbor College, Spring Arbor, MI [*OCLC symbol*] (OCLC) ... EES
Spring Arbor College, Spring Arbor, MI [*Library symbol Library of Congress*] (LCLS) ... MiSaS
Spring Arbor, MI [*AM radio station call letters*] ... KTGG
Spring Arbor, MI [*FM radio station call letters*] ... WSAE
Spring Back (ADA) ... SB
Spring City, TN [*FM radio station call letters*] ... WAYA
Spring City, TN [*AM radio station call letters*] ... WXQK
Spring Conditions [*Skiing*] ... SC
Spring Creek Elementary School, Rockford, IL [*Library symbol*] [*Library of Congress*] (LCLS) ... IRoScE
Spring Evaluation Analysis and Design (MCD) ... SPREAD
Spring Garden College, Philadelphia, PA [*OCLC symbol*] (OCLC) ... PAG
Spring Garden College, Philadelphia, PA [*Library symbol Library of Congress*] (LCLS) ... PPSG
Spring Garden Institute ... SGI
Spring Grove, MN [*FM radio station call letters*] ... KQYB
Spring Grove State Hospital, Catonsville, MD [*Library symbol Library of Congress*] (LCLS) ... MdCatSG
Spring Hill [*Alabama*] [*Seismograph station code, US Geological Survey*] (SEIS) ... SHA
Spring Hill College [*Mobile, AL*] ... SHC
Spring Hill College, Mobile, AL [*Library symbol Library of Congress*] (LCLS) ... AMobS
Spring Hill College, Mobile, AL [*OCLC symbol*] (OCLC) ... ASH
Spring Hill College, Spring Hill, AL [*Library symbol Library of Congress*] (LCLS) ... AShC
Spring Hope Public Library, Spring Hope, NC [*Library symbol Library of Congress*] (LCLS) ... NcSph
Spring Industries, Inc. [*Associated Press*] (SAG) ... Springs
Spring Inflow-River Inflow [*Geology*] ... S-R
Spring Joint Computer Conference [*American Federation of Information Processing Societies*] ... SJCC
Spring Knife Trade Federation [*A union*] [*British*] ... SKTF
Spring Lake, NC [*AM radio station call letters*] ... WCIE
Spring Lake Public Library, Spring Lake, NJ [*Library symbol Library of Congress*] (LCLS) ... NjSpl
Spring Manufacturers Institute (EA) ... SMI
Spring Opening ... SO
Spring Point [*Bahamas*] [*Airport symbol*] (OAG) ... AXP
Spring Point [*Bahamas*] [*ICAO location identifier*] (ICLI) ... MYAP
Spring Research and Manufacturers' Association (EAIO) ... SRAMA
Spring Research Institute (EA) ... SRI
Spring, Summer, Autumn, Winter, and Snow [*Pronounced "zausu"*] [*Another name for Skidome, an indoor ski center*] (ECON) ... SSAWS
Spring Tide ... Sp
Spring Tide (WDAA) ... ST
Spring Trap Makers' Society [*A union*] [*British*] ... STMS
Spring Trapmakers' Society [*British*] (DCTA) ... STS
Spring Valley Consolidated Community School District 99, Spring Valley, IL [*Library symbol Library of Congress*] (LCLS) ... ISprvSD
Spring Valley, IL [*FM radio station call letters*] ... WAIV
Spring Valley, MN [*FM radio station call letters*] ... KNFX-FM
Spring Valley, MN [*FM radio station call letters*] (RBYB) ... KVGO-FM
Spring Valley, NY [*AM radio station call letters*] ... WLIR
Spring Valley Public Library, Spring Valley, IL [*Library symbol Library of Congress*] (LCLS) ... ISprv
Spring Viremia of Carp ... SVC
Spring Yearling ... SY
Springbank Aviation Ltd. [*Canada ICAO designator*] (FAAC) ... SAQ
Springboard (NVT) ... SPBD
Springboard Resources Ltd. [*Vancouver Stock Exchange symbol*] ... SPB
Springbok [*South Africa*] [*ICAO location identifier*] (ICLI) ... FASB
Springbok [*South Africa*] [*Airport symbol*] (OAG) ... SBU
Spring-Burned [*Ecology*] ... S
Springdale [*Arkansas*] [*Airport symbol*] (OAG) ... SPZ
Springdale Air Services, Inc. [*ICAO designator*] (FAAC) ... SPG
Springdale, AR [*FM radio station call letters*] ... KBRS
Springdale, AR [*Television station call letters*] ... KSBN
Springdale, AR [*AM radio station call letters*] ... KZRA
Springdale Public Library, Newfoundland [*Library symbol National Library of Canada*] (NLC) ... NFSP
Springdale Public Library, Springdale, NF, Canada [*Library symbol Library of Congress*] (LCLS) ... CaNfSp
Springender Bogen [*Bouncing Bow*] [*Music*] ... SPR BOG
Springer Public Library, Springer, NM [*Library symbol Library of Congress*] (LCLS) ... NmSp
Springer Public Library, Springer, NM [*Library symbol*] [*Library of Congress*] (LCLS) ... NmSpP
Springer Resources [*Vancouver Stock Exchange symbol*] ... SPR
Springerville, AZ [*Location identifier FAA*] (FAAL) ... CYH
Springerville Public Library, Springerville, AZ [*Library symbol Library of Congress*] (LCLS) ... AzSp
Springerville-Eager, AZ [*FM radio station call letters*] ... KQAZ
Springerville-Eager, AZ [*AM radio station call letters*] ... KRVZ
Springfield [*Diocesan abbreviation*] [*Illinois*] (TOCD) ... SFD
Springfield [*Missouri*] [*Airport symbol*] (OAG) ... SGF
Springfield [*Ohio*] [*Airport symbol*] (AD) ... SGH
Springfield [*Illinois*] [*Airport symbol*] (OAG) ... SPI
Springfield [*Diocesan abbreviation*] [*Massachusetts*] (TOCD) ... SPR
Springfield [*Vermont*] [*Airport symbol*] (OAG) ... VSF
Springfield Armory [*Army*] ... SA
Springfield City Library, Springfield, MA [*Library symbol Library of Congress*] (LCLS) ... MS
Springfield College (GAGS) ... Springfield C
Springfield College, Springfield, MA [*Library symbol Library of Congress*] (LCLS) ... MSC
Springfield, FL [*FM radio station call letters*] ... WRBA
Springfield, FL [*FM radio station call letters*] ... WYOO
Springfield Free Public Library, Springfield, NJ [*Library symbol Library of Congress*] (LCLS) ... NjSp
Springfield, GA [*FM radio station call letters*] (RBYB) ... WSGF
Springfield Hospital, Medical Center Library, Springfield, MA [*Library symbol Library of Congress*] (LCLS) ... MSSH
Springfield, IL [*Location identifier FAA*] (FAAL) ... CAP
Springfield, IL [*Location identifier FAA*] (FAAL) ... LQY
Springfield, IL [*Television station call letters*] ... WCFN
Springfield, IL [*FM radio station call letters*] ... WDBR
Springfield, IL [*AM radio station call letters*] ... WFMB
Springfield, IL [*FM radio station call letters*] ... WFMB-FM
Springfield, IL [*Television station call letters*] ... WICS
Springfield, IL [*FM radio station call letters*] (RBYB) ... WLGM
Springfield, IL [*AM radio station call letters*] ... WMAY
Springfield, IL [*FM radio station call letters*] ... WNNS
Springfield, IL [*FM radio station call letters*] ... WQNA
Springfield, IL [*FM radio station call letters*] ... WQQL
Springfield, IL [*Television station call letters*] ... WRSP
Springfield, IL [*FM radio station call letters*] ... WSCT
Springfield, IL [*AM radio station call letters*] ... WTAX
Springfield, IL [*FM radio station call letters*] (RBYB) ... WUIS
Springfield Instit'n for Svgs [*NASDAQ symbol*] (TTSB) ... SISB
Springfield Institution for Savings [*NASDAQ symbol*] (SAG) ... SISB
Springfield Institution for Savings [*Associated Press*] (SAG) ... SprfldSv
Springfield, KY [*FM radio station call letters*] (RBYB) ... WAKY-FM
Springfield, KY [*FM radio station call letters*] ... WMQQ
Springfield, MA [*FM radio station call letters*] ... WAIC
Springfield, MA [*FM radio station call letters*] ... WAQY
Springfield, MA [*Television station call letters*] ... WGBY
Springfield, MA [*Television station call letters*] ... WGGB
Springfield, MA [*AM radio station call letters*] ... WHYN
Springfield, MA [*FM radio station call letters*] ... WHYN-FM
Springfield, MA [*AM radio station call letters*] ... WMAS
Springfield, MA [*FM radio station call letters*] ... WMAS-FM
Springfield, MA [*FM radio station call letters*] ... WNEK
Springfield, MA [*FM radio station call letters*] ... WSCB
Springfield, MA [*AM radio station call letters*] ... WSPR

Springfield, MA [*FM radio station call letters*] .... WTCC
Springfield, MA [*Television station call letters*] .... WWLP
Springfield, MN [*FM radio station call letters*] (RBYB) .... KNSG
Springfield, MO [*Location identifier FAA*] (FAAL) .... ILJ
Springfield, MO [*FM radio station call letters*] (RBYB) .... KAKU-FM
Springfield, MO [*Television station call letters*] .... KDEB
Springfield, MO [*AM radio station call letters*] .... KGMY
Springfield, MO [*AM radio station call letters*] .... KIDS
Springfield, MO [*AM radio station call letters*] .... KLFJ
Springfield, MO [*Television station call letters*] .... KOLR
Springfield, MO [*Television station call letters*] .... KOZK
Springfield, MO [*FM radio station call letters*] .... KSMU
Springfield, MO [*Television station call letters*] .... KSPR
Springfield, MO [*AM radio station call letters*] .... KTOZ
Springfield, MO [*AM radio station call letters*] .... KTTS
Springfield, MO [*FM radio station call letters*] .... KTTS-FM
Springfield, MO [*FM radio station call letters*] .... KTXR
Springfield, MO [*FM radio station call letters*] .... KWFC
Springfield, MO [*FM radio station call letters*] .... KWND
Springfield, MO [*AM radio station call letters*] .... KWTO
Springfield, MO [*FM radio station call letters*] .... KWTO-FM
Springfield, MO [*FM radio station call letters*] .... KXUS
Springfield, MO [*Television station call letters*] .... KYTV
Springfield, MO [*Location identifier FAA*] (FAAL) .... RIN
Springfield, MO [*Location identifier FAA*] (FAAL) .... SGF
Springfield, OH [*Location identifier FAA*] (FAAL) .... CCJ
Springfield, OH [*Location identifier FAA*] (FAAL) .... SGH
Springfield, OH [*AM radio station call letters*] .... WBLY
Springfield, OH [*FM radio station call letters*] .... WEEC
Springfield, OH [*FM radio station call letters*] (RBYB) .... WING-FM
Springfield, OH [*AM radio station call letters*] .... WIZE
Springfield, OH [*Television station call letters*] .... WTJC
Springfield, OH [*FM radio station call letters*] .... WUSO
Springfield, OH [*Location identifier FAA*] (FAAL) .... XSF
Springfield, OR [*AM radio station call letters*] (RBYB) .... KNRQ
Springfield, OR [*FM radio station call letters*] .... KQFE
Springfield Public Library, Springfield, OR [*Library symbol Library of Congress*] (LCLS) .... OrSp
Springfield Resources [*Vancouver Stock Exchange symbol*] .... SPF
Springfield State Hospital, Sykesville, MD [*Library symbol Library of Congress*] (LCLS) .... MdSyH
Springfield Technical Community College [*Massachusetts*] .... STCC
Springfield Technical Community College, Springfield, MA [*Library symbol Library of Congress*] (LCLS) .... MSST
Springfield Terminal Railway Co. [*Later, ST*] [*AAR code*] .... SPGT
Springfield Terminal Railway Co. [*AAR code*] .... ST
Springfield, TN [*Location identifier FAA*] (FAAL) .... PED
Springfield, TN [*AM radio station call letters*] .... WDBL
Springfield, TN [*FM radio station call letters*] .... WDBL-FM
Springfield, TN [*AM radio station call letters*] .... WSGI
Springfield, VT [*Location identifier FAA*] (FAAL) .... SXD
Springfield, VT [*Location identifier FAA*] (FAAL) .... VSF
Springfield, VT [*AM radio station call letters*] .... WCFR
Springfield, VT [*FM radio station call letters*] .... WCFR-FM
Springfield-Cape Girardeau [*Diocesan abbreviation*] [*Missouri*] (TOCD) .... SPC
Springfield-Eugene, OR [*FM radio station call letters*] .... KKNU
Springfield-Eugene, OR [*AM radio station call letters*] .... KORE
Springfield-Greene County Library, Springfield, MO [*OCLC symbol*] (OCLC) .... MOS
Springfields Nuclear Laboratories [*British*] (NUCP) .... SNL
Springfields Nuclear Power Development Laboratories [*British*] (NUCP) .... SNPDL
Springhill, LA [*AM radio station call letters*] .... KBSF
Springhill, LA [*FM radio station call letters*] .... KTKC
Springhill, LA [*Location identifier FAA*] (FAAL) .... SPH
Springlfied City Library, Springfield, MA [*Library symbol*] [*Library of Congress*] (LCLS) .... MSCL
Spring-Loaded Ball Plunger .... SLBP
Spring-Loaded Pulley .... SLP
Springs [*South Africa*] [*ICAO location identifier*] (ICLI) .... FASI
Springs .... SPGS
Springs (MCD) .... SPGS
Springs [*Commonly used*] (OPSA) .... SPNGS
Springs [*Commonly used*] (OPSA) .... SPRINGS
Springs [*Commonly used*] (OPSA) .... SPRNGS
Springs Industries, Inc. [*Formerly, Springs Mills, Incorporated*] [*NYSE symbol*] (SPSG) .... SMI
Springs Industries'A' [*NYSE symbol*] (TTSB) .... SMI
Springs Valley Herald, French Lick, IN [*Library symbol Library of Congress*] (LCLS) .... InFrenSH
Springtown, TX [*FM radio station call letters*] (RBYB) .... KMQX
Springvale [*Queensland*] [*Airport symbol*] (AD) .... ZVG
Springville City Library, Springville, UT [*Library symbol Library of Congress*] (LCLS) .... USp
Springville, NY [*Television station call letters*] .... WNGS
Springville, NY [*AM radio station call letters*] .... WSPQ
Springville Public Library, Springville, IA [*Library symbol Library of Congress*] (LCLS) .... IaSpr
Sprinkle [*NWS*] (FAAC) .... SPKL
Sprinkled [*Bookbinding*] (DGA) .... Spr
Sprinkled Edge [*Bookbinding*] (DGA) .... SE
Sprinkler (WGA) .... SPKR
Sprinkler (AAG) .... SPR
Sprinkler Irrigation Association [*Later, IA*] (EA) .... SIA
Sprinkler Leakage [*Insurance*] .... SL
Sprinkling (MSA) .... SPRG
Sprinkling [*Freight*] .... SPRKLG
SPRINT Air-Directed Defense [*Army*] .... SPAD
SPRINT Air-Directed Defense System [*Army*] (AABC) .... SPADS
Sprint Corp 8.25%'DECS' 2000 [*NYSE symbol*] (TTSB) .... FXN
Sprint Corp. [*NYSE symbol*] (SAG) .... FON
Sprint Corp. [*NYSE symbol*] (SAG) .... FXN
Sprint Corp. [*Associated Press*] (SAG) .... Sprint
Sprint Corp. [*Associated Press*] (SAG) Sprint00
Sprint Corp. $1.50 CV Ser 1 Pfd [*NYSE symbol*] (TTSB) .... FONPr
Sprint Corp. $1.50 Cv Ser 2 Pfd [*NYSE symbol*] (TTSB) .... FONPrA
SPRINT Early Missile Test RADAR [*Army*] (AABC) .... SEMTR
SPRINT Electromagnetic Radiation Evaluation [*Army*] (AABC) .... SEMRE
SPRINT Engagement Simulation [*Missile system evaluation*] [*Army*] (RDA) .... SES
SPRINT [*Solid-Propellant Rocket Intercept*] **Extra Pulse Out of Tail** [*Army*] .... SEXPOT
SPRINT Missile Electromagnetic Radiation Evaluation [*Army*] (AABC) .... SMERE
SPRINT Missile Engineering/Service Course [*Army*] (AABC) .... SME/SC
SPRINT [*Solid-Propellant Rocket Intercept*] **Missile Subsystem** [*Army*] .... SMS
SPRINT Operations Shelter [*Army*] .... SOS
SPRINT [*Solid-Propellant Rocket Intercept*] **Service Vehicle** [*Army*] .... SSV
Sprite-Midget Owners Group (EA) .... SMOG
Spritsail [*Ship's rigging*] (ROG) .... SPL
Spritsail [*Ship's rigging*] (DS) .... Spt
Sprocket .... SPKT
Sprocket (MSA) .... SPRKT
Sprocket Feed (ECII) .... SF
Spruce (VRA) .... spr
Spruce Budworm .... SBW
Spruce Canyon Correctional Center, Resident Library, Colville, WA [*Library symbol Library of Congress*] (LCLS) .... WaClvSC-R
Spruce Canyon Correctional Center, Staff Library, Colville, WA [*Library symbol Library of Congress*] (LCLS) .... WaClvSC
Spruce Fall Power & Paper [*AAR code*] .... SFPP
Spruce Grove Public Library, Alberta [*Library symbol National Library of Canada*] (NLC) .... ASG
Spruce Grove Public Library, Spruce Grove, AB, Canada [*Library symbol*] [*Library of Congress*] (LCLS) .... CaASg
Spruce Pine, NC [*AM radio station call letters*] .... WTOE
Spruce-Fast [*Forestry*] .... SF
SPS Technologies [*NYSE symbol*] (TTSB) .... ST
SPS Technologies, Inc. [*Formerly, Standard Pressed Steel Co.*] (MCD) .... SPS
SPS Technologies, Inc. [*Associated Press*] (SAG) .... SPSTec
SPS Technologies, Inc. [*Formerly, Standard Pressed Steel Co.*] [*NYSE symbol*] (SPSG) .... ST
SPS Transaction Services [*NYSE symbol*] (SAG) .... PAY
SPS Transaction Services, Inc. [*Associated Press*] (SAG) .... SPS Trns
SPSS, Inc. [*NASDAQ symbol*] (SAG) .... SPSS
Spun Soy Fiber [*Food technology*] .... SSF
Spur [*Postal Service standard*] (OPSA) .... SPUR
Spur Stepover Gear .... SSOG
Spur Ventures [*Vancouver Stock Exchange symbol*] .... SVU
Spuria Iris Society (EA) .... SIS
Spurious Emission Detection Acquisition System (MCD) .... SEDAS
Spurious Response Rejection .... SRR
Spurling Aviation [*ICAO designator*] (FAAC) .... ASL
Spurs [*Horse racing*] .... S
Spurs [*Commonly used*] (OPSA) .... SPURS
Spurwing Airlines (Pty) Ltd. [*South Africa ICAO designator*] (FAAC) .... PUR
Sputter Auger Electron Spectroscopy (IAA) .... SAES
Sputtered Iridium Oxide Film (PDAA) .... SIROF
Sputtered Neutral Mass Spectrometry [*Surface analysis*] .... SNMS
Sputter-Induced Photon Spectroscopy (MCD) .... SIPS
Sputter-Initiated Resonance Ionization Spectrometry .... SIRIS
Sputum .... SPT
Sputum [*Medicine*] (DAVI) .... SPUT
SPX Corp. [*Formerly, Sealed Power Corp.*] [*NYSE symbol*] (SPSG) .... SPW
SPX Corp. [*Formerly, Sealed Power Corp.*] [*Associated Press*] (SAG) .... SPX Cp
Spy Against Pollution [*An association*] .... SAP
Spyglass, Inc. [*NASDAQ symbol*] (SAG) .... SPYG
Spyglass, Inc. [*Associated Press*] (SAG) .... Spyglss
SQA, Inc [*NASDAQ symbol*] (SAG) .... SQAX
SQA, Inc. [*Associated Press*] (SAG) .... SQA
SQA Inc. [*NASDAQ symbol*] (TTSB) .... SQAX
SQL [*Structured Query Language*] **Windows Application Language** [*Computer science*] .... SAL
SQT [*Ship's Qualification Trial*] **Requirements Alert Message** .... SRAM
Squad (AABC) .... SQD
Squad Assault Weapon [*Marine Corps*] (DOMA) .... SAW
Squad Automatic Weapon [*Army*] .... SAW
Squad Automatic Weapon System [*Army*] .... SAWS
Squad Combat Operations Exercise, Simulation [*Military*] .... SCOPES
Squad Combat Qualification Exercise [*Army*] (INF) .... SCQE
Squad Engagement Training System [*Army*] (INF) .... SETS
Squad Radio Set .... SRS
Squad Weapon Analytical Trainer (MCD) .... SWAT
Squadron (MUGU) .... RON
Squadron .... S
Squadron .... SQ
Squadron (NVT) .... SQD
Squadron (AAG) .... SQDN
Squadron (NATG) .... SQN
Squadron .... SQUAD
Squadron Accountant Officer [*Navy British*] .... SAO
Squadron Aid Post (ADA) .... SAP

Squadron Airfield (NATG)	SQNA
Squadron Augmentation Unit [*Navy*] (DOMA)	SAU
Squadron Command Officer (AAG)	SCO
Squadron Constructor Officer [*Navy British*]	SCO
Squadron Control Center (AAG)	SCC
Squadron Corporal-Major [*British military*] (DMA)	SCM
Squadron Duty Officer [*Navy*] (NVT)	SDO
Squadron Exercises [*Canadian Navy*]	SQUADEX
Squadron Gunnery Officer	SGO
Squadron Headquarters [*British military*] (DMA)	SHQ
Squadron Landing Team [*Marine Corps*] (DOMA)	SLT
Squadron Leader [*British military*] (DMA)	S/Ldr
Squadron Maintenance Area	SMA
Squadron Manning Document (NVT)	SQMD
Squadron Medical Element	SME
Squadron Medical Officer	SMO
Squadron Observer [*British military*] (DMA)	Sqn Obs
Squadron Officer	SQO
Squadron Officers School [*Air Force*]	SOS
Squadron Operational Report	SOR
Squadron Operational Support [*Military*] (AFIT)	SOS
Squadron Operational Support Kit (MCD)	SOSK
Squadron Operational Support Package [*Military*] (AFIT)	SOSP
Squadron Operations Center [*Air Force*]	SOC
Squadron or Flotilla Flag [*Navy British*]	SF
Squadron Performance Effectiveness Analysis Representation (MCD)	SPEAR
Squadron Quartermaster-Corporal [*British military*] (DMA)	SQMC
Squadron Quartermaster-Serjeant [*Military British*] (ROG)	SQMS
Squadron Recreation Officer [*Navy British*]	SRO
Squadron Sergeant Major	SSM
Squadron Sergeant-Major Instructor in Fencing and Gymnastics [*Military British*] (ROG)	SSMIF & G
Squadron Service Unit [*Aircraft*]	SSU
Squadron Signals Officer [*Navy British*]	SSO
Squadron Supervisory and Control Equipment (SAA)	SSCE
Squadron Supervisory Console [*Air Force*]	SSC
Squadron Support Center (AAG)	SSC
Squadron Tactical Analysis Board [*Military*] (CAAL)	STAB
Squadron Training (NVT)	SQTNG
Squadron Wireless Officer [*Navy British*]	SWO
Squadron-Leader [*Military*]	SL
Squadron-Leader [*British military*] (DMA)	Sqdn Ldr
Squadron-Leader [*British military*] (DMA)	Sqn Ldr
Squadron-Officer [*British military*] (DMA)	Sqn Offr
Squadron-Officer [*British military*] (DSUE)	SQUO
Squadron-Officer [*British military*] (DSUE)	SQUOFF
Squalene-Binding Protein [*Biochemistry*]	SBP
Squall [*Meteorology*]	SQ
Squalls [*Meteorology*] (BARN)	Q
Squamish, BC [*Television station call letters*] (RBYB)	CHAN-3
Squamish, BC [*FM radio station call letters*]	CISQ
Squamish Public Library, British Columbia [*Library symbol National Library of Canada*] (NLC)	BSO
Squamish Valley Museum, Garibaldi Highlands, British Columbia [*Library symbol National Library of Canada*] (NLC)	BGHS
Squamocolumnar Junction [*Medicine*] (MAE)	SCJ
Squamous [*Cell*] [*Oncology*]	SQ
Squamous [*Cell*] [*Oncology*] (DAVI)	SQU
Squamous [*Cell*] [*Oncology*] (DAVI)	SQUAM
Squamous Cell Carcinoma [*Also, SCC*] [*Medicine*]	SC
Squamous Cell Carcinoma [*Also, SC*] [*Medicine*]	SCC
Squamous Cell Carcinoma [*Endocrinology*] (CPH)	Sq Ca
Squamous Cell Carcinoma [*Medicine*] (MAE)	sq cell ca
Squamous Cell Cervical Carcinoma [*Medicine*] (DMAA)	SCCC
Squamous Epithelial Cells [*Medicine*] (MEDA)	SEC
Squamous Epithelium [*Medicine*] (CPH)	Sq Epith
Squamous Intraepithelial Lesion [*Medicine*]	SIL
Squamous Intraepithelial Neoplastic [*Oncology*]	SIN
Squamous-Cell Carcinoma [*Oncology*] (DAVI)	SCCa
Squamous-Cell Carcinoma [*Oncology*] (DAVI)	Sq CCa
Squamous-Cell Carcinoma [*Medicine*] (MEDA)	SqCCA
Square (EY)	SQ
Square (VRA)	sq
Square (DD)	Sq
Square (IDOE)	sq
Square	SQ
Square (ODBW)	sq
Square	SQR
Square [*Commonly used*] (OPSA)	SQRE
Square (BJA)	Squ
Square [*Commonly used*] (OPSA)	SQUARE
Square [*Ship's rigging*] (ROG)	SR
Square Back [*Bookbinding*] (DGA)	Sq Bk
Square Cartridge Heater	SCH
Square Centimeter (IDOE)	cm²
Square Centimeter	CM²
Square Centimeter (ROG)	CMR₂
Square Centimeter (MSA)	SQCM
Square Chain (BARN)	sq ch
Square Corners [*Bookbinding*] (DGA)	SC
Square Corners [*Bookbinding*] (DGA)	Sq C
Square Corners Plain Edges [*Bookbinding*] (DGA)	SCPE
Square Corners Silver Bevelled Deckle Edges [*Bookbinding*] (DGA)	SCSBDE
Square Corners Silver Edges [*Bookbinding*] (DGA)	SCSE
Square Corners Silver-Bevelled Edges [*Bookbinding*] (DGA)	SCSBE
Square Dance Callers Association [*Australia*]	SDCA
Square Dance Callers Club [*British*] (DBA)	SDC
Squared Decimeter (ROG)	Dm²
Square Dekameter	DAM²
Square Dekameter	Dkm²
Square Die Bushing	SDB
Square Feet	ft2
Square Feet per Hour	FT²/H
Square Feet per Second	FT²/S
Square Foot	FT²
Square Foot	SF
Square Foot (MSA)	SQFT
Square Foot per Minute (WDAA)	FT²/MIN
Square Head [*Bolt*]	SQH
Square Hectometer	HM²
Square Hollow Section [*Metal industry*]	SHS
Square Inch	IN²
Square Inch (MCD)	SI
Square Inch (MSA)	SQIN
Square Industries [*NASDAQ symbol*] (TTSB)	SQAI
Square Industries, Inc. [*NASDAQ symbol*] (NQ)	SQAI
Square Industries, Inc. [*Associated Press*] (SAG)	SquareI
Square Kilometer (CDAI)	km²
Square Kilometer	km2
Square Kilometer (MSA)	SQKM
Square Law Detection	SLD
Square Law Detector [*Telecommunications*] (OA)	SD
Square Loop Antenna	SLA
Square Mesh Tracking [*Air Force*]	SMT
Square Meter	m2
Square Meter	M²
Square Meter (IDOE)	m²
Square Meter	SM
Square Meter	SQM
Square Meters per Second	M²/S
Square Micrometer (WDAA)	MU M²
Square Mile (CDAI)	mi²
Square Mile (CDAI)	sq mi
Square Millimeter	MM²
Square Millimeter (MAE)	sq mm
Square Nautical Mile (NVT)	SNM
Square of the Hatch [*Stowage*] (DNAB)	SQ/H
Square Planar [*Organic chemistry*]	SP
Square Punch	SP
Square Pyramidal [*Organic chemistry*]	SPY
Square Rod (CDAI)	rd²
Square Rod (CDAI)	sq rd
Square Root [*Computer science*]	SQR
Square Root	SQRT
Square Root Mode [*Computer science*]	SRM
Square Root of the Sum of the Squares (NRCH)	SRSS
Square Rooter (IDOE)	SQR
Square Tank [*Liquid gas carriers*]	sq
Square Yard (CDAI)	sq yd
Square Yard	SY
Square Yard (CDAI)	yd²
Square Yards Equivalent (DICI)	SYE
Squared Multiple Correlation [*Psychology*]	SMC
Squared Successive Differences [*Computer science*]	SSD
Squared Sum of Errors [*Statistics*]	SSE
Squared Up [*Typography*] (DGA)	S/U
Squared Up Halftone [*Typography*] (DGA)	SUHT
Squared-Mean to Variance	SM/V
Square-Edge and Sound (DAC)	SqE & S
Square-Edge Siding (DAC)	SE Sdg
Square-Root Function (IDOE)	SQR
Squares [*Commonly used*] (OPSA)	SQRS
Squares [*Postal Service standard*] (OPSA)	SQS
Squares	SQS
Squares [*Commonly used*] (OPSA)	SQUARES
Squarewave (MSA)	SQW
Squarewave	SQWV
Squarewave Amplitude Modulation	SAM
Squarewave Generator	SWG
Squarewave Oscillator	SWO
Squarewave Voltammetry [*Electrochemistry*]	SWV
Squaric Acid Dibutylester [*Medicine*] (MEDA)	SADBE
Squaring Amplifier	SQA
Squash Australia	SA
Squash Leaf Curl Virus	SLCV
Squash Mosaic Virus	SQMV
Squash Rackets Association [*British*]	SRA
Squash Rackets Professionals Association [*British*] (DBA)	SRPA
Squaw Lake School, Squaw Lake, MN [*Library symbol*] [*Library of Congress*] (LCLS)	MnSqlS
Squaw Peak [*Utah*] [*Seismograph station code, US Geological Survey*] (SEIS)	SQU
Squawk (DA)	MS
Squawk [*Aviation*] (FAAC)	SQK
Squawk Mode Code [*Aviation*] (FAAC)	SMC
Squawk Sheet (KSC)	SS
Squeeze Film Test	SFT
Squeeze Grip	SQZGR
Squeezed Files [*Computer science*]	SQ
Squeezed Files [*Computer science*] (MHDI)	USQ

Squelch ..... SQL
Squib Fuse Electrical Assembly (KSC) ..... SFEA
Squib Simulator Console ..... SSC
Squibb Canada, Inc., Montreal, PQ, Canada [*Library symbol*] [*Library of Congress*] (LCLS) ..... CaQMSQC
Squibb Canada, Inc., Montreal, Quebec [*Library symbol National Library of Canada*] (NLC) ..... QMSQC
Squibb on Auctioneers [*2nd ed.*] [*1891*] [*A publication*] (DLA) ..... Squibb Auc
Squibb-Beechnut, Inc., New Brunswick, NJ [*Library symbol Library of Congress*] (LCLS) ..... NjNbSI
Squint Quoin [*Construction*] (IAA) ..... SQ
Squire (WGA) ..... Sq
Squirrel Cage (IAA) ..... SC
Squirrel Cage [*Electricity*] ..... SQCG
Squirrel Fibroma Virus [*Medicine*] (DMAA) ..... SFV
Squirrel Monkey Retravirus ..... SMRV
S-R Advocate News, Wilton Junction, IA [*Library symbol Library of Congress*] (LCLS) ..... IaWijS
SR Telecom, Inc. [*Toronto Stock Exchange symbol*] ..... SRX
SRAM Equivalent Volume (MCD) ..... SEV
SRB [*Solid-Rocket Booster*] **Storage Facility** [*NASA*] (NASA) ..... SSF
SRC Network (NITA) ..... SRCNET
S-Receptor Kinase [*An enzyme*] ..... SRK
Srednekan [*Later, MGD*] [*Former USSR Geomagnetic observatory code*] ..... SRE
Sredniy Kalar [*Former USSR Seismograph station code, US Geological Survey*] (SEIS) ..... SRK
Sri Aurobindo Association (EA) ..... SAA
Sri Chinmoy Oneness-Home Peace Run [*An association*] (EA) ..... SCPR
Sri Kapila Humanitarian Society (EAIO) ..... SKHS
Sri Lanka [*Aircraft nationality and registration mark*] (FAAC) 4R
Sri Lanka [*IYRU nationality code*] (IYR) ..... CY
Sri Lanka [*ANSI two-letter standard code*] (CNC) ..... LK
Sri Lanka [*ANSI three-letter standard code*] (CNC) ..... LKA
Sri Lanka Freedom Party [*Political party*] (PPW) ..... SLFP
Sri Lanka Navy ..... SLN
Sri Lanka People's Party [*Political party*] (PPW) ..... SLPP
Sri Lanka Rupee [*Monetary unit*] (IMH) ..... Rs
Sri Lanka Trade Union Federation [*Sri Lanka Vurthiya Samithi Sammelanaya*] ..... SLTUF
Sriharikota Island Launch Complex [*India*] ..... SHAR
Srinagar [*India*] [*Airport symbol*] (OAG) ..... SXR
Srinagar [*India*] [*ICAO location identifier*] (ICLI) ..... VISR
Srinivasan's Reports of Income Tax Cases [*India*] [*1886-*] [*A publication*] (ILCA) ..... ITC
SRO Entertainment [*Vancouver Stock Exchange symbol*] ..... SOT
Srpska Akademija Nauka i Umetnosti [*Belgrade, Yugoslavia*] ..... SAN
Srpska Demokratska Stranka [*Serb Democratic Party*] [*Political party*] ..... SDS
Srpska Radikalna Stranka [*Serbian Radical Party*] [*Former Yugoslavia*] [*Political party*] (PPE) ..... SRS
Srpska Zemljoradnicka Stranka [*Serbian Agrarian Party*] [*Former Yugoslavia*] [*Political party*] (PPE) ..... SZS
Srpski Pokret Obnove [*Serbian Renaissance Movement*] [*Political party*] (EY) ..... SPO
SRS Labs, Inc. [*Associated Press*] (SAG) ..... SRS Lbs
SRS Labs, Inc. [*NASDAQ symbol*] (SAG) ..... SRSL
SS1 [*Nevada*] [*Seismograph station code, US Geological Survey Closed*] (SEIS) ..... SSX
SSE Telecom [*NASDAQ symbol*] (TTSB) ..... SSET
SSE Telecom, Inc. [*Associated Press*] (SAG) ..... SSE Tl
SSE Telecom, Inc. [*NASDAQ symbol*] (SAG) ..... SSET
SSIE Number (NITA) ..... SN
SSM/I Land Products Working Team (USDC) ..... SPWT
SSM/I [*Special Sensor Microwave/Imager*] **Land Products Working Team** [*Marine science*] (OSRA) ..... SPWT
SSRC [*Social Science Research Council*] **Research Unit on Ethnic Relations** [*Research center British*] (IRC) ..... RUER
SSV [*Space Shuttle Vehicle*] **Integrated Test** [*NASA*] (NASA) ..... SIT
St Augustine Beach, FL [*AM radio station call letters*] ..... WKLN
St George, UT [*FM radio station call letters*] ..... KSGI-FM
St Joseph, MN [*FM radio station call letters*] ..... KKJM
St Louis [*Branch in the Federal Reserve regional banking system*] (BARN) ..... H
St Louis, MO [*AM radio station call letters*] ..... KSD
St Mark's Review [*A publication*] (APTA) ..... SMR
STAAR Surgical [*NASDAQ symbol*] (TTSB) ..... STAA
Staar Surgical Co. [*NASDAQ symbol*] (NQ) ..... STAA
Staar Surgical Co. [*Associated Press*] (SAG) ..... StaarSur
Staatkundig Gereformeerde Partij [*Netherlands Political party Benelux*] ..... SGP
Staatliche Gesellschaft zur Erfassung von Ruestungsgut [*German Public Corporation for the Collection and Distribution of War Materials*] ..... STEG
Staatliche Zentrale fuer Strahlenschutz Berlin [*East Germany*] ..... SZS
Staats- und Universitatsbibliothek Hamburg, Hamburg, Germany [*Library symbol Library of Congress*] (LCLS) ..... GyHaS
Staatsbibliothek Preuss. Kulturbesitz - Gesamtkat. U. Dok., Berlin, Federal Republic of Germany [*OCLC symbol*] (OCLC) ..... SBG
Staatsbibliothek und Universitatsbibliothek, Breitenweg, Bremen, Germany [*Library symbol Library of Congress*] (LCLS) ..... GyBrSU
Staatsblad [*Official Bulletin*] [*Netherlands*] (ILCA) ..... Stb
Staatssicherheitsdienst [*State Security Service*] [*Germany*] ..... SSD
Staatsuitgeverij Christoffel Plantijnstaat (State Printing Office), The Hague, Netherlands [*Library symbol Library of Congress*] (LCLS) ..... NeHSU
Stab Wound [*Medicine*] (MAE) ..... SW
Stab Wound of the Throat (DAVI) ..... SWT
Stabell Resources [*Vancouver Stock Exchange symbol*] ..... SLR
Stability (IDOE) ..... stab
Stability (MSA) ..... STABY
Stability and Frequency Response ..... S & FR
Stability and Safety Screening [*Sailing terminology*] ..... SSS
Stability Augmentation [*Aviation*] (MCD) ..... STAB AUG
Stability Augmentation Attitude Hold System [*Aviation*] ..... SAAHS
Stability Augmentation System [*or Subsystem*] [*FAA*] ..... SAS
Stability Augmentation System with Control Stick Steering (PDAA) ..... SAS/CSS
Stability, Control, and Load Maneuvers [*Aerospace*] (MCD) ..... SCLM
Stability Control Augmentation System (NVT) ..... SCAS
Stability Enhancement Function [*Aviation*] (GFGA) ..... SEF
Stability Margin ..... SM
Stability Operations ..... STOPS
Stability Regulated Controlled Rectifier ..... SRCR
Stability Return Loss [*Telecommunications*] (TEL) ..... SRL
Stabilization [*or Stabilizer*] (IAA) ..... STAB
Stabilization (IDOE) ..... stab
Stabilization (MSA) ..... STBLN
Stabilization, Acquisition, Tracking, and Pointing ..... SATP
Stabilization and Control [*Aerospace*] (KSC) ..... S & C
Stabilization and Control [*Aerospace*] (GFGA) ..... S/C
Stabilization and Control System [*or Subsystem*] [*NASA*] ..... SCS
Stabilization and Control System Control Panel (IAA) ..... SCPA
Stabilization Assurance Test (IEEE) ..... SAT
Stabilization/Attitude Control [*NASA*] (NASA) ..... S/AC
Stabilization Control Electronics ..... SCE
Stabilization Data Computer ..... SDC
Stabilization Network Group ..... SNG
Stabilization of Export Earnings [*Program of the EEC*] ..... STABEX
Stabilization Reference Package (MCD) ..... SRP
Stabilization Reference Package / Position Determination System [*Military*] ..... SRP/PDS
Stabilization Reserve Account [*Health insurance*] (GHCT) ..... SRA
Stabilization/Solidification (FFDE) ..... S/S
Stabilization System (AAG) ..... SS
Stabilize [*or Stabilizer*] [*Aviation*] (AAG) ..... STAB
Stabilize (AABC) ..... STBLZ
Stabilized Assay Meter (NRCH) ..... SAM
Stabilized Bombing Approach Equipment [*Navy*] ..... SBAE
Stabilized Breakdown ..... SB
Stabilized Carbon Dioxide LASER ..... SCDL
Stabilized Core Composite [*Materials science*] ..... SCC
Stabilized Flight Operations Manual ..... SFOM
Stabilized Fuming Nitric Acid ..... SFNA
Stabilized Glide Slope Indicator (NVT) ..... SGSI
Stabilized Ground Cloud [*NASA*] (MCD) ..... SGC
Stabilized Gyro Platform ..... SGP
Stabilized Line-of-Sight Tracker ..... SLOT
Stabilized Local Oscillator [*RADAR*] ..... STALO
Stabilized March Technique ..... SMT
Stabilized Master Oscillator ..... SMO
Stabilized Member [*NASA*] (KSC) ..... SM
Stabilized Member Assembly [*NASA*] ..... SMA
Stabilized Night Sight ..... SNS
Stabilized Optical Sight ..... SOS
Stabilized Optical Tracking Device (SAA) ..... SOTD
Stabilized Optical Viewing Device ..... SOVD
Stabilized Platform Airborne LASER (RDA) ..... SPAL
Stabilized Platform Subsystem (KSC) ..... SPS
Stabilized Routing for Afloat Commands (MCD) ..... STROFAC
Stabilized Screen (IAA) ..... SS
Stabilized Ship Detector [*Navy*] ..... SSD
Stabilized Shunt [*Electricity*] ..... STSH
Stabilized Sight Unit (MCD) ..... SSU
Stabilized Sighting System ..... SSS
Stabilized Telescope System ..... STS
Stabilized Temperature Platform Furnace ..... STPF
Stabilized Terrain Optical Position Sensor [*Army*] ..... STOPS
Stabilized Tracking Tripod Module (RDA) ..... STTM
Stabilized Translation and Maneuvering Propulsion System (IAA) ..... STAMPS
Stabilized Tunable Local Oscillator ..... STALOS
Stabilized Twin-Gyro Attitude Reference System ..... STARS
Stabilized Viewing System ..... SVS
Stabilizer (IDOE) ..... stab
Stabilizer Gyro Circuit ..... SGC
Stabilizing Amplifier [*Telecommunications*] (IAA) ..... STABAMP
Stabilizing Automatic Bomb Sight ..... SABS
Stable ..... ST
Stable [*Army*] ..... Stab
Stable (MSA) ..... STB
Stable ..... STBL
Stable Auroral Red [*Arc*] [*Geophysics*] ..... SAR
Stable Axis Platform Follow-Up System ..... STAPFUS
Stable Carbon Isotope Ratio Analysis [*For determining material source*] ..... SCIRA
Stable Continental Region [*Geology*] ..... SCR
Stable Control Unit ..... SCU
Stable Element ..... SE
Stable Element Panel ..... SEP
Stable Factor [*Medicine*] (DMAA) ..... SF
Stable Isotope Dilution Assay [*Analytical chemistry*] ..... SIDA
Stable Isotope Mass Spectrometer ..... SIMS
Stable Isotope Ratio Analysis ..... SIRA
Stable Isotope Ratio Mass Spectrometer [*or Spectrometry*] ..... SIRMS
Stable Isotopes Resource ..... SIR
Stable Lads' Association [*British*] (ECON) ..... SLA
Stable Master Oscillator ..... STAMO
Stable Matrix Form ..... SMF

Stable Ocean Platform	STOP
Stable Parachute	STARUTE
Stable Plasma Protein Solution [*Medicine*]	SPPS
Stable Platform	SP
Stable Platform Alignment Unit	SPAU
Stable Platform Housing	SPH
Stable Plurilamellar Vesicle [*Pharmacology*]	SPLV
Stable Production Low Leach Glass [*For nuclear wastes*]	SPLLG
Stable Radio Frequency	SRF
Stable Reactor, General, Atomic	SRGA
Stable Recipient [*Medicine*] (DAVI)	SR
Stable Sarcoidosis [*Medicine*]	SS
Stable Super-Active Scavenger [*Color film technology*]	SSAS
Stable Tubule Only Polypeptide [*Biochemistry*]	STOP
Stable X-Ray Transmitter	SXT
Stable-Orbit Rendezvous [*NASA*]	SOR
Stable-Price Economic and Monetary Union [*Europe*]	SPEMU
Stabo Air Ltd. [*Zambia*] [*FAA designator*] (FAAC)	SBO
Stac Electronics [*NASDAQ symbol*] (SAG)	STAC
Stac Inc. [*NASDAQ symbol*] (TTSB)	STAC
Staccato [*Detached, Distinct*] [*Music*]	STAC
Staccato [*Detached, Distinct*] [*Music*]	STACC
Staccato Syndrome [*Medicine*] (DAVI)	SS
Staceys Buffet [*NASDAQ symbol*] (SAG)	SBUF
Staceys Buffet [*Commercial firm Associated Press*] (SAG)	Staceys
Staceys Buffet [*Commercial firm Associated Press*] (SAG)	Stacys
Staceys Buffet Wrrt [*NASDAQ symbol*] (TTSB)	SBUFW
Stacia Ventures [*Vancouver Stock Exchange symbol*]	STA
Stack	S
Stack (MSA)	STK
Stack Access (MHDI)	SA
Stack Access Block	SAB
Stack Address Register (IAA)	SAR
Stack and Play Hub [*Intellicom, Inc.*] [*Telecommunication switching device*] (PCM)	SP
[*A*] Stack Based Abstraction Language [*1978*] [*Computer science*] (CSR)	ASBAL
Stack Control Block	SCB
Stack Empty (MHDI)	SE
Stack Entry Time [*Aviation*] (FAAC)	SET
Stack Full (MHDI)	SF
Stack Gas Reheat [*Air pollution control*]	SGR
Stack Mark (IAA)	SM
Stack (Pipe) Cut [*Sanitation*] [*British*] (ROG)	SC
Stack Pointer [*Computer science*]	SP
Stack Pool [*Computer memory*] (PCM)	SP
Stack Segment [*Computer science*]	S
Stackable Container (DCTA)	SS
Stacked Dipole Aerial Array	SDAA
Stacked Dipole Array	SDA
Stacked Gate Injection Metal-Oxide Semiconductor [*Computer science*] (IAA)	SIMOS
Stacked Job Processing (IAA)	SJP
Stacked-Gate Avalanche Injection Type Metal-Oxide Semiconductor (IAA)	SAMOS
Stacking Fault Energy [*Alloy*]	SFE
Stacking Fault Tetrahedra [*Metals*]	SFT
Stacking Gel [*Biochemistry*]	SG
Stack-Oriented Interactive Compiler [*Computer science*] (MHDI)	STOIC
Stackpool Resources Ltd. [*Vancouver Stock Exchange symbol*]	SKL
Stactic Gel Strength [*Well drilling technology*]	SGS
Stacy Design and Development, Inc. [*Telecommunications service*] (TSSD)	SDD
Stadia [*Speedways, race tracks, etc.*] [*Public-performance tariff class*] [*British*]	Z
Stadler Herter, Montreal, PQ, Canada [*Library symbol Library of Congress*] (LCLS)	CaQMSHE
Stadler Hurter, Montreal, Quebec [*Library symbol National Library of Canada*] (NLC)	QMSHE
Stadskanaal [*Netherlands ICAO location identifier*] (ICLI)	EHST
Stadt u Universitatsbibliothek, Senckenbergische Bibliothek Fernleihe, Frankfurt/Main, Federal Republic of Germany [*Library symbol Library of Congress*] (LCLS)	GyFmSU
Stadt- und Universitaetsbibliothek Frankfurt [*Database producer*]	STUB
Stadtbibliothek Vadiana, St. Gallen, Switzerland [*Library symbol Library of Congress*] (LCLS)	SzStg
Stadtbucherei Salzgitter, Joachim Campe, Salzgitter, Germany [*Library symbol Library of Congress*] (LCLS)	GySalS
Stadtbucherei Witten, Witten, Germany [*Library symbol Library of Congress*] (LCLS)	GyWitS
Stadtlohn/Wenningfeld [*Germany ICAO location identifier*] (ICLI)	EDLS
Staff	S
Staff [*License plate code assigned to foreign diplomats in the US*]	S
Staff	STAF
Staff (AFM)	STF
Staff Accounting Bulletins (TDOB)	SAB
Staff Activity System (IAA)	SAS
Staff Administrative Assistant [*Army*] (AABC)	SAA
Staff Administrative Office [*Military*]	SAO
Staff Administrative Specialist [*Military*]	SAS
Staff and Educational Development Association (AIE)	SEDA
Staff and Faculty	S & F
Staff and Faculty Development Elements	SFDE
Staff Assessment of Readiness Report (MCD)	STARR
Staff Association of Catholic Secondary Schools [*Australia*]	SACSS
Staff Association of the Organization of American States (EA)	SAOAS
Staff Builders 'A' [*NASDAQ symbol*] (TTSB)	SBLI
Staff Builders, Inc. [*NASDAQ symbol*] (NQ)	SBLI
Staff Builders, Inc. [*Associated Press*] (SAG)	StafBld
Staff Burn-Out Scale [*Medicine*] (MEDA)	SBS
Staff Captain [*Military British*]	SC
Staff Car [*British*]	SC
Staff Civil Engineer [*Military*] (DNAB)	SCE
Staff Civil Engineer and Public Works Department (DNAB)	SCE & PWD
Staff Civilian Personnel Division [*Army*]	SCPD
Staff Civilian Personnel Division, Office, Chief of Staff, Army (AABC)	SCPD OCSA
Staff College [*Military*]	SC
Staff Committee on Mediation, Arbitration, and Inquiry [*American Library Association*]	SCMAI
Staff Communications Division, Office, Chief of Staff, Army (AABC)	SCD OC of SA
Staff Communications Division, Office, Chief of Staff, Army (AABC)	SCD OCSA
Staff Communications Office [*Army*]	SCO
Staff Communications Office, Office of the Chief of Staff [*Army*]	CSSCO
Staff Corporal [*British military*] (DMA)	S/Corp
Staff Corporal [*British military*] (DMA)	S/Cpl
Staff Corporal of Horse [*British military*] (DMA)	SCOH
Staff Corps	SC
Staff Counterintelligence Officer [*Military*] (NVT)	SCIO
Staff Development (ADA)	SD
Staff Development and Training	SD & T
Staff Development for School Improvement Program (EDAC)	SDSI
Staff Development Management System (AIE)	SDMS
Staff Duties [*Military British*]	SD
Staff Duties and Training [*British military*] (DMA)	SD & T
Staff Duty Noncommissioned Officer [*Army*]	SDNCO
Staff Duty Officer [*Army*]	SDO
Staff Engineer [*Navy British*] (ROG)	SE
Staff Evaluation Coordinators (MCD)	SEC
Staff Exercises [*NATO*] (NATG)	STAFEX
Staff Inspector	SI
Staff Judge Advocate [*Military*]	SJA
Staff Judge Advocate Office Institute (SAA)	SJAOI
Staff Legal Officer [*Navy*] (DNAB)	SLO
Staff Library, Baycrest Centre for Geriatric Care, Toronto, Ontario [*Library symbol National Library of Canada*] (BIB)	OTBCGC
Staff Library, Glenrose Provincial General Hospital, Edmonton, Alberta [*Library symbol National Library of Canada*] (NLC)	AEG
Staff Library, Lakehead Psychiatric Hospital, Thunder Bay, Ontario [*Library symbol National Library of Canada*] (NLC)	OTBLP
Staff Library, North Bay Psychiatric Hospital, Ontario [*Library symbol National Library of Canada*] (NLC)	ONBP
Staff Management Division, Office, Chief of Staff [*Army*]	SMD, OCOFS
Staff Management Division, Office, Chief of Staff, Army (AABC)	SMD OC of SA
Staff Management Division, Office, Chief of Staff, Army (AABC)	SMD OCSA
Staff Manager [*Insurance*]	SM
Staff Medical Library, G. F. Strong Rehabilitation Centre, Vancouver, British Columbia [*Library symbol National Library of Canada*] (BIB)	BVAGF
Staff Memorandum	SM
Staff Message Control [*Military*]	SMC
Staff Meteorological Officer [*NATO*] (NATG)	SMETO
Staff Meteorologist [*AFSC*]	WE
Staff Model Health Maintenance Organization [*Insurance*] (WYGK)	SMHMO
Staff Noncommissioned Officer [*Military*]	SNCO
Staff Nurse (MEDA)	SN
Staff Nurse (DAVI)	SN
Staff Nurse Advisory Board (MEDA)	SNAB
Staff Nurse Executive Committee (MEDA)	SNEC
Staff of Chief of Defence Staff [*British*]	SCDS
Staff of Chief of Personnel and Logistics [*British military*] (DMA)	SCPL
Staff of the Production Executive Committee [*of the WPB*] [*Obsolete*]	SPEC
Staff Office [*Marine science*] (OSRA)	SO
Staff Officer	SO
Staff Officer, Administration [*British military*] (DMA)	SOA
Staff Officer, Air Defence [*British military*] (DMA)	SOAD
Staff Officer Construction Engineering	SOCE
Staff Officer for Civil Affairs [*British World War II*]	SOCA
Staff Officer for Communications [*Air Force*] (DMA)	A4
Staff Officer for Intelligence [*Army*] [*Marine Corps*] (DOMA)	G2
Staff Officer for Operations [*Army*] [*Marine Corps*] (DOMA)	G3
Staff Officer for Operations and Plans [*Air Force*] (DOMA)	A3
Staff Officer for Personnel [*Army*] [*Marine Corps*] (DOMA)	G1
Staff Officer for Planning [*Army*] [*Marine Corps*] (DOMA)	G5
Staff Officer for Supply/Logistics [*Army*] [*Marine Corps*] (DOMA)	G4
Staff Officer Navigation Instructor (IAA)	SONI
Staff Officer of Pensioners [*Army British*] (ROG)	SOP
Staff Officer Operations [*British*]	SOO
Staff Officer Radio Instructor (IAA)	SORI
Staff Officers Association of America (EA)	SOAA
Staff Operations Division [*NASA*] (MCD)	SOD
Staff Organization and Regulation	SOAR
Staff Organizations Round Table [*American Library Association*]	SORT
Staff Paymaster [*Navy British*] (ROG)	SP
Staff Payroll Allocation and Record (OA)	SPAR
Staff Planner [*DoD*]	SP
Staff Planning Evaluation Group (AAG)	SPEG
Staff Procurement Activity Requirement [*Military*]	SPAR
Staff Qualified [*Military British*]	SQ
Staff Quartermaster Sergeant	SQMS
Staff Report	SR

Staff Returns [*Marine Corps*] ... S/RS
Staff Security Officer (AAG) ... SSO
Staff Selection Committee [*UN Food and Agriculture Organization*] ... SSC
Staff Sergeant [*Air Force*] ... E5
Staff Sergeant [*Army, Marine Corps*] ... E6
Staff Sergeant [*Military British*] (ROG) ... SS
Staff Sergeant [*Army*] (AABC) ... SSG
Staff Sergeant [*Military*] ... SSGT
Staff Sergeant [*Marine Corps*] ... STFSGT
Staff Sergeant Instructor [*Military British*] ... SSI
Staff Sergeant Major [*Army*] ... E9
Staff Sergeant Major [*Military*] ... SSM
Staff Service Center (MCD) ... SSC
Staff Signals Officer [*British military*] (DMA) ... SSO
Staff Site Position [*Nuclear energy*] (NRCH) ... SSP
Staff Specialist [*Military*] ... SS
Staff Squadron Major [*Military British*] ... SSM
Staff Summary Sheet (MCD) ... SSS
Staff Supermarket Associates, Inc., Jericho, NY [*Library symbol Library of Congress*] (LCLS) ... NJerS
Staff Supply Assistant [*Military*] (AABC) ... SSA
Staff Support Agencies [*Military*] ... SSA
Staff Support Room [*NASA*] ... SSR
Staff Surgeon ... SS
Staff Tactical Watch Officer (DOMA) ... STWO
Staff Technical Representative ... STR
Staff Training Assistant [*Army*] (AABC) ... STA
Staff Training Exercise for Programming Supervisor (SAA) ... STEPS
Staff Training Extramural Programs [*National Institutes of Health*] ... STEP
Staff Transport [*When V is the first of two letters in a military aircraft designation*] ... V
Staff Watch Officer (NVT) ... SWO
Staff Weather Officer [*Military*] ... SWO
Staff Weather Officer [*NASA*] (KSC) ... SWXO
Staff Working Group ... SWG
Staff Years (OICC) ... SY
Staffing Guides [*Army*] (AABC) ... STFG
Staffing Needs Assessment Process ... SNAP
Staffing of African Institutions for Legal Education and Research [*Later, International Legal Center*] [*An association*] ... SAILER
Stafford Road [*Wolverhampton*] [*British depot code*] ... SRD
Stafford's Reports [*69-71 Vermont*] [*A publication*] (DLA) ... Stafford
Staffordshire [*County in England*] ... STAFF
Staffordshire [*County in England*] ... STAFFS
Staffordshire [*County in England*] (ODBW) ... Staffs
Staffordshire Imperial Yeomanry [*British military*] (DMA) ... SIY
Staffordshire Terrier Club of America (EA) ... STCA
Stage ... ST
Stage [*of Disease*] (DAVI) ... st
Stage ... STGE
Stage and Arena Guild of America ... SAGA
Stage Assembly and Maintenance [*Building*] ... SAM
Stage Calibration Equipment (SAA) ... SCE
Stage Center [*A stage direction*] ... SC
Stage Direction ... SD
Stage Door [*Theatrical slang*] ... SD
Stage Golfing Society [*British*] (BI) ... SGS
Stage Handling Manual [*NASA*] (KSC) ... SHM
Stage II Apparel [*AMEX symbol*] (TTSB) ... SA
Stage II Apparel Corp. [*AMEX symbol*] (SPSG) ... SA
Stage II Apparel Corp. [*Associated Press*] (SAG) ... Stage
Stage Inert Mass ... SIM
Stage Interface Simulator (IAA) ... SIS
Stage Interface Substitute ... SIS
Stage Left [*A stage direction*] ... SL
Stage Loose Equipment Hardware (SAA) ... SLEH
Stage Management Association [*British*] ... SMA
Stage Manager ... SM
Stage Manager [*Theater term*] (DSUE) ... STAG-MAG
Stage of Exhaustion [*of gas*] [*Medicine*] ... SE
Stage of Resistance [*in General-Adaptation Syndrome*] ... SR
Stage Operating Manual [*NASA*] (KSC) ... SOM
Stage Operations Engineer ... SOE
Stage Right [*Theater*] (WDMC) ... R1
Stage Right [*A stage direction*] ... SR
Stage Scanning Microscope ... SSM
Stage Separation Subsystem [*NASA*] (NASA) ... SSS
Stage Stores, Inc. [*NASDAQ symbol*] (SAG) ... STGE
Stage Stores, Inc. [*Associated Press*] (SAG) ... StgeStrs
Stage Systems Engineer ... SSE
Staged Assessment in Learning (AIE) ... SAIL
Staged Combustion Compound Engine [*Automotive engineering*] ... SCCE
Staged Field Experiment [*Gas production*] ... SFE
Staged in Orbit ... SIO
Staged Turbulent Bed Process [*Chevron Corp.*] [*Oil shale pyrolysis*] ... STB
Staged-Cascade Fluidized Bed Combustion ... SCFBC
Stages of Concern Questionnaire [*Educational test*] ... SOCQ
Stage-Specific Embryonic Antigen [*Immunology*] ... SSEA
Stagger Tuned Antenna ... STA
Staggered Phase Carrier Cancellation ... SPCC
Staggered Quadraphase Phase Shift Key Modulation [*Computer science*] (PDAA) ... SQPSK
Staggered Quadriphase Pseudorandom Noise (MCD) ... SQPN
Staggered Spondaic Word ... SSW
Staggered Spondiac World Test [*Speech and language therapy*] (DAVI) ... SSW
Staging (AABC) ... STG
Staging (AAG) ... STGG
Staging and Support Area [*NASA*] (KSC) ... SSA
Staging Area [*Military*] ... STGAR
Staging Base [*Military*] ... STGB
Staging Connections, Inc. [*Telecommunications service*] (TSSD) ... SCI
Staging Velocity [*NASA*] (NASA) ... VS
Stagnation [*NWS*] (FAAC) ... STAGN
Stagnation Line ... SL
Stagnation Pressure (WDAA) ... Q
Stain (WGA) ... ST
Stain [*Deltiology*] ... STN
Stain Release Rating [*Textile technology*] ... SRR
Stained (WGA) ... STND
Stained Glass ... SG
Stained Glass (VRA) ... stdgls
Stained Glass Association of America (EA) ... SGAA
Stained Glass Overlay [*Commercial firm British*] ... SGO
Stained Glass Professionals Association [*Inactive*] (EA) ... SGPA
Stained Pollen [*Botany*] ... SP
Stained Urinary Sediment [*Medicine*] (MAE) ... SUS
Stainless ... STN
Stainless (MSA) ... STNLS
Stainless ... STNLS
Stainless Steel (VRA) ... ss
Stainless Steel ... SS
Stainless Steel ... SST
Stainless Steel Crown [*Dentistry*] (DAVI) ... SSC
Stainless Steel Crown [*Dentistry*] ... SSCr
Stainless Steel Development Association [*British*] (BI) ... SSDA
Stainless Steel Fabricators' Association of Great Britain (BI) ... SSFA
Stainless Steel Fastenings ... SF
Stainless Steel Fiber ... SSF
Stainless Steel Helium Bottle ... SSHB
Stainless Steel Helium Sphere ... SSHS
Stainless Steel Plumbing Fixture Council [*Defunct*] (EA) ... SSPFC
Stainless Steel Propeller (DS) ... SSP
Stainless Steel Sink [*Classified advertising*] (ADA) ... SSS
Stainless Steel Sink Council [*Defunct*] (EA) ... SSSC
Stainless Steel with Molybdenum [*Devices*] [*Orthopedics*] (DAVI) ... SMo
Stair Public Library, Morenci, MI [*Library symbol Library of Congress*] (LCLS) ... MiMor
Staircase Function Generator ... SFG
Stair's Decisions of the Lords of Council and Session [*1661-81*] [*Scotland*] [*A publication*] (DLA) ... Stair
Stair's Decisions, Scotch Court of Session [*A publication*] (DLA) ... St
Stair's Decisions, Scotch Court of Session [*A publication*] (DLA) ... Stair Rep
Stair's Institutes [*5th ed.*] [*1832*] [*A publication*] (DLA) ... St
Stair's Institutes [*5th ed.*] [*1832*] [*A publication*] (ILCA) ... St Inst
Stair's Institutes [*5 eds.*] [*1681-1832*] [*A publication*] (DLA) ... Stair I
Stair's Institutes [*5 eds.*] [*1681-1832*] [*A publication*] (DLA) ... Stair Inst
Stair's Principles of the Laws of Scotland [*A publication*] (DLA) ... Stair Prin
Stairway (AAG) ... STWY
Stake and Platform [*Technical drawings*] ... S & P
Stake Technology Ltd. [*Associated Press*] (SAG) ... StakeTc
Stake Technology Ltd. [*Oakville, ON*] [*NASDAQ symbol*] (NQ) ... STKL
Stake Technology Ltd [*NASDAQ symbol*] (TTSB) ... STKLF
Stakes (ROG) ... STKS
Stakes Race [*Horse racing*] ... STK
Staking Tool (AAG) ... STTO
Stalactite/Stalagmite Formation (DSUE) ... STAL
Stalk Median Eminence [*Anatomy*] ... SME
Stall (WGA) ... STL
Stall Inhibitor System [*Aviation*] (GFGA) ... SIS
Stall Lake Mines [*Vancouver Stock Exchange symbol*] ... SAK
Stall Warning and Margin Indicator ... SWAMI
Stall Warning Computer (MCD) ... SWC
Stall Warning Indicator ... SWI
Stall Warning System (MCD) ... SW
Stalling Speed in a Specified Flight Configuration (GAVI) ... VSI
Stalling Speed in the Landing Configuration (GAVI) ... VSO
Stallion Resources Ltd. [*Vancouver Stock Exchange symbol*] ... STZ
Stalman on Election and Satisfaction [*1827*] [*A publication*] (DLA) ... Stal Elect
STA-Mali [*ICAO designator*] (FAAC) ... SBA
Stamen [*Botany*] ... St
Stamford [*Connecticut*] [*Airport symbol*] (AD) ... SCC
Stamford, CT [*FM radio station call letters*] ... WEDW
Stamford, CT [*FM radio station call letters*] ... WKHL
Stamford, CT [*AM radio station call letters*] ... WSTC
Stamford Public Library and Museum, Stamford, United Kingdom [*Library symbol Library of Congress*] (LCLS) ... UkSta
Stamford Public Library, Stamford, CT [*Library symbol Library of Congress*] (LCLS) ... CtS
Stamford, TX [*AM radio station call letters*] ... KVRP
Stamford Ukrainian [*Diocesan abbreviation*] [*Connecticut*] (TOCD) ... STF
Stammlager [*Prisoner-of-war camp*] [*German*] ... STALAG
Stammlagerluft [*Prisoner-of-war camp for airmen*] [*German*] ... STALAGLUFT
Stamp ... STMP
Stamp (MSA) ... STP
Stamp Behaviour Study Technique [*Psychology*] ... BST
Stamp Cancelling Machine (DCTA) ... SCM
Stamp Collectors' Association [*British*] (BI) ... SCA
Stamp Duties Rulings [*Australia A publication*] ... SD Rulings
Stamp Duty ... SD
Stamp Office [*British*] (ROG) ... SO

Stamp Out Drug Addiction .... SODA
Stamp Out Regulatory Excesses [*An association*] (EA) .... SORE
Stamp Out Stupidity [*Student group opposing drug abuse*] .... SOS
Stamp Seal (BJA) .... StS
Stamp Vending Machine (DCTA) .... SVM
Stamp Ventures [*Printer of U.S. postage stamps*] (BARN) .... SVS
Stampe Club International (EA) .... SCI
Stamped [*Stocks*] (MHDW) .... sd
Stamped [*Stock exchange term*] (SPSG) .... ST
Stamped .... STA
Stamped (ROG) .... STPD
Stamped Addressed Envelope .... SAE
Stamped Addressed Envelope (ODBW) .... sae
Stamped Envelope .... SE
Stamped Self-Addressed Envelope (WDMC) .... SSAE
Stampede Pass, WA [*Location identifier FAA*] (FAAL) .... SMP
Stampeder Exploration Ltd. [*NYSE symbol*] (SAG) .... SDX
Stampeder Exploration Ltd. [*Associated Press*] (SAG) .... StamEx
Stamping .... STAMPG
Stamping (ROG) .... STPG
Stamping Ground, KY [*FM radio station call letters*] .... WKYI
Stamps, AR [*FM radio station call letters*] .... KZHE
Stamps for the Wounded (EA) .... SFTW
Stamps on Stamps - Centenary Unit (EA) .... SOSCU
Stan West Mining Corp. [*Toronto Stock Exchange symbol*] .... SWM
Stanborough [*England*] .... STANB
Stanchion .... STAN
Stand .... S
Stand (WGA) .... ST
Stand Alone Executive (MHDI) .... SAE
Stand Alone Support Program .... SASP
Stand Alone Terminal (IAA) .... SALT
Stand Down (MCD) .... STDWN
Stand for Exchange of Product Model Data [*Computer-assisted engineering*] .... STEP
Stand Magazine [*A publication*] (BRI) .... Stand
Stand on Leg, Eyes Closed [*Equilibrium test*] .... SOLEC
Stand-Alone Computer Unit .... SCU
Stand-Alone Digital Communications Unit (MCD) .... SACU
Stand-Alone Diplay Unit .... SDU
Stand-Alone Engine Simulator (NASA) .... SAES
Stand-Alone Information System [*National Library of Medicine*] .... SIS
Stand-Alone Intelligent Terminal (MHDI) .... SIT
Stand-Alone Low-Frequency Active Sonar (DOMA) .... SALFAS
Stand-Alone Mudmixing System .... SAMS
Standalone Prediction System .... SAPS
Stand-Alone Self-Test Program [*NASA*] (MCD) .... SASTP
Standard .... S
Standard .... ST
Standard (WGA) .... STAN
Standard .... STAND
Standard .... STAND
Standard (AAGC) .... Stand
Standard (WDMC) .... std
Standard (AFM) .... STD
Standard .... STDR
Standard [*Legal shorthand*] (LWAP) .... STND
Standard Acceptance Limits .... SAL
Standard Acceptance Value .... SAV
Standard Access and Format [*Reference Technology, Inc. software*] .... STA/F
Standard Accounting and Reporting Systems (MCD) .... STARS
Standard Accounting, Budgeting, and Reporting System [*Military*] (GFGA) .... SABRS
Standard Accuracy [*Analytical chemistry*] .... SA
Standard Acid Reflux Test [*Clinical chemistry*] .... SART
Standard Addition .... SA
Standard Addition Method [*Mathematics*] .... SAM
Standard Address Generator (IEEE) .... SAG
Standard Address Number [*Publishing*] .... SAN
Standard Advanced Dewar Assembly [*Army*] .... SADA
Standard Advanced Infrared Sensor [*Military*] .... STAIRS
Standard Advertising Unit [*System introduced to make national newspaper advertising pages uniform in size and format*] .... SAU
Standard Agena [*NASA*] (KSC) .... SA
Standard Agena Clamshell [*NASA*] (KSC) .... SAC
Standard Air Carrier Delay Reporting System .... SACDRS
Standard Air Munitions Package .... STAMP
Standard Aircraft Characteristics .... SAC
Standard Aircraft Navigation System .... STANS
Standard Aircraft Weapon Monitor and Release Control System (NG) .... SAWMARCS
Standard Allowed Hours .... SAH
Standard American Diet (DAVI) .... SAD
Standard Analysis Method .... SAM
Standard Analysis Software System [*Astronomy*] .... SASS
Standard Analytical Reference Material (MCD) .... SARM
Standard and Nuclear Propulsion Module .... SNPM
Standard & Poor's (DFIT) .... S&P
Standard & Poor's 100 Stock Index (DFIT) .... OEX
Standard & Poor's 500 Index Subordinated Notes .... SPIN
Standard and Poor's Compustat Services (NITA) .... SPCS
Standard & Poor's COMPUSTAT Services, Inc. [*Also, an information service or system*] (IID) .... SPCS
Standard & Poor's Corp. .... S & P
Standard & Poor's Corp., New York, NY [*Library symbol Library of Congress*] (LCLS) .... NNSPo
Standard & Poor's Dep Receipts [*AMEX symbol*] (TTSB) .... SPY
Standard & Poor's Deposit Receipts [*AMEX symbol*] (SPSG) .... SPY
Standard & Poors Depositary Receipts [*Associated Press*] (SAG) .... SPDR
Standard and Poor's Index - Composite [*Stock market*] .... SPIC
Standard and Poor's Index - Industrials [*Stock market*] .... SPII
Standard and Poor's Index - Rails [*Stock market*] .... SPIR
Standard and Poor's Index - Utilities [*Stock market*] .... SPIU
Standard and Poor's Indexed Note (TDOB) .... SPIN
Standard & Poor's MidCap 400 Depository Receipts [*AMEX symbol*] (SAG) .... MDY
Standard & Poor's MidCap 400 Depository Receipts [*Associated Press*] (SAG) .... SPMid
Standard & Poor's MidCap Dep Rc [*AMEX symbol*] (TTSB) .... MDY
Standard & Poor's Trading Systems [*Standard & Poor's Corp.*] [*Information service or system*] (IID) .... S & PTS
Standard Antiradiation Missile (MCD) .... SARM
Standard Apple Numerics Environment [*Software*] [*Apple Computers, Inc.*] .... SANE
Standard Area of Tinplate [*100,000 square inches*] .... SAT
Standard Army Ammunition System (AABC) .... SAAS
Standard Army Automated Contracting System (RDA) .... SAACONS
Standard Army Civilian Pay System .... STARCIPS
Standard Army Civilian Pay System Redesign (GFGA) .... STARCIPS-R
Standard Army Commissary Operating Manual .... STACOM
Standard Army Data Elements Systems (MCD) .... STADES
Standard Army Financial Inventory Accounting and Reporting System .... STARFIARS
Standard Army Intermediate Level Supply System [*or Subsystem*] .... SAILS
Standard Army Logistics System .... SALS
Standard Army Maintenance System (AABC) .... SAMS
Standard Army Management Information System (MCD) .... SAMIS
Standard Army Management Information System .... STAMIS
Standard Army Management Language (AABC) .... SAML
Standard Army Management System - Supply Support Arrangement .... SAMSA
Standard Army Multicommand Management Information System (MCD) .... STAMMIS
Standard Army Nonappropriated System (MCD) .... STANS
Standard Army Publications System .... STARPUBS
Standard Army Retail Supply System .... SARSS
Standard Army Retail Supply System/Objective Supply Capability (RDA) .... SARSS/OSC
Standard Army Supply System .... SASS
Standard Army Vetronics Architecture (RDA) .... SAVA
Standard Assembly Module [*Eastman Kodak Co.*] .... SAM
Standard Asset Management and Disposition Agreement [*Resolution Trust Corp.*] .... SAMDA
Standard Atmosphere .... AS
Standard Attitude Heading Reference System (MCD) .... SAHRS
Standard Australian English .... SAE
Standard Automated Financial System [*Navy*] (GFGA) .... STAFS
Standard Automated Material Management System [*DoD*] .... SAMM
Standard Automated Materiel Management System [*DoD*] .... SAMMS
Standard Average European .... SAE
Standard Average Hour (HGAA) .... SAH
Standard Avionics Integrated Fuzing [*Air Force*] .... SAIF
Standard Avionics Module (MCD) .... SAM
Standard Babylonian (BJA) .... SB
Standard Base Supply System [*Military*] (AFIT) .... SBSS
Standard Battery Grade .... SBG
Standard Battle Plan Emplacement [*Military*] .... SBPE
Standard Bead .... SB
Standard Beam Approach [*British aircraft landing method*] .... SBA
Standard Bibliographic Description .... SBD
Standard Bicarbonate [*Pharmacology*] (DAVI) .... SBC
Standard Big Bang Nucleosynthesis [*Cosmology*] .... SBBN
Standard Book Number .... SBN
Standard Boundary Condition .... SBC
Standard Brands Paint Co. [*NYSE symbol*] (SPSG) .... SBP
Standard Brands Paint Co. [*Associated Press*] (SAG) .... StBPt
Standard Broadcasting Corp. Ltd. [*Toronto Stock Exchange symbol*] .... STR
Standard Buried Collector [*Circuit*] .... SBC
Standard Buried Collector Integrated Circuit (IAA) .... SBCIC
Standard Business Software Award (NITA) .... SBSA
Standard Businessowners Policy [*Insurance*] .... SBP
Standard Busy Rate (NATG) .... SBR
Standard Calomel Electrode .... SCE
Standard Candle [*Power*] .... SC
Standard Capacitance (IDOE) .... C_S
Standard Capital Superannuation Benefit [*British*] .... SCSB
Standard Card Enclosure [*Business term*] (MHDI) .... SCE
Standard Cardiopulmonary Resuscitation .... SCPR
Standard Carriers Alpha Code (MCD) .... SCAC
Standard Cascade Form (IAA) .... SCF
Standard Central Air Data Computer .... SCADC
Standard Change Integration and Tracking (NASA) .... SCIT
Standard Channel (IAA) .... SC
Standard Charge Factor (NASA) .... SCF
Standard Chartered [*International bank*] [*British*] .... STANCHART
Standard Chartered Bank Australia Ltd. (ADA) .... SCBAL
Standard Chartered Leasing (NITA) .... SCL
Standard Chartered Merchant Bank [*Singapore*] .... SCMB
Standard Civilian Personnel Management Information System [*Army*] .... SCIPMIS

Standard Classification List [Military] .... SCL
Standard Combat Oriented Recurring Evaluation System [Military] .... SCORES
Standard Command Supply Review System - SAILS .... SCSRS-S
Standard Commands for Programmable Controllers (ACII) .... SCPI
Standard Commercial [NYSE symbol] (TTSB) .... STW
Standard Commercial Corp. [Associated Press] (SAG) .... StdCm
Standard Commercial Corp. [NYSE symbol] (SPSG) .... STW
Standard Commodity Classification [Military] .... SCC
Standard Commodity Classification System (NG) .... SCC
Standard Commodity Codes (MCD) .... SCE
Standard Communication Environment (DOMA) .... SCE
Standard Compliance Review Report (AAGC) .... SCRR
Standard Computer Output Microform [Army] .... STACOM
Standard Computer Software Number .... SCSN
Standard COMSEC [Communications Security] Facility Equipment List ... SCFEL
Standard Conditions .... SC
Standard Configuration and Modification Program [Military] .... SCAMP
Standard Configuration Management Systems [Military] (AFIT) ... SCMS
Standard Consolidated Area [Bureau of Census] .... SCA
Standard Consolidated Statistical Area [Census Bureau] .... SCSA
Standard Consultative Commission [for resolving compliance disputes arising
　from SALT 1 accord] .... SCC
Standard Controlled Heteroydne Oscillator .... SCHO
Standard Conventional Load .... SCL
Standard Coordinate System (KSC) .... SCS
Standard Corporate Protocol [Telecommunications] .... SCP
Standard Corps-Army-MACOM [Major Army Command] Personnel System
　(AABC) .... SCAMPERS
Standard Costing of Laboratory Resources .... SCOLAR
Standard Cross-Cultural Sample [Human Relations Area Files] [Information
　retrieval] .... SCCS
Standard Cubic Centimeter (KSC) .... SCC
Standard Cubic Centimeters per Hour (MCD) .... SCCH
Standard Cubic Centimeters per Minute (NASA) .... SCCM
Standard Cubic Centimeters per Second (NASA) .... SCCS
Standard Cubic Feet (WDAA) .... STDFT³
Standard Cubic Feet per Day .... SCFD
Standard Cubic Feet per Hour (AAG) .... SCFH
Standard Cubic Feet per Minute (DAVI) .... scf/min
Standard Cubic Feet per Minute .... SCFM
Standard Cubic Feet per Second (AAG) .... SCFS
Standard Cubic Foot .... SCF
Standard Cubic Inches per Minute (AAG) .... SCIM
Standard Cubic Inches per Second (NASA) .... SCIS
Standard Cubic Meter .... SCM
Standard Data Chain .... SDC
Standard Data Element [Army] (AABC) .... SDE
Standard Data Element and Codes [Air Force] .... SDE & C
Standard Data Elements System (MCD) .... STADES
Standard Data Format [Computer science] (CDE) .... SDF
Standard Data Interface [Computer science] .... SDI
Standard Data Processor (SSD) .... SDP
Standard Data Terminal .... SDT
Standard Decision (MCD) .... SD
Standard Deduction .... SD
Standard Definition [Electronics] .... SD
Standard Delivery Date [Military] .... SDD
Standard Depot Level Maintenance (MCD) .... SDLM
Standard Depot Management Information System [Army] ... SDMIS
Standard Depot System [Army] .... SDS
Standard Design [of a vessel] (DS) .... SD
Standard Design Platform .... SPD
Standard Deviation [Also, SD] [Statistics] .... s
Standard Deviation [Also, s] .... SD
Standard Deviation (MCD) .... STD/DEV
Standard Deviation above the Mean [Statistics] .... SDAM
Standard Deviation Interval [Medicine] .... SDI
Standard Deviation of Means [Statistics] .... SDOM
Standard Deviation of Standard Deviation [Statistics] ... SDOSD
Standard Deviation of the Logarithm [Statistics] .... SDL
Standard Deviation of the Mean (AAMN) .... SDM
Standard Deviation of the Regression [Statistics] .... SDR
Standard Deviation Unit [Statistics] (MAE) .... SDU
Standard Deviation Waveform [Physics] .... STDW
Standard Device Byte (IAA) .... SDB
Standard d'Exchange et de Transfert [Computer graphics] [French] ... SET
Standard Digital Data Recorder (DWSG) .... SDDR
Standard Dimension Ratio (DAC) .... SDR
Standard Disk Filing System .... SDFS
Standard Distance File (DOMA) .... SDF
Standard Distance Package (DOMA) .... SDP
Standard Distribution Format [Computer science] .... SDF
Standard Distribution List [NASA] .... SDL
Standard Distribution List [NASA] (NASA) .... STDL
Standard Document Interchange Format [Telecommunications] ... SD
Standard Dress [Military British] .... SD
Standard Dress Blue [Navy] (DOMA) .... SDB
Standard Drive Interface [Computer science] (CDE) ...... SDI
Standard Drug File [Derwent Publications Ltd.] [Database] ... SDF
Standard Earth Observation Satellite (MCD) .... S/EOS
Standard Electric Kirk (NITA) .... SEK
Standard Electric Puhelinteollisius (NITA) .... SEP
Standard Electrica, Sociedad Anonima [Brazilian affiliate of ITT] ... SESA
Standard Electrik Hellas (NITA) .... SEH
Standard Electronic Accounting Language [Computer science] (BUR) ... SEAL

Standard Electronic Assembly .... SEA
Standard Electronic Automatic Computer (IAA) .... SEAC
Standard Electronic Module (CAAL) .... SEM
Standard Electronic Module RADAR (PDAA) .... SEMR
Standard Electronic Module-E Format (MCD) .... SEM-E
Standard Electronic Package .... SEP
Standard Electronics Module Program (MCD) .... SEMP
Standard Elektrik Lorenz AG [Germany] .... SEL
Standard ELINT Data System Codes and Format (NVT) ... SEDSCAF
Standard End Effector (NASA) .... SEE
Standard Engineering Practice (AAG) .... SEP
Standard English .... SE
[The] Standard English Language Typewriter Keyboard (BARN) ..... QWERTY
Standard Entry/Exit System [Army] .... SEES
Standard Equipment Modules [Navy] (DOMA) .... SEM
Standard Equipment Nomenclature List [Military] .... SENL
Standard Equipment Practice (IAA) .... STEP
Standard Error .... SE
Standard Error of Calibration .... SEC
Standard Error of Estimate .... SEE
Standard Error of Measurement [Testing] .... SEM
Standard Error of Prediction .... SEP
Standard Error of the Mean .... SEM
Standard Estimating Module (IEEE) .... SEM
Standard Etac Corp. [Toronto Stock Exchange symbol] ... SDE
Standard Evaluation Cylinder (MCD) .... SEC
Standard Evaluation Procedure [Environmental Protection Agency] ... SEP
Standard Excess Profits Tax Reporter [Commerce Clearing House]
　[A publication] (DLA) .... Stand Ex Prof Tax Rep
Standard External Cardiopulmonary Resuscitation .... SECPR
Standard External File .... SEF
Standard Facility Equipment Card [Electronics] .... SFEC
Standard Facility Equipment List [Electronics] .... SFEL
Standard Facility Material List [Electronics] .... SFML
Standard Facility Years [FAA] .... SFY
Standard Fading Hour [National Institute of Standards and Technology] ... SFH
Standard Family Interaction Test [Psychology] .... SFIT
Standard Fdg Corp. [NASDAQ symbol] (TTSB) .... SFUN
Standard Federal Bancorp [Associated Press] (SAG) ... StdFdBcp
Standard Federal Bank [NYSE symbol] (SPSG) .... SFB
Standard Federal Tax Reporter [Commerce Clearing House] [A publication]
　(DLA) .... Stand Fed Tax Rep
Standard Federal Tax Reporter (Commerce Clearing House)
　[A publication] (DLA) .... CCH Stand Fed Tax Rep
Standard Fedl Bancorp'n [NYSE symbol] (TTSB) .... SFB
Standard File Format .... SFF
Standard Finance System Redesign [DoD] (GFGA) .... STANFINS-R
Standard Financial [NASDAQ symbol] (SAG) .... STND
Standard Financial Co. [Associated Press] (SAG) ...... StdFincl
Standard Financial System [Military] (AABC) .... STANFINS
Standard Firing Unit [NASA] (NASA) .... SFU
Standard Fixation Preference Test [Laboratory science] (DAVI) ... SFPT
Standard Flight Data Recorder .... SFDR
Standard for the Exchange of Product Data [Materials science] ... STEP
Standard for the Uniform Scheduling of Drugs and Poisons (EERA) ... SUSDP
Standard Form .... SF
Standard Format for Exchange of MAPMOPP Data among Data Centers
　(MSC) .... SYNDARC
Standard Forms Bureau Form [Insurance] (IIA) .... SFBF
Standard Freight Trade Classification [Council for Mutual Economic
　Assistance] (DS) .... SFTC
Standard Frequency .... SF
Standard Frequency and Time Signals (IEEE) .... SFTS
Standard Frequency Station [ITU designation] .... SS
Standard Fuel Assembly [Nuclear energy] (NRCH) ...... SFA
Standard Fuel Savings Advisor System .... SFSAS
Standard Funding Corp. [NASDAQ symbol] (SAG) ...... SFUN
Standard Funding Corp. [Associated Press] (SAG) ..... StdFndg
Standard (Galilean) Telescopes [Instrumentation] ...... STS
Standard Generalized Markup Language [Also, GSML] [International
　Standards Organization] .... SGML
Standard Geographical Classification [Canada] .... SGC
Standard Geographical Unit (WDMC) .... SGU
Standard Georgia Practice [A publication] (DLA) ...... Stand GA Prac
Standard Glucose Tolerance Test [Medicine] (DMAA) ... SGTT
Standard Gold Mines Ltd. [Vancouver Stock Exchange symbol] ... SDA
Standard Government Travel Request .... SGTR
Standard Graphic Interface [XOR Systems] .... SGI
Standard Ground Support Equipment .... SGSE
Standard Guidance Package .... SGP
Standard Hardware Interface Program .... SHIP
Standard Hardware Program [Military] .... SHP
Standard Heavy Spanwire [Military] (CAAL) .... SHS
Standard High-Level Query Language .... SQL
Standard Holding Pattern [Aviation] .... SHP
Standard Holding Pattern [Aviation] .... SP
Standard Holding Procedure [Aviation] .... SHP
Standard Hourly Rate .... SHR
Standard Hydrogen Electrode [Electrochemistry] .... SHE
Standard Identification for Individuals [Social security] [American National
　Standards Institute] .... SII
Standard Image Format [Computer science] .... SIF
Standard Independent Data Format Association .... SIDF
Standard Index Base (DNAB) .... SIB
Standard Indexing System [DoD] .... SIS

Standard Industrial Classification [*File indexing code*] [*Also, an information service or system*] .... SIC
Standard Industrial Classification 72 (NITA) .... SIC 72
Standard Industrial Trade Classification [*United Nations*] .... SITC
Standard Industry Code (PCM) .... SIC
Standard Information Display System [*Military*] (CAAL) .... SIDS
Standard Information Retrieval Capability for Users [*Army*] .... SIRCUS
Standard Initial Provisioning System (MCD) .... SIP
Standard Injection Method [*Laboratory science*] .... SIM
Standard Input/Output (MCD) .... SIO
Standard Inside Diameter Dimension Ratio (DAC) .... SIDD
Standard Inspection Criteria .... SIC
Standard Inspection Procedure [*Military*] .... SIP
Standard Installation/Division Personnel System [*Military*] (AABC) .... SIDPERS
Standard Installation Instruction Technical Order (SAA) .... SIITO
Standard Instruction Set (MSA) .... SIS
Standard Instrument Approach [*RADAR*] [*Aviation*] .... SIA
Standard Instrument Approach [*RADAR*] [*Aviation*] .... STIAP
Standard Instrument Approach Procedure [*Aviation*] .... SIAP
Standard Instrument Departure [*RADAR*] [*Aviation*] .... SID
Standard Integrated Supply/Transportation Manifest System [*Military*] (AABC) .... SISTMS
Standard Integrated Support Management System [*Joint Chiefs of Staff*] .... SISMS
Standard Interchange Data Form [*Computer science*] (MHDI) .... SIDF
Standard Interchange Format .... SIF
Standard Interest Profile .... SIP
Standard Interface (IAA) .... SIF
Standard Interface Adapter .... SIA
Standard Interface Connector (SSD) .... SIC
Standard Interface Control Electronics (ECII) .... SICE
Standard Interface Document (NASA) .... SID
Standard Interface Specification [*NASA*] (GFGA) .... SIS
Standard Interline Passenger Procedures Manual [*Air Traffic Conference of America*] [*IATA*] (DS) .... SIPP
Standard International Trade Classification .... SITC
Standard International Unit (IAA) .... SI
Standard Interpretation and Compilation System (IAA) .... STICO
Standard Iron Bar (MSA) .... SIB
Standard Item Location Index .... SILI
Standard Jack and Jennet Registry of America (EA) .... SJJR
Standard Jet Penetration [*Aviation*] .... SJP
Standard Jewish Encyclopedia [*A publication*] .... SJE
Standard Label [*Computer science*] .... SL
Standard Laboratory Module .... SLM
Standard Landing Craft Unit [*Military*] .... SLCU
Standard Landing Craft Unit [*Military*] .... STANLANCRU
Standard Lap Turn Method (NVT) .... SLTM
Standard Launch Complex (KSC) .... SLC
Standard Launch Vehicle .... SLV
Standard Length .... SL
Standard Level User Charge .... SLUC
Standard Library Identification Number .... SLIN
Standard Life Association (EA) .... SLA
Standard Light Rail Vehicle [*Mass transit*] .... SLRV
Standard Light Source (IAA) .... SLT
Standard Light Spanwire [*Military*] (CAAL) .... SLS
Standard Lightweight Avionics Equipment [*Army*] (RDA) .... SLAE
Standard Line Item Number [*Army*] (AABC) .... SLIN
Standard Listen Output Program (IAA) .... SLOP
Standard Load [*Automotive engineering*] .... SL
Standard Location [*Civil Defense*] .... SL
Standard Location Area [*Civil Defense*] .... SLA
Standard Location Codes .... SLC
Standard Long Play [*VHS recorder playing time mode*] (NTCM) .... SLP
Standard Low-Frequency Range Approach .... SLRAP
Standard Machinery Control Console [*Canadian Navy*] .... SMCC
Standard Maintenance Allowance .... SMA
Standard Maintenance Management System [*Military*] (CAAL) .... SMMS
Standard Maintenance Procedure .... SMP
Standard Malaysian Rubber [*Grade of natural rubber*] .... SMR
Standard Management [*NASDAQ symbol*] (TTSB) .... SMAN
Standard Management Corp. [*NASDAQ symbol*] (SAG) .... SMAN
Standard Management Corp. [*Associated Press*] (SAG) .... StdMgt
Standard Manned Space Flight Initiator [*Later, NSI-I*] [*NASA*] (NASA) .... SMSI
Standard Markup Language [*Computer science*] .... SML
Standard Matched .... SM
Standard Matched (DAC) .... StdM
Standard Material Specification (MCD) .... SMS
Standard Materials Worksheet [*NASA*] (NASA) .... SMW
Standard Mean Chord [*Aviation*] (AIA) .... SMC
Standard Mean Ocean Water .... SMOW
Standard Measurement Technique [*Navy*] .... SMT
Standard Measuring Instrument .... SMI
Standard Mechanical Interface (NITA) .... SMIF
Standard Medical Examination [*Military*] .... SME
Standard Medium-Accuracy Navigator .... SMAN
Standard Memoranda (AAG) .... SM
Standard Memory Loader Verifier (DWSG) .... SMLV
Standard Merchants Bank [*British*] .... SMB
Standard Message Trunk Design System [*Telecommunications*] (TEL) .... SMETDS
Standard Messaging Format [*Computer science*] (CDE) .... SMF
Standard Metal Window (WDAA) .... SMW
Standard Meteorological Station (SAA) .... SMS
Standard Method of Measurement (IEEE) .... SMM

Standard Method of Measurement for Civil Engineering Quantities (PDAA) .... SMMCEQ
Standard Methods .... SM
Standard Methods Agar [*Microbiology*] .... SMA
Standard Methods of Measuring Performance (IEEE) .... SMMP
Standard Metropolitan Statistical Area [*Later, MSA*] [*Census Bureau*] .... SMSA
Standard Mgmt 11% Cv 'S' Pfd [*NASDAQ symbol*] (TTSB) .... SMANP
Standard Microfilm Reproductions Ltd., Scarborough, ON, Canada [*Library symbol Library of Congress*] (LCLS) .... XmC
Standard Microsystems [*NASDAQ symbol*] (TTSB) .... SMSC
Standard Microsystems Corp. [*NASDAQ symbol*] (NQ) .... SMSC
Standard Microsystems Corp. [*Associated Press*] (SAG) .... StdMic
Standard MIDI [*Musical Instrument Digital Interface*] **File** .... SMF
Standard Mineral Base [*Medium*] [*Medicine*] .... SMB
Standard Mirror Hybrid (MCD) .... SMH
Standard Missile .... SM
Standard Missile Correlation Task Group [*Military*] .... SMCTG
Standard Missile Medium-Range (SAA) .... SMMR
Standard Mixed Cargo Harness (NASA) .... SMCH
Standard Modular System .... SMS
Standard Modular System Card [*Computer science*] (BUR) .... SMSC
Standard Molding Corp. .... SMC
Standard Molecular System .... SMS
Standard Monthly Maintenance Charge (NITA) .... SMMC
Standard Morbidity Ratio (MAE) .... SMR
Standard Mortality Rate .... SMR
Standard Motor Prod [*NYSE symbol*] (TTSB) .... SMP
Standard Motor Products, Inc. [*NYSE symbol*] (SPSG) .... SMP
Standard Motor Products, Inc. [*Associated Press*] (SAG) .... StMotr
Standard Motor Pump .... SMP
Standard Motorists Centre [*Automotive sales and service chain*] [*British*] .... SMC
Standard Municipal Library, Alberta [*Library symbol National Library of Canada*] (NLC) .... ASTM
Standard Municipal Library, Standard, AB, Canada [*Library symbol Library of Congress*] (LCLS) .... CaAStM
Standard Music Description Language [*Computer science*] .... SMDL
Standard Name Line [*Military*] .... SNL
Standard National Account [*Economics*] .... SNA
Standard Navigation Computer .... SNC
Standard Navy Accounting Procedures .... SNAP
Standard Navy Distribution List .... SNDL
Standard Navy Maintenance and Material Management Information System .... SNMMMIS
Standard Navy Maintenance and Material Management System .... SNMMMS
Standard Navy Maintenance Data Collection System .... SNMDCS
Standard Navy Stock List .... SNSL
Standard Navy Stock Number .... SNSN
Standard Network Access Protocol [*Computer science*] .... SNAP
Standard Network Interconnection [*Telecommunications*] .... SNI
Standard Nine Score [*Military*] .... STANINE
Standard Nomenclature .... SN
Standard Nomenclature List [*Military*] .... SNDL
Standard Nomenclature List [*Military*] .... SNL
Standard Nomenclature of Athletic Injuries [*Medicine*] (MAE) .... SNAI
Standard Nomenclature of Diseases and Operations [*Medicine*] .... SNDO
Standard Nomenclature of Diseases and Operations [*Medicine*] (DHSM) .... SNODO
Standard Nomenclature of Pathology [*College of American Pathologists*] .... SNOP
Standard Normal Distribution [*Mathematics*] .... SND
Standard Normal Ocean Water .... SNOW
Standard Notes and Parts Selection (TEL) .... SNAPS
Standard Occupational Classifications (OICC) .... SOC
Standard of Automotive Engineers (IAA) .... SAE
Standard of Living .... SL
Standard of Living .... SOL
Standard of Training, Certification, and Watchkeeping Convention (DS) .... STCW
Standard Oil [*Trademark in foreign use only; superseded in US, 1973, by Exxon*] .... ESSO
Standard Oil Co. .... SOC
Standard Oil Co. (Indiana) .... STANOLIND
Standard Oil Co. (Indiana), Central Research Library, Naperville, IL [*OCLC symbol*] (OCLC) .... JAW
Standard Oil Co. (New Jersey), New York, NY [*Library symbol Library of Congress*] (LCLS) .... NNStOD
Standard Oil Co. of California .... SOCAL
Standard Oil Co. of California .... SOCO
Standard Oil Co. of California .... STANCAL
Standard Oil Co. of California, San Francisco, CA [*Library symbol Library of Congress*] (LCLS) .... CSfSO
Standard Oil Co. of New York [*Socony Mobil is now official name of firm*] .... SOCONY
Standard Oil Co. of Texas, Houston, TX [*Library symbol Library of Congress*] (LCLS) .... TxHSOC
Standard Oil Co. (Ohio) .... SOHIO
Standard Oil Research Center, Naperville, IL [*Library symbol Library of Congress*] (LCLS) .... INapS
Standard Omnirange Approach .... SORAP
Standard Online Module (NITA) .... SOM
Standard Operating Instruction (KSC) .... SOI
Standard Operating Manual [*NASA*] (NASA) .... SOM
Standard Operating Plan (OICC) .... SOP
Standard [*or Standing*] Operating Procedure .... SOP
Standard Operating Procedure Amplified (GAVI) .... SOPA
Standard Operating Procedure/Maintenance Requirement (MCD) .... SOP/MR

Standard Operating Report ... SOR
Standard Operating Rules ... SOR
Standard Operations and Maintenance Squadron (DNAB) ... SOMS
Standard Optical Test Equipment ... SOTE
Standard Option Equipment (DOMA) ... SOE
Standard or Peculiar (NASA) ... SP
Standard Orbital Parameter Message [*NASA*] (KSC) ... SOPM
Standard Pacific [*NYSE symbol*] (TTSB) ... SPF
Standard Page Description Language [*ISO/IEC*] [*Computer science*] ... SPDL
Standard Page Specification Association (BTTJ) ... SPSA
Standard Parallel Port [*Computer science*] (CDE) ... SPP
Standard Payload Display and Control Interface (NASA) ... SPDCI
Standard Payload Interface Facility [*NASA*] (MCD) ... SPIF
Standard Payload Module (MCD) ... SPM
Standard Penetration Test [*Nuclear energy*] (NRCH) ... SPT
Standard Pennsylvania Practice [*A publication*] (DLA) ... PA Prac
Standard Pennsylvania Practice [*A publication*] (DLA) ... Stan PA Prac
Standard Pennsylvania Practice [*A publication*] (DLA) ... Stand PA Prac
Standard Performance Indicator [*Army*] ... SPI
Standard Performance Indicator Dictionary [*Army*] ... SPID
Standard Performance Summary Charts (AAG) ... SPSC
Standard Perfusion Fluid [*Medicine*] (DMAA) ... SPF
Standard Periodical Database [*Oxbridge Communications, Inc.*] [*Information service or system*] (CRD) ... SPD
Standard Periodical Directory [*A publication*] ... SPD
Standard Peripherals (IAA) ... SP
Standard Personnel Information Retrieval System [*Military*] ... SPIRES
Standard Pesticide File [*Derwent Publications Ltd.*] [*Database*] ... SPF
Standard Phase-Locked Loop ... SPLL
Standard Pile [*Nuclear reactor*] ... SP
Standard Pipe Size ... SPS
Standard Plate Agar [*Microbiology*] (OA) ... SPA
Standard Plate Count [*Microbiology*] ... SPC
Standard Platinum Resistance Thermometer ... SPRT
Standard Play [*Video technology*] ... SP
Standard Point Location Code [*American Trucking Association and Association of American Railroads*] ... SPLC
Standard Police Automated Resource Management Information System ... SPARMIS
Standard Polishing Index ... SPE
Standard Port System (MCD) ... SPS
Standard Positioning Service ... SPS
Standard Positioning Service ... SPS
Standard Potential [*Symbol*] [*Physics*] (DAVI) ... E
Standard Practice [*or Procedure*] ... SP
Standard Practice Amendment (AAG) ... SPA
Standard Practice Bulletin (MCD) ... SPB
Standard Practice Directive [*NASA*] (NASA) ... SPD
Standard Practice Instructions (MCD) ... SPI
Standard Practice Memo (MCD) ... SPM
Standard Practice Procedures (MCD) ... SPP
Standard Precision Navigator ... SPN
Standard Precision Navigator/Gimbaled Electrostatic-Gyro Aircraft Navigation System (MCD) ... SPN/GEANS
Standard Precision Navigator/Gimballed Electrostatic Aircraft Navigation System ... SPN/GEANS
Standard Preparation Method ... SPM
Standard Pressure (IAA) ... SP
Standard Price ... SP
Standard Procedure Instructions (KSC) ... SPIN
Standard Procedure Manual (AAG) ... SPM
Standard Procedure Monitor Chart (PDAA) ... SPMC
Standard Process Manual ... SPM
Standard Process Specification (MCD) ... SPS
Standard Procurement System (AAGC) ... SPS
Standard Product Numbering System (PDAA) ... SPNS
Standard Production Information Systems (NITA) ... SPIS
Standard Products [*NYSE symbol*] (TTSB) ... SPD
Standard Products Committee [*Navy*] ... SPC
Standard Products Co. [*NYSE symbol*] (SPSG) ... SPD
Standard Products Co. [*Associated Press*] (SAG) ... StdProd
Standard Program [*Computer science*] (BUR) ... SP
Standard Program [*Computer science*] (IAA) ... STP
Standard Program Device (NITA) ... SPD
Standard Program Facility (NITA) ... SPF
Standard Programming Logic [*Computer science*] (IAA) ... SPL
Standard Progressive Matrices [*Also, Raven's Coloured Progressive Matrices*] [*A type of intelligence test*] (PAZ) ... SPM
Standard Project Flood [*Nuclear energy*] (NRCH) ... SPF
Standard Project Storm [*Nuclear energy*] (NRCH) ... SPS
Standard Property Book System [*Army*] ... SPBS
Standard Property Book System - Redesign [*or Redesigned*] [*Army*] ... SPBS-R
Standard Proportionate Mortality Ratio [*Medicine*] (DMAA) ... SPMR
Standard Propulsion Unit (IAA) ... SPU
Standard Protective Item ... SPI
Standard Prototype Microcomputer (NITA) ... SPM
Standard Psychiatric [*Medicine*] (DMAA) ... StanPsych
Standard Pulse LASER ... SPL
Standard Quantum Limit [*Physics*] ... SQL
Standard Quarter Horse Association (EA) ... SQHA
Standard Query Language [*Computer science*] ... SQL
Standard RADAR Environment ... SRE
Standard Radio & Telefon (NITA) ... SRT
Standard Random Sample ... SRS
Standard Range Approach [*Aviation*] ... SR
Standard Range Approach [*Aviation*] ... SRAP
Standard Rate and Data (IAA) ... SRD
Standard Rate and Data Service, Inc. [*Information service or system*] (MCD) ... SRDS
Standard Rate Turn (NVT) ... SRT
Standard Raven's Progressive Matrix [*Psychiatry*] (DAVI) ... SRPM
Standard Reactor Island Design [*Nuclear energy*] (NRCH) ... STRIDE
Standard Recovery Completion Time ... SRCT
Standard Reference Aerosol (PDAA) ... SRA
Standard Reference Data ... SRD
Standard Reference Data Center ... SRDC
Standard Reference Data System (DIT) ... SRDS
Standard Reference Library ... SRL
Standard Reference Material [*National Institute of Standards and Technology*] ... SRM
Standard Reference Module ... SRM
Standard Reference Section ... SRS
Standard Reference Water Sample [*US Geological Survey*] ... SRWS
Standard Register [*NYSE symbol*] (TTSB) ... SR
[*The*] **Standard Register Co.** [*NASDAQ symbol*] (NQ) ... SREG
Standard Register Co. [*Associated Press*] (SAG) ... StdReg
Standard Register Co., Engineering and Research Library, Dayton, OH [*Library symbol Library of Congress*] (LCLS) ... ODaSR
Standard Relative Power ... SRP
Standard Remote Terminal ... SRT
Standard Repair (AAG) ... SR
Standard Repair Design [*Navy*] (MCD) ... SRD
Standard Repair Manual (MCD) ... SRM
Standard Repair Procedures ... SRP
Standard Repair Specification (MCD) ... SRS
Standard Reporting Designator (MCD) ... SRD
Standard Requirement ... SR
Standard Requirements Code [*Military*] ... SRC
Standard Requisition and Issue Procedures [*Military*] (CINC) ... STRIP
Standard Research Institute (MCD) ... SRI
Standard Resistor (IAA) ... SR
Standard Review Plan [*Nuclear energy*] (NRCH) ... SRP
Standard Routine (IAA) ... STAR
Standard Safety Analysis Report [*Nuclear energy*] (NRCH) ... SSAR
Standard Saline Citrate ... SSC
Standard Saline Citrate Phosphate [*A buffer*] ... SSCP
Standard Saybolt Furol [*Oil viscosity*] ... SSF
Standard Saybolt Universal [*Oil viscosity*] ... SSU
Standard Scalable and Portable [*Standard High-Level Query Language*] [*Benchmark test for relational database systems*] (PCM) ... AS3AP
Standard Schedule Message (DA) ... SSM
Standard Schnauzer Club of America (EA) ... SSCA
Standard Score [*Psychology*] ... SS
Standard Score [*Psychology*] ... Z
Standard Scratch Score [*Golf*] ... SSS
Standard Seawater Service [*British*] ... SSS
Standard Security Operating Procedure (SSD) ... SSOP
Standard Serial Numbers (DIT) ... SSN
Standard Shipboard Inspection and Testing Form [*Navy*] (DNAB) ... SSITF
Standard Ship's Organization and Regulations Manual [*Navy*] (NVT) ... SSORM
Standard Shop Practice (MCD) ... SSP
Standard Signal Generator (IAA) ... SSG
Standard Single Account (INF) ... SSA
Standard Single Account File [*Number*] (MCD) ... SSAF
Standard Size (ADA) ... SS
Standard Small Launch Vehicle (DOMA) ... SSLV
Standard Software Base (MCD) ... SSB
Standard Source Data Package (AFIT) ... SSDP
Standard Space Guidance System ... SSGS
Standard Space Launch System [*BSD*] ... SSLS
Standard Space Launch Vehicle ... SSLV
Standard Speed Radial [*Automobile tires*] ... SR
Standard Spending Assessment [*Department of the Environment*] [*British*] ... SSA
Standard Stability Prediction (MCD) ... SSP
Standard Statistical Establishment List [*Bureau of the Census*] ... SSEL
Standard Study Number [*Military*] ... SSN
Standard Study Numbering System [*Military*] (AABC) ... SSNS
Standard Subject Identification Code (NVT) ... SSIC
Standard Submarine Operations and Regulations Manual (DOMA) ... SSORM
Standard Subroutine Package ... SSP
Standard Supply System [*Army*] (RDA) ... 3S
Standard Supply System [*Army*] (AABC) ... SSS
Standard Supply Transportation Manifest System ... SSTMS
Standard Support and Environmental Impact Statement [*Environmental Protection Agency*] (GFGA) ... SSEIS
Standard Surfacing Mat [*Fiberglass*] ... SSM
Standard Switch Panel (MCD) ... SSP
Standard System Applications [*Military*] ... SSA
Standard Systems Center [*Military*] ... SSC
Standard Systems Command (AAGC) ... SSC
Standard Systems Improvement Program ... SSIP
Standard Tachymetric Anti-Aircraft Gun [*British military*] (DMA) ... STAAG
Standard Tactical Operating Condition ... STOC
Standard Tanks, Racks, Adapter, and Pylon Packages (MCD) ... STRAPP
Standard Tape Executive Package [*or Program*] [*NCR Corp.*] ... STEP
Standard Tape Executive System (NITA) ... STEP
Standard Tape Print Program [*Computer science*] (IAA) ... STAPP
Standard Taped Routines for Image Processing [*National Institute of Standards and Technology*] ... STRIP
Standard Tariff Agents Code ... STAC

Standard Taxiway Routing .... STR
Standard Technical Data Management Information System (CAAL) .... STEDMIS
Standard Technical Equipment Development Division [*National Security Agen cy*] [*Obsolete*] .... STED
Standard Technical Institute (SSD) .... STI
Standard Technical Report Number .... STRN
Standard Technical Specifications [*Nuclear energy*] (NRCH) .... STS
Standard Techniques for Reporting Information on Value Engineering .... STRIVE
Standard Telecommunications Automatic Recognizer [*Computer science*] .... STAR
Standard Telecommunications Laboratory (IAA) .... STL
Standard Telegraph Level [*Telecommunications*] (TEL) .... STL
Standard Telephon und Radio [*Switzerland*] (NITA) .... STR
Standard Telephone and Cable [*IT & T affiliate*] [*Research center British*] .... STC
Standard Telephones Electronic Computer (MCD) .... STANTEC
Standard Temperature (IAA) .... ST
Standard Temperature and Pressure .... STP
Standard Temperature and Pressure, Dry .... STPD
Standard [*Normal*] **Temperature and Pulse** [*Medicine*] .... STP
Standard Tensioned Alongside Receiver [*Navy*] (NVT) .... STAR
Standard Tensioned Replenishment Alongside Method [*Military*] (NVT) .... STREAM
Standard Terminal Arrival Route [*Aviation*] .... STAR
Standard Terminal Arrival Routes [*Aviation*] (MCD) .... STARS
Standard Terminal Automation Replacement System [*FAA*] (TAG) .... STARS
Standard Terminal Equipment [*Computer science*] (HGAA) .... STE
Standard Terminal Program [*Computer science*] (IEEE) .... STEP
Standard Terrestrial Navigation System (MCD) .... STENS
Standard Test and Administrative Form (SAA) .... STAF
Standard Test Authorization and Report System [*Navy*] .... STAR
Standard Test Chamber (MCD) .... STC
Standard Test Configuration [*NASA*] (NASA) .... STC
Standard Test Dose .... STD
Standard Test Equipment / Internal Combustion Engine .... STE/ICE
Standard Test Equipment Procedure (NG) .... STEP
Standard Test for Syphilis [*Medicine*] .... STS
Standard Test Key [*Computer science*] .... STK
Standard Test Methods Bulletins [*A publication*] (EAAP) .... STM
Standard Test Procedure .... STP
Standard Test Processing Language (NITA) .... STPL
Standard Test Vehicle .... STV
Standard Theater Army Command and Control System (RDA) .... STACCS
Standard Thermal Profile .... STP
Standard Threshold Shift .... STS
Standard Time .... ST
Standard Time and Rate Setting (MHDB) .... STARS
Standard Tool Request .... STR
Standard Torsion Bar (MCD) .... STB
Standard Towing Equipment for Aircraft Maintenance (MCD) .... STEAM
Standard Tractor, Universal with Dozer [*Army*] .... STUD
Standard, TRADOC Automated Retrieval System (MCD) .... STARS
Standard Training Requirements [*Navy*] (NVT) .... STR
Standard Transfer Order .... STATRAFO
Standard Transfer Order .... STO
Standard Transmission Code [*Computer science*] .... STC
Standard Transportation Commodity Classification [*or Code*] .... STCC
Standard Transportation Operations Personnel Property (MCD) .... STOPPS
Standard Transportation Operations Property System (MCD) .... STOPS
Standard Triple Therapy [*For hypertension*] .... STT
Standard Trustco Ltd. [*Toronto Stock Exchange symbol*] .... STD
Standard Tube Feeding [*Gastroenterology*] (DAVI) .... STD TF
Standard Type Material (MCD) .... STM
Standard Type Process (MCD) .... STP
Standard Umbilical Retraction System (NASA) .... SURS
Standard Underwater Research Vehicle .... SURV
Standard Unit of Accounting [*Computer science*] .... SUA
Standard Unit of Processing [*Computer science*] .... SUP
Standard Units and Nomenclature (MCD) .... SUN
Standard Universal Identifier (NITA) .... SUI
Standard Universal Identifying Number .... SUI
Standard UNREP [*Underway Replenishment*] **Receiving Fixture** [*Navy*] (NVT) .... SURF
Standard Upkeep .... SU
Standard Usage Rate Modifier .... SURM
Standard USAREUR Munitions System .... SUMS
Standard User Labels [*Computer science*] .... SUL
Standard Utility Means for Information Transformation [*Computer science*] .... SUMIT
Standard Vacuum Oil Co. .... STANVAC
Standard Vehicle Mounted Launcher [*Army*] .... SVML
Standard Vented Furnace .... SVF
Standard Version Acceptance Test (MCD) .... SVAT
Standard Volume Flow (IAA) .... SVF
Standard Wafer Array Programming .... SWAP
Standard Weapon Station [*Nuclear arms control*] .... SWS
Standard Weather Messages Command and Control System (MCD) .... SWMCCS
Standard Web Offset Press [*Computer science*] (PCM) .... SWOP
Standard Winter .... SW
Standard Wire Gauge [*Telecommunications*] .... SWG
Standard Work Ordering and Reporting Data System [*Army*] .... SWORDS
Standard Work Procedure (SAA) .... SWP
Standard Work Unit (EG) .... SWU
Standard/Working Group (MCD) .... SWG
Standard Working Home [*Pet-adoption terminology*] .... SWH
Standard Wozniak Integrated Machine [*Computer science*] .... SWIM
Standard Written Agreement [*Military*] .... SWAG
Standard Yiddish (BJA) .... StY
Standardbred Owners Association (EA) .... SOA
Standard-Dose Epinephrine [*Medicine*] .... SDE
Standard-Frequency Oscillator (IDOE) .... SFO
Standardised Minimum Rules [*For the treatment of prisoners*] [*Australia*] .... SMR
Standard-Italo Americana Petroli .... SIAP
Standardization [*or Standardized*] (DAVI) .... standard
Standardization (AFM) .... STDN
Standardization (AABC) .... STDZN
Standardization Agreement [*NATO*] .... STANAG
Standardization Agreement [*NATO*] .... STNAG
Standardization and Evaluation Assistance Team [*Military*] .... SEAT
Standardization and Interoperability .... SI
Standardization and Parts Control Program .... SPCP
Standardization Control of Industry Quality Tools [*Military*] (INF) .... SCIT
Standardization Data .... SD
Standardization Data Management Information System .... SDMIS
Standardization Design Memoranda (IEEE) .... SDM
Standardization Directory .... SD
Standardization/Evaluation (AFM) .... S/E
Standardization/Evaluation .... STAN/EVAL
Standardization Evaluation Flight Examiner .... SEFE
Standardization Evaluation Group (AFM) .... SEG
Standardization/Evaluation Review Panel (AFIT) .... SERP
Standardization Field Panel for Artillery and Naval Gunfire Support [*Army*] (AABC) .... SFP-ANGS
Standardization Flight [*Naval Air Training and Operating Procedures Standardization*] (DNAB) .... STANFLT
Standardization Group [*Air Force*] (AFM) .... SG
Standardization Instructor Pilot [*Military*] (AABC) .... SIP
Standardization Management Policy Group .... SMPG
Standardization of Certain Aspects of Operations and Logistics [*Military*] .... SOLOG
Standardization of Tar Products Test Committee .... STPTC
Standardization Order [*Navy*] (NG) .... STANORD
Standardization, Policy, and Coordination Committee [*NATO*] (NATG) .... SPCC
Standardization Report .... SR
Standardization Status Code [*DoD*] .... SSC
Standardized Abnormality Ratio (WDAA) .... SAR
Standardized Admissions Ratios [*Hospital activity analysis*] .... SAR
Standardized Advanced Infrared System [*Army*] .... SAIRS
Standardized Aeronautical Navigation/Guidance [*Program*] [*Air Force*] .... SANG
Standardized Air Quality Monitoring [*Environmental Protection Agency*] .... SAQM
Standardized Army Refueling System (DOMA) .... SARS
Standardized Assessment of Depressive Disorders [*Medicine*] (DMAA) .... SADD
Standardized Care Plans [*for hospitals*] .... SCP
Standardized Cost Categories .... SCC
Standardized Curriculum Oriented Pupil Evaluation (EDAC) .... SCOPE
Standardized Delay Reporting System [*FAA*] (TAG) .... SDRS
Standardized Device (DAVI) .... z
Standardized Discharge Instructions [*for hospital patients*] .... SDI
Standardized Discriminant Function Coefficient .... SDFC
Standardized Distributed Energy Release (MCD) .... SDER
Standardized Environmental Technical Specifications [*Nuclear energy*] (NRCH) .... SETS
Standardized Field Sobriety Test [*NHTSA*] (TAG) .... SFST
Standardized Government Travel Regulations .... SGTR
Standardized Incidence Ratio .... SMI
Standardized Inertial Guidance Multiple Application .... SIGMA
Standardized Integrated Command Post System [*Army*] (INF) .... SICPS
Standardized Job Control Language (PDAA) .... SJCL
Standardized Launcher Vehicle (IAA) .... SLV
Standardized Military Drawing Program (AAGC) .... SMD
Standardized Military Drawings [*Army*] .... SMD
Standardized Mortality Ratio .... SMR
Standardized Mortality Ratio .... SMR
Standardized Normal Distribution .... SND
Standardized Nuclear Unit Power Plant System [*Nuclear reactor combine*] .... SNUPPS
Standardized Operation Research Management System (MCD) .... STORMS
Standardized Oscillator (IDOE) .... stalo
Standardized Performance Battery [*Acoustics*] .... SPB
Standardized Proportional Incidence Ratio [*Epidemiology*] .... SPIR
Standardized Rate Ratio (DMAA) .... SRR
Standardized Solution [*Pharmacy*] .... SS
Standardized Test [*Psychology*] .... ST
Standardized Test of Essential Writing Skills (EDAC) .... STEWS
Standardized Test of Fitness [*Canadian Association of Sports Sciences*] .... STF
Standardized Test Program .... STP
Standard-Modern Technologies Corp. [*Toronto Stock Exchange symbol*] .... SMC
Standard-Pacific Corp. [*NYSE symbol*] (SPSG) .... SPF
Standard-Pacific Corp. [*Associated Press*] (SAG) .... StdPac
Standard-Range Juno [*Survey meter for radiation*] .... SRJ
Standards [*Timber measurement*] (EY) .... STDS
Standards and Calibration Laboratory (KSC) .... SACL
Standards and Control .... S & C
Standards and Ethics Commission [*American Occupational Therapy Association*] .... SEC
Standards and Interface Specification Document .... SISD
Standards and Limits .... S & L
Standards & Practices Division (ACII) .... S&P
Standards and Recommended Practices .... SARP

Standards and Recommended Practices [*International Civil Aviation Organization*] .... SARPS
Standards and Security Compliance Section [*Social Security Administration*] .... SSCS
Standards Association of Australia (BARN) .... SAA
Standards Australia .... SA
Standards Completion Program [*Analytical method procedure, OSHA and NIOSH requirements*] .... SCP
Standards Council of Canada [*See also CCNO*] .... SCC
Standards Council of Canada [*See also CCNO*] .... STCC
Standards Council of Canada [*See also CCNO*] .... STDC
Standards Council of Canada, Ottawa, Ontario [*Library symbol National Library of Canada*] (BIB) .... OOST
Standards Developing Organization .... SDO
Standards Development (IEEE) .... SD
Standards Development Organization .... SDO
Standards Eastern [*or Electronic*] Automatic Computer [*National Institute of Standards and Technology*] .... SEAC
Standards Engineering Society (EA) .... SES
Standards for Management Advisory Services (TDOB) .... SSMAS
Standards in Training Commission [*Army*] (INF) .... STRAC
Standards Information Center of China [*Library*] .... SICC
Standards Information Service [*Standards Council of Canada*] [*Information service or system*] (IID) .... SIS
Standards Information Service [*National Institute of Standards and Technology*] (IID) .... SIS
Standards Institution [*Telecommunications*] .... SI
Standards Laboratory Information Manual (NG) .... SLIM
Standards Manual .... SM
Standards, Methods, and Planning .... SMP
Standards of Conduct Office (AAGC) .... SOCO
Standards of Grade Authorization [*Military*] .... SGA
Standards of Official Conduct [*A publication*] (DLA) .... SOC
Standards of Performance for New Sources [*Power*] (DICI) .... SPNS
Standards of Readiness and Availability (NATG) .... SRA
Standards Parts Listing (MCD) .... SPL
Standards Planning and Requirements Committee [*ANSI*] .... SPARC
Standards Policy Panel (ACII) .... SPP
Standards Promotion Application Group [*Telecommunications*] .... SPAG
Standards Referenced in Federal Legislation [*Standards Council of Canada*] [*Information service or system*] (CRD) .... FED-STAN
Standards Review Committee [*American Occupational Therapy Association*] .... SRC
Standards Starts Index [*Horse racing*] (DICI) .... SSI
Standards Steering Committee [*ANSI*] .... SSC
Standards Support Document [*Environmental Protection Agency*] (GFGA) ...... SSD
Standards Technical Advisory Group .... STAG
Standards Tool Master (MCD) .... STM
Standards Western Automatic Computer [*National Institute of Standards and Technology*] .... SWAC
Standarization, Interoperability, and Readiness [*NATO*] (MCD) .... SIR
Standby .... SB
Standby [*Airlines*] .... SBY
Standby .... SDBY
Standby (AAG) .... STBY
Standby (NVT) .... STDBY
Standby Advisory Board [*Army*] (INF) .... SAI
Standby Airspeed [*or Attitude*] Indicator (MCD) .... SARI
Standby Altitude Reference Indicator (MCD) .... SBA
Stand-By Assistance [*Medicine*] (MEDA) .... SBA
Stand-By Assistance (DAVI) .... SBA
Standby Auxiliary Feed Water Pump (IEEE) .... SBAFWP
Standby Base [*Air Force*] (AFM) .... SB
Standby Compatible One-Tape [*System*] .... SCOT
Standby Core Cooling System [*Nuclear energy*] (NRCH) .... SCCS
Standby Fighter Director Ship [*Navy*] .... SFDS
Standby Filter Unit (IEEE) .... SBFU
Standby Flying [*British military*] (DMA) .... SBF
Standby Gas Treatment [*Nuclear energy*] (GFGA) .... SBGT
Standby Gas Treatment System [*Nuclear energy*] (NRCH) .... SBGTS
Standby Gas Treatment System [*Nuclear energy*] (NRCH) .... SGTS
Standby Liquid Control [*Nuclear energy*] (NRCH) .... SBLC
Standby Liquid Control [*Nuclear energy*] (NRCH) .... SLC
Standby Liquid Control System [*Nuclear energy*] (NRCH) .... SLCS
Standby Local Early Warning and Control Center (PDAA) .... SLEW
Standby Note Issuance Facility [*Finance*] .... SNIF
Standby Power .... SP
Standby Power Source [*Electronics*] .... SPS
Standby Power Supply (PCM) .... SPS
Standby Pressure Control [*Nuclear energy*] (NRCH) .... SPC
Standby Request for Information [*Military*] (AABC) .... SRI
Standby Reserve of the Armed Forces .... SRAF
Standby Salvage Ship [*Navy*] (NVT) .... STSALV
Standby Service Water [*Nuclear energy*] (NRCH) .... SSW
Standby Service Water [*Nuclear energy*] (NRCH) .... SW
Standby Service Water System [*Nuclear energy*] (NRCH) .... SSWS
Standby Shutdown Facility [*Nuclear energy*] (NRCH) .... SSF
Standby Status (AAG) .... SBS
Standby Status Panel .... SSP
Standby Supply Relay [*Telecommunications*] (IAA) .... SSR
Standby Time (MCD) .... ST
Standby Township [*Navy*] (NVT) .... SBTOW
Standby Warning Panel (MCD) .... SWP
Standerton [*South Africa*] [*ICAO location identifier*] (ICLI) .... FASR
Standex International Corp. [*Associated Press*] (SAG) .... Standex

Standex International Corp. [*NYSE symbol*] (SPSG) .... SXI
Standex Intl [*NYSE symbol*] (TTSB) .... SXI
Standforward Jamming [*Military*] (LAIN) .... SFJ
Standiford Field [*FAA*] (TAG) .... SDF
Standing (AABC) .... STD
Standing [*Numismatics*] .... STG
Standing Administrative Instruction for Air Attaches (AFM) .... STADINAIR
Standing Administrative Instruction for Army Attaches (AABC) .... STADIN
Standing Advisory Committee for Scientific Advice [*Oslo Commission*] (DCTA) .... SACSA
Standing Advisory Committee on Fisheries of the Caribbean Organization .... SAFCO
Standing Advisory Committee on Private Pilot Licensing [*British*] (AIA) .... SACPPL
Standing Advisory Council for Religious Education (AIE) .... SACRE
Standing Advisory Panel on Library Automation (NITA) .... SAPLA
Standing Air Emissions Work Group [*Environmental Protection Agency*] (GFGA) .... SAEWG
Standing Air Monitoring Work Group [*Environmental Protection Agency*] (GFGA) .... SAMWG
Standing Armaments Committee [*NATO*] (NATG) .... SAC
Standing Authority Release [*For perishables*] [*Business term*] .... SAR
Standing Balance: Eyes Closed [*Test*] [*Occupational therapy*] .... SBC
Standing Balance: Eyes Open [*Test*] [*Occupational therapy*] .... SBO
Standing British Army .... SBA
Standing Commission on Church Music (EA) .... SCCM
Standing Commission on Ecumenical Relations of the Episcopal Church (EA) .... SCER
Standing Committee (ADA) .... SC
Standing Committee for Controlled Thermonuclear Research [*AEC*] .... CTR
Standing Committee for Controlled Thermonuclear Research [*Terminated, 1973*] [*AEC*] (EGAO) .... SCCTR
Standing Committee for International Cooperation within the Field of Non-Destructive Testing (EA) .... SCICFNDT
Standing Committee for Nobel Prize Winners' Congresses (EA) .... SCNPWC
Standing Committee for the Study of Scientific Principles of Standardization [*ISO*] .... STACO
Standing Committee of Consumer Affairs Ministers .... SCCAM
Standing Committee of French-Speaking Ethnical Communities (EA) .... SCFSEC
Standing Committee of Nature Conservation Ministers [*Australia*] .... SCNCM
Standing Committee of the Murray-Darling Basin Ministerial Council [*Australia*] .... SCMDBMC
Standing Committee on Archival Information Exchange [*Society of American Archivists*] [*Information service or system*] (IID) .... CAIE
Standing Committee on Army Organization [*British*] .... SCAO
Standing Committee on Education and Training (ACII) .... SCET
Standing Committee on Education in Librarianship .... SCEL
Standing Committee on Library Education [*American Library Association*] .... SCOLE
Standing Committee on National Defence and Veterans Affairs [*Canada*] .... SCNDVA
Standing Committee on Personnel Training and Readiness [*Navy*] .... SCPTR
Standing Committee on Professional Education (NITA) .... SCOPE
Standing Committee on Professional Institutions (ACII) .... SCPI
Standing Committee on Regulatory Effectiveness [*Nuclear Regulatory Commission*] (NRCH) .... SCORE
Standing Committee on Research and Statistics [*UN Food and Agriculture Organization*] .... STACRES
Standing Committee on Social Sciences, Economic, and Legal Aspects [*Great Lakes Research Advisory Board*] .... SSELA
Standing Committee on Submarine Escape [*British military*] (DMA) .... SCOSE
Standing Committee on the Economic and Social Work of the United Nations .... SCESWUN
Standing Committee on the Free Circulation of Scientists [*International Council of Scientific Unions*] .... SCFCS
Standing Committee on the Safeguard of the Pursuit of Science [*International Council of Scientific Unions*] .... SCSPS
Standing Committee on Water Resources [*Australia*] .... SCWR
Standing Conference for Amateur Music [*British*] .... SCAM
Standing Conference for Europe of the International Basketball Federation (EAIO) .... SCEIBF
Standing Conference for the Advancement of Training and Supervision [*British*] (DBA) .... SCATS
Standing Conference of African University Libraries [*Lagos, Nigeria*] .... SCAUL
Standing Conference of African University Libraries (EAIO) .... SCAULWA
Standing Conference of Arts and Social Sciences [*British*] (DBA) .... SCASS
Standing Conference of Associations for Guidance in Education Settings (AIE) .... SCAGES
Standing Conference of Atlantic Organisations [*British*] (EAIO) .... SCAO
Standing Conference of Co-Operative Library and Information Services [*British*] .... SCOCLIS
Standing Conference of Employers of Graduates [*British*] .... SCOEG
Standing Conference of Institutions of Printing Education (DGA) .... SCOPE
Standing Conference of Principals and Directors of Colleges and Institutes of Higher Education (AIE) .... SCPDCIHE
Standing Conference of Principals of Tertiary and Sixth Form Colleges [*British*] (AIE) .... SCOTVIC
Standing Conference of Regional Advisory Councils for Further Education .... SCRAC
Standing Conference of Regional Arts Associations [*British*] (DI) .... SCRAA
Standing Conference of the Canonical Orthodox Bishops in the Americas (EA) .... SCOBA
Standing Conference of University Appointments Services [*British*] .... SCUAS
Standing Conference of University Drama Departments (AIE) .... SCUDD
Standing Conference of University Information Officers [*British*] .... SCUIO

Standing Conference of Youth Organisations (AIE) .... SCOYO
Standing Conference on Dance in Higher Education [*British*] (DBA) .... SCODHE
Standing Conference on Education Development (AIE) .... SCED
Standing Conference on Education for International Understanding [*British*] (DBA) .... SCEIU
Standing Conference on Library Materials on Africa [*British*] .... SCOLMA
Standing Conference on National and University Libraries [*British*] .... SCNUL
Standing Conference on National and University Libraries [*British*] .... SCONUL
Standing Conference on Refugees [*British*] .... SCOR
Standing Conference on School Science and Technology [*British*] .... SCSST
Standing Conference on Telecommunications Research (IAA) .... SCTR
Standing Conference on Television Viewing [*British*] .... SCTV
Standing Conference on Theological and Philosophical Libraries in London .... SCOTAPLL
Standing Conference on University Entrance [*British*] (DI) .... SCUE
Standing Conference on University Teaching and Research in the Education of Adults [*British*] (DI) .... SCUTREA
Standing Consultative Commission [*SALT agreements*] [*US/USSR*] .... SCC
Standing Crop .... SC
Standing Detonation Wave .... SDW
Standing EEC [*European Economic Community*] **Committee of the International Association of the Soap and Detergent Industry** [*See also CPCEAISD*] [*Brussels, Belgium*] (EAIO) .... SEECCIASDI
Standing Group .... SG
Standing Group Communication Security and Evaluation Agency Washington .... SECAN
Standing Group Communications-Electronics Committee [*Later, MCEWG*] [*NATO*] (NATG) .... SGCEC
Standing Group Liaison Officer to the North Atlantic Council .... SGLO
Standing Group Memorandum [*Obsolete NATO*] (NATG) .... SGM
Standing Group Meteorological Committee [*Obsolete NATO*] (NATG) .... SGMC
Standing Group, North Atlantic Treaty Organization .... SGN
Standing Group Representative [*NASA*] .... SGREP
Standing Group Representative Communication to the Private Office of the NATO Secretary General [*Obsolete*] (NATG) .... SGPO
Standing Group Representative Liaison Paper to the International Staff [*Obsolete NATO*] (NATG) .... SGLP
Standing Group Security Committee [*Obsolete NATO*] (NATG) .... SGSC
Standing Group Technical Intelligence Agency [*NATO*] (NATG) .... SGTIA
Standing Group Working Memorandum [*NATO*] (NATG) .... SGWM
Standing Instruction (MSA) .... SI
Standing Interdepartmental Committee on Censorship [*War Cabinet*] [*British*] .... SCC
Standing Joint Committee .... SJC
Standing Joint Pacifist Committee [*Defunct*] (EAIO) .... SJPC
Standing Lenticular Altocumulus [*Meteorology*] .... ACSL
Standing Liaison Committee .... SLC
Standing Liaison Committee of Physiotherapists within the EEC [*European Economic Community*] [*See also CPLK*] [*Copenhagen, Denmark*] (EAIO) .... SLCP
Standing Naval Force, Atlantic (MCD) .... SNFL
Standing Naval Force, Atlantic (ANA) .... STANAVFORLANT
Standing Naval Force, Channel [*NATO*] (NATG) .... STANAVFORCHAN
Standing Naval Force Mediterranean [*NATO*] (DOMA) .... STANAVFORMED
Standing Operating and Landing .... STOL
Standing Operating Procedure - Meteorological Plan (NATG) .... SOPMET
Standing Operating Procedure Regulation [*Navy*] (MCD) .... SOPR
Standing Order .... SO
Standing Order [*Business term*] (DCTA) .... STO
Standing Order Advance Payment .... SOAP
Standing Order Confirmation [*Publishing*] .... SOC
Standing Order Microfiche Service .... SRIM
Standing Orders (NITA) .... STO
Standing Orders Committee [*British*] (DCTA) .... SOC
Standing Procedure (NATG) .... SP
Standing Register [*Civil Service*] .... SREG
Standing Representative Committee for Medical Laboratory Technology in the EEC [*European Econommic Community*] [*England*] (EAIO) .... SRCMLT
Standing Request for Information (MCD) .... SRI
Standing Results Review Committee [*Nuclear energy*] (NRCH) .... SRRC
Standing Room Only [*Theater*] .... SRO
Standing Route Order [*Army*] (AABC) .... SRO
Standing Signal Instructions [*Military*] .... SSI
Standing Spin Wave Mode (MCD) .... SSWM
Standing State Advisory Committee [*Terminated, 1977*] [*of Water Resources Council*] (EGAO) .... SSAC
Standing Submarine Operations and Repair Manual [*Navy*] (DNAB) .... SSORM
Standing Technical Advisory Committee on Water Quality [*Department of the Environment*] [*British*] .... STACWV
Standing Technical Committee [*British*] (DCTA) .... STC
Standing Technical Committee on Disposal of Sewage Sludge [*British*] (DCTA) .... STCDSS
Standing Tool Order (KSC) .... STO
Standing Wave (IAA) .... SW
Standing Wave Apparatus .... SWA
Standing Wave Area Monitor Indicator (MUGU) .... SWAMI
Standing Wave Detector .... SWD
Standing Wave Impedance Probe [*Geophysical instrument*] .... SWIP
Standing Wave Indicator .... SWI
Standing Wave Ratio [*Voltage*] [*Electronics*] .... SWR
Standing Wave Ratio Bridge [*Electronics*] .... SWRB
Standing Wave Ratio Meter [*Electronics*] .... SWRM
Standing Wave Read-Only Memory [*Computer science*] .... SWROM
Standing Wave Signal Ratio (IAA) .... SWSR
Standing Wave Voltage Ratio [*Electronics*] (IAA) .... SWVR
Standing with Eyes Closed [*Equilibrium test*] .... SEC
Standing-Shock Equilibrium Expansion .... SSEE
Standing-Wave Acoustic Parametric Source (PDAA) .... SWAPS
Standing-Wave Fluorescence Microscopy .... SWFM
Standish Care [*NASDAQ symbol*] (TTSB) .... STAN
Standish Care Co. [*NASDAQ symbol*] (SAG) .... STAN
Standish Care Co. [*Associated Press*] (SAG) .... Standsh
Standish, ME [*FM radio station call letters*] .... WSJB
Standish, MI [*FM radio station call letters*] .... WSTD
Standoff .... STDF
Standoff/Attack Weapons Guidance Utility Study (MCD) .... SAWGUS
Standoff Cluster Munitions .... SOCM
Stand-off, High Altitude, Long Endurance (PDAA) .... SHALE
Standoff Imaging Sensor System (MCD) .... SISS
Standoff Jammer (NVT) .... SOJ
Standoff Jammer Interceptor Missile (MCD) .... SOJIM
Standoff Jammer Suppression (MCD) .... SOJS
Standoff Jammer Suppression Missile (MCD) .... SOJSM
Standoff Jammer System (MCD) .... SOJS
Standoff Land Attack Missile [*Military*] .... SLAM
Standoff Mine Detection Ground [*Army*] (DOMA) .... SMDG
Standoff Minefield Detection System [*Military*] (INF) .... STAMIDS
Standoff Missile (MCD) .... SOM
Stand-Off Modular Missile (PDAA) .... SOMM
Standoff Munitions Disrupter System (MCD) .... SMUD
Standoff Precision Attack [*Military*] (CAAL) .... SOPA
Standoff Range (MCD) .... SOR
Standoff Target Acquisition and Surveillance System [*Army*] .... SOTASS
Standoff Target Acquisition/Attack System .... SOTAS
Standoff Target Acquisition Reconnaissance Surveillance System (MCD) .... SOTARSS
Standoff Techniques for Parachute Insertion (MCD) .... STOTINS
Standoff Weapons (MCD) .... SOW
Standpipe (MSA) .... SP
Standpipe .... S'PIPE
Stands Detached [*Freight*] .... SD
Stand's Georgia Practice [*A publication*] (DLA) .... GA Prac
Standup Extravehicular Activity [*Aerospace*] .... SEVA
Stanfield Public Library, Stanfield, OR [*Library symbol*] [*Library of Congress*] (LCLS) .... OrStf
Stanford [*California*] [*Seismograph station code, US Geological Survey*] (SEIS) .... SFT
Stanford Achievement Test [*Education*] .... SAT
Stanford Achievement Test, Special Edition for Hearing Impaired Students (EDAC) .... SAT-HI
Stanford Artificial Intelligence Laboratory [*Stanford University*] .... SAIL
Stanford Artificial Intelligence Language (NITA) .... SAIL
Stanford Automated Bibliographic Systems (NITA) .... SABS
Stanford, CA [*FM radio station call letters*] .... KZSU
Stanford Center for Chicano Research [*Stanford University*] [*Research center*] (RCD) .... SCCR
Stanford Center for Chicano Research, Stanford, CA [*Library symbol*] [*Library of Congress*] (LCLS) .... CStCC
Stanford Center for Health Care Research [*Closed, 1978*] .... SCHCR
Stanford Center for Information Processing [*Stanford University*] [*Later, CIT*] .... SCIP
Stanford Center for RADAR Astronomy .... SCRA
Stanford Center for Reservoir Forecasting [*Stanford University*] [*Research center*] (RCD) .... SCRF
Stanford Community Against Reagan University [*Group opposed to proposed Ronald Reagan presidential library at Stanford University*] .... SCAReU
Stanford Computer Industry Project .... SCIP
Stanford Diagnostic Arithmetic Test .... SDAT
Stanford Diagnostic Mathematics Test [*Education*] .... SDMT
Stanford Diagnostic Reading Test [*Education*] .... SDRT
Stanford Early School Achievement Test [*Educational test*] .... SESAT
Stanford Electronics Laboratory [*Stanford University*] [*Research center*] (MCD) .... SEL
Stanford Humanities Center [*Stanford University*] [*Research center*] (RCD) .... SHC
Stanford Hypnotic Susceptibility Scale [*Psychology*] .... SHSS
Stanford Integrated Manufacturing Association [*Stanford University*] [*Research center*] (RCD) .... SIMA
Stanford International Development Education Center [*Stanford University*] .... SIDEC
Stanford, KY [*AM radio station call letters*] .... WRSL
Stanford, KY [*FM radio station call letters*] .... WRSL-FM
Stanford Linear Accelerator Center [*Stanford, CA*] [*Department of Energy*] .... SLAC
Stanford Linear Accelerator Computer [*Stanford University*] [*Department of Energy*] (IAA) .... SLAC
Stanford Linear Collider [*High-energy physics*] .... SLC
Stanford Magnetic Resonance Laboratory [*Stanford University*] [*Research center*] (RCD) .... SMRL
Stanford Parent Questionnaire [*Psychology*] .... SPQ
Stanford Positron-Electron Axisymmetric Ring .... SPEAR
Stanford Preschool Internality-Externality Scale (EDAC) .... SPIES
Stanford Profile Scales of Hypnotic Susceptibility [*Psychology*] .... SPSHS
Stanford Program on International and Cross Cultural Education [*Stanford University*] [*Research center*] (RCD) .... SPICE
Stanford Public Information Retrieval System [*Stanford University Libraries*] [*Stanford, CA Bibliographic database management system*] [*Information service or system*] .... SPIRES
Stanford Research Institute [*Later, SRI International*] [*Databank originator*] .... SRI
Stanford Research Institute Lead Time Analysis .... SRILTA

Stanford Research Institute Library, Menlo Park, CA [*Library symbol Library of Congress*] (LCLS) .... CMenSR
Stanford Research Institute Problem Solver [*Computer system*] .... STRIPS
Stanford Research Institute, South Pasadena, CA [*Library symbol Library of Congress*] (LCLS) .... CSpSR
Stanford Resources Ltd. [*Toronto Stock Exchange symbol*] .... STF
Stanford School Scheduling System S4
Stanford Sleepiness Scale .... SSS
Stanford Synchrotron Radiation Laboratory [*Stanford, CA*] [*Department of Energy*] .... SSRL
Stanford Synchrotron Radiation Project .... SSRP
Stanford Telecommun [*NASDAQ symbol*] (TTSB) .... STII
Stanford Telecommunications, Inc. [*Associated Press*] (SAG) .... StanfTI
Stanford Telecommunications, Inc. [*NASDAQ symbol*] (NQ) .... STII
Stanford University (GAGS) .... Stanford U
Stanford University [*California*] .... SU
Stanford University, Branner Earth Sciences Library, Systems Office, Stanford, CA [*Library symbol*] [*Library of Congress*] (LCLS) .... CSt-ES
Stanford University, Department of Aeronautics and Astronautics (MCD) .... SUDAER
Stanford University Division of Aero Engineering (AAG) .... SUNDAE
Stanford University, Graduate School of Business, Stanford, CA [*Library symbol Library of Congress*] (LCLS) .... CSt-B
Stanford University, Hoover Institution on War, Revolution, and Peace, Stanford,CA [*Library symbol Library of Congress*] (LCLS) .... CSt-H
Stanford University Institute for Plasma Research .... SUI
Stanford University, Lane Medical Library, Stanford, CA [*Library symbol Library of Congress*] (LCLS) .... CSt-L
Stanford University, Law Library, Stanford, CA [*Library symbol Library of Congress*] (LCLS) .... CSt-Law
Stanford University Medical Center .... SUMC
Stanford University Medical Experimental Computer Project [*Stanford University*] [*Research center*] (RCD) .... SUMEX
Stanford University Medical Experiment-Applications of Artificial Intelligence to Medical Research (NITA) .... SUMEXAIM
Stanford University Modified Markers and Cell Method .... SUMMAC
Stanford University, Music Library, Stanford, CA [*Library symbol Library of Congress*] (LCLS) .... CSt-Mus
Stanford University, Nathan Van Patten Library, Stanford, CA [*Library symbol Library of Congress*] (LCLS) .... CSt-V
Stanford University Network for Space Telescience Applications Research [*Research center*] (RCD) .... SUNSTAR
Stanford University Press (DGA) .... SUP
Stanford University, Stanford, CA [*Library symbol Library of Congress*] (LCLS) .... CSt
Stanford Workshop on Political and Social Issues [*Stanford University*] .... SWOPSI
Stanford Worldwide Acquisition of Meteorological Information [*Weather prediction system*] .... SWAMI
Stanford-Binet [*Intelligence test*] [*Education*] .... SB
Stanford-Binet Intelligence Scale [*Psychology*] (DAVI) .... SBIS
Stanford's Compendium of Geography and Travel [*A publication*] .... SCGT
Stanford's English Pleas of the Crown [*A publication*] (DLA) .... Stanford
Stanforth Junior High School, Sewanhaka, NY [*Library symbol Library of Congress*] (LCLS) .... NSewSJ
Stanhome, Inc. [*Associated Press*] (SAG) .... Stanhm
Stanhome, Inc. [*NYSE symbol*] (SPSG) .... STH
Staniel Cay, Exuma Island [*Bahamas*] [*ICAO location identifier*] (ICLI) .... MYEL
Stanislaus County Free Library, Modesto, CA [*OCLC symbol*] (OCLC) .... CFL
Stanislaus County Free Library, Modesto, CA [*Library symbol Library of Congress*] (LCLS) .... CMS
Stanislaus County Law Library, Modesto, CA [*Library symbol Library of Congress*] (LCLS) .... CML
Stanislaus County Medical Library, Modesto, CA [*Library symbol Library of Congress*] (LCLS) .... CMSM
Stankovyi Goryunova 1943 Medium Machine Gun [*Soviet made*] (VNW) .... SG43 MMG
Stanlabs, Inc. [*Research code symbol*] .... AR
Stanley Airport [*Falkland Islands*] [*ICAO location identifier*] (ICLI) .... SFAL
Stanley Associates Engineering Ltd., Edmonton, AB, Canada [*Library symbol Library of Congress*] (LCLS) .... CaAESAE
Stanley Associates Engineering Ltd., Edmonton, Alberta [*Library symbol National Library of Canada*] (NLC) .... AESAE
Stanley City Library, Stanley, ID [*Library symbol*] [*Library of Congress*] (LCLS) .... IdSt
Stanley Furniture [*NASDAQ symbol*] (TTSB) .... STLY
Stanley Furniture Co. [*Associated Press*] (SAG) .... StanlFrn
Stanley Furniture Co. [*NASDAQ symbol*] (SAG) .... STLY
Stanley Resources [*Vancouver Stock Exchange symbol*] .... SAY
[The] Stanley Works [*Associated Press*] (SAG) .... StanlWk
[The] Stanley Works [*NYSE symbol*] (SPSG) .... SWK
Stanly Technical Institute, Albemarle, NC [*Library symbol Library of Congress*] (LCLS) .... NcAlbS
Stanmar Resources Ltd. [*Vancouver Stock Exchange symbol*] .... SMR
Stanmore Park [*British ICAO location identifier*] (ICLI) .... EGWS
Stannum [*Tin*] [*Chemical element*] .... Sn
STANO [*Surveillance, Target Acquisition, and Night Observation*] **System Manager** [*Army*] (RDA) .... STANSM
Stansbury Island [*Utah*] [*Seismograph station code, US Geological Survey Closed*] (SEIS) .... SBU
Stanstead [*England*] .... STAN
Stanstead Historial Society, Quebec [*Library symbol National Library of Canada*] (NLC) .... QSH
Stanstead Historical Society, Stanstead, PQ, Canada [*Library symbol Library of Congress*] (LCLS) .... CaQSH

Stanstead Journal, Quebec [*Library symbol National Library of Canada*] (NLC) .... QSJ
Stanstead Journal, Stanstead, PQ, Canada [*Library symbol Library of Congress*] (LCLS) .... CaQSJ
Stansted [*England*] [*Airport symbol*] (OAG) .... STN
Stant Corp. [*Associated Press*] (SAG) .... Stant
Stant Corp. [*NASDAQ symbol*] (SAG) .... STNT
Stanton Community Library, Stanton, IA [*Library symbol Library of Congress*] (LCLS) .... IaStan
Stanton Foundation (EA) .... KCSF
Stanton Foundation [*Later, KCSF*] (EA) .... SF
Stanton, KY [*AM radio station call letters*] .... WBFC
Stanton, KY [*FM radio station call letters*] .... WSKV
Stanton, MN [*Location identifier FAA*] (FAAL) .... SYN
Stanton Number [*IUPAC*] .... St
Stanton Public Library, Stanton, MI [*Library symbol Library of Congress*] (LCLS) .... MiStan
Stanton Viking, Stanton, IA [*Library symbol*] [*Library of Congress*] (LCLS) .... IaStanV
Stanton's Kentucky Digest [*A publication*] (DLA) .... Stan Dig
Stanton's Reports [*11-13 Ohio*] [*A publication*] (DLA) .... Stanton
Stanton's Revised Kentucky Statutes [*A publication*] (DLA) .... Stanton's Rev St
Stanwood Public Library, Stanwood, IA [*Library symbol*] [*Library of Congress*] (LCLS) .... IaStaw
Stanza (WDMC) .... st
Stanza .... ST
Staodyn, Inc. [*NASDAQ symbol*] (NQ) .... SDYN
Staodyn, Inc. [*Associated Press*] (SAG) .... Staody
Staodyn, Inc. [*Associated Press*] (SAG) .... Staodyn
Staodyn Inc. Wrrt'Il' [*NASDAQ symbol*] (TTSB) .... SDYNZ
Stapedius Muscle [*Anatomy*] (DAVI) .... SM
Staphylococcal Bacteriophage Lysate .... SBL
Staphylococcal Clumping Test [*Medicine*] (AAMN) .... SCT
Staphylococcal Enterotoxin A [*Medicine*] .... SEA
Staphylococcal Enterotoxin B [*Medicine*] .... SEB
Staphylococcal Enterotoxin B Antisera [*Medicine*] .... SEBA
Staphylococcal Enterotoxin D [*Medicine*] .... SED
Staphylococcal Enterotoxin E [*Medicine*] .... SEE
Staphylococcal Hemagglutinating Antibody [*Medicine*] (DMAA) .... SHA
Staphylococcal Nuclease [*An enzyme*] .... SNase
Staphylococcal Phage Lysate [*Biochemistry*] .... SPL
Staphylococcal Protease [*Medicine*] (DMAA) .... SP
Staphylococcal Protein A [*Biochemistry*] (DAVI) .... SP
Staphylococcal Protein A [*Immunochemistry*] .... SPA
Staphylococcal Scalded Skin Syndrome [*Medicine*] .... SSSS
Staphylococcal Toxic Shock Syndrome [*Medicine*] (DMAA) .... STSS
Staphylococcus [*Medicine*] (MAE) .... S
Staphylococcus [*Medicine*] .... STAPH
Staphylococcus Adherence Test [*Clinical chemistry*] .... SAT
Staphylococcus Aureus [*Microbiology*] .... SA
Staphylococcus Aureus Cervan [*Microbiology*] .... SAC
Staphylococcus Aureus Enterotoxin F [*Toxic shock toxin*] .... SEF
Staphylococcus aureus Protease [*An enzyme*] .... SAP
Staphylococcus Epidermidis [*A bacterium*] (DAVI) .... Staph Epi
Staphylococcus Medium [*Microbiology*] .... SM
Staple and Stapling Machine Manufacturers Association [*Defunct*] .... SSMMA
Stapleford [*British ICAO location identifier*] (ICLI) .... EGSG
Stapleford Flight Center [*British ICAO designator*] (FAAC) .... STL
Staples High School, Staples, MN [*Library symbol*] [*Library of Congress*] (LCLS) .... MnStHS
Staples, Inc. [*NASDAQ symbol*] (NQ) .... SPLS
Staples, Inc. [*Associated Press*] (SAG) .... Staples
Staples, MN [*AM radio station call letters*] .... KNSP
Staples, MN [*FM radio station call letters*] .... KNSP-FM
Staples, MN [*FM radio station call letters*] .... KSKK
Staples, MN [*Location identifier FAA*] (FAAL) .... SAZ
Staples Public Library, Staples, MN [*Library symbol*] [*Library of Congress*] (LCLS) .... MnSt
Staples Technical Institute, Staples, MN [*Library symbol*] [*Library of Congress*] (LCLS) .... MnStT
Stapleton [*England*] .... STAP
Stapleton International Airport [*FAA*] (TAG) .... DEN
Staploe [*England*] .... STAP
Star [*Mauritania*] [*Airport symbol*] (AD) .... ATR
Star (NASA) .... S
Star Air IS [*Denmark ICAO designator*] (FAAC) .... SRR
Star Airways [*ICAO designator*] (AD) .... ZR
Star Alliance Foundation (EA) .... SAF
Star and Crescent [*Steamship*] (MHDW) .... S & C
Star and Wave, Cape May, NJ [*Library symbol Library of Congress*] (LCLS) .... NjCapS
Star Asia [*Philippines*] [*FAA designator*] (FAAC) .... TIM
Star Aviation [*British ICAO designator*] (FAAC) .... STA
Star Banc Corp. [*Associated Press*] (SAG) .... StarBc
Star Banc Corp. [*NYSE symbol*] (SAG) .... STB
Star Chamber Cases [*England*] [*A publication*] (DLA) .... St Ch Cas
Star Chamber Cases [*1477-1648*] [*England*] [*A publication*] (DLA) .... Star Ch Ca
Star Chamber Cases [*1477-1648*] [*England*] [*A publication*] (DLA) .... Star Ch Cas
Star Chamber Cases, by Crompton [*A publication*] (DLA) .... Cromp
Star Chamber Cases, by Crompton [*A publication*] (DLA) .... Crompt
Star Chamber Proceedings [*England*] [*A publication*] (DLA) .... Burn
STAR [*Self Testing and Reporting*] **Computer Assembly Language** .... SCAL
Star/Earth Horizon Sightings .... SEH
Star/Earth Landmark Sightings .... SEL
Star Epitaxial Planar (MSA) .... SEP

Star Field (MCD) ... SF
Star Field (MCD) ... STRFLD
Star Field Camera [*NASA*] ... SFC
Star Field Scanning Device ... SFSD
Star Field Sensor ... SFS
Star Formation Rate [*Astronomy*] ... SFR
Star Gas Partners L.P. SBI [*NASDAQ symbol*] (SAG) ... SGAS
Star Gas Partners L.P. SBI [*Associated Press*] (SAG) ... StarGas
Star Gas Ptnrs L.P. [*NASDAQ symbol*] (TTSB) ... SGASZ
Star Gazette, Hackettstown, NJ [*Library symbol Library of Congress*] (LCLS) ... NjHaS
Star Gazette, Hackettstown, NJ [*Library symbol*] [*Library of Congress*] (LCLS) ... NjHaSG
Star Identification Program, Mariner [*NASA*] ... SIPM
Star Line ... SL
Star Line-of-Sight (MCD) ... SLOS
Star Line-of-Sight (KSC) ... STLOS
Star Magnitude (NASA) ... SMAG
Star Multi Care Services, Inc. [*NASDAQ symbol*] (SAG) ... SMCS
Star Multi Care Services, Inc. [*Associated Press*] (SAG) ... StarMC
Star Multi Care Svcs [*NASDAQ symbol*] (TTSB) ... SMCS
Star of Asia [*Kyrgyzstan*] [*FAA designator*] (FAAC) ... SSA
Star of Courage [*Award*] [*British*] ... SC
Star of India ... SI
Star of Valour [*British*] (ADA) ... SV
Star One Resources, Inc. [*Vancouver Stock Exchange symbol*] ... SOQ
Star Petroleum Refinery Complex [*Thailand*] ... SPRC
Star Point Transfer [*Photography*] (OA) ... SPT
Star Present (NASA) ... SPRES
Star Resources Corp. [*NASDAQ symbol*] (SAG) ... SRRC
Star Resources Corp. [*Associated Press*] (SAG) ... StarRes
Star Route [*A type of rural postal delivery route*] ... SR
Star Service International [*France ICAO designator*] (FAAC) ... SSD
Star Session Cases [*1824-25*] [*A publication*] (DLA) ... Star SC
Star Shot (SAA) ... STARS
Star, Starling, Stuart, and Briton Car Register (EA) ... SSSBCR
Star Technologies [*NASDAQ symbol*] (TTSB) ... STRR
Star Technologies, Inc. [*Associated Press*] (SAG) ... StarTc
Star Technologies, Inc. [*Sterling, VA*] [*NASDAQ symbol*] (NQ) ... STRR
Star Tracker [*NASA*] (AAG) ... ST
Star Tracker (NASA) ... STRK
Star Tracker Electronics [*Apollo*] [*NASA*] ... STE
Star Tracker for Economical Long Life Attitude Reference [*NASA*] ... STELLAR
Star Tracker Unit [*NASA*] (MCD) ... STU
Star [*or Stellar*] **Tracking Rocket Attitude Positioning** [*System*] [*NASA*] ... STRAP
Star Trek, the Next Generation [*Television program*] ... STTNG
Star Trek Welcommittee (EA) ... STW
Star Valley [*Idaho*] [*Seismograph station code, US Geological Survey*] (SEIS) ... STI
Star Valley Resources [*Vancouver Stock Exchange symbol*] ... SVL
Star Vector Calibration Sensor [*Aviation*] (OA) ... SVCS
Stara Dala [*Czechoslovakia*] [*Later, HRB*] [*Geomagnetic observatory code*] ... STA
Stara Zagora [*Bulgaria*] [*ICAO location identifier*] (ICLI) ... LBSZ
STARAN [*Stellar Attitude Reference and Navigation*] **Control Module** (OA) ... SCM
STARAN Debug Module ... SDM
STARAN Evaluation and Training Facility ... SETF
Starbase Corp. [*NASDAQ symbol*] (SAG) ... SBAS
Starbase Corp. [*Associated Press*] (SAG) ... Starbase
Starboard ... S
Starboard (DS) ... sor
Starboard ... STBD
Starboard Flag [*Navy British*] ... ST
Starboard Out, Port Home [*Variation of POSH*] ... SOPH
Starboard Side/Forward [*Stowage*] (DNAB) ... SS/F
Starboard Side Light (MCD) ... SSLT
Starbucks Corp. [*NASDAQ symbol*] (SAG) ... SBUX
Starbucks Corp. [*Associated Press*] (SAG) ... Starbcks
Starburst Energy [*Vancouver Stock Exchange symbol*] ... SBR
Starburst Galaxy [*Astronomy*] ... SBG
Starburst Giant Cells [*Cytology*] ... SGC
Starch Equivalent ... SE
Starch Gel Electrophoresis (OA) ... SGE
Starch-Branching Enzyme I [*Plant genetics*] ... SBEI
Starch-Free [*Pharmacy*] ... St F
Starcke [*Queensland*] [*Airport symbol*] (AD) ... SUR
Starcraft Automotive Corp. [*Associated Press*] (SAG) ... Starcraft
Starcraft Automotive Corp. [*NASDAQ symbol*] (SAG) ... STCR
Starcraft Campers Club (EA) ... SCC
Starcraft Corp. [*NASDAQ symbol*] (TTSB) ... STCR
Stardust Ventures [*Vancouver Stock Exchange symbol*] ... SDZ
Starfield Image Generator ... SIG
Starfire Optical Range [*Air Force*] ... SOR
Starfire Resources Ltd. [*Vancouver Stock Exchange symbol*] ... SFI
Starfish Radiation [*Satellite*] [*NASA*] ... STARAD
Starfleet Command [*An association*] (EA) ... SC
Starfleet Command (EA) ... SFC
Starfleet Operations [*An association*] (EA) ... SOSA
Stargardt Disease [*Medicine*] ... STGT
Stargazer Resources Ltd. [*Vancouver Stock Exchange symbol*] ... SZR
Stark County District Library, Canton, OH [*Library symbol Library of Congress*] (LCLS) ... OCanS
Stark County District Library, Canton, OH [*OCLC symbol*] (OCLC) ... SDL
Stark Quadratic Zeeman Effect [*Physics*] ... SQZE
Starke County Historical Museum, Knox, IN [*Library symbol Library of Congress*] (LCLS) ... InKnoCHi
Starke County Recorder's Office, Knox, IN [*Library symbol Library of Congress*] (LCLS) ... InKnoCR
Starke, FL [*FM radio station call letters*] ... WTLG
Starkie on Evidence [*A publication*] (DLA) ... Stark Ev
Starkie on Evidence [*A publication*] (DLA) ... Starkie Ev
Starkie on Libel [*A publication*] (DLA) ... Stark Lib
Starkie on Slander and Libel [*A publication*] (DLA) ... Stark Sl & L
Starkie on Slander and Libel [*A publication*] (DLA) ... Starkie Sland & L
Starkie on Trial by Jury [*A publication*] (DLA) ... Stark Jury Tr
Starkie's Criminal Law [*A publication*] (DLA) ... Stark CL
Starkie's Criminal Pleading [*A publication*] (DLA) ... Stark Cr Pl
Starkie's English Nisi Prius Reports [*A publication*] (DLA) ... Star
Starkie's English Nisi Prius Reports [*1815-22*] [*A publication*] (DLA) ... Stark
Starkie's English Nisi Prius Reports [*A publication*] (DLA) ... Stark NP
Starkie's English Nisi Prius Reports [*A publication*] (DLA) ... Starkie
Starkie's English Nisi Prius Reports [*171 English Reprint*] [*A publication*] (DLA) ... Starkie (Eng)
Starkville, MS [*Location identifier FAA*] (FAAL) ... STF
Starkville, MS [*AM radio station call letters*] ... WKOR
Starkville, MS [*FM radio station call letters*] ... WMSU
Starkville, MS [*FM radio station call letters*] ... WMSV
Starkville, MS [*FM radio station call letters*] ... WMXU
Starkville, MS [*AM radio station call letters*] ... WSSO
Starlight Energy [*Vancouver Stock Exchange symbol*] ... SEY
Starlight Foundation (EA) ... SF
Starlight Scope ... SS
Starlight Scope [*Night sighting device*] [*Military*] (VNW) ... SSS
Starling's East India Criminal Law and Procedure [*A publication*] (DLA) ... Starl I Cr Law
Starlog Franchise [*NASDAQ symbol*] (TTSB) ... SIFI
Star-Oriented Real-Time Teaching Instrument (AAG) ... SORTI
Star-Oriented Real-Time Tracking Instrument [*Aerospace*] (IAA) ... SORTI
Starptautiskas Apmainas Centrs [*International Exchange Center*] [*Latvia*] (EAIO) ... SAC
Starr and Curtis' Annotated Statutes [*Illinois*] [*A publication*] (DLA) ... Starr & C Ann St
Starr Center Association, Philadelphia, PA [*Library symbol Library of Congress Obsolete*] (LCLS) ... PPStarr
Starr-Edwards [*Prosthesis*] (AAMN) ... S-E
Starrett [*L. S.*] **Co.** [*NYSE symbol*] (SPSG) ... SCX
Starrett [*L.S.*] **Co.** [*Associated Press*] (SAG) ... Starret
Starrett Corp. [*AMEX symbol*] (TTSB) ... SHO
Starrett Corp. [*Associated Press*] (SAG) ... StarrtCp
Starrett Housing Corp. [*AMEX symbol*] (SPSG) ... SHO
Starrett (L.S.)'A' [*NYSE symbol*] (TTSB) ... SCX
Starrex Mining Corp. Ltd. [*Toronto Stock Exchange symbol*] ... STX
Stars of David (EA) ... SD
Stars of David International (EAIO) ... SDI
Stars of the Stage [*A publication*] ... SSA
Stars Organisation for Spastics [*British television awards program*] ... SOS
StarSight Telecast [*NASDAQ symbol*] (TTSB) ... SGHT
StarSight Telecast, Inc. [*NASDAQ symbol*] (SAG) ... SGHT
StarSight Telecast, Inc. [*Associated Press*] (SAG) ... StarTel
Starsky Operupolnomochennyy [*Senior Case Officer*] [*Soviet military rank*] ... ST
Star-Spangled Banner Flag House Association (EA) ... SSBFH
Starspeed Ltd. [*British ICAO designator*] (FAAC) ... SSP
Start (KSC) ... S
Start ... ST
Start (WDMC) ... st
Start ... STRT
Start Acknowledge [*Computer science*] (MHDI) ... STACK
Start Action Request [*Environmental Protection Agency*] ... SAR
Start Address [*Telecommunications*] (TEL) ... STAD
Start Address Register [*Telecommunications*] (IAA) ... STR
Start and Stop ... ST & SP
Start Breguet Cruise [*SST*] ... SBC
Start Checkout [*NASA*] (NASA) ... SCO
Start Climb [*Aviation*] (FAAC) ... STCLB
Start Computer ... SC
Start Conversion [*Computer science*] ... SC
Start Date (NITA) ... SD
Start Delimiter [*Computer science*] (TNIG) ... SD
Start Descent [*Aviation*] (FAAC) ... STDST
Start Device (IAA) ... SDV
Start Early and Walk [*Fictitious railroad initialism used to indicate one of the most reliable modes of rural transportation*] ... SE & W
Start Frame Delimiter (TNIG) ... SFD
Start Input/Output ... SIO
Start Interpretive Execution (HGAA) ... SIE
Start Launch Sequence [*Military*] ... SLS
Start Line ... SL
Start Manual Input (IAA) ... SMI
Start of Active Profile (PDAA) ... SAP
Start of Address ... SOA
Start of Anesthesia (DAVI) ... X
Start of Answer [*Telecommunications*] (TEL) ... AS
Start of Block ... SOB
Start of Climb [*Aviation*] (DA) ... SOC
Start of Construction [*Military*] (AFIT) ... SOC
Start of Conversion [*Navy*] ... SOC
Start of Data Block (MCD) ... SODB
Start of Entry [*Computer science*] ... SOE
Start of Frame ... SOF
Start of Header [*or Heading*] [*Transmission control character*] [*Computer science*] ... SOH

Start of Injection [*Fuel systems*] [*Automotive engineering*] .... SOI

Start of Line Block (CET) .... SOLB

Start of Manual Message (BUR) .... SMM

Start of Message [*Telecommunications*] .... SOM

Start of Message (NITA) .... SOM

Start of Minor Frame (MCD) .... SOMF

Start of Record (MUGU) .... SOR

Start of Significance [*Computer science*] (BUR) .... SOS

Start of Tape .... SOT

Start of Text .... SOT

Start of Text [*Telecommunications*] (OSI) .... STX

Start of Text Character [*Keyboard*] [*Computer science*] .... STX

Start of the Exercise (MCD) .... STARTEX

Start of Word .... SOW

Start of Work .... SOW

Start Permission (KSC) .... SP

Start Rendezvous Point (MCD) .... SRP

Start Sample Command Delayed .... SSCD

Start Signal Indicator [*Telecommunications*] (TEL) .... SSI

Start/Stop .... S/S

Start Tank (AAG) .... S/T

Start Tank Discharge Valve (KSC) .... STDV

Start Time (IAA) .... STT

Start Timing .... ST

Start Tromping on Pedal [*Facetious interpretation of the traffic sign*] .... STOP

Start Unload Address Register .... SUAR

Start Up [*of a relay, power switchgear*] (IEEE) .... SU

Start-Data-Traffic [*Computer science*] (IBMDP) .... SDT

Startec Marketing [*Vancouver Stock Exchange symbol*] .... SQE

Started (ADA) .... STD

Starter (MCD) .... ST

Starter [*Automotive engineering*] .... STRTR

Starter Corp. [*NYSE symbol*] (SPSG) .... STA

Starter Corp. [*Associated Press*] (SAG) .... Starter

Starter Electrode .... SE

Starter or Ground, Thermoplastic [*Automotive engineering*] .... SGT

Starting (MSA) .... STG

Starting Address Register (ECII) .... SAR

Starting Air Compressor (CAAL) .... SAC

Starting Air Receiver (AAG) .... SAR

Starting Charge [*Bookbinding*] (DGA) .... SC

Starting, Lighting, and Ignition [*Automobile system*] .... SLI

Starting Point .... SP

Starting Point Code (NASA) .... SPC

Starting Point Counter [*NASA*] (IAA) .... SPC

Starting Price .... SP

Starting Relay (DEN) .... SR

Starting Resistor (IAA) .... SR

Startled Falcon [*Book written by Thomas Dunn English (1844)*] .... SF

Start-of-Cycle [*Engineering*] .... SOC

Start-of-Format Control [*Computer science*] .... SOF

Start-of-Message - High Precedence (CET) .... SOM-H

Start-of-Message - Low Precedence (CET) .... SOM-L

Start-of-Message - Priority .... SOM-P

Start-of-Run [*Engineering*] .... SOR

Start-Over Dad .... SOD

Startover Data Transfer and Processing [*Program*] .... SDTP

Startover Data Transfer and Processing Program .... SDTP PROGRM

Start-Promoting Factor [*Cytology*] .... SPF

Start-Stop-Restart System [*NASA*] (KSC) .... SSRS

Startup [*Nuclear energy*] (NRCH) .... S/U

Start-Up Costs [*Business term*] (MHDB) .... SUC

Start-Up Rate (NRCH) .... SUR

Startup System [*Nuclear energy*] (NRCH) .... SUS

Start-Up Transformer (NRCH) .... SUT

Star-Vaporizing Millisecond Pulsar [*Cosmology*] .... SVP

Starved Feed Reactor [*for Polymerization*] .... SFR

Starved Rock Library System [*Library network*] .... SRLS

Starved Rock Library System, Ottawa, IL [*OCLC symbol*] (OCLC) .... IEF

Starved Rock Library System, Ottawa, IL [*Library symbol Library of Congress*] (LCLS) .... IOtS

Starview, PA [*FM radio station call letters*] (RBYB) .... WEGK-FM

Starview, PA [*FM radio station call letters*] .... WHTF

Starways SA [*Switzerland ICAO designator*] (FAAC) .... STW

Starwelt Airways [*Burundi*] [*ICAO designator*] (FAAC) .... SBU

Starwood Lodging Tr [*NYSE symbol*] (TTSB) .... HOT

Starwood Lodging Trust [*NYSE symbol*] (SAG) .... HOT

Starwood Lodging Trust [*AMEX symbol*] (SAG) .... HOT

Starwood Lodging Trust [*Associated Press*] (SAG) .... Starwd

Starwood Lodging Trust [*Associated Press*] (SAG) .... StarwdLT

Stat [*Unit of radioactive disintegration rate*] .... s

STAT Healthcare [*NASDAQ symbol*] (TTSB) .... ERDR

Stat Healthcare, Inc. [*NASDAQ symbol*] (SAG) .... ERDR

Stat Healthcare, Inc. [*Associated Press*] (SAG) .... StatHlt

Stat Healthcare, Inc. [*Associated Press*] (SAG) .... StatHlth

Stat Healthcare Wrrt'A' [*NASDAQ symbol*] (TTSB) .... ERDRW

Statampere [*Also, statA*] [*Unit of electric current*] .... sA

Statampere [*Also, sA*] [*Unit of electric current*] .... statA

Statcoulomb [*Also, Fr, statC*] [*Unit of electric charge*] .... sC

Statcoulomb [*Also, sC*] [*Unit of electric charge*] .... statC

State [*Telecommunications*] .... S

State .... ST

State (WDMC) .... st

State .... STAT

State Aboriginal Affairs [*South Australia*] .... SAA

State Acid Rain Projects [*Environmental Protection Agency*] (GFGA) .... STAR

State Actuary and Insurance Commissioner [*Queensland, Australia*] .... SAIC

State Administration of Exchange Control [*China*] .... SAEC

State Administrative Agency (GFGA) .... SAA

State Administrative Expense Funds .... SAEF

State Advisory Committee [*Department of Education*] .... SAC

State Advisory Councils for Vocational Education (EDAC) .... SACVE

State Agency [*Formerly, the Disability Determination Services*] [*Social Security Administration*] (OICC) .... SA

State Agency for Surplus Property .... SASP

State Agency Issuance [*Employment and Training Administration*] (OICC) .... SAI

State Agency Libraries of Texas [*Library network*] .... SALT

State Agent [*Insurance*] .... S/A

State Agricultural Experiment Station .... SAES

State Air Resources Board .... SARB

State Airport System Plan [*Department of Transportation*] .... SASP

State Alcoholism and Drug Abuse Profile [*Public Health Service*] [*Information service or system*] (IID) .... SADAP

State Alcoholism Profile Information System [*Public Health Service*] (IID) .... SAPIS

State and Function Control Unit [*Computer science*] (MHDI) .... SFCU

State and Local Air Monitoring Stations [*Environmental Protection Agency*] .... SLAMS

State and Local Air Pollution Control Official [*Environmental Protection Agency*] (ERG) .... STALAPCO

State and Local Assistance Act .... SLAA

State and Local Documents Task Force [*Government Documents Round Table*] [*American Library Association*] .... SLDTF

State and Local Officials for Soviet Jews (EA) .... SLOSJ

State and Local Planning Division [*Environmental Protection Agency*] (GFGA) .... SLPD

State and Local Program Support [*Nuclear energy*] (NRCH) .... SLPS

State and Local Tax Service (Prentice-Hall, Inc.) [*A publication*] (DLA) .... St & Loc Tax Serv (P-H)

State and Local Taxes (Bureau of National Affairs) [*A publication*] (DLA) .... St & Loc Taxes (BNA)

State and Metropolitan Analyses of Regional Transportation [*BTS*] (TAG) .... SMART

State and Metropolitan Area Data Book [*Bureau of the Census*] (GFGA) .... SAMADB

State and National Apprenticeship Program Statistics [*Bureau of Apprenticeship and Training*] [*Department of Labor*] .... SNAPS

State and Regional Associations of the United States [*A publication*] .... SRA

State and Regional Defense Airlift Plan [*FAA, Civil Defense*] .... SARDA

State and Regional Indicators Archive [*University of New Hampshire*] [*Information service or system*] (IID) .... SRIA

State and Territorial Air Pollution Program Administrators (EA) .... STAPPA

State Applicant Agency (GFGA) .... SAA

State Apprenticeship Council [*Bureau of Apprenticeship and Training*] [*Department of Labor*] .... SAC

State Approving Agency [*Bureau of Apprenticeship and Training*] [*Department of Labor*] .... SAA

State Archives [*Australia*] .... SA

State Area Commands (MCD) .... STARC

State, Army, Navy, Air (AABC) .... SANA

State Assisted Academic Library Council of Kentucky [*Library network*] .... SAALCK

State Association President [*American Occupational Therapy Association*] .... SAP

State Auditors Coordinating Committee (EA) .... SACC

State Auto Financial [*NASDAQ symbol*] (TTSB) .... STFC

State Auto Financial Corp. [*Associated Press*] (SAG) .... StatAut

State Auto Financial Corp. [*NASDAQ symbol*] (SPSG) .... STFC

State Aviation Liaison Official (NOAA) .... SALO

State Bancorp, Inc. [*Associated Press*] (SAG) .... StateBcp

State Bancorp, Inc. [*NASDAQ symbol*] (SAG) .... STBC

State Bancorp NY [*NASDAQ symbol*] (TTSB) .... STBC

State Bank of India (PDAA) .... SBI

State Bank of New South Wales [*Australia*] .... SBNSW

State Bank of Pakistan .... SBP

State Bank of South Australia .... SBSA

State Bank of Victoria [*Australia*] .... SBV

State Bar Journal of California [*A publication*] (DLA) .... S Bar J

State Bar Review [*A publication*] (DLA) .... St Bar Rev

State Board of Education (OICC) .... SBE

State Board of Health (MAE) .... SBH

State Board of Medical Examiners (NADA) .... SBME

State Board of Vocational Education [*State Board of Education*] (OICC) .... SBVE

State Boards Test Pool Examination [*Medicine*] (DMAA) .... SBTPE

State Business and Corporate Affairs Office [*South Australia*] .... SBCAO

State Capacity Building (EDAC) .... SCB

State Casual Employees Superannuation Board [*Victoria, Australia*] .... SCESB

State Center Enterprise, State Center, IA [*Library symbol*] [*Library of Congress*] (LCLS) .... IaStcE

State Central Information Reception Agency .... SCIRA

State Chamber of Commerce [*New South Wales*] [*Australia*] .... SCC(NSW)

State Chamber of Commerce [*Queensland*] [*Australia*] .... SCC(Q)

State Change Algorithm Translator .... SCAT

State Civil Defense .... SCD

State Coastal Zone (NOAA) .... SCZ

State College [*Pennsylvania*] [*Airport symbol*] (OAG) .... SCE

State College [*Pennsylvania*] [*Seismograph station code, US Geological Survey*] (SEIS) .... SCP

State College of Arkansas, Conway, AR [*Library symbol Library of Congress*] (LCLS) .... ArCT

State College of Washington .... SCW

State College, PA [*Location identifier FAA*] (FAAL) .... SCE
State College, PA [*Location identifier FAA*] (FAAL) .... UNV
State College, PA [*FM radio station call letters*] .... WBHV
State College, PA [*FM radio station call letters*] .... WFGI
State College, PA [*FM radio station call letters*] (RBYB) ..... WKPS
State College, PA [*AM radio station call letters*] .... WMAJ
State College, PA [*FM radio station call letters*] .... WPSU
State College, PA [*AM radio station call letters*] .... WQWK
State College, PA [*AM radio station call letters*] .... WRSC
State College, PA [*FM radio station call letters*] .... WTLR
State Commission Against Discrimination .... SCAD
State Commission for Space Exploration [*Former USSR*] .... SCSE
State Committee on the Utilization of Atomic Energy [*Former USSR*] ...... SCUAE
State Community College of East St. Louis, Learning Resources Center, East St. Louis, IL [*Library symbol Library of Congress*] (LCLS) ...... IEsSC
State Contracts Control Board [*New South Wales, Australia*] ..... SCCB
State Controller and System Services [*NASA*] .... SCSS
State Cooperative Extension Service .... SCES
State Coordinating Officer [*Federal disaster planning*] .... SCO
State Coordination Committee [*Responsible for administering the Work Incentive Program at the state level*] .... SCC
State Coroners' Office [*Australia*] .... SCO
State Corporation Commission .... SCC
State Correctional Institute at Camp Hill, Camp Hill, PA [*OCLC symbol*] (OCLC) PI1
State Correctional Institute at Dallas, Dallas, PA [*OCLC symbol*] (OCLC) PI2
State Correctional Institute at Grateford, Grateford, PA [*OCLC symbol*] (OCLC) PI3
State Correctional Institute at Huntingdon, Huntingdon, PA [*OCLC symbol*] (OCLC) PI4
State Correctional Institute at Muncy, Muncy, PA [*OCLC symbol*] (OCLC) PI5
State Correctional Institute at Pittsburgh, Pittsburgh, PA [*OCLC symbol*] (OCLC) PI6
State Cost Accounting System (OICC) .... SCAS
State Criminal Justice Communications .... STACOM
State Data Center [*Bureau of the Census*] (GFGA) .... SDC
State Data Program [*Information service or system*] (IID) .... SDP
State Defense Council .... SDC
State Defense Force Association of the United States (EA) ..... SDFAUS
State, Defense Liaison Office [*Federal government*] (AABC) .... SDLO
State Department .... SD
State Department of Education (DAVI) .... SDE
State Department of Education (OICC) .... SDOE
State Department of Education-Information System [*Minnesota*] (EDAC) .... SDE-IS
State Department Reports [*A publication*] (DLA) .... St Dept
State Department Telegram (NATG) .... DEPTEL
State Dependent State Variable Feedback [*Rocket engine*] [*NASA*] ..... SDSVF
State Development Bank [*Hungary*] .... SDB
State Development Company (AAGC) .... SDC
State Difference Equation (IAA) .... SDE
State Director .... SD
State Disability (DAVI) .... SD
State Disability Insurance .... SDI
State Disability Insurance - Unemployment Compensation .... SDI/UC
State Disability Service (DAVI) .... SDS
State Disasters Committee [*Australia*] .... SDC
State Document (WDAA) .... S DOC
State Earnings-Related Pension Scheme [*British*] .... SERPS
State Earthquake Administration [*China*] [*Marine science*] (OSRA) .... SEA
State Economic Area [*Bureau of Economic Analysis*] [*Department of Commerce*] .... SEA
State Economic Information Management System [*State Department*] [*Database*] .... SEIMS
State Economic Opportunity Office .... SEOO
State Education Agency [*Department of Education*] .... SEA
State Education Research Clearinghouse [*California*] (EDAC) .... SERCH
State Emergency Communications Committee [*National Oceanic and Atmospheric Administration*] (GFGA) .... SECC
State Emergency Defense Airlift .... SEDA
State Emergency Management Committee [*New South Wales, Australia*] .... SEMC
State Emergency Management Organisation [*New South Wales, Australia*] .... SEMO
State Emergency Operations Centre [*New South Wales, Australia*] .... SEOC
State Emergency Planning Director [*Civil Defense*] .... SEPD
State Emergency Response Commission [*Environmental science*] .... SERC
State Emergency Response Committee [*Environmental Protection Agency*] .... SERC
State Employees' Retirement Benefits Board [*Australia*] .... SERBB
State Employees Retirement System .... SERS
State Employment Security Agency .... SESA
State Energy Conservation Program .... SECP
State Energy Data System [*Department of Energy*] [*Database*] .... SEDS
State Energy Office .... SEO
State Energy Research Advisory Committee [*Australia*] .... SERAC
State Energy Research and Development Fund [*New South Wales, Australia*] .... SERDF
State Enforcement Agreement [*Environmental Protection Agency*] (GFGA) ..... SEA
State Engineer's Office, Cheyenne, WY [*Library symbol Library of Congress*] (LCLS) .... WyCSE
State Enrolled Nurse [*British*] .... SEN
State Enrolled Nurse (Mental Nursing) [*British*] (DBQ) .... SEN(M)
State Enrolled Nurse (Mental Subnormal Nursing) [*British*] (DBQ) .... SEN(MS)
State Environmental Education Coordinators Association [*Defunct*] (EA) .... SEECA

State Equalized Value [*Real estate*] .... SEV
State Estimation Algorithm for Small-Scale System (PDAA) .... SEAS
State Executive Director .... SED
State Experiment Stations Division [*of ARS, Department of Agriculture*] .... SES
State Extension Management Information System [*Department of Agriculture*] .... SEMIS
State Farm Insurance Co., Bloomington, IL [*Library symbol*] [*Library of Congress*] (LCLS) .... IBIoSF
State/Federal Fisheries Management Program [*National Marine Fisheries Service*] .... SFFMP
State FIFRA [*Federal Insecticide, Fungicide, and Rodenticide Act*] Issues Research and Evaluation Group [*Environmental Protection Agency*] (EGAO) .... SFIREG
State Film Centre of Victoria [*Australia*] .... SFCV
State Financial Services Corp. [*NASDAQ symbol*] (SAG) .... SFSW
State Financial Services Corp. [*Associated Press*] (SAG) .... StFncl
State Financial Svcs 'A' [*NASDAQ symbol*] (TTSB) .... SFSW
State Fire Commission of Tasmania [*Australia*] .... SFCT
State Fleet Services [*New South Wales, Australia*] .... SFS
State Flight Academy of Ukraine [*FAA designator*] (FAAC) .... UFA
State Forces [*India*] [*Army*] .... SF
State Fund Chairmen [*Red Cross*] .... SFC
State Fund Vice Chairmen [*Red Cross*] .... SFVC
State Government Research Directory [*A publication*] .... SGRD
State Governmental Affairs Council (EA) .... SGAC
State Grants Commission [*Tasmania, Australia*] .... SGC
State Guaranteed Agency (GFGA) .... SGA
State Hazardous Materials Enforcement Development [*Nuclear energy*] (NRCH) .... SHMED
State Health Plan [*Generic term*] (DHSM) .... SHP
State Health Planning and Development Agency .... SHPDA
State Higher Education Executive Officers Association (EA) .... SHEEO
State Highway Agency [*MOCD*] (TAG) .... SHA
State Highway Departments [*A publication*] (AAGC) .... SHD
State Highway Safety Agencies [*NHTSA*] (TAG) .... SHSA
State Historic Preservation Office .... SHPO
State Historic Preservation Officer .... SHPO
State Historical Society of Iowa, Iowa City, IA [*Library symbol Library of Congress*] (LCLS) .... IaHi
State Historical Society of North Dakota, Bismarck, ND [*OCLC symbol*] (OCLC) .... HND
State Historical Society of North Dakota, Bismarck, ND [*Library symbol Library of Congress*] (LCLS) .... NdHi
State Historical Society of Wisconsin, Madison, WI [*Library symbol Library of Congress*] (LCLS) .... WHi
State Historical Society of Wisconsin, Madison, WI [*OCLC symbol*] (OCLC) .... WIH
State Hospital (MAE) .... SH
State Hospital, Jamestown, ND [*Library symbol Library of Congress*] (LCLS) .... NdJSH
State Hospital South, Medical Library, Blackfoot, ID [*Library symbol*] [*Library of Congress*] (LCLS) .... IdBfH
State Implementation and Enforcement Program [*Environmental Protection Agency*] .... SIEP
State Implementation Grant .... SIG
State Implementation Plan [*Environmental Protection Agency*] .... SIP
State Implementation Plan System [*Environmental Protection Agency*] .... SIPS
State Income Tax (AAGC) .... SIT
State Income Tax Withheld .... SITW
State Industry Advisory Committee [*Civil Defense*] .... SIAC
State Information Service [*Australia*] .... SIS
State Information Technology [*Western Australia*] .... SIT
State Interagency Coordinating Council .... SICC
State Job Training Coordinating Council (OICC) .... SJTCC
State Judicial Information System (OICC) .... SJIS
State Labor Relations Board .... SLRB
State Lamb Producers' Association [*Queensland, Australia*] .... SLPA
State Law and Order Restoration Council [*Myanmar*] .... SLORC
State Law Library of Montana, Helena, MT [*OCLC symbol*] (OCLC) .... MTS
State Legalization Impact Assistance Grant [*Department of Health and Human Services*] .... SLIAG
State Legislative Committee .... SLC
State Level Electricity Demand [*Model*] [*Nuclear Regulatory Commission*] .... SLED
State Liaison Officer .... SLO
State Library Agency Section [*Association of Specialized and Cooperative Library Agencies*] .... SLAS
State Library Commission of Iowa, Des Moines, IA [*OCLC symbol*] (OCLC) .... IOZ
State Library of Florida, Bureau of Book Processing, Tallahassee, FL [*OCLC symbol*] (OCLC) .... FBN
State Library of Florida, Tallahassee, FL [*OCLC symbol*] (OCLC) .... FBA
State Library of Ohio .... SLO
State Library of Ohio, Catalog Center, Columbus, OH [*OCLC symbol*] (OCLC) .... SLC
State Library of Ohio, Columbus, OH [*OCLC symbol*] (OCLC) .... OHI
State Library of Pennsylvania, Harrisburg, PA [*OCLC symbol*] (OCLC) .... PHA
State Library of Queensland, Brisbane, QLD, Australia [*Library symbol Library of Congress*] (LCLS) .... AuBrS
State Library of Queensland, Oxley Memorial Library, Brisbane, QLD, Australia [*Library symbol Library of Congress*] (LCLS) .... AuBrS-O
State Library of Tasmania, Hobart, TAS, Australia [*Library symbol Library of Congress*] (LCLS) .... AuHS
State Library of Victoria [*State*] (EERA) .... VSL
State Library of Victoria, Melbourne, V, Australia [*Library symbol Library of Congress*] (LCLS) .... AuMS

State Library, Pretoria, South Africa [*Library symbol Library of Congress*] (LCLS) ... SaPSL
State Library Resource Center - Maryland Interlibrary Organization [*Library network*] ... SLRC/MILO
State Line End Point (DNAB) ... SLEP
State Liquor Authority ... SLA
State Loan Repayment Program [*Department of Health and Human Services*] (GFGA) ... SLRP
State Local Government Relations Unit [*South Australia*] ... SLGRU
State Maintenance Office [*or Officer*] [*Military*] ... SMO
State Manpower Coordinating Committee [*Department of Labor*] ... SMCC
State Manpower Service Council [*Department of Labor*] ... SMSC
State Medicaid Directors Association (EA) ... SMDA
State Medical Facilities Plan [*Generic term*] (DHSM) ... SMFP
State Medical Journal Advertising Bureau (DAVI) ... SMJAB
State Medical Society (DAVI) ... SMS
State Medical Society (MAE) ... SMS
State Mental Health Agency (DMAA) ... SMHA
State Meteorlogy Administration [*China*] [*Marine science*] (OSRA) ... SMA
State Microscopical Society of Illinois (EA) ... SMSI
State Militia [*e.g., NJSM - New Jersey State Militia*] ... SM
State Minerals Advisory Council [*Australia*] ... SMAC
State Monopoly Capitalism ... STAMOCAP
State Motor Carrier Guide [*Commerce Clearing House*] [*A publication*] (DLA) ... State Mot Carr Guide
State Motor Carrier Guide (Commerce Clearing House) [*A publication*] (DLA) ... St Mot Carr Guide (CCH)
State Music Trust [*Record label*] [*Former USSR*] ... USSR
State Music Trust [*78 RPM*] [*Record label*] [*Former USSR*] ... USSRM
State Mutual Life Assurance Co. of America ... SMA
State Narcotic Law ... SNL
State Normal and Industrial School, Ellendale, ND [*Library symbol Library of Congress Obsolete*] (LCLS) ... NdEIN
State Occupational Information Coordinating Committee ... SOICC
State Oceanic Administration [*China*] [*Marine science*] (OSRA) ... SOA
State of Alert ... SOA
State of California Answering Network [*Information service or system*] (IID) ... SCAN
State of Charge ... SOC
State of Charge ... SOC
State of Consciousness ... SoC
State of Environment [*Australia*] ... SOE
State of Illinois, Institute of Natural Resources, Division of Environmental Management, Chicago, IL [*Library symbol Library of Congress*] (LCLS) ... ISNR-E
State of Illinois, Institute of Natural Resources, Energy Information Library, Springfield, IL [*Library symbol Library of Congress*] (LCLS) ... ISNR
State of Louisiana: Acts of the Legislature [*A publication*] (DLA) ... LA Acts
State of Missouri Code of State Regulations Annotated [*A publication*] (AAGC) ... Mo Code Regs
State of North Carolina, Governor's Press Office State Capital Building, Raleigh, NC [*Library symbol*] [*Library of Congress*] (LCLS) ... NcRGP
State of Ohio: Legislative Acts Passed and Joint Resolutions Adopted [*A publication*] (DLA) ... Ohio Laws
State of Origin [*Soccer*] ... SOO
State of Polarization ... SOP
State of Readiness (MCD) ... SOR
State of Stimulus Overinclusion [*Schizophrenia*] ... SOI
State of Termination [*Telecommunications*] (TEL) ... SOT
State of the Art ... SOA
State of the Art ... SOTA
State of the Art, Inc. [*NASDAQ symbol*] (SPSG) ... SOTA
State of the Art, Inc. [*Associated Press*] (SAG) ... SteArt
State of the Environment (EERA) ... SOE
State of the Environment Report (EERA) ... SOER
State of the Forests Report (EERA) ... SOFR
State of the Marine Environment Reporting [*Commonwealth*] (EERA) ... SOMER
State of the Total Army Report Team ... START
State of Utah Bulletin [*A publication*] (DLA) ... Utah Admin Bull
State of Vermont, Department of Libraries, Montpelier, VT [*Library symbol Library of Congress*] (LCLS) ... Vt
State of Vietnam Ribbon of Friendship [*Presidential unit commendation*] ... SOVNROF
State of Vietnam Ribbon of Friendship [*Military decoration*] (AABC) ... SVNRF
State of Washington Department of General Administration, Division of Archives and Records Management, Olympia, WA [*Library symbol Library of Congress*] (LCLS) ... WaOAr
State of Washington Department of Labor and Industries Libraries, Olympia, WA [*Library symbol Library of Congress*] (LCLS) ... WaOLI
State Officer ... SO
State On-the-Job Training Agencies [*Department of Labor*] ... SOJTA
State Opera of South Australia ... SOSA
State Operating Permit Program [*Environmental Protection Agency*] ... SOPP
State Operations Manual [*Home Health Agency Program*] [*Department of Health and Human Services*] (GFGA) ... SOM
State Operator and Result [*Computer program*] ... SOAR
State or Local Government ... SLG
State Papers [*A publication*] (DLA) ... St P
State Park [*State*] (EERA) ... SP
State per Pupil Expenditure [*Education*] (GFGA) ... SPPE
State Permit System [*Environmental Protection Agency*] (GFGA) ... SPS
State Plan (OICC) ... SP
State Plane Coordinate System [*National Geodetic Survey Division*] [*National Oceanic and Atmospheric Administration*] ... SPCS
State Planning Agency [*Department of Justice*] ... SPA
State Planning Office, Library, Baton Rouge, LA [*Library symbol Library of Congress*] (LCLS) ... LBrSP
State Plantations Impact Study [*Victoria, Australia*] ... SPIS
State Pollution Control Commission [*of New South Wales*] [*State*] (EERA) ... SPCC
State Power Authority (IAA) ... SPA
State Programs Division [*Environmental Protection Agency*] (GFGA) ... SPD
State Property Agency [*Hungary*] (ECON) ... SPA
State Public Historical Library, Moscow, Soviet Union [*Library symbol Library of Congress*] (LCLS) ... RuMHi
State Public Services Federation Victoria [*Australia*] ... SPSFV
State Purchasing and Sales Division [*Tasmania, Australia*] ... SPSD
State Recreation Area [*State*] (EERA) ... SRA
State Recycling Organizations [*Environment*] (GNE) ... SRO
State Regional Correctional Facility at Mercer, Mercer, PA [*OCLC symbol*] (OCLC) ... PIQ
State Regional Correctional Facility, Greensburg, PA [*OCLC symbol*] (OCLC) ... PI7
State Register ... SR
State Registered Dietitian ... SRD
State Registered Nurse [*British*] ... SRN
State Registered Physiotherapist [*British*] ... SRP
State Regulation Report: Toxics [*Business Publishers, Inc.*] [*Information service or system*] (CRD) ... SRR
State Reporter [*A publication*] (DLA) ... St Rep
State Reports [*A publication*] (DLA) ... St Rep
State Required Public Notification of Standards Exceedances [*Environmental Protection Agency*] ... SRPNSE
State Research Bureau [*Secret police*] [*Uganda*] ... SRB
State Revenue Board [*Victoria, Australia*] ... SRB
State Revenue Society (EA) ... SRS
State Revolving Fund [*Environmental Protection Agency*] (GFGA) ... SRF
State Rivers and Estuaries Policy [*New South Wales*] (EERA) ... SREP
State Rural Assistance Scheme [*New South Wales*] [*State*] (EERA) ... SRAS
State Rural Development Councils (USGC) ... SRDC
State School (ADA) ... SS
State Science and Technology Commission [*China*] ... SSTC
State Science, Engineering, and Technology Program [*National Science Foundation*] ... SSET
State Seismological Bureau [*China*] ... SSB
State Seismological Bureau [*China*] ... SSB
State Servants and Allied Motoring Association [*British*] (DBA) ... SSMA
State Service Center Program (OICC) ... SSCP
State Services Group [*Information service or system*] (IID) ... SSG
State Sports Council [*Victoria, Australia*] ... SSC
State Str Boston [*NYSE symbol*] (TTSB) ... STT
State Street Boston, Inc. [*Associated Press*] (SAG) ... StaSTBos
State Street Boston, Inc. [*NYSE symbol*] (SAG) ... STT
State Student Assessment Test [*Florida*] (EDAC) ... SSAT
State Student Incentive Grant [*Department of Education*] ... SSIG
State Superfund Contract [*Environmental Protection Agency*] ... SSC
State Supervisor ... SS
State Supplementary Payment [*Department of Health and Human Services*] ... SSP
State Supply Board [*South Australia*] ... SSB
State Supply Commission [*Western Australia*] ... SSC
State Supply Service [*Victoria, Australia*] ... SSS
State Tax Cases [*Commerce Clearing House*] [*A publication*] (DLA) ... STC
State Tax Cases Reporter [*Commerce Clearing House*] [*A publication*] (DLA) ... State Tax Cas Rep
State Tax Cases Reporter (Commerce Clearing House) [*A publication*] (DLA) ... St Tax Cas Rep (CCH)
State Tax Cases Reports (Commerce Clearing House) [*A publication*] (DLA) ... CCH State Tax Cas Rep
State Tax Management System [*Price Waterhouse & Co.*] (PCM) ... STMS
State Tax Reporter (Commerce Clearing House) [*A publication*] (DLA) ... St Tax Rep (CCH)
State Tax Review (Commerce Clearing House) [*A publication*] (DLA) ... CCH State Tax Rev
State Taxation Department [*Western Australia*] ... STD
State Taxation Office [*Australia*] ... STO
State Teachers College ... STC
State Teachers' College, Hyannis, MA [*Library symbol Library of Congress Obsolete*] (LCLS) ... MHyT
State Technical Assistance (OICC) ... STA
State Technical Institute ... STI
State Technical Institute and Rehabilitation Center, Plainwell, MI [*Library symbol Library of Congress*] (LCLS) ... MiPIS
State Technical Institute at Memphis, Memphis, TN [*Library symbol Library of Congress*] (LCLS) ... TMTI
State Technical Services [*Abolished, 1970*] ... STS
State Technical Services Act ... STSA
State Technology Extension Program [*National Institute of Standards and Technology*] ... STEP
State Tender Board [*Victoria, Australia*] ... STB
State/Territorial Operational Guidelines [*Australia*] ... STOG
State/Territories Consultative Committee [*Australia*] ... SCC
State Theatre of Victoria [*Australia*] ... STOV
State Total Cost [*Bookselling*] (DGA) ... STC
State Transit Authority Plan [*Victoria, Australia*] ... STAP
State Transition Matrix ... STM
State, Treasury, War, Attorney General, Postmaster General, Navy, Interior, Agriculture, Commerce, Labor [*Pre-1947 mnemonic guide to names of the departments in the President's Cabinet, in order of creation*] [*Obsolete*] ... ST. WAPNIACL

State Trials [*Legal*] [*British*] ... ST
State Trials [*A publication*] (DLA) ... St Tri
State Trials (Howell) [*England*] [*A publication*] (DLA) ... State Tr
State Trials, New Series, Edited by Macdonell [*England*] [*A publication*] (DLA) ... State Tr NS
State Unemployment Disability Insurance (AAG) ... SUDI
State Unemployment Tax (MCD) ... SUT
State Universities Association [*Later, NASULGC*] ... SUA
State University Computation Center [*Iowa State University*] [*Research center*] (RCD) ... SUCC
State University of Iowa [*Later, University of Iowa*] ... SUI
State University of Iowa Hospitals (DAVI) ... SUIH
State University of Nebraska ... SUN
State University of New York [*Computer retrieval and control projects*] [*Albany, NY*] ... SUNY
State University of New York, Agricultural and Technical College at Alfred, Alfred, NY [*Library symbol Library of Congress*] (LCLS) ... NAlfUA
State University of New York, Agricultural and Technical College at Alfred, Alfred, NY [*OCLC symbol*] (OCLC) ... ZAM
State University of New York, Agricultural and Technical College at Canton, Canton, NY [*OCLC symbol*] (OCLC) ... ZCM
State University of New York, Agricultural and Technical College at Cobleskill, Cobleskill, NY [*Library symbol Library of Congress*] (LCLS) ... NCobUA
State University of New York, Agricultural and Technical College at Delhi, Delhi, NY [*Library symbol Library of Congress*] (LCLS) ... NDeUA
State University of New York, Agricultural and Technical College at Delhi, Delhi, NY [*OCLC symbol*] (OCLC) ... XDM
State University of New York, Agricultural and Technical College at Farmingdale,Farmingdale, NY [*Library symbol Library of Congress*] (LCLS) ... NFarUA
State University of New York, Agricultural and Technical College at Farmingdale,Farmingdale, NY [*OCLC symbol*] (OCLC) ... YFM
State University of New York, Agricultural and Technical College at Morrisville,Morrisville, NY [*Library symbol Library of Congress*] (LCLS) ... NMvUA
State University of New York, Agricultural and Technical College at Morrisville,Morrisville, NY [*OCLC symbol*] (OCLC) ... XMM
State University of New York, Agricultural and Technical College, Canton, NY [*Library symbol Library of Congress*] (LCLS) ... NCaUA
State University of New York, Agricultural and Technical College, Cobleskill, Cobleskill, NY [*OCLC symbol*] (OCLC) ... WKM
State University of New York, Albany Library School, Albany, NY [*OCLC symbol*] (OCLC) ... ZAL
State University of New York at Albany (GAGS) ... SUNY (Albany)
State University of New York at Albany ... SUNYA
State University of New York at Albany, Albany, NY [*Library symbol Library of Congress*] (LCLS) ... NAlU
State University of New York at Albany, Albany, NY [*OCLC symbol*] (OCLC) ... NAM
State University of New York at Albany, Filmdex, Albany, NY [*Library symbol Library of Congress*] (LCLS) ... NAlU-F
State University of New York at Albany, Graduate School of Public Affairs, Albany, NY [*Library symbol Library of Congress*] (LCLS) ... NAlU-PA
State University of New York at Albany Library School, Albany, NY [*Library symbol Library of Congress*] (LCLS) ... NAlU-L
State University of New York at Binghampton (GAGS) ... SUNY (Binghampton)
State University of New York at Binghamton, Binghamton, NY [*OCLC symbol*] (OCLC) ... BNG
State University of New York at Binghamton, Binghamton, NY [*Library symbol Library of Congress*] (LCLS) ... NBiSU
State University of New York at Brooklyn, Medical Research Library, Brooklyn, NY [*Library symbol*] [*Library of Congress*] (LCLS) ... NBSU-M
State University of New York at Buffalo (GAGS) ... SUNY (Buffalo)
State University of New York at Buffalo ... SUNYAB
State University of New York at Buffalo, Archives, Buffalo, NY [*Library symbol Library of Congress*] (LCLS) ... NBuU-AR
State University of New York at Buffalo, Art Library, Buffalo, NY [*Library symbol Library of Congress*] (LCLS) ... NBuU-A
State University of New York at Buffalo, Bell Annex, Buffalo, NY [*Library symbol Library of Congress*] (LCLS) ... NBuU-BA
State University of New York at Buffalo, Bell Science Library, Buffalo, NY [*Library symbol Library of Congress*] (LCLS) ... NBuU-BS
State University of New York at Buffalo, Buffalo, NY [*OCLC symbol*] (OCLC) ... BUF
State University of New York at Buffalo, Buffalo, NY [*Library symbol Library of Congress*] (LCLS) ... NBuU
State University of New York at Buffalo, Chemistry Library, Buffalo, NY [*Library symbol Library of Congress*] (LCLS) ... NBuU-C
State University of New York at Buffalo, Documents Library, Buffalo, NY [*Library symbol Library of Congress*] (LCLS) ... NBuU-D
State University of New York at Buffalo, Educational Opportunity Center, Buffalo, NY [*Library symbol Library of Congress*] (LCLS) ... NBuU-E
State University of New York at Buffalo, Harriman Library, Buffalo, NY [*Library symbol Library of Congress*] (LCLS) ... NBuU-HA
State University of New York at Buffalo, Health Sciences Library, Buffalo, NY [*Library symbol Library of Congress*] (LCLS) ... NBuU-H
State University of New York at Buffalo, Law Library, Buffalo, NY [*Library symbol Library of Congress*] (LCLS) ... NBuU-L
State University of New York at Buffalo, Law Library, Buffalo, NY [*OCLC symbol*] (OCLC) ... SBL
State University of New York at Buffalo, Library Literature Library, Buffalo, NY [*Library symbol Library of Congress*] (LCLS) ... NBuU-LL
State University of New York at Buffalo, Library Science Library, Buffalo, NY [*Library symbol Library of Congress*] (LCLS) ... NBuU-LS
State University of New York at Buffalo, Music Library, Buffalo, NY [*Library symbol Library of Congress*] (LCLS) ... NBuU-Mu
State University of New York at Buffalo, Physics Library, Buffalo, NY [*Library symbol Library of Congress*] (LCLS) ... NBuU-P
State University of New York at Buffalo, Poetry Library, Buffalo, NY [*Library symbol Library of Congress*] (LCLS) ... NBuU-PO
State University of New York at Buffalo, Reference, Buffalo, NY [*Library symbol Library of Congress*] (LCLS) ... NBuU-R
State University of New York at Buffalo, Ridge Lea, Buffalo, NY [*Library symbol Library of Congress*] (LCLS) ... NBuU-RL
State University of New York at Buffalo, Roswell Park Memorial Institute, Buffalo, NY [*Library symbol Library of Congress*] (LCLS) ... NBuU-RP
State University of New York at Buffalo, Science and Engineering Library, Buffalo, NY [*Library symbol Library of Congress*] (LCLS) ... NBuU-SE
State University of New York at Stony Brook (GAGS) ... SUNY (Stony Brook)
State University of New York at Stony Brook, Health Sciences Library, Stony Brook, NY [*Library symbol Library of Congress*] (LCLS) ... NSbSU-H
State University of New York at Stony Brook, Health Sciences Library, Stony Brook, NY [*OCLC symbol*] (OCLC) ... VZB
State University of New York at Stony Brook, Stony Brook, NY [*Library symbol Library of Congress*] (LCLS) ... NSbSU
State University of New York at Stony Brook, Stony Brook, NY [*OCLC symbol*] (OCLC) ... YSM
State University of New York Biomedical Communication Network (EA) ... SUNY BCN
State University of New York, Central Administration, Albany, NY [*OCLC symbol*] (OCLC) ... ZJC
State University of New York College at Brockport (GAGS) ... SUNYC (Brockport)
State University of New York, College at Brockport, Brockport, NY [*Library symbol Library of Congress*] (LCLS) ... NBrockU
State University of New York, College at Brockport, Brockport, NY [*OCLC symbol*] (OCLC) ... XBM
State University of New York College at Buffalo (GAGS) ... SUNYC (Buffalo)
State University of New York, College at Buffalo, Buffalo, NY [*Library symbol Library of Congress*] (LCLS) ... NBuC
State University of New York, College at Buffalo, Buffalo, NY [*OCLC symbol*] (OCLC) ... YBM
State University of New York College at Cortland (GAGS) ... SUNYC (Cortland)
State University of New York, College at Cortland, Cortland, NY [*Library symbol Library of Congress*] (LCLS) ... NCortU
State University of New York, College at Cortland, Cortland, NY [*OCLC symbol*] (OCLC) ... YCM
State University of New York College at Fredonia (GAGS) ... SUNYC (Fredonia)
State University of New York, College at Fredonia, Fredonia, NY [*Library symbol Library of Congress*] (LCLS) ... NFredU
State University of New York, College at Fredonia, Fredonia, NY [*OCLC symbol*] (OCLC) ... XFM
State University of New York College at Geneseo (GAGS) ... SUNYC (Geneseo)
State University of New York, College at Geneseo, Geneseo, NY [*Library symbol Library of Congress*] (LCLS) ... NGenoU
State University of New York, College at Geneseo, Geneseo, NY [*OCLC symbol*] (OCLC) ... YGM
State University of New York College at New Paltz (GAGS) ... SUNYC (New Paltz)
State University of New York, College at New Paltz, New Paltz, NY [*Library symbol Library of Congress*] (LCLS) ... NNepaSU
State University of New York, College at New Paltz, New Paltz, NY [*OCLC symbol*] (OCLC) ... ZLM
State University of New York, College at Old Westbury, Old Westbury, NY [*OCLC symbol*] (OCLC) ... ZOW
State University of New York, College at Old Westbury, Oyster Bay, NY [*Library symbol Library of Congress*] (LCLS) ... NOwU
State University of New York College at Oneonta (GAGS) ... SUNYC (Oneonta)
State University of New York, College at Oneonta, Oneonta, NY [*Library symbol Library of Congress*] (LCLS) ... NOneoU
State University of New York, College at Oneonta, Oneonta, NY [*OCLC symbol*] (OCLC) ... ZBM
State University of New York College at Oswego (GAGS) ... SUNYC (Oswego)
State University of New York, College at Oswego, Oswego, NY [*Library symbol Library of Congress*] (LCLS) ... NOsU
State University of New York, College at Oswego, Oswego, NY [*OCLC symbol*] (OCLC) ... YOM
State University of New York College at Plattsburg (GAGS) ... SUNYC (Plattsburg)
State University of New York, College at Plattsburgh, Plattsburgh, NY [*Library symbol Library of Congress*] (LCLS) ... NPlaU
State University of New York, College at Plattsburgh, Plattsburgh, NY [*OCLC symbol*] (OCLC) ... YPM
State University of New York College at Potsdam (GAGS) ... SUNYC (Potsdam)
State University of New York, College at Potsdam, Potsdam, NY [*Library symbol Library of Congress*] (LCLS) ... NPotU
State University of New York, College at Potsdam, Potsdam, NY [*OCLC symbol*] (OCLC) ... ZQM
State University of New York, College at Purchase, Purchase, NY [*Library symbol Library of Congress*] (LCLS) ... NPurU
State University of New York, College at Purchase, Purchase, NY [*OCLC symbol*] (OCLC) ... ZPM
State University of New York, College at Utica-Rome, Utica, NY [*Library symbol Library of Congress*] (LCLS) ... NUtSU
State University of New York, College at Utica-Rome, Utica, NY [*OCLC symbol*] (OCLC) ... YTM
State University of New York, College of Ceramics at Alfred University, Alfred, NY [*Library symbol Library of Congress*] (LCLS) ... NAlfC
State University of New York, College of Ceramics at Alfred University, Alfred, NY [*OCLC symbol*] (OCLC) ... YDM
State University of New York College of Environmental Science and Forestry at Syracuse (GAGS) ... SUNYC Environ Sci & For (Syracuse)

State University of New York, College of Environmental Science and Forestry, Syracuse, NY [*OCLC symbol*] (OCLC) ... VXF
State University of New York, College of Environmental Sciences and Forestry at Syracuse University, Syracuse, NY [*Library symbol Library of Congress*] (LCLS) ... NSySU-F
State University of New York, College of Optometry, New York, NY [*Library symbol Library of Congress*] (LCLS) ... NNSU-Op
State University of New York, College of Optometry, New York, NY [*OCLC symbol*] (OCLC) ... VXP
State University of New York Health Science Center at Brooklyn (GAGS) ... SUNY H Sci Cent
State University of New York Health Science Center at Syracuse (GAGS) ... SUNY H Sci Cent
State University of New York, Health Sciences Library, Buffalo, NY [*OCLC symbol*] (OCLC) ... SBH
State University of New York, Maritime College, Bronx, NY [*OCLC symbol*] (OCLC) ... ZMM
State University of New York, Maritime College, Fort Schuyler, Bronx, NY [*Library symbol Library of Congress*] (LCLS) ... NNSU-MC
State University of New York, OCLC [*Online Computer Library Center*], Albany, NY [*OCLC symbol*] (OCLC) ... TQW
State University of New York, OCLC [*Online Computer Library Center*], Albany, NY [*OCLC symbol*] (OCLC) ... TQX
State University of New York Online Computer Library Center [*Library network*] ... SUNY/OCLC
State University of New York Press, Albany, NY [*Library symbol Library of Congress*] (LCLS) ... SunyP
State University of New York, Union List of Serials, Albany, NY [*Library symbol Library of Congress*] (LCLS) ... NAISU
State University of New York, Union List of Serials, Albany, NY [*OCLC symbol*] (OCLC) ... SUL
State University of New York, Upstate Medical Center, Syracuse, NY [*Library symbol Library of Congress*] (LCLS) ... NSySU-M
State University of South Dakota ... SUSD
State University Railroad Co. [*AAR code*] ... SUR
State University Railroad Co. [*Later, SUR*] [*AAR code*] ... SUY
State University Research Center at Oswego [*State University College at Oswego*] [*Research center*] (RCD) ... SURCO
State University System of Florida (NOAA) ... SUSF
State University System of Florida Institute of Oceanography (NOAA) ... SUSIO
State Variable Estimation and Accuracy Determination ... SVEAD
State Variable Filter ... SVF
State Vector (KSC) ... SV
State Vehicular Recreation Area ... SVRA
State Veterans Employment Representative [*Department of Labor*] ... SVER
State, War, Navy Coordinating Committee [*Later, SANAAC*] ... SWNCC
State Water Project [*California*] (ECON) ... SWP
State Water Resources Control Board (DOGT) ... SWRCB
State Welfare Agency [*Social Security Administration*] (OICC) ... SWA
State Wildlife Reserve [*State*] (EERA) ... SWR
State Worker's Compensation Law (OICC) ... SWCL
State-Army-Navy Communications Intelligence Board [*Later, USCIB*] ... STANCIB
State-Army-Navy-Air Force Coordinating Committee [*Terminated, 1949*] (EGAO) ... SANACC
State-Certified Midwife [*British*] ... SCM
Stated Redemption Price at Maturity [*of debt instruments*] ... SRPM
State-Defense Military Information Control Committee (AFM) ... S-DMICC
State-Dependent Learning [*Psychology*] ... SDL
State-Dependent Retrieval [*Psychology*] ... SDR
State-EPA [*Environmental Protection Agency*] **Agreements** (EG) ... SEA
State-Event Matrix [*Computer science*] ... SEM
StateFed Financial [*NASDAQ symbol*] (TTSB) ... SFFC
Statefed Financial Corp. [*NASDAQ symbol*] (SAG) ... SFFC
Statefed Financial Corp. [*Associated Press*] (SAG) ... StateFn
State-Federal Crop Reporting Service ... SFCRS
State-Federal Information Clearinghouse for Exceptional Children ... SFICEC
Statement (WDAA) ... ST
Statement ... STATT
Statement (ECII) ... STM
Statement (IAA) ... STMNT
Statement (AFM) ... STMT
Statement Level Simulator [*NASA*] (NASA) ... SLS
Statement Match Unit (IAA) ... SMU
Statement of Additional Information [*Finances*] (BARN) ... SAI
Statement of Assurance ... SOA
Statement of Auditing Standards ... SAS
Statement of Billing ... SB
Statement of Capability [*NASA*] ... SC
Statement of Capability (MCD) ... SOC
Statement of Charges [*Army*] ... S/C
Statement of Charges ... SOC
Statement of Compatibility [*NASA*] (MCD) ... SC
Statement of Condition and Recommendation [*Military*] (AABC) ... SOCAR
Statement of Conditions ... SOC
Statement of Differences ... S/D
Statement of Essential Need (AAGC) ... SEN
Statement of Financial Accounting Concepts ... SFAC
Statement of Financial Accounting Standards ... SFAS
Statement of Functions (NATG) ... SF
Statement of Guidance ... SOG
Statement of Intelligence Interest [*Army*] (RDA) ... SII
Statement of Intent ... SOI
Statement of Inventory Transaction [*Military*] ... SIT
Statement of Logistical Needs [*Air Force*] ... SLN
Statement of Material Requirements ... SMR
Statement of Need - Clothing and Individual Equipment [*Military*] ... SN-CIE
Statement of Objectives (AAGC) ... SOO
Statement of Operational Need ... SON
Statement of Operational Requirements Document (AAGC) ... SORD
Statement of Personal History [*Military*] ... SPH
Statement of Policy [*SEC*] ... SOP
Statement of Policy or Interpretation [*Food and Drug Administration*] ... SPI
Statement of Position (TDOB) ... SOP
Statement of Prior Submission (NASA) ... SPS
Statement of Procedural Rules [*A publication*] (DLA) ... SPR
Statement of Provisioning Policy [*Military*] (AFIT) ... SOPP
Statement of Quality and Support (MCD) ... SOQAS
Statement of Recommended Practice [*Accounting*] [*British*] ... SORP
Statement of Requirement [*Military*] (AFIT) ... SOR
Statement of Requirements [*NASA*] (MCD) ... SR
Statement of Service [*Military*] ... S/S
Statement of Service [*Military*] ... SOS
Statement of Service [*Military*] ... STMT of SVC
Statement of Standard Accounting Practice ... SSAP
Statement of Supply ... SOS
Statement of Technology Needs [*Air Force*] ... STN
Statement of Work (MCD) ... SOW
Statement of Work/Specifications and Design ... SOW/S & D
Statement on Auditing Procedure ... SAP
Statement on Standards for Accounting and Review Services (TDOB) ... SSARS
Statements of Responsibilites in Tax Practice (TDOB) ... SRPT
Statements on Quality Control Standards (TDOB) ... SQCS
State-Municipal Income Tax Evaluation System (PDAA) ... SMITES
Staten Island ... SI
Staten Island Community College, Staten Island, NY [*Library symbol Library of Congress Obsolete*] (LCLS) ... NSiC
Staten Island Historical Society, New York, NY [*Library symbol Library of Congress*] (LCLS) ... NNSIHi
Staten Island Institute of Arts and Sciences, New York, NY [*Library symbol Library of Congress*] (LCLS) ... NNSII
Staten Island, NY [*FM radio station call letters*] ... WSIA
[*The*] **Staten Island Railroad Corp.** [*AAR code*] ... SIRC
Staten Island Rapid Transit Railway Co. [*Later, SIRC*] [*AAR code*] ... SIR
Staten Island Rapid Transit Railway Co. [*Later, SIRC*] ... SIRT
Statens Avtalsverk [*Sweden*] ... SAV
Statens Jaernvaegar [*Sweden*] ... SJ
Statens Offentliga Utredningar [*Sweden*] ... SOU
Statens Psykologisk-Pedagogiska Bibliotek [*National Library for Psychology and Education*] [*Sweden*] [*Information service or system*] (IID) ... SPPB
Statens Rad for Vetenskaplig Information och Dokumentation [*Swedish Council for Scientific Information and Documentation*] (IID) ... SINFDOK
Statens Trafikkflygerskole [*Norway ICAO designator*] (FAAC) ... FBD
Statens Vag- och Trafikinstitut [*Swedish Road and Traffic Research Institute*] [*Linkoping*] [*Information service or system*] (IID) ... VTI
State-of-the-Art Car [*Transit*] [*Department of Transportation*] ... SOAC
State-of-the-Art Car [*Transit*] [*Department of Transportation*] ... SOTAC
State-of-the-Art Contingency Analysis System [*Science Applications International Corp.*] (MCD) ... SOTACA
State-of-the-Art Medium Terminal ... SAMT
State-of-the-Art Report [*Navy*] ... SOAR
State-of-the-Art Vehicle Engineering Documentation (MCD) ... SAVED
State-of-the-Atmosphere Variables (USDC) ... SAV
State-Operated Contracts ... SOC
State-Operated Program [*Department of Education*] (GFGA) ... SOP
State-Owned Corporation ... SOC
State-Owned Enterprise ... SOE
Stateroom (MSA) ... SR
State's Attorney ... SA
States Audiovisual Education Study ... SAVES
States Exploration Ltd. [*Toronto Stock Exchange symbol*] ... SAX
States Information Center [*Council of State Governments*] (IID) ... SIC
States Marine Lines ... SML
State's Urban Development Something-or-Other [*Slang for Urban Development Corporation, New York*] ... SUDS
Statesboro, GA [*Location identifier FAA*] (FAAL) ... TBR
Statesboro, GA [*FM radio station call letters*] ... WMCD
Statesboro, GA [*FM radio station call letters*] (RBYB) ... WPMX
Statesboro, GA [*AM radio station call letters*] ... WPTB
Statesboro, GA [*FM radio station call letters*] ... WVGS
Statesboro, GA [*AM radio station call letters*] ... WWNS
Stateside Energy Corp. [*Vancouver Stock Exchange symbol*] ... SSE
Statesman [*or Stateswoman*] ... states
Statesman (WGA) ... STSM
Statesman Series [*A publication*] ... SS
Statesman's Yearbook [*A publication*] ... SYB
Statesville, NC [*Location identifier FAA*] (FAAL) ... SVH
Statesville, NC [*FM radio station call letters*] ... WFMX
Statesville, NC [*AM radio station call letters*] ... WHYM
Statesville, NC [*AM radio station call letters*] ... WSIC
Statesville, NC [*FM radio station call letters*] ... WTDR
Stateswest Airlines [*ICAO designator*] (AD) ... YW
StatesWest Airlines, Inc. [*ICAO designator*] (FAAC) ... SWJ
State-Trait Anxiety Inventory [*Psychology*] ... STAI
State-Trait Anxiety Inventory for Children [*Psychology*] ... STAIC
State-Transition Diagram [*Computer science*] ... STD
Statewide Comprehensive Outdoor Recreation Plan ... SCORP
Statewide Course Numbering System [*Florida*] (EDAC) ... SCNS
Statewide Ear Health Advisory Committee [*Australia*] ... SWEHAC
Statewide Financial [*NASDAQ symbol*] (TTSB) ... SFIN
Statewide Financial Corp. [*NASDAQ symbol*] (SAG) ... SFIN

Statewide Financial Corp. [*Associated Press*] (SAG) .... StateF
Statewide Financial Corp. [*Associated Press*] (SAG) .... StatewdeF
Statewide Health Coordinating Council .... SHCC
Statewide Individual Referral System (OICC) .... SIRS
Statewide Information Steering Committee [*California*] .... SISC
Statewide Instructional Computing Network [*New York*] (EDAC) .... SICN
Statewide Library Computer System [*University of Illinois*] [*Information service or system*] (IID) .... LCS
Statewide Operating Plan .... SOP
Statewide Operations Center .... SOC
Statewide Planning and Research Cooperative System [*New York State Department of Health*] [*Albany*] [*Information service or system*] (IID) .... SPARCS
Statewide Public Library Interlibrary Loan and Reference Network [*Library network*] .... SPPL
Statewide Resource Information and Accounting System [*State*] (EERA) .... SRAIS
Statewide Transportation Improvements Program [*MOCD*] (TAG) .... STIP
Statfarad [*Also, statF*] [*Unit of capacitance*] .... sF
Statfarad [*Also, sF*] [*Unit of capacitance*] .... statF
Statfjord-A [*Norway ICAO location identifier*] (ICLI) .... ENSF
Statham's Abridgment [*A publication*] (DLA) .... St Ab
Statham's Abridgment [*A publication*] (DSA) .... Sta
Statham's Abridgment [*A publication*] (DLA) .... Stath Abr
Stathenry [*Also, statH*] [*Unit of inductance*] .... sH
Stathenry [*Also, sH*] [*Unit of inductance*] .... statH
Statherin (DMAA) .... STATH
Static .... S
Static (KSC) .... ST
Static (AAG) .... STAT
Static Adjustable Speed Drive .... SASD
Static Air Temperature .... SAT
Static Allegation Analyzer [*Computer science*] .... SAA
Static and Transient Analysis, Nonlinear, Shells [*Computer program*] [*Navy*] .... SATANS
Static Automatic Reporting System (MCD) .... SARS
Static Card Reader .... SCR
Static Checkout Unit (KSC) .... SCU
Static Column Decode [*Computer science*] .... SCD
Static Column Dynamic Random-Access Memory [*Computer science*] (EECA) .... SCRAM
Static Column Isoelectric Focusing [*Materials processing*] .... SCIF
Static Complementary Logic (ECII) .... SCL
Static Compliance (MAE) .... Cst
Static Design Factor .... SDF
Static Dielectric Constant .... SDC
Static Direction Finder .... SDF
Static/Dynamic Load Technology (SSD) .... SDLT
Static Error Analysis .... SEA
Static Feed Water Electrolysis Module [*NASA*] .... SFWEM
Static Firing [*NASA*] (NASA) .... SF
Static Firing Test [*NASA*] (NASA) .... SFT
Static Firing Test Facility [*NASA*] (NASA) .... SFTF
Static Friction .... STICTION
Static Induction Transistor [*Telecommunications*] (TEL) .... SIT
Static Induction Transistor Logic (NITA) .... SITL
Static Line Regulation .... SLR
Static Load Error Washout .... SLEW
Static Loaded Radius [*Automotive engineering*] .... SLR
Static Lund Compliance [*Medicine*] (DAVI) .... C Stat
Static Magnetic Field .... SMF
Static Margin .... SM
Static Memory Board [*Computer science*] (BYTE) .... SMB
Static Memory Interface [*Computer science*] (MDG) .... SMI
Static Mercury Drop Electrode [*Electrochemistry*] .... SMDE
Static Mission Equivalent (IAA) .... SME
Static Nibble Access Path [*Computer science*] .... SNAP
Static No Delivery .... SND
Static Nonlinear Analysis of Shells of Revolution [*Computer program*].... SNASOR
Static Phase Error [*NASA*] .... SPE
Static Phase Error [*NASA*] (NASA) .... STPH
Static Pointer [*Computer science*] .... SP
Static Power Conservers (MCD) .... SPC
Static Power Conversion System .... SPCS
Static Power Converter (IAA) .... SPC
Static Power Inverter (DWSG) .... STPI
Static Power System .... SPS
Static Presentation Mode .... SPM
Static Pressure .... PS
Static Pressure .... SP
Static Pressure Compensation .... SPC
Static Pressure Distribution .... SPD
Static Pressure System .... SPS
Static Pressure Transducer .... SPT
Static Random Access Memory [*Computer science*] .... SRAM
Static Round Jet .... SRJ
Static Secondary Ion Mass Spectroscopy .... SSIM
Static Secondary Ion Mass Spectroscopy .... SSIMS
Static Self-Verification .... SSV
Static Sensitive Device [*Electronics*] (EECA) .... SSD
Static Shift Register .... SSR
Static Sodium Pot [*Nuclear energy*] (NRCH) .... SSP
Static Source Error Correction .... SSEC
Static Spontaneous Potential (IAA) .... SSP
Static Squelch Range .... SSR
Static Stability Augmentation System [*Aviation*] .... SSAS
Static Standby Computer [*Mission Control Center*] [*NASA*] .... SSC
Static Strength Prediction Program [*Ergonmetrics*] .... SSPP
Static Stretching [*Medicine*] .... SS
Static Technology Office Information Analysis Center (NITA) .... STOIAC
Static Test .... ST
Static Test Article (NASA) .... STA
Static Test Facility (KSC) .... STF
Static Test Model (MCD) .... STM
Static Test Stand .... STS
Static Test Unit (KSC) .... STU
Static Thrust .... ST
Static, TN [*AM radio station call letters*] .... WSBI
Static Transpulmonary Pressure at a Specific Lung Volume [*Medicine*] (DAVI) .... Pst
Static Water Supply (ADA) .... SWS
Static-Dynamic Ullage Simulation Unit .... STA-DYNULSIMU
Statim [*Immediately*] [*Latin*] (ROG) .... ST
Statim [*Immediately*] [*Latin*] .... STAT
Statine Congener of Renin Inhibitory Peptide [*Biochemistry*] .... SCRIP
Station .... S
Station [*Medicine*] .... ST
Station [*Telecommunications*] .... STA
Station (VRA) .... sta
Station .... STA
Station (IDOE) .... sta
Station .... STAT
Station [*Commonly used*] (OPSA) .... STATION
Station [*Commonly used*] (OPSA) .... STATN
Station (IDOE) .... stn
Station (DD) .... Stn
Station .... STN
Station 2 [*Nevada*] [*Seismograph station code, US Geological Survey Closed*] (SEIS) .... STX
Station Accommodation Test Set (SSD) .... SATS
Station Acquisition Marketing Plan [*PBS*] (NTCM) .... SAM
Station Address [*Computer science*] (BUR) .... SA
Station Address Directory [*Army*] .... SAD
Station Administrator (FAAC) .... STADMR
Station Air System [*Nuclear energy*] (NRCH) .... SAS
Station Airline Ticket Office (MCD) .... SATO
Station Allowance Unit (NATG) .... SAL
Station Buffer Unit [*Computer science*] .... SBU
Station Cable Equalizer (IAA) .... SCE
Station Casinos [*NASDAQ symbol*] (TTSB) .... STCI
Station Casinos $3.50 Cv Pfd [*NASDAQ symbol*] (TTSB) .... STCIP
Station Casinos, Inc. [*Associated Press*] (SAG) .... StatCas
Station Casinos, Inc. [*Associated Press*] (SAG) .... StatnCas
Station Casinos, Inc. [*NASDAQ symbol*] (SAG) .... STCI
Station Casinos, Inc. [*NYSE symbol*] (SAG) .... STN
Station Code File .... SCF
Station Communications Control Group [*Ground Communications Facility, NASA*] .... SCCG
Station Communications Processor .... SCP
Station Complement [*Army*] .... Sta Com
Station Conferencing and Monitoring Arrangement [*NASA*] .... SCAMA
Station Configuration Requirement List [*NASA*] (MCD) .... SCRL
Station Construction Engineering Officer .... SCEO
Station Control and Monitoring .... SCAM
Station Control Block [*Computer science*] (IBMDP) .... SCB
Station Control Unit .... SCU
Station Data Acquisition and Control [*NASA*] (NASA) .... STADAC
Station Data Processing .... SDP
Station Digital Command System (IAA) .... SDCS
Station Director [*Deep Space Instrumentation Facility, NASA*] .... SD
Station Directory Control (SAA) .... SDC
Station Display Unit .... SDU
Station Duty Officer [*Navy*] .... SDO
Station Engineering Control Office [*Telecommunications*] (TEL) .... SECO
Station Engineering Manual [*Telecommunications*] (TEL) .... SEM
Station Federale d'Essais Agricoles, Lausanne, Switzerland [*Library symbol Library of Congress*] (LCLS) .... SzLaS
Station Headquarters .... SHQ
Station Hospital [*Military*] .... SH
Station House .... SH
Station Housing Allowance [*Military*] (MCD) .... SHA
Station Identification .... SI
Station Identification .... STAID
Station Identification Store [*Bell Laboratories*] .... SIS
Station Independence Program [*Public television project*] (NTCM) .... SIP
Station Infomation Management System [*Navy*] (DOMA) .... SIMS
Station Interface Adapter (SSD) .... SIA
Station Interface Unit [*Computer science*] (ECII) .... SIU
Station Keeping Light (NFPA) .... SKLT
Station Liaison Engineer [*NASA*] .... SLE
Station List Publishing Co., St. Louis MO [*STAC*] .... SLL
Station Management .... SMT
Station Manager [*Broadcasting*] (NTCM) .... SM
Station Manager [*Deep Space Instrumentation Facility, NASA*] .... SM
Station Manager (FAAC) .... STMGR
Station Master (WDAA) .... SM
Station Message Detail Recorder (NITA) .... SMDR
Station Message Detail Recording [*Formerly, MDR*] [*Telecommunications*] .... SMDR
Station of Initial Assignment .... SIA
Station Officer [*British police*] .... SO

Station Open Exclusively to the Correspondence of a Private Agency [*ITU designation*] (CET) CV
Station Open from Sunrise to Sunset [*ITU designation*] (CET) .... HJ
Station Open to Limited Public Correspondence [*ITU designation*] .... CR
Station Open to Official Correspondence Exclusively [*ITU designation*] .... CO
Station Open to Public Correspondence [*ITU designation*] .... CP
Station Operating Plan (AAG) .... SOP
Station Operating Supervisor (IEEE) .... SOS
Station Operations and Engineering Squadron [*Marine Corps*] .... SOES
Station Operations Console (MCD) .... SOC
Station Operations Review Committee [*Nuclear energy*] (NRCH) .... SORC
Station/Platform LIDAR Facility (SSD) .... S/PLF
Station Police [*British military*] (DMA) .... SP
Station Program Cooperative [*Public television*] .... SPC
Station Program Identification [*Telecommunications*] (TEL) .... SPI
Station Project Engineer [*NASA*] .... SPE
Station Quality Control [*RADAR*] .... SQC
Station Radio [*British*] .... SR
Station Readiness Test .... SRT
Station Regulation .... SR
Station Reliability Coordinator .... SRC
Station Representatives Association (EA) .... SRA
Station Resources and Planning [*Navy*] (DNAB) .... SR & P
Station Resources and Planning Office [*Navy*] (DNAB) .... SR & PO
Station Routine Order (IAA) .... SRO
Station Selected Display [*Electronics*] (ECII) .... SSD
Station Selection Code [*Western Union*] (BUR) .... SSC
Station Serial Number (CET) .... SSN
Station Service Transformer [*Nuclear energy*] (NRCH) .... SST
Station Service Water Pump [*Nuclear energy*] (NRCH) .... SSWP
Station Set [*NASA*] (NASA) .... SS
Station Set Handbook [*NASA*] (NASA) .... SSHB
Station Set Requirement [*NASA*] (NASA) .... SSR
Station Set Requirements Document [*NASA*] (NASA) .... SSRD
Station Set Requirements Review [*NASA*] (NASA) .... SSRR
Station Set Specification [*NASA*] (NASA) .... SSS
Station Ship [*Navy*] (NVT) .... STASHIP
Station Ship [*Coast Guard symbol*] (DNAB) .... WYTM
Station Sick Quarters .... SSQ
Station Signaling and Announcement Subsystem [*Telecommunications*] (TEL) .... SSAS
Station Staff Officer [*British military*] (DMA) .... SSO
Station Supervision .... SS
Station Technical Control [*Telecommunications*] (TEL) .... STC
Station Test and Calibration .... STC
Station Test Equipment [*Deep Space Instrumentation Facility, NASA*] .... STE
Station to Station .... S to S
Station to Station .... STS
Station to Station Send Paid [*Telecommunications*] (TEL) .... SSSP
Station Transmission Link [*Telecommunications*] (IAA) .... STL
Station Unit [*Telecommunications*] (OA) .... SU
Station Wagon [*Car*] .... SW
Station Warrant Officer [*Air Force British*] .... SWO
Stationary .... S
Stationary (MSA) .... STA
Stationary (IDOE) .... sta
Stationary [*Chemistry*] .... STAT
Stationary .... STATNRY
Stationary (WGA) .... STATY
Stationary .... STNR
Stationary Afterglow [*Chemical kinetic*] .... SA
Stationary Attachment and Flexible Endoskeleton .... SAFE
Stationary Automatic Tank Target System (MCD) .... STATTS
Stationary Automotive Road Simulator .... STARS
Stationary Catalytic Basket Reactor [*Chemical engineering*] .... SCBR
Stationary Combustion Process [*Automotive engineering*] .... SCP
Stationary Control Variable Speed (IAA) .... SVS
Stationary Cosmic Ray Gas .... SCRG
Stationary Digital Audio Tape .... SDAT
Stationary Eddy .... SE
Stationary Engine Society (EA) .... SES
Stationary Engineer .... Sta Eng
Stationary Gaussian Markov [*Telecommunications*] (IAA) .... SGM
Stationary [*or Strategic*] **High-Altitude Relay Platform** [*Microwave airplane*] [*Canada*] .... SHARP
Stationary High-Power [*Reactor*] (NRCH) .... SH
Stationary LASER Site [*NASA*] .... STALAS
Stationary Low-Power [*Reactor*] [*Dismantled*] (NRCH) .... SL
Stationary Media (GAAI) .... SM
Stationary Medium-Power [*Reactor*] [*Nuclear energy*] .... SM
Stationary Meteorological Satellite [*NASA*] .... SMS
Stationary Orbit (IAA) .... SO
Stationary Plasma Motor .... SPM
Stationary Reflector/Tracking Absorber [*Solar power*] (DICI) .... SRTA
Stationary Remotely Piloted Vehicle (MCD) .... SRPV
Stationary Satellite (IAA) .... SS
Stationary Source [*Environmental Protection Agency*] .... SS
Stationary Source Compliance Division [*Environmental Protection Agency*] (GFGA) .... SSCD
Stationary Source Emissions and Inventory System [*Environmental Protection Agency*] (GFGA) .... SSEIS
Stationary Source Simulator Facility [*Environmental science*] .... SSSF
Stationary Tank Automatic Target System (MCD) .... STATS
Stationary Time Series .... STS
Stationary Wave (IAA) .... SW
Stationary-State Hypothesis [*Chemistry*] .... SSH
Station-Control and Monitor Console Subsystem [*Deep Space Instrumentation Facility, NASA*] .... SMC
Stationer .... STATNR
Stationers and Publishers Board of Trade [*Later, Stationery and Office Equipment Board of Trade*] .... SPBOT
Stationery and Office Equipment Board of Trade (EA) .... SOEBT
Stationery Industry Exhibition [*British*] (ITD) .... STATINDEX
Stationery Office [*British*] .... SO
Stationery Office [*British*] .... STAT
Stationery Request (MCD) .... SR
Stationing Analysis Model [*Military*] (GFGA) .... SAM
Stationing and Installations Planning Committee [*Military*] .... SIPC
Stationing Capability System [*Army*] (AABC) .... SCS
Stationing Flag [*Navy British*] .... SN
Station-Keeping .... SK
Station-Keeping and Mobile Platform [*Robot sailboat*] .... SKAMP
Station-Keeping Assistance (DS) .... SKA
Station-Keeping Distance [*British military*] (DMA) .... SKD
Station-Keeping Equipment .... SKE
Station-Keeping Position .... SKP
Station-Keeping RADAR .... SKR
Station-Keeping Ship .... SKS
Stations Legers d'Infrastructures [*Light infrastructures*] [*French*] .... SLI
Stations Open Exclusively to Operational Traffic of the Services Concerned [*ITU designation*] (CET) .... OT
Statisitcal Pattern Recognition [*Computer science*] .... SPR
Statistic (AFM) .... STAT
Statistical [*Army*] .... Statl
Statistical Abstract of the World [*A publication*] .... SAW
Statistical Adiabatic Channel Model [*Physical chemistry*] .... SACM
Statistical Advisory Committee [*UN Food and Agriculture Organization*] .... SAC
Statistical Analog Monitor (PDAA) .... STAM
Statistical Analysis and Quality Control .... SAQC
Statistical Analysis and Reports Division [*Administrative Office of the U S Courts*] [*Washington, DC*] (GRD) .... SARD
Statistical Analysis Center (OICC) .... SAC
Statistical Analysis Group in Education (EDAC) .... SAGE
Statistical Analysis of a Series of Events (PDAA) .... SASE
Statistical Analysis of Documentation Files (PDAA) .... SADF
Statistical Analysis of Files (IAA) .... STAF
Statistical Analysis of Network .... STATNET
Statistical Analysis Routine (IAA) .... STAR
Statistical Analysis System [*Programming language*] [*1966*] .... SAS
Statistical Analysis Unit .... SAU
Statistical and Economic Information Bulletin for Africa [*A publication*] .... SEIB
Statistical and Social Enqiry Society of Ireland .... SSESI
Statistical and Social Inquiry Society of Ireland (DBA) .... SSISI
Statistical Annals (DLA) .... STAT AN
Statistical Approach to Investment Appraisal to Evaluate Risk (MHDW) .... SATIATER
Statistical Bulletin .... SB
Statistical Bulletin .... STBU
Statistical Calculation and Analysis of Engine Removal [*Navy*] .... SCALER
Statistical Clearance Liaison Officer [*Army*] (AABC) .... SCLO
Statistical Collection File (NASA) .... SCF
Statistical Computing Library [*Bell System*] .... STATLIB
[*A*] **Statistical Computing Procedure** .... ASCOP
Statistical Context-Aided Testing [*North-Holland Publishing Co.*] [*Software package*] (NCC) .... STATCAT
Statistical Control .... SC
Statistical Control and Operations Records Unit [*Air Force*] .... SCORU
Statistical Control Office [*or Officer*] [*Military*] .... SCO
Statistical Control System .... SCS
Statistical Control Unit [*Military*] .... SCU
Statistical Data Collection Program .... STADACOL
Statistical Data Recorder [*Computer science*] (MDG) .... SDR
Statistical Delta Modulation .... SDM
Statistical Distribution Analyzer .... SDA
Statistical, Economic, and Social Research and Training Center for Islamic Countries [*Research center Turkey*] (IRC) .... SESRTCIC
Statistical Energy Analysis [*or Approach*] [*Vibration analysis*] .... SEA
Statistical Engine Test Work Group [*Lubricants testing*] [*Automotive engineering*] .... SETWEG
Statistical Engineering Institute (MCD) .... SEI
Statistical Estimation Fault Isolation Procedure (MCD) .... SEFIP
Statistical Fine Structure [*Physics*] .... SFS
Statistical Forecasts of the United States [*A publication*] .... SFUS
Statistical Historical Input/Output Error Rate Utility [*Sperry UNIVAC*] .... SHIOER
Statistical Hurricane Intensity Prediction Scheme [*Marine science*] (OSRA) .... SHIPS
Statistical Hurricane Intensity Prediction Scheme (USDC) .... SHIPS
Statistical Information Retrieval .... SIR
Statistical Information System [*Bundesamt fuer Statistik*] [*Switzerland Information service or system*] (CRD) .... STATINF
Statistical Information System Data (NITA) .... SISDATA
Statistical Institute for Asia and the Pacific [*United Nations*] (ECON) .... SIAP
Statistical Interactive Programming System .... SIPS
Statistical Interpretive Language [*Computer science*] (MDG) .... STIL
Statistical Isolinear MultiCategory Analysis [*Data analysis*] [*Computer science*] .... SIMCA
Statistical Language for Microcomputers (IID) .... SL-MICRO
Statistical Learning Model (IEEE) .... SLM
Statistical List .... SL
Statistical Methods Division [*Bureau of the Census*] (OICC) .... SMD

Statistical Model of Overlap .... SMO
Statistical Modeling and Estimation Review of Functioning Software [*Science Applications International Corp.*] .... SMERFS
Statistical Multiplexer (MCD) .... SM
Statistical Multiplexer [*Computer science*] .... STATMUX
Statistical Multiplexing [*Telecommunications*] .... STM
Statistical Network Processor .... SNP
Statistical Office of the European Communities [*Commission of the European Communities*] (EAIO) .... EUROSTAT
Statistical Office of the European Communities (DCTA) .... SOEC
Statistical Package (MHDI) .... STAT-PACK
Statistical Package for the Social Sciences [*Programming language*] [*1970*] .... SPSS
Statistical Parametric Mapping [*Data treatment*] .... SPM
Statistical Passenger Data Collection System [*MTMC*] (TAG) .... STATCO
Statistical Performance Standards [*Navy*] (NG) .... SPS
Statistical Policy Division [*Office of Management and Budget*] .... SPD
Statistical Process Control .... SPC
Statistical Process Control Society (EA) .... SPCS
Statistical Process Control Toolbox (RDA) .... SPCT
Statistical Process/Statistical Quality Control .... SPC/SQC
Statistical Processing and Analysis [*Computer science*] .... SPAN
Statistical Profile of Old Norse .... SPON
Statistical Property Estimation and Regeneration (MCD) .... SPEAR
Statistical Quality Analysis Report (MHDB) .... SQUARE
Statistical Quality Control .... SQC
Statistical Quality Control Procedure .... SQCP
Statistical Quality Control System [*Military*] .... STAQC
Statistical Record of Asian Americans [*A publication*] .... SRAA
Statistical Record of Black America [*A publication*] .... SRBA
Statistical Record of Children [*A publication*] .... SRC
Statistical Record of Health and Medicine [*A publication*] .... SRHM
Statistical Record of Hispanic Americans [*A publication*] .... SRHA
Statistical Record of Native North Americans [*A publication*] .... SRNNA
Statistical Record of Older Americans [*A publication*] .... SROA
Statistical Record of Religion in America [*A publication*] .... SRRA
Statistical Record of the Environment [*A publication*] .... SRE
Statistical Record of the Environment [*A publication*] .... SROE
Statistical Record of Women Worldwide [*A publication*] .... SROWW
Statistical Reference Index [*A publication*] .... SRI
Statistical Reporting Service [*Later, ESCS*] [*Department of Agriculture*] .... SRS
Statistical Research Division [*Census*] (OICC) .... SRD
Statistical Research Group [*Princeton University*] (MCD) .... SRG
Statistical, Sampling Inventory Method [*Military*] (AABC) .... SSIM
Statistical Service Office [*Military*] .... SSO
Statistical Service Office [*Supreme Headquarters Allied Powers Europe*] (NATG) .... STATSERVOFF
Statistical Service Unit [*Military*] .... SSU
Statistical Services (MUGU) .... STATSVS
Statistical Society of Australia. Newsletter [*A publication*]..... Newsl Statist Soc Aust
Statistical Society of Canada [*Societe Statistique du Canada*] .... SSC
Statistical Software Package [*Computer science*] (EERA) .... S-Plus
Statistical Standards .... SS
Statistical Subdivision (EERA) .... SSD
Statistical Summary Report (AAG) .... SSR
Statistical Table Assembly and Retrieval System [*Proposed for Social Security Administration*] .... STAR
Statistical Time Division Multiplexer [*or Multiplexing*] .... STDM
Statistical Training Programme for Africa [*United Nations*] (EY) .... STPA
Statistical Trajectory Estimation Program [*NASA*] .... STEP
Statistical Treatment of Aircraft Returns (MCD) .... STAR
Statistical Unit [*UNRISD*] [*United Nations*] (DUND) .... SU
Statistical Utility Program .... SUP
Statistical Vibration Analysis .... SVA
Statistical Weight [*Symbol*] [*IUPAC*] .... g
Statistical-Dynamical Model .... SDM
Statistically Oriented Matrix Program (IEEE) .... STORM
Statistically Significant (MAE) .... SS
Statistically-Tensioned Extension Mast (DNAB) .... STEM
Statistics .... STATIS
Statistics (DD) .... Stats
Statistics and Analysis Branch [*Public Health Service*] [*Information service or system*] (IID) .... SAB
Statistics and Market Intelligence Library [*Department of Trade*] [*British*] (DCTA) .... SMIL
Statistics Canada .... SC
Statistics Canada [*Statistics Canada Library*] [*Information service or system*] .... StatCan
Statistics Canada .... Stats Can
Statistics Canada, Census Library, Ottawa, ON, Canada [*Library symbol Library of Congress*] (LCLS) .... CaOOSCL
Statistics Canada, Census Map Library, Ottawa, ON, Canada [*Library symbol Library of Congress*] (LCLS) .... CaOOSCM
Statistics Canada, Edmonton, AB, Canada [*Library symbol Library of Congress*] (LCLS) .... CaAES
Statistics Canada [*Statistique Canada*] **Edmonton, Alberta** [*Library symbol National Library of Canada*] (NLC) .... AES
Statistics Canada, Montreal, PQ, Canada [*Library symbol Library of Congress*] (LCLS) .... CaQMSCa
Statistics Canada [*Statistique Canada*] **Montreal, Quebec** [*Library symbol National Library of Canada*] (NLC) .... QMSCA
Statistics Canada, Ottawa, ON, Canada [*Library symbol Library of Congress*] (LCLS) .... CaOOS
Statistics Canada [*Statistique Canada*] **Ottawa Ontario** [*Library symbol National Library of Canada*] (NLC) .... OOS
Statistics Canada, Toronto, ON, Canada [*Library symbol Library of Congress*] (LCLS) .... CaOTS
Statistics Canada [*Statistique Canada*] **Toronto, Ontario** [*Library symbol National Library of Canada*] (NLC) .... OTS
Statistics Gathering System [*NASA*] .... SGS
Statistics Indexing and Retrieval Project (NITA) .... STIR
Statistics of Income [*IRS*] .... SOI
Statistics of Naval Shipyards .... SONS
Statistics on the North Atlantic [*Fisheries*] [*UN Food and Agriculture Organization*] .... STANA
Statistics Package [*Computer program*] (IEEE) .... STATPAC
Statistics Sources [*A publication*] .... SS
Statistische Quellenwerke der Schweiz [*Switzerland*] .... SQS
Statistiske Meddelelser [*Denmark*] .... SM
Statius [*First century AD*] [*Classical studies*] (OCD) .... Stat
Stative (BJA) .... Stat
Statni Knihovna Ceske Socialisticke Republiky [*State Library of the Czech S ocialist Republic*], Klementinum, Czechoslovakia [*Library symbol*] [*Library of Congress*] (LCLS) .... CzP
Statni Technicka Knihova, Ustredi Vedeckych, Technickych a Ekonomickych Informaci, Prague, Czechoslovakia [*Library symbol Library of Congress*] (LCLS) .... CzPS
Statni Vedecka Knihova [*State Scientific Library*], Brno, Czechoslovakia [*Library symbol Library of Congress*] (LCLS) .... CzBrS
Statocyst Anlage .... SA
Statoersted (IDOE) .... statOe
Stator (WGA) .... STA
Stator .... STTR
Stator Interstage Seal .... SIS
Stator Pivot Seal .... SPS
Statsbiblioteket i Arhus Universitetsbiblioteket [*State and Arhus University Library*], Arhus, Denmark [*Library symbol Library of Congress*] (LCLS) ...... DnAu
Statsiemens [*Also, statS*] [*Unit of electric conductance, admittance, and susceptance*] .... sS
Statsiemens [*Also, sS*] [*Unit of electric conductance, admittance, and susceptance*] .... statS
Statstjanstemannens Riksforbund [*National Association of Salaried Employees in Government Service*] [*Sweden*] .... SR
Stattesla [*Unit of magnetic flux density*] .... statT
Statuary .... STAT
Statue (ADA) .... S
Statue (WDMC) .... ST
Statue (WDMC) .... st
Statue of Liberty - Ellis Island Centennial Commission (EA) .... SLEICC
Statue of Liberty - Ellis Island Foundation (EA) .... SLEIF
Statue of Liberty National Monument .... STLI
Status .... ST
Status [*Online database field identifier*] (AABC) .... STA
Status (MSA) .... STAT
Status [*ICAO designator*] (FAAC) .... STS
Status Absolutus .... StAbs
Status Advisory Display (MCD) .... SAD
Status and Alert (AAG) .... S/A
Status and Capability (SAA) .... STACAP
Status and Telling (SAA) .... STL
Status and Verification System [*NASA*] (KSC) .... SAVS
Status Application Resource (HGAA) .... STAR
Status Board [*Automated*] (MCD) .... SB
Status Change Character (IAA) .... SCC
Status Constructus (BJA) .... StatConst
Status Constructus (BJA) .... StC
Status Control Alert and Reporting (MCD) .... SCAR
Status Control Alert Reporting System (NATG) .... SCARS
Status Control of Rejections (MCD) .... SCOR
Status Disable [*Computer science*] (MHDI) .... STATDSB
Status Display Support (MCD) .... SDS
Status During Minimize Required (MCD) .... STAMINRQ
Status Enquiry [*British*] .... SE
Status Entry Device [*Telecommunications*] (TEL) .... SED
Status Entry Device Multiplexer [*Telecommunications*] (TEL) .... SEDM
Status Epilepticus [*Medicine*] .... SE
Status Fill-In Unit [*Telecommunications*] (TEL) .... SFU
Status Indicator (IAA) .... SI
Status Inventory Data Management System (MCD) .... SIDMS
Status Memory and Real Time System [*AT & T*] .... SMARTS
Status Monitor .... SM
Status Monitor Software .... SMS
Status Monitoring Routine .... SMR
Status of Electronic Test Equipment (MCD) .... SETE
Status of Equipment [*Army*] (AABC) .... SOE
Status of Forces .... SOF
Status of Forces Agreement [*International treaty*] .... SOFA
Status of Forces Treaty .... SOFT
Status of Implementation Chart .... SIC
Status of Logistics Offensive [*Military*] (AABC) .... SOLO
Status Of Readiness and Training System (DOMA) .... SORTS
Status of Resources and Training System Report [*Military*] .... SORTS
Status of Support Information System .... SOSIS
Status of United States Air Force Equipment .... SOUSAFE
Status of Women [*Canada*] .... SW
Status of Women Canada [*Condition Feminine Canada*] **Ottawa, Ontario** [*Library symbol National Library of Canada*] (NLC) .... OOSW
Status or Operating Resources (MCD) .... SOR
Status Panel (CAAL) .... SP
Status Positive [*Medicine*] (CPH) .... SP

Status Post [*Medicine*] .... S/P
Status Post Myocardial Infarction [*Cardiology*] (DAVI) .... SPMI
Status Post Transurethral Resection of the Prostate [*Medicine*] (DAVI) .... SPTURP
Status Postoperative [*Surgery*] (DAVI) .... SPO
Status Projection System .... SPS
Status Register [*Computer science*] .... SR
Status Register [*Computer science*] .... STR
Status Report .... SR
Status Report [*IRS*] .... STREP
Status Report Panels (SAA) .... SRP
Status Request Field [*Computer science*] (IAA) .... SRQ
Status Required [*Civil Service*] .... S
Status Review [*NASA*] (NASA) .... SR
Status Select [*Army*] .... STAT-SEL
Status Statement [*Online database field identifier*] .... SC
Status Strobe (MHDI) .... STSTB
Status, Time, Attrition, Planning Methodology .... STAPLAN
Status Valid .... SV
Status Word .... SW
Status Word Enable .... SWE
Statute .... S
Statute .... ST
Statute (WGA) .... STA
Statute .... STAT
Statute .... STE
Statute Book (ADA) .... SB
Statute Expired [*IRS*] .... STEX
Statute Law Revision [*A publication*] (DLA) .... SLR
Statute Mile .... SM
Statute Mile [*Nautical charts*] .... St Mi
Statute Mile .... Sta Mi
Statute Mile .... STM
Statute Miles .... SMI
Statute of Distribution [*Legal shorthand*] (LWAP) .... SOD
Statute of Fraud [*Legal shorthand*] (LWAP) .... SOF
Statute of Frauds [*Business term*] .... S/F
Statute of Gloucester [*First statute to give costs in actions*] [*A publication*] (DLA) .... St Gloc
Statute of Gloucester [*First statute to give costs in actions*] [*A publication*] (DLA) .... Stat Glo
Statute of Limitations (OICC) .... S/L
Statute of Limitations [*Legal shorthand*] (LWAP) .... SOL
Statute of Limitations [*A publication*] (DLA) .... St Lim
Statute of Marlborough [*A publication*] (DSA) .... Marl
Statute of Marlbridge [*A publication*] (DLA) .... St Marlb
Statute of Marlbridge [*A publication*] (DLA) .... Stat Marl
Statute of Merton [*A publication*] (DLA) .... St Mert
Statute of Merton [*A publication*] (DLA) .... Stat Mer
Statute of Merton [*A publication*] (DLA) .... Stat Mert
Statute of the International Court of Justice [*A publication*] (DLA) .... Stat ICJ
Statute of Uses [*Legal shorthand*] (LWAP) .... SOU
Statute of Westminster [*A publication*] (DLA) .... St Westm
Statute of Westminster [*A publication*] (DLA) .... Stat Westm
Statute of Winchester [*A publication*] (DLA) .... Stat Winch
Statutes .... STAS
Statutes and Amendments to the Code of California [*A publication*] (DLA) .... Cal Stat
Statutes at Large [*A publication*] (DLA) .... St at Large
[*United States*] **Statutes at Large** (USGC) .... Stat
Statutes at Large, Ruffhead's Edition [*England*] [*A publication*] (DLA) .... Ruff
Statutes at Large, Runnington's Edition [*England*] [*A publication*] (DLA) .... Runn
Statutes, Laws, of the Province of Massachusetts [*A publication*] (DLA) .... Prov St
Statutes of Alberta [*Canada Information service or system*] (IID) .... SA
Statutes of British Columbia [*British Columbia Attorney General's Ministry*] [*Information service or system A publication*] (CRD) .... SBC
Statutes of California [*A publication*] (DLA) .... Cal Stats
Statutes of Canada [*A publication*] (DLA) .... Can Stat
Statutes of Canada [*A publication*] (DLA) .... S of C
Statutes of Canada .... SC
Statutes of Connecticut, Compilation of 1854 [*A publication*] (DLA) .... RS Comp
Statutes of Nevada [*A publication*] (DLA) .... Nev Stats
Statutes of New Brunswick [*Database*] [*Department of Justice*] [*Information service or system*] (CRD) .... SNB
Statutes of New Zealand [*A publication*] (DLA) .... NZ Stat
Statutes of New Zealand [*A publication*] (DLA) .... Stat NZ
Statutes of Newfoundland [*A publication*] (ILCA) .... SN
Statutes of Ontario [*QL Systems Ltd.*] [*Information service or system*] (CRD) .... SO
Statutes of Quebec in the Reign of Victoria [*A publication*] (DLA) .... Q Vic
Statutes of the Province of Canada [*A publication*] (DLA) .... Prov Can Stat
Statutes of the Realm [*England*] [*A publication*] (DLA) .... Stat Realm
Statutes Revised [*A publication*] (DLA) .... SR
Statutory (ROG) .... STATY
Statutory Declaration .... SD
Statutory Definition [*Legal term*] (DLA) .... Stat Def
Statutory Instruments [*A publication*] (DLA) .... Stat Inst
Statutory Invention Registration [*Patents*] .... SIR
Statutory Licensing Authority [*Embryology*] [*British*] .... SLA
Statutory Long Service Leave (ADA) .... SLSL
Statutory Marketing Authority .... SMA
Statutory Maternity Pay [*British*] .... SMP
Statutory Minimum Remuneration [*British*] (DI) .... SMR
Statutory Orders and Regulations [*Canada A publication*] (DLA) .... Can Stat O & Regs
Statutory Orders and Regulations (NITA) .... SOR
Statutory Orders and Regulations [*Canada*] [*A publication*] (DLA) .... Stat O & R
Statutory Orders and Regulations of Canada [*Canada Department of Justice*] [*Information service or system*] .... SOR
Statutory Regulations [*New Zealand*] [*A publication*] (DLA) .... Stat Reg NZ
Statutory Rule (ADA) .... SR
Statutory Rules and Orders [*England*] [*A publication*] (DLA) .... SR & O
Statutory Rules and Orders .... SRO
Statutory Rules and Orders [*1890-1947*] [*England*] [*A publication*] (DLA) .... Stat R & O
Statutory Rules and Orders and Statutory Instruments Revised [*England*] [*A publication*] (DLA) .... SR & O and SI Rev
Statutory Rules and Orders and Statutory Instruments Revised [*England*] [*A publication*] (DLA) .... Stat R & O & Stat Inst Rev
Statutory Rules and Orders of Northern Ireland [*A publication*] (DLA) .... Stat R & ONI
Statutory Sick Pay [*British*] .... SSP
Statutory Tenant (DSUE) .... STAT
Statuts Revises du Canada [*Revised Statutes of Canada*] [*Database Federal Department of Justice*] [*Information service or system*] (CRD) .... SRC
Statvolt [*Also, sV*] [*Electrostatic unit of potential difference*] .... statV
Statvolt [*Also, statV*] [*Electrostatic unit of potential difference*] .... sV
Statweber [*Unit of magnetic flux*] .... statWb
Stauffer Chemical Co. [*Research code symbol*] .... N
Stauffer Chemical Co. [*Research code symbol*] .... R
Stauffer Chemical Co., Eastern Research Center, Dobbs Ferry, NY [*Library symbol Library of Congress*] (LCLS) .... NDfS
Stauffer Chemical Co., Information Services, Dobbs Ferry, NY [*OCLC symbol*] (OCLC) .... ZSC
Stauffer Chemical Co., Richmond, CA [*Library symbol Library of Congress*] (LCLS) .... CRicS
Staundeforde's Exposition of the King's Prerogative [*A publication*] (DLA) .... St Pr
Staundeforde's Exposition of the King's Prerogative [*A publication*] (DSA) .... Sta Pr
Staundeforde's Exposition of the King's Prerogative [*A publication*] (DLA) .... Staundef
Staundeforde's Exposition of the King's Prerogative [*A publication*] (DLA) .... Staundf Prerog
Staundeforde's Exposition of the King's Prerogative [*A publication*] (DLA) .... Staunf Pr
Staundeforde's Pleas of Crown [*A publication*] (DLA) .... St Pl Cr
Staundeforde's Pleas of Crown [*A publication*] (DSA) .... Sta P C
Staundeforde's Pleas of Crown [*A publication*] (DLA) .... Staund Pl
Stauning [*Denmark ICAO location identifier*] (ICLI) .... EKVJ
Stauning [*Denmark*] [*Airport symbol*] (OAG) .... STA
Staunton [*Virginia*] [*Airport symbol*] (OAG) .... SHD
Staunton Public Library, Staunton, IL [*Library symbol Library of Congress*] (LCLS) .... IStau
Staunton Public Library, Staunton, VA [*Library symbol Library of Congress*] (LCLS) .... ViSt
Staunton, VA [*FM radio station call letters*] .... WBGT
Staunton, VA [*AM radio station call letters*] .... WINF
Staunton, VA [*AM radio station call letters*] (RBYB) .... WKDW-AM
Staunton, VA [*FM radio station call letters*] (RBYB) .... WSVO-FM
Staunton, VA [*AM radio station call letters*] .... WTON
Staunton, VA [*FM radio station call letters*] .... WTON-FM
Staunton, VA [*FM radio station call letters*] .... WVAO
Staunton, VA [*Television station call letters*] .... WVPT
Staunton/Waynesboro/Harrisonburg, VA [*Location identifier FAA*] (FAAL) .... SHD
Stavanger [*Norway ICAO location identifier*] (ICLI) .... ENSV
Stavanger [*Norway*] [*Airport symbol*] (OAG) .... SVG
Stavanger/Sola [*Norway ICAO location identifier*] (ICLI) .... ENZV
Stavely Public Library, Alberta [*Library symbol National Library of Canada*] (NLC) .... ASTA
Staverton [*England*] [*Airport symbol*] (AD) .... STV
Stawell [*Australia Airport symbol*] (OAG) .... SWC
Stay at Work, Earn Extra Time [*United Auto Workers*] .... SWEET
Stay Out [*Official leave from Eton College*] [*British*] .... SO
Stay Time Extension Module [*NASA*] .... STEM
Staying Healthy after Fifty [*Project*] [*AARP*] .... SHAF
Stayner Public Library, Ontario [*Library symbol National Library of Canada*] (NLC) .... OSTA
Stayton, OR [*AM radio station call letters*] .... KCKX
Stayton Public Library, Stayton, OR [*Library symbol Library of Congress*] (LCLS) .... OrSt
STB Systems [*NASDAQ symbol*] (TTSB) .... STBI
STB Systems, Inc. [*Associated Press*] (SAG) .... STB Sy
STB Systems, Inc. [*NASDAQ symbol*] (SAG) .... STBI
STC Communications Subsystem Distribution Interface Cabinet (MCD) .... SDIC
STD Terrestrial Navigation System (MCD) .... STENS
STDN [*Space Tracking and Data Network*] **Ranging Equipment** [*NASA*] (GFGA) .... SRE
Steady (MSA) .... STDY
Steady Initial Climb Speed [*Aviation code*] (AIA) V4
Steady Magnetospheric Convection .... SMC
Steady, Oscillatory, and Unsteady, Subsonic, and Supersonic Aerodynamics [*NASA*] .... SOUSSA
Steady Potential (MAE) .... SP
Steady Potential Shift .... SPS
Steady State .... SS
Steady State Adiabatic Reactor [*Chemical engineering*] .... SSAR
Steady State Determining Routine .... SSDR
Steady State Diffusing Lung Capacity for Carbon Monoxide (MAE) .... DLCO-SS
Steady State Distribution (IAA) .... SSD

Steady State Evoked Potential [*Neurophysiology*] ..... SSEP
Steady State Plasma Glucose [*Medicine*] (DMAA) ..... SSPG
Steady State Plasma Insulin [*Medicine*] (DMAA) ..... SSPI
Steady-State Advanced TOKAMAK [*Toroidal Kamera Magnetic*] [*Plasma physics*] ..... SSAT
Steady-State Fermi Level ..... SSFL
Steady-State Free Precession [*Magnetic resonance imaging*] [*Radiology*] (DAVI) ..... SSFP
Steady-State Irradiation [*Nuclear energy*] (NRCH) ..... SSI
Steady-State Isotopic Transient Kinetic Analysis [*Chemical physics*] ..... SSITKA
Steady-State Oscillation ..... SSO
Steady-State Power Level (IEEE) ..... SSPL
Steady-State Pulse [*Telecommunications*] (IAA) ..... SSP
Steady-State Rate [*of production*] [*Medicine*] ..... SSR
Steady-State/Transient Analysis [*Nuclear energy*] (NRCH) ..... SS/T
Steak ..... STK
Stealth Aircraft, Sea-Launched Cruise Missiles, SDI [*Strategic Defense Initiative*]-Like Devices, Space Systems [*High-tech weaponry*] ..... 4S's
Stealth Club of America (EA) ..... SCA
Steam (AAG) ..... ST
Steam ..... STM
Steam ..... STM
Steam and Electric Cogeneration [*Power source*] ..... SECO
Steam and Feedwater Line Rupture Control System [*Nuclear energy*] (NRCH) ..... SFRCS
Steam and Feedwater Rupture Control System (IAA) ..... SAFCS
Steam and Feedwater System [*Nuclear energy*] (NRCH) ..... SFS
Steam and Gas [*Turbine*] ..... STAG
Steam Automobile Club of America (EA) ..... SACA
Steam Bypass Control System [*Nuclear energy*] (NRCH) ..... SBCS
Steam Condensing Mode [*Nuclear energy*] (NRCH) ..... SCM
Steam Derrick [*Coast Guard symbol*] (DNAB) ..... WYTM
Steam Distillation Extracton ..... SDE
Steam Dump Bypass Control System [*Nuclear energy*] (NRCH) ..... SDBCS
Steam Dump System [*Nuclear energy*] (NRCH) ..... SDS
Steam Electric Evaluating and Recording (IAA) ..... SEER
Steam Electric Station [*Nuclear energy*] (NRCH) ..... SES
Steam Emulsion ..... SE
Steam Emulsion Number ..... SEN
Steam Emulsion Number ..... SENO
Steam Engine Direct Connected (MSA) ..... SEDC
Steam Engine Makers' Society [*A union*] [*British*] ..... SEMS
Steam Engine Systems Corp. ..... SES
Steam Explosion in Containment [*Nuclear energy*] (NRCH) ..... CSE
Steam Explosion in Vessel [*Nuclear energy*] (NRCH) ..... VSE
Steam Gas Recycle [*Shale oil process*] ..... SGR
Steam Generator (NRCH) ..... SG
Steam Generator ..... STGEN
Steam Generator Auxiliary Heat Removal System [*Nuclear energy*] (NRCH) ..... SGAHRS
Steam Generator Available Signal [*Nuclear energy*] (NRCH) ..... SGAS
Steam Generator Blowdown [*Nuclear energy*] (NRCH) ..... SGB
Steam Generator Blowdown [*Nuclear energy*] (NRCH) ..... SGBD
Steam Generator Blowdown Processing System [*Nuclear energy*] (NRCH) ..... SGBPS
Steam Generator Blowdown System [*Nuclear energy*] (NRCH) ..... SGBS
Steam Generator Building [*Nuclear energy*] (NRCH) ..... SGB
Steam Generator Feed Pump (IEEE) ..... SGFP
Steam Generator Feedwater (DNAB) ..... SGF
Steam Generator Isolation Signal (IEEE) ..... SGIS
Steam Generator Level Instrumentation Cabinet [*Nuclear energy*] (NRCH) ..... SGLIC
Steam Generator Maximum Steam Rate [*Nuclear energy*] (NRCH) ..... SGMSR
Steam Generator Stop Valve Dump Valve (IEEE) ..... SGSVDV
Steam Generator System [*Nuclear energy*] (NRCH) ..... SGS
Steam Generator Test Facility [*Nuclear energy*] (NRCH) ..... SGTF
Steam Generator Test Rig [*Nuclear energy*] (NRCH) ..... SGTR
Steam Generator Tube Rupture [*Nuclear energy*] (NRCH) ..... SGTR
Steam Generator Water Level Control [*Nuclear energy*] (NRCH) ..... SGWLC
Steam Generators Owners Group [*Nuclear energy*] (NRCH) ..... SGOG
Steam Gunboat [*British military*] (DMA) ..... SGB
Steam Heating Equipment Manufacturers Association [*Defunct*] (EA) ..... SHEMA
Steam Isolation Line (IEEE) ..... SIL
Steam Jet Air Ejector [*Nuclear energy*] (NRCH) ..... SJAE
Steam Lava Flow Deflector (MCD) ..... SLFD
Steam Line Break (NRCH) ..... SLB
Steam Line Isolation [*Nuclear energy*] (NRCH) ..... SLI
Steam Line Isolation Valve [*Nuclear energy*] (NRCH) ..... SLIV
Steam Navigation ..... SN
Steam Pipe Rupture Detector System (IEEE) ..... SPRDS
Steam Plant Automation and Results Computer ..... SPARC
Steam Plant Gauge (DNAB) ..... SPGE
Steam Propulsion Control Panel (DNAB) ..... SPCP
Steam Railway Traction Society [*British*] (BI) ..... SRTS
Steam Service Pressure ..... SSP
Steam Tank Vessel (DNAB) ..... STV
Steam Tanker ..... ST
Steam Trawler ..... ST
Steam Tug ..... ST
Steam Turbine (DS) ..... S Turb
Steam Turbine (MCD) ..... ST
Steam Vacuum Pulse ..... SVP
Steam Valve ..... SV
Steam Wagon [*British*] ..... SW
Steam Working Pressure (MSA) ..... STWP
Steam Yacht (ROG) ..... SY
Steamboat ..... SB
Steamboat (ADA) ..... STBT
Steamboat Association [*British*] (DBA) ..... SBA
Steamboat Bay, AK [*Location identifier FAA*] (FAAL) ..... WSB
Steamboat Springs [*Colorado*] [*Airport symbol Obsolete*] (OAG) ..... HDN
Steamboat Springs [*Colorado*] [*Airport symbol*] (OAG) ..... SBS
Steamboat Springs, CO [*AM radio station call letters*] ..... KBCR
Steamboat Springs, CO [*FM radio station call letters*] (RBYB) ..... KBCR-FM
Steamboat Springs, CO [*Television station call letters*] ..... KSBS
Steamboat Springs, CO [*FM radio station call letters*] ..... KSBT
[*The*] **Steamboaters** (EA) ..... TS
Steam-Conditioning Valve ..... SCV
Steam-Cooled Breeder Reactor [*Nuclear energy*] ..... SCBR
Steam-Cooled Deuteriated Water-Moderated Reactor [*Nuclear energy*] ..... SCDMR
Steam-Cooled Fast Breeder Reactor [*Nuclear energy*] ..... SCFBR
Steam-Cooled Heavy-Water Reactor ..... SCHWR
Steamer ..... S
Steamer (ROG) ..... ST
Steamer ..... STMR
Steamer ..... STR
Steamer Pays Dues [*Shipping*] ..... SPD
Steamfitter (WGA) ..... STMFR
Steam-Generating, Heavy-Water [*Reactor*] [*British Nuclear energy*] (NRCH) ..... SGHW
Steam-Generating, Heavy-Water Reactor [*British Nuclear energy*] (NRCH) ..... SGHWR
Steaming (MSA) ..... STMG
Steam-Injected Gas Turbine ..... STIG
Steam-In-Place [*Sterilization process*] ..... SIP
Steam-Jacketed Kettle ..... SJK
Steam-Methane Reforming [*Chemical engineering*] ..... SMR
Steampipe Survey ..... SPS
Steamship (DS) ..... S
Steamship ..... SS
Steamship Bill of Lading [*Shipping*] ..... SSB/L
Steamship Freight Brokers Association ..... SFBA
Steamship Historical Society of America (EA) ..... SSHSA
Ste-Anne's Hospital, Ste-Anne-De-Bellevue, Quebec [*Library symbol National Library of Canada*] (NLC) ..... QSTAH
Stearic/Oleic Acid Ratio [*Clinical chemistry*] ..... SOR
Stearman Restorers Association (EA) ..... SRA
Stearns & Lehman, Inc. [*NASDAQ symbol*] (SAG) ..... SLHN
Stearns & Lehman, Inc. [*Associated Press*] (SAG) ..... StrLhmn
Stearns/Benton Counties Law Library, St. Cloud, MN [*Library symbol*] [*Library of Congress*] (LCLS) ..... MnStclSC
Stearns County Historical Society, St. Cloud, MN [*Library symbol*] [*Library of Congress*] (LCLS) ..... MnStclHi
Stearn's Real Actions [*A publication*] (DLA) ..... Stearns RA
Stearn's Real Actions [*A publication*] (DLA) ..... Stearns Real Act
Stearns-Roger Corp., Denver, CO [*Library symbol Library of Congress*] (LCLS) ..... CoDSR
Stearyldimethylbenzylammonium Chloride [*Organic chemistry*] ..... STEDBAC
Steatite (VRA) ..... steat
Steatite Insulation Material ..... SIM
Steatite Manufacturers Association [*Later, DPCSMA*] (EA) ..... SMA
Stebbins [*Alaska*] [*Airport symbol*] (OAG) ..... WBB
Stebbins, AK [*Location identifier FAA*] (FAAL) ..... WBB
Stecher's Cases on Agency and Partnership [*A publication*] (DLA) ..... Stecher Agency & Partnership
Steck-Vaughn Publishing [*NASDAQ symbol*] (TTSB) ..... STEK
Steck-Vaughn Publishing Corp. [*Associated Press*] (SAG) ..... SteckVn
Steck-Vaughn Publishing Corp. [*NASDAQ symbol*] (SAG) ..... STEK
Steed Ventures Corp. [*Formerly, Poney Explorations Ltd.*] [*Vancouver Stock Exchange symbol*] ..... SVJ
Steel ..... S
Steel [*Technical drawings*] ..... ST
Steel (KSC) ..... STL
Steel ..... STL
Steel (VRA) ..... stl
Steel, Aluminum, Polyethylene [*Components of a type of telecommunications cable*] ..... STALPETH
Steel Authority of India Ltd. [*Commercial firm*] ..... SAIL
Steel Bar Mills Association [*Later, SMA*] (EA) ..... SBMA
Steel Basement Window ..... SBW
Steel Beam Design [*Modray Ltd.*] [*Software package*] (NCC) ..... SBD
Steel Boiler Institute [*Defunct*] ..... SBI
Steel Building System ..... SBS
Steel Cadmium Plated ..... SCDP
Steel Can Recycling Association (EA) ..... SCRA
Steel Car of Tomorrow ..... SCOT
Steel Carriers Conference [*Later, RDCC*] [*An association*] (EA) ..... SCC
Steel Carriers Group [*Later, RDCC*] [*Defunct*] (EA) ..... SCG
Steel Carriers Tariff Association, Inc. [*Riverdale, MD*] ..... SCTA
Steel Carriers Tariff Association, Inc., East Riverdale MD [*STAC*] ..... STA
Steel Casting ..... SC
Steel Castings Association [*British*] (BI) ..... SCA
Steel Castings Research and Trade Association [*Sheffield, England*] (EAIO) ..... SCRATA
Steel Castings Research and Trade Association [*British*] ..... SCRTA
Steel Column [*Camutek*] [*Software package*] (NCC) ..... STCOL
Steel Co. of Canada ..... STELCO
Steel Co. of Canada, Hamilton, ON, Canada [*Library symbol Library of Congress*] (LCLS) ..... CaOHSCC

Steel Company of Canada, Hamilton, Ontario [*Library symbol National Library of Canada*] (NLC) .... OHSCC
Steel Construction Institute [*British*] (IRUK) .... SCI
Steel Containment Vessel [*Nuclear energy*] (NRCH) .... SCV
Steel Cored [*Conductors*] .... SC
Steel Deck (ADA) .... SD
Steel Deck Institute (EA) .... SDI
Steel Door Institute (EA) .... SDI
Steel Fork Grinders' Association [*A union*] [*British*] .... SFGA
Steel Fork Makers' Association [*A union*] [*British*] .... SFMA
Steel Founders' Society of America (EA) .... SFSA
Steel Girder [*Bridges*] .... SG
Steel Heads .... SH
Steel Industry Compliance Extension Act of 1981 .... SICEA
Steel Industry Management Association [*Trade union*] [*British*] .... SIMA
Steel Joist Institute (EA) .... SJI
Steel Kitchen Cabinet Manufacturers Association (EA) .... SKCMA
Steel Labor Relations Board [*New Deal*] .... SLRB
Steel Lintel Manufacturers Association [*British*] (DBA) .... SLMA
Steel Locus Factor [*Genetics*] .... SLF
Steel Management in Action [*Bethlehem Steel Co.*] .... SMIA
Steel Manufacturers Association (EA) .... SMA
Steel Memorial Hospital, Salmon, ID [*Library symbol*] [*Library of Congress*] (LCLS) .... IdSalH
Steel Nail Association [*British*] (BI) .... SNA
Steel Non-Watertight [*Shipfitting*] .... SNWT
Steel of West Virginia [*NASDAQ symbol*] (TTSB) .... SWVA
Steel of West Virginia, Inc. [*NASDAQ symbol*] (NQ) .... SWVA
Steel or Steel and Wood [*Freight*] .... STL STL and WD
Steel or Wire [*Freight*] .... STL WI
Steel or Wood [*Freight*] .... STL WD
Steel Plants Information System [*German Iron and Steel Engineers Association*] [*Dusseldorf*] [*Information service or system*] (IID) .... PLANTFACTS
Steel Plate Fabricators Association (EA) .... SPFA
Steel Plate Ordering Technique (IAA) .... SPOT
Steel Products Engineering Co. .... SPECO
Steel Products Warehouse Association .... SPWA
Steel Radiator and Convector Manufacturers' Association [*British*] (BI) .... SRCMA
Steel Sash .... SS
Steel Scaffolding and Shoring Institute [*Later, SSFI*] (EA) .... SSSI
Steel Service Center Institute (EA) .... SSCI
Steel Sheet information and Developement Association [*British*] (BI) .... SSIDA
Steel Shipping Container Institute (EA) .... SSCI
Steel Sleeper Association [*British*] (BI) .... SSA
Steel Structures Painting Council (EA) .... SSPC
Steel Tank Institute (EA) .... STI
Steel Tape Armored [*Cables*] .... STA
Steel Technologies [*NASDAQ symbol*] (TTSB) .... STTX
Steel Technologies, Inc. [*Associated Press*] (SAG) .... SteelTch
Steel Technologies, Inc. [*Louisville, KY*] [*NASDAQ symbol*] (NQ) .... STTX
Steel Truss [*Bridges*] .... ST
Steel Tube Institute .... STI
Steel Tube Institute of North America (EA) .... STINA
Steel User Service [*British*] (BI) .... SUS
Steel Watertight [*Shipfitting*] .... SWT
Steel West Virginia [*NASDAQ symbol*] (SAG) .... SWVA
Steel West Virginia, Inc. [*Associated Press*] (SAG) .... StlWVa
Steel Window Association [*British*] (DBA) .... SWA
Steel Window Institute (EA) .... SWI
Steel Wire (IAA) .... SW
Steel Wire Rope .... SWR
Steel Wool Manufacturers' Association [*British*] (BI) .... SWMA
Steel Workers Organizing Committee [*Became United Steelworkers of America*] .... SWOC
Steel Works Plant Association [*British*] (BI) .... SWPA
Steel-Cored Aluminum (IAA) .... SCAL
Steel-Cored Aluminum Conductor (IAA) .... SCALC
Steel-Cored Copper (IAA) .... SCCO
Steel-Cored Copper Conductor (IAA) .... SCCOC
Steel-Cored-Aluminium .... SCA
Steele Elementary School, Baldwin, NY [*Library symbol Library of Congress*] (LCLS) .... NBaldStE
Steele Memorial Library of Elmira and Chemung County, Elmira, NY [*Library symbol Library of Congress*] (LCLS) .... NEIm
Steele-Richardson-Olszewski Syndrome [*Medicine*] .... SRO
Steelhawk Resources Ltd. [*Vancouver Stock Exchange symbol*] .... SWU
Steelhead Resources Ltd. [*Vancouver Stock Exchange symbol*] .... SHZ
Steelton & Highspire Railroad Co. [*AAR code*] .... SH
Steelworker [*Navy rating*] .... SW
Steelworker Erector [*Navy rating*] .... SWE
Steelworker Fabricator [*Navy rating*] .... SWF
Steelworker, First Class [*Navy rating*] SW1
Steelworker, Second Class [*Navy rating*] SW2
Steelworker, Third Class [*Navy rating*] SW3
Steenbock Memorial Library, Madison, WI [*OCLC symbol*] (OCLC) .... WIX
Steenkol/Bintuni [*Indonesia*] [*ICAO location identifier*] (ICLI) .... WASB
Steenkool [*West Irian, Indonesia*] [*Airport symbol*] (AD) .... ZKL
Steep Glide Slope [*NASA*] .... SGS
Steep Rock Resources, Inc. [*Toronto Stock Exchange symbol*] .... SR
Steeple (DS) .... STPL
Steeplechase .... SCHASE
Steep-Spectrum Compact Sources [*of galactic radio waves*] .... SSCS
Steep-Spectrum Radio Quasar [*Galaxy*] .... SSRQ
Steer, Inc. [*An association*] (EA) .... SI

Steer on Parish Law [*6th ed.*] [*1899*] [*A publication*] (DLA) .... Steer PL
Steerable Adaptive Broadcast Reception Equipment (PDAA) .... SABRE
Steerable Antenna Focusing Technique .... STAFT
Steerable Array for RADAR and Communications (CET) .... SARAC
Steerable Array RADAR .... STAR
Steerable Hydrophone Array, Nonlinear Element .... SHANE
Steerable LASER Radiometer (MCD) .... SLAR
Steerable Low-Light-Level Television (PDAA) .... STV
Steerable Null Antenna Processor (RDA) .... SNAP
Steerable Paraboloid Azimuth Radio Reflector (IAA) .... SPARR
Steerable Right-Angle Drive (DNAB) .... SRAD
Steerable Telemetry Antenna Receiving Equipment .... STARE
Steered Directional Transmission (MCD) .... SDT
Steered Vertical Line Array [*Military*] (CAAL) .... SVLA
Steering (AAG) .... STRG
Steering .... STRNG
Steering and Hydroplane [*British*] .... S & H
Steering Angle Error .... SAE
Steering Axis Inclination [*Automotive engineering*] .... SAI
Steering Column and Occupant Response Simulation [*Automotive safety*] [*Computer-aided design*] .... SCORES
Steering Committee (NATG) .... SC
Steering Committee for Sustainable Agriculture [*Later, CSA*] (EA) .... SCSA
Steering Committee on Crossborder Data Exchange in Science and Technology (NITA) .... SCCDEST
Steering Committee on Pilotage (DS) .... SCOP
Steering Control Console (DNAB) .... SCC
Steering Control Unit .... SCU
Steering Damping System [*Aerospace*] (MCD) .... SDS
Steering Gear [*Automotive engineering*] .... S/GR
Steering Gear Dual Emergency (MSA) .... SGDE
Steering Group (MCD) .... SG
Steering Hover Indicator Unit (MCD) .... SHIU
Steering Intelligence (MCD) .... SI
Steering Knuckle [*Automotive engineering*] .... S/KNU
Steering Pressure Sensor [*Automotive engineering*] .... SPS
Steering Reversal Rate .... SRR
Steering Safety .... SS
Steering System .... SS
Steering Task Group .... STG
Steering Wheel Anti-Theft [*Device*] [*Auto Alarm*] .... SWAT
Stefan Resources, Inc. [*Vancouver Stock Exchange symbol*] .... SFN
Stefanovikion [*Greece*] [*ICAO location identifier*] (ICLI) .... LGSV
Steger-South Chicago Heights Library District, South Chicago Heights, IL [*Library symbol Library of Congress*] (LCLS) .... ISch
Stein & Day [*Publishers*] .... SD
Stein Collectors International (EA) .... SCI
Stein Mart [*NASDAQ symbol*] (TTSB) .... SMRT
Stein Mart, Inc. [*NASDAQ symbol*] (SAG) .... SMRT
Stein Mart, Inc. [*Associated Press*] (SAG) .... SteinMrt
Steinbach [*Federal Republic of Germany*] [*Seismograph station code, US Geological Survey*] (SEIS) .... STB
Steinbach Bible College, Manitoba [*Library symbol National Library of Canada*] (BIB) .... MSBC
Steinbach, MB [*AM radio station call letters*] .... CHSM
Steinbach Public Library, Manitoba [*Library symbol National Library of Canada*] (NLC) .... MSTE
Steinbach Public Library, Steinbach, MB, Canada [*Library symbol Library of Congress*] (LCLS) .... CaMSte
Steinbeck Center Foundation (EA) .... SCF
Steinberg, Inc. [*Toronto Stock Exchange symbol*] .... SBG
Steiner Minimum Tree [*Mathematics*] (BARN) .... SMT
Steinkohlen-Elektrizitaet AG [*West Germany*] .... STEAG
Stein-Leventhal Syndrome [*Medicine*] (DMAA) .... SLS
Steinman Aviation, Inc. [*FAA designator*] (FAAC) .... SBB
Stelco, Inc. [*Toronto Stock Exchange symbol Vancouver Stock Exchange symbol*] .... STE
Stelco Inc.'A' [*TS symbol*] (TTSB) .... STE.A
Stella Branch, Lennox and Addington County Library, Ontario [*Library symbol National Library of Canada*] (NLC) .... OSLA
Stella Hill Memorial Library, Alto, TX [*Library symbol Library of Congress*] (LCLS) .... TxAI
Stella Maris [*Bahamas*] [*Airport symbol*] (OAG) .... SML
Stella Maris, Long Island [*Bahamas*] [*ICAO location identifier*] (ICLI) .... MYLS
Stellacyanin .... Sc
Steliair [*France ICAO designator*] (FAAC) .... STR
Stellar Acquisition Flight Feasibility .... STAFF
Stellar Attitude Reference .... STAR
Stellar Attitude Reference and Navigation .... STARAN
Stellar Attitude Reference Study .... SARS
Stellar Camera .... SC
Stellar Image Monitor .... SIM
Stellar Inertial Bombing System .... SIBS
Stellar Inertial Doppler System .... SIDS
Stellar Inertial Guidance Signal .... SIG
Stellar Inertial Guidance System [*Air Force*] (AAG) .... SIGS
Stellar Inertial Guidance System [*Air Force*] .... STRINGS
Stellar Inertial Guidance System (DNAB) .... STRINGS
Stellar Inertial Measurement System [*NASA*] .... SIMS
Stellar Inertial Measuring Unit (IAA) .... SIMU
Stellar Inertial Navigation System (IAA) .... SINS
Stellar Mass Ejection .... SME
Stellar Simulation Complex (OA) .... SSC
Stellar Television Monitor Equipment .... STME
Stellar Tracker Evaluation Missile .... STEM

Stellar Tracking Attitude Reference System ... STARS
Stellar X-Ray Spectra ... SXS
Stellate Ganglion [*Neuroanatomy*] ... SG
Stellate Ganglion Blockade [*Anesthesiology*] ... SGB
[*The*] **Stelle Group** (EA) ... TSG
Stellenbosch [*South Africa*] [*ICAO location identifier*] (ICLI) ... FASH
Stellite [*Metallurgy*] ... STLT
Stelway Food [*Vancouver Stock Exchange symbol*] ... SWF
Stem ... S
Stem [*Linguistics*] [*Botany*] ... ST
Stem Cell Activating Factor [*Biochemistry*] ... SAF
Stem Cell Factor [*Genetics*] ... SCF
Stem Cell Inhibitor [*Cytology*] ... SCI
Stem Cell Leukaemia [*Hematology*] ... SCL
Stem Elevated Camera System ... SECS
Stem End Rot [*Plant pathology*] ... SER
Stem Pubescence [*Botany*] ... STPUB
Stem Tolerance Index [*Botany*] ... STI
Stemming and Closure Panel [*Terminated, 1975*] [*DoD*] (EGAO) ... SACPAN
Stencil ... ST
Stencil ... STEN
Stencil (VRA) ... stncl
Stenciled Weight ... SW
Stenographer [*British military*] (DMA) ... ST
Stenographer ... STEN
Stenographer (MUGU) ... STENO
Stenographer and Typist [*Examination*] [*Civil Service Commission*] ... S & T
Stenographer, Medical [*Navy*] ... STT
Stenosing Peripheral Arterial Disease [*Medicine*] (DMAA) ... SPAD
Stent [*Let Them Stand*] [*Latin*] (MAE) ... st
Stenton. Rolls of the Justices in Eyre [*A publication*] (ILCA) ... Stenton
Step Adjustable Antenna ... SAA
Step by Step Switch (NITA) ... SXS
Step Climb (GAVI) ... S/C
Step Control Table (CMD) ... SCT
Step Counter (IAA) ... SC
Step Down Amplifier ... SDA
Step Down Fix [*Aviation*] (DA) ... SDF
Step Down Unit [*Medicine*] (CPH) ... SDU
Step Family Foundation (EA) ... SFF
Step Function Input ... SFI
Step in Place ... SIP
Step Index [*Nuclear energy*] (NUCP) ... SI
Step Index (NITA) ... SI
STEP [*Scientific and Technical Exploitation Program*] **Information Subsystem** ... SIS
Step Input/Output (NITA) ... SIO
Step Recovery Diode ... SRD
Step Recovery Transistor ... SRT
Step Recovery Varactor ... SRV
Step Size (IAA) ... SS
Step Timing Control [*Truck engineering*] ... STC
Step Up ... STU
Stepan Chemical Co. [*AMEX symbol*] (SPSG) ... SCL
Stepan Co. [*NYSE symbol*] (TTSB) ... SCL
Stepan Co. 5.50% Cv Pfd [*NYSE symbol*] (TTSB) ... SCLPr
Stepanavan [*Former USSR Seismograph station code, US Geological Survey Closed*] (SEIS) ... STE
Step-by-Step Monitor and Selector Hold [*Telecommunications*] (TEL) ... SMASH
Step-by-Step Precedents and Procedures. Companies, Trusts, Superannuation Funds [*Australia A publication*] ... LSPP
Step-by-Step Switching System [*Telecommunications*] ... SxS
Step-by-Step Test (IAA) ... SST
Stepchild [*or Children*] (DNAB) ... SC
Stepchild ... STC
StepClimb (GAVI) ... STEPCLB
Stepdown ... STPDN
Step-Down and Step-Up (MSA) ... SDN & SU
Step-Down Transformer ... SDT
Stepfamily Association of America (EA) ... SAA
Step-Father (DAVI) ... STFA
Stephan Co. [*Associated Press*] (SAG) ... Stepan
Stephan Co. [*Associated Press*] (SAG) ... Stephan
Stephan Co. [*AMEX symbol*] (SAG) ... TSC
Stephanus Bertrandus [*Flourished, 16th century*] [*Authority cited in pre-1607 legal work*] (DSA) ... Stepha Bertrand
Stephanus Pragensis [*Flourished, 14th century*] [*Authority cited in pre-1607 legal work*] (DSA) ... Steph
Stephanus Provincialis [*Flourished, 1290-97*] [*Authority cited in pre-1607 legal work*] (DSA) ... S
Stephanus Provincialis [*Flourished, 1290-97*] [*Authority cited in pre-1607 legal work*] (DSA) ... Ste
Stephanus Tornacensis [*Deceased, 1203*] [*Authority cited in pre-1607 legal work*] (DSA) ... Ste
Stephanus Tornacensis [*Deceased, 1203*] [*Authority cited in pre-1607 legal work*] (DSA) ... Steph
Step-Height Ratio [*Crystallography*] ... SHR
Stephen and Benecke on Average [*A publication*] (DLA) ... Ben Av
Stephen Elementary School, Stpehen, MN [*Library symbol*] [*Library of Congress*] (LCLS) ... MnSteE
Stephen F. Austin State University (GAGS) ... S F Austin St U
Stephen F. Austin State University, Nacogdoches, TX [*Library symbol Library of Congress*] (LCLS) ... TxNacS
Stephen F. Austin University, Nacogdoches, TX [*OCLC symbol*] (OCLC) ... TXK
Stephen Greene Press ... SGP
Stephen High School, Stephen, MN [*Library symbol*] [*Library of Congress*] (LCLS) ... MnSteH
Stephen Madden Ltd. [*NASDAQ symbol*] (SAG) ... SHOO
Stephen on Pleading [*A publication*] (DLA) ... Steph Pl
Stephens College, Columbia, MO [*Library symbol Library of Congress*] (LCLS) ... MoCoS
Stephens College, Columbia, MO [*OCLC symbol*] (OCLC) ... MOV
Stephen's Commentaries on the Laws of England [*21st ed.*] [*1950*] [*A publication*] (DLA) ... St C
Stephen's Commentaries on the Laws of England [*A publication*] (DLA) ... Steph Com
Stephen's Commentaries on the Laws of England [*A publication*] (DLA) ... Steph Comm
Stephens Creek [*Australia Seismograph station code, US Geological Survey*] (SEIS) ... STK
Stephen's Digest, New Brunswick Reports [*A publication*] (DLA) ... Steph Dig
Stephen's Digest of Criminal Procedure [*9th ed.*] [*1950*] [*A publication*] (DLA) ... Dig Crim Proc
Stephen's Digest of the Criminal Law [*A publication*] (DLA) ... Steph Cr
Stephen's Digest of the Criminal Law [*A publication*] (DLA) ... Steph Crim Dig
Stephen's Digest of the Criminal Law [*A publication*] (DLA) ... Steph Dig Cr L
Stephen's Digest of the Criminal Law [*A publication*] (DLA) ... Steph Dig Cr Law
Stephen's Digest of the Law of Evidence [*A publication*] (DLA) ... Steph Dig Ev
Stephen's Digest of the Law of Evidence [*A publication*] (DLA) ... Steph Ev
Stephen's General View of the Criminal Law [*2nd ed.*] [*1890*] [*A publication*] (DLA) ... Gen View Cr L
Stephen's General View of the Criminal Law [*9 eds.*] [*1877-1950*] [*A publication*] (DLA) ... Steph Cr L
Stephen's General View of the Criminal Law [*A publication*] (DLA) ... Steph Cr Law
Stephen's General View of the Criminal Law [*2nd ed.*] [*1890*] [*A publication*] (DLA) ... Steph Gen View
Stephens Glacier [*Alaska*] [*Seismograph station code, US Geological Survey Closed*] (SEIS) ... SGA
Stephen's History of Criminal Law [*A publication*] (DLA) ... Stephen HCL
Stephen's Law of Nisi Prius [*A publication*] (DLA) ... Steph NP
Stephen's Lectures on the History of France [*A publication*] (DLA) ... Steph Lect
Stephens on Clergy [*1848*] [*A publication*] (DLA) ... Steph Cl
Stephens on Elections [*1840*] [*A publication*] (DLA) ... Steph Elect
Stephens on Procurations [*A publication*] (DLA) ... Steph Proc
Stephens on Slavery [*A publication*] (DLA) ... Steph Slav
Stephens on the English Constitution [*A publication*] (DLA) ... Steph Const
Stephens Owners Registry [*Defunct*] (EA) ... SOR
Stephens' Supreme Court Decisions [*1774-1923*] [*Jamaica*] [*A publication*] (DLA) ... Steph
Stephens-Adamson, Belleville, ON, Canada [*Library symbol*] [*Library of Congress*] (LCLS) ... CaOBESA
Stephens-Adamson, Belleville, Ontario [*Library symbol National Library of Canada*] (NLC) ... OBESA
Stephenson Locomotive Society [*British*] (BI) ... SLS
Stephenson Public Library, Marinette, WI [*Library symbol*] [*Library of Congress*] (LCLS) ... WMari
Stephenville [*Canada*] [*Airport symbol*] (OAG) ... YJT
Stephenville Crossing Public Library, Newfoundland [*Library symbol National Library of Canada*] (NLC) ... NFSTC
Stephenville Crossing Public Library, Stephenville Crossing, NF, Canada [*Library symbol Library of Congress*] (LCLS) ... CaNfStC
Stephenville, NF [*Television station call letters*] ... CBYT-1
Stephenville, NF [*AM radio station call letters*] ... CFSX
Stephenville, NF [*FM radio station call letters*] ... CIOS
Stephenville, NF [*Television station call letters*] ... CJSV
Stephenville, NF [*ICAO location identifier*] (ICLI) ... CYJT
Stephenville, TX [*FM radio station call letters*] ... KCUB
Stephenville, TX [*AM radio station call letters*] ... KSTV
Stephenville, TX [*Location identifier FAA*] (FAAL) ... SEP
Stepheville Aviation Services [*Canada ICAO designator*] (FAAC) ... XSN
Steph's Joint-Stock Companies in Canada [*A publication*] (DLA) ... Steph J St Comp
Step-Mother (DAVI) ... STMO
Stepped Atomic Time [*National Institute of Standards and Technology*] ... SAT
Stepped Care [*Medicine*] ... SC
Stepped Electrode Transistor ... SET
Stepped Impedance Transformer (IAA) ... SIT
Stepped Piston Crossover (PDAA) ... SPX
Stepped Potential Electrode [*Electrode chemistry*] ... SPE
Stepped-Bore Wheel Cylinder [*Automotive brake systems*] ... SBWC
Stepped-Frequency Microwave Radiometer [*For measuring rain rate and wind speed*] ... SFMR
Stepped-Temperature Stress-Rupture [*Ceramics*] (DICI) ... STSR
Stepper [*Motor*] [*Electronics*] ... STPR
Stepper Central Office Tester (NITA) ... SCOT
Stepper Motor Control ... SMC
Stepping (WGA) ... STP
Stepping (MSA) ... STPG
Stepping Switch Counter (AAG) ... SSC
Stepping Switch Scanner ... SSS
Steps to Abstract Reasoning ... STAR
Steps Up Developmental Screening Program [*Child development test*] [*Psychology*] ... SUDS
Step-Through Latencies ... STL
Step-Wise Cracking (MCD) ... SWC
Stepwise Discriminant Analysis ... SDA
Step-Wise Discriminant Analysis ... SWDA
Stepwise Linear Regression (IAA) ... SLREG
Stepwise Multiple Linear Regression [*Mathematics*] ... SMLR
Stepwise Refinement (IAA) ... SWR

Stepwise Regression Analysis (PDAA) .... SWRA
Stepwise Thermal Desorption [Surface analysis] .... STD
Steradian [Symbol] [SI unit of solid angle] .... sr
Steradian .... STER
Sterba Curtain Antenna .... SCA
Stere [Metric measure of volume] .... S
Stere [Metric measure of volume] .... st
Stereo (CDAI) .... S
Stereo (VRA) .... ster
Stereo .... STER
Stereo Broadcast [British] .... S
Stereo Dimensional Array .... SDA
Stereo Directional .... SD
Stereo Electro-Optical Tracking System (MCD) .... SETS
Stereo Imaging (SSD) .... SI
Stereo Lithography .... STL
Stereo Photographers, Collectors, and Enthusiasts Club (EA) .... SPCEC
Stereo Photographic System .... SPS
Stereo Radio Cassette .... SRC
Stereo Review [A publication] (BRI) .... Stereo
Stereo Routes [Aviation] (FAAC) .... STRO
Stereo Synthetic Aperture RADAR (SSD) .... SSAR
Stereo Tape Club of America .... STC
Stereo Wave Observation Project (IAA) .... SWOP
Stereo Zoom Microscope .... SZM
Stereochemical Descriptor (NITA) .... ST
Stereochemistry Fragment (NITA) .... STF
Stereocilia [Zoology] .... ST
Stereogram [Radiology] (DAVI) .... Stereo
Stereo-Image Alternator (PDAA) .... SIA
Stereolithography [Desktop manufacturing] .... SLA
Stereolithography / Rapid Prototyping [Design] (RDA) .... SLA/RP
Stereonet Analysis Program (PDAA) .... SNAP
Stereophonic (MSA) .... STEREO
Stereophotogrammetry [Medicine] .... SPG
Stereoquadraphonic [Record playing system] [CBS] .... SQ
Stereoscan Electron Microscope .... SEM
Stereoscope [or Stereoscopic] .... STEREO
Stereoscopic Society [Chessington, Surrey, England] (EAIO) .... SS
Stereoscopic Society - American Branch (EA) .... SS
Stereospecifically Numbered [Biochemistry] .... sn
Stereotactic Subcaudate Tractotomy [Medicine] (DMAA) .... SSCT
Stereotype .... STER
Stereotype [Refers to old news] [Slang] (DSUE) .... STEREO
Stereotyped Behavior [Medicine] (DMAA) .... SB
Stereoview (VRA) .... STER
Steric Hindrance Enzyme Immunoassay [Clinical chemistry] .... SHEIA
Stericycle, Inc. [NASDAQ symbol] (SAG) .... SRCL
Stericycle, Inc. [Associated Press] (SAG) .... Stricycle
Sterile Aqueous Suspension .... SAS
Sterile Concepts [NYSE symbol] (TTSB) .... SYS
Sterile Concepts Holdings, Inc. [Associated Press] (SAG) .... SterileC
Sterile Concepts Holdings, Inc. [NYSE symbol] (SAG) .... SYS
Sterile Connection Device [Medicine] .... SCD
Sterile Disposable Device Committee [Defunct] .... SDDC
Sterile Distilled Water .... SDW
Sterile Dressing [Medicine] (MEDA) .... SD
Sterile Dressing [Surgery] (DAVI) .... SD
Sterile Dry Dressing [Surgery] (DAVI) .... SDD
Sterile Environmental Control Technology Applications to Medicine .... SECTAM
Sterile Females [Genetics] .... SF
Sterile Injectable Suspension .... SIS
Sterile Insect Release Method .... SIRM
Sterile Insect Technology .... SIT
Sterile Nitrogen Atmosphere Processing .... SNAP
Sterile Preparation Area (MCD) .... SPA
Sterile Recoveries, Inc. [Associated Press] (SAG) .... SterRecv
Sterile Recoveries, Inc. [NASDAQ symbol] (SAG) .... STRC
Sterile Saline Soak .... SSS
Sterile Solution .... SS
Sterile Supply Unit (MAE) .... SSU
Sterile Vaginal Examination [Obstetrics] (DAVI) .... SVE
Sterile Water .... SW
Sterile Water for Injection [Pharmacology] (DAVI) .... SWFI
Sterile Water for Injection [Pharmacology] (DAVI) .... SWI
Sterilised Cat Gut Manufacturers' Association [British] (BI) .... SCMA
Sterilised Suture Manufacturers Association [British] (DBA) .... SSMA
Sterility Research Center [Public Health Service] (GRD) .... SRC
Sterilizable Potting Compound .... SPC
Sterilization Aerospace Ground Equipment (KSC) .... SAGE
Sterilization and Bath .... S & B
Sterilization Assembly Development Laboratory [NASA] .... SADL
Sterilization Assembly Facility .... SAF
Sterilization Qualification Tests .... SQT
Sterilization Test Program .... STP
Sterilize (AABC) .... STER
Steris Corp. [Associated Press] (SAG) .... Steris
Steris Corp. [NASDAQ symbol] (SAG) .... STRL
Sterivet Laboratories Ltd. [Toronto Stock Exchange symbol] .... SVB
Sterling .... STER
Sterling (ODBW) .... ster
Sterling (ADA) .... STERL
Sterling .... STG
Sterling (ODBW) .... stg
Sterling (WGA) .... STLG

Sterling .... STRLNG
Sterling Airways Ltd. [Denmark ICAO designator] (FAAC) .... SAW
Sterling and Decimal Invoicing Electronically (IEEE) .... SADIE
Sterling and Francine Clark Art Institute, Williamstown, MA [Library symbol Library of Congress] (LCLS) .... MWiCA
Sterling Bancorp [NYSE symbol] (SPSG) .... STL
Sterling Bancorp [Associated Press] (SAG) .... StrlBcp
Sterling Bancshares [NASDAQ symbol] (TTSB) .... SBIB
Sterling Bancshares, Inc. [NASDAQ symbol] (SAG) .... SBIB
Sterling Bancshares, Inc. [Associated Press] (SAG) .... StrlBnc
Sterling Capital [AMEX symbol] (TTSB) .... SPR
Sterling Capital Corp. [AMEX symbol] (SPSG) .... SPR
Sterling Capital Corp. [Associated Press] (SAG) .... StrlCap
Sterling Central Union List of Serials, Sterling, KS [OCLC symbol] (OCLC) .... KUL
Sterling Chemicals [NYSE symbol] (TTSB) .... STX
Sterling Chemicals, Inc. [Associated Press] (SAG) .... StrlCh
Sterling Chemicals, Inc. [NYSE symbol] (CTT) .... STX
Sterling City, TX [FM radio station call letters] (RBYB) .... KAKR-FM
Sterling, CO [Location identifier FAA] (FAAL) .... BAJ
Sterling, CO [FM radio station call letters] .... KNNG
Sterling, CO [FM radio station call letters] .... KPMX
Sterling, CO [AM radio station call letters] .... KSTC
Sterling, CO [Television station call letters] .... KTVS
Sterling, CO [Location identifier FAA] (FAAL) .... STK
Sterling College, Sterling, KS [OCLC symbol] (OCLC) .... KKQ
Sterling College, Sterling, KS [Library symbol Library of Congress] (LCLS) .... KSteC
Sterling Commerce [NYSE symbol] (TTSB) .... SE
Sterling Drug Ltd., Aurora, Ontario [Library symbol National Library of Canada] (BIB) .... OAUS
Sterling Electronics (IAA) .... SE
Sterling Electronics [NYSE symbol] (TTSB) .... SEC
Sterling Electronics Corp. [NYSE symbol] (SAG) .... SEC
Sterling Electronics Corp. [Associated Press] (SAG) .... SterlEl
Sterling Energy Corp. [Vancouver Stock Exchange symbol] .... SNG
Sterling Financial Corp. [Associated Press] (SAG) .... StrlF
Sterling Financial Corp. [Associated Press] (SAG) .... StrlFnWA
Sterling Financial Corp. [NASDAQ symbol] (SAG) .... STSA
Sterling Finl $1.8125 Cv Pfd [NASDAQ symbol] (TTSB) .... STSAP
Sterling Finl (WA) [NASDAQ symbol] (TTSB) .... STSA
Sterling Forest [New York] [Seismograph station code, US Geological Survey] (SEIS) .... SFO
Sterling Healthcare Group [NASDAQ symbol] (SAG) .... STER
Sterling Healthcare Group [Associated Press] (SAG) .... SterlHlth
Sterling Heights, MI [AM radio station call letters] .... WUFL
Sterling Heights Public Library, Sterling Heights, MI [Library symbol Library of Congress] (LCLS) .... MiSth
Sterling House [AMEX symbol] (TTSB) .... SGH
Sterling House Corp. [AMEX symbol] (SAG) .... SGH
Sterling House Corp. [Associated Press] (SAG) .... SterlHous
Sterling House Corp. [Associated Press] (SAG) .... SterlHs
Sterling, IL [FM radio station call letters] (RBYB) .... WNIQ-FM
Sterling, IL [AM radio station call letters] .... WSDR
Sterling, IL [FM radio station call letters] .... WSSQ
Sterling, KS [FM radio station call letters] (RBYB) .... KGGG
Sterling Lord Literistic, Inc. [Literary agency] [British] .... SLL
Sterling Municipal Library, Baytown, TX [Library symbol Library of Congress] (LCLS) .... TxBy
Sterling Nuclear Plant (NRCH) .... SN
Sterling Public Library, Sterling, CO [Library symbol Library of Congress] (LCLS) .... CoSt
Sterling Public Library, Sterling IL [Library symbol] [Library of Congress] (LCLS) .... ISter
Sterling Public Library, Sterling, VA [Library symbol Library of Congress] (LCLS) .... ViSte
Sterling/Rock Falls [Illinois] [Airport symbol] (OAG) .... SQI
Sterling Rockfalls, IL [Location identifier FAA] (FAAL) .... BOZ
Sterling Silver (VRA) .... strl si
Sterling Silversmiths Guild of America (EA) .... SSGA
Sterling Software [NYSE symbol] (TTSB) .... SSW
Sterling Software, Inc. [NYSE symbol] (SPSG) .... SSW
Sterling Software, Inc. [Associated Press] (SAG) .... SterlSft
Sterling Transferable Accruing Government Securities (TDOB) .... STAGS
Sterling Transferable Accruing Government Securities (ODBW) .... STAGS
Sterling Vision [NASDAQ symbol] (TTSB) .... ISEE
Sterling Vision, Inc. [NASDAQ symbol] (SAG) .... ISEE
Sterling Vision, Inc. [Associated Press] (SAG) .... StrlVis
Sterling Warrant into Gilt-Edged Stock [British] .... SWING
Sterling West Bancorp [Associated Press] (SAG) .... StrlWst
Sterling West Bancorp [NASDAQ symbol] (SAG) .... SWBC
Sterling-Winthrop Research Institute, Rensselaer, NY [Library symbol Library of Congress] (LCLS) .... NRenSW
Stern Activities Index [Psychology] .... SAI
Stern Air, Inc. [ICAO designator] (FAAC) .... SNA
Stern Discharge .... SD
Stern Diving .... STDVG
Stern Environment Indexes [Psychology] .... SEI
Stern Loading .... SL
Stern Plane .... STPL
Stern Post .... SP
Stern Reference Point [Navy] (DNAB) .... SRP
Stern Teacher Preference Schedule .... STPS
Stern Telecommunications Corp. [New York, NY] [Telecommunications] (TSSD) .... STC

Stern Thruster [*Type of ship*] (DS) ... ST
Stern Wheel [*of a ship*] (DS) ... STW
Sternair, Inc. [*FAA designator*] (FAAC) ... JJW
Sternal Angie [*Anatomy*] (DAVI) ... SA
Sternal Border [*Anatomy*] ... SB
Sternal Notch [*Anatomy*] (DAVI) ... SN
Sternal-Occipital-Mandibular Immobilization [*Medicine*] ... SOMI
Stern-Gerlach [*Experiment for measuring atomic magnetism*] ... SG
Sternoclavicular [*Joint*] [*Anatomy*] ... SC
Sternoclavicular Joints [*Anatomy*] (DAVI) ... SCJ
Sternocleidomastoid [*Anatomy*] ... SCM
Sternocostoclavicular Hyperostosis [*Medicine*] (DMAA) ... SCCH
Sternocostoclavicular Hyperostosis [*Medicine*] (DMAA) ... SCCHO
Sternothyroid [*Anatomy*] ... ST
Sternotomy [*Medicine*] ... ST
Sternutamentum [*Snuff*] [*Pharmacy*] ... STERNUT
Steroid Action Aid Group [*British*] (DBA) ... SAAG
Steroid Protein Activity Index [*Medicine*] (MAE) ... SPAI
Steroid Receptor [*Endocrinology*] ... SR
Steroid Receptor Coactivator [*Endocrenalogy*] ... SRC
Steroid Score [*Immunology*] ... SS
Steroid Sulfatase Deficiency Disease [*Medicine*] (DMAA) ... SSDD
Steroid Sulfurylation (AAMN) ... SS
Steroid-Binding Assay [*Clinical chemistry*] ... SBA
Steroid-Binding Plasma Protein ... SBP
Steroid-Dependent Asthmatic [*Medicine*] ... SDA
Steroidogenesis Activator Polypeptide ... SAP
Steroidogenesis-Stimulating Protein [*Physiology*] ... STP
Steroid-Responsive Nephrotic Syndrome [*Medicine*] ... SRNS
Steroid-Sensitive Nephrotic Syndrome [*Medicine*] (DMAA) ... SSNS
Sterol Biosynthesis Inhibitors [*Chemotherapentic agent*] ... SBI
Sterol Carrier Protein ... SCP
Sterol Regulatory Element [*Genetics*] ... SRE
Sterol Regulatory Element Binding Protein [*Biochemistry*] ... SREBP
Sterol-sulphatase [*An enzyme*] ... STS
Ste-Rose Regional Library, Manitoba [*Library symbol National Library of Canada*] (NLC) ... MSTR
Stet [*Let It Stand*] [*Latin*] ... ST
Stet Societa Finaziaria Telefonica PA [*Associated Press*] (SAG) ... SSFnTA
Stet Societa Finaziaria Telefonica PA [*Associated Press*] (SAG) ... SSFnTel
Stet Societa Finaziaria Telefonica PA [*NYSE symbol*] (SAG) ... STE
STET-Societa Fin Tel Ord ADS [*NYSE symbol*] (TTSB) ... STE
STET-Societa Fin Tele Svg ADS [*NYSE symbol*] (TTSB) ... STE A
Stetson Hat [*After John Batterson Stetson, 19th-century American hat manufacturer*] [*Slang*] ... JB
Stetson Reading-Spelling Vocabulary Test [*Educational test*] ... RSVT
Stetson University (GAGS) ... Stetson U
Stetson University College of Law (DLA) ... SUCL
Stetson University College of Law, St. Petersburg, FL [*Library symbol Library of Congress*] (LCLS) ... FDS-L
Stetson University, De Land, FL [*Library symbol Library of Congress*] (LCLS) ... FDS
Stettler, AB [*AM radio station call letters*] ... CKSQ
Stettler Public Library, Alberta [*Library symbol National Library of Canada*] (NLC) ... AST
Steuben Society of America (EA) ... SSA
Steubenville [*Diocesan abbreviation*] [*Ohio*] (TOCD) ... STU
Steubenville, OH [*AM radio station call letters*] ... WDIG
Steubenville, OH [*FM radio station call letters*] ... WRKY
Steubenville, OH [*AM radio station call letters*] ... WSTV
Steubenville, OH [*Television station call letters*] ... WTOV
Steuerordnung [*Tax Law*] [*German*] (ILCA) ... StO
Steve Cochran Fan Club (EA) ... SCFC
Steve Earle and Dukes Fan Organization (EA) ... SEDFC
Steve Long Fan Club [*Defunct*] (EA) ... SLFC
Steve Miller Band [*Pop music group*] ... SMB
Stevedore ... STEV
Stevedore (DS) ... stvdr
Stevedoring Barge [*Navy symbol Obsolete*] ... YS
Steven Marshall, Edward Calamy, Thomas Young, Matthew Newcomen, William Spurstow [*Collective author of 17th-century antiepiscopal tract*] ... SMECTYMNUS
Steven Spielberg Film Society (EA) ... SSFS
Stevengraph Collectors' Association (EA) ... SCA
Stevens and Benecke on Insurance [*A publication*] (DLA) ... Stev & Ben Ins
Stevens and Graham's Reports [*98-139 Georgia*] [*A publication*] (DLA) ... Stev & G
Stevens and Graham's Reports [*98-139 Georgia*] [*A publication*] (DLA) ... Stevens & G
Stevens Creek [*California*] [*Seismograph station code, US Geological Survey*] (SEIS) ... SEC
Stevens Institute of Technology [*Hoboken, NJ*] ... SIT
Stevens Institute of Technology (GAGS) ... Stevens Inst Tech
Stevens Institute of Technology, Hoboken, NJ [*Library symbol Library of Congress*] (LCLS) ... NjHoS
Stevens International, Inc. [*Associated Press*] (SAG) ... StevInt
Stevens International, Inc. [*AMEX symbol*] (SPSG) ... SVG
Stevens Intl Cl'A' [*AMEX symbol*] (TTSB) ... SVG.A
Stevens Intl Cl'B' [*AMEX symbol*] (TTSB) ... SVG.B
Stevens Memorial Library, Attica, NY [*Library symbol Library of Congress*] (LCLS) ... NAtt
Stevens' New Brunswick Digest [*A publication*] (DLA) ... Stev Dig
Stevens on Arbitration [*2nd ed.*] [*1835*] [*A publication*] (DLA) ... Stev Arb
Stevens on Average [*5th ed.*] [*1835*] [*A publication*] (DLA) ... Stev Av
Stevens Point [*Wisconsin*] [*Airport symbol Obsolete*] (OAG) ... STE
Stevens Point, WI [*AM radio station call letters*] ... WSPO
Stevens Point, WI [*FM radio station call letters*] ... WSPT
Stevens Point, WI [*AM radio station call letters*] (RBYB) ... WSPT-AM
Stevens Point, WI [*FM radio station call letters*] ... WWSP
Stevens Trade School, Lancaster, PA [*OCLC symbol*] (OCLC) ... PIS
Stevens Village [*Alaska*] [*Airport symbol*] (OAG) ... SVS
Stevens-Duryea Associates (EA) ... SDA
Stevens-Johnson Syndrome [*Medicine*] (AAMN) ... S-J
Stevens-Johnson Syndrome [*Medicine*] (DMAA) ... SJS
Stevenson, AL [*FM radio station call letters*] (RBYB) ... WMXN
Stevenson, ON [*Television station call letters*] ... CIII-22
Steveston Museum, Richmond, British Columbia [*Library symbol National Library of Canada*] (NLC) ... BRSM
Steward [*Navy rating*] ... SD
Steward [*British*] ... STD
Steward, First Class [*Navy rating*] ... SD1
Steward of Meeting [*Auto racing*] ... SOM
Steward, Second Class [*Navy rating*] ... SD2
Steward, Technical [*Marine Corps*] ... STET
Steward, Third Class [*Navy rating*] ... SD3
Stewardesses for Women's Rights ... SFWR
Steward's Assistant [*Navy*] ... STDA
Steward's Branch [*Marine Corps*] ... STDB
Steward's Mate [*Navy rating*] ... STM
Stewardship Incentive Program [*Forestry*] ... SIP
Stewardsman [*Nonrated enlisted man*] [*Navy*] ... TN
Stewardsman Apprentice, Steward, Striker [*Navy rating*] ... SDTA
Stewardsman Recruit [*Navy*] ... TR
Stewardsman, Steward, Striker [*Navy rating*] ... SDTN
Stewart [*Canada*] [*Airport symbol*] (OAG) ... ZST
Stewart and Porter's Alabama Reports [*A publication*] (DLA) ... S & P (Ala) Rep
Stewart and Porter's Alabama Reports [*A publication*] (DLA) ... St & P
Stewart and Porter's Alabama Reports [*A publication*] (DLA) ... St and Port
Stewart and Porter's Alabama Reports [*A publication*] (DLA) ... Stew & P Rep
Stewart and Porter's Alabama Reports [*A publication*] (DLA) ... Stew and Porter
Stewart and Porter's Alabama Supreme Court Reports [*1831-34*] [*A publication*] (DLA) ... Stew & P
Stewart & Stevenson [*NASDAQ symbol*] (TTSB) ... SSSS
Stewart & Stevenson Services, Inc. [*NASDAQ symbol*] (NQ) ... SSSS
Stewart & Stevenson Services, Inc. [*Associated Press*] (SAG) ... StwStv
Stewart Avenue Elementary School, Garden City, NY [*Library symbol*] [*Library of Congress*] (LCLS) ... NGcSE
Stewart Aviation Services, Inc. [*ICAO designator*] (FAAC) ... YBE
Stewart Elementary School, Elmont, NY [*Library symbol Library of Congress*] (LCLS) ... NElmoSE
Stewart Enterprises, Inc. [*NASDAQ symbol*] (SPSG) ... STEI
Stewart Enterprises'A' [*NASDAQ symbol*] (TTSB) ... STEI
Stewart Evaluation of Nursing Scale (DMAA) ... SENS
Stewart Historical Museum, British Columbia [*Library symbol National Library of Canada*] (NLC) ... BSTHM
Stewart Information Services [*Associated Press*] (SAG) ... StewInfo
Stewart Information Services Corp. [*NYSE symbol*] (SPSG) ... STC
Stewart Information Sv [*NYSE symbol*] (TTSB) ... STC
Stewart Island [*ICAO designator*] (AD) ... SJ
Stewart Island [*New Zealand*] [*Airport symbol*] (OAG) ... SZS
Stewart Lake Resources, Inc. [*Toronto Stock Exchange symbol*] ... SWK
Stewart, MacKeen & Covert, Halifax, NS, Canada [*Library symbol Library of Congress*] (LCLS) ... CaNSHSMC
Stewart, MacKeen & Covert Law Firm, Halifax, Nova Scotia [*Library symbol National Library of Canada*] (NLC) ... NSHSMC
Stewart Public Library, Grinnell, IA [*Library symbol Library of Congress*] (LCLS) ... IaG
Stewart Public Schools, Stewart, MN [*Library symbol*] [*Library of Congress*] (LCLS) ... MnStwPS
Stewart, Tabori & Chang [*Publisher*] ... STC
Stewart Warner Microcircuits (IAA) ... SWM
Stewart-Brown's Cases in the Court of the Star Chamber [*1455-1547*] [*A publication*] (DLA) ... St Brown
Stewart-Brown's Lancashire and Cheshire Cases in the Court of Star Chamber [*A publication*] (DLA) ... Stewart-Brown
Stewart's Alabama Reports [*1827-31*] [*A publication*] (DLA) ... Stew
Stewart's Alabama Reports [*A publication*] (DLA) ... Stew (Ala)
Stewart's Alabama Reports [*1827-31*] [*A publication*] (DLA) ... Stewart
Stewart's Alabama Reports [*A publication*] (DLA) ... Stewart (Ala)
Stewart's Alabama Reports [*A publication*] (DLA) ... Stewart R
Stewart's Alabama Reports [*A publication*] (DLA) ... Stewt Rep
Stewart's Answers to Dirleton's Doubts [*2 eds.*] [*1715, 1762 Scotland*] [*A publication*] (DLA) ... Stew Ans
Stewart's Digest of Decisions of Law and Equity [*New Jersey*] [*A publication*] (ILCA) ... Stew Dig
Stewart's Equity Reports [*28-45 New Jersey*] [*A publication*] (DLA) ... Stew
Stewart's Equity Reports [*28-45 New Jersey*] [*A publication*] (DLA) ... Stew Eq
Stewart's Equity Reports [*28-45 New Jersey*] [*A publication*] (DLA) ... Stewart
Stewart's Nova Scotia Admiralty Reports [*A publication*] (DLA) ... Stew
Stewart's Nova Scotia Admiralty Reports [*A publication*] (DLA) ... Stew Admr
Stewart's Nova Scotia Admiralty Reports [*A publication*] (DLA) ... Stew N Sc
Stewart's Nova Scotia Admiralty Reports [*A publication*] (DLA) ... Stewart
Stewart's Nova Scotia Vice-Admiralty Reports [*1803-13*] [*A publication*] (DLA) ... Stew Adm
Stewart's Nova Scotia Vice-Admiralty Reports [*A publication*] (DLA) ... Stew VA
Stewart's Reports [*1-10 South Dakota*] [*A publication*] (DLA) ... Stew
Stewart's Reports [*1-10 South Dakota*] [*A publication*] (DLA) ... Stewart
[*The*] **Stewartstown Railroad Co.** [*AAR code*] ... STRT
Stewartville, MN [*FM radio station call letters*] ... KYBA
Stewart-Warner Array Program [*Electronics*] (EECA) ... SWAP

Stewart-Warner Corp. ... SW
Steyr-Daimler-Puch [*Manufacturing firm*] [*Automotive engineering*] ... SDP
Sthene [*Absolute unit of force*] ... sn
Stheneboea [*of Euripides*] [*Classical studies*] (OCD) ... Sthen
Stibium [*Antimony*] [*Chemical element*] ... Sb
Stich (VRA) ... sti
Stichting Mondiaal Alternatief [*Foundation for Ecological Development Alternatives*] [*Netherlands*] (EAIO) ... SMA
Stichting Nederlands Orgaan voor de Bevordering van de Informatieverzorging [*Netherlands Organization for Information Policy*] [*Information service or system Defunct*] (IID) ... NOBIN
Stichting Oecumenische Hulp aan Kerken en Vluchtelingen [*Netherlands*] ... SOH
Stichting Plurale Samenlevingen [*Foundation for the Study of Plural Societies - FSPS*] (EAIO) ... SPS
Stichting Technisch Centrum Waalsteen [*Research center Netherlands*] (IRC) ... STCW
Stichting Tool [*Tool Foundation - TF*] [*Amsterdam, Netherlands*] (EAIO) ... ST
Stichting Waakzaamheid Persoonregistratie [*Netherlands*] ... SWP
Stichting Werkgroep Indianen Projekt [*Netherlands*] ... SWIP
Stichus [*of Plautus*] [*Classical studies*] (OCD) ... Stich
Stick Positioning Device (MCD) ... SPD
Stick Sensor Assembly (MCD) ... SSA
Stick Shift [*Automotive advertising*] ... STK
Stick to Rudder Interconnect (MCD) ... SRI
Stickler Syndrome [*Medicine*] (DMAA) ... SS
Stickney-Forest View Library District, Stickney, IL [*Library symbol Library of Congress*] (LCLS) ... ISt
Sticky [*Quality of the bottom*] [*Nautical charts*] ... stk
Sticky (WGA) ... SY
Sticky Type [*Bomb*] ... ST
Stifel Financial [*NYSE symbol*] (TTSB) ... SF
Stifel Financial Corp. [*NYSE symbol*] (SPSG) ... SF
Stifel Financial Corp. [*Associated Press*] (SAG) ... Stifel
Stiff [*Quality of the bottom*] [*Nautical charts*] ... stf
Stiff Circuit Analysis Program [*Computer science*] ... STICAP
Stiffened Cylindrical Shell ... SCS
Stiffened Super-Tough [*Polymer technology*] ... SST
Stiffener [*Civil engineering*] ... STIF
Stiff-Leg Derrick (NASA) ... SLD
Stiff-Man Syndrome [*Medicine*] ... SMS
Stiftung Wissenschaft und Politik [*Foundation for Science and Politics*] [*Information service or system*] (IID) ... SWP
Stigma [*Botany*] ... ST
Stigmastanyl(phosphorylcholine) [*Biochemistry*] ... SPC
Stigmata of Recent Hemorrhage [*Medicine*] ... SRH
Stigmatine Fathers and Brothers (TOCD) ... CSS
Stigmatine Fathers and Brothers, Congregation of the Sacred Stigmata (TOCD) ... css
Stikine Silver [*Vancouver Stock Exchange symbol*] ... STV
Stilb [*Unit of luminance*] ... sb
Stilbite [*A zeolite*] ... STI
Stile (WGA) ... STL
Stiles Elementary School, Rockford, Il [*Library symbol*] [*Library of Congress*] (LCLS) ... IRoStE
Stiles' Reports [*22-29 Iowa*] [*A publication*] (DLA) ... Stiles
Stiles' Reports [*22-29 Iowa*] [*A publication*] (DLA) ... Stiles (IA)
Still Another Response Averager ... SARA
Still Bank Collectors Club of America (EA) ... SBCCA
Still in the Seventies [*Lifestyle classification*] ... SITS
Still Out of Luck [*Army Slang*] ... Sol
Still Picture Projector (MSA) ... SPP
Still Traffic Camera ... STC
Still Video Camera ... SVC
Still Water Level ... SWL
Still Water Surface ... SWS
Still Waters Foundation (EA) ... SWF
Stillatim [*By Drops or In Small Quantities*] [*Pharmacy*] ... STILLAT
Stillbirth and Neonatal Death Society [*British*] (EAIO) ... SANDS
Stillbirth and Neonatal Death Society [*British*] (EAIO) ... SNDS
Stillbirth-Mummification, Embryonic-Death, Infertility Syndrome [*Medicine*] (DMAA) ... SMEDI
Stillborn [*Medicine*] ... SB
Stillborn [*Medicine*] ... STB
Stillborn [*Medicine*] ... STILLB
Still-Camera Video System [*Canon, Inc.*] ... SVS
Stillingfleet's Discourse on Ecclesiastical Law [*A publication*] (DLA) ... Still Ecc Law
Stillingfleet's English Ecclesiastical Cases [*A publication*] (DLA) ... St Cas
Stillingfleet's English Ecclesiastical Cases [*A publication*] (DLA) ... St Eccl Cas
Stillingfleet's English Ecclesiastical Cases [*1702-04*] [*A publication*] (DLA) ... Stil
Stillingfleet's English Ecclesiastical Cases [*A publication*] (DLA) ... Still Eccl Cas
Stillman College, Tuscaloosa, AL [*Library symbol Library of Congress*] (LCLS) ... ATuS
Stillman College, Tuscaloosa, AL [*OCLC symbol*] (OCLC) ... SCM
Still-Picture Camera (DNAB) ... SPC
Stillwater [*Oklahoma*] [*Airport symbol*] (OAG) ... SWO
Still-Water Bending Moment (PDAA) ... SWBM
Stillwater Mining [*NASDAQ symbol*] (TTSB) ... PGMS
Stillwater Mining Co. [*NASDAQ symbol*] (SAG) ... PGMS
Stillwater Mining Co. [*Associated Press*] (SAG) ... StillwtrM
Stillwater, MN [*AM radio station call letters*] ... WIMN
Stillwater, NJ [*Location identifier FAA*] (FAAL) ... STW
Stillwater, NY [*FM radio station call letters*] ... WJKE
Stillwater, OK [*FM radio station call letters*] ... KGFY
Stillwater, OK [*FM radio station call letters*] ... KOSU
Stillwater, OK [*AM radio station call letters*] ... KSPI
Stillwater, OK [*FM radio station call letters*] ... KSPI-FM
Stillwater, OK [*FM radio station call letters*] (RBYB) ... KXPX
Stillwater Public Library, Stillwater, OK [*Library symbol Library of Congress*] (LCLS) ... OkSt
Stillwater Public Library, Stillwater, OK [*OCLC symbol*] (OCLC) ... STW
Stilton Cheese Makers Association [*British*] (DBA) ... SCMA
Stimmen der Zeit (BJA) ... SDZ
Stimmen der Zeit [*A publication*] (BJA) ... StiZ
Stimmen Orient und Uebersee [*A publication*] (BJA) ... StOU
Stimsonite Corp. [*NASDAQ symbol*] (SAG) ... STIM
Stimsonite Corp. [*Associated Press*] (SAG) ... Stimson
Stimson's Law Glossary [*A publication*] (DLA) ... Stim Gloss
Stimson's Law Glossary [*A publication*] (DLA) ... Stim L Gl
Stimson's Law Glossary [*A publication*] (DLA) ... Stim Law Gloss
Stimson's Law Glossary [*A publication*] (DLA) ... Stimson
Stimulant (DSUE) ... STIM
Stimulant to Sustain Performance (RDA) ... STIMSUP
Stimulate (MSA) ... STML
Stimulated Brillouin Scattering ... SBS
Stimulated Compton Scattering [*Spectroscopy*] ... SCS
Stimulated Echo Acquisition Mode [*Medicine*] (DMAA) ... STEAM
Stimulated Emission of Energetic Particles [*Experiment for study of radio waves*] ... SEEP
Stimulated Emission Pumping [*Spectroscopy*] ... SEP
Stimulated Emission Spectroscopy ... SES
Stimulated Fibrinolytic Activity [*Medicine*] (DMAA) ... SFA
Stimulated Learning by Automated Typewriter Environment ... SLATE
Stimulated Protein Synthesis [*Medicine*] (DMAA) ... SPS
Stimulated Raman Gain [*Spectroscopy*] ... SRG
Stimulated Raman Gain Spectroscopy (PDAA) ... SRGS
Stimulated Raman Scattering [*Spectrometry*] ... SRS
Stimulated Rayleigh Scattering (IAA) ... SRS
Stimulated Thermal Rayleigh Scattering (PDAA) ... STRS
Stimulated Thermal Scattering [*Photonics*] ... STS
Stimulating (ROG) ... STIM
Stimulation (DAVI) ... stimn
Stimulation des Cooperations Internationaux et des Echanges Necessaires aux Chercheurs Europeennes [*Stimulation of International Cooperation and the Necessary Exchanges of European Scientists*] [*EEC*] ... SCIENCE
Stimulation Index [*Cytochemistry*] ... SI
Stimulation Value [*Psychology*] ... SV
Stimulation-Bound Behavior [*Medicine*] (DMAA) ... SBB
Stimulation-Induced Hypalgesia [*Medicine*] (DMAA) ... SIH
Stimulation-Produced Analgesia ... SPA
Stimulator of DNA Synthesis [*Immunochemistry*] ... SDS
Stimulator, Planetary Instrument Alignment ... SPINAL
Stimulator Substance [*Liver regeneration*] ... SS
Stimuli Analog Refresh Table [*NASA*] (MCD) ... SART
Stimuli and Measurements (KSC) ... SAM
Stimulus ... S
Stimulus [*Medicine*] ... ST
Stimulus ... stim
Stimulus, Conditioned (AAMN) ... SC
Stimulus, Discriminative (MAE) ... Sd
Stimulus Drive (MAE) ... Sd
Stimulus Evaluation/Response Selection Test [*Medicine*] (DMAA) ... SERS
Stimulus Onset Asynchrony [*Psychology*] ... SOA
Stimulus Onset Interval ... SOI
Stimulus/Response Measurements Catalog (NASA) ... SRMC
Stimulus Train-Induced Bursting [*Neuroscience*] ... STIB
Stimulus Valve [*Medicine*] (BABM) ... SV
Stimulus Valve [*Medicine*] (DAVI) ... SV
Stimulus-Bound Repetition [*Medicine*] ... SBR
Stimulus-Organism-Response ... S-O-R
Stimulus-Response ... S-R
Stina Resources Ltd. [*Vancouver Stock Exchange symbol*] ... SQA
Stiness' Reports [*20-34 Rhode Island*] [*A publication*] (DLA) ... Stiness
STING [*Swift Target Identification Notification Grid*] **Array** [*Computer system*] ... STAR
Stinger Launch Simulator (MCD) ... STILS
Stinger Training Launch Simulator (MCD) ... STLS
Stinson [*ICAO aircraft manufacturer identifier*] (ICAO) ... ST
Stinson [*Record label*] ... Sti
Stipend [*or Stipendiary*] ... STIP
Stipendiary Magistrate ... SM
Stipendiary Magistrate [*British*] (DSUE) ... STIPE
Stipendiary Magistrates Association, Queensland [*Australia*] ... SMAQ
Stipites [*Stalk*] [*Latin*] ... Stip
Stipulation (DAS) ... STIP
Stipule [*Botany*] ... SP
Stirling, NJ [*AM radio station call letters*] ... WKMB
Stirling, ON [*ICAO location identifier*] (ICLI) ... CUQC
Stirling Public Library, Alberta [*Library symbol National Library of Canada*] (NLC) ... ASTI
Stirling Public Library, Ontario [*Library symbol National Library of Canada*] (BIB) ... OSTIR
Stirred-Tank Fermentors [*Chemical engineering*] ... STF
Stirred-Tank Reactor (IAA) ... SR
Stirred-Tank Reactor [*Chemical engineering*] ... STR
Stirrer Drive Assembly ... SDA
Stirrup (WGA) ... STIR
Stirrup Pump ... SP
Stitch ... ST

Stitch (MSA) ... STCH
Stites, McElwain & Fowler, Bellarmine College Library, Louisville, KY [*OCLC symbol*] (OCLC) ... KBS
Stittsville Branch, Goulbourn Township Public Library, Ontario [*Library symbol National Library of Canada*] (NLC) ... OSGS
STM Publishers (NITA) ... STM
STM Wireless [*NASDAQ symbol*] (TTSB) ... STMI
STM Wireless, Inc. [*NASDAQ symbol*] (SAG) ... STMI
STM Wireless, Inc. [*Associated Press*] (SAG) ... STMWire
STN Shop Television Network Ltd. [*Vancouver Stock Exchange symbol*] ... SPV
Stochastic Adaptive Sequential Information Dissemination System ... SASIDS
Stochastic Boundary Molecular Dynamics [*Force energy simulation method*] ... SBMD
Stochastic Context-Free Grammar (PDAA) ... SCFG
Stochastic Dominance with Respect to Function [*Statistics*] ... SDWRF
Stochastic Electrodynamics [*Quantum physics*] ... SED
Stochastic Evolutionary Adoption Model (PDAA) ... STEAM
Stochastic Liouville Equation [*Statistical mechanics*] ... SLE
Stochastic Network Adaptive Kinematics Evaluator ... SNAKE
Stochastic Queuing System ... SQS
Stochastic Resonance [*Dynamical systems*] ... SR
Stochastic Self-Propagating Star Formation ... SSPSF
Stochastic Sequential Machine (IAA) ... SSM
Stock ... S
Stock ... STCK
Stock (VRA) ... stk
Stock (AAG) ... STK
Stock and Fixtures ... S & F
Stock and Machinery ... S & M
Stock and Station Agents' Association of New South Wales [*Australia*] ... SSAANSW
Stock Appreciation Relief [*British*] ... SAR
Stock Appreciation Rights [*Method of compensation for top executives*] ... SAR
Stock Appreciation Rights (TDOB) ... SAR
Stock Assessment and Fishery Investigations [*National Marine Fisheries Service*] (NOAA) ... SAFE
Stock Assessment and Fishery Investigations Program [*National Oceanic and Atmospheric Administration*] (GFGA) ... SAFI
Stock at Valuation ... SAV
Stock at Valuation (ODBW) ... sav
Stock Balance and Consumption Report (AFM) ... SB & CR
Stock Balance and Consumption Report (NASA) ... SBCR
Stock Brick Manufacturers Association [*British*] (BI) ... SBMA
Stock Car Racing [*A publication*] ... SCR
Stock Certificate [*Investment term*] ... SC
Stock Change Voucher [*Military*] (AFIT) ... SCV
Stock Clearing Corp. [*NYSE*] ... SCC
Stock Company Association [*Defunct*] (EA) ... SCA
Stock Control Activity (AFIT) ... SCA
Stock Control and Analysis (BUR) ... SCAN
Stock Control and Distribution (AFM) ... SC & D
Stock Control Center [*Army*] ... SCC
Stock Control Number ... SCN
Stock Control Package (IAA) ... STOKPAC
Stock Corporation Law [*A publication*] (DLA) ... SCL
Stock Dividend [*Investment term*] ... SD
Stock Exchange ... SE
Stock Exchange ... STK EX
Stock Exchange Automated Quotation (NITA) ... SEAQ
Stock Exchange Automated Quotation System [*British*] ... SEAQ
Stock Exchange Automated Trading ... SEAT
Stock Exchange Automatic Execution Facility ... SAEF
Stock Exchange Computer Managers Association (MHDW) ... SECMA
Stock Exchange Council [*British*] ... SEC
Stock Exchange of Singapore Dealing and Automated Quotation System ... SESDAQ
Stock Exchange of Singapore Index (ODBW) ... SESI
Stock Exchange of Thailand [*Thailand*] ... SET
Stock Feed Manufacturers' Association of New South Wales [*Australia*] ... SFMANSW
Stock Feed Manufacturers' Association of Queensland [*Australia*] ... SFMAQ
Stock Feed Manufacturers' Association of South Australia ... SFMASA
Stock Feed Manufacturers' Association of Victoria [*Australia*] ... SFMAV
Stock Feed Manufacturers' Association of Western Australia ... SFMAWA
Stock Fund (AFM) ... SF
Stock Fund [*Military*] ... STKF
Stock Fund Accounting [*Military*] ... STKFA
Stock Fund/Financial Inventory Accounting ... SF/FIA
Stock Fund Inventory Management Record [*Military*] (AFIT) ... SFIMR
Stock Fund Statement [*Military*] ... STKFS
Stock Funding Depot - Level Repairables [*Army*] ... SFDLR
Stock Index Futures Fund ... SIFF
Stock Item Catalog (MCD) ... SIC
Stock Keeping Unit [*Merchandising system*] ... SKU
Stock Ledger Control ... SLC
Stock Length [*Construction or manufacturing materials*] ... SL
Stock Level (AFM) ... SL
Stock Line Inventory Management (MHDW) ... SLIM
Stock List (MCD) ... SL
Stock List Price [*Military*] (AFIT) ... SLP
Stock Management Description Pattern ... SMDP
Stock Management Report [*Military*] ... SMR
Stock Market ... SM
Stock Market Computer Answering Network [*British*] ... SCAN
Stock Material (SAA) ... SM
Stock Material Order (SAA) ... SMO
Stock Medicines Board [*Australia*] ... SMB
Stock Medicines Board of South Australia ... SMBSA
Stock Not Listed (AAG) ... SNL
Stock Number (MCD) ... SN
Stock Number (MSA) ... SNO
Stock Number ... STK NO
Stock Number Action Bulletin ... SNAB
Stock Number Assignment Control System [*Air Force*] (AFM) ... SNACS
Stock Number Data Section (MCD) ... SNDS
Stock Number Identification Table ... SNIT
Stock Number Sequence Listing (MSA) ... SNSL
Stock Number Source Code (MCD) ... SN/SC
Stock Number User Directory [*Air Force*] (AFM) ... SNUD
Stock on Non Compotes Mentis [*A publication*] (DLA) ... Stock Non Com
Stock Option [*Investment term*] ... SO
Stock Option Plan ... SOP
Stock Option Writers Association [*Defunct*] (EA) ... SOWA
Stock Order (AAG) ... SO
Stock Order Shipment ... SOS
Stock Outboard [*Powerboat*] ... SO
Stock Point ADP [*Automatic Data Processing*] **Replacement Program** [*Navy*] (GFGA) ... SPAR
Stock Point Interrogation/Requirements Technique ... SPIRT
Stock Point Logistics Integrated Communications Environment Project [*Navy*] ... SPLICE
Stock Positioning and Transportation Study [*DoD*] ... SPTS
Stock Purchase Plan [*Offered by a company to its employees*] ... SPP
Stock Purchase Warrant (MHDW) ... SPW
Stock Quality [*Pisciculture*] ... S-Q
Stock Ratio Optimizing (MHDB) ... STROP
Stock Record Account (AFM) ... SRA
Stock Record Account Number (AFM) ... SRAN
Stock Record Card [*Military*] ... SRC
Stock Record Officer ... SRO
Stock Removal Grinding (MCD) ... SRG
Stock Replacement (AAG) ... SR
Stock Report ... SR
Stock Request Number ... SRNR
Stock Segregation Notice [*DoD*] ... SSN
Stock Shortage Control (SAA) ... SSC
Stock Shot (NTCM) ... SS
Stock Size Template (MCD) ... SST
Stock Split-Down [*Investment term*] ... SSD
Stock Status Balance Card (NG) ... SSBC
Stock Status Lag Time (AABC) ... SSLT
Stock Status Report ... SSR
Stock Tank Oil Initially in Place [*Petroleum technology*] ... STOIIP
Stock Technical Analysis Reports [*Innovest Systems, Inc.*] [*Database*] ... STAR
Stock, Time Limitation (DNAB) ... STL
Stock Trading System ... STS
Stock Transfer ... ST
Stock Transfer Association [*New York, NY*] (EA) ... STA
Stock Trust Certificate [*Investment term*] ... STC
Stock Turn-In and Replenishment Invoicing Procedures ... STRIP
Stock Updating Sales Invoicing Electronically (IEEE) ... SUSIE
Stock Valuation Adjustment [*Business term*] (ADA) ... SVA
Stock Volume (DAVI) ... SV
Stock Width [*Construction or manufacturing materials*] ... SW
Stockade (AABC) ... STKD
Stockage List [*Military*] ... STL
Stockage List Code [*Military*] (AABC) ... SLC
Stockage List Item [*Military*] ... STLI
Stockage Objectives [*Military*] ... SO
Stockage Priority Code [*Military*] (AFIT) ... SPC
Stockbridge Library Association, Stockbridge, MA [*Library symbol Library of Congress*] (LCLS) ... MStoc
Stockbroker ... S
Stockbroker ... SB
Stocked and Issued (AFM) ... S & I
Stocker & Yale [*NASDAQ symbol*] (TTSB) ... STKR
Stockett's Reports [*27-53 Maryland*] [*A publication*] (DLA) ... Stockett
Stockholder ... SH
Stockholder ... STCKHLDR
Stockholder of Record ... SOR
Stockholder Relations Society of New York (EA) ... SRSNY
Stockholders Sovereignty Society [*Later, FFSR*] (EA) ... SSS
Stockholm [*Sweden ICAO location identifier*] (ICLI) ... ESCC
Stockholm [*Sweden ICAO location identifier*] (ICLI) ... ESKI
Stockholm [*Sweden ICAO location identifier*] (ICLI) ... ESOS
Stockholm [*Sweden*] [*Airport symbol*] (OAG) ... STO
Stockholm Aeronautical Fixed Telecommunication Network Center [*Sweden ICAO location identifier*] (ICLI) ... ESSS
Stockholm/Arlanda [*Sweden ICAO location identifier*] (ICLI) ... ESSA
Stockholm [*Sweden*] **Arlanda Airport** [*Airport symbol*] (OAG) ... ARN
Stockholm/Barkarby [*Sweden ICAO location identifier*] (ICLI) ... ESKB
Stockholm/Bromma [*Sweden ICAO location identifier*] (ICLI) ... ESSB
Stockholm [*Sweden*] **Bromma Airport** [*Airport symbol*] (OAG) ... BMA
Stockholm Environment Institute ... SEI
Stockholm/Gamla Stan [*Sweden ICAO location identifier*] (ICLI) ... ESHG
Stockholm/Huddinge Hospital [*Sweden ICAO location identifier*] (ICLI) ... ESHL
Stockholm International Peace Research Institute [*Solna, Sweden*] (EAIO) ... SIPRI
Stockholm Radio [*Sweden ICAO location identifier*] (ICLI) ... ESKR
Stockholm/Ska-Edeby [*Sweden ICAO location identifier*] (ICLI) ... ESSE

Stockholm/Southern Hospital [Sweden ICAO location identifier] (ICLI) .... ESHC
Stockholm Stock Exchange .... SSE
Stockholm/Tullinge [Sweden ICAO location identifier] (ICLI) .... ESCN
Stockholm University Computing Center [Sweden] (TSSD) .... QZ
Stockholmia [Stockholm] [Imprint] (ROG) .... STOCKH
Stockholms Universitetsbiblioteket, Stockholm, Sweden [Library symbol Library of Congress] (LCLS) .... SwSU
Stockmen's Memorial Foundation, Calgary, AB, Canada [Library symbol] [Library of Congress] (LCLS) .... CaACSM
Stockmen's Memorial Foundation, Calgary, Alberta [Library symbol National Library of Canada] (NLC) .... ACSM
Stockpile Emergency Verification [DoD] .... SEV
Stockpile Entry Inspection [Navy] (NG) .... SEI
Stockpile Evaluation and Reliability Assessment Program .... SEARA
Stockpile Flight Tests .... SFT
Stockpile Laboratory Tests .... SLT
Stockpile Reliability/Survivability Program .... SRSP
Stockpile Stewardship and Management Programmatic Environmental Impact Statement .... SSM PEIS
Stockpile Surveillance Inspection .... SSI
Stockpile-to-Target (AFM) .... STOT
Stockpile-to-Target Sequence [Military] .... STS
Stockport [Postcode] (ODBW) .... SK
Stockroom (AABC) .... STKR
Stocks, Bonds, Bills, and Inflation [Investment term] .... SBBI
Stock-Tank Barrel [Petroleum industry] .... STB
Stockton [California] [Airport symbol] (OAG) .... SCK
Stockton [Diocesan abbreviation] [California] (TOCD) .... STO
Stockton and San Joaquin County Public Library, Stockton, CA [OCLC symbol] (OCLC) .... CSP
Stockton and San Joaquin County Public Library, Stockton, CA [Library symbol Library of Congress] (LCLS) .... CSto
Stockton, CA [FM radio station call letters] .... KCJH
Stockton, CA [Television station call letters] .... KFTL
Stockton, CA [AM radio station call letters] .... KJAX
Stockton, CA [FM radio station call letters] .... KJOY
Stockton, CA [Television station call letters] .... KOVR
Stockton, CA [Television station call letters] (RBYB) .... KQCA
Stockton, CA [FM radio station call letters] .... KQOD
Stockton, CA [FM radio station call letters] .... KSJC
Stockton, CA [AM radio station call letters] .... KSTN
Stockton, CA [FM radio station call letters] .... KSTN-FM
Stockton, CA [FM radio station call letters] .... KUOP
Stockton, CA [AM radio station call letters] .... KWG
Stockton, CA [Location identifier FAA] (FAAL) .... SCK
Stockton Geriatric Rating Scale [Psychology] .... SGRS
Stockton State College, Pomona, NJ [OCLC symbol] (OCLC) .... NJS
Stockton State Hospital, Stockton, CA [Library symbol Library of Congress] (LCLS) .... CStoSH
Stockton/Stockton Metropolitan [California] [ICAO location identifier] (ICLI) .... KSCK
Stockton Terminal & Eastern Railroad [AAR code] .... STE
Stockton's New Brunswick Vice-Admiralty Reports [1879-91] [A publication] (DLA) .... Stock
Stockton's New Brunswick Vice-Admiralty Reports [A publication] (DLA) .... Stock Adm
Stockton's New Brunswick Vice-Admiralty Reports [A publication] (DLA) .... Stockt Vice-Adm
Stockton's New Brunswick Vice-Admiralty Reports [A publication] (DLA) .... Stockton
Stockton's New Brunswick Vice-Admiralty Reports [A publication] (DLA) .... Stockton Adm (New Br)
Stockton's New Jersey Equity Reports [A publication] (DLA) .... Stock
Stockton's New Jersey Equity Reports [9-11 New Jersey] [A publication] (DLA) .... Stockt
Stockton's New Jersey Equity Reports [9-11 New Jersey] [A publication] (DLA) .... Stockt Ch
Stockyard .... STKYD
Stodden [England] .... STOD
Stoel, Rives, Bolly, Jones & Grey, Law Library, Seattle, WA [Library symbol] [Library of Congress] (LCLS) .... WaSSRB
Stoelmanseiland [Surinam] [ICAO location identifier] (ICLI) .... SMST
Stoelmanseiland [Surinam] [Airport symbol] (OAG) .... SMZ
Stoichiometric Ratio [Chemistry] .... SR
Stoicorum Veterum Fragmenta [A publication] (OCD) .... SVF
Stoke (IAA) .... S
Stoke (IAA) .... ST
Stokely USA [NASDAQ symbol] (TTSB) .... STKY
Stokely USA, Inc. [Oconomowoc, WI] [NASDAQ symbol] (NQ) .... STKY
Stokely USA, Inc. [Associated Press] (SAG) .... Stokely
Stokely-Van Camp 5% Pref [NYSE symbol] (TTSB) .... SVCPr
Stokely-Van Camp, Inc. [Associated Press] (SAG) .... StkVC
Stokely-Van Camp, Inc. [NYSE symbol] (SPSG) .... SVC
Stoke-On-Trent [City in England] .... S-O-T
Stoke-on-Trent [Postcode] (ODBW) .... ST
Stoker [Navy British] .... STKR
Stoker [Navy British] .... STO
Stoker Manufacturers Association (EA) .... SMA
Stoker Petty Officer [Navy British] (DSUE) .... SPO
Stokes [Unit of kinematic viscosity] .... St
Stokes County Public Library, Danbury, NC [Library symbol Library of Congress] (LCLS) .... NcDan
Stokes on Lien of Attorneys and Solicitors [1860] [A publication] (DLA) .... Sto Att Lien
Stokes on Liens of Attorneys [A publication] (DLA) .... Stokes L of Att

Stokes-Adams [Syndrome] [Medicine] .... SA
Stokes-Adams Attack [Medicine] (MAE) .... SAA
Stokley Van Camp [Associated Press] (SAG) .... StkVC
Stokley Van Camp [NYSE symbol] (SAG) .... SVC
Stokmarknes [Norway] [Airport symbol] (OAG) .... SKN
Stokmarknes [Norway] [Airport symbol] (AD) .... ZTK
Stokmarknes/Skagen [Norway ICAO location identifier] (ICLI) .... ENSK
STOL Navigation and Landing System (MCD) .... STOLAND
STOL Support Ship [Navy] (CAAL) .... SSS
Stoleczny Komitet Samopomocy Spolecznej [Warsaw] (BJA) .... SKSS
Stolen Base [Baseball] .... S
Stolen Base [Baseball] .... SB
Stolen Children Information Exchange (EA) .... SCIE
Stollet [Sweden] [Seismograph station code, US Geological Survey] (SEIS) .... SLL
Stolt Comex Seaway [NASDAQ symbol] (TTSB) .... SCSWF
Stolt Comex Seaway SA [NASDAQ symbol] (SAG) .... SCSW
Stolt Comex Seaway SA [Associated Press] (SAG) .... StoltCmx
Stolt Nielsen SA [Associated Press] (SAG) .... Stolt
Stolt Nielson SA [NASDAQ symbol] (SAG) .... STLTF
Stolt Tankers & Terminals SA (MHDW) .... STLTF
Stolt-Nielsen, SA [Associated Press] (SAG) .... StoltNiel
Stolt-Nielsen S.A. ADS [NASDAQ symbol] (TTSB) .... STLBY
Stomach (MAE) .... St
Stomach and Duodenum (CPH) .... S & D
Stomach Rumble [Medicine] (AAMN) .... SR
Stomachic [To Strengthen the Stomach] [Medicine] (ROG) .... STOM
Stomach-Partitioning Gastrojejunostomy [Surgery] .... SPGJ
Stomatocytes [Hematology] (DAVI) .... STOM
Stomatogastric Ganglion [Neuroanatomy] .... STG
Stomatogastric Nerve [Neuroanatomy] .... STN
Stomatogastric Nervous System [Neuroanatomy] .... STS
Stomodeal Lip [Endocrinology] .... SL
Stomount, Dundas & Glengarry County Public Library, Alexandria Branch, Alexandria, ON, Canada [Library symbol] [Library of Congress] (LCLS) .... CaOASDG
Stone (VRA) .... st
Stone [Unit of weight] (ODBW) .... st
Stone [Unit of weight] .... ST
Stone [Unit of weight] (AAG) .... STN
Stone .... STN
Stone and Graham's Court of Referees Reports [England] [A publication] (DLA) .... S & G
Stone and Graham's Private Bills Decisions [1865] [A publication] (DLA) .... Sto & G
Stone and Graham's Private Bills Reports [England] [A publication] (DLA) .... S & G
Stone & Webster [NYSE symbol] (TTSB) .... SW
Stone & Webster, Inc. [Associated Press] (SAG) .... StneWb
Stone & Webster, Inc. [NYSE symbol] (SPSG) .... SW
Stone and Webster Standard Safety Analysis Report [Nuclear energy] (NRCH) .... SWESSAR
Stone Arch [Bridges] .... SA
Stone Canyon Observatory [California] [Seismograph station code, US Geological Survey] (SEIS) .... STC
Stone Carvers Trade Association [A union] [British] .... SCTA
Stone Child Community College, Box Elder, MT [Library symbol] [Library of Congress] (LCLS) .... MtBeS
Stone Container [NYSE symbol] (TTSB) .... STO
Stone Container Corp. [NYSE symbol] (SPSG) .... STO
Stone Container Corp. [Associated Press] (SAG) .... StonC
Stone Container Corp. [Associated Press] (SAG) .... StoneC
Stone Container Cv Ex Pfd [NYSE symbol] (TTSB) .... STOPrE
Stone Deflector [Automotive engineering] .... S/DEFL
Stone Disintegration [Urology] .... SD
Stone Energy [NYSE symbol] (TTSB) .... SGY
Stone Energy Corp. [NYSE symbol] (SPSG) .... SGY
Stone Energy Corp. [Associated Press] (SAG) .... StoneEn
Stone Groundwood [Pulp and paper technology] .... SGW
Stone Roller [Ichthyology] .... ST
Stone Shop Museum, Grimsby, ON, Canada [Library symbol Library of Congress] (LCLS) .... CaOGriSM
Stone Shop Museum, Grimsby, Ontario [Library symbol National Library of Canada] (NLC) .... OGSM
Stone Street Bancorp [AMEX symbol] (TTSB) .... SSM
Stone Street Bancorp, Inc. [AMEX symbol] (SAG) .... SSM
Stone Street Bancorp, Inc. [Associated Press] (SAG) .... StoneStB
Stonebridge, Inc. [Toronto Stock Exchange symbol] .... SBF
Stonecat [Ichthyology] .... Sc
Stonehenge Study Group (EA) .... SSG
Stonehill College, North Easton, MA [Library symbol Library of Congress] (LCLS) .... MNoeS
Stonehill College, North Easton, MA [OCLC symbol] (OCLC) .... STO
Stonehouse [England] .... STONEH
Stones [Quality of the bottom] [Nautical charts] .... St
Stone's Benefit Building Societies [1851] [A publication] (DLA) .... Stone Ben Bdg Soc
Stone's Justices' Manual (Annual) [A publication] (DLA) .... Stone
Stone's Justices' Manual (Annual) [A publication] (DLA) .... Stone Just Man
Stones River National Battlefield .... STRI
Stoneville Public Library, Stoneville, NC [Library symbol] [Library of Congress] (LCLS) .... NcEdR-S
Stonewall Jackson Regional Library, Buckhannon, WV [Library symbol Library of Congress] (LCLS) .... WvBu
Stonewall Resources [Vancouver Stock Exchange symbol] .... SWR
Stonewall, TX [Location identifier FAA] (FAAL) .... STV

Stoneware [Freight] .... STNWRE
Stoneware (VRA) .... stwr
Stoney Hill [Jamaica] [Seismograph station code, US Geological Survey] (SEIS) .... STH
Stoney Rapids [Canada] [Airport symbol] (OAG) .... YSF
Stonington, CT [FM radio station call letters] .... WVVE
Stony Brook Institute for Advanced Studies of World Religions, Stony Brook, NY [OCLC symbol] (OCLC) .... VZI
Stony Brook, NY [FM radio station call letters] .... WUSB
Stony Mountain Institution Library, Winnipeg, Manitoba [Library symbol National Library of Canada] (NLC) .... MWSM
Stony Mountain Institution Library, Winnipeg, MB, Canada [Library symbol Library of Congress] (LCLS) .... CaMWSM
Stony Plain Public Libary, Alberta [Library symbol National Library of Canada] (NLC) .... ASP
Stony Plain Public Library, Stony Plain, AB, Canada [Library symbol] [Library of Congress] (LCLS) .... CaASpl
Stony Rapids, SK [ICAO location identifier] (ICLI) .... CYSF
Stony River [Alaska] [Airport symbol] (OAG) .... SRV
Stony River [Alaska] [Seismograph station code, US Geological Survey] (SEIS) .... STY
Stony Soil [Agronomy] .... ST
Stonyfork, PA [Location identifier FAA] (FAAL) .... SFK
Stonyhurst [Blackburn] [England] [Seismograph station code, US Geological Survey] [Closed] (SEIS) .... STO
Stool [Gastroenterology] (DAVI) .... st
Stool Preservative [Medicine] .... SP
Stop Abuse by Counselors (EA) .... STOP ABC
Stop Acknowledge (CMD) .... SAK
Stop Addiction through Voluntary Effort .... SAVE
Stop All Racist Tours [An association British] .... SART
[The] Stop & Shop Companies, Inc. [NYSE symbol] (SPSG) .... SHP
[The] Stop & Shop Companies, Inc. [Associated Press] (SAG) .... StopSh
Stop & Shop Cos. [NYSE symbol] (TTSB) .... SHP
Stop at Expiration [Magazine subscriptions] .... SAE
Stop Authorization and Lift Order (AAG) .... SALO
Stop Bar (DA) .... STB
Stop Bath [Photography] (DGA) .... SB
Stop Character [Computer science] .... STP
Stop Control Braking System [Lucas Girling] .... SCS
Stop Element [Computer science] (EECA) .... SE
Stop Equal Rights Amendment [An association Defunct] (EA) .... SERA
Stop for Tea [British] .... SFT
Stop forced busing; Teach children, not bus them; Operate neighborhood schools for those in the neighborhood wishing to attend them; Put an end to government interference in the parent-child relationship [An association] (EA) .... STOP
Stop Hospital and Medical Errors .... SHAME
Stop Immorality on Television [An association] .... SIT
Stop Inflation Now [Variation on the anti-inflation WIN slogan of President Gerald Ford] .... SIN
Stop Lamp [Automotive engineering] .... S/LP
Stop Merchandising Alcohol on Radio and Television .... SMART
Stop Motion Detector .... SMD
Stop Order (MCD) .... SO
Stop Payment [Banking] .... SP
Stop Planned Parenthood [An association] (EA) .... STOPP
Stop Press (ADA) .... SP
Stop Project ELF [Extremely Low Frequency system] [Defunct] (EA) .... SPE
Stop Sale, Use and Removal Order [Environmental Protection Agency] (GFGA) .... SSURO
Stop Scan (IAA) .... SS
Stop Tap .... ST
Stop Teen-Age Addiction to Tobacco (EA) .... STAT
Stop the Act Coalition [An association] .... STAC
Stop the Arms Race [Women's International League for Peace and Freedom] .... STAR
Stop the Oil Profiteers [Antioil price slogan] .... STOP
Stop the Olympic Prison [Lake Placid Olympics, 1980] [Opposed possible later use of an Olympic building as a prison] [Defunct] .... STOP
Stop the Pentagon/Serve the People (EA) .... STP
Stop the Robberies, Enjoy Safe Streets [Detroit police unit] [Disbanded] .... STRESS
Stop This Outrageous Purge [Group opposed to extremist measures used by segregationists in Arkansas; opposed by CROSS] .... STOP
Stop Transfer Effector [Genetics] .... STE
Stop Unnecessary Spending .... SUS
Stop Valve (IAA) .... SV
Stop War Toys Campaign (EA) .... SWTC
Stop without Pay .... SWOP
Stop Work Order .... SWO
Stopcock .... SC
Stop-Continue (DEN) .... SC
Stoplamp [Automotive engineering] .... SL
Stop-Limit Order [Business term] .... SLO
Stop-Loss Order [Business term] .... SLO
Stopover [Slang] .... SO
Stoppage (AABC) .... STP
Stopped Bonds [Stock exchange term] (MHDB) .... STOP
Stopped Diapason [Organ stop] [Music] .... ST D
Stopped Diapason [Organ stop] [Music] .... ST DIAP
Stopped Flow Pressure .... SFP
Stopped Stock (MHDB) .... SS
Stopped-Flow [Spectroscopy] .... SF
Stopped-Flow Analyzer [Chemical analysis] .... SFA

Stopped-Flow Circular Dichroism [Spectroscopy] .... SFCD
Stopped-Flow Multimixing Spectroflourimeter .... SF-MX
Stopped-Flow/Unsegmented Storage Analyzer [Chemical analysis] .... SF/USA
Stopped-Flow Wavelength Scanning [Spectrometry] .... SFWS
Stopping (MSA) .... STPNG
Stopping Distance Factor (MCD) .... SDF
Stopping in Transit .... SIT
Stopping Power .... S
Stop-Start [Telecommunications] (TEL) .... STPST
Stop-Transfer [Genetics] .... ST
Stopway .... SWY
Stopway Light [Aviation] (FAAC) .... STWL
Storable Fluid Management Experiment (NASA) .... SFME
Storable Tubular Extendable Member .... STEM
Storable Tubular Extendable Member Fabrication .... STEMFAB
Storage .... S
Storage .... STG
Storage (AAGC) .... Stg
Storage .... STGE
Storage (IDOE) .... STO
Storage (AFM) .... STOR
Storage Access Channel (CMD) .... SAC
Storage Access Control [Computer science] .... SAC
Storage Access Counter (IAA) .... SAC
Storage Activity .... SA
Storage Address Counter (IAA) .... SAC
Storage Address Register [Telecommunications] .... SAR
Storage Address Register [Telecommunications] (IAA) .... STAR
Storage Address Switch (IAA) .... SAS
Storage Aids Systems [Air Force] (DOMA) .... SAS
Storage Allocator [Telecommunications] (TEL) .... SA
Storage and Assembly Building [NASA] (NASA) .... SAB
Storage and Distribution .... S & D
Storage and Distribution Point [Military] (AFM) .... SDP
Storage and Handling Equipment Distributors Association [British] (DBA) .... SHEDA
Storage and Information Retrieval System [Computer science] (CDE) .... STAIRS
Storage and Information Retrieval System [IBM Corp.] .... STAIRS
Storage and Information Retrieval System/Virtual Storage [IBM Corp.] .... STAIRS/VS
Storage and Inspection (IAA) .... SAI
Storage and Processing Control System .... SPCS
Storage and Repair (MCD) .... SR
Storage and Retrieval [Computer science] .... S & R
Storage and Retrieval [Computer science] .... STORET
Storage and Retrieval for Water Quality Data [Databank] [Environmental Protection Agency] (MSC) .... STORET
Storage and Retrieval of Aerometric Data [Database] [Sigma Data Services Corp.] [Information service or system] (CRD) .... SAROAD
Storage and Retrieval of Bibliographic References Program (EDAC) .... SRBR
Storage and Retrieval Processor (MCD) .... SARP
Storage Area (KSC) .... S/A
Storage Array Tester and Analyzer (PDAA) .... SATAN
Storage Battery Electric Energy Demonstration .... SBEED
Storage Buffer Register .... SBR
Storage Bus in Register .... SBIR
Storage Capacity (AAG) .... SC
Storage, Checkout, and Transportation [Rack] [Aerospace] .... SCAT
Storage Circuit (IAA) .... SC
Storage Computer [AMEX symbol] (TTSB) .... SOS
Storage Computer Corp. [AMEX symbol] (SAG) .... SCS
Storage Computer Corp. [AMEX symbol] (SAG) .... SOS
Storage Computer Corp. [Associated Press] (SAG) .... StrCmp
Storage Computer Corp. [Associated Press] (SAG) .... StrgCmp
Storage Connecting Circuit [Teletype] .... SCC
Storage Container (MCD) .... STC
Storage Control Processor (NOAA) .... SCP
Storage Control Unit .... SCU
Storage Data Acceleration [Computer science] .... SDX
Storage Data Acceleration [Computer science] .... SDX
Storage Data Bus .... SDB
Storage Data Bus-In [Computer science] (MHDB) .... SDBI
Storage Data Bus-Out [Computer science] (MHDB) .... SDBO
Storage Data Recorder (NITA) .... SDR
Storage Data Register (MCD) .... SDR
Storage Element (MCD) .... SE
Storage Equipment Manufacturers Association [British] (DBA) .... SEMA
Storage Extension Frame (NITA) .... SEF
Storage Facility Cable Spreading Room [Nuclear energy] (NRCH) .... SFCSR
Storage Facility Control Room [Nuclear energy] (NRCH) .... SFCR
Storage Facility Manual (MCD) .... SFM
Storage, Handling, and Retrieval of Technical Data in Image Formation [Computer science] (IEEE) .... SHIRTDIF
Storage Immediate .... SI
Storage in Transit .... SIT
Storage Inspection Test [Navy] (NG) .... SIT
Storage Instantaneous Audimeter [Measures television viewing] .... SIA
Storage Interface Facility .... SIF
Storage Limits Register .... SLR
Storage Location .... SL
Storage Management Service [Telecommunications] (PCM) .... SMS
Storage Management System (IAA) .... SMS
Storage Mark [Computer science] (OA) .... SM
Storage Module Controller .... SMC
Storage Module Device [Computer science] .... SMD

Storage Module Drive	SMD
Storage Module Drive - Enhanced [Computer science] (BTTJ)	SMD-E
Storage Multiple Access Control (NITA)	SMAL
Storage Online Automatic Retrieval (NITA)	SOLAR
Storage Operations Module [SAILS] (MCD)	SOM
Storage or Distribution	S/D
Storage Oscilloscope Fragments	SOF
Storage Planning and Allocation [Computer science]	SPAN
Storage Planning Centre [Shipping]	SPC
Storage Pool Disease	SPD
Storage Process Vent [Nuclear energy] (NRCH)	SPV
Storage Process Vent Room [Nuclear energy] (NRCH)	SPVR
Storage Processor	STO
Storage Program Computer (IAA)	SPC
Storage Properties, Inc. [AMEX symbol] (SPSG)	PSA
Storage Properties, Inc. [AMEX symbol] (SAG)	STG
Storage Properties, Inc. [Associated Press] (SAG)	StorPr
Storage Protect Violation (CMD)	SPV
Storage Protection (IAA)	SP
Storage Protection Key [Computer science] (IAA)	SPK
Storage Protection Register	SPR
Storage Protector [Computer science] (IAA)	STOP
Storage Protein [Food industry]	SP
Storage Protein Isolate [Food industry]	SPI
Storage Queue	STOQ
Storage Rack	SR
Storage Rack (MCD)	STR
Storage Register	SR
Storage Room	SR
Storage Serviceability Standard [Army]	SSS
Storage Structure Language	SSL
Storage Target Date	STD
Storage Technology [NYSE symbol] (TTSB)	STK
Storage Technology Corp. (IAA)	STC
Storage Technology Corp. [NYSE symbol] (SPSG)	STK
Storage Technology Corp. [Associated Press] (SAG)	StorTc
Storage Technology Corp. [Associated Press] (SAG)	StorTch
Storage Technology for Operational Readiness	STORE
Storage Time Limit (DNAB)	STL
Storage to Storage (MCD)	SS
Storage Triacylglycerol [Biochemistry]	STG
Storage Trust Realty [NYSE symbol] (SAG)	SEA
Storage Trust Reaity [Associated Press] (SAG)	StorTRlt
Storage Tube	ST
Storage Tube Display	STD
Storage Tube Processor	STP
Storage Unit [Computer science]	SU
Storage USA [NYSE symbol] (TTSB)	SUS
Storage USA, Inc. [Associated Press] (SAG)	StroUSA
Storage USA, Inc. [NYSE symbol] (SAG)	SUS
Storage-Command Pulse [Computer science] (ECII)	SCP
Storage-Handling Facility [Nuclear energy] (NRCH)	SHF
Storage-on-Site [Grolier Electronic Publishing, Inc.]	SOS
Storage-to-Storage Instruction (IEEE)	SSI
Stord [Norway ICAO location identifier] (ICLI)	ENSO
Storden-Jeffers Elementary School, Storden, MN [Library symbol] [Library of Congress] (LCLS)	MnStoES
Storden-Jeffers Junior Senior High School, Jeffers, MN [Library symbol] [Library of Congress] (LCLS)	MnJeJSH
Store (IAA)	S
Store (AAG)	ST
Store (IDOE)	STO
Store	STR
Store	STR
Store Access Bus Recording Equipment [Telecommunications] (TEL)	SABRE
Store Access Controller (NITA)	SAC
Store Access Director (NITA)	SAD
Store Accumulator	STA
Store Address	SA
Store Address (SAA)	STA
Store Address Director	SAD
Store and Clear	SAC
Store and Clear Accumulator [Computer science]	SAC
Store and Forward Element [Telecommunications] (TEL)	SAFE
Store and Forward Facsimile	SAFF
Store Answer (NITA)	STA
Store Automation	SA
Store Block Control Journal [Military] (AABC)	SBCJ
Store Channel (SAA)	SCH
Store Decrement (SAA)	STD
Store Door Delivery	SDD
Store Index in Decrement (SAA)	SXD
Store Indicators (SAA)	STI
Store Input-Output [Computer science] (IAA)	STIO
Store Interface Link	SIL
Store Labor and Inventory Management (MHDW)	SLIM
Store Level Communications Controller (MHDI)	SLCC
Store Logical Word	SLW
Store Monitor Unit	SMU
Store Multiple [Computer command] (PCM)	STM
Store Multiple Access Control (MHDI)	SMAC
Store or Office Fixture [s] [Freight]	STR OFF FIXT
Store Overstocked [Inventory]	SOS
Store Port Allocation Register (PDAA)	SPAR
Store Release Evaluation System (MCD)	STRES

Store Room (VRA)	strm
Store Ship [Navy symbol]	AF
Store Station Control Unit (MCD)	SSCU
Store Tag (SAA)	STT
Store Transfer (IAA)	ST
Store Word [Computer science] (IAA)	STW
Store Zero [Computer science] (IAA)	STZ
Store-and-Forward [Data communications]	S/F
Storecast Carrier Authorization [Broadcasting] (WDMC)	SCA
Stored	STRD
Stored Address [Computer science]	STORAD
Stored Chemical Energy Propulsion System	SCEPS
Stored Cold Gas	SCG
Stored Command	SC
Stored Controlled Energy	SCE
Stored Data Definition and Translation Task Group	SDDTTG
Stored Data Definition Language	SDDL
Stored Data Description	SDD
Stored Energy Actuated Lift System	SEALS
Stored Energy Rotary Drive	SERD
Stored Flight Plan Program [Aviation] (FAAC)	SFPP
Stored Heading (MCD)	SH
Stored Index to Address	SXA
Stored Information Loss Tree	SILT
Stored Information System (IAA)	SIS
Stored Logic Adaptable Metal Oxide (IAA)	SLAM
Stored Logic Array	SLA
Stored Program Alphanumerics [FAA]	SPAN
Stored Program Buffer	SPB
Stored Program CAMAC [Computer-Aided Measurement and Control] Channel [Computer science]	SPCC
Stored Program Command [or Control] [Computer science]	SPC
Stored Program Command Word [Computer science] (NASA)	SPCW
Stored Program Control [Telecommunications] (IAA)	SPC
Stored Program Controlled Network [Telecommunications]	SPCN
Stored Program Data Compressor [Computer science] (IAA)	SPDC
Stored Program Data Processor (KSC)	SPDP
Stored Program Decoder [or Decommutation]	SPD
Stored Program Educational Computer	SPEC
Stored Program Educational Transistorized Automatic Computer	SPEDTAC
Stored Program Electronic Switching System [Telecommunications] (TEL)	SPESS
Stored Program Element	SPE
Stored Program Element System [Computer science] (IEEE)	SPES
Stored Program Numeric Control [Computer science] (IAA)	SNC
Stored Program Real-Time Commands (MCD)	SRTC
Stored Program Simulator	SPS
Stored Program Universal Demonstrator	SPUD
Stored Response Chain [Computer science] (BARN)	SRC
Stored Thermal Energy Propulsion System	STEPS
Stored Time	ST
Stored Time Command	STC
Stored Wave Inverse Fourier Transform [Spectrometry]	SWIFT
Stored-Charge Diode (IAA)	SCD
Stored-Energy Transmission (PDAA)	SET
Storekeeper [Navy rating]	SK
Storekeeper [Coast Guard]	STO
Storekeeper	STRKP
Storekeeper, Aviation [Navy rating]	SKV
Storekeeper, Construction Battalion, Stevedore [Navy rating]	SKCB
Storekeeper, Disbursing [Navy rating]	SKD
Storekeeper, First Class [Navy rating]	SK1
Storekeeper, Second Class [Navy rating]	SK2
Storekeeper, Technical [Navy rating]	SKT
Storekeeper, Third Class [Navy rating]	SK3
Storeman's Action Copy (DNAB)	SAC
Storer and Heard on Criminal Abortion [A publication] (DLA)	St & H Abor
Storer and Heard on Criminal Abortion [A publication] (DLA)	Sto & H Cr Ab
Storer and Heard on Criminal Abortion [A publication] (DLA)	Stor & H Abor
Storeroom (MSA)	STRM
Storeroom Item (DNAB)	SRI
Stores [British military] (DMA)	S
Stores Account Material Management Afloat (NG)	SAMMA
Stores Account Material Management Afloat / Ship Authorization Level (DNAB)	SAMMA/SAL
Stores Accountant [British military] (DMA)	SA
Stores and Clothing Research and Development Establishment [British]	SCRDE
Stores Assistant [British military] (DMA)	SA
Stores Depot [British military] (DMA)	SD
Stores Locator System (MCD)	SLS
Stores Locator System Adjustment (MCD)	SLSADJ
Stores Management Multiplex Bus [Computer science] (MCD)	SMMB
Stores Management Process (MCD)	SMP
Stores Management Sea [Navy]	SMS
Stores Management System (MCD)	SMS
Stores Officer [British military] (DMA)	SO
Stores Select Panel (SAA)	SSP
Stores Ship [Military Sea Transportation Service] (CINC)	TAF
Stores Ship	TAFS
Stores Stock Catalog	SSC
Stores Stressed Platform [Military British]	SSP
Storey's Delaware Reports [A publication] (DLA)	Sto
Storm and Combined Sewer Program (GNE)	SCSP
Storm and Tempest (ADA)	S & T

Storm Cell Identification and Tracking [*Algorithm*] (USDC) .... SCIT
Storm Cell Identification and Tracking [*Algorithm*] [*Marine science*] (OSRA) .... SCIT
Storm Deck [*Naval engineering*] .... SD
Storm Detection [*RADAR*] .... SD
Storm Drain [*Technical drawings*] .... SD
Storm Evasion [*Navy*] (NVT) .... STMEV
STORM [*Stormscale Operational and Research Meteorology*] **Fronts Experiment Systems Test** [*Marine science*] (OSRA) .... STORM-FEST
STORM [*Stormscal Operational and Research Meteorology*] **Fronts Experiment Systems Test** (USDC) .... STORM-FEST
Storm Lake, IA [*AM radio station call letters*] .... KAYL
Storm Lake, IA [*FM radio station call letters*] .... KAYL-FM
Storm Lake, IA [*Location identifier FAA*] (FAAL) .... SLB
Storm Lake Pilot-Tribune, Storm Lake, IA [*Library symbol*] [*Library of Congress*] (LCLS) .... IaSIPT
Storm Lake Public Library, Storm Lake, IA [*Library symbol Library of Congress*] (LCLS) .... IaSl
Storm of Drifting Snow [*Meteorology*] (WDAA) .... KS
Storm Prediction Center [*Marine science*] (OSRA) .... SPC
Storm RADAR Data Processor [*ESD*] .... STRADAP
Storm Satellite (MCD) .... STORMSAT
Storm Signal Station [*Nautical charts*] .... S Sig Sta
Storm Track Prediction (MCD) .... STP
Storm Vulcan .... SV
Storm Water .... STW
Storm Water Pollution Prevention Plan [*Environmental science*] .... SWPPP
Stormedia 'A' [*NASDAQ symbol*] (TTSB) .... STMD
Stormedia, Inc. [*NASDAQ symbol*] (SAG) .... STMD
Stormedia, Inc. [*Associated Press*] (SAG) .... Stormda
Stormont, Dundas, and Glengarry County Public Library, Cornwall, Ontario [*Library symbol National Library of Canada*] (NLC) .... OCSDG
Stormont, Dundas and Glengarry Highlanders [*British military*] (DMA) .... SDG
Stormont, Dundas, and Glengarry Law Association, Cornwall, Ontario [*Library symbol National Library of Canada*] (BIB) .... OCSDGL
Stormont-Vail Hospital, Topeka, KS [*Library symbol Library of Congress*] (LCLS) .... KTSV
Stormount, Dundas and Glengarry County Library, Crysler Branch, Crysler, ON, Canada [*Library symbol*] [*Library of Congress*] (LCLS) .... CaOCrSDG
Stormount, Dundas and Glengarry County Library, Ingleside Branch, Ingleside, ON,Canada [*Library symbol*] [*Library of Congress*] (LCLS) .... CaOInSDG
Stormount, Dundas & Glengarry County Library, Lancaster Branch, Lancaster, ON, Canada [*Library symbol*] [*Library of Congress*] (LCLS) .... CaOLSDG
Stormount, Dundas & Glengarry County Library, Williamstown Branch, Williamstown,ON, Canada [*Library symbol*] [*Library of Congress*] (LCLS) .... CaOWISDG
Stormouth's Dictionary of the English Language [*A publication*] (DLA) .... Stor Dict
Storm-Relative Environmental Helicity (USDC) .... SREH
Storm-Relative Environmental Helicity [*Marine science*] (OSRA) .... SREH
Storms Prediction Center (USDC) .... SPC
Stormscale Operational and Research Meteorology [*National Oceanic and Atmospheric Administration*] .... STORM
Stormwater Channel .... SWC
Stormwater Drain .... SWD
Stornaway Central Development [*Vancouver Stock Exchange symbol*] .... SDP
Stornaway Resources Corp. [*Vancouver Stock Exchange symbol*] .... SWY
Stornoway [*British ICAO location identifier*] (ICLI) .... EGPO
Stornoway [*Scotland*] [*Airport symbol*] (OAG) .... SYY
Storrington Branch, Frontenac County Library, Ontario [*Library symbol National Library of Canada*] (BIB) .... OSTFC
Storrs, CT [*FM radio station call letters*] .... WHUS
Story (ROG) .... ST
Story (WGA) .... STO
Story [*Journalism*] .... Sty
Story City Herald, Story City, IA [*Library symbol*] [*Library of Congress*] (LCLS) .... IaStocH
Story City Public Library, Story City, IA [*Library symbol Library of Congress*] (LCLS) .... IaStoc
Story of Exploration Series [*A publication*] .... SES
Story of the Empire Series [*A publication*] .... SESA
Story of the Nations [*A publication*] .... SN
Story on Agency [*A publication*] (DLA) .... Sto Ag
Story on Agency [*A publication*] (DLA) .... Story Ag
Story on Bailments [*A publication*] (DLA) .... Sto Bailm
Story on Bailments [*A publication*] (DLA) .... Story Bailm
Story on Bills [*A publication*] (DLA) .... Sto Bills
Story on Conflict of Laws [*A publication*] (DLA) .... Sto Conf Law
Story on Conflict of Laws [*A publication*] (DLA) .... Story Confl Laws
Story on Contracts [*A publication*] (DLA) .... Sto Con
Story on Contracts [*A publication*] (DLA) .... Sto Cont
Story on Contracts [*A publication*] (DLA) .... Story Cont
Story on Equity Jurisprudence [*A publication*] (DLA) .... Sto Eq Jur
Story on Equity Jurisprudence [*1836-1920*] [*A publication*] (DLA) .... Story
Story on Equity Jurisprudence [*A publication*] (DLA) .... Story Eq Jur
Story on Equity Pleadings [*A publication*] (DLA) .... Sto Eq Pl
Story on Partnership [*A publication*] (DLA) .... Sto Part
Story on Partnership [*A publication*] (DLA) .... Story Partn
Story on Prize Courts [*A publication*] (DLA) .... Sto Pr
Story on Promissory Notes [*A publication*] (DLA) .... Sto Pr Notes
Story on Promissory Notes [*A publication*] (DLA) .... Story Prom Notes
Story on Sales of Personal Property [*A publication*] (DLA) .... Sto Sales
Story on Sales of Personal Property [*A publication*] (DLA) .... Story Sales
Story's Abridgment of the Constitution [*A publication*] (DLA) .... Sto Abr Const
Story's Civil Pleading [*A publication*] (DLA) .... Sto Pl
Story's Commentaries on the Constitution of the United States [*A publication*] (DLA) .... Sto Comm
Story's Commentaries on the Constitution of the United States [*A publication*] (DLA) .... Sto Const
Story's Commentaries on the Constitution of the United States [*A publication*] (DLA) .... Story Comm Const
Story's Commentaries on the Constitution of the United States [*A publication*] (DLA) .... Story Const
Story's Constitutional Class Book [*A publication*] (DLA) .... Sto Const Cl B
Story's Equity Planning [*A publication*] (DLA) .... Story Eq Pl
Story's Laws of the United States [*A publication*] (DLA) .... Sto Laws
Story's Laws of the United States [*A publication*] (DLA) .... Sto US Laws
Story's Laws of the United States [*A publication*] (DLA) .... Story Laws
Story's Laws of the United States [*A publication*] (DLA) .... Story US Laws
Story's Miscellaneous Writings [*A publication*] (DLA) .... Sto Miscel Writ
Story's United States Circuit Court Reports [*A publication*] (DLA) .... St
Story's United States Circuit Court Reports [*A publication*] (DLA) .... Sto
Story's United States Circuit Court Reports [*A publication*] (DLA) .... Sto CC
Story's United States Circuit Court Reports [*A publication*] (DLA) .... Story
Story's United States Circuit Court Reports [*First Circuit*] [*A publication*] (DLA) .... Story R
Story's United States Circuit Court Reports [*First Circuit*] [*A publication*] (DLA) .... Story's Circuit CR
Story's United States Circuit Court Reports [*A publication*] (DLA) .... Story's Rep
Story's United States Laws [*A publication*] (DLA) .... Story's Laws
Story-Telling Automatic Reading Tutor .... START
Stotinki [*Monetary unit*] [*Bulgaria*] .... ST
Stourbridge [*British depot code*] .... STB
Stove [*Classified advertising*] (ADA) .... STV
Stove Bolt .... SB
Stove, Furnace, and Allied Appliance Workers International Union of North America [*AFL-CIO*] .... SFAAW
Stove, Furnace, and Allied Appliance Workers International Union of North America [*AFL-CIO*] .... SFAW
Stove Grate Workers' Society [*A union*] [*British*] .... SGWS
Stove Mounters International Union of North America [*Later, Stove, Furnace, Allied Appliance Workers International Union of North America*] .... SMIU
Stove or Range .... SR
Stove Rod .... SROD
Stovins' Law Respecting Horses [*A publication*] (DLA) .... Stov Hors
Stow (NASA) .... STO
Stow Resources [*Vancouver Stock Exchange symbol*] .... SWW
Stowable Aircrew Vehicle Escape Rotoseat (MCD) .... SAVER
Stowage (AAG) .... STOW
Stowage (MSA) .... STWG
Stowage and Repair .... S & R
Stowage Container .... S/C
Stowage Drawer .... SD
Stowage Factor [*Shipping*] .... SF
Stowage Launch Adapter Container .... SLAC
Stowage Launch Adapter, Lower .... SLAL
Stowage Launch Adapter, Middle .... SLAM
Stowage Launch Adapter, Upper .... SLAU
Stowage List and Hardware Tracking System [*NASA*] (MCD) .... SLAHTS
Stowe Elementary School, Duluth, MN [*Library symbol*] [*Library of Congress*] (LCLS) .... MnDuSE
Stowe, VT [*FM radio station call letters*] .... WVMX
Stowe-Day Foundation (EA) .... SDF
Stowe-Day Memorial Library and Historical Foundation, Hartford, CT [*Library symbol Library of Congress*] (LCLS) .... CtHSD
Stoy Hayward [*Venture capital group*] [*British*] .... SH
Strabismus [*Medicine*] .... Sb
Strabismus [*Medicine*] .... STRAB
Strabo [*First century BC*] [*Classical studies*] (OCD) .... Strab
Strachan-Scott [*Syndrome*] [*Medicine*] (DAVI) .... SS
Strachey and McIlroy [*in SAM/76, a programming language named after its authors and developed in 1976*] (CSR) .... SAM
Straddle the Market [*Investment term*] (MHDW) .... STM
Stradivari [*Record label*] .... Strad
Stradivarius Violin [*Music*] (DSUE) .... STRAD
Strafgesetzbuch [*Penal Code*] [*German*] .... StGB
Straggler .... STRAG
Straggler Line [*Military*] .... STRAGL
Strahan's Domat's Civil Law [*A publication*] (DLA) .... Strah Domat
Strahan's Reports [*19 Oregon*] [*A publication*] (DLA) .... Strahan
Straight .... S
Straight (AAMN) .... st
Straight .... STGHT
Straight (AAG) .... STR
Straight Bag Drainage [*Medicine*] (MAE) .... SBD
Straight Binary .... SB
Straight Binary Second .... SBS
Straight Cactus [*Horticulture*] .... STC
Straight Channel Tape Print [*Computer science*] (KSC) .... SCTP
Straight Channel Tape Print Program [*Computer science*] (KSC) .... SCTPP
Straight Chiropractic Academic Standards Association (EA) .... SCASA
Straight Cut Control System (IAA) .... SCCS
Straight Drainage [*Medicine*] (MEDA) .... SD
Straight Duty .... SD
Straight Edge [*Philately*] .... SE
Straight Filament [*Biochemistry*] .... SSF

Straight Fixed Price .... SFP
Straight Gravity Drainage [Surgery] (DAVI) .... SGD
Straight in Approach [Aviation] (DA) .... STA
Straight, Inc. (EA) .... SI
Straight Leg Raising [Medicine] .... SLR
Straight Leg Raising Test [or Tenderness] [Medicine] ... SLRT
Straight Lengths [Freight] .... STR LGTHS
Straight Line .... SL
Straight Line [Freight] .... STR L
Straight Line Depreciation [Telecommunications] (TEL) ... SLD
Straight Partners [Defunct] (EA) .... SP
Straight Path Penetration .... SPP
Straight Shank [Screw] .... SS
Straight Sided .... SS
Straight Time .... S/T
Straight Times Index [Singapore Stock Exchange] .... STI
Straight Tip [Fiber connector for coaxial cable] [Telecommunications] (PCM) ... ST
Straight to Services Economy .... SSE
Straight Wire Antenna .... SWA
Straight-Flow [Water turbine] .... STRAFLO
Straight-In Approach [Aviation] .... SI
Straight-In Approach [Aviation] .... SIAP
Straight-Line Capacitance [or Capacity] .... SLC
Straight-Line Capacitor (IAA) .... SLC
Straight-Line Frequency .... SLF
Straight-Line (Linear) Accelerator [Nuclear energy] ... SLAC
Straight-Line Wavelength .... SLW
Straight-Line Wavelength (MSA) .... SLWL
Straightpath Elementary School, Wyandanch, NY [Library symbol] [Library of
    Congress] (LCLS) .... NWyaSE
Straight-Talking American Government [Comedian Pat Paulsen's political
    party] .... STAG
Strain Arrestor Plate [NASA] (NASA) .... SAP
Strain Gauge (KSC) .... SG
Strain Gauge Bridge .... SGB
Strain Gauge Load Cell .... SGLC
Strain Gauge Signal Conditioner [NASA] (MCD) .... SGSC
Strain Gauge Thrust Meter .... SGTM
Strain Gauge Transient Dosimetry .... STD
Strain Isolator Pad [Aerospace] .... SIP
Strained-Layer Superlattices [Crystalline materials] ... SLS
Strainer (DAC) .... ST
Strainer (AAG) .... STR
Strainer (AAG) .... STRNR
Strain-Transport-Time [Geology] .... STT
Strait .... ST
Strait [Maps and charts] .... STR
Strait [Board on Geographic Names] .... STRT
Strait of Gibraltar (DOMA) .... STROG
Straits Air Freight Express [Australia] .... SAFE
Straits Law Journal [1888-92] [Malasia] [A publication] (DLA) ... SLJ
Straits Law Journal and Reporter [A publication] (DLA) ... Straits LJ & Rep
Straits Law Reports, New Series [Malasia] [A publication] (DLA) ... SLRNS
Straits Oil & Gas [Vancouver Stock Exchange symbol] ... SOG
Straits Settlements [in Malaya] .... SS
Straits Settlements Law Reports [A publication] (DLA) ... SSLR
Straits Settlements Law Reports, Supplement [1897-99] [Malasia]
    [A publication] (DLA) .... SSLR Supp
Straits Settlements Volunteer Force [British military] (DMA) ... SSVF
Strake [Mining engineering] .... STK
Stralak Resources [Vancouver Stock Exchange symbol] ... SRK
Strand [Engineering] .... STRD
Strand Burning Rate (MCD) .... SBR
Strand Resources [Vancouver Stock Exchange symbol] ... SQL
Strange [Quark] [Atomic physics] .... s
Strange's Cases of Evidence [1698-1732] [England] [A publication] (DLA) ... Str
Strange's Cases of Evidence [1698-1732] [England] [A publication]
    (DLA) .... Str Ev
Strange's Cases of Evidence ("Octavo Strange") [A publication]
    (DLA) .... Str Cas Ev
Strange's English Court Reports [A publication] (DLA) ... Strange
Strange's English Courts Reports [93 English Reprint] [A publication]
    (DLA) .... Strange (Eng)
Strange's English King's Bench Reports [1716-49] [A publication] (DLA) ... Str
Strange's Hindoo Law [A publication] (DLA) .... Str HL
Strange's Notes of Cases, Madras [1798-1816] [A publication] (DLA) ... NC Str
Strange's Notes of Cases, Madras [A publication] (DLA) ... Strange Madras
Strangeways Research Laboratory [British] (IRUK) ..... SRL
Strangnas [Sweden ICAO location identifier] (ICLI) .... ESKS
Stranka Demokratskih Reformi [Party of Democratic Reform] [Slovenia]
    [Political party] (EY) .... SDP
Stranka Demokratske Akcije [Party of Democratic Action] [Bosnia-
    Herzegovina] [Political party] (EY) .... SDA
Stranraer, SK [Television station call letters] CBKST-1
Stranraer, SK [Television station call letters] CFQC-1
Strap .... STRP
Strap-Around Unit [NASA] (NASA) .... SAU
Strapdown Electrically Suspended Gyro (KSC) ...... SDESG
Strapdown Electrically Suspended Gyro Aerospace Navigation
    [System] .... SEAN
Strapdown Gyroscope (SAA) .... SDG
Strapdown Inertial Guidance .... SIG
Strapdown Inertial Guidance and Navigation (MCD) ... SIGN
Strapdown Inertial Measuring Unit (MCD) .... SDIMU
Strapdown Inertial Reference Assembly (MCD) .... SIRA

Strapdown Inertial Reference Unit [Navigation] .... SIRU
Strapdown Navigator .... SDN
Strap-On Motor .... SOM
Strap-On Tank [NASA] (NASA) .... SOT
Strapped, Corded, and Sealed [As, of a package or bale] ... SC & S
Strapped, Corded and Sealed (MHDB) .... SCC
Straps [JETDS nomenclature] [Military] (CET) .... ST
Strasbourg [France] [Seismograph station code, US Geological Survey]
    (SEIS) .... STR
Strasbourg [Imprint] (ROG) .... STRASB
Strasbourg [France] [Airport symbol] (OAG) .... SXB
Strasbourg/Entzheim [France ICAO location identifier] (ICLI) ... LFST
Strasbourg/Neuhof [France ICAO location identifier] (ICLI) ... LFGC
Strasburg, CO [FM radio station call letters] .... KAGM
Strasburg Railroad Co. [AAR code] .... SRC
Strasburg, VA [FM radio station call letters] .... WBPP
Strassburger Israelitisch Wochenschrift [A publication] (BJA) ... SIW
Strasse [Street] [German] .... STR
Strata and Tenancy Commissioner's Office [New South Wales, Australia] ... STCO
Strata Energy Corp. [Vancouver Stock Exchange symbol] ... SGC
Strata Titles Board [New South Wales, Australia] .... STB
Stratacom, Inc. [Associated Press] (SAG) .... Stratcm
Stratacom, Inc. [NASDAQ symbol] (SAG) .... STRM
Stratas Corp. [Vancouver Stock Exchange symbol] ...... SRZ
Stratasys, Inc. [NASDAQ symbol] (SAG) .... SSYS
Stratasys, Inc. [Associated Press] (SAG) .... Stratasys
STRATCOM Program Automated Data System [Army] ... SPADS
Strategemata [of Frontinus] [Classical studies] (OCD) ..... Str
Strategic (AFM) .... STRAT
Strategic .... STRTGC
Strategic Advantages Profile .... SAP
Strategic Aerospace Division [Air Force] (AFM) ...... STRAD
Strategic Aerospace Division [Air Force] .... STRATAD
Strategic Aerospace Squadron [Air Force] .... SASq
Strategic Aerospace Summary .... SAS
Strategic Aerospace Wing [Air Force] .... SAW
Strategic Aerospace Wing [Air Force] (AFM) .... SAWg
Strategic Air Combat Operations Staff .... STRACOS
Strategic Air Command [Air Force] .... SAC
Strategic Air Command [Air Force] .... STRATCOM
Strategic Air Command Automated Command Control System
    (AFM) .... SACACCS
Strategic Air Command Channel and Traffic Control Agency (IAA) ... SCTCA
Strategic Air Command Command Control Network ... SACCON
Strategic Air Command Command Post .... SACCP
Strategic Air Command Communications (MCD) ... SACCOM
Strategic Air Command Communications Network ... SACCOMNET
Strategic Air Command Communications [or Control] System [Military] ... SACCS
Strategic Air Command Communications-Electronics Instruction ... SACCEI
Strategic Air Command Digital Information Network (MCD) ... SACDIN
Strategic Air Command Headquarters (AAG) .... SACHQ
Strategic Air Command Liaison Officer .... SACLO
Strategic Air Command Low-Altitude Missile Program [Air Force] ... SACLAMP
Strategic Air Command Manual (IAA) .... SACM
Strategic Air Command/Minuteman Education Program (AFM) ... SAC/MEP
Strategic Air Command Missile (IAA) .... SACM
Strategic Air Command Office of Operations Analysis ... SAC-OA
Strategic Air Command Operational Planning System (MCD) ... SACOPS
Strategic Air Command Project Office (AAG) .... SACP
Strategic Air Command Regulations (AAG) .... SACR
Strategic Air Command Telephone Network (IAA) ...... STN
Strategic Air Command Teletype Network .... SACTTYNET
Strategic Air Force .... SAF
Strategic Air Force, Pacific Ocean Area .... STRAFPOA
Strategic Air Force, Pacific Ocean Area .... STRAIRPOA
Strategic Air Relocatable Photographic Facility (CINC) ... SARPF
Strategic Airborne Surveillance System [Military] ...... SASS
Strategic Aircraft Reconstitution Team [Air Force] (DOMA) ... SART
Strategic Alert Cadre (NVT) .... SAC
Strategic Alerting Sound System (AAG) .... SASS
Strategic American Traveler .... SAT
Strategic Analysis Guidance and Estimate (MCD) .... SAGE
Strategic Analysis Support Group [Navy] (DNAB) ... STRATANALSUPPGRU
Strategic and Critical Materials [Military] .... S & CM
Strategic and Critical Raw Material [Military] .... S & C
Strategic Antimissile Barrage Objects .... SAMBO
Strategic Area Study (MCD) .... SAS
Strategic Area Task Force (SAA) .... SATF
Strategic Arms Limitation .... SAL
Strategic Arms Limitation Treaty (MCD) .... SALT
Strategic Arms Reduction Talks (USGC) .... START
Strategic Arms Reduction Talks (AAGC) .... START
Strategic Arms Reduction Treaty .... START
Strategic Army Command and Control Software [Computer science Army]
    (RDA) .... SACCS
Strategic Army Command Network .... STARCOM
Strategic Army Communications System .... STARCOM
Strategic Army Corps [Acronym has come to mean "ordered" or "neat"] ... STRAC
Strategic Army Forces .... STRAF
Strategic Army Forces Readiness Improvement Program (AABC) ... STRAFIP
Strategic Artificially Intelligent Nuclear Transport [Robot series designation
    in 1986 movie "Short Circuit"] .... SAINT
Strategic Assessment Branch [Office of Oceanography and Marine
    Assessment] [National Oceanic and Atmospheric Administration] ... SAB
Strategic Audit Plan .... SAP

Strategic Automatic Message-Switching Operational Network [Canada] (MCD) .... SAMSON
Strategic Avionics Crewstation Design Evaluation Facility .... SACDEF
Strategic Balkan Services [World War II] .... SBS
Strategic Base Air Defense [Military] (AABC) .... STRABAD
Strategic Bomb Wing [Military] .... SBWG
Strategic Bombardment Training Squadron .... SBTS
Strategic Bomber Enhancement (MCD) .... SBE
Strategic Bomber Group .... SBG
Strategic Bomber Group .... SBGP
Strategic Bomber Penetration Decoy [Air Force] .... SCAD
Strategic Bombing Survey .... SBS
Strategic Business Segment .... SBS
Strategic Business Unit .... SBU
Strategic Cislunar Advanced Retaliatory Force (IAA) ..... SCARF
Strategic Communication and Alerting System .... SCAAS
Strategic Communications [Army] (IAA) .... STRATCOM
Strategic Communications Command [Army] (MCD) .... SCC
Strategic Communications Command [Army] (RDA) ..... STRATCOM
Strategic Communications Command Advanced Concepts Office [Army] .... SCC-ACO
Strategic Communications Command Equipment Applications Directorate [Army] .... SCCEA
Strategic Communications Command - Test and Evaluation Directorate [Army] .... SCC-TED
Strategic Communications Division [Military] .... SCD
Strategic Communications Ltd. [Vancouver Stock Exchange symbol] .... SAG
Strategic Communications Military Exchange [Army] (IAA) .... STRATCOMMEX
Strategic Communications Network [Military] (LAIN) ...... SCN
Strategic Concepts Development Center [National Defense University] .... SCDC
Strategic Confirmation of Optical Phenomenology .... SCOOP
Strategic Conventional Standoff Capability (MCD) .... SCSC
Strategic Cruise Missile (MCD) .... SCM
Strategic Cruise Missile Carrier .... SCMC
Strategic Defense Command [Military] (SDI) .... SDC
Strategic Defense Initiative [Commonly known as "Starwars"] [Facetiously translated as "Silly Damn Idea"] .... SDI
Strategic Defense Initiative Advisory Council [Military] (SDI) .... SDIAC
Strategic Defense Initiative Institute [Military] (SDI) .... SDII
Strategic Defense Initiative Office [DoD] .... SDIO
Strategic Defense Initiative Organization [Washington, DC DoD] (GRD) .... SDIO
Strategic Defense Initiative System Effectiveness Model [Military] .... SDISM
Strategic Defense Initiative System Evaluation Model .... SDISEM
Strategic Defense System [DoD] .... SDS
Strategic Defensive Forces [Army] (AABC) .... SDF
Strategic Diagnostics, Inc. [NASDAQ symbol] (SAG) .... SDIX
Strategic Diagnostics, Inc. [Associated Press] (SAG) ..... StrtDiag
Strategic Direction Center (MCD) .... SDC
Strategic Distribution [NASDAQ symbol] (SAG) .... STRD
Strategic Distribution [Associated Press] (SAG) .... StrtgDist
Strategic Earth Orbit System (IAA) .... SEOS
Strategic Engineering Survey [Navy] .... SES
Strategic Environmental Assessment System [Environmental Protection Agency] .... SEAS
Strategic Environmental Research and Development Program [National Center for Atmospheric Research] .... SERDP
Strategic Environmental Research Program [DoD Department of Energy] .... SERP
Strategic Facilities Initiative [Oak Ridge National Laboratory] .... SFI
Strategic Facsimile Network (IAA) .... SFN
Strategic Global Income Fd [NYSE symbol] (TTSB) .... SGL
Strategic Global Income Fund [NYSE symbol] (SPSG) ...... SGL
Strategic Global Income Fund [Associated Press] (SAG) ..... StrGlob
Strategic Group [Military] .... SG
Strategic Guidance Memo [Navy] .... SGM
Strategic High Altitude Relay Platform [Aviation] .... SHARP
Strategic High-Altitude Orbital Bomber (IAA) .... SHAOB
Strategic Highway Corridor Network [BTS] [MTMC] (TAG) ..... STRAHNET
Strategic Highway Research Program .... SHRP
Strategic Highway Research Program [National Research Council] .... SHRP
Strategic Impact and Assumptions Identification Method .... SIAM
Strategic Impediments Initiative [MHDW] .... SII
Strategic Industries Association (EA) .... SIA
Strategic Information Plan (SSD) .... SIP
Strategic Information Review (NITA) .... SIR
Strategic Integrated Management System [American Occupational Therapy Association] .... SIMS
Strategic Integrated Operational Plan [Nuclear warfare] .... SIOP
Strategic Intelligence/Business Research Corp. .... SI/BRC
Strategic Intelligence Digests [Military] (AABC) .... SID
Strategic Intelligence Research and Analysis .... SIRA
Strategic Intelligence School [Military] .... SIS
Strategic Intelligence Summary [Military] (NATG) ...... SIS
Strategic Intelligence Systems, Inc. [Also, an information service or system] (IID) .... SIS
Strategic Intelligence Wing (MCD) .... SIW
Strategic Intermediate Planner (PDAA) .... STRIP
Strategic Issue Competitive Information System (PDAA) ..... SICIS
Strategic LASER Communications [Military] (CAAL) ...... SLC
Strategic Lawsuit Against Public Participation [Term coined by George Pring and Penelope Canan] .... SLAPP
Strategic Locations Planning [Information service or system] (IID) .... SLP
Strategic Logistic Program [Army] (RDA) .... SLP
Strategic Logistics Agency [Army] (RDA) .... SLA
Strategic Low Attitude Missile .... SLAM
Strategic Low-Orbit Bomber (AAG) .... SLOB

Strategic Lunar System (IAA) .... SLS
Strategic Management Accounting (ADA) .... SMA
Strategic Management Society [British] .... SMS
Strategic Material Management Information Program (PDAA) ...... SMMIP
Strategic Metals Recovery Research Facility [University of Arizona] (RCD) .... SMRRF
Strategic Military Intelligence Detachment [Army] (MCD) ...... STRATMID
Strategic Missile (NATG) .... SM
Strategic Missile Division [Military] .... STRMD
Strategic Missile Evaluation Committee [Air Force] .... SMEC
Strategic Missile Evaluation Squadron .... SMES
Strategic Missile Group [Air Force] .... SMGP
Strategic Missile Squadron [Air Force] .... SMS
Strategic Missile Squadron [Air Force] .... SMSq
Strategic Missile Squadron Munitions Section [Air Force] (AAG) .... SMSMS
Strategic Missile Support Base [Air Force] (AFM) ...... SMSB
Strategic Missile Wing [Air Force] .... SMW
Strategic Missile Wing [Air Force] .... SMWG
Strategic Missiles Materials Technology (MCD) .... SMMT
Strategic Mission Data Preparation System [Air Force] (DOMA) .... SMDPS
Strategic Mission Support Study [DoD] .... SMSS
Strategic Mobility Analysis [Military] .... SMA
Strategic Mobility [Planning and] Analysis System [Military] (NVT) ...... STRATMAS
Strategic Mobility Simulation Model .... SMOBSMOD
Strategic Mobility Work Project [Army] (AABC) .... SMWP
Strategic Mobilization Requirements and Program (MCD) .... SMRP
Strategic Network Environment (NITA) .... SNE
Strategic Nuclear Delivery Vehicle [Army] (AABC) ...... SNDV
Strategic Nuclear Launch Vehicle .... SNLV
Strategic Nuclear Weapon .... SNW
Strategic Objectives Plan .... SOP
Strategic Offensive Delivery Systems (DOMA) .... SODS
Strategic Offensive Forces [Army] (AABC) .... SOF
Strategic Orbit Point (KSC) .... SOP
Strategic Orbit Point (AFM) .... STOP
Strategic Orbital System (AAG) .... SOS
Strategic Orbital System Study (AAG) .... SOSS
Strategic Outline Chart [Air Force] .... SO
Strategic Petroleum Reserve [Department of Energy] .... SPR
Strategic Planning and Management System [Environmental Protection Agency] (GFGA) .... SPMS
Strategic Planning Chart [Air Force] .... SP
Strategic Planning Initiative [Environmental Protection Agency] (GFGA) .... SPI
Strategic Planning Institute [Cambridge, MA] .... SPI
Strategic Planning Review (SSD) .... SPR
Strategic Planning Society [See also SPS] [London, England] (EAIO) .... SP
Strategic Planning Society [Formerly, Society for Strategic and Long Range Planning] (EA) .... SPS
Strategic Planning Staff [Social Security Administration] .... SPS
Strategic Plans and Resource Analysis Agency (DOMA) ...... SPRAA
Strategic Platform Defense Study [DoD] .... SPDS
Strategic Posture Analysis [Army] (AABC) .... SPA
Strategic Posture Display (MCD) .... SPD
Strategic Program for Innovative Research on AIDS Treatment [The National Institute of Allergy and Infectious Diseases] .... SPIRAT
Strategic Programme for Innovation and Technology Transfer [European Commission] .... SPRINT
Strategic Protection Force .... SPF
Strategic Quality Management (AIE) .... SQM
Strategic Rail Corridor Network [MTMC] (TAG) .... STRACNET
Strategic Ready Reserve [Military] .... SRR
Strategic Reconnaissance [Military] .... SR
Strategic Reconnaissance (DOMA) .... SR
Strategic Reconnaissance Center [Air Force] (DOMA) ...... SRC
Strategic Reconnaissance Missile .... SRM
Strategic Reconnaissance Squadron .... SR Sq
Strategic Reconnaissance Squadron (MCD) .... SRS
Strategic Reconnaissance Training Squadron .... SRTS
Strategic Reconnaissance Wing [Air Force] (MCD) ...... SRW
Strategic Reconnaissance Wing [Air Force] (AFM) ...... SRWg
Strategic Relocatable Target [DoD] .... SRT
Strategic Research (MCD) .... SR
Strategic Research and Management Service .... SRMS
Strategic Reserve Forces (MCD) .... SRF
Strategic Resource Area (PDAA) .... SRA
Strategic Retaliatory Forces (AAG) .... SRF
Strategic Rocket Forces (MCD) .... SRF
Strategic Rocket Troops (NATG) .... SRT
Strategic Satellite System (MCD) .... SSS
Strategic Satellite System [Air Force Telecommunications] (TEL) .... STRATSAT
Strategic Sealift Contingency Planning System [Army] (AABC) .... SEACOP
Strategic Services Unit [Formerly, OSS] .... SSU
Strategic Special Nuclear Materials .... SSNM
Strategic Squadron .... SS
Strategic Standardization Board .... SSB
Strategic Studies Advisory Group [Army] (AABC) .... SSAG
Strategic Studies Group [Naval War College] (DOMA) ...... SSG
Strategic Studies Institute (MCD) .... SSI
Strategic Studies Staff [Environmental Protection Agency] (GFGA) .... SSS
Strategic Study [Military] .... SS
Strategic Support Squadron [Air Force] .... SSS
Strategic Systems Committee [DoD] (DOMA) .... SSC
Strategic Systems Committee (AAGC) .... SSC
Strategic Systems Project [Office] [Navy] .... SSP
Strategic Systems Project Office [Navy] .... SSPO

Strategic Systems Project Office, Technical Representative [Navy] (DNAB) .... SSPOTR
Strategic Systems Project Office, Washington, DC [OCLC symbol] (OCLC) .... NPO
Strategic/Tactical Area Test System (MCD) .... STATS
Strategic Talks on Prevention [of accidental atomic war and nuclear weapons proliferation] [Proposed by Sen. Gary Hart, 1982] .... STOP
Strategic Target Data System (SSD) .... STDS
Strategic Target System [Rocket] .... STARS
Strategic Targets Product Office [Army] (RDA) .... STPO
Strategic Technical Directorate [South Vietnamese studies and observations group] (VNW) .... STD
Strategic Technical Service (CINC) .... STS
Strategic Technologies for the Army .... STAR
Strategic Technology Leveraging .... STL
Strategic Technology Office [Arlington, VA] [DoD] (GRD) .... STO
Strategic Technology Office Information Analysis Center [Battelle Memorial Institute] (MCD) .... STOIAC
Strategic Training Range (MCD) .... STR
Strategic Training Squadron (MCD) .... STS
Strategic Transport [Aircraft] [Military] .... ST
Strategic Transportation Analysis [MTMC] (TAG) .... STA
Strategic Transportation Analysis Decision Support System [MTMC] (TAG) .... STADSS
Strategic Transportation Analysis System [MTMC] (TAG) .... STAS
Strategic Transportation Research Study [FHWA] (TAG) .... STRS
Strategic War Planning System [Air Force] .... SWPS
Strategic Warning (MCD) .... SW
Strategic Warning Staff .... SWS
Strategic Weapon System [Military] (CAAL) .... SWS
Strategic Weapons Loader (DWSG) .... SWL
Strategic Wing [Military] .... SW
Strategical Planning Section [Joint Planning Staff] [World War II] .... SPS
Strategically Targeted Activities for Results System ...... STARS
Strategies and Air Standards Division [Environmental Protection Agency] (GFGA) .... SASD
Strategies and Errors in Secondary Mathematics [Project] (AIE) .... SESM
Strategies and Policies for Informatics [Intergovernmental Bureau for Informatics] .... SPIN
Strategies for Today's Environmental Partnership .... STEP
Strategy and Force Evaluation (MCD) .... SAFE
Strategy and Options Review (DOMA) .... SOR
Strategy and Planning Committee [Military] .... SPC
Strategy and Policy Group [War Department] [World War II] ...... S & P
Strategy and Tactics Analysis Group [Later, Concepts Analysis Agency] [Army] (KSC) .... STAG
Strategy Evaluator and Planning-Production System (PDAA) .... STEPS
Strategy for Exploration of the Inner Planets (IAA) ...... SEIP
Strategy Gaming Society (EA) .... SGS
Strategy, Research & Action [Commercial firm British] ...... SR & A
Stratford [England] .... STRATF
Stratford [New Zealand] [Seismograph station code, US Geological Survey Closed] (SEIS) .... STZ
Stratford Airways Ltd. [Canada ICAO designator] (FAAC) .... FCA
Stratford American Corp. [Vancouver Stock Exchange symbol] ...... SQS
Stratford Avenue Elementary School, Garden City, NY [Library symbol] [Library of Congress] (LCLS) .... NGcSAE
Stratford College, Danville, VA [Library symbol Library of Congress] (LCLS) .... ViDS
Stratford, CT [Location identifier FAA] (FAAL) .... JSD
Stratford Library Association, Stratford, CT [Library symbol Library of Congress] (LCLS) .... CtStr
Stratford, ON [AM radio station call letters] .... CJCS
Stratford Public Library, Ontario [Library symbol National Library of Canada] (NLC) .... OST
Stratford Public Library, Stratford, CT [OCLC symbol] (OCLC) ..... SSA
Stratford Public Library, Stratford, ON, Canada [Library symbol Library of Congress] (LCLS) .... CaOST
Stratford-on-Avon [British] .... SonA
Stratford-On-Avon, England .... S on A
Stratford-Perth Archives Board, Ontario [Library symbol National Library of Canada] (BIB) .... OSTPA
Strathclyde Institute [Glasgow, Scotland] .... SI
Strathcona Resources Industries Ltd. [Toronto Stock Exchange symbol] ..... SRH
Strathearn House Group Ltd. [Toronto Stock Exchange symbol] ..... SRN
Strathelyde Graduate Business School [Toulouse, France] (ECON) ..... SGBS
Strathfield Oil & Gas Ltd. [Toronto Stock Exchange symbol] .... SFO
Strathgordon [Tasmania] [Seismograph station code, US Geological Survey] (SEIS) .... STG
Strathmore Municipal Library, Alberta [Library symbol National Library of Canada] (NLC) .... ASM
Strathmore Municipal Library, Strathmore, AB, Canada [Library symbol Library of Congress] (LCLS) .... CaASM
Strathroy Middlesex Museum, Strathroy, Ontario [Library symbol National Library of Canada] (BIB) .... OSTMM
Strathroy Public Library, Ontario [Library symbol National Library of Canada] (NLC) .... OSTP
Strathroy Public Library, Strathroy, ON, Canada [Library symbol Library of Congress] (LCLS) .... CaOStrP
Stratified Charge [Automotive engineering] .... SC
Stratified Charge, Omnivorous Rotary Engine [Automotive engineering] ..... SCORE
Stratified Charge Rotary Engine (DWSG) .... SCRE
Stratified Fuel-Water Injection [Automotive engineering] .... SWFI
Stratified Indexing and Retrieval [Japan Computer science] .... SIR
Stratified-Charge Engine [Auto engine] .... SCE

Stratiform [NWS] (FAAC) .... STFRM
Stratigraphic .... STRAT
Stratocumulus [Cloud] [Meteorology] .... SC
Stratocumulus [Cloud] [Meteorology] (AIA) .... StCu
Stratocumulus-Topped Boundary Layer (USDC) .... SMBL
Stratocumulus-Topped Boundary Layer [Marine science] (OSRA) .... SMBL
Stratofortress strategic bomber [Boeing Co.] B-52
Stratosphere .... St
Stratosphere (AFM) .... STRATO
Stratosphere (WGA) .... STRSPH
Stratosphere Corp. [Associated Press] (SAG) .... StratCp
Stratosphere Corp. [Associated Press] (SAG) .... StrtCp
Stratosphere Corp. [NASDAQ symbol] (SAG) .... TOWV
Stratosphere Sulfate Aerosol [Meteorology] .... SSA
Stratosphere Telescope (IAA) .... STRATOSCOPE
Stratosphere-Troposphere [Radar] [Marine science] (OSRA) ..... ST
Stratosphere-Troposphere [Radar] (USDC) .... ST
Stratosphere-Troposphere Exchange Project [NASA] .... STEP
Stratosphere-Troposphere Interactions and the Biosphere (EERA) ...... STIB
Stratospheric Aerosol Gas Experiment .... SAGE
Stratospheric Aerosol Measurement [or Monitor] [Meteorology] .... SAM
Stratospheric and Mesospheric Sounder .... SAMS
Stratospheric Circulation Index [Geophysics] .... SCI
Stratospheric Composition (MCD) .... STRATCOM
Stratospheric Cruise Emissions Reduction Program (DICI) ..... SCERP
Stratospheric Dust Particle .... SDP
Stratospheric Gravity Waves [Planetary science] .... SGW
Stratospheric Observatory for Infrared Astronomy [NASA] ..... SOFIA
Stratospheric Ozone Review Group [British] (DBA) ...... SORG
Stratospheric Photochemistry Aerosols, and Dynamics Expedition [Meteorology] .... SPADE
Stratospheric Processes and their Role in Climate (EERA) ..... SPARC
Stratospheric Processes and their Role in Climate [Marine science] (OSRA) .... SPARC
Stratospheric Research Program .... SRP
Stratospheric Sounding Unit [Telecommunications] (TEL) .... SSU
Stratospheric Tracers of Atmospheric Transport [Marine science] (OSRA) .... STAT
Stratospheric Tracers of Atmospheric Transport (USDC) .... STAT
Stratospheric Warming .... STRATWARM
Strattec Security [NASDAQ symbol] (TTSB) .... STRT
Strattec Security Corp. [Associated Press] (SAG) ...... Strattec
Strattec Security Corp. [NASDAQ symbol] (SAG) .... STRT
Stratton [England] .... STRAT
Stratton Public Library, Stratton, CO [Library symbol Library of Congress] (LCLS) .... CoStr
Stratton's Reports [12-14 Oregon] [A publication] (DLA) ..... Stratton
Stratum (BJA) .... S
Stratum Corneum [Skin membrane] .... SC
Stratum Super Stratum [Layer Over Layer] [Latin] .... SSS
Stratus [Meteorology] .... S
Stratus [Meteorology] .... ST
Stratus Computer [NYSE symbol] (TTSB) .... SRA
Stratus Computer, Inc. [NYSE symbol] (SPSG) .... SRA
Stratus Computer, Inc. [Associated Press] (SAG) ...... Stratus
Straubing/Mitterharthausen [Germany ICAO location identifier] (ICLI) .... EDPS
Straubing/Wallmuehle [Germany ICAO location identifier] (ICLI) .... EDMS
Stravenue .... STRA
Stravenue [Postal Service standard] (OPSA) .... STRA
Stravenue [Commonly used] (OPSA) .... STRAV
Stravenue [Commonly used] (OPSA) .... STRAVE
Stravenue [Commonly used] (OPSA) .... STRAVEN
Stravenue [Commonly used] (OPSA) .... STRAVENUE
Stravenue [Commonly used] (OPSA) .... STRAVN
Stravenue [Commonly used] (OPSA) .... STRVN
Stravenue [Commonly used] (OPSA) .... STRVNUE
Straw [Colored] [Laboratory science] (DAVI) .... STRW
Straw Boss (MHDB) .... SB
Strawberry Crinkle Virus [Plant pathology] .... STCV
Strawberry Latent Ringspot Virus [Plant pathology] .... SLRV
Strawberry Point Press-Journal, Strawberry Point, IA [Library symbol Library of Congress] (LCLS) .... IaStrpP
Strawberry Point Public Library, Strawberry Point, IA [Library symbol Library of Congress] (LCLS) .... IaStrp
Strawberry Vein Banding Virus [Plant pathology] .... SVBV
Strawbery Banke, Portsmouth, NH [Library symbol Library of Congress] (LCLS) .... NhPoS
Strawboard [Shipping] .... SBD
Strawboard [Shipping] .... STWBRD
Strawbridge & Clothier [NASDAQ symbol] (NQ) .... STRW
Strawbridge Clothier [Associated Press] (SAG) .... StrwbCl
Strawbridge/Clothier'A' [NASDAQ symbol] (TTSB) ..... STRWA
Stray Energy Detector .... SED
Stray Energy Indicator .... SEI
Stray Energy Monitor .... SEM
Stray Energy Monitor Device .... SEMD
Stray Energy Monitor System .... SEMS
Stray Field Test (NVT) .... STFT
Stray Horse Resources, Inc. [Vancouver Stock Exchange symbol] ..... STH
Stray Radiant Energy .... SRE
Stray Radiant Power .... SRP
Stray Radiant Power Ratio .... SRPR
Stray Radiation Chamber .... SRC
Stray Voltage Tester .... SVT
Strayer Education, Inc. [NASDAQ symbol] (SAG) .... STRA

Strayer Education, Inc. [*Associated Press*] (SAG) .... Strayer
STRC [*Science and Technology Research Center*] **Inverted File Search System** [*Search system*] .... STRC-IVS
Streak .... STR
Streaky [*Quality of the bottom*] [*Nautical charts*] .... str
Streaky Bay [*Australia Airport symbol*] (OAG) .... KBY
Stream [*Board on Geographic Names*] .... STM
Stream [*Maps and charts*] .... STR
Stream [*Commonly used*] (OPSA) .... STREAM
Stream [*Commonly used*] (OPSA) .... STREME
Stream .... STRM
Stream .... STRM
Stream Editor [*Computer science*] (CDE) .... sed
Stream Generation Statement [*Computer science*] .... SGS
Stream of Thought .... SOT
Stream Routing [*Computer science*] .... STR
Stream Support Team (MCD) .... SST
Stream Tension Actuated Remotely [*Navy*] (DOMA) .... STAR
Stream Tree Data (PDAA) .... STD
Streamflow Synthesis and Reservoir Regulation [*Computer science*] .... SSARR
Streaming Current Detector .... SCD
Streaming Data Procedure [*Computer science*] (CDE) .... SDP
Streaming Tape Backup Unit .... STB
Streamline .... SL
Streamline (MSA) .... STRLN
Streamline Aviation [*British ICAO designator*] (FAAC) .... STM
Streamline Curvature Method [*Computer program*] .... SCM
Streamlined Acquisition Requirements System [*DoD*] .... STAR
Streamlined Alternative Logistics Transmission System (DOMA) .... SALTS
Streamlined Automated Logistics Transmission System .... SALTS
Streamlined Inspection System [*USDA meat standards*] .... SIS
StreamLogic Corp. [*NASDAQ symbol*] (SAG) .... STLC
StreamLogic Corp. [*NASDAQ symbol*] (TTSB) .... STLC
StreamLogic Corp. [*Associated Press*] (SAG) .... StrmLog
Streamtube Curvature .... STC
Streator Elementary School District 45, Streator, IL [*Library symbol Library of Congress*] (LCLS) .... IStrSD
Streator, IL [*Location identifier FAA*] (FAAL) .... STQ
Streator, IL [*AM radio station call letters*] .... WIZZ
Streator, IL [*FM radio station call letters*] .... WSTQ
Streator, IL [*FM radio station call letters*] (RBYB) .... WYYS
Streator Public Library, Streator, IL [*Library symbol Library of Congress*] (LCLS) .... IStr
Streator Township High School District 40, Streator, IL [*Library symbol Library of Congress*] (LCLS) .... IStrHSD
Street [*Bureau of the Census*] .... S
Street (EY) .... ST
Street (VRA) .... st
Street (DD) .... St
Street (WDMC) .... st
Street (ODBW) .... St
Street .... STR
Street [*Commonly used*] (OPSA) .... STREET
Street .... STRET
Street [*Commonly used*] (OPSA) .... STRT
Street Address Record [*Telecommunications*] (TEL) .... SAR
Street and Highway Safety Lighting Bureau [*Defunct*] (EA) .... SHSLB
Street Corner Offense Reduction Experiment .... SCORE
Street Crime Unit [*Criminology*] (LAIN) .... SCU
Street Legal Performance [*Auto model designation*] .... SLP
Street Narcotics Unit [*Criminology*] (LAIN) .... SNU
Street Price (ROG) .... SP
Street Railway Law [*United States*] [*A publication*] (DLA) .... Rosenberger
Street Railway Reports [*United States*] [*A publication*] (DLA) .... St Ry Rep
Street Railway Reports [*A publication*] (DLA) .... Street Ry Rep
Street Rod [*Automobile modification*] .... SR
Street Rod Equipment Association (EA) .... SREA
Streets [*Commonly used*] (OPSA) .... STREETS
Streets [*Postal Service standard*] (OPSA) .... STS
Streets .... STS
Streets and Highways Code [*A publication*] (DLA) .... Str & HC
Streetsboro, OH [*FM radio station call letters*] .... WSTB
Streetsville Public Library, Ontario [*Library symbol National Library of Canada*] (NLC) .... OSTR
Streetsville Public Library, Streetsville, ON, Canada [*Library symbol Library of Congress*] (LCLS) .... CaOStr
StreetTalk Directory Assistance [*VINES*] [*Computer science*] (PCM) .... STDA
Streich, Lang, Weeks & Cardon, Phoenix, AZ [*Library symbol*] [*Library of Congress*] (LCLS) .... AzPhS
Streicher Mobile Fueling, Inc. [*NASDAQ symbol*] (SAG) .... FUEL
Streicher Mobile Fueling, Inc. [*Associated Press*] (SAG) .... StrchMb
Streicher Mobile Fueling, Inc. [*Associated Press*] (SAG) .... StrMb
Streichinstrumente [*Stringed Instruments*] [*Music*] .... STR
Strela Antiaircraft Missiles .... SAM
Strength (DS) .... S
Strength (AFM) .... STR
Strength (AAG) .... STRN
Strength and Dynamics Branch [*Air Force*] .... SDB
Strength Differential [*Steel*] .... SD
Strength, Interference, Noise, Propagation, and Overall Merit Code [*Signal reception quality rating*] (NTCM) .... SINPO
Strength of Pole [*Chemistry*] (DAVI) .... M
Strength of Radio Frequency (IAA) .... SRF
Strength of Wings Including Flutter .... SWIFT
Strength Power and Communications Cable .... SPCC
Strength, Toughness, Pride .... STP
Strength-Duration (Curve) [*Prosthesis*] .... SD
Strengthened (ROG) .... STRENGTHD
Strengthening Developing Institutions Program [*HEW*] .... SDIP
Strengths, Weaknesses, Alternatives, Threats [*Analysis*] (ADA) .... SWAT
Strengths, Weaknesses, Opportunities, Threats [*Analysis for organizations*] .... SWOT
Strepsiptera [*Entomology*] .... Strep
Streptococcal Acidic Glycoprotein [*Antineoplastic drug*] .... SAGP
Streptococcal Cell Membrane [*Microbiology*] .... SCM
Streptococcal Chemotactic Factor Inhibitor [*Immunochemistry*] .... SCFI
Streptococcal Enterotoxin [*Medicine*] .... SPE
Streptococcal Pyrogenic Exotoxin A [*Immunochemistry*] .... SPEA
Streptococcal Pyrogenic Exotoxin B [*Immunochemistry*] .... SPEB
Streptococcal Pyrogenic Exotoxin C [*Immunochemistry*] .... SPEC
Streptococcal Superantigen [*Immunochemistry*] .... SSA
Streptococcus [*Medicine*] (MAE) .... S
Streptococcus [*Medicine*] .... STR
Streptococcus [*Medicine*] .... STREP
Streptococcus [*A bacterium*] [*Medicine*] (DAVI) .... strept
Streptococcus faecilis [*Microbiology*] .... SF
Streptococcus lactis R Factor [*Biochemistry*] .... SLR
Streptococcus Lactis, Resistant [*Immunology*] (DAVI) .... SLR
Streptodornase [*An enzyme*] .... SD
Streptokinase [*An enzyme*] .... SK
Streptokinase [*An enzyme*] (AAMN) .... STK
Streptokinase Streptodornase [*An enzyme mixture*] [*Medicine*] .... SKSD
Streptolysin [*Hematology*] .... SL
Streptolysin O [*Hematology*] .... SLO
Streptomycin [*An antibiotic*] .... S
Streptomycin [*An antibiotic*] .... SM
Streptomycin [*An antibiotic*] (AAMN) .... STM
Streptomycin [*An antibiotic*] (DSUE) .... STREPTO
Streptomycin Phosphotransferase [*An enzyme*] .... SPT
Streptomycin Resistance [*Genetics*] .... Smr
Streptonigrin [*Antineoplastic drug*] (DAVI) .... SN
Streptonigrin, Thioguanine, Endoxan [*Cyclophosphamide*], Actinomycin, Mitomycin C [*Antineoplastic drug regimen*] .... STEAM
Streptozocin [*Antineoplastic drug*] .... S
Streptozocin [*Antineoplastic drug*] .... STZ
Streptozocin [*Antineoplastic drug*] .... SZ
Streptozocin [*Antineoplastic drug*] .... SZN
Streptozocin, Adriamycin, Methyl-CCNU [*or Semustine*] [*Antineoplastic drug regimen*] (DAVI) .... SAM
Streptozocin, CCNU [*Lomustine*], Adriamycin, Bleomycin [*Antineoplastic drug regimen*] .... SCAB
Streptozocin, Mitomycin C, Fluorouracil [*Antineoplastic drug regimen*] .... SMF
Stress Analysis and Computer-Aided Design [*Computer science*] (WDAA) .... SACAD
Stress Analysis of Axisymmetric Solids (MCD) .... SAAS
Stress and Arousal Adjective Checklist (PDAA) .... SACL
Stress and Degraded Mode Test (CAAL) .... SDMT
Stress Anneal (KSC) .... SA
Stress Concentration Factor (MCD) .... SCF
Stress Corrosion Cracking [*Metals*] .... SCC
Stress Cracking [*Metallurgy*] .... SC
Stress Degree Day [*Crop inventory*] .... SDD
Stress Distribution Factor [*Medicine*] (DMAA) .... SDF
Stress Electrocardiography [*Cardiology*] (DMAA) .... SECG
Stress Evaluation Inventory [*Test*] .... SEI
Stress Fiber-Like Structure [*Biology*] .... SFLS
Stress Formula .... SF
Stress Hypertensive Rats .... StHR
Stress Incontinence [*Urology*] (DAVI) .... SI
Stress Intensity Factor (MCD) .... SIF
Stress Limit Tests .... SLT
Stress Loading Facility [*Fort Huachuca, AZ*] [*United States Army Electronic Proving Ground*] (GRD) .... SLF
Stress Memo Manual .... SMM
Stress Number (NASA) .... S-N
Stress on Analytical Reasoning .... SOAR
Stress Relaxation Processability Tester (PDAA) .... SRPT
Stress Relief Tool .... SRT
Stress Relieved Annealed [*Metallurgical engineering*] .... SRA
Stress Relieving Liner (KSC) .... SRL
Stress/Strain Controlled Fatigue (MCD) .... SSCF
Stress Survival Matrix Test (PDAA) .... SSMT
Stress Testing [*Medicine*] .... ST
Stress Urinary Incontinence [*Medicine*] (DMAA) .... SUI
Stress Wave Analysis Technique .... SWAT
Stress Wave Analyzing Program .... SWAP
Stress Wave Emission .... SWE
Stress Wave in Layered Arbitrary Media (SAA) .... SLAM
Stress Wave Riveter [*Metal forming*] .... SWR
Stress-Activated Protein Kinase [*An enzyme*] .... SAPK
Stress-Activated Protein Kinases [*An enzyme*] .... SAPK
Stressed Panel Fasteners .... SPF
Stressed-Skin Insulated-Core Panels [*Construction technology*] (PS) .... SSIC
Stress-Induced Analgesia [*Medicine*] .... SIA
Stress-Induced Pseudoelasticity (PDAA) .... STRIPE
Stress-Oriented Hydrogen-Induced Cracking [*Metallurgy*] .... SOHIC
Stress-Related Mucosal Damage [*Medicine*] (DMAA) .... SMRD
Stress-Related Mucosal Damage [*Medicine*] .... SRMD
Stress-Rupture (MCD) .... SR
Stretch [*Horse racing*] .... STR

Stretch (AAG) ..... STRCH
Stretch Assembly Program [*IBM Corp.*] ..... STRAP
Stretch Block (MCD) ..... STB
Stretch Block Template Set (MCD) ..... SBTS
Stretch Chuck Jaws (MCD) ..... SCJ
Stretch Glass Society (EA) ..... SGS
Stretch Inhibitor ..... SI
Stretch Receptor Neuron ..... SRN
Stretch Reflex (MAE) ..... SR
Stretch-Activated Ion Channel ..... SA
Stretched Upper Deck (AIA) ..... SUD
Stretcher (VRA) ..... stret
Stretcher Form [*Tool*] (AAG) ..... STFM
Stretcher Jaws [*Tool*] (AAG) ..... STJW
Stretcher Party ..... SP
Stretcher-Bearer ..... SB
Stretch-Inactivated Ion Channel ..... SI
Stretching-Yawning Syndrome [*Medicine*] (DMAA) ..... SYS
Stria Medullaris [*Neuroanatomy*] ..... SM
Striae Keratopathy [*Ophthalmology*] (DAVI) ..... SK
Striated Microtubule-Associated Components [*Botanical cytology*] ..... SMAC
Striatum [*Brain anatomy*] [*Also, ST*] ..... Str
Stricken Aircraft Reclamation and Disposal Program [*Navy*] (NG) ..... SARDIP
Strickland on Evidence [*1830*] [*A publication*] (DLA) ..... Strick Ev
STRICOM [*Strike Command*] **Command and Control System** [*Army*] (AABC) ..... SCCS
Strict [*Medicine*] ..... ST
Strict Baptist Historical Society [*British*] (DBA) ..... SBHS
Strict Bed Confinement [*Medicine*] ..... SBC
Strict Bed Rest [*Medicine*] ..... SBR
Strict Good Middling (IAA) ..... SGM
Strict Good Ordinary (IAA) ..... SGO
Strict Middling (IAA) ..... SM
Strictly Confined to Bed [*Medicine*] ..... SCB
Strictly Out of Luck (IIA) ..... SOL
Strictly Wild Guess (SAA) ..... SWG
Stride Rite [*NYSE symbol*] (TTSB) ..... SRR
Stride Rite Corp. [*NYSE symbol*] (SPSG) ..... SRR
Stride Rite Corp. [*Associated Press*] (SAG) ..... StrideRt
Strike [*or Stroke*] ..... Sk
Strike [*Navy*] (DOMA) ..... STK
Strike [*Bowling symbol*] X
Strike Aircraft Test Directorate [*Military*] (CAAL) ..... SATD
Strike and Terrain Following RADAR [*Military*] (PDAA) ..... SATF
Strike Anywhere [*Match*] ..... SAW
Strike Assault Boat [*Navy symbol*] ..... STAB
Strike Attack [*Military*] ..... SATK
Strike Attack Vector [*Navy*] (ANA) ..... SAV
Strike Benefits (MHBD) ..... SB
Strike Camera (MCD) ..... SCAM
Strike Command [*Military*] ..... SC
Strike Command [*Military*] ..... STRICOM
Strike Command Alternate Headquarters [*Military*] (AABC) ..... SALTHQ
Strike Command Integrated Communications System [*British*] ..... STCICS
Strike Control and Reconnaissance [*Aircraft*] ..... SCAR
Strike Energy, Inc. [*Vancouver Stock Exchange symbol*] ..... SEN
Strike Exercise [*Navy NATO*] (NATG) ..... STRIKEX
Strike Fighter Advanced Readiness Program [*Navy*] (DOMA) ..... SFARP
Strike for Peace [*Later, WDFP*] (EA) ..... SFP
Strike Force Data System (NVT) ..... SFDS
Strike Improved Display System (MCD) ..... SIDS
Strike/Interdiction (MCD) ..... S/I
Strike Leader Attack Training [*Navy*] (DOMA) ..... SLAT
Strike Leader Attack Training School [*Navy*] (DOMA) ..... SLATS
Strike Operations [*Military*] (NVT) ..... STRIKEOPS
Strike Operations Coordinator [*Navy*] (NVT) ..... SOC
Strike Options Comparison (MCD) ..... SOC
Strike Planning and Damage Estimator [*Military*] ..... SPADE
Strike Projection Evaluation and Anti-War Warfare Research (DOMA) ..... SPEAR
Strike Rate (ADA) ..... SR
Strike Reporting System ..... SRS
Strike Route Information Book [*Strategic Air Command*] (AABC) ..... SRIB
Strike Support Ship [*Navy*] (NVT) ..... SSS
Strike, Transfers, Acquisitions, or Removals [*Navy*] (NG) ..... STAR
Strike Warning Message [*Army*] (ADDR) ..... STRIKWARN
Strikeout [*Baseball symbol*] ..... K
Strikeouts [*Baseball*] ..... SO
Striker [*Automotive engineering*] ..... STRKR
Striker Industries [*NASDAQ symbol*] (SAG) ..... SKRI
Striker Industries [*Associated Press*] (SAG) ..... Striker
Strikes, Riots, and Civil Commotions [*Insurance*] ..... SRCC
Striking (WGA) ..... STR
Striking and Support Forces Southern Europe [*Navy*] ..... STRIKFORSOUTH
Striking Fleet Atlantic [*Military*] ..... STRIKFLTLANT
Striking Fleet Atlantic Representative in Europe [*NATO*] (NATG) ..... STRIKFTLANTREPEUR
String ..... STR
String (NASA) ..... STRG
String (VRA) ..... strg
String Analysis (IAA) ..... SA
String and Character Recording Oriented Logogrammatic Language [*1970*] [*Computer science*] (CSR) ..... SCROLL
String Array [*Computer system*] (MCD) ..... STAR
String Array Processor ..... STAR
String Control Language [*Computer science*] ..... SCL

String Length [*Computer science*] (PCM) ..... STRLEN
String or Wind [*Freight*] ..... STRG WND
String Polling Multiple Access (PDAA) ..... SPMA
String Process System (NITA) ..... SPS
String Processing Language [*Computer science*] (DIT) ..... STRIP
String Processing System [*Word processing software*] ..... SPS
Stringcourse (VRA) ..... strgcr
Stringendo [*Hastening*] [*Music*] ..... STR
Stringendo [*Hastening*] [*Music*] ..... STRING
Stringendo [*Hastening*] [*Music*] (ROG) ..... STRINO
Stringer (AAG) ..... STGR
Stringfellow's Reports [*9-11 Missouri*] [*A publication*] (DLA) ..... Stringf
Stringfellow's Reports [*9-11 Missouri*] [*A publication*] (DLA) ..... Stringfellow
String-Oriented Symbolic Language [*1963*] [*Computer science*] ..... SNOBOL
Strings [*of an orchestra*] ..... STR
Strio-Pallido-Dentate Calcinosis [*Medicine*] (DMAA) ..... SPDC
Strip ..... STP
Strip (AAG) ..... STR
Strip Chart [*Recorder*] [*NASA*] (NASA) ..... S/C
Strip Chart Recorder [*NASA*] ..... SCR
Strip Chart Recorder System [*NASA*] ..... SCRS
Strip Chart Viewer ..... SCV
Strip Delay Line ..... SDL
Strip Domain Resonance ..... SDR
Strip Electron Beam ..... SEB
Strip Immunoblot Assay [*Immunology*] ..... SIA
Strip Mine ..... SM
Strip Shunt Transmission Line Antenna [*Aviation*] (AIA) ..... SSTLA
Strip Transmission Line Adapter [*or Assembly*] ..... STLA
Strip-Buried Heterostructure [*Telecommunications*] (TEL) ..... SBH
Stripe Rot [*Plant pathology*] ..... SR
Striped Peak [*Washington*] [*Seismograph station code, US Geological Survey*] (SEIS) ..... STW
Striped Shiner [*Ichthyology*] ..... Ss
Stripers Unlimited (EA) ..... SU
Stripes for Exceptional Performers [*Air Force*] (DOMA) ..... STEP
Stripline ..... SLA
Stripline Opposed Emitter (IAA) ..... SOE
Stripline Tunnel Diode ..... STD
Stripline Tunnel Diode Amplifier ..... STDA
Stripline with Stud (IAA) ..... SWS
Stripped (MSA) ..... STPD
Stripper ..... STPR
Stripping Film (DGA) ..... SF
Stripping Voltammetry [*Electroanalytical chemistry*] ..... SV
Stripping Yield [*Agriculture*] (OA) ..... SY
Strip-Tin (MSA) ..... S-T
Strobe [*NASA*] (IAA) ..... STR
Strobe (NASA) ..... STRB
Strobe Intersection Deghoster ..... SIND
Strobed Single Channel Analyzer [*Electronics*] (OA) ..... SSCA
Strobel, E. H., Saint Louis MO [*STAC*] ..... SEH
Strober Organization [*NASDAQ symbol*] (TTSB) ..... STRB
[*The*] Strober Organization, Inc. [*Brooklyn, NY*] [*NASDAQ symbol*] (NQ) ..... STRB
Strober Organization, Inc. [*Associated Press*] (SAG) ..... Strober
Strobes Against Troops at Night (MCD) ..... SATAN
Strobhart's South Carolina Equity Reports [*A publication*] (DLA) ..... Strob Ch
Strobhart's South Carolina Equity Reports [*1846-50*] [*A publication*] (DLA) ..... Strob Eq
Strobhart's South Carolina Equity Reports [*A publication*] (DLA) ..... Strobh Eq (SC)
Strobhart's South Carolina Law Reports [*1846-50*] [*A publication*] (DLA) ..... Strob
Strobhart's South Carolina Law Reports [*A publication*] (DLA) ..... Strobh L (SC)
Stroboscope [*Engineering*] ..... STBSCP
Stroboscopic ..... STROBE
Stroboscopic Analyzing Monitor [*Instrumentation*] ..... SAM
Stroke ..... STR
Stroke (MSA) ..... STRK
Stroke Club International (EA) ..... SCI
Stroke in Evolution [*Medicine*] (MEDA) ..... SIE
Stroke in Patients with Atrial Fibrillation ..... SPAF
Stroke Index ..... SI
Stroke of Piston in Inches [*Railroad term*] ..... S
Stroke Rehabilitation Technician (MAE) ..... SRT
Stroke Volume [*Physiology*] ..... SV
Stroke Volume Index [*Medicine*] ..... SVI
Stroke with Full Recovery [*Neurology*] (DAVI) ..... SFR
Stroke with Minimum Residuum [*Medicine*] (DMAA) ..... SMR
Stroke Work [*Cardiology*] ..... SW
Stroke Work Index [*Neurology*] ..... SWI
Strokes per Minute ..... SPM
Strollad ar Vro [*Country Party*] [*France Political party*] (PPW) ..... SAV
Stroma [*Medicine*] ..... ST
Stroma-Free Hemoglobin [*Hematology*] ..... SFHb
Stroma-Free Hemoglobin Pyridoxylated [*Clinical chemistry*] ..... SFH-P
Stromal Cell-Derived Factor [*Biochemistry*] ..... SDF
Stromateis [*of Clemens Alexandrinus*] [*Classical studies*] (OCD) ..... Strom
Stromberg [*Automotive engineering*] ..... STROM
Stromberg Central Operations Panel - Electric ..... SCOPE
Stromberg Dexterity Test [*Education*] ..... SDT
Stromberg-Carlson Automatic Test Equipment ..... SCATE
Stromberg-Carlson Corp., Rochester, NY [*Library symbol Library of Congress*] (LCLS) ..... NRGD-SC
Stromberg-Carlson Practices [*Telecommunications*] (TEL) ..... SCP
Stromberg-Datagraphix, San Diego, CA [*Library symbol Library of Congress*] (LCLS) ..... CSdSC

Stromboli-Ginostra [*Italy*] [*Seismograph station code, US Geological Survey*] (SEIS) ... GIN
Stromstad/Nasinge [*Sweden ICAO location identifier*] (ICLI) ... ESGS
Strong (MSA) ... STRG
Strong Absorption Model [*Nuclear physics*] (OA) ... SAM
Strong Acid Leach (PDAA) ... SAL
Strong Acid Number (IAA) ... SAN
Strong Anion Exchanger [*Chemistry*] ... SAX
Strong Anthropic Principle [*Term coined by authors John Barrow and Frank Tipler in their book, "The Anthropic Cosmological Principle"*] ... SAP
Strong Base Number (IAA) ... SBN
Strong Black Liquor [*Pulp and paper technology*] ... SBL
Strong Black Liquor Oxidation [*Pulp and paper technology*] ... SBLO
Strong Cation Exchanger [*Chemistry*] ... SCX
Strong Equivalence Principle [*Thermodynamics*] ... SEP
Strong Exchange Degeneracy [*Physics*] (OA) ... SED
Strong Metal-Support Interaction [*Catalysis*] ... SMSI
Strong No-Trump After Passing [*Bridge card games*] (BARN) ... SNAP
Strong Partial Maternal Behavior [*Psychology*] ... SPMB
Strong Point/Obstacle System [*Military*] (NVT) ... SPOS
Strong Reactive [*Laboratory science*] (DAVI) ... SR
Strong Safety [*Football*] ... SS
Strong Soap Solution ... SSS
Strong Ultraviolet Index ... SUVI
Strong Vocational Interest Blank [*Psychology*] ... SVIB
Strongback ... STRBK
Strong-Campbell Interest Inventory [*Vocational guidance*] ... SCII
Strong-Campbell Interest Inventory (DMAA) ... SCII
Strongly Implicit Procedure ... SIP
Strongpoint Obstacle System [*Military*] (VNW) ... SOS
Strongsville Savings Bank [*NASDAQ symbol*] (SAG) ... SSBK
Strongsville Savings Bank [*Associated Press*] (SAG) ... StrongSv
Strongsville Svgs Bk Ohio [*NASDAQ symbol*] (TTSB) ... SSBK
Strongyloidiasis with Massive Hyperinfection [*Medicine*] (DMAA) ... SMH
Stronnictwo Chlopskie [*Peasants' Party*] [*Poland Political party*] (PPE) ... SC
Stronnictwo Chrzescijanskiej Demokracji [*Christian Democratic Party*] [*Poland*] (PPE) ... CHADECJA
Stronnictwo Demokratyczne [*Democratic Party*] [*Poland Political party*] (PPE) ... SD
Stronnictwo Ludowe [*Peasant Party*] [*Poland Political party*] (PPE) ... SL
Stronnictwo Ludowe-Wola Ludu [*Peasant Party-People's Will*] [*Poland Political party*] (PPE) ... SL-Wola Ludu
Stronnictwo Narodowe [*Nationalist Party*] [*Poland Political party*] (PPE) ... SN
Stronnictwo Narodowej Demokracji [*Nationalist Democratic Party*] [*Poland*] (PPE) ... ENDECJA
Stronnictwo Pracy [*Labour Party*] [*Poland Political party*] (EY) ... SP
Stronsay [*Scotland*] [*Airport symbol*] (OAG) ... SOY
Strontium [*Chemical element*] ... Sr
Strontium Beryllium Boron Oxide [*Inorganic chemistry*] ... SBBO
Strontium Chromium Gallium Oxide [*Inorganic chemistry*] ... SCGO
Strontium Unit Equivalent ... SUE
Strontium Units [*Nuclear energy*] ... SU
Strontium-Barium-Niobidium [*Inorganic chemistry*] ... SBN
Stroop Color-Word Test [*Psychology*] (DAVI) ... SCWT
Strophe [*Poetry*] (ROG) ... ST
Strophe [*Classical studies*] (OCD) ... STR
Stroposcopic Pulse Radiolysis [*Physical chemistry*] ... SPR
Stroud Branch, Township of Innisfil Public Library, Ontario [*Library symbol National Library of Canada*] (NLC) ... OSTRO
Stroud, OK [*Location identifier FAA*] (FAAL) ... SUD
Stroud on Slavery [*A publication*] (DLA) ... Stroud Sl
Stroud Resources Ltd. [*Toronto Stock Exchange symbol*] ... SDR
Strouds Creek & Muddlety Railroad [*AAR code*] ... SCM
Strouds, Inc. [*NASDAQ symbol*] (SAG) ... STRO
Strouds, Inc. [*Associated Press*] (SAG) ... Strouds
Stroudsburg, PA [*FM radio station call letters*] ... WSBG
Stroudsburg, PA [*AM radio station call letters*] ... WVPO
Strouhal Number [*Sound*] ... SN
Strouhal Number [*IUPAC*] ... Sr
Stround Branch Library, Stround, ON, Canada [*Library symbol Library of Congress*] (LCLS) ... CaOStro
Strowger Automatic Toll Ticketing [*Telecommunications*] ... SATT
Strubby [*British ICAO location identifier*] (ICLI) ... EGCG
Struck off Charge [*British military*] (DMA) ... SOC
Struck off Strength [*British military*] (DMA) ... SOS
Structural (NASA) ... ST
Structural [*Lumber*] ... STR
Structural ... STRL
Structural ... STRL
Structural ... STRTL
Structural Acoustic Monitor ... SAM
Structural Adhesive Bond ... SAB
Structural Adjustment Facility [*Finance*] ... SAF
Structural Adjustment Loan [*World Bank*] ... SAL
Structural Adjustment Package [*Australia*] ... SAP
Structural Analysis and Matrix Interpretive System (IAA) ... SAMIS
Structural Analysis and Matrix Inversion System [*Nuclear energy*] (NRCH) ... SAMIS
Structural Analysis Consultant (MCD) ... SACON
Structural Analysis, Frailty Evaluation and Redesign (MHDB) ... SAFER
Structural Analysis Interpretive Routine ... STAIR
Structural Analysis Method for Evaluation of Complex Structures (PDAA) ... SAMECS
Structural Analysis Numerical Design System ... SANDS
Structural Analysis of General Shells ... STAGS
Structural Analysis of Layered Orthotropic Ring-Stiffened Shells [*Computer program*] [*NASA*] ... SALORS
Structural Analysis of Social Behavior ... SASB
Structural Analysis Package ... STRAP
Structural Analysis Program (MCD) ... SAP
Structural Analysis Technologies, Inc. ... SAT
Structural Analytical Interpreter ... STRAIN
Structural Assembly Demonstration Experiment (MCD) ... SADE
Structural Assembly Model [*NASA*] ... SAM
Structural Biology and Design Applications [*bbscrc-Biotechnology and Biological Sciences Research Council*] [*British*] ... SBDA
Structural Board Association (EA) ... SBA
Structural Carbon Steel Hard ... SCSH
Structural Carbon Steel Medium ... SCSM
Structural Carbon Steel Soft ... SCSS
Structural Cement-Fiber Products Association [*Defunct*] (EA) ... SCFPA
Structural Ceramic Analysis and Reliability Evaluation [*NASA*] ... SCARE
Structural Ceramic Panel ... SCP
Structural Clay Products Institute [*Later, BIA*] (EA) ... SCPI
Structural Clay Products Research Foundation [*BIA*] [*Absorbed by*] (EA) ... SCPRF
Structural Clay Tile [*Technical drawings*] ... SCT
Structural Computer-Aided Logic Design ... SCALD
Structural Concrete Consortium [*British*] (DBA) ... SCC
Structural Design Criteria [*Nuclear energy*] ... SDC
Structural Design Gross Weight ... SDGW
Structural Design Language [*Computer science*] (MCD) ... STRUDL
Structural Design Language Dynamic Analysis [*Computer science*] ... STRUDLDYNAL
Structural Design Language for Transmission Tower ... STRUDLTOWER
Structural Design Language Output Plots ... STRUDLPLOTS
Structural Detail (AAG) ... SD
Structural Development Model ... SDM
Structural Dynamic Test [*NASA*] (NASA) ... SDT
Structural Dynamic Test Article [*NASA*] (NASA) ... SDTA
Structural Dynamics (KSC) ... SD
Structural Dynamics Malfunction ... SDF
Structural Dynamics Modification ... SDM
Structural Dynamics Res [*NASDAQ symbol*] (TTSB) ... SDRC
Structural Dynamics Research Corp. [*NASDAQ symbol*] (NQ) ... SDRC
Structural Dynamics Research Corp. [*Associated Press*] (SAG) ... StrucD
Structural Econometric Model [*Statistics*] ... SEM
Structural Econometric Modeling Time Series Analysis [*Statistics*] ... SEMTSA
Structural Engineering Bulletin [*Department of Housing and Urban Development*] [*A publication*] (GFGA) ... SEB
Structural Engineering Systems Solver [*Programming language*] [*1962*] ... STRESS
Structural Engineers Association of California (EA) ... SEAOC
Structural Engineers Councils (KSC) ... SEC
Structural Fatigue Test (MCD) ... STF
Structural Fatigue Test Article [*NASA*] (NASA) ... SFTA
Structural Feedback ... SFB
Structural Fire Protection Association [*British*] ... SFPA
Structural Firing Test [*Military*] (CAAL) ... SFT
Structural Foam [*Plastics*] (DICI) ... SF
Structural Formula [*Chemistry*] [*Computer science*] ... STRUFO
Structural Gene ... SG
Structural Glass ... SG
Structural Impediments Initiative [*US-Japan trade negotiations*] ... SII
Structural Influence Coefficient ... SIC
Structural Instrumentation, Inc. [*NASDAQ symbol*] (SAG) ... SISI
Structural Instrumentation, Inc. [*Associated Press*] (SAG) ... StrctIns
Structural Insulated Panel ... SIP
Structural Integrity Monitoring (MCD) ... SIM
Structural Inventory and Appraisal [*Of roads and bridges*] ... SIA
Structural Lander Test Model ... SLTM
Structural Liquid Composite Molding [*Plastics technology*] ... SLCM
Structural Loads on Reentry Vehicles (MCD) ... SLORV
Structural Macroassembly Language ... SMAL
Structural Maintenance and Repair Team (MCD) ... SMART
Structural Maintenance of Chromosome [*Cytology*] ... SMC
Structural Margin Beyond Design Basis [*Nuclear energy*] (NRCH) ... SMBDB
Structural Materials Property Manual [*NASA*] (NASA) ... SMPM
Structural Mechanical (MCD) ... SM
Structural Mode Control System (MCD) ... SMCS
Structural Modeling Oriented Graphics [*Module*] ... SMOG
Structural Network Analysis Program ... SNAP
Structural Operations Technology Group (SSD) ... SOT
Structural Programming Technique ... SPT
Structural Reaction Injection Molding [*Plastics*] ... SRIM
Structural Repair Handbook (DNAB) ... SRH
Structural Repair Manual ... SRM
Structural Repeating Unit [*Polymer nomenclature system*] ... SRU
Structural Research Series ... SRS
Structural Return Loss [*Telecommunications*] (TEL) ... SRL
Structural Significant Item (MCD) ... SSI
Structural Stability Research Council (EA) ... SSRC
Structural Static Test [*NASA*] (NASA) ... SST
Structural Test Article (NASA) ... STA
Structural Test Model ... STM
Structural Test Plan (ACII) ... STP
Structural Test Vehicle [*NASA*] (KSC) ... STV
Structural Testing, Analysis, and Reporting ... STAR
Structural Thinking Experiential Learning Laboratory with Animation [*Software*] ... STELLA

Structural Tracking and Engine Monitoring System (MCD) .... STEMS
Structural Transition Section [*NASA*] (MCD) .... STS
Structural Unemployed [*Business term*] (MHDW) .... SU
Structural Weight Optimization Program [*NASA*] (KSC) .... SWOP
Structural Wood Fiber Products Association [*Later, SCFPA*] (EA) .... SWFPA
Structurally Conserved Region [*Biochemistry*] .... SCR
Structurally Integrated Thruster (MCD) .... SIT
Structurally Oriented Simulation System [*NASA*] .... SOSS
Structure (AABC) .... STRUC
Structure (AAG) .... STRUCT
Structure Activity Relationship .... SAR
Structure and Composition System [*Military*] (AABC) .... SACS
Structure and Nomenclature Search System [*Formerly, SSS*] [*Chemical Information Systems, Inc.*] [*Information service or system*] .... SANSS
Structure and Parity Observing Output Function .... SPOOF
Structure and Reference Analyzer [*IBM Corp.*] [*Chemistry*] .... SANDRA
Structure Borne Acoustics (KSC) .... SBA
Structure Building Language (PDAA) .... SBL
Structure Function .... SF
Structure Isolation Dynamics [*Vehicle development*] [*Automotive engineering*] .... SID
Structure Manning Decision Review .... SMDR
Structure Memory .... SM
Structure Memory Information Processor .... SMIP
Structure Module Qualification Test (MCD) .... SMQ
Structure Mold Line (MCD) .... SML
Structure of Instruction Rating Scale (EDAC) .... SIRS
Structure of Intellect [*Education*] (AEE) .... SOI
Structure of Intellect-Learning Abilities Test (EDAC) .... SOI-LA
Structure of Management Information .... SMI
Structure Preserving Estimation (ADA) .... SPREE
Structure Resonance Modulation Spectroscopy .... SRMS
Structure Tee (AAG) .... ST
Structure Tests, English Language [*Educational test*] .... STEL
Structure-Based Drug Design [*Organic chemistry*] .... SBDD
Structure-Carcinogenic Activity Relationship [*Biochemistry*] .... SCAR
Structure-Chart Diagramer [*Computer science*] .... SCD
Structured .... STRCTRD
Structured Analysis [*Programming language*] [*1977*] (CSR) .... SA
Structured Analysis and Design Technique [*Programming language*] [*1978*] .... SADT
Structured Analysis, Design and Implementation of information Systems (MHDI) .... STRADIS
Structured Analysis, Design, and Programming [*Computer science*] .... SADP
Structured Analysis/Structured Design (MCD) .... SA/SD
Structured and Scaled Interview to Assess Maladjustment [*Psychometrics*] .... SSIAM
Structured Assembly Language .... SAL
Structured Basic Language [*Computer science*] (CSR) .... STRUBAL
Structured Block Diagram [*Computer science*] (MHDB) .... SBD
Structured Case Review Blank .... SCRB
Structured Clinical Interview .... SCI
Structured Clinical Interview for DSM-III .... SCID
Structured Common Business-Oriented Language .... SCOBOL
Structured Design Strategy (NITA) .... SDS
Structured Development Strategy (NITA) .... SDS
Structured Document Handbook [*Computer science*] .... SDH
Structured Doll Play Test [*Psychology*] .... SDPT
Structured English Query Language [*1974*] [*Computer science*] (CSR) .... SEQUEL
Structured Environment for the Emotionally Disturbed Project (EDAC) .... SEED
Structured Exploratory Data Analysis .... SEDA
Structured Keyword Out of Context (NITA) .... SKWOC
Structured Learning Therapy .... SLT
Structured Markov Algorithm (MHDI) .... SMA
Structured On-the-Job Training (MCD) .... SOJT
Structured Pediatric Psychosocial Interview (EDAC) .... SPPI
Structured Programming [*Computer science*] (BUR) .... SP
Structured Programming Facility [*Computer science*] .... SPF
Structured Programming Processor [*Computer science*] (IAA) .... SPP
Structured Query Language [*IBM Corp.*] .... SQL
Structured Query Language (GAVI) .... SQL
Structured Query Language/Data System [*IBM Corp.*] .... SQL/DS
Structured Soy Protein Fiber [*Food industry*] .... SSPF
Structured Surfactant Formulation [*Solvent technology*] .... SSF
Structured Systems Analysis (NITA) .... SSA
Structured Systems Analysis and Design Method [*British*] .... SSADM
Structured Systems Design (NITA) .... SSD
Structured-Objective Rorschach Test [*Psychology*] .... SORT
Structure-Metabolism Relationship [*For drug design prediction*] .... SMR
Structure-Nomenclature Notation [*Chemistry*] .... SNN
Structure-of-Intellect [*Model*] .... SI
Structure-Oriented Description and Simulation (IEEE) .... SODAS
Structure-Preserved Error-Correcting Tree Automata (MHDI) .... SPECTA
Structure-Property Relationship [*Chemistry*] .... SPR
Structures and Materials (MCD) .... S & M
Structures and Mechanical System [*Skylab*] [*NASA*] .... SMS
Structures and Mechanics Division [*NASA*] .... SMD
Structures Assembly Deployment and Operations Technology (SSD) .... SADOT
Structures for Orbiting Radio Telescope (MCD) .... SORT
Structures Heating Facility .... SHF
Structures Laboratory [*Army*] (GRD) .... SL
Structures Memorandum .... SM
Structures Research Associates .... SRA
Structures, Structural Dynamics, and Materials (MCD) .... SDM
Structures Subsystem (KSC) .... SSS
Structures, Systems, and Components [*Nuclear energy*] (NRCH) .... SSC
Structures Technology Experiments Platform (MCD) .... STEP
Structures with Error Expurgation Program .... SWEEP
Structure-Specific Recognition Protein [*Biochemistry*] .... SSRP
Structure-Superstructure [*Economics*] .... SS
Strumech Engineering Electronic Developments (NITA) .... SEED
Strumpell-Marie [*Disease*] [*Also, Rheumatoid Spondylitis*] [*Medicine*] (DAVI) .... SM
Struthers Industries [*AMEX symbol*] (SPSG) .... SIR
Struthers Industries [*Associated Press*] (SAG) .... Struther
Struthers, OH [*FM radio station call letters*] .... WKTL
Struthers Wells Corp. (IAA) .... SW
Struve's Washington Territory Reports [*1854-88*] [*A publication*] (DLA) .... Struve
Strybing Arboretum Society of Golden Gate Park, San Francisco, CA [*Library symbol Library of Congress*] (LCLS) .... CSfSA
Strychnina [*Strychnine*] [*Pharmacy*] (ROG) .... STRYCH
Stryker Corp. [*NASDAQ symbol*] (NQ) .... STRY
Stryker Corp. [*Associated Press*] (SAG) .... Stryker
Stryker Resources Ltd. [*Vancouver Stock Exchange symbol*] .... SRY
STS [*Space Transportation System*] **Cargo Operations** [*Kennedy Space Center Directorate*] [*NASA*] (NASA) .... CS
STS [*Space Transportation System*] **Data Select Switch** (MCD) .... SDSS
STS [*Shuttle Test Station*] **Integrated Schedule Working Group** [*NASA*] (GFGA) .... SISWG
STS Payload Requirements and Analysis Group [*NASA*] (NASA) .... SPRAG
Sts. Peter and Paul Elementary School Library, Richmond, MN [*Library symbol*] [*Library of Congress*] (LCLS) .... MnRmS
Sts. Peter & Paul Middle Schol, St. Cloud, MN [*Library symbol*] [*Library of Congress*] (LCLS) .... MnStclSP
Sts. Peter & Paul Primary School, St. Cloud, MN [*Library symbol*] [*Library of Congress*] (LCLS) .... MnStclP
STS [*Shuttle Test Station*] **Planning and Operations Management** [*NASA*] (GFGA) .... SPOM
STS [*Shuttle Test Station*] **Processing Control Center** [*NASA*] (GFGA) .... SPCC
Stuart (ROG) .... STU
Stuart [*Florida*] [*Airport symbol*] (OAG) .... SUA
Stuart [*or Stewart*] **and Porter's Alabama Reports** [*A publication*] (DLA) .... Stuart & Por
Stuart [*or Stewart*] **and Porter's Alabama Reports** [*A publication*] (DLA) .... Stuart & Porter
Stuart [*or Stewart*] **and Porter's Alabama Reports** [*A publication*] (DLA) .... Stur & Porter
Stuart Co., Pasadena, CA [*Library symbol Library of Congress*] (LCLS) .... CPS
Stuart Co., Pasadena, CA [*Library symbol*] [*Library of Congress*] (LCLS) .... CPSC
Stuart Entertainment [*NASDAQ symbol*] (SPSG) .... STUA
Stuart Entertainment, Inc. [*Associated Press*] (SAG) .... SturtEn
Stuart, FL [*Location identifier FAA*] (FAAL) .... SUA
Stuart, FL [*AM radio station call letters*] .... WSTU
Stuart, FL [*FM radio station call letters*] .... WZZR
Stuart Herald, Stuart, IA [*Library symbol*] [*Library of Congress*] (LCLS) .... IaStuH
Stuart, IA [*FM radio station call letters*] .... KKRF
Stuart [*D. A.*] **Ltd.** [*Toronto Stock Exchange symbol*] .... STU
Stuart, Milne, and Peddie's Scotch Court of Session Cases [*A publication*] (DLA) .... St
Stuart, Milne, and Peddie's Scotch Court of Session Cases [*A publication*] (DLA) .... Stuart
Stuart, Milne, and Peddie's Scotch Court of Session Cases [*1851-53*] [*A publication*] (DLA) .... Stuart M & P
Stuart, Milne, and Peddie's Scotch Court of Sessions Reports [*A publication*] (DLA) .... Stu M & P
Stuart, Milne, and Peddie's Scotch Court of Sessions Reports [*A publication*] (DLA) .... Stu Mil & Ped
Stuart Plastics Ltd., New Westminster, British Columbia [*Library symbol National Library of Canada*] (NLC) .... BNWSP
Stuart, VA [*AM radio station call letters*] .... WHEO
Stuart's Lower Canada Appeal Cases [*1810-35*] [*A publication*] (DLA) .... SLC
Stuart's Lower Canada Appeal Cases [*A publication*] (DLA) .... SLC App
Stuart's Lower Canada Appeal Cases [*Quebec*] [*A publication*] (DLA) .... St R
Stuart's Lower Canada King's Bench Reports [*1810-35*] [*A publication*] (DLA) .... Stu KB
Stuart's Lower Canada King's Bench Reports [*1810-35*] [*A publication*] (DLA) .... Stu LC
Stuart's Lower Canada King's Bench Reports [*1810-25*] [*Quebec*] [*A publication*] (DLA) .... Stuart KB
Stuart's Lower Canada King's Bench Reports [*Quebec*] [*A publication*] (DLA) .... Stuart KB (Quebec)
Stuart's Lower Canada King's Bench Reports [*A publication*] (DLA) .... Stuart LCKB
Stuart's Lower Canada King's Bench Reports, Appeal Cases [*A publication*] (DLA) .... Stu Ap
Stuart's Lower Canada King's Bench Reports, Appeal Cases [*Quebec*] [*A publication*] (DLA) .... Stuart's R
Stuart's Lower Canada Reports [*A publication*] (DLA) .... SRC
Stuart's Lower Canada Reports [*A publication*] (DLA) .... Stuart
Stuart's Lower Canada Vice-Admiralty Reports [*A publication*] (DLA) .... Stu Adm
Stuart's Lower Canada Vice-Admiralty Reports [*A publication*] (ILCA) .... Stu VA
Stuart's Lower Canada Vice-Admiralty Reports [*A publication*] (DLA) .... Stuart
Stuart's Lower Canada Vice-Admiralty Reports [*A publication*] (DLA) .... Stuart LCVA
Stuart's Lower Canada Vice-Admiralty Reports [*A publication*] (DLA) .... Stuart Vice-Adm
Stuart's Lower Canada Vice-Admiralty Reports [*A publication*] (DLA) .... Stuart's Adm
Stuart's Lower Canada Vice-Admiralty Reports [*A publication*] (DLA) .... SVAR
Stuart's Lower Canada Vice-Admiralty Reports, New Series [*A publication*] (DLA) .... St Adm NS

Stuart's Lower Canada Vice-Admiralty Reports, New Series [*A publication*] (DLA) ... Stu Adm NS
Stuart's Lower Canada Vice-Admiralty Reports, New Series [*A publication*] (DLA) ... Stuart Adm NS
Stuart's Select Cases [*1860*] [*Bengal, India*] [*A publication*] (DLA) ... Stuart Beng
Stubb's Constitutional History [*A publication*] (DLA) ... Stubbs CH
Stubbs Public Library, Holstein, IA [*Library symbol Library of Congress*] (LCLS) ... IaHol
Stubb's Select Charters [*A publication*] (DLA) ... Stubbs Sel Ch
Stubs Wire Gauge ... SWG
Stucco (VRA) ... stu
Stucco Manufacturers Association (EA) ... SMA
Stuchbery Elementary School, Houston, TX [*Library symbol*] [*Library of Congress*] (LCLS) ... TxHSE
Stud and Girt (DAC) ... S & G
Stud Welding Outfit ... SWO
Stud-Arc Welding ... SW
Studded Panel Fastener (DNAB) ... SPF
Studebaker [*Automotive engineering*] ... STUDE
Studebaker Automobile Club of America (EA) ... SACA
Studebaker Driver's Club (EA) ... SDC
Studebaker-Packard [*Automobile manufacturer*] ... S-P
Studebaker's Resource Development Ltd. [*Formerly, Rio Blanco Resources Ltd.*] [*Vancouver Stock Exchange symbol*] ... SDK
Student ... SDNT
Student ... STDNT
Student (AFM) ... STU
Student ... STUD
Student Access Centre [*Australia*] ... SAC
Student Achievement Monitoring [*Vocational guidance*] ... SAM
Student Action Corps for Animals (EA) ... SACA
Student Action for Education [*Defunct*] (EA) ... SAE
Student Action Voters for Ecology ... SAVE
Student Admission Records Administration (IAA) ... SARA
Student Agitation [*FBI*] ... STAG
Student Aid Index [*Department of Education*] (GFGA) ... SAI
Student Aid Project ... SAP
Student Aid Report [*Department of Education*] ... SAR
Student Air Travel Association ... SATA
Student Alliance for Christian Renewal in America ... SACRA
Student Alternatives to Violence [*Defunct*] (EA) ... SAV
Student American Medical Association [*Later, AMSA*] (EA) ... SAMA
Student American Pharmaceutical Association [*Later, APhA-ASP*] (EA) ... SAPhA
Student Association for the Rights of Students [*Australia*] ... SARS
Student Association for the Study of Hallucinogens [*Defunct*] (EA) ... STASH
Student Association for the Study of Hallucinogens, Madison, WI [*Library symbol Library of Congress*] (LCLS) ... WMaS
Student at Staff College [*Army British*] (ROG) ... SS
Student Book Exchange ... SBX
Student Career Automated Network (IEEE) ... SCAN
Student Census-Date Report File (EDAC) ... STUCENFL
Student Christian Movement [*British*] ... SCM
Student Coalition Against Drug Abuse ... SCADA
Student Coalition for the Right to Drink [*Defunct*] (EA) ... SCRD
Student Coalition for Truth (EA) ... SCT
Student Committee for Economic Education (EA) ... SCEE
Student Committee for the Right to Bear Arms [*Defunct*] (EA) ... SCRBA
Student Competitions on Relevant Engineering ... SCORE
Student Conference on United States Affairs ... SCUSA
Student Conservation Association (EA) ... SCA
Student Contact Book [*A publication*] ... SCB
Student Contact Hours (EDAC) ... SCH
Student Council for Exceptional Children (AEBS) ... SCEC
Student Council on Pollution and the Environment [*Association conceived in late 1969 by then Secretary of the Interior Walter J. Hickel*] ... SCOPE
Student Credit Hours ... SCH
Student Description Form [*Psychology*] ... SDF
Student Description Questionnaire ... SDQ
Student Developmental Task Inventory [*Educational test*] ... SDTI
Student Education Loan Fund [*Minnesota*] ... SELF
Student Education Program ... STEP
Student Eligibility Report (EDAC) ... SER
Student Empowerment Training Project (EA) ... SET
Student Enhancement Program [*Army*] ... SEP
Student Evaluation Scale [*Student attitudes test*] ... SES
Student Expense Program [*Civil Defense*] ... SEP
Student Explorer Demonstration Initiative [*NASA*] ... STEDI
Student Exposition on Energy Resources [*Project*] ... SEER
Student Flight [*Military*] ... STUF
Student Foreign Missions Fellowship [*Later, IVMF*] (EA) ... SFMF
Student Government Information Service (EA) ... SGIS
Student Group [*Military*] ... STUG
Student Guide ... SG
Student Handout [*Military training document*] (INF) ... SH
Student Health (MAE) ... SH
Student Health Organizations [*Defunct*] ... SHO
Student Health Service (DAVI) ... SHS
Student Homelessness Rate [*Australia*] ... SHR
Student Homophile League [*Superseded by Gay People at Columbia*] (EA) ... SHL
Student in Theology [*British*] ... STH
Student Information Record System (AEBS) ... SIRS
Student Instruction Sheet [*Military*] ... SIS
Student Instructional Report [*Test of teacher performance*] ... SIR
Student Insurance Producers Association (EA) ... SIP
Student Intellectual Property Law Association (AAGC) ... SIPLA
Student Interactive Training System ... SITS
Student Interests Quarterly [*A publication*] ... SIQ
Student International Service [*Foundation*] ... SIS
Student Interracial Ministry [*Defunct*] ... SIM
Student Investigator (KSC) ... SI
Student Law Review [*A publication*] (DLA) ... Student L Rev
Student Lawyer Journal [*A publication*] (DLA) ... Student Law J
Student Lesson Sheets ... SLS
Student Letter Exchange (EA) ... SLE
Student Ln Mktg Adj Rt A Pfd [*NYSE symbol*] (TTSB) ... SLMPrA
Student Load ... SL
Student Loan Corp. [*NYSE symbol*] (SPSG) ... STU
Student Loan Corp. [*Associated Press*] (SAG) ... StuLnCp
Student Loan Guaranty Program ... SLGP
Student Loan Insurance Fund [*Department of Health and Human Services*] (GFGA) ... SLIF
Student Loan Marketing [*Associated Press*] (SAG) ... SallieM
Student Loan Marketing Association [*See also SLMA*] ... SALLIE MAE
Student Loan Marketing Association [*Sallie Mae*] [*Associated Press*] (SAG) ... SallM
Student Loan Marketing Association [*NYSE symbol*] (SPSG) ... SLM
Student Loan Marketing Association [*Government-chartered private corporation*] [*Nickname: "Sallie Mae"*] ... SLMA
Student Loan Mktg [*NYSE symbol*] (TTSB) ... SLM
Student Manual [*Civil Defense*] ... SM
Student Medical Technologist (MEDA) ... SMT
Student Member of the Institute of Business and Technical Management [*British*] (DBQ) ... StudInstBTM
Student Member of the Institute of Manufacturing [*British*] (DBQ) ... StudIManf
Student Missions Fellowship [*Later, IVMF*] (EA) ... SMF
Student Mobilization Committee [*to End the War in Vietnam*] [*Defunct*] (EA) ... SMC
Student Monitoring System [*Vocational guidance*] ... SMS
Student National Coordinating Committee [*Pronounced "snick"*] (EA) ... SNCC
Student National Dental Association (EA) ... SNDA
Student National Education Association (EA) ... SNEA
Student National Medical Association (EA) ... SNMA
Student National Podiatric Medical Association (EA) ... SNPMA
Student Naval Aviation Pilot ... SNAP
Student Naval Aviation Pilot (Glider) ... SNAP(G)
Student Naval Aviator ... SNA
Student Naval Flight Officer ... SNFO
Student Naval Flight Surgeon ... SNFS
Student Need Analysis System ... SNAS
Student Nurse ... SN
Student Nurses' Association (DAVI) ... SNA
Student Nursing Assistant Program ... SNAP
Student Occupational Competency Achievement Testing [*Educational test*] ... SOCAT
Student of Codrington College [*Barbados*] ... SCC
Student of the Civil Law ... SCL
Student of the Institute of British Bakers (DBQ) ... SInstBB
Student of the Institute of Management Specialists [*British*] (DBQ) ... StudIMS
Student of the Institute of Petroleum [*British*] (DBQ) ... SInstPet
Student of the Institution of Electrical and Electronic Incorporated Engineers [*British*] (DBQ) ... StudentIElecIE
Student of the Institution of Works and Highways Technician Engineers [*British*] (DBQ) ... StudentIWHTE
Student of the Society of Certified Professionals [*British*] (DBQ) ... StudSCP
Student of the Society of Engineers [*British*] (DBQ) ... StudSE
Student of the Society of Licensed Aircraft Engineers and Technologists [*British*] (DBQ) ... StudSLAET
Student of the Welding Institute [*British*] (DBQ) ... StudWeldI
Student Organization Development (EDAC) ... SOD
Student Organization for Black Unity ... SOBU
Student Organization for Latin America [*University of Notre Dame*] [*Research center*] (RCD) ... SOLA
Student Orientation Assistant ... SOA
Student Orientations Survey [*Student attitudes test*] ... SOS
Student Osteopathic Medical Association (EA) ... SOMA
Student Overseas Flights for Americans ... SOFA
Student Peace Union [*Defunct*] (EA) ... SPU
Student Performance Evaluation Form ... SPEF
Student Personnel Association for Teacher Education [*Later, AHEAD*] (EA) ... SPATE
Student Pilot Disposition (DNAB) ... SPD
Student Pilot's Licence (AIA) ... SPL
Student Potential Life Achievement Test [*Parody of Scholastic Aptitude Test preparation books*] ... SPLAT
Student Practical Nurse (AAMN) ... SPN
Student Press Law Center (EA) ... SPLC
Student Product Assessment Form (EDAC) ... SPAF
Student Proficiency Rating Scale ... SPRS
Student Profile and Assessment Record [*Student attitudes test*] ... SPAR
Student Profile Section [*of the American College Testing Test Battery*] ... SPS
Student Progress Questionnaire (AIE) ... SPQ
Student Project for International Responsibility ... SPIR
Student Pugwash USA [*An association*] (EA) ... SP-USA
Student Reaction to College [*Student attitudes test*] ... SRC
Student Record System [*Australia*] ... SRS
Student Registered Nurse (MAE) ... SRN
Student Religious Liberals [*Later, SRL, A Free Religious Fellowship*] [*Defunct*] ... SRL
Student Response System [*Automated group instruction*] ... SRS
Student Response Unit ... SRU

Student Role Expectation Inventory .... SREI
Student Science Training [Program] [National Science Foundation]
  [Defunct] .... SST
Student Science Training Program [National Science Foundation Defunct].... SSTP
Student Semester Hours (EDAC) .... SSH
Student Ski Association (EA) .... SSA
Student Squadron .... STUS
Student Struggle for Soviet Jewry (EA) .... SSSJ
Student/Supervisor Instructions [Army Training Extension Course] (INF) .... SSI
Student Support and Parent Awareness [Australia] .... SSPA
Student Support Services Program [Department of Education] (GFGA) .... SSS
Student Taskforce Against Telecommunication Information Concealment
  [Student legal action organization] .... STATIC
Student/Teacher Organization to Prevent Nuclear War [Defunct] (EA) .... STOP
Student Teacher Performance Profile .... STPP
Student Teachers' Attitude Questionnaire .... STAQ
Student Teams-Achievement Division (AEE) .... STAD
Student Teams-Achievement Divisions (EDAC) .... STAD
Student Training [Navy] (DNAB) .... STUTNG
Student Transfer Education Plan [National Urban League] [Defunct] .... STEP
Student Travel School .... STS
Student Union .... SU
Student Union Building [Canada] .... SUB
Student Ward Secretary [Hospital administration] (DAVI) .... SWS
Student Woodlawn Area Project [Chicago, IL] .... SWAP
Student Zionist Organization [Defunct] (EA) ...... SZO
Studenta Tutmonda Esperantista Liga [World League of Esperanto-Speaking
  Students] .... STEL
Studentenes og Akademikernes Internasjonale Hjelpefond [Norway] .... SAIH
Student-Faculty Evaluation .... SFE
Student-Newman-Keuls [Statistical procedure] .... SNK
Student-Originated Studies [National Science Foundation] .... SOS
Students Against Driving Drunk (EA) .... SADD
Students Against Famine Everywhere [Defunct] (EA) ...... SAFE
Students Against Faulty Tires Ripping in Pieces [Student legal action
  organization] .... SAFE TRIP
Students Against Fires [International student engineering project for 1972-73
  sponsored by Student Competitions on Relevant Engineering - SCORE] ..... SAF
Students Against Misleading Enterprises [Student legal action
  organization] .... SAME
Students Against Nuclear Suicide [Defunct] (EA) .... SANS
Students Against Violence, Injustice, and Guns .... SAVING
Students Against Volvo Exaggerations [Student legal action organization].... SAVE
Students' and Teachers' Integrated Learning Environment (AIE) .... STILE
Students Army Training Corps .... SATC
Students at Risk [Australia] .... SAR
Students Audio Visual Interface (PDAA) .... SAVI
Students Challenging Regulatory Agency Proceedings [Student legal action
  organization] .... SCRAP
Students Committee on Human Rights .... SCOHR
Students Concerned about Legal Prices [Student legal action
  organization] .... SCALP
Students Concerned with Public Health [Defunct] (EA) .... SCWPH
Student's Confidential Statement [Education] .... SCS
Students for a Democratic Society [Defunct] (EA) .... SDS
Students for a Democratic University [Canada] .... SDU
Students for a Libertarian Society (EA) .... SLS
Students for America (EA) .... SA
Students for America (EA) .... SFA
Students for Data Education (IEEE) .... SDE
Students for Democratic Action .... SDA
Students for Ecological Action .... SEA
Students for Economic Democracy (EA) .... SED
Students for Labeling of Alcoholic Beverages [Student legal action
  organization] .... SLAB
Students for Origins Research (EA) .... SOR
Students for Peace (EA) .... SFP
Students for Promotion of Identity on Campus [New York group promoting
  ethnic pride among Latin American students] .... SPIC
Students for Social Responsibility (EA) .... SSR
Students for the Exploration and Development of Space (EA) .... SEDS
Students for the Right to Bear Arms (EA) .... SRBA
Students Guide to Childcare [British] .... SGC
Students' Health and Welfare Centers Organization .... SHAWCO
Students Hot on Conserving Kilowatts [Student legal action
  organization] .... SHOCK
Students in Free Enterprise (EA) .... SFE
Students in Free Enterprise [Bolivar, MO] (EA) .... SIFE
Students' International Meditation Society .... SIMS
Students' International Travel Association .... SITA
Students League for Industrial Democracy [Later, Students for a Democratic
  Society] .... SLID
Students Litigating Against Injurious Can Edges [Student legal action
  organization] .... SLICE
Students Mobilizing on Auto Safety Hazards [Student legal action
  organization] (EA) .... SMASH
Students Naturally Opposed to Outrageous Prying [Student legal action
  organization] (EA) .... SNOOP
Students Older than Average .... SOTA
Students Opposed to Advertised Pollutants [Student legal action
  organization] .... SOAP
Students Opposed to Unfair Practices [in advertising] [Student legal action
  organization] .... SOUP
Student's Own Record of Education (AIE) .... STORE
Student's Perception of Ability Scale (EDAC) .... SPAS

Students' Pocket Law Lexicon [A publication] (DLA) .... Stud Law Lex
Students Protesting Illegal Real Estate Operators [Student legal action
  organization] (EA) .... SPIRO
Students' Representative Council [British] .... SRC
Students Resisting Aerosol Flurocarbon Emissions [Student legal action
  organization] (EA) .... STRAFE
Students' Series of Historical and Comparative Grammars
  [A publication] .... SSHCG
Students Tackle Ocean Plastics .... STOP
Students Taking Action with Recognition [Kentucky] (EDAC) .... STAR
Students Taught Awareness and Resistance [An association] .... STAR
Students to Observe Retail Establishments [Student legal action
  organization] (EA) .... STORE
Students to Oppose Participation in the National Student Association
  (EA) .... STOP-NSA
Students to Save Baltic and Mediterranean Avenues [Defunct] (EA) .... SSBMA
Students toward Environmental Participation [UNESCO and National Park
  Service] .... STEP
Student's t-Test [Statistical mathematics] .... ST
Students Wildly Indignant about Nearly Everything [Group in "L'il Abner"
  comic strip] .... SWINE
Students with Disabilities .... SwD
Studi di Urbanistica Antica [A publication] (OCD) .... Stud Urb
Studi Etruschi [Firenze] [A publication] (OCD) .... Stud Etr
Studi Italiani di Filologia Classica [A publication] (OCD) .... Stud Ital
Studi Storici per l'Antichita Classica [A publication] (OCD) .... Studi Stor
Studia ad Corpus Hellenisticum Novi Testamenti (BJA) .... SCH
Studia Anselmiana [Rome] [A publication] .... StAns
Studia Biblica et Orientalia [Rome] [A publication] (BJA) .... SBO
Studia Catholica [Nijmegen] [A publication] (BJA) .... StCath
Studia et Documenta ad Iura Orientis Antiqui Pertinenta [Leiden]
  [A publication] (BJA) .... SD
Studia et Documenta Historiae et Iuris [Rome] [A publication]
  (OCD) .... Stud Doc Hist Iur
Studia Fransisci Scholten Memorial Dicata (BJA) .... SFSMD
Studia Rosenthaliana [A publication] (BJA) .... SRo
Studie- en Informatiecentrum TNO voor Milieu-Onderzoek [TNO Study and
  Information Center on Environmental Research] [Information service or
  system] (IID) .... SCMO
Studiecentrum voor Kernenergie [Also, CEEN, NERC] [Center for Nuclear
  Energy Studies] [Belgium] (NRCH) .... SCK
Studiegroup voor Europese Politiek (EA) .... SEP
Studien zur Geschichte und Kultur des Altertums [A publication]
  (OCD) .... Stud Gesch Kult Alt
Studien zur Geschichte und Kultur des Alterums [A publication] (BJA) .... SGKA
Studien zur Palaeographie und Papyruskunde [C. Wessely] [A publication]
  (BJA) .... SPPK
Studiengesellschaft fuer Atomenergie [Implements Austria's nuclear
  program] (NRCH) .... SGAE
Studies .... STUD
Studies, Analysis, and Gaming Agency [Military] .... SAGA
Studies and Expansion Society [See also SEE] (EAIO) .... SES
Studies and Observations Group [Military] .... SOG
Studies in Ancient Technology [A publication] (OCD) .... Stud Anc Technol
Studies in Continuing Education [A publication] .... Stud Cont Ed
Studies in Criminal Law and Procedure [A publication] (DLA) .... Studies Crim L
Studies in Greek and Roman History [A publication] (OCD) .... Stud Gr Rom Hist
Studies in History, Economics, and Public Law [A publication] (DLA) .... Stud Hist
Studies in Law and Economic Development [A publication]
  (DLA) .... Stud L & Econ Dev
Studies in Old Testament Prophecy Presented to T. H. Robinson
  [A publication] (BJA) .... StOTPr
Studies in Philosophy and Education [A publication] (AEBS) .... SPE
Studies in Process [Jet Propulsion Laboratory, NASA] .... SIP
Studies in Short Fiction [A publication] (BRI) .... SSF
Studies in the Decorative Arts [A publication] (BRI) .... SDA
Studies in the History of Christian Thought [A publication] (BJA) .... SHCT
Studies in the Political Economy of Canada [Society] .... SPEC
Studies in Theology [A publication] .... ST
Studies in Western Australian History [A publication] .... Stud W Aust Hist
Studies in Western Australian History [A publication] .... SWAH
Studies of Coastal and Estuarine Environments [National Oceanic and
  Atmospheric Administration] (MSC) .... SCENE
Studies of Left Ventricular Dysfunction [National Heart, Lung, and Blood
  Institute] .... SOLVD
Studies of Ocean Upper Layers (MSC) .... SOUL
Studies on East Asia Tectonics and Resources [Marine science]
  (MSC) .... SEATAR
Studies on International Fiscal Law [A publication] (DLA) .... Stud Int'l Fiscal L
Studies on Smoking, Inc. [Research center] (RCD) .... SOS
Studies on the Texts of the Desert of Judah [J. Van Der Ploeg] [Leiden]
  [A publication] (BJA) .... StTDJ
Studii Biblici Franciscani. Liber Annuus [A publication] (BJA) .... SBFLA
Studio .... STD
Studio Address (WDMC) .... SA
Studio Address (WDMC) .... SA
Studio Collector's Club (EA) .... SCC
Studio Lighting Equipment .... SLE
Studio Location .... SL
Studio Plus Hotels [NASDAQ symbol] (TTSB) .... SPHI
Studio Plus Hotels, Inc. [NASDAQ symbol] (SAG) .... SPHI
Studio Plus Hotels, Inc. [Associated Press] (SAG) .... StudioP
Studio Plus Hotels, Inc. [Associated Press] (SAG) .... StudioPH
Studio Reference Disc [Prosonus] [Electronic music] .... SRD
Studio SM [Record label] [France] .... SM

Studio Suppliers Association (EA) .... SSA
Studio to Transmitter (IAA) .... ST
Studio-to-Headend Link [*Transmitter site relay*] (NTCM) .... SHL
Studio-Transmitter Link .... STL
Studio-Transmitter Link-Television .... STLT
Studium Franciscain de Theologie, Montreal, PQ, Canada [*Library symbol Library of Congress*] (LCLS) .... CaQMFran
Studium Franciscain de Theologie, Montreal, Quebec [*Library symbol National Library of Canada*] (NLC) .... QMFRAN
Studium Spraw Polskich (Wielka Brytania) [*Information Centre for Polish Affairs*] (EAIO) .... SSPWB
Study (VRA) .... sdy
Study .... STUD
Study Advisory Committee on Aeronautics [*National Academy of Engineering*] .... SACA
Study Advisory Group [*Army*] .... SAG
Study and Action Course in District Management [*LIMRA*] .... SACDM
Study and Analysis Center (AAGC) .... S & A
Study and Performance Efficiency in Entry Design .... SPEED
Study and Review [*Reports*] (RDA) .... SAR
Study Attitudes and Methods Survey [*Study skills test*] .... SAMS
Study Behavior Inventory (EDAC) .... SBI
Study Centre for Christian-Jewish Relations [*Roman Catholic Church*] [*British*] (CB) .... CJR
Study Circles Resource Center (EA) .... SCRC
Study Commission on Ocean Data Stations [*Marine science*] (MSC) .... SCODS
Study Committee on Analysis of Research, Development, and Engineering .... SCARDE
Study Course in Agency Management [*LIMRA*] .... SCAM
Study Director (MCD) .... SD
Study Group [*NATO*] .... STG
Study Group for Mathematical Learning (EA) .... SGML
Study Group on Environmental Monitoring [*National Research Council*] .... SGEM
Study Group on Labor and Working Class History (EA) .... SGLWCH
Study Group on Legal Aspects of Intermodal Transportation [*National Research Council*] .... SLAIT
Study Group on Social Security [*Defunct*] (EA) .... SGSS
Study Item Number [*Army*] (AABC) .... SIN
Study of Accreditation of Selected Health Educational Programs .... SASHEP
Study of American Markets [*US News and World Report*] .... SAM
Study of Appeal Tribunals [*British*] .... SAT
Study of Army Test and Evaluation (MCD) .... SATE
Study of Automation of the Logistic System [*Military*] .... STALOG
Study of Cataloguing Computer Software (AIE) .... SoCCS
Study of Children's Learning Styles (EDAC) .... SCLS
Study of Computer Cataloguing Software (NITA) .... SOCCS
Study of Critical Environmental Problems [*MIT*] .... SCEP
Study of Education at Stanford [*Stanford University*] .... SES
Study of Energy Release in Flares [*International Council of Scientific Unions*] .... SERF
Study of Environmental Quality Information Programs (KSC) .... SEQUIP
Study of Lunar Orbiter Photographic Evaluation (MCD) .... SLOPE
Study of Management Information Systems Support [*Army*] .... SOMISS
Study of Man's Impact on Climate .... SMIC
Study of Mathematically Precocious Youth (EDAC) .... SMPY
Study of Media & Markets [*Simmons Market Research Bureau, Inc.*] [*Information service or system*] (CRD) .... SMM
Study of One-Atmosphere Manned Underwater Structures .... SOAMUS
[*A*] **Study of Schooling** (EDAC) .... ASOS
Study of Tactical Airborne RADAR System .... STARS
Study of the Enhanced Radiation Belt [*NASA*] .... SERB
Study of Travelling Interplanetary Phenomena [*Meteorology*] .... STIP
Study of Utilization Systems, Policies, and Techniques (MCD) .... SUNSPOT
Study of Values .... SOV
Study of Values [*Psychology*] .... SV
Study of Values: British Edition [*Psychology*] .... SV:B
Study of Western Palestine: Jerusalem [*C. Warren and C. R. Conder*] [*A publication*] (BJA) .... SWPJ
Study on Sea-Air Exchanges [*USA*] [*Marine science*] (OSRA) .... SEAREX
Study on Surgical Services in the United States [*Medicine*] .... SOSSUS
Study on the Efficacy of Nosocomial Infection Control (MEDA) .... SENIC
Study Organization Plan (BUR) .... SOP
Study Plan .... SP
Study Planning and Coordinating Committee [*Army*] .... SPCC
Study Planning Guide (MCD) .... SPG
Study Reference List (AFM) .... SRL
Study Regulation (MCD) .... SR
Study Requirement [*Air Force*] .... SR
Study Skills Counseling Evaluation Reading (AEBS) .... SSCE
Study Skills Surveys [*Educational test*] .... SSS
Study Skills Unit (AIE) .... SSU
Study Techniques for Advanced RADAR Requirements .... STARR
Study to Align AMC [*Now DAR COM*] **Functions** (MCD) .... STAAF
Study to Assess and Validate Essential Reports [*Military*] (AABC) .... SAVER
Study to Understand Prognoses and Preferences for Outcomes and Risks of Treatments .... SUPPORT
Study With a Teacher Program [*Ohio*] (EDAC) .... SWAT
Stuff .... STFF
Stuffed Indirect Reference Word [*Computer science*] (MHDI) .... SIRW
Stuffed Toy Manufacturers Association .... STMA
Stuffing (MSA) .... STFG
Stuffing Box .... SB
Stumped [*Cricket*] .... ST
Stumped (WGA) .... STPD
Stumper [*Freight*] .... STPR
Stump-Tailed Macaque Virus (PDAA) .... STMV
Stumpwork Society (EA) .... SS
Stung [*by bees*] [*Medicine*] .... S
Stung Treng [*Cambodia*] [*ICAO location identifier*] (ICLI) .... VDST
Stunt Women of America [*Later, SAMP*] (EA) .... SWA
Stuntmen's Association of Motion Pictures (EA) .... SAMP
Stunts Unlimited (EA) .... SU
Stuntwomen's Association of Motion Pictures (EA) .... SAMP
Stupid Error Message [*Computer science*] .... SEM
Sturctural Analysis via Generalized Interactive Graphics (PDAA) .... STAGING
Sturgate [*British ICAO location identifier*] (ICLI) .... EGCS
Sturge-Kalische-Weber [*Syndrome*] [*or Sturge-Weber Syndrome*] [*Medicine*] (DAVI) .... SKW
Sturgeon. Bankrupt Acts [*A publication*] (ILCA) .... Sturg BL
Sturgeon Bay, WI [*Location identifier FAA*] (FAAL) .... EDH
Sturgeon Bay, WI [*Location identifier FAA*] (FAAL) III
Sturgeon Bay, WI [*Location identifier FAA*] (FAAL) .... SUE
Sturgeon Bay, WI [*AM radio station call letters*] .... WDOR
Sturgeon Bay, WI [*FM radio station call letters*] .... WDOR-FM
Sturgeon Bay, WI [*FM radio station call letters*] .... WGEE
Sturgeon Bay, WI [*FM radio station call letters*] .... WPFF
Sturgeon Bay, WI [*FM radio station call letters*] (RBYB) .... WSRG
Sturgeon Falls Branch of the Algonquin Regional Library System, Ontario [*Library symbol National Library of Canada*] (NLC) .... OSFAR
Sturgeon Falls, ON [*Television station call letters*] CBLFT-1
Sturgeon Falls Public Library, Sturgeon Falls, ON, Canada [*Library symbol Library of Congress*] (LCLS) .... CaOStu
Sturgeon's Insolvent Debtors Act [*1842*] [*A publication*] (DLA) .... Sturg Ins D
Sturge-Weber Foundation (EA) .... SWF
Sturge-Weber Syndrome [*Medicine*] (DAVI) .... SWS
Sturgis, KY [*Location identifier FAA*] (FAAL) .... TWT
Sturgis, MI [*Location identifier FAA*] (FAAL) .... IRS
Sturgis, MI [*AM radio station call letters*] .... WMSH
Sturgis, MI [*FM radio station call letters*] .... WMSH-FM
Sturgis Public Library, Sturgis, MI [*Library symbol Library of Congress*] (LCLS) .... MiStu
Sturgis Public Library, Sturgis, SD [*Library symbol Library of Congress*] (LCLS) .... SdSt
Sturgis, SD [*AM radio station call letters*] .... KBHB
Sturgis, SD [*FM radio station call letters*] .... KRCS
Sturm Ruger [*NYSE symbol*] (TTSB) .... RGR
Sturm Ruger & Co. [*NYSE symbol*] (SPSG) .... RGR
Sturm Ruger & Co. [*Associated Press*] (SAG) .... SturmR
Sturmabteilung [*German Political party*] (PPE) .... SA
Sturmgeschuetz [*Self-propelled assault gun*] [*German military - World War II*] .... STUG
Sturmgewehr [*Storm Rifle*] [*German military - World War II*] .... STG
Sturminster [*England*] .... STURM
Sturmkanone [*Self-propelled assault gun*] [*German military - World War II*] .... STK
Sturmkanone [*Self-propelled assault gun*] [*German military - World War II*] .... STUK
Sturtevant, WI [*FM radio station call letters*] .... WZXA
Sturzkampfflugzeug [*Dive bomber*] [*German military - World War II*] .... STUKA
Sturzkampfgeschwader [*Dive-bomber wing*] [*German military - World War II*] .... STKG
Stuttering Prediction Instruction [*Speech and language therapy*] (DAVI) .... SPI
Stuttering Severity Index [*Speech and language therapy*] (DAVI) .... SSI
Stuttgart [*Germany ICAO location identifier*] (ICLI) .... EDDS
Stuttgart [*Germany Airport symbol*] (OAG) .... STR
Stuttgart [*Federal Republic of Germany*] [*Seismograph station code, US Geological Survey*] (SEIS) .... STU
Stuttgart, AR [*AM radio station call letters*] .... KWAK
Stuttgart, AR [*FM radio station call letters*] .... KWAK-FM
Stuttgart, AR [*Location identifier FAA*] (FAAL) .... SGT
Stuttgarter Bibelstudien. Katholisches Bibelwerk [*Stuttgart*] [*A publication*] (BJA) .... SBS
STV Group [*NASDAQ symbol*] (TTSB) .... STVI
STV Group, Inc. [*Associated Press*] (SAG) .... STV
STV Group, Inc. [*NASDAQ symbol*] (SAG) .... STVI
STwo Golf, Inc. [*NASDAQ symbol*] (SAG) .... GOLF
STwo Golf, Inc. [*Associated Press*] (SAG) .... S2 Glf
Stykkisholmur [*Iceland*] [*ICAO location identifier*] (ICLI) .... BIST
Stykkisholmur [*Iceland*] [*Airport symbol*] (OAG) .... SYK
Style .... STYL
Style Manual for Biological Journals .... SMBJ
Style of Learning and Thinking [*Occupational therapy*] .... SOLAT
Style of Mind Inventory [*Psychology*] .... SMI
Style Sac .... SS
Style Sac Artery .... SSA
Style Sac Flap .... SSF
Style's English King's Bench Reports [*1646-55*] [*A publication*] (DLA) .... Mod
Style's English King's Bench Reports [*1646-55*] [*A publication*] (DLA) .... Mod Rep
Style's English King's Bench Reports [*1646-55*] [*A publication*] (DLA) .... Sty
Style's English King's Bench Reports [*A publication*] (DLA) .... Style
Styles of Leadership Survey [*Test*] .... SLS
Styles of Management Inventory [*Test*] .... SMI
Styles on Video [*AMEX symbol*] (TTSB) .... SOV
Styles on Video, Inc. [*AMEX symbol*] (SPSG) .... SOV
Styles On Video, Inc. [*Associated Press*] (SAG) .... StyleVid
Style's Practical Register [*England*] [*A publication*] (DLA) .... St Pr Reg
Style's Practical Register [*1657-1710*] [*A publication*] (DLA) .... Sty Pr Reg
Style's Practical Register [*A publication*] (DLA) .... Style Pr Reg
Styling .... STYLG
Styling Data Handling .... SDH
Styling Research Vehicle [*Automotive engineering*] .... SRV
Stylist .... STYLST

Stylomastoid Artery [*Anatomy*] ... SMA
Stylus (VRA) ... sty
Styptic [*Stopping Bleeding*] [*Medicine*] (ROG) ... STYP
Styrelsen foer Teknisk Utveckling [*Swedish Board for Technical Development*] ... STU
Styrelserepresentationsutredningen [*Sweden*] ... STRU
Styrene [*Also, Sty*] [*Organic chemistry*] ... St
Styrene [*Also, St*] [*Organic chemistry*] ... Sty
Styrene/Allyl Glycidyl Ether [*Organic chemistry*] ... SAGE
Styrene and Ethylbenzene Association (EA) ... SEA
Styrene Block Copolymer [*Plastics technology*] ... SBC
Styrene Butadiene [*Organic chemistry*] ... SB
Styrene Butadiene Latex Manufacturers Council (EA) ... SBLMC
Styrene Information and Research Center (EA) ... SIRC
Styrene Maleic Acid Neocarzinostatin [*Antineoplastic drug*] ... SMANCS
Styrene Methylstyrene [*Organic chemistry*] ... SMS
Styrene Rubber ... SR
Styrene Rubber Butadiene (NG) ... SRB
Styrene-Acrylonitrile [*Also, SAN*] [*Organic chemistry*] ... SA
Styrene-Acrylonitrile [*Also, SA*] [*Organic chemistry*] ... SAN
Styrene-Butadiene Latexes [*Organic chemistry*] ... SBL
Styrene-Butadiene Rubber [*Also, GR-S*] [*Synthetic rubber*] ... SBR
Styrene-Butadiene-Styrene [*Copolymer*] ... SBS
Styrene-Divinylbenzene [*Organic chemistry*] ... S-DVB
Styrene-Isoprene Rubber ... SIR
Styrene-Isoprene-Butadiene Rubber [*Materials science*] ... SIBR
Styrene-Isoprene-Styrene [*Organic chemistry*] ... SIS
Styrene-Maleic Anhydride [*Organic chemistry*] ... SMA
Su Cuenta [*Your Account*] [*Business term Spanish*] ... SC
Su Favor [*Your Favor*] [*Spanish*] ... SF
Su Giro [*Your Draft*] [*Spanish Business term*] ... S/G
Su Remesa [*Your Remittance*] [*Spanish Business term*] ... SR
Sua Eccellenza Reverendissima [*His Eminence*] (EY) ... SER
Suai [*East Timor*] [*ICAO location identifier*] (ICLI) ... WPDB
Suao [*Republic of China*] [*Seismograph station code, US Geological Survey*] (SEIS) ... TWC
Suasoriae [*of Seneca the Elder*] [*Classical studies*] (OCD) ... Suas
Sub Anno [*Under the Year*] [*Latin*] ... SA
Sub BIT [*Binary Digit*] **Encoder** (MCD) ... SBE
Sub Board of Inspection and Survey of Atlantic and Pacific [*Navy*] (ANA) ... SUBINSURV (LANT) (PAC)
Sub Branch [*Banking*] ... SB
Sub Carrier Demodulation, Automatic (PDAA) ... SCDAuto
Sub Center Visibility (MCD) ... SCV
Sub Clutter Visibility ... SCV
Sub Critical Carbon-Moderated Reactor Assembly for Plutonium Investigations [*British*] (NUCP) ... SCORPIO
Sub Finem [*Near the End*] [*Latin*] ... SF
Sub Finem Coctionis [*When the Boiling Is Nearly Finished*] (ROG) ... SUBFIN COCT
Sub Hoc Voce [*or Sub Hoc Verbo*] [*Under This Word*] [*Latin*] ... SHV
Sub Initio [*At the Beginning*] [*Latin*] (ROG) ... S IN
Sub Initio [*At the Beginning*] [*Latin*] ... Sub Init
Sub Judice [*Under Consideration*] [*Latin*] ... SJ
Sub Nanosecond (IAA) ... SN
Sub Nomine [*Under the Name*] [*Latin*] (DLA) ... sub nom
Sub Petito Remissionis [*With Request for Return*] [*Latin*] ... SPR
Sub Postmaster [*British*] (DCTA) ... SPMR
Sub Signo Veneni [*Under a Poison Label*] [*Pharmacy*] ... SSV
Sub Tuner (IAA) ... ST
Sub Verbo [*or Sub Voce*] [*Under the Word*] [*Latin*] ... SV
Sub Vi [*Under Compulsion*] [*Latin*] ... sv
Sub Vocibus [*Latin*] ... svv
Subaccount (NASA) ... SA
Subacoustic Warfare System ... SAWS
Subacute [*Medicine*] (DMAA) ... Subac
Subacute Bacterial Endocarditis [*Medicine*] ... SBE
Subacute Bacterial Peritonitis (DAVI) ... SBP
Subacute Combined Degeneration [*of spinal cord*] [*Medicine*] (AAMN) ... SACD
Subacute Combined Degeneration [*of spinal cord*] [*Medicine*] ... SCD
Subacute Cutaneous Lupus Erythematosus [*Medicine*] ... SCLE
Subacute Hepatic Necrosis [*Medicine*] (DMAA) ... SHN
Subacute Hepatitis with Bridging [*Medicine*] ... SHB
Subacute Hepatitis with Multilobular Necrosis [*Medicine*] ... SHMN
Subacute Infectious Arthritis [*Medicine*] (DMAA) ... SIA
Subacute Myeloid Leukemia [*Oncology*] ... SML
Subacute Myelo-Optic Neuropathy [*Medicine*] ... SMON
Subacute Necrotizing Encephalomyelopathy [*Medicine*] ... SNE
Subacute Sclerosing Leukoencephalitis [*Medicine*] ... SSLE
Subacute Sclerosing Panencephalitis [*Medicine*] (DAVI) ... SSP
Subacute Sclerosing Panencephalitis [*Medicine*] ... SSPE
Subacute Spongiform Virus Encephalopathies [*Medicine*] ... SSVE
Subacute Thyroiditis [*Medicine*] ... SAT
Subaddressing [*Telecommunications*] (DOM) ... SUB
Subaltern ... SUB
Subangular Blocky Soil [*Agriculture*] ... sbk
Subantarctic Mode Water [*Marine science*] (OSRA) ... SAMW
Sub-Antarctic Surface Water [*Marine science*] (MSC) ... SAASW
Subantarctic Water ... SAW
Subaortic Stenosis [*Medicine*] (DMAA) ... SAS
Subaortic Stenosis [*Medicine*] (MAE) ... SS
Sub-Aqua Association [*British*] (DBA) ... SAA
Subaqueous Sound Ranging (IAA) ... SASR
Subaqueous Sound Ranging Development Installation (IAA) ... SASRDI
Subarachnoid [*Medicine*] ... SA
Subarachnoid Bleed [*Neurology*] (DAVI) ... SAB
Subarachnoid Block [*Medicine*] (MAE) ... SAB
Subarachnoid Hemorrhage [*Medicine*] ... SAH
Subarchitectural Interface ... SAI
Subarea Advisory Council [*Generic term*] (DHSM) ... SAC
Subarea Petroleum Office [*Military*] ... SAPO
Subarea Petroleum Office, Vietnam [*Military*] ... SAPOV
Subarea Routing Manager (IAA) ... SRM
Subarray Beam Former [*Computer science*] (MHDI) ... SABF
Subarray Electronics Module [*Computer science*] ... SEM
Subaru-Isuzu Automotive ... SIA
Subassembly ... SA
Subassembly ... SUBASSY
Subassembly Precision (MCD) ... SAP
Subassembly Repairable Unit (MCD) ... SRU
Subassembly Template (MCD) ... SAT
Subaud [*Understand*] [*Latin*] ... SUB
Subauroral Red [*Arc*] [*Geophysics*] ... SAR
Subauroral Red Arc [*Geophysics*] ... SARARC
Subbit Error Rate ... SBER
Subbituminous ... SB
Subcable (KSC) ... S/C
Subcaliber ... SUBCAL
Subcaliber Aircraft Rocket ... SCAR
Subcaliber Rocket Trainer [*Army*] (INF) ... SRT
Subcaliber Tracer Bullet Trainer [*Army*] (INF) ... STBT
Subcaliber Training Device [*Military*] (AABC) ... SCTD
Subcarrier (AAG) ... S/C
Subcarrier Amplitude Modulation (IAA) ... SCAM
Subcarrier Authorization (MSA) ... SCA
Subcarrier Channel [*Telecommunications*] ... SCA
Sub-Carrier Channels (NITA) ... SCC
Subcarrier Delay Unit ... SDU
Subcarrier Demodulator Assembly [*Deep Space Instrumentation Facility, NASA*] ... SDA
Subcarrier Discriminator ... SCD
Subcarrier Frequency Modulation [*Telecommunications*] (TEL) ... SCFM
Subcarrier Frequency Shift (IAA) ... SCFS
Subcarrier Oscillator ... SCO
Subcarrier Oscillator (IDOE) ... sco
Subcarrier Oscillator Rack ... SOR
Subcell Address Register [*Computer science*] (MHDB) ... SCAR
Subchannel (IAA) ... SC
Subchannel Adapter ... SCA
Subchannel Data Distributor (KSC) ... SDD
Subchapter (DNAB) ... SUBCH
Sub-Chief Ranger [*Ancient Order of Foresters*] ... SCR
Subchorionic Fibrin [*Obstetrics*] ... SCF
Subclavian [*Anatomy*] ... SC
Subclavian Artery [*Medicine*] (DMAA) ... SCA
Subclavian Intravenous Injection [*Medicine*] ... SCIV
Subclavian Vein [*Anatomy*] ... SCLV
Subclavian Vein [*Cardiology*] ... SV
Subclavian Vein Thrombosis [*Medicine*] (DMAA) ... SVT
Subcommand Data Management Office [*Military*] (AFIT) ... SDMO
Subcommission for Tectonic Maps of the Commission for the Geological Map of the World (EAIO) ... STMCGMW
Subcommissural Organ [*Neuroanatomy*] ... SCO
Subcommittee ... SC
Subcommittee (DLA) ... Sub
Subcommittee ... SUBCOM
Subcommittee on Accreditation of the American Association of Blood Banks (DAVI) ... SAAABB
Subcommittee on Chemical Abstracts Service [*American Chemical Society*] ... SOCAS
Subcommittee on Department Operations, Research, and Foreign Agriculture [*Congress*] ... DORFA
Subcommittee on Frequency Allocations ... SFA
Subcommittee on Interzonal Trade [*Allied German Occupation Forces*] ... SCIT
Subcommittee on Programming Technology (NITA) ... SCOPT
Subcommittee on Use of Radioactivity Standards [*National Research Council*] ... SOURS
Subcommutator Identification [*NASA*] ... SCID
Subcompact [*Car size*] ... S
Subconjunctival [*Ophthalmology*] (DAVI) ... subconj
Sub-Continental Lithospheric Mantle ... SCLM
Subcontract ... S/C
Subcontract Agreement (MCD) ... SA
Subcontract Authorization (AAG) ... SCA
Subcontract Change Authorization (AAG) ... SCCA
Subcontract [*or Subcontractor*] **Change Notice** (KSC) ... SCCN
Subcontract Consignment Order ... SCO
Subcontract Data Requirement ... SDR
Subcontract Deviation ... SCD
Subcontract Engineers (MCD) ... SE
Subcontract Item Definition ... SID
Subcontract Management Team [*NASA*] (SSD) ... SCMT
Subcontract Material Availability Schedule ... SMAS
Subcontract Material Sales Order ... SMSO
Subcontract Plans Committee ... SPC
Subcontract Proposal (AAG) ... SCP
Subcontract Schedule and Procurement Request ... SSPR
Subcontract Task Group Procurement ... STGP
Subcontract Work Breakdown Structure (MCD) ... SWBS
Subcontractor (NATG) ... SC
Subcontractor (SAA) ... SCR

Subcontractor (WGA) .... SUB
Subcontractor Bid Document (MCD) .... SBD
Subcontractor Change Request (MCD) .... SCCR
Subcontractor Critical Design Review [NASA] .... SCDR
Subcontractor Data .... SD
Subcontractor Data Item .... SDI
Subcontractor Data Requirements List (DNAB) .... SCDRL
Subcontractor Data Requirements List .... SDRL
Subcontractor Data Status Reporting System (MCD) .... SDSRS
Subcontractor Engineering Change Proposal (MCD) .... SECP
Subcontractor Engineering Memorandum (MCD) .... SEM
Subcontractor Furnished [NASA] (NASA) .... SF
Subcontractor Information Request .... SIR
Subcontractor Interceptor Transporter/Loader Intermediate Level Maintenance Course .... SITLILM
Subcontractor Organizational Intermediate Level Maintenance (NASA) .... SOITLM
Subcontractor Performance Review [NASA] (NASA) .... SPR
Subcontractor Statement of Work (MCD) .... SSOW
Subcontractor's Data Catalog (MCD) .... SDC
Subcorneal [Ophthalmology] (AAMN) .... SC
Subcorneal Pustular Dermatosis [Sneddon-Wilkinson disease] [Dermatology] .... SPD
Subcortical Arteriosclerotic Encephalopathy [Medicine] .... SAE
Subcortical White Matter [Medicine] (DMAA) .... SCWM
Subcostal Right Ventricle Outflow View [Medicine] (DMAA) .... SCOT
Subcours .... SC
Subcrepitant [Medicine] .... subcrep
Subcritical Assembly (DEN) .... SCA
Subcritical Carbon-Moderated Reactor Assembly for Plutonium Investigations (MCD) .... SCORPI
Subcritical Experiment [Nuclear energy] .... SE
Subcritical Fluid Chromatography .... SFC
Subcutaneous [Pharmacology] (DAVI) .... S
Subcutaneous [Beneath the Skin] [Medicine] .... SC
Subcutaneous [Beneath the Skin] [Medicine] .... SQ
Subcutaneous [Beneath the Skin] [Medicine] .... SUB Q
Subcutaneous [Beneath the Skin] [Medicine] .... SUBCU
Subcutaneous [Beneath the Skin] [Medicine] .... subcut
Subcutaneous Abdominal [Block] [Anesthesiology] (DAVI) .... SCA
Subcutaneous Fat Class .... FC
Subcutaneous Histamine Test [Medicine] (MAE) .... SHT
Subcutaneous Intravenous [Medicine] (DMAA) .... SCIV
Subcutaneous Lupus Erythematosus [Medicine] (DAVI) .... SCLE
Subcutaneous Nerve Stimulation [For treatment of pain] .... SCNS
Subcutaneous Peritoneal Access Device [Nephrology] (DAVI) .... SPAD
Subcutaneous Vaginal [Block] [Anesthesiology] (DAVI) .... SCV
Subcuticular [Medicine] (DAVI) .... subcu
Subcuticular [Medicine] (DAVI) .... Sub-Q
Subdeacon .... SDN
Subdistrict Headquarters Induction and Recruiting Station [Navy] .... SDHIRS
Subdivision (DLA) .... Subd
Subdivision and Map Plotting System (MHDB) .... SAMPS
Subdivision Flag [Navy British] .... SV
Subdivision Manager .... SDM
Subdivision of Work [NASA] (NASA) .... SOW
Subdivision of Work Authorization Document [NASA] (NASA) .... SWAD
Subdrift (IAA) .... SUB
Subduction Zone [Geology] .... SZ
Subdural [Anatomy] .... SD
Subdural Empyema [Medicine] (DMAA) .... SDE
Subdural Hematoma [Medicine] .... SDH
Subeditor .... SUB
Subendocardial Myocardial Infarction [Cardiology] (MAE) .... SEMI
Subendocardial Myocardial Injury [Cardiology] (MAE) .... SEMI
Subendothelial Space [Medicine] (DMAA) .... SES
Subependymal Giant Cell Astrocytoma [Medicine] (DMAA) .... SGCA
Subependymal Hemorrhage [Medicine] .... SEH
Suberin Lamella [Botany] .... SL
Subesophageal Ganglion [Anatomy] .... SEG
Subfile (NITA) .... SF
Subfloor (BARN) .... sub
Subfornical Organ [Brain anatomy] .... SFO
Subframe .... SF
Sub-Functional Code (DNAB) .... SFC
Subgeneric (WDAA) .... S-G
Subgenual Organ [Entomology] .... SGO
Subgenus (WDAA) .... S-G
Subgenus .... subg
Subgenus .... SUBGEN
Subglottic Foreign Body [Medicine] (DMAA) .... SFG
Subgroup Modern Terminal .... SGMT
Sub-Group of Experts on Marine Pollution Monitoring [Marine science] (MSC) .... MARPOLMON
Subgroup on Assessment of Weapons [NATO] (NATG) .... SGAW
Subgroup on Nuclear Export Coordination [Nuclear Regulatory Commission] (GFGA) .... SNEC
Subharmonic (IAA) .... SH
Subharmonic Parametic Oscillator (IAA) .... SHPO
Subhuman Primate Model [Medicine] (DMAA) .... SPM
Subic Bay [Philippines] [Seismograph station code, US Geological Survey Closed] (SEIS) .... SBP
Subic Bay Freeport .... SBF
Subic Bay Metropolitan Authority [Philippines] .... SBMA
Subic Bay News [A publication] (DNAB) .... SBN
Sub-Interface Generator (NITA) .... SIG

Subionospheric Latitude .... SILAT
Subionospheric Longitude .... SILON
Subito [Immediately; Suddenly] [Music] .... S
Subject [Psychology] .... S
Subject [of a proposition in logic] .... S
Subject [of an Experiment] (DAVI) .... S
Subject [Online database field identifier] .... SU
Subject .... SUB
Subject (AFM) .... SUBJ
Subject Access Project .... SAP
Subject Activity Monitor [Device used in biological research] .... SAM
Subject Analysis Systems Collection [University of Toronto] [Information service or system] (IID) .... SASC
Subject as Above [Military] (AABC) .... SAB
Subject Authority Cooperative Program [American Library Association] .... SACO
Subject Authority File, Washington, DC [UTLAS symbol] .... SAF
Subject Authority List [NASA] .... SAL
Subject Classification [Library science] .... SC
Subject Code (NITA) .... SC
Subject Codes for Intelligence Management (MCD) .... SCIM
Subject Directory of Special Libraries and Information Centers [A publication] .... SDSL
Subject Guide to Books in Print [A publication] .... SGBIP
Subject Heading (NITA) .... SH
Subject Heading Authority List [Computer science] .... SHAL
Subject Heading Authority Unit (NITA) .... SHAU
Subject Heading Language [Classification and indexing] [Association for Library Collections and Technical Services] .... SHL
Subject Headings for Engineering [A publication] .... SHE
Subject Headings Used in the Dictionary Catalog [Later, LCSH] [A publication] .... SHDC
Subject Identification Module [NASA] .... SID
Subject Index to Sources of Comparative International Statistics [A publication] .... SISCIS
Subject Indication Number .... SIN
Subject Interface Box (KSC) .... SIB
Subject Issue .... S/I
Subject Matter Area (AFM) .... SMA
Subject Matter Expert (NVT) .... SME
Subject Matter Specialist .... SMS
Subject Matter Trainer (SAA) .... SMT
Subject Name (NITA) .... SN
Subject Named Member (NVT) .... SNM
Subject Profile Index [Computer-based] .... SPINDEX
Subject Ratio .... SR
Subject Specialists Section [Association of College and Research Libraries] .... SSS
Subject Standardized Test .... SST
Subject Summary Table File [US Census Bureau] .... SSTF
Subject To [ICAO designator] (FAAC) .... SUBJ
Subject to Approval .... SA
Subject to Approval No Risk .... SANR
Subject to Correction (DNAB) .... SUBCOR
Subject to Finance (ADA) .... STF
Subject to Mortgage (ADA) .... STM
Subject to No Known or Reported Losses [Insurance] (AIA) .... SNKORL
Subject to Non-Renewal [Advertising] (DOAD) .... SNR
Subject to Particular Average [Insurance] .... SPA
Subject to Permission to Deal [Finance] (WDAA) .... SPD
Subject to the Availability of Funds (MCD) .... SAF
Subject Travel Was Necessary at This Time and Time Consumed in Administrative Channels Prevented Written Orders Being Issued .... TRAVNEC
Subject Word (NITA) .... SW
Subject Word out of Context [Computer science] (DIT) .... SWOC
Subject-Content-Oriented Retriever for Processing Information On-Line [Congressional Research Service] .... SCORPIO
Subject-Field Reference Code (ADA) .... SRC
Subjective [findings] (DAVI) .... S
Subjective (ROG) .... SUBJ
Subjective Expected Utility [Concept] [Theory used for decision making] .... SEU
Subjective, Objective, Assessment, and Plan [Medicine] .... SOAP
Subjective, Objective, Assessment, Plan, Implementation, and Evaluation [Medicine] (DMAA) .... SOAPIE
Subjective Optical Vertical .... SOV
Subjective Posttraumatic Syndrome [Medicine] (DMAA) .... SPTS
Subjective Probability Distribution .... SPD
Subjective Quality Factor (OA) .... SQF
Subjective Scale Value .... SSV
Subjective Stress Scale .... SSS
Subjective Transfer Function (MCD) .... STF
Subjective Units of Disturbance .... SUDS
Subjective Vertical [Neurology] .... SV
Subjective Weakness [Medicine] .... SW
Subjective Well-Being [Psychology] .... SWB
Subject-Predicate .... SP
Subject's Treatment Emergent Symptom Scale [Medicine] (DMAA) .... STESS
Subject-Subject [Education of the hearing-impaired] .... SS
Subject-Verb [Education of the hearing-impaired] .... SV
Subject-Verb-Object [Education of the hearing-impaired] .... SVO
Subjunctive [Grammar] (WGA) .... SBJ
Subjunctive [Grammar] .... SUB
Subjunctive [Grammar] .... SUBJ
Subjunctive [Grammar] (WGA) .... SUBJV
Sublentiform Nucleus (DMAA) .... SLN

Subler, Carl, Agent, Versailles OH [*STAC*] .... SUBC
Sublethal Damage Repair [*Medicine*] (DMAA) .... SLDR
Sublette County Library, Pinedale, WY [*Library symbol Library of Congress*]
  (LCLS) .... WyPdS
Sublevel (IAA) .... SUB
Sub-Lieutenant [*British military*] (DMA) .... S Lt
Sub-Lieutenant [*British military*] .... SL
Sub-Lieutenant [*British military*] (DMA) .... Sub-Lt
Sublimation Point (IAA) .... SUBL
Sublime [*or Subliming*] .... SUBL
Sublime Power of the Royal Secret [*Freemasonry*] (ROG) .... SPRS
Subliminal Perception .... SP
Subliminal Self [*Psychical research*] .... SS
Sub-Line Item Number (MCD) .... SLIN
Sublingual [*Medicine*] .... SL
Sublingual [*Medicine*] .... subling
Sublingual Cleft [*Medicine*] .... SLC
Sublingual Tablet [*Medicine*] (MEDA) .... ST
Subluxation [*Chiropractic*] .... S
Sub-Machine Carbine [*British military*] (DMA) .... SMC
Submachine Gun .... SMG
Submachine Gun [*Named after Sheppard, Turpin and England, its Inventors*]
  (BARN) .... Sten
Submandibular [*Anatomy*] (DAVI) .... SM
Submandibular [*Medicine*] .... submand
Submandibular Gland [*Anatomy*] .... SMG
Submandibular Gland Renin [*Endocrinology*] .... SGR
Submanubrial Dullness [*Medicine*] .... SMD
Submarine .... S
Submarine [*British*] .... S/M
Submarine [*Navy symbol*] .... SS
Submarine (AFM) .... SUB
Submarine (WGA) .... SUBM
Submarine Acceleration and Velocity System .... SAAVS
Submarine Acoustic Warfare System [*Navy*] (MCD) ...... SAWS
Submarine Active Detection System .... SADS
Submarine Active Detection System - Transmit Group [*Navy*] .... SADS-TG
Submarine Advanced [*or Active*] Combat System .... SUBACS
Submarine Advanced Reactive Tactical Training System .... SMARTS
Submarine Advanced Reactor .... SAR
Submarine Advanced Signal Training System (DNAB) ..... SASITS
Submarine Air Defense .... SUBAD
Submarine Air Frequency Plan (DNAB) .... SAFEPLAN
Submarine Air Optical Communications System (MCD) .... SAOCS
Submarine Alerting and Loading System .... SAL
Submarine Alerting and Locating [*Navy*] .... SAL
Submarine Allied Command, Atlantic [*NATO*] (NATG) .... SUBACLANT
Submarine Analysis Group [*Navy*] (CAAL) .... SAG
Submarine Analytic Search Program [*Navy*] (CAAL) ...... SASP
Submarine Anomaly Detection [*Navy*] (NVT) .... SAD
Submarine Antenna Improvement Program [*Military*] ...... SAIP
Submarine Antenna Quality Assurance Directory [*Navy*] (DNAB) .... SAQAD
Submarine Antenna Quality Assurance Facility [*Navy*] (DNAB) .... SAQAF
Submarine Area Frequency Plan [*Navy*] .... SAFPLAN
Submarine Automatic Remote Television Inspection Equipment
  (PDAA) .... SMARTIE
Submarine, Ballistic Missile [*Diesel*] [*NATO*] .... SSB
Submarine Basaltic Glasses [*Geology*] .... SBG
Submarine Base [*Navy*] .... SB
Submarine Base [*Navy*] .... SUBASE
Submarine Base, New London [*Connecticut*] [*Navy*] ...... SBNL
Submarine Base, Pearl Harbor [*Navy*] (DNAB) .... SBPH
Submarine Bases, Atlantic [*Navy*] .... SUBASELANT
Submarine Bases, Pacific [*Navy*] .... SUBASEPAC
Submarine Bathythermograph .... SBT
Submarine Boat [*British*] (ROG) .... SB
Submarine Bubble Target [*British military*] (DMA) .... SBT
Submarine Celestial Altitude Recorder [*Navy*] .... SCAR
Submarine Chaser [*Navy symbol*] .... MC
Submarine Chaser [*173 foot*] [*Navy symbol Obsolete*] .... PC
Submarine Chaser .... PCS
Submarine Chaser [*110 foot*] .... SC
Submarine Chaser (Air Cushion) (MCD) .... PCS(A)
Submarine Chaser (Control) [*173 foot*] [*Navy symbol Obsolete*] .... PC(C)
Submarine Chaser (Control) [*110 foot*] [*Obsolete*] .... SC(C)
Submarine Chaser Escort .... PCE
Submarine Chaser (Hydrofoil) (MCD) .... PCS(H)
Submarine Chaser Training Center [*Navy*] .... SCTC
Submarine Chaser Training Center [*Navy*] .... SCTRACEN
Submarine Classification and Tracking .... SCAT
Submarine Contact Analysis and Evaluation Center (NVT) .... SCAEC
Submarine Coxswain [*British military*] (DMA) .... S/C
Submarine Craft for Ocean Repair, Positioning, Inspection, and
  Observation (PDAA) .... SCORPIO
Submarine Data Extraction System [*Navy*] (CAAL) .... SDES
Submarine Defense Identification Zone .... SDIZ
Submarine Defense Identification Zone .... SUBDIZ
Submarine Departure Approval Request (DNAB) .... SDAR
Submarine Detecting System .... SUDS
Submarine Detector (ADA) .... SD
Submarine Detector Instructor [*British military*] (DMA) .... SDI
Submarine Development Group One [*San Diego*] ..... SUBDEVGRUONE
Submarine Development Group Two [*New York*] ..... SUBDEVGRUTWO
Submarine Division [*Navy*] .... SUBDIV
Submarine Electromagnetic Deception System .... SUBED

Submarine Element Coordinator (NVT) .... SEC
Submarine Emergency Buoyancy System .... SEBS
Submarine Emergency Communications Transmitter ...... SECT
Submarine Emergency Identification Signal (NG) .... SEIS
Submarine Engineering Technical .... SET
Submarine Escape Immersion Equipment .... SEIE
Submarine Escape Training Centre [*British military*] (DMA) .... SETC
Submarine Escape Training Tank .... SETT
Submarine Exercise (NATG) .... SUBEX
Submarine Exercise Area Coordinator [*Navy*] (NVT) ...... SEAC
Submarine Expendable Bathythermograph [*Marine science*] (MSC) .... SSXBT
Submarine Explosive Echo Ranging .... SEER
Submarine Extended Operating Cycle (NVT) .... SEOC
Submarine Extremely Low Frequency Radio [*Navy*] .... SELF
Submarine Flag [*Navy British*] .... SM
Submarine Fleet Reactor .... SFR
Submarine Flotilla [*Navy*] .... SUBFLOT
Submarine Fog Bell [*Mechanical*] [*Maps and charts*] .... SB
Submarine Fog Bell [*Mechanical*] .... SUB-BELL
Submarine Fog Oscillator [*Maps and charts*] .... SFO
Submarine Force, Atlantic Fleet .... SUBLANT
Submarine Force, Eastern Atlantic [*NATO*] .... SUBEASTLANT
Submarine Force, Pacific Fleet .... SUBPAC
Submarine Force, Pacific Fleet Administration .... SUBAD
Submarine Force, Pacific Fleet Administration, Mare Island .... SUBADMI
Submarine Force, Pacific Fleet, Administrative Command .... SUBPACAD
Submarine Force, Pacific Fleet, Subordinate Command ...... SUBPACSUBORDCOM
Submarine Force, Western Atlantic Area [*NATO*] (NATG) .... SUBWESTLANT
Submarine Ground Water Discharge [*Geophysics*] .... SGWD
Submarine Group .... SUBGRU
Submarine Inertial Navigation System (IAA) .... SINS
Submarine Integrated Antenna System (MCD) .... SIAS
Submarine Integrated Attack Center (MCD) .... SIAC
Submarine Integrated Control Systems .... SUBIC
Submarine Integrated SONAR .... SIS
Submarine Integrated SONAR System .... SISS
Submarine Intended Movement (NVT) .... SIM
Submarine Intermediate Reactor [*Nuclear energy*] .... SIR
Submarine Kit Allowance [*British military*] (DMA) .... S/KA
Submarine LASER Communications .... SLC
Submarine LASER Communications Satellite (MCD) ..... SLCSAT
Submarine Launched One-Way Transmitter [*AN/BRT-1*] (DOMA) .... SLOT
Submarine Liaison Officer [*Navy*] (NVT) .... SLO
Submarine Lightwave Cable [*AT & T*] [*Telecommunications*] .... SL
Submarine Material Identification and Control [*Navy*] (DNAB) .... SMIC
Submarine Medical Center [*Navy*] .... SUBMEDCEN
Submarine Medical Research Laboratory .... SMRL
Submarine Mine Depot .... SMD
Submarine, Minelaying [*Obsolete*] .... SM
Submarine Miners [*British military*] (DMA) .... SMM
Submarine Missing [*Navy*] (NVT) .... SUBMISS
Submarine Missing/Presumed Sunk [*Navy*] ...... SUBMIS/SUBSUNK
Submarine Movement Advisory Authority (NVT) .... SMAA
Submarine Net Controller (MCD) .... SNC
Submarine Notice (MCD) .... SUBNOT
Submarine Notice [*Navy*] (NVT) .... SUBNOTE
Submarine (Nuclear-Powered) [*Navy symbol*] (NVT) ...... SSN
Submarine (Nuclear-Powered) in Direct Support [*Navy symbol*] (NVT) .... SSN(DS)
Submarine Oceanographic Digital Data System [*Navy*] (DNAB) .... SODDS
Submarine Oceanographic Observation Program .... SOOP
Submarine Off-Board Mine Search System (DOMA) ...... SOMSS
Submarine Officer Advanced Course [*Navy*] (DNAB) ...... SOAC
Submarine Officer Basic Course [*Navy*] (DOMA) .... SOBC
Submarine Oiler [*Navy ship symbol*] [*Obsolete*] .... AO(SS)
Submarine Oiler [*Navy ship symbol*] .... SSO
Submarine One-Way Satellite [*Navy*] (CAAL) .... SOSAT
Submarine Operating Area [*Navy*] .... SSOA
Submarine Operating Authority [*Navy*] (NVT) .... SUBOPAUTH
Submarine Operational Readiness Assessment and Training .... SORAT
Submarine Operational Update Program [*Canadian Navy*] .... SOUP
Submarine Operations Control Center [*Navy*] (CAAL) ..... SOCC
Submarine Operations Research Group [*Navy*] .... SORG
Submarine Operations Research Report [*Navy*] .... SORR
Submarine Oscillator (DEN) .... SO
Submarine Oscillator .... SUB-OSC
Submarine Overhaul Allowance Parts [*Navy*] (DNAB) ..... SOAP
Submarine Overhaul and Refueling Building [*Navy*] (DNAB) .... SORB
Submarine Overhaul Work Requirement [*Navy*] (DNAB) .... SOWR
Submarine Overhaul Work Requirement Authorization [*Navy*] (DNAB) .... SOWRA
Submarine Patrol [*Navy*] .... SP
Submarine Patrol Area [*Navy*] (NVT) .... SPA
Submarine Patrol Area Definition (MCD) .... SPAD
Submarine Patrol Zone [*Navy*] (NVT) .... SPZ
Submarine Pay .... S/M
Submarine Pay [*British military*] (DMA) .... S/P
Submarine Piloting and Navigation [*Navy*] .... SPAN
Submarine Piping System .... SPS
Submarine Program Information Notebook .... SPIN
Submarine Qualification [*Navy*] .... SS
Submarine Qualification Lapsed [*Navy*] .... SL
Submarine Quickened Response .... SQUIRE
Submarine Range Prediction System [*Navy*] (NVT) .... SUBRAP
Submarine Range-Finder .... SRF
Submarine Reactor Small .... SRS
Submarine Recorder [*British military*] (DMA) .... SR

Submarine Repair and Berthing Barge [*Non-self-propelled*] [*Navy symbol*] .... YRB
Submarine Repair, Berthing, and Messing Barge [*Non-self-propelled*] [*Navy symbol*] .... YRBM
Submarine Repair, Berthing, and Messing Barge (Large) [*Navy symbol*] .... YRBM(L)
Submarine Repair Facility .... SRF
Submarine Repair Unit .... SRU
Submarine Repair Unit .... SUBRU
Submarine Reportback Processor Unit (DWSG) .... SBRP
Submarine Rescue Chamber (MCD) .... SRC
Submarine Rescue Chamber [*Navy symbol*] .... YRC
Submarine Rescue Ship [*Navy symbol*] .... ASR
Submarine Rocket .... SUBROC
Submarine Rocket (IAA) .... SUBROCK
Submarine Safety [*Program*] .... SUBSAFE
Submarine Safety Center [*Navy*] .... SUBSAFECEN
Submarine Safety Certification [*Navy*] (DNAB) .... SUBCERT
Submarine Safety Certification Boundary (Book) [*Navy*] (DNAB) .... SSCB(B)
Submarine Safety Monitoring System .... SSMS
Submarine Salvage Exercise [*Navy*] (DNAB) .... SUBSALVEX
Submarine Sand Recovery System .... SSRS
Submarine Satellite Information Exchange [*Geosynchronous communications satellite*] .... SSIX
Submarine Satellite Information Exchange System (MCD) .... SSIXS
Submarine School Graduate [*Navy*] (DNAB) .... SU
Submarine Schoolship [*Navy*] (NVT) .... SUBSS
Submarine Schoolship [*Navy*] (NVT) .... SUSS
Submarine Scout .... SS
Submarine Scout Experimental [*British military*] (DMA) .... SSE
Submarine Scout Patrol (DMA) .... SSP
Submarine Scout Twin-Type [*British military*] (DMA) .... SST
Submarine Search Attack Unit (NVT) .... SSAU
Submarine Sensor to Weapon Alignment Steering Group .... SWASG
Submarine Shock Test Vehicle .... SSTV
Submarine SONAR Calibration Set .... SSCS
Submarine SONAR Subjective Analysis (NVT) .... SSSA
Submarine Squadron [*Navy*] .... SUBRON
Submarine Studies [*SORG*] .... SS
Submarine Sunk [*Navy*] (NVT) .... SUBSUNK
Submarine Supply Center .... SSC
Submarine Supply Office .... SSO
Submarine Support Division (Fleet Support) [*Navy*] (DNAB) .... SSD(F)
Submarine Support Division (Shore Facilities) [*Navy*] (DNAB) .... SSD(S)
Submarine Support Division (Staff Support) [*Navy*] (DNAB) .... SSD(ST)
Submarine Surface-to-Air Missile [*Military*] (LAIN) .... SUBSAM
Submarine Surveillance Equipment Program (NVT) .... SSEP
Submarine Tactical Acoustic Communications [*Navy*] (ANA) .... STAC
Submarine Tactical Advanced Missile (MCD) .... STAM
Submarine Tactical Array SONAR System .... STASS
Submarine Tactical Data Display Subsystem (MCD) .... STDDS
Submarine Tactical Data Link (NVT) .... STDL
Submarine Tactical Data System (MCD) .... STDS
Submarine Tactical Group [*NATO*] (NATG) .... SUBTACGRU
Submarine Tactics Analysis Group .... SUBTAG
Submarine Target Vessel (NVT) .... STV
Submarine Technical Repair Standard [*Navy*] (DNAB) .... STRS
Submarine Technology Program [*Defense Advanced Research Projects Agency*] (DOMA) .... STP
Submarine Telegraph [*Military*] (IAA) .... SUBTEL
Submarine Telephone [*Military*] (IAA) .... SUBTEL
Submarine Tender [*Navy symbol*] .... AS
Submarine Tender Availability .... STA
Submarine Tender Availability Arrival/Departure [*Obsolete*] .... STAAD
Submarine Tender Availability Document .... STAD
Submarine Tender (Fleet Ballistic Missile) [*Navy symbol*] .... AS(FBM)
Submarine Tender Load List .... STLL
Submarine Tender (Small) [*Navy ship symbol*] (NATG) .... ASL
Submarine Test and Research (MCD) .... STAR
Submarine Test Reactor .... STR
Submarine Test Unit .... STU
Submarine Thermal Reactor [*Nuclear energy*] .... STR
Submarine Towed Array SONAR System [*Navy*] .... STASS
Submarine Training Facility .... SUBTRAFAC
Submarine Transit Identification Zones (NVT) .... STIZ
Submarine Transport [*Navy symbol Obsolete*] .... SSP
Submarine Volcano [*Nautical charts*] .... Sub Vol
Submarine Warfare (MCD) .... SBW
Submarine Warfare Operations Research Department (DOMA) .... SWORD
Submarine Water Reactor [*Nuclear energy*] (NRCH) .... SWR
Submarine Wire Dispenser .... SWD
Submarine-Antisubmarine Warfare Exercise (NVT) .... SUBASWEX
Submarine-Exhaust Detector [*Navy British*] .... ASH
Submarine-Launched Air Missile .... SLAM
Submarine-Launched Antiship Torpedo .... SLAST
Submarine-Launched Assault Missile Exercise (NVT) .... SLAMEX
Submarine-Launched Ballistic Missile Detection and Warning System (IEEE) .... SLBMDWS
Submarine-Launched Ballistic Missile Warning (IAA) .... SLBMW
Submarine-Launched Cruise Missile (IEEE) .... SLCM
Submarine-Launched Inertial Missile .... SLIM
Submarine-Launched Missile .... SLM
Submarine-Launched Mobile Mine (MCD) .... SLMM
Submarine-Launched One-Way Tactical [*Buoy*] (NVT) .... SLOT
Submarine-Rocket Technical Advisory Group .... STAG
Submarines, Atlantic Fleet .... SUBSLANT
Submarines, Experimental .... SSX
Submarines Mediterranean [*NATO*] (NATG) .... SUBMED
Submarines Northeast Mediterranean [*NATO*] (NATG) .... SUBMEDNOREAST
Submarines, Pacific Fleet .... SUBSPAC
Submarines Scouting Force [*Pacific Fleet*] .... SUBSCOFOR
Submarines, Southwest Pacific Force .... SUBSSOWESPAC
Submarine-to-Aircraft Communications .... STAC
Submarine-Towed Array Surveillance System (NVT) .... STASS
Submaximal Treadmill Exercise Test (AAMN) .... STET
Submaximal Working Capacity (DMAA) .... SWC
Submento-Vertex [*View*] [*Radiology*] (DAVI) .... SMV
Submerge [*or Submersible*] (KSC) .... SBM
Submerged .... SUB
Submerged .... SUBM
Submerged (MSA) .... SUBMG
Submerged Anchor Leg Mooring [*Engineering*] .... SUALM
Submerged Aquatic Vegetation .... SAV
Submerged Arc (OA) .... SA
Submerged Arc Weld .... SAW
Submerged Celestial Altitude Recorder (IAA) .... SCAR
Submerged Demineralizer System [*Water purification*] .... SDS
Submerged Floating Tunnell .... SFT
Submerged Injection Process [*Steelmaking*] .... SIP
Submerged Launched Surface-to-Surface Missile (MCD) .... SLSSM
Submerged Metal Arc Weld [*Nuclear energy*] (NRCH) .... SMAW
Submerged Metal Arc Welding .... SMA
Submerged Object Locating and Retrieving Identification System .... SOLARIS
Submerged Object Recovery Device .... SORD
Submerged Ordnance Recovery Device [*Navy*] .... SORD
Submerged Production System [*Deepwater platform*] [*Humble Oil*] .... SPS
Submerged Pump [*Liquid gas carriers*] .... s
Submerged Quick Intervention Device [*Human-powered submarine*] .... SQUID
Submerged Repeater Monitoring Equipment [*RADAR*] .... SMRE
Submerged Research Vehicle .... SRV
Submerged Unmanned Recovery Platform (NVT) .... SURP
Submerged Well [*Nautical charts*] .... Subm W
Submersible Craft [*Self-propelled*] [*Navy ship symbol*] X
Submersible Craft Acoustic Navigation and Track Indication Equipment (PDAA) .... SCANTIE
Submersible Craft Assisting Repair and Burial [*Autonomous underwater vehicle*] .... SCARAB
Submersible Decompression Chamber [*Underwater tank*] .... SDC
Submersible Diving Capsule [*Oceanography*] .... SDC
Submersible Mining Device .... SMD
Submersible Oriented Platform for Deep Ocean Sediment Studies [*Marine science*] (MSC) .... SOPDOSS
Submersible Pipe Alignment Rig [*Deep-sea diving*] .... SPAR
Submersible Portable Inflatable Dwelling .... SPID
Submersible Research Vehicle (Nuclear Propulsion) [*Navy ship symbol*] .... NR
Submersible System Used to Assess Vented Emissions (USDC) .... SUAVE
Submersible Test Rack .... STR
Submersible Test Unit [*Navy*] .... STU
Submersible Training Platform [*Marine science*] (MSC) .... SUBTRAP
Submersible, Transportable Utility, Marine Pump (PDAA) .... STUMP
Submersible [*System*] **Used to Assess Vented Emissions** [*Marine science*] (OSRA) .... SUAVE
Submersible Wastewater Pump Association (EA) .... SWPA
Submersible Water Pump .... SWP
Submersible Work Chamber .... SWC
Submetacentric [*Botany*] .... sm
Submicrometer Metal-Oxide Semiconductor (IAA) .... SMOS
Submicron Aerosol Collector .... SMAC
SubMicron Systems [*NASDAQ symbol*] (TTSB) .... SUBM
SubMicron Systems Corp. [*NASDAQ symbol*] (SAG) .... SUBM
SubMicron Systems Corp. [*Associated Press*] (SAG) .... SubMicr
Submillimeter Array [*Telescope*] .... SMA
Submillimeter Common-User Bolometer Array [*Instrumentation*] .... SCUBA
Submillimeter Wave (MCD) .... SMMW
Submillimeter Wave Astronomy Satellite [*Military*] .... SWAS
Subminiature (IAA) .... SM
Subminiature .... SUBMIN
Subminiature Displacement Gyroscope .... SDG
Subminiature Integrated Antenna .... SIA
Subminiature Microwave Delay Line .... SMDL
Subminiature Rotary Actuator .... SRA
Submission [*or Submit*] (AFM) .... SUBM
Submission (ROG) .... SUBMON
Submission and Delivery Entity [*Telecommunications*] (OSI) .... SDE
Submission Control Code (MCD) .... SCC
Submit (AABC) .... SBM
Submit (ROG) .... SMIT
Submit New Duty Station [*Navy*] (DNAB) .... SUBNEWSTA
Submit Requisition (NOAA) .... SUREQ
Submit to Naval Personnel (DNAB) .... SUBNAVPERS
Submitochondrial Particle [*Cytology*] .... SMP
Submitted Package Sequence Number (MCD) .... SPSN
Submitting Activity Code .... SAC
Submitting Office Number [*Navy*] (DNAB) .... SON
Submodel .... SBMDL
Submodule and Operator Controller [*For sequence of telephonic operations*] .... SMOC
Submucosal [*Anatomy*] (DAVI) .... SM
Submucous [*Medicine*] (MAE) .... SM
Submucous Resection [*Medicine*] .... SMR
Submucous Resection and Rhinoplasty [*Medicine*] (MAE) .... SMRR

Submultiplex (IAA) ... SMX
Submultiplexer Unit ... SMX
Submuscular Aponeurotic System [*Medicine*] ... SMAS
Subnetwork (IAA) ... SN
Subnetwork Access Point (TNIG) ... SNAP
Subnetwork Access Protocol [*Telecommunications*] (OSI) ... SNACP
Subnetwork Dependent Convergence Function [*Telecommunications*] (OSI) ... SNDCF
Subnetwork Dependent Convergence Protocol [*Telecommunications*] (OSI) ... SNDCP
Subnetwork Independent Convergence Protocol [*Telecommunications*] (OSI) ... SNICP
Subnetwork Point of Attachment [*Telecommunications*] (OSI) ... SNPA
Subnormal ... SN
Sub-Occipito Bregma [*Medicine*] (ROG) ... SOB
Sub-Occipito Frontal [*Medicine*] (ROG) ... SOF
Suboffice ... SO
Suborbital Mission [*NASA*] (SAA) ... SOM
Suborbital Offense Systems Group [*NASA*] (SAA) ... SOOSE
Suborbital Reentry Test Integrated Environment [*NASA*] (IAA) ... SORTIE
Suborbital Sequence [*NASA*] ... SOS
Suborbital Tank Separation [*NASA*] (MCD) ... SOTS
Subordinate (DSUE) ... SUB
Subordinate (AFM) ... SUBOR
Subordinate [*Linguistics*] ... SUBORD
Subordinate Army Field Services ... SARFS
Subordinate Command ... SUBORCOM
Subordinate Command, [*US*] Naval Forces, Eastern Atlantic and Mediterranean ... SUBCOMNELM
Subordinate Command, Service Force, Atlantic Fleet ... SUBORCOMDSERVLANT
Subordinate Command, Service Force, Pacific Fleet ... SUBCOM
Subordinate Command, Service Force, Pacific Fleet ... SUBORCOMDSERVPAC
Subordinate Operations Control Center ... SOCC
Subordinate Operations Data System (NVT) ... SODS
Subparagraph (DLA) ... Subpar
Subparagraph ... SUBPARA
Subpart (WDAA) ... SUBPT
Subplate [*Neurology*] ... SP
Subpoena [*Legal term*] ... SPA
Subpoena [*Legal shorthand*] (LWAP) ... SUBP
Subpoena ad Testificandum [*Subpoena to Testify*] [*Latin*] (ROG) ... SPA ad TEST
Subpoena Duces Tecum [*Legal term Latin*] (HGAA) ... SDT
Subpoena Duces Tecum [*Legal*] [*Latin*] (ROG) ... SPA DT
Subpolar Intermediate Water [*Oceanography*] ... SIW
Subpolar Mode Water [*Marine science*] (OSRA) ... SPMW
Subpool Queue Element (MHDI) ... SPQE
Subport of Embarkation ... SPE
Subprocessor with Dynamic Microprogramming ... SPDM
Subprofessional [*Civil Service employees designation*] ... SP
Subprogram (IAA) ... SP
Subprogram Change Affect Diagram (MHDB) ... SCAD
Subpurchase Order (AAG) ... SPO
Subpurchase Order Change Notice (AAG) ... SPOCN
Subrate Data Multiplexer [*Telecommunications*] (TEL) ... SRDM
Subregional Headquarters [*Military British*] ... SRHQ
Sub-Registered Publications Issuing Office ... SUBRPIO
Subrequirement ... SUBRQMT
Subretinal Fluid [*Ophthalmology*] (MAE) ... SRF
Subretinal Neovascularization [*Ophthalmology*] (DAVI) ... SRN
Subretinal Neovascularization [*Ophthalmology*] ... SRNV
Subrogation ... SUBRO
Subroutine [*Computer science*] (AAG) ... SR
Subroutine ... SUB
Subroutine Call Table [*Computer science*] ... SCT
Subroutine Recipe Entry Pointer Table ... SRET
Subsagittal [*Medicine*] ... SS
Sub-Saharan African [*MARC language code Library of Congress*] (LCCP) ... ssa
Sub-Saharan African Country ... SSA
Subsatellite Point [*Telecommunications*] (TEL) ... SSP
Subscale ... SS
Subscale Subsonic Targets (MCD) ... SSSST
Subscapularis [*Muscle*] [*Anatomy*] (DAVI) ... SS
Subscribed (ROG) ... SUBSCD
Subscriber [*Finance*] ... Sub
Subscriber Access Terminal ... SAT
Subscriber Busy [*Telecommunications*] (TEL) ... SSB
Subscriber Carrier Terminal [*Telecommunications*] (TEL) ... SCT
Subscriber Channel Unit (IAA) ... SCU
Subscriber Computer (MHDI) ... SC
Subscriber Digital Access Unit [*Telecommunications*] ... SDAU
Subscriber Group Equipment [*Telecommunications*] ... SGE
Subscriber Group Plant (IAA) ... SGP
Subscriber Identification (CAAL) ... SID
Subscriber Interface Control (DOMA) ... SIC
Subscriber Line Access Protocol (IAA) ... SLAP
Subscriber Line Audio Processing Circuit [*Telecommunications*] (EECA) ... SLAC
Subscriber Line Audio Processor Circuit (NITA) ... SLAC
Subscriber Line Circuit [*Telecommunications*] (IAA) ... SLC
Subscriber Line Unit [*Telecommunications*] (IAA) ... SLU
Subscriber Line Use [*Telecommunications*] ... SLU
Subscriber Loop Analysis Program System [*Bell System*] ... SLAPS
Subscriber Loop Carrier [*Telecommunications*] (TEL) ... SLC
Subscriber Loop Interface Circuit (NITA) ... SLIC
Subscriber Loop Multiplex [*Bell System*] ... SLM
Subscriber Network Interface [*Computer science*] (CDE) ... SNI
Subscriber Originating Trunk [*Telecommunications*] (TEL) ... SOT
Subscriber Plant Factor [*Telecommunications*] ... SPF
Subscriber Premises Network [*Telecommunications*] ... SPN
Subscriber Register ... SR
Subscriber Set (CET) ... SUBSET
Subscriber Switching [*Telecommunications*] (TEL) ... SS
Subscriber Switching Grid (IAA) ... SSG
Subscriber Switching Unit [*Telecommunications*] (TEL) ... SSU
Subscriber Toll Dialing [*Telecommunications*] (TSSD) ... STD
Subscriber Transferred [*Telecommunications*] (TEL) ... SST
Subscriber Trunk Dialing [*Telephone communications*] ... STD
Subscriber Unit [*RADA*] [*Army*] (RDA) ... SU
Subscriber-Response System [*Study of cable television*] [*Hughes Aircraft Co.*] ... SRS
Subscriber-Response Unit (IAA) ... SRU
Subscribers' Apparatus Line Tester [*Telecommunications*] (TEL) ... SALT
Subscribers' Call Processing (Subsystem) [*Telecommunications*] (TEL) ... SCP(S)
Subscribers' Circuit Routine Tester [*Telecommunications*] (TEL) ... SCRT
Subscribers' Concentration Module [*Telecommunications*] (TEL) ... SCM
Subscribers' Concentrator Unit [*Telecommunications*] (TEL) ... SCU
Subscriber's Directory Number [*Telecommunications*] (TEL) ... SDN
Subscriber's Line Interface Circuit [*Telecommunications*] (TEL) ... SLIC
Subscriber's Line Use System [*AT & T*] [*Telecommunications*] (TEL) ... SLUS
Subscriber's Loop [*Telecommunications*] (TEL) ... SL
Subscriber's Private Meter [*Telecommunications*] (TEL) ... SPM
Subscriber's Switching Subsystem [*Telecommunications*] (TEL) ... SSS
Subscribers' Trunk Unit [*Telecommunications*] (TEL) ... STU
Subscript Character [*Computer science*] ... SBS
Subscription [*Finance*] ... SUB
Subscription (WGA) ... SUBS
Subscription (DLA) ... Subsc
Subscription [*Finance*] (ROG) ... SUBSCR
Subscription ... SUBSCR
Subscription [*Finance*] (ROG) ... SUBSCRON
Subscription Book (DGA) ... Sub Bk
Subscription Fulfillment Managers Association [*Later, FMA*] (EA) ... SFMA
Subscription Item ... SI
Subscription Television ... STV
Subscription Television Association (NTCM) ... STA
Subscription Television Association [*Defunct*] (EA) ... STVA
Subscription Television Authority [*FCC*] (NTCM) ... STV
Subscription TV, Inc. (NTCM) ... STV
Subsea Beacon/Transponder ... SBX
Subsea Equipment Associates Ltd. [*Bermuda*] ... SEAL
Subsea Production System [*Petroleum technology*] ... SPS
Subsea Test Tree (PDAA) ... SSTT
Sub-Seabed Disposal Program [*National Science Foundation*] (NUCP) ... SDP
Subsection ... SUBSEC
Subsection [*Legal shorthand*] (LWAP) ... SUBSECT
Subsegmental [*Medicine*] (DAVI) ... SS
Subsequent (AABC) ... SUBQ
Subsequent (ROG) ... SUBSEQ
Subsequent Access (BYTE) ... SA
Subsequent Address Message [*Telecommunications*] (TEL) ... SAM
Subsequent Application Review ... SAR
Subsequent Contrast Application Review (MCD) ... SCAR
Subsequent Coupons Attached ... SCA
Subsequent Maintenance Assessment ... SMA
Subsequent Notification of an Aircraft Accident [*Aviation code*] ... ACCIDSUB
Subsequent Opinion (HGAA) ... sub opn
Subsequent Sibling (DAVI) ... SS
Subsequent Signal Unit [*Group of BITS*] [*Telecommunications*] (TEL) ... SSU
Subsequently (ROG) ... SUBSLY
Subsequently (ADA) ... SUBSQ
Subset Extraction and Association Measurement ... SEAM
Subset-Specified Sequential Machine [*Air Force*] ... SSSM
Subshock Insulin [*Pharmacology*] (DAVI) ... SSI
Sub-Shop Replaceable Assembly ... SUB-SRA
Subsidiary [*Business term*] ... SUB
Subsidiary [*Business term*] ... SUBS
Subsidiary [*Business term*] (ROG) ... SUBSID
Subsidiary [*Business term*] ... Suby
Subsidiary ... SUBY
Subsidiary Account Number ... SAN
Subsidiary/Affiliate Order (MCD) ... SAO
Subsidiary Channel Authorization (IAA) ... SCA
Subsidiary Communications Allocation (IAA) ... SCA
Subsidiary Communications Authorization [*Facilities used to transmit background music to subscribing customers*] ... SCA
Subsidiary Communications Multiplex Operation [*FM radio frequency unused portion*] ... SCMO
Subsidiary Company (MHDB) ... SC
Subsidiary Heading (DGA) ... Sub Hdg
Subsidiary Learning Net (IAA) ... SLN
Subsidiary Legislation [*India*] [*A publication*] (DLA) ... India Subs Leg
Subsidiary Legislation of the Australian Capital Territory [*A publication*] (DLA) ... Austl Cap Terr Subs Leg
Subsistence (WDAA) ... SUB
Subsistence (AABC) ... SUBS
Subsistence (AFM) ... SUBSIS
Subsistence Allowance ... SA
Subsistence Operations Review Board [*Military*] (AABC) ... SORB
Subsistence Preparation by Electronic Energy Diffusion ... SPEED
Subsisting Elsewhere ... SUBSELS
Subsod Injection [*Waste treatment*] (DICI) ... SSI

Subsoil Drain [Technical drawings] ..... SSD
Subsolar [NASA] (KSC) ..... SS
Subsolar Point [Aerospace] ..... SSP
Subsonic Aerodynamic Testing Association (MCD) ..... SATA
Subsonic Cruise Armed Decoy [Air Force] ..... SCAD
Subsonic Cruise Armed Missile/Decoy [Air Force] (MCD) ..... SCAM
Subsonic Cruise Armed Missile/Decoy [Air Force] ..... SCAM/D
Subsonic Cruise Unarmed Decoy [Air Force] (MCD) ..... SCUD
Subsonic [or Supersonic] Jet Transport ..... SJT
Subspecialty Codes (DOMA) ..... SSC
Subspecialty Requirements Board [Navy] (DNAB) ..... SRB
Subspecies [Also, ssp] ..... SSP
Subspecies [Plural form] [Also, sspp] ..... SSPP
Subspecies ..... SUBSP
Subspecies [Plural form] ..... subspp
Subspecies Nova [New Subspecies] [Biology] ..... ssp nov
Substance ..... SBSTNC
Substance (ROG) ..... SUBST
Substance Abuse and Mental Health Services Administration [Formerly, ADAMHA] [Department of Health and Human Services] ..... SAMHSA
Substance Abuse Coordinator [Navy] (DNAB) ..... SAC
Substance Abuse Facility Information System [Department of Health and Human Services] (GFGA) ..... SAFIS
Substance Abuse Librarians and Information Specialists (EA) ..... SALIS
Substance Abuse Problem Checklist ..... SAPC
Substance Abuse Quarterly Report [Navy] (DNAB) ..... SAQR
Substance Abuse Report [Navy] (DNAB) ..... SAR
Substance Abuse Technology, Inc. [AMEX symbol] (SAG) ..... SAU
Substance Abuse Technology, Inc. [Associated Press] (SAG) ..... SubstAb
Substance Abuse Technology, Inc. [Associated Press] (SAG) ..... SubstAbus
Substance Abuse Treatment [Health insurance] (GHCT) ..... SAT
Substance Hazard Index [Environmental science] ..... SHI
Substance K [Biochemistry] ..... SK
Substance Of ..... S/O
Substance P [A peptide] [Biochemistry] ..... SP
Substance P Antagonist [Biochemistry] ..... SPA
Substance P Receptor [Biochemistry] ..... SPR
Substance P-Like Immunoreactivity ..... SPLI
Substance-K Receptor [Biochemistry] ..... SKR
Substances Immunologically Cross-Reactive with Insulin ..... SICRI
Substandard (WGA) ..... Substand
Substandard (DAVI) ..... substd
Substantia Gelatinosa [Anatomy] ..... SG
Substantia Gelatinosa Rolandi [Medicine] (DMAA) ..... SGR
Substantia Nigra [Brain anatomy] ..... SN
Substantia Nigra [pars] Compacta [Brain anatomy] ..... SNC
Substantia Nigra Pars Reticulata [Brain anatomy] ..... SNr
Substantial Gainful Activity [Social Security Administration] (OICC) ..... SGA
Substantial Stockholder ..... SSH
Substantive ..... S
Substantive ..... SB
Substantive (WDAA) ..... SUB
Substantive [Grammar] ..... SUBS
Substantive (ROG) ..... SUBST
Substation (IAA) ..... SS
Substation ..... SUBSTA
Substernal [Anatomy] (DAVI) ..... SS
Substitute ..... SUB
Substitute ..... SUB
Substitute ..... SUBS
Substitute (AAG) ..... SUBST
Substitute Alloy Material [Nuclear energy] ..... SAM
Substitute Blank (IAA) ..... SB
Substitute Character [Keyboard] (AFM) ..... SUB
Substitute for Morphine [Pharmacology] (DAVI) ..... SM
Substitute Fragment (NITA) ..... SF
Substitute Materials [British] ..... SM
Substitute [or Synthetic] Natural Gas ..... SNG
Substitute Optical Landing System (NG) ..... SOL
Substitute Optical Landing System (MCD) ..... SOLS
Substitute Part Authorization (AAG) ..... SPA
Substitute Route Structure ..... SRS
Substitute Standard [Army] ..... SUB-STD
Substituted (ROG) ..... SUBSTD
Substituted ..... SUBSTTD
Substituted Accounting Period ..... SAP
Substituted Anilines Task Force (EA) ..... SATF
Substituted Metabolites [Biochemistry] (DAVI) ..... SM
Substitutes [Sports] ..... SS
Substitutes Not Desired [Military] ..... SUBNO
Substituting (AAG) ..... SUBSTG
Substitution (IAA) ..... SUB
Substitution ..... SUBSTN
Substitution Acceptable [Military] ..... SUBOK
Substitution Approval Request (MCD) ..... SAR
Substitution Authorization (AAG) ..... SA
Substitution Oscillator (IAA) ..... SO
Substitution Theorem [Logic] ..... ST
Substorm Current Wedge ..... SCW
Substrate (IAA) ..... S
Substrate [Electronics] ..... SBSTR
Substrate Adhesion Molecule [Cytology] ..... SAM
Substrate Fed Logic ..... SFL
Substrate, Free [Enzyme kinetics] ..... S
Substrate Hot Electron (IAA) ..... SHE

Substrate-Attached Material [Cytology] ..... SAM
Substrate-Labeled Fluorescent Immunoassay ..... SLFIA
Substratum ..... SUB
Substructure [Computer science] ..... ss
Substructure (AAG) ..... SUBSTR
Substructure Search System [Later, SANSS] [NIH/EPA] ..... SSS
Subsumed Abilities Test [Student attitudes test] ..... SAT
Subsurface Geological Laboratory, Regina, Saskatchewan [Library symbol National Library of Canada] (NLC) ..... SRSG
Subsurface Geological Laboratory, Regina, SK, Canada [Library symbol Library of Congress] (LCLS) ..... CaSRSG
Subsurface Interface RADAR [A trademark] ..... SIR
Subsurface Ocean Area (NVT) ..... SSOA
Subsurface Probe Data and Control Unit ..... SPDCU
Subsurface Propulsion Unit ..... SPU
Subsynaptic Membrane [Anatomy] ..... SSM
Subsynaptic Plate Perforation [Neurophysiology] ..... SSPP
Subsynchronous Resonance (IEEE) ..... SSR
Subsynoptic Advection Model ..... SAM
Subsystem (NASA) ..... S/SYS
Subsystem (AAG) ..... SS
Subsystem (AAG) ..... SUBSYS
Subsystem (IAA) ..... SUSY
Subsystem Action Message [Military] ..... SAM
Subsystem and Vehicle Number (SAA) ..... SSVN
Subsystem Capability Impact Reporting [Military] (NVT) ..... SCIR
Subsystem Computer (MCD) ..... SSC
Subsystem Computer Application Software (MCD) ..... SCAS
Subsystem Computer Operating System [NASA] (NASA) ..... SCOS
Subsystem Configuration Management [or Monitoring] [NASA] (NASA) ..... SCM
Subsystem Configuration Management Board [NASA] (GFGA) ..... SCMB
Subsystem Control of Required Equipment (MCD) ..... SCORE
Subsystem Controller Definition Record [Computer science] (IBMDP) ..... SCDR
Subsystem Critical Design Review ..... SSCDR
Subsystem Data Handbook [NASA] (NASA) ..... SSDH
Subsystem Design Description (MCD) ..... SDD
Subsystem Design Manual [NASA] (MCD) ..... SDM
Subsystem Design Review ..... SSDR
Subsystem Development Requirement (AFM) ..... SSDR
Subsystem Element [NASA] (NASA) ..... SSE
Subsystem Executive Control Program (IAA) ..... SSEC
Subsystem Fault Tree Analysis Report ..... SFTAR
Subsystem for the Control of Operations and Plan Evaluation ..... SCOPE
Subsystem Ground Test (MCD) ..... SGT
Subsystem Ground Test (MCD) ..... SSGT
Subsystem Hazard Analysis ..... SSHA
Subsystem Identification [Electronics] ..... SID
Subsystem Integration Plan (IAA) ..... SSIP
Subsystem Interface Module ..... SIM
Subsystem Interface Unit (MCD) ..... SSIU
Subsystem Library [Computer science] (IBMDP) ..... SLIB
Subsystem Manager [NASA] (NASA) ..... SSM
Subsystem Measurement Management [NASA] (NASA) ..... SMM
Subsystem Operating and Checkout System [NASA] (MCD) ..... SOCS
Subsystem Operating Program (NASA) ..... SOP
Subsystem Operation [in Spacelab] [NASA] (MCD) ..... SSO
Subsystem Postioning Aid Device (NASA) ..... SPAD
Subsystem Power Distribution Box (MCD) ..... SPDB
Subsystem Power Distribution Box (MCD) ..... SSPDB
Subsystem Preliminary Design Review ..... SSPDR
Subsystem Program Preparation Support [Programming language] [Computer science] ..... SPPS
Subsystem Project Manager [NASA] (NASA) ..... SPM
Subsystem Readiness Test (KSC) ..... SSRT
Subsystem Replacement ..... SURE
Subsystem Requirements Review ..... SRR
Subsystem Response Message [Military] ..... SRM
Subsystem Segment [NASA] (NASA) ..... SSS
Subsystem Sequence Controller [NASA] (NASA) ..... SSC
Subsystem: Short-Term Integrating Model [Department of Energy] (GFGA) ..... STIM
Subsystem: Short-Term Price Forecasting Model [Department of Energy] (GFGA) ..... STPFM
Subsystem Software Group ..... SSG
Subsystem Software Program (MCD) ..... S/SP
Subsystem Status Block (MCD) ..... SSB
Subsystem Support Equipment [NASA] (MCD) ..... SSE
Subsystem Support Service (BUR) ..... SSS
Subsystem Tactical Equipment Verification Site ..... STEVS
Sub-System Technical Specification ..... SSTS
Subsystem Terminal on Spacelab [NASA] (MCD) ..... SST
Subsystem Test Plan [NASA] (NASA) ..... STP
Subsystems Functional Verification Test [NASA] ..... SSFVT
Subsystems Integration Program [or Project] [NATO] (NATG) ..... SSIP
Subsystems Operating Procedure [NASA] (NASA) ..... SOP
Subsystems Requirements Definition Handbook [NASA] (NASA) ..... SRDH
Subsystems Requirements Handbook [NASA] (NASA) ..... SRH
Subsystems Test (KSC) ..... SST
Subsystems Test Bed (MCD) ..... STB
Subsystems Test Procedure (KSC) ..... SSTP
Subtalar [Medicine] (MAE) ..... ST
Subtalar Joint [Anatomy] (DAVI) ..... STJ
Subtask ABEND [Abnormal End] Intercept [Computer science] (BUR) ..... STAI
Subtask Control Block [Computer science] (IBMDP) ..... STCB
Subtelocentric [Botany] ..... st

Subtentacular [Zoology] ..... ST
Subterranean Clover Mottle Virus [Plant pathology] ..... SCMOV
Subterranean Clover Red Leaf Virus ..... SCRLV
Subterranean Exploration Agency ..... SEA
Subterranean Sociological Association (EA) ..... SSA
Subthalamic Nucleus [Neurobiology] ..... STN
Subthalamus [Anatomy] ..... STh
Subtotal (MAE) ..... ST
Subtotal Discectomy [Medicine] ..... SD
Subtotal Hysterectomy [Medicine] ..... STH
Subtotal Integration Mode ..... SIM
Subtotal Lymphoid Irradiation [Medicine] (DMAA) ..... STLI
Subtotal Nodal Irradiation [Oncology] ..... STNI
Subtotal Villose Atrophy [Medicine] (MAE) ..... STVA
Subtract ..... SUB
Subtract BCD [Binary Coded Decimal] Number [Computer science] ..... SBCD
Subtract Binary Number [Computer science] ..... SUB
Subtract Contents (NITA) ..... SBC
Subtract Magnitude (IAA) ..... SBM
Subtract with Borrow [Computer science] (PCM) ..... SBB
Subtraction (MSA) ..... SUBTR
Subtraction, Addition, Multiplication ..... SAM
Subtractively Normalized Interfacial FTIR [Fourier Transform Infrared]
   Spectroscopy ..... SNIFTIRS
Subtropical ..... subtrop
Subtropical Agricultural Research Laboratory [Weslaco, TX] [Department of
   Agriculture] (GRD) ..... SARL
Subtropical Atlantic Climate Studies [National Oceanic and Atmospheric
   Administration] ..... STACS
Subtropical Convergence [Oceanography] ..... STC
Subtropical Jet Stream (ADA) ..... STJ
Subtropical Mode Water [Oceanography] ..... STMW
Sub-tropical Seedgrowers' Association [Australia] ..... STSA
Subtropical Underwater [Marine science] (OSRA) ..... STUW
Subtropical Water ..... STW
Subtype (MAE) ..... St
Subud International Cultural Association (EA) ..... SICA
Subud Youth Association (EA) ..... SYA
Sub-Unit (DNAB) ..... SU
Sub-Unit Evaluation (MCD) ..... SUE
Subunit Test ..... SUT
Suburban ..... SUB
Suburban ..... SUBN
Suburban Action Institute [Later, MAI] (EA) ..... SAI
Suburban Air Freight, Inc. [ICAO designator] (FAAC) ..... SRB
Suburban Airlines [ICAO designator] (AD) ..... UQ
Suburban Audio-Visual Service, La Grange Park, IL (LCLS) ..... ILagpS
Suburban Bancorp [NASDAQ symbol] (SAG) ..... SBCN
Suburban Bancorp [Associated Press] (SAG) ..... SubBncp
Suburban Bancorp Inc. [NASDAQ symbol] (TTSB) ..... SBCN
Suburban Bancsharees, Inc. [NASDAQ symbol] (SAG) ..... SBNK
Suburban Bancshares [NASDAQ symbol] (TTSB) ..... SBNK
Suburban Bancshares, Inc. [Associated Press] (SAG) ..... SubBn
Suburban Bancshares, Inc. [Associated Press] (SAG) ..... SubBnc
Suburban Bancshares, Inc. [Associated Press] (SAG) ..... SubBncsh
Suburban Library System [Library network] ..... SLS
Suburban Library System, Burr Ridge, IL [Library symbol Library of
   Congress] (LCLS) ..... IBrS
Suburban Library System, Burr Ridge, IL [OCLC symbol] (OCLC) ..... IED
Suburban Library System, Hinsdale, IL [Library symbol Library of Congress]
   (LCLS) ..... IHS
Suburban Lodges America [NASDAQ symbol] (TTSB) ..... SLAM
Suburban Lodges of America, Inc. [NASDAQ symbol] (SAG) ..... SLAM
Suburban Lodges of America, Inc. [Associated Press] (SAG) ..... SubLdgs
Suburban News, Franklin Lakes, NJ [Library symbol Library of Congress]
   (LCLS) ..... NjFraS
Suburban Newspaper Group, Cherry Hill, NJ [Library symbol Library of
   Congress] (LCLS) ..... NjChSN
Suburban Newspapers of America (EA) ..... SNA
Suburban Ostomy Supply Co., Inc. [NASDAQ symbol] (SAG) ..... SOSC
Suburban Ostomy Supply Co., Inc. [Associated Press] (SAG) ..... SubOstm
Suburban Propane Ptnrs L.P. [NYSE symbol] (TTSB) ..... SPH
Suburban Publishing Co., Union, NJ [Library symbol Library of Congress]
   (LCLS) ..... NjUS
Suburban Service (DD) ..... SS
Suburbfed Financial Corp. [NASDAQ symbol] (SAG) ..... SFSB
Suburbfed Financial Corp. [Associated Press] (SAG) ..... Subrfed
Suburbfed Finl [NASDAQ symbol] (TTSB) ..... SFSB
Subvalvular Aortic Obstruction [Medicine] (DMAA) ..... SAO
Subvent Datenbank Systeme [Innovationstechnik GmbH & Co.] [Hamburg,
   Federal Republic of Germany] [Information service or system] (IID) ..... SDS
Subventricular Zone [Anatomy] ..... SVZ
Subversion (AABC) ..... SUBV
Subversion and Espionage Directed Against US Army and Deliberate
   Security Violations (AABC) ..... SAEDA
Subversive Activities Control Act of 1950 ..... SACA
Subversive Activities Control Board [Later, Federal Internal Security
   Board] ..... SACB
Subversive Operations, Mediterranean Theatre of Operations [World War
   II] ..... SOMTO
Subvert (ROG) ..... SVERT
Subway ..... SBWY
Subway (AAG) ..... SUB
Sub-Working Group ..... SWG
Subxiphoid Pericardial Window [Medicine] (DMAA) ..... SPW

Subzonal Sperm Insertion [In-vitro fertilization] (PAZ) ..... SZI
Succeeded ..... S
Succeeding (MSA) ..... SUC
Succentor [Ecclesiastical] (ROG) ..... SUCC
Success Factor ..... SF
Success Management System ..... SMS
Success Motivation Institute ..... SMI
Successful Effort (DICI) ..... SE
Successful Flight (MCD) ..... SF
Successful Magazine Publishers Group [Defunct] (EA) ..... SMPG
Succession (ROG) ..... SUCCN
Succession ..... SUCCON
Succession Duties Reports [A publication] (ILCA) ..... SDR
Successive Accelerated Replacement ..... SAR
Successive Approximation (IEEE) ..... SA
Successive Approximation (IEEE) ..... SUPROX
Successive Approximation Register [Computer science] ..... SAR
Successive Approximation Technique (NOAA) ..... SAT
Successive Block Overrelaxation (IAA) ..... SBOR
Successive Discrimination Reversal ..... SDR
Successive Line Overrelaxation (IAA) ..... SLOR
Successive Linear Approximation at Minimum Step (SAA) ..... SLAMS
Successive Organization of Perception [Pilot behavior] ..... SOP
Successive Overrelaxation ..... SOR
Successive Planometric [A discrimination task] ..... SP
Successive, Proportionate, Additive Numeration [Decision making] ..... SPAN
Successive Quadratic Programming [Algorithm] [Computer science] ..... SQP
Successive Stereometric [A discrimination task] ..... SS
Successive Subtraction with Total Recognition Accuracy [Algorithm] ..... SSTRA
Successively Truncated Expectation of the Reciprocal [Statistics] ..... STER
Successor ..... S
Successor (ADA) ..... SUC
Successor (ROG) ..... SUCC
Successor ..... SUCCR
Successor (WGA) ..... SUCR
Successor Contracting Officer (MCD) ..... SCO
Successor Event Number (DNAB) ..... SEN
Successor Instruction Set (IAA) ..... SIS
Successories, Inc. [NASDAQ symbol] (SAG) ..... SCES
Successories, Inc. [Associated Press] (SAG) ..... Success
Succinate ..... SUCC
Succinate-Semialdehyde Dehydrogenase [An enzyme] ..... SSADH
Succinic Acid - Dimethylhydrazide [Plant growth retardant] ..... SADH
Succinic Dehydrogenase [An enzyme] ..... SDH
Succinic Dehydrogenase Activity ..... SDA
Succinimidyl Diphenyl Phosphate [Organic chemistry] ..... SDPP
Succinimidyl (Maleimidomethyl)cyclohexanecarboxylate [Organic
   chemistry] ..... SMCC
Succinimidyl (Maleimidophenyl)butyrate [Organic chemistry] ..... SMPB
Succinimidyl(pyridyldithio)propionate [Organic chemistry] ..... SPDP
Succinoaminoimidazolecarboxamide Ribonucleotide [Biochemistry] ..... SAICAR
Succinoyl [Biochemistry] ..... Suc
Succinum [Amber] [Latin] (ROG) ..... SUCC
Succinyl CAMP [Biochemistry] ..... SCAMP
Succinyl CAMP Tyrosine Methyl Ester [Biochemistry] ..... SCAMPTME
Succinylacetone [Organic chemistry] ..... SA
Succinyl-Alanyl-para-Nitroanilide [Biochemistry] ..... SAPNA
Succinylcholine [Biochemistry] (MAE) ..... SC
Succinylcholine [Biochemistry] ..... SCh
Succinylcholine [A muscle relaxant] (DAVI) ..... SUX
Succinyldehydrogenase (DMAA) ..... SUDH
Succinyldicholine [Biochemistry] (MAE) ..... SDC
Succinyl-L-alanyl-L-alanyl-L-alanine-p-nitroanilide [Biochemistry] ..... SLAPN
Succinylmonocholine [Biochemistry] (MAE) ..... SMC
Succinyl-poly-DL-alanine Poly-L-lysine [Biochemical analysis] ..... SPAL
Succinyl-Poly-L-Lysine [Biochemical analysis] ..... SPL
Succursale (DD) ..... succ
Succursale d'Embrun, Bibliotheque Publique du Canton de Russell
   [Embrun Branch, Russell Township Public Library] Ontario [Library symbol
   National Library of Canada] (BIB) ..... OERT
Succus [Juice] [Pharmacy] ..... SUC
Suceava [Romania] [Airport symbol] (OAG) ..... SCV
Suceava/Salcea [Romania] [ICAO location identifier] (ICLI) ..... LRSV
Such As ..... S/A
Such Systems (NITA) ..... SUSY
Such Transportation as Available ..... SUCHTRANSAVAIL
Such Transportation as Command Indicated Designates ..... SUCHTRANS
Sucker Creek Indian Band Public Library, Little Current, Ontario [Library
   symbol National Library of Canada] (NLC) ..... OLICUS
Sucker, Low-Brow, Idiot, Goodwill-Buster [Acronym used as word meaning
   "act of discourtesy or stupid criticism"] [World War II] ..... SLIG
Suckling [Medicine] (DMAA) ..... S
Suckling Airways [Airline flight code] (ODBW) ..... CB
Suckling Airways [British ICAO designator] (FAAC) ..... SAY
Suckling Hamster [Medicine] (DMAA) ..... sHa
Suckling Hill [Alaska] [Seismograph station code, US Geological Survey]
   (SEIS) ..... SUK
Suckling Mice ..... SM
Suckling Mouse Brain [Microbiology] (DMAA) ..... sMb
Suckling Mouse Cataract Agent [Microbiology] ..... SMCA
Suckling Mouse Mean Lethal Dose [Microbiology] ..... SMLD
Sucrase to Lactase Ratio (DAVI) ..... S:L
Sucre [Monetary unit] [Ecuador] ..... S
Sucre [Bolivia] [ICAO location identifier] (ICLI) ..... SLSU
Sucre [Bolivia] [Airport symbol] (OAG) ..... SRE

Sucre [*Bolivia*] [*Seismograph station code, US Geological Survey Closed*] (SEIS) ... SUC
Sucro-Sac-Ologists Society International [*Defunct*] (EA) ... SSI
Sucrose [*Organic chemistry*] ... SUC
Sucrose Acetate Isobutyrate [*Organic chemistry*] ... SAIB
Sucrose Density Gradient Analysis [*Clinical chemistry*] ... SDGA
Sucrose Density Gradients ... SDG
Sucrose Medium [*Microbiology*] (DAVI) ... SM
Sucrose, Phosphate, Glutamate [*A culture medium*] ... SPG
Sucrose Polyester [*Pharmacology*] ... SPE
Sucrose Tallowate (OA) ... ST
Sucrose-Isomaltose Deficiency [*Medicine*] ... SIM
Sucrose-Phosphate Synthase [*An enzyme*] ... SPS
Sucrose-Phosphate-Citrate [*A culture medium*] ... SPC
Suction (ADA) ... SUC
Suction (AAG) ... SUCT
Suction [*Surgery*] (DAVI) ... sx
Suction [*Surgery*] (DAVI) ... SZ
Suction and Irrigation [*Surgery*] (DAVI) ... S & I
Suction Infusion Tissue Extractor [*Ophthalmology*] ... SITE
Suction Line Filter ... SLF
Suction Method [*Medicine*] (MAE) ... SM
Suction, Oxygen, Apparatus, Pharmaceuticals, Saline [*Mnemonic device for anesthetists*] (AAMN) ... SOAPS
Suction Socket (AAMN) ... SS
Sucua [*Ecuador*] [*ICAO location identifier*] (ICLI) ... SESC
Sud [*South*] [*French*] (ROG) ... S
Sud Air Transport SA [*Guinea*] [*ICAO designator*] (FAAC) ... GID
Sudan [*MARC geographic area code Library of Congress*] (LCCP) ... f-sj--
Sudan [*ANSI two-letter standard code*] (CNC) ... SD
Sudan [*ANSI three-letter standard code*] (CNC) ... SDN
Sudan [*MARC country of publication code Library of Congress*] (LCCP) ... sj
Sudan African Closed Districts National Union ... SACDNU
Sudan African Freedom Fighters' Union of Conservatives ... SAFFUC
Sudan African Liberation Front ... SALF
Sudan African National Union [*Political party*] ... SANU
Sudan Airways [*ICAO designator*] (AD) ... SD
Sudan Airways [*ICAO designator*] (FAAC) ... SUD
Sudan Defence Force [*British*] ... SDF
Sudan Interior Mission ... SIM
Sudan Law Journal and Reports [*A publication*] (DLA) ... SLJR
Sudan Law Journal and Reports [*Khartoum*] [*A publication*] (DLA) ... Sudan LJ & Rep
Sudan News Agency (BJA) ... SNA
Sudan News Agency ... SUNA
Sudan Notes and Records [*A publication*] ... SNR
Sudan People's Liberation Army ... SPLA
Sudan (Region) [*MARC geographic area code Library of Congress*] (LCCP) ... fn----
Sudanese Aeronautical Services Co. Ltd. [*Sudan*] [*ICAO designator*] (FAAC) ... SAC
Sudanese Aeronautical Services Co. Ltd. [*Sudan*] [*ICAO designator*] (FAAC) ... SASCO
Sudanese African Congress [*Political party*] (MENA) ... SAC
Sudanese African People's Congress [*Political party*] (EY) ... SAPCO
Sudanese Communist Party [*Political party*] (PD) ... SCP
Sudanese Flight [*Sudan*] [*ICAO designator*] (FAAC) ... SFT
Sudanese National Front [*Political party*] (PD) ... SNF
Sudanese National Party [*Political party*] (EY) ... SNP
Sudanese National Research Council ... SNRC
Sudanese People's Federal Party [*Sudan*] [*Political party*] (MENA) ... SPFP
Sudanese Pound (IMH) ... LS
Sudanese Youth Union ... SYU
Sudania Aviation Co. [*Sudan*] [*ICAO designator*] (FAAC) ... ASK
Sudania Aviation Co. [*Sudan*] [*ICAO designator*] (FAAC) ... SAC
Sudania Aviation Co. [*Sudan*] [*ICAO designator*] (FAAC) ... SAV
Sudanian Satellite ... SUDOSAT
Sudbury [*Ontario*] [*Seismograph station code, US Geological Survey*] (SEIS) ... SUD
Sudbury [*Canada*] [*Airport symbol*] (OAG) ... YSB
Sudbury Board of Education [*UTLAS symbol*] ... SUD
Sudbury Contact Mines Ltd. [*Toronto Stock Exchange symbol*] ... SUD
Sudbury General Hospital, Ontario [*Library symbol National Library of Canada*] (NLC) ... OSUGH
Sudbury General Hospital, Sudbury, ON, Canada [*Library symbol Library of Congress*] (LCLS) ... CaOSuGH
Sudbury Igneous Complex [*Geology*] ... SIC
Sudbury, Inc. [*Associated Press*] (SAG) ... Sudbury
Sudbury, Inc. [*NASDAQ symbol*] (NQ) ... SUDS
Sudbury, MA [*FM radio station call letters*] ... WYAJ
Sudbury Neutrino Observatory [*Proposed joint US-Canadian project*] ... SNO
Sudbury, ON [*FM radio station call letters*] ... CBCS
Sudbury, ON [*Television station call letters*] ... CBLFT-2
Sudbury, ON [*FM radio station call letters*] ... CBON
Sudbury, ON [*AM radio station call letters*] ... CHNO
Sudbury, ON [*AM radio station call letters*] ... CHYC
Sudbury, ON [*Television station call letters*] ... CICI
Sudbury, ON [*Television station call letters*] ... CICO-19
Sudbury, ON [*AM radio station call letters*] ... CIGM
Sudbury, ON [*FM radio station call letters*] ... CJMX
Sudbury, ON [*FM radio station call letters*] ... CJRQ
Sudbury, ON [*Television station call letters*] ... CKNC
Sudbury, ON [*ICAO location identifier*] (ICLI) ... CYSB
Sudbury Public Library, Information and Reference, Sudbury, ON, Canada [*Library symbol*] [*Library of Congress*] (LCLS) ... CaOSUCS
Sudbury Public Library, Ontario [*Library symbol National Library of Canada*] (NLC) ... OSU
Sudbury Public Library, Sudbury, ON, Canada [*Library symbol Library of Congress*] (LCLS) ... CaOSu
Sudden Auroral Intensity ... SAI
Sudden Cardiac Death [*Medicine*] ... SCD
Sudden Changes in the Integrated Intensity of Atmospherics (PDAA) ... SCIIA
Sudden Commencement ... SC
Sudden Coronary Death (MAE) ... SCD
Sudden Cosmic-Noise Absorption ... SCNA
Sudden Death [*Medicine*] ... SD
Sudden Death [*Tiebreaking in sports*] ... S-D
Sudden Death Syndrome [*in children*] [*Medicine*] ... SDS
Sudden Drowning Syndrome ... SDS
Sudden Enhancement of Atmospherics [*NASA*] ... SEA
Sudden Expansion ... SUE
Sudden Frequency Deviation ... SFD
Sudden Heart Death [*Medicine*] (DMAA) ... SHD
Sudden Increase of Solar Particles ... SISP
Sudden Infant Death [*Syndrome*] [*Medicine*] ... SID
Sudden Infant Death Syndrome [*Medicine*] ... SIDS
Sudden Infant Death Syndrome Act of 1974 ... SIDSA
Sudden Infant Death Syndrome Alliance (PAZ) ... SIDS Alliance
Sudden Ionospheric Disturbance [*Geophysics*] ... SID
Sudden Phase Anomaly [*Radio engineering*] ... SPA
Sudden Pressure Relay ... SPR
Sudden Shortwave Fade ... SSWF
Sudden Sniffing Death (DAVI) ... SSD
Sudden Storm Commencement [*Physics*] ... SSC
Sudden Stratospheric Warming (EERA) ... SSW
Sudden Tetanus of Prey [*Biology*] ... STOP
Sudden Unexpected [*or Unexplained*] **Death** [*Medicine*] ... SUD
Sudden Unexpected Death in Infancy [*Medicine*] (DMAA) ... SUDI
Sudden Unexpected Infant Death [*Medicine*] ... SUID
Sudden Unexpected Nocturnal Death Syndrome [*Medicine*] (ECON) ... SUNDS
Sudden, Unexpected, Unexplained Death (DAVI) ... SUUD
Sudden Unexplained Death in Epilepsy [*Medicine*] ... SUDEP
Sudden Unexplained Infant Death [*Neonatology*] (DAVI) ... SUID
Sudden Wave Fade Out (IAA) ... SWF
Sudden-Death Heart Disease [*Medicine*] ... SDHD
Sudden-Death Ischemic Heart Disease [*Medicine*] ... SDIHD
Sudden-Dosage Onset [*Pharmacology*] (DAVI) ... SOD
Sudder Dewanny Adawlut [*or Sadr Diwani Adalat*] **Reports** [*India*] [*A publication*] (DLA) ... Sud Dew Ad
Sudder Dewanny [*or Sadr Diwani*] **Reports, Northwest Province** [*India*] [*A publication*] (DLA) ... Sud Dew Rep
Sudeten German Party ... SGP
Sudetendeutsche Partei [*Sudeten German Party*] [*Former Czechoslovakia*] [*Political party*] (PPE) ... SdP
Sudflug Suddeutsche Fluggesellschaft MbH [*Germany ICAO designator*] (FAAC) ... SFG
Sud-Ghoubbet [*Djibouti*] [*Seismograph station code, US Geological Survey*] (SEIS) ... SGH
Sudorific [*Causing Sweat*] [*Pharmacy*] (ROG) ... SUD
Sudost-Bahn [*Swiss Southeastern Railway*] ... SOB
Sudtiroler Volkspartei [*South Tyrolean People's Party*] [*Italy Political party*] (EAIO) ... SVP
Sudureyri [*Iceland*] [*Airport symbol*] (OAG) ... SUY
Sue and Labor Charges [*Insurance*] ... SL
Sue and Labor Clause [*Business term*] ... SLC
Sue Bennett College [*London, KY*] ... SBC
Sueddeutsche Juristenzeitung [*German*] (ILCA) ... SJZ
Sueddeutsche Kalkstickstoffwerke [*AG*] ... SKW
Sueddeutscher Rundfunk [*South German Radio Network*] ... SDR
Suede and Leather Refinishers of America [*Defunct*] (EA) ... SLRA
Suedschleswigscher Waehlerverband [*South Schleswig Voter's League*] [*Also, SSV*] [*Germany*] [*Political party*] (PPE) ... SSW
Suedwestfunk [*Radio network*] [*West Germany*] ... SWF
Suetonius [*First century AD*] [*Classical studies*] (OCD) ... Suet
Suez Canal [*MARC geographic area code Library of Congress*] (LCCP) ... fu----
Suez Canal Users Association (NATG) ... SCUA
Suez Petroleum Corp. [*Vancouver Stock Exchange symbol*] ... SUZ
Suez-Mediterranean [*Pipeline*] ... SUMED
Sufentanil [*or Sulfentanyl*] [*An analgesic*] ... Su
Suffern Free Library, Suffern, NY [*Library symbol Library of Congress*] (LCLS) ... NSuf
Sufficient (AFM) ... SUF
Sufficient ... SUFF
Sufficient ... SUFFT
Sufficient Feasibility Test ... SFT
Sufficient Funding (MCD) ... SF
Sufficiently (ROG) ... SUFFTY
Sufficit [*Suffices*] [*Latin*] ... SUFF
Suffield [*Alberta*] [*Seismograph station code, US Geological Survey*] (SEIS) ... SES
Suffield, AB [*ICAO location identifier*] (ICLI) ... CYSD
Suffield Experimental Station [*Canada*] ... SES
Suffix (AAG) ... SUFF
Suffolk [*County in England*] ... SUFF
Suffolk Academy of Medicine, Hauppauge, NY [*Library symbol Library of Congress*] (LCLS) ... NHapSA
Suffolk and Cambridgeshire Regiment [*British military*] (DMA) ... SC
Suffolk Bancorp [*Riverhead, NY*] [*NASDAQ symbol*] (NQ) ... SUBK
Suffolk Bancorp [*Associated Press*] (SAG) ... SuffBnc
Suffolk Cooperative Library System, Bellport, NY [*Library symbol Library of Congress*] (LCLS) ... NBelS

Suffolk County Community College, Eastern Campus, Riverhead, NY
   [Library symbol Library of Congress] (LCLS) .... NSelC-E
Suffolk County Community College, Selden, NY [Library symbol Library of
   Congress] (LCLS) .... NSelC
Suffolk County Community College, Western Campus, Brentwood, NY
   [Library symbol Library of Congress] (LCLS) .... NSelC-W
Suffolk County Court House, Boston, MA [Library symbol Library of
   Congress] (LCLS) .... MBSufC
Suffolk County Department of Health Service, Hauppauge, NY [Library
   symbol] [Library of Congress] (LCLS) .... NHapS
Suffolk County Department of Health Service, Hauppauge, NY [Library
   symbol Library of Congress] (LCLS) .... NHauS
Suffolk County Historical Society, Riverhead, NY [Library symbol Library of
   Congress] (LCLS) .... NRvS
Suffolk Marine Museum, West Sayville, NY [Library symbol Library of
   Congress] (LCLS) .... NWesyM
Suffolk Museum at Stony Brook, Stony Brook, NY [Library symbol Library of
   Congress] (LCLS) .... NSbSM
Suffolk State School, Melville, NY [Library symbol Library of Congress]
   (LCLS) .... NMelS
Suffolk University (GAGS) .... Suffolk U
Suffolk University, Boston, MA [Library symbol Library of Congress]
   (LCLS) .... MBSuf
Suffolk University, Boston, MA [OCLC symbol] (OCLC) .... SUF
Suffolk University, Law Library, Boston, MA [OCLC symbol] (OCLC) ..... SLL
Suffolk, VA [Location identifier FAA] (FAAL) .... SFQ
Suffolk, VA [FM radio station call letters] .... WAFX
Suffolk, VA [FM radio station call letters] .... WFOG
Suffolk, VA [AM radio station call letters] .... WLPM
Suffragan [Ecclesiastical] (ROG) .... SUFF
Suffragan [Ecclesiastical] (WGA) .... SUFFR
Sufonylurea Receptor [Biochemistry] .... SUR
Sufuric Acid Terrahydrate [Inorganic chemistry] .... SAT
Sugar [Phonetic alphabet] [Royal Navy World War I Pre-World War II] [World
   War II] (DSUE) .... S
Sugar .... SUG
Sugar .... SUG
Sugar, Acetone, Diacetic Acid [Test] [Medicine] .... SAD
Sugar and Acetone [Medicine] .... S & A
Sugar and Acetone Determination [Endocrinology] (DAVI) ..... SAD
Sugar Association .... SA
Sugar Association, Inc. (EA) .... SAI
Sugar Association of the Caribbean [Port Of Spain, Trinidad] (EAIO) ..... SAC
Sugar Beet Pulp (PDAA) .... SBP
Sugar Cane Downy Mildew [Plant pathology] .... SDM
Sugar Cane Mosaic Virus .... SCMV
Sugar Determination .... SD
Sugar Flotation [Soil testing] .... SF
Sugar Hotel Alpha Victor Echo [Apollo 10 astronauts' code for shaving
   operation] .... SHAVE
Sugar Industry Adjustment Assistance Program [Australia] ..... SIAAP
Sugar Industry Manufacturers and Service Group of Australia ..... SIMSGA
Sugar Industry Technologists (EA) .... SIT
Sugar Information, Inc. [Defunct] (EA) .... SII
Sugar Island [Michigan] [Seismograph station code, US Geological Survey
   Closed] (SEIS) .... SUG
Sugar Land [Texas] [Airport symbol] (OAG) .... SGR
Sugar Packet Club (EA) .... SPC
Sugar Packet Collectors Club (EA) .... SPCC
Sugar Phosphate [Biochemistry] .... SP
Sugar Processing Research, Inc. .... SPRI
Sugar Rationing Administration [Department of Agriculture] [Ceased
   functions, 1948] .... SRA
Sugar Requirements and Quotas .... SR
Sugar Research and Development Corp. (EERA) .... SRDC
Sugar Research Foundation, Inc. [Later, ISRF] (EA) .... SRFI
Sugar Research Institute [Australia] .... SRI
Sugar Salem School/Community Library, Sugar City, ID [Library symbol]
   [Library of Congress] (LCLS) .... IdSc
Sugar Snap [Peas] (DICI) .... SS
Sugar, Tobacco, Alcohol, Fat, and Salt .... STAFS
Sugar-Coated [Pharmacy] .... SC
Sugar-Coated Tablet .... SCT
Sugar-Free [Pharmacy] .... SF
Sugar-Tong Splint [Medicine] (MEDA) .... STS
Sugary [A gene in sweet corn] .... su
Sugary Enhancer [A gene in sweet corn] .... se
Sugden on Powers [8 eds.] [1808-61] [A publication] (DLA) ..... Sug Pow
Sugden on Powers [A publication] (DLA) .... Sugd Powers
Sugden on Property Statutes [A publication] (DLA) .... Sug Pr St
Sugden on the Law of Estates [A publication] (DLA) .... Sug Est
Sugden on the Law of Property [A publication] (DLA) .... Sug Pr
Sugden on the Law of Property as Administered by the House of Lords
   [A publication] (DLA) .... Sug Prop
Sugden on Vendors and Purchasers [14 eds.] [1805-62] [A publication]
   (DLA) .... Sug V & P
Sugden on Vendors and Purchasers [A publication] (DLA) ..... Sug Vend
Sugden on Vendors and Purchasers [A publication] (DLA) ..... Sugd Vend
Sugden's Hand-Book of Property Law [A publication] (DLA) ..... Sug Hd Bk
SUGEN, Inc. [Associated Press] (SAG) .... SUGEN
SUGEN, Inc. [NASDAQ symbol] (SAG) .... SUGN
Sugendus [To Be Sucked] [Pharmacy] .... SUGEND
Suggest (AFM) .... SUG
Suggested for Mature Audiences [Motion pictures] .... SMA
Suggested No Adverse Risk Levels [Environmental Protection Agency] ..... SNARL

Suggested Retail Price .... SRP
Suggested Retail Price (WDMC) .... SRP
Suggested State Regulations for the Control of Radiation [Nuclear
   Regulatory Commission] (NRCH) .... SSRCR
Suggestion (ROG) .... SUGG
Suggestion Program Data System [Military] .... SPDS
Suggestive-Accelerative Learning and Teaching (EDAC) .... SALT
Sugluk [Canada] [Airport symbol] (OAG) .... YZG
Sui [Pakistan] [ICAO location identifier] (ICLI) .... OPSU
Sui [Pakistan] [Airport symbol] (OAG) .... SUL
Sui Generis Degree .... SGD
Suia-Missu [Brazil] [Airport symbol] (OAG) .... SWM
Suicidal/Homicidal [Ideation] [Psychiatry] (DAVI) .... S/H
Suicidal Ideation [Psychiatry] (DAVI) .... SI
Suicide Information and Education [Suicide Information and Education
   Center] [Canada Information service or system] (CRD) ..... SIE
Suicide Information and Education Centre [Canadian Mental Health
   Association] [Information service or system] (IID) .... SIEC
[The] Suicide Information and Education Centre, Calgary, Alberta [Library
   symbol National Library of Canada] (NLC) .... ACSIEC
Suicide Precaution (MAE) .... SP
Suicide Prevention Association [Australia] .... SPA
Suicide Prevention Center (IIA) .... SPC
Suicide Probability Scale [Personality development test] [Psychology] ..... SPS
Suid-Afrikaanse Lugmag [South African Air Force] [See also SALM, SAAF] ..... SAL
Suider Afrikaanse Katolieke Biskopsraad [Southern African Catholic Bishops'
   Conference - SACBC] (EAIO) .... SAKB
Suider-Afrika Padfederasie [Southern Africa Road Federation - SARF]
   (EAIO) .... SAPF
Suihwa [Republic of China] [Seismograph station code, US Geological
   Survey] (SEIS) .... SUI
Suinn Test Anxiety Behavior Scale [Psychology] .... STABS
Suippes [France ICAO location identifier] (ICLI) .... LFFS
Suit .... S
Suit (DNAB) .... SU
Suit Communication System [for spacesuits] [NASA] .... SCS
Suit, Contamination Avoidance, and Liquid Protection [Army] ..... SCALP
Suit Cooling Unit (IAA) .... SCU
Suit Umbilical System (MCD) .... SUS
Suit Ventilation System [Aerospace] (MCD) .... SVS
Suitability (CAAL) .... S
Suitability Evaluation Team (MCD) .... SET
Suitability Index [Fishery science] .... SI
Suitability Test [Military] (CAAL) .... S (Test)
Suitability Test Evaluation (AAG) .... STE
Suitable Occupation for a Sloane [British Slang] .... SOFAS
Suitcase Emergency Procedures Trainer (MCD) .... SCEPTR
Suite .... STE
Suite .... Su
Suivant [Following] [French] .... SUIV
Suiza Foods [NASDAQ symbol] (TTSB) .... SWZA
Suiza Foods Corp. [Associated Press] (SAG) .... SuizaF
Suiza Foods Corp. [NASDAQ symbol] (SAG) .... SWZA
Sukes Enterprises [NASDAQ symbol] (TTSB) .... SYKE
Sukhoy [Aircraft] .... SU
Sukhumi [USSR] [Airport symbol] (AD) .... SUI
Sukhumi [Former USSR ICAO location identifier] (ICLI) ...... UGSS
Suki [Papua New Guinea] [Airport symbol] (OAG) .... SKC
Sukkah (BJA) .... Suk
Sukkertoppen [Greenland] [ICAO location identifier] (ICLI) .... BGST
Sukkertoppen [Greenland] [Airport symbol] (AD) .... JSU
Sukkur [Pakistan] [ICAO location identifier] (ICLI) .... OPSK
Sukkur [Pakistan] [Airport symbol] (OAG) .... SKZ
Sukuma [MARC language code Library of Congress] (LCCP) ..... suk
Sukuma Exploration [Vancouver Stock Exchange symbol] ..... SMA
Sul Ross State College [Later, SRSU] [Texas] .... SRSC
Sul Ross State University [Texas] .... SRSU
Sul Ross State University (GAGS) .... Sul Ross St U
Sul Ross State University, Alpine, TX [Library symbol Library of Congress]
   (LCLS) .... TxAlpS
Sul Ross State University, Library, Alpine, TX [OCLC symbol] (OCLC) ..... SUR
Sulaco [Honduras] [Airport symbol] (AD) .... SCD
Sulamethoxazole and Trimethoprim [Antibiotics] (DAVI) ..... SMZTMP
Sulawesi Regional Development Project [Coordinated by Indonesian and
   Canadian governments] (ECON) .... SRDP
Sulayel [Saudi Arabia] [ICAO location identifier] (ICLI) ...... OESL
Sulayel [Saudi Arabia] [Airport symbol] (AD) .... SLF
Sulbactam (DMAA) .... SBT
Sulcus [Brain anatomy] .... Su
Sulcus Computer [AMEX symbol] (TTSB) .... SUL
Sulcus Computer Corp. [AMEX symbol] (SPSG) .... SUL
Sulcus Computer Corp. [Associated Press] (SAG) .... Sulcus
Sule [Papua New Guinea] [Airport symbol] (OAG) .... ULE
Sulf South Medical Supply [Associated Press] (SAG) .... GulfSou
Sulfabromomethazine [Antibacterial] [Veterinary medicine] .... SBZ
Sulfachloropyridazine [Antibacterial] .... SCP
Sulfadiazine [Antibiotic] .... SDA
Sulfadiazine [Microbiology] (DAVI) .... SPS
Sulfadimethoxine [Antibacterial] [Veterinary medicine] .... SDM
Sulfamethazine [Antibacterial] [Veterinary medicine] .... SMZ
Sulfamethoxazole [Also, SMX, SMZ] [Antibacterial compound] ..... S
Sulfamethoxazole [Also, S, SMZ] [Antibacterial compound] .... SMX
Sulfamethoxazole [or Sulphamethoxazole] [An antibacterial] (DAVI) ..... SMX
Sulfamethoxazole [Also, S, SMX] [Antibacterial compound] .... SMZ
Sulfamethoxazole [An antibacterial] (DAVI) .... SXT

Sulfamethoxazole and Trimethoprim [*Medicine*] (DMAA) ... SULF-PRIM
Sulfamethoxypyridazine [*Antimicrobial compound*] ... SMP
Sulfanilamide [*Antimicrobial compound*] ... SNM
Sulfaquinoxaline [*or (Sulfanilamido)quinoxaline*] [*Animal antibiotic*] ... SQX
Sulfarsphenamine [*or Sulpharsphenamine*] [*Chemistry*] (DAVI) ... Sar
Sulfasalazine [*Pharmacology*] (DAVI) ... SAS
Sulfasalazine (MEDA) ... SS
Sulfate ... S
Sulfate (GNE) ... SO_4
Sulfate [*or Sulphate*] [*Chemistry*] (DAVI) ... sulf
Sulfate of Potash [*Fertilizer*] ... SOP
Sulfate of Potash Magnesia Export Association (EA) ... SkMg
Sulfate of Potash Magnesia Export Association (EA) ... SPMEA
Sulfate Reducing Bacteria ... SRB
Sulfate Reduction Index [*Environmental chemistry*] ... SRI
Sulfate-Binding Protein [*Biochemistry*] ... SBP
Sulfated Acid Mucopolysaccharide [*Medicine*] (MAE) ... SAM
Sulfated Ethoxylated Alcohol [*Surfactants*] ... SEA
Sulfated Glycoprotein [*Biochemistry*] ... SGP
Sulfated Hydrogenated Castor Oil (MAE) ... SHCO
Sulfated Polysaccharide-Peptoglycan [*Biochemistry*] ... SP-PG
Sulfation Factor [*of blood serum*] ... SF
Sulfhemoglobin [*Medicine*] (MAE) ... S Hb
Sulfhemoglobin [*Also, Sulfmethemoglobin*] [*Biochemistry*] (DAVI) ... SULFHB
Sulfhydryl [*Chemistry*] ... SH
Sulfide Production, Indole Production, and Motility [*Growth medium*] ... SIM
Sulfide Stress Corrosion Cracking (MCD) ... SSCC
Sulfinpyrazone [*Uricosuric compound*] ... SPZ
Sulfisoxazole [*An antibiotic*] ... SSX
Sulfite Evaporator Condensate [*Pulp and paper technolgy*] ... SEC
Sulfite Oxidase [*An enzyme*] ... SOase
Sulfite Sensitive Asthmatic ... SSA
Sulfite Waste Liquor ... SWL
Sulfite-Polymyxin-Sulfadiazine [*Agar*] [*Microbiology*] ... SPS
Sulfocyanate [*Organic chemistry*] (DAVI) ... CNS
Sulfofluorescein Diacetate [*Biological stain*] ... SFDA
Sulfo-Iduronate Sulfatase (DMAA) ... SIDS
Sulfomethoxine [*Medicine*] (MAE) ... SOM
Sulfonamide ... SA
Sulfonamide [*An antibiotic*] (DAVI) ... SU
Sulfonamide-Resistant [*Microbiology*] ... SR
Sulfonated Chemimechanical Pulp [*Pulp and paper technology*] ... SCMP
Sulfonium Compounds Containing Expellable Sophisticated Sidegroups [*Photoresists*] ... SUCCESS
Sulfonyldiphenol [*Organic chemistry*] ... SDP
(Sulfophenylazo)dihydroxynaphthalene-disulfonate [*Organic chemistry*] ... SPADNS
Sulfophosphovanillin (Reaction) [*Clinical chemistry*] ... SPV
Sulfopropyl [*Organic chemistry*] ... SP
Sulforicinoleic Acid [*Organic chemistry*] ... SRA
Sulfosalicylic Acid [*Organic chemistry*] ... SSA
Sulfotransferase [*An enzyme*] ... ST
Sulfur [*Chemical element*] ... S
Sulfur [*Chemical element*] (DAVI) ... SULF
Sulfur and Nitrogen Emissions (GNE) ... SANE
Sulfur Chemiluminescence Detector ... SCD
Sulfur Colloid [*Chemistry*] (DAVI) ... SC
Sulfur Development Institute of Canada ... SUDIC
Sulfur Dioxide [*Organic chemistry*] (DAVI) ... SO_2
Sulfur Dioxide ... SO2
Sulfur Hexafluoride [*Used in fluid-gas exchange*] [*Ophthalmology*] (DAVI) ... SF-6
Sulfur Oxide ... SOX
Sulfur Oxide Control Technology Assessment Panel [*Federal interagency committee*] ... SOCTAP
Sulfur Oxidizing Bacteria ... SOB
Sulfur, Phosphorus, Emission Detector [*Chromatograph accessory*] ... SPED
Sulfur Recovery Unit [*Chemical engineering*] ... SRU
Sulfur Reducing Bacteria [*Diesel fuels*] ... SRB
Sulfur Trioxide Chlorsulfonic Acid [*Inorganic chemistry*] ... FS
Sulfur-Asphalt Module [*Road-paving technology*] ... SAM
Sulfur-Coated Urea [*Chemical technology*] ... SCU
Sulfur-Disproportionating Bacteria ... SDB
Sulfuric Acid (GNE) ... H_2SO_4
Sulfuric Acid [*Chemistry*] (DAVI) ... H_2SO_4
Sulfuric Acid Concentrate (MCD) ... SAC
Sulfuric Acid Regenerator (MCD) ... SAR
Sulfur-Lead Analyzer ... SLA
Sulgi Hymn A (BJA) ... SHa
Sulgi Hymn D (BJA) ... SHd
Sulla [*of Plutarch*] [*Classical studies*] (OCD) ... Sull
Sullana [*Peru*] [*ICAO location identifier*] (ICLI) ... SPAN
Sullins College, Bristol, VA [*Library symbol Library of Congress*] (LCLS) ... ViBS
Sullivan County Community College, South Fallsburg, NY [*Library symbol Library of Congress*] (LCLS) ... NSfSC
Sullivan County Historical Society, Sullivan, IN [*Library symbol Library of Congress*] (LCLS) ... InSuHi
Sullivan County Public Library, Sullivan, IN [*Library symbol Library of Congress*] (LCLS) ... InSu
Sullivan County Public Library, Sullivan, IN [*Library symbol*] [*Library of Congress*] (LCLS) ... InSuC
Sullivan County Recorder's Office, Sullivan, IN [*Library symbol Library of Congress*] (LCLS) ... InSuCR
Sullivan Daily Times, Sullivan, IN [*Library symbol Library of Congress*] (LCLS) ... InSuT
Sullivan Dental Products [*NASDAQ symbol*] (SAG) ... SULL
Sullivan Dental Products [*Associated Press*] (SAG) ... Sull Dnt
Sullivan, IL [*FM radio station call letters*] (RBYB) ... WZNX
Sullivan, IN [*Location identifier FAA*] (FAAL) ... SIV
Sullivan, IN [*AM radio station call letters*] ... WNDI
Sullivan, IN [*FM radio station call letters*] ... WNDI-FM
Sullivan Mines, Inc. [*Toronto Stock Exchange symbol*] ... SUM
Sullivan, MO [*AM radio station call letters*] ... KTUI
Sullivan, MO [*FM radio station call letters*] ... KTUI-FM
Sullivan Museum, Zionsville, IN [*Library symbol Library of Congress*] (LCLS) ... InZSM
Sullivans Cove Development Authority [*Tasmania, Australia*] ... SCDA
Sullivan's Land Titles in Massachusetts [*A publication*] (DLA) ... Sull Ld Tit
Sullivan's Lectures on Constitution and Laws of England [*A publication*] (DLA) ... Sull Lect
Sullom Voe [*British ICAO location identifier*] (ICLI) ... EGRS
Sully-Potter County Library, Gettysburg, SD [*Library symbol Library of Congress*] (LCLS) ... SdGe
Sulpetro Ltd. [*Toronto Stock Exchange symbol*] ... SUL
Sulphate [*or Sulfate*] [*Chemistry*] (DAVI) ... sulph
Sulphate Regional Experiment [*Electric Power Research Institute*] ... SURE
Sulphate Resisting Portland Cement ... SRPC
Sulphite Pulp Manufacturers' Research League (EA) ... SPMRL
Sulphocynogen [*Pharmacy*] (ROG) ... CSY
Sulphonamide [*or Sulfonamide*] [*An antibacterial*] (DAVI) ... sulpha
Sulphur ... SLPHR
Sulphur Creek [*New Britain*] [*Seismograph station code, US Geological Survey*] (SEIS) ... SUL
Sulphur Development Institute of Canada ... SUDIC
Sulphur Development Institute of Canada, Calgary, AB, Canada [*Library symbol Library of Congress*] (LCLS) ... CaACSDI
Sulphur Development Institute of Canada, Calgary, Alberta [*Library symbol National Library of Canada*] (NLC) ... ACSDI
Sulphur Export Corp. [*An association*] (EA) ... SEC
Sulphur Export Corp. [*An association*] (EA) ... SuLEXCo
Sulphur Extended Asphalt [*Paving material*] ... SEA
Sulphur Institute (EA) ... SI
Sulphur, LA [*AM radio station call letters*] ... KEZM
Sulphur, LA [*FM radio station call letters*] ... KKGB
Sulphur, OK [*FM radio station call letters*] ... KFXT
Sulphur Oxides [*Chemical*] (EERA) ... SOx
Sulphur Springs, TX [*Location identifier FAA*] (FAAL) ... BHG
Sulphur Springs, TX [*FM radio station call letters*] ... KDXE
Sulphur Springs, TX [*AM radio station call letters*] ... KSST
Sulphur Springs, TX [*Location identifier FAA*] (FAAL) ... SLR
Sulphurets Gold [*Vancouver Stock Exchange symbol*] ... SLE
Sulphurized Mineral Oil (IAA) ... SM
Sulpician Archives Baltimore, Baltimore, MD [*Library symbol Library of Congress*] (LCLS) ... MdBSAr
Sulpician Seminary Theological College, Washington, DC [*Library symbol Library of Congress*] (LCLS) ... DTheolC
Sultan ... SULT
Sultanate of Oman Air Force ... SOAF
Sultan-Mazar [*Former USSR Seismograph station code, US Geological Survey Closed*] (SEIS) ... SMT
Sulzer Canada, Inc., Toronto, ON, Canada [*Library symbol*] [*Library of Congress*] (LCLS) ... CaOTSCI
Sulzer Canada, Inc., Toronto, Ontario [*Library symbol National Library of Canada*] (NLC) ... OTSCI
Sum (MAE) ... S
Sum Frequency Generation ... SFG
Sum Insured (ODBW) ... si
Sum of Absolute Residuals [*Mathematics*] ... SAR
Sum of Adjacent Spans ... SAS
Sum of All Repairable Subassemblies ... SRS
Sum of Digits (SAA) ... SD
Sum of Magnitudes of Pitch Matrix - Correlator ... SMPC
Sum of Magnitudes of Pitch Matrix - Skin ... SMPS
Sum of Magnitudes of Sum [*Channel Matrix*] **Correlator** ... SMSC
Sum of Magnitudes of Sum [*Channel Matrix*] **Skin** ... SMSS
Sum of Pain Intensity Differences ... SPID
Sum of Square Deviation (MAE) ... SSD
Sum of Squared Errors [*Statistics*] ... SSE
Sum of the Squared Residuals [*Econometrics*] ... SSR
Sum of the Squares (IAA) ... SSQ
Sum of the Year's Digits [*Statistics*] ... SYD
Sum of the Years' Digits Method [*Finance*] ... SOYD
Sum of Vector Elements (IAA) ... SVE
Sum over States [*Physics*] ... SOS
Sum Total and Nosegear (MCD) ... STAN
Suma Four [*NASDAQ symbol*] (TTSB) ... SUMA
Suma Industries [*NASDAQ symbol*] (SAG) ... SUMX
Sumac Ventures, Inc. [*Vancouver Stock Exchange symbol*] ... SSV
Sumantur [*Let It Be Taken*] [*Latin*] [*Pharmacy*] (DAVI) ... SUM
Sumat [*Let Him Take, Let the Person Take*] [*Latin*] [*Pharmacy*] (DAVI) ... SUM
Sumat Talem [*Take One Like This*] [*Pharmacy*] ... SUM TAL
Sumatra ... Sum
Sumatra (VRA) ... Sumat
Sumbawa [*Indonesia*] [*Airport symbol*] (AD) ... SWQ
Sumbawa/Sumbawa Besar [*Indonesia*] [*ICAO location identifier*] (ICLI) ... WRRS
Sumbawanga [*Tanzania*] [*ICAO location identifier*] (ICLI) ... HTSU
Sumbe [*Angola*] [*Airport symbol*] (OAG) ... NDD
Sumburgh [*British ICAO location identifier*] (ICLI) ... EGPB
Sume [*Take*] [*Pharmacy*] ... SUM
Sumendum [*To Be Taken*] [*Latin*] [*Pharmacy*] (DAVI) ... SUM
Sumendus [*To Be Taken*] [*Pharmacy*] ... S

Sumenep/Trunojoyo [*Indonesia*] [*ICAO location identifier*] (ICLI) .... WRST
Sumerian (BJA) .... Sum
Sumerian [*MARC language code Library of Congress*] (LCCP) .... sux
Sumerian and Babylonian Psalms [*A publication*] (BJA) .... SBP
Sumerian Animal Proverbs (BJA) .... SAP
Sumerian Laws (BJA) .... SL
Sumerian Mythology [*S. N. Kramer*] [*A publication*] (BJA) .... SM
Sumerian Proverbs (BJA) .... SP
Sumerian Texts of Varied Context [*E. Chiera*] [*A publication*] .... STVC
Sumerisch-Babylonische Hymnen [*A publication*] (BJA) .... SBH
Sumerische Kultlieder aus Altbabylonischer Zeit [*A publication*] (BJA) .... SK
Sumerisches Glossar [*A publication*] (BJA) .... SGI
Sumet [*Let Him, or Her, Take*] [*Pharmacy*] .... Su
Sumi-E Society of America (EA) .... SSA
Sumika Technical Information Service, Inc. [*Information service or system*] (IID) .... STIS
Sumitomo Atomic Energy Commission [*Japan*] .... SAEC
Sumitomo Atomic Energy Industries Ltd. [*Japan*] .... SAEI
Sumitomo Bank (CA) [*NASDAQ symbol*] (TTSB) .... SUMI
Sumitomo Bank CA Dep'A'Pfd [*NASDAQ symbol*] (TTSB) .... SUMIZ
Sumitomo Bank of California [*NASDAQ symbol*] (NQ) .... SUMI
Sumitomo Bank of California [*Associated Press*] (SAG) .... Sumito
Sumitomo Chemical Co. [*Japan*] [*Research code symbol*] .... CS
Sumitomo Chemical Co. [*Japan*] [*Research code symbol*] .... ID
Sumitomo Chemical Co. [*Japan*] [*Research code symbol*] .... PC
Sumitomo Electric Industries [*Auto inudustry supplier*] .... SEI
SumitomoBank of California [*Associated Press*] (SAG) .... Sumito
Sumiton, AL [*AM radio station call letters*] .... WRSM
Summa [*or Summe*] [*Sum or Total*] [*Latin*] .... Sa
Summa Four, Inc. [*NASDAQ symbol*] (SAG) .... SUMA
Summa Four, Inc. [*Associated Press*] (SAG) .... SummaF
Summa Industries [*Associated Press*] (SAG) .... Summa
Summa Industries [*NASDAQ symbol*] (SAG) .... SUMX
Summa Industries [*NASDAQ symbol*] (TTSB) .... SUMX
Summagraphics [*NASDAQ symbol*] (TTSB) .... SUGR
Summagraphics Corp. [*NASDAQ symbol*] (NQ) .... SUGR
Summagraphics Corp. [*Associated Press*] (SAG) .... Sumgph
Summarize (IAA) .... SUMM
Summarized Spares Requirement .... SSR
Summary .... S
Summary (FAAC) .... SMRY
Summary (MSA) .... SMY
Summary (AABC) .... SUM
Summary .... SUMM
Summary Accounting for Low-Dollar Turnover Items [*Army*] .... SALTI
Summary Activity Account [*Army*] (AABC) .... SAA
Summary Analysis Report (NASA) .... SAR
Summary and Charge Number .... SCN
Summary Annual Report .... SAR
Summary Area Problem Report (AAG) .... SAPR
Summary Billing Card (AFM) .... SBC
Summary Control Report [*Planning and Production*] [*Navy*] .... SCR
Summary Cost Account [*Military*] (AABC) .... SCA
Summary Court [*Navy*] .... SC
Summary Court-Martial [*Army*] .... SCM
Summary Court-Martial .... SUMCM
Summary Court-Martial Order [*Army*] .... SCMO
Summary Court-Martial Order .... SUMCMO
Summary Court-Martial Order .... SUMMCO
Summary Decisions [*Bengal, India*] [*A publication*] (DLA) .... Sum Dec
Summary Decisions [*Bengal, India*] [*A publication*] (ILCA) .... Summ Dec
Summary Development Cost Plan [*NASA*] (NASA) .... SDCP
Summary Earnings Record [*Social Security Administration*] (GFGA) .... SER
Summary Engineering Assessment Report (MCD) .... SEAR
Summary Financial Program .... SFP
Summary Flight Plan (MCD) .... SFP
Summary Flight Test Report (MCD) .... SFTR
Summary Format of Family Functioning .... SFFF
Summary Language (NITA) .... SL
Summary Management Data Report [*DoD*] .... SMDR
Summary Maneuver Plan .... SMP
Summary Memorandum .... SM
Summary Message Enable Keyboard .... SMEK
Summary of Component Control Status [*Nuclear energy*] (NRCH) .... SOCCS
Summary of Effective Allowance Parts List [*Navy*] .... SOEAP
Summary of Effective Allowance Parts List [*Navy*] (DNAB) .... SOEAPL
Summary of Engagements (MCD) .... SOE
Summary of Information on Film and Television [*British*] .... SIFT
Summary of Installation Control Status [*Nuclear energy*] (NRCH) .... SOICS
Summary of Monthly Aerological Reports [*Navy*] (DNAB) .... SMAR
Summary of Navy Approved Programs .... SNAP
Summary of Pennsylvania Jurisprudence [*A publication*] (DLA) .... PA Summary
Summary of Proceedings and Debate [*of House of Representatives*] .... SOPAD
Summary of Radiation Tolerant Electronics .... SORTE
Summary of Reported Defects, Incidents and Delays (MHDB) .... SORDID
Summary of Supplemental Type Certificates .... SSTC
Summary of Synoptic Meteorological Observations [*National Oceanic and Atmospheric Administration*] (MSC) .... SSMO
Summary of the Law of Nisi Prius [*A publication*] (DLA) .... Summ NP
Summary of World Broadcasts [*British Broadcasting Corporation*] .... SWB
Summary Parts List .... SPL
Summary Performance Measure (MCD) .... SUMPM
Summary Plan Description .... SPD
Summary Plot Board (SAA) .... SPB
Summary Plotter [*RADAR*] .... SP

Summary Punch [*Computer science*] (OA) .... SP
Summary Punch Control [*Computer science*] (IAA) .... SPC
Summary Punch IBM [*International Business Machines*] **Collector** .... SPIC
Summary Reference File (DOMA) .... SRF
Summary Report .... SR
Summary Requirements List (MCD) .... SRL
Summary Sheet .... SS
Summary Sheet Bar Chart [*NASA*] (NASA) .... SSBC
Summary Statistical Data [*Federal government*] .... SUMSTAT
Summary Status Entry (SAA) .... SSE
Summary Tape Assistance, Research, and Training .... START
Summary Tape File [*Bureau of the Census*] (GFGA) .... STF
Summary Tape Operations Rental [*Bureau of the Census*] .... STOR
Summary Task Planning Sheet .... STPS
Summary Technical Report .... STR
Summating Potential [*Hearing*] .... SP
Summation (AAMN) .... SUM
Summation Check [*Communications transmissions*] .... CHECKSUM
Summation Gallop [*Cardiology*] .... SG
Summation Sound .... SS
Summator (IAA) .... SUM
Summed Pain Intensity Difference [*Medicine*] (DMAA) .... SPID
Summer [*Vessel load line mark*] .... LS
Summer [*Vessel load line mark*] .... S
Summer .... SUM
Summer .... SUMM
Summer and Casual Furniture Manufacturers Association (EA) .... SCFMA
Summer Campus, Advanced Mathematics Program [*Institute for Defense Analysis*] .... SCAMP
Summer Community Organization and Political Education Program .... SCOPE
Summer Computer Simulation Conference .... SCSC
Summer Cultural Opportunities for Teams and Children [*National music program*] .... SCOTCH
Summer Educational Enrichment .... SEE
Summer Emergency [*Vessel load line mark*] .... SE
Summer Employment for Science Students .... SESS
Summer Employment Youth [*DoD*] .... SEY
Summer Experiment Group [*Summer work for engineering undergraduates*] .... SEX
Summer Food Service Program [*Department of Agriculture*] (GFGA) .... SFSP
Summer Institute of Linguistics .... SIL
Summer Program for Economically Disadvantaged Youth [*Department of Labor*] .... SPEDY
Summer Time [*Daylight saving time*] .... ST
Summer Training Employment Program (MCD) .... STEP
Summer Work Program .... SWP
Summer Youth Employment Program [*Department of Labor*] .... SYEP
Summer Youth Recreation Program .... SYRP
Summerdale Elementary School, Rockford, IL [*Library symbol*] [*Library of Congress*] (LCLS) .... IRoSuE
Summerdale, PA [*FM radio station call letters*] .... WJAZ
Summerfield's Reports [*21 Nevada*] [*A publication*] (DLA) .... Summerfield
Summerford Public Library, Newfoundland [*Library symbol National Library of Canada*] (NLC) .... NFSU
Summerford Public Library, Summerford, NF, Canada [*Library symbol Library of Congress*] (LCLS) .... CaNfSu
Summerland, BC [*AM radio station call letters*] .... CHOR
Summerland Key, FL [*FM radio station call letters*] .... WPIK
Summerland Museum, British Columbia [*Library symbol National Library of Canada*] (NLC) .... BSUM
Summerside [*Prince Edward Island*] [*Airport symbol*] (AD) .... YSU
Summerside Canadian Forces Base, PE [*ICAO location identifier*] (ICLI) .... CYSU
Summerside, PE [*AM radio station call letters*] .... CJRW
Summersville School District 79, Mount Vernon, IL [*Library symbol Library of Congress*] (LCLS) .... IMtvSD
Summersville, WV [*Location identifier FAA*] (FAAL) .... IJZ
Summersville, WV [*Location identifier FAA*] (FAAL) .... SXL
Summersville, WV [*FM radio station call letters*] .... WCWV
Summersville, WV [*FM radio station call letters*] .... WMLJ
Summerton [*South Carolina*] [*Seismograph station code, US Geological Survey Closed*] (SEIS) .... SMA
Summerville, GA [*AM radio station call letters*] .... WGTA
Summerville, SC [*AM radio station call letters*] .... WAZS
Summerville, SC [*FM radio station call letters*] .... WWWZ
Summing .... SUM
Summing Amplifier .... SA
Summing Selector (MSA) .... SS
Summit (MCD) .... SMT
Summit .... SMT
Summit [*Commonly used*] (OPSA) .... SUMIT
Summit [*Commonly used*] (OPSA) .... SUMITT
Summit [*Commonly used*] (OPSA) .... SUMMIT
Summit Airlines [*ICAO designator*] (FAAC) .... SMM
Summit, AK [*Location identifier FAA*] (FAAL) .... UMM
Summit Bancorp [*NYSE symbol*] (TTSB) .... SUB
Summit Bancorp New Jersey [*Associated Press*] (SAG) .... SumitB
[*The*] Summit Bancorporation [*NASDAQ symbol*] (NQ) .... SUBN
Summit Bancshares [*NASDAQ symbol*] (TTSB) .... SBIT
Summit Bancshares Texas [*NASDAQ symbol*] (SAG) .... SBIT
Summit Bancshares Texas [*Associated Press*] (SAG) .... SmtBTX
Summit Bancshares TX [*Associated Press*] (SAG) .... SumtBTX
Summit Bank Corp. [*NASDAQ symbol*] (SAG) .... SBGA
Summit Bank Corp. (GA) [*Associated Press*] (SAG) .... SmtBGA
Summit Bcp Adj B Pfd [*NYSE symbol*] (TTSB) .... SUBPrB
Summit Books [*Publisher's imprint*] .... S
Summit Care [*NASDAQ symbol*] (TTSB) .... SUMC

Summit Care Corp. [*NASDAQ symbol*] (SAG) .... SUMC
Summit Care Corp. [*Associated Press*] (SAG) .... SumtCre
Summit City Clerk, Summit, NJ [*Library symbol Library of Congress*] (LCLS) .... NjSCC
Summit County Public Library, Frisco, CO [*Library symbol Library of Congress*] (LCLS) .... CoFr
Summit Design, Inc. [*NASDAQ symbol*] (SAG) .... SMMT
Summit Design, Inc. [*Associated Press*] (SAG) .... SumtDsg
Summit Family Restaurants [*NASDAQ symbol*] (TTSB) .... SMFR
Summit Family Restaurants, Inc. [*NASDAQ symbol*] (SAG) ...... SMFR
Summit Family Restaurants, Inc. [*Associated Press*] (SAG) .... SumitFR
Summit Financial [*NASDAQ symbol*] (SAG) .... SUMM
Summit Financial [*Associated Press*] (SAG) .... SumtFn
Summit Free Public Library, Summit, NJ [*Library symbol Library of Congress*] (LCLS) .... NjS
Summit Herald, Summit, NJ [*Library symbol Library of Congress*] (LCLS) ...... NjSH
Summit, IL [*FM radio station call letters*] .... WARG
Summit: Journal of the Liturgical Commission [*of the Archdiocese of Melbourne*] [*A publication*] (APTA) .... Sum
Summit Lane Elementary School, Levittown, NY [*Library symbol*] [*Library of Congress*] (LCLS) .... NLevSLE
Summit Medical System [*NASDAQ symbol*] (TTSB) .... SUMT
Summit Medical Systems, Inc. [*NASDAQ symbol*] (SAG) .... SUMT
Summit Medical Systems, Inc. [*Associated Press*] (SAG) ..... SumtMd
Summit Power Station [*Nuclear energy*] (NRCH) .... SPS
Summit Properties [*NYSE symbol*] (TTSB) .... SMT
Summit Properties, Inc. [*NYSE symbol*] (SAG) .... SMT
Summit Properties, Inc. [*Associated Press*] (SAG) .... SumtPrp
Summit Resources Ltd. [*Toronto Stock Exchange symbol*] .... SUI
Summit Tax Exempt Bond [*AMEX symbol*] (TTSB) .... SUA
Summit Tax Exempt Bond Fund Ltd. [*AMEX symbol*] (SPSG) ..... SUA
Summit Tax Exempt Bond Fund Ltd. [*Associated Press*] (SAG) .. SumtTx
Summit Technical Center [*Celanese Research Co.*] .... STC
Summit Technology [*NASDAQ symbol*] (TTSB) .... BEAM
Summit Technology, Inc. [*NASDAQ symbol*] (NQ) .... BEAM
Summit Technology, Inc. [*Associated Press*] (SAG) .... SumitTc
Summit-Argo Public Library, Summit, IL [*Library symbol Library of Congress*] (LCLS) .... ISu
Summitatis [*Summits or Tops*] [*Pharmacy*] (ROG) .... SUMM
Summoned .... SUM
Summons (ROG) .... SS
Summons [*Legal shorthand*] (LWAP) .... SUMM
Summons (ROG) .... SUMNS
Summons (ROG) .... SUMS
Summus Pontifex [*Supreme Pontiff, Pope*] [*Latin*] .... SP
Sumner, WA [*AM radio station call letters*] .... KZIZ
Sumner's Edition of Vesey's Reports [*A publication*] (DLA) .... Sum Ves
Sumner's Edition of Vesey's Reports [*A publication*] (DLA) ... Sumn Ves
Sumner's United States Circuit Court Reports [*A publication*] (DLA) ...... Sum
Sumner's United States Circuit Court Reports [*A publication*] (DLA) ...... Sum Rep
Sumner's United States Circuit Court Reports [*A publication*] (DLA).... Sum UCCR
Sumner's United States Circuit Court Reports [*A publication*] (DLA) ...... Sumn
Sumner's United States Circuit Court Reports [*A publication*] (DLA) ...... Sumner
Sum-of-Products [*Computer science*] (OA) .... SOP
Sum-of-the-Squares .... SOS
Sum-of-the-Squares .... SS
Sum-of-the-Squares of the Differences [*Mathematics*] .... SSD
Sum-of-the-Years Digit [*Statistics*] (IAA) .... SOD
Sumoto [*Japan*] [*Seismograph station code, US Geological Survey*] (SEIS) ..... SUM
Sump and Sewage Pump Manufacturers Association (EA) ...... SSPMA
Sump Pump Manufacturers Association [*Later, SSPMA*] (EA) .... SPMA
Sump Tank .... SMTK
Sumpter Valley Railway [*AAR code*] .... SUV
Sumptuary (VRA) .... sumpt
Sumter [*South Carolina*] [*Airport symbol*] (OAG) .... SUM
Sumter & Choctaw Railway Co. [*AAR code*] .... SC
Sumter County Library, Sumter, SC [*Library symbol Library of Congress*] (LCLS) .... ScSu
Sumter, SC [*Location identifier FAA*] (FAAL) .... JWU
Sumter, SC [*Location identifier FAA*] (FAAL) .... SMS
Sumter, SC [*Location identifier FAA*] (FAAL) .... SSC
Sumter, SC [*AM radio station call letters*] .... WDXY
Sumter, SC [*FM radio station call letters*] .... WICI
Sumter, SC [*AM radio station call letters*] .... WQMC
Sumter, SC [*FM radio station call letters*] .... WRJA
Sumter, SC [*Television station call letters*] .... WRJA-TV
Sumter, SC [*AM radio station call letters*] .... WSSC
Sumter, SC [*FM radio station call letters*] .... WWDM
Sumter/Shaw Air Force Base [*South Carolina*] [*ICAO location identifier*] (ICLI) .... KSSC
Sumter Technical College, Sumter, SC [*Library symbol*] [*Library of Congress*] (LCLS) .... ScSuTC
Sun .... S
Sun Air Aviation Services [*Canada ICAO designator*] (FAAC) .... SNX
Sun Artificial Intelligence Workstation .... SAIW
Sun Bancorp [*NASDAQ symbol*] (TTSB) .... SUBI
Sun Bancorp, Inc. [*NASDAQ symbol*] (SAG) .... SUBI
Sun Bancorp, Inc. [*Associated Press*] (SAG) .... SunBanc
Sun Bancorp, Inc. [*Associated Press*] (SAG) .... SunBcp
Sun Bay Recovery - International Missing Children's Division (EA) ..... SBRIMCD
Sun Belt Institute (EA) .... SBI
Sun Bulletin, Ridgefield Park, NJ [*Library symbol Library of Congress*] (LCLS) .... NjRpS
Sun City [*South Africa*] [*Airport symbol*] (OAG) .... NTY
Sun City, AZ [*FM radio station call letters*] .... KEDJ

Sun City Branch Library, Sun City, CA [*Library symbol Library of Congress*] (LCLS) .... CSuc
Sun City, CA [*FM radio station call letters*] .... KWXH
Sun City, CA [*FM radio station call letters*] (RBYB) .... KXFG-FM
Sun City Indus [*AMEX symbol*] (TTSB) .... SNI
Sun City Industries, Inc. [*AMEX symbol*] (SPSG) .... SNI
Sun City Industries, Inc. [*Associated Press*] (SAG) .... SunCty
Sun City Public Library, Sun City, AZ [*Library symbol Library of Congress*] (LCLS) .... AzSu
Sun Coast Indus [*NYSE symbol*] (TTSB) .... SN
Sun Coast Industries [*Formerly, Sun Coast Plastics*] [*NYSE symbol*] (SPSG) .... SN
Sun Coast Industries, Inc. [*Associated Press*] (SAG) .... SunCoast
Sun Communities [*NYSE symbol*] (SPSG) .... SUI
Sun Communities [*Associated Press*] (SAG) .... SunCmts
Sun Co. [*NYSE symbol*] (TTSB) .... SUN
Sun Co.'A'Dep'TARGETS' [*NYSE symbol*] (TTSB) .... SUNPrD
Sun Co., Inc. [*NYSE symbol*] (SPSG) .... SUN
Sun Co., Inc. [*Associated Press*] (SAG) .... SunCo
Sun Country Airlines, Inc. [*ICAO designator*] (FAAC) .... SCX
Sun Distributors Ltd. [*Associated Press*] (SAG) .... SunDis
Sun Distributors Ltd. [*Associated Press*] (SAG) .... SunDist
Sun Distributors Ltd. Class A [*NYSE symbol*] (SPSG) .... SDP
Sun Earth Explorer [*Satellite*] [*NASA*] .... SEE
Sun Energy Partners Ltd. [*Associated Press*] (SAG) .... SunEng
Sun Energy Partners LP [*NYSE symbol*] (SPSG) .... SLP
Sun Energy Ptnrs L.P. [*NYSE symbol*] (TTSB) .... SLP
Sun Entertainment [*Vancouver Stock Exchange symbol*] .... SED
Sun Factor (ADA) .... SF
Sun Finder Assembly [*NASA*] .... SFA
Sun Gate .... SG
Sun Glass Institute of America [*Defunct*] (EA) .... SGIA
Sun Hawkeye Record, Mount Vernon, IA [*Library symbol Library of Congress*] (LCLS) .... IaMvS
Sun Healthcare Group [*NYSE symbol*] (SPSG) .... SHG
Sun Healthcare Group, Inc. [*Associated Press*] (SAG) .... SunHltcr
Sun Hydraulics Corp. [*NASDAQ symbol*] (SAG) .... SNHY
Sun Hydraulics Corp. [*Associated Press*] (SAG) .... SunHydr
Sun Ice Ltd. [*Toronto Stock Exchange symbol*] .... SIH
Sun International [*NASDAQ symbol*] (SAG) .... SIHBF
Sun International [*NASDAQ symbol*] (SAG) .... SIHL
Sun International [*Associated Press*] (SAG) .... SunInt
Sun International [*Associated Press*] (SAG) .... SunIntl
Sun International Hotels .... SIH
Sun Intl Hotels Ord [*NYSE symbol*] (TTSB) .... SIH
Sun Jet International Airlines, Inc. [*ICAO designator*] (FAAC) ... SJI
Sun Life Assurance Co. of Canada [*UTLAS symbol*] .... SUN
Sun Life Assurance Co. of Canada, Montreal, PQ, Canada [*Library symbol Library of Congress*] (LCLS) .... CaQMS
Sun Life of Canada [*Sun Life du Canada*] Montreal, Quebec [*Library symbol National Library of Canada*] (NLC) .... QMS
Sun Life of Canada, Reference Library, Toronto, ON, Canada [*Library symbol Library of Congress*] (LCLS) .... CaOTSLR
Sun Life of Canada, Toronto, Ontario [*Library symbol National Library of Canada*] (NLC) .... OTSLI
Sun Line-of-Sight .... SLOS
Sun Marine Employees Association (EA) .... SMEA
Sun Microsystems [*NASDAQ symbol*] (TTSB) .... SUNW
Sun Microsystems, Inc. [*Associated Press*] (SAG) .... SunMic
Sun Microsystems, Inc. [*Mountain View, CA*] [*NASDAQ symbol*] (NQ) .... SUNW
Sun News, Lowden, IA [*Library symbol Library of Congress*] (LCLS) .... IaLowS
Sun Oil Co. [*Later, Sun Co., Inc.*] .... SUNOCO
Sun Oil Co., Calgary, AB, Canada [*Library symbol Library of Congress*] (LCLS) .... CaACSO
Sun Oil Co., General Office Library, Philadelphia, PA [*Library symbol Library of Congress Obsolete*] (LCLS) .... PPSOPR
Sun Oil Co., Marcus Hook, PA [*Library symbol Library of Congress*] (LCLS) .... PMarhSO
Sun Oil Co. of Radnor [*Pennsylvania*] .... SUNCOR
Sun Oil Co., Richardson, TX [*Library symbol Library of Congress*] (LCLS) .... TxRiS
Sun Position Indicator (IAA) .... SPI
Sun Prairie, WI [*AM radio station call letters*] .... WMAD
Sun Prairie, WI [*FM radio station call letters*] .... WMAD-FM
Sun Present - Horizon Lost .... SP-HL
Sun Probe near Limb of Venus [*Angle*] .... SPV
Sun Probe-Mars [*NASA*] .... SPM
Sun Protection Required [*Identification system for heat-sensitive cargo*] [*Shipping*] (DCTA) .... SPR
Sun Pumped LASER (MCD) .... SPL
Sun River [*Oregon*] [*Airport symbol Obsolete*] (OAG) .... SUO
Sun River Gold Corp. [*Vancouver Stock Exchange symbol*] .... SRF
Sun, Sand, Sea, Sex [*Used in advertising by travel agencies*] .... 4S's
Sun Seeker (AAG) .... SS
Sun Sensor .... SS
Sun Sensor Attitude Angle Transducer .... SSAAT
Sun Shadow Device .... SSD
Sun Shipbuilding & Dry Dock Co., Chester, PA [*Library symbol Library of Congress*] (LCLS) .... PCS
Sun Simulator (MCD) .... SS
Sun Sportswear [*NASDAQ symbol*] (TTSB) .... SSPW
Sun Sportswear, Inc. [*NASDAQ symbol*] (NQ) .... SSPW
Sun Sportswear, Inc. [*Associated Press*] (SAG) .... SunSpt
Sun Synchronous Day/Night (SSD) .... SSD/N
Sun Television & Appliances [*NASDAQ symbol*] (SAG) .... SNTV
Sun Television & Appliances, Inc. [*Associated Press*] (SAG) .... SunTV
Sun User Group [*An association*] .... SUG

Sun Valley [*Idaho*] [*Airport symbol*] (OAG) .... SUN
Sun Valley Gold Mines Ltd. [*Vancouver Stock Exchange symbol*] .... SVG
Sun Valley, ID [*FM radio station call letters*] .... KECH
Sun Valley, ID [*FM radio station call letters*] .... KSKI
Sun Valley, ID [*FM radio station call letters*] .... KWRV
Sun Valley, NV [*AM radio station call letters*] (RBYB) .... KIRS
Sun West [*ICAO designator*] (AD) .... KY
Sun, Wind, Dust [*Goggles*] (MCD) .... SWD
Sun, Wind, Dust Goggles [*Military*] (INF) .... SWDG
Sun World [*ICAO designator*] (AD) .... JK
Sunair Electronics [*AMEX symbol*] (TTSB) .... SNR
Sunair Electronics, Inc. [*AMEX symbol*] (SPSG) .... SNR
Sunair Electronics, Inc. [*Associated Press*] (SAG) .... Sunair
Sun-Air of Scandinavia [*ICAO designator*] (AD) .... EZ
Sun-Air of Scandinavia AS [*Denmark ICAO designator*] (FAAC) .... SUS
Sunaire Lines [*ICAO designator*] (AD) .... OO
SunAmer Cap 9.95% 'TOPrS' [*NYSE symbol*] (TTSB) .... SAIPrT
SunAmer Cap II 8.35%'TOPrS' [*NYSE symbol*] (TTSB) .... SAIPrV
SunAmerica 9 1/4% cm'B'Pfd [*NYSE symbol*] (TTSB) .... SAIPrB
Sunamerica Capital Trust [*NYSE symbol*] (SAG) .... SAI
Sunamerica Capital Trust [*Associated Press*] (SAG) .... SunaC
Sunamerica Capital Trust II [*NYSE symbol*] (SAG) .... SAI
Sunamerica Capital Trust II [*Associated Press*] (SAG) .... SunaC
Sunamerica Capital Trust III [*NYSE symbol*] (SAG) .... SAI
Sunamerica Capital Trust III [*Associated Press*] (SAG) .... SunaC
SunAmerica Dep'E'Pfd [*NYSE symbol*] (TTSB) .... SAIPrE
SunAmerica, Inc. [*Formerly, Broad, Inc.*] [*NYSE symbol*] (SPSG) .... SAI
Sunamerica, Inc. [*Associated Press*] (SAG) .... Suna
Sunamerica, Inc. [*Associated Press*] (SAG) .... Sunamer
Sunatco Development Corp. [*Vancouver Stock Exchange symbol*] .... SNC
Sun-Bank Newspapers, Nutley, NJ [*Library symbol Library of Congress*] (LCLS) .... NjNuS
Sunbase Asia [*NASDAQ symbol*] (TTSB) .... ASIA
Sunbeam Alpine Club (EA) .... SAC
Sunbeam Car Club [*Defunct*] (EA) .... SCC
Sunbeam Corp. [*NYSE symbol*] (SAG) .... SOC
Sunbeam Corp. [*Associated Press*] (SAG) .... Sunbeam
Sunbeam Publishing Co., Salem, NJ [*Library symbol Library of Congress*] (LCLS) .... NjSalS
Sunbeam-Talbot-Darracq [*Automobile manufacturer*] .... STD
Sunbelt Companies [*NASDAQ symbol*] (SAG) .... SBLT
Sunbelt Companies [*Associated Press*] (SAG) .... Sunbelt
Sunbelt Nursery Group [*AMEX symbol*] (TTSB) .... SBN
Sunbelt Nursery Group, Inc. [*AMEX symbol*] (SPSG) .... SBN
Sunbelt Nursery Group, Inc. [*Associated Press*] (SAG) .... SunNur
Sunberg Elementary School, Sunberg, MN [*Library symbol*] [*Library of Congress*] (LCLS) .... MnSuES
Sunbird [*ICAO designator*] (AD) .... ED
Sunbird [*ICAO designator*] (AD) .... QP
Sunburn Cell [*For measuring phototoxicity*] .... SC
Sunburst Exploration Ltd. [*Toronto Stock Exchange symbol*] .... SNX
Sunbury, PA [*AM radio station call letters*] .... WKOK
Sunbury, PA [*FM radio station call letters*] .... WQKX
Sunbury West Historical Society, Fredericton Junction, New Brunswick [*Library symbol National Library of Canada*] (NLC) .... NBFJS
Sunchon [*North Korea ICAO location identifier*] (ICLI) .... ZKSC
Suncoast Aviation, Inc. [*ICAO designator*] (FAAC) .... SNT
Suncoast Petroleum [*Vancouver Stock Exchange symbol*] .... SUC
Suncoast S & L Assn FSA [*NASDAQ symbol*] (TTSB) .... SCSL
Suncoast S&L 8% Cv Pfd [*NASDAQ symbol*] (TTSB) .... SCSLP
Suncoast Savings & Loan Association [*Hollywood, FL*] [*NASDAQ symbol*] (NQ) .... SCSL
Suncoast Savings & Loan Association [*Associated Press*] (SAG) .... SunSav
Suncoast Savings & Loan Association [*Associated Press*] (SAG) .... SunSv
Suncor, Inc. [*Toronto Stock Exchange symbol AMEX symbol*] .... SU
Suncor, Inc. [*Associated Press*] (SAG) .... Suncor
SUNCOR Inc., Calgary, Alberta [*Library symbol National Library of Canada*] (NLC) .... ACSO
SUNCOR, Inc., Resources Group, Information Centre, Fort McMurray, AB, Canada [*Library symbol Library of Congress*] (LCLS) .... CaAFmSI
Suncorp Insurance and Finance [*Commercial firm Australia*] .... SIF
Sundance Air Operations, Inc. [*FAA designator*] (FAAC) .... BNC
Sundance Gold Mining Ltd. [*Vancouver Stock Exchange symbol*] .... SDG
Sundance Homes [*NASDAQ symbol*] (TTSB) .... SUNH
Sundance Homes, Inc. [*Associated Press*] (SAG) .... SundHme
Sundance Homes, Inc. [*NASDAQ symbol*] (SAG) .... SUNH
Sundance Institute (EA) .... SI
Sundance, WY [*FM radio station call letters*] (RBYB) .... KYDT-FM
Sundance, WY [*Location identifier FAA*] (FAAL) .... SUC
Sundanese [*MARC language code Library of Congress*] (LCCP) .... sun
Sundata Corp. [*NASDAQ symbol*] (SAG) .... SNDT
Sundata Corp. [*Associated Press*] (SAG) .... SunGrd
Sunday .... S
Sunday .... SU
Sunday (AFM) .... SUN
Sunday (ODBW) .... Sun
Sunday .... SUND
Sunday Herald [*Melbourne*] [*A publication*] .... Sund H
Sunday League (EA) .... SL
Sunday Nation [*A publication*] .... SN
Sunday Newspaper Distibutors' Association (DGA) .... SNDA
Sunday Review [*A publication*] .... Sunday Rev
Sunday School .... SS
Sunday School Board of the Southern Baptist Convention, Nashville, TN [*Library symbol*] [*Library of Congress*] (LCLS) .... TNSB-S
Sunday School Union .... SSU
Sunday Shakespeare Society [*British*] .... SSS
Sunday Sport [*A publication*] .... SS
Sunday Times [*A publication*] .... S Times
[*The*] **Sunday Times Atlantic Riband** [*Award offered by a London newspaper to any sailboat beating the 1905 record for a transatlantic crossing*] .... STAR
Sundays and Holidays .... S & H
Sundays and Holidays Excepted .... S/HE
Sundays and Holidays Excepted [*Business term*] .... SHEX
Sundays and Holidays Excepted in Lay Days (DS) .... S & H/exct
Sundays and Holidays Included [*Business term*] .... SHINC
Sundbro [*Sweden ICAO location identifier*] (ICLI) .... ESKC
Sunderland, VT [*FM radio station call letters*] .... WJAN
Sun-Diamond Growers of California (EA) .... SDGC
Sundor International Air Services Ltd. [*Israel*] [*ICAO designator*] (FAAC) .... ERO
Sundorph Aeronautical, Corp. [*ICAO designator*] (FAAC) .... SDF
Sundre Public Library, Alberta [*Library symbol National Library of Canada*] (NLC) .... ASUN
Sundridge & Strong Union Public Library, Sundridge, Ontario [*Library symbol National Library of Canada*] (NLC) .... OSSU
Sundries .... SUND
Sundries (ROG) .... SUNDS
Sundries Pack [*Field troops military issue*] (VNW) .... SP
Sundry .... SNDRY
Sundry Persons' Account [*Banking*] .... SPA
Sundstand Data Control Corp., Sundstrand Corp., Redmond, WA [*Library symbol*] [*Library of Congress*] (LCLS) .... WaRedSu
Sundstrand Aviation, Engineering Library, Rockford, IL [*Library symbol Library of Congress*] (LCLS) .... IRoSA
Sundstrand Corp. [*NYSE symbol*] (TTSB) .... SNS
Sundstrand Corp. [*NYSE symbol*] (SPSG) .... SNS
Sundstrand Corp. [*Associated Press*] (SAG) .... Sunstrnd
Sundstrand Corp., Denver Division, Engineering Department Library, Denver, CO [*Library symbol Library of Congress*] (LCLS) .... CoDS
Sundstrand Processing Language Internally Translated .... SPLIT
Sundstrand-Turbo Division (AAG) .... SUN
Sundsvall [*Sweden ICAO location identifier*] (ICLI) .... ESUN
Sundsvall [*Sweden*] [*Airport symbol*] (OAG) .... SDL
Sundsvall-Harnosand [*Sweden ICAO location identifier*] (ICLI) .... ESNN
Sun-Earth Observatory and Climatology Satellite .... SEOCS
Sun-End Work Station [*NASA*] (KSC) .... SEWS
Sun-Energy Collecting Satellite .... SUNSAT
Suneva Resources [*Vancouver Stock Exchange symbol*] .... SNV
Sunfield District Library, Sunfield, MI [*Library symbol Library of Congress*] (LCLS) .... MiSun
Sunflower Airlines Ltd. [*Fiji*] [*ICAO designator*] (FAAC) .... SUF
Sunflower Army Ammunition Plant (AABC) .... SFAAP
Sunflower Association of America [*Later, NSA*] (EA) .... SAA
Sunflower County Library, Sunflower, MS [*Library symbol Library of Congress*] (LCLS) .... MsSu
Sunflower Ordnance Works [*Military*] .... SOW
Sunflower Seed Oil .... SSO
Sunflower Seed Oil Assistance Program [*Department of Agriculture*] .... SOAP
Sunflower Space Power System (IAA) .... SSPS
Sungai Penuh/Depati Parbo [*Indonesia*] [*ICAO location identifier*] (ICLI) .... WIPH
SunGard Data Systems [*NASDAQ symbol*] (TTSB) .... SNDT
Sungei Patani [*Malaysia*] [*ICAO location identifier*] (ICLI) .... WMBB
Sunglass Association of America (EA) .... SAA
Sunglass Hut International, Inc. [*NASDAQ symbol*] (SAG) .... RAYS
Sunglass Hut International, Inc. [*Associated Press*] (SAG) .... Sunglss
Sunglass Hut Intl [*NASDAQ symbol*] (TTSB) .... RAYS
Sunglasses .... SGL
Sun-Health, Inc., Charlotte, NC [*Library symbol*] [*Library of Congress*] (LCLS) .... NcCSH
Sun-Improved Frequency Response .... SIFR
Sun-Jupiter-Probe [*Angle*] .... SJP
Sunk Face [*Construction*] .... SF
Sunk or Damaged [*Navy*] .... SUDAM
Sunkist Growers (EA) .... SG
Sunland Center, Tallahassee, FL [*Library symbol Library of Congress*] (LCLS) .... FTaS
Sunlit Period .... SP
Sun-Load Sensor [*Automotive engineering*] .... SLS
Sun-Maid Growers of California (EA) .... SMGC
Sun-Maid Raisin Growers of California (EA) .... SMRGC
Sunmask Petroleum [*Vancouver Stock Exchange symbol*] .... SNM
Sunmount Development Center, Staff Library, Tupper Lake, NY [*Library symbol Library of Congress*] (LCLS) .... NTuPSC
Sunna Air Ltd. [*Iceland*] [*ICAO designator*] (FAAC) .... VOR
Sunne [*Poland ICAO location identifier*] (ICLI) .... ESKU
Sunn-Hemp Mosaic Virus [*Plant pathology*] .... SHMV
Sunnidale Township Public Library, New Lowell, Ontario [*Library symbol National Library of Canada*] (BIB) .... ONLS
Sunny [*Meteorology*] (ADA) .... S
Sunny (MSA) .... SNY
Sunny Point Army Terminal .... SPART
Sunny Von Bulow National Victim Advocacy Center [*Later, NVC*] (EA) .... NVAC
Sunny Von Bulow National Victim Advocacy Center [*Later, NVC*] (EA) .... SVNVAC
Sunnybrook Medical Centre, Toronto [*UTLAS symbol*] .... SMC
Sunnybrook Medical Centre, Toronto, ON, Canada [*Library symbol Library of Congress*] (LCLS) .... CaOTSMC
Sunnybrook Medical Centre, Toronto, Ontario [*Library symbol National Library of Canada*] (NLC) .... OTSMC

Sunnyside [Utah] [Seismograph station code, US Geological Survey Closed] (SEIS) .... SUN
Sunnyside Medical Library, Clackamas, OR [Library symbol Library of Congress] (LCLS) .... OrCIS
Sunnyside Mine [Utah] [Seismograph station code, US Geological Survey Closed] (SEIS) .... SMU
Sunnyside, WA [AM radio station call letters] .... KREW
Sunnyside, WA [FM radio station call letters] .... KREW-FM
Sunnyside, WA [FM radio station call letters] (RBYB) .... KZTB-FM
Sunnyvale Control Facility [California] [NASA] (NASA) .... SCF
Sunnyvale Public Library, Sunnyvale, CA [Library symbol Library of Congress] (LCLS) .... CSv
Sunnyvale Public Library, Sunnyvale, CA [OCLC symbol] (OCLC) .... SXP
Sun-Orbiting Relativity Experiment Satellite .... SOREL
Sunpapers Library, Baltimore, MD [Library symbol Library of Congress] (LCLS) .... MdBSp
Sunpapers Library, Baltimore, MD [Library symbol] [Library of Congress] (LCLS) .... MdBSup
SunPharm Corp. [NASDAQ symbol] (SAG) .... SUNP
SunPharm Corp. [Associated Press] (SAG) .... SunPh
SunPharm Corp. [Associated Press] (SAG) .... SunPhm
Sunpharm Corp. Wrrt [NASDAQ symbol] (TTSB) .... SUNPW
Sun-Planet-Earth [Astronomy] .... SPE
Sunport Med [NASDAQ symbol] (TTSB) .... SMQCF
Sunport Medical Corp. [NASDAQ symbol] (SAG) .... SMQC
Sunport Medical Corp. [Associated Press] (SAG) .... Sunport
Sun-Protection Factor [Cosmetics industry] .... SPF
Sunquest Information Sys [NASDAQ symbol] (TTSB) .... SUNQ
Sunquest Information Systems, Inc. [NASDAQ symbol] (SAG) .... SUNQ
Sunquest Information Systems, Inc. [Associated Press] (SAG) .... Sunquest
Sunresorts Ltd. NV [NASDAQ symbol] (SAG) .... RSTA
Sunresorts Ltd. NV [Associated Press] (SAG) .... Sunrst
Sunresorts Ltd NV 'A' [NASDAQ symbol] (TTSB) .... RSTAF
Sunrise .... SNRS
Sunrise Assisted Living [NASDAQ symbol] (TTSB) .... SNRZ
Sunrise Assisted Living, Inc. [NASDAQ symbol] (SAG) .... SNRZ
Sunrise Assisted Living, Inc. [Associated Press] (SAG) .... SunrAss
Sunrise Bancorp [NASDAQ symbol] (NQ) .... SRBC
Sunrise Bancorp [Associated Press] (SAG) .... SunBCA
Sunrise Bancorp, Inc. New York [NASDAQ symbol] (SAG) .... SUNY
Sunrise Bancorp, Inc. NY [Associated Press] (SAG) .... SunBcNY
Sunrise, FL [FM radio station call letters] .... WKPX
Sunrise Group Home, Ephrata, WA [Library symbol Library of Congress] (LCLS) .... WaEpS
Sunrise Medical [NYSE symbol] (TTSB) .... SMD
Sunrise Medical, Inc. [NYSE symbol] (SPSG) .... SMD
Sunrise Medical, Inc. [Associated Press] (SAG) .... SunMed
Sunrise Metals [Vancouver Stock Exchange symbol] .... SRS
Sunrise Park Elementary School, Wantagh, NY [Library symbol Library of Congress] (LCLS) .... NWanSPE
Sunrise Preschools [NASDAQ symbol] (TTSB) .... SUNR
Sunrise Preschools Cv'C' Pfd [NASDAQ symbol] (TTSB) .... SUNRP
Sunrise Preschools, Inc. [NASDAQ symbol] (SAG) .... SUNR
Sunrise Preschools, Inc. [Associated Press] (SAG) .... Sunrise
Sunrise Resources [NASDAQ symbol] (TTSB) .... SUNL
Sunrise Resources, Inc. [NASDAQ symbol] (SAG) .... SUNL
Sunrise Resources, Inc. [Associated Press] (SAG) .... SunResc
Sunrise to Sunset [ICAO] (FAAC) .... HJ
Sunrise-Sunset (DA) .... SR-SS
SunRiver Corp. [NASDAQ symbol] (TTSB) .... SRVC
SunRiver Corp. [NASDAQ symbol] (SAG) .... SRVC
SunRiver Corp. [Associated Press] (SAG) .... SunRiver
SunRiver Corp. Wrrt [NASDAQ symbol] (TTSB) .... SRVCW
Sun's Declensions [Astronomy] (ROG) .... SD
Sun's Parallax [Astronomy] (ROG) .... SP
Sun's Right Ascension [Astrology] (ROG) .... SRA
Sun's True Bearing [Navigation] .... STB
Sunset .... SNST
Sunset Coast Sub-tropical Fruits Association [Queensland, Australia] .... SCSFA
Sunset Crater National Monument [Arizona] [Seismograph station code, US Geological Survey] (SEIS) .... SCN
Sunset Crater National Monument .... SUCR
Sunset Gun [Military ceremonial] .... SG
Sunset Hill School, Kansas City, MO [Library symbol Library of Congress] (LCLS) .... MoKSH
Sunset Lake [Pennsylvania] [Seismograph station code, US Geological Survey Closed] (SEIS) .... SSL
Sunset Magazine Reference Library, Menlo Park, CA [Library symbol Library of Congress] (LCLS) .... CMenS
Sunset Railway Co. [AAR code] .... SUN
Sunset to Sunrise [ICAO] (FAAC) .... HN
Sunshine .... SNSHN
Sunshine [Alaska] [Seismograph station code, US Geological Survey] (SEIS) .... SSH
Sunshine Act (GNE) .... SA
Sunshine Airlines [Airline code] [Australia] .... PI
Sunshine Aviation SA [Switzerland ICAO designator] (FAAC) .... SHS
Sunshine Columbia [Vancouver Stock Exchange symbol] .... SUS
Sunshine Foundation (EA) .... SF
Sunshine Hall Free Library, Eldred, NY [Library symbol Library of Congress] (LCLS) .... NEld
Sunshine Mining & Refining Co. [NASDAQ symbol] (SAG) .... SILV
Sunshine Mining & Refining [Formerly, Sunshine Mining] Co. [NYSE symbol] (SPSG) .... SSC
Sunshine Mining & Refining Co. [Associated Press] (SAG) .... SunM

Sunshine Mining & Refining Co. [Associated Press] (SAG) .... SunMn
Sunshine Mining & Refining Co. [Associated Press] (SAG) .... SunsMn
Sunshine Mining & Refining Wrrt [NASDAQ symbol] (TTSB) .... SIVZV
Sunshine Mng & Refining Wrrt [NASDAQ symbol] (TTSB) .... SILVW
Sunshine Music - Jan and Dean Collectors Club (EA) .... SM-JDCC
Sunshine Point [Alaska] [Seismograph station code, US Geological Survey] (SEIS) .... SNH
Sunshine-Jr Stores, Inc. [Associated Press] (SAG) .... SunshJr
Sunsource L.P. [NYSE symbol] (SAG) .... SDP
Sunsource LP [Associated Press] (SAG) .... Sunsource
Sunsource LP [Associated Press] (SAG) .... SunsrceB
Sunsource L.P.'A' [NYSE symbol] (TTSB) .... SDP
Sunsource L.P.'B' [NYSE symbol] (TTSB) .... SDP.B
Sunstar Foods, Inc. (MHDW) .... SUNF
SunStar Healthcare [NASDAQ symbol] (TTSB) .... SUNS
SunStar Healthcare, Inc. [NASDAQ symbol] (SAG) .... SUNS
SunStar Healthcare, Inc. [Associated Press] (SAG) .... SunStar
Sunstates $3.75 cm Pfd [NASDAQ symbol] (TTSB) .... SUSTP
Sunstates Corp. [Associated Press] (SAG) .... Sunstat
Sunstates Corp. [Associated Press] (SAG) .... Sunstate
Sunstates Corp. [NASDAQ symbol] (SAG) .... SUST
Sunstates Corp. [NASDAQ symbol] (TTSB) .... SUSTE
Sunstone Hotel Investors [NASDAQ symbol] (TTSB) .... SSHI
Sunstone Hotel Investors, Inc. [NASDAQ symbol] (SAG) .... SSHI
Sunstone Hotel Investors, Inc. [NYSE symbol] (SAG) .... SSI
Sunstone Hotel Investors, Inc. [Associated Press] (SAG) .... SunstH
Sunstone Hotel Investors, Inc. [Associated Press] (SAG) .... SunstoneH
Sunsweet Growers (EA) .... SG
Suntac Minerals [Vancouver Stock Exchange symbol] .... SUJ
Suntanning Association for Education (EA) .... SAFE
Suntec Ventures Ltd. [Vancouver Stock Exchange symbol] .... SUN
Suntech Library and Information Center, Marcus Hook, PA [OCLC symbol] (OCLC) .... SUN
Suntory Toyota International Centre for Economics and Related Disciplines [London School of Economics and Political Science] [British] (CB) .... ST/ICERD
SunTrust Banks [NYSE symbol] (TTSB) .... STI
SunTrust Banks, Inc. [NYSE symbol] (SPSG) .... STI
SunTrust Banks, Inc. [Associated Press] (SAG) .... SunTrst
Sunwapta Shores Public Library, Alberta [Library symbol National Library of Canada] (NLC) .... ASUNW
Sunwest Airlines Ltd. [Canada ICAO designator] (FAAC) .... SST
Sunwest International Aviation [Canada] [FAA designator] (FAAC) .... CNK
Sunworld International Airways, Inc. [ICAO designator] (FAAC) .... SWI
Sunyani [Ghana] [ICAO location identifier] (ICLI) .... DGSN
Sunyani [Ghana] [Airport symbol] (OAG) .... NYI
Suo Loco [In Its Place] [Latin] (WGA) .... sl
Suomen Kansan Demokraattinen Liitto [Finnish People's Democratic League] [Political party] (PPW) .... SKDL
Suomen Kansan Yhtenaeisyyden Puolue [People's Unity Party] [Finland Political party] (PPW) .... SKYP
Suomen Kommunistinen Puolue [Communist Party of Finland] [Political party] (PPW) .... SKP
Suomen Konsulttitoimistojen Liitto [Finnish Association of Consulting Firms] (EY) .... SKOI
Suomen Konsulttitoimistojen Liitto [Finnish Association of Consulting Firms] (EY) .... SKOL
Suomen Kristillinen Liitto [Finnish Christian League] [Political party] (PPE) .... SKL
Suomen Maaseudun Puolue [Finnish Rural Party] [Political party] (PPW) .... SMP
Suomen Perustuslaillinen Kansanpuolue [Finnish Constitutional People's Party] [Political party] (PPW) .... SPKP
Suomen Sosialidemokraattinen Puolue [Finnish Social Democratic Party] [Political party] (EAIO) .... SDP
Suomen Sosialidemokraattinen Puolue [Finnish Social Democratic Party] [Political party] (PPW) .... SSDP
Suomen Standardisomisliitto [Finnish Standards Association] [Information service or system] (IID) .... SFS
Suomen Tietotoimisto-Finska Notisbyran [Press agency] [Finland] .... STT-FNB
Suomen Valtakunnan Uhreiluliitto [Finnish Central Sports Federation] .... SVUL
Suomen Yksityisyrittaejaein Puoluejaerjesto [Finnish Private Entrepreneurs' Party] [Political party] (PPE) .... SYP
Suomi College, Hancock, MI [Library symbol Library of Congress] (LCLS) .... MiHanS
Suomi, Eesti, Latvija, Lietuva [Finland, Estonia, Latvia, Lithuania] .... SELL
Suomussalmi [Finland ICAO location identifier] (ICLI) .... EFSU
Suore della Carita Cristiana [Sisters of Christian Charity] [Italy] (EAIO) .... SCC
Suore di Carita delle Sante Bartolomea Capitanio e Vincenza Gerosa [Sisters of Charity of Saints Bartholomew Capitanio And Vincent Gerosa] [Italy] (EAIO) .... SCSBCVG
Suore di San Giovanni Baptista [Sisters of St. John the Baptist - SSJB] [Rome, Italy] (EAIO) .... SSGB
Suore Francescane di Dillingen [Sisters of St. Francis of Dillingen - SSFD] [Italy] (EAIO) .... SFD
Suore Missionarie dell'Apostolato Cattolico [Missionary Sisters of the Catholic Apostolate] [Rome, Italy] (EAIO) .... SAC
Super .... S
Super .... SPR
Super (WDMC) .... sup
Super .... SUP
Super Abrasion Furnace [Carbon black manufacture] .... SAF
Super Accuracy Simplex (IAA) .... SAS
Super America [Automobile model, Ferrari Motors] .... SA
Super Bit Mapping [Compact-disc technology] (PS) .... SBM
Super Buffer FET Logic (NITA) .... SBFL
Super Caster [Monotype] (DGA) .... SC

Super Chevys Limited [*Defunct*] (EA) ... SCL
Super Cobra Jet [*Automotive engineering*] ... SCJ
Super Computer (IAA) ... SC
Super Computer Automotive Applications Partnership ... SCAAP
Super Conducting Super Collider Liability Library, Dallas, TX [*Library symbol*] [*Library of Congress*] (LCLS) ... TxDaSSC
Super Coupe [*Model of automobile*] ... SC
Super Critical (MCD) ... SUPCRIT
Super Current (IAA) ... SC
Super Data Interchange [*Computer science*] (HGAA) ... SDI
Super Density [*Computer science*] ... SD
Super Diesel [*Automotive engineering*] ... SD
Super Duty [*Automotive engineering*] ... SD
Super Eight [*Motion picture*] (VRA) ... SUPE
Super Einspritz [*Super, Injection*] [*Mercedes-Benz automotive model designation*] ... SE
Super Einspritz Lang [*Fuel-injection, long wheelbase*] [*As in 450 SEL, the model number of a Mercedes-Benz automobile*] ... SEL
Super Extra [*Bookbinding*] (DGA) ... SUP X
Super Flash X-Ray (MCD) ... SFXR
Super Flat Pack ... SFP
Super Flux Harness ... SFH
Super Food Services [*NYSE symbol*] (TTSB) ... SFS
Super Food Services, Inc. [*NYSE symbol*] (SPSG) ... SFS
Super Food Services, Inc. [*Associated Press*] (SAG) ... SuprFd
Super Gossypium [*On Cotton Wool*] [*Pharmacy*] ... SUP GOSSYP
Super Group (NATG) ... SG
Super Guppy (KSC) ... SG
Super Harvard Architecture Computer ... SHARC
Super High Frequency [*Radio wave*] ... SHF
Super High Frequency (DOMA) ... SHF
Super High Output [*Model of Ford automobile*] ... SHO
Super Highband [*Radio frequency*] (NTCM) ... SHB
Super High-Performance Diesel [*Fuel*] ... SHPD
Super Highway (TEL) ... SHWY
Super Intercontinental Ballistic Missile (IAA) ... SICBM
Super Joint Academic Network [*UK*] (EERA) ... SuperJANET
Super Knowledge Information Processing Intelligence [*Computer science*] ... SKIPI
Super Knowledge, Processing Interaction [*Concept advanced by Timothy Leary*] ... SKPI
Super Large-Scale Integration ... SLSI
Super Linear Accelerator [*Space flight simulator*] ... SULINAC
Super Linear Variable Capacitor (PDAA) ... SLVC
Super Linteum [*On Lint*] [*Pharmacy*] ... SUP LINT
Super Long Play [*Video technology*] ... SLP
Super Maneuverable Aircraft ... SM
Super Mare [*On Sea*] [*In place names*] [*Latin*] (ROG) ... S/M
Super Market Institute [*Later, FMI*] (EA) ... SMI
Super Ninendo Entertainment System ... SNES
Super Oak Leaf Online [*Santa Rosa Junior College online conference*] ... SOLO
Super Orbit Entry ... SOE
Super Plastic Formed [*Metal fabrication*] ... SPF
Super Power [*Water boiler*] [*Nuclear reactor*] ... SUPO
Super Power Electron Tube ... SPET
Super Pressure - High Temperature ... SPHT
Super Proton Synchrotron [*Particle physics*] ... SPS
Super Quick Point Detonating ... SQPD
Super Rapid Bloom Off Board Chaff [*Navy*] (NVT) ... SRBOC
Super Rapid Gun Mounting [*Military*] ... SRGM
Super Search (MCD) ... SS
Super Serial Card [*Apple Computer, Inc.*] ... SSC
[*The*] **Super Show** (ITD) ... TSS
Super Show & Tell [*Ask Me Multimedia Center software*] [*Computer science*] (PCM) ... SST
Super Small-Scale Cook-Off Bomb (MCD) ... SSCB
Super Smart Vehicle System [*FHWA*] (TAG) ... SSVS
Super Smoothing Technology [*Apple Computer, Inc.*] ... SST
Super Sonic Car ... SCC
Super Speed ... SS
Super Speed Logic [*Computer science*] (IAA) ... SSL
Super Sport [*In automobile model name*] ... SS
Super Sport Kurz [*Super, Sport, Short chassis*] [*Mercedes-Benz automotive model designation*] ... SSK
Super Star Cluster [*Astronomy*] ... SSC
Super Stock [*Automotive classification*] ... SS
Super Sunfish Class Association [*Defunct*] (EA) ... SSCA
Super Sunfish Racing Class Association (EA) ... SSRCA
Super Surface Treatment (IAA) ... SST
Super Symmetric [*Particle physics*] ... SS
Super System Code (NRCH) ... SSC
Super Tampella [*Explosive*] (INF) ... ST
Super Tension Cables Group [*British*] (DBA) ... STCG
Super Tractor Oil-Universal [*Lubricants*] ... STOU
Super Transportable RADAR ... STR
Super Unleaded (Gasoline) ... SU
Super Vernier Auto Alert [*Military*] (CAAL) ... SVAA
Super Video Graphics Array [*Computer science*] ... SVGA
Super Video Home System [*Japan Victor Co.*] ... SVHS
Super Video Recorder ... SVR
Super Vision International [*NASDAQ symbol*] (SAG) ... SUPV
Super Vision International [*Associated Press*] (SAG) ... SupVs
Super Vision International [*Associated Press*] (SAG) ... SupVsn
Super Vision Intl Wrrt'A' [*NASDAQ symbol*] (TTSB) ... SUPVW
Super Vision Intl Wrrt'B' [*NASDAQ symbol*] (TTSB) ... SUPVZ
Super Vision Intl'A' [*NASDAQ symbol*] (TTSB) ... SUPVA
Super Volkswagen [*Auto racing*] ... SV
Super Wozniak Integrated Machine [*Computer science*] ... SWIM
Super-Abrasion-Resistant [*Lucite glazing material*] ... SAR
Superabsorbent Polymer [*Organic chemistry*] ... SAP
Superannuation ... SUP
Superannuation ... SUPER
Superannuation Division, Compensation Services Branch, Department of Supply and Services [*Division des Pensions de Retraite, Direction des Services de Renumeration, Ministere des Approvisionnements et Services*] **Ottawa, Ontario** [*Library symbol National Library of Canada*] (NLC) ... OODPS
Superannuation Funds Office [*Inland Revenue*] [*British*] ... SFO
Superannuation Guarantee Levy ... SGL
Superannuation, Home, and Overseas Allowances [*Civil Service*] [*British*] ... SHOA
Superannuation Law Bulletin [*A publication*] ... SLB
Superantigen [*Immunology*] ... SAG
Superb ... S
Superb [*Philately*] ... Su
Superbananas ... SB
Superburn Systems Ltd. [*Vancouver Stock Exchange symbol*] ... SBS
Supercalendered [*Paper*] ... SC
Supercalendered (NTCM) ... SUPER
Supercalendered Web-Offset [*Paper*] (DGA) ... SCWO
Super-Caliber Rocket-Assisted Projectile (IEEE) ... SCRAP
Supercat Race Association International (EA) ... SRAI
Supercharge ... SCHG
Supercharge ... SPCHG
Supercharge (FAAC) ... SUPCHG
Supercharged Ejector Ramjet [*Aircraft engine*] ... SERJ
Supercharger [*Automotive engineering*] ... SC
Supercharger (AAG) ... SPCHGR
Supercharger (IAA) ... SPCHR
Super-Chilled Seawater ... SCSW
Supercircular Orbital Reentry Test Integrated Environment [*NASA*] (IAA) ... SORTIE
Supercircular Reentry Research (IAA) ... SCRR
Supercommutation (SAA) ... SU
Supercomputer Computations Research Institute [*Florida State University*] [*Research center*] (RCD) ... SCRI
Supercomputer Project Research Experiment in Advanced Development [*Lawrence Livermore Laboratory, Los Alamos National Laboratory, and SRI*] ... SPREAD
Superconducting Cavity Stabilized Oscillator [*For clocks*] ... SCSO
Superconducting Electromagnetic Propulsion (ECON) ... SEMP
Superconducting Flux-Flow Transistor [*Physics*] ... SFFT
Superconducting Low-Inductance Undulatory Galvanometer ... SLUG
Superconducting Magnet (IEEE) ... SCM
Superconducting Magnet (SSD) ... SUPERMAG
Superconducting Magnetic (MCD) ... S/C
Superconducting Magnetic Energy Storage (NASA) ... SMES
Superconducting Magnetic Mirror Apparatus ... SUMMA
Superconducting Power Transmission Line (PDAA) ... SPTL
Superconducting Quantum Interference Detector [*or Device*] [*For study of magnetic fields*] ... SQUID
Superconducting Quantum Interference Device [*Physics*] ... SQUID
Superconducting Super Collider [*Particle accelerator*] ... SSC
Superconducting Supercollider (AAGC) ... SSC
Superconducting Tunnel Junction [*Physics*] ... STJ
Superconducting Tunnel Junction [*Physics*] ... STJ
Superconductive Materials Data Center (KSC) ... SMDC
Superconductive Precision Inertial Navigation ... SPIN
Superconductive Tunneling Device (IAA) ... STD
Superconductivity Information System [*Department of Energy*] [*Information service or system*] (IID) ... SIS
Superconductor Applications Association (EA) ... SCAA
Superconductor/Normal Metal/Superconductor [*Physics*] ... SNS
Superconductor Technologies [*NASDAQ symbol*] (SAG) ... SCON
Superconductor Technologies [*Commercial firm Associated Press*] (SAG) ... SupTech
Superconductor-Insulator-Superconductor [*Transistor technology*] ... SIS
Super-Cooled Infrared Multispectral Survey and Analysis [*Traces mineral deposits*] ... SMSA
Supercooled Liquid Water (USDC) ... SLW
Supercooled Liquid Water [*Marine science*] (OSRA) ... SLW
Supercritical Antisolvent [*Chemical engineering*] ... SAS
Supercritical Chromatography ... SC
Super-Critical Cryogenics (SAA) ... SCC
Supercritical Extract [*Separation technology*] ... SCE
Supercritical Fluid ... SCF
Supercritical Fluid Chromatography ... SFC
Supercritical Fluid Desorption [*Chemical engineering*] ... SFD
Supercritical Fluid Extraction [*Also, SFE*] [*Chemical engineering*] ... SCFE
Supercritical Fluid Extraction [*Also, SCFE*] [*Chemical engineering*] ... SFE
Supercritical Gas Extraction ... SCG
Super-Critical Gas Extraction [*Chemical engineering*] ... SGE
Super-Critical Gas Storage System [*NASA*] (KSC) ... SCGSS
Supercritical Helium (KSC) ... SHE
Supercritical Hydrogen [*NASA*] (NASA) ... SH_2
Super-Critical, Once-Thru Tube Reactor [*Experiment*] [*General Electric Co.*] ... SCOTT-R
Supercritical Oxygen (MCD) ... SCO
Supercritical Oxygen [*NASA*] (KSC) ... SOX
Supercritical Water ... SCW
Supercritical Water Oxidation [*Waste disposal technology*] ... SCWO

Supercritical Water Reactor ..... SCWR
Super-Critical Wing ..... SCW
Supercuts, Inc. [*NASDAQ symbol*] (SPSG) ..... CUTS
Supercuts, Inc. [*Associated Press*] (SAG) ..... Supercut
Superelastic LASER Energy Conversion (MCD) ..... SELEC
Superexcited Electronic State [*Chemistry*] (OA) ..... SES
Superfast Train ..... SFT
Superficial ..... S
Superficial (AAMN) ..... SUP
Superficial ..... SUPER
Superficial (ROG) ..... SUPERFL
Superficial Distal Axillary [*Lymph node*] ..... SDA
Superficial Epithelial Infiltrates [*Ophthalmology*] (DAVI) ..... SEI
Superficial Extensor Motoneuron [*Neurology*] ..... SEMN
Superficial Femoral Artery [*Anatomy*] ..... SFA
Superficial Flexor Motoneuron [*Neurology*] ..... SFMN
Superficial Image Emphasis Lithography (NITA) ..... SIEL
Superficial Musculoaponeurotic System [*Plastic surgery*] ..... SMAS
Superficial Occipital Artery to Middle Cerebral Artery [*Medicine*] (MAE) ..... SOA-MCA
Superficial Pineal Organ [*Neuroanatomy*] ..... SP
Superficial Punctate Erosions [*Ophthalmology*] (DAVI) ..... SPE
Superficial Punctate Keratitis [*Ophthalmology*] ..... SPK
Superficial Rays of the Sun [*In reference to suntanning, supposedly occuring before 10am and after 2pm*] [*See also BROTS*] ..... SROTS
Superficial Reflex [*Neurology*] (DAVI) ..... SR
Superficial Spreading Melanoma [*Oncology*] ..... SSM
Superficial Spreading Type (Melanoma) [*Oncology*] ..... SST
Superficial Temporal Artery [*Anatomy*] ..... STA
Superficial Temporal Artery to Middle Cerebral Artery [*Anatomy*] (MAE) ..... STA-MCA
Superficial-Femoral Artery Occlusive Disease [*Medicine*] ..... SFAOD
Superfine ..... SUP
Superfine ..... SUPER
Superfluid-Helium Gyroscope ..... SHEG
Superfund [*Environmental Protection Agency*] (GFGA) ..... SF
Superfund Amendment and Reauthorization Act [*1986*] ..... SARA
Superfund Community Relations Coordinator [*Environmental Protection Agency*] (GFGA) ..... SCRC
Superfund Community Relations Program [*Environmental Protection Agency*] (GFGA) ..... SCRP
Superfund Comprehensive Accomplishment Plan [*Environmental Protection Agency*] (GFGA) ..... SCAP
Superfund Financial Assessment System [*Environmental Protection Agency*] (GFGA) ..... SFFAS
Superfund Innovative Technologies Evaluation Program [*Environmental Protection Agency*] ..... SITE
Superfund Memorandum of Agreement [*Environmental Protection Agency*] ..... SMOA
Superfund Surcharge [*Environmental Protection Agency*] (GFGA) ..... SS
SuperGen, Inc. [*Associated Press*] (SAG) ..... SuperG
SuperGen, Inc. [*Associated Press*] (SAG) ..... SuperGn
SuperGen, Inc. [*NASDAQ symbol*] (SAG) ..... SUPG
SuperGen Inc. [*NASDAQ symbol*] (TTSB) ..... SUPG
SuperGen Inc. Wrrt [*NASDAQ symbol*] (TTSB) ..... SUPGW
Supergroup Connector [*Telecommunications*] (TEL) ..... SGC
Supergroup Distribution Frame [*Telecommunications*] (TEL) ..... SDF
Supergroup Distribution Frame [*Telecommunications*] (TEL) ..... SGDF
Supergroup Distribution Frame [*Telecommunications*] (OSI) ..... SGDS
Supergroup Translation Equipment ..... STE
Super-Hard Extremely-Low Frequency (MCD) ..... SHELF
Superheat Advanced Demonstration Experiment [*Nuclear energy*] ..... SADE
Superheat Control [*Boilers*] ..... SHC
Superheat Limit Explosion ..... SLE
Superheat Power Experiment [*Nuclear energy*] ..... SPX
Superheated (AAG) ..... SUPHTD
Superheated Aerosol (DAVI) ..... SHA
Superheated Steam ..... SHS
Superheated Superconducting Colloid Detector [*Particle physics*] ..... SSCD
Superheater (AAG) ..... SUPHTR
Superheater Protection Device (DNAB) ..... SPD
Superheavy Element [*Nuclear physics*] ..... SHE
Superheterodyne ..... SUPERHET
Superhigh Frequency (WDMC) ..... shf
Super-High Frequency/Extremely-High Frequency (MCD) ..... SHF/EHF
Super-High Resolution Ion Microprobe [*Analytical chemistry*] ..... SHRIMP
Superhigh Speed Steel (IAA) ..... SHSS
Super-High-Frequency [*Radio wave*] (NG) ..... SH
Super-High-Frequency - Ground Mobile Forces Satellite Communications (MCD) ..... SHF-GMFSC
Super-High-Frequency - Time Division Multiple Access - MODEM (MCD) ..... SHF-TDMA-MODEM
Super-High-Intensity Vulnerability Assessor ..... SHIVA
Superhybrid Composite [*Laminate*] ..... SHC
Superhyperfine Structure ..... SHFS
Superimpose (MDG) ..... SI
Superimpose (IAA) ..... SM
Superimpose ..... SUPER
Superimposed Coding [*Computer science*] (DIT) ..... SC
Superimposed Current ..... SC
Superimposed Current ..... SUPCUR
Superimposed Integrated Trajectory Error [*Aviation*] ..... S-ITED
Superimposed Panoramic RADAR Display ..... SPANRAD
Superimposed Pregnancy-Induced Hypertension [*Obstetrics*] (DMAA) ..... SPIH
Superimposed Surface Wave Modes ..... SSWM
Superimposition (NTCM) ..... SUPER
Superintendencia da Agricultura e Producao [*Brazil*] ..... SUDAP
Superintendencia de Servicos Medicos [*Brazil*] ..... SUSEME
Superintendencia de Urbanizacao e Saneamento [*Brazil*] ..... SURSAN
Superintendencia do Desenvolvimento do Nordeste [*Brazil*] ..... SUDENE
Superintendencia do Desenvolvimento Economico e Cultural [*Brazil*] ..... SUDEC
Superintendencia do Plano de Valorizacao Economica da Amazonia [*Brazil*] ..... SPVEA
Superintendent (ADA) ..... SUPDT
Superintendent ..... SUPER
Superintendent (ROG) ..... SUPR
Superintendent (EY) ..... SUPT
Superintendent (DD) ..... supt
Superintendent ..... SUPT
Superintendent, Naval Observatory ..... SUPTNAVOBSY
Superintendent of Car Service ..... SCS
Superintendent of Contract Work [*Navy*] ..... SCW
Superintendent of Document/Item (NITA) ..... SI
Superintendent of Documents [*US Government Printing Office*] ..... SD
Superintendent of Documents [*US Government Printing Office*] ..... SOD
Superintendent of Documents, Government Printing Office (DLA) ..... Su Doc
Superintendent of Documents-Government Printing Office (TAG) ..... SUPDOC
Superintendent of Government Printing, India (ROG) ..... SGPI
Superintendent of Instruction [*British military*] (DMA) ..... S of I
Superintendent of Mine Design (WDAA) ..... SMD
Superintendent of Public Instruction (OICC) ..... SOPI
Superintendent of Public Instruction (DNAB) ..... SPI
Superintendent [*or Supervisor*] **of Range Operations** [*NASA*] ..... SRO
Superintendent of Shipbuilding [*Navy*] (AAGC) ..... SUPSHIPS
Superintendent of Technical Applications of Metals [*Ministry of Supply*] [*British World War II*] ..... STAM
Superintendent of Transportation ..... S of T
Superintendent of Transportation ..... ST
Superintending Armament Supply Officer [*British military*] (DMA) ..... SASO
Superintending Cartographer [*Navy British*] ..... SC
Superintending Civil Engineer [*British*] ..... SCE
Superintending Constructor ..... SUPCON
Superintending Engineer (ADA) ..... SE
Superintending Naval Stores Officer [*British military*] (DMA) ..... SNSO
Superintending Scientist [*British*] (ADA) ..... SS
Superintending Sea Transport Officer [*British military*] (DMA) ..... SSTO
Superintending Sister [*Navy British*] ..... SS
Superintending Veterinary Investigation Officer [*Ministry of Agriculture, Fisheries, and Food*] [*British*] ..... SVIO
Superintending Victualling Stores Officer [*British*] ..... SVSO
Superior ..... S
Superior (AFM) ..... SUP
Superior (WDMC) ..... sup
Superior ..... SUPER
Superior ..... SUPER
Superior (AABC) ..... SUPR
Superior Acceptance Corp. Ltd. [*Toronto Stock Exchange symbol*] ..... SUA
Superior Atrial Septum [*Anatomy*] ..... SAS
Superior Aviation, Inc. [*ICAO designator*] (FAAC) ..... HKA
Superior Carnegie Library, Superior, NE [*Library symbol Library of Congress*] (LCLS) ..... NbSu
Superior Cerebellar Artery [*Anatomy*] ..... SCA
Superior Cervical Ganglion [*Anatomy*] ..... SCG
Superior Cervical Sympathetic Ganglia [*Anatomy*] ..... SCSG
Superior Colliculus [*Brain anatomy*] ..... SC
Superior Consultant Holdings Corp. [*NASDAQ symbol*] (SAG) ..... SUPC
Superior Consultant Holdings Corp. [*Associated Press*] (SAG) ..... SupConsl
Superior Court (DLA) ..... SC
Superior Court (DLA) ..... Su
Superior Court (BARN) ..... Sup C
Superior Court (DLA) ..... Super
Superior Court (DLA) ..... Super Ct
Superior Court, Appellate Division (DLA) ..... Super Ct App Div
Superior Court, Chancery Division (DLA) ..... Super Ct Ch Div
Superior Court, Law Division (DLA) ..... Super Ct Law Div
Superior Court Reports [*A publication*] (DLA) ..... Super
Superior Court Reports [*New York, Pennsylvania, etc.*] [*A publication*] (DLA) ..... Super Ct Rep
Superior Electric (IAA) ..... SE
Superior Energy Services, Inc. [*NASDAQ symbol*] (SAG) ..... SESI
Superior Energy Services, Inc. [*Associated Press*] (SAG) ..... SupE
Superior Energy Services, Inc. [*Associated Press*] (SAG) ..... SupEnrgy
Superior Energy Svcs [*NASDAQ symbol*] (TTSB) ..... SESI
Superior Energy Svcs Wrrt [*NASDAQ symbol*] (TTSB) ..... SESIW
Superior Energy Svcs Wrrt'B' [*NASDAQ symbol*] (TTSB) ..... SESIZ
Superior Fine Cognac ..... SFC
Superior Geniculate Artery [*Anatomy*] ..... SGA
Superior Geocentric Conjunction ..... SGC
Superior Heliocentric Conjunction ..... SHC
Superior Indus Intl [*NYSE symbol*] (TTSB) ..... SUP
Superior Industries International, Inc. [*NYSE symbol*] (SPSG) ..... SUP
Superior Industries International, Inc. [*Associated Press*] (SAG) ..... SuperInd
Superior Internal Quality (WDAA) ..... SIQ
Superior Laryngeal Nerve [*Neuroanatomy*] ..... SLN
Superior Limbic Keratoconjunctivitis [*Ophthalmology*] ..... SLK
Superior Limbic Keratoconjunctivitis [*Ophthalmology*] (MAE) ..... SLKC
Superior Mesenteric [*Anatomy*] (DAVI) ..... SM
Superior Mesenteric Artery [*Anatomy*] ..... SMA
Superior Mesenteric Artery Blood Flow [*Medicine*] (DMAA) ..... SMABF
Superior Mesenteric Artery Embolus [*Medicine*] ..... SMAE

Superior Mesenteric Artery Flow ... SMAF
Superior Mesenteric Artery Occlusion [*Medicine*] (DMAA) ... SMAO
Superior Mesenteric Artery Thrombosis [*Medicine*] ... SMAT
Superior Mesenteric Blood Flow [*Physiology*] ... SMBF
Superior Mesenteric Vein [*Anatomy*] ... SMV
Superior National Insurance Group, Inc. [*NASDAQ symbol*] (SAG) ... SNTL
Superior National Insurance Group, Inc. [*Associated Press*] (SAG) ... SupNatl
Superior Natl Insurance Grp [*NASDAQ symbol*] (TTSB) ... SNTL
Superior, NE [*AM radio station call letters*] ... KRFS
Superior, NE [*FM radio station call letters*] ... KRFS-FM
Superior, NE [*Television station call letters*] ... KSNB
Superior Oblique [*Muscle*] [*Anatomy*] ... SO
Superior Oblique Muscle [*Eye anatomy*] ... SOM
Superior Official Bureaucrat [*Satirical bureaucracy term*] ... SOB
Superior Oil Co., Exploration Library, Houston, TX [*OCLC symbol*] (OCLC) ... SUP
Superior Oil Exploration Library, Houston, TX [*Library symbol Library of Congress*] (LCLS) ... TxHSU
Superior Old [*Spirits*] ... SO
Superior Old Marsala ... SOM
Superior Orbital Fissure [*Eye anatomy*] ... SOF
Superior Parietal Lobule [*Neuroanatomy*] ... SPL
Superior Performance Proficiency Pay (MCD) ... SPPP
Superior Public Library, Superior, WI [*OCLC symbol*] (OCLC) ... WNW
Superior Public Library, Superior, WI [*Library symbol Library of Congress*] (LCLS) ... WS
Superior Rectus [*Ophthalmology*] (MAE) ... SR
Superior Rectus Muscle [*Eye anatomy*] ... SRM
Superior Sagittal Sinus Blood Velocity [*Medicine*] (AAMN) ... SSSV
Superior Services [*NASDAQ symbol*] (TTSB) ... SUPR
Superior Services, Inc. [*NASDAQ symbol*] (SAG) ... SUPR
Superior Services, Inc. [*Associated Press*] (SAG) ... SupServ
Superior Shore Systems [*An association*] (EA) ... SSS
Superior Surgical [*AMEX symbol*] (TTSB) ... SGC
Superior Surgical Manufacturing Co., Inc. [*AMEX symbol*] (SPSG) ... SGC
Superior Surgical Manufacturing Co., Inc. [*Associated Press*] (SAG) ... SuprSrg
Superior Temporal Artery [*Anatomy*] ... STA
Superior Temporal Quadrant [*Medicine*] (DMAA) ... STQ
Superior Temporal Sulcus [*Brain anatomy*] ... STS
Superior Temporal Vein [*Medicine*] (DMAA) ... STV
Superior Turbinate [*Otorhinolaryngology*] (DAVI) ... ST
Superior Vena Cava [*Anatomy*] ... SVC
Superior Vena Cava Obstruction [*Cardiology*] (DAVI) ... SVCO
Superior Vena Cava - Right Pulmonary Artery Shunt [*Anatomy*] (MAE) ... SVC-RPA
Superior Vena Caval Syndrome [*Medicine*] ... SVCS
Superior White Crystal [*Sugar*] ... SWC
Superior, WI [*Television station call letters*] ... KBJR
Superior, WI [*FM radio station call letters*] (RBYB) ... KRBR-FM
Superior, WI [*FM radio station call letters*] ... KUWS
Superior, WI [*AM radio station call letters*] ... KXTP
Superior, WI [*FM radio station call letters*] ... KZIO
Superior, WI [*Location identifier FAA*] (FAAL) ... SUW
Superior, WI [*AM radio station call letters*] ... WDSM
Superiorland Library Cooperative, Marquette, MI [*OCLC symbol*] (OCLC) ... EZP
Superiorland Library Cooperative System, Marquette, MI [*Library symbol Library of Congress*] (LCLS) ... MiMarqS
Superlative ... SUP
Superlative ... SUPERL
Superlattice [*Solid state physics*] ... SL
Super-Low-Frequency (MCD) ... SLF
Superluminal [*Galaxy*] ... SL
Superluminescent Diode [*Tomography*] ... SLD
Supermarket (WDMC) ... SM
Supermarket ... SPRMRKT
Supermarket Allocation and Recorder Technique (IAA) ... SMART
Supermarket Computer Answering Service (OA) ... SCAN
Supermarket Subsystem Definition Record [*Computer science*] (IBMDP) ... SSDR
Supermassive Black Hole [*Cosmology*] ... SBH
Supermassive Object [*Cosmology*] ... SMO
Supermedial Thigh [*Flap for plastic surgery*] ... SMT
Super-Metal Rich [*Astronomy*] ... SMR
Super-Module Unit [*Telecommunications*] (TEL) ... SMU
Supermolecular Information Processor ... SIP
Super-Multi-Coating [*Camera lenses*] ... SMC
Supernatant [*Protein*] [*Cytology*] ... S
Supernatant [*Chemistry*] ... SN
Supernatant Treatment System [*Nuclear energy*] (NUCP) ... STS
Super-Normal Attitude Kinetic Enhancement [*Later, Enhanced Fighter Maneuverability*] [*X-31 experimental aircraft under development by Rockwell International Corp. and Messerschmitt-Boelkow-Blohm GmbH*] ... SNAKE
Supernova ... SN
Supernova Remnant [*Astronomy*] ... SNR
Supernumerary ... SUPER
Super-Open-Frame Low Voltage (IEEE) ... SOLV
Super-Orbital Reentry Test Integrated Environment (MUGU) ... SORTIE
Superoxide Anion [*Chemistry*] ... SOA
Superoxide Dismutase [*Also, SODI*] [*An enzyme*] ... SOD
Superoxide Dismutase [*SOD*] [*Absorbed by An enzyme*] ... SODI
Super-Packed Capillary Column [*Spectroscopy*] ... SPCC
Superparamagnetic [*Fraction in rock*] [*Geophysics*] ... SP
Superparamagnetic [*Fraction in rock*] [*Geophysics*] ... SPM
Superphantom (IAA) ... SPH
Superphosphate Manufacturers' Association [*British*] (BI) ... SMA
Superphosphoric Acid [*Fertilizer*] ... SPA
Superplastic Forming [*Materials science*] ... SPF
Superplastic Forming/Diffusion Bonding [*Materials science*] ... SPF/DB
Superplastic Metal Alloy ... SMA
Superposed Panoramic RADAR Display (IAA) ... SPANRAD
Superposition of Configuration [*Atomic physics*] ... SOC
Superprecipitation Response [*Medicine*] (DMAA) ... SPPT
Super-Precision Approach RADAR ... SPAR
Superquick [*Fuse*] ... SQ
Superquick and Delay [*Fuse*] (SAA) ... SQ-DEL
Superquick Sensor (MCD) ... SQS
Super-Radiant Diode ... SRD
Supersatellite Vehicle ... SSV
Supersaturated (MAE) ... SS
Supersearch-Online Friendly Interface [*Computer science*] ... SOFI
Supersede (WGA) ... SUP
Supersede (MUGU) ... SUPER
Supersede (AFM) ... SUPSD
Superseded [*New regulation or order substituted for an existing one*] [*Used in Shepard's Citations*] [*Legal term*] (DLA) ... S
Superseded in Part [*New matter substituted for part of an existing regulation or order*] [*Used in Shepard's Citations*] [*Legal term*] (DLA) ... SP
Supersensitive (AAG) ... SS
Supersensitive ... SUPSENS
Supersensitivity Perception ... SSP
SuperSerial Technology [*Equinox Systems, Inc.*] [*Telecommunications*] ... SST
Supersized and Calendered [*Paper*] ... SS & C
Supersonic ... SS
Supersonic Aerophysics Laboratory (MCD) ... SAL
Supersonic Airborne Infrared Measurement System (MCD) ... SAIMS
Supersonic Aircraft Engine ... SAE
Supersonic Antiship Missile (MCD) ... SASM
Supersonic Attack Seaplane ... SAS
Supersonic Balloon (IAA) ... SSB
Supersonic Combustion Ramjet ... SCR
Supersonic Combustion Ramjet ... SCRAMJET
Supersonic Combustion Ramjet ... SCRJ
Supersonic Combustion Ramjet Missile ... SCRAM
Supersonic Commercial Air Transport [*NASA*] ... SCAT
Supersonic Cruise Aircraft (PDAA) ... SCA
Supersonic Cruise Aircraft [*or Airplane*] **Research** [*NASA*] ... SCAR
Supersonic Cruise Attack Fighter (MCD) ... SCAF
Supersonic Cruise Intermediate Range Missile (MCD) ... SCRIM
Supersonic Cruise Missile ... SCV
Supersonic Expendable Turbojet Engine (MCD) ... SETE
Supersonic Frequency (IAA) ... SSF
Supersonic Gas Jet ... SGJ
Supersonic Gas Jet ... SSGJ
Supersonic High-Altitude Parachute Experiment [*NASA*] ... SHAPE
Supersonic Infantry Projectile ... SIP
Supersonic Infantry Rocket ... SIR
Supersonic Jet [*Gas stream*] ... SJ
Supersonic Jet Flow ... SJF
Supersonic Jet Noise ... SJN
Supersonic Local Pressure ... SLP
Supersonic Low Activities Target (MCD) ... SLAT
Supersonic Low-Altitude Attack Aircraft System (MCD) ... SLAAS
Supersonic Low-Altitude Missile [*Later, LASV*] [*NATO*] (NATG) ... SLAM
Supersonic Low-Altitude Target [*Navy*] ... SLAT
Supersonic Military Air Research Track ... SMART
Supersonic Missile and Rocket Track ... SMART
Supersonic Naval Ordnance Research Track [*China Lake, CA*] ... SNORT
Supersonic Nonequilibrium Analysis Program (MCD) ... SNAP
Supersonic Parachute Test Vehicle (IAA) ... SPTV
Supersonic Planetary Entry Decelerator (KSC) ... SPED
Supersonic Split Line (KSC) ... SSSL
Supersonic Tactical Missile (MCD) ... STM
Supersonic Target System ... STS
Supersonic Telegraphy [*British military*] (DMA) ... SS/T
Supersonic Test Vehicle (AAG) ... STV
Supersonic Test Vehicles ... SSV
Supersonic Tests of Aerodynamic Bombs (MUGU) ... STAB
Supersonic Transition Locus [*Galactic winds*] ... STL
Supersonic Transport ... SST
Supersonic Transport Advisory Board ... STAB
Supersonic Transport Evaluation Group ... STEG
Supersonic Transport Optimization Program [*NASA*] ... STOP
Supersonic Transport Panel [*International Civil Aviation Organization*] ... SSTP
Supersonic Tunnel Association (EA) ... STA
Supersonic Wind Tunnel (MCD) ... SWT
Superstar Ice Hockey [*Computer game*] ... SIH
Superstition Mountain Historical Society (EA) ... SMHS
Superstructure ... SUPERSTR
Superstructure (AAG) ... SUPRSTR
Superstructure Heater (DS) ... SH
Superstructure Heater Safety Valve (DS) ... SHSV
Supersymmetric Theories [*Particle physics*] ... SUSY's
Supertech Industries [*Vancouver Stock Exchange symbol*] ... SPU
Supertel Hospitality [*NASDAQ symbol*] (TTSB) ... SPPR
Supertel Hospitality, Inc. [*NASDAQ symbol*] (SAG) ... SPPR
Supertel Hospitality, Inc. [*Associated Press*] (SAG) ... Supertel
Supertex, Inc. [*Associated Press*] (SAG) ... Suprtex
Supertex, Inc. [*NASDAQ symbol*] (NQ) ... SUPX
Supertropical Bleach [*Sanitizing agent*] ... STB
Supertrust Trust Index Trust [*Associated Press*] (SAG) ... SpU/In
Supertrust Trust Money Market Trust [*Associated Press*] (SAG) ... SpU/MM

Supertwisted Birefringence Effect (NITA) .... SBE
SuperTwisted Nematic [Electronics] (CDE) .... STN
Supervalu, Inc. [Associated Press] (SAG) .... Supval
Supervalu Inc. [NYSE symbol] (TTSB) .... SVU
Supervised Agency (DLA) .... S/Ag
Supervised On-the-Job Training .... SOJT
Supervising .... SUPVG
Supervising Customs Agent [U.S. Customs Service] (BARN) .... SCA
Supervising Inspector of Naval Material .... SUPINSMAT
Supervising Teacher Behavior Description Questionnaire (EDAC) .... STBDQ
Supervision (MSA) .... SPVN
Supervision .... SUPRVSN
Supervision .... SUPVSN
Supervision Control Module [Telecommunications] (TEL) .... SCM
Supervision, Inspection, and Overhead (AFM) .... SIOH
Supervision, Inspection, Engineering, and Services (NASA) .... SIES
Supervision Through Educational Management by Objectives and
  Results (EDAC) .... STEMBOR
Supervisor (IAA) .... S
Supervisor (ECII) .... SPV
Supervisor .... Spvsr
Supervisor (TEL) .... SR
Supervisor (IAA) .... SUP
Supervisor (WDMC) .... sup
Supervisor (DSUE) .... SUPER
Supervisor .... SUPR
Supervisor (AAG) .... SUPV
Supervisor (AFM) .... SUPVR
Supervisor (DD) .... supvr
Supervisor .... SUPVSR
Supervisor (IAA) .... SV
Supervisor Call (IAA) .... SC
Supervisor Call (NASA) .... SVC
Supervisor Call Address Table (IAA) .... SVCT
Supervisor Call Instruction (IAA) .... SCI
Supervisor Control Console .... SCC
Supervisor Executive Program [NASA] (KSC) .... SEP
Supervisor Information on Civilian Career Management [Navy] (DNAB)..... SICCM
Supervisor of Diving [Navy] .... SUPDIV
Supervisor of Diving [Navy] .... SUPDIVE
Supervisor of Flying (MCD) .... SOF
Supervisor of Loan Fund Companies [New South Wales, Australia] .... SLFC
Supervisor of Multiprogramming, Multiprocessing, Interactive Time
  Sharing [Computer science] (IEEE) .... SUMMIT
Supervisor of Salvage [Navy] .... SUPSAL
Supervisor of Salvage [Navy] .... SUPSALV
Supervisor of Salvage Representative, West Coast [Navy]
  (DNAB) .... SUPSALREPWCOAST
Supervisor of Shipbuilding [Navy] .... SOS
Supervisor of Shipbuilding [Navy] .... SUPSHIP
Supervisor of Shipbuilding, Conversion, and Repair [Navy] (DNAB) .... SOSCAR
Supervisor Program Over Other Kinds [Computer science] .... SPOOK
Supervisor Range Operations (MCD) .... SRO
Supervisor Request Block [Computer science] (BUR) .... SVRB
Supervisor Training Conference Outline [Air Force] (MCD) .... STCO
Supervisor's Console .... SC
Supervisor's Control Panel .... SCP
Supervisor's Evaluation of Research Personnel (AEBS) .... SERP
Supervisors Section [American Association of School Librarians] .... SPVS
Supervisors Section [American Association of School Librarians] .... SS
Supervisory (MHDW) .... supvry
Supervisory .... SUPVRY
Supervisory (DEN) .... SUPY
Supervisory, Administrative, and Technical Association [Union of Ship
  Distribution and Allied Workers] [British] (DCTA) .... SATA
Supervisory Air Traffic Control Organization [FAA] .... SATCO
Supervisory Airplane Pilot .... SAP
Supervisory Aptitude Development [In George Lee Walker novel "The
  Chronicles of Doodah"] .... SAD
Supervisory Authority .... SA
Supervisory Behavior Description Questionnaire (EDAC) .... SBDQ
Supervisory Change Relations Test .... SCHR
Supervisory Circuit Breaker (IAA) .... SCB
Supervisory Coaching Relations Test .... SCORE
Supervisory Communication Relations Test .... SCOM
Supervisory Control .... SC
Supervisory Control and Data (IAA) .... SCADA
Supervisory Control and Data Acquisition (IEEE) .... SCADA
Supervisory Control And Data Acquisition [Industrial engineering] [Computer
  science] .... SCADA
Supervisory Control Conference (KSC) .... SCC
Supervisory Control Language [Computer science] (MHDI) .... SCL
Supervisory Control of Program Execution (MCD) .... SCOPE
Supervisory Control Program [Burroughs Corp.] .... SCP
Supervisory Control System (MCD) .... SCS
Supervisory Cost Inspector [Navy] .... SCI
Supervisory Cost Inspector [Navy] .... SUPCOSTINS
Supervisory Electronic Engineer [Radio] .... SEER
Supervisory Electronic Installation Technician .... SEIT
Supervisory Electronic Maintenance Technician [Relief] .... SEMTR
Supervisory Electronics Specialist .... SES
Supervisory Field Representative [Department of Commerce] (GFGA) .... SFR
Supervisory Human Relations Test .... SHR
Supervisory Immigrant Inspector [Immigration and Naturalization Service] .... SII

Supervisory Immigration Patrol Inspector [Immigration and Naturalization
  Service] .... SIPI
Supervisory Inventory on Communication [Test] .... SIC
Supervisory Inventory on Human Relations [Test] .... SIHR
Supervisory Inventory on Safety [Test] .... SIS
Supervisory Job Discipline Test .... SJD
Supervisory Job Instruction Test .... SJI
Supervisory Job Safety Test .... SJS
Supervisory Middle Management .... SMM
Supervisory Package (OA) .... SP
Supervisory Performance Appraisal [Civil Service] .... SPA
Supervisory Potential Test .... SPT
Supervisory Practices Inventory [Test] .... SPI
Supervisory Printer [Computer science] (OA) .... SP
Supervisory Printer Read [Computer science] (OA) .... SPR
Supervisory Process [Telecommunications] (TEL) .... SP
Supervisory Radio Station (IAA) .... SUPRVRADSTA
Supervisory Signal (IAA) .... SVS
Supervisory Surveillance Program [DoD] .... SSP
Supervisory Tape Executive Program [Computer science] .... STEP
Supervisory Time Frame .... STF
Supervisory Union Relations Test .... SUR
Super-Weight Improvement Program [Navy] (NG) .... SWIP
Superwomen Anonymous [Later, Overachievers Anonymous] (EA) .... SA
Superwomen's Anonymous (EA) .... SWA
Supima Association of America (EA) .... SAA
Supination [or Supinator] [Medicine] (DAVI) .... SUP
Supination [Medicine] (DMAA) .... supin
Supination, External Rotation - Type IV Fracture .... SER-IV
Supine .... SUP
Supine and Upright (MEDA) .... S & U
Supine and Upright (DAVI) .... S & U
Supine Diastolic Blood Pressure [Medicine] .... SDBP
Supplement .... SP
Supplement (BJA) .... Spl
Supplement (AFM) .... SUP
Supplement (WDMC) .... sup
Supplement (AAGC) .... Supp
Supplement (KSC) .... SUPP
Supplement (AABC) .... SUPPL
Supplement Aviation Spares Report (MCD) .... SASS
Supplement on Aging [to the 1984 National Health Interview Survey]
  [Department of Health and Human Services] (GFGA) .... SOA
Supplement to 4 Swabey and Tristram's Probate and Divorce Reports
  [England] [A publication] (DLA) .... Trist
Supplement to Petersdorff's Abridgment [A publication] (DLA) .... Pet Suppl
Supplement to Safety Evaluation Report [Nuclear energy] (NRCH) .... SSER
Supplement to Sayles' Annotated Civil Statutes [Texas] [A publication]
  (DLA) .... Sayles' Supp
Supplement to the Code [A publication] (DLA) .... Code Supp
Supplement to the Compiled Statutes [A publication] (DLA) .... CS Supp
Supplement to the Revised Statutes [A publication] (DLA) .... RS Supp
Supplement to the Revised Statutes [A publication] (DLA) .... Supp Rev St
Supplement to the Revised Statutes [A publication] (GFGA) .... Supp Rev Stat
Supplement to the Revision [A publication] (DLA) .... Supp Rev
Supplement to Vesey, Junior's, English Chancery Reports, by Hovenden
  [34 English Reprint] [A publication] (DLA) .... Ves Jr Suppl
Supplement to Vesey, Junior's, English Chancery Reports, by Hovenden
  [34 English Reprint] [A publication] (DLA) .... Ves Jun Supp
Supplement to Vesey, Junior's, English Chancery Reports, by Hovenden
  [34 English Reprint] [A publication] (DLA) .... Ves Jun Supp (Eng)
Supplement to Vesey, Junior's, English Chancery Reports, by Hovenden
  [34 English Reprint] [1789-1817] [A publication] (DLA) .... Ves Supp
Supplement to Vesey, Junior's, Reports [A publication] (DLA) .... Supp Ves Jun
Supplement to Vesey, Senior's, English Chancery Reports [28 English
  Reprint] [A publication] (DLA) .... Ves Sen Supp
Supplement to Vesey, Senior's, English Chancery Reports [28 English
  Reprint] [1747-56] [A publication] (DLA) .... Ves Sr Supp
Supplement to Vesey, Senior's, English Chancery Reports [28 English
  Reprint] [A publication] (DLA) .... Ves Sr Supp (Eng)
Supplement to Viner's Abridgment of Law and Equity [England]
  [A publication] (DLA) .... Vin Abr
Supplement to Viner's Abridgment of Law and Equity [A publication]
  (DLA) .... Vin Supp
Supplemental .... SUPMTL
Supplemental Advance Notice of Proposed Rulemaking [RSPA]
  (TAG) .... SANPRM
Supplemental Agreement (NG) .... SA
Supplemental Air Carrier (MCD) .... SAC
Supplemental Air Carrier Conference [Defunct] (EA) .... SACC
Supplemental Assistance for Facilities to Assist the Homeless [Department
  of Housing and Urban Development] (GFGA) .... SAFAH
Supplemental Basic Allowance for Subsistence [Military] (DNAB) .... SUPP BAS
Supplemental Budget Request .... SBR
Supplemental Contract (AAG) .... SC
Supplemental Conventional Reading Program [Education] .... SCRP
Supplemental Data Sheet .... SDS
Supplemental Educational Opportunity Grant [Department of Education] .... SEOG
Supplemental Environmental Impact Statement [Department of
  Agriculture] .... SEIS
Supplemental Environmental Projects [Policy] [Environmental Protection
  Agency] .... SEP
Supplemental Executive Retirement Plan [Human resources] (WYGK) .... SERP
Supplemental Flight Test .... SFT

Supplemental Health Manpower Shortage Area Placement Opportunity List [Department of Health and Human Services] (GFGA) .... SHPOL
Supplemental Heat Rejection Devices (NASA) .... SHRD
Supplemental Income Plan .... SIP
Supplemental Indian Appeals, Law Reports [A publication] (DLA) .... Ind App Supp
Supplemental Inflatable Restraint System [Automotive engineering] ... SIRS
Supplemental Knowledge Incentive Notes [Scrip offered to students for good performance] [Experimental learning program] .... SKINS
Supplemental Layoff Benefits (MCD) .... SLOB
Supplemental Loans for Students [Department of Education] .... SLS
Supplemental Maintenance and Repair Parts Instruction .... SUMARPI
Supplemental Maintenance Appraisal .... SMA
Supplemental Medical Expense Reimbursement Plan .... SMERP
Supplemental Medical Report .... SMR
Supplemental Minimal Medium [Microbiology] .... SMM
Supplemental Notice of Proposed Rulemaking .... SNPRM
Supplemental Oxygen Package (MCD) .... SOP
Supplemental Oxygen System (MCD) .... SOS
Supplemental Pack [Field troops military issue] (VNW) .... SP
Supplemental Planning Card (AAG) .... SPC
Supplemental Plot (MCD) .... SUPPLOT
Supplemental Preclaims Assistance [Department of Education] (GFGA) .... SPA
Supplemental Procurement Instrument Identification Number [DoD] ..... SPIIN
Supplemental Production Order (AAG) .... SPO
Supplemental Program Directive (AFIT) .... SPD
Supplemental Provisioning Technical Documentation [NASA] (NASA) .... SPTD
Supplemental Quality Assurance Provision [Military] .... SQAP
Supplemental Recreational Activities Overseas [Red Cross] .... SRAO
Supplemental Report .... SR
Supplemental Reporting Code .... SUPPREP
Supplemental Restraint System [Automotive engineering] .... SRS
Supplemental Retirement Annuities .... SRA
Supplemental Security Income [Social Security Administration] .... SSI
Supplemental Security Income Program (USGC) .... SSI
Supplemental Security Income/State Supplemental Payment (DAVI) ..... SSI/SSP
Supplemental Security Insurance [Program] .... SSI
Supplemental Security Record [Social Security Administration] (GFGA) ..... SSR
Supplemental Standard Practice (AAG) .... SSP
Supplemental Support Evaluation .... SSE
Supplemental Training and Employment Program (OICC) .... STEP
Supplemental Training and Readiness Program .... STARP
Supplemental Type Certificate .... STC
Supplemental Unemployment Assistance .... SUA
Supplemental Unemployment Benefits .... SUB
Supplemental Vacation Plan .... SVP
Supplemental Vocational Education Assistance (OICC) .... SVEA
Supplemental Weather Service Location [Aviation] (FAAC) .... SWSL
Supplementary (DLA) .... Suppl
Supplementary Address (MCD) .... SUPAD
Supplementary Application Forms Required [Civil Service] .... SAFR
Supplementary Aviation Information Display .... SAID
Supplementary Aviation Weather Reporting Station (FAAC) .... SAWRS
Supplementary Benefits .... SB
Supplementary Benefits Commission [Department of Employment] [British] .... SBC
Supplementary Checkout Trailer .... SCOT
Supplementary Control Strategy [System] [Environmental] (GNE) ..... SCS
Supplementary Development Plan .... SDP
Supplementary Experiment Data Record [Aerospace] .... SEDR
Supplementary Failure Analysis [NASA] (KSC) .... SFA
Supplementary Financing Facility [International Monetary Fund] .... SFF
Supplementary Flight Information Documentation (IAA) .... SFID
Supplementary Flight Plan Message [Aviation code] .... SPL
Supplementary Frequency (DA) .... S
Supplementary Heat Removal System (IEEE) .... SHRS
Supplementary Information [Telecommunications] (TEL) .... SC
Supplementary Intelligence Report [Military] (AABC) .... SUPINTREP
Supplementary Interim Medium Antitank System [Army] (INF) .... SIMATS
Supplementary Leak Collection and Release System [Nuclear energy] (IAA) .... SLAE
Supplementary Leak Collection and Release System [Nuclear energy] (NRCH) .... SLCRS
Supplementary List [Navy British] .... SL
Supplementary Medical Insurance .... SMI
Supplementary Monophonic Transmission (ADA) .... SMT
Supplementary Motor Area [Anatomy] .... SMA
Supplementary Ophthalmic Service [Medicine] .... SOS
Supplementary Patent Certificate [European Community] .... SPC
Supplementary Pay Appeals Tribunal [British] (DI) .... SPAT
Supplementary Petroleum Duty [Tax] [British] .... SPD
Supplementary Photographic Interpretation Report [Military] .... SUPIR
Supplementary Power Supply (IAA) .... SPS
Supplementary Power Supply Set (IAA) .... SPSS
Supplementary Progress Report .... SPR
Supplementary Protection Certificates [For European patents] .... SPC
Supplementary Protection System [Nuclear energy] (NRCH) .... SPS
Supplementary Quality Assurance Provisions .... SQUAP
Supplementary Radio (NG) .... SUPRAD
Supplementary Regulation .... SR
Supplementary Reserve [British military] (DMA) .... SR
Supplementary Reserve of Officers [Military British] .... SRO
Supplementary Reserve Regulations [Army British] .... SRR
Supplementary Service Exchange (NITA) .... SSX
Supplementary Service Tariff [British] (DCTA) .... SST
Supplementary Special Deposit [British] .... SSD

Supplementary Statement Required [Civil Service] .... SSR
Supplementary Strategies Working Group (EERA) .... SSWG
Supplementary Teaching Assistance in Reading (AEBS) .... STAR
Supplementary Technical Manual [Military] .... STM
Supplementary Term [Online database field identifier] .... ST
Supplementary Test Site [Nuclear energy] (IID) .... STS
Supplemented Eagle's Minimum Essential Medium [Medicine] (DMAA) ... SMEM
Supplementing [New matter added to an existing regulation or order] [Used in Shepard's Citations] [Legal term] (DLA) .... Sg
Supplementum Aeschyleum [A publication] (OCD) .... Supp Aesch
Supplemtary Meteorological Office (BARN) .... SMO
Supplices [of Euripides] [Classical studies] (OCD) .... Supp
Supplices Contra Thebas [of Aeschylus] [Classical studies] (OCD) ..... Supp
Supplier Assurance Test Procedures .... SATP
Supplier Capability Information Retrieval Technique (PDAA) .... SCIRT
Supplier Change Proposal (MCD) .... SCP
Supplier Corrective Action Request .... SCAR
Supplier Corrective Action Request .... SCAR
Supplier Cost Reduction Effort [Auto industry, project management] ... SCORE
Supplier Data Approval [Nuclear energy] (NRCH) .... SDA
Supplier Data Control Information System (MCD) .... SDCIS
Supplier Data Item (MCD) .... SDI
Supplier Data Item Description (MCD) .... SDID
Supplier Data Management System (MCD) .... SDMS
Supplier Data Package (NASA) .... SDP
Supplier Data Requirements Description (NASA) .... SDRD
Supplier Data Requirements List (NASA) .... SDRL
Supplier Data Review Notice (DNAB) .... SDRN
Supplier Data Sheet .... SDS
Supplier Data Transmittal (MCD) .... SDT
Supplier Delivery Schedules [Chrysler Corp.] .... SDS
Supplier Documentation (NASA) .... SD
Supplier Documentation Checklist (NASA) .... SDCL
Supplier Documentation Group [NASA] (NASA) .... SDG
Supplier Documentation Review Board [NASA] (NASA) .... SDRB
Supplier Documentation Review Data (NASA) .... SDRD
Supplier Identification System [London Enterprise Agency] [Information service or system] (IID) .... SIS
Supplier Interface Control Drawing (MCD) .... SICD
Supplier Item Control List (MCD) .... SICL
Supplier Item Engineering Order (MCD) .... SIED
Supplier Letter (MCD) .... SL
Supplier Loaned Property (MCD) .... SLP
Supplier Loaned Property Request (MCD) .... SLPR
Supplier Material Review Record (MCD) .... SMRR
Supplier Nonconformance Report [Nuclear energy] (NRCH) .... SNR
Supplier Operating Procedure (MCD) .... SOP
Supplier Performance Evaluation and Corrective Action (PDAA) .... SPECA
Supplier Performance Evaluation and Reporting [or Review] [General Motors quality award] .... SPEAR
Supplier Quality Assurance .... SQA
Supplier Quality Assurance Assistance .... SQAA
Supplier Quality Assurance Representative .... SQAR
Supplier Quality Engineering (MCD) .... SQE
Supplier Quality Engineering .... SQE
Supplier Quality Improvement .... SQI
Supplier Quality Rating .... SQR
Supplier Quality Representative [Nuclear energy] (NRCH) .... SQR
Supplier Quality System Survey Evaluations (MCD) .... SQSSE
Supplier Rating Incentive Program .... SRIP
Supplier Rating Report (SAA) .... SRR
Supplier Request for Engineering Approval .... SREA
Supplier Request for Product Change .... SRPC
Supplier Transmittal and Approval Request (MCD) .... STAR
Supplier-Allied-Price [Automobile content legislation] .... SAP
Supplier-Outside-Price [Automobile content legislation] .... SOP
Suppliers and Equipment Information Retrieval System [International Civil Aviation Organization] [Databank] [Information service or system] (IID).... SEIRS
Supplier's Contract Property (MCD) .... SCP
Suppliers Information Request .... SIR
Suppliers of Advanced Composite Materials .... SACMA
Suppliers of Advanced Composite Materials Association [Arlington, VA] (EA) .... SACMA
Suppliers Quality Identification Classification .... SQIC
Supplies (WGA) .... SUPLS
Supplies and Accounts .... S & A
Supplies and Accounts .... SANDA
Supplies and Equipage [Military] (CINC) .... S & E
Supplies, Equipment, and Training [Civil Defense] .... SE & T
Supplies in Liberated Areas [British World War II] .... SLA
Supplies Information System (NITA) .... SIS
Supplies Invoice Generation Network (PDAA) .... SIGNET
Supply [Department aboard a carrier] [Navy] .... S
Supply [Economics] .... S
Supply (MSA) .... SPLY
Supply [Business term] .... SU
Supply [Business term] (AFM) .... SUP
Supply .... SUPL
Supply .... SUPP
Supply [Business term] .... SY
Supply Accountant [Navy British] .... SA
Supply Acquisition Regulation Supplement [Navy] .... SUPARS
Supply Action Will Be Taken .... SAWBET
Supply Activity .... SA
Supply Administration Center [DoD] (MCD) .... SAC

Supply and Equipment Management Officer (AAGC) ... SEMO
Supply and Equipment Report [*Army*] (AABC) ... SEPORT
Supply and Fiscal Officer ... S & FO
Supply and Logistics ... S & L
Supply and Logistics (IAA) ... SAL
Supply and Maintenance [*Army*] (AABC) ... S & M
Supply and Maintenance Agency [*System*] [*Army*] ... S & MA
Supply and Maintenance Assessment and Review Team [*Army*] ... SMART
Supply and Maintenance Career Program ... SMCP
Supply and Maintenance Command [*Army*] ... SMC
Supply and Maintenance Command Packaging Storage and Transportability Center [*Army*] ... SMCPSTC
Supply and Maintenance Control Point ... SMCP
Supply and Maintenance Management Information System [*Army*] ... S & MMIS
Supply and Maintenance Plan and Report [*Army*] (AABC) ... SMPR
Supply and Repair Parts (DNAB) ... SRP
Supply and Repair Parts Specification (DNAB) ... SRPS
Supply and Service [*Army*] (AABC) ... S & S
Supply and Services Canada ... SSC
Supply and Training Mission [*Military*] (CINC) ... SATM
Supply and Training Mission [*Military*] (CINC) ... STRA
Supply and Transport [*Military*] ... S & T
Supply and Transport Corps [*British*] (DMA) ... S & T
Supply and Transportation Operations [*NASA*] (NASA) ... SATO
Supply Annex ... SUPANX
Supply Assistant (WDAA) ... SA
Supply Availability Card (MCD) ... SAC
Supply Bulletin [*Military*] ... SB
Supply Catalog [*Military*] (AABC) ... SC
Supply Catalog Components List [*Military*] ... SCCL
Supply Cataloging Program ... SCP
Supply Categories of Material (MCD) ... SCM
Supply Category of Material Code ... SCMC
Supply Center ... SUPCEN
Supply, Commissary, and Disbursing [*Navy*] ... SCD
Supply Contract (AAGC) ... SUP
Supply Control [*Military*] ... SC
Supply Control Center [*Military*] ... SCC
Supply Control Plan [*World War II*] ... SCP
Supply Control Study ... SCS
Supply Corps ... SC
Supply Corps, Navy ... SCN
Supply Corps Officer Refresher Training [*Navy*] (DNAB) ... SORT
Supply Cost (AAGC) ... SC
Supply Demand Control Point [*Military*] ... SDCP
Supply Department [*Navy*] ... SD
Supply Depot ... SD
Supply Depot ... SUPDEP
Supply Detachment [*British military*] (DMA) ... SD
Supply Distribution Center [*Military*] (AFIT) ... SDC
Supply Distribution Point ... SDP
Supply Duct [*Nuclear energy*] (NRCH) ... SD
Supply Executive Committee [*NATO*] (NATG) ... SEC
Supply Fan (AAG) ... SF
Supply from Stock on Hand or Due In ... SUPOHDU
Supply Improvement Program ... SIP
Supply Information Letter (MCD) ... SIL
Supply Information Management System [*Air Force*] (GFGA) ... SIMS
Supply Inspection [*Navy*] (NVT) ... SUPINSP
Supply Instruction [*Marine Corps*] ... SI
Supply Item Change Record ... SICR
Supply Item Design Change [*Navy*] (NG) ... SIDC
Supply Item Provisioning Document [*Navy*] (NG) ... SIPD
Supply Item Status ... SIS
Supply Item Status and Order Reporting System ... SISORS
Supply Item Status Order Reporting [*Army*] ... SISOR
Supply Left of Baseline (MCD) ... SLOB
Supply Line Inventory Management System [*Bell System*] ... SLIMS
Supply Loading Airfield ... SLA
Supply, Maintenance and Readiness Management Information System [*Logistics Management Information System*] [*Military*] (AABC) ... SMR/MIS
Supply, Maintenance, and Recoverability Code [*Army*] ... SMR
Supply, Maintenance, and Transportation [*Directorate*] [*Army*] (RDA) ... SMT
Supply Management Date and Price List [*Navy*] ... SMDPL
Supply Management Grouping Designator [*Navy*] (NG) ... SMGD
Supply Management Information Center [*Military*] (CAAL) ... SMIC
Supply Management Information System ... SMIS
Supply Management Inspection (NVT) ... SMI
Supply Management Office [*Air Force*] (AFM) ... SMO
Supply Management Report ... SMR
Supply Manual [*Military*] ... SM
Supply Master Plan ... SMP
Supply Module (SSD) ... SM
Supply of Essential Engineering Data ... SEED
Supply Officer [*Army*] ... S4
Supply Officer ... SO
Supply Officer ... SUPO
Supply Officer-in-Charge [*Navy*] ... SOINC
Supply Officer-in-Command [*Military*] ... SOIC
Supply OK [*i.e., Authorized*] ... SOK
Supply on Hand or Due In ... SUPOH DI
Supply Online Management Information System [*Computer science*] (PDAA) ... SOLMIS
Supply On-Line Option [*IMS America Ltd.*] [*Database*] ... SOLO
Supply Operations [*DoD*] ... SUPOPS
Supply Operations Assistance Program [*Military*] ... SOAP
Supply Overhaul (MCD) ... SOH
Supply Overhaul Coordinator (MCD) ... SOC
Supply Performance Report (CINC) ... SPR
Supply Petty Officer [*British military*] (DMA) ... Sy PO
Supply Pier [*Navy*] ... SUPIER
Supply Platoon [*Military*] (DNAB) ... SUPPLT
Supply Point [*Military*] (NATG) ... SP
Supply Point [*Military*] ... SUPPT
Supply Point Simulation (MCD) ... SPS
Supply Point Simulation Model (MCD) ... SPSM
Supply, Priorities, and Allocations Board [*World War II*] ... SPAB
Supply Railhead ... SRH
Supply Readiness Milestone Plan [*Military*] (CAAL) ... SRMP
Supply Readiness Program [*Air Force*] ... SRP
Supply Refuelling Point [*Air Force British*] ... SRP
Supply Requisition Inquiry ... SRI
Supply Response Section [*Navy*] ... SRS
Supply Response Time ... SRT
Supply Room ... SR
Supply Screening Section [*Navy*] ... SSS
Supply Selective Treatment and Review System ... SUPSTARS
Supply Sergeant [*Marine Corps*] ... SUPSGT
Supply Ship (MCD) ... SS
Supply Significant Items List (MCD) ... SSIL
Supply Spectrum Generator ... SSG
Supply Squadron ... SUPS
Supply Status Code [*Army*] (AABC) ... SSC
Supply Status File (MCD) ... SSF
Supply Support Activity [*Military*] (AABC) ... SSA
Supply Support Arrangements [*A bilateral agreement between the United States and a friendly foreign government*] ... SSA
Supply Support Center [*Navy*] ... SSC
Supply Support Element Manager ... SSEM
Supply Support Index (CAAL) ... SSI
Supply Support Management ... SSM
Supply Support Management Plan [*Military*] (CAAL) ... SSMP
Supply Support Request [*or Requirement*] [*Military*] (AFM) ... SSR
Supply System Command [*Navy*] (MCD) ... SSC
Supply System Command [*Navy*] ... SUPSYSCOM
Supply System, Security Group [*Navy*] (DNAB) ... SUPSYSECGRU
Supply Systems Redevelopment Branch [*Australian Defence Force*] ... SSRB
Supply/Utilization Accounts [*FAO*] [*Information service or system United Nations*] (DUND) ... SUA
Supply Valve (MCD) ... S/V
Supply Working Party of Official Committee on Armistice Terms and Civil Administration [*World War II*] ... SWP
Supply-Voltage Rejection (IEEE) ... SVR
Support ... SP
Support ... SPPRT
Support (MSA) ... SPRT
Support (AFM) ... SPT
Support (IAA) ... SU
Support ... SUP
Support (AAG) ... SUPP
Support (CINC) ... SUPT
Support Acronym Definition [*Computer science*] ... SAD
Support Action Center [*NASA*] (MCD) ... SAC
Support Action Form (MCD) ... SAF
Support Activities Building [*National Security Agency*] ... SAB
Support Activities Staffing Review (MCD) ... SASTAR
Support Activity (MCD) ... SA
Support Activity ... SUPPACT
Support Agency [*NASA*] (KSC) ... SA
Support Air Direction [*Navy*] ... SAD
Support Air Observation [*Navy*] ... SAO
Support Air Request [*Net*] [*Navy communications*] ... SAR
Support Amplifier Station [*Telecommunications*] (OA) ... SAS
Support Analysis Test ... SAT
Support and Electronic Test Equipment ... SETE
Support and Encouragement for Talent - Gateway to Opportunity [*Project*] (EA) ... SET-GO
Support and Logistics Areas [*NASA*] (MCD) ... SLA
Support and Range Development (MUGU) ... SARD
Support and Stimulation [*Medicine*] (DAVI) ... S & S
Support and Sustaining Implications of Increased POMCUS Levels [*Military*] ... SSIPL
Support Area [*NASA*] (MCD) ... SA
Support Assessment Capability ... SAC
Support Availability Multisystem Operational Model ... SAMSOM
Support Base Activation (AAG) ... SBA
Support Box ... SB
Support by Fire [*Military*] (INF) ... SBF
Support Cambodia Out of Thailand [*Military operation*] (VNW) ... SCOOT
Support Careers Advisory Committee [*Environmental Protection Agency*] (EPA) ... SCAC
Support Carrier Force ... SCF
Support Center ... SC
Support Center [*Army*] ... SPTCEN
Support Center International Logistics [*Army*] ... SCIL
Support Center Management Plan (AAG) ... SCMP
Support Centers of America [*An association*] (EA) ... SCA
Support Chief ... SC
Support Command [*Army*] ... SC
Support Command [*Army*] ... SUPCOM

Support Command Operations Center [*Military*] ..... SCOC
Support Concept Economic Evaluation Technique (MCD) ..... SCEET
Support Concept Manual [*Marine Corps*] ..... SC
Support Contractor (MCD) ..... SC
Support Control Program (IAA) ..... SCP
Support Control Room [*NASA*] (KSC) ..... SCR
Support Controller [*NASA*] (KSC) ..... SC
Support Coordinator (AAG) ..... SC
Support Data Engineering (MCD) ..... SDE
Support Data Sheet [*Military*] ..... SDS
Support Design Change ..... SDC
Support Directive (KSC) ..... SD
Support Directive Instruction (KSC) ..... SDI
Support [*or Supporting*] Document (KSC) ..... SD
Support Dogs for the Handicapped (EA) ..... SDH
Support Electronics Assembly [*Military*] ..... SEA
Support Engineering Manhour Summary (MCD) ..... SEMS
Support Equipment (AFM) ..... SE
Support Equipment Abbreviated Items Description [*NASA*] (NASA) ..... SEAID
Support Equipment Acquisition Planning Group [*NASA*] (NASA) ..... SEAPG
Support Equipment Assembly and Checkout Facility [*NASA*] (NASA) ..... SEACF
Support Equipment Asset Management Subsystem (MCD) ..... SEAMS
Support Equipment Avionics System ..... SEAS
Support Equipment Building [*NASA*] (NASA) ..... SEB
Support Equipment Bulletin (MCD) ..... SEB
Support Equipment Change (MCD) ..... SEC
Support Equipment Concept Approval Data ..... SECAD
Support Equipment Cost Effectiveness Model (MCD) ..... SECEM
Support Equipment Critical Item (MCD) ..... SECI
Support Equipment Data Acquisition and Control System (MCD) ..... SEDACS
Support Equipment Data System (MCD) ..... SEDS
Support Equipment Delivery Schedule Delinquency Report (MCD) ..... SEDSDR
Support Equipment End Item (MCD) ..... SEEI
Support Equipment End Item Funding Report (MCD) ..... SEIFR
Support Equipment Exhibit (MCD) ..... SEE
Support Equipment/Facility [*NASA*] (NASA) ..... SE/FAC
Support Equipment Field Modification (AAG) ..... SEFM
Support Equipment for Robot (DWSG) ..... SEFR
Support Equipment Illustration (MCD) ..... SEI
Support Equipment Illustration Data (MCD) ..... SEID
Support Equipment Installation [*NASA*] (NASA) ..... SEI
Support Equipment Installation and Checkout [*NASA*] (NASA) ..... SEICO
Support Equipment List [*Navy*] ..... SEL
Support Equipment List Requirement (MCD) ..... SELR
Support Equipment Management Report (MCD) ..... SEMR
Support Equipment Package [*NASA*] (NASA) ..... SEP
Support Equipment Recommendation Data [*NASA*] (KSC) ..... SERD
Support Equipment Requirement ..... SER
Support Equipment Requirements Data ..... SERD
Support Equipment Requirements Sheet ..... SERS
Support Equipment Rework Management Information System [*Navy*] (GFGA) ..... SERMIS
Support Equipment Subsystem ..... SES
Support Equipment Utilization List (NASA) ..... SEUL
Support Facility Annex [*Army*] ..... SFA
Support Flight [*Military*] ..... SPTF
Support for Creative Independent Production Talent [*EC*] (ECED) ..... SCRIPT
Support for East European Democracies Act [*1989*] ..... SEED
Support for Engineer Development Priorities (MCD) ..... SEDP
Support for Industry (NITA) ..... SFI
Support for Innovation Project (AIE) ..... SIP
Support for Projects Under Research [*British*] ..... SPUR
Support for Promoting the Utilization of Resources [*Esso Education Foundation*] ..... SPUR
Support for the Analysts' File Environment (MCD) ..... SAFE
Support Force ..... SPORTFOR
Support Group [*Military*] ..... SPTG
Support Group Europe [*Military*] ..... SGE
Support Harness Assembly ..... SHA
Support Helicopter Flight NI [*British ICAO designator*] (FAAC) ..... SHF
Support, Help, and Empowerment ..... SHE
Support Identification Code (SSD) ..... SIC
Support Information Network ..... SIN
Support Installation (MCD) ..... SI
Support Instrumentation Requirements Document [*NASA*] ..... SIRD
Support Integrated Data System (MCD) ..... SIDS
Support Issue Development Committee [*Military*] (CAAL) ..... SIDC
Support Item Requirement List (MCD) ..... SIRL
Support Items List (MCD) ..... SIL
Support Jamming [*Military*] (LAIN) ..... SJ
Support Landing Boat [*Navy symbol Obsolete*] ..... LES
Support Landing Ship (Large) MK III ..... LSSL
Support Line [*Military*] ..... SL
Support Line [*Military*] ..... SPTL
Support List Allowance Card ..... SIAC
Support List Allowance Card (MCD) ..... SLAC
Support List Allowance Master ..... SLAM
Support List Allowance Tape (MCD) ..... SLAT
Support Maintenance Management System [*Army*] ..... SMMS
Support Management Area [*Mission Control Center*] [*NASA*] ..... SMA
Support Material List ..... SML
Support Module [*NASA*] (NASA) ..... SM
Support of Nuclear Operations with Conventional Air Tactics (NATG) ..... SNOWCAT

Support of Other Nations [*Military support furnished certain nations and funded by the Air Force*] ..... SON
Support of Positive Youth [*Australia*] ..... SOPY
Support of User Records and Files [*Computer science*] ..... SURF
Support on Site [*Computer science*] ..... SOS
Support Operations ..... SO
Support Operations Automated Training System [*NASA*] (NASA) ..... SOATS
Support Operations Center ..... SOC
Support Organization for Trisomy 18/13 (EA) ..... SOFT 18/13
Support Organization for Trisomy 18, 13 and Related Disorders (PAZ) ..... SOFT
Support Our Aging Religious, Inc. ..... SOAR
Support Our Soldiers [*Network of antiwar-oriented coffee houses located near military bases*] (EA) ..... SOS
Support Package for Aerospace Computer Emulation (MCD) ..... SPACE
Support Period Requirement ..... SPR
Support Plan (MCD) ..... SP
Support Plan (MCD) ..... SPLAN
Support Plan to Continuity of Operations Plan [*Military*] ..... SCOOP
Support Planning Analysis Reporting and Control [*Navy*] (NG) ..... SPARC
Support Planning Identification File [*NASA*] (MCD) ..... SPIDF
Support Plans and Requirements ..... SPR
Support Platoon Leader [*Military*] (INF) ..... SPL
Support Program for Remote Entry of Alphanumeric Displays (NITA) ..... SPREAD
Support Program Management ..... SPM
Support Publications (AAG) ..... SP
Support Reaction Load (NRCH) ..... SR
Support Request [*or Requirement*] (KSC) ..... SR
Support Requirement System [*NASA*] (NASA) ..... SRS
Support Requirements Analysis [*NASA*] (NASA) ..... SRA
Support Requirements Letter (CET) ..... SRL
Support Requirements Records [*Navy*] (NG) ..... SRR
Support Research Branch [*Springfield Armory*] ..... SRB
Support Resource Unit (MCD) ..... SRU
Support Review Code (MCD) ..... SRC
Support Room (MCD) ..... SR
Support Services Alliance [*Schoharie, NY*] (EA) ..... SSA
Support Services Control Center [*NASA*] (MCD) ..... SSCC
Support Services Management Information System [*Army*] ..... SSMIS
Support Services Office [*Environmental Protection Agency*] (GFGA) ..... SSO
Support Site Activation Data Package (MCD) ..... SSADP
Support Software (MCD) ..... SSW
Support Software Center ..... SSC
Support Software Documentation (MCD) ..... SSD
Support Software Package (MCD) ..... SSP
Support Squadron [*Air Force*] ..... SPTS
Support Squadron [*Air Force*] ..... SPTSq
Support Squadron Eastern Flank [*British military*] (DMA) ..... SSEF
Support Staff Interests Round Table [*American Library Association*] ..... SSIRT
Support Staff Rooms (SAA) ..... SSR
Support Status List (MCD) ..... SSL
Support Subsystem Manager ..... SSM
Support System [*Air Force*] ..... SS
Support System Concept Document ..... SSCD
Support System Design Integration (AAG) ..... SSDI
Support System Evaluation ..... SSE
Support System for OEX [*Orbiter Experiments*] (NASA) ..... SSO
Support System Language [*Computer science*] (IAA) ..... SSL
Support System Project Engineer ..... SSPE
Support System Task Analysis (AAG) ..... SSTA
Support Systems Engineering [*Boeing*] ..... SSE
Support Systems Module [*NASA*] ..... SSM
Support Table Load ..... STL
Support Teacher Learning Difficulties ..... STLD
Support Test Equipment (MCD) ..... STE
Support Test Manager (NASA) ..... STM
Support to Aftermarket Repairs [*Toyota automobile service repair program*] ..... STAR
Support to Total Force Analysis [*TRADOC*] (MCD) ..... STFAS
Support Tracking Analysis Reporting Systems (MCD) ..... STARS
Support Unit [*NASA*] (NASA) ..... SU
Support Unit Improvement Program (MCD) ..... SUIP
Support Unit Vehicle Automatic Tester ..... SUVAT
Support Validation Laboratory [*Army*] ..... SVL
Support Vehicle [*British military*] (DMA) ..... SV
Support Work Authorization [*NASA*] (MCD) ..... SWA
Support Work Order (AAG) ..... SWO
Support Your Local Police ..... SYLP
Supportability Assurance Program ..... SAP
Supportability, Maintainability, and Repairability (SSD) ..... SMR
Supportable Technology for Affordable Fighter Structures [*Air Force*] (DOMA) ..... STAFS
Support-Coated Open-Tubular [*Column*] [*Chromatography*] ..... SCOT
Supported Activities Supply System [*Marine Corps*] ..... SASSY
Supported Aqueous-Phase Catalysis [*Chemistry*] ..... SAPC
Supported Drift Tube Klystron ..... SDTK
Supported Liquid Membrane [*Separation science and technology*] ..... SLM
Supported Liquid Phase Catalyst [*Chemical engineering*] ..... SLPC
Supported Ring Frame ..... SRF
Supporters of Silkwood [*Defunct*] (EA) ..... SOS
Supporting (AAG) ..... SUPTG
Supporting Administrative Contracting Officer (AFIT) ..... SACO
Supporting Applied Research and Exploratory Development [*National Weather Service*] ..... SARED
Supporting Arms [*Navy A publication*] ..... SA
Supporting Arms Coordination Center [*Air Force*] ..... SACC

Supporting Arms Coordination Exercise (DOMA) .... SACEX
Supporting Arms Coordinator [*Air Force*] (NVT) .... SAC
Supporting Arms Coordinator (Airborne) [*Marine Corps*] (DOMA) .... SAC(A)
Supporting Arms Department [*Navy*] (DNAB) .... SAD
Supporting Arms Liaison Team [*Army*] (INF) .... SALT
Supporting Assistance Bureau [*Agency for International Development*] .... SAB
Supporting Cells [*Zoology*] .... SC
Supporting Checkout .... SCH
Supporting Data Analysis .... SDA
Supporting Document List .... SDL
Supporting Facilities and Services .... SF & S
Supporting Gunnery Ship [*Navy symbol Obsolete*] .... APG
Supporting Research [*Military*] .... SR
Supporting Research and Advanced Development .... SR/AD
Supporting Research and Technology (AAGC) .... SR&T
Supporting Research and Technology (MCD) .... SRT
Supporting Technologies [*Military*] (RDA) .... ST
Supporting Technology Development (KSC) .... STD
Supportive Council on Preventive Effort [*Ohio*] .... SCOPE
Supportive Housing Demonstration Program [*Department of Housing and Urban Development*] (GFGA) .... SHDP
Supportive Older Women's Network [*An association*] .... SOWN
Supportive Service (OICC) .... SS
Supposedly Noiseless Infrared Detector .... SNIRD
Suppositorium [*Suppository*] [*Pharmacy*] .... SUPP
Suppository [*Pharmacy*] .... SUPPOS
Suppresor [*Electronics*] (ECII) .... SUP
Suppress (DEN) .... SUP
Suppress .... SUPR
Suppress Leading Zero [*Computer science*] .... SLZ
Suppress Length Indication (BUR) .... SLI
Suppress Normal End (IAA) .... SNE
Suppress, Obscure, Secure, and Reduce [*Military*] (INF) .... SOSR
Suppressed Carrier (IEEE) .... SC
Suppressed Carrier Double Sideband [*Transmission*] (IAA) .... SCDSB
Suppressed Electrical Discharge (IAA) .... SED
Suppressed-Carrier Modulation .... SCM
Suppressing Line Operands and Translating to Hexadecimal [*Telecommunications*] (TEL) .... SLOTH
Suppression (IDOE) .... sup
Suppression (MSA) .... SUPPR
Suppression .... SUPRN
Suppression of Air Defense System (MCD) .... SUPADS
Suppression of Enemy Air Defenses (AABC) .... SEAD
Suppression Pool Makeup System [*Nuclear energy*] (NRCH) .... SPMS
Suppression Pool Retention Analysis [*Nuclear energy*] .... SUPRA
Suppressor [*Electronics*] (MDG) .... SU
Suppressor (IDOE) .... sup
Suppressor Activating Factor [*Immunology*] .... SAF
Suppressor Cell Activating Factor [*Biochemistry*] .... SCAF
Suppressor Cell Activity [*Medicine*] (DMAA) .... SCA
Suppressor Grid Orbitron Gauge .... SGOG
Suppressor Receptor [*Embryology*] .... SR
Suppressor Sensitive [*Laboratory scienc*] (DAVI) .... SUS
Suppressor T Lymphocyte [*Immunology*] .... STL
Suppurative [*Medicine*] .... supp
Supr Einspritz Coupe [*Super, Fuel Injection, Coupe*] [*Mercedes-Benz automotive model designation*] .... SEC
Supra [*Above*] [*Latin*] .... SUP
Supra Citato [*Cited Above*] [*Latin*] (DAVI) .... supra cit
Supra Scriptum [*Written Above*] [*Latin*] .... SS
Suprachiasmatic Nucleus [*or Nuclei*] [*of the hypothalamus Anatomy*] .... SCN
Supracondylar/Suprapatellar [*Prosthesis*] .... SC/SP
Supracondylar Tibial Prosthesis [*Medicine*] .... STP
Suprahepatic Vena Cava [*Medicine*] (AAMN) .... SVC
Supra-High Frequency [*Radio wavelength*] (IAA) .... SHF
Supralaryngeal Vocal Tract [*Anatomy*] .... SVT
Supramamillary [*Neurology*] (DAVI) .... SM
Supraoesophageal Ganglion [*Invertebrate nuerology*] .... SOG
Supraoptic [*Nucleus*] [*Ophtalmology*] (DAVI) .... SO
Supraoptic Hypothalamic Nucleus [*Medicine*] (DMAA) .... SOHN
Supraoptic Nucleus [*Brain anatomy*] .... SON
Supraoptic-Hypophyseal Diabetes Insipidus [*Endocrinology*] .... SHDI
Supraorbital Artery Test [*Neurological evaluation*] (CPH) .... SOA
Supraphon [*Record label*] [*Former Czechoslovakia*] .... Sup
Supraprotest .... SP
Suprapubic [*Medicine*] .... SP
Suprapubic Aspiration [*Medicine*] .... SPA
Suprapubic Bladder Tap [*Medicine*] (MEDA) .... SPBT
Suprapubic Prostatectomy [*Medicine*] .... SPP
Suprapublic Bladder Tap [*Urology*] (DAVI) .... SPBT
Suprasellar Arachnoid Cyst [*Medicine*] .... SSAC
Suprasonic Transport [*Aviation*] (DAVI) .... STS
Suprasternal Notch [*Anatomy*] .... SN
Supra-Subduction Zone [*Geology*] .... SSZ
Suprathermal Ion Detector (PDAA) .... SID
Suprathermal-Ion-Detector Experiment [*Apollo*] [*NASA*] .... SIDE
Supravalvular Aortic Stenosis [*Cardiology*] .... SAS
Supravalvular Aortic Stenosis [*Cardiology*] (MAE) .... SVAS
Supraventricular [*Cardiology*] .... SV
Supraventricular Aortic Stenosis [*Medicine*] (DMAA) .... SVAS
Supraventricular Ectopic [*Beat*] [*Cardiology*] .... SVE
Supraventricular Paroxysmal Tachycardia [*Cardiology*] (DAVI) .... SVPT
Supraventricular Premature Beats [*Cardiology*] .... SVPB
Supraventricular Tachyarrhythmia [*Cardiology*] (DAVI) .... SVT
Supraventricular Tachycardia [*Cardiology*] .... SVT
Supravergence (AAMN) .... S
Supravital [*Medicine*] (MAE) .... SV
Suprema Specialities, Inc. [*NASDAQ symbol*] (SAG) .... CHEZ
Suprema Specialities, Inc. [*Associated Press*] (SAG) .... SupSpcl
Suprema Specialties [*NASDAQ symbol*] (TTSB) .... CHEZ
Supreme .... SPRM
Supreme .... SUP
Supreme .... SUPR
Supreme Allied Atlantic Command Anti-Submarine Warfare Research Centre [*NATO*] [*Italy*] .... SACLANTCEN
Supreme Allied Command [*or Commander*] [*Headquarters in London*] [*World War II*] .... SAC
Supreme Allied Command, Europe [*World War II*] (NADA) .... SACEUR
Supreme Allied Command [*or Commander*], Southeast Asia .... SACSEA
Supreme Allied Commander, Atlantic [*NATO*] .... SACLANT
Supreme Allied Commander, Atlantic, Antisubmarine Warfare Research Center [*NATO*] .... SACLANTCEN
Supreme Allied Commander, Atlantic, Representative in Europe [*NATO*] .... SACLANTREPEUR
Supreme Allied Commander, Europe [*NATO*] .... SACEUR
Supreme Allied Commander, Europe Representative [*NATO*] (NATG) .... SACEUREP
Supreme Allied Commander, Mediterranean [*World War II*] .... SACMED
Supreme Allied Headquarters [*World War II*] .... SAH
Supreme and Exchequer Courts Act [*Canada*] (ILCA) .... SCA
Supreme Assembly for the Islamic Revolution in Iraq [*Political party*] (ECON) .... SAIRI
Supreme Assembly, International Order of Rainbow for Girls [*Freemasonry*] (EA) .... SAIORG
Supreme Bench [*Legal term*] (DLA) .... SB
Supreme Caldron, Daughters of Mokanna (EA) .... D of M
Supreme Camp of the American Woodmen (EA) .... SCAW
Supreme Circle Brotherhood of America (EA) .... SCBA
Supreme Command .... SUPCOM
Supreme Commander, Allied Expeditionary Force [*World War II*] .... SCAEF
Supreme Commander, Allied Powers [*World War II*] (MUGU) .... SCAP
Supreme Commander of Allied Forces (ADA) .... SCAF
Supreme Commandery Knights of St. John (EA) .... SCKSJ
Supreme Committee for the Liberation of Lithuania [*Defunct*] (EA) .... SCLL
Supreme Cossack Representation in Exile (EA) .... SCRE
Supreme Council [*Freemasonry*] (ROG) .... SC
Supreme Council, Ancient Accepted Scottish Rite of Freemasonry - Northern Masonic Jurisdiction (EA) .... AASR-NMJ
Supreme Council, Ancient Accepted Scottish Rite of Freemasonry - Southern Masonic Jurisdiction (EA) .... AASR-SMJ
Supreme Council for National Reconstruction [*South Korea*] .... SCNR
Supreme Council for Sport in Africa [*See also CSSA*] [*Yaounde, Cameroon*] (EAIO) .... SCSA
Supreme Council, Mystic Order Veiled Prophets of Enchanted Realm (EA) .... MOVPER
Supreme Council of the Independent Associated Spiritualists [*Defunct*] (EA) .... SCIAS
Supreme Council of the Royal Arcanum [*Boston, MA*] (EA) .... SCRA
Supreme Council of the Western Catholic Union [*Later, Western Catholic Union*] (EA) .... SCWCU
Supreme Council Order of the Amaranth (EA) .... SCOA
Supreme Council Sovereign Grand Inspectors General [*Freemasonry*] .... SCSGIG
Supreme Court .... SC
Supreme Court (BARN) .... Sup C
Supreme Court (DLA) .... Sup Ct
Supreme Court Appeals [*India*] [*A publication*] (ILCA) .... SCA
Supreme Court Appeals [*India*] [*A publication*] (DLA) .... Sup Ct App
Supreme Court Appellate Term (DLA) .... App T
Supreme Court Cases [*A publication*] (DLA) .... SC Cas
Supreme Court Cases [*India*] [*A publication*] (DLA) .... SCC
Supreme Court Circular [*Ceylon*] [*A publication*] (ILCA) .... SCC
Supreme Court Decisions, by J. E. R. Stephens [*A publication*] (DLA) .... Stephens
Supreme Court Decisions (St. Vincent) [*1928-36*] [*A publication*] (DLA) .... SCD (St V)
Supreme Court, Fifth Judicial District, Law Library, Utica, NY [*OCLC symbol*] (OCLC) .... ZUM
Supreme Court Historical Society (EA) .... SCHS
Supreme Court in Banco [*Canada*] [*A publication*] (DLA) .... SC in Banco
Supreme Court, Individual Slip Opinions .... SCISO
Supreme Court Journal [*India*] [*A publication*] (DLA) .... SC J
Supreme Court Journal [*India*] [*A publication*] (DLA) .... Sup Ct J
Supreme Court Judgments by Clark [*1917-32*] [*Jamaica*] [*A publication*] (DLA) .... Clark
Supreme Court Law Library, Tenth Judical District, Riverhead, NY [*Library symbol Library of Congress*] (LCLS) .... NRvSL
Supreme Court Law Library-Elmira, Elmira, NY [*Library symbol*] [*Library of Congress*] (LCLS) .... NElmSC
Supreme Court Library at Saratoga Springs, Saratoga Springs, NY [*Library symbol*] [*Library of Congress*] (LCLS) .... NSsSC
Supreme Court Monthly Review [*India*] [*A publication*] (DLA) .... Sup Ct MR
Supreme Court of Canada .... SCC
Supreme Court of Canada Judgements [*Canada Department of Justice*] [*Information service or system*] (CRD) .... SCCJ
Supreme Court of Canada, Ottawa, ON, Canada [*Library symbol Library of Congress*] (LCLS) .... CaOOSC
Supreme Court of Canada [*Cour Supreme du Canada*] **Ottawa, Ontario** [*Library symbol National Library of Canada*] (NLC) .... OOSC
Supreme Court of Christmas Island [*Australia*] .... SCCI
Supreme Court of Cocos (Keeling) Islands [*Australia*] .... SCC(K)I

Supreme Court of Justice [*British*] (ROG) .... SCJ
Supreme Court of New South Wales [*Australia*] .... SCNSW
Supreme Court of New York, Library, Syracuse, NY [*OCLC symbol*] (OCLC) .... ZVD
Supreme Court of Norfolk Island [*Australia*] .... SCNI
Supreme Court of Quebec, Reports [*A publication*] (DLA) .... SR
Supreme Court of the Australian Capital Territory .... SCACT
Supreme Court of the Northern Territory [*Australia*] .... SCNT
Supreme Court of the State of Oregon Advance Sheets [*A publication*] (DLA) .... Or Ad Sh
Supreme Court of the United States (WDAA) .... SCOTUS
Supreme Court of the United States .... SCUS
Supreme Court of Western Australia .... SCWA
Supreme Court Practice [*A publication*] (DLA) .... Sup Ct Pr
Supreme Court, Preliminary Prints .... SCPP
Supreme Court Reporter [*A publication*] (DLA) .... S
Supreme Court Reporter [*A publication*] (DLA) .... S Ct
Supreme Court Reporter [*National Reporter System*] [*A publication*] (DLA) .... SC
Supreme Court Reporter (BARN) .... Sup C
Supreme Court Reporter [*A publication*] (DLA) .... Sup Court Rep
Supreme Court Reporter [*National Reporter System*] [*A publication*] (DLA) .... Sup Ct
Supreme Court Reporter [*A publication*] (DLA) .... Sup Ct Rep
Supreme Court Reporter [*A publication*] (DLA) .... Sup Ct Repr
Supreme Court Reporter [*A publication*] (DLA) .... Supr Ct Rep
Supreme Court Reporter [*A publication*] (DLA) .... US Sup Ct Reps
Supreme Court Reports [*India*] [*A publication*] (DLA) .... SCR
Supreme Court Reports [*1928-41, 1946-51*] [*Sarawak*] [*A publication*] (DLA) .... SCR
Supreme Court Reports [*Canada Department of Justice*] [*Information service or system*] (CRD) .... SCR
Supreme Court Reports .... SCt
Supreme Court Reports [*India*] [*A publication*] (DLA) .... Sup Ct R
Supreme Court Reports, Cape Colony [*1880-1910*] [*South Africa*] [*A publication*] (DLA) .... Cape SCR
Supreme Court Reports, District of Columbia [*A publication*] (DLA) .... SCDC
Supreme Court Reports, District of Columbia, New Series [*A publication*] (DLA) .... SCDCNS
Supreme Court Reports, Lawyer's Edition [*A publication*] (NTCM) .... L Ed US
Supreme Court Reports, Transvaal [*1885-88*] [*South Africa*] [*A publication*] (DLA) .... Kotze & B
Supreme Court Reports, Transvaal [*1885-88*] [*South Africa*] [*A publication*] (DLA) .... Kotze & Barb
Supreme Court Review [*A publication*] (ILCA) .... Su Ct Rev
Supreme Emblem Club of the United States (EA) .... SECUS
Supreme Forest Woodmen Circle [*Later, Woodmen of the World Life Insurance Society*] (EA) .... SFWC
Supreme Grand Royal Arch Chapter [*Freemasonry*] (ROG) .... SGRAC
Supreme Headquarters .... SHQ
Supreme Headquarters, Alien Defense Organization [*in television program "UFO"*] .... SHADO
Supreme Headquarters, Allied Expeditionary Force [*Europe*] [*World War II*] .... SHAEF
Supreme Headquarters, Allied Powers Europe [*NATO*] .... SHAPE
Supreme Headquarters, Chief of Staff [*World War II*] .... SHCOS
Supreme Headquarters, International Espionage Law-Enforcement Division [*Organization in comic book "Nick Fury, Agent of SHIELD"*] .... SHIELD
Supreme Headquarters, Secretary General Staff [*World War II*] .... SHSGS
Supreme Headquarters, Supreme Allied Commander [*World War II*] .... SHSAC
Supreme High Command of the Soviet Armed Forces [*Russian*] (MCD) .... STAVRA
Supreme Indus Wrrt [*AMEX symbol*] (TTSB) .... STS.WS
Supreme Industries [*AMEX symbol*] (SAG) .... MOD
Supreme Industries [*Formerly, ESI Industries Corp.*] [*AMEX symbol*] (SPSG) .... STS
Supreme Industries [*Associated Press*] (SAG) .... SupIn
Supreme Industries [*Associated Press*] (SAG) .... SuprmInd
Supreme Industries'A' [*AMEX symbol*] (TTSB) .... STS
Supreme International [*NASDAQ symbol*] (TTSB) .... SUPI
Supreme International Corp. [*NASDAQ symbol*] (SAG) .... SUPI
Supreme International Corp. [*Associated Press*] (SAG) .... SupIntl
Supreme Judicial Court .... SJC
Supreme Judicial Court [*Massachusetts*] (DLA) .... Sup Jud Ct
Supreme Knight of the Knights of Columbus of America .... SKKCA
Supreme Ladies Auxiliary Knights of St. John (EA) .... SLAKSJ
Supreme Lodge Knights of Pythias (EA) .... SLKP
Supreme Lodge of the Danish Sisterhood of America (EA) .... DSA
Supreme Master Ching Hai Meditation Association (EA) .... SMCHMA
Supreme National Council [*Cambodia*] .... SNC
Supreme People's Assembly [*Political party North Korea*] (FEA) .... SPA
Supreme Pup Tent, Military Order of the Cootie (EA) .... MOC
Supreme Resources, Inc. [*Vancouver Stock Exchange symbol*] .... SUP
Supreme Royal Zuanna, Ladies of the Orient [*Defunct*] (EA) .... SRZLO
Supreme Shrine of the Order of the White Shrine of Jerusalem (EA) .... SSOWSJ
Supreme Temple Order Pythian Sisters (EA) .... STOPS
Supreme Unsurpassable Engineers of the Universe [*Rank in Junior Woodchucks organization mentioned in Donald Duck comic by Carl Barks*] .... SUEOTU
Supreme War Council [*World War II*] .... SWC
Sur [*Oman*] [*ICAO location identifier*] (ICLI) .... OOSR
Sur [*On*] [*French*] .... S
Sur Antizana [*Ecuador*] [*ICAO location identifier*] (ICLI) .... SESZ
Sur Cayambe [*Ecuador*] [*ICAO location identifier*] (ICLI) .... SESY
Sur Iliniza [*Ecuador*] [*ICAO location identifier*] (ICLI) .... SESI
Surabaya [*Indonesia*] [*Airport symbol*] (OAG) .... SUB
Surabaya/Gedangan [*Indonesia*] [*ICAO location identifier*] (ICLI) .... WRSS
Surabaya/Juanda [*Indonesia*] [*ICAO location identifier*] (ICLI) .... WRSJ
Surabaya/Perak [*Indonesia*] [*ICAO location identifier*] (ICLI) .... WRSP
Sural Nerve .... Sur
Surallah/Allah Valley, Cotabato (South) [*Philippines*] [*ICAO location identifier*] (ICLI) .... RPWA
Suramin [*Antineoplastic drug*] (CDI) .... SUR
Surat [*India*] [*ICAO location identifier*] (ICLI) .... VASU
Surat Thani [*Thailand*] [*Airport symbol*] (OAG) .... URT
Surat Thani [*Thailand*] [*ICAO location identifier*] (ICLI) .... VTSB
Surat Thani/Don Nok [*Thailand*] [*ICAO location identifier*] (ICLI) .... VTSO
Surcharge [*Business term*] (ROG) .... SUR
Sure out of Luck [*Bowdlerized version*] .... SOL
Sure Shot International, Inc. [*NASDAQ symbol*] (SAG) .... HOOP
Sure Shot International, Inc. [*Associated Press*] (SAG) .... SureSh
Sure Shot International, Inc. [*Associated Press*] (SAG) .... SurShot
Sure Shot Intl Inc. [*NASDAQ symbol*] (TTSB) .... HOOP
Sure Shot Intl Wrrt [*NASDAQ symbol*] (TTSB) .... HOOPW
Surefire Fan Club [*Defunct*] (EA) .... SFC
Surete du Quebec, Montreal, PQ, Canada [*Library symbol Library of Congress*] (LCLS) .... CaQMSU
Surete du Quebec, Montreal, Quebec [*Library symbol National Library of Canada*] (NLC) .... QMSU
Surety (DLA) .... Sur
Surety Agents Promotional Society [*Defunct*] (EA) .... SAPS
Surety and Operational Inspection [*Military*] (AFIT) .... SOI
Surety Association of America [*Iselin, NJ*] (EA) .... SAA
Surety Bond (MHDB) .... SB
Surety Bond Waiver [*SBA program*] (AAGC) .... SBW
Surety Capital [*AMEX symbol*] (TTSB) .... SRY
Surety Capital Corp. [*AMEX symbol*] (SAG) .... SRY
Surety Capital Corp. [*Associated Press*] (SAG) .... SuretyC
Suretyship [*Legal shorthand*] (LWAP) .... SURSHIP
Surewin Resources Corp. [*Vancouver Stock Exchange symbol*] .... SWC
Surf Code (DNAB) .... SURFCO
Surf Inlet Mines [*Vancouver Stock Exchange symbol*] .... SFE
Surf Observation Report [*Navy*] (NVT) .... SUROB
Surf Zone (DOMA) .... SZ
Surf Zone Process .... SZP
Surface (AFM) .... SFC
Surface .... SFCE
Surface (AABC) .... SUR
Surface (WDMC) .... sur
Surface (VRA) .... sur
Surface .... SURF
Surface .... SURFC
Surface Acoustic Wave [*Engineering*] .... SAW
Surface Acoustic Wave [*Microwave system*] .... SAW
Surface Acoustic Wave Delay Line Oscillator (PDAA) .... SAWDLO
Surface Acoustic Wave Device (PDAA) .... SAWD
Surface Acoustic Wave Oscillator [*Telecommunications*] (TEL) .... SAWO
Surface Action Group [*Military*] (NVT) .... SAG
Surface Active Agents (ADA) .... SAA
Surface Active Substances (IEEE) .... SAS
Surface Aerospace Technology .... SAT
Surface/Air (NATG) .... SA
Surface Air System Integration .... SASI
Surface Air Temperature [*Climatology*] .... SAT
Surface Aligned Photochemistry [*Physics*] .... SAP
Surface Alloy Diffused-Base Transistor .... SADT
Surface Alloy Transistor (IAA) .... SAT
Surface Ammunition Malfunction Control (DNAB) .... SAMC
Surface Analysis by LASER Ionization .... SALI
Surface Analysis by Resonance Ionization of Sputtered Atoms .... SARISA
Surface and Underwater Target (MCD) .... SUT
Surface Antenna Terminal (MCD) .... SAT
Surface Antigen [*Immunology*] (DAVI) .... SA
Surface Antigen [*Medicine*] (DMAA) .... SAX
Surface Area .... S
Surface Area .... SA
Surface Area Decay [*Plant pathology*] .... SAD
Surface Attack [*Missile mission symbol*] .... G
Surface Attack Group [*Navy*] (CAAL) .... SAG
Surface Attack Guided Missile (MCD) .... SAGMI
Surface Attack Unit .... SAU
Surface Barrier Detector .... SBD
Surface Barrier Diffused Transistor .... SBDT
Surface Barrier Transistor .... SBT
Surface Based (WDAA) .... S/B
Surface Binding [*Immunochemistry*] .... SB
Surface Boundary Layer (MCD) .... SBL
Surface Burst Fuze .... SBF
Surface Charge Density Wave [*Physics*] .... SCDW
Surface Charge Transistor [*Electronics*] (OA) .... SCT
Surface Coating Synthetic Resin Manufacturers Association [*British*] (BI) .... SCSRMA
Surface Coatings Abstracts [*Paint Research Association of Great Britain*] [*Bibliographic database*] .... SCA
Surface Coil Rotating Frame [*Medicine*] (DMAA) .... SCRF
Surface Combat Air Patrol (DOMA) .... SUCAP
Surface Combat Condition (DNAB) .... SCC
Surface Combatant Airborne Tactical System (MCD) .... SCATS
Surface Combatant Force Requirements Study [*Navy*] (DOMA) .... SCFRS
Surface Combustion [*Reducing gas process*] .... SC
Surface Command [*NASA*] (MCD) .... SC

Surface Composition by Analysis of Neutral and Ion Impact Radiation [*Qualitative analysis*] .... SCANIIR
Surface Composition Mapping Radiometer [*NASA*] .... SCMR
Surface Composition Strengthened .... SCS
Surface Condition Analyzer (MCD) .... SCAN
Surface Contamination Module (DWSG) .... SCM
Surface Control Unit .... SCU
Surface Crack Opening Displacement (PDAA) .... SCOD
Surface Danger Zone [*Military*] (INF) .... SDZ
Surface Deformation Pattern .... SDP
Surface Demand Diving Equipment .... SDDE
Surface Design Association (EA) .... SDA
Surface Design Journal [*A publication*] (BRI) .... Surface DJ
Surface Detector/Tracker [*Navy*] (CAAL) .... SD/T
Surface Detector/Tracker [*Navy*] (CAAL) .... SURF DET TRKR
Surface Direct Fire [*Navy*] (CAAL) .... SDF
Surface Discharge Spark Gap (IAA) .... SSG
Surface Drone Unit [*Navy*] (CAAL) .... SDU
Surface Duct [*Navy*] (CAAL) .... SD
Surface Effect Cruiser Escort (DNAB) .... SECF
Surface Effect Fast Sea Lift Ship [*MTMC*] (TAG) .... SFS
Surface Effect Rescue Vessel [*Coast Guard*] .... SERV
Surface Effect Ship .... SEF
Surface Effect Ship for Ocean Commerce .... SESOC
Surface Effect Ship Project [*Navy*] (DNAB) .... SESPROJ
Surface Effect Ship Test Facility [*Navy*] (DNAB) .... SESTF
Surface Effect Ships Project Office [*Navy*] .... SESPO
Surface Effect Takeoff and Land System [*Naval aviation*] .... SETOLS
Surface Effects Ship [*Navy symbol*] .... SES
Surface Effects Vehicle [*Military*] .... SEV
Surface Electrical Property [*Apollo*] [*NASA*] .... SEP
Surface Electrical Resistivity .... SER
Surface Electromagnetic Wave .... SEW
Surface Electromagnetic Wave Spectroscopy .... SEWS
Surface Electronic Warfare Officer [*Course*] (DOMA) .... SURF EWO
Surface Emitter Detection, Identification System [*Navy*] .... SEDIS
Surface Emitting LASER .... SEL
Surface Environment and Mining Program .... SEAM
Surface Environmental Sample Container [*Apollo*] [*NASA*] .... SESC
Surface Evaluation and Definition .... SUEDE
Surface Experiments [*NASA*] .... SEP
Surface Export Cargo System [*Military*] (AABC) .... SURS
Surface Extravehicular Activity [*Lunar exploration*] .... SEVA
Surface Feet per Minute .... SFPM
Surface Feet per Minute .... SFPM
Surface Fibroblast Antigen [*Cytochemistry*] .... SFA
Surface Field Effect Transistor (IAA) .... SFET
Surface Fixed Priority .... SFP
Surface Foot .... SF
Surface Force Apparatus [*Physical chemistry*] .... SFA
Surface Force Pacific (MCD) .... SUFPAC
Surface Forces Apparatus [*For study of bilayers*] [*Physical chemistry*] .... SFA
Surface Ground Zero .... SGZ
Surface Heat Budget of the Arctic (USDC) .... SHEBA
Surface Heat Budget of the Arctic [*Marine science*] (OSRA) .... SHEBA
Surface Imaging and Sounding Package .... SISP
Surface Immunoglobulin [*Immunochemistry*] .... sIg
Surface Impoundment (EG) .... SI
Surface Impulsion Propulsion (PDAA) .... SIP
Surface Integrated Control (MCD) .... SURIC
Surface Integrity .... SI
Surface Ionization [*Physics*] .... SI
Surface Ionization Detector [*Instrumentation*] .... SID
Surface Ionization Engine .... SIE
Surface Ionization Organic Mass Spectrometry .... SIOMS
Surface Laboratory System [*NASA*] (KSC) .... SLS
Surface Launch (MUGU) .... SL
Surface Launch Cruise Missile .... SLCM
Surface Launch Platform (NVT) .... SLP
Surface Launcher Air-Targeted [*Weapon*] (MCD) .... SLAT
Surface Layer Quality .... SLQ
Surface Layout Release .... SLR
Surface Light Emitting Diode [*Electronics*] .... SLED
Surface Linking Number [*Genetics*] .... SLk
Surface Look-Alike Mine .... SLAM
Surface Look-Alike Mine System (MCD) .... SLAMS
Surface Magnetic Confinement (MCD) .... SURMAC
Surface Magnetooptic Kerr Effect [*Surface analysis*] .... SMOKE
Surface Mail Air Lifted (ADA) .... SAL
Surface Measure .... SM
Surface Measuring Equipment .... SME
Surface Membrane Immunoglobulin [*Immunochemistry*] .... SmIg
Surface Metastable Quenching [*Surface analysis*] .... SMQ
Surface Mine Countermeasures [*Navy*] (DOMA) .... SMCM
Surface Mining and Environment Information System [*University of Arizona*] (IID) .... SEAMINFO
Surface Mining Control and Reclamation Act [*1977*] .... SMCRA
Surface Mining Office [*Department of the Interior*] (OICC) .... SMO
Surface Miss Distance Indicator [*Navy*] (CAAL) .... SMDI
Surface Missile (AAG) .... SM
Surface Missile Compatibility Test Group [*Military*] .... SMCTG
Surface Missile, Extended Range .... SM-ER
Surface Missile, Medium Range .... SM-MR
Surface Missile Processing Description (MCD) .... SMPD
Surface Missile Proficiency Inspection (MCD) .... SMPI

Surface Missile Ship (MUGU) .... SMS
Surface Missile Ship Improvement Program (MCD) .... SMSIP
Surface Missile System [*NASA*] .... SMS
Surface Missile System Availability Evaluation [*NASA*] (KSC) .... SMSAE
Surface Missile Test [*Navy*] (CAAL) .... SMT
Surface Mixed Layer Experiment (NOAA) .... SMILE
Surface Modification and Characterization Collaborative Research Center [*Oak Ridge, TN*] [*Oak Ridge National Laboratory*] [*Department of Energy*] (GRD) .... SMAC/CRC
Surface Modulating Assembly [*Cytology*] .... SMA
Surface Mount [*Electronics*] (EECA) .... SM
Surface Mount Component [*Environmental science*] .... SMC
Surface Mount Equipment Manufacturers Association (EA) .... SMEMA
Surface Mount Technology Association (EA) .... SMTA
Surface Mountable Device (NITA) .... SMD
Surface Mounted Device [*Microelectronics*] .... SMD
Surface Mounted Technology (NITA) .... SMT
Surface Mounting Applicator (NITA) .... SMA
Surface Movement Control [*Aviation*] .... SMC
Surface Movement Element (AFIT) .... SME
Surface Movement Guidance and Control [*FAA*] (TAG) .... SMGC
Surface Movement RADAR .... SMR
Surface Navy Association (DOMA) .... SNA
Surface Oil Pickup .... SOP
Surface Operations [*Navy*] (CAAL) .... SO
Surface Ordnance Technician [*Navy*] (DNAB) .... SURORDTECH
Surface Photovoltage [*Photovoltaic energy systems*] .... SPV
Surface Picture [*AMVER*] [*Coast Guard*] .... SURPIC
Surface Plasma Wave .... SPW
Surface Plasmon Microscopy [*Physics*] .... SPM
Surface Plasmon Resonance [*Physics*] .... SPR
Surface Position Indicator (NASA) .... SPI
Surface RADAR and Navigation Operation .... SURANO
Surface Radiation (USDC) .... SURFRAD
Surface Radiation [*Marine science*] (OSRA) .... SURFRAD
Surface Radiation Budget [*Marine science*] (OSRA) .... SRB
Surface Raid Reporting Control Ship [*Navy*] (NVT) .... SRRCS
Surface Recombination Velocity (DEN) .... SRV
Surface Recording Terminal (MCD) .... SRT
Surface Reflected Bottom Reflected (IAA) .... SRBR
Surface Refractivity (CET) .... Ns
Surface Roughness .... SR
Surface Roughness Factor [*Telecommunications*] (TEL) .... SRF
Surface Roughness Indicator .... SRI
Surface Roving Vehicle [*NASA*] (KSC) .... SRV
Surface Sampler Control Assembly [*NASA*] (NASA) .... SSCA
Surface Sampler Device [*NASA*] .... SSD
Surface Sampler Processing and Distribution Assembly .... SSPDA
Surface Science Western [*University of Western Ontario*] [*Research center*] (RCD) .... SSW
Surface Screen Unit [*Navy*] (NVT) .... SSU
Surface Search RADAR (SAA) .... SSR
Surface Ship .... SS
Surface Ship Advance Sonar [*Navy*] (LAIN) .... SSAS
Surface Ship Electromagnetic Jammer .... SUREJ
Surface Ship Electromagnetic Passive Intercept System .... SUREPI
Surface Ship Integrated Control System [*Obsolete Navy*] .... SURIC
Surface Ship SONAR Modernization Program (MCD) .... SSSMP
Surface Ship Torpedo Defense [*Navy*] (CAAL) .... SSTD
Surface Ship Slip Resistance .... SSR
Surface Stabilized Ferroelectric Liquid Crystal [*Physical chemistry*] .... SSFLC
Surface Strike Warfare [*Navy*] (CAAL) .... SSW
Surface/Subsurface Control [*Navy*] (CAAL) .... SSSC
Surface/Subsurface Surveillance Center [*Navy*] (NVT) .... SSSC
Surface/Subsurface Surveillance Coordinator [*Navy*] .... SSSC
Surface/Subsurface Surveillance Coordinator [*Navy*] (CAAL) .... SSSSC
Surface/Subsurface Warfare [*Navy*] (CAAL) .... SSSW
Surface/Subsurface Warfare Coordinator [*Navy*] (CAAL) .... SSWC
Surface Supplied Breathing Apparatus .... SSBA
Surface Support Equipment .... SSE
Surface Target [*Navy*] (CAAL) .... ST
Surface Target Acquisition Model (MCD) .... STAM
Surface Target Attack Comparison Model (MCD) .... STAC
Surface Target Simulator [*Navy*] (DNAB) .... STS
Surface Targets of Interest (MCD) .... STI
Surface Temperature Measuring System .... SURTEMS
Surface Tension .... ST
Surface Tension [*Physics*] (WDAA) .... T
Surface to Underwater (IAA) .... SU
Surface Tracker [*Navy*] (CAAL) .... ST
Surface Traffic Control System (MCD) .... STRACS
Surface Transport Loading Data [*MTMC*] (TAG) .... STLD
Surface Transportation and Uniform Relocation Assistance Act [*1987*] .... STURAA
Surface Transportation Assistance Act [*1978*] .... STAA
Surface Transportation Board [*Formerly, the ICC - Interstate Commerce Commission, 1996*] .... STB
Surface Transportation Board [*Department of Transportation*] .... STB
Surface Transportation Policy Project [*Military*] .... STPP
Surface Transportation Program [*MOCD*] (TAG) .... STP
Surface Treatment Enhancement Council [*Metallurgy*] .... STEC
Surface/Underwater Ship Intercept Equipment (DNAB) .... SUSIE
Surface Vehicle Power Adapter .... SPA
Surface Vehicular Unit .... SVU
Surface Velocity Program [*Marine science*] (OSRA) .... SVP

Surface Velocity Programme (USDC) ... SVP
Surface Vessel ... SV
Surface Vessel Torpedo Tube (NVT) ... SVTT
Surface/Volume [*Ratio*] ... S/V
Surface/Volume Ratio ... SVR
Surface Warfare (NVT) ... SUW
Surface Warfare (MCD) ... SW
Surface Warfare Coordinator [*Also, SWC*] (NVT) ... SUWC
Surface Warfare Coordinator [*Also, SUWC*] (NVT) ... SWC
Surface Warfare Development Group [*Also, SWDG*] [*Navy*] ... SURFWARDEVGRU
Surface Warfare Development Group [*Also, SURFWARDEVGRU*] [*Navy*] ... SWDG
Surface Warfare Officer [*Navy*] (NVT) ... SWO
Surface Warfare Officer, Personnel Qualification Standards [*Navy*] (DNAB) ... SWOAPQS
Surface Warfare Officer's School [*Navy*] (NVT) ... SWOS
Surface Warfare Officer's School Command [*Navy*] (NVT) ... SWOSCOLCOM
Surface Warfare Officer's School Command Detachment [*Navy*] (DNAB) ... SWOSCOLCOMDET
Surface Warfare Plan [*Navy*] (CAAL) ... SWP
Surface Water Acidification Project [*Joint venture involving Norway, Sweden, and Great Britain*] ... SWAP
Surface Water Automatic Computer (AAG) ... SURWAC
Surface Water Improvement and Management (MCD) ... SWIM
Surface Water Supply Index [*to measure drought*] ... SWSI
Surface Water Treatment Rule [*Environmental Protection Agency*] ... SWTR
Surface Wave Delay Line ... SWDL
Surface Wave Dielectrometer ... SWD
Surface Wave Independent Tap Transducer (IEEE) ... SWITT
Surface Wave Line ... SWL
Surface Wave Mode ... SWM
Surface Wave Phenomena ... SWP
Surface Wave Transmission Line ... SWTL
Surface Weapons Control ... SWC
Surface Weapons Coordinator [*Navy*] (CAAL) ... SWC
Surface Weapons Fire Control ... SWFC
Surface Wind [*Meteorology*] (DA) ... S/W
Surface Wire Grounding System [*Electronics*] (RDA) ... SWGS
Surface X-Ray Scattering [*Physics*] ... SXS
Surface Zero [*Navy*] (NVT) ... SZ
Surface-Active Material ... SAM
Surface-Air-Generated Electronic Environment (SAA) ... SAGEE
Surface-Area-Center [*Mechanical engineering*] ... SAC
Surface-Contour RADAR ... SCR
Surface-Controlled Avalanche Transistor ... SCAT
Surface-Controlled Oxide Unipolar Transistor ... SCOUT
Surface-Controlled Transistor (IAA) ... SCT
Surfaced ... S
Surfaced and Matched [*Lumber*] ... S & M
Surfaced Dry [*Lumber*] ... S-DRY
Surfaced Four Sides [*Technical drawings*] ... SFS
Surfaced Four Sides and Caulking Seam [*Lumber*] (DAC) ... S4S & CS
Surfaced Green [*Lumber*] ... S-GRN
Surfaced One Edge [*Technical drawings*] ... S1E
Surfaced One Side and Edge [*Lumber*] (DAC) ... S & E
Surfaced One Side and Two Edges [*Lumber*] (DAC) ... S1S2E
Surfaced or Dressed Four Sides [*Technical drawings*] ... S4S
Surfaced or Dressed One Side [*Technical drawings*] ... S1S
Surfaced or Dressed One Side and One Edge [*Technical drawings*] ... S1S1E
Surfaced or Dressed Two Sides [*Technical drawings*] ... S2S
Surfaced Two Edges [*Lumber*] (DAC) ... S2E
Surfaced Two Sides and Center Matched [*Lumber*] (DAC) ... S2S & CM
Surfaced Two Sides and One Edge [*Lumber*] (DAC) ... S2S1E
Surfaced Two Sides and Shiplapped [*Technical drawings*] (DAC) ... S2S & SL
Surface-Enhanced Raman Optical Data Storage Technology [*Developed at Oak Ridge National Laboratory*] ... SERODS
Surface-Enhanced Raman Scattering [*Spectroscopy*] ... SERS
Surface-Enhanced Resonance Raman Scattering [*Spectroscopy*] ... SERRS
Surface-Extended X-Ray Absorption Fine Structure ... SEXAFS
Surface-Free Energy ... SFE
Surface-Induced Dissociation [*Physics*] ... SID
Surface-Launched Air Missile ... SLAM
Surface-Launched Guided Missile ... SLGM
Surface-Launched Low-Volume Ramjet ... SLVRJ
Surface-Launched Missile [*Navy*] (CAAL) ... SLM
Surface-Launched Missile System ... SLMS
Surface-Launched Unit, Fire Area Equipment (MCD) ... SLUFAE
Surface-Launched Unit, Fuel-Air Explosive Mine Neutralizer [*Army*] (RDA) ... SLUFAE
Surface-Launched Unit, Mine Layer (MCD) ... SLUMINE
Surface-Mount Technology [*Electronics*] ... SMT
Surface-Oriented Diode (IAA) ... SOD
Surface-Sized [*Paper*] ... SS
Surface-Supported Diving System (CAAL) ... SSDS
Surface-to-Air Beam Rider (MCD) ... SABER
Surface-to-Air Guided Weapon [*British*] ... SAGW
Surface-to-Air Missile ... SAM
Surface-to-Air Missile Availability Report (NG) ... SAMAR
Surface-to-Air Missile Capability (PDAA) ... SAMCAP
Surface-to-Air Missile Development ... SAMD
Surface-to-Air Missile Exercise (NVT) ... SAMEX
Surface-to-Air Missile Improvement Program (MCD) ... SAMIP
Surface-to-Air Missile Intercept Development ... SAMID
Surface-to-Air Missile Servicing, Assembly, and Test ... SAMSAT
Surface-to-Air Missile Simulation Model (MCD) ... SAMSIM
Surface-to-Air Missile-Development, Contract Definition (SAA) ... SAM-D/CDP
Surface-to-Air Missle System [*Military*] ... SAMS
Surface-to-Air Recovery ... STAR
Surface-to-Air Recovery System ... STARS
Surface-to-Air, Surface-to-Surface Missile (MCD) ... SASSM
Surface-to-Surface (NATG) ... SS
Surface-to-Surface Guided Weapon (NATG) ... SSGW
Surface-to-Surface Missile ... SSM
Surface-to-Surface Missile Order of Battle (MCD) ... SSMOB
Surface-to-Surface Mission [*Military*] (AABC) ... SSMSN
Surface-to-Surface Strategic Ballistic Missile System (IAA) ... SSBS
Surface-to-Target-to-Missile ... STM
Surface-to-Target-to-Surface-to-Missile ... STSM
Surface-to-Underwater Missile ... SUM
Surface-Water Modeling System ... SMS
Surfactant ... surf
Surfdale [*Waiheke Island, New Zealand*] [*Airport symbol*] (AD) ... SFU
Surfrider Foundation (EA) ... SF
Surfside Beach-Garden City, SC [*AM radio station call letters*] (RBYB) ... WCKN
Surfside Beach-Garden City, SC [*FM radio station call letters*] ... WYAK-FM
Surge (MSA) ... SRG
Surge Components, Inc. [*NASDAQ symbol*] (SAG) ... SRGE
Surge Components, Inc. [*Associated Press*] (SAG) ... SurgeC
Surge Components, Inc. [*Associated Press*] (SAG) ... SurgeCm
Surge Impedance Loading ... SIL
Surge Protective Device (MCD) ... SPD
Surge Voltage Protection (IAA) ... SVP
Surge Withstand Capability (IEEE) ... SWC
Surgeon [*Navy British*] (ROG) ... S
Surgeon ... SG
Surgeon [*Military British*] ... SGN
Surgeon ... SRGN
Surgeon [*or Surgery or Surgical*] (AFM) ... SURG
Surgeon ... SURGN
[*The*] **Surgeon General** [*Army, Air Force*] ... SG
Surgeon General (GFGA) ... Surg Gen
[*The*] **Surgeon General** [*Army, Air Force*] ... SURGEN
[*The*] **Surgeon General** [*Army*] ... TSG
Surgeon General of the Navy ... SGN
Surgeon General's Office ... SGO
Surgeon Lieutenant [*British military*] ... Surg Lt
Surgeon Lieutenant-Commander [*British military*] (DMA) ... Sg L Cr
Surgeon Lieutenant-Commander [*British military*] ... SLC
Surgeon Major ... SM
Surgeon Rear-Admiral [*British military*] (DMA) ... Sg RA
Surgeon Rear-Admiral [*British military*] ... SRA
Surgeon Vice-Admiral [*British military*] (DMA) ... Sg VA
Surgeon-Captain [*British military*] ... SC
Surgeon-Captain [*British military*] (DMA) ... Sg C
Surgeon-Commander [*British military*] ... SC
Surgeon-Commander [*British military*] (DMA) ... Sg Cr
Surgeon-Commander [*British military*] ... Surg Cdr
Surgeon-in-Chief (WDAA) ... S in C
Surgeon's Assistant [*Medicine*] ... SA
Surgeries (DAVI) ... SX
Surgery [*Medical Officer designation*] [*British*] ... S
Surgery (DAVI) ... SU
Surgery ... SUR
Surgery ... SURG
Surgery Expandable Unit (SAA) ... SEU
Surgery, Gynecology, and Obstetrics (MAE) ... SGO
Surgery Recovery Room [*Medicine*] (DMAA) ... SRR
Surgical ... SURGCL
Surgical Achilles Tendon Lengthening [*Medicine*] ... SATL
Surgical Anastomosis [*Medicine*] ... SA
Surgical and Anesthesia Service (HCT) ... SA
Surgical Capsule [*of prostate gland*] ... SC
Surgical Care Affiliates, Inc. [*NYSE symbol*] (SPSG) ... SCA
Surgical Care Affiliates, Inc. [*Nashville, TN*] [*Associated Press*] (SAG) ... SurgAf
Surgical Drain (DAVI) ... SD
Surgical Dressing Manufacturers Association [*British*] (BI) ... SDMA
Surgical Dressing Room (DAVI) ... SDR
Surgical Emergency Officer (DAVI) ... SEO
Surgical Emergency Officer (MEDA) ... SEO
Surgical Eye Expeditions International (EAIO) ... SEE
Surgical Hernia [*Medicine*] (WDAA) ... SH
Surgical History [*Medicine*] ... SH
Surgical Hospital [*Medicine*] ... SGH
Surgical Hypoparathyroidism [*Medicine*] (MAE) ... SHP
Surgical Infection Society (EA) ... SIS
Surgical Intensive Care Unit [*Medicine*] ... SICU
Surgical Intensive Therapy Unit ... SITU
Surgical Laser Tech [*NASDAQ symbol*] (TTSB) ... SLTI
Surgical Laser Technologies, Inc. [*NASDAQ symbol*] (NQ) ... SLTI
Surgical Laser Technologies, Inc. [*Associated Press*] (SAG) ... SurgLsr
Surgical Officer of the Day (DAVI) ... SOD
Surgical Operations Database [*Medicine*] ... SOD
Surgical Outpatient [*Medicine*] ... SOP
Surgical Postcaval Shunt [*Medicine*] ... SPCS
Surgical Removal (DAVI) ... SR
Surgical Research Society [*British*] ... SRS
Surgical Resident's Admission Note (DAVI) ... SRAN
Surgical Specialist ... SSP
Surgical Technician ... ST
Surgical Technologies [*NASDAQ symbol*] (TTSB) ... SGTI

Surgical Technologies, Inc. [*NASDAQ symbol*] (SAG) .... SGTI
Surgical Technologies, Inc. [*Associated Press*] (SAG) .... SurgTc
Surgical Technologist (DAVI) .... ST
Surgical Textiles Conference [*British*] (DBA) .... STC
Surgical-Evaluative Staging of Cancer [*Classification of malignant tumors*] [*T refers to the size of the tumor, N refers to the status of the nodes, and M refers to metastases*] (DAVI) .... sTNM
Surging Sine [*Mathematics*] (DAVI) .... SS
Surgoinsville, TN [*FM radio station call letters*] .... WEYE
Surgut [*Former USSR ICAO location identifier*] (ICLI) .... USRR
Surgut Commodity and Raw Materials Exchange [*Russian Federation*] (EY) .... SCME
Suria [*Papua New Guinea*] [*Airport symbol*] (OAG) .... SUZ
Surigao [*Philippines*] [*Airport symbol*] (OAG) .... SUG
Surigao, Surigao Del Norte [*Philippines*] [*ICAO location identifier*] (ICLI) .... RPWS
Surinaams Nieuws Agentschap [*Surinam News Agency*] (EY) .... SNA
Surinaamse Luchtvaart Maatschappij NV [*Surinam*] [*ICAO designator*] (FAAC) .... SLM
Surinaamse Partij van de Arvid [*Suriname Labour Party*] [*Political party*] (EY) .... SPA
Surinaamse Televisie Sichtung [*Television network*] [*Surinam*] .... STVS
Surinaamse Televisie Stichtig (EY) .... STVS
Surinam [*Aircraft nationality and registration mark*] (FAAC) .... PZ
Surinam [*MARC country of publication code Library of Congress*] (LCCP) .... sr
Surinam [*ANSI two-letter standard code*] (CNC) .... SR
Surinam [*MARC geographic area code Library of Congress*] (LCCP) .... s-sr--
Surinam [*ANSI three-letter standard code*] (CNC) .... SUR
Surinam Airways [*ICAO designator*] (AD) .... PY
Surinam Florin [*Monetary unit in Surinam*] .... SFL
Suriname [*International vehicle registration*] (ODBW) .... SME
Suriname Freedom Union (EA) .... SFU
Suring, WI [*FM radio station call letters*] .... WRVM
Suring, WI [*Television station call letters*] .... WSCO
Surjet [*Knitting*] [*French*] (BARN) .... surj
Surkhet [*Nepal*] [*Airport symbol*] (OAG) .... SKH
Surkhet [*Nepal*] [*Airport symbol*] (AD) .... SUS
Surkhet [*Nepal*] [*ICAO location identifier*] (ICLI) .... VNSK
Surlari [*Romania*] [*Geomagnetic observatory code*] .... SUR
Surma Valley Light Horse [*British military*] (DMA) .... SVLH
Surpassing All Previous Foul Ups [*Military slang*] [*Bowdlerized version*] .... SAPFU
Surpine (DAVI) .... S
Surplus .... S
Surplus [*Business term*] .... SUR
Surplus .... SURPL
Surplus .... Surps
Surplus Agricultural Commodities Disposal Act of 1982 .... SACDA
Surplus Budget .... SB
Surplus Distribution List (AAG) .... SDL
Surplus Facilities Management Program [*Department of Energy*] .... SFMP
Surplus Land for Community Development .... SLCD
Surplus Marketing Administration [*New Deal*] .... SMA
Surplus Materials Division (AAGC) .... SMD
Surplus Personal Property .... SPP
Surplus Property Board .... SPB
Surplus Property Office [*Transferred to War Assets Administration, 1947*] .... SPO
Surplus Record Information Services (IID) .... SRIS
Surplus Release Date (AAGC) .... SRD
Surplus Review Record (SAA) .... SRR
Surplus Termination Material Requisition (MCD) .... S/T-MR
Surplus to Immediate Requirements (ADA) .... STIR
Surplus to Requirements (ADA) .... STR
Surplus War Property Administration [*Terminated, 1944*] .... SWPA
Surplus War Property Board [*Terminated, 1945*] .... SWPB
Surprise Security Inspection [*Navy*] (NVT) .... SSI
Surprised Middle-Aged Person [*Lifestyle classification*] .... Smap
Surratt Society (EA) .... SS
Surrender (DNAB) .... SUR
Surrender (AABC) .... SURR
Surrender Value [*Insurance*] .... S/V
Surrender Value (ODBW) .... sv
Surrendered (WGA) .... SUR
Surrendered (ROG) .... SURRD
Surrendered Enemy Personnel .... SEP
Surrey [*County in England*] .... SURR
Surrey [*County in England*] .... SY
Surrey and Sussex Libraries in Cooperation (NITA) .... SASLIC
Surrey and Sussex Yeomanry [*British military*] (DMA) .... S & Sx Yeo
Surrey Centennial Museum, British Columbia [*Library symbol National Library of Canada*] (NLC) .... BSURCM
Surrey Commercial Dock [*British*] .... SCD
Surrey Investigation Group into Aerial Phenomena [*British*] .... SIGAP
Surrey Library Interactive Circulation Experiment (NITA) .... SLICE
Surrey Local Militia [*British military*] (DMA) .... SLM
Surrey Public Library, British Columbia [*Library symbol National Library of Canada*] (NLC) .... BSUR
Surrey Public Library, Surrey, BC, Canada [*Library symbol*] [*Library of Congress*] (LCLS) .... CaBSur
Surrey Volunteer Training Corps [*British military*] (DMA) .... SVTC
Surridge Dawson [*Commercial firm British*] .... SD
Surrogate .... S
Surrogate .... SURR
Surrogate (ADA) .... SURRO
Surrogate Acquilla Training System [*Army*] .... SATS
Surrogate Embryo Transfer [*Gynecology*] (CPH) .... SET
Surrogate Fast Attack Vehicle [*Two-passenger wheeled vehicle*] (INF) .... SFAV
Surrogate Parent Foundation (EA) .... SPF
Surrogate Research Vehicle [*Army Tank-Automotive Command*] .... SRV
Surrogates by Choice (EA) .... SBC
Surrogates by Choice [*Defunct*] (EA) .... SC
Surrogate's Court (DLA) .... Sur Ct
Surrogate's Court Procedure Act [*A publication*] (DLA) .... Surr Ct Proc Act
Surround .... SUR
Surrounding Combustion Process [*Automotive engineering*] .... SCP
Surry Community College, Dobson, NC [*Library symbol Library of Congress*] (LCLS) .... NcDoS
Surry County-Dobson Library, Dobson, NC [*Library symbol Library of Congress*] (LCLS) .... NcDo
SURTASS Measurement System [*Navy*] (CAAL) .... SMS
SURTASS Probability Area [*Navy*] (CAAL) .... SPA
Surtax (WDAA) .... ST
Surtax Rate (MHDW) .... SR
Surveillance (DA) .... SRV
Surveillance (AAG) .... SURV
Surveillance .... SURVI
Surveillance (AFM) .... SURVL
Surveillance, Acquisition, and Tracking [*Military*] (RDA) .... SAT
Surveillance, Acquisition, Tracking, and Kill Assessment [*Section of SDI - Strategic Defense Initiative*] .... SATKA
Surveillance Aided Intercept (NVT) .... SAI
Surveillance Aircraft Company [*Army*] (VNW) .... SURV
Surveillance Airplane Company [*Army*] (VNW) .... SAC
Surveillance and Accountability (NRCH) .... S & A
Surveillance and Accountability Control Team (MCD) .... SAACT
Surveillance and Analysis [*Environmental Protection Agency*] (GFGA) .... S & A
Surveillance and Battle Damage Assessment Device [*Military*] .... SBDAD
Surveillance and Control Data Link [*Military*] .... SCDL
Surveillance and Control of Transmission Systems [*Bell Laboratories*] .... SCOTS
Surveillance and Entry .... S & E
Surveillance and Identification .... S & ID
Surveillance and In-Service Inspection [*Nuclear energy*] (NRCH) .... SISI
Surveillance and Inspection (AAG) .... S & I
Surveillance and Inspection (IAA) .... SAI
Surveillance and Maintenance [*Army*] (AABC) .... SURVM
Surveillance and Missile Observation System [*Military*] (IAA) .... SAMOS
Surveillance and Precision Approach RADAR (NATG) .... SPAR
Surveillance and Reconnaissance Ground Equipment .... SARGE
Surveillance and Target Acquisition [*Marine Corps*] (DOMA) .... STA
Surveillance and Target Acquisition Aircraft System (AFM) .... STAAS
Surveillance and Target Acquisition RADAR for Tank Location and Engagement [*Army*] (MCD) .... STARTLE
Surveillance Approach (FAAC) .... SA
Surveillance Calibration Satellite .... SURCAL
Surveillance Communication Processor [*Aviation*] (OA) .... SCP
Surveillance Compliance [*Nuclear energy*] (NRCH) .... SC
Surveillance Control and Driver Information [*Traffic system*] .... SCANDI
Surveillance Coordination Center (NATG) .... SCC
Surveillance Criticality Designator [*DoD*] .... SCD
Surveillance Data Transmission .... SDT
Surveillance Direction System (DOMA) .... SDS
Surveillance Drone [*Air Force*] .... SD
Surveillance Environmental Acoustic Support [*Military*] (CAAL) .... SEAS
Surveillance Environmental Acoustic Support Project [*Naval Ocean Research and Development Activity*] [*Mississippi*] .... SEAS
Surveillance, Epidemiology, and End-Results [*Program*] [*National Cancer Institute*] .... SEER
Surveillance Facility [*Navy*] .... SURFAC
Surveillance Force (DNAB) .... SURVFOR
Surveillance Helicopter Co. [*Army*] (AABC) .... SHC
Surveillance Imagery Fast Access Recording (MCD) .... SIFAR
Surveillance Inspection [*Nuclear energy*] (NRCH) .... SI
Surveillance Intelligence and Reconnaissance Mission [*Military*] (CAAL) .... SIM
Surveillance Licence [*Importing*] [*British*] (DS) .... SL
Surveillance Officer .... SO
Surveillance Operations [*Military*] (NVT) .... SRVEILOPS
Surveillance, Patrol, Reconnaissance, Intelligence Gathering, Target Designation, and Electronic Warfare [*Unmanned aircraft*] [*Military*] .... SPRITE
Surveillance Procedure (NRCH) .... SP
Surveillance RADAR [*Air Force*] .... SR
Surveillance RADAR (MCD) .... SRAD
Surveillance RADAR Approach .... SRA
Surveillance RADAR Element .... SRE
Surveillance RADAR Equipment .... SRE
Surveillance RADAR Station [*ITU designation*] (CET) .... RLS
Surveillance RADAR Station .... SRS
Surveillance RADAR Test Set .... SRTS
Surveillance RADAR Zone (DA) .... SRZ
Surveillance Range Acoustics Prediction System (MCD) .... SURVRAP
Surveillance, Reconnaissance, and Intelligence [*Marine Corps*] (DOMA) .... SRI
Surveillance, Reconnaissance, and Intelligence Group [*Marine Corps*] (DOMA) .... SRIG
Surveillance Requirement [*Nuclear Regulatory Commission*] (GFGA) .... SR
Surveillance Situation Display .... SSD
Surveillance Squadron .... SURS
Surveillance Station [*RADAR*] .... SS
Surveillance Summary Reports (NVT) .... SURVSUM
Surveillance Tactical (MCD) .... SURTAC
Surveillance, Target Acquisition, and Night Observation [*DoD*] .... STANO
Surveillance, Target Acquisition, and Reconnaissance .... STAR
Surveillance, Target Acquisition, Night Observation, and Counter - Surveillance [*British*] (MCD) .... STANOC

Surveillance Target Acquisition Support System (IAA) ... STASS
Surveillance Target Attack RADAR System ... STARS
Surveillance Television (AFM) ... STV
Surveillance Test (NATG) ... ST
Surveillance Test Set (MCD) ... STS
Surveillance Towed Array Sensor System (USDC) ... SURTASS
Surveillance Towed Array Sensor System [*Marine science*] (OSRA) ... SURTASS
Surveillance Towed Array SONAR System ... SURTASS
Surveillance Training and Operating Procedures Standardization [*Military*] (CAAL) ... SURTOPS
Surveillance/Vantage Point [*Military*] (INF) ... S/VP
Survey ... S
Survey ... SRVY
Survey (AABC) ... SURV
Survey ... SVY
Survey ... SY
Survey and Investigation Staff [*Navy*] (NVT) ... S & IS
Survey and Reports Branch [*Division of Biometry and Applied Sciences, National Institute of Mental Health*] (GFGA) ... SRB
Survey Control Point [*Military*] ... SCP
Survey Craft [*Navy symbol*] ... YGS
Survey Data Analysis [*Computer science*] ... SUDAAN
Survey Data Processing ... SDP
Survey Electronics Distance Measuring Equipment (MCD) ... SEDME
Survey Entry ... SENTRY
Survey Information Center [*Military*] ... SIC
Survey Instrument, Azimuth Gyroscope, Lightweight (MCD) ... SIAGL
Survey, Liaison, and Reconnaissance Party [*Navy*] (ANA) ... SLRP
Survey Methodology Information System [*Inter-University Consortium for Political & Social Research*] [*Database*] ... SMIS
Survey Number ... SN
Survey of Adults and Markets of Affluence [*Monroe Mendelsohn Research, Inc.*] [*Information service or system*] (CRD) ... SAMA
Survey of Agency Opinion [*LIMRA*] ... SAO
Survey of American Indians and Alaska Natives [*Department of Health and Human Services*] (GFGA) ... SAIAN
Survey of Basic Competencies [*Achievement test*] ... SBC
Survey of Basic Skills [*Achievement test*] ... SBS
Survey of California Law [*A publication*] (DLA) ... Survey Calif L
Survey of Change and Residential Finance [*Census Bureau*] ... SCARF
Survey of Clerical Skills (AEBS) ... SOCS
Survey of Doctorate Recipients [*National Research Council*] [*Database*] ... SDR
Survey of Eastern Palestine [*A publication*] (BJA) ... SEP
Survey of Income and Program Participation Awareness Program [*Bureau of the Census*] (GFGA) ... SIPPAP
Survey of India [*India*] (EERA) ... SOI
Survey of Inmates of Local Jails [*Department of Justice*] (GFGA) ... SILJ
Survey of Interpersonal Values [*Psychology*] ... SIV
Survey of Market Absorption [*Department of Housing and Urban Development*] (GFGA) ... SOMA
Survey of Motor Freight Transportation and Public Warehousing [*BTS*] (TAG) ... WATS
Survey of Motor Vehicle Use (EERA) ... SMVU
Survey of Next of Kin [*Department of Health and Human Services*] (GFGA) ... SNK
[*A*] **Survey of Old Testament Introductions** [*Gleason L. Archer*] [*A publication*] (BJA) ... SOTI
Survey of Personal Attitude [*Psychology*] ... SPA
Survey of Personal Values [*Psychology*] ... SPV
Survey of Primary Reading Development (AEBS) ... SPRD
Survey of Pupil Opinion (EDAC) ... SURPO
Survey of School Attitudes [*Student attitudes test*] ... SSA
Survey of Student Personnel Objectives (EDAC) ... SSPO
[*A*] **Survey of Students' Educational Talents and Skills** [*Educational test*] ... ASSETS
Survey of Study Habits and Attitudes [*Education*] ... SSHA
Survey of Teacher Demand and Shortage [*Department of Education*] (GFGA) ... STDS
Survey of the Chronic Sick and Handicapped [*British*] ... SCSH
Survey of Use Permits [*Bureau of the Census*] (GFGA) ... SOP
Survey of Western Palestine [*C. R. Conder et al*] [*A publication*] (BJA) ... SWP
Survey of Western Palestine: Memoirs [*C. R. Conder*] [*A publication*] (BJA) ... SWPM
Survey of Western Palestine: Special Papers [*A publication*] (BJA) ... SWPSP
Survey on Income and Program Participation [*Census Bureau, Department of Health and Human Services*] ... SIPP
Survey Operations [*Navy*] (NVT) ... SURVOPS
Survey, Question, Read, Review, Recite [*Psychology*] ... SQ3R
Survey Records Branch, Ontario Ministry of Natural Resources, Toronto, Ontario [*Library symbol National Library of Canada*] (BIB) ... OTNR
Survey Research Center [*Oregon State University*] [*Research center*] (RCD) ... SRC
Survey Research Center [*University of Kentucky*] [*Research center*] (RCD) ... SRC
Survey Research Consultants International, Inc. [*Information service or system*] (IID) ... SRCI
Survey Research Laboratory [*University of Illinois*] [*Information service or system*] (IID) ... SRL
Survey Research Service [*National Opinion Research Center, University of Chicago*] [*Research center*] ... SRS
Survey Research Singapore (Pte) Ltd. [*Information service or system*] (IID) ... SRS
Survey Sampling, Inc. [*Information service or system*] (IID) ... SSI
Survey Satellite [*NASA*] ... SURSAT
Survey Science Centre [*A consortium of European oranizations*] ... SSC
Survey System (IAA) ... SUSY
Survey Tabulation Services, Inc. [*Information service or system*] (IID) ... STS
Survey Test of Algebraic Aptitude [*Education*] (AEBS) ... STAA
Survey Udara (Penas) PT [*Indonesia*] [*ICAO designator*] (FAAC) ... PNS
Surveyed Before Shipment [*Business term*] (MHDB) ... SBS
Surveyer, Nenninger & Chenevert, Inc., Montreal, PQ, Canada [*Library symbol Library of Congress*] (LCLS) ... CaQMSNC
Surveying and Mapping Industry Council (EERA) ... SMIC
Surveying and Mapping Library, Cartographic Information and Distribution Centre,Energy, Mines, and Resources Canada [*Bibliotheque des Leves et de Cartograph ies, Centre d'Information et de Distribution Cartographiques, Energie, Mines, et Ressources Canada*] **Ottawa, Ontario** [*Library symbol National Library of Canada*] (NLC) ... OOSM
Surveying and Mapping Victoria [*Australia*] ... SMV
Surveying Equipment Distance Measuring Electronic (MCD) ... SEDME
Surveying Recorder [*Navy rating British*] ... SR
Surveying Ship [*Navy symbol*] ... AGS
Surveyor [*British military*] (DMA) ... SR
Surveyor ... SURV
Surveyor ... SURVR
Surveyor ... SURVYR
Surveyor Command Preparation Program [*Aerospace*] ... SCPP
Surveyor Flight Control Section ... SFCS
Surveyor Lunar Roving Vehicle [*Aerospace*] (MCD) ... SLRV
Surveyor Payload Mechanism Section ... SPMS
Surveyor Project Policy and Procedure Manual [*NASA*] ... SPPPM
Surveyor Quality Assurance ... SQA
Surveyor Quality Assurance Directive ... SQAD
Surveyor Retro Nozzle Structure ... SRNS
Surveyor Scientific Evaluation Advisory Team [*NASA*] ... SSEAT
Surveyor Test Equipment Assembly ... STEA
Surveyor Thermal Control Section ... STCS
Surveyor Vehicle Department ... SVD
Surveyors Appointments Consultancy [*Royal Institute of Chartered Surveyors*] [*British*] ... SAC
Surveyors' Board of Queensland [*Australia*] ... SBQ
Surveyors Historical Society (EA) ... SHS
Surveys and Investigation ... S & I
Surveys and Investigations of the House Appropriations Committee (AAGC) ... S&I
Surveys and Mapping Library [*Canada Energy Mines and Resources*] [*UTLAS symbol*] ... EMS
Surveys of Minority-Owned Business Enterprises [*Bureau of the Census*] (GFGA) ... SMOBE
Survivability and Hardening (MCD) ... S & H
Survivability and Vulnerability Improvement Modification [*Army*] (RDA) ... SAVIM
Survivability/Crash Flight Data Recorder (MCD) ... S/CFDR
Survivability, Lethality, and Key Technologies (SDI) ... SLKT
Survivability Management Office [*Adelphi, MD*] [*Army*] ... SMO
Survivability Management Operation ... SMO
Survivability Management Steering Group [*DoD*] ... SMSG
Survivability Optimization Model (MCD) ... SOM
Survivability System [*Military*] ... SS
Survivability Test Advisory Panel [*Military*] (CAAL) ... STAP
Survivability/Vulnerability [*Applied to ability of weapon systems to survive attacks*] [*Military*] ... S/V
Survivability/Vulnerability Information Analysis Center [*Wright-Patterson Air Force Base, OH*] [*DoD*] (MCD) ... SURVIAC
Survivable and Effective Airbreathing Defense [*Study*] (MCD) ... SEADS
Survivable Collective Projected System ... SCPS
Survivable Collective Protection System [*Air Force*] (DOMA) ... SCPS
Survivable Collision Protection System (DWSG) ... SCPS
Survivable Communications Integration System ... SCIS
Survivable Electronic Air Defense ... SEAD
Survivable Enduring Command and Control ... SECC
Survivable Flight Control Electronic Set [*Aviation*] (PDAA) ... SFCES
Survivable Flight Control System [*Military*] ... SFCS
Survivable Low-Frequency Communications [*Air Force*] ... SLFC
Survivable Low-Frequency Communications System [*Air Force*] ... SLFCS
Survivable Optical Forward Acquisition Sensor ... SOFAS
Survivable Optical Forward Acquisition System (MCD) ... SOFAS
Survivable Radio Guidance System [*Military*] ... SRGS
Survivable Satellite ... SURVSAT
Survivable Satellite Communications ... SUR/SATCOM
Survivable Satellite Communications System (MCD) ... SURVSA
Survivable Satellite Communications System ... SURVSATCOM
Survivable Satellite System (MCD) ... SSS
Survivable Tactical Army Generator (RDA) ... STAG
Survivable-MOS [*Metal-Oxide Semiconductor*] **Array Computer** [*Air Force*] ... SMARC
Survival ... S
Survival (MSA) ... SRVL
Survival (AFM) ... SURV
Survival Air-to-Air (MCD) ... SAA
Survival [*formerly, Space*] **and Flight Equipment Association** [*Later, SAFE Association*] ... SAFE
Survival and Flight Equipment Association [*Later, SAFE Association*] (EA) ... SAFEA
Survival [*formerly, Space*] **and Flight Equipment Association** [*Later, SAFE Association*] ... SFEA
Survival and Ventricular Enlargement [*Medicine*] ... SAVE
Survival Army Recovery Vest, Insert, and Pockets ... SARVIP
Survival Assistance Director [*Federal disaster planning*] ... SAD
Survival Assistance Officer [*Army*] (AABC) ... SAO
Survival Avionics System [*Military*] (CAAL) ... SAS
Survival Dose ... SD
Survival Education Association [*Defunct*] (EA) ... SEA

Survival, Escape, and Evasion Kit [*Navy*] (NG) .... SEEK
Survival, Evasion, and Escape [*Military*] .... SEE
Survival, Evasion, Resistance, and Escape [*Military*] (AFM) .... SERE
Survival in Target Area (MCD) .... STA
Survival International [*British*] (EAIO) .... SI
Survival International, USA [*Defunct*] (EA) .... SIUSA
Survival Kit Air-Droppable [*Military Canada*] .... SKAD
Survival Motor Neuron [*Genetics*] .... SMN
Survival of American Indians Association (EA) .... SAIA
Survival Probability Function .... SPF
Survival Probability Hazard in a Nuclear Exchange .... SPHINX
Survival Quotient (ADA) .... SQ
Survival, Recovery, and Reconstitution [*Military*] (AFM) .... SRR
Survival Research Foundation (EA) .... SRF
Survival School [*Air Force*] .... SRVLSCH
Survival Sited Casualty Treatment Assemblage (AFM) .... SCATA
Survival Stabilator Actuator Package [*Hydraulic power*] .... SSAP
Survival Support Device (NVT) .... SSD
Survival Surface-to-Air (MCD) .... SSA
Survival Technology [*NASDAQ symbol*] (TTSB) .... STIQ
Survival Technology, Inc. [*NASDAQ symbol*] (SAG) .... STIQ
Survival Technology, Inc. [*Associated Press*] (SAG) .... SurvTc
Survival Time .... ST
Survive Tomorrow, Inc. [*Commercial firm*] (EA) .... STI
Surviving .... SURV
Surviving Capability Plan [*Military*] .... SURCAP
Surviving Propagules [*Botany*] .... SP
Surviving Today's Experiences and Problems Successfully Curriculum [*West Virginia*] (EDAC) .... STEPS
Survivor (DNAB) .... SUR
Survivor .... Surv
Survivor .... SURVOR
Survivor (AAG) .... SURVR
Survivor Benefit Plan [*For survivors of retired military personnel*] .... SBP
Survivor Income Benefit Insurance (DICI) .... SIBI
Survivors Network of Those Abused by Priests [*An association*] .... SNAP
Survivors of a Person with AIDS [*An association*] (CPH) .... SOPWA
Survivors of Incest Anonymous (EA) .... SIA
Survivors of Sacrifice [*Defunct*] (EA) .... SOS
Survivors of Stalking .... SOS
Survivors of Suicide .... SOS
Survivorship Agreement [*Legal term*] (DLA) .... S/A
Susaek [*South Korea ICAO location identifier*] (ICLI) .... RKSK
Susaki [*Mitsui*] [*Japan*] [*Seismograph station code, US Geological Survey*] [*Closed*] (SEIS) .... SUS
Susan B. Anthony Dollar .... SBA
Susan B. Anthony Women's Spirituality Education Forum (EA) .... SBAWSEF
Susan G. Komen Foundation (EA) .... SGKF
Susan Hayward Collectors Club (EA) .... SHCC
Susanna [*Apocryphya*] (BJA) .... Sus
Susanne Severeid Fan Club (EA) .... SSFC
Susanville, CA [*FM radio station call letters*] .... KJDX
Susanville, CA [*AM radio station call letters*] .... KSUE
Susanville, CA [*Location identifier FAA*] (FAAL) .... SVE
Susara [*Romania*] [*Seismograph station code, US Geological Survey*] (SEIS) .... SSR
Susceptance [*Symbol*] [*IUPAC*] .... B
Susceptible .... S
Susceptible, Exposed, Infected or Immune, Recovered [*Epidemiological model*] .... SEIR
Susceptor Meus Dominus [*God Is My Protector*] [*Motto of Jacob, Margrave of Baden-Hochberg (1562-90); Georg Friedrich, Margrave of Baden-Hochberg (1573-1638)*] [*Latin*] .... SMD
Susitna [*Alaska*] [*Seismograph station code, US Geological Survey Closed*] (SEIS) .... SST
Susitna [*Alaska*] [*Seismograph station code, US Geological Survey*] (SEIS) .... SUA
Susitna Valley, AK [*Location identifier FAA*] (FAAL) .... TXR
Suspect .... SUS
Suspect Chemicals Sourcebook [*Roytech Publications*] [*Information service or system*] (CRD) .... SCS
Suspect Index [*British*] .... SI
Suspecta Lectio [*Double Reading*] [*Latin*] (ROG) .... SUSP L
Suspected [*Passage or line of a work*] [*Literary criticism*] (ROG) .... SUSP
Suspected Child Abuse and Neglect [*Medicine*] (DMAA) .... SCAN
Suspected Child Abuse and Neglect (DAVI) .... SCAN
Suspected Duplicate .... SUS DUP
Suspected, Not Proved .... SNP
Suspect-Variant Anomalous Mental Condition .... SV-AMC
Suspend (NASA) .... SPND
Suspend [*or Suspension*] (AFM) .... SUSP
Suspend from Issue and Use as Suspect Material .... SIUSM
Suspend Issue and Use of Following Lots .... SIUFL
Suspend Other Service [*Business term*] .... SOS
Suspendatur per Collum [*Let Him Be Hanged by the Neck*] [*Latin*] .... Sus Per Coll
Suspended [*Regulation or order suspended*] [*Used in Shepard's Citations*] [*Legal term*] (DLA) .... Sd
Suspended [*Technical drawings*] .... SUS
Suspended .... SUSPD
Suspended Access Equipment Manufacturers Association [*British*] (DBA) .... SAEMA
Suspended Acoustical-Plaster Ceiling [*Technical drawings*] .... SAPC
Suspended Acoustical-Tile Ceiling [*Technical drawings*] .... SATC
Suspended Aluminosilicate .... SAS
Suspended and Canceled Pesticides [*Environmental Protection Agency*] (GFGA) .... SAC
Suspended Array Surveillance System [*To detect submarines*] .... SASS
Suspended Array System [*To detect submarines*] .... SAS
Suspended Ceilings Association [*British*] (DBA) .... SCA
Suspended Dust (DICI) .... SD
Suspended from Issue, Movement, and Use [*Army*] (ADDR) .... SIMU
Suspended in Part [*Regulation or order suspended in part*] [*Legal term*] (DLA) .... Sdp
Suspended Maneuvering System [*McDonnell Douglas Corp.*] (MCD) .... SMS
Suspended Matter [*Chemistry*] .... SM
Suspended Organic Carbon [*Chemistry*] .... SOC
Suspended Particulate Matter .... SPM
Suspended Particulate Organic Material [*Environmental chemistry*] .... SPOM
Suspended Plaster Ceiling [*Technical drawings*] .... SPC
Suspended Sentence .... SS
Suspended Solids [*Wastewater treatment*] .... SS
Suspended Sprayed Acoustical Ceiling [*Technical drawings*] .... SSAC
Suspended-Particle Display [*Glazing technology*] .... SPD
Suspending [*Freight*] .... SUSPDNG
Suspensio per Collum [*Execution by Hanging*] [*Latin*] .... Sus Per Col
Suspensio per Collum [*Hanged by the Neck*] [*Latin*] .... SUS per COLL
Suspension (MSA) .... SPNSN
Suspension .... SUSPNSN
Suspension and Release Units (AFM) .... SRU
Suspension of Expendable Penetration Aids by Kite [*Military*] .... SEPAK
Suspension of Service [*Pilots' strike*] .... SOS
Suspension Specialists Association (EA) .... SSA
Suspension Technology Demonstrator [*Army*] (RDA) .... STD
Suspension Unit (AFM) .... SUU
Suspension Unit Universal [*Weaponry*] [*Air Force*] (INF) .... SUU
Suspicion [*FBI standardized term*] .... SUSP
Suspicion Law [*Statute permitting policemen to detain individuals suspected of criminal activity*] [*British*] .... SUS
Suspicious Person .... SP
Susquehanna [*ICAO designator*] (AD) .... FR
Susquehanna Bancshares [*NASDAQ symbol*] (TTSB) .... SUSQU
Susquehanna Bancshares, Inc. [*Lititz, PA*] [*NASDAQ symbol*] (NQ) .... SUSQ
Susquehanna Bancshares, Inc. [*Associated Press*] (SAG) .... SusqBnc
Susquehanna Environmental Advocates (NRCH) .... SEA
Susquehanna Leading Chronicle [*Pennsylvania*] [*A publication*] (DLA) .... Susq LC
Susquehanna Legal Chronicle [*Pennsylvania*] [*A publication*] (DLA) .... Sus Leg Chron
Susquehanna Legal Chronicle [*Pennsylvania*] [*A publication*] (DLA) .... Susq L Chron
Susquehanna Legal Chronicle [*Pennsylvania*] [*A publication*] (DLA) .... Susq Leg Chron
Susquehanna Legal Chronicle [*Pennsylvania*] [*A publication*] (DLA) .... Susq Legal Chron
Susquehanna Legal Chronicle [*Pennsylvania*] [*A publication*] (DLA) .... Susquehanna Leg Chron (PA)
Susquehanna Library Cooperative [*Library network*] .... SLC
Susquehanna, PA [*FM radio station call letters*] .... WKGB
Susquehanna River Basin Commission [*Federal government*] (EGAO) .... SRBC
Susquehanna River Basin Compact [*Maryland, Pennsylvania, New York*] .... SRBC
Susquehanna Steam Electric Station [*Nuclear energy*] (NRCH) .... SSES
Susquehanna University, Selinsgrove, PA [*Library symbol Library of Congress*] (LCLS) .... PSelS
Susquehanna University, Selinsgrove, PA [*OCLC symbol*] (OCLC) .... SUS
Sussex [*County in England*] .... SUSS
Sussex [*County in England*] .... SX
Sussex Cattle Association of America (EA) .... SCAA
Sussex Cattle Society (EAIO) .... SCS
Sussex County Clerk, Newton, NJ [*Library symbol Library of Congress*] (LCLS) .... NjNetCoC
Sussex County Historical Society, Newton, NJ [*Library symbol Library of Congress*] (LCLS) .... NjNetSHi
Sussex County Library, Newton, NJ [*Library symbol Library of Congress*] (LCLS) .... NjNetS
Sussex European Research Centre [*Research center British*] (IRC) .... SERC
Sussex Imperial Yeomanry [*British military*] (DMA) .... SIY
Sussex Library, Canada Institute for Scientific and Technical Information [*Bibliotheque Sussex, Institut Canadien de l'Information Scientifique et Technique*] **Ottawa, Ontario** [*Library symbol National Library of Canada*] (NLC) .... OONS
Sussex, NB [*AM radio station call letters*] .... CJCW
Sussex, NJ [*FM radio station call letters*] .... WNJP
Sussex Public Library, New Brunswick [*Library symbol National Library of Canada*] (NLC) .... NBSUS
Sussex Public Library, Sussex, NB, Canada [*Library symbol*] [*Library of Congress*] (LCLS) .... CaNBSuS
Sussex, WI [*AM radio station call letters*] .... WKSH
Sussex Yeomanry [*British military*] (DMA) .... SY
Sustain [*Legal*] (ROG) .... SUSTN
Sustain Our Schools .... SOS
Sustainability Predictions for Army Spare Component Requirements for Combat (RDA) .... SPARC
Sustainable Biosphere Initiative (GNE) .... SBI
Sustainable Business Entity .... SIBE
Sustainable Energy and Environment Division [*United Nations*] .... SEED
Sustainable Equilibrium Exchange Rate [*Economics*] .... SEER
Sustainable National Domestic Product (EERA) .... SNDP
Sustainable Net National Expenditure (EERA) .... SNNE
Sustainable Non-Inflationary Growth (ODBW) .... SNIG
Sustainable Social Net National Product (EERA) .... SSNNP
Sustained [*Legal*] (ROG) .... SUSTD
Sustained Abdominal Compression [*Gastroenterology*] .... SAC

Sustained Action [Pharmacy] .... SA
Sustained Airborne Training [Army] (INF) .... SAT
Sustained Breakdown (IAA) .... SB
Sustained Competitive Motivation .... SCM
Sustained Electron Bombardment-Induced Conductivity ...... SEBIC
Sustained Ethanol Release Tube [Pharmacology] .... SERT
Sustained Fire [Military] (INF) .... SF
Sustained Load Crack [Titanium alloy] .... SLC
Sustained Maximal Inspiration [Physiology] .... SMI
Sustained Medication [Pharmacology] .... SM
Sustained Monomorphic Ventricular Tachycardia [Cardiology] (DAVI) .... SMVT
Sustained Naval Aviation Operations in Chemical, Biological, and
    Radiological Warfare Conditions [Military] .... SNAO/CWC
Sustained Noninflationary Market-Oriented Growth .... SNIMOG
Sustained Operational Date (AFM) .... SOD
Sustained Operations [Study of soldier performance in extended combat
    situation] [Army] .... SUSOPS
Sustained Operations Control (IAA) .... SOCR
Sustained Operations Control Room [NASA] (KSC) .... SOCR
Sustained Operations Manual .... SOM
Sustained Operations Model .... SOM
Sustained Operations Support Area [NASA] (KSC) .... SOSA
Sustained Peak Low-Cycle Fatigue (PDAA) .... SPLCF
Sustained Rate of Fire [Military] (INF) .... SROF
Sustained Re-Entrant Ventricular Tachyarrhythmia [Cardiology] (DMAA) .... SRVT
Sustained Release [Pharmacy] .... SR
Sustained Release Nitroglycerin (DMAA) .... SRNG
Sustained Release Theophylline [Medicine] .... SRT
Sustained Silent Reading [Education] (AEE) .... SSR
Sustained Superior Performance [Military] .... SSP
Sustained-Attrition Minefield Evaluation Model (DNAB) ...... SAMEM
Sustained-Release Capsule [Pharmacology] .... SRC
Sustained-Yield Tropical Agroecosystem .... SYTA
Sustainer (AAG) .... SUS
Sustainer .... SUST
Sustainer Engine (AAG) .... SE
Sustainer Firing Package .... SFP
Sustainer Gas Generator .... SGG
Sustainer Pitch (AAG) .... SP
Sustainer Yaw (AAG) .... SY
Sustainer-Engine Cutoff [Aerospace] .... SECO
Sustaining .... STNG
Sustaining Base Army Network (GFGA) .... STARNET
Sustaining Base Automation [Army] (RDA) .... SBA
Sustaining Base Information Service [or System] [Army] (RDA) .... SBIS
Sustaining Engineering .... SE
Sustaining Engineering Services .... SES
Sustaining Fiber .... SF
Sustaining Support Increment [Military] .... SSI
Sustainment Training Program [Army] (INF) .... STP
Sustentation [Ecclesiastical] (ROG) .... SUSTN
Susu [MARC language code Library of Congress] (LCCP) .... sus
Sutherland [South Africa] [ICAO location identifier] (ICLI) .... FASL
Sutherland [South Africa] [Seismograph station code, US Geological Survey]
    (SEIS) .... SUR
Sutherland [County in Scotland] .... SUTH
Sutherland on Statutes and Statutory Construction [A publication]
    (DLA) .... Suth St Const
Sutherland on Statutes and Statutory Construction [A publication]
    (DLA) .... Suth Stat Const
Sutherland on the Law of Damages [A publication] (DLA) .... Suth Dam
Sutherland Resources [Vancouver Stock Exchange symbol] .... SRD
Sutherland's Appeal Reports, Small Causes Court [1861-65] [Bengal, India]
    [A publication] (DLA) .... Suth App
Sutherland's Bengal Full Bench Reports [India] [A publication] (DLA) .... Suth FBR
Sutherland's Bengal High Court Reports [India] [A publication]
    (DLA) .... Suth Bengal
Sutherland's Calcutta Reports [India] [A publication] (DLA) .... Suth
Sutherland's Privy Council Appeals [A publication] (DLA) .... Suth PCA
Sutherland's Privy Council Judgments [A publication] (DLA) .... Suth PCJ
Sutherland's Special Number of Weekly Reporter [A publication]
    (DLA) .... Suth Sp N
Sutherland's Weekly Report [India] [A publication] (DLA) .... WR
Sutherland's Weekly Reporter, Calcutta [1864-76] [A publication]
    (DLA) .... Suth WR
Sutherland's Weekly Reporter, Calcutta [India] [A publication] (DLA) ...... WR Calc
Sutherland's Weekly Reports, Miscellaneous Appeals [India]
    [A publication] (DLA) .... Suth WR Mis
Sutter Antigen [Of Kell system blood group] [Hematology] (DAVI) .... Jsᵃ
Sutter County Free Library, Yuba City, CA [Library symbol Library of
    Congress] (LCLS) .... CYcCL
Sutter Creek, CA [FM radio station call letters] .... KRAZ
Sutter Creek, CA [FM radio station call letters] (RBYB) ...... KSAC
Sutter's Fort State Monument, Sacramento, CA [Library symbol Library of
    Congress] (LCLS) .... CSSF
Sutton [Postcode] (ODBW) .... SM
Sutton Avian Research Center .... SARC
Sutton on Personal Actions at Common Law [A publication] (DLA) ...... Sutton
Sutton Resource Ltd. [NASDAQ symbol] (SAG) .... STTZ
Sutton Resource Ltd. [Associated Press] (SAG) .... SuttRsc
Sutton Resources [NASDAQ symbol] (TTSB) .... STTZF
Sutton Resources Ltd. [Vancouver Stock Exchange symbol] .... STT
Sutton, WV [FM radio station call letters] .... WCKA
Sutton, WV [AM radio station call letters] .... WSGB
Suttsu [Japan] [Seismograph station code, US Geological Survey] (SEIS) ...... SUT

Suture Removal [Surgery] (DAVI) .... SR
Suus [His] [Latin] .... S
Suva [Fiji] [Airport symbol] (OAG) .... SUV
Suva [Fiji] [Seismograph station code, US Geological Survey] (SEIS) ...... SUV
Suva [Fiji] [Seismograph station code, US Geological Survey] (SEIS) ...... SVA
Suva/Nausori [Fiji] [ICAO location identifier] (ICLI) .... NFSU
Suwannee River Regional Library, Live Oak, FL [Library symbol Library of
    Congress] (LCLS) .... FLiS
Suwon [South Korea ICAO location identifier] (ICLI) .... RKSW
Suzie Mining Exploration [Vancouver Stock Exchange symbol] .... SUE
Suzuki Association of the Americas (EA) .... SAA
Suzuki Continuously-Variable Transmission [Automotive powertrain] ...... SCVT
Svalbard and Jan Mayen [MARC geographic area code Library of Congress]
    (LCCP) .... lnsb--
Svalbard and Jan Mayen [MARC country of publication code Library of
    Congress] (LCCP) .... sb
Svalbard and Jan Mayen Islands [ANSI two-letter standard code] (CNC) ...... SJ
Svalbard and Jan Mayen Islands [ANSI three-letter standard code] (CNC) ..... SJM
Svalbard/Longyear [Norway ICAO location identifier] (ICLI) ...... ENSB
Svartnes [Norway ICAO location identifier] (ICLI) .... ENSS
Svedberg Flotation Unit (AAMN) .... Sf
Svedberg Unit [Physical chemistry] .... S
Sveg [Sweden ICAO location identifier] (ICLI) .... ESND
Svensk Biblisk Uppslagverk [A publication] (BJA) .... SBU
Svenska Aeroplan Aktiebolaget [Swedish automobile manufacturer; acronym
    used as name of its cars] .... SAAB
Svenska Arbetsgivareforeningen [An employers' confederation] [Sweden] ..... SAF
Svenska Folkpartiet [Swedish People's Party] [Finland Political party] (PPE) .... SFP
Svenska Institutet foer Opinionsundersoekningar .... SIFO
Svenska Kullager Frabikon [Swedish Ball Bearing Manufacturing] ..... SKF
Svenska Kullagerfabriken AB [Swedish manufacturer, especially of ball
    bearings; active in many countries] .... SKF
Svenska Utvecklingsaktiebolaget [Swedish Corporation for Development] .... SUAB
Svenski Indianska Foerbundet [Sweden] .... SVIF
Svensk-Internationella Pressbyran [Swedish-International Press Bureau]
    (EY) .... SIP
Sverdlovsk [Former USSR Geomagnetic observatory code] .... SVD
Sverdlovsk [Ekaterinburg] [Former USSR Seismograph station code, US
    Geological Survey] (SEIS) .... SVE
Sverdlovsk [Former USSR ICAO location identifier] (ICLI) .... USSS
Sverdlovsk Airline [Russian Federation] [ICAO designator] (FAAC) ...... SVR
Sverdlovsk (Arti) [Former USSR Geomagnetic observatory code] ...... ARS
SverigeAmerika Stiftelsen [Sweden-American Foundation] (EAIO) ...... SAS
Sveriges Akademikers Centralorganisation [Swedish Confederation of
    Professional Associations] .... SACO
Sveriges Arbetarepartiet Kommunisterna [Swedish Workers' Communist
    Party] [Political party] (PPW) .... SAK
Sveriges Arbetares Centralorganisation [Central Organization of Swedish
    Workers] .... SAC
Sveriges Geologiska Undersokning [Geological Survey of Sweden] [Uppsala]
    [Information service or system] (IID) .... SGU
Sveriges Kommunistiska Partiet [Communist Party of Sweden] [Political
    party] (PPE) .... SKP
Sveriges Radio .... SR
Sveriges Socialdemokratiska Arbetareparti [Swedish Social Democratic
    Labor Party] [Political party] (PPW) .... SAP
Sveriges Standardiseringskommission [Swedish Standards Institution] [Also,
    an information service or system] (IID) .... SIS
Svetoveho Kongresu Slovakov [Canada] (EAIO) .... SKS
Svolvaer [Norway] [Airport symbol] (OAG) .... SVJ
Svolvaer/Helle [Norway ICAO location identifier] (ICLI) .... ENSH
SW Electricity Board [British ICAO designator] (FAAC) .... ELE
Swabey and Tristram's Probate and Divorce Reports [1858-65]
    [A publication] (DLA) .... S & T
Swabey and Tristram's Probate and Divorce Reports [164 English Reprint]
    [A publication] (DLA) .... Sw & Tr
Swabey and Tristram's Probate and Divorce Reports [164 English Reprint]
    [A publication] (DLA) .... Swab & T
Swabey and Tristram's Probate and Divorce Reports [164 English Reprint]
    [A publication] (DLA) .... Swab & Tr
Swabey and Tristram's Probate and Divorce Reports [164 English Reports]
    [A publication] (DLA) .... Swabey & T (Eng)
Swabey on Divorce and Matrimonial Causes [3rd ed.] [1859]
    [A publication] (DLA) .... Swab Div
Swabey's English Admiralty Reports [A publication] (DLA) ...... Sw
Swabey's English Admiralty Reports [166 English Reprint] [A publication]
    (DLA) .... Swab Admr
Swabey's English Admiralty Reports [166 English Reprint] [1855-59]
    [A publication] (DLA) .... Swabey Adm
Swabey's English Admiralty Reports [166 English Reprint] [A publication]
    (DLA) .... Swabey Adm (Eng)
Swabey's English Ecclesiastical Reports [1855-59] [A publication] (DLA) ...... Sw
Swabey's English Ecclesiastical Reports [1855-59] [A publication] (DLA) .... Swab
Swaging Die [Tool] .... SGDI
Swaging Mandel .... SGMD
Swahili [MARC language code Library of Congress] (LCCP) .... swa
Swainsboro, GA [Location identifier FAA] (FAAL) .... SBO
Swainsboro, GA [AM radio station call letters] .... WJAT
Swainsboro, GA [FM radio station call letters] .... WJAT-FM
Swainsboro, GA [AM radio station call letters] .... WXRS
Swainsboro, GA [FM radio station call letters] .... WXRS-FM
Swakopmund [Namibia] [ICAO location identifier] (ICLI) .... FASM
Swakopmund [South-West Africa] [Airport symbol] (AD) .... SWP
SWALCAP Library Services Ltd. [Information service or system] (IID) ...... SLS
Swaleureniddwharfeairecalderdon [British town] .... SUNWACD

Swallow Sidecar [*Automobile manufacturer*] [*Forerunner to Jaguar*] ... SS
Swamp [*Maps and charts*] ... sw
Swamp (ADA) ... SWP
Swamp Creek [*Montana*] [*Seismograph station code, US Geological Survey Closed*] (SEIS) ... SWP
Swamp Glider ... SG
Swan and Critchfield's Revised Statutes [*Ohio*] [*A publication*] (DLA) ... S & C
Swan and Critchfield's Revised Statutes [*Ohio*] [*A publication*] (DLA) ... S & C Rev St
Swan and Critchfield's Revised Statutes [*Ohio*] [*A publication*] (DLA) ... Swan & CR St
Swan and Sayler's Revised Statutes of Ohio [*A publication*] (DLA) ... S & S
Swan and Sayler's Supplement to the Revised Statutes [*Ohio*] [*A publication*] (DLA) ... Swan & S St
Swan Hill [*Victoria, Australia*] [*Airport symbol*] (AD) ... SWH
Swan Hills Public Library, Alberta [*Library symbol National Library of Canada*] (NLC) ... ASH
Swan Hills Public Library, Swan Hills, AB, Canada [*Library symbol*] [*Library of Congress*] (LCLS) ... CaASh
Swan Island [*Seismograph station code, US Geological Survey Closed*] (SEIS) ... SWA
Swan Islands [*ICAO location identifier*] (ICLI) ... KSWA
Swan Islands [*MARC geographic area code Library of Congress*] (LCCP) ... nwsv--
Swan Islands [*used in records cataloged after January 1978*] [*MARC country of publication code Library of Congress*] (LCCP) ... sv
Swan Library, Albion, NY [*Library symbol Library of Congress*] (LCLS) ... NAlbi
Swan on Pleading and Practice [*Ohio*] [*A publication*] (DLA) ... Swan Pl & Pr
Swan on Practice [*Ohio*] [*A publication*] (DLA) ... Swan Pr
Swan View [*Australia Seismograph station code, US Geological Survey*] (SEIS) ... SWV
Swan Wooster Engineering Co., Vancouver, BC, Canada [*Library symbol Library of Congress*] (LCLS) ... CaBVaSW
Swan Wooster Engineering Co., Vancouver, British Columbia [*Library symbol National Library of Canada*] (NLC) ... BVASW
Swan-Ganz [*Catheter*] [*Cardiology*] (DAVI) ... SG
Swan-Ganz [*Catheter*] [*Medicine*] (MEDA) ... SG
Swank, Inc. [*NASDAQ symbol*] (NQ) ... SNKI
Swank Inc. [*NASDAQ symbol*] (TTSB) ... SNKIE
Swank, Inc. [*Associated Press*] (SAG) ... Swank
Swann [*Blood group*] ... Sw
Swannanoa Public Library, Swannanoa, NC [*Library symbol Library of Congress*] (LCLS) ... NcSw
Swanquarter, NC [*FM radio station call letters*] ... WHYC
Swan's Ecclesiastical Courts [*1830*] [*A publication*] (DLA) ... Swan Eccl C
Swan's Justice [*Ohio*] [*A publication*] (DLA) ... Swan Just
Swan's Ohio Statutes [*A publication*] (DLA) ... Swan's St
Swan's Ohio Treatise [*A publication*] (DLA) ... Swan Tr
Swan's Tennessee Reports [*31, 32 Tennessee*] [*A publication*] (DLA) ... Sw
Swan's Tennessee Reports [*A publication*] (DLA) ... Swan's
Swan's Tennessee Reports [*A publication*] (DLA) ... Swan's R
Swan's Tennessee Supreme Court Reports [*1851-53*] [*A publication*] (DLA) ... Swan
Swansboro, NC [*Location identifier FAA*] (FAAL) ... NJM
Swansea [*British ICAO location identifier*] (ICLI) ... EGFH
Swansea [*Wales*] [*Airport symbol*] (OAG) ... SWS
Swansea East Dock [*Welsh depot code*] ... SED
Swansea Free Public Library, Swansea, MA [*Library symbol*] [*Library of Congress*] (LCLS) ... MSs
Swansea Harbour Trust [*Wales*] ... SHT
Swansea Public Library, Swansea, United Kingdom [*Library symbol Library of Congress*] (LCLS) ... UkSw
Swanston's English Chancery Reports [*A publication*] (DLA) ... Sw
Swanston's English Chancery Reports [*A publication*] (DLA) ... Swan
Swanston's English Chancery Reports [*A publication*] (DLA) ... Swan Ch
Swanston's English Chancery Reports [*A publication*] (DLA) ... Swans
Swanston's English Chancery Reports [*36 English Reprint*] [*A publication*] (DLA) ... Swanst
Swanston's English Chancery Reports [*36 English Reprint*] [*A publication*] (DLA) ... Swanst (Eng)
Swanton, OH [*FM radio station call letters*] (RBYB) ... WJUC
Swanville Elementary School, Swanville, MN [*Library symbol*] [*Library of Congress*] (LCLS) ... MnSwE
Swanville High School, Swanville, MN [*Library symbol*] [*Library of Congress*] (LCLS) ... MnSwH
Swanville Public Library, Swanville, MN [*Library symbol*] [*Library of Congress*] (LCLS) ... MnSw
Swap Byte [*Computer science*] (NHD) ... SWAB
SWAP [*Salesmen with a Purpose*] **Club International** [*Arvada, CO*] (EA) ... SWAP
Swap Control Table [*Computer science*] (BYTE) ... SCT
Swap Transferring Risk with Participating Element [*Finance*] ... STRIPE
Swap-In [*Computer science*] ... SI
Swap-Out [*Computer science*] ... SOUT
Swarthmore College Peace Collection, Swarthmore, PA [*Library symbol Library of Congress*] (LCLS) ... PSC-P
Swarthmore College Peace Collection, Swarthmore, PA [*OCLC symbol*] (OCLC) ... PSP
Swarthmore College, Swarthmore, PA [*Library symbol Library of Congress OCLC symbol*] (LCLS) ... PSC
Swarthmore, PA [*FM radio station call letters*] ... WSRN
Swarthmore Public Library, Swarthmore, PA [*Library symbol Library of Congress*] (LCLS) ... PS
Swartkop [*South Africa*] [*ICAO location identifier*] (ICLI) ... FASK
Swash ... SW
Swash Bulkhead ... SWBHD
Swastika Branch, Kirkland Lake Public Library, Ontario [*Library symbol National Library of Canada*] (BIB) ... OSKL
Swatch (WGA) ... SW
Swath-Sounding Sonar (BARN) ... SASS
Swayzee Public Library, Swayzee, IN [*Library symbol Library of Congress*] (LCLS) ... InSw
Swazi Air Charter (Pty) Ltd. [*Swaziland*] [*ICAO designator*] (FAAC) ... HWK
Swaziland [*Aircraft nationality and registration mark*] (FAAC) ... 3D
Swaziland [*MARC geographic area code Library of Congress*] (LCCP) ... f-sq--
Swaziland ... SD
Swaziland [*MARC country of publication code Library of Congress*] (LCCP) ... sq
Swaziland (WDAA) ... SWAZ
Swaziland ... Swazil
Swaziland [*Swaziland*] [*Seismograph station code, US Geological Survey*] (SEIS) ... SWD
Swaziland [*ANSI three-letter standard code*] (CNC) ... SWZ
Swaziland (VRA) ... Swzld
Swaziland [*ANSI two-letter standard code*] (CNC) ... SZ
Swaziland Democratic Party ... SDP
Swaziland Progressive Party ... SPP
Swaziland United Front ... SUF
Swea City Public Library, Swea City, IA [*Library symbol Library of Congress*] (LCLS) ... IaSwc
Swear ... SW
Swearingen Aircraft [*ICAO aircraft manufacturer identifier*] (ICAO) ... SW
Sweat ... SWT
Swedair [*ICAO designator*] (AD) ... JG
Swedair AB [*Sweden ICAO designator*] (FAAC) ... SWE
Sweden [*MARC geographic area code Library of Congress*] (LCCP) ... e-sw--
Sweden [*IYRU nationality code*] ... S
Sweden [*ANSI two-letter standard code*] (CNC) ... SE
Sweden [*MARC country of publication code Library of Congress*] (LCCP) ... sw
Sweden (ODBW) ... Sw
Sweden (VRA) ... Swe
Sweden [*ANSI three-letter standard code*] (CNC) ... SWE
Sweden [*or Swedish*] ... SWED
Sweden Airways [*ICAO designator*] (FAAC) ... SWB
Sweden and Britain RADAR Auroral Experiment [*Ionospheric physics*] ... SABRE
Sweden Integrated Banking On-Line (IAA) ... SIBOL
Swedenborg Foundation (EA) ... SF
Swedenborg School of Religion, Newton, MA [*Library symbol Library of Congress*] (LCLS) ... MNtS
Swedesboro Free Public Library, Swedesboro, NJ [*Library symbol Library of Congress*] (LCLS) ... NjSw
Swedesboro News, Swedesboro, NJ [*Library symbol Library of Congress*] (LCLS) ... NjSwN
Swedish (ODBW) ... Sw
Swedish [*MARC language code Library of Congress*] (LCCP) ... swe
Swedish Agency for Administrative Development (NITA) ... SAFAD
Swedish Air Ambulance [*ICAO designator*] (FAAC) ... SAG
Swedish Air Force ... SAF
Swedish Airforce [*ICAO designator*] (FAAC) ... SDC
Swedish American Museum Association of Chicago (EA) ... SAMAC
Swedish Antarctic Expedition [*1901-04*] ... SwedAE
Swedish Aspirin Low-Dose Trial ... SALT
Swedish Behavioural Sciences [*Database*] [*National Library for Psychology and Education*] [*Information service or system*] (CRD) ... SBS
Swedish Cement and Concrete Research Institute (MCD) ... SCCRI
Swedish Chamber of Commerce for the United Kingdom (DS) ... SCCUK
Swedish Chamber of Commerce of the United States [*Later, Swedish-American Chamber of Commerce*] ... SCCUS
Swedish Colonial Society (EA) ... SCS
Swedish Council of America (EA) ... SCA
Swedish Defense Forces ... SDF
Swedish Drug Information System [*Swedish National Board of Health and Welfare*] [*Databank*] (IID) ... SWEDIS
Swedish Environmental Research Index [*Swedish National Environmental Protection Board*] [*Database*] (IID) ... SERIX
Swedish Export Credit Corp. [*Associated Press*] (SAG) ... SEHK
Swedish Export Credit Corp. [*NYSE symbol*] (SAG) ... SEP
Swedish Export Credit Corp. [*Associated Press*] (SAG) ... SwdEC
Swedish Export Credit Corp. [*AMEX symbol*] (SAG) ... SYC
Swedish Export Credit Corp. [*AMEX symbol*] (SAG) ... SYP
Swedish Hospital Medical Center, Seattle, WA [*Library symbol Library of Congress*] (LCLS) ... WaSSH
Swedish Hospital Medical Center, Seattle, WA [*Library symbol*] [*Library of Congress*] (LCLS) ... WaSSwH
Swedish Hospital, Medical Staff Library, Englewood, CO [*Library symbol Library of Congress*] (LCLS) ... CoEnS-M
Swedish Information Service, New York, NY [*Library symbol*] [*Library of Congress*] (LCLS) ... NNSIS
Swedish Inteplanetary Society (IAA) ... SIS
Swedish International Development Agency ... SIDA
Swedish Ionosonde Network ... SIN
Swedish Journalists Association of America (EA) ... SJAA
Swedish Krona [*Monetary unit*] ... S KR
Swedish Krona [*Monetary unit*] (ODBW) ... Skr
Swedish Krona [*Monetary unit*] ... SW KR
Swedish Low-Energy Experimental Pile [*Nuclear energy*] ... SLEEP
Swedish Match [*Associated Press*] (SAG) ... SwdMtch
Swedish Match [*NASDAQ symbol*] (SAG) ... SWMA
Swedish Match AB ADR [*NASDAQ symbol*] (TTSB) ... SWMAY
Swedish Medical Center, Denver, CO [*Library symbol Library of Congress*] (LCLS) ... CoDSMC

Swedish Medical Literature [Database] [Karolinska Institute Library and Information Center/Medical Information Center] [Information service or system] (CRD) .... SWEMED
Swedish National Commission for UNESCO (EAIO) .... SNCUNESCO
Swedish Pioneer Historical Society (EA) .... SPHS
Swedish Post Defense Forces .... SPDF
Swedish Question Answering Project (NITA) .... SQAP
Swedish Society Against Painful Experiments on Animals (EAIO) .... SSAPEA
Swedish Society, Discofil [Record label] [Sweden] .... SS
Swedish Space Research Committee .... SSRC
Swedish Standards Institution (IID) .... SIS
Swedish State Power Board [Nuclear energy] .... SSPB
Swedish Tactical Attack RADAR .... STAR
Swedish Tank Agility/Survivability Test (MCD) .... STAGS
Swedish Telecommunications Administration [Telecommunications] .... STA
Swedish Telecoms International AB [Telecommunications] .... SWEDTEL
Swedish Trade Office (EA) .... STO
Swedish Trial in Old Patients with Hypertension .... STOP-H
[The] Swedish University Network (TNIG) .... SUNET
Swedish Warmblood Association (EA) .... SWA
Swedish Women's Educational Association, International (EA) .... SWEA
Swedish-American Association (NADA) .... SAA
Swedish-American Historical Society (EA) .... SAHS
Swedish-American Hospital, Rockford, IL [Library symbol Library of Congress] (LCLS) .... IRoSH
Swedish-English Literary Translators Association [British] (DBA) .... SELTA
Swedish-ESO Submillimetre Telescope [Observatory] .... SEST
Sweeney's New York Superior Court Reports [A publication] (DLA) .... Sw
Sweeney's New York Superior Court Reports [31-32 New York] [1869-70] [A publication] (DLA) .... Sween
Sweeney's New York Superior Court Reports [31-32 New York] [A publication] (DLA) .... Sweeney (NY)
Sweeney's New York Superior Court Reports [31-32 New York] [A publication] (DLA) .... Sweeny
Sweeney's New York Superior Court Reports [31-32 New York] [A publication] (DLA) .... Swen
Sweep .... SWP
Sweep .... SWP
Sweep, Acoustic [British military] (DMA) .... SA
Sweep Back Station (MCD) .... SBS
Sweep Driver .... SD
Sweep Frequency, Continuous Wave .... SFCW
Sweep Generator .... SG
Sweep Integrator (AAG) .... SWINGR
Sweep Signal Generator .... SSG
Sweep Stop Alarm Jam (MCD) .... SSAJ
Sweep Stop Alarm Target [Military] (CAAL) .... SSAT
Sweeper Device [Navy symbol] .... XMAP
Sweeping Current Supply .... SCS
Sweet .... SWT
Sweet Adelines (EA) .... SA
Sweet Briar College [Virginia] .... SBC
Sweet Briar College Library, Sweet Briar, VA [OCLC symbol] (OCLC) .... VSB
Sweet Briar College, Sweet Briar, VA [Library symbol Library of Congress] (LCLS) .... ViSwC
Sweet Bugger All [An exclamation] [Slang British] (DSUE) .... SBA
Sweet Clover Necrotic Mosaic Virus [Plant pathology] .... SCNMV
Sweet Damn All [Nothing At All] [Slang] .... SDA
Sweet Dough .... SDGH
Sweet Dough Stabilizer [Brand of bakery product from H. C. Brill Co., Inc.] ...... SDS
Sweet Home, OR [AM radio station call letters] .... KFIR
Sweet Home, OR [FM radio station call letters] .... KSKD
Sweet on the Limited Liability Act [A publication] (DLA) .... Sweet
Sweet on the Limited Liability Act [A publication] (DLA) .... Sweet LL
Sweet on Wills [A publication] (DLA) .... Sweet
Sweet Potato Council of the United States (EA) .... SPCUS
Sweet Potato Feather Mottle Virus .... SPFMV
Sweet Potato Mild Mottle Virus [Plant pathology] .... SPMMV
Sweet Syndrome [Medicine] (DMAA) .... SS
Sweet Valley, PA [FM radio station call letters] .... WRGN
Sweet Yet Simple [Computer science] .... SYS
Sweet Young Thing [An attractive girl] [Slang] .... SYT
Sweetener Users Association (EA) .... SUA
Sweetens Computer Services [British] .... SCS
Sweetheart Contract [Business term] (MHDB) .... SC
Sweet's Dictionary of English Law [1882] [A publication] (DLA) .... Sweet LD
Sweet's Law Dictionary [A publication] (DLA) .... Sweet
Sweet's Marriage Settlement Cases [A publication] (DLA) .... Sweet
Sweet's Marriage Settlement Cases [England] [A publication] (DLA) .... Sweet M Sett Cas
Sweet's Precedents in Conveyancing [A publication] (DLA) .... Sweet
Sweet's Precedents in Conveyancing [4th ed.] [1886] [A publication] (DLA) .... Sweet Pr Conv
Sweet's Technical Information Test [Vocational guidance test] .... STIT
Sweetwater [Texas] [Airport symbol] (AD) .... SWW
Sweetwater City-County Library, Sweetwater, TX [Library symbol Library of Congress] (LCLS) .... TxSw
SweetWater, Inc. [Associated Press] (SAG) .... SweetW
SweetWater, Inc. [NASDAQ symbol] (SAG) .... SWWT
Sweetwater Inc. [NASDAQ symbol] (TTSB) .... SWWT
Sweetwater Library, Gypsum, CO [Library symbol Library of Congress] (LCLS) .... CoGyS
Sweetwater, TN [AM radio station call letters] .... WDEH
Sweetwater, TN [FM radio station call letters] .... WDEH-FM
Sweetwater, TX [Television station call letters] .... KTXS

Sweetwater, TX [AM radio station call letters] .... KXOX
Sweetwater, TX [FM radio station call letters] .... KXOX-FM
Sweetwater, TX [Location identifier FAA] (FAAL) .... SWW
Swell Organ .... SW
Swellendam [South Africa] [ICAO location identifier] (ICLI) .... FASX
Swelling of Ankles [Medicine] (DMAA) .... SOA
Swelling Power [Food technology] .... SP
Swelling, Tenderness, Limitation of Movement [Medicine] .... STL
Swensen's, Inc. [Vancouver Stock Exchange symbol] .... SWE
Swept Angle Retarding Ion Mass Spectrometer (PDAA) .... SARIMS
Swept Area [Automotive engineering] .... SA
Swept Delta Wing .... SDW
Swept Forward Wing [Aviation] (PDAA) .... SFW
Swept Frequency Continuous Wave Illumination (MCD) .... SFCW(I)
Swept Frequency Jamming .... SFJ
Swept Frequency Modulation .... SFM
Swept Frequency Radiometer System .... SFRS
Swept Frequency Topside Sounder (SAA) .... SFTS
Swept Frequency Transform (CAAL) .... SWT
Swept Gain Control (DA) .... SGC
Swept Local Oscillator (IEEE) .... SLO
Swept Local Oscillator .... SLOS
Swept Local Oscillator Receiver (NG) .... SLOR
Swept Square Wave (MCD) .... SSW
Swept Tone .... ST
Swept Volume .... SV
Swept Volume Efficiency [Air Force] .... SVE
Swept Wing with Inboard Flap for Trim [Hang glider] (PS) .... SWIFT
Swets Automated Independant Library System (NITA) .... SAILS
Swift & Company, Research Laboratory Library, Chicago, IL [Library symbol Library of Congress] (LCLS) .... ICSC
Swift Current [Saskatchewan] [Airport symbol] (AD) .... YYN
Swift Current, SK [FM radio station call letters] .... CIMG
Swift Current, SK [Television station call letters] .... CJFB
Swift Current, SK [Television station call letters] .... CKMC
Swift Current, SK [AM radio station call letters] .... CKSW
Swift Current, SK [ICAO location identifier] (ICLI) .... CYYN
Swift Energy [NYSE symbol] (TTSB) .... SFY
Swift Energy Co. [NYSE symbol] (SPSG) .... SFY
Swift Energy Co. [Associated Press] (SAG) .... SwftEng
SWIFT [Society for Worldwide Interbank Financial Telecommunications] Interface Device .... SID
Swift Minerals Ltd. [Vancouver Stock Exchange symbol] .... SWS
Swift Museum Foundation (EA) .... SMF
Swift on Evidence, and Bills and Notes [A publication] (DLA) .... Swift Ev
Swift River Valley Historical Society, New Salem, MA [Library symbol Library of Congress] (LCLS) .... MNSaS
Swift Target Identification Notification Grid (MCD) .... STING
Swift Transportation [NASDAQ symbol] (TTSB) .... SWFT
Swift Transportation Co. [NASDAQ symbol] (SAG) .... SWFT
Swift Transportation Co. [Associated Press] (SAG) .... SwiftT
Swiftair Cargo Ltd. [Canada ICAO designator] (FAAC) .... SCL
Swiftair SA [Spain ICAO designator] (FAAC) .... SWT
Swift-Aire Lines [ICAO designator] (AD) .... WI
Swift-Eckrich, Research and Development Information Center Library, Oak Brook, IL [Library symbol] [Library of Congress] (LCLS) .... IObSE
Swiftlines Ltd. [Kenya] [ICAO designator] (FAAC) .... SLC
Swift's Connecticut Digest [A publication] (DLA) .... Swift Dig
Swift's System of the Laws of Connecticut [A publication] (DLA) .... Swift Sys
Swim Criteria .... SWIMCRIT
Swim the Ontario Waterways [Personal incentive program for fitness swimmers] [Ontario Masters Swimming Club] .... STOW
Swimmer and Navigation System [Navy] (CAAL) .... SANS
Swimmer Delivery Vehicle [Navy symbol Obsolete] (MCD) .... SDV
Swimmer Delivery Vehicle Support Craft (DNAB) .... ASDV
Swimmer Distress Signal [Navy] (CAAL) .... SDS
Swimmer Life Support System [Navy] (CAAL) .... SLSS
Swimmer Support Boat .... SSB
Swimmer-Canoeist [British military] (DMA) .... SC
Swimmer's Air Breathing Apparatus [Deep-sea diving] .... SABA
Swimming Club .... SC
Swimming Pool and Allied Trades Association [British] (DBA) .... SPATA
Swimming Pool and Spa Association of Australia .... SPSAA
Swimming Teachers' Association [British] .... STA
Swinburne Film and Television School [Australia] .... SFTS
Swinburne Institute of Technology [Australia] .... SIT
Swinburne on Descents [1825] [A publication] (DLA) .... Swinb Desc
Swinburne on Married Women [1846] [A publication] (DLA) .... Swinb Mar
Swinburne on Spousals [A publication] (DLA) .... Swinb Spo
Swinburne on Wills [10 eds.] [1590-1803] [A publication] (DLA) .... Swin
Swinburne on Wills [A publication] (DLA) .... Swinb Wills
Swinburne University of Technology [Australia] .... SUT
Swinderby [British ICAO location identifier] (ICLI) .... EGXS
Swinderby FTU [British ICAO designator] (FAAC) .... SWD
Swindon [British depot code] .... SDN
Swine [Veterinary medicine] (DAVI) .... Sw
Swine Vesicular Disease [Medicine] (DMAA) .... SVD
Swinehead [England] .... SWIN
Swing (MSA) .... SWG
Swing Arm (KSC) .... SA
Swing Grip Thermal Stripper .... SGTS
Swing [Parachute] Landing Trainer [Military] (INF) .... SLT
Swing Rate Discriminator (IAA) .... SRD
Swing-Arm Beam Erector (MCD) .... SABER
Swinging Door .... SWGD

Swing-N-Slide [*Associated Press*] (SAG) ... SwingNSl
Swing-N-Slide Corp. [*AMEX symbol*] (SAG) ... SWG
Swing-N-Slide Corp. [*Associated Press*] (SAG) ... SwingSl
Swink Public Library, Swink, CO [*Library symbol Library of Congress*] (LCLS) ... CoSw
Swinton's Scotch Justiciary Cases [*A publication*] (DLA) ... Sw
Swinton's Scotch Justiciary Cases [*A publication*] (DLA) ... Swin Jus Cas
Swinton's Scotch Justiciary Cases [*A publication*] (DLA) ... Swint
Swinton's Scotch Justiciary Reports [*1835-41*] [*A publication*] (DLA) ... Swin
Swinton's Scotch Registration Appeal Cases [*1835-41*] [*A publication*] (DLA) ... Swin Reg App
Swirl Control Valve [*Automotive engine design*] ... SCV
Swirl Jet ... SJ
Swirling Circulating Fluidized Bed ... SCFB
Swisher International [*Commercial firm Associated Press*] (SAG) ... Swish
Swisher International [*Commercial firm Associated Press*] (SAG) ... Swisher
Swisher International [*NASDAQ symbol*] (SAG) ... SWSH
Swisher International Group ... SWR
Swisher Intl Wrrt [*NASDAQ symbol*] (TTSB) ... SWSHW
Swiss ... SW
Swiss Agammaglobulinemia [*Medicine*] (MAE) ... SAG
Swiss Air Defense System ... SADS
Swiss Air-Ambulance Ltd. [*ICAO designator*] (FAAC) ... SAZ
Swiss Army Brands [*NASDAQ symbol*] (TTSB) ... SABI
Swiss Association for Friendship with China (EAIO) ... SAFC
Swiss Association of Autonomous Unions ... SAAU
Swiss Bank Corp. ... SBC
Swiss Bank Corp. International ... SBCI
Swiss Bank Corp./O'Connor & Associates Services (ECON) ... SBC/OC
Swiss Benevolent Society of New York (EA) ... SBS
Swiss Broadcasting Corp. ... SBC
Swiss Center of Documentation in Microtechnology [*Information service or system*] (IID) ... CENTREDOC
Swiss Federal Institute of Technology (IAA) ... SFIT
Swiss Federation of National-Christian Trade Unions ... SFNCTU
Swiss Federation of Protestant Trade Unions ... SFPTU
Swiss Federation of Watch Manufacturers (EA) ... SFWM
Swiss Franc [*Monetary unit*] ... S FR
Swiss Franc [*Monetary unit*] ... SF
Swiss Helvetia Fund [*NYSE symbol*] (SPSG) ... SWZ
Swiss Helvetia Fund, Inc. [*Associated Press*] (SAG) ... SwHelv
Swiss Institute for Nuclear Research ... SINR
Swiss Institute for Technical Information [*Information service or system*] (IID) ... SITI
Swiss Institute of Nuclear Research - Eidgenoessische Technische Hochschule ... SIN-ETH
Swiss Intellectual Property Office [*Bern*] [*Information service or system*] (IID) ... SIPO
Swiss Market Index (ECON) ... SMI
Swiss Mouse [*Medicine*] (DMAA) ... S
Swiss Mouse Embryo Tissue Culture ... SMETC
Swiss National Bank ... SNB
Swiss National Tourist Office (EA) ... SNTO
Swiss Nonvaleurs Club [*Later, Scripophila Helvetica - SH*] (EAIO) ... SNC
Swiss Options and Financial Futures Exchange ... SOFFEX
Swiss Party of Labour ... SPL
Swiss Radio International ... SRI
Swiss Railways Society [*British*] (DBA) ... SRS
Swiss Red Cross ... SRC
Swiss Review of World Affairs [*A publication*] ... SRWA
Swiss Society of Engineers and Architects (IAA) ... SIA
Swiss Society of New York (EA) ... SSNY
Swiss Videotex Industry Association [*Information service or system*] (IID) ... SVIPA
Swiss Viewdata Information Providers Association [*Zurich*] [*Telecommunications*] ... SVIPA
Swiss Volksbank [*Bank*] ... V
Swiss Watch ... SWATCH
Swiss Webster Mouse [*Medicine*] (DMAA) ... SW
Swiss Wildlife Information Service [*Zurich*] [*Information service or system*] (IID) ... SWIS
Swiss Yiddish (BJA) ... SWY
Swissair [*Airline*] [*ICAO designator*] ... SR
Swissair [*Airline*] (MCD) ... SWA
Swissair (Societe Anonyme Switzerland pour la Navigation Aerienne) [*ICAO designator*] (FAAC) ... SWR
Swiss-American Aircraft Corp. (IAA) ... SAAC
Swiss-American Historical Society (EA) ... SAHS
Swiss-Australian Chamber of Commerce and Industry [*Australia*] ... SACCI
Swissray International, Inc. [*NASDAQ symbol*] (SAG) ... SRMI
Swissray International, Inc. [*Associated Press*] (SAG) ... Swissray
SWISSRAY Intl [*NASDAQ symbol*] (TTSB) ... SRMI
Switch ... S
Switch (AAG) ... SW
Switch (IDOE) ... sw
Switch (MCD) ... SWCH
Switch Action Interrupt Count ... SAIC
Switch Alarm (AAG) ... SWALM
Switch and Cable Distribution Unit (AAG) ... S & CDU
Switch and Cable Distribution Unit (IAA) ... SACDU
Switch Busy Hour [*Telecommunications*] (IEEE) ... SBH
Switch Closure In (MCD) ... SCI
Switch Closure Out (MCD) ... SCO
Switch Control Assembly ... SCA
Switch Control Unit (MCD) ... SCU
Switch Driver ... SD
Switch Element Controller [*Telecommunications*] ... SEC
Switch Group Assembly ... SGA
Switch Handler [*Telecommunications*] (TEL) ... SH
Switch Hook (HGAA) ... SH
Switch Interpretation (IAA) ... SI
Switch Maintenance Center [*Telecommunications*] (TEL) ... SMC
Switch Matrix (MCD) ... SWMAT
Switch Mode Power Amplifier (DWSG) ... SMPA
Switch Mode Power Supply (EECA) ... SMPS
Switch, Modular, Attenuator (IAA) ... SMA
Switch Off Assembly (MCD) ... SOA
Switch Panel ... SP
Switch Port [*Telecommunications*] ... SP
Switch Processing Element (NITA) ... SPE
Switch Rails ... SWR
Switch Register ... SR
Switch Scan (MCD) ... SWS
Switch Selector (KSC) ... SS
Switch Selector Update ... SSU
Switch Stand ... SWS
Switch Tail Interceptor Missile (MCD) ... SWIM
Switch Tail Ring Counter ... STRC
Switch Ties ... SWT
Switchable Acoustic Filter ... SAF
Switchable Acoustic Matched Filter ... SAMF
Switchable Matched Filter ... SMF
Switchable-Input Operational Amplifier [*Electronics*] (EECA) ... SWOP AMP
Switch-Backup Entry [*NASA*] (KSC) ... SBUE
Switchband Wound [*Relay*] ... SW
Switchblade Knife Act ... SKA
Switchboard [*Telecommunications*] (TEL) ... S
Switchboard ... SB
Switchboard (NATG) ... SWB
Switchboard (AAG) ... SWBD
Switchboard Detachment (IAA) ... SBDET
Switchboard Operation Detachment (IAA) ... SBOPERDET
Switchboard Operator [*Navy*] ... SB
Switchboard Operator (IAA) ... SWBDOP
Switchboard Operator [*British military*] (DMA) ... SWOP
Switchboard Panel [*Telecommunications*] (TEL) ... PAN
Switched Access Remote Test System [*Bell System*] ... SARTS
Switched Access System [*Telecommunications*] (TEL) ... SAS
Switched Capacitor [*Electronics*] (IAA) ... SC
Switched Circuit Automatic Network [*Army*] ... SCAN
Switched Collector Impedance [*Electronics*] (OA) ... SCI
Switched Data Access Line ... SDAL
Switched Data Service Unit [*Computer science*] (MHDI) ... SDSU
Switched Digital Data Service [*Southern New England Telephone*] ... SDDS
Switched Digital International [*AT&T*] (CDE) ... SDI
Switched Ground Discrete Input (MCD) ... SGDI
Switched Ground Discrete Output (MCD) ... SGDO
Switched in for Checkout [*NASA*] (KSC) ... SICO
Switched In-Flight (KSC) ... SIF
Switched Maintenance Access System [*Bell System*] ... SMAS
Switched Multimegabit Data Service [*Telecommunications*] (PCM) ... SMDS
Switched Multiple Instruction, Multiple Data Stream [*Computer science*] (MHDI) ... SMIMD
Switched Network Backup [*Computer science*] (IBMDP) ... SNBU
Switched Network Server [*Tylink Corp.*] ... SNS
Switched out for Checkout [*NASA*] (KSC) ... SOCO
Switched Private Network Service [*ITT service mark*] ... SPNS
Switched Programmable Read-Only Memory ... SPROM
Switched Proton Electron Challeltron Spectrometer (BARN) ... SPECS
Switched Public Network [*Telecommunications*] (IAA) ... SPN
Switched Reluctance ... SR
Switched Reluctance Motor (ECON) ... SRM
Switched Service Network [*Telecommunications*] ... SSN
Switched Telecommunications Network ... STN
Switched Virtual Call [*Telecommunications*] (NITA) ... SVC
Switched Virtual Circuit ... SVC
Switched-Mode Power Supply (PDAA) ... SMPS
Switcher [*Broadcasting*] (WDMC) ... SW
Switchgear ... SWGR
Switchgear Block (MSA) ... SGB
Switching (WGA) ... SWG
Switching (WGA) ... SWTG
Switching and Maintenance Set ... SMS
Switching and Processing Center [*EFTS*] [*Banking*] ... SPC
Switching Assembly (IAA) ... SA
Switching Cell (IEEE) ... SC
Switching Central [*Telecommunications*] (AABC) ... SWCENT
Switching, Conferencing, and Monitoring Arrangement [*NASA*] ... SCAMA
Switching Control [*Telecommunications*] (IAA) ... SWC
Switching Control Center [*Bell System*] ... SCC
Switching Control Center System [*Telecommunications*] (TEL) ... SCCS
Switching Devices [*JETDS nomenclature*] [*Military*] (CET) ... SA
Switching Element (IAA) ... SE
Switching Equipment Congestion [*Telecommunications*] (TEL) ... SEC
Switching Filter Connector ... SFC
Switching Linear Amplifier ... SLA
Switching Logic Unit (CAAL) ... SLU
Switching Mode Frequency Multipliers ... SFM
Switching Mode Regulator ... SMR
Switching Network Analysis Program [*Bell System*] ... SNAP

Switching Network Junction [*Telecommunications*] (OA) .... SNJ
Switching Node and Processing Sites [*ITT*] (TEL) .... SNAPS
Switching Oscilloscope .... SO
Switching Selector Repeater (PDAA) .... SSR
Switching Service Operations Center [*Telecommunications*] .... SSOC
Switching System Engineer (IAA) .... SSE
Switching, Transmitting, Receiving, and Distribution .... STRAD
Switching Unit .... SU
Switching Unit .... SUN
Switchman (WGA) .... SWCHMN
Switchman's Local Test [*Telecommunications*] (TEL) .... SLT
Switchmen's Union of North America [*Later, United Transportation Union*] .... SUNA
Switchover .... SO
Switchover .... SW/O
Switchover (MSA) .... SWOV
Switch-to-Computer Applications Interface (CDE) .... SCAI
Switch-to-Computer Link (CDE) .... SCL
Switchyard Relay House [*Nuclear energy*] (NRCH) .... SRH
Switzerland [*ANSI two-letter standard code*] (CNC) .... CH
Switzerland [*ANSI three-letter standard code*] (CNC) .... CHE
Switzerland [*MARC geographic area code Library of Congress*] (LCCP) .... e-sz--
Switzerland .... SW
Switzerland .... SWIT
Switzerland .... SWITZ
Switzerland (VRA) .... Switz
Switzerland .... SWTZ
Switzerland [*MARC country of publication code Library of Congress*] (LCCP) .... sz
Switzerland [*IYRU nationality code*] (IYR) .... Z
Switzerland Cheese Association [*Defunct*] (EA) .... SCA
Switzerland County Public Library, Vevay, IN [*Library symbol Library of Congress*] (LCLS) .... InVe
Switzerland County Recorder's Office, Vevay, IN [*Library symbol Library of Congress*] (LCLS) .... InVeCR
Switzerland Democrat, Vevay, IN [*Library symbol Library of Congress*] (LCLS) .... InVeSD
Swivel (AAG) .... SWV
Swivel (MSA) .... SWVL
Swiveling Gunner's Station .... SGS
Swiveling Jet Engine .... SJE
Sword and Sorcery .... S & S
Swordsmen and Sorcerers' Guild of America (EA) .... SSGA
Sworn (ROG) .... SWN
Sworn Statement .... SS
SX-70 (VRA) SX70
SXT Resources Ltd. [*Vancouver Stock Exchange symbol*] .... SX
S.Y. Bancorp [*Associated Press*] (SAG) .... SY Bcp
S.Y. Bancorp [*NASDAQ symbol*] (SAG) .... SYBA
Syanboche [*Nepal*] [*ICAO location identifier*] (ICLI) .... VNSB
Sybase, Inc. [*Associated Press*] (SAG) .... Sybase
Sybase, Inc. [*NASDAQ symbol*] (SPSG) .... SYBS
Sybron Chemical Industries [*Associated Press*] (SAG) .... Sybron
Sybron Chemicals [*NASDAQ symbol*] (TTSB) .... SYCM
Sybron Chemicals, Inc. [*NASDAQ symbol*] (SPSG) .... SYCM
Sybron Corp., Medical Products Division Library, Rochester, NY [*OCLC symbol*] (OCLC) .... RVK
Sybron Corp., Pfaudler Division Technical Library, Henrietta, NY [*OCLC symbol*] (OCLC) .... RVL
Sybron Corp., Rochester, NY [*Library symbol Library of Congress*] (LCLS) .... NRRP
Sybron Corp., Taylor Division Research Library, Rochester, NY [*OCLC symbol*] (OCLC) .... RVM
Sybron International Co. [*Formerly, Sybron Corp.*] [*NYSE symbol*] (SAG) .... SYB
Sybron International Co. [*Formerly, Sybron Corp.*] [*Associated Press*] (SAG) .... SybronInt
Sybron Intl [*NYSE symbol*] (TTSB) .... SYB
Sycamore (AAG) .... SYC
Sycamore, IL [*AM radio station call letters*] .... WSQR
Sycamore Public Library, Sycamore, IL [*Library symbol Library of Congress*] (LCLS) .... ISy
Sycamore Test Procedure [*Aerospace*] (AAG) .... STP
Sychronize (IAA) .... SYCR
Sydaero [*ICAO designator*] (AD) .... UF
Sydenham Branch, Frontenac County Library, Ontario [*Library symbol National Library of Canada*] (BIB) .... OSYFC
Syder [*Bulgaria*] [*ICAO designator*] (FAAC) .... SDR
Sydfyn/Tasinge [*Denmark ICAO location identifier*] (ICLI) .... EKST
Sydney [*Australia ICAO location identifier*] (ICLI) .... ASKS
Sydney [*Australia ICAO location identifier*] (ICLI) .... ASRF
Sydney [*Australia ICAO location identifier*] (ICLI) .... ASSR
Sydney [*Australia ICAO location identifier*] (ICLI) .... ASSS
Sydney [*Australia ICAO location identifier*] (ICLI) .... ASSX
Sydney [*Australia Airport symbol*] (OAG) .... LBH
Sydney [*Australia Airport symbol*] (OAG) .... SYD
Sydney [*Australia Seismograph station code, US Geological Survey Closed*] (SEIS) .... SYD
Sydney [*Canada*] [*Airport symbol*] (OAG) .... YQY
Sydney & Louisburg Railway Co. [*AAR code*] .... SL
Sydney Anglican Schools Corp. [*Commercial firm*] .... SASC
Sydney/Bankstown [*Australia ICAO location identifier*] (ICLI) .... ASBK
Sydney Basketball Council [*Australia*] .... SBC
Sydney College of the Arts [*Australia*] .... SCOA
Sydney Computerised Overnight Market [*Australia*] .... SYCOM
Sydney Conservatorium of Music [*Australia*] .... SCM
Sydney Coordinated Adaptive Traffic System [*FHWA*] (TAG) .... SCATS
Sydney Entertainment Centre [*Australia*] .... SEC
Sydney Esperanto Society [*Australia*] .... SES
Sydney Fire District [*Australia*] .... SFD
Sydney Garden Festival [*Australia*] .... SGF
Sydney Godolphin Osborne [*Literary signature of 19th-century British writer*] .... SGO
Sydney Greens [*Political party Australia*] .... SG
Sydney Harbour National Park [*Australia*] .... SHNP
Sydney Indochinese Refugee Youth Support Group [*Australia*] .... SICRYS
Sydney Journalists' Club [*Australia*] .... SJC
Sydney Junior Chamber of Commerce [*Australia*] .... SJCC
Sydney/Kingsford Smith International [*Australia ICAO location identifier*] (ICLI) .... ASSY
Sydney Metropolitan Area [*Australia*] .... SMA
Sydney Morning Herald [*Database*] .... SMH
Sydney, NS [*Television station call letters*] CBHFT-3
Sydney, NS [*AM radio station call letters*] .... CBI
Sydney, NS [*FM radio station call letters*] .... CBI-FM
Sydney, NS [*Television station call letters*] .... CBIT
Sydney, NS [*AM radio station call letters*] .... CHER
Sydney, NS [*AM radio station call letters*] .... CJCB
Sydney, NS [*Television station call letters*] .... CJCB-TV
Sydney, NS [*FM radio station call letters*] .... CKPE
Sydney, NS [*ICAO location identifier*] (ICLI) .... CYQY
Sydney Ocean Meeting Point [*Navy*] .... SOMP
Sydney Paralympic Organising Committee [*Australia*] .... SPOC
Sydney Rainforest Action Group (EERA) .... SRAG
Sydney Regional Environmental Plan [*Australia*] .... SREP
Sydney Regional Planning Authority [*Proposed*] [*Australia*] .... SRPA
Sydney Review [*A publication*] .... Syd R
Sydney Statistical Division [*Australia*] .... SSD
Sydney Stock Exchange [*Australia*] (ADA) .... SSE
Sydney Transport Coordination Advisory Council [*New South Wales, Australia*] .... STCAC
Sydney University [*State*] (EERA) .... SU
Sydney University. Gazette [*A publication*] .... Sydney Univ Gaz
Sydney University Press [*Australia*] (ADA) .... SUP
Sydney University. Review [*A publication*] .... Sydney Univ Rev
Sydney UNIX Network (TNIG) .... SUN III
Sydney Wastewater Action Program [*Australia*] .... SWAP
Sydney-Rose Bay [*Australia Airport symbol*] (OAG) .... RSE
Sydslesvigsk Vaelgerforening [*South Schleswig Voters' Association*] [*Also, SSW*] [*Germany*] [*Political party*] (PPW) .... SSV
SYFA Concurrent Logic Operating System .... SYCLOPS
SYFA Current Logic Operating System (NITA) .... SYCLOPS
Syferfontein [*South Africa*] [*ICAO location identifier*] (ICLI) .... FASY
Sykepleiernes Samarbeid i Norden [*Northern Nurses Federation - NNF*] (EAIO) .... SSN
Sykes Enterprises, Inc. (PCM) .... SEI
Sykes Enterprises Inc. [*NASDAQ symbol*] (SAG) .... SYKE
Sykes Enterprises Inc. [*Associated Press*] (SAG) .... SykesEn
Syktyvkar [*Former USSR ICAO location identifier*] (ICLI) .... UUYY
Sylacauga, AL [*Location identifier FAA*] (FAAL) .... SCD
Sylacauga, AL [*FM radio station call letters*] .... WAWV
Sylacauga, AL [*AM radio station call letters*] .... WFEB
Sylacauga, AL [*AM radio station call letters*] .... WYEA
Sylhet [*Bangladesh*] [*Airport symbol*] (OAG) .... ZYL
Sylhet Osmani [*Bangladesh*] [*ICAO location identifier*] (ICLI) .... VGSY
[*The*] **Syllabi** [*A publication*] (DLA) .... Syl
Syllable (ADA) .... SYL
Syllable .... SYLL
Syllable Duration [*Entomology*] .... SD
Syllable Hyphen Character [*Computer science*] .... SHY
Syllable Number [*Entomology*] .... SN
Syllable Period [*Entomology*] .... SP
Syllable Repetition Interval [*Entomology*] .... SRI
Syllabus (WDAA) .... SYL
Sylloge Inscriptionum Religionis Isiacae et Sarapiacae [*A publication*] (BJA) .... SIRIS
Sylva, NC [*AM radio station call letters*] .... WRGC
Sylvan Foods Holdings, Inc. [*Associated Press*] (SAG) .... Sylvan
Sylvan, Inc. [*NASDAQ symbol*] (SAG) .... SYLN
Sylvan Lake Public Library, Alberta [*Library symbol National Library of Canada*] (NLC) .... ASYL
Sylvan Learning Systems [*Montgomery, AL*] [*NASDAQ symbol*] (NQ) .... SLVN
Sylvan Learning Systems [*Commercial firm Associated Press*] (SAG) .... SylvnLrn
Sylvania Central Railroad (IIA) .... SC
Sylvania Electric Products, Inc. (KSC) .... SEPI
Sylvania Electronic Systems (SAA) .... SES
Sylvania Electronics Systems, Inc., Mountain View, CA [*Library symbol Library of Congress*] (LCLS) .... CMvS
Sylvania, GA [*AM radio station call letters*] .... WSYL
Sylvania, GA [*FM radio station call letters*] .... WZBX
Sylvania High-Intelligence Electronic Defense (MCD) .... SHIELD
Sylvania Multimode Tracking [*Aerospace*] (MCD) .... SYMMTRAC
Sylvania, OH [*FM radio station call letters*] .... WWWM
Sylvania Schools, Sylvania, OH [*Library symbol*] [*Library of Congress*] (LCLS) .... OSyS
Sylvania Ultrahigh-Level Logic (IEEE) .... SUHL
Sylvania Universal High-Level Logic (IAA) .... SUHL
Sylvania-Corning Nuclear Corp. .... SCN
Sylvester, GA [*Location identifier FAA*] (FAAL) .... SYV
Sylvester, GA [*FM radio station call letters*] .... WRXZ
Sylvester, GA [*FM radio station call letters*] .... WWSG

Sylvester Memorial Wellston Public Library, Wellston, OH [*Library symbol Library of Congress*] (LCLS) .... OWel
Sylvia Fan Club (EA) .... SFC
Sylvia Packard Junior High School, North Massapequa, NY [*Library symbol*] [*Library of Congress*] (LCLS) .... NNomPJ
Symantec Antivirus for Macintosh [*Computer science*] (CDE) .... SAM
Symantec Corp. [*NASDAQ symbol*] (NQ) .... SYMC
Symantec Corp. [*Associated Press*] (SAG) .... Symntc
Symantec Utilities for Macintosh [*Computer software*] (CDE) .... SUM
Symbionese Liberation Army [*Defunct*] (EA) .... SLA
Symbionics On-Line Information System [*Computer science*] .... SOLIS
Symbiont .... SYM
Symbiotic Bacteria [*Ecology*] .... SB
Symbol (IAA) .... SY
Symbol [*Spain ICAO designator*] (FAAC) .... SYB
Symbol [*or Symbolic*] (AAG) .... SYM
Symbol (IDOE) .... sym
Symbol .... SYMB
Symbol Acquisition Routine .... SAR
Symbol Conversion Program (NITA) .... SCP
Symbol Correspondence Element [*Computer science*] (PCM) .... SYC
Symbol Elaboration Test [*Psychology*] .... SET
Symbol Element [*Computer science*] (PCM) .... SYE
Symbol Generation and Storage [*Computer science*] .... SGS
Symbol Generator .... SG
Symbol Graph [*Computer science*] (PCM) .... SYG
Symbol Location Point (NITA) .... SLP
Symbol Manipulation [*Computer science*] .... SYMAN
Symbol Processing Machine (IEEE) .... SPM
Symbol Programmer (MUGU) .... SP
Symbol, SA [*Spain*] [*FAA designator*] (FAAC) .... ANS
Symbol Sink - Matched Filter .... SSMF
Symbol Synchronizer Assembly [*NASA*] .... SSA
Symbol Table (IAA) .... ST
Symbol Table Counter [*Computer science*] (IAA) .... STC
Symbol Technologies [*NYSE symbol*] (TTSB) .... SBL
Symbol Technologies, Inc. [*NYSE symbol*] (SPSG) .... SBL
Symbol Technologies, Inc. [*Associated Press*] (SAG) .... SyblTc
Symbol Time Recovery (NITA) .... STR
Symbol Value [*Computer science*] (PCM) .... SYV
Symbolae Philologicae [*O. A.*] **Danielsson Octogenario Dicatae** [*Uppsala*] [*A publication*] (OCD) .... Symb Philol Danielsson
Symbolic Address Program .... SAP
Symbolic Algebraic Language [*Computer science*] .... SYMBAL
Symbolic Algebraic Language Translator [*Computer science*] .... SALT
Symbolic and Algebraic Manipulation (IEEE) .... SAM
Symbolic Application Debugging Environment .... SADE
Symbolic Assembler (IEEE) .... SA
Symbolic Assembler for Binary Relocatable Programs .... SABR
Symbolic Assembly Language [*Computer science*] (DIT) .... SAL
Symbolic Assembly Program [*Computer science*] .... SAP
Symbolic Automatic Integrator .... SAINT
Symbolic Code (AAG) .... SC
Symbolic Conversion Program (BUR) .... SCP
Symbolic Correction Loader .... SCL
Symbolic Corrector (SAA) .... SYC
Symbolic Debugger [*Also, SOLD, SYMDEB*] [*Computer science*] (BYTE) .... sdb
Symbolic Debugger [*Also, sdb, SYMDEB*] [*Computer science*] .... SOLD
Symbolic Debugger [*Computer science*] (MHDI) .... SYMBUG
Symbolic Debugger [*Also, sdb, SOLD*] [*Computer science*] .... SYMDEB
Symbolic Device Address .... SDA
Symbolic Disk Address (AFM) .... SDA
Symbolic Displays, Inc. (MCD) .... SDI
Symbolic Equations Program (IAA) .... SEP
Symbolic File Directory [*Computer science*] (HGAA) .... SFD
Symbolic File Support .... SFS
Symbolic Flowchart Language (IAA) .... SFL
Symbolic Hierarchical Automated Reliability and Performance Evaluator .... SHARPE
Symbolic Horribly Optimizing Assembly Program (IAA) .... SHOAP
Symbolic Information Retrieval (IAA) .... SIRE
Symbolic Input [*Computer science*] .... SI
Symbolic Input Program [*Computer science*] (BUR) .... SIP
Symbolic Input Routine [*Computer science*] (DIT) .... SIR
Symbolic Integrated Maintenance (IAA) .... SIM
Symbolic Integrated Maintenance Manual (MCD) .... SIMM
Symbolic Integrated Maintenance System .... SIMS
Symbolic Integrator .... SIN
Symbolic Language Adapted for Microcomputers .... SLAM
Symbolic Language Assembly Program [*Computer science*] (KSC) .... SLAP
Symbolic Layout System (MCD) .... SLS
Symbolic Link [*Data format*] .... SYLK
Symbolic List Processing (NITA) .... SLISP
Symbolic List Processor .... SLIP
Symbolic Machine Language [*Computer science*] .... SML
Symbolic Manipulation [*Computer science*] .... SM
Symbolic Manipulation Language [*Computer science*] (CSR) .... SYMBOLANG
Symbolic Mathematics Program .... SMP
Symbolic Matrix Interpretation System .... SMIS
Symbolic Modeling [*Computer science*] .... SYMMOD
Symbolic Operating System [*Computer science*] .... SOS
Symbolic Optimum Assembly Programming [*IBM Corp.*] [*Computer science*] .... SOAP
Symbolic Optimum Program .... SOP
Symbolic Output [*Computer science*] .... SO
Symbolic Pictorial Indicator (MCD) .... SPI
Symbolic Play Test [*Child development test*] .... SPT
Symbolic Processing Array [*Computer science*] .... SPA
Symbolic Processing Using RISC [*Reduced Instruction Set Computer*] .... SPUR
Symbolic Program Assembly Routine [*Computer science*] .... SPAR
Symbolic Program for Automatic Control .... SYMPAC
Symbolic Program System (NITA) .... SPS
Symbolic Program Tape [*Computer science*] (IEEE) .... SPT
Symbolic Program Translator [*Computer science*] (IEEE) .... SPT
Symbolic Programming Anyone Can Enjoy .... SPACE
Symbolic Programming Language [*Computer science*] (IAA) .... SPL
Symbolic Programming System [*Computer science*] .... SPS
Symbolic Representations for Image Understanding System (MHDI) .... SYRIUS
Symbolic Shorthand System .... SSS
Symbolic Stream Generator [*Computer science*] .... SSG
Symbolic Unit (IAA) .... SU
Symbolic Unit Number [*Computer science*] (WDAA) .... SUN
Symbolic Utilities Revenue Environment [*IBM Corp.*] .... SURE
Symbolization All Series (ADA) .... SYMBAS
Symbollon Corp. [*Associated Press*] (SAG) .... Symb
Symbollon Corp. [*NASDAQ symbol*] (TTSB) .... SYMBA
Symbollon Corp. [*Associated Press*] (SAG) .... Symbl
Symbollon Corp. [*Associated Press*] (SAG) .... Symboln
Symbollon Corp. Wrrt'A' [*NASDAQ symbol*] (TTSB) .... SYMBW
Symbollon Corp. Wrrt'B' [*NASDAQ symbol*] (TTSB) .... SYMBZ
Symbology Annotation (MCD) .... SYM/ANNOT
Symbols per Second [*Computer science*] .... SPS
Symbols, Units, and Nomenclature [*Commission*] [*IUPAC*] .... SUN
Symbols-Digits-Alphabetics .... SDA
Symbral Foundation (EA) .... SF
Symes Resources [*Vancouver Stock Exchange symbol*] .... SYI
Syme's Scotch Justiciary Reports [*1826-30*] [*A publication*] (DLA) .... Syme
Symetrics Industries [*NASDAQ symbol*] (TTSB) .... SYMT
Symetrics Industries, Inc. [*Associated Press*] (SAG) .... Symetr
Symetrics Industries, Inc. [*NASDAQ symbol*] (NQ) .... SYMT
Symfoni & Artist [*Record label*] [*Sweden*] .... Symf
Symix Systems [*Associated Press*] (SAG) .... Symix
Symix Systems [*NASDAQ symbol*] (SPSG) .... SYMX
Symmachus (BJA) .... Sy
Symmachus' Greek Translation of the Bible [*A publication*] (BJA) .... Sym
Symmetric Clipper .... SCL
Symmetric Exchange of Symmetry [*Spectrometry*] .... SEOS
Symmetric List Interpretive Program [*Computer science*] .... SLIP
Symmetric List Processor [*FORTRAN extension*] .... SLIP
Symmetric Multiprocessing .... SMP
Symmetric Multiprocessing (PCM) .... SMP
Symmetric Multiprocessor [*Computer science*] .... SMP
Symmetric Self Electrooptic Effect Device [*Optical Computing*] .... S-SEED
Symmetric Tonic Neck Reflex [*Medicine*] (DMAA) .... STNR
Symmetrical [*Also, sym*] [*Chemistry*] .... s
Symmetrical [*Also, s*] [*Chemistry*] .... sym
Symmetrical (MSA) .... SYMM
Symmetrical Balanced Incomplete Block Designs (MCD) .... SBIBD
Symmetrical Digital Single Line (DMAA) .... SDSL
Symmetrical Disubstituted Ethoxy Propane [*Organic chemistry*] (MCD) .... SYEP
Symmetrical Emitter Coupled Logic (IAA) .... SECL
Symmetrical Strength [*Neurology*] (DAVI) .... SS
Symmetrical Switching Function .... SSF
Symmetrical TOKAMAK .... ST
Symmetrical-Dimthylhydrazine [*Organic chemistry*] .... SDMH
Symmetrically Configured AC [*Alternating Current*] **Light-Emitting** [*Device*] .... SCALE
Symmetrically Cyclically Magnetized (IAA) .... SCM
Symmetrically Substituted (IAA) .... S
Symmetrically-Operated Emitter Coupled Logic (IAA) .... SECL
Symmetricom, Inc. [*Associated Press*] (SAG) .... Symetric
Symmetricom, Inc. [*NASDAQ symbol*] (SAG) .... SYMM
Symmetrized Logarithmic Derivative (IAA) .... SLD
Symmetrizing and Transformation Line (IAA) .... STL
Symmetrizing Line (IAA) .... SL
Symmetry [*or Symmetrical*] (DAVI) .... SY
Symmetry (IDOE) .... sym
Symmetry .... SYM
Symmetry Number [*Symbol*] [*IUPAC*] .... s
Symmetry, Orbitals, and Spectra [*Atomic physics*] .... SOS
Symmetry-Adapted Function .... SAF
Symmetry-Adapted Perturbation Theory [*Physical chemistry*] .... SAPT
Symmetry-Adapted Spherical-Harmonic [*Mathematics*] .... SASH
Symmetry-Restricted-Multiconfiguration Annihilation of Single Excitations [*Physics*] .... SRMCASE
Symonds Picture-Story Test [*Psychology*] .... SPST
Sympalmograph (VRA) .... SYMGR
Sympathetic [*Neurology*] .... sympat
Sympathetic [*Neurology*] (DAVI) .... sympath
Sympathetic Activity [*Physiology*] .... SA
Sympathetic Aerial Detonation [*Air Force*] .... SAD
Sympathetic Efferent Nerve Activity .... SENA
Sympathetic Firing Device [*Military*] (CAAL) .... SFD
Sympathetic Nervous System [*Physiology*] .... SNS
Sympathetic Ophthalmia [*Medicine*] .... SO
Sympathetic Orthostatic Hypotension [*Medicine*] (DMAA) .... SOH
Sympathetic Post-Ganglionic Neurone [*Neurology*] .... SPGN
Sympathetic Preganglionic Neuron [*Anatomy*] .... SPN
Sympathetically Stimulated [*Physiology*] .... SS
Symphonic Popular [*Armed Forces Radio-Televsion*] (DNAB) .... SP

Symphony ... SYM
Symphony (ADA) ... SYMPH
Symphony Command Language [*Computer science*] ... SCL
Symphony for United Nations (EA) ... SUN
Symphony Foundation of America (EA) ... SFA
Symphony Orchestra ... SO
Symphony Orchestra Library Information [*Sinfonia Software*] [*Piedmont, CA*] ... SOLI
Symphony Recording Co. [*Record label*] ... Sym
Symphysis Pubica [*Anatomy*] ... SP
Symposium [*of Plato*] [*Classical studies*] (OCD) ... Symp
Symposium (MSA) ... SYMP
Symposium. Association de Jeune Barreau de Montreal [*A publication*] (DLA) ... Symposum Jun Bar
Symposium of Software for Computer Control (MHDI) ... SOCOCO
Symposium on Applications of Ferroelectrics [*IEEE*] ... SAF
Symposium on Computer Applications in Medical Care [*Baltimore, MD*] ... SCAMC
Symposium on Image Display and Recording ... SIDAR
Symposium on the Numerical Solution of Partial Differential Equations [*Book title, Academic Press*] ... SYNSPADE
Symposium on the Preventability of Perinatal Injury ... SPPI
Symptom [*Medicine*] (MAE) ... SM
Symptom [*Medicine*] (CPH) ... sym
Symptom [*Medicine*] (AAMN) ... SYMP
Symptom [*Medicine*] ... sympt
Symptom Checklist [*Medicine*] (DMAA) ... SCL
Symptom Distress Check List [*Medicine*] (MAE) ... SDCL
Symptom Evaluation Survey (EDAC) ... SES
Symptom Interpretation Questionnaire [*Medicine*] (DMAA) ... SIQ
Symptom Medication Diary [*Medicine*] ... SMD
Symptom Pattern Observation Technique [*Aviation*] ... SPOT
Symptom Sign Inventory [*Psychology*] ... SSI
Symptomatic Diffuse Esophageal Spasm [*Medicine*] (DMAA) ... SDES
Symptomatic Urinary Tract Infection [*Medicine*] (DMAA) ... SUTI
Symptomatic Volunteer [*In drug studies*] ... SV
Symptom-Cause-Test ... SYCATE
Symptom-Free [*Medicine*] (DAVI) ... SF
Symptomless Autoimmune Thyroiditis [*Medicine*] (DMAA) ... SAT
Symptom-Limited Graded Exercise Test [*Cardiology*] (DAVI) ... SLGXT
Symptoms [*Medicine*] (WGA) ... Sx
Symptoms [*Medicine*] ... Sy
Symptoms, Observations, Assessment, Plan ... SOAP
Syms' Code of English Law [*1870*] [*A publication*] (DLA) ... Sym Code
Syms Corp. [*NYSE symbol*] (SPSG) ... SYM
Syms Corp. [*Associated Press*] (SAG) ... SymsCp
Synagogue (BJA) ... Sng
Synagogue ... SYN
Synagogue Council of America (EA) ... SCA
Synagraphic Mapping System [*Computer-made maps*] ... SYMAP
Synagro Tech Unit [*NASDAQ symbol*] (TTSB) ... SYGRU
Synagro Technologies, Inc. [*NASDAQ symbol*] (SAG) ... SYGR
Synagro Technologies, Inc. [*Associated Press*] (SAG) ... Synagro
Synagro Technologies, Inc. [*Associated Press*] (SAG) ... Syngro
Synagro Technologies Wrrt [*NASDAQ symbol*] (TTSB) ... SYGRW
Synalbumin-Insulin Antagonism [*Medicine*] ... SIA
Synalloy Corp. [*Associated Press*] (SAG) ... Synaloy
Synalloy Corp. [*NASDAQ symbol*] (SAG) ... SYNC
Synanon Church (EA) ... SC
Synanon Committee for a Responsible American Press (EA) ... SCRAP
Synanon Committee for Responsible American Media [*Later, SCRAP*] ... SCRAM
Synaptec, a Knowledge Engineering Corp. [*Vancouver Stock Exchange symbol*] ... SYN
Synaptic Membrane [*Medicine*] (DMAA) ... SM
Synaptic Pharmaceutical [*NASDAQ symbol*] (TTSB) ... SNAP
Synaptic Pharmaceutical Corp. [*NASDAQ symbol*] (SAG) ... SNAP
Synaptic Pharmaceutical Corp. [*Associated Press*] (SAG) ... SynapPhm
Synaptic Plasma Membrane [*Neurophysiology*] ... SPM
Synaptic Transporter Current [*Neurochemistry*] ... STC
Synaptic Vesicle [*Neurobiology*] ... SV
Synaptic Vesicle Amine Transporter [*Biochemistry*] ... SVAT
Synaptonemal Complex [*Botanical cytology*] ... SC
Synaptosomal Plasma Membrane [*Neurobiology*] ... SPM
Synaptosomal-Associated Protein [*Biochemistry*] ... SNAP
Synaptotagmin [*Neurochemistry*] ... SYT
Synbiotics Corp. [*NASDAQ symbol*] (NQ) ... SBIO
Synbiotics Corp. ... Syn
Synbiotics Corp. [*Associated Press*] (SAG) ... Synbio
Sync (IDOE) ... S
Sync Address Bus (IAA) ... SAB
Sync Research [*NASDAQ symbol*] (TTSB) ... SYNX
Sync Research, Inc. [*Associated Press*] (SAG) ... SyncRes
Sync Research, Inc. [*NASDAQ symbol*] (SAG) ... SYNX
SYNCH [*Synchronize*] **and MUX** [*Multiplex*] (MCD) ... S & M
Synchonous Dynamic Random Access Memory [*Computer science*] ... SDRAM
Synchro Amplifier ... SA
Synchro and Resolver Transmission ... SRT
Synchro Azimuth Converter ... SAC
Synchro Error Tester ... SET
Synchro Loop Closure ... SLC
Synchro Null Pulse ... SNP
Synchro Resolver Zeroing Fixture ... SRZF
Synchro Signal Amplifier ... SSA
Synchro Standard ... SS
Synchro Switch [*Electronics*] ... SSW
Synchro Tie ... SYNTI
Synchro Zeroing Procedure ... SZP
Synchro-Cyclotron ... SC
Synchro-Digital/Digital-Synchro (CAAL) ... SD/DS
Synchromechanism ... SYNC
Synchromesh [*Automotive engineering*] ... SYNCRO
Synchronism (IDOE) ... sync
Synchronization (IDOE) ... sync
Synchronization Base [*NASA*] (NASA) ... SB
Synchronization Bit (MSA) ... SB
Synchronization Code (IAA) ... SYNCCODE
Synchronization Coefficient ... SC
Synchronization Input [*Computer science*] (IAA) ... SYNCIN
Synchronization Output (IAA) ... SYNCOUT
Synchronization Pulse Generator (IAA) ... SPG
Synchronization Separator and Digitizer ... SS & D
Synchronization Signal Unit [*Telecommunications*] ... SYU
Synchronize (IAA) ... SYN
Synchronize (AAG) ... SYNC
Synchronize ... SYNCH
Synchronized (MDG) ... SY
Synchronized (AAG) ... SYNCD
Synchronized Accumulating Radioisotope Detection ... SARD
Synchronized Digital Network [*Telecommunications*] (TEL) ... SDN
Synchronized Framing Camera ... SFC
Synchronized Intermittent Mandatory Ventilation [*Medicine*] (DAVI) ... SIMV
Synchronized Maneuver Countermeasures Model (MCD) ... SMC
Synchronized Multimedia Integration Language [*Computer science*] ... SMIL
Synchronized Parallel Displacement [*Automotive engineering*] ... SPD
Synchronized Power On (MHDI) ... SPO
Synchronized Sleep ... S
Synchronized Time, Automated Reporting System ... STARS
Synchronizer (AAG) ... SYNCR
Synchronizer for Peripheral Devices ... SPD
Synchronizers [*JETDS nomenclature*] [*Military*] (CET) ... SN
Synchronizing (AAG) ... SYNCG
Synchronizing Character [*Computer science*] (IAA) ... SYNC
Synchroniztion Table (IAA) ... ST
Synchronoscope (IAA) ... SY
Synchronoscope (IAA) ... SYNCSCP
Synchronous ... S
Synchronous (AAG) ... SYN
Synchronous (AAG) ... SYNCS
Synchronous Altitude Communications Satellite ... SACS
Synchronous Altitude Gravity Gradient Experiment ... SAGGE
Synchronous Altitude Meteorological Satellite (IAA) ... SMS
Synchronous Altitude Spin-Stabilized Experiment ... SASSE
Synchronous Amplitude Modulation ... SAM
Synchronous Astro Compass (SAA) ... SAC
Synchronous Automatic Dial Language ... SADL
Synchronous Bus Interface [*Computer science*] (HGAA) ... SBI
Synchronous Communication Satellite [*Telecommunications*] (IAA) ... SYNCOM
Synchronous Communications [*Satellite*] [*GSFC*] ... SYCOM
Synchronous Communications [*Hughes Aircraft Co.*] ... SYNCOM
Synchronous Communications Access Method ... SCAM
Synchronous Communications Adapter ... SCA
Synchronous Communications Controller ... SCC
Synchronous Continuous Orbital Three-Dimensional Tracking ... SCOTT
Synchronous Controller Unit ... SCU
Synchronous Data Link Control [*Telecommunications*] ... SDLC
Synchronous Data Modern Equipment ... SDME
Synchronous Data Set (NOAA) ... SDS
Synchronous Detector [*Electronics*] (OA) ... SD
Synchronous Digital Hierarchy [*Computer science*] ... SDH
Synchronous Digital Machine ... SDM
Synchronous Earth Observatory Satellite [*NASA*] ... SEOS
Synchronous Equatorial Orbit [*or Orbiter*] [*NASA*] (KSC) ... SEO
Synchronous Generator (IAA) ... SG
Synchronous Graphics RAM [*Random Access Memory*] (PCM) ... SGRAM
Synchronous Halo Monitor [*NASA*] ... SHALOM
Synchronous Hubbing Regeneration (MHDI) ... SHR
Synchronous Identification System (DNAB) ... SID
Synchronous Identification System (MCD) ... SIS
Synchronous Identification System Study ... SISS
Synchronous Idle [*Transmission control character*] [*Computer science*] ... SYN
Synchronous Interface Module ... SIM
Synchronous Line Adapter ... SLA
Synchronous Line Control Unit ... SLCU
Synchronous Line Control Unit [*Computer science*] (MHDI) ... SYLCU
Synchronous Line Driver ... SLD
Synchronous Line Group (BUR) ... SLG
Synchronous Line Interface ... SLI
Synchronous Line, Low, Load (BUR) ... SLLL
Synchronous Line Medium Speed (BUR) ... SL
Synchronous Line Medium Speed with Clock (BUR) ... SLC
Synchronous Line Module ... SLM
Synchronous Link Control [*Computer science*] ... SLC
Synchronous Meteorological Satellite [*NASA*] ... SMS
Synchronous Meteorological Test Satellite [*NASA*] ... SMTS
Synchronous Missile Alarm System ... SYNMAS
Synchronous MODEM ... SM
Synchronous Modulator-Demodulator (MCD) ... SMD
Synchronous Multiline Communications Coupler (NITA) ... SMLCC
Synchronous Network Processor ... SNP
Synchronous, Operational Meteorological Satellite ... SOMS

Synchronous Optical Network [*Computer science*] ..... SONET
Synchronous Orbit Communication Relay (MCD) ..... SOCR
Synchronous Orbit Data Relay Satellite ..... SODRS
Synchronous Orbit Satellite (AAG) ..... SOS
Synchronous Orbiting Solar Observatory ..... SOSO
Synchronous Orbiting Tracking Stations (MCD) ..... SOTS
Synchronous Phase Demodulator ..... SPD
Synchronous Position Altitude Recorder ..... SPAR
Synchronous Program Supervisor (IAA) ..... SPS
Synchronous Relay Satellite [*Telecommunications*] (TEL) ..... SRS
Synchronous Remote Control ..... SRC
Synchronous Satellite Communications System ..... SSCS
Synchronous Satellite Military Communication System ..... SSMCS
Synchronous Serial Data Adapter ..... SSDA
Synchronous Single-Line Controller ..... SSLC
Synchronous Stable Relaying (IEEE) ..... SSR
Synchronous System [*on a ship*] (DS) ..... Sy
Synchronous System Trap ..... SST
Synchronous Systems Interface ..... SSI
Synchronous Time-Division Multiplexing [*Computer science*] (MDG) ..... STDM
Synchronous Transistor Logic (MDG) ..... STL
Synchronous Transmission [*Computer science*] (TSSD) ..... SYNCH
Synchronous Transmit Receive (NITA) ..... STR
Synchronous Transmit Receive Access Method (CMD) ..... STRAM
Synchronous Transmitter Receiver [*Computer science*] ..... STR
Synchronous Transport Signal [*Computer science*] ..... STS
Synchronous Voltage (OA) ..... SV
Synchronous Wave Device ..... SWD
Synchronously Programmed User Terminal and Network Interface Control [*Computer science*] (MHDI) ..... SPUTNIC
Synchronous-Orbiting Communications Satellite [*GSFC*] ..... SYNCOM
Synchrony ..... sync
Synchrony Service and Transport System [*Ascom Timeplex, Inc.*] ..... STS
Synchroscope (KSC) ..... SYNSCP
Synchrotron Orbital Radiation [*High-energy physics*] ..... SOR
Synchrotron Orbital Radiation Technology [*High-energy physics*] ..... SORTEC
Synchrotron Radiation [*High-energy physics*] ..... SR
Synchrotron Radiation Center [*University of Wisconsin - Madison*] [*Research center*] (RCD) ..... SRC
Synchrotron Radiation Source [*High-energy physics*] ..... SRS
Synchrotron Self-Compton [*X-ray emission*] ..... SSC
Synchrotron Ultraviolet Radiation Facility [*National Institute of Standards and Technology*] ..... SURF
Synchrotron X-Ray Fluorescence [*Spectrometry*] ..... SXRF
Synclinal [*Geology*] ..... SC
Syncline Ridge [*Nevada*] [*Seismograph station code, US Geological Survey Closed*] (SEIS) ..... NYS
Sync-link DRAM [*Display Random Access Memory*] [*Computer science*] ..... SLDRAM
Synco Development [*Vancouver Stock Exchange symbol*] ..... SYC
Syncopated Time (WDAA) ..... ST
Syncor International Corp. [*NASDAQ symbol*] (NQ) ..... SCOR
Syncor International Corp. [*Associated Press*] (SAG) ..... Syncor
Syncor Int'l [*NASDAQ symbol*] (TTSB) ..... SCOR
Syncrude Canada Ltd. [*ICAO designator*] (FAAC) ..... SYN
Syncrude Canada Ltd., Edmonton, AB, Canada [*Library symbol Library of Congress*] (LCLS) ..... CaAESC
Syncrude Canada Ltd., Edmonton, Alberta [*Library symbol National Library of Canada*] (NLC) ..... AESC
Sync-Stream Manager (PCM) ..... SSM
Syncytiovascular Membrane [*Medicine*] (MAE) ..... SVM
Syncytium Inducing [*Cytology*] ..... SI
Syncytium-Forming Units [*Biochemistry*] ..... SFU
Syndicat Autonome des Fonctionnaires d'Oubangi-Chari [*Autonomous Union of the Workers of Ubangi-Shari*] ..... SAFOC
Syndicat Autonome des Travailleurs de la Alimentation de Madagascar [*Autonomous Union of Food Workers of Madagascar*] ..... SATAM
Syndicat Canadien de la Fonction Publique [*Canadian Union of Public Employees - CUPE*] ..... SCFP
Syndicat Canadien des Communications, de l'Energie et du Papier (AC) ..... SCEP
Syndicat Canadien des Employes de Bureau [*Canadian Office Employees Union - COEU*] ..... SCEB
Syndicat Canadien des Employes Professionnels et Techniques (AC) ..... SCEPT
Syndicat Canadien des Travailleurs Agricoles (AC) ..... SCTA
Syndicat Canadien des Travailleurs du Papier [*Canadian Paperworkers Union - CPU*] ..... SCTP
Syndicat de l'Emploi et de l'Immigration du Canada ..... SEIC
Syndicat des Commercants Importateurs et Exportateurs de l'Ouest African [*Union of Commercial Importers and Exporters of West Africa*] ..... SCIMPEX
Syndicat des Communications Canada ..... SCC
Syndicat des Controleurs de Circulation Ferroviaire du Canada [*Union of Rail Canada Traffic Controllers - RCTC*] ..... CCFC
Syndicat des Employes Indigenes du Commerce du Togo [*Union of Indigenous Employees of Commerce of Togo*] ..... SECIT
Syndicat des Enseignants Africains du Niger [*African Union of Teachers of Niger*] ..... SEAN
Syndicat des Enseignants du Togo [*Union of Togolese Teachers*] ..... SET
Syndicat des Fonctionnaires [*Lao Civil Servants' Union*] ..... SF
Syndicat des Medecins, Veterinaires, Pharmaciens, et Sages Femmes Africains du Mali [*Union of African Doctors, Pharmacists, Midwives, and Veterinarians of the Mali Federation*] ..... SYMEVETOPHARSA
Syndicat des Postiers du Canada [*Canadian Union of Postal Workers - CUPW*] ..... SPC
Syndicat des Travailleurs de l'Administration Generale du Dahomey [*Dahomean Union of General Administration Workers*] ..... STAGD
Syndicat des Travailleurs de l'Energie Electrique et de Distribution d'Eau du Togo [*Union of Electrical and Water Distribution Workers of Togo*] ..... SYNTEEDISETO
Syndicat des Travailleurs de l'Energie et de la Chimie [*Energy and Chemical Workers Union - ECWU*] [*Canada*] ..... STEC
Syndicat des Travailleurs de Transport et de la Navigation du Togo [*Union of Transport and Navigation Workers of Togo*] ..... STANAVITO
Syndicat des Travailleurs des Entreprises, Privees, Travaux Publics et Batiments [*Union of Workers of Private Enterprises, Public Works and Buildings*] [*Togo*] ..... SENTRAB
Syndicat des Travailleurs des Industries Reunies du Togo [*Union of Workers of United Industries of Togo*] ..... SYNTIRT
Syndicat des Travailleurs en Communication du Canada ..... STCC
Syndicat des Travailleurs en Communication, Electronique, Electricite, Techniciens, et Salaries du Canada [*Communications, Electronic, Electrical, Technical, and Salaried Workers of Canada - CWC*] ..... STCC
Syndicat des Travailleurs en Telecommunications [*Telecommunications Workers Union - TWU*] [*Canada*] ..... STT
Syndicat d'Etudes de l'Energie Nucleaire [*Belgium*] ..... SEEN
Syndicat du Personnel Africain de l'Aeronautique Civile [*African Union for Civil Aviation Employees*] ..... SPAAC
Syndicat du Personnel de l'Aeronautique Civile du Gabon [*Union of Civil Aviation Employees of Gabon*] ..... SPACG
Syndicat Europeen des Travailleurs de l'Alimentation, de l'Hotellerie, et des Branches Connexes dans l'UITA [*European Committee of Food, Catering, and Allied Workers' Unions within the IUF - ECF-IUF*] (EAIO) ..... SETA-UITA
Syndicat International des Debardeurs et Magasiniers [*International Longshoremen's and Warehousemen's Union ILWU*] [*Canada*] ..... SIDM
Syndicat International des Gens de Mer du Canada ..... SIGM
Syndicat International des Marins Canadiens [*Seafarers' International Union of Canada - SIU*] ..... SIMC
Syndicat International des Travailleurs Unis de l'Automobile, de l'Aerospatiale,et de l'Outillage Agricole d'Amerique [*International Union, United Automobile, Aerospace, and Agricultural Implement Workers of America - UAW*] [*Canada*] ..... TUA
Syndicat National de la Fonction Publique Provinciale [*National Union of Provincial Government Employees - NUPGE*] [*Canada*] ..... SNFPP
Syndicat National de l'Edition [*French publishers' association*] ..... SNE
Syndicat National de l'Enseignement Secondaire [*National Union of Secondary Schoolteachers*] [*France*] ..... SNES
Syndicat National de l'Enseignement Technique [*National Union of Technical School Teachers*] [*France*] ..... SNET
Syndicat National des Enseignants de Guinee [*National Union of Guinean Teachers*] ..... SNEG
Syndicat National des Enseignants du Second Degre de Cote d'Ivoire ..... SYNESCI
Syndicat National des Instituteurs [*National Union of Teachers*] [*France*] ..... SNI
Syndicat National des Transporteurs de Cameroun [*National Union of Cameroonese Transportation Workers*] ..... SNTC
Syndicat National des Travailleurs Congolais [*National Union of Congolese Workers*] [*Leopoldville*] ..... SNTC
Syndicat National des Travailleurs de l'Amiante d'Asbestos [*Canada*] ..... SNAA
Syndicat National du Cinema [*National Syndicate of Motion Pictures*] ..... SNC
Syndicat Togolais du Personnel de la Meteorologie [*Togolese Union of Meteorological Personnel*] ..... STPM
Syndicat Uni du Transport [*United Transportation Union - UTU*] [*Canada*] ..... SUT
Syndicat Unique des Enseignants de Mauritanie [*Unitary Union of Mauritanian Teachers*] ..... SUEM
Syndicate (ROG) ..... SYN
Syndicate ..... SYND
Syndicate (WDMC) ..... synd
Syndicate for Fabrication of Fuel Elements [*French Acronym is based on foreign phrase*] ..... SICN
Syndicate of North Germany Electric Utilities [*Germany*] [*Acronym is based on foreign phrase*] ..... SKW
Syndicated Exclusivity [*FCC*] ..... SYNDEX
Syndicated Note-Issuance Facility [*Banking*] (ADA) ..... SNIF
Syndicated Program Analysis (NTCM) ..... SPA
Syndiotactic Polystyrene [*Organic chemistry*] ..... SPS
Syndiotactic Polystyrene ..... SPS
Syndrome [*Medicine*] ..... synd
Syndrome of Inappropriate Antidiuretic Hormone [*Endocrinology*] ..... SIADH
Syndrome of Primary Aldosteronism [*Medicine*] (DMAA) ..... SOPA
Syndrome of Primary Ciliary Dyskinesia [*Medicine*] (DMAA) ..... SPCD
Syndrome of the Trephined [*Medicine*] (DMAA) ..... ST
Syne Unit [*Telecommunications*] (OA) ..... SU
Synecdoche (WDAA) ..... SYNEC
Synergetic Society (EA) ..... SS
Synergist (WGA) ..... SYN
Synergist Erection System [*Medicine*] ..... SES
Synergistic Hldg [*NASDAQ symbol*] (TTSB) ..... SYNH
Synergistic Hldg Wrrt [*NASDAQ symbol*] (TTSB) ..... SYNHW
Synergistic Holding Corp. [*NASDAQ symbol*] (SAG) ..... SALX
Synergistic Holding Corp. [*NASDAQ symbol*] (SAG) ..... SYNH
Synergistic Holding Corp. [*Associated Press*] (SAG) ..... SynHld
Synergistic Holding Corp. [*Associated Press*] (SAG) ..... SynHold
Synergistic Strike System S3
Synergistics Industries Ltd. [*Toronto Stock Exchange symbol*] ..... SGX
Synergy International [*Vancouver Stock Exchange symbol*] ..... SYG
Synergy Power Institute [*Defunct*] (EA) ..... SPI
Synetic, Inc. [*NASDAQ symbol*] (NQ) ..... SNTC
Synetic, Inc. [*Associated Press*] (SAG) ..... Synetic

Synex International, Inc. [*Toronto Stock Exchange symbol*] .... SXI
Synfuels Bibliography and Index [*A publication*] .... SBI
Syngeneic Graft-Versus-Host Disease [*Medicine*] (DMAA) .... SGVHD
Syngold Exploration, Inc. [*Toronto Stock Exchange symbol*] .... SIN
Synod .... SYN
Synod of Evangelical Lutheran Churches (IIA) .... SELC
Synod Office, Diocese of Algoma, Anglican Church of Canada, Sault Ste. Marie, Ontario [*Library symbol National Library of Canada*] (NLC) .... OSTMAAS
Synod Office, Diocese of Brandon, Anglican Church of Canada, Manitoba [*Library symbol National Library of Canada*] (NLC) .... MBABS
Synod Office, Diocese of British Columbia, Anglican Church of Canada, Victoria, British Columbia [*Library symbol National Library of Canada*] (NLC) .... BVIABS
Synod Office, Diocese of Caledonia, Anglican Church of Canada, Prince Rupert, British Columbia [*Library symbol National Library of Canada*] (NLC) .... BPRACS
Synod Office, Diocese of Keewatin, Anglican Church of Canada, Kenora, Ontario [*Library symbol National Library of Canada*] (NLC) .... OKAKS
Synod Office, Diocese of Moosonee, Anglican Church of Canada, Schumacher, Ontario [*Library symbol National Library of Canada*] (NLC) .... OSAMS
Synod Office, Diocese of Nova Scotia, Anglican Church of Canada, Halifax, Nova Scotia [*Library symbol National Library of Canada*] (NLC) .... NSHANSS
Synod Office, Diocese of Ontario, Anglican Church of Canada, Kingston, Ontario [*Library symbol National Library of Canada*] (NLC) .... OKAOS
Synod Office, Diocese of Quebec, Anglican Church of Canada, Quebec, Quebec [*Library symbol National Library of Canada*] (NLC) .... QQAQS
Synod Office, Diocese of Rupert's Land, Anglican Church of Canada, Winnipeg, Manitoba [*Library symbol National Library of Canada*] (NLC) .... MWARS
Synod Office, Diocese of Saskatchewan, Angelican Church of Canada, Prince Albert, Saskatchewan [*Library symbol National Library of Canada*] (NLC) .... SPAASS
Synod Office, Ecclesiastical Province of British Columbia, Anglican Church of Canada, Vancouver, British Columbia [*Library symbol National Library of Canada*] (NLC) .... BVAABS
Synomospondia Ergaton Kyprou [*Cyprus Workers' Confederation*] [*"Free Labour Syndicats"*] .... SEK
Synonym .... SYN
Synonym (ROG) .... SYNON
Synonyms (NITA) .... SY
Synopic Reporting of the Location of Sources of Atmospherics [*Aviation*] (DA) .... SFLOC
Synopsis (DLA) .... Syn
Synopsis (AABC) .... SYNOP
Synopsis (MSA) .... SYNS
Synopsis Information System (AAGC) .... SIS
Synopsis Series of the United States Treasury Decisions [*A publication*] (DLA) .... SS
Synopsis Series of the United States Treasury Decisions [*A publication*] (DLA) .... STD
Synopsis Series of the United States Treasury Decisions [*A publication*] (DLA) .... Syn Ser
Synopsys, Inc. [*NASDAQ symbol*] (SAG) .... SNPS
Synopsys, Inc. [*Associated Press*] (SAG) .... Synopsy
Synoptic [*Meteorology*] .... S
Synoptic [*or Synoptist*] (BJA) .... Synpt
Synoptic Meteorological Sounding .... SMS
Synoptic Oceanographic Data Acquisition System [*Marine science*] (MSC) .... SODAS
Synoptic Properties Code (MCD) .... SPC
Synoptic Random Access Measurement System (NOAA) .... SYNRAMS
Synoptic-Scale Subprogramme Data Centre [*Marine science*] (MSC) .... SSDC
Synoptische Studien fuer A. Wikenhauser [*1953*] [*A publication*] (BJA) .... SStW
Synovial [*Fluid*] [*Medicine*] .... syn
Synovial Fluid [*Medicine*] .... SF
Synovial Fluid [*Medicine*] (MAE) .... syn fl
Synovial Fluid Lymphocyte [*Medicine*] (DMAA) .... SFI
Synovial Membrane [*Anatomy*] (DAVI) .... SM
Synovitis [*Medicine*] .... syn
Synovus Financial [*NYSE symbol*] (TTSB) .... SNV
Synovus Financial Corp. [*NYSE symbol*] (SPSG) .... SNV
Synovus Financial Corp. [*Associated Press*] (SAG) .... Synovus
Synperiplanar [*Chemistry*] .... SP
Synpolydactyly [*Medicine*] .... SPD
Syntactic Density Score (EDAC) .... SDS
Syntactic Tracer Organized Retrospective Enquiry System [*Instituut voor Wiskunde, Informatiewerk, en Statistiek*] [*Computer science Netherlands*] .... STORES
Syntagmatic Organization Language [*Computer science*] .... SYNTOL
Syntax Analyzer Generator (PDAA) .... SAG
Syntax and Semantics (IEEE) .... SYNSEM
Syntax Directed Editor (NITA) .... SDE
Syntax Improving Device (IEEE) .... SID
Syntax Macro Preprocessor for Language Evaluation [*Computer science*] (PDAA) .... SYMPLE
Syntax Translation [*Computer science*] (DIT) .... SYNTRAN
Syntax-Controlled Acoustic Classifier [*Computer science*] (MHDI) .... SCAC
Syntax-Directed Translation [*Computer science*] (MHDI) .... SDT
Syntax-Directed Translation Scheme [*Computer science*] (MHDI) .... SDTS
Syntax-Oriented Translator (PDAA) .... SORTRAN
Syntax-Oriented Translator (IEEE) .... SOT
Syntech International, Inc. (MHDW) .... SYNEP
Syntellect, Inc. [*NASDAQ symbol*] (SAG) .... SYNL
Syntellect, Inc. [*Associated Press*] (SAG) .... Syntlct
Syntex Corp., Palo Alto, CA [*OCLC symbol*] (OCLC) .... SYN
Syntex Corp., Research Library, Palo Alto, CA [*Library symbol Library of Congress*] (LCLS) .... CPaS
Syntex, Inc., Medical Library, Mississauga, ON, Canada [*Library symbol Library of Congress*] (LCLS) .... CaOMSM
Syntex Laboratories, Inc. [*Research code symbol*] .... RS
Synthesewerk Schwarzheide [*Former East German chemical company*] (ECON) .... SYS
Synthesis [*Phase in mitosis*] [*Cytology*] .... S
Synthesis and Modeling Working Group [*Marine science*] (OSRA) .... SMWG
Synthesis Center of the Institute for Wholistic Education (EA) .... SCIWE
Synthesis Measurement Plan (IAA) .... SMP
Synthesis of Aircraft (MCD) .... SYNAC
Synthesis of Impact Acceleration Technology (MCD) .... SIAT
Synthesis Telescope .... ST
Synthesis-Phase Fraction [*Medicine*] (CDI) .... SPF
Synthesized Hydrocarbon (PDAA) .... SHC
Synthesized Hydrocarbon Fluid [*Petroleum engineering*] .... SHF
Synthesized User-Based Terminology Index Language (NITA) .... SUBTIL
Synthesizer .... SYN
Synthesizer .... SYNTH
Synthesizer Frequency .... SYNFRQ
Synthetech, Inc. [*NASDAQ symbol*] (NQ) .... NZYM
Synthetech, Inc. [*Associated Press*] (SAG) .... Synthe
Synthetic (AAG) .... SYN
Synthetic .... SYNT
Synthetic (VRA) .... synt
Synthetic .... SYNTH
Synthetic Aircraft Turbine Oil .... SATO
Synthetic Algal Nutrient Medium .... SANM
Synthetic Amorphous Silica and Silicates Industry Association (EA) .... SASSI
Synthetic Amorphous Silica and Silicates Industry Association (EA) .... SASSIA
Synthetic Amorphous Silicas [*Inorganic Chemistry*] .... SAS
Synthetic Aperture Focusing Technique [*Computer imaging*] .... SAFT
Synthetic Aperture High Altitude RADAR (AAG) .... SAHARA
Synthetic Aperture LASER RADAR .... SALR
Synthetic Aperture Precision Processor High Reliability (MCD) .... SAPPHIRE
Synthetic Aperture RADAR .... SAR
Synthetic Aperture RADAR [*Computer imaging*] .... SAR
Synthetic Aperture RADAR .... SAR
Synthetic Aperture RADAR - C-Band (SSD) .... SAR-C
Synthetic Aperture RADAR Guidance (MCD) .... SARG
Synthetic Aperture RADAR Gun [*NASA*] .... SARGUN
Synthetic Aperture RADAR Interpretation System [*NASA*] (MCD) .... SARIS
Synthetic Aperture RADAR Satellite [*NASA*] (SSD) .... SARSAT
Synthetic Aperture RADAR Signature Experiment [*Oceanography*] .... SARSEX
Synthetic Aperture Retransmission Guidance (MCD) .... SARG
Synthetic Armed Aircraft Training System (SAA) .... SATS
Synthetic Array Data Processor .... SADP
Synthetic Array RADAR Command Air-Launched Missile .... SARCALM
Synthetic Array RADAR System .... SARS
Synthetic Bathymetric Profiling System [*Naval Oceanographic Office*] .... SYNBAPS
Synthetic Cell [*Biological research*] .... SYNCELL
Synthetic Combinatorial Library [*Biochemistry*] .... SCL
Synthetic Crude .... SYNCRUDE
Synthetic Crude Oil [*Fuel technology*] .... SCO
Synthetic Detergent (BARN) .... syndet
Synthetic Detergents .... SYNDETS
Synthetic Dextrose [*Biochemistry*] .... SD
Synthetic Drying Oil .... SDO
Synthetic Dynamic Display [*Aviation*] (OA) .... SDD
Synthetic English (MHDI) .... SYNGLISH
Synthetic Environment .... SE
Synthetic Enzymes .... SYNZYMES
Synthetic Fermented Egg [*Animal repellent*] .... SFE
Synthetic Flight Training Simulator .... SFTS
Synthetic Flight Training System [*Army*] .... SFTS
Synthetic Fuel (BARN) .... synfuel
Synthetic Fuels .... SYNFUELS
Synthetic Fuels Commercialization Program [*Also, SFCP*] [*Energy Resources Council*] .... SCP
Synthetic Fuels Commercialization Program [*Also, SCP*] [*Energy Resources Council*] .... SFCP
Synthetic Fuels Corp. [*Sponsored by the federal government*] .... SFC
Synthetic Fuels Update [*A publication*] .... SFU
Synthetic Gas (BARN) .... syngas
Synthetic Human Gastrin [*Medicine*] (MAE) .... SHG
Synthetic Hydrocarbons [*Lubricants*] .... SHC
Synthetic Interstitial Fluid [*Biochemistry*] .... SIF
Synthetic Medium [*Microbiology*] .... SM
Synthetic Medium Old Tuberculin Trichloroacetic Acid Precipitated [*Later, PPD, Purified Protein Derivative*] [*Immunology*] .... SOTT
Synthetic Mineral Fiber .... SMF
Synthetic Model Interferometric LASER Imaging (PDAA) .... SMILI
Synthetic Multiple-Interaction [*For chiral separation*] .... SMI
Synthetic Natural Gas (IEEE) .... SNG
Synthetic Navigation Trainer .... SNT
Synthetic Ocean Water .... SOW
Synthetic Organic Chemical .... SOC
Synthetic Organic Chemical Manufacturers Association (EA) .... SOCMA
Synthetic Organic Chemical Manufacturing Industry [*Environmental Protection Agency*] .... SOCMI
Synthetic Phase Isolation [*Telemetry*] .... SPI
Synthetic Phenolic Foam .... SPF

Synthetic Plasma Membrane [*Biochemistry*] ... SPM
Synthetic Resin Bonded Paper (IAA) ... SRBP
Synthetic Rock [*For storage of nuclear waste*] ... SYNROC
Synthetic Sentence Indentification [*Speech and language Therapy*] (DAVI) ... SSI
Synthetic Sodium Aluminosilicate [*Inorganic chemistry*] ... SSAS
Synthetic Tactics ... SYNTAC
Synthetic Theater of War [*Army*] ... STOW
Synthetic Theater of War-Systems Engineering, Integration, and Demonstration [*Military*] (RDA) ... STOW-SKID
Synthetic Timing Mode ... STM
Synthetic Turf Council [*Defunct*] (EA) ... STC
Synthetic Unrandomization of Randomized Fragments [*Chemistry*] ... SURF
Synthetic Vision Systems, Inc. ... SVS
Synthetic Zeolite Molecule ... SZM
Synthetic-Aperture Imaging RADAR [*System*] ... SIR
Syntype ... SYN
Syosset Hospital, Syosset, NY [*Library symbol Library of Congress*] (LCLS) ... NSyoH
Syosset, NY [*FM radio station call letters*] ... WKWZ
Syosset Public Library, Syosset, NY [*Library symbol Library of Congress*] (LCLS) ... NSyo
Syosset Senior High School, Syosset, NY [*Library symbol*] [*Library of Congress*] (LCLS) ... NSyoSH
Syowa [*Ongul*] [*Antarctica*] [*Seismograph station code, US Geological Survey*] (SEIS) ... SYO
Syowa Base [*Antarctica*] [*Geomagnetic observatory code*] ... SYO
Syphilis [*Medicine*] ... SY
Syphilis (DSUE) ... SYPH
Syphilis, Toxoplasmosis, Other Agents Rubella, Cytomegalovirus, and Herpes [*Medicine*] (DAVI) ... STORCH
Syphilis, Toxoplasmosis, Rubella, Cytomegalovirus, and Herpesvirus [*Medicine*] (DMAA) ... STORCH
Syphilitic [*Medicine*] (DMAA) ... SY
Syphilology [*or Syphilologist*] [*Medicine*] (DAVI) ... Syph
SyQuest Technology [*NASDAQ symbol*] (TTSB) ... SYQT
SyQuest Technology, Inc. [*Associated Press*] (SAG) ... SyQstTc
SyQuest Technology, Inc. [*NASDAQ symbol*] (SPSG) ... SYQT
Syracuse [*Diocesan abbreviation*] [*New York*] (TOCD) ... SY
Syracuse [*New York*] [*Airport symbol*] ... SYR
Syracuse Air Defense Sector (SAA) ... SYADS
Syracuse/Hancock International [*New York*] [*ICAO location identifier*] (ICLI) ... KSYR
Syracuse, IN [*FM radio station call letters*] ... WAWC
Syracuse Information Retrieval Experiments (NITA) ... SIRE
Syracuse Journal of International Law [*A publication*] (DLA) ... Syracuse J Int'l L
Syracuse Microfilm Co., Syracuse, NY [*Library symbol*] [*Library of Congress*] (LCLS) ... SyMC
Syracuse, NY [*Location identifier FAA*] (FAAL) ... MRZ
Syracuse, NY [*FM radio station call letters*] ... WAER
Syracuse, NY [*FM radio station call letters*] ... WCNY
Syracuse, NY [*Television station call letters*] ... WCNY-TV
Syracuse, NY [*AM radio station call letters*] ... WDCW
Syracuse, NY [*AM radio station call letters*] ... WHEN
Syracuse, NY [*FM radio station call letters*] ... WHEN-FM
Syracuse, NY [*Television station call letters*] ... WIXT
Syracuse, NY [*FM radio station call letters*] ... WJPZ
Syracuse, NY [*FM radio station call letters*] ... WMHR
Syracuse, NY [*AM radio station call letters*] ... WNDR
Syracuse, NY [*AM radio station call letters*] (RBYB) ... WNSS-AM
Syracuse, NY [*FM radio station call letters*] ... WNTQ
Syracuse, NY [*Television station call letters*] ... WNYS
Syracuse, NY [*AM radio station call letters*] ... WOLF
Syracuse, NY [*FM radio station call letters*] (RBYB) ... WRVD-FM
Syracuse, NY [*Television station call letters*] ... WSTM
Syracuse, NY [*AM radio station call letters*] ... WSYR
Syracuse, NY [*Television station call letters*] ... WSYT
Syracuse, NY [*Television station call letters*] ... WTVH
Syracuse, NY [*FM radio station call letters*] (RBYB) ... WWHT-FM
Syracuse, NY [*FM radio station call letters*] ... WYYY
Syracuse Public Library, Syracuse, IN [*Library symbol Library of Congress*] (LCLS) ... InSy
Syracuse Research Corp. [*New York*] [*Information service or system*] (IID) ... SRC
Syracuse Research Corp., Library, Syracuse, NY [*OCLC symbol*] (OCLC) ... ZVB
Syracuse Research Corp., Syracuse, NY [*Library symbol*] [*Library of Congress*] (LCLS) ... NSyR
Syracuse Research Corp., Syracuse, NY [*Library symbol Library of Congress*] (LCLS) ... NSyR
Syracuse Scales of Social Relations [*Education*] ... SSSR
Syracuse University [*New York*] ... SU
Syracuse University (GAGS) ... Syracuse U
Syracuse University College of Law (DLA) ... SYRUCL
Syracuse University, Educational Resources Center of the All-University Gerontology Center, Syracuse, NY [*Library symbol Library of Congress*] (LCLS) ... NSyU-G
Syracuse University Libraries' Information Retrieval System (NITA) ... SULIRS
Syracuse University Libraries Information System [*Syracuse University Libraries*] [*New York*] [*Information service or system*] (IID) ... SULIS
Syracuse University, Library of Continuing Education at Syracuse, Syracuse, NY [*Library symbol Library of Congress*] (LCLS) ... NSyU-CE
Syracuse University Press (DGA) ... SUP
Syracuse University Psychological Abstracts Retrieval Service (NITA) ... SUPARS
Syracuse University Publications in Continuing Education (EA) ... SUPCE
Syracuse University Research Corp. ... SURC
Syracuse University Research Institute (MCD) ... SURI
Syracuse University Resources for Educators of Adults (EDAC) ... SUREA
Syracuse University, Syracuse, NY [*Library symbol Library of Congress*] (LCLS) ... NSyU
Syracuse University, Syracuse, NY [*OCLC symbol*] (OCLC) ... SYB
Syratech Corp. [*NYSE symbol*] (SPSG) ... SYR
Syratech Corp. [*Associated Press*] (SAG) ... Syratch
Syrene-Chloroprene Rubber ... SCR
Syria [*License plate code assigned to foreign diplomats in the US*] ... AQ
Syria [*MARC geographic area code Library of Congress*] (LCCP) ... a-sy--
Syria (BARN) ... S
Syria [*or Syrian Arab Republic*] [*ANSI two-letter standard code*] (CNC) ... SY
Syria [*MARC country of publication code Library of Congress*] (LCCP) ... sy
Syria [*or Syrian Arab Republic*] [*ANSI three-letter standard code*] (CNC) ... SYR
Syria (VRA) ... Syr
Syria and Lebanon ... SL
Syriac [*MARC language code Library of Congress*] (LCCP) ... syr
Syriac Version in Walton's Polyglot (BJA) ... SyrW
Syrian [*Language, etc.*] (ROG) ... SYR
Syrian Air Force (BJA) ... SAF
Syrian Arab Airlines ... SAA
Syrian Arab Airlines [*ICAO designator*] (FAAC) ... SYR
Syrian Arab News Agency ... SANA
Syrian Arab Republic ... SAR
Syrian Communist Party [*Political party*] (PPW) ... SCP
Syrian Hamster [*Medicine*] (DMAA) ... SYR
Syrian Hamster Embryonic [*Cells*] ... SHE
Syrian News Agency (BJA) ... SNA
Syrian Telecommunications Establishment [*Syrian Arab Republic*] (TSSD) ... STE
Syringe (DNAB) ... SG
Syringe ... SRNG
Syringe [*Medicine*] ... SYR
Syringe Exchange Program [*To prevent infectious disease*] ... SEP
Syrohexapla (BJA) ... Syh
Syro-Mesopotamian Studies [*Malibu, CA*] [*A publication*] (BJA) ... SMS
Syropalaestinum (BJA) ... Syp
Syrtis Major Plantia [*A filamentary mark on Mars*] ... SMP
Syrup (WGA) ... SY
Syrupus [*Syrup*] [*Pharmacy*] ... SYR
Sysco Corp. [*Associated Press*] (SAG) ... Sysco
Sysco Corp. [*NYSE symbol*] (SPSG) ... SYY
System ... S
System ... SY
System (MDG) ... SYM
System (AFM) ... SYS
System ... SYST
System ... SYST
System Access Layer [*Computer science*] ... SAL
System Access Technique [*Sperry UNIVAC*] ... SAT
System Access Terminal AT&T (NITA) ... SAT
System Accuracy Model ... SAM
System Acquisition Decision Memorandum (MCD) ... SADM
System Acquisition Report ... SAR
System Acquisition Review Council [*Army*] ... SARC
System Acquisition Review Memorandum [*Army*] ... SARM
System Acquisition School (MCD) ... SAS
System Activity Monitor [*Computer science*] ... SAM
System Administration Manager [*Hewlett-Packard Co.*] (PCM) ... SAM
System Administration Menu [*Hewlett-Packard Co.*] ... SAM
System Administrator [*Computer science*] ... SA
System Administrator [*Computer science*] ... SYSADMIN
System Administrator Tool for Analyzing Networks ... SATAN
System Advisory Board ... SAB
System Advisory Notice ... SAN
System Alignment Procedure (NATG) ... SAP
System Alignment Test (NVT) ... SAT
System Allocation Document [*NASA*] (NASA) ... SAD
System Amendment Detail(s) (NITA) ... SAD
System Analysis and Integration Model (IAA) ... SAIM
System Analysis - Building Block Approach [*Ge Cae International and Gen-Red Ltd.*] [*Software package*] (NCC) ... SABBA
System Analysis Drawing ... SAD
System Analysis Indicator (MCD) ... SAI
System Analysis Machine (IAA) ... SAM
System Analysis of Manned Space Operations (MCD) ... SAMSON
System Analysis of Vulnerability and Effectiveness (IAA) ... SAVE
System Analysis Report ... SAR
System Analysis Research Unit ... SARU
System Analysis Study ... SAS
System Analysis Table (IAA) ... SAT
System and Computer Evaluation Revision Technique ... SCERT
System and Logistics ... S & L
System Application Architecture [*IBM Corp.*] ... SAA
System Application Group (SAA) ... SAG
System Application Software [*Computer science*] (BUR) ... SAS
System Approach to Training for Transfer Effectiveness Evaluation (DNAB) ... SAT for TEE
System Architecture Design Package ... SADP
System Architecture Development Study [*NATO Integrated Communications System*] (NATG) ... SADS
System, Area, Function, Equipment ... SAFE
System Array RADAR (KSC) ... SAR
System Assessment ... SA
System Assessment Capability ... SAC
System Assistance Visit [*Army*] ... SAV
System Automation Corp. [*Information service or system*] (IID) ... SAC

System Automation Software, Inc. .... SASI
System Availability and Reliability Analysis (MHDB) .... SARA
System Availability Calculation Tool [*Science Applications International Corp.*] (MCD) .... SACT
System Availability Estimator .... SAVE
System Availability Report .... SAR
System [*or Subsystem*] Availability Unit .... SAU
System Avionics Value Estimation .... SAVE
System Balance Measure (BUR) .... SBM
System Billing Unit (NITA) .... SBU
System Breakdown Structure [*Military*] (AFIT) .... SBS
System Buffer Element (NITA) .... SBE
System Builder Kit [*Digital Research, Inc.*] [*Computer science*] (PCM) .... SBK
System Building Block [*Computer science*] .... SBB
System Burning Time .... SBT
System Bus Controller (NITA) .... SBC
System Calibration, Repair, and Maintenance Model [*Military*] (CAAL) .... SCRAMM
System Calibration Support Plan [*Air Force*] (CET) .... SCSP
System Capability .... SC
System Casualty Control Console [*Military*] (CAAL) .... SCCC
System Catalog [*Computer science*] (ECII) .... SYSCTLG
System Category Code (NITA) .... SC
System Centre, Saskatchewan Revenue Supply and Services, Regina, Saskatchewan [*Library symbol National Library of Canada*] (NLC) .... SRSC
System Change Failure (SAA) .... SCF
System Change Notice .... SCN
System Change Package .... SCP
System Change Request .... SCR
System Change Review Group [*George C. Marshall Space Flight Center*] (NASA) .... SCRG
System Check and Utility Master (MCD) .... SUM
System Checkout Automatic Network Simulator .... SCANS
System Check-Out Computer (PDAA) .... SCO
System Checkout Test Set (MCD) .... SCOTS
System Circuit Test .... SCT
System Cold Wire Tests .... SCWT
System/Command Accounting/Monitoring of Projects (DNAB) .... SCAMP
System Command Language [*Computer science*] .... SCL
System Commonality Analysis Tool (SSD) .... SCAT
System Communication (MHDI) .... SCOM
System Communication Area (ECII) .... SCA
System Communication Controller .... SCC
System Communication Pamphlet (IEEE) .... SCP
System Communications .... SYSCOM
System Comparison Analysis [*Bell System*] .... SCA
System Compatibility and Performance Evaluation [*Military*] (CAAL) .... SCAPE
System Compatibility Tests .... SCT
System Compatibility Vehicle .... SCV
System Component Test (IAA) .... SCT
System Component Verification .... SCV
System Components Test Station (MCD) .... SCTS
System Computerized for Economical Performance, Tracking, Recording and Evaluation [*North Central Airlines*] .... SCEPTRE
System Concept Development Working Group .... SCDWG
System Concept Paper [*Army*] (RDA) .... SCP
System Conceptual Requirement (SSD) .... SCR
System Configuration Acceptance Test (IAA) .... SCAT
System Configuration Management Board (SSD) .... SCMB
System Configuration Table (IAA) .... SCT
System Configuration Unit (MCD) .... SCU
System Conformance Statement [*Telecommunications*] ... SCS
System Contents Directory [*Computer science*] (MHDB) ... SCD
System Contractor Management Plan [*NASA*] (NASA) ...... SCMP
System Control Adapter (IAA) .... SCA
System Control and Monitor [*Telecommunications*] (TSSD) .... SCM
System Control and Receiving Station [*Air Force*] .... SCARS
System Control Area .... SCA
System Control Audit Review File [*Computer science*] .... SCARF
System Control Code (MCD) .... SCC
System Control Console (MCD) .... SCC
System Control Distribution Computer (MHDB) .... SCDC
System Control Incorporated Identification Program [*Navy*] .... SCIDNT
System Control Interface .... SCI
System Control Interface Package [*Computer science*] (MHDI) .... SCIP
System Control Module [*NASA*] (GFGA) .... SCM
System Control Number .... SCN
System Control Panel (IAA) .... SCP
System Control Processor [*Honeywell, Inc.*] .... SCP
System Control Program (NITA) .... SCP
System Control Programming [*Computer science*] .... SCP
System Control Record (NITA) .... SCR
System Control Registers [*Computer science*] .... SCR
System Control Routine .... SCR
System Control Signal Unit (NITA) .... SCSU
System Control Unit .... SCU
System Controller [*Military*] (CAAL) .... SC
System Controller .... SC
System Controlling Research Image Processing Tasks (MCD) ... SCRIPT
System Coordinate Center [*Military*] (CAAL) .... SCC
System Coordination Document .... SCD
System Coordination for SAGE [*Semiautomatic Ground Environment*] Computer Programming [*Military*] (IAA) .... SCSCP
System Coordinator / Anomaly Handler (SSD) .... SC/AH
System Core Image Library Maintenance Program [*Computer science*] (IAA) .... SYSCMA

System Cost and Operational Resource Evaluation (MCD) ... SCORE
System Counterpart Officer [*Military*] (AFIT) .... SCO
System Data Acquisition System .... SYDAS
System Data Buffer (MCD) .... SDB
System Data Flow Diagram (IAA) .... SDFD
System Data Format [*Computer science*] .... SDF
System Data Link Control [*Telecommunications*] .... SDLC
System Data Module (IAA) .... SDM
System Data Record .... SDR
System Data Synthesizer (KSC) .... SDS
System Database .... SDB
System Debugging Aids (NITA) .... SDAID
System Decision Manager (IAA) .... SDM
System Decision Paper .... SDP
System Definition Manual [*NASA*] (NASA) .... SDM
System Definition Record [*Computer science*] (IBMDP) ... SDR
System Definition Requirements .... SDR
System Demonstration [*Military*] .... SD
System Demonstration Flight Test [*DoD*] .... SDFT
System Description .... SD
System Description and Implementation Plan [*Navy*] ...... SDIP
System Descriptive Language [*Computer science*] (IEEE) ... SDL
System Design Agency [*Bell Telephone Laboratory*] (MCD) ... SDA
System Design Agency-Subcontractor Design Direction (MCD) ... SDA-S
System Design and Development Environment .... SDDE
System Design and Performance Requirements .... SDPR
System Design Confirmation .... SDC
System Design Description [*Nuclear energy*] (NRCH) ...... SDD
System Design Document [*NASA*] (MCD) .... SDD
System Design Group (MCD) .... SDG
System Design Kit .... SDK
System Design Language .... SDL
System Design Proposal [*Navy*] .... SDP
System Design Report [*NATO*] (NATG) .... SDR
System Design Review [*NASA*] (NASA) .... SDR
System Design Specification .... SDS
System Designator (AFIT) .... SD
System Designator Code (AFM) .... SDC
System Developer Interface Activity [*Computer science*] ... SYDIA
System Developers' Kit [*Computer hardware*] [*Microsoft, Inc.*] (PCM) ... SDK
System Development and Integration (MCD) .... SD & I
System Development and Performance .... SDAP
System Development Breadboard Facility .... SDBF
System Development Corp. [*Information service or system*] (IID) ... SDC
System Development Corp., Technical Information Center Library, Santa Monica, CA [*Library symbol Library of Congress*] (LCLS) ... CStmoS
System Development Engine (NITA) .... SDE
System Development Facility [*NASA*] (KSC) .... SDF
System Development Handbook [*NASA*] (NASA) .... SDH
System Development Language [*1971*] [*Computer science*] (CSR) ... SDL
System Development Life Cycle .... SDLC
System Development Notification .... SDN
System Development Requirement [*Air Force*] .... SDR
System Diagram Index (IAA) .... SDI
System Directory List [*Computer science*] (BUR) .... SDL
System Discrepancy Report .... SDR
System Drawer .... SD
System Dynamic Tester .... SDT
System Effective Data Rate (BUR) .... SEDR
System Effectiveness [*Army*] (AABC) .... SE
System Effectiveness Assurance Management System (MCD) ... SEAMS
System Effectiveness Data System [*Air Force*] .... SEDS
System Effectiveness Engineering Section .... SEES
System Effectiveness Forecast Report .... SEFR
System Effectiveness Information Central .... SEIC
System Effectiveness Measure (IAA) .... SEM
System Effectiveness Model (CAAL) .... SEM
System Electronics Laboratory (MCD) .... SEL
System Element (NASA) .... SE
System Employment and Organizational Plan [*Army*] ...... SEOP
System Engineering (IAA) .... SE
System Engineering Analysis .... SEA
System Engineering Analysis Facility (MCD) .... SEAFAC
System Engineering Analysis Report .... SEAR
System Engineering Communication (IAA) .... SECOM
System Engineering Cost Reduction Assistance Contractor (PDAA) ... SECRAC
System Engineering Division [*Apollo Spacecraft Program Office*] ... SED
System Engineering Groundrule [*NASA*] (NASA) .... SEG
System Engineering Implementation Plan .... SEIP
System Engineering Instrumentation (NASA) .... SEI
System Engineering Integration and Test (MCD) .... SEIT
System Engineering Laboratories (MCD) .... SEL
System Engineering Management [*NASA*] .... SEM
System Engineering Management Plan .... SEMP
System Engineering Management Standard .... SEMS
System Engineering Release Order (MCD) .... SERO
System Enhancement and Support [*Military*] (CAAL) ...... SEAS
System Entry Date [*Military*] (AFIT) .... SED
System Environment Qualification Test .... SEQT
System Environment Recording (BUR) .... SER
System Environment Recording and Edit Program [*Computer science*] (IAA) ... SEREP
System Environment Recording, Editing, and Printing [*Computer science*] ... SEREP
System Equalizer (IAA) .... SE

System/Equipment Inventory ... SEI
System/Equipment Population Summary ... SEPS
System Error Analysis ... SEA
System Error Bridge ... SEB
System Error Notification [*Computer science*] ... SEN
System Error Record Editing Program [*Computer science*] ... SEREP
System Evaluation and Reliability Checker ... SEARCH
System Evaluation, Integration, and Test (MCD) ... SEIT
System Evaluation Planning and Assessment Model (MCD) ... SEPA
System Evaluation Program (IAA) ... SEVA
System Evaluation System (MCD) ... SES
System Evaluation Technique (IAA) ... SET
System Evaluation Test Equipment [*Military*] (CAAL) ... SETE
System Executive (MHDB) ... SYSEX
System Expansion [*In "Macintosh SE"*] [*Apple Computer, Inc.*] ... SE
System Experience Correlation and Analysis Program (IAA) ... SECAP
System Extension Test ... SET
System External Storage ... SES
System Failure Analysis Report (IEEE) ... SFAR
System Failure Summaries [*NASA*] (KSC) ... SFS
System Fault Tolerant [*Novell, Inc.*] [*Orem, UT*] [*Telecommunications*] ... SFT
System Fielding Readiness Analysis [*Army*] ... SFRA
System Fielding Readiness Assessment [*Army*] ... SFRA
System for Access [*Computer science*] (IAA) ... SYFA
System for Access Network [*Wespac*] (TSSD) ... SYFANET
System for Aiding Man-Machine Interaction [*Prime Computer (UK) Ltd. and Prime Computers CAD/CAM Ltd.*] [*Software package*] (NCC) ... SAMMIE
System for Aircrew Flight Extension and Return (PDAA) ... SAFER
System for Analysis, Research, and Training (USDC) ... START
System for Analysis, Research and Training (EERA) ... START
System for Anesthetic and Respiratory Analysis ... SARA
System for Application [*Computer science*] ... SYFA
System for Automated Flight Efficiency (PDAA) ... SAFE
System for Automatic Generation and Analysis ... SAGA
System for Automatic Message Switching [*Telecommunications*] (TSSD) ... SAM
System for Automatic Value Exchange [*Computer science*] ... SAVE
System for Automation of Materiel Plan for Army Materiel/Budget (AABC) ... SAMBUD
System for Automation of Materiel Plans for Army Material (MCD) ... SAMPAM
System for Autonomous Bodies Reporting and Evaluation [*Joint project of the Government of Bangladesh and United Nations Department of Technical Co-operation for Development*] [*Information service or system*] ... SABRE
System for Business Automation (IAA) ... SBA
System for Capacity and Orders Planning and Enquiries (PDAA) ... SCOPE
System for Circuit Evaluation and Prediction of Transient Radiation Effect (MCD) ... SCEPTRE
System for Collection and Analysis of Near-Collision Reports (AAG) ... SCAN
System for Comparative Analysis of Community Action Programs [*Information service or system*] (AEBS) ... SCANCAP
System for Comparative Analysis of Programs For Educational Development [*Information service or system*] (AEBS) ... SCANPED
System for Computer Automated Typesetting (PDAA) ... SCAT
System for Computerization of Office Processes (MHDI) ... SCOOP
System for Computerized Application Analysis [*Automotive engineering*] ... SCAAN
System for Computerized Olympic Results and Events [*Texas Instruments, Inc.*] ... SCORE
System for Computerized Reporting of Information for Better Education (MHDI) ... SCRIBE
System for Conceptual Information Summarization, Organization, and Retrieval [*Software package*] (IT) ... SCISOR
System for Constant Elevation Precipitation Transmission and Recording ... SCEPTRE
System for Controlling Returns in Inventory and Production Data [*IRS*] ... SCRIP
System for Correspondence Recording and Interrogation by EDP [*Electronic Data Processing*] ... SCRIBE
System for Countering Interdiction Missiles and Targets RADARs (MCD) ... SCIMITAR
System for Data Calculation [*Information retrieval*] ... SDC
System for Data Retrieval [*Information retrieval*] ... SDR
System for Documentation and Information in Metallurgy [*Fachinformationszentrum Werkstoffe eV*] [*Information service or system*] (IID) ... SDIM
System for Electronic Analysis and Retrieval of Criminal Histories [*Project succeeded by National Crime Information Center*] [*Department of Justice*] ... SEARCH
System for Electronic Evaluation and Retrieval [*Computer science*] ... SEER
System for Emission Sampling and Measurement [*Automotive engineering*] ... SESAM
System for Equipment Requirements Forecasting (MHDB) ... SERF
System for Estimating Wartime Attrition and Replacement Requirements (AABC) ... SYMWAR
System for Evaluation of Tactical Information on Missile Destroyers ... SATIR
System for Exploring Alternative Resource Commitments in Higher Education [*Computer science*] ... SEARCH
System for Holding and Retrieving Wanted Data (IAA) ... SHREWD
System for Hospital Uniform Reporting ... SHUR
System for Improved Acoustic Performance ... SIAP
System for Improved Acquisition of Material (MCD) ... SIAM
System for Inertial Experiment Priority and Attitude Control (MCD) ... SIXPAC
System for Information Management and Program Logic for Education and Research (IAA) ... SIMPLER
System for Information on Grey Literature in Europe [*European Association for Grey Literature Exploitation*] [*Commission of the European Communities*] [*Information service or system*] (IID) ... SIGLE
System for Information Storage and Retrieval and Analysis ... SISTRAN
System for Instructional Response Analysis ... SIRA
System for Integrated Maintenance and Program Language Extension ... SIMPLE
System for Interactive Guidance and Information [*Computerized career-counseling service offered by the Educational Testing Service*] [*Princeton, NJ*] ... SIGI
System for Interactive Test Editing, Analysis, and Retrieval (IAA) ... SITAR
System for International Literature Information on Ceramics and Glass [*Fachinformationszentrum Werkstoffe*] [*Database*] ... SILICA
System for Locating Eruptive Underwater Turbidity and Hydrography [*Marine science*] (OSRA) ... SLEUTH
System for Locating Eruptive Underwater Turbidity and Hydrography (USDC) ... SLEUTH
System for Management and Allocation of Resources Technique [*Computer science*] ... SMART
System for Manipulation and Retrieval of Text ... SMART
System for Mass Balancing in Off-line (IAA) ... SYMBOL
System for Mineral Products [*European Community*] (MHDB) ... SYSMIN
System for Nuclear Auxiliary Power (IAA) ... SNAP
System for Nuclear Observation of Possible Explosives [*Science Applications International Corp.*] [*Aviation*] ... SNOOPE
System for Online Optimization [*Computer science*] (PDAA) ... SOLO
System for Ordinary Life Operations [*Insurance*] ... SOLO
System for Organizing Content to Review and Teach Educational Subjects ... SOCRATES
System for Organizing Current Reports to Aid Technologists and Scientists (NITA) ... SOCRATES
System for Organizing Current Reports to Aid Technology and Science ... SOCRATES
System for Personnel Automated Reports, Transactions, and Notices [*Census Bureau, NASA*] ... SPARTAN
System for Pinpointed, Exhaustive and Expeditious Dissemination of Subjects (PDAA) ... SPEEDS
System for Precise Navigation [*Later, DNSS*] (MCD) ... SSPN
System for Private Access for Reservations and Travel Agents [*British*] (DI) ... SPARTA
System for Processing Educational Data Electronically ... SPEDE
[*A*] **System for Programmers** ... ASP
System for Projecting Ammunition Repairable End Items [*Military*] ... SPARE
System for Projection and Analysis ... SPAN
System for Pupil and Program Evaluation and Development (EDAC) ... SPPED
System for Quick Ultra-Fiche-Based Information Retrieval [*Computer science*] (PDAA) ... SQUIRE
System for Resources Management [*Jet Propulsion Laboratory, NASA*] ... SRM
System for Safeguarding and Developing Mineral Production [*EC*] (ECED) ... SYSMIN
System for Takeoff Weight ... STOW
System for Telephone Administrative Response [*Computer science*] ... STAR
System for Testing Evaluation of Potential [*Employee evaluation software*] [*London House, Inc.*] ... STEP
System for the Automated Management of Text from a Hierarchical Arrangement ... SAMANTHA
System for the Mechanical Analysis and Retrieval of Text ... SMART
System for Thermal Diagnostic Studies ... STDS
System for Time and Accomplishment Reporting (MCD) ... STAR
System for Upper Atmosphere Sounding (MCD) ... SUAS
System Function Description (IEEE) ... SFD
System Function Description Algorithmic Language (IAA) ... SFDALGOL
System Functional Design Specification (MCD) ... SFDS
System Functional Diagram [*or Drawing*] (KSC) ... SFD
System Gain ... SG
System Generation Cross-Reference Index [*NASA*] ... SGINDEX
System Generation Language (IAA) ... SGL
System Generator Program (NITA) ... SYSGEN
System Ground Data Equipment [*RADAR*] ... SGDE
System Hazard Analyses [*NASA*] (NASA) ... SHA
System - Hydraulic, Electrical, Mechanical, Pneumatic ... S-HEMP
System Identification Data List [*Navy*] (NG) ... SIDL
System Identification from Tracking (MCD) ... SIFT
System Implementation Language [*Computer science*] ... SIL
System Improvement Plan (INF) ... SIP
System Independent Data Format [*Computer science*] (PCM) ... SIDF
System Information [*Computer science*] (PCM) ... SI
System Information Processing Program (MCD) ... SIPP
System Information Reports Formatting (MCD) ... SIRF
System Informatise pour Biblitheques [*Information System for Libraries*] (EAIO) ... SIBIL
System Initialization Routine ... SIR
System Initialize Program (IAA) ... SIP
System Input [*Computer science*] (MDG) ... SYSIN
System Input/Output Adapter (CAAL) ... SIOA
System Input Stream [*or Unit*] [*Computer science*] (MHDI) ... SYSIPT
System Input Unit I [*Computer science*] (AEBS) ... SSINI
System Integrated Access Method (IAA) ... SIAM
System Integration ... SI
System Integration Area (MCD) ... SIA
System Integration Board (SSD) ... SIB
System Integration Computer (MCD) ... SIC
System Integration Equipment (KSC) ... SIE
System Integration Laboratory and Test Facility ... SILTF
System Integration of Triad Technology (IAA) ... SITT

System Integration Receiver [*System*] .... SIR
System Integration Receiver System (MCD) .... SIRS
System Integration Schedule [*NASA*] (NASA) .... SIS
System Integration Support .... SIS
System Integration Support Service .... SISS
System Integration Test .... SIT
System Integration Test Program .... SITP
System Integration Test Program Board .... SITPB
System Integration Test Service .... SITS
System Integration Test Site [*Military*] (CAAL) .... SITS
System Integration Test Vehicle .... SITV
System Integration Unit (IAA) .... SIU
System Integrational Diagnostic (IAA) .... SID
System Interconnect Bus [*Computer science*] .... SIB
System Interface Document [*NASA*] (NASA) .... SID
System Interface Requirements (NASA) .... SIR
System [*or Subsystem*] Interface Unit .... SIU
System Internal Performance Evaluator (IAA) .... SIPE
System International (IAA) .... SI
System International Tinplate Area .... SITA
System Interrupt Supervisor .... SIS
System Inventory [*or Review of Systems*] (DAVI) .... SI
System Investigation Equipment (KSC) .... SIE
System Junction Module [*Deep Space Instrumentation Facility, NASA*] .... SJM
System Language .... SL
System Level Requirement [*Military*] (CAAL) .... SLR
System Library [*Computer science*] (MDG) .... SYSLIB
System Library File [*Computer science*] (BUR) .... SLF
System Life Cycle .... SLC
System Life Cycle Estimation .... SLICE
System Line Image Composer .... SLIC
System Line Item Number (MCD) .... SLIN
System Load and Initialization [*NASA*] (NASA) .... SL & I
System Loader [*Computer science*] .... SLDR
System Log [*Computer science*] .... SYSLOG
System Logic and Algorithm Development .... SLAD
System Maintenance Manual .... SMM
System Maintenance Monitor [*Telecommunications*] (IAA) .... SMM
System Maintenance Monitor Console [*FAA*] .... SMMC
System Maintenance Program (IAA) .... SMP
System Maintenance Test .... SMT
System Maintenance Trainer (MCD) .... SMT
System Maintenance Unit [*Computer science*] .... SMU
System Malfunction Analysis Reinforcement Trainer .... SMART
System Malfunction Report .... SMR
System Management and Control .... SMAC
System Management and Review Technique (HGAA) .... SMART
System Management Application Entity .... SMAE
System Management Application Process [*or Protocol*] [*Telecommunications*] .... SMAP
System Management Directive (AFM) .... SMD
System Management Facility [*IBM Corp.*] .... SMF
System Management Interface Tool [*IBM Corp.*] .... SMIT
System Management Interrupt [*Computer science*] (PCM) .... SMI
System Management Mode [*Computer science*] (PCM) .... SMM
System Management Office (AFIT) .... SMO
System Management/Performance Monitor [*NASA*] (NASA) .... SM/PM
System Management/Performance Monitor .... SW/PM
System Management Plan .... SMP
System Management Research Operation (DIT) .... SYMRO
System Management Work Group .... SMWG
System Manager [*Military*] (AFM) .... SM
System Manager or Item Manager (AFIT) .... SM/IM
System MANPRINT [*Manpower and Personnel Integration*] Management Plan [*Army*] .... SMMP
System Manual (IAA) .... SM
System Master Tape (IAA) .... SMT
System Material Analysis List .... SMAL
System Measurement Facility [*Computer science*] (IEEE) .... SMF
System Measurement Software (IAA) .... SMS
System Mechanical Performance .... SMP
System Mechanics .... SM
System/Memory Control Unit (NITA) .... SCU
System Memory Interface [*Computer science*] .... SMI
System Memory Pool (PCM) .... SMP
System Message Block [*Telecommunications*] (PCM) .... SMB
System Migration Section [*Social Security Administration*] .... SMS
System Modification Program [*Computer science*] .... SMP
System Modulation Transfer [*Acutance*] [*Photography*] .... SMT
System Monitor .... SM
System Monitor Board .... SMB
System Monitor Console (CAAL) .... SMC
System Monitor Controller (NITA) .... SMC
System Monitor Kernal (MHDI) .... SMK
System Monitoring and Coordinating Center [*National Weather Service*] (USDC) .... SMCC
System Monitoring and Coordinating Center [*Marine science*] (OSRA) .... SMCC
System Monitoring and Reporting Tool (HGAA) .... SMART
System Monitoring Unit .... SMU
System Net Activity Program (NITA) .... SNAP
System Network Activity Program [*Sperry UNIVAC*] .... SNAP
System Network Computer Center [*Louisiana State University*] [*Research center*] (RCD) .... SNCC
System Network Online Operations Information [*Suggested name for the Library of Congress computer system*] .... SNOOPI

System Network Processor .... SNP
System Noise Figure .... SNF
System Noise Temperature .... SNT
System Numerical Attributes (IAA) .... SNA
System Object Model [*Computer science*] (PCM) .... SOM
System Object Model/Distributed System Object Model [*Computer science*] .... SOM/DSOM
System of Analysis and Assignment of Operations according to Capacities (MHDI) .... SAAOC
System of Automatic Processing and Indexing of Reports .... SAPIR
System of Cellular Radio for Traffic Efficiency and Safety [*FHWA*] (TAG) .... SOCRATES
System of Circuit Analysis Program .... SYSCAP
System of Computerized Processing of Scientific Information [*Technical University of Wroclaw*] [*Information service or system*] (IID) .... APIN
System of Electronic Marks' Interrogation, Registration, and Administration [*Database*] [*WIPO*] [*United Nations*] (DUND) .... SEMIRA
System of Information Processing for Professional Societies .... SIPPS
System of Information Retrieval and Analysis, Planning [*Army Information service or system*] (IID) .... SIRAP
System of Multi-Cultural Pluralistic Assessment [*Psychiatry*] (DAVI) .... SMCPA
System of Multicultural Pluralistic Assessment [*Psychological and educational testing*] .... SOMPA
System of National Accounts [*United Nations*] .... SNA
System of National Accounts (EERA) .... SNA
System of National Accounts and System of Material Product Balances [*United Nations Statistical Office*] [*Information service or system*] (CRD) .... NAMAST
System of Operational Buoys in the North Atlantic [*Marine science*] (OSRA) .... SOBA
System of Operational Requirements Document [*Air Force*] (DOMA) .... SORD
System of Radio Communications Using a Satellite [*Telecommunications*] (TSSD) .... SYRACUSE
System of Reinforcement-Inhibition (PDAA) .... SRI
System of Social and Demographic Statistics (EERA) .... SSDS
System of Transportation Applying Rendezvous Technique (MCD) .... START
System on Automotive Safety Information [*General Motors Corp.*] [*Information service or system*] .... SASI
System Operational Complex .... SOC
System Operational Concept .... SOC
System Operational Readiness Test (MCD) .... SORT
System Operational Specification [*Military*] (CAAL) .... SOS
System Operational Test Evaluation (SAA) .... SOTE
System Operations Control [*Canadian Airlines International*] .... SOC
System Operations Panel (SSD) .... SOP
System Operator [*Computer networking*] .... SYSOP
System Operator Manual [*Military*] (CAAL) .... SOM
System Optical Quality (MCD) .... SOQ
System Optimization and Design Algorithm (HGAA) .... SODA
System Option Controller [*NASA*] (NASA) .... SOC
System Ordnance Safing Device [*Military*] .... SOSD
System Oriented Language .... SOL
System Output [*Computer science*] (IBMDP) .... SYSOUT
System Output Unit 1 [*IBM Corp.*] (MDG) SSOU1
System Overhaul Test Program .... SOTP
System Override (AAG) .... SO
System Package Plan [*or Program*] [*Military*] .... SPP
System Page Table [*Telecommunications*] (TEL) .... SPT
System Parameter (KSC) .... SP
System Parameter Record [*Computer science*] (IBMDP) .... SPR
System Parameter Table [*Computer science*] (IBMDP) .... SPT
System Parametric Allocation of Resources and Cost (MCD) .... SPARC
System Partitioning Unit [*Computer science*] .... SPU
System Peculiar Non-Repairable .... SPNR
System Performance Analyzer [*Motorola, Inc.*] .... SPA
System Performance and Activity Software Monitor [*Computer science*] (IEEE) .... SPASM
System Performance and Repeatability Test [*Military*] (CAAL) .... SPRT
System Performance Check Compound .... SPCC
System Performance Demonstration .... SPD
System Performance Evaluation (KSC) .... SPE
System Performance Factor [*Telecommunications*] (TEL) .... SPF
System Performance Indicator .... SPI
System Performance Measure (MCD) .... SYSPM
System Performance Model .... SPM
System Performance Rating .... SPR
System Performance Score [*Telecommunications*] (TEL) .... SPS
System Performance Simulation .... SPS
System Peripheral Output Utility [*Nuclear energy*] (NRCH) .... SPOUT
System Phasing Group (MCD) .... SPG
System Planning Team [*Military*] (AFIT) .... SPT
System Power Unit .... SPU
System Power Up .... SPU
System Probatoire d'Observation de la Terre [*of France*] [*Instrument*] (EERA) .... SPOT
System Problem Area (SAA) .... SPA
System Problem Report (MCD) .... SPR
System Processor (IEEE) .... SP
System Productivity Facility [*Computer science*] .... SPF
System Professional Computer (HGAA) .... SPC
System Program Assessment Review [*Air Force*] .... SPAR
System Program Directive (AFIT) .... SPD
System Program Director [*Air Force*] (MCD) .... SPD
System Program Loader .... SPL
System Program Management Surveys [*Air Force*] .... SPMS

System Program [or Project] Office [Military] .... SPO
System Program Office/Project Office [Air Force] (AFIT) .... SPO-PO
System Program Offices (IAA) .... SPOS
System Program Review [Military] (AABC) .... SPR
System Programmed Operator [Computer science] (MHDB) ...... SYSOPO
System Programmed Operators [Computer science] (MDG) ...... SYSPOP
System Programming Interface [Computer science] .... SPI
System Programming Language [Computer science] (NASA) ...... SPL
System/Project Management .... S/PM
System Punch [Computer science] (MHDI) .... SYSPCH
System Purchase of Long Lead Time Material .... SYSPLLTM
System Qualification Test Phase .... SQTP
System Qualification Tests .... SQT
System Queue Area [Computer science] (BUR) .... SQA
System Reaction Analysis [Bell System] .... SRA
System Reaction Time (KSC) .... SRT
System Reader [Computer science] (MHDI) .... SYSRDR
System Readiness Objective .... SRO
System Readiness Review (MCD) .... SRR
System Readiness Verification .... SRV
System Recovery Factor .... SRF
System Reference Library (HGAA) .... SRL
System Rehabilitation and Modernization (MCD) .... SRAM
System Reliability Analysis .... SRA
System Reliability Test .... SRT
System Replaceable Unit .... SRU
System Request [Computer science] (CDE) .... SysReq
System Requirement (SSD) .... SR
System Requirements Analysis .... SRA
System Requirements Review [NASA] .... SRR
System Requirements Specification (MCD) .... SRS
System Research and Planning Division [NASA] (KSC) ...... SRPD
System Residence [Computer science] .... SYSRES
System Resource and Status Table [Computer science] (IAA) ...... SRST
System Resource Manager [IBM Corp.] (BUR) .... SRM
System Resource Unit [Environmental Protection Agency] (GFGA) ...... SRU
System Response Time [Computer order entry] .... ST
System Review Board (MCD) .... SRB
System Routing Guide [Military] (CAAL) .... SRG
System Run Control Record .... SRCR
System Safety Assessment [Army] .... SSA
System Safety Development Center (IAA) .... SSDC
System Safety Engineering (AFM) .... SSE
System Safety Engineering Analysis (MCD) .... SSEA
System Safety Engineering Plan (AFM) .... SSEP
System Safety Group [Air Force] .... SSG
System Safety Group [Air Force] (AFM) .... SSGp
System Safety Hazard Analysis [Military] .... SSHA
System Safety Plan (MCD) .... SSP
System Safety Program Plan [Navy] .... SSPP
System Safety Risk Analysis [Army] .... SSRA
System Safety Society (EA) .... SSS
System Safety Working Group .... SSWG
System Science Institute [IBM Corp.] .... SSI
System Sclerosis [or Scleroderma] [Rheumatology] (DAVI) ...... SS
System Security Control Officer [Military] (GFGA) .... SSCO
System Security Manager [Military] (GFGA) .... SSM
System Security Officer .... SSO
System Security Plan .... SSP
System Segment (MCD) .... SS
System Segment Design Document .... SSDD
System Segment Specification (MCD) .... SSS
System Segment Table .... SST
System Selector Extension Unit .... SSEU
System Selector Unit .... SSU
System Sensitivity .... SS
System Service Order [Bell System] .... SSO
System Service Program [Computer science] (IAA) .... SSP
System Services Control Point [Computer science] .... SSCP
System Setup Indicator Panel .... SSIP
System Sign Inventory (DAVI) .... SSI
System Simulation Center .... SSC
System/Site Control (DOMA) .... SS
System Software [NASA] (MCD) .... SSAX
System Software [NASDAQ symbol] (TTSB) .... SSAX
System Software [Computer science] (IAA) .... SYSTSW
System Software Associates [Associated Press] (SAG) ...... SystSft
System Software Associates, Inc. [NASDAQ symbol] (NQ) ...... SSAX
System Software Associates, Inc. [Associated Press] (SAG) ...... SystSftw
System Software Loader (NASA) .... SSL
System Software Message [Computer science] (IAA) .... SSM
System Software Package Component List (MCD) .... SSPCL
System Software Reference Number [NASA] (NASA) ...... SSRN
System Software Requirement Review (MCD) .... SSRR
System Source Selection Board [Air Force] .... SSSB
System Source Selection Board Procedure [Air Force] ...... SSSBP
System Source Selection Procedure [Air Force] .... SSSP
System Specification (AAGC) .... A SPEC
System Specification Language .... SSL
System Specification Verification (IEEE) .... SYSVER
System Staff Office .... SSO
System Staff Office [or Officer] .... SYSTO
System Status Display .... SSD
System Status Evaluation [Army] (AABC) .... SSE
System Status Index (IAA) .... SSI

System Status Indicator [Bell System] .... SSI
System Status Panel .... SSP
System Status Report .... SSR
System Status Review .... SSR
System Stock List (NATG) .... SSL
System Study Requirement (AAG) .... SSR
System Subroutines (SAA) .... SS
System/Subsystem/Subject Number (MCD) .... S/S/SN
System Summary [NASA] (MCD) .... SS
System Summary Display [NASA] (MCD) .... SSD
System Supervisor .... SS
System Supply Manager .... SSM
System Support Controller (NITA) .... SSC
System Support Engineering .... SSE
System Support Equipment .... SSE
System Support Facility .... SSF
System Support Machine [Telecommunications] .... SSM
System Support Management [or Manager] [Military] (AFM) ...... SSM/IM
System Support Manager/Inventory Manager (MCD) .... SSM/IM
System Support Package Component List (MCD) .... SSPCL
System Support Package List (MCD) .... SSPL
System Support Processor (NITA) .... SSP
System Support Program (AFM) .... SSP
System Support Program-Interactive Communication Feature [Computer
   science] (MHDI) .... SSP-ICF
System Support Record .... SSR
System Support Technical Manager [Navy] (NG) .... SSTM
System Support Test Evaluation Program .... SSTEP
System Support Unification (MCD) .... SSU
System Support Unification Subsystem (MCD) .... SSUS
System Survey Team [Military] (AFIT) .... SST
System Synthesizer and Evaluation Center .... SYSEC
System Table (IAA) .... ST
System Tape Writer [Computer science] (IAA) .... STW
System Technical Control .... STC
System Technical Coordinator Technician (SAA) .... STCT
System Technical Services .... STS
System Technology Demonstration Program (RDA) .... STD
System Technology Test Facility (MCD) .... STTF
System Telecommunications Access Method [NCR Corp.] ...... STAM
System Ten European Language Ledger Accounting (PDAA) ...... STELLA
System Termination and Display Unit (MCD) .... STADU
System Test .... ST
System Test and Astronaut Requirement Simulation .... STARS
System Test and Evaluation .... STE
System Test and Operations Manual .... STOM
System Test and Operations Report .... STOR
System [or Subsystem] Test Bed [NASA] (KSC) .... STB
System Test Complex (IAA) .... STC
System Test Complex Data System .... STCDS
System Test Complex Equipment .... STCE
System Test Configuration .... STC
System Test Console .... STC
System Test Engineer [NASA] (NASA) .... STE
System Test Environment Input .... STEIN
System Test Equipment Mission [NASA] (KSC) .... STEM
System Test, Evaluation, and Assembly .... STEA
System Test Experiments Tape .... STET
System Test Facility .... STF
System Test Facility Data Display Control (SAA) .... STF DDC
System Test Loop (IEEE) .... STL
System Test Manufacturing Information System (IEEE) ...... STMIS
System Test Objective (IAA) .... STO
System Test Objectives .... STO
System Test Operator (IAA) .... STO
System Test Plan .... STP
System Test Procedure [Nuclear energy] (GFGA) .... STP
System Test Program [Navy] (CAAL) .... STP
System Test Report [Military] .... STR
System Test Review [NASA] (NASA) .... STR
System Test Set .... STS
System Test Software (CAAL) .... STS
System Test Station (SAA) .... STS
System Test Summary Report [NASA] (NASA) .... STSR
System Thermal Air Platform Reconnaissance Signature (MCD) ...... STARS
System Threat Assessment Report [Army] .... STAR
System Time Code Word .... STCW
System Time Unit (NITA) .... STU
System Time-Domain Simulation Program [Computer science] (PDAA) ..... SYSTID
System Timing Element (ECII) .... STE
System Timing Unit .... STU
System to Accumulate and Retrieve Financial Information with Random
   Extraction [Computer science] .... STARFIRE
System to Automate Records (NITA) .... STAR
System to Coordinate the Operation of Peripheral Equipment ...... SCOPE
System to Retrieve Information from Drug Evidence [Drug Enforcement
   Administration] .... STRIDE
System to Uncover Facts Fast .... STUFF
System Training Application Requirements .... STAR
System Training Equipment Requirement .... STER
System Training Exercise (SAA) .... STE
System Training Management Plan (MCD) .... STMP
System Training Mission (AFM) .... STM
System Training Plan .... STRAP
System Training Production Department (SAA) .... STPD

System Training Section (SAA) ... STS
System Training Specialist (SAA) ... STS
System Transatlantic [*Foreign language translator*] (EECA) ... SYSTRAN
System Transfer Constant ... STC
System Transition Unit [*Computer science*] ... STU
System Transmission Unit (NITA) ... STU
System Trouble Shooting ... STS
System Trouble Survey (CET) ... STS
System under Test (AAG) ... SUT
System Used for Prediction and Evaluation of Reliability [*Computer science*] (MHDI) ... SUPER
System User Engineered (IAA) ... SUE
System Utility Facility for Easy Recovery [*NASA*] ... SUFFER
System Utilization Monitor [*Computer science*] ... SUM
System Utilization Procedural Guide ... SUPG
System Utilization Procedure ... SUP
System Utilization Reporting Facility (HGAA) ... SURF
System Utilizing Signal-Processing for Automatic Navigation (MCD) ... SUSAN
System V Interface Definition (NITA) ... SVID
System Validation Model (NVT) ... SVM
System Validation Testing ... SVT
System Valve Engineering ... SVE
System Verification Installation ... SVI
System Verification Test [*Automotive engineering*] ... SVT
System Verification Unit ... SVU
System Weapons Coordinator [*Navy*] (CAAL) ... SWC
System Work Area ... SWA
System Work List Item Number (DNAB) ... SWLIN
System Work Team (MCD) ... SWT
System Workshops in Forecasting Techniques [*Bell System*] ... SWIFT
Systema Malykh [*Small System*] [*Russian Computer science*] ... SM
Systema Nervosum Vegetativo [*Obsolete term for the autonomic nervous system*] [*Medicine*] ... SNV
Systematic Activity Modeling Method (MHDB) ... SAMM
Systematic Aid to Flow on Existing Roads [*Traffic-control system*] ... SAFER
Systematic Alien Verification for Entitlements [*Immigration and Naturalization Service*] ... SAVE
Systematic Approach to Group Technology (PDAA) ... SAGT
Systematic Approach to Multidimensional Occupational Analysis (MCD) ... SAMOA
Systematic Assertiveness Training ... SAT
Systematic Assessment of Licensee Performance [*Nuclear energy*] (NRCH) ... SALP
Systematic Communications of Range Effectiveness (MUGU) ... SCORE
Systematic Control of Range Effectiveness (IAA) ... SCORE
Systematic Design Language [*Computer science*] ... SDL
Systematic Design Language [*Computer science*] ... SDS
Systematic Effort to Analyze Results ... SEAR
Systematic Equipment Analysis and Cost Optimization Scanning Technique (MHDB) ... SEACOST
Systematic Evaluation and Analysis of a LASER in a Test Environment (MCD) ... SEALITE
Systematic Evaluation Program [*Nuclear Regulatory Commission*] ... SEP
Systematic Evolution of Ligands by Exponential Enrichment [*Genetics*] ... SELEX
Systematic Exploration and Mapping Program [*National Oceanic and Atmospheric Administration*] (MSC) ... SEAMAP
Systematic Interaction Model (PDAA) ... SYSTIM
Systematic Layout Planning [*Industrial engineering*] ... SLP
Systematic Machinery and Equipment Selection (PDAA) ... SYMES
Systematic National Acquisitions Programme [*Public Archives of Canada*] ... SNAP
Systematic Organizational Design ... SORD
Systematic Planning for the Integration of Defense Engineering and Research [*Program*] ... SPIDER
Systematic Plotting and Evaluation of Enumerated Data [*National Institute of Standards and Technology Computer science*] ... SPEED
Systematic Pulmono/Cardiac Anaphylaxis Resusitation Kit (MCD) ... SPARK
Systematic Software Development and Maintenance [*Computer science*] (MHDI) ... SSDM
Systematic Tabular Analysis of Requirements Technique (IEEE) ... START
Systematic Teaching and Measuring Mathematics [*Education*] ... STAMM
Systematic Training for Effective Parenting ... STEP
Systematized Assertive Therapy [*Psychology*] (DAVI) ... SAT
Systematized Nomenclature of Medicine ... SNOMed
Systematized Nomenclature of Pathology [*NCI*] ... SNOP
Systeme Communautaire d'Acces a la Documentation [*Database*] [*EC*] (ECED) ... SCAD
Systeme d'Acces a la Banque Informatique des Nomenclatures Europeennes [*Database*] [*EC*] (ECED) ... SABINE
Systeme d'Atterrissage a Trajectoires Multiples [*Aviation*] ... SATRAM
Systeme de Reference pour la Determination de l'Affaiblissement Equivalent pour la Nettete [*Master telephone transmission reference system*] ... SRAEN
Systeme Economique Latino-Americain [*Latin American Economic System - LAES*] [*French*] ... SELA
Systeme Electronique Couleur avec Memoire [*French broadcast color standard*] ... SECAM
Systeme Fundamental Europeen de Reference pour la Transmission Telephonique [*European master telephone reference system*] ... SFERT
Systeme Informatique pour la Conjoncture [*Information System for the Economy*] [*INSEE*] [*France*] [*Information service or system*] (IID) ... SIC
Systeme Integre de Gestion Informatise des Ressources Documentaires [*Integrated System for the Management of Documentary Resources*] [*University of Quebec, Montreal*] [*Information service or system*] (IID) ... SIGIRD
Systeme Integre pour les Bibliotheques Universitaires de Lausanne [*Integrated System for the University of Lausanne Libraries*] [*Switzerland*] (IID) ... SIBIL
Systeme International (NITA) ... SI
Systeme International d'Unites [*International System of Units*] [*Also, SIU*] ... SI
Systeme International d'Unites [*International System of Units*] [*Also, SI*] ... SIU
Systemed [*NASDAQ symbol*] (SAG) ... SYSM
SysteMed Inc. [*NASDAQ symbol*] (TTSB) ... SYSM
Systemed, Inc. [*Associated Press*] (SAG) ... Systmd
System-Generated Electromagnetic Pulse [*Army*] ... SGEMP
Systemhouse Ltd. [*Toronto Stock Exchange symbol*] ... SHS
Systemhouse Ltd., Technical Library, Ottawa, ON, Canada [*Library symbol*] [*Library of Congress*] (LCLS) ... CaOOSHT
System-Human Interaction ... S-HI
Systemic [*Medicine*] (DAVI) ... sys
Systemic [*Medicine*] ... syst
Systemic Acquired Resistance [*Biology*] ... SAR
Systemic Antibiotic [*Medicine*] ... SA
Systemic Arterial Hypertension [*Cardiology*] (DAVI) ... SAH
Systemic Arterial Pressure [*Medicine*] ... SAP
Systemic Arterial Resistance [*Medicine*] ... SAR
Systemic Aspergillosis [*Medicine*] (DMAA) ... SA
Systemic Availability Ratio [*Physiology*] ... SAR
Systemic Bacterial Infection (DAVI) ... SBI
Systemic Blood Pressure [*Medicine*] (MAE) ... SBP
Systemic Capillary Leak Syndrome [*Medicine*] (DMAA) ... SCLS
Systemic Inflammatory Response Syndrome [*Medicine*] ... SIRS
Systemic Lupus Erythematosus [*Medicine*] ... SLE
Systemic Lupus Erythematosus Activity Measure [*Medicine*] (DMAA) ... SLAM
Systemic Mastocytosis [*Medicine*] ... SM
Systemic Necrotizing Vasculitis [*Medicine*] (CPH) ... SNV
Systemic Peripheral Vascular Resistance [*Cardiology*] (DAVI) ... SPVR
Systemic Progressive Sclerosis [*Medicine*] (AAMN) ... SPS
Systemic Resistance [*Medicine*] (MAE) ... SR
Systemic Side Effects [*Pharmacology*] (DAVI) ... SSE
Systemic Transformation Facility [*Former USSR*] (ECON) ... STF
Systemic Vascular Resistance [*Medicine*] ... SVR
Systemic Vascular Resistance Index ... SVRI
SyStemix, Inc. [*NASDAQ symbol*] (SPSG) ... STMX
Systemix, Inc. [*Associated Press*] (SAG) ... Systemix
Systemized Excerpt Abstracts and Reviews of Chemical Headlines (NITA) ... SEARCH
System-Level Engineering Document (SSD) ... SLED
Systems Acceptance Tests (KSC) ... SAT
Systems Acquisition and Implementation Program [*Environmental Protection Agency*] (GFGA) ... SAIP
Systems Acquisition Career ... SAC
Systems Acquisition Career Management Personnel Center [*DoD*] ... SACMPC
Systems Acquisition Career Management Program for Civilians (AAGC) ... SACMPC
Systems Acquisition Career Management Program for Civilians [*Air Force*] (DOMA) ... SACPMC
Systems Acquisition Contracting Course (AAGC) ... SACC
Systems Acquisition Management (AAGC) ... SAM
Systems Acquisition Management (DOMA) ... SAM
Systems Acquisition Management Inspection ... SAMI
Systems Acquisition Officer [*Military*] (AFIT) ... SAO
Systems Adapter Module ... SAM
Systems Adaptor Module (NITA) ... SAM
Systems Address ... SA
Systems Adviser ... SYSAD
Systems Alterations Status ... SALTS
Systems Analysis ... SA
Systems Analysis and Battle Management [*Military*] (RDA) ... SA/BM
Systems Analysis and Data Processing Office ... SADPO
Systems Analysis and Design (NITA) ... SAD
Systems Analysis and Engineering Development [*Naval Air Development Center*] (MCD) ... SAED
Systems Analysis and Integration Model (MCD) ... SAIM
Systems Analysis and Research Corp. ... SARC
Systems Analysis and Resource Accounting [*Data processing system*] ... SARA
Systems Analysis Branch (IAA) ... SAB
Systems Analysis Document (MCD) ... SAD
Systems Analysis for Integrated Relief Variation [*Engineering*] ... SAFIRE
Systems Analysis Group ... SAG
Systems Analysis Module (IEEE) ... SAM
Systems Analysis of an Integrated Network of Tasks [*Air Force*] ... SAINT
Systems Analysis of Manned Space Operations (MCD) ... SAMSO
Systems Analysis Office ... SAO
Systems Analysis Translator [*Computer science*] ... SYSTRAN
Systems Analyst ... SA
Systems Analyst Aptitude Test ... SAAT
Systems & Computer Tech [*NASDAQ symbol*] (TTSB) ... SCTC
Systems and Computer Technology (IAA) ... SCT
Systems & Computer Technology Corp. [*NASDAQ symbol*] (NQ) ... SCTC
Systems & Computer Technology Corp. [*Associated Press*] (SAG) ... SystCpt
Systems and Computers Evaluation and Review Technique [*Computer science*] ... SCERT
Systems and Control Technology Panel (ACII) ... SCTP
Systems and Data Service (IAA) ... SDS
Systems and Logistics (IAA) ... SAL
Systems and Management Panel (ACII) ... SMP
Systems and Procedures ... S-P
Systems and Procedures Association [*Later, ASM*] (EA) ... SPA
Systems and Procedures Association of America (IAA) ... SPAA

Systems and Procedures Exchange Center [*Association of Research Libraries*] .... SPEC

Systems and Services Section [*Library Administration and Management Association*] .... SASS

Systems and Software Simulator S3

Systems Application Architecture / Common User Access [*Computer science*] .... SAA/CUA

Systems Applications of Millimeter Wave Contact Seeker (MCD) .... SAMICS

Systems Applications Project Operation Action Detail (IAA) .... SAPOAD

Systems Approach to Managing BUSHIPS [*Bureau of Ships; later, NESC or ESC*]Acquisition [*Navy*] (MCD) .... SAMBA

Systems Approach to Training [*NASA*] (MCD) .... SAT

Systems Architecture [*British*] .... SA

Systems Assembly Language [*Computer science*] (IEEE) .... SAL

Systems Assessment Review [*NASA*] (KSC) .... SAR

Systems Assurance Program [*IBM Corp.*] .... SAP

Systems Auditability and Control [*Computer science*] .... SAC

Systems Automation Division [*Navy*] (DNAB) .... SAD

Systems Builders Association (EA) .... SBA

Systems Certification and Integration Facility .... SCIF

Systems Change Control Procedure [*Social Security Administration*] .... SCCP

Systems Change Impact Analysis [*Social Security Administration*] .... SCIA

Systems Change Proposal (AFM) .... SCP

Systems Command [*Air Force*] .... SC

Systems Command .... SYCOM

Systems Command [*Navy*] .... SYSCOM

Systems Communications Management Association (IAA) .... SCMA

Systems Component List (KSC) .... SCL

Systems, Components, and Displays .... SCD

Systems Concepts and Procedures .... SCAP

Systems Consolidation of Accessions and Trainees [*Military*] (AABC) .... SCAT

Systems Control [*Military*] (AABC) .... SYSCON

Systems Control Center .... SCC

Systems Control, Incorporated Computerized Library Operations [*Information service or system*] (IID) .... SCICLOPS

Systems Control Language [*Computer science*] .... SCL

Systems Control Microprocessor .... SCM

Systems Coordinative Reporting (MCD) .... SCORE

Systems Data Analysis .... SDA

Systems Data Analysis Section .... SDAS

Systems Definition Directive [*Military*] (AFM) .... SDD

Systems Design Laboratory (IAA) .... SDL

Systems Design Methodology [*Computer science*] (HGAA) .... SDM

Systems Designers [*Software manufacturer*] [*British*] .... SD

Systems Designers International Ltd. [*British*] (IRUK) .... SDI

Systems Designers Ltd. [*Research center British*] .... SDL

Systems Designers Ltd. (NITA) .... SDL

Systems Development (MCD) .... SD

Systems Development (NOAA) .... SYSDEV

Systems Development Analysis Program .... SDAP

Systems Development and Acquisition Plan (MCD) .... SDAP

Systems Development Branch [*Space Environmental Laboratory*] (USDC) .... SDB

Systems Development Branch [*Marine science*] (OSRA) .... SDB

Systems Development Department [*David W. Taylor Naval Ship Research and Development Center*] .... SDD

Systems Development Dictionary (NITA) .... SDD

Systems Development District (AAG) .... SDC

Systems Development Division [*Marine science*] (OSRA) .... SDD

Systems Development Laboratories (MCD) .... SDL

Systems Development Methodology [*Computer science*] (HGAA) .... SDM

Systems Development (Montreal), Information Resource Centre (Systemes-Applications Practiques (Montreal), Centre d'Information Specialise), Montreal, PQ, Canada [*Library symbol*] [*Library of Congress*] (LCLS) .... CaQMSD

Systems Development Office [*National Weather Service*] .... SDO

Systems Development Package [*or Plan*] [*Military*] (NG) .... SDP

Systems Directorate [*Army*] (RDA) .... SD

Systems Display [*Vancouver Stock Exchange symbol*] .... SMD

Systems Division [*Department of Commerce*] [*Information service or system*] (IID) .... SD

Systems Dynamic Analyzer .... SDA

Systems Effectiveness Analyzer (IEEE) .... SEA

Systems Effectiveness Demonstration (NG) .... SED

Systems Effectiveness Engineering (MCD) .... SEE

Systems Effectiveness Evaluation (NG) .... SEE

Systems Effectiveness Evaluation/Analyzer (DNAB) .... SEE/AN

Systems Effectiveness Plan .... SEP

Systems Effects Test [*Nuclear energy*] (GFGA) .... SET

Systems Efficiency Expert .... SEE

Systems Engineer [*or Engineering*] [*Computer science*] .... SE

Systems Engineer (NITA) .... SE

Systems Engineering and Integration .... SE & I

Systems Engineering and Management Operations [*Military*] .... SEMO

Systems Engineering and Management Support [*Air Force*] .... SEMS

Systems Engineering and Technical Assistance (MCD) .... SETA

Systems Engineering and Technical Assistance Contract .... SETAC

Systems Engineering and Technical Direction (AAG) .... SE & TD

Systems Engineering and Technical Direction (AAGC) .... SE/TD

Systems Engineering Branch [*NASA*] (NASA) .... SEB

Systems Engineering Department Report (IEEE) .... SEDR

Systems Engineering Detailed Schedule .... SEDS

Systems Engineering, Evaluation, and Research (MCD) .... SEER

Systems Engineering Facility [*Defense Communications Agency*] (RDA) .... SEF

Systems Engineering Group [*Air Force*] .... SEG

Systems Engineering Group/Research and Technology [*Air Force*] .... SEG/R & T

Systems Engineering Laboratories Data Bus (NITA) .... SELBUS

Systems Engineering Laboratory Circuit-Drawing Program (PDAA) .... SELCIR

Systems Engineering/Logistics Management (MCD) .... SE/LM

Systems Engineering Master Schedule .... SEMS

Systems Engineering Notice .... SEN

Systems Engineering, Policy Analysis and Management [*Delft University of Technology, Netherlands*] .... SEPA

Systems Engineering Process .... SEP

Systems Engineering Respecting Acquisition and Propagation of Heuristic Instructional Materials [*Chemistry*] .... SERAPHIM

Systems Engineering Review Board [*NASA*] (NASA) .... SERB

Systems Engineering Study .... SES

Systems Engineering Study on Atmospheric Measurements and Equipment (NOAA) .... SESAME

Systems Engineering Summary of Installation and Program Planning (IAA) .... SESIP

Systems Engineering Support .... SES

Systems Engineering Support and Management Integration (MCD) .... SESMI

Systems Engineering/Systems Integration (SDI) .... SE/SI

Systems Engineering Test (CET) .... SET

Systems Engineering Work Statement .... SES

Systems Equipment Engineer [*Telecommunications*] (TEL) .... SEE

Systems/Equipment/Munitions [*Army*] (AFIT) .... S-E-M

Systems Evaluation and Development Division [*NASA*] .... SEDD

Systems Evaluation and Exchange of Knowledge [*Computer science*] .... SEEK

Systems Evaluation Code Under Radiation Environment .... SECURE

Systems Evaluation Code Under Radiation Environment (IEEE) .... SEURE

Systems Evaluation Experiment (MCD) .... SEEX

Systems Evaluation Group .... SEG

Systems Evaluation Squadron [*Air Force*] .... SES

Systems Exchange [*Computer science*] (IAA) .... SYSX

Systems Experiment Correlation and Analysis Program (MCD) .... SECAP

Systems Extension Plan .... SEP

Systems Flexowriter Double Case .... SFD

Systems for Heat and Radiation Energy [*Nuclear energy*] .... SHARE

Systems for Nuclear Auxiliary Power .... SNAP

Systems for Nuclear Auxiliary Power Transient .... SNAPTRAN

Systems for Test Output Consolidation [*Computer science*] .... STOC

Systems for Tools and Equipment Management [*Military*] (AFIT) .... STEM

Systems Gauge [*Tool*] (AAG) .... SYGA

Systems Generator [*or Generation*] [*Computer science*] .... SYSGEN

Systems Group, Inc. [*Telecommunications service*] (TSSD) .... SGI

Systems Housekeeping .... SHK

Systems Identification Data Cost .... SIDC

Systems Implementation Plan [*Military*] .... SIP

Systems Improved Numerical Differencing Analyses [*Database*] .... SINDA

Systems Information Bulletin [*Computer science*] .... SIB

Systems Information Processing Analysis (EDAC) .... SIPA

Systems Integrated Test Plan [*Military*] (CAAL) .... SITP

Systems Integration and Checkout .... SICO

Systems Integration and Deployment [*Program*] [*Department of Transportation*] .... SID

Systems Integration Contractor .... SIC

Systems Integration Demonstrator [*Aircraft*] .... SID

Systems Integration Laboratory [*NASA*] (MCD) .... SIL

Systems Integration Management Review [*NASA*] (MCD) .... SIMR

Systems Integration Model (MCD) .... SIM

Systems Integration Office [*NASA*] (NASA) .... SIO

Systems Integration Review [*NASA*] (NASA) .... SIR

Systems Interface Test (NVT) .... SIT

Systems Language .... SLANG

Systems Library Subscription Service [*Computer science*] (IBMDP) .... SLSS

Systems Maintenance Management [*Computer science*] .... SMM

Systems Maintenance Procedure (MCD) .... SMP

Systems Maintenance Service (MCD) .... SMS

Systems, Man, and Cybernetics (MCD) .... SMC

Systems Management [*NASA*] (MCD) .... SM

Systems Management Analysis Group (MCD) .... SMAG

Systems Management Analysis Project (MCD) .... SMAP

Systems Management Analysis, Research, and Testing (MCD) .... SMART

Systems Management and Sequencing (NASA) .... SM & S

Systems Management Application Service Element [*Telecommunications*] (OSI) .... SMASE

Systems Management Branch [*Space Environmental Laboratory*] (USDC) .... SMB

Systems Management Branch [*Marine science*] (OSRA) .... SMB

Systems Management Processor (IAA) .... SMP

Systems Management Responsibility (SAA) .... SMR

Systems Management Server [*Microsoft Corp.*] (PCM) .... SMS

Systems Managers Administrative Rating Test [*Simulation game*] .... SMART

Systems Manufacturing Division [*IBM Corp.*] .... SMD

Systems Manufacturing Technology [*San Marcos, CA*] .... SMT

Systems Measurement Instrument [*Computer science*] .... SMI

Systems Measuring Device (KSC) .... SMD

Systems Memory [*Computer science*] (BUR) .... SM

Systems Methodology Office .... SMO

Systems Modernization Plan [*Social Security Administration*] .... SMP

Systems Monitor Display .... SMD

Systems Monitoring Panel (NVT) .... SMP

Systems Network Analysis Process [*Computer science*] (AEBS) .... SNAP

Systems Network Architecture [*IBM Corp.*] [*Computer science*] .... SNA

Systems Network Architecture and Transdata Coupling of Hosts [*IBM Corp.*] (IAA) .... SNATCH

Systems Network Architecture/Local Entry Networking (NITA) .... SNA/LEN

Systems Operating Test .... SOT

Systems Operation Center .... SOC

Systems Operation Plan [*NASA*] (KSC) .... SOP
Systems Operational Analysis Plan .... SOAP
Systems Operational Compatibility Assessment Review [*NASA*] .... SOCAR
Systems Operational Description [*or Design*] .... SOD
Systems Operational Requirement .... SOR
Systems Operator (EERA) .... SYSOP
Systems Optimization and Monitoring Services (MHDI) .... SOMS
Systems Orientation .... SO
Systems Parameters Document (AAG) .... SPD
Systems Performance/Design Requirements .... SP/DR
Systems Performance Effectiveness .... SPE
Systems Performance Effectiveness Conference .... SPECON
Systems Personnel Branch (SAA) .... SPB
Systems Planning and Effectiveness Evaluation Device (MCD) .... SPEED
Systems Planning and Integration Office [*NASA*] .... SPIO
Systems Planning Approach - North Atlantic [*FAA*] .... SPANAT
Systems Program Documentation .... SPD
Systems Program Manager .... SPM
Systems Program Office Cadre (MCD) .... SPOC
Systems Programming Aptitude Test .... SPAT
Systems Programming Ltd. (IAA) .... SPL
Systems Readiness Test (KSC) .... SRT
Systems Release Certification [*Social Security Administration*] .... SRC
Systems Reliability Service (NUCP) .... SRS
Systems Reproduction Order (MCD) .... SRO
Systems Requirements Document [*NASA*] .... SRD
Systems Research (DAVI) .... SR
Systems Research and Applications Corp. [*Arlington, VA*] (TSSD) .... SRA
Systems Research and Development Service [*FAA*] (MCD) .... SRDS
Systems Research Configuration .... SRC
Systems Research Group (CINC) .... SRG
Systems Research Integration Office [*Army Air Mobility Research and Development Laboratory*] [*St. Louis, MO*] .... SRIO
Systems Research Laboratory .... SRL
Systems Review [*Medicine*] .... SR
Systems Science and Cybernetics (MCD) .... SSC
Systems, Science, and Software .... SSS
Systems Simulation Research Laboratory .... SSRL
Systems Software Avionics Command Support (MCD) .... SACS
Systems Software Interface Processing [*NASA*] (MCD) .... SSIP
Systems Specifications [*NASA*] (NG) .... SS
Systems Support Center (BUR) .... SSC
Systems Support Division [*Air Force*] .... SSD
Systems Support Module [*NASA*] (MCD) .... SSM
Systems Support Module Equipment Section [*NASA*] (SSD) .... SSMES
Systems Support Service Module (SSD) .... SSSM
Systems Support Tape .... SST
Systems Tape Addition and Maintenance Program [*Computer science*] (IEEE) .... STAMP
Systems Techniques Laboratory [*Stanford University*] (MCD) .... STL
Systems Technology (IAA) .... ST
Systems Technology Forum [*Fairfax, VA*] [*Telecommunications*] (TSSD) .... STF
Systems Technology Inc. .... STI
Systems Technology Program (MCD) .... STP
Systems Technology Project Office .... STPO
Systems Technology RADAR (MCD) .... STR
Systems Technology Reentry Experiment Program [*Military*] .... STREP
Systems Technology Report (MCD) .... STR
Systems, Test, and Checkout Report (DICI) .... STCR
Systems Test and Evaluation Plan [*Military*] (AABC) .... SYSTEP
Systems Test and Operation Language .... STOL
Systems Test Area .... STA
Systems Test Bed for Avionics Research .... STAR
Systems Test Complex [*NASA*] .... STC
Systems Test Equipment Program (MCD) .... STEP

Systems Test Planning Section (SAA) .... STPS
Systems Test Unit (KSC) .... STU
Systems Testing Branch [*Social Security Administration*] .... STB
Systems Training and Exercise Module (MCD) .... STEM
Systems Training Program [*RADAR*] .... STP
Systems Training Program Exercise (AABC) .... STPX
Systems Unit Method [*Medical transcription*] .... SUM
Systems Weapon Improvement Program [*A-6 Intruder*] (DOMA) .... SWIP
Systems West Consultants Ltd. [*Vancouver Stock Exchange symbol*] ..... SSW
Systems Work Assignment Group (SAA) .... SWAG
Systems Worthiness Analysis Program [*FAA*] .... SWAP
System-Segment [*Computer science*] .... SSEG
Systemsoft Corp. [*NASDAQ symbol*] (SAG) .... SYSF
Systemsoft Corp. [*Associated Press*] (SAG) .... SystmSft
System-Wide Medium-Term Environment Programme (GNE) .... SWMTEP
System-Wide On-Line Network for Information Control [*Computer science*] .... SONIC
Systemwide Program Committee [*Individually-guided education*] (AEE) .... SPC
Systemwide Project for Electronic Equipment at Depots [*Military*] (AABC) .... SPEED
Systemwide Project for Electronic Equipment at Depots Extended [*Military*] (AABC) .... SPEEDEX
Systmatic Productivity Improvement Review In TRADOC [*Training and Doctrine Command*] [*Army*] .... SPIRIT
Systolic [*Cardiology*] (DAVI) .... s
Systolic [*Cardiology*] .... syst
Systolic Anterior Motion [*Cardiology*] .... SAM
Systolic Blood Pressure [*Medicine*] .... SBP
Systolic Click [*Cardiology*] .... SC
Systolic Discharge [*Cardiology*] .... SD
Systolic Ejection Murmur [*Cardiology*] .... SEM
Systolic Ejection Murmur, Left Sternal Border [*Cardiovascular*] (DAVI) ..... SEMLSB
Systolic Ejection Period [*Cardiology*] .... SEP
Systolic Ejection Rate [*Cardiology*] (MAE) .... SER
Systolic Ejection Time [*Cardiology*] (MAE) .... SET
Systolic, First Heart Sound [*S2 is second heart sound, etc., through S4*] [*Cardiology*] (DAVI) S1
Systolic Hypertension in the Elderly Program [*Medicine*] .... SHEP
Systolic Mean [*Cardiology*] .... SM
Systolic Murmur [*Cardiology*] .... SM
Systolic Murmur [*Cardiology*] (BABM) .... SYST M
Systolic Murmur [*Cardiology*] (DAVI) .... syst m
Systolic Pressure [*Cardiology*] .... SP
Systolic Pressure Time Index [*Cardiology*] (DAVI) .... SPTI
Systolic Threshold Pressure [*Cardiology*] .... SPTH
Systolic Time Interval [*Cardiology*] .... STI
Systolic to Diastolic [*Cardiology*] (MAE) .... S/D
Systolic Wall Stress [*Cardiology*] .... SWS
Syuhurei [*South Korea*] [*Seismograph station code, US Geological Survey Closed*] (SEIS) .... SYU
SYVA Co., Palo Alto, CA [*Library symbol Library of Congress*] (LCLS) .... CPaSy
Syva Research Library, Palo Alto, CA [*OCLC symbol*] (OCLC) .... SYV
Syzygy Mathematics (WDAA) .... SM
Szabad Demokratak Szovetsege [*Alliance of Free Democrats*] [*Hungary Political party*] (EY) .... SzDSz
Szakszervezetek Orszagos Tanacsa [*National Trade Union Council*] [*Hungary*] .... SZOT
Szczecin [*Poland*] [*Airport symbol*] (OAG) .... SZZ
Szechuan Province [*China, Mainland*] [*MARC geographic area code Library of Congress*] (LCCP) .... a-cc-sz
Szeged [*Hungary*] [*Seismograph station code, US Geological Survey Closed*] (SEIS) .... SZE
Szegedi Orvostudomanyi Egyetem, Szeged, Hungary [*Library symbol Library of Congress*] (LCLS) .... HuSzOE
SZL Sportsight [*Vancouver Stock Exchange symbol*] .... SZL
Szondi Test [*Psychology*] .... ST

T

By Meaning

T & H Resources Ltd. [*Toronto Stock Exchange symbol*] .... THE
T. B. Monroe's Kentucky Reports [*17-23 Kentucky*] [*A publication*]
   (DLA) .... Mon T B
T. B. Monroe's Kentucky Reports [*17-23 Kentucky*] [*A publication*]
   (DLA) .... T B Mon (KY)
T. B. Monroe's Kentucky Supreme Court Reports [*17-23 Kentucky*] [*1824-
28*] [*A publication*] (DLA) .... T B Mon
T. B. Scott Free Library, Merril, WI [*Library symbol Library of Congress*]
   (LCLS) .... WMer
T B Wood's [*NYSE symbol*] (TTSB) .... TBW
T Cell Sciences [*NASDAQ symbol*] (TTSB) .... TCEL
T Cell Sciences, Inc. [*Associated Press*] (SAG) .... T Cell
T Cell Sciences, Inc. [*Cambridge, MA*] [*NASDAQ symbol*] (NQ) ..... TCEL
T Early Alpha [*Genetics*] .... TEA
T. Finch's Precedents in English Chancery [*1689-1722*] [*A publication*]
   (DLA) .... Fin T
T. G. Sheppard International Fan Club (EA) .... TGSIFC
'T Heiling Land [*Nijmegen*] [*A publication*] (BJA) .... 'tHL
T J Cinnamons Wrrt'A' [*NASDAQ symbol*] (TTSB) .... TJCIW
T J Cinnamons Wrrt'B' [*NASDAQ symbol*] (TTSB) .... TJCIZ
T J International [*NASDAQ symbol*] (TTSB) .... TJCO
T. Jones' English King's Bench Reports [*84 English Reprint*] [*A publication*]
   (DLA) .... T Jo
T. Jones' English King's Bench Reports [*84 English Reprint*] [*A publication*]
   (DLA) .... T Jones
T. Jones' English King's Bench Reports [*84 English Reprint*] [*A publication*]
   (DLA) .... T Jones (Eng)
T. J.'s [*Tom Jones*] Fans of Soul (EA) .... TJFS
T. L. L. Temple Memorial Library, Diboll, TX [*Library symbol Library of
Congress*] (LCLS) .... TxDib
T R Financial [*NASDAQ symbol*] (TTSB) .... ROSE
T. Rowe Price Associates, Inc. [*Baltimore, MD*] [*NASDAQ symbol*] (NQ) ..... TROW
T/SF Communications [*AMEX symbol*] (TTSB) .... TCM
T/SF Communications Corp. [*AMEX symbol*] (SPSG) .... TCM
T/SF Communications Corp. [*Associated Press*] (SAG) ...... TSF
T Suppressor [*Cell*] [*Immunology*] .... Ts
T Switch Cell [*Immunology*] .... TSW
T Tauri Infrared Companion [*Object believed to be first planet sighted that is
not in our solar system*] .... TIRC
T. U. P. Charlton's Georgia Reports [*A publication*] (DLA) ..... T U P Charlt
T. U. P. Charlton's Georgia Reports [*A publication*] (DLA) ..... TUPC
T V G Technologies Wrrt'A' [*NASDAQ symbol*] (TTSB) ...... TVGWF
T V G Technologies Wrrt'B' [*NASDAQ symbol*] (TTSB) ...... TVGZF
T V G Technologies Wrrt'C' [*NASDAQ symbol*] (TTSB) ...... TVGLF
T. W. Cape and Associates [*Atlanta, GA*] [*Telecommunications service*]
   (TSSD) .... TWCA
T. W. Josey High School, Augusta, GA [*Library symbol Library of Congress*]
   (LCLS) .... GAuJ
T-18 Builders and Owners Association (EA) .... TBOA
Ta Ta for Now .... TTFN
TAAG Linhas Aereas de Angola [*Angola*] [*ICAO designator*] (ICDA) ..... DT
TAAG, Linhas Aereas de Angola [*ICAO designator*] (FAAC) ..... DTA
TAAG-Angola Airlines [*ICAO designator*] (AD) .... DT
Ta'anith (BJA) .... Ta
Ta'anith (BJA) .... Ta'an
Tab Card Punch Control .... TCPC
Tab Card Reader .... TCR
Tab Products [*AMEX symbol*] (TTSB) .... TBP
Tab Products Co. [*Associated Press*] (SAG) .... TabPrd
Tab Products Co. [*AMEX symbol*] (SPSG) .... TBP
Tab Sequence Format .... TSF
Tab Set [*Typography*] (WDMC) .... TS
Tab Set [*Typesetting*] (WDMC) .... ts
Tabas [*Iran*] [*ICAO location identifier*] (ICLI) .... OIMT
Tabatinga [*Brazil*] [*Airport symbol*] (OAG) .... TBT
Tabatinga/Internacional [*Brazil ICAO location identifier*] (ICLI) ..... SBTT
Tab-automated Bonded [*Computer science*] (PCM) .... TAB
Tabele [*Papua New Guinea*] [*Seismograph station code, US Geological
Survey*] (SEIS) .... TBL
Tabella [*Tablet*] [*Pharmacy*] .... TAB
Tabella [*Tablet*] [*Pharmacy*] (ROG) .... TABEL
Taber, AB [*AM radio station call letters*] .... CKTA
Taber Public Library, Alberta [*Library symbol National Library of Canada*]
   (NLC) .... ATA
Tabernacle (VRA) .... tbnle
Tabibuga [*Papua New Guinea*] [*Airport symbol*] (OAG) ...... TBA

Tabiki [*Surinam*] [*ICAO location identifier*] (ICLI) .... SMTA
Tabiteuea (North) [*Kiribati*] [*ICAO location identifier*] (ICLI) ..... NGTE
Tabiteuea North [*Kiribati*] [*Airport symbol*] (OAG) .... TBF
Tabiteuea (South) [*Kiribati*] [*ICAO location identifier*] (ICLI) ..... NGTS
Tabiteuea South [*Kiribati*] [*Airport symbol*] (OAG) .... TSU
Tablas [*Philippines*] [*Airport symbol*] (OAG) .... TBH
Table .... T
Table .... TAB
Table .... TBL
Table .... TBL
Table and Art Glassware Manufacturers [*Defunct*] (EA) ..... TAGM
Table and Item Documentation System .... TIDOS
Table and Item Inventory (SAA) .... TII
Table Base Register .... TBR
Table Data Organization and Reductions .... TADOR
Table Editing Process .... TEP
Table Fashion Institute (EA) .... TFI
Table Grape Advisory Committee [*Western Australia*] .... TGAC
Table Indicator [*Computer science*] .... TI
Table Input to Memory .... TIM
Table Input to Memory/Table Output from Memory (NITA) ..... TIM/TOM
Table Jellies Association (DBA) .... TJA
Table Look Up [*Computer science*] .... TLU
Table Lookaside Buffer [*Computer science*] (MHDB) .... TLB
Table Maintenance (NASA) .... TM
Table Maintenance Block Update (NASA) .... TMBU
Table Manipulation Language (MHDB) .... TAMALAN
Table Mountain [*California*] [*Seismograph station code, US Geological Survey
Closed*] (SEIS) .... TMC
Table Mountain Observatory (USDC) .... TMO
Table Mountain Observatory [*Marine science*] (OSRA) .... TMO
Table Mountain Radio Astronomy Observatory .... TMRAO
Table of Allowances (MCD) .... TA
Table of Allowances (DOMA) .... TOA
Table of Allowances .... TOA
Table of Authorization .... TA
Table of Authorized Personnel (NATG) .... TAP
Table of Coincidences [*Telecommunications*] (TEL) .... TOC
Table of Contents (IT) .... TC
Table of Contents .... TOC
Table of Contents Editor Processor [*Computer science*] ..... TOCED
Table of Distribution [*Military*] .... TD
Table of Distribution and Allowances [*Military*] (AABC) ..... TDA
Table of Distribution-Augmentation [*Military*] .... TDA
Table of Equipment [*Army*] .... TE
Table of Equipment Ready Issue [*Navy*] (ANA) .... TERI
Table of Organization .... TO
Table of Organization and Allowance .... TOA
Table of Organization and Equipment Working Group [*Army*] ..... TOEWG
Table of Organization and Management .... TOM
Table of Organization Equipment .... TOE
Table of Organization (Tentative) .... T/OT
Table of Output Products .... TOP
Table of Personnel Distribution (NATG) .... T/PD
Table of Replaceable Parts .... TRP
Table Producing Language [*1971*] [*Computer science*] (IID) ..... TPL
Table Rock [*New York*] [*Seismograph station code, US Geological Survey*]
   (SEIS) .... TBR
Table Ronde Internationale pour le Developpement de l'Orientation
[*International Round Table for the Advancement of Counselling - IRTAC*]
   (EAIO) .... TRIDO
Table Simulation [*or Simulator*] (IAA) .... TABSIM
Table Structure Overview [*NASA*] .... TSO
Table Tennis Association of Wales (DBA) .... TTAW
Table Top Rotaprint (DGA) .... TTR
Tableaux Entrees-Sorties [*Database*] [*EC*] (ECED) .... TES
Tabled Agreement [*in labor relations*] .... TA
Tableland [*Western Australia*] [*Airport symbol*] (AD) .... TBL
Tables and Charts through Extended Character Sets [*Computer
science*] .... TACTECS
Tables for Approximation of Midpoints for Exponential Regression
   (MCD) .... TAMPER
Tables of Basic Allowances [*Previously, Basic Tables of Commissioning
Allowances*] [*Navy*] .... TBA
Tables of Distribution and Allowances Mobilization Troop Basis [*Army*]
   (AABC) .... TDAMTB

Tables of Distribution Mobilization Troop Basis [*Army*] (AABC) .... TDMTB
Tables of Organization and Equipment [*Military*] (AAG) .... TO & E
Tables of Organization and Equipment [*Military*] .... TOE
Tables of Organization and Equipment Mobilization Troop Basis [*Army*]
(AABC) .... TOEMTB
Tables of Redemption Values for US Savings Bonds .... TRVB
Tablespoon [*Measure*] .... T
Tablespoon [*Measure*] (WGA) .... tb
Tablespoon [*Measurement*] (DAVI) .... tbl
Tablespoon .... TBLSP
Tablespoon .... TBS
Tablespoon .... TBSP
Tablespoonful (ODBW) .... tbsp
Tablet (WGA) .... T
Tablet (ADA) .... TA
Tablet (WDAA) .... TAB
Tablet Triturate [*Pharmacy*] .... TT
Tablet-Shaped [*As in "T-grains"*] [*Photography*] .... T
Tablettes Cappadociennes [*Paris*] [*A publication*] (BJA) .... TC
Tablettes Sumeriennes Archaiques [*A publication*] (BJA) .... TSA
Tabligbo [*Togo*] [*ICAO location identifier*] (ICLI) .... DXTA
Tabloid (NTCM) .... TAB
Tabloid Lithographers, Inc., Avenel, NJ [*Library symbol Library of
Congress*] (LCLS) .... NjAveT
Tablon de Tamara [*Colombia*] [*Airport symbol*] (AD) .... TTM
Tabloncillo [*Race of maize*] .... TAB
Tabloncillo Perla [*Race of maize*] .... T-P
Taboga [*Costa Rica*] [*ICAO location identifier*] (ICLI) .... MRTG
Taboo Search [*Optimization method*] .... TS
Tabor City, NC [*AM radio station call letters*] .... WTAB
Tabor City, NC [*FM radio station call letters*] .... WYNA
Tabor College, Hillsboro, KS [*Library symbol Library of Congress*] (LCLS) .... KHiIT
Tabora [*Tanzania*] [*ICAO location identifier*] (ICLI) .... HTTB
Tabora [*Tanzania*] [*Airport symbol*] (OAG) .... TBO
Tabou [*Ivory Coast*] [*ICAO location identifier*] (ICLI) .... DITB
Tabou [*Ivory Coast*] [*Airport symbol*] (OAG) .... TXU
Tabriz [*Iran*] [*ICAO location identifier*] (ICLI) .... OITT
Tabriz [*Iran*] [*ICAO location identifier*] (ICLI) .... OITV
Tabriz [*Iran*] [*Seismograph station code, US Geological Survey*] (SEIS) .... TAB
Tabriz [*Iran*] [*Airport symbol*] (OAG) .... TBZ
Tab-Tronic Recorder (DIT) .... TTR
Tabubil [*Papua New Guinea*] [*Airport symbol*] (OAG) .... TBG
Tabubil [*Papua New Guinea*] [*Seismograph station code, US Geological
Survey*] (SEIS) .... TZZ
Tabueran Island [*Fanning Islands*] [*Kiribati*] [*ICAO location identifier*] (ICLI)..... PLFA
Tabuk [*Saudi Arabia*] [*ICAO location identifier*] (ICLI) .... OETB
Tabuk [*Saudi Arabia*] [*Airport symbol*] (OAG) .... TUU
Tabula [*Plate*] [*Latin*] .... t
Tabular Data (BUR) .... TD
Tabular Firing Table [*Military*] (AABC) .... TFT
Tabular Language [*Computer science*] (IEEE) .... TAB
Tabular List of Parts (AAG) .... TLP
Tabular Parts List .... TPL
Tabular Sequence Control .... TASC
Tabular System Reliability Analysis .... TASRA
Tabular Systems-Oriented Language [*General Electric Co.*] [*British*] .... TABSOL
Tabular [*or Tabulator*] Tape Processor [*Computer science*] (IAA) .... TTP
Tabulate (AAG) .... TAB
Tabulated Assembly Technical Data List .... TATDL
Tabulated Drawing (MSA) .... TADR
Tabulated [*or Charted*] LORAN Reading [*Long-Range Aid to Navigation*] .... T
Tabulated Numerical Technical Data List .... TNTDL
Tabulating Card .... TAB-CD
Tabulating Card (AAG) .... TC
Tabulating Card Manufacturers Association [*Later, IOSA*] (EA) .... TCMA
Tabulating Form (AAG) .... TF
Tabulating Machine (IAA) .... TAB
Tabulating Simulator (NITA) .... TABSIM
Tabulation (NITA) .... TAB
Tabulation Block (MSA) .... TB
Tabulator Character (IAA) .... TABC
Tabulator Simulator .... TABSIM
Tabulator Stops (AAG) .... TABS
Tabun [*Nerve gas*] [*Army symbol*] .... GA
Taburiente [*Canary Islands*] [*Seismograph station code, US Geological
Survey*] (SEIS) .... TBT
TACA International Airlines SA [*El Salvador*] [*ICAO designator*] (ICDA) .... TA
TACA International Airlines SA [*El Salvador*] [*ICAO designator*] (FAAC) .... TAI
TACAMO [*Take Charge and Move Out*] Improvement Program .... TIP
TACAN [*Tactical Air Navigation*] Antenna System (DWSG) .... TAS
TACAN [*Tactical Air Navigation*] Distance Indicator .... TDI
TACAN [*Tactical Air Navigation*] Guidance Augmentation System [*Military*]
(CAAL) .... TGAS
TACAN [*Tactical Air Navigation*] RADAR Altimeter (NASA) .... TAC/RA
Tace [*Be Silent*] .... T
TACFIRE [*Tactical Fire*] Ad Hoc Group on Testing and Analysis
(MCD) .... TAGOTA
TACFIRE [*Tactical Fire*] Advanced Training Program [*Army*] .... TATP
TACFIRE Remote Terminal (MCD) .... TRT
TACFIRE Software Specialist (MCD) .... TSS
TACFIRE Training Assistance Team (MCD) .... TTAT
TACFIRE Training System (MCD) .... TTS
Tachikawa [*Japan ICAO location identifier*] (ICLI) .... RJTC
Tachilek [*Myanmar*] [*Airport symbol*] (OAG) .... THL
Tachilek [*Myanmar*] [*ICAO location identifier*] (ICLI) .... VBTL

Tachistoscope (WDMC) .... t-scope
Tachometer (IDOE) .... tach
Tachometer (AAG) .... TACH
Tachometer (DSUE) .... TACHO
Tachometer Calibration (DNAB) .... TAKCAL
Tachometer Generator (IAA) .... TACH
Tachometer Voltmeter .... TVM
Tachycardia [*Cardiology*] (DAVI) .... tach
Tachycardia [*Cardiology*] (AAMN) .... TACHY
Tachyelectromagnetic Pulse .... TEMP
Tachykinin Receptor [*Medicine*] (DMAA) .... TACR
Tachykinin-Like Immunoreactivity [*Laboratory science*] (DAVI) .... TKLI
Tacitus [*First century AD*] [*Classical studies*] (OCD) .... Tac
TACJAM [*Tactical Communications Jamming System*] Quickfix, Trail Blazer
Maintenance Trainer [*Army*] .... TQTMT
Tack Welded Joint .... TWJ
Tackapausha Museum, Seaford, NY [*Library symbol Library of Congress*]
(LCLS) .... NSeaTM
Tackboard [*Technical drawings*] .... TKBD
Tackle [*Football*] .... T
Tackle .... TCKL
Tackle [*Mechanical engineering*] .... TKL
Tackle and Shooting Sports Agents Association (EA) .... TSSA
Tackle and Shooting Sports Agents Association (EA) .... TSSAA
Tackle Representatives Association (EA) .... TRA
Tackle Representatives Association International [*Later, TSSAA*]
(EA) .... TRA INT'L
Tackle Representatives Association International [*Later, TSSAA*] (EA) .... TRAI
Tackled Attempting to Pass [*Football*] .... TAP
Tackline [*British naval signaling*] .... TL
Tackstrip [*Technical drawings*] .... TKS
Tacloban [*Philippines*] [*Airport symbol*] (OAG) .... TAC
Tacloban/Daniel Z. Romualdez, Leyte [*Philippines*] [*ICAO location identifier*]
(ICLI) .... RPVA
Tacna [*Peru*] [*ICAO location identifier*] (ICLI) .... SPTN
Tacna [*Peru*] [*Airport symbol*] (OAG) .... TCQ
Taco Cabana, Inc. [*NASDAQ symbol*] (SAG) .... TACO
Taco Cabana, Inc. [*Associated Press*] (SAG) .... TacoCab
Taco Cabana 'A' [*NASDAQ symbol*] (TTSB) .... TACO
TACOM [*Tank Automotive Command*] Scientific Advisory Group [*DoD*]
(EGAO) .... TASAG
Tacoma [*Washington*] [*Airport symbol*] (AD) .... TIW
Tacoma Branch Genealogical Library, Tacoma, WA [*Library symbol Library
of Congress*] (LCLS) .... WaTG
Tacoma Community College, Tacoma, WA [*Library symbol Library of
Congress*] (LCLS) .... WaTCC
Tacoma/Fort Lewis, WA [*Location identifier FAA*] (FAAL) .... GRF
Tacoma General Hospital, Pierce County Medical Library, Tacoma, WA
[*Library symbol Library of Congress*] (LCLS) .... WaTGH
Tacoma/McChord Air Force Base [*Washington*] [*ICAO location identifier*]
(ICLI) .... KTCM
Tacoma Municipal Belt Line Railway [*AAR code*] .... TMBL
Tacoma Public Library, Tacoma, WA [*Library symbol Library of Congress*]
(LCLS) .... WaT
Tacoma Public Schools, Professional and Curriculum Library, Tacoma, WA
[*Library symbol Library of Congress*] (LCLS) .... WaTPS
Tacoma, WA [*FM radio station call letters*] (RBYB) .... KBKS-FM
Tacoma, WA [*FM radio station call letters*] .... KBSG
Tacoma, WA [*FM radio station call letters*] .... KBTC
Tacoma, WA [*Television station call letters*] .... KBTC-TV
Tacoma, WA [*FM radio station call letters*] (RBYB) .... KCIN
Tacoma, WA [*Television station call letters*] .... KCPQ
Tacoma, WA [*AM radio station call letters*] (RBYB) .... KHHO-AM
Tacoma, WA [*AM radio station call letters*] .... KKMO
Tacoma, WA [*AM radio station call letters*] .... KMTT
Tacoma, WA [*FM radio station call letters*] .... KMTT-FM
Tacoma, WA [*FM radio station call letters*] .... KPLU
Tacoma, WA [*FM radio station call letters*] .... KRPM
Tacoma, WA [*Television station call letters*] .... KSTW
Tacoma, WA [*Television station call letters*] .... KTBW
Tacoma, WA [*FM radio station call letters*] .... KUPS
Tacoma, WA [*FM radio station call letters*] .... KVTI
Tacoma, WA [*Television station call letters*] .... KWDK
Tacoma, WA [*Location identifier FAA*] (FAAL) .... MAR
Tacoma, WA [*Location identifier FAA*] (FAAL) .... TCM
Tacoma, WA [*Location identifier FAA*] (FAAL) .... TIW
Tacon [*Flamenco dance term*] .... TAC
TACS/TADS OED [*Tactical Air Control System/Tactical Air Defense System
Operational Effectiveness Demonstration*] Special Study Group
[*Military*] .... TOSSG
TACSATCOM Management Office .... TSMO
TACSATCOM Single Channel Vehicular Terminal System (MCD) .... TSCVT
Tactica [*of Arrian*] [*Classical studies*] (OCD) .... Tact
Tactical (AAG) .... TAC
Tactical .... TACT
Tactical (AAG) .... TACTL
Tactical (AAG) .... TCTL
Tactical Action Display [*SAGE*] .... TAD
Tactical Action Observer [*Military*] (CAAL) .... TAO
Tactical Action Officer [*Navy*] (NVT) .... TAO
Tactical Action Programs .... TAP
Tactical Action Situation Display .... TASD
Tactical Advanced Combat Direction and Electronic Warfare (MCD) ...... TACDEW
Tactical Advanced Combat Direction and Electronic Warfare
Environmental Generation Control System [*Navy*] .... TACDEW/EGCS

Tactical Advisory [*Military*] (CAAL) .... TACAD
Tactical Advisory Service [*Department of Commerce*] .... TAS
Tactical Aerial Reconnaissance Pod System (MCD) .... TARPS
Tactical Aerial Surveillance and Reconnaissance Operational Capability Objectives [*1995*] (MCD) .... TASROCO
Tactical Aerial Targets Squadron (MCD) .... TATS
Tactical Aeromed Evacuation (CINC) .... TAE
Tactical Aeromedical Evacuation System .... TAES
Tactical Air [*Military*] (AABC) .... TACAIR
Tactical Air Against First and Following Enemy Echelons (MCD) .... TAAFFEE
Tactical Air Against First and Follow-On Eschelon (MCD) .... TAFFE
Tactical Air Armament Study (MCD) .... TAAS
Tactical Air Army (NATG) .... TAA
Tactical Air Base (AFM) .... TAB
Tactical Air Base Weather .... TABWX
Tactical Air Base Weather Dissemination System [*Air Force*] .... TABWDS
Tactical Air Base Weather Element [*Air Force*] .... TABWE
Tactical Air Beacon Command and Surveillance System (MCD) .... TABCASS
Tactical Air Combat Operations Staff (MCD) .... TACOPS
Tactical Air Combat Operations Staff .... TACOS
Tactical Air Combat Simulation (NATG) .... TACOS
Tactical Air Command [*Air Force*] .... TAC
Tactical Air Command/Air Force Systems Command .... TAC/AFSC
Tactical Air Command Aircraft Profiler Capability [*Air Force*] .... TACAP
Tactical Air Command and Control [*Air Force*] .... TACC
Tactical Air Command Center [*Air Force*] (NVT) .... TACC
Tactical Air Command, Central .... TACC
Tactical Air Command Control System (MCD) .... TACCS
Tactical Air Command, Deputy Commander for Air Defense (MCD) .... ADTAC
Tactical Air Command Letter [*Air Force*] .... TACL
Tactical Air Command Liaison Officer (FAAC) .... TACLO
Tactical Air Command Manual [*Air Force*] .... TACM
Tactical Air Command Office of Operations Analysis [*Langley Air Force Base, VA*] .... TAC-OA
Tactical Air Command Pamphlet [*Air Force*] .... TACP
Tactical Air Command Post [*Air Force*] (MCD) .... TACP
Tactical Air Command Regulation [*Air Force*] .... TACR
Tactical Air Communications [*or Control*] System Improvements [*Air Force*] (MCD) .... TACSI
Tactical Air Control and Landing System [*Military*] (IAA) .... TACALS
Tactical Air Control and Navigation .... TACTAN
Tactical Air Control Center [*Air Force*] .... TACC
Tactical Air Control Center Operations (NVT) .... TACCOPS
Tactical Air Control Center Squadron .... TACCS
Tactical Air Control Coordinator .... TACCO
Tactical Air Control Flight [*Military*] .... TAIRCF
Tactical Air Control Group [*Military*] .... TACG
Tactical Air Control Group [*Military*] .... TACGP
Tactical Air Control Group [*Military*] (NVT) .... TACGRU
Tactical Air Control Group [*Military*] (AFIT) .... TAIRCG
Tactical Air Control Operation Center .... TACOC
Tactical Air Control Party [*Air Force*] .... TACP
Tactical Air Control Point .... TACP
Tactical Air Control Squadron [*Military*] .... TACRON
Tactical Air Control Squadron [*Air Force*] .... TACSQ
Tactical Air Control Squadron [*Air Force*] .... TAIRCS
Tactical Air Control System [*Air Force*] .... TACS
Tactical Air Control System/Tactical Air Defense System .... TACS/TADS
Tactical Air Control/Tactical Air Defense System [*Military*] (CAAL) .... TAC/TADS
Tactical Air Control Training .... TACT
Tactical Air Control Wing [*Air Force*] .... TAIRCW
Tactical Air Controller (NVT) .... TAC
Tactical Air Coordination Center [*Military*] (CAAL) .... TACC
Tactical Air Coordination Element .... TACE
Tactical Air Coordinator (SAA) .... TAC
Tactical Air Coordinator [*or Controller*] (Airborne) [*Military*] (NVT) .... TAC(A)
Tactical Air Cover .... TAC
Tactical Air Defense (MCD) .... TAD
Tactical Air Defense Alerting System [*Army*] .... TADAS
Tactical Air Defense Systems (RDA) .... TADS
Tactical Air Designation Grid System [*Tactical Air Command*] .... TADGC
Tactical Air Direction [*Military*] .... TAD
Tactical Air Direction Center [*Military*] .... TADC
Tactical Air Direction Post [*Military*] .... TADP
Tactical Air Exercise (CINC) .... TAX
Tactical Air Force .... TAF
Tactical Air Force Headquarters .... TAFHQ
Tactical Air Force Initiative (MCD) .... TAFIN
Tactical Air Force Integrated Information Systems (MCD) .... TAFIIS
Tactical Air Force Maintenance Management (MCD) .... TAFMM
Tactical Air Force Required Operational Capability (MCD) .... TAFROC
Tactical Air Force Systems Engineering Group (MCD) .... TAFSEG
Tactical Air Forces Intelligence Exploitation System .... TAFIES
Tactical Air Forces Interoperability Group [*Air Force*] .... TAFIG
Tactical Air Group [*MTMC*] (TAG) .... TAG
Tactical Air Intelligence Data Handling System (NATG) .... TAIDHS
Tactical Air Intelligence System [*Military*] (MCD) .... TAIS
Tactical Air Launched Decoy (DOMA) .... TALD
Tactical Air Liaison Officer [*Air Force*] .... TALO
Tactical Air Missile .... TA
Tactical Air Missile .... TAM
Tactical Air Mission [*Air Force*] .... TAM
Tactical Air Navigation [*System*] .... TACAN
Tactical Air Navigation .... TACAN
Tactical Air Navigation Control Center (DNAB) .... TACANCEN

Tactical Air Navigation Distance Measuring Equipment .... TACAN-DME
Tactical Air Navigation System [*Helicopter*] .... TANS
Tactical Air Observation [*or Observer*] (NATG) .... TAO
Tactical Air Officer (NVT) .... TAO
Tactical Air Operations .... TAO
Tactical Air Operations Center .... TAOC
Tactical Air Operations Control Center (NATG) .... TAOCC
Tactical Air Operations Module/Modular Control Equipment [*Military*] (RDA) .... TAOM/MCE
Tactical Air Operations Officer [*Tactical Air Command*] .... TAOO
Tactical Air Power Evaluation [*Air Force*] .... TAPE
Tactical Air Reconnaissance (AFM) .... TAR
Tactical Air Reconnaissance and Aerial Battlefield Surveillance System [*Military*] .... TARABS
Tactical Air Reconnaissance and Electronic Warfare Support (MCD) .... TAREWS
Tactical Air Reconnaissance Center [*Shaw Air Force Base*] .... TARC
Tactical Air Reconnaissance Center Office of Operations Analysis [*Shaw Air Force Base, SC*] .... TARC-OA
Tactical Air Reconnaissance School [*Air Force*] .... TARS
Tactical Air Request (NVT) .... TAR
Tactical Air Request Net [*Army*] (DOMA) .... TARN
Tactical Air Research and Survey Office [*Air Force*] .... TARS
Tactical Air Squadron (DOMA) .... TACRON
Tactical Air Strike Force [*Air Force*] .... TASF
Tactical Air Support [*Tactical Air Command*] .... TAS
Tactical Air Support Aircraft .... TASA
Tactical Air Support Center (CINC) .... TASC
Tactical Air Support Control System [*Military*] (PDAA) .... TASCS
Tactical Air Support Coordination Center (MCD) .... TASCC
Tactical Air Support Element [*Military*] (AABC) .... TASE
Tactical Air Support for Maritime Operations [*Navy*] (NVT) .... TASMO
Tactical Air Support Force [*Air Force*] .... TASF
Tactical Air Support Group [*Air Force*] (AFIT) .... TASG
Tactical Air Support Section [*Military*] .... TASS
Tactical Air Support Squadron [*Military*] .... TASS
Tactical Air Support Squadron [*Military*] (AFM) .... TASSq
Tactical Air Support Training Group [*Air Force*] .... TASTG
Tactical Air Support Training Squadron [*Air Force*] .... TASTNGSq
Tactical Air Support Training Squadron [*Air Force*] .... TASTS
Tactical Air Target Recommender .... TATR
Tactical Air Threat Environment Description (MCD) .... TACAIR TED
Tactical Air Traffic Control (NVT) .... TATC
Tactical Air Warfare Center [*Air Force*] .... TAWC
Tactical Air Warfare Group .... TAWG
Tactical Air Weapons Control System .... TAWCS
Tactical Air [*or Airlift*] Wing .... TAW
Tactical Airborne Beacon System (AFM) .... TABS
Tactical Airborne Command, Control, and Surveillance .... TACCS
Tactical Airborne Controller Aircraft [*Military*] (CAAL) .... TACA
Tactical Airborne Countermeasures or Strike [*Air Force*] .... TACOS
Tactical Airborne Information Document (NVT) .... TACAID
Tactical Airborne Laser Communication (DOMA) .... TALC
Tactical Airborne Laser Communications [*Military*] (LAIN) .... TALC
Tactical Airborne LORAN Navigation System [*Model*] (MCD) .... TALONS
Tactical Airborne Processing, Interpretation, and Transmission System [*Military*] .... TAPITS
Tactical Airborne Reconnaissance Pod .... TARP
Tactical Airborne Recording Package .... TARP
Tactical Airborne SIGINT Support Improvement Acquisition Plan (MCD) .... TASSI
Tactical Airborne Signal Exploitation System (MCD) .... TASES
Tactical Airborne SONAR Decision Aid .... TASDA
Tactical Airborne Warning and Control System (AFM) .... TAWACS
Tactical Airborne Weather Stations (MCD) .... TABWS
Tactical Aircraft .... TA
Tactical Aircraft Guidance System [*Air Force*] .... TAGS
Tactical Aircraft Mission Planning System (DOMA) .... TAMPS
Tactical Aircraft Recovery (CINC) .... TAR
Tactical Aircraft Support Model (MCD) .... TASMOL
Tactical Aircrew Combat Training System (NVT) .... TACTS
Tactical Aircrew Combat Training System/Air Combat Maneuvering Instrumentation (MCD) .... TACTS/ACMI
Tactical Airfield Fuel Dispensing System (NG) .... TAFDS
Tactical Air-Land Operations (MCD) .... TALON
Tactical Air-Launched Cruise Missile (MCD) .... TALCM
Tactical Air-Launched Missile (MCD) .... TALM
Tactical Airlift [*Tactical Air Command*] .... T/A
Tactical Airlift Center (AFM) .... TALC
Tactical Airlift Center Office of Operations Analysis [*Pope Air Force Base, NC*] .... TALC-OA
Tactical Airlift Duty Officer (AFM) .... TADO
Tactical Airlift Group (MCD) .... TAG
Tactical Airlift Modernization .... TAM
Tactical Airlift Squadron [*Air Force*] .... TACAIRLIFTSq
Tactical Airlift Squadron [*Air Force*] .... TAS
Tactical Airlift Squadron [*Air Force*] .... TASQ
Tactical Airlift Training Group [*Air Force*] .... TATG
Tactical Airlift Training Squadron [*Air Force*] .... TACAIRLIFTTNGSq
Tactical Airlift Training Squadron [*Air Force*] .... TATS
Tactical Air-to-Air Mission Evaluation (MCD) .... TAME
Tactical Air-to-Surface Missile (NATG) .... TASM
Tactical Alert Zone (NATG) .... TAZ
Tactical All Weather Attack Requirements [*Air Force*] (MCD) .... TAWAR
Tactical Analysis Branch [*Military*] (DNAB) .... TAB
Tactical Analysis Group [*Military*] (CAAL) .... TAG

Tactical Analysis Team [*Military drug interdiction program*] ... TAT
Tactical and Environmental Support System [*Military*] (CAAL) ... TESS
Tactical and Staff Duties [*British military*] (DMA) ... TSD
Tactical and Technical Fire Control (MCD) ... TTFC
Tactical Antimissile Measurement Program [*Military*] (IAA) ... TAMP
Tactical Antiradiation Tracker [*Military*] (CAAL) ... TART
Tactical Antiship Missile (MCD) ... TASM
Tactical Approach and Landing RADAR [*NASA*] ... TALAR
Tactical Area Communications System (MCD) ... TACOM
Tactical Area Defense Alerting RADAR (MCD) ... TADAR
Tactical Area Files [*Military*] (CAAL) ... TAF
Tactical Area of Interest [*Military*] (INF) ... TAI
Tactical Area of Interest [*Military*] ... TAOI
Tactical Area of Responsibility [*Military*] (AFM) ... TAOR
Tactical Area Positioning System [*Military*] ... TAPS
Tactical Area Switching ... TAS
Tactical Area Weather Sensor (MCD) ... TAWS
Tactical Armament Master Plan (MCD) ... TAMP
Tactical Armament Plan (MCD) ... TAP
Tactical Armament Turret (NG) ... TAT
Tactical Armament Turret System ... TATS
Tactical Armored Weapons Carrier (MCD) ... TAWC
Tactical Army Aircraft Landing Systems ... TAALS
Tactical Army Automation (MCD) ... TAA
Tactical Army Combat Service Support (DOMA) ... TACSS
Tactical Army Combat Service Support Computer System ... TACCS
Tactical Articulated Swimmable Carrier (OA) ... TASC
Tactical Assault Supply Transport (MCD) ... TAST
Tactical Assault Weapon ... TAW
Tactical Assembly Area [*Army*] (INF) ... TAA
Tactical Assembly Area [*Army*] (DOMA) ... TAA
Tactical Assignment Console ... TAC
Tactical ASW [*Antisubmarine Warfare*] **Environmental Acoustic Support** [*Navy*] (CAAL) ... TAEAS
Tactical Atomic Demolition [*Munitions*] [*Obsolete Military*] (NG) ... TAD
Tactical Atomic Demolition Munitions [*Obsolete Military*] (AABC) ... TADM
Tactical Attack RADAR and Navigation ... TARAN
Tactical Automated Data Processing System ... TACADS
Tactical Automated Maintenance Facility ... TAMF
Tactical Automated Situation Receiver [*Military*] ... TASR
Tactical Automated System (MCD) ... TAS
Tactical Automatic Data Information Links (MCD) ... TADILS
Tactical Automatic Digital Switch [*Military*] ... TADS
Tactical Automatic Digital Switching System ... TADSS
Tactical Automatic Landing System [*Aviation*] (NG) ... TAILS
Tactical Automatic Switch [*Military*] (AABC) ... TAS
Tactical Automatic Switch Control Office ... TASCO
Tactical Automatic Telephone Central Office [*Military*] ... TATCO
Tactical Automatic Weather Station [*Buoy*] (MSC) ... TAWS
Tactical Automation Appraisal (MCD) ... TAA
Tactical Automation Program Review [*Military*] ... TAPR
Tactical Aviation Maintenance Co. [*Army*] ... TAMC
Tactical Aviation Model ... TACAV
Tactical Avionics Maintenance Simulation (KSC) ... TAMS
Tactical Avionics System Simulator [*Army*] (MCD) ... TASS
Tactical Ballistic Missile [*Military*] (CAAL) ... TBM
Tactical Ballistic Missile Defense (DOMA) ... TBMD
Tactical Ballistic Missile Experiment ... TBMX
Tactical Ballistic Missile, Experimental ... TBX
Tactical Bare Base Support Study [*Air Force*] ... TABBSS
Tactical Battle Drill [*Army*] (INF) ... TBD
Tactical Bomb Group [*Air Force*] ... TBGP
Tactical Bomb Line (NVT) ... TBL
Tactical Bomb Squadron [*Air Force*] ... TACBOMBSq
Tactical Bomb Squadron [*Air Force*] ... TBS
Tactical Bomb Wing [*Air Force*] ... TBWG
Tactical Call Sign (IAA) ... TCS
Tactical Channel Assignment Panel [*Military radio*] ... TCAP
Tactical Combat Aircraft (IEEE) ... TCA
Tactical Combat Operations ... TCO
Tactical Combat Training System [*Navy*] ... TCTS
Tactical Command (NATG) ... TC
Tactical Command and Control Procedures Standardization Working Group [*Army*] (AABC) ... TCCPSWG
Tactical Command Center (DOMA) ... TCC
Tactical Command Control (MCD) ... TCC
Tactical Command, Control, and Communications System [*Canada*] ... TCCCS
Tactical Command Post [*Army*] (INF) ... TAC
Tactical Command Post [*Army*] ... TACCP
Tactical Command Readiness Program [*Army*] ... TCRP
Tactical Command Ship [*Navy symbol*] ... CC
Tactical Command Ship [*Navy symbol*] ... CLC
Tactical Commander's Terrain Analysis [*Military*] (AABC) ... TACCTA
Tactical Communications (MCD) ... TACCOM
Tactical Communications (AFM) ... TACOM
Tactical Communications [*Military*] (AABC) ... TACOMM
Tactical Communications [*Military*] (DWSG) ... TC
Tactical Communications Area ... TCA
Tactical Communications Center ... TCC
Tactical Communications Control Facility [*Air Force*] (MCD) ... TCCF
Tactical Communications Control Terminal (MCD) ... TCCT
Tactical Communications Division [*Military*] ... TCD
Tactical Communications Emitter Location and Identification System [*Army*] (MCD) ... TACELIS
Tactical Communications Jamming [*Military*] (CAAL) ... TCJ
Tactical Communications Location Identification Navigation and Control System [*Military*] (ECON) ... TACLINC
Tactical Communications Plan [*NATO*] ... TACOMPLAN
Tactical Communications Satellite [*Also, TACSAT*] [*DoD*] ... TACOMSAT
Tactical Communications Satellite [*Also, TACOMSAT*] [*DoD*] ... TACSAT
Tactical Communications Satellite Program [*DoD*] (MCD) ... TCSP
Tactical Communications Simulator ... TACCOMSIM
Tactical Communications System ... TACOS
Tactical Communications Systems Requirements (MCD) ... TACSYR
Tactical Communications Systems Technical Standards [*Military*] ... TCTS
Tactical Communications Terminal ... TCT
Tactical Communications Vulnerability Assessment of Combat Electronics Warfare Intelligence System (MCD) ... TACVA/CEWIS
Tactical Communications-Electronics Simulation and Support System ... TACESS
Tactical Computer (IEEE) ... TC
Tactical Computer Modeling Analysis and Simulation (SSD) ... TACMAS
Tactical Computer Processor ... TCP
Tactical Computer System [*Army*] (MCD) ... TCS
Tactical Computer Terminal [*Army*] (MCD) ... TCT
Tactical Container Shelter System [*Rockwell International Corp.*] ... TACOSS
Tactical Control [*Military*] (CAAL) ... TACON
Tactical Control Center [*Military*] ... TCC
Tactical Control Computer (AAG) ... TCC
Tactical Control Console (NATG) ... TCC
Tactical Control Flight ... TCF
Tactical Control Flight ... TCFlt
Tactical Control Group [*Air Force*] ... TCG
Tactical Control Group [*Air Force*] (AFM) ... TCGp
Tactical Control Officer [*Army*] (AABC) ... TACCO
Tactical Control Officer [*Army*] ... TCO
Tactical Control Panel (MCD) ... TCP
Tactical Control RADAR (IAA) ... TCR
Tactical Control Squadron [*Air Force*] ... TACCONSq
Tactical Control Squadron ... TCS
Tactical Control Surveillance System ... TCSS
Tactical Control Unit (MCD) ... TCU
Tactical Control Wing [*Air Force*] ... TCW
Tactical Coordinator (NVT) ... T/C
Tactical Coordinator (NATG) ... TAC
Tactical Coordinator (NG) ... TACO
Tactical Countermeasure ... TAC COUNT
Tactical Cruise Missile (MCD) ... TCM
Tactical Cryptologic Program [*DoD*] ... TCP
Tactical Data Automation System (IAA) ... TDAS
Tactical Data Base Manager (DOMA) ... TDBM
Tactical Data Communications Center ... TDCC
Tactical Data Converter ... TDC
Tactical Data Display ... TDD
Tactical Data Display System (MCD) ... TDDS
Tactical Data Entry [*Army*] (IAA) ... TACDEN
Tactical Data Entry Unit [*Army*] ... TACDEN
Tactical Data Information Exchange Subsystem [*Navy*] (ANA) ... TADIX
Tactical Data Information Exchange Subsystem ... TADIXS
Tactical Data Information Exchange System-B (DOMA) ... TADSIXS-B
Tactical Data Information Link [*DoD*] ... TADIL
Tactical Data Information Link-JTIDS [*Joint Tactical Information Distribution System*] [*DoD*] ... TADIL-J
Tactical Data Link ... TDL
Tactical Data Processor (DOMA) ... TDP
Tactical Data Replay System (NVT) ... TADREPS
Tactical Data System ... TDS
Tactical Data System Development Testbed ... TDSDT
Tactical Data Systems Management Office [*Fort Leavenworth*] [*Army*] (MCD) ... TDSMO
Tactical Data Terminal (MCD) ... TDT
Tactical Data Transfer System (NATG) ... TDTS
Tactical Database Management System ... TDBMS
Tactical Deception (MCD) ... TAC-D
Tactical Deception Element (NVT) ... TDE
Tactical Deception Unit (NVT) ... TDU
Tactical Decision Aid ... TDA
Tactical Decision Game [*Marine Corps*] (DOMA) ... TDG
Tactical Defense Alerting RADAR ... TDAR
Tactical Defense Communications Satellite Program (MCD) ... TDCSP
Tactical Deployment Control Squadron ... TDCS
Tactical Deployment Support ... TDS
Tactical Development Agent [*Military*] (CAAL) ... TDA
Tactical Development and Evaluation [*Military*] (CAAL) ... TAC D & E
Tactical Development Group [*Military*] (CAAL) ... TDG
Tactical Digital Computer (MCD) ... TDC
Tactical Digital Facsimile (MCD) ... TDF
Tactical Digital Facsimile Equipment (MCD) ... TACFAX
Tactical Digital Information Link ... TADIL
Tactical Digital Information Link - Joint ... TADIL-J
Tactical Digital Systems Office [*Navy*] (MCD) ... TADSO
Tactical Director [*Military*] (GFGA) ... TD
Tactical Display Engagement Control Console [*Military*] (RDA) ... TDECC
Tactical Display Plotting Board ... TDPB
Tactical Display System (CAAL) ... TDS
Tactical Display Unit (NVT) ... TDU
Tactical Division [*Air Force*] ... TD
Tactical Document Copier (MCD) ... TDC
Tactical Drone Group (MCD) ... TDG
Tactical Drone Squadron ... TDS

Tactical Early Warning ... TEW
Tactical Effectiveness of Minefields in Antiarmor Warfare Systems [*Army*] (INF) ... TEMAW
Tactical Effectiveness of Minefields in Antiarmor Warfare Systems [*Army*] ... TEMAWS
Tactical Effectiveness of Minefields in the Antiarmor Weapons System (PDAA) ... TEMANS
Tactical Effectiveness of Weapons Systems [*Army*] (AABC) ... TEWS
Tactical Effectiveness Testing of Antitank Missiles [*DoD*] ... TETAM
Tactical Electromagnetic Coordinator (IEEE) ... TEC
Tactical Electromagnetic Project Office [*Military*] (CAAL) ... TEMPO
Tactical Electromagnetic Readiness Advisory Council (MCD) ... TERAC
Tactical Electromagnetic Reconnaissance [*Air Force*] (IAA) ... TEREC
Tactical Electromagnetic Systems Study (IEEE) ... TESS
Tactical Electromagnetic Systems Study Action Council [*Navy*] (ANA) ... TESSAC
Tactical Electronic Intelligence [*Navy*] (ANA) ... TACELINT
Tactical Electronic Locating and Targeting System (MCD) ... TELATS
Tactical Electronic Reconnaissance [*Aircraft*] ... TEREC
Tactical Electronic Reconnaissance Processing and Evaluation [*Air Force*] (MCD) ... TERPE
Tactical Electronic Reconnaissance Processing and Evaluation System (MCD) ... TERPES
Tactical Electronic Reconnaissance Processing (and Evaluation) System [*Navy*] (DOMA) ... TERPS
Tactical Electronic Reconnaissance System (IEEE) ... TERS
Tactical Electronic Warfare [*Aircraft*] (NATG) ... TEW
Tactical Electronic Warfare Deception System (MCD) ... TEWDS
Tactical Electronic Warfare Group [*Military*] ... TEWG
Tactical Electronic Warfare Group [*Air Force*] (AFM) ... TEWGp
Tactical Electronic Warfare Set ... TEWS
Tactical Electronic Warfare Squadron [*Air Force*] (DNAB) ... TACELECRON
Tactical Electronic Warfare Squadron [*Navy*] (ANA) ... TACELRON
Tactical Electronic Warfare Squadron [*Air Force*] ... TEWS
Tactical Electronic Warfare Squadron [*Air Force*] ... TEWSq
Tactical Electronic Warfare Squadron [*Navy symbol*] (DNAB) ... VAQ
Tactical Electronic Warfare Squadron Detachment [*Air Force*] (DNAB) ... TACELECRONDET
Tactical Electronic Warfare Support (MCD) ... TEWS
Tactical Electronic Warfare System (DOMA) ... TEWS
Tactical Electronic Warfare Training Squadron ... TEWTS
Tactical Electronics Squadron ... TACES
Tactical ELINT Processor (MCD) ... TEP
Tactical Emergency [*Army*] ... T/E
Tactical Emergency [*Army*] ... TAC-E
Tactical Emitter Operational Support System (MCD) ... TEOSS
Tactical Employment Guide [*Military*] (CAAL) ... TEG
Tactical Endurance Synthetic Aperture RADAR [*Army*] (RDA) ... TESAR
Tactical Energy Requirements and Supply System (MCD) ... TERAS
Tactical Engagement and Range [*Army*] ... TE & R
Tactical Engagement Close Combat System [*Army*] ... TECCS
Tactical Engagement Simulation System [*Developed by Sandia National Laboratories for the Defense Nuclear Agency*] ... TESS
Tactical Environment Satellite Readout (MCD) ... TESR
Tactical Environment Simulator [*Navy*] (MCD) ... TES
Tactical Environment System [*Navy*] ... TES
Tactical Environmental Dissemination and Display System (MCD) ... TEDDS
Tactical Evaluation (MCD) ... TACEVAL
Tactical Event Reporting System (DOMA) ... TERS
Tactical Exchange Automation System (MCD) ... TEXAS
Tactical Executive ... TACEXEC
Tactical Exercise Controller [*Marine Corps*] (MCD) ... TEC
Tactical Exercise Evaluation Control Group [*Marine Corps*] (DOMA) ... TEECG
Tactical Exercise Simulator and Evaluator (NVT) ... TESE
Tactical Exercise without Troops ... TEWT
Tactical Expendable Drone System (MCD) ... TEDS
Tactical Exploitation Collection and Coordination Element (MCD) ... TECCE
Tactical Exploitation of National Space Capabilities ... TENCAP
Tactical Explosive System [*Military*] (RDA) ... TEXS
Tactical Ferret Display System ... TFDS
Tactical Fiber Optic Cable Assembly [*Army*] ... TFOCA
Tactical Field Exchange [*Air Force*] (DOMA) ... TFE
Tactical Fighter (AFM) ... TF
Tactical Fighter Defense Munitions [*Air Force*] ... TFDM
Tactical Fighter Dispenser (MCD) ... TFD
Tactical Fighter Dispenser Test Bed ... TFDTB
Tactical Fighter Dispensing Munition (AFM) ... TFDM
Tactical Fighter Display Systems [*Air Force*] ... TFDS
Tactical Fighter Experimental [*Air Force*] ... TFX
Tactical Fighter Experimental - Navy ... TFX-N
Tactical Fighter Experimental - Offensive ... TFX-O
Tactical Fighter Experimental - Reconnaissance ... TFX-R
Tactical Fighter Force (ADA) ... TFF
Tactical Fighter Group [*Air Force*] ... TFG
Tactical Fighter Group [*Air Force*] ... TFGP
Tactical Fighter Replacement Squadron [*Air Force*] ... TACFTRRSq
Tactical Fighter Squadron [*Air Force*] ... TFS
Tactical Fighter Squadron [*Air Force*] ... TFSQ
Tactical Fighter Training Aggressor Squadron [*Air Force*] ... TFTAS
Tactical Fighter Training Aggressor Squadron [*Air Force*] ... TFTASq
Tactical Fighter Training Group [*Military*] ... TFTG
Tactical Fighter Training Squadron [*Air Force*] ... TFTNGSq
Tactical Fighter Training Squadron [*Air Force*] (MCD) ... TFTS
Tactical Fighter Training Wing [*Air Force*] (MCD) ... TFTW
Tactical Fighter Weapon School [*Air Force*] (MCD) ... TFWS
Tactical Fighter Weapons Center [*Air Force*] (AFM) ... TFWC
Tactical Fighter Weapons Center Range Group [*Military*] ... TFWCRG
Tactical Fighter Wing [*Air Force*] ... TFW
Tactical Fighter Wing [*Air Force*] ... TFWG
Tactical Fire [*Military*] ... TACFIRE
Tactical Fire Control (MCD) ... TFC
Tactical Fire Direction Center [*Army*] (AABC) ... TACFDC
Tactical Flag Command Center [*Navy*] ... TFCC
Tactical Flag Command Center System [*Navy*] ... TFCCS
Tactical Flag Commander (MCD) ... TFC
Tactical Flag Data System (NG) ... TFDS
Tactical Flight Control ... TFC
Tactical Flight Management (MCD) ... TFM
Tactical Forecast Unit ... TFU
Tactical Frequency Management System (MCD) ... TFMS
Tactical Fusion Center (MCD) ... TFC
Tactical Generic Cable Replacement ... TGCR
Tactical Generic Multiplex ... TGM
Tactical Global Positioning System Guidance (MCD) ... TGPSG
Tactical Ground Intercept Facility [*Air Force*] (DOMA) ... TGIF
Tactical Ground Sensor System/Unattended Ground Sensor (MCD) ... TGSS/UGS
Tactical Ground Support Equipment ... TGSE
Tactical Group [*Military*] ... TACG
Tactical High-Altitude Penetration (MCD) ... THAP
Tactical High-Mobility Terminal (DOMA) ... THMT
Tactical Homing and Warning System ... THAWS
Tactical Hybrid Switch (LAIN) ... THS
Tactical Identification and Acquisition [*Navy*] (NG) ... TIA
Tactical Imagery Interpretation Facility [*Military*] ... TIIF
Tactical Imagery Processing Laboratory [*Army*] (MCD) ... TIPL
Tactical Imagery Processing Set ... TIPS
Tactical Implementation Time ... TIP
Tactical Improvement Program [*Military*] ... TIP
Tactical Incapacitating Munitions System (MCD) ... TIMS
Tactical Inertial Performance Requirements ... TIPR
Tactical Inertial Performance Requirements (MCD) ... TIPRE
Tactical Infantry Load Carrier Amphibious Remote [*Military*] (PDAA) ... TILCAR
Tactical Information about Perilous Situations [*New York City Fire Department program*] ... TIPS
Tactical Information Broadcast System [*Air Force*] (DOMA) ... TIBS
Tactical Information Coordinator (DOMA) ... TIC
Tactical Information Display ... TID
Tactical Information Distribution Systems [*Army*] (RDA) ... TIDS
Tactical Information Exchange System [*Navy United Nations*] (MCD) ... TIES
Tactical Information Processing and Interpretation [*Military*] (AFM) ... TIPI
Tactical Information Processing and Interpretation Total Environment Facility (MCD) ... TIPITEF
Tactical Information Processing Laboratory [*Army*] (MCD) ... TIPL
Tactical Information Processing System [*Military*] (CAAL) ... TIPS
Tactical Information Recording System [*Military*] (CAAL) ... TIRS
Tactical Initialization [*Computer software*] [*Military*] ... TACI
Tactical Instrument Landing (MCD) ... TACLAND
Tactical Instrument Landing System ... TILS
Tactical Instrument Steep Approach and Landing System (MCD) ... TISAL
Tactical Instrumental Missile (MCD) ... TIM
Tactical Integrated Mission Planning Station (MCD) ... TACIMPS
Tactical Integrated Ocean Surveillance [*Military*] (CAAL) ... TIOS
Tactical Integrity Loss Factor ... TILF
Tactical Intelligence and Related Activity ... TIARA
Tactical Intelligence Collection Team [*Military*] (AFM) ... TICT
Tactical Intelligence Concepts (MCD) ... TIC
Tactical Intelligence Group [*Military*] ... TIG
Tactical Intelligence Information Exchange System (NVT) ... TACINTEL
Tactical Intelligence Processing and Interpretation System Program Office [*Air Force*] (PDAA) ... TIPISPO
Tactical Intelligence Squadron (MCD) ... TIS
Tactical Intelligence Squadron [*Air Force*] ... TISq
Tactical Intelligence Transfer System ... TINTS
Tactical Intelligence Wing [*Military*] ... TIW
Tactical Intercom Assembly [*Ground Communications Facility, NASA*] ... TICA
Tactical Intercom Systems (MCD) ... TIC
Tactical Interdiction System ... TIS
Tactical Intermediate Support System [*Military*] (MCD) ... TISS
Tactical International Data Exchange (NG) ... TIDE
Tactical Intrusion Detectors (MCD) ... TID
Tactical Jammer [*Military*] (CAAL) ... TJR
Tactical Jamming ... TACJAM
Tactical Jamming Pod [*Military*] (CAAL) ... TJP
Tactical Jamming System ... TJS
Tactical Jamming Transmitter [*Navy*] ... TJT
Tactical Landing ... T/L
Tactical Landing System ... TLS
Tactical Landing System Guidance Techniques (MCD) ... TLSGT
Tactical LASER Beam Recorder (MCD) ... TLBR
Tactical Law Enforcement Teams [*Coast Guard*] ... TACLET
Tactical Leadership Course [*Army*] (INF) ... TLC
Tactical Leadership Program [*Military*] ... TLP
Tactical Life Support System [*G-suit developed by Boeing Co.*] ... TLSS
Tactical Light Shot Simulation (MCD) ... TALISSI
Tactical Link Control Facility [*Military*] (CAAL) ... TLCF
Tactical Loader [*Preparation software*] [*Army*] ... TACL
Tactical Logical and Air Simulation ... TLAS
[*A*] **Tactical, Logistical, and Air Simulation** [*NATO*] (NATG) ... ATLAS
Tactical Maintenance Control System ... TMCS
Tactical Management Information System [*Army*] (RDA) ... TACMIS
Tactical Manager [*Military*] (CAAL) ... TM

Tactical Manuals [*Aircraft*] (MCD) .... TACMAN
Tactical Marine Petroleum Terminal (MCD) .... TMPT
Tactical Marine Terminal (MCD) .... TMT
Tactical Medical Center .... TMC
Tactical Memorandum [*Navy*] (ANA) .... TACMEMO
Tactical Memory Address Register [*Computer science*] (IAA) .... TACMAR
Tactical Metrology Device (DWSG) .... TMD
Tactical Microwave Radio .... TMR
Tactical Mid-Range Air Defense Program [*Army*] (AABC) .... TAMIRAD
Tactical Miniature Crystal Oscillator .... TMXO
Tactical Missile [*Air Force*] .... TM
Tactical Missile Defense [*Army*] (DOMA) .... TMD
Tactical Missile Defense Initiative (DOMA) .... TMDI
Tactical Missile Electrical Simulator [*Obsolete*] .... TMES
Tactical Missile Encounter [*Air Force*] (KSC) .... TAME
Tactical Missile Experimental (IAA) .... TMX
Tactical Missile Group [*Air Force*] .... TMG
Tactical Missile Maintenance Squadron [*Air Force*] .... TMMS
Tactical Missile Receiver .... TMR
Tactical Missile Squadron [*Air Force*] .... TMS
Tactical Missile Squadron [*Air Force*] .... TMSq
Tactical Missile System [*Provisional*] [*Army*] (RDA) .... TACMS
Tactical Missile Training Group [*Military*] .... TMTG
Tactical Missile Training Squadron [*Air Force*] .... TMTS
Tactical Missile Wing [*Air Force*] .... TMW
Tactical Mission Data [*Military*] (AFM) .... TMD
Tactical Mobile Unit [*Police*] .... TMU
Tactical Modular Display [*Army*] (PDAA) .... TACMOD
Tactical Monitor .... TM
Tactical Moving Map Display (MCD) .... TMMD
Tactical Multifunction Array RADAR [*Air Force*] .... TACMAR
Tactical Multinet Gateway [*Computer science Military*] (RDA) .... TMG
Tactical Multipurpose Automated Platform [*Military*] .... TMAP
Tactical Munitions Dispenser (MCD) .... TMD
Tactical Navigation and Collision Avoidance [*Military*] (CAAL) .... TANCAV
Tactical Navigation System .... NAVTAC
Tactical Navigation System .... TACNAV
Tactical Navigation System (DWSG) .... TNS
Tactical Navigational Display System .... TNDS
Tactical/Navigational Modernization [*Navy*] .... TACNAVMOD
Tactical Notice (NVT) .... TACNOTE
Tactical Nuclear Force (MCD) .... TNF
Tactical Nuclear Warfare (MCD) .... TNW
Tactical Nuclear Warfare/Chemical Warfare (MCD) .... TNW/CW
Tactical Nuclear Weapon .... TNW
Tactical Nuclear Weapons Requirements (CINC) .... TANWERE
Tactical Nuclear Weapons Requirements Methodology .... TANREM
Tactical Observer .... TO
Tactical Observing Weather Element [*Air Force*] .... TOBWE
Tactical Ocean Surveillance Coordinator [*Military*] (CAAL) .... TOSC
Tactical Offense Subsystem .... TOS
Tactical Officer [*Military*] (RDA) .... TO
Tactical Operation Simulator .... TOS
Tactical Operational Readiness Trainer .... TORT
Tactical Operational Requirement [*Military*] (CAAL) .... TOR
Tactical Operational Scoring System (MCD) .... TOSS
Tactical Operations Center [*Military*] .... TOC
Tactical Operations Center/Command Post [*Military*] .... TOC/CP
Tactical Operations Control Center Weather Element [*Air Force*] .... TOCCWE
Tactical Operations Initiation .... TOI
Tactical Operations Plot [*Military*] (CAAL) .... TOP
Tactical Operations Room [*Air Force*] .... TOR
Tactical Operations Squadron [*Air Force*] .... TACOPNSSq
Tactical Operations Squadron [*Air Force*] .... TOS
Tactical Operations Support System (MCD) .... TOSS
Tactical Operations System [*ADSAF*] .... TOS
Tactical Operations System Operable Segment (MCD) TOS2
Tactical Operations System/Operations and Intelligence Tactical Data Systems [*Military*] (RDA) .... TOS/OITDS
Tactical Optical Projection System (NVT) .... TOPS
Tactical Organization .... T
Tactical Organization Paperless System [*Army*] .... TACOPS
Tactical Packet Switching System [*Army*] (RDA) .... TACPACS
Tactical Paint Scheme (MCD) .... TPS
Tactical Patrol Force [*Police*] .... TPF
Tactical Patrol Unit [*Military*] (LAIN) .... TPU
Tactical Penetration Aids Rocket .... TPAR
Tactical Performance Evaluation .... TPE
Tactical Peripherals Equipment Monitor [*Military*] .... TPEM
Tactical Petroleum Terminal .... TPT
Tactical Photographic Image Transmission .... TAPIT
Tactical Photographic Image Transmission System .... TAPITS
Tactical Pilotage Chart .... TPC
Tactical Probe System (SAA) .... TPS
Tactical Procedure Oriented Language [*Computer science*] (CSR) .... TACPOL
Tactical Protective Structures (MCD) .... TAPS
Tactical Quiet Generator (RDA) .... TQG
Tactical RADAR [*Military*] (IAA) .... TR
Tactical Radar Correlator [*Army*] (DOMA) .... TRAC
Tactical RADAR System .... TRS
Tactical RADAR Target Analysis [*Military*] (CAAL) .... TARTA
Tactical RADAR Threat Generator (MCD) .... TRTG
Tactical Radio Analysis, Division Restructuring [*Army*] .... TRADR
Tactical Radio Communications Equipment .... TRCE
Tactical Radio Communications System .... TRCS
Tactical Radio Set .... TRS
Tactical Range Ballistic Missile [*Military*] (IAA) .... TBX
Tactical Range Landing Force Support Weapon .... TRLFSW
Tactical Range Prediction System .... TACRAPS
Tactical Range Recorder [*Navy*] .... TRR
Tactical Range Ship-to-Shore Missile (IAA) .... TRSSM
Tactical Range Surface-to-Surface Guided Missile .... TRSSGM
Tactical Range Surface-to-Surface Missile .... TRSSM
Tactical Rapid Access Processing System (KSC) .... TRAPS
Tactical Reaction Reconnaissance .... TRR
Tactical Readiness and Checkout Equipment .... TRACE
Tactical Readiness Drill [*Military*] (DNAB) .... TACREDD
Tactical Readiness Evaluation [*Submarines*] (DOMA) .... TRE
Tactical Receive Element (DOMA) .... TRE
Tactical Receive Equipment (DOMA) .... TRE
Tactical Reconnaissance .... TAC/R
Tactical Reconnaissance (NATG) .... TR
Tactical Reconnaissance and Surveillance - 1975 [*Army*] TARS-75
Tactical Reconnaissance Data Link (MCD) .... TRDL
Tactical Reconnaissance Data Marking .... TRDM
Tactical Reconnaissance Group .... TRG
Tactical Reconnaissance Group [*Air Force*] .... TRGP
Tactical Reconnaissance Information Processing and Interpretation (SAA) .... TRIPI
Tactical Reconnaissance/Intelligence [*Air Force*] (AFM) .... TRI
Tactical Reconnaissance Intelligence Support Squadron .... TRISS
Tactical Reconnaissance Intelligence System Enhancement [*Air Force*] .... TAC RISE
Tactical Reconnaissance Reaction Aircraft (MCD) .... TACREACT
Tactical Reconnaissance Squadron [*Air Force*] .... TRS
Tactical Reconnaissance Squadron [*Air Force*] (AFM) .... TRSq
Tactical Reconnaissance System .... TRS
Tactical Reconnaissance Task Force (CINC) .... TRTF
Tactical Reconnaissance Training Squadron .... TRTS
Tactical Reconnaissance Wing [*Air Force*] (MCD) .... TRW
Tactical Reconnaissance Wing [*Air Force*] .... TRWG
Tactical Reconstruction Information Pod [*Navy*] (ANA) .... TRIPOD
Tactical Record Traffic Center (MCD) .... TRTC
Tactical Record Traffic Facsimile (MCD) .... TRTF
Tactical Record Traffic System (MCD) .... TRTS
Tactical Record Traffic Terminal [*Army*] (MCD) .... TRTT
Tactical Recovery of Aircraft and Personnel .... TRAP
Tactical Reflected and Emitted Energy Suppression System .... TREESS
Tactical Remote Sensor System (DWSG) .... TRSS
Tactical Report (DOMA) .... TACREP
Tactical Resources and Combat Effectiveness Model (MCD) .... TRACE
Tactical Review Board [*Military*] (CAAL) .... TRB
Tactical Satellite [*Military*] (IAA) .... TACSAT
Tactical Satellite Communications [*Military*] .... TACSATCOM
Tactical Satellite Communications Executive Steering Group .... TSEG
Tactical Satellite Communications Program (SAA) .... TSCP
Tactical Satellite Communications System [*Air Force*] (CET) .... TSCS
Tactical Satellite Executive Steering Group .... TSESG
Tactical Satellite Signal Processor (RDA) .... TSSP
Tactical Schoolship [*Navy*] (NVT) .... TACSS
Tactical Secure Data Communication [*Air Force*] (DOMA) .... TASDAC
Tactical Security Support Equipment [*Military*] .... TSSE
Tactical Shelter System (DOMA) .... TSS
Tactical Signal Simulator [*Canadian Astronautics Ltd. RADAR threat simulation system*] .... TASS
Tactical Simulation .... TACSIM
Tactical Situation Display .... TSD
Tactical Situation Display Indicator .... TSDI
Tactical Software Control Site [*Missile system evaluation*] (RDA) .... TSCS
Tactical Software Development Facility .... TSDF
Tactical SONAR Range (NVT) .... TSR
Tactical Special Security Office [*Army*] (AABC) .... TASSO
Tactical Standing Operating Procedure [*Army*] (INF) .... TACSOP
Tactical Standing Operating Procedure [*Army*] .... TSOP
Tactical Strike and Reconnaissance .... TSR
Tactical Strike Fighter (MCD) .... TSF
Tactical Strike System .... TSS
Tactical Studies Rules [*In corporation name TSR, Inc.*] .... TSR
Tactical Support Center .... TSC
Tactical Support Center Information Exchange Subsystem .... TSCIXS
Tactical Support Element (AFM) .... TSE
Tactical Support Equipment .... TASE
Tactical Support Equipment [*Military*] (MCD) .... TSE
Tactical Support Functional Components (NVT) .... TSFC
Tactical Surveillance Officer (MCD) .... TSO
Tactical Surveillance, Reconnaissance, and Target Acquisition Mission Area Analysis (MCD) .... TSRTAMAA
Tactical Surveillance Sonobuoy (MCD) .... TSS
Tactical Survey Meter .... TSM
Tactical Synchronous Satellite Communication System .... TSSCS
Tactical Target Illustration (AFM) .... TTI
Tactical Target Materials .... TTM
Tactical Target Materials Catalogue (MCD) .... TTMC
Tactical Targeting Program (AFM) .... TTP
Tactical Targets Materials Program (AFM) .... TTMP
Tactical Task Force (AFM) .... TTF
Tactical Technical Requirements (RDA) .... TTR
Tactical Technology Information Analysis Center [*Columbus, OH*] [*DoD*] (GRD) .... TACTEC
Tactical Technology Office [*Arlington, VA*] [*DoD*] (GRD) .... TTO

Tactical Telemetry ... TTM
Tactical Telephone Central [*Telecommunications*] (IAA) ... TTC
Tactical Telephone Numbering Plan (MCD) ... TTNP
Tactical Terrain Analysis Database [*Army*] ... TTADB
Tactical Terrain Data [*Army*] ... TTD
Tactical Test [*Military*] (NVT) ... TACEST
Tactical Test Data Translator (MUGU) ... TTDT
Tactical Test Set (MCD) ... TTS
Tactical Tone and Acoustic Surveillance System [*Military*] (CAAL) ... TACTASS
Tactical [*Software*] **Tools** ... TACTOOL
Tactical Torpedo Evaluation Program [*Navy*] ... TTEP
Tactical Towed Array Sensor [*Formerly, ETAS*] [*Navy*] ... TACTAS
Tactical Towed Array SONAR [*Navy*] ... TACTAS
Tactical Towed Array Surveillance System [*Military*] (MCD) ... TACTLASS
Tactical Towed-Array Surveillance System (DOMA) ... TACTASS
Tactical Traffic and System Analysis (MCD) ... TTSA
Tactical Training [*Followed by location*] [*Military*] ... TT
Tactical Training Flight [*Military*] ... TTF
Tactical Training Group [*Military*] ... TTG
Tactical Training Group, Atlantic [*Military*] (DNAB) ... TACTRAGRULANT
Tactical Training Group, Pacific [*Military*] (DNAB) ... TACTRAGRUPAC
Tactical Training Officer [*Army*] ... TTO
Tactical Training Squadron ... TTS
Tactical Training Team [*Military*] (CAAL) ... TTT
Tactical Training Wing [*Air Force*] ... TTW
Tactical Transmission System Summary (KSC) ... TATS
Tactical Transport [*Aircraft*] ... TACT
Tactical Transport Group [*Military*] ... TTG
Tactical Transport Medium Range [*Aircraft*] ... TAC T MR
Tactical Transport Short Range [*Aircraft*] ... TAC T SR
Tactical Undercover Function [*Chicago police operation*] ... TUF
Tactical Unit Financial Management Information System ... TUFMIS
Tactical Unit Location and Communication System (MCD) ... TULACS
Tactical Unit Operations Center (AFM) ... TUOC
Tactical Unmanned Ground Vehicle [*Army*] (PS) ... TUGV
Tactical Unmanned Vehicle [*Military*] (INF) ... TUV
Tactical Utilization Working Committee [*Navy*] (MCD) ... TUWC
Tactical Vehicle Fleet Simulation (MCD) ... TVFS
Tactical Vehicle Review Board [*Army*] (AABC) ... TVRB
Tactical Vehicle Special Program [*Army*] (RDA) ... TVSP
Tactical Vocoder System ... TVS
Tactical Vulnerability Assessment [*Military*] (MCD) ... TACVA
Tactical Warfare Analysis and Evaluation System (MCD) ... TWAES
Tactical Warfare Center [*Army*] (AABC) ... TAWS
Tactical Warfare (Model) [*Army*] ... TACWAR
Tactical Warfare Research Advisory Committee [*Military*] (RDA) ... TACRAC
Tactical Warfare Simulation, Evaluation, and Analysis System [*Marine Corps*] (MCD) ... TWSEAS
Tactical Warfare Simulation Program ... TWSP
Tactical Warning (MCD) ... TW
Tactical Warning/Attack Assessment ... TW/AA
Tactical Warning System (AAG) ... TWS
Tactical Water Distribution System (MCD) ... TWDS
Tactical Weapon System (NG) ... TWS
Tactical Weapon Systems Operation ... TWSO
Tactical Weapons Delivery ... TWD
Tactical Weapons Unit [*British military*] (DMA) ... TWU
Tactical Weapons Unit Diagnostics ... TWUD
Tactical Weather Analysis Center (MCD) ... TWAC
Tactical Weather RADAR ... TWR
Tactical Weather Station [*Military*] ... TWS
Tactical Weather System (MCD) ... TACWE
Tactical Wheeled Vehicle ... TMV
Tactical Wheeled Vehicle (DOMA) ... TWV
Tactical Wheeled Vehicle Modernization Program [*Army*] ... TWVMP
Tactical Wheeled Vehicles Remanufacture Program [*Army*] (RDA) ... TWVRP
Tactical Work Program ... TWP
Tactical Zone [*Military*] (AABC) ... TZ
Tactical-Logistical [*Army*] (AABC) ... TACLOG
Tactical-Logistics Control Group [*Military*] ... TACLOG GP
Tactical-Technical Assignment [*Army*] (RDA) ... TTZ
Tactics Certification Course [*Army*] (INF) ... TCC
Tactics Development and Evaluation [*Military*] (MCD) ... TDAE
Tactics Development Evaluation (MCD) ... TDE
Tactics, Equipment, and Logistics Conference [*between US, Great Britain, Australia, and Canada*] [*Developed "duck" designations for Mallard and Gander military communications systems*] ... TEAL
Tactics Guide Issued (CAAL) ... TGI
Tactics Guide Not Required (CAAL) ... TGNR
Tactics Inspection Procedures Report ... TIPR
Tactics Inspection Results Report ... TIRR
Tactics, Techniques, and Procedures ... TTP
Tactile Afferent [*Medicine*] (DMAA) ... TA
Tactile Communicator [*Device which aids the deaf by translating certain sounds into coded vibrations*] ... TC
Tactile Fremitus [*Medicine*] ... TF
Tactile Information Presentation [*Biotechnology*] ... TIP
Tactile Procedure-Oriented Language (CSR) ... TACPOL
Tactile Tension [*Ophthalmology*] ... TT
Tactile Vision Substitution System (PDAA) ... TVSS
Tactile Vocal Fremitus [*Medicine*] ... TVF
Tactual ... T
Tacuarembo [*Uruguay*] [*ICAO location identifier*] (ICLI) ... SUTB
Tacubaya [*Mexico*] [*Seismograph station code, US Geological Survey*] (SEIS) ... TAC
Tacurong/Kenram, Cotabato [*Philippines*] [*ICAO location identifier*] (ICLI) ... RPWK
Tadair SA [*Spain ICAO designator*] (FAAC) ... TDC
Tadcaster Volunteer Rifles [*British military*] (DMA) ... TVR
Tadiran Limited [*NYSE symbol*] (SPSG) ... TAD
Tadiran Ltd. [*Associated Press*] (SAG) ... Tadiran
Tadiran Limited ADS [*NYSE symbol*] (TTSB) ... TAD
Tadiran Telecomm [*NASDAQ symbol*] (TTSB) ... TTELF
Tadji [*Papua New Guinea*] [*Airport symbol*] (OAG) ... TAJ
Tadjoura [*Djibouti*] [*Seismograph station code, US Geological Survey*] (SEIS) ... TDJ
Tadjoura [*Djibouti*] [*Airport symbol*] (OAG) ... TDJ
Tadotu [*Japan*] [*Seismograph station code, US Geological Survey Closed*] (SEIS) ... TAD
Tadpole Edema Virus [*Medicine*] (DMAA) ... TEV
TADS [*Target Acquisition Designation Sight*] **Electronics Unit Card** [*Army*] ... TEUC
Tadzhik Soviet Socialist Republic ... TadzhSSR
Tadzhik Soviet Socialist Republic [*MARC country of publication code Library of Congress*] (LCCP) ... tar
Taegu [*South Korea ICAO location identifier*] (ICLI) ... RKTN
Taegu [*South Korea ICAO location identifier*] (ICLI) ... RKTT
Taegu [*South Korea*] [*Seismograph station code, US Geological Survey Closed*] (SEIS) ... TAE
Taegu [*South Korea*] (ECON) ... TK
Taehti [*Record label*] [*Finland*] ... Tah
Taejon [*South Korea ICAO location identifier*] (ICLI) ... RKTD
Taenia [*Medicine*] (MAE) ... T
Taeria Foundation (EA) ... TF
TAES [*Tecnicas Aereas de Estudios y Servicios SA*] [*Spain ICAO designator*] (FAAC) ... ESS
TAF Helicopters SA [*Spain ICAO designator*] (FAAC) ... HET
TAFE (Technical and Further Education) and People with Disabilities [*Australia*] ... TPD
Tafel (BJA) ... Tf
Tafelberg/Rudi Kappel [*Surinam*] [*ICAO location identifier*] (ICLI) ... SMTB
Taff Vale Railway [*Wales*] ... TV
TAFIES [*Tactical Air Force Intelligence Exploitation System*] **Microfilm Subsystem** (MCD) ... TAMICSS
Taforalt [*Morocco*] [*Seismograph station code, US Geological Survey*] (SEIS) ... TAF
Tafresh [*Iran*] [*ICAO location identifier*] (ICLI) ... OIHF
Taft [*Iran*] [*ICAO location identifier*] (ICLI) ... OIYF
Taft, CA [*AM radio station call letters*] ... KMYX
Taft, CA [*FM radio station call letters*] ... KMYX-FM
Taft College, Taft, CA [*Library symbol Library of Congress*] (LCLS) ... CTaf
Taft Information System [*Provides information on private foundations*] (IID) ... TIS
Taft Institute for Two-Party Government [*Later, TTI*] (EA) ... TITPG
Taft, OK [*FM radio station call letters*] ... KHJM
Taft Sanitary Engineering Center ... TSEC
Taftan [*Pakistan*] [*ICAO location identifier*] (ICLI) ... OPTT
Taft-Hartley [*Act*] ... T-H
Taft-Hartley Act [*1947*] ... THA
Taft-Hartley Labor Relations Act (OICC) ... THLRA
Taft's Foundation Reporter [*A publication*] ... TFR
Tafuna, AS [*Location identifier FAA*] (FAAL) ... TUT
Tag [*Computer science*] [*Telecommunications*] ... t
Tag and Label Manufacturers Association (DGA) ... TLMA
Tag and Label Manufacturers Institute (EA) ... TLMI
Tag Closed Cup [*Flash point test*] ... TCC
Tag Code (NITA) ... TC
Tag Distribution Protocol [*Computer science*] ... TDP
Tag Heuer International SA [*Associated Press*] (SAG) ... TagHeur
Tag Heuer International SA [*NYSE symbol*] (SAG) ... THW
Tag Open Cup [*Flash point test*] ... TOC
Tag Vector Display Register ... TVDR
Tag Vector Response (NITA) ... TVR
Tag Vector Word (NITA) ... TVW
Tagalog [*MARC language code Library of Congress*] (LCCP) ... tag
Tagbilaran [*Philippines*] [*Army*] (OAG) ... TAG
Tagbilaran, Bohol [*Philippines*] [*ICAO location identifier*] (ICLI) ... RPVT
Tagesarbeitsnormen [*Workday Standards*] [*German*] ... TN
Tageseinfluesse [*Weather factors, a gunnery term*] [*German military - World War II*] ... TE
Tagged Image File [*Computer science*] (PCM) ... TIF
Tagged Image File Format [*Computer science*] ... TIFF
Tagged Image File Format [*Computer science*] ... tiff
Tagged Material Detector (DWSG) ... TMD
Taghi Ghambar [*Iran*] [*Seismograph station code, US Geological Survey*] (SEIS) ... TGI
Tagliabue Closed Cup [*Analytical chemistry*] ... TCC
Tagliabue Open Cup [*Analytical chemistry*] ... TOC
Taguatinga [*Brazil*] [*Airport symbol*] (AD) ... TGX
Tagula [*Papua New Guinea*] [*Airport symbol*] (OAG) ... TGL
Tahiti [*French Polynesia*] [*ICAO location identifier*] (ICLI) ... NTTT
Tahiti [*Society Islands*] [*Seismograph station code, US Geological Survey Closed*] (SEIS) ... TAH
Tahiti Conquest Airlines [*France ICAO designator*] (FAAC) ... TCA
Tahiti/FAAA [*French Polynesia*] [*ICAO location identifier*] (ICLI) ... NTAA
Tahlequah, OK [*FM radio station call letters*] ... KEOK
Tahlequah, OK [*AM radio station call letters*] ... KTLQ
Tahlequah, OK [*Location identifier FAA*] (FAAL) ... TQH
Tahneta Pass Lodge, AK [*Location identifier FAA*] (FAAL) ... HNE
Tahoe City, CA [*FM radio station call letters*] (RBYB) ... KKTO-FM
Tahoe City, CA [*FM radio station call letters*] ... KRZQ
Tahoe City, CA [*FM radio station call letters*] ... KXKB
Tahoka, TX [*FM radio station call letters*] ... KZUB

Tahoua [*Niger*] [*ICAO location identifier*] (ICLI) .... DRRT
Tahoua [*Niger*] [*Airport symbol*] (OAG) .... THZ
Tahun Vivere Pericoloso [*The Year of Living Dangerously*] [*President Sukarno's national policy in 1964 Indonesia*] .... TAVIP
Tahuna/Naha [*Indonesia*] [*ICAO location identifier*] (ICLI) .... WAMH
Tai Chi and Chi Kung Academy [*Australia*] .... TCCKA
Tai Chi Chuan/Shaolin Chuan Association (EA) .... TCC/SCA
Tai Hei Yo Bashi [*Bridge over the Great Ocean*] (EA) .... THYB
Taian [*Republic of China*] [*Seismograph station code, US Geological Survey*] (SEIS) .... TIA
Taibei City/Taibei International Airport [*China*] [*ICAO location identifier*] (ICLI) .... RCTP
Taibei/Songshan [*China*] [*ICAO location identifier*] (ICLI) .... RCSS
Taichung [*Taityu*] [*Republic of China*] [*Seismograph station code, US Geological Survey*] (SEIS) .... TCU
Taichung [*Formosa*] [*Airport symbol*] (AD) .... TXG
Taidong/Fengnian [*China*] [*ICAO location identifier*] (ICLI) .... RCFN
Taidong/Zhihang [*China*] [*ICAO location identifier*] (ICLI) .... RCQS
Taif [*Saudi Arabia*] [*ICAO location identifier*] (ICLI) .... OETF
Taif [*Saudi Arabia*] [*Airport symbol*] (OAG) .... TIF
Taiheiyo Hoso Kyokai [*Pacific Broadcasting Association*] [*Japan*] (EAIO) .... THK
Tail Back [*Football*] .... TB
Tail Bomb Fuse (KSC) .... TBF
Tail Clamp .... TC
Tail Damping Power Factor [*Aviation*] .... TDPF
Tail Damping Ratio [*Aviation*] .... TDR
Tail Fuze (MSA) .... TFZ
Tail Gate .... TGT
Tail Gear .... TG
Tail Lamp [*Automotive engineering*] .... T/LP
Tail Lamp [*Automotive engineering*] .... TL
Tail Landing Gear .... TLG
Tail Number Change [*Air Force*] (AFIT) .... TNC
Tail Number Configuration List [*Navy*] (NG) .... TNCL
Tail Pipe Temperature (NG) .... TPT
Tail RADAR Acquisition and Tracking System (MCD) .... TAILRATS
Tail Rotor Gearbox [*Aviation*] (DA) .... TRGB
Tail Section Test Stand (AAG) .... TSTS
Tail Service Mast [*NASA*] (KSC) .... TSM
Tail Stop and Turning [*Automotive engineering*] .... TST
Tail Wags Dog [*Airspace effects*] .... TWD
Tail Warning [*RADAR*] (NATG) .... TW
Tail Warning (Indicator) [*RADAR*] (DEN) .... TW(I)
Tail Warning Set [*or System*] [*Aerospace*] (MCD) .... TWS
Tail Wheel [*Aviation*] .... TWHL
Tail Wind .... TW
Taildragger Pilots Association (EA) .... TPA
Tail-Flick Latency .... TFL
Tail-Gas Treating Unit [*Petroleum engineering*] .... TGTU
Tailhook Association (EA) .... TA
Tail-Lift [*of trucks and vans*] (DCTA) .... TL
Tailor (MSA) .... TAL
Tailor .... TLR
Tailor .... TLR
Tailored Abstracts (NITA) .... TABS
Tailored Exhaust Velocity Rocket .... TEVROC
Tailored Exhaust Velocity Rocket .... TEVROK
Tailored List of Base Spares [*Military*] (AFIT) .... TLOBS
Tailored List of Spares [*Military*] (AFIT) .... TLOS
Tailored Master Cross Reference List [*Military*] (AABC) .... TMCRL
Tailored Outfitting List (MCD) .... TOL
Tailored Owner Protection System [*Automotive optional warranty*] .... TOPS
Tailored Performance Test Vehicle (SAA) .... TAPER
Tailored Probability Forecast .... TPF
Tailored Reliable Integrated Modular .... TRIM
Tailored Requirements Items List (MCD) .... TRIL
Tailored Retrieval and Information Management .... TRIM
Tailored Ship Training Availability [*Navy*] (DOMA) .... TSTA
Tailored Upper Stage (MCD) .... TUS
Tailoring .... TLRG
Tailor-Made (DSUE) .... TM
Tailpiece .... TLPC
Tail-Pinch Stress .... TP
Tailshaft .... TLSFT
Tailshaft Renewed .... TSN
Tailshaft Survey .... TS
Tailspike Protein [*Biochemistry*] .... TSP
Tail-to-Tail [*Polymer structure*] .... TT
Tailwater .... TW
Tailwater Quality Numerical Model [*Army Corps of Engineers*] .... TWQM
Tainan [*China*] [*ICAO location identifier*] (ICLI) .... RCNN
Tainan [*Republic of China*] [*Seismograph station code, US Geological Survey*] (SEIS) .... TAI
Tainan [*Taiwan*] [*Airport symbol*] (OAG) .... TNN
Taino Tours [*Dominican Republic*] [*ICAO designator*] (FAAC) .... TIN
Taipei [*Taihoku*] [*Taiwan*] [*Seismograph station code, US Geological Survey*] (SEIS) .... TAP
Taipei [*Taiwan*] [*Seismograph station code, US Geological Survey*] (SEIS) .... TATO
Taipei [*Taiwan*] [*Airport symbol*] (OAG) .... TPE
Taipei Stock Exchange [*Taiwan*] .... TSE
Taipei World Trade Center .... TWTC
Taipei-Sung Shan [*Taiwan*] [*Airport symbol*] (OAG) .... TSA
Taiping [*China*] [*Airport symbol*] (AD) .... TPG
Taiping [*Malaysia*] [*ICAO location identifier*] (ICLI) .... WMBI
Taisha [*Ecudaor*] [*ICAO location identifier*] (ICLI) .... SETH
Tait on Evidence [*A publication*] (DLA) .... Tait Ev
Taitron Components, Inc. Class A [*NASDAQ symbol*] (SAG) .... TAIT
Taitron Components, Inc. Class A [*Associated Press*] (SAG) .... Taitron
Taitron Components'A' [*NASDAQ symbol*] (TTSB) .... TAIT
Tait's Index to Morison's Dictionary [*Scotland*] [*A publication*] (DLA) .... Tait
Tait's Index to Scotch Session Cases [*1823*] [*A publication*] (DLA) .... Tait
Tait's Index to Scotch Session Cases [*1823*] [*A publication*] (DLA) .... Tait Ind
Tait's Justice of the Peace [*A publication*] (DLA) .... Tait JP
Tait's Justice of the Peace [*A publication*] (DLA) .... TJ
Tait's Manuscript Decisions, Scotch Session Cases [*A publication*] (DLA) .... Tait
Taitung [*Taito*] [*Republic of China*] [*Seismograph station code, US Geological Survey*] (SEIS) .... TTN
Taitung [*Taiwan*] [*Airport symbol*] (OAG) .... TTT
Taitung [*Republic of China*] [*Seismograph station code, US Geological Survey*] (SEIS) .... TWG
Taiwan [*International vehicle registration*] (ODBW) .... RC
Taiwan .... Tai
Taiwan (VRA) .... Taiw
Taiwan [*ANSI two-letter standard code*] (CNC) .... TW
Taiwan [*ANSI three-letter standard code*] (CNC) .... TWN
Taiwan Acute Respiratory Disease [*Pneumonia-causing chlamydia strain named after the ailment that results from it*] .... TWAR
Taiwan Aerospace Corp. (ECON) .... TAC
Taiwan Base Command (CINC) .... TBC
Taiwan Defense Command (MCD) .... TDC
Taiwan Equity Fd [*NYSE symbol*] (TTSB) .... TYW
Taiwan Equity Fund, Inc. [*Associated Press*] (SAG) .... TaiwanE
Taiwan Equity Fund, Inc. [*NYSE symbol*] (SAG) .... TYW
Taiwan Federation of Labor [*Nationalist China*] .... TFL
Taiwan Fund [*NYSE symbol*] (TTSB) .... TWN
Taiwan Fund, Inc. [*Associated Press*] (SAG) .... Taiwan
Taiwan Fund, Inc. [*NYSE symbol*] (SPSG) .... TWN
Taiwan International Standard Electronics Ltd. (NITA) .... TAISEL
Taiwan Land Development Corp. .... TLDC
Taiwan Maintenance Agency [*Military*] (AABC) .... TMA
Taiwan New PC [*Personal Computer*] **Consortium** [*Computer science*] .... TNPC
Taiwan Open Pool Reactor .... TOPR
Taiwan Relations Act [*1979*] (DOMA) .... TRA
Taiwan Semiconductor Manufacturing Co. .... TSMC
Taiwan Television Enterprise (EY) .... TTV
Taiwanese Association of America (EA) .... TAA
Taiwanese Oscilliation Network [*For solar observation*] .... TON
Taiwanese-American Society (EA) .... TAS
Taiyuan [*China*] [*Airport symbol*] (OAG) .... TYN
Taiyuan [*China*] [*Seismograph station code, US Geological Survey*] (SEIS) .... TYN
Taiyuan/Wusu [*China*] [*ICAO location identifier*] (ICLI) .... ZBYN
Taiz [*Yemen Arab Republic*] [*Airport symbol*] (OAG) .... TAI
Taiz/Ganad [*Yemen*] [*ICAO location identifier*] (ICLI) .... OYTZ
Taizhong [*China*] [*ICAO location identifier*] (ICLI) .... RCLG
Tajee Resources Ltd. [*Vancouver Stock Exchange symbol*] .... TJR
Tajik [*MARC language code Library of Congress*] (LCCP) .... taj
Tajik Soviet Socialist Republic [*MARC geographic area code Library of Congress*] (LCCP) .... e-ur-ta
Tajikair [*Tajikistan*] [*ICAO designator*] (FAAC) .... TJK
Tajikistan [*ICAO designator*] (FAAC) .... TZK
Tajikistan International Airlines [*FAA designator*] (FAAC) .... TIL
Tak [*Thailand*] [*Airport symbol*] (AD) .... TKL
Tak [*Thailand*] [*ICAO location identifier*] (ICLI) .... VTPT
Tak/Mae Sot [*Thailand*] [*ICAO location identifier*] (ICLI) .... VTPM
Tak/Sam Ngao [*Thailand*] [*ICAO location identifier*] (ICLI) .... VTPY
Takab [*Iran*] [*ICAO location identifier*] (ICLI) .... OICQ
Takada [*Japan*] [*Seismograph station code, US Geological Survey*] (SEIS) .... TKD
Takaka [*New Zealand*] [*Seismograph station code, US Geological Survey Closed*] (SEIS) .... TAK
Takamatsu [*Japan ICAO location identifier*] (ICLI) .... RJOT
Takamatsu [*Japan*] [*Airport symbol*] (OAG) .... TAK
Takamatsu [*Japan*] [*Seismograph station code, US Geological Survey*] (SEIS) .... TKM
Takapoto [*French Polynesia*] [*ICAO location identifier*] (ICLI) .... NTGT
Takapoto Island [*French Polynesia*] [*Airport symbol*] (OAG) .... TKP
Takaroa [*French Polynesia*] [*ICAO location identifier*] (ICLI) .... NTKR
Takayama [*Japan*] [*Seismograph station code, US Geological Survey*] (SEIS) .... TKY
Takayasu's Disease (DAVI) .... TD
Takayasuyama [*Japan*] [*Seismograph station code, US Geological Survey*] (SEIS) .... TKU
Take a Look Foundation (EA) .... TALF
Take Care of Business [*Slang*] .... TCB
Take Charge and Move Out Aircraft [*Military*] .... TACAMO
Take Five Australia [*An association*] .... TFA
Take It Somewhere Else [*The Solid Waste Syndrome*] (GNE) .... TISE
Take Off and Die [*Surfers' slang for a very dangerous wave*] .... TOAD
Take Off and Die Syndrome .... TOADS
Take Off/Go Around (MCD) .... TOGA
Take off Performance Monitoring System .... TOPMS
Take Off Pounds Sensibly (EA) .... TOPS
Take Off Weight (IAA) .... TOWT
Take Over (MCD) .... T/O
Take Pride in America Program [*Forest Service*] (GFGA) .... TPIA
Take Real Result [*Computer science*] (IAA) .... TRR
Take Your Own Gadgets .... TYOG
Take-a-Look-See (MCD) .... TALC
Takeda Pharm. Industries [*Japan*] [*Research code symbol*] .... B
Take-Home Pay (MHDB) .... THP
Taken .... T

Taken	TAK
Taken and Offered [*Sporting*] [*British*]	T & O
Taken Care Of (MCD)	TCO
Taken into Consideration	TIC
Taken on Strength [*British military*] (DMA)	TOS
Taken Out of Service [*Telecommunications*] (TEL)	TOS
Taken Without Owner's Consent	TWOC
Takenaka Aqua-Reactive Chemical Soil-Stabilisation System [*Nuclear energy*] (NUCP)	TACSS
Takeoff (GAVI)	T/O
Takeoff [*Aviation*]	TKOF
Takeoff [*Aviation*]	TO
Take-Off (IAA)	TO
Takeoff and Landing Analysis [*Air Force*]	TOLA
Takeoff and Landing Clear Air Turbulence [*Aviation*]	TOLCAT
Takeoff and Landing Critical Atmosphere Turbulence [*Aviation*] (MCD)	TOLCAT
Takeoff Boost [*Aviation*]	TOB
Takeoff Cruise Landing [*Aviation*]	TCL
Takeoff Decision Speed [*Aviation*]	V₁
Takeoff Distance Available [*FAA*] (TAG)	TODA
Take-Off Distance Available [*ICAO*] (FAAC)	TODA
Takeoff Distance Required [*Aviation*] (AIA)	TODR
Takeoff Engine Pressure Ratio (GAVI)	TO EPR
Takeoff Field Length [*Aviation*]	TOFL
Takeoff Gross [*Weight*] [*Aviation*]	TOG
Takeoff Gross Weight [*Aviation*]	TOGW
Takeoff Horsepower [*Aviation*]	TOHP
Take-Off Mass (SAA)	TM
Takeoff Performance Monitor [*Aviation*] (DA)	TOPM
Takeoff Rotation Velocity (GAVI)	VR
Take-Off Run Available [*FAA*] (TAG)	TORA
Takeoff Run Required [*Aviation*] (AIA)	TORR
Takeoff Safety Speed [*Aviation*]	V₂
Takeoff Space Available [*Aviation*] (DA)	TOSA
Takeoff Speed Over Screen [*Aviation code*] (AIA)	V3
Takeoff Time [*Aviation*]	PX Out
Takeoff Trim [*Aviation*] (MCD)	TOT
Takeoff Weight [*Aviation*]	TOW
Takes [*As in K x B - King Takes Bishop*] [*Chess*]	x
Takestan [*Iran*] [*ICAO location identifier*] (ICLI)	OIHA
Take-Up (IAA)	TU
Takigahara [*Japan ICAO location identifier*] (ICLI)	RJAT
Taking and Driving Away [*Motoring offense*] [*British*] (DI)	TDA
Taking Care of Business [*Brand name of Alberto-Culver Co.*]	TCB
Taking Care of Elvis [*Motto of Elvis Presley fans*]	TCE
Takoma Park, MD [*FM radio station call letters*]	WGTS
Takoradi [*Ghana*] [*ICAO location identifier*] (ICLI)	DGTK
Takoradi [*Ghana*] [*Airport symbol*]	TKD
Takotna [*Alaska*] [*Airport symbol*] (OAG)	TCT
Takotna, AK [*Location identifier FAA*] (FAAL)	TCT
Taku Lodge, AK [*Location identifier FAA*] (FAAL)	TKL
Tala [*Monetary unit in Western Samoa*]	T
Tala Pozo [*Argentina*] [*Seismograph station code, US Geological Survey Closed*] (SEIS)	TPA
Talair [*ICAO designator*] (AD)	GV
Talair Pty Ltd. [*New Guinea*] [*ICAO designator*] (FAAC)	TAL
Talang [*Sumatra*] [*Seismograph station code, US Geological Survey Closed*] (SEIS)	TLN
Talanta [*A publication*]	TA
Talar Tilt [*Angle of ankle joint*]	TT
Talara [*Peru*] [*Seismograph station code, US Geological Survey*] (SEIS)	TAL
Talara [*Peru*] [*Airport symbol*] (OAG)	TYL
Talara/Capitan Montes [*Peru*] [*ICAO location identifier*] (ICLI)	SPYL
Talara/El Pato [*Peru*] [*ICAO location identifier*] (ICLI)	SPTP
Talasea [*New Britain*] [*Seismograph station code, US Geological Survey*] (SEIS)	TLS
Talasea [*New Britain, New Guinea*] [*Airport symbol*] (AD)	TLW
Talbot Brook [*Australia Seismograph station code, US Geological Survey*] (SEIS)	WA3
Talbot County Free Library, Easton, MD [*Library symbol Library of Congress*] (LCLS)	MdEa
Talbot's Cases in Equity [*1734-38*] [*A publication*] (DLA)	Tal
Talbot's Cases in Equity [*1734-38*] [*A publication*] (DLA)	Talb
Talbots, Inc. [*Associated Press*] (SAG)	Talbots
Talbots, Inc. [*NYSE symbol*] (SPSG)	TLB
Talc	T
Talcorp Ltd. [*Toronto Stock Exchange symbol*]	TAL
Talcott Free Public Library, Rockton, IL [*Library symbol Library of Congress*] (LCLS)	IRockt
Talcott Mountain [*Connecticut*] [*Seismograph station code, US Geological Survey Closed*] (SEIS)	TMT
Talcott Mountain Science Center for Student Involvement, Inc. [*Avon, CT*] [*Telecommunications service*] (TSSD)	TMSC
Tale Quale [*Of Conditions on Arrival*] [*Latin*]	TQ
Talemon Investments Ltd. [*Vancouver Stock Exchange symbol*]	TLV
Talent, OR [*AM radio station call letters*]	KSJK
Talented and Gifted (EDAC)	TAG
Talent-Keyhole [*Satellite photography*] [*Military*] (LAIN)	TK
Talgar [*Also, TLG*] [*Alma-Ata*] [*Former USSR*] [*Seismograph station code, US Geological Survey*] (SEIS)	AAB
Talgar [*Also, AAB*] [*Alma-Ata*] [*Former USSR Seismograph station code, US Geological Survey*] (SEIS)	TLG
Talgarno [*Western Australia*] [*Airport symbol*] (AD)	TLR
Talhar [*Pakistan*] [*ICAO location identifier*] (ICLI)	OPTH

Talia Airlines [*Turkey*] [*ICAO designator*] (FAAC)	TAY
Taliabu [*Indonesia*] [*ICAO location identifier*] (ICLI)	WAPT
Taligent Application Environment [*Taligent, Inc.*] [*Computer science*]	TAE
Taligent Object Services [*Taligent, Inc.*] [*Computer science*]	TOS
Talipes Equinovarus [*Anatomy*]	TEV
Talipes Varus [*Orthopedics*] (DAVI)	TV
Talis [*Such*] [*Pharmacy*]	TAL
Talis Qualis [*Such As It Is*] [*Latin*] (ROG)	TAL QUAL
Talith and Tefillin (BJA)	TT
Talk and Listen Beacon [*Radio*]	TALBE
Talk Back [*NASA*] (KSC)	TB
Talk[*ing*] Club	TC
Talk Jockey [*Radio*]	TJ
Talk/Listen (NASA)	T/L
Talk/Monitor (NASA)	T
Talk Only (IAA)	TON
Talk to U Later [*Internet language*] [*Computer science*]	TTUL
Talk to You Later [*Internet language*] [*Computer science*]	TTYL
Talk to You Later (EERA)	TTYL
Talk-between-Ships [*which are tactically maneuvering; also, the VHF radio equipment used for this purpose*]	TBS
Talkeetna [*Alaska*] [*ICAO location identifier*] (ICLI)	PATK
Talkeetna, AK [*FM radio station call letters*]	KTNA
Talkeetna, AK [*Location identifier FAA*] (FAAL)	PEE
Talkeetna, AK [*Location identifier FAA*] (FAAL)	TKA
Talkeetna Mountains [*Alaska*] [*Seismograph station code, US Geological Survey*] (SEIS)	TLK
Talkeetna Mountains, AK [*Location identifier FAA*] (FAAL)	AAW
Talker Active State [*Telecommunications*] (IAA)	TACS
Talker Commission Error (MUGU)	TCE
Talker Communication Error (IAA)	TCE
Talker Function [*Telecommunications*] (IAA)	TF
Talker Idle State [*Telecommunications*] (IAA)	TIDS
Talker Listener Adapter (NITA)	TLA
Talker Omission Error (MUGU)	TOE
Talker per Megacycle (SAA)	T/MC
Talking [*Telecommunications*] (TEL)	TLK
Talking Directory Display System [*FTA*] (TAG)	TDDS
Talking Machine	TM
Talking Newspaper Association, United Kingdom	TNAUK
Talking Newspaper Week [*British*]	TNW
Talking Screen Textwriting Program (EDAC)	TSTP
Tall Building Syndrome	TBS
Tall Cedars of Lebanon of North America (EA)	TCLNA
Tall Clubs International (EA)	TCI
Tall Copy [*Publishing*] (DGA)	TC
Tall, Dark, and Gruesome [*Slang*]	TD & G
Tall, Dark, and Handsome [*Slang*]	TD & H
Tall Fashion Promotions of Australia	TFPA
Tall Oil Fatty Acids [*Organic chemistry*]	TOFA
Tall Oil Rosin [*Organic chemistry*]	TOR
Tall Salicornia Zone [*Ecology*]	TS
Tall Timbers [*An association*] (EA)	TTR
Talladega, AL [*Location identifier FAA*] (FAAL)	ASN
Talladega, AL [*Location identifier FAA*] (FAAL)	TDG
Talladega, AL [*FM radio station call letters*]	WEYY
Talladega, AL [*AM radio station call letters*]	WNUZ
Talladega, AL [*AM radio station call letters*]	WSSY
Talladega College, Talladega, AL [*Library symbol Library of Congress*] (LCLS)	ATaT
Talladega College, Talladega, AL [*OCLC symbol*] (OCLC)	TAL
Tallahassee [*Florida*] [*Airport symbol*] (OAG)	TLH
Tallahassee Community College, Tallahassee, FL [*Library symbol Library of Congress*] (LCLS)	FTaT
Tallahassee/Dale Mabry Field [*Florida*] [*ICAO location identifier*] (ICLI)	KTLH
Tallahassee, FL [*Location identifier FAA*] (FAAL)	PLQ
Tallahassee, FL [*FM radio station call letters*] (RBYB)	WAIB
Tallahassee, FL [*FM radio station call letters*]	WAMF
Tallahassee, FL [*AM radio station call letters*]	WANM
Tallahassee, FL [*FM radio station call letters*]	WBZE
Tallahassee, FL [*AM radio station call letters*]	WCVC
Tallahassee, FL [*FM radio station call letters*]	WFSQ
Tallahassee, FL [*FM radio station call letters*]	WFSU
Tallahassee, FL [*Television station call letters*]	WFSU-TV
Tallahassee, FL [*FM radio station call letters*]	WGLF
Tallahassee, FL [*AM radio station call letters*]	WHBT
Tallahassee, FL [*AM radio station call letters*]	WHBX
Tallahassee, FL [*FM radio station call letters*]	WNLS
Tallahassee, FL [*FM radio station call letters*]	WRZK
Tallahassee, FL [*FM radio station call letters*]	WTAL
Tallahassee, FL [*FM radio station call letters*]	WTNT
Tallahassee, FL [*Television station call letters*]	WTWC
Tallahassee, FL [*Television station call letters*]	WTXL
Tallahassee, FL [*Television station call letters*]	WVFS
Tallahassee, FL [*FM radio station call letters*] (RBYB)	WWLD-FM
Tallahatchie County Library, Charleston, MS [*Library symbol Library of Congress*] (LCLS)	MsCh
Tallapoosa, GA [*AM radio station call letters*]	WKNG
Tallassee, AL [*AM radio station call letters*]	WACQ
Tallassee, AL [*AM radio station call letters*]	WTLS
Talley Indus [*NYSE symbol*] (TTSB)	TAL
Talley Indus,$1.00 Cv B Pfd [*NYSE symbol*] (TTSB)	TALPrB
Talley Industries, Inc. [*NYSE symbol*] (SPSG)	TAL
Talley Industries, Inc. [*Associated Press*] (SAG)	Talley
Tallgrass Prairie Alliance (EA)	TPA

Tallin [*Former USSR ICAO location identifier*] (ICLI) ... ULTT
Tallinn [*Former USSR Airport symbol*] (OAG) ... TLL
Tallow Alkyl Sulfate [*Surfactant*] ... TAS
Tallow Amine Ethoxylate ... TAE
Tallulah Falls Railway Co. [*AAR code*] ... TF
Tallulah, LA [*AM radio station call letters*] ... KBYO
Tallulah, LA [*FM radio station call letters*] ... KBYO-FM
Tallulah, LA [*Location identifier FAA*] (FAAL) ... TTT
Tally ... TLY
Tally Ho [*Air Force*] ... TH
Tally Resources [*Vancouver Stock Exchange symbol*] ... TLR
Tally-Ho Explorations Ltd. [*Vancouver Stock Exchange symbol*] ... THL
Tallyman ... tlymn
Talmud ... TAL
Talmud Bavli (BJA) ... TB
Talmud Jerushalmi (BJA) ... TJ
Talmud Torah (BJA) ... TT
Talmud Yerushalmi (BJA) ... TY
Talmudic Encyclopedia [*A publication*] (BJA) ... TE
Talmudical Academy (BJA) ... TA
Talmudische Archaeologie [*A publication*] (BJA) ... TA
Talon [*Heel of the Bow*] [*Music*] ... T
TALON Reporting and Information Processing System (NITA) ... TRIPS
Talos Activity Report (MCD) ... TALAR
Talos Adaptable Computer System [*Navy*] ... TACOS
Talos Conversion Equipment (MCD) ... TACE
Talos Defense Unit (SAA) ... TDU
Talos Discrepancy Report (MCD) ... TDR
Talos Integration Investigation ... TII
Talos [*Missile*] **Tactical Test Equipment** ... TATTE
Talos-Terrier-Recruit [*Flight-test vehicle*] ... TATER
Talpa [*New Mexico*] [*Airport symbol*] (AD) ... TLP
Taltal [*Chile*] [*Airport symbol*] (AD) ... TTC
Taluqan [*Afghanistan*] [*ICAO location identifier*] (ICLI) ... OATQ
Talx Corp [*Associated Press*] (SAG) ... TalxCp
Talx Corp. [*NASDAQ symbol*] (SAG) ... TALX
Talyllyn Railway [*Wales*] ... TR
TAM Ceramics, Inc., Niagara Falls, NY [*Library symbol Library of Congress*] (LCLS) ... NNiaTC
Tama County Historical Society, Elberon, IA [*Library symbol Library of Congress*] (LCLS) ... IaElbTHi
Tamale [*Ghana*] [*ICAO location identifier*] (ICLI) ... DGLE
Tamale [*Ghana*] [*Airport symbol*] (OAG) ... TML
Tamana [*Kiribati*] [*ICAO location identifier*] (ICLI) ... NGTM
Tamana [*Kiribati*] [*Airport symbol*] (OAG) ... TMN
Tamanrasset [*Algeria*] [*ICAO location identifier*] (ICLI) ... DAAT
Tamanrasset [*Algeria*] [*Seismograph station code, US Geological Survey*] (SEIS) ... TAM
Tamanrasset [*Algeria*] [*Airport symbol*] (OAG) ... TMR
Tamaqua, PA [*FM radio station call letters*] ... WMGH
Tamara Resources, Inc. [*Vancouver Stock Exchange symbol*] ... TAM
[*The*] **Tamarind Book of Lithography** ... TBL
Tamarind Institute (EA) ... TI
Tamarind Institute Workshop [*Graphic arts school*] [*New Mexico*] ... TIW
Tamarindo [*Costa Rica*] [*Airport symbol*] (OAG) ... TNO
Tamarindo de Bagaces [*Costa Rica*] [*ICAO location identifier*] (ICLI) ... MRTA
Tamarindo de Santa Cruz [*Costa Rica*] [*ICAO location identifier*] (ICLI) ... MRTM
Tamas Darida Enterprise [*Hungary ICAO designator*] (FAAC) ... DTE
Tamatave [*Madagascar*] [*Airport symbol*] (OAG) ... TMM
Tamavack Resources, Inc. [*Vancouver Stock Exchange symbol*] ... TKS
Tambacounda [*Senegal*] [*ICAO location identifier*] (ICLI) ... GOTT
Tambacounda [*Senegal*] [*Airport symbol*] (OAG) ... TUD
Tambankulu [*Swaziland*] [*ICAO location identifier*] (ICLI) ... FDTM
Tambao [*Burkina Faso*] [*ICAO location identifier*] (ICLI) ... DHEM
Tambao [*Upper Volta*] [*Airport symbol*] (AD) ... TMQ
Tambaram [*India*] [*ICAO location identifier*] (ICLI) ... VOTX
Tambohorano [*Madagascar*] [*ICAO location identifier*] (ICLI) ... FMMU
Tambohorano [*Madagascar*] [*Airport symbol*] (OAG) ... WTA
Tambolaka [*Indonesia*] [*Airport symbol*] (OAG) ... TMC
Tambor [*Costa Rica*] [*ICAO location identifier*] (ICLI) ... MRTR
Tambrands, Inc. [*Associated Press*] (SAG) ... Tambd
Tambrands, Inc. [*NYSE symbol*] (SPSG) ... TMB
Tamburitza Association of America (EA) ... TAA
Tambyah's Reports [*Ceylon*] [*A publication*] (DLA) ... Tamb
Tamchakett [*Mauritania*] [*ICAO location identifier*] (ICLI) ... GQNT
Tamdy-Bulak [*Former USSR ICAO location identifier*] (ICLI) ... UTSM
Tame [*Colorado ICAO location identifier*] (ICLI) ... SKTM
Tame [*Colombia*] [*Airport symbol*] (OAG) ... TME
Tamerton [*England*] ... TAM
Tamid (BJA) ... Tam
Tamil [*Language, etc.*] (ROG) ... TAM
Tamil [*MARC language code Library of Congress*] (LCCP) ... tam
Tamil Eelam International Research and Documentation Centre [*Canada*] ... TEIRDC
Tamil Eelam Liberation Front [*Sri Lanka*] [*Political party*] (PPW) ... TELF
Tamil Eelam Liberation Organization [*Sri Lanka*] [*Political party*] ... TELO
Tamil United Liberation Front [*Sri Lanka*] (PD) ... TULF
Tamil Vimukhti Peramena [*Sri Lanka*] [*Political party*] (PPW) ... TVP
Tamiment Institute (EA) ... TI
[*The*] **Taming of the Shrew** [*Shakespearean work*] ... Shr
[*The*] **Taming of the Shrew** [*Shakespearean work*] (BARN) ... Tam Shr
Tamlyn's English Rolls Court Reports [*48 English Reprint*] [*A publication*] (DLA) ... Tam
Tamlyn's English Rolls Court Reports [*48 English Reprint*] [*A publication*] (DLA) ... Taml
Tamlyn's English Rolls Court Reports [*48 English Reprint*] [*A publication*] (DLA) ... Tamlyn
Tamlyn's English Rolls Court Reports [*48 English Reprint*] [*A publication*] (DLA) ... Tamlyn Ch
Tamlyn's English Rolls Court Reports [*A publication*] (DLA) ... Tamlyn (Eng)
Tamlyn's Evidence in Chancery [*2nd ed.*] [*1846*] [*A publication*] (DLA) ... Taml Ev
Tamlyn's Terms of Years [*1825*] [*A publication*] (DLA) ... Taml TY
Tammy Graham Fan Club (EA) ... TGFC
Tammy Wynette International Fan Club (EA) ... TWIFC
Tamoxifen [*Antineoplastic drug*] ... T
Tamoxifen [*Antineoplastic drug*] ... TAM
Tamoxifen [*Antineoplastic drug*] ... TMX
Tamoxifen, Adriamycin, Cyclophosphamide [*Antineoplastic drug regimen*] ... TAC
Tamoxifen, Adriamycin, Cyclophosphamide, Oncovin [*Vincristine*] [*Antineoplastic drug regimen*] ... TACO
Tampa Bay Library Consortium, Tampa, FL [*Library symbol*] [*Library of Congress*] (LCLS) ... FTLC
Tampa Bay Medical Library Network [*Library network*] ... TABAMLN
Tampa Bay-Ruskin, FL [*Location identifier FAA*] (FAAL) ... TBW
Tampa Blue Print Co., Tampa, FL [*Library symbol Library of Congress*] (LCLS) ... TbP
Tampa, FL [*Location identifier FAA*] (FAAL) ... AMP
Tampa, FL [*Location identifier FAA*] (FAAL) ... GBZ
Tampa, FL [*Location identifier FAA*] (FAAL) ... JRT
Tampa, FL [*Location identifier FAA*] (FAAL) ... MCF
Tampa, FL [*Location identifier FAA*] (FAAL) ... TPF
Tampa, FL [*AM radio station call letters*] ... WAMA
Tampa, FL [*Television station call letters*] ... WBHS
Tampa, FL [*FM radio station call letters*] ... WBVM
Tampa, FL [*AM radio station call letters*] ... WDAE
Tampa, FL [*Television station call letters*] ... WEDU
Tampa, FL [*AM radio station call letters*] ... WFLA
Tampa, FL [*Television station call letters*] ... WFLA-TV
Tampa, FL [*FM radio station call letters*] ... WFLZ
Tampa, FL [*Television station call letters*] ... WFTS
Tampa, FL [*FM radio station call letters*] ... WMNF
Tampa, FL [*FM radio station call letters*] ... WRBQ
Tampa, FL [*AM radio station call letters*] ... WTIS
Tampa, FL [*Television station call letters*] ... WTVT
Tampa, FL [*FM radio station call letters*] ... WUSA
Tampa, FL [*FM radio station call letters*] ... WUSF
Tampa, FL [*Television station call letters*] ... WUSF-TV
Tampa, FL [*FM radio station call letters*] ... WWRM
Tampa/International [*Florida*] [*ICAO location identifier*] (ICLI) ... KTPA
Tampa/MacDill Air Force Base [*Florida*] [*ICAO location identifier*] (ICLI) ... KMCF
Tampa/St. Petersburg/Clearwater [*Florida*] [*Airport symbol*] ... TPA
Tampa Southern Railroad [*AAR code*] ... TAS
Tampa-Hillsborough County Public Library, Tampa, FL [*Library symbol Library of Congress*] (LCLS) ... FT
Tampa-Hillsborough County Public Library, Tampa, FL [*OCLC symbol*] (OCLC) ... TNH
Tamper (NFPA) ... T
Tamper Attempt Board ... TAB
Tamper Evident ... TE
Tamper Resistant Packaging [*Food and Drug Administration*] ... TRP
Tamper Switch [*NFPA pre-fire planning symbol*] (NFPA) ... TS
Tampere [*Finland ICAO location identifier*] (ICLI) ... EFES
Tampere [*Finland*] [*Airport symbol*] (OAG) ... TMP
Tampere-Pirkkala [*Finland ICAO location identifier*] (ICLI) ... EFTP
Tampering [*FBI standardized term*] ... TAMP
Tamper-Protected Recording [*3M Co.*] ... TPR
Tamper-Resistant Unattended Safeguard Technique (PDAA) ... TRUST
Tampico [*Mexico*] [*Airport symbol*] (OAG) ... TAM
Tampico/General Francisco Javier Mina Internacional [*Mexico ICAO location identifier*] (ICLI) ... MMTM
Tamuin [*Mexico ICAO location identifier*] (ICLI) ... MMTN
Tamuning, GU [*Television station call letters*] ... KTGM
Tamworth [*Australia ICAO location identifier*] (ICLI) ... ASTW
Tamworth [*Australia Airport symbol*] (OAG) ... TMW
Tamworth Branch, Lennox and Addington County Library, Ontario [*Library symbol National Library of Canada*] (BIB) ... OTLAC
Tamworth Swine Association (EA) ... TSA
Tan Son Nhut [*Air base*] [*Vietnam*] ... TSN
Tan Tan [*Morocco*] [*Airport symbol*] (OAG) ... TTA
Tana Toraja [*Indonesia*] [*Airport symbol*] (OAG) ... TTR
Tanabe Seiyaku Co. Ltd. [*Japan*] [*Research code symbol*] ... CRD
Tanabe Seiyaku Co. Ltd. [*Japan*] [*Research code symbol*] ... TA
Tanabu [*Japan*] [*Seismograph station code, US Geological Survey Closed*] (SEIS) ... TNB
Tanacross, AK [*Location identifier FAA*] (FAAL) ... TSG
Tanagra [*Greece*] [*ICAO location identifier*] (ICLI) ... LGTG
Tanah Grogot [*Indonesia*] [*ICAO location identifier*] (ICLI) ... WRLH
Tanah Merah [*Indonesia*] [*ICAO location identifier*] (ICLI) ... WAKT
Tanahmerah [*Indonesia*] [*Airport symbol*] (OAG) ... TMH
Tanai [*Myanmar*] [*ICAO location identifier*] (ICLI) ... VBTN
Tanaka [*New Britain*] [*Seismograph station code, US Geological Survey*] (SEIS) ... TKA
Tanalian Point, AK [*Location identifier FAA*] (FAAL) ... TPO
Tanana [*Alaska*] [*ICAO location identifier*] (ICLI) ... PATA
Tanana [*Alaska*] [*Airport symbol*] (OAG) ... TAL
Tanana [*Alaska*] [*Seismograph station code, US Geological Survey*] (SEIS) ... TNN
Tanana Air Service [*ICAO designator*] (FAAC) ... TNR
Tananarive [*Madagascar*] [*Seismograph station code, US Geological Survey*] (SEIS) ... TAN
Tananarive [*Malagasy*] [*Airport symbol*] (AD) ... TNR

Tanandava-Samangoky [*Madagascar*] [*ICAO location identifier*] (ICLI) .... FMSN
Tanavco Airways Ltd. [*Tanzania*] [*ICAO designator*] (FAAC) .... TNA
Tanbar [*Queensland*] [*Airport symbol*] (AD) .... TXR
Tancos [*Portugal ICAO location identifier*] (ICLI) .... LPTN
Tancred. Quo Warranto [*A publication*] (ILCA) .... Tanc QW
Tancredus [*Deceased circa 1236*] [*Authority cited in pre-1607 legal work*] (DSA) .... Tan
Tancredus [*Deceased circa 1236*] [*Authority cited in pre-1607 legal work*] (DSA) .... Tanc
Tancredus [*Deceased circa 1236*] [*Authority cited in pre-1607 legal work*] (DSA) .... Tancre
Tancredus [*Deceased circa 1236*] [*Authority cited in pre-1607 legal work*] (DSA) .... Tancred
Tandag [*Philippines*] [*Airport symbol*] (OAG) .... TDG
Tandag, Surigao Del Sur [*Philippines*] [*ICAO location identifier*] (ICLI) .... RPWW
Tandala [*Zaire*] [*ICAO location identifier*] (ICLI) .... FZFT
Tandapi [*Ecuador*] [*ICAO location identifier*] (ICLI) .... SETP
Tandem (AAG) .... TAN
Tandem (AAG) .... TDM
Tandem Accelerator Mass Spectrometry .... TAMS
Tandem Accelerator Superconducting Cyclotron Facility [*Canadian nuclear physics facility*] .... TASCC
Tandem Cantilevered Axle .... TAXLE
Tandem Club of America (EA) .... TCA
Tandem Computers [*NYSE symbol*] (TTSB) .... TDM
Tandem Computers, Inc. [*Associated Press*] (SAG) .... Tandem
Tandem Computers, Inc. [*NYSE symbol*] (SPSG) .... TDM
Tandem Cross-Section Program [*Bell System*] .... TCSP
Tandem Mass Spectroscopy .... MS-MS
Tandem Matching Loss [*Telecommunications*] (TEL) .... TML
Tandem Mirror Experiment [*Atomic fusion*] .... TMX
Tandem Mirror Hybrid Reactor (PDAA) .... TMHR
Tandem Mirror Reactor (MCD) .... TMR
Tandem Outlet .... TO
Tandem Propeller Submarine .... TPS
Tandem Razor and Cartridge [*Gillette Co.*] .... TRAC
Tandem Recursive Algorithm Process (HGAA) .... TRAP
Tandem Resources [*Vancouver Stock Exchange symbol*] .... TDM
Tandem Rotary Activator .... TRA
Tandem Scanning Microscope .... TSM
Tandem Scanning Reflected Light Microscopy .... TSRLM
Tandem Signal Unit [*Telecommunications*] (TEL) .... TSU
Tandem Tie Trunk Network (PDAA) .... TTTN
Tandem Truck Safety Act [*1984*] (GFGA) .... TTSA
Tandem Wing in Sound Effect (MCD) .... TWIG
Tandem-Rocket Dual-Combustion Ramjet (MCD) .... TRDCR
Tandil [*Argentina ICAO location identifier*] (ICLI) .... SAZT
Tandil [*Argentina*] [*Airport symbol*] (OAG) .... TDL
Tandy Brands Accessories [*NASDAQ symbol*] (TTSB) .... TBAC
Tandy Brands Accessories, Inc. [*Associated Press*] (SAG) .... TandyBr
Tandy Brands Accessories, Inc. [*NASDAQ symbol*] (SAG) .... TBAC
Tandy Corp. [*NYSE symbol*] (SPSG) .... TAN
Tandy Corp. [*Associated Press*] (SAG) .... Tandy
Tandy [*Corp.*] **High-Performance Optical Recording System** [*Dye-polymer technology*] (PCM) .... THOR
Tandy Radio Shack (NITA) .... TRS
Tandycrafts, Inc. [*NYSE symbol*] (SPSG) .... TAC
Tandycrafts, Inc. [*Associated Press*] (SAG) .... Tndycft
Tanegashima [*Japan ICAO location identifier*] (ICLI) .... RJFG
Tanegashima [*Ryukyu Islands*] [*Seismograph station code, US Geological Survey*] (SEIS) .... TAJ
Tanegashima [*Japan*] [*Airport symbol*] (OAG) .... TNE
Taney County, MO [*A lake at Branson, MO*] .... TANEYCOMO
Taney's United States Circuit Court Reports [*A publication*] (DLA) .... Tan
Taney's United States Circuit Court Reports [*A publication*] (DLA) .... Taney
Taney's United States Circuit Court Reports [*A publication*] (DLA) .... Taney's CC Dec
Taney's United States Circuit Court Reports [*A publication*] (DLA) .... Taney's Dec (USCC)
Tanga [*Tanzania*] [*ICAO location identifier*] (ICLI) .... HTTG
Tanga [*Tanzania*] [*Airport symbol*] (OAG) .... TGT
Tanganyika African National Union [*Political party*] .... TANU
Tanganyika African Postal Union .... TAPU
Tanganyika Federation of Labor .... TFL
Tanganyika Law Reports [*1921-52*] [*A publication*] (DLA) .... TLR
Tanganyika Law Reports (Revised) [*1921-52*] [*A publication*] (DLA) .... TLR (R)
Tanganyika Notes and Records [*A publication*] .... TNR
Tanganyika Plantation Workers Union .... TPWU
Tanganyika Railway African Union .... TRAU
Tanganyika Territory .... TT
Tanganyika Territory Law Reports [*A publication*] (DLA) .... Tan LR
Tanganyika Territory Law Reports [*1921-47*] [*A publication*] (DLA) .... TTLR
Tanganyika Union of Public Employees .... TUPE
Tangent [*Mathematics*] .... TAN
Tangent (IDOE) .... tan
Tangent [*Mathematics*] (ODBW) .... tan
Tangent [*Mathematics*] (IAA) .... TG
Tangent Altitude [*Photography*] .... TAN ALT
Tangent Approximating Manifold .... TAM
Tangent Elevation (MSA) .... TE
Tangent Group (EA) .... TG
Tangent, Hyperbolic .... TANH
Tangent Latitude Computer .... TLC
Tangent Latitude Computer Amplifier .... TLCA
Tangent Line to Tangent Line [*Engineering*] .... TL to TL
Tangent Mechanism .... TM
Tangent Oil & Gas [*Vancouver Stock Exchange symbol*] .... TGL
Tangent Plane System (MUGU) .... TPS
Tangent to Spiral .... TS
Tangential (AAG) .... TANG
Tangential Abrasive Dehulling Device [*for grains*] .... TADD
Tangential Bomb Suspension (MCD) .... TABS
Tangential Bracket .... TB
Tangential Cell [*Neurology*] .... TAN
Tangential Flow Filtration .... TFF
Tangential Flow Torch [*For plasma generation*] .... TFT
Tangential Force Variation [*Automotive fire testing*] .... TFV
Tangential Inlet Manifold .... TIM
Tangential Period Correction .... TPC
Tangential Signal Sensitivity .... TSS
Tanger [*Morocco*] [*Airport symbol*] (OAG) .... TNG
Tanger/Boukhalf [*Morocco*] [*ICAO location identifier*] (ICLI) .... GMTT
Tanger Fac Outlt Cv Dep Pfd [*NYSE symbol*] (TTSB) .... SKTPrA
Tanger Factory Outlet Centers [*Associated Press*] (SAG) .... Tanger
Tanger Factory Outlet Centers [*Associated Press*] (SAG) .... Tangr
Tanger Factory Outlet Centers, Inc. [*NYSE symbol*] (SPSG) .... SKT
Tanger Factory Outlet Ctrs [*NYSE symbol*] (TTSB) .... SKT
Tangerang [*Java*] [*Seismograph station code, US Geological Survey*] (SEIS) .... TNG
Tangerang/Budiarto [*Indonesia*] [*ICAO location identifier*] (ICLI) .... WIIA
Tangible Asset .... TA
Tangible Property [*Business*] (MHDW) .... TP
Tangible Reinforcement Operant Conditioning Audiometry .... TROCA
Tangible Research Property [*Business*] .... TRP
Tangier American Legation Museum Society (EA) .... TALMS
Tangier, VA [*Location identifier FAA*] (FAAL) .... TGI
Tangipahoa & Eastern [*AAR code*] .... TAEA
Tangipahoa Parish Library, Amite, LA [*Library symbol Library of Congress*] (LCLS) .... LAmT
Tangkuban-Prahu [*Java*] [*Seismograph station code, US Geological Survey Closed*] (SEIS) .... TPJ
Tanglewood Consolidated Resources, Inc. [*Toronto Stock Exchange symbol*] .... TAN
Tango [*Phonetic alphabet*] [*International*] (DSUE) .... T
Tangram Enterprise Solutions, Inc. [*Associated Press*] (SAG) .... TangEnt
Tangram Enterprise Solutions, Inc. [*NASDAQ symbol*] (SAG) .... TESI
Tanheim [*Germany ICAO location identifier*] (ICLI) .... EDMT
Tanhuma (BJA) .... T
Tanhuma (BJA) .... Tan
Tanhuma (BJA) .... Tanh
Tanjore [*India*] [*ICAO location identifier*] (ICLI) .... VOTJ
Tanjung Balai/Sungai Bati [*Indonesia*] [*ICAO location identifier*] (ICLI) .... WIBT
Tanjung Enim/Bangko [*Indonesia*] [*ICAO location identifier*] (ICLI) .... WIPE
Tanjung Karang/Branti [*Indonesia*] [*ICAO location identifier*] (ICLI) .... WIIT
Tanjung Pandan [*Indonesia*] [*Airport symbol*] (OAG) .... TJQ
Tanjung Pandan/Bulu Tumbang [*Indonesia*] [*ICAO location identifier*] (ICLI) .... WIKD
Tanjung Pinang [*Indonesia*] [*Airport symbol*] (OAG) .... TNJ
Tanjung Pinang/Kijang [*Indonesia*] [*ICAO location identifier*] (ICLI) .... WIKN
Tanjung Redep/Kalimarau [*Indonesia*] [*ICAO location identifier*] (ICLI) .... WRLK
Tanjung Santan [*Indonesia*] [*ICAO location identifier*] (ICLI) .... WRLT
Tanjung Selor/Tanjung Harapan [*Indonesia*] [*ICAO location identifier*] (ICLI) .... WRLG
Tanjung/Warukin [*Indonesia*] [*ICAO location identifier*] (ICLI) .... WRBN
Tank [*Trains*] [*British*] .... T
Tank (AAG) .... TK
Tank (AAG) .... TNK
Tank and Antitank [*Artillery and ammunition*] (NATG) .... T & AT
Tank and Orbiter Weight [*NASA*] (MCD) .... TOW
Tank and Pump Unit [*Mechanized infantry battalion*] (DWSG) .... T & P
Tank and Pump Unit [*Mechanized infantry battalion*] (INF) .... TPU
Tank, Antitank, and Assault Weapons Study [*or System*] [*Army*] .... TATAWS
Tank Appended Crew Evaluation Device (MCD) .... TACED
Tank Army (MCD) .... TA
Tank Arrangement Thermal Efficiency [*Computer program*] (KSC) .... TATE
Tank/Attack Helicopter Operational Performance (MCD) .... TAHOP
Tank Battalion [*Army*] .... TANKBAT
Tank Battalion [*Army*] .... TB
Tank Battalion [*Marine Corps*] .... TKBN
Tank Battle War Game .... TABWAG
Tank Cannon Launched Beam Rider Projectile (MCD) .... TCLBRP
Tank Car .... TC
Tank Car Committee [*RSPA*] (TAG) .... TCC
Tank Checkout Facility [*NASA*] (NASA) .... TCF
Tank Circuit (IAA) .... TC
Tank Cleaning Vessel (ADA) .... TCV
Tank Commander (RDA) .... TC
Tank Company [*Military*] (MCD) .... TC
Tank Corps .... TC
Tank Crew Qualification Course [*Army*] .... TCQC
Tank Crew Turret Simulator (MCD) .... TCTS
Tank Destroyer [*Military*] .... TD
Tank Destroyer [*Military*] .... TkDtyr
Tank Destroyer Armed with Missiles (INF) .... TDM
Tank Destroyer Center [*Army*] .... TDC
Tank Destroyer Replacement Training Center .... TDRTC
Tank Destroyer Tactical and Firing Center .... TDT/FC
Tank Destroyers Division [*Army*] .... TDDn
Tank Development Program [*Military*] .... TDP
Tank Division (MCD) .... TD
Tank Driver Trainer [*Army*] .... TDT

Tank Engine Exhaust Smoke System (MCD) .... TEESS
Tank Equipment Manufacturers Association (NUCP) .... TEMA
Tank Exchange Model .... TXM
Tank Exchange Ratio (MCD) .... TXR
Tank Extended Range Munition [Army] .... TERM
Tank Farm (NATG) .... TF
Tank Field Exercise (NVT) .... TANKEX
Tank Fire Combat Computer .... TFCC
Tank Fire Control .... TFC
Tank Fire Control System .... TFCS
Tank Force Management Group [Army] .... TFMG
Tank Forces Management Office [Army] .... TFMO
Tank Gunnery and Missile Tracking System .... TGMTS
Tank Infrared Elbow [Night vision device] [Army] (RDA) .... TIRE
Tank Landing Craft [Navy symbol Obsolete] .... ATL
Tank Landing Craft [Army British] .... TLC
Tank LASER Sight (MCD) .... TLS
Tank, Laying, Aiming, and Firing Trainer (MCD) .... TALAFIT
Tank Lease (ADA) .... TL
Tank Level Indicator (DNAB) .... TLI
Tank Lighter .... TLL
Tank Lighter (Medium Tank-Well Type) .... TLLW
Tank Main Armament Development (MCD) .... TMAD
Tank Main Armament Development Working Group [Army] .... TMADWG
Tank Main Armament Systems (RDA) .... TMAS
Tank Management Information System (MCD) .... TMIS
Tank Master Mechanic (MCD) .... TMM
Tank Nitrogen Supply (AAG) .... TNS
Tank Parliament [British] .... TP
Tank Petroleum Unit [Army] (INF) .... TPU
Tank Piercing [Ammunition] [Military] .... TP
Tank Precision Gunnery in Bore Device [Army] .... TPGID
Tank Pressure (DS) .... TP
Tank Pressure Sensing (AAG) .... TPS
Tank Pressurizing Orifice (KSC) .... TPO
Tank, Racks, Adapters, Pylons [Military] .... TRAP
Tank Range-Finder .... TRF
Tank Range-Finder Kit .... TRK
Tank Recovery Vehicle [Army] (AABC) .... TRV
Tank Regiment (MCD) .... TR
Tank Scope (DNAB) .... TS
Tank [Missile] Sight Improvement Program [Army] .... TSIP
Tank Steamer .... TS
Tank Surveillance Service [Military Traffic Management Command] .... TSS
Tank Tainers [Shipping] (DCTA) .... TA
Tank Technology (WDAA) .... TT
Tank Thermal Site .... TTS
Tank Top (DS) .... TT
Tank Track Test [Army] T3
Tank Training Devices (MCD) .... TTD
Tank Transporter [Military] (AABC) .... TKTRANSR
Tank Truck [Freight] .... TT
Tank Turret Camouflage System [Army] .... TTCS
Tank Turret Organizational Maintenance Trainer [Army] .... TTOMT
Tank Turret Safety Adapter [Army] .... TTSA
Tank Weapons Gunnery Simulation System (MCD) .... TWGSS
Tank-Automotive Command [Warren, MI] [Army] (MCD) .... TACOM
Tank-Automotive Concepts Laboratory [Army] (RDA) .... TACL
Tank-Automotive Integrated Database (MCD) .... TAIDB
Tank-Automotive Logistics Command [Army] .... TALC
Tank-Automotive Materiel Readiness Command [Army] .... TARCOM
Tank-Automotive Materiel Readiness Command, Selfridge Activity (MCD) .... TARCOMSA
Tank-Automotive Research and Development Command [Army] .... TARADCOM
Tank-Automotive Research, Development, and Engineering Center [Army] (RDA) .... TARDEC
Tank-Automotive Systems Development Center [Army] .... TASDC
Tanker [Designation for all US military aircraft] .... K
Tanker [Shipping] (DCTA) .... TA
Tanker .... TK
Tanker (AAG) .... TKR
Tanker [Army symbol] .... Y
Tanker and Bulk Carrier .... TBC
Tanker Motor Vessel [Shipping] (DS) .... TMV
Tanker Oil & Gas [Vancouver Stock Exchange symbol] .... TKL
Tanker Operating Instructions (DNAB) .... TANKOPINS
Tanker Operational Circular .... TOC
Tanker Owners Voluntary Agreement on Liability for Oil Pollution .... TOVALOP
Tanker Recovery Team [Air Force] (DOMA) .... TRT
Tanker Safety and Pollution Prevention .... TSPP
Tanker Service Committee .... TSC
Tanker Task Force .... TKTF
Tanker Task Force (AFM) .... TTF
Tanker, Transport, Bomber [Requirements] [Air Force] .... TTB
Tanker Transport Training System [Air Force] .... TTTS
Tanker-Transport Trailer System (MCD) .... TTTS
Tank-Fired Guided Missile (MCD) .... TFGM
Tanking (AAG) .... TKG
Tanking Control System (AAG) .... TCS
Tanking Unit (AAG) .... TU
Tanknology Environmental [NASDAQ symbol] (SPSG) .... TANK
Tankology Environmental, Inc. [Associated Press] (SAG) .... Tanklgy
Tanks and Mechanized Infantry Experiment (MCD) .... TAMI
Tankwagon .... TW
Tanna (BJA) .... T

Tanna di-be Eliahu (BJA) .... TdbE
Tanna Island [Vanuata] [Airport symbol] (OAG) .... TAH
Tanned (MSA) .... TAN
Tanned Red Cell [Clinical chemistry] .... TRC
Tanned Red Cell Hemagglutination [Immunology] (MAE) .... TRCH
Tanned Red Cell Hemagglutination Inhibition Immunoasay [Immunology] (PDAA) .... TRCHII
Tanned Red Cell Hemagglutination Inhibition Test [Immunology] .... TRCHI
Tanned-Cell Hemagglutination Test [Immunology] .... TCHT
Tanner Eclectic Stuttering Therapy Program .... TEST
Tanner's Council of America [Later, LIA] (EA) .... TCA
Tanner's Reports [8-14 Indiana] [A publication] (DLA) .... Tann
Tanner's Reports [13-17 Utah] [A publication] (DLA) .... Tann
Tanner's Reports [13-17 Utah] [A publication] (DLA) .... Tanner
Tanner's Reports [8-14 Indiana] [A publication] (DLA) .... Tanner
Tanners' Union [British] .... TU
Tannery .... TNRY
Tannic Acid [Urology] (DAVI) .... TA
Tannic Acid Agar [Culture media] .... TAA
Tannic Acid Equivalent [Analytical chemistry] .... TAE
Tannic Acid, Phosphomolybdic Acid, Amido Acid Black [A staining technique] .... TPA
Tanning .... TAN
Tanos Petroleum Corp. [Vancouver Stock Exchange symbol] .... TNS
Tanout [Niger] [ICAO location identifier] (ICLI) .... DRZT
Tanqueray [Gin] and Tonic .... T & T
Tanquery Resources Ltd. [Vancouver Stock Exchange symbol] .... TQY
Tansavio [ICAO designator] (AD) .... TD
Tanscend Services, Inc. [Associated Press] (SAG) .... Transcnd
Tansy Resources, Inc. [Vancouver Stock Exchange symbol] .... TAR
Tantalum [Chemical element] .... Ta
Tantalum Capacitor (IEEE) .... TC
Tantalum Carbon Bond .... TCB
Tantalum Foil Capacitor .... TFC
Tantalum Integrated Circuit [Electronics] (PDAA) .... TIC
Tantalum Producers Association [Defunct] (EA) .... TPA
Tantalum Producers International Study Center [Later, Tantalum-Niobium International Study Center] (EAIO) .... TIC
Tantalum-Controlled Rectifier .... TCR
Tantalus Resources Ltd. [Vancouver Stock Exchange symbol] .... TTU
Tan-Tan/Plage Blanche [Morocco] [ICAO location identifier] (ICLI) .... GMAT
Tantato Resources, Inc. [Vancouver Stock Exchange symbol] .... TT
Tantawangalo Catchment Protection Association (EERA) .... TCPA
TANU [Tanganyika African National Union] Youth League [Tanganyika] .... TYL
Tanya Roberts Fan Club (EA) .... TRFC
Tanya Tucker Fan Club (EA) .... TTFC
Tanyang [Myanmar] [ICAO location identifier] (ICLI) .... VBTY
Tanzania [International vehicle registration] (ODBW) .... EAT
Tanzania [MARC geographic area code Library of Congress] (LCCP) .... f-tz--
Tanzania (WDAA) .... TAN
Tanzania .... Tanz
Tanzania [MARC country of publication code Library of Congress] (LCCP) .... tz
Tanzania Electric Supply Co. .... TANESCO
Tanzania Gazette Law Reports [A publication] (DLA) .... TLR
Tanzania National Documentation Centre [National Central Library] [Information service or system] (IID) .... TANDOC
Tanzanian Shilling [Monetary unit] (ODBW) .... TSh
Tanzania-Zambia [Railway] .... TAN-ZAM
Tanzania-Zambia Railway .... TAZARA
Tanzania-Zambia Railway (PDAA) .... TZR
Tanzer 22 Class Association (EA) .... TCA
TAO [Tropical Atmosphere-Ocean] Implementation Panel [Marine science] (OSRA) .... TIP
Taoist Sanctuary [Later, DS] (EA) .... TS
Taos, NM [FM radio station call letters] (RBYB) .... KAPF-FM
Taos, NM [AM radio station call letters] .... KKIT
Taos, NM [FM radio station call letters] .... KTAO
Taos, NM [Location identifier FAA] (FAAL) .... SKX
Taos, NM [Location identifier FAA] (FAAL) .... TAS
Taoudenni [Mali] [ICAO location identifier] (ICLI) .... GATN
Taoyuan [China] [ICAO location identifier] (ICLI) .... RCGM
Tap Changing Under Load (MSA) .... TCUL
Tap Water [Medicine] .... TW
Tap Water Agar [Microbiology] .... TWA
Tap Water Enema [Medicine] .... TWE
Tapachula [Mexico ICAO location identifier] (ICLI) .... MMTP
Tapachula [Mexico] [Airport symbol] (OAG) .... TAP
Tapak Tuan/Teuku Cut Ali [Indonesia] [ICAO location identifier] (ICLI) .... WITA
Tape (IAA) .... TA
Tape (BUR) .... TP
Tape (WDMC) .... tp
Tape Adapter .... TA
Tape Adapter Cabinet (IAA) .... TAC
Tape Adapter Unit [Computer science] (IAA) .... TAU
Tape Address Register [Demography] .... TAR
Tape Address Register File [Bureau of the Census] (GFGA) .... TAR
Tape Advance (AAG) .... TA
Tape Alteration Subroutine .... TAS
Tape and Buffer System [Computer science] .... TBS
Tape Archive [Computer science] (DOM) .... TAR
Tape Armored [Telecommunications] (TEL) .... TA
Tape Automated Bonding [Integrated circuit technology] .... TdbB
Tape Automatic Positioning and Control .... TAPAC
Tape Automatic Preparation Equipment .... TAPE
Tape Backup Unit .... TB

Tape Block	TPBK
Tape Carrier Package (PCM)	TCP
Tape Carrier Packaging [Computer science]	TCP
Tape Cassette Recorder	TCR
Tape Command	TC
Tape Compare [Computer science] (IAA)	TPCOMP
Tape Compare Processor [Computer science]	TCOMP
Tape Control Block [Computer science] (IAA)	TCB
Tape Control Unit	TCU
Tape Control via Console	TCVC
Tape Conversion Program [Computer science] (MDG)	TCP
Tape Core	TC
Tape Data Control Sheet [Computer science]	TDCS
Tape Data Family	TDF
Tape Data Handling System	TDHS
Tape Data Register	TDR
Tape Data Selector	TDS
Tape Deblock	TPDB
Tape Decal System	TDS
Tape Degausser	TD
Tape Direct Memory Access	TDMA
Tape Direct Memory Address (NITA)	TDMA
Tape Disk Operating System [Computer science]	TDOS
Tape Distributor [Computer science] (IAA)	TD
Tape Distributor (MSA)	TDISTR
Tape Drive	TD
Tape Dump and Utility Monitor [Computer science]	TDUM
Tape Duplicate [Computer science] (IAA)	TPDUP
Tape Edit Processor [Computer science]	TEP
Tape Editing Equipment	TEE
Tape Error [Computer science] (IAA)	TE
Tape Error Block [Computer science] (IAA)	TEB
Tape Error Recovery [Routine] [Computer science] (ECII)	TER
Tape Executive Program (SAA)	TAPEX
Tape Feed	TF
Tape File Management	TFM
Tape File Octal Load	TFOL
Tape File Supervisor	TFS
Tape Gauge	TG
Tape Identification Card	TIC
Tape Identification Unit	TIU
Tape Indicator [Computer science] (IAA)	TI
Tape Initializer [Computer science] (IAA)	TPINIT
Tape Input and Output [Computer science] (DNAB)	TAPIO
Tape Input - Tape Output [Honeywell, Inc.] [Computer science]	TIPTOP
Tape Interface Direct Memory Access	TIDMA
Tape Intersystem Connection [Computer science]	TIC
Tape Inventory File (IEEE)	TIF
Tape Inverter	TI
Tape Label [Information] [Computer science]	TPLAB
Tape Librarian System	TLS
Tape Library (BUR)	TL
Tape Library [National Center for Atmospheric Research]	TLIB
Tape Library Management System	TLMS
Tape Loop Recorder	TLR
Tape Management Catalog	TMC
Tape Management Software [Computer science] (IAA)	TMS
Tape Management System (MCD)	TMS
Tape Manufacturers Group [British] (DBA)	TMG
Tape Mark [Computer science] (BUR)	TM
Tape Module (DEN)	TM
Tape Operating System [IBM Corp.] [Computer science]	TOS
Tape Output Test Rack Autonetics Diode	TOTRAD
Tape Overlap Emulator [Computer science] (IAA)	TOE
Tape Phase Inverter	TPI
Tape Playback BIT [Binary Digit] [Computer science]	TPB
Tape Playback Discriminator	TPD
Tape Playback Discriminator System	TPDS
Tape Plotting System	TPS
Tape Post-Processing System	TPPS
Tape Preparation Unit	TPU
Tape Preventive Maintenance	TPM
Tape Processing Machine	TPM
Tape Processing System (CMD)	TPS
Tape Programmed Automatic Tester	TAPAT
Tape Programmed Row [Data scanner]	TPR
Tape Programming System (NITA)	TPS
Tape Pulse Amplifier	TPA
Tape Punch Subassembly	TPS
Tape Punch Subassembly Panel	TPSP
Tape Read and Write Library	TRAWL
Tape Read Register	TRR
Tape Reader	TR
Tape Reader Calibrator	TRC
Tape Reader Control	TRC
Tape Reader Emulator Module	TREM
Tape Reading Typing Relay (IAA)	TTR
Tape Record Coordinator [Computer science]	TRC
Tape Recorder	TR
Tape Recorder Action Plan [Committee] [NASA/Air Force]	TRAP
Tape Recorder Amplifier	TRA
Tape Recorder Control Panel (MCD)	TRCS
Tape Recorder Subsystem	TRS
Tape Register	TR
Tape Relay Center (NATG)	TRC
Tape Repeating Automatic Data Integration System	TRADIS
Tape Resident	TR
Tape Resident Operating System [Computer science] (IEEE)	TROS
Tape Search System	TSS
Tape Search Unit (CET)	TSU
Tape Serial Number [Computer science]	TSN
Tape Station Conversion (CET)	TSC
Tape Status [Computer science] (OA)	TS
Tape Storage System	TSS
Tape System Output Converter [Computer science] (IAA)	TSOC
Tape to Card	TTC
Tape Transport Cassette	TTC
Tape Unit	TU
Tape Unit Group [Telecommunications] (TEL)	TUG
Tape Update of Formatted Files-Format Table Tape Updater and Generator [Computer science]	TUFF-TUG
Tape Velocity Fluctuation	TVF
Tape Wrapping Machine	TWM
Tape Write Register	TWR
Tape-Controlled Automatic Testing	TCAT
Tape-Controlled Reckoning and Checkout Equipment [Component of automatic pilot] [Aviation] (IAA)	TRACE
Tape-Controlled Recording Automatic Checkout Equipment [Component of automatic pilot] [Aviation]	TRACE
Taped Commentary [On a bus tour] [British]	T
Tape-Handler [Computer science] (IAA)	TH
Tape-Handling Equipment	THE
Tape-Handling Operational System [Computer science] (IEEE)	THOPS
Tape-Handling Optional Routines [Honeywell, Inc.]	THOR
Tapeless Rotorless On-Line Cryptographic Equipment (NATG)	TROL
Tape-Pack	TAPAK
Tape-Position Indicator (DEN)	TPI
Taper	T
Taper (MSA)	TPR
TAPER Isolated Dynamic Gain (IAA)	TIDG
Taper Shank [Screw]	TS
Taper Sided	TS
Tape-Reading Tripping Relay	TTR
Tapered Aperture Horn Antenna	TAHA
Tapered Bearing Simulator [Lubricant testing]	TBS
Tapered Channel [Wave power technology]	TAPCHAN
Tapered Double Cantilever Beam (MCD)	TDCB
Tapered Element Oscillating Microbalance	TEOM
Tapered Hatchway [on a ship] (DS)	T
Tapered Link Pin	TLP
Tapered Roller Bearing	TRB
Tapered Steel Transmission Pole Institute [Defunct] (EA)	TSTPI
Taper-Faced Napier Ring [Automobile engines]	TFNR
Tapes and Recording Wires [JETDS nomenclature] [Military] (CET)	TW
Tapes for the Blind [Defunct] (EA)	TB
Tapestry (ADA)	TAP
Tapestry (VRA)	tap
Tapestry (ADA)	TPY
Tapetochoroidal Dystrophy [Ophthalmology]	TCD
Tape-to-File Recorder	TFR
Tape-to-Print	TTP
Tape-to-Printer [Computer science] (IAA)	TPPR
Tape-to-Random Access [Computer science] (IAA)	TPRA
Tape-to-Tape [Computer science] (IAA)	TPTP
Tape-Wound Nylon Phenolic (SAA)	TWNP
Tapia House Movement [Trinidad and Tobago] [Political party] (PPW)	THM
Taping for the Blind (EA)	TFTB
Tapini [Papua New Guinea] [Airport symbol] (OAG)	TPI
Tapini [Papua New Guinea] [Seismograph station code, US Geological Survey Closed] (SEIS)	TPN
Tapistron International, Inc. [NASDAQ symbol] (SAG)	TAPI
Tapistron International, Inc. [Associated Press] (SAG)	Tapist
Tapistron International, Inc. [Associated Press] (SAG)	Tapistrn
Tapistron Intl [NASDAQ symbol] (TTSB)	TAPI
Tapistron Intl Wrrt [NASDAQ symbol] (TTSB)	TAPIW
Taplejung [Nepal] [ICAO location identifier] (ICLI)	VNTJ
Tapp on Maintenance and Champerty [1861] [A publication] (ILCA)	Tapp M & Ch
Tappahannock, VA [AM radio station call letters]	WRAR
Tappahannock, VA [FM radio station call letters]	WRAR-FM
Tappan Free Library, Tappan, NY [Library symbol Library of Congress] (LCLS)	NTap
Tappan Zee Fin'l [NASDAQ symbol] (TTSB)	TPNZ
Tappan's Ohio Common Pleas Reports [A publication] (DLA)	T
Tappan's Ohio Common Pleas Reports [A publication] (DLA)	Tap
Tappan's Ohio Common Pleas Reports [A publication] (DLA)	Tapp
Tappan's Ohio Common Pleas Reports [A publication] (DLA)	Tappan
Tappan's Ohio Common Pleas Reports [A publication] (DLA)	Tappan (Ohio)
Tappan's Ohio Common Pleas Reports [A publication] (DLA)	Tappan's Ohio Rep
Tappan's Ohio Common Pleas Reports [A publication] (DLA)	Tappan's R
Tapped (MSA)	TPD
Tapped Delay Line	TDL
Tappen Zee Financial, Inc. [Associated Press] (SAG)	TapZee
Tappen Zee Financial, Inc. [NASDAQ symbol] (SAG)	TPNZ
Tappet [Mechanical engineering]	TPT
Tapping	TPG
Tapping Achievement Potential Project (EDAC)	TAP
Tapping Fixture	TAFX
Tapping on the Writ of Mandamus [1848] [A publication] (DLA)	Tap Man
Tapping on the Writ of Mandamus [A publication] (DLA)	Tapping

Tapping Plate [*Automotive engineering*] .... T/PLT
Tapping's Copyholder's Manual [*A publication*] (DLA) .... Tap CM
Tappit Resources [*Vancouver Stock Exchange symbol*] .... TPT
Taps and Dies (WDAA) .... T & D
Tapuruquara [*Brazil ICAO location identifier*] (ICLI) .... SBTC
Taputuquara [*Brazil*] [*Airport symbol*] (AD) .... TPU
Tapwater (DAVI) .... TW
Tapwater Enema Till Clear [*Pharmacology*] (DAVI) .... TWETC
Tapwater Wet Dressing [*Surgery*] (DAVI) .... TWWD
Tar and Nicotine [*In cigarettes*] .... T/N
Tar Heel Aviation, Inc. [*ICAO designator*] (FAAC) .... THC
Tar Macadam .... TARMAC
Tara [*Queensland*] [*Airport symbol*] (AD) .... XTR
Tara Air Line [*Iran*] [*FAA designator*] (FAAC) .... IRR
Tara Branch, Bruce County Public Library, Ontario [*Library symbol National Library of Canada*] (NLC) .... OT
Tara Collectors Club (EA) .... TCC
Tara Exploration & Development Co. Ltd. [*Toronto Stock Exchange symbol*] .... TAR
Taracua [*Brazil*] [*Airport symbol*] (AD) .... TAJ
Taradale [*New Zealand*] [*Seismograph station code, US Geological Survey*] (SEIS) .... TRZ
Tarakan [*Indonesia*] [*Airport symbol*] (OAG) .... TRK
Taraken [*Indonesia*] [*ICAO location identifier*] (ICLI) .... WRLR
Tarakeshwar [*India*] [*ICAO location identifier*] (ICLI) .... VETK
Tarama [*Ryukyu Islands*] [*ICAO location identifier*] (ICLI) .... RORT
Taramajima [*Japan*] [*Airport symbol*] (OAG) .... TRA
TARAN [*Tactical Attack RADAR and Navigation*] System Data .... TSD
Taranto [*Italy*] [*Seismograph station code, US Geological Survey*] (SEIS) .... TAR
Taranto [*Italy*] [*Airport symbol*] (AD) .... TAR
Tarapoa [*Ecuador*] [*ICAO location identifier*] (ICLI) .... SETR
Tarapoto [*Peru*] [*ICAO location identifier*] (ICLI) .... SPST
Tarapoto [*Peru*] [*Airport symbol*] (OAG) .... TPP
Tarapur Atomic Power Station [*India*] .... TAPS
Tarata [*New Zealand*] [*Seismograph station code, US Geological Survey*] (SEIS) .... TNZ
Tarauaca [*Brazil ICAO location identifier*] (ICLI) .... SBTK
Tarauaca [*Brazil*] [*Airport symbol*] (AD) .... TRQ
Taravao [*Society Islands*] [*Seismograph station code, US Geological Survey*] (SEIS) .... TVO
Tarawa [*Kiribati*] [*Airport symbol*] (OAG) .... TRW
Tarawa/Betio [*Kiribati*] [*ICAO location identifier*] (ICLI) .... NGTT
Tarawa/Bonriki International [*Kiribati*] [*ICAO location identifier*] (ICLI) .... NGTA
Tarbes [*France*] [*Airport symbol*] (AD) .... TFR
Tarbes/Laloubere [*France ICAO location identifier*] (ICLI) .... LFDT
Tarbes/Ossun-Lourdes [*France ICAO location identifier*] (ICLI) .... LFBT
Tarbiz. Jerusalem (BJA) .... Tarb
Tarboro, NC [*AM radio station call letters*] .... WCPS
Tarboro, NC [*FM radio station call letters*] .... WFXK
Tardeable Emmission Rights (EERA) .... TER
Tardive Dyskinesia [*Medicine*] .... TD
Tardive Dyskinesia [*Neurology*] (DAVI) .... TDK
Tardive Dyskinesia/Tardive Dystonia National Association (EA) .... TD/TDNA
Tare [*Phonetic alphabet*] [*World War II*] (DSUE) .... T
Tare (ROG) .... TR
Taree [*Australia Airport symbol*] (OAG) .... TRO
Tarfaya [*Morocco*] [*Airport symbol*] (AD) .... TFY
Target .... T
Target (DEN) .... TA
Target .... TAR
Target (AAG) .... TGT
Target (AAG) .... TRGT
Target Abilities Test [*Psychometrics*] .... TAT
Target Acquisition (MCD) .... TA
Target Acquisition and Data Collection System .... TACDACS
Target Acquisition and Data Collection System .... TACDAS
Target Acquisition and Data System [*Army*] (DOMA) .... TADS
Target Acquisition and Designation System (MCD) .... TADS
Target Acquisition and Track System (MUGU) .... TATS
Target Acquisition Battalion [*Military*] .... TAB
Target Acquisition Battery (MCD) .... TAB
Target Acquisition Center [*Army*] .... TAC
Target Acquisition Console [*Military*] (CAAL) .... TAC
Target Acquisition Data .... TAD
Target Acquisition/Designation Aerial Reconnaissance System (MCD) .... TADARS
Target Acquisition/Designation Reconnaissance System (MCD) .... TADRS
Target Acquisition Designation Sight [*Army*] .... TADS
Target Acquisition Designation System/Pilot Night Vision System [*Army*] (RDA) .... TADS/PNVS
Target Acquisition Laboratory .... TAL
Target Acquisition Model [*Military*] .... TAM
Target Acquisition Reconnaissance and Surveillance System (SAA) .... TARS
Target Acquisition System .... TAS
Target Acquisition System / Infrared Automatic System [*Military*] (DNAB) .... TAS/IRAS
Target Acquisition System / Integrated [*Military*] (DNAB) .... TAS/I
Target Acquisition System / RADAR Automatic System [*Military*] (DNAB) .... TAS/RAS
Target Acquisition Systems Force Mix Analysis [*Military*] .... TASFMA
Target Acquisition Systems Force Mix Evaluation Analysis .... TASFMEA
Target Acquisition Sytem / RADAR Manual System [*Military*] (DNAB) .... TAS/RMS
Target Acquisition Weapon Delivery System [*Air Force*] (MCD) .... TAWDS
Target Acquisition Working Group [*Air Force*] .... TAWG
Target Activated Munition [*Air-delivered land mines*] .... TAM

Target Activated Munitions System .... TAMS
Target Activation Date (AAG) .... TAD
Target Aim Points .... TAP
Target Aircraft (MUGU) .... TA
Target Aircraft Transmitter .... TAT
Target Alert Data Display Set (MCD) .... TADD
Target Alert Data Display Set (RDA) .... TADDS
Target Analysis and Planning [*Computer system*] [*Military*] .... TAP
Target and Activity Display System [*Military*] .... TADS
Target and Background Signal-to-Noise Evaluation (MUGU) .... TABSTONE
Target and Background Signal-to-Noise Experiment (IAA) .... TABSTONE
Target and Penetration (IAA) .... TAP
Target and Training Submarine [*Self-propelled*] [*Navy symbol*] .... SST
Target Angular Position [*Photonics*] .... TAP
Target Antisubmarine Patrol (NVT) .... TASP
Target Area [*Military*] (AFM) .... TA
Target Area Advisory Council (OICC) .... TAAC
Target Area Analysis-RADAR .... TAAR
Target Area Analysis-Repair (MCD) .... TAAR
Target Area Designator [*Air Force*] .... TAD
Target Area of Interest [*Army intelligence matrix*] (INF) .... TAI
Target Area Sequential Correlator (MCD) .... TASC
Target Assignment Panel .... TAP
Target Attaching Globulin [*Medicine*] (AAMN) .... TAG
Target Attitude Group [*Advertising*] .... TAG
Target Audience Description [*Army*] .... TAD
Target Barge [*Navy symbol*] .... YGTN
Target Bearing Designator [*Navy*] .... TBD
Target Bearing Indicator [*Military*] .... TBI
Target Bearing Transmitter .... TBT
Target Benefit Plan [*Human resources*] (WYGK) .... TBP
Target Cell [*Immunology*] .... TC
Target Center Display .... TCD
Target Class Assignment .... TCA
Target Cleanup Level [*Environmental science*] (ERG) .... TCL
Target Combat Air Patrol [*Navy*] .... TARCAP
Target Concentration [*or Toxic*] (GNE) .... TC
Target Control (MCD) .... TC
Target Control Box [*Army*] .... TCB
Target Control System .... TCS
Target Control Unit (IAA) .... TCU
Target Coordinate Data (IEEE) .... TACODA
Target Coordinate Map Locator [*Military*] (PDAA) .... TCML
Target Coordination Center .... TCC
Target Cost plus Target Fee .... TCPTF
Target Cost System .... TCS
Target Data Collection .... TDC
Target Data Communicator (DWSG) .... TDC
Target Data Control Unit (AAG) .... TDCU
Target Data Input Computer .... TDIC
Target Data Input Unit .... TDIU
Target Data Inventory [*Military*] (AFM) .... TDI
Target Data Inventory Master Tape Preparation [*Military*] (IAA) .... TDIPRE
Target Data Planning File (SAA) .... TDPF
Target Data Processor (NVT) .... TDP
Target Data Sheet (MCD) .... TDS
Target Designation System [*Navy*] .... TADS
Target Designation System [*Navy*] .... TDS
Target Designation Transmitter .... TDT
Target Designation Transmitter and Control Unit .... TDT and CU
Target Designator (MCD) .... TD
Target Designator Control (MCD) .... TDC
Target Designator Control Unit (MCD) .... TDCU
Target Detecting Device .... TDD
Target Detection and Recognition (MCD) .... TDR
Target Detection, Identification, and Location .... TDIL
Target Detection Unit .... TDU
Target Detection-Conversion Sensor .... TDCS
Target Development Facility [*Proposed, 1986, for fusion research*] .... TDF
Target Development Laboratory [*Eglin AFB*] (AAG) .... TDL
Target Director Post [*RADAR*] [*Military*] .... TDP
Target Discrimination .... TD
Target Discrimination RADAR (IEEE) .... TDR
Target Docking Adapter [*NASA*] (KSC) .... TDA
Target Docking Trainer [*NASA*] (KSC) .... TDT
Target Doppler Indicator [*RADAR*] .... TDI
Target Doppler Nullifier [*RADAR*] .... TDN
Target Doppler Reference Frequency .... TDRF
Target Drone .... TD
Target Echo Signature Generator [*SONAR*] .... TESG
Target Effluent Detection System (MCD) .... TEDS
Target Engagement Console .... TEC
Target Engagement Evaluation [*Military*] .... TEVAL
Target Engagement Message (NVT) .... TEM
Target Engagement Proficiency Exercise [*Military*] .... TEPE
Target Engagement Simulator [*Military*] (MCD) .... TES
Target Entry Console .... TEC
Target Evaluation and Weapon Assignment (MCD) .... TEWA
Target Evaluation Maintenance .... TEM
Target Exploitation [*Military*] (AABC) .... TAREX
Target Factor Analysis [*Statistical technique*] .... TFA
Target File (MCD) .... TF
Target Fiscal Year (MCD) .... TFY
Target Gate (CAAL) .... TG
Target Generating System .... TGS

Target Ground Elapsed Time ..... TGET
Target Group Index [*British Market Research Bureau Ltd.*] [*Information service or system*] ..... TGI
Target Health Hazard Program [*Occupational Safety and Health Administration*] ..... THHP
Target Heart Rate [*Exercise*] (INF) ..... THR
Target Height Finding (MCD) ..... THF
Target Holding Mechanism, Tank Gunnery ..... THMTG
Target Homing Correlator ..... THC
Target Homing System ..... THS
Target Identification ..... TI
Target Identification and Acquisition System ..... TIAS
Target Identification Device [*Military*] (CAAL) ..... TID
Target Identification Equipment (MCD) ..... TIE
Target Identification Navigation RADAR ..... TINR
Target Identification Point (NATG) ..... TIP
Target Identification Software [*Military*] (CAAL) ..... TIS
Target Identification System, Electro-Optical [*Air Force*] ..... TISEO
Target Illuminating RADAR [*Air Force*] ..... TIR
Target Illumination and Recovery Aid ..... TIARA
Target Illumination/Target Tracking RADAR (MCD) ..... TI/TTR
Target Image Generator ..... TIG
Target Impact Point ..... TIP
Target Index Reference System [*Army*] (DOMA) ..... TIRS
Target Indication Officer [*Navy*] ..... TIO
Target Indication Room [*Navy*] ..... TIR
Target Indication Unit [*Navy*] ..... TIU
Target Indicator ..... TI
Target Indicator Kit ..... TIK
Target Industries [*Industry segments which have been selected by the US Department of Commerce for special trade promotion emphasis*] ..... TIR
Target Industries Program [*Occupational Safety and Health Administration*] ..... TIP
Target Information Officer [*Marine Corps*] (DOMA) ..... TIO
Target Information Sheet [*Air Force*] ..... TIS
Target Information System ..... TIS
Target Input Panel ..... TIP
Target Input Panel and Target Assign Panel ..... TIP/TAP
Target Instruction Register ..... TIR
Target Integration Center (MCD) ..... TIC
Target Intelligence (MCD) ..... TI
Target Intelligence File (CINC) ..... TIF
Target Intelligence Handbook (MCD) ..... TIHB
Target Intelligence Material (MCD) ..... TIM
Target Intelligence Package (MCD) ..... TIP
Target Intelligence Production Program ..... TIPP
Target Intensifier ..... TGI
Target Intensifier Vidicon ..... TIV
Target Intercept Computer [*Military*] ..... TIC
Target Intercept Timer (MCD) ..... TINT
Target Jamming System ..... TJS
Target Language ..... TL
Target Launch Vehicle [*NASA*] ..... TLV
Target Launch Zone ..... TLZ
Target Letter Position [*Psychology*] ..... TLP
Target Level of Safety (DA) ..... TLS
Target List Review Group (CINC) ..... TLRG
Target Locating System [*Military*] (MCD) ..... TARLOCS
Target Location Error [*Military*] (AABC) ..... TLE
Target Location System ..... TLS
Target Logistics Support Costs ..... TLSC
Target Loss (OA) ..... TL
Target Map Coordinate Locator [*Military*] ..... TMCL
Target Marker Air Droppable (MCD) ..... TMAD
Target Marker and Dispenser (MCD) ..... TMAD
Target Market Coverage [*Advertising*] (BARN) ..... TMC
Target Marking System ..... TMS
Target Material Production Instruction [*Air Force*] ..... TMPI
Target Materials Program [*DoD*] ..... TMP
Target Materials Squadron (MCD) ..... TMS
Target [*or Total*] **Maximum Operating Time** ..... TMOT
Target Mechanism (MCD) ..... TM
Target Motion Analyzer ..... TMA
Target Network Television [*Cable television network*] (NTCM) ..... TNT
Target Occulting Processor (MCD) ..... TOP
Target of Interest [*Military*] (CAAL) ..... TOI
Target of Opportunity ..... T/O
Target of Opportunity [*Military*] (CAAL) ..... TOO
Target on Wire [*British military*] (DMA) ..... TOW
Target Opportunity Generator (KSC) ..... TOG
Target Organ [*Medicine*] (AAMN) ..... TO
Target Organizational Maintenance Trainer (MCD) ..... TOMT
Target Planning Worksheet (DOMA) ..... TPW
Target Point ..... TP
Target Population ..... TP
Target Position ..... T-POS
Target Position Analyzer [*Military*] (CAAL) ..... TPA
Target Position Indicator ..... TPI
Target Position Location (MCD) ..... TPL
Target Practice [*Military*] ..... TP
Target Practice Cone Stabilized Discarding Sabot with Tracer [*Army*] (DOMA) ..... TPCSDS-T
Target Practice Discarding Sabot-Tracer [*Projectile*] (MCD) ..... TPDS-T
Target Practice Round (SAA) ..... TPR
Target Practice Round, Aerobee (SAA) ..... TPRA
Target Practice [*Ammunition*] **with Tracer** ..... TPT
Target Presentation Area [*Army*] (RDA) ..... TPA
Target Profile Examination Technique [*RADAR analysis concept*] [*Air Force*] ..... TAPE
Target Radiant Intensity, Aerobee (SAA) ..... TRIA
Target Radiant Intensity Measurement (MCD) ..... TRIM
Target Radiant Spectral Intensity Measurements from a Spin-Stabilized Vehicle (SAA) ..... TRIS
Target Radiation Measurement Program (IAA) ..... TRAMP
Target Radiation Ultraviolet Measurement Program (AAG) ..... TRUMP
Target Range Servo ..... TRS
Target Ranging RADAR ..... TRR
Target Rating Point [*Television*] (WDMC) ..... TRP
Target Recognition (AFM) ..... TR
Target Recognition Attack Multisensor [*DoD*] ..... TRAM
Target Recognition through Integral Spectrum Analysis Techniques (MCD) ..... TRISAT
Target Reference Material List [*Air Force*] ..... TRML
Target Reference Point (AABC) ..... TRP
Target Reporting Parameters (MCD) ..... TRP
Target Research Analysis Center (CINC) ..... TRAC
Target Resolution and Discrimination Experiment [*ARPA*] ..... TRADEX
Target Resolution Extraction of Statistical Invariances ..... TRESI
Target Resolving Information Augmentation Device (MCD) ..... TRIAD
Target Review and Adjustment for Continuous Control (MCD) ..... TRACC
Target Rifle (WDAA) ..... TR
Target Satellite Controlled Approach (MUGU) ..... TSCA
Target Seeker ..... T/S
Target Seeker-Azimuth ..... TSAZ
Target Selection and Seeking Console ..... TSSC
Target Selection and Tracking Console ..... TSTC
Target Selection Console (MCD) ..... TSC
Target Selection Standard [*Military*] (INF) ..... TSS
Target Selector Azimuth (IAA) ..... TSAZ
Target Selector Switch ..... TSS
Target Selector-Elevation (SAA) ..... T/S-EL
Target Sensing Switch ..... TSS
Target Service Agent [*Computer science*] ..... TSA
Target Service Agents [*Computer science*] (PCM) ..... TSA
Target Service Ship [*Navy symbol*] (DNAB) ..... AGT
Target Service Task Craft [*Navy symbol*] ..... YGT
Target Signature Analysis ..... TSA
Target Signature Analysis Center (MCD) ..... TSAC
Target Signature Investigation ..... TSI
Target Signature Model ..... TSM
Target Skin Distance ..... TSD
Target State Estimator (MCD) ..... TSE
Target Strength ..... TS
Target Support Element (MCD) ..... TSE
Target System Alternatives (MCD) ..... TSA
Target System Data File ..... TSDF
Target System Data Update ..... TSDU
Target System Service Charge (NG) ..... TSSC
Target Systems Office [*Army Materiel Command*] (RDA) ..... TSO
Target Tech Inc. [*NASDAQ symbol*] (TTSB) ..... CFON
Target Technologies, Inc. [*NASDAQ symbol*] (SAG) ..... CFON
Target Technologies, Inc. [*Associated Press*] (SAG) ..... TargTch
Target Therapeutics [*NASDAQ symbol*] (TTSB) ..... TGET
Target Therapeutics, Inc. [*Associated Press*] (SAG) ..... TargetT
Target Therapeutics, Inc. [*NASDAQ symbol*] (SAG) ..... TGET
Target Token Rotation Time [*Computer science*] ..... TTRT
Target Towing Aircraft [*Navy*] ..... TT
Target Towing Flight [*British military*] (DMA) ..... TTF
Target Track Central ..... TTC
Target Track [*or Tracking*] **RADAR** [*Air Force*] ..... TTR
Target Tracking and Control System (MCD) ..... TTCS
Target Tracking Console (MCD) ..... TTC
Target Tracking Receiver [*Military*] (CAAL) ..... TTR
Target Trajectory Sensor ..... TTS
Target Transfer Unit (MCD) ..... TTU
Target Transformation Factor Analysis [*Environmental Protection Agency*] (GFGA) ..... TTFA
Target Triggered Burst ..... TTB
Target Value Analysis [*Army*] (ADDR) ..... TVA
Target Value Kills (MCD) ..... TVK
Target Valve (MCD) ..... TV
Target Vehicle [*Air Force*] (AAG) ..... T/V
Target Vehicle Experimental [*Air Force*] ..... TVX
Target Velocity ..... TV
Target Velocity ..... TVEL
Target Velocity, North ..... TVN
Target Verification Test [*Military*] (CAAL) ..... TVT
Target Via Missile [*Aviation*] ..... TVM
Target Vulnerability (MCD) ..... TV
Target Weather Information ..... TARWI
Target Year ..... TY
Targeted Amortization-Class Bond [*Investment term*] ..... TAC
Targeted Export Assistance Program [*Later, MAP*] [*Department of Agriculture*] ..... TEA
Targeted Genetics [*NASDAQ symbol*] (TTSB) ..... TGEN
Targeted Genetics Corp. [*Associated Press*] (SAG) ..... TargGene
Targeted Genetics Corp. [*NASDAQ symbol*] (SAG) ..... TGEN
Targeted Industry Categories (AAGC) ..... TIC
Targeted Jobs Credit [*Tax credit*] ..... TJC
Targeted Jobs Demonstration Program (EDAC) ..... TJDP
Targeted Jobs Tax Credit Coalition (EA) ..... TJTCC

Targeted Jobs Tax Credits [*Federal program*] .... TJTC
Targeted Outreach Program [*Department of Labor*] .... TOP
Targeted Selection Criteria (GFGA) .... TSC
Targeting Agent [*Medicine*] .... TA
Targeting and Control (IAA) .... TAC
Targeting/Optimization for Solar Electric Propulsion [*NASA*] .... TOPSEP
Target-Observer-Gun [*Method*] [*Army*] .... TOG
Target-on-Threshold Speed [*Aviation*] .... VT
Target-Organ Damage [*Medicine*] .... TOD
Target-Recognizing Domain [*Genetics*] .... TRD
Targets and Timetables .... T & T
Targets for Excellence .... TFE
Targets Management Office [*MIRCOM*] (RDA) .... TMO
Targets, Receivers, Impacts, and Methods .... TRIM
Target-to-Film Distance [*X-Ray machine*] [*Navy*] .... TFD
Target-to-Surface-to-Missile Path .... TSM
Targhee Sheep Association (EA) .... TSA
Targovishte [*Bulgaria*] [*Airport symbol*] (OAG) .... TGV
Targum (BJA) .... Targ
Targum Jonathan (BJA) .... TargJon
Targum Jonathan (BJA) .... TJ
Targum Onkelos (BJA) .... Onk
Targum Onkelos (BJA) .... TargOnk
Targum Onkelos (BJA) .... TO
Targum Yerusahlmi (BJA) .... TargYer
Tari [*Papua New Guinea*] [*Airport symbol*] (OAG) .... TIZ
Tarif Douanier Commun [*Common Customs Tariff*] .... TDC
Tarif Exterieur Commun [*Common External Tariff*] [*for EEC countries*] .... TEC
Tariff .... TRF
Tariff Act [*1930*] .... TA
Tariff and Trade Data Files (NITA) .... TTDF
Tariff Board [*Canada*] .... TRFB
Tariff Bureau .... TB
Tariff Circular .... TC
Tariff Commission [*Later, International Trade Commission*] .... TC
Tariff Commission Publications [*A publication*] (DLA) .... TC Pub
Tariff Item .... TI
Tariff Number .... TN
Tariff Programs and Appraisals [*Canada Customs*] .... TPA
Tariff Reform .... TR
Tariff Reform League [*British*] (ROG) .... TRL
Tariff Rules of the Interstate Commerce Commission .... TRICC
Tariff Schedules of the United States [*Later, HTSUS*] .... TSUS
Tariff Schedules of the United States, Annotated .... TSA
Tariff Schedules of the United States, Annotated .... TSUSA
Tariff Selection Unit (OA) .... TSU
Tarija [*Bolivia*] [*ICAO location identifier*] (ICLI) .... SLTJ
Tarija [*Bolivia*] [*Airport symbol*] (OAG) .... TJA
Tarija [*Bolivia*] [*Seismograph station code, US Geological Survey*] (SEIS) .... TRJ
Tarkio College, Tarkio, MO [*OCLC symbol*] (OCLC) .... MOT
Tarkio College, Tarkio, MO [*Library symbol Library of Congress*] (LCLS) .... MoTaC
Tarkio, MO [*FM radio station call letters*] .... KTRX
Tarl Town Reports [*New South Wales*] [*A publication*] (DLA) .... TTR
Tarlac (Crow Valley) [*Philippines*] [*ICAO location identifier*] (ICLI) .... RPXC
Tarleton State College [*Later, TSU*] [*Texas*] .... TSC
Tarleton State University (GAGS) .... Tarleton St U
Tarleton State University [*Formerly, TSC*] [*Texas*] .... TSU
Tarleton State University, Dick Smith Library, Stephenville, TX [*OCLC symbol*] (OCLC) .... TTS
Tarleton State University, Stephenville, TX [*Library symbol Library of Congress*] (LCLS) .... TxSvT
Tarmac Plc [*British ICAO designator*] (FAAC) .... TMC
Tarn Pure Technology Corp. [*Vancouver Stock Exchange symbol*] .... TPU
Tarnished Plant Bug [*Entomology*] .... TPB
Taro Industries Ltd. [*Toronto Stock Exchange symbol*] .... TIN
Taro Pharmaceutical Ind [*NASDAQ symbol*] (TTSB) .... TAROF
Taro Pharmaceutical Industries [*NASDAQ symbol*] (SAG) .... TARO
Taro Pharmaceutical Industries [*Associated Press*] (SAG) .... TaroPh
Tarom, Romanian Air Transport [*ICAO designator*] (FAAC) .... ROT
Taroom [*Queensland*] [*Airport symbol*] (AD) .... XTO
Taroudant [*Morocco*] [*ICAO location identifier*] (ICLI) .... GMMO
Tarpaulin (VRA) .... tarp
Tarpaulin (AAG) .... TARP
Tarpon Springs, FL [*FM radio station call letters*] .... WYFE
Tarragon Oil & Gas Ltd. [*Toronto Stock Exchange symbol*] .... TN
Tarragona [*Spain*] [*Airport symbol*] (AD) .... TGN
Tarraleah [*Tasmania*] [*Seismograph station code, US Geological Survey*] (SEIS) .... TRR
Tarrant Apparel Group [*NASDAQ symbol*] (SAG) .... TAGS
Tarrant Apparel Group [*Associated Press*] (SAG) .... Tarrant
Tarrant County Junior College District, Hurst, TX [*Library symbol Library of Congress*] (LCLS) .... TxHurT
Tarrant County Junior College, Fort Worth, TX [*Library symbol Library of Congress*] (LCLS) .... TxFT
Tarrant County Junior College, Hurst, TX [*OCLC symbol*] (OCLC) .... TCJ
Tarrant County Junior College, Northeast Campus, Hurst, TX [*Library symbol Library of Congress*] (LCLS) .... TxFT-NE
Tarrant County Junior College, South Campus, Fort Worth, TX [*Library symbol Library of Congress*] (LCLS) .... TxFT-S
Tarron Industry [*Vancouver Stock Exchange symbol*] .... TRO
Tarsis Oculorum [*To the Eyelids*] [*Pharmacy*] .... TARS OCUL
Tarsometatarsal [*Joint*] [*Anatomy*] (DAVI) .... TMT
Tartagal [*Argentina*] [*Airport symbol*] (AD) .... TTG
Tartagal/Gral Mosconi [*Argentina ICAO location identifier*] (ICLI) .... SAST
Tartan Educational and Cultural Association (EA) .... TECA
Tartana [*Ship's rigging*] (ROG) .... TA
Tartar Reliability Improvement Plan [*Military*] .... TRIP
Tartar Weapons System .... TWS
Tartar-Talos-Terrier-Typhon [*Military*] (DNAB) .... TTTT
Tartarum [*Tartar*] [*Pharmacy*] (ROG) .... TART
Tartrate .... TART
Tartrate Resistant Acid Phosphatase [*An enzyme*] .... TRAP
Tartu [*Dorpat, Jurjeio*] [*Former USSR Seismograph station code, US Geological Survey Closed*] (SEIS) .... TTU
Tarvisio [*Italy ICAO location identifier*] (ICLI) .... LIVO
Tarxien International, Inc. [*Toronto Stock Exchange symbol*] .... TAX
TAS Aviation, Inc. [*ICAO designator*] (FAAC) .... RMS
TASAMS [*The Army Supply and Maintenance System*] **Coordination Field Office** (AABC) .... TACFO
Taschereau's Criminal Law Acts [*Canada A publication*] (DLA) .... Tasch Cr Acts
TASD (Transporti Aerei Speciali) [*Italy ICAO designator*] (FAAC) .... TTS
Taseko Mines [*NASDAQ symbol*] (TTSB) .... TKOCF
Taseko Mines Ltd. [*Associated Press*] (SAG) .... Taseko
Taseko Mines Ltd. [*Vancouver Stock Exchange symbol*] .... TKO
Taseko Mines Ltd. [*NASDAQ symbol*] (SAG) .... TKOC
Tashkent [*Former USSR Seismograph station code, US Geological Survey*] (SEIS) .... TAS
Tashkent [*Former USSR Airport symbol*] (OAG) .... TAS
Tashkent [*Former USSR Geomagnetic observatory code*] .... TKT
Tashkent/Yuzhny [*Former USSR ICAO location identifier*] (ICLI) .... UTTT
Tashkurghan [*Afghanistan*] [*ICAO location identifier*] (ICLI) .... OATG
Tashota-Nipigon Mines [*Vancouver Stock Exchange symbol*] .... TNM
Tasikmalaya/Cibeureum [*Indonesia*] [*ICAO location identifier*] (ICLI) .... WIAM
Task .... TSK
Task Analysis .... TA
Task Analysis Form .... TAF
Task Analysis/Operational Sequence Diagram .... TA/OSD
Task Analysis Reduction Technique [*Navy*] .... TART
Task and Skill Analysis (AAG) .... T & SA
Task and Skill Analysis [*Military*] (AABC) .... TASA
Task Area Plan .... TAP
Task Assignment (AAG) .... TA
Task Assignment and Directive (MCD) .... TAAD
Task Assignment Directive (KSC) .... TAD
Task Assignment Drawing (MCD) .... TAD
Task Assignment Queue Table (MCD) .... TAQT
Task Assignment Queue Table Display (MCD) .... TAQTD
Task Assignment Queue Table Update (MCD) .... TAQTU
Task Assignment Table (MCD) .... TAT
Task Assignment Table Display (MCD) .... TATD
Task Attribution Questionnaire (EDAC) .... TAQ
Task Authorization Notice .... TAN
Task Breakdown Structure (NASA) .... TBS
Task Budget Allocation (MCD) .... TBA
Task Builder [*Computer science*] (MHDI) .... TKB
Task Change Proposal (AAG) .... TCP
Task Change Request [*Army*] .... TCR
Task Completion Date (AAG) .... TCD
Task Control Area (IAA) .... TCA
Task Control Block [*Computer science*] .... TCB
Task Control Character (CMD) .... TCC
Task Control Packet (NASA) .... TCP
Task Control Program .... TCP
Task Database [*Computer science*] (PCM) .... TDB
Task Deletion Form [*Nuclear energy*] (NRCH) .... TDF
Task Description (AAG) .... TD
Task Description Document (NASA) .... TDD
Task Description Item (MCD) .... TDI
Task Description Memo (MCD) .... TDM
Task Direction Order [*Military*] .... TDO
Task Directive (AAG) .... TD
Task Dispatch Table [*Computer science*] (OA) .... TDT
Task Element .... TE
Task Equipment Analysis .... TEA
Task Execution Language .... TEL
Task Extension Area [*Computer science*] (IAA) .... TXA
Task Flotilla .... TASKFLOT
Task Force .... TF
Task Force A .... TFA
Task Force Against Nuclear Pollution (EA) .... TFANP
Task Force Air Defense (MUGU) .... TAFAD
Task Force Alpha [*DoD*] .... TFA
Task Force Command Center [*Navy*] (DOMA) .... TFCC
Task Force Commander [*Navy*] (DNAB) .... TFC
Task Force Commander, North Norway [*NATO*] (NATG) .... TFCNN
Task Force Final Report [*DoD*] .... TFFR
Task Force for Child Survival (EA) .... TFCS
Task Force for Community Broadcasting (EA) .... TCB
Task Force for European Digital Road-mapping Association .... TFEDRA
Task Force on Alternatives in Print (EA) .... TFAIP
Task Force on Children Out of School (EA) .... TFCOS
Task Force on Emphysema and Chronic Bronchitis [*Public Health Service and National Lung Association*] (EA) .... TFECB
Task Force on Equality of Women in Judaism [*Defunct*] (EA) .... TFEWJ
Task Force on Families in Crisis (EA) .... TFFC
Task Force on Scientific Uses of the Space Station [*NASA*] .... TFSUSS
Task Force on Service to the Public [*Canada*] .... TFSP
Task Force on Teaching as a Profession [*Defunct*] (EA) .... TFTP
Task Force on the Environment [*American Library Association*] .... TFOE
Task Force on Women in Sports [*of NOW*] (EA) .... TFWS

Task Force on Women's Rights and Responsibilities [*National Council on Family Relations*] (EA) .... TFWRR
Task Force on Youth Allowance Administration [*Australia*] .... TFYAA
Task Force Operations [*Navy*] (NVT) .... TFOPS
Task Force Planning Group [*DoD*] .... TFPG
Task Force Pro Libra Ltd. (IID) .... TFPL
Task Force/Task Group .... TF/TG
Task Group [*Military*] .... TG
Task Group Delta (MCD) .... TGD
Task Group Leader .... TGL
Task Group Lung Model [*ICRP*] .... TGLM
Task Group Manager (CAAL) .... TGM
Task Group Operations [*Navy*] (NVT) .... TGOPS
Task Guidance .... TG
Task Identification and Analysis .... TI & A
Task Identification and Analysis (MCD) .... TIAA
Task Implementation Notice .... TIN
Task Initiation and Prediction .... TIP
Task Initiation Date (WDAA) .... TID
Task Initiation Force [*Nuclear energy*] (NRCH) .... TIF
Task Initiation Form [*Nuclear energy*] (NRCH) .... TIF
Task Input/Output Table [*Computer science*] (BUR) .... TIOT
Task Input Parameter Synthesizer .... TIPSY
Task Input Queue [*Computer science*] (IBMDP) .... TIQ
Task Item Authorization (MCD) .... TIA
Task Leader (NRCH) .... TL
Task Level Controller .... TLC
Task List (KSC) .... T/L
Task Maintenance Burden .... TMB
Task Memory [*Computer science*] (IAA) .... TM
Task Number [*Computer science*] (IAA) .... TN
Task of Public Education Questionnaire (AEBS) .... TPE
Task Order (MCD) .... TO
Task Order Contract .... TOC
Task Oriented Plant Practice (MHDI) .... TOPP
Task Oriented Training (MCD) .... TOT
Task Parameter Interpretation .... TPI
Task Parameter Synthesizer .... TPS
Task Parameter Synthesizer (SAA) .... TPSY
Task Plan Change Notice (MCD) .... TPCN
Task Plan Change Request (MCD) .... TPCR
Task Processing Unit .... TPU
Task Processor [*Telecommunications*] (TSSD) .... TP
Task Ready Queue .... TRQ
Task Register [*Computer science*] (BYTE) .... TR
Task Related Instructional Methodology (PDAA) .... TRIM
Task Reporting and Current Evaluation .... TRACE
Task Response Module [*Office furniture*] .... TRM
Task, Schedule, and Status Control Plan (AAG) .... TS & SCP
Task Schedule Change Form [*Nuclear energy*] (NRCH) .... TSCF
Task Sequence Number (IAA) .... TSN
Task Statement (MCD) .... TS
Task Status Index [*Computer science*] (OA) .... TSI
Task Status Word (NITA) .... TSW
Task Table (MHDB) .... TTBL
Task Termination Notice [*Computer science*] (MHDB) .... TKTN
Task Training Exercise .... TTE
Task Training Remedial Exercise [*Army*] .... TTRE
Task Unit [*Military*] .... TU
Task Work Package (KSC) .... TWP
Task-Directed Learning .... TDL
Tasking Requirements and Tasking File (MCD) .... TRTF
Task-Oriented Costing [*Telecommunications*] (TEL) .... TOC
Tasks of Emotional Development Test [*Psychology*] .... TED
Task-Specific Utility .... TSU
Task-State Segment [*Operating system data structure*] [*Computer science*] ..... TSS
Task-Switched (BYTE) .... TS
Tasman Air Services [*New Zealand*] [*FAA designator*] (FAAC) .... TAN
Tasman Empire Airways Ltd. [*Australia*] (ADA) .... TEAL
Tasmania [*State*] (EERA) .... T
Tasmania (ODBW) .... Tas
Tasmania (ROG) .... TASM
Tasmania [*MARC geographic area code Library of Congress*] (LCCP) .... u-at-tm
Tasmania Acts of Parliament [*A publication*] (DLA) .... Tasm Acts
Tasmania Fellowship of Australia Writers [*Australia*] .... TFAW
Tasmania House of Assembly - Journals [*A publication*] .... THAJ
Tasmania Museum and Art Gallery, Tasmania [*State*] (EERA) .... TMH
Tasmania Sashimi Tuna Fisherman's Association (EERA) .... TSTFA
Tasmania University [*Tasmania*] [*Seismograph station code, US Geological Survey*] (SEIS) .... TAU
Tasmanian AIDS [*Acquired Immune Deficiency Syndrome*] Council [*Australia*] .... TAC
Tasmanian AIDS [*Acquired Immune Deficiency Syndrome*] Council [*Australia*] .... TAIDSC
Tasmanian Amateur Diving Association [*Australia*] .... TADA
Tasmanian Amateur Gymnastics Association [*Australia*] .... TAGA
Tasmanian Amateur Walking Club [*Australia*] .... TAWC
Tasmanian Ambulance Service [*Australia*] .... TAS
Tasmanian Apple and Pear Growers' Association [*Australia*] .... TAPGA
Tasmanian Arts Advisory Board [*Australia*] .... TAAB
Tasmanian Association for Sustainable Agriculture [*Australia*] .... TASA
Tasmanian Association of Children's Services [*Australia*] .... TACS
Tasmanian Badminton Association [*Australia*] .... TBA
Tasmanian Bank [*Australia Commercial firm*] .... TB

Tasmanian Bar Association [*Australia*] .... TBA
Tasmanian Baseball League [*Australia*] .... TBL
Tasmanian Basketball Association [*Australia*] .... TBA
Tasmanian Beekeepers' Association [*Australia*] .... TBA
Tasmanian Bookmakers' Association [*Australia*] .... TBA
Tasmanian Bowls Council [*Australia*] .... TBC
Tasmanian Bridge Association [*Australia*] .... TBA
Tasmanian Builder [*A publication*] .... Tas Build
Tasmanian Building and Construction Industry Training Committee [*Australia*] .... TBCITC
Tasmanian Building Journal [*A publication*] .... Tas Build J
Tasmanian Caledonian Society [*Australia*] .... TCS
Tasmanian Cancer Committee [*Australia*] .... TCC
Tasmanian Canine Defence League [*Australia*] .... TCDL
Tasmanian Canoe Association [*Australia*] .... TCA
Tasmanian Carpet Wool Growers' Ltd. [*Commercial firm Australia*] .... TCWG
Tasmanian Catholic Education Employees' Association [*Australia*] .... TCEEA
Tasmanian Chamber of Commerce [*Australia*] .... TCC
Tasmanian Chamber of Mines [*Australia*] .... TCM
Tasmanian Chicken Growers' Association [*Australia*] .... TCGA
Tasmanian College of Hospitality [*Australia*] .... TCH
Tasmanian Commercial Egg Producers' Association [*Australia*] .... TCEPA
Tasmanian Community Health Association [*Australia*] .... TCHA
Tasmanian Confederation of Industries [*Australia*] .... TCI
Tasmanian Conservation Trust [*State*] (EERA) .... TCT
Tasmanian Convention Bureau [*Australia*] .... TCB
Tasmanian Council for Adult Literacy [*Australia*] .... TCAL
Tasmanian Council of Churches World Christian Action [*Australia*] .... TCCWCA
Tasmanian Council of Social Service [*Australia*] .... TCOSS
Tasmanian Council of Social Service [*Australia*] .... TCSS
Tasmanian Council on the Ageing [*Australia*] .... TCA
Tasmanian Country Music Jamboree Association [*Australia*] .... TCMJA
Tasmanian Croquet Association [*Australia*] .... TCA
Tasmanian Cycling Federation [*Australia*] .... TCF
Tasmanian Dairy Industry Authority [*Australia*] .... TDIA
Tasmanian Deaf Society [*Australia*] .... TDS
Tasmanian Department of Primary Industry [*State*] (EERA) .... TDPI
Tasmanian Department of Sea Fisheries [*Australia*] .... TDSF
Tasmanian Earth Resources Satellite Station [*Commonwealth*] [*State*] (EERA) .... TERSS
Tasmanian Environment Centre [*State*] (EERA) .... TEC
Tasmanian Federation of Cooperative Housing Societies [*Australia*] .... TFCHS
Tasmanian Field and Game Association [*Australia*] .... TFGA
Tasmanian Field Naturalists' Club [*Australia*] .... TFNC
Tasmanian Fine Merino Breeders' Association [*Australia*] .... TFMBA
Tasmanian Fire Service [*Australia*] .... TFS
Tasmanian Fishing Industry Council (EERA) .... TAFIC
Tasmanian Fishing Industry Council [*Australia*] .... TFIC
Tasmanian Fishing Industry Training Council [*Australia*] .... TFITC
Tasmanian Floricultural Association [*Australia*] .... TFA
Tasmanian Food Industry Training Council [*Australia*] .... TFITC
Tasmanian Football League [*Australia*] .... TFL
Tasmanian Forest Industries Training Council [*Australia*] .... TFITC
Tasmanian Forestry Commission [*State*] (EERA) .... TFC
Tasmanian Forests and Forest Industry Strategy [*Australia*] .... TFFIS
Tasmanian Furniture Industry Training Council [*Australia*] .... TFITC
Tasmanian Game Fishing Association [*Australia*] .... TGFA
Tasmanian Gaming Commission [*Australia*] .... TGC
Tasmanian Golf Council [*Australia*] .... TGC
Tasmanian Government Printing Office [*Australia*] .... TGPO
Tasmanian Grain Elevators Board [*Australia*] .... TGEB
Tasmanian Greens [*Australia Political party*] .... TG
Tasmanian Guild of Furniture Manufacturers [*Australia*] .... TGFM
Tasmanian Historical Research Association. Papers and Proceedings [*A publication*] .... THRAPP
Tasmanian Hockey Association [*Australia*] .... THA
Tasmanian Hospitality Group Apprenticeship Scheme [*Australia*] .... THGAS
Tasmanian Imperial Bushmen [*British military*] (DMA) .... TIB
Tasmanian Institute of Senior Educational Administrators [*Australia*] .... TISEA
Tasmanian Irregular Notes [*A publication*] .... Irr N
Tasmanian Irregular Notes [*A publication*] .... Tas Irreg Notes
Tasmanian Journal of Natural Science [*A publication*] .... Tasmanian J
Tasmanian Labour Adjustment Package [*Australia*] .... TASLAP
Tasmanian Law Newsletter [*A publication*] .... Tas LN
Tasmanian Law Newsletter [*A publication*] .... TLN
Tasmanian Licensed Fruit Exporters [*Australia*] .... TLFE
Tasmanian Meat Industry Advisory Council [*Australia*] .... TMIAC
Tasmanian Museum and Art Gallery [*Australia*] .... TMAG
Tasmanian Music Industry Association [*Australia*] .... TMIA
Tasmanian Netball Association [*Australia*] .... TNA
Tasmanian Olympic Council [*Australia*] .... TOC
Tasmanian Parks and Wildlife Service [*State*] (EERA) .... TASPAWS
Tasmanian Peace Trust [*Australia*] .... TPT
Tasmanian Police [*Australia*] .... TP
Tasmanian Public Finance Corp. [*Commercial firm Australia*] .... TASCORP
Tasmanian Public Finance Corp. [*Australia Commercial firm*] .... TPFC
Tasmanian Racing Authority [*Australia*] .... TRA
Tasmanian Registered Teachers' Association [*Australia*] .... TRTA
Tasmanian Retail Industry Training Board [*Australia*] .... TRITB
Tasmanian Rifle Association [*Australia*] .... TRA
Tasmanian Road Transport Industry Training Council [*Australia*] .... TRTITC
Tasmanian Rowing Council [*Australia*] .... TRC
Tasmanian Rugby Union [*Australia*] .... TRU
Tasmanian Rural Counselling [*Australia*] .... TRC
Tasmanian Rural Industry Training Board [*Australia*] .... TRITB

Tasmanian Sawmillers' Industrial Association .... TSIA
Tasmanian Shellfish Quality Assurance Program (EERA) .... TSQAP
Tasmanian Shippers' Association [Australia] .... TSA
Tasmanian Small Bore and Air Rifle Association [Australia] .... TSBARA
Tasmanian Soccer Association [Australia] .... TSA
Tasmanian Soccer Federation [Australia] .... TSF
Tasmanian Soft Drink Association [Australia] .... TSDA
Tasmanian Stone Fruit Growers' Association [Australia] .... TSFGA
Tasmanian Swimming Inc. [Commercial firm Australia] .... TS
Tasmanian Timber Promotion Board [Australia] .... TTPB
Tasmanian Totalisator Agency Board [Australia] .... TTAB
Tasmanian Touch Association [Australia] .... TTA
Tasmanian Trades Union Council [Australia] .... TTUC
Tasmanian Wilderness Society (EERA) .... TWS
Tasmanian Wilderness World Heritage Area .... TWWHA
Tasmanian Wool Brokers' Association [Australia] .... TWBA
Tasmanian Wool Selling Brokers' Association [Australia] .... TWSBA
TASS [Towed Array SONAR System] Probability Area (NVT) .... TPA
Taste Receptor Cell [Biochemistry] .... TRC
Tasto [Touch, Key, Fingerboard] [Music] .... T
Tasto Solo [Bass without Accompaniment] [Music] .... TS
Tasty Baking [AMEX symbol] (TTSB) .... TBC
Tasty Baking Co. [Associated Press] (SAG) .... Tasty
Tasty Baking Co. [AMEX symbol] (SPSG) .... TBC
Tasu Resources Ltd. [Vancouver Stock Exchange symbol] .... TAS
Taswell-Langmead's English Constitutional History [10th ed.] [1946]
    [A publication] (DLA) .... Tasw Lang Hist
TAT Technologies [Associated Press] (SAG) .... TAT Tch
TAT Technologies [NASDAQ symbol] (SAG) .... TATTF
TAT Technologies Ltd [NASDAQ symbol] (TTSB) .... TATTF
TATA Box-Binding Protein (DOG) .... TBP
Tata Energy Research Institute [New Delhi, India] (ECON) .... TERI
Tata Engineering & Locomotive Co. [India] .... TELCO
Tata Institute for Fundamental Research [British] .... TIFR
Tata Iron and Steel Co. (ECON) .... TISCO
Tata Workers' Union [India] .... TWU
Tatakoto [French Polynesia] [ICAO location identifier] (ICLI) .... NTGO
Tatakoto [French Polynesia] [Airport symbol] (OAG) .... TKV
Tatalina [Alaska] [Airport symbol] (OAG) .... TLJ
Tatalina [Alaska] [Seismograph station code, US Geological Survey] (SEIS) ..... TTA
Tatalina [Alaska] [Seismograph station code, US Geological Survey Closed]
    (SEIS) .... TTL
Tatalina Air Force Station [Alaska] [ICAO location identifier] (ICLI) .... PATL
Tatalina, AK [Location identifier FAA] (FAAL) .... TLJ
Tatar [MARC language code Library of Congress] (LCCP) .... tar
Tat-Binding Protein [Genetics] .... TBP
Tate Integrated Systems .... TIS
Tatenhill [British ICAO location identifier] (ICLI) .... EGBM
Tate's Digest of Laws [Virginia] [A publication] (DLA) .... Tate's Dig
Tateyama [Japan ICAO location identifier] (ICLI) .... RJTE
Tateyama [Japan] [Seismograph station code, US Geological Survey] (SEIS) .... TAT
Tatham Offshore [NASDAQ symbol] (TTSB) .... TOFF
Tatham Offshore, Inc. [Associated Press] (SAG) .... Tatham
Tatham Offshore, Inc. [NASDAQ symbol] (SAG) .... TOFF
Tatiko-Tekhnicheskye-Trebovaniya [Tactical Technical Requirement] [for
    military materiel] [Former USSR] (RDA) .... TTT
Tatin Experimental [British military] (DMA) .... TE
Tatlar Resources Ltd. [Vancouver Stock Exchange symbol] .... TLA
Tatonduk Outfitters Ltd. [FAA designator] (FAAC) .... FXG
Tatoo-a-Pet [Commercial firm] (EA) .... PSU
Tatra Air [Slovakia] [ICAO designator] (FAAC) .... TTR
Tatry/Poprad [Former Czechoslovakia] [Airport symbol] (OAG) .... TAT
Tattletale Beginner's All-Purpose Symbolic Instruction Code [Computer
    science] .... TTBASIC
Tattoo Club of America (EA) .... TCA
Tatung [Republic of China] [Seismograph station code, US Geological
    Survey] (SEIS) .... TTC
Tatuoca [Brazil] [Geomagnetic observatory code] .... TTB
Tau [Nineteenth letter of the Greek alphabet] (DAVI) .... T
Tau [American Samoa] [Airport symbol] (OAG) .... TAV
Tau Beta Pi Association .... TBP
Tau Epsilon Phi [Fraternity] .... TEP
Tau Epsilon Rho [Fraternity] .... TER
Tau Epsilon Xi [Text Formatter] [Computer science] .... TEX
Tau Kappa Epsilon [Fraternity] (EA) .... TEKE
Tau Kappa Epsilon [Fraternity] [Later, TEKE] .... TKE
Taubman Centers [NYSE symbol] (TTSB) .... TCO
Taubman Centers Co., Inc. [Associated Press] (SAG) .... Taubmn
Taubman Centers, Inc. [NYSE symbol] (SPSG) .... TCO
Tauchnitz [Bibliography] (ROG) .... TAUCH
Tauern Air Gesellschaft GmbH [Austria ICAO designator] (FAAC) .... FAN
Taunton [British depot code] .... TN
Taunton, MA [Location identifier FAA] (FAAL) .... TAN
Taunton, MA [AM radio station call letters] .... WPEP
Taunton, MA [FM radio station call letters] .... WSNE
Taunton Municipal Lighting Plant [Nuclear energy] (NRCH) .... TAML
Taunton Public Library, Taunton, MA [Library symbol Library of Congress]
    (LCLS) .... MTa
Taunton's English Common Pleas Reports [A publication] (DLA) .... Taun
Taunton's English Common Pleas Reports [127, 129 English Reprint]
    [A publication] (DLA) .... Taunt (Eng)
Taunton's English Common Pleas Reports [A publication] (DLA) .... Taunt
Taunus [Federal Republic of Germany] [Seismograph station code, US
    Geological Survey] (SEIS) .... TNS
Taupo [New Zealand] [ICAO location identifier] (ICLI) .... NZAP

Taupo [New Zealand] [Airport symbol] (OAG) .... TUO
Taupo Volcanic Zone [Geology] .... TVZ
Taura [Ecuador] [ICAO location identifier] (ICLI) .... SETA
Tauramena [Colombia] [Airport symbol] (AD) .... TAU
Tauranga [New Zealand] [ICAO location identifier] (ICLI) .... NZTG
Tauranga [New Zealand] [Airport symbol] (OAG) .... TRG
Tauranga Aero Club, Inc. [New Zealand] [ICAO designator] (FAAC) .... PGS
Taurine Bibliophiles of America (EA) .... TBA
Taurine Mustard [Antineoplastic drug] .... TM
Taurochenodeoxycholate [Biochemistry] .... TCDC
Taurocholate [Microbiology] (MAE) .... TC
Taurocholate-Gelatin Agar [Microbiology] .... TGA
Taurodeoxycholate [or Taurodeoxycholic] Acid [Biochemistry] .... TDC
Tauroursodeoxycholate [Biochemistry] .... TUDC
Tauroursodeoxycholic Acid [Biochemistry] .... TUDCA
Taurus [Constellation] .... Tau
Taurus [Constellation] .... Taur
Taurus Footwear, Inc. [Toronto Stock Exchange symbol] .... TFI
Taurus MuniCalif Hldgs [NYSE symbol] (TTSB) .... MCF
Taurus Municipal California Holdings [NYSE symbol] (SPSG) .... MCF
Taurus Municipal California Holdings [Associated Press] (SAG) .... TauCA
Taurus Municipal New York Holdings [NYSE symbol] (SPSG) .... MNY
Taurus Municipal New York Holdings [Associated Press] (SAG) .... TauNY
Taurus MuniNewYork Hldgs [NYSE symbol] (TTSB) .... MNY
Taurus Resources [Vancouver Stock Exchange symbol] .... TRU
Taut Band Suspension (IAA) .... TBS
Tautology (ADA) .... TAUT
Tavaj Transportes Aereos Regulares, SA [Brazil] [FAA designator] (FAAC) .... TVJ
Tavares & Gulf R. R. [AAR code] .... TVG
Tavern (ROG) .... TAV
Tavern .... TRVN
Tavern .... TVRN
Tavern and Guild Association [Division of Homophile Effort for Legal
    Protection] (EA) .... TAG
Taverny [France ICAO location identifier] (ICLI) .... LFPJ
Taveuni [Fiji] [Airport symbol] (OAG) .... TVU
Tavil-Dara [Former USSR Seismograph station code, US Geological Survey
    Closed] (SEIS) .... TDT
Tavistock [England] .... TAV
Tavistock Institute of Medical Psychology [British] .... TIMP
Tavoy [Myanmar] [Airport symbol] (OAG) .... TVY
Tavoy [Myanmar] [ICAO location identifier] (ICLI) .... VBTV
Tavrey, Aircompany [Ukraine] [FAA designator] (FAAC) .... TVR
Tavria-Mak [Ukraine] [FAA designator] (FAAC) .... TVM
Tavurvur [New Britain] [Seismograph station code, US Geological Survey]
    (SEIS) .... TAV
Tawas City, MI [FM radio station call letters] (RBYB) .... WAOU
Tawas City, MI [FM radio station call letters] .... WHST
Tawas City, MI [AM radio station call letters] .... WIOS
Tawas City, MI [FM radio station call letters] .... WKJC
Tawau [Malaysia] [Airport symbol] (OAG) .... TWU
Tawau [Malaysia] [ICAO location identifier] (ICLI) .... WBKW
Tawi-Tawi [Philippines] [Airport symbol] (OAG) .... TWT
Tawton [England] .... TAWT
Tawu [Republic of China] [Seismograph station code, US Geological Survey]
    (SEIS) .... TAW
Tax .... TX
Tax Abatement .... TA
Tax Action Digest [Australia A publication] .... ADIG
Tax Administration System [Internal Revenue Service] .... TAS
Tax Administrators News [Federation of Tax Administrators] [A publication] .... TAN
Tax Administrators News [A publication] (DLA) .... Tax Adm'rs News
Tax Advance Rulings [Database] [Taxation Canada] [Information service or
    system] (CRD) .... TAR
Tax Agent .... TA
Tax Amortization [Plan] .... TA
Tax and Insurance Payment [Banking] .... T & I
Tax and Price Index .... TPI
Tax and Tip .... T & T
Tax Anticipation Bill [Obligation] [Department of the Treasury] .... TAB
Tax Anticipation Note [Obligation] [State or local government] .... TAN
Tax Anticipation Notes .... TANS
Tax Board Memorandum [Internal Revenue Bulletin] [United States]
    [A publication] (DLA) .... TBM
Tax Cases [A publication] (DLA) .... Tax Cas
Tax Cases [Legal] [British] .... TC
Tax Cases Leaflets [Legal] [British] .... L(TC)
Tax Certificate .... TC
Tax Code [A publication] (AAGC) .... TC
Tax Council (EA) .... TC
Tax Counseling for the Elderly [Internal Revenue Service] .... TCE
Tax Court [of the United States] [Also, TCUS Later, United States Tax Court] ..... TC
Tax Court Memorandum Decisions [Commerce Clearing House]
    [A publication] (DLA) .... Tax Ct Mem Dec
Tax Court Memorandum Decisions [Commerce Clearing House or Prentice-
    Hall, Inc.] [A publication] (DLA) .... TC Memo
Tax Court Memorandum Decisions [Commerce Clearing House or Prentice-
    Hall, Inc.] [A publication] (DLA) .... TCM
Tax Court Memorandum Decisions (Commerce Clearing House)
    [A publication] (DLA) .... CCH Tax Ct Mem
Tax Court Memorandum Decisions (Commerce Clearing House)
    [A publication] (DLA) .... TCM (CCH)
Tax Court Memorandum Decisions (Prentice-Hall, Inc.) [A publication]
    (DLA) .... P-H Tax Ct Mem

Tax Court Memorandum Decisions (Prentice-Hall, Inc.) [*A publication*] (DLA) ... TCM (P-H)
Tax Court of Canada [*Cour Canadienne de l'Impot*] **Ottawa, Ontario** [*Library symbol National Library of Canada*] (NLC) ... OOTR
Tax Court of the United States [*Also, TC*] [*Later, United States Tax Court*] ... TCUS
Tax Court of the United States, Memorandum [*A publication*] (DLA) ... T Ct Mem
Tax Court of the United States, Reports [*A publication*] (DLA) ... T Ct
Tax Court of the United States Reports [*A publication*] ... TAC
Tax Court Reported and Memorandum Decisions (Prentice-Hall, Inc.) [*A publication*] (DLA) ... P-H Tax Ct Rep & Mem Dec
Tax Court Reported and Memorandum Decisions (Prentice-Hall, Inc.) [*A publication*] (DLA) ... Tax Ct Rep & Mem Dec (P-H)
Tax Court Reported Decisions [*Prentice-Hall, Inc.*] [*A publication*] (DLA) ... Tax Ct Rep Dec
Tax Court Reporter [*Commerce Clearing House*] [*A publication*] (DLA) ... Tax Ct Rep
Tax Court Reporter (Commerce Clearing House) [*A publication*] (DLA) ... CCH Tax Ct Rep
Tax Deferred Annuity [*Insurance*] ... TDA
Tax Deposit Account [*Banking*] (MHDW) ... TDA
Tax Detectable to the Extent Allowed by Law ... TDTTEABL
Tax Equity and Fiscal Responsibility Act (AAGC) ... TEFRA
Tax Equity and Fiscal Responsibility Act of 1982 ... TEFRA
Tax Equity and Responsibility Act of 1982 (WYGK) ... TERA
Tax Exchange Format [*Computer science*] (PCM) ... TXF
Tax Executives Institute (EA) ... TEI
Tax Exempt Special Savings Account [*British*] (ODBW) ... Tessa
Tax Foundation (EA) ... TF
Tax Foundation, Inc. ... TFI
Tax Foundation, Inc., New York, NY [*Library symbol Library of Congress*] (LCLS) ... NNTax
Tax Free (WDAA) ... TF
Tax Free America (EA) ... TFA
Tax Free Shopping ... TFS
Tax Haven (MHDW) ... TH
Tax Identification Number System [*IRS*] ... TINS
Tax Increment Financing ... TIF
Tax Information Circular [*Canada*] (IID) ... TIC
Tax Information Exchange Agreement (ECON) ... TIEA
Tax Information Plan and Total Owed Purchase Accounting ... TIP TOP
Tax Installment Deduction ... TID
Tax Institute of America [*Later, NTA-TIA*] (EA) ... TIA
Tax Interpretation Bulletins [*Canada*] (IID) ... TIB
Tax Law Reporter [*A publication*] (DLA) ... Tax L Rep
Tax Law Reporter [*A publication*] (DLA) ... Tax Law Rep
Tax Law Reporter [*A publication*] (DLA) ... Tax LR
Tax Lawyer [*A publication*] (ILCA) ... T Lawyr
Tax Limitation/Balanced Budget Coalition [*Defunct*] (EA) ... TL/BBC
Tax Magazine [*A publication*] (DLA) ... Tax Mag
Tax Magazine [*A publication*] (DLA) ... Taxes
Tax Magazine [*A publication*] (DLA) ... TM
Tax Management [*A publication*] (DLA) ... Tax Man
Tax Management [*Bureau of National Affairs*] [*A publication*] (DLA) ... Tax Mngm't
Tax Management [*A publication*] (DLA) ... TM
Tax Management (Bureau of National Affairs) [*A publication*] (DLA) ... Tax Mgmt (BNA)
Tax Management International Journal [*A publication*] (DLA) ... Tax Mgmt Int'l J
Tax Management Memorandum [*Bureau of National Affairs*] [*A publication*] (DLA) ... TMM
Tax Management Weekly Report [*Bureau of National Affairs*] [*Information service or system*] (CRD) ... TMWR
Tax Matters Newsletter [*Australia A publication*] ... TMN
Tax Memo [*A publication*] (DLA) ... TM
Tax Module [*IRS*] ... TM
Tax Notes Highlights [*Tax Analysts*] [*Information service or system*] (CRD) ... TNH
Tax Notes Today [*Database*] [*Tax Analysts*] [*Information service or system*] (CRD) ... TNT
Tax on Value Added [*European manufacturing tax*] ... TVA
Tax Paid Wine Bottling House ... TPWBH
Tax Payers United [*Australia*] ... TPU
Tax Period ... TXPRD
Tax Planning [*A publication*] (DLA) ... TP
Tax Planning Ideas [*A publication*] (DLA) ... TPI
Tax Planning International [*A publication*] (DLA) ... Tax Pl Int
Tax Planning Review [*A publication*] (DLA) ... Tax Pl Rev
Tax Practitioner Master File [*IRS*] ... TPMF
Tax Practitioners Forum [*A publication*] (DLA) ... Tax Pract Forum
Tax Rate ... TR
Tax Reduction Act Stock Ownership Plan ... TRASOP
Tax Reduction and Simplification Act of 1977 ... TRSA
Tax Reduction Option ... TRO
Tax Reform Act [*1969, 1976, 1984, 1986*] ... TRA
Tax Reform Action Coalition (EA) ... TRAC
Tax Reform Australia ... TRA
Tax Reform Immediately (EA) ... TRIM
Tax Reform Information Materials ... TRIM
Tax Reform Research Group [*Defunct*] (EA) ... TRRG
Tax Resisters' Penalty Fund (EA) ... TRPF
Tax Return Avoidance Syndrome ... TRAS
Tax Revenue Anticipation Note [*Finance*] ... TRAN
Tax Review Board [*Canada*] ... TRB
Tax Review Board, Ottawa, ON, Canada [*Library symbol Library of Congress*] (LCLS) ... CaOOTR
Tax Services, Canada Trust Co., London, Ontario [*Library symbol National Library of Canada*] (BIB) ... OLCT
Tax Shelter ... TS
Tax Shelter Insider [*Newsletter Management Corp.*] [*Defunct Information service or system*] (CRD) ... TSI
Tax Straddle (MHDW) ... TS
Tax Year ... TY
Taxa Referencial de Juros [*Brazil*] (ECON) ... TR
Taxa Referencial Diaria [*Brazil*] (ECON) ... TRD
Taxable ... TXBL
Taxable Adjustment Column (AAGC) ... TAC
Taxable Income ... TI
Taxation [*Economics*] ... T
Taxation (DD) ... tax
Taxation (ROG) ... TAXN
Taxation ... TXN
Taxation and Revenue (DLA) ... Tax & Rev
Taxation Assessment Notice ... TAN
Taxation Division, Department of National Revenue [*Division de l'Impot, Ministere du Revenu National*] **Ottawa, Ontario** [*Library symbol National Library of Canada*] (NLC) ... OONRT
Taxation Employment Number [*Canada*] ... TEMP
Taxation for Accountants [*A publication*] (DLA) ... Tax Acct
Taxation in Australia [*A publication*] ... Tax Aust
Taxation Institute of Australia (EERA) ... TIA
Taxation Reports [*England*] [*A publication*] (DLA) ... Tax R
Taxation Reports [*England*] [*A publication*] (DLA) ... TR
Tax-Based Incomes Policy ... TIP
Tax-Benefit Transfer (WGA) ... TBT
Taxe a la Valeur Ajoutee [*Value-Added Tax*] [*French Business term*] ... TVA
Tax-Equivalent (TDOB) ... TE
Taxes (DLA) ... T
Tax-Exempt Bond [*Investment term*] ... TEB
Tax-Exempt Dividend (MHDW) ... TED
Tax-Exempt Equity Fund ... TEEF
Tax-Exempt Investor Program [*Investment term*] ... TEIP
Tax-Exempt Money Market Fund [*Investment term*] ... TEMMF
Tax-Exempt Special Savings Account [*British*] ... TESSA
Tax-Free Investment [*Finance*] ... TFI
Taxi Aereo de Jimulco SA de CV [*Mexico ICAO designator*] (FAAC) ... JML
Taxi Aereo de Mexico [*ICAO designator*] (FAAC) ... TXM
Taxi Aereo de Veracruz [*Mexico ICAO designator*] (FAAC) ... VRC
Taxi Air Group, Inc. ... TAG
Taxi and Runway Surveillance RADAR ... TRSR
Taxi Drivers' Association [*Australia*] ... TDA
Taxi Fleet Operators' Federation [*British*] (BI) ... TFOF
Taxicab Industry Group (EA) ... TIG
Taxicrinic Unit [*Computer science*] ... TU
Taxidermy ... TXDRMY
Taxiing [*Aviation*] ... TAX
Taxiing and Routing of Aircraft Coordinating Equipment (MCD) ... TRACE
Taxiing Guidance System [*Aviation*] ... TGS
Taxilane [*FAA*] (TAG) ... TL
Taximeter Cabriolet ... taxi
Taxirey SA de CV [*Mexico ICAO designator*] (FAAC) ... TXR
Taxis Aereos del Noroeste SA de CV [*Mexico ICAO designator*] (FAAC) ... TNE
Taxis Aereos del Pacifico, SA de CV [*Mexico*] [*FAA designator*] (FAAC) ... TPF
Taxiway [*Aviation*] ... TW
Taxiway [*Aviation*] (AAG) ... TWY
Taxiway Centerline Lighting [*Aviation*] (DA) ... TC
Taxiway Edge Lighting [*Aviation*] (DA) ... TE
Taxiway Routing and Coordination Equipment [*Aviation*] ... TRACE
Taxiway Safety Area [*FAA*] (TAG) ... TSA
Taxiway-Link [*Aviation*] ... TWYL
Tax-Offset Pension [*Account*] ... TOP
Taxol (DMAA) ... TAX
Taxonometric Intra-Cellular Analytic System (OA) ... TICAS
Taxonomic Code (NITA) ... TC
Taxonomic Databases Working Group for Plant Sciences (EERA) ... TDWG
Taxonomic Descriptor (NITA) ... TX
Taxonomic Information Retrieval [*Computer science*] (DIT) ... TAXIR
Taxonomic Literature, edition 2 [*Index*] (EERA) ... TL2
Taxonomy ... TAXON
Taxpayer ... TP
Taxpayer [*Legal shorthand*] (LWAP) ... TXP
Taxpayer ... TXPYR
Taxpayer Compliance Measurement Program [*IRS*] ... TCMP
Taxpayer Delinquency Investigation Notice File [*IRS*] ... TDINF
Taxpayer Delinquent Account [*IRS*] ... TDA
Taxpayer Delinquent Account Information Record [*IRS*] ... TDAIR
Taxpayer Delinquent Investigation [*IRS*] ... TDI
Taxpayer Identification Number [*IRS*] ... TIN
Taxpayer Identification Number/File Source [*IRS*] ... TIN/FS
Taxpayer Information File [*IRS*] ... TIF
Taxpayer Information Processing [*IRS*] ... TIP
Taxpayer Inquiry [*IRS*] ... TPI
Taxpayer Inquiry Lookup Table [*IRS*] ... TILT
Taxpayer Service [*IRS*] ... TXS
Taxpayers Against Fraud [*Washington, DC*] (AAGC) ... TAF
Taxpayers Against Fraud Quarterly Review (AAGC) ... TAF QR
Taxpayers' Association of Australia ... TAA
Taxpayers' Association of New South Wales [*Australia*] ... TANSW
Taxpayers' Association of South Australia [*Australia*] ... TASA
Taxpayers' Association of Tasmania [*Australia*] ... TAT
Taxpayers' Association of Victoria [*Australia*] ... TAV

Taxpayers' Committee [*Defunct*] (EA) ... TC
Taxpayers Education Lobby (EA) ... TEL
Taxpayers' Society [*British*] ... TS
Tax-Response Element [*Genetics*] ... TRE
Tax-Sheltered Annuity ... TSA
Tay River Petroleum [*Vancouver Stock Exchange symbol*] ... TRM
Taybad [*Iran*] [*ICAO location identifier*] (ICLI) ... OIMP
Tayflight Ltd. [*British ICAO designator*] (FAAC) ... TFL
Taylor [*Arizona*] [*Airport symbol Obsolete*] (OAG) ... TYZ
Taylor and Bell's Bengal Reports [*India*] [*A publication*] (DLA) ... Tay & B
Taylor and Bell's Calcutta Supreme Court Reports [*India*] [*A publication*] (DLA) ... T & B
Taylor County Court House, Perry, FL [*Library symbol*] [*Library of Congress*] (LCLS) ... FPerCC
Taylor Devices [*NASDAQ symbol*] (TTSB) ... TAYD
Taylor Devices, Inc. [*NASDAQ symbol*] (NQ) ... TAYD
Taylor Devices, Inc. [*Associated Press*] (SAG) ... TaylrDv
Taylor Elementary School, Palisade, CO [*Library symbol Library of Congress*] (LCLS) ... CoPalTE
Taylor Falls Public Library, Taylor Falls, MN [*Library symbol*] [*Library of Congress*] (LCLS) ... MnTf
Taylor Falls School, Taylor Falls, MN [*Library symbol*] [*Library of Congress*] (LCLS) ... MnTfS
Taylor, FL [*Location identifier FAA*] (FAAL) ... TAY
Taylor Instrument Cos., Rochester, NY [*Library symbol Library of Congress*] (LCLS) ... NRT
Taylor Manifest Anxiety State [*Psychology*] ... TMAS
Taylor, MI [*AM radio station call letters*] ... WCHB
Taylor Model Basin [*Navy*] ... TMB
Taylor Mountain [*Idaho*] [*Seismograph station code, US Geological Survey*] (SEIS) ... TMI
Taylor on Civil Law [*A publication*] (DLA) ... Tayl Civil Law
Taylor on Equity Jurisprudence [*A publication*] (DLA) ... Tay Eq Jur
Taylor on Evidence [*12th ed.*] [*1931*] [*A publication*] (DLA) ... T Ev
Taylor on Evidence [*12th ed.*] [*1931*] [*A publication*] (DLA) ... Tay Ev
Taylor on Evidence [*A publication*] (DLA) ... Tayl Ev
Taylor on Government [*A publication*] (DLA) ... Tay Gov
Taylor on Poisons [*3rd ed.*] [*1875*] [*A publication*] (DLA) ... Tay Poi
Taylor on Private Corporations [*A publication*] (DLA) ... Tayl Corp
Taylor on Private Corporations [*A publication*] (DLA) ... Tayl Priv Corp
Taylor on the Bankruptcy Law [*A publication*] (DLA) ... Tay Bank L
Taylor on Tithe Commutation [*1876*] [*A publication*] (DLA) ... Tay Tit
Taylor Ranch [*California*] [*Seismograph station code, US Geological Survey*] (SEIS) ... TRC
Taylor Series Correction Method ... TSCM
Taylor, TX [*AM radio station call letters*] ... KTAE
Taylor University, Upland, IN [*Library symbol Library of Congress*] (LCLS) ... InUpT
Taylor University, Upland, IN [*OCLC symbol*] (OCLC) ... ITU
Taylor Vortex Flow [*Fluid mechanics*] ... TVF
Taylor Woodrow Management & Engineering Ltd. [*British*] (IRUK) ... TAYMEL
Taylor Woodrow Research Laboratories [*Research center British*] (IRUK) ... TWRL
Taylor-Carlisle Bookseller [*ACCORD*] [*UTLAS symbol*] ... TCB
Taylorcraft [*ICAO aircraft manufacturer identifier*] (ICAO) ... TC
Tayloreed Corporation, Rochester, NY [*Library symbol Library of Congress*] (LCLS) ... TrC
Taylor-Johnson Temperament Analysis [*Psychology*] ... TJTA
Taylor's Book of Rights [*1833*] [*A publication*] (DLA) ... Tay Bk R
Taylor's Customary Laws of Rembau [*1903-28*] [*Malaya*] [*A publication*] (DLA) ... Taylor
Taylor's Customary Laws of Rembau [*1903-28*] [*Malaya*] [*A publication*] (DLA) ... Taylor (Malaya)
Taylor's Elements of Civil Law [*A publication*] (DLA) ... Tay Civ L
Taylor's Encyclopedia of Government Officials [*A publication*] ... TEGO
Taylor's Landlord and Tenant [*A publication*] (DLA) ... Tay L & T
Taylor's Landlord and Tenant [*A publication*] (DLA) ... Tayl Landl & Ten
Taylor's Law Glossary [*2nd ed.*] [*1823*] [*A publication*] (DLA) ... Tay Glos
Taylor's Law Glossary [*A publication*] (DLA) ... Tay L Gl
Taylor's Law Glossary [*A publication*] (DLA) ... Tayl Gloss
Taylor's Medical Jurisprudence [*12th ed.*] [*1966*] [*A publication*] (DLA) ... Tay Med Jur
Taylor's Medical Jurisprudence [*A publication*] (DLA) ... Tayl Med Jur
Taylor's North Carolina Reports [*1 North Carolina*] [*1798-1802*] [*A publication*] (DLA) ... Tay
Taylor's North Carolina Reports [*1 North Carolina*] [*A publication*] (DLA) ... Tay NC
Taylor's North Carolina Reports [*1 North Carolina*] [*A publication*] (DLA) ... Tay Rep
Taylor's North Carolina Reports [*1 North Carolina*] [*A publication*] (DLA) ... Tayl NC
Taylor's North Carolina Reports [*1 North Carolina*] [*A publication*] (DLA) ... Taylor
Taylor's North Carolina Term Reports [*A publication*] (DLA) ... NCTR
Taylor's North Carolina Term Reports [*4 North Carolina*] [*A publication*] (DLA) ... Taylor
Taylor's North Carolina Term Reports [*A publication*] (DLA) ... Term NC
Taylor's North Carolina Term Reports [*4 North Carolina*] [*A publication*] (DLA) ... Term Rep (NC)
Taylor's Precedents of Wills [*A publication*] (DLA) ... Tay Wills
Taylor's Reports [*Bengal, India*] [*A publication*] (DLA) ... Taylor
Taylor's Revised Statutes [*Wisconsin*] [*A publication*] (DLA) ... Tayl St
Taylor's Supreme Court Reports [*1847-48*] [*Bengal, India*] [*A publication*] (DLA) ... Tay
Taylor's Upper Canada King's Bench Reports [*1823-1827*] [*A publication*] (DLA) ... Tay
Taylor's Upper Canada King's Bench Reports [*1 vol.*] [*1823-27*] [*A publication*] (DLA) ... Tay UC
Taylor's Upper Canada King's Bench Reports [*A publication*] (DLA) ... Taylor
Taylor's Upper Canada King's Bench Reports [*A publication*] (DLA) ... Taylor KB (Can)
Taylor's Upper Canada King's Bench Reports [*A publication*] (DLA) ... Taylor UC
Taylor's Wisconsin Statutes [*A publication*] (DLA) ... Tay Wis Stat
Taylor-Schechter Collection. University Library [*Cambridge, England*] (BJA) ... TS
Taylorsville, MS [*FM radio station call letters*] ... WBBN
Taylorsville, NC [*AM radio station call letters*] ... WACB
Taylorsville, NC [*AM radio station call letters*] ... WTLK
Taylorville, IL [*Location identifier FAA*] (FAAL) ... TAZ
Taylorville, IL [*FM radio station call letters*] (RBYB) ... WMKR-FM
Taylorville, IL [*FM radio station call letters*] ... WQLZ
Taylorville, IL [*AM radio station call letters*] ... WTIM
Taymouth Township Library, Burt, MI [*Library symbol Library of Congress*] (LCLS) ... MiBu
Tay-Sachs Disease [*Medicine*] ... TSD
Tayside [*Scotland*] (WGA) ... Tay
Tayside Aviation Ltd. [*British ICAO designator*] (FAAC) ... TFY
Tayside Rehabilitation Engineering Services [*British*] (IRUK) ... TRES
Tayson Systems, Inc. [*Telecommunications service*] (TSSD) ... TSI
Tayu Center (EA) ... TC
Tayu Fellowship (EA) ... TF
Tay-Victoria Harbour Union Library, Victoria Harbour, Ontario [*Library symbol National Library of Canada*] (BIB) ... OVHT
Taywin Resources Ltd. [*Vancouver Stock Exchange symbol*] ... TYN
Taza [*Morocco*] [*ICAO location identifier*] (ICLI) ... GMFZ
Tazewell, TN [*Location identifier FAA*] (FAAL) ... AWE
Tazewell, TN [*FM radio station call letters*] ... WCTU
Tazewell, TN [*AM radio station call letters*] ... WNTT
Tazewell, VA [*AM radio station call letters*] ... WTZE
Tazewell, VA [*FM radio station call letters*] ... WTZE-FM
TB Woods Corp. [*Associated Press*] (SAG) ... TB Wood
TB Woods Corp. [*NYSE symbol*] (SAG) ... TBW
TBC Corp. [*Associated Press*] (SAG) ... TBC
TBC Corp. [*NASDAQ symbol*] (NQ) ... TBCC
Tbessa [*Algeria*] [*Airport symbol*] (OAG) ... TEE
Tbilisi [*Former USSR Airport symbol*] (OAG) ... TBS
Tbilisi [*Former USSR Geomagnetic observatory code*] ... TFS
Tbilisi/Novoalexeyevka [*Former USSR ICAO location identifier*] (ICLI) ... UGGG
TBM NT Corp. [*Toronto Stock Exchange symbol*] ... TBM
TCA Cable TV, Inc. [*Associated Press*] (SAG) ... TCA
TCA Cable TV, Inc. [*NASDAQ symbol*] (NQ) ... TCAT
TCAM-Information Management System/Virtual Storage (NITA) ... TCAM-IMS/VS
T-Carrier [*Telecommunications*] (TEL) ... TC
T-Carrier Administration System [*Minicomputer*] [*Bell System*] ... TCAS
T-Carrier Restoration Control Center [*Bell System*] ... TRCC
TCATA [*TRADOC Combined Arms Test Activity*] **Automated Field InstrumentationSystem** (MCD) ... TAFIS
TCB [*Taking Care of Business*] **for Elvis Fan Club** (EA) ... TCBEFC
TCBY Enterprises [*NYSE symbol*] (TTSB) ... TBY
TCBY Enterprises, Inc. [*NYSE symbol*] (CTT) ... TBY
TCBY Enterprises, Inc. [*Associated Press*] (SAG) ... TCBY
TCC Beverages Ltd. [*Toronto Stock Exchange symbol*] ... KOC
TCC Industries [*NYSE symbol*] (TTSB) ... TEL
TCC Industries, Inc. [*Formerly, Telecom Corp.*] [*Associated Press*] (SAG) ... TCC Inds
TCC Industries, Inc. [*Formerly, Telecom Corp.*] [*NYSE symbol*] (SAG) ... TEL
T-Cell Acute Lymphoblastic Leukemia [*Oncology*] ... T-ALL
T-Cell Antigen Receptor [*Medicine*] (DMAA) ... TCAR
T-Cell Chronic Lymphoblastic Leukemia [*Medicine*] (DMAA) ... TCCL
T-Cell Chronic Lymphocytic Leukemia [*Oncology*] ... TCLL
T-Cell Clone [*Cytology*] ... TCC
T-Cell, Delayed Type [*Immunology*] ... Td
T-Cell Growth Factor [*See also IL-2*] [*Biochemistry*] ... TCGF
T-Cell, Helper Type [*Immunology*] ... Th
T-Cell, Killer Type [*Immunology*] ... Tk
T-Cell Line Adapted [*Cytology*] ... TCLA
T-Cell Lymphoblastic Lymphoma [*Oncology*] ... T-LL
T-Cell Lymphosarcoma Cell Leukemia [*Oncology*] ... T-LCL
T-Cell Marker [*Biochemistry*] ... TM
T-Cell Prolymphocytic Leukemia [*Oncology*] ... T-PLL
T-Cell Reactivity ... TCR
T-Cell Rearranging Gene [*Genetics*] ... TRG
T-Cell Receptor [*Immunology*] ... TCR
T-Cell Receptor Alpha (DMAA) ... TCRA
T-Cell Receptor Beta (DMAA) ... TCRB
T-Cell Receptor Delta (DMAA) ... TCRD
T-Cell Receptor Z (DMAA) ... TCRZ
T-Cell Recovery Column [*Chromatography*] ... TCR
T-Cell Replacing Factor [*Biochemistry*] ... TRF
T-Cell Rosette [*Medicine*] (DMAA) ... TCR
T-Cell-Activating Protein [*Biochemistry*] ... TAP
TCF Financial [*NYSE symbol*] (TTSB) ... TCB
TCF Financial Corp. [*NYSE symbol*] (SAG) ... TCB
TCF Financial Corp. [*Associated Press*] (SAG) ... TCF
TCF Financial Corp. [*Associated Press*] (SAG) ... TCF Fn
Tchaikazan Enterprises, Inc. [*Vancouver Stock Exchange symbol*] ... TZN
Tchibanga [*Gabon*] [*ICAO location identifier*] (ICLI) ... FOOT
Tchibanga [*Gabon*] [*Airport symbol*] (OAG) ... TCH
Tchien [*Liberia*] [*ICAO location identifier*] (ICLI) ... GLTN
Tchien [*Liberia*] [*Airport symbol*] (OAG) ... THC
Tchimkent [*Former USSR Seismograph station code, US Geological Survey Closed*] (SEIS) ... TCH
Tchoupitoulas [*Virus*] ... TCH

TCI Commun Fin 1 8.72%'TOPrS' [*NYSE symbol*] (TTSB) .... TFIPr
TCI Communications Financing I [*Associated Press*] (SAG) .... TCI Cm
TCI Communications Financing I [*NYSE symbol*] (SAG) .... TFI
TCI Communications Financing II [*Associated Press*] (SAG) .... TCICm
TCI Communications Financing II [*NYSE symbol*] (SAG) .... TFI
TCI International, Inc. [*Associated Press*] (SAG) .... TCI Int
TCI International, Inc. [*NASDAQ symbol*] (NQ) .... TCII
TCI Intl [*NASDAQ symbol*] (TTSB) .... TCII
TCI Pacific Communications [*Associated Press*] (SAG) .... TCI Pac
TCI Pacific Communications [*NASDAQ symbol*] (SAG) .... TPAC
TCI Satellite Entertainment .... TSATA
TCI Satellite Entertainment, Inc. [*Associated Press*] (SAG) .... TCI Sat
TCI Satellite Entertainment, Inc. [*NASDAQ symbol*] (SAG) .... TSAT
TCI: The Business of Entertainment Technology and Design [*A publication*] (BRI) .... TCI
T-Colony-Stimulating Factor (DMAA) .... TCSF
TCPL Resources Ltd., Calgary, AB, Canada [*Library symbol*] [*Library of Congress*] (LCLS) .... CaACTC
TCPL Resources Ltd., Calgary, Alberta [*Library symbol National Library of Canada*] (NLC) .... ACTC
TCSI Corp. [*NASDAQ symbol*] (SAG) .... TCSI
TCSI Corp. [*NASDAQ symbol*] (TTSB) .... TCSI
TCSI Corp. [*Associated Press*] (SAG) .... TCSI Cp
TCW Conv Sec Fund [*NYSE symbol*] (TTSB) .... CVT
TCW Convertible Security Fund [*NYSE symbol*] (SPSG) .... CVT
TCW Convertible Security Fund [*Associated Press*] (SAG) .... TCW
TCW/DW Emerg Mkt Opp Tr [*NYSE symbol*] (TTSB) .... EMO
TCW/DW Emerging Markets Opportunities Trust [*NYSE symbol*] (SAG) .... EMO
TCW/DW Emerging Markets Opportunities Trust [*Associated Press*] (SAG) .... TCWEM
TCW/DW Term Trust 2000 [*Associated Press*] (SAG) .... TCW 00
TCW/DW Term Trust 2000 [*NYSE symbol*] (SPSG) .... TDT
TCW/DW Term Trust 2002 [*Associated Press*] (SAG) .... TCW 02
TCW/DW Term Trust 2002 [*NYSE symbol*] (SPSG) .... TRM
TCW/DW Term Trust 2003 [*Associated Press*] (SAG) .... TCW 03
TCW/DW Term Trust 2003 [*NYSE symbol*] (SPSG) .... TMT
TDA [*Taxpayer Delinquent Account*] **Report Edit Data** [*IRS*] .... TRED
TDCC [*Transportation Data Coordinating Committee*]: the Electronic Data Interchange Association [*Telecommunications service*] (TSSD) .... TDCC/EDIA
T-Dependent [*Immunology*] .... TD
TDK Corp. [*NYSE symbol*] (SPSG) .... TDK
TDK Corp. ADS [*NYSE symbol*] (TTSB) .... TDK
TDR: The Drama Review [*A publication*] (BRI) .... TDR
TDRS Command Interface (MCD) .... TCI
TDRS [*Tracking and Data Relay Satellite*] **Operations** [*NASA*] (SSD) .... TO
TDRSS [*Tracking and Data Relay Satellite System*] **Interface Prepocessor Into TELOPS** [*Telemetry Online Processing System*] .... TIPIT
TDRSS/NASCOM [*Tracking and Data Relay Satellite System/NASA Communications Network*] **Interface Panel** (SSD) .... TNIP
TDRSS [*Tracking and Data Relay Satellite System*] **Network** [*NASA*] (SSD) .... TN
TDRSS [*Tracking and Data Relay Satellite System*] **Operations Control Center** [*NASA*] .... TOCC
Te Anau [*New Zealand*] [*Airport symbol*] (OAG) .... TEU
Te Deum [*Music*] .... TeD
Tea and Dinner [*Slang British*] (DSUE) .... TINNER
Tea Association of the USA [*Defunct*] (EA) .... TA
Tea Brokers' Association [*British*] (DBA) .... TBA
Tea Buyers' Association [*British*] (EAIO) .... TBA
Tea Buying Brokers' Association [*British*] (DBA) .... TBBA
Tea Clearing House [*British*] (DBA) .... TCH
Tea Council of the United States of America (EA) .... TC
Tea Cyprus Ltd. [*ICAO designator*] (FAAC) .... TEC
Tea Leaf Club International (EA) .... TLCI
Tea Operators' and General Labourers' Association [*A union*] [*British*] .... TOGLA
Tea Plantation Workers' Union [*Kenya*] .... TPWU
Tea Research Foundation (Central Africa) [*Malawi*] (EAIO) .... TRFCA
TEA (UK) Ltd. [*British ICAO designator*] (FAAC) .... TUK
Teach Cable Assembly [*Robot technology*] .... TCA
Teach Each Customer How [*Tire repair training seminar*] [*Technical Rubber Co.*] .... TECH
Teach for America .... TFA
Teach Information Processing Language .... TIPL
Teachable Language Comprehender (PDAA) .... TLC
Teacher .... T
Teacher .... TCHR
Teacher .... TEACH
Teacher Assessment (AIE) .... TA
Teacher Assessment of Leverage (EDAC) .... TAL
Teacher Attitude Inventory [*Teacher evaluation test*] .... TAI
Teacher Author League of America [*Formerly, TALNY*] (EA) .... TALA
Teacher Author League of New York [*Later, TALA*] (EA) .... TALNY
Teacher Authoring System (EDAC) .... TAS
Teacher Characteristics Schedule .... TCS
Teacher Concerns Questionnaire (EDAC) .... TCQ
Teacher Contact Ratio (AIE) .... TCR
Teacher Demand and Shortage Survey [*Department of Education*] (GFGA) .... TDS
Teacher Demonstration Rating (OA) .... TDR
Teacher Development in Desegregating Schools [*Office of Education*] .... TDDS
Teacher Education and Mathematics Project (EDAC) .... TEAM
Teacher Education and Media [*Project*] .... TEAM
Teacher Education Center (EDAC) .... TEC
Teacher Education Division [*Council for Exceptional Children*] .... TED
Teacher Educators and Advisers in Media Education (AIE) .... TEAME
Teacher Effectiveness Training [*A course of study*] .... TET
Teacher Equity and Choice Act [*Proposed*] .... TEACH
Teacher Examiner Mark Sheet (AIE) .... TEMS
Teacher Follow-Up Survey [*Department of Education*] (GFGA) .... TFS
Teacher Housing Authority of New South Wales [*Australia*] .... THANSW
Teacher in Charge (ADA) .... TIC
Teacher Information Center (EA) .... TIC
Teacher Interactive Computer System (IEEE) .... TICS
Teacher Investigator Awards .... TIA
Teacher Occupational Stress Factor Questionnaire (EDAC) .... TOSFQ
Teacher of Electrotherapy [*British*] .... TE
Teacher of Electrotherapy [*British*] .... TET
Teacher of Hydrotherapy [*British*] .... TH
Teacher of Hydrotherapy [*British*] .... THT
Teacher of Massage and Medical Gymnastics [*British*] .... TMMG
Teacher of Medical Electricity [*British*] .... TME
Teacher Organized Training for the Acquisition of Language (EDAC) .... TOTAL
Teacher Organizing Project (EA) .... TOP
Teacher Participation Project (EDAC) .... TPP
Teacher Performance Assessment Instruments (EDAC) .... TPAI
Teacher Performance Evaluation (EDAC) .... TPE
Teacher Programming Language [*Computer science*] (PDAA) .... TPL
Teacher Rating Form (EDAC) .... TRF
Teacher Recruitment for Educational Excellence (EDAC) .... TREE
Teacher Resource Center, Rockford, IL [*Library symbol*] [*Library of Congress*] (LCLS) .... IRoRC
Teacher Resources for Urban Education (AEBS) .... TRUE
Teacher Situation Reaction Test .... TSRT
Teacher Stress Scale (EDAC) .... TSS
Teacher Survey .... TS
Teacher Training .... TT
Teacher Training College .... TTC
Teacher Training in Developing Institutions .... TTDI
Teacher-Aiding Electronic Learning Link (PDAA) .... TELL
Teacher-Based Instruction (EDAC) .... TBI
Teacher-Pupil Question Inventory .... TPQI
Teacher-Pupil Relationship Inventory .... TPRI
Teachers' Advisory Council on Alcohol and Drug Education [*British*] .... TACADE
Teacher's Aide Program .... TAP
Teachers and Schools Registration Board [*Australia*] .... TSRB
Teachers Audio Placement System .... TAPS
Teachers' Benevolent Fund (AIE) .... TBF
Teachers' Centers Exchange (EA) .... TCE
Teachers' Central Register [*Australia*] .... TCR
Teachers' Centre (AIE) .... TC
Teacher's Certificate [*British*] .... TC
Teacher's Certificate [*British*] (DBQ) .... TCert
Teachers' Certification Board [*Australia*] .... TCB
Teachers' Christian Fellowship of New South Wales [*Australia*] .... TCFNSW
Teachers College .... TC
Teachers College, Columbia University, New York, NY [*OCLC symbol*] (OCLC) .... VVT
Teachers College, New York, NY [*Library symbol Library of Congress*] (LCLS) .... NNTC
Teachers College of Connecticut .... TCC
Teachers College of Kansas City, Kansas City, MO [*Library symbol Library of Congress Obsolete*] (LCLS) .... MoKT
Teachers College Press .... TCP
Teachers College Record [*A publication*] (BRI) .... TCR
Teachers' Committee on Central America (EA) .... TCCA
Teacher's Diploma [*British*] .... TD
Teacher's Diploma of the College of Radiographers [*British*] (DBQ) .... TDCR
Teachers Educational Council - National Association Cosmetology Schools .... TEC-NACS
Teachers for Peace (EAIO) .... TFP
Teachers Freedom Party (EA) .... TFP
Teachers' Guild of New South Wales [*Australia*] .... TGNSW
Teachers Have More Fun - They Should - They Get Stewed Enough [*Slogan*] [*Bowdlerized version*] .... THMF-TS-TGSE
[*The*] **Teachers, Inc.** (EA) .... TTI
Teachers Instructional Plan .... TIP
Teachers Insurance and Annuity Association [*New York, NY*] (EA) .... TIAA
Teachers Insurance and Annuity Association of America, New York, NY [*Library symbol*] [*Library of Congress*] (LCLS) .... NNTIA
Teachers Insurance and Annuity Association-College Retirement Equities Fund (AEE) .... TIAA-CREF
Teachers' Labour League [*British*] (AIE) .... TLL
Teachers' Library and Resource Centre, Winnipeg School Division No. 1, Manitoba [*Library symbol National Library of Canada*] (NLC) .... MWSD
Teachers of English to Speakers of Other Languages (EA) .... TESOL
Teachers' Resource Center, Duluth, MN [*Library symbol*] [*Library of Congress*] (LCLS) .... MnDuTRC
Teachers Section [*Library Education Division*] [*American Library Association*] .... TS
Teacher's Self-Control Rating Scale .... TSCRS
Teachers Training Diploma .... TTD
Teaching .... TCHG
Teaching .... TCHNG
Teaching Aids Kit [*Red Cross Youth*] .... TAKIT
Teaching and Learning Support (AIE) .... TLS
Teaching and Research [*Medicine*] .... TR
Teaching and Research in Bicultural Education [*Indian organization in Maine*] .... TRIBE
Teaching and Research Reactor .... TRR
Teaching and Teacher Education [*Educational Resources Information Center (ERIC) Clearinghouse*] [*American Association of Colleges for Teacher Education*] (PAZ) .... SP
Teaching as a Career [*British*] .... TASC

Teaching Assistant [*in a university*] .... TA
Teaching Career Month .... TCM
Teaching Certificate .... TEACHCERT
Teaching Certificate for Teachers of Art [*British*] .... TCTA
Teaching Company Scheme [*British*] .... TCS
Teaching Company Scheme (AIE) .... TCS
Teaching Curriculum Association [*A generic term; not the name of a specific organization*] .... TCA
Teaching Each Other about Conquering Handicaps (EA) .... TEACH
Teaching English as a Foreign Language .... TEFL
Teaching English as a Second Language .... TESL
Teaching English to the Non-English Speaking .... TENES
Teaching Events Stress Inventory (EDAC) .... TESI
Teaching Family Model [*Psychology*] .... TFM
Teaching Fellow .... TF
Teaching Hospital [*British*] .... TH
Teaching Improvement Project System [*University of Kentucky*] [*Research center*] (RCD) .... TIPS
Teaching Individual Protective Strategies and Teaching Individual Positive Solutions [*In association name TIPS Program*] (EA) .... TIPS
Teaching Information Processing System .... TIPS
Teaching, Learning and Curriculum Model (EDAC) .... TLC
Teaching Music [*A publication*] (BRI) .... Teach Mus
Teaching of English as a Foreign Language .... TOEFL
Teaching of English to Adult Speakers of Other Languages [*Australia*] .... TEASOL
Teaching Practice .... TP
Teaching Resources (AEBS) .... TR
Teaching Sample Table (PDAA) .... TESAT
Teaching Usefulness Classification [*of a hospital patient*] .... TUC
Teaching-Learning Unit (AEE) .... TLU
Teachta Dala [*Member of Parliament*] [*Ireland*] .... TD
Teague Elementary School, Pasadena, TX [*Library symbol*] [*Library of Congress*] (LCLS) .... TxPTE
Teal Industry Ltd. [*Vancouver Stock Exchange symbol*] .... TEO
Tealto Dail [*Member of the Dail*] [*Irish*] (ILCA) .... TD
Team (AABC) .... TM
Team Acceptance Review (SAA) .... TAR
Team Acceptance Review Notice (SAA) .... TARN
Team Activity Chart .... TAC
Team Apache Systems [*Army*] .... TAS
Team Approach to Better Schools [*National Education Association program*] .... TABS
Team Effectiveness Survey [*Test*] .... TES
Team, Inc. [*Associated Press*] (SAG) .... Team
Team, Inc. [*AMEX symbol*] (SPSG) .... TMI
Team Integrated Avionic System (MHDI) .... TIAS
Team Leader (AABC) .... TL
Team Management by Objectives [*Management technique*] (ADA) .... TMBO
Team Manager .... TM
Team Member .... TM
Team Nursing .... TN
Team of Advocates for Special Kids .... TASK
Team Power Rating [*Hockey*] .... TPR
Team Recorder [*Sports*] .... TR
Team Rental Group [*NASDAQ symbol*] (SAG) .... TBUD
Team Rental Group [*Associated Press*] (SAG) .... TeamRn
Team Rental Group'A' [*NQS*] (TTSB) .... TBUD
Team Surtees [*Automobile manufacturer*] .... TS
Team to Advance Research for Gas Energy Transformation [*Group of US gas and gas-electric companies*] .... TARGET
Team Trainer, Pearl Harbor .... TTPH
Team Training Launch Station (AAG) .... TTLS
Team-Assisted Individualization (EDAC) .... TAI
Teaming Analysis Model Personnel Selector (MCD) .... TAMPS
Teams of Our Lady [*See also END*] (EAIO) .... TOOL
Teams-Games-Tournaments [*Education*] (AEE) .... TGT
Teamster Economic Action Mobilization .... TEAM
Teamsters for a Democratic Union (EA) .... TDU
Teamster's International Terminal and Accounting Network (IAA) .... TITAN
Teamwork (MSA) .... TW
Teamwork, Enthusiasm, Stamina, Tenacity, Initiative, Courage, Loyalty, Excellence, and a Sense of Humor [*Military slang*] (VNW) .... TESTICLES
Teaneck, NJ [*FM radio station call letters*] .... WFDU
Teaneck Public Library, Teaneck, NJ [*Library symbol Library of Congress*] (LCLS) .... NjTea
Tear [*Phonetic alphabet*] [*World War II*] .... T
Tear [*Deltiology*] .... TR
Tear Drop Golf Co. [*Associated Press*] (SAG) .... TrDrpG
Tear Efficiency Factor [*Textiles*] .... TEF
Tear Fund [*An association*] (EA) .... TF
Tear Gas [*US Chemical Corps symbol*] .... CS
Teardown Compliance .... TC
Teardown Deficiency (MCD) .... TDD
Teardown Deficiency Report .... TDR
Teardown Inspection .... TDI
Teardown Inspection .... TI
TearDrop Golf Co. [*NASDAQ symbol*] (SAG) .... TDRP
TearDrop Golf Co. [*Associated Press*] (SAG) .... TrDrpGf
Teased Fibers [*Neurology*] .... TF
Teaspoon [*Measure*] .... t
Teaspoon [*Measure*] (WGA) .... ts
Teaspoon [*Measure*] (WGA) .... tspn
Teaspoonful .... teasp
Teaspoonful (GPO) .... TSP
Teaspoonful (ODBW) .... tsp
Teatr Voennykh Deistvii [*Theater of Military Operations*] [*Former USSR*] .... TVD
Teatro Popolare Italiano [*Italian theatrical troupe*] .... TPI
Tebellong [*Lesotho*] [*ICAO location identifier*] (ICLI) .... FXTB
Tebessa [*Algeria*] [*ICAO location identifier*] (ICLI) .... DABS
Tebessa [*Algeria*] [*Airport symbol*] (AD) .... TSS
Tebing Tingci/Pabatu [*Indonesia*] [*ICAO location identifier*] (ICLI) .... WIMT
Tebtunis Papyri [*A publication*] (OCD) .... PTeb
Tebul [*or Tevul*] **Yom** (BJA) .... TY
Tec Tech [*Vancouver Stock Exchange symbol*] .... TCH
Tech Base Executive Steering Committee [*Army*] (RDA) .... TBESC
Tech Data Corp. [*Clearwater, FL*] [*NASDAQ symbol*] (NQ) .... TECD
Tech Data Corp. [*Associated Press*] (SAG) .... TechData
Tech Electro Industries [*NASDAQ symbol*] (TTSB) .... TELE
Tech Electro Industries, Inc. [*Associated Press*] (SAG) .... TchElec
Tech Electro Industries, Inc. [*Associated Press*] (SAG) .... TechEl
Tech Electro Industries, Inc. [*NASDAQ symbol*] (SAG) .... TELE
Tech Electro Industries Unit [*NASDAQ symbol*] (TTSB) .... TELEU
Tech Electro Industries Wrrt [*NASDAQ symbol*] (TTSB) .... TELEW
Tech Force Corp. [*Associated Press*] (SAG) .... TechFrce
Tech/Ops Sevcon [*AMEX symbol*] (TTSB) .... TO
Tech/Ops Sevcon, Inc. [*Associated Press*] (SAG) .... TecOpS
Tech-Base Enhancement for Autonomous Machines [*Military*] (RDA) .... TEAM
Techbyte, Inc. [*Vancouver Stock Exchange symbol*] .... TB
Techdyne, Inc. [*NASDAQ symbol*] (SAG) .... TCDN
Techdyne, Inc. [*Associated Press*] (SAG) .... Tchdyn
Techdyne, Inc. [*Associated Press*] (SAG) .... Tchdyne
Teche Holding [*AMEX symbol*] (TTSB) .... TSH
Teche Holding Co. [*Associated Press*] (SAG) .... Teche
Teche Holding Co. [*AMEX symbol*] (SAG) .... TSH
TechForce Corp. [*NASDAQ symbol*] (TTSB) .... TFRC
TechForce Corp. [*NASDAQ symbol*] (SAG) .... TFRC
Techicas Aereas de Estudios y Servicios SA [*Spain ICAO designator*] (FAAC) .... TAES
Techknits, Inc. [*NASDAQ symbol*] (SAG) .... KNIT
TechKnits, Inc. [*Associated Press*] (SAG) .... Techknit
Techman Engineering Ltd., Calgary, AB, Canada [*Library symbol Library of Congress*] (LCLS) .... CaACTE
Techman Engineering Ltd., Calgary, Alberta [*Library symbol National Library of Canada*] (NLC) .... ACTE
Technalysis Corp. [*Associated Press*] (SAG) .... Tchnal
Technalysis Corp. [*NASDAQ symbol*] (NQ) .... TECN
Techne Corp. [*NASDAQ symbol*] (SAG) .... TECH
Techne Corp. [*Associated Press*] (SAG) .... Techne
Technetium [*Chemical element*] .... Tc
Technetium Albumin Study [*Radiology*] (DAVI) .... TECA
Technetium Hepatoiminodiacetic Acid [*Scan*] [*Radiology*] (DAVI) .... TcHIDA
Technetium Iminodiacetic Acid [*Clinical chemistry*] .... Tc-IDA
Technetium Methylene Diphosphonate [*Organic chemistry*] .... TMDP
Technetium Pertechnetate/N-Paraisoproplyacetanilide-Iminodiacetic Acid Scan [*Radiology*] (DAVI) .... Tc-PIPIDA
Technetium Stannous Pyrophosphate [*Radiochemistry*] .... TSPP
Technetium Sulfur Colloid [*Medicine*] (MAE) .... TSC
Technetium-99 .... Tc-99
Technical [*or Technician*] .... T
Technical .... TEC
Technical (AAG) .... TECH
Technical .... TECHL
Technical .... TECHL
Technical (EY) .... TECHN
Technical Abstract Bulletin [*ASTIA*] [*A publication*] .... TAB
Technical Acceptance Date (AAG) .... TAD
Technical Acceptance Demonstration (IAA) .... TAD
Technical Acceptance Team [*NASA*] (AAG) .... TAT
Technical Achievement Plan [*NASA*] (NASA) .... TAP
Technical Acknowledgment Message [*Aviation*] .... TAM
Technical Action Panel [*Department of Agriculture*] .... TAP
Technical Action Program (OICC) .... TAP
Technical Action Request [*Army*] (AABC) .... TAR
Technical Activities Board (MCD) .... TAB
Technical Activities Committee (SAA) .... TAC
Technical Activity Steering Committee [*Nuclear energy*] (NRCH) .... TASC
Technical Adjutant [*British military*] (DMA) .... Tech Adj
Technical, Administrative, and Supervisory Section [*Amalgamated Union of Engineering Workers - Engineering Section*] [*British*] .... TASS
Technical Advanced Training for Units (MCD) .... TATU
Technical Advice Memorandum .... TAM
Technical Advisor (MCD) .... TA
Technical Advisor [*Navy*] .... TECHAD
Technical Advisory [*Military*] (CAAL) .... TECAD
Technical Advisory Board (IAA) .... TAB
Technical Advisory Center [*National Bureau of Standards*] .... TAC
Technical Advisory Committee .... TAC
Technical Advisory Committee on Inland Transport .... TACIT
Technical Advisory Committee to Influence Congress [*Federation of American Scientists*] .... TACTIC
Technical Advisory Group (EERA) .... TAC
Technical Advisory Group (EERA) .... TAG
Technical Advisory Group (IAA) .... TAG
Technical Advisory Panel [*United Nations*] .... TAP
Technical Advisory Panel for Electronics [*Air Force*] .... TAPE
Technical Advisory Service for Attorneys [*Technical Advisory Service, Inc.*] [*Information service or system*] .... TASA
Technical Advisory Services [*Army*] (RDA) .... TAS
Technical Advisory Unit (OICC) .... TAU

Technical Air Intelligence Center [*Navy*] ... TAIC
Technical Aircraft Instrument Unit [*Navy*] ... TAIU
Technical Aircraft Reliability Statistics (IAA) ... TARS
Technical Air-to-Ground (NASA) ... TAG
Technical Amendment Regulation [*Federal government*] (EG) ... TAR
Technical Ammunition ... TAM
Technical Analysis (NG) ... TA
Technical Analysis and Advisory Group [*Navy*] (MCD) ... TAAG
Technical Analysis Division [*National Bureau of Standards*] ... TAD
Technical Analysis of Cost Proposals [*DoD*] ... TACP
Technical Analysis Office (MCD) ... TAO
Technical Analysis Order ... TAO
Technical Analysis Positions System ... TAPS
Technical Analysis Request [*NASA*] (KSC) ... TAR
Technical Analysis Work Sheet (AAG) ... TAWS
Technical and Administrative Support Division [*Marine science*] (OSRA) ... TASD
Technical and Adminstrative Support Division [*Pacific Marine Environmental Laboratory*] (USDC) ... TASD
Technical and Agricultural College (AIE) ... TAC
Technical and Business Service ... TABS
Technical and Cost Reduction Assistance Contract ... TACRAC
Technical and Engineering Acquisition Support [*Air Force*] ... TEAS
Technical and Further Education (ODBW) ... TAFE
Technical and Further Education Commission New South Wales [*Australia*] ... TAFECNSW
Technical and Further Education Discipline Appeals Board [*Victoria, Australia*] ... TAFEDAB
Technical and Further Education External Studies College [*Western Australia*] ... TAFEESC
Technical and Further Education National Centre for Research and Development [*Australia*] ... TAFENCRD
Technical and Further Education Rural Studies [*South Australia*] ... TAFERS
Technical and Further Education Teachers' Association of New South Wales [*Australia*] ... TAFETANSW
Technical and Further Education Teaching Service Appeals Board [*Victoria, Australia*] ... TAFETSAB
Technical and Management Advisory Service [*ADPA*] (MCD) ... TMAS
Technical and Management Information System (SSD) ... TMIS
Technical and Management Note (IEEE) ... TMN
Technical and Managerial Support Environment (DOMA) ... TEMSE
Technical and Miscellaneous Revenue Act of 1988 ... TAMRA
Technical and Miscellanous Revenue Act (MHDB) ... TMRA
Technical and Office Protocol [*Data communications standards*] ... TOP
Technical and Operations Control Center [*INTELSAT*] ... TOCC
Technical and Schedule Performance Report [*NASA*] (NASA) ... TASPR
Technical and Scholastic Test [*Vocational guidance test*] ... TST
Technical and Scientific Advisory Panel for GOOS (EERA) ... TSAP GOOS
Technical and Scientific Information [*United Nations Development Program*] ... T and S
Technical and Vocational Education Initiative [*Manpower Services Commission*] [*British*] ... TVEI
Technical and Vocational Education Initiative: Pilot (AIE) ... TVEI(P)
Technical Appliance Corp. (IAA) ... TACO
Technical Applications [*Branch*] [*Marine science*] (OSRA) ... TA
Technical Applications [*Branch*] [*Forecast Systems Laboratory*] (USDC) ... TA
Technical Applications Center [*Air Force*] ... TAC
Technical Applications for Southeast Asia [*Air Force*] ... TAFSEA
Technical Approach Demonstration ... TAD
Technical Approval Demonstration (AAG) ... TAD
Technical Approval Team ... TAT
Technical Architecture [*Computer science*] (RDA) ... TA
Technical Architecture Framework for Information Management [*Army*] (RDA) ... TAFIM
Technical Architecture Framework for Information Management [*Army*] ... TAFIM
Technical Area Coordinator ... TAC
Technical Area Integration Manager (SSD) ... TAIM
Technical Area Manager ... TAM
Technical Area Plan [*Navy*] (MCD) ... TAP
Technical Art Group ... TAG
Technical Assembly System ... TASS
Technical Assessment and Fraud Prevention Division [*Environmental Protection Agency*] (GFGA) ... TAFPD
Technical Assessment Group [*Navy*] ... TAG
Technical Assessor ... TA
Technical Assignment Control [*Nuclear energy*] (NRCH) ... TAC
Technical Assignment Control System [*Nuclear energy*] (NRCH) ... TACS
Technical Assistance [*or Assistant*] ... TA
Technical Assistance Administration [*United Nations*] ... TAA
Technical Assistance Agreement [*NASA*] (NASA) ... TAA
Technical Assistance and Management Services [*General Services Administration*] (GFGA) ... TAMS
Technical Assistance and Manufacturing Agreement ... TAMA
Technical Assistance and Manufacturing License Agreement ... TAMLA
Technical Assistance and Technology Transfer (NOAA) ... TATT
Technical Assistance and Training ... TAT
Technical Assistance and Training Survey [*Department of Labor*] (OICC) ... TATS
Technical Assistance Board [*United Nations*] ... TAB
Technical Assistance Bureau [*ICAO*] (DA) ... TAB
Technical Assistance Center [*Telecommunications*] ... TAC
Technical Assistance Center [*State University College at Plattsburgh*] [*Research center*] (RCD) ... TAC
Technical Assistance Center [*Operated by the Helen Keller National Center for Deaf-Blind Youths and Adults (HKNC)*] (PAZ) ... TAC
Technical Assistance Committee [*of the Economic and Social Council of the United Nations*] ... TAC
Technical Assistance Consortium to Improve College Services [*Defunct*] (EA) ... TACTICS
Technical Assistance Contract [*Nuclear energy*] (NRCH) ... TAC
Technical Assistance Data ... TADS
Technical Assistance Field Team (MCD) ... TAFT
Technical Assistance for Parents Program [*Established under the EHC (Education for all Handicapped Children act)*] (PAZ) ... TAPP
Technical Assistance Grant ... TAG
Technical Assistance Group [*NASA*] (KSC) ... TAG
Technical Assistance Guides (OICC) ... TAG
Technical Assistance Information Clearing House [*of ACVAFS*] [*Information service or system*] (EA) ... TAICH
Technical Assistance Information Clearing House, New York, NY [*Library symbol Library of Congress*] (LCLS) ... NNTAICH
Technical Assistance of the United Nations ... TAUN
Technical Assistance Office ... TAO
Technical Assistance Operations [*United Nations*] ... TAO
Technical Assistance Order (KSC) ... TAO
Technical Assistance Program [*Environmental Protection Agency*] (GFGA) ... TAP
Technical Assistance Project (EA) ... TAP
Technical Assistance Recruitment Service [*United Nations*] ... TARS
Technical Assistance Request [*Nuclear energy*] (NRCH) ... TAR
Technical Assistance Team [*Air Force*] (AFM) ... TAT
Technical Assistance to Commonwealth of Independent States ... TACIS
Technical Assistance Visit (MCD) ... TAV
Technical Assistant, Royal Artillery [*British military*] (DMA) ... TARA
Technical Associate of the Geological Society [*British*] (DBQ) ... TechGeol
Technical Association of the Fur Industry ... TAFI
Technical Association of the Graphic Arts (EA) ... TAGA
Technical Association of the Pulp and Paper Industry (EA) ... TAPPI
Technical Availability [*Navy*] (NG) ... TAV
Technical Availability [*Navy*] (NVT) ... TECHAV
Technical Availability/Restricted Availability [*Navy*] (NVT) ... TA/RA
Technical Benzene Hexachloride [*Organic chemistry*] ... TBH
Technical Book Review Index ... TBRI
Technical Bulletin [*Military*] ... TB
Technical Center [*Environmental Protection Agency*] (GFGA) ... TC
Technical Ceramics Manufacturers Association (EA) ... TECMA
Technical Change Analysis (MCD) ... TCA
Technical Change Centre [*British*] (CB) ... TCC
Technical Change Proposal ... TCP
Technical Change Request ... TCR
Technical Change Summary [*NASA*] (MCD) ... TCS
Technical Changes to Technical Orders ... TCTO
Technical Characteristics [*Military*] (AABC) ... TC
Technical Characteristics Review ... TCR
Technical Checkout [*Nuclear*] (MCD) ... TCO
Technical Chemicals & Products [*NASDAQ symbol*] (SAG) ... TCPI
Technical Chemicals & Products [*Associated Press*] (SAG) ... TechChm
Technical Chemicals & Products Co. [*Associated Press*] (SAG) ... TechCh
Technical Circular ... TC
Technical Classification of Soils [*For pine plantations*] [*Australia*] ... TCS
Technical College [*British*] ... T
Technical College ... TC
Technical Command Informal Reports [*Army*] (MCD) ... TCIR
Technical Commission for Marine Meteorology [*WHO*] [*Geneva, Switzerland*] (EAIO) ... CMM
Technical Committee ... TC
Technical Committee Minutes [*Military*] (AFIT) ... TCM
Technical Committee on Agricultural Chemicals (EERA) ... TCAC
Technical Committee on Communications Satellites ... TCCS
Technical Committee on Fish Diseases [*Australia*] ... TCFD
Technical Committee on High Energy Physics [*of the Federal Council for Science and Technology*] ... TCHEP
Technical Committee on Industrial Classification [*Office of Management and Budget*] [*Washington, DC*] (EGAO) ... TCIC
Technical Committee on Veterinary Drugs (EERA) ... TCVD
Technical Communication ... TC
Technical Communications [*NASDAQ symbol*] (TTSB) ... TCCO
Technical Communications Corp. [*NASDAQ symbol*] (NQ) ... TCCO
Technical Communications Corp. [*Associated Press*] (SAG) ... TchCom
Technical Compliance Record ... TCR
Technical Component Industries [*Aerospace British*] ... TCI
Technical Computing Center (IEEE) ... TCC
Technical Concurrence Sheets [*NASA*] (NASA) ... TCS
Technical Conference of the Observation and Measurement of Atmospheric Pollution [*Helsinki, 1973*] ... TECOMAP
Technical Contract Administrator ... TCA
Technical Contracting Office [*Navy*] ... TCO
Technical Contracts Department ... TCD
Technical Control (MSA) ... TC
Technical Control and Analysis Center ... TCAC
Technical Control and Analysis Center - Division ... TCAC-D
Technical Control and Analysis Element (INF) ... TCAE
Technical Control and Analysis System (MCD) ... TCAS
Technical Control and Management Subsystem (MCD) ... TCMS
Technical Control Center ... TCC
Technical Control Facility [*or Function*] ... TCF
Technical Cooperation ... TC
Technical Cooperation Administration [*Transferred to Foreign Operations Administration, 1953*] ... TCA
Technical Cooperation among Developing Countries [*United Nations*] ... TCDC
Technical Co-Operation Committee [*OECD*] (DS) ... TECO
[*The*] **Technical Cooperation Committee** [*Army*] (AABC) ... TTCC
Technical Cooperation Fund (EERA) ... TCF

Technical Cooperation Officer [*British*] .... TCO
[*The*] **Technical Cooperation Program** [*US, UK, Canada, Australia*] [*Research*] .... TTCP
Technical Coordination Group (MCD) .... TCG
Technical Coordination Meeting (MCD) .... TCM
Technical Coordination Program [*Military*] (AFIT) .... TCP
Technical Coordinator Bulletin [*NASA*] (KSC) .... TCB
Technical Corrigendum [*Correction*] (OSI) .... TC
Technical Cost Proposal (AAG) .... TCP
Technical Cost Review (SSD) .... TCR
Technical Countdown Sequences (KSC) .... TCS
Technical Critical Item (NASA) .... TCI
Technical Data .... TD
Technical Data [*DoD*] .... TECHDATA
Technical Data Center [*Department of Labor*] [*Information service or system*] (IID) .... TDC
Technical Data Change Notice (MCD) .... TDCN
Technical Data Change Request [*NASA*] (KSC) .... TDCR
Technical Data/Configuration Management System (MCD) .... TD/CMS
Technical Data Contract Requirement (MCD) .... TDCR
Technical Data Control Centre, Edmonton, AB, Canada [*Library symbol Library of Congress*] (LCLS) .... CaAENI
Technical Data Control Centre, Edmonton, Alberta [*Library symbol National Library of Canada*] (NLC) .... AENI
Technical Data Department Report [*NASA*] (KSC) .... TDDR
Technical Data Digest [*Air Force*] .... TDD
Technical Data Engineer (MCD) .... TDE
Technical Data Evaluation .... TDE
Technical Data Impact Summary (MCD) .... TDIS
Technical Data International [*Information service or system*] (IID) .... TDI
Technical Data Justification Code [*Army*] .... TDJC
Technical Data Laboratory [*National Weather Service*] .... TDL
Technical Data Management Center [*Department of Energy*] [*Information service or system Defunct*] (IID) .... TDMC
Technical Data Management Office [*Navy*] .... TDMO
Technical Data Management Program [*Navy*] .... TDMP
Technical Data Package [*Military*] .... TDP
Technical Data Package Automated System .... TEDPAS
Technical Data Package Depository [*Army*] .... TDPD
Technical Data Package List [*Military*] (AABC) .... TDPL
Technical Data Package Management Plan [*Army*] .... TDPMP
Technical Data Relay (IEEE) .... TDR
Technical Data Report .... TDR
Technical Data Requests .... TDR
Technical Data Requirement Review Board .... TDRRB
Technical Data Requirements Sheet .... TDRS
Technical Data Resource Centre, Transport Canada [*Centre de la Documentation Technique, Transports Canada*], Ottawa, Ontario [*Library symbol National Library of Canada*] (NLC) .... OOTTD
Technical Data Specialist .... TDS
Technical Data Status Accounting (MCD) .... TDSA
Technical Data Support Facility .... TDSF
Technical Data Support Package [*Navy*] .... TDSP
Technical Data System (KSC) .... TDS
Technical Data Usage Program .... TDUP
Technical Database Services, Inc. [*Information service or system*] (IID) .... TDS
Technical Deficiency Report .... TDR
Technical Demonstration (AAG) .... TD
Technical Description Sheet .... TDS
Technical Design (AAG) .... TD
Technical Design Guide .... TDG
Technical Design Review (NASA) .... TDR
Technical Developing Group [*of the Publishers' Association*] [*British*] .... TDG
Technical Development (WDAA) .... TD
Technical Development Capital (IAA) .... TDC
Technical Development Center .... TDC
Technical Development Contractor .... TDC
Technical Development Evaluation Center .... TDEC
Technical Development Objective .... TDO
Technical Development Plan .... TDP
Technical Development Requirement .... TDR
Technical Directing Agency .... TDA
Technical Direction [*or Directive*] .... TD
Technical Direction Contract Effort .... TDCE
Technical Direction Order .... TDO
Technical Directive Bulletin (MCD) .... TDB
Technical Directive Compliance (MCD) .... TDC
Technical Directive Compliance Form (NVT) .... TDCF
Technical Directive Records (NG) .... TDR
Technical Directive Status Accounting .... TDSA
Technical Directive System (MCD) .... TDS
Technical Directives Ordnance (NG) .... TDO
Technical Director [*Television*] .... TD
Technical Directorate Assistance Team [*South Vietnamese studies and observation group team*] (VNW) .... TDAT
Technical Discussion .... TD
Technical Division .... TD
Technical Division and Engineering Center [*FAA*] (MCD) .... TDEC
Technical Division Manager .... TDM
Technical Division Memo Report [*Army World War II*] .... TDMR
Technical Divisions Office [*Jet Propulsion Laboratory, NASA*] .... TDO
Technical Document (DNAB) .... TDOC
Technical Document Center .... TDC
Technical Document Change (MCD) .... TDC
Technical Document List .... TDL
Technical Documentary Report .... TDR
Technical Documentation [*DoD*] .... TECDOC
Technical Documentation and Graphic Services .... TD & GS
Technical Documentation for Provisioning [*Military*] (AFIT) .... TDP
Technical Documents Division [*Naval Air Systems Command*] .... TDD
Technical Drawing .... TD
Technical Edit Unit [*Navy*] (DNAB) .... TEU
Technical Editing and Composition System [*Computer science*] (DGA) .... TECS
Technical Editor (DGA) .... Tech Ed
Technical Education Center .... TEC
Technical Education Center .... TEDC
Technical Education Institute (AIE) .... TEI
Technical Education Program (OICC) .... TEP
Technical Education Research Centers, Inc. [*Cambridge, MA*] [*Research center*] .... TERC
Technical Effort Locator and Technical Interest Profile System [*Army*] (PDAA) .... TELTIPS
Technical Electronic Management Planning Organization .... TEMPO
Technical Electronic Office [*Data General Corp.*] .... TEO
Technical Electronic Product Radiation Safety Standards Committee (MCD) .... TEPRSSC
Technical Enforcement Guidance Document [*Environmental Protection Agency*] .... TEGD
Technical Enforcement Support [*Environmental Protection Agency*] (GFGA) .... TES
Technical Engagement Simulation .... TES
Technical Engineer .... TE
Technical Engineer-Architect Management (MCD) .... TEAM
Technical Engineering and Maintenance .... TEAM
Technical Engineering and Spacelift Services [*Air Force*] (AAGC) .... TESS
Technical Engineering Item (MCD) .... TEI
Technical Engineering Management Support [*Air Force*] .... TEMS
Technical Engineers Association (EA) .... TEA
Technical Engineers Association .... TENG
Technical Enquiry Service [*British*] (DCTA) .... TES
Technical Equipment Planning Information .... TEPI
Technical Error Message [*Aviation*] .... TEM
Technical Escort Center [*Army*] (RDA) .... TEC
Technical Escort Unit [*Army*] (AABC) .... TEU
Technical Evaluation [*Army*] .... TE
Technical Evaluation [*Navy*] (NG) .... TECHEVAL
Technical Evaluation and Acquisition Management Support [*Air Force*] .... TEAMS
Technical Evaluation and Countermeasures Assignment .... TECA
Technical Evaluation Committee [*Environmental Protection Agency*] (GFGA) .... TEC
Technical Evaluation Panel [*In various federal government agencies*] (NASA) .... TEP
Technical Evaluation Report [*Nuclear energy*] (NRCH) .... TER
Technical Evaluation Team (MCD) .... TET
Technical Evaluation Test (MCD) .... TET
Technical Exchange .... TE
Technical Exchange (MHDI) .... TECH EX
Technical Exchange Agreement .... TEA
Technical Exhibition for Florists [*Brussels International Trade Fair*] .... FLOREX
Technical Facilities Subsystem [*Space Flight Operations Facility, NASA*] .... TFSS
Technical Facility Change Procedure (AAG) .... TFCP
Technical Facility Modification Authorization (AAG) .... TFMA
Technical Feasibility Demonstration Model .... TFDM
Technical Feasibility Testing [*Army*] .... TFT
Technical Feedback Report (DNAB) .... TFBR
Technical File (MCD) .... TF
Technical Grade Active Constituent (EERA) .... TGAC
Technical Guidance Directions .... TGD
Technical Guidance Unit (NVT) .... TGU
Technical Handbook Distribution Code (MCD) .... THDC
Technical Help to Exporters [*British Standards Institution*] .... THE
Technical High School (ADA) .... THS
Technical Idea Exchange (MCD) .... TIE
Technical Illustrators Management Association [*Later, IG*] .... TIMA
Technical Improvement Program .... TIP
Technical Independent Evaluator [*Army*] .... TIE
Technical Indexes Ltd. [*Information service or system*] (IID) .... ti
Technical Indexes Ltd. (NITA) .... TIL
Technical Industrial Cooperation Contract .... TICC
Technical Industrial Intelligence Committee [*US Military Government, Germany*] .... TIIC
Technical Industrial Intelligence Division [*Allied Board set up to send experts into Germany to ferret out Germany's war-developed scientific secrets*] [*Post-World War II*] .... TIID
Technical Industrial Liaison Office .... TILO
Technical Information [*DoD*] .... TECHINFO
Technical Information (CINC) .... TI
Technical Information Advisory Committee [*AEC*] .... TIAC
Technical Information Analysis Centers .... TIAC
Technical Information & Liaison Service [*Information service or system*] (IID) .... TILS
Technical Information and Library Services [*Ministry of Technology*] [*British*] .... TIL
Technical Information and Product Service .... TIPS
Technical Information Base (MCD) .... TIB
Technical Information Branch [*US Public Health Service*] [*Information service or system*] (IID) .... TIB
Technical Information Bulletin [*Cincinnati, OH*] (AAG) .... TIB
Technical Information Bulletin. National Information Service on Drug Abuse [*A publication*] .... Tech Inf Bull

Technical Information Bureau [*British*] ... TIB
Technical Information Capability ... TIC
Technical Information Center [*Department of Energy*] ... TIC
Technical Information Center Administration [*Conference*] ... TICA
Technical Information Centre, 3M Canada, Inc., London, Ontario [*Library symbol National Library of Canada*] (NLC) ... OLTMC
Technical Information Centre, Bank of Montreal, Willowdale, Ontario [*Library symbol National Library of Canada*] (NLC) ... OTBM
Technical Information Centre, Reed Ltd., Quebec, Quebec [*Library symbol National Library of Canada*] (NLC) ... QQR
Technical Information Centre, Transport Canada Training Institute [*Centre d'Information Technique, Institut de Formation Transports Canada*], Cornwall, Ontario [*Library symbol National Library of Canada*] (NLC) ... OOTI
Technical Information Contact Officer [*Navy*] (DNAB) ... TICO
Technical Information Coordinator [*Environmental Protection Agency*] (GFGA) ... TIC
Technical Information Directive Update Panel ... TIDUP
Technical Information Distribution Service [*Publisher*] ... TIDS
Technical Information Division [*Romar Consultants, Inc.*] [*Information service or system*] (IID) ... TID
Technical Information Documentation Center [*Advisory Group for Aerospace Research and Development*] (NATG) ... TIDOC
Technical Information Exchange [*National Bureau of Standards*] ... TIE
Technical Information Facility, Canadien Imperial Bank of Commerce, Toronto, Ontario [*Library symbol National Library of Canada*] (NLC) ... OTBCO
Technical Information File ... TIF
Technical Information for Product Safety [*Consumer Product Safety Commission*] (IID) ... TIPS
Technical Information Handbook ... TIH
Technical Information Maintenance Instruction ... TIMI
Technical Information Management System ... TIMS
Technical Information Manager [*Environmental Protection Agency*] (GFGA) ... TIM
Technical Information Manual ... TIM
Technical Information Office ... TIO
Technical Information on Microfilm [*British*] (DIT) ... TIM
Technical Information on Patents [*Swiss Intellectual Property Office*] [*Bern*] [*Information service or system*] (IID) ... TIPAT
Technical Information Panel [*Terminated, 1971*] [*AEC*] ... TIP
Technical Information Periodicals Service [*General Electric Co.*] ... TIPS
Technical Information Pilot [*A publication Obsolete*] ... TIP
Technical Information Pilot (DOMA) ... TIP
Technical Information Pool ... TIP
Technical Information Processing (IEEE) ... TIP
Technical Information Processing System [*Rockwell International Corp.*] [*Downey, CA*] (AFM) ... TIPS
Technical Information Program ... TIP
Technical Information Project [*MIT*] ... TIP
Technical Information Release ... TIR
Technical Information Report (IEEE) ... TIR
Technical Information Reports for Music-Media Specialists [*Music Library Association publication series*] ... TIRMMS
Technical Information Retrieval and Analysis System (CAAL) ... TIRAS
Technical Information Section [*Navy*] ... TIS
Technical Information Series (IAA) ... TIS
Technical Information Service [*American Institute of Aeronautics and Astronautics*] (IID) ... TIS
Technical Information Service [*Caribbean Industrial Research Institute*] [*Trinidad and Tobago*] ... TIS
Technical Information Service (IAA) ... TISE
Technical Information Service Extension (SAA) ... TISE
Technical Information Service - of American Institute of Aeronautics and Astronautics (EA) ... AIAA-TIS
Technical Information Services [*Acurex Corp.*] (IID) ... TIS
Technical Information Staff [*Environmental Protection Agency*] (GFGA) ... TIS
Technical Information Support Activities [*Army*] ... TISA
Technical Information Support Activities Project [*Army*] (DIT) ... TISAP
Technical Information Support Personnel [*Department of Labor*] ... TISP
Technical Information System for Carrier Aviation [*Navy*] (MCD) ... TISCA
Technical Information Systems [*Department of Agriculture*] ... TIS
Technical Input Checklist/Evaluation Report (MCD) ... TICLER
Technical Inspection [*Military*] ... TI
Technical Inspection Field Office, Office of the Inspector General ... TIFO
Technical Inspection/Quality Control (MCD) ... TI/QC
Technical Institute ... TI
Technical Institute Council (EA) ... TIC
Technical Institute of Alamance, Burlington, NC [*Library symbol Library of Congress*] (LCLS) ... NcBurT
Technical Instruction [*or Instructor*] ... TI
Technical Instructors Course [*Air Force*] (AFM) ... TIC
Technical Integration [*NASA*] (NASA) ... TI
Technical Integration and Evaluation [*Apollo*] [*NASA*] ... TIE
Technical Integration Panel [*NASA*] (SSD) ... TIP
Technical Intelligence [*Spy satellites, etc.*] ... TECHINT
Technical Intelligence [*Military*] ... TI
Technical Intelligence Branch [*National Coal Board*] (PDAA) ... TIB
Technical Intelligence Center [*Navy*] ... TIC
Technical Intelligence Center Allied Command Europe [*NATO*] (NATG) ... TICACE
Technical Intelligence Coordination Center [*NATO*] (NATG) ... TICC
Technical Intelligence Data Extraction (MCD) ... TIDE
Technical Intelligence Report ... TIR
Technical Interchange (KSC) ... TI
Technical Interchange Meeting (NASA) ... TIM
Technical Interest Profiles (SAA) ... TIPS
Technical Interface Concepts (RDA) ... TIC
Technical Interface Design Plan - Test Edition (RDA) ... TIDP-TE
Technical Interface Design Plans ... TIDP
Technical Interface Specification (NATG) ... TIS
Technical Journal (MCD) ... TJ
Technical Knockout [*Boxing*] ... TKO
Technical Letter ... TL
Technical Liaison Engineer ... TLE
Technical Liaison Memo ... TLM
Technical Liaison Office [*Military*] ... TLO
Technical Library ... TL
Technical Library AAFBAA, Flight Services Directorate, Transport Canada [*Bibliotheque Technique AAFBAA, Direction Generale du Service des Vols, Transports Canada*], Ottawa, Ontario [*Library symbol National Library of Canada*] (NLC) ... OOTFS
Technical Library, Alcan Smelters Chemicals Ltd., Kitimat, British Columbia [*Library symbol National Library of Canada*] (NLC) ... BKAS
Technical Library, Boeing of Canada Ltd., Winnipeg, Manitoba [*Library symbol National Library of Canada*] (NLC) ... MWBC
Technical Library, Microtel Pacific Research Ltd., Burnaby, British Columbia [*Library symbol National Library of Canada*] (NLC) ... BBMT
Technical Library, Novacor Chemicals Ltd., Calgary, Alberta [*Library symbol National Library of Canada*] (BIB) ... ACNCT
Technical Library, Novatel Communications Ltd., Calgary, Alberta [*Library symbol National Library of Canada*] (NLC) ... ACNOC
Technical Library, Petro-Canada Products, Mississauga, Ontario [*Library symbol National Library of Canada*] (NLC) ... OMGCR
Technical Library, Potash Corp. of Saskatchewan, Saskatoon, Saskatchewan [*Library symbol National Library of Canada*] (NLC) ... SSPCT
Technical Library Service (IID) ... TLS
Technical Library Services Section ... TLSS
Technical Library, Shell Canada Resources Ltd., Calgary, Alberta [*Library symbol National Library of Canada*] (NLC) ... ACSC
Technical Library, Systemhouse Ltd., Ottawa, Ontario [*Library symbol National Library of Canada*] (NLC) ... OOSHT
Technical Limit ... TL
Technical Logistics Data [*Army*] (AABC) ... TLD
Technical Logistics Data and Information [*Army*] (AABC) ... TLDI
Technical Logistics Data Information Program ... TLDIP
Technical Logistics Data Program [*Navy*] (DNAB) ... TLDP
Technical Maintenance Repair Center (MCD) ... TMRC
Technical Management (AAGC) ... TM
Technical Management Items (NASA) ... TMI
Technical Management Requirements Document ... TMRD
Technical Management Requirements Document Change Notice (MCD) ... TMCN
Technical Manager ... TM
Technical Manual (DNAB) ... TECHMAN
Technical Manual ... TM
Technical Manual Audit and Requirement Reporting System (MCD) ... TMARS
Technical Manual Change Number [*Army*] ... TM CHG
Technical Manual Change Request [*or Requirement*] ... TMCR
Technical Manual Contract Requirement ... TMCR
Technical Manual Control Panel (IAA) ... TMCP
Technical Manual Data Cards [*DoD*] (MCD) ... TMDC
Technical Manual Data List [*DoD*] ... TMDL
Technical Manual Data Record [*DoD*] (MCD) ... TMDR
Technical Manual Designation ... TMD
Technical Manual - Engineering [*Marine Corps*] ... TM-ENG
Technical Manual Evaluation Record (MCD) ... TMER
Technical Manual Functional Group Code ... TMFGC
Technical Manual Identification Numbering System (MCD) ... TMINS
Technical Manual Indenture Code [*Army*] ... TMINDCD
Technical Manual Index [*Navy*] ... TMI
Technical Manual Integrated Management Information Systems [*DoD*] ... TMIMIS
Technical Manual List (MCD) ... TML
Technical Manual Management Agent ... TMA
Technical Manual Management Information System [*Navy*] (DNAB) ... TMMIS
Technical Manual Management Program [*Navy*] (NVT) ... TMMP
Technical Manual Management Team [*DoD*] ... TMMT
Technical Manual Ordtask Requirement (MCD) ... TMOR
Technical Manual Parts [*Army*] (AABC) ... TMP
Technical Manual Plan [*DoD*] ... TMP
Technical Manual Quality Assurance Plan [*Navy*] (DNAB) ... TMQAP
Technical Manual Specifications and Standards [*Military*] (AFIT) ... TMSS
Technical Manual Status and Schedule Report (MCD) ... TMSSR
Technical Manual Status Report (MCD) ... TMSR
Technical Manual Work Request ... TMWR
Technical Manual Work Requirement (MCD) ... TMWR
Technical Marketing Society of America (EA) ... TMSA
Technical Medical Information System (DAVI) ... TMIS
Technical Meetings Information Service ... TMIS
Technical Memorandum (MHDB) ... TECH MEMO
Technical Memorandum ... TM
Technical Memorandum Report ... TMR
Technical Military Planning Operation (AAG) ... TEMPO
Technical Minutes ... TM
Technical Missions, Structures and Career Development [*Military*] ... TECSTAR
Technical Monograph ... TM
Technical Munitions Safety Study [*Air Force*] ... TMSS
Technical News Bulletin [*National Bureau of Standards*] ... TNB
Technical Newsletter ... TNL
Technical Note [*or Notice*] (DNAB) ... TECHNOTE
Technical Note ... TN
Technical Nuclear Safety (MCD) ... TNSA
Technical Objective ... TO
Technical Objective Directive [*or Document*] [*Air Force*] (MCD) ... TOD

Technical Observer ... TO
Technical, Office, and Professional Department [*UAW*] ... TOP
Technical Officer [*Military British*] ... TO
Technical On-Site Inspection ... TOSI
Technical Operating Center [*Telecommunications*] (TSSD) ... TOC
Technical Operating Procedure ... TOP
Technical Operating Report ... TOR
Technical Operation Instruction (KSC) ... TOI
Technical Operational Evaluation ... TECHOPEVAL
Technical Operational Support ... TOS
Technical Operations and Systems Support (AAGC) ... TOSS
Technical Operations Department ... TOD
Technical Operations Group [*Air Force*] ... TCHOG
Technical Operations Group [*Air Force*] ... TOG
Technical Operations, Inc. (MCD) ... TOI
Technical Operations Manager [*Navy*] ... TOM
Technical Operations Research (KSC) ... TOR
Technical Operations Squadron [*Air Force*] ... TCHOS
Technical Operations Squadron [*Air Force*] ... TOS
Technical Order ... TO
Technical Order Change Notice [*Air Force*] (MCD) ... TOCN
Technical Order Compliance [*Military*] ... TOC
Technical Order Compliance/Engineering Change Proposal [*Military*] (AFIT) ... TOC/ECP
Technical Order Dilemma (SAA) ... TOD
Technical Order Distribution Activity ... TODA
Technical Order Distribution Code [*Air Force*] ... TODC
Technical Order Distribution Office [*or Officer*] ... TODO
Technical Order Field Change Notice [*Air Force*] (MCD) ... TOFCN
Technical Order Identification (MCD) ... TOID
Technical Order Management Agency [*Military*] (AFIT) ... TOMA
Technical Order Notification and Completion System (AAG) ... TONAC
Technical Order Page Supplement [*Air Force*] ... TOPS
Technical Order Status Report (MCD) ... TOSR
Technical Order System Publication Deficiency Report [*Military*] (AFIT) ... TOSPDR
Technical Organizational Memory Bank (RDA) ... TOMB
Technical Oriented Disk System [*Computer science*] (ECII) ... TODS
Technical Override ... TOR
Technical Oversight Representative ... TOR
Technical Pamphlet ... TP
Technical Panel for International Broadcast (NTCM) ... TPIB
Technical Panel on the Earth Satellite Program ... TPESP
Technical Paper ... TP
Technical Paper / Author Cross-Index System (DNAB) ... TECHAUTHIND
Technical Papers for the Bible Translator [*A publication*] (BJA) ... TPBT
Technical Performance (MCD) ... TP
Technical Performance Audit ... TPA
Technical Performance Criteria (SSD) ... TPC
Technical Performance Management ... TPM
Technical Performance Measurement (AAGC) ... TPM
Technical Performance Measurement System [*NASA*] ... TPM
Technical Performance Module (MCD) ... TPM
Technical Performance Parameter (MCD) ... TPP
Technical Planning Office ... TPO
Technical Practice Aid (ADA) ... TPA
Technical Prime Contractor ... TPC
Technical Problem ... TP
Technical Processing and Reporting Unit (CAAL) ... TPRU
Technical Professional ... TP
Technical Proficiency Inspection [*Military*] ... TPI
Technical Program Planning Division [*Air Force*] (MCD) ... TPPD
Technical Program Planning Document [*Air Force*] (IAA) ... TPPD
Technical Program Review ... TPR
Technical Programs Division [*Environmental Protection Agency*] (GFGA) ... TPD
Technical Progress Committee [*British*] (DCTA) ... TPC
Technical Progress Report ... TPR
Technical Project Officer ... TPO
Technical Proposal ... TP
Technical Proposal Requirement (MCD) ... TPR
Technical Protein Colloid ... TPC
Technical Publication ... TP
Technical Publications - Administration [*Naval Facilities Engineering Command Publications*] ... TP-AD
Technical Publications Agent (MCD) ... TPA
Technical Publications Announcement ... TPA
Technical Publications Documentation [*Army*] ... TPD
Technical Publications Library (MCD) ... TPL
Technical Publications - Maintenance Operation [*Naval Facilities Engineering Command Publications*] ... TP-MO
Technical Publications - Planning [*Naval Facilities Engineering Command Publications*] ... TP-PL
Technical Publications - Public Utilities [*Naval Facilities Engineering Command Publications*] ... TP-PU
Technical Publishing Society [*Later, STC*] ... TPS
Technical Publishing Software [*Interleaf, Inc.*] ... TPS
Technical Quality Control [*Telecommunications*] (TEL) ... TQC
Technical Quality Evaluation [*Polaris*] ... TQE
Technical Quartermaster Sergeant ... TQMS
Technical Readiness ... TR
Technical Reason [*Aviation*] ... TECR
Technical Reconnaissance and Surveillance (MCD) ... TECRAS
Technical Records Office [*or Officer*] [*British*] ... TRO
Technical Reference Branch [*Department of Transportation*] (IID) ... TRB
Technical Reference File ... TRF
Technical Reference Handbook ... TRH
Technical Reference Model [*Army*] (RDA) ... TRM
Technical Reference Model ... TRM
Technical Regulation ... TR
Technical Repair Center [*Air Force*] (AFIT) ... TRC
Technical Repair Standards ... TRS
Technical Replacement Factor ... TRF
Technical Report (MHDI) ... TECH REPT
Technical Report ... TR
Technical Report ... TRP
Technical Report Analysis, Condensation, Evaluation ... TRACE
Technical Report Instruction (AAG) ... TRI
Technical Report Program (NITA) ... TR
Technical Report Request ... TRR
Technical Reporter [*World Council of Credit Unions*] [*A publication*] ... TR
Technical Reporting of Automated Configuration Electrical Requirements ... TRACER
Technical Reports Announcement Checklist ... TRAC
Technical Reports Automated Cataloging - Yes [*National Oceanic and Atmospheric Administration*] ... TRACY
Technical Reports Indexing Project (KSC) ... TRIP
Technical Representative [*Military*] ... TECHREP
Technical Representative ... TR
Technical Representative of the Contracting Officer (MCD) ... TRCO
Technical Requirement (AABC) ... TECR
Technical Requirement (MCD) ... TR
Technical Requirement Analysis (OA) ... TRA
Technical Requirements Document ... TRD
Technical Requirements Identification Matrix (MCD) ... TRIM
Technical Requirements Management System ... TRMS
Technical Requirements Package (MCD) ... TRP
Technical Requirements Review (MCD) ... TRR
Technical Requirements Specification (MCD) ... TRS
Technical Research Center (MCD) ... TRC
Technical Research Centre of Finland ... VIT
Technical Research Centre of Finland, Espoo, Finland [*OCLC symbol*] (OCLC) ... TIS
Technical Research Centre of Finland, Information Service, Espoo, Vuorimiehentie, Finland [*Library symbol*] [*Library of Congress*] (LCLS) ... FiVTRC
Technical Research Group, Inc. (MCD) ... TRG
Technical Research Institute [*Japan*] ... TRI
Technical Research Note (IEEE) ... TRN
Technical Research Ship [*Navy symbol*] ... AGTR
Technical Research Ship ... TRS
Technical Research Ship Special Communications [*System*] [*Pronounced "triss-com"*] [*Navy*] ... TRSSCOMM
Technical Research Sub-Department [*French Acronym is based on foreign phrase*] ... SDRT
Technical Resource Centre, Department of Public Works and Highways, Government of the Northwest Territories, Yellowknife, Northwest Territories [*Library symbol National Library of Canada*] (BIB) ... NWYPW
Technical Resource Document ... TRD
Technical Resources Center [*Syracuse University*] [*Research center*] ... TRC
Technical Review [*Nuclear energy*] (NRCH) ... TR
Technical Review and Analysis ... TRA
Technical Review Board [*NASA*] (KSC) ... TRB
Technical Review Committee [*International Atomic Energy Agency*] (NRCH) ... TRC
Technical Review Committee [*Environmental Protection Agency*] (GFGA) ... TRC
Technical Review Committee ... TRC
Technical Review Criteria (ERG) ... TRC
Technical Review Document (GNE) ... TRD
Technical Review Group ... TRG
Technical Review Team [*Nuclear energy*] (NRCH) ... TRT
Technical Review Updated Manuals and Publications (MCD) ... TRUMP
Technical Reviewing Office (AFM) ... TRO
Technical Risk Assessment (MCD) ... TRA
Technical Risk Reduction [*Military*] ... TRR
Technical Sales Representative ... TSR
Technical Sales Seminars [*Department of Commerce*] ... TSS
Technical School [*Air Force*] ... TECHS
Technical School (ADA) ... TS
Technical School Squadron [*Army*] ... TSS
Technical, Scientific, and Medical Publishing (WDMC) ... tsm publishing
Technical Scope of Work ... TSW
Technical Secretariat (NATG) ... TS
Technical Sergeant [*Air Force*] ... E6
Technical Sergeant [*Military*] ... TSGT
Technical Sergeant (Commissary) [*Marine Corps*] ... TSGT(C)
Technical Service Bulletin ... TSB
Technical Service Career Development Program [*Military*] ... TSCDP
Technical Service Group (IAA) ... TSG
Technical Service Guild of Australia ... TSGA
Technical Service Intelligence Team [*Military*] ... TSIT
Technical Service Order [*Aviation*] (DA) ... TSO
Technical Service Organization [*A generic term*] ... TSO
Technical Service Unit ... TSU
Technical Service Unit [*Military*] ... TU
Technical Services [*Army*] ... TECHSVS
Technical Services Center, Memphis, Tenn (AAGC) ... TSC
Technical Services Co. ... TS
Technical Services, Joseph E. Seagram & Sons Ltd., La Salle, Quebec [*Library symbol National Library of Canada*] (NLC) ... QMJES
Technical Services Quarterly [*A publication*] ... TSQ
Technical Services Report [*A publication*] (EAAP) ... TSR

Technical Services Representative (MCD) ... TSR
Technical Services Staff [*Environmental Protection Agency*] (GFGA) ... TSS
Technical Shop (NASA) ... TESH
Technical Simulation and Evaluation System ... TSES
Technical Skill Reenlistment Incentive ... TSRI
Technical Specialty Group [*AIAA*] ... TSG
Technical Specification (MCD) ... TS
Technical Specification ... TSP
Technical Specification Order ... TSO
Technical Specification Sheet ... TSS
Technical Specifications (IAA) ... TECHSPECS
Technical Staff Officer ... TSO
Technical Staff Surveillance [*Military*] (IAA) ... TSS
Technical Standard Operating Procedure [*NASA*] (KSC) ... TSOP
Technical Standard Order [*FAA*] ... TSO
Technical Standard Order Authorization (MCD) ... TSOA
Technical Standardization Inspection [*Military*] ... TSI
Technical Standards Division, Ontario Ministry of Consumer and Commercial Relations, Toronto, Ontario [*Library symbol National Library of Canada*] (NLC) ... OTCCRT
Technical Standards for Library Automation ... TESLA
Technical Standing Order (KSC) ... TSO
Technical Status Review [*NASA*] (NASA) ... TSR
Technical Steering Group (OICC) ... TSG
Technical Study Implementation Plan (SSD) ... TSIP
Technical Study Report ... TSR
Technical Subcommittee ... TSC
Technical Subgroup (NATG) ... TSG
Technical Summary Report ... TSR
Technical Supplemental Allowance [*Military*] ... TSA
Technical Supply Management Code ... TSMC
Technical Support (NASA) ... TS
Technical Support Activity [*Army*] (RDA) ... TSA
Technical Support Agent (MCD) ... TSA
Technical Support Alliance [*Computer science*] (PCM) ... TSA
Technical Support Asset ... TSA
Technical Support Center [*Nuclear energy*] (NRCH) ... TSC
Technical Support Division [*Environmental Protection Agency*] (GFGA) ... TSD
Technical Support Document ... TSD
Technical Support Effort ... TSE
Technical Support Equipment ... TSE
Technical Support Organization [*AEC*] ... TSO
Technical Support Package [*NASA*] ... TSP
Technical Support Real Property ... TSRP
Technical Support Review (SSD) ... TSR
Technical Support Services ... TSS
Technical Support Staff [*Environmental Protection Agency*] (GFGA) ... TSS
Technical Support Unit (IAA) ... TSU
Technical Surgical Assistance [*Medicine*] (MAE) ... TSA
Technical Surveillance Countermeasures [*Program*] [*Air Force*] ... TSCM
Technical System for Continued Emissions Reduction [*Environmental Protection Agency*] ... TSFCER
Technical Systems, Inc. (IAA) ... TSI
Technical Team ... TT
Technical Test ... TT
Technical Test and Evaluation ... TT & E
Technical Test Battery [*Aptitude test*] ... TTB
Technical Test Director ... TTD
Technical Test Readiness Review [*Army*] ... TTRR
Technical Test Support Divisions [*Army*] (RDA) ... TTSD
Technical Testing/Initial Operator Test and Evaluation [*Army*] ... TT/IOTE
Technical Testing/Operational Testing Evaluation [*Army*] ... TT/OTE
Technical Training (NVT) ... TECHTNG
Technical Training (OICC) ... TT
Technical Training Air Force ... TECHTAF
Technical Training Air Force ... TTAF
Technical Training Center [*Air Force*] ... TTC
Technical Training Command [*Army Air Forces*] [*World War II*] ... TTC
Technical Training Detachment ... TTD
Technical Training Engineer ... TTE
Technical [*or Tactical*] **Training Equipment** (MCD) ... TTE
Technical Training Squadron [*Air Force*] ... TCHTS
Technical Training Squadron [*Air Force*] ... TECHTNGSq
Technical Training Squadron (MCD) ... TTS
Technical Training Wing [*Air Force*] ... TCHTW
Technical Translation [*A publication Obsolete*] ... TT
Technical Translation Group (IEEE) ... TTG
Technical Transmitter Holding Fixture ... TMF
Technical Transmitter Holding Future (MCD) ... TMF
Technical University in Munich [*Germany*] ... TUM
Technical University of Nova Scotia [*UTLAS symbol*] ... TUN
Technical University of Nova Scotia, Halifax, Nova Scotia [*Library symbol National Library of Canada*] (NLC) ... NSHT
Technical User Performance Specifications [*US Independent Telephone Association*] [*Telecommunications*] (TEL) ... TUPS
Technical Value Committee (BARN) ... TVC
Technical Win [*Boxing*] (DICI) ... TW
Technical Working Group [*of the Conference on the Discontinuance of Nuclear Weapon Tests*] ... TWG
Technical Working Group (EERA) ... TWG
Technical Works [*Air Force*] (MCD) ... TW
Technical Writing Improvement Society ... TWIS
Technical Writing Unit [*NASA*] ... TWU
Technical-Engineering-Science Training for Secretaries ... TESTS
Technically Advanced Family (PS) ... TAFY
Technically Classified (BARN) ... TC
Technically Enhanced Naturally Radioactive (NRCH) ... TENR
Technically Enhanced Naturally Radioactive Product (NRCH) ... TENRAP
Technically Improved Interference Prediction System (IEEE) ... TIIPS
Technically Specified Natural Rubber ... TSR
Technically Workable Ideal System [*Industrial engineering*] ... TWIS
Technicals and Turnovers [*Basketball*] ... T & T
Technician [*Communications*] [*Navy rating*] ... TE
Technician ... TECH
Technician ... TECHN
Technician ... TECHN
Technician Aeronautical Engineering (IAA) ... TAE
Technician Affiliate Group [*of American Chemical Society*] ... TAG
Technician (Council of Engineering Institutions) [*British*] (DI) ... Tech(CEI)
Technician Education Council [*British*] (DI) ... TEC
Technician Engineer [*British*] (DBQ) ... TEng
Technician Engineer of the Institution of Metallurgists [*British*] (DBQ) ... TEngAMIN
Technician Fifth Grade [*Army*] ... T/5
Technician in Costing and Accounting [*British*] (DBQ) ... TCA
Technician Maintenance Information System (MHDB) ... TMIS
Technician Member of the Chartered Institute of Building [*British*] (DI) ... TMCIOB
Technician Member of the Institute of Water Pollution Control [*British*] (DI) ... TechMIWPC
Technician Member of the Institution of Mechanical and General Technician Engineers [*British*] (DI) ... TMIMGTechE
Technician of the Construction Surveyor's Institute [*British*] (DBQ) ... TnCSI
Technician of the Institute of Municipal Building Management [*British*] (DBQ) ... TnIMBM
Technician of the Society of Licensed Aircraft Engineers and Technologists [*British*] (DBQ) ... TSLAET
Technician of the Welding Institute [*British*] (DBQ) ... TechWeldI
Technician, Second Grade [*Military*] ... T2G
Technician-in-Training (ADA) ... TIT
Technician's Certificate [*British*] (DI) ... TC
Technician's Diploma [*British*] (DI) ... TD
Techniclone International Corp. [*NASDAQ symbol*] (SAG) ... TCLN
Techniclone International Corp. [*Associated Press*] (SAG) ... Techclne
Techniclone Intl [*NASDAQ symbol*] (TTSB) ... TCLN
Technicolor (KSC) ... TC
Technicolor, Inc., Burbank, CA [*Library symbol Library of Congress*] (LCLS) ... CBbT
Technicon Integrator/Calculator ... TIC
Technigen Corp. [*Associated Press*] (SAG) ... Technign
Technigen Corp. [*NASDAQ symbol*] (SAG) ... TGPA
Technigen Corp. [*NASDAQ symbol*] (TTSB) ... TGPAF
Technigen Platinum Corp. [*Vancouver Stock Exchange symbol*] ... TGP
Technion News Bulletin [*Haifa*] [*A publication*] (BJA) ... TNB
Technique ... TECH
Technique ... TECHNQ
Technique for Assessing Comparative Force Modernization [*Army*] ... TASCFORM
Technique for Econometric Modeling Program (BUR) ... TEMP
Technique for Establishing Personnel Performance Standards [*Navy*] ... TEPPS
Technique for Evaluation and Analysis of Maintainability ... TEAM
Technique for Extreme Point Optimization (BUR) ... TEMPO
Technique for Human Error Rate Prediction ... THERP
Technique for Information Management and Employment ... TIME
Technique for Interactive Systems Analysis (NVT) ... TISA
Technique for Report and Index Management [*No longer available*] [*Information service or system*] (IID) ... TRIM
Technique for Responsive Inventory Management (MHDB) ... TRIM
Technique for the Optimum Placement of Activities in Zones (PDAA) ... TOPAZ
Technique of Operations Review [*Engineering*] ... TOR
Technique to Retrieve Information from Abstracts of Literature [*Computer science*] ... TRIAL
Techniques for Determining RADAR Cross Section [*Air Force*] ... TRCS
Techniques for Effective Alcohol Management [*NHTSA*] (TAG) ... TEAM
Techniques in Product Selection [*National Association of Manufacturers*] ... TIPS
Techniques of Alcohol Management [*Campaign, sponsored in part by the National Licensed Beverage Association, to prevent drunk driving*] ... TAM
Techniques to Counter Air Defense Suppression (MCD) ... TECADS
Technisch Documentatie Centrum voor der Krijgsmacht [*Netherland Armed Services Technical Documentation and Information Center*] (MCD) ... TDCK
Technische Akademie der Luftwaffe [*Germany*] (MCD) ... TAL
Technische Arbeitsnorm ... TAN
Technische Hochschule [*Technical College*] [*German*] ... TH
Technische Hogeschool Delft, Delft, Netherlands [*Library symbol Library of Congress*] (LCLS) ... NeDTH
Technische Hogeschool te Eindhoven, Eindhoven, Netherlands, [*Library symbol Library of Congress*] (LCLS) ... NeEinT
Technische Informationsbibliothek [*Technical Information Library*] [*Germany*] ... TIB
Technische Kontrollorganisation ... TKO
Technische Universitat [*Technical University*] [*German*] ... TU
Technische Universitat Berlin, Berlin, Germany [*Library symbol Library of Congress*] (LCLS) ... GyBTU
Technische Universitat Carolo Wilhelmina zu Braunschweig, Braunschweig, Federal Republic of Germany [*Library symbol Library of Congress*] (LCLS) ... GyBraTU
Technische Universitat Graz, Graz, Austria [*Library symbol Library of Congress*] (LCLS) ... AsGTU
Technischer Ueberwachungs-Verein [*Technical Watch-Over Association*] [*European product safety organization*] (CDE) ... TUV

Technischord [*Record label*] ... Tec
Techniscope Development [*Vancouver Stock Exchange symbol*] ... TSC
Technisonic [*Record label*] ... TMS
Technitrol, Inc. [*Associated Press*] (SAG) ... Technitrl
Technitrol, Inc. [*AMEX symbol*] (SPSG) ... TNL
Techno Venture Management [*Germany*] ... TVM
Techno-Economic-Environmental Model (EERA) ... TEEM
Technographic Publication ... TP
Technologic ... TECHNOL
Technological ... TCHHNLGCL
Technological ... TECHGL
Technological Adjustment Pay ... TAP
Technological Aid to Creative Thought (PDAA) ... TACT
Technological Aides to Creative Thoughts (IAA) ... TOCS
Technological American Party (EA) ... TAP
Technological and Applied Studies ... TAS
Technological Capabilities Panel (LAIN) ... TCP
Technological Change Committee (EERA) ... TCC
Technological Dependence ... TD
Technological, Economic, Military, and Political Evaluation Routine [*Computer-based simulation model*] ... TEMPER
Technological Education Clearinghouse ... TECH
Technological Engineer [*A publication*] ... TE
Technological Excellence Commission ... TEC
Technological Forecasting ... TF
Technological Forecasting and Simulation for Program Selection (MCD) ... TEFORS
Technological Hierarchy for the Removal of Undesirables and the Subjugation of Humanity [*Fictitious organization in "The Man from UNCLE" television series*] ... THRUSH
Technological Information Exchange System [*UNIDO*] [*United Nations*] ... TIES
Technological Market Segmentation ... TMS
Technological Qualification in Microscopy, Royal Microscopical Society [*British*] (DBQ) ... TechRMS
Technological Service [*Queen's Award*] [*British*] ... T
Technological Services Delivery System [*UNIDO*] ... TSDS
Technological War Plan ... TWP
Technologically Advanced Family [*Lifestyle classification*] ... Taffie
Technologico De Monterrey [*Mexico*] [*Seismograph station code, US Geological Survey*] (SEIS) ... TMM
Technologie Zentrum Steyr [*Steyr Technology Center*] [*German*] ... TZS
Technologie-Centrum Hannover GmbH [*Database producer*] (IID) ... TCH
Technologies ... Technols
Technologies and Innovations in Training Equipment ... TITE
Technologies Network [*Database*] [*EC*] (ECED) ... TECNET
Technologist ... TECH
Technologist Section of the Society of Nuclear Medicine (EA) ... TSSNM
Technology (AAG) ... TECH
Technology (DD) ... tech
Technology ... TECHLGY
Technology ... TECHN
Technology Access Fund [*Chrysler Corp.*] ... TAF
Technology Adaptation Program [*Massachusetts Institute of Technology*] [*Research center*] (RCD) ... TAP
Technology Alert Network (GNE) ... TAN
Technology & Business Communications, Inc. [*Information service or system*] (IID) ... TBC
Technology and Culture [*A publication*] (BRI) ... T&C
Technology and Information Policy Program [*Syracuse University*] [*Research center*] (RCD) ... TIPP
Technology and Innovation Council [*Information Industry Association*] ... TIC
Technology and Livelihood Resource Center [*Philippines*] [*Information service or system*] (IID) ... TLRC
Technology and Physical Science History Associates (IID) ... TAPSHA
Technology and Pollution Control Committee [*Environmental Protection Agency*] ... TAPCC
Technology and Social Change [*Australia*] ... TASC
Technology Application Center [*University of New Mexico*] [*Albuquerque, NM*] ... TAC
Technology Application Program Management [*Air Force*] ... TAPM
Technology Application Team [*NASA*] ... TAT
Technology Applications Group [*Commercial firm*] (IID) ... TAG
Technology Applications Information System ... TAIS
Technology Applications Office [*NASA*] ... TAO
Technology Applications Program [*University of Kentucky*] [*Lexington, KY*] [*NASA*] ... TAP
Technology Area Description (MCD) ... TAD
Technology Assessment Advisory Council [*Washington, DC*] (EGAO) ... TAAC
Technology Assessment Annex (MCD) ... TAA
Technology Assessment Board [*Washington, DC*] (EGAO) ... TAB
Technology Assessment Database [*Fachinformationszentrum Karlsruhe GmbH*] [*Germany Information service or system*] (CRD) ... TA
Technology Assistance Officer [*Small Business Administration*] ... TAO
Technology Assistance Program [*Army*] ... TAP
Technology Availability Date (MCD) ... TAD
Technology Base Enhancement Project ... TBEP
Technology Base Executive Steering Commitee [*Army*] (RDA) ... TBESC
Technology Base Investment Strategy [*Army*] ... TBIS
Technology Catalysts, Inc. [*Information service or system*] (IID) ... TCI
Technology Club of Syracuse, Syracuse, NY [*Library symbol Library of Congress*] (LCLS) ... NSyT
Technology Commercialization Center [*Minority Business Development Administration*] ... TCC
Technology Communications, Inc. ... TCI
Technology Computer-Aided Design [*Computer science*] ... TCAD
Technology Concepts, Inc. [*Sudbury, MA*] [*Telecommunications*] (TSSD) ... TCI
Technology Coordinating Paper ... TCP
Technology Delivery System (NUCP) ... TDS
Technology Demonstration [*NASA*] (RDA) ... TD
Technology Demonstration Satellite [*NASA*] (NASA) ... TDS
Technology Development Advocacy Group [*NASA*] (SSD) ... TDAG
Technology Development and Integration ... TD & I
Technology Development Corp. ... TDC
Technology Development Mission [*NASA*] (SSD) ... TDM
Technology Development Mission Polar [*Canada*] (SSD) ... TDMP
Technology Development Missions Working Group [*NASA*] (SSD) ... TDMWG
Technology Development Vehicle (IEEE) ... TDV
Technology Document (KSC) ... TD
Technology Dynamics Institute [*Telecommunications service*] (TSSD) ... TDI
Technology Education for Children Council (EA) ... TECC
Technology, Entertainment and Design [*Conference*] ... TED
Technology Evaluation and Acquisition Method ... TEAM
Technology Evaluation and Integration (MCD) ... TE & I
Technology for Business (NITA) ... TFB
Technology for Children [*Vocational program*] ... T4C
Technology for Communications International ... TCI
Technology for Communications International, Inc. (AAGC) ... TCI
Technology for Energy Corporation (NRCH) ... TEC
Technology for Object-Oriented Linking and Sharing [*Computer science*] ... TOOLS
Technology for the Automated Generation of Systems (NITA) ... TAGS
Technology Forecasting and Assessment (IAA) ... TFA
Technology Gap ... TG
Technology, Immediate-Diagnosis, Mammography Effective Treatment ... TIME
Technology in Production (IAA) ... TIP
Technology in Public Libraries Section [*Public Library Association*] ... TPLS
Technology in Retrospect and Critical Events in Science [*IITRI*] ... TRACES
Technology in Training [*DoD*] ... TIT
Technology Incubator ... TI
Technology, Information, and Society ... TIS
Technology Information Division [*Department of Energy, Mines, and Resources*] (IID) ... TID
Technology Information Exchange (IID) ... TIE
Technology Information Exchange-Innovation Network [*Ohio State Department of Development*] [*Information service or system*] (IID) ... TIE-IN
Technology Information System [*Lawrence Livermore National Laboratory*] [*University of California*] (IID) ... TIS
Technology Innovation Center [*University of Iowa*] [*Research center*] (RCD) ... TIC
Technology Innovation Office [*Environmental Protection Agency*] ... TIO
Technology Insertion [*Military*] (RDA) ... TI
Technology Integration of Missile Subsystems (MCD) ... TIMS
Technology Integration Office [*Army*] (RDA) ... TIO
Technology Integration Steering Committee [*Army*] (RDA) ... TISC
Technology Internship Program [*Oak Ridge National Laboratory*] ... TIP
Technology Life Cycle (NITA) ... TLC
Technology Management Office [*Army*] ... TMO
Technology Management Review [*Military*] (AFIT) ... TMR
Technology Mobilization and Reemployment Program [*Department of Labor*] ... TMRP
Technology Modernization (AAGC) ... TECHMOD
Technology Modernization (MCD) ... TECMOD
Technology Modernization Program [*DoD*] ... TECHMOD
Technology Needs (MCD) ... TN
Technology Parameter ... TP
Technology Partnerships Canada [*Science and technology strategy*] ... TPC
Technology, People, Environment [*National Science Foundation project*] ... TPE
Technology Performance Requirements Guideline ... TPRG
Technology Planning and Research Division [*Central Electricity Generating Board*] [*British*] (IRUK) ... TPRD
Technology Planning Guide [*Military*] (AFIT) ... TPG
Technology Planning Objectives (MCD) ... TPO
Technology Policy and Assessment Center [*Georgia Institute of Technology*] [*Research center*] (RCD) ... TPAC
Technology Policy Statement [*1982*] [*India*] ... TPS
Technology Program Plan [*Military*] (AFIT) ... TPP
Technology Reinvestment Project [*for converting military to civilian applications*] ... TRP
Technology Reports Centre [*British*] ... TRC
Technology Requirement and Definition Study ... TRADES
Technology Research [*NASDAQ symbol*] (TTSB) ... TRCI
Technology Research Corp. [*Associated Press*] (SAG) ... TchRsh
Technology Research Corp. [*Clearwater, FL*] [*NASDAQ symbol*] (NQ) ... TRCI
Technology Resource Center [*Information service or system Phillipines*] (IID) ... TRC
Technology Review [*A publication*] (BRI) ... Tec R
Technology Satellite (MCD) ... TECHSAT
Technology/Scientific Services, Inc. ... T/SSI
Technology Security Technical Assessment [*DoD*] ... TSTA
Technology Service Group, Inc. [*Associated Press*] (SAG) ... TechSvc
Technology Service Group, Inc. [*NASDAQ symbol*] (SAG) ... TSGI
Technology Service Grp [*NASDAQ symbol*] (TTSB) ... TSGI
Technology Service Grp Wrrt [*NASDAQ symbol*] (TTSB) ... TSGIW
Technology Solutions [*NASDAQ symbol*] (TTSB) ... TSCC
Technology Solutions Co. [*Associated Press*] (SAG) ... TechSol
Technology Solutions Co. [*NASDAQ symbol*] (SPSG) ... TSCC
Technology Student Association (EA) ... TSA
Technology Support Group ... TSG
Technology through Electricity, Electronics, and Microelectronics (AIE) ... TEEM
Technology Training Corporation (AAGC) ... TTC

Technology Transfer (DS) .... TT
Technology Transfer Component Qualification Facility (SSD) .... TTCQF
Technology Transfer Data Bank [*California State University*] [*Sacramento*] [*Information service or system*] (IID) .... TECTRA
Technology Transfer, Fabrication, and Test (RDA) .... TTF & T
Technology Transfer Institute [*Santa Monica, CA*] [*Telecommunications*] (TSSD) .... TTI
Technology Transfer Network [*Michigan State Department of Commerce*] [*Lansing, MI*] [*Information service or system*] (IID) .... TTN
Technology Transfer Society (EA) T2S
Technology Use Studies Center [*Southeastern State College*] .... TUSC
Technology Utilization .... TU
Technology Utilization Center .... TUC
Technology Utilization Division [*NASA*] (IEEE) .... TUD
Technology Utilization Office [*NASA*] .... TUO
Technology Utilization Program [*Defunct*] .... TUP
Technology Validation Experiment (SDI) .... TVE
Technology Without an Interesting Name [*Computer science*] .... TWAIN
Technology-Assisted Learning Market Information Services [*Educational Programming Systems, Inc.*] .... TALMIS
Technology-Based Regional Economic Development .... TRED
Technonet Asia (EA) .... TA
Technoogy Innovation (IAA) .... TI
Technopaegnion [*of Ausonius*] [*Classical studies*] (OCD) .... Technop
Technophility Index [*Mining technology*] .... TP
Technopolymer Structure [*Engineering plastics*] .... TPS
Technoserve, Norwalk, CT [*Library symbol Library of Congress*] (LCLS) .... CtNowaT
Technoserve's World Harvest Fund (EA) .... TWHF
Tech-Ops Sevcon, Inc. [*Associated Press*] (SAG) .... TecOpsSv
Tech-Ops Sevcon, Inc. [*AMEX symbol*] (SAG) .... TO
Tech-Sym [*NYSE symbol*] (TTSB) .... TSY
Tech-Sym Corp. [*Associated Press*] (SAG) .... TchSym
Tech-Sym Corp. [*NYSE symbol*] (SPSG) .... TSY
Teck Centennial Public Library, Kirkland Lake, ON, Canada [*Library symbol Library of Congress*] (LCLS) .... CaOKIT
Teck Centennial Public Library, Kirkland Lake, Ontario [*Library symbol National Library of Canada*] (NLC) .... OKLT
Teck Corp Cl'A' [*TS symbol*] (TTSB) .... TEK A
Teck Corp. [*Toronto Stock Exchange symbol Vancouver Stock Exchange symbol*] .... TEK
Teck Mining Group Ltd., Elizabeth Watson Library, Vancouver, BC, Canada [*Library symbol Library of Congress*] (LCLS) .... CaBVaTE
Tecmar Music Synthesis System .... TMSS
Tecnavia [*France ICAO designator*] (FAAC) .... TNV
Tecnol Medical Products [*NASDAQ symbol*] (SPSG) .... TCNL
Tecnol Medical Products, Inc. [*Associated Press*] (SAG) .... TecnolM
Tecnomatix Technologies Ltd. [*NASDAQ symbol*] (SAG) .... TCNO
Tecnomatix Technologies Ltd. [*Associated Press*] (SAG) .... Tecnmtx
Tecnomatix Technologies Ltd [*NASDAQ symbol*] (TTSB) .... TCNOF
TECO Energy [*NYSE symbol*] (TTSB) .... TE
TECO Energy, Inc. [*NYSE symbol*] (SPSG) .... TE
TECO Energy, Inc. [*Associated Press*] (SAG) .... TECO
Tecrad, Inc., Ancienne-Lorette, Quebec [*Library symbol National Library of Canada*] (NLC) .... QQTE
TECSULT, Montreal, Quebec [*Library symbol National Library of Canada*] (NLC) .... QMABB
TecSyn International [*TS Symbol*] (TTSB) .... TSN
Tecsyn International, Inc. [*Toronto Stock Exchange symbol*] .... TSN
Tectonic Surface Uplift Rate [*Biology*] .... TSUR
Tectoreticular Neuron [*Neurology*] .... TRN
Tectorial Membrane [*of the cochlea*] [*Ear anatomy*] .... TM
Tecumseh, MI [*Location identifier FAA*] (FAAL) .... TCU
Tecumseh Products Cl'A' [*NASDAQ symbol*] (TTSB) .... TECUA
Tecumseh Products Cl'B' [*NASDAQ symbol*] (TTSB) .... TECUB
Tecumseh Products Co. [*NASDAQ symbol*] (NQ) .... TECU
Tecumseh Products Co. [*Associated Press*] (SAG) .... Tecum
Tecumseh Public Library, Tecumseh, MI [*Library symbol Library of Congress*] (LCLS) .... MiTe
Tecumseh Township Public Library, Bond Head, Ontario [*Library symbol National Library of Canada*] (BIB) .... OBHT
Ted McGinley Fan Club (EA) .... TMFC
Ted Nugent United Sportsmen of America .... TNUSA
Ted Smith Aircraft [*ICAO aircraft manufacturer identifier*] (ICAO) .... TS
Teddy Air AS [*Norway ICAO designator*] (FAAC) .... TED
Teddy Boy (ODBW) .... Ted
Tee [*Piping joint, etc.*] [*Technical drawings*] .... T
Tee Com Electronics, Inc. [*Associated Press*] (SAG) .... TeeCom
Tee Comm Electronics, Inc. [*Associated Press*] (SAG) .... TeeCm
Tee Comm Electronics, Inc. [*NASDAQ symbol*] (SAG) .... TENWF
Tee Comm Electronics, Inc. [*NASDAQ symbol*] (SAG) .... TENX
Tee-Comm Electronics [*NASDAQ symbol*] (TTSB) .... TENXF
Tee-Comm Electronics, Inc. [*Toronto Stock Exchange symbol*] .... TEN
Teekay Shipping [*NYSE symbol*] (TTSB) .... TK
Teekay Shipping Corp. [*Associated Press*] (SAG) .... Teekay
Teekay Shipping Corp. [*NYSE symbol*] (SAG) .... TK
Teekin [*Tonga*] [*Seismograph station code, US Geological Survey*] (SEIS) .... TEK
Teen Age Republican [*Lifestyle classification*] .... TAR
Teen Age Republicans .... TARS
Teen Association of Model Railroading (EA) .... TAMR
Teen International Entomology Group [*Later, YES*] (EA) .... TIEG
Teen Missions International (EA) .... TMI
Teen-Age Assembly of America (EA) .... TAAA
Teenage Attitudes and Practices Survey [*Centers for Disease Control*] .... TAPS
Teen-Age Employment Skills Training, Inc. .... TEST
Teenage Health Education Teaching Assistants [*National Foundation for the Prevention of Oral Disease*] .... THETA
Teenage, Infants, and Girls' Fashion Fair Organisation [*British*] (BI) .... TIGFFO
Teen-Age Mutant Ninja Turtles [*Name of comic book and cartoon characters and line of toys by Playmates Toys*] .... TMNT
Teens for Retarded Youth [*Program in Fairfax County, Virginia*] .... TRY
Teens with a Positive Attitude .... TWAPA
Teeples Ranch [*Montana*] [*Seismograph station code, US Geological Survey Closed*] (SEIS) .... TEE
Teeshin Resources Ltd. [*Vancouver Stock Exchange symbol*] .... TEE
Teeside Automated Library (NITA) .... TEAL
Tees-Side [*British ICAO location identifier*] (ICLI) .... EGNV
Tees-Side [*England*] [*Airport symbol*] (OAG) .... MME
Teeswater Branch, Bruce County Public Library, Ontario [*Library symbol National Library of Canada*] (NLC) .... OTEE
Teeswater Sheep Breeders Association [*British*] (DBA) .... TSBA
Teeth [*Technical drawings*] .... T
Teeth per Inch [*of cog wheels*] .... TPI
Teetotaler [*Slang*] .... TT
Tefe [*Brazil ICAO location identifier*] (ICLI) .... SBTF
Tefe [*Brazil*] [*Airport symbol*] (OAG) .... TFF
Tefillin (BJA) .... Tef
TEFLON Bonding Kit .... TBK
TEFLON Dielectric Capacitor .... TDC
TEFLON Insulation Material .... TIM
TEFLON-Coated Aluminum Foil .... TCAF
TEFLON-Insulated Wire .... TIW
Tegal Corp. [*Associated Press*] (SAG) .... Tegal
Tegal Corp. [*NASDAQ symbol*] (SAG) .... TGAL
TEGAS Extended Simulator Behavioral (NITA) .... TEXSIM/B
Tegra Enterprises, Inc. [*Vancouver Stock Exchange symbol*] .... TEA
Tegucigalpa [*Honduras*] [*Airport symbol*] (OAG) .... TGU
Tegucigalpa/Toncontin Internacional [*Honduras*] [*ICAO location identifier*] (ICLI) .... MHTG
Tegula [*Entomology*] .... Teg
Tehachapi, CA [*FM radio station call letters*] .... KTPI
Tehachapi, CA [*Location identifier FAA*] (FAAL) .... TSP
Tehama County Free Library, Red Bluff, CA [*Library symbol Library of Congress*] (LCLS) .... CRbCL
Tehillim (BJA) .... Teh
Tehran [*Iran*] [*ICAO location identifier*] (ICLI) .... OIIT
Tehran [*Iran*] [*ICAO location identifier*] (ICLI) .... OIIX
Tehran [*Iran*] [*Seismograph station code, US Geological Survey*] (SEIS) .... TEH
Tehran [*Iran*] [*Airport symbol*] (OAG) .... THR
Tehran Area Support Center [*Military*] (MCD) .... TASC
Tehran/Doshan Tappeh [*Iran*] [*ICAO location identifier*] (ICLI) .... OIID
Tehran/Ghaleh Morghi [*Iran*] [*ICAO location identifier*] (ICLI) .... OIIG
Tehran/Mehrabad International [*Iran*] [*ICAO location identifier*] (ICLI) .... OIII
Tehran Union Catalogue of Scientific Periodicals [*A publication*] .... TUCOSP
Tehrik-i-Istiqlal [*Solidarity Party*] [*See also TIP Pakistan*] [*Political party*] (FEA) .... TI
Tehrik-i-Istiqlal [*Solidarity Party*] [*See also TI Pakistan*] [*Political party*] (FEA) .... TIP
Tehua [*Race of maize*] .... TEH
Tehuacan [*Mexico ICAO location identifier*] (ICLI) .... MMHC
Teich [*Pond*] [*German military*] .... T
Teichoic Acid Crude Extract [*Medicine*] (DMAA) .... TACE
Teichoic Acids [*Biochemistry*] .... TA
Teichuronic Acid [*Biochemistry*] .... TUA
Teignbridge [*England*] .... TEIGNBR
Teignmouth [*Urban district in England*] .... TEIGN
Teikyo Marycrest University (GAGS) .... Teikyo Marycrest U
Teilhard Centre for the Future of Man (EAIO) .... TCFM
Teisko [*Finland ICAO location identifier*] (ICLI) .... EFTS
Teissler's Court of Appeal, Parish of Orleans, Reports [*1903-17*] [*A publication*] (DLA) .... Teiss
Teissler's Court of Appeal, Parish of Orleans, Reports [*1903-17*] [*A publication*] (DLA) .... Teissler
Tejas Airlines [*ICAO designator*] (AD) .... TB
Tejas Gas 5.25% Cv Dep Pfd [*NYSE symbol*] (TTSB) .... TEJPrA
Tejas Gas Corp. [*NYSE symbol*] (SPSG) .... TEJ
Tejas Gas Corp. [*Associated Press*] (SAG) .... Tejas
Tejas Gas Corp. [*Associated Press*] (SAG) .... TejasGas
Tejas Gas Corp. [*Associated Press*] (SAG) .... TejasGs
Tejas Gas Cp 9.96% Dep Pfd [*NYSE symbol*] (TTSB) .... TEJPr
Tejas Power [*Associated Press*] (SAG) .... TejasPw
Tejas Power Corp. [*AMEX symbol*] (SPSG) .... TPC
Tejon Ranch [*AMEX symbol*] (TTSB) .... TRC
Tejon Ranch Co. [*Associated Press*] (SAG) .... TejnR
Tejon Ranch Co. [*AMEX symbol*] (SPSG) .... TRC
Tekakwitha Conference National Center [*Later, TCNC*] (EA) .... TC
Tekakwitha Conference National Center (EA) .... TCNC
Tekamah Carnegie Public Library, Tekamah, NE [*Library symbol Library of Congress*] (LCLS) .... NbTe
Tekamah, NE [*Location identifier FAA*] (FAAL) .... TQE
TEKELEC [*Calabasas, CA*] [*NASDAQ symbol*] (NQ) .... TKLC
Tekelec, Inc. [*Associated Press*] (SAG) .... Tekelec
Teknekron Communications Systems [*NASDAQ symbol*] (SPSG) .... TCSI
Tek-Net International Ltd. (Canada) [*Vancouver Stock Exchange symbol*] .... TKN
Teknikvetenskapliga FoskningsRadet [*Swedish Research Council for Engineering Sciences*] .... TFR
Tekniska Litteratursallskapet (NITA) .... TLS
Tekniska Nomenklaturcentralen [*Swedish Center for Technical Terminology*] [*Information service or system*] (IID) .... TNC
Tekniska Rapporter (NITA) .... TR

Tekonsha Public Library, Tekonsha, MI [*Library symbol Library of Congress*] (LCLS) .... MiTek
Tekst en Uitleg (BJA) .... TeU
Tektronix Development Co. (NITA) .... TDC
Tektronix, Inc. [*NYSE symbol*] (SPSG) .... TEK
Tektronix, Inc. [*Associated Press*] (SAG) .... Tektrnx
Tektronix, Inc., Beaverton, OR [*Library symbol Library of Congress*] (LCLS) .... OrBT
Tel Argentina-France Tel'B'ADS [*NYSE symbol*] (TTSB) .... TEO
Tel Aviv [*Israel*] [*ICAO location identifier*] (ICLI) .... LLTA
Tel Aviv [*Israel*] (BJA) .... TA
Tel Aviv/D. Ben Gurion [*Israel*] [*ICAO location identifier*] (ICLI) .... LLBG
Tel Aviv/Sde Dov [*Israel*] [*ICAO location identifier*] (ICLI) .... LLSD
Tel Aviv Stock Exchange [*Israel*] (IMH) .... TASE
Tel Aviv University [*Israel*] .... TAU
Tel Aviv University Studies in Law [*Tel-Aviv, Israel*] [*A publication*] (DLA) .... Tel Aviv Univ Stud L
Tel Aviv University, Tel Aviv, Israel [*Library symbol Library of Congress*] (LCLS) .... IsTU
Tel Aviv University Ultra-Violet Explorer [*Israel*] .... TAUVEX
Tel Aviv/Yafo [*Israel*] [*Airport symbol*] (OAG) .... SDV
Tel Aviv-Yafo [*Israel*] [*Airport symbol*] (OAG) .... TLV
TEL Electronics, Inc. [*American Fork, UT*] [*NASDAQ symbol*] (NQ) .... TELS
TEL Offshore Tr UBI [*NASDAQ symbol*] (TTSB) .... TELOZ
TEL Offshore Trust [*Associated Press*] (SAG) .... TEL Off
Tel Offshore Trust [*NASDAQ symbol*] (NQ) .... TELO
Tela [*Honduras*] [*ICAO location identifier*] (ICLI) .... MHTE
Tela [*Honduras*] [*Airport symbol*] (AD) .... TEA
Telamarketing Communications, Inc. [*Louisville, KY*] [*Telecommunications*] (TSSD) .... TMC
Tel-Aviv University Studies in Law [*Tel-Aviv, Israel*] [*A publication*] (DLA) .... Tel-Aviv U Stud L
Telco Group, Inc. [*Telecommunications service*] (TSSD) .... TGI
Telco Systems [*NASDAQ symbol*] (TTSB) .... TELC
Telco Systems, Inc. [*NASDAQ symbol*] (NQ) .... TELC
Telco Systems, Inc. [*Associated Press*] (SAG) .... Telco
TelCom Semiconductor, Inc. [*Associated Press*] (SAG) .... TelCSm
TelCom Semiconductor, Inc. [*NASDAQ symbol*] (SAG) .... TLCM
TelCom Seminconductor [*NASDAQ symbol*] (TTSB) .... TLCM
Tel-Com Wireless Cable TV [*NASDAQ symbol*] (TTSB) .... TCTV
Tel-Com Wireless Cable TV Corp. [*NASDAQ symbol*] (SAG) .... TCTV
Tel-Com Wireless Cable TV Corp. [*Associated Press*] (SAG) .... TelCTV
Tel-Com Wireless CATV Wrrt [*NASDAQ symbol*] (TTSB) .... TCTVW
Tel-Communications [*Associated Press*] (SAG) .... TelCm
Tele Danmark A/S ADS [*NYSE symbol*] (TTSB) .... TLD
Tele Danmark Co. [*Associated Press*] (SAG) .... TeleDan
Tele Danmark Co. [*NYSE symbol*] (SAG) .... TLD
Tele Video Systems, Inc. [*Associated Press*] (SAG) .... Telvid
Teleactive Shock Electronic Repulsion [*Nonlethal weapon*] .... TASER
Teleautograph [*ICAO designator*] (FAAC) .... TELAU
Telebase Systems, Inc. [*Information service or system*] (IID) .... TSI
Telebit Corp. [*NASDAQ symbol*] (SAG) .... TBIT
Telebit Corp. [*Associated Press*] (SAG) .... Telebit
Telechips Corp. [*NASDAQ symbol*] (SAG) .... TCHP
Telechips Corp. [*Associated Press*] (SAG) .... Telech
Telechips Corp. [*Associated Press*] (SAG) .... Telechps
Telechips Corp. Wrrt [*NASDAQ symbol*] (TTSB) .... TCHPW
Telecine .... T/C
Telecom Analysis Systems, Inc. .... TAS
Telecom Argentina Stet France Telecom SA [*NYSE symbol*] (SAG) .... TEO
Telecom Argentina Stet France Telecom SA [*Associated Press*] (SAG) .... TlcmArg
Telecom Broadcasting, Inc. [*Oceanside, CA*] [*Telecommunications service*] (TSSD) .... TBI
Telecom Canada Remote Interface Monitoring and Management System .... TRIMMS
Telecom Corp. New Zealand [*NYSE symbol*] (SPSG) .... NZT
Telecom Corp. New Zealand ADS [*NYSE symbol*] (TTSB) .... NZT
Telecom Corp. of New Zealand [*Associated Press*] (SAG) .... TelcNZ
Telecom Eireann [*Dublin, Ireland*] [*Telecommunications service*] (TSSD) .... TE
Telecom Gold (NITA) .... TG
Telecom Publishing Group (IID) .... TPG
Telecom Securitor Cellular Radio Ltd. [*British*] .... TSCR
Telecom Small Enterprise Policy Panel [*Australia*] .... TSEPP
Telecom Technology Showcase [*British*] .... TTS
Tele-Comm Inc. 'A' Liberty Media [*NASDAQ symbol*] (TTSB) .... LBTYA
TeleComm TCI Grp 6% Exch Pfd [*NASDAQ symbol*] (TTSB) .... TCOMP
Telecommand (NASA) .... TLC
Telecommanded Inertially Referenced Attitude Control System (MCD) .... TIRACS
Tele-Comm'B'Liberty Media [*NASDAQ symbol*] (TTSB) .... LBTYB
Telecommunicacoes Aeronauticas SA [*Brazil*] [*ICAO designator*] (FAAC) .... TASA
Telecommunicacoes Brasilerias SA Telebras [*NYSE symbol*] (SAG) .... TBR
Telecommunicacoes Brasilerias SA Telebras [*Associated Press*] (SAG) .... TelBrasl
Tele-Communic'ATCI Group [*NASDAQ symbol*] (TTSB) .... TCOMA
Telecommunicatinos Products Information Retrieval and Simulation (MHDI) .... TPIS
Telecommunication .... TELEC
Telecommunication .... TELECC
Telecommunication Alarm Surveillance and Control [*AT & T*] .... TASC
Telecommunication Authority [*ICAO designator*] (ICDA) .... YT
Telecommunication/Data Management System .... TCDMS
Telecommunication Engineering and Manufacturing Association [*British*] (IAA) .... TEMA
Telecommunication Equipment Low-Cost Acquisition Method [*Navy*] .... TELCAM
Telecommunication Industry .... TI
Telecommunication Information Control System .... TICS
Telecommunication Interference Filter [*Computer science*] .... TIF
Telecommunication Laboratories [*Taiwan*] .... TCL
Telecommunication Liaison Staff (IEEE) .... TLS
Telecommunication Management and Control [*AT & T*] .... TMAC
Telecommunication Network (OSI) .... TELNET
Telecommunication Products Plus Technology [*Pennwell Publishing Co.*] [*Littleton, MA*] (TSSD) .... TPT
Telecommunication Program Generator .... TPG
Telecommunication Switching System .... TSS
Telecommunication Traffic Association [*British*] (BI) .... TTA
Telecommunication Training Centre [*Fiji*] [*Telecommunications*] .... TTC
Telecommunication Working Group .... TCWG
Telecommunications .... TC
Telecommunications (NASA) .... TELCOM
Telecommunications (AFM) .... TELECOM
Telecommunications .... TELECOM
Telecommunications (DD) .... telecommun
Telecommunications Access Language .... TAL
Telecommunications Access Method .... TAM
Telecommunications Access Method [*IBM Corp.*] [*Computer science*] .... TCAM
Telecommunications Advisory Board .... TAB
Telecommunications and Command and Control Program [*Air Force*] (AFIT) .... T & CCP
Telecommunications and Electronics, Canadian Air Transportation Administration, Transport Canada [*Telecommunications et Electronique, Administration Canadienne des Transports Aeriens, Transports Canada*] **Edmonton, Alberta** [*Library symbol National Library of Canada*] (NLC) .... AETATE
Telecommunications and Electronics Directorate, Transport Canada [*Direction des Telecommunications et de l'Electronique, Transports Canada*] **Ottawa, Ontario** [*Library symbol Obsolete National Library of Canada*] (NLC) .... OOTTE
Telecommunications and Information Infrastructure Assistance Program .... TIIAP
Telecommunications and Information Infrastructure Assistance Program [*Department of Commerce*] .... TIIAP
Telecommunications and Information Systems Laboratory [*University of Kansas*] [*Research center*] (RCD) .... TISL
Telecommunications and Network Management .... TNM
Telecommunications and Telephone Association [*Arlington, VA*] [*Telecommunications service*] (TSSD) .... TTA
Tele-Communications Association (EA) .... TCA
Telecommunications Authority [*FAA designator*] (FAAC) .... YTY
Telecommunications Authority of Singapore (TSSD) .... TELECOMS
Telecommunications Authority Singapore .... TAS
Telecommunications Automation Directorate [*Army*] (RDA) .... TAD
Telecommunications Carrier System (NITA) .... T-carrier system
Telecommunications Censorship Technician [*Navy*] .... ESK
Telecommunications Censorship Technician, Chief [*Navy*] .... ESKC
Telecommunications Censorship Technician, Master Chief [*Navy*] .... ESKCM
Telecommunications Censorship Technician, Senior Chief [*Navy*] .... ESKCS
Telecommunications Center (CET) .... TCC
Telecommunications Certifying Officer [*Air Force*] (AFIT) .... TCO
Tele-Communications Class A [*NASDAQ symbol*] (SAG) .... LBTY
Tele-Communications Class A [*Associated Press*] (SAG) .... TCA LM
Tele-Communications Class A [*Associated Press*] (SAG) .... TCB LM
Tele-Communications Class A [*NASDAQ symbol*] (SAG) .... TCOM
Tele-Communications Class A [*Associated Press*] (SAG) .... TelC
Tele-Communications Class A [*Associated Press*] (SAG) .... TeleCom
Telecommunications, Command, Control, and Computer System TC3
Telecommunications/Communications Terminal (MCD) .... TCC/CT
Telecommunications Consulting Group, Inc. [*Washington, DC*] (TSSD) .... TCG
Telecommunications Consulting Services [*Richard A. Eisner & Co.*] [*New York, NY*] (TSSD) .... TCS
Telecommunications Consumer Coalition [*Defunct*] (EA) .... TCC
Telecommunications Control System [*Toshiba Corp.*] [*Computer science*] .... TCS
Telecommunications Control System-Advanced Function (MHDI) .... TCS-AF
Telecommunications Control Unit (NITA) .... TCU
Telecommunications Cooperative Network (EA) .... TCN
Telecommunications Coordinating Committee [*Department of State*] .... TCC
Telecommunications Counselor [*Voice & Data Resources, Inc.*] [*Information service or system Defunct*] (IID) .... TC
Telecommunications Data Interface .... TDI
Telecommunications Data-Link Monitor (CET) .... TDM
Telecommunications Dealers Association (EA) .... TDA
Telecommunications Development Bureau [*United Nations*] (DUND) .... BDT
Telecommunications Device for the Deaf .... TDD
Telecommunications Documentation (NITA) .... TELEDOC
Telecommunications Electronic Reviews [*A publication*] .... TER
Telecommunications Engineering (WDAA) .... TE
Telecommunications Engineering Establishment [*British*] .... TEE
Telecommunications Engineering, Inc. [*Dallas, TX*] (TSSD) .... TEI
Telecommunications Executive Management Institute of Canada (TSSD) .... TEMIC
Telecommunications Facility .... TELEFAC
Telecommunications Flying Unit [*British*] .... TFU
Telecommunications for the Deaf and Disabled .... TDD
Telecommunications for the Deaf, Inc. (EA) .... TDI
Telecommunications Group [*Range Commanders Council*] [*NASA*] .... TCG
Telecommunications Headquarters (NITA) .... THQ
Tele-Communications, Inc. [*Brookpark, OH*] (TSSD) .... TCI
Tele-Communications, Inc. [*NASDAQ symbol*] (NQ) .... TCOM
Telecommunications Industry Association (EA) .... TIA
Telecommunications Industry Forum (EA) .... TCIF

Telecommunications Industry Research [British] (ECON) .... TIR
Telecommunications Information Center [George Washington University] [Information service or system] (IID) .... TIC
Telecommunications Information Centre-Telecommunications Office for Consumers (NITA) .... TIC-TOC
Telecommunications Instruction Module System (IAA) .... TIMS
Tele-Communications International, Inc. [Associated Press] (SAG) .... TelC Int
Tele-Communications International, Inc. [NASDAQ symbol] (SAG) .... TINTA
Telecommunications International Union [Defunct] (EA) .... TIU
Tele-Communications Intl [NASDAQ symbol] (TTSB) .... TINTA
Telecommunications Library, Transport Canada [Bibliotheque de Telecommunications, Transports Canada], Ottawa, Ontario [Library symbol National Library of Canada] (NLC) .... OOTCO
Telecommunications Management Association (NITA) .... TMA
Telecommunications Management College (NITA) .... TMC
Telecommunications Management Corp. [Needham Heights, MA] (TSSD) ..... TMC
Telecommunications Management, Inc. [Oakbrook, IL] [Telecommunications] (TSSD) .... TMI
Telecommunications Management Network (MCD) .... TMN
Telecommunications Management System (MHDI) .... TCMS
Telecommunications Manager (MHDB) .... TCM
Telecommunications Managers Association [Orpington, England] (TSSD) .... TMA
Telecommunications Managers Association - Belgium .... TMAB
Telecommunications Managers Association of the Capital Area (TSSD) .... TMACA
Telecommunications Marketing Corp. [Bay Shore, NY] (TSSD) .... TMC
Telecommunications Marketing Resource Ltd. [Telecommunications service] (TSSD) .... TMR
Telecommunications Marketing/Sales Association [Defunct] (EA) .... TMSA
Telecommunications Message Switcher .... TMS
Telecommunications Modernization Project (AAGC) .... TMP
Telecommunications Monitor .... TCM
Telecommunications Network Architects [Telecommunications service] (TSSD) .... TNA
Telecommunications Network for the Deaf .... TND
Telecommunications Network Services [Data Resources] [Information service or system] (CRD) .... TNS
Telecommunications of Jamaica [Commercial firm] (ECON) .... TOJ
Telecommunications Officers' Association [Australia] .... TOA
Telecommunications Performance and Interface Document (MCD) .... TPID
Telecommunications Planning Committee [Civil Defense] .... TPC
Telecommunications Processing Unit .... TPU
Telecommunications Processor (IAA) .... TCP
Telecommunications Processor [FAA] (TAG) .... TP
Telecommunications Program and Control (IAA) .... TPC
Telecommunications Program Objective [Army] (AABC) .... TPO
Telecommunications Programming Language (IAA) .... TPL
Telecommunications Programming System .... TPS
Telecommunications Relay Service [Hearing-impaired technology] .... TRS
Telecommunications Requirements (MCD) .... TELER
Telecommunications Research and Action Center [Washington, DC] [Information service or system Telecommunications] (TSSD) .... TRAC
Telecommunications Research Center [University of Louisville] [Research center] (RCD) .... TRC
Telecommunications Research Establishment [British military] (DMA) .... TRE
Telecommunications Research Group [Culver City, CA] [Telecommunications] (TSSD) .... TRG
Telecommunications Sales Superintendents' Association [A union] [British] .... TSSA
Telecommunications Satellite .... TELESAT
Telecommunications Security [Army] (AABC) .... TSEC
Telecommunications Security System (MCD) .... TSS
Telecommunications Service Order [Telecommunications] (TEL) .... TSO
Telecommunications Service Request (CET) .... TSR
Telecommunications Service System (NITA) .... TSS
Telecommunications Software User's Network [Telesun Corp.] [Englewood, OH] (TSSD) .... TELESUN
Telecommunications Strategy Group [Australia] .... TSG
Telecommunications Study Unit [American Topical Association] [Defunct] (EA) .... TSU
Telecommunications System .... TCS
Telecommunications System .... TS
Telecommunications Systems Architecture Planning Group (DNAB) .... TSAPG
Telecommunications Systems Corp. (IAA) .... TSC
Telecommunications Systems Engineering (IAA) .... TSE
Telecommunications Technical Officer [British] .... TTO
Telecommunications Technician [British military] (DMA) .... TT
Telecommunications Techniques Corp. .... TTC
Telecommunications Terminal Systems .... TTS
Telecommunications Traffic and Supervisory Officers' Association [Australia] .... TTSOA
Telecommunications Translator (IAA) .... TLT
Telecommunications Users' Association (TSSD) .... TUA
Telecommunications Users Coalition (EA) .... TUC
Telecommunications Users Group [Montclair, NJ] [Telecommunications service] (TSSD) .... TUG
Telecommunications Workers Union [Canada] .... TWU
Tele-Communic'B'TCI Group [NASDAQ symbol] (TTSB) .... TCOMB
TeleCommuting Report [Electronic Services Unlimited] [Information service or system] (CRD) .... TC
Telecomputer Applications Group .... TAG
Telecomputer Research, Inc. [Bala Cynwyd, PA] [Information service or system Telecommunications] (TSSD) .... TRI
Telecomputing Corp. (IAA) .... TC
Telecomputing Corporation of America (NITA) .... TCA

TELECOMS Authorities Cryptographic Algorithm [Bell Telephone encryption chip] .... TACA
TELECOMS On-Line Data System [Telecommunications] (TEL) .... TOLD
Telecomun Brasil-Telbras ADS [NYSE symbol] (TTSB) .... TBR
Telecomunicacoes Aeronauticas SA [Brazil] [ICAO designator] (FAAC) .... XLT
Telecomunicacoes Aeronauticas Sociedada Anonima (TASA) [Brazil ICAO designator] (ICDA) XL
Teleconcepts in Communications, Inc. [New York, NY] [Telecommunications] (TSSD) .... TCC
Teleconference Association of Canada [Toronto, ON] [Information service or system] (TSSD) .... TAC
Teleconference Network [University of Nebraska Medical Center] [Omaha, NE] [Telecommunications] (TSSD) .... TCN
Teleconference Network of Texas [University of Texas] [San Antonio] [Telecommunications] (TSSD) .... TNT
Teleconference System [Memorial University of Newfoundland] [St. John's, NF] [Telecommunications] (TSSD) .... TCS
Teleconferencing Systems Canada Ltd. [Etobicoke, ON] [Telecommunications service] (TSSD) .... TSC
Teleconferencing Systems International, Inc. [Elk Grove Village, IL] [Telecommunications] (TSSD) .... TCI
Teleconferencing Systems International, Inc. [Elk Grove Village, IL] (TSSD) .... TSI
Teledata Communication [NASDAQ symbol] (TTSB) .... TLDCF
Teledata Communications [Associated Press] (SAG) .... Teledta
Teledata Communications [NASDAQ symbol] (SAG) .... TLDC
Teledata Processing .... TDP
Teledate Equipment [Military] .... TELD
Telediffusion de France [Broadcasting agency] [French] .... TDF
Teledifusao de Macau [Radio and television broadcasting company] [Macau] (FEA) .... TDM
Teledyne Airborne Geophysical Services .... TAGS
Teledyne CAE Engineering Library, Toledo, OH [Library symbol Library of Congress] (LCLS) .... OTT
Teledyne Canada Ltd. [Toronto Stock Exchange symbol] .... TDC
Teledyne Continental Motors [ICAO designator] (FAAC) .... TCM
Teledyne Electrically-Alterable Digital Differential Analyzer (IAA) .... TEADDA
Teledyne Geotech Alexandria Laboratories .... TGAL
Teledyne, Inc. [NYSE symbol] (SPSG) .... TDY
Teledyne, Inc. [Associated Press] (SAG) .... Teldy
Teledyne, Inc. [Associated Press] (SAG) .... Teldyn
Teledyne Inc. Sr'E' Pfd [NYSE symbol] (TTSB) .... TDYPrE
Teledyne Materials Research (IAA) .... TMR
Teledyne Systems Corp. .... TSC
Teledyne-Wah Chang Albany, Albany, OR (LCLS) .... OrAIT
Tele-Engineering Corp. [Telecommunications service] (TSSD) .... TE
Tele-Engineering Corp. [Framingham, MA] [Telecommunications] (TSSD) .... TEC
Telefiche Image Processor (NITA) .... TIP
Teleflex, Inc. [Associated Press] (SAG) .... Teleflex
Teleflex, Inc. [NYSE symbol] (SAG) .... TFX
Teleflora Australia .... TA
Teleflora Delivery Service (EA) .... TDS
Telefomin [Papua New Guinea] [Airport symbol] (OAG) .... TFM
Telefonica De Argentina ADS [NYSE symbol] (TTSB) .... TAR
Telefonica de Argentina SA [NYSE symbol] (SAG) .... TAR
Telefonica de Argentina SA [Associated Press] (SAG) .... TelArg
Telefonica de Espana ADS [NYSE symbol] (TTSB) .... TEF
Telefonica de Espana SA [NYSE symbol] (SPSG) .... TEF
Telefonica de Espana SA [Associated Press] (SAG) .... Telef
Telefonica de Espana SA [Associated Press] (SAG) .... TelefEsp
Telefonica del Peru SA [NYSE symbol] (SAG) .... TDP
Telefonica del Peru SA [Associated Press] (SAG) .... TelPeru
Telefonos de Mexico [Associated Press] (SAG) .... TelefMex
Telefonos de Mexico [NYSE symbol] (SAG) .... TMX
Telefonos de Mexico SA [Associated Press] .... TelMex
Telefonos de Mexico SA de CV [NASDAQ symbol] (NQ) .... TFON
Telefonos de Mexico'A'ADR [NASDAQ symbol] (TTSB) .... TFONY
Telefonos de Mexico'L'ADS [NYSE symbol] (TTSB) .... TMX
Telefunken [Record label] [Germany, etc.] .... T
Telefunken Computer AG (IAA) .... TC
Telefunken Microelectronik .... TEMIC
Telefunken (Pressed by Decca) [Record label] [Great Britain] .... DT
Telefunken Variable Microgroove [Record label] [Germany] .... TV
Telefunken-Decca [Video disk system] .... TeD
Telefunken-Decca [Video disk system] (IAA) .... TELDEC
Telegen Corp. [Associated Press] (SAG) .... Telegen
Telegen Corp. [NASDAQ symbol] (SAG) .... TLGN
Teleglobe Canada .... TELC
Teleglobe Canada .... TELEC
Teleglobe Canada .... TGC
Teleglobe Canada, Montreal, PQ, Canada [Library symbol Library of Congress] (LCLS) .... CaQMTGC
Teleglobe Canada, Montreal, Quebec [Library symbol National Library of Canada] (NLC) .... QMTGC
Telegrafska Agencija Nove Jugoslavije [Press agency] [Yugoslavia] .... TANJUG
Telegram (BJA) .... T
Telegram .... TE
Telegram .... TEL
Telegram (WDMC) .... tel
Telegram .... TELE
Telegram .... TELEG
Telegram .... TELG
Telegram (ROG) .... TELM
Telegram .... TG
Telegram (ROG) .... TGM

Telegram (IAA) ... TLG
Telegram for Delivery by Telephone ... TF
Telegram Identification Group [*Telecommunications*] (TEL) ... TIG
Telegramme Multiple [*Telegram with Multiple Addresses*] [*French*] (ROG) ... TM
Telegraph [*JETDS nomenclature*] ... G
Telegraph (ROG) ... T
Telegraph ... TEL
Telegraph (WDMC) ... tel
Telegraph ... TELE
Telegraph ... TELEG
Telegraph ... TELG
Telegraph ... TG
Telegraph (IAA) ... TH
Telegraph (AAG) ... TLG
Telegraph and Data Message Generator (MCD) ... TDMG
Telegraph and Data Signals Analyzer (MCD) ... TDSA
Telegraph and Public Address [*JETDS nomenclature*] ... IA
Telegraph Apparatus [*JETDS nomenclature*] [*Military*] (CET) ... TH
Telegraph Automatic Routing in the Field (IAA) ... TARIT
Telegraph Bureau ... TB
Telegraph Communic Ltd [*NASDAQ symbol*] (TTSB) ... TELGF
Telegraph Communications [*Commercial firm Associated Press*] (SAG) ... TelC
Telegraph Communications [*Commercial firm Associated Press*] (SAG) ... TelegCm
Telegraph Communications [*NASDAQ symbol*] (SAG) ... TELG
Telegraph Communications [*NASDAQ symbol*] (SAG) ... TLGZ
Telegraph Communications Wrrt [*NASDAQ symbol*] (TTSB) ... TLGZF
Telegraph Condenser Co. (IAA) ... TCC
Telegraph Construction and Maintenance (IAA) ... TCAM
Telegraph Delivery Order ... TDO
Telegraph Department ... TD
Telegraph Distortion Measuring System ... TDMS
Telegraph Editor [*Journalism*] (WDMC) ... TE
Telegraph Exchange [*Telecommunications*] (IAA) ... TELEX
Telegraph Florists Delivery Service ... TELEFLORA
Telegraph Form (ROG) ... TF
Telegraph Input-Output Multiplexer [*Telecommunications*] (OA) ... TIOM
Telegraph Line Pair (BUR) ... TLP
Telegraph Money Order ... TMO
Telegraph Multiplexer (MHDB) ... TELEMUX
Telegraph Office ... Tel Off
Telegraph Office ... TO
Telegraph on Radio [*Telecommunications*] (TEL) ... TOR
Telegraph Repeater [*Telecommunications*] (IAA) ... TR
Telegraph System (MSA) ... TS
Telegraph System Analyzer ... TSA
Telegraphe Restant [*Telegram to Be Called for at a Telegraph Office*] [*French*] (ROG) ... TR
Telegrapher [*Navy*] ... T
Telegraphic (NTCM) ... TEL
Telegraphic Address ... TA
Telegraphic Address (DS) ... Tel Add
Telegraphic Approval Requested (NOAA) ... TGARQ
Telegraphic Authority Requested (NOAA) ... TGURG
Telegraphic Automatic Relay [*or Routing*] **Equipment** (NG) ... TARE
Telegraphic Automatic Routing in the Field (MCD) ... TARIF
Telegraphic Distortion Measuring Set (IAA) ... TDMS
Telegraphic Message (MSA) ... TWX
Telegraphic Order (WDAA) ... TO
Telegraphic Transfer [*of funds*] [*Banking*] ... TT
Telegraphist (DSUE) ... TELIST
Telegraphist Air Gunner [*British military*] (DMA) ... TAG
Telegraphist Air Gunner's Association [*Navy British*] ... TAGA
Telegraphist Detector [*British military*] (DMA) ... TD
Telegraphist Detector Instructor [*British military*] (DMA) ... TDI
Telegraphist-Lieutenant [*Navy British*] ... TL
Telegraphnoye Agentstvo Sovyetskovo Soyuza [*Telegraph Agency of the Soviet Union*] [*News agency*] ... TASS
Telegraphy Channel Reliability Analyzer [*Telecommunications*] (OA) ... TCRA
Telegraphy with Automatic Switching [*Telecommunications*] (IAA) ... TAS
Telegraphy with Manual Switching [*Telecommunications*] (IAA) ... TMS
Telegu Desam Party [*India*] [*Political party*] ... TDP
Teleguard System International [*Vancouver Stock Exchange symbol*] ... TSI
Telehop, Inc. [*Fresno, CA*] [*Telecommunications*] (TSSD) ... THI
Teleilaet Ghassul (BJA) ... TG
Tele-Link, Inc. [*Miami, FL*] [*Telecommunications service*] (TSSD) ... TLC
Telemail International Licensees' Association (TSSD) ... TILA
Teleman [*Navy rating British*] ... TE
TeleManagement Associates [*Telecommunications service*] (TSSD) ... TMA
Telemanagement Resources, Inc. [*Charlotte, NC*] [*Telecommunications*] (TSSD) ... TMR
Telemanagement Resources International, Inc. (TSSD) ... TRI
Telemarketing ... TELMKTG
Telemarketing Corp. of America [*Phoenix, AZ*] (TSSD) ... TCA
Telemarketing Sales Representative ... TSR
Telemarketing Service Representative (WDMC) ... TSR
Telematica, Inc. [*Telecommunications service*] (TSSD) ... TmI
Telemation Program Services ... TPS
Telemedia Communication Television [*Cable-television system*] ... TCTV
Telemedia, Inc. [*Toronto Stock Exchange symbol*] ... TMD
Telemedicine for Ontario [*Toronto, ON*] [*Telecommunications*] (TSSD) ... TFO
Telemessage (DS) ... TMESS
Telemeter [*or Telemetry*] [*Telecommunications*] (IAA) ... T
Telemeter [*or Telemetry*] (AAG) ... TLM
Telemeter Magnetics, Inc. (IAA) ... TMI
Telemeter Set/Synthesized (DWSG) ... TS/S
Telemeter Transmitter (IAA) ... TMS
Telemeter Transmitter ... TMX
Telemetered Data (AAG) ... TMD
Telemetered Data Reduction (AAG) ... TEDAR
Telemetered Ultrasonic Liquid Interface Plotting System (PDAA) ... TULIPS
Telemetering [*JETDS*] ... K
Telemetering (AAG) ... TLMG
Telemetering Control Assembly (AAG) ... TCA
Telemetering Control Indicator ... TMCI
Telemetering Data Recording Set (CAAL) ... TDRS
Telemetering Fixed Station [*ITU designation*] (CET) ... FXE
Telemetering Land Station [*ITU designation*] (CET) ... FLE
Telemetering Mobile Station [*ITU designation*] ... MOE
Telemetering Ocean Bottom Seismometer [*Marine science*] (MSC) ... TOBS
Telemetering Oscillator Voltage ... TOV
Telemetering Package ... TELEPAK
Telemetric Automated Microbial Identification System ... TAMIS
Telemetric Data Analyzer ... TDA
Telemetric Data Converter ... TELEDAC
Telemetric Data Monitor ... TDM
Telemetric Universal Sensor ... TELUS
Tele-Metropole, Inc. [*Toronto Stock Exchange symbol*] ... TM
Telemetry (KSC) ... TEL
Telemetry [*Cardiology*] (DAVI) ... tele
Telemetry (MSA) ... TLMY
Telemetry ... TM
Telemetry Acceptance Pattern (KSC) ... TAP
Telemetry Analog to Digital [*Information converter*] ... TAD
Telemetry Analog-Digital Information Converter ... TADIC
Telemetry Analysis and Simulation Program [*Spacecraft*] [*NASA*] ... TASP
Telemetry and Command (SSD) ... T & C
Telemetry and Command (MCD) ... TAC
Telemetry and Command ... TEC
Telemetry and Command Data (KSC) ... TCD
Telemetry and Command Processor Assembly [*Deep Space Instrumentation Facility, NASA*] ... TCP
Telemetry and Command Station [*Aerospace*] (MCD) ... TCS
Telemetry and Command Subsystem [*Deep Space Instrumentation Facility, NASA*] ... TCO
Telemetry and Command System (MCD) ... TACS
Telemetry & Communications Division (ACII) ... TELCOM
Telemetry and Communications Systems Division [*Apollo*] [*NASA*] ... TCSD
Telemetry and Data [*Telecommunications*] (IAA) ... TAD
Telemetry and Remote Control (IEEE) ... TRC
Telemetry Antenna ... Telem Ant
Telemetry Antenna Pedestal ... TAP
Telemetry Antenna Positions System [*Military*] (CAAL) ... TAPS
Telemetry Antenna Subsystem (NASA) ... TAS
Telemetry Auto Following Equipment ... TAFE
Telemetry Automatic Reduction Equipment ... TARE
Telemetry Buffer Unit (SSD) ... TBU
Telemetry Carrier Acquisition and Recovery (MCD) ... TELECAR
Telemetry Checkout Equipment (KSC) ... TCE
Telemetry Code Modulation ... TCM
Telemetry Components Information (KSC) ... TCI
Telemetry Compression Routine ... TCR
Telemetry Computation ... TMCOMP
Telemetry Control and Monitoring ... TC & M
Telemetry Control Panel (IAA) ... TLMCTLPNL
Telemetry Data ... TD
Telemetry Data Buffer ... TLMB
Telemetry Data Digitizer ... TDD
Telemetry Data Evaluation System ... TEDES
Telemetry Data Format Control Handbook (KSC) ... TDFCHB
Telemetry Data Generation ... TDG
Telemetry Data Link [*Telecommunications*] (IAA) ... TDL
Telemetry Data Monitor Set ... TDMS
Telemetry Data Processing Unit (CAAL) ... TDPU
Telemetry Data Signal Simulator (MCD) ... TDSS
Telemetry Decommutation System ... TDS
Telemetry Downlist Receiving Site (NASA) ... TDRS
Telemetry Equipment Unit ... TEU
Telemetry Evaluation Station ... TES
Telemetry Event [*Telecommunications*] (IAA) ... TE
Telemetry Format Load (MCD) ... TFL
Telemetry Format Selection (NASA) ... TFS
Telemetry Ground Station ... TGS
Telemetry Ground Support Equipment [*NASA*] (KSC) ... TGSE
Telemetry Ground System (NASA) ... TGS
Telemetry Guidance System [*From computer game "Hacker II"*] ... TGS
Telemetry Impact Prediction System [*Air Force*] ... TIPS
Telemetry Input System ... TIS
Telemetry Instruction Conference (KSC) ... TIC
Telemetry Instrumentation Controller ... TIC
Telemetry Integrated Processing System [*Air Force*] ... TIPS
Telemetry Intelligence ... TELINT
Telemetry Listing Submodule ... TLS
Telemetry Manufacturers' Association (IAA) ... TMA
Telemetry Modulation System ... TMS
Telemetry Module Facility ... TMF
Telemetry Multiplex System ... TMS
Telemetry On-Line Monitoring Compression and Transmission ... TOMCAT
Telemetry Online Processing System [*Computer science*] ... TELOPS
Telemetry On-Line Processing System [*Computer science*] ... TOPS
Telemetry Oscillator (IAA) ... TO

Telemetry Output Buffer [*Computer science*] ... TOB
Telemetry Power Amplifier ... TPA
Telemetry Preprocessing Computer (MCD) ... TPC
Telemetry Processing ... TMPROC
Telemetry Processing Facility (MCD) ... TPF
Telemetry Processing System [*Space Flight Operations Facility, NASA*] ... TPS
Telemetry Processing System Buffer [*Space Flight Operations Facility, NASA*] ... TPSB
Telemetry Processor ... TP
Telemetry Processor Module ... TPM
Telemetry/Radio Frequency ... TM/RF
Telemetry Range Instrumentation Aircraft ... TRIA
Telemetry Redundancy Analyzer System ... TRANS
Telemetry Simulation Program ... TSP
Telemetry Simulation Submodule ... TSIMS
Telemetry Simulation Terminal ... TST
Telemetry Standards Coordination Committee (HGAA) ... TCC
Telemetry Standards Coordination Committee ... TSCC
Telemetry Station System [*Telecommunications*] (IAA) ... TELSTATS
Telemetry Subcarrier Spectrum Analyzer ... TSSA
Telemetry Support Equipment (IAA) ... TSE
Telemetry System Analysis Group ... TAG
Telemetry System Application Requirements ... TSAR
Telemetry Technical Analysis Position (MCD) ... TTAP
Telemetry Tracking [*Telecommunications*] (IAA) ... TELTRAC
Telemetry, Tracking, and Command (NASA) ... TTC
Telemetry, Tracking, Command, and Monitoring ... TTC & M
Telemetry Traffic Control (SSD) ... TTC
Telemetry Transmission System ... TTS
Telemetry Van ... TMV
Telemetry Video Spectrum ... TVS
Telemetry Working Group ... TWG
Telemetry-Computer Translator [*Bell Laboratories*] ... TCT
Telemetry-Surveillance-Communications ... TELSCOM
TeleMonteCarlo [*Private television operation*] [*Italy*] ... TMC
Telemotor ... TELMTR
Telemundo Group 'A' [*NASDAQ symbol*] (TTSB) ... TLMD
Telemundo Group, Inc. [*Associated Press*] (SAG) ... Telmn
Telemundo Group, Inc. [*Associated Press*] (SAG) ... Telmun
Telemundo Group, Inc. [*NASDAQ symbol*] (SAG) ... TLMD
Telemundo Group Wrrt [*NASDAQ symbol*] (TTSB) ... TLMDW
TELENET Access Controller ... TAC
TELENET Communications Corp. [*GTE*] (TEL) ... TELENET
TELENET Interface Processor ... TIP
Telenoticiosa Americana [*Press agency*] [*Argentina*] ... Telan
Teleoperated Mobile Antiarmor Platform [*Army*] (INF) ... TMAP
Teleoperator and Robotic System Simulation (MCD) ... TRSS
Teleoperator Assembler (SSD) ... TA
Teleoperator for Operations, Maintenance, and Construction Using Advanced Technology ... TOMCAT
Teleoperator Ground Operations Working Group [*NASA*] (NASA) ... TGOWG
Teleoperator Maneuvering System (MCD) ... TMS
Teleoperator Retrieval/Skylab Boost System [*Aerospace*] (MCD) ... TR/SBS
Teleoperator Retrieval System [*NASA*] ... TRS
Teleordering Users' Council [*British*] ... TUC
Teleos Institute (EA) ... TI
Telepad Corp. [*Associated Press*] (SAG) ... Telepad
Telepad Corp. [*Associated Press*] (SAG) ... Tlepd
Telepad Corp. [*NASDAQ symbol*] (SAG) ... TPAD
TelePad Corp. 'A' [*NASDAQ symbol*] (TTSB) ... TPADA
TelePad Corp. Unit [*NASDAQ symbol*] (TTSB) ... TPADU
TelePad Corp. Wrrt 'D' [*NASDAQ symbol*] (TTSB) ... TPADL
TelePad Corp. Wrrt'A' [*NASDAQ symbol*] (TTSB) ... TPADW
TelePad Corp. Wrrt'B' [*NASDAQ symbol*] (TTSB) ... TPADZ
TelePad Corp. Wrrt'C' [*NASDAQ symbol*] (TTSB) ... TPADM
Telepanel, Inc. [*Vancouver Stock Exchange symbol*] ... TPA
Telepanel Systems [*Toronto Stock Exchange symbol*] (SPSG) ... TLS
Telepanel Systems [*NASDAQ symbol*] (TTSB) ... TLSIF
Telepanel Systems, Inc. [*Associated Press*] (SAG) ... Telepanel
Telepanel Systems, Inc. [*NASDAQ symbol*] (SAG) ... TLSI
Telephone (NTCM) ... PHONE
Telephone ... T
Telephone (AAG) ... TEL
Telephone ... TEL
Telephone (ODBW) ... Tel
Telephone ... TELE
Telephone ... TELEPH
Telephone (IAA) ... TELN
Telephone (NATG) ... TF
Telephone (NATG) ... TN
Telephone (CET) ... TP
Telephone & Data Sys [*AMEX symbol*] (TTSB) ... TDS
Telephone & Data Systems, Inc. [*AMEX symbol*] (SPSG) ... TDS
Telephone & Data Systems, Inc. [*Associated Press*] (SAG) ... TelDta
Telephone and Telegraph (IAA) ... TAT
Telephone and Telegraph (IAA) ... TELATEL
Telephone Answering and Recording Machine (NITA) ... TARM
Telephone Answering Device ... TAD
Telephone Answering Machine (IEEE) ... TAM
Telephone Answering Service (NITA) ... TAN
Telephone Answering Service [*or System*] ... TAS
Telephone Apparatus [*JETDS nomenclature*] [*Military*] (CET) ... TA
Telephone Area Billing System ... TABS
Telephone Area Office [*British*] ... TAO
Telephone Area Staff [*British*] ... TAS
Telephone Artifacts Association (EA) ... TAA
Telephone as Soon as Possible (NOAA) ... TPHASAP
Telephone at [*Followed by time*] (NOAA) ... TPHAT
Telephone at Your Convenience (NOAA) ... TPHAYC
Telephone Automated Briefing Service (DA) ... TABS
Telephone Booth ... TELB
Telephone Cable Makers' Association [*British*] (BI) ... TCMA
Telephone Cable Process Controller (MHDB) ... TCPC
Telephone Cables Ltd. [*British*] ... TCL
Telephone Center (IAA) ... TC
Telephone Central Office (IAA) ... TC
Telephone Central Office ... TELCO
Telephone Channel Monitor ... TCM
Telephone Collectors International (EA) ... TCI
Telephone Communications (IAA) ... TELCO
Telephone Company [*ICAO designator*] (FAAC) ... TELCO
Telephone Co. Engineered [*Telecommunications*] (TEL) ... TCE
Telephone Conference [*or Conversation*] ... FONECON
Telephone Conference [*or Conversation*] (AAG) ... TELCON
Telephone [*or Teletype*] **Conference** [*or Conversation*] (AFM) ... TELECON
Telephone Conference Summary (NRCH) ... TCS
Telephone Consultants of America [*Bergenfield, NJ*] [*Telecommunications*] (TSSD) ... TCA
Telephone Contract Officers' Association [*A union*] [*British*] ... TCOA
Telephone Conversation (MCD) ... FONCON
Telephone Conversation [*or Conference*] ... PHONCON
Telephone Conversation ... TELECONV
Telephone, Data, and Special Audio (NASA) ... TD & SA
Telephone Department ... TD
Telephone Depot (IAA) ... TD
Telephone Device for the Deaf ... TDD
Telephone Directory ... TD
Telephone Engineer [*Telecommunications*] (IAA) ... TELENGR
Telephone Engineering Center [*Telecommunications*] (TEL) ... TEC
Telephone Equipment Order [*Telecommunications*] (TEL) ... TEO
Telephone Equipment Room [*NFPA pre-fire planning symbol*] (NFPA) ... TE
Telephone Exchange (NITA) ... TX
Telephone Exchange (Crossbar) [*Telecommunications*] (TEL) ... TXK
Telephone Exchange (Digital) [*Telecommunications*] (TEL) ... TXD
Telephone Exchange (Electronics) [*Telecommunications*] (IEEE) ... TXE
Telephone Exchange (Equipment) [*Telecommunications*] ... TXE
Telephone Exchange (Strowger) [*Telecommunications*] (TEL) ... TXS
Telephone Executive Leader for a Day [*New England Telephone Co. program for high school students*] ... TELFAD
Telephone Group (IAA) ... TEL
Telephone Influence Factor ... TIF
Telephone Information and Management Systems (ADA) ... TIMS
Telephone Information Processing (MCD) ... TIP
Telephone Information Services [*Commercial firm*] [*British*] ... TIS
Telephone Installation and Requisition Application (MCD) ... TIARA
Telephone Interface Unit [*Telecommunications*] ... TIU
Telephone Interference Factor (DEN) ... TIF
Telephone Jack (DEN) ... TJ
Telephone Line Digital Error Checking ... TDEC
Telephone Line Doubler (IAA) ... TLD
Telephone Line Interface (IEEE) ... TLI
Telephone Line Patch ... TLP
Telephone Management and Accounting (HGAA) ... TMA
Telephone Management System ... TELEMAN
Telephone Management System (HGAA) ... TMS
Telephone Manufacturing Company (IAA) ... TMC
Telephone Museum (EA) ... TM
Telephone Number (IAA) ... TELNO
Telephone Number ... TN
Telephone Office ... TO
Telephone Office Planning and Engineering System [*Telecommunications*] (TEL) ... TOPES
Telephone Operating Co. [*Also, TELOP*] ... TELCO
Telephone Operating Co. [*Also, TELCO*] ... TELOP
Telephone Operations and Standards Division [*Rural Electrification Administration*] [*Telecommunications*] (TEL) ... TOSD
Telephone Order [*Medicine*] ... TO
Telephone Order Dispatch Notice ... TODN
Telephone Order Entry System (AAGC) ... TOES
Telephone Order Personalities and Smiles [*Organization of chief telephone operators*] ... TOPS
Telephone Order Processing System ... TOPS
Telephone Order Purchasing System (MCD) ... TOPS
Telephone Organization of Thailand (NITA) ... TOT
Telephone Package ... TELPAK
Telephone Pickup Coil ... TPC
Telephone Pickup Coil ... TPUC
Telephone Pioneers of America (EA) ... TPA
Telephone Provincial Clerical and Contract Officers' Association [*A union*] [*British*] ... TPCCOA
Telephone Rationalization by Computer (PDAA) ... TERCO
Telephone Relay Coupler (HGAA) ... TRC
Telephone Rentals [*Commercial firm*] ... TR
Telephone Repeater Station (IAA) ... TRS
Telephone Sales Representative (WDMC) ... TSR
Telephone Satellite, Experimental ... TSX
Telephone Service Attitude Measurement [*Telephone interviews*] [*AT & T*] ... TELSAM
Telephone Service Fitting ... TSF
Telephone Service Observation [*Telecommunications*] (TEL) ... TSO

Telephone Set (IAA) ... TS
Telephone Signal Unit [*Telecommunications*] (TEL) ... TSU
Telephone Software Connection, Inc. ... TSC
Telephone Station (IAA) ... TEL
Telephone Support Request ... TSR
Telephone Survey (MUGU) ... TEL SUR
Telephone Switchboard (LAIN) ... TS
Telephone Switching Planning (ADA) ... TSP
Telephone System ... TEL-SYS
Telephone System Interface Unit ... TSIU
Telephone Systems Programming Language [*Computer science*] (MHDB) ... TSPL
Telephone Tape (IAA) ... TELTAP
Telephone Terminal Cables (KSC) ... TTC
Telephone Terminal Equipment ... TTE
Telephone Toll Call (IAA) ... TTC
Telephone Tracking System Directory (MCD) ... TTSD
Telephone Trunk Call [*British*] (ROG) ... T
Telephone Users Association (EA) ... TUA
Telephone Video System [*NEC America, Inc.*] [*Wood Dale, IL*] [*Telecommunications*] (TSSD) ... TVS
Telephonic (NTCM) ... TEL
Telephonie sans Fil [*Wireless Telephony*] ... TPSF
Telephony (NTCM) ... TEL
Telephony Application Programming Interface [*Microsoft Corp.*] (PCM) ... TAPI
Telephony Preprocessor [*Telecommunications*] (TEL) ... TPP
Telephony Services Application Programming Interface [*Novell, Inc.*] (PCM) ... TSAPI
Telephony [*or Telephone*] **User Part** [*Telecommunications*] (TEL) ... TUP
Telephoto (NTCM) ... TELE
Telephoto Transmission Measuring Set ... TTMS
Telephotograph ... TPHO
Teleport Communications Group, Inc. [*NASDAQ symbol*] (SAG) ... TCGI
Teleport Communications Group, Inc. [*Associated Press*] (SAG) ... TeleprtC
Teleprensa [*Press agency*] [*Colombia*] ... TP
Telepresence-Controlled Remotely-Operated Vehicle [*NASA*] ... TROV
Telepresent Rapid Aiming Platform [*Remotely operated rifle*] ... TRAP
Teleprinter ... TP
Teleprinter (AAG) ... TPR
Teleprinter Automatic Switching System (NITA) ... TASS
Teleprinter Coordinator ... TPCO
Teleprinter Error Correction Equipment ... TECE
Teleprinter Error Detector (IAA) ... TED
Teleprinter Exchange [*Telecommunications*] (IAA) ... TELEX
Teleprinter Exchange Service [*Telecommunications*] (IAA) ... TEX
Teleprinter Load Tables (KSC) ... TLT
Teleprinter Message Pool ... TMP
Teleprinter on Multiplex [*Telecommunications*] (IAA) ... TOM
Teleprinter on Radio [*Telecommunications*] (TSSD) ... TOR
Teleprinter Over Radio (NITA) ... TOR
Teleprinter Planning Table ... TPT
Teleprinter Retransmitting [*Telecommunications*] (IAA) ... TER
Teleprocessed Record and Card Entry Reporting System (MCD) ... TRACERS
Teleprocessing [*Computer science*] (MCD) ... TP
Teleprocessing Access Method [*Telecommunications*] (IAA) ... TAM
Teleprocessing Access Method ... TPAM
Teleprocessing Analysis and Design Program [*Computer science*] (IAA) ... TPAD
Teleprocessing Design Center [*Army*] (PDAA) ... TDS
Teleprocessing Executive [*Telecommunications*] (IAA) ... TELEX
Teleprocessing Monitor ... TPM
Teleprocessing Multiplexer Module ... TPMM
Teleprocessing Network Simulator ... TPNS
Teleprocessing Online Test (NITA) ... TOLTE
Teleprocessing On-Line Test Executive [*Computer science*] (IBMDP) ... TOTE
Teleprocessing On-Line Test Executive Program [*IBM Corp.*] ... TOLTEP
Teleprocessing Recording for Analysis by the Customer ... TRAC
Teleprocessing Recording for Analysis by the Customer (IEEE) ... TRACE
Teleprocessing Remote Access Control System (HGAA) ... TRACS
Teleprocessing Services Program [*General Service Administration*] ... TSP
Teleprocessing System [*Computer science*] (IAA) ... TPS
Teleprocessing Test Center (MHDI) ... TPTC
Teleprocessing Virtual Machine (MHDI) ... TPVM
Teleprogrammer Assembly System [*Computer science*] (IAA) ... TAS
Tele-Radio Systems Ltd. [*Toronto Stock Exchange symbol*] ... TRF
Telerail Automated Information Network [*Association of American Railroads*] ... TRAIN
Teleram Users Group (EA) ... TUG
Teleregister Omni Processing and Switching [*Computer science*] ... TOPS
Tele-Research Item Movement, Inc. [*Commercial firm*] (WDMC) ... TRIM
Telergma [*Algeria*] [*ICAO location identifier*] (ICLI) ... DAAM
Telesat Canada, Ottawa, Ontario [*Library symbol National Library of Canada*] (NLC) ... OOTEL
Telescan, Inc. [*Associated Press*] (SAG) ... Telescan
Telescan, Inc. [*NASDAQ symbol*] (SAG) ... TSCN
Telescope (AAG) ... TEL
Telescope (KSC) ... TLS
Telescope (MSA) ... TLSCP
Telescope and Electron Telescope ... TET
Telescope Assembly (KSC) ... TA
Telescope Precision Angle Counter ... TPAC
Telescope Sight Unit (MCD) ... TSU
Telescoped ... TELSCPD
Telescopes in Education ... TIE
Telescopic Photographic Recorder ... TPR
Telescoping Collar (OA) ... TC
Telescoping Rotor Aircraft Concept (MCD) ... TRAC
Telescopium [*Constellation*] ... Tel
Telescopium [*Constellation*] ... Tele
TeleService Resources ... TSR
Telesoft Corp. [*Associated Press*] (SAG) ... Telesoft
Telesoft Corp. [*NASDAQ symbol*] (SAG) ... TSFT
Telesoftware (NITA) ... TSW
TeleSpectrum Worldwide, Inc. [*Associated Press*] (SAG) ... TeleSpec
TeleSpectrum Worldwide, Inc. [*NASDAQ symbol*] (SAG) ... TLSP
Tele-Systems Associates, Inc. [*Bloomington, MN*] [*Telecommunications service*] (TSSD) ... TSA
Teletape Video ... TTV
Teleteach Expanded Delivery System [*US Air Force*] [*Wright-Patterson AFB, OH*] [*Telecommunications*] (TSSD) ... TEDS
Teletec Development, Inc. [*Vancouver Stock Exchange symbol*] ... TDI
TeleTech Holdings, Inc. [*Associated Press*] (SAG) ... TeleTech
TeleTech Holdings, Inc. [*NASDAQ symbol*] (SAG) ... TTEC
Tele-Tech Services [*McAfee, NJ*] [*Information service or system Telecommunications*] (TSSD) ... TTS
Teletek, Inc. [*Associated Press*] (SAG) ... Teletek
Teletek, Inc. [*NASDAQ symbol*] (NQ) ... TLTK
Teleterminals Expandable Added Memory ... TEAM
Teletex [*Telecommunications*] ... TTX
Teletex Access Unit [*Telecommunications*] (OSI) ... TTXAU
Teletext Output of Price Information by Computer [*London Stock Exchange*] ... TOPIC
Teletherapy Treatment Quality Assurance Program [*Nuclear energy*] (NRCH) ... TTQAP
Telethon Institute of Genetics and Medicine [*Italy*] ... TIGEM
Teletouch Communications, Inc. [*Associated Press*] (SAG) ... Teletch
Teletouch Communications, Inc. [*Associated Press*] (SAG) ... Teletouch
Teletouch Communications, Inc. [*NASDAQ symbol*] (SAG) ... TELL
Teletouch Communicns Wrrt'A' [*NASDAQ symbol*] (TTSB) ... TELLW
Teletype [*JETDS nomenclature*] ... G
Teletype ... T
Teletype (NTCM) ... TEL
Teletype (IAA) ... TLTP
Teletype ... TLTYP
Teletype ... TT
Teletype (CAAL) ... TTY
Teletype Alert Network (NVT) ... TAN
Teletype Center [*Telecommunications*] (IAA) ... TTC
Teletype Communications Unit (NVT) ... TCU
Teletype Conversion Device (DWSG) ... TCD
Teletype Exchange (NITA) ... TELEX
Teletype Exchange ... TEX
Teletype Input (IAA) ... TTI
Teletype Input Generator ... TIG
Teletype Input Processing ... TIP
Teletype Interpreter (PDAA) ... TINT
Teletype, Line Printer, Card Reader Controller (NOAA) ... TLC
Teletype Message Converter [*Telecommunications*] (IAA) ... TTC
Teletype Modulator Interface Units (MCD) ... TMIU
Teletype on Radio [*Telecommunications*] (IAA) ... TOR
Teletype Optical Projection System (IEEE) ... TOPS
Teletype Output [*Telecommunications*] (IAA) ... TTO
Teletype Page Printer ... TPP
Teletype Point-To-Point Online Communications Driver (NITA) ... TTYPP
Teletype Preamble Generator ... TPG
Teletype Service Without Voice Communication [*Telecommunications*] (IAA) ... TWC
Teletype Switching System [*or Subsystem*] ... TSS
Teletype Telling ... TTL
Teletype Test Instruction (KSC) ... TTI
Teletype Translator [*Telecommunications*] (IAA) ... TTR
Teletypesetter ... TTS
Teletypesetting (NITA) ... TTS
Teletypesetting Code (NITA) ... TTS
Teletypewriter [*Telecommunications*] (NOAA) ... TEL
Teletypewriter [*Telecommunications*] ... TELETYPE
Teletypewriter [*International telex abbreviation*] (WDMC) ... TPR
Teletypewriter [*Telecommunications*] ... TT
Teletypewriter [*Telecommunications*] ... TTW
Teletypewriter [*Telecommunications*] ... TTY
Teletypewriter [*Telecommunications*] (IAA) ... TY
Teletypewriter and Facsimile Apparatus [*JETDS nomenclature*] [*Military*] (CET) ... TT
Teletypewriter Assembly ... TTYA
Teletypewriter Automatic Dispatch System ... TADS
Teletypewriter Buffer (CET) ... TTB
Teletypewriter Center [*Military*] ... TTC
Teletypewriter Communications out of Service (FAAC) ... TYPNO
Teletypewriter Communications Returned to Service (FAAC) ... TYPOK
Teletypewriter Conference (IAA) ... TELECON
Teletypewriter Control Unit (CET) ... TCU
Teletypewriter Control Unit (AABC) ... TTCU
Teletypewriter Distribution (NATG) ... TELEDIS
Teletypewriter Equipment (IAA) ... TTY
Teletypewriter Exchange Service ... TWS
Teletypewriter Exchange Service [*Western Union*] [*Term also used generically for teletypewriter message*] ... TWX
Teletypewriter Identification (NOAA) ... TELID
Teletypewriter Integrated Display (NVT) ... TIDY
Teletypewriter Message ... TWIX
Teletypewriter, Private Line ... TWPL
Teletypewriter Query-Reply Subsystem (CET) ... TTYQ/RSS

Teletypewriter Simulation [*or Simulator*] ..... TELSIM
Teletypewriter Simulator ..... TELESIM
Teletypewriter System ..... TTS
Teletypewriter Technician ..... TTEC
Teletypewriter Terminal Assembly ..... TTTA
Teletypewriter Translator (CET) ..... TTR
Teletypewriter Wire Transmission ..... TWX
Tele-Typewriters for the Deaf [*An association*] ..... TTYD
Tele-Universite [*University of Quebec*] [*Telecommunications service*] (TSSD) ..... TELUQ
Tele-Universite, Universite du Quebec, Montreal, Quebec [*Library symbol National Library of Canada*] (NLC) ..... QMUQTM
Tele-Universite, Universite du Quebec, Quebec, Quebec [*Library symbol National Library of Canada*] (NLC) ..... QQUQT
Tele-Universite (University of Quebec) [*Quebec, PQ*] [*Telecommunications*] (TSSD) ..... TELUQ
Televideo Consultants, Inc. [*Evanston, IL*] [*Telecommunications*] (TSSD) ..... TVC
TeleVideo Systems [*NASDAQ symbol*] (TTSB) ..... TELV
TeleVideo Systems, Inc. [*NASDAQ symbol*] (NQ) ..... TELV
Televisao Nacional de Cabo Verde [*National Television of Cape Verde*] (EY) ..... TNCV
Televised Images of Gaseous Region in Interplanetary Space ..... TIGRIS
Televisi Republik Indonesia [*Indonesian television network*] (FEA) ..... TVRI
Television [*FCC*] (NTCM) ..... T
Television (IAA) ..... TEL
Television (ADA) ..... TELE
Television (IAA) ..... TLV
Television ..... TV
Television ..... TV
Television Accessory Manufacturers Institute (NTCM) ..... TAMI
Television Action Committee for Today and Tomorrow [*Later, American Council forBetter Broadcasts*] (AEBS) ..... TACT
Television Advertisers' Report [*A publication*] (DOAD) ..... TVAR
Television Advertising Council [*Australia*] ..... TAC
Television Advertising Duty ..... TAD
Television Advisory Committee [*British*] (DEN) ..... TAC
Television Advisory Committee for Educational Television (NTCM) ..... TACET
Television Advisory Committee of Mexican Americans (NTCM) ..... TACOMA
Television Air Trainer ..... TVAT
Television Allocation Research Committee [*or Council*] ..... TARC
Television Allocations Study Organization [*Defunct*] ..... TASO
Television and Computer (EECA) ..... TELEPUTER
Television and Electronics Service Association ..... TESA
Television and Inertial Guidance ..... TVIG
Television and Infrared Observation Satellite [*NASA*] ..... TIROS
Television and Infrared Observation Satellite - Meteorological [*NASA*] (DNAB) ..... TIROS-M
Television and RADAR Navigation System (MUGU) ..... TELERAN
Television and Radio Industry Club [*British*] (DBA) ..... TRIC
Television and Radio Political Action Committee [*National Association of Broadcasters*] ..... TARPAC
Television and Radio Suppression [*Electronics*] ..... TVRS
Television and Video Switching Subsystem (MCD) ..... TVSS
Television Angle Rate Bombing System (MCD) ..... TV-ARBS
Television Appliance Association ..... TAA
Television Associates [*Mountain View, CA*] (TSSD) ..... TA
Television Associates Network [*Canada*] ..... TvA
Television Audience Measurement ..... TAM
Television Audience Program Evaluation ..... TAPE
Television Audio Support Activity [*Army*] ..... TASA
Television Australia Ltd. ..... TVA
Television Automatic Sequence Control ..... TASCON
Television Awareness Training ..... TAT
Television Briefing Console ..... TBC
Television Broadcast Satellite [*NASA*] ..... TVBS
Television Broadcasting (CET) ..... TELECAST
Television Broadcasting Station [*ITU designation*] (CET) ..... BCT
Television Broadcasts [*Hong Kong television company*] (ECON) ..... TVB
Television Bureau of Advertising ..... TBA
Television Bureau of Advertising (DOAD) ..... TVB
Television Camera (MDG) ..... TELECAMRA
Television Camera (MHDB) ..... TVC
Television Camera and Control Equipment ..... TVCAM
Television Camera System ..... TCS
Television Cathode Ray (IAA) ..... TCR
Television Center for Business and Industry ..... TCBI
Television Communications Subsystem ..... TVCS
Television Confirming Sensor (MCD) ..... TECS
Television Control Center ..... TCC
Television Control Set ..... TCS
Television Critics Association (EA) ..... TCA
Television Data Acquisition System (MCD) ..... TELEDAQ
Television Data Display System (KSC) ..... TDDS
Television Deflection Yoke ..... TVDY
Television Disc (NITA) ..... TED
Television Display (MCD) ..... TVD
Television Esmeraldena Compania de Economia Mixta [*Ecuador*] (EY) ..... TESEM
Television Espanola [*Television network*] [*Spain*] ..... TVE
Television Evaluation and Renewal Standards [*Student legal action organization*] ..... TVERS
Television Experiment Interconnecting Station [*NASA*] (NASA) ..... TVEXPIS
Television Facility Test Position [*Telecommunications*] (TEL) ..... TFTP
Television Facsimile (NTCM) ..... TELEFAC
Television Feasibility Demonstration [*NASA*] (KSC) ..... TFD
Television Film Exhibit (NTCM) ..... TFE
Television Film Recorder ..... TFR
Television Flyback Transformer ..... TVFT
Television Food Network ..... TVFN
Television Frame Identification Data [*NASA*] ..... TVID
Television Francophone par Satellite [*France*] (EAIO) TV5
Television Ground Data Handling System [*NASA*] ..... TVGDHS
Television Household [*Ratings*] (NTCM) ..... TVHH
Television Information Office [*Defunct*] (EA) ..... TIO
Television Information Storage (IAA) ..... TVIS
Television Information Storage Tube ..... TVIST
Television Infrared Observational Satellite [*Marine science*] (OSRA) ..... TIROS
Television Infrared-Observation Satellite NOAA [*National Oceanographic and Atmospheric Administration*] [*Navy*] (ANA) ..... TIROS-N
Television Input Converter ..... TVIC
Television Intercity [*FCC*] (NTCM) ..... TI
Television Interface (ECII) ..... TVI
Television Interference [*Communications*] ..... TVI
Television Interference Committee ..... TVIC
Television LASER Link ..... TLL
Television Licensing and Records Office [*Post Office*] [*British*] ..... TVLRO
Television Licensing Center [*Defunct*] (EA) ..... TLC
Television Listener (IDOE) ..... TVL
Television Listening (IDOE) ..... TVL
Television Malta ..... TVM
Television Management Information System (IAA) ..... TMIS
Television Measurement [*or Metering*] **Information System** (OA) ..... TMIS
Television Microwave Link [*FAA*] (TAG) ..... TML
Television Monitor [*Video only*] ..... TVM
Television News, Inc. ..... TVN
Television Observation Post (CET) ..... TVOP
Television of Thailand (FEA) ..... TVT
Television Operating Center ..... TOC
Television Operations Center [*NASA*] (KSC) ..... TVOC
Television Operators Caucus (EA) ..... TOC
Television Optical (NTCM) ..... TELOP
Television Ordnance Scoring System (MCD) ..... TOSS
Television Pickup [*FCC*] (NTCM) ..... TP
Television Picture Generator (MCD) ..... TEPIGEN
Television Program Export Association (EA) ..... TPEA
Television Program Standard ..... TPS
Television Quarterly [*A publication*] (BRI) ..... TV Q
Television, Radio, and Audio-Visuals of the Presbyterian Church in the United States (NTCM) ..... TRAV
Television, Radio and Film Communications [*of the Methodist Church*] ..... TRAFCO
Television Rating ..... TVR
Television Reading Program ..... TVRP
Television Receive Only [*Telecommunications*] ..... TVRO
Television Receiver/Monitor ..... TVRM
Television Recording (WDMC) ..... TVR
Television Relay Using Small Terminals (MCD) ..... TRUST
Television Remote Pickup ..... TRP
Television Resource Teachers [*Canada*] ..... TRT
Television Satellite (NTCM) ..... TELSAT
Television Scan Converter ..... TSC
Television Series for United Nations [*A foundation formed to produce, and telecast on a commercial basis, dramatized descriptions of UN activities*] ..... TELSUN
Television Service Dealers' Association (IAA) ..... TSDA
Television Services International [*British*] ..... TSI
Television Sight Unit ..... TVSU
Television Sight Unit Identification (MCD) ..... TVID
Television Signal Generator ..... TVSG
Television Signal Tracer (DEN) ..... TST
Television, Sound Channel ..... TS
Television Space Observatory ..... TVSO
Television Studio-Transmitter-Link [*FCC*] (NTCM) ..... TS
Television Subsystem [*Spacecraft*] ..... TVS
Television Subsystem Interconnecting Station [*NASA*] (NASA) ..... TVSSIS
Television System (IAA) ..... TVSYS
Television System Monitor ..... TVSM
Television Systems Section ..... TVSS
Television Technicians' Association (IAA) ..... TTA
Television Terminal (CMD) ..... TVT
Television Tower [*Mast*] ..... TV TR
Television Trainer/Tapes (MCD) ..... TVT
Television Training Centre Ltd. [*British*] (CB) ..... TTC
Television Transcription (NTCM) ..... Telescription
Television Typewriter ..... TVT
Television Video Generator ..... TVG
Television Video Recording System (MCD) ..... TVRS
Television Videotape Satellite Communications [*Group W Productions*] [*Pittsburgh, PA*] (TSSD) ..... TVSC
Television, Vision Channel ..... TV
Television Writer's Guild (NTCM) ..... TWG
Televisora Nacional [*Television network*] [*Venezuela*] ..... TVN
TeleWest Communications Ltd. [*NASDAQ symbol*] (SAG) ..... TWST
TeleWest Communications PLC [*Associated Press*] (SAG) ..... TeleWest
TeleWest PLC ADS [*NASDAQ symbol*] (TTSB) ..... TWSTY
TELEX ..... TEX
TELEX [*Automated Teletypewriter Exchange Service*] [*Western Union Corp.*] ..... TLX
Telex ..... TLX
TELEX ..... TX
Telex Chile SA [*Associated Press*] (SAG) ..... TelexChil
Telex Chile SA [*NYSE symbol*] (SAG) ..... TL
Telex Communications Service (NITA) ..... TCS

TELEX Computer Inquiry Service .... TCIS
TELEX Extended Memory (IAA) .... TEM
TELEX File Adapter (IAA) .... TFA
TELEX Line Adapter (IAA) .... TLA
TELEX Main Memories [*Telecommunications*] (IAA) .... TMM
Telex Management Systems (NITA) .... TMS
Telex Network Adapter (MHDB) .... TA
Telex World Letter [*MCI International, Inc.*] [*Rye Brook, NY*] (TSSD) .... TWL
TELEX-Type [*Terminal*] .... TTY
Telfer [*Australia Airport symbol*] (OAG) .... TEF
Telford Aviation, Inc. [*ICAO designator*] (FAAC) .... TEL
Telivision Infrared Orbital Satellite [*Instrument*] (EERA) .... TITOS
Tell Abu Huwam (BJA) .... TAH
Tell Asmar [*Iraq*] (BJA) .... TA
Tell Beit Mirsim (BJA) .... TBM
Tell City, IN [*Location identifier FAA*] (FAAL) .... TEL
Tell City, IN [*AM radio station call letters*] .... WTCJ
Tell City News, Tell City, IN [*Library symbol Library of Congress*] (LCLS) .... InTcN
Tell City-Perry County Public Library, Tell City, IN [*Library symbol Library of Congress*] (LCLS) .... InTc
Tell el-Obed (BJA) .... TO
Tell en-Nasbeh (BJA) .... TN
Tell Halaf (BJA) .... TH
Tell Me About Yourself [*Interviewing technique*] .... TMAY
Tell Taanach (BJA) .... TT
Tellabs Co. [*Associated Press*] (SAG) .... Tellabs
Tellabs, Inc. [*NASDAQ symbol*] (NQ) .... TLAB
Tell-Amarna [*Egypt*] (BJA) .... TA
Teller [*Alaska*] [*Airport symbol*] (OAG) .... TLA
Teller .... TLR
Teller, AK [*Location identifier FAA*] (FAAL) .... TLA
Teller Mission, AK [*Location identifier FAA*] (FAAL) .... KTS
Teller of the Exchequer [*British*] (ROG) .... TE
Teller Register Unit Monitoring Program (IEEE) .... TRUMP
Teller Terminal (MHDW) .... TT
"Tell-Me-A-Story" Thematic Appreciation Test (EDAC) .... TEMAS
Tell-Rimah (BJA) .... TR
Telluraheptadecanoic Acid [*Organic chemistry*] .... THDA
Tellurian, Inc. [*Associated Press*] (SAG) .... Tellurn
Tellurian, Inc. [*NASDAQ symbol*] (SAG) .... TLRN
Telluride Association (EA) .... TA
Telluride, CO [*FM radio station call letters*] .... KOTO
Telluride, CO [*FM radio station call letters*] .... KRYD
Telluride Elementary School, Telluride, CO [*Library symbol*] [*Library of Congress*] (LCLS) .... CoTeE
Telluride High School, Telluride, CO [*Library symbol*] [*Library of Congress*] (LCLS) .... CoTeS
Tellurite, Taurocholate, and Gelatin [*Microbiology*] (DMAA) .... TTG
Tellurite-Polymyxin-Egg Yolk [*Agar*] [*Microbiology*] .... TPEY
Tellurite-Taurocholate-Gelatin Agar [*Microbiology*] .... TTGA
Tellurium [*Chemical element*] .... Te
Tellurium Diethyldithiocarbamate [*Organic chemistry*] .... TEDC
Tellus Industries, Inc. [*Associated Press*] (SAG) .... Tellus
Tellus Industries, Inc. [*Sacramento, CA*] [*NASDAQ symbol*] (NQ) .... TLLS
TelMed, Inc. [*Associated Press*] (SAG) .... TelMd
TelMed, Inc. [*Associated Press*] (SAG) .... TelMed
TelMed, Inc. [*NASDAQ symbol*] (SAG) .... TEMD
TelMed Inc. Wrrt [*NASDAQ symbol*] (TTSB) .... TEMDW
Telnet [*Internet*] .... T
Telocator Network of America (EA) .... TNA
Telocentric .... t
Telomere Position Effect [*Genetics*] .... TPE
Telomere Repeat Amplification Protocol [*Analytical biochemistry*] .... TRAP
Telomeric Repeat Amplification Protocol [*Analytical biochemistry*] .... TRAP
Telomeric Repeat-Binding Factor [*Genetics*] .... TRF
Telophase Society [*Commercial firm*] (EA) .... TS
Telor Ophthalmic Pharm [*NASDAQ symbol*] (TTSB) .... TELR
Telor Ophthalmic Pharmaceuticals [*NASDAQ symbol*] (SAG) .... TELR
Telor Ophthalmic Pharmaceuticals [*Commercial firm Associated Press*] (SAG) .... TelrOph
TELS Corp. [*Associated Press*] (SAG) .... TELS
TELS Corp. [*NASDAQ symbol*] (SAG) .... TELS
Tel-Save Holdings [*NASDAQ symbol*] (TTSB) .... TALK
Tel-Save Holdings, Inc. [*NASDAQ symbol*] (SAG) .... TALK
Tel-Save Holdings, Inc. [*Associated Press*] (SAG) .... TelSave
Telscape International, Inc. [*Associated Press*] (SAG) .... Telscape
Telscape International, Inc. [*Associated Press*] (SAG) .... Telscpe
Telscape International, Inc. [*NASDAQ symbol*] (SAG) .... TSCP
Telstar Resource Corp. [*Vancouver Stock Exchange symbol*] .... TLT
Teltrend, Inc. [*Associated Press*] (SAG) .... Teltrnd
Teltrend, Inc. [*NASDAQ symbol*] (SAG) .... TLTN
Teltronics, Inc. [*NASDAQ symbol*] (NQ) .... TELT
Teltronics, Inc. [*Associated Press*] (SAG) .... Teltron
Telugu [*MARC language code Library of Congress*] (LCCP) .... tel
Teluk Kepayang [*Indonesia*] [*ICAO location identifier*] (ICLI) .... WRBT
Telukbetung [*Sumatra, Indonesia*] [*Airport symbol*] (AD) .... TKG
Telular Corp. [*Associated Press*] (SAG) .... Telular
Telular Corp. [*NASDAQ symbol*] (SAG) .... WRLS
Telxon Corp. [*Associated Press*] (SAG) .... Telxon
Telxon Corp. [*NASDAQ symbol*] (NQ) .... TLXN
TEM Enterprises [*ICAO designator*] (FAAC) .... CXP
Tema [*Ghana*] [*ICAO location identifier*] (ICLI) .... DGAT
Temagami Community Library, Ontario [*Library symbol National Library of Canada*] (NLC) .... OTEMAC
Temagami Oil & Gas Ltd. [*Toronto Stock Exchange symbol*] .... TOG
Temazepam [*Tranquilizer*] .... TMP
Tembagapura [*Indonesia*] [*Airport symbol*] (OAG) .... TIM
Tembec Inc. [*Toronto Stock Exchange symbol*] .... TBC
Temecula, CA [*FM radio station call letters*] .... KRTM
Temerloh [*Malaysia*] [*ICAO location identifier*] (ICLI) .... WMBE
Temifibre, Inc., Temiscaming, PQ, Canada [*Library symbol*] [*Library of Congress*] (LCLS) .... CaQTeTF
Temifibre, Inc., Temiscaming, Quebec [*Library symbol National Library of Canada*] (NLC) .... QTTF
Teminabuan [*West Irian, Indonesia*] [*Airport symbol*] (AD) .... TXM
Teminabuan [*Indonesia*] [*ICAO location identifier*] (ICLI) .... WAST
Temiscaming, PQ [*Television station call letters*] CBFST-2
Temiskaming & Northern Ontario Railway [*AAR code*] .... TEM
Temiskaming & Northern Ontario Railway .... TNOR
Temne [*MARC language code Library of Congress*] (LCCP) .... tem
Temo Resources Ltd. [*Vancouver Stock Exchange symbol*] .... TMR
Temora [*Australia Airport symbol*] (OAG) .... TEM
Temora [*New South Wales*] [*Airport symbol*] (AD) .... TMT
Tempe, AZ [*AM radio station call letters*] .... KCWW
Tempe, AZ [*AM radio station call letters*] .... KUKQ
Tempe, AZ [*FM radio station call letters*] .... KUPD
Tempe Public Library, Tempe, AZ [*Library symbol Library of Congress*] (LCLS) .... AzTe
Tempelhof Airways, Inc. [*Germany ICAO designator*] (FAAC) .... TEH
Tempelhof Automatic System (DWSG) .... TAS
Tempelhof Central Airport [*West Berlin*] .... TCA
Tempelurkunden aus Tello [*A publication*] (BJA) .... TT
[*Egg*] **Tempera** (VRA) .... temp
Temperament and Values Inventory [*Interpersonal skills and attitudes test*] .... TVI
Temperament Comparator [*Psychology*] .... TC
Temperance [*i.e., entitled to a daily rum ration but voluntarily not drawing it and receiving money instead*] [*See also G, UA*] [*Navy*] [*British*] .... T
Temperance (ADA) .... TEMP
Temperance and Social Welfare [*Free Church*] [*British*] .... T & SW
Temperance Collegiate Association [*British*] (AEBS) .... TCA
Temperance Education Foundation [*Defunct*] (EA) .... TEF
Temperance, Grog, or Underage [*British military*] .... TG or UA
Temperate Zone .... TEMP
Temperate Zone Phase .... TZP
Temperature .... T
Temperature (DEN) .... TEM
Temperature (AAG) .... TEMP
Temperature .... TEMP
Temperature (BUR) .... TMP
Temperature (MDG) .... TMT
Temperature (DAVI) .... TPR
Temperature Acceleration Vibration Environmental Tester .... TAVET
Temperature Alarm [*Engineering*] .... TA
Temperature Altitude Chamber .... TAC
Temperature and Dew Point (NASA) .... TAD
Temperature and Dew Point (KSC) .... TDP
Temperature and Liquid Level Monitor [*Nuclear energy*] (NRCH) .... TLLM
Temperature and Pressure [*Medicine*] .... TP
Temperature and Pressure [*Temporoparietal*] [*Anatomy*] (DAVI) .... TP
Temperature and Pulse [*Medicine*] .... T + P
Temperature Auto Stabilizing Regime (IAA) .... TASR
Temperature Autostabilizing Nonlinear Dielectric Element (IAA) .... TANDEL
Temperature Average (IAA) .... TAVG
Temperature, Axillary .... TA
Temperature Capability .... TC
Temperature Change [*Refrigeration*] .... TC
Temperature Coefficient .... TC
Temperature Coefficient of Breakdown Voltage .... TCBV
Temperature Coefficient of Capacitance .... TCC
Temperature Coefficient of Expansion .... TCE
Temperature Coefficient of Offset (IAA) .... TCO
Temperature Coefficient of Resistance .... TCR
Temperature Coefficient of Sensitivity (IAA) .... TCS
Temperature Coefficient of Voltage .... TCV
Temperature Compensating (MSA) .... TC
Temperature Compensating Resistors (NATG) .... TEMPISTORS
Temperature Control .... TC
Temperature Control Amplifier (IAA) .... TCA
Temperature Control Assembly (KSC) .... TCA
Temperature Control Circuit .... TCC
Temperature Control Device for Crystal Units (IAA) .... TCD
Temperature Control Flux Monitor [*NASA*] .... TCFM
Temperature Control Instrument .... TCI
Temperature Control Model .... TCM
Temperature Control Reference .... TCR
Temperature Control Subsystem (KSC) .... TCS
Temperature Control Unit .... TCU
Temperature Control Valve (AAG) .... TCV
Temperature Controlled Storage and Distribution Exhibition [*British*] (ITD) .... TCS & D
Temperature Controller [*Nuclear energy*] (NRCH) .... TC
Temperature Datum (NG) .... T/D
Temperature Density Computer .... TDC
Temperature Density Plotter .... TDP
Temperature Depth Recorder .... TDR
Temperature Differential (MSA) .... TD
Temperature Element [*Nuclear energy*] (NRCH) .... TE
Temperature Excess (PDAA) .... TEX
Temperature Extreme Pressure (DNAB) .... TEP
Temperature Factor .... TF

Temperature Gauge [*Automotive engineering*] ... T/GA
Temperature Gradient Lamp [*Spectroscopy*] ... TGL
Temperature in Degrees Centigrade (IAA) ... TC
Temperature Independent [*Ferrite computer memory core*] ... TIN
Temperature Independent Material (IAA) ... TIM
Temperature Indicating Alarm [*Engineering*] ... TIA
Temperature Indicating Label ... TIL
Temperature Indicating Switch ... TIS
Temperature Indicator ... TI
Temperature Indicator Controller ... TIC
Temperature Indicator Monitor ... TIM
Temperature Indicator Recorder (ECII) ... TIR
Temperature Indicator Recorder Controller (ECII) ... TIRC
Temperature Jump-Stopped Flow [*Spectroscopy*] ... TJSF
Temperature Junction (MCD) ... TJ
Temperature Level Control (IAA) ... TLC
Temperature Management Station ... TMS
Temperature Maximum (DAVI) ... T-MAX
Temperature, Mean ... TM
Temperature Measurement Society ... TMS
Temperature Measurement Unit (NASA) ... TMU
Temperature Measuring Equipment (IAA) ... TME
Temperature Meter ... TM
Temperature Monitor (NRCH) ... TM
Temperature Monitoring Apparatus ... TMA
Temperature Monitoring Power Supply ... TMPS
Temperature Normal [*Medicine*] ... TN
Temperature of Cabin [*Aerospace*] (MCD) ... TCAB
Temperature of Hot-Channel Sodium [*Nuclear energy*] (NRCH) ... THCS
Temperature of Injectate ... Ti
Temperature of Maximum Density ... TMD
Temperature, Oral [*Medicine*] ... TO
Temperature Pressure Test Chamber (IAA) ... TPTC
Temperature Probe (AAG) ... TP
Temperature Profile Recorder (AAG) ... TPR
Temperature Programmed Hydrogenation [*Chemical engineering*] ... TPH
Temperature, Pulse, Respiration [*Medicine*] ... TPR
Temperature Range ... TR
Temperature Rate Flight Control System ... TRFCS
Temperature Recorder ... TR
Temperature Recording Alarm [*Engineering*] ... TRA
Temperature Recording Controller ... TRC
Temperature, Rectal [*Medicine*] ... TR
Temperature Regualtor and Missile Power Supply (IAA) ... TRMPS
Temperature Regulating Power Supply ... TRPS
Temperature Regulation and Monitor Panel ... TRAMP
Temperature Regulator and Missile Power Supply ... TRAMPS
Temperature Removable Instrument Assembly [*Nuclear energy*] (NRCH) ... TRIA
Temperature Rising Elution Fractionation [*Analytical chemistry*] ... TREF
Temperature Sensing Transducer ... TST
Temperature Sensitive ... TS
Temperature Sensitive Mutation [*Genetics*] (DOG) ... ts mutation
Temperature Swing Adsorption [*Chemical engineering*] ... TSA
Temperature Switch ... TS
Temperature Switch (MSA) ... TSW
Temperature Switch, High [*Nuclear energy*] (NRCH) ... TSH
Temperature Test Chamber ... TTC
Temperature Test Model ... TTM
Temperature Test Set ... TTS
Temperature to Precipitation Ratio [*Botany*] ... T/P
Temperature Transmitter [*Nuclear energy*] (NRCH) ... TT
Temperature Valve Control ... TVC
Temperature Variation of Resistance [*Electricity*] ... TVR
Temperature Well (MSA) ... TW
Temperature-Activated Vacuum [*Automotive engineering*] ... TAV
Temperature-Actuated Switch (IEEE) ... TAS
Temperature-Compensated Crystal Oscillator (MCD) ... TCCO
Temperature-Compensated Crystal Oscillator ... TCXO
Temperature-Compensated Mask (IAA) ... TCM
Temperature-Compensated Reference Element ... TCRE
Temperature-Compensated Zener Diode ... TCZD
Temperature-Compensation (IAA) ... TCM
Temperature-Controlled Animal ... TCA
Temperature-Controlled Crystal Oscillator (IAA) ... TCCO
Temperature-Controlled Crystal Oscillator ... TCXO
Temperature-Controlled Test Chamber [*EPA engine test*] ... TCTC
Temperature-Dependent Resistor (BYTE) ... TDR
Temperature-Dependent Sex Determination ... TSD
Temperature-Dependent Sex Determination [*Reptile Embryology*] ... TSD
Temperature-Depth-Salinity [*Oceanography*] ... TDS
Temperature-Determined Sex [*Laboratory science*] (DAVI) ... TDS
Temperature-Enhanced Displacement Effect ... TEDE
Temperature-Gradient Gel Electrophoresis [*Analytical biochemistry*] ... TGGE
Temperature-Gradient Zone-Melting [*Chemistry*] ... TGZM
Temperature-Gradient Zone-Melting Process [*Chemistry*] (IAA) ... TGZMP
Temperature-Humidity Index ... THI
Temperature-Humidity Infrared Radiometer ... THIR
Temperature-Independent Paramagnetism ... TIP
Temperature-Limited Emission ... TLE
Temperature-Modulated Air Cleaner [*Automotive engineering*] ... TMAC
Temperature-Programmed Analysis ... TPA
Temperature-Programmed Desorption [*Catalysis*] ... TPD
Temperature-Programmed Gas Chromatography ... TPGC
Temperature-Programmed Oxidation [*For surface analysis*] ... TPO
Temperature-Programmed Reaction [*Chemistry*] ... TPR
Temperature-Programmed Reaction Spectroscopy ... TPRS
Temperature-Programmed Reaction System ... TPRS
Temperature-Programmed Reduction [*For analysis of surfaces*] ... TPR
Temperature-Resistant Element (DNAB) ... TRE
Temperature-Salinity [*Oceanography*] ... T-S
Temperature-Salinity Data [*Oceanography*] (MCD) ... TEMPSAL
Temperature-Salinity-Currents [*Oceanography*] (IID) ... TESAC
Temperature-Salinity-Density-Depth [*Oceanography*] ... TSD
Temperature-Salinity-Density-Depth (IEEE) ... TSDD
Temperature-Sensitive Period ... TSP
Temperature-to-Voltage (IDOE) ... T/V
Temperature-Viscosity Index (DAVI) ... TVI
Temperature-Voltage-Gases (DNAB) ... TVG
Tempered (DEN) ... TEM
Tempered (AAG) ... TEMP
Tempered (MSA) ... TMPD
Tempered Safety Glass [*Automotive engineering*] ... TSG
Tempered Water ... TW
Tempering ... TMPRG
[*The*] **Tempest** [*Shakespearean work*] (BARN) ... Temp
[*The*] **Tempest** [*Shakespearean work*] ... Tmp
TEMPEST Automated Data Acquisition and Analysis System ... TADAAS
[*The*] **Templar** [*1788-79*] [*London*] [*A publication*] (DLA) ... Tem
Templar Mining [*Vancouver Stock Exchange symbol*] ... TEG
Template (DEN) ... TEM
Template (AAG) ... TEMP
Template [*Engineering*] ... TEMPL
Template Descriptor Memory ... TDM
Template Graphics Software ... TGS
Template Set-Up (MCD) ... TS
Template Set-Up Check Fixture (MCD) ... TSCF
Template Tracing Technique (DA) ... TTT
Template-Assisted Intelligence Report Fusion Process ... TEMPRO
Template-Assisted Synthetic Protein [*Biochemistry*] ... TASP
Temple ... TMPL
Temple (VRA) ... tmpl
Temple [*Texas*] [*Airport symbol*] (OAG) ... TPL
Temple and Mew's English Criminal Appeal Cases [*A publication*] (DLA) ... T & M
Temple and Mew's English Crown Cases [*1848-51*] [*A publication*] (DLA) ... T & M
Temple and Mew's English Crown Cases [*1848-51*] [*A publication*] (DLA) ... Temp & M
Temple and Mew's English Crown Cases [*A publication*] (DLA) ... Temple & M
Temple and Mew's English Crown Cases [*A publication*] (DLA) ... Temple & M (Eng)
Temple Autobiographies [*A publication*] ... TA
Temple, Barker & Sloane, Inc. [*Lexington, MA*] [*Telecommunications service*] (TSSD) ... TBS
Temple Beth Israel, Portland, OR [*Library symbol Library of Congress*] (LCLS) ... OrPT
Temple Biographies [*A publication*] ... TB
Temple Classics [*A publication*] ... TC
Temple Cyclopaedic Primers [*A publication*] ... TCP
Temple Israel Library, White Plains, NY [*Library symbol Library of Congress*] (LCLS) ... NWhpTI
Temple Junior College [*Texas*] ... TJC
Temple Junior College, Temple, TX [*Library symbol Library of Congress*] (LCLS) ... TxTemC
Temple Library, Tiffereth Israel Congregation, Cleveland, OH [*Library symbol Library of Congress*] (LCLS) ... OClTem
Temple Magazine [*A publication*] (ROG) ... TM
Temple Name (BJA) ... TN
Temple of Man (EA) ... TM
Temple Opportunity Program [*Temple University*] (EA) ... TOP
Temple Terrace, FL [*AM radio station call letters*] ... WQBN
Temple Terrace, FL [*AM radio station call letters*] ... WTMP
Temple, TX [*Television station call letters*] ... KCEN
Temple, TX [*FM radio station call letters*] (RBYB) ... KKIK
Temple, TX [*FM radio station call letters*] ... KLTD
Temple, TX [*AM radio station call letters*] ... KTEM
Temple, TX [*Location identifier FAA*] (FAAL) ... TPL
Temple University (GAGS) ... Temple U
Temple University, Ambler Campus, Ambler, PA [*Library symbol Library of Congress*] (LCLS) ... PAmC
Temple University, Dental-Pharmacy School, Philadelphia, PA [*Library symbol Library of Congress*] (LCLS) ... PPT-D
Temple University. Law Quarterly [*A publication*] (DLA) ... Temp Univ LQ
Temple University, Law School, Philadelphia, PA [*Library symbol Library of Congress*] (LCLS) ... PPT-L
Temple University, Medical School, Philadelphia, PA [*Library symbol Library of Congress*] (LCLS) ... PPT-M
Temple University, Philadelphia, PA [*Library symbol Library of Congress*] (LCLS) ... PPT
Temple University, Philadelphia, PA [*OCLC symbol*] (OCLC) ... TEU
Temple University Press ... TUP
Temple University, School of Theology, Philadelphia, PA [*Library symbol Library of Congress*] (LCLS) ... PPT-T
Temple University Short Syntax Inventory [*Educational test*] ... TUSSI
Temple Youth Group [*Local groups of National Federation of Temple Youth, sometimes called TYG-ers, pronounced "tigers"*] ... TYG
Temple-Inland [*NYSE symbol*] (TTSB) ... TIN
Temple-Inland, Inc. [*Associated Press*] (SAG) ... TempII
Temple-Inland, Inc. [*NYSE symbol*] (SPSG) ... TIN
Templeton China World Fd [*NYSE symbol*] (TTSB) ... TCH

Templeton China World Fund [*NYSE symbol*] (SPSG) .... TCH
Templeton China World Fund [*Associated Press*] (SAG) .... TmpChin
Templeton Dragon Fd [*NYSE symbol*] (TTSB) .... TDF
Templeton Dragon Fund [*NYSE symbol*] (SAG) .... TDF
Templeton Dragon Fund [*Associated Press*] (SAG) .... TmpDrgn
Templeton Emerg Mkts [*NYSE symbol*] (TTSB) .... EMF
Templeton Emerg Mkts Income [*NYSE symbol*] (TTSB) .... TEI
Templeton Emerging Market Appreciation Fund [*NYSE symbol*] (SAG) .... TEA
Templeton Emerging Market Appreciation Fund [*Associated Press*] (SAG) .... TEMAF
Templeton Emerging Market Fund, Inc. [*Associated Press*] (SAG) .... TEMFI
Templeton Emerging Markets Fund, Inc. [*NYSE symbol*] (SPSG) .... EMF
Templeton Emerging Markets Income Fund [*NYSE symbol*] (SPSG) .... TEI
Templeton Emerging Markets Income Fund [*Associated Press*] (SAG) .... TEMIF
Templeton Energ Mkts Apprec [*NYSE symbol*] (TTSB) .... TEA
Templeton Engineering, Winnipeg, MB, Canada [*Library symbol Library of Congress*] (LCLS) .... CaMWTE
Templeton Global Government Income Trust [*NYSE symbol*] (CTT) .... TGG
Templeton Global Governments Income Trust [*Associated Press*] (SAG) .... TpGGv
Templeton Global Gvts [*NYSE symbol*] (TTSB) .... TGG
Templeton Global Income [*NYSE symbol*] (SPSG) .... GIM
Templeton Global Income Fund [*Associated Press*] (SAG) .... TmpGlb
Templeton Global Utilities, Inc. [*Associated Press*] (SAG) .... TempGu
Templeton Global Utilities, Inc. [*AMEX symbol*] (SPSG) .... TGU
Templeton Russia Fund [*Associated Press*] (SAG) .... TmpRus
Templeton Russia Fund [*Associated Press*] (SAG) .... TmpRuss
Templeton Russia Fund [*NYSE symbol*] (SAG) .... TRF
Templeton Vietnam Opport Fd [*NYSE symbol*] (TTSB) .... TVF
Templeton Vietnam Opportunities Fund [*Associated Press*] (SAG) .... TmpViet
Templeton Vietnam Opportunities Fund [*NYSE symbol*] (SAG) .... TVF
Templin Darley Test of Articulation [*Speech and language therapy*] (DAVI) .... TDTA
Tempo .... T
Tempo [*Record label*] [*Germany*] .... Tem
Tempo [*Music*] .... TEM
Tempo [*Music*] .... TEMP
Tempo [*Record label*] [*Germany*] .... Tpo
Tempo di Restituzione Termica [*Thermal Restitution Test*] [*Italian*] [*Medicine*] .... TRT
Tempo of Operations (MCD) .... OPTEMPO
Tempo Primo [*Original Tempo*] [*Music*] .... TEMP PRIM
Tempo Primo [*Original Tempo*] [*Music*] .... TP
Temporal .... T
Temporal .... TEMP
Temporal Analysis of Products [*System developed by Monsanto Chemical Co.*] .... TAP
Temporal Arteritis [*Medicine*] .... TA
Temporal Bone Banks [*Otology*] (EA) .... TBB
Temporal Fourier Hologram (PDAA) .... TFH
Temporal Lobe Epilepsy [*Medicine*] .... TLE
Temporal Stem [*Brain anatomy*] .... TS
Temporaries Food for All Seasons Foundation (EA) .... TFFASF
Temporarily (MDG) .... TMPRLY
Temporarily Able-Bodied .... TAB
Temporarily Attached [*Navy*] (DNAB) .... TEMPATT
Temporarily Disconnected at Subscriber's Request [*Telecommunications*] (TEL) .... TDR
Temporarily Discontinued [*Fog signal*] .... TD
Temporarily Mounted User Set [*Computer science*] (ADA) .... TMUS
Temporarily Out of Print .... TOP
Temporarily Out of Service (DEN) .... TOS
Temporarily Out of Stock [*Business term*] .... TOS
Temporarily Replaced by Lighted Buoy Showing Same Characteristic [*Maps and charts*] .... TRLB
Temporarily Replaced by Unlighted Buoy [*Maps and charts*] .... TRUB
Temporarily Transferred [*Telecommunications*] (TEL) .... TT
Temporary .... T
Temporary .... TEMP
Temporary (AAG) .... TEMPO
Temporary .... TEMPY
Temporary .... TEMPY
Temporary (BARN) .... tmp
Temporary (AFM) .... TMPRY
Temporary .... Ty
Temporary Access Authorization (NASA) .... TAA
Temporary Accumulator (IAA) .... TAR
Temporary Accumulator Register (IAA) .... TAR
Temporary Active Duty .... TEMAC
Temporary Active Duty [*Navy*] .... TEMACDU
Temporary Active Duty in a Flying Status Involving Operational or Training Flights [*Navy*] .... TEMACDIFOT
Temporary Active Duty in a Flying Status Involving Proficiency Flying [*Navy*] (DNAB) .... TACDIFPRO
Temporary Active Duty under Instruction [*Navy*] .... TEMACINS
Temporary Active Duty under Instruction in a Flying Status Involving Operationalor Training Flights [*Navy*] .... TEMACDIFOTINS
Temporary Active Duty under Instruction in a Flying Status Involving ProficiencyFlying [*Navy*] (DNAB) .... TACDIFINSPRO
Temporary Active Reserve (DNAB) .... TAR
Temporary Additional Duty [*Military*] .... TAD
Temporary Additional Duty [*Navy*] .... TEMADD
Temporary Additional Duty in Connection with [*Specified activity*] [*Navy*] .... TEMADDCON
Temporary Additional Duty under Instruction [*Navy*] .... TEMADDINS
Temporary Air Transport Advisory Committee [*NATO*] (NATG) .... TATAC
Temporary Alteration Control Form (IAA) .... TACF
Temporary Ambulance Train [*British military*] (DMA) .... TAT
Temporary Appointment Pending Establishment of a Register [*Civil Service*] .... TAPER
Temporary Assembled Skeleton [*Computer science*] (IAA) .... TASK
Temporary Assigned Duty [*Military*] (VNW) .... TAD
Temporary Assigned Skeleton [*Computer science*] .... TASK
Temporary Assistance for Needy Families .... TANF
Temporary Assistance to Needy Families [*An association*] .... TANF
Temporary Assistant (WDAA) .... T/A
Temporary Attached Duty .... TAD
Temporary Augmentation for Command and Control [*Navy*] (ANA) .... TACC
Temporary Authorization [*Personnel*] (OICC) .... TAU
Temporary Base Activation Instruction (AAG) .... TBAI
Temporary Base Register [*Computer science*] (IAA) .... TBR
Temporary Bench Mark .... TBM
Temporary Buoy [*Nautical charts*] .... TB
Temporary Care Arrangement .... TCA
Temporary Certificate (MHDW) .... Temp Ctf
Temporary Change of Station [*Military*] .... TCS
Temporary Change Procedure (AAG) .... TCP
Temporary Chaplain [*British military*] (DMA) .... TC
Temporary Chaplain to the Forces [*British*] .... TCF
Temporary Chaplain to the Royal Navy [*British*] .... TCRN
Temporary Conditioning Station [*Nuclear energy*] (NRCH) .... TCS
Temporary Constable .... TC
Temporary Construction Hole [*Technical drawings*] .... TCH
Temporary Container Discharge Facility .... TCDF
Temporary Correction .... TC
Temporary Correction Sheet (MCD) .... TCS
Temporary Council Committee [*NATO*] .... TCC
Temporary Customs Impost [*British*] .... TCI
Temporary Danger Area (DA) .... TDA
Temporary Detached Duty [*Navy*] (DNAB) .... TEMPDETD
Temporary Detective Constable [*Scotland Yard*] .... TDC
Temporary Detention Facility .... TDF
Temporary Detention of Pay .... TDP
Temporary Disability .... TD
Temporary Disability Benefits [*Insurance*] .... TDB
Temporary Disability Insurance [*Unemployment*] .... TDI
Temporary Disability Retired List [*Military*] .... TDRL
Temporary Dummy Symbol B [*NASDAQ symbol*] (SAG) .... TEMPB
Temporary Dummy Symbol B [*Associated Press*] (SAG) .... TempSymbB
Temporary Duty .... TD
Temporary Duty .... TDY
Temporary Duty [*Navy*] .... TEMDU
Temporary Duty (MCD) .... TYD
Temporary Duty as a Patient [*Navy*] (DNAB) .... TEMDU PAT
Temporary Duty Awaiting [*Specified event*] [*Navy*] .... TEMWAIT
Temporary Duty Connection [*Navy*] (DNAB) .... TEMCON
Temporary Duty Connection, Separation Processing. Upon Completion and When Directed Detach; Proceed Home for Release from Active Duty in Accordance with Instructions [*Navy*] .... TEMSEPRAD
Temporary Duty for Further Assignment [*Navy*] (DNAB) .... TEMDU FFA
Temporary Duty for Further Transfer [*Navy*] (DNAB) .... TEMDU FFT
Temporary Duty in a Flying Status Involving Operational or Training Flights [*Navy*] .... TEMDIFOT
Temporary Duty in a Flying Status Involving Proficiency Flying [*Navy*] (DNAB) .... TEMDIFPRO
Temporary Duty in Connection With [*Specified activity*] [*Navy*] .... TEMDUCON
Temporary Duty Involving Flying [*Navy*] .... TEMFLY
Temporary Duty Involving Flying under Instruction [*Navy*] .... TEMFLYINS
Temporary Duty Pending Disciplinary Action [*Navy*] (DNAB) .... TEMDU DIS
Temporary Duty Pending Further Orders [*Military*] .... TDPFO
Temporary Duty Pending Separation [*Navy*] (DNAB) .... TEMDU SEP
Temporary Duty - Programmed Student Input [*Navy*] (DNAB) .... TEMDU PSI
Temporary Duty Station [*Air Force*] (AFM) .... TDS
Temporary Duty under Instruction [*Navy*] .... TEMDUINS
Temporary Duty under Instruction [*Navy*] .... TEMINS
Temporary Duty under Instruction in a Flying Status Involving Operational or Training Flights [*Navy*] .... TEMDIFOTINS
Temporary Duty Will Cover Approximately [*Navy*] .... TEMPROX
Temporary Early Retirement Authority (DOMA) .... TERA
Temporary Emergency Court of Appeals .... TECA
Temporary Emergency Court of Appeals [*United States*] (DLA) .... Temp Emer Ct App
Temporary Emergency Food Assistance Program [*Department of Agriculture*] .... TEFAP
Temporary Employee [*Business term*] (MHDB) .... TE
Temporary Employment Assistance .... TEA
Temporary Employment Subsidy [*British*] (DCTA) .... TES
Temporary Employment Subsidy Scheme [*Department of Employment*] [*British*] .... TESS
Temporary Engineering Change (AAG) .... TEC
Temporary Engineering Instruction [*Navy*] (NG) .... TEI
Temporary Entry Permit .... TEP
Temporary Equipment Recovery Mission (CINC) .... TERM
Temporary Expedient Equipment List [*Army*] (AABC) .... TEEL
Temporary Extended Compensation [*Labor*] .... TEC
Temporary Extended Unemployment Compensation [*Labor*] .... TEUC
Temporary Facility Tool (SAA) .... TFT
Temporary Fix (AAG) .... TF
Temporary Forfeiture of Pay .... TFP
Temporary Full-Time (GFGA) .... TFT

Temporary Full-Time Equivalent (GFGA) ... TFTE
Temporary Gentleman [*British slang term for officer for duration of the war*] [*World War I*] ... TG
Temporary Geographic Grid ... TGG
Temporary Guidebase [*Oil*] (DICI) ... TGB
Temporary Hold ... TH
Temporary Identification Number [*Military*] ... TIN
Temporary Importation Bond (MCD) ... TIB
Temporary Incapacity Allowance ... TIA
Temporary Instruction [*Nuclear energy*] (NRCH) ... TI
Temporary Instruction Notice ... TIN
Temporary Instructor Lieutenant [*Navy British*] ... TIL
Temporary Intermittent (GNE) ... TI
Temporary/Intermittent Employee ... TIE
Temporary International Council for Educational Reconstruction (DLA) ... TICER
Temporary Joint Committee on Deficit Reduction ... TJCDR
Temporary Light [*Navigation signal*] ... Temp
Temporary Lighted Buoy [*Maps and charts*] ... TLB
Temporary Living Expenses ... TLE
Temporary Loading Facilities (MCD) ... TLF
Temporary Lodging Allowance [*Military*] ... TLA
Temporary Lodging Entitlement (DOMA) ... TLE
Temporary Lodging Expense (DOMA) ... TLE
Temporary Lodging Expense [*DoD*] ... TLE
Temporary Lodging Facility ... TLF
Temporary Lodging Quarters [*Military*] (DNAB) ... TLQ
Temporary Minor Change (MCD) ... TMC
Temporary Missile Assembly Building (AAG) ... TMAB
Temporary Mortgage Assistance Payments Program [*HUD*] ... TMAP
Temporary National Commission on Supplies and Shortages [*Initiated 1974*] ... TNCSS
Temporary National Economic Committee [*Congressional committee which studied the American economic system*] [*World War II*] ... TNEC
Temporary Occupation License (EERA) ... TOL
Temporary Pacemaker [*Cardiology*] (MEDA) ... TPM
Temporary Part Time [*Personnel*] (MCD) ... TPT
Temporary Partial Disablement [*Insurance*] (AIA) ... TPD
Temporary Patient [*British*] ... TP
Temporary Pay Record for a Retired Member [*Called to Active Duty*] [*Navy*] (DNAB) ... TEM-RET
Temporary Price Reduction ... TPR
Temporary Printing Officer (DGA) ... TPO
Temporary Program File [*Computer science*] ... TPF
Temporary Rank [*Army slang*] ... MEX
Temporary Record Number ... TRN
Temporary Regulation (AAGC) ... TR
Temporary Rental Allowance ... TRA
Temporary Reserved Airspace [*ICAO designator*] (FAAC) ... TRA
Temporary Resident ... TR
Temporary Restraining Order ... TRO
Temporary Restricted Area [*Former USSR*] (NATG) ... TRA
Temporary Short-Time Working Compensation Scheme (AIE) ... TSTWCS
Temporary Sort Number [*Computer science*] ... TSN
Temporary Standard Practice [*or Procedure*] (AAG) ... TSP
Temporary Storage Location ... TSL
Temporary Storage Register ... TSR
Temporary Storage Site [*DoD*] ... TSS
Temporary Stowage Bag [*NASA*] (KSC) ... TSB
Temporary Substitution Approval ... TSA
Temporary Test Equipment (AAG) ... TTE
Temporary Text Delay ... TTD
Temporary Threshold Shift ... TTS
Temporary Threshold Shift Reduction (SAA) ... TTSR
Temporary Total Disablement [*Insurance*] (AIA) ... TTD
Temporary Tour of Active Duty [*Military*] ... TTAD
Temporary Transmission Permit [*Australia*] ... TTP
Temporary Transvenous Pacemaker [*Cardiology*] (DAVI) ... TTVP
Temporary Travel Document (NATG) ... TTD
Temporary Unattached Register [*Employment*] [*British*] ... TUR
Temporary Unemployment Compensation [*Labor*] ... TUC
Temporary Unlighted Buoy [*Maps and charts*] ... TUB
Temporary Variance Authority [*or Authorization*] [*NASA*] (AAG) ... TVA
Temporary Volume Allowance ... TVA
Temporary Voluntary Allowance ... TVA
Temporary Warrant ... TW
Temporary Worker ... TEMP
Temporary-Casuality Pay Record [*Navy*] (DNAB) ... TEM-CAS
Temporary-General [*Navy*] (DNAB) ... TEM-GEN
Temporary-Help Supplier Personnel ... THSP
Tempore [*In the Time of*] [*Latin*] ... T
Tempore [*In the Time Of*] [*Latin*] (DLA) ... Tem
Tempore [*In the Time Of*] [*Latin*] (GPO) ... temp
Tempore Paschale [*At Easter Time*] [*Latin*] ... TP
Tempore Regis [*In the Time of the King*] [*Latin*] ... TR
Tempore Regis Edwardi [*In the Time of King Edward*] [*Latin*] (DLA) ... TRE
Tempori Sinistro [*To the Left Temple*] [*Pharmacy*] (ADA) ... TEMP SINIST
Temporomandibular [*Anatomy*] ... TM
Temporomandibular Joint [*Anatomy*] (DAVI) ... TMJ
Temporomandibular Joint [*Dentistry*] (DAVI) ... TMJ
Temporomandibular Joint Disorder [*Medicine*] ... TMJ
Temporomandibular Joint Syndrome [*Medicine*] ... TMJS
Temporomandibular Pain and Dysfunction Syndrome [*Medicine*] (DMAA) ... TMPDS
Temporomandibular Syndrome [*Medicine*] ... TMS
Temps Atomique International [*International Atomic Time*] [*Telecommunications*] ... TAI
Temps Dynamique Barycentrique [*Barycentric Dynamical Time*] [*French*] ... TDB
Tempus Dextra [*Right Temple*] [*Medicine*] ... TEMP DEXT
Temsco Airlines [*ICAO designator*] (AD) ... KN
Temsco Helicopters, Inc. [*ICAO designator*] (FAAC) ... TMS
Temtex Indus [*NASDAQ symbol*] (TTSB) ... TMTX
Temtex Industries, Inc. [*Associated Press*] (SAG) ... Temtex
Temtex Industries, Inc. [*NASDAQ symbol*] (NQ) ... TMTX
Temuco [*Chile*] [*Seismograph station code, US Geological Survey Closed*] (SEIS) ... TEM
Temuco [*Chile*] [*Seismograph station code, US Geological Survey*] (SEIS) ... TMU
Temuco [*Chile*] [*Airport symbol*] (AD) ... ZCO
Temuco/Maquehue [*Chile*] [*ICAO location identifier*] (ICLI) ... SCTC
Ten [*Roman numeral*] ... X
Ten Call Seconds [*Telecommunications*] (TEL) ... XCS
Ten Class Association (EA) ... TCA
Ten High-Day [*Telecommunications*] ... 10HD
Ten Nation Committee on Disarmament [*Defunct, 1960*] ... TNCD
Ten Outstanding Young Men of America [*Jaycees' program*] ... TOYM
TEN Private Cable Systems, Inc. [*Vancouver Stock Exchange symbol*] ... TCB
Ten Silhouettes [*Psychological testing*] ... TS
Ten Year Plan for Ocean Exploration [*National Council on Marine Resources and Engineering Development*] (MSC) ... TYPOE
Tena [*Ecuador*] [*ICAO location identifier*] (ICLI) ... SETE
Tenacious [*Quality of the bottom*] [*Nautical charts*] ... ten
Tenaculum [*Medicine*] (MAE) ... tenac
Tenado [*Burkina Faso*] [*ICAO location identifier*] (ICLI) ... DHCT
Tenafly Public Library, Tenafly, NJ [*Library symbol Library of Congress*] (LCLS) ... NjTen
Tenajon Resources Corp. [*Formerly, Tenajon Silver*] [*Vancouver Stock Exchange symbol*] ... TJS
Tenakee [*Alaska*] [*Airport symbol*] (OAG) ... TKE
Tenakee Springs, AK [*Location identifier FAA*] (FAAL) ... TKE
Tenancy (ROG) ... TENCY
Tenancy Advice Service [*Australia*] ... TAS
Tenancy in Common (MHDB) ... TIC
Tenancy Service [*New South Wales, Australia*] ... TS
Tenant [*Legal shorthand*] (LWAP) ... T
Tenant (WDAA) ... TEN
Tenant (ROG) ... TENT
Tenant by the Entirety [*Legal shorthand*] (LWAP) ... TBE
Tenant Farmers' Association [*British*] (DBA) ... TFA
Tenants by the Entirety [*Legal term*] ... TE
Tenants in Common (MHDB) ... TEN COM
Tenants' Union of Tasmania [*Australia*] ... TUT
Tencor Instruments [*NASDAQ symbol*] (TTSB) ... TNCR
Tencor Instruments, Inc. [*Associated Press*] (SAG) ... Tencor
Tencor Instruments, Inc. [*NASDAQ symbol*] (SAG) ... TNCR
Tendaho [*Ethiopia*] [*ICAO location identifier*] (ICLI) ... HATO
Tendency (FAAC) ... TNDCY
Tendency to Seek Help Questionnaire (EDAC) ... TSH
Tender [*Horticulture*] ... T
Tender [*Navy*] (NVT) ... TDR
Tender and Repair Ship Load List [*Navy*] (NG) ... TARSLL
Tender Assist Minimum Platform Arrangement (PDAA) ... TAMPA
Tender Availability [*Navy*] ... TAV
Tender Load List ... TLL
Tender Load Quantities (DNAB) ... TLQ
Tender Loving Care ... TLC
Tender Master Equipment List ... TMEL
Tender Option Bond [*Finance*] ... TOB
Tender Production Management Program ... TPMP
Tender Support Equipment ... TSE
Tender to Contract and Forward Exchange Supplement [*Export Credits Guarantee Department*] [*British*] (DS) ... TTC/FES
Tender to Contract Policy [*Export Credits Guarantee Department*] [*British*] ... TTC
Tenderizer ... TNDZR
Tenderness, Guarding, Rigidity [*On abdominal examination*] [*Medicine*] (DAVI) ... TGR
Tenders Electronic Daily [*Office for Official Publications of the European Communities*] [*Database Luxembourg*] ... TED
Tendo Achilis Reflex [*Neurology*] (DAVI) ... TA
Tendo Achillis Lengthening [*Orthopedics*] (DAVI) ... TAL
Tendon Graft [*Orthopedics*] (DAVI) ... TG
Tendon Jerk [*Neurology*] (DAVI) ... TJ
Tendon Transfer [*Surgery*] ... TT
Tendre [*Tender*] [*Music*] ... T
Tendring [*England*] ... TENDR
Tenebrio Unit [*Endocrinology*] ... TU
Tenement (ROG) ... TENEMT
Tenement (ROG) ... TENT
Tenement House Smell [*British*] (ROG) ... THS
Tenera, Inc. [*AMEX symbol*] (SAG) ... TNR
Tenera Ltd. [*Associated Press*] (SAG) ... Tenera
Tenerife [*Canary Islands*] [*ICAO location identifier*] (ICLI) ... GCXO
Tenerife [*Canary Islands*] [*Airport symbol*] (OAG) ... TCI
Tenerife [*Canary Islands*] [*Seismograph station code, US Geological Survey*] (SEIS) ... TEN
Tenerife-Reina Sofia [*Canary Islands*] [*ICAO location identifier*] (ICLI) ... GCTS
Tenerife-Reina Sofia [*Canary Islands*] [*Airport symbol*] (OAG) ... TFS
Tenero [*Tender*] ... T
Tenet Healthcare [*NYSE symbol*] (TTSB) ... THC
Tenet Healthcare Corp. [*Associated Press*] (SAG) ... TenetHlt
Tenet Healthcare Corp. [*NYSE symbol*] (SAG) ... THC

Tengah [*Singapore*] [*ICAO location identifier*] (ICLI) .... WSAT
Tenguel [*Ecuador*] [*ICAO location identifier*] (ICLI) .... SETG
Teniente Ortiz [*Ecuador*] [*ICAO location identifier*] (ICLI) .... SETT
Teniposide [*Antineoplastic drug regimen*] (DAVI) .... PTG
Tenkodogo [*Burkina Faso*] [*ICAO location identifier*] (ICLI) .... DHET
Tenkodogo [*Upper Volta*] [*Airport symbol*] (AD) .... TEG
Tenn Val Auth 7.50%'QUIDS' [*NYSE symbol*] (TTSB) .... TVB
Tenn Val Auth 8.00%'QUIDS' [*NYSE symbol*] (TTSB) .... TVA
Tennant Co. [*NASDAQ symbol*] (NQ) .... TANT
Tennant Co. [*Associated Press*] (SAG) .... Tennant
Tennant Creek [*Australia ICAO location identifier*] (ICLI) .... ADTC
Tennant Creek [*Australia Airport symbol*] (OAG) .... TCA
Tenneco $7.40 cm Pfd [*NYSE symbol*] (TTSB) .... TENPrB
Tenneco Chemicals, Inc., Pasadena, TX [*Library symbol Library of Congress*] (LCLS) .... TxPT
Tenneco, Inc [*Formerly, Tennessee Gas Transmission Co.*] [*Associated Press*] (SAG) .... Tnco
Tenneco Inc. [*NYSE symbol*] (SAG) .... TEN
Tenneco, Inc. [*Formerly, Tennessee Gas Transmission Co.*] [*Associated Press*] (SAG) .... Tennco
Tenneco Oil Co., Exploration Research Library, Houston, TX [*Library symbol Library of Congress*] (LCLS) .... TxHTO
Tennessee [*MARC geographic area code Library of Congress*] (LCCP) .... n-us-tn
Tennessee (ROG) .... TEN
Tennessee (AAG) .... TENN
Tennessee (ODBW) .... Tenn
Tennessee [*Postal code*] .... TN
Tennessee [*MARC country of publication code Library of Congress*] (LCCP) .... tnu
Tennessee Administrative Register [*A publication*] (AAGC) .... TAR
Tennessee Administrative Register [*A publication*] (DLA) .... Tenn Admin Reg
Tennessee Air National Guard (164th Airlift Group) [*FAA designator*] (FAAC) .... TNG
Tennessee Airways [*ICAO designator*] (AD) .... ZN
Tennessee Airways, Inc. [*ICAO designator*] (FAAC) .... TEN
Tennessee, Alabama & Georgia Railway Co. [*AAR code*] .... TAG
Tennessee & North Carolina [*Railroad*] (MHDB) .... T & NC
Tennessee & North Carolina Railroad (IIA) .... T & NC
Tennessee Appeals Reports [*A publication*] (DLA) .... Ten App
Tennessee Appeals Reports [*A publication*] (DLA) .... Tenn App
Tennessee Appeals Reports [*A publication*] (DLA) .... Tenn App R
Tennessee Appeals Reports [*A publication*] (DLA) .... Tenn Appeals
Tennessee Appeals Reports [*A publication*] (DLA) .... TN A
Tennessee Appellate Bulletin [*A publication*] (DLA) .... Tenn App
Tennessee Appellate Bulletin [*A publication*] (DLA) .... Tenn App Bull
Tennessee Automated Clearing House Association .... TACHA
Tennessee Business Education Association (EDAC) .... TBEA
Tennessee Central Railway Co. [*AAR code*] .... TC
Tennessee Chancery Appeals [*A publication*] (DLA) .... Tenn Ch A
Tennessee Chancery Appeals Decisions [*1895-1907*] [*A publication*] (DLA) .... Tenn Ch App Dec
Tennessee Chancery Appeals Reports (Wright) [*A publication*] (DLA) .... Tenn Chancery App
Tennessee Chancery Appeals (Wright) [*A publication*] (DLA) .... Tenn Ch App
Tennessee Chancery Reports (Cooper) [*A publication*] (DLA) .... Coop Chy
Tennessee Chancery Reports (Cooper) [*A publication*] (DLA) .... Tenn Ch R
Tennessee Chancery Reports (Cooper) [*A publication*] (DLA) .... Tenn Chancery
Tennessee Civil Appeals [*A publication*] (DLA) .... Tenn Civ A
Tennessee Civil Appeals [*A publication*] (DLA) .... Tenn Civ App
Tennessee Civil Appeals Reports [*A publication*] (DLA) .... Tenn App
Tennessee Code Annotated [*A publication*] .... TCA
Tennessee Code, Annotated [*A publication*] (DLA) .... Tenn Code Ann
Tennessee Court of Civil Appeals (DLA) .... Tenn CCA
Tennessee Criminal Appeals [*A publication*] (DLA) .... Tenn Cr App
Tennessee Criminal Appeals Reports [*A publication*] (DLA) .... Tenn Crim App
Tennessee Criminal Appeals Reports [*A publication*] (DLA) .... TN Cr
Tennessee Department of Environmental Conservation .... TDEC
Tennessee Department of Environmental Conservation .... TDEC
Tennessee Department of Environmental Conservation (DOGT) .... TDEC
Tennessee Department of Public Health, Nashville, TN [*Library symbol Library of Congress*] (LCLS) .... TNPH
Tennessee Folklore Society (EA) .... TFS
Tennessee Gas Pipeline Co., Houston, TX [*Library symbol Library of Congress*] (LCLS) .... TxHTGP
Tennessee Gas Transmission Co., Houston, TX [*Library symbol Library of Congress*] (LCLS) .... TxHTen
Tennessee Health Science Library Association [*Library network*] .... THESLA
Tennessee Historical Society, Nashville, TN [*Library symbol Library of Congress*] (LCLS) .... THi
Tennessee Hospital Association, Nashville, TN [*Library symbol Library of Congress*] (LCLS) .... TNTHA
Tennessee Jurisprudence [*A publication*] (DLA) .... Tenn Jur
Tennessee Jurisprudence [*A publication*] (DLA) .... Tenn Juris
Tennessee Lawyer [*A publication*] (DLA) .... Tenn Law
Tennessee Legal Reporter [*A publication*] (DLA) .... Tenn Leg Rep
Tennessee Microfilms, Nashville, TN [*Library symbol Library of Congress*] (LCLS) .... TeM
Tennessee Open Records [*An association*] .... TENOR
Tennessee Polytechnic Institute .... TPI
Tennessee Psychiatric Hospital and Institute, Memphis, TN [*Library symbol Library of Congress*] (LCLS) .... TMTP
Tennessee Railway Co. [*AAR code*] .... TENN
Tennessee Reports [*A publication*] (DLA) .... Law Tenn Rep
Tennessee Reports [*A publication*] (ILCA) .... Ten
Tennessee Reports [*A publication*] (DLA) .... Tenn R
Tennessee Reports [*A publication*] (DLA) .... Tenn Rep
Tennessee Reports [*A publication*] (DLA) .... Tennessee R
Tennessee Reports [*A publication*] (DLA) .... Tennessee Rep
Tennessee Reports [*A publication*] (DLA) .... TN
Tennessee Self-Concept Scale [*Psychology*] .... TSCS
Tennessee State Data Center [*Tennessee State Planning Office*] [*Nashville*] [*Information service or system*] (IID) .... TSDC
Tennessee State Law Library, Jackson, TN [*Library symbol Library of Congress*] (LCLS) .... TJaLaw
Tennessee State Law Library, Knoxville, TN [*Library symbol Library of Congress*] (LCLS) .... TKLaw
Tennessee State Law Library, Nashville, TN [*Library symbol Library of Congress*] (LCLS) .... T-L
Tennessee State Library and Archives, Nashville, TN [*Library symbol Library of Congress*] (LCLS) .... T
Tennessee State Library and Archives, Nashville, TN [*OCLC symbol*] (OCLC) .... TNS
Tennessee State Supreme Court Law Library, Knoxville, TN [*Library symbol Library of Congress Obsolete*] (LCLS) .... TK-SC
Tennessee State University (GAGS) .... Tenn St U
Tennessee State University, Downtown Campus, Nashville, TN [*OCLC symbol*] (OCLC) .... TUN
Tennessee State University, Nashville, TN [*Library symbol Library of Congress OCLC symbol*] (LCLS) .... TSU
Tennessee Study of State Science Policy [*National Science Foundation*] (EA) .... TSSSP
Tennessee Supreme Court Reports [*A publication*] (DLA) .... Tenn
Tennessee Technical University, Cookville, TN [*OCLC symbol*] (OCLC) .... TTU
Tennessee Technological University (GAGS) .... Tenn Tech U
Tennessee Technological University, Cookeville, TN [*Library symbol Library of Congress*] (LCLS) .... TCooP
Tennessee Temple Schools, Chattanooga, TN [*Library symbol Library of Congress*] (LCLS) .... TCT
Tennessee Temple University, Chattanooga, TN [*OCLC symbol*] (OCLC) .... TCT
Tennessee Valley Authority [*NYSE symbol*] (SAG) .... TVA
Tennessee Valley Authority [*Also, an information service or system*] .... TVA
Tennessee Valley Authority [*Associated Press*] (SAG) .... TVA 45
Tennessee Valley Authority [*Associated Press*] (SAG) .... TVA 46
Tennessee Valley Authority [*NYSE symbol*] (SAG) .... TVB
Tennessee Valley Authority, Knoxville, TN [*Library symbol Library of Congress*] (LCLS) .... TKTVA
Tennessee Valley Authority, Technical Library, Chattanooga, TN [*Library symbol Library of Congress*] (LCLS) .... TCTVA
Tennessee Valley Authority, Technical Library, Knoxville, TN [*OCLC symbol*] (OCLC) .... TVA
Tennessee Valley Authority, Technical Library, Muscle Shoals, AL [*Library symbol Library of Congress*] (LCLS) .... ATVA
Tennessee Valley Public Power Association (EA) .... TVPPA
Tennessee Valley Region .... TVR
Tennessee Walking Horse Breeders' and Exhibitors' Association (EA) .... TWHBEA
Tennessee Walking Horse Breeders' and Exhibitors' Association of America [*Later, TWHBEA*] (EA) .... TWHBEAA
Tennessee Walking Horse Trainers' Association [*Later, Walking Horse Trainers Association*] .... TWHTA
Tennessee Water Resources Research Center [*Knoxville, TN*] [*Department of the Interior*] (GRD) .... TNWRRI
Tennessee Wesleyan College .... TWC
Tennessee Wesleyan College, Athens, TN [*Library symbol Library of Congress*] (LCLS) .... TAW
Tennessee-Tombigbee [*Proposed waterway*] .... TENN-TOM
Tennille, GA [*FM radio station call letters*] .... WJFL
Tennis .... TEN
Tennis and Rackets Association [*British*] (DBA) .... T and RA
Tennis Australia .... TA
Tennis Club .... TC
Tennis Coaches' Association of Victoria [*Australia*] .... TCAV
Tennis Coaches' Association of Western Australia .... TCAWA
Tennis Elbow [*Medicine*] (DMAA) .... TE
Tennis Foundation of North America [*Later, ATF*] (EA) .... TFNA
Tennis Manufacturers Association [*Later, ATF*] (EA) .... TMA
Tennis Professionals Association [*Canada*] .... TPA
Tennyson (BARN) .... Tenn
Tennyson Society (EA) .... TS
Teno [*or Tendo*] **Achillis Lengthening and Toe Flexor Release** [*Orthopedics*] (DAVI) .... TALTER
Tenor .... T
Tenor [*Genotype of Phlox paniculata*] .... T
Tenor .... TEN
Tenor, Baritone, Bass .... TBB
Tenor, Bass (CDAI) .... TB
Tenore Oil & Gas [*Vancouver Stock Exchange symbol*] .... TNO
Tenpin Bowling Association of Victoria [*Australia*] .... TBAV
Tenquille Resources Ltd. [*Vancouver Stock Exchange symbol*] .... TQR
Tensas Parish Library, St. Joseph, LA [*Library symbol Library of Congress*] (LCLS) .... LStjT
Tense .... T
Tensile .... TENS
Tensile .... TNSL
Tensile Adhesion Test [*for coatings*] .... TAT
Tensile Bond Strength [*Materials science*] .... TBS
Tensile Energy Absorption [*Physics*] .... TEA
Tensile Properties (MCD) .... TP
Tensile Safety Index [*Engineering design*] .... TSI
Tensile Shear Specimen [*Plastics technology*] .... TSS
Tensile Strength .... TS

Tensile Strength (IDOE) ... ts
Tensile Strength Retention [*Textile technology*] ... TSR
Tensile Stress ... TS
Tensile Yield Strength ... TYS
Tension ... T
Tension [*Intraocular*] [*Opthalmology*] (DAVI) ... T
Tension (AAG) ... TENS
Tension (MSA) ... TNSN
Tension Arterielle [*Blood Pressure*] [*Medicine*] ... TA
Tension by Applanation [*Ophthalmology*] ... TA
Tension by Applanation [*Ophthalmology*] ... TAP
Tension Control Optimisation Theory [*Tire manufacturing*] ... TCOT
Tension Equalizer [*Electrical*] **Wave** ... TE
Tension, Schiotz [*Opthalmology*] (DAVI) ... T_s
Tension Time Index (AAMN) ... TTI
Tension Truss Antenna Concept ... TETRAC
Tensional Integrity [*Construction principle named by Buckminster Fuller*] ... TENSEGRITY
Tensioned Replacement Alongside Method (MCD) ... TRAM
Tension-Leg Platform [*Oil exploration*] ... TLP
Tension-Time Index per Beat [*Neurology*] (DAVI) ... TTIB
Tensor ... T
Tensor Fascia Lata [*Anatomy*] ... TFL
Tensor Meson Dominance [*Physics*] (OA) ... TMD
Tensor Society of Great Britain ... TSGB
Tensor Surface Harmonic [*Physics*] ... TSH
Ten-Statement FORTRAN [*Computer science*] (IEEE) ... TSF
Tent City Bravo [*Area near Tan Son Nhut Air Base, formerly site of USAR headquarters*] ... TCB
Tent, Extendable, Modular, Personnel [*DoD*] ... TEMPER
Tentage and Organizational Equipment B ranch [*US Army Natick Research, Development, and Engineering Center*] ... T & OE
Tentative (AAG) ... TENT
Tentative (AFM) ... TNTV
Tentative Acceptance Sampling Procedure [*Army*] ... TASP
Tentative Airworthiness Standards for Supersonic Transports ... TASST
Tentative Annual Planning Estimate (NVT) ... TAPE
Tentative Basis of Issue [*Army*] (AABC) ... TBOI
Tentative Basis of Issue Plan [*Army*] (AABC) ... TBOIP
Tentative Basis of Issue Plan Feedback Data [*Army*] ... TBOIPFD
Tentative Calculated Landing Time [*FAA*] (TAG) ... TCLT
Tentative Cancellation Request ... TCR
Tentative Classification of Damage ... TCD
Tentative Classification of Defects (NG) ... TCD
Tentative Classification of Documents ... TCD
Tentative Clean Up (MCD) ... TCU
Tentative CNO [*Chief of Naval Operations*] **Program Analysis Memorandum** (NVT) ... TCPAM
Tentative Drainage Tomorrow [*Surgery*] (DAVI) ... TDT
Tentative Final Monograph [*Food and Drug Administration*] ... TFM
Tentative Findings and Recommendations ... TFAR
Tentative Fiscal Guidance (MCD) ... TFG
Tentative Fiscal Guidance Memorandum [*Military*] (AFIT) ... TFGM
Tentative Force Guidance (NG) ... TFG
Tentative Logistics Guidance (MCD) ... TLG
Tentative OMA [*Operations and Maintenance Army*] **Program Analysis Memorandum** ... T-OPAM
Tentative Operational Requirement ... TOR
Tentative Pamphlet ... TP
Tentative Planning and Programming Guidance Memorandum [*Navy*] (NVT) ... TPPGM
Tentative Program Objectives [*Navy*] ... TPO
Tentative Program Objectives Memorandum [*Military*] (CAAL) ... TPOM
Tentative Qualitative Quantitative Personnel Requirements Information [*Army*] ... TQQPRI
Tentative Safe Exposure Level [*Toxicology*] ... TSEL
Tentative Specific Operational Requirement [*Military*] ... TSOR
Tentative Specification ... TS
Tentative Standard Method [*of analysis*] ... TSM
Tentative Summary CPAM [*Military*] (CAAL) ... TSCPAM
Tentative Tables of Equipment ... TTE
Tentative Tables of Organization and Equipment [*Army*] ... TTOE
Tentative Target ... T
Tentative Unit Allowance List [*Air Force*] (AFM) ... TUAL
Tentatively Identified Compounds (GNE) ... TIC
Tentena [*Indonesia*] [*ICAO location identifier*] (ICLI) ... WAMC
Tenth Molar [*Solute concentration by volume*] [*Chemistry*] (DAVI) ... M/10
Tenth Thickness Value [*Nuclear energy*] (NRCH) ... TTV
Tenth Value Layer ... TVL
Tenth-Power Width ... TPW
Ten-to-Twelve-Year Oscillation [*Meteorology*] ... TTO
Tenu'at Ha-Moshavim (BJA) ... TM
Tenuazonic Acid [*Biochemistry*] ... TA
Tenure Administration System [*Queensland*] [*State*] (EERA) ... TAS
Tenuto [*Held, Sustained*] [*Music*] ... TEN
Ten-Year Chinese Dong Tang [*Turmoil*] **Cycle** [*Reference to the Kuomintang's defeat in 1946-48, Mao's Great Leap Forward in 1956, the Cultural Revolution in 1966, the Gang of Four's fall in 1976*] [*Term coined by William Safire*] ... T-YCDT
Ten-Year Device [*Military decoration*] ... XYrDev
Ten-Year Oceanographic Program [*Navy*] ... TENOC
Teodoro Sampaio/Usina Porto Primavera [*Brazil ICAO location identifier*] (ICLI) ... SBAV
Teologinen Aikakauskirja [*Helsinki*] [*A publication*] (BJA) ... TA
Teoloyucan [*Mexico*] [*Geomagnetic observatory code*] ... TEO
Teoponte [*Bolivia*] [*ICAO location identifier*] (ICLI) ... SLTE
Tepecintle [*Race of maize*] ... TEP
Tephrosia Symptomless Virus [*Plant pathology*] ... TESV
TEPI [*Technical Equipment Planning Information*] **Approved Letter** ... TAL
Tepic [*Mexico ICAO location identifier*] (ICLI) ... MMEP
Tepic [*Mexico*] [*Airport symbol*] ... TPQ
Tepidarium (VRA) ... tepid
Tepidus [*Lukewarm*] [*Pharmacy*] (ROG) ... TEPID
Tepoe [*Surinam*] [*ICAO location identifier*] (ICLI) ... SMTP
Tepoztlan [*Mexico*] [*Seismograph station code, US Geological Survey*] (SEIS) ... TPM
Teppco Partners Ltd. [*Associated Press*] (SAG) ... Tepco
Teppco Partners Ltd. [*NYSE symbol*] (SPSG) ... TPP
Teppco Ptnrs L.P. [*NYSE symbol*] (TTSB) ... TPP
Teptep [*Papua New Guinea*] [*Airport symbol*] (OAG) ... TEP
Tequesquitengo [*Mexico ICAO location identifier*] (ICLI) ... MMTQ
Tequesta, FL [*Television station call letters*] ... WPBF
Ter [*Three Times*] [*Pharmacy*] ... T
Ter in Die [*Three Times a Day*] [*Symbol*] [*Pharmacology*] (DAVI) ... iii
Ter in Die [*Three Times a Day*] [*Pharmacy*] ... TD
Ter in Die [*Three Times a Day*] [*Pharmacy*] ... TID
Ter in Die Sumendum [*To Be Taken Three Times a Day*] [*Pharmacy*] ... TDS
Ter in Nocte [*Three Times a Night*] [*Pharmacy*] ... TIN
Ter Quaterve in Die [*Three or Four Times a Day*] [*Pharmacy*] ... TQD
Tera [*Niger*] [*ICAO location identifier*] (ICLI) ... DRRE
Tera [*A prefix meaning multiplied by 10^{12}*] [*SI symbol*] ... T
Tera Computer [*NASDAQ symbol*] (TTSB) ... TERA
Tera Computer Co. [*NASDAQ symbol*] (SAG) ... TERA
Tera Computer Co. [*Associated Press*] (SAG) ... TeraCo
Tera Computer Wrrt [*NASDAQ symbol*] (TTSB) ... TERAW
Tera Mines Ltd. [*Toronto Stock Exchange symbol*] ... TER
TeraBIT [*Binary Digit*] [*10^{12} BITs*] ... Tb
TeraBIT [*Binary Digit*] **Memory** [*Computer science*] ... TBM
TeraBIT Memory Operating System (NOAA) ... TBMOS
Terabits per Second (EECA) ... TBPS
Terabyte [*10^{12} bytes*] ... TB
Terabyte [*Computer science*] (EERA) ... Tb
Terabyte [*Computer science*] (EERA) ... Tbyte
Teracycle (BUR) ... T
Teracycle ... TC
Teradyne, Inc. [*NYSE symbol*] (SPSG) ... TER
Terahertz ... THz
Terahertz Optical Asymmetric Demultiplexer [*Optical computing*] ... TOAD
Terajoule [*SI unit of energy*] ... TJ
Terapascal [*Pressure unit*] ... TPa
Terapo [*Papua New Guinea*] [*Airport symbol*] (OAG) ... TEO
Terato Resources Ltd. [*Toronto Stock Exchange symbol*] ... TEO
Teratology (ROG) ... TERAT
Teratology Society (EA) ... TS
Terawatt ... TW
Terawatt Hour (ADA) ... TWh
Terbela [*Pakistan*] [*ICAO location identifier*] (ICLI) ... OPTA
Terbium [*Chemical element*] ... Tb
Terbium [*Symbol is Tb*] [*Chemical element*] (ROG) ... TR
Terbium Iron Garnet (IEEE) ... TbIG
Terceira [*Azores*] [*Airport symbol*] (OAG) ... TER
Terciarios Capuchinos de Nostra Signora de los Dolores [*Tertiary Capuchins of Our Lady of Sorrows*] [*Italy*] (EAIO) ... TC
TERCOM [*Terrain Contour Mapping*] **Aircraft Positioning Systems** [*Air Force*] ... TAPS
TERCOM [*Terrain Contour Mapping*]-**Assisted Inertial Navigation System** (MCD) ... TAINS
Tere [*Rub*] [*Pharmacy*] ... TER
Tere Simul [*Rub Together*] [*Latin*] (ADA) ... TER SIM
Terebinthinae Oleum [*Oil of Turpentine*] [*Pharmacology*] (ROG) ... TEREBINTH
TEREC [*Tactical Electronic Reconnaissance*] **Remote Terminal** (DWSG) ... TRT
Tereen [*Afghanistan*] [*ICAO location identifier*] (ICLI) ... OATN
Terence [*Second century BC*] [*Classical studies*] (OCD) ... Ter
Tereno [*MARC language code Library of Congress*] (LCCP) ... ter
Terentius Clemens [*Flourished, 2nd century*] [*Authority cited in pre-1607 legal work*] (DSA) ... Terent
Terephthalic Acid [*Also, TPA*] [*Organic chemistry*] ... TA
Terephthalic Acid [*Also, TA*] [*Organic chemistry*] ... TPA
Terephthalyl Bis(butylaniline) [*Organic chemistry*] ... TBBA
Teresa Brewer Fan Club (EA) ... TBFC
Teresian Apostolic Movement [*See also MTA*] [*Italy*] (EAIO) ... TAM
Teresian Institute (EA) ... TI
Teresina [*Brazil ICAO location identifier*] (ICLI) ... SBTE
Teresina [*Brazil*] [*Airport symbol*] (OAG) ... THE
Teresita [*Peru*] [*ICAO location identifier*] (ICLI) ... SPTE
Terex Corp. [*Associated Press*] (SAG) ... Terex
Terex Corp. [*NYSE symbol*] (SPSG) ... TEX
Terex Equipment Ltd. ... TEL
Tergotrochanteral Muscle Motoneuron [*Zoology*] ... TTMM
Teriton Resources Ltd. [*Vancouver Stock Exchange symbol*] ... TRN
Term [*Medicine*] ... T
Term [*Mathematics*] (WDAA) ... T
Term Availability Plan (IAA) ... TAP
Term Birth, Living Child [*Medicine*] ... TBLC
Term Birth, Living Infant [*Obstetrics*] (DAVI) ... TBLI
Term Coordination (NITA) ... TC
Term Lease Plan (IAA) ... TLP
Term Life Insurance ... TLI
Term Normal Delivery [*Obstetrics*] (MAE) ... TND
Term of Enlistment [*Military*] ... TOE

Term of Induction [*Military*] .... TOI
Term of Service [*Military*] .... TOS
Term Pass (AAG) .... TP
Term Reports [*North Carolina*] [*1816-18*] [*A publication*] (DLA) .... Term
Term Reports [*Legal*] [*British*] .... TR
Term Reports [*99-101 English Reprint*] [*A publication*] (DLA) .... TR (Eng)
Term Reports, English King's Bench [*Durnford and East's Reports*] [*England*]
  [*A publication*] (DLA) .... TR
Term Reports, English King's Bench (Durnford and East's Reports)
  [*A publication*] (DLA) .... Term
Term Reports, English King's Bench (Durnford and East's Reports)
  [*A publication*] (DLA) .... Term R
Term Reports, English King's Bench (Durnford and East's Reports)
  [*England*] [*A publication*] (DLA) .... Term Rep
Termex Resources, Inc. [*Vancouver Stock Exchange symbol*] .... TME
Termex [*USSR*] [*Airport symbol*] (AD) .... TMZ
Termez [*Former USSR ICAO location identifier*] (ICLI) .... UTST
Terminal .... T
Terminal [*Computer science*] (IAA) .... TE
Terminal (AAG) .... TERM
Terminal (AABC) .... TML
Terminal (AFM) .... TRML
Terminal .... TRMNL
Terminal Access Controller [*Advanced Research Projects Agency Network*]
  [*DoD*] .... TAC
Terminal Access Method .... TAM
Terminal Access Point [*Telecommunications*] (OSI) .... TAP
Terminal Access Processor .... TAP
Terminal Access System (MCD) .... TAS
Terminal Access to Batch Service [*Computer science*] (BUR) .... TABS
Terminal Activated Channel Test .... TACT
Terminal Adapter [*Telecommunications*] .... TA
Terminal Address (IAA) .... TA
Terminal Address Designator .... TAD
Terminal Address Register .... TAR
Terminal Address Selector .... TAS
Terminal Advanced Automation System [*Aviation*] .... TAAS
Terminal Aerodrome Forecast [*Also, TAFOR*] .... TAF
Terminal Aerodrome Forecast [*Also, TAF*] .... TAFOR
Terminal Aerodrome Forecast Verification .... TAFVER
Terminal Air Surveillance System [*FAA*] (TAG) .... TASS
Terminal Air Traffic Control .... TATC
Terminal Air Traffic Control Automation [*FAA*] (TAG) .... TATCA
Terminal Air Traffic Control Automation (GAVI) .... TATCA
Terminal Air Traffic Control Element .... TATCE
Terminal Air Traffic Control Facility .... TATCF
Terminal Air Traffic Control System .... TATCS
Terminal Airspace Visualization Tool [*FAA*] (TAG) .... TAVT
Terminal and Computer Network (MHDI) .... TNET
Terminal and Enroute Navigation (PDAA) .... TERN
Terminal Application Language .... TAL
Terminal Application Processing System .... TAPS
Terminal Application Program System [*Computer science*] .... TAPS
Terminal Application Support System (MCD) .... TASS
Terminal Applications Group, Inc. .... TAG
Terminal Applications Package (IEEE) .... TAP
Terminal Applications Program Generator [*Computer science*] (MHDI) .... TAPGEN
Terminal Area Altitude Monitoring (PDAA) .... TAAM
Terminal Area Chart [*Followed by identification*] [*Aviation*] .... T
Terminal Area Distribution Processing .... TAD/P
Terminal Area Energy Management [*NASA*] (NASA) .... TAEM
Terminal Area Impact Point (MUGU) .... TAIP
Terminal Area Instrumentation RADAR (MCD) .... TAIR
Terminal Area Navigation System .... TANS
Terminal Area Positive Separation [*FAA*] .... TAPS
Terminal Area Productivity (GAVI) .... TAP
Terminal Area RADAR/Moving Aircraft (KSC) .... TARMAC
Terminal Area Security Officer [*Military*] (AABC) .... TASO
Terminal Area Sequencing and Control .... TASC
Terminal Area Surveillance RADAR .... TAR
Terminal Area Surveillance RADAR .... TASR
Terminal Area Weapon Delivery Simulator (MCD) .... TAWDS
Terminal Atrial Contraction [*Cardiology*] (DAVI) .... TAC
Terminal Automated RADAR Services [*Aviation*] (FAAC) .... TARS
Terminal Automatic Monitoring System .... TAMOS
Terminal Auto-Operator and Monitor System (NITA) .... TAMOS
Terminal Ballistic Missile Defense [*Army*] (AABC) .... TBMD
Terminal Ballistic Track .... TBT
Terminal Ballistics Laboratory [*Army*] .... TBL
Terminal Base (MCD) .... TB
Terminal Block [*Automotive engineering*] .... T/BLK
Terminal Block .... TB
Terminal Board .... TB
Terminal Board Assembly (MSA) .... TBA
Terminal Bomber Defense [*Army*] (AABC) .... TBD
Terminal Bronchiole [*Medicine*] (MAE) .... TB
Terminal Buffer Controller (NASA) .... TBC
Terminal Buffer Unit [*Telecommunications*] (TEL) .... TBU
Terminal Business System [*Computer science*] (IAA) .... TBS
Terminal Business-Oriented Language .... TEBOL
Terminal Cancer [*Medicine*] .... TCA
Terminal Capacity Matrix (OA) .... TCM
Terminal Carcinoma [*Oncology*] (DAVI) .... TCA
Terminal Cluster Unit .... TCU
Terminal Command Language [*Applied Digital Data Systems*] .... TCL

Terminal Communication Adapter .... TCA
Terminal Communication Facility [*Telecommunications*] (TSSD) .... TCF
Terminal Communications Interface .... TCI
Terminal Communications Interface Test Program (MCD) .... TCITP
Terminal Communications Subsystem .... TCS
Terminal Computer (BUR) .... TC
Terminal Computer Identification (KSC) .... TCID
Terminal Computer System (BUR) .... TCS
Terminal Concentrator .... TC
Terminal Configuration Facility [*Computer science*] .... TCF
Terminal Congestion [*Telecommunications*] (TEL) .... TC
Terminal Control (NITA) .... TC
Terminal Control (DA) .... TMC
Terminal Control Area [*Aviation*] (AFM) .... TCA
Terminal Control Block [*Computer science*] (OA) .... TCB
Terminal Control Corridor [*Aviation*] .... TCC
Terminal Control Element (CAAL) .... TCE
Terminal Control Language .... TCL
Terminal Control Office [*or Officer*] .... TCO
Terminal Control Program .... TCP
Terminal Control System [*Hewlett-Packard Co.*] .... TCS
Terminal Control Table [*Computer science*] (IAA) .... TCT
Terminal Control Unit (MCD) .... TCU
Terminal Controller .... TC
Terminal Count [*Flight readiness count*] (MCD) .... T-COUNT
Terminal Count Sequence (IAA) .... TCS
Terminal Countdown Demonstration .... TCD
Terminal Countdown Sequencer [*or Sequences*] [*NASA*] (KSC) .... TCS
Terminal Cretaceous Event [*Geology*] .... TCE
Terminal Data Corp. [*Information service or system*] (IID) .... TDC
Terminal Data Input System (MCD) .... TDIS
Terminal Death Time (OA) .... TDT
Terminal Defense Interceptor Subsystem [*DoD*] .... TDIS
Terminal Defense Program [*Military*] .... TDP
Terminal Delivered Vehicle [*Army*] .... TDV
Terminal Deoxynucleotidyl Transferase [*An enzyme*] .... TDT
Terminal Deoxytransferase [*An enzyme*] (DAVI) .... TDT
Terminal Descent and Landing RADAR .... TDLR
Terminal Device [*of a prosthesis*] .... TD
Terminal Digit [*Telecommunications*] (TEL) .... TD
Terminal Digit Fitting System [*Military*] (AABC) .... TDFS
Terminal Digit Requested [*Telecommunications*] (TEL) .... TDR
Terminal Display (BUR) .... TD
Terminal Distributor (KSC) .... TD
Terminal Doppler Weather RADAR (DWSG) .... TDWR
Terminal Duct Lobular Unit [*Of mammary gland*] .... TDLU
Terminal Editing System [*Computer science*] (PDAA) .... TESY
Terminal Editor (ADA) .... TED
Terminal Effects and Experimentation (MCD) .... TEE
Terminal Effects Research and Analysis Group [*New Mexico Institute of
  Mining and Technology*] [*Research center*] (RCD) .... TERA
Terminal Elevator Grain Merchants Association (EA) .... TEGMA
Terminal Encounter System .... TES
Terminal Endpoint Identifier (TNIG) .... TEPI
Terminal Enquiry/Response Programming System [*British*] .... TERPS
Terminal Environment Module [*Computer science*] (MHDB) .... TEMOD
Terminal Equipment .... TE
Terminal Equipment Replacement Program [*Electronic communications
  system*] [*Department of State*] .... TERP
Terminal Equipment Test Facility [*Army*] (RDA) .... TETF
Terminal Equipment Vehicle [*British military*] (DMA) .... TEV
Terminal Error Program .... TEP
Terminal Exchange (MCD) .... TE
Terminal Exchange Area [*Computer science*] (MHDB) .... TXA
Terminal Executive [*Computer science*] (MHDB) .... TX
Terminal Facilities Guide [*DoD*] .... TFG
Terminal Flight Control (NATG) .... TFC
Terminal Flight Evaluation .... TFE
Terminal Forecast .... TF
Terminal Forecast Manual .... TFM
Terminal Forecasts [*Symbol*] [*National Weather Service*] .... FT
Terminal Frame (NATG) .... TF
Terminal Framing Bits [*Telecommunications*] (ACRL) .... Ft
Terminal Guidance .... TG
Terminal Guidance Environmental Effects Program (MCD) .... TGEEP
Terminal Guidance for Lunar Vehicles [*Aerospace*] (AAG) .... TGLVQ
Terminal Guidance Indirect Fire (MCD) .... TGIF
Terminal Guidance Sensor [*or System*] .... TGS
Terminal Guidance Sensor System .... TGSS
Terminal Handling Processor .... THP
Terminal High Altitude .... T-HA
Terminal Holding Power [*Advertising*] (IIA) .... THP
Terminal Homing Vehicle .... THV
Terminal Identification Code .... TIC
Terminal Ileum [*Gastroenterology*] (DAVI) .... TI
Terminal Imaging RADAR [*Military*] (RDA) .... TIR
Terminal Impact Prediction .... TIP
Terminal Independent Format .... TIF
Terminal Independent Graphics System .... TIGS
Terminal Information Processing [*Aviation*] (FAAC) .... TIPS
Terminal Innervation Ratio [*Psychiatry*] .... TIR
Terminal Input/Output (NITA) .... TIO
Terminal Input/Output Controller (NITA) .... TIOC
Terminal Input/Output Coordinator [*Computer science*] (IBMDP) .... TIOC
Terminal Input/Output Module [*Computer science*] .... TIOM

Terminal Input/Output Wait Queue [*Computer science*] .... TIOWQ
Terminal Instruction (System) for Managed Education .... TIME
Terminal Instrument Procedure [*Aviation*] .... TERP
Terminal Instrument Procedures [*Military*] .... TERPS
Terminal Interactive Access Method [*Computer science*] (IAA) .... TIAM
Terminal Interface .... TI
Terminal Interface Equipment .... TIE
Terminal Interface Monitor (IAA) .... TIM
Terminal Interface Package [*Computer science*] .... TIP
Terminal Interface [*Message*] Processor [*Computer science DoD*] .... TIP
Terminal Interface Program (NITA) .... TIP
Terminal Interface Subsystem [*Telecommunications*] (TEL) .... TIS
Terminal Interface Table (MCD) .... TIT
Terminal Interface Unit [*Bell System*] .... TIU
Terminal Island [*San Pedro*] [*Navy base*] .... TI
Terminal Job Identification (BUR) .... TJID
Terminal Junction System .... TJS
Terminal Landing System (KSC) .... TLS
Terminal Launch Facility .... TLF
Terminal Leaf Area [*Botany*] .... TAREA
Terminal Learning Objective .... TLO
Terminal Limen .... TL
Terminal List Table (IAA) .... TLT
Terminal Logic Unit [*Telecommunications*] (TEL) .... TLU
Terminal Low Altitude .... TLA
Terminal Management System [*Military*] (AABC) .... TERMS
Terminal Maneuvering Area [*Aviation*] .... TMA
Terminal Monitor Program [*Computer science*] (BUR) .... TMP
Terminal Monitor Program [*Computer science*] (MDG) .... TMT
Terminal Multiplexer [*Computer science*] (IAA) .... TM
Terminal Navy Post Office (AFM) .... TNPO
Terminal Net Loss .... TNL
Terminal Network Controller .... TNC
Terminal Node .... TN
Terminal Node Controller [*Computer science*] .... TNC
Terminal Office [*Computer science*] (IAA) .... TO
Terminal On-Line Availability Reporting .... TOLAR
Terminal Operations and Movements Management System (MCD) .... TOMMS
Terminal Operations Control System .... TOCS
Terminal or Computer Originated Mail Systems, Inc. [*Washington, DC*] (TSSD) .... TCOM
Terminal Oriental Real-Time Operating System [*Computer science*] (IAA) .... TORTOS
Terminal Panel (NASA) .... TMP
Terminal per Line [*Telecommunications*] .... TPL
Terminal Performance Specification .... TPS
Terminal Phalanx [*Anatomy*] .... TP
Terminal Phase Finalization [*or Finish*] [*NASA*] (KSC) .... TPF
Terminal Phase Ignition [*NASA*] .... TPI
Terminal Phase Initiate [*NASA*] (KSC) .... TPI
Terminal Phase Insertion [*NASA*] .... TPI
Terminal Phase Intercept .... TEPI
Terminal Phase Maneuver [*Aerospace*] (MCD) .... TPM
Terminal Phase Midcourse [*Aerospace*] (MCD) .... TPM
Terminal Pin Fault Insertion .... TPFI
Terminal Planning System [*Military*] .... TERPS
Terminal Point (NATG) .... TP
Terminal Pole [*Telecommunications*] (TEL) .... TP
Terminal Polling System .... TPS
Terminal Portability [*Telecommunications*] (DOM) .... TP
Terminal Position Location System .... TPLS
Terminal Primary and Secondary RADAR System (DA) .... TPSRS
Terminal Processing Language .... TPL
Terminal Processing Unit [*Computer science*] (IAA) .... TPU
Terminal Processor .... TP
Terminal Profile Security File [*IRS*] .... TPSF
Terminal Program Testing Guide .... TPTG
Terminal Programming Language [*Computer science*] (IAA) .... TPL
Terminal Programming System [*Computer science*] (ECII) .... TPS
Terminal Protective Device (MSA) .... TPD
Terminal Protocol (MHDI) .... TP
Terminal RADAR [*Aviation*] (FAAC) .... TRAD
Terminal RADAR Approach Control [*FAA*] .... TRACON
Terminal RADAR Approach Control Facility [*Aviation*] (FAAC) .... TRACON
Terminal RADAR Approach Control in Tower Cab [*Aviation*] (FAAC) .... TRACAB
Terminal RADAR Control (IAA) .... TRACON
Terminal RADAR Service Area [*Aviation*] (FAAC) .... TRSA
Terminal Radar Service Area [*FAA*] (TAG) .... TRSA
Terminal Radiation Airborne Program [*Air Force*] .... TRAP
Terminal Radiation Airborne Program Translator [*Air Force*] (IAA) .... TTR
Terminal Railroad Association Historical and Technical Society (EA) .... TRRA H & TS
Terminal Railroad Association of St. Louis .... TRR of ST L
Terminal Railroad Association of St. Louis [*AAR code*] .... TRRA
Terminal Railway, Alabama State Docks [*AAR code*] .... TASD
Terminal Ready [*Computer science*] .... TR
Terminal Release Order [*Military*] (AFIT) .... TRO
Terminal Renal Failure [*Medicine*] .... TRF
Terminal Rendezvous .... TR
Terminal Rendezvous Phase .... TRP
Terminal Repeat [*Genetics*] .... TR
Terminal Repeat Array [*Genetics*] .... TRA
Terminal Repeller Unconstrained Subenergy Tunneling [*An algorithm for global optimization*] .... TRUST
Terminal Replacement and Enquiry System (NITA) .... TRES

Terminal Response Monitor .... TRM
Terminal Restriction Fragment [*Genetics*] .... TRF
Terminal Restriction Fragment [*Cytology*] .... TRF
Terminal Retrieval and Enquiry Services [*Department of Employment*] [*British*] .... TRES
Terminal Secondary RADAR Beacon [*Aviation*] (FAAC) .... TSEC
Terminal Security System [*Computer science*] .... TSS
Terminal Send Side .... TSS
Terminal [*or Greater*] Sensation .... TS
Terminal Series (IAA) .... TS
Terminal Service .... TS
Terminal Source Editor .... TSE
Terminal Stage Vehicle .... TSV
Terminal Station (IAA) .... TS
Terminal Status Block [*Computer science*] (IBMDP) .... TSB
Terminal Sterilization Chamber .... TSC
Terminal Sterilization Facility .... TSF
Terminal Strip (DEN) .... TS
Terminal Student (OICC) .... TS
Terminal Support Module .... TSM
Terminal Support Processor [*Computer science*] (PDAA) .... TSP
Terminal Support Subsystems (NITA) .... TSS
Terminal Support System .... TSS
Terminal Tax Filing Time Trauma .... TTFTT
Terminal Testing Section [*Social Security Administration*] .... TTS
Terminal Threat Warning System .... TTWS
Terminal Timing (KSC) .... T/T
Terminal Timing Unit [*NASA*] (KSC) .... TTU
Terminal Tracking Telescope .... TETRA
Terminal Training Objective [*Army*] (INF) .... TTO
Terminal Trajectory Telescope (IAA) .... TTO
Terminal Translator (KSC) .... TERMTRAN
Terminal Transparent Delay Language (NITA) .... TTDL
Terminal Transparent Display Language [*Computer science*] (MHDI) .... TTDL
Terminal Transportation Unit [*Military*] (GFGA) .... TTU
Terminal Unit .... TU
Terminal Uridylyl Transferase [*An enzyme*] .... TUTase
Terminal Usage Charge [*Computer science*] (HGAA) .... TUC
Terminal Usage Reporting System [*Computer science*] .... TURS
Terminal User's Manual .... TUM
Terminal Vector Display Unit .... TVDP
Terminal Velocity [*Navy*] .... TV
Terminal Very High Frequency Omnirange (IAA) .... TVOR
Terminal VHF [*Very-High Frequency*] Omnidirectional Range .... TVOR
Terminal Visual Omnirange .... TVOR
Terminal Weather Doppler Radar [*FAA*] (TAG) .... TWDR
Terminal-Based Electronic Mail .... TBEM
Terminal-Configured Vehicle [*NASA*] .... TCV
Terminal-Configured Vehicles and Avionics [*Program*] [*NASA*] .... TCVA
Terminalischer Reiz [*Terminal Stimulus*] [*German Psychology*] .... TR
Terminally (Guided) Anti-Armor Mortar Projectile [*Navy*] (DOMA) .... TAMP
Terminally Guided Submissile (MCD) .... TGSM
Terminally Guided Submunitions (MCD) .... TGSM
Terminally Guided Warhead [*or Weapon*] .... TGW
Terminal-Modified RADAR Video Data Processor [*Noise control*] .... TMRVDP
Terminal-Operated Production Language (IAA) .... TOPL
Terminal-Operated Production Program (BUR) .... TOPP
Terminal-Oriented Administrative Data System .... TOADS
Terminal-Oriented Computer System .... TOCS
Terminal-Oriented Control Applications Program .... TOCAP
Terminal-Oriented Data Analysis and Retrieval System [*National Institute of Standards and Technology*] .... TODARS
Terminal-Oriented Planning System (MCD) .... TOPS
Terminal-Oriented Service Language .... TOSL
Terminal-Oriented Software [*Computer science*] (IEEE) .... TOS
Terminal-Oriented Support System .... TOSS
Terminal-Oriented System [*Computer science*] (IEEE) .... TOS
Terminals per Station [*Telecommunications*] .... TPS
Terminal-to-Computer Multiplexer .... TCM
Terminate (AFM) .... TERM
Terminate and Stay Resident [*Computer science*] .... TSR
Terminate Task Key .... TTK
Terminate with Extreme Prejudice [*To kill*] [*Counterintelligence*] .... TWEP
Terminating Amber Codon [*Genetics*] .... TAG
Terminating and Grounding .... TAG
Terminating Contracting Officer (AAGC) .... TC
Terminating Signal Unit [*Electronics*] (ECII) .... TSU
Terminating System (IAA) .... TS
Terminating Toll Center (DEN) .... TTC
Terminating Toll Operator [*Telecommunications*] (TEL) .... TX
Terminating Unfair Broadcasting Excesses [*Student legal action organization*] (EA) .... TUBE
Termination .... T
Termination (ECII) .... TERM
Termination (ROG) .... TERMINON
Termination .... TERMN
Termination Accountable Property Officer .... TAPO
Termination Check [*NASA*] (NASA) .... T/C
Termination Contracting Officer [*Military*] .... TCO
Termination Date (NITA) .... TD
Termination Design Change .... TDC
Termination for Convenience [*DoD*] .... T/C
Termination for Convenience (AAGC) T4C
Termination for Default (MCD) .... T (for) D
Termination Instruction .... TI

Termination Inventory Schedule (SAA) .... TIS
Termination of Centralized Management (MCD) .... TCM
Termination of Parental Rights (PAZ) .... TPR
Termination of Pregnancy (MAE) .... TOP
Termination, Test, and Verification (NASA) .... TTV
Terminator [*Genetics*] .... T
Terminator 2 [*Motion picture*] T2
Terminator Group .... TG
Terminator Group Controller (IAA) .... TGC
Terminator Interrupt [*Computer science*] (IAA) .... TI
Terminator Kit Assembly [*Robot*] .... TKA
Terminator Power [*Computer science*] .... TERM PWR
Terminator Sensor Output .... TSO
Terminological Data Bank .... TDB
Terminology .... TERM
Terminology, Administrative, Logistical, and Operational Procedures [*Military*] .... TALOP
Terminology, Aids, References, Applications, and Coordination (IAA) .... TARAC
Terminology and Documentation Branch, Translation Bureau, Department of the Secretary of State [*Direction generale de la Terminologie et de la Documentation,Bureau des Traductions, Secretariat d'Etat*] **Ottawa, Ontario** [*Library symbol National Library of Canada*] (NLC) .... OOSSTE
Terminology Database (NITA) .... TDB
Terminology Evaluation and Acquisition Method .... TEAM
Terminology Library [*Computer science*] (IAA) .... TL
Terminology Library, Information Resource Services Directorate, Secretary of State [*Bibliotheque de la Terminologie, Direction Info-Ressources, Secretariat d'Etat*], Ottawa, Ontario [*Library symbol National Library of Canada*] (NLC) .... OOSSTE
Terminus [*Biochemistry*] .... T
Terminus Paschae [*Easter Term*] [*Latin Legal term*] (DLA) .... Pas
Terminus Technicus (BJA) .... tt
Termite (ADA) .... TERM
Termite .... TRMT
Termite and Ant Detection Dog [*In TADD Services Corp.*] .... TADD
Term-Limit Pricing [*Agreement*] [*Price Commission*] .... TLP
Termo Fibertek, Inc. [*AMEX symbol*] (SPSG) .... TFT
Termoli [*Italy ICAO location identifier*] (ICLI) .... LIBT
Terms and Conditions .... T & C
Terms of Agreement (NATG) .... T of A
Terms of Agreement [*Army*] (AABC) .... TOA
Terms of Reference [*Army*] (AABC) .... TOR
Terms of Reference .... TR
Terms of the Common Laws and Statutes Expounded and Explained by John Rastell [*1685*] [*A publication*] (DLA) .... Termes de la Ley
Terms of Trade .... TOT
Terms of Trade (MHDW) .... TT
Tern Island Station (SAA) .... TIS
Ternary Compound Semiconductor .... TCS
Ternary Delta Modulation .... TDM
Ternary Digit (IAA) .... TIT
Ternary Eutectic Chloride [*Fire extinguishing agent*] .... TEC
Ternary Mobile Phase [*Physical chemistry*] .... TMP
Ternate [*Indonesia*] [*Airport symbol*] (OAG) .... TTE
Ternate/Babullah [*Indonesia*] [*ICAO location identifier*] (ICLI) .... WAMT
Terneplate [*Materials*] .... TRPL
Ternhill [*British ICAO location identifier*] (ICLI) .... EGOE
Terohmmeter (IEEE) .... TOHM
Teroson Europe Technical Centre [*Research center Germany*] .... TETC
Terpin Hydrate and Codeine [*Medicine*] .... TH & C
Terra Cotta [*Technical drawings*] .... TC
Terra Cotta [*Pronounced "tee-ko"*] [*Type of American art pottery*] .... TECO
Terra Industries [*NYSE symbol*] (TTSB) .... TRA
Terra Industries, Inc. [*Associated Press*] (SAG) .... Terra
Terra Industries, Inc. [*Formerly, Inspiration Resources Corp.*] [*NYSE symbol*] (SPSG) .... TRA
Terra Lliure [*Free Land*] [*Spanish terrorist group*] .... TL
Terra Mines Ltd. [*Toronto Stock Exchange symbol Vancouver Stock Exchange symbol*] .... TER
Terra Nitrogen Co. Ltd. [*Formerly, Agricultural Minerals Ltd.*] [*Associated Press*] (SAG) .... TerraNit
Terra Nitrogen Co. Ltd.[*Formerly, Agricultural Minerals Ltd.*] [*NYSE symbol*] (SAG) .... TNH
Terra Nitrogen L.P. [*NYSE symbol*] (TTSB) .... TNH
Terra Nova Bermuda Holdings Ltd. [*Associated Press*] (SAG) .... TerrNov
Terra Nova Bermuda Holdings Ltd. [*NYSE symbol*] (SAG) .... TNA
Terra Nova (Bermuda)Hldg [*NYSE symbol*] (TTSB) .... TNA
Terra Nova Energy [*Vancouver Stock Exchange symbol*] .... TNE
Terra Sancta Tourist Co. Ltd. [*Jordan*] .... testco
Terra Santa [*Jerusalem*] (BJA) .... TerS
Terra Santa [*Jerusalem*] [*A publication*] (BJA) .... TS
Terracamp Development [*Vancouver Stock Exchange symbol*] .... TPD
Terrace (ROG) .... TCE
Terrace .... TER
Terrace .... TER
Terrace (DD) .... Terr
Terrace (VRA) .... terr
Terrace .... TERR
Terrace [*Commonly used*] (OPSA) .... TERRACE
Terrace [*Classified advertising*] (ADA) .... TRCE
Terrace [*Canada*] [*Airport symbol*] (OAG) .... YXT
Terrace Bay [*Canada*] [*Airport symbol*] (OAG) .... YTJ
Terrace Bay Public Library, Ontario [*Library symbol National Library of Canada*] (NLC) .... OTBA
Terrace Bay Public Library, Terrace Bay, ON, Canada [*Library symbol Library of Congress*] (LCLS) .... CaOTbA
Terrace Bay Resources [*Vancouver Stock Exchange symbol*] .... TBY
Terrace, BC [*Television station call letters*] CBUFT-3
Terrace, BC [*AM radio station call letters*] .... CFTK
Terrace, BC [*Television station call letters*] .... CFTK-TV
Terrace, BC [*FM radio station call letters*] .... CJFW
Terrace, BC [*ICAO location identifier*] (ICLI) .... CYXT
Terrace Holdings [*NASDAQ symbol*] (TTSB) .... THIS
Terrace Holdings, Inc. [*Associated Press*] (SAG) .... Terrace
Terrace Holdings, Inc. [*NASDAQ symbol*] (SAG) .... THIS
Terrace Holdings Wrrt [*NASDAQ symbol*] (TTSB) .... THISW
Terrace Plaza Branch Library, Alberta Research Council, Edmonton, Alberta [*Library symbol National Library of Canada*] (NLC) .... AERTP
Terrace Public Library, British Columbia [*Library symbol National Library of Canada*] (NLC) .... BTE
Terraced Heterostructure (NITA) .... TH
Terracotta (VRA) .... ter
Terracotta Roofing Tile Association [*Australia*] .... TCRTA
Terracotta Tile [*Classified advertising*] (ADA) .... TCT
Terradyne, Inc. [*Associated Press*] (SAG) .... Terdyn
Terrain .... T
Terrain Analog RADAR Simulator .... TARS
Terrain Analysis Center [*Army*] (RDA) .... TAC
Terrain Analysis Program [*Military*] .... TAP
Terrain Analyst Work Station [*Army*] (RDA) .... TAWS
Terrain Analyst's Synthesizer Station [*Army*] (RDA) .... TASS
Terrain and Obstacle Warning and Avoidance .... TOWA
Terrain and RADAR Simulator (IAA) .... TARS
Terrain Avoidance [*Helicopter*] .... TA
Terrain Avoidance Accessory Device .... TAAD
Terrain Avoidance Override (MCD) .... TAO
Terrain Avoidance RADAR .... TAR
Terrain Avoidance RADAR (IAA) .... TARA
Terrain Avoidance RADAR System (MCD) .... TARS
Terrain Clearance [*Military*] (NG) .... TC
Terrain Clearance Altitude [*Aviation*] (DA) .... T
Terrain Clearance Indicator .... TCI
Terrain Clearance Measurement .... TCM
Terrain Clearance RADAR .... TCR
Terrain Contour Mapping (MCD) .... TERCOM
Terrain Contour Matching [*Navigation system*] [*Air Force*] .... TERCOM
Terrain Correlation (MCD) .... TC
Terrain Correlation Method .... TERCOM
Terrain Data Base [*Army*] (RDA) .... TDB
Terrain Elevation (SAA) .... TERREL
Terrain Elevation Retrieval Program (IEEE) .... TERP
Terrain Evaluation and Retrieval for Road Alignment (IAA) .... TERRA
Terrain Following/Terrain Avoidance (MCD) .... TF/TA
Terrain Height (MCD) .... TH
Terrain Index Reference System [*Army*] (INF) .... TIRS
Terrain Information System .... TIS
Terrain Integration Rough Earth Model .... TIREM
Terrain Mortar Positioning [*Military*] (INF) .... TMP
Terrain Profile Matching [*British*] .... TERPROM
Terrain Profile Recorder .... TPR
Terrain SDP SA [*Spain ICAO designator*] (FAAC) .... SDT
Terrain Trend System (MCD) .... TTS
Terrain-Following [*Helicopter*] .... TF
Terrain-Following Display .... TFD
Terrain-Following Evaluator .... TFE
Terrain-Following Flight .... TFF
Terrain-Following Flight Evaluator .... TFFE
Terrain-Following RADAR .... TFR
Terrain-Following System .... TFS
Terrain-Intelligence Integration Prototype [*Army*] (RDA) .... TIIP
Terrain-Referenced Navigation System [*Navy*] .... TRNS
Terrain-Related Accident [*Aviation*] .... TRA
Terramar Resources Corp. [*Toronto Stock Exchange symbol Vancouver Stock Exchange symbol*] .... TEM
Terramycin Capsule [*Antibacterial, trademark of Pfizer, Inc.*] .... TMC
Terranova [*Guatemala*] [*Seismograph station code, US Geological Survey*] (SEIS) .... TER
TERRAP [*Territorial Apprehensiveness*] **Programs** [*Commercial firm*] (EA) .... TERRAP
Terrarium Association (EA) .... TA
Terrasse (DD) .... tsse
Terratech Resources, Inc. [*Toronto Stock Exchange symbol*] .... TRE
Terrawest [*Vancouver Stock Exchange symbol*] .... TAW
Terraza .... TERR
Terrazo [*Technical drawings*] .... TZ
Terrazzo .... TER
Terrazzo [*Classified advertising*] (ADA) .... TRZO
Terrazzo Base .... TERB
Terre Adelie [*Antarctica*] [*Seismograph station code, US Geological Survey Closed*] (SEIS) .... TAA
Terre des Hommes [*An international organization*] .... TDH
Terre Haute [*Indiana*] [*Airport symbol*] (OAG) .... HUF
Terre Haute [*Indiana*] [*Seismograph station code, US Geological Survey*] (SEIS) .... THI
Terre Haute & Peoria Railroad [*Nickname: Take Hold and Push*] .... TH & P
Terre Haute, IN [*FM radio station call letters*] (RBYB) .... WAPC-FM
Terre Haute, IN [*Television station call letters*] .... WBAK
Terre Haute, IN [*AM radio station call letters*] .... WBOW
Terre Haute, IN [*FM radio station call letters*] .... WCRT

Terre Haute, IN [*FM radio station call letters*] ... WISU
Terre Haute, IN [*AM radio station call letters*] ... WJSH
Terre Haute, IN [*FM radio station call letters*] ... WLEZ
Terre Haute, IN [*FM radio station call letters*] ... WMGI
Terre Haute, IN [*FM radio station call letters*] ... WMHD
Terre Haute, IN [*AM radio station call letters*] ... WTHI
Terre Haute, IN [*FM radio station call letters*] ... WTHI-FM
Terre Haute, IN [*Television station call letters*] ... WTHI-TV
Terre Haute, IN [*Television station call letters*] ... WTWO
Terre Haute, IN [*AM radio station call letters*] (RBYB) ... WZZQ
Terre Haute, IN [*FM radio station call letters*] ... WZZQ-FM
Terre Haute Spectator, Terre Haute, IN [*Library symbol Library of Congress*] (LCLS) ... InTS
Terre Haute Tribune-Star, Terre Haute, IN [*Library symbol Library of Congress*] (LCLS) ... InTTS
Terre Ocean Atmosphere [*Marine science*] (OSRA) ... TOA
Terre Sainte (BJA) ... TeS
Terrebonne Parish Library, Houma, LA [*Library symbol Library of Congress*] (LCLS) ... LHouT
Terrell and Walker's Reports [*38-51 Texas*] [*A publication*] (DLA) ... Terr & Wal
Terrell and Walker's Reports [*38-51 Texas*] [*A publication*] (DLA) ... Terr & Walk
Terrell Hills, TX [*FM radio station call letters*] (RBYB) ... KCJZ
Terrell Hills, TX [*AM radio station call letters*] ... KLUP
Terrell, TX [*AM radio station call letters*] ... KPYK
Terrell, TX [*FM radio station call letters*] ... KTLR
Terrell, TX [*Location identifier FAA*] (FAAL) ... TRL
Terrell's Laboratories Medical Library, Fort Worth, TX [*Library symbol Library of Congress*] (LCLS) ... TxFTM
Terrell's Reports [*38-71 Texas*] [*A publication*] (DLA) ... Terr
Terrestrial Application of Solar Technology and Research (MCD) ... TERRESTAR
Terrestrial Auxiliary Power ... TAP
Terrestrial Background Infrared Detection (SAA) ... TBIRD
Terrestrial Ballistic Infrared Development (SAA) ... T-BIRD
Terrestrial Biogeochemical Model [*for climate effects*] ... TBM
Terrestrial Carbon Model [*Earth science*] ... TCM
Terrestrial Dust Belt ... TDB
Terrestrial Dynamic Time (WGA) ... TDT
Terrestrial Ecosystem Model [*for climate effects*] ... TEM
Terrestrial Environmental Services [*Army*] (AABC) ... TERENVSVC
Terrestrial Initiative in Global Environmental Research [*UK government research program*] ... TIGER
Terrestrial Interference (WDMC) ... TI
Terrestrial Kilometric Radiation [*Physics*] ... TKR
Terrestrial Low-Power Reactor ... TLPR
Terrestrial Magnetic Guidance System [*Aerospace*] (AAG) ... TMGS
Terrestrial Microcosm Chamber [*For environmental studies*] ... TMC
Terrestrial Microwave Link ... TML
Terrestrial Myriametric Radiation [*Physics*] ... TMR
Terrestrial Observation Panel (EERA) ... TOP
Terrestrial Planet Finder [*Proposed*] ... TPF
Terrestrial Plants ... TP
Terrestrial Radio Frequency ... TRF
Terrestrial Radio System ... TRS
Terrestrial Science Center (MCD) ... TSC
Terrestrial Unattended Reactor Power System ... TURPS
Terret Communications [*Whitehouse Station, NJ*] (TSSD) ... T-Comm
Terri Gibbs Fan Club (EA) ... TGFC
Terri LaVelle Fan Club (EA) ... TLFC
Terricide-Escape by Rethinking, Research, Action [*An association*] ... TERRA
Terridic Reactor Isotope Separator To Analze Nuclides [*Brookhaven National Laboratory*] ... TRISTAN
Terrier Advanced RADAR (DNAB) ... TAR
Terrier Land Weapon System ... TLWS
Terrier Operation Proof High-Altitude Target (MUGU) ... TOPHAT
Terrier RADAR and Beacon Orientation Test (MUGU) ... TRABOT
Terrier/Tartar Reliability Improvement Program (SAA) ... TRIP
Terrier Weapons System ... TWS
Territoire Francaise des Afars et des Issas [*French Territory of the Afars and Issas*] ... TFAI
Territorial Airlines, Inc. [*ICAO designator*] (FAAC) ... TER
Territorial and Army Volunteer Reserve [*British*] ... T & AVR
Territorial and Auxiliary Forces Association [*British military*] (DMA) ... TAFA
Territorial Army ... TA
Territorial Army and Air Force Association [*British military*] (DMA) ... TAAFA
Territorial Army Association [*British*] ... TAA
Territorial Army Nursing Service [*British*] ... TANS
Territorial Army Regulations [*British military*] (DMA) ... TAR
Territorial Army Reserve of Officers [*British*] ... TARO
Territorial Army Rifle Association [*British military*] (DMA) ... TARA
Territorial Auxiliary and Volunteer Reserve Association [*British Armed Forces*] ... TAVRA
Territorial Cadet Force [*British military*] (DMA) ... TCF
Territorial College of Guam ... TCG
Territorial Command Net ... TCN
Territorial Decoration [*Military British*] ... TD
Territorial Experiment Stations Division [*of ARS, Department of Agriculture*] ... TES
Territorial Force [*Military British*] ... TF
Territorial Force Nursing Service ... TFNS
Territorial Force Reserve [*British*] ... TFR
Territorial Fund Campaign [*Red Cross*] ... TFC
Territorial Highway System [*FHWA*] (TAG) ... THS
Territorial Long Service Medal [*Military British*] ... TLS
Territorial Party [*Northern Marianas*] (PPW) ... TP
Territorial Petroleum [*Vancouver Stock Exchange symbol*] ... TTV
Territorial Production Complex [*Russian*] ... TPC
Territorial Reserve [*British military*] (DMA) ... TR
Territorial Residents ... TERRES
Territorial Rhine Coordination [*NATO*] (NATG) ... TERRHICO
Territorial Staff Course [*British military*] (DMA) ... tsc
Territorial Support Group [*Scotland Yard*] [*British*] ... TSG
Territorial Teacher Training Assistance Program [*Department of Education*] (GFGA) ... TTTAP
Territorial Yeomanry [*British military*] (DMA) ... TY
Territories Law [*Northwest Territories*] [*A publication*] (DLA) ... Terr L
Territories Law Reports [*1885-1907*] [*Canada*] [*A publication*] (DLA) ... Can Terr
Territories Law Reports [*1885-1907*] [*Canada*] [*A publication*] (DLA) ... Terr L (Can)
Territories Law Reports [*1885-1907*] [*Canada*] [*A publication*] (DLA) ... Terr LR
Territory ... T
Territory ... TER
Territory (AFM) ... TERR
Territory ... TERRIT
Territory ... TY
Territory (ODBW) ... Ty
Territory Airlines [*Australia*] ... TAL
Territory Anti-Litter Committee [*Northern Territory, Australia*] ... TALC
Territory Enterprises Proprietary ... TEP
Territory of Hawaii [*to 1959*] ... TH
Territory of Papua and New Guinea ... TPNG
Territory Parks and Wildlife Advisory Council [*Northern Territory, Australia*] ... TPWAC
Territory Wildlife Park [*Northern Territory, Australia*] ... TWP
Terror Bay [*Alaska*] [*Airport symbol*] (OAG) ... KTY
Terror Bay, AK [*Location identifier FAA*] (FAAL) ... KTY
Terrorism and Guerrilla Warfare [*Israel*] ... Terrorilla
Terrorism Incident Working Group [*Bureau of Diplomatic Security*] [*Department of State*] (EGAO) ... TIWG
Terrorisme, Radicalisme, Extremisme, Violence Internationale [*International anti-terrorist group*] [*Belgium*] ... TREVI
Terrorist [*Slang term used by whites in Zimbabwe to refer to a black nationalist guerrilla*] ... Terr
Terrorist Action Team [*Military*] (MCD) ... TAT
Terrorist and Disruptive Activities Act [*India*] (ECON) ... TADA
Terrorist Intelligence Gathering Evaluation and Review [*British*] ... TIGER
Terry and the Pirates [*Pop music group*] ... T & TP
Terry and the Pirates Fan Club (EA) ... TTPFC
Terry Fox Canadian Youth Centre ... TFCYC
Terry's Delaware Reports [*A publication*] (DLA) ... Ter
Terrytown, NE [*FM radio station call letters*] ... KCMI
Terrytown, NE [*AM radio station call letters*] ... KOAQ
Tert-Butylbicyclophosphorothionate [*Biochemistry*] ... TBPS
tert-Butyloxycarbonyl [*Also, t-Boc*] [*Organic chemistry*] ... t-BOC
Tertbutyl-P-Cresol (DICI) ... TBPC
Tertiary [*Also, tert*] [*Chemistry*] ... t
Tertiary (KSC) ... TER
Tertiary [*Also, t*] [*Chemistry*] ... tert
Tertiary [*Period, era, or system*] [*Geology*] ... TERT
Tertiary Amyl Ethyl Ether [*Gasoline*] [*Organic chemistry*] ... TAEE
Tertiary Butyl Acetate [*Organic chemistry*] ... TBA
Tertiary Butyl Acetate [*USAN*] [*Organic chemistry*] ... TEBUTATE
Tertiary Butyl Alcohol [*Gasoline additive*] ... TBA
Tertiary Butyl Mercaptan [*Organic chemistry*] ... TBM
Tertiary Butyl Phosphine [*Organic chemistry*] ... TBP
Tertiary Butylphenyl Salicylate [*Food packaging*] ... TBS
Tertiary Colleges Association [*British*] (DBA) ... TCA
Tertiary Data Set [*Computer science*] (OA) ... TDS
Tertiary Dodecyl Mercaplan (OA) ... TDM
Tertiary Education Research Centre [*British*] (AIE) ... TERC
Tertiary Leucine (BABM) ... Terleu
Tertiary of the Order of St. Dominic [*Roman Catholic religious order*] ... TSD
Tertiary of Third Order of St. Francis [*Later, SFO*] [*Roman Catholic religious order*] ... TOSF
Tertiary Operation ... TOP
Tertiary Orientation Program [*Australia*] ... TOP
Tertiary Research Group [*British*] ... TRG
Tertiary Sand [*Agronomy*] ... TERTSD
Tertiary-Amyl Alcohol [*Organic chemistry*] ... TAA
Tertiary-Amyl Methyl Ether [*Gasoline additive*] ... TAME
Tertiary-Amylphenol [*Disinfectant*] ... TAMP
Tertiary-Butyl Hydroperoxide [*Organic chemistry*] ... TBHP
Tertiary-Butyl Perbenzoate [*Organic chemistry*] ... TBPB
Tertiary-Butylacetyl Chloride [*Organic chemistry*] ... TBAC
Tertiary-Butylamine [*Organic chemistry*] ... TBA
Tertiary-Butylarsine [*Organic chemistry*] ... TBA
Tertiary-Butylcatechol [*Organic chemistry*] ... TBC
Tertiary-Butyldimethylsilyl [*Organic chemistry*] ... TBDMS
Tertiary-Butyldimethylsilyl [*Also, TBDMS, TBDPS*] [*Organic chemistry*] ... TBS
Tertiary-Butyldimethylsilyl Chloride [*Also, TBSCl*] [*Organic chemistry*] ... TBDMSCl
Tertiary-Butyldimethylsilyl Chloride [*Also, TBDMSCl*] [*Organic chemistry*] ... TBSCl
Tertiary-Butyldimethylsilylimidazole [*Organic chemistry*] ... TBDMIM
Tertiary-Butyldiphenysilyl [*Also, TBDMS, TBS*] [*Organic chemistry*] ... TBDPS
Tertiary-Butylhydroperioxide [*Organic chemistry*] ... TBHP
Tertiary-Butylhydroquinone [*Also, MTBHQ*] [*Organic chemistry*] ... TBHQ
Tertiary-Butylnaphthalene [*Organic chemistry*] ... TBN
Tertiary-Butylstyrene [*Organic chemistry*] ... TBS
Tertiary-Pentylphenol [*Organic chemistry*] ... TPP
Tertius [*Third*] [*Latin*] ... TERT
Tertullian [*160-240AD*] [*Classical studies*] (OCD) ... Tert

Tertullianus [*Flourished, 2nd-3rd century*] [*Authority cited in pre-1607 legal work*] (DSA) .... Tertul

Terumot (BJA) .... Ter

Teruvenkatachariar's Railway Cases [*India*] [*A publication*] (DLA) .... Teruv

Tervola [*Finland ICAO location identifier*] (ICLI) .... EFTE

Teryl Resources Corp. [*Vancouver Stock Exchange symbol*] .... TRC

Terza Posizione [*Third Position*] [*Italy*] .... TP

Terz'Ordine dei Minimi [*Third Order of Minimi*] [*Italy*] (EAIO) .... TOM

Tesak [*Afghanistan*] [*ICAO location identifier*] (ICLI) .... OATZ

Tescorp 10% 1990 Cv Pfd [*NASDAQ symbol*] (TTSB) .... TESCP

Tescorp, Inc. [*NASDAQ symbol*] (SAG) .... TESC

Tescorp, Inc. [*Associated Press*] (SAG) .... Tescp

Tescorp, Inc. [*Associated Press*] (SAG) .... Tescrp

Tesero Oolite Horizon [*Geology*] .... TOH

Teshmount Consultants, Winnipeg, Manitoba [*Library symbol National Library of Canada*] (NLC) .... MWTC

Teshmount Consultants, Winnipeg, MB, Canada [*Library symbol Library of Congress*] (LCLS) .... CaMWTC

Tesis [*Russian Federation*] [*ICAO designator*] (FAAC) .... TIS

Tesla [*Symbol*] [*SI unit of flux density*] .... T

Tesla Coil Builders Association (EA) .... TCBA

Tesla Memorial Society (EA) .... TMS

Teslin, YT [*ICAO location identifier*] (ICLI) .... CYZW

Tesma International, Inc. [*Associated Press*] (SAG) .... Tesma

Tesma International, Inc. [*NASDAQ symbol*] (SAG) .... TSMAF

Tesma Intl'A' [*NASDAQ symbol*] (TTSB) .... TSMAF

Tesoro Petroleum [*NYSE symbol*] (TTSB) .... TSO

Tesoro Petroleum Corp. [*Associated Press*] (SAG) .... Tesor

Tesoro Petroleum Corp. [*Associated Press*] (SAG) .... Tesoro

Tesoro Petroleum Corp. [*NYSE symbol*] (SPSG) .... TSO

Tessalit [*Mali*] [*ICAO location identifier*] (ICLI) .... GATS

Tessaoua [*Niger*] [*ICAO location identifier*] (ICLI) .... DRRA

Tessaral Harmonic Resonance of Orbital Elements (PDAA) .... THROE

TESSCO Technologies [*NASDAQ symbol*] (TTSB) .... TESS

TESSCO Technologies, Inc. [*NASDAQ symbol*] (SAG) .... TESS

TESSCO Technologies, Inc. [*Associated Press*] (SAG) .... TESSCO

Tessenei [*Ethiopia*] [*ICAO location identifier*] (ICLI) .... HATS

Tessenei [*Ethiopia*] [*Airport symbol*] (AD) .... tes

Tessera (VRA) .... T

Test (MSA) .... T

Test .... TS

Test (AAG) .... TST

Test a BIT [*Binary Digit*] and Change [*Computer science*] .... BCHG

Test a BIT [*Binary Digit*] and Clear [*Computer science*] .... BCLR

Test a BIT [*Binary Digit*] and Set [*Computer science*] .... BSET

Test Acceptance Document [*Computer science*] (IAA) .... TAD

Test Access [*Telecommunications*] (TEL) .... TA

Test Access Control [*Telecommunications*] (TEL) .... TAC

Test Access Control Interface [*Telecommunications*] (TEL) .... TACI

Test Access Line Termination Circuit [*Telecommunications*] (TEL) .... TALTC

Test Access Multiplexer [*Telecommunications*] (TEL) .... TAM

Test Access Selector [*Telecommunications*] (TEL) .... TAS

Test Access Signaling Conversion Circuit [*Telecommunications*] (TEL) .... TASCC

Test Access Unit [*Telecommunications*] (TEL) .... TAU

Test Accessory (AAG) .... TA

Test Acquisition Module Self Check (CAAL) .... TSC

Test Action Requirement (NASA) .... TAR

Test Administration Plan (NASA) .... TAP

Test Advisory Committee (MUGU) .... TAC

Test Agency Report (NASA) .... TAR

Test Analysis Guide .... TAG

Test Analysis Outline .... TAO

Test Analysis Report .... TAR

Test, Analyze, and Fix (AAGC) .... TAAF

Test, Analyze, and Fix Program [*Navy*] (MCD) .... TAAF

Test, Analyze, Fix (MCD) .... TAF

Test Analyzer System [*Electronics*] .... TAS

Test and Adjust (SSD) .... T & A

Test and Checkout [*NASA*] (GFGA) .... TCO

Test and Checkout Operations [*NASA*] (NASA) .... TACO

Test and Checkout Plan [*NASA*] (KSC) .... TCOP

Test and Checkout Procedure [*NASA*] (KSC) .... TCP

Test and Checkout Requirements Document [*NASA*] (KSC) .... TCRD

Test and Checkout Requirements Specification Documentation [*NASA*] (NASA) .... TCRSD

Test and County Cricket Board [*British*] .... TCCB

Test and Crossmatch [*Medicine*] (MAH) .... T & C

Test and Debug System (HGAA) .... TADS

Test and Development (MCD) .... TAD

Test and Development Work Order .... TDWO

Test and Diagnostic Language (MCD) .... TDL

Test and Diagnostics (IAA) .... TD

Test and Engineering (MCD) .... TE

Test and Evaluation [*Navy*] (NG) .... T & E

Test and Evaluation (MCD) .... TAE

Test and Evaluation Advisory Council [*Military*] (CAAL) .... TEAC

Test and Evaluation Agency .... TEA

Test and Evaluation, Aircraft Survivability .... TEAS

Test and Evaluation Command [*Army*] .... T & EC

Test and Evaluation Command [*Aberdeen Proving Ground, MD*] [*Army*] .... TECOM

Test and Evaluation Committee [*DoD*] (RDA) .... TEC

Test and Evaluation Coordinating Group [*Military*] (CAAL) .... TECG

Test and Evaluation Division [*National Weather Service*] .... TED

Test and Evaluation Facility [*Nuclear energy*] (NUCP) .... TEF

Test and Evaluation Flight [*Military*] .... TEF

Test and Evaluation Management Agency [*Army*] (RDA) .... TEMA

Test and Evaluation Management Course (MCD) .... TEMC

Test and Evaluation Management Office [*Army*] (RDA) .... TEMO

Test and Evaluation Management Plan [*Army*] .... TEMP

Test and Evaluation Objectives Annex (MCD) .... TEOA

Test and Evaluation of Air Mobility .... TEAM

Test and Evaluation Plan [*Military*] (CAAL) .... TEP

Test and Evaluation Planning Committee [*Military*] (CAAL) .... TEPC

Test and Evaluation Squadron .... TES

Test and Evaluation Support .... TES

Test and Evaluation Support Resource Plan (MCD) .... TESRP

Test and Evaluation Task Group Manager .... T & ETGM

Test and Evaluation Task Group Manager (MCD) .... TAETGM

Test and Evaluation Technical Support Services [*Army*] .... TETSS

Test and Evaluation Work Group [*Military*] (CAAL) .... TEWG

Test and Experimentation Command [*TRADOC*] [*Fort Hood, TX*] .... TEXCOM

Test and Handling [*Equipment*] (NG) .... T & H

Test and Maintenance (WDAA) .... T & M

Test and Measurement [*Quality control*] .... T & M

Test & Measurement Division (ACII) .... TMD

Test and Measurement Equipment (MCD) .... TME

Test and Measurement Equipment for Maintenance Calibration .... TMEMC

Test and Monitor (CAAL) .... T & M

Test and Monitoring Station .... TMS

Test and Monitoring System (MCD) .... TAMS

Test and Operation [*NASA*] (KSC) .... T & O

Test and Operation (IAA) .... TAO

Test and Operations Plan .... TOP

Test and Quality Assurance (IAA) .... TAQA

Test and Repair [*or Replace*] as Necessary .... TARAN

Test and Repair Processor [*Computer science*] .... TARP

Test and Repair Station .... TARS

Test and Research Reactor [*Nuclear energy*] (NRCH) .... TRR

Test and Return (IAA) .... TAR

Test and Set [*Computer science*] .... TAS

Test and Set [*Computer science*] (IAA) .... TS

Test and Switching Gear [*NASA*] (KSC) .... TSG

Test and Timesharing Facility [*Social Security Administration*] .... TTSF

Test and Training Monitor (AAG) .... T/TM

Test and Training Satellite [*Also, TETR, TTS*] [*NASA*] .... TATS

Test and Training Satellite [*Also, TATS, TTS*] [*NASA*] .... TETR

Test and Training Satellite [*Also, TATS, TETR*] [*NASA*] .... TTS

Test and Validation (KSC) .... TAV

Test and Verification Environment for Remote Network Systems (SSD) .... TAVERNS

Test and Verify Programs [*Computer science*] (MDG) .... T & V

Test Announcer (IAA) .... TA

Test Answer Document Reader .... TADR

Test Answer Sheets .... TAS

Test Anxiety Inventory [*Educational test*] .... TAI

Test Anxiety Profile [*Educational test*] .... TAP

Test Anxiety Scale for Children [*Psychology*] .... TASC

Test Area North [*AEC*] .... TAN

Test Area Support Assembly .... TASA

Test Article (NASA) .... TA

Test Article Engineering Order (MCD) .... TAEO

Test Article Signal Translator (MCD) .... TAST

Test Article Specification (NASA) .... TAS

Test Assembly Conditioning Station [*Nuclear energy*] (NRCH) .... TACS

Test Assembly Grapple [*Nuclear energy*] (NRCH) .... TAG

Test Assembly Inspection Record [*NASA*] (NASA) .... TAIR

Test Assembly Unloading Fixture [*Nuclear energy*] (NRCH) .... TAUF

Test Assistance Program [*Sperry UNIVAC*] .... TAP

Test ASW [*Antisubmarine Warfare*] Missile [*Navy*] (CAAL) .... TASWM

Test Automation Growth .... TAG

Test Base Dispatch Service (AAG) .... TBDS

Test Base Material Operation (AAG) .... TBMO

Test Base Support Group (AAG) .... TBSG

Test Bed (MCD) .... TB

Test Bed Aircraft .... TBA

Test Bed Harness (MCD) .... TBH

Test Bed Installation (MCD) .... TBI

Test Bed Mode Control .... TBMC

Test Before Using (MCD) .... TBU

Test Bench Harness (NG) .... TBH

Test Bench Installation (NG) .... TBI

Test Bench Set (MCD) .... TBS

Test Boring Association (EA) .... TBA

Test Boring Contractors Association [*Later, TBA*] (EA) .... TBCA

Test Bulletin .... TB

Test Call Answer Relay Set (PDAA) .... TCARS

Test Call Generator [*Telecommunications*] (TEL) .... TCG

Test Call Module [*Telecommunications*] (TEL) .... TCM

Test Call Sender (NITA) .... TCS

Test Case Specification (IAA) .... TC

Test Change Notice [*NASA*] (MCD) .... TCN

Test Change Proposal (CAAL) .... TCP

Test Checkout Panel .... TCP

Test Checkout Support Plan (KSC) .... TCSP

Test Chief .... TC

Test Collection [*Educational Testing Service*] [*Information service or system*] (IID) .... TC

Test Command Defense Nuclear Agency [*Military*] (AABC) .... TESTCOMDNA

Test Communications Division (SAA) .... TCD

Test Compare Results (MCD) .... TCR

Test Completion Date (NASA) .... TCD
Test Computer Unit .... TCU
Test Condition Requirements [Army] .... TCR
Test Conductor (AAG) .... TC
Test Conductor (MCD) .... TCR
Test Conductor Console (AAG) .... TCC
Test Configuration Identifier (NASA) .... TCID
Test Connection Equipment (IAA) .... TCE
Test Console .... TC
Test Constraints Review [NASA] (MCD) .... TCR
Test Control Center [NASA] .... TCC
Test Control Commission [NATO] .... TCC
Test Control Document [NASA] (MCD) .... TCD
Test Control Drawings (MCD) .... TCD
Test Control Fixture (MCD) .... TCF
Test Control Group [NASA] (NASA) .... TCG
Test Control Instruction (KSC) .... TCI
Test Control Noncommissioned Officer (AFM) .. TCNCO
Test Control Officer [Military] .... TCO
Test Control Package (NASA) .... TCP
Test Control Supervisor (NASA) .... TCS
Test Control System (NASA) .... TCS
Test Control Unit (NASA) .... TCU
Test Controller .... TC
Test Controller Computer (MCD) .... TCC
Test Controller Console (KSC) .... TCC
Test Coordinating Center [Army] .... TCC
Test Coordinator .... TC
Test Coordinator Console (CAAL) .... TCC
Test Coverage Analysis Tool (IEEE) .... TCAT
Test Data .... TD
Test Data Division (SAA) .... TDD
Test Data Generating Language (MHDB) .... TDGL
Test Data Generation Section [Social Security Administration] ...... TDGS
Test Data Generator (BUR) .... TDG
Test Data Interpolation .... TDI
Test Data Memorandum (AAG) .... TDM
Test Data Recorder .... TDR
Test Data Recording and Retrieval (NASA) ...... TDRR
Test Data Report (AAG) .... TDR
Test Data Sheet (KSC) .... TDS
Test Data Specification (IAA) .... TDS
Test Data System (NASA) .... TDS
Test Data Van (NASA) .... TDV
Test Data Variation .... TDV
Test de Bon Fonctionnement [Spacelab] (MCD) .... TBF
Test Deficiency Change Request [Nuclear energy] (NRCH) ...... TDCR
Test Deficiency Report [Nuclear energy] (NRCH) .... TDR
Test Definition Document .... TDD
Test Description Log (MCD) .... TDL
Test Design and Evaluation .... TD & E
Test Design and Evaluation (MCD) .... TDAE
Test Design Description [Nuclear energy] (NRCH) .... TDD
Test Design In-Process Review (MCD) .... TDIPR
Test Design Plan [Army] .... TDP
Test Design Specification (IEEE) .... TD
Test Development Activity [Army] .... TDA
Test Development Agent (CAAL) .... TDA
Test Development Director .... TDD
Test Development Manager [Military] (CAAL) .... TDM
Test, Diagnostic, and Measurement Equipment (MCD) .... TDME
Test Direction Team .... TDT
Test Directive (AAG) .... TD
Test Director .... TD
Test Director Console .... TDC
Test Director Console Operator [Navy] (CAAL) .. TDCO
Test Disable/Reset (AAG) .... TD/R
Test Discount Rate .... TDR
Test Discrepancy Report (MCD) .... TDR
Test Display Generator .... TDG
Test Distributor [Telecommunications] (TEL) ... TD
Test Documentation Booklet [Navy] (CAAL) ..... TDB
Test Documentation Group .... TDG
Test Drawing (MCD) .... TD
Test Dwell Time .... TDT
Test Ear [Otorhinolaryngology] (DAVI) .... TE
Test Effectiveness Ratio [Computer science] .... TER
Test Element Group .... TEG
Test Engineer Readiness List [NASA] (NASA) ... TERL
Test Engineering Division [Navy] .... TED
Test Engineering Documentation (MCD) .... TED
Test Engineer's Assistant [Computer-aided design tool] .... TEA
Test Equipment (NG) .... T
Test Equipment .... TE
Test Equipment .... TSTEQ
Test Equipment Accessory (MCD) .... TEA
Test Equipment Analysis .... TEA
Test Equipment Center [NASA] (NASA) .... TEC
Test Equipment Change Requirement (NATG) ... TECR
Test Equipment Committee (AAG) .... TEC
Test Equipment Commodity Manager .... TECM
Test Equipment Configuration Log [NASA] (KSC) .... TECL
Test Equipment Documentation Scheduling Committee .... TEDSCO
Test Equipment Engineering (AAG) .... TEE
Test Equipment Error Analysis Report (IAA) ..... TEEAR

Test Equipment for Rapid Automatic Checkout and Evaluation [Pan American Airways] .... TRACE
Test Equipment Kit .... TEK
Test Equipment Logistics Information Source [Army] .... TELIS
Test Equipment Maintenance Set .... TEMS
Test Equipment Modernization [Army] (RDA) ... TEMOD
Test Equipment Operator .... TEO
Test Equipment Readiness [NASA] (NASA) .... TER
Test Equipment Readiness List [NASA] (NASA) .... TERL
Test Equipment Status Report .... TESR
Test Equipment Team (AAG) .... TET
Test Equipment Technical Adviser .... TETA
Test Equipment Tool (AAG) .... TET
Test Equivocal, Possible Low Titer [Laboratory science] (DAVI) .... TEQU
Test, Evaluation, Analysis, and Management Uniformity Plan [or Procedure] [Army] .... TEAM-UP
Test, Evaluation, Analysis, and Modeling [Army] (RDA) .... TEAM
Test Evaluation and Control (IAA) .... TEC
Test, Evaluation, and Development (MUGU) ...... TED
Test Evaluation and Monitoring System .... TEAMS
Test Evaluation Master Plan (MCD) .... TEMP
Test Evaluation Planning Group (MCD) .... TEPG
Test Evaluation Report [NASA] (KSC) .... TER
Test Evaluation Team [NASA] (KSC) .... TET
Test Event Sequencing, Simulating, and Recording System (PDAA) .... TESSAR
Test Exception [Nuclear energy] (NRCH) .... TE
Test Executive Processor (NITA) .... TEP
Test Explicit .... TE
Test Facilities Requirements Document .... TFRD
Test Facility .... TESTFAC
Test Facility [NASA] (NASA) .... TF
Test Facility Master Plan [DoD] (RDA) .... TFMP
Test Facility Program [NASA] (KSC) .... TFP
Test Facility Utilization [NASA] (NASA) .... TFU
Test Failure Report (CAAL) .... TFR
Test File Generator [Computer science] .... TFG
Test Fixture (KSC) .... TF
Test Flight [Air Force] .... TF
Test Flow Diagram (MCD) .... TFD
Test for Auditory Comprehension of Language [Speech and language therapy] (DAVI) .... TACL
Test for Auditory Figure-Ground Discrimination .... TAFD
Test for Entrance into Teacher Education Programs [Achievement test] .... TETEP
Test for Examining Expressive Morphology [Educational test] .... TEEM
Test for Oral Language Production [Educational test] .... TOLP
Test for the Necessity of Therapy [Medicine] ... TNT
Test for The Necessity of Therapy for Seniors [Medicine] .... TNT-S
Test Frame [Telecommunications] (TEL) .... TF
Test Generation and Simulation .... TEGAS
Test Group [Military] .... TESTG
Test Group .... TG
Test Group Support Facility .... TGSF
Test Guaranteed .... TG
Test Header (Fire Pump) [NFPA pre-fire planning symbol] (NFPA) .... TH
Test Identify (CAAL) .... TID
Test Implicit .... TI
Test Incidence and Reporting System .... TIR
Test Incident Report (IAA) .... TIR
Test Incoming Trunk [Telecommunications] (IAA) .... TSTICT
Test Index (CAAL) .... TI
Test Information Processing System [Air Force] .... TIPS
Test Information Sheet (MCD) .... TIS
Test Input/Output [Computer science] .... TIO
Test Instruction (MCD) .... TI
Test Instruction Record of Discussion (MCD) ... TIROD
Test Instrumentation .... TI
Test Instrumentation Data Link .... TIDL
Test Instrumentation System .... TIS
Test Instrumented Missile [Army] .... TIM
Test Integration Working Group [Military] (GFGA) .... TIWG
Test Interactive Management System .... TIMS
Test Interface and Control Module (MCD) .... TICM
Test Interface Assembly .... TIA
Test Interface Module (CAAL) .... TIM
Test Interface Subsystem (NASA) .... TIS
Test Interface Summary (MCD) .... TIS
Test Item Malfunction (MCD) .... TIM
Test Item Simulator [Fort Huachuca, AZ] [United States Army Electronic Proving Ground] (GRD) .... TIS
Test Item Taker .... TIT
Test Item Transmittal Form (IAA) .... TITF
Test Items [JETDS nomenclature] [Military] (CET) .... TS
Test Jack (DEN) .... TJ
Test Jack Field [Telecommunications] (IAA) ..... TJF
Test Kit (AAG) .... TSKT
Test Laboratory (AFM) .... TL
Test Laboratory Engineer (IAA) .... TLE
Test Launch Vehicle (MCD) .... TLV
Test Line Signal (IAA) .... TLS
Test Link .... TL
Test Link (IEEE) .... TLK
Test Listening Accuracy in Children [Educational test] .... TLAC
Test Load .... TL
Test Load Wire .... TLW
Test Log .... TEL

Test Log (IEEE) ... TL
Test Macro [*Computer science*] (IAA) ... TEMA
Test Maintenance Equipment [*Computer science*] ... TME
Test Maintenance Panel [*Computer science*] ... TMP
Test Maintenance Panel Subassembly [*Computer science*] ... TMPS
Test Maintenance Unit [*Computer science*] ... TMU
Test Malfunction Report ... TMR
Test Management and Diagnostic Equipment [*Army*] ... TMDE
Test, Management, and Diagnostic Equipment Support Group [*Army*] (MCD) ... TMDESG
Test Management Information System ... TMIC
Test Management Protocol [*Telecommunications*] (OSI) ... TMP
Test Manual ... TM
Test Manufacturing Order (NASA) ... TMO
Test Market Plan [*Advertising*] (NTCM) ... TMP
Test Market Profile [*Advertising*] (NTCM) ... TMP
Test Marketing Exemption [*Environmental Protection Agency*] ... TME
Test, Measurement, and Diagnostic Equipment Modernization [*Military*] (RDA) ... TEMOD
Test, Measurement, and Diagnostic Equipment Support Equipment [*Army*] ... TMDESE
Test, Measurement, and Diagnostic Systems [*Army*] (RDA) ... TMDS
Test, Measuring, and Diagnostic Equipment [*Later, TMDE*] [*Army*] (AABC) ... TM & DE
Test, Measuring [*or Measurement*], and Diagnostic Equipment [*Formerly, TM & DE*] [*Army*] (AABC) ... TMDE
Test Message Monitor ... TMM
Test Methods and Procedures ... TMP
Test Mode ... TM
Test Mode Fail [*Apollo*] [*NASA*] ... TMF
Test Model [*NASA*] ... TM
Test, Monitor, and Control [*Aviation*] ... TMC
Test Monitor System ... TMS
Test Monitoring Center [*ASTM*] [*Engineering standards*] ... TMC
Test Monitoring Console (NASA) ... TMC
Test Narrative (CAAL) ... TN
Test Negative [*Clinical chemistry*] ... TN
Test Number (AAG) ... TN
Test Observation and Training Room [*Military*] (CAAL) ... TOTR
Test of Academic Skills [*Sanford University*] (EDAC) ... TASK
Test of Adolescent Language ... TOAL
Test of Adult College Aptitude ... TACA
Test of Articulation Performance - Diagnostic ... TAP-D
Test of Articulation Performance - Screen ... TAP-S
Test of Auditory Comprehension ... TAC
Test of Auditory-Perceptual Skills ... TAP
Test of Basic Assumptions [*Psychology*] ... TBA
Test of Basic Experiences [*Child development test*] ... TOBE
Test of Basic Information [*Education*] ... TOBI
Test of Behavioral Rigidity [*Psychology*] ... TBR
Test of Cognitive Skills [*Achievement test*] ... TCS
Test of Cognitive Style in Mathematics [*Educational test*] ... TCSM
Test of Concept Utilization [*Psychometrics*] ... TCU
Test of Creative Potential ... TCP
Test of Cure [*Medicine*] ... TOC
Test of Diabetes Knowledge ... TDK
Test of Early Language Development ... TELD
Test of Early Learning Skills [*Child development test*] ... TELS
Test of Early Mathematics Ability ... TEMA
Test of Early Reading Ability ... TERA
Test of Early Socioemotional Development [*Child development test*] ... TOESD
Test of Ecology Comprehension (EDAC) ... TEC
Test of Economic Literacy [*Educational test*] ... TEL
Test of Economic Understanding ... TEU
Test of Elementary Training (WDAA) ... TOET
Test of Energy Concepts and Values (EDAC) ... TECV
Test of English as a Foreign Language ... TOEFL
Test of English as a Foreign Language (GAGS) ... TOEFL
Test of English for International Communication ... TOEIC
Test of Gross Motor Development [*Sensorimotor skills test*] ... TGMD
Test of Integrated Process Skills (EDAC) ... TIPS
Test of Language Competence [*Educational test*] ... TLC
Test of Language Development [*Education*] ... TOLD
Test of Logical Thinking (EDAC) ... TOLT
Test of Mathematical Abilities ... TOMA
Test of Minimal Articulation Competence [*Speech evaluation test*] ... T-MAC
Test of Multiple Corridor Identification System (IAA) ... TOMCIS
Test of Nonverbal Intelligence ... TONI
Test of Oral Structures and Functions [*Speech evaluation test*] ... TOSF
Test of Orientation for Rehabilitation Patients [*Occupational therapy*] ... TORP
Test of Perceptual Organization [*Neuropsychology test*] ... TPO
Test of Performance in Computational Skills [*Educational test*] ... TOPICS
Test of Practical Knowledge ... TPK
Test of Problem Solving [*Intelligence test*] ... TOPS
Test of Reading Affective Cues [*Psychology*] ... TRAC
Test of Reading Comprehension ... TORC
Test of Retail Sales Insight ... TRSI
Test of Scholastic Abilities [*Achievement test*] ... TOSCA
Test of Selected Topics in Physics ... TSTP
Test of Significance [*Medicine*] (MAE) ... t
Test of Social Insight [*Psychology*] ... TSI
Test of Spoken English ... TSE
Test of Standard Written English ... TSWE
Test of Syntactic Abilities [*Speech and language therapy*] (DAVI) ... TSA
Test of Understanding of College Economics ... TUCE
Test of Visual-Motor Skills [*Sensorimotor skills test*] ... TVMS
Test of Visual-Perceptual Skills ... TVPS
Test of Work Competency and Stability [*Psychology*] ... TWCS
Test of Written English [*Educational test*] ... TWE
Test of Written English (GAGS) ... TWE
Test of Written Language ... TOWL
Test of Written Spelling [*Education*] ... TWS
Test on Understanding Science ... TOUS
Test One BIT [*Binary Digit*] (SAA) ... TOB
Test Operating Procedure ... TOP
Test Operating System (MCD) ... TOS
Test Operating Time Log ... TOTL
Test Operation (AAG) ... TO
Test Operation Report (KSC) ... TOR
Test Operation Support Segment ... TOSS
Test Operations and Policy Office [*TECOM*] (RDA) ... TOPO
Test Operations Center [*NASA*] (NASA) ... TOC
Test Operations Change [*NASA*] (NASA) ... TOC
Test Operations Control Center [*NASA*] ... TOCC
Test Operations Directorate (RDA) ... TOD
Test Operations Facility [*NASA*] (MCD) ... TOF
Test Operations Order [*NASA*] ... TOO
Test Operations Planning System ... TOPSY
Test Operations Procedures [*Army*] (RDA) ... TOPS
Test Oscilloscope [*JETDS nomenclature*] [*Military*] (CET) ... OS
Test Outline (CAAL) ... TO
Test Outline Plan [*Army*] (AABC) ... TOP
Test Package Set (DOMA) ... TPS
Test Panel (AAG) ... T/P
Test Parts List ... TPL
Test Performance Management [*Army*] ... TPM
Test Performance Recorder ... TPR
Test Phase Report ... TPR
Test Pilot School [*Navy*] ... TPS
Test Pilot Training ... TPT
Test Pilot Training Division ... TPTD
Test Plan ... TP
Test Plan (CAAL) ... TPL
Test Plan Log (MCD) ... TPL
Test Plan of the Day ... TPOD
Test Planning and Evaluation ... TPE
Test Planning and Status Checker [*Computer science*] ... TPSC
Test Planning Liaison Drawing (AAG) ... TPLD
Test Planning Manager [*NASA*] (KSC) ... TPM
Test Planning Working Group [*Military*] ... TPWG
Test Plans and Analysis ... TPA
Test Plasma Produced by Discharge (MCD) ... TPD
Test Plotting System ... TPS
Test Point ... TP
Test Point Access (IAA) ... TPA
Test Point Algorithm Technique (MCD) ... TPAT
Test Point Controller ... TPC
Test Point Data ... TPD
Test Point Data Chart [*Military*] ... TPDC
Test Point Logic ... TPL
Test Point Pace (KSC) ... TPP
Test Point Prelaunch Automatic Checkout Equipment [*NASA*] (IAA) ... TPP
Test Point Selector ... TPS
Test Port (KSC) ... TP
Test Position ... TP
Test Positive [*Clinical chemistry*] ... TP
Test Power Control Unit (IAA) ... TPCU
Test Preparation Area [*NASA*] (KSC) ... TPA
Test Preparation Sheet [*NASA*] (AAG) ... TPS
Test Pressure [*Nuclear energy*] (NRCH) ... TP
Test Problem Report [*NASA*] (NASA) ... TPR
Test Procedure (NATG) ... TP
Test Procedure Change Authorization (NATG) ... TPCA
Test Procedure Deviation [*Nuclear energy*] (NRCH) ... TPD
Test Procedure Drawing [*NASA*] (KSC) ... TPD
Test Procedure Record (NATG) ... TPR
Test Procedure Specification [*NASA*] (IAA) ... TPROC
Test Procedure Specification [*NASA*] (KSC) ... TPS
Test Procedure Update Notice (NASA) ... TPUN
Test Procedures and Results Report ... TPRR
Test Procedures Development System (NASA) ... TPDS
Test Process ... TP
Test Program ... TP
Test Program Instruction (MCD) ... TPI
Test Program Interaction (MCD) ... TPI
Test Program Logic Computer (DWSG) ... TPLC
Test Program Operating System ... TEPOS
Test Program Outline [*Military*] ... TPO
Test Program Plan (MCD) ... TPP
Test Program Report ... TPR
Test Program Set [*Aviation*] (MCD) ... TPS
Test Program Set Management Plan ... TPSMP
Test Program Tape (MCD) ... TPT
Test Project Agreement (NG) ... TPA
Test Project Engineer (NASA) ... TPE
Test Reactor ... T
Test Reactor Area ... TRA
Test Readiness Certificate (AAG) ... TRC
Test Readiness Design Review ... TRDR
Test Readiness List [*NASA*] (NASA) ... TRL

Test Readiness Review [*NASA*] (NASA) .... TRR
Test Readiness Review Board [*NASA*] .... TRRB
Test Reference System .... TRS
Test Regulation (MCD) .... TR
Test Reliability and Maintenance Program [*Navy*] (NVT) .... TRAM
Test Replaceable Unit .... TRU
Test Report .... TR
Test Report Management Forms (MCD) .... TRMF
Test Request .... TR
Test Request Message [*Computer science*] .... TRM
Test Requirement Analysis (CAAL) .... TRA
Test Requirement Bulletins [*NASA*] (KSC) .... TRB
Test Requirement Identification (DNAB) .... TRI
Test Requirement Implementation Plan (CAAL) .... TRIP
Test Requirement Specification (MCD) .... TRS
Test Requirements Document [*NASA*] (AAG) .... TRD
Test Requirements Handbook (MUGU) .... TRH
Test Requirements Manual .... TRM
Test Requirements Outline .... TRO
Test Requirements/Specification Document [*NASA*] (MCD) .... TRSD
Test Requirements Summary (MUGU) .... TRS
Test Research Service [*Defunct*] (EA) .... TRS
Test Research Station .... TRS
Test Resource Management System [*TECOM*] (RDA) .... TRMS
Test Resources Improvement Advisory Council [*Military*] .... TRIAC
Test Resources Review Committee [*DoD*] .... TRRC
Test Response Spectrum (IEEE) .... TRS
Test Responsibility Matrix (MCD) .... TRM
Test Results Review Team [*Nuclear energy*] (NRCH) .... TRRT
Test Retrieval and Memory Print [*Computer science*] .... TRAMP
Test Review Board [*NASA*] (NASA) .... TRB
Test Routine (AAG) .... TR
Test Rules for Inventory Management .... TRIM
Test Run .... TR
Test Schedule and Review Committee [*Army*] (AABC) .... TSARC
Test Schedule Request .... TSR
Test Score Category [*DoD*] .... TSC
Test Scorer and Statistical Analyzer [*Computer science*] .... TSSA
Test Scoring Equipment .... TSE
Test Sequence Document (SAA) .... TSD
Test Sequence Generator Program [*European Space Research and Technology Center*] (NASA) .... TSGP
Test Sequence Network (CAAL) .... TSN
Test Set .... T
Test Set (KSC) .... TS
Test Set Computer .... TSC
Test Set Connection .... TSC
Test Set Electrical .... TSE
Test Set Fault (AAG) .... TSTFLT
Test Set Guided Missile Set [*or System*] .... TSGMS
Test Set Logic .... TSL
Test Set Operational Signal Converter (AAG) .... TSOSC
Test Set, Overall Missile (IAA) .... TOM
Test Set Simulator .... TSS
Test Setup Complete [*NASA*] (NASA) .... TSC
Test Shipping Cask [*Nuclear energy*] (NRCH) .... TSC
Test Shop .... TESH
Test Signal [*Telegraphy*] (IDOE) VVV
Test Signal Analyser (NITA) .... TSA
Test Signal Generator .... TSG
Test Signal Switching Unit (MCD) .... TSSU
Test Signal Unit [*Telecommunications*] (TEL) .... TSU
Test Site [*NASA*] (NASA) .... TS
Test Site Activation [*NASA*] (KSC) .... TSA
Test Site Data Source Matrix .... TSDSM
Test Site Manager [*Army*] .... TSM
Test Site Office [*NASA*] .... TSO
Test Site Position [*NASA*] (KSC) .... TSP
Test Site Support Activity [*NASA*] .... TSSA
Test Site Tool Order [*NASA*] (AAG) .... TSTO
Test Software (MCD) .... TSW
Test Software Program [*NASA*] (NASA) .... TSP
Test Solution [*of a chemical*] [*Medicine*] .... TS
Test Source Library .... TSL
Test Specification (MSA) .... TS
Test Specification (MSA) .... TSPEC
Test Specification and Criteria Document (MCD) .... TSCD
Test Squadron [*Air Force*] .... TES
Test Squadron (MCD) .... TESTS
Test Stand (AAG) .... T/S
Test Stand Adapter Kit .... TSAK
Test Stand Level (AAG) .... TSL
Test Standards Module .... TSM
Test Start Approval [*NASA*] (NASA) .... TSA
Test Start Date [*NASA*] (NASA) .... TSD
Test Station [*NASA*] (MCD) .... TS
Test Station Configuration Model (MCD) .... TSCM
Test Status Panel (MCD) .... TSP
Test Status Report [*NASA*] (NASA) .... TSR
Test Steering Committee [*Military*] .... TSC
Test Stimulus .... TS
Test Structure Input (NITA) .... TSI
Test Suite Structure and Test Purpose [*Telecommunications*] .... TSS & TP
Test Summary .... TS
Test Summary Report (IAA) .... TSR

Test Support Agent (MCD) .... TSA
Test Support Building .... TSB
Test Support Center High-Level Terminal (CAAL) .... TSCHLT
Test Support Control Center [*NASA*] (KSC) .... TSCC
Test Support Controller [*or Coordinator*] [*NASA*] (KSC) .... TSC
Test Support Coordination Office [*NASA*] (MCD) .... TSCO
Test Support Coordinator (NASA) .... TSCO
Test Support Equipment [*NASA*] .... TSE
Test Support Equipment Evaluation (MCD) .... TSEE
Test Support Instructions [*NASA*] (KSC) .... TSI
Test Support List (CAAL) .... TSL
Test Support Manager [*NASA*] (KSC) .... TSM
Test Support Operations [*NASA*] (KSC) .... TSO
Test Support Package .... TSP
Test Support Plan [*Army*] .... TSP
Test Support Position .... TSP
Test Support Program .... TSP
Test Support Requirements (KSC) .... TSR
Test Support Table .... TST
Test Switch .... TSW
Test Switch Thrust Termination .... TSWTT
Test System .... TS
Test System Analysis Directorate [*Army*] (MCD) .... TSAD
Test Target Array (AFM) .... TTA
Test Target Generator .... TTG
Test Technology Information Center (MCD) .... TTIC
Test Temperature [*Nuclear energy*] (NRCH) .... TT
Test Terminator (IAA) .... TT
Test [*or Testing*] Time (IAA) .... TT
Test to Failure (SAA) .... TF
Test to Failure (NATG) .... TTF
Test Tone to Noise Ratio [*Telecommunications*] (TEL) .... TT/N
Test Transfer Cask [*Nuclear energy*] (NRCH) .... TTC
Test Transfer Port [*Nuclear energy*] (GFGA) .... TTP
Test Translator [*Computer science*] .... TESTRAN
Test Tube (IAA) .... TT
Test Tube and Ring-Shaped Forms [*AIDS cytology*] .... TRF
Test Tube Turbidity Test [*Laboratory science*] (DAVI) .... TTTT
Test Two Bits (IAA) .... TTB
Test Unit .... TU
Test Unit Adapter [*Aviation*] .... TUA
Test Variance (NASA) .... TVAR
Test Vector Generator .... TVG
Test Vehicle .... TV
Test Vehicle Engine (AAG) .... TVE
Test Verification Network [*NASA*] (NASA) .... TVN
Test Verification Program [*NASA*] (NASA) .... TVP
Test Voltage (IAA) .... TV
Test Volts, Direct Current .... TVDC
Test Ware Instrument (PDAA) .... TWIN
Test Weight .... TW
Test Wing [*Military*] .... TESTW
Test Work Release (MCD) .... TWR
Test Working Group [*in various federal government agencies*] (KSC) .... TWG
Testa Rossa [*Red engine cylinder head*] [*Ferrari automotive model designation*] [*Italian*] .... TR
Testa Rossa Sport .... TRS
Testable Read Only Memory Programmed [*Computer science*] (DGA) .... TROMP
Testament (ROG) .... T
Testament .... TEST
Testament .... TESTT
Testament of Abraham [*Pseudepigrapha*] (BJA) .... TestAbr
Testament of Asher [*Pseudepigrapha*] (BJA) .... TestAsh
Testament of Benjamin [*Pseudepigrapha*] (BJA) .... TestBen
Testament of Issachar [*Pseudepigrapha*] (BJA) .... TestIss
Testament of Joseph [*Pseudepigrapha*] (BJA) .... TestJos
Testament of Judah [*Pseudepigrapha*] (BJA) .... TestJud
Testament of Levi [*Pseudepigrapha*] (BJA) .... TestLevi
Testament of Levi from Qumran. Cave Four (BJA) 4QTLevi
Testament of Naphtali [*Pseudepigrapha*] (BJA) .... TestNaph
Testament of Reuben [*Pseudepigrapha*] (BJA) .... TestReub
Testament of Simeon [*Pseudepigrapha*] (BJA) .... TestSim
Testament of Zebulun [*Pseudepigrapha*] (BJA) .... TestZeb
Testamentary [*Legal term*] (DLA) .... Test
Testamentary (ROG) .... TESTY
Testamentary Trust [*Legal term*] .... TT
Testaments of the Twelve Patriarchs [*Pseudepigrapha*] (BJA) .... TestXII
Testaments of the Twelve Patriarchs [*Pseudepigrapha*] .... XII P
Testamentsgesetz [*Law on Wills*] [*German*] (ILCA) .... TG
Testamentum [*Will*] [*Latin*] .... T
Testantibus Actis [*As the Records Show*] [*Latin*] .... TA
Testator [*Legal term*] .... T
Testator (ADA) .... TEST
Testator (ROG) .... TESTOR
Testatrix (WDAA) .... TEST
Testatrix (ROG) .... TESTRIX
Tested Extra (MCD) .... TX
Tested Overhead Projection Series [*Education*] .... TOPS
Tester (MSA) .... TSTR
Test-Estrin Time(d) Action [*Pharmacology*] (DAVI) .... TETA
Testicular Blood Flow [*Physiology*] .... TBF
Testicular Feminization [*Endocrinology*] .... TFM
Testicular Feminization Syndrome [*Endocrinology*] .... TFS
Testicular Hypothermia Device [*Medicine*] .... THD
Testicular Interstitial Fluid [*Physiology*] .... TIF

Testicular Self-Examination .... TSE
Testigo [*Witness*] [*Latin*] (ADA) .... TESTO
[*The*] **Testimonia from Qumran. Cave Four** (BJA) 4QTest
Testimonial (ADA) .... TEST
Testing .... TEST
Testing (MSA) .... TSTG
Testing .... TSTNG
Testing Accessories (AAG) .... TSAC
Testing, Adjusting, and Balancing [*Heating and cooling technology*] .... TAB
Testing and Analysis of Local Area Optical Networks (NITA) .... TALON
Testing and Development Division [*Coast Guard*] .... TD
Testing and Operating System .... TOPS
Testing and Popping (SAA) .... TS & POP
Testing and Regulating Department [*Especially, in a wire communications maintenance division*] .... T & R
Testing Complete (CAAL) .... TC
Testing Device (MSA) .... TD
Testing Difficulty Estimator .... TDE
Testing Facilities Branch [*Social Security Administration*] .... TFB
Testing Methods and Techniques [*Telecommunications*] (TEL) .... TMT
Testing Orientation and Work Evaluation for Rehabilitation .... TOWER
Testing the Limits for Sex [*Psychology*] .... TLS
Testing Tool (AAG) .... TSTO
Testing-Teaching Module of Auditory Discrimination [*Child development test*] .... TTMAD
Testis-Determining Factor [*Genetics*] .... TDF
Testo Unico [*Consolidated Statutes*] [*Italian*] (ILCA) .... TU
Testolactone [*Antineoplastic drug*] .... TESLAC
Testolactone [*Biochemistry*] .... TL
Test-Operator-Test-Exit [*Unit*] [*Psychology*] .... TOTE
Test-Oriented Disk System (IEEE) .... TODS
Test-Oriented Language [*Computer science*] .... TOL
Test-Oriented Operated Language [*Programming language*] [*Computer science*] .... TOOL
Test-Oriented Paper-Tape System [*Computer science*] (IEEE) .... TOPTS
Testosterone [*Endocrinology*] (DAVI) .... TESTOS
Testosterone Binding Globulin [*Endocrinology*] (AAMN) .... TeBG
Testosterone Glucuronide [*Medicine*] (MAE) .... TG
Testosterone Production Rate [*Endocrinology*] (MAE) .... TPR
Testosterone Propionate [*Endocrinology*] .... TP
Testosterone Sterilized Rat .... TSR
Testosterone-Binding Affinity [*Endocrinology*] (MAE) .... TBA
Testosterone-Binding Globulin [*Endocrinology*] .... TBG
Testosterone-Binding Protein [*Endocrinology*] (MAE) .... TBP
Testosterone-Estradiol Binding Globulin [*Endocrinology*] .... TeBG
Test-Retest .... TR
Tests for Everyday Living [*Educational test*] .... TEL
Tests of Achievement and Proficiency [*Educational test*] .... TAP
Tests of Achievement in Basic Skills [*Educational test*] .... TABS
Tests of Adult Basic Education [*Achievement test*] .... TABE
Tests of Elementary Training [*Military British*] .... TSOET
Tests of Engineering Aptitude, Mathematics, and Science .... TEAMS
Tests of General Ability [*Education*] (AEBS) .... TOGA
Tests of Reasonable Quantitative Understanding of the Environment [*Education*] .... TORQUE
Tests of Social Intelligence [*Psychology*] .... TSI
Test-Section Melt-Down Accident [*Nuclear energy*] (NRCH) .... TSMDA
Tesuque Peak [*New Mexico*] [*Seismograph station code, US Geological Survey*] (SEIS) .... TSP
Tetanic Contraction [*Neurology*] (DAVI) .... ADTe
Tetanus [*Medicine*] (WGA) .... Te
Tetanus [*Medicine*] .... Tet
Tetanus and Diphtheria [*Toxoids*] [*Medicine*] .... TD
Tetanus Antitoxin [*Medicine*] .... TAT
Tetanus Antitoxin Skin Test [*Medicine*] (MAE) .... TATST
Tetanus Immune Globulin [*Immunology*] .... TIG
Tetanus Immune Globulin (Human) [*Immunology*] .... TIG(H)
Tetanus Toxin (WDAA) .... TET TOX
Tetanus Toxoid [*Medicine*] (CPH) .... Tet Tox
Tetanus Toxoid [*Medicine*] .... TT
Tetbury [*England*] .... TETB
Tete [*Mozambique*] [*ICAO location identifier*] (ICLI) .... FQTE
Tete [*Mozambique*] [*Seismograph station code, US Geological Survey*] (SEIS) .... TET
Tete [*Mozambique*] [*Airport symbol*] (OAG) .... TET
Tete A La Baleine [*Canada*] [*Airport symbol*] (OAG) .... ZTB
Tete/Chingozi [*Mozambique*] [*ICAO location identifier*] (ICLI) .... FQTT
Tetebedi [*Papua New Guinea*] [*Airport symbol*] (OAG) .... TDB
Teterboro [*New Jersey*] [*ICAO location identifier*] (ICLI) .... KTEB
Teterboro [*New Jersey*] [*Airport symbol*] (AD) .... TEB
Teterboro, NJ [*Location identifier FAA*] (FAAL) .... TEB
Tethered Aerostat RADAR System [*Aviation*] (FAAC) .... TARS
Tethered Buoyed Platform [*Petroleum engineering*] .... TBP
Tethered Communications, Inc. [*Westinghouse subsidiary*] .... TCOM
Tethered Free-Floating Worker .... TFW
Tethered Lighter-than-Air (KSC) .... TELTA
Tethered Meteorological Balloon (IAA) .... TETROON
Tethered Orbiting Satellite Simulator .... TOSS
Tethered RADAR Reflector .... TRR
Tethered Remotely Operational Vehicle [*Marine science*] (MSC) .... TROV
Tethered Rover for Atmospheric Measurement [*Ozone measurement*] .... TRAM
Tethered Satellite System (MCD) .... TSS
Tethys Circumglobal Current [*Paleooceanography*] .... TCC
Tetiaroa [*French Polynesia*] [*ICAO location identifier*] (ICLI) .... NTTE
Tetilla Peak [*New Mexico*] [*Seismograph station code, US Geological Survey*] (SEIS) .... TTP
Tetouan/Sania R'Mel [*Morocco*] [*ICAO location identifier*] (ICLI) .... GMTN
Tetra [*Prefix meaning four*] (DAVI) .... T
Tetra Tech [*NASDAQ symbol*] (TTSB) .... WATR
Tetra Tech, Inc. [*Associated Press*] (SAG) .... TetraTc
Tetra Tech, Inc. [*NASDAQ symbol*] (SPSG) .... WATR
TETRA Technologies [*NASDAQ symbol*] (TTSB) .... TTRA
Tetra Technologies, Inc. [*Associated Press*] (SAG) .... Tetra
Tetra Technologies, Inc. [*NASDAQ symbol*] (SAG) .... TTRA
Tetraacetylethylenediamine [*Laundry bleaching agent*] .... TAED
Tetraalkyllead [*Organic chemistry*] .... TAL
Tetraaminobenzophenone [*Organic chemistry*] .... TABP
Tetraaminobiphenyl [*Organic chemistry*] .... TAB
Tetraaminodiphenylether [*Organic chemistry*] .... TADE
Tetrabenazine [*Tranquilizer*] .... TBZ
Tetrabenzonaphthalene [*Organic chemistry*] .... TBN
Tetrabromobisphenol-A [*Organic chemistry*] .... TBBPA
Tetrabromodibenzo-p-dioxin [*Organic chemistry*] .... TBDD
Tetrabromoethane [*Microscopy*] .... TBE
Tetrabromophthalic Anhydride [*Flame retardant*] [*Organic chemistry*] .... TBPA
Tetrabutyl Titanate [*Organic chemistry*] .... TBT
Tetrabutylammonium Bromide [*Organic chemistry*] .... TBAB
Tetrabutylammonium Chlorochromate [*Organic chemistry*] .... TBACC
Tetrabutylammonium Fluoride [*Organic chemistry*] .... TBAF
Tetrabutylammonium Fluoroborate [*Organic chemistry*] .... TBAF
Tetrabutylammonium Hydrogen Sulfate [*Organic chemistry*] .... TBAHS
Tetrabutylammonium Hydroxide [*Organic chemistry*] .... TBAH
Tetrabutylammoniumperchlorate [*Photovoltaic energy systems*] .... TBAP
Tetrabutylperoxyhydroxide [*Organic chemistry*] .... TBPH
Tetrabutylthiuram Disulfide [*Organic chemistry*] .... TBTD
Tetrachloride [*Chemistry*] (AAG) .... TET
Tetrachloroazobenzene [*Organic chemistry*] .... TCAB
Tetrachloroazoxybenzene [*Organic chemistry*] .... TCAOB
Tetrachlorobiphenyl [*Organic chemistry*] .... TCB
Tetrachlorobiphenyl [*Organic chemistry*] .... TCP
Tetrachlorocatechol [*Organic chemistry*] .... TCC
Tetrachlorodibenzodioxin [*Organic chemistry*] .... TCDD
Tetrachlorodibenzofuran [*Organic chemistry*] .... TCDF
Tetrachloro-Diphenyl- Ethane [*An insecticide*] (DAVI) .... TCE
Tetrachlorodiphenylethane [*Also, DDD*] [*Insecticide*] .... TDE
Tetrachloroethylene [*Also, P*] [*Organic chemistry*] .... TCE
Tetrachlorohydroquinone [*Organic chemistry*] .... TCH
Tetrachloromercurate [*Inorganic chemistry*] .... TCM
Tetrachlorophenol [*Organic chemistry*] .... TCP
(Tetrachlorophenyl)pyrrole [*Organic chemistry*] .... TCPP
Tetrachlorophthalic Anhydride [*Flame retardant*] [*Organic chemistry*] .... TCPA
Tetrachlorophthalodinitrile [*Organic chemistry*] .... TPN
Tetrachlororesourcinol [*Organic chemistry*] .... TCR
Tetrachlorosalicylanilide [*Organic chemistry*] .... TCSA
Tetrachlorothiophene [*Organic chemistry*] .... TCTP
Tetrachlorotrifluoromethylbenzimidazole [*Organic chemistry*] .... TTFB
Tetrachoric Correlation [*Psychology*] .... Rt
Tetracyanoanthracene [*Organic chemistry*] .... TCA
Tetracyanobenzene [*Organic chemistry*] .... TCNB
Tetracyanoethylene [*Organic chemistry*] .... TCNE
Tetracyanoethylene Oxide [*Organic chemistry*] .... TCNEO
Tetracyanoplatinate [*Inorganic chemistry*] .... TCP
Tetracyanopyrazine [*Organic chemistry*] .... TCP
Tetracyanoquinodimethane [*Organic chemistry*] .... TCNQ
Tetracyanoquionodimethane [*Organic chemistry*] (SAA) .... TCQM
Tetracycline [*Antibiotic compound*] .... T
Tetracycline [*Antibiotic compound*] .... TC
Tetracycline [*Antibiotic*] .... TCN
Tetracycline [*Antibiotic compound*] .... TE
Tetracycline [*Antibiotic compound*] .... Tet
Tetracycline [*An Antibiotic*] [*Pharmacology*] (DAVI) .... TETCYC
Tetracycline-Induced Steatosis [*Medicine*] .... TIS
Tetradecadiene [*Organic chemistry*] .... TDD
Tetradecadienyl Acetate [*Biochemistry*] .... TDDA
Tetradecanol [*Organic chemistry*] .... TDOL
Tetradecanoylphorbolacetate [*Also, PMA, PTA*] [*Organic chemistry*] .... TPA
Tetradecanylglutarate [*Biochemistry*] .... TDG
Tetradecenal [*Biochemistry*] .... TDAL
Tetradecenyl Acetate [*Organic chemistry*] .... TDA
Tetradecyltrimethylammonium Bromide [*Organic chemistry*] .... TTAB
Tetradichlorozylene (GNE) .... TOC
Tetra-Electron Volt .... TeV
Tetraethoxypropane [*Organic chemistry*] .... TEP
Tetraethoxysilane [*Organic radical*] .... TEOS
Tetraethyl Dithionopyrophosphate [*Organic chemistry*] .... TEDP
Tetraethyl Orthosilicate [*Organic chemistry*] (NASA) .... TEOS
Tetraethyl Pyrophosphate [*Insecticide*] [*Pharmacology*] (IAA) .... TEP
Tetraethyl Pyrophosphate [*Insecticide*] [*Pharmacology*] .... TEPP
Tetraethyl Urea [*Organic chemistry*] .... TEU
Tetraethylammonium [*Organic chemistry*] .... TEA
Tetraethylammonium Bromide [*Organic chemistry*] .... TEAB
Tetraethylammonium Chloride [*Organic chemistry*] .... TEAC
Tetraethylammonium Perchlorate [*Organic chemistry*] .... TEAP
Tetraethylene Glycol [*Organic chemistry*] .... TEG
Tetraethylene Glycol Diacrylate [*Organic chemistry*] .... TTEGDA
Tetraethylene Glycol Dimethyl Ether [*Organic chemistry*] .... TEGDME
Tetraethylenepentamine [*Organic chemistry*] .... TEPA
Tetraethyllead [*Organic chemistry*] .... TEL
Tetraethylsulfamide [*Organic chemistry*] .... TES

Tetraethylthiuram Disulfide [Also, TTD] [Organic chemistry] .... TETD
Tetraethylthiuram Disulfide [Also, TETD] [Organic chemistry] .... TTD
Tetraethylthiuram Monosulfide [Organic chemistry] .... TETM
Tetrafluorethylene [Organic chemistry] .... TETFLEYNE
Tetrafluoroethanedisulfonic Acid [Organic chemistry] .... TFEDSA
Tetrafluoroethylene [Organic chemistry] .... TFE
Tetrafluoroethylene Oxide [Organic chemistry] .... TFEO
Tetrafluoroethylene Resin [Du Pont] .... TEFLON
Tetrafluoroethylene-Epoxide [Organic chemistry] .... TFEO
Tetraglycidyl(diaminodiphenyl)methane [Organic chemistry] .... TGDDM
Tetraglycine (DAVI) .... TG
Tetragonal .... TETR
Tetragonal Tungsten Bronze .... TTB
Tetrahedral [Molecular geometry] .... Td
Tetrahedral Balloon [Meteorology] .... TETROON
Tetrahedral Cubic [Metallography] .... TC
Tetrahedral Research Satellite .... TRS
Tetrahexylammonium Benzoate [Organic chemistry] .... THAB
Tetrahydraisoquinolon (DAVI) .... THIQ
Tetrahydro [Biochemistry] H4
Tetrahydro F [Also, called tetrahydrocortisone] [Endocrinology] (DAVI) .... THF
Tetrahydro-11-Deoxycortisol .... THS
Tetrahydroaminoacridine [Pharmacology] .... THA
Tetrahydroanthraquinone [Organic chemistry] .... THAQ
Tetrahydrobenzopyrene [Organic chemistry] .... THBP
Tetrahydrobiopterin [Biochemistry] BH4
Tetrahydrocannabinol [Active principle of marijuana] .... THC
Tetrahydrocannabinol Cross-Reacting-Cannabinoid [Active principle of marijuana] (PDAA) .... THC-CRC
Tetrahydro-Compound S [Organic chemistry] (MAE) .... THS
Tetrahydrocortisol (MAE) .... TH
Tetrahydrocortisol .... THC
Tetrahydrocortisol [Endocrinology] (DAVI) .... THF
Tetrahydrocortisone [Endocrinology] .... THE
Tetrahydrocorynantheine [Biochemistry] .... THCN
Tetrahydrodeoxycorticosterone [Biochemistry] .... THDOC
Tetrahydrofluorenone [Organic chemistry] .... THF
Tetrahydrofolate [Biochemistry] H4folate
Tetrahydrofolate [Biochemistry] .... THF
Tetrahydrofolic Acid [Also, THFA] [Organic chemistry] .... THF
Tetrahydrofolic Acid [Biochemistry] .... THFA
Tetrahydrofuran [Organic chemistry] H4furan
Tetrahydrofuran [Organic chemistry] .... THF
Tetrahydrofurfuryl Alcohol [Organic chemistry] .... THFA
Tetrahydrohomofolate [Organic chemistry] .... THHF
Tetrahydroimidazobenzodiazepin [Antiviral] .... TIBO
Tetrahydroisooxazolopyridineol [Organic chemistry] .... THIP
Tetrahydroisoquinoline [Biochemistry] .... TIQ
Tetrahydroisoquinoline Sulfonamide [A drug] .... TIS
Tetrahydromethanopterin [Biochemistry] .... THMP
Tetrahydropalmatine [Organic chemistry] .... THP
Tetrahydropapaveroline [Biochemistry] .... THP
Tetrahydrophthalic Anhydride [Organic chemistry] .... THPA
Tetrahydrophthalimide [Organic chemistry] .... THPI
Tetrahydropteric Acid [Organic chemistry] (MAE) .... THPA
Tetrahydropyranyl [Organic chemistry] H4pyran
Tetrahydropyranyl [Organic chemistry] .... thp
Tetrahydropyranyldoxorubicin [Antineoplastic drug] .... THPDX
((Tetrahydrotetramethylnaphthalenyl)propenyl)benzoic Acid [Antineoplastic drug] .... TTNPB
(Tetrahydrotetramethylnaphthyl) Naphthoic Acid [Antineoplastic drug] .... TTNN
Tetrahydrothiophene [Organic chemistry] .... THT
Tetrahydroxyethylethylenediamine [Organic chemistry] .... THEED
Tetrahydroxyquinone [Chemical indicator] .... THQ
Tetraiodophenolphthalein Sodium [Pharmacology] .... TIPPS
Tetraiodothyroacetic Acid [Medicine] (MAE) TA4
Tetraiodothyroacetic Acid [Organic chemistry] (MAH) .... TETRAC
Tetraisopropyl Titanate [Organic chemistry] .... TPT
Tetrakis Dimethylamino Ethylene [Organic chemistry] .... TDAE
Tetrakis(acetoxymercuri)methane [Organic chemistry] .... TAMM
Tetrakis(dimethylamino)ethylene [Also, TKDE, TMAE] [Organic chemistry] .... TDAE
Tetrakis(dimethylamino)ethylene [Organic chemistry] .... TKDE
Tetrakis(dimethylamino)ethylene [Organic chemistry] .... TMAE
Tetrakis(ethylhexoxy)silane [Organic chemistry] .... TEHOS
Tetrakis(hydroxymethyl)phosphonium [Organic chemistry] .... THP
Tetrakis(hydroxymethyl)phosphonium Chloride [Flame retardant] .... THPC
Tetrakis(hydroxymethyl)phosphonium Sulfate [Flame retardant] [Organic chemistry] .... THPS
Tetrakis(pyridylmethyl)ethylenediamine [Organic chemistry] .... TPEN
Tetralogy [Medicine] .... Tet
Tetralogy of Fallot [Neonatology] (DAVI) .... TEF
Tetralogy of Fallot [Neonatology] (DAVI) .... TET
Tetralogy of Fallot [Cardiology] .... TF
Tetralogy of Fallot [Cardiology] .... TOF
Tetramesitylporphyrin [Organic chemistry] .... TMP
Tetramethoxypropane [Organic chemistry] .... TMP
Tetramethoxysilane [Organic chemistry] .... TMOS
Tetramethoxysilane [Organic chemistry] .... TMS
Tetramethyl Lead (MCD) .... TML
Tetramethyl Rhodamine Isothiocyanate [Organic chemistry] .... TRITC
Tetramethylammonium [Organic chemistry] .... TMA
Tetramethylammonium Borohydride [Organic chemistry] .... TMAB
Tetramethylammonium Hydroxide [Organic chemistry] .... TMAH
Tetramethylammonium Iodide [Organic chemistry] .... TMAI

Tetramethylammonium Manganese Chloride [Organic chemistry] .... TMMC
Tetramethylbenzene [Organic chemistry] .... TMB
Tetramethylbenzidine [Organic chemistry] .... TMB
Tetramethylbutanediamine [Also, TMBDA] .... TMBD
Tetramethylbutanediamine [Organic chemistry] .... TMBDA
(Tetramethylbutyl)phenol [Organic chemistry] .... TMBP
Tetramethylcyclooctatetraene [Organic chemistry] .... TMCOT
Tetramethyldioxetane [Organic chemistry] .... TMD
Tetramethyldisilazane [Organic chemistry] .... TMDS
Tetramethylene-bis-Acetamide [Biochemistry] .... TMBA
Tetramethyleneglutaric Acid [Organic chemistry] .... TMGA
Tetramethylethylene [Organic chemistry] .... TME
Tetramethylethylenediamine [Also, TMED, TMEDA] [Organic chemistry] .... TEMED
Tetramethylethylenediamine [Also, TEMED, TMEDA] [Organic chemistry] .... TMED
Tetramethylethylenediamine [Also, TEMED, TMED] [Organic chemistry] .... TMEDA
Tetramethylguanidine [Organic chemistry] .... TMG
Tetramethyl-para-phenylenediamine [Analytical chemistry] .... TMPD
Tetramethylpiperidine [Organic chemistry] .... TMP
Tetramethylpiperidinol N-oxyl [Organic chemistry] .... TEMPO
Tetramethylpiperidinol N-oxyl [Organic chemistry] .... TMPN
Tetramethylpyrazine [Biochemistry] .... TMPZ
Tetramethylrhodamine [Fluorescent dye] .... TMR
Tetramethylrhodamine Isothiocyanate [Analytical biochemistry] .... TMRI
Tetramethylrhodamine-Maleimide [Organic chemistry] .... TMRM
Tetramethylrhodamino-Isothiocyanate [Organic chemistry] (MAH) .... TRMC
Tetramethylsilane [Organic chemistry] .... TMS
Tetramethyltetraselenafulvene [Organic chemistry] .... TMTSF
Tetramethylthiourea [Also, TMTU] [Organic chemistry] .... TMT
Tetramethylthiourea [Also, TMT] [Organic chemistry] .... TMTU
Tetramethylthiuram Disulfide [Also, THTMS, TMTDS] [Organic chemistry] .... TMTD
Tetramethylthiuram Disulfide [Also, TMTD, THTMS] [Organic chemistry] .... TMTDS
Tetramethylthiuram Monosulfide [Also, TMTD] [Organic chemistry] .... THTMS
Tetramethylurea [Organic chemistry] .... TMU
Tetramethylxylene Diisocyanate [Organic chemistry] .... TMXDI
Tetranitro Blue Tetrazolium [A dye] [Organic chemistry] .... TNBT
Tetranitroadamantane [Explosive] [Organic chemistry] .... TNA
Tetranitroaniline [Organic chemistry] .... TNA
Tetranitrodiphenyl [Organic chemistry] .... TNDP
(Tetranitrofluorylideneaminooxy)propionic Acid .... TAPA
Tetranitromethane [Organic chemistry] .... TNM
Tetra-N-Propylammonium Perruthenate [Organic chemistry] .... TRAP
Tetraphenyl Tetrazolium [Histochemical stain] (AAMN) .... TPT
Tetraphenylboron [Analytical chemistry] .... TBP
Tetraphenylbutadiene [Organic chemistry] .... TPB
Tetraphenylbutane [Organic chemistry] .... TPB
Tetraphenylcyclopentadienone [Organic chemistry] .... TPCD
Tetraphenylethylene [Organic chemistry] .... TPE
Tetraphenylfuran [Organic chemistry] .... TPF
Tetraphenylporphine [Organic chemistry] .... TPP
Tetraphenylporphinesulfonate [Reagent] .... TPPS
Tetraphenylporphyrin [Biochemistry] .... TPP
Tetraploid [Genetics] .... tetra
Tetrapotassium Pyrophosphate [Organic chemistry] (DICI) .... TKPP
Tetrapropylammonium [Chemical radical] .... TPA
Tetrapropylammonium Hydroxide [Organic chemistry] .... TPAOH
Tetrapropylenbenzenesulfonate [Organic chemistry] .... TPBS
Tetrapropylene Alkylbenesulfonate [Surfactant] [Organic chemistry] .... TBS
Tetrapyrrole Group [British] (EAIO) .... TG
Tetraselenofulvalene [Organic chemistry] .... TSF
Tetrasodium Pyrophosphate [Inorganic chemistry] .... TSPP
Tetratellurafulvalene [Organic chemistry] .... TTeF
Tetrathiafulvene-Tetracyanoquinodimethane [Organic chemistry] .... TTF-TCNQ
Tetrathiofulvalene [Organic chemistry] .... TTF
Tetrathionate [Nutrient broth] [Microbiology] .... TT
Tetrathiotetracene [Organic chemistry] .... TTT
Tetratricopeptide Repeat [Genetics] .... TPR
Tetra(trifluoromethyl)thiophene [Organic chemistry] .... TTFT
Tetrazol (MAE) .... TT
Tetrazolium Chloride Agar [Biological stain] .... TZC
Tetrazolium Reduction (MAE) .... TR
Tetrazolium Reduction Inhibition (MAE) .... TRI
Tetrazolium Violet [Also, TZV] .... TV
Tetrazolium Violet [Also, TV] .... TZV
Tetrhydrouridine [Biochemistry] .... THU
Tetrode [Electronics] .... TET
Tetrode [Electronics] (IAA) .... TR
Tetrodotoxin [A poison] [Biochemistry] .... TTX
Tetuan [Morocco] [Airport symbol] (OAG) .... TTU
Teubners Bibliotheca Scriptorum Graecorum et Romanorum (BJA) .... TBG
Teuton .... TEUT
Teuton Resources Corp. [Vancouver Stock Exchange symbol] .... TUO
Teutopolis Community Unit, School District 50, Teutopolis, IL [Library symbol Library of Congress] (LCLS) .... ITeuSD
Teutopolis, IL [FM radio station call letters] .... WAES
Teva Pharm Indus ADR [NASDAQ symbol] (TTSB) .... TEVIY
Teva Pharmaceutical Industries Ltd. [Associated Press] (SAG) .... Teva
Teva Pharmaceutical Industries Ltd. [NASDAQ symbol] (NQ) .... TEVI
Tewara [Afghanistan] [ICAO location identifier] (ICLI) .... OATW
Tewkesbury [Municipal borough in England] .... TEWK
TEWS [Tactical Electronic Warfare System] Intermediate Age Commercial System .... TIACS
TEWS [Tactical Electronic Warfare System] Intermediate Test Equipment [Military] .... TITE
Tex [Formerly, den] [Linear density] [SI unit] .... tex

Tex Johnston, Inc. ... TJI

Tex Jones Fan Club [*Defunct*] (EA) ... TJFC

Tex Ritter Fan Club (EA) ... TRFC

Texaco Canada, Inc., Don Mills, Ontario [*Library symbol National Library of Canada*] (NLC) ... OTTEX

Texaco Canada Inc., Don Mills, Toronto, ON, Canada [*Library symbol Library of Congress*] (LCLS) ... CaOTTex

Texaco Canada Resources Ltd., Calgary, AB, Canada [*Library symbol Library of Congress*] (LCLS) ... CaACTCR

Texaco Canada Resources Ltd., Calgary, Alberta [*Library symbol National Library of Canada*] (NLC) ... ACTCR

Texaco Cap LLC'B'Adj MIPS [*NYSE symbol*] (TTSB) ... TXCPrB

Texaco Capital [*Associated Press*] (SAG) ... TxCap

Texaco Capital LLC [*NYSE symbol*] (SPSG) ... TXC

Texaco Capital LLC 'MIPS' [*NYSE symbol*] (TTSB) ... TXCPrA

Texaco Combustion Process [*Automotive engineering*] ... TCP

Texaco Continuous Grease Unit ... TCGU

Texaco, Humble, Union, Mobil, and Shell [*Petroleum companies*] ... THUMS

Texaco, Inc. [*Associated Press*] (SAG) ... Texaco

Texaco, Inc. [*NYSE symbol*] (SPSG) ... TX

Texaco, Inc., Bellaire, TX [*Library symbol Library of Congress*] (LCLS) ... TxBIT

Texaco Inc., Corp. Library, White Plains, NY [*Library symbol*] [*Library of Congress*] (LCLS) ... NWhpT

Texaco Lubricants Co. [*Automotive industry supplier*] ... TLC

Texaco Overseas Tankerships ... TOT

Texair Charter, Inc. [*ICAO designator*] (FAAC) ... TXA

Texarkana [*Arkansas*] [*Airport symbol*] (OAG) ... TXK

Texarkana, AR [*AM radio station call letters*] ... KKYR

Texarkana, AR [*FM radio station call letters*] ... KTWN-FM

Texarkana, AR [*FM radio station call letters*] (RBYB) ... KYGL

Texarkana College, Texarkana, TX [*Library symbol Library of Congress*] (LCLS) ... TxTeC

Texarkana First Financial [*AMEX symbol*] (TTSB) ... FTF

Texarkana First Financial Corp. [*AMEX symbol*] (SAG) ... FTF

Texarkana First Financial Corp. [*Associated Press*] (SAG) ... TexarkF

Texarkana/Municipal-Webb Field [*Arkansas*] [*ICAO location identifier*] (ICLI) ... KTXK

Texarkana Public Library, Texarkana, TX [*Library symbol Library of Congress*] (LCLS) ... TxTe

Texarkana, TX [*AM radio station call letters*] ... KCMC

Texarkana, TX [*AM radio station call letters*] ... KHSP

Texarkana, TX [*FM radio station call letters*] ... KKYR-FM

Texarkana, TX [*FM radio station call letters*] ... KTAL

Texarkana, TX [*Television station call letters*] ... KTAL-TV

Texarkana, TX [*AM radio station call letters*] (RBYB) ... KTFS-AM

Texarkana, TX [*AM radio station call letters*] ... KTWN

Texarkana, TX [*FM radio station call letters*] ... KTXK

Texarkana Union Station Trust [*AAR code*] ... TUST

Texas [*MARC geographic area code Library of Congress*] (LCCP) ... n-us-tx

Texas (AAG) ... TEX

Texas (ODBW) ... Tex

Texas [*Postal code*] ... TX

Texas [*MARC country of publication code Library of Congress*] (LCCP) ... txu

Texas A & I University at Corpus Christi, Corpus Christi, TX [*Library symbol Library of Congress*] (LCLS) ... TxCcT

Texas A & I University, Kingsville, TX [*Library symbol Library of Congress*] (LCLS) ... TxKT

Texas A & M University [*College Station, TX*] ... TAM

Texas A & M University ... TAMU

Texas A & M University at Galveston, Galveston, TX [*OCLC symbol*] (OCLC) ... TAG

Texas A & M University, College Station, TX [*OCLC symbol*] (OCLC) ... TXA

Texas A & M University, College Station, TX [*Library symbol Library of Congress*] (LCLS) ... TxCM

Texas A & M University, Medical Sciences Library, College Station, TX [*OCLC symbol*] (OCLC) ... TMV

Texas A & M University, Medical Sciences Library, College Station, TX [*Library symbol Library of Congress*] (LCLS) ... TxCM-M

Texas A & M University, Moody College of Marine Sciences and Maritime Resources,Galveston, TX [*Library symbol Library of Congress*] (LCLS) ... TxGML

Texas A & M University Variable Energy Cyclotron ... TAMVEC

Texas A&I University (GAGS) ... Tex A&I U

Texas A&M University, College Station (USDC) ... TAMU

Texas Academic Skills Program ... TASP

[*Official*] **Texas Administrative Code** (AAGC) ... TAC

Texas Administrative Code [*A publication*] (DLA) ... Tex Admin Code

Texas Agricultural and Mechanical University (GAGS) ... Tex A&M U

Texas Agricultural Experiment Station [*Texas A & M University*] [*Research center*] (RCD) ... TAES

Texas Airlines, Inc. [*ICAO designator*] (FAAC) ... TXS

Texas and Mexico [*Refers to fashion, food, language, or lifestyle that has characteristics of these two regions*] ... TexMex

Texas & New Orleans R. R. [*AAR code*] ... TNO

Texas & Northern Railway Co. [*AAR code*] ... TN

[*The*] **Texas & Pacific Railway Co.** [*Absorbed into Missouri Pacific System*] ... T and P

[*The*] **Texas & Pacific Railway Co.** [*Absorbed into Missouri Pacific System*] [*AAR code*] ... TP

Texas and Southwestern Cattle Raisers Association (EA) ... TSCRA

Texas Arkansas Louisiana Oklahoma, New Mexico (NITA) ... TALON

Texas Armadillo Association [*Commercial firm*] (EA) ... TAA

Texas Assesment Modeling Systems (EDAC) ... TAMS

Texas Assessment of Academic Skills ... TAAS

Texas Assessment of Basic Skills (EDAC) ... TABS

Texas Association for Bilingual Education (EDAC) ... TABE

Texas Association for Community Service and Continuing Education (EDAC) ... TACSCE

Texas Association for Educational Data Systems (EDAC) ... TAEDS

Texas Barbed Wire Collectors Association (EA) ... TBWCA

Texas Biotechnology [*AMEX symbol*] (TTSB) ... TXB

Texas Biotechnology Corp. [*Associated Press*] (SAG) ... TexBi

Texas Biotechnology Corp. [*Associated Press*] (SAG) ... TexBiotch

Texas Biotechnology Corp. [*AMEX symbol*] (SAG) ... TXB

Texas Biotechnology Wrrt [*AMEX symbol*] (TTSB) ... TXB.WS

Texas Business Corporation Act, Annotated [*A publication*] (DLA) ... Tex Bus Corp Act Ann

Texas Butadine & Chemical Corp., Channelview, TX [*Library symbol Library of Congress*] (LCLS) ... TxCvT

Texas Centennial Society (EA) ... TCS

Texas Center for Policy Studies (CROSS) ... TCPS

Texas Center for Superconductivity, University of Houston [*Research center*] (RCD) ... TCSUH

Texas Central Railroad Co. ... TC

Texas Central Railroad Co. [*AAR code*] ... TEXC

Texas Chiropractic College, Pasadena, TX [*Library symbol*] [*Library of Congress*] (LCLS) ... TxPTC

Texas Christian University [*Fort Worth, TX*] ... TCU

Texas Christian University (GAGS) ... Tex Christ U

Texas Christian University Computer Center [*Research center*] (RCD) ... TCUCC

Texas Christian University, Fort Worth, TX [*OCLC symbol*] (OCLC) ... ICU

Texas Christian University, Fort Worth, TX [*Library symbol Library of Congress*] (LCLS) ... TxFTC

Texas City Terminal Railway Co. [*AAR code*] ... TCT

Texas City, TX [*AM radio station call letters*] ... KYST

Texas Civil Appeals Cases [*A publication*] (DLA) ... Tex App

Texas Civil Appeals Reports [*A publication*] (DLA) ... Civ

Texas Civil Appeals Reports [*A publication*] (DLA) ... Tex Civ App

Texas Civil Appeals Reports [*A publication*] (DLA) ... Tex Civ Rep

Texas Civil Appeals Reports [*A publication*] (DLA) ... Texas Civ

Texas Civil Appeals Reports [*A publication*] (DLA) ... Texas Civ App

Texas Civil Appeals Reports [*A publication*] (DLA) ... TX Ci

Texas Civil Cases [*A publication*] (DLA) ... App CC

Texas Civil Cases [*A publication*] (DLA) ... App CC (White & W)

Texas Civil Cases [*A publication*] (DLA) ... App CC (Willson)

Texas Civil Cases [*A publication*] (DLA) ... App Civ Cases

Texas Civil Cases [*A publication*] (DLA) ... Ct App CC

Texas Civil Cases [*A publication*] (DLA) ... Tex Ct App Civ

Texas Civil Cases [*A publication*] (DLA) ... Tex Ct App Dec Civ

Texas Civil Cases [*A publication*] (DLA) ... Texas Ct App Civ Cas

Texas Civil Cases [*A publication*] (DLA) ... White & W Civil Cases Ct App

Texas Civil Cases [*A publication*] (DLA) ... White & Willson

Texas Civil Cases [*A publication*] (DLA) ... Will Con Rep

Texas Civil Cases [*A publication*] (DLA) ... Willson's CC

Texas Climatological Model [*Environmental Protection Agency*] (GFGA) ... TCM

Texas Code of Criminal Procedure, Annotated [*A publication*] (DLA) ... Tex Code Crim Proc Ann

Texas Codes, Annotated [*A publication*] (DLA) ... Tex Code Ann

Texas College of Osteopathic Medicine ... TCOM

Texas College of Osteopathic Medicine, Fort Worth, TX [*OCLC symbol*] (OCLC) ... TOM

Texas College of Osteopathic Medicine, Fort Worth, TX [*Library symbol Library of Congress*] (LCLS) ... TxFCO

Texas College, Tyler, TX [*OCLC symbol*] (OCLC) ... TTT

Texas College, Tyler, TX [*Library symbol Library of Congress*] (LCLS) ... TxTyT

Texas Co. ... TEXACO

Texas Computer Education Association (EDAC) ... TCEA

Texas Cooperative Wildlife Collections [*Texas A & M University*] [*Research center*] (RCD) ... TCWC

Texas Council of Industrial Arts Supervisors (EDAC) ... TCIAS

Texas Council on Industrial Arts Teacher Education (EDAC) ... TCIATE

Texas Court of Appeal Civil Cases (Wilson) [*or Willson*] [*A publication*] (DLA) ... Tex A Civ Cas (Wilson)

Texas Court of Appeals Decisions, Civil Cases (White and Wilson) [*or Willson*] [*1876-92*] [*A publication*] (DLA) ... Tex Civ Cas

Texas Court of Appeals Reports [*A publication*] (DLA) ... App

Texas Court of Appeals Reports [*A publication*] (DLA) ... Court Appeals

Texas Court of Appeals Reports [*A publication*] (DLA) ... Ct App CC

Texas Court of Appeals Reports [*A publication*] (DLA) ... Ct Apps

Texas Court of Appeals Reports [*A publication*] (DLA) ... Tex Ct App

Texas Court of Appeals Reports [*A publication*] (DLA) ... Tex Ct App R

Texas Court of Appeals Reports [*A publication*] (DLA) ... Texas Cr App

Texas Court of Appeals Reports [*A publication*] (DLA) ... Texas Ct App

Texas Court of Appeals Reports [*A publication*] (DLA) ... Texas Ct of App

Texas Court of Appeals Reports (Criminal Cases) [*A publication*] (DLA) ... Cr

Texas Court of Appeals Reports (Criminal Cases) [*A publication*] (DLA) ... Tex App

Texas Court Reporter [*A publication*] (DLA) ... Tex Ct Rep

Texas Court Reporter [*1900-1908*] [*A publication*] (DLA) ... Texas Ct Rep

Texas Criminal [*A publication*] (DLA) ... Tex Cr

Texas Criminal Appeals Reports [*A publication*] (DLA) ... Tex Cr App

Texas Criminal Appeals Reports [*A publication*] (DLA) ... Tex Cr R

Texas Criminal Appeals Reports [*A publication*] (DLA) ... Texas Crim App

Texas Criminal Appeals Reports [*A publication*] (DLA) ... TX Cr

Texas Criminal Reports [*A publication*] (DLA) ... Cr

Texas Criminal Reports [*A publication*] (DLA) ... Tex Cr Rpts

Texas Criminal Reports [*A publication*] (DLA) ... Tex Crim

Texas Criminal Reports [*A publication*] (DLA) ... Tex Crim Rep

Texas Criminal Reports [*A publication*] (DLA) ... Texas Cr Rep

Texas Criminal Reports [*A publication*] (DLA) ... Texas Crim

Texas Criminal Reports [*A publication*] (DLA) .... Texas Crim Rep
Texas Data Base System (EDAC) .... TDBS
Texas Date Nail Collectors Association (EA) .... TDNCA
Texas Decisions [*A publication*] (DLA) .... Tex Dec
Texas Delaine Sheep Association (EA) .... TDSA
Texas Delaine-Merino Record Association [*Later, TDSA*] (EA) .... TDMRA
Texas Department of Mental Health and Mental Retardation, Austin, TX [*Library symbol Library of Congress*] (LCLS) .... TxAuMH
Texas Department of Parks and Wildlife, Austin, TX [*Library symbol Library of Congress*] (LCLS) .... TxAuPW
Texas Digest [*A publication*] (DLA) .... Texas Dig
Texas Eastern Transmission Corp., Houston, TX [*Library symbol Library of Congress*] (LCLS) .... TxHTE
Texas Eastern Transmission Corp., Shreveport, LA [*Library symbol Library of Congress*] (LCLS) .... LShTE
Texas Eastern University, Tyler, TX [*Library symbol Library of Congress*] (LCLS) .... TxTyC
Texas Education Agency, Austin, TX [*Library symbol Library of Congress*] (LCLS) .... TxAuEd
Texas Education Computer Cooperative [*Houston*] [*Information service or system*] (IID) .... TECC
[*The*] **Texas Education Network** [*A data communications network*] (TNIG) .... TENET
Texas Educational Assessment of Minimum Skills .... TEAMS
Texas Educational Computer Courseware Database [*Texas Education Computer Cooperative*] [*Information service or system Defunct*] (CRD) .... TECC
Texas Educational Microwave Project .... TEMP
Texas Election Code, Annotated [*A publication*] (DLA) .... Tex Elec Code Ann
Texas Electric Service Co., Fort Worth, TX [*Library symbol Library of Congress*] (LCLS) .... TxFTE
Texas Engineering Experiment Station [*Texas A & M University*] [*Research center*] .... TEES
Texas Episodic Model [*Environmental Protection Agency*] (GFGA) .... TEM
Texas Experimental TOKAMAK [*Atomic physics*] .... TEXT
Texas Export [*AAR code*] .... TXRC
Texas Foreign Language Association (EDAC) .... TFLA
Texas Forest Products Laboratory .... TFPL
Texas Forest Service, Forest Products Laboratory Library, Lufkin, TX [*Library symbol Library of Congress*] (LCLS) .... TxLufFS
Texas Gas Exploration Co., Houston, TX [*Library symbol Library of Congress*] (LCLS) .... TxHTexG
Texas Group [*Navy*] (DNAB) .... TEXGRP
Texas Gulf Sulphur Co., Inc., Houston, TX [*Library symbol Library of Congress*] (LCLS) .... TxHTGS
Texas Gun Collectors Association .... TGCA
Texas Heart Institute [*University of Texas*] [*Research center*] (RCD) .... THI
Texas, Inc., New Orleans, LA [*Library symbol*] [*Library of Congress*] (LCLS) .... LNTex
Texas Independent Producers and Royalty Owners Association (EA) .... TIPRO
Texas Indus [*NYSE symbol*] (TTSB) .... TXI
Texas Industries, Inc. [*Associated Press*] (SAG) .... TexInd
Texas Industries, Inc. [*NYSE symbol*] (SPSG) .... TXI
Texas Information Exchange .... TIE
Texas Institute for Computational Mechanics [*University of Texas at Austin*] [*Research center*] (RCD) .... TICOM
Texas Institute of Rehabilitation and Research (BABM) .... TIRR
Texas Instructional Media Project [*Education*] .... TIMP
Texas Instruments (NITA) .... TI
Texas Instruments [*NYSE symbol*] (TTSB) .... TXN
Texas Instruments Automatic Computer .... TIAC
Texas Instruments Bourdon Tube Pressure Gauge .... TIBTPG
Texas Instruments, Canon, Hewlett-Packard [*Joint Venture*] .... TECH
Texas Instruments Cassette Operating Language (IAA) .... TIOL
Texas Instruments Co. .... TIC
Texas Instruments Digital Analog Readout .... TIDAR
Texas Instruments, Inc. [*Associated Press*] (SAG) .... TexInst
Texas Instruments, Inc. .... TI
Texas Instruments, Inc. .... TII
Texas Instruments, Inc. [*NYSE symbol*] (SPSG) .... TXN
Texas Instruments, Inc., Apparatus Division Library, Dallas, TX [*Library symbol Library of Congress*] (LCLS) .... TxDaTI-A
Texas Instruments, Inc., Austin Site Library, Austin, TX [*Library symbol*] [*Library of Congress*] (LCLS) .... TxAuTI
Texas Instruments, Inc., Central Library Services, Dallas, TX [*OCLC symbol*] (OCLC) .... TIM
Texas Instruments, Inc., Central Research and Engineering Library, Dallas, TX [*Library symbol Library of Congress*] (LCLS) .... TxDaTI-C
Texas Instruments, Inc., Forest Lane Technical Library, Dallas, TX [*Library symbol*] [*Library of Congress*] (LCLS) .... TxDaTI-F
Texas Instruments, Inc., Houston, TX [*Library symbol Library of Congress*] (LCLS) .... TxHTI
Texas Instruments, Inc., Industrial Products Division, Houston, TX [*Library symbol Library of Congress*] (LCLS) .... TxHTI-I
Texas Instruments, Incorporated, IS & S Library, Dallas, TX [*OCLC symbol*] (OCLC) .... TII
Texas Instruments, Inc., IS & S Library, Dallas, TX [*Library symbol Library of Congress*] (LCLS) .... TxDaTI-IS
Texas Instruments, Inc., Johnson City Technical Library, Johnson City, TX [*Library symbol*] [*Library of Congress*] (LCLS) .... TxJoTI
Texas Instruments, Inc., Lewisville Technical Library, Lewisville, TX [*Library symbol*] [*Library of Congress*] (LCLS) .... TxLvTI
Texas Instruments, Inc., McKinney Technical Library, McKinney, TX [*Library symbol*] [*Library of Congress*] (LCLS) .... TxMckTI
Texas Instruments, Inc., North Building Library, Dallas, TX [*Library symbol*] [*Library of Congress*] (LCLS) .... TxDaTI-N
Texas Instruments, Inc., Research Building Library, Dallas, TX [*Library symbol*] [*Library of Congress*] (LCLS) .... TxDaTI-R
Texas Instruments, Inc., Science Services Division, Dallas, TX [*Library symbol Library of Congress*] (LCLS) .... TxDaTI-SS
Texas Instruments, Inc., Semiconductor Division, Dallas, TX [*Library symbol Library of Congress*] (LCLS) .... TxDaTI-S
Texas Instruments, Inc., Sherman Technical Library, Sherman, TX [*Library symbol*] [*Library of Congress*] (LCLS) .... TxShTI
Texas Instruments Index Access Method .... TINDX
Texas Instruments Language Translator [*Computer science*] (IAA) .... TILT
Texas Instruments Minicomputer Information Exchange (IAA) .... TIMIX
Texas Instruments Online Reporting System [*Computer science*] .... TIOLR
Texas Instruments Planning and Control System .... TIPACS
Texas Instruments Plotter (NITA) .... TEXPLOT
Texas Instruments Pressure Controller .... TIPC
Texas Instruments Registration and Identification System [*Auto theft deterrent*] .... TIRIS
Texas Instruments Registration and Identification System [*Texas Instruments, Inc.*] [*Automobile anti-theft protection*] .... TIRIS
Texas Instruments Transistor Transistor Logic (IAA) .... TITTI
Texas Instruments Universal Command Language (NITA) .... TI UCL
Texas Instruments Vidicon (IAA) .... TIVICON
Texas Insurance Code, Annotated [*A publication*] (DLA) .... Tex Ins Code Ann
Texas International (GAVI) .... TI
Texas International Airlines [*ICAO designator*] (AD) .... TI
Texas International Airlines, Inc. [*Air carrier designation symbol*] .... TXI
Texas Intersection Air Quality Model [*Environmental Protection Agency*] (GFGA) .... TEXIN
Texas Israel Exchange [*A trade and research venture*] .... TIE
Texas Jurisprudence [*A publication*] (DLA) .... Tex Jur
Texas Jurisprudence [*2nd ed.*] [*A publication*] (DLA) .... Tex Jur 2d
Texas Law and Legislation [*A publication*] (DLA) .... Tex Law & Leg
Texas Law Journal [*A publication*] (DLA) .... Tex LJ
Texas Law Journal [*A publication*] (DLA) .... TX LJ
Texas Law Reporter [*1882-84*] [*A publication*] (DLA) .... Tex L Rep
Texas Lawman [*A publication*] (DLA) .... Tex Law
Texas League [*Baseball*] .... TL
Texas Lexicon [*Slang*] .... TexLex
Texas Longhorn Breeders Association of America (EA) .... TLBAA
Texas Lutheran College .... TLC
Texas Lutheran College, Seguin, TX [*Library symbol Library of Congress*] (LCLS) .... TxSeTL
Texas Male Sterility Cytoplasm [*Agriculture*] (OA) .... TMSC
Texas Manufacturers Association, Houston, TX [*Library symbol Library of Congress*] (LCLS) .... TxHTM
Texas Medical Association, Austin, TX [*Library symbol Library of Congress*] (LCLS) .... TxAuM
Texas Meridian Resources [*AMEX symbol*] (TTSB) .... TMR
Texas Meridian Resources Ltd. [*Associated Press*] (SAG) .... TexMer
Texas Meridian Resources Ltd. [*AMEX symbol*] (SPSG) .... TMR
Texas Mexican Railway Co. .... TEX MEX
Texas Mexican Railway Co. [*AAR code*] .... TM
Texas Microelectronics, Inc. (IAA) .... TMI
Texas National Airlines [*ICAO designator*] (FAAC) .... TXN
Texas Natural Resource Conservation Commission .... TNRCC
Texas Natural Resources Conservation Council (DOGT) .... TNRCC
Texas Natural Resources Information System [*Austin*] [*Information service or system*] (IID) .... TNRIS
Texas Northern Oil & Gas [*Vancouver Stock Exchange symbol*] .... TXN
Texas Nuclear Corp. (KSC) .... TNC
Texas, Oklahoma & Eastern Railroad Co. [*AAR code*] .... TOE
Texas Onboard Program of Computer Assisted Training (NITA) .... TOPCAT
Texas Opera Theatre .... TOT
Texas Outlaw Midget Automobile Racing Association [*Car racing*] .... TOMARA
Texas Pac Ld Tr [*NYSE symbol*] (TTSB) .... TPL
Texas Pacific Land Trust [*NYSE symbol*] (SPSG) .... TPL
Texas Pacific Land Trust [*Associated Press*] (SAG) .... TxPac
Texas Pacific-Missouri Pacific Terminal [*Railroad of New Orleans*] [*AAR code*] .... TPMP
Texas Panhandle Library System [*Library network*] .... TPLS
Texas Petroleum Corp. [*Vancouver Stock Exchange symbol*] .... TPC
Texas Preschool Screening Inventory (EDAC) .... TPSI
Texas Reconfigurable Array Computer .... TRAC
Texas Red-Conjugated Dextran [*Analytical biochemistry*] .... TRD
Texas Red-Labeled Dextran [*Analytical biochemistry*] .... TRDx
Texas Regional Banc'A' [*NASDAQ symbol*] (TTSB) .... TRBS
Texas Regional Bancshares, Inc. [*Associated Press*] (SAG) .... TexRegl
Texas Regional Bancshares, Inc. [*NASDAQ symbol*] (SAG) .... TRBS
Texas Regional Library, Division for the Blind and Physically Handicapped, Austin, TX [*Library symbol Library of Congress*] (LCLS) .... Tx-BPH
Texas Reports [*A publication*] (DLA) .... Texas R
Texas Reports [*A publication*] (DLA) .... Texas Rep
Texas Reports [*A publication*] (DLA) .... TX
Texas Research Foundation, Renner, TX [*Library symbol Library of Congress*] (LCLS) .... TxReTR
Texas Research Institute of Mental Sciences, Houston, TX [*Library symbol Library of Congress*] (LCLS) .... TxHP
Texas Revised Civil Statutes, Annotated (Vernon) [*A publication*] (DLA) .... Tex Rev Civ Stat Ann (Vernon)
Texas Satellite Network [*Telecommunications service*] (TSSD) .... TXN
Texas Session Law Service (Vernon) [*A publication*] (DLA) .... Tex Sess Law Serv
Texas Short Line Railway [*AAR code*] .... TSL
Texas Shrimp Association (EA) .... TSA
Texas South-Eastern Railroad Co. [*AAR code*] .... TSE

Texas Southern Intramural Law Review [*A publication*] (DLA) ..... Tex So Intra L Rev
Texas Southern University (GAGS) ..... Tex So U
Texas Southern University ..... TSU
Texas Southern University, Houston, TX [*Library symbol Library of Congress*] (LCLS) ..... TxHTSU
Texas Southern University, Houston, TX [*OCLC symbol*] (OCLC) ..... TXT
Texas Southern University, Law Library, Houston, TX [*Library symbol*] [*Library of Congress*] (LCLS) ..... TxHTSU-L
Texas Southmost College ..... TSC
Texas Southmost College, Brownsville, TX [*Library symbol Library of Congress*] (LCLS) ..... TxBS
Texas Star Resources [*NASDAQ symbol*] (TTSB) ..... TEXSF
Texas Star Resources Corp. [*NASDAQ symbol*] (SAG) ..... TEXS
Texas Star Resources Corp. [*Associated Press*] (SAG) ..... TexStar
Texas Star Resources Corp. [*Vancouver Stock Exchange symbol*] ..... TXS
Texas State Department of Highways and Public Transportation, Materials and Tests Research Library, Austin, TX [*Library symbol Library of Congress*] (LCLS) ..... TxAuHi
Texas State Law Library, Austin, TX [*Library symbol Library of Congress*] (LCLS) ..... Tx-SC
Texas State Library and Historical Commission, Austin, TX [*OCLC symbol*] (OCLC) ..... IKM
Texas State Library and Historical Commission, Austin, TX [*Library symbol Library of Congress*] (LCLS) ..... Tx
Texas State Library Communication Network [*Library network*] ..... TSLCN
Texas State Medical Library, Austin, TX [*Library symbol Library of Congress*] (LCLS) ..... Tx-M
Texas Statutes, Annotated [*A publication*] (DLA) ..... Tex Stat Ann
Texas Student Information System (EDAC) ..... TEXSIS
Texas Supplement [*A publication*] (DLA) ..... Tex Supp
Texas Supplement [*A publication*] (DLA) ..... Tex Suppl
Texas Supreme Court Reporter [*A publication*] (DLA) ..... Tex S Ct
Texas Supreme Court Reports [*A publication*] (DLA) ..... Tex
Texas Supreme Court Reports, Supplement [*A publication*] (DLA) ..... Tex S
Texas Tax-General, Annotated [*A publication*] (DLA) ..... Tex Tax-Gen Ann
Texas Tech University (GAGS) ..... Tex Tech U
Texas Tech University, Lubbock, TX [*OCLC symbol*] (OCLC) ..... ILU
Texas Tech University, Lubbock, TX [*Library symbol Library of Congress*] (LCLS) ..... TxLT
Texas Tech University, Regional Academic Health Center, El Paso, TX [*Library symbol*] [*Library of Congress*] (LCLS) ..... TxLTM-E
Texas Tech University, School of Law Library, Lubbock, TX [*OCLC symbol*] (OCLC) ..... TTL
Texas Tech University, School of Medicine at Lubbock, Library of the Health Science, Lubbock, TX [*OCLC symbol*] (OCLC) ..... TML
Texas Tech University, School of Medicine at Lubbock, Lubbock, TX [*Library symbol Library of Congress*] (LCLS) ..... TxLTM
Texas Tech University, Southwest Collection, Lubbock, TX [*Library symbol*] [*Library of Congress*] (LCLS) ..... TxLT-SW
Texas Technological University (PDAA) ..... TTU
Texas Tower (SAA) ..... TT
Texas Transportation Institute [*Texas A & M University*] [*Research center*] ..... TTI
Texas Unreported Cases [*A publication*] (DLA) ..... Posey UC
Texas Util Elec Dep Pfd [*NYSE symbol*] (TTSB) ..... TUEPr
Texas Util Elec'A'Dep Pfd [*NYSE symbol*] (TTSB) ..... TUEPrA
Texas Util Elec'B'Dep Pfd [*NYSE symbol*] (TTSB) ..... TUEPrB
Texas Utilities [*NYSE symbol*] (TTSB) ..... TXU
Texas Utilities Co. [*Associated Press*] (SAG) ..... TexUtil
Texas Utilities Co. [*NYSE symbol*] (SPSG) ..... TXU
Texas Utilities Electric [*Associated Press*] (SAG) ..... TxUtEl
Texas Utilities Electric Co. [*NYSE symbol*] (SPSG) ..... TUE
Texas Water Development Board, Austin, TX [*Library symbol Library of Congress*] (LCLS) ..... TxAuW
Texas Water Resources Institute [*Texas A & M University*] [*Department of the Interior Research center*] (RCD) ..... TWRI
Texas Wesleyan College ..... TWC
Texas Wesleyan College, Fort Worth, TX [*OCLC symbol*] (OCLC) ..... TWC
Texas Wesleyan College, Fort Worth, TX [*Library symbol Library of Congress*] (LCLS) ..... TxFTW
Texas Western College [*Later, UTEP*] ..... TWC
Texas Woman's University (GAGS) ..... Tex Woman's U
Texas Woman's University ..... TWU
Texas Woman's University, Denton, TX [*OCLC symbol*] (OCLC) ..... IWU
Texas Woman's University, Denton, TX [*Library symbol Library of Congress*] (LCLS) ..... TxDW
Texas World Speedway [*Auto racing*] ..... TWS
Texasgulf Oil & Gas Co., Houston, TX [*Library symbol Library of Congress*] (LCLS) ..... TxHTexO
Texas-Louisiana Freight Bureau ..... TLFB
Texas-Louisiana Freight Bureau, St. Louis MO [*STAC*] ..... TLB
Texas-New Mexico Railway Co. [*AAR code*] ..... TNM
Texas-United States Chemical Co., Process Engineering Section, R and D Library, Port Neches, TX [*Library symbol Library of Congress*] (LCLS) ..... TxPnT
Texcan Technology Corp. [*Vancouver Stock Exchange symbol*] ..... TCN
TEXCOM [*Test and Experimentation Command*] **Automated Field Instrumentation System** [*Army*] ..... TAFIS
Texeira [*Portugal*] [*Airport symbol*] (AD) ..... TXA
Texel [*Netherlands ICAO location identifier*] (ICLI) ..... EHTX
Texfi Indus [*NYSE symbol*] (TTSB) ..... TXF
Texfi Industries, Inc. [*Associated Press*] (SAG) ..... Texfi
Texfi Industries, Inc. [*NYSE symbol*] (SPSG) ..... TXF
Texico, NM [*Location identifier FAA*] (FAAL) ..... TXO
Texoil, Inc. [*Associated Press*] (SAG) ..... Texo
Texoil, Inc. [*Associated Press*] (SAG) ..... Texoil
Texoil, Inc. [*NASDAQ symbol*] (SAG) ..... TXLI
Texoil Inc. Wrrt'A' [*NASDAQ symbol*] (TTSB) ..... TXLIW
Texoil Inc. Wrrt'B' [*NASDAQ symbol*] (TTSB) ..... TXLIZ
Texoro Resources Ltd. [*Vancouver Stock Exchange symbol*] ..... TXU
Text ..... TXT
Text and Date Messaging (HGAA) ..... TDM
Text and File Management System ..... TFMS
Text and Graphics System [*or Subsystem*] (NASA) ..... TAGS
Text Change [*Computer science*] (PCM) ..... TG
Text Check [*Computer science*] ..... TCHK
Text Data Retrieval System (NITA) ..... TDRS
Text Editing and Composition System [*Computer science*] (DGA) ..... TECS
Text Editing System ..... TES
Text Editor [*Computer science*] ..... TE
Text Editor [*Computer science*] (MHDI) ..... TED
Text Editor ..... TX
Text Editor and Corrector [*Computer science*] (MHDI) ..... TECO
Text Encoding Initiative [*Computer science*] ..... TEI
Text Entry and Edit (DGA) ..... TEE
Text Excursion Module (IAA) ..... TEM
Text File Device Driver [*Computer science*] (PCM) ..... TFDD
Text Indexing and Retrieval [*Computer science*] ..... TEXTIR
Text Information and Management System [*Computer science*] ..... TIMS
Text Information Processing System ..... TIPS
Text Information Retrieval and Management Program System [*Computer science*] (IAA) ..... TRAMPS
Text Interchange Format [*Telecommunications*] (OSI) ..... TIF
Text Maintenance [*Computer science*] (MHDB) ..... TXTM
Text Matter Depth [*Typography*] (DGA) ..... TMD
Text Message System (MCD) ..... TMS
Text on Microform [*Information Access Co. - IAC*] [*Information service or system*] (IID) ..... TOM
Text Online (NITA) ..... TEXTLINE
Text or ASCII File [*Computer science*] ..... txt
Text Preparation and Interchange [*Telecommunications*] ..... TPI
Text Processing (NITA) ..... TP
Text Processing Language [*Computer science*] ..... TPL
Text Processing Utility [*Computer science*] ..... TPU
Text Processor ..... TP
Text Reckoning and Compiling [*Computer science*] ..... TRAC
Text Retrieval Conference [*Sponsored by National Institute of Standards and Technology*] ..... TREC
Text Retrieval Terminal [*Computer science*] (DGA) ..... TRT
Text Setting [*Computer science*] (PCM) ..... TS
Text Telephone [*Hearing-impaired technology*] [*See also TDD*] ..... TT
Text Typewriter (PAZ) ..... TT
Text User Interface [*Computer science*] ..... TUI
Text Word(s) (NITA) ..... TW
Text-Based Management Systems [*Computer science*] ..... TBMS
Textbook Authors Association (EA) ..... TAA
Textbook Information and Exchange Service [*Regional clearinghouses for used textbooks*] ..... TIES
[*A*] **Text-Book of North-Semitic Inscriptions** [*A publication*] (BJA) ..... TNSI
Text-Books of Physical Chemistry [*A publication*] ..... TBPC
Text-Books of Science [*A publication*] ..... TBS
Textbuch zur Geschichte Israels [*A publication*] (BJA) ..... TGI
Texte de Louvre [*Paris*]: Monuments de Ninive et de Babylone [*A publication*] (BJA) ..... MNB
Texte und Arbeiten [*Beuron*] [*A publication*] (BJA) ..... TuA
Texte und Materialien der Frau Professor Hilprecht Collection of Babylonian Antiquities im Eigentum der Univerișitaet Jena [*A publication*] (BJA) ..... TuM
Texte und Materialien der Frau Professor Hilprecht Collection of Babylonian Antiquities im Eigentum der Universitaet Jena (BJA) ..... TMH
Textes Arameens d'Egypte [*A publication*] (BJA) ..... TAE
Textes Cuneiformes. Departement des Antiquites Orientales. Musee du Louvre [*A publication*] (BJA) ..... TCL
Textes et Monuments Figures Relatifs aux Mysteres de Mithra [*A publication*] (BJA) ..... TMMM
Textes Mathematiques Babyloniens [*A publication*] (BJA) ..... TMB
Textes Religieux Sumeriens du Louvre [*A publication*] (BJA) ..... TRS
Textes Sogdiens. Edites. Traduits et Commentes [*A publication*] (BJA) ..... TS
Text-Fiche ..... TF
Textile (AABC) ..... TEX
Textile ..... TEXT
Textile (MSA) ..... TXTL
Textile (VRA) ..... txtl
Textile ..... TXTL
Textile ..... TXTLE
Textile and Clothing Contractors' Association [*British*] (BI) ..... TCCA
Textile Association of Los Angeles (EA) ..... TALA
Textile Bag and Packaging Association (EA) ..... TBPA
Textile Bag Manufacturers Association (EA) ..... TBMA
Textile Care Allied Trades Association (EA) ..... TCATA
Textile Care and Rental Industry Council for Education (AIE) ..... TRICE
Textile Chemical Manufacturers Association [*Later, IOSA*] (EA) ..... TCMA
Textile Clothing and Footwear Council of Australia ..... TCFCA
Textile, Clothing, and Footwear Industries Committee [*British*] (DCTA) ..... TCFIC
Textile Color Card Association of the US [*Later, CAUS*] ..... TCCA
Textile Converters Association (EA) ..... TCA
Textile Data Processing Association [*Later, ATMI*] (EA) ..... TDPA
Textile Dealers Association of America (EA) ..... TEXDEALAM
Textile Designers Guild (EA) ..... TDG
Textile Distributors Association (EA) ..... TDA
Textile Dye Institute [*Later, American Dye Manufacturers Institute*] ..... TDI
Textile Economics Bureau ..... TEB

Textile Educators' Association [*Australia*] ... TEA
Textile Export Association of the US (EA) ... TEA
Textile Fabric Distributors Association [*Later, TDA*] (EA) ... TFDA
Textile Fiber Products Identification Act [*1960*] ... TFPIA
Textile Fibers and By-Products Association [*Charlotte, NC*] ... TFBA
Textile Fibers and By-Products Association (EA) ... TFBPA
Textile Finishers Association (DBA) ... TFA
Textile Foremen's Guild ... TFG
Textile Foundation, Inc. ... TFI
Textile History Society [*Defunct*] (EA) ... THS
Textile Industry (IAA) ... TEXTINDY
Textile Industry (WDAA) ... TI
Textile Industry Product Safety [*A publication*] ... TIPS
Textile Industry Support Campaign [*British*] (DBA) ... TISC
Textile Information Retrieval Program (NITA) ... TIRP
Textile Information Treatment Users' Service [*French Textile Institute*] [*Bibliographic database*] [*Information service or system*] (IID) ... TITUS
Textile Information Users Council (EA) ... TIUC
Textile Institute [*Manchester, England*] (EAIO) ... TI
Textile Labor Association [*India*] ... TLA
Textile Labor Relations Board [*Terminated, 1937; functions absorbed by US Conciliation Service, Department of Labor*] ... TLRB
Textile Laundry Council (EA) ... TLC
Textile Machinery and Accessory Manufacturers Association [*British*] (BI) ... TMAMA
Textile Market Studies [*British*] ... TMS
Textile Operational Control System [*Computer science*] ... TOCS
Textile Printers and Dyers Labor Relations Institute (EA) ... TPDLRI
Textile Quality Control Association (EA) ... TQCA
Textile Refinishers Association (EA) ... TRA
Textile Rental and Laundry Association [*Australia*] ... TRLA
Textile Rental and Laundry Association of New South Wales [*Australia*] ... TRLA(NSW)
Textile Rental and Laundry Association of Western Australia ... TRLAWA
Textile Rental and Laundry Association (Queensland) [*Australia*] ... TRLA(Q)
Textile Rental and Laundry Association (Victoria) [*Australia*] ... TRLA(V)
Textile Rental Services Association of America (EA) ... TRSA
Textile Research Council [*British*] ... TRC
Textile Research Institute (EA) ... TRI
Textile Research Institute, Princeton, NJ [*Library symbol Library of Congress*] (LCLS) ... NjPTe
Textile Resource and Research Center (EA) ... TRRC
Textile Salesmen's Association [*Defunct*] (EA) ... TSA
Textile Services Association [*British*] (DBA) ... TSA
Textile Supplies and Credit Association (EA) ... TSCA
Textile Technology Centre (AC) ... TTC
Textile Technology Digest Keyterm Index (NITA) ... TTD keyterm index
Textile Veterans Association (EA) ... TVA
Textile Veterans Association Hospitalized Veterans Fund [*Defunct*] (EA) ... TVAHVF
Textile Waste Association [*Later, Textile Fibers and By-Products Association*] (EA) ... TWA
Textile Waste Exchange [*Later, Textile Fibers and By-Products Association*] ... TWE
Textile Work Assignment Boards [*Terminated, 1935*] ... TWAB
Textile Workers Union of America [*Later, ACTWU*] ... TWUA
Textiles Surveillance Body [*Textile trade agreement*] ... TSB
Textil-Wirtschaft [*Textile Industry*] [*Deutscher Fachverlag GmbH*] [*Information service or system*] (IID) ... TW
Textron, $1.40 Cv B Pfd [*NYSE symbol*] (TTSB) ... TXTPrB
Textron, $2.08 Cv A Pfd [*NYSE symbol*] (TTSB) ... TXTPrA
Textron Aero-Structures, Nashville, TN [*Library symbol*] [*Library of Congress*] (LCLS) ... TNTA
Textron Cap 1 7.92% Tr Sec [*NYSE symbol*] (TTSB) ... TXTPrT
Textron, Inc. [*Associated Press*] (SAG) ... Textr
Textron, Inc. [*Associated Press*] (SAG) ... Textron
Textron, Inc. [*NYSE symbol*] (SPSG) ... TXT
Textron, Inc., Dalmo Victor Co., Belmont, CA [*Library symbol Library of Congress*] (LCLS) ... CBelmD
Texts and Studies [*Cambridge*] [*A publication*] (BJA) ... TS
Texts and Studies [*A publication*] (BJA) ... TSt
Texts from Cuneiform Sources [*A publication*] (BJA) ... TCS
Text-to-Speech [*Computer science*] ... TTS
Texture (VRA) ... text
Texture Analysis System [*Image analysis for biochemistry*] ... TAS
Texture Profile Analysis [*Food technology*] ... TPA
Textured Peanut Protein [*Food industry*] ... TPP
Textured Soy Flour ... TSF
Textured Soy Protein [*Food industry*] ... TSP
Textured Vegetable Protein [*Trademark of Archer Daniels Midland Co. for soybean product*] ... TVP
Textured Yarn Association of America (EA) ... TYAA
Textus Receptus [*The Received Text*] [*Latin*] ... TEXT REC
Textus Receptus (BJA) ... TR
Tezpur [*India*] [*Airport symbol*] (OAG) ... TEZ
Tezu [*India*] [*ICAO location identifier*] (ICLI) ... VETJ
TF Financial [*NASDAQ symbol*] (TTSB) ... THRD
TF Financial Corp. [*Associated Press*] (SAG) ... TF Fincl
TF Financial Corp. [*NASDAQ symbol*] (SAG) ... THRD
TFC Enterprises [*NASDAQ symbol*] (TTSB) ... TFCE
TFC Enterprises, Inc. [*Associated Press*] (SAG) ... TFC Ent
TFC Enterprises, Inc. [*NASDAQ symbol*] (SAG) ... TFCE
TFTR [*Tokamak Fusion Test Reactor*] **Flexibility Modification** ... TFM
TG Aviation Ltd. [*British ICAO designator*] (FAAC) ... TGC
TGC Industries [*NASDAQ symbol*] (TTSB) ... TGCI
TGC Industries, Inc. [*Associated Press*] (SAG) ... TGC In
TGC Industries, Inc. [*Associated Press*] (SAG) ... TGC Ind
TGC Industries, Inc. [*Associated Press*] (SAG) ... TGC Inds
TGC Industries, Inc. [*NASDAQ symbol*] (SAG) ... TGCI
TGV Software, Inc. [*Associated Press*] (SAG) ... TGV Sft
TGV Software, Inc. [*NASDAQ symbol*] (SAG) ... TGVI
Thaad Information Management System ... TIMS
Thaba Tseka [*Lesotho*] [*ICAO location identifier*] (ICLI) ... FXTA
Thaba Tseka [*Lesotho*] [*Airport symbol*] (OAG) ... THB
Thacher's Criminal Cases [*1823-42*] [*Massachusetts*] [*A publication*] (DLA) ... Th CC
Thacher's Criminal Cases [*1823-42*] [*Massachusetts*] [*A publication*] (DLA) ... Thac Cr Cas
Thacher's Criminal Cases [*Massachusetts*] [*A publication*] (DLA) ... Thach Cr
Thacher's Criminal Cases [*Massachusetts*] [*A publication*] (DLA) ... Thacher Cr
Thacher's Criminal Cases [*Massachusetts*] [*A publication*] (DLA) ... Thacher Cr Cas
Thacher's Criminal Cases [*Massachusetts*] [*A publication*] (DLA) ... Thacher Crim Cas (Mass)
Thackeray Corp. [*Associated Press*] (SAG) ... Thack
Thackeray Corp. [*NYSE symbol*] (SPSG) ... THK
Thai [*MARC language code Library of Congress*] (LCCP) ... tha
Thai Aerospace Services Co. Ltd. [*FAA designator*] (FAAC) ... EGP
Thai Airways [*ICAO designator*] (AD) ... TG
Thai Airways [*ICAO designator*] (AD) ... TH
Thai Airways Co. Ltd. [*Later, Thai Airways International*] [*ICAO designator*] (FAAC) ... TAC
Thai Airways International (MCD) ... TAI
Thai Airways International ... THAI
Thai Airways International Ltd. [*Thailand*] [*ICAO designator*] (FAAC) ... THA
Thai Aquatic Sciences and Fisheries Information System [*Marine science*] (OSRA) ... TFIS
Thai Capital Fund [*NYSE symbol*] (TTSB) ... TC
Thai Capital Fund, Inc. [*NYSE symbol*] (SPSG) ... TC
Thai Capital Fund, Inc. [*Associated Press*] (SAG) ... ThaiCF
Thai Computer Science Network (TNIG) ... TCSnet
Thai Development Information Service (EAIO) ... TDIS
Thai Environmental and Community Development Association (EERA) ... TECDA
Thai Exiles Association (CINC) ... TEA
Thai Farmers' Bank ... TFB
Thai Flying Helicopter Service Co. Ltd. [*Thailand*] [*ICAO designator*] (FAAC) ... TFH
Thai Fund [*Associated Press*] (SAG) ... Thai
Thai Fund [*NYSE symbol*] (SPSG) ... TTF
Thai Information Center (EA) ... TIC
Thai National Documentation Center (IID) ... TNDC
Thai National Documentation Centre (NITA) ... TNDC
Thai Patriotic Front [*Communist-directed activity outside Thailand*] [*Merged with TIM*] ... TPF
Thai People's Liberation Armed Forces [*Thailand*] ... TPLAF
Thai Petro-chemical Industry ... TPI
Thai Support Foundation (EA) ... TSF
Thai-American Business [*A publication*] (IMH) ... T-AB
Thai-American Treaty of Amity and Economic Relations (IMH) ... AER
Thailand [*MARC geographic area code Library of Congress*] (LCCP) ... a-th--
Thailand [*International civil aircraft marking*] (ODBW) ... HS
Thailand [*IYRU nationality code*] [*ANSI two-letter standard code*] (CNC) ... TH
Thailand [*MARC country of publication code Library of Congress*] (LCCP) ... th
Thailand [*ANSI three-letter standard code*] (CNC) ... THA
Thailand ... Thai
Thailand ... Thail
Thailand Ammunition Manufacturing Plant (CINC) ... TAMP
Thailand Atomic Energy Commission for Peace ... TAEC
Thailand Independence Movement [*Communist-directed activity outside Thailand*] [*Merged with TPF*] ... TIM
Thailand Informations und Solidaritaetskomitee [*Germany*] ... TISK
Thailand National Police (CINC) ... TNP
Thailand Research Reactor ... TRR
Thailand-UNESCO Fundamental Education Centre ... TUFEC
Thakhek [*Laos*] [*Airport symbol*] (AD) ... THK
Thakhek [*Laos*] [*ICAO location identifier*] (ICLI) ... VLTK
Thakuragaon [*Bangladesh*] [*ICAO location identifier*] (ICLI) ... VGSG
Thakurgaon [*Bangladesh*] [*Airport symbol*] (AD) ... TKR
Thalamic Projection Neurons [*Neurology*] ... TPN
Thalamic Radiation [*Neurology*] ... TR
Thalamocortical Axon [*Neurophysiology*] ... TCA
Thalamocortical Relay [*Neurology*] ... TCR
Thalassa Research Associates, Victoria, BC, Canada [*Library symbol*] [*Library of Congress*] (LCLS) ... CaBViTRA
Thalassa Research Associates, Victoria, British Columbia [*Library symbol National Library of Canada*] (NLC) ... BVITRA
Thalassemia [*Medicine*] ... Thal
Thalassemia Action Group [*Organization concerned with Cooley's anemia*] (PAZ) ... TAG
Thalassemia Intermedia [*Hematology*] ... TI
Thalassemia Major [*Hematology*] ... TM
Thaler [*or Talari*] [*Monetary unit Ethiopia*] ... T
Thaler [*Numismatics*] ... THLR
Thallium [*Chemical element*] ... Tl
Thallium Acetate ... TIA
Thallium Beam Tube ... TBT
Thallium Calcium Barium Copper Oxide [*Inorganic chemistry*] ... TCBCO
Thallium Chloride [*A radioactive isotope*] (DAVI) ... TICI
Thallium Myocardial Perfusion [*Test*] [*Cardiology*] (DAVI) ... TMP
Thallium Myocardial Scintigraphy [*Cardiology*] ... TMS
Thallium Trifluoroacetate [*Organic chemistry*] ... TTFA

Thallium-Activated Sodium Iodide [*Scintillation detector*] [*Medicine*]
(MEDA) .... NaI (TI)

Thalner Electronic Laboratories, Inc. [*Ann Arbor, MI*] (TSSD) ...... TEL

Thames Action and Resources Group for Education and Training [*British*]
(AIE) .... TARGET

Thames Air Services & Charter Ltd. [*Nigeria*] [*ICAO designator*] (FAAC) ...... TMQ

Thames and Chilterns Tourist Board [*British*] (DCTA) .... T & CTB

Thames & Hudson [*Publisher*] .... T & H

Thames Arts Centre, Chatham, ON, Canada [*Library symbol Library of Congress*] (LCLS) .... CaOChaT

Thames Arts Centre, Chatham, Ontario [*Library symbol National Library of Canada*] (NLC) .... OCHAT

Thames Boating Trades' Association [*British*] (BI) .... TBTA

Thames Conservancy [*British*] (BI) .... TC

Thames Measurement [*Formula for rating yachts*] [*British*] .... TM

Thames Navigation Service [*British*] (DS) .... TNS

Thames Ontario Library Service Board [*UTLAS symbol*] .... THA

Thames Rowing Club [*British*] (DI) .... TRC

Thames Valley [*England*] .... TV

Thames Water Authority [*British*] .... TWA

Thames Yacht Club [*Later, RTYC*] [*British*] (DI) .... TYC

Than .... T

Thanatophoric Dysplasia [*Lethal dwarfism*] .... TD

Thangool [*Queensland*] [*Airport symbol*] (AD) .... THG

Thank God It's Friday [*Meaning work-week is nearly over*] .... TGIF

Thank God It's Friday - Only Two More Work Days Until Monday [*Pentagon saying*] .... TGIF-OTMWDUM

Thank God It's Summer .... TGIS

Thank You [*Communications operator's procedural remark*] .... TU

Thank You .... TY

Thank You for Shopping Our K-Mart [*or Kresge's*] [*Slogan of K-Mart Corp.*] .... TYFSOK

Thank You Very Much .... TYVM

Thanks (ADA) .... TKS

Thanks (IAA) .... TN

Thanks [*Communications operator's procedural remark*] .... TNX

Thanks for Coming By [*Exxon slogan*] .... TFCB

Thanks in Advance [*Internet language*] [*Computer science*] .... TIA

Thanks to Scandinavia (EA) .... TTS

Thapsigargin [*Organic chemistry*] .... TG

Thargomindah [*Queensland*] [*Airport symbol*] (AD) .... XTG

Tharsis Region [*A filamentary mark on Mars*] .... TH

That .... T

That Bloody Woman [*Nickname given to British Prime Minister Margaret Thatcher*] .... TBW

That Is [*Id est*] [*Latin*] (WDMC) .... ie

That Looks about Right [*Aviation*] .... T-LAR

That Was The Week That Was [*Also, TWTWTW*] [*Television program of English origin*] TW3

That Was The Week That Was [*Also, TW3*] [*Television program of English origin*] .... TWTWTW

Thatcher, AZ [*FM radio station call letters*] .... KFMM

That's Entertainment, Part 2 [*Initialism is shortened form of movie title*] TE2

Thayer, MO [*AM radio station call letters*] .... KALM

Thayer-Martin Medium [*Medicine*] (DMAA) .... TM

Thayer's Preliminary Treatise on Evidence [*A publication*]
(DLA) .... Thayer Prelim Treatise Ev

Thayer's Reports [*18 Oregon*] [*A publication*] (DLA) .... Thayer

THC Homecare, Inc. [*Associated Press*] (SAG) .... THC

THC Homecare, Inc. [*Associated Press*] (SAG) .... THC Hm

THC Homecare, Inc. [*NASDAQ symbol*] (SAG) .... THCI

The Association for Persons with Severe Handicaps (PAZ) .... TASH

The Association for the Severely Handicapped [*Later, TASH: the Association for Persons with Severe Handicaps*] (EA) .... TASH

The Baseball Network .... TBN

#The Basic School [*Marine Corps*] (DOMA) .... TBS

The Berkeley Internet Name Domain .... BIND

The Brigittine Sisters (TOCD) .... OSSS

The Canadian Orthoptic Society (AC) .... TCOS

The Center for International Climate and Environmental Research - Oslo [*University of Oslo*] [*Norway*] .... CICERO

The Church of the Brethren Homes and Hospitals Association [*Later, BHOAM*] (EA) .... TCBHHA

The Dalles, OR [*Location identifier FAA*] (FAAL) .... DLS

The Dalles, OR [*AM radio station call letters*] .... KACI

The Dalles, OR [*FM radio station call letters*] .... KACI-FM

The Dalles, OR [*FM radio station call letters*] .... KMCQ

The Dalles, OR [*AM radio station call letters*] .... KODL

#The Early Retirement Authority .... TERA

The Easy Animator [*Computer software*] .... TEA

The Entertainment Network (NITA) .... TEN

The Ethics Bulletin Board System (AAGC) .... TEBBS

The Expert System Shell (NITA) .... TESS

The Gambia [*International civil aircraft marking*] (ODBW) .... WAG

The Glenmary Home Missioners (TOCD) .... glmy

The Information System (NITA) .... TIS

The Intelligent Machine Model (NITA) .... TIMM

The International English School (AIE) .... TIES

The Internet Product Site .... TIPS

The Learning Co. .... TLC

The Library Corp. .... TLC

The Library-Hattisburg, Petal Forrest County, Hattiesburg, MS [*Library symbol*] [*Library of Congress*] (LCLS) .... MsHaP

The Maintenance Council .... TMC

The Methodist Museum, St. Simons Island, GA [*Library symbol*] [*Library of Congress*] (LCLS) .... GSsiM

[*The*] The Michigan Educational Research Network [*Computer science*]
(TNIG) .... MERIT

#The Military Coalition .... TMC

The Monastic Fraternity of Jerusalem (TOCD) .... fmj

The Muskokas, ON [*Television station call letters*] CKCO-4

The National Alliance of Professional and Executive Women's Networks [*Later, TIA*] (EA) .... TNA

The National Association for the Craniofacially Handicapped (PAZ) .... FACES

The Netherlands Insitute for MBA Studies .... NIMBAS

The New York Times Online (NITA) .... TNYT

The Next Big Thing .... TNBT

The Next Generation .... TNG

The Nurturing Network (PAZ) .... TNN

The Office Manager (NITA) .... TOM

The Online Publishing System (NITA) .... TOPS

The Pas, MB [*AM radio station call letters*] .... CJAR

The Pas, MB [*ICAO location identifier*] (ICLI) .... CYQD

The Pas, MB [*Canada*] [*Airport symbol*] (OAG) .... YQD

The Pas Public Library, Manitoba [*Library symbol National Library of Canada*] (NLC) .... MTP

The Pas Public Library, The Pas, MB, Canada [*Library symbol Library of Congress*] (LCLS) .... CaMTp

The Searchers Workbench (NITA) .... TSW

The Sisters of St. Francis of Assisi (TOCD) .... OSF

The Sisters of St. Francis of Philadelphia (TOCD) .... OSF

The Times Network for Schools (NITA) .... TTNS

The Well Oiled Machine (NITA) .... TWOM

The Writers Union of Canada [*Canada*] (WWLA) .... TWUC

Theodore Roosevelt Elementary School, Roosevelt, NY [*Library symbol*] [*Library of Congress*] (LCLS) .... NRoosRE

Theaetetus [*of Plato*] [*Classical studies*] (OCD) .... Tht

Theater (AFM) .... THTR

Theater .... THTR

Theater Accounting and Finance Office [*Military*] (AFM) .... TAFO

Theater Administrative Zone [*Military*] .... TAZ

Theater Air Base Survivability [*Air Force*] .... TABS

Theater Air Base Vulnerability [*Air Force*] .... TAB VEE

Theater Air Base Vulnerability [*Air Force*] (AFM) .... TABV

Theater Air Command and Control Simulator Facility [*Air Force*] .... TACCSF

Theater Air Defense [*Military*] .... TAD

Theater Air Transportation Board .... TATB

Theater Air-Ground Warfare Simulation (MCD) .... TAGS

Theater Area Communications Systems [*Military*] .... TACS

Theater Army .... TA

Theater Army Air Defense Command (AABC) .... TAADC

Theater Army Air Defense Command (AABC) .... TAADCOM

Theater Army Area Command (AABC) .... TAACOM

Theater Army Civil Affairs Command (AABC) .... TACAC

Theater Army Communications System (MCD) .... TACS

Theater Army Headquarters .... TAHQ

Theater Army Logistical Command .... TALOG

Theater Army Materiel Management Center .... TAMMC

Theater Army Medical Management Information System (GFGA) .... TAMMIS

Theater Army Medical Management Information System - Division .... TAMMIS-D

Theater Army Personnel (MCD) .... TAPER

Theater Army Personnel Operations Center .... TAPOC

Theater Army Repair Program .... TARP

Theater Army Replacement and Training Command .... TARTC

Theater Army Replacement Command .... TARC

Theater Army Replacement System (AABC) .... TARS

Theater Army Replacement System / Southeast Asia (SAA) .... TARS/SEA

Theater Army Signal System (IAA) .... TASS

Theater Army Special Operations Support Command .... TASOSC

Theater Army Support Command [*Terminated, 1975*] [*West Germany*]
(AABC) .... TASCOM

Theater Army Support Command (Supply) .... TASCOM(S)

Theater Authorized Consumption List [*Army*] (AABC) .... TACL

Theater Authorized Stockage List [*Military*] (AABC) .... TASL

Theater Automated Command and Control Information Management System (MCD) .... TACCIMS

Theater Automated Command and Control System - Korea (MCD) .... TACCS-K

Theater Aviation Maintenance Program [*Army*] (DOMA) .... TAMP

Theater Ballistic Missile .... TBM

Theater Ballistic Missile Defense (DOMA) .... TBMD

Theater Battle Model (MCD) .... TBM

Theater Combat Model (NATG) .... TCM

Theater Commander's Approval [*Military*] .... TCA

Theater Communications Center (MCD) .... TCC

Theater Communications Command (MCD) .... TCC

Theater Communications System (MCD) .... TCS

Theater COMSEC [*Communications Security*] Logistic Support Center [*Army*] (AABC) .... TCLSC

Theater COMSEC Logistics Support Center - Europe (MCD) .... TCLSC-E

Theater Container Management Agency .... TCMA

Theater Force Evaluation by Combat Simulation (MCD) .... TFECS

Theater Ground Command [*Military*] .... TGC

Theater Headquarters [*Military*] .... THQ

Theater High-Altitude Area Defense [*Military*] .... THAAD

Theater Information and Engagement System [*Military*] (MCD) .... TIES

Theater Integrated Warfare Scenarios Study .... TIWSS

Theater Intelligence Architecture Program (DOMA) .... TIAP

Theater Intelligence Section [*Navy*] .... TIS

Theater Inventory Control Point [*Military*] (AABC) .... TICP

Theater Joint Air Defense Command [Military] (AABC) ... TJADC
Theater Joint Operations Center [Military] ... TJOC
Theater Level Scenario [Military] ... TLS
Theater Materiel Management Center [Military] (AABC) ... TMMC
Theater Medical Information System (DOMA) ... TMIS
Theater Missile Defense ... TMD
Theater Missile Defense Initiative [Army] (DOMA) ... TMDI
Theater Mission Planning Center (AAGC) ... TMPC
Theater Mission Planning System [Military] (CAAL) ... TMPS
Theater Movement Control Center [Military] (AABC) ... TMCC
Theater Naval Commander ... TNC
Theater Navy Headquarters ... TNHQ
Theater Network Analysis Model [Europe] (MCD) ... TNAM
Theater Network Television (IAA) ... TNT
Theater Nuclear Forces ... TNF
Theater Nuclear Forces Security [DoD] ... TNF/S
Theater Nuclear Forces Survivability (MCD) ... TNFS
Theater Nuclear Forces Survivability and Security (MCD) ... TNFSS
Theater Nuclear Forces, Survivability, Security, and Safety (MCD) ... TNFS3
Theater Nuclear Weapon ... TNW
Theater of All Possibilities [International touring company of actor-authors] ... TAP
Theater of Operations [Military] ... T of OPNS
Theater of Operations [Military] ... TO
Theater of Operations [Military] ... TOPNS
Theater of Operations Command [Military] ... TOC
Theater of Operations Medical Support System [Military] (MCD) ... TOMSS
Theater of Operations Missile Continuous-Wave Antitank Weapon ... TOMCAT
Theater Operations and Tactical Evaluation Model ... TOTEM
Theater Owners Booking Association [Vaudeville] [Facetious translation: Tough on Black Artists] ... TOBA
Theater Prisoner of War Information Center ... TPWIC
Theater Production Service (AEBS) ... TPS
Theater Rate Consolidation Data File [Military] ... TRCONS
Theater Rate Mapping Data File [Military] ... TRMAP
Theater Rates Model [Military] ... TRM
Theater Readiness Monitoring Equipment (MCD) ... TRME
Theater Readiness Monitoring Facility [Missile testing] ... TRMF
Theater Realignment of Traffic Transportation Support (MCD) ... TROTTS
Theater Reserve [Army] (DOMA) ... TR
Theater Reserve Unit/Army Readiness Package, South ... TRU/ARPS
Theater Service Area (MCD) ... TSA
Theater Service Forces, European Theater [World War II] ... TSFET
Theater Shipping Document [Military] ... TSD
Theater Sterile Supply Unit [Surgery] (DAVI) ... TSSU
Theater Stock Status Report [Military] ... TSSR
Theater Storage Area [Military] ... TSA
Theater Targets Product Office [Army] (RDA) ... TTPO
Theater Transition and Sustainment Model ... TTSM
Theater War Reserves [Army] ... TWR
Theater Watch Intelligence Condition (NATG) ... TWIC
Theater Weather Central [Military] ... TWC
Theater-Oriented Depot [Military] ... TOD
Theater-Oriented Depot Complex [Military] (AABC) ... TODC
Theater-Type Mobilization Corps Force Capabilities [Military] ... TTMCFC
Theater-Type Mobilization Corps Force Objective [Military] ... TTMCFO
Theatine Fathers (TOCD) ... CR
Theatine Fathers (TOCD) ... cr
Theatine Sisters of the Immaculate Conception (TOCD) ... RT
Theatre (ROG) ... TH
Theatre (VRA) ... thtr
Theatre about Glasgow [Acting company] (ECON) ... TAG
Theatre Arts Society [British] ... TAS
Theatre Authority (EA) ... TA
Theatre Ballet of Canada ... TBC
Theatre Committee for Eugene O'Neill (EA) ... TCEO
Theatre Communications Group (EA) ... TCG
Theatre Development Fund (EA) ... TDF
Theatre/Drama, and Speech Information Center (IID) ... TDSIC
Theatre Education Society (EA) ... TES
Theatre Equipment and Supply Manufacturers Association [Later, TEA] (EA) ... TESMA
Theatre Equipment Association (EA) ... TEA
Theatre Equipment Dealers Association [Later, TEA] (EA) ... TEDA
Theatre, Film, and Television Biographies Master Index [A publication] ... TF & T
Theatre for Ideas [Defunct] (EA) ... TFI
Theatre Guild (EA) ... TG
Theatre Guild-American Theatre Society (EA) ... TG-ATS
Theatre Historical Society (EA) ... THS
Theatre History Studies [A publication] (BRI) ... THS
Theatre in Education (EA) ... TE
Theatre Journal [A publication] (BRI) ... Theat J
Theatre Library Association (EA) ... TLA
Theatre Managers' Association [Australia] ... TMA
Theatre Mask Ensemble ... TME
Theatre National Populaire [France] ... TNP
Theatre of Latin America [Defunct] (EA) ... TOLA
Theatre Ontario [Canada] (WWLA) ... TO
Theatre Organ Preservation Society [British] ... TOPS
Theatre Owners of America [Later, NATO] (EA) ... TOA
Theatre Recording Society (EA) ... TRS
Theatre Royal (ROG) ... TR
Theatre Television Authority (EA) ... TTA
Theatre Writers' Union [British] (DBA) ... TWU
Theatres [Public-performance tariff class] [British] ... T
Theatres Advisory Committee [British] ... TAC

Theatres National Committee [British] (DBA) ... TNC
Theatre-Screen Advertising Bureau [Defunct] ... TSAB
Theatrical ... THEA
Theatrical ... THEAT
Theatrical Management Association [British] (DBA) ... TMA
Theatrical Mutual Association (EA) ... TMA
Theatrical Traders Association Ltd. [British] (BI) ... TTA
Theatrum Orbis Terrarum [Dutch firm] ... TOT
Thebacha College Library, Fort Smith, Northwest Territories [Library symbol National Library of Canada] (NLC) ... NWFST
Thebais [of Statius] [Classical studies] (OCD) ... Theb
[The] Theban Tombs Series [London] [A publication] (BJA) ... TTS
Theda Clark Memorial Hospital, Neenah, WI [Library symbol Library of Congress] (LCLS) ... WNTC
Thedford, NE [Location identifier FAA] (FAAL) ... TDD
Theft ... T
Theft and Pilferage ... T and P
Theft from Interstate Shipment [FBI standardized term] ... TFIS
Theft of Government Property [FBI standardized term] ... TGP
Theft, Pilferage, and Nondelivery [Insurance] ... TPND
Theiler's Murine Encephalitis Virus ... TMEV
Theiler's Original [Strain of mouse encephalitis virus] ... TO
Their (ROG) ... THR
Their Highnesses (ADA) ... TH
Their Imperial Highnesses ... TIH
Their Majesties ... TM
Their Royal Highnesses [British] (ROG) ... THR
Their Royal Highnesses ... TRH
Their Serene Highnesses ... TSH
Theistic Evolutionist ... TE
Thelma Dingus Bryant Library, Wallace, NC [Library symbol Library of Congress] (LCLS) ... NcWal
Theioall's Le Digest des Briefs [2 eds.] [1579, 1687] [A publication] (DLA) ... Thel
T-Helper [Immunology] ... Th
Thematic Apperception Test [Psychology] ... TAT
Thematic Content Modification Program (DMAA) ... TCMP
Thematic Mapper [Satellite technology] ... TM
Thematic Mapper Simulator [for aerial photography] ... TMS
Thematic Resource Nomination [National Register of Historic Places] ... TR
Themes and Topics of Literature Criticism [A publication] ... TTLC
Themes Concerning Blacks [Personality development test] [Psychology] ... TCB
Themistocles [of Plutarch] [Classical studies] (OCD) ... Them
Thenar [Anatomy] ... Th
Thenardite [CIPW classification] [Geology] ... th
(Thenoylthio)propionylglycine [Biochemistry] ... TTPG
Thenoyltrifluoroacetone [Also, TTB] [Organic chemistry] ... TTA
Theobald on Wills [13th ed.] [1971] [A publication] (DLA) ... Theo Wills
Theobald on Wills [11 eds.] [1876-1954] [A publication] (DLA) ... Theobald
Theobald's Act for the Amendment of the Law [A publication] (DLA) ... Theo Am A
Theobald's Principal and Surety [1832] [A publication] (DLA) ... Theo Pr & S
Theocritus [Third century BC] [Classical studies] (OCD) ... Theoc
Theodolite Measuring Point (MUGU) ... TMP
Theodor Herzl Institute (EA) ... THI
Theodore [Queensland] [Airport symbol] (AD) ... THJ
Theodore A. Hungerford Memorial Library, Harwinton, CT [Library symbol Library of Congress] (LCLS) ... CtHa
Theodore Army Terminal ... TART
Theodore Army Terminal ... THART
Theodore Austin Cutler Memorial Library, St. Louis, MI [Library symbol Library of Congress] (LCLS) ... MiStlo
Theodore F. Jenkins Memorial Law Library, Philadelphia, PA [Library symbol Library of Congress] (LCLS) ... PPTJ
Theodore Francis Green State Airport [FAA] (TAG) ... PVD
Theodore Roethke Memorial Foundation (EA) ... TRMF
Theodore [Teddy] Roosevelt [US president, 1858-1919] ... TR
Theodore Roosevelt Association (EA) ... TRA
Theodore Roosevelt Association, New York, NY [Library symbol Library of Congress] (LCLS) ... NNRo
Theodore Roosevelt Birthplace National Historic Site ... THRB
Theodore Roosevelt Centennial Commission [Government agency] [Terminated, 1959] ... TRCC
Theodore Roosevelt Elementary School, Oyster Bay, NY [Library symbol] [Library of Congress] (LCLS) ... NOyRE
Theodore Roosevelt National Memorial Park ... THRO
Theodore Von Karman Memorial Foundation (EA) ... TVKMF
Theodosian Code (BJA) ... CTh
Theodotion (BJA) ... Th
Theodotion (BJA) ... Theod
Theogonia [of Hesiod] [Classical studies] (OCD) ... Th
Theogonia [of Hesiod] [Classical studies] (OCD) ... Theog
Theologia [Theology] [Latin] (BARN) ... Thia
Theologiae Apud Remonstrantes Professorem, Tyrannidis Osorem, Limburgium Amstelodamensem [Pseudonym used by John Locke] ... TARPTOLA
Theologiae Baccalaureas [Bachelor of Theology] ... Th B
Theologiae Doctor [Doctor of Theology] ... Th D
Theologiae Magister [Master of Theology] ... Th M
Theologiai Szemle [Budapest] [A publication] (BJA) ... ThSzemle
Theological ... THEOL
Theological Associate, King's College [London] ... TAKC
Theological College of the Canadian Reformed Churches, Hamilton, ON, Canada [Library symbol] [Library of Congress] (LCLS) ... CaOHTR
Theological College of the Canadian Reformed Churches, Hamilton, Ontario [Library symbol National Library of Canada] (NLC) ... OHTR

Theological Dictionary of the New Testament [*A publication*] (BJA) ... TDNT
Theological Education Association of Mid-America, Library Section [*Library network*] ... TEAM A
Theological Education by Extension [*Church of England*] ... TEE
Theological Educator [*A publication*] ... TE
Theological Examination ... TE
Theological School Inventory [*Psychology*] ... TSI
Theological Students Fellowship [*Defunct*] (EA) ... TSF
Theological Studies [*A publication*] (BRI) ... Theol St
Theological Translation Library [*A publication*] ... TTL
Theologicka Priloha (Krestanske Revue) [*A publication*] (BJA) ... TPKrR
Theologie des Alten Testaments [*A publication*] (BJA) ... ThAT
Theologie en Practijk [*Rotterdam*] [*A publication*] (BJA) ... ThPract
Theologische Arbeiten [*A publication*] (BJA) ... TheolArb
Theologische Buecherei. Neudrucke und Berichte aus dem 20 Jahrhundert [*Munich*] [*A publication*] (BJA) ... ThB
Theologische Existenz Heute [*Munich*] [*A publication*] (BJA) ... ThE
Theologische Existenz Heute. Neue Folge [*A publication*] (BJA) ... ThExNF
Theologische Realenzyklopaedie [*A publication*] ... TRE
Theologische Studien [*Utrecht*] [*A publication*] (BJA) ... TS
Theologischer Hand-Kommentar zum Neuen Testament [*A publication*] (BJA) ... ThHK
Theologischer Literaturbericht [*A publication*] (BJA) ... ThlBer
Theologisches Woerterbuch zum Alten Testament [*A publication*] (BJA) ... ThWAT
Theologisches Woerterbuch zum Neuen Testament [*A publication*] (BJA) ... ThW
Theologisches Woerterbuch zum Neuen Testament [*A publication*] (BJA) ... ThWB
Theologisches Woerterbuch zum Neuen Testament [*A publication*] (BJA) ... ThWBNT
Theologisches Woerterbuch zum Neuen Testament [*A publication*] (BJA) ... ThWNT
Theologisches Woerterbuch zum Neuen Testament [*A publication*] (BJA) ... TWBNT
Theologisches Woerterbuch zum Neuen Testament [*A publication*] (BJA) ... TWNT
Theologisch-Praktische Monatsschrift [*A publication*] (BJA) ... ThPrM
Theology ... TH
Theology ... THEO
Theology Student (DSUE) ... THEOLOG
Theology Today [*A publication*] (BRI) ... TT
Theomonistic Licensee ... Theom L
Theophilus [*Sixth century*] [*Early Christian bishop*] (BARN) ... Theoph
Theophilus [*Flourished, 6th century*] [*Authority cited in pre-1607 legal work*] (DSA) ... Theophil
Theophrastus [*Third Century BC*] [*Classical studies*] (BARN) ... Theoph
Theophrastus [*Third century BC*] [*Classical studies*] (OCD) ... Theophr
Theophylline [*Pharmacology*] ... T
Theophylline [*Pharmacology*] (DAVI) ... TH
Theophylline [*Pharmacology*] ... THEO
Theophylline, Proxyphylline, and Dyphylline [*Antineoplastic drug regimen*] ... TPD
Theopompus Historicus [*Fourth century BC*] [*Classical studies*] (OCD) ... Theopomp
Theorem (ROG) ... THEOR
Theoretical ... THEO
Theoretical (AAG) ... THEOR
Theoretical and Applied Mechanics (IAA) ... TAAM
Theoretical and Experimental Beam-Plasma Physics ... TEBPP
Theoretical Astrophysics Centre ... TAC
Theoretical Chemistry Institute [*University of Wisconsin - Madison*] [*Research center*] (RCD) ... TCI
Theoretical Density [*Nuclear energy*] (NRCH) ... TD
Theoretical Earth Utilization System (PDAA) ... THEUS
Theoretical Final Route [*Telecommunications*] (TEL) ... TFR
Theoretical First Unit [*Economics*] ... TFU
Theoretical First Unit Cost ... TFUC
Theoretical Indoor Relative Humidity ... TIRH
Theoretical Lethality Index (MCD) ... TLI
Theoretical Line of Escape (WDAA) ... TLE
Theoretical Linear Solvation Energy Relationship [*Physical chemistry*] ... TLSER
Theoretical Maximum Daily Intake [*Toxicology*] ... TMDI
Theoretical Maximum Density ... TMD
Theoretical Maximum Residue Contribution [*to acceptable daily intake*] [*Environmental Protection Agency*] ... TMRC
Theoretical Oxygen Demand [*Analytical biochemistry*] ... TOD
Theoretical Platers per Meter [*Chromatography*] ... TPM
Theoretical Point of Fog (MSA) ... TPF
Theoretical Renal Phosphorus Threshold [*Medicine*] (MAE) ... TRPT
Theoretical Research Report ... TRR
Theory (VRA) ... thry
Theory of Everything [*Cosmology*] ... TOE
Theory of Neuronal Group Selection [*Neurology*] ... TNGS
Theory of Presumptive Proof [*A publication*] (DLA) ... Theo Pres Pr
Theory of Signal Detection ... TSD
Theory of Signal Detection Analysis ... TSDA
THEOS [*They Help Each Other Spiritually*] **Foundation** (EA) ... TF
Theosophical Book Association for the Blind (EA) ... TBAB
Theosophical Publishing House ... TPH
Theosophical Review [*A publication*] (ROG) ... THEOS R
Theosophical Society ... TS
Theosophical Society, Atlanta, GA [*Library symbol Library of Congress*] (LCLS) ... GAThS
Theosophical Society in America (EA) ... TS in A
Theosophical Society in Australia ... TSA
Theosophical Society, Philadelphia, PA [*Library symbol Library of Congress Obsolete*] (LCLS) ... PPT
Theosophical Society, San Francisco, CA [*Library symbol Library of Congress*] (LCLS) ... CSfTheo
Theosophical University, Altadena, CA [*Library symbol Library of Congress*] (LCLS) ... CAltT
Theosophy ... THEOS
Theragenics Corp. [*Associated Press*] (SAG) ... Thrgen
Theragenics Corp. [*NASDAQ symbol*] (NQ) ... THRX
Therapeutic ... THER
Therapeutic [*Range*] [*Laboratory science*] (DAVI) ... THER
Therapeutic ... THERAP
Therapeutic Abortion [*Medicine*] ... TA
Therapeutic Abortion [*Medicine*] (MEDA) ... TAB
Therapeutic Abortion, Dilation, Aspiration, Curettage [*Medicine*] (MAE) ... TADAC
Therapeutic Activities Specialist [*Physical therapy*] (DAVI) ... TAS
Therapeutic Communities of America (EA) ... TCA
Therapeutic Concentration [*Pharmacology*] ... TC
Therapeutic Contact Lens [*Opthalomology*] (DAVI) ... T-lens
Therapeutic Continuous Penicillin [*Medicine*] (MAE) ... TCP
Therapeutic Device Evaluation Committee [*Australia*] ... TDEC
Therapeutic Discovery Corp. [*NASDAQ symbol*] (SAG) ... TDCA
Therapeutic Discovery Corp. [*Associated Press*] (SAG) ... TherD
Therapeutic Discovery Corp. [*Associated Press*] (SAG) ... TherDiscA
Therapeutic Donor Insemination [*Obstetrics*] ... TDI
Therapeutic Drug Monitoring ... TDM
Therapeutic Drug Utilization Review [*Insurance*] (WYGK) ... TDUR
Therapeutic Electrical Stimulation ... TES
Therapeutic Exercise [*Physical therapy*] (DAVI) ... Ther Ex
Therapeutic Gain Factor [*Medicine*] ... TGF
Therapeutic Gazette [*Philadelphia*] [*A publication*] (ROG) ... TH GAZ
Therapeutic Goods Administration (EERA) ... TGA
Therapeutic Goods Administration [*Australia*] ... TGA
Therapeutic Goods Advertising Code [*Australia*] ... TGAC
Therapeutic Goods Committee [*Australia*] ... TGC
Therapeutic Index [*Medicine*] (DMAA) ... TI
Therapeutic Intervention Scoring System (MEDA) ... TISS
Therapeutic Learning Program [*Psychology*] ... TLP
Therapeutic Level [*Medicine*] ... TL
Therapeutic Plasma Exchange [*Hematology*] (CPH) ... TPE
Therapeutic Radiology ... TR
Therapeutic Recreation Associate [*Rehabilitation*] (DAVI) ... TRA
Therapeutic Referral Center (DAVI) ... TRC
Therapeutic Residential Center (DAVI) ... TRC
Therapeutic Work Aid Station for Physically Inactive Thinkers (MCD) ... TWASPIT
Therapist ... THRP
Therapist ... THRPST
Theraplix [*France*] [*Research code symbol*] ... TH
Therapy (DAVI) ... Rx
Therapy [*Medicine*] (DHSM) ... TH
Therapy (DAVI) ... THER
Therapy ... THRPY
Therapy ... THRPY
Therapy [*Medicine*] ... Tx
Therapy Attitude Inventory [*Test*] [*Psychology*] ... TAI
Therapy [*or Treatment*] **Discontinued** [*Medicine*] ... TD
Therapy Dogs International (EA) ... TDI
TheraTech, Inc. [*NASDAQ symbol*] (SAG) ... THRT
TheraTech, Inc. [*Associated Press*] (SAG) ... ThrTch
TheraTx, Inc. [*Associated Press*] (SAG) ... TheraTx
TheraTx, Inc. [*NASDAQ symbol*] (SAG) ... THTX
There (ROG) ... THR
There Ain't No Such Thing As a Free Lunch [*Principle of economics indicating that one cannot get something for nothing*] [*See also TINSTAAFL*] ... TANSTAAFL
There Is a Radical Alternative [*Parliamentary slang*] [*British*] (DI) ... TIARA
There Is No Alternative [*Nickname given to British Prime Minister Margaret Thatcher because she so often uses this phrase to defend her government's economic policies*] ... TINA
There Is No Excuse (ECON) ... TINE
There Is No Opposition [*Parliamentary slang*] [*British*] (DI) ... TINO
There Is No Possible Other Tactic [*Parliamentary slang*] [*British*] (DI) ... TINPOT
There Is No Such Thing as a Free Lunch [*Principle of economics indicating that one cannot get something for nothing*] [*See also TANSTAAFL*] ... TINSTAAFL
THERE Programming Language [*Computer science*] ... TPL
Thereabouts [*Legal term British*] ... THABTS
Thereabouts [*Legal term British*] (ROG) ... THRABTS
Thereafter [*Legal term British*] (ROG) ... THRAR
Thereafter (FAAC) ... THRFTR
Thereat [*Legal term British*] (ROG) ... THRAT
Thereby ... THBY
Therefor [*Legal term British*] (ROG) ... THFOR
Therefrom [*Legal term British*] ... THFM
Therefrom [*Legal term British*] (ROG) ... THFROM
Therein ... THRIN
Thereinafter [*Legal term British*] (ROG) ... THRINAR
Thereinbefore [*Legal term British*] (ROG) ... THRINBEFE
Thereof ... THOF
Thereof ... THROF
Thereon [*Legal term British*] ... THON
Thereon [*Legal term British*] (ROG) ... THRON
Thereout [*Legal term British*] (ROG) ... THROUT
Thereto ... THTO

Thereupon [*Legal term British*] (ROG) .... THRUPON
Therewith [*Legal term British*] (ROG) .... THW
Therewith [*Legal term British*] (ROG) .... THWITH
Theriaca [*of Nicander*] [*Classical studies*] (OCD) .... Ther
Therm (MSA) .... THM
Therm Advanced Research (SAA) .... TAR
Thermactor Air Bypass [*Automotive engineering*] .... TAB
Thermactor Air Diverter [*Automotive engineering*] .... TAD
Thermactor Emission [*Automotive engineering*] .... TE
Thermactor Idle Vacuum [*Automotive engineering*] .... TIV
Thermadyne Holdings [*NASDAQ symbol*] (TTSB) .... TDHC
Thermadyne Holdings Corp. [*NASDAQ symbol*] (SAG) .... TDHC
Thermadyne Holdings Corp. [*Associated Press*] (SAG) .... Thrmady
Thermafor Pyrolytic Cracking [*A chemical process developed by Surface Combustion*] .... TPC
Thermagenesis Corp. [*NASDAQ symbol*] (SAG) .... KOOL
Thermal .... TH
Thermal (DEN) .... THERM
Thermal (AAG) .... THRM
Thermal Accelerated Short Time Evaporator [*Facetious term used in orange juice industry*] .... TASTE
Thermal Activation [*Physics*] .... TA
Thermal Activation-Strain Rate Analysis .... TASRA
Thermal Advanced Gas-Cooled Reactor Exploiting Thorium [*Nuclear energy*] (IAA) .... TAGRET
Thermal Advanced Reactor, Gas-Cooled, Exploiting Thorium [*Nuclear energy*] .... TARGET
Thermal Analysis .... TA
Thermal Analysis Data .... TAD
Thermal Analysis Data Station .... TADS
Thermal Analysis Mass Spectrometry .... TA-MS
Thermal Analysis of Substrates and Intergrated Circuits (PDAA) .... TASIC
Thermal Analysis Program [*Nuclear energy*] .... TAP
Thermal Analytical Model [*Apollo*] [*NASA*] .... TAM
Thermal and Hydraulic [*Nuclear energy*] (NRCH) .... T/H
Thermal and Hydrodynamic Experiment Research Module in Orbit (MCD) .... THERMO
Thermal Anti-Ice (GAVI) .... TAI
Thermal Arc Jet .... TAJ
Thermal Array for the Ocean (USDC) .... TAO
Thermal Bakeout .... TBO
Thermal Barrier Coating (RDA) .... TBC
Thermal Bypass Valve .... TBV
Thermal, CA [*Location identifier FAA*] (FAAL) .... TRM
Thermal calibration (CDE) .... T-cal
Thermal Canister Experiment [*Space shuttle*] [*NASA*] .... TCE
Thermal Capacitor (MCD) .... T/CAP
Thermal Case Penetrator - External (MCD) .... TCP-E
Thermal Case Penetrator - Internal (MCD) .... TCP-I
Thermal Catalyst Aging Tester [*Chemical engineering*] .... TCAT
Thermal Chromatography/Mass Spectrometry .... TC-MS
Thermal Coefficient of Expansion .... TCE
Thermal Coefficient of Linear Expansion [*Rocket motor stress*] .... TCLE
Thermal Coefficient of Resistance (IAA) .... TCR
Thermal Compression Bond .... TCB
Thermal Concept Review (NASA) .... TCR
Thermal Conditioning Service (IAA) .... TCS
Thermal Conditioning System (KSC) .... TCS
Thermal Conduction Module [*IBM Corp.*] .... TCM
Thermal Conductivity [*Symbol*] [*IUPAC*] .... k
Thermal Conductivity .... TC
Thermal Conductivity Detector [*Analytical instrumentation*] .... TCD
Thermal Control (KSC) .... TC
Thermal Control Coating .... TCC
Thermal Control Coating Material .... TCCM
Thermal Control Subsystem Segment [*NASA*] (NASA) .... TCSSS
Thermal Control System [*or Subsystem*] .... TCS
Thermal Control Unit .... TCU
Thermal Converter (MSA) .... THC
Thermal Cracker [*Chemical engineering*] .... TC
Thermal Critical Assembly [*Nuclear energy*] .... TCA
Thermal Cutting [*Welding*] .... TC
Thermal Death Time [*Bacteriological testing*] .... TDT
Thermal Death-Point .... TDP
Thermal Decomposition Analytical System [*For study of incineration*] .... TDAS
Thermal Degradation Sample [*Apollo*] .... TDS
Thermal Demand Transmitter (MSA) .... TDX
Thermal Depolarization Analysis .... TDA
Thermal Desorption [*from surfaces*] .... TD
Thermal Desorption Mass Spectroscopy .... TDMS
Thermal Desorption Spectroscopy .... TDS
Thermal Development Model .... TDM
Thermal Diffusion Chamber .... TDC
Thermal Diffusion Coefficient [*Nuclear energy*] (NRCH) .... TDC
Thermal Diffusion Method .... TDM
Thermal Diffusivity [*Symbol*] [*Thermodynamics*] .... a
Thermal Dilution Cardiac Output .... TDCO
Thermal Effect of Exercise (MEDA) .... TEE
Thermal Effect of Food (MEDA) .... TEF
Thermal Effects Tests Model .... TETM
Thermal Efficiency .... TE
Thermal Elastic Model Study .... TEMS
Thermal Element (KSC) .... TE
Thermal Emission Spectrometer .... TES
Thermal End Cover .... TEC
Thermal Energy Analysis [*or Analyzer*] .... TEA
Thermal Energy Management Process (MCD) .... TEMP
Thermal Energy Storage .... TES
Thermal Enhancement Ratio .... TER
Thermal Enzyme Probe .... TEP
Thermal Expansion Coefficient .... TEC
Thermal Expansion Load [*Nuclear energy*] (NRCH) .... TE
Thermal Expansion Molding (MCD) .... TEM
Thermal Expansion Resin Transfer Molding .... TERTM
Thermal Fatigue Test .... TFT
Thermal Field Emission (IAA) .... TFE
Thermal Hartree-Fock Approximation (PDAA) .... THFA
Thermal Helium Desorption Spectrometry (MCD) .... THDS
Thermal Hydraulic Test Facility [*Nuclear energy*] (NRCH) .... THTF
Thermal Hydrodealkylation [*Petroleum technology*] .... THDA
Thermal Hysteresis Factor .... THF
Thermal Hysteresis Proteins [*Biochemistry*] .... THP
Thermal Identification Device .... TID
Thermal Image Camera (PDAA) .... TIC
Thermal Imagery Kit (DWSG) .... TIK
Thermal Imaging [*Criminology*] (LAIN) .... TI
Thermal Imaging, Airborne LASER Designator [*Royal Air Force*] [*British*] .... TIALD
Thermal Imaging Common Modules .... TICM
Thermal Imaging Devices (MCD) .... TID
Thermal Imaging Navigation Set [*Hughes Aircraft Co.*] [*Navy*] (ECON) .... TINS
Thermal Imaging Scanner .... TIS
Thermal Imaging Sensor System .... TISS
Thermal Imaging Sight [*Artillery*] [*Army*] (INF) .... TIS
Thermal Imaging System - Reticle .... TIS-RET
Thermal Inactivation Point [*Medicine*] (DMAA) .... TIP
Thermal Inactivation Time .... TIT
Thermal Industries [*NASDAQ symbol*] (TTSB) .... THMP
Thermal Industries, Inc. [*NASDAQ symbol*] (NQ) .... THMP
Thermal Industries, Inc. [*Associated Press*] (SAG) .... Thrmln
Thermal Infrared (PDAA) .... TIR
Thermal Infrared Mapping Spectrometer (SSD) .... TIMS
Thermal Infrared Multispectral Scanner [*Airborne instrument for geological applications*] .... TIMS
Thermal Infrared Scanner (RDA) .... TIRS
Thermal Insulation Contractors' Association [*British*] (BI) .... TICA
Thermal Insulation Manufacturers and Suppliers Association (DBA) .... TIMSA
Thermal Insulation System .... TIS
Thermal Internal Boundary Layer (GFGA) .... TIBL
Thermal Ionization Mass Spectrometry .... TIMS
Thermal Joining .... THJ
Thermal Junction (KSC) .... TJ
Thermal Kilowatts .... TKW
Thermal Liquefaction [*Chemical engineering*] .... TL
Thermal Liquid Junction Potential (PDAA) .... TLJP
Thermal Management System [*Dell Computer Corp.*] (PCM) .... TMS
Thermal Maneuvering System (SSD) .... TMS
Thermal Mapper .... TM
Thermal Margin beyond Design Basis [*Nuclear energy*] (NRCH) .... TMBDB
Thermal Margin/Low Pressure [*Nuclear energy*] (NRCH) .... TM/LP
Thermal Marrow Expansion [*Roentgenology*] .... TME
Thermal Mass Penalty (KSC) .... TMP
Thermal Mathematical Model .... TMM
Thermal Measurement Treatment .... TMT
Thermal Mechanical Controlled Processing (PDAA) .... TMCP
Thermal/Mechanical Enzyme [*Fermentation*] .... TME
Thermal Megawatt [*Also, TMW*] .... Mwt
Thermal Megawatt [*Also, Mwt*] .... TMW
Thermal Meteoroid [*or Micrometeoroid*] **Garment** [*NASA*] (KSC) .... TMG
Thermal Micrometeoroid Cover (MCD) .... TMC
Thermal Microscope Stage .... TS
Thermal Modeling and Analysis Project [*Marine science*] (OSRA) .... TMAP
Thermal Modeling and Analysis Project (USDC) .... TMAP
Thermal Modeling Program .... TMP
Thermal Necrosis [*Roentgenology*] .... NT
Thermal Neutron Activation [*FAA*] .... TNA
Thermal Neutron Analysis [*For detection of explosives*] .... TNA
Thermal Night Site .... TNS
Thermal Night Vision System .... TNVS
Thermal Noise Optical Optimization Communication System [*NASA*] .... TOPS
Thermal Nuclear Analyzer .... TNA
Thermal Observation and Gunnery Sights [*British*] .... TOGS
Thermal Optical Analysis .... TOA
Thermal Overload Relay (IAA) .... TOR
Thermal Oxide Reprocessing Plant [*Nuclear energy*] .... THORP
Thermal Polyaspartate [*Organic chemistry*] .... TPA
Thermal Power Monitor [*Nuclear energy*] (NRCH) .... TPM
Thermal Power Plant (CINC) .... TPP
Thermal Preconditioning Unit .... TPCU
Thermal Protection and Control (NASA) .... TP & C
Thermal Protection Investigation .... TPI
Thermal Protection Material .... TPM
Thermal Protection Panel .... TPP
Thermal Protection Subsystem Experiments (NASA) .... TPSE
Thermal Protection System [*or Subsystem*] .... TPS
Thermal Protection System Selection .... TPSS
Thermal Radiation at Microwave Frequencies .... TRF
Thermal Radiation Simulator .... TRS
Thermal Reactor Safety [*Nuclear energy*] (NRCH) .... TRS
Thermal Receiver Unit [*Army*] .... TRU
Thermal Regenerative Cracking [*Hydrocarbon pyrolysis process*] .... TRC

Thermal Remanent Magnetization [*Geophysics*] (IEEE) .... TRM
Thermal Residue Stress (MCD) .... TRS
Thermal Resistance (IDOE) .... R_T
Thermal Resistance (IAA) .... TR
Thermal Resistance Measurement .... TRM
Thermal Resistance of Unit Area [*Heat transmission symbol*] .... RA
Thermal Resistor .... THERMISTOR
Thermal Scale Model (MCD) .... TSM
Thermal Sciences and Propulsion Center [*Purdue University*] [*Research center*] (RCD) .... TSPC
Thermal Sensitive Vote [*Automotive interior comfort survey*] .... TSV
Thermal Shape Control (SSD) .... TSC
Thermal Shock Rig [*Nuclear energy*] (NRCH) .... TSR
Thermal Sight Test Set [*Army*] .... TSTS
Thermal Single-Determinant Approximation (PDAA) .... TSDA
Thermal Spray [*Also, TS*] [*Coating technology*] .... THSP
Thermal Spray [*Also, THSP*] [*Coating technology*] .... TS
Thermal Stethoscope [*Medical instrumentation*] .... TS
Thermal Stress Crack [*Plastics*] .... TSC
Thermal Stress Relief [*Mechanical engineering*] .... TSR
Thermal Structure Monitoring Program in the Pacific [*Marine science*] (MSC) .... TRANSPAC
Thermal Surface Coating .... TSC
Thermal Swing Adsorption [*Chemical engineering*] .... TSA
Thermal Synchrotron [*High-energy physics*] .... TS
Thermal Systems Unit (KSC) .... TSU
Thermal Test Model .... TTM
Thermal Test Reactor [*Nuclear energy*] (AAG) .... TTR
Thermal Test Vehicle .... TTV
Thermal Time Distribution [*Chemical engineering*] .... TTD
Thermal Timing Relay .... TTR
Thermal Transfer Equipment (IAA) .... TTE
Thermal Transfer Standard .... TTS
Thermal Transfer Voltmeter .... TTVM
Thermal Transient Equipment [*Nuclear energy*] (NRCH) .... TTE
Thermal Transient Histogram Equivalent [*Nuclear energy*] (NRCH) .... TTHE
Thermal Transmittance per Unit of Area [*Heat transmission symbol*] .... U
Thermal Transpiration Ratio .... TTR
Thermal Unit .... TU
Thermal Unit End Cover (MCD) .... TEC
Thermal Uplink Data Display [*Computer science*] .... THUDD
Thermal Utilization Factor (MCD) .... TUF
Thermal Vacuum .... TV
Thermal Vacuum Chamber (NASA) .... TVC
Thermal Vacuum Environment .... TVE
Thermal [*or Thermostatic*] **Vacuum Switch** [*Automotive engineering*] .... TVS
Thermal Vacuum Test .... TVT
Thermal Vacuum Test Article (NASA) .... TVTA
Thermal Vacuum Valve [*Automotive engineering*] .... TVV
Thermal Vapor Recompressors [*For evaporators*] .... TVR
Thermal Vent Valve [*Automotive engineering*] .... TVV
Thermal Voltage Converter .... TVC
Thermal Voltaic Detection [*Analytical chemistry*] .... TVD
Thermal Warning Device (MCD) .... TWD
Thermal Weapon Sight [*Army*] (INF) .... TWS
Thermal Wire (KSC) .... TW
Thermal Wire Stripper .... TWS
Thermal-Hydraulic Out-of-Reactor Safety Facility [*Department of Energy*] .... THORS
Thermally Activated Delayed Fluorescence [*Analytical chemistry*] .... TADF
Thermally Activated Flux Flow [*Physics*] .... TAFF
Thermally and Oxidatively Stable .... TOS
Thermally and Oxidatively Stable Resin .... TOSR
Thermally Induced Phase Separation [*Chemistry*] .... TIPS
Thermally Initiated Venting System (MCD) .... TIVS
Thermally Operated Plasma System .... TOPSY
Thermally Optimized Die .... TOPDIE
Thermally Processed Silver (NITA) .... TPS
Thermally Protected Composite .... TPC
Thermally Protected Plastic .... TPP
Thermally Pulsing, Asymptotic Giant Branch [*Astronomy*] .... TP-AGB
Thermally Regenerative Alloy Cell .... TRAC
Thermally Regenerative Electrochemical System [*Power source*] .... TRES
Thermally Released Volatile Aromatics [*i.e., odors*] [*Slang*] .... TRVA
Thermally Stabilized Burner [*Engineering*] .... TSB
Thermally Stable Fuel (MCD) .... TSF
Thermally Stable Resin .... TSR
Thermally Stimulated Capacitance [*Photovoltaic energy systems*] .... TSCAP
Thermally Stimulated Charge [*Analytical chemistry*] .... TCS
Thermally Stimulated Conductivity [*or Currents*] .... TSC
Thermally Stimulated Depolarization [*Chemistry*] .... TSD
Thermally Stimulated Discharge Current [*Voltage-induced polarization*] .... TSDC
Thermally Stimulated Exoelectron Emission [*Dosimetry*] .... TSEE
Thermally Tuned (IAA) .... TT
Thermally-Stimulated Luminescence (PDAA) .... TSL
Thermal-Mechanical Unit .... TMU
Thermal-Tow .... TT
Thermal-Transfer Printing .... TTP
Thermatrix, Inc. [*Associated Press*] (SAG) .... Thermat
Thermatrix, Inc. [*NASDAQ symbol*] (SAG) .... TMXI
Thermedics, Inc. [*Associated Press*] (SAG) .... Thermed
Thermedics, Inc. [*AMEX symbol*] (SPSG) .... TMD
Thermionic Electrical Power Generator (IEEE) .... TEPG
Thermionic Emission Detector [*For gas chromatography*] .... TED
Thermionic Emission Technique .... TET
Thermionic Energy Converter (RDA) .... TEC
Thermionic Field (IAA) .... TF
Thermionic Fuel Element [*Nuclear energy*] .... TFE
Thermionic Integrated Circuit [*Electronics*] .... TIC
Thermionic Integrated Micromodule .... TIMM
Thermionic Ionization Detector [*Instrumentation*] .... TID
Thermionic Power Generator .... TPG
Thermionic Reactor Critical Experiment [*NASA*] .... TRCE
Thermionic Reactor for Installed Oceanic Service (KSC) .... TRIOS
Thermionic Specific Detector [*Analytical instrumentation*] .... TSD
Thermistor [*Electronics*] .... THMS
Thermistor (AAG) .... TMTR
Thermistor Detector Package .... TDP
Thermistor Micropower Resistor .... TMR
Thermistor Sterilization Test .... TST
Thermistor Sterilization Test Program .... TSTP
Thermistor Test Program .... TTP
Thermit Welding .... TW
Thermo Bioanalysis Corp. [*AMEX symbol*] (SAG) .... TBA
Thermo Bioanalysis Corp. [*Associated Press*] (SAG) .... ThrmBio
Thermo Cardio Systems, Inc. [*AMEX symbol*] (SAG) .... TCA
Thermo Cardiosystems [*AMEX symbol*] (TTSB) .... TCA
Thermo Cardiosystems, Inc. (PS) .... TCI
Thermo Cardiosystems, Inc. [*Associated Press*] (SAG) .... ThCar
Thermo Cardiosystems, Inc. [*Associated Press*] (SAG) .... ThmoCrd
Thermo Ecotek [*AMEX symbol*] (TTSB) .... TCK
Thermo Ecotek Corp. [*AMEX symbol*] (SAG) .... TCK
Thermo Ecotek Corp. [*Associated Press*] (SAG) .... TmEco
Thermo Electron [*NYSE symbol*] (TTSB) .... TMO
Thermo Electron Corp. [*Associated Press*] (SAG) .... TherEl
Thermo Electron Corp. [*NYSE symbol*] (SPSG) .... TMO
Thermo Fibergen, Inc. [*AMEX symbol*] (SAG) .... TFG
Thermo Fibergen, Inc. [*Associated Press*] (SAG) .... ThrFibr
Thermo Fibertek [*AMEX symbol*] (TTSB) .... TFT
Thermo Fibertek, Inc. [*Associated Press*] (SAG) .... ThmFib
Thermo Instrument Sys [*AMEX symbol*] (TTSB) .... THI
Thermo Instrument Systems, Inc. [*AMEX symbol*] (SPSG) .... THI
Thermo Instrument Systems, Inc. [*Associated Press*] (SAG) .... ThrInst
Thermo Magnetic Printing (HGAA) .... TMP
Thermo Mechanical Pulp (EERA) .... TMP
Thermo Opportunity Fund, Inc. [*Associated Press*] (SAG) .... ThmoOp
Thermo Opportunity Fund, Inc. [*AMEX symbol*] (SAG) .... TMF
Thermo Optek Corp. [*Associated Press*] (SAG) .... ThrOptk
Thermo Optek Corp. [*AMEX symbol*] (SAG) .... TOC
Thermo Power [*AMEX symbol*] (TTSB) .... THP
Thermo Power Corp. [*Formerly, Tecogen, Inc.*] [*AMEX symbol*] (SPSG) .... THP
Thermo Power Corp. [*Associated Press*] (SAG) .... ThrmPw
Thermo Process Systems, Inc. [*Associated Press*] (SAG) .... ThrmP
Thermo Process Systems, Inc. [*AMEX symbol*] (SPSG) .... TPI
Thermo Remediation [*Associated Press*] (SAG) .... TherRe
Thermo Remediation [*AMEX symbol*] (SPSG) .... THN
Thermo Remediation [*Associated Press*] (SAG) .... ThrmRe
Thermo Sentron [*AMEX symbol*] (TTSB) .... TSR
Thermo Sentron, Inc. [*Associated Press*] (SAG) .... ThrSent
Thermo Sentron, Inc. [*AMEX symbol*] (SAG) .... TSR
Thermo Spectra Corp. [*Associated Press*] (SAG) .... ThrSpect
Thermo Tech Technologies [*Associated Press*] (SAG) .... ThrmTch
Thermo Tech Technologies [*NASDAQ symbol*] (SAG) .... TTRI
Thermo Tech Technologies Inc. [*NASDAQ symbol*] (TTSB) .... TTRIF
Thermo Technology International [*Vancouver Stock Exchange symbol*] .... TTJ
Thermo Terratech [*Associated Press*] (SAG) .... ThrmTer
Thermo Terratech [*AMEX symbol*] (SAG) .... TTT
Thermo Terratech [*AMEX symbol*] (TTSB) .... TTT
Thermo Voltek [*AMEX symbol*] (TTSB) .... TVL
Thermo Voltek Corp. [*Associated Press*] (SAG) .... ThrVolt
Thermo Voltek Corp. [*AMEX symbol*] (SAG) .... TVL
Thermoacidurans Agar Modified [*Microbiology*] (DAVI) .... TAM
Thermoacoustic Sensing Technique (IEEE) .... TAST
Thermobarometer .... TB
Thermocentrifugometric Analysis [*Analytical chemistry*] .... TCA
Thermochemical Deposition .... TCD
Thermochemical Environmental Energy System [*Service mark*] [*Battelle Development Corp.*] .... TEES
Thermochemical Recuperator [*Proposed heat recovery system*] .... TCR
Thermochemical Remanent Magnetization .... TCRM
Thermochemical Sulfate Reduction [*Chemistry*] .... TSR
Thermochemical-Kinetic .... TCK
Thermochemistry (BARN) .... thermochem
Thermochromic Liquid Crystal .... TLC
Thermocompression Bonding Equipment .... TCBE
Thermocouple .... TC
Thermocouple Data Acquisition System .... TDAS
Thermocouple Gauge Control .... TGC
Thermocouple Gauge Tube .... TGT
Thermocouple Junction .... TCJ
Thermocouple/Lead Detector [*Nuclear energy*] (NRCH) .... TC/LD
Thermocouple Meter (IDOE) .... TCM
Thermocouple Open Circuit Detection (IAA) .... TCOCD
Thermocouple Reference Junction .... TCRJ
Thermocouple Reference Junction .... TRJ
Thermocurrent (IEEE) .... TC
Thermodifferential Analysis .... TDA
Thermodilution .... TD
Thermodynamic Activity [*Chemistry*] (DAVI) .... a
Thermodynamic Kelvin Temperature Scale .... TKTS

Thermodynamic Molding ..... TDM
Thermodynamic Ocean Prediction System [*Navy*] (GFGA) ..... TOPS
Thermodynamic Properties of Metals and Alloys (KSC) ..... TPMA
Thermodynamic Property Values Database [*Chemical Information Systems, Inc.*] [*Information service or system*] (CRD) ..... THERMO
Thermodynamic Suppression Head ..... TSH
Thermodynamic Temperature [*Symbol*] [*IUPAC*] ..... T
Thermodynamics (AAG) ..... THERMODYN
Thermodynamics and Physical Properties Package (NITA) ..... TAP
Thermodynamics Research Center [*College Station, TX*] [*Department of Commerce*] (GRD) ..... TRC
Thermodynamics Research Laboratory [*National Institute of Standards and Technology*] (MCD) ..... TRL
Thermoelectric ..... TE
Thermoelectric Cooler (IAA) ..... TEC
Thermoelectric Device ..... TED
Thermoelectric Environmental Control Unit ..... TECU
Thermoelectric Generator ..... TEG
Thermoelectric Heat Pump (MCD) ..... TEHP
Thermoelectric Module ..... TEM
Thermoelectric Outer Planet Spacecraft [*NASA*] ..... TOPS
Thermoelectric Power [*Physics*] (BARN) ..... Q
Thermoelectric Power [*Thermodynamics*] ..... TEP
Thermoelectric Quartz Crystal Microbalance ..... TQCM
Thermoelectric Voltage ..... TEV
Thermoelectronic LASER Energy Converter ..... TELEC
Thermofit Zap Gun ..... TZG
Thermo-Fluid Mechanics Research Centre [*University of Sussex*] [*British*] (CB) ..... TFMRC
Thermoform Continuous Percolation (IAA) ..... TCP
Thermoform, Fill, and Seal [*Pharmaceutical packaging*] ..... TFFS
Thermogenesis Corp. [*NASDAQ symbol*] (SAG) ..... KOOL
Thermogenesis Corp. [*Associated Press*] (SAG) ..... Thrmogn
Thermogravimetric [*or Thermogravimetry*] **Analysis** [*Instrumentation*] ..... TGA
Thermogravimetric [*or Thermogravimetry*] **System** [*Instrumentation*] ..... TGS
Thermogravimetry ..... TG
Thermogravimetry - Mass Spectrometry ..... TG-MS
Thermogrip Electric Glue Gun ..... TEGG
Thermohaline Circulation [*Oceanography*] ..... THC
Thermohaline Circulation [*Marine science*] (OSRA) ..... THC
Thermoid (SAA) ..... TH
Thermoisolation Technique ..... TIT
Thermokeratoplasty [*Medicine*] (CPH) ..... TKP
Thermokinetic Analysis ..... TKA
Thermolase Corp. [*Associated Press*] (SAG) ..... Thmolse
Thermolase Corp. [*Associated Press*] (SAG) ..... Thrmolse
Thermolase Corp. [*AMEX symbol*] (SAG) ..... TLZ
Thermoluminescence [*Also, TL*] ..... THL
Thermoluminescence [*Also, THL*] ..... TL
Thermoluminescent Device ..... TLD
Thermoluminescent Dosimeter [*or Dosimetry*] ..... TLD
Thermolysin [*An enzyme*] ..... TLN
Thermomagnetic Analysis [*Analytical chemistry*] ..... TMA
Thermomagnetic Optical Disk ..... TMO
Thermomagnetic Treatment (IAA) ..... TT
Thermomagnetic-Galvanic Effect ..... TMGE
Thermomagnetometry [*Analytical chemistry*] ..... TMG
Thermomagneto-Optic (MCD) ..... TMO
Thermomechanical Analysis [*or Analyzer*] ..... TMA
Thermomechanical Loading ..... TML
Thermomechanical Model Software Development Center [*Research center*] (RCD) ..... TMSDC
Thermomechanical Processing ..... TMP
Thermomechanical Pulps ..... TMP
Thermomechanical System [*Instrumentation*] ..... TMS
Thermomechanical Test Area [*NASA*] (NASA) ..... TTA
Thermomechanical Treatment ..... TMT
Thermometer ..... T
Thermometer (DAVI) ..... THER
Thermometer (AAG) ..... THERM
Thermometer Collectors Club of America (EA) ..... TCCA
Thermometeroid Garnet (IAA) ..... TMG
Thermometric Enthalpy Titration [*Analytical chemistry*] ..... TET
Thermometric Enzyme-Linked Immunosorbent Assay [*Analytical biochemistry*] ..... TELISA
Thermometric Titrimetry ..... TT
Thermomicrophotometry ..... TMP
Thermo-Mizer Env Wrrt [*NASDAQ symbol*] (TTSB) ..... THMZW
Thermo-Mizer Environmental [*NASDAQ symbol*] (TTSB) ..... THMZ
Thermo-Mizer Environmental Corp. [*Associated Press*] (SAG) ..... ThmoM
Thermo-Mizer Environmental Corp. [*Associated Press*] (SAG) ..... ThmoMz
Thermo-Mizer Environmental Corp. [*NASDAQ symbol*] (SAG) ..... THMZ
Thermoneutral Zone ..... TNZ
Thermonuclear ..... TN
Thermonuclear TOKAMAK Demonstration Reactor [*Particle physics*] ..... TNTDR
Thermonuclear Weapon (WDAA) ..... TN WP
Thermophilic Actinomyces [*Microbiology*] ..... TA
Thermophotovoltaic ..... TPV
Thermo-Photo-Voltaic ..... TVP
Thermophysical and Electronic Properties Information Analysis Center [*Later, HTMIAC*] [*Purdue University*] ..... TEPIAC
Thermophysical Properties Information Center [*Purdue University*] (PDAA) ..... TPIC
Thermophysical Properties Research Center [*DoD*] ..... TPRC
Thermophysical Properties Research Laboratory [*Purdue University*] [*Research center*] (RCD) ..... TPRL
Thermoplastic [*Also, TP*] [*Plastics technology*] (MSA) ..... T
Thermoplastic [*Also, T*] [*Plastics technology*] ..... TP
Thermoplastic Cellular Molding [*Plastics technology*] ..... TCM
Thermoplastic Covered Fixture Wire Flexible Stranding (IAA) ..... TFF
Thermoplastic Elastomer [*Plastics technology*] ..... TPE
Thermoplastic Fan Wheel ..... TFW
Thermoplastic Fan Wheel ..... TPFW
Thermoplastic, Heat-Resistant, High-Temperature, Nylon-Jacketed [*Electric cable*] ..... THHN
Thermoplastic, Heat-Resistant, Wet-Location [*Electric cable*] ..... THW
Thermoplastic, Heat-Resistant, Wet-Location, Nylon-Jacketed [*Electric cable*] ..... THWN
Thermoplastic Imide [*Plastics*] ..... TPI
Thermoplastic Olefinic [*Elastomer*] ..... TPO
Thermoplastic Optical Phase Recorder (IAA) ..... TOPR
Thermoplastic Photoconductor Device ..... TPD
Thermoplastic Polyester [*Materials science*] ..... TPPE
Thermoplastic Polyimide ..... TPI
Thermoplastic Polyolefin [*Materials science*] ..... TPO
Thermoplastic Recording ..... TPR
Thermoplastic Rubber ..... TPR
Thermoplastic Solid Molding [*Materials science*] ..... TSM
Thermoplastic Storage ..... TPS
Thermoplastic Structural Foam (MCD) ..... TSF
Thermoplastic Urethane [*or Polyurethane*] [*Plastics technology*] ..... TPU
Thermoplastic Vulcanizate [*Plastics technology*] ..... TPV
Thermoplastic Wire ..... TW
Thermopolis, WY [*AM radio station call letters*] ..... KTHE
Thermopolis, WY [*Location identifier FAA*] (FAAL) ..... THP
Thermoquest Corp. [*Associated Press*] (SAG) ..... Thmqst
Thermoquest Corp. [*AMEX symbol*] (SAG) ..... TMQ
ThermoQuest Corp. [*AMEX symbol*] (TTSB) ..... TMQ
Thermoradiotherapy [*Radiation therapy*] (DAVI) ..... TRT
Thermo-Reactive Deposition [*Metal treating*] ..... TRD
Thermoremanence ..... TRM
Thermoremanent Magnetism [*or Magnetization*] ..... TRM
Thermoset Elastomer Styrene Plastic [*Materials science*] ..... TES
Thermosetting (MSA) ..... TMOS
Thermosetting [*Plastics technology*] ..... TS
Thermosiphoning Air Pan ..... TAP
ThermoSpectra Corp. [*Associated Press*] (SAG) ..... ThrSpec
ThermoSpectra Corp. [*AMEX symbol*] (SAG) ..... THS
Thermosphere Probe ..... TP
Thermospray [*Also, TSP*] [*Ionization Physics*] ..... TS
Thermospray [*Also, TS*] [*Ionization Physics*] ..... TSP
Thermospray-Electron Ionization [*Chemistry*] ..... TS-EI
Thermostabilized (NASA) ..... T
Thermostable E-Rosetting [*Cells*] [*Medicine*] ..... TE-R
Thermostat (DEN) ..... THERM
Thermostat (AAG) ..... THERMO
Thermostat ..... THRMST
Thermostat Switch ..... THS
Thermostat Switch (IAA) ..... TT
Thermostatic (MSA) ..... THRMSTC
Thermostatic Air Cleaner [*Automotive engineering*] ..... TAC
Thermostatic Expansion Valve [*Refrigeration*] ..... TEV
Thermostatic Ignition Control [*Automotive engineering*] ..... TIC
Thermostatic Vacuum Switching Valve [*Automotive engineering*] ..... TVSV
Thermostatic Vacuum Transmitting Valve [*Automotive engineering*] ..... TVTV
Thermo-Time Switch [*Electronics*] ..... TTS
Thermotolerance Ratio [*Roentgenology*] ..... TTR
Thermotrex Corp. [*Associated Press*] (SAG) ..... Thrmotx
Thermotrex Corp. [*Associated Press*] (SAG) ..... Thrmtx
Thermotrex Corp. [*AMEX symbol*] (SPSG) ..... TKN
Thermoviscoelastic Analysis Program (MCD) ..... TAP
Thermus Aquaticus [*Bacteria*] ..... Taq
Thermwood Corp. [*AMEX symbol*] (SPSG) ..... THM
Thermwood Corp. [*Associated Press*] (SAG) ..... Thrmwd
Therofor Catalytic Cracking ..... TCC
Theron Airways [*ICAO designator*] (AD) ..... LU
Theron Airways [*South Africa ICAO designator*] (FAAC) ..... TRN
Thesaurus Alphabetical Up to Date (NITA) ..... TAU
Thesaurus at Play [*Acronym is trademark for word game*] ..... TAP
Thesaurus Brevium [*2 eds.*] [*1661, 1687*] [*A publication*] (DLA) ..... Th Br
Thesaurus of Engineering and Scientific Terms [*A publication*] ..... TEST
Thesaurus Syriacus [*R. Paine Smith*] [*A publication*] (BJA) ..... PSm
Thesaurus-Oriented Retrieval [*Information service or system*] ..... THOR
Theses of Economics and Business in Finland [*Helsinki School of Economics Library*] [*Information service or system*] (CRD) ..... THES
Theseus [*of Plutarch*] [*Classical studies*] (OCD) ..... Thes
Thesis (ADA) ..... THES
Thesmophoriazusae [*of Aristophanes*] [*Classical studies*] (OCD) ..... Thesm
Thessalon Union Public Library, Ontario [*Library symbol National Library of Canada*] (NLC) ..... OTHE
Thessalonians [*New Testament book*] (BJA) ..... Th
Thessalonians [*New Testament book*] ..... Thes
Thessalonians [*New Testament book*] ..... Thess
Thessaloniki [*Greece*] [*ICAO location identifier*] (ICLI) ..... LGTS
Thessaloniki [*Greece*] [*Airport symbol*] (OAG) ..... SKG
Thessaly [*District of both ancient and modern Greece*] (BARN) ..... Thess
Theta Kappa Phi [*Fraternity*] ..... TKP
Theta Phi Alpha [*Sorority*] ..... TPA
Theta Rho Girls' Club (EA) ..... TRGC

Theta Sigma Phi [*Later, Women in Communications*] .... TSP
Theta-Burst Stimulation [*Neurophysiology*] .... TBS
Theta-Sensitive Regulatory Cell [*Hypothetical*] [*Hematology*] .... TSRC
Thetford Mines, PQ [*FM radio station call letters*] .... CFJO
Thetford Mines, PQ [*AM radio station call letters*] .... CKLD
Theux-Verviers [*Belgium ICAO location identifier*] (ICLI) .... EBTX
Thexylborane [*Organic chemistry*] .... TB
Thexylborane-N, N-Diethylaniline [*Organic chemistry*] .... TBDA
They Help Each Other Spiritually [*Motto of THEOS Foundation*] .... THEOS
They Might Be Giants Information Club (EA) .... TMBGIC
Thiabendazole [*or Thiazolyl*] Benzimidazole [*Pesticide*] .... TBZ
Thiamine Cobalt Chlorophyllin [*Antiulcer*] .... TCC
Thiamine Deficient (OA) .... TD
Thiamine Diphosphate [*Also, DPT, TPP*] [*Biochemistry*] .... TDP
Thiamine Diphosphate [*Biochemistry*] .... ThDP
Thiamine Hydrochloride [*Pharmacology*] (DAVI) .... B_1
Thiamine Propyl Disulfide (MAE) .... TPD
Thiamine Pyrophosphate [*Also, DPT, TDP*] [*Biochemistry*] .... TPP
Thiamine Tetrahydrofurfuryl Disulfide [*Pharmacology*] .... TTFD
Thiamphenicol [*Antimicrobial compound*] .... TP
Thiamylal [*An anesthetic*] (DAVI) .... THIA
Thiazole Orange [*Organic chemistry*] .... TO
Thiazolylazonaphthol [*An indicator*] [*Chemistry*] .... TAN
Thiazoylethylamine [*Organic chemistry*] .... TEA
Thibodaux, LA [*FM radio station call letters*] .... KNSU
Thibodaux, LA [*AM radio station call letters*] .... KTIB
Thibodaux, LA [*FM radio station call letters*] (RBYB) .... KTLN
Thibodaux, LA [*FM radio station call letters*] .... KXOR
Thibodaux, LA [*Location identifier FAA*] (FAAL) .... TBD
Thick [*Automotive engineering*] .... TH
Thick [*or Thickness*] (AAG) .... THK
Thick (ROG) .... TK
Thick [*Aviation*] (DA) .... TKH
Thick Ascending Limb of Henle's Loop [*Medicine*] (DMAA) .... TALH
Thick Film (MSA) .... THKF
Thick Film Ignition [*System*] [*Ford Motor Co.*] [*Automotive engineering*] .. TFI
Thick Fog [*Navigation*] .... FF
Thick Molding Compound .... TMC
Thick Molding Compound [*Plastics technology*] .... TMC
Thick Paper Copy (DGA) .... Th PC
Thick Paper Copy (DGA) .... TPC
Thicker (MSA) .... THKR
Thick-Film Hybrid .... TFH
Thick-Film Hybrid Circuit (IAA) .... TFHC
Thick-Film Integrated [*Electronics*] .... TFI
Thickness .... T
Thickness .... THKNS
Thickness Chord Wing [*Aviation*] (AIA) .... TC
Thickness Data Acquisition System [*Southwest Research Institute*] ...... TDAS
Thickness Readout Module .... TRM
Thickness-Insensitive Solar Paint [*Coating technology*] .... TISP
Thickness-Sensitive Solar Paint [*Coating technology*] .... TSSP
Thickness-Shear-Mode [*Instrumentation*] .... TSM
Thief .... T
Thief River Falls [*Minnesota*] [*Airport symbol*] (OAG) .... TVF
Thief River Falls, MN [*Location identifier FAA*] (FAAL) .... HYZ
Thief River Falls, MN [*Television station call letters*] .... KBRR
Thief River Falls, MN [*AM radio station call letters*] .... KKAQ
Thief River Falls, MN [*FM radio station call letters*] .... KKDQ
Thief River Falls, MN [*FM radio station call letters*] .... KNTN
Thief River Falls, MN [*FM radio station call letters*] .... KQMN
Thief River Falls, MN [*FM radio station call letters*] .... KSNR
Thief River Falls, MN [*FM radio station call letters*] .... KSRQ
Thief River Falls, MN [*AM radio station call letters*] .... KTRF
Thief River Falls Public Library, Thief River Falls, MN [*Library symbol*]
  [*Library of Congress*] (LCLS) .... MnTP
Thiel College, Greenville, PA [*Library symbol Library of Congress*]
  (LCLS) .... PGrevT
Thienyl(cyclohexyl)piperidine [*Biochemistry*] .... TCP
Thienylmalonic Acid [*Organic chemistry*] .... TMA
Thigh Brachial Pressure Index .... TBPI
Thimble .... TMB
Thimble Collectors International (EA) .... TCI
Thin [*Philately*] .... Th
Thin Base Laminate .... TBL
Thin Basement Membrane Nephropathy [*Medicine*] (DMAA) .... TBMN
Thin Charcoal Layer .... TCL
Thin Dielectric Film .... TDF
Thin Elastic Shell .... TES
Thin Film Deposition Unit .... TFDU
Thin Film Integrated Optics (PDAA) .... TFIO
Thin Glass Laminate .... TGL
Thin Iron Film .... TIF
Thin Leading Edge .... TLE
Thin Line Array Handling Equipment (DWSG) .... TAHE
Thin Line Handling System (DWSG) .... TLHS
Thin Line Towed Array [*Navy*] (CAAL) .... TLTA
Thin Lipid Membrane (OA) .... TLM
Thin Liquid Stillage [*Fermentation byproduct*] .... TLS
Thin Nickel Film .... TNF
Thin Nickel Iron .... TNI
Thin Nickel Iron Film .... TNIF
Thin Region Integral Method .... TRIM
Thin Shock Layer .... TSL
Thin Small-Outline Package [*Computer science*] .... TSOP

Thin Solid Films (IEEE) .... TSF
Thin Wire Analysis Program [*Air Force*] .... TWAP
Thin-Film .... TF
Thin-Film Active Device (IAA) .... TFAD
Thin-Film Barrier .... TFB
Thin-Film Capacitor .... TFC
Thin-Film Cell .... TFC
Thin-Film Cell Array .... TFCA
Thin-Film Circuit .... TFC
Thin-Film Crystal Growth .... TFCG
Thin-Film Diode Descriptor Electronics .... TFD
Thin-Film Distillation .... TFD
Thin-Film Electrode [*Electrochemistry*] .... TFE
Thin-Film Electroluminescence .... TFEL
Thin-Film FET [*Field-Effect Transistor*] (IAA) .... TFF
Thin-Film Field-Effect Transistor (IAA) .... TFFET
Thin-Film Field-Effect Transistor .... TFT
Thin-Film Ignition [*Automotive engineering*] .... TFI-I
Thin-Film Integrated Circuit (IAA) .... TFIC
Thin-Film Interface Barrier .... TFIB
Thin-Film Mercury Electrode [*Electrochemistry*] .... TFME
Thin-Film Microelectronics .... TFM
Thin-Film Oxygen Uptake Test .... TFOUT
Thin-Film Personal Communications and Telemetry System (MCD) ...... TFPCTS
Thin-Film Personal Communications and Telemetry System (MCD) ...... TFPECTS
Thin-Film Photovoltaic Cell .... TFPC
Thin-Film Photovoltaic Cell Array .... TFPCA
Thin-Film Resist .... TFR
Thin-Film Spreading Agent [*For enhanced oil recovery*] .... TFSA
Thin-Film Technique .... TFT
Thin-Film Technology .... TFT
Thin-Film Thermocouple (IAA) .... TFTC
Thin-Film Transducer .... TFT
Thin-Film Transistor .... TFT
Thing .... THNG
Thingeyri [*Iceland*] [*ICAO location identifier*] (ICLI) .... BITE
Thingeyri [*Iceland*] [*Airport symbol*] (OAG) .... TEY
Things Are Fouled Up Beyond All Recognition [*Military slang*] [*Bowdlerized
  version*] .... TAFUBAR
Things Are Really Fouled Up [*Military slang*] [*Bowdlerized version*] ...... TARFU
Things Are So Fouled Up It's Really Amazing [*Military slang*] [*Bowdlerized
  version*] .... TASFUIRA
Things Falling Off Aircraft (MCD) .... TFOA
Things Gone Right [*Measure of automobile customer satisfaction*] .... TGR
Things Gone Wrong [*Measure of automobile customer satisfaction*] ...... TGW
Things to Do .... TTD
Think for Yourself and Question Authority [*Term coined by Dr. Timothy
  Leary*] .... TFYQA
Think Ink [*An association*] (EA) .... TI
Think New Ideas, Inc. [*Associated Press*] (SAG) .... ThinkNw
Think New Ideas, Inc. [*NASDAQ symbol*] (SAG) .... THNK
Think Time [*Computer order entry*] .... TT
Thinking Cap [*Layman's term for neocortex*] .... TC
Thinking Creatively in Action and Movement [*Test*] .... TCAM
Thinking Creatively with Sounds and Words [*Educational test*] .... TCSW
Thinking Tools, Inc. [*Associated Press*] (SAG) .... ThkTools
Thinking Tools, Inc. [*NASDAQ symbol*] (SAG) .... TSIM
Thin-Layer Activation [*Engine wear testing*] .... TLA
Thin-Layer Chromatography [*Analytical chemistry*] .... TLC
Thin-Layer Chromatography/Infrared [*Analytical chemistry*] .... TLC/IR
Thin-Layer Electrophoresis [*Analytical chemistry*] .... TLE
Thin-Layer Explosive (MCD) .... TLX
Thin-Layer Field Effect Transistor (IAA) .... TIFET
Thin-layer Field-Effect Transistor (IAA) .... TFET
Thin-Layer Gel [*Filtration*] [*Analytical chemistry*] .... TLG
Thin-Layer Immunoassay [*Analytical biochemistry*] .... TIA
Thin-Layer Isoelectric Focusing [*Analytical chemistry*] .... TLIEF
Thin-Line Communications Connectivity .... TLCC
Thinned Aperture Computed Lens (IEEE) .... TACOL
Thinned Aperture Telescope .... TAT
Thinner [*Freight*] .... THNR
Thinner .... TNR
Thinner Than [*Freight*] .... THNR T
Thio [*or Mercapto*] [*As substituent on nucleoside*] [*Biochemistry*] .... s
Thioacetamide [*Organic chemistry*] .... TAA
Thiobarbituric Acid [*Organic chemistry*] .... TBA
Thiobarbituric Acid Reactive Substance [*Analytical chemistry*] .... TBARS
Thiobisdichlorophenol [*Pharmacology*] .... TBP
Thiocarbamyl-nitro-blue Tetrazolium [*Organic chemistry*] .... TC-NBT
Thiocarbanidin [*Pharmacology*] .... THC
Thiocarbanilide [*Organic chemistry*] .... TCA
Thiocarbohydrazide [*Organic chemistry*] .... TCH
Thiocyanate [*Organic chemistry*] (DAVI) .... SCND
(Thiocyanomethylthio)benzothiazole [*Fungicide*] [*Organic chemistry*] .... TCMTB
Thio(deaza)guanine [*Antineoplastic drug*] .... TDG
Thiodiethanethiol [*Organic chemistry*] .... TDT
Thiodigalactoside [*Organic chemistry*] .... TDG
Thiodiglycol [*Organic chemistry*] .... TDG
Thiodiphenol [*Organic chemistry*] .... TDP
Thiodipropionic Acid [*Organic chemistry*] .... TDPA
Thioesterase [*An enzyme*] .... TE
Thioglucose [*Biochemistry*] .... TG
Thioglycolate [*Biochemistry*] .... TG
Thioglycolic Acid [*Organic chemistry*] .... TGA
Thioguanine [*Also, TG*] [*Antineoplastic drug*] .... T

Thioguanine [*Also, T*] [*Antineoplastic drug*] .... TG
Thioguanine, ara-C, Daunomycin [*Daunorubicin*] [*Antineoplastic drug regimen*] .... TAD
Thioguanine, Oncovin [*Vincristine*], ara-C, Prednisone [*Antineoplastic drug regimen*] .... TOAP
Thioguanine Riboside [*Antineoplastic drug*] (DAVI) 6-TGR
Thioguanine, Rubidomycin [*Daunorubicin*], ara-C, Methotrexate, Prednisolone, Cyclophosphamide, Oncovin [*Vincristine*] [*Antineoplastic drug regimen*] .... TRAMPCO
Thioguanine, Rubidomycin [*Daunorubicin*], ara-C, Methotrexate, Prednisolone, Cyclophosphamide, Oncovin , L-Asparaginase [*Vincristine*] [*Antineoplastic drug regimen*] .... TRAMPCOL
Thioguanine, Rubidomycin [*Daunorubicin*], Cytosine arabinoside , Prednisone [*ara-C*] [*Antineoplastic drug regimen*] .... TRAP
Thioinosine [*One-letter symbol; see Slno, Sno*] .... M
Thioinosine [*Also, Sno, M*] [*A nucleoside*] .... Slno
Thioinosine [*Also, Slno, M*] [*A nucleoside*] .... Sno
Thiokol Chemical Corp. [*Later, Thiokol Corp.*] (AAG) .... TCC
Thiokol Chemical Corp., Utah Division, Brigham City, UT [*Library symbol Library of Congress*] (LCLS) .... UBcT
Thiokol Corp. [*Associated Press*] (SAG) .... Thiokl
Thiokol Corp. [*NYSE symbol*] (SPSG) .... TKC
Thiokol Nuclear Development Center; Allison Division, General Motors; Linde Division, Union Carbide; and Nuclear Development Corp. Team (SAA) .... TALANT
Thiol Alkaline Phosphatase [*An enzyme*] .... TAP
Thiolacetoxybenzanilide [*Organic chemistry*] .... TAB
Thiomalic Acid [*Organic chemistry*] .... TMA
Thiomethylgalactoside [*Organic chemistry*] .... TMG
Thionaphthenecarboxylic Acid [*Organic chemistry*] .... TNCA
Thionine [*Organic chemistry*] .... TH
Thio(nitro)benzoic Acid [*Analytical biochemistry*] .... TNB
Thionville/Yutz [*France ICAO location identifier*] (ICLI) .... LFGV
Thiopental [*An anesthetic*] .... T
Thiopental [*An anesthetic*] .... Th
Thiopental [*An anesthetic*] .... THIO
Thiopental [*An anesthetic*] .... TP
Thioperazine [*or Thioproperazine*] [*Tranquilizer*] .... TPZ
Thiophosphoryl Triamide [*Fertilizer technology*] .... TPTA
Thioredoxin [*Also, TR, Trx*] [*Biochemistry*] .... TD
Thioredoxin [*Also, TD, Trx*] [*Biochemistry*] .... TR
Thioredoxin [*Also, TD, TR*] [*Biochemistry*] .... Trx
Thioredoxin Reductase [*An enzyme*] .... TR
Thioredoxin Reductase [*An enzyme*] .... TRR
Thioridazine [*Tranquilizer*] .... TDZ
Thioridazine [*Tranquilizer*] .... TRZ
Thios Resources, Inc. [*Vancouver Stock Exchange symbol*] .... THI
Thiosemicarbazide [*Organic chemistry*] .... TSC
Thiosulfate-Citrate-Bile Salt Sucrose [*Growth medium*] .... TCBS
Thiothiazolidinecarboxylic Acid [*Organic chemistry*] .... TTCA
Thiothixene [*Tranquilizer*] .... TTX
Thiouracil [*Also, SUra*] [*Biochemistry*] .... Sur
Thiouracil [*Also, Sur*] [*Biochemistry*] .... SUra
Thiouracil [*Biochemistry*] (MAE) .... TU
Thiouridine [*One-letter symbol; see Srd*] .... S
Thiouridine [*Also, S, SU*] [*A nucleoside*] .... Srd
Thiouridine [*Two-letter symbol; see Srd*] .... SU
Thioxanthone [*Organic chemistry*] .... TIXA
Thira [*Greece*] [*Airport symbol*] (AD) .... JTR
Third Air Force .... TAF
Third Attack [*Men's lacrosse position, until 1933*] .... TA
Third Base [*or Baseman*] [*Baseball*] 3B
Third Canadian General Investment Trust Ltd. [*Toronto Stock Exchange symbol*] .... THD
Third Cervical Nerve [*Anatomy*] (DMAA) C3
Third Cervical Vertebra [*Anatomy*] (DMAA) C3
Third Circuit Court of Appeals, Wilmington, DE [*Library symbol Library of Congress*] (LCLS) .... DeWTC
Third Class Mail Association (EA) .... TCMA
Third Component of Complement (DMAA) C3
Third Continental Congress (EA) .... TCC
Third Defense [*Men's lacrosse position, until 1933*] .... TD
[*The*] Third Degree [*A publication*] (EAAP) .... TTD
Third Financial [*NASDAQ symbol*] (TTSB) .... THIR
Third Financial Corp. [*NASDAQ symbol*] (SAG) .... THIR
Third Financial Corp. [*Associated Press*] (SAG) .... ThrdFn
Third Generation (EA) .... TG
Third Generation Antitank [*Army*] .... TRIGAT
Third Generation Gyro (MCD) .... TGG
Third International Mathematics and Science Study [*Education research*] .... TIMSS
Third International Mathematics and Science Study .... TIMSS
Third Level Thermal Margin [*Nuclear energy*] (NRCH) .... TLTM
Third Market [*Securities*] .... TM
Third Moment of Frequency (PDAA) .... TMF
Third Mortgage (MHDW) .... TM
Third Normal Form [*Databases*] .... TNF
Third Officer [*British military*] (DMA) 3/O
Third Order of Mary (EA) .... TOM
Third Order of Saint Dominic [*Rome, Italy*] (EAIO) .... TOSD
Third Order Regular of St. Francis [*Roman Catholic men's religious order*] .... TOR
Third Order Regular of Saint Francis (TOCD) .... tor
Third Party [*Legal shorthand*] (LWAP) 3P
Third Party (ADA) .... T/P
Third Party [*Insurance*] (ODBW) .... TP

Third Party Administrator .... TPA
Third Party Beneficiary [*Legal shorthand*] (LWAP) 3PB
Third Party Bodily Injury [*Insurance*] (AIA) .... TPBI
Third Party Liability [*Insurance*] .... TPL
Third Party Prescription Program .... TPPP
Third Party Reimbursement (HCT) .... TPR
Third Party Traffic [*Radio*] .... TPC
Third Readiness State (AAG) .... TRS
Third Reich Study Group (EA) .... TRSG
Third Soviet-American Gas and Aerosol [*Experiment*] (USDC) SAGA-3
Third Soviet-American Gas and Aerosol [*Experiment*] [*Marine science*] (OSRA) SAGA-3
Third Stage [*Aerospace*] (AAG) .... T/S
Third Stage Test Set [*Aerospace*] (MCD) .... TSTS
Third Survey of Veterans [*Veterans Administration*] (GFGA) .... SOVIII
Third United States Army [*Terminated, 1973*] .... TUSA
Third Wave Civilization [*Title of record album by Ian Lloyd*] 3WC
Third Word Designator [*Computer science*] .... T
Third World Academy of Sciences [*Trieste, Italy*] (EAIO) .... TWAS
Third World Conference Fund .... TWCF
Third World Education Outreach (EA) .... TEO
Third World First [*An association British*] 3W1
Third World Forum [*Cairo, Egypt*] (EAIO) .... TWF
Third World Foundation [*British*] (EAIO) .... TWF
Third World Information Network [*British*] (EAIO) .... TWIN
Third World Institute of Theatre Arts Studies .... TWITAS
Third World Movement Against the Exploitation of Women [*Quezon City, Philippines*] (EAIO) .... TW-MAE-W
Third World Moving Images Project (EA) .... TWMIP
Third World Network (EERA) .... TWN
Third World Resources [*A publication*] (BRI) .... TWR
Third World Women's Project [*Defunct*] (EA) .... TWWP
Third-Class Post Office .... TCPO
Third-Class Ship in Lloyd's Register (BARN) .... AE
Third-Degree Stochastic Dominance [*Agricultural statistics*] .... TSD
Third-Harmonic Band .... THB
Third-Harmonic Distortion [*Physics*] (IAA) .... THC
Third-Harmonic Distortion [*Physics*] (IAA) .... THD
Third-Harmonic Generation [*Physics*] .... THG
Third-Octave Digital Analyzer .... TODA
Third-Party Maintenance (BTTJ) .... TPM
Third-Party Transaction [*Business term*] .... TPT
Thirst Quencher TQ2
Thirteenth Coast Guard District [*Seattle, WA*] [*USCG*] (TAG) D13
Thirty-Five New Guys [*Group of new astronauts*] [*NASA*] .... TFNG
This Day Tonight (ADA) .... TDT
This I Believe Test [*Education*] .... TIB
This Is Not a Legally Enforceable Agreement [*Legal term*] (NUCP) .... TINALEA
This Mode of Transportation has been Determined to be More Advantageous to the Government .... TMDAG
This Office Has No Record Of [*Army*] (AABC) .... RECNO
This Scherzo Is a Joke [*Used by American composer Charles Edward Ives*] .... TSIAJ
This Side Up .... TSU
This Umbrella Folds Itself [*Trademark for type of umbrella*] .... TUFI
This Week at Headquarters [*Military publication*] (DNAB) .... TWAH
This Week in Baseball [*Television program*] .... TWIB
This Week Only (ADA) .... TWO
Thisted [*Denmark ICAO location identifier*] (ICLI) .... EKTS
Thisted [*Denmark*] [*Airport symbol*] (OAG) .... TED
Thistle Class Association (EA) .... TCA
Thistle Mottle Virus [*Plant pathology*] .... THMOV
Thistletown Regional Centre for Children and Adolescents, Rexdale, ON, Canada [*Library symbol*] [*Library of Congress*] (LCLS) .... CaOTTRCC
Thistletown Regional Centre for Children and Adolescents, Rexdale, Ontario [*Library symbol National Library of Canada*] (NLC) .... OTTRC
Thitec Recovery [*Vancouver Stock Exchange symbol*] .... TCR
Thogoto Virus [*Virology*] .... THO
Thohoyandou [*South Africa*] [*ICAO location identifier*] (ICLI) .... FATH
Thom Bierdz International Fan Club (EA) .... TBIFC
Thom Christopher Fan Club (EA) .... TCFC
Thomas A. Dooley Foundation [*Later, Dooley Foundation/Intermed-USA*] .... TADF
Thomas Aloysius Dorgan [*Satirical cartoonist*] .... TAD
Thomas & Betts [*NYSE symbol*] (TTSB) .... TNB
Thomas & Betts Corp. [*Associated Press*] (SAG) .... ThmBet
Thomas & Betts Corp. [*NYSE symbol*] (SPSG) .... TNB
Thomas and Franklin's Chancery Reports [*1 Maryland*] [*A publication*] (DLA) .... Thom & Fr
Thomas Aquinas [*Deceased, 1274*] [*Authority cited in pre-1607 legal work*] (DSA) .... Tho
Thomas Branigan Memorial Library, Las Cruces, NM [*Library symbol Library of Congress*] (LCLS) .... NmLc
Thomas Branigan Memorial Library, Las Cruces, NM [*OCLC symbol*] (OCLC) .... TBL
Thomas C. Calvin [*Character in TV series "Magnum, P.I."*] .... TC
Thomas Campegius [*Deceased, 1564*] [*Authority cited in pre-1607 legal work*] (DSA) .... Thom Camp
Thomas Crane Public Library, Quincy, MA [*Library symbol Library of Congress*] (LCLS) .... MQ
Thomas Crane Public Library, Quincy, MA [*OCLC symbol*] (OCLC) .... QUI
Thomas de Elya [*Authority cited in pre-1607 legal work*] (DSA) .... Tho de Lya
Thomas de Formaginis [*Flourished, 1331-38*] [*Authority cited in pre-1607 legal work*] (DSA) .... Tho de For
Thomas de Formaginis [*Flourished, 1331-38*] [*Authority cited in pre-1607 legal work*] (DSA) .... Tho For

Thomas de Formaginis [*Flourished, 1331-38*] (DSA) .... Tho Form
Thomas de Formaginis [*Flourished, 1331-38*] [*Authority cited in pre-1607 legal work*] (DSA) .... To de For
Thomas de Formaginis [*Flourished, 1331-38*] [*Authority cited in pre-1607 legal work*] (DSA) .... To For
Thomas de Piperata [*Flourished, 1268-72*] [*Authority cited in pre-1607 legal work*] (DSA) .... Th
Thomas de Piperata [*Flourished, 1268-72*] [*Authority cited in pre-1607 legal work*] (DSA) .... Tho
Thomas Dolby Fan Club (EA) .... TDFC
Thomas E. Ryan Public Library, East Williston, NY [*Library symbol Library of Congress*] (LCLS) .... NEw
Thomas' Edition of Coke upon Littleton [*A publication*] (DLA) .... Thom Co Lit
Thomas' Edition of Coke upon Littleton [*A publication*] (DLA) .... Thom Co Litt
Thomas' Edition of Coke upon Littleton [*A publication*] (DLA) .... Thos Co Lit
Thomas Edmund Dewey [*Republican candidate for President, 1948*] .... TED
Thomas Edward Lawrence [*Lawrence of Arabia*] [*British archaeologist, soldier, and writer, 1888-1935*] .... TEL
Thomas Fisher Rare Book Library, University of Toronto, Ontario [*Library symbol National Library of Canada*] (NLC) .... OTUTF
Thomas Fleschner Memorial Library, Birch Run, MI [*Library symbol Library of Congress*] (LCLS) .... MiBicr
Thomas Ford Memorial Library, Western Springs, IL [*Library symbol Library of Congress*] (LCLS) .... IWesp
Thomas Foroliviensis [*Authority cited in pre-1607 legal work*] (DSA) .... Tho Foroli
Thomas Gilcrease Institute of American History and Art, Tulsa, OK [*Library symbol Library of Congress*] (LCLS) .... OkTG
Thomas Grammaticus [*Flourished, 16th century*] [*Authority cited in pre-1607 legal work*] (DSA) .... Tho Grama
Thomas Group [*NASDAQ symbol*] (TTSB) .... TGIS
Thomas Group, Inc. [*NASDAQ symbol*] (SAG) .... TGIS
Thomas Group, Inc. [*Associated Press*] (SAG) .... ThomasG
Thomas Hackney Braswell Memorial Library, Rocky Mount, NC [*Library symbol Library of Congress*] (LCLS) .... NcRm
Thomas Hardy Society (EAIO) .... THS
Thomas Hardy Society of America [*Defunct*] (EA) .... THSA
Thomas Hewett Edward Cat [*In TV series "T.H.E. Cat"*] .... THE
Thomas Indus [*NYSE symbol*] (TTSB) .... TII
Thomas Industries, Inc. [*Associated Press*] (SAG) .... ThomIn
Thomas Industries, Inc. [*NYSE symbol*] (SPSG) .... TII
Thomas J. Lipton, Inc., Englewood Cliffs, NJ [*Library symbol Library of Congress*] (LCLS) .... NjEncL
Thomas Jefferson [*US president, 1743-1826*] .... TJ
Thomas Jefferson Center (EA) .... TJC
Thomas Jefferson Equal Tax Society (EA) .... TJETS
Thomas Jefferson Institute for the Study of Religious Freedom (EA) .... TJISRF
Thomas Jefferson Junior/Senior High School Library, Rochester, NY [*OCLC symbol*] (OCLC) .... RXJ
Thomas Jefferson Library System, Jefferson City, MO [*Library symbol Library of Congress*] (LCLS) .... MoJc
Thomas Jefferson Research Center [*Later, TJC*] (EA) .... TJRC
Thomas Jefferson University (GAGS) .... Thom Jefferson U
Thomas Jefferson University, Philadelphia, PA [*Library symbol Library of Congress*] (LCLS) .... PPJ
Thomas Jefferson University, Philadelphia, PA [*OCLC symbol*] (OCLC) .... TVJ
Thomas Jefferson University, Scott Memorial Library, Philadelphia, PA [*Library symbol Library of Congress*] (LCLS) .... PPJ-S
Thomas' Leading Cases in Constitutional Law [*A publication*] (DLA) .... Th Ca Const Law
Thomas' Leading Cases on Constitutional Law [*A publication*] (DLA) .... Th C Const Law
Thomas' Leading Cases on Constitutional Law [*A publication*] (DLA) .... Thom Const L
Thomas' Leading Cases on Constitutional Law [*A publication*] (DLA) .... Thom LC
Thomas' Leading Statutes Summarized [*A publication*] (DLA) .... Thom St Sum
Thomas Legal Defense Fund (EA) .... TLDF
Thomas M. Cooley Law School (GAGS) .... Thom Cooley Law
Thomas M. Cooley Law School, Lansing, MI [*Library symbol Library of Congress*] (LCLS) .... MiLTC
Thomas Marketing Information Center [*Thomas Publishing Co.*] [*Information service or system*] (IID) .... TMIC
Thomas Micro-Catalogs .... TM-C
Thomas Mieres [*Flourished, 1429-39*] [*Authority cited in pre-1607 legal work*] (DSA) .... T
Thomas Mieres [*Flourished, 1429-39*] [*Authority cited in pre-1607 legal work*] (DSA) .... Tho
Thomas More Association (EA) .... TMA
Thomas More College, Fort Mitchell, KY [*OCLC symbol*] (OCLC) .... KTM
Thomas More College, Fort Mitchell, KY [*Library symbol Library of Congress*] (LCLS) .... KyFmTM
Thomas More Society of America (EA) .... TMSA
Thomas Nast Society (EA) .... TNS
Thomas Nelson [*NYSE symbol*] (TTSB) .... TNM
Thomas Nelson - Australia [*Publisher*] .... TNA
Thomas Nelson 'B' [*NYSE symbol*] (TTSB) .... TNM.B
Thomas Nelson Community College, Hampton, VA [*Library symbol Library of Congress*] (LCLS) .... ViHaT
Thomas Nelson - United Kingdom [*Publisher*] .... TNUK
Thomas on Mortgages [*A publication*] (DLA) .... Thom Mort
Thomas on Mortgages [*A publication*] (DLA) .... Thomas Mortg
Thomas on Negligence [*A publication*] (DLA) .... Thomas Negl
Thomas Paine Society [*Nottingham, England*] (EAIO) .... TPS
Thomas Parpalea [*Flourished, 16th century*] [*Authority cited in pre-1607 legal work*] (DSA) .... Tho Parpal
Thomas Power [*"Tay Pay"*] **O'Connor** [*Irish journalist and politician, 1848-1929*] .... TP
Thomas Register Catalog File [*A publication*] .... THOMCAT
Thomas' Reports [*1 Wyoming*] [*A publication*] (DLA) .... Thom
Thomas' Reports [*1 Wyoming*] [*A publication*] (DLA) .... Thomas
Thomas Roderick Fraser and Andrew Dewar [*Pseudonym*] .... TRFAD
Thomas Self-Concept Values Test [*Psychology*] .... TSCVT
Thomas Tallis Society [*British*] .... TTS
Thomas Thorpe [*Publisher of a 1609 edition of Shakespeare's sonnets*] .... TT
Thomas' Universal Jurisprudence [*2nd ed.*] [*1829*] [*A publication*] (DLA) .... Thom Un Jur
Thomas Wolfe Society (EA) .... TWS
Thomas-Binetti [*Test*] [*Laboratory science*] (DAVI) .... T-B
Thomason, Richland, and Martens [*Air-charter business*] .... TRM
Thomasons Ltd., London, United Kingdom [*Library symbol Library of Congress*] (LCLS) .... UkLTh
Thomaston, GA [*AM radio station call letters*] .... WSFT
Thomaston, GA [*AM radio station call letters*] .... WTGA
Thomaston, GA [*FM radio station call letters*] .... WTGA-FM
Thomaston, ME [*FM radio station call letters*] .... WAVX
Thomaston Mills Class B [*Associated Press*] (SAG) .... ThomMA
Thomaston Mills Class B [*Associated Press*] (SAG) .... ThomMB
Thomaston Mills, Inc. [*NASDAQ symbol*] (NQ) .... TMST
Thomaston Mills'A' [*NASDAQ symbol*] (TTSB) .... TMSTA
Thomaston Mills'B' [*NASDAQ symbol*] (TTSB) .... TMSTB
Thomasville Aircraft and Warning Station (IAA) .... TAWS
Thomasville, AL [*AM radio station call letters*] .... WJDB
Thomasville, AL [*FM radio station call letters*] .... WJDB-FM
Thomasville, GA [*Location identifier FAA*] (FAAL) .... TVI
Thomasville, GA [*Television station call letters*] .... WCTV
Thomasville, GA [*AM radio station call letters*] .... WHGH
Thomasville, GA [*AM radio station call letters*] .... WPAX
Thomasville, GA [*FM radio station call letters*] .... WSNI
Thomasville, GA [*AM radio station call letters*] .... WSTT
Thomasville, NC [*FM radio station call letters*] .... WFAZ
Thomasville, NC [*AM radio station call letters*] .... WTNC
Thomasville Public Library, Thomasville, NC [*Library symbol Library of Congress*] (LCLS) .... NcTh
Thompson [*Canada*] [*Airport symbol*] (OAG) .... YTH
Thompson and Cook's New York Supreme Court Reports [*A publication*] (DLA) .... NY Sup Ct Rep
Thompson and Cook's New York Supreme Court Reports [*A publication*] (DLA) .... NY Sup Ct (T & C)
Thompson and Cook's New York Supreme Court Reports [*A publication*] (DLA) .... NYSC
Thompson and Cook's New York Supreme Court Reports [*A publication*] (DLA) .... SC (T & C)
Thompson and Cook's New York Supreme Court Reports [*A publication*] (DLA) .... T & C
Thompson and Cook's New York Supreme Court Reports [*1873-75*] [*A publication*] (DLA) .... Th & C
Thompson and Cook's New York Supreme Court Reports [*A publication*] (DLA) .... Thomp & C
Thompson and Cook's New York Supreme Court Reports [*A publication*] (DLA) .... Thomp & Cook
Thompson and Cook's New York Supreme Court Reports [*A publication*] (DLA) .... Thompson & C
Thompson and Merriam on Juries [*A publication*] (DLA) .... Thomp & M Jur
Thompson and Steger's Code [*Tennessee*] [*A publication*] (DLA) .... Thomp & St
Thompson and Steger's Code [*Tennessee*] [*A publication*] (DLA) .... Thomp & St Code
Thompson. Benefit Building Societies [*A publication*] (ILCA) .... Thom BBS
Thompson Elementary School, Rockford, IL [*Library symbol*] [*Library of Congress*] (LCLS) .... IRoTE
Thompson Falls, MT [*Location identifier FAA*] (FAAL) .... THM
Thompson Falls Public Library, Thompson Falls, MT [*Library symbol*] [*Library of Congress*] (LCLS) .... MtTf
Thompson Falls Schools, Thompson Falls, MT [*Library symbol*] [*Library of Congress*] (LCLS) .... MtTfS
Thompson Home Library, Ithaca, MI [*Library symbol Library of Congress*] (LCLS) .... MiIt
Thompson, MB [*FM radio station call letters*] .... CBWK
Thompson, MB [*AM radio station call letters*] .... CHTM
Thompson, MB [*FM radio station call letters*] (RBYB) .... CINC
Thompson, MB [*ICAO location identifier*] (ICLI) .... CYTH
Thompson, OH [*FM radio station call lettes*] (RBYB) .... WKSV-FM
Thompson on Carriers [*A publication*] (DLA) .... Thomp Car
Thompson on Charging the Jury [*A publication*] (DLA) .... Thomp Ch Jur
Thompson on Homesteads and Exemptions [*A publication*] (DLA) .... Thomp H & Ex
Thompson on Liability of Officers of Corporations [*A publication*] (DLA) .... Thomp Liab Off
Thompson on Liability of Stockholders [*A publication*] (DLA) .... Thomp Liab St
Thompson on Liability of Stockholders [*A publication*] (DLA) .... Thomp Liab Stockh
Thompson on Patent Laws of All Countries [*13th ed.*] [*1905*] [*A publication*] (DLA) .... Thomp Pat
Thompson on the Law of Highways [*A publication*] (DLA) .... Thomp High
Thompson on Trials [*A publication*] (DLA) .... Thomp Trials
Thompson PBE [*NASDAQ symbol*] (TTSB) .... THOM
Thompson PBE, Inc. [*Associated Press*] (SAG) .... ThmPBE
Thompson PBE, Inc. [*NASDAQ symbol*] (SAG) .... THOM
Thompson Products, Inc. [*Later, Thompson Ramo Woolridge, Inc.*] .... TAPCO
Thompson Public Library, Manitoba [*Library symbol National Library of Canada*] (NLC) .... MTH

Thompson Public Library, Thompson, MB, Canada [*Library symbol Library of Congress*] (LCLS) .... CaMTh
Thompson R2-J School District, Loveland, CO [*Library symbol*] [*Library of Congress*] (LCLS) .... CoLovT
Thompson Submachine Gun .... TSMG
Thompson-Huston Co. of France .... THCF
Thompson-Lundmark Gold Mines Ltd. [*Toronto Stock Exchange symbol*] .... TOM
Thompson-Ramo-Wooldridge, Inc., Canoga Park, CA [*Library symbol Library of Congress*] (LCLS) .... CCpT
Thompson's Cases [*Tennessee*] [*A publication*] (DLA) .... Thomp Cas
Thompson's Cases on Negligence [*A publication*] (DLA) .... Thomp Neg
Thompson's Commentaries on Law of Private Corporations [*A publication*] (DLA) .... Thomp Corp
Thompson's Digest of Laws [*Florida*] [*A publication*] (DLA) .... Dig Fla
Thompson's Digest of Laws [*Florida*] [*A publication*] (DLA) .... Fla Dig
Thompson's Digest of Laws [*Florida*] [*A publication*] (DLA) .... Thomp Dig
Thompson's Digest of Laws [*Florida*] [*A publication*] (DLA) .... Thompson's Fla Dig
Thompson's Entries [*A publication*] (DLA) .... Thomp Ent
Thompson's Law of the Farm [*A publication*] (DLA) .... Thomp Farm
Thompson's National Bank Cases [*A publication*] (DLA) .... Thomp NB Cas
Thompson's Ohio Citations [*A publication*] (DLA) .... Thomp Cit
Thompson's Provisional Remedies [*A publication*] (DLA) .... Thomp Prov Rem
Thompson's Reports [*39, 40 California*] [*A publication*] (DLA) .... Thomp Cal
Thompson's Reports [*39, 40 California*] [*A publication*] (DLA) .... Thompson
Thompson's Tennessee Cases [*A publication*] (DLA) .... Thomps Cas
Thompson's Unreported Cases (Pennsylvania) [*A publication*] (DLA) .... Thompson Unrep (PA)
Thompson's Unreported Tennessee Cases [*A publication*] (DLA) .... Ten Cas
Thompson's Unreported Tennessee Cases [*1847-69*] [*A publication*] (DLA) .... Tenn Cas (Shannon)
Thompson's Unreported Tennessee Cases [*A publication*] (DLA) .... Thomp Tenn Cas
Thoms' Judicial Factors [*A publication*] (DLA) .... Thoms Jud Fac
Thoms Rehabilitation Hospital, Medical Library, Asheville, NC [*Library symbol*] [*Library of Congress*] (LCLS) .... NcATH
Thomson & Rogers, Barristers and Solicitors, Toronto, ON, Canada [*Library symbol Library of Congress*] (LCLS) .... CaOTTR
Thomson and Steger's Tennessee Statutes [*A publication*] (ILCA) .... T & S
Thomson Book/Reference Group [*The Thomson Corp.*] [*Publishing*] .... TBRG
Thomson Business Information [*The Thomson Corp.*] [*Publishing*] .... TBI
Thomson CEA Industries [*France*] (ECON) .... TCI
Thomson Corp. [*TS symbol*] (TTSB) .... TOC
[*The*] **Thomson Corp.** .... TTC
Thomson CSF SA [*Associated Press*] (SAG) .... Thmsn
Thomson Financial Services [*The Thomson Corp.*] [*Publishing*] .... TFS
Thomson, GA [*Location identifier FAA*] (FAAL) .... THG
Thomson, GA [*FM radio station call letters*] .... WTHO
Thomson, GA [*AM radio station call letters*] .... WTWA
Thomson Gold Co. [*Vancouver Stock Exchange symbol*] .... TGV
Thomson Information/Publishing Group [*The Thomson Corp.*] .... TIPG
Thomson Information Services Ltd. [*The Thomson Corp.*] [*Publishing*] .... TISL
Thomson Newspapers Ltd. [*Toronto Stock Exchange symbol*] .... THM
Thomson on Bills and Notes [*A publication*] (DLA) .... Thom B & N
Thomson on Bills and Notes [*A publication*] (DLA) .... Thom Bills
Thomson Press (India) Ltd. [*Publisher*] .... TP
Thomson Professional Publishing [*The Thomson Corp.*] .... TPP
Thomson Regional Newspapers [*The Thomson Corp.*] [*Publishing*] .... TRN
Thomson, Rogers, Barristers & Solicitors, Toronto, Ontario [*Library symbol National Library of Canada*] (NLC) .... OTTR
Thomson T-Line [*Commercial firm British*] .... TTL
Thomson-CSF [*France NASDAQ symbol*] .... TCSF
Thomson-CSF ADS [*NASDAQ symbol*] (TTSB) .... TCSFY
Thomsonite [*A zeolite*] .... THO
Thomson's Loss-Making Consumer-Electronics [*France*] (ECON) .... TCE
Thomson's Nova Scotia Reports [*A publication*] (DLA) .... NSR Thom
Thomson's Nova Scotia Reports [*A publication*] (DLA) .... Thom
Thomson's Nova Scotia Reports [*1834-52*] [*A publication*] (DLA) .... Thom Dec
Thomson's Nova Scotia Reports [*1834-51, 1856-59*] [*Canada*] [*A publication*] (DLA) .... Thom N Sc
Thomson's Nova Scotia Reports [*A publication*] (DLA) .... Thom Rep
Thomson's Nova Scotia Select Decisions [*A publication*] (DLA) .... Thom Sel Dec
Thomson's Scotch Acts [*A publication*] (DLA) .... Thom Sc Acts
Thor Explorations [*Vancouver Stock Exchange symbol*] .... THX
Thor Industries [*NYSE symbol*] (TTSB) .... THO
Thor Industries, Inc. [*NYSE symbol*] (SPSG) .... THO
Thor Industries, Inc. [*Associated Press*] (SAG) .... ThorInd
Thoracentesis [*Fluid*] [*Medicine*] (DAVI) .... THOR
Thoraci [*To the Throat*] [*Pharmacy*] .... THORAC
Thoracic [*Anatomy*] .... T
Thoracic [*Anatomy*] (MAE) .... th
Thoracic Aorta [*Medicine*] .... ThA
Thoracic Aortic Aneurysm [*Cardiology*] .... TAA
Thoracic Asphyxiant Dystrophy [*Medicine*] (MAE) .... TAD
Thoracic Cage [*Medicine*] .... TC
Thoracic Cage Volume [*Medicine*] .... TCV
Thoracic Duct [*Anatomy*] .... TD
Thoracic Duct Drainage [*Medicine*] .... TDD
Thoracic Duct Fistula [*Medicine*] (MAE) .... TDF
Thoracic Duct Flow [*Medicine*] (MAE) .... TDF
Thoracic Duct Lining Cells Antigen [*Immunology*] .... TDLCA
Thoracic Duct Lymphocyte [*Immunochemistry*] .... TDL
Thoracic Duct Pressure [*Medicine*] (MAE) .... TDP
Thoracic Ganglion [*Neuroanatomy*] .... TG
Thoracic Gas Volume [*Medicine*] (AAMN) .... TGV
Thoracic Index [*Medicine*] (MAE) .... TI
Thoracic Inferior Vena Cava [*Medicine*] (MAE) .... TIVC
Thoracic Lymph Duct [*Medicine*] (MAE) .... TLD
Thoracic Outlet Syndrome [*Medicine*] .... TOS
Thoracic Surgery [*Medicine*] .... TH
Thoracic Surgery [*Medicine*] .... TS
Thoracic Trauma Index [*Automotive safety research*] .... TTI
Thoracic Vena Cava [*Medicine*] .... TVC
Thoracic Vertebra [*Medicine*] .... THV
Thoracoabdominal Aortic Aneurysm [*Cardiology*] .... TAAA
Thoracoabdominal Stapler [*Surgery*] (DAVI) .... TA
Thoracolumbosacral [*Drain*] [*Surgery*] (DAVI) .... TLS
Thoracolumbosacral Orthosis [*Medicine*] .... TLSO
Thor-Agena D [*Rocket*] [*NASA*] .... THORAD
Thor-Agena Vibration Experiment [*NASA*] .... TAVE
Thorah Eldon Historical Society, Inc., Beaverton, ON, Canada [*Library symbol Library of Congress*] (LCLS) .... CaOBeaTE
Thoratec Labs Corp. [*NASDAQ symbol*] (SAG) .... THOR
Thoratec Labs Corp. [*Associated Press*] (SAG) .... Thoratc
Thorax [*Anatomy*] (MAE) .... T
Thorax [*Anatomy*] (DAVI) .... Th
Thorax [*Anatomy*] (DAVI) .... Thor
Thorborn on Bankers' Law [*A publication*] (DLA) .... Thor Bank
Thorcheron Hunter Association [*Defunct*] (EA) .... THA
Thorco Resources, Inc. [*Toronto Stock Exchange symbol*] .... THO
Thor-Delta [*Satellite*] .... TD
Thoreau Fellowship (EA) .... TF
Thoreau Lyceum (EA) .... TL
Thoreau, NM [*FM radio station call letters*] .... KXTC
Thoreau Society (EA) .... TS
Thorhild Municipal Library, Alberta [*Library symbol National Library of Canada*] (NLC) .... ATHOM
Thorhild Municipal Library, Thorhild, AB, Canada [*Library symbol*] [*Library of Congress*] (LCLS) .... CaAThoM
Thoria Dispersed [*Nickel*] .... TD
Thoriated-Tungsten Filament (SAA) .... TTF
Thorington's Reports [*107 Alabama*] [*A publication*] (DLA) .... Thor
Thorium [*Chemical element*] .... Th
Thorium Dioxide (DAVI) .... ThO_2
Thorium Extraction (GAAI) .... THOREX
Thorium High Temperature Reactor Association (IAA) .... THTRA
Thorium High-Temperature Reactor [*Nuclear energy*] .... THTR
Thorium High-Temperature Reactor Association .... THIRA
Thorium, Uranium, Deuterium .... THUD
Thorium-Uranium Fuel Cycle Development Facility [*Nuclear energy*] .... TUFCDF
Thorium-Uranium Recycle Facility [*Oak Ridge National Laboratory*] .... TURF
Thorn Apple Valley [*NASDAQ symbol*] (TTSB) .... TAVI
Thorn Apple Valley, Inc. [*Southfield, MI*] [*NASDAQ symbol*] (NQ) .... TAVI
Thorn Apple Valley, Inc. [*Associated Press*] (SAG) .... ThrnAV
Thorn Color [*Botany*] .... THCOL
Thorn Curvature [*Botany*] .... THCUR
Thorn Length [*Botany*] .... THLEN
Thorn Security and Electronics [*A division of Thorn EMI Corp.*] (ECON) .... TSE
Thornburg Mortgage Asset [*NYSE symbol*] (TTSB) .... TMA
Thornburg Mortgage Asset Corp. [*Associated Press*] (SAG) .... Thornbg
Thornburg Mortgage Asset Corp. [*NYSE symbol*] (SPSG) .... TMA
Thornbury [*England*] .... THORNB
Thornbury Public Library, Ontario [*Library symbol National Library of Canada*] (NLC) .... OTHO
Thornbury Public Library, Thronbury, ON, Canada [*Library symbol*] [*Library of Congress*] (LCLS) .... CaOTHO
Thorndike Dimensions of Temperament [*Psychology*] .... TDOT
Thorne Ecological Institute (EA) .... TEI
Thorne River, AK [*Location identifier FAA*] (FAAL) .... KTB
Thorne-Zytkow Object [*Astronomy*] .... TZO
Thornhill Public Library, Ontario [*Library symbol National Library of Canada*] (NLC) .... OTHOR
Thornhill Public Library, Thornhill, ON, Canada [*Library symbol Library of Congress*] (LCLS) .... CaOThor
Thornicroft's Mounted Infantry [*Military British*] (ROG) .... TMI
Thornton Academy, Saco, ME [*Library symbol Library of Congress*] (LCLS) .... MeSacoT
Thornton and Blackledge's Law Relating to Building and Loan Associations [*A publication*] (DLA) .... Thornt & Bl Bldg & Loan Ass'ns
Thornton Aviation Fuel Lubricity Evaluator [*Fuels and lubricants testing*] .... TAFLE
Thornton, CO [*AM radio station call letters*] .... KTLK
Thornton Community College, South Holland, IL [*Library symbol Library of Congress*] (LCLS) .... IShoT
Thornton Junior College [*Illinois*] .... TJC
Thornton on Gifts and Advancements [*A publication*] (DLA) .... Thornton Gifts
Thornton Pacific Investment Fund .... TPIF
Thornton Public Library, Thornton, IL [*Library symbol Library of Congress*] (LCLS) .... ITh
Thornton's Conveyancing [*A publication*] (DLA) .... Thorn Conv
Thornton's Notes of Ecclesiastical and Maritime Cases [*1841-50*] [*A publication*] (DLA) .... Thorn
Thorntown Public Library, Thorntown, IN [*Library symbol Library of Congress*] (LCLS) .... InTho
Thornwell Orphanage, Clinton, SC [*Library symbol Library of Congress*] (LCLS) .... ScClTO
Thorold Public Library, Ontario [*Library symbol National Library of Canada*] (BIB) .... OTHORO
Thorotrast-Associated Angiosarcoma [*Oncology*] .... TAAS
Thorotrast-Associated Cholangiocarcinoma [*Oncology*] .... TACC
Thoroughbred .... TB
Thoroughbred (WGA) .... TH

Thoroughbred Breeders' Association [*British*] (BI) ... TBA
Thoroughbred Club of America (EA) ... TCA
Thoroughbred Half-Bred Registry (EA) ... THBR
Thoroughbred Owners and Breeders Association (EA) ... TOBA
Thoroughbred Racehorse Owners' Association [*Australia*] ... TROA
Thoroughbred Racing Associations (EA) ... TRA
Thoroughbred Racing Communications [*An association*] (EA) ... TRC
Thoroughbred Racing Protective Bureau (EA) ... TRPB
Thoroughfare [*Maps and charts*] ... Thoro
Thorpe's Ancient Laws of England [*A publication*] (DLA) ... Thorpe Anc L
Thorpe's Annual Reports [*52 Louisiana*] [*A publication*] (DLA) ... Thorpe
Thorsby Municipal Library, Alberta [*Library symbol National Library of Canada*] (NLC) ... ATM
Thorsen Memorial Public Library, Elbow Lake, MN [*Library symbol*] [*Library of Congress*] (LCLS) ... MnElb
Thorshofn [*Iceland*] [*ICAO location identifier*] (ICLI) ... BITH
Thorshofn [*Iceland*] [*Airport symbol*] (OAG) ... THO
Thorvald Hansen [*Steamship*] (MHDW) ... TH
Those Hags Encourage Neuterism [*Organization opposed to NOW (National Organization for Women)*] ... THEN
Thouars [*France ICAO location identifier*] (ICLI) ... LFCT
Though ... THO
Thought ... THOT
Thought Organizer [*Computer program produced by Fastware, Inc.*] ... THOR
Thought Quality [*Psychology*] ... TQ
Thousand (ADA) ... K
Thousand ... /M
Thousand (AFM) ... THOU
Thousand (NASA) ... THOUS
Thousand Acre-Feet [*Measurement*] ... TAF
Thousand Astronomical Units ... TAU
Thousand Barrels (EG) ... MBBL
Thousand Barrels per Day [*Also, TBD*] ... KBD
Thousand Barrels per Day [*Also, KBD*] ... TBD
Thousand Board Feet [*Lumber*] ... MBF
Thousand Characters per Second ... KCS
Thousand Circular Mils ... MCM
Thousand Cubic Feet ... KCF
Thousand Cubic Feet ... MCF
Thousand Cubic Feet per Day ... MCFD
Thousand Cubic Feet per Hour ... MCFH
Thousand Feet Board Measure [*Lumber*] (GPO) ... MBM
Thousand Feet Board Measure [*Lumber*] ... MFBM
Thousand Feet Surface Measure [*Lumber*] ... MSM
Thousand Foot-Pounds ... KIP-FT
Thousand Gallons (EG) ... MGAL
Thousand Kilograms (EG) ... KKG
Thousand Metric Tons (IMH) ... TMT
Thousand Oaks, CA [*AM radio station call letters*] (RBYB) ... KAHS
Thousand Oaks, CA [*FM radio station call letters*] ... KCLU
Thousand Oaks, CA [*FM radio station call letters*] ... KCPB
Thousand Oaks, CA [*FM radio station call letters*] ... KNJO
Thousand Palms, CA [*FM radio station call letters*] ... KLOB
Thousand Palms, CA [*AM radio station call letters*] ... KNWZ
Thousand Palms, CA [*AM radio station call letters*] ... KPSL
Thousand Pieces (EG) ... MPC
Thousand Pounds ... KIP
Thousand Standard Bushels (EG) ... MSBu
Thousand Standard Cubic Feet ... KSCF
Thousands (10^3) of Characters (NITA) ... M chs
Thousands of Amperes ... KA
Thousands of Barrels (MCD) ... MBBLS
Thousands of BTU per Hour ... MBH
Thousands of Delivered Machine Instructions [*Computer science*] ... KDMI
Thousands of Delivered Source Instructions [*Computer science*] ... KDSI
Thousands of Delivered Source Lines of Code [*Computer science*] ... KDSL
Thousands of Instructions Per Second (NITA) ... TIPS
Thousands of Operations per Second (NASA) ... KOPS
Thousands Position (IAA) ... THP
THQ, Inc. [*Associated Press*] (SAG) ... THQ
THQ, Inc. [*NASDAQ symbol*] (SAG) ... TOYH
T-HQ Inc. [*NASDAQ symbol*] (TTSB) ... TOYH
Thrace Requirements Analysis [*Military*] ... TRA
Thrall Library, Middletown, NY [*Library symbol Library of Congress*] (LCLS) ... NMi
Thread ... T
Thread (AAG) ... THD
Thread ... THD
Thread ... thrd
Thread (VRA) ... THRD
Thread ... TRD
Thread (AAG) ... TRD
Thread Both Ends (MSA) ... TBE
Thread Cutting (MSA) ... TC
Thread Die ... THDI
Thread Forming (MSA) ... TF
Thread Gauge ... THGA
Thread Identifier [*Computer science*] ... TID
Thread Institute [*Defunct*] (EA) ... TI
Thread Mate System [*Dentistry*] ... TMS
Thread One End (MSA) ... TOE
Thread Tap ... THTA
Threaded Blind Insert ... TBI
Threaded Neck ... THDNK
Threaded Nut Connector (IAA) ... TNC
Threaded Rod ... TR
Threaded Stud ... TS
Threaded-Neill-Concelman (DOM) ... TNC
Threaded-Nut Coupling [*Electronics*] (EECA) ... TNC
Threading Tool (AAG) ... THTO
Threadpiece ... THDPC
Threads No Couplings ... TNOC
Threads per Inch ... TPI
Threat ... TH
Threat [*or Threatening*] [*FBI standardized term*] ... THRT
Threat Alert Collision Avoidance System ... T/CAS
Threat Analysis (MCD) ... TA
Threat Artillery Preparation Against Thermal Sights (MCD) ... TAPATS
Threat Assessment and Control Receiver [*Air Force*] ... TACOR
Threat Avoidance Receiver (MCD) ... TAR
Threat Axis [*Military*] (NVT) ... TA
Threat Coordinating Group [*DoD*] ... TCG
Threat Detection RADAR [*Military*] (CAAL) ... TDR
Threat Determination (MCD) ... TD
Threat Determination and Resource Allocation ... TD & RA
Threat Determination and Resource Allocation (MCD) ... TDARA
Threat Display Control Unit (MCD) ... TDCU
Threat Display Unit (MCD) ... TDU
Threat Evaluation (NVT) ... TE
Threat Evaluation and Action Selection [*Civilian defense program*] ... TEAS
Threat Evaluation and Weapon Selection [*Military*] (CAAL) ... TEWS
Threat Evaluation and Weapons Assignment (NVT) ... TEWA
Threat Evaluation Equipment Zone of Interior (SAA) ... TEEZI
Threat Integrated Staff Officer [*Army*] ... TISO
Threat Orientation Protection Posture [*Military equipment*] ... TOPP
Threat Platform Simulator [*Military*] (CAAL) ... TPS
Threat Reaction [*Military*] (CAAL) ... TR
Threat Reaction System ... TRS
Threat Reaction Upgrade Modernization (MCD) ... TRUMP
Threat Reactive Integrated Combat System ... TRICS
Threat Recognition Processor [*Navy*] (MCD) ... TRP
Threat Recognizer Programmer ... TRP
Threat Responsive Weapon Control [*Military*] (CAAL) ... TRWC
Threat Simulation System Terminal [*Military*] ... TSST
Threat Simulator Project Office [*Army Intelligence Agency*] (RDA) ... TSPO
Threat Summary Message (MCD) ... THRSUM
Threat Support Package [*DoD*] ... TSP
Threat Support Plan (MCD) ... TSP
Threat to Army Mission Areas ... TAMA
Threat Warning Information [*Air Force*] ... TWI
Threat Warning Information Display System (MCD) ... TWIDS
Threat Warning RADAR ... TWR
Threat Warning Receiver ... TWR
Threatened Myocardial Infarction [*Cardiology*] (MEDA) ... TMI
Threatened Plants Unit (EERA) ... TPU
Threatened Species Strategy (EERA) ... TSS
Three Axis Rotational Flight Simulator [*Military*] (RDA) ... TARFS
Three CI Complete Compliance Corp. [*Associated Press*] (SAG) ... 3 CI
Three CI Complete Compliance Corp. [*NASDAQ symbol*] (SAG) ... TCCC
Three Com Corp. [*Associated Press*] (SAG) ... 3Com
Three Com Corp. [*NASDAQ symbol*] (SAG) ... COMS
Three Concept View [*Medicine*] (DMAA) ... TCV
Three Counties Agricultural Society [*British*] ... TCAS
Three D Departments, Inc. [*AMEX symbol*] (SPSG) ... TDD
Three D Departments, Inc. [*Associated Press*] (SAG) ... ThrD
Three D Depts Cv Cl'B' [*AMEX symbol*] (TTSB) ... TDD.B
Three D Geophysical, Inc. [*Associated Press*] (SAG) ... 3DGeo
Three D Geophysical, Inc. [*NASDAQ symbol*] (SAG) ... TDGO
Three D Systems [*NASDAQ symbol*] (SAG) ... TDSC
Three D Systems, Inc. [*Associated Press*] (SAG) ... 3D Sys
Three Day Event [*Horseriding*] [*British*] (DI) ... TDE
Three Depts Cl'A' [*AMEX symbol*] (TTSB) ... TDDA
Three Dimensional [*Also, 3D*] (DAVI) ... DDD
Three Do Co. [*Associated Press*] (SAG) ... 3DO Co
Three Do Co. [*NASDAQ symbol*] (SAG) ... THDO
Three Factor Contribution Method [*Insurance*] ... TFCM
Three Five Systems Co. [*NYSE symbol*] (SAG) ... TFS
Three Five Systems Co. [*Associated Press*] (SAG) ... ThreeFS
Three Hills Municipal Library, Alberta [*Library symbol National Library of Canada*] (NLC) ... ATHM
Three Hills Municipal Library, Three Hills, AB, Canada [*Library symbol Library of Congress*] (LCLS) ... CaAThM
Three Hundred Mile Zone ... THMZ
Three Lakes, WI [*FM radio station call letters*] ... WHTD
Three Letter Acronym ... TLA
Three M (3M) Co., Business Information Service, St. Paul, MN [*Library symbol*] [*Library of Congress*] (LCLS) ... MnSTM-B
Three M (3M) Co., Engineering Information Services, St. Paul, MN [*Library symbol Library of Congress*] (LCLS) ... MnSTM-E
Three M (3M) Co., Health Care Library, St. Paul, MN [*Library symbol*] [*Library of Congress*] (LCLS) ... MnSTM-H
Three M (3M) Co., St. Paul, MN [*Library symbol*] [*Library of Congress*] (LCLS) ... MnSTM
Three M (3M) Co., St. Paul, MN [*Library symbol*] [*Library of Congress*] (LCLS) ... MnSTM-A
Three M (3M) Co., St. Paul, MN [*Library symbol*] [*Library of Congress*] (LCLS) ... MnSTM-G
Three M (3M) Co., St. Paul, MN [*Library symbol*] [*Library of Congress*] (LCLS) ... MnSTM-M
Three M (3M) Co., St. Paul, MN [*Library symbol*] [*Library of Congress*] (LCLS) ... MnSTM-P

Three M (3M) Co., St. Paul, MN [*Library symbol*] [*Library of Congress*] (LCLS) .... MnSTM-T
Three M Canada, Inc., Technical Information Centre, London, ON, Canada [*Library symbol Library of Congress*] (LCLS) .... CaOLTMC
Three Mile Island [*Pennsylvania*] [*Site of nuclear reactor accident, 1979*] .... TMI
Three Mile Island Alert (EA) .... TMIA
Three Mile Island Nuclear Station (NRCH) .... TMINS
Three R Microfilm Service, Record Retention & Retrieval Corp., Lynbrook, NY [*Library symbol*] [*Library of Congress*] (LCLS) .... TrM
Three Rivers Community College, Poplar Bluff, MO [*Library symbol Library of Congress*] (LCLS) .... MoPobT
Three Rivers Financial Corp. [*AMEX symbol*] (SAG) .... THR
Three Rivers Financial Corp. [*Associated Press*] (SAG) .... ThrRvF
Three Rivers Finl [*AMEX symbol*] (TTSB) .... THR
Three Rivers, MI [*Location identifier FAA*] (FAAL) .... HAI
Three Rivers, MI [*AM radio station call letters*] .... WLKM
Three Rivers, MI [*FM radio station call letters*] .... WLKM-FM
Three Rivers Public Library, Three Rivers, MI [*Library symbol Library of Congress*] (LCLS) .... MiThr
Three Rivers, TX [*Location identifier FAA*] (FAAL) .... THX
Three Sigma Market Newspaper Audiences [*Three Sigma Research Center, Inc.*] [*Information service or system*] (CRD) .... SIG
Three Stooges Club (EA) .... TS
Three Times [*Pharmacy*] (DAVI) .... TER
Three Times a Week [*Pharmacology*] .... tiw
Three Ton Range and Azimuth Only (IAA) .... TRZON
Three (TRI) Dimensional Error Correcting Code (NITA) .... TRIDECC
Three Year Plan [*From George Orwell's novel, "1984"*] 3YP
Three-Acetylpiridine [*Biochemistry*] (DAVI) 3-AP
Three-Astronaut Space System Experimental Laboratory (MCD) .... TASSEL
Three-Axis (IAA) .... TRAX
Three-Axis Accelerometer .... TAA
Three-Axis Antenna Positioner .... TAAP
Three-Axis Attitude Sensor (IEEE) .... TAAS
Three-Axis Manual Attitude Controller .... TAMAC
Three-Axis Package .... TAP
Three-Axis Reference System [*Used in reference to Titan missile*] .... TARS
Three-Axis Reference System Checkout Console [*Used in reference to Titan missile*] .... TARSCC
Three-Axis Rotational Control-Direct (SAA) .... TRD
Three-Axis Rotational Control-Normal (SAA) .... TRN
Three-Axis Rout Byro Inertial Tracker (IAA) .... TARBIT
Three-Axis Stabilization (AAG) .... TAS
Three-Base Hit [*Baseball*] 3B
Three-Base Hit [*Baseball*] 3BH
Three-Channel Decoder .... TCD
Three-Conductor [*Wire or cable*] 3/C
Three-Conductor Cables [*JETDS nomenclature*] [*Military*] (CET) .... WT
Three-Conductor, Heat and Flame Resistant, Armor Cable .... THFA
Three-Conductor, Heat and Flame Resistant, Radio Cable .... THFR
Three-Conductor, Shipboard, General Use, Armor Cable .... TSGA
ThreeD Labs, Inc. Ltd. [*Associated Press*] (SAG) .... 3D Labs
ThreeD Labs, Inc. Ltd. [*NASDAQ symbol*] (SAG) .... TDDD
Three-Dimensional [*Pictures or films*] 3-D
Three-Dimensional Analog Computer [*British*] (MCD) .... TRIDAC
Three-Dimensional Antenna Pattern Analyzer [*Air Force*] .... TAPA
Three-Dimensional Direction Finding [*Navigation systems*] 3DF
Three-Dimensional Electron Gas [*Physics*] 3DEG
Three-Dimensional Geometry File [*Computer science*] (DOM) 3-DGF
Three-Dimensional Laminate 3DL
Three-Dimensional OPFOR [*Opposing Force*] **Plastic Individual Target** [*Army*] (INF) .... TOPI
Three-Dimensional Optics [*Multimedia electronics corporation*] (ECON) 3DO
Three-Dimensional Reconstruction and Display (MHDB) .... THREAD
ThreeDX Technologies, Inc. [*Associated Press*] (SAG) .... 3DX Tch
ThreeDX Technologies, Inc. [*NASDAQ symbol*] (SAG) .... TDXT
Three-Five Systems [*NYSE symbol*] (TTSB) .... TFS
Threefold (DAVI) .... TER
Three-Letter Acronym [*Computer hacker terminology*] (NHD) .... TLA
Three-Mile Limit .... TML
Three-Mirror X-Ray Telescope [*NASA*] .... TMXRT
Three-Mode Control (AAG) .... TMC
Three-Party Service [*Telecommunications*] (DOM) 3PTY
Threepenny Review [*A publication*] (BRI) .... TPR
Three-Phase 3PH
Three-Phase Aquatic Microcosms [*Technique for study of waters*] .... TPAM
Three-Phase Full Wave .... TPFW
Three-Phase Half Wave .... TPHW
Three-Phase Modulation Modified [*Telecommunications*] (OSI) 3PMM
Three-Phase Radionuclide Bone Scanning [*Radiology*] (DAVI) .... TPBS
Three-Phase Star Connection [*Symbol*] (DEN) .... Y
Three-Pole [*or Triple Pole*] [*Switch*] 3P
Three-Pulse Image Photon Echo [*Spectroscopy*] 3PIE
Three-Pulse Stimulated Photon Echo [*Spectroscopy*] 3PSE
Three-Quarter Midget [*Horse racing*] .... TQ
Three-Quarter Size [*Car racing*] .... TQ
Three-Stage Least Squares [*Econometrics*] .... THS
Three-State [*Computer science*] (IAA) .... TS
Three-State Control [*Computer science*] .... TSC
Three-State Logic [*Computer science*] (IAA) .... TSL
Three-State Transceiver [*Computer science*] (IAA) .... TTS
Three-Way Catalyst [*Vehicle exhaust control*] .... TWC
Three-Way Valve [*Hydraulics*] .... TWV
Three-Wheeler [*Type of motorcycle*] .... T-W
Three-Wire (MSA) 3W
Threni (BJA) .... Thr
Threonine [*One-letter symbol; see Thr*] [*An amino acid*] .... T
Threonine [*Also, T*] [*An amino acid*] .... Thr
Threonine [*An amino acid*] (DOG) .... thr
Threshold (WGA) .... TH
Threshold .... THLD
Threshold (NASA) .... THOLD
Threshold .... THR
Threshold (IAA) .... THRES
Threshold by Identification of Pictures (DAVI) .... TIP
Threshold Circuit [*Telecommunications*] (OA) .... TC
Threshold Control Unit (CET) .... TCU
Threshold Crossing Height [*Aviation*] (FAAC) .... TCH
Threshold Crossing Height [*FAA*] (TAG) .... TCH
Threshold Crossing Height Downwind [*Aviation*] (FAAC) .... TCHD
Threshold Crossing Height Upwind [*Aviation*] (FAAC) .... TCHU
Threshold Damage Level .... TDL
Threshold Decoding [*Computer science*] (IAA) .... TD
Threshold Detection .... TD
Threshold Detection Level .... TDL
Threshold Dose [*Medicine*] .... TD
Threshold Electron Secondary Ion Coincidence [*Spectroscopy*] .... TESICO
Threshold Element (IAA) .... TE
Threshold Energy [*Medicine*] (MAE) .... TE
Threshold Erythema Dose [*Medicine*] .... TED
Threshold Exceeded .... TE
Threshold Extension Demodulator .... TED
Threshold Factor (OA) .... TF
Threshold Failure Temperatures .... TFT
Threshold Function (IAA) .... TF
Threshold Ignition Energy (MCD) .... TIE
Threshold Lactose Load [*Clinical chemistry*] .... TLL
Threshold Learning Process (IEEE) .... TLP
Threshold Lighting [*Aviation*] (DA) .... T
Threshold Lights [*Aviation*] (DA) .... Thr
Threshold Limit Value [*Industrial hygiene*] .... TLV
Threshold Limit Value - Ceiling [*Industrial hygiene*] (PDAA) .... TLV-C
Threshold Limit Value - Short Term Exposure Limit [*Industrial hygiene*] (PDAA) .... TLV-STEL
Threshold Limit Value - Time-Weighted Average [*Industrial hygiene*] (PDAA) .... TLV-TWA
Threshold Logic Unit .... TLU
Threshold Management Center [*Environmental Protection Agency*] (GFGA) .... TMC
Threshold Odor Number [*Water analysis*] .... TON
Threshold of Discomfort [*Medicine*] (MAE) .... TD
Threshold of Odor (NASA) .... TOO
Threshold of Regulation [*FDA*] .... TOR
Threshold Photoelectron [*Spectroscopy*] .... TPE
Threshold Photoelectron Spectroscopy [*Physics*] .... TPES
Threshold Planning Quantity (ERG) .... TPQ
Threshold Planning Quantity [*Hazardous substances*] .... TPQ
Threshold Potential (MAE) .... TP
Threshold Quality Factor .... TQF
Threshold Setting Tracer .... TST
Threshold Signal-to-Interference Ratio (IEEE) .... TSI
Threshold Soot Index .... TSI
Threshold Test Ban Treaty [*1974*] .... TTBT
Threshold Value (NITA) .... TV
Threshold Voltage Generator .... TVG
Thrift .... THRFT
Thrift & Loans [*Industrial loan company*] .... T & L
Thrift Depositor Protection Oversight Board (BARN) .... TDPOB
Thrift Industry Recovery Act [*1987*] .... TIRA
Thrift Institutions Restructuring Act [*1982*] .... TIRA
Thrift Savings Plan [*Office of Personnel Management*] (GFGA) .... TSP
Thrifty .... THRFTY
Thrifty Payless Hldg'B' [*NYSE symbol*] (TTSB) .... TPD
Thrill [*Cardiology*] (DAVI) .... T
Thrill [*Cardiology*] (DAVI) .... TH
Thring on Joint Stock Companies [*5th ed.*] [*1889*] [*A publication*] (DLA) .... Thring J St Com
Thring on the Land Drainage Act [*1862*] [*A publication*] (DLA) .... Thring LD
Thriplow [*England*] .... THRIP
Throat .... THRT
Throat Culture [*Clinical chemistry*] .... TC
Throat Culture [*Medicine*] (DAVI) .... TH-CULT
Throgmorton Secured Growth Trust [*Commercial firm British*] .... TSGT
Thrombin Clotting Time [*Clinical chemistry*] .... TCT
Thrombin Control [*Hematology*] (DAVI) .... THR-CT
Thrombin Receptor Activating Peptide [*Biochemistry*] .... TRAP
Thrombin Time [*Hematology*] .... TT
Thrombin Time Tritium [*Hematology*] (DAVI) .... THROMB
Thromboangitis Obliterans [*Cardiology*] .... TAO
Thrombocytopenia with Absent Radii [*Medicine*] .... TAR
Thrombocytopenic Purpura [*Medicine*] .... TP
Thromboelastogram [*or Thromboelastograph*] [*Medicine*] .... TEG
Thromboembolic [*Medicine*] .... TE
Thromboembolic Cerebrovascular Accident [*Cardiology*] (DAVI) .... TCVA
Thromboembolic Disease [*Medicine*] .... TED
Thromboembolic Disease Stockings [*Cardiology*] (DAVI) .... TEDS
Thromboembolic Pulmonary Hypertension [*Medicine*] (CPH) .... TEPH
Thromboembolic Pulmonary Hypertension [*Medicine*] .... TPH
Thromboembolus Deterrant Stocking (MEDA) .... TEDS
Thromboendarterectomy [*Medicine*] (DMAA) .... TEA
Thromboendophlebectomy [*Medicine*] (MAE) .... TEP

Thromboglobulin [*Clinical chemistry*] ... TG
Thromboloysis and Angioplasty in Myocardial Infarction [*Cardiology study*] ... TAMI
Thrombolysis Early in Acute Heart Attack Trial [*Cardiology study*] ... TEAHAT
Thrombolysis in Myocardial Infarction (Study) [*Medicine*] ... TIMI
Thrombophlebitis [*Medicine*] (DAVI) ... thrombo
Thrombophlebitis [*Medicine*] ... TP
Thromboplastic Activity of Amniotic Fluid [*Medicine*] ... TAAF
Thromboplastic Cell Component [*Hematology*] ... TCC
Thromboplastic Plasma Component [*Factor VIII*] [*Also, AHF, AHG, PTF Hematology*] ... TPC
Thromboplastin Activation Test [*Clinical chemistry*] ... TAT
Thromboplastin Activation Time [*Clinical chemistry*] (DAVI) ... TAT
Thromboplastin Generation Test [*Hematology*] ... TGT
Thromboplastin Generation Time [*Hematology*] (MAE) ... TGT
Thrombopoietic Stimulating Factor [*Medicine*] ... TSF
Thrombopoietin [*Hematology*] ... TPO
Thrombosis (AAMN) ... THROM
Thrombosis (CPH) ... thromb
Thrombosis [*Medicine*] (BARN) ... thrombo
Thrombosis Research Center [*Temple University*] [*Research center*] (RCD) ... TRC
Thrombospondin [*or Thrombin-Sensitive Protein*] [*Hematology*] ... TSP
Thrombospondin-Related Anonymous Protein [*Biochemistry*] ... TRAP
Thrombotic Microangiopathy [*Nephrology*] ... TMA
Thrombotic Thrombocytopenic Purpura [*Medicine*] ... TTP
Thromboxane [*Also, TA, Tx, TX*] [*Biochemistry*] ... T
Thromboxane [*Also, T, Tx, TX*] [*Biochemistry*] ... TA
Thromboxane [*Also, T, TA, Tx*] [*Biochemistry*] ... TX
Thromboxane A [*Also, TxA, TXA*] [*Biochemistry*] ... TA
Thromboxane A [*Also, TA, TxA*] [*Biochemistry*] ... TXA
Thromboxane B [*Also, TxB, TXB*] [*Biochemistry*] ... TB
Thromboxane B [*Also, TB, TxB*] [*Biochemistry*] ... TXB
Thromboxane B_2 [*Hematology*] (DAVI) ... TBX_2
Thrombus-Free Surface [*Hematology*] ... TFS
Throop on the Validity of Verbal Agreements [*A publication*] (DLA) ... Thr Verb Agr
Throop's Treatise on Public Officers [*A publication*] (DLA) ... Throop Pub Off
Throttle (AAG) ... THROT
Throttle Body [*Automotive engineering*] ... TB
Throttle Body Fuel Injection [*Fuel systems*] [*Automotive engineering*] ... TBFI
Throttle Body Fuel Injection [*Automotive engineering*] ... TBI
Throttle Command (NASA) ... T
Throttle Control [*Automotive engineering*] ... T/CONT
Throttle Control Valve ... TCV
Throttle Governor Control ... TGC
Throttle Hold (GAVI) ... THR HOLD
Throttle Kicker Actuator [*Automotive engineering*] ... TKA
Throttle Kicker Solenoid [*Automotive engineering*] ... TKS
Throttle Lever Angle (MCD) ... TLA
Throttle Lever Setting (KSC) ... TLS
Throttle Position Sensor [*Automotive engineering*] ... TPS
Throttle Positioner [*Automotive engineering*] ... TP
Throttle Potentiometer [*Automotive engineering*] ... TP
Throttle Reset ... TRST
Throttle Resolver Angle (MCD) ... TRA
Throttle Solenoid Positioner [*Automotive engineering*] ... TSP
Throttle Valve ... TV
Throttle Valve Control ... TVC
Throttle Valve Opening [*Automotive engineering*] ... TVO
Throttleable Solid Augmented Rocket (MCD) ... TSAR
Throttled Homogeneous Combustion ... THC
Throttling Expansion Valve [*Automotive air conditioning*] ... TXV
Through (ADA) ... THR
Through ... THRO
Through (AAG) ... THRU
Through Air Waybill [*Shipping*] (DS) ... TAWB
Through Axis Rotational Control [*Aerospace*] (MCD) ... TARC
Through Back of Loop [*Knitting*] ... TBL
Through Bill of Lading [*Shipping*] ... TBL
Through Bill of Lading [*Shipping*] ... ThroBL
Through Bolt (DAC) ... TB
Through Deck Cruisers [*British*] ... TDC
Through Flow Line ... TFL
Through Government Bill of Lading [*Military*] (AABC) ... TGBL
Through Group Filter [*Telecommunications*] (TEL) ... TGF
Through Hole Probe ... THP
Through Ice Bathymetry System (EERA) ... TIBS
Through Knee [*Medicine*] ... TK
Through Ownership [*Shipping*] ... TO
Through Plated Hole [*Printed circuit board feature*] (IAA) ... TPH
Through Supergroup Filter (IAA) ... TSF
Through the Hole Plating [*Electronics*] (EECA) ... THP
Through the Lens [*Trademark of Spiratone, Inc.*] ... TTL
Through the Skin (DAVI) ... TTS
Through-Axis Navigational Control ... TANC
Through-Bulkhead Initiator [*Military*] (MCD) ... TBI
Through-Camera-Lens ... TCL
Through-Connected Circuit [*Telecommunications*] (TEL) ... TCC
Through-Hole [*Computer science*] ... TH
Throughput ... THR
Throughput Efficiency (CAAL) ... TE
Throughput Rate ... THR
Throughput Time Average [*Compression algorithm*] (MCD) ... TTA
Throughput Transmitted Algorithm ... TTA
Throughput X-Cellerator [*Celeritas Technologies*] [*Cellular data transmission*] (PCM) ... TX-CEL
Through-Surface Hardening [*Metallurgy*] ... TSH
Through-the-Lens Light Metering (MCD) ... TTLM
Through-Transmission Ultrasound [*Materials testing*] (RDA) ... TTU
Through-Water Communications System [*Navy*] (CAAL) ... TWCS
Throughway [*Commonly used*] (OPSA) ... THROUGHWAY
Throughway [*Postal Service standard*] (OPSA) ... TRWY
Throughway ... TRWY
Throw Away ... TA
Throw Away Detector [*Space shuttle*] [*NASA*] ... TAD
Throw Away Detector (PDAA) ... TADS
Throw Away Maintenance ... TAM
Throw Away/Repair Implications on Maintenance ... TRIM
Throw the Hypocritical Rascals Out [*An association*] ... THRO
Thrower ... THWR
Throwout [*Mechanical engineering*] ... THWT
Throws Left-Handed [*Baseball*] ... TL
Throws Right-Handed [*Baseball*] ... TR
Thru-Axis Rotational Control ... TARC
Thru-Mode [*or Tri-Mode*] **Tape Converter** ... TMTC
Thrupp's Historical Law Tracts [*A publication*] (DLA) ... Thr Hist Tr
Thru-Sight Video [*Army training device*] (INF) ... TSV
Thrust (IAA) ... T
Thrust (AAG) ... THR
Thrust Augmented Long Tank Thor (MCD) ... TALTT
Thrust Chamber [*Air Force, NASA*] ... TC
Thrust Chamber Assembly [*Missile technology*] ... TCA
Thrust Chamber Fuel Purge (SAA) ... TCFP
Thrust Chamber Oxidizer Purge (SAA) ... TCOP
Thrust Chamber Pressure [*Aerospace*] (IEEE) ... TCP
Thrust Chamber Valve (MCD) ... TCV
Thrust Control Exploratory Development (KSC) ... TCED
Thrust Control Unit ... TCU
Thrust Control Valve ... TCV
Thrust Cutoff (NVT) ... TCO
Thrust Floated Gyroscope (PDAA) ... TFG
Thrust Hand Controller [*NASA*] (KSC) ... THC
Thrust Horsepower [*Jet engines*] ... THP
Thrust Inlet Pressure (MCD) ... TIP
Thrust Level (NASA) ... TL
Thrust Line ... TL
Thrust Magnitude Control (KSC) ... TMC
Thrust Management Computer (GAVI) ... TMC
Thrust Management Control Analysis ... TMCA
Thrust Management Function (GAVI) ... TMF
Thrust Measuring System ... TMS
Thrust Monopropellant Engine ... TME
Thrust of Propeller [*Naval engineering*] (DAS) ... T
Thrust Okay [*NASA*] (KSC) ... TOK
Thrust Reduction Altitude (GAVI) ... TRA
Thrust Reduction Valve ... TRV
Thrust Required for Level Flight [*Aviation*] (MCD) ... TLF
Thrust Resources, Inc. [*Vancouver Stock Exchange symbol*] ... THT
Thrust Reverser (MCD) ... TR
Thrust Section Blower (AAG) ... TSB
Thrust Section Observer (AAG) ... TSO
Thrust Shell ... THRSHL
Thrust Specific Fuel Consumption ... TSFC
Thrust Stand System ... TSS
Thrust Structure Test Stand (AAG) ... TSTS
Thrust Subsystem Design Team [*NASA*] ... TSSDT
Thrust Termination ... TT
Thrust Termination Assembly ... TTA
Thrust Termination Initiator Test Set ... TTITS
Thrust Termination Unit (MSA) ... TTU
Thrust to Earth Weight Ratio (IAA) ... TEWR
Thrust/Translation Control Assembly [*NASA*] (KSC) ... T/TCA
Thrust Vector [*Aerospace*] (NASA) ... TV
Thrust Vector Activation Control [*Aerospace*] ... TVAC
Thrust Vector Actuator ... TVA
Thrust Vector Alignment [*Aerospace*] (MCD) ... TVA
Thrust Vector Control [*Aerospace*] ... TVC
Thrust Vector Control Actuator [*Aerospace*] (NASA) ... TVCA
Thrust Vector Control Assembly [*Aerospace*] ... TVCA
Thrust Vector Control Driver [*Aerospace*] (NASA) ... TVCD
Thrust Vector Control/Jet Interaction Control ... TVC/JIC
Thrust Vector Control System [*Aerospace*] (KSC) ... TVCS
Thrust Vector/Jet Interaction ... TV/JI
Thrust Vector Position Servo Amplifier [*Aerospace*] ... TVSA
Thrust Vector System [*Aerospace*] ... TVS
Thrust Vectoring Motor [*Aerospace*] (MUGU) ... TVM
Thrust-Assisted Orbiter Shuttle [*NASA*] ... TAOS
Thrust-Augmented Delta [*NASA*] ... TAD
Thrust-Augmented Improved Delta [*Launch vehicle*] [*NASA*] ... TAID
Thrust-Augmented Rocket [*NASA*] ... TAR
Thrust-Augmented Thor [*NASA*] ... TAT
Thrust-Augmented Wing [*NASA*] (MCD) ... TAW
Thruster [*of a ship*] (DS) ... T
Thruster Attitude Control System [*NASA*] ... TACS
Thruster Subsystem Module [*NASA*] ... TSSM
Thruster-Assisted Mooring System [*of a ship*] (DS) ... TAMS
Thrustmaster, Inc. [*Associated Press*] (SAG) ... Thrust
Thrustmaster, Inc. [*NASDAQ symbol*] (SAG) ... TMSR
Thrust-to-Weight ... T/W

Thruway .... THRWY
Thruway (BARN) .... Thwy
Thruxton [*British ICAO location identifier*] (ICLI) .... EGHO
THT, Inc. [*Associated Press*] (SAG) .... THT
THT, Inc. [*Formerly, Texas Hitech, Inc.*] [*NASDAQ symbol*] (NQ) .... TXHI
Thucydides [*Greek historian, c. 460-400BC*] [*Classical studies*] (ROG) .... THUC
Thule [*Denmark*] [*Geomagnetic observatory code*] .... THL
Thule [*Greenland*] [*Seismograph station code, US Geological Survey Closed*] (SEIS) .... THU
Thule Air Base [*Greenland*] [*ICAO location identifier*] (ICLI) .... BGTL
Thule Tracking Station (MCD) .... TTS
Thulium [*Chemical element*] .... Tm
Thulium [*Symbol is Tm*] [*Chemical element*] (ROG) .... TU
Thumb Wheel Encoder .... TWE
Thumba Equatorial Launching Station [*Indian rocket station*] .... TERLS
Thumbwheel (MCD) .... TW
Thumrait [*Oman*] [*ICAO location identifier*] (ICLI) .... OOTH
Thun [*Switzerland ICAO location identifier*] (ICLI) .... LSZW
Thunder .... TH
Thunder Bay [*Ontario*] [*Airport symbol*] (AD) .... YGT
Thunder Bay [*Canada*] [*Airport symbol*] (OAG) .... YQT
Thunder Bay District Health Council, Thunder Bay, ON, Canada [*Library symbol Library of Congress*] (LCLS) .... CaOTBDHC
Thunder Bay District Health Council, Thunder Bay, Ontario [*Library symbol National Library of Canada*] (NLC) .... OTBDHC
Thunder Bay Historical Museum Society, Ontario [*Library symbol National Library of Canada*] (NLC) .... OTBH
Thunder Bay Historical Society, Thunder Bay, ON, Canada [*Library symbol Library of Congress*] (LCLS) .... CaOTBH
Thunder Bay, ON [*FM radio station call letters*] .... CBQ
Thunder Bay, ON [*FM radio station call letters*] .... CBQT
Thunder Bay, ON [*Television station call letters*] .... CHFD
Thunder Bay, ON [*Television station call letters*] CICO-9
Thunder Bay, ON [*AM radio station call letters*] .... CJLB
Thunder Bay, ON [*FM radio station call letters*] .... CJSD
Thunder Bay, ON [*AM radio station call letters*] .... CKPR
Thunder Bay, ON [*Television station call letters*] .... CKPR-TV
Thunder Bay, ON [*ICAO location identifier*] (ICLI) .... CYQT
Thunder Bay Public Library, Thunder Bay, ON, Canada [*Library symbol Library of Congress*] (LCLS) .... CaOTB
Thunder Engines Corp. [*Vancouver Stock Exchange symbol*] .... TE
Thunder Explorations [*Vancouver Stock Exchange symbol*] .... THU
Thunder Mountain Elementary School Library, Grand Junction, CO [*Library symbol Library of Congress*] (LCLS) .... CoGjThE
Thunderbird [*Automobile*] .... T/B
Thunderbird [*Automobile*] (DSUE) .... T (Bird)
Thunderbird American Indian Dancers (EA) .... TAID
Thunderbird Tours [*Canada*] [*FAA designator*] (FAAC) .... TBD
Thunderbirds of America (EA) .... TA
ThunderBYTE Anti-Virus [*Computer software*] (PCM) .... TBAV
Thunderstorm [*Meteorology*] .... T
Thunderstorm Research International Project [*Meteorology*] .... TRIP
Thunderstorm Research Project [*Environmental Science Services Administration*] .... TRP
Thunderstorm with Hail [*Meteorology*] .... TSGR
Thunderstorm with Ice Pellets [*ICAO*] (FAAC) .... TSPE
Thunderstorm with Rain [*ICAO*] (FAAC) .... TSRA
Thunderstorm with Sandstorm [*Meteorology*] .... TSSA
Thurber Consultants Ltd., Victoria, British Columbia [*Library symbol National Library of Canada*] (NLC) .... BVIT
Thurgood Marshall Law Journal [*A publication*] (DLA) .... TMLJ
Thurgood Marshall Law Review [*A publication*] (DLA) .... Thur Mar L Rev
Thurgood Marshall Law Review [*A publication*] (DLA) .... TML Rev
Thurman, CO [*Location identifier FAA*] (FAAL) .... TXC
Thurmont, MD [*Location identifier FAA*] (FAAL) .... DVD
Thurmont, MD [*AM radio station call letters*] .... WTHU
Thursday (WGA) .... T
Thursday .... TH
Thursday (AFM) .... THU
Thursday (WGA) .... Thur
Thursday .... THURS
Thursday (ODBW) .... Thurs
Thursday Island [*Australia ICAO location identifier*] (ICLI) .... ABTD
Thursday Island [*Australia Airport symbol*] (OAG) .... TIS
Thursdays Only [*British railroad term*] .... THO
Thurstable [*England*] .... THURST
Thurston Aviation Ltd. [*British ICAO designator*] (FAAC) .... THG
Thurstone Temperament Schedule [*Psychology*] .... TTS
Thwartship (DS) .... Thw
Thylungra [*Queensland*] [*Airport symbol*] (AD) .... THY
Thymic Alymphoplasia [*Medicine*] (MAE) .... TAL
Thymic Epithelial Cell [*Cytology*] .... TEC
Thymic Epithelial Supernatant [*Endocrinology*] .... TES
Thymic Factor X [*Endocrinology*] .... TFX
Thymic Humoral Factor [*Endocrinology*] .... THF
Thymic Hypocalcemic Factor [*Biochemistry*] .... THF
Thymic Lymphoma [*Medicine*] .... TL
Thymic Nurse Cell [*Cytology*] .... TNC
Thymic Polypeptide [*Endocrinology*] .... TP
Thymidine [*Medicine*] (MAE) .... T
Thymidine [*Genetics*] (DAVI) .... TdR
Thymidine Diphosphate [*Biochemistry*] .... TDP
Thymidine Diphosphorhamnose [*Biochemistry*] .... TDPRha
Thymidine Factor [*Endocrinology*] .... TF
Thymidine Kinase [*An enzyme*] .... TK
Thymidine Kinase (Activity) Transforming Unit [*Biochemistry*] .... TKTU
Thymidine Kinase Deficiency [*Medicine*] (DMAA) .... TKD
Thymidine Monophosphate [*Biochemistry*] .... TMP
Thymidine Phosphorylase [*An enzyme*] .... TP
Thymidine Triphosphate [*Biochemistry*] .... TTP
Thymidine-Labeling Index [*Biochemical analysis*] .... TI
Thymidine-Labeling Index [*Oncology*] .... TLI
Thymidylate Synthase [*Also, TS*] [*An enzyme*] .... ThS
Thymidylate Synthase [*Also, ThS*] [*An enzyme*] .... TS
Thymidylate Synthetase Dihydrofolate Reductase [*Biochemistry*] .... TS-DHFR
Thymine [*Also, Thy*] [*Biochemistry*] .... T
Thymine [*Also, T*] [*Biochemistry*] .... Thy
Thymine, Adenine, Guanine [*Laboratory science*] (DAVI) .... TAG
Thymine Ribonucleoside-5-Phosphate [*Genetics*] (DAVI) .... TMP
Thymocyte [*Clinical chemistry*] .... THY
Thymocyte Mitogenic Protein [*Immunology*] .... TMP
Thymol Blue [*An indicator*] .... TB
Thymol Flocculation [*Clinical chemistry*] .... TF
Thymol Turbidity [*Clinical chemistry*] (CPH) .... Thym Turb
Thymol Turbidity [*Clinical chemistry*] .... TT
Thymol Turbidity Test [*Clinical chemistry*] .... TTT
Thymolphthalein [*Organic chemistry*] .... TP
Thymolphthalein complexone [*Analytical reagent*] .... TPC
Thymolphthalein Monophosphate [*Biochemistry*] .... TMP
Thymopentin [*Biochemistry*] .... TP
Thymopoietin .... TP
Thymosin [*A thymus hormone*] .... TSN
Thymostimulin [*Endocrinology*] .... TS
Thymus [*Medicine*] .... T
Thymus Cell Growth Factor [*Cytology*] .... TCGF
Thymus Cell Replacing Factor [*Immunology*] .... TRF
Thymus Dependent [*Cells*] [*Hematology*] .... TD
Thymus Derived [*Hematology*] .... T
Thymus Epithelial [*Cell*] [*Immunology*] (DAVI) .... TE
Thymus Independent [*Cells*] [*Hematology*] .... TI
Thymus Leukemia [*Hematology*] .... TL
Thymus Permeability Factor .... TPF
Thymus Protein .... TP
Thymus-Dependent Cell-Replacing Factor [*Hematology*] (DAVI) .... TRF
Thymus-Dependent Lymphocyte [*Hematology*] .... TDL
Thymus-Dependent Lymphocyte [*Hematology*] (DAVI) .... T-L
Thymus-Dependent Zone [*Hematology*] (MAE) .... TDZ
Thymus-Derived Lymphocyte [*Hematology*] .... TL
Thyratron [*Electronics*] (IAA) .... THY
Thyratron (IDOE) .... thy
Thyratron Core Driver .... TCD
Thyratron Motor Control [*Electronics*] (IAA) .... THOMOTROL
Thyratron Motor Control [*Electronics*] (MCD) .... THYMOTRO
Thyratron Motor Control [*Electronics*] .... THYMOTROL
Thyristor [*Electronics*] .... THYR
Thyristor Power Supply [*Electronics*] (IAA) .... TPS
Thyrocalcitonin [*Endocrinology*] (MAE) .... TC
Thyrocalcitonin [*Also, CT, TCT*] [*Endocrinology*] .... TCA
Thyrocalcitonin [*Also, CT, TCA*] [*Endocrinology*] .... TCT
Thyroglobulin [*Endocrinology*] (DAVI) .... TBG
Thyroglobulin [*Also, Thg*] [*Endocrinology*] .... TG
Thyroglobulin [*Also, TG*] [*Endocrinology*] .... Thg
Thyroglobulin Antibody .... TGAb
Thyroglobulin Auto-Precipitation [*Endocrinology*] (AAMN) .... TA
Thyrohyoid [*Medicine*] (MAE) .... TH
Thyroid [*Medicine*] .... T
Thyroid Autoantibody [*Endrocrinology*] (DAVI) .... TA
Thyroid Function Test [*Endocrinology*] (DAVI) .... TFT
Thyroid Hormone [*Thyroxine*] [*Endocrinology*] .... TH
Thyroid Hormone Binding Inhibitor [*Clinical chemistry*] .... THBI
Thyroid Hormone Binding Ratio [*Clinical chemistry*] .... THBR
Thyroid Hormone Receptor [*Endocrinology*] .... TR
Thyroid Hormone Response Element [*Endocrinology*] .... TRE
Thyroid Hormone Secretion Rate (OA) .... TSR
Thyroid Hormone Uptake Test [*Clinical chemistry*] .... THUT
Thyroid Microsomal Antibody [*Immunology*] .... TMA
Thyroid Microsomal Autoantibody [*Immunology*] .... TMaab
Thyroid Peroxidase [*An enzyme*] .... TPO
Thyroid Radioisotope Assay (BABM) .... TyRIA
Thyroid:Serum [*Radioiodide ratio*] .... T/S
Thyroid Transcription Factor [*Genetics*] .... TTF
Thyroid Vein [*Medicine*] (PDAA) .... TV
Thyroidectomy [*Medicine*] .... Tx
Thyroid-Parathyroidectomy [*Endocrinology*] (DAVI) .... TPTX
Thyroid-Responsive Element [*Genetics*] .... TRE
Thyroid-Stimulating Antibodies [*Endocrinology*] .... TSAb
Thyroid-Stimulating Autoantibody [*Endocrinology*] .... TSaab
Thyroid-Stimulating Hormone [*Thyrotrophin*] [*Also, TTH Endocrinology*] .... TSH
[*TSH*] **Thyroid-stimulating hormone Binding Inhibitory Immunoglobulin** [*Endocrinology*] (DAVI) .... TBII
Thyroid-Stimulating Hormone of the Prepituitary Gland [*Endocrinology*] .... TSP
Thyroid-Stimulating Hormone-Displacing Antibody [*Medicine*] (DMAA) .... TDA
Thyroid-Stimulating Hormone-Releasing Factor [*Endocrinology*] (MAE) .... TSH-RF
Thyroid-Stimulating Hormone-Releasing Factor [*Endocrinology*] (CPH) .... TSH-RH
Thyroid-Stimulating Immunoglobulin [*Endocrinology*] .... TSI
Thyroid-to-Serum Ratio [*Medicine*] (MAE) .... TSR
Thyroparathyroidectomized [*Medicine*] .... TPTX
Thyrotroph Embryonic Factor [*Genetics*] .... TEF
Thyrotrophic Hormone [*Also, TSH*] [*Endocrinology*] .... TTH
Thyrotrophic Hormone-Releasing Factor [*Endocrinology*] .... THRF

Thyrotrophin-Releasing Factor [*Later, TRH*] [*Endocrinology*] .... TRF
Thyrotrophin-Releasing Hormone [*Formerly, TRF*] [*Endocrinology*] .... TRH
Thyrotrophin-Releasing Hormone Receptor [*Endocrinology*] .... TRH-R
Thyrotropin-Binding Inhibitor Immunoglobulin .... TBII
Thyrotropin-Stimmulating Hormone Receptor [*Endocrinology*] .... TSHR
Thyroxine [*Also, Thx, Ty*] [*An amino acid Endocrinology*] T4
Thyroxine [*Also, T4, Ty*] [*An amino acid Endocrinology*] .... THX
Thyroxine [*Also, T4, Thx*] [*An amino acid Endocrinology*] .... Ty
Thyroxine Radioisotope Assay [*Endocrinology*] (DAVI) .... T_4RIA
Thyroxine-Binding Albumin [*Biochemistry*] (MAE) .... TBA
Thyroxine-Binding Capacity [*Biochemistry*] .... TBC
Thyroxine-Binding Capacity of Thyroxine-Binding Globulin Assays [*Endrocrinology*] (DAVI) .... TBG cap
Thyroxine-Binding Coagulin [*Biochemistry*] (MAE) .... TBC
Thyroxine-Binding Globulin [*Biochemistry*] .... TBG
Thyroxine-Binding Index [*Biochemistry*] (MAE) .... TBI
Thyroxine-Binding Prealbumin [*Biochemistry*] .... TBPA
Thyroxine-Binding Protein [*Biochemistry*] .... TBP
Thyroxine-Specific Activity [*Medicine*] (MAE) .... T_4SA
Thyssen Henschel .... TH
Thyssen-Bornemisza Group NV [*Netherlands*] .... TBG
TI Diskette Operating System (NITA) .... TXDS
TI [*Texas Instruments, Inc.*] **Graphics Architecture** [*Computer science*] .... TIGA
TI [*Texas Instruments*] **Programmable Calculator Club** (EA) .... TIPCC
TI Travel International, Inc. [*Vancouver Stock Exchange symbol*] .... TI
Tian Hua Fen [*Chinese herbal medicine*] .... THF
Tianjin [*China*] [*Airport symbol*] (OAG) .... TSN
Tianjin/Zhangguizhuang [*China*] [*ICAO location identifier*] (ICLI) .... ZBTJ
Tiaprofenic Acid .... TIA
Tiara Enterprises Ltd. [*Vancouver Stock Exchange symbol*] .... TIK
Tiaret [*Algeria*] [*ICAO location identifier*] (ICLI) .... DAOB
Tiaret [*Algeria*] [*Airport symbol*] (AD) .... TRT
Tibaldstone [*England*] .... TIBALD
Tibati [*Cameroon*] [*ICAO location identifier*] (ICLI) .... FKKT
Tiber Energy Corp. [*Toronto Stock Exchange symbol*] .... TBE
Tiberius [*of Suetonius*] [*Classical studies*] (OCD) .... Tib
Tiberius Gracchus [*of Plutarch*] [*Classical studies*] (OCD) .... Ti Gracch
Tibet (VRA) .... Tib
Tibet Fund (EA) .... TF
Tibet Society (EA) .... TS
Tibetan [*MARC language code Library of Congress*] (LCCP) .... tib
Tibetan Aid Project (EA) .... TAP
Tibetan Autonomous Region [*China, Mainland*] [*MARC geographic area code Library of Congress*] (LCCP) .... a-cc-ti
Tibetan Terrier Club of America (EA) .... TTCA
Tibetan Youth Sponsorship Programs (EA) .... TYSP
Tibi Aderit Numen Divinum, Expecta Modo [*God Will Help Thee - Only Wait*] [*Motto of Elisabeth Ernestine Antonie, Duchess of Saxony (1681-1766)*] [*Latin*] .... TANDEM
Tibia [*Anatomy*] (DAVI) .... Tib
Tibia and Fibula (DSUE) .... TIB and FIB
Tibial Dyschondroplasia [*Medicine*] .... TD
Tibial Torsion [*Orthopedics*] (DAVI) .... TT
Tibial Tubercle [*Anatomy*] .... TT
Tibialis [*Muscle*] (DAVI) .... tib
Tibialis Anterior [*A muscle*] .... TA
Tibialis Posterior [*Anatomy*] .... TP
Tibiti [*Surinam*] [*ICAO location identifier*] (ICLI) .... SMTI
Tibooburra [*New South Wales*] [*Airport symbol*] (AD) .... TYB
Tibullus [*First century BC*] [*Classical studies*] (OCD) .... Tib
Tiburon Petroleum [*Vancouver Stock Exchange symbol*] .... TIP
Ticaban [*Costa Rica*] [*ICAO location identifier*] (ICLI) .... MRTB
Tical [*Monetary unit in Thailand*] .... TC
Ticarcillin and Tobramycin [*Antibacterial mixture*] .... TT
Tice, FL [*FM radio station call letters*] .... WAAD
Tice, FL [*Television station call letters*] .... WRXY
Tichitt [*Mauritania*] [*ICAO location identifier*] (ICLI) .... GQNC
Tick-Borne Encephalitis .... TBE
Ticked Off [*Slang*] .... TO
Ticker Tape Information Processing System [*Online stock information service*] .... TTIPS
Ticker Tape Resources Ltd. [*Vancouver Stock Exchange symbol*] .... TKT
Ticket .... TKT
Ticket Agents' Association [*British*] .... TAA
Ticket Board (DGA) .... TB
Ticket Information Data .... TID
Ticket Issue Machines .... TIM
Ticket of Leave (ADA) .... TL
Ticket of Leave .... TOL
Ticket Reservation Systems, Inc. .... TRS
Ticket-Granting Server .... TGS
Ticket-Granting Ticket [*Computer science*] .... TGT
Ticketmaster Group, Inc. [*Associated Press*] (SAG) .... Ticktmst
Ticketmaster Group, Inc. [*NASDAQ symbol*] (SAG) .... TKTM
Ticking (VRA) .... tik
Ticknor & Fields [*Publisher*] .... T & F
Ticonderoga, NY [*FM radio station call letters*] .... WANC
Ticonderoga, NY [*AM radio station call letters*] .... WIPS
Tidal [*Volume*] [*Laboratory science*] (DAVI) .... TD
Tidal and Current Survey (NOAA) .... TICUS
Tidal Constants [*Marine science*] (MSC) .... TC
Tidal Current Survey System [*National Oceanic and Atmospheric Administration*] .... TICUS
Tidal Disruption [*Astronomy*] .... TD
Tidal Electric Station .... TES
Tidal Gas [*Respiration*] [*Medicine*] .... T
Tidal Regenerator Engine .... TRE
Tidal Volume [*Amount of air that moves in and out of lungs under given conditions*] [*Physiology*] .... TV
Tidal Volume [*Medicine*] (DAVI) .... Vt
Tidal Zone .... TZ
Tidbinbilla Deep Space Communications Complex .... TDSCC
Tidd's Costs [*A publication*] (DLA) .... Tidd
Tidd's Costs [*A publication*] (DLA) .... Tidd Co
Tidd's Practice [*A publication*] (DLA) .... Tidd
Tidd's Practice [*A publication*] (DLA) .... Tidd Pr
Tidd's Practice [*A publication*] (DLA) .... Tidd Prac
Tidd's Practice [*A publication*] (DLA) .... Tidd's Pract
Tide Communication Control Ship (NATG) .... TCCS
Tide Gauge System .... TGS
Tide Net Controller (NATG) .... TNC
Tide Rips [*Navigation*] .... T
Tide Surveyor [*British*] (ROG) .... TS
Tide West Oil [*NASDAQ symbol*] (TTSB) .... TIDE
Tide West Oil Co. [*NASDAQ symbol*] (NQ) .... TIDE
Tide West Oil Co. [*Associated Press*] (SAG) .... TideWst
Tidelands Rlty Tr B SBI [*NASDAQ symbol*] (TTSB) .... TIRTZ
Tidelands Royalty [*Associated Press*] (SAG) .... TideR
Tidelands Royalty Class B [*Associated Press*] (SAG) .... TideR
Tidelands Royalty Trust "B" [*NASDAQ symbol*] (NQ) .... TIRT
TideMark Bancorp [*Associated Press*] (SAG) .... TideMrk
Tide-Measuring Buoy .... TMB
Tidewater Community College, Chesapeake, VA [*Library symbol*] [*Library of Congress*] (LCLS) .... ViCheC
Tidewater Consortium, Librarians' Networking Committee [*Library network*] .... VTCCHE
Tidewater, Inc. [*NYSE symbol*] (SPSG) .... TDW
Tidewater, Inc. [*Associated Press*] (SAG) .... Tidwtr
Tidewater Nicaragua Project Foundation (EA) .... TNPF
Tidewater Southern Railway Co. [*AAR code*] .... TS
Tidewater Virginia Development Council .... TVDC
Tidioute, PA [*Location identifier FAA*] (FAAL) .... TDT
Tidjikja [*Mauritania*] [*ICAO location identifier*] (ICLI) .... GQND
Tidjikja [*Mauritania*] [*Airport symbol*] (OAG) .... TIY
Tidningarnas Telegrambyra [*Press agency*] [*Sweden*] .... TT
Tidy Britain Group [*An association*] (EAIO) .... TBG
Tie [*Sports*] .... T
Tie Bus Fault .... TBF
TIE Communications, Inc. [*AMEX symbol*] (SPSG) .... TIE
Tie Connector (MCD) .... TC
Tie Control Relay (MCD) .... TCR
Tie Fabrics Association [*Defunct*] (EA) .... TFA
Tie In (MCD) .... TI
Tie Line [*Communication channel*] .... TL
Tie Line Bias Control [*Telecommunications*] (IAA) .... TBC
Tie Plate [*Technical drawings*] .... TP
Tie Point .... TP
TIE/Telecommunications Canada Ltd. [*Toronto Stock Exchange symbol*] .... TTI
Tie Trunk [*Telecommunications*] .... TTK
Tied .... TD
Tiedeman on Real Property [*A publication*] (DLA) .... Tiedeman Real Prop
Tiedeman's Treatise on Municipal Corporations [*A publication*] (DLA) .... Tied Mun Corp
Tiedeman's Treatise on the Limitations of Police Power in the United States [*A publication*] (DLA) .... Tied Lim Police Power
Tienshan Mountain Region [*MARC geographic area code Library of Congress*] (LCCP) .... at---
Tienshui [*Republic of China*] [*Seismograph station code, US Geological Survey*] (SEIS) .... TNH
Tientsin [*Republic of China*] [*Seismograph station code, US Geological Survey*] (SEIS) .... TIE
Tientsin [*China*] [*Airport symbol*] (AD) .... TSN
Tientsin Volunteer Corps [*British military*] (DMA) .... TVC
Tier [*Psychology*] .... T
Tierce [*Unit of measurement*] .... TC
Tierce [*Unit of measurement*] (ROG) .... TIER
Tierce [*Unit of measurement*] .... TRC
Tiered Premium System [*Insurance*] (WYGK) .... TPS
Tierp [*Sweden ICAO location identifier*] (ICLI) .... ESKT
Tierras Morenas [*Costa Rica*] [*Seismograph station code, US Geological Survey*] (SEIS) AR3
Tiers Ordre Carmelitaine [*Carmelite Third Order*] [*An association Italy*] (EAIO) .... TOC
Tieteellisen Informoinnin Neuvosto [*Finnish Council for Scientific Information and Research Libraries*] (EAIO) .... TINFO
Tiferet Israel (BJA) .... TI
Tiffany and Bullard on Trusts and Trustees [*A publication*] (DLA) .... Law of Trusts Tiff & Bul
Tiffany and Bullard on Trusts and Trustees [*A publication*] (DLA) .... Tif & Bul Tr
Tiffany & Co. [*NYSE symbol*] (SPSG) .... TIF
Tiffany & Co. [*Associated Press*] (SAG) .... Tifany
Tiffany and Smith's New York Practice [*A publication*] (DLA) .... Tif & Sm Pr
Tiffany on Government and Constitutional Law [*A publication*] (DLA) .... Tif Gov
Tiffany on Landlord and Tenant [*A publication*] (DLA) .... Tiffany Landl & T
Tiffany on Landlord and Tenant [*A publication*] (DLA) .... Tiffany Landlord & Ten
Tiffany on Real Property [*A publication*] (DLA) .... Tiffany Real Prop
Tiffany Resources, Inc. [*Vancouver Stock Exchange symbol*] .... TFO
Tiffany's Reports [*28-39 New York Court of Appeals*] [*A publication*] (DLA) .... Tiff
Tiffany's Reports [*28-39 New York Court of Appeals*] [*A publication*] (DLA) .... Tiffany

Tiffin, OH [*Location identifier FAA*] (FAAL) .... TII
Tiffin, OH [*FM radio station call letters*] .... WHEI
Tiffin, OH [*AM radio station call letters*] .... WTTF
Tiffin, OH [*FM radio station call letters*] .... WTTF-FM
Tiffin Seneca Public Library, Tiffin, OH [*Library symbol Library of Congress*]
    (LCLS) .... OTif
Tiflis [*Tbilisi*] [*Former USSR Seismograph station code, US Geological
    Survey*] (SEIS) .... TIF
Tift College, Forsyth, GA [*Library symbol Library of Congress*] (LCLS) .... GForsT
Tifton, GA [*Location identifier FAA*] (FAAL) .... IFM
Tifton, GA [*Location identifier FAA*] (FAAL) .... TMA
Tifton, GA [*FM radio station call letters*] .... WABR
Tifton, GA [*FM radio station call letters*] .... WOBB
Tifton, GA [*FM radio station call letters*] .... WPLH
Tifton, GA [*AM radio station call letters*] .... WTIF
Tifton, GA [*AM radio station call letters*] .... WWGS
Tifton Loamy Soil [*Agronomy*] .... TLS
TIG Holdings [*NYSE symbol*] (TTSB) .... TIG
TIG Holdings, Inc. [*NYSE symbol*] (SPSG) .... TIG
TIG Holdings,Inc. [*Associated Press*] (SAG) .... TIG Hd
Tiga [*Loyalty Islands*] [*Airport symbol*] (OAG) .... TGJ
Tiga, Iles Loyaute [*New Caledonia*] [*ICAO location identifier*] (ICLI) .... NWWA
TIGA Sailboard Class Association [*Defunct*] (EA) .... TSCA
Tigard, OR [*AM radio station call letters*] .... KEZF
Tigard Public Library, Tigard, OR [*Library symbol Library of Congress*]
    (LCLS) .... OrTig
Tiger Cat Association [*Defunct*] (EA) .... TCA
Tigerfly [*British ICAO designator*] (FAAC) .... MOH
Tigers East/Alpines East (EA) .... TE/AE
Tight Building Syndrome [*Air quality*] .... TBS
Tight Close-Up [*Cinematography*] (NTCM) .... TCU
Tight End [*Football*] .... TE
Tight Filum Terminale [*Medicine*] (DMAA) .... TFT
Tight Fingertip [*Medicine*] .... TFT
Tight Little Unit [*Ski-bum slang*] .... TLU
Tight Model Series (MCD) .... TMS
Tight Money (MHDW) .... TM
Tight Tape Contact .... TTC
Tight Torso [*Women's fashions*] .... TT
Tight Wrapped (MSA) .... TW
Tightening (MSA) .... TTNG
TIGIN Ltd. [*ICAO designator*] (FAAC) .... XNV
Tigre (BJA) .... Te
Tigre [*MARC language code Library of Congress*] (LCCP) .... tig
Tigre People's Liberation Front [*Ethiopia*] [*Political party*] (PD) .... TPLF
Tigrina [*MARC language code Library of Congress*] (LCCP) .... tir
Tigrinya (BJA) .... Tna
Tigris Minerals [*Vancouver Stock Exchange symbol*] .... TIG
Tiguipa [*Bolivia*] [*ICAO location identifier*] (ICLI) .... SLTY
Tihany [*Hungary*] [*Geomagnetic observatory code*] .... TYH
TII Indus [*NASDAQ symbol*] (TTSB) .... TIII
TII Industries, Inc. [*Associated Press*] (SAG) .... TII
TII Industries, Inc. [*Associated Press*] (SAG) .... TII Inds
TII Industries, Inc. [*NASDAQ symbol*] (SAG) .... TIII
Tijuana [*Mexico*] [*Airport symbol*] (OAG) .... TIJ
Tijuana [*Mexico*] [*Airport symbol*] (AD) .... TIJ
Tijuana [*Mexico*] .... TJ
Tijuana & Tecate Railway Co. (IIA) .... T & T
Tijuana & Tecate Railway Co. [*Later, TTR*] [*AAR code*] .... TITE
Tijuana & Tecate Railway Co. [*AAR code*] .... TTR
Tijuana Brass [*Musical group*] .... TJB
Tijuana/General Abelardo L. Rodriguez Internacional [*Mexico ICAO location
    identifier*] (ICLI) .... MMTJ
Tikapur [*Nepal*] [*ICAO location identifier*] (ICLI) .... VNTP
Tikehau [*French Polynesia*] [*ICAO location identifier*] (ICLI) .... NTGC
Tikehau [*French Polynesia*] [*Airport symbol*] (OAG) .... TIH
Tikhaya Bay [*Later, HIS*] [*Former USSR Geomagnetic observatory code*] .... TKH
Tiko [*Cameroon*] [*ICAO location identifier*] (ICLI) .... FKKC
Tiko [*Cameroon*] [*Airport symbol*] (AD) .... TKC
Tiksi [*Former USSR Seismograph station code, US Geological Survey*]
    (SEIS) .... TIK
Tilabery [*Niger*] [*ICAO location identifier*] (ICLI) .... DRRL
Tilapia International Association (EAIO) .... TIA
Tilapia International Foundation (EA) .... TIF
Tilbury & Southend Railway [*British*] (ROG) .... T & SER
Tilbury Docks (ROG) .... TD
Tilbury Public Library, Ontario [*Library symbol National Library of Canada*]
    (NLC) .... OTIL
Tilbury Public Library, Tilbury, ON, Canada [*Library symbol Library of
    Congress*] (LCLS) .... CaOTil
Til-Chatel [*France ICAO location identifier*] (ICLI) .... LFET
Tile Base [*Technical drawings*] .... TB
Tile Block [*Technical drawings*] .... T/B
Tile Contractors' Association of America (EA) .... TCAA
Tile Council of America (EA) .... TCA
Tile Drain [*Technical drawings*] .... TD
Tile Floor [*Technical drawings*] .... TF
Tile Manufacturers Association (EA) .... TMA
Tile, Marble, and Terrazzo Finishers and Shopmen International Union .... TMTF
Tile Threshold (MSA) .... TT
Tile Wainscot [*Technical drawings*] .... TW
Tiled [*Classified advertising*] (ADA) .... TLD
Tiler [*Freemasonry*] .... T
Tiler [*Freemasonry*] .... TLR
Tile-Shingle Roof [*Technical drawings*] .... TSR

Tilic Subgroup [*Ilmenite, titanite, perofskite, rutile*] [*CIPW classification
    Geology*] .... T
Tilimsen [*Algeria*] [*Airport symbol*] (OAG) .... TLM
Till All Taken [*Pharmacy*] (DAVI) .... TAT
Till Cancelled [*Press advertisements*] (DGA) .... TC
Till Counterbalanced .... T/C
Till Countermanded .... TC
Till Forbidden [*i.e., repeat until forbidden to do so*] [*Advertising*] .... TF
Till Further Notice .... TFN
Till Sale .... TS
Tillamook County Library, Tillamook, OR [*OCLC symbol*] (OCLC) .... TCO
Tillamook, OR [*AM radio station call letters*] .... KMBD
Tillamook, OR [*FM radio station call letters*] .... KTIL-FM
Tiller (MSA) .... TLR
Tilletia controversa Kuehn [*Wheat fungus*] .... TCK
Tilley Public Library, Alberta [*Library symbol National Library of Canada*]
    (NLC) .... ATI
Tilley Public Library, Tilley, AB, Canada [*Library symbol*] [*Library of
    Congress*] (LCLS) .... CaATi
Tillicum Industry [*Vancouver Stock Exchange symbol*] .... TLC
Tillinghast and Shearman's New York Practice [*A publication*] (DLA) ...... T & S Pr
Tillinghast and Shearman's New York Practice [*A publication*]
    (DLA) .... Til & Sh Pr
Tillinghast and Yates on Appeals [*A publication*] (DLA) .... Till & Yates App
Tillinghast's Precedents [*A publication*] (DLA) .... Til Prec
Tillman's Reports [*68, 69, 71, 73, 75 Alabama*] [*A publication*] (DLA) .... Tillman
Tillonsburg and District Historical Museum Society, Tillonsburg, ON,
    Canada [*Library symbol*] [*Library of Congress*] (LCLS) .... CaOTiHM
Tillotson Equation of State [*Physical chemistry*] .... TEOS
Tillsonburg and District Historical Museum Society, Tillsonburg, Ontario
    [*Library symbol National Library of Canada*] (NLC) .... OTIHM
Tillsonburg, ON [*AM radio station call letters*] .... CKOT
Tillsonburg, ON [*FM radio station call letters*] .... CKOT-FM
Tillsonburg Public Library, Ontario [*Library symbol National Library of
    Canada*] (NLC) .... OTIP
Tillsonburg Public Library, Tillsonburg, ON, Canada [*Library symbol Library
    of Congress*] (LCLS) .... CaOTiP
Tilrempt/Hassi R'Mel [*Algeria*] [*ICAO location identifier*] (ICLI) .... DAFH
Tilsley on Stamp Laws [*3rd ed.*] [*1871*] [*A publication*] (DLA) .... Tils St L
Tilt and Shift [*Camera lens*] (DICI) .... TS
Tilt Board Reach [*Test*] [*Occupational therapy*] .... TBR
Tilt Board Tip [*Test*] [*Occupational therapy*] .... TBT
Tilt Correction .... N
Tilt Covered [*Truck*] (DCTA) .... TC
Tilt Isolation Platform .... TIP
Tilt Rotor Research Aircraft .... TRRA
Tilt Table [*Orthopedics*] (DAVI) .... TT
Tilt Table Angle [*Vehicle rollover*] [*Automotive safety*] .... TTA
Tilt Trailers (DCTA) .... TT
Tilted Electric Field (PDAA) .... TEF
Tilting (PDAA) .... TLG
Tilting Journal Bearing .... TJB
Tilting Wind-Water Tunnel [*Environmental technology*] .... TWWT
Tilton Library, South Deerfield, MA [*Library symbol Library of Congress*]
    (LCLS) .... MSde
Tilt-Up Concrete Association (EA) .... TCA
Tilt-Up Concrete Association (EA) .... TUCA
Tim Donut Ltd. [*Canada ICAO designator*] (FAAC) .... TND
Timaeus [*of Plato*] [*Classical studies*] (OCD) .... Ti
Timaru [*New Zealand*] [*ICAO location identifier*] (ICLI) .... NZTU
Timaru [*New Zealand*] [*Airport symbol*] (OAG) .... TIU
Timballes [*Kettle drum*] .... TIMB
Timbedra [*Mauritania*] [*ICAO location identifier*] (ICLI) .... GQNH
Timbedra [*Mauritania*] [*Airport symbol*] (AD) .... TMD
Timbedra/Dahara [*Mauritania*] [*ICAO location identifier*] (ICLI) .... GQNM
Timber [*Lumber*] [*Vessel load line mark*] L
Timber (ADA) .... TIMB
Timber (AAG) .... TMBR
Timber .... TMBR
Timber and Building Materials Association [*New South Wales, Australia*].... TBMA
Timber Arbitrators Association [*British*] (DBA) .... TAA
Timber Development Association (New South Wales) [*Australia*] .... TDANSW
Timber Development Association of South Australia .... TDASA
Timber Drying Association [*British*] (DBA) .... TDA
Timber Importers Association of America .... TIAA
Timber Industry Strategy [*Victoria, Australia*] .... TIS
Timber Information Keyword Retrieval [*Timber Research and Development
    Association*] [*Information service or system*] (IID) .... TINKER
Timber Lodge Steakhouse [*NASDAQ symbol*] (TTSB) .... TBRL
Timber Lodge Steakhouse, Inc. [*NASDAQ symbol*] (SAG) .... TBRL
Timber Lodge Steakhouse, Inc. [*Associated Press*] (SAG) .... TimbLdg
Timber Management Decision System (PDAA) .... TIMADS
Timber Management Policy Reform Program (GNE) .... TMPEP
Timber Management Research [*Department of Agriculture*] (GRD) .... TMR
Timber Merchants' Association of South Australia .... TMASA
Timber Merchants' Association of Victoria [*Australia*] .... TMAV
Timber Mountain [*Nevada*] [*Seismograph station code, US Geological
    Survey*] (SEIS) .... TMN
Timber Operators Council (EA) .... TOC
Timber Preservers' Association of Australia .... TPAA
Timber Producers Association of Michigan and Wisconsin (EA) .... TPA
Timber Products Manufacturers (EA) .... TPM
Timber Products Manufacturers Association [*Later, TPM*] .... TPMA
Timber Promotion Council [*Victoria, Australia*] .... TPC
Timber Research and Development Advisory Council [*Australia*] .... TRDAC

Timber Research and Development Association [*Research center British*] (IRC) .... TRADA
Timber Rights Purchase .... TRP
Timber Sales Program Information Reporting System [*Department of the Interior*] .... TSPIRS
Timber Stand Improvement (DICI) .... TSI
Timber Trade Industrial Association [*Australia*] .... TTIA
Timber Trade Training Association [*British*] (DBA) .... TTTA
Timber Trades' Benevolent Society [*British*] (BI) .... TTBS
Timber Trades Federation (DAS) .... TTF
Timberland Co. [*NYSE symbol*] (SPSG) .... TBL
Timberland Co. [*Associated Press*] (SAG) .... TimbCo
Timberland Co. Cl'A' [*NYSE symbol*] (TTSB) .... TBL
Timberland Regional Library, Olympia, WA [*Library symbol Library of Congress*] (LCLS) .... WaO
Timberline Software [*NASDAQ symbol*] (TTSB) .... TMBS
Timberline Software Corp. [*Associated Press*] (SAG) .... TimbSf
Timberline Software Corp. [*NASDAQ symbol*] (NQ) .... TMBS
Timbre [*Ecuador*] [*ICAO location identifier*] (ICLI) .... SETB
Timbre Poste [*Postage Stamp*] [*French*] .... T-P
Time .... T
Time [*Symbol*] [*IUPAC*] .... t
Time (FAAC) .... TM
Time Action Calendar [*Management*] .... TAC
Time Actual (NASA) .... TA
Time after Lift-Off .... TALO
Time Air Corp. [*Toronto Stock Exchange symbol*] .... TMI
Time Air Ltd. [*Canada ICAO designator*] (FAAC) .... TAF
Time Air Speed (NATG) .... TAS
Time Analysis and Billing System (BUR) .... TABS
Time Analysis of Program Status .... TAPS
Time and Allowance .... T & A
Time and Altitude Over [*Aviation*] (FAAC) .... TAO
Time and Amount (DMAA) .... T/A
Time and Attendance .... TA
Time and Attendance (IAA) .... TAA
Time and Attendance (USDC) .... T&A
Time and Attendance, Payroll, and Personnel (GFGA) .... TAPP
Time and Attendance Terminal (MHDI) .... TAT
Time and Charges [*Telecommunications*] (TEL) .... T & C
Time and Charges [*Telecommunications*] (IAA) .... TAC
Time and Charges, Operate .... TCO
Time and Cycle Log [*NASA*] (KSC) .... TACL
Time and Cycle Log [*NASA*] (KSC) .... TCL
Time and Cycle Record [*NASA*] (KSC) .... TACR
Time and Cycle Record Card [*NASA*] (KSC) .... TCRC
Time and Effort Measurement through Periodic Observation (MCD) .... TEMPO
Time and Event (IAA) .... TAE
Time and Event Recorder (IAA) .... TAEREC
Time and Event Recorder .... TER
Time and Events (AAG) .... T & E
Time and Frequency (MHDB) .... TAF
Time and Frequency Standard .... TFS
Time and Frequency Unit (ECII) .... TFU
Time and Materials .... T & M
Time and Materials (MCD) .... TAM
Time and Motion Study (NG) .... TMS
Time and Relative Dimensions in Space [*Acronym is name of spaceship in British TV series "Dr. Who"*] .... TARDIS
Time and Space Processing (MCD) .... TSP
Time and Super Quick .... TSQ
Time and Temperature .... T & T
Time Arrive Guarantee (AAG) .... TAG
Time Assessment Interview Schedule (DMAA) .... TAIS
Time Assigned Data Interpolation (HGAA) .... TADI
Time Assignment Speech Interpolation [*Timesharing technique*] [*Telecommunications*] .... TASI
Time at Completion (MCD) .... TAC
Time Australia [*A publication*] (APTA) .... Time A
Time Automated Grid .... TAG
Time Available for Delivery (CET) .... TAD
Time Averaged Clutter Coherent (MCD) .... TACC
Time Averaged Clutter Coherent Airborne RADAR .... TACCAR
Time, Azimuth, Elevation, and Range [*Aerospace*] .... TAER
Time Band-Width (IAA) .... TBW
Time Base .... TB
Time Base Corrector [*Videotape recording element*] [*Early processing device*] .... TBC
Time Base Corrector (NITA) .... TBC
Time Base Error .... TBE
Time Base Error Difference [*Computer science*] (IAA) .... TBED
Time Base Unit .... TBU
Time between Failures [*Quality control*] (AFIT) .... TBF
Time between Inspections [*Quality control*] .... TBI
Time Between Oil Changes [*Automotive servicing*] .... TBO
Time between Overhauls [*of engine, or other equipment*] .... TBO
Time between Points [*Experimentation*] .... TB
Time between Scheduled Visits (MCD) .... TBSV
Time Buffered Coarse Fine (IAA) .... TBCE
Time, Bulb, Instantaneous [*Initials on certain Kodak cameras*] .... TBI
Time Called [*Baseball*] .... Tc
Time Certificate of Deposit [*Banking*] .... TC
Time Change Item (MCD) .... TCI
Time Change Unit (MCD) .... TCU
Time Charter [*Shipping*] .... T/C
Time Check .... TC
Time Clock .... TC
Time Closing (MSA) .... TC
Time Code (NTCM) .... TC
Time Code Generator .... TCG
Time Code Reader .... TCR
Time Code Translator .... TCT
Time Code Word .... TCW
Time Compensation .... TC
Time Compliance Directive [*Air Force*] (MCD) .... TCD
Time Compliance Technical Instruction (NASA) .... TCTI
Time Compliance Technical Order [*NASA*] (AAG) .... TCTO
Time Compression [*Computer science*] (IAA) .... TC
Time Compression Coding .... TCC
Time Compression Display System (NVT) .... TICODS
Time Compression Multiplex (IAA) .... TCM
Time Compression Tactical Communications .... TICTAC
Time Consistent Busy Hour (NITA) .... TCBH
Time Constant (IAA) .... T
Time Constant (MSA) .... TC
Time Consumed in Playing Game [*Baseball*] .... T
Time Controlled [*Computer science*] (IAA) .... TC
Time Controlled Gain (AAG) .... TCG
Time Correction Factor (ADA) .... TCF
Time Correlation Buffer (MCD) .... TCB
Time Correlation Data .... TCD
Time, Cost, and Performance .... TCP
Time Critical Requirements (MCD) .... TCR
Time Data Card (AAG) .... TDC
Time Delay .... TD
Time Delay (FAAC) .... TDEL
Time Delay Amplifier .... TDA
Time Delay and Integration (MCD) .... TDI
Time Delay Array RADAR .... TIDAR
Time Delay Closing .... TDC
Time Delay Compression Network .... TDCN
Time Delay Dropout [*Relay*] (AAG) .... TDDO
Time Delay Generator .... TDG
Time Delay Neural Network [*Computer science*] .... TDNN
Time Delay of Arrival (MCD) .... TDOA
Time Delay Opening .... TDO
Time Delay Receiver (NITA) .... TDR
Time Delay Relay .... T/DRLY
Time Delay Relay .... TDR
Time Delay Relay [*Computer science*] (IAA) .... TR
Time Delay Squib [*Navy*] .... TDSQB
Time Delay Switch .... TDS
Time Deposit [*Banking*] .... TD
Time Deposit, Open Account [*Banking*] .... TDOA
Time Difference [*or Differential*] .... TD
Time Difference of Arrival and Differential Doppler (MCD) .... TDOA/DD
Time Difference of Arrival / Distance Measuring Equipment (PDAA) .... TDOA/DME
Time Difference of Arrrival .... TDOA
Time Differential Perturbed Angular Correlation [*Physics*] .... TDPAC
Time Differential Phase-Shift Keying .... TDPSK
Time Dilution of Precision .... TDOP
Time Disintegration (MEDA) .... TD
Time Displacement Error (IAA) .... TDE
Time Display Unit (NASA) .... TDU
Time Distance [*Military*] (AABC) .... TDIS
Time, Distance, Speed .... TDS
Time Distance Terminal Data Input System (MCD) .... TDIS
Time Distributed Multiple Access (IAA) .... TDMA
Time Distribution Card (AAG) .... TDC
Time Distribution System (MCD) .... TDS
Time Dividing Spectrum Stabilization [*Electronics*] (OA) .... TDSS
Time Division (SAA) .... TD
Time Division Multiple Access .... TDMA
Time Division Multiplex [*Electronics*] .... TDM
Time Division Multiplexing [*Telecommunications*] .... TDM
Time Docket (DGA) .... TD
Time Domain Harmonic Scaling [*Telecommunications*] (LAIN) .... TDHS
Time Domain Reflectometer (NITA) .... TDR
Time Domain Reflectometry [*or Reflectometer*] .... TDR
Time Dose Fractionation Factor [*Roentgenology*] .... TDF
Time Driven Monitor (MHDI) .... TDM
Time Duration Modulation (DEN) .... TDM
Time Duration of Burn (MCD) .... TB
Time Earliest/Expected (NASA) .... TE
Time Elapsed After Study (MHDI) .... TEAS
Time Electronics (GFGA) .... TE
Time, Elevation, Azimuth, Range (MCD) .... TEAR
Time Encoded Speech [*Telecommunications*] (TEL) .... TES
Time Equipment (IAA) .... TE
Time Error in Psychophysical Judgments [*Psychology*] .... TE
Time Error Indicated .... TEI
Time Estimating Relationship (NASA) .... TER
Time Estimation (DAVI) .... TE
Time Expanded Video .... TEV
Time Expired (ADA) .... T/E
Time Exposure [*Photography*] .... TEXP
Time Factor (CAAL) .... TF
Time Frame .... TF
Time Frequency (IAA) .... TF
Time Frequency Collision Avoidance System .... TF-CAS

Time Frequency Digitizer (MCD) ... TFD
Time Frequency Shift Keying [*Computer science*] (IAA) ... TFSK
Time from Cutoff [*NASA*] (NASA) ... TFC
Time from Event [*NASA*] (KSC) ... TFE
Time from Ignition [*Apollo*] [*NASA*] ... TFI
Time from Launch [*NASA*] ... TFL
Time Gain Compensation [*Radiology*] (DAVI) ... TGC
Time Gain Control (IAA) ... TGC
Time Generation and Simulation [*Telecommunications*] (TEL) ... TEGAS
Time Handed In [*Navy*] ... THI
Time Homogenous Data Set (MCD) ... THDS
Time in Deadband Digital Attitude Control ... TIDDAC
Time in Grade [*Air Force*] ... TIG
Time in Grade [*Army*] ... TIMIG
Time in Grade [*Navy*] ... TMIG
Time in Hold (SAA) ... TIH
Time in Mode (EG) ... TIM
Time in Rate ... TIR
Time in Seconds [*Aerospace*] ... t
Time in Service [*Military*] (DOMA) ... TIS
Time in View ... TIV
Time Index ... TI
Time Indicator (IAA) ... TIM
Time Indicator, Miniature (MUGU) ... TIM
Time Initiator Monitor (SAA) ... TIM
Time Integral Cost Effectiveness ... TICE
Time Interval (IEEE) ... TI
Time Interval (AABC) ... TIMINT
Time Interval Counter ... TIC
Time Interval Distribution ... TID
Time Interval Error [*Telecommunications*] (TEL) ... TIE
Time Interval Gage of Relays [*Telecommunications*] (IAA) ... TIGOR
Time Interval Measurement ... TIM
Time Interval Meter ... TIM
Time Interval Miss Distance Acoustical Scoring System (MCD) ... TIMASS
Time Interval Monitor (NASA) ... TIM
Time Interval Optimization (IEEE) ... TIO
Time Isolation Unit ... TIU
Time Lapse (MAE) ... TL
Time Latest (NASA) ... TL
Time Lengths ... TL
Time Limit ... TL
Time Limited Correlation Processing ... TCP
Time Line ... TL
Time Line Analysis ... TLA
Time Line Controller ... TLC
Time Line Form ... TLF
Time Line Sheet [*NASA*] ... TLS
Time Loan [*Banking*] ... T/L
Time Location System [*Navy*] ... TIMATION
Time Maintenance Began [*Military*] (AFIT) ... TMB
Time Management (MCD) ... TM
Time Management Processor (NASA) ... TMP
Time Manager International [*Commercial firm British*] ... TMI
Time Mark Generator ... TMG
Time Marker Frequency ... TMF
Time Measurement Unit [*Industrial engineering*] ... TMU
Time Meter (AAG) ... TIM
Time Meter Reading ... TMR
Time, Mission ... TM
Time Modulation ... TM
Time Monitor ... TM
Time Motion Technique ... TM
Time Multiplexed Analogue Radio Control (PDAA) ... TIMARC
Time Multiplexed Switching [*Telecommunications*] ... TMS
Time Multiplication Factor [*Offshore racing*] ... TMF
Time of Arrival (AFM) ... TOA
Time of Check to Time of Use (MHDI) ... TOCTTOU
Time of Closest Approach [*Aerospace*] ... TCA
Time of Correlation (MCD) ... TOC
Time of Day ... TOD
Time of Day Clock (IAA) ... TDC
Time of Delivery ... TOD
Time of Departure ... TD
Time of Departure (NVT) ... TOD
Time of Despatch [*British*] ... TOD
Time of Entry (MCD) ... TOE
Time of Event [*Military*] (CAAL) ... TOE
Time of Expiration (MHDB) ... TOX
Time of Fail (MSA) ... T/F
Time of Fall (SAA) ... T/F
Time of Filing ... TOF
Time of Fire [*Military*] (CAAL) ... TOF
Time of First Call [*Navy*] ... TFC
Time of Flight [*Ballistics*] ... TF
Time of Flight (MSA) ... TMFL
Time of Flight ... TOF
Time of Flight Diffraction [*Nuclear energy*] (NUCP) ... TOFD
Time of Flight Diffraction [*Ultrasonic imaging*] ... TOFD
Time of Flight to Intercept [*Military*] (CAAL) ... T2
Time of Free Fall [*NASA*] (KSC) ... TFF
Time of Ignition ... TIG
Time of Ignition ... TIGN
Time of Intercept [*Military*] (CAAL) ... TOI
Time of Landing ... TL
Time of Last Update ... TLU
Time of Launch [*NASA*] ... L
Time of Launch [*NASA*] (KSC) ... T-O
Time of Lockout (SAA) ... TOLO
Time of Main Engine Cutoff [*Aerospace*] (MCD) ... TMECO
Time of Maneuver ... M
Time of Maximum [*Particle physics*] ... TOM
Time of Maximum Concentration [*Laboratory science*] (DAVI) ... T_{max}
Time of Nearest Approach ... TNA
Time of Origin [*Communications*] ... TOO
Time of Receipt [*Military*] (AABC) ... TOR
Time of Reception [*Communications*] ... TOR
Time of Retrofire [*NASA*] (KSC) ... TORF
Time of Rise (MSA) ... T/R
Time of Sunrise ... TESR
Time of Sunset ... TESS
Time of Takeoff [*Air Force*] (AFIT) ... TOT
Time of Transmission [*Communications*] ... TOT
Time of Travel (MCD) ... TOT
Time of Use [*Utility rates*] ... TOU
Time of Useful Consciousness [*Medicine*] ... TUC
Time of Useful Function [*Computer science*] (MHDB) ... TUF
Time of Wait [*Vehicle location systems*] ... TOW
Time of Week (SSD) ... TOW
Time Off in Lieu ... TOIL
Time on Jamming (IAA) ... TOJ
Time on Risk [*Insurance*] (AIA) ... TOR
Time on Tape [*Military*] ... TOT
Time on Target [*Artillery support*] ... TOT
Time on Track ... TOT
Time Only Emitter Location System (MCD) ... TOEL
Time Opening ... TO
Time Optimal Control (MCD) ... TOC
Time Out ... TMO
Time Out Circuit (MHDI) ... TOC
Time Out of Area (MCD) ... TOA
Time out of View ... TOV
Time Out to Enjoy (EA) ... TOTE
Time Over (IAA) ... TO
Time over Target [*Air support*] ... TOT
Time Overhead (NVT) ... TOH
Time Perception Inventory [*Test*] ... TPI
Time Period Tape [*Database*] [*Arbitron Ratings Co.*] [*Information service or system*] (CRD) ... TPT
Time Phasing Program [*NASA*] (KSC) ... TIPP
Time, Place, and Person ... TP & P
Time Polarity Control ... TPC
Time Postintegration (NASA) ... T+
Time Prior to Launch [*Usually followed by a number*] [*NASA*] (KSC) ... T
Time Priority Table ... TPT
Time Prism Filter [*Telecommunications*] (TEL) ... TPF
Time Problems Inventory [*Test*] ... TPRI
Time Processing Unit [*Automotive engineering Electronics*] ... TPU
Time Projection Chamber [*High-energy physics*] ... TPC
Time Pulse ... TP
Time Pulse Distributor (MCD) ... TPD
Time, Quality, Cost ... TQC
Time Quantized Frequency Modulation [*Telecommunications*] (IAA) ... TFM
Time Radius and Velocity Vector ... TRVV
Time Rate [*Payment system*] ... TR
Time Ratio Control (IAA) ... TRC
Time Ratio Modulation ... TRM
Time Record (MCD) ... TR
Time Recovery Loop [*Navy Navigation Satellite System*] (DNAB) ... TRL
Time Reference Scanning Beam [*Aviation*] ... TRSB
Time Reference Scanning Beam Microwave Landing System [*Aviation*] (OA) ... TRSBMLS
Time Reference System (MCD) ... TRS
Time Release (MAE) ... TR
Time Release Mechanism [*Martin-Baker seat system*] [*Aviation*] (NG) ... TRM
Time Release Unit (MCD) ... TRU
Time Remaining until Dive [*Air Force*] ... TRUD
Time Remaining until Transition [*Air Force*] ... TRUT
Time Repetitive Analog Contour Equipment (PDAA) ... TRACE
Time Resolved [*Fluoroscopy*] ... TR
Time Resolved Fluorescence Spectroscopy ... TRFO
Time Resolved X-Ray Absorption Spectroscopy ... TRXAS
Time Resources Corp. [*Vancouver Stock Exchange symbol*] ... TIS
Time Response Approximation ... TRAP
Time Routine [*Computer science*] (IAA) ... TR
Time Scheduled (NASA) ... TS
Time Scheduled Maintenance ... TSM
Time Sequenced [*NASA*] (KSC) ... TSEQ
Time Series Analysis ... TSA
Time Series Analysis and Modeling [*Software*] ... TSAM
Time Series Analysis Package ... TSAP
Time Series Generation System ... TSGS
Time Series Language (MHDB) ... TSL
Time Series Modeling System (MHDB) ... TSMS
Time Series Oriented Database ... TSODB
Time Series Package [*Bell System*] ... TSPAK
Time Series Processor Software [*Bureau of the Census*] (GFGA) ... TSP
Time Service (IAA) ... TS
Time Shack [*NAS operations desk*] ... TS

Time Share International Data Communications Network [*Telecommunications*] (IAA) .... TIMNET
Time Sharing Resources, Inc. [*Information service or system*] (IID) .... TSR
Time Sharing Services Management System (GFGA) .... TSSMS
Time Sharing System Performance Activity Recorder (PDAA) .... TS/SPAR
Time Shift Keying .... TSK
Time Signal Generator .... TSG
Time Since Last Inspection (MCD) .... TSLI
Time since New [*Navy*] (NG) .... TSN
Time Since Overhaul [*of engine, or other equipment*] .... TSO
Time Slice End [*Computer science*] (OA) .... TSE
Time Slot [*Telecommunications*] (TEL) .... TS
Time Slot Access .... TSA
Time Slot Access Unit [*Telecommunications*] (TEL) .... TSAU
Time Slot Assignment Circuit [*Telecommunications*] (TEL) .... TSAC
Time Slot Input [*Telecommunications*] (IAA) .... TSI
Time Slot Interchange [*Telecommunications*] (TEL) .... TSI
Time Slot Interchange Circuit [*Telecommunications*] (IAA) .... TSIC
Time Slot Zero [*Telecommunications*] (IAA) .... TSO
Time Sorting Program .... TSP
Time Sows and Reaps [*Acronym used in name of Tsar Publishing Co.*] .... TSAR
Time, Space, and Matter [*Princeton University course title*] (AEE) .... TSM
Time Spent Listening (WDMC) .... TSL
Time Standard Unit .... TSU
Time Status Register .... TSR
Time Sterile Indicator .... TSI
Time Study Analysis .... TSA
Time Switch (MSA) .... TS
Time Switch [*Telecommunications*] (TEL) .... TSW
Time Synchronization Device .... TSD
Time Temperature Indicator (IEEE) .... TTI
Time Temperature Transformation .... TTT
Time, Temperature, Turbulence [*Fuel technology*] .... TTT
Time Template Indicator .... TTI
Time to Apogee [*Aerospace*] (MCD) .... TTA
Time to Blackout .... TTB
Time to Circular (MCD) .... TC
Time to Circularize Orbit (MCD) .... TTC
Time to Closest Point of Approach [*Navigation*] .... TCPA
Time to Computation .... TC
Time to Control .... TTC
Time to Echo [*Medicine*] .... TE
Time to Emplacement [*Military*] .... T(EMP)
Time to End .... TTE
Time to Equipment Reset [*Computer science*] (MDG) .... TX
Time to Event [*NASA*] (KSC) .... TTE
Time to Failure .... TTF
Time to Failure Location .... TFL
Time to Fire [*Military*] (CAAL) .... TTF
Time to First Fix [*Quality control*] .... TTFF
Time to First System Failure (MHDI) .... TFSF
Time to Function .... TF
Time to Go [*Apollo*] [*NASA*] .... TGO
Time to Go (SAA) .... TOGO
Time to Go [*Air Force*] .... TTG
Time to Intercept [*Missiles*] (NG) .... TTI
Time to Launch [*Navy*] (CAAL) .... TL
Time to Peak Filling Rate [*Cardiology*] .... TPFR
Time to Peak Flow Velocity [*Cardiology*] .... TPV
Time to Peak Tension .... TPT
Time to Perigee (MCD) .... TP
Time to Perigee (MCD) .... TTP
Time to Reach Peak Tension .... TRPT
Time to Repair [*Military*] (CAAL) .... TTR
Time to Repair Part .... TRP
Time to Repetition [*Medicine*] .... TR
Time to Retrofire .... TR
Time to Station (DA) .... TTS
Time to Subsequent Fix [*Quality control*] .... TTSF
Time to Sustained Respirations [*Obstetrics*] .... TSR
Time to Target (AAG) .... TTT
Time to Turn [*Ship or aircraft*] .... TTT
Time Trial .... T
Time until in Range .... TUIR
Time Urgent Hard Target Kill Potential (MCD) .... TUHTKP
Time Use Analysis [*Test*] .... TUA
Time Variable Parameter (IAA) .... TVP
Time Variable Reflectivity (MCD) .... TVR
Time Variant Automation (IAA) .... TVA
Time Variation of Gain .... TV
Time Variation of Gain .... TVG
Time Variation of Loss (IAA) .... TVL
Time Video Information Services, Inc. (IID) .... TVIS
Time War Cp 1 8.78% Pfd Tr Sec [*NYSE symbol*] (TTSB) .... TWXPrT
Time Warner Capital I [*Associated Press*] (SAG) .... TWCap
Time Warner Capital I [*NYSE symbol*] (SAG) .... TWX
Time Warner Entertainment (ECON) .... TWE
Time Warner Fin Tr'PERCS' [*NYSE symbol*] (TTSB) .... THA
Time Warner Financing Trust PERCS [*NYSE symbol*] (SAG) .... THA
Time Warner Financing Trust PERCS [*Associated Press*] (SAG) .... TW Fin
Time Warner, Inc. [*Associated Press*] (SAG) .... TimeWa
Time Warner, Inc. [*NYSE symbol*] (SPSG) .... TWX
Time Warner, Inc. Holding Co. [*Associated Press*] (SAG) .... TimeWarn
Time Weighted Average [*Data sampling*] .... TWA
Time Wire Transmission (IAA) .... TWT

Time Wire Transmission .... TWX
Time without Symptoms of Disease and Systemic Treatment [*Medicine*] (CDI) .... TWSST
Time Word .... TW
Time Zero (MCD) T-0
Time Zero .... TZ
Time Zero Pulse .... TZP
Time-Adjusted Rate of Return .... TARR
Time-Authenticated Cryptographic Identity Transmission [*Military*] .... TACIT
Time-Bandwidth .... TB
Time-Based Competition [*Business term*] .... TBC
Time-Based Recurring Cost .... TBRC
Time-Compensated Gain [*Cardiology*] .... TCG
Time-Consistent Busy Hour [*Telecommunications*] (EECA) .... TCBM
Time-Constrained [*Computer science*] .... TC
Time-Correlated Photon Counting [*Spectrometry*] .... TCPC
Time-Correlated Single Photon Counting [*Analytical chemistry*] .... TCSPC
Time-Critical Shipment Committee [*Defunct*] (EA) .... TCSC
Time-Critical, Unspecified Area .... TCUA
Timed (MSA) .... TMD
Timed Access to Pertinent Excerpts .... TAPE
Timed Disintegration [*Pharmacy*] .... TD
Timed Environment Multipartitioned Operating System .... TEMPOS
Timed Forced Expiratory Volume [*Laboratory science*] (DAVI) .... TFEV
Timed Induction with Supercharge [*Automotive engineering*] .... TISC
Timed Scanned Array RADAR .... TSAR
Timed Vital Capacity .... TVC
Timed Wire Service (WDAA) .... TWS
Time-Dependence Fluorescence [*Chemistry*] .... TDF
Time-Dependent Stokes Shift [*Physical chemistry*] .... TDSS
Time-Division Circuit Switching [*Telecommunications*] .... TDCS
Time-Division Data Link [*Radio*] .... TDDL
Time-Division Data Link Print-Out [*Telecommunications*] (IAA) .... TDDLPO
Time-Division Digital Multiplexer (MCD) .... TDDM
Time-Division Electronics Switching System (KSC) .... TIDES
Time-Division Exchange .... TDX
Time-Division [*or Time-Domain*] **Multiple Access** [*Computer control system*] .... TDMA
Time-Division Multiplex Device [*Radio*] .... TDMD
Time-Division Multiplex System [*Radio*] (MCD) .... TDMS
Time-Division Multiplex - Variable Destination Multiple Access [*Telecommunications*] (TEL) .... TDM-VDMA
Time-Division Multiplexed Analogue Components (NITA) .... TMAC
Time-Division Multiplexor [*Computer science*] (DOM) .... TDM
Time-Division Switching [*Telecommunications*] .... TDS
Time-Domain Automatic Network Analyzer [*National Institute of Standards and Technology*] .... TDANA
Time-Domain Coding .... TDC
Time-Domain Coding Technique .... TDCT
Time-Domain Electromagnetics [*Technique for searching for underground water*] .... TDEM
Time-Domain Filter .... TDF
Time-Domain Prony Method (IAA) .... TDPM
Time-Domain Reflectometry Microcomputer .... TDRM
Time-Domain Spectroscopy (IEEE) .... TDS
Timed-Release [*Pharmacy*] .... TR
Time-Exposure Setting [*Photography*] (WDMC) .... T-setting
Time-Focused Crystal Analyzer [*Spectrometer*] .... TFXA
Time-Frequency Dissemination (IEEE) .... TF/D
Time-Independent Escape Sequence [*Computer science*] (CDE) .... TIES
Timekeeper [*Sports*] .... T
Timekeeper (WGA) .... TMKPR
Time-Lapse Cinematography .... TLC
Time-Life Books [*Publisher*] .... T-L
Time-Life Books .... TLB
Time-Life Education .... TLE
Time-Life International .... TLI
Time-Limited Impulse Response [*Telecommunications*] (IAA) .... TLIR
Time-Limited Signal .... TLS
Timeline (MCD) .... TL
Timeline, Inc. [*Associated Press*] (SAG) .... Timeline
Timeline, Inc. [*Associated Press*] (SAG) .... TimeIn
Timeline, Inc. [*NASDAQ symbol*] (SAG) .... TMLN
Timely [*Record label*] .... Tim
Timely Responsive Integrated Multiuse System (MCD) .... TRIM
Time-Modulated Antenna .... TMA
Time-Multiplexer Communications Channels .... TMCC
Time-Multiplexer Unit [*Telecommunications*] (IAA) .... TMU
Time-of-Flight Aerosol Beam Spectrometry .... TOFABS
Time-of-Flight and Absorbance [*Physics*] .... TOFA
Time-of-Flight Isochronous Spectrometer .... TOFI
Time-of-Flight Mass Spectrometer .... TOFMS
Time-of-Flight Scattering and Recoiling Spectrometry .... TOFSARS
Time-of-Flight Secondary Ion Mass Spectrometry .... TOFSIMS
Time-of-Flight Spectrometer [*or Spectroscopy*] .... TOFS
Time-of-Update .... TU
Time-on-Station [*Military*] (INF) .... TOS
Time-On-Stream [*Theory*] [*Engineering*] .... TOS
Time-Ordered Programmer Integrated Circuit [*NASA*] .... TOPIC
Time-Ordered Reporting System (MCD) .... TORS
Time-Ordered System (MCD) .... TOS
Time-Ordered Techniques Experiment System .... TOTES
Time-Oriented Metropolitan Model (MCD) .... TOMM
Time-Out .... TO
Time-Phased Allocation (MCD) .... TPA

Time-Phased Downgrading and Reclassification System [*Military*] (DNAB) .... TPDRS
Time-Phased Force Deployment Data [*Military*] (AABC) .... TPFDD
Time-Phased Force Deployment List [*Military*] (AFM) .... TPFDL
Time-Phased Transportation Requirements List [*Military*] (AABC) .... TPTRL
Time-Phased-Action Plan [*DoD*] .... TPAP
Timer (IAA) .... T
Timer (AAG) .... TMR
Timer, Actuator, Fin, Fuze (DWSG) .... TAFF
Timer Demodulator .... TIDE
Timer Queue Element .... TQE
Time-Resolved Electron Energy-Loss Spectroscopy .... TREELS
Time-Resolved Emission Spectra .... TRES
Time-Resolved Europium Excitation Spectroscopy .... TREES
Time-Resolved Immunofluorometric Assay [*Clinical chemistry*] .... triFMA
Time-Resolved Liquid Scintillation Counting [*Analytical procedure*] .... TRLSC
Time-Resolved Liquid Scintillation Counting [*Instrumentation*] .... TR-LSC
Time-Resolved Microwave Conductivity [*Physical chemistry*] .... TRMC
Time-Resolved Phosphorimetry [*Analytical chemistry*] .... TRP
Time-Resolved Spectrometry .... TRS
Time-Resolved X-Ray Diffraction .... TRXRD
Time-Reversal [*Atomic physics*] .... T
Time-Reversal Invariance [*Physics*] .... TRI
Time-Reversal Mirrors [*For acoustic study*] .... TRM
Times [*Multiplication sign*] [*Mathematics*] X
Times Advertising Printing Co., Pemberton, NJ [*Library symbol Library of Congress*] (LCLS) .... NjPeT
Times at Bat [*Baseball*] .... TB
Times Beacon Co., Manahawkin, NJ [*Library symbol Library of Congress*] (LCLS) .... NjManhT
Times British Colonies Review [*London*] [*A publication*] .... TBCR
Times Educational Supplement [*A publication*] (BRI) .... TES
Times Educational Supplement Scotland (AIE) .... TESS
Times, Elevations, Azimuths, Ranges, and Range Rates [*Aerospace*] .... TEARR
Times Higher Education Supplement (AIE) .... THES
Times Journal, Vineland, NJ [*Library symbol Library of Congress*] (LCLS) .... NjVT
Times Law Reports [*England*] [*A publication*] (DLA) .... Times L (Eng)
Times Law Reports [*England*] [*A publication*] (DLA) .... Times L Rep
Times Law Reports [*Ceylon*] [*A publication*] (DLA) .... Times L Rep
Times Law Reports [*England*] [*A publication*] (DLA) .... Times LR
Times Law Reports [*Ceylon*] [*A publication*] (DLA) .... Times LR
Times Law Reports [*1884-1952*] [*England*] [*A publication*] (DLA) .... TLR
Times Literary Supplement [*A publication*] (BRI) .... TLS
Times Mirror 4.25%'PEPS'2001 [*NYSE symbol*] (TTSB) .... TME
Times Mirror 'A' [*NYSE symbol*] (TTSB) .... TMC
Times Mirror cm Sr'B'Pfd [*NYSE symbol*] (TTSB) .... TMCPrP
Times Mirror Co. [*Associated Press*] (SAG) .... TimM
Times Mirror Co. [*Associated Press*] (SAG) TimM01
Times Mirror Co. [*Associated Press*] (SAG) .... TimMir
Times Mirror Co. [*NYSE symbol*] (SAG) .... TMC
Times Mirror Co. [*NYSE symbol*] (SAG) .... TME
Times Mirror Magazines [*A publication*] .... TMM
Times Mirror Press .... TMP
Times Mirror Videotex Services, Inc. [*Information service or system Inactive*] (IID) .... TMVS
Times Network for Schools (NITA) .... TNS
Times Newspapers Ltd. [*British*] .... TNL
Times of Increased Probability [*Earthquake prediction*] .... TIP
Times On-Line Services [*Information service or system*] (IID) .... TOLS
Times Roman [*Typography*] (DGA) .... TR
Times, Scotch Plains, NJ [*Library symbol Library of Congress*] (LCLS) .... NjScpT
Times Square Energy Resource Ltd. [*Vancouver Stock Exchange symbol*] .... TMS
Times Three [*Referring to orientation to time, place, and person*] [*Neurology*] (DAVI) X3
Times-Bulletin, Boonton, NJ [*Library symbol Library of Congress*] (LCLS) .... NjBooT
Timeshare Developers Association [*British*] (DBA) .... TDA
Timeshare, Inc. Network [*Telecommunications*] (TEL) .... TYMNET
Time-Share Peripherals [*Computer science*] (IAA) .... TSP
Time-Shared Amplifier .... TSA
Time-Shared Data Management [*System*] [*Computer science*] (IEEE) .... TSDM
Time-Shared/Data Management System .... TDMS
Time-Shared/Data Management System .... TS/DMS
Time-Shared Disk Operating System [*Computer science*] (IEEE) .... TSDOS
Time-Shared Executive [*Computer science*] (IAA) .... TSEXEC
Time-Shared General Accounting System [*Computer science*] (MHDI) .... TSGAS
Time-Shared Input/Output [*Data processing*] .... TSIO
Time-Shared Interactive Computer-Controlled Information Television [*System*] [*Mitre Corp. Brigham Young University 1971*] .... TICCIT
Time-Shared Monitor System [*Computer science*] (IEEE) .... TMS
Time-Shared Monitor System [*Computer science*] (IEEE) .... TSM
Time-Shared Reactive On-Line Laboratory [*Computer science*] (MHDI) .... TROLL
Time-Shared Relational Associative Memory Program [*Computer science*] (IEEE) .... TRAMP
Time-Shared Routines for Analysis, Classification, and Evaluation (DIT) .... TRACE
Time-Shared Supervisory System (IAA) .... TSS
Time-Shared System (NITA) .... TSS
Time-Shared Terminal [*Computer science*] (IAA) .... TST
Timesharer Developers' Group [*British*] .... TDG
Time-Sharing [*Computer science*] .... TS
Time-Sharing Accounting Package (MHDB) .... TAP
Time-Sharing Activity Report System [*Computer science*] (IAA) .... TSAR
Time-Sharing and Multiplexing Numerical Control [*Telecommunications*] (IAA) .... TSNC
Time-Sharing Assembly Program [*Computer science*] (DIT) .... TAP
Time-Sharing Business Package [*Computer science*] (IAA) .... TSBP
Time-Sharing Control (NITA) .... TSC
Time-Sharing Control Task [*Computer science*] (BUR) .... TSC
Time-Sharing Control Task (NITA) .... TSCT
Time-Sharing Execution [*Computer science*] (IAA) .... TSX
Time-Sharing Executive [*Modular Computer Systems*] [*Computer science*] .... TSX
Time-Sharing Executive System [*Computer science*] (IAA) .... TSX
Time-Sharing Job Control Block [*Computer science*] (IBMDP) .... TJB
Time-Sharing Multiplex [*Telecommunications*] (IAA) .... TSM
Time-Sharing Multiplex Unit [*Telecommunications*] (IAA) .... TSMU
Time-Sharing Operating Control System [*Computer science*] (IAA) .... TSOC
Time-Sharing Operating System [*Computer science*] .... TOPS
Time-Sharing Operating System [*Computer science*] (IAA) .... TOS
Time-Sharing Operating System [*Computer science*] (IEEE) .... TSOS
Time-Sharing Operation of Product Structure Directory System (PDAA) .... TOPSY
Time-Sharing Option [*Computer science*] .... TSO
Time-Sharing Option Extensions (HGAA) .... TSO/E
Time-Sharing Option for the Virtual Telecommunications Access Method [*Computer science*] (MHDI) .... TSO/VTAM
Time-Sharing Programming System [*Computer science*] (IEEE) .... TSPS
Time-Sharing Real-Time Operating System (IAA) .... TROS
Time-Sharing System [*Computer science*] .... TSS
Time-Sharing System Message Control Program (NITA) .... TSSMCP
Time-Sharing Terminals, Inc. .... TST
Time-Sharing - Virtual System [*Computer science*] (MCD) .... TSVS
Time-Significant Item (MCD) .... TSI
Time-Significant Item List (AAG) .... TSIL
Timeslips III Accounting Link [*Computer science*] .... TAL
Timeslot Generator [*Telecommunications*] (TEL) .... TSG
Time-Space-Position-Information (MCD) .... TSPI
Time-Space-Space-Space-Time [*Telecommunications*] (TEL) .... TSSST
Time-Space-Time [*Digital switching*] [*Telecommunications*] (TEL) .... TST
Time-Span-of-Discretion (PDAA) .... TSD
Time-Speed-Distance [*Vehicle testing*] .... TSD
Timetable (DS) .... TT
Time-Tagged Event [*Remote sensing*] .... TTE
Time-Temperature Index .... TTI
Time-Temperature Recorder .... TTR
Time-Temperature Recorder and Integrator (MCD) .... TTRI
Time-to-Amplitude Converter .... TAC
Time-to-Autoignition [*NASA*] (KSC) .... TAI
Time-to-Digital Converter [*Instrumentation*] .... TDC
Time-to-Frequency Transformation [*Electronics*] (OA) .... TFT
Time-to-Go Dial .... TTGD
Time-to-Go Rating [*Air Force*] (IAA) .... TTGR
Time-to-Intercept .... TI
Time-to-Jitter Flag .... TJF
Time-to-Live (TNIG) .... TTL
Time-to-Peak [*tension*] [*Neurology*] (DAVI) .... TTP
Time-to-Peak Tension (DAVI) .... tp
Time-to-Pulse Height Converter .... TPHC
Time-to-Retrograde [*NASA*] (KSC) .... TR
Time-Varying Adaptive Correlation .... TVAC
Time-Varying Coefficient .... TVC
Time-Varying Sequential Measuring [*Device*] .... TVSM
Time-Varying Signal Measurement (IAA) .... TVSM
Time-Varying Spectral Display .... TVSD
Time-Weighted Average Concentration [*Toxicology*] .... TWAC
Time-Weighted Average Exposure [*Toxicology*] .... TWAE
Timika/Tembagapura [*Indonesia*] [*ICAO location identifier*] (ICLI) .... WABP
Timimoun [*Algeria*] [*ICAO location identifier*] (ICLI) .... DAUT
Timimoun [*Algeria*] [*Airport symbol*] (AD) .... TMX
Timing .... TMG
Timing and Control Panel .... TCP
Timing and Countdown [*NASA*] (NASA) .... T & CD
Timing and Injection Rate Control System [*Diesel engines*] .... TICS
Timing and Telemetry .... T/T
Timing Belt Pulley .... TBP
Timing Channel .... TC
Timing Control Unit .... TCU
Timing Cover and Seal Set [*Automotive engineering*] .... TCS
Timing Cover Gasket [*Automotive engineering*] .... TC
Timing Data Distributor (IAA) .... TDD
Timing Data Input-Output .... TDIO
Timing Defense Depot (SAA) .... TDD
Timing Device .... TD
Timing Devices (MSA) .... TMGD
Timing Electronics (KSC) .... TE
Timing Filter Analyzer .... TFA
Timing Gage (IAA) .... TG
Timing Gate (AAG) .... TG
Timing Level Generator (IAA) .... TLG
Timing Negative Film .... TNF
Timing of Movements [*Physiology*] .... TM
Timing Operation Center .... TOC
Timing Point (AFM) .... TP
Timing Pulse Generator .... TPG
Timing Pulse Idler .... TPI
Timing Read Error .... TRE
Timing Relay Valve .... TRV
Timing Release Pin .... TRP
Timing Results and Competition Knowledge [*Auto racing*] .... TRACK
Timing Selector .... TS

Timing Single-Channel Analyzer .... TSCA
Timing System (MCD) .... TS
Timing Systems Group [*NASA*] .... TSG
Timing Terminal Unit (NASA) .... TTU
Timing Unit .... TU
Timiskaming [*Quebec*] [*Seismograph station code, US Geological Survey Closed*] (SEIS) .... TMK
Timisoara [*Romania*] [*Seismograph station code, US Geological Survey*] (SEIS) .... TIM
Timisoara [*Romania*] [*Airport symbol*] (OAG) .... TSR
Timisoara/Giarmata [*Romania*] [*ICAO location identifier*] (ICLI) .... LRTR
TI-MIX [*Texas Instruments Mini/Microcomputer Information Exchange*] **Europe** (EA) .... TiMixE
[*The*] **Timken Co.** [*Associated Press*] (SAG) .... Timken
[*The*] **Timken Co.** [*Formerly, TDX*] [*NYSE symbol*] (SPSG) .... TKR
Timken Co., Research Library, Canton, OH [*OCLC symbol*] (OCLC) .... OTM
Timken Tapered Roller Bearing .... TTRB
Timminco Ltd. [*Toronto Stock Exchange symbol*] .... TIM
Timmins [*Canada*] [*Airport symbol*] (OAG) .... YTS
Timmins Museum, South Porcupine, ON, Canada [*Library symbol*] [*Library of Congress*] (LCLS) .... CaOSpTM
Timmins Museum, South Porcupine, Ontario [*Library symbol National Library of Canada*] (BIB) .... OSPTM
Timmins, ON [*Television station call letters*] CBLFT-3
Timmins, ON [*Television station call letters*] .... CFCL
Timmins, ON [*Television station call letters*] .... CITO
Timmins, ON [*FM radio station call letters*] .... CJQQ
Timmins, ON [*AM radio station call letters*] .... CKGB
Timmins, ON [*AM radio station call letters*] .... CKOY
Timmins, ON [*ICAO location identifier*] (ICLI) .... CYTS
Timmins Public Library, Ontario [*Library symbol National Library of Canada*] (NLC) .... OTI
Timmins Public Library, Timmins, ON, Canada [*Library symbol Library of Congress*] (LCLS) .... CaOTi
Timoleon [*of Plutarch*] [*Classical studies*] (OCD) .... Tim
Timon of Athens [*Shakespearean work*] .... Tim
Timothy [*New Testament book*] .... Tim
Timothy [*New Testament book*] .... Tm
Timothy Grass Pollen [*Immunology*] .... TGP
Timpani [*Kettle drum*] .... TIMP
Timpano [*Music*] .... TP
Timpanogos Cave National Monument .... TiCA
Timrod Library, Summerville, SC [*Library symbol Library of Congress*] (LCLS) .... ScSum
Timrod Library, Summerville, SC [*Library symbol*] [*Library of Congress*] (LCLS) .... ScSumL
Tin [*Chemical*] (EERA) .... Sn
Tin [*Chemical element*] (DOG) .... Sn
Tin .... TN
Tin Can Sailors (EA) .... TCS
Tin Can Tourists of the World (EA) .... TCT
Tin City [*Alaska*] [*Seismograph station code, US Geological Survey*] (SEIS) .... TNA
Tin City [*Alaska*] [*Airport symbol*] (OAG) .... TNC
Tin City Air Force Station [*Alaska*] [*ICAO location identifier*] (ICLI) .... PATC
Tin City, AK [*Location identifier FAA*] (FAAL) .... TNC
Tin Container Collectors Association (EA) .... TCCA
Tin Decorating Co. .... TINDECO
Tin Plate .... TP
Tin Research Institute (EA) .... TRI
Tin Telluride Crystal .... TTC
Tin Triphenyl [*or Triphenyltin*] **Acetate** [*Organic chemistry*] .... TPTA
Tinak [*Marshall Islands*] [*Airport symbol*] (OAG) .... TIC
Tinctura [*Tincture*] [*Latin*] .... Tct
Tinctura [*tincture*] [*Latin*] [*Pharmacology*] (DAVI) .... tinc
Tinctura [*Tincture*] [*Pharmacy*] .... TINCT
Tinctura [*Tincture*] [*Pharmacy*] .... TR
Tinctura [*Tincture*] [*Pharmacy*] (ROG) .... TRA
Tinctura Opii [*Tincture of Opium*] .... TO
Tinctura Opii Camphorata [*Paregoric Elixir*] [*Pharmacy*] (ROG) .... TOC
Tincture (ADA) .... TINC
Tincture [*Pharmacy*] (DAVI) .... TR
Tincture of Green Soap [*Medicine*] (DMAA) .... TGS
Tincture of Opium [*Pharmacology*] (DAVI) .... TO
Tincture of Time [*Medical slang for treatment of problems that are better left alone*] .... TOT
Tindal [*Australia ICAO location identifier*] (ICLI) .... ADTN
Tindouf [*Algeria*] [*ICAO location identifier*] (ICLI) .... DAOF
Tindouf [*Algeria*] [*Airport symbol*] (OAG) .... TIN
Tinemaha [*California*] [*Seismograph station code, US Geological Survey*] (SEIS) .... TIN
Tin-Free Steel .... TFS
Tin-Free Steel Chromium-Type (PDAA) .... TFS-CT
Tingi-Tingi [*Zaire*] [*ICAO location identifier*] (ICLI) .... FZOB
Tingmiarmiut [*Greenland*] [*ICAO location identifier*] (ICLI) .... BGTM
Tingo Maria [*Peru*] [*ICAO location identifier*] (ICLI) .... SPGM
Tingo Maria [*Peru*] [*Airport symbol*] (OAG) .... TGI
Tinian [*Mariana Islands*] [*Airport symbol*] (OAG) .... TIQ
Tiniteqilaq [*Greenland*] [*ICAO location identifier*] (ICLI) .... BGTN
Tinkers Knob [*California*] [*Seismograph station code, US Geological Survey*] (SEIS) .... TNK
Tinley Park Mental Health Center, Tinley Park, IL [*Library symbol Library of Congress*] (LCLS) .... ITpM
Tinley Park Public Library, Tinley Park, IL [*Library symbol Library of Congress*] (LCLS) .... ITp
Tinned .... TD
Tinned .... TND
Tinned Copper .... TC
Tinned Copper .... TDCU
Tinned Copper Weld .... TCW
Tinny and Buzzing [*Sounds*] .... TIZZY
Tinogasta [*Argentina ICAO location identifier*] (ICLI) .... SANI
Tinplate Stockholders' and Merchants' Association [*British*] (BI) .... TSMA
Tinsley Laboratories, Inc. [*NASDAQ symbol*] (NQ) .... TNSL
Tinsley Labs [*NASDAQ symbol*] (TTSB) .... TNSL
Tinsley Labs, Inc. [*Associated Press*] (SAG) .... Tinsley
Tint (VRA) .... tnt
Tinted Glass .... TG
Tinted Printing [*Paper*] (DGA) .... TP
Tintina Mines Ltd. [*Toronto Stock Exchange symbol*] .... TTS
Tinting Strength [*Dye chemistry*] .... TS
Tinto Gold Corp. [*Vancouver Stock Exchange symbol*] .... TNT
Tintype (VRA) .... TTYP
Tinwald's Reports, Scotch Court of Session [*A publication*] (DLA) .... Tinw
Tiny Humans Underground Military Bureau [*Government organization in TV cartoon series "Tom of T.H.U.M.B."*] .... THUMB
Tiny Income, Parents Supporting [*Lifestyle classification*] .... Tips
Tioga, LA [*FM radio station call letters*] .... KLAA
Tioga, ND [*AM radio station call letters*] .... KTGO
Tioga, ND [*Location identifier FAA*] (FAAL) .... VEX
Tioga, PA [*FM radio station call letters*] .... WPHD
Tioman [*Malaysia*] [*Airport symbol*] (OAG) .... TOD
Tiong Chong [*Indonesia*] [*ICAO location identifier*] (ICLI) .... WRLI
Tiouine [*Morocco*] [*Seismograph station code, US Geological Survey*] (SEIS) .... TIO
Tioxide Canada, Inc., Sorel, Quebec [*Library symbol National Library of Canada*] (NLC) .... QSTC
Tip [*Switchboard plug*] [*Telecommunications*] (TEL) .... T
Tip Air Mass Injection [*Helicopter*] .... TAMI
Tip Speed .... TS
Tiphook PCL [*British ICAO designator*] (FAAC) .... BOX
Tip-of-Tongue Phenomenon [*Medicine*] .... TOT
Tippecanoe Battleground National Historical Landmark (EA) .... TBNHL
Tippecanoe County Historical Association, Lafayette, IN [*Library symbol Library of Congress*] (LCLS) .... InLTHi
tippecanoe County Public Library, Lafayette, IN [*Library symbol*] [*Library of Congress*] (LCLS) .... InL
Tipped In (DGA) .... Tpd I
Tipper [*Shipping*] (DS) .... T
Tipperary [*County in Ireland*] (WGA) .... Tip
Tipperary [*County in Ireland*] .... TIPP
Tipperary Corp. [*Associated Press*] (SAG) .... Tippery
Tipperary Corp. [*AMEX symbol*] (SAG) .... TPY
Tippers [*Shipping*] (DCTA) .... TS
Tippers Anonymous (EA) .... TA
Tippers International (EA) .... TI
Tippi [*Ethiopia*] [*ICAO location identifier*] (ICLI) .... HATP
Tippi [*Ethiopia*] [*Airport symbol*] (OAG) .... TIE
Tipping Bucket Gauge (NOAA) .... TBG
Tipron Public Library, Tipron, IA [*Library symbol Library of Congress*] (LCLS) .... IaTip
Tipton, CA [*FM radio station call letters*] (RBYB) .... KZZC-FM
Tipton County Hospital, Covington, TN [*Library symbol Library of Congress*] (LCLS) .... TCovH
Tipton County Public Library, Tipton, IN [*Library symbol Library of Congress*] (LCLS) .... InTi
Tipton County Public Library, Tipton, IN [*Library symbol*] [*Library of Congress*] (LCLS) .... InTip
Tiptonville [*Tennessee*] [*Seismograph station code, US Geological Survey Closed*] (SEIS) DY3
Tiptonville, TN [*FM radio station call letters*] .... WAAT
Tipuani [*Bolivia*] [*ICAO location identifier*] (ICLI) .... SLTP
Tiputa [*Tuamotu Archipelago*] [*Seismograph station code, US Geological Survey*] (SEIS) .... TPT
Tiputini [*Ecuador*] [*ICAO location identifier*] (ICLI) .... SETI
Tir Systems Ltd. [*Vancouver Stock Exchange symbol*] .... TIY
Tiraid Community Unit, School District 2, St. Jacob, IL [*Library symbol Library of Congress*] (LCLS) .... IStJSD
Tirailleur Regiments [*Military*] .... TR
Tirana [*Albania*] [*Airport symbol*] (OAG) .... TIA
Tirana [*Albania*] [*Seismograph station code, US Geological Survey*] (SEIS) .... TIR
Tiravita Munnerrat Kalam .... TMK
Tire and Rim Association (EA) .... TRA
Tire Control System [*Automotive engineering*] .... TCS
Tire Degradation Monitor (MCD) .... TDM
Tire Industry Safety Council (EA) .... TISC
Tire Inflation Label [*Automotive engineering*] .... TIL
Tire Management Terminal [*Automotive engineering*] .... TMT
Tire Performance Criteria [*General Motors Corp.*] .... TPC
Tire Pressure [*Automotive engineering*] .... TP
Tire Pressure Indicating System (MCD) .... TPI
Tire Pressure Indicating System (MCD) .... TPIS
Tire Retread Information Bureau (EA) .... TRIB
Tire Retreading Institute (EA) .... TRI
Tire Uniformity Grading [*Automotive engineering*] .... TUG
Tired Bureaucrat Syndrome .... TBS
Tiree [*British ICAO location identifier*] (ICLI) .... EGPU
Tiree Island [*Scotland*] [*Airport symbol*] (AD) .... TIR
Tiree Island [*Scotland*] [*Airport symbol*] (OAG) .... TRE
Tires as Imaginative Recreation Equipment .... TIRE
Tires, Batteries, and Accessories .... TBA
Tirgu Mures [*Romania*] [*Airport symbol*] (OAG) .... TGM

Tirgu Mures/Vidrasau [*Romania*] [*ICAO location identifier*] (ICLI) ... LRTM

TIROS [*Television and Infrared Observation Satellite*] **Ice Reconnaissance** [*NASA*] ... TIREC

TIROS [*Television and Infrared Observation Satellite*] **Information Processor** [*Telecommunications*] ... TIP

TIROS [*Television and Infrared Observation Satellite*] **Operational Satellite** [*NASA*] ... TOS

TIROS [*Television and Infrared Observation Satellite*] **Operational Satellite System** [*NASA*] ... TOSS

TIROS [*Television Infrared Observational Satellite*] **Operational System** [*Marine science*] (OSRA) ... TOS

TIROS [*Television and Infrared Observation Satellite*] **Operational System** (USDC) ... TOS

TIROS [*Television and Infrared Observation Satellite*] **Operational VerticalSounder** [*NASA*] ... TOVS

Tirstrup [*Denmark ICAO location identifier*] (ICLI) ... EKAH

Tiruchchirappalli [*India*] [*ICAO location identifier*] (ICLI) ... VOTR

Tiruchirappalli [*India*] [*Airport symbol*] (OAG) ... TRZ

Tirupati [*India*] [*Airport symbol*] (OAG) ... TIR

Tirupeti [*India*] [*ICAO location identifier*] (ICLI) ... VOTP

TIS Mortgage Investment Co. [*NYSE symbol*] (CTT) ... TIS

TIS Mortgage Investors Co. [*Associated Press*] (SAG) ... TIS

TIS Mtge Investment [*NYSE symbol*] (TTSB) ... TIS

Tisbury, MA [*FM radio station call letters*] ... WMVY

Tiselius Electrophoresis Apparatus ... TEA

TISEO RADAR Logic Unit [*Air Force*] (MCD) ... TRLU

Tishomingo, OK [*FM radio station call letters*] ... KTSH

Tiskilwa Community Unit, School District 300, Tiskilwa, IL [*Library symbol Library of Congress*] (LCLS) ... ITisSD

Tiskilwa Township Library, Tiskilwa, IL [*Library symbol Library of Congress*] (LCLS) ... ITis

Tissu Musculaire Specifique [*France*] [*Medicine*] ... TMS

Tissue (ADA) ... TIS

Tissue (VRA) ... tis

Tissue Angiogenesis Factor [*Medicine*] (DMAA) ... TAF

Tissue Banks International [*An association*] (EA) ... TBI

Tissue Coding Factor [*Medicine*] (DMAA) ... TCF

Tissue Culture [*Microbiology*] ... TC

Tissue Culture Association (EA) ... TCA

Tissue Culture Association, Lake Placid, NY [*Library symbol Library of Congress*] (LCLS) ... NLpT

Tissue Culture Dose (AAMN) ... TCD

Tissue Culture Dose, 50% Infectivity ... TCD_{50}

Tissue Culture for Crops Project [*Colorado State University*] [*Research center*] (RCD) ... TCCP

Tissue Culture Infectious [*or Infective*] **Dose** ... TCID

Tissue Culture Medium ... TCM

Tissue Equivalent Ionization Chamber ... TEIC

Tissue Equivalent Proportional Counter (PDAA) ... TEPC

Tissue Factor [*Clinical chemistry*] ... TF

Tissue Factor Pathway Inhibitor [*Biochemistry*] ... TFPI

Tissue Glucose Threshold [*Medicine*] (BARN) ... TGT

Tissue Inhibitor of Metalloproteinases [*Biochemistry*] ... TIMP

Tissue Plasminogen Activator [*Anticlotting agent*] ... TPA

Tissue Polypeptide Antigen [*Immunochemistry*] ... TPA

Tissue Resistance [*Laboratory science*] (DAVI) ... Rti

Tissue Respiratory Factors [*Medicine*] ... TRF

Tissue Tolerance Dose (MAE) ... TTD

Tissue Type Specific [*Antigen*] ... TTS

Tissue Volume [*Laboratory science*] (DAVI) ... V_T

Tissue-Coding Factor [*Clinical chemistry*] (MAE) ... TSF

Tissue-Damaging Factor [*Medicine*] (MAE) ... TF

Tissue-Equivalent [*Medicine*] (MAE) ... TE

Tissue-Specific Antigens [*Immunology*] (DAVI) ... TSA

Tissue-Specific Extinguisher 1 [*Genetics*] ... TSE1

Tit for Tat [*Slang*] ... TFT

Tital Pharmaceuticals, Inc. [*Associated Press*] (SAG) ... TitalPh

Titan [*Record label*] ... Tit

Titan Airways Ltd. [*British ICAO designator*] (FAAC) ... AWC

Titan Corp. [*Associated Press*] (SAG) ... TitanCp

[*The*] **Titan Corp.** [*NYSE symbol*] (SPSG) ... TTN

Titan Corp. [*NYSE symbol*] (TTSB) ... TTN

Titan Corp., $1.cm Cv Pfd [*NYSE symbol*] (TTSB) ... TTNPr

Titan Exploration, Inc. [*NASDAQ symbol*] (SAG) ... TEXP

Titan Exploration, Inc. [*Associated Press*] (SAG) ... TitanEx

Titan Holdings [*NYSE symbol*] (TTSB) ... TH

Titan Holdings, Inc. [*NYSE symbol*] (SAG) ... TH

Titan Holdings, Inc. [*Associated Press*] (SAG) ... TitanHld

Titan Missile Contractor (AAG) ... TMC

Titan Pharmaceuticals [*NASDAQ symbol*] (TTSB) ... TTNP

Titan Pharmaceuticals, Inc. [*NASDAQ symbol*] (SAG) ... TTNP

Titan Pharmaceuticals Unit [*NASDAQ symbol*] (TTSB) ... TTNPU

Titan Resources Ltd. [*Vancouver Stock Exchange symbol*] ... TNR

Titan Society (EA) ... TS

Titan Standardized Space Launch System (SAA) ... TSSLS

Titan Wheel International [*Associated Press*] (SAG) ... TitanW

Titan Wheel International Co. [*NYSE symbol*] (SAG) ... TWI

Titan Wheel Intl [*NYSE symbol*] (TTSB) ... TWI

Titanic Enthusiasts of America [*Later, THS*] (EA) ... TEA

Titanic Historical Society (EA) ... THS

Titanite [*CIPW classification*] [*Geology*] ... tn

Titanium [*Chemical element*] ... Ti

Titanium Butt Weld ... TBW

Titanium Chloride [*Inorganic chemistry*] ... TM

Titanium Development Association (EA) ... TDA

Titanium Dioxide Manufacturers Sector Group (EAIO) ... SGTM

Titanium Elevon Track ... TET

Titanium Mesh [*Medicine*] ... TIM

Titanium Metallurgical Laboratory (MCD) ... TML

Titanium Metals Corp. [*NASDAQ symbol*] (SAG) ... TIMT

Titanium Metals Corp. [*Associated Press*] (SAG) ... TitanMet

Titanium Metals Corp. of America ... TMCA

Titanium Optimized Design [*Plate*] [*Orthopedics*] (DAVI) ... TOD

Titanium Proximal Loading-6-Inch Stem [*Total hip system*] [*Orthopedics*] (DAVI) ... TPL-6

Titanium Sublimation Pump (OA) ... TSP

Titanium Tetrachloride [*Inorganic chemistry*] ... FM

Titanium Toroidal Propellant Container ... TTPC

Titanium-Lead-Zinc ... TLZ

Titanium-Zirconium-Molybdenum [*Alloy*] ... TZM

Titao [*Burkina Faso*] [*ICAO location identifier*] (ICLI) ... DHCI

Tite [*Guinea-Bissau*] [*ICAO location identifier*] (ICLI) ... GGTT

Tithe (ILCA) ... Tit

Tithe Annuity ... TA

Tithe Commutation Act [*British*] ... TCA

Tithe Rent-Charge ... TRC

Tithing [*Geographical division*] [*British*] ... T

Tithing [*Church of England*] ... TG

Titizima [*Bonin Islands*] [*Seismograph station code, US Geological Survey Closed*] (SEIS) ... TTZ

Title [*Bibliography*] ... T

Title [*Online database field identifier*] [*Computer science*] ... TI

Title [*Bibliography*] ... TIT

Title ... TITL

Title [*Online database field identifier*] [*Computer science*] ... TTL

[*Journal*] **Title Abbreviation** (NITA) ... TA

Title Abstract Bulletin (IAA) ... TAB

Title Analytic [*Bibliography*] ... TAN

Title Annotation (NITA) ... TA

Title Announcement Bulletin ... TAB

Title Block (SAA) ... T/B

Title Card (NTCM) ... TC

Title Certificate Book [*A publication*] (DLA) ... TCB

Title I Evaluation and Reporting System [*Department of Education*] ... TIERS

Title Information [*Publishing*] ... TI

Title Insurance & Trust Co., Los Angeles, CA [*Library symbol Library of Congress*] (LCLS) ... CLTI

Title List ... TL

Title Page [*Bibliography*] ... TP

Title Page (WDMC) ... tp

Title, Page, and Index ... TPI

Title Page Mutilated ... TPM

Title Page Wanting ... TPW

Title plus Last Name ... TLN

Title, Subtitle, and Caption ... TSAC

Title Tech, Inc. [*Vancouver Stock Exchange symbol*] ... TTH

Title Terms (NITA) ... TT

Title Verso [*Publishing*] (WDMC) ... TV

Title Wave Stores, Inc. [*Associated Press*] (SAG) ... TitleWve

Titles Alphabetically Listed by Keyword (KSC) ... TALK

Titles Automated Register and Document Information System [*Australian*] (EERA) ... TARDIS

Titles Now Troublesome [*School books*] [*American Library Association*] ... TNT

Titmus Stereocuity Test [*Medicine*] (DAVI) ... TST

Titograd [*Former Yugoslavia*] [*ICAO location identifier*] (ICLI) ... LYTI

Titograd [*Former Yugoslavia*] [*Airport symbol*] (OAG) ... TGD

Titograd [*Yugoslavia*] [*Seismograph station code, US Geological Survey*] (SEIS) ... TTG

Titonka Public Library, Titonka, IA [*Library symbol Library of Congress*] (LCLS) ... IaTit

Titratable Acid [*Clinical chemistry*] ... TA

Titratable Base Number [*Analytical chemistry*] ... TBN

Titrate [*Analytical chemistry*] ... titr

Titrated Initial Dose (AAMN) ... TID

Titrated Water (DAVI) ... TH_2O

Titrated Water [*Laboratory science*] (DAVI) ... THO

Titration Alkalinity [*Oceanography*] ... TA

Titration System Software [*Metter Instruments*] ... TS

Titular (WDAA) ... TIT

Tituli Asiae Minoris [*Vienna*] [*A publication*] (OCD) ... TAM

Titus [*New Testament book*] ... Ti

Titus [*New Testament book*] ... Tit

Titus [*New Testament book*] (BJA) ... Tt

Titus Andronicus [*Shakespearean work*] ... Tit

Titus Andronicus [*Shakespearean work*] (BARN) ... Tit A

Titusville [*Florida*] [*Airport symbol*] (AD) ... TIX

Titusville, FL [*Location identifier FAA*] (FAAL) ... GGL

Titusville, FL [*Location identifier FAA*] (FAAL) ... TIX

Titusville, FL [*AM radio station call letters*] ... WAMT

Titusville, FL [*FM radio station call letters*] ... WGNE

Titusville, FL [*FM radio station call letters*] ... WPIO

Titusville, PA [*AM radio station call letters*] ... WTIV

Tivat [*Former Yugoslavia*] [*ICAO location identifier*] (ICLI) ... LYTV

Tivat [*Former Yugoslavia*] [*Airport symbol*] (OAG) ... TIV

Tiverton [*Municipal borough in England*] ... TIV

Tiverton Branch, Bruce County Public Library, Ontario [*Library symbol National Library of Canada*] (NLC) ... OTIV

Tiverton, OH [*Location identifier FAA*] (FAAL) ... TVT

Tiverton Petroleums Ltd. [*Toronto Stock Exchange symbol*] ... TIV

Tivoli Inds Wrrt'A' [*NASDAQ symbol*] (TTSB) ... TVLIW

Tivoli Inds Wrrt'B' [*NASDAQ symbol*] (TTSB) .... TVLIZ
Tivoli Indus Inc. [*NASDAQ symbol*] (TTSB) .... TVLI
Tivoli Industries, Inc. [*Associated Press*] (SAG) .... Tivoli
Tivoli Industries, Inc. [*NASDAQ symbol*] (SAG) .... TVLI
Tivoli Music Hall [*London*] (DSUE) .... TIV
Tivoli Systems, Inc. [*Associated Press*] (SAG) .... TivoliSy
Tivoli Systems, Inc. [*NASDAQ symbol*] (SAG) .... TIVS
Tixie [*Former USSR Geomagnetic observatory code*] .... TIK
T.J. Cinnamons [*NASDAQ symbol*] (TTSB) .... TJCI
TJ Cinnamons, Inc. [*Associated Press*] (SAG) .... TJ Cinn
TJ Cinnamons, Inc. [*Associated Press*] (SAG) .... TJ Cn
TJ Cinnamons, Inc. [*NASDAQ symbol*] (SAG) .... TJCI
TJ International, Inc. [*Associated Press*] (SAG) .... TJ Intl
TJ International, Inc. [*NASDAQ symbol*] (NQ) .... TJCO
TJ Systems Corp. [*Associated Press*] (SAG) .... TJ Sys
Tjaenstemaennens Centralorganisation [*Central Organization of Salaried
    Employees*] [*Sweden*] .... TCO
TJT, Inc. [*NASDAQ symbol*] (SAG) .... AXLE
T.J.T. Inc. [*NASDAQ symbol*] (TTSB) .... AXLE
TJT, Inc. [*Associated Press*] (SAG) .... TJT
T.J.T. Inc. Wrrt [*NASDAQ symbol*] (TTSB) .... AXLEW
Tjumenaviatrans [*Russian Federation*] [*ICAO designator*] (FAAC) .... TMN
Tjuringa: an Australasian Benedictine Review [*A publication*] (APTA) .... Tju
TJX Companies [*NYSE symbol*] (SPSG) .... TJX
TJX Companies [*Associated Press*] (SAG) .... TJX
TJX Co's $3.125 cm Cv'C'Pfd [*NYSE symbol*] (TTSB) .... TJXPrC
TK Travel Ltd. [*Gambia*] [*ICAO designator*] (FAAC) .... RDA
Tlaxcala [*Mexico ICAO location identifier*] .... MMTA
TLB [*Translation - Lookaside - Buffers*] Identifier .... TLBID
TLC Air, Inc. [*ICAO designator*] (FAAC) .... TLS
Tlemcen [*Algeria*] [*Seismograph station code, US Geological Survey*] (SEIS) .... TEC
Tlemcen/Zenata [*Algeria*] [*ICAO location identifier*] (ICLI) .... DAON
Tlingit [*MARC language code Library of Congress*] (LCCP) .... tli
T-Logic, Inc. [*Information service or system*] (IID) .... TLI
Tlokoeng [*Lesotho*] [*ICAO location identifier*] (ICLI) .... FXTK
T-Lymphocyte Chemotactic Factor .... TCF
T-Lymphocyte Clones [*Immunology*] .... TLC
T-Lymphocyte-Associated Antigen [*Hematology*] (DAVI) .... TLAA
TM Century [*NASDAQ symbol*] (NQ) .... TMCI
TM Century, Inc. [*Associated Press*] (SAG) .... TM Cent
TMA [*Tobacco Merchants Association*] Bibliographic Index to the Tobacco
    Scene [*Database*] .... TMA BITS
TMBR/Sharp Drilling [*NASDAQ symbol*] (TTSB) .... TBDI
TMBR Sharp Drilling, Inc. [*NASDAQ symbol*] (SAG) .... TBDI
TMBR Sharp Drilling, Inc. [*Associated Press*] (SAG) .... TMBR Sh
TMCI Electronics [*NASDAQ symbol*] (TTSB) .... TMEI
TMCI Electronics, Inc. [*Associated Press*] (SAG) .... TMCIEI
TMCI Electronics, Inc. [*NASDAQ symbol*] (SAG) .... TMEI
TMCI Electronics Wrrt [*NASDAQ symbol*] (TTSB) .... TMEIW
TMDE [*Test, Measuring, and Diagnostic Equipment*] Modernization [*Army*]
    (RDA) .... TMOD
TME Resources, Inc. [*Vancouver Stock Exchange symbol*] .... TME
TMIS [*Technical and Management Information System*] Control Board
    [*NASA*] (SSD) .... TCB
TMP Worldwide, Inc. [*Associated Press*] (SAG) .... TMP Wr
TMP Worldwide, Inc. [*NASDAQ symbol*] (SAG) .... TMPW
T-Netix, Inc. [*Associated Press*] (SAG) .... TNetix
T-Netix, Inc. [*NASDAQ symbol*] (SAG) .... TNTX
TNP Enterprises [*NYSE symbol*] (TTSB) .... TNP
TNP Enterprises, Inc. [*NYSE symbol*] (SPSG) .... TNP
TNT Freightways Corp. [*Associated Press*] (SAG) .... TNT Frt
TNT Freightways Corp. [*NASDAQ symbol*] (SAG) .... TNTF
TNT Tariff Agents, Inc., New York NY [*STAC*] .... TNT
Tnu'at 'Aliyah (BJA) .... TA
To Accompany Troops .... TAT
To Be Absorbed [*Pharmacology*] (DAVI) .... TBA
To Be Activated [*Military*] .... TBA
To Be Added (AAG) .... TBA
To Be Admitted [*Medicine*] (DAVI) .... TBA
To Be Advised (AIA) .... TBAD
To Be Agreed (AIA) .... TBA
To Be Agreed (AIA) .... TBAG
To Be Announced .... TBA
To Be Announced [*Army*] (AABC) .... TBAN
To Be Assigned .... TBA
To Be Avoided [*Slang*] .... TBA
To Be Called For [*British Rail parcel service*] [*Obsolete*] (DI) .... TCF
To Be Continued [*Polish underground publishing house begun by author
    Czeslaw Bielecki*] [*Acronym represents Polish phrase*] .... CDN
To Be Cooked [*Food*] .... TBC
To Be Declassified (AAG) .... TBD
To Be Defined .... TBD
To Be Designated (MCD) .... TBD
To Be Designated Later (CINC) .... TBDL
To Be Determined (AFM) .... TBD
To Be Developed (NASA) .... TBD
To Be Disbanded .... TBD
To Be Done (AAG) .... TBD
To Be Evaluated (NASA) .... TBE
To Be Expended (AAG) .... TBE
To Be Funded [*Contracting*] [*Military*] .... TBF
To Be Inactivated .... TBI
To Be Indicated (AIA) .... TBI
To Be Initiated (IAA) .... TBI
To Be Negotiated (NASA) .... TBN

To Be Nominated .... TBN
To Be Picked Up [*Postal service marking*] [*British*] .... TBPU
To Be Planned (MCD) .... TBP
To Be Provided (NASA) .... TBP
To be Published .... TBP
To be Released (SAA) .... TBR
To be Resolved (SSD) .... TBR
To Be Selected (KSC) .... TBS
To Be Specified (NASA) .... TBS
To Be Superseded (NASA) .... TBS
To Be Supplied (KSC) .... TBS
To Be Withheld .... TBW
To Come Again [*in a given number of days*] [*Medicine*] .... TCA
To Come In [*to hospital*] [*Medicine*] .... TCI
"To Complete" Performance Index (MCD) .... TCPI
To Consider (DAVI) .... T/C
To Contain [*Pipet calibration*] .... TC
To Deliver [*Pipet calibration*] .... TD
To Derive a Total (IDOE) .... tot
To Duty Assigned By [*Military*] .... DUSIGN
To Expiry Only (AIA) .... TEO
To Fill .... TF
To Follow .... TF
To Insure Promptness .... TIP
To Keep Needle Open [*Pharmacology*] (DAVI) .... TKNO
To Keep Open [*Medicine*] .... TKO
To Kum [*i.e., To Come*] [*Publishing*] .... TK
To My Knowledge [*Computer science*] (DOM) .... TMK
To Oblige (AIA) .... T/O
To Order From .... TOF
To Order Only [*Commerce*] (ODBW) .... TOO
To Other Service Center [*IRS*] .... TOSC
To Pay (ADA) .... TP
To Restore American Independence Now [*An association*] .... TRAIN
To Take Leave .... TTL
To Take Out [*Medicine*] .... TTO
To the Best of You [*An association*] (EA) .... TTBOY
To Whom It May Concern .... TWIMC
Toa Domestic Airlines [*ICAO designator*] (AD) .... JD
Toamasina [*Madagascar*] [*ICAO location identifier*] (ICLI) .... FMMT
Toarcian [*Geology*] .... T
Toastmaster, inc. [*NYSE symbol*] (SPSG) .... TM
Toastmaster, Inc. [*Associated Press*] (SAG) .... Toastmst
Toastmasters and Masters of Ceremonies Federation [*British*] (BI) .... TMCF
Toastmasters International (EA) .... TI
Tobacco (ADA) .... TOB
Tobacco .... TOB
Tobacco Advisory Council [*British*] .... TAC
Tobacco and Associated Farmers' Cooperative of Victoria [*Australia*] .... TAFCV
Tobacco and Health Information Services (NITA) .... THIS
Tobacco Associates (EA) .... TA
Tobacco Association of United States (EA) .... TAUS
Tobacco Black-Shank Nematode [*Plant pathology*] .... TBS
Tobacco Branch, Internal Revenue Bureau [*United States*] (DLA) .... Tob
Tobacco Bud Worm [*Agronomy*] .... TBW
Tobacco Cyst Nematode [*Plant pathology*] .... TCN
Tobacco Etch Virus .... TEV
Tobacco Free Young America Project (EA) .... TFYAP
Tobacco Glycoprotein [*Biochemistry*] .... TGP
Tobacco Growers' Council of Australia .... TGCA
Tobacco Growers' Information Committee (EA) .... TGIC
Tobacco Growers of Victoria [*Australia*] .... TGV
Tobacco Industry Labor/Management Committee (EA) .... TILMC
Tobacco Industry Research Committee (EA) .... TIRC
Tobacco Inspection Service [*Philippines*] .... TIS
Tobacco Institute (EA) .... TI
Tobacco Leaf Curl Virus [*Plant pathology*] .... TLCV
Tobacco Leaf Marketing Board [*Australia*] .... TLMB
Tobacco Mechanics' Association [*A union*] [*British*] (DCTA) .... TMA
Tobacco Merchants Association of the United States, New York, NY
    [*Library symbol Library of Congress*] (LCLS) .... NNTM
Tobacco Merchants Association of United States (EA) .... TMA
Tobacco Mosaic Virus .... TMV
Tobacco Mosaic Virus Protein .... TMVP
Tobacco Necrosis Virus .... TNV
Tobacco Necrotic Dwarf Virus [*Plant pathology*] .... TNDV
Tobacco Products Liability Project (EA) .... TPLP
Tobacco Quota Committee [*Australia*] .... TQC
Tobacco Rattle Virus .... TRV
Tobacco Research and Development Council [*Australia*] .... TRDC
Tobacco Research Council [*British*] (BI) .... TRC
Tobacco Ring Spot Virus .... TobRV
Tobacco Ring Spot Virus .... TRSV
Tobacco Salesmen's Association of America (EA) .... TSAA
Tobacco Streak Virus .... TSV
Tobacco Strippers Mutual Society [*A union*] [*British*] .... TSMS
Tobacco Tax Council (EA) .... TTC
Tobacco Tax Guide [*Internal Revenue Service*] .... TTG
Tobacco Tax Ruling, Internal Revenue Bureau [*United States*]
    [*A publication*] (DLA) .... T
Tobacco Tax Ruling Term (DLA) .... TT
Tobacco Trade Travellers' Association [*British*] (BI) .... TTTA
Tobacco Vein Mottling Virus .... TVMV
Tobacco Workers International Union [*Later, BCTWIU*] (EA) .... TWIU
Tobacco Workers' Mutual Assistance Society [*A union*] [*British*] .... TWMAS

Tobacco Workers' Union [British] (DCTA) .... TWU
Tobacco Yellow Dwarf Virus [Plant pathology] .... TYDV
Tobacconists' Association of America (EA) .... TAA
Tobacco-Specific Nitrosamine [Biochemistry] .... TSNA
Tobago [Trinidad and Tobago] [Airport symbol] (OAG) .... TAB
Tobe, CO [Location identifier FAA] (FAAL) .... TBE
Tobermory Branch, Bruce County Public Library, Ontario [Library symbol
    National Library of Canada] (NLC) .... OTOB
Tobex Resources Ltd. [Vancouver Stock Exchange symbol] .... TBB
Tobey's Reports [9, 10 Rhode Island] [A publication] (DLA) .... Tobey
Tobias [Old Testament book] [Douay version] .... TOB
Tobit [Old Testament book] [Roman Catholic canon] .... Tb
Tobit [Old Testament book] [Roman Catholic canon] (ROG) .... TOB
Toboggan .... TOB
Tobramycin [An antibiotic] .... TM
Tobramycin Peak [An antibiotic] (DAVI) .... TOBP
Tobramycin, Ticarcillin, and Cephalothin .... TTC
Tobramycin, Trough [An antibiotic] (DAVI) .... TOBT
Tobramycin-Clindamycin [Antibiotic compound] .... TC
Tobramycin-Nafcillin-Ticarcillin [Antibiotic combination] .... TNT
Tobramycin-Ticarcillin [Antibiotic combination] .... TT
Tobruk [Libya] [Airport symbol] (OAG) .... TOB
Toby Creek Resources Ltd. [Vancouver Stock Exchange symbol] ... TYC
Tobyhanna Army Depot [Pennsylvania] (AABC) .... TOAD
Tobyhanna Army Depot, Library, Tobyhanna, PA [OCLC symbol] (OCLC) .... TAD
Tobyhanna, PA [FM radio station call letters] (RBYB) .... WKRF
Toc [Phonetic alphabet] [Pre-World War II] (DSUE) .... T
Tocache [Peru] [ICAO location identifier] (ICLI) .... SPCH
Tocantina [Goias, Brazil] [Airport symbol] (AD) .... TOX
Tocantinopolis [Brazil] [Airport symbol] (AD) .... TPY
Toccoa Falls College [Georgia] .... TFC
Toccoa Falls, GA [FM radio station call letters] .... WRAF
Toccoa, GA [Location identifier FAA] (FAAL) .... TOC
Toccoa, GA [AM radio station call letters] .... WLET
Toccoa, GA [FM radio station call letters] .... WLET-FM
Toccoa, GA [AM radio station call letters] .... WNEG
Toccoa, GA [Television station call letters] .... WNEG-TV
Tocharian [Language group] (BARN) .... Toch
Tochas Affen Tish [In television production company name "TAT Productions."
    Words are Yiddish and translate figuratively as "Let's Be Honest"] ...... TAT
Tocix Chemicals Committee (EERA) .... TCC
Tocklai [India] [Seismograph station code, US Geological Survey] (SEIS) ... TOC
Toconce [Chile] [Seismograph station code, US Geological Survey] (SEIS) ... TCN
Tocopherol [Biochemistry] .... T
Tocopherol Equivalent [Nutrition] .... TE
Tocopherol Polyethylene Glycol Succinate [Organic chemistry] ..... TPGS
Tocopherolquinone [Vitamin E] [Biochemistry] .... TQ
Tocopilla [Chile] [Seismograph station code, US Geological Survey Closed]
    (SEIS) .... TCP
Tocopilla [Chile] [Airport symbol] (AD) .... TOQ
Tocopilla [Chile] [Seismograph station code, US Geological Survey] (SEIS) ... TPL
Tocotrienol [Biochemistry] T-3
Tocotrienolquinone [Biochemistry] TQ-3
Tocumen/General Omar Torrijos H. [Panama] [ICAO location identifier]
    (ICLI) .... MPTO
Tocumwal [Australia Airport symbol] (OAG) .... TCW
Tod [Unit of weight] .... TD
Tod und Leben nach der Vorstellungen der Babylonier [A publication]
    (BJA) .... TuL
Todai International Science Network .... TISN
Today (FAAC) .... TDA
Today Show [Television program] .... TS
Today's Bancorp [NASDAQ symbol] (TTSB) .... TDAY
Todays Bancorp, Inc. [NASDAQ symbol] (SAG) .... TDAY
Todays Bancorp, Inc. [Associated Press] (SAG) .... TodaysBc
Today's Child, Tomorrow's Victim [Book title] .... TCTV
Today's Computers [A publication] .... TC
Today's English Version [of the Bible] .... TEV
Today's Insurance Woman [National Association of Insurance Women
    (International)] [A publication] .... TIW
Today's Man [NASDAQ symbol] (TTSB) .... TMANQ
Todays Man, Inc. [NASDAQ symbol] (SAG) .... TMAN
Today's Man, Inc. [Associated Press] (SAG) .... TodayM
Todd AO Corp. [Associated Press] (SAG) .... ToddAO
Todd County Historical Society, Long Prairie, MN [Library symbol] [Library of
    Congress] (LCLS) .... MnLpHi
Todd Shipyards [NYSE symbol] (TTSB) .... TOD
Todd Shipyards Corp. [NYSE symbol] (SAG) .... TOD
Todd Shipyards Corp. [Associated Press] (SAG) .... ToddShp
Todd Unit [Medicine] (MAE) .... TU
Todd-American Optical Co. [Wide-screen system used by producer Michael
    Todd and the American Optical Co.] .... TODD-AO
[The] Todd-AO Corp. [NASDAQ symbol] (NQ) .... TODD
Todd-AO Corp.'A' [NASDAQ symbol] (TTSB) .... TODDA
Todhunter International, Inc. [NASDAQ symbol] (SAG) .... TODH
Todhunter International, Inc. [Associated Press] (SAG) ..... Todhuntr
Todhunter Intl [NASDAQ symbol] (TTSB) .... TODH
Todoroki [Japan] [Seismograph station code, US Geological Survey Closed]
    (SEIS) .... TDR
Todos Santos [Bolivia] [ICAO location identifier] (ICLI) .... SLTS
Todos Santos Ambulance Fund [An association] (EA) .... TSAF
Todwind Development Corp. [Vancouver Stock Exchange symbol] ... TND
Toe .... T
TOE [Table of Organization and Equipment] Army Authorization Document
    System .... TAADS

Toe Goes in First [As is "You're so dumb you have TGIF on your shoes"] ...... TGIF
Toensberg [Norway] [Airport symbol] (AD) .... TNS
Toe-Out-in-Turns [Automotive engineering] .... TOT
Tofield Public Library, Alberta [Library symbol National Library of Canada]
    (NLC) .... ATOF
Tofield Public Library, Tofield, AB, Canada [Library symbol] [Library of
    Congress] (LCLS) .... CaATof
Tofino, BC [ICAO location identifier] (ICLI) .... CYAZ
Tofranil [Also, called imipramine hydrochloride] [An antidepressant] [Geigy
    Pharmaceuticals] (DAVI) .... TOFRAN
Tofutti Brands [AMEX symbol] (TTSB) .... TOF
Tofutti Brands, Inc. [AMEX symbol] (SPSG) .... TOF
Tofutti Brands, Inc. [Associated Press] (SAG) .... Tofutti
TOGA [Tropical Ocean Global Atmosphere Program] Coupled Ocean-
    Atmosphere Response Experiment (EERA) .... TOGA COARE
TOGA [Tropical Ocean and Global Atmosphere] Heat Exchange Program
    [Marine science] (OSRA) .... THEP
TOGA [Tropical Ocean and Global Atmosphere] Program on Prediction
    [Marine science] (OSRA) .... T-POP
TOGA [Tropical Ocean-Global Atmosphere] Program on Prediction
    (USDC) .... T-POP
TOGA [Tropical Ocean-Atmosphere] Sea Level Center (USDC) .... TSLC
TOGA [Tropical Ocean and Global Atmosphere] Sea Level Center [Marine
    science] (OSRA) .... TSLC
TOGA [Tropical Ocean and Global Atmosphere] Subsurface Data Center
    [Marine science] (OSRA) .... TSDC
Togane [Japan] [Seismograph station code, US Geological Survey Closed]
    (SEIS) .... TOG
Together .... TOG
Together (ROG) .... TOGR
Together Everyone Achieves More .... TEAM
Together, Inc. (EA) .... TI
Together International/Anti-Soviet Research Center [Defunct] (EA) ...... TI
Together Women in Neighborhoods .... TWIN
Toggle [Telecommunications] (IAA) .... T
Toggle (AAG) .... TGL
Toggle .... TOG
Toggle Buffer (MCD) .... TB
Toggle Flip-Flop [Computer science] (IAA) .... TFF
Togiak [Alaska] [Airport symbol] (OAG) .... TOG
Togiak Village, AK [Location identifier FAA] (FAAL) .... TOG
Togo [MARC geographic area code Library of Congress] (LCCP) ..... f-tg--
Togo [MARC country of publication code Library of Congress] (LCCP) ..... tg
Togo [ANSI two-letter standard code] (CNC) .... TG
Togo [ANSI three-letter standard code] (CNC) .... TGO
Togo Airlines [ICAO designator] (FAAC) .... TGA
Togo School, Togo, MN [Library symbol] [Library of Congress] (LCLS) ...... MnToS
Togoland Congress [Ghana] [Political party] .... TC
Tohoku University, Sendai, Japan [Library symbol] [Library of Congress]
    (LCLS) .... JSeTU
Tohoku University, Sendai, Japan [Library symbol Library of Congress]
    (LCLS) .... JSTU
Tohoroth [or Toharoth] (BJA) .... Toh
Tohoroth [or Toharoth] (BJA) .... Toho
Toilet (MSA) .... T
Toilet .... TLT
Toilet .... TOIL
Toilet [Slang] X
Toilet Case (MSA) .... TC
Toilet Exhaust (OA) .... TX
Toilet Goods Association [Later, CTFA] (EA) .... TGA
Toilet Paper [To be "TP'd" is to have your yard covertly decorated with u
    nrolled toilet paper] [Slang] .... TP
Toilet Paper Dispenser [Technical drawings] .... TPD
Toilet Partition [Technical drawings] .... TPTN
Toilet Preparations Federation [British] (BI) .... TPF
Toilet-Paper Holder .... TH
Toiletry Merchandising Association [Later, NASM] (EA) .... TMA
Toimihenkilo - ja Virkamiesjarjestojen Keskusliitto [Confederation of
    Intellectual and Government Workers] [Finland] .... TVK
Toivola-Meadowlands School, Meadowlands, MN [Library symbol] [Library of
    Congress] (LCLS) .... MnMeaS
Tok, AK [FM radio station call letters] (RBYB) .... KUDU-FM
Tok, AK [Location identifier FAA] (FAAL) .... TKJ
Tokachi [Japan ICAO location identifier] (ICLI) .... RJCT
TOKAMAK [Toroidal Kamera Magnetic] at Fontenay-aux-Roses ..... TFR
TOKAMAK [Toroidal Kamera Magnetic] Chauffage Alfven [Plasma physics
    instrumentation] .... TCA
TOKAMAK [Toroidal Kamera Magnetic] Chauffage Variable [Plasma physics
    instrumentation] .... TCV
TOKAMAK [Toroidal Kamera Magnetic] Experiment for Technical Oriented
    Research [Oak Ridge National Laboratory] .... TEXTOR
TOKAMAK [Toroidal Kamera Magnetic] Fusion Core Experiment [Plasma
    physics] .... TFCX
TOKAMAK [Toroidal Kamera Magnetic] Fusion Test Reactor [Princeton,
    NJ] .... TFTR
Tokelau Islands [MARC geographic area code Library of Congress]
    (LCCP) .... potl--
Tokelau Islands [ANSI two-letter standard code] (CNC) .... TK
Tokelau Islands [ANSI three-letter standard code] (CNC) .... TKL
Tokelau Islands [MARC country of publication code Library of Congress]
    (LCCP) .... tl
Token and Medal Society (EA) .... TAMS
Token Bus Controller [Motorola, Inc.] .... TBC
Token Corresponding Society [British] (DBA) .... TCS

Token Economy Program [*Psychiatry*] ... TEP
Token Kenkyu Kai [*Defunct*] (EA) ... TKK
Token/Net Interface Module [*Telecommunications*] (TSSD) ... TIM
Token Ring Controller ... TRC
Token Ring Interface Coupler (PCM) ... TIC
Token Test (EDAC) ... TT
Token-Holding Time [*Computer science*] ... THT
Tokheim Corp. [*NYSE symbol*] (SPSG) ... TOK
Tokheim Corp. [*Associated Press*] (SAG) ... Tokhem
[*The*] **Tokio Marine & Fire Insurance Co.** (MHDW) ... TKIOY
[*The*] **Tokio Marine & Fire Insurance Co. Ltd.** [*NASDAQ symbol*] (NQ) ... TKIO
Tokio Marine & Fire Insurance Co. Ltd. [*Associated Press*] (SAG) ... TokioF
Tokio Marine/Fire ADR [*NASDAQ symbol*] (TTSB) ... TKIOY
Tokodynagraph ... TKG
Tokodynamometer [*Obstetrics*] (DAVI) ... TK
Tokodynamometer ... TKD
Tokos Medical Corp. [*NASDAQ symbol*] (SAG) ... TKOS
Tokos Medical Corp. [*Associated Press*] (SAG) ... TokosMd
Toksook [*Alaska*] [*Airport symbol*] (OAG) ... OOK
Tokuno Shima [*Japan*] [*Airport symbol*] (OAG) ... TKN
Tokunoshima Island [*Japan ICAO location identifier*] (ICLI) ... RJKN
Tokushima [*Japan ICAO location identifier*] (ICLI) ... RJOS
Tokushima [*Japan*] [*Airport symbol*] (OAG) ... TKS
Tokushima [*Japan*] [*Seismograph station code, US Geological Survey*] (SEIS) ... TKS
Tokyo [*Japan ICAO location identifier*] (ICLI) ... RJTD
Tokyo [*Japan ICAO location identifier*] (ICLI) ... RJTG
Tokyo [*Japan ICAO location identifier*] (ICLI) ... RJTI
Tokyo [*Japan*] [*Seismograph station code, US Geological Survey*] (SEIS) ... TOK
Tokyo [*Japan*] [*Airport symbol*] (OAG) ... TYO
Tokyo Astronomical Observatory ... TAO
Tokyo Atomic Industrial Consortium ... TAIC
Tokyo Automatic Computer (IAA) ... TAC
Tokyo Broadcasting System ... TBS
Tokyo Commodity Exchange for Industry [*Japan*] (ECON) ... TOCOM
Tokyo Denki Kagaku [*Tokyo Electronics and Chemical Co.*] [*Initialism is now name of recording tape manufacturer and brand name of its products*] ... TDK
Tokyo Electric Power Co. (ECON) ... TEPCO
Tokyo Electro Acoustical Co. [*Acronym is now name of electronics company and brand name of its products*] ... TEAC
Tokyo Electron Ltd. (IAA) ... TEL
Tokyo Electronics Corp. ... TEC
Tokyo Financial Wire [*COMLINE International Corp.*] [*Japan Information service or system*] (CRD) ... TFW
Tokyo [*Japan*] **Haneda Airport** [*Airport symbol*] (OAG) ... HND
Tokyo/International [*Japan ICAO location identifier*] (ICLI) ... RJTT
Tokyo International Film Festival [*Japan*] ... TIFF
Tokyo Kikai Seisakusho [*Japan*] ... TKS
Tokyo/New Tokyo International [*Japan ICAO location identifier*] (ICLI) ... RJAA
Tokyo Shoko Research Ltd. [*Database producer*] [*Japan*] ... TSR
Tokyo Stock Exchange [*Japan*] ... TSE
Tokyo Stock Price Index [*Japan*] (ECON) ... TOPIX
Tokyo Tsushin Kogyo [*Tokyo Telecommunications Engineering Co.*] ... TTK
Tokyo-Narita [*Japan*] [*Airport symbol*] (OAG) ... NRT
Tol [*Papua New Guinea*] [*Airport symbol*] (OAG) ... TLO
Tolagnaro [*Madagascar*] [*ICAO location identifier*] (ICLI) ... FMSD
Tol-Air Services, Inc. [*ICAO designator*] (FAAC) ... TOL
Tolbutamide [*Pharmacology*] (DAVI) ... D 860
Tolbutamide - Tolerance Test [*Clinical chemistry*] (MAE) ... TBT
Tolbutamide Tolerance Test [*Clinical chemistry*] ... TTT
Toledo [*Spain*] [*Seismograph station code, US Geological Survey*] (SEIS) ... TLO
Toledo [*Spain*] [*Seismograph station code, US Geological Survey*] (SEIS) ... TOL
Toledo [*Ohio*] [*Airport symbol*] (OAG) ... TOL
[*The*] **Toledo, Angola & Western Railway Co.** [*AAR code*] ... TAW
Toledo Bird Association, Zebra Finch Club of America (EA) ... TBAZFCA
Toledo Chronicle, Toledo, IA [*Library symbol*] [*Library of Congress*] (LCLS) ... IaToC
Toledo Ed 8.84%cm Pfd [*NYSE symbol*] (TTSB) ... TEDPrE
Toledo Edison 4 1/4% Pfd [*AMEX symbol*] (TTSB) ... TEPrB
Toledo Edison 10% Pfd [*AMEX symbol*] (TTSB) ... TEDPrD
Toledo Edison 7.76% Pfd [*AMEX symbol*] (TTSB) ... TEDPrC
Toledo Edison 8.32% Pfd [*AMEX symbol*] (TTSB) ... TEDPrA
Toledo Edison $2.365 Pfd [*NYSE symbol*] (TTSB) ... TEDPrF
Toledo Edison Adj A Pfd [*NYSE symbol*] (TTSB) ... TEDPrK
Toledo Edison Adj Rt B Pfd [*NYSE symbol*] (TTSB) ... TEDPrL
Toledo Edison Co. [*AMEX symbol*] (SAG) ... TED
Toledo Edison Co. [*NYSE symbol*] (SPSG) ... TED
Toledo Edison Co. [*Associated Press*] (SAG) ... TolE
Toledo Museum of Art, Toledo, OH [*Library symbol Library of Congress*] (LCLS) ... OTM
Toledo, OH [*Location identifier FAA*] (FAAL) ... BQE
Toledo, OH [*Location identifier FAA*] (FAAL) ... EXF
Toledo, OH [*Location identifier FAA*] (FAAL) ... TDZ
Toledo, OH [*AM radio station call letters*] ... WCWA
Toledo, OH [*FM radio station call letters*] ... WGTE
Toledo, OH [*Television station call letters*] ... WGTE-TV
Toledo, OH [*FM radio station call letters*] ... WIOT
Toledo, OH [*FM radio station call letters*] ... WKKO
Toledo, OH [*Television station call letters*] ... WLMB
Toledo, OH [*FM radio station call letters*] ... WLQR
Toledo, OH [*Television station call letters*] ... WNWO
Toledo, OH [*FM radio station call letters*] ... WOTL
Toledo, OH [*FM radio station call letters*] (RBYB) ... WRVF
Toledo, OH [*AM radio station call letters*] ... WSPD
Toledo, OH [*AM radio station call letters*] ... WTOD
Toledo, OH [*Television station call letters*] ... WTOL
Toledo, OH [*Television station call letters*] ... WTVG
Toledo, OH [*Television station call letters*] ... WUPW
Toledo, OH [*FM radio station call letters*] ... WVKS
Toledo, OH [*AM radio station call letters*] ... WVOI
Toledo, OH [*FM radio station call letters*] ... WXTS
Toledo, OH [*FM radio station call letters*] ... WXUT
Toledo, OR [*AM radio station call letters*] ... KZUS
Toledo, OR [*FM radio station call letters*] ... KZUS-FM
Toledo, Peoria & Western Railroad Co. ... TP & W
Toledo, Peoria & Western Railroad Co. [*AAR code*] ... TPW
Toledo Progressive Party [*Belize*] [*Political party*] (PPW) ... TPP
Toledo Public Library, Toledo, IA [*Library symbol Library of Congress*] (LCLS) ... IaTo
Toledo, St. Louis & Kansas City Railroad ... TStL & KC
[*The*] **Toledo Terminal Railroad Co.** [*AAR code*] ... TT
Toledo, WA [*Location identifier FAA*] (FAAL) ... TDO
Toledo-Lucas County Public Library, Toledo, OH [*Library symbol Library of Congress*] (LCLS) ... OT
Toledo-Lucas County Public Library, Toledo, OH [*OCLC symbol*] (OCLC) ... TLM
Tolerable Daily Intake [*Toxicology*] ... TDI
Tolerance (FAAC) ... TLRNC
Tolerance (AAG) ... TOL
Tolerance Detector ... TD
Tolerance in Radius ... TIR
Tolerance of Unrealistic Experience [*Psychometrics*] ... TUE
Tolerant Majority [*An association Defunct*] (EA) ... TM
Tolerated (DAVI) ... tol
Toli Toli/Lalos [*Indonesia*] [*ICAO location identifier*] (ICLI) ... WAMI
Toliara [*Madagascar*] [*ICAO location identifier*] (ICLI) ... FMST
Tolitoli [*Indonesia*] [*Airport symbol*] (OAG) ... TLI
Tolkien Fellowships [*Defunct*] (EA) ... TF
Tolkien Society [*Hove, East Sussex, England*] (EAIO) ... TS
Tolkien Society of America ... TSA
Toll ... T
Toll Alternatives Studies Program [*Telecommunications*] (TEL) ... TASP
Toll Brothers [*NYSE symbol*] (TTSB) ... TOL
Toll Brothers, Inc. [*NYSE symbol*] (SPSG) ... TOL
Toll Brothers, Inc. [*Associated Press*] (SAG) ... TollBro
Toll Center [*Telecommunications*] ... TC
Toll Centering and Metropolitan Sectoring [*AT & T*] [*Telecommunications*] (TEL) ... TCMS
Toll Centre Code (NITA) ... TCC
Toll Circuit Layout [*Telecommunications*] (TEL) ... TCL
Toll Circuit Layout Record [*Telecommunications*] (TEL) ... TCLR
Toll Completing [*Telecommunications*] ... TC
Toll Connecting Trunk [*Telecommunications*] (TEL) ... TCT
Toll Dial Assistance [*Telecommunications*] (TEL) ... TDA
Toll Line Release ... TLR
Toll Point [*Telecommunications*] (TEL) ... TP
Toll Pole Line [*Telecommunications*] (TEL) ... TPL
Toll Prefix [*Telecommunications*] (TEL) ... TP
Toll Pulse Accepter [*Telecommunications*] (TEL) ... TPA
Toll Restricted [*Telecommunications*] (TEL) ... TOLR
Toll Room Switch [*Telecommunications*] (TEL) ... TRS
Toll Service Results Plan [*Bell System*] ... TSRP
Toll Switching [*Trunk*] [*Telecommunications*] (TEL) ... TS
Toll Switching System [*Telecommunications*] (TEL) ... TSS
Toll Testboard [*Telecommunications*] (TEL) ... TTB
Tolland Bank [*AMEX symbol*] (SPSG) ... TBK
Tolland Bank [*Associated Press*] (SAG) ... Tolland
Toller on Executors [*A publication*] (ILCA) ... Toll Ex
Toller on Executors [*A publication*] (DLA) ... Toller
Tollerford [*England*] ... TOLL
Tolleson, AZ [*Television station call letters*] (RBYB) ... KAJW
Tolleson, AZ [*AM radio station call letters*] ... KRDS
Tolleson, AZ [*AM radio station call letters*] ... KXEG
Tolleson Public Library, Tolleson, AZ [*Library symbol Library of Congress*] (LCLS) ... AzTol
Tollgate [*Maps and charts*] ... TG
Tollgrade Communications [*NASDAQ symbol*] (TTSB) ... TLGD
Tolls Recording and Computing Equipment (IEEE) ... TRACE
Tolmetin Glycine Amide [*Biochemistry*] ... TGA
Tolmezzo [*Italy*] [*Seismograph station code, US Geological Survey*] (SEIS) ... TLM
Tololo Astronomical Observatory [*Chile*] [*Seismograph station code, US Geological Survey*] (SEIS) ... TLL
Tolono Township Library, Tolono, IL [*Library symbol Library of Congress*] (LCLS) ... ITolo
Tolsona [*Alaska*] [*Seismograph station code, US Geological Survey*] (SEIS) ... TOA
Tolstoy Foundation (EA) ... TF
Tolstoy on Divorce and Matrimonial Causes [*A publication*] (DLA) ... Tolst Div
Tolu [*Colombia*] [*Airport symbol*] (OAG) ... TLU
Toluca [*Mexico ICAO location identifier*] (ICLI) ... MMTO
Toluca City Library, Toluca, IL [*Library symbol Library of Congress*] (LCLS) ... ITol
Toluca Community Unit, School District 2306, Toluca, IL [*Library symbol Library of Congress*] (LCLS) ... ITolSD
Toluene [*or Tolylene*] **Diisocyanate** [*Organic chemistry*] ... TDI
Toluene Disproportionation Process [*Organic chemistry*] ... TDP
Toluene Hydrodealkylation [*Organic chemistry*] ... THDA
Toluene-Cellosolve [*Scintillation solvent*] ... TC
Toluenediamine [*Organic chemistry*] ... TDA
Toluene-Dioxane-Ethanol [*Scintillation solvent*] ... TDE
Toluene-Ethanol [*Scintillation solvent*] ... TE
Toluene-Hyamine [*Scintillation solvent*] ... TH

Toluene-Methanol-Dioxane [*Scintillation solvent*] ... TMD
Toluenesulfonic Acid [*Organic chemistry*] ... TSA
Toluenesulfonyl Hydrazide [*Organic chemistry*] ... TSH
Toluenesulfonylmethyl Isocyanide [*or Tosylmethylisocyanide*] [*Organic chemistry*] ... TOSMIC
(Toluenesulfonyl)nitroimidazole [*Organic chemistry*] ... TSNI
(Toluenesulfonyl)nitrotriazole [*Organic chemistry*] ... TSNT
Toluene-Sulfo-Trypsin Arginine Methyl Ester [*Organic chemistry*] (MAE) ... TAME
Toluene-Xylene-Dioxane-Ethanol [*Scintillation solvent*] ... TXDE
Toluic Acid Phenylhydrazide [*Organic chemistry*] ... TAPH
Toluidine Blue [*Organic chemistry*] ... TB
Toluidine Red Unheated Serum Test ... TRUST
Toluidinylnaphthalene Sulfonate [*Organic chemistry*] ... TNS
Toluoyl Chloride Phenylhydrazine [*Drug for sheep*] ... TCPH
Tolyl(mono)isocyanate [*Organic chemistry*] ... TMI
Tolylsulfonyl [*Organic chemistry*] ... Tosyl
Tolyltriazole [*Organic chemistry*] ... TTA
Tolytriazole [*Organic chemistry*] ... TT
Tom Baker Cancer Centre [*University of Calgary*] [*Formerly, Southern Alberta Cancer Centre*] [*Research center*] (RCD) ... TBCC
Tom Baker Cancer Centre, Medical Library, Calgary, AB, Canada [*Library symbol Library of Congress*] (LCLS) ... CaACTBC
Tom Baker Friendship Group (EAIO) ... TBFG
Tom Brown [*NASDAQ symbol*] (TTSB) ... TMBR
Tom Burford Fan Club (EA) ... TBFC
Tom Cruise Fan Club (EA) ... TCFC
Tom Dooley Youth League [*Defunct*] ... TADYL
Tom Green County Library, San Angelo, TX [*Library symbol Library of Congress*] (LCLS) ... TxSal
Tom Jones Appreciation Society (EAIO) ... TJAS
Tom Jones Fan Club (EA) ... TJFC
Tom Jones Gadabouts (EA) ... TJG
Tom Jones "Tom Terrific" Fan Club (EA) ... TJTTFC
Tom Mix International Fan Club (EA) ... TMIFC
Tom Price [*Australia Airport symbol*] ... TPR
Tom Robinson Band ... TRB
Tom Skinner Associates (EA) ... TSA
Tom Sneva Fan Club (EA) ... TSFC
Tom Swift and His Electric Rifle [*Electronic "stun gun"*] [*A trademark*] ... TASER
Tom T. Hall Fan Club [*Defunct*] (EA) ... TTHFC
Tom Thomson Memorial Gallery, Owen Sound, ON, Canada [*Library symbol Library of Congress*] (LCLS) ... CaOOwT
Tom Thomson Memorial Gallery, Owen Sound, Ontario [*Library symbol National Library of Canada*] (NLC) ... OOWT
Tom Walkinshaw Racing [*Auto racing*] ... TWR
Tom Wopat Fan Club (EA) ... TWFC
Tomah, WI [*FM radio station call letters*] ... WBOG
Tomah, WI [*AM radio station call letters*] ... WTMB
Tomah, WI [*FM radio station call letters*] ... WUSK
Tomah, WI [*FM radio station call letters*] ... WVCX
Tomahawk Air Field Attack Missile (MCD) ... TAAM
Tomahawk Airways, Inc. [*ICAO designator*] (FAAC) ... TMK
Tomahawk Antiship Missile (MCD) ... TASM
Tomahawk Antiship Missile Guidance Set (MCD) ... TASMGS
Tomahawk Baseline Improvement Program (DOMA) ... TBIP
Tomahawk Experimental Reaction [*Navy*] ... TEPR
Tomahawk Land Attack Missile (MCD) ... TLAM
Tomahawk Land Attack Missile/Conventional [*Navy*] (ANA) ... TLAM/C
Tomahawk Land Attack Missile - Nuclear (MCD) ... TLAM-N
Tomahawk Multi-Mission Missile (DOMA) ... TMMM
Tomahawk Public Library, Alberta [*Library symbol National Library of Canada*] (NLC) ... ATO
Tomahawk Resources [*Vancouver Stock Exchange symbol*] ... TMH
Tomahawk System Test Set ... TSTS
Tomahawk Tactical Commanders Course (DOMA) ... TTCC
Tomahawk Test Missile (MCD) ... TOTEM
Tomahawk Weapon Control System (DOMA) ... TWCS
Tomahawk, WI [*AM radio station call letters*] ... WJJQ
Tomahawk, WI [*FM radio station call letters*] ... WJJQ-FM
Tomakomai [*Japan*] [*Seismograph station code, US Geological Survey*] (SEIS) ... TMR
Tomanggong [*Malaysia*] [*Airport symbol*] (OAG) ... TMG
Tomato (BARN) ... tom
Tomato Aspermy Virus ... TAV
Tomato Black Ring Virus [*Plant pathology*] ... TBRV
Tomato Bushy Stunt Virus ... TBSV
Tomato Etch Virus ... TEV
Tomato Extract Medium (OA) ... TEM
Tomato Genetics Cooperative (EA) ... TGC
Tomato Golden Mosaic Virus ... TGMV
Tomato Golden Mosaic Virus [*Plant pathology*] ... TOGMV
Tomato Intercellular Fluid ... TIF
Tomato Juice ... TJ
Tomato Mosaic Virus [*Plant pathology*] ... TOMV
Tomato Necrotic Dwarf Virus ... TomNDV
Tomato (Peru) Mosaic Virus ... TPMV
Tomato Ringspot Virus ... TmRSV
Tomato Ringspot Virus ... TomRSV
Tomato Ringspot Virus [*Plant pathology*] ... TORSV
Tomato Ringspot Virus - Seed Borne ... TomRSV-S
Tomato Spotted Wilt Virus ... TSWV
Tomato Top Necrosis Virus [*Plant pathology*] ... TTNV
Tomato Yellow Dwarf Virus [*Plant pathology*] ... TOYDV
Tomato Yellow Leaf Curl [*Plant pathology*] ... TYLC
Tomato Yellow Leaf Curl Virus ... TYLCV
Tomato Yellow Mosaic Virus [*Plant pathology*] ... TOYMV
Tomato Yellow Top Virus ... TYTV
Tomb (VRA) ... tb
Tomb of the Unknown Soldier Identification Badge [*Military decoration*] (GFGA) ... TUSIDBAD
Tomball, TX [*AM radio station call letters*] ... KSEV
Tombigbee Regional Library, West Point, MS [*Library symbol Library of Congress*] (LCLS) ... MsWp
Tombill Mines Ltd. [*Toronto Stock Exchange symbol*] ... TBL
Tombouctou [*Mali*] [*ICAO location identifier*] (ICLI) ... GATB
Tombouctou [*Mali*] [*Airport symbol*] (OAG) ... TOM
Tombstone-Cochise County Library, Tombstone, AZ [*Library symbol Library of Congress*] (LCLS) ... AzTo
Tomenson Alexander Ltd., Montreal, Quebec [*Library symbol National Library of Canada*] (NLC) ... QMTA
Tomenson-Aletander Ltd., Montreal, PQ, Canada [*Library symbol Library of Congress*] (LCLS) ... CaQMTA
Tomie [*Japan*] [*Seismograph station code, US Geological Survey Closed*] (SEIS) ... TOM
Tomisaki [*Mera*] [*Japan*] [*Seismograph station code, US Geological Survey*] [*Closed*] (SEIS) ... TMS
Tomkins and Jenckens' Compendium of the Modern Roman Law [*A publication*] (DLA) ... Tom & J Comp
Tomkins and Jencken's Compendium of the Modern Roman Law [*A publication*] (DLA) ... Tomkins & J Mod Rom Law
Tomkins and Lemon's Translation of Gaius [*A publication*] (DLA) ... Tom & Lem Gai
Tomkins' Institutes of Roman Law [*A publication*] (DLA) ... Tom Inst
Tomkins Ltd. [*Associated Press*] (SAG) ... Tmk Plc
Tomkins PLC [*NYSE symbol*] (SAG) ... TKS
Tomkins PLC [*Associated Press*] (SAG) ... Tmk plc
Tomkins plc ADS [*NYSE symbol*] (TTSB) ... TKS
Tomlin's Criminal Law [*A publication*] (DLA) ... Toml Cr L
Tomlins' Election Cases [*1689-1795*] [*A publication*] (DLA) ... Toml
Tomlins' Election Cases [*1689-1795*] [*A publication*] (DLA) ... Toml Cas
Tomlins' Law Dictionary [*A publication*] (DLA) ... Toml Law Dict
Tomlins' Law Dictionary [*A publication*] (DLA) ... Toml LD
Tomlins' Law Dictionary [*A publication*] (DLA) ... Tomlins
Tomlins' Supplement to Brown's Parliamentary Cases [*A publication*] (DLA) ... Toml Supp Br
Tomlinson-Holman Cross-Over [*Motion picture theater sound system*] ... THX
Tommy [*Phonetic alphabet*] [*Royal Navy World War I*] (DSUE) ... T
Tommy Cash Fan Club [*Defunct*] (EA) ... TCFC
Tommy Hilfiger [*Fashion designer*] ... TH
Tommy Hilfiger [*NYSE symbol*] (TTSB) ... TOM
Tommy Hilfiger, Inc. [*NYSE symbol*] (SPSG) ... TOM
Tommy Hilfiger Sportwear, Inc. [*Associated Press*] (SAG) ... THilfgr
Tommy John [*Baseball pitcher*] ... TJ
Tomo [*Volume*] [*Italian*] (ILCA) ... T
Tomogram [*Radiology*] (DAVI) ... TOMO
Tomogram with Oscillating Bucky [*Radiology*] (DAVI) ... B
Tomography [*Radiology*] (DAVI) ... TOMO
Tomorrow (ROG) ... TOMR
Tompkins City Trustco [*NASDAQ symbol*] (TTSB) ... TCTC
Tompkins County Public Library, Ithaca, NY [*Library symbol Library of Congress*] (LCLS) ... NI
Tompkins County Trust [*Associated Press*] (SAG) ... Tompkn
Tompkins County Trust Co. [*Ithaca, NY*] [*NASDAQ symbol*] (NQ) ... TCTC
Tompkins-Cortland Community College, Division of Instructional and Learning Resources, Dryden, NY [*Library symbol Library of Congress*] (LCLS) ... NDryT
Tompkins-Cortland Community College, Dryden, NY [*OCLC symbol*] (OCLC) ... VXT
Tompkins-Cortland Community College, Groton, NY [*Library symbol Library of Congress Obsolete*] (LCLS) ... NGroT
Tompkins-Seneca-Tioga Board of Cooperative Educational Services, Ithaca, NY [*Library symbol*] [*Library of Congress*] (LCLS) ... NITB
Tompkinsville, KY [*AM radio station call letters*] ... WTKY
Tompkinsville, KY [*FM radio station call letters*] ... WTKY-FM
Tom's Look of Love (EA) ... TLL
Tom's Love Connection (EA) ... TLC
Toms River, NJ [*Location identifier FAA*] (FAAL) ... MJX
Toms River, NJ [*AM radio station call letters*] ... WJRZ
Toms River, NJ [*FM radio station call letters*] ... WOBM
Toms River Signal Laboratory [*Army*] (MCD) ... TRSL
Tomsk [*Former USSR Geomagnetic observatory code*] ... TMK
Tomus [*Volume*] ... T
Tomus [*Volume*] [*Latin*] ... Tom
Tomy Jennings Fan Club (EA) ... TJFC
Ton ... T
Ton ... TN
Ton Equivalent of Coal ... TEC
Ton Load ... TL
Ton of Oil Equivalent [*Energy equivalent*] ... TOE
Ton Statute Mile (AAG) ... TSM
Tonalite-Trondhjemite-Granodiorite [*Geology*] ... TTG
Tonb Island [*Iran*] [*ICAO location identifier*] (ICLI) ... OIBX
Tonbridge [*Postcode*] (ODBW) ... TN
Tonder [*Denmark ICAO location identifier*] (ICLI) ... EKTD
Tondu [*British depot code*] ... TDU
Tone (IAA) ... T
Tone (MSA) ... TN
Tone Answer Back [*Telecommunications*] (IAA) ... TAB
Tone Burst ... TB
Tone Burst Amplitude Modulation ... TBAM

Tone Burst Modulation .... TBM
Tone Call Squelch [*Telecommunications*] (IAA) .... TCS
Tone Code Modulation (IAA) .... TCM
Tone Control [*Telecommunications*] (IAA) .... TC
Tone Decay [*Audiometry*] (MAE) .... TD
Tone Decay Test [*Audiometry*] .... TDT
Tone Dial Receiver .... TDR
Tone Dial Switching System Control (IAA) .... TDSSC
Tone Digital Command (IAA) .... TDC
Tone Encoded Burst .... TEB
Tone Generator and Master Alarm (KSC) .... TGMA
Tone Generator Panel .... TGP
Tone Modulation .... TM
Tone Multiplex Apollo Command System [*NASA*] (KSC) .... TMACS
Tone Not Relevant .... TNR
Tone Off [*Telecommunications*] (TEL) .... TOF
Tone On [*Telecommunications*] (TEL) .... TON
Tone Relevant .... TR
Tone Reproduction and Neutral Determination [*Chart*] [*Printing technology*] .... TRAND
Tone Telegraph Filter .... TTF
Tone-Count Audiometric Computer (PDAA) .... TCAC
Tonecraft Realty, Inc. [*Toronto Stock Exchange symbol*] .... TCR
Toned (VRA) .... tn
Tone-Operated Net Loss Adjuster Receiving .... TONLAR
Tong [*Sudan*] [*ICAO location identifier*] (ICLI) .... HSTO
Tonga [*Aircraft nationality and registration mark*] (FAAC) A3
Tonga [*MARC geographic area code Library of Congress*] (LCCP) .... poto--
Tonga [*MARC country of publication code Library of Congress*] (LCCP) .... to
Tonga [*ANSI two-letter standard code*] (CNC) .... TO
Tonga [*ANSI three-letter standard code*] (CNC) .... TON
Tonga Air Service [*ICAO designator*] (AD) .... DH
Tonga and Tin Can Mail Study Circle (EA) .... TTCMSC
Tonga Defence Force [*British military*] (DMA) .... TDF
Tongariro [*New Zealand*] [*Seismograph station code, US Geological Survey Closed*] (SEIS) .... TON
Tongass Historical Society Museum, Ketchikan, AK [*Library symbol Library of Congress*] (LCLS) .... AkKTHi
Tongass National Forest, Petersburg, AK [*Library symbol Library of Congress*] (LCLS) .... AkPT
Tongass [*National Forest*] Timber Reform Act .... TTRA
Tongass [*National Forest*] Timber Supply Fund [*Department of the Interior*] .... TTSF
Tongatapu [*Tonga Island*] [*Airport symbol*] (OAG) .... TBU
Tongatapu/Fua'Amotu International [*Tonga*] [*ICAO location identifier*] (ICLI) .... NFTF
Tongkang [*Ship's rigging*] (ROG) .... TKG
Tongliao [*China*] [*Airport symbol*] (OAG) .... TGO
Tongo [*Sierra Leone*] [*ICAO location identifier*] (ICLI) .... GFTO
Tongo [*Sierra Leone*] [*Airport symbol*] (AD) .... TNQ
Tongoa [*Vanuatu*] [*ICAO location identifier*] (ICLI) .... NVST
Tongoa [*Vanuatu*] [*Airport symbol*] (OAG) .... TGH
Tongoucheon [*South Korea ICAO location identifier*] (ICLI) .... RKST
Tongue (MSA) .... TNG
Tongue and Groove [*Lumber*] .... T & G
Tongue and Groove [*Lumber*] (IAA) .... TAG
Tongue of the Ocean [*Area of the Bahama Islands*] [*Navy*] .... TOTO
Tongued, Grooved, and Beaded [*Lumber*] .... TGB
Tongueless .... TGLS
Tongue-Retaining Device [*Medicine*] .... TRD
Tonic [*Permanently Strengthening*] [*Pharmacy*] (ROG) .... TON
Tonic Hind Limb Extension (BABM) .... THE
Tonic Immobility [*Neurophysiology*] .... TI
Tonic Neck Reflex [*Physiology*] .... TNR
Tonic Sol-Fa College [*London*] .... TSC
Tonic Vibration Reflex [*or Response*] [*Medicine*] .... TVR
Tonica Consolidated Community School District 79 and Consolidated High School District 360, Tonica, IL [*Library symbol Library of Congress*] (LCLS) .... ITonSD
Tonically Active Neurons [*Neurobiology*] .... TAN
Tonight (DAVI) .... TONOC
Tonight Only [*Newspapers*] (DGA) .... TO
Tonkabon [*Iran*] [*ICAO location identifier*] (ICLI) .... OINV
Tonkawa, OK [*FM radio station call letters*] .... KAYE
Tonkawa Public Library, Tonkawa, OK [*Library symbol Library of Congress*] (LCLS) .... OkTo
Ton-Kilometer Performed .... TKP
Ton-Mile Per Hour [*Heavy tires*] (DICI) .... TMPH
Ton-Miles .... TM
Ton-Miles per Gallon [*Automotive fuel*] .... TMPG
Tonnage [*Shipping*] .... T
Tonnage [*Shipping*] .... TNGE
Tonnage [*Shipping*] .... TONN
Tonnage Mark [*Found on each side of the ship aft*] (DS) .... TMK
Tonnage Opening (DS) .... TO
Tonne [*Metric*] .... t
Tonnerre-Moulins [*France ICAO location identifier*] (ICLI) .... LFFO
Tono [*Zaire*] [*ICAO location identifier*] (ICLI) .... FZDE
Tonometer Reading [*Medicine*] (MEDA) .... T
Tonopah [*Nevada*] [*Seismograph station code, US Geological Survey*] (SEIS) .... TNP
Tonopah [*Nevada*] [*Seismograph station code, US Geological Survey*] (SEIS) .... TPH
Tonopah [*Nevada*] [*Airport symbol*] (AD) .... TPH

Tonopah [*Nevada*] [*Seismograph station code, US Geological Survey Closed*] (SEIS) .... TPV
Tonopah & Goldfield Railroad (IIA) .... T & G
Tonopah, NV [*FM radio station call letters*] .... KHWK
Tonopah, NV [*FM radio station call letters*] .... KTPH
Tonopah, NV [*Location identifier FAA*] (FAAL) .... TNX
Tonopah, NV [*Location identifier FAA*] (FAAL) .... TPH
Tonopah, NV [*Location identifier FAA*] (FAAL) .... XSD
Tonopah Resources, Inc. [*Vancouver Stock Exchange symbol*] .... TON
Tonopah Test Range .... TTR
Tons Deadweight (DS) .... TDW
Tons Deadweight (DS) .... TS D/W
Tons Equivalent of Petroleum [*Fuel measure*] .... TEP
Tons of Coal Equivalent .... TCE
Tons of Cubic Capacity Bale Space [*Shipping*] .... TCCBL
Tons of Oil Equivalent .... TOE
Tons of Paper In [*Computer science*] (IAA) .... TOPI
Tons of Paper Out [*Computer science*] (IAA) .... TOPO
Tons per Annum (ADA) .... TPA
Tons per Centimeter (DCTA) .... TPC
Tons per Day .... TD
Tons per Day .... TPD
Tons per Hour .... TPH
Tons per Hour .... TPHR
Tons per Inch .... TPI
Tons per Man-Hour .... TMH
Tons per Minute .... TM
Tons per Minute .... TPM
Tons per Month .... TPM
Tons per Square Foot .... TON/FT^2
Tons per Square Inch (MCD) .... TSI
Tons per Week .... TPW
Tons per Workable Hatch per Day [*Shipping*] .... TWHD
Tons per Year .... TPY
Tons Poids Lourd [*Deadweight Tons*] [*French*] .... TPL
Tons Registered [*Shipping*] .... TR
Tonsillectomy [*Medicine*] (DAVI) .... TE
Tonsillectomy and Adenoidectomy [*or Tonsils and Adenoids*] [*Medicine*] .... T & A
Tonsils Excised [*Medicine*] (DAVI) .... TE
Tonto Forest Array [*Arizona*] [*Seismograph station code, US Geological Survey Closed*] (SEIS) .... TFO
Tonto Forest Seismological Observatory [*Arizona*] .... TFSO
Tonto Hills Observatory [*Arizona*] [*Seismograph station code, US Geological Survey Closed*] (SEIS) .... THO
Tonto National Monument .... TONT
Tony Booth Fan Club (EA) .... TBFC
Tony Orlando Fan Club [*Defunct*] (EA) .... TOFC
Tony, Oscar, Emmy [*Refers to actors who have won these three major awards, for stage, film, and television work, respectively*] .... TOE
Too Badly Decomposed .... TBD
Too Badly Decomposed/Technician Destroyed Animal [*Laboratory testing*] .... TBD/TDA
Too Good to be True [*Internet language*] [*Computer science*] .... TGTBT
Too Hard to Do (CAAL) .... THTD
Too Hot to Handle .... THTH
Too Long to Print (FAAC) .... TLTP
Too Many Birthdays (MEDA) .... TMB
Too Many Metaphors [*Used in correcting manuscripts, etc.*] .... TMM
Too Many to Count [*Laboratory science*] (DAVI) ...... TMTC
Too Numerous to Count .... TNC
Too Numerous to Count [*Microbiology*] .... TNTC
Too Short [*Symbol stamped in shoes which are not actually of the size marked*] .... TS
Too Tacky for Words [*Slang*] .... TTFW
Too Well Known .... TWK
Toodoggone Gold [*Vancouver Stock Exchange symbol*] .... TDG
Tooele Army Depot [*Utah*] .... TAD
Tooele Army Depot [*Utah*] (AABC) .... TEAD
Tooele Public Library, Tooele, UT [*Library symbol Library of Congress*] (LCLS) .... UT
Tooele, UT [*FM radio station call letters*] .... KTLE
Tooele, UT [*AM radio station call letters*] .... KTUR
Tooele Valley Railway Co. [*AAR code*] .... TOV
Tool Accessory (AAG) .... TOAC
Tool and Cutter Grinding Equipment (MCD) .... TCGE
Tool and Cutter Grinding Tool (MCD) .... TCGT
Tool and Die Institute (KSC) .... TDI
Tool and Operation Liaison Order (AAG) .... TOLO
Tool and Production Change Planning Record (SAA) .... TPCRP
Tool and Production Planning (SAA) .... TPP
Tool and Production Planning Change Record (SAA) .... TPPCR
Tool and Stainless Steel Industry Committee (EA) ...... TSSIC
Tool and Test Equipment [*DoD*] .... TTE
Tool and Test Equipment List [*NASA*] (NASA) .... TTEL
Tool and Trades History Society (EAIO) .... TATHS
Tool Available .... TA
Tool Center Point [*Robotics*] .... TCP
Tool Change Order (MCD) .... TCO
Tool Change Time .... TCT
Tool Clearance Slip (AAG) .... TCS
Tool Command Language [*Computer science*] .... TCL
Tool Completion Report .... TCR
Tool Control List [*Military*] (AFIT) .... TCL
Tool Coordinate System .... TCS
Tool Cost Transportation [*MTMC*] (TAG) .... TCT

Tool Data Sheet (MCD) ... TDS
Tool Design ... TD
Tool Design Manual (MCD) ... TDM
Tool Design Request (KSC) ... TDR
Tool Design Service (MCD) ... TDS
Tool Design Study (MCD) ... TDS
Tool Detail (AAG) ... TODT
Tool Disposition ... TD
Tool Drawing (MCD) ... TD
Tool Fabrication (SAA) ... TF
Tool Fabrication Instruction Manual (MCD) ... TFIM
Tool Fabrication Manual (MCD) ... TFM
Tool Follow Up ... TFU
Tool for Automatic Conversion of Operational Software ... TACOS
Tool Foundation [*See also ST*] [*Amsterdam, Netherlands*] (EAIO) ... TF
Tool Handling Vehicle (MCD) ... THV
Tool Inspection Small Tools Historical Record (MCD) ... TISTHR
Tool Inventors Program [*Automobile tool design*] ... TIP
Tool Investigation and Disposition Report (SAA) ... TIDR
Tool Issue Center [*Military*] (AFIT) ... TIC
Tool Kits [*JETDS nomenclature*] [*Military*] (CET) ... TK
Tool Liaison Request (AAG) ... TLR
Tool Life ... TL
Tool List ... TL
Tool Management Culture ... TMC
Tool Manufacturing Instruction (AAG) ... TMI
Tool Manufacturing Order [*NASA*] (NASA) ... TMO
Tool Offset (IAA) ... TO
Tool Order ... TO
Tool Order Control System (MCD) ... TOCS
Tool Order Release (SAA) ... TOR
Tool Order-Reporting and Cost Control System (SAA) ... TORACCS
Tool Package (IAA) ... TOP
Tool Performance Report [*Navy*] (DNAB) ... TPR
Tool Process Instruction Manual (MCD) ... TPIM
Tool Record Accountability System [*NASA*] (NASA) ... TRACS
Tool Requirement Code [*Army*] ... TOOL CD
Tool Resistant [*Rating for safes*] ... TR
Tool Room Lathe ... TRL
Tool Sharpness ... TS
Tool Shed (IIA) ... TS
Tool Specification Control Drawing (MCD) ... TSCD
Tool Steel ... TS
Tool Storage ... TS
Tool Strength (ADA) ... TS
Tool Subcontract Authorization (AAG) ... TSCA
Tool Truck ... TLTK
Tool Usage Instructions (MCD) ... TUI
Tool Wear Rate ... TWR
Tool Welders Kit ... TWK
Toolangi [*Australia Seismograph station code, US Geological Survey*] (SEIS) ... TOO
ToolBook [*Computer format*] (PCM) ... TBK
Toole County Free Library, Shelby, MT [*Library symbol*] [*Library of Congress*] (LCLS) ... MtSh
Tooled (BARN) ... tld
Toolex-Alpha [*NASDAQ symbol*] (SAG) ... TLXA
Toolex-Alpha [*Associated Press*] (SAG) ... ToolAlph
Toolex-Alpha N.V. [*NASDAQ symbol*] (TTSB) ... TLXAF
Toolik, AK [*Location identifier FAA*] (FAAL) ... MUY
Tooling Advance Material Order (MCD) ... TAMO
Tooling and Manufacturing Association (EA) ... TMA
Tooling Automated Direct Labor Reporting (MCD) ... TADLR
Tooling Change Request ... TCR
Tooling Component Manufacturers Association (EA) ... TCMA
Tooling Contour Check Tool (MCD) ... TCCT
Tooling Coordination Group (AAG) ... TCG
Tooling Design Change ... TDC
Tooling Expenditure Control Order (MCD) ... TECO
Tooling Form (AAG) ... TOFM
Tooling Gauge (AAG) ... TOGA
Tooling Impound Notice ... TIN
Tooling Inspection Instrumentation (NASA) ... TII
Tooling Investigation Report ... TIR
Tooling Layout (AAG) ... TOLO
Tooling Machine Control Medium (MCD) ... TMCM
Tooling Manufacturing Outline ... TMO
Tooling Order Change ... TOC
Tooling Pattern ... TOPA
Tooling Project Data Sheet Assembly Sequence Record ... TPDSASR
Tooling Rejection and Rework Laboratory ... TRRL
Tooling Rejection and Rework Tag ... TRRT
Tooling Samples ... TOSE
Tooling Supplement to Contract (SAA) ... TS-C
Tooling Tag (SAA) ... TT
Tooling Template ... TOTP
Tooling Template (MCD) ... TT
Tooling Test Equipment Team (AAG) ... TTEM
Tooling Work Authorization ... TWA
Tooling Work Order (MCD) ... TWO
Toolkit for Interoperable Privacy-Enhanced Messaging [*RSA Data Security, Inc.*] ... TIPEM
Toolmanager [*Computer science*] (IAA) ... TOM
Tools [*JETDS nomenclature*] [*Military*] (CET) ... TL
Tools for Designing Office Information Systems (NITA) ... TODOS
Tools for Self Reliance [*British*] (EAIO) ... TFSR
Toorghondi [*Afghanistan*] [*ICAO location identifier*] (ICLI) ... OATD
Tootal Broadhurst Lee [*Textile testing*] [*Obsolete*] ... TBL
Tooth ... T
Tooth Extracted (MAE) ... TE
Tooth Treatment [*Dentistry*] (DAVI) ... TT
Toothbrushing Instruction [*Dentistry*] (DMAA) ... TBI
Toothed Ring [*Technical drawings*] ... TR
Toothpick ... TP
Tooth-to-Tooth Composite Error ... TTCE
Tootsie Roll Indus [*NYSE symbol*] (TTSB) ... TR
Tootsie Roll Industries, Inc. [*Associated Press*] (SAG) ... TootsRI
Tootsie Roll Industries, Inc. [*NYSE symbol*] (SPSG) ... TR
Toowoomba [*Australia Airport symbol*] (OAG) ... TWB
Toowoomba Newspapers Publishers Ltd., Toowoomba, QLD, Australia [*Library symbol Library of Congress*] (LCLS) ... AuTooT
Tooyserkan [*Iran*] [*ICAO location identifier*] (ICLI) ... OIHU
Top ... T
Top ... TP
Top Air Havacilik Sanayi Ve Ticaret, AS [*Turkey*] [*FAA designator*] (FAAC) ... TOP
Top Air Manufacturing, Inc. [*Associated Press*] (SAG) ... TopAir
Top Air Manufacturing, Inc. [*NASDAQ symbol*] (NQ) ... TOPM
Top Air Mfg [*NASDAQ symbol*] (TTSB) ... TOPM
Top and Bottom [*Technical drawings*] ... T & B
Top and Bottom (IAA) ... TAB
Top and Bottom Bolt [*Technical drawings*] ... T & BB
Top Assembly ... TA
Top Assembly Drawing ... TAD
Top Baseband Frequency ... TBBF
Top Blacks in Law Enforcement [*Later, BLE*] (EA) ... TBLE
Top, Bottom, and Sides [*Lumber*] ... TB & S
Top Boy [*British*] (DSUE) ... TB
Top Cap (IAA) ... TC
Top Carnivore ... TC
Top Cat [*Cartoon character*] ... TC
Top Center [*Valve position*] ... TC
Top Chord ... TC
Top Computer Executive (MHDB) ... TCE
Top Contact [*Valve*] (DEN) ... TC
Top Dead Center ... TDC
Top Desk Computer (IAA) ... TDC
Top Down ... TD
Top Down Development (MHDB) ... TDD
Top Down Structured Programming (MHDB) ... TDSP
Top Drawing Breakdown (AAG) ... TDB
Top Edge Gilt [*Bookbinding*] ... TEG
Top Electronic Security Systems [*Commercial firm British*] ... TESS
Top Eliminator [*Automobile racing*] (DICI) ... TE
Top End Aboriginal Music Association [*Australia*] ... TEAMA
Top European Advertising Media ... TEAM
Top Farmers of America Association [*Defunct*] (EA) ... TFA
Top Flight Air Service, Inc. [*ICAO designator*] (FAAC) ... CHE
Top Flight Club [*Northwest Airlines' club for frequent flyers*] (EA) ... TFC
Top Fuel Motorcycle Riders Association (EA) ... TFMRA
Top Gear Switch [*Automotive engineering*] ... TGS
Top Grille (OA) ... TG
Top Groove Fill [*Lubricating oil test*] ... TGF
Top Image Systems Ltd. [*NASDAQ symbol*] (SAG) ... TISA
Top Image Systems Ltd. [*Associated Press*] (SAG) ... TopIm
Top Image Systems Ltd. [*Associated Press*] (SAG) ... TopImge
Top Kit Drawing ... TKD
Top Left Side (MCD) ... TLS
Top Level Computer Software Component ... TLCSC
Top Level Requirements [*Navy*] ... TLR
Top Level Specification [*Military*] (CAAL) ... TLS
Top Load Pad (NRCH) ... TLP
Top Load Plane [*Nuclear energy*] (NRCH) ... TLP
Top Loading Air Cleaner (MCD) ... TLAC
Top Man ... TM
Top Management ... TM
Top Management Program ... TMP
Top Management Simulation [*Game*] ... TMS
Top of Active Fuel [*Nuclear energy*] (NRCH) ... TAF
Top of Alabama Regional Council of Governments ... TARCOG
Top of Climb [*Aviation*] ... TOC
Top of Column ... TC
Top of Descent (GAVI) ... TOD
Top of Duct (OA) ... TOD
Top of Edge (AAG) ... TOE
Top of File ... TOF
Top of Form [*Computer science*] ... TOF
Top of Frame (AAG) ... T/FR
Top of Grade (MCD) ... TOG
Top of Potentiometer [*Electronics*] (IAA) ... TOP
Top of Slab [*Technical drawings*] ... TSL
Top of Stack [*Computer science*] ... TOS
Top of Stack Control Word [*Computer science*] (MHDI) ... TOSCW
Top of Stack Pointer (MHDB) ... TOSP
Top of Steel [*Flooring*] (AAG) ... TOS
Top of the Atmosphere [*Meterology*] ... TOA
Top of the News [*A publication*] ... TON
Top of the Pops [*Television program*] [*British*] ... TOTP
Top of Wall [*Technical drawings*] ... TW
Top One Percent Society (EA) ... TOPS
Top Priority ... TP

Top Pumparound [*Chemical engineering*] ..... TPA
Top [*or Truth*] **(Quark)** [*Atomic physics*] ..... t
Top Register (OA) ..... TR
Top Right Side (MCD) ..... TRS
Top Salaries Review Board [*British*] ..... TSRB
Top Secret ..... T
Top Secret [*Security classification*] ..... TOPSEC
Top Secret ..... TS
Top Secret (MCD) ..... TSEC
Top Secret Codeword (MCD) ..... TSCW
Top Secret Control (MCD) ..... TSC
Top Secret Control Agency (MCD) ..... TSCA
Top Secret Control Channels [*Military*] ..... TSCC
Top Secret Control Officer [*Military*] ..... TSCO
Top Secret Control Proceeding [*Navy*] ..... TSCP
Top Secret Control Section [*Navy*] ..... TSCS
Top Secret Cover Folder (AAG) ..... TSCF
Top Source, Inc. [*Associated Press*] (SAG) ..... TopSrce
Top Source, Inc. [*AMEX symbol*] (SPSG) ..... TPS
Top Source Technol [*AMEX symbol*] (TTSB) ..... TPS
Top Spare ..... TS
Top Surface Imaging [*Microlithography*] ..... TSI
Top to Bottom ..... T/B
Top Value Television [*Group of 26 young people who photographed the 1972 Democratic convention and presented it on TV*] ..... TVTV
Top Visual Quality ..... TVQ
Top Water Level ..... TWL
Topair Ltd. [*Czechoslovakia*] [*ICAO designator*] (FAAC) ..... TPI
Topaz Exploration Ltd. [*Vancouver Stock Exchange symbol*] ..... TZE
Top-Blown Rotary Converter [*Nonferrous metallurgy*] ..... TBRC
Topcliffe [*British ICAO location identifier*] (ICLI) ..... EGXZ
Topcliffe FTU [*British ICAO designator*] (FAAC) ..... TOF
Top-Down Greedy ..... TDG
Top-Down Parsing Language ..... TDPL
Tope Elementary School, Grand Junction, CO [*Library symbol Library of Congress*] (LCLS) ..... CoGjTE
Top-Edge Gilt [*Bookbinding*] (WDMC) ..... teg
Topeka [*Kansas*] [*Airport symbol*] (OAG) ..... TOP
Topeka [*Kansas*] **Forbes** [*Airport symbol*] (OAG) ..... FOE
Topeka/Forbes Air Force Base [*Kansas*] [*ICAO location identifier*] (ICLI) ..... KFOE
Topeka, KS [*Location identifier FAA*] (FAAL) ..... FOE
Topeka, KS [*FM radio station call letters*] ..... KBUZ
Topeka, KS [*FM radio station call letters*] ..... KDVV
Topeka, KS [*FM radio station call letters*] ..... KJTY
Topeka, KS [*AM radio station call letters*] ..... KMAJ
Topeka, KS [*FM radio station call letters*] ..... KMAJ-FM
Topeka, KS [*Television station call letters*] ..... KSNT
Topeka, KS [*Television station call letters*] ..... KTKA
Topeka, KS [*AM radio station call letters*] ..... KTOP
Topeka, KS [*FM radio station call letters*] ..... KTPK
Topeka, KS [*Television station call letters*] ..... KTWU
Topeka, KS [*FM radio station call letters*] ..... KWIC
Topeka, KS [*Location identifier FAA*] (FAAL) ..... OPE
Topeka, KS [*Location identifier FAA*] (FAAL) ..... TOP
Topeka, KS [*AM radio station call letters*] ..... WIBW
Topeka, KS [*FM radio station call letters*] ..... WIBW-FM
Topeka, KS [*Television station call letters*] ..... WIBW-TV
Topeka, KS [*AM radio station call letters*] (RBYB) ..... WREN
Topeka Public Library, Topeka, KS [*Library symbol Library of Congress*] (LCLS) ..... KT
Topeka State Hospital, Topeka, KS [*Library symbol Library of Congress*] (LCLS) ..... KTSH
Topel [*Turkey ICAO location identifier*] (ICLI) ..... LTBQ
Topic [*Record label*] [*Great Britain*] ..... Top
Topic [*Record label*] [*Great Britain*] ..... TRC
Topic Indexing Matrix ..... TIM
Topic Statement (WGA) ..... TS
Topica [*of Aristotle*] [*Classical studies*] (OCD) ..... Top
Topical (ADA) ..... T
Topical ..... top
Topical Hazard Evaluation Program [*Toxicology*] [*Military*] (RDA) ..... THEP
Topical Magnetic Resonance [*Medical diagnostic technique*] ..... TMR
Topical Nitrogen Mustard [*Dermatology*] ..... TNM
Topical Numismatic Society (EA) ..... TNS
Topical Numismatic Society (EA) ..... TONS
Topical Pulmonary Chemotherapy [*Medicine*] ..... TPC
Topical Reference Books [*A publication*] ..... TRB
Topical Report [*Nuclear energy*] (NRCH) ..... TR
Topical Report Request [*or Review*] [*Nuclear energy*] (NRCH) ..... TRR
Topical Time [*A publication*] ..... TT
Topics in Australasian Library and Information Studies [*A publication*] ..... TALIS
Topinabee Public Library, Topinabee, MI [*Library symbol Library of Congress*] (LCLS) ..... MiTop
Top-Level Demonstration [*Military*] (INF) ..... TLD
Top-Level Domain [*Internet Name*] ..... TLD
Toplumcu Kurtulus Partisi [*Communal Liberation Party*] [*Cyprus*] [*Political party*] (EY) ..... TKP
Top-of-Climb (GAVI) ..... T/C
Top-of-Descent (GAVI) ..... T/D
Topographic ..... TOP
Topographic Center [*Defense Mapping Agency*] ..... TC
Topographic Center [*Defense Mapping Agency*] ..... TPC
Topographic Command [*Army*] ..... TOPOCOM
Topographic Data Library System ..... TDLS
Topographic Developments Laboratory [*Fort Belvoir, VA*] [*United States Army Engineer Topographic Laboratories*] (GRD) ..... TDL
Topographic Draftsman [*Navy*] ..... TD
Topographic Engineering Center [*Ft. Belvoir, VA*] [*Army*] (RDA) ..... TEC
Topographic Experiment [*Proposed oceanographic satellite*] ..... TOPEX
Topographic Map Inventory Control Point [*Army*] (AABC) ..... TMICP
Topographic Platoon (DNAB) ..... TOPOPLT
Topographic Scientific Advisory Committee [*Terminated, 1973*] [*Army*] (EGAO) ..... TSAC
Topographic Support System [*Army*] (RDA) ..... TSS
Topographical Engineer ..... TE
Topographical Engineer ..... TOPOENGR
Topographical Infrared Operations Satellite (NASA) ..... TIROS
Topographically Integrated Geographic Referencing[*and Coding System*] [*Electronic map used for political demography*] ..... TIGR
Topographie Historique de la Syrie Antique et Medievale [*A publication*] (BJA) ..... THSAM
Topography (AFM) ..... TOPO
Topography ..... TOPOG
Topoisomerase [*An enzyme*] ..... TOP
Topolino Register of North America (EA) ..... TRNA
Topological Optimization Module [*Computer science*] (OA) ..... TOM
Topological Representation of Synthetic and Analytical Relations of Concepts (PDAA) ..... TOSAR
Topologically Integrated Geographic Encoding and Referencing [*Bureau of the Census*] ..... TIGER
Topologically Integrated Geographic Encoding Referencing ..... TIGER
Topology ..... TOP
Topolovo [*Former USSR Seismograph station code, US Geological Survey*] (SEIS) ..... TOP
Toponymic [*Anatomy*] ..... TOP
Topotactic Reaction [*Inorganic synthesis*] ..... TR
Topped Long Resid [*Petroleum technology*] ..... TLR
Toppenish, WA [*AM radio station call letters*] ..... KENE
Toppenish, WA [*FM radio station call letters*] ..... KXXS
Topping (MSA) ..... TOPG
Topping (AAG) ..... TPNG
Topping Control Unit (AAG) ..... TCU
Topps Co. [*NASDAQ symbol*] (TTSB) ..... TOPP
[*The*] **Topps Co., Inc.** [*NASDAQ symbol*] (NQ) ..... TOPP
Topps Co., Inc. [*Associated Press*] (SAG) ..... Topps
Topro, Inc. [*Associated Press*] (SAG) ..... Topro
Topro, Inc. [*NASDAQ symbol*] (SAG) ..... TPRO
Topro Inc. Wrrt [*NASDAQ symbol*] (TTSB) ..... TPROW
Tops and Accessories [*Show business slang*] [*Bowdlerized version*] ..... T & A
Tops Appliance City [*NASDAQ symbol*] (SAG) ..... TOPS
Tops Appliance City [*Associated Press*] (SAG) ..... TopsApl
Tops Order (MCD) ..... TO
Topsail [*Ship's rigging*] (ROG) ..... TPL
Topsail Beach, NC [*FM radio station call letters*] ..... WZXS
Topsail Campus Resource Centre, Cabot Institute of Applied Arts and Technology, St. John's, Newfoundland [*Library symbol National Library of Canada*] (NLC) ..... NFSCTM
Topsham, ME [*FM radio station call letters*] ..... WXGL
Topside Sounder, Ionosphere [*NASA*] ..... TOPSI
Top-to-Top (IAA) ..... TT
Torah Atmosphere (BJA) ..... TA
Torah Nebi'im Ketubim [*Teaching, prophets, writing*] [*Pronounced Tanakh*] [*The Hebrew Bible*] ..... TNK
Torah Shelemah [*A publication*] (BJA) ..... TSh
Torah Umesorah - National Society for Hebrew Day Schools [*Defunct*] (EA) ..... TU
Torah Umesorah - National Society for Hebrew Day Schools ..... TuM
Torah Va'Avodah (BJA) ..... TVA
Torah, Veni'im, Ketubim (BJA) ..... Tenakh
Torath Kohanim (BJA) ..... TK
Torbat-E-Heidarieh [*Iran*] [*ICAO location identifier*] (ICLI) ..... OIMH
Torbat-E-Jam [*Iran*] [*ICAO location identifier*] (ICLI) ..... OIMA
Torbay Public Library, Newfoundland [*Library symbol National Library of Canada*] (NLC) ..... NFTO
Torbay Public Library, Torbay, NF, Canada [*Library symbol Library of Congress*] (LCLS) ..... CaNfTo
Tor-Cal Resources Ltd. [*Toronto Stock Exchange symbol*] ..... TCD
Torch Bible Commentaries [*A publication*] (BJA) ..... TB
Torch Bible Commentaries [*New York/London*] [*A publication*] (BJA) ..... TBC
Torch Brazing ..... TB
Torch Energy Royalty Trust [*Associated Press*] (SAG) ..... TorchEn
Torch Energy Royalty Trust [*NYSE symbol*] (SPSG) ..... TRU
Torch Soldering ..... TS
Torchbearers for Legacy in Western Australia ..... TFLWA
Torchmark Capital LLC, Inc. [*Associated Press*] (SAG) ..... TmkCa
Torchmark Capital 'MIPS' [*NYSE symbol*] (TTSB) ..... TMKPrM
Torchmark Corp. [*NYSE symbol*] (SPSG) ..... TMK
Torchmark Corp. [*Associated Press*] (SAG) ..... Trchmrk
Toreador Royalty [*NASDAQ symbol*] (TTSB) ..... TRGL
Toreador Royalty Corp. [*Associated Press*] (SAG) ..... TorRoy
Toreador Royalty Corp. [*NASDAQ symbol*] (NQ) ..... TRGL
Torero-Matador [*Said to have been coined by Georges Bizet for opera "Carmen"*] ..... TOREADOR
Torex Minerals Ltd. [*Vancouver Stock Exchange symbol*] ..... TXI
Torhsen Energy Corp. [*Vancouver Stock Exchange symbol*] ..... TOR
Tories Against Cruise and Trident [*Missiles*] [*British*] (DI) ..... TACT
Torino [*Italy ICAO location identifier*] (ICLI) ..... LIMA
Torino [*Italy*] [*Seismograph station code, US Geological Survey*] (SEIS) ..... TNO
Torino/Bric Della Croce [*Italy ICAO location identifier*] (ICLI) ..... LIMK

Torino/Caselle [*Italy ICAO location identifier*] (ICLI) ... LIMF
Torishima [*Japan*] [*Seismograph station code, US Geological Survey Closed*] (SEIS) ... TOR
Torit [*Sudan*] [*ICAO location identifier*] (ICLI) ... HSTR
Tormentor [*Theater*] (WDMC) ... torm
Tornado ... TDO
Tornado Detection Algorithm [*Marine science*] (OSRA) ... TDA
Tornado Electronic Messaging System [*Computer science*] ... TEMS
Tornado Operational Conversion Unit [*British military*] (DMA) ... TOCU
Tornado Vortex Signature [*Marine science*] (OSRA) ... TVS
Tornado Vortex Signature (USDC) ... TVS
Tornisterempfaenger [*Pack-type portable receiver*] [*German military - World War II*] ... TE
Tornquist-Teisseyre Zone [*Geology*] ... TTZ
Toro Co. [*NYSE symbol*] (TTSB) ... TTC
Toro Corp. [*Associated Press*] (SAG) ... Toro
Toro Corp. [*NYSE symbol*] (SPSG) ... TTC
Toroidal Carbohydrate Module [*i.e., doughnut*] [*Slang*] ... TCM
Toroidal Combustion Chamber ... TCC
Toroidal Field (MCD) ... TF
Toroidal Fusion Test Reactor [*Nuclear energy*] (MCD) ... TFTR
Toroidal Kamera Magnetic [*Thermonuclear-fusion system*] [*Acronym formed from the Russian*] ... TOKAMAK
Toroidal Magnetic Chamber (DI) ... TOMAC
Toroidal Propellant Container ... TRC
Toroidal Space Station ... TSS
Toroidal Support Submarine ... TSS
Torokina [*Papua New Guinea*] [*Airport symbol*] (OAG) ... TOK
Toromont Industries Ltd. [*Toronto Stock Exchange symbol*] ... TIH
Torontair [*ICAO designator*] (AD) ... WJ
Toronto [*Ontario*] [*Seismograph station code, US Geological Survey Closed*] (SEIS) ... TNT
Toronto ... TO
Toronto (ROG) ... TOR
Toronto [*Canada*] [*Airport symbol*] (OAG) ... YTZ
Toronto [*Canada*] [*Airport symbol*] (OAG) ... YYZ
Toronto Airways Ltd. [*Canada ICAO designator*] (FAAC) ... TOR
Toronto Anti-Draft Programme [*Defunct*] (EA) ... TADP
Toronto Art Students' League [*1886-1903*] [*Canada*] (NGC) ... TASL
Toronto Baptist Seminary ... TBS
Toronto Biculture Test of Nonverbal Reasoning [*Speech and language therapy*] (DAVI) ... TBTNR
Toronto Board of Education, Education Centre, Toronto, ON, Canada [*Library symbol Library of Congress*] (LCLS) ... CaOTEC
Toronto Board of Education, Professional Library [*UTLAS symbol*] ... TBE
Toronto Board of Education, Secondary Schools [*UTLAS symbol*] ... TBS
Toronto [*Canada*] **Buttonville Airport** [*Airport symbol*] (OAG) ... YKZ
Toronto/Buttonville, ON [*ICAO location identifier*] (ICLI) ... CYKZ
Toronto City Planning Board Library, Ontario, [*Library symbol National Library of Canada*] (NLC) ... OTCPB
Toronto City Planning Board, Toronto, ON, Canada [*Library symbol Library of Congress*] (LCLS) ... CaOTCPB
Toronto Dance Theatre ... TDT
Toronto Dominion Bank [*Toronto Stock Exchange symbol Vancouver Stock Exchange symbol*] ... TD
Toronto Dominion Bank, Toronto, ON, Canada [*Library symbol Library of Congress*] (LCLS) ... CaOTTDB
Toronto/Downsview, ON [*ICAO location identifier*] (ICLI) ... CYZD
Toronto Game [*Simulation game*] ... TOG
[*The*] **Toronto, Hamilton & Buffalo Railway Co.** [*Nickname: To Hell and Back*] ... TH & B
[*The*] **Toronto, Hamilton & Buffalo Railway Co.** [*AAR code*] ... THB
Toronto Historical Society, Ontario [*Library symbol National Library of Canada*] (BIB) ... OTHB
Toronto International Furniture Market [*Canada*] (ITD) ... TFM
Toronto/International, ON [*ICAO location identifier*] (ICLI) ... CYYZ
Toronto Island, ON [*ICAO location identifier*] (ICLI) ... CYTZ
Toronto Musicians Association [*Canada*] (WWLA) ... TMA
Toronto Normal School ... TNS
Toronto, ON [*AM radio station call letters*] ... CBL
Toronto, ON [*FM radio station call letters*] ... CBL-FM
Toronto, ON [*Television station call letters*] ... CBLFT
Toronto, ON [*Television station call letters*] ... CBLT
Toronto, ON [*Television station call letters*] ... CFMT
Toronto, ON [*AM radio station call letters*] ... CFRB
Toronto, ON [*Television station call letters*] ... CFTO
Toronto, ON [*AM radio station call letters*] ... CFTR
Toronto, ON [*FM radio station call letters*] ... CHFI
Toronto, ON [*AM radio station call letters*] ... CHIN
Toronto, ON [*FM radio station call letters*] ... CHIN-FM
Toronto, ON [*FM radio station call letters*] ... CHRY
Toronto, ON [*AM radio station call letters*] ... CHUM
Toronto, ON [*FM radio station call letters*] ... CHUM-FM
Toronto, ON [*Television station call letters*] ... CICA
Toronto, ON [*Television station call letters*] ... CIII-41
Toronto, ON [*FM radio station call letters*] ... CILQ
Toronto, ON [*FM radio station call letters*] ... CIRV
Toronto, ON [*FM radio station call letters*] ... CISS
Toronto, ON [*Television station call letters*] ... CITY
Toronto, ON [*FM radio station call letters*] ... CIUT
Toronto, ON [*AM radio station call letters*] ... CJBC
Toronto, ON [*AM radio station call letters*] ... CJCL
Toronto, ON [*FM radio station call letters*] ... CJEZ
Toronto, ON [*FM radio station call letters*] ... CJRT
Toronto, ON [*FM radio station call letters*] ... CKFM
Toronto, ON [*FM radio station call letters*] (RBYB) ... CKLN
Toronto, ON [*AM radio station call letters*] ... CKYC
Toronto, ON [*ICAO location identifier*] (ICLI) ... CWTO
Toronto, ON [*ICAO location identifier*] (ICLI) ... CZYZ
Toronto, Ottawa, Montreal [*Derogatory reference to people in these cities; used by other Canadians who think people living in these cities "run things"*] ... TOM
Toronto PET Users Group [*Canada*] ... TPUG
Toronto Public Libraries, Fine Arts Libraries, Northern District, Toronto, ON, Canada [*Library symbol Library of Congress*] (LCLS) ... CaOTPFA
Toronto Public Libraries, Ontario [*Library symbol National Library of Canada*] (NLC) ... OTP
Toronto Public Library [*UTLAS symbol*] ... TPL
Toronto Public Library, Metropolitan Bibliographic Centre, Toronto, ON, Canada [*Library symbol Library of Congress*] (LCLS) ... CaOTP
Toronto Railway ... TRY
Toronto Region Aggregation of Computer Enthusiasts [*Canada*] ... TRACE
Toronto Regional Office, Department of Justice Canada [*Bureau Regional de Toronto, Ministere de la Justice du Canada*] **Toronto, Ontario** [*Library symbol National Library of Canada*] (NLC) ... OTJ
Toronto School of Theology Library, University of Toronto [*UTLAS symbol*] ... STH
Toronto School of Theology, Toronto, Ontario [*Library symbol National Library of Canada*] (NLC) ... OTTST
Toronto Stock Exchange ... T
Toronto Stock Exchange [*Toronto, ON*] ... TSE
Toronto Stock Exchange - Gold ... TSEG
Toronto Stock Exchange - Industrials ... TSEI
Toronto Stock Exchange Library, Ontario [*Library symbol National Library of Canada*] (BIB) ... OTSE
Toronto Stock Exchange Library, Toronto, ON, Canada [*Library symbol*] [*Library of Congress*] (LCLS) ... CaOTSE
Toronto Stock Exchange - Mines ... TSEM
Toronto Stock Exchange - Oils ... TSEO
Toronto Sun Publishing Corp. [*Toronto Stock Exchange symbol*] ... TSP
Toronto Symphony Orchestra (CDAI) ... TSO
Toronto Teachers' College, Ontario [*Library symbol National Library of Canada*] (NLC) ... OTTEC
Toronto Teachers' College, Toronto, ON, Canada [*Library symbol Library of Congress*] (LCLS) ... CaOTTeC
Toronto Theatre Alliance [*Canada*] (WWLA) ... TTA
Toronto Transit Commission [*Canada*] (BARN) ... TTC
Toronto Transit Commission, Ontario [*Library symbol National Library of Canada*] (NLC) ... OTT
Toronto Transportation Commission, Toronto, ON, Canada [*Library symbol Library of Congress*] (LCLS) ... CaOTT
Toronto University. Faculty Law Review [*Canada*] [*A publication*] (DLA) ... Toronto U Faculty L Rev
Toronto Western Hospital [*UTLAS symbol*] ... TWH
Toronto Women in Film and Theatre [*Canada*] (WWLA) ... TWIFT
Toronto-Dominion Bank, Toronto, Ontario [*Library symbol National Library of Canada*] (NLC) ... OTTDB
Toronto-Dominion Bk [*TS symbol*] (TTSB) ... TD
Tororo [*Uganda*] [*ICAO location identifier*] (ICLI) ... HUTO
Tororo [*Uganda*] [*Airport symbol*] (AD) ... TOW
Tororo [*Uganda*] [*Airport symbol*] (OAG) ... TRY
Toros Airlines [*Turkey*] [*ICAO designator*] (FAAC) ... TAU
Torotel, Inc. [*Associated Press*] (SAG) ... Tortel
Torotel, Inc. [*AMEX symbol*] (SPSG) ... TTL
Torp [*Norway ICAO location identifier*] (ICLI) ... ENTO
Torpedo [*Obsolete Navy British*] (ROG) ... T
Torpedo [*Army*] ... Tor
Torpedo (AABC) ... TORP
Torpedo Acquisition ... TORAC
Torpedo and Antisubmarine [*Obsolete Navy British*] ... TAS
Torpedo and Anti-Submarine Instructor [*British military*] (DMA) ... TASI
Torpedo, Anti-Submarine, and Mine Warfare Division [*British military*] (DMA) ... TASWD
Torpedo Attack Teacher [*Navy*] ... TAT
Torpedo Boat [*German symbol*] ... E
Torpedo Boat [*Navy symbol Obsolete*] ... TB
Torpedo Bomber [*or Bombing*] ... TB
Torpedo Bomber Fighter (NATG) ... TBF
Torpedo Bomber Reconnaissance Aircraft [*Navy*] ... TBR
Torpedo Certification Program [*Military*] (CAAL) ... TCP
Torpedo Control [*British military*] (DMA) ... TC
Torpedo Control Officer [*British military*] (DMA) ... TCO
Torpedo Control Unit ... TCU
Torpedo Countermeasures (NVT) ... TCM
Torpedo Countermeasures and Deception ... TORPCM
Torpedo Coxswain [*British military*] (DMA) ... TC
Torpedo Danger Area (NVT) ... TDA
Torpedo Danger Zone (NVT) ... TDZ
Torpedo Data Computer [*Navy*] (NVT) ... TDC
Torpedo Data Computer Operator [*Navy*] ... TDCO
Torpedo Deflection Sight ... TDS
Torpedo Destruction System ... TDS
Torpedo Detection Modification [*SONAR*] ... TDM
Torpedo Development Unit [*Ministry of Technology*] [*British*] ... TDU
Torpedo Dive Bomber Aircraft ... TD
Torpedo Effective Range Indicator ... TERI
Torpedo Ejection Pump (DNAB) ... TEP
Torpedo Evasive Maneuvering (MCD) ... TEAM
Torpedo Evasive Maneuvering [*Navy*] ... TEM
Torpedo Exercise (NVT) ... TORPEX

Torpedo Experimental Establishment [*British*] ..... TEE
Torpedo Fighter Aircraft [*Navy*] ..... TF
Torpedo Fire Control ..... TFC
Torpedo Fire Control System ..... TFCS
Torpedo Firing System (DNAB) ..... TFS
Torpedo Group ..... TG
Torpedo Gunboat (ROG) ..... TGB
Torpedo Gunner's Mate [*Obsolete Navy British*] ..... TGM
Torpedo Installation and Exercise System [*Military*] (DWSG) ..... TIES
Torpedo Instructor [*British military*] (DMA) ..... TI
Torpedo Landplane [*Navy*] ..... TLP
Torpedo Lieutenant [*Navy British*] ..... TL
Torpedo Lieutenant's Writer [*British military*] (DMA) ..... TLW
Torpedo Main Assembly ..... TMA
Torpedo Officer [*Obsolete Navy British*] ..... TO
Torpedo Part of Beam (MSA) ..... TP
Torpedo Plane [*Navy symbol*] ..... VT
Torpedo Prize Money [*British military*] (DMA) ..... TPM
Torpedo Readiness Assistance Team ..... TRAT
Torpedo Reconnaissance Aircraft [*Navy*] ..... TR
Torpedo Recovery Boat ..... TRB
Torpedo Retriever [*Navy symbol*] (DNAB) ..... YPT
Torpedo Rocket Thrown ..... TRT
Torpedo Seaplane [*Navy*] ..... TSP
Torpedo Setting Panel [*Military*] (CAAL) ..... TSP
Torpedo Ship Ranging Vessel [*Canadian Navy*] ..... TSRV
Torpedo Squadron ..... TORPRON
Torpedo Station (MCD) ..... TS
Torpedo Testing Barge [*Navy symbol Obsolete*] ..... YTT
Torpedo Transportation Lighter [*Navy symbol Obsolete*] ..... YFT
Torpedo Tube ..... TT
Torpedo Tube Acceptance Trials [*Navy*] (NG) ..... TTAT
Torpedo Tube Missile (MCD) ..... TTM
Torpedo Tube Pump Ejection System [*Navy*] (CAAL) ..... TTPES
Torpedo Water ..... TW
Torpedo Water Tube ..... TWT
Torpedo Weapons Receiver ..... TWR
Torpedo Wire Dispenser ..... TWD
Torpedo-Boat Destroyer [*Obsolete*] ..... TBD
Torpedo-Bombing Plane [*Navy symbol*] ..... VTB
Torpedoman [*Navy British*] ..... T
Torpedoman's Mate [*Navy rating*] ..... TM
Torpedoman's Mate, Aviation [*Navy rating*] ..... TMV
Torpedoman's Mate, Electrical [*Navy rating*] ..... TME
Torpedoman's Mate, First Class [*Navy rating*] TM1
Torpedoman's Mate, Second Class [*Navy rating*] TM2
Torpedoman's Mate, Third Class [*Navy rating*] TM3
Torpedo-Recovery Vessel [*Navy British*] ..... TRV
Torpedo-Spotter Reconnaissance [*Obsolete Military British*] ..... TSR
Torquay [*England*] ..... TORQ
Torquay [*Postcode*] (ODBW) ..... TQ
Torquay Pottery Collectors' Society (EA) ..... TPCS
Torque ..... T
Torque (AAG) ..... TOR
Torque [*Automotive engineering*] ..... TORQ
Torque (AAG) ..... TRQ
Torque Arm Speed Reducer ..... TASR
Torque Control Isolation [*Automotive engineering*] ..... TCI
Torque Converter [*Automotive engineering*] ..... T/CONV
Torque Converter Clutch [*Automotive engineering*] ..... TCC
Torque Equilibrium Attitude (SSD) ..... TEA
Torque Generator (IAA) ..... TG
Torque/Inertia ..... T/I
Torque Meter (NG) ..... T/M
Torque Motor ..... TM
Torque Motor Beam Steerer (MCD) ..... TMBS
Torque Motor Pilot Valve (NASA) ..... TMPV
Torque, Nip, and Tension [*Winding technology*] ..... TNT
Torque Oil Pressure [*Air Force*] ..... TOP
Torque Overload Switch (NRCH) ..... TOOS
Torque Overload Switch [*Nuclear energy*] (NRCH) ..... TOS
Torque Pressure in Pounds per Square Inch ..... TPSI
Torque Proportioning Differential [*Automotive engineering*] ..... TPD
Torque Receiver (IAA) ..... TR
Torque Repeater (IAA) ..... TR
Torque Screwdriver ..... TSD
Torque Screwdriver Kit ..... TSDK
Torque Screwdriver Kit ..... TSK
Torque Sensing Differential [*Audi*] [*Automotive engineering*] ..... TORSEN
Torque Synchro Receiver (MUGU) ..... TR
Torque Synchro Transmitter (IAA) ..... TS
Torque Transmitter (IAA) ..... TS
Torque Transmitter ..... TX
Torque-Differential Receiver (MUGU) ..... TDR
Torque-Differential Transmitter (MUGU) ..... TDX
Torque-Limiting Nut ..... TLN
Torque-Limiting Screwdriver ..... TLSD
Torquemeter ..... TORM
Torque-Regulated Speed Follower ..... TRSF
Torque-to-Yield [*Automotive engineering*] ..... TTY
Torrance [*California*] ..... TOR
Torrance, CA [*Location identifier FAA*] (FAAL) ..... TOA
Torrance Public Library, Torrance, CA [*Library symbol Library of Congress*] (LCLS) ..... CT
Torrance Public Library, Torrance, CA [*Library symbol*] [*Library of Congress*] (LCLS) ..... CTorr
Torrance State Hospital, Torrance, PA [*OCLC symbol*] (OCLC) ..... PHT
Torrance Tests of Creative Thinking [*Educational test*] ..... TTCT
Torrent Resources Ltd. [*Vancouver Stock Exchange symbol*] ..... TTL
Torreon [*Mexico ICAO location identifier*] (ICLI) ..... MMTC
Torreon [*Mexico*] [*Airport symbol*] (OAG) ..... TRC
Torres Strait Defence Force [*Australia*] ..... TSDF
Torres Strait Islander Advisory Board [*Australia*] ..... TSIAB
Torres Strait Islander Media Association [*Australia*] ..... TSIMA
Torres Strait Protected Zone [*Commonwealth*] (EERA) ..... TSPZ
Torres Strait Protected Zone Authority [*Australia*] ..... TSPZA
Torres Strait Regional Authority [*Australia*] ..... TSRA
Torres Strait Treaty (EERA) ..... TST
Torres United Party [*Australia Political party*] ..... TUP
Torrey Botanical Club (EA) ..... TBC
Torrez Resources Ltd. [*Vancouver Stock Exchange symbol*] ..... TZR
Torricelli [*Unit of pressure*] ..... TORR
Torrid Zone (BARN) ..... Tor
Torrington [*England*] ..... TORR
Torrington, CT [*FM radio station call letters*] (RBYB) ..... WAPJ-FM
Torrington, CT [*AM radio station call letters*] ..... WSNG
Torrington, WY [*FM radio station call letters*] ..... KERM
Torrington, WY [*AM radio station call letters*] ..... KGOS
Torrington, WY [*Location identifier FAA*] (FAAL) ..... TOR
Torry Research Station [*British*] ..... TRS
Torsade de Pointes [*Fringe of Pointed Tips*] [*Found on electrocardiograms*] [*Cardiology*] (DAVI) ..... TdP
Torsatron/Stellarator Laboratory [*University of Wisconsin - Madison*] [*Research center*] (RCD) ..... TSL
Torsby/Fryklanda [*Sweden ICAO location identifier*] (ICLI) ..... ESST
Torsion [*Automotive engineering*] ..... TORS
Torsion (MSA) ..... TRSN
Torsion Bar [*Automotive engineering*] ..... TB
Torsion Bar Spring [*Automotive engineering*] ..... TBS
Torsion Constant [*Physics*] (BARN) ..... k
Torsion Dystonia [*Medicine*] (AAMN) ..... TD
Torsion Head Wattmeter ..... THW
Torsion Reaction Integrating ..... TRI
Torsional ..... TORNL
Torsional Braid Analysis [*Instrumentation*] ..... TBA
Torsional Simple Shear Device [*Nuclear energy*] (NUCP) ..... TSSD
Torsional Vibration Characteristics ..... TVC
Torsional-Bending Vibration Damper [*Mechanical engineering*] ..... TBVD
Torso Back Protective Armor (PDAA) ..... TBPA
Torso Limb Suit Assembly (MCD) ..... TLSA
Torso Restraint Assembly with Integrated Flotation ..... TRAIF
Torstar Corp. [*Toronto Stock Exchange symbol*] ..... TS
Tortilla Industry Association (EA) ..... TIA
Tortoise (VRA) ..... tort
Tortola [*British Virgin Islands*] [*Airport symbol*] (OAG) ..... EIS
Tortola [*British Virgin Islands*] [*Airport symbol*] (AD) ..... TLB
Torus Fontenay AWY-Roses ..... TFR
Torus Longitudinalis [*Anatomy*] ..... TL
Torus Oxygen Monitoring System (IEEE) ..... TOMS
Torus Water Storage Tank (IEEE) ..... TWST
Torwood [*Australia Airport symbol Obsolete*] (OAG) ..... TWP
Tory Legacy Plus World Depression [*British*] (DI) ..... TLPWD
Tory Reform Group [*British*] (DBA) ..... TRG
Tory, Tory, DesLauriers & Binnington, Toronto, Ontario [*Library symbol National Library of Canada*] (BIB) ..... OTTT
TOS [*TIROS Operational Satellite*] **Checkout Center** [*Goddard Space Flight Center*] (NOAA) ..... TCC
TOS [*TIROS Operational Satellite*] **Communications System** (NOAA) ..... TOSCOM
TOS [*TIROS Operational Satellite*] **Operations Center** (NOAA) ..... TOC
TOS [*TIROS Operational Satellite*] **Test Evaluation Center** [*Goddard Space Flight Center*] (NOAA) ..... TEC
Tosafoth (BJA) ..... Tos
Tosafoth (BJA) ..... Tosaf
Tosco Corp. [*NYSE symbol*] (SPSG) ..... TOS
Tosco Corp. [*Associated Press*] (SAG) ..... Tosco
Tosco Corp., Los Angeles, CA [*OCLC symbol*] (OCLC) ..... TOS
Tosco Corp., Technical Information Center, Golden, CO [*Library symbol Library of Congress*] (LCLS) ..... CoGT
Tosefta (BJA) ..... T
Tosefta (BJA) ..... Tos
Tosefta (BJA) ..... Tosef
Tosephta (BJA) ..... Toseph
Toshiba Minicomputer Complex System ..... TMCS
Toshiba Scientific and Business Automatic Computer [*Toshiba Corp.*] ..... TOSBAC
Toshiba Training Reactor [*Japan*] (NRCH) ..... TTR
Toss Bomb Computer ..... TBC
Tosyl [*Also, Ts*] [*Organic chemistry*] ..... Tos
Tosyl [*Also, Tos*] [*Organic chemistry*] ..... Ts
Tosyl Phenylalanine Chloromethyl Ketone [*Biochemistry*] ..... TPCK
Tosylaminophenylethyl Chloromethyl Ketone [*Organic chemistry*] ..... TPCK
Tosylarginine Methyl Ester [*Also, TAME*] [*Biochemistry*] ..... TosArgOMe
Tosyl-L-arginine Methyl Ester [*Also, TosArgOMe*] [*Biochemical analysis*] ..... TAME
Tosyl-L-arginyl Sarcosine Methyl Ester [*Biochemistry*] ..... TASME
Tosyllysine Chloromethyl Ketone [*Biochemistry*] ..... TLCK
Tosylmethyl Isocyanide [*Organic chemistry*] ..... TOSMIC
Tosylphenylalanine Chloromethyl Ketone [*Biochemistry*] ..... $TosPheCH_2Cl$
Totable Tornado Observatory [*National Oceanic and Atmospheric Administration*] ..... TOTO

Total	T
Total	TL
Total (AAG)	TOT
Total (WDMC)	tot
Total [Associated Press] (SAG)	Total
Total	TTL
Total Abdominal Hysterectomy [Medicine]	TAH
Total Abdominal Hysterectomy Bilateral Salpingo-Oophorectomy [Medicine] (MAH)	TAHBSO
Total Aboard (FAAC)	TA
Total Absorption Nuclear Cascade	TANC
Total Absorption Shower Cascade	TASC
Total Abstinence Brotherhood	TAB
Total Abstinence - No Smoking [On social invitations]	TA-NS
Total Access Communications System [Commercial firm British]	TACS
Total Accomplishment Requirement (DNAB)	TAR
Total Acid Number [Oil analysis]	TAN
Total Acid Output [Clinical chemistry]	TAO
Total Acidity (DAVI)	a
Total Action Against Poverty [A federal government program]	TAP
Total Active Aircraft Authorized (MCD)	TAAA
Total Active Aircraft Inventory (MCD)	TAAI
Total Active Federal Commissioned Service to Date [Military]	TAFCSD
Total Active Federal Military Service (DNAB)	TAFMS
Total Active Federal Military Service to Date	TAFMSD
Total Active Inventory (MCD)	TAI
Total Active Military Service (AFM)	TAMS
Total Active Motion [Orthopedics]	TAM
Total Active Preventive Maintenance Time (MCD)	TPM
Total Active Vitamin C [Nutrition]	TAVC
Total Adenine [Nucleotide pool] [Medicine]	TA
Total Adenine Nucleotide [Medicine]	TAN
Total Administrative and Logistics Downtime (MCD)	TALDT
Total Aerobic Bacteria Counts	TABC
Total Aerospace Vehicle [or Aircraft] Authorization	TAA
Total Age-Specific Fertility Rate [Population studies]	TAFR
Total Air Pressure (NASA)	TAP
Total Air Temperature (NASA)	TAT
Total Air Temperature Indicator	TATI
Total Airborne Weapon Systems (MUGU)	TAWS
Total Aircraft Authorized (MCD)	TAA
Total Aircraft Inventory	TAI
Total Aircraft Time (MCD)	TAT
Total Alert Time	TAT
Total Alkalinity [Marine science] (OSRA)	TAlk
Total Alkaloids [Medicine]	TA
Total Alkaloids of Cinchona [Medicine]	TAC
Total Allowable Catch [Fishing regulation proposed by EEC]	TAC
Total Allowable Level of Foreign Fishing	TALFF
Total Allowance Level of Foreign Fishing [Marine science] (OSRA)	TALFF
Total Ammonia Nitrogen	TAN
Total Analysis System for Production, Accounting, and Control [Computer science]	TAS-PAC
Total Angular Momentum Quantum Number of a Single Particle [Symbol] [Spectroscopy]	j
Total Angular Momentum Quantum Number of a System [Symbol] [Spectroscopy]	J
Total Ankle Arthroplasty [Medicine] (DMAA)	TAA
Total Ankle Replacement [Orthopedics] (DAVI)	TAR
Total Annual Benzene-in-Waste [Environmental Protection Agency]	TAB
Total Annual Variable Cost	TVC
Total Annualized Cost	TAC
Total Annualized Profit	TAP
Total Anomalous Pulmonary Venous Connection [Cardiology]	TAPVC
Total Anomalous Pulmonary Venous Drainage [Cardiology] (AAMN)	TAPVD
Total Anomalous Pulmonary Venous Return [Cardiology]	TAPVR
Total Antioxidant Activity [Chemistry]	TAA
Total Antitryptic Activity [Medicine] (MAE)	TAT
Total Application of Prerecorded Evidence	TAPE
Total Armament Weapons System (MUGU)	TAWS
Total Army Analysis (AABC)	TAA
Total Army Authorization	TAA
Total Army Basing Study (DOMA)	TABS
Total Army Career Counselor [Inservice recruiter] (INF)	TACC
Total Army Equipment Distribution Program (AABC)	TAEDP
Total Army Equipment Distribution System (MCD)	TAEDS
Total Army Inventory Management [Army]	TAIM
Total Army Personnel Agency (INF)	TAPA
Total Army Personnel Command (DOMA)	TAPC
Total Army Personnel Database (GFGA)	TAPDB
Total Army Personnel Evaluation System	TAPES
Total Army Personnel System	TAPSYS
Total Army Requirements Program	TARP
Total Army School System (INF)	TASS
Total Army Training System Course (INF)	TATSC
Total Articular Replacement Arthroplasty [Orthopedics]	TARA
Total Artificial Heart	TAH
Total Artificial Heart [Cardiology] (DMAA)	TAH
Total Asset Visibility [Army]	TAV
Total Assets Reporting (MCD)	TAR
Total Associates Guest Satisfaction	TAGS
Total Atoll Production System (NOAA)	TAPS
Total Audience [Television ratings]	TA
Total Audience Listening Output [Television ratings] (WDMC)	TALO
Total Audience Plan [Radio advertising] (NTCM)	TAP

Total Audit Concept Technique (PDAA)	TACT
Total Automatic Banking System [Trademark of Diebold, Inc.]	TABS
Total Automatic Color (IAA)	TAC
Total Automotive Management Service	TAMS
Total Autonomic Blockage [Medicine] (DMAA)	TAB
Total Available Residual Chlorine [Water quality]	TARC
Total Average Cost (KSC)	TAC
Total Average Dollar Inventory	A
Total Avionic Support Capability	TASC
Total Axial Lymph Node Irradiation [Medicine]	TANI
TOTAL 'B' ADS [NYSE symbol] (TTSB)	TOT
Total Bandwidth	TBW
Total Base Number [Automotive engineering]	TBN
Total Bases	TB
Total Bed Rest [Medicine] (MEDA)	TBR
Total Bile-Duct Ligation [Medicine]	TBDL
Total Bilirubin [Clinical chemistry] (MAE)	T Bili
Total Bilirubin [Clinical chemistry]	TB
Total Bilirubin [Clinical chemistry]	TBIL
Total Bilirubin [Gastroenterology] (DAVI)	TBR
Total Binding Energy (IAA)	TBE
Total Blackout (IIA)	TBO
Total Blank [Entertainment slang for poor show town]	TB
Total Blood Granulocyte Pool [Hematology]	TBGP
Total Blood Out [Medicine] (DMAA)	TBO
Total Blood Volume [Physiology]	TBV
Total Blood Volume Predicted from Body Surface [Physiology] (MAH)	TBV_P
Total Body [Nuclear energy] (NRCH)	TB
Total Body [Medicine] (DAVI)	TB
Total Body Bone Mineral	TBBM
Total Body Calcium	TBC
Total Body Carbon	TBC
Total Body Clearance (MAE)	Qb
Total Body Density [Medicine] (MAE)	TBD
Total Body Ergometer	TBE
Total Body Fat	TBF
Total Body Hematocrit [Medicine] (MAE)	TBH
Total Body Irradiation [Medicine]	TBI
Total Body Irradiation [Radiation therapy] (DAVI)	TBX
Total Body Length [Of Crustacea]	TL
Total Body Neutron Activation (AAMN)	TBNA
Total Body Neutron Activation Analysis	TBNAA
Total Body Nitrogen [Medicine] (DMAA)	TBN
Total Body Potassium [Clinical chemistry]	TBK
Total Body Protein Turnover [Medicine] (DMAA)	TBPT
Total Body Solute [Biochemistry]	TBS
Total Body Surface [Medicine]	TBS
Total Body Surface Area [Medicine]	TBSA
Total Body Water [Man]	TBW
Total Body Water	TW
Total Body Weight [Medicine]	TBW
Total Bolivia [Bolivia] [ICAO location identifier] (ICLI)	SLTT
Total Bouts [Boxing]	TB
Total Breech Extraction [Gynecology]	TBE
Total Burn	TB
Total Burn Size [Medicine] (DMAA)	TBS
Total Burn Surface Area (DAVI)	TBSA
Total Business System Review (AAGC)	TBSR
Total Calcium [Clinical chemistry]	TCa
Total Calorimeter (KSC)	TCAL
Total Canada Oil & Gas Ltd. [Later, Rigel Energy] [AMEX symbol] (SPSG)	TOG
Total Capacity [Lung]	TC
Total Capacity of the Lung [Medicine] (DMAA)	TCL
Total Car Coefficient [Formula] [Automobile analysis]	TCC
Total Carbon	TC
Total Cardiopulmonary Bypass [Medicine] (MAE)	TCB
Total Catchment Management (EERA)	TCM
Total Cavopulmonary Shunt [Medicine] (DMAA)	TCPS
Total Cell Protein [Biochemistry]	TCP
Total Cellular Receptor Pool (DMAA)	TCRP
Total Cerebral Ischemia	TCI
Total Chances	TC
Total Cholesterol [Medicine]	TC
Total Circulating Albumin [Medicine] (DMAA)	TCA
Total Circulating Hemoglobin [Medicine] (MAE)	TCH
Total Circulating Protein [Medicine] (DMAA)	TCP
Total Clottable Protein [Clinical chemistry]	TCP
Total COBOL [Common Business-Oriented Language] Capability [Computer science] (IAA)	TCC
Total Colonoscopy [Proctoscopy]	TC
Total Colonoscopy plus Polypectomy [Proctoscopy]	TC + P
Total Commissioned Service (DOMA)	TCS
Total Communication Systems [Pittsburgh, PA] [Telecommunications service] (TSSD)	TCS
Total Comparative Costs [Army]	TCC
Total Composite Error	TCE
Total Composite Tolerance	TCT
Total Concept Engineering	TCE
Total Containment [NASDAQ symbol] (SAG)	TCIX
Total Containment Co. [Associated Press] (SAG)	TotCont
Total Containment Vessel (CAAL)	TCV
Total Contractual Requirements (MCD)	TCR
Total Control (PCM)	TC
Total Control Racing [Road-racing game] [Ideal Toy Corp.]	TCR
Total Controlled Return (WDAA)	TCR

Total Controlled Tabulation (WDAA) .... TCT
Total Core Recovery [*Nuclear energy*] (NUCP) .... TCR
Total Coronary Flow [*Medicine*] (MAE) .... TCF
Total Corp. [*NYSE symbol*] (SAG) .... TOT
Total Correlation Spectroscopy .... TOCSY
Total Cost .... TC
Total Cost Approach to Distribution .... TCD
Total Cost of Ownership (PCM) .... TCO
Total Counts of Successive Fractions [*Chromatography*] .... TCSF
Total Creatine [*Pool*] .... TCr
Total Current Spectroscopy .... TCS
Total Daily Energy [*Requirement*] [*Dietary*] (DAVI) .... TDE
Total Damage [*Meteorology*] .... TD
Total Data Entry .... TDE
Total Data Network System (TEL) .... TDNS
Total Defect Rate .... TDR
Total Delay Time .... TDT
Total Denier [*Textile technology*] .... TD
Total Density [*Ecology*] .... TDEN
Total Depth .... TD
Total Design Concept [*Sarcastic reference to a completely coordinated wardrobe, decorating scheme, etc.*] [*Slang*] .... TDC
Total Development Plan .... TDP
Total Dictatorship .... TD
Total Diet Research Center [*Public Health Service*] (GRD) .... TDRC
Total Dietary Calories [*Dietetics*] (DAVI) .... TDC
Total Differential Equation .... TDE
Total Digestible Energy [*Nutrition*] .... TDE
Total Digestible Nutrients .... TDN
Total Digitalizing Dose [*Medicine*] (MEDA) .... TDD
Total Disability [*Medicine*] .... TD
Total Disability Benefit (DLA) .... TDB
Total Disability Income Provisions [*Military*] (AABC) .... TDIP
Total Discectomy [*Medicine*] .... TD
Total Dissolvable Manganese [*Chemistry*] .... TDM
Total Dissolved Arsenic .... TDA
Total Dissolved Inorganic Carbon [*Environmental chemistry*] .... TDIC
Total Dissolved Solids .... TDS
Total Dissolved Solids .... TDS
Total Distributed Control [*Computer science*] .... TDC
Total Distribution Action Plan .... TDAP
Total Distribution Advanced Technology Demonstration [*Army*] .... TDATD
Total Domestic Incomes [*Department of Employment*] [*British*] .... TDI
Total Dose [*of radiation*] .... TD
Total Dose/Dose Rate Simulator .... TDDRS
Total Dose Infusion [*Medicine*] (MAE) .... TDI
Total Downtime .... TDT
Total Downtime for Corrective Unscheduled Maintenance [*Quality control*] (MCD) .... TCM
Total Downtime for Preventive Scheduled Maintenance [*Quality control*] (MCD) .... TPM
Total Duration-Specific Fertility Rate [*Population studies*] .... TDFR
Total Dynamic Head (AAG) .... TDH
Total Earnings (MHDB) .... TE
Total Earth Resources System for the Shuttle Era [*NASA*] .... TERSSE
Total Economic Value .... TEV
Total Effective Exposure [*Advertising*] .... TEE
Total Effective Fare (PDAA) .... TEF
Total Elapsed Time (KSC) .... TET
Total Elbow Arthroplasty [*Medicine*] (DMAA) .... TEA
Total Electromechanical Systole [*Cardiology*] (DAVI) QS2
Total Electron Content (MCD) .... TEC
Total Electron Yield [*Spectroscopy*] .... TEY
Total Electronic Advanced Microprocessing Maneuvers and Tactics Equipment [*A game*] .... TEAMMATE
Total Emergency Medical Services System .... TEMSS
Total Endarterectomy [*Cardiology*] (DAVI) .... TEA
Total Endoplasmic Reticulum [*Cytology*] .... TER
TOTAL Energold Corp. [*Toronto Stock Exchange symbol*] .... TDG
Total Energy (ROG) .... H
Total Energy Control System .... TECS
Total Energy Detector .... TED
Total Energy Feasibility (IAA) .... TEF
Total Energy Loss (IAA) .... TEL
Total Energy Management Professionals [*Defunct*] (EA) .... TEMP
Total Energy Ratio [*Mechanical engineering*] .... TER
Total Energy Suppression Shield Array [*Nuclear structure*] .... TESSA
Total Energy Systems Service (IAA) .... TESS
Total Engagement Quality [*Computer science*] .... TEQ
Total Engineering Support System (HGAA) .... TESS
Total Enteral Nutrition .... TEN
Total Entertainment Network [*Online gaming service*] .... TEN
Total Environment Analysis and Management (EERA) .... TEAM
Total Environment Centre (EERA) .... TEC
Total Environment Facility (SAA) .... TEF
Total Environmental Action Foundation [*Defunct*] (EA) .... TEAF
Total Environmental Control System [*Army*] (RDA) .... TECS
Total Environmental Remediation Contracts (AAGC) .... TERC
Total Environmental Warming Impact .... TEWI
Total Eosinophil Count [*Hematology*] .... TEC
Total Equivalent Warming Impact [*Greenhouse gases*] .... TEWI
Total Equivalent Weight .... TEW
Total Erickson Resources Ltd. [*Toronto Stock Exchange symbol Vancouver Stock Exchange symbol*] .... TLE
Total Essential Fatty Acid [*of foodstuffs*] .... TEFA
Total Esterified Fatty Acid .... TEFA
Total Estimated Cost .... TEC
Total Estrogen [*Medicine*] (MAE) .... TE
Total Estrogens After Zinc and Hydrochloric Acid [*Zn-HCl Treatment*] [*Laboratory*] (DAVI) .... Tzn
Total Evaluation of Management and Production Output .... TEMPO
Total Evaporative Emissions [*Automotive engineering*] .... TEV
Total Excreted [*or Excretory*] **Nitrogen** .... TEN
Total Expenditure .... TE
Total Exposure Assessment Methodology [*or Monitoring*] [*Environmental chemistry*] .... TEAM
Total External Reflection .... TER
Total Extractable Organic [*Analytical chemistry*] .... TEO
Total Extractable Protein [*Food technology*] .... TEP
Total Factor Productivity [*Economics*] .... TFP
Total Fatty Acids .... TFA
Total Fecal Nitrogen .... TFN
Total Federal Commissioned Service to Date [*Military*] .... TFCSD
Total Federal Officer Service [*Military*] (AABC) .... TFOS
Total Feedwater Flow .... TFF
Total Fertility Rate [*Medicine*] .... TFR
Total Field Detection Only Processor (CAAL) .... TFDOP
Total Field of View (MCD) .... TFOV
Total Fielding Chances per Game [*Baseball*] .... TC/G
Total Final Cost [*Business term*] .... TFC
Total Final Reports .... TFR
Total Finish Positions [*Horse racing*] .... TFP
Total Fixed Cost .... TFC
Total Fixed Nitrogen [*Chemistry*] .... TFN
Total Float (IAA) .... TF
Total Flow (MAE) .... TF
Total Flow Control [*Automotive engineering*] .... TFC
Total Flowers [*Plant pathology*] .... TF
Total Fly-By Energy .... TFE
Total Follicular Response (OA) .... TFR
Total Force Manpower Management System [*Navy*] (GFGA) .... TFMMS
Total Force Policy [*DoD*] .... TFP
Total Forfeiture [*of all pay and allowances*] [*Army*] (AABC) .... TF
Total Forfeiture [*of all pay and allowances*] [*Army*] (AABC) .... TOTFORF
Total Frequency Deviation (AAG) .... TFD
Total Fruit Number [*Botany*] .... TFN
Total Fuel Consumption (KSC) .... TFC
Total Gaseous Mercury [*Environmental chemistry*] .... TGM
Total Gaseous Non-Methane Organic [*Environmental chemistry*] .... TGNMO
Total Gas-Phase Carbon [*Environmental chemistry*] .... TGC
Total Gate Leakage Current .... TGLC
Total Glycoalkaloids [*Analytical biochemistry*] .... TGA
Total Graft Area Rejected [*Medicine*] (MAE) .... TGAR
Total Graph (OA) .... TG
Total Gross Output (GNE) .... TGO
Total Haloacetic Acid [*Environmental chemistry*] .... THAA
Total Harmonic Distortion [*Electronics*] .... THD
Total Heart Volume [*Physiology*] .... THV
Total Heat Rejection (IAA) .... THR
Total Height Expansion .... THE
Total Height Index (OA) .... THI
Total Heme Mass [*Medicine*] (MAE) .... THM
Total Hepatic Blood Flow .... THBF
Total Hepatic Plasma Flow [*Physiology*] .... THPF
Total Hip Arthroplasty [*Orthopedics*] .... THA
Total Hip Articular Replacement with Internal Eccentric Shells [*Orthopedics*] .... THARIES
Total Hip Replacement [*Medicine*] .... THR
Total Homing Time .... THT
Total Homocysteine [*Clinical chemistry*] .... tHcy
Total Hospital Operating and Medical Information System .... THOMIS
Total Hydrocarbon .... THC
Total Hydrocarbon Analyzer .... THA
Total Hydrocarbon Reforming [*Hydrogen production*] .... THR
Total Hydroxyapatite [*Clinical chemistry*] (MAE) .... THA
Total Hydroxyproline [*Clinical chemistry*] (MAE) .... THP
Total Hydroxyproline [*Clinical chemistry*] .... THYP
Total Hypophysectomy [*Medicine*] .... THX
Total Hysterectomy [*Medicine*] .... TH
Total Image Readout .... TIR
Total Immersion [*Language study*] .... TI
Total Immunoreaction [*Immunochemistry*] .... TIR
Total Improved Frequency Response .... TIFR
Total Inactive Aerospace Vehicle [*or Aircraft*] **Authorization** .... TIA
Total Inactive Aerospace Vehicle [*or Aircraft*] **Inventory** .... TII
Total Indicated Runout .... TIR
Total Indication Time (MCD) .... TIT
Total Indicator Reading .... TIR
Total Indicator Variation (IAA) .... TIV
Total Industry Simulation [*Game*] .... INDUSSIM
Total In-Flight Simulation [*or Simulator*] [*Air Force*] .... TIFS
Total Information for Educational Systems [*Saint Paul, MN*] (BUR) .... TIES
Total Information Gathering and Executive Reporting [*International Computers Ltd.*] .... TIGER
Total Information Management (NITA) .... TIM
Total Information Processing (BUR) .... TIP
Total Information Processing System [*Veterans Administration*] .... TIPS
Total Information System [*Computer science*] .... TIS
Total In-House Publication Production System (MCD) .... TIPPS
Total Initial Lamp Lumens .... TILL

Total Inorganic Carbon [Chemistry] .... TIC
Total Insertion Time .... TIT
Total Installed Cost [Engineering] .... TIC
Total Installed Horsepower .... TIH
Total Installed Horsepower .... TIHP
Total Integrated Dose [Nuclear energy] (NRCH) .... TID
Total Integrated Engineering System .... TIES
Total Integrated Manpower Management System .... TIMMS
Total Integrated Pneumatic System (MCD) .... TIPS
Total Integrated Radial Peaking Factor (IEEE) .... TIRPF
Total Internal Reflecting .... TIR
Total Internal Reflection Face-Pumped LASER .... TIR-FPL
Total Internal Reflection Fluorescence .... TIRF
Total Internal Reflection Prism .... TIRP
Total Internal Reflection Technique .... TIRT
Total Internal Reflectiona Fluorescence Microscopy .... TIRFM
Total Intrauterine Volume [Gynecology] .... TIUV
Total Inventory (DOMA) .... TI
Total Investment for Return (MHDW) .... TIFR
Total Ion Chromatography .... TIC
Total Ion Current [Spectroscopy] .... TIC
Total Ion Detector (OA) .... TID
Total Ion Measurement Source .... TIMS
Total Ion Scanning Mode [Spectroscopy] .... TIM
Total Ionic Strength Adjustment Buffer (PDAA) .... TISAB
Total Iron-Binding Capacity [Hematology] .... TIBC
Total Isomerization Process [Petroleum refining] .... TIP
Total Item Change (NASA) .... TIC
Total Item Record (MCD) .... TIR
Total Joint Replacement [Orthopedics] (DAVI) .... TJR
Total Kinetic Energy .... TKE
Total Kjeldahl Nitrogen [Organic analysis] .... TKN
Total Knee Arthroplasty [Medicine] .... TKA
Total Knee Replacement [Medicine] .... TKR
Total Language Processor [Computer science] (IEEE) .... TLP
Total L-Chain Concentration .... TLC
Total Length .... TL
[A] Total Library Automation System .... ATLAS
Total Library Computerization .... TLC
Total Library System [OCLC] .... TLS
Total Life Cycle Competition Plan [Army] .... TLCCP
Total Life Cycle Competition Strategy [Army] .... TLCCS
Total Life Cycle Time .... TLCT
Total Light Chain Concentration [Immunology] (DAVI) .... TLC
Total Lipid Extract [Biochemistry] .... TLE
Total Lipids [Clinical chemistry] .... TL
Total Liquid Product [Chemical engineering] .... TLP
Total Living Quotient (MAE) .... TLQ
Total Load [Engineering] .... TL
Total Load .... TLLD
Total Load .... W
Total Load Control (MCD) .... TLC
Total Loan-to-Value [Real estate] (EMRF) .... TLTV
Total Logic Solution .... TLS
Total Logistic Readiness/Sustainability Analysis [Military] .... TLR/S
Total Loss [Insurance] .... TL
Total Loss [Insurance] (ODBW) .... tl
Total Loss of Pay [Court-martial sentence] [Military] .... TLP
Total Loss Only .... TLO
Total Loss Only [Insurance] (ODBW) .... tlo
Total Luminescence [Spectroscopy] .... TL
Total Luminescence Spectroscopy .... TLS
Total Lung Capacity [Physiology] .... TLC
Total Lung Compliance [Medicine] (DAVI) .... CLT
Total Lung Compliance [Medicine] .... TLC
Total Lung Volume [Physiology] .... TLV
Total Lung Water [Medicine] (DMAA) .... TLW
Total Lymphocyte Count [Clinical chemistry] .... TLC
Total Lymphoid Irradiation .... TLI
Total Maintenance Actions (MCD) .... TMA
Total Maintenance Effort per Flight Hour [Navy] (NG) .... TME/FH
Total Maintenance Time (MCD) .... TMT
Total Management Information System .... TMIS
Total Manufacturing Cost (MHDB) .... TMC
Total Market Coverage [Advertising] (NTCM) .... TMA
Total Market Coverage [Advertising] .... TMC
Total Market Estimate (ADA) .... TME
Total Material Package [Military] (DNAB) .... TMP
Total Materiel Assets [Military] .... TMA
Total Materiel Objective [Military] .... TMO
Total Materiel Procurement Objective [Military] .... TMPO
Total Materiel Requirement [Military] (AABC) .... TMR
Total Matrix Formation Rate (DAVI) .... R_{tmf}
Total Maximum Daily Load [Environmental Protection Agency] .... TMDL
Total Mean Downtime [Computer science] (IAA) .... TMD
Total Mean Downtime .... TMDT
Total Metabolizable Energy [Nutrition] .... TME
Total Metal Removed .... TMR
Total Military Service to Date .... TMSD
Total Milk Proteinate [Trademark of New Zealand Milk Products, Inc.] .... TMP
Total Mission Recorder [Navy] .... TMR
Total Mission Time .... TMT
Total Molecular Surface Area .... TSA
Total Molecular Volume [Chemistry] .... TMV
Total Negative (MAE) .... TN

Total Net Value .... TNV
Total Network Data System [Bell System] .... TNDS
Total Network Operations Plan [Telecommunications] (TEL) .... TNOP
Total Network Recall [Systems Enhancement Corp.] [Computer science] (PCM) .... TNR
Total Nitrogen [Analytical chemistry] .... TN
Total Nodal Irradiation [Oncology] .... TNI
Total Noise Equivalent Power [Electronics] (EECA) .... TNEP
Total Noise Exposure Level (DA) .... TNEL
Total Nonstructural Carbohydrates .... TNC
Total Nonvolatile [Chemistry] .... TNV
Total Not Operating Time .... TNOT
Total Not-Mission Capable, Supply [Air Force] (DOMA) .... TNMCS
Total Nucleic Acid .... TNA
Total Numerical Control (IAA) .... TNC
Total Nutrient Admixtures [Parenteral emulsions] .... TNA
Total Objective Plan for Career Airmen Personnel [Air Force] (AFM) .... TOPCAP
Total Objective Plan for Reserve Personnel [Air Force] (AFM) .... TOPREP
Total Obligational Authority [Military] .... TOA
Total Obscuring Power [Smoke cloud] .... TOP
Total Ocean Profiling System (USDC) .... TOPS
Total Ocean Profiling System [Marine science] (OSRA) .... TOPS
Total Office Products Group [Commercial firm British] .... TOP
Total Office Support System (HGAA) .... TOSS
Total Officer Personnel Management [Army] (RDA) .... TOPMIS
Total Officer Personnel Objective Structure for the Line Officer Force (DNAB) .... TOPLINE
Total Online Medical Material Integration [Computer science] .... TOMMI
Total On-Line Program and Information Control System [Japan] .... TOPICS
Total On-Line Searching and Cataloging Activities [Information service or system] .... TOSCA
Total On-Line Testing System [Honeywell, Inc.] .... TOLTS
Total Operating Expense .... TOE
Total Operating Traffic System [Bell System] .... TOTS
Total Operational Cost [Engineering] .... TOC
Total Operational Flying Duty Credit [Military] (AABC) .... TOFDC
Total Operations Processing System [Computer science] .... TOPS
Total Operations Processing System (NITA) .... TOPS
Total Optical Color [Photography] (OA) .... TOC
Total Ordnance Alteration Application List [Navy] .... TOAL
Total Organ Perfusion System .... TOPS
Total Organic Carbon .... TOC
Total Organic Chlorine [Analytical chemistry] .... TOCI
Total Organic Compound [Organic chemistry] (DAVI) .... TOC
Total Organic Halide (ACII) .... TOX
Total Ossicular Replacement Prosthesis .... TORP
Total Outage Time (IAA) .... TOT
Total Overall Aerospace Vehicle [or Aircraft] Authorization .... TOAA
Total Overall Aerospace Vehicle [or Aircraft] Inventory .... TOAI
Total Oxidants .... TOX
Total Oxygen Demand [Analytical chemistry] .... TOD
Total Ozone Mapping Spectrometer (MCD) .... TOMS
Total Ozone Mapping Spectrophotometer [Marine science] (OSRA) .... TOMS
Total Ozone Mapping System [Meteorology] .... TOMS
Total Ozone Measurement Scanner (SSD) .... TOMS
Total Ozone Portable Spectroradiometer [Measures ozone layer] (ECON) .... TOPS
Total Package Contract .... TPC
Total Package Fielding [Army] .... TPF
Total Package Fielding - Activation [Military] .... TPF-A
Total Package Fielding-(Unit)Conversion [Military] .... TPF-C
Total Package Procurement [Government contracting] .... TPP
Total Package Procurement Concept [Government contracting] .... TPPC
Total Package Unit Material Fielding [Army] .... TRUMF
Total Package/Unit Materiel Fielding [Army] (RDA) .... TP/UMF
Total Packed Cell Volume [Hematology] (DMAA) .... TPCV
Total Pain Relief [Medicine] .... TOTPAR
Total Pancreatectomy [Medicine] .... TPX
Total Parameter Space [Statistics] .... TPS
Total Parathyroid Hormone Secretion [Endocrinology] (MAE) .... TPTHS
Total Parenteral Alimentation [Medicine] (DMAA) .... TPA
Total Parenteral Nutrition .... TPN
Total Particulate Matter [BTS] (TAG) .... TP
Total Particulate Matter [The "tar" of cigar and cigarette smoke] .... TPM
Total Parts .... TP
Total Passive Motion .... TPM
Total Patient Care [Nursing] (DAVI) .... TPC
Total Peak Loss (IAA) .... TPL
Total Peaking Factor [Nuclear energy] (NRCH) .... TPF
Total Peripheral Parenteral Nutrition .... TPPN
Total Peripheral Resistance .... TPR
Total Peripheral Resistance Index .... TPRI
Total Permanent Disability [or Disablement] [Insurance] (AIA) .... TPD
Total Personnel Service .... TOPS
Total Petroleum Hydrocarbon [Analytical chemistry] .... TPH
Total Petroleum (North America) Ltd. [Associated Press] (SAG) .... TotlPet
Total Petroleum (North America) Ltd. [AMEX symbol Toronto Stock Exchange symbol] (SPSG) .... TPN
Total Petroleum (North America) Ltd., Calgary, Alberta [Library symbol National Library of Canada] (NLC) .... ACTP
Total Petroleum (North American) Ltd., Calgary, AB, Canada [Library symbol Library of Congress] (LCLS) .... CaACTP
Total Petrol'm NA [AMEX symbol] (TTSB) .... TPN
Total Phenolic Levels [Chemistry] .... TP
Total Phosphorus [Analytical chemistry] .... TP
Total Plasma Catecholamines [Hematology] (DMAA) .... TPC

Total Plasma Cholesterol [*Clinical chemistry*] ... TPC
Total Points ... TP
Total Polar Material [*Analytical chemistry*] ... TPM
Total Population Management [*Department of Agriculture*] ... TPM
Total Pore Volume [*Geology*] ... TPV
Total Positive Income [*IRS*] ... TPI
Total Positives [*Medicine*] (DMAA) ... TP
Total Possessed Hours (MCD) ... TPH
Total Potential Energy ... TPE
Total Power ... TP
Total Pressure ... PT
Total Pressure ... TP
Total Pressure Gauge ... TPG
Total Pressure Transducer ... TPT
Total Preventative Maintenance [*Manufacturing*] ... TPM
Total Primary Energy Requirement [*BTS*] (TAG) ... TPER
Total Prime Time (WDMC) ... TPT
Total Print Control [*Computer science*] (IAA) ... TPC
Total Product Support ... TPS
Total Production [*or Product*] [*Ecology*] ... TP
Total Productive Maintenance [*Japanese industrialization theory*] ... TPM
Total Program Costs (KSC) ... TPC
Total Program Diagnostic [*Computer science*] (IAA) ... TPD
Total Program Planning/Procurement ... TPP
Total Project Cost (DOMA) ... TPC
Total Protective Environment [*Immunology*] (DAVI) ... TPE
Total Protein (MAE) ... tot prot
Total Protein ... TP
Total Protein Concentration ... TPC
Total Protein Tuberculin [*Medicine*] (MAE) ... TPT
Total Publishing Environment [*Computer science*] (IAA) ... TPE
Total Pulmonary Blood Flow [*Physiology*] ... TPBF
Total Pulmonary Resistance [*Medicine*] (DAVI) ... R_L
Total Pulmonary Resistance [*Medicine*] (DAVI) ... R_T
Total Pulmonary Resistance [*Cardiology*] ... TPR
Total Pulmonary Vascular Resistance (AAMN) ... TPVR
Total Purity by Difference [*Gas analysis*] ... TPD
Total Quality ... TQ
Total Quality and Productivity ... TQP
Total Quality Assurance (OA) ... TQA
Total Quality Control ... TQC
Total Quality Design (RDA) ... TQD
Total Quality Leadership ... TQL
Total Quality Management ... TQM
Total Quality Management System (MCD) ... TQMS
Total Quality Planning and Producibility (MCD) ... TQPP
Total Quality Service ... TQS
Total Quantity Recommended [*Army*] ... TQTYREC
Total Radiance Spectral Distribution ... TRSD
Total Radiance Spectral Polarization ... TRSP
Total Radiation Absolute Radiometer [*NASA*] ... TRAR
Total Rare Earths (NRCH) ... TRE
Total Rate Imaging with X-Rays ... TRIX
Total Rated Service Date [*Air Force*] (AFM) ... TRSD
Total Reactance (IDOE) ... X_T
Total Reactance (IDOE) ... X_t
Total Reaction (DA) ... TR
Total Reconnaissance Intelligence System Evaluation and Comparison Technique (MCD) ... TRISECT
Total Record Access Control (SAA) ... TRAC
Total Recoverable Petroleum Hydrocarbon ... TRPH
Total Recycle Unit (OA) ... TRU
Total Recycling Advisory Committee [*Northern Territory, Australia*] ... TRAC
Total Red Cell Volume [*Medicine*] (DMAA) ... TCRV
Total Red Cell Volume [*Immunology*] (DAVI) ... TRCV
Total Reduced Sulfur [*Environmental chemistry*] ... TRS
Total Reducing Sugars [*Food science*] ... TRS
Total Reevaluation Under SPRINT Thrust [*Army*] ... TRUST
Total Refinement and Integration of Maintenance Management Systems [*Army*] ... TRIMMS
Total Reflection Angle X-Ray Spectroscopy ... TRAXS
Total Refractory Period (MAE) ... TRP
Total Regulation ... TR
Total Relaxation Time [*Cardiology*] ... TRT
Total Relevant Cost ... TRC
Total Remote Access Center (MHDI) ... TRACE
Total Renal Blood Flow [*Medicine*] ... TRBF
Total Renal Care Hldgs [*NYSE symbol*] (TTSB) ... TRL
Total Renal Care Holdings, Inc. [*Associated Press*] (SAG) ... TotRenl
Total Renal Care Holdings, Inc. [*NYSE symbol*] (SAG) ... TRL
Total Renin Activity [*Medicine*] (DMAA) ... TRA
Total Renin Concentration [*Laboratory science*] (DAVI) ... TRC
Total Repair Time [*Automotive maintenance*] ... TRT
Total Replenishment Inventory Program (PDAA) ... TRIP
Total Requirements (AAG) ... TRQ
Total Research [*NASDAQ symbol*] (TTSB) ... TOTL
Total Research Corp. [*Associated Press*] (SAG) ... TotalRs
Total Research Corp. [*NASDAQ symbol*] (NQ) ... TOTL
Total Reserves ... RT
Total Residual Chlorine [*Environmental chemistry*] ... TRC
Total Resistance (IDOE) ... R_t
Total Resistance (MAE) ... TR
Total Resource Allocation Cost Estimating (RDA) ... TRACE
Total Resource Effectiveness Index [*Environmental Protection Agency*] ... TRE
Total Response [*Medicine*] (MAE) ... TR
Total Response Index [*Psychology*] ... TRI
Total Revenue ... TR
Total Reverse Triiodothyronine ... TrT_3
Total Revision and Upgrading of Maintenance Procedures [*Marine Corps*] ... TRUMP
Total Ridge Count [*Anthropology*] ... TRC
Total Risk Assessing Cost Estimate [*Army*] (RDA) ... TRACE
Total Risk Assessing Cost Estimate - Production [*Army*] (RDA) ... TRACE-P
Total Rosette-Forming Cell [*Medicine*] (DMAA) ... TREC
Total Rosette-Forming Cell [*Laboratory science*] (DAVI) ... TRFC
Total Run Time [*Robotic assay*] ... TT
Total Running Time [*Broadcasting*] (WDMC) ... TRT
Total Scan Area (OA) ... TSA
Total Scheduled Maintenance [*Army*] ... TSM
Total Serum Bile Acid [*Clinical chemistry*] ... TBSA
Total Serum Prostatic Acid Phosphatase [*Medicine*] (MAE) ... TSPAP
Total Serum Protein [*Medicine*] ... TSP
Total Serum Thyroxine Iodine Also, called tri-iodothyronine [*Endocrinology*] (DAVI) ... T_4I
Total Service Life [*Telecommunications*] (TEL) ... TSL
Total Severity Assessment Score (DAVI) ... TSAS
Total Shielding Effectiveness (IAA) ... TSE
Total Ship Simulation Model ... TSSM
Total Ship Survivability (DOMA) ... TSS
Total Ship Test Director [*Navy*] (CAAL) ... TSTD
Total Ship Test Program [*Navy*] (CAAL) ... TSTP
Total Ship Test Program/Active Fleet Surface Ships [*Navy*] (CAAL) ... TSTP/AFS
Total Ship Test Program/Ship Production [*Navy*] (CAAL) ... TSTP/SP
Total Shoulder Arthroplasty [*Medicine*] (DMAA) ... TSA
Total Shoulder Arthroplasty [*Orthopedics*] (DAVI) ... TSA
Total Shoulder Replacement [*Medicine*] ... TSR
Total Signal Lines (IAA) ... TSL
Total Skin Electron Beam [*Medicine*] (DMAA) ... TSEB
Total Skin Examination [*Dermatology*] (DAVI) ... TSE
Total Solar Radiation [*Botany*] ... TSR
Total Solids [*Medicine*] ... TS
Total Soluble Inorganic Nitrogen [*Analytical chemistry*] ... TSIN
Total Soluble Sulfur [*Analytical chemistry*] ... TSS
Total Specifications Information System ... TSIS
Total Spectral Density ... TSD
Total Squared Distance ... TSD
Total Story Time [*Broadcasting*] (WDMC) ... TST
Total Stress Range [*Nuclear energy*] (NUCP) ... TSR
Total Subscriber Satisfaction [*HBO (Home Box Office) rating system*] ... TSS
Total Subsystem Evaluation ... TSE
Total Sum Insured (AIA) ... TSI
Total Sum of Squares ... TSS
Total Support Requirements List (AAG) ... TSRL
Total Surface Area [*Chemistry*] ... TSA
Total Surface Tested ... TST
Total Survey Area (WDMC) ... TSA
Total Suspended Matter [*Environmental science*] ... TSM
Total Suspended Particulate Matter ... TSPM
Total Suspended Particulates ... TSP
Total Suspended Solids [*Environmental chemistry*] ... TSS
Total System Acquistion Management Methodology [*Army*] (RDA) ... $TSAM^2$
Total System Analyzer (IAA) ... TSA
Total System Control [*Architecture*] ... TSC
Total System Cost [*Aviation*] ... TSC
Total System Integration Responsibility ... TSIR
Total System Life Cycle Cost-Effectiveness ... TSLCC-E
Total System Management Concept (MCD) ... TSM
Total System Requirements Analysis (NASA) ... TSRA
Total System Responsibility ... TSR
Total System Services, Inc. [*Associated Press*] (SAG) ... TotlSys
Total System Svcs [*NYSE symbol*] (TTSB) ... TSS
Total Systemic Vascular Resistance ... TSVR
Total Systems Performance [*MODCOMP*] ... TSP
Total Systems Performance Reliability [*or Responsibility*] (MCD) ... TSPR
Total Systems Services, Inc. [*NYSE symbol*] (SPSG) ... TSS
Total Tangible Assets [*Business term*] (ADA) ... TTA
Total Tank Requirement ... TTR
Total Tank System Study [*Army*] ... T2S2
Total Task Chaining [*Psychology*] ... TT
Total Tax Expenditures [*Economics*] ... TTE
Total Taxable Pay ... TTP
Total Taxable Pay Earned ... TTPE
Total Tectonic Subsidence ... TTS
Total Tel USA Communications [*NASDAQ symbol*] (SAG) ... TELU
Total Tel USA Communications [*Associated Press*] (SAG) ... TotlTel
Total Temperature (MCD) ... TT
Total Temperature and Weight ... TTW
Total Temperature Probe (MCD) ... TTP
Total Threshold Limit Concentration [*Environmental chemistry*] ... TTLC
Total Thyroxine [*Endocrinology*] ... TT
Total Thyroxine [*Endocrinology*] ... TT4
Total Time (MSA) ... TT
Total Time Management [*Industrial engineering*] ... TTM
Total Time Spent Listening [*Radio*] (WDMC) ... TTSL
Total Time to Doctorate ... TTD
Total Time to Launch [*NASA*] (KSC) ... TTL
Total Titratable Acidity [*Analytical chemistry*] ... TTA
Total Toe Arthroplasty [*Medicine*] (DMAA) ... TTA
Total Towed Vehicle Weight [*Automotive engineering*] ... TTVW
Total Toxic Organics [*Environmental chemistry*] ... TTO

Total Transportation Expenditure [*Department of Transportation*] ... TTE
Total Trihalomethane [*Analytical chemistry*] ... TTHM
Total Triiodothyronine [*Endocrinology*] ... TT_3
Total Underground Distribution (IAA) ... TUD
Total Unemployment Rate ... TUR
Total Unsaturated Fatty Acid [*of foodstuffs*] ... TUFA
Total Unscheduled Maintenance Time ... TUM
Total Urethral Discharge [*Medicine*] ... TUD
Total Urinary Gonadotropin [*Clinical chemistry*] ... TUG
Total Vaginal Hysterectomy [*Gynecology*] ... TVH
Total Value ... TV
Total Value of Ownership ... TVO
Total Variable Cost Curve [*Economics*] ... TVC
Total Variable Costs ... TVC
Total Variable Factor Curve [*Economics*] ... TVF
Total Vascular Resistance [*Medicine*] (DMAA) ... TVR
Total Vegetative Control Agents [*Agriculture*] ... TVCA
Total Ventricular Weight [*Cardiology*] ... TVW
Total Vertical Error [*Aviation*] (DA) ... TVE
Total Viable Cells [*Microbiology*] ... TVC
Total Virus Defense [*Computer Security System*] ... TVD
Total Virus Defense [*McAfee*] [*Computer science*] ... TVD
Total Vision, Inc. [*Houston, TX*] (TSSD) ... TVI
Total Vital Capacity [*Medicine*] (DAVI) ... TVC
Total Volatile Bases [*Chemistry*] ... TVB
Total Volatile Basic Nitrogen [*Food analysis*] ... TVBN
Total Volatile Fatty Acid [*of foodstuffs*] ... TVFA
Total Volatile Nitrogen [*Analytical chemistry*] ... TVN
Total Volatile Solids [*Analytical chemistry*] ... TVS
Total Volume ... TV
Total Volume Capacity [*Physiology*] ... TVC
Total Volume Urine [*in 24 hours*] ... TVU
Total Warrant Officer System [*Army*] ... TWOS
Total Water Burden [*Environmental science*] ... TWB
Total Wave Pressure ... TWP
Total Wear Coefficient [*Materials science*] ... TWC
Total Weight ... TW
Total Weight Loss (MCD) ... TWL
Total Weighted Pollutant Load (ERG) ... TWPL
Total White and Differential Count [*Hematology*] ... TWD
Total White Blood Cells [*Medicine*] ... TWBC
Total Woman [*Title of a 1973 book by Marabel Morgan and of TV seminars based on this book*] ... TW
Total Work ... TW
Total Work Package Budget (MCD) ... TWPB
Total World Telecommunications, Inc. [*Associated Press*] (SAG) ... TtlWrld
Total World Telecommunications, Inc. [*NASDAQ symbol*] (SAG) ... TWTI
Total Wrist Replacement [*Medicine*] ... TWR
Total Years Service Date ... TYSD
Total Yield (AABC) ... TY
Totalisator Agency Board of New South Wales [*Australia*] ... TABNSW
Totalisator Employees' Association of Victoria [*Australia*] ... TEAV
Totalization (ECII) ... TOTLN
Totalize ... TOTLZ
Totalized Interface Subroutine and Post Processor [*Computer science*] (BUR) ... TISAP
Totalizer Agency Board (IAA) ... TAB
Totalizing Relay ... TOR
Totally Accurate Clock ... TAC
Totally Advanced Communications Technology ... TACTEC
Totally and Permanently Disabled Soldiers' Association [*Australia*] ... TPDSA
Totally and Permanently Incapacitated [*Insurance*] (ADA) ... T & PI
Totally Automated Method Development [*High-performance liquid chromatography*] ... TAMED
Totally Automated Programming Equipment ... TAPE
Totally Chlorine-Free [*Pulp and paper processing*] ... TCF
Totally Decentralized Control (IAA) ... TDC
Totally Embedded (DAVI) ... TE
Totally Enclosed (MSA) ... TE
Totally Enclosed - Closed-Air Circuit ... TECA
Totally Enclosed - Fan Cooled ... TEFC
Totally Enclosed - Nonventilated ... TENV
Totally Hilarious Incredibly Neat Games of Skill [*Milton-Bradley product*] ... THINGS
Totally Implantable Artificial Heart ... TIAH
Totally Positive ... TP
Totally Reflective Mirror ... TRM
Totally Self-Checking ... TSC
Totally Smutted [*Plant pathology*] ... TS
Totally Synthetic Organic Chemical [*or Compound*] (GNE) ... TSOC
Totally Unified Theories [*Cosmology*] ... TUT's
Totally User Friendly ... TUF
Totally-Enclosed Air Water-Cooled Reactor [*Nuclear energy*] (IAA) ... TEAWC
Totally-Enclosed Force-Cooled Reactor [*Nuclear energy*] (IAA) ... TEFC
Totally-Enclosed (Separately) Fan-Cooled [*Reactor*] (DEN) ... TE(S)FC
Totally-Enclosed Water-Cooled [*Reactor*] (DEN) ... TEWC
Total-Reflection X-Ray Fluorescence [*Analytical chemistry*] ... TXRF
Total-Response Chromatogram ... TRC
Totals to Date (MCD) ... TTD
Total-Tel USA Communic [*NASDAQ symbol*] (TTSB) ... TELU
Totegegie [*French Polynesia*] [*ICAO location identifier*] (ICLI) ... NTGJ
Totem Capital Corp. [*Vancouver Stock Exchange symbol*] ... TOM
Totem Industries [*Vancouver Stock Exchange symbol*] ... TOT
Tothill's English Chancery Reports [*A publication*] (DLA) ... Tot
Tothill's English Chancery Reports [*A publication*] (DLA) ... Toth
Tothill's English Chancery Reports [*A publication*] (DLA) ... Tothill (Eng)
Tothill's Transactions in Chancery [*21 English Reprint*] [*A publication*] (DLA) ... Tot
Tothill's Transactions in Chancery [*21 English Reprint*] [*A publication*] (DSA) ... Toth
Tothill's Transactions in Chancery [*21 English Reprint*] [*A publication*] (DLA) ... Tothill (Eng)
Totipotent Hematopoietic Stem Cell [*Hematology*] (MAE) ... THSC
Totma [*Former USSR ICAO location identifier*] (ICLI) ... ULWT
Totnes [*Municipal borough in England*] ... TOT
Toto [*Angola*] [*ICAO location identifier*] (ICLI) ... FNTO
Totta & Acores Financing Ltd. [*NYSE symbol*] (SAG) ... BTA
Totta & Acores Financing Ltd. [*Associated Press*] (SAG) ... TottaAc
Tottenham Public Library, Ontario [*Library symbol National Library of Canada*] (NLC) ... OTO
Tottenham Public Library, Tottenham, ON, Canada [*Library symbol Library of Congress*] (LCLS) ... CaOTo
Tottori [*Japan ICAO location identifier*] (ICLI) ... RJOR
Tottori [*Japan*] [*Seismograph station code, US Geological Survey*] (SEIS) ... TOT
Tottori [*Japan*] [*Airport symbol*] (OAG) ... TTJ
Totul pentru Tara [*"All for the Fatherland"*] [*Romania*] [*Political party*] (PPE) ... TPT
Totus Tuus [*All Yours*] [*Latin*] ... TT
Touahar [*Morocco*] [*ICAO location identifier*] (ICLI) ... GMFT
Touba [*Ivory Coast*] [*Airport symbol*] (OAG) ... TOZ
Touba/Mahana [*Ivory Coast*] [*ICAO location identifier*] (ICLI) ... DITM
Touch ... TCH
Touch and Concern [*Legal shorthand*] (LWAP) ... T & C
Touch and Go [*Landings*] [*Aviation*] (MCD) ... T & G
Touch and Go Landings [*Aviation*] ... TGL
Touch and Go Ltd. [*Former USSR*] [*FAA designator*] (FAAC) ... TUG
Touch and Learn Computer ... TLC
Touch and Stay ... T and S
Touch and Tone [*Neurology*] (DAVI) ... T & T
Touch Calling Multifrequency (IEEE) ... TCMF
Touch for Health Foundation (EA) ... TFH
Touch Information Display ... TID
Touch Input Device [*Computer science*] (IAA) ... TID
Touch Logic Controlled [*Electronics*] ... TLC
Touch N' Go [*Computer Interface*] [*Touch N' Go Systems, Inc*] (PCM) ... TNG
[*A*] **Touch of Days** [*An association*] (EA) ... ATD
Touch Sensitive Digitizer [*Electronics*] (OA) ... TSD
Touch Tone America [*NASDAQ symbol*] (TTSB) ... TONE
Touch Tone America, Inc. [*NASDAQ symbol*] (SAG) ... TONE
Touch Tone America, Inc. [*Associated Press*] (SAG) ... TouTne
Touch Tone America, Inc. [*Associated Press*] (SAG) ... TouTone
Touch Tone America Wrrt [*NASDAQ symbol*] (TTSB) ... TONEW
Touch Wire Display (PDAA) ... TWD
Touchdown [*NASA*] (NASA) ... T/D
Touchdown [*Football*] ... TD
Touchdown Lift-Off Surface [*OST*] (TAG) ... TLOF
Touchdown Protection [*Military*] (MCD) ... TDP
Touchdown Rate of Descent Indicator [*Aviation*] ... TRODI
Touchdown Velocity [*Aviation*] ... TDV
Touch-Down Weight-Bearing [*Orthopedics and rehabilitation*] (DAVI) ... TDWB
Touchdown Zone/Centerline [*Aviation*] (DNAB) ... TDZ/CL
Touchdown Zone Elevation [*Aviation*] (DA) ... TDZE
Touchdown Zone Light System [*Aviation*] (FAAC) ... TDZL
Touchdowns Passing [*Football*] ... TP
Touchdowns Running [*Football*] ... TR
Touche Remnant [*Investment firm*] [*British*] ... TR
Touche Remnant Natural Resources [*Investment fund*] [*British*] ... TRNR
Touche Ross & Co., Calgary, AB, Canada [*Library symbol*] [*Library of Congress*] (LCLS) ... CaACTR
Touche Ross & Co., Calgary, Alberta [*Library symbol National Library of Canada*] (NLC) ... ACTR
Touche Ross and Co., Toronto, ON, Canada [*Library symbol*] [*Library of Congress*] (LCLS) ... CaOTTRC
Touche Ross & Co., Toronto, Ontario [*Library symbol National Library of Canada*] (NLC) ... OTTRC
Touche Ross & Co., Vancouver, BC, Canada [*Library symbol*] [*Library of Congress*] (LCLS) ... CaBVaTR
Touch-Operated Selector Control ... TOSC
Touchstone Applied Science [*NASDAQ symbol*] (TTSB) ... TASA
Touchstone Applied Sciences [*NASDAQ symbol*] (SAG) ... TASA
Touchstone Applied Sciences [*Associated Press*] (SAG) ... TchA
Touchstone Applied Sciences [*Associated Press*] (SAG) ... TchApld
TouchStone Software [*NASDAQ symbol*] (TTSB) ... TSSW
TouchStone Software Corp. [*Associated Press*] (SAG) ... TouchSt
TouchStone Software Corp. [*NASDAQ symbol*] (SAG) ... TSSW
Touch-Tone [*Telecommunications*] (IAA) ... TT
Touch-Tone Multifrequency (CET) ... TTMF
Touch-Tone Receiver [*Telecommunications*] (IAA) ... TTR
Tougaloo College, Tougaloo, MS [*Library symbol Library of Congress*] (LCLS) ... MsToT
Tougaloo College, Tougaloo, MS [*OCLC symbol*] (OCLC) ... TGC
Tougan [*Burkina Faso*] [*ICAO location identifier*] (ICLI) ... DHOT
Tougan [*Upper Volta*] [*Airport symbol*] (AD) ... TUQ
Touggourt [*Algeria*] [*Airport symbol*] (OAG) ... TGR
Touggourt/Sidi Mahdi [*Algeria*] [*ICAO location identifier*] (ICLI) ... DAUK
Tough Jeans Territory [*Sears, Roebuck & Co. advertising slogan*] ... TJT
Tough on Black Actors [*Facetious translation of acronym for Theater Owners Booking Association*] ... TOBA
Tough Orthodox Rabbis and Hassidim [*An association*] ... TORAH
Tough Plastic-Sheathed ... TPS
Tough Rubber-Sheathed [*Cable*] (DEN) ... TRS

Tough Rubber-Sheathed Cable .... TRC
Tough Situation [*Bowdlerized version*] .... TS
Tough Stuff .... TS
Touho [*New Caledonia*] [*ICAO location identifier*] (ICLI) .... NWWU
Touho [*New Caledonia*] [*Airport symbol*] (OAG) .... TOU
Toul/Rosieres [*France ICAO location identifier*] (ICLI) .... LFSL
Toullier's Droit Civil Francais [*A publication*] (DLA) .... Toull
Toulomne County Museum, Sonora, CA [*Library symbol*] [*Library of Congress*] (LCLS) .... CSoM
Toulon [*France ICAO location identifier*] (ICLI) .... LFTC
Toulon [*France ICAO location identifier*] (ICLI) .... LFTS
Toulon [*France*] (BARN) .... Tou
Toulon/Hyeres [*France*] [*Airport symbol*] (OAG) .... TLN
Toulon Public Library, Toulon, IL [*OCLC symbol*] (OCLC) .... ISW
Toulon Public Library, Toulon, IL [*Library symbol Library of Congress*] (LCLS) .... ITou
Toulon/Saint-Mandrier [*France ICAO location identifier*] (ICLI) .... LFTR
Toulouse [*France ICAO location identifier*] (ICLI) .... LFBQ
Toulouse [*France*] [*Airport symbol*] (OAG) .... TLS
Toulouse/Blagnac [*France ICAO location identifier*] (ICLI) .... LFBO
Toulouse/Francazal [*France ICAO location identifier*] (ICLI) .... LFBF
Toulouse/Lasbordes [*France ICAO location identifier*] (ICLI) .... LFCL
Toulouse-Bourg-Saint-Bernard [*France ICAO location identifier*] (ICLI) .... LFIT
Toulx Ste. Croix [*France*] [*Seismograph station code, US Geological Survey*] (SEIS) .... TCF
Toumodi [*Ivory Coast*] [*Seismograph station code, US Geological Survey*] (SEIS) .... TIC
Tour Advisory Review Panel [*Army National Guard*] (INF) .... TARP
Tour Basing Fare [*Air travel term*] .... TBF
Tour Completion Date .... TCD
Tour du Monde [*World Tour*] [*French*] ('JA) .... TM
Tour Operators Integrated Computer System [*Airline ticket system*] .... TROPICS
Touraine [*South Vietnam*] [*Airport symbol*] (AD) .... TOU
Touraine Air Transport [*ICAO designator*] (AD) .... IJ
Touraine Air Transport [*Private airline*] [*French*] (EY) .... TAT
TourBase Hotel-/Unterkunftsdaten [*Jaeger-Verlag GmbH*] [*Germany Information service or system*] (CRD) .... TBH
TourBase Ortsdaten [*Jaeger-Verlag GmbH*] [*Germany Information service or system*] (CRD) .... TBO
Tour-Based Fare [*Airline fare code*] .... IT
Toured Sea Duty (DNAB) .... TSD
Tourette Syndrome [*Neurology*] .... TS
Tourette Syndrome Association (EA) .... TSA
Tourgee's North Carolina Digest [*A publication*] (DLA) .... Tourg Dig
Touring Car Drivers Association [*Automobile racing*] .... TCDA
Touring Club .... TC
Touring Diesel [*Automobile model, Mercedes-Benz Motors*] .... TD
Touring Riders Emergency Kare [*An association*] .... TREK
Touring Sedan [*As in Olds 98 TS*] .... TS
Touring Sport [*Automobile model*] .... TS
Touring Sport Extra-4WD [*In automotive name Ghia Vignale TSX-4*] TSX-4
Touring Twin Carburetor [*Automobile model*] .... TT
Touring Twin Carburetor Sport [*Automobile model*] .... TTS
Tourism and Travel Research Development Council [*Australia*] .... TTRDC
Tourism Brisbane [*Australia*] .... TB
Tourism Council of the South Pacific (EERA) .... TCSP
Tourism Industry Association of Canada .... TIAC
Tourism Ministers Council (EERA) .... TMC
Tourism Reference and Documentation, Regional Industrial Expansion [*Centre deReference et de Documentation Touristique, Expansion Industrielle Regionale*] **, Ottawa, Ontario** [*Library symbol National Library of Canada*] (NLC) .... OOTB
Tourism South Australia .... TSA
Tourism Tasmania [*Australia*] .... TT
Tourism Training Australia .... TTA
Tourism Training Queensland [*Australia*] .... TTQ
Tourismo Internationale [*International Touring*] [*Italian*] .... TI
Tourismo Internationale Injection [*International Touring-fuel Injection*] [*Italian*] .... TII
Tourist [*Rate*] [*Value of the English pound*] .... T
Tourist Authority of Thailand (ECON) .... TAT
Tourist Class Passengers [*British*] .... TOUR
Tourist Development Corp. of Malaysia .... TDC
Tourist Hospitality Service [*British*] .... THS
Tourist House Association of America (EA) .... THAA
Tourist Information [*Traffic sign*] [*British*] i
Tourist Information Board (WDAA) .... TIB
Tourist Information Facts and Abstracts [*Economic Documentation and Information Ltd.*] [*Ringmer Near Lewes, East Sussex, England*] [*Information service or system*] (IID) .... TIFA
Tourist Observation and Underwater Research Submarine (PDAA) .... TOURS
Tourist Organization of Thailand (DS) .... TOT
Tourist Railway Association, Inc. (EA) .... TRAIN
Tourist Trophy [*Motorcycle racing*] [*British*] .... TT
Touristische Gemeinschaft der Alpenlander [*Alpine Tourist Commission - ATC*] [*Zurich, Switzerland*] (EAIO) .... TGA
Tourist-Oriented-Directional [*Traffic sign*] .... TOD
Tournai/Maubray [*Belgium ICAO location identifier*] (ICLI) .... EBTY
Tournament .... TOURN
Tournament Golf International .... TGI
Tournament of Champions .... T of C
Tournament of Roses Association (EA) .... TOR
Tournament of Roses Association [*Later, TOR*] (EA) .... TRA
Tournament Players Association (EA) .... TPA
Tournament Players Championship .... TPC
Tournament Players Division of the Professional Golfers Association of America [*Later, TPA*] .... TPD
Tournavista [*Peru*] [*ICAO location identifier*] (ICLI) .... SPTR
Tournez s'il Vous Plait [*Please Turn Over*] [*See also PTO*] [*French*] .... TSVP
Tournigan Mining Explorations Ltd. [*Vancouver Stock Exchange symbol*] .... TGN
Tourniquet [*Medicine*] (MAE) .... Tq
Tournus-Cuisery [*France ICAO location identifier*] (ICLI) .... LFFX
Touro College (GAGS) .... Touro C
Touro Law Library, New York, NY [*OCLC symbol*] (OCLC) .... ZTL
Tours [*France*] [*Airport symbol*] (OAG) .... TUF
Tours/Cinq-Mars La Pile [*France ICAO location identifier*] (ICLI) .... LFXO
Tours par Minute [*Revolutions per Minute*] [*French*] .... TPM
Tours/Saint-Symphorien [*France ICAO location identifier*] (ICLI) .... LFOT
Tours/Sorigny [*France ICAO location identifier*] (ICLI) .... LFEN
Toussus-Le-Noble [*France ICAO location identifier*] (ICLI) .... LFPN
Tovarystvo Ukrainskykh Progresyvistiv [*Ukrainian Progressive Association*] [*Russian Political party*] (PPE) .... TUP
TOW Against Helicopter Operational Equipment (RDA) .... TAHOE
Tow Bar (MCD) .... TOB
Tow/Bushmaster Armored Turret [*Military*] .... TBAT
TOW [*Tube-Launched, Optically-Tracked, Wire-Guided Weapon*] **Control Box** (INF) .... TCB
TOW [*Tube-Launched, Optically-Tracked, Wire-Guided Weapon*] **Cooler Kit** (DWSG) .... TCK
TOW [*Tube-Launched, Optically Tracked, Wire-Guided (Weapon)*] **Cover Artillery Protection** .... TOW CAP
TOW [*Tube-Launched, Optically Tracked, Wire-Guided (Weapon)*] **Crew Evaluator** [*Military*] (INF) .... TCE
TOW [*Tube-launched, Optically-tracked, Wire-guided*] **Field Tactical Trainer** [*Army*] (INF) .... TFTT
TOW [*Tube-Launched, Optically Tracked, Wire-Guided (Weapon)*] **Field Test Set** (MCD) .... TFTS
TOW [*Tube-launched, Optically Tracked, Wire-Guided (weapon)*] **Gunnery Trainer** [*Army*] (INF) .... TGT
TOW [*Tube-Launched, Optically Tracked, Wire-Guided (Weapon)*] **Light Antitank Battalion** (MCD) .... TLAT
TOW [*Tube-Launched, Optically Tracked, Wire-Guided (Weapon)*] **Missile SightVideo Camera System** (MCD) .... TMSVCS
TOW [*Tube-Launched, Optically Tracked, Wire-Guided (Weapon)*] **Missile System** (RDA) .... TMS
TOW [*Tube-Launched, Optically Tracked, Wire-Guided (Weapon)*] **Missile Transporter** (MCD) .... TMT
TOW [*Tube-Launched, Optically Tracked, Wire-Guided (Weapon)*] **Protective Shelters** (MCD) .... TOWPROS
TOW [*Tube-Launched, Optically Tracked, Wire-Guided (Weapon)*] **Subsystem** [*Army*] .... TSS
Tow Target Cable .... TTC
Tow Test Vehicle [*Aerospace*] .... TTV
TOW [*Tube-Launched, Optically Tracked, Wire-Guided (Weapon)*] **Thermal NightSight** [*Night vision device*] [*Army*] (RDA) .... TTNS
Tow Truck .... TT
TOW [*Tube-Launched, Optically Tracked, Wire-Guided (Weapon)*] **Vehicle PowerConditioner** (MCD) .... TVPC
TOW [*Tube-Launched, Optically Tracked, Wire-Guided (Weapon)*] **Visual Module** [*Army*] .... TVM
Towanda, PA [*AM radio station call letters*] .... WTTC
Towanda, PA [*FM radio station call letters*] .... WTTC-FM
Towanda-Monroeton Shippers Lifeline, Inc. [*AAR code*] .... TMSS
Toward [*Altitude difference*] .... T
Toward .... TA
Toward (VRA) .... towd
Toward .... TWD
Toward Affective Development [*Educational tool*] .... TAD
Toward, Away, versus Selection System [*Psychology*] (AEBS) .... TAV
Toward Freedom (EA) .... TF
Toward Liberal Education [*In book title*] .... TLE
Toward Other Planetary Systems [*NASA*] .... TOPS
Toward Utility Rate Normalization .... TURN
Towards .... TOW
Towards (ROG) .... TRDS
Towards (ROG) .... TRJ
Towards Racial Justice [*British*] .... TRJ
Towarzystwo Niesienia Pomocy Zydom Ofiarom Wojny [*A publication*] (BJA) .... TNPZOW
Towarzystwo Ochrony Zdrowia [*A publication*] (BJA) .... TOZ
Towboat and Harbor Carriers Association of New York and New Jersey (EA) .... T & HCA
Towed Acoustic Monitor (PDAA) .... TAM
Towed Acoustic Surveillance System [*Marine science*] (MSC) .... TASS
Towed Array RADAR .... TAR
Towed Array SONAR .... TAS
Towed Array SONAR System .... TASOS
Towed Array SONAR System .... TASS
Towed Array Surveillance Range Prediction (MCD) .... TASSRAP
Towed Array Surveillance System [*Navy*] (CAAL) .... TASS
Towed Assault Bridge [*Army*] .... TAB
Towed Buoy Antenna .... TBA
Towed Cable [*Telecommunications*] (IAA) .... TC
Towed Flexible Barge (PDAA) .... TFB
Towed Ocean Bottom Instrument [*Oceanography*] .... TOBI
Towed Oceanographic Data Acquisition System (MSC) .... TODAS
Towed Optical Assessment Device [*Marine science*] (MSC) .... TOAD
Towed SONAR Body .... TSB
Towed SONAR Response .... TSR
Towed Unit [*Aerial Target*] (CAAL) .... TDU
Towed Universal Glider .... TUG

Towed Vehicle Brake ... TWB
Towed Vehicle Weight [*Automotive engineering*] ... TVW
Towel Bar [*Technical drawings*] ... TB
Towel Rack (MSA) ... TR
Tower ... TR
Tower (AAG) ... TWR
Tower (VRA) ... twr
Tower Air [*NASDAQ symbol*] (TTSB) ... TOWR
Tower Air, Inc. [*ICAO designator*] (FAAC) ... TOW
Tower Air, Inc. [*NASDAQ symbol*] (SAG) ... TOWR
Tower Air, Inc. [*Associated Press*] (SAG) ... TowrAir
Tower Automated Ground Surveillance System (MCD) ... TAGS
Tower Automotive [*NASDAQ symbol*] (TTSB) ... TWER
Tower Automotive, Inc. [*NASDAQ symbol*] (SAG) ... TWER
Tower Automotive, Inc. [*Associated Press*] (SAG) ... TwrAuto
Tower Aviation Weather Reporting Station (NOAA) ... TAWRS
Tower Cab Digital Display (PDAA) ... TCDD
Tower Control Computer Complex [*Aviation*] ... TCCC
Tower Data-Link Services [*FAA*] (TAG) ... TDLS
Tower Disconnect Technician (SAA) ... TDT
Tower en Route Control [*Aviation*] (FAAC) ... TEC
Tower en Route Control Area [*Aviation*] (FAAC) ... TECA
Tower Hamlets Reading Initiative via Exploration [*British*] (AIE) ... THRIVE
Tower Hill School, Wilmington, DE [*OCLC symbol*] (OCLC) ... THA
Tower Integrated Display System [*FAA*] (TAG) ... TIDS
Tower Jettison Command (SAA) ... TJC
Tower Jettison Motor ... TJM
Tower Lighting Equipment ... TLE
Tower of London ... TL
Tower of London ... TOL
Tower Operator Training System [*Air traffic control*] ... TOTS
Tower Proof [*Gunpowder*] (DICI) ... TP
Tower Restoral Vehicle and Surveillance Restoral Vehicle [*Air Force*] (DOMA) ... TRV/SRV
Tower Semiconductor [*NASDAQ symbol*] (TTSB) ... TSEMF
Tower Semiconductor Ltd. [*Associated Press*] (SAG) ... TowerS
Tower Semiconductor Ltd. [*NASDAQ symbol*] (SAG) ... TSEM
Tower Shielding Facility [*Nuclear energy*] ... TSF
Tower Shielding Reactor [*Nuclear energy*] ... TSR
Tower Station ... TS
Tower Tech [*NASDAQ symbol*] (TTSB) ... TTMT
Tower Tech, Inc. [*Associated Press*] (SAG) ... TowrTch
Tower Tech, Inc. [*NASDAQ symbol*] (SAG) ... TTMT
Towering Cumulus [*Meteorology*] ... TCU
Towers ... TWRS
Towers, Perrin, Forster & Crosby [*Compensation and actuarial consulting company*] ... TPF & C
Towers Perrin Forster & Crosby, Vancouver, BC, Canada [*Library symbol*] [*Library of Congress*] (LCLS) ... CaBVaTPF
Towers, Perrin, Forster & Crosby, Vancouver, British Columbia [*Library symbol National Library of Canada*] (NLC) ... BVATPF
Towet ... TWR
Towing ... TOW
Towing ... TWNG
Towing and Recovery Association of America (EA) ... TRAA
Towing Chock [*Shipfitting*] ... Tc
Towing Light (AAG) ... TOLT
Towle's Analysis of the United States Constitution [*A publication*] (DLA) ... Towle Const
Town ... T
Town ... TN
Town (MCD) ... TWN
Town ... TWN
Town & Country [*A publication*] ... T & C
Town & Country Cl'A' [*AMEX symbol*] (TTSB) ... TNC
Town & Country Corporate Trust [*NYSE symbol*] (SPSG) ... TCT
Town & Country Corp. [*AMEX symbol*] (SPSG) ... TNC
Town & Country Jewelry Corp. [*Associated Press*] (SAG) ... TownCty
Town and Country Planning Act [*British*] ... TCP
Town and Country Planning Association [*British*] ... TCPA
Town and Country Planning (Churches, Places of Religious Worship, and Burial Grounds) Regulations [*British*] ... TCP(CPRW)R
Town and Country Planning Commission [*Tasmania, Australia*] ... TCPC
Town and Country Planning (Compensation and Certificates) Regulations [*British*] ... TCP(CC)R
Town and Country Planning General Regulations [*British*] ... TCPGR
Town and Country Planning (Minerals) Regulations [*British*] ... TCP(M)R
Town & Country Trust [*NYSE symbol*] (TTSB) ... TCT
Town & Country Trust [*Associated Press*] (SAG) ... TwnCtry
Town and Village Enterprise (EERA) ... TVE
Town Campers' Housing and Infrastructure Program [*Australia*] ... TCHIP
Town Center Library at Tanasbourne, Portland, OR [*Library symbol Library of Congress*] (LCLS) ... OrPTC
Town Clerk [*or Councillor*] ... TC
Town Development Act [*Town planning*] [*British*] ... TDA
Town Hall (ROG) ... TH
Town Hall (VRA) ... town ha
Town Hall, Collins Canada, Toronto, Ontario [*Library symbol National Library of Canada*] (NLC) ... OTCTH
Town Major [*British military*] (DMA) ... TM
Town News, Paramus, NJ [*Library symbol Library of Congress*] (LCLS) ... NjParT
Town of Caledon Public Libraries, Albion-Bolton Branch, Bolton, ON, Canada [*Library symbol Library of Congress*] (LCLS) ... CaOBCAB
Town of Haldimand Public Libraries, Caledonia, ON, Canada [*Library symbol Library of Congress*] (LCLS) ... CaOCTH
Town of Haldimand Public Libraries, Caledonia, Ontario [*Library symbol National Library of Canada*] (NLC) ... OCTH
Town Planning Institute [*Later, Royal Town Planning Institute*] [*British*] (ILCA) ... TPI
Town Planning Institute of Canada ... TPIC
Town Suboffice ... TSO
Town Topics, Inc., Princeton, NJ [*Library symbol Library of Congress*] (LCLS) ... NjPTT
Towne ... TWNE
Townhouse ... TH
Townsend on Commercial Law [*A publication*] (DLA) ... Town Com Law
Townsend Plan National Lobby (EA) ... TPNL
Townsend Thoreson [*Company running English Channel ferries*] ... TT
Townsend's Judgment [*A publication*] (DLA) ... Town Jud
Townsend's Modern State Trials [*1850*] [*A publication*] (DLA) ... Town St Tr
Townshend on Slander and Libel [*A publication*] (DLA) ... Town Sl & Lib
Townshend on Slander and Libel [*A publication*] (DLA) ... Townsh Sland & L
Townshend's Code [*A publication*] (DLA) ... Town Co
Townshend's Pleading [*A publication*] (DLA) ... Town Pl
Townshend's Pleading [*A publication*] (DLA) ... Townsh Pl
Townshend's Practice [*A publication*] (DLA) ... Town Pr
Townshend's Precedents of Pleading [*A publication*] (DLA) ... Town Pr Pl
Townshend's Summary Landlord and Tenant Process [*A publication*] (DLA) ... Town Sum Proc
Township ... T
Township ... TO
Township ... TP
Township ... TWP
Township ... TWP
Township (DD) ... Twp
Township and Village Enterprise [*People's Republic of China*] (ECON) ... TVE
Township of Armstrong Public Library [*Bibliotheque Publique Canton Armstrong*], Earlton, Ontario [*Library symbol National Library of Canada*] (BIB) ... OETA
Township of Muskoka Lakes Public Library Board, Port Carling, Ontario [*Library symbol National Library of Canada*] (BIB) ... OPCML
Township of Norfolk Public Library, Langston, ON, Canada [*Library symbol Library of Congress*] (LCLS) ... CaOLaTN
Township of Norfolk Public Library, Langton, Ontario [*Library symbol National Library of Canada*] (NLC) ... OLATN
Townsville [*Australia ICAO location identifier*] (ICLI) ... ABTL
Townsville [*Australia ICAO location identifier*] (ICLI) ... ABTT
Townsville [*Australia ICAO location identifier*] (ICLI) ... ABTV
Townsville [*Australia Airport symbol*] (OAG) ... TSV
Townsville [*Australia Seismograph station code, US Geological Survey Closed*] (SEIS) ... TVL
Towson, MD [*AM radio station call letters*] ... WKDB
Towson, MD [*FM radio station call letters*] ... WTMD
Towson State University (GAGS) ... Towson St U
Towson State University, Baltimore, MD [*Library symbol Library of Congress*] (LCLS) ... MdBT
Towson State University, Towson, MD [*OCLC symbol*] (OCLC) ... TSC
Toxemia (BARN) ... tox
Toxic (CPH) ... tox
Toxic Air Contaminant ... TAC
Toxic Air Monitoring System [*Environmental Protection Agency*] (GFGA) ... TAMS
Toxic Air Monitoring Technical Advisory Committee [*Environmental Protection Agency*] (GFGA) ... TAMTAC
Toxic Air Pollutant ... TAP
Toxic Air Pollutant Data System [*Environmental Protection Agency*] (GFGA) ... TAPDS
Toxic Altitude Propulsion Research (MCD) ... TAPR
Toxic and Hazardous Materials Agency [*Army*] (RDA) ... THAMA
Toxic Characteristic Leaching Procedure ... TCLP
Toxic Characteristics Leaching Procedure [*Environmental Protection Agency*] ... TCLP
Toxic Chemical Munitions [*Army*] ... TCM
Toxic Chemical Munitions/Agents (MCD) ... TCM/A
Toxic Chemical Release Form ... TCRF
Toxic Chemical Release Inventory (GNE) ... TCRI
Toxic Chemical Release Inventory [*National Library of Medicine*] [*Information service or system*] (CRD) ... TRI
Toxic Colds [*Medicine*] ... T (Colds)
Toxic Concentration Low (ERG) ... TC^{Lo}
Toxic Dose (EG) ... TD
Toxic Dose High (OA) ... TDH
Toxic Dose Low (OA) ... TDL
Toxic Dose Low (ERG) ... TD^{Lo}
Toxic Epidermal Necrolysis [*Medicine*] ... TEN
Toxic Equivalency Factor [*Environmental Protection Agency*] ... TEF
Toxic, Explosive, Corrosive, Hazardous Cargo [*Shipping*] (DS) ... TECH
Toxic Goiter [*Medicine*] (MAE) ... TG
Toxic Granulation [*Laboratory science*] (DAVI) ... TOXI
Toxic Granulation-Differential [*Laboratory science*] (DAVI) ... TOXGR
Toxic Hazards Research Unit [*NASA*] (KSC) ... THRU
Toxic Incident Report ... TOXREP
Toxic Incident Report (MUGU) ... TOXREPT
Toxic Integration Program [*Environmental Protection Agency*] ... TIP
Toxic Materials Control Activity [*General Motors Corp.*] ... TMCA
Toxic Materials Information Center [*Oak Ridge National Laboratory*] (IID) ... TMIC
Toxic Materials Transport [*Business Publishers, Inc.*] [*Information service or system*] (CRD) ... TMT
Toxic Oil Epidemic Syndrome [*Medicine*] (DMAA) ... TOES
Toxic Oil Syndrome [*Medicine*] ... TOS
Toxic Organic Management Plan [*Pollution prevention*] ... TOMP

Toxic Pregnancy [*Gynecology*] ... TP
Toxic Regulatory Listings [*American Petroleum Institute*] [*Information service or system*] (CRD) ... TOXLIST
Toxic Release Inventory [*Environmental Protection Agency*] ... TRI
Toxic Release Inventory Program (GNE) ... TRIP
Toxic Release Inventory System [*Environmental Protection Agency*] ... TRIS
Toxic Shock Antigen [*Immunology*] (DAVI) ... TSA
Toxic Shock Syndrome [*Medicine*] ... TSS
Toxic Shock Syndrome Exotoxin ... TSSE
Toxic Shock Syndrome Toxin [*Medicine*] ... TSST
Toxic Shock Toxin [*Biochemistry*] ... TST
Toxic Shock-Associated Protein [*Biochemistry*] (DAVI) ... TSAP
Toxic Shock-Like Syndrome [*Medicine*] ... TSLS
Toxic Substance (MAE) ... TS
Toxic Substances Bulletin [*A publication*] ... TSB
Toxic Substances Control Act [*1976*] ... TOSCA
Toxic Substances Control Act [*1976*] ... TSCA
Toxic Substances Control Act Interagency Testing Committee [*Environmental Protection Agency*] (GFGA) ... TITC
Toxic Substances Control Act Plant and Production Data [*Chemical Information Systems, Inc.*] [*Information service or system*] ... TSCAPP
Toxic Substances Control Act Test Submissions [*Database*] [*Environmental Protection Agency*] ... TSCATS
Toxic Substances Coordinating Committee [*Environmental Protection Agency*] (GFGA) ... TSCC
Toxic Substances Coordinator [*Environmental Protection Agency*] (GFGA) ... TSC
Toxic Substances Dialogue Group [*Environmental Protection Agency*] (GFGA) ... TSDG
Toxic Substances Priority Committee [*Terminated, 1984*] [*Environmental Protection Agency*] (EGAO) ... TSPC
Toxic Substances Strategy Committee [*Nuclear energy*] (NRCH) ... TSSC
Toxic Unit [*Medicine*] ... TU
Toxic Use Reduction [*Manufacturing*] ... TUR
Toxic Vapor Detection System (SAA) ... TVDS
Toxic Vapor Detector ... TVD
Toxic Vapor Disposal [*NASA*] (KSC) ... TVD
Toxic Vapor Suit [*NASA*] (NASA) ... TVS
Toxic Victims Compensation Legislation ... TVCL
Toxic Waste Incinerator ... TWI
Toxicant Extraction Procedure ... TEP
Toxicity (MAE) ... T
Toxicity Bibliography [*MEDLARS*] ... TOBI
Toxicity Bibliography [*MEDLARS*] ... TOXBIB
Toxicity Characteristic [*Environmental Protection Agency*] ... TC
Toxicity Characteristic Leaching Procedure [*Environmental Protection Agency*] ... TCLP
Toxicity Characteristic Leading Procedure [*Hazardous materials control*] ... TCLP
Toxicity Equivalent ... TEQ
Toxicity Identification Evaluation ... TIE
Toxicity Prediction by Komputer Assisted Technology ... TOPKAT
Toxicity Reduction Evaluation ... TRE
Toxicological Agent Protective Item [*or Suit*] (MCD) ... TAP
Toxicological Research (SAA) ... TORES
Toxicologically Insignificant Usage ... TIU
Toxicology ... TOX
Toxicology ... TOXICOL
Toxicology and Microbiology Division [*Cincinnati, OH*] [*Environmental Protection Agency*] (GRD) ... TMD
Toxicology Data Bank [*National Library of Medicine*] [*Information service or system*] (IID) ... TDB
Toxicology Data Management System [*Department of Health and Human Services*] (GFGA) ... TDMS
Toxicology Data Network [*National Library of Medicine*] [*Information service or system*] (IID) ... TOXNET
Toxicology Forum (EA) ... TF
Toxicology Information Backup (NITA) ... TOXBACK
Toxicology Information Brief [*Environmental*] (GNE) ... TIB
Toxicology Information Conversational On-Line Network [*National Library of Medicine*] [*Later, TOXLINE*] ... TOXICON
Toxicology Information On-Line [*National Library of Medicine*] [*Bethesda, MD Bibliographic database*] ... TOXLINE
Toxicology Information Program [*National Library of Medicine*] [*Bethesda, MD*] ... TIP
Toxicology Information Query Response Center [*National Library of Medicine*] ... TIQRC
Toxicology Information Research Center [*Department of Energy*] [*Oak Ridge National Laboratory Oak Ridge, TN*] ... TIRC
Toxicology Information Response Center [*Information service or system*] (IID) ... TIRC
Toxicology Information Working Party (PDAA) ... TIWP
Toxicology Research and Testing Program [*National Institutes of Health*] ... TRTP
Toxicology Testing in Progress (NITA) ... TOXTIPS
Toxics and Pesticides Division [*Environmental Protection Agency*] (GFGA) ... TPD
Toxics and Waste Management Division [*Environmental Protection Agency*] (GFGA) ... TWMD
Toxics Release Inventory [*Environmental Protection Agency*] ... TRI
Toxics Testing and Assessment Research Committee [*Terminated, 1984*] [*Environmental Protection Agency*] (EGAO) ... TARC
Toxics Use Reduction [*Environmental science*] ... TUR
Toxics Use Reduction Institute [*University of Massachusetts, Lowell*] [*Research center*] (RCD) ... TURI
Toxin (CPH) ... tox
Toxin-Antitoxin [*Also, TAT*] [*Immunology*] ... TA
Toxin-Antitoxin [*Medicine*] (DMAA) ... T-A
Toxin-Antitoxin [*Also, TA*] [*Immunology*] ... TAT
Toxin-Coregulated Pili [*Biochemistry*] ... TCP
TOXLINE Back-File ... TOXBACK
TOXLINE Chemical Dictionary [*A publication*] ... TCD
Toxoid-Antitoxin Floccules [*Immunology*] ... TAF
Toxoid-Antitoxin Mixture [*Immunology*] ... TAM
Toxoplasma Encephalitis [*Neurology*] (DAVI) ... TE
Toxoplasma, Other [*Viruses*], Rubella, Cytomegaloviruses, Herpes [*Virus*] ... TORCH
Toxoplasmosis [*Medicine*] ... TOXO
Toxoplasmosis, Other Viruses, Rubella, Cytomegalovirus, Herpes Virus, and Syphilis [*Titer*] (DAVI) ... TORCHS
Toxteth (ROG) ... TOXT
Toy and Giftware Importers Association [*British*] (DBA) ... TGIA
Toy and Hobby Retailer [*A publication*] ... TH
Toy Biz, Inc. [*NYSE symbol*] (SAG) ... TBZ
Toy Biz, Inc. [*Associated Press*] (SAG) ... Toy Biz
Toy Biz'A' [*NYSE symbol*] (TTSB) ... TBZ
Toy Knights of America (EA) ... TKA
Toy Libraries Association [*British*] ... TLA
Toy Manufacturers of America (EA) ... TMA
Toy Manufacturers of the United States ... TMUS
Toy Preference Test [*Psychology*] (AEBS) ... TPT
Toy Press Publishers, Editors, and Reporters ... TOPPER
Toy Safety Act (MHDB) ... TSA
Toy Stores Steiff Collectors Club (EA) ... TSSCC
Toy Train Collectors Society (EA) ... TTCS
Toy Train Operating Society (EA) ... TTOS
Toy Wholesalers Association of America (EA) ... TWA
Toy World Test [*Psychology*] ... TWT
Toyama [*Japan ICAO location identifier*] (ICLI) ... RJNT
Toyama [*Japan*] [*Seismograph station code, US Geological Survey*] (SEIS) ... TOY
Toyo Kogyo Co. [*Auto manufacturer*] ... TKK
Toyon Research Corp. ... TRC
Toyooka [*Japan*] [*Seismograph station code, US Geological Survey*] (SEIS) ... TYK
Toyota Atlantic Championship [*Auto racing*] ... TAC
Toyota Canada, Inc. [*ICAO designator*] (FAAC) ... TOY
Toyota Celica Supra Club (EA) ... TCSC
Toyota Diffusion/Deposition ... TD
Toyota Electronically Modulated Suspension [*Automotive engineering*] ... TEMS
Toyota Industrial Engine Operations [*Torrance, CA*] ... TIEO
Toyota Industrial Equipment ... TIE
Toyota Manufacturing Australia Ltd. ... TMA
Toyota Motor Co. [*Associated Press*] (SAG) ... Toyota
Toyota Motor Corp. ... TMC
Toyota Motor Corp. [*NASDAQ symbol*] (NQ) ... TOYO
Toyota Motor Corp. ADR [*NASDAQ symbol*] (TTSB) ... TOYOY
Toyota Motor Manufacturing of North America ... TMMNA
Toyota Motor Marketing and Engineering [*Automotive industry, corporate subsidiary*] ... TMME
Toyota Motor Sales, Inc. ... TMS
Toyota Motor Workers' Union ... TMW
Toyota Owners Association (EA) ... TOA
Toyota Production System [*Innovative lean-production manufacturing*] (ECON) ... TPS
Toyota Racing Development [*Toyota Motor Corp.*] ... TRD
Toyota Reflex Burn [*Automotive engineering*] ... TRB
Toyota Technical Education Network ... T-TEN
Toyota Total Clean-Lean [*Automotive engineering*] ... TTC-L
Toyota's Computer-Controlled System (ADA) ... TCCS
Toyota's Variable Induction System [*Automotive engineering*] ... T-VIS
Toys R Us [*NYSE symbol*] (TTSB) ... TOY
Toys R Us, Inc. [*NYSE symbol*] (SPSG) ... TOY
Toys R Us, Inc. [*Associated Press*] (SAG) ... ToyRU
Tozeur [*Tunisia*] [*Airport symbol*] (OAG) ... TOE
Tozeur/Nefta [*Tunisia*] [*ICAO location identifier*] (ICLI) ... DTTZ
TP Monitor [*Computer science*] ... TPM
TPC Corp. [*AMEX symbol*] (TTSB) ... TPC
TPFDD Interface ... T/I
TPI Enterprises [*NASDAQ symbol*] (TTSB) ... TPIE
TPI Enterprises, Inc. [*Associated Press*] (SAG) ... TPI En
TPI Enterprises, Inc. [*NASDAQ symbol*] (NQ) ... TPIE
T-Platform Electric Van [*Chrysler*] [*Automotive engineering*] ... TEV
T-Pulse Effectiveness [*Neurology*] ... TPE
T-Pulse Response [*Telecommunications*] (IAA) ... TPR
TR Financial Corp. [*NASDAQ symbol*] (SAG) ... ROSE
TR Financial Corp. [*Associated Press*] (SAG) ... TR Fnc
TR-1 [*Aircraft*] **Ground Station** [*Air Force*] (DOMA) ... TRIGS
TR8 Car Club of America (EA) ... TR8CCA
Trabaccolo [*Small coasting vessel of the Adriatic*] (DS) ... TRB
Trabajos Aereos SA [*Spain ICAO designator*] (FAAC) ... TGE
Trabajos Aereos y Enlaces SA [*Spain ICAO designator*] (ICDA) ... JK
Trabeated (VRA) ... trab
Trabecular Bone Volume ... TBV
Trabecular Meshwork (DAVI) ... TM
Traben-Trarbach [*Germany ICAO location identifier*] (ICLI) ... EDZX
Trabzon [*Turkey ICAO location identifier*] (ICLI) ... LTCG
Trabzon [*Turkey*] [*Airport symbol*] (OAG) ... TZX
Trac Industries, Inc. [*Toronto Stock Exchange symbol Vancouver Stock Exchange symbol*] ... TCS
Tracan Oil & Gas [*Vancouver Stock Exchange symbol*] ... TRA
Trace (DAVI) ... T
Trace ... TR
Trace [*Commonly used*] (OPSA) ... TRACE
Trace [*Commonly used*] (OPSA) ... TRACES
Trace ... TRCE

Trace	TRCE
Trace Acceptance Tester	TAT
Trace Analysis Research Centre [*Dalhousie University*] [*Canada*] (IRC)	TARC
Trace Atmospheric Gas Analyser [*Instrument*]	TAGA
Trace Contaminant Control System	TCCS
Trace Contamination Analysis	TCA
Trace Element Analyzer Based on LASER Ablation and Selectivity (MCD)	TABLASER
Trace Element Doping	TED
Trace Element Pattern (KSC)	TEP
Trace Elements [*Chemistry*] (DAVI)	TE
Trace Elements in Man and Animals [*An international symposium*]	TEMA
Trace Fuselage Station (MCD)	TRFS
Trace Gas Acquisition System	TGAS
Trace Gas Analysis	TGA
Trace Hierarchy of Requirements [*Science Applications International Corp.*]	THOR
Trace Junior-Senior High School, Tracy, MN [*Library symbol*] [*Library of Congress*] (LCLS)	MnTrJSH
Trace Last Reference Position (IAA)	TLRP
Trace Material Generation Rate Simulator	TMGRS
Trace Metals Analyzer	TMA
Trace Metals Detection Technique	TMDT
Trace Narcotics Detector	TND
Trace of Precipitation [*Less than 0.005 inch of rain or 0.05 inch of snow*]	T
Trace of/Trace of Referring to findings of traces of different substances on tests (DAVI)	T/T
Trace Operate Unit	TOU
Trace Organic Analysis [*Environmental Protection Agency*] (GFGA)	TOA
Trace Remote Atmospheric Chemical Evaluation [*National Center for Atmospheric Research*]	TRACE
Trace Test and Evaluation	TRATE
Trace to Destination and Advise [*Military*]	TRADAD
Trace Watch Unit (IAA)	TWU
Traceability and Reporting System	TRS
Traceability Code (NASA)	TC
Tracer [*Ammunition*] (NATG)	T
Tracer (AAG)	TCR
Tracer	TR
Tracer (AABC)	TRAC
Tracer (MSA)	TRCR
Tracer Bullet	TB
Tracer Burst Obscuration System [*Weaponry simulation*] [*Military*] (INF)	TBOS
Tracer Control Chassis	TCCH
Tracer, Number as Indicated. Furnish Information Immediately or Advise	TRACINFO
Tracer Pete Wrrt [*NASDAQ symbol*] (TTSB)	TCXWF
Tracer Petroleum [*NASDAQ symbol*] (TTSB)	TCXXF
Tracer Petroleum Corp. [*NASDAQ symbol*] (SAG)	TCXW
Tracer Petroleum Corp. [*NASDAQ symbol*] (SAG)	TCXXF
Tracer Petroleum Corp. [*Associated Press*] (SAG)	TracrP
Tracer Petroleum Corp. [*Associated Press*] (SAG)	TracrP
Tracer Resources [*Vancouver Stock Exchange symbol*]	TUC
Tracer Test Unit (IAA)	TTU
Tracers Association [*A union*] [*British*]	TA
Tracery (VRA)	trac
Traces (VRA)	tr
Tracewell and Mitchell's United States Comptroller's Decisions [*A publication*] (DLA)	Trace & M
Tracewell, Bowers, and Mitchell's United States Comptroller's Decisions [*A publication*] (DLA)	TB & M
Tracey's Cases on Evidence [*A publication*] (DLA)	Tracey Evidence
Trachea [*Anatomy*]	T
Trachea [*or Tracheotomy*] [*Medicine*]	TRACH
Tracheal Antimicrobial Peptide [*Biochemistry*]	TAp
Tracheal Aspiration (CPH)	Trach Asp
Tracheal Cellular Score [*Medicine*]	TCS
Tracheal Fistula [*Otorhinolaryngology*] (DAVI)	TF
Tracheal Sound [*Medicine*] (AAMN)	TS
Tracheal-Bronchiolar [*Region*] [*Medicine*]	TB
Tracheary Element [*Botany*]	TE
Tracheobronchial Lymph Node [*Anatomy*]	TBLN
Tracheobronchial Toilet [*Medicine*] (MAE)	TBT
Tracheobronchitis [*Medicine*]	TB
Tracheoesophageal [*Also, TOE*] [*Medicine*]	TE
Tracheoesophageal [*Also, TE*] [*Medicine*]	TOE
Tracheoesophageal Fistula [*Medicine*]	TEF
Tracheo-Esophageal Fistula [*Medicine*] (DAVI)	TOF
Tracheo-Esophageal Puncture [*Medicine*]	TEP
Tracheo-Oesophageal [*Medicine*] (DAVI)	TO
Tracheostomy [*Medicine*] (DAVI)	Trach
Tracheosyringeal [*Neuroanatomy of birds*]	ts
Tracheotomy (DSUE)	TRACHY
Tracheotomy Set (CPH)	T
Trachiniae [*of Sophocles*] [*Classical studies*] (OCD)	Trach
Trachoma-Inclusion Conjunctivitis [*Ophthalmology*]	TRIC
Traci Lords Fan Club [*Defunct*] (EA)	TLFC
Tracing Change Notice	TCN
Tracing Dye (OA)	TD
Tracing-Hold	TH
Track	T
Track [*or Tracking*] (AAG)	TCK
Track	TK
Track	TR
Track [*Commonly used*] (OPSA)	TRACK

Track [*Postal Service standard*] (OPSA)	TRAK
Track	TRAK
Track (AAG)	TRK
Track [*Commonly used*] (OPSA)	TRKS
Track Accelerator [*Missile simulator*]	TA
Track Address (IAA)	TA
Track Address Register	TAR
Track Adjusting Link [*Army*] (RDA)	TAL
Track and Field Association of the United States of America (EA)	TFA/USA
Track and Field Athletes of America	TFAA
Track and Store [*Computer science*] (IAA)	TRS
Track Angle Error	TKE
Track Channel Number (SAA)	TCN
Track Circuit (DCTA)	TC
Track Combat Status (SAA)	TCMS
Track Commander [*Army*] (INF)	TC
Track Confirmation Word [*Computer science*]	TCW
Track Continuity Area (NATG)	TCA
Track Crossing Altitude [*or Attitude*]	TCA
Track Crossing Angle	TCA
Track Data	TD
Track Data Center	TDC
Track Data Central	TDC
Track Data Central Tables (SAA)	TDCT
Track Data Corp. [*Software firm*] [*Information service or system*] (IID)	TDC
Track Data Corp. [*NASDAQ symbol*] (TTSB)	TRAC
Track Data Corp. [*NASDAQ symbol*] (SAG)	TRAC
Track Data Corp. [*Associated Press*] (SAG)	TrackD
Track Data Corp. Wrrt [*NASDAQ symbol*] (TTSB)	TRACW
Track Data Request (CAAL)	TDR
Track Data Simulator	TDS
Track Data Storage	TDS
Track Data Storage (MSA)	TDST
Track Database (MCD)	TDB
Track Detection Circuit [*Electronics*] (OA)	TDC
Track Display	TD
Track Dog [*Dog show term*]	TD
Track Entry Console (MCD)	TEC
Track Evaluation System [*Canadian National Railways*]	TEST
Track File Number (CAAL)	TFN
Track Geometry [*In TG-01, an Austrian built subway inspection car*]	TG
Track Identity	TI
Track Identity	TIDY
Track Identity	TRID
Track Imitation (MSA)	TIM
Track Initiation and Prediction [*RADAR*]	TIP
Track, Initiation, Monitoring Overlap Technician (SAA)	TIMOT
Track Initiation Supervisor (SAA)	TIS
Track Initiator	TI
Track Initiator Monitor (CAAL)	TIM
Track Last Reference Position	TLRP
Track Levitated Vehicle [*Department of Transportation*]	TLV
Track Made Good [*Aviation*]	TMG
Track Magnetic [*Aviation*] (DA)	TrM
Track Monitor (CAAL)	TM
Track Monitor Supervisor (IAA)	TMS
Track Navigation Computer	TNC
Track No Conversion	TNC
Track Number	TN
Track Number Conversion (IAA)	TNC
Track Number Sorted Table (SAA)	TNS
Track on Jamming	TOJ
Track Path Length [*Army*] (RDA)	TPL
Track Position	TPOS
Track Processing Special (SAA)	TPS
Track Production Area [*Air Force*]	TPA
Track Production Officer [*NATO Air Defense Ground Environment*] (NATG)	TPO
Track Quality	TQ
Track RADAR Simulation Group [*Military*] (CAAL)	TRSG
Track RADAR Test Set (MCD)	TRTS
Track Reference Number (IAA)	TRN
Track Reference Printout	TRPO
Track Retrieve and Account for Configuration of Equipment (MCD)	TRACE
Track Sector Identification	TSID
Track Security Element [*Military*] (INF)	TSE
Track Situation Display	TSD
Track Store Switch (IAA)	TSS
Track Store Unit (IAA)	TS
Track Subsystem Analyst (MUGU)	TSA
Track Supervisor (CAAL)	TK SUP
Track Supply Association	TSA
Track Suspension System [*MTMC*] (TAG)	TSS
Track Synthesis Frequency	TSF
Track True [*Aviation*] (DA)	TrT
Track Velocity	TVEL
Track Width Mine Plow (MCD)	TWMP
Tracked	TRKD
Tracked Air Cushion Vehicle Powered by Linear Induction Motor (PDAA)	TACV/LIM
Tracked Air-Cushion Research Vehicle [*DoD*]	TACRV
Tracked Air-Cushion Vehicle [*High-speed ground transportation*]	TACV
Tracked Combat Vehicle (MCD)	TCV
Tracked Levitated Research Vehicle	TLRV
Tracked Vehicle (AABC)	TRVEH
Tracker [*British military*] (DMA)	T

Tracker	TRKR
Tracker Analysis Program (MCD)	TRAP
Tracker Lock [*NASA*] (KSC)	TL
Tracker Test Set [*Dragon*] (MCD)	TTS
Tracker Test Set Supplemental Unit (MCD)	TTSU
Tracking (AAG)	TRKG
Tracking Accuracy Control	TAC
Tracking Adjunct System [*I-HAWK*] (MCD)	TAS
Tracking Adjunct Systems Trainer	TAST
Tracking Air with Circularly Polarized Radar [*Marine science*] (OSRA)	TRACIR
Tracking Air with Circularly Polarized Radar (USDC)	TRACIR
Tracking Alarms Processor [*Space Flight Operations Facility, NASA*]	TAP
Tracking Altitude (MCD)	TALT
Tracking and Communication Component	TCC
Tracking and Communications [*Aviation*] (IAA)	TRAC
Tracking and Communications, Extraterrestrial	TRACE
Tracking and Control Center	TCC
Tracking and Data Acquisition (IAA)	TADA
Tracking and Data Acquisition	TDA
Tracking and Data Acquisition/Advanced Engineering	TDA/AE
Tracking and Data Acquisition Satellite (SSD)	TDAS
Tracking and Data Acquisition Satellite System (SSD)	TDASS
Tracking and Data Acquisition System	TDAS
Tracking and Data Relay [*NASA*]	TDR
Tracking and Data Relay Experiment [*Telecommunications*] (TEL)	TDRE
Tracking and Data Relay Satellite [*NASA*]	TDRS
Tracking and Data Relay Satellite Services [*or System*] [*NASA*]	TDRSS
Tracking and Data Relay Satellite System [*Instrument*] (EERA)	TDRSS
Tracking and Data System [*NASA*]	TDS
Tracking and Display Processor (CAAL)	TDP
Tracking and Display System	TADS
Tracking and Evolution of Solar Active Regions (USDC)	TELSAR
Tracking and Evolution of Solar Active Regions [*Marine science*] (OSRA)	TELSAR
Tracking and Ground Instrumentation System (DNAB)	TAGIS
Tracking and Ground Instrumentation Unit [*NASA*]	TAGIU
Tracking and Guidance	TG
Tracking and Injection Station	TIS
Tracking and Reporting Format [*Military*] (CAAL)	TARF
Tracking and Reporting Format Extended [*Military*] (CAAL)	TARFX
Tracking Antenna Pedestal System (IAA)	TPS
Tracking Antenna System	TAS
Tracking Asynchronous RADAR Data (DA)	TARAD
Tracking Band Width (MCD)	TBW
Tracking Camera	TC
Tracking Comparison	TRACOMP
Tracking Computer Controls (MCD)	TCC
Tracking Console	TC
Tracking Data Analysis	TDA
Tracking Data Editing Program [*NASA*]	TDEP
Tracking Data Handling	TDH
Tracking Data Message (SSD)	TDM
Tracking Data Processor	TDP
Tracking Data Processor System (MCD)	TDPS
Tracking Display Unit	TDU
Tracking Dog	TD
Tracking Dog Excellent	TDX
Tracking Enhancement (MCD)	TE
Tracking/Erosion Resistance Tester	TERT
Tracking Error Detector (MCD)	TED
Tracking Errors and Simulation Evaluation [*RADAR*]	TEASE
Tracking Exercise [*Navy*] (NVT)	TRACKEX
Tracking Filter	TF
Tracking Head (IAA)	TH
Tracking Impact Prediction [*of satellites*]	TIP
Tracking in an Active and Passive RADAR Environment	TAPRE
Tracking Information Memorandum	TIM
Tracking Instruction Manual	TIM
Tracking Instrument Mount (MUGU)	TIM
Tracking Instrumentation Subsystem (MCD)	TIS
Tracking Light Electronics (KSC)	TLE
Tracking Local Oscillator	TLO
Tracking Loop Test Set	TLTS
Tracking Merit Interception	TMI
Tracking Modifier Power Supply	TMPS
Tracking [*or Transit*] **Network** [*Navy*]	TRANET
Tracking Officer (IAA)	TO
Tracking Operation Memorandum [*Obsolete*]	TOM
Tracking Program (MUGU)	TP
Tracking RADAR	TR
Tracking RADAR Angle Deception Equipment (NG)	TRADE
Tracking RADAR Automatic Monitoring (AFM)	TRAM
Tracking RADAR Central Control Console [*BMEWS*]	TRCCC
Tracking RADAR Data Takeoff	TRDTO
Tracking RADAR Electronic Component (AFM)	TREC
Tracking RADAR Experiment (IAA)	TRADEX
Tracking RADAR Input and Correlation (MSA)	TRIC
Tracking RADAR Instrumentation Ship (SAA)	TRIS
Tracking, RADAR-Input, and Correlation	TRC
Tracking Range Instrumented Aircraft (PDAA)	TRIA
Tracking Scope	TS
Tracking Servobridge Detector (MCD)	TSBD
Tracking Signal Generator	TSG
Tracking Signal Processor (LAIN)	TSP
Tracking Supervisor (SAA)	TS
Tracking System (AAG)	TS
Tracking System Analysis Group [*NASA*]	TSAG
Tracking System Analytical Calibration	TSAC
Tracking System Test Set (AAG)	TSTS
Tracking System Test Stand (IAA)	TSTS
Tracking Technician (SAA)	TT
Tracking, Telemetry, and Command [*AEC*] (IAA)	TTAC
Tracking, Telemetry, and Command	TTC
Tracking, Telemetry, and Control [*NASA*] (NASA)	TTC
Tracking, Telemetry, Command, and Voice [*Aerospace*]	TTCV
Tracking Telemetry Data Receiver (AAG)	TTDR
Tracking Telescope	TT
Tracking through Telemetry [*Air Force*]	TRATEL
Track-Laying Air-Cushion Vehicle	TLACV
Trackless Trolley [*Freight*]	TRAK TROL
Track-on-Jam Valid [*Military*]	TOJV
Track-on-Repeater [*Military*]	TOR
Track-Rich Grains [*s*] [*Cosmic-ray path in meteorites*]	TRG
Tracks per Inch [*Magnetic storage devices*] [*Computer science*]	TPI
Tracks per Second (WGA)	TPS
Track-Via-Missile	TVM
Track-via-Missile Analog Processor [*Military*]	TVMAP
Trackway	TRWA
Track-while-Scan [*Communications*]	TWS
Track-while-Scan on Receive Only (NG)	TWSRO
Track-while-Scan RADAR	TWSR
Track-while-Scan RADAR Simulator	TWSRS
TRACON Traffic Management Advisor [*FAA*] (TAG)	TTMA
Tracor, Inc. [*Associated Press*] (SAG)	Tracor
Tracor, Inc. [*NASDAQ symbol*] (SAG)	TTRR
Tracor, Inc., Technical Library, Austin, TX [*Library symbol Library of Congress*] (LCLS)	TxAuT
Tracor Inc.Wrrt'A' [*NASDAQ symbol*] (TTSB)	TTRRW
Tract	TR
Tract Evaluation Computer (NATG)	TEC
Tractatus in Evangelium Iohannis [*of Augustine*] [*Classical studies*] (OCD)	In Evang Iohan
Traction [*Orthopedics*] (DAVI)	tr
Traction	tract
Traction [*Medicine*]	TX
Traction Assist [*Automotive engineering*]	TA
Traction Asynchronous Motor (PDAA)	TAM
Traction Control [*Mitsubishi*] [*Transmission systems*]	TCL
Traction Control System [*Alfred Teves GmbH*] [*Automotive engineering*]	TCS
Traction Engine [*British*]	TE
Traction Retinal Detachment [*Ophthalmology*] (DAVI)	TRD
Traction-Immune Track Circuits [*Railway signals system*] [*British*]	TITC
Tractive Effort to Weight Ratio (MCD)	TE/W
Tractor (AAG)	TRAC
Tractor	TRCR
Tractor	TRCTR
Tractor and Machinery Association of Australia	TMAA
Tractor Biplane	TB
Tractor Computing Corp. (IAA)	TCC
Tractor/Loader/Backhoe	TLB
Tractor Monoplane	TM
Tractor, Rubber-Tired, Articulated, Multipurpose (DOMA)	TRAM
Tractor Supply [*NASDAQ symbol*] (SAG)	TSCO
Tractor Supply Co. [*Associated Press*] (SAG)	TracSup
Tractor Truck, Six Wheel [*Automotive engineering*]	TTSW
Tractor Vaporizing Oil [*Automotive engineering*]	TVO
Tractor-Drawn	TD
Tractor-Drawn	TRACDR
Tracy, CA [*FM radio station call letters*] (RBYB)	KMIX
Tracy Defense Depot (SAA)	TDD
Tracy Elementary School, Tracy, MN [*Library symbol*] [*Library of Congress*] (LCLS)	MnTrES
Tracy, MN [*FM radio station call letters*]	KARL
Tradable Emission Reduction Assessments [*Environmental Protection Agency*]	TERA
Trade	TR
Trade	TRD
Trade (BARN)	Trd
Trade Acceptance [*Business term*]	T/A
Trade Acceptance [*Investment term*] (DFIT)	TA
Trade Action Monitoring System [*Office of the United States Trade Representative*] (GFGA)	TAMS
Trade Adjustment Act	TAA
Trade Adjustment Assistance [*Department of Commerce*]	TAA
Trade Adjustment Assistance Center [*Department of Commerce*]	TAAC
Trade Adjustment Assistance Program [*Department of Commerce*]	TAAP
Trade Agreements Act	TA
Trade Agreements Act	TAA
Trade Agreements Act of 1979 (AAGC)	TAA
Trade Agreements Committee [*An interagency committee of the executive branch of US government*] [*Terminated, 1963*]	TAC
Trade and Development Agency (USGC)	TDA
Trade and Development Board [*United Nations Conference on Trade and Development*]	TDB
Trade and Development Program [*US International Development Cooperation Agency*]	TDP
Trade and Industrial Education (AEE)	T and I
Trade and Industry Index [*Information Access Corp.*] [*Information service or system*] (IID)	TI
Trade and Professional Exhibits Directory [*Later, TSW*] [*A publication*]	TPED

Trade and Tourism Alliance [*Defunct*] (EA) .... TTA
Trade Aptitude Test [*Vocational guidance test*] .... TRAT
Trade Assistance and Planning Office (AAGC) .... TAPA
Trade Association (DCTA) .... TA
Trade Association of Proprietary Plants (EA) .... TAPP
Trade Cases [*Commerce Clearing House*] [*A publication*] (DLA) .... TC
Trade Cases [*Commerce Clearing House*] [*A publication*] (DLA) .... Trade Cas
Trade Commission of Norway (EA) .... TCN
Trade Commission of Spain (EA) .... TCS
Trade Control Measures Information System [*UNCTAD*] [*United Nations*] (DUND) .... TCMIS
Trade Data Element Exchange .... TRADEX
Trade Data Elements Directory (DS) .... TDED
Trade Data Interchange (DS) .... TDI
Trade Data Interchange System [*Telecommunications*] (OSI) .... TEDIS
Trade Development (AAGC) .... TD
Trade Development Assistance Division [*Bureau of East-West Trade*] [*Former USSR*] (IMH) .... TDAD
Trade Development Bank [*Subsidiary of American Express Bank*] .... TDB
Trade Development Corp. [*South Australia*] [*Commercial firm*] .... TDC
Trade Development Council (EERA) .... TDC
Trade Development Zone (ADA) .... TDZ
Trade Development Zone Authority [*Northern Territory, Australia*] .... TDZA
Trade Dispute (OICC) .... TD
Trade Division [*British military*] (DMA) .... TD
Trade Effluent Joint Advisory Committee [*British*] (DCTA) .... TEJAC
Trade Expansion Act [*1962*] .... TEA
Trade Expansion Act Advisory Committee [*Terminated, 1975*] (EGAO) .... TEAAC
Trade Expenses [*Business term*] .... TE
Trade Information Committee [*Department of State*] (EA) .... TIC
Trade Information Research Unit [*ITC*] [*United Nations*] (DUND) .... TIRU
Trade Information Service [*ESCAP*] [*United Nations*] (DUND) .... TIS
Trade Information Supply Unit [*ITC*] [*United Nations*] (DUND) .... TISU
Trade International (BARN) .... TI
Trade List (ODBW) .... tl
Trade List (IIA) .... TL
Trade Mark Bulletin, New Series [*A publication*] (DLA) .... TM Bull
Trade Mark Record [*United States*] [*A publication*] (DLA) .... TM Rec
Trade Marks Opposition Board [*Information service or system*] (IID) .... TMOB
Trade Marks, Patents, and Designs Federation [*British*] (DBA) .... TMPDF
Trade Mission .... TM
Trade Movement Society of Carpenters and Joiners [*A union*] [*British*] .... TMSCJ
Trade Name (DEN) .... TN
Trade Name (MSA) .... TRN
Trade Names Database [*Information service or system*] (IID) .... TND
Trade Names Dictionary [*Later, BTC*] [*A publication*] .... TND
Trade Names Dictionary: Company Index [*Later, CTB*] [*A publication*] .... TND:CI
Trade Negotiations among Developing Countries (IMH) .... TNDC
Trade Negotiations Committee [*Australia*] .... TNC
Trade Negotiations Office, External Affairs Canada [*Affaires Exterieures Canada*] **Ottawa, Ontario** [*Library symbol National Library of Canada*] (NLC) .... OOTN
Trade Opportunities Program [*Departments of State and Commerce*] .... TOP
Trade Opportunity Referral Service [*Department of Agriculture*] [*Information service or system*] (IID) .... TORS
Trade Pattern (MSA) .... TRP
Trade Policy Committee [*Advisory to President*] [*Abolished, 1963*] .... TPC
Trade Policy Research Centre [*British*] (ECON) .... TPRC
Trade Policy Staff Committee [*Federal interagency group*] .... TPSC
Trade Practices Commission (EERA) .... TPC
Trade Practices Reports [*Australia A publication*] .... TPR
Trade Promotion Coordinating Committee [*Department of Commerce*] (EGAO) .... TPCC
Trade Promotion Organisation .... TPO
Trade Promotion Services Group [*British*] .... TPS
Trade Protection Service [*or Society*] [*British*] .... TP
Trade Readjustment Allowance [*or Assistance*] .... TRA
Trade Records Analysis of Flora and Fauna in Commerce [*An association*] .... TRAFFIC
Trade Records Analysis of Flora and Fauna in Commerce (GNE) .... TRAFFIC
Trade Recovery Act .... TRA
Trade Reform Action Coalition [*Defunct*] (EA) .... TRAC
Trade Regulation Reporter [*Commerce Clearing House*] [*A publication*] (DLA) .... Trade Reg Rep
Trade Regulation Reporter [*A publication*] (DLA) .... TRR
Trade Regulation Review [*A publication*] (DLA) .... Trade Reg Rev
Trade Regulation Rule (MHDW) .... TRR
Trade Relations Association (EA) .... TRA
Trade Relations Council of the United States (EA) .... TRC
Trade Remedy Assistance Office (AAGC) .... TRAO
Trade Representative (MHDW) .... TR
Trade Show Bureau (EA) .... TSB
Trade Show Services Association [*Defunct*] (EA) .... TSSA
Trade Shows and Professional Exhibits Directory [*Formerly, TPED*] [*Later, TSW*] [*A publication*] .... TSPED
Trade Shows Worldwide [*Formerly, TSPED*] [*A publication*] .... TSW
Trade Society of Iron Foundry Labourers [*A union*] [*British*] .... TSIFL
Trade Specialty Qualification (MCD) .... TSQ
Trade Standards Advisory Council [*Australia*] .... TSAC
Trade Study (MCD) .... TS
Trade Study Management (NASA) .... TSM
Trade Study Report .... TSR
Trade Support System (MHDW) .... TSS
Trade Union .... TU
Trade Union Advisory Committee [*British*] (DAS) .... TUAC
Trade Union Advisory Committee (EERA) .... TUAC
Trade Union Advisory Committee to the Organization for Economic Cooperation and Development [*Paris, France*] (EAIO) .... TUAC OECD
Trade Union and Labour Relations Act [*1974 and 1976*] [*British*] (DCTA) .... TULRA
Trade Union Badge Collectors Society [*British*] (DBA) .... TUBCS
Trade [*or Trades*] **Union Council** .... TUC
Trade Union Council of South Africa .... TUCSA
Trade Union Educational League .... TUEL
Trade Union Federation [*British*] (EY) .... TUF
Trade Union Immunities [*British*] .... TUI
Trade Union International .... TUI
Trade Union International Research and Education Group [*England*] (EAIO) .... TUIREC
Trade Union Leadership Council (EA) .... TULC
Trade Union Unity League .... TUUL
Trade Union Women of African Heritage (EA) .... TUWAH
Trade Unionists' Defence Committee [*Australia*] .... TUDC
Trade Unionists for Labour [*British*] .... TUFL
Trade Unions' Industrial Council [*Australia*] .... TUIC
Trade Unions International of Agriculture, Forestry, and Plantation Workers [*See also UISTAFP*] [*Prague, Czechoslovakia*] (EAIO) .... TUIAFPW
Trade Unions International of Miners and Workers in Energy [*See also UISMTE*] (EAIO) .... TUIMWE
Trade Unions International of Public and Allied Employees [*Berlin, Federal Republic of Germany*] (EAIO) .... TUIPAE
Trade Unions International of Transport Workers (EAIO) .... TUI
Trade Unions International of Transport Workers (EAIO) .... TUITW
Trade Unions International of Workers in Commerce [*Prague, Czechoslovakia*] (EAIO) .... TUIWC
Trade Unions International of Workers of Building, Wood, and Building Materials Industries .... UIBWM
Trade Valuers Institute [*British*] (DBA) .... TVI
Trade Wind Zone Oceanography .... TWZO
Trade Winds Resources [*Vancouver Stock Exchange symbol*] .... TRW
Traded .... T
Traded Options Market [*London Stock Exchange*] .... TO
Trade-Last .... TL
Trademark .... TM
Trademark .... TRDMRK
Trademark Bulletin. United States Trademark Association (New Series) [*New York*] [*A publication*] (DLA) .... Trademark Bull (NS)
Trademark Examining Procedure Directives [*A publication*] .... TEPD
Trademark Manual of Examining Procedure [*A publication*] (DLA) .... TMEP
Trademark Registration Treaty .... TRT
Trademark Rules of Practice [*A publication*] (DLA) .... TMR Prac
Trademark Section, Official Gazette [*Federal government*] .... TMS
Trademark Society (EA) .... TMS
Trademark Society (EA) .... TS
Trademark Society, Inc. .... TRSOC
Trademark Trial and Appeal Board [*of Patent Office*] .... TTAB
Trade-Off Analysis [*Military*] .... TOA
Trade-Off Analysis Systems/Force Mix (MCD) .... TRANSLOC
Trade-Off Analysis - Systems/Force Mix Analysis [*Military*] .... TRANSFORM
Trade-Off and Technology .... TOT
Trade-Off Determination [*Military*] (AABC) .... TOD
Trade-Off Evaluation System .... TOES
Tradeoff Study Suggestion (SSD) .... TSS
Trade-Offs for Lifting Reentry Vehicle Evaluation and Nominal Design .... TREND
Trader Resource Corp. [*Toronto Stock Exchange symbol*] .... TRR
Trade-Related Aspects of Intellectual Property Right .... TRIP
Trade-Related Intellectual Property (ECON) .... TRIPS
Trade-Related Investment Measures [*International finance*] (ECON) .... TRIMS
Traders and Contacts .... TAC
Traders Group Ltd. [*Toronto Stock Exchange symbol Vancouver Stock Exchange symbol*] .... TG
Traders' Road Transport Association [*British*] (BARN) .... TRTA
Trades Advisory Council [*British*] .... TAC
Trades and Labour Congress of Canada [*1883-1956*] .... TLC(C)
Trades and Labour Council of Queensland [*Australia*] .... TLCQ
Trades and Labour Council of the Australian Capital Territory .... TLCACT
Trades and Labour Council of Western Australia .... TLCWA
Trades and Labour Council of Western Australia .... WATLC
Trades Councils' Joint Consultative Committee [*British*] (DCTA) .... TCJCC
Trades Union Congress [*British*] .... TUC
Trades Union Congress of Nigeria .... TUCN
Trades Union Digest [*A publication*] .... Trad Un Dig
Trades Union Movement .... TUM
Trades Union Research Centre (AIE) .... TURC
Tradesman [*British military*] (DMA) .... T
Tradesman [*British military*] .... TD
Tradesman .... TRDSMAN
TRADEVMAN [*Training Devices Man*] [*Navy rating*] .... TD
TRADEVMAN [*Training Devices Man*], First Class [*Navy rating*] TD1
TRADEVMAN [*Training Devices Man*], Seaman [*Navy rating*] .... TDSN
TRADEVMAN [*Training Devices Man*], Seaman Apprentice [*Navy rating*] .... TDSA
TRADEVMAN [*Training Devices Man*], Second Class [*Navy rating*] TD2
TRADEVMAN [*Training Devices Man*], Third Class [*Navy rating*] TD3
Trade-Weighted Index (ADA) .... TWI
Tradewinds Aviation Ltd. [*Canada ICAO designator*] (FAAC) .... TWL
Trading (DCTA) .... TDG
Trading .... TRADE
Trading (DCTA) .... TRDG
Trading & Development Bank Ltd. [*Liberia*] .... TRADEVCO
Trading As .... TA

Trading As (AAGC) ... ta
Trading Bank ... TB
Trading Bay, AK [*Location identifier FAA*] (FAAL) ... TDY
Trading Expert ... TE
Trading Index [*Short term*] (MHDW) ... TRIN
Trading Information System [*AutEx Systems*] [*Information service or system*] (CRD) ... TIS
Trading Law [*British*] ... TRL
Trading Limit ... TL
Trading Partner Agreement (AAGC) ... TPA
Trading Stamp Institute of America (EA) ... TSIA
Trading Standards Officer (ODBW) ... TSO
Trading with the Enemy Act ... TWEA
Tradition ... TRAD
Traditional (BJA) ... T
Traditional Aboriginal Teacher Education [*Australia*] ... TATE
Traditional Acupuncture Foundation (EA) ... TAF
Traditional Acupuncture Society [*Stratford-Upon-Avon, Warwickshire, England*] (EAIO) ... TAS
Traditional Birth Attendant ... TBA
Traditional Chinese Medicine ... TCM
Traditional Hi-Bye Function [*Army*] ... THBF
Traditional Instruction ... TI
Traditional Life Cycle (PDAA) ... TLC
Traditional Medical Practice ... TMP
Traditional Neighborhood Development Ordinance ... TND
Traditional Organized Crime ... TOC
Traditional Orthography [*Writing system*] ... TO
Traditional Products Line (MHDI) ... TPL
Traditional Siamese Breeders and Fanciers Association (EA) ... TSBFA
Traditional Small Craft Association (EA) ... TSCA
Traditional Wooden Boat Society [*Defunct*] (EA) ... TWBS
Traditionally Administered Instruction (BUR) ... TAI
Traditionally Black Institutions (EDAC) ... TBI
TRADOC Analysis Command ... TRAC
TRADOC [*Training and Doctrine Command*] **Analysis Command - Fort Leavenworth** [*Kansas*] [*Army*] ... TRAC-F
TRADOC [*Training and Doctrine Command*] **Analysis Command - White Sands Missile Range** [*New Mexico*] [*Army*] ... TRAC-WSMR
TRADOC [*Training and Doctrine Command*] **Analysis Command-Monterey** [*California*] [*Army*] (GRD) ... TRAC-MTRY
TRADOC Combined Arms Test Activity [*Army*] (MCD) ... TCATA
TRADOC [*Training and Doctrine Command*] **Combined Arms Test Agency** [*Army*] ... TCATA
TRADOC [*Training and Doctrine Command*] **Command Management Information System** [*Military*] ... TCMIS
TRADOC Data Evaluation Study (MCD) ... TRADES
TRADOC Educational Data System ... TREDS
TRADOC [*Training and Doctrine Command*] **Educational Data System - Nonresident Instruction** [*Army*] ... TREDS-NRI
TRADOC [*Training and Doctrine Command*] **Engineer Management Information System** [*Army*] ... TEMIS
TRADOC [*Training and Doctrine Command*] **Instrumentation Review Committee** [*Army*] ... TIRC
TRADOC [*Training and Doctrine Command*] **Integration Staff Officer** [*Army*] ... TISO
TRADOC Library Information Network (MCD) ... TRALINET
TRADOC [*Training and Doctrine Command*] **Management Engineering Activity** [*Military*] ... TRAMEA
TRADOC [*Training and Doctrine Command*] **Management Information System** [*Army*] ... TRAMIS
TRADOC Master Priority List (MCD) ... TRAMPL
/TRADOC Material Development and Readiness Council [*Development and Readiness Communications*] [*Training and Doctrine Command*] [*Army*] (MCD) ... FDTMDRC
TRADOC [*Training and Doctrine Command*] **Materiel Evaluation Committee** [*Army*] ... TMEC
TRADOC [*Training and Doctrine Command*] **Mobilization and Operations Planning System** [*Military*] ... TMOPS
TRADOC [*Training and Doctrine Command*] **Operations Research Activity** [*Military*] ... TORA
TRADOC Procurement Instruction (MCD) ... TPI
TRADOC Program Analysis and Resource Review [*Military*] (MCD) ... TPARR
TRADOC [*Training and Doctrine Command*] **Research and Analysis Center** [*Army*] ... TRAC
TRADOC Research Center [*Monterey, CA*] [*Army*] (GRD) ... TREM
TRADOC Resources Management (MCD) ... TRM
TRADOC [*Training and Doctrine Command*] **Review of Manpower** ... TRM
TRADOC System Manager [*Army*] ... TSM
TRADOC [*Training and Doctrine Command*] **Systems Analysis Activity** [*White Sands Missile Range, NM*] [*Army*] ... TRASANA
TRADOC [*Training and Doctrine Command*] **Systems Analysis Agency** [*Army*] ... TRASANA
TRADOC Systems Management Office [*Military*] (RDA) ... TSMO
TRADOC Systems Staff Officer [*or Office*] [*Army*] ... TRASSO
TRADOC Troop List (MCD) ... TTL
Traductrice (IAA) ... TRAD
Traer Star-Clipper, Traer, IA [*Library symbol*] [*Library of Congress*] (LCLS) ... IaTraS
Trafalgar [*On army list*] [*British*] (ROG) ... T
Trafalgar Brookmount [*British*] ... TB
Trafalgar Resources, Inc. [*Vancouver Stock Exchange symbol*] ... TFR
Traffic ... TFC
Traffic ... TRAF
Traffic (ROG) ... TRAFF
Traffic (MSA) ... TRFC
Traffic ... TRFC
Traffic Accident (DAVI) ... TA
Traffic Accident Data [*Project*] [*National Safety Council*] ... TAD
Traffic Account Analysis System [*Military British*] ... TAAS
Traffic Agent [*or Auditor*] ... TA
Traffic Alert and Collision Avoidance Detection [*Aviation*] ... TACAD
Traffic Alert and Collision Avoidance Device [*Aviation*] (DA) ... TCAD
Traffic Alert and Collision Avoidance System [*Aviation*] ... TCAS
Traffic Analysis [*National Security Agency*] ... T/A
Traffic Analysis Survey (MCD) ... TAS
Traffic Analysis Zone [*Bureau of the Census*] (GFGA) ... TAZ
Traffic and Incident Management System ... TIMS
Traffic Audit Bureau [*Later, TABMM*] (EA) ... TAB
Traffic Audit Bureau for Media Measurement (EA) ... TABMM
Traffic Bureau ... TB
Traffic Camera Office [*Victoria, Australia*] ... TCO
Traffic Cases [*A publication*] (DLA) ... T
Traffic Clubs International (EA) ... TCI
Traffic Collision ... TC
Traffic Commissioner [*or Consultant*] ... TC
Traffic Consultant (WGA) ... TC
Traffic Control (NG) ... TFC
Traffic Control and Landing [*Aviation*] (IAA) ... TRACAL
Traffic Control and Landing System [*Aviation*] (IAA) ... TRACALS
Traffic Control Approach and Landing System [*Aviation electronics*] ... TRACALS
Traffic Control Area [*Aviation*] ... TCA
Traffic Control Center ... TCC
Traffic Control Complex (SAA) ... TCC
Traffic Control Devices [*MOCD*] (TAG) ... TCD
Traffic Control Point [*or Post*] [*Military*] ... TCP
Traffic Control RADAR ... TCR
Traffic Control Satellite ... TCS
Traffic Control Station ... TCS
Traffic Control System [*Army*] ... TCS
Traffic Control Transponder ... TCT
Traffic Controller (CAAL) ... TC
Traffic Count and Listing [*Aviation*] (DA) ... TRC
Traffic Court Program of the American Bar Association (EA) ... ABA/TCP
Traffic Data Administration System [*Bell System*] ... TDAS
Traffic Data Collection System (MCD) ... TDCS
Traffic Data Processing ... TDP
Traffic Data Processing Program (MCD) ... TDPP
Traffic Data Record (DA) ... TDR
Traffic Data Recording System [*Bell System*] ... TDRS
Traffic Decisions [*Interstate Commerce Commission*] ... TD
Traffic Demand Predictor [*Aviation*] ... TDP
Traffic Department [*Scotland Yard*] ... TD
Traffic Director ... TD
Traffic Engineering for Automatic Route Selection (PDAA) ... TEARS
Traffic Executives Association, Eastern Railroads [*Later, ERA*] ... TEA-ER
Traffic Facilities Management System [*Australia*] ... TFMS
Traffic Flow Management [*FAA*] (TAG) ... TFM
Traffic Flow Management (GAVI) ... TFM
Traffic Flow Planning Simulation [*FAA*] (TAG) ... FLOWSIM
Traffic Flow Security [*Telecommunications*] (TEL) ... TFS
Traffic Flow Visualization and Control [*FHWA*] (TAG) ... TFVC
Traffic Flow Visualization and Control ... TFVC
Traffic Forecasting System [*Telecommunications*] (TEL) ... TFS
Traffic Guidance [*Aviation*] ... TG
Traffic Headquarters ... T
Traffic Identification ... TI
Traffic Improvement Association ... TIA
Traffic Information Broadcast by Aircraft (DA) ... TIBA
Traffic Information System ... TIS
Traffic Information Zone (DA) ... TIZ
Traffic Injury Research Foundation of Canada [*Research center*] (RCD) ... TIRF
Traffic Injury Research Foundation of Canada [*Fondation de Recherches sur lesBlessures de la Route au Canada*] **Ottawa, Ontario** [*Library symbol National Library of Canada*] (NLC) ... OOTIR
Traffic Law Enforcement ... TLE
Traffic Loading Device (CAAL) ... TLD
Traffic Management Advisor [*FAA*] (TAG) ... TMA
Traffic Management Advisor (GAVI) ... TMA
Traffic Management Agency (CINC) ... TMA
Traffic Management and Proceedings Office [*CONUS*] (MCD) ... TMPO
Traffic Management Center [*Highway operations*] ... TMC
Traffic Management Channel [*Navigation and driver information systems*] ... TMC
Traffic Management Computer Complex [*FAA*] (TAG) ... TMCC
Traffic Management Information Letter [*MTMC*] (TAG) ... TMIL
Traffic Management Laboratory [*FHWA*] (TAG) ... TML
Traffic Management Office [*or Officer*] [*Air Force*] (AFM) ... TMO
Traffic Management Program Alert [*Aviation*] (FAAC) ... TMPA
Traffic Management System [*FAA*] (TAG) ... TMS
Traffic Management Unit [*FAA*] (TAG) ... TMU
Traffic Management Unit (GAVI) ... TMU
Traffic Manager [*or Management*] ... TM
Traffic Measure and Path Search [*Telecommunications*] (TEL) ... TRAMPS
Traffic Measurement System ... TMS
Traffic Measuring and Recording System [*Telecommunications*] (TEL) ... TMRS
Traffic Message Channel [*FHWA*] (TAG) ... TMC
Traffic Message Channel ... TMC
Traffic Model (NASA) ... TM
Traffic Monitoring Guide [*FHWA*] (TAG) ... TMG
Traffic Monitoring System [*FHWA*] (TAG) ... TMS

Traffic Noise Index [*Department of Transportation*] ... TNI
Traffic Officer ... TO
Traffic on Request [*Aviation*] (FAAC) ... TOR
Traffic Operations to Increase Capacity and Safety [*Department of Transportation*] ... TOPICS
Traffic Operator Position System [*Telecommunications*] (TEL) ... TOPS
Traffic Order Change (SAA) ... TOC
Traffic Orientation Scheme (DA) ... TOS
Traffic Overload Reroute Control ... TORC
Traffic Pattern Altitude [*Aviation*] ... TPA
Traffic Post ... TP
Traffic Received (FAAC) ... TFRCD
Traffic Records Committee (EA) ... TRC
Traffic Records Criminal Justice Information System (OICC) ... TRACIS
Traffic Regulation Point [*Military*] ... TRP
Traffic Reporting and Control System (IAA) ... TRACS
Traffic Reporting and Control System (NITA) ... TRCS
Traffic Responsive Advance Green [*Control strategy*] ... TRAG
Traffic Retrieval Analysis Validation and Information System [*Telecommunications*] (TEL) ... TRAVIS
Traffic Route [*Telecommunications*] (TEL) ... TR
Traffic Route Testing [*Telecommunications*] (TEL) ... TRT
Traffic Routing and Control Equipment (MCD) ... TRACE
Traffic Routing and Management System (NITA) ... TRAMS
Traffic Safety Now [*Defunct*] (EA) ... TSN
Traffic Safety Training Program ... TSTP
Traffic Separation Scheme ... TSS
Traffic Service Position [*Telephone*] ... TSP
Traffic Service Position System [*Telecommunications*] ... TSPS
Traffic Service Position System Real-Time Capacity Program [*Telecommunications*] (TEL) ... TSPSCAP
Traffic Situation [*Status*] **Display** ... TSD
Traffic Superintendent [*British*] (DCTA) ... TS
Traffic Surveillance System [*Traffic management*] ... TSS
Traffic Tester [*Telecommunications*] (TEL) ... TT
Traffic/Traffic Management and Control [*British*] ... T/TMC
Traffic Trunk Administration [*Telecommunications*] (TEL) ... TTA
Traffic Trunk Order [*Telecommunications*] (TEL) ... TTO
Traffic Unit ... TU
Traffic Usage Recorder [*Telecommunications*] ... TUR
Traffic Volume Trends [*BTS*] (TAG) ... TVT
Traffic Zone (FAAC) ... TFZ
Traffic-Guidance Long-Range Aid to Navigation (DEN) ... TG-LORAN
Trafficway [*Commonly used*] (OPSA) ... TRAFFICWAY
Trafficway [*Postal Service standard*] (OPSA) ... TRFY
Trafficway ... TRFY
Tragedy ... TR
Tragedy ... TRAG
Trager's Medium [*Chemically defined culture medium*] ... TM
Tragicorum Graecorum Fragmenta [*A publication*] (OCD) ... TGF
Tragicorum Romanorum Fragmenta [*A publication*] (OCD) ... TRF
Tragoedopodagra [*of Lucian*] [*Classical studies*] (OCD) ... Trag
Trail [*Commonly used*] (OPSA) ... TR
Trail [*Commonly used*] (OPSA) ... TRAIL
Trail [*Commonly used*] (OPSA) ... TRAILS
Trail ... TRL
Trail (MCD) ... TRL
Trail [*Commonly used*] (OPSA) ... TRLS
Trail, BC [*AM radio station call letters*] ... CJAT
Trail, BC [*FM radio station call letters*] (RBYB) ... CJAT-FM
Trail, BC [*Television station call letters*] ... CKTN
Trail Blazer Library System [*Library network*] ... TBLS
Trail City Archives, British Columbia [*Library symbol National Library of Canada*] (NLC) ... BTCA
Trail Lake Flying Service, Inc. [*ICAO designator*] (FAAC) ... HBA
Trail Making Test [*Psychiatry*] (DAVI) ... TMT
Trail Museum, British Columbia [*Library symbol National Library of Canada*] (NLC) ... BTM
Trail Museum, Trail, BC, Canada [*Library symbol*] [*Library of Congress*] (LCLS) ... CaBTM
Trail Pilot Sensor ... TPS
Trail Public Library, British Columbia [*Library symbol National Library of Canada*] (NLC) ... BT
Trail Riders of the Canadian Rockies (EA) ... TRCR
Trail Riders of the Wilderness [*Later, AFA*] (EA) ... TRW
Trail Riders of Today (EA) ... TROT
Trail Termination Line (MCD) ... TTL
Trail Watcher (CINC) ... TW
Trailer (AAG) ... TLR
Trailer (AAG) ... TR
Trailer ... TRLR
Trailer ... TRLR
Trailer Coach Association [*Later, Manufactured Housing Institute*] (EA) ... TCA
Trailer Container [*MTMC*] (TAG) ... TCON
Trailer Height [*Automotive engineering*] ... TH
Trailer Hitch Manufacturers Association (EA) ... THMA
Trailer Launch Bridge (DWSG) ... TLB
Trailer Length [*Specifications*] [*Automotive engineering*] ... TL
Trailer Manufacturers Association [*Later, NAMPS*] (EA) ... TMA
Trailer Mounted ... TLRMTD
Trailer on Flatcar [*Railroad*] ... TOFC
Trailer Point [*MTMC*] (TAG) ... TP
Trailer Test Equipment (AAG) ... TTE
Trailer Transfer Point ... TTP
Trailer Van Mount ... TVM
Trailerable Aids to Navigation Boat [*USCG*] (TAG) ... TANB
Trailerable Intracoastal Waterway Aids to Navigation [*Boat*] ... TICWAN
Trailerless Collective Protection Station [*Military*] ... TCPS
Trailerless Collective Protection System (DWSG) ... TRACOPS
Trailer-Mounted Power Support System (DWSG) ... TMPSS
Trailfinders [*Travel agency*] [*British*] ... TF
Trailing (AAG) ... TRG
Trailing Edge [*Aviation*] ... TE
Trailing Edge Down [*Aviation*] (MCD) ... TED
Trailing Edge Radius (MSA) ... TE/R
Trailing Edge Tracking [*Aviation*] (LAIN) ... TET
Trailing Edge Up ... TEU
Trailing Wire Antenna [*on aircraft*] ... TWA
Trailing-Arm-Drive ... TAD
Trailing-Throttle Oversteer [*Automobile driving*] ... TTO
Trailokya Bauddha Mahasangha [*Friends of the Western Buddhist Order*] [*British*] (EAIO) ... TBM
Trailokya Bauddha Mahasangha Sahayaka Gana [*Friends of the Western Buddhist Order*] [*British*] (EAIO) ... TBMSG
Trails Regional Library, Johnson County-Lafayette County Library, Warrensburg, MO [*Library symbol Library of Congress*] (LCLS) ... MoWarbTR
Trails, Roads, and Interdiction Missions [*or Multisensor*] **Program** [*Navy*] ... TRIM
Train (AAG) ... TN
Train (ADA) ... TR
Train a Grande Vitesse [*High-speed train*] ... TGV
Train America's Workforce [*An association*] (WYGK) ... TAW
Train and Heard's Precedents of Indictment [*A publication*] (DLA) ... Tr & H Prec Ind
Train Axis Optical Cube ... TAOC
Train Collectors Association (EA) ... TCA
Train Conducting Officer [*British military*] (DMA) ... TCO
Train Printer [*Computer science*] (IAA) ... TP
Train Regulation Advisory Control (PDAA) ... TRAC
Train Supervisory System (IAA) ... TSS
Trainable Adaptive Network ... TAN
Trainable Bow Propeller ... TBP
Trainable Mentally Handicapped ... TMH
Trainable Mentally Retarded ... TMR
Trainable Retractable Bow Propeller ... TRBP
Trainable Retractable Propeller ... TRP
Trainborne Operational Equipment ... TOE
Trained Aide [*Medicine*] ... TA
Trained in Minesweeping [*British military*] (DMA) ... TM/S
Trained Man [*British military*] (DMA) ... TM
Trained Operator [*British military*] (DMA) ... TO
Trained Personnel Requirements [*Air Force*] ... TPR
Trained Profile Panel [*Sensory testing*] ... TPP
Trained Soldier [*British military*] (DMA) ... TS
Trainee (WDAA) ... TR
Trainee ... TRN
Trainee (AABC) ... TRNE
Trainee Discharge Program [*Army*] ... TDP
Trainee Enrolled Nurse ... TEN
Trainee Management System (MCD) ... TMS
Trainee Mobility Assistance [*Australia*] ... TMA
Trainees, Transients, Patients, and Students Program [*Military*] ... TTP & S
Train-Elevated Guideway Interaction (PDAA) ... TEGI
Trainer [*Designation for all US military aircraft*] ... T
Trainer (AAG) ... TNR
Trainer (AAG) ... TR
Trainer (AAG) ... TRNR
Trainer ... TRNR
Trainer Aircraft Designation [*MTMC*] (TAG) ... T
Trainer Appraisal Kit ... TAK
Trainer Change Proposal [*Military*] (AFIT) ... TCP
Trainer Change Request [*Military*] ... TCR
Trainer Control and Simulation Computer ... TCSC
Trainer Digital Self-Test Program ... TDSTP
Trainer Facilities Report [*Army*] ... TFR
Trainer Fighter ... TF
Trainer Flight Equipment (MCD) ... TFE
Trainer Installation Requirements Report ... TIRR
Trainer Jet Exhaust Decontamination System ... TJEDS
Trainer Operator Console (SAA) ... TOC
Trainer Parts Fabrication (AAG) ... TPF
Trainer Power Control Panel ... TPCP
Trainer Software Support System [*Military*] ... TSSS
Trainer Specification Change Notice (MCD) ... TSCN
Trainer System Software ... TSS
Trainer Test Procedure [*Army*] ... TTP
Trainer Test Procedures and Results [*Army*] ... TTPR
Trainer Test Procedures and Results Report [*DoD*] ... TTPRR
Trainer Training Assistance [*Australia*] ... TTA
Trainer Unique Equipment [*Navy*] ... TUE
Trainfire ... TNF
Training (AAG) ... TNG
Training (ROG) ... TR
Training ... TRA
Training ... train
Training ... TRAIN
Training ... TRG
Training ... TRNG
Training Access Point (AIE) ... TAP
Training Advisor (WDAA) ... TA
Training Agency (EERA) ... TA

Training Agency Intelligence Unit (AIE) .... TAIU
Training Aid and Device [*Military*] .... TAD
Training Aid Bulletins [*Navy*] .... TAB
Training Aid, Device, Simulation and Simulator [*Military*] .... TADSS
Training Aid Feasibility Studies (AAG) .... TAFS
Training Aid for MOBIDIC Console Operations .... TAMCO
Training Aids Division [*Navy*] .... TAD
Training Aids Guide [*Navy*] .... TAG
Training Aids Library [*Navy*] .... TAL
Training Aids Management Agency [*Army*] (AABC) .... TAMA
Training Aids Management Office [*Army*] (AABC) .... TAMO
Training Aids Research Laboratory [*Air Force*] (MCD) .... TARL
Training Aids Section [*Navy*] .... TAS
Training Aids Service Office [*Army*] (AABC) .... TASO
Training Aids Support Center [*Army*] .... TASC
Training Aircraft [*Lighter-than-Air*] [*Navy symbol*] (MUGU) .... ZT
Training Aircraft Carrier [*Navy symbol*] .... CVT
Training Alarm Controller .... TAC
Training Allowance [*British military*] (DMA) .... TA
Training Ammunition Authorization Committee (MCD) .... TAAC
Training Ammunition Management Information System (MCD) .... TAMIS
Training Ammunition Management Study [*Army*] (MCD) .... TAMS
Training Analysis and Evaluation Group [*Navy*] .... TAEG
Training Analysis and Feedback (MCD) .... TAF
Training Analyst (HGAA) .... TA
Training Anchorage [*Navy*] (NVT) .... TNGANCH
Training and Administration of the Reserve .... TAR
Training and Administrative Reserves [*on permanent active duty*] .... TARS
Training and Approaches to Careers Education [*Project*] (AIE) .... TRACE
Training and Audio-Visual Support Activity - Europe (MCD) .... TASAE
Training and Audiovisual Support Center [*Army*] .... TASC
Training and Audiovisual Support Center [*Army*] .... TAVSC
Training and Audiovisual Support Center/Subcommunity [*Army*] .... TASC/SC
Training and Audiovisual Support Officer [*Military*] .... TASO
Training and Battle Simulation [*SAGE*] .... TBS
Training and Detention (ADA) .... T & D
Training and Development Alert [*Advanced Personnel Systems*] [*Information service or system*] (CRD) .... TDA
Training and Development in Australia [*A publication*] .... Tra Devel Aust
Training and Development Lead Body (AIE) .... TDLB
Training and Distribution Center [*Navy*] .... T & DC
Training and Distribution Center [*Navy*] .... TADC
Training and Doctrine Command [*Army*] .... TRADOC
Training and Doctrine Command Mission Area Manager [*Army*] .... TMAM
Training and Doctrine Command Regulation [*Army*] .... TRADOC-R
Training and Doctrine Command System Manager [*Army*] (MCD) .... TSM
Training and Education .... T & E
Training and Education Activities Clearing House [*Military*] .... TEACH
Training and Education Group (NITA) .... TEG
Training and Education in Adoption Methods [*Conference sponsored by the North American Council on Adoptable Children*] .... TEAM
Training and Enterprise Council [*British*] .... TEC
Training and Evaluation (OICC) .... TE
Training and Evaluation Group [*Navy*] (MCD) .... TAEG
Training and Evaluation Outline .... T & EO
Training and Experience [*Military*] (AFM) .... TRAEX
Training and Operations [*Military*] .... T & O
Training and Performance Data Center [*Military*] .... TPDC
Training and Personnel Systems Technology (MCD) .... TPST
Training and Readiness [*Marine Corps*] (DOMA) .... T & R
Training and Retention as Permanent Party [*Army*] (AABC) .... TRAPP
Training and Riot Control Agent .... CN
Training and Skills Program .... TASK
Training and Technical Assistance (OICC) .... T & TA
Training and Technology .... TAT
Training and Test Lung [*Simulator*] [*Medicine*] (DAVI) .... TTL
Training and Training Equipment (MCD) .... TTEP
Training As .... T/A
Training Assessment Exercise .... TAX
Training Atlantic Fleet [*Navy*] .... TRAINLANT
Training Availability [*Navy*] (NVT) .... TRAV
Training Back [*Main parachute*] .... TB
Training Balloon [*Navy symbol*] .... ZKN
Training Base Force, Pacific Fleet [*Navy*] .... TRAINBASEFOR
Training Base Review (MCD) .... TBR
Training Battalion [*British military*] (DMA) .... TB
Training Capability [*Military*] .... TRNCAP
Training Carrier .... AVT
Training Center [*Military*] .... TC
Training Center .... TRACEN
Training Center for Experimental Aerodynamics [*NATO*] .... TCEA
Training Centre Brigade of Gurkhas [*British military*] (DMA) .... TCBG
Training Certification Management System [*NASA*] .... TCMS
Training Check Frame [*Computer science*] .... TCF
Training Chest [*Emergency parachute*] .... TC
Training Circular [*Military*] .... TC
Training Command (AAG) .... TC
Training Command [*Navy*] (DNAB) .... TRACOMD
Training Command Amphibious Forces .... PHIBTRA
Training Command Amphibious Forces, US Atlantic Fleet .... PHIBTRAINLANT
Training Command Amphibious Forces, US Atlantic Fleet .... PHIBTRALANT
Training Command Amphibious Forces, US Pacific Fleet .... PHIBSTRAPAC
Training Command Amphibious Forces, US Pacific Fleet .... PHIBTRAINPAC
Training Command Amphibious Forces, US Pacific Fleet .... PHIBTRAPAC
Training Command, Atlantic Fleet [*Navy*] .... TRACOMDLANT
Training Command, Pacific Fleet [*Navy*] .... TRACOMDPAC
Training Command, Submarines, Pacific Fleet [*Navy*] .... TRACOMDSUBPAC
Training Command, West Coast [*Navy*] .... TRACOMDWESTCOAST
Training Conference (MCD) .... TRAINCON
Training Controller Panel .... TCP
Training/Conversion/Replacement (MCD) .... TCR
Training Corps [*British military*] (DMA) .... TC
Training Cruiser (MCD) .... CT
Training Data and Analysis Center .... TDAC
Training Department, Iron Ore Co. of Canada, Labrador City, Newfoundland [*Library symbol National Library of Canada*] (NLC) .... NFLIO
Training Depot Brigade of Gurkhas [*British military*] (DMA) .... TDBG
Training Depot Station [*British military*] (DMA) .... TDS
Training Destroyer [*Navy symbol*] .... DDT
Training Detachment .... TD
Training Detachment [*Navy*] .... TRADET
Training Development Action Plan (DOMA) .... TDAP
Training Development Advisors (MCD) .... TDA
Training Development and Improvement Program [*Department of Education*] .... TDI
Training Development Information System [*Army*] .... TDIS
Training Development Office [*Army*] .... TDO
Training Development Officer [*British*] .... TDO
Training Developments .... TD
Training Developments Institute [*Army*] .... TDI
Training Developments Study .... TDS
Training Device (MCD) .... TD
Training Device Acquisition Management Model (MCD) .... TDAMM
Training Device Acquisition Strategy .... TDAS
Training Device Center .... TDC
Training Device Computer (DNAB) .... TRADEC
Training Device Development Management [*Model*] (MCD) .... TDDM
Training Device Letter of Agreement .... TDLOA
Training Device Letter Requirement [*Military*] .... TDLR
Training Device Needs Statement [*Army*] .... TDNS
Training Device Requirement [*Army*] (AABC) .... TDR
Training Device Requirements Review Committee [*Army*] .... TDRRC
Training Device Supply Office [*Navy*] (DNAB) .... TDSO
Training Device Support Center [*Army*] .... TDSC
Training Devices (RDA) .... TRADE
Training Devices and Equipment .... TRADE
Training Devices Man [*Navy rating*] .... TRADEVMAN
Training Devices Requirements Office [*TRADOC*] (MCD) .... TRADER
Training Directors' Forum [*An association*] (EA) .... TDF
Training Directors Seminar [*LIMRA*] .... TDS
Training Directory for Business and Industry [*A publication*] .... TDBI
Training Division [*Canadian Navy*] .... TRAINDIV
Training, Education, and Mutual Assistance (USDC) .... TEMA
Training, Education and Mutual Assistance [*Marine science*] (OSRA) .... TEMA
Training, Education, and Mutual Assistance in the Marine Sciences [*IOC working committee*] (MSC) .... TEMA
Training Effectiveness Analysis .... TEA
Training Effectiveness Analysis - Tube-Launched Optically Tracked Wire-Guided (MCD) .... TEA-TOW
Training Effectiveness Evaluation .... TEE
Training Element Need Statement .... TENS
Training/Employment of Automotive Mechanics [*Project*] .... TEAM
Training Equipment .... TE
Training Equipment (KSC) .... TRE
Training Equipment and Maintenance [*Aviation*] (DA) .... TEAM
Training Equipment Change Directives [*Navy*] .... TECD
Training Equipment Checkout Procedure .... TECP
Training Equipment Cost Effectiveness Prediction Techniques [*Navy*] .... TECEPT
Training Equipment Development [*Military*] .... TED
Training Equipment Item Specification (MCD) .... TEIS
Training Equipment List .... TEL
Training Equipment Plan .... TEP
Training Equipment Planning Information [*Military*] (AFM) .... TEPI
Training Equipment Progress Report .... TEPR
Training Equipment Requirements Guide (KSC) .... TERG
Training Equipment Requirements Plan .... TER
Training Equipment Summary (MCD) .... TES
Training Establishment [*British military*] (DMA) .... TE
Training Evaluation and Control .... TEC
Training Exercise Coordinator [*Military*] (NVT) .... TEC
Training Extension Course [*Army*] .... TEC
Training Facility [*Navy*] (DNAB) .... TRAFAC
Training Film [*Military*] .... TF
Training Film and Video Association (NITA) .... TFVA
Training Film Production Laboratory [*Military*] .... TFPL
Training Flight [*British military*] (DMA) .... TF
Training for Aboriginals Program Scheme [*Australia*] .... TAPS
Training for [*US Military Academy*] **Cadets** (NVT) .... TRACAD
Training for Life [*Young Men's Christian Association*] [*British*] .... TFL
Training for [*US Naval Academy/Naval Reserve Officers Training Corps*] **Midshipmen** (NVT) .... TRAMID
Training for Opportunities in Programming (IAA) .... TOP
Training for Skill Ownership (AIE) .... TSO
Training Frigate [*Navy symbol*] .... FFT
Training Glider [*Navy symbol*] .... VLN
Training Group (WDAA) .... TG
Training Group Pacific Headquarters [*Canadian Navy*] .... TRAINPACHQ
Training Group, Royal Marines [*British*] .... TrgGpRM
Training Guarantee Fund [*Australia*] .... TGF
Training - Guided Air Missile (MUGU) .... T-GAM

Training Guided Missile [*Air Force*] .... TGM
Training Hazardous Condition (MCD) .... TRHAZCON
Training ICON Environment .... TIE
Training Implementation Plan [*Military*] .... TIP
Training Improvement Board [*Military*] (CAAL) .... TIB
Training in Expanded Auxiliary Management .... TEAM
Training in Urban Environment [*Navy*] (DOMA) .... TRUE
Training Instructor .... TI
Training Instrumentation Evaluation (MCD) .... TIE
Training Integrator [*or Integration*] (MCD) .... TI
Training Launch Control Center (IAA) .... TLCC
Training Launch Station (MCD) .... TLS
Training Liaison Officer [*Ministry of Agriculture, Fisheries, and Food*]
   [*British*] .... TLO
Training Literature .... T/L
Training Literature [*Military*] .... TNGLIT
Training Management [*Navy*] (DNAB) .... TRAINMAN
Training Management Control System [*Army*] (INF) .... TMACS
Training Management Development Office [*Army*] .... TMDO
Training Management Instruction Packet .... TMIP
Training Manual [*Military*] .... TM
Training Material Support .... TMS
Training Material Support Detachment [*Army*] .... TMSD
Training Media Association (EA) .... TMA
Training Media Database [*Access Innovations, Inc.*] [*Information service or
   system*] (CRD) .... TMD
Training Media Distributors Association [*Later, TMA*] (EA) .... TMDA
Training Media Services .... TMS
Training Memorandum (DAS) .... TM
Training Missions [*Air Force*] .... TM
Training Name and Address File [*IRS*] .... TNAF
Training Name and Address Key Index File [*IRS*] .... TKIF
Training Needs Analysis (AIE) .... TNA
Training Occupational Classification (AIE) .... TOC
Training of Documentalists .... TD
Training of Teacher Trainers .... TTT
Training on the Job .... TOTJ
Training Operation Plan [*Military*] (CAAL) .... TOP
Training Operations and Planning Station (MCD) .... TOPS
Training Opportunities Schemes [*Department of Employment*] [*British*] .... TOPS
Training Outside Public Practice (PDAA) .... TOPP
Training Package System Planning (IAA) .... TPS
Training Parts List (AAG) .... TPL
Training Period [*Military*] (AFM) .... TP
Training Place in Industry (AIE) .... TPI
Training Plan (NASA) .... TP
Training Plan Information (MCD) .... TPI
Training Plane [*Navy symbol*] .... VN
Training Plane, 2-Engine [*Navy symbol*] .... VSN(M)
Training Plans Conference .... TPC
Training, Practicing [*Ammunition*] .... TP
Training Priority Requirements Index .... TPRI
Training Problem Analysis (MCD) .... TPA
Training Proficiency Test [*Army*] (INF) .... TPT
Training Program and Planning .... TPP
Training Program and Planning Guidance .... TPPG
Training Programs Directorate [*Army*] .... TPD
Training Quality Index [*Military*] (CAAL) .... TQI
Training Reactor, Isotopes General Atomic [*Nuclear energy*] .... TRIGA
Training Readiness Analysis Monitor (MCD) .... TRAM
Training Readiness Condition .... TRC
Training Readiness Evaluation (MCD) .... TRE
Training Readiness Squadron .... TRNGRS
Training Readjustment Allowance (OICC) .... TRA
Training Regulations [*Military*] .... TR
Training Relation and Instruction Mission [*Vietnam, France, United States*]
   [*Military*] .... TRIM
Training Requirement Priority Index .... TRPI
Training Requirements .... TR
Training Requirements Analysis [*NASA*] (NASA) .... TRA
Training Requirements Analysis Directorate [*Army*] .... TRAD
Training Requirements Analysis Model (MCD) .... TRAMOD
Training Requirements Analysis System [*Army*] .... TRAS
Training Requirements and Information Management System [*Navy*] .... TRIM
Training Requirements and Information Management System (MCD) .... TRIMS
Training Requirements and Planning Subsystem [*Military*] ...... TRAPS
Training Research and Development (IAA) .... TRAD
Training Research Laboratory [*Army Research Institute for the Behavioral and
   Social Sciences*] (RDA) .... TRL
Training Reservation System (MCD) .... TRS
Training Review File [*IRS*] .... TRRF
Training Review Panel (CAAL) .... TRP
Training School (DAVI) .... TS
[*The*] Training School at Vineland [*An association*] (EA) .... TTS
Training Services [*Navy*] (NVT) .... TNGSVCS
Training Services [*Job Training and Partnership Act*] (OICC) .... TSS
Training Services Agency [*Department of Employment*] [*British*] .... TSA
Training Set, Fire Observation (MCD) .... TSFO
Training Set, Forward Observer [*Army*] .... TSFO
Training Ship .... TS
Training Simulator Control Panel [*NASA*] (MCD) .... TSCP
Training Simulators Engineering Department .... TSED
Training Site Manager (MCD) .... TSM
Training Site Requirements Study [*DoD*] .... TSRS
Training Situation Analysis [*Navy*] .... TSA

Training Squadron [*Later, SERRON*] [*Navy*] .... TRAINRON
Training Squadron .... TRARON
Training Squadron [*British military*] (DMA) .... TS
Training Squadron [*Navy symbol*] (NVT) .... VT
Training Standards Advisory Service (AIE) .... TSAS
Training Station [*Navy*] .... TRASTA
Training Subject .... TngS
Training Submarine [*Navy symbol*] .... SST
Training Subsystem (MCD) .... TSS
Training Subsystem Effectiveness Analysis .... TSEA
Training Support [*Navy*] (NVT) .... TNGSUP
Training Support Activity - Europe (MCD) .... TSAE
Training Support Activity - Korea (MCD) .... TSAK
Training Support Agency [*Army*] .... TSA
Training Support Center [*Army*] (MCD) .... TSC
Training Support Requirements [*Military*] .... TSR
Training Support Requirements Analysis (MCD) .... TSRA
Training Support Service [*ILO*] [*United Nations*] (DUND) .... TSS
Training Support Working Group [*Army*] .... TSWG
Training Surface-to-Air Missile .... TSAM
Training System Manager (MCD) .... TSM
Training System Procurement Package .... TSPP
Training System Program Requirements (MCD) .... TSPR
Training System Requirements Analysis (DOMA) .... TRSA
Training System Resource Management Plan [*Army*] ...... TSRMP
Training System Test and Evaluation (MCD) .... TSTE
Training Task Force .... TTF
Training Task Indentification Guide .... TTIG
Training Taxpayer Information File [*IRS*] .... TTIF
Training Technology Centers [*Army*] .... TTC
Training Technology Field Activity [*Army*] .... TTFA
Training Technology Transfer Act of 1984 (WYGK) .... TTTA
Training Test Support Package [*Army*] .... TTSP
Training Text .... TT
Training, Transient and Patient .... TT & P
Training Unit [*Army*] .... TU
Training with Industry Program [*Army*] (RDA) .... TWI
Training-Related Expenses [*Work Incentive Program*] .... TRE
Training-Testing Intervals .... TTI
Trainmaster [*Railroading*] .... TM
Trains Inertial Navigation System (IAA) .... TINS
Train-the-Trainer [*Army*] .... T_3
Trait Evaluation Index [*Psychology*] .... TEI
Traite de Grammaire Syriaque [*A publication*] (BJA) .... TGS
Traitement Automatique des Donnees [*Automatic Data Processing*]
   [*French*] .... TAD
Traitement Electronique des Donnees [*Electronic Data Processing - EDP*]
   [*French*] .... TED
Traitement Industrial des Gadoues [*French company*] .... TRIGA
Traitement Integral des Galaxies par l'Etude de leurs Raies [*An integral field
   spectrograph*] .... TIGER
Traitement Integre des Donnees [*Integrated Data Processing - IDP*]
   [*French*] .... TID
Trajectory (AABC) .... TJ
Trajectory (AAG) .... TRAJ
Trajectory Accuracy Prediction System [*Air Force*] .... TAPS
Trajectory Analysis Program (MCD) .... TAP
Trajectory Analysis Room [*NASA*] (KSC) .... TAR
Trajectory and Guidance Data .... TGD
Trajectory Application Method (MCD) .... TAM
Trajectory Chart .... TJC
Trajectory Correction Maneuver .... TCM
Trajectory Determination and Acquisition Computation .... TRADAC
Trajectory Diagram [*Army*] (MCD) .... TD
Trajectory Diagram .... TJD
Trajectory Engineer .... TE
Trajectory Error Analysis Program [*NASA*] .... TEAP
Trajectory Incremental Correction System (MCD) .... TRICS
Trajectory Integration (CAAL) .... TI
Trajectory Integration Program (PDAA) .... TRIP
Trajectory Optimization and Linearized Pitch [*Computer program*] .... TOLIP
Trajectory Optimization Program for Comparing Advanced Technology
   (MCD) .... TOPCAT
Trajectory/Parametric Study (SAA) .... TRAJ/PS
Trajectory Velocity RADAR (MCD) .... TVR
Trajectory-Sensitive Arming Device (SAA) .... TSAD
Trak Auto [*NASDAQ symbol*] (TTSB) .... TRKA
Trak-Auto Corp. [*Associated Press*] (SAG) .... TrakAu
Trak-Auto Corp. [*NASDAQ symbol*] (NQ) .... TRKA
Trakehner Breed Association and Registry of America [*Defunct*] (EA) ..... TBARA
Tramford International Ltd. [*NASDAQ symbol*] (SAG) .... TRFD
Tramford International Ltd. [*NASDAQ symbol*] (SAG) .... TRFW
Tramford International Ltd. [*Associated Press*] (SAG) .... Trmfrd
Tramiel Operating System [*Atari, Inc.*] .... TOS
Tramp Power Supply .... TPS
Tramson Ltd. [*Sudan*] [*ICAO designator*] (FAAC) .... TRR
Tramway (ROG) .... TR
Tramway and Light Railway Society [*British*] (BI) .... TLRS
[*The*] Tramway Museum Society [*British*] (DCTA) .... TMS
Trane Air Conditioning Economics [*The Trane Co.*] .... TRACE
Trang [*Thailand*] [*Airport symbol*] (OAG) .... TST
Trang [*Thailand*] [*ICAO location identifier*] (ICLI) .... VTST
Tranquility Base [*Moon landing site*] .... TB
Tranquilize(r) [*Pharmacology*] (DAVI) .... tranq
Tranquillo [*Quietly*] [*Music*] (ROG) .... TRANQ

Trans [*Chemical conformation*] .... t
Trans Air Bretagne [*France ICAO designator*] (FAAC) .... TRB
Trans Air Charter, Inc. [*ICAO designator*] (FAAC) .... TRC
Trans Air Valtologia [*Moldova*] [*ICAO designator*] (FAAC) .... VLG
Trans Air Welwitchia [*Angola*] [*FAA designator*] (FAAC) .... TWW
Trans Am [*Model of automobile*] .... TA
Trans Am Club USA (EA) .... TCUSA
Trans Am Compania Ltda. [*Ecuador*] [*ICAO designator*] (FAAC) .... RTM
Trans America Airlines, Inc. [*ICAO designator*] (FAAC) .... TVA
Trans America Industries [*Vancouver Stock Exchange symbol*] .... TSA
Trans American Airways, Inc. [*ICAO designator*] (FAAC) .... CLR
Trans Arabian Air Transport [*Sudan*] [*ICAO designator*] (FAAC) .... TRT
Trans Asian Resources [*Vancouver Stock Exchange symbol*] .... TAQ
Trans Atlantic Resources, Inc. [*Vancouver Stock Exchange symbol*] .... TAT
Trans Border Energy [*Vancouver Stock Exchange symbol*] .... TBD
Trans Canada Glass Ltd. [*Toronto Stock Exchange symbol Vancouver Stock Exchange symbol*] .... TCG
Trans Canada Options [*Stock exchange network of VSE, TSE, and MSE*] .... TCO
Trans Catalina Airlines [*ICAO designator*] (AD) .... DC
Trans Continental Air Transport [*Air carrier designation symbol*] .... TCAX
Trans Continental Airlines [*ICAO designator*] (FAAC) .... TCN
Trans Energy [*NASDAQ symbol*] (TTSB) .... TSRG
Trans Energy, Inc. [*Associated Press*] (SAG) .... TrnsEn
Trans Energy, Inc. [*NASDAQ symbol*] (SAG) .... TSRG
Trans Equatorial Propagation .... TEP
Trans European Airways [*Belgium ICAO designator*] (FAAC) .... TEA
Trans European Airways [*Switzerland ICAO designator*] (FAAC) .... TSW
Trans European Airways SA [*France ICAO designator*] (FAAC) .... TFR
Trans European Policy Studies Association (EA) .... TEPSA
Trans Fatty Acids .... TFA
Trans Financial [*NASDAQ symbol*] (TTSB) .... TRFI
Trans Financial Bancorp, Inc. [*Bowling Green, KY*] [*NASDAQ symbol*] (NQ) .... TRFI
Trans Financial, Inc. [*Associated Press*] (SAG) .... TrnsFin
Trans Global Airlines [*FAA*] (TAG) .... TGA
Trans Global Services, Inc. [*NASDAQ symbol*] (SAG) .... TGSI
Trans Global Services, Inc. [*Associated Press*] (SAG) .... TrnGlb
Trans Global Services, Inc. [*Associated Press*] (SAG) .... TrnsGlbl
Trans Global Svcs [*NASDAQ symbol*] (TTSB) .... TGSI
Trans Global Svcs Wrrt [*NASDAQ symbol*] (TTSB) .... TGSIW
Trans Golgi Network [*Cytology*] .... TGN
Trans International Airlines [*ICAO designator*] (FAAC) .... TIA
Trans International Airlines [*Air carrier designation symbol*] .... TIAX
Trans International Airlines .... TRIN
Trans International Gold [*Vancouver Stock Exchange symbol*] .... TNI
Trans Island Air [*Barbados*] [*ICAO designator*] (FAAC) .... TRD
Trans Jamaican Airlines Ltd. [*ICAO designator*] (FAAC) .... JQA
Trans Korea Pipeline .... TKP
Trans Leasing International, Inc. [*Northbrook, IL*] [*NASDAQ symbol*] (NQ) .... TLII
Trans Leasing International, Inc. [*Associated Press*] (SAG) .... TrnLsg
Trans Leasing Intl. [*NASDAQ symbol*] (TTSB) .... TLII
Trans Mediterranean [*ICAO designator*] (AD) .... TL
Trans Mediterranean Airlines [*Lebanon*] [*ICAO designator*] (FAAC) .... TMA
Trans Midwest Airlines, Inc. [*ICAO designator*] (FAAC) .... TMT
Trans Mo Airlines [*ICAO designator*] (AD) .... XU
Trans Mountain Airlines [*ICAO designator*] (AD) .... OW
Trans Mountain Pipe Line Co. Ltd. [*Toronto Stock Exchange symbol Vancouver Stock Exchange symbol*] .... TMP
Trans Mountain Pipe Line Co. Ltd., Vancouver, British Columbia [*Library symbol National Library of Canada*] (NLC) .... BVATM
Trans New York [*ICAO designator*] (AD) .... YH
Trans North Turbo Air Ltd. [*Canada ICAO designator*] (FAAC) .... TNT
Trans Oceanic Airways Ltd. [*British*] .... TOA
Trans Pennsylvania Airlines [*ICAO designator*] (AD) .... PF
Trans Quebec & Maritimes, Montreal, Quebec [*Library symbol National Library of Canada*] (NLC) .... QMTQM
Trans Rampart Industry [*Vancouver Stock Exchange symbol*] .... TPS
Trans Service Airlift [*Zaire*] [*ICAO designator*] (FAAC) .... TSR
Trans Siberian Landbridge (DS) .... TSL
Trans States Airlines, Inc. [*ICAO designator*] (FAAC) .... LOF
Trans Tasman Recognition Arrangement for Qualifications and Skills [*Australia*] .... TRAQS
Trans Unsaturated Fatty Acids .... TUFA
Trans West African Airlines Ltd. [*Gambia*] [*ICAO designator*] (FAAC) .... TWS
Trans Western Airlines of Utah [*ICAO designator*] (FAAC) .... TRW
Trans Western Airlines of Utah [*ICAO designator*] (AD) .... WZ
Trans Wings AS [*Norway ICAO designator*] (FAAC) .... TWG
Trans World Airlines [*Associated Press*] (SAG) .... TWA
Trans World Airlines, Inc. [*ICAO designator*] .... TW
Trans World Airlines, Inc. [*Humorously interpreted as "Try Walking Across" and "Teeny Weeny Airlines"*] [*AMEX symbol*] (SPSG) .... TWA
Trans World Airlines, Inc. [*ICAO designator*] (FAAC) .... TWA
Trans World Airlines Wrrt [*AMEX symbol*] (TTSB) .... TWA.WS
Trans World Entertainment [*Movie production*] .... TWE
Trans World Entertainment [*NASDAQ symbol*] (TTSB) .... TWMC
Trans World Entertainment Corp. [*Associated Press*] (SAG) .... TrnWEnt
Trans World Entertainment Corp. [*NASDAQ symbol*] (NQ) .... TWMC
Trans World Express, Inc. [*ICAO designator*] (FAAC) .... RBD
Trans World Gaming [*NASDAQ symbol*] (TTSB) .... IBET
Trans World Gaming Corp. [*NASDAQ symbol*] (SAG) .... IBET
Trans World Gaming Corp. [*Associated Press*] (SAG) .... TW Gam
Trans World Gaming Wrrt [*NASDAQ symbol*] (TTSB) .... IBETW
Trans World News Service (NTCM) .... TWNS
Trans World Radio Pacific [*Guam*] (FEA) .... TWR
Transabdominal Hysterectomy [*Medicine*] (MAE) .... TAH
TRANSAC [*Transistorized Automatic Computer*] **Assembler Compiler** .... TAC
TRANSAC [*Transistorized Automatic Computer*] **Users Group** .... TUG
TransAct Technologies .... TACT
TransAct Technologies Inc. [*NASDAQ symbol*] (SAG) .... TACT
TransAct Technologies Inc. [*Associated Press*] (SAG) .... TransAct
Trans-Acting Responsive Sequence [*Genetics*] .... TAR
Transaction .... T
Transaction .... TR
Transaction .... TRAN
Transaction .... TRANS
Transaction (MSA) .... TRANSA
Transaction .... TRX
Transaction, Accounting, Control, and Endorsing (PDAA) .... TRACE
Transaction Application Drive [*Computer Technology, Inc.*] .... TAD
Transaction Application Language [*Computer science*] (MHDB) .... TAL
Transaction Application Program [*Computer science*] .... TAP
Transaction Area (IAA) .... TAR
Transaction Code [*Military*] .... TC
Transaction Control and Encoding (IAA) .... TRACE
Transaction Control System [*Hitachi Ltd.*] .... TCS
Transaction Cost Estimator (MHDI) .... TCE
Transaction Data Recorder (DNAB) .... TRADAR
Transaction Definition Language .... TDL
Transaction Diaries [*Bureau of the Census*] (GFGA) .... TD
Transaction Distribution System .... TDS
Transaction Driven (IAA) .... TD
Transaction Driven System [*Honeywell, Inc.*] .... TDS
Transaction Exception Code [*Military*] (AFIT) .... TEX
Transaction Executive (IAA) .... TRANEX
Transaction Facility .... TAF
Transaction Flow Auditing (ADA) .... TFA
Transaction Formatting Routines .... TFR
Transaction Forwarding System [*Computer science*] .... TFS
Transaction Identification Code [*Military*] (AFIT) .... TIC
Transaction Identification Code [*Military*] (AFIT) .... TRIC
Transaction Identification Number (AFM) .... TIN
Transaction Information Systems .... TIS
Transaction Interface Package [*Sperry UNIVAC*] [*Computer science*] .... TIP
Transaction Interface Processor .... TIP
Transaction Interpretation (MCD) .... TI
Transaction Item Report [*Navy*] (NG) .... TIR
Transaction Item Reporting / Serial Lot Item Tracking [*Navy*] (DNAB) .... TIR/SLIT
Transaction Language .... TL
Transaction Listing (AFM) .... TL
Transaction Log Analysis .... TLA
Transaction Management System (BUR) .... TMS
Transaction Manager [*Computer science*] .... TM
Transaction Mode (IAA) .... TM
Transaction Monitoring Facility [*Tandem Computers*] .... TMF
Transaction Network Service [*AT & T*] .... TNS
Transaction Network Service Planning Model [*Telecommunications*] (TEL) .... TRANSPLAN
Transaction Network Services [*NASDAQ symbol*] (SAG) .... TNSI
Transaction Network Services [*Associated Press*] (SAG) .... TrnNtw
Transaction Network Svcs [*NASDAQ symbol*] (TTSB) .... TNSI
Transaction Processing [*Computer science*] .... TP
Transaction Processing [*Computer science*] .... TRAN-PRO
Transaction Processing Application Service Element [*Telecommunications*] (OSI) .... TP-ASE
Transaction Processing Applications Program (MHDI) .... TPAP
Transaction Processing Executive (MCD) .... TPE
Transaction Processing Facility (HGAA) .... TPF
Transaction Processing Management System (NITA) .... TPMS
Transaction Processing Performance Council (EA) .... TPC
Transaction Processing Performance Council (BTTJ) .... TPPC
Transaction Processing Service Element [*Telecommunications*] .... TPSE
Transaction Processing Service User [*Telecommunications*] .... TPSU
Transaction Processing System [*Trademark of Software Consulting Service, Inc.*] .... TPS
Transaction Program [*Computer science*] (BYTE) .... TP
Transaction Provider (WDMC) .... TP
Transaction Record .... TR
Transaction Reporting and Control System (MCD) .... TRAC
Transaction Routing and Form Formatting in COBOL [*Common Business-Oriented Language*] [*Computer science*] (MHDI) .... TRAFFIC
Transaction Routing Index .... TRI
Transaction Services (MCD) .... TS
Transaction Step Task .... TST
Transaction Sys Architects'A' [*NYSE symbol*] (TTSB) .... TSAI
Transaction System Architects, Inc. [*Associated Press*] (SAG) .... TrnSyA
Transaction Systems Architects, Inc. [*NASDAQ symbol*] (SAG) .... TSAI
Transaction Technology, Inc., Technical Library, Los Angeles, CA [*OCLC symbol*] (OCLC) .... CTR
Transaction Terminal (BUR) .... TT
Transaction Terminal System (NITA) .... TTS
Transaction Tracking System (PCM) .... TTS
Transaction Work Area .... TWA
Transactional Analysis [*System of psychotherapy developed by Eric Berne, MD*] .... TA
Transactional Analysis Control Technique [*Training program*] [*American Airlines*] .... TACT
Transactional Analysis Life Position Survey [*Psychology*] .... TALPS
Transactional Analysis of Personality and Environment [*Psychology*] (AEBS) .... TAPE
Transactional Analysis Systems Institute .... TASI

Transactional Document Recorder (NITA) .... TDR
Transaction-Oriented Operating System (IAA) .... TOOS
Transactions and Proceedings. Royal Society of South Australia
  [*A publication*] .... Trans & Proc Roy Soc SA
Transactions and Proceedings. Royal Society of Victoria [*Australia A
  publication*] .... Trans & Proc Roy Soc Vic
Transactions. Australian Medical Congress
  [*A publication*] .... Trans Aust Med Congress
Transactions by Others [*Military*] .... TBO
Transactions Editorial Executive Committee (ACII) .... TEEC
Transactions for Others [*Military*] .... TFO
Transactions. Geological Society of South Africa [*A publication*] .... TGSSA
Transactions. Grotius Society [*England*] [*A publication*] (DLA) .... Grot Soc'y
Transactions. Historical Society of Ghana [*A publication*] .... THSG
Transactions. Institution of Engineers of Australia
  [*A publication*] .... Trans Instn Eng Aust
Transactions. International Congress of Orientalists [*A publication*]
  (BJA) .... TICO
Transactions. International Law Association [*1873-1924*] [*A publication*]
  (DLA) .... Trans ILA
Transactions. Medico-Legal Society [*A publication*] (ILCA) .... Med Leg Soc Trans
Transactions of the American Association of Electrical Engineers
  (IAA) .... TRANSAIEE
Transactions of the High Court of Chancery (Tothill's Reports)
  [*A publication*] (DLA) .... Tr Ch
Transactions of the Society of Biblical Archaeology [*London*]
  [*A publication*] (BJA) .... TSBA
Transactions on Database Systems .... TODS
Transactions on Mathematical Software .... TOMS
Transactions on Programming Languages and Systems (MCD) .... TOPLAS
Transactions per Second .... TPS
Transactions. Philosophical Institute of Victoria [*Australia A
  publication*] .... Trans Phil Inst Vic
Transactions. Philosophical Society of New South Wales [*Australia A
  publication*] .... Trans Phil Soc NSW
Transactions. Queensland Philosophical Society [*Australia A
  publication*] .... Trans Qld Phil Soc
Transactions. Royal Society of New South Wales [*Australia A
  publication*] .... Trans Roy Soc NSW
Transactions. Royal Society of South Australia
  [*A publication*] .... Trans Roy Soc SA
Transactions. Society of Biblical Archaeology [*London*] [*A publication*]
  (BJA) .... TransSBA
Trans-Activator [*Genetics*] .... TAT
Trans-Activator Response Element [*Genetics*] .... TAR
Transactivator-Responsive Region [*Genetics*] .... TAR
Transaero Airlines [*Former USSR ICAO designator*] (FAAC) .... TSO
TransAfrica Forum (EA) .... TF
Transair France [*ICAO designator*] (FAAC) .... TSA
Trans-Air Link Corp. [*ICAO designator*] (FAAC) .... GJB
Transair Mali SA [*ICAO designator*] (FAAC) .... TSM
Trans-Air Services Ltd. [*Nigeria*] [*ICAO designator*] (FAAC) ...... TSN
Trans-Alaska Pipeline .... TAP
Trans-Alaska Pipeline .... TAPLINE
Trans-Alaska Pipeline Authorization Act .... TAPA
Trans-Alaska Pipeline Liability Fund .... TAPLF
Trans-Alaska Pipeline System [*Department of Energy*] .... TAPS
Trans-Alaskan Pipeline [*Marine science*] (OSRA) .... TAPS
Trans-Alaskan Pipeline (USDC) .... TAPS
Transaldolase [*An enzyme*] (AAMN) .... TA
Transaldolase [*An enzyme*] (MAE) .... TRA
Transall-Normen (MCD) .... TAN
TransAlpine [*Pipeline*] [*Western Europe*] .... TAL
Transalsace [*France*] [*FAA designator*] (FAAC) .... TAS
Transalta Corp. [*TS symbol*] (TTSB) .... TA
Transalta Resources Corp. [*Toronto Stock Exchange symbol*] ...... TA
Transalta Utilities, Calgary, AB, Canada [*Library symbol Library of
  Congress*] (LCLS) .... CaACTU
Transalta Utilities, Calgary, Alberta [*Library symbol National Library of
  Canada*] (NLC) .... ACTU
Transalta Utilities Corp. [*Toronto Stock Exchange symbol*] .... TAU
Transamerica [*ICAO designator*] (AD) .... TV
Transamerica 8.50% Dep Pfd [*NYSE symbol*] (TTSB) .... TAPrD
Transamerica Corp. [*NYSE symbol*] (SPSG) .... TA
Transamerica Corp. [*Associated Press*] (SAG) .... Transm
Transamerica Corp. [*Associated Press*] (SAG) .... Trnsm
Transamerica Del L.P.'MIPS' [*NYSE symbol*] (TTSB) .... TAPrA
Transamerica Delaware Ltd. [*NYSE symbol*] (SAG) .... TA
Transamerica Delaware Ltd. [*Associated Press*] (SAG) .... TrnDE
Transamerica Electronic Scoring Technique [*Credit risk evaluation*] .... TEST
Transamerica Income Shares, Inc. [*NYSE symbol*] (SPSG) ...... TAI
Transamerica Income Shares, Inc. [*Associated Press*] (SAG) ...... TranInc
TransAmerica Inc. Shrs [*NYSE symbol*] (TTSB) .... TAI
TransAmerica Solar Auto Run [*In name of solar-powered car TSAR
  Phoenix*] .... TSAR
Trans-American Airline .... TAA
Transamerican Trailer Transport .... TTT
Transamerican Waste Inds Wrrt'A' [*NASDAQ symbol*] (TTSB) .... WSTEW
Transamerican Waste Inds Wrrt'B' [*NASDAQ symbol*] (TTSB) .... WSTEZ
TransAmerican Waste Indus [*NASDAQ symbol*] (TTSB) .... WSTE
TransAmerican Waste Industries [*Associated Press*] (SAG) .... TrnsWste
TransAmerican Waste Industries, Inc. [*Associated Press*] (SAG) ...... TA Wst
TransAmerican Waste Industries, Inc. [*Associated Press*] (SAG) ...... TrnsWst
TransAmerican Waste Industries, Inc. [*NASDAQ symbol*] (SAG) ...... WSTE
Trans-Aminocrotonic Acid [*Also, TACA*] [*Organic chemistry*] .... TAC

Trans-Aminocrotonic Acid [*Also, TAC*] [*Organic chemistry*] .... TACA
Transannular Patch [*Cardiology*] .... TP
Trans-Antarctic Association [*British*] .... TAA
Transantarctic Expedition (ADA) .... TAE
Transantarctic Mountains .... TAM
Transantral [*Medicine*] (AAMN) .... TA
Trans-Arabian Investment Bank (MENA) .... TAIB
Trans-Arabian Pipeline .... TAPLINE
Transatlantic (SSD) .... TAL
Trans-Atlantic [*Aviation*] (FAAC) .... TSATLC
Transatlantic Air Safety Service Organization .... TASSO
Trans-Atlantic Airlines Ltd. [*Gambia*] [*ICAO designator*] (FAAC) ...... TGL
Transatlantic Book Service [*British*] .... TABS
Transatlantic Brides and Parents Association (EA) .... TBPA
Transatlantic Broadcasting Co. [*In TV series "W.E.B."*] .... TAB
Transatlantic Carriers Ltd. [*Steamship line*] (MHDW) .... TCL
Trans-Atlantic Geotraverse [*Project*] [*National Oceanic and Atmospheric
  Administration*] .... TAG
Transatlantic Geotraverse [*Geology*] .... TAG
Transatlantic Holdings [*NYSE symbol*] (SPSG) .... TRH
Transatlantic Holdings [*Associated Press*] (SAG) .... TrnatH
Transatlantic Landing .... TAL
Trans-Atlantic Passenger Steamship Conference [*Later, IPSA*] (EA) .... TAPSC
Transatlantic Telecommunications 8 (NITA) .... TAT 8
Transatlantic Telephone [*Cable*] .... TAT
Transatlantic Telephone Cable (IEEE) .... TATC
Transatlantic Training Exercise (MCD) .... TRANSLANTEX
Trans-Atlantic Universities Speech Association .... TAUSA
Transatmospheric Vehicle [*Proposed futuristic plane capable of flying at
  hypersonic speeds*] .... TAV
Trans-Australia Airlines (ADA) .... TAA
Trans-Australia Airlines [*ICAO designator*] (AD) .... TN
Transavia Holland BV [*Netherlands ICAO designator*] (FAAC) ...... TRA
Transavia Ltd. [*Romania*] [*FAA designator*] (FAAC) .... IRS
Transavia (Pty) Ltd. [*South Africa ICAO designator*] (FAAC) ...... TRV
Transaviaexport [*Belarus*] [*ICAO designator*] (FAAC) .... TXC
Transaviation, SA [*Spain*] [*FAA designator*] (FAAC) .... TVT
Transaxel Fluid (IAA) .... TAF
Transborder Data Flows [*Also, TDF*] [*Telecommunications*] ...... TBDF
Transborder Data Flows [*Also, TBDF*] [*Telecommunications*] ...... TDF
Transbrasil [*ICAO designator*] (AD) .... TR
Transbrasil SA Linhas Aereas [*Brazil ICAO designator*] (ICDA) .... QD
Transbrasil SA Linhas Aereas [*Brazil*] [*ICAO designator*] (FAAC) ...... TBA
Transbronchial Aspiration Needle [*Medicine*] (DMAA) .... TBAN
Transbronchial Biopsy [*Medicine*] .... TBB
Transbronchial Lung Biopsy [*Medicine*] (DMAA) .... TBLB
Transbronchial Lung Brush [*Medicine*] (DAVI) .... TBLB
Transbronchial Needle Aspiration [*Medicine*] (DMAA) .... TBNA
Trans-California [*ICAO designator*] (AD) .... ZO
Trans-Canada Airlines [*Facetious translation: "Two Crashes Apiece"*] ...... TCA
TransCanada Computer Communications Network (IAA) .... TCCN
Trans-Canada Highway .... TCH
TransCanada Pipeline Ltd. [*Associated Press*] (SAG) .... TrCda
TransCanada Pipeline Ltd. [*NYSE symbol Toronto Stock Exchange symbol
  Vancouver Stock Exchange symbol*] (SPSG) .... TRP
TransCanada Pipeline Ltd. Capital [*Associated Press*] (SAG) ...... TCdaC
TransCanada Pipeline Ltd. Capital [*NYSE symbol*] (SAG) .... TCL
Trans-Canada Pipelines, Calgary, AB, Canada [*Library symbol Library of
  Congress*] (LCLS) .... CaACTCP
Trans-Canada Pipelines, Calgary, Alberta [*Library symbol National Library of
  Canada*] (NLC) .... ACTCP
TransCanada Pipelines Ltd. [*Commercial firm*] .... TCPL
TransCanada P.L. [*NYSE symbol*] (TTSB) .... TRP
Trans-Canada Resources Ltd. [*Toronto Stock Exchange symbol*] ...... TCO
TransCanada Telephone System [*Later, Telecom Canada*] (TSSD) ...... TCS
Trans-Canada Telephone System (MCD) .... TCTS
TransCanada Telephone System, Ottawa, ON, Canada [*Library symbol
  Library of Congress*] (LCLS) .... CaOOTCT
TransCanada Telephone System, Ottawa, Ontario [*Library symbol National
  Library of Canada*] (NLC) .... OOTCT
Transcapillary Escape Rate .... TER
Transcapillary Escape Route [*Medicine*] (DAVI) .... TER
Transcarga SA [*Costa Rica*] [*ICAO designator*] (FAAC) .... TDA
Transcaribbean (MCD) .... TRC
Trans-Caribbean Airways (IIA) .... TCA
Transcaribe [*Airline*] [*Colorado*] .... TABA
Transcarpathian Yiddish (BJA) .... TCpY
Transcatheter Arterial Embolization [*Medicine*] .... TAE
Transcatheter Hepatic Artery Embolization [*Medicine*] .... THAE
Transcaucasian Soviet Federation Socialist Republic .... TSFSR
Transceiver .... T/R
Transceiver (AABC) .... TCR
Transceiver (CET) .... TCVR
Transceiver (CET) .... TRCVR
Transceiver (AAG) .... XCVR
Transceiver Code [*Navy*] .... TC
Transceiver Transmitter Receiver (IAA) .... TRCVR
Transcend Services [*NASDAQ symbol*] (TTSB) .... TRCR
Transcend Services, Inc. [*Associated Press*] (SAG) .... Transcnd
Transcend Services, Inc. [*NASDAQ symbol*] (SAG) .... TRCR
Transcendental Meditation .... TM
Transcendental Network [*Centram Systems West, Inc.*] [*Berkeley, CA*]
  [*Telecommunications*] (TSSD) .... TOPS
Trans-Central [*ICAO designator*] (AD) .... ZM
Transcerebral Electrotherapy .... TCET

Transcervical Endometrial Resection [*Medicine*] .... TCRE
Trans-Charter [*Former USSR*] [*FAA designator*] (FAAC) .... TCH
TRANS-CIS Commodities [*Monte Carlo*] (ECON) .... TCC
Transcisco Indus [*AMEX symbol*] (TTSB) .... TNI
Transcisco Industries [*AMEX symbol*] (SPSG) .... TNI
Transcisco Industries [*Associated Press*] (SAG) .... Transcis
Transcobalamin [*Biochemistry*] .... TC
Transcolombiana de Aviacion SA [*Colombia*] [*ICAO designator*] (FAAC) .... TVN
Trans-Colorado [*ICAO designator*] (AD) .... VJ
Trans-Colorado Airlines, Inc. [*ICAO designator*] (FAAC) .... TCE
Transcom International Ltd. [*Associated Press*] (SAG) .... Transcm
Transcom International Ltd. [*NASDAQ symbol*] (SAG) .... TRIX
TRANSCOM [*Transportation Command*] **Siting and Readiness** [*Model*] .... TSAR
Transcona Public Library, Manitoba [*Library symbol National Library of Canada*] (NLC) .... MT
Transcona Public Library, Transcona, MB, Canada [*Library symbol Library of Congress*] (LCLS) .... CaMT
Transcontinental (DOAD) .... TC
Transcontinental (MCD) .... TRANSCON
Transcontinental Air Transport .... TAT
Transcontinental & Western Airlines [*Later, Trans World Airlines, Inc.*] .... TWA
Transcontinental Ballistic Missile [*Air Force*] .... TCBM
Transcontinental Control Area [*Aviation*] (DA) .... TCA
Transcontinental Corps [*Amateur radio*] .... TCC
Transcontinental Dislocation Zone [*Geology*] .... TDZ
Trans-Continental Freight Bureau .... TCFB
Trans-Continental Freight Bureau, Chicago IL [*STAC*] .... TCB
Transcontinental Gas Pipe Line Corp., Houston, TX [*Library symbol Library of Congress*] (LCLS) .... TxHTC
Transcontinental Geophysical Survey (NOAA) .... TGS
Trans-Continental Railroad Passenger Association [*Defunct*] (EA) .... TCRPA
Transcontinental Realty Investors [*NYSE symbol*] (SPSG) .... TCI
Transcontinental Realty Investors [*Associated Press*] (SAG) .... TrnsRty
Transcontinental Resources [*Vancouver Stock Exchange symbol*] .... TR
Transcontinental Rlty [*NYSE symbol*] (TTSB) .... TCI
Trans-Continental Weighing and Inspection Bureau .... T-CW & IB
Transcor Waste Services [*NASDAQ symbol*] (TTSB) .... TRCW
Transcor Waste Services, Inc. [*Associated Press*] (SAG) .... Transcor
Transcor Waste Services, Inc. [*NASDAQ symbol*] (SAG) .... TRCW
Transcorp Airways [*British ICAO designator*] (FAAC) .... TCP
Transcranial Color-Coded Doppler [*Medicine*] (DMAA) .... TCCD
Transcranial Color-Coded Sonography [*Medicine*] (DMAA) .... TCCS
Transcranial Magnetic Stimulation [*Proposed therapy for depression*] .... TMS
Transcribe (IAA) .... TRANSC
Transcribe (MSA) .... TRSCB
Transcribed .... TRANSCR
Transcribed Weather Broadcast .... TWEB
Transcriber (MSA) .... TRSBR
Transcribing (MSA) .... TRSBG
Transcript (DLA) .... Tr
Transcript (ADA) .... TRANS
Transcript Appeals [*New York*] [*1867-68*] [*A publication*] (DLA) .... Tr App
Transcript Appeals [*New York*] [*1867-68*] [*A publication*] (DLA) .... Trans Ap
Transcript Appeals [*New York*] [*A publication*] (DLA) .... Trans App
Transcript Appeals [*New York*] [*A publication*] (DLA) .... Transc A
Transcript Appeals [*New York*] [*A publication*] (DLA) .... Transcr A
Transcript of Absentee's Account .... TAA
Transcript of Data Extraction (DNAB) .... TODE
Transcript of Data Extraction System (MCD) .... TODES
Transcript/Video Index [*A publication*] .... TVI
Transcription .... T
Transcription (IAA) .... TRANSC
Transcription (ROG) .... TRANSCRON
Transcription Activating Protein [*Biochemistry*] .... TAP
Transcription Activation Function [*Genetics*] .... TAF
Transcription Factor [*Genetics*] .... TF
Transcription Factor Database (EERA) .... TFD
Transcription Termination Factor [*Genetics*] .... TTF
Transcription-Coupled Repair [*Genetics*] .... TCR
Transcription-Repair Coupling Factor [*Genetics*] .... TRCF
Transcrypt International, Inc. [*NASDAQ symbol*] (SAG) .... TRII
Transcrypt International, Inc. [*Associated Press*] (SAG) .... Trscrypt
Transcultural Mental Health Centre [*Australia*] .... TMHC
Transcutaneous .... TC
Transcutaneous Carbon Dioxide [*Monitor*] [*Medicine*] (DAVI) .... TC CO_2
Transcutaneous Cranial Electrical Stimulation [*Medicine*] .... TCES
Transcutaneous Electrical Nerve Stimulation [*Also, TES, TNS*] [*A method of pain control*] [*Medicine*] .... TENS
Transcutaneous Electrical Stimulation [*Also, TENS, TNS*] [*A method of pain control*] [*Medicine*] .... TES
Transcutaneous Endomyocardial Biopsy [*Cardiology*] (CPH) .... TEB
Transcutaneous [*Oxygen*] **Monitoring** [*Medicine*] .... TCM
Transcutaneous Nerve Stimulation [*Medicine*] (MAE) .... TCNS
Transcutaneous Nerve Stimulation [*Also, TENS, TES*] [*A method of pain control*] [*Medicine*] .... TNS
Transcutaneous Oxygen Monitor [*Laboratory Science*] (DAVI) .... TCOM
Transcutaneous Partial Pressure of Oxygen [*Monitor*] [*Medicine*] (DAVI) .... TC pO_2
Transcutaneous Random Electrical Nerve Stimulator [*Medicine*] .... TRENS
Transcutaneous Stimulation .... TCS
Transdermal (DAVI) .... TD
Transdermal Drug Delivery [*Medicine*] .... TDD
Transdermal Drug Delivery Research .... TDDR
Transdermal Estradiol [*Pharmacology*] .... TDE
Transdermal Nitroglycerine Patch [*Medicine*] .... TNG
Transdermal Therapeutic System [*Medicine*] .... TTS
Transdiaphragmatic [*Pressure*] .... Pdi
Transdihydrolisuride [*Biochemistry*] .... TDHL
Trans-Dominion Energy Corp. [*Toronto Stock Exchange symbol*] .... TDE
Transducer .... T
Transducer [*Electronics*] (IAA) .... TD
Transducer (AAG) .... XDCR
Transducer .... XDER
Transducer (AAG) .... XDR
Transducer .... XDUCER
Transducer Calibration System .... TCS
Transducer Evaluation Facility .... TRANSDEF
Transducer Excitation Unit .... TEU
Transducer Information Center (MCD) .... TIC
Transducer Kit (MCD) .... TK
Transducer Power Programmer .... TPP
Transducer Read Only Storage (IAA) .... TROS
Transducer Repair Facility .... TRF
Transducer Tubing System .... TTS
Transducers [*JETDS nomenclature*] [*Military*] (CET) .... TR
Transduodenal Pancreatic Sphincteroplasty .... TPS
Transearth (SAA) .... TE
Transearth Coast [*AEC*] .... TEC
Transearth Injection [*AEC*] .... TEI
Transearth Injection Geometry (SAA) .... TIG
Trans-East African Highway Authority (EA) .... TEAHA
Trans-Eastern Airlines Ltd. [*Kenya*] [*ICAO designator*] (FAAC) .... TRE
Transepidermal Water Loss [*Physiology*] .... TEWL
Transepidermal Water Loss [*Physiology*] (MAE) .... TWL
Transepithelial Electrical Resistance [*Cytology*] .... TER
Transept (VRA) .... trsp
Transequatorial [*Scatter*] .... TE
Transesophageal Echocardiography .... TEE
Trans-European Automated Real-Time Gross-Settlement Express Transfer [*Banking*] .... TARGET
Trans-European Exchange and Transfer Consortium (AIE) .... TEXT
Trans-European Mobility Scheme for Unversity Students [*EC*] (ECED) .... TEMPUS
Trans-European Network [*European Union*] (ECON) .... TEN
Trans-European Research and Education Networking Association [*Formed from merger of Reseaux Associes pour le Recherche Europeenne and European Academic and Research Network*] [*Internet*] .... TERENA
Trans-Europ-Express [*Continental high-speed train*] .... TEE
Trans-Europ-Express-Marchandises [*Continental high-speed train*] .... TEEM
Transfer [*Genetics*] .... t
Transfer (IAA) .... TF
Transfer .... TFER
Transfer .... TFR
Transfer (DEN) .... TR
Transfer .... TRA
Transfer (AAG) .... TRANS
Transfer (ODBW) .... trans
Transfer (VRA) .... transf
Transfer (AABC) .... TRF
Transfer (DEN) .... TRN
Transfer (KSC) .... TRNFR
Transfer .... TRNSFR
Transfer (ADA) .... TRS
Transfer (AFM) .... TSFR
Transfer (AAG) .... XFER
Transfer .... XFR
Transfer Accounting, Lodging for Investments, and Stock Management for Jobbers [*Stock exchange term British*] .... TALISMAN
Transfer Agent [*Business term*] .... TA
Transfer Agent [*Business term*] (MHDB) .... TAG
Transfer Aisle (NRCH) .... TA
Transfer Alignment Set (DNAB) .... TAS
Transfer and Accountability (IAA) .... TAA
Transfer and Automated Registration of Uncertificated Stock [*London Stock Exchange computer project*] (ECON) .... TAURUS
Transfer and Set Index (SAA) .... TSX
Transfer and Void (MCD) .... TV
Transfer Barge [*Navy symbol*] (DNAB) .... YWN
Transfer Building .... TB
Transfer Canal [*Nuclear energy*] (NRCH) .... TC
Transfer Carry Subtract .... TCS
Transfer Channel Control (IEEE) .... TCC
Transfer Charge [*Telecommunications*] (TEL) .... XFC
Transfer Chemical LASER (IEEE) .... TCL
Transfer Clerk .... TC
Transfer Control [*or Controller*] (HGAA) .... TC
Transfer Control A Register (SAA) .... TCA
Transfer Control Block .... TCB
Transfer Control Register .... TCR
Transfer Count (MHDB) .... TC
Transfer Dolly [*Bottom-loading transfer cask*] [*Nuclear energy*] (NRCH) .... TD
Transfer Effective Date [*Military*] (AFM) .... TED
Transfer Effectiveness Ratio .... TER
Transfer Factor [*Immunochemistry*] .... TF
Transfer Factor Test [*Medicine*] (DAVI) .... TFT
Transfer Fee [*Banking*] .... TF
Transfer Following Enlisted Personnel .... TRAFOLPERS
Transfer Function (AAG) .... TF
Transfer Function Analyzer .... TFA
Transfer Function Computer .... TFC

Transfer Function, Cumulative .... TFC
Transfer Function Hazard .... TFH
Transfer Function Response .... TFR
Transfer Gate (IAA) .... TG
Transfer Gear Case (MCD) .... TGC
Transfer Generator System (IAA) .... TGS
Transfer if Indicators Off (SAA) .... TIF
Transfer Impedance (IEEE) .... TI
Transfer in Channel .... TCH
Transfer in Lieu of Layoff (MCD) .... TILLO
Transfer Income Model [Department of Health and Human Services]
  (GFGA) .... TRIM
Transfer Line [Manufacturing] .... TL
Transfer Memorandum .... TM
Transfer Mold Forming (MCD) .... TMF
Transfer of Accountability .... T/A
Transfer of Control .... TOC
Transfer of Control Cancellation Message [Aviation] .... TCX
Transfer of Control Card .... TOCC
Transfer of Control Point [Aviation] (FAAC) .... TCP
Transfer of Electrostatic Images [Electrophotography] .... TESI
Transfer of Function [Military] (AFM) .... T/F
Transfer of Function (MCD) .... TOF
Transfer of Heat Reduced Magnetically .... THERMA
Transfer of Know-How Through Expatriate Nationals [Council of Scientific
  and Industrial Research] [India] .... TOKTEN
Transfer of Know-How through Expatriate Nationals [British] (DI) .... TOKTEN
Transfer of Master Scheduled Item .... TOMSI
Transfer of Pay Account [Military] .... TPA
Transfer of Program Management Responsibility .... TPMR
Transfer of Technology [Telecommunications] (TEL) .... TOT
Transfer on Channel in Operation (IAA) .... TCO
Transfer on Channel Not in Operation (SAA) .... TCN
Transfer on Death [Finance] .... TOD
Transfer on End of File (SAA) .... TEF
Transfer on Error Indication .... TEI
Transfer on Index [Telecommunications] (IAA) .... TIX
Transfer on Index High .... TXH
Transfer on Index Low (IAA) .... TXL
Transfer on Less than Zero .... TLZ
Transfer on Minus (SAA) .... TMI
Transfer on Negative .... TN
Transfer on No Index (SAA) .... TNX
Transfer on No Overflow .... TNF
Transfer on No Overflow (SAA) .... TNO
Transfer on No Zero (IAA) .... TNZ
Transfer on Nonzero .... TNZ
Transfer on Overflow (IAA) .... TOV
Transfer on Plus (SAA) .... TPL
Transfer on Positive .... TP
Transfer on Zero .... TZE
Transfer Orbit Stage [Satellite booster] .... TOS
Transfer Orbit Stage - Shortened Version [Space technology] .... TOS-S
Transfer Orbital Insertion [NASA] .... TOI
Transfer Order .... TO
Transfer Payments [Economics] .... R
Transfer Phase Final (MCD) .... TPF
Transfer Phase Midcourse [Aerospace] (MCD) .... TPM
Transfer Rate of Information BITs [Binary Digits] [Dial telephone network
  American National Standards Institute] .... TRIB
Transfer Register .... TR
Transfer Relay Rack (CAAL) .... TRR
Transfer Reset .... TR
Transfer Resistor .... TRANSISTOR
Transfer Ribonucleic Acid (CPH) .... tRNA
Transfer Scheme Handbook (AIE) .... TSH
Transfer Set .... TS
Transfer Summary Dictated [Followed by date] [Medical records] (DAVI) .... TSD
Transfer Switch .... TSW
Transfer Switch Unit (AAG) .... TSU
Transfer System C (SAA) .... TSC
Transfer to Higher Rated Job in Lieu of Layoff (MCD) .... THRILLO
Transfer Trip [Telecommunications] (IAA) .... TT
Transfer Unconditionally .... TU
Transfer Unconditionally .... TUN
Transfer Underwater Pressure Chamber (DNAB) .... TUPC
Transfer Unit (AAG) .... TU
Transfer Varnish (DGA) .... TV
Transfer Vector .... TV
Transfer Vector (NITA) .... TV
Transfer Voucher (AFM) .... TV
Transfer with Index Incremented .... TXI
Transfer Working Group (MCD) .... TWG
Transferable Account Area [Business term] (DCTA) .... TAA
Transferable Assets Program .... TAP
Transferable Atom Equivalent [Chemical modeling] .... TAE
Transferable Development Credit .... TDC
Transferable Development Rights [Community planning] .... TDR
Transferable Loan Certificate .... TLC
Transferable Loan Instrument (MHDW) .... TLI
Transferable Notice [Business term] .... TN
Transferable Revolving Underwriting Facility [Finance] (ADA) .... TRUF
Transferable Rouble [International Bank for Economic Co-Operation] (EY) .... TR
Transfer-Deoxyribonucleic Acid .... T-DNA
Transfer-In Channel (CMD) .... TIC

Transfer-Line Exchanger [Manufacturing technology] .... TLX
Transferline Heat Exchanger [Chemical engineering] .... TLE
Transfer-of-Training .... TOT
Transferred [Navy] .... T
Transferred .... TRANSF
Transferred (ROG) .... TRANSFD
Transferred (ROG) .... TRD
Transferred [Army] .... Trfd
Transferred .... TRSD
Transferred (ECII) .... XFRD
Transferred Charge Call (NITA) .... XFC
Transferred Electron Amplifier .... TEA
Transferred Electron Device [Air Force] .... TED
Transferred Electron Logic Device (IAA) .... TELD
Transferred Electron Oscillator .... TEO
Transferred on Assembly (IAA) .... TOA
Transferred to Fleet Reserve (DNAB) .... TR/FLRES
Transferred-Electron-Device Logic (MSA) .... TEDL
Transferrin [Also, TF, TRF] [Biochemistry] .... T
Transferrin [Also, T, TRF] [Biochemistry] .... TF
Transferrin [Also, T, TF] [Biochemistry] .... TRF
Transferrin Binding Protein [Biochemistry] .... TFBP
Transferrin, Common Form [or Siderophilin] (DAVI) .... TFC
Transferrin Receptor [Immunology] .... TfR
Transferrin-Bound Iron [Biochemistry] (MAE) .... Tf-Fe
Transfert de la Technologie de l'Energie dans les Batiments [Buildings
  Energy Technology Transfer Program] [Canada] .... TTEB
Trans-Fiberoptic-Photographic [Electron microscopy] .... TFP
Transfield (NSW) Pty. Ltd. [Transavia Division] [Australia ICAO aircraft
  manufacturer identifier] (ICAO) .... TN
Transfiguration .... TRANSFIG
Transfiguration Prison Ministries (EA) .... TPM
Trans-Florida Airlines, Inc. [ICAO designator] (FAAC) .... TFA
Transfluxor, Constant Board Assembly (AAG) .... T-CBA
Transfluxor Constants Matrix (AAG) .... TCM
Transform Domain .... TD
Transform Fault Effect [Geology] .... TFE
Transformation and Identification Program [Commercial & Industrial
  Development Bureau] [Software package] (NCC) .... TRIP
Transformation Definition Language [Computer science] (IBMDP) .... TDL
Transformation Line [Telecommunications] (IAA) .... TL
Transformation of Imagery [Computer science NASA] .... TRIM
Transformation Ratio .... TR
Transformation Research Network [Canada Research center] (RCD) .... TRN
Transformation Rule [Linguistics] .... T
Transformation Toughened (MCD) .... TT
Transformation Toughened Alumina (MCD) .... TTA
Transformation Toughened Zirconia [Metallurgy] .... TTZ
Transformational Grammar .... TG
Transformational Grammar Tester (IAA) .... TGT
Transformational-Generative [Linguistics] .... T-G
Transformation-Associated Protein [Biochemistry] .... TAP
Transformation-Associated Recombination [Genetics] .... TAR
Transformation-Induced Plasticity [Steel] .... TRIP
Transformation-Induced Plasticity (Steel) .... TRIPS
Transformed Mink Fibroblast [Cell line] [Laboratory science] (DAVI) .... TMF
Transformed Special Index of the External Standard [Scintillation
  analysis] .... TSIE
Transformer .... T
Transformer .... TFORMR
Transformer (DEN) .... TR
Transformer (IAA) .... TRAFO
Transformer .... TRAN
Transformer (AFM) .... TRANS
Transformer (IDOE) .... trans
Transformer (AAG) .... TRANSF
Transformer .... TRANSFRMR
Transformer .... TX
Transformer (IDOE) .... xfmr
Transformer (AAG) .... XFORMER
Transformer (IDOE) .... xformer
Transformer (AAG) .... XFRMR
Transformer (AAG) .... XMFR
Transformer Analog Computer .... TAC
Transformer Analog Polynomial Equation Solver (PDAA) .... TAPES
Transformer Design Engineer (IAA) .... TRANSFDESENGR
Transformer Differential (IAA) .... TDF
Transformer Environment Overcurrent Monitor (IEEE) .... TEOM
Transformer Interface .... XFMI
Transformer LASER (IAA) .... TRASER
Transformer Load (NASA) .... T/L
Transformer Load Management (IAA) .... TLM
Transformer Read Only Storage .... TROS
Transformerless (IAA) .... TFL
Transformer-Rectifier .... T-R
Transformer-Rectifier Unit (MCD) .... TRU
Transformers [JETDS nomenclature] [Military] (CET) .... TF
Transforming Growth Factor .... TGF
Transforming Growth Factor - Alpha .... TGF-A
Transforming Lens .... TL
Transforming Principle [Bacteriology] .... TP
Transfrigoroute International (EA) .... TI
Transfrontal (AAMN) .... TF
Transfusion [Medicine] .... T
Transfusion [Medicine] (CPH) .... Tx

Transfusion Associated	TA
Transfusion Reaction [*Medicine*]	TR
Transfusion Receptors [*Oncology*]	TR
Transgenic [*Genetics*]	TG
Trans-Global Resource NL ADR [*NASDAQ symbol*] (TTSB)	TGBRY
Trans-Global Resources NL [*NASDAQ symbol*] (NQ)	TGBR
Trans-Global Resources NL [*Associated Press*] (SAG)	TrnGlbR
Transglobe Energy [*NASDAQ symbol*] (TTSB)	TGLEF
Transglobe Energy Corp. [*NASDAQ symbol*] (SAG)	TGLE
Transglobe Energy Corp. [*Associated Press*] (SAG)	TrnsglbE
Transglobe Resources [*Vancouver Stock Exchange symbol*]	TSG
Transglutaminase [*An enzyme*]	TG
Transgranular [*Metallurgy*]	TG
Transhepatic Cholangiogram [*Medicine*]	THC
Transhepatic Embolization [*Medicine*]	THE
Trans-Hudson Orogen [*Geology*]	THO
Transhybrid Loss [*Telecommunications*] (TEL)	THL
Transhydro (AABC)	T-H
Trans-Hydroxycrotonic Acid [*Organic chemistry*]	T-HCA
Transient [*Bureau of the Census*]	T
Transient (AABC)	TRAN
Transient (AFIT)	TRANS
Transient Abnormal Q Wave [*Medicine*] (DMAA)	TAQW
Transient Abnormal Q Waves [*Medicine*] (AAMN)	TAQW
Transient Absorption Anisotropy [*Physics*]	TAA
Transient Acoustic Radiation Program	TARP
Transient Airman Quarters [*Air Force*] (AFM)	TAQ
Transient Alert (MCD)	TA
Transient Analysis Array Program	TAAP
Transient Analysis Generator	TAG
Transient and/or Steady State [*Nuclear energy*] (NRCH)	TOSS
Transient Center [*Marine Corps*]	TRANC
Transient Cerebral Ischemia [*Medicine*]	TCI
Transient Cerebral Ischemic Episode [*Medicine*] (MAE)	TCIE
Transient Circuit Analysis Program [*Computer science*]	TRACAP
Transient Combustion Chamber [*Analysis*] (MCD)	TCC
Transient Data Input Area [*Computer science*] (IAA)	TDIA
Transient Detector	TD
Transient Early Curvature [*Orthopedics*]	TEC
Transient Eddy	TE
Transient Electric Birefringence [*Physics*]	TEB
Transient Electromagnetic Pulse Emanation Standard (MCD)	TEMPEST
Transient Electro-Optic Raman Scattering [*Physics*]	TEORS
Transient Erythroblastopenia of Childhood [*Hematology*]	TEC
Transient Event [*Nuclear energy*] (NRCH)	TE
Transient Fault Locator	TFL
Transient Global Amnesia [*Medicine*]	TGA
Transient Hemispheric Attack [*Medicine*] (DAVI)	THA
Transient Hyperammonemia of Newborn [*Neonatology*] (DAVI)	THAN
Transient Hyperphosphatasemia [*Medicine*]	TH
Transient Hypogammaglobulinemia of Infancy [*Immunology*] (DAVI)	THI
Transient [*or Traveling or Traversing*] In-Core Probe [*Nuclear energy*] (NRCH)	TIP
Transient Infrared Emission Spectroscopy	TIRES
Transient Installation Confinement Facility [*Military*] (AABC)	TICF
Transient Intermodulation [*Distortion*]	TIM
Transient Ischemic Attack [*Medicine*]	TIA
Transient Ischemic Attack-Incomplete Recovery [*Cardiology*] (DAVI)	TIA-IR
Transient Ischemic Episode [*Medicine*]	TIE
Transient Late Curvature [*Orthopedics*]	TLC
Transient Load (MCD)	TL
Transient Lunar Phenomena	TLP
Transient Mass Distribution Code [*Nuclear energy*] (NRCH)	TMD
Transient Monitoring Unit (DNAB)	TRANSMONUNIT
Transient Monocular Blindness [*Medicine*]	TMB
Transient Neonatal Pustular Melanosis [*Medicine*] (MEDA)	TNPM
Transient Network Analyzer (IEEE)	TNA
Transient Nuclear Test	TNT
Transient On-State Characteristics (PDAA)	TONC
Transient or Steady-State Analysis [*Computer science*]	TOSSA
Transient Osteoporosis of Hip [*Medicine*] (DMAA)	TOH
Transient Overpower Accident [*Nuclear energy*]	TOP
Transient Peak Reverse Voltage	TPRV
Transient Personnel Unit [*Navy*] (DNAB)	TPU
Transient Photodichroism [*Physics*]	TPD
Transient Program Area	TPA
Transient Radiation Analysis by Computer (KSC)	TRAC
Transient Radiation Effect on Radiation (SAA)	TRER
Transient Radiation Effects	TRE
Transient Radiation Effects Automated Tabulation	TREAT
Transient Radiation Effects on Electronic Systems [*Air Force*] (MCD)	TREES
Transient Radiation Effects on Electronics [*Military*]	TREE
Transient Radiation Effects Recorder (MCD)	TRADER
Transient Reactor Analysis Code (NRCH)	TRAC
Transient Reactor Test Facility	TREAT
Transient Recovery Voltage (IEEE)	TRV
Transient Response (IEEE)	TR
Transient Signal Detector	TSD
Transient Source	TS
Transient State (AAG)	TS
Transient Synovitis [*Medicine*]	TS
Transient Tachypnea [*Medicine*] (DMAA)	TT
Transient Tachypnea of Newborn [*Gynecology*]	TTN
Transient Tachypnea of the Newborn [*Medicine*] (MEDA)	TTNB
Transient Temperature Control	TTC

Transient Temperature Control Instrument	TTCI
Transient Thermal Radiation	TTR
Transient Time Flowmeter [*Nuclear energy*] (NRCH)	TTF
Transient Undercooling Accident [*Nuclear energy*]	TUCA
Transient Voltage Indicator	TVI
Transient Voltage Suppressor	TVS
Transient Voltage Surge Suppression	TVSS
Transient-Mode Liquid Epitaxy	TMLE
Transients, Patients, and Prisoners [*Military*]	TPP
Transillumination	TI
Transilluminator [*Chromatography*]	TR
Transimpedance Amplifier [*Instrumentation*]	TIA
Transimpedence Receiver Circuit	TIRC
Trans-Industries, Inc. [*Associated Press*] (SAG)	TranIn
Trans-Industries, Inc. [*NASDAQ symbol*] (NQ)	TRNI
Trans-Ionospheric Sensing System (DWSG)	TISS
Trans-Israel Pipeline	TIP
Transistor [*Electronics*] (IAA)	T
Transistor [*Electronics*] (EECA)	TR
Transistor (ADA)	TRANS
Transistor (AAG)	TSTR
Transistor [*Symbol*] (DEN)	X
Transistor (IDOE)	xistor
Transistor (AAG)	XSTR
Transistor Analysis Recording Equipment	TARE
Transistor and Component Tester	TACT
Transistor and Nixie Tube (IAA)	TRIXIE
Transistor Chopper Driver	TCD
Transistor Contact Land	TCL
Transistor Coupled Logic	TCL
Transistor Current Switching Logic [*Electronics*] (IAA)	TCSL
Transistor Digital Circuit (IAA)	TDC
Transistor Digital Computer	TRADIC
Transistor Digital Control (IAA)	TDC
Transistor Dip Oscillator (IAA)	TDO
Transistor Display and Data-Handling System [*Computer science*] (MDG)	TDS
Transistor Driver Core Memory	TDCM
Transistor Equivalent [*Electronics*] (IAA)	TE
Transistor Evaluation Test	TET
Transistor Feedback Amplifier	TFA
Transistor Information Microfile	TIM
Transistor Logic (IAA)	TL
Transistor Magnetic-Pulse Amplifier	TMA
Transistor Mounting Kit	TMK
Transistor Mounting Pad	TMP
Transistor Noise Analyzer (IAA)	TNA
Transistor Oscillator Multiplier (IAA)	TOM
Transistor Outline (IEEE)	TO
Transistor Output Buffer (DNAB)	TOB
Transistor Photo Control	TPC
Transistor Power Amplifier (LAIN)	TPA
Transistor Qualification Program	TQP
Transistor Qualification Test	TQT
Transistor Qualification Test Program	TQTP
Transistor Radiation Effects Compilation [*Program*] (MCD)	TREC
Transistor Radio Automatic Circuit Evaluator	TRACE
Transistor Resistor Logic	TRL
Transistor Saturable Reactor	TSR
Transistor Servo Simulator	TSS
Transistor Specialities, Inc. (IAA)	TSI
Transistor Telegraph Relay [*Telecommunications*] (IAA)	TTR
Transistor Test Fixture	TTF
Transistor under Test (IEEE)	TUT
Transistor Volt-Ohmmeter (IDOE)	TVO
Transistor Volt-Ohmmeter (IDOE)	TVOM
Transistor-Amplifier-Multiplier (IIA)	TAM
Transistor-Assisted Circuit (ADA)	TAC
Transistor-Controlled Delay (MCD)	TCD
Transistorized (MSA)	TSTRZ
Transistorized Airborne Digital Computer [*Air Force*]	TRADIC
Transistorized Automatic Computer (IAA)	TAC
Transistorized Automatic Computer	TRANSAC
Transistorized Automatic Computer Users' Group (IAA)	TUG
Transistorized Automatic Control	TAC
Transistorized Car Radio (IAA)	TCR
Transistorized Carrier	TC
Transistorized Digital Computer [*Air Force*] (IAA)	TRADIC
Transistorized Digital Readout	TDR
Transistorized Frequency Converter	TFC
Transistorized High-Speed Operations Recorder	THOR
Transistorized High-Speed Operations Recorder Advanced (IAA)	THORAD
Transistorized Image Orthicon	TIO
Transistorized Image Orthicon Camera (IAA)	TIO
Transistorized Inverter Power Supply	TIPS
Transistorized Operational Phone System (MCD)	TOPS
Transistorized Portable Laboratory	TPL
Transistorized RADAR (IAA)	TRANSRA
Transistorized Real-Time Incremental Computer	TRICE
Transistorized Real-Time Incremental Computer Expandable (IAA)	TRICE
Transistorized Thyratron Ring Counter	TTRC
Transistorized Universal Logic Elements	TULE
Transistorized Volt Ohm Milliammeter (IAA)	TVOM
Transistorized Voltmeter	TRVM
Transistorized Voltmeter	TVM
Transistor-Operated Voltage Divider	TOVD

Transistor-Resistor-Transistor Logic (IEEE) ..... TRTL
Transistor-to-Transistor-to-Transistor Logic (HGAA) ..... TTTL
Transistor-Transistor Logic [Also, TTL] ..... T²L
Transistor-Transistor Logic (IDOE) ..... T²L
Transistor-Transistor Logic [Also, T²L] ..... TTL
Transistor-Transistor Logic - Schottky ..... TTL-S
Transistor-Transistor Logic Schottky Barrier (IEEE) ..... TTS
Transistor-Transistor Micrologic (IAA) ..... TTML
Transit ..... T
Transit ..... TRAN
Transit ..... TRAN
Transit (ODBW) ..... trans
Transit Advertising Association [Washington, DC] (EA) ..... TAA
Transit Air Cargo Manifest ..... TACM
Transit Atlantic [By ship or aircraft] (DOMA) ..... TRANSLANT
Transit Authority ..... TA
Transit Canal (NVT) ..... TC
Transit Commission Reports [New York] [A publication] (DLA) ..... TCR
Transit Control Center (SAA) ..... TCC
Transit Cooperative Research Program [FTA] (TAG) ..... TCRP
Transit Data Transmission System (SAA) ..... TRADAT
Transit Development Program [TRB] (TAG) ..... TDP
Transit Exercise (NVT) ..... TRANSITEX
Transit Financial Holdings, Inc. [Toronto Stock Exchange symbol] ..... TFH
Transit Improvement Program [Satellite] (MCD) ..... TIP
Transit Injection Station (IAA) ..... TIS
Transit Injector Polaris Derived (AAG) ..... TRIPOD
Transit Injector Polaris Derived ..... TRIPOLD
Transit Missile Hold Facility [Military] (IAA) ..... TMHF
Transit Network Route Decision Aid [FHWA] (TAG) ..... TNRDA
Transit Nuclear Radiation ..... TNR
Transit Nuclear Radiation Effect ..... TNRE
Transit Research and Attitude Control [Navy satellite] ..... TRAAC
Transit Research and Attitude Control Satellite [Navy] (IEEE) ..... TRAACS
Transit Research Information Center [Department of Transportation] [Washington, DC] (GRD) ..... TRIC
Transit Routing Domain (TNIG) ..... TRD
Transit Simplified Receiver [Satellite navigation system] ..... TRANSIM
Transit Storage ..... TS
Transit Switching Center [Telecommunications] (TEL) ..... CT
Transit Switching Center [Telecommunications] (TEL) ..... TSC
Transit Time [of blood through heart and lungs] ..... TT
Transit Time Accelerometer ..... TTA
Transit Time Magnetic Pumping ..... TTMP
Transit Time Modulation (DEN) ..... TTM
Transit Tracers in the Ocean [Oceanography] ..... TTO
Transit Without Visa ..... TRWOV
Transit Working [Telecommunications] (TEL) ..... TW
Transition ..... T
Transition (ROG) ..... TRANS
Transition [A publication] ..... Transn
Transition (AABC) ..... TRNS
Transition (MSA) ..... TRNSN
Transition Agreement ..... TA
Transition Altitude ..... TA
Transition Altitude [Aviation] (DA) ..... TRANSALT
Transition Area [For chart use only] [Aviation] ..... TA
Transition Assistance for Needy Families [Welfare program] ..... TANF
Transition Assistance Management Program [Army] ..... TAMP
Transition Assistance Office [Army] (INF) ..... TAO
Transition Assistance Program [Military] ..... TAP
Transition Day [Based on the expected transition from a two-front to a one-front war] [World War II] ..... T (Day)
Transition Education ..... TRANSED
Transition Education Advisory Committee (AIE) ..... TEAC
Transition Layer ..... TLa
Transition Level (DA) ..... TL
Transition Level ..... TLv
Transition Level (DA) ..... TRANSLEV
Transition Level [Aviation] (FAAC) ..... TRLVL
Transition Management ..... TM
Transition Metal (MCD) ..... TM
Transition Metal Oxide (MCD) ..... TMO
Transition Metal-Metalloid [Physical chemistry] ..... TMM
Transition Period (NASA) ..... TP
Transition Plans (MCD) ..... TP
Transition point (DAVI) ..... T
Transition Program for Refugee Children [Department of Education] (GFGA) ..... TPRC
Transition Quarter [Between fiscal years 1976 and 1977] ..... TQ
Transition Radiation and Ionization Calorimeter (SSD) ..... TRIC
Transition Region and Coronal Explorer [Satellite] ..... TRACE
Transition State [Physical chemistry] ..... TS
Transition State Analog ..... TSA
Transition State Spectroscopy [Physics] ..... TSS
Transition State Theory [Physical chemistry] ..... TST
Transition Systems [NASDAQ symbol] (TTSB) ..... TSIX
Transition Systems, Inc. [Associated Press] (SAG) ..... TransSys
Transition Systems, Inc. [NASDAQ symbol] (SAG) ..... TSIX
Transition to Working Life [Project] (AIE) ..... TWL
Transition Training Squadron, Atlantic [Navy] ..... TTSA
Transition Training Squadron, Pacific [Navy] ..... TTSP
Transition Work Group ..... TWG
Transition Zone [in plant growth] [Botany] ..... TZ
Transitional (DLA) ..... Transtl

Transitional Antarctic Coastal Air Mass [Meteorology] (BARN) ..... nA
Transitional Butterworth Modified Ultraspherical Filter (PDAA) ..... TBMU
Transitional Butterworth Thomson (IAA) ..... TBT
Transitional Butterworth Ultraspherical Filter (PDAA) ..... TBU
Transitional Cell Carcinoma ..... TCC
Transitional Control (IAA) ..... TC
Transitional Engineering (MCD) ..... TE
Transitional Environmental Working Group (EERA) ..... TEWG
Transitional Executive Council [Implemented in 1993 to work with the Cabinet and ensure fair political campaigning] [South Africa] (ECON) ..... TEC
Transitional Flight Training (NVT) ..... TRANSFLTNG
Transitional Government of National Unity [South Africa] ..... TGNU
Transitional Hospitals Corp. [NYSE symbol] (SAG) ..... THY
Transitional Hospitals Corp. [Associated Press] (SAG) ..... TransHosp
Transitional Low-Emission Truck ..... TLET
Transitional Low-Emission Vehicle ..... TLEV
Transitional Manpower Program [Navy] (DNAB) ..... TMP
"Transitional" Mucosa [Oncology] ..... TM
Transitional Testing [Aircraft] ..... Y
Transitional Ultraspherical-Ultraspherical Filter (PDAA) ..... TUU
Transitional Year Program [Brandeis University] (EA) ..... TYP
Transitional-Cell Carcinoma of Bladder [Oncology] (DAVI) ..... TCCB
Transitive ..... T
Transitive ..... TR
Transitive ..... TRANS
Transitory ..... TRANS
Transit-Time LIDAR (MCD) ..... TTL
Transit-without-Visa ..... TWOV
Trans-Jamaican Airlines [ICAO designator] (AD) ..... JQ
Trans-Jordan (BJA) ..... TJ
Trans-Jordan Frontier Force [British military] (DMA) ..... TJFF
Transjugular Intrahepatic Portosystemic Shunt ..... TIPS
Transkaryotic Therapies, Inc. [NASDAQ symbol] (SAG) ..... TKTX
Transkaryotic Therapies, Inc. [Associated Press] (SAG) ..... Trnskry
Transkei Airways [ICAO designator] (AD) ..... KV
Transkei Airways [South Africa ICAO designator] (FAAC) ..... TAK
Transkei Defence Force [South Africa] ..... TDF
Transkei National Party [Political party] (EY) ..... TNP
Transkei People's Freedom Party [South Africa] [Political party] (PPW) ..... TPFP
Transketolase [An enzyme] ..... TK
Transketolase [An enzyme] (MAE) ..... TRK
Transketolase Activity [Medicine] (MAE) ..... TKA
Translate [or Translation, or Translator] ..... TR
Translate and Test (IAA) ..... TRT
Translated (ROG) ..... T
Translater Mixer Amplifier (DWSG) ..... TMA
Translating Research into Practice ..... TRIP
Translation ..... T
Translation (IAA) ..... TR
Translation ..... TRANS
Translation (AAG) ..... TRANSL
Translation (BJA) ..... Translat
Translation (IAA) ..... TRN
Translation ..... XLATION
Translation (NASA) ..... XLTN
Translation and Docking Simulator [Navy] (KSC) ..... TDS
Translation and Docking Trainer ..... TDT
Translation Bureau, Canada Department of the Secretary of State [Bureau des Traductions, Secretariat d'Etat] Montreal, Quebec [Library symbol National Library of Canada] (NLC) ..... QMBD
Translation Bureau Library, Secretary of State [UTLAS symbol] ..... BTO
Translation Control Ribonucleic Acid (MAE) ..... tcRNA
Translation Controller ..... TC
Translation Controller Assembly (NASA) ..... TCA
Translation Definition Language ..... TDL
Translation Director (IEEE) ..... TRANDIR
Translation Error Detector (DIT) ..... TED
Translation Hand Controller [NASA] ..... THC
Translation Hand Controller X-Axis Direction (MCD) ..... TX
Translation Hand Controller Y-Axis Direction (MCD) ..... TY
Translation Hand Controller Z-Axis Direction (NASA) ..... TZ
[A] Translation in the Language of the People (1950) [Charles B. Williams] [A publication] (BJA) ..... CBW
Translation Inhibitory Protein ..... TIP
Translation Lookaside Buffer [Computer science] (CMD) ..... TLAB
Translation Lookaside Buffer [Computer science] (BUR) ..... TLB
Translation of Brook's New Cases [1515-58] [A publication] (DLA) ..... March NC
Translation Register ..... TR
Translation Research Institute (EA) ..... TRI
Translation Review [A publication] (BRI) ..... TranslRev
Translation Review Supplement [A publication] (BRI) ..... TranslRevS
Translation Service ..... TS
Translation Services Branch, Translation Bureau, Department of the Secretary of State [Direction Generale des Services de Traduction, Bureau des Traductions, Secretariat d'Etat] Ottawa, Ontario [Library symbol National Library of Canada] (NLC) ..... OOSSTR
Translation Thrust Control ..... TTC
Translational Control (SAA) ..... TCO
Translational Electromagnetic Environment Chamber (MCD) ..... TEMEC
Translational Vestibulo-Ocular Reflex [Ophthalmology] ..... TVOR
Translations Activities Committee [Special Libraries Association] ..... TAC
Translations Register - Index (MCD) ..... TR-I
Translator (AFM) ..... TLTR
Translator ..... tr
Translator (DLA) ..... Trans

Translator [*MARC relator code*] [*Library of Congress*] (LCCP) ... trl
Translator (IAA) ... TSL
Translator (MSA) ... XLTR
Translator and Code Treatment Frame (IEEE) ... TCT
Translator, Assembler, Compiler ... TAC
Translator Bail Switch ... TBS
Translator CAM [*Computer-Aided Manufacturing*] **Magnet** (IAA) ... TCM
Translator Code Magnet (IAA) ... TM
Translator Command Module [*Fluorescence technique*] ... TCM
Translator for Structured FORTRAN [*Formula translation*] [*Computer science*] (MHDI) ... TRANSFOR
Translator Generator System (IEEE) ... TGS
Translator Language [*Computer science*] ... TRANSLANG
Translator Octal Mnemonic ... TOM
Translator Synthesizer (DWSG) ... TS
Translator Writing System [*Computer science*] (IAA) ... TWS
Translators' and Interpreters' Educational Society (EA) ... TIES
Translators' Guild (WDAA) ... TG
Translator's Note ... TN
Translift Airways Ltd. [*British ICAO designator*] (FAAC) ... TLA
Transliteration ... TRANSLIT
Translocated Basilic Vein Arteriovenous Fistula [*Surgery*] ... TBAVF
Translocated in Liposarcoma [*Genetics*] ... TLS
Translocating Chain Associating Membrane [*Biochemistry*] ... TRAM
Translocation ... T
Translocation Crossover [*Geology*] ... TCO
Translocation Defect [*Medicine*] ... TL
Translucent (VRA) ... transl
Translucent Aluminum Oxide [*Ceramic*] ... LUCALOX
Translucent Paper (ADA) ... TP
Translumbar Aortogram [*Medicine*] ... TLA
Transluminal Angioplasty [*Cardiology*] (DAVI) ... TLA
Transluminal Balloon Valvuloplasty [*Cardiology*] (DAVI) ... TBV
Transluminal Coronary Angioplasty [*Cardiology*] ... TCA
Translunar Coast [*Aerospace*] ... TLC
Translunar Injection [*Aerospace*] ... TLI
Translunar Propulsion Stage [*Aerospace*] (AAG) ... TPS
Translunar Trajectory Characteristics [*AEC*] (IAA) ... TTC
Trans-Lux [*AMEX symbol*] (TTSB) ... TLX
Trans-Lux Corp. [*AMEX symbol*] (SPSG) ... TLX
Trans-Lux Corp. [*Associated Press*] (SAG) ... TrnsLx
Transmanche-Link [*Eurotunnel*] (ECON) ... TML
Trans-Mars Injection [*Aerospace*] ... TMI
Transmatic Money Service ... TMS
Transmation, Inc. [*NASDAQ symbol*] (NQ) ... TRNS
Transmation, Inc. [*Associated Press*] (SAG) ... Trnsmt
Transmed Airlines [*Egypt*] [*ICAO designator*] (FAAC) ... TMD
Transmedia Asia Pacific [*NASDAQ symbol*] (TTSB) ... TMNA
Transmedia Asia Pacific, Inc. [*NASDAQ symbol*] (SAG) ... TMNA
Transmedia Asia Pacific, Inc. [*Associated Press*] (SAG) ... TrnAsia
Transmedia Enterprises, Inc. [*Vancouver Stock Exchange symbol*] ... TMC
Transmedia Europe, Inc. [*NASDAQ symbol*] (SAG) ... TMNE
Transmedia Europe, Inc. [*Associated Press*] (SAG) ... TrnmdEu
Transmedia Network [*NYSE symbol*] (TTSB) ... TMN
Transmedia Network, Inc. [*NYSE symbol*] (SAG) ... TMN
Transmedia Network, Inc. [*Associated Press*] (SAG) ... Trnmedia
Trans-Mediterranean Airways (BJA) ... TMA
Transmedullary [*Anatomy*] ... TM
Transmembrane Activation Voltage [*Biochemistry*] (DAVI) ... MAV
Transmembrane Domain [*Genetics*] ... TM
Transmembrane Domain [*Genetics*] ... TMD
Transmembrane Potential [*Biochemistry*] ... TMP
Transmembrane Potential Gradient (DAVI) ... TPG
Transmembrane Pressure [*Biomedicine*] ... TMP
Transmembrane Protein [*Biochemistry*] ... TMP
Transmembrane Receptors [*Biochemistry*] ... TMR
Transmembrane Substitution Mutants [*Genetics*] ... TM
Transmetatarsal [*Anatomy*] ... TM
Transmetatarsal Amputation [*Medicine*] ... TMA
Transmile Air Service (M) Sdn, Bhd. [*Malaysia*] [*FAA designator*] (FAAC) ... TSE
Transmissable Virus Dementia [*Psychiatry*] ... TVD
Transmissible Gastroenteritis [*Virus*] ... TG
Transmissible Gastroenteritis [*Virus*] ... TGE
Transmissible Gastroenteritis Virus [*Virology*] ... TGEV
Transmissible Mink Encephalopathy ... TME
Transmissible Spongiform Encephalothi [*Medicine*] ... TSE
Transmissible Venereal Virus [*Infectious diseases*] (DAVI) ... TVV
Transmission [*Telecommunications*] (IAA) ... T
Transmission (AFM) ... TMN
Transmission ... TRANS
Transmission ... TRANS
Transmission (AFM) ... TRANSM
Transmission (ROG) ... TRANSMON
Transmission (IDOE) ... xmission
Transmission ... xmn
Transmission (AAG) ... XMSN
Transmission Access Processor [*Newbridge Networks, Inc.*] ... TAP
Transmission Adapter (MDG) ... XA
Transmission and Distribution ... T & D
Transmission and Distribution (IAA) ... TAD
Transmission and Drive Train Oil ... TDTO
Transmission and Information Exchange System ... TIES
Transmission and Processing Model ... TPM
Transmission and Signaling Test Plan and Analysis Concept [*Telecommunications*] (TEL) ... TSTPAC
Transmission Authenticator [*Telecommunications*] (TEL) ... TA
Transmission Computer-Assisted Tomography [*Medicine*] (DAVI) ... TCAT
Transmission Control [*Telecommunications*] (IAA) ... TC
Transmission Control Character [*Telecommunications*] (TEL) ... TCC
Transmission Control Program [*Telecommunications*] (OSI) ... TCP
Transmission Control Protocol [*Telecommunications*] (PCM) ... TCP
Transmission Control Protocol [*Advanced Research Projects Agency Network*] [*DoD*] ... TCP
Transmission Control Protocol [*or Program*] **and Internet Protocol** (PCM) ... TCP/IP
Transmission Control Protocol/Internet Protocol [*Computer science*] (EERA) ... TCP/IP
Transmission Control Protocol/Internet Protocol [*Computer science*] (DOM) ... TCP/IP
Transmission Control System (IAA) ... TCS
Transmission Control Unit ... TCU
Transmission Control Unit ... TCU
Transmission Controlled Spark (MCD) ... TCS
Transmission Controller ... TC
Transmission Disequilibrium Test [*Genetics*] ... TDT
Transmission Distortion Measuring Set ... TDMS
Transmission Distribution Center (IAA) ... TDC
Transmission Distributor (NITA) ... TD
Transmission Electron Diffraction (MCD) ... TED
Transmission Electron Micrograph ... TEM
Transmission Electron Microscope [*or Microscopy*] ... TEM
Transmission Electron Microscopy and Microprobe Analysis (PDAA) ... TEMMA
Transmission Electronic Control [*Bradley Fighting Vehicle*] [*Army*] (DWSG) ... TEC
Transmission Engineering Memorandum (IAA) ... TEM
Transmission Engineering Recommendation [*Telecommunications*] (IAA) ... TER
Transmission Equivalent Resistance (IEEE) ... TER
Transmission Error [*Automotive engineering*] ... TE
Transmission Fault Control [*Telecommunications*] (TEL) ... TFC
Transmission Gear Selection Switch [*Automotive engineering*] ... TGSS
Transmission Group (IAA) ... TG
Transmission Group Identifier [*Telecommunications*] (MHDI) ... TGID
Transmission Header [*Computer science*] (IBMDP) ... TH
Transmission Hydraulic Switch [*Automotive engineering*] ... THS
Transmission Identification (NG) ... TI
Transmission Identification Number [*Automotive engineering*] ... TIN
Transmission Impairment Measuring Set [*Telecommunications*] (TEL) ... TIMS
Transmission Impairment Measuring Set [*Telecommunications*] (IAA) ... TMIS
Transmission Impairment Measuring System (IAA) ... TIMS
Transmission Infrared [*Spectroscopy*] ... TIR
Transmission Integrated Rotor ... TIGR
Transmission Intercept and Landing Terminated (MCD) ... TILT
Transmission Interface Converter (IAA) ... TRI
Transmission Interface Converter ... XIC
Transmission Level [*or Line*] ... TL
Transmission Level Point [*Telecommunications*] ... TLP
Transmission Line [*Telecommunications*] (IAA) ... TL
Transmission Line Adapter [*or Assembly*] ... TLA
Transmission Line Conditioning Equipment (MCD) ... TLCE
Transmission Line Method [*Photovoltaic energy systems*] ... TLM
Transmission Loss [*Telecommunications*] (IAA) ... TL
Transmission Maintenance Center [*Telecommunications*] (TEL) ... TMC
Transmission Matrix (IEEE) ... TM
Transmission Measuring Set [*Bell Laboratories*] ... TMS
Transmission Message Unit ... TMU
Transmission Monitoring Facility (NITA) ... TMF
Transmission Multiplexer (NITA) ... TRANSMUX
Transmission Oil Temperature [*Automotive engineering*] ... TOT
Transmission Only [*Telecommunications*] ... TO
Transmission Oscillator Ultrasonic Spectrometer ... TOUS
Transmission Parity Error [*Computer science*] (IAA) ... TPE
Transmission Performance Index [*Telecommunications*] (TEL) ... TPI
Transmission Products Association [*Defunct*] (EA) ... TPA
Transmission Project Group (IAA) ... TPG
Transmission Ratio Distortion [*Genetics*] ... TRD
Transmission Release Code (DNAB) ... TRC
Transmission Reliability Analysis Program ... TRAP
Transmission Report [*Telecommunications*] (TEL) ... TR
Transmission Resource Management System [*Australia*] ... TRMS
Transmission Scheme Translator (MCD) ... TST
Transmission Secondary Electron Multiplication [*Physics*] (IAA) ... TSEM
Transmission Secondary Emission [*Physics*] ... TSE
Transmission Secondary Emission Multiplier [*Physics*] ... TSEM
Transmission Security [*Communications*] ... TRANSEC
Transmission Security Analysis Report (AFM) ... TSAR
Transmission Service [*Telecommunications*] ... TS
Transmission Set ... TS
Transmission, Signaling, and Test Access ... TSTA
Transmission Spark Control Valve [*Automotive engineering*] ... TSCV
Transmission Stop (NTCM) ... T
Transmission Surveillance System [*Bell System*] ... TSS
Transmission Surveillance System - Cable [*Telecommunications*] (TEL) ... TSS-C
Transmission System Optimum Relief Tool [*Telecommunications*] (TEL) ... TSORT
Transmission System Test (MCD) ... TST
Transmission Temperature Switch [*Automotive engineering*] ... TTS
Transmission Test Rack (NITA) ... TTR
Transmission Test Set (IEEE) ... TTS
Transmission Unit [*Telecommunications*] ... TU
Transmission-Controlled Speed (IIA) ... TCS
Transmission-Engine Communication Link [*Automotive engineering*] ... TECL

Transmission-Keying Indicator Buffer (DNAB) .... TKIBU
Transmission-Operating Gear Switch [Automotive engineering] .... TOGS
Transmission-Regulated Spark [Automotive engineering] .... TRS
Trans-Mississippi Philatelic Society (EA) .... TMPS
Transmissivity (FFDE) .... T
Transmit [or Transmitting] .... T
Transmit .... TRAN
Transmit (IDOE) .... trans
Transmit (NITA) .... TRC
Transmit (BUR) .... TRN
Transmit [or Transmitter] (IAA) .... TS
Transmit .... TSMT
Transmit (NITA) .... TX
Transmit X
Transmit [or Transmitter] .... XMIT
Transmit (IDOE) .... xmit
Transmit (IDOE) .... xmt
Transmit (WDMC) .... XMT
Transmit (MSA) .... XMT
Transmit and Receive (WDMC) .... T/R
Transmit and Receive (IAA) .... TAR
Transmit Carry and Clear .... TCC
Transmit Clock (IAA) .... TCL
Transmit Data (IEEE) .... TD
Transmit Data [Computer science] .... TXD
Transmit Data Register [Computer science] (MDG) .... TDR
Transmit Electronically Location Shippers' Car Advice Reports .... TELSCAR
Transmit Filter (MHDB) .... TF
Transmit First-In First-Out [Computer science] .... TFIFO
Transmit Format Generator .... TFG
Transmit Frame Acquisition [Telecommunications] (LAIN) .... TFA
Transmit Frame Memory .... TFM
Transmit Gain Control (MSA) .... TGC
Transmit Level Control (PDAA) .... TLC
Transmit, Receive, and Guard (MSA) .... T/R & G
Transmit/Receive Control Unit .... TRC
Transmit/Receive Control Unit-Asynchronous Start/Stop .... TRC-AS
Transmit/Receive Control Unit-Synchronous Character .... TRC-SC
Transmit/Receive Control Unit-Synchronous Framing .... TRC-SF
Transmit Reference Equivalent (NITA) .... TRE
Transmit [or Transmitting] Variolosser (IAA) .... TVL
Transmit-Receive .... T-R
Transmit-Receive (IDOE) .... TR
Transmit-Receive (AAG) .... XMT-REC
Transmit-Receive Image System (DNAB) .... TRIS
Transmit-Receive Switch (IAA) .... TRS
Transmit-Receive Unit .... TRU
Transmittal (IEEE) .... XMTL
Transmittal Control Record [Computer science] .... TCR
Transmittal Engineering Order .... TEO
Transmittal Header Record [Computer science] .... THR
Transmittal Letter (AAG) .... TL
Transmittal Locator Number [Computer science] .... TLN
Transmittal Memorandum (MCD) .... TM
Transmittal Sheet [Military] .... TS
Transmittance [A symbol used in spectrophotometry] (DAVI) .... T
Transmittance (AAG) .... TRANS
Transmitted (MCD) .... XMTD
Transmitted Light [Microscopy] .... TrL
Transmitted Light Microscope .... TLM
Transmitted Optical Microscopy .... TOM
Transmitted Reference Phase Shift Keying [Computer science] (IAA) .... TRPSK
Transmitted Shock .... TS
Transmitted-Reflected-Reflected [Wave mechanics] .... TRR
Transmitter .... T
Transmitter .... TMTR
Transmitter .... TR
Transmitter (IDOE) .... trans
Transmitter .... TRNSMT
Transmitter (IAA) .... TRS
Transmitter (DA) .... TSMTR
Transmitter .... TX
Transmitter (ADDR) .... XMITR
Transmitter (NTCM) .... XMITTER
Transmitter (IDOE) .... xmitter
Transmitter (IDOE) .... xmtr
Transmitter .... XMTR
Transmitter Assembler Compiler [Telecommunications] (IAA) .... TAC
Transmitter Buffer [Telecommunications] (IAA) .... TB
Transmitter Buffer Empty [Computer science] .... TBE
Transmitter Buffer Empty [Computer science] .... TBMT
Transmitter Circuit (IAA) .... TRC
Transmitter Control and Display Panel .... TCDP
Transmitter Control Pulse (NITA) .... TCP
Transmitter Controller [Electronics] (ECII) .... TC
Transmitter Experiment Package .... TEP
Transmitter Frequency .... TF
Transmitter Frequency Multiplier .... TFM
Transmitter Holding Register (MHDB) .... THP
Transmitter Holding Register .... THR
Transmitter Interface Module [Army] .... XMIM
Transmitter Location .... TL
Transmitter Off (BUR) .... XOFF
Transmitter On (BUR) .... XON
Transmitter Oscillator .... TO

Transmitter Power Output (NTCM) .... TPO
Transmitter Power Rating .... TPR
Transmitter Receiver (IAA) .... TR
Transmitter/Responder [Telecommunications] (EECA) .... TRANSPONDER
Transmitter Signal Element Timing (IAA) .... TSET
Transmitter Start Code [Bell System] .... TSC
Transmitter Station .... TS
Transmitter Tuning Circuit [Telecommunications] (IAA) .... TC
Transmitter Turn-Off .... TTO
Transmitter Underflow .... TUF
Transmitter Zone [Telecommunications] (TEL) .... TZ
Transmitter-Blocker (DEN) .... TB
Transmitter-Distributor .... T-D
Transmitter-Receiver (NATG) .... TRANSCEIVER
Transmitter-Receiver (IAA) .... TSRC
Transmitter-Receiver .... TXRX
Transmitter-Receiver .... XMTR-REC
Transmitting .... TRANSMTG
Transmitting .... XMTG
Transmitting and Receiving Equipment Development (MCD) .... TRED
Transmitting Circuit [Telecommunications] (OA) .... TC
Transmitting Elementary Dipole with Optional Polarity (MCD) .... XELEDOP
Transmitting Information by Optical Electronics (KSC) .... TIBOE
Transmitting Objective Loudness Rating [of telephone connections]
  (IEEE) .... TOLR
Transmitting Slide Wire .... TSW
Transmitting Subscriber Information [Computer science] .... TSI
Transmitting Subscriber's Identification (NITA) .... TSI
Transmitting Switch Control (IAA) .... TSC
Transmitting Tract [Botany] .... TT
Transmitting Typewriter [Telecommunications] (IAA) .... TT
Transmitting Typewriter with Card Punch (IAA) .... TTCP
Transmitting Typewriter with Tape Punch (IAA) .... TTTP
Transmontaigne Oil Co. [AMEX symbol] (SAG) .... TMG
Transmultiplexer (LAIN) .... TMUX
Transmural Colitis [Crohn's disease] (CPH) .... TMC
Transmural Electrical Field Stimulation [Medicine] (DMAA) .... TEFS
Transmural Electrical Stimulation .... TES
Transmural Enteritis [Medicine] .... TME
Transmural Myocardial Infarction [Cardiology] .... TMI
Transnasal Butorphanol [Analgesic] .... TNB
Transnational (DLA) .... Transnatl
Trans-National Communications, Inc. .... TNC
Transnational Corp. .... TNC
Transnational Data and Communicative Report [A publication] (TSSD) .... TDR
Transnational Data Reporting Service, Inc. [Springfield, VA]
  [Telecommunications service] (TSSD) .... TDRS
Transnational European Rural Network [Belgium] (EAIO) .... TERN
Transnational Institute [Netherlands] .... TNI
Transnational Network for Appropriate/Alternative Technologies .... TRANET
Transnational Operation (EERA) .... TNC
Transnational Prospectives [A publication] .... TP
Transnational Re Corp. [NASDAQ symbol] (SAG) .... TREX
Transnational Re Corp. [Associated Press] (SAG) .... TrnReCp
Transnational Re'A' [NASDAQ symbol] (TTSB) .... TREX
Transnational Reporter [A publication] (DLA) .... Transnat'l Rep
Transnational Terrorism (ADA) .... TNT
Transnationals Information Exchange .... TIE
TransNet [NASDAQ symbol] (TTSB) .... TRNT
TransNet Corp. [Associated Press] (SAG) .... Trnsnt
TransNet Corp. [NASDAQ symbol] (NQ) .... TRNT
Transocean Air Lines .... TAL
Transocean Marine Paint Association [Netherlands] (EAIO) .... TMPA
Transocean Offshore, Inc. [NYSE symbol] (SAG) .... RIG
Transocean Offshore, Inc. [Associated Press] (SAG) .... Transocn
Transoceanic Abort Landing (NASA) .... TAL
Transoceanic Airborne Environment .... TAE
Trans-Oceanic Geophysical Investigations [Marine science] (MSC) .... TOGI
Transom (MSA) .... TR
Transonabuoy Automatic Weather System (SAA) .... TAWS
Transonic Aerodynamic Characteristics .... TAC
Transonic Aerodynamic Nozzle .... TAN
Transonic Aircraft Technology [Program] [NASA and Air Force] .... TACT
Transonic Armament Technology (MCD) .... TART
Transonic Dynamic Tunnel [NASA] .... TDT
Transonic Dynamic Wind Tunnel [NASA] (KSC) .... TDWT
Transonic Gasdynamics Facility [Air Force] .... TGF
Transonic Model Tunnel [NASA] .... TMT
Transonic Pressure Tunnel [NASA] .... TPT
Transonic Research Tunnel (MCD) .... TRT
Transonic Tunnel [NASA] .... TT
Transonic Wind Tunnel [NASA] (AAG) .... TWT
Transort of Equatorial Waters [Project] [Marine science] (OSRA) .... TEW
Transovarial Passage [Virology] .... TOP
Transovarial Transmission [Virology] .... TOT
Transpacific .... TRANSPAC
Trans-Pacific Airlines Ltd. .... TPA
Trans-Pacific Freight Conference of Japan/Korea Agent, San Francisco CA
  [STAC] .... TPC
Trans-Pacific Magnetic Anomaly Study [National Oceanic and Atmospheric
  Administration] (NOAA) .... TRANSPACMAG
Trans-Pacific Passenger Conference [Later, PCC] (EA) .... TPPC
Trans-Pacific Profiler Network [Marine science] (OSRA) .... TPPN
Trans-Pacific Profiler Network (USDC) .... TPPN
Transpacific Resources, Inc. [Toronto Stock Exchange symbol] .... TRI

Trans-Pacific Sections [*Marine science*] (OSRA) .... TPS
Transpacific Westbound Rate Agreement (DS) .... TWRA
Transparency (VRA) .... trans
Transparency (AAG) .... TRANSP
Transparency [*Photography*] (WDMC) .... TX
Transparent (MSA) .... TRANS
Transparent Anatomical Manikin [*An exhibit at the Chicago Museum of Science and Industry*] .... TAM
Transparent Armor Kit .... TAK
Transparent Asynchronous Transceiver Interface .... TAXI
Transparent Computing Facility .... TCF
Transparent Conducting Polymers [*Photovoltaic energy systems*] .... TCP
Transparent Conductive Coating [*Organic chemistry*] .... TCC
Transparent Conductive Oxide [*Photovoltaic energy systems*] .... TCO
Transparent Data Link (SSD) .... TDL
Transparent Electrophotographic (NITA) .... TEP
Transparent Electrophotography [*Proposed archival storage medium*] .... TEP
Transparent Ferroelectric Ceramics [*Physics*] .... TFC
Transparent Hull Submersible [*Navy*] .... THS
Transparent Infrared Material .... TIRM
Transparent Intelligent Network .... TI-NET
Transparent LAN [*Local Area Network*] Service (TNIG) .... TLS
Transparent Line Sharing Adapter .... TLSA
Transparent Network Transport [*Computer science*] (CDE) .... TNT
Transparent Office Manager [*Computer science*] (IAA) .... TOM
Transparent Operating System [*Computer science*] (CDE) .... TOPS
Transparent Organic Light-Emitting Device [*Photonics*] .... TOLED
Transparent Rotating Disk Electrode [*Electrochemistry*] .... TRDE
Transparent Semiconductor Shutter .... TSS
Transparent Substrate [*Materials science*] .... TS
Transpatent [*German*] (DLA) .... TrP
Transperineal Urethral Resection [*Medicine*] (DAVI) .... TPUR
Transpersonal Consciousness [*Parapsychology*] .... TC
Transpiration [*Botany*] .... T
Transpiration-Cooled Nose Tip .... TCNT
Transpiration-Cooled Stacked Platelet Injection (MCD) .... TRANSPIRE
Transplacental Gradient [*Obstetrics*] (MAE) .... TPG
Transplacental Hemorrhage [*Obstetrics*] (MAE) .... TPH
Transplant .... TP
Transplant .... transpl
Transplant [*or Transplantation*] [*Medicine*] .... Tx
Transplant Organ Procurement Foundation (EA) .... TOPF
Transplant Recipients International Organization (EA) .... TRIO
Transplantation Antigen [*Medicine*] .... TA
Transplantation Society (EA) .... TS
Transplantation Society of Australia and New Zealand .... TSANZ
Trans-Pluto Probe .... TPP
Transponder (IAA) .... T
Transponder (KSC) .... TPX
Transponder .... TSP
Transponder (MUGU) .... XPDR
Transponder (AAG) .... XPNDR
Transponder .... XPONDER
Transponder (IDOE) .... xponder
Transponder Access Program [*Satellite Business Systems*] [*McLean, VA*] [*Telecommunications*] (TSSD) .... TAP
Transponder Array Location by Co-Planar Ranges [*Oceanography*] (DICI) .... TALCOR
Transponder Component (MCD) .... TC
Transponder Control Group .... TCG
Transponder Inoperative [*Aviation*] (FAAC) .... TINOP
Transponder Interrogation and Decoding Equipment [*Telecommunications*] (IAA) .... TIDE
Transponder Interrogation SONAR .... TIS
Transponder, Interrogator, Pinger, and Echo Sounder .... TIPE
Transponder Interrogator Processor .... TIP
Transponder Location by Surface Positioning [*RADAR*] .... TLSP
Transponder Miss Distance Indicator .... TMDI
Transponder On-Off .... TROO
Transponder RADAR (IAA) .... TR
Transponder Receiver Isolation .... TRI
Transponder Test Set .... TTS
Transponder Transmitter Detector .... TTD
Transponder-Hopping .... TH
Transport [*Navy ship symbol*] .... AP
Transport [*Fitted to evacuate wounded*] [*Navy ship symbol*] [*Obsolete*] .... APH
Transport [*Russian aircraft symbol*] .... PS
Transport [*Naval aircraft designation*] .... R
Transport (NATG) .... T
Transport .... TN
Transport .... TPORT
Transport .... TPT
Transport .... TR
Transport .... TRAN
Transport [*or Transportation*] (AAG) .... TRANS
Transport [*or Transportation*] (AFM) .... TRNSP
Transport .... TRNSPRT
Transport (WGA) .... TSPT
Transport 2000 International [*British*] (EAIO) T2000I
Transport Accident Commission Insurance [*Victoria, Australia*] .... TACI
Transport Air Centre [*France ICAO designator*] (FAAC) .... CTR
Trans-Port Air Drop and Jettison Test [*Air Force, Army*] .... TADJET
Transport Air Group [*Joint Army, Navy, and Marine Corps*] .... TAG
Transport Airlift Estimator [*Air Force*] .... TRAE
Transport Airworthiness Reports Committee [*AIA*] (MCD) .... TARC

Transport and Aircraft Ferry [*Navy symbol Obsolete*] .... APV
Transport and Atmospheric Chemistry Near the Equator .... TRACE
Transport and Communications [*Department of Employment*] [*British*] .... TC
Transport and Communications Commission [*United Nations*] (WDAA) .... TCC
Transport and Communications Division, United Nations ESCAP [*Economic and Social Commission for Asia and the Pacific*] [*Thailand*] (EAIO) .... TACD
Transport and Dock Workers' Union [*India*] .... TDWU
Transport and General Workers' Union [*British*] .... TGWU
Transport and Road Abstracting and Cataloguing System (NITA) .... TRACS
Transport and Road Research Laboratory [*Departments of the Environment and Transport*] [*Information service or system*] (IID) .... TRRL
Transport and Supply .... TS
Transport Approach and Landing Simulator .... TALS
Transport Association [*British*] (DBA) .... TA
Transport Aviation [*Soviet-Russian*] (DOMA) .... VTA
Transport Canada [*Government regulatory agency*] .... TC
Transport Canada, Canadian Air Transportation Administration, Telecommunicationsand Electronics, Edmonton, AB, Canada [*Library symbol Library of Congress*] (LCLS) .... CaAETATE
Transport Canada Library, Ottawa [*UTLAS symbol*] .... TCL
Transport Canada [*Transports Canada*] Ottawa, Ontario [*Library symbol National Library of Canada*] (NLC) .... OOT
Transport Cargo (NATG) .... TC
Transport Code for Computer (IAA) .... TDC
Transport Combine [*Combined Transport*] [*French Business term*] .... TC
Transport Command [*British military*] (DMA) .... TC
Transport Command Development Unit [*British military*] (DMA) .... TCDU
Transport Command Police [*British military*] (DMA) .... TCP
Transport Control Center [*Air Force*] .... TCC
Transport Control Protocol [*Telecommunications*] .... TCP
Transport Conversion Unit [*British military*] (DMA) .... TCU
Transport Corp. Amer [*NASDAQ symbol*] (TTSB) .... TCAM
Transport Corp. of America, Inc. [*NASDAQ symbol*] (SAG) .... TCAM
Transport Corp. of America, Inc. [*Associated Press*] (SAG) .... TrnspAm
Transport Development Group Ltd. [*British*] .... TDG
Transport Disengaging Height [*Fluidized beds of particles*] .... TDH
Transport Distribution Analysis (DCTA) .... TDA
Transport Division [*Navy*] .... TRANSDIV
Transport Documentation (NITA) .... TRANSDOC
Transport Driver (NOAA) .... TD
Transport Empty .... TE
Transport Environment Monitoring System [*NASA*] (MCD) .... TEMS
Transport Ferry Service [*English Channel*] .... TFS
Transport for Christ International (EA) .... TFC
Transport, Four-Engine, Landplane [*Navy symbol*] .... VR(HL)
Transport, Four-Engine, Seaplane [*Navy symbol*] .... VR(HS)
Transport, General and Port Workers' Union [*Aden*] .... TGPWU
Transport Glider [*Navy symbol*] .... VLR
Transport Group, South Pacific Force [*Navy*] .... TRANSGRPSOPAC
Transport Holdings, Inc. [*NASDAQ symbol*] (SAG) .... TLIC
Transport Holdings'A' [*NASDAQ symbol*] (TTSB) .... TLIC
Transport Index [*Nuclear energy*] (NUCP) .... TI
Transport Individuel Publique [*Also known as PROCOTIP*] [*French auto cooperative*] .... TIP
Transport Industries Committee [*Trades Union Congress*] [*British*] (DCTA) .... TIC
Transport Infrastructure Programme [*EDF*] .... TRIP
Transport International Aerien [*Belgium ICAO designator*] (FAAC) .... TRS
Transport International par Fer [*International Transport of Goods by Railway*] [*French*] .... TIF
Transport International Routier [*International Transport of Goods by Road*] [*French*] .... TIR
Transport Issues Group Australia (EERA) .... TIGA
Transport Landplane [*Navy*] .... TRLP
Transport Layer Interface [*Computer science*] (PCM) .... TLI
Transport Layer Interface [*Application program interface*] (TNIG) .... TLI
Transport Management Survey (MCD) .... TMS
Transport Maximum [*Physiology*] (DAVI) .... Tm
Transport Mechanism [*Physiology*] .... TM
Transport Medium [*Laboratory science*] (DAVI) .... TM
Transport Messenger [*Laboratory science*] (DAVI) .... TM
Transport Movement Control [*Military*] (AFM) .... TMC
Transport Museum Association (EA) .... TMA
Transport Network Controller .... TNC
Transport Number [*Symbol*] [*Electrochemistry*] .... t
Transport Number [*Chemistry*] (BARN) .... t
Transport Oiler [*Navy*] (MCD) .... AOT
Transport Oiler Ship .... TAOT
Transport Pack .... TP
Transport Pilot .... TP
Transport Plane [*Multiengine*] [*Navy symbol*] .... VR
Transport Plane Commander .... TPC
Transport Planning and Economics [*British*] .... TPE
Transport - Planning Board European Inland Surface Transport (NATG) .... T(PBEIST)
Transport - Planning Board Ocean Shipping (NATG) .... T(PBOS)
Transport Policies and Programme [*British*] (DCTA) .... TPP
Transport Protein [*Superseded by SC, Secretory Component*] [*Immunology*] .... TP
Transport Protocol [*Computer science*] .... TP
Transport Protocol Data Unit [*Telecommunications*] (OSI) .... TPDU
Transport Quartermaster .... TQM
Transport Research and Development Command [*Army*] (MCD) .... TRDC
Transport Salaried Staff's Association [*A union*] [*British*] (DCTA) .... TSSA
Transport Seaplane [*Navy*] .... TRSP
Transport Service (ROG) .... TS
Transport Service Access Point [*Telecommunications*] .... TSAP

Transport Service Data Unit [Telecommunications] .... TSDU
Transport Ship [Military Sea Transportation Service] (CINC) ...... TAP
Transport Ship (ROG) .... TS
Transport Squadron [Navy] .... TRANSRON
Transport Squadron [Navy symbol] .... VR
Transport Studies and Inquiries [British] .... TSI
Transport, Submarine [Later, SSP] [Navy symbol] .... APS
Transport, Submarine [Later, LPSS] [Navy symbol Obsolete] ... APSS
Transport, Submarine [Later, LPSS] [Navy symbol Obsolete] ... ASSP
Transport Submarine (MCD) .... SSLP
Transport Supplement Grant [British] .... TSG
Transport Systems Research Facility (GAVI) .... TSRV
Transport Systems Research Vehicle .... TSRV
Transport Ticket Society [British] (DBA) .... TTS
Transport Trust [British] [An association] (DBA) .... TT
Transport, Two-Engine, Landplane [Navy symbol] .... VR(ML)
Transport, Two-Engine, Seaplane [Navy symbol] .... VR(MS)
Transport Unit (MCD) .... TU
Transport Users' Consultative Council [British] (ILCA) ..... TUCC
Transport Vehicle [Military] .... TV
Transport, Wages, Maintenance, and Care .... TWMC
Transport Workers' Union [British] .... TWU
Transport Workers Union of America (EA) .... TWU
Transport Workers' Union of Australia .... TWUA
Transport Working Group [Australia] .... TWG
Transportability Analysis Reports Generator [Military] (MCD) ... TARGET
Transportability Approval [Army] .... TA
Transportability Clearance Diagram (MCD) .... TCD
Transportability Engineering Analysis [Army] .... TEA
Transportability Engineering Focal Point .... TEFP
Transportability Focal Point [Army] (MCD) .... TFP
Transportability Guidance Manual .... TGM
Transportability Guidance Technical Manual .... TGTM
Transportability Report [Army] .... TR
Transportability Report/Transportability Engineering Analysis [Army] ... TR/TEA
Transportability Summary Manual [MTMC] (TAG) .... TSM
Transportable Automated Control Environment .... TRACE
Transportable Automated Electromagnetic Measurement System
   (MCD) .... TAEMS
Transportable Automated Intelligence Processing and Interpretation
   System (MCD) .... TIPI
Transportable Automatic Digital Switch (PDAA) .... TADS
Transportable Blood Transfusion Shipment Center (DWSG) ... TBTC
Transportable Calibration Laboratory .... TCL
Transportable Cassette Converter (IAA) .... TCC
Transportable Cassette Recorder (IAA) .... TCR
Transportable Collective Protection System (DWSG) .... TCPS
Transportable Communications .... TRANSCOM
Transportable Communications System .... TCS
Transportable Computer Unit .... TCU
Transportable Database [Telecommunications] .... TDB
Transportable Earth Station [British] .... TES
Transportable Electromagnetic Pulse Simulator (RDA) .... TEMPS
Transportable Electronic Receiving Antenna Group (DWSG) ... TERAG
Transportable Electronic Tower (MCD) .... TET
Transportable Equation Program (DNAB) .... TEP
Transportable Field Calibration Unit .... TFCU
Transportable Ground Communications Station .... TGCS
Transportable Ground Control Approach (IAA) .... TGCA
Transportable Ground Intercept Facility .... TGIF
Transportable Ground Station .... TGS
Transportable Group Control Approach (NG) .... TGCA
Transportable Helicopter Enclosure (RDA) .... THE
Transportable Horizontal Gravity Gradiometer .... THGG
Transportable LASER Ranging Station [for measurement of earth
   movement] .... TLRS
Transportable LASER Unit .... TLU
Transportable Link Terminal [AMC] .... TLT
Transportable LORAN-C (MCD) .... TRANSLOC
Transportable Measurement Package (MCD) .... TMP
Transportable Medium-Range Ballistic Missile .... TMRBM
Transportable Mobile Ground Station (MCD) .... TMGS
Transportable Moisture Limit [Shipping] (DS) .... TML
Transportable Operations Tactical Equipment (NITA) ..... TOTE
Transportable RADAR Approach Control [Army] .... TRAPCON
Transportable Radio Unit [Military] .... TRU
Transportable Relay Station .... TRS
Transportable Reliable Acoustic Path SONAR (MCD) ..... TRAPS
Transportable Reliable Acoustic Path Sonobuoy (NVT) .. TRRAPS
Transportable Satellite Communications Link Terminal ... TSCLT
Transportable Satellite Communications Terminal .... TSCT
Transportable Satellite Earth Station .... TSES
Transportable Surveillance RADAR (MCD) .... TSR
Transportable Telemetry Set .... TTS
Transportable Treatment Unit .... TTU
Transportable Understanding Mechanism Package [Software system]
   (IT) .... TRUMP
Transportable Units and Self-Sufficient Teams (MCD) ... TRUST
Transportable Vehicle Refuelling Equipment (PDAA) ..... TVRE
Transportable Vertical Erectable Launcher .... TRAVEL
Transportable Very-Low-Frequency [Transmitter] .... TVLF
Transportacion Aerea Mexicana [Mexico ICAO designator] (FAAC) ... TAM
Transportacion Aerea Mexicana [Mexico ICAO designator] (FAAC) ... TMX
Transportacion Maritima ADS [NYSE symbol] (TTSB) .... TMM
Transportacion Maritima Mexicana [NYSE symbol] (SPSG) ... TMM

Transportacion Maritima Mexicana [Associated Press] (SAG) ... TMMexA
Transportacion Maritima Mexicana [Associated Press] (SAG) ... TrMMex
Transportadora De Gas ADS [NYSE symbol] (TTSB) .... TGS
Transportadora de Gas Del Sur SA [NYSE symbol] (SAG) ... TGS
Transportadora de Gas Del Sur SA [Associated Press] (SAG) ... TrGasSur
Transportadora Fruyleg, SA de CV [Mexico] [FAA designator] (FAAC) ... FRU
Transportation .... TN
Transportation (CINC) .... TNSP
Transportation (DD) .... trans
Transportation (VRA) .... transp
Transportation .... TRANSP
Transportation (KSC) .... TRNSPN
Transportation .... TRNSPRTN
Transportation .... TRPN
Transportation Accident Research Graduate Education and Training ... TARGET
Transportation Account Code [Military] (AFM) .... TAC
Transportation Account Code (AFM) .... TRAC
Transportation Accounts Receivable and Payment System [GSA] (TAG) ... TARP
Transportation Acquisition Circular (AAGC) .... TAC
Transportation Acquisition Manual [A publication] (AAGC) ... TAM
[Department of] Transportation Acquisition Procurement Regulation
   [A publication] (AAGC) .... TAPR
[Department of] Transportation Acquisition Regulation [A publication]
   (AAGC) .... TAR
Transportation Acronym Guide [BTS] (TAG) .... TAG
Transportation Act of 1989 (WYGK) .... TA
Transportation Agent .... TA
Transportation Aircraft Maintenance Company [Army] ... TAMC
Transportation Aircraft Rebuild Shops [National Guard] (MCD) ... TARS
Transportation Aircraft Test and Support Activity [Military] ... TATSA
Transportation Allocations, Priorities, and Controls Committee
   [Military] .... TAPAC
Transportation Alternatives (EA) .... TA
Transportation Alternatives Group [Transportation 2000] [MTMC] (TAG) ... TAG
Transportation America Corp. [ICAO designator] (FAAC) ... DEE
Transportation Analysis Zone [MM] (TAG) .... TAZ
Transportation and Communications Service [of GSA] [Abolished, 1972] ... TCS
Transportation and Docking (MCD) .... TD
Transportation and Handling [Army] .... T/H
Transportation and Handling Procedure .... T & HP
Transportation and Land Use Study [Michigan] .... TALUS
Transportation and Public Utilities Service [Later, part of Transportation and
   Communication Service, GSA] .... TPUS
Transportation and Recruiting Naval Personnel [Budget appropriation
   title] .... T & RNP
Transportation and Transportability .... T & T
Transportation Applications Office [Jet Propulsion Laboratory, NASA] ... TAO
Transportation Army Aviation Maintenance .... TAAM
Transportation Association of America (EA) .... TAA
Transportation Association of Canada (EAIO) .... TAC
Transportation Authorization (AAG) .... TA
Transportation Authorized in Accordance with BUPERS Manual, Article
   .... TABPM
Transportation Automated Material Movements System [Army]
   (PDAA) .... TRAMMS
Transportation Aviation Supply Support System TAS3
Transportation Aviation Test and Support .... TATSU
Transportation Branch [Navy] (DNAB) .... TRBR
Transportation Brokers Conference of America (EA) ..... TBCA
Transportation Cargo Manifest Document .... TCMD
Transportation Claims and Prevention Council (EA) ...... TCPC
Transportation Club of the Petroleum Industry (EA) ..... TCPI
Transportation Clubs International (EA) .... TCI
Transportation Command [Army] .... TRANSCOM
Transportation Commodity Classification Code .... TCC
Transportation, Communications, and Utilities .... TCU
Transportation Communications International Union (EA) ... TCIU
Transportation Community Awareness and Emergency
   Response .... TRANSCAER
Transportation Community Awareness and Emergency
   Response .... TRANSCAER
Transportation Co. [Army] .... TCO
Transportation Component Command (DOMA) .... TCC
Transportation Computer Assisted Design [MTMC] (TAG) ... TRANSCAD
Transportation Constructor [MTMC] (TAG) .... TCON
Transportation Consulting & Service Corp., Chicago IL [STAC] ... TCS
Transportation Control and Movement Document [Military] ... TCMD
Transportation Control Card [Military] .... TCC
Transportation Control Center .... TCC
Transportation Control Committee [Navy] .... TCC
Transportation Control Measure [Environmental Protection Agency]
   (GFGA) .... TCM
Transportation Control Number [Air Force] (AFM) .... TCN
Transportation Control Officer [Air Force] (AFM) .... TCO
Transportation Control Plan [Environmental Protection Agency] (GFGA) ... TCP
Transportation Control Unit [MTMC] (TAG) .... TCU
Transportation Coordination [or Coordinator] Automated Command and
   ControlInformation System [Military] .... TC ACCIS
Transportation Coordinator's Automated Information for Movement
   System (DOMA) .... TC-AIMS
Transportation Corps [Military] .... TC
Transportation Corps Release [Military] .... TCR
Transportation Corps Research and Development Command
   [Army] .... TRADCOM
Transportation Corps Supply Maintenance Command [Army] ... TCSMC

Transportation Corps Technical Committee [*Army*] ..... TCTC
Transportation Corridor Agencies ..... TCA
Transportation Costing Service [*Database*] [*A. T. Kearney, Inc.*] [*Information service or system*] (CRD) ..... TCS
Transportation Data Coordinating Committee [*Later, EDIA*] ..... TDCC
Transportation Data Sampler [*BTS*] (TAG) ..... TDS
Transportation Data Xchange, Inc. (IID) ..... TDX
Transportation Demand Management [*MOCD*] (TAG) ..... TDM
Transportation Department ..... TD
Transportation Development Agency [*British*] ..... TDA
Transportation Development Center [*Cambridge, MA*] [*Department of Transportation Formerly, NASA Electronic Research Center*] ..... TDC
Transportation Development Centre [*Transport Canada*] [*Research center*] (RCD) ..... TDC
Transportation Development Centre Library [*UTLAS symbol*] ..... TDC
Transportation Development Centre, Transport Canada [*Centre de Developpement des Transports, Transports Canada*] **Montreal, Quebec** [*Library symbol National Library of Canada*] (NLC) ..... QMTD
Transportation Disadvantaged [*MOCD*] (TAG) ..... TD
Transportation Discrepancy Report [*MTMC*] (TAG) ..... TDR
Transportation Displays, Inc. [*A company*] [*Advertising*] [*New York, NY*] (WDMC) ..... TDI
Transportation Employees' Canadian Union ..... TECU
Transportation Engineer Magazine [*A publication*] (EAAP) ..... TE
Transportation Environmental Measurement and Recording System (MCD) ..... TEMARS
Transportation Facilitation Center [*Department of Transportation*] ..... TFC
Transportation Factor (MCD) ..... TF
Transportation Feasibility Estimator ..... TFE
Transportation Financial Management [*Army*] ..... TFM
Transportation Flight [*Military*] ..... TRNSPF
Transportation Group Amphibious Forces [*Navy*] ..... TRANSGRPPHIBFOR
Transportation Horoscope of Trade Goods (PDAA) ..... THOT
Transportation Improvement Program ..... TIP
Transportation in America [*BTS*] (TAG) ..... TIA
Transportation Induced Pollution Surveillance [*Marine science*] (MSC) ..... TIPS
Transportation Institute [*Camp Springs, MD*] (EA) ..... TI
Transportation Insurance Rating Bureau [*Later, AAIS*] (EA) ..... TIRB
Transportation Integrated Management System [*Air Force*] ..... TRIMS
Transportation Intelligence Agency (AAG) ..... TIA
Transportation Intelligent Planning System [*MTMC*] (TAG) ..... TRIPS
Transportation Interface and Reporting System [*GSA*] (TAG) ..... TIRES
Transportation Lawyers Association (EA) ..... TLA
Transportation Legislative Data Base [*Battelle Memorial Institute*] [*Department of Energy Information service or system*] (IID) ..... TLDB
Transportation Liaison Flight [*Military*] ..... TRNSPLF
Transportation Library [*National Academy of Sciences*] [*Information service or system*] (IID) ..... TLIB
Transportation Management Association ..... TMA
Transportation Management Bulletin [*NASA*] (NASA) ..... TMB
Transportation Management Center ..... TMC
Transportation Management Officer (AAGC) ..... TMO
Transportation Management School [*Navy*] ..... TMS
Transportation Management School [*Navy*] (DNAB) ..... TRANSMGTSCOL
Transportation Materiel Command [*AMC - Mobility*] ..... TMC
Transportation Model [*Military*] ..... TRANSMO
Transportation Motor Pool [*Military*] (AABC) ..... TMP
Transportation Motor Transport [*Military*] (AABC) ..... TMT
Transportation Movement Document Control (MCD) ..... TMDC
Transportation Movement Planing System (SAA) ..... TRAMPS
Transportation Movement Requirements Data (MCD) ..... TMRD
Transportation Movements Office [*or Officer*] [*Military*] ..... TMO
Transportation Movements Release [*Military*] (AABC) ..... TMR
Transportation News Ticker [*Knight-Ridder Business Information Services*] [*Information service or system*] (CRD) ..... TNT
Transportation Noise Research Information Service [*Department of Transportation*] ..... TNRIS
Transportation of Dangerous Goods [*International symposium*] ..... TDG
Transportation of Dependents [*Navy*] (DNAB) ..... TRANS/DEP
Transportation Office Network System [*Department of Transportation*] (GFGA) ..... TONS
Transportation Office Will Furnish the Necessary Transportation [*Military*] ..... TOT
Transportation Officer [*Military*] ..... TO
Transportation Officer ..... TRO
Transportation Operating Agencies (AFM) ..... TOA
Transportation Operating Command [*MTMC*] (TAG) ..... TOC
Transportation Operational Personal Property System [*Army*] ..... TOPS
Transportation Operations Authority (MCD) ..... TOA
Transportation Operations Center ..... TOC
Transportation Operations Coordinating Committee [*FHWA*] (TAG) ..... TRANSCOM
Transportation Operations Squadron ..... TRNSPOPS
Transportation Packaging Order (AFM) ..... TPO
Transportation Payment Act of 1972 (AAGC) ..... TPA
Transportation Planning Suite [*MVA Systematica*] [*Software package*] (NCC) ..... TRIPS
Transportation Planning Support Information System [*TRB*] (TAG) ..... TPSIS
Transportation Priority [*Military*] (AFM) ..... TP
Transportation Protective Service [*MTMC*] (TAG) ..... TPS
Transportation Reform Alliance ..... TRA
Transportation [*or Travel*] **Request** [*Military*] ..... TR
Transportation Research Activities Information Service [*Department of Transportation*] ..... TRAIS
Transportation Research and Engineering Command (MUGU) ..... TRECOM
Transportation Research Board (EA) ..... TRB
Transportation Research Center [*Ohio*] ..... TRC
Transportation Research Command [*Army*] (MCD) ..... TCREC
Transportation Research Command [*Army*] (IAA) ..... TRC
Transportation Research Command [*Army*] (KSC) ..... TRCO
Transportation Research Command [*Fort Eustis, VA*] [*Army*] ..... TRECOM
Transportation Research Forum (EA) ..... TRF
Transportation Research Foundation ..... TRF
Transportation Research Information Services [*National Academy of Sciences*] [*Bibliographic database*] [*Washington, DC*] ..... TRIS
Transportation Research Information Services Network [*Department of Transportation*] [*Library network*] ..... TRISNET
Transportation Research Institute [*Carnegie-Mellon University*] ..... TRI
Transportation Research Institute [*Oregon State University*] [*Research center*] (RCD) ..... TRI
Transportation Research Laboratory ..... TRL
Transportation Safeguards Division ..... TSD
Transportation Safety Equipment Institute (EA) ..... TSEI
Transportation Safety Information System [*Department of Transportation*] (IID) ..... TRANSIS
Transportation Safety Institute [*Department of Transportation*] ..... TSI
Transportation Service, Army ..... TSA
Transportation Service for the Army in the Field (MCD) ..... TSAF
Transportation Services Branch [*Air Force*] ..... TSB
Transportation Simulation for Estimating Requirements (DNAB) ..... TRANSFER
Transportation Simulator (DNAB) ..... TRANSIM
Transportation Squadron ..... TRNSPS
Transportation Standardization Agency [*DoD*] ..... TSA
Transportation Statistics Annual Report [*BTS*] (TAG) ..... TSAR
Transportation Stores Assignment [*British*] ..... TSA
Transportation Stores Depot [*British military*] (DMA) ..... TSD
Transportation Supply and Maintenance Command ..... TSMC
Transportation Supply Officer [*Military*] ..... TSO
Transportation Support Equipment (NASA) ..... TSE
Transportation Support Field Office [*Federal disaster planning*] ..... TSFO
Transportation System Capability Study [*MTMC*] (TAG) ..... TSCS
Transportation System Utilization Program [*Department of Energy*] ..... TSU
Transportation Systems Center [*Department of Transportation*] [*Cambridge, MA*] ..... TSC
Transportation Systems, Inc. [*FAA designator*] (FAAC) ..... WAE
Transportation Systems Management ..... TSM
Transportation Systems Review Committee [*MTMC*] (TAG) ..... TSRC
Transportation Technical Data [*Army*] ..... TTD
Transportation Terminal Command Europe [*MTMC*] (TAG) ..... TTCE
Transportation Terminal Command Far East [*MTMC*] (TAG) ..... TTFE
Transportation Terminal Unit [*Army*] ..... TTU
Transportation Test Center [*Department of Transportation*] [*Pueblo, CO*] (GRD) ..... TTC
Transportation, Utilities, Communications ..... TUC
Transportation Zone [*Department of Transportation*] ..... TZ
Transportation-Communication Employees Union [*Later, TCIU*] ..... TCE
Transportation-Communication Employees Union (MHDB) ..... TCEU
Transportation-Communication Employees Union [*Later, TCIU*] ..... TCU
Transportation-Works Department, Regional Municipality of Ottawa-Carleton, Ottawa, Ontario [*Library symbol National Library of Canada*] (NLC) ..... OORMT
Transporte Aereco Dominicano [*Dominican Republic*] [*ICAO designator*] (FAAC) ..... TDO
Transporte Aereo Andino SA [*Venezuela*] [*ICAO designator*] (FAAC) ..... EAA
Transporte Aereo Andino SA [*Venezuela*] [*ICAO designator*] (FAAC) ..... TAAN
Transporte Aereo de la Amazonia [*Colombia*] [*ICAO designator*] (FAAC) ..... TAZ
Transporte Aereo Dominicano [*Dominican Republic*] [*ICAO designator*] (FAAC) ..... TRADO
Transporte Aereo Dominicano SA [*Dominican Republic*] [*ICAO designator*] (FAAC) ..... TAD
Transporte Aereo Rioplatense [*Argentina ICAO designator*] (FAAC) ..... HRT
Transporte Combinado [*Combined Transport*] [*Spanish Business term*] ..... TC
Transporte de Carga Aeropacifico SA de CV [*Mexico ICAO designator*] (FAAC) ..... APF
Transporte del Caribe [*Colombia*] [*ICAO designator*] (FAAC) ..... TCB
Transporte e Trabalho Aero [*Mozambique*] [*ICAO designator*] (FAAC) ..... TTA
Transported ..... TPTD
Transporter (DCTA) ..... TP
Transporter ..... TPTR
Transporter (KSC) ..... TRNSPR
Transporter Air Lock [*Nuclear energy*] (NRCH) ..... TAL
Transporter Associated with Antigen Processing [*Biochemistry*] ..... TAP
Transporter/Launcher [*NASA*] (KSC) ..... T/L
Transporter/Loader (MCD) ..... T/L
Transporter, Loader, Launcher ..... TLL
Transporter - Loader Vehicle [*NASA*] (NASA) ..... TLV
Transporter Maintenance Facility [*NASA*] (NASA) ..... TMF
Transporter-Erector [*NASA*] (KSC) ..... T/E
Transporter-Erector-Launcher [*Air Force*] ..... TEL
Transporter-Erector-Launcher and RADAR (MCD) ..... TELAR
Transportes, Aduanas, y Consignaciones SA [*Shipping company*] [*Spain*] (EY) ..... TAC
Transportes Aereos Boliviands [*Bolivia*] [*ICAO designator*] (FAAC) ..... TAB
Transportes Aereos Coyhaique [*Chile*] [*ICAO designator*] (FAAC) ..... COY
Transportes Aereos Coyhaique [*Chile*] [*ICAO designator*] (FAAC) ..... TAC
Transportes Aereos da Bacia Amazonica [*Airline*] [*Brazil*] ..... TABA
Transportes Aereos da Bacia Amazonica SA [*Brazil*] [*ICAO designator*] (FAAC) ..... TAB
Transportes Aereos de Cabo Verde [*Cape Verde*] [*ICAO designator*] (FAAC) ..... TACV

Transportes Aereos de Cabo Verde [*Cape Verde*] [*ICAO designator*] (FAAC) .... TCV

Transportes Aereos de Cabo Verde [*ICAO designator*] (AD) .... VR

Transportes Aereos de El Salvador SA de CV [*ICAO designator*] (FAAC) .... TAES

Transportes Aereos de El Salvador SA de CV [*ICAO designator*] (FAAC) ...... TES

Transportes Aereos de Xalapa, SA de CV [*Mexico*] [*FAA designator*] (FAAC) .... TPX

Transportes Aereos Fueguino [*Argentina ICAO designator*] (FAAC) .... STU

Transportes Aereos Mercantiles Panamericanos [*National airlines*] [*Colorado*] (EY) .... Tampa

Transportes Aereos Mercantiles Panamericanos [*Colombia*] [*ICAO designator*] (FAAC) .... TPA

Transportes Aereos Mexicano, Sociedad Anonima .... TAMSA

Transportes Aereos Militares Ecatorianos CA [*Ecuador*] [*ICAO designator*] (FAAC) .... TAE

Transportes Aereos Nacionales [*ICAO designator*] (AD) .... TX

Transportes Aereos Nacionales Ecuatorianas [*Airline*] [*Ecuador*] .... TANE

Transportes Aereos Nacionales, SA [*TAN Airlines*] .... TAN

Transportes Aereos Neuquen [*Argentina ICAO designator*] (FAAC) .... NQN

Transportes Aereos Neuquinos Sociedad de Estado [*Argentina ICAO designator*] (FAAC) .... NEU

Transportes Aereos Neuquinos Sociedad de Estado [*Argentina ICAO designator*] (FAAC) .... TANSE

Transportes Aereos Norte-Sur Ltda. [*Chile*] [*ICAO designator*] (FAAC) .... ANS

Transportes Aereos Pegaso SA de CV [*Mexico ICAO designator*] (FAAC) ...... TPG

Transportes Aereos Portugueses EP [*Portugal ICAO designator*] (FAAC) ...... TAP

Transportes Aereos Portugueses, SARL [*Portuguese Air Transport*] .... TAP

Transportes Aereos Ranquetes, Sociedad Anonima [*Argentina*] .... TARSA

Transportes Aereos Regionais [*Airline*] [*Brazil*] .... TAR

Transportes Aereos Regionais SA [*Brazil*] [*ICAO designator*] (FAAC) .... TAM

Transportes Aereos Regionais (TAR) SA [*Brazil ICAO designator*] (ICDA) .... TF

Transportes Aereos Salvador [*Brazil*] .... TAS

Transportes Aereos Tamaulipas, SA de CV [*Mexico*] [*FAA designator*] (FAAC) .... ETM

Transportes Aeromar [*Mexico ICAO designator*] (FAAC) .... TAO

Transportes Aeros Boliviands [*Bolivia*] [*ICAO designator*] (FAAC) .... BOL

Transportes Aeros Ejecutivos SA de CV [*Mexico ICAO designator*] (FAAC) .... TEJ

Transportes Aeros Nacionales [*National Air Line*] [*Honduras*] (PDAA) .... TAN

Transportes Aeroside Timor [*Portuguese Timor*] .... TAT

Transportes de Carga Aerea Especializada y Servicios Aeronauticos [*Mexico ICAO designator*] (FAAC) .... TCS

Transportes La Paz SA de CV [*Mexico ICAO designator*] (FAAC) .... TPZ

Transport-Independendt Remote Procedure Call [*Computer science*] .... TIRPC

Transporto Combinato [*Combined Transport*] [*Italian Business term*] .... TC

Transports Aeriens de la Guinee-Bissau [*Guinea-Bissau*] [*ICAO designator*] (FAAC) .... GBU

Transports Aeriens du Benin [*Benin*] (EY) .... TAB

Transports Aeriens du Benin [*ICAO designator*] (FAAC) .... TSB

Transports Aeriens Intercontinentaux [*Privately owned French airline*] .... TAI

Transports Aeriens Mediterraneens [*France ICAO designator*] (FAAC) .... TRM

Transports Aeros Hispanos SA [*Spain ICAO designator*] (FAAC) .... THS

Transports, Amphibious Force, Atlantic Fleet [*Navy*] .... TRANSPHIBLANT

Transports, Amphibious Force, Pacific Fleet [*Navy*] .... TRANSPHIBPAC

Transports, Atlantic Fleet [*Navy*] .... TRANSLANT

Transporturi Aeriene Romane [*Romanian Air Transport*] .... TAROM

Transposable Element [*Genetics*] .... TE

Transpose .... TR

Transpose [*Proofreading*] (WDMC) .... tr

Transpose [*Proofreading*] .... TRANS

Transpose (MSA) .... TRNPS

Transpose (ROG) .... TRS

Transposed .... TRSD

Transposition (AAG) .... TPSN

Transposition and Docking [*NASA*] (KSC) .... T & D

Transposition, Docking, and Ejection [*NASA*] (KSC) .... TD & E

Transposition of Aorta [*Cardiology*] (MAE) .... T of A

Transposition of Great Arteries [*Cardiology*] .... TGA

Transposition of the Great Vessels [*Cardiology*] .... TGV

Transposition of the Great Vessels [*Medicine*] (DAVI) .... TOGV

Transposon [*Genetics*] (DOG) .... Tn

Transposon Yeast [*Genetics*] .... TY

Transpro, Inc. [*NYSE symbol*] (SAG) .... TPR

Transpro, Inc. [*Associated Press*] (SAG) .... Trnspro

Trans-Provincial Airlines [*ICAO designator*] (AD) .... CD

Trans-Provincial Airlines Ltd. [*Canada ICAO designator*] (FAAC) .... TPY

Transpt'n Marit Part Ctfs ADS [*NYSE symbol*] (TTSB) .... TMM.A

Transpulmonary Pressure [*Cardiology*] (DAVI) .... P$_L$

Transpulmonary Pressure (MAE) .... Ptp

Transputer Module [*Computer science*] .... TRAM

Trans-Quebec & Maritimes, Montreal, PQ, Canada [*Library symbol Library of Congress*] (LCLS) .... CaQMTQM

Transracial Adoption .... TRA

Transrectal Ultra Sounds [*Medicine*] .... TRUS

Transrectal Ultrasonography [*Medicine*] .... TRUS

Trans-Service Inc., Bala-Cynwyd PA [*STAC*] .... TSI

Transsexual (DAVI) .... transsex

Transsexual (DAVI) .... TRX

Transsexual [*Medicine*] .... TS

Transshipment Point (AFM) .... TSP

Trans-Siberian Railway .... TSR

Trans-Species Unlimited [*Later, ARM*] (EA) .... TSU

Transtage [*Upper stage for Titan III C rocket*] .... T/S

TransTechnology [*NYSE symbol*] (TTSB) .... TT

TransTechnology Corp. [*Associated Press*] (SAG) .... TrnsTec

TransTechnology Corp. [*NYSE symbol*] (SPSG) .... TT

Transtex Universal Gateway [*Computer science*] .... TUG

Trans-Texas Airways .... TT

Trans-Texas Airways .... TTA

TransTexas Gas [*NASDAQ symbol*] (TTSB) .... TTXG

Transtexas Gas Corp. [*Associated Press*] (SAG) .... TranstxGs

Transtexas Gas Corp. [*NASDAQ symbol*] (SAG) .... TTXG

Transthoracic [*Medicine*] .... TT

Transthoracic Endoscopic Sympathectomy .... TES

Transthoracic Impedance [*Medicine*] .... TTI

Transthoracic Intracardiac Monitoring [*Medicine*] (DMAA) .... TIM

Transthoracic Pressure [*Medicine*] (DAVI) .... Pw

Transthyretin [*Biochemistry*] .... TTR

Transtracheal [*Medicine*] (DAVI) .... TT

Transtracheal Aspiration [*Medicine*] .... TTA

Transtracheal Selective Bronchial Brushing [*Medicine*] (AAMN) .... TSBB

Transuranic [*or Transuranium*] [*Chemistry*] .... TRU

Transuranic Waste (GAAI) .... TRUW

Transuranium [*Chemistry*] .... TU

Transuranium Extraction .... TRUEX

Transuranium Processing Plant .... TPP

Transuranium Processing Plant (NRCH) .... TRU

Transuranium Research Laboratory [*AEC*] .... TRL

Trans-Urban Bicentennial Exposition .... TUBE

Transurethral Incision of the Prostate [*Medicine*] .... TUIP

Transurethral Resection [*of prostate gland*] .... TUR

Transurethral Resection of Bladder Neck [*Medicine*] (DAVI) .... TURBN

Transurethral Resection of Bladder Tumor [*Medicine*] (MAH) .... TURBT

Transurethral Resection of the Bladder [*Medicine*] (AAMN) .... TURB

Transurethral Resection of the Prostate [*Medicine*] .... TURP

Transurethral Resection of Valves [*Urology*] (DAVI) .... TURV

Transurethral Ultrasonic Uterolithotripsy [*Urology*] .... TUUL

Transurethral Ultrasound - Guided LASER-Induced Prostatectomy [*Medicine*] .... TULIP

Transvaal [*South Africa*] (ROG) .... TRANSV

Transvaal [*South Africa*] .... Tvl

Transvaal and Natal Native Appeal and Divorce Court Decisions [*A publication*] (DLA) .... NA & DT & N

Transvaal and Witwatersrand Reports [*A publication*] (DLA) .... Trans & Wit

Transvaal Cadets [*British military*] (DMA) .... TC

Transvaal Court Reports [*A publication*] (DLA) .... Kotze & Barber

Transvaal Horse Artillery [*British military*] (DMA) .... THA

Transvaal Indian Congress [*South Africa*] (PD) .... TIC

Transvaal Mounted Rifles [*British military*] (DMA) .... TMR

Transvaal Province [*Republic of South Africa*] .... TP

Transvaal Provincial Division Reports [*South Africa*] [*A publication*] (DLA) .... T

Transvaal Reports, by Kolze [*A publication*] (DLA) .... Kolze

Transvaal Supreme Court Reports [*South Africa*] [*A publication*] (DLA) .... TP

Transvaal Supreme Court Reports [*South Africa*] [*A publication*] (DLA) .... TS

Transvaginal Cone [*Medicine*] (MAE) .... TVC

Transvaginal Hysterectomy [*Gynecology*] (DAVI) .... TVH

Transvascular Protein Clearance [*Medicine*] .... TPC

Transvenous (DAVI) .... TV

Transvenous Pacemaker [*Cardiology*] (DAVI) .... TVP

Transversal Filter (IAA) .... TF

Transversale Spyder [*Ferrari automotive model designation*] .... TS

Transverse (AAMN) .... T

Transverse (DEN) .... TR

Transverse (IDOE) .... TRANS

Transverse (AAG) .... trans

Transverse [*Referring to sections*] [*Pathology*] (DAVI) X

Transverse (AAG) .... TRANSV

Transverse Abdominal Diameter (DAVI) .... XVERS

Transverse Acoustic .... TAD

Transverse Air Spring .... TA

Transverse Alternating Field Electrophoresis .... TAS

Transverse Cross Section [*Medicine*] (CPH) .... TAFE

Transverse Cylindrical Orthomorphic Chart .... T-SECT

Transverse Diameter [*Of heart*] [*Anatomy*] .... TCOC

Transverse Diameter [*Anatomy*] (CPH) .... TD

Transverse Direction .... Trans D

Transverse Division [*Cytology*] .... TD

Transverse Electric [*or Electrostatic*] [*Wave propagation mode*] .... TD

Transverse Electric Field .... TE

Transverse Electromagnetic [*Wave*] [*Radio*] .... TEF

Transverse Electromagnetic Mode [*Telecommunications*] (IAA) .... TEM

Transverse Electrostatic (IAA) .... TEM

Transverse Exitation Mode [*or Electrostatic*] (NITA) .... TE

Transverse Expansion Joint [*Technical drawings*] .... TEM

Transverse Fascicular Area [*Neuroanatomy*] .... TEJ

Transverse Feed System .... TFA

Transverse Field Modulator .... TFS

Transverse Film Attenuator .... TFM

Transverse Flow Fan .... TFA

Transverse Inlet [*Medicine*] (MAE) .... TFF

Transverse Junction Stripe (MCD) .... TI

Transverse Magnetic .... TJS

Transverse Magnetic Circular X-Ray Dichroism [*Physics*] .... TM

Transverse Magnetic Wave [*Radio*] .... TMCXD

Transverse Nerve [*Neuroanatomy*] .... TMW

Transverse Optic .... TN

Transverse Optical Pumping (MCD) .... TO

Transverse Pallial Vein .... TOP

Transverse Process [*Neurosurgery*] (DAVI) .... TPV

Transverse Propulsion Unit (PDAA) .... TP

.... TPU

Transverse Rectus Abdominis Myocutaneous [*Breast reconstruction*] (DAVI) ... TRAM
Transverse Redundancy Check [*Computer science*] (IBMDP) ... TRC
Transverse Relaxation Time Constant [*On magnetic resonance imaging (MRI) scans*] [*Also called spin-spin relaxation time constant*] [*Radiology*] (DAVI) ... T2
Transverse Rupture Strength [*Metallurgy*] ... TRS
Transverse Section [*Medicine*] (AAMN) ... Trans Sect
Transverse Section [*Medicine*] ... TS
Transverse Shear Force ... TSF
Transverse Spinal Sclerosis [*Orthopedics*] (DAVI) ... TSS
Transverse Staggering (IAA) ... TS
Transverse System [*Cytology*] ... TS
Transverse Thrust Propeller ... TTP
Transverse Tubular System (DAVI) ... TS
Transverse Tubule [*Muscle neurobiology*] ... T
Transverse Vertical Longitudinal ... TVL
Transversely Adjusted Gap (IEEE) ... TSG
Transversely Excited Atmospheric [*LASER*] (RDA) ... TEA
Transversely Excited Atmospheric LASER (RDA) ... TEAL
Transversely Excited Atmospheric Pressure ... TEAP
Transversely Magnetized Plasma ... TMP
Transverse-Mounted Engine ... TME
Transverse-Mounted Engine Propulsion System ... TMEPS
Transversion [*Molecular biology*] ... TV
Transverter (AAG) ... XVTR
Transvesical Prostatectomy [*Urology*] (DAVI) ... TVP
Transvestite [*Medicine*] ... TV
Transway Air Services, Inc. [*Liberia*] [*ICAO designator*] (FAAC) ... TAW
Transwede [*Sweden ICAO designator*] (FAAC) ... TWE
Trans-West [*ICAO designator*] (AD) ... WW
Trans-Western Exploration, Inc. [*Toronto Stock Exchange symbol*] ... TWE
TranSwitch Corp. [*Associated Press*] (SAG) ... TrnSwtc
TranSwitch Corp. [*NASDAQ symbol*] (SAG) ... TXCC
Transworld Advertising Agency Network [*Englewood, CO*] (EA) ... TAAN
Transworld Bancorp [*Associated Press*] (SAG) ... TrwlBc
Transworld Bancorp [*NASDAQ symbol*] (NQ) ... TWBC
Transworld Home HealthCare, Inc. [*NASDAQ symbol*] (SAG) ... TWHH
Transworld Home HealthCare, Inc. [*Associated Press*] (SAG) ... TwldH
Transworld Home HealthCare, Inc. [*Associated Press*] (SAG) ... TwldHH
Transworld Home Hlthcare [*NASDAQ symbol*] (TTSB) ... TWHH
Transworld Home Hlthcr Wrrt [*NASDAQ symbol*] (TTSB) ... TWHHW
TransWorld Radio (EA) ... TWR
Transylvania County Library, Brevard, NC [*Library symbol Library of Congress*] (LCLS) ... NcBre
Transylvania University, Lexington, KY [*OCLC symbol*] (OCLC) ... KTU
Transylvania University, Lexington, KY [*Library symbol Library of Congress*] (LCLS) ... KyLxT
Transylvanian World Federation (EAIO) ... TWF
Tranylcypromine [*Organic chemistry*] ... TCP
Tranzonic Cos. [*AMEX symbol*] (SPSG) ... TNZ
Tranzonic Cos. [*Associated Press*] (SAG) ... Trnzn
Tranzonic Cos 'A' [*AMEX symbol*] (TTSB) ... TNZ.A
Tranzonic Cos Cl'B' [*AMEX symbol*] (TTSB) ... TNZ.B
Trap Control Line ... TCL
Trap Designator Register ... TDR
Trap Designator Set ... TDS
Trap Flag [*Computer memory language*] (PCM) ... TF
Trap on Overflow BIT [*Binary Digit*] **Set** [*Computer science*] ... TRAPV
Trap Oxidizer-Continuous [*Automotive engineering*] ... TOC
Trap Oxidizer-Periodic [*Automotive engineering*] ... TOP
Trap Processing Line ... TPL
Trapani [*Italy*] [*Airport symbol*] (OAG) ... TPS
Trapani/Birgi [*Italy ICAO location identifier*] (ICLI) ... LICT
Trapezius [*Muscle*] [*Anatomy*] (DAVI) ... trap
Trapezoid (MSA) ... TRAP
Trapezoid Body [*Audiometry*] ... TB
Traphagen School of Fashion, New York, NY [*Library symbol Library of Congress*] (LCLS) ... NNTF
Trapped Air Cushion ... TAC
Trapped Air Volume [*Medicine*] (DMAA) ... TAV
Trapped Domain (IAA) ... TD
Trapped Plasma Avalanche Transit Time [*Bell Laboratories*] (IAA) ... TRAPATT
Trapped Plasma Avalanche Triggered Transit [*Bell Laboratories*] ... TRAPATT
Trapped Pressure Ratio [*Gas analysis*] ... TPR
Trapped Radiation Belt ... TRB
Trapped Radiation Detector ... TRD
Trapping (VRA) ... trap
Trapping Layer [*NWS*] (FAAC) ... TRPLYR
Trasco Wind-Force [*Vancouver Stock Exchange symbol*] ... TWF
Trascranial Magnetic Stimulation [*Medicine*] ... TMS
Trash Disposal System ... TDS
Trash Disposal Unit (DNAB) ... TDU
Trash Remover and Satellite Hauler [*Proposed device to remove orbiting space debris*] ... TRASH
Traskei Airways Corp. [*South Africa*] (EY) ... TAC
Trasport Device Interface [*Computer science*] ... TDI
Trattenuto [*Music*] ... Tratt
Trau, Schau, Wem [*Trust, but Be Careful Whom*] [*Motto of Christian I, Elector of Saxony (1560-91)*] [*German*] ... TSW
Trauma (DAVI) ... trau
Trauma Action Group [*Defunct*] (EA) ... TAG
Trauma and Emergency Center [*Medicine*] ... T & EC
Trauma Care Unit [*Medicine*] (DMAA) ... TCU
Trauma Intensive Care Unit [*Medicine*] ... TICU
Traumatic (DAVI) ... trau
Traumatic Brain Injury [*Medicine*] ... TBI
Traumatic Epiphyseal Coxa Vara [*Medicine*] (DMAA) ... TECV
Traumatic Surgery [*Medical specialty*] (DHSM) ... TRS
Trausdorf [*Austria ICAO location identifier*] (ICLI) ... LOAT
Travail Canada [*Labour Canada - LC*] ... TRAVC
Travail Force [*Penal Servitude*] [*French*] ... TF
Travailleurs Unis des Transports [*United Transportation Union - UTU*] [*Canada*] ... TUT
Travailleurs Unis du Telegraphe [*United Telegraph Workers - UTW*] [*Canada*] ... TUT
Travail-Quebec, Montreal, PQ, Canada [*Library symbol Library of Congress*] (LCLS) ... CaQMIMO
Travancore [*India*] (ROG) ... TRAV
Travancore Law Journal [*India*] [*A publication*] (DLA) ... TLJ
Travancore Law Journal [*India*] [*A publication*] (DLA) ... Trav LJ
Travancore Law Reports [*India*] [*A publication*] (DLA) ... TLR
Travancore Law Reports [*India*] [*A publication*] (DLA) ... Trav LR
Travancore Law Times [*India*] [*A publication*] (DLA) ... TLT
Travancore Law Times [*India*] [*A publication*] (DLA) ... Trav LT
Travaux. Centre de Recherche sur le Proche-Orient et la Grece Antiques. Universite de Sciences Humaines de Strasbourg [*A publication*] (BJA) ... TCR
Travaux. Faculte de Philosophie et Lettres. Universite Catholique de Louvain [*A publication*] (BJA) ... TFP
Travaux Forces a Perpetuite [*Penal Servitude for Life*] [*French*] ... TP
Travaux. Institut Catholique de Paris [*A publication*] (BJA) ... TICP
Travaux Publics [*Public Works*] [*French*] ... TP
Travaux Publics Canada [*Public Works Canada - PWC*] ... TPC
Travel ... TRVL
Travel (AABC) ... TVL
Travel Accounting Control System [*Citicorp Diners Club*] ... TRACS
Travel Advance Payment [*TDY*] ... TVLADVP
Travel Agents Computer Society [*Defunct*] (EA) ... TACOS
Travel Agents Guild of America (EA) ... TAGA
Travel Agents' Licensing Authority [*Victoria, Australia*] ... TALA
Travel Agents' Licensing Board [*Australia*] ... TALB
Travel Air Club (EA) ... TAC
Travel Alberta, Edmonton, AB, Canada [*Library symbol Library of Congress Obsolete*] (LCLS) ... CaAETA
Travel Allowance ... TA
Travel Allowance Advance [*in PCS*] ... TVLALWADV
Travel Allowance on Separation [*Military*] ... TAOS
Travel Allowance on Separation [*Army*] ... TVLALWS
Travel and Entertainment [*IRS*] ... T & E
Travel and Living Allowance [*Military*] (AABC) ... TLA
Travel and Relocation ... TR
Travel and Tourism (EERA) ... T&T
Travel and Tourism Association (EA) ... TTA
Travel and Tourism Government Affairs Council (EA) ... TTGAC
Travel and Tourism Program [*Association of Independent Colleges and Schools specialization code*] ... TT
Travel and Tourism Research Association (EA) ... TTRA
Travel and Transportation Order ... TTO
Travel Arrangements Without Government Expense (FAAC) ... TAWOG
Travel as Directed Is Necessary in the Military Service (MUGU) ... TDN
Travel [*or Trip*] **Authorization** (MCD) ... TA
Travel Authorized via Privately-Owned Vehicle with Understanding No Additional Cost to Government Involved ... PRIVAUTH
Travel by Government Automobile Authorized ... TBGAA
Travel by Government Transportation Authorized [*Military*] (AABC) ... TBGTA
Travel by Military Aircraft Authorized ... TBMAA
Travel by Military Aircraft, Military and/or Naval Water Carrier, Commercial Rail and/or Bus Is Authorized [*Army*] (AABC) ... TBAWRBA
Travel by Personal Auto Authorized [*Military*] ... TPA
Travel by Privately-Owned Conveyance Permitted for Convenience [*Military*] (AFM) ... TPC
Travel Centre of New South Wales [*Australia*] ... TCNSW
Travel Classification Code ... TCC
Travel Consultants, Inc. ... TCI
Travel Correction Calculator (MSA) ... TCC
Travel Cost Method ... TCM
[*US*] **Travel Data Center** [*BTS*] (TAG) ... TDC
Travel Document and Issuance System [*US passport*] [*Department of State*] ... TDIS
Travel Economic Impact Model [*Department of Commerce*] ... TEIM
Travel Expense Report (SAA) ... TER
Travel for Industry [*Commercial firm*] [*British*] ... tfi
Travel for Tomorrow Council (EA) ... TTC
Travel Group Charter [*Airline fare*] ... TGC
Travel Industry and Disabled Exchange (EA) ... TIDE
Travel Industry Association of America (EA) ... TIA
Travel Industry Association of America ... TIAA
Travel [*later, Tourism*] **Industry Association of Canada** ... TIAC
Travel Industry for the Environment ... TIE
Travel Industry Network, Inc. [*Winter Springs, FL*] [*Telecommunications*] (TSSD) ... TINET
Travel Industry School (AIE) ... TRAVIS
Travel Industry Systems Standards Group [*British*] ... TISSG
Travel Information ... TRAVINFO
Travel Information Center [*An association*] (EA) ... TIC
Travel Information Processing System (NITA) ... TRIPS
Travel Information Service (EA) ... TIS
Travel Journalists Guild (EA) ... TJG
Travel Limit ... TRVLMT
Travel Management Center [*General Services Administration*] (GFGA) ... TMC
Travel Managers International (EA) ... TMI

Travel Model Improvement Program [*BTS*] (TAG) .... TMIP
Travel More Advantageous to the Government (AAG) .... TMAG
Travel News [*Wire service code*] (NTCM) .... T
Travel of Dependents and Household Goods Authorized [*Military*] (AABC) .... TDHGA
Travel Order .... TO
Travel Ports Amer [*NASDAQ symbol*] (TTSB) .... TPOA
Travel Ports of America, Inc. [*NASDAQ symbol*] (SAG) .... TPOA
Travel Ports of America, Inc. [*Associated Press*] (SAG) .... TravPrt
Travel Professionals Association (EA) .... TPA
Travel Related Services Co., Inc. .... TRS
Travel Request .... T/R
Travel Required [*Civil Service*] .... TR
Travel Security Guide [*Control Risks Information Services - CRIS*] [*British Information service or system*] (IID) .... TSG
Travel Supplement [*Publishing*] .... TS
Travel Time Authorized .... TTA
Travel to Interview Scheme (AIE) .... TIS
Travel to Work Area (AIE) .... TTWA
Travel/Tourism .... T/T
Travel Trends International [*Commercial firm British*] .... TTI
Travel via Commercial Aircraft Is Directed [*Where Government Aircraft Is Not Available*] (MCD) .... COMLAIRDIR
Travel via Commercial Transportation Authorized [*Military*] .... COMLTRANSAUTH
Travel via Government Aircraft Authorized Outside CONUS [*Military*] .... GOVAIRAUTHOUT
Travel via Government Aircraft Authorized Outside CONUS Where Available [*Military*] .... GOVAIRAUTHVATL
Travel via Government Aircraft Is Directed Outside CONUS [*Military*] .... GOVAIRDIROUT
Travel via Government Aircraft Is Directed Outside CONUS Where Available [*Military*] .... GOVAIRDIRVAIL
Travel via Government Aircraft Is Directed Where Necessary [*Military*] .... GOVAIRDIR
Travel via Government Aircraft Outside CONUS Class ____ Priority Certified [*Military*] .... GOVAIRPRI
Travel via Government and/or Commercial Aircraft Authorized Where Necessary to Expedite Completion of Duty [*Military*] .... GOVCOMLAIRAUTH
Travel via Government Transportation Directed Outside CONUS [*Military*] .... GOVTRANSDIROUT
Travel via Government Transportation Directed Outside CONUS Where Available [*Military*] .... GOVTRANSDIRVAIL
Travel Voucher (GFGA) .... TV
Travel Warrant .... TW
Travel Will Be Performed at No Expense to the Government [*Military*] .... TPNEG
Travel with Troops .... TWT
Travel with Troops Going .... TTG
Travel with Troops Returning .... TTR
Travel without Troops .... TW/OT
Travel Writer [*A publication*] (EAAP) .... TW
Travel-Agent Discount [*For air travel*] .... AD
Travelair GmbH [*Germany ICAO designator*] (FAAC) .... TAX
Travelair Goteborg [*ICAO designator*] (AD) .... RF
Travelcraft Ambassadors Club [*Defunct*] (EA) .... TAC
Traveler (MSA) .... TRVLR
Traveler/Failure Report [*Deep Space Instrumentation Facility, NASA*] .... TFR
Traveler Group, Inc. Capital I [*NYSE symbol*] (SAG) .... TRV
Traveler's Advisory [*Weather information*] .... TA
Travelers/Aetna Prop Casual'A' [*NYSE symbol*] (TTSB) .... TAP
Travelers Aetna Property Casualty Corp. [*NYSE symbol*] (SAG) .... TAP
Travelers Aetna Property Casualty Corp. [*Associated Press*] (SAG) .... TravAet
Travelers Aid Association of America [*Defunct*] (EA) .... TAAA
Travelers Aid - International Social Service of America [*Later, ISS/AB*] .... TAISSA
Travelers Canada, Toronto, Ontario [*Library symbol National Library of Canada*] (BIB) .... OTTRAC
Travelers' Century Club (EA) .... TCC
[*The*] **Travelers Corp.** [*Associated Press*] (SAG) .... Travelrs
[*The*] **Travelers Corp.** [*Associated Press*] (SAG) .... Travl
Travelers Corp. P & C Capital I [*NYSE symbol*] (SAG) .... TAP
Travelers Corp. P & C Capital I [*Associated Press*] (SAG) .... TravPC
Travelers Corp. P & C Capital II [*NYSE symbol*] (SAG) .... TAP
Travelers Corp. P & C Capital II [*Associated Press*] (SAG) .... TrvPC
Travelers, Defect Route Sheet (DNAB) .... TDRS
Traveler's Diarrhea [*Medicine*] (DMAA) .... TD
Travelers Emergency Transportation Association [*Sought to pool transportation of salesmen traveling similar routes*] [*World War II*] .... TETA
Travelers Group [*NYSE symbol*] (TTSB) .... TRV
[*The*] **Travelers Group, Inc.** [*Associated Press*] (SAG) .... Travel
Travelers Group, Inc. [*Associated Press*] (SAG) .... Travelrs
Travelers Grp 9.25% Dep Pfd [*NYSE symbol*] (TTSB) .... TRVPrD
Travelers Grp 8.125%'A'Dep Pfd [*NYSE symbol*] (TTSB) .... TRVPrA
Travelers Grp Wrrt [*NYSE symbol*] (TTSB) .... TRV.WS
Travelers Health Institute [*Later, ITHI*] .... THI
[*The*] **Travelers, Inc.** [*NYSE symbol*] (SAG) .... TRV
Travelers Information Service [*Oracle Corp.*] [*Information service or system*] (IID) .... TIS
Travelers P&C Cap 1 8.08% Pfd [*NYSE symbol*] (TTSB) .... TAPPrA
Travelers P&C Cap II 8.00% Pfd [*NYS*] (TTSB) .... TAPPrB
Travelers Protective Association of America [*St. Louis, MO*] (EA) .... TPA
Travelers Protective Association of America (EA) .... TPAA
Travelers Research Center [*Oceanography*] .... TRC
Travelers Rest, SC [*AM radio station call letters*] .... WDAB
TravelersGrp5.5%CV'B'Pfd [*NYSE symbol*] (TTSB) .... TRVPrB
Travel-Holiday [*A publication*] (BRI) .... Trav
Traveling (MSA) .... TRVLG
Traveling Around Drunk .... TAD
Traveling Businesswomen's Network (EA) .... TBN
Traveling Hat Salesmen's Association [*Defunct*] (EA) .... THSA
Traveling Heater Method .... THM
Traveling Image Storage Tube (MCD) .... TRIST
Traveling in Core Probe (IAA) .... TIP
Traveling Industrial Gaseous Emission Research [*Vehicle*] [*Exxon Corp.*] .... TIGER
Traveling Ionospheric Disturbance .... TID
Traveling Post Office .... TPO
Traveling Salesman Problem [*Mathematics*] .... TSP
Traveling Salesman Problem Library [*Electronic mail*] .... TSPLIB
Traveling Scholar Program (EA) .... TSP
Traveling Stock Reserve .... TSR
Traveling Ticket Inspector (DCTA) .... TTI
Traveling Trickle Irrigation System .... TTIS
Traveling Wave .... TW
Traveling-Wave Amplifier .... TWA
Traveling-Wave Amplifier Tube .... TWAT
Traveling-Wave Beam [*LASER*] .... TWB
Traveling-Wave Cathode-Ray Tube (IEEE) .... TWCRT
Traveling-Wave Klystron .... TWK
Traveling-Wave LASER .... TWL
Traveling-Wave Magnetron (IAA) .... TWM
Traveling-Wave MASER .... TWM
Traveling-Wave Multiple-Beam Klystron (MSA) .... TWMBK
Traveling-Wave Optical MASER .... TWOM
Traveling-Wave Parametric Amplifier .... TWPA
Traveling-Wave Phase Sifter .... TWPS
Traveling-Wave Phototube .... TWP
Traveling-Wave Resonator .... TWR
Traveling-Wave Tube (IAA) .... TET
Traveling-Wave Tube [*Radio*] .... TWT
Traveling-Wave Tube Amplifier [*Radio*] .... TWTA
Travellers' Aid Society of New South Wales [*Australia*] .... TASNSW
Travellers' Aid Society of Victoria [*Australia*] .... TASV
Travellers Cheque [*British*] (ADA) .... TC
Travellers Cheque Association Ltd. [*British*] .... TCA
Travellers Fare [*Train catering service*] [*British*] .... TF
Travelling and Meal Allowance .... TMA
Travelling Convection Vortices .... TCV
Travelling Showmen [*Public-performance tariff class*] [*British*] .... TS
Travelling-Wave Oscillator .... TWO
Travelmaster Travel Club [*Defunct*] (EA) .... TTC
Travels [*or Traveler*] .... TRAV
Travelwriter Marketletter [*Information service or system*] (IID) .... TM
Travenol Laboratories [*of Baxter Travenol Laboratories, Inc.*] [*Research code symbol*] .... BAX
Travenol Laboratories, Morton Grove, IL [*Library symbol Library of Congress*] (LCLS) .... IMgT
Travenol Laboratories, Morton Grove, IL [*OCLC symbol*] (OCLC) .... JAY
Traverisng In-Core Probe .... TIP
Travers and Twiss on Law of Nations [*A publication*] (DLA) .... Trav & Tw L of N
Travers Pensions [*Formerly, Naval Knights of Windsor*] [*Military British*] (ROG) .... TP
Traverse (AABC) .... TRAV
Traverse .... TRV
Traverse (IEEE) .... TV
Traverse and Elevation [*Weapons*] [*Army*] (INF) .... T & E
Traverse City [*Michigan*] [*Airport symbol*] (OAG) .... TVC
Traverse City, MI [*Location identifier FAA*] (FAAL) .... CXM
Traverse City, MI [*Location identifier FAA*] (FAAL) .... SRP
Traverse City, MI [*AM radio station call letters*] .... WCCW
Traverse City, MI [*FM radio station call letters*] .... WCCW-FM
Traverse City, MI [*Television station call letters*] .... WGTU
Traverse City, MI [*FM radio station call letters*] .... WLDR
Traverse City, MI [*FM radio station call letters*] .... WLJN
Traverse City, MI [*FM radio station call letters*] .... WNMC
Traverse City, MI [*Television station call letters*] .... WPBN
Traverse City, MI [*AM radio station call letters*] .... WTCM
Traverse City, MI [*FM radio station call letters*] .... WTCM-FM
Traverse City Public Library, Traverse City, MI [*Library symbol Library of Congress*] (LCLS) .... MiT
Traverse des Sioux Library System, Mankato, MN [*Library symbol Library of Congress*] (LCLS) .... MnManTD
Traverse des Sioux Library System, Mankato MN [*OCLC symbol*] (OCLC) .... TDS
Traverse Displacement Unit (DNAB) .... TDU
Traverse Gravimeter Experiment (KSC) .... TGE
Traversing Infrared Inspection System (MCD) .... TIRIS
Travertine (VRA) .... trvtn
Travis Air Force Base [*California*] .... TAFB
Travis Boats & Motors, Inc. [*Associated Press*] (SAG) .... TravBt
Travis Boats & Motors, Inc. [*NASDAQ symbol*] (SAG) .... TRVS
Travis County Law Library, Austin, TX [*Library symbol*] [*Library of Congress*] (LCLS) .... TxAuTL
Travnik [*Yugoslavia*] [*Seismograph station code, US Geological Survey Closed*] (SEIS) .... TRA
Trawl Efficiency Device (USDC) .... TED
Trawl Efficiency Device [*Marine science*] (OSRA) .... TED
Trawler .... TR
Trawler Owners' Association of Australia .... TOAA
Trawler Petroleum Explorations Ltd. [*Vancouver Stock Exchange symbol*] .... TWP
Trawling .... T
Trax Petroleums [*Vancouver Stock Exchange symbol*] .... TRL
Tray (WGA) .... TR

Trayner's Latin Maxims and Phrases [*A publication*] (ILCA) ... Tray Leg Max
Trayner's Latin Maxims and Phrases, Etc. [*A publication*] (DLA) ... Tray Lat Max
TRC, Companies [*Associated Press*] (SAG) ... TRC
TRC Cos. [*NYSE symbol*] (TTSB) ... TRR
TRC Cos., Inc. [*NYSE symbol*] (SPSG) ... TRR
Tre Corde [*With Three Strings, or Release the Soft Pedal*] [*Music*] ... TC
Tre Lateral Load Transfer Distribution ... TLLTD
Treacher Collins Foundation (EA) ... TCF
Treacher Collins Syndrome [*Medicine*] (DMAA) ... TC
Tread [*Stair details*] [*Technical drawings*] ... T
Tread (WGA) ... TR
Tread ... TRD
Tread Rubber Manufacturers Group (EA) ... TRMG
Treadco, Inc. [*Associated Press*] (SAG) ... Treadco
Treadco, Inc. [*NASDAQ symbol*] (SPSG) ... TRED
Treadmill Exercise (DAVI) ... TE
Treadmill Exercise Test [*Physiology*] (CPH) ... TET
Treadmill Exercise Test [*Medicine*] (DMAA) ... TMET
Treadmill Score [*Medicine*] (DMAA) ... TS
Treadmill Stress Test [*or Study*] [*Cardiology*] (DAVI) ... TMST
Treadmill Stress Testing [*Physiology*] ... TST
Treadway's South Carolina Constitutional Reports [*A publication*] (DLA) ... Tread
Treadway's South Carolina Constitutional Reports [*A publication*] (DLA) ... Tread Const
Treadway's South Carolina Constitutional Reports [*A publication*] (DLA) ... Treadway Const (SC)
Treadway's South Carolina Law Reports [*1812-16*] [*A publication*] (DLA) ... Tread
Treasure ... TREAS
Treasure Cay [*Bahamas*] [*Airport symbol*] (OAG) ... TCB
Treasure Cay, Abaco Island [*Bahamas*] [*ICAO location identifier*] (ICLI) ... MYAT
Treasure Hunter Research and Information Center (EA) ... THRIC
Treasure Island [*San Francisco Bay*] [*Navy base*] ... TI
Treasure Island Naval Shipyard [*San Francisco Bay*] ... TINSY
Treasure Island Resources [*Vancouver Stock Exchange symbol*] ... TRS
Treasure Trove Club (EA) ... TTC
Treasure Valley Community College, Ontario, OR [*Library symbol Library of Congress*] (LCLS) ... OrOnT
Treasurer ... T
Treasurer ... TR
Treasurer (EY) ... TREAS
Treasurer (DD) ... treas
Treasurer ... TRES
Treasurer of the United States (AFM) ... TUS
Treasury [*As in T-Bill, T-Bond, T-Note*] ... T
Treasury ... TRE
Treasury (ROG) ... TREAS
Treasury (VRA) ... treas
Treasury ... TRSRY
Treasury (AABC) ... TRSY
Treasury Acquisition/Procurement Regulation (AAGC) ... TAPR
Treasury Bill ... TB
Treasury Bill (TDOB) ... T-bill
Treasury Bill Rate (MHDW) ... TBR
Treasury Board Advisory Committee on Federal Land Management [*Canada*] ... TBAC/FLM
Treasury Board Manual [*Canada*] (AAGC) ... TBM
Treasury Board, Ottawa, ON, Canada [*Library symbol Library of Congress*] (LCLS) ... CaOOTRB
Treasury Board Secretariat [*Canada*] ... TB
Treasury Board Secretariat [*Canada*] ... TBS
Treasury Bulletin ... TRBU
Treasury Circular ... TC
Treasury Corp. Victoria [*Australia*] ... TCV
Treasury Decision [*In references to rulings*] ... TD
Treasury Decisions under Customs and Other Laws [*United States*] [*A publication*] (DLA) ... Treas Dec
Treasury Decisions under Internal Revenue Laws [*A publication*] (DLA) ... Treas Dec Int Rev
Treasury Department ... TD
Treasury Department Circular [*United States*] [*A publication*] (DLA) ... DC
Treasury Department Circular [*A publication*] (DLA) ... TDC
Treasury Department Circular [*A publication*] (DLA) ... Treas Dept Cir
Treasury Department, Comptroller of the Currency, Washington, DC [*OCLC symbol*] (OCLC) ... CTC
Treasury Department Decision (AFIT) ... TDD
Treasury Department Order [*A publication*] (DLA) ... TDO
Treasury Deposit Receipt ... TDR
Treasury Enforcement Agent ... TEA
Treasury Enforcement Communications System [*Customs Service*] ... TECS
Treasury Financial Communication System [*Department of the Treasury*] ... TFCS
Treasury General Account [*Department of the Treasury*] ... TGA
Treasury Gold License (MCD) ... TGL
Treasury Guard Force ... TGF
Treasury Historical Association (EA) ... THA
Treasury Indexed Bond (ADA) ... TIB
Treasury Instruction (ADA) ... TI
Treasury Inter-Services Committee [*British military*] (DMA) ... TISC
Treasury Investment Growth Receipt (MHDW) ... TIGER
Treasury Investment Growth Receipts [*Merrill Lynch & Co.*] [*Finance*] ... TIGR
Treasury Law Enforcement Information and Communications System ... TLEICS
Treasury Management Association ... TMA
Treasury Management Services [*British*] ... TMS
Treasury Market Securities (MHDW) ... TMS
Treasury Multi-User Acquisition Contract (AAGC) ... TMAC
Treasury Northern Territory [*Australia*] ... TNT
Treasury Obligation [*Finance*] ... TO
Treasury of Great American Quotations [*A publication*] ... TGAQ
Treasury of Jewish Quotations [*A publication*] ... TJQ
Treasury Order [*British*] (ROG) ... TO
Treasury Payroll/Personnel Information System ... TPPIS
Treasury Receipt ... TR
Treasury Regional Disbursing Office (AAGC) ... TRDO
Treasury Relief Aid Project ... TRAP
Treasury Security Force [*Department of the Treasury*] ... TSF
Treasury Solicitor [*British*] ... TS
Treasury Stock ... TS
Treasury Tax and Loan Account [*Banking*] ... TT & L
Treasury's Inflation Protection Securities ... TIPS
Treasury's Inflation Protection Securities ... TIPS
Treat, Scates, and Blackwell's Compiled Illinois Statutes [*A publication*] (DLA) ... Scates' Comp St
Treated ... T
Treated (MSA) ... TRTD
Treated but Not Admitted [*Medicine*] ... TBNA
Treated Hard-Pressed Fiberboard [*Technical drawings*] ... THPFB
Treated Paper Copier [*Reprography*] ... TPC
Treated Versus Cured [*Medicine*] ... T/C
Treaties and Other International Acts ... TIA
Treaties and Other International Agreements of the United States of America [*A publication*] (DLA) ... TI Agree
Treaties in Force [*A publication*] (DLA) ... TIF
Treating ... TRTG
Treatise (ROG) ... TR
Treatise on Trover and Conversion [*A publication*] (DLA) ... Treat Tro
Treatment ... T
Treatment [*Medicine*] ... TMT
Treatment [*Medicine*] (AAMN) ... TR
Treatment (AAG) ... TREAT
Treatment (AFM) ... TRMT
Treatment [*Medicine*] ... trt
Treatment ... TRTMNT
Treatment (MSA) ... TRTMT
Treatment ... TX
Treatment Action Group [*for AIDS medication*] [*FDA*] ... TAG
Treatment Alternatives to Street Crime [*Antidrug program*] ... TASC
Treatment Charge [*Metallurgy*] ... T/C
Treatment Code (NITA) ... TC
Treatment Completed [*Medicine*] (MEDA) ... TC
Treatment Control Unit [*Medicine*] (DMAA) ... TCU
Treatment Day ... TD
Treatment Development and Assessment Committee [*National Institutes of Health*] (EGAO) ... TDA
Treatment Discontinued [*Medicine*] ... T/D
Treatment of Emergent Symptom [*Medicine*] (MEDA) ... TES
Treatment of Mild Hypertension Study ... TOMHS
Treatment of War Gas Casualties (MCD) ... TWGC
Treatment Rating Assessment Matrix [*Medicine*] (MAE) ... TRAM
Treatment Response Assessment Method [*Medicine*] (MAE) ... TRAM
Treatment Selection Team (DOGT) ... TST
Treatment Services Control ... TSC
Treatment, Storage, and Disposal (GAAI) ... T/S/D
Treatment, Storage and Disposal Facilities (AAGC) ... TSD
Treatment, Storage, and Disposal Facility [*Hazardous waste*] ... TSDF
Treatment, Storage, Disposal, or Recycling [*Hazardous waste management*] ... TSDR
Treatment, Storage, or Disposal [*Hazardous waste management*] ... TSD
Treatment System [*Nuclear energy*] (NRCH) ... TS
Treatment System Support ... TSS
Treatment Works Treating Domestic Sewage [*Environmental Protection Agency*] ... TWTDS
Treatment Zone (GNE) ... TZ
Treatment-Authorization Request [*Medicine*] (MEDA) ... TAR
Treats, Inc. [*Toronto Stock Exchange symbol*] ... TTZ
Treaty [*Legal shorthand*] (LWAP) ... T
Treaty (ROG) ... TR
Treaty Limited Equipment (DOMA) ... TLE
Treaty of Friendship, Commerce, and Navigation [*Indonesia*] (IMH) ... FCN
Treaty Port ... TP
Treaty Series [*A publication*] (DLA) ... Tr Ser
Treaty Series [*A publication*] (ILCA) ... TS
Treble [*Music*] (ROG) ... T
Treble [*Knitting*] ... TR
Treble [*Music*] ... TR
Treble ... TRB
Treble (ROG) ... TREB
Treble Black [*Pencil*] ... BBB
Treble Cash Ruling [*Business term*] ... TX
Treble Crochet ... trc
Tredegar Indus [*NYSE symbol*] (TTSB) ... TG
Tredegar Industries [*Associated Press*] (SAG) ... Tredgar
Tredegar Industries, Inc. [*NYSE symbol*] (SPSG) ... TG
Tredegar Industries, Inc. [*Associated Press*] (SAG) ... Tredgar
Tredgold's Cape Colony Reports [*A publication*] (DLA) ... Tred
Tree and Tabular Combined Notation [*Telecommunications*] (OSI) ... TTCN
Tree Crops Database ... TREDAT
Tree Island Industries Ltd. [*Toronto Stock Exchange symbol Vancouver Stock Exchange symbol*] ... TIL
Tree of Life [*Internet phylogeny project originating from the University of Arizona, Tucson*] ... TOL
Tree Point, AK [*Location identifier FAA*] (FAAL) ... TRP

Tree Preservation Order [*Town planning*] [*British*] ... TPO
Tree Project (EA) ... TP
Tree Pruning System ... TPS
Tree Searching Language [*Computer science*] (PDAA) ... TSL
Tree Sparrow [*Ornithology*] ... TS
Tree Structured Attribute (IAA) ... TSA
Tree Test [*Psychology*] ... TT
Tree Tops ... TT
Tree-Adjoining Grammar [*Artificial intelligence*] ... TAG
Treehouse Books, Calgary, AB, Canada [*Library symbol*] [*Library of Congress*] (LCLS) ... CaACT
Treehouse Books, Calgary, Alberta [*Library symbol National Library of Canada*] (NLC) ... ACT
Treeing Walker Breeders and Fanciers Association (EA) ... TWBFA
TreePeople (EA) ... TP
Tree-Ring Society (EA) ... TRS
Trees [*Ecology*] ... TR
Trees for Life [*An association*] (EA) ... TFL
Trees for Tomorrow (EA) ... TT
Trees on Farms Program (EERA) ... TFP
Tree-Walking Pushdown Transducer (MHDI) ... TPDT
Trehalose Dimycolate [*Biochemistry*] ... TDM
Trehaven Aviation Ltd. [*British ICAO designator*] (ICDA) ... JF
Treherbert [*Cardiff*] [*Welsh depot code*] ... TRT
Treinta Y Tres [*Uruguay*] [*ICAO location identifier*] (ICLI) ... SUTR
Trek Airways [*South Africa ICAO designator*] (FAAC) ... TKE
Trek Magazine [*Generic term for a publication of interest to fans of the television program "Star Trek"*] ... TREKZINE
Trekville USA (EA) ... TUSA
Trelew [*Argentina*] [*Airport symbol*] (OAG) ... REL
Trelew [*Argentina*] [*Geomagnetic observatory code*] ... TWA
Trelew/Almirante Zar [*Argentina ICAO location identifier*] (ICLI) ... SAVT
Trelleborg [*Sweden ICAO location identifier*] (ICLI) ... ESMR
Trellis-Coded Modulation [*Data transmission*] (BYTE) ... TCM
Tremaine's Pleas of the Crown [*England*] [*A publication*] (DLA) ... Trem
Tremaine's Pleas of the Crown [*England*] [*A publication*] (DLA) ... Trem PC
Tremendously High Frequency [*Telecommunications*] (TEL) ... THF
Treminco Resources Ltd. [*Toronto Stock Exchange symbol Vancouver Stock Exchange symbol*] ... TMO
Tremolo [*Tremulous*] [*Music*] (WGA) ... trem
Tremont & Gulf Railroad (IIA) ... T & G
Tremont Corp. [*NYSE symbol*] (SPSG) ... TRE
Tremont Corp. [*Associated Press*] (SAG) ... Tremnt
Tremonton, UT [*AM radio station call letters*] ... KNFL
Tremonton, UT [*FM radio station call letters*] ... KNFL-FM
Tremor [*Medicine*] (AAMN) ... TR
Trempealeau, WI [*FM radio station call letters*] ... WKBH
Trench Feet [*or Fever*] ... TF
Trench Fighter [*British military*] (DMA) ... TF
Trench Junction Box ... TJB
Trench Mortar ... TM
Trench Mortar Battery [*British military*] (DMA) ... TMB
Trench-Metal Oxide Silicon [*Transistor*] ... T-MOS
Trend Analysis Program [*American Council of Life Insurance*] [*Washington, DC Information service or system*] (IID) ... TAP
Trend and Error Analysis Methodology System (MCD) ... TEAMS
Trend Asignment File [*Computer science*] (ECII) ... TAF
Trend Evaluation and Monitoring [*Congressional Clearinghouse on the Future*] (EA) ... TEAM
Trend Impact Analysis [*The Futures Group, Inc.*] [*Information service or system*] (IID) ... TIA
Trend Landing Forecast [*Aviation*] (DA) ... t
Trend Type Forecast (ADA) ... TTF
Trendelenburg [*Position*] [*Surgery*] (DAVI) ... tren
Trendelenburg (MEDA) ... Trend
Trend-Lines, Inc. [*Associated Press*] (SAG) ... TrendL
Trend-Lines, Inc. [*NASDAQ symbol*] (SAG) ... TRND
Trend-Lines'A'Inc. [*NASDAQ symbol*] (TTSB) ... TRND
Trends in Microbiology [*A publication*] ... TIM
Trends in Online Computer Control Systems (PDAA) ... TOLCCS
Trends in Pharmacological Sciences [*A publication*] ... TIPS
Trends, Indicators, and Analyses [*on the Southeast Asia war*] [*Classified Air Force document*] ... TIA
Trend-Set Industry [*Vancouver Stock Exchange symbol*] ... TSS
Trennzahl Values [*For carrier gas flow rates*] [*Chromatography*] ... TZ
Trent Audio Library Services, Trent University, Peterborough, Ontario [*Library symbol National Library of Canada*] (NLC) ... OPETAL
Trent Canal Office, Peterborough, Ontario [*Library symbol National Library of Canada*] (BIB) ... OPETC
Trent Institute for the Study of Popular Culture [*Trent University*] [*Canada Research center*] (RCD) ... TISPOC
Trent Interlibrary Loan and Communication Network [*Canada Information service or system*] (IID) ... TRESNET
Trent Regional Library System [*UTLAS symbol*] ... TRT
Trent Resource Sharing Network [*Ontario Library Service Trent*] [*Richmond Hill, ON*] [*Telecommunications*] (TSSD) ... TRESNET
Trent University [*UTLAS symbol*] ... TRE
Trent University Archives, Peterborough, ON, Canada [*Library symbol Library of Congress*] (LCLS) ... CaOPeTA
Trent University Archives, Peterborough, Ontario [*Library symbol National Library of Canada*] (NLC) ... OPETA
Trent University, Map Library, Peterborough, ON, Canada [*Library symbol Library of Congress*] (LCLS) ... CaOPeTM
Trent University, Peterborough, ON, Canada [*Library symbol Library of Congress*] (LCLS) ... CaOPeT
Trent University, Peterborough, Ontario [*Library symbol National Library of Canada*] (NLC) ... OPET
Trent University, Trent Audio Library Services, Peterborough, ON, Canada [*Library symbol*] [*Library of Congress*] (LCLS) ... CaOPeTAL
Trente [*Italy*] [*Seismograph station code, US Geological Survey Closed*] (SEIS) ... TRE
Trentiner Tiroler Volkspartei [*Trentino Tirol People's Party*] [*Italy Political party*] (PPE) ... TTVP
Trenton [*Diocesan abbreviation*] [*New Jersey*] (TOCD) ... TR
Trenton [*New Jersey*] [*Airport symbol*] (OAG) ... TTN
Trenton Canadian Forces Base, ON [*ICAO location identifier*] (ICLI) ... CYTR
Trenton, FL [*FM radio station call letters*] ... WDJY
Trenton Free Public Library, Trenton, NJ [*Library symbol Library of Congress*] (LCLS) ... NjT
Trenton, GA [*FM radio station call letters*] ... WBDX
Trenton, GA [*AM radio station call letters*] (RBYB) ... WKWN
Trenton/Mercer County [*New Jersey*] [*ICAO location identifier*] (ICLI) ... KTTN
Trenton, MO [*AM radio station call letters*] ... KTTN
Trenton, MO [*FM radio station call letters*] ... KTTN-FM
Trenton, MO [*Location identifier FAA*] (FAAL) ... TRX
Trenton, NJ [*Location identifier FAA*] (FAAL) ... TTN
Trenton, NJ [*AM radio station call letters*] ... WBUD
Trenton, NJ [*FM radio station call letters*] ... WCHR
Trenton, NJ [*FM radio station call letters*] ... WKXW
Trenton, NJ [*Television station call letters*] ... WNJT
Trenton, NJ [*FM radio station call letters*] ... WNJT-FM
Trenton, NJ [*FM radio station call letters*] ... WPST
Trenton, NJ [*FM radio station call letters*] ... WTSR
Trenton, NJ [*AM radio station call letters*] ... WTTM
Trenton, NJ [*FM radio station call letters*] ... WWFM
Trenton, ON [*AM radio station call letters*] ... CJTN
Trenton Public Library, Ontario [*Library symbol National Library of Canada*] (NLC) ... OTRE
Trenton Public Library, Trenton, IL [*Library symbol Library of Congress*] (LCLS) ... ITre
Trenton Savings Bank [*Associated Press*] (SAG) ... TrentS
Trenton Savings Bank [*NASDAQ symbol*] (SAG) ... TSBS
Trenton State College (GAGS) ... Trenton St C
Trenton State College, Trenton, NJ [*OCLC symbol*] (OCLC) ... NJT
Trenton State College, Trenton, NJ [*Library symbol Library of Congress*] (LCLS) ... NjTS
Trenton Times Newspapers, Trenton, NJ [*Library symbol Library of Congress*] (LCLS) ... NjTTT
Trenton, TN [*Location identifier FAA*] (FAAL) ... TGC
Trenton, TN [*AM radio station call letters*] ... WTNE
Trenton, TN [*FM radio station call letters*] ... WWEZ
Trentonian, Trenton, NJ [*Library symbol Library of Congress*] (LCLS) ... NjTTr
Trenton-Princeton Traction Co. [*Absorbed into Consolidated Rail Corp.*] [*AAR code*] ... TPT
Trenwick Group [*NASDAQ symbol*] (TTSB) ... TREN
Trenwick Group, Inc. [*NASDAQ symbol*] (NQ) ... TREN
Trenwick Group, Inc. [*Associated Press*] (SAG) ... Trnwck
Trepassey Public Library, Newfoundland [*Library symbol National Library of Canada*] (NLC) ... NFTR
Trepassey Public Library, Trepassey, NF, Canada [*Library symbol Library of Congress*] (LCLS) ... CaNfTr
Treponema [*Microbiology*] (AAMN) ... T
Treponema [*Microbiology*] ... Trep
Treponema Immobilization Test [*Clinical chemistry*] ... TIT
Treponema Immobilization Test [*Clinical chemistry*] (MAE) ... TPI
Treponema Pallidum [*A spirochete*] [*Clinical chemistry*] ... TP
Treponema Pallidum Agglutination [*Medicine*] (DAVI) ... TPA
Treponema Pallidum Complement [*Clinical chemistry*] (MAE) ... TPC
Treponema Pallidum Complement Fixation [*Clinical chemistry*] ... TPCF
Treponema Pallidum Cryolysis Complement Fixation [*Test for Syphilis*] (DAVI) ... TPCP
Treponema Pallidum Hemagglutination ... TPHA
Treponema Pallidum Immobilization [*or Immobilizing*] [*Clinical chemistry*] ... TPI
Treponema Pallidum Immune Adherence [*Clinical chemistry*] ... TPIA
Tres Arroyos [*Argentina*] [*Airport symbol*] (OAG) ... OYO
Tres Arroyos [*Argentina ICAO location identifier*] (ICLI) ... SAZH
Tres Esquinas [*Colombia*] [*Airport symbol*] (OAG) ... TQS
Tres Lagoas [*Brazil*] [*Airport symbol*] (AD) ... TLG
Tres Sage [*Wisest*] [*Presiding officer in the French rite Freemasonry*] ... TS
TresCom International [*NASDAQ symbol*] (TTSB) ... TRES
TresCom International, Inc. [*NASDAQ symbol*] (SAG) ... TRES
TresCom International, Inc. [*Associated Press*] (SAG) ... TresCom
Trespass [*Legal shorthand*] (LWAP) ... TPSS
Trestle (WGA) ... TRES
Tretes [*Java*] [*Seismograph station code, US Geological Survey*] (SEIS) ... TRT
Treu und Bestaendig [*Faithful and Steadfast*] [*Motto of Johann Georg, Margrave of Brandenburg (1577-1624)*] [*German*] ... TVB
Trevecca Nazarene College [*Tennessee*] ... TNC
Trevecca Nazarene College, Nashville, TN [*Library symbol Library of Congress*] (LCLS) ... TNTN
Trevecca Nazarene College, Nashville, TN [*OCLC symbol*] (OCLC) ... TTN
Trevico [*Italy ICAO location identifier*] (ICLI) ... LIRT
Treviso [*Italy*] [*Seismograph station code, US Geological Survey Closed*] (SEIS) ... TRV
Treviso [*Italy*] [*Airport symbol*] (AD) ... TRY
Treviso/Istrana [*Italy ICAO location identifier*] (ICLI) ... LIPS
Treviso/San Angelo [*Italy ICAO location identifier*] (ICLI) ... LIPH
Trevor (Wilkinson) [*Sports car named for its designer*] [*British*] ... TVR
Trevor's Taxes on Succession [*4th ed.*] [*1881*] [*A publication*] (DLA) ... Trev Tax Suc

Trex Medical Corp. [*Associated Press*] (SAG) ... TrexMed
Trex Medical Corp. [*AMEX symbol*] (SAG) ... TXM
Tri City, OR [*FM radio station call letters*] ... KKMX
Tri- [*or Triple*] **Coincidence Navigation** (IAA) ... TRICO
Tri County Bancorp [*NASDAQ symbol*] (SAG) ... TRIC
Tri County Bancorp [*Associated Press*] (SAG) ... TriCnty
Tri County Times, Slater, IA [*Library symbol*] [*Library of Congress*] (LCLS) ... IaSlaT
Tri Gold Industry [*Vancouver Stock Exchange symbol*] ... TGU
Tri Polyta Indonesia [*NASDAQ symbol*] (SAG) ... TPIFY
Tri Polyta Indonesia [*Associated Press*] (SAG) ... TriPolyta
Tri Star Airlines, Inc. [*FAA designator*] (FAAC) ... TRY
Tri Town Topics, Arcadia, IN [*Library symbol Library of Congress*] (LCLS) ... InArcT
Triacetin [*Antifungal compound*] [*Organic chemistry*] ... TA
Triacetoneamine Nitroxide [*Organic chemistry*] ... TANO
Triacetylhexahydrotriazine [*Organic chemistry*] ... TRAT
Triacetylole-Andomycin [*Medicine*] (DMAA) ... TAO
Triacontanol [*Plant growth regulator*] ... TRIA
Triactor Resources Corp. [*Vancouver Stock Exchange symbol*] ... TCC
Triacylglycerol [*Food technology*] ... TAG
Triad Computer Systems (DOMA) ... TRICOMS
Triad Guaranty [*NASDAQ symbol*] (TTSB) ... TGIC
Triad Guaranty, Inc. [*NASDAQ symbol*] (SAG) ... TGIC
Triad Guaranty, Inc. [*Associated Press*] (SAG) ... TriadGty
Triad Systems [*NASDAQ symbol*] (TTSB) ... TRSC
Triad Systems Corp. [*Associated Press*] (SAG) ... TriadSy
Triad Systems Corp. [*NASDAQ symbol*] (NQ) ... TRSC
Triad Systems Integration Corp. ... TSI
Triadal Equated Personality Inventory [*Psychology*] ... TEPI
Triafol ... TN
Trial ... TL
Trial (ROG) ... TR
Trial (ROG) ... TRL
Trial Advocate Quarterly [*A publication*] (DLA) ... Trial Advoc Q
Trial and Error ... TE
Trial and Tort Trends [*A publication*] (DLA) ... Tr & TT
Trial Assessment Procedure Scale [*Medicine*] (DMAA) ... TAPS
Trial Attorney's Litigation File (AAGC) ... TALF
Trial Balance [*Bookkeeping*] (ODBW) ... tb
Trial Balance [*Bookkeeping*] ... TB
Trial Balloon ... TB
Trial Boll Weevil Eradication Program [*Department of Agriculture*] ... TBWEP
Trial Counsel [*Military*] ... TC
Trial Court [*Legal shorthand*] (LWAP) ... TCT
Trial for Early Alcohol Treatment ... TrEAT
Trial Installation (MCD) ... TI
Trial Judge Advocate [*Army*] ... TJA
Trial Judges' Journal [*A publication*] (DLA) ... Tr Judge J
Trial Kit Installation (CAAL) ... TKI
Trial Lawyers for Public Justice (EA) ... TLPJ
Trial Lawyers Forum [*A publication*] (DLA) ... Trial Law Forum
Trial Lawyers Marketing Association (EA) ... TLMA
Trial Modification (SAA) ... TM
Trial of Antihypertensive Interventions and Management [*Medicine*] ... TAIM
Trial of John Fries (Treason) [*A publication*] (DLA) ... Fries Tr
Trial of Labor [*Gynecology*] ... TOL
Trial of Professor Webster for Murder [*A publication*] (DLA) ... Web Tr
Trial of the Earl of Coventry [*A publication*] (DLA) ... E of Cov
Trial of the Earl of Coventry [*A publication*] (DLA) ... Tri E of Cov
Trial of the Savannah Privateers [*A publication*] (DLA) ... Sav Priv
Trial of the Seven Bishops [*A publication*] (DLA) ... Tri Bish
Trial of Warren Hastings [*A publication*] (DLA) ... Hast Tr
Trial Preparation (LAIN) ... TP
Trial Report ... TR
Trial Run Model (SAA) ... TRM
Trial Shot Point ... TSP
Trial Visit (AAMN) ... TV
Trial Work Period [*Social Security Administration*] (OICC) ... TWP
Trial Y-Plane ... TY-P
Trial-Dependent-Forgetting [*Process*] [*Psychology*] ... TDF
Trialkoxycitrate [*Organic chemistry*] ... TAC
Trialkoxyglyceryl Ether [*Organic chemistry*] ... TGE
Trialkoxytricarballylate [*Organic chemistry*] ... TATCA
Trialkylamine [*Organic chemistry*] ... TAM
Trialkylphosphine Oxide [*Organic chemistry*] ... TRPO
Trialkylstannylmaleate [*Organic chemistry*] ... TASM
Triallyl Cyanurate [*Organic chemistry*] ... TAC
Triallylisocyanurate [*Organic chemistry*] ... TAIC
Trials of Hypertension Prevention [*Medicine*] ... TOHP
Trials per Pais [*A publication*] (DLA) ... Tri per P
Trials Recording and Analysis Console (PDAA) ... TRAC
Triamcinolone [*Synthetic steroidal drug*] ... TMC
Triamcinolone Acetonide [*Also, TAA*] [*Synthetic steroidal drug*] ... TA
Triamcinolone Acetonide [*Also, TA*] [*Synthetic steroidal drug*] ... TAA
Triamcinolone Cream [*Anti-inflammatory steroid*] ... TAC
Triaminobenzene [*Organic chemistry*] ... TRAB
Triaminoguanidine Nitrate [*Propellant ingredient*] ... TAGN
Triaminopyrimidine [*Organic chemistry*] ... TAP
Triaminotrinitrobenzene [*Organic chemistry*] ... TAT
Triaminotrinitrobenzene [*Organic chemistry*] ... TATB
Triamterene [*Diuretic*] ... TAT
Trian Equities Ltd. [*Vancouver Stock Exchange symbol*] ... TEQ
Triangle ... T
Triangle (BARN) ... trg
Triangle ... TRI
Triangle (MSA) ... TRNGL
Triangle Airline (Uganda) Ltd. [*FAA designator*] (FAAC) ... TRU
Triangle Amplitude Modulation ... TAM
Triangle Bancorp [*NASDAQ symbol*] (SAG) ... TRBC
Triangle Bancorp [*Associated Press*] (SAG) ... TrianBc
Triangle Below Canal Street [*Artists' colony in New York City*] [*See also NoHo, SoHo, SoSo*] ... TriBeCa
Triangle Coalition for Science and Technology Education (EA) ... TCSTE
Triangle Fraternity Education Fund ... TFEF
Triangle Pacific [*NASDAQ symbol*] (TTSB) ... TRIP
Triangle Pacific Corp. [*NASDAQ symbol*] (SAG) ... TRIP
Triangle Pacific Corp. [*Associated Press*] (SAG) ... TriPacf
Triangle Resources, Inc. [*Vancouver Stock Exchange symbol*] ... TLI
Triangle Universities Computation Center [*Durham, NC*] ... TUCC
Triangle Universities Nuclear Laboratory [*Research center*] (RCD) ... TUNL
Triangle University Library Cooperative Committee [*Library network*] ... TULCC
Triangular Fibrocartilage Complex [*Anatomy*] ... TFCC
Triangular Guide Line ... TGL
Triangulated Irregular Network (EERA) ... TIN
Triangulation ... Tri
Triangulation (AABC) ... TRIG
Triangulation Ranging and Crossfix System [*Military*] (CAAL) ... TRACS
Triangulation-Listening-Ranging [*SONAR*] ... TLR
Triangulum [*Constellation*] ... Tri
Triangulum [*Constellation*] ... Tria
Triangulum Australe [*Constellation*] ... TrA
Triangulum Australe [*Constellation*] ... TrAu
Triannual Review (NATG) ... TAR
Triarc Co. [*Associated Press*] (SAG) ... Triarc
Triarc Co., Inc. [*Formerly, DWG Corp.*] [*NYSE symbol*] (SPSG) ... TRY
Triarc Cos Cl'A' [*NYSE symbol*] (TTSB) ... TRY
Tri-Arc Energy Ltd. [*Vancouver Stock Exchange symbol*] ... TRY
Triassic [*Period, era, or system*] [*Geology*] ... TRI
Triathalon Broadcasting Co. [*NASDAQ symbol*] (SAG) ... TBCOA
Triathalon Broadcasting Co. [*Associated Press*] (SAG) ... TriathB
Triathlon Association of Victoria [*Australia*] ... TAV
Triathlon Brdcst 9% Pfd [*NASDAQ symbol*] (TTSB) ... TBCOL
Triathlon Broadcasting 'A' [*NASDAQ symbol*] (TTSB) ... TBCOA
Triathlon Federation of Australia ... TFA
Triathlon Federation/USA (EA) ... TRI-FED
Triathlon Federation/USA [*Later, TRI-FED*] (EA) ... TRIFED/USA
Triax Airlines Ltd. [*Nigeria*] [*ICAO designator*] (FAAC) ... TIX
Triaxial Earth Ellipsoid ... TEE
Triaxial Recording Accelerometer ... TRA
Triazabicydo-decene [*Organic chemistry*] ... TBD
Triazacyclononane [*Organic chemistry*] ... TACN
Triazinate [*Antineoplastic drug*] (CDI) ... TZT
Triazolam [*Tranquilizer*] ... TAZ
Triazolopyridazine [*Potential antianxiety drug*] ... TZP
Triazolo-Thiadiazine [*Organic chemistry*] ... TTD
(Triazolyl-Azo) diaminotoluene [*Organic chemistry*] ... TrADAT
Tribal ... TRIB
Tribal Class Update and Modernization Project [*Canadian Navy*] ... TRUMP
Tribal Employment Rights Office ... TERO
Tribal Indian Land Rights Association (EA) ... TILRA
Tribal Liaison Program [*Bureau of the Census*] (GFGA) ... TLP
Tribal Sovereignty Program [*Later, SGFID*] (EA) ... TSP
Tribal Trust Land [*Zimbabwe*] ... TTL
Tribally Controlled Colleges and Universities ... TCCU
Tri-Basin Resources Ltd. [*Vancouver Stock Exchange symbol*] ... TIA
Tribological Experiments in Zero Gravity ... TEZG
Tribology Centre [*British*] ... TC
Triboluminescence [*Atomic physics*] ... TL
Tribothermoluminescence ... TTL
Tribromo(hydroxy)benzoic Acid [*Organic chemistry*] ... TBHBA
Tribromosalicylanilide [*or Tribromsalan*] [*Organic chemistry*] ... TBS
Tribulation (DSUE) ... TRIB
Tribuna di North Jersey, Newark, NJ [*Library symbol Library of Congress*] (LCLS) ... NjNT
Tribunal ... Tbnl
Tribunal ... Trib
Tribunal Administratif [*Administrative Court*] [*French*] (ILCA) ... TA
Tribunal Arbitral du Sport [*Court of Arbitration of Sport - CAS*] [*Switzerland*] (EAIO) ... TAS
Tribunal Correctionnel [*Court of First Instance in Penal Matters*] [*Belgium*] (ILCA) ... Corr
Tribunal des Conflits [*Tribunal of Conflicts*] [*French*] (ILCA) ... TC
Tribunale [*Ordinary Court of First Instance*] [*Italian*] (DLA) ... Trib
Tribune Books [*A publication*] (BRI) ... Trib Bks
[*The*] **Tribune Co.** [*NYSE symbol*] (SPSG) ... TRB
[*The*] **Tribune Co.** [*Associated Press*] (SAG) ... Tribune
Tribune de St. Gervais [*A publication*] ... TG
Tribune Internationale des Jeunes Interpretes [*International Rostrum of Young Performers - IRP*] (EAIO) ... TIJI
Tribunicia Potestas [*Latin*] (OCD) ... TRIB POT
Tribunus [*Tribune*] [*Latin*] ... Trb
Tribunus [*Tribune*] [*Latin*] (OCD) ... TRIB
Tribus [*Tribe*] [*Latin*] ... trib
Tributary (ROG) ... TR
Tributary ... TRIB
Tributary Team [*Military*] ... TT
Tribute (ADA) ... TRIB
Tri(butoxyethyl) Phosphate [*Organic chemistry*] ... TBEP
Tributyl Phosphate [*Organic chemistry*] ... TBF

Tributyl Phosphate [*Organic chemistry*] ... TBP
Tributyl Phosphate Task Force (EA) ... TPTF
Tributyl Phosphine [*Organic chemistry*] ... TBP
Tributyl Tin [*Chemical*] (EERA) ... TBT
Tributyl Trithiophosphate [*Defoliant*] [*Organic chemistry*] ... TBTP
Tributylamine [*Organic chemistry*] ... TBA
Tributylmethylammonium Chloride [*Organic chemistry*] ... TBMAC
Tributylphosphine [*Organic chemistry*] ... TBUP
Tributylstannylmaleate [*Organic chemistry*] ... TBSM
Tributylthiourea [*Organic chemistry*] ... TBTU
Tributyltin [*Anitimicrobial agent*] ... TBT
Tributyltin Fluoride [*Antimicrobial agent*] ... TBTF
Tributyltin Hydride [*Organic chemistry*] ... TBTH
Tributyltin Oxide [*Organic chemistry*] ... TBTO
Tributyltin Sulfide [*Organic chemistry*] ... TBTS
Tricaine Methane Sulphonate [*Chemistry*] (DAVI) ... mS-222
Tricalcium Aluminate [*Inorganic chemistry*] (MAE) ... TCA
Tricalcium Phosphate [*Inorganic chemistry*] ... TCP
Tricalcium Phosphate Ceramic [*Inorganic chemistry*] ... TPC
Tri-Camera (IAA) ... TRIC
Tricapped Triangular Prism ... TCTP
Tricarboxylic Acid [*Cycle*] [*Biochemistry*] ... TCA
Triceps Jerk ... TJ
Triceps Skinfold [*Medicine*] ... TSF
Triceps Skinfold Thickness [*Medicine*] ... TST
Trichinopoli Cigar (DSUE) ... TRICI
Trichinopoly [*India*] [*Airport symbol*] (AD) ... TRZ
Trichinosis [*Gastroenterology*] (DAVI) ... TRICH
Trichlorethylene-Extracted Soybean Oil Meal ... TCESOM
Trichloroacetate [*Organic chemistry*] ... TCA
Trichloroacetic Acid [*Also, TCAA*] [*Organic chemistry*] ... TCA
Trichloroacetic Acid [*Also, TCA*] [*Organic chemistry*] ... TCAA
Trichloroanisole [*Organic chemistry*] ... TCA
Trichlorobenzene [*Organic chemistry*] ... TCB
Trichlorobenzoic Acid [*Herbicide*] [*Organic chemistry*] ... TBA
Trichlorobenzoquinoneimine [*Reagent*] ... TCQ
Trichlorobenzyl Chloride [*Organic chemistry*] ... TCBC
Trichlorobiphenyl [*Chemistry*] (DAVI) ... triCB
Trichlorobutylene Oxide [*Organic chemistry*] ... TCBO
Trichlorocarbanilide [*Organic chemistry*] ... TCC
Trichloroethane [*Organic chemistry*] ... TCEA
Trichloroethanol [*Organic chemistry*] ... TCE
Trichloroethanol [*An anesthetic and hypnotic*] [*Pharmacology*] (DAVI) ... TCE
Trichloroethylene [*Also, TRI*] [*Organic chemistry*] ... TCE
Trichloroethylene [*Anesthesiology*] ... TRI
Trichloroethylene [*A solvent*] [*Chemistry*] (DAVI) ... TRI
Trichloroethylene [*A solvent*] [*Chemistry*] (DAVI) ... TRIC
Trichloroethylene Finishing ... TF
Trichloroisocyanuric Acid [*Organic chemistry*] ... TCCA
Trichloromethiazide [*Diuretic*] ... TCMZ
Trichloromethyltriazine ... TCT
Trichlorophenol [*Organic chemistry*] ... TCP
(Trichlorophenoxy)acetic Acid [*Also known as 2,4,5-T*] [*Herbicide*] ... TCP
(Trichlorophenoxy)propionic Acid [*Plant hormone*] [*Herbicide*] ... TCPPA
Trichlorophenylacetic Acid [*Herbicide*] [*Organic chemistry*] ... TCPA
Trichloropropane [*Organic chemistry*] ... TCP
Trichlorosilane [*Inorganic chemistry*] ... TCS
Trichlorotrifluoroethane [*Organic chemistry*] ... TCTFE
Trichlorotrinitrobenzene [*Organic chemistry*] ... TCTNB
Trichome [*Botany*] ... T
Trichomonas [*A parasite*] (DAVI) ... T
Trichomonas [*A protozoan*] [*Medicine*] ... Trich
Trichomonas and Monilia [*cultures*] (DAVI) ... T & M
Trichomonas vaginalis [*A protozoan*] [*Medicine*] ... TV
Trichomonas Vaginitis [*A parasite*] (DAVI) ... Trich V
Trichomonas Vaginitis [*A parasitic infection*] (DAVI) ... TV
Trichophyton [*Medicine*] (MAE) ... T
Trichoptera [*Entomology*] ... Trich
Trichorhinophalangeal [*Syndrome*] (DAVI) ... TRP
Trichorhinophalangeal Syndrome (DAVI) ... TRPS
Trichosanic Acid [*Biochemistry*] ... TCA
Trichosanthin [*Botany*] ... TCS
Trichothiodystrophy [*Medicine*] ... TTD
Trichothiodystrophy [*Medicine*] ... TTD
Trichromatic (DGA) ... Tr-Cro
Trichromatic (DGA) ... Tri-Chro
Tri-City Airport [*Tennessee*] [*Airport symbol*] (OAG) ... TRI
Trick Wheel ... TRKWHL
Trickle Ammonia Process [*for drying grain feedstuffs*] ... TAP
Trickle Bed Reactor [*Chemical engineering*] ... TBR
Trickle Up Program (EA) ... TUP
Tricks for Research in Cancer ... TRIC
Trick-Taking Potential [*Statistics*] ... TTP
Triclinic [*Crystallography*] (IAA) ... TRI
Triclinic [*Crystallography*] ... TRIC
Triclinic ... TRICL
Triclinium (VRA) ... tricl
Triclocarban [*Pharmacology*] ... TCC
Trico Bancshares [*NASDAQ symbol*] (SAG) ... TCBK
Trico Bancshares [*Commercial firm Associated Press*] (SAG) ... TriCoBn
Trico Marine Services, Inc. [*NASDAQ symbol*] (SAG) ... TMAR
Trico Marine Services, Inc. [*Associated Press*] (SAG) ... TricoMr
Trico Marine Svcs [*NASDAQ symbol*] (TTSB) ... TMAR
Tri-College Library, Moorhead, MN [*OCLC symbol*] (OCLC) ... TRI
Tri-College University Library Consortium [*Library network*] ... TCU
Tri-color Visual Approach Slope Indicator [*Aviation*] (FAAC) ... TRCV
Tricommand Review Panel [*Military*] (AFIT) ... TRP
Tri-Community Library, Fernwood, ID [*Library symbol*] [*Library of Congress*] (LCLS) ... IdFe
Tri-Cone Support Structure [*NASA*] ... TCSS
Triconix Control Application Language (NITA) ... T-Cal
Tri-Continental [*NYSE symbol*] (TTSB) ... TY
Tri-Continental, $2.50 Pfd [*NYSE symbol*] (TTSB) ... TYPr
Tri-Continental Corp. [*Associated Press*] (SAG) ... TriCn
Tri-Continental Corp. [*Associated Press*] (SAG) ... TriCon
Tri-Continental Corp. [*NYSE symbol*] (SPSG) ... TY
Tricord Systems [*NASDAQ symbol*] (TTSB) ... TRCD
Tricord Systems, Inc. [*NASDAQ symbol*] (SAG) ... TRCD
Tricord Systems, Inc. [*Associated Press*] (SAG) ... Tricord
Tricot Institute of America [*Defunct*] (EA) ... TIA
Tri-County High School, Karlstad, MN [*Library symbol*] [*Library of Congress*] (LCLS) ... MnKarH
Tri-County Library Council, Inc. [*Library network*] ... TLC
Tri-County Memorial Hospital, Gowanda, NY [*Library symbol Library of Congress*] (LCLS) ... NGowH
Tri-County Mental Health Center, Salisbury, NC [*Library symbol*] [*Library of Congress*] (LCLS) ... NcSalTM
Tri-County News, South Bend, IN [*Library symbol Library of Congress*] (LCLS) ... InSTN
Tri-County News, Zearing, IA [*Library symbol Library of Congress*] (LCLS) ... IaZN
Tri-County Public Library District, Augusta, IL [*Library symbol Library of Congress*] (LCLS) ... IAug
Tri-County Regional Library, Rome, GA [*Library symbol Library of Congress*] (LCLS) ... GRT
Tri-County Regional Planning Commission [*Information service or system*] (IID) ... TCRPC
Tri-County Technical College, Pendleton, SC [*Library symbol*] [*Library of Congress*] (LCLS) ... ScPT
Tri-County Technical Institute, Murphy, NC [*Library symbol Library of Congress*] (LCLS) ... NcMuT
Tricresyl Phosphate [*Organic chemistry*] ... TCP
Tricuspid Atresia [*Cardiology*] ... TA
Tricuspid Atresia [*Cardiology*] (DAVI) ... TCA
Tricuspid Closure [*Cardiology*] ... TC
Tricuspid First Heart Sound [*Cardiology*] ... T_1
Tricuspid First Sound [*Cardiology*] (DAVI) ... T_1
Tricuspid Incompetence [*Cardiology*] (MAE) ... TI
Tricuspid Insufficiency [*Medicine*] (MEDA) ... TCI
Tricuspid Insufficiency [*Cardiology*] ... TI
Tricuspid Regurgitation [*Cardiology*] ... TR
Tricuspid Second Heart Sound [*Cardiology*] ... T_2
Tricuspid Stenosis [*Cardiology*] ... TS
Tricuspid Valve [*Anatomy*] ... TV
Tricuspid Valve Echophonocardiogram [*Cardiology*] ... TVE
Tricuspid Valve Opening [*Cardiology*] ... TO
Tricuspid Valve Prolapse [*Cardiology*] ... TVP
Tricuspid Valve Replacement [*Cardiology*] ... TVR
Tricyanoaminopropene [*Organic chemistry*] ... TCAP
Tricycle (AAG) ... TRI
Tricycle [*A publication*] ... Tric
Tricycle and Tail Skid [*Aerospace*] (AAG) ... TT
Tricycle Association [*British*] (DBA) ... TA
Tricycle Club [*British*] ... TC
Tricycle Racing Club of America ... TRCA
Tricyclic Antidepressant [*Medicine*] ... TCA
Tricyclic Antidepressant [*Pharmacology*] (DAVI) ... TCAD
Tridecylcyclohexane [*Organic chemistry*] ... TDC
Tridecylcyclohexane [*Organic chemistry*] ... TDCH
Tridel Enterprises, Inc. [*Toronto Stock Exchange symbol*] ... TDZ
Trident Aircraft Ltd. [*Canada ICAO aircraft manufacturer identifier*] (ICAO) ... TR
Trident Command and Control Systems Maintenance Facility (DNAB) ... TRICCSMA
Trident Intl [*NASDAQ symbol*] (TTSB) ... TRDT
Trident Microsystems [*NASDAQ symbol*] (SAG) ... TRID
Trident Microsystems, Inc. [*Associated Press*] (SAG) ... TridMic
Trident NGL Holdings, Inc. [*NYSE symbol*] (SPSG) ... NGL
Trident Planned Equipment Replacement (DNAB) ... TRIPER
Trident Refit Facility (DNAB) ... TRIREFFAC
Trident Rowan Group [*NASDAQ symbol*] (SAG) ... TRGI
Trident Rowan Group [*Associated Press*] (SAG) ... TridentR
Trident SONAR Maintenance Trainer (DWSG) ... TSMT
Trident Technical College, Palmer Campus, Charleston, SC [*Library symbol Library of Congress*] (LCLS) ... ScCT
Trident Training Facility (DNAB) ... TRITRAFAC
Tridex Corp. [*AMEX symbol*] (SPSG) ... TDX
Tridex Corp. [*NASDAQ symbol*] (SAG) ... TRDX
Tridex Corp. [*Associated Press*] (SAG) ... Tridex
Tridodecylmethylammonium Chloride [*Organic chemistry*] ... TDMAC
Tridont Health Care, Inc. [*Toronto Stock Exchange symbol*] ... THC
Tridoppler ... TRIDOP
Triduum [*Three Days*] [*Latin*] (ADA) ... TRID
Triengen [*Switzerland ICAO location identifier*] (ICLI) ... LSPN
Triennial Cycle (BJA) ... TC
Trienoic/Tetraenoic [*Ratio of unsaturated chemicals*] ... T/T
Trier [*Germany ICAO location identifier*] (ICLI) ... EDZI
Trier/Foehren [*Germany ICAO location identifier*] (ICLI) ... EDRT
Trierer Theologische Studien [*Trier*] [*A publication*] (BJA) ... TTSt
Trieste [*Italy ICAO location identifier*] (ICLI) ... LIVT
Trieste [*Grotta Gigante*] [*Italy*] [*Seismograph station code, US Geological Survey*] (SEIS) ... TRI

Trieste [*Italy*] [*Seismograph station code, US Geological Survey Closed*] (SEIS) .... TRS
Trieste [*Italy*] [*Airport symbol*] (OAG) .... TRS
Trieste United States Troops .... TRUST
Triethanolamine [*Organic chemistry*] .... TEA
Triethanolamine [*Organic chemistry*] .... TEOA
Triethanolamine [*Medicine*] (DMAA) .... TREA
Triethanolamine [*USAN*] [*Organic chemistry*] .... TROLAMINE
Triethanolamine Lauryl Sulfate [*Organic chemistry*] .... TEALS
Triethanolamine Phosphoric Acid [*Organic chemistry*] .... TEAPA
Triethanolamine-Buffered Saline [*Organic chemistry*] (MAE) .... TBS
Triethoxymethoxy Propanes [*Organic chemistry*] .... TEMP
Triethyl Gallium [*Organic chemistry*] .... TEG
Triethyl Orthoformate [*Organic chemistry*] .... TEOF
Triethylaluminum [*Organic chemistry*] .... TEA
Triethylamine [*Organic chemistry*] .... TEA
Triethylaminoethyl [*Organic chemistry*] .... TEAE
Triethylammonium [*Organic chemistry*] .... TEA
Triethylammonium Acetate [*Organic chemistry*] .... TEAA
Triethylammonium Formate [*Organic chemistry*] .... TEAF
Triethylammonium Phosphate [*Organic chemistry*] .... TEAP
Triethylbenylammonium Chloride [*Organic chemistry*] .... TEBAC
Triethylbenzene [*Organic chemistry*] .... TEB
Triethylborane [*Organic chemistry*] .... TEB
Triethylene Dimethacrylate [*Organic chemistry*] .... TEDMA
Triethylene Glycol [*Organic chemistry*] .... TEG
Triethylene Glycol Diglycidyl Ether [*Medicine*] .... TDE
Triethylene Glycol Dimethacrylate [*Organic chemistry*] (MCD) .... TEGMA
Triethylene Glycol Dimethyl Ether [*Organic chemistry*] .... TRIGLYME
Triethylene Glycol Dinitrate [*An explosive*] .... TEGDN
Triethylene Melamine [*An arizidine mutagen*] [*Genetics*] (DOG) .... tem
Triethylenediamine [*Organic chemistry*] .... TEDA
Triethyleneiminobenzoquinone [*Organic chemistry*] (MAE) .... TEIB
Triethylenemelamine [*Organic chemistry*] .... TEM
Triethylenephosphoramide [*Also, APO*] [*Organic chemistry*] .... TEPA
Triethylenetetramine [*Organic chemistry*] .... TETA
Triethylenetetraminehexaacetic Acid [*Organic chemistry*] .... TTHA
Triethylenethiophosphoramide [*Antineoplastic drug*] (DAVI) .... TESPA
Triethylenethiophosphoramide [*Also, ThioTepa, TSPA*] [*Antineoplastic drug*] (DAVI) .... Thio-T
Triethylenethiophosphoramide [*Also, TSPA*] [*Antineoplastic drug*] .... THioTEPA
Triethylenethiophosphoramide [*Also, THioTEPA*] [*Antineoplastic drug*] .... TSPA
Triethylenethiophosphoramide [*Antineoplastic drug*] (MAE) .... TTPA
Triethyl-Phosphine [*Organic chemistry*] .... TEP
Triethylsilyl [*Organic chemistry*] .... TES
Triethylstannylmaleate [*Organic chemistry*] .... TESM
Triex Resources Ltd. [*Vancouver Stock Exchange symbol*] .... TXR
Trifascicular Block [*Medicine*] (AAMN) .... TFB
Trifluoperazine [*Also, Trifluoroperazine*] [*Organic chemistry*] .... TFP
Trifluoroacetic [*or Trifluoroacetyl*] **Acid** [*Organic chemistry*] .... TFA
Trifluoroacetic Anhydride [*Organic chemistry*] .... TFA
Trifluoroacetic Anhydride [*Organic chemistry*] .... TFAA
Trifluoroacetyl [*Organic chemistry*] .... TFA
Trifluoroacetylimidazole [*Organic chemistry*] .... TFAI
Trifluoroacetylprolyl Chloride (BARN) .... TFAP
Trifluoroethanol [*Organic chemistry*] .... TFE
Trifluoromethanesulfonate [*Organic chemistry*] .... TRIFLATE
Trifluoromethanesulfonic [*Organic chemistry*] .... TRIFLIC
Trifluoromethanesulfonic Acid [*Organic chemistry*] .... TFMSA
Trifluoromethyldichlorocarbanilide [*Organic chemistry*] .... TFC
Trifluoromethyl(iodophenyl)deazirine [*Biochemistry*] .... TID
Trifluoromethylnitrophenol [*Organic chemistry*] .... TFM
Trifluoromethyl(phenyl)piperazine [*Organic chemistry*] .... TFMPP
Trifluoroperazine [*Also, Trifluoperazine*] [*Organic chemistry*] .... TFP
Trifluoro(thienyl)butanedione [*Also, TTA*] [*Organic chemistry*] .... TTB
Trifluorothymidine [*Pharmacology*] .... TFT
Trifluroperazine [*Tranquilizer*] .... TFZ
Triforium (VRA) .... trifr
Triganglioside [*Chemistry*] .... GT
Trigeminal Ganglion [*Neuroanatomy*] .... TG
Trigeminal Mesencephalic Nucleus [*Neuroanatomy*] .... TMN
Trigeminal Neuralgia [*Medicine*] .... TGN
Trigeminal Neuralgia Association (EA) .... TNA
Trigen Energy [*NYSE symbol*] (TTSB) .... TGN
Trigen Energy Corp. [*NYSE symbol*] (SAG) .... TGN
Trigen Energy Corp. [*Associated Press*] (SAG) .... TrigenE
Trigesimo-Secundo [*Book from 10 to 12-1/2 centimeters in height*] [*Bibliography*] .... TT
Trigger (IAA) .... T
Trigger (IAA) .... TG
Trigger (AAG) .... TRIG
Trigger and Monitor Panel (IAA) .... TAMPNL
Trigger Delay Unit .... TDU
Trigger Generator .... TG
Trigger Inverter Module .... TIM
Trigger Inverter Unit .... TIU
Trigger Point [*Medicine*] (DMAA) .... TP
Trigger Pricing Mechanism .... TPM
Trigger Pulse [*Telecommunications*] (IAA) .... TP
Triggered [*Cardiology*] .... T
Triggered Reconnection Adiabatically Compressed Torus (MCD) .... TRACT
Triggered Spark Gap (IAA) .... TSG
Triggered Vacuum Gap .... TVG
Trigger-Price System [*Department of the Treasury*] .... TPS
Triglyceride [*Biochemistry*] .... TG
Triglyceride [*Biochemistry*] (MAE) .... TGL
Triglyceride Fatty Acid [*Biochemistry*] .... TGFA
Triglyceride Lipase [*Clinical chemistry*] .... TGL
Triglyceride Secretion Rate [*Physiology*] .... TGSR
Triglycerides [*Clinical chemistry*] .... TGL
Triglycerides [*Clinical chemistry*] .... trig
Triglycerides Incalculable [*Laboratory science*] (DAVI) .... TRGI
Triglycidyl Isocyanurate [*Organic chemistry*] .... TGIC
Triglycidylurazol [*Antineoplastic drug*] .... TGU
Triglycine Fluoberyllate [*Ferroelectrics*] .... TGF
Triglycine Sulfate [*Ferroelectrics*] .... TGS
Triglycollamic Acid [*Organic chemistry*] .... TGA
Trigon Tech, Inc. [*Vancouver Stock Exchange symbol*] .... TTE
Trigonal [*Molecular geometry*] .... TR
Trigonal [*Crystallography*] .... TRIG
Trigonal Bipyramidal [*Geometry of molecular structure*] .... TBP
Trigonometric (IDOE) .... trig
Trigonometric Function Computer .... TFC
Trigonometrischer Punkt [*Triangulation Point*] [*German military - World War II*] .... TP
Trigonometry .... TRIG
Trigonometry (IDOE) .... trig
Trigonometry (ROG) .... TRIGON
Trihalomethane [*Organic chemistry*] .... THM
Trihalomethane Formation Potential [*Environmental chemistry*] .... THMFP
Trihexphenidyl Hydrochloride [*An anti-cholinergic*] (DAVI) .... THP
Trihydroxybutyrophenone [*Antioxidant*] [*Organic chemistry*] .... TBHP
Trihydroxycholestanoic Acid [*Biochemistry*] .... THCA
Trihydroxycoprostanic Acid [*Biochemistry*] .... THCA
Trihydroxyglutamic Acid [*Organic chemistry*] .... THGA
Trihydroxyglutaric Acid [*Organic chemistry*] .... THGA
Trihydroxyindol [*Organic chemistry*] .... THI
Trihydroxynaphthalene [*Organic chemistry*] .... THN
Trihydroxypropane [*Organic chemistry*] .... THP
Tri-Institutional Library, Philadelphia, PA [*Library symbol Library of Congress*] (LCLS) .... PPTri
Triiodobenzoic Acid [*Plant growth regulator*] .... TIBA
Triiodothyroacetic Acid [*Endocrinology*] .... TRIAC
Triiodothyronine [*Also, TITh*] [*Endocrinology*] .... T_3
Triiodothyronine [*Endocrinology*] (MAE) .... TIT
Triiodothyronine [*Also, T_3*] [*Endocrinology*] .... TITh
Triiodothyronine [*Endocrinology*] (MAE) .... TRIT
Triiodothyronine, Amino Acids, Glucagon, and Heparin [*Medicine*] (DMAA) .... TAGH
Triiodothyronine Radioimmunoassay [*Endocrinology*] (DAVI) .... T_3RIA
Triiodothyronine Resin Uptake [*Endocrinology*] (MAE) .... T_3RU
Triiodothyronine Serum Uptake [*Endocrinolgy*] (CPH) .... T_3SU
Triiodothyronine Uptake [*Endocrinology*] .... T_3U
Tri-Iodothyronine Uptake [*Endocrinology*] (DAVI) .... T_3UP
Triiodothyronine Uptake Radio [*Endocrinology*] (DAVI) .... T_3UR
Triisobutylaluminum [*Organic chemistry*] .... TIBA
Triisobutylamine [*Organic chemistry*] .... TIBA
Triisononyl Trimellitate [*Organic chemistry*] .... TINTM
Triisooctyl Trimellitate [*Organic chemistry*] .... TIOTM
Triisopropanolamine [*Organic chemistry*] .... TIPA
Triisopropylbenzene [*Also, TIPB*] [*Organic chemistry*] .... TIB
Triisopropylbenzene [*Also, TIB*] [*Organic chemistry*] .... TIPB
Triisopropylbenzenesulfonyl Tetrazolide [*Organic chemistry*] .... TPSTe
Triisopropysilyl [*Organic chemistry*] .... TIPS
Tri-Junction Transistor (IAA) .... TJT
Tri-Lake Health Centre, Killarney, Manitoba [*Library symbol National Library of Canada*] (NLC) .... MKTLH
Tri-Lake Health Centre, Killarney, MB, Canada [*Library symbol Library of Congress*] (LCLS) .... CaMKTLH
Tri-Lake Regional Library, Hot Springs, AR [*Library symbol*] [*Library of Congress*] (LCLS) .... ArHsT
Trilanguage Education Learning Environment Program [*New York City*] (EDAC) .... TELE
Trilateral Commission (EA) .... TC
Trilateral Commission [*International study group*] .... TLC
Trilateral Range and Range Rate System .... TRRR
Trilateral Tracking Technique .... TTT
Tri-Line Expressways Ltd. [*Toronto Stock Exchange symbol*] .... TLX
Trilineage Myelodysplasia Syndrome [*Medicine*] .... TMDS
Tri-Lite, Inc. [*AMEX symbol*] (SPSG) .... NRG
Tri-Lite, Inc. [*Associated Press*] (SAG) .... Tri-Lite
Trillion [*10^{12}*] .... T
Trillion 10^{12} (IDOE) .... tera-
Trillion Cubic Feet .... TCF
Trillion Cubic Feet (WDAA) .... TFT^3
Trillion Electron Volts .... TeV
Trillium Telephone Systems, Inc. [*Toronto Stock Exchange symbol*] .... TLM
Trillo [*Trill*] [*Music*] .... T
Trillo [*Trill*] [*Music*] .... TR
Trillo [*Trill*] [*Music*] (ROG) .... TRL
Trilobita-Crustacea-Chelicerata [*Evolution history*] .... TCC
Trilogy Resource Corp. [*Toronto Stock Exchange symbol*] .... TRG
Trilogy Screening Technique .... TST
Trilon Financial Corp. [*Toronto Stock Exchange symbol Vancouver Stock Exchange symbol*] .... TFC
Trim after Forming (MSA) .... TAF
Trim and Drain Pump [*Navy*] (CAAL) .... TDP
Trim and Drill Fixture (MCD) .... TDF
Trim and Drill Template (MCD) .... TRDT
Trim Coil (AAG) .... TC

Trim Control System ... TCS
Trim Die (AAG) ... TRDI
Trim Fuel System (MCD) ... TFS
Tri-M Music Honor Society [*Modern Music Masters Society*] [*Acronym is based on former name,*] (EA) ... TRI-M
Trim, Neat, and Terrific [*Slang*] ... TNT
Trim on Assembly (MCD) ... TOA
Trim Panel [*Automotive engineering*] ... T/PNL
Trim Position Indicator ... TPI
Trim Power Assembly ... TPA
Trim Shell ... TRSH
Trim Template (MCD) ... TRT
Trimac Ltd. [*Toronto Stock Exchange symbol*] ... TMA
Trimark Holdings [*NASDAQ symbol*] (TTSB) ... TMRK
Trimark Holdings, Inc. [*NASDAQ symbol*] (SPSG) ... TMRK
Trimark Holdings, Inc. [*Associated Press*] (SAG) ... Trimark
TriMas Corp. [*NYSE symbol*] (SPSG) ... TMS
TriMas Corp. [*Associated Press*] (SAG) ... Trimas
Tri-Mask Process (IAA) ... TRIM
Trimble Navigation Ltd. [*Associated Press*] (SAG) ... Trimble
Trimble Navigation Ltd. [*NASDAQ symbol*] (SAG) ... TRMB
Trimedyne, Inc. [*NASDAQ symbol*] (NQ) ... TMED
Trimedyne, Inc. [*Associated Press*] (SAG) ... Trimed
Trimel Corp. [*Toronto Stock Exchange symbol*] ... TXM
Trimellitic Acid [*Organic chemistry*] ... TMA
Trimellitic Anhydride ... TMA
Trimellitic Anhydride [*Chemistry*] ... TMA
Trimellitic Anhydride Chloride [*Organic chemistry*] ... TMAC
Trimetaphosphate [*Organic chemistry*] ... TMP
Trimethallyl Isocyanurate [*Organic chemistry*] ... TMAIC
Trimethoprim [*Also, TMP*] [*Antibacterial compound*] ... T
Trimethoprim [*Also, T*] [*Antibacterial compound*] ... TMP
Trimethoprim and Sulfamethoxazole [*Antibacterials*] (DAVI) ... TMS
Trimethoprim Sulfamethoxazole ... T/S
Trimethoprim, Sulfamethoxazole, Nystatin [*Medicine*] ... TSN
Trimethoprim-Sulfamethoxazole [*Antibacterial*] [*Antineoplastic drug*] ... TMP/SMX
Trimethoprim-Sulfamethoxazole [*Antineoplastic drug*] (MEDA) ... TMP-SMZ
Trimethoprim-Sulfamethoxazole [*Medicine*] (DMAA) ... TRM-SMX
Trimethoprim-Sulfamethoxazole-Double-Strength [*Antineoplastic drug*] (MEDA) ... TMP-SMZ-DS
Trimethoxyamphetamine [*Organic chemistry*] (MAE) ... TMA
Trimethoxyboroxine [*Organic chemistry*] ... TMB
Trimethoxyethane [*Organic chemistry*] ... TMOE
Trimethoxyphenyl Aminopropane [*Organic chemistry*] (MAE) ... TMA
Trimethyl Colchicinic Acid [*Organic chemistry*] (MAE) ... TMCA
Trimethyl Phosphate [*Organic chemistry*] ... TMP
Trimethyladenine [*Biochemistry*] ... TMA
Trimethylaluminum [*Organic chemistry*] ... TMA
Trimethylamine [*Organic chemistry*] ... TMA
Trimethylamine Alane [*Organic chemistry*] ... TMAA
Trimethylamine N-Oxide [*Organic chemistry*] ... TMO
Trimethylamine Oxide [*Organic chemistry*] ... TMAO
Trimethylaminoethylpiperazine [*Organic chemistry*] ... TAP
Trimethylammonium [*Organic chemistry*] ... TMA
Trimethylbenzaldehyde [*Organic chemistry*] ... TMBA
Trimethylbenzanthracene [*Carcinogen*] ... TMBA
Trimethylbenzene [*Organic chemistry*] ... TMB
Trimethylbenzylammonium Chloride [*Also, BTM*] [*Organic chemistry*] ... TMBAC
Trimethylcetylammonium Pentachlorphenate [*Organic chemistry*] ... TCAP
Trimethylchlorosilane [*Organic chemistry*] ... TMCS
Trimethylcyclododecatriene [*Organic chemistry*] ... TMCDT
Trimethylcyclohexanol [*Organic chemistry*] ... TMC
Trimethylcyclopentanone [*Organic chemistry*] ... TMCP
Trimethylcyclopropenyl(nitrophenyl)malononitrile [*Organic chemistry*] ... TCNM
Trimethyldihydronapthalene [*Organic chemistry*] ... TDN
Trimethyldihydroquinoline Polymer [*Organic chemistry*] ... TDQP
Trimethyldodecatetraene [*Organic chemistry*] ... TMDT
Trimethylenediamine [*Organic chemistry*] ... TMEDA
Trimethylenemethane [*Organic chemistry*] ... TMM
Trimethylethyllead [*Organic chemistry*] ... TMEL
Trimethylgallium [*Organic chemistry*] ... TMG
Trimethylguanosine [*Biochemistry*] ... TMG
Trimethylhexamethylene Diamine [*Organic chemistry*] ... TMD
Trimethylhexamethylene Diisocyanate [*Organic chemistry*] ... TMDI
Trimethylhexane [*Organic chemistry*] ... TMH
(Trimethylhydrazinium) Propionate [*Biochemistry*] ... THP
Trimethylindium [*Organic chemistry*] ... TMI
Trimethylolethane [*Organic chemistry*] ... TME
Trimethylolethane [*Organic chemistry*] ... TRIMET
Trimethylolethane Trinitrate [*Organic chemistry*] ... TMETN
Trimethylolmelamine [*Organic chemistry*] ... TMM
Trimethylolpropane [*Organic chemistry*] ... TMOP
Trimethylolpropane [*Organic chemistry*] ... TMP
Trimethylolpropane Triacrylate [*Organic chemistry*] ... TMPTA
Trimethylolpropane Trimethacrylate [*Organic chemistry*] ... TMPTMA
Trimethylpentane [*Organic chemistry*] ... TMP
Trimethylpentanediol [*Organic chemistry*] ... TMPD
Trimethylphosphine [*Organic chemistry*] ... TMP
Trimethylphosphoramide [*Organic chemistry*] ... TMPA
Trimethylpsoralen [*Photochemotherapeutic compound*] ... TMeP
Trimethylpsoralen [*Photochemotherapeutic compound*] (AAMN) ... TMP
Trimethylsilyl [*Organic chemistry*] ... TMS
Trimethylsilyl Azide [*Organic chemistry*] ... TMSA
Trimethylsilyl Chloride [*Organic chemistry*] ... TMSCl
Trimethylsilyl Propionate [*Organic chemistry*] ... TSP
Trimethylsilylacetonitrile [*Organic chemistry*] ... TMSAN
Trimethylsilylated Controlled-Pore Glass [*Packing for chromatography*] ... TMS-CPG
Trimethylsilylcyanide [*Organic chemistry*] ... TMSCN
Trimethylsilyldiethylamine [*Organic chemistry*] ... TMSDEA
(Trimethylsilyl)imidazole [*Also, TSIM*] [*Organic chemistry*] ... TMSIM
(Trimethylsilyl)imidazole [*Also, TMSIM*] [*Organic chemistry*] ... TSIM
Trimethylstannylmaleate [*Organic chemistry*] ... TMSM
Trimethylxylene Diisocyanate [*Organic chemistry*] ... TMXDI
Trimmable Horizontal Stabilizer [*Aviation*] ... THS
Trimmed ... TRMD
Trimmed Complete [*Automotive engineering*] ... T/COMP
Trimmed Element Analysis Method [*Computer modeling*] ... TEAM
Trimmed in Bunkers [*Shipping*] (DS) ... TIB
Trimmer (IAA) ... T
Trimmer [*British military*] (DMA) ... Tmr
Trimmer [*Mining engineering*] ... TRIM
Trimmer [*Mining engineering*] ... TRMR
Trimmers, Firemen, and Foundry Labourers Union [*British*] ... TFFLU
Trimming ... TRMG
Tri-National Tornado Training Establishment [*British military*] (DMA) ... TTTE
Tri-N-Butyl Phosphate [*Organic chemistry*] (AAMN) ... TNBP
Trincomalee [*Sri Lanka port city*] (DSUE) ... TRINCO
Trincomalee [*Ceylon*] [*Airport symbol*] (AD) ... TRR
Trincomalee/China Bay [*Sri Lanka*] [*ICAO location identifier*] (ICLI) ... VCCT
Trinet Corporate Realty Trust [*NYSE symbol*] (SPSG) ... TRI
Trinet Corporate Realty Trust [*Associated Press*] (SAG) ... TriNet
Trinidad [*Cuba ICAO location identifier*] (ICLI) ... MUTD
Trinidad [*Colorado ICAO location identifier*] (ICLI) ... SKTD
Trinidad [*Bolivia*] [*ICAO location identifier*] (ICLI) ... SLTR
Trinidad [*Colorado*] [*Airport symbol Obsolete*] (OAG) ... TAD
Trinidad [*Brigand Hill*] [*Trinidad-Tobago*] [*Seismograph station code, US Geological Survey*] (SEIS) ... TBH
Trinidad [*Colombia*] [*Airport symbol*] (AD) ... TDA
Trinidad [*Colorado*] [*Seismograph station code, US Geological Survey Closed*] (SEIS) ... TDC
Trinidad [*Bolivia*] [*Airport symbol*] (OAG) ... TDD
Trinidad [*Colorado*] [*Seismograph station code, US Geological Survey*] (SEIS) ... TJC
Trinidad [*Cuba*] [*Airport symbol*] (AD) ... TND
Trinidad [*Pointe-A-Pierre*] [*Trinidad-Tobago*] [*Seismograph station code, US Geological Survey*] (SEIS) ... TPP
Trinidad (BARN) ... Trd
Trinidad ... Trin
Trinidad [*Trinidad-Tobago*] [*Seismograph station code, US Geological Survey*] (SEIS) ... TRN
Trinidad and Tobago [*Aircraft nationality and registration mark*] (FAAC) ... 9Y
Trinidad and Tobago [*IYRU nationality code*] (IYR) ... KT
Trinidad and Tobago [*MARC geographic area code Library of Congress*] (LCCP) ... nwtr--
Trinidad and Tobago ... TD
Trinidad and Tobago [*MARC country of publication code Library of Congress*] (LCCP) ... tr
Trinidad and Tobago [*ANSI two-letter standard code*] (CNC) ... TT
Trinidad and Tobago [*ANSI three-letter standard code*] (CNC) ... TTO
Trinidad and Tobago Air Services [*ICAO designator*] (AD) ... HU
Trinidad and Tobago Airways Corp. [*Trinidad and Tobago*] [*ICAO designator*] (ICDA) ... BW
Trinidad and Tobago Airways Corp. [*ICAO designator*] (FAAC) ... BWA
Trinidad & Tobago Electricity Commission ... T & TEC
Trinidad and Tobago National Alliance [*Political party*] (PPW) ... TTNA
Trinidad and Tobago Supreme Court Judgments [*A publication*] (ILCA) ... T & T Sup
Trinidad & Tobago Television Co. ... TTT
Trinidad Artillery [*British military*] (DMA) ... TA
Trinidad Base Command [*World War II*] ... TBC
Trinidad Carnegie Public Library, Trinidad, CO [*Library symbol Library of Congress*] (LCLS) ... CoT
Trinidad, CO [*AM radio station call letters*] ... KCRT
Trinidad, CO [*FM radio station call letters*] ... KCRT-FM
Trinidad Law Reports [*A publication*] (DLA) ... Tr LR
Trinidad Law Reports [*A publication*] (DLA) ... Trinidad LR
Trinidad Light Infantry [*British military*] (DMA) ... TLI
Trinidad Sector [*World War II*] ... TS
Trinidad State Junior College [*Colorado*] ... TSJC
Trinidad State Junior College, Trinidad, CO [*Library symbol Library of Congress*] (LCLS) ... CoTJ
Trinidad Volunteers [*British military*] (DMA) ... TV
Trinitarian Bible Society [*British*] ... TBS
Trinitas [*The Trinity*] ... T
Trinitech Systems [*AMEX symbol*] (TTSB) ... TSI
Trinitech Systems, Inc. [*Associated Press*] (SAG) ... Trinitech
Trinitech Systems, Inc. [*AMEX symbol*] (SPSG) ... TSI
Trinitroaniline [*Organic chemistry*] ... TNA
Trinitroazetidine [*An explosive*] ... TNAZ
Trinitrobenzene [*Explosive*] ... TNB
Trinitrobenzenesulfonic Acid [*Biochemistry*] ... TNBS
Trinitrocellulose [*Organic chemistry*] ... TNC
Trinitroethyl Formal [*An explosive*] ... TNEF
Trinitroethyl Orthocarbonate [*An explosive*] ... TNEOC
Trinitroethyl Orthoformate [*An explosive*] ... TNEOF
Trinitrofluorenone [*Organic chemistry*] ... TNF
Trinitroglycerin [*Also, TNT*] (DAVI) ... TNG
Trinitrophenol [*or Trinitrophenyl*] [*Organic chemistry*] ... TNP
Trinitrophenyl Keyhole Limpet Hemocyanin [*Immunology*] ... TNP-KLH

Trinitrotoluene [Explosive] ... TNT
Trinitrotoluene and Black Powder (SAA) ... TNTBP
Trinitroxylene [Organic chemistry] ... TNX
Trinity ... TRIN
Trinity ... TRNTY
Trinity Air Bahamas [ICAO designator] (FAAC) ... TBH
Trinity, AL [FM radio station call letters] (RBYB) ... WWXQ
Trinity Bible Institute, Ellendale, ND [Library symbol Library of Congress] (LCLS) ... NdEIT
Trinity Bible Institute, Ellendale, ND [OCLC symbol] (OCLC) ... TBI
Trinity Biotech [NASDAQ symbol] (SAG) ... TRIB
Trinity Biotech [NASDAQ symbol] (SAG) ... TRIW
Trinity Biotech [NASDAQ symbol] (SAG) ... TRIZ
Trinity Biotech [Associated Press] (SAG) ... TrnB
Trinity Biotech [Associated Press] (SAG) ... TrnBi
Trinity Biotech [Associated Press] (SAG) ... TrnBio
Trinity Biotech plc ADS [NASDAQ symbol] (TTSB) ... TRIBY
Trinity Biotech plc Wrrt'A' [NASDAQ symbol] (TTSB) ... TRIWF
Trinity Biotech plc Wrrt'B' [NASDAQ symbol] (TTSB) ... TRIZF
Trinity Broadcasting Network [Cable-television system] ... TBN
Trinity Christian Academy, Addison, TX [Library symbol] [Library of Congress] (LCLS) ... TxAdTC
Trinity College (GAGS) ... Trinity C
Trinity College, Burlington, VT [Library symbol Library of Congress] (LCLS) ... VtBT
Trinity College, Deerfield, IL [OCLC symbol] (OCLC) ... ICT
Trinity College, Dublin [Ireland] ... TCD
Trinity College, Hartford, CT [Library symbol Library of Congress] (LCLS) ... CtHT
Trinity College, Hartford, CT [OCLC symbol] (OCLC) ... TYC
Trinity College Library, University of Toronto [UTLAS symbol] ... KTC
Trinity College, London ... TCL
Trinity College, Oxford [British] (DAS) ... TCO
Trinity College, Sioux City, IA [Library symbol Library of Congress Obsolete] (LCLS) ... IaScT
Trinity College, University of Dublin, Dublin, Ireland [Library symbol Library of Congress] (LCLS) ... IreDT
Trinity College, Washington, DC [Library symbol Library of Congress] (LCLS) ... DTr
Trinity College, Watkinson Library, Hartford, CT [Library symbol Library of Congress] (LCLS) ... CtHT-W
Trinity County Free Library, Weaverville, CA [Library symbol Library of Congress] (LCLS) ... CWeT
Trinity Engineering Co. [Huxley, IA] [Telecommunications service] (TSSD) ... TECO
Trinity Episcopal School, Ambridge, PA [Library symbol] [Library of Congress] (LCLS) ... PAmbT
Trinity Evangelical Divinity School, Deerfield, IL [Library symbol Library of Congress] (LCLS) ... IDfT
Trinity Evangelical Divinity School, Deerfield, IL [Library symbol Library of Congress] (LCLS) ... IDfTD
Trinity Evangelical Divinity School, Rolfing Memorial Library, Deerfield, IL [OCLC symbol] (OCLC) ... IHT
Trinity High-Water Mark ... THWM
Trinity House [British] (BARN) ... TH
Trinity Indus [NYSE symbol] (TTSB) ... TRN
Trinity Industries, Inc. [Associated Press] (SAG) ... TrinityIn
Trinity Industries, Inc. [NYSE symbol] (SPSG) ... TRN
Trinity International Holdings [British] ... TIH
Trinity Low-Water Mark ... TLWM
Trinity Lutheran Hospital, Kansas City, MO [Library symbol Library of Congress] (LCLS) ... MoKTrL
Trinity Lutheran School, Johnson, MN [Library symbol] [Library of Congress] (LCLS) ... MnJoTS
Trinity Lutheran School, Long Prairie, MN [Library symbol Library of Congress] (LCLS) ... MnLpT
Trinity Lutheran School, Sauk Rapids, MN [Library symbol Library of Congress] (LCLS) ... MnSrT
Trinity Lutheran Seminary, Columbus, OH [OCLC symbol] (OCLC) ... LTS
Trinity Medical Center, August Cameron Medical Library, Minot, ND [Library symbol Library of Congress] (LCLS) ... NdMinT-M
Trinity Medical Center, School of Nursing, Minot, ND [Library symbol Library of Congress] (LCLS) ... NdMinT-N
Trinity Memorial Hospital, Cudahy, WI [Library symbol Library of Congress] (LCLS) ... WCT
Trinity Ministries Center (EA) ... TMC
Trinity Occasional Papers [A publication] ... TOP
Trinity Peninsula Group [Geology] ... TPG
Trinity Resources Ltd. [Toronto Stock Exchange symbol] ... TRT
Trinity Term [British Legal term] (DLA) ... Trin
Trinity Term [British Legal term] (DLA) ... Trint T
Trinity Term ... TT
Trinity University (GAGS) ... Trinity U
Trinity University, Library, San Antonio, TX [OCLC symbol] (OCLC) ... TNY
Trinity University, San Antonio, TX [Library symbol Library of Congress] (LCLS) ... TxSaT
Trinity University, Whitsett Library Museum, San Antonio, TX [Library symbol Library of Congress] (LCLS) ... TxSaT-W
Trinity Western College, Langley, BC, Canada [Library symbol Library of Congress] (LCLS) ... CaBLTW
Trinity Western College, Langley, British Columbia [Library symbol National Library of Canada] (NLC) ... BLTW
Tri-n-Octyl Phosphine Oxide [Organic chemistry] ... TOPO
Tri-Normal-Butylaluminum [Organic chemistry] ... TNBA
Tri-normal-butylamine [Organic chemistry] ... TNBA
Tri-Normal-Propylaluminum [Organic chemistry] ... TNPA
Tri-normal-propylamine [Organic chemistry] ... TNPA

Trinova Corp. [NYSE symbol] (SPSG) ... TNV
Trinova Corp. [Associated Press] (SAG) ... Trinova
Trinucleotide Repeat Sequence [Genetics] ... TNR
Trio Archean Developments [Vancouver Stock Exchange symbol] ... TAD
Trioctyl Trimellitate [Chemistry] ... TOTM
Trioctylmethylammonium Chloride [Organic chemistry] ... TOMAC
Trioctylphosphine Oxide [Organic chemistry] ... TOPO
Trioctylphosphorine Oxide/Methyl Isobutyl Keton [Solvent mixture] ... TOPO-MIBK
Trioctyltin [Organic chemistry] ... TOT
Triode ... T
Triode (AAG) ... TRI
Triode Alternating Current (IAA) ... TRIAC
Triode Alternating Current Semiconductor Switch ... TRIAC
Triode Cavity Oscillator ... TCO
Triode-Tetrode (IAA) ... TRITET
Triodyne, Inc., Information Center, Skokie, IL [OCLC symbol] (OCLC) ... IVF
Triodyne, Skokie, IL [Library symbol Library of Congress] (LCLS) ... ISkT
Triola [Record label] [Finland] ... Trla
Trion, GA [FM radio station call letters] ... WATG
Trion, GA [AM radio station call letters] (RBYB) ... WSAF
Trion, Inc. [Associated Press] (SAG) ... Trion
Trion, Inc. [NASDAQ symbol] (NQ) ... TRON
Trionics Technology Ltd. [Vancouver Stock Exchange symbol] ... TNC
Tri-ortho-cresyl Phosphate [Organic chemistry] ... TOCP
Triorthotolylphosphate [Organic chemistry] ... TOTP
Triose Phosphate Isomerase [An enzyme] ... TIM
Triosephosphate Isomerase [An enzyme] ... TPI
Trio-Tech International [Associated Press] (SAG) ... TrioTch
Trio-Tech International [NASDAQ symbol] (SAG) ... TRTC
Trio-Tech Intl [NASDAQ symbol] (TTSB) ... TRTC
Trip Authorization ... TA
Trip Cell (IAA) ... TC
Trip Coil ... TC
Trip Reduction Ordinance [MOCD] (TAG) ... TRO
Trip Report ... TR
Trip Valve [Railroad term] ... TV
Tri-Pacific Resources Ltd. [Vancouver Stock Exchange symbol] ... TPF
Tripanel, Convoluted, Y-Strap [A knee immobilizer] [Orthopedics] (DAVI) ... TCS
Tripara [having borne three children] [Gynecology and obstetrics] (DAVI) ... Para III
Tri-para-anisylchloroethylene [Estrogen] ... TACE
Triparanol [Pharmacology] [A cholesterol biosynthesis inhibitor removed from market due to side effects] (DAVI) ... MER-29
Tripartite Commission for the Restitution of Monetary Gold [Belgium] (EAIO) ... TCRMG
Tripartite Engineering Committee [Allied German Occupation Forces] ... TEC
Tripartite Leader [Genetics] ... TPL
Tripartite Naval Commission [Allied German Occupation Forces] ... TNC
Tripartite Nuclear Cross-Sections Committee [British, Canadian, and US] ... TNCC
Tripartite Research Coordination Committee (SAA) ... TRCC
Tripartite Technical Cooperation Program [Military] (NG) ... TTCP
Tripartite Technical Procedures Committee (SAA) ... TTPC
Tri-Party Agreement (DOGT) ... TPA
Triphenyl Phosphite [Organic chemistry] ... TPP
Triphenylamine [Organic chemistry] ... TPA
Triphenylbenzene [Organic chemistry] ... TPB
Triphenylguanidine [Organic chemistry] ... TPG
Triphenyllead Acetate [Organic chemistry] ... TPLA
Triphenylmethane [Class of organic dyes] [Organic chemistry] ... TPM
Triphenylmethyl Methacrylate [Organic chemistry] ... TPMM
Triphenylphosphine [Organic chemistry] ... TPP
Triphenylphosphine Trisulphonate [Organic chemistry] ... TPPTS
Triphenylstibine Oxide [Organic chemistry] ... TPSO
Triphenylsulfonium Chloride [Organic chemistry] ... TPS
Triphenyltetrazolium Chloride [Also, RT, TTC] [Chemical indicator] ... TPTZ
Triphenyltetrazolium Chloride [Also, RT, TPTZ] [Chemical indicator] ... TTC
Triphenyltin Chloride [Organic chemistry] ... TPTC
Triphenyltin Hydroxide [Organic chemistry] ... TPTH
Triphosphate (MAE) ... TP
Triphosphoinositide [Biochemistry] ... TPI
Triphosphopyridine Nucleotide [See NADP] [Biochemistry] ... TPN
Triphosphopyridine Nucleotide (Reduced) [See NADPH] [Biochemistry] ... TPNH
Triplane Elevated Evaluation System [Army] (RDA) ... T-PEES
Triplate Module ... TPM
Triple ... T
Triple (MSA) ... TPL
Triple ... TRPL
Triple A and Gvt Ser'97(New) [AMEX symbol] (TTSB) ... TGB
Triple A Government Series 1997, Inc. [AMEX symbol] (SAG) ... TGB
Triple A Government Series 1997, Inc. [Associated Press] (SAG) ... TrpAG97
Triple Antibiotic [Bacitracin, neomycin, and polymyxin] [Pharmacology] (DAVI) ... TAB
Triple Antigen [Medicine] ... TA
Triple Axis Inertial Drift Erection Test ... TAIDET
Triple Axis Spectrometer [Biochemistry] ... TAS
Triple Capability [Army] ... TRICAP
Triple Capacity Division [Army] (VNW) ... TRICAP
Triple Conductor, Heat, Oil, and Flame Resistant (IAA) ... THOF
Triple Coronary Artery Bypass Graft [Cardiology] ... TCABG
Triple Cotton-Covered [Wire insulation] ... TCC
Triple Crown Electronics, Inc. [Toronto Stock Exchange symbol] ... TPE
Triple Diffused Emitter-Follower Logic (MDG) ... 3DEFL
Triple Ejection [or Ejector] Rack (NVT) ... TER
Triple Erasure Correction ... TEC
Triple Excellent ... XXX
Triple Expansion (DS) ... TE

Triple Frequency	TF
Triple Fronted [Classified advertising] (ADA)	TF
Triple Hard [Pencil leads]	HHH
Triple Lindy [Dance step]	TL
Triple Missile Mount (MCD)	TRIMM
Triple Modular Redundancy [Computer science]	TMR
Triple Molecular Collision	TMC
Triple Nine Society (EA)	TNS
Triple Overriding Dual Control (IAA)	TODC
Triple P [NASDAQ symbol] (SAG)	TPPP
Triple P [Associated Press] (SAG)	TripleP
Triple P N.V. [NASDAQ symbol] (TTSB)	TPPPF
Triple Paper-Covered [Wire insulation] (DEN)	TPC
Triple Phosphate (DAVI)	TRPC
Triple Play [Baseball]	TP
Triple Pole [Switch]	TP
Triple Pole and Neutral [Switch]	TP & N
Triple Polio Vaccine [Medicine]	TPV
Triple Quadrupole Mass Spectrometer	TQMS
Triple Reduction (DS)	TR
Triple Redundancy Incorporating Self-Adaptive Failure Exclusion (MCD)	TRISAFE
Triple Redundant Timing Systems (MCD)	TRTS
Triple Revolving Fund Account (AABC)	TRFA
Triple Rotating Directional Transmission [Military] (CAAL)	TRDT
Triple S Plastics [NASDAQ symbol] (SAG)	TSSS
Triple S Plastics Co. [Associated Press] (SAG)	TripleS
Triple Screw [Shipping] (DS)	TR
Triple Screw	TRPSC
Triple Screw Ship	TRSS
Triple Stage Quadrupole [Instrumentation]	TSQ
Triple Strength	TS
Triple Sugar-Iron [Agar] [Microbiology]	TSI
Triple Sugar-Iron Agar [Microbiology]	TSIA
Triple Sugar-Urea Base [Agar] [Microbiology]	TSU
Triple Supertwist Nematic [Video technology] (PCM)	TSTN
Triple Thermoplastic (SAA)	TT
Triple Thin Film [Electronics]	TFT
Triple Throw [Switch]	3T
Triple Transit Suppression (IAA)	TTS
Triple Vessel Disease with Abnormal Left Ventricle [Cardiology]	TVDALV
Triple Voiding Cystogram [Medicine]	TVC
Triple Wall	TPLW
Triple-Braid Weatherproof (IAA)	TBWP
Triple-Braided (CET)	TB
Triple-Crown Resources [Vancouver Stock Exchange symbol]	TCW
Triple-Diffusion Process (MDG)	3-D
Triple-Layer [Pharmacy]	TL
Triple-Pole, Double-Throw [Switch] (MUGU)	3PDT
Triple-Pole, Double-Throw [Switch]	TPDT
Triple-Pole, Single-Throw [Switch] (MUGU)	3PST
Triple-Pole, Single-Throw [Switch]	TPST
Triple-Product Convolver [Acousto-optic technology] (RDA)	TPC
Tripler Army Medical Center (AABC)	TAMC
Tripler General Hospital [Army] (GFGA)	TGH
Triple-Sequence Diffusion	TSD
Triple-Super Phosphates	TSP
Triplet Connection (EA)	TC
Triplet Metastable Helium Level	TMHL
Triplet Recall [Neuropsychology test]	TRIPREC
Triplet-Doublet Resonance [Physics]	TDR
Triplets [Slang] (DSUE)	TRIPS
Triplet-Triplet Annihilation [Spectroscopy]	TTA
Triplet-Triplet Resonance [Physics]	TTR
Triple-Vessel Disease [Cardiology] (DAVI)	TVD
Triplex [Paper] (DGA)	tpx
Triplex	TRX
Triplex Annealed	TA
Triplex Flight Control System [or Subsystem] [NASA] (NASA)	TFCS
Triplex-Forming Oligonucleotide [Biochemistry]	TFO
Triplicate (AABC)	TRIP
Triplicate (WGA)	Tripl
Triplicate (WDMC)	trpl
Triplicated Majority Voting (IAA)	TMV
Tripoli [Libya] [ICAO location identifier] (ICLI)	HLLL
Tripoli [Lebanon] [ICAO location identifier] (ICLI)	OLKK
Tripoli [Lebanon] [ICAO location identifier] (ICLI)	OLKV
Tripoli [Libya] [Airport symbol] (OAG)	TIP
Tripoli	Trip
Tripoli/International [Libya] [ICAO location identifier] (ICLI)	HLLT
Tripoli Leader, Tripoli, IA [Library symbol] [Library of Congress] (LCLS)	IaTriL
Tripoli Rocketry Association (EA)	TRA
Tripoli Science Association (EA)	TSA
Tripoli Trots [Term used by entertainers in World War II]	TT's
Tripolis [Greece] [ICAO location identifier] (ICLI)	LGTP
Tripolitania [Libya] (BJA)	Trip
Tripolyphosphate [Food industry]	TPP
Tripos, Inc. [Associated Press] (SAG)	Tripos
Tripos, Inc. [NASDAQ symbol] (SAG)	TRPS
Tri-Power Petroleum Corp. [Toronto Stock Exchange symbol]	TPP
Tripp County Library, Winner, SD [Library symbol Library of Congress] (LCLS)	SdWinT
Tripped	TRP
Tripped Automatic Gain Control	TAGC
Tripp's Reports [5, 6 Dakota] [A publication] (DLA)	Tripp

Tripropylamine [Organic chemistry]	TPA
Tripropylene Glycol Diacrylate [Organic chemistry]	TRPGDA
Triptych (VRA)	tpyt
TriQuint Semiconductor [NASDAQ symbol] (TTSB)	TQNT
Triquint Semiconductor, Inc. [NASDAQ symbol] (SAG)	TQNT
Triquint Semiconductor, Inc. [Associated Press] (SAG)	Triquint
Trireme Trust USA [An association] (EA)	TTUSA
TRIS, HEPES, Mannitol [A buffer]	THM
TRIS, Potassium Chloride, Magnesium Chloride [A buffer]	TKM
TRIS, Sodium Chloride, EDTA [A buffer]	TNE
Tris(2,3-dibromopropyl)phosphate [Also, TDBP, TDBPP, Tris-BP] [Flame retardant, mutagen]	Tris
Tris(2,3-dibromopropyl)phosphate [Also, TDBP, TDBPP, Tris] [Flame retardant, mutagen]	Tris-BP
TRIS-Acetate-Buffered Saline [Clinical chemistry]	TABS
Tris-Acetate-EDTA [Ethylenediaminetetraacetate] [Buffer]	TAE
Tris(aminoethyl)amine [Organic chemistry]	tren
Tris(aziridinyl)phosphine Oxide [Organic chemistry]	APO
Trisbicyclo Thexabenzene [Organic chemistry]	TBHB
Tris-Borate Buffer Electrophoresis	TBE
Tris-Borate-EDTA [Ethylenediaminetetraacetate] [Buffer]	TBE
TRIS-Buffered Saline [Solution]	TBS
TRIS-Buffered Saline Azide [Culture media]	TBSA
Tris(chloroethyl)phosphite [Organic chemistry]	TCEP
Tris(cyanoethoxy)propane [Organic chemistry]	TCEP
Tris(dibromopropyl) Phosphate [Also, TDBPP, Tris, T ris-BP] [Flame retardant, mutagen]	TDBP
Tris(dibromopropyl) Phosphate [Also, TDBP, Tris, Tris-BP] [Flame retardant, mutagen]	TDBPP
Tris(epoxypropyl)isocyanurate [Organic chemistry]	TEPIC
Tri-Service Contracting Officer (AAGC)	TSCO
Tri-Service Fighter, Experimental (MCD)	TFX
Tri-Service Group [NATO]	TSG
Tri-Service Group on Air Defense [NATO] (NATG)	TSGAD
Tri-Service Group on Communications and Electronic Equipment [NATO] (NATG)	TSGCEE
Triservice LASER	TSL
Triservice LASER Seeker [DoD]	TSLS
Tri-Service Medical Information Systems [Military]	TRIMIS
Triservice Program [Military]	TSP
Tri-Service Standoff Attack Missile [Military]	TSSAM
Tri-Service Support Center [Military] (MCD)	TSC
Tri-Service Tactical Communications System [DoD]	TRITAC
Triservice Tactical Switch	TRITAC
Tris-Ethylenediaminetetra-Acetate Borate [Organic chemistry] (MAH)	TEB
Tris(hydroxyethyl)isocyanurate [Organic chemistry]	THEIC
Tris(hydroxymethyl)aminomethane [Also, TRIS] [Biochemical analysis]	THAM
Tris(hydroxymethyl)aminomethane [Also, THAM] [Biochemical analysis]	TRIS
Tris(hydroxymethyl)methylamino Propanesulfonic Acid	TAPS
Tris(hydroxymethyl)methylaminoethanesulfonic Acid [A buffer]	TES
Tris(hydroxymethyl)methylglycine [Biochemical analysis]	TRICINE
Tris(hydroxymethyl)phosphine [Organic chemistry]	THP
Tris(hydroxymethyl)phosphine Oxide [Organic chemistry]	THPO
Triskaidekaphobia Illuminatus Society (EA)	TIS
Tris(I-aziridinyl) Phosphine Oxide [Organic chemistry]	TAPO
Trism, Inc. [Associated Press] (SAG)	Trism
Trism, Inc. [NASDAQ symbol] (SAG)	TRSM
Tris(methoxy)mercaptopropylsilane [Organic chemistry]	TMMPS
Tris(methylethylene)phosphoric Triamide [Organic chemistry]	METEPA
Tris(nonylphenyl) Phosphite [Organic chemistry]	TNPP
Trisodium Edetate [Inorganic chemistry] (MAE)	TSE
Trisodium Phosphate [Inorganic chemistry]	TSP
Trisodium Phosphate - Zephiran [Clinical chemistry]	TSP-Z
Tris-ortho-thymotide [Organic chemistry]	TOT
Tris(pyridyl)-s-triazine [Analytical chemistry]	TPTZ
Tristan da Cunha Island [MARC geographic area code Library of Congress] (LCCP)	lstd--
Tristan De Cunha [South Africa] [ICAO location identifier] (ICLI)	FATC
Tristan Rogers Fan Club [Defunct] (EA)	TRFC
Tristar Corp. [Associated Press] (SAG)	Tristar
Tristar Corp. [NASDAQ symbol] (SAG)	TSAR
Tri-Star Resources [Vancouver Stock Exchange symbol]	TSR
Tristate [Electronics] (IAA)	TS
Tri-State Automated Clearing House Association (MHDB)	TRI-SACH
Tri-State College Library Cooperative [Rosemont College Library] [Rosemont, PA] [Library network]	TCLC
Tristate Control [Electronics] (IAA)	TSC
Tristate Data Consultants, Inc. [Database producer] (IID)	TDC
Tristate Logic [Electronics]	TSL
Tri-State Motor Tariff Service	TSMTS
Tri-State Resources Ltd. [Vancouver Stock Exchange symbol]	TRX
Tri-State University, Angola, IN [Library symbol Library of Congress] (LCLS)	InAngT
Tri-State University, Angola, IN [OCLC symbol] (OCLC)	ITS
Tristia [of Ovid] [Classical studies] (OCD)	Tr
Tristram's Consistory Judgments [England] [A publication] (DLA)	Tr
Tristram's Consistory Judgments [1872-90] [England] [A publication] (DLA)	Tr Consist J
Tristram's Consistory Judgments [England] [A publication] (DLA)	Trist
Tristram's Consistory Judgments [1872-90] [A publication] (DLA)	Tristram
Tristram's Probate Practice [25th ed.] [1978] [A publication] (DLA)	Tris Pr Pr
Tristram's Probate Practice [25th ed.] [1978] [A publication] (DLA)	Tristram
Tristram's Supplement to 4 Swabey and Tristram [A publication] (DLA)	Tristram
Trisyllable (ROG)	TRISYLL

TriTeal Corp. [*NASDAQ symbol*] (SAG) .... TEAL
TriTeal Corp. [*Associated Press*] (SAG) .... TriTeal
Tritiated Thymidine [*Genetics*] (DAVI) .... TdR-³H
Tritiated Thymidine (MAE) .... TTH
Tritiated Waste Treatment [*Subsystem*] (MCD) .... TWT
Triticale Association of Australia .... TAA
Tritium [*Also, T*] [*Radioisotope of hydrogen*] .... H₃
Tritium [*Also, H₃*] [*Radioisotope of hydrogen*] .... T
Tritium Fluoride .... TF
Tritium Nuclear Magnetic Resonance [*Spectrometry*] .... TNMR
Tritium Ratio [*Measure of tritium activity*] [*AEC*] .... TR
Tritium Recovery [*Nuclear energy*] (NRCH) .... TR
Tritium Removal with Organic Compound [*Nuclear energy*] .... TROC
Tritium Supply and Recycling Programmatic Environmental Impact
    Statement .... TSR PEIS
Tritium Systems Test Assembly (MCD) .... TSTA
Tritium Unit [*Nuclear energy*] .... TU
Tritium-Labeled Water [*Laboratory Science*] (DAVI) .... THO
Tritocerebral Commissure, Giant [*Zoology*] .... TCG
Trito-Isaiah (BJA) .... TrIs
Tritolylamine [*Organic chemistry*] .... TTA
Triton [*A nuclear particle*] .... t
Triton Acid Urea .... TAU
Triton Airlines, Inc. [*Canada ICAO designator*] (FAAC) .... DRC
Triton Canada Resources Ltd. [*Toronto Stock Exchange symbol*] .... TTN
Triton College, River Grove, IL [*OCLC symbol*] (OCLC) .... IAW
Triton College, River Grove, IL [*Library symbol Library of Congress*]
    (LCLS) .... IRivgT
Triton Corp. (EA) .... TC
Triton Energy [*NYSE symbol*] (TTSB) .... OIL
Triton Energy Corp. [*Toronto Stock Exchange symbol*] .... EGY
Triton Energy Corp. [*NYSE symbol*] (SPSG) .... OIL
Triton Energy Corp. [*Associated Press*] (SAG) .... TritEng
Triton Group Ltd. [*AMEX symbol*] (SPSG) .... TGL
Triton Group Ltd. [*Associated Press*] (SAG) .... Triton
Triton Group Ltd Wrrt [*AMEX symbol*] (TTSB) .... TGL.WS
Triton Industries, Inc. [*Toronto Stock Exchange symbol*] .... T
Triton Research Group (EA) .... TRG
Tri-Township Library, Troy, IL [*Library symbol Library of Congress*] (LCLS) .... ITro
Tritura [*Triturate*] [*Pharmacy*] .... TRIT
Trityl [*Organic chemistry*] .... Tr
Trityl [*Biochemistry*] .... Trt
(Tritylphenyl)sulfonylethanol [*Organic chemistry*] .... TPSE
(Tritylphenyl)thioethanol [*Organic chemistry*] .... TPTE
Triumph [*Automobile model*] .... TR
Triumph Adler Assembler (IAA) .... TRIASS
Triumph Adler Computer Series (NITA) .... TA
Triumph International Owners Club (EA) .... TIOC
Triumph Petroleums Ltd. [*Vancouver Stock Exchange symbol*] .... TPL
Triumph Register of America (EA) .... TRA
Triumph Resources Corp. [*Vancouver Stock Exchange symbol*] .... TPH
Triumph Roadster Club (EA) .... TRC
Triumph Sports Owners Association (EA) .... TSOA
Triumphal Arch (VRA) .... trim arh
Tri-University-Meson Facility [*Nuclear research facility at the University of British Columbia*] .... TRIUMF
Trivalent Oral Poliomyelitis Vaccine [*Medicine*] .... TOPV
Trivalent Sodium Antimony Gluconate [*Pharmacology*] .... TSAG
Trivandrum [*India*] [*Seismograph station code, US Geological Survey*]
    (SEIS) .... TRD
Trivandrum [*India*] [*Airport symbol*] (OAG) .... TRV
Trivandrum [*India*] [*ICAO location identifier*] (ICLI) .... VOTV
Trivial File Transfer Protocol (BYTE) .... TFTP
Trivial Problem Discriminator [*Computer science*] (IAA) .... TPD
Tri-West Resources Ltd. [*Vancouver Stock Exchange symbol*] .... TWT
Trizec Corp. Ltd. [*Toronto Stock Exchange symbol*] .... TZC
Trizec Corp. Ltd'A'Wrrt [*NYSE symbol*] (TTSB) .... TZC.WS
Trizec Hahn Corp. [*Associated Press*] (SAG) .... TrizecH
Trizec Hahn Corp. [*Associated Press*] (SAG) .... TrizecHhn
Trizec Hahn Corp. [*NYSE symbol*] (SAG) .... TZH
TRM Copy Centers [*NASDAQ symbol*] (TTSB) .... TRMM
TRM Copy Centers Corp. [*Associated Press*] (SAG) .... TRMCpy
TRM Copy Centers Corp. [*NASDAQ symbol*] (SPSG) .... TRMM
Trnasport Holdings, Inc. [*Associated Press*] (SAG) .... TransH
TrNet Corporate Rlty Tr [*NYSE symbol*] (TTSB) .... TRI
TRO Learning [*NASDAQ symbol*] (TTSB) .... TUTR
TRO Learning, Inc. [*Associated Press*] (SAG) .... TRO Lrn
TRO Learning, Inc. [*NASDAQ symbol*] (SAG) .... TUTR
Troades [*of Euripides*] [*Classical studies*] (OCD) .... Tro
Trocadero [*London*] (DSUE) .... TROC
Trocaire College, Buffalo, NY [*Library symbol Library of Congress*]
    (LCLS) .... NBuTC
Troche [*Lozenge*] [*Pharmacy*] (DAVI) .... TROCH
Trochiscus [*Lozenge*] [*Pharmacy*] (ROG) .... TROC
Trochiscus [*Lozenge*] [*Pharmacy*] .... TROCH
Trochu Municipal Library, Alberta [*Library symbol National Library of Canada*] (NLC) .... ATRM
Trochu Municipal Library, Trochu, AB, Canada [*Library symbol Library of Congress*] (LCLS) .... CaATrM
Troell-Junet [*Syndrome*] [*Genetics*] (DAVI) .... TJ
Trogen [*Switzerland ICAO location identifier*] (ICLI) .... LSXT
Troilus and Cressida [*Shakespearean work*] (BARN) .... Tr & Cr
Troilus and Cressida [*Shakespearean work*] .... Tro
Trois Fois Salut [*Thrice Greeting*] [*Freemasonry*] [*French*] (ROG) .... SSS
Trois Rivieres [*Quebec*] [*Airport symbol*] (AD) .... YRQ

Trois Rivieres, PQ [*FM radio station call letters*] CBF-FM-1
Trois Rivieres, PQ [*Television station call letters*] .... CHEM
Trois Rivieres, PQ [*FM radio station call letters*] .... CHEY
Trois Rivieres, PQ [*AM radio station call letters*] .... CHLN
Trois Rivieres, PQ [*FM radio station call letters*] .... CIGB
Trois-Rivieres High School, Quebec [*Library symbol National Library of Canada*] (NLC) .... QTT
Trois-Rivieres High School, Trois-Rivieres, PQ, Canada [*Library symbol Library of Congress*] (LCLS) .... CaQTT
Trois-Rivieres, PQ [*Television station call letters*] .... CFKM
Trois-Rivieres, PQ [*Television station call letters*] CIVC
Trois-Rivieres, PQ [*Television station call letters*] .... CKTM
Trois-Rivieres, PQ [*ICAO location identifier*] (ICLI) .... CYRQ
Troitskoye [*Former USSR ICAO location identifier*] (ICLI) .... UHHO
Trojan Energy Corp. [*Vancouver Stock Exchange symbol*] .... TJE
Trojan Nuclear Plant (NRCH) .... TNP
Troland [*Unit of light intensity at the retina*] .... Trol
Troleandomycin [*Formerly, Triacetyloleandomycin*] [*Antibacterial compound*] .... TAO
Trolley .... TRLY
Trolley Coach News [*A publication*] (EAAP) .... TCN
Trolleybus Bulletin [*A publication*] (EAAP) .... TBB
Trolley-Mounted Hoist (NRCH) .... TMH
Trollhattan [*Sweden*] [*Airport symbol*] (OAG) .... THN
Trollhattan/Vanersborg [*Sweden ICAO location identifier*] (ICLI) .... ESGT
Tromba [*Trumpet*] [*Music*] (ROG) .... TROMB
Trombone [*Music*] .... TRB
Trombone [*Music*] .... TRBN
Trombone .... TROM
Trombone .... TROMB
Trombone, Muted .... TM
Tromboni [*Trombones*] .... TBI
Trompette [*Trumpets*] [*Music*] .... TROMP
Troms Fylkes Dampskipsselskap [*Shipping line*] [*Norway*] .... TFDS
Tromso [*Norway ICAO location identifier*] (ICLI) .... ENVN
Tromso [*Norway*] [*Airport symbol*] (OAG) .... TOS
Tromso/Langnes [*Norway ICAO location identifier*] (ICLI) .... ENTC
Tromsoe [*Norway*] [*Airport symbol*] (AD) .... TOA
Tromsoe [*Norway*] [*Seismograph station code, US Geological Survey*]
    (SEIS) .... TRO
TRON [*The Real-Time Operating System Nucleus*] **Universal Language System** [*Computer science*] .... TULS
Trona Railway Co. [*AAR code*] .... TRC
Trondheim [*Norway ICAO location identifier*] (ICLI) .... ENTR
Trondheim [*Norway*] [*Airport symbol*] (OAG) .... TRD
Trondheim/Vaernes [*Norway ICAO location identifier*] (ICLI) .... ENVA
Trondhjemite-Tonalite-Dacite [*Geology*] .... TTD
Trondhjemite-Tonalite-Granodiorite [*Geology*] .... TTG
Troop .... TP
Troop .... TR
Troop (AFM) .... TRP
Troop Airlift Squadron (CINC) .... TAS
Troop Airlift Wing (CINC) .... TAW
Troop Barge, Class A [*Navy symbol Obsolete*] .... APP
Troop Barge, Class B [*Navy symbol Obsolete*] .... APT
Troop Basis [*Military*] .... TB
Troop Basis (MUGU) .... TRB
Troop Carrier [*Air Force*] .... TC
Troop Carrier [*Military*] (CINC) .... TRPCAR
Troop Carrier Command [*World War II*] .... TCC
Troop Carrier Forces [*Military*] .... TCF
Troop Carrier (Medium) (CINC) .... TRPCAR(M)
Troop Carrier Squadron [*Military*] (CINC) .... TCS
Troop Carrier Squadron [*Air Force*] (AFM) .... TCSq
Troop Carrier Squadron [*Air Force*] .... TRPCSq
Troop Carrier Wing [*Military*] (CINC) .... TCW
Troop Carrier Wing [*Air Force*] (AFM) .... TCWg
Troop Carrying Vehicle .... TCV
Troop Corporal-Major [*British military*] (DMA) .... TCM
Troop Evaluation Tests [*Army*] .... TET
Troop Exercise Director (CINC) .... TED
Troop Headquarters .... THQ
Troop Housing [*Army*] (AABC) .... TPHSG
Troop Information .... TI
Troop Information and Education .... TI & E
Troop Information and Education Division .... TIED
Troop Information Officer .... TIO
Troop Information Program .... TIP
Troop Issue Subsistence Activity [*Military*] (AABC) .... TISA
Troop Issue Subsistence Officer [*Military*] (AABC) .... TISO
Troop Issue Support Agency (MCD) .... TISA
Troop Issue Support System [*Army*] .... TISS
Troop List for Operations and Supply .... TLOS
Troop Movement Action Officer .... TMAO
Troop Movement Assignment Order .... TMAO
Troop Proficiency Trainer .... TPT
Troop Program [*Military*] (AABC) .... TP
Troop Program Field Deployment List [*Military*] .... TPFDL
Troop Program List [*Army*] .... TPL
Troop Program Sequence Number [*Military*] .... TPSN
Troop Program Unit [*Army*] (AABC) .... TPU
Troop Quartermaster-Sergeant [*British military*] (DMA) .... TQMS
Troop Reaction and Posture Sequence (MCD) .... TRAPS
Troop Recognition and Detection (MCD) .... TREAD
Troop Safety Line .... TSL
Troop Sergeant-Major [*British military*] (DMA) .... TSM

Troop Support Agency [*Army*] (AABC) .... TSA
Troop Support Agency Bagger Fund (MCD) .... TSABF
Troop Support and Aviation Materiel Readiness Command [*Army*] .... TSARCOM
Troop Support Center [*Army*] .... TSC
Troop Support Command [*Formerly, MECOM*] [*St. Louis, MO*] [*Army*] .... TROSCOM
Troop Support Command [*Formerly, MECOM*] [*Army*] .... TSC
Troop Test .... TT
Troop Unit Basis [*Military*] .... TUB
Troop Unit Change Request .... TUCR
Trooper .... TPR
Trooper .... TRPR
Troop-Leading Procedure [*Military*] (INF) .... TLP
Troops [*Military British*] .... TPS
Troops .... TRPS
Troops In, Troops Out .... TITO
Troops-in-Contact .... TIC
Tropair Airservices [*British ICAO designator*] (FAAC) .... TSV
Tropendienstunfaehig [*Unfit for service in tropics*] [*German military - World War II*] .... TDU
Trophic Unit [*Analytical biochemistry*] .... TU
Trophoblast Antigen [*Immunochemistry*] .... TA
Trophoblast Antigen One [*Immunochemistry*] TA1
Trophoblast/Lymphocyte Cross-Reactive (Antigens) [*Immunochemistry*] .... TLX
Trophoblastic Basement Membrane (PDAA) .... TBM
Trophy .... TROPH
Trophy Dealers and Manufacturers Association (EA) .... TDMA
Tropic Air [*ICAO designator*] (AD) .... CN
Tropic Air Services [*ICAO designator*] (AD) .... EP
Tropic Higher High Water [*Tides*] .... TCHHW
Tropic Higher High-Water Interval [*Tides*] .... TCHHWI
Tropic Higher Low Water [*Tides*] .... TCHLW
Tropic Lower High Water [*Tides*] .... TCLHW
Tropic Lower Low Water [*Tides*] .... TCLLW
Tropic Lower Low-Water Interval [*Tides*] .... TCLLWI
Tropic of Cancer (WDAA) .... TROP CAN
Tropic of Capricorn (WDAA) .... TROP CAP
Tropic Test Center [*Army*] (MCD) .... TTC
Tropicair Cargo [*Burundi*] [*FAA designator*] (FAAC) .... TPK
Tropical [*Load line mark, or air mass*] .... T
Tropical [*Broadcasting antenna*] .... TRO
Tropical .... TROP
Tropical (WGA) .... TRP
Tropical [*NWS*] (FAAC) .... TRPCL
Tropical .... TRPCL
Tropical Africa Advisory Group [*British Overseas Trade Board*] (DS) .... TAAG
Tropical Agriculture [*A publication*] .... Trop
Tropical Agriculture [*Royal Tropical Institute*] [*Bibliographic database*] [*Netherlands*] .... TROPAG
Tropical Air Services [*Belize*] [*ICAO designator*] (FAAC) .... TOS
Tropical Analysis and Real-Time Display [*National Oceanic and Atmospheric Administration*] .... TARDIS
Tropical Array Ocean .... TAO
Tropical Assimilation and Prognosis System (EERA) .... TAPS
Tropical Atlantic Biological Laboratory .... TABL
Tropical Atmosphere/Ocean [*Array*] (USDC) .... TAO
Tropical Atmosphere-Ocean [*Marine science*] (OSRA) .... TAO
Tropical Biennial Oscillation [*Climatology*] .... TBO
Tropical Botanical Garden and Research Institute [*India*] .... TBGR
Tropical Canine Pancytopenia (RDA) .... TCP
Tropical Chocolate Bar [*Military issue*] (VNW) .... TCB
Tropical Conservation Program (GNE) .... TCP
Tropical Constant-Level Balloon System [*Meteorology*] .... TCLBS
Tropical Continental [*American air mass*] .... TC
Tropical Continental [*Meteorology*] (FAAC) .... TRPCD
Tropical Cyclone (ADA) .... TC
Tropical Cyclone Aircraft Reconnaissance Coordinator [*Navy*] (DNAB) .... TCARC
Tropical Depression [*Meteorology*] .... TD
Tropical Deterioration Administrative Committee [*of NDRC*] [*World War II*] .... TDAC
Tropical Deterioration Committee Reports [*of NDRC*] [*World War II*] .... TD
Tropical Development and Research Institute (PDAA) .... TDaRI
Tropical Development and Research Institute [*Research center British*] (IRC) .... TDRI
Tropical Disease Research [*WHO*] .... TDR
Tropical Environmental Data .... TREND
Tropical Experiment [*Proposed by BOMEX*] .... TROPEX
Tropical Experiment Board [*of World Meteorological Organization and International Council on Scientific Unions*] .... TEB
Tropical Experiment Council [*of World Meteorological Organization and International Council on Scientific Unions*] .... TEC
Tropical Experimental Unit [*British military*] (DMA) .... TEU
Tropical Fish Hobbyist [*A publication*] .... Trop F H
Tropical Forest Action Group (EA) .... TFAG
Tropical Forest Foundation (EA) .... TFF
Tropical Forest Initiative (EERA) .... TFI
Tropical Forest Program (EERA) .... TRF
Tropical Forestry Action Plan [*World Bank, UN, and other groups*] .... TFAP
Tropical Forestry Contact Group [*Australia*] .... TFCG
Tropical Fresh Water [*Vessel load line mark*] .... TF
Tropical Fresh Water .... TFW
Tropical Growers' Association (EAIO) .... TGA
Tropical Gulf [*American air mass*] .... TG
Tropical Hypereosinophilia [*Medicine*] (DMAA) .... THE
Tropical Instability Wave Experiment (USDC) .... TIWE
Tropical Instability Wave Experiment [*Marine science*] (OSRA) .... TIWE
Tropical Livestock Unit [*Ratio of livestock to humans*] .... TLU
Tropical Man [*Leiden*] [*A publication*] .... TROPM
Tropical Maritime .... TM
Tropical Maritime Cold Air Mass [*Meteorology*] (BARN) .... mtk
Tropical Maritime Warm Air Mass [*Meteorology*] (BARN) .... mtw
Tropical Medicine .... TM
Tropical Medicine (DAVI) .... TropMed
Tropical Meteorology Research Programme [*Marine science*] (OSRA) .... TMRP
Tropical Ocean Climate Study [*Marine science*] (OSRA) .... TOCS
Tropical Ocean Global Atmosphere Program (EERA) .... TOGA
Tropical Ocean Global Atmosphere Program Numerical Experiment Group (EERA) .... TOGA NEG
Tropical Ocean-Atmosphere Newsletter [*Now Tropical Ocean-Global Atmosphere Notes*] (USDC) .... TO-AN
Tropical Ocean-Atmosphere Newsletter [*Marine science*] (OSRA) .... TOAN
Tropical Ocean-Global Atmosphere [*Program*] (USDC) .... TOGA
Tropical Oceanographic and Meteorological Experiment [*National Science Foundation*] .... TROMEX
Tropical Oceans and Global Atmosphere Project [*World Meteorological Organization*] .... TOGA
Tropical Pacific [*American air mass*] .... TP
Tropical Pacific Thermal Monitoring System [*Marine science*] (OSRA) .... TPTMS
Tropical Pacific Upper Ocean Heat and Mass Budgets [*USA*] [*Marine science*] (OSRA) .... TROPIC HEAT
Tropical Pancreatic Diabetes [*Endocrinology*] (DAVI) .... TPD
Tropical Pesticides Research Unit [*Later, Centre for Overseas Pest Research*] [*British*] .... TPRU
Tropical Products Institute [*Overseas Development Administration*] [*British*] (DS) .... TPI
Tropical Radio Telegraph [*Telecommunications*] (IAA) .... TRT
Tropical Rain Mapping Radar [*Instrument*] (EERA) .... TRAMAR
Tropical Rainfall Explorer Mission (MCD) .... TREM
Tropical Rainfall Measurement Mission [*NASA*] [*Marine science*] (OSRA) .... TRMM
Tropical Rainfall Measuring Mission [*Proposed satellite*] .... TRMM
Tropical Rainforest Ecology Experiment [*Marine science*] (OSRA) .... TREE
Tropical Rainforest Ecology Experiment (USDC) .... TREE
Tropical Rainforest Society [*Australia*] .... TRS
Tropical Regional Analysis [*National Weather Service*] .... TROPRAN
Tropical Research Institute [*Smithsonian Institution*] .... TRI
Tropical Research Medical Laboratory [*Army*] .... TRML
Tropical Resources for Agricultural Development Information System [*Overseas Development Natural Resources Institute*] [*British Information service or system*] (IID) .... TRADIS
Tropical Resources Institute [*Yale University*] [*Research center*] (RCD) .... TRI
Tropical Revolving Storm [*Meteorology*] .... TRS
Tropical Sea Airlines [*Thailand*] [*ICAO designator*] (FAAC) .... TSS
Tropical Spastic Paraparesis [*Neurology*] .... TSP
Tropical Splenomegaly Syndrome [*Medicine*] (MAE) .... TSS
Tropical Sprue [*Medicine*] (MAE) .... TS
Tropical Stored Products Centre [*Tropical Products Institute*] [*Overseas Development Administration*] [*British*] (DS) .... TSPC
Tropical Summer Winter [*Vessel load line mark*] .... TSW
Tropical Timber Information Center [*College of Environmental Science and Forestry at Syracuse*] [*Research center*] (RCD) .... TTIC
Tropical Upper Tropospheric Trough [*Meteorology*] .... TUTT
Tropical Vegetable Information Service [*Asian Vegetable Research and Development Center*] [*Information service or system*] (IID) .... TVIS
Tropical Western Pacific (USDC) .... TWP
Tropical Western Pacific [*Marine science*] (OSRA) .... TWP
Tropical Wind, Energy Conversion, and Reference Level [*National Science Foundation*] .... TWERL
Tropical Wind, Energy Conversion, and Reference Level Experiment [*National Science Foundation*] .... TWERLE
Tropical Wind, Energy Conversion and Reference Level Experiment [*Marine science*] (OSRA) .... TWERLE
Tropical Wind Observing Ships [*Marine science*] (MSC) .... TWOS
Tropical Worsted Uniform [*Army*] (VNW) .... TW
Tropical Zodiac .... TZ
Tropicalized (MSA) .... TPL
Tropicana Development Corp. [*Vancouver Stock Exchange symbol*] .... TNA
Tropics [*MARC geographic area code Library of Congress*] (LCCP) .... w-----
Tropocollagen [*Genetics*] (DAVI) .... TC
Tropomyosin [*Biochemistry*] .... TM
Troponin [*Biochemistry*] .... TN
Troponin C [*Biochemistry*] .... TnC
Troponin I [*Biochemistry*] .... TnI
Troponin T [*Biochemistry*] .... TnT
Troponwerke Dinklage & Co. [*Germany*] [*Research code symbol*] .... D
Troposcatter Communications Link .... TCL
Troposcatter Communications System .... TCS
Troposheric Gravity Wave [*Planetary science*] .... TGW
Tropospheric .... TROPO
Tropospheric Chemistry Systems Model (MCD) .... TCSM
Tropospheric Emission Sensor .... TES
Tropospheric Frontal Zone .... TFZ
Tropospheric Scatter Radio Equipment (AAG) .... TSRE
Tropospheric Scatter System .... TSS
Trott Vocational High School, Niagara Falls, NY [*Library symbol Library of Congress*] (LCLS) .... NNiaTV
Trotter .... T
Trotting Horse Museum (EA) .... THM
Troubat and Haly's Pennsylvania Practice [*A publication*] (DLA) .... T & H Prac
Troubat and Haly's Pennsylvania Practice [*A publication*] (DLA) .... Tr & H Pr
Troubat and Haly's Pennsylvania Practice [*A publication*] (DLA) .... Troub & H Prac

Troubat on Limited Partnership [*A publication*] (DLA) .... Troub Lim Partn
Trouble [*Telecommunications*] (TEL) .... TBL
Trouble (IAA) .... TBLE
Trouble Analysis Chart .... TAC
Trouble Analysis System or Subsystem [*Telecommunications*] (TEL) .... TASS
Trouble and Failure Report [*Army*] .... TAFR
Trouble and Failure Report [*NASA*] .... TFR
Trouble and Failure Report/Corrective Action Report .... TFR/CAR
Trouble Came Back [*Computer hacker terminology*] (NHD) .... TCB
Trouble Detection (IAA) .... TRDET
Trouble Detection and Monitoring .... TDM
Trouble Indicator Trunk [*Telecommunications*] (IAA) .... TIT
Trouble Location Problem (AAG) .... TLP
Trouble Recorder (IAA) .... TRR
Trouble Report .... TR
Trouble Report Evaluation and Analysis Tool (MCD) .... TREAT
Trouble Reporting Desk [*NASA*] (KSC) .... TRD
Trouble Reporting Operations Center [*Federal Telecommunications System*] (GFGA) .... TROC
Trouble Shooting Manual (IAA) .... TSM
Troubles d'Apprentissage - Association Canadienne [*Learning Disabilities Association of Canada*] (EAIO) .... TAAC
Troubles/Requests Logging and Coordination [*Staff*] [*Computer science*] ..... TLC
Troubleshoot (MCD) .... TS
Troubleshooting .... TBST'G
Troubleshooting (NASA) .... TRBL
Troubleshooting Aid (MCD) .... TSA
Troubleshooting Block Diagram .... TBD
Trouble-Shooting Checklist [*Test for academic institutions*] .... TSC
Troubleshooting Guide (MCD) .... TSG
Troubleshooting Logic Diagram (NASA) .... TSLD
Troubleshooting Loop .... TSL
Troubleshooting Record Sheet [*NASA*] (NASA) .... TRS
Troubleshooting Time (SAA) .... TST
Troudor Resources, Inc. [*Vancouver Stock Exchange symbol*] .... TRD
Trough (ADA) .... TR
Trough [*Freight*] .... TRGH
Trough Serum Concentration [*Immunology*] (DAVI) .... CPmin
Troup County Archives, La Grange, GA [*Library symbol*] [*Library of Congress*] (LCLS) .... GLagTAr
Troupe (ROG) .... TR
Trousdale County Public Library, Hartsville, TN [*Library symbol*] [*Library of Congress*] (LCLS) .... THav
Trouser Institute of America [*Absorbed by NOSA*] (EA) .... TIA
Trout Creek Community Library, Ontario [*Library symbol National Library of Canada*] (NLC) .... OTRCR
Trout Creek Elementary School, Trout Creek, MT [*Library symbol*] [*Library of Congress*] (LCLS) .... MtTcES
Trout Farmers' Association of Australia .... TFAA
Trout Unlimited (EA) .... TU
Troutdale, OR [*Location identifier FAA*] (FAAL) .... TTD
Trove Resources [*Vancouver Stock Exchange symbol*] .... TRV
Trow [*Ship's rigging*] (ROG) .... TW
T.Rowe Price Assoc [*NASDAQ symbol*] (TTSB) .... TROW
Trower's Debtor and Creditor [*1860*] [*A publication*] (DLA) .... Trow D & Cr
Trower's Manual of the Prevalance of Equity [*1876*] [*A publication*] (DLA) .... Trow Eq
Troy [*A system of weights for precious metals*] .... T
Troy [*New York*] [*Seismograph station code, US Geological Survey*] (SEIS) ..... TRY
Troy, AL [*Location identifier FAA*] (FAAL) .... TOI
Troy, AL [*Television station call letters*] .... WRJM-TV
Troy, AL [*AM radio station call letters*] .... WTBF
Troy, AL [*FM radio station call letters*] .... WTSU
Troy, AL [*FM radio station call letters*] .... WZHT
Troy Hess Fan Club (EA) .... THFC
Troy Hill Bancorp [*NASDAQ symbol*] (TTSB) .... THBC
Troy Hill Bancorp, Inc. [*NASDAQ symbol*] (SAG) .... THBC
Troy Hill Bancorp, Inc. [*Associated Press*] (SAG) .... TroyHill
Troy, IL [*Location identifier FAA*] (FAAL) .... TOY
Troy Mineral & Tech [*Vancouver Stock Exchange symbol*] .... TMT
Troy, MO [*FM radio station call letters*] .... KZMM
Troy, NC [*AM radio station call letters*] .... WJRM
Troy, NY [*FM radio station call letters*] .... WFLY
Troy, NY [*AM radio station call letters*] .... WHAZ
Troy, NY [*FM radio station call letters*] .... WRPI
Troy, NY [*AM radio station call letters*] .... WTRY
Troy, OH [*FM radio station call letters*] .... WTRJ
Troy Ounce .... TO
Troy, PA [*AM radio station call letters*] .... WHGL
Troy Public Library, Troy, MI [*Library symbol Library of Congress*] (LCLS) ...... MiTr
Troy Public Library, Troy, NY [*Library symbol Library of Congress*] (LCLS) .... NT
Troy Senior High School, Troy, MT [*Library symbol*] [*Library of Congress*] (LCLS) .... MtTyrSH
Troy State University (GAGS) .... Troy St U
Troy State University at Dorhan (GAGS) .... Troy St U (Dorhan)
Troy State University at Dothan, Dothan, AL [*Library symbol*] [*Library of Congress*] (LCLS) .... ADoT
Troy State University at Fort Rucker, Fort Rucker, AL [*Library symbol Library of Congress*] (LCLS) .... AFrT
Troy State University at Montgomery, Montgomery, AL [*Library symbol Library of Congress*] (LCLS) .... AMT
Troy State University, School of Nursing, Montgomery, AL [*Library symbol Library of Congress*] (LCLS) .... ATrT-N
Troy State University, Troy, AL [*OCLC symbol*] (OCLC) .... ADA
Troy State University, Troy, AL [*Library symbol Library of Congress*] (LCLS) .... ATrT
Troyes/Barberey [*France ICAO location identifier*] (ICLI) .... LFQB
Troy-Miami County Public Library, Troy, OH [*Library symbol Library of Congress*] (LCLS) .... OTr
Troy-Miami County Public Library, Troy, OH [*Library symbol*] [*Library of Congress*] (LCLS) .... OTrL
Truancy [*FBI standardized term*] .... TRU
Truce .... T
Truce Day .... T (Day)
Trucial Oman Levies [*British military*] (DMA) .... TOL
Trucial Oman Scouts [*British military*] (DMA) .... TOS
Trucial States [*United Arab Emirates*] [*MARC geographic area code Library of Congress*] (LCCP) .... a-ts--
Trucial States [*United Arab Emirates*] [*MARC country of publication code Library of Congress*] (LCCP) .... ts
Truck (AAG) .... TK
Truck .... TR
Truck .... TRCK
Truck (AAG) .... TRK
Truck, Airplane, Boat (SAA) .... TAB
Truck and Bus .... T & B
Truck and Heavy Equipment Claims Council (EA) .... THECC
Truck & Off-Highway Industries [*A publication*] .... T & OHI
Truck and Rail .... TAR
Truck and Rail Van .... TARVAN
Truck and Recreation Products Office .... TRPO
Truck Assembly .... TA
Truck Assembly Plants .... TAP
Truck Body and Equipment Association [*Defunct*] (EA) .... TBEA
Truck Cap Industry Association (EA) .... TCIA
Truck Commander [*Military*] (INF) .... TC
Truck Components Marketing [*Eaton Corp.*] .... TCM
Truck Computer Analysis of Performance and Economy .... TCAPE
Truck Crash Analysis Data System [*FHWA*] (TAG) .... TCADS
Truck Design Optimization Project [*Railroads*] .... TDOP
Truck Discharge Point Jet (NATG) .... TDPJ
Truck Discharge Point Mogas (NATG) .... TDPM
Truck Driving Program [*Association of Independent Colleges and Schools specialization code*] .... TD
Truck Electrical Center [*Volvo White Truck Corp.*] .... TEC
Truck Equipment and Body Distributor Association [*Later, NTEA*] (EA).... TEBDA
Truck Expense Analysis and Management [*Computer science*] .... TEAM
Truck Head .... TRKHD
Truck Hub Unit [*Suspension*] [*Automotive engineering*] .... THU
Truck Inventory and Use Survey [*BTS*] (TAG) .... TIUS
Truck Loading Point (NATG) .... TLP
Truck Lock [*Nuclear energy*] (NRCH) .... TL
Truck Manufacturers Association .... TMA
Truck Master Association [*Auto enthusiast organization*] .... TMA
Truck Mixer Manufacturers Bureau (EA) .... TMMB
Truck Operation Analysis .... TOA
Truck Operator Road Test [*Part of TORQUE*] .... TORT
Truck Operators Road Qualifying Exam [*National Highway Traffic Safety Administration*] .... TORQUE
Truck Ordering and Pricing System .... TOPS
Truck Performance Analysis .... TPA
Truck Renting and Leasing Association (EA) .... TRALA
Truck Renting and Leasing Association (EA) .... TRLA
Truck Route Order [*Army*] (AABC) .... TRO
Truck Routing Improvement Program (IAA) .... TRIP
Truck Technical Operations [*Automobile manufacturer corporate structure*] .... TTO
Truck Trailer Manufacturers Association (EA) .... TTMA
Truck Transportable Communications Station .... TTCS
Truck Writers of North America [*An association*] (EA) .... TWNA
Truck-Drawn .... TRKDR
Truckee, CA [*Location identifier FAA*] (FAAL) .... TRK
Truckee Public Library, Truckee, CA [*Library symbol*] [*Library of Congress*] (LCLS) .... CTr
Trucker with Upscale Living Quarters in His or Her Vehicle [*Lifestyle classification*] .... Truppie
Truckers Against Drunk Drivers [*Defunct*] (EA) .... TADD
Truck-Frame and Axle Repair Association (EA) .... TARA
Trucking .... TRCKNG
Trucking Employers, Inc. [*Later, TMI*] .... TEI
Trucking Management, Inc. (EA) .... TMI
Trucking Research Institute [*Research center*] (RCD) .... TRI
Truckload [*24,000 pounds or more*] .... TL
Truck-Mounted (AABC) .... TRKMTD
Trucks Involved in Fatal Accidents [*NHTSA*] (TAG) .... TIFA
Tru-Cut Needle Biopsy [*Surgery*] (DAVI) .... TNB
Trudeau Early Retirement Fund [*Established 1982 by Canadians who hoped t hat the money would persuade their prime minister to retire from office*] [*Defunct*] .... TERF
Trudeau Institute, Saranac Lake, NY [*Library symbol Library of Congress*] (LCLS) .... NSIT
Trudeau, R. G., Bloomfield Hills MI [*STAC*] .... TRG
True [*Direction*] .... T
True (GAVI) .... TRU
True Air Temperature (AFM) .... TAT
True Airspeed .... TAS
True Airspeed Computer .... TAC
True Airspeed Computer .... TASC
True Altitude [*Height*] [*Navigation*] .... TA
True and Relative Motion Plotting System (IAA) .... TARPS

True Angle of Attack (MCD) ... AOAT
True Anomaly ... TA
True Azimuth [*Symbol*] (MUGU) ... Zn
True Bearing [*Navigation*] ... TB
True Blood Loss ... TBL
True Blue [*A fluorescent dye*] ... TB
True Boiling Point ... TBP
True Centerline Tested ... TCT
True Color (CDE) ... TC
True Complement ... T/C
True Conjugate [*Ophthalmology*] (DAVI) ... TC
True Conservative Party [*British*] (ECON) ... TCP
True Course ... TC
True Date-Time Group [*Military*] ... TDTG
True Depth [*Diamond drilling*] ... TD
True Dipole Moment [*Geodesy*] ... TDM
True Economic Depreciation ... TED
True/False (CDAI) ... T/F
True Fibrous Involution [*Medicine*] ... TFI
True Ground Speed (IAA) ... TGS
True Ground Track (MCD) ... TGT
True Heading ... TH
True Heading (GAVI) ... THDG
True Heading Computer (DNAB) ... THC
True Height Above Aerodrome Level [*Aviation*] (AIA) ... TER
True Indicated Airspeed (GAVI) ... TIAS
True Indicated Radius (IAA) ... TIR
True Interest Cost [*Finance*] ... TIC
True Involute Form ... TIF
True Life Institute (EA) ... TLI
True Mach Number ... TMN
True Mean ... TM
True Mean Value ... TMV
True Metabolizable Energy ... TME
True Money Rate [*Finance*] ... TMR
True Motion [*RADAR*] (DEN) ... TM
True Motion RADAR (IAA) ... TMR
True Name ... T/N
[*The*] **True Nature Network** (EA) ... TTNN
True Negative [*Medicine*] ... TN
True Negative Rate [*Medicine*] (DAVI) ... TNR
True North ... TN
True North Communications, Inc. [*Formerly, Foote, Cone & Belding*] [*NYSE symbol*] (SAG) ... TNO
True North Communications, Inc. [*Formerly, Foote, Cone & Belding*] [*Associated Press*] (SAG) ... TrueNrth
True North Communicns [*NYSE symbol*] (TTSB) ... TNO
True North Film [*Vancouver Stock Exchange symbol*] ... TNF
True Path Party [*Turkey Political party*] ... TPP
True Personal Identification Number [*Banking*] ... TPIN
True Polar Wandering [*Geophysics*] ... TPW
True Position ... TP
True Position Dimensioning and Tolerancing (PDAA) ... TPDT
True Position Tolerance (MSA) ... TPTOL
True Positive [*Medicine*] ... TP
True Positive Rate [*Medicine*] (DMAA) ... TPR
True Positive Stress Test [*Medicine*] (DMAA) ... TPST
True Profile [*Technical drawings*] ... TP
True Radiation Emittance ... TRE
True Rate of Return [*Finance*] (ADA) ... TRR
True Root Mean Square [*Statistics*] ... TRMS
True Seed Exchange [*Later, SSE*] (EA) ... TSX
True Sounds of Liberty [*Musical group*] ... TSOL
True Speed Indicator (IAA) ... TSI
True Tape Motion Monitor ... TTMM
True Temperature Tunnel [*Acronym pronounced, "Triple T"*] ... TRIPLTEE
True Temperature Tunnel ... TTT
True to Scale ... TTS
True Total Ion ... TTI
True Ultimate Tensile Strength (MCD) ... TUTS
True Unidentified Flying Objects ... TRUFOS
True Vapor Pressure ... TVP
True Vertical Depth [*Diamonds*] ... TVD
True Vocal Cord (MEDA) ... TVC
True Watt (MSA) ... TW
True Whig Party [*Liberia*] (AF) ... TWP
True Zenith Distance [*Navigation*] ... TZD
Truebner's Simplified Grammars [*A publication*] ... TSG
Trueman's New Brunswick Equity Cases [*1876-93*] [*A publication*] (DLA) ... Tru
Trueman's New Brunswick Equity Cases [*A publication*] (DLA) ... Truem Eq Cas
Trueman's New Brunswick Equity Cases [*A publication*] (DLA) ... Trueman Eq Cas
Trueman's New Brunswick Reports [*A publication*] (DLA) ... NBR Tru
Trueman's New Brunswick Reports [*A publication*] (DLA) ... True
True-Motion, Anti-Collision System (PDAA) ... TM/ACS
True-Motion, Basic Collision Avoidance (PDAA) ... TM/BAC
TrueType Font [*Computer science*] (CDE) ... TTF
Truevision Advanced Raster Graphics Adapter [*AT & T*] ... TARGA
Truevision Image Processing Software [*AT & T*] ... TIPS
Truevision, Inc. [*Associated Press*] (SAG) ... Truevision
Truevision, Inc. [*NASDAQ symbol*] (SAG) ... TRUV
Trufocus [*Lamp base type*] (NTCM) ... Tf
Trujillo [*Honduras*] [*ICAO location identifier*] (ICLI) ... MHTJ
Trujillo [*Honduras*] [*Airport symbol*] (AD) ... TJI
Trujillo [*Peru*] [*Seismograph station code, US Geological Survey*] (SEIS) ... TRP
Trujillo [*Peru*] [*Airport symbol*] (OAG) ... TRU
Trujillo/Capitan Carlos Martinez de Pinillos - Huanchaco [*Peru*] [*ICAO location identifier*] (ICLI) ... SPRU
Truk [*Caroline Islands*] [*ICAO location identifier*] (ICLI) ... PTKK
Truk [*Caroline Islands*] [*Airport symbol*] (OAG) ... TKK
Truk [*Caroline Islands*] [*Seismograph station code, US Geological Survey Closed*] (SEIS) ... TRU
Truly (ROG) ... TRY
Truly ... TY
Truly Fast Fourier Transform (PDAA) ... TFFT
Truman College, Chicago, IL [*Library symbol Library of Congress*] (LCLS) ... ICTr
Truman Philatelic and Historical Association (EA) ... TPHA
Trumann, AR [*FM radio station call letters*] (RBYB) ... KKCN
Trumann Southern Railroad (IIA) ... TS
Truman's American Railway Reports [*A publication*] (DLA) ... Tru Railw Rep
Trumansburg, NY [*AM radio station call letters*] ... WPIE
Trumark Resource Corp. [*Vancouver Stock Exchange symbol*] ... TMK
Trumbull County Law Library, Warren, OH [*Library symbol Library of Congress*] (LCLS) ... OWLaw
Trumeau (VRA) ... trum
Trump Hotels & Casino Resorts [*NYSE symbol*] (TTSB) ... DJT
Trump Hotels & Casino Resorts, Inc. [*NYSE symbol*] (SAG) ... DJT
Trump Hotels & Casino Resorts, Inc. [*Associated Press*] (SAG) ... Trump
Trump Shuttle [*ICAO designator*] (AD) ... TB
Trumpet ... TP
Trumpet ... TPT
Trumpet ... TR
Trumpeter ... TPTR
[*The*] **Trumpeter Swan Society** (EA) ... TTSS
Truncal Vagotomy [*Medicine*] (DMAA) ... TV
Truncated Cone [*Golf balls*] ... TC
Truncated Icosahedra [*Crystallography*] ... TICOS
Truncated Sequential Probability Ratio Test (PDAA) ... TSPRT
Truncated Sequential Probability Ratio Test for Reliability (PDAA) ... TSPRTR
Truncated Sequential Test (PDAA) ... TST
Truncated Variant [*Genetics*] ... TRU
Truncated Whitworth, British Standard Pipe (Parallel) [*Thread*] ... TWPP
Truncated Whitworth Coarse [*Thread*] (MSA) ... TWC
Truncated Whitworth Fine [*Thread*] (MSA) ... TWF
Truncated Whitworth Special [*Thread*] (MSA) ... TWS
Truncation Mutant ... TM
Truncation Safety Factor [*In biological systems*] ... TSF
Truncus Arteriosus [*Medicine*] (DMAA) ... TA
Trunk (IAA) ... T
Trunk (IAA) ... TK
Trunk (AAG) ... TRK
Trunk Access Unit ... TAU
Trunk Amplifier (IAA) ... TA
Trunk and Facilities Maintenance System [*Telecommunications*] (TEL) ... TFMS
Trunk and Junction Routing [*Telecommunications*] (TEL) ... TJR
Trunk Barrier [*Telecommunications*] (IAA) ... TB
Trunk Block Connector ... TBC
Trunk Class of Service [*Telecommunications*] (TEL) ... TCOS
Trunk Coin Telephone (OA) ... TCT
Trunk Control ... TC
Trunk Cross Sectional Area [*of a tree*] ... TCSA
Trunk Cut-In ... TCI
Trunk Cutoff ... TCO
Trunk Destination Words (CET) ... TDW
Trunk Distribution Frame (DEN) ... TDF
Trunk Encryption Device [*Telecommunications*] (TEL) ... TED
Trunk Equalizer [*Telecommunications*] (OA) ... TE
Trunk Equipment [*Telecommunications*] (TEL) ... TK
Trunk Extension-Flexion [*Medicine*] (DMAA) ... TEF
Trunk Forecasting System [*Telecommunications*] (TEL) ... TFS
Trunk Frame [*Telecommunications*] (TEL) ... TF
Trunk Group Identification [*Telecommunications*] (TEL) ... TGID
Trunk Group Multiplexer [*Telecommunications*] (TEL) ... TGM
Trunk Group Number [*Telecommunications*] (TEL) ... TGN
Trunk Interface Handler ... TIH
Trunk Interface Module for Data Links [*Telecommunications*] ... TIM/DL
Trunk Intermediate Distribution Frame [*Telecommunications*] (TEL) ... TIDF
Trunk Junctor [*Telecommunications*] (IAA) ... TJ
Trunk Line Association ... TLA
Trunk Line Network ... TLN
Trunk Line Tariff Bureau ... TLTB
Trunk Line Test Panel [*Telecommunications*] (TEL) ... TLTP
Trunk Line-Central Passenger Committee ... TLCPC
Trunk Line-Central Territory Railroad Tariff Bureau ... TL-CTR
Trunk Link Frame [*Telecommunications*] (TEL) ... TLF
Trunk Load [*Telecommunications*] (IAA) ... TL
Trunk Maintenance Files [*Telecommunications*] (TEL) ... TMF
Trunk Mark [*Telecommunications*] (IAA) ... TM
Trunk Offer [*Telecommunications*] (TEL) ... TKO
Trunk Offering (NITA) ... TKO
Trunk Piston Engine Oil [*Automotive lubricants*] ... TPEO
Trunk Processing Unit [*Bell System*] ... TPU
Trunk Register Link [*Telecommunications*] (TEL) ... TRL
Trunk Servicing Forecasting System [*Telecommunications*] (TEL) ... TSFS
Trunk Servicing System [*Bell System*] ... TSS
Trunk Supervisor [*Telecommunications*] (IAA) ... TSUP
Trunk Switching Unit (NITA) ... TSU
Trunk Test [*Telecommunications*] (IAA) ... TT
Trunk Test Rack (NITA) ... TTR
Trunked Private Mobile Radio ... TPMR

Trunkline Gas Co., Houston, TX [*Library symbol Library of Congress*] (LCLS) ..... TxHTG
Trunks Integrated Record Keeping System [*Bell System*] ..... TIRKS
Trunnion [*Pivot*] ..... TR
Trunnion (NASA) ..... TRN
Trunnion [*Pivot*] (KSC) ..... TRUN
Trunnion Angle (KSC) ..... TA
Trunnion Angle (MCD) ..... TRUNANG
Trunnion Drive Axis (SAA) ..... TDA
Trunnion Pin Attachment Device [*NASA*] ..... TPAD
Truppenentgiftungskompanie [*Personnel decontamination company*] [*German military - World War II*] ..... TEK
Truro [*British depot code*] ..... TR
Truro [*Postcode*] (ODBW) ..... TR
Truro, MA [*FM radio station call letters*] ..... WCDJ
Truro, NS [*AM radio station call letters*] ..... CKCL
Truro, NS [*FM radio station call letters*] ..... CKTO
Truronensis [*Signature of the Bishop of Truro*] [*Latin*] (ROG) ..... TRURON
Trus-Joist I-Beam ..... TJI
Truss (AAG) ..... T
Truss (MSA) ..... TR
Truss [*Shipping*] ..... TRS
Truss Connector Bulletin [*Department of Housing and Urban Development*] [*A publication*] (GFGA) ..... TCB
Truss Head [*Engineering*] ..... TRH
Truss Plate Institute (EA) ..... TPI
Trussville, AL [*FM radio station call letters*] (RBYB) ..... WRAX-FM
Trussville, AL [*FM radio station call letters*] ..... WWBR
Trust ..... TR
Trust ..... TRST
Trust ..... TST
Trust Chamber [*NASA*] (KSC) ..... TCH
Trust Chamber Pressure [*Missile technology*] (KSC) ..... TCP
Trust Companies Magazine [*1904-38*] [*A publication*] (DLA) ..... Trust Co Mag
Trust Company (MHDB) ..... Tr Co
Trust Co. of New Jersey [*NASDAQ symbol*] (NQ) ..... TCNJ
Trust Co. of New Jersey [*Associated Press*] (SAG) ..... TrustNJ
Trust Deed ..... TD
Trust for Education on the United Nations (EA) ..... TEUN
Trust for Investments in Mortgages (MHDW) ..... TIMS
Trust for Public Land (EA) ..... TPL
Trust Fund ..... TF
Trust House [*British*] ..... TH
Trust Houses Forte Ltd. [*Hotel empire*] ..... THF
Trust Investment Committee Memorandum [*A publication*] (DLA) ..... TICM
Trust Letter. American Bankers Association [*A publication*] (ILCA) ..... Trust Lett
Trust Officers Committee Minutes [*A publication*] (DLA) ..... TOCM
Trust or Complement (MHDI) ..... T/C
Trust Originated Preferred Securities [*Finance*] ..... TOPrS
Trust Receipt [*Banking*] ..... T/R
Trust Secretary ..... TS
Trust Termination ..... TT
Trust Territories ..... TT
Trust Territory of the Pacific Islands [*MARC geographic area code Library of Congress*] (LCCP) ..... pott--
Trust Territory of the Pacific Islands ..... TERPACIS
Trust Territory of the Pacific Islands [*Postal code*] ..... TT
Trust Territory of the Pacific Islands [*MARC country of publication code Library of Congress*] (LCCP) ..... tt
Trust Territory of the Pacific Islands ..... TTPI
Trust Territory Reports [*A publication*] (DLA) ..... Trust Terr
Trust Territory Reports of Pacific Island [*A publication*] (DLA) ..... TTR
Trustco Bank Corp. New York [*NASDAQ symbol*] (SAG) ..... TRST
Trustco Bank Corp. New York [*Associated Press*] (SAG) ..... TrstNY
Trusted Computer System Evaluation Criteria (MCD) ..... TCSEC
Trusted Computing Base ..... TCB
Trusted Information Systems [*Commercial firm*] ..... TIS
Trusted Information Systems, Inc. [*NASDAQ symbol*] (SAG) ..... TISX
Trusted Information Systems, Inc. [*Associated Press*] (SAG) ..... TrustInf
Trustee ..... TR
Trustee ..... TR
Trustee ..... TREE
Trustee ..... TRU
Trustee (WGA) ..... TSTEE
Trustee ..... TTEE
Trustee ..... TTEE
Trustee, Administration, and Physician's Institute [*Seminar*] ..... TAP
Trustee Companies' Association of Australia ..... TCAA
Trustee Companies Officers' Association [*Australia*] ..... TCOA
Trustee Savings Bank [*British*] ..... TSB
Trustee Savings Bank (Channel Islands) [*British*] ..... TSB(CI)
Trustee under Agreement [*Legal term*] (DLA) ..... T/U/Ag
Trustee under Agreement [*Legal term*] (DLA) ..... TA
Trustee under Will [*Legal term*] (DLA) ..... TUW
Trustee under Will [*Legal term*] (DLA) ..... TW
Trustees ..... TRS
Trustees for Conservation [*Defunct*] (EA) ..... TFC
Trustees of the California State University and Colleges, Chancellor's Office Library, Long Beach, CA [*Library symbol Library of Congress*] (LCLS) ..... CLobT
Trustees of the Franklin Delano Roosevelt Library [*Abolished, 1958*] [*Library is now operated by the General Services Administration*] ..... TFDRL
Trusteeship [*Legal shorthand*] (LWAP) ..... TREESHIP
Trusteeship Council [*of the United Nations*] ..... TC
Trusteeship Council of the United Nations ..... TC(UN)
Trusteeship Institute (EA) ..... TI
Trusteeship Institute, Inc. (EA) ..... TII
Trustmark Corp. [*NASDAQ symbol*] (SPSG) ..... TRMK
Trustmark Corp. [*Associated Press*] (SAG) ..... TrUstmk
Trustworthy Interface Unit [*Telecommunications*] (OSI) ..... TIU
Trustworthy Network Interface Unit [*Telecommunications*] (OSI) ..... TNIU
Trustworthy Terminal Interface Unit [*Telecommunications*] (OSI) ..... TTIU
Truth about Civil Turmoil [*An association Defunct*] (EA) ..... TACT
Truth Data Acquisition, Recording, and Display System ..... TDARDS
Truth, Esteem, Attitude, and Motivation [*Name of actor Chuck Norris' anti-gang project*] ..... TEAM
Truth in Advertising [*An association Defunct*] (EA) ..... TA
Truth in Mileage Act of 1986 ..... TIMA
Truth in Negotiations Act ..... TINA
Truth Missionaries Chapter of Positive Accord (EA) ..... TMCA
Truth Or Consequences/Municipal [*New Mexico*] [*ICAO location identifier*] (ICLI) ..... KTCS
Truth or Consequences, NM [*AM radio station call letters*] ..... KCHS
Truth or Consequences, NM [*FM radio station call letters*] ..... KSNM
Truth Or Consequences, NM [*Location identifier FAA*] (FAAL) ..... TCS
Truth Or Consequences Public Library, Truth Or Consequences, NM [*Library symbol Library of Congress*] (LCLS) ..... NmTr
Truth-in-Lending Act [*1968*] ..... T-i-L
Truth-in-Lending Act [*1968*] ..... TILA
Truth-in-Lending Simplification and Reform Act [*1980*] ..... TILSRA
Truth-Maintenance System [*Artificial intelligence*] (ECON) ..... TMS
Tru-Wall Group Ltd. [*Toronto Stock Exchange symbol*] ..... TW
TRV Minerals Corp. [*Vancouver Stock Exchange symbol*] ..... TVM
TRW Advanced Steering [*Automotive components*] ..... TAS
TRW Environmental Safety Systems, Inc. (GAAI) ..... TESS
TRW, Inc. [*Formerly, Thompson Ramo Wooldridge, Inc.*] [*NYSE symbol*] (SPSG) ..... TRW
TRW Inc.,$4.40 Cv II Pref [*NYSE symbol*] (TTSB) ..... TRWPrB
TRW Inc.,$4.50 Cv II Pref [*NYSE symbol*] (TTSB) ..... TRWPrD
TRW Information Networks Division [*TRW, Inc.*] [*Torrance, CA*] (TSSD) ..... TRW IND
TRW Systems Group, Houston, TX [*Library symbol Library of Congress*] (LCLS) ..... TxHTRW
TRW Systems Group, Redondo Beach, CA [*Library symbol Library of Congress*] (LCLS) ..... CRdbT
Try Again [*Telecommunications*] (TEL) ..... AG
Try Repeating Dose [*Medicine*] ..... TRD
Trye's Jus Filizarii [*A publication*] (ILCA) ..... Trye Jus Filiz
Tryon, NC [*AM radio station call letters*] ..... WKJT
Tryout Employment [*Job Training and Partnership Act*] (OICC) ..... TOE
Trypan Blue [*Biological stain*] ..... TpB
Trypanosoma [*Medicine*] (MAE) ..... T
Trypanosome Lytic Factor [*Biochemistry*] ..... TLF
Trypsin (MAE) ..... TPS
Trypsin [*An enzyme*] (DAVI) ..... TRYPSN
Trypsin Inhibitor [*Food technology*] ..... TI
Trypsin Inhibitor Activity [*Food technology*] ..... TIA
Trypsin Inhibitory Capacity [*Biochemistry*] ..... TIC
Trypsin Inhibitory Unit [*Food analysis*] ..... TIU
Trypsin Units Inhibited [*Food technology*] ..... TUI
Trypsin-Aldehyde-Fuchsin [*Medicine*] (MAE) ..... TAF
Trypsin-Insoluble Segment [*Cytochemistry*] ..... TIS
Trypsin-Modulating Oostatic Factor [*Biochemistry*] ..... TMOF
Tryptamine Chemical Delivery System [*Pharmacology*] ..... TCDS
Trypticase, Peptone, Glucose ..... TPG
Trypticase Soy [*Plate*] [*Laboratory*] (DAVI) ..... TS
Trypticase Soy Agar [*Cell growth medium*] ..... TSA
Trypticase Soy Broth [*Cell growth medium*] ..... TSB
Trypticase Soy Yeast [*Cell growth medium*] (MAE) ..... TSY
Trypticase, Yeast-Extract, Glucose [*Cell growth medium*] ..... TYG
Trypticose-Peptone-Glucose-Yeast Extract-Trypsin [*Medium*] [*Microbiology*] (DAVI) ..... TPGY
Tryptone Broth [*Culture medium*] ..... TB
Tryptone Glucose Extract [*Cell growth medium*] ..... TGE
Tryptone Glucose Yeast [*Cell growth medium*] (MAE) ..... TGY
Tryptone Glucose Yeast Agar [*Cell growth medium*] [*Medicine*] (DMAA) ..... TGYA
Tryptone Phosphate Broth ..... TPB
Tryptone Sulfite Neomycin (OA) ..... TSN
Tryptophan [*An amino acid*] (MAE) ..... TP
Tryptophan [*Also, W*] [*An amino acid*] ..... Trp
Tryptophan [*An amino acid*] (DOG) ..... trp
Tryptophan [*An amino acid*] (MAE) ..... Try
Tryptophan (MEDA) ..... Tryp
Tryptophan [*One-letter symbol; see Trp*] ..... W
Tryptophan Oxygenase [*Also, TP, TPO*] [*An enzyme*] ..... TO
Tryptophan Oxygenase [*Also, TO, TP*] [*An enzyme*] ..... TPO
Tryptophan Peptone Glucose [*Broth*] [*Microbiology*] (DAVI) ..... TPG
Tryptophan Peptone Sulfide Neomycin [*Agar*] (MAE) ..... TSN
Tryptophan Peroxidase [*An enzyme*] (AAMN) ..... TPO
Tryptophan Pyrrolase [*Also, TPO*] [*An enzyme*] ..... TP
Tryptophan Tryptophylquinone [*Biochemistry*] ..... TTQ
Tryptophane Acid (AAMN) ..... TA
Tryptophane Synthetase [*An enzyme*] (DAVI) ..... T'ASE
Tryptophan-Rich Prealbumin [*Biochemistry*] ..... TRPA
Tryptose Agar [*Medicine*] (DMAA) ..... TA
Tryptose Blood Agar Base [*Medicine*] (DMAA) ..... TBAB
Tryptose-Sulfite Cyclosterone [*Agar*] [*Microbiology*] (DAVI) ..... TSC
Tryptose-Sulphite Cyclosterone [*Agar*] (BABM) ..... TSC
TS Communications [*Springfield, IL*] [*Telecommunications*] (TSSD) ..... TSCOM
Tsaile [*Navajo Community College*] [*Arizona*] [*Seismograph station code, US Geological Survey*] (SEIS) ..... TSL

Tsaratanana [*Madagascar*] [*ICAO location identifier*] (ICLI) .... FMNT
Tsaratanana [*Madagascar*] [*Airport symbol*] (OAG) .... TTS
TSC Shannock Corp. [*Toronto Stock Exchange symbol Vancouver Stock Exchange symbol*] .... TSH
TSCA [*Toxic Substances Control Act*] **Assistance Office** [*Environmental Protection Agency*] (GFGA) .... TAO
TSCA [*Toxic Substances Control Act*] **Experimental Release Application** [*Environmental Protection Agency*] .... TERA
Tse Bonito, NM [*AM radio station call letters*] .... KHAC
Tseng Labs [*NASDAQ symbol*] (TTSB) .... TSNG
Tseng Labs, Inc. [*Associated Press*] (SAG) .... Tseng
Tseng Labs, Inc. [*Newtown, PA*] [*NASDAQ symbol*] (NQ) .... TSNG
Tsentar za Nauchna Informacija po Meditsina i Zdraveopazvane [*Center for Scientific Information in Medicine and Public Health*] [*Medical Academy*] [*Information service or system*] (IID) .... CNIMZ
Tsentralniya Suvet na Profesionalnite Suyuzi [*Central Council of Trade Unions*] [*Bulgaria*] .... TSSPS
Tsentralyni Aero-Gidrodinamichescky Institute [*Institute of Aeronautical Research*] [*Former USSR*] .... TsAGI
TSH [*Thyroid-Stimulating Hormone*] **Displacing Immunoglobulin** [*Endocrinology*] .... TDI
Tshabong [*Botswana*] [*ICAO location identifier*] (ICLI) .... FBTS
Tshane [*Botswana*] [*ICAO location identifier*] (ICLI) .... FBTE
Tshaneni [*Swaziland*] [*ICAO location identifier*] (ICLI) .... FDTS
Tshela [*Zaire*] [*ICAO location identifier*] (ICLI) .... FZAH
Tshibala [*Zaire*] [*ICAO location identifier*] (ICLI) .... FZUR
Tshikaji [*Zaire*] [*ICAO location identifier*] (ICLI) .... FZUS
Tshikapa [*Zaire*] [*ICAO location identifier*] (ICLI) .... FZUK
Tshikapa [*Zaire*] [*Airport symbol*] (OAG) .... TSH
TSHIRTS: [*The*] **Society Handling the Interchange of Remarkable T-Shirts** [*Defunct*] (EA) .... TSHIRTS
Tshumbe [*Zaire*] [*ICAO location identifier*] (ICLI) .... FZVJ
TSI, Inc. [*Associated Press*] (SAG) .... TSI Inc
TSI, Inc. [*NASDAQ symbol*] (NQ) .... TSII
Tsimshian [*MARC language code Library of Congress*] (LCCP) .... tsi
Tsing Hua Open-Pool Reactor [*Formosa*] .... THOR
Tsinghai Province [*China, Mainland*] [*MARC geographic area code Library of Congress*] (LCCP) .... a-cc-ts
Tsingtau [*Republic of China*] [*Seismograph station code, US Geological Survey*] (SEIS) .... TSN
Tsiroanomandidy [*Madagascar*] [*ICAO location identifier*] (ICLI) .... FMMX
Tsiroanomandidy [*Madagascar*] [*Airport symbol*] (OAG) .... WTS
TSR, Inc. [*Associated Press*] (SAG) .... TSR
TSR, Inc. [*Hauppauge, NY*] [*NASDAQ symbol*] (NQ) .... TSRI
TST Impreso, Inc. [*NASDAQ symbol*] (SAG) .... TSTI
TST Impreso, Inc. [*Associated Press*] (SAG) .... TSTImp
TST/Impresso [*NASDAQ symbol*] (TTSB) .... TSTI
Tsu [*Japan*] [*Seismograph station code, US Geological Survey*] (SEIS) .... TSU
Tsuiki [*Japan ICAO location identifier*] (ICLI) .... RJFZ
Tsukuba - Telemeter [*Japan*] [*Seismograph station code, US Geological Survey*] (SEIS) .... TSK
Tsumeb [*Namibia*] [*ICAO location identifier*] (ICLI) .... FATM
Tsumeb [*Namibia*] [*Airport symbol*] (OAG) .... TSB
Tsumeb [*South-West Africa*] [*Geomagnetic observatory code*] .... TSU
Tsumkwe [*Namibia*] [*ICAO location identifier*] (ICLI) .... FATK
Tsunami Hazard Reduction Using System Technology (USDC) .... THRUST
Tsunami Hazard Reduction Using Systems Technology [*Marine science*] (OSRA) .... THRUST
Tsunami Inundation Modeling Exchange Project [*Marine science*] (OSRA) .... TIME
Tsunami Research Advisory System of Hawaii .... TRASH
Tsunami Risk Evaluation through Seismic Moment from Real-Time System [*Marine science*] (OSRA) .... TREMORS
Tsunami Warning System [*National Oceanic and Atmospheric Administration*] .... TWS
T-Suppressor-Cell Growth Factor [*Immunology*] .... TSGF
Tsuruga [*Japan*] [*Seismograph station code, US Geological Survey*] (SEIS) .... TSR
Tsurugisan [*Anabuki*] [*Japan*] [*Seismograph station code, US Geological Survey*] (SEIS) .... TSS
Tsushima [*Japan ICAO location identifier*] (ICLI) .... RJDT
Tsushima [*Japan*] [*Airport symbol*] (OAG) .... TSJ
Tswana [*MARC language code Library of Congress*] (LCCP) .... tsw
TSX Corp. [*Associated Press*] (SAG) .... TSX Cp
TSX Corp. [*NASDAQ symbol*] (SAG) .... TSXX
T-Ten Class Association (EA) .... TTCA
TTY Controller (NITA) .... TTYC
TU Elec Cap II 8.00%'QUIPS' [*NYSE symbol*] (TTSB) .... TUEPrO
TU Electric Cap 1 8.25%'TOPrS' [*NYSE symbol*] (TTSB) .... TUEPrM
TU Electric Cap II 9.00%'TOPrS' [*NYSE symbol*] (TTSB) .... TUEPrN
TU Electric Capital I [*NYSE symbol*] (SAG) .... TUE
TU Electric Capital I [*Associated Press*] (SAG) .... TxUtEl
TU Electric Capital II [*NYSE symbol*] (SAG) .... TUE
TU Electric Capital II [*Associated Press*] (SAG) .... TxUtEl
TU Electric Capital III [*NYSE symbol*] (SAG) .... TUE
TU Electric Capital III [*Associated Press*] (SAG) .... TxUtEl
Tuai [*New Zealand*] [*Seismograph station code, US Geological Survey*] (SEIS) .... TUA
Tualatin Public Library, Tualatin, OR [*Library symbol Library of Congress*] (LCLS) .... OrTua
Tuality Community Hospital, Hillsboro, OR [*Library symbol Library of Congress*] (LCLS) .... OrHilT
Tuality Health Information Resource Center, Hillsboro, OR [*Library symbol*] [*Library of Congress*] (LCLS) .... OrHilHI
Tuba [*Music*] .... TBA
Tuba .... TU
Tuba City, AZ [*FM radio station call letters*] .... KGHR
Tuba City, AZ [*AM radio station call letters*] .... KTBA
Tuba City, AZ [*Location identifier FAA*] (FAAL) .... TBC
Tuba City Public Library, Tuba City, AZ [*Library symbol Library of Congress*] (LCLS) .... AzTu
Tubal Embryo Stage Transfer .... TEST
Tubal Embryo Stage Transfer [*Alternative to traditional in-vitro fertilization (IVF)*] [*Also, TEST*] (PAZ) .... TET
Tubal Ligation [*Medicine*] .... TL
Tubala [*Panama*] [*Airport symbol*] (OAG) .... TUW
Tubarao [*Brazil*] [*Airport symbol*] (AD) .... TUB
Tubby's, Inc. [*Associated Press*] (SAG) .... Tubbys
Tubby's, Inc. [*NASDAQ symbol*] (SAG) .... TUBY
Tube (IAA) .... T
Tube .... TU
Tube Agglutination [*Medicine*] (MAE) .... TA
Tube and Pipe Fabricators Association, International (EA) .... TPF
Tube and Pipe Fabricators Association, International (EAIO) .... TPFA
Tube Axial .... TBAX
Tube Bending Chart .... TBC
Tube Bending Data (MCD) .... TBD
Tube Broke [*Organic chemistry*] (DAVI) .... BROK
Tube Cooling Supply .... TCS
Tube Council of North America (EA) .... TCNA
Tube Deflection Coil .... TDC
Tube Earphone and Microphone (DNAB) .... TEAM
Tube Engineering Panel Advisory Council [*Defunct*] (EA) .... TEPAC
Tube Evaluation Program .... TEP
Tube Expander .... TBEX
Tube Failure Alarm .... TFA
Tube Feeding [*Medicine*] (DMAA) .... TF
Tube Fixture [*Tool*] (AAG) .... TBFX
Tube Flood and Drain .... TFD
Tube Form Die (MCD) .... TFD
Tube Heat Dissipator .... THD
Tube Heat Exchanger .... THE
Tube Heating and Cooling Control .... THCC
Tube Heating Supply .... THS
Tube Humidity Control .... THC
Tube Investments Ltd. [*British*] .... TI
Tube Moisture Control .... TMC
Tube over Bar [*Suspension*] (MCD) .... TOB
Tube Pin Straightener .... TPS
Tube Plate Drilling Program [*Kongsberg Vaapenfabrikk*] [*Software package*] (NCC) .... TUDRIP
Tube Precipitin [*Laboratory science*] (DAVI) .... TP
Tube Propagation d'Ondes Magnetron .... TPOM
Tube/Sea Differential Pressure Subsystem .... T/SDPS
Tube Sheet (MSA) .... TS
Tube Sheet Inlet and Outlet Head (MSA) .... TSI-OH
Tube Support Assembly [*Nuclear energy*] (NRCH) .... TSA
Tube Support Plate [*Nuclear energy*] (NRCH) .... TSP
Tube Temperature Control .... TTC
Tube Temperature Indication and Alarm .... TTIA
Tube Template (MCD) .... TUT
Tube Tester [*JETDS nomenclature*] [*Military*] (CET) .... TV
Tube under Test (MSA) .... TUT
Tube Voltmeter (IAA) .... TV
Tube-Excited X-Ray Fluorescence Analyzer .... TEFA
Tube-Fed Food [*Medicine*] (DMAA) .... TFF
Tube-Generated X-Ray .... TGX
Tubelair [*Tunisia*] [*FAA designator*] (FAAC) .... TBR
Tube-Launched Guided Projectiles (MCD) .... TLGB
Tube-Launched Missile (MCD) .... TLM
Tube-Launched, Optically Tracked, Wire-Guided [*Weapon*] .... TOW
Tubeless Steel Disc [*Wheel*] [*Automotive engineering*] .... TSD
Tubemakers of Australia Ltd. [*Commercial firm*] .... TOA
Tuberal Magnocellular [*Nuclei, neuroanatomy*] .... TM
Tubercle [*Anatomy*] [*Medicine*] .... Tu
Tubercle Bacillus [*Bacteriology*] .... TB
Tubercle Bacillus [*Bacteriology*] .... TBC
Tubercle Bacillus Vaccine [*Medicine*] .... TBV
Tubercular Rueckstand [*Medicine*] .... TR
Tuberculin [*or Tuberculosis*] (AABC) .... TB
Tuberculin Albumose-Frei [*Albumose-Free Tuberculin*] [*German Medicine*] .... TAF
Tuberculin, Alkaline [*Medicine*] .... TA
Tuberculin Bacillen Emulsion [*Medicine*] .... TBE
Tuberculin Filtrate [*Medicine*] .... TF
Tuberculin Ober [*Supernatant portion*] [*Medicine*] .... TO
Tuberculin Old [*or Original*] [*Also, OT*] [*Medicine*] .... TO
Tuberculin Precipitation [*Medicine*] .... TP
Tuberculin R [*Also called new tuberculin*] [*Infectious diseases*] (DAVI) .... TR
Tuberculin Residue [*Medicine*] .... TR
Tuberculin Rest [*Infectious diseases*] (DAVI) .... TR
Tuberculin Skin Test [*Medicine*] (PDAA) .... TST
Tuberculin Tested [*Milk*] .... TT
Tuberculin Time Test [*Medicine*] (DMAA) .... TBTT
Tuberculin Unit .... TU
Tuberculin Volutin [*Medicine*] (MAE) .... TV
Tuberculin Zymoplastiche [*Medicine*] (MAE) .... TZ
Tuberculosis .... TBC
Tuberculosis [*Medicine*] .... tuberc
Tuberculosis and Brucellosis [*Medicine*] (ADA) .... TB & B
Tuberculosis, Contagious [*Medicine*] (AAMN) .... TC
Tuberculosis Nursing Advisory Service (DAVI) .... TNAS

Tuberculosis - Respiratory Disease (MAE) ... TB-RD
Tuberculosis Surveillance Research Unit [*Netherlands*] (EAIO) ... TSRU
Tuberculosis Welfare League [*Defunct*] (EA) ... TWL
Tuberculous Diseases Diploma [*British*] ... TDD
Tuberculous Meningitis [*Medicine*] ... TBM
Tuberculous Peritonitis [*Medicine*] (DAVI) ... TBP
Tuberoinfundibular Dopaminergic [*Neurons*] [*Neurology*] ... TD
Tuberoinfundibular Dopaminergic System [*Medicine*] (DMAA) ... TIDA
Tuberous Sclerosis [*Medicine*] ... TS
Tuberous Sclerosis Association of America [*Also known as American Tuberous Sclerosis Association and Asociacion de Esclerosis Tuberosa de America*] (EA) ... TSAA
Tuberous Sclerosis Association of Great Britain ... TSA
Tuberous Sclerosis Complex [*Medicine*] ... TSC
Tubeshaft (DS) ... TBS
Tube-Slide Agglutination Test [*Clinical chemistry*] ... TSAT
Tube-Vehicle System (MCD) ... TVS
Tubing (MSA) ... TBG
Tubing (AAG) ... TUB
Tubing (VRA) ... tub
Tubing Connector [*Instrumentation*] ... TC
Tubing Connector Manifold [*Instrumentation*] ... TCM
Tubing Connector Reducer [*Instrumentation*] ... TCR
Tubingen [*Federal Republic of Germany*] [*Seismograph station code, US Geological Survey*] (SEIS) ... TUB
Tubists Universal Brotherhood Association (EA) ... TUBA
Tubocurarine [*Muscle relaxant*] ... TC
Tubolare Zagato [*Automotive model designation*] [*Alfa-Romeo*] ... TZ
Tubo-Ovarian [*Medicine*] (MAE) ... TO
Tubo-Ovarian Abscess [*Medicine*] ... TOA
Tubo-Ovarian Complex [*Anatomy*] (DAVI) ... TOC
Tuboreticular Inclusions [*Hematology*] ... TRI
Tuboreticular Structure [*Cytology*] ... TRS
Tubos de Acero de Mexico [*AMEX symbol*] (SPSG) ... TAM
Tubos De Acero De Mexico [*Associated Press*] (SAG) ... TubMex
Tuboscope Vetco International [*NASDAQ symbol*] (SAG) ... TUBO
Tuboscope Vetco International Corp. [*Associated Press*] (SAG) ... Tubscp
Tuboscope Vetco Intl [*NASDAQ symbol*] (TTSB) ... TUBO
TubosDeAceroMex ADR [*AMEX symbol*] (TTSB) ... TAM
Tubouterine [*Junction*] [*Gynecology*] (DAVI) ... TUB
Tubouterine Junction [*Anatomy*] ... TUJ
Tub-Sized [*Paper*] ... TS
Tub-Sized Air-Dried [*Paper*] (DGA) ... TSAD
Tubuai [*Tubuai Islands*] [*Seismograph station code, US Geological Survey*] (SEIS) ... TBI
Tubuai Island [*Austral Islands*] [*Airport symbol*] (OAG) ... TUB
Tubuai/Mataura [*French Polynesia*] [*ICAO location identifier*] (ICLI) ... NTAT
Tubular (IAA) ... T
Tubular [*Automotive engineering*] ... TUB
Tubular (VRA) ... tub
Tubular [*Freight*] ... TUBLR
Tubular and Split Rivet Council [*Later, TRMI*] (EA) ... TSRC
Tubular Atrophy [*Nephrology*] ... TA
Tubular Basement Membrane ... TBM
Tubular Carbon Electrode ... TCE
Tubular Exchanger Manufacturers Association (EA) ... TEMA
Tubular Extendible Element (PDAA) ... TEE
Tubular Finishers and Processors Association [*Defunct*] (EA) ... TFPA
Tubular Flow Reactor ... TFR
Tubular Fluid [*Medicine*] (MAE) ... TF
Tubular Fluid Plasma [*Medicine*] (MAE) ... TF/P
Tubular Maximum for Para-Aminohippuric Acid [*Biochemistry*] (MAE) ... Tmpah
Tubular Maximum Reabsorption Rate for Glucose [*of Kidney*] [*Nephrology*] (DAVI) ... TMG
Tubular Products Manual [*A publication*] (EAAP) ... TPM
Tubular Reabsorption [*Medicine*] (MAE) ... TR
Tubular Reabsorption [*or Resorption*] **of Phosphate** ... TRP
Tubular Reactor Assembly [*Nuclear energy*] (NRCH) ... TRA
Tubular Rivet and Machine Institute (EA) ... TRMI
Tubular [*Tracheal*] **Sound** ... TS
Tubular Tires [*Cyclist term*] [*British*] (DSUE) ... TUBS
Tubular Zippered Jacket ... TZJ
Tubule Fluid-to-Plasma [*Ratio*] [*Medicine*] (DAVI) ... TF/P
Tubule Fluid-to-Plasma Insulin Ratio [*Medicine*] (DAVI) ... (TF/P)In
Tubulin [*A protein*] ... T
Tubulinyl Tyrosine Carboxypeptidase ... TTC
Tubulinyl Tyrosine Ligase ... TTL
Tubulointerstitial Nephritis [*Nephrology*] ... TIN
Tubuloreticular Inclusion [*Medicine*] (DAVI) ... TRI
Tucana [*Constellation*] ... Tuc
Tucana [*Constellation*] ... Tucn
Tucavaca [*Bolivia*] [*ICAO location identifier*] (ICLI) ... SLTU
Tuck in Back [*Sit up straight*] [*Slang British*] (DI) ... TIB
Tuck Tummy In [*Slang*] ... TTI
Tuckahoe Financial Corp. [*Toronto Stock Exchange symbol*] ... TUK
Tuckahoe Public Library, Tuckahoe, NY [*Library symbol Library of Congress*] (LCLS) ... NTuc
Tucker and Clephane's Reports [*21 District of Columbia*] [*1892-93*] [*A publication*] (DLA) ... Tuck
Tucker and Clephane's Reports [*21 District of Columbia*] [*A publication*] (DLA) ... Tuck & C
Tucker and Clephane's Reports [*21 District of Columbia*] [*1892-93*] [*A publication*] (DLA) ... Tuck & Cl
Tucker Automobile Club of America (EA) ... TACA
Tucker Drilling [*NASDAQ symbol*] (TTSB) ... TUCK
Tucker Drilling Co., Inc. [*NASDAQ symbol*] (NQ) ... TUCK
Tucker Drilling Co., Inc. [*Associated Press*] (SAG) ... TuckDr
Tucker Free Library, Henniker, NH [*Library symbol Library of Congress*] (LCLS) ... NhHen
Tucker Properties [*NYSE symbol*] (SPSG) ... TUC
Tucker Properties [*Associated Press*] (SAG) ... TuckerPr
Tucker's Blackstone's Commentaries [*A publication*] (DLA) ... Tuck Bl Com
Tucker's Blackstone's Commentaries [*A publication*] (DLA) ... Tucker's Blackstone
Tucker's District of Columbia Appeals [*A publication*] (DLA) ... Tuck Dist of Col
Tucker's Lectures [*A publication*] (DLA) ... Tuck Lect
Tucker's New York Surrogate's Court Reports [*A publication*] (DLA) ... Tuck
Tucker's New York Surrogate's Court Reports [*A publication*] (DLA) ... Tucker
Tucker's Pleadings [*A publication*] (DLA) ... Tuck Pl
Tucker's Reports [*156-175 Massachusetts*] [*A publication*] (DLA) ... Tuck
Tucker's Reports [*District of Columbia*] [*A publication*] (DLA) ... Tuck
Tucker's Select Cases [*Newfoundland*] [*A publication*] (DLA) ... Tuck
Tucker's Select Cases [*1817-28*] [*Newfoundland*] [*A publication*] (DLA) ... Tuck Sel Cas
Tucker's Surrogate Reports, City of New York [*A publication*] (DLA) ... Tuck Sur
Tucker's Surrogate Reports, City of New York [*A publication*] (DLA) ... Tuck Surr
Tuckerton, NJ [*FM radio station call letters*] ... WTUC
Tucson [*Arizona*] [*Seismograph station code, US Geological Survey*] (SEIS) ... TUC
Tucson [*Arizona*] [*Airport symbol*] (OAG) ... TUS
Tucson, AZ [*Location identifier FAA*] (FAAL) ... DMA
Tucson, AZ [*Location identifier FAA*] (FAAL) ... IVI
Tucson, AZ [*AM radio station call letters*] ... KCEE
Tucson, AZ [*FM radio station call letters*] ... KCRZ
Tucson, AZ [*AM radio station call letters*] ... KCUB
Tucson, AZ [*AM radio station call letters*] (RBYB) ... KFFN-AM
Tucson, AZ [*AM radio station call letters*] ... KFLT
Tucson, AZ [*Television station call letters*] ... KGUN
Tucson, AZ [*Television station call letters*] ... KHRR
Tucson, AZ [*FM radio station call letters*] (RBYB) ... KHYT-FM
Tucson, AZ [*FM radio station call letters*] ... KIIM
Tucson, AZ [*FM radio station call letters*] ... KKHG
Tucson, AZ [*AM radio station call letters*] (RBYB) ... KKND
Tucson, AZ [*FM radio station call letters*] ... KLPX
Tucson, AZ [*Television station call letters*] ... KMSB
Tucson, AZ [*FM radio station call letters*] (RBYB) ... KMXZ-FM
Tucson, AZ [*AM radio station call letters*] ... KNST
Tucson, AZ [*Television station call letters*] ... KOLD
Tucson, AZ [*FM radio station call letters*] ... KRQQ
Tucson, AZ [*AM radio station call letters*] ... KSAZ
Tucson, AZ [*AM radio station call letters*] ... KTKT
Tucson, AZ [*Television station call letters*] ... KTTU
Tucson, AZ [*AM radio station call letters*] ... KTUC
Tucson, AZ [*AM radio station call letters*] ... KTZR
Tucson, AZ [*Television station call letters*] ... KUAS
Tucson, AZ [*AM radio station call letters*] ... KUAT
Tucson, AZ [*FM radio station call letters*] ... KUAT-FM
Tucson, AZ [*Television station call letters*] ... KUAT-TV
Tucson, AZ [*FM radio station call letters*] ... KUAZ
Tucson, AZ [*Television station call letters*] ... KVOA
Tucson, AZ [*FM radio station call letters*] ... KWFM-FM
Tucson, AZ [*FM radio station call letters*] ... KXCI
Tucson, AZ [*Location identifier FAA*] (FAAL) ... RBJ
Tucson, AZ [*Location identifier FAA*] (FAAL) ... RYN
Tucson, Cornelia & Gila Bend Railroad Co. [*AAR code*] ... TCG
Tucson/Davis Monthan Air Force Base [*Arizona*] [*ICAO location identifier*] (ICLI) ... KDMA
Tucson Ele Power(New) [*NYSE symbol*] (TTSB) ... TEP
Tucson Electric Power Co. [*NYSE symbol*] (SPSG) ... TEP
Tucson Electric Power Co. [*Associated Press*] (SAG) ... TucsEP
Tucson/International [*Arizona*] [*ICAO location identifier*] (ICLI) ... KTUS
Tucson Observatory [*Arizona*] [*Seismograph station code, US Geological Survey*] (SEIS) ... TUO
Tucson Public Library, Tucson, AZ [*Library symbol Library of Congress*] (LCLS) ... AzT
Tucson Public Library, Tucson, AZ [*OCLC symbol*] (OCLC) ... AZT
Tucson - Telemeter [*Arizona*] [*Seismograph station code, US Geological Survey Closed*] (SEIS) ... TUT
Tucson Unified School District, Tucson, AZ [*Library symbol*] [*Library of Congress*] (LCLS) ... AzTS
Tucuman [*Argentina*] [*Seismograph station code, US Geological Survey Closed*] (SEIS) ... TCM
Tucuman [*Argentina*] [*Airport symbol*] (OAG) ... TUC
Tucuman/Teniente Benjamim Matienzo [*Argentina ICAO location identifier*] (ICLI) ... SANT
Tucumcari [*New Mexico*] [*ICAO location identifier*] (ICLI) ... KTCC
Tucumcari, NM [*FM radio station call letters*] ... KQAY
Tucumcari, NM [*AM radio station call letters*] ... KTNM
Tucumcari, NM [*Location identifier FAA*] (FAAL) ... TCC
Tucumcari Public Library, Tucumcari, NM [*Library symbol Library of Congress*] (LCLS) ... NmTu
Tucupita [*Venezuela*] [*Airport symbol*] (OAG) ... TUV
Tucupita, T. F. Delta Amacuro [*Venezuela ICAO location identifier*] (ICLI) ... SVTC
Tucurui [*Brazil ICAO location identifier*] (ICLI) ... SBTU
Tucurui [*Brazil*] [*Airport symbol*] (OAG) ... TUR
Tudor (ROG) ... TU
Tudor and Cashel Public Library, Gilmour, Ontario [*Library symbol National Library of Canada*] (BIB) ... OGTC
Tudor Corp. Ltd. [*Toronto Stock Exchange symbol*] ... TDR
Tudor's Charitable Trusts [*2nd ed.*] [*1871*] [*A publication*] (DLA) ... Tud Char Tr
Tudor's Charitable Trusts [*2nd ed.*] [*1871*] [*A publication*] (DLA) ... Tud Char Trusts

Tudor's Leading Cases on Mercantile Law [*3 eds.*] [*1860-84*] [*A publication*] (DLA) .... Tud Cas Merc Law
Tudor's Leading Cases on Mercantile Law [*A publication*] (DLA) .... Tudor's LCML
Tudor's Leading Cases on Real Property [*4 eds.*] [*1856-98*] [*A publication*] (DLA) .... Tud Cas RP
Tudor's Leading Cases on Real Property [*A publication*] (DLA) .... Tudor Lead Cas Real Prop
Tudor's Leading Cases on Real Property [*A publication*] (DLA) .... Tudor's LCRP
Tuebinger Zeitschrift fuer Theologie [*A publication*] (BJA) .... TZTh
Tuesday .... T
Tuesday .... TU
Tuesday (AFM) .... TUE
Tuesday (ODBW) .... Tue
Tuesday (ODBW) .... Tues
Tuesday (EY) .... TUES
Tuesday Downtown Operators and Observers [*An association*] (EA) .... TDO
Tuesday Morning [*NASDAQ symbol*] (TTSB) .... TUES
Tuesday Morning Corp. [*NASDAQ symbol*] (NQ) .... TUES
Tuesday Morning Corp. [*Associated Press*] (SAG) .... TuesM
Tuesday, Thursday, Saturday (BARN) .... TTS
Tuesdays Only [*British railroad term*] .... TO
Tufa [*Quality of the bottom*] [*Nautical charts*] .... T
Tufco Technologies [*NASDAQ symbol*] (SAG) .... TFCO
Tufco Technologies [*Associated Press*] (SAG) .... Tufco
Tufi [*Papua New Guinea*] [*Airport symbol*] (OAG) .... TFI
Tufted Carpet Manufacturers' Association [*British*] (BI) .... TCMA
Tufted Textile Manufacturers Association [*Later, CRI*] (EA) .... TTMA
Tufted Titmouse [*Ornithology*] .... TT
Tufts Assessment of Motor Performance [*Occupational therapy*] .... TAMP
Tufts University (GAGS) .... Tufts U
Tufts University, Eliot Pearson Department of Child Study, Medford, MA [*Library symbol Library of Congress*] (LCLS) .... MMeT-EP
Tufts University, Fletcher School of Law and Diplomacy, Medford, MA [*Library symbol Library of Congress*] (LCLS) .... MMeT-F
Tufts University, Health Sciences Library, Boston, MA [*OCLC symbol*] (OCLC) .... TFH
Tufts University, Medford, MA [*Library symbol Library of Congress*] (LCLS) .... MMeT
Tufts University, Medford, MA [*OCLC symbol*] (OCLC) .... TFW
Tufts University, Medical and Dental School, Boston, MA [*Library symbol Library of Congress*] (LCLS) .... MMeT-M
Tufts University, Universalist Historical Society, Medford, MA [*Library symbol Library of Congress*] (LCLS) .... MMeT-Hi
Tug [*Navy*] .... T
Tug, Ocean-Going [*Navy symbol*] .... AT
Tug Processing Facility [*NASA*] (NASA) .... TPF
Tug Rotational System [*NASA*] (NASA) .... TRS
Tug Structural Support [*NASA*] (NASA) .... TSS
Tugboat Underwriting Syndicate [*Defunct*] (EA) .... TUS
Tugboatmen's Union [*British*] .... TU
Tug-of-War International Federation [*Zevenhuizen, Netherlands*] (EAIO) .... TWIF
Tugold Resources, Inc. [*Vancouver Stock Exchange symbol*] .... TUD
Tugrik [*Monetary unit*] [*Mongolia*] (BARN) .... Tug
Tuguegarao [*Philippines*] [*Airport symbol*] (OAG) .... TUG
Tuguegarao, Cagayan [*Philippines*] [*ICAO location identifier*] (ICLI) .... RPUT
Tuition .... TU
Tuition (DSUE) .... TUI
Tuition Assistance Program [*New York*] (EDAC) .... TAP
Tuktoyaktuk [*Canada*] [*Airport symbol*] (OAG) .... YUB
Tuktoyaktuk, NT [*AM radio station call letters*] .... CFCT
Tuktoyaktuk, NT [*ICAO location identifier*] (ICLI) .... CYUB
Tukulti-Ninurta (BJA) .... Tn
Tula Peak, New Mexico [*Spaceflight Tracking and Data Network*] [*NASA*] .... TUL
Tulancingo [*Mexico ICAO location identifier*] (ICLI) .... MMTL
Tulane Civil Law Forum [*A publication*] (DLA) .... Tu Civ LF
Tulane Civil Law Forum [*A publication*] (DLA) .... Tul Civ LF
Tulane Computer Laboratory [*Tulane University*] [*Research center*] (RCD) .... TCL
Tulane Factors of Liberalism-Conservatism [*Psychology*] .... TFLC
Tulane University [*New Orleans, LA*] .... TU
Tulane University (GAGS) .... Tulane U
Tulane University, Graduate School of Business Administration, New Orleans, LA [*Library symbol Library of Congress*] (LCLS) .... LNT-BA
Tulane University, Law Library, New Orleans, LA [*Library symbol Library of Congress*] (LCLS) .... LNT-L
Tulane University, Law Library, New Orleans, LA [*OCLC symbol*] (OCLC) .... LRL
Tulane University, Medical Library, New Orleans, LA [*Library symbol Library of Congress*] (LCLS) .... LNT-M
Tulane University, New Orleans, LA [*Library symbol Library of Congress*] (LCLS) .... LNT
Tulane University, New Orleans, LA [*OCLC symbol*] (OCLC) .... LRU
Tulare Apple Mosaic Virus [*Plant pathology*] .... TAMV
Tulare, CA [*FM radio station call letters*] .... KBOS
Tulare, CA [*AM radio station call letters*] .... KGEN
Tulare, CA [*AM radio station call letters*] .... KJUG
Tulare, CA [*FM radio station call letters*] .... KJUG-FM
Tulare, CA [*Location identifier FAA*] (FAAL) .... TLR
Tulare County Free Library System, Visalia, CA [*OCLC symbol*] (OCLC) .... TCB
Tulare County Free Library, Visalia, CA [*Library symbol Library of Congress*] (LCLS) CViCL
Tulare Free Public Library, Tulare, CA [*Library symbol Library of Congress*] (LCLS) .... CTul
Tulare Free Public Library, Tulare, CA [*OCLC symbol*] (OCLC) .... TPK
Tularemia [*An infectious, plague-like disease*] (DAVI) .... TULAR
Tulcan [*Ecuador*] [*ICAO location identifier*] (ICLI) .... SETU
Tulcan [*Ecuador*] [*Airport symbol*] (OAG) .... TUA
Tulcea [*Romania*] [*Airport symbol*] (OAG) .... TCE
Tulcea/Cataloi [*Romania*] [*ICAO location identifier*] (ICLI) .... LRTC
Tule Lake Aster Yellows [*Plant pathology*] .... TAY
Tule Lake Aster Yellows [*Plant pathology*] .... TLAY
Tulear [*Madagascar*] [*Airport symbol*] (OAG) .... TLE
Tulelake, CA [*FM radio station call letters*] .... KFLS
Tuli Lodge [*Botswana*] [*ICAO location identifier*] (ICLI) .... FBTL
Tulia, TX [*FM radio station call letters*] .... KJMX
Tulia, TX [*AM radio station call letters*] .... KTUE
Tulip (VRA) .... tlp
Tulip Air [*Netherlands ICAO designator*] (FAAC) .... TLP
Tulip Breaking Virus [*Plant pathology*] .... TBV
Tulip Virus X [*Plant pathology*] .... TUVX
Tulip Virus X .... TVX
Tuliptree Flower Spiroplasma [*Plant pathology*] .... TFS
Tullahoma [*Tennessee*] [*Airport symbol*] (AD) .... THA
Tullahoma, TN [*Location identifier FAA*] (FAAL) .... THA
Tullahoma, TN [*Location identifier FAA*] (FAAL) .... TUH
Tullahoma, TN [*AM radio station call letters*] .... WJIG
Tullahoma, TN [*FM radio station call letters*] (RBYB) .... WPZM
Tulloch Resources [*Vancouver Stock Exchange symbol*] .... TLH
Tulsa [*Diocesan abbreviation*] [*Oklahoma*] (TOCD) .... TLS
Tulsa [*Oklahoma*] [*Seismograph station code, US Geological Survey Closed*] (SEIS) .... TSO
Tulsa [*Oklahoma*] [*Airport symbol*] (OAG) .... TUL
Tulsa [*Oklahoma*] [*Seismograph station code, US Geological Survey*] (SEIS) .... TUL
Tulsa Ballet Theatre .... TBT
Tulsa City-County Library System, Tulsa, OK [*Library symbol Library of Congress*] (LCLS) .... OkT
Tulsa City-County Library System, Tulsa, OK [*OCLC symbol*] (OCLC) .... TUL
Tulsa/International [*Oklahoma*] [*ICAO location identifier*] (ICLI) .... KTUL
Tulsa, OK [*Location identifier FAA*] (FAAL) .... DWE
Tulsa, OK [*Location identifier FAA*] (FAAL) .... GNP
Tulsa, OK [*AM radio station call letters*] .... KAKC
Tulsa, OK [*FM radio station call letters*] .... KBEZ
Tulsa, OK [*AM radio station call letters*] .... KCFO
Tulsa, OK [*AM radio station call letters*] .... KGTO
Tulsa, OK [*Television station call letters*] .... KJRH
Tulsa, OK [*FM radio station call letters*] (RBYB) .... KJSR
Tulsa, OK [*FM radio station call letters*] .... KMOD
Tulsa, OK [*Television station call letters*] .... KOED
Tulsa, OK [*Television station call letters*] .... KOKI
Tulsa, OK [*Television station call letters*] .... KOTV
Tulsa, OK [*AM radio station call letters*] .... KQLL
Tulsa, OK [*FM radio station call letters*] .... KRAV
Tulsa, OK [*AM radio station call letters*] .... KRMG
Tulsa, OK [*Television station call letters*] .... KTFO
Tulsa, OK [*Television station call letters*] .... KTUL
Tulsa, OK [*AM radio station call letters*] .... KVOO
Tulsa, OK [*FM radio station call letters*] .... KVOO-FM
Tulsa, OK [*FM radio station call letters*] .... KWEN
Tulsa, OK [*FM radio station call letters*] .... KWGS
Tulsa, OK [*Television station call letters*] .... KWHB
Tulsa, OK [*Television station call letters*] .... KWMJ
Tulsa, OK [*Location identifier FAA*] (FAAL) .... RVS
Tulsa, OK [*Location identifier FAA*] (FAAL) .... TJY
Tulsa Studies in Women's Literature [*A publication*] (BRI) .... TSWL
Tulsa University [*Oklahoma*] (PDAA) .... TU
Tulsa-Sapulpa Union Railway Co. [*AAR code*] .... TSU
Tultex Corp. [*NYSE symbol*] (SPSG) .... TTX
Tultex Corp. [*Associated Press*] (SAG) .... Tultex
Tulua [*Colombia*] [*Airport symbol*] (OAG) .... ULQ
Tuluksak [*Alaska*] [*Airport symbol*] (OAG) .... TLT
Tuluksak, AK [*Location identifier FAA*] (FAAL) .... TLT
Tulum [*Mexico*] [*Airport symbol Obsolete*] (OAG) .... TUY
Tum [*Ethiopia*] [*Airport symbol*] (OAG) .... TUJ
Tumacacori National Monument .... TUMA
Tumaco [*Colombia*] [*Airport symbol*] (OAG) .... TCO
Tumaco/La Florida [*Colorado ICAO location identifier*] (ICLI) .... SKCO
Tumbes [*Peru*] [*Airport symbol*] (OAG) .... TBP
Tumbes/Pedro Canga [*Peru*] [*ICAO location identifier*] (ICLI) .... SPME
Tumble (MSA) .... TMB
Tumbler (MSA) .... TBLR
Tumbler Ridge Public Library, British Columbia [*Library symbol National Library of Canada*] (BIB) .... BTR
Tumbleweed Diagnostic Vehicle .... TDV
Tumbleweed High-Altitude Samples (MUGU) .... THAS
Tumbling Explorer [*Aerospace*] .... TEX
Tumbura [*Sudan*] [*ICAO location identifier*] (ICLI) .... HSTU
Tumeremo [*Venezuela*] [*Airport symbol*] (OAG) .... TMO
Tumeremo, Bolivar [*Venezuela ICAO location identifier*] (ICLI) .... SVTM
Tumichucua [*Bolivia*] [*ICAO location identifier*] (ICLI) .... SLTH
Tumlingtar [*Nepal*] [*Airport symbol*] (OAG) .... TMI
Tumlingtar [*Nepal*] [*ICAO location identifier*] (ICLI) .... VNTR
Tumor [*Oncology*] .... T
Tumor Acquisition, Processing, and Preservation [*Oncology*] .... TAPP
Tumor Activity Test [*Medicine*] (DMAA) .... TAT
Tumor Associated [*Medicine*] (DMAA) .... TA
Tumor Cell Burden [*Oncology*] .... TCB
Tumor Cell Detection [*Medicine*] .... TCD
Tumor Colony-Forming Unit [*Oncology*] .... TCFU
Tumor Control Dose [*Oncology*] .... TCD
Tumor Dose [*Radiation therapy*] (DAVI) .... TD
Tumor Dose Fractionation [*Oncology*] [*Radiation therapy*] (DAVI) .... TDF
Tumor Doubling Time [*Cytology*] .... TDT

Tumor Glycoprotein Assay [*Medicine*] (DMAA) ... TGA
Tumor Growth Factor [*Oncology*] ... TGF
Tumor in Situ [*Oncology*] ... TIS
Tumor Infiltrating Lymphocyte [*Oncology*] ... TIL
Tumor Inhibitory Factor [*Oncology*] ... TIF
Tumor Inhibitory Principle [*Oncology*] ... TIP
Tumor Lethal Dose [*Medicine*] (MAE) ... TLD
Tumor Necrosis Factor [*Immunology*] [*Antineoplastic drug*] ... TNF
Tumor Necrosis Factor Receptor [*Immunology*] ... TNFR
Tumor Necrosis Factor-Alpha ... TNF-A
Tumor Necrosis Serum (PDAA) ... TNS
Tumor Neurosis Factor [*Biochemistry*] ... TNF
Tumor Neurosis Factor Receptor-Associated Factor [*Biochemistry*] ... TRAF
Tumor, Node, and Metastasis [*Criteria for staging*] [*Pathology*] (DAVI) ... TNM
Tumor, Node, Metastases [*System*] [*Medicine*] (HCT) ... TNM
Tumor Polypeptide Antigen [*Oncology*] (DAVI) ... TPA
Tumor Polysaccharidal Substance [*Oncology*] ... TPS
Tumor Site, T-Stage, N-Stage [*Oncology*] ... TTN
Tumor Skin Test [*Medicine*] (MAE) ... TST
Tumor Specific [*Medicine*] ... TS
Tumor Virus Epidemiology Repository [*National Institutes of Health*] ... TVER
Tumor Volume Doubling Time [*Cytology*] ... TVDT
Tumor-Angiogenesis Factor [*Medicine*] ... TAF
Tumor-Associated Antibody [*Medicine*] (DAVI) ... TAA
Tumor-Associated Antigen [*Immunology*] ... TAA
Tumor-Associated Macrophages [*Immunology*] ... TAM
Tumor-Associated Rejection Antigen [*Immunology*] (MAE) ... TARA
Tumor-Associated Surface Antigen [*Immunology*] ... TASA
Tumor-Associated Transplantation Antigen [*Medicine*] (DMAA) ... TATA
Tumor-Associated Trypsin Inhibitor [*Medicine*] ... TATI
Tumor-Bearing [*Animal*] ... TB
Tumor-Bearing Animal (AAMN) ... TBA
Tumor-Bearing Rabbit Serum [*Immunology*] ... TBR
Tumor-Cell Migratory Inhibition Factor [*Immunology*] ... TMIF
Tumor-Derived Activated Cell [*Oncology*] ... TDAC
Tumor-Direct Cell-Mediated Hypersensitivity [*Oncology*] (DAVI) ... TCMH
Tumor-Induced Angiogenesis [*Immunology*] ... TIA
Tumor-Induced Cytatocity [*Medicine*] (DAVI) ... TIMC
Tumor-inducing [*Plasmids*] [*Plant cytology*] ... Ti
Tumor-Inducing Factor [*Oncology*] ... TIF
Tumor-Inducing Principle [*Plant cytology*] ... TIP
Tumor-infiltrating Lymphocyte [*Immunotherapy*] ... TIF
Tumor-Producing Dose [*Virology*] ... TPD
Tumor-Specific Antibody [*Immunology*] (DAVI) ... TSA
Tumor-Specific Antigens [*Immunology*] ... TSA
Tumor-Specific Glycoprotein [*Biochemistry*] (DAVI) ... TSG
Tumor-Specific Surface Antigen [*Immunology*] ... TSSA
Tumor-Specific Tissue Antigen [*Immunology*] (DAVI) ... TSTA
Tumor-Specific Transplantation Antigen [*Immunology*] ... TSTA
Tumut [*Australia Airport symbol*] (OAG) ... TUM
Tumwater [*Washington*] [*Seismograph station code, US Geological Survey*] (SEIS) ... TUM
Tumwater, WA [*AM radio station call letters*] ... KVSN
Tun [*Unit of liquid capacity*] ... T
Tuna Boat Owners' Association [*Defunct*] (EA) ... TBOA
Tuna Boat Owners' Association of Australia ... TBOAA
Tuna Boat Owners' Association of South Australia ... TBOASA
Tuna Research Foundation (EA) ... TRF
Tunable Atomic Line Molecular Spectroscopy ... TALMS
Tunable Attribute Display Subsystem (CAAL) ... TUNA
Tunable Compound Phase-Locked Demodulator (IAA) ... TCPLD
Tunable Control Frequency ... TCF
Tunable Diode LASER [*Also, SDL*] ... TDL
Tunable Diode LASER Absorption Spectrometry ... TDLAS
Tunable Electron Amplifier for Stimulated Emission of Radiation (MCD) ... TEASER
Tunable Etalon Filter ... TEF
Tunable Frequency Range ... TFR
Tunable Frequency Source ... TFS
Tunable Infrared Photomission Sensor ... TIPS
Tunable Noise Source ... TNS
Tunable Parametric Amplifier ... TPA
Tunable Pulsed LASER ... TPL
Tunable Pulsed LASER System ... TPLS
Tunable Ultraviolet Generation ... TUG
Tundra Biome [*Ecological biogeographic study*] ... TB
Tundra Gold Mines [*Vancouver Stock Exchange symbol*] ... TDA
Tunduru [*Tanzania*] [*ICAO location identifier*] (ICLI) ... HTTU
Tune-Controlled Gain ... TCG
Tuned Anode Tuned Grid (DEN) ... TATG
Tuned Aperiodic Tuned (IAA) ... TAT
Tuned Backward Wave Oscillator ... TBWO
Tuned Circuit [*Telecommunications*] (IAA) ... TC
Tuned Grid (KSC) ... TG
Tuned Grid Oscillator ... TGO
Tuned Grid Tuned Plate [*Electronic plate*] (IAA) ... TGTP
Tuned Hybrid Lattice ... THL
Tuned Integrated Circuit ... TIC
Tuned LASER Differential Spectrometry (IAA) ... TDS
Tuned Plate (DEN) ... TP
Tuned Plate Oscillator ... TPO
Tuned Plate Tuned Grid [*Electronic tube*] ... TPTG
Tuned Port Fuel Injection ... TPI
Tuned Radio Frequency ... TRF
Tuned Radio Frequency (IDOE) ... trf
Tuned Receiver Tuner ... TRT
Tuned Rotor Gyro (MCD) ... TRG
Tuned Vertical Array (CAAL) ... TVA
Tuned Viscoelastic Damper ... TVD
Tuned Viscoelastic Damper ... TVED
Tuned-Not-Tuned (IAA) ... TNT
Tuneful Viewer's Society for the Preservation of Television Theme Songs ... TV SPOTTS
Tune-In, Question, Listen, Review Technique [*Education*] (EDAC) ... TQLR
Tune-Up Manufacturers Institute (EA) ... TMI
Tung Research and Development League [*Defunct*] (EA) ... TR & DL
Tung Yeun Feng [*Republic of China*] [*Seismograph station code, US Geological Survey*] (SEIS) ... TYF
Tungco Resources Corp. [*Vancouver Stock Exchange symbol*] ... TNG
Tungshih [*Republic of China*] [*Seismograph station code, US Geological Survey*] (SEIS) ... TWQ
Tungsten (AAG) ... TUNG
Tungsten [*Chemical element*] (DOG) ... W
Tungsten Carbide (IAA) ... TC
Tungsten Electron Snatcher ... TES
Tungsten Institute [*Defunct*] (EA) ... TI
Tungsten Water Moderated Reactor (KSC) ... TWMR
Tungsten-Inert-Gas ... TIG
Tunica Vaginalis [*Anatomy*] ... TV
Tunica Vaginalis Testis [*Anatomy*] ... TVT
Tunicamycin [*Biochemistry*] ... TM
Tunicatae [*Coated*] [*Pharmacy*] ... TUNICAT
Tuning (IAA) ... TN
Tuning (AAG) ... TUN
Tuning Device Assembly ... TDA
Tuning Eye ... TE
Tuning Fork (AAMN) ... TF
Tuning Fork Filter ... TFF
Tuning Fork Oscillator ... TFO
Tuning Indicator (DEN) ... TI
Tuning Inductance (IAA) ... TI
Tuning Meter (DEN) ... TM
Tuning Meter Indicator (IAA) ... TMI
Tuning Stability ... TS
Tuning Unit [*JETDS nomenclature*] [*Military*] (CET) ... TN
Tuning Unit [*JETDS nomenclature*] [*Military*] (IAA) ... TU
Tuning Unit Member (IEEE) ... TUM
Tuninter [*Tunisia*] [*ICAO designator*] (FAAC) ... TUI
Tunis [*Tunisia*] [*ICAO location identifier*] (ICLI) ... DTTC
Tunis [*Tunisia*] [*ICAO location identifier*] (ICLI) ... DTTV
Tunis [*Tunisia*] [*Seismograph station code, US Geological Survey Closed*] (SEIS) ... TUN
Tunis [*Tunisia*] [*Airport symbol*] (OAG) ... TUN
Tunis Airline (DS) ... TU
Tunis Air-Societe Tunisienne de l'Air [*Tunisia*] [*ICAO designator*] (FAAC) ... TAR
Tunis/Carthage [*Tunisia*] [*ICAO location identifier*] (ICLI) ... DTTA
Tunis-Afrique Presse [*Press agency*] [*Tunisia*] ... TAP
Tunisavia - Societe de Transport, Services et Travaux Aeriens [*Tunisia*] [*ICAO designator*] (FAAC) ... TAJ
Tunisia [*MARC geographic area code Library of Congress*] (LCCP) ... f-ti--
Tunisia [*MARC country of publication code Library of Congress*] (LCCP) ... ti
Tunisia [*IYRU nationality code*] [*ANSI two-letter standard code*] (CNC) ... TN
Tunisia [*ANSI three-letter standard code*] (CNC) ... TUN
Tunisia (VRA) ... Tun
Tunison Laboratory of Fish Nutrition [*Cortland, NY*] [*Department of the Interior*] (GRD) ... TLFN
Tunkhannock, PA [*AM radio station call letters*] ... WEMR
Tunkhannock, PA [*FM radio station call letters*] (RBYB) ... WEMR-FM
Tunkwa Copper Mining [*Vancouver Stock Exchange symbol*] ... TNK
Tunnel (MSA) ... TNL
Tunnel [*Commonly used*] (OPSA) ... TUNEL
Tunnel ... TUNL
Tunnel ... TUNL
Tunnel [*Commonly used*] (OPSA) ... TUNLS
Tunnel [*Commonly used*] (OPSA) ... TUNNEL
Tunnel [*Commonly used*] (OPSA) ... TUNNELS
Tunnel [*Commonly used*] (OPSA) ... TUNNL
Tunnel Boring Machine ... TBM
Tunnel Destruct System ... TDS
Tunnel Detection System (MCD) ... TUDS
Tunnel Diode ... TD
Tunnel Diode [*Electronics*] ... TNLDIO
Tunnel Diode Tunnel Logic (NITA) ... TDTL
Tunnel Exploration Kit [*Army*] (VNW) ... TEK
Tunnel Explorer, Locator and Communications System [*Army*] (VNW) ... TELACS
Tunnel Lining Manufacturers Association [*British*] (DBA) ... TLMA
Tunnel Luminescence [*Physics*] ... TnL
Tunnel Rectifier ... TR
Tunnel Thermal Control (NASA) ... TTC
Tunnel Transit Time (IAA) ... TUNNET
Tunnel-Diode Amplifier ... TDA
Tunnel-Diode Amplifier System ... TDAS
Tunnel-Diode Arithmetic Tester (IAA) ... TUDAT
Tunnel-Diode Charge Transformer ... TDCT
Tunnel-Diode Charge-Transformer Logic ... TDCTL
Tunnel-Diode FET [*Field-Effect Transistor*] **Logic** (IAA) ... TDFL
Tunnel-Diode Logic ... TDL
Tunnel-Diode Mixer ... TDM
Tunnel-Diode Transducer ... TDT
Tunnel-Diode Transistor Logic ... TDTL

Tunnel-Emission Amplifier (IEEE) ... TEA
Tunneling Hot-Electron Transfer Amplifier [*Semiconductor technology*] ... THETA
Tunneling Stabilized Magnetic Force Microscopy [*Physics*] ... TSMFM
Tunnels, Mines, and Booby Trap School [*Army*] (VNW) ... TM & B
Tuns Library, Halifax, NS, Canada [*Library symbol Library of Congress*] (LCLS) ... CaNSHTU
Tuntatuliak [*Alaska*] [*Airport symbol*] (OAG) ... WTL
Tununak [*Alaska*] [*Airport symbol*] (OAG) ... TNK
Tunxi [*China*] [*Airport symbol*] (OAG) ... TXN
Tuolumne County Free Public Library, Sonora, CA [*Library symbol Library of Congress*] (LCLS) ... CSoCL
Tupelo [*Mississippi*] [*Airport symbol*] (OAG) ... TUP
Tupelo, MS [*Location identifier FAA*] (FAAL) ... LON
Tupelo, MS [*FM radio station call letters*] ... WAFR
Tupelo, MS [*FM radio station call letters*] (RBYB) ... WAJS
Tupelo, MS [*AM radio station call letters*] ... WELO
Tupelo, MS [*AM radio station call letters*] (RBYB) ... WNRX
Tupelo, MS [*AM radio station call letters*] ... WTUP
Tupelo, MS [*Television station call letters*] ... WTVA
Tupelo, MS [*FM radio station call letters*] ... WZLQ
Tupelo National Battlefield ... TUPE
Tupik [*Former USSR Seismograph station code, US Geological Survey*] (SEIS) ... TUP
Tupile [*Panama*] [*Airport symbol*] (OAG) ... TUE
Tupiza [*Bolivia*] [*ICAO location identifier*] (ICLI) ... SLTZ
Tupolev [*Former USSR ICAO aircraft manufacturer identifier*] (ICAO) ... TU
Tupper Lake, NY [*FM radio station call letters*] ... WRGR
Tupper's Appeal Reports [*Ontario*] [*A publication*] (DLA) ... Tup App
Tupper's Appeal Reports [*Ontario*] [*A publication*] (DLA) ... Tupp
Tupper's Appeal Reports [*Ontario*] [*A publication*] (DLA) ... Tupp App
Tupper's Appeal Reports [*Ontario*] [*A publication*] (DLA) ... Tupper
Tupper's Upper Canada Practice Reports [*A publication*] (DLA) ... Tupp
Tupper's Upper Canada Practice Reports [*A publication*] (DLA) ... Tupper
Tupperware Corp. [*NYSE symbol*] (TTSB) ... TUP
Tur Avrupa Havayollari AS [*Turkey*] [*ICAO designator*] (FAAC) ... TCT
Turaif [*Saudi Arabia*] [*ICAO location identifier*] (ICLI) ... OETR
Turaif [*Saudi Arabia*] [*Airport symbol*] (OAG) ... TUI
Turan Air [*Azerbaijan*] [*FAA designator*] (FAAC) ... URN
Turavia [*Poland ICAO designator*] (FAAC) ... TUV
Turbat [*Pakistan*] [*ICAO location identifier*] (ICLI) ... OPTU
Turbat [*Pakistan*] [*Airport symbol*] (OAG) ... TUK
Turbat [*Former USSR Seismograph station code, US Geological Survey Closed*] (SEIS) ... TUR
Turbid Creamy Layer on Top [*Laboratory science*] (DAVI) ... TCT
Turbid No Creamy Layer [*Laboratory science*] (DAVI) ... TNC
Turbidimetric Immunoassay [*Immunology*] ... TIA
Turbidity (AAMN) ... TURB
Turbidity Reducing (AAMN) ... TR
Turbidity Reducing Unit (AAMN) ... TRU
Turbidity Unit ... TU
Turbinate [*Medicine*] (DAVI) ... TURB
Turbine ... TUR
Turbine (AAG) ... TURB
Turbine Alternator Assembly ... TAA
Turbine and Jet Aircraft Engine Type Designation System ... TJAETDS
Turbine Area Ventilation System [*Nuclear energy*] (NRCH) ... TAVS
Turbine Automated Design System ... TADSYS
Turbine Automatic Control Equipment (IAA) ... TACE
Turbine Building [*Nuclear energy*] (NRCH) ... TB
Turbine Building Secondary Closed Cooling Water [*Nuclear energy*] (NRCH) ... TBSCCW
Turbine Building Ventilation [*Nuclear energy*] (NRCH) ... TBV
Turbine Bypass System [*Nuclear energy*] (NRCH) ... TBS
Turbine Close Coupled (MSA) ... TCC
Turbine Control System [*Nuclear energy*] (NRCH) ... TCS
Turbine Control Unit ... TCU
Turbine Control Valve [*Nuclear energy*] (NRCH) ... TCV
Turbine Direct ... TD
Turbine Disk Integrity [*Nuclear energy*] (NRCH) ... TDI
Turbine Drive [*or Driven*] ... TD
Turbine Electric Drive ... TE
Turbine Electric Drive ... TED
Turbine Electric Reduction Drive ... TERD
Turbine Engine (WDAA) ... TE
Turbine Engine Analysis Check (AABC) ... TEAC
Turbine Engine Checkout ... TECO
Turbine Engine Diagnosis [*Army*] ... TED
Turbine Engine Division [*Air Force*] ... TED
Turbine Engine Loads Simulator ... TELS
Turbine Engine Monitoring and Control [*ASMAP Electronics Ltd.*] [*Software package*] (NCC) ... TEMAC
Turbine Engine Monitoring System ... TEMS
Turbine Engine Power Plant (DWSG) ... TEPP
Turbine Engine Reliability Program (PDAA) ... TERP
Turbine Entry Temperature [*Aviation*] ... TET
Turbine Extreme Pressure (MCD) ... TEP
Turbine First Stage [*Nuclear energy*] (NRCH) ... TFS
Turbine Flow Function ... TFF
Turbine Flow Meter (KSC) ... TFM
Turbine Flow Sensor ... TFS
Turbine Gas Temperature (NATG) ... TGT
Turbine Generator (NRCH) ... TG
Turbine Generator Building [*Nuclear energy*] (NRCH) ... TGB
Turbine Generator Emergency Power [*Nuclear energy*] (NRCH) ... TGEP
Turbine Generator Management ... TGM
Turbine Generator System [*Nuclear energy*] (NRCH) ... TGS
Turbine Gland Sealing System [*Nuclear energy*] (NRCH) ... TGSS
Turbine Governor Valve [*Nuclear energy*] (NRCH) ... TGV
Turbine Heat Rate (DNAB) ... THR
Turbine Helicopters Ltd. [*British*] [*FAA designator*] (FAAC) ... TBN
Turbine Inlet Gas Temperature [*Aviation*] ... TIGT
Turbine Inlet Pressure (MSA) ... TIP
Turbine Inlet Temperature ... TIT
Turbine Integral Propellant (MCD) ... TIP
Turbine Interstage Temperature ... TIT
Turbine Lube Oil Storage Tank [*Nuclear energy*] (NRCH) ... TLOST
Turbine Lube Oil (System) [*Nuclear energy*] (NRCH) ... TLO(S)
Turbine Management Station ... TMS
Turbine Oil Stability Test [*Lubricant testing*] [*Automotive engineering*] ... TOST
Turbine Outlet Temperature (NG) ... TOT
Turbine Oxidation Stability Test (OA) ... TOST
Turbine Power Control Valve ... TPCV
Turbine Propelled (WDAA) ... TURBOPROP
Turbine Rate (NVT) ... TR
Turbine Reduction Drive ... TRD
Turbine Shaft Rate [*Military*] (CAAL) ... TSR
Turbine Steam Ship ... TSS
Turbine Steamship (WDAA) ... TS
Turbine Stop Valve [*Nuclear energy*] (NRCH) ... TSV
Turbine Supersonic Speed (ERG) ... TSS
Turbine Tanker ... TT
Turbine Transport Evaluation Team [*FAA*] (MUGU) ... TTET
Turbine Trip (IEEE) ... TT
Turbine Trip and Throttle Valve [*Nuclear energy*] (IAA) ... TAT
Turbine Trip with Bypass [*Nuclear energy*] (NRCH) ... TTWB
Turbine Vibration Indication System (NG) ... TVIS
Turbine-Alternator Assembly (MCD) ... TTA
Turbine-Building Closed Cooling Water [*Nuclear energy*] (NRCH) ... TBCCW
Turbine-Building Exhaust System Isolation [*Nuclear energy*] (NRCH) ... TBESI
Turbine-Building Service Water [*Nuclear energy*] (NRCH) ... TSW
Turbine-Driven Auxiliary Feed Pump [*Nuclear energy*] (NRCH) ... TDAFP
Turbine-Driven Auxiliary Feedwater Pump [*Nuclear energy*] (NRCH) ... TDAFWP
Turbine-Driven Blower ... TDB
Turbine-Driven Emergency Feedwater Pump [*Nuclear energy*] (NRCH) ... TDEFWP
Turbine-Electric Drive Submarine (DNAB) ... TEDS
Turbine-Integrated Geared Rotor ... TIGR
Turbine-Operated Suspension System [*NASA*] ... TOSS
Turbine-Powered Catapult ... TURBOCAT
Turbo [*Colombia*] [*Airport symbol*] (OAG) ... TRB
Turbo Assembler [*Computer science*] ... TASM
Turbo Debugger for Windows [*Computer science*] (PCM) ... TDW
Turbo, Gonzalo Mejia [*Colorado ICAO location identifier*] (ICLI) ... SKTU
Turbo Hydramatic [*Automotive engineering*] ... THM
Turbo Pascal for Windows [*Computer science*] ... TPW
Turbo Pascal Unit [*Borland International*] [*Computer science*] (PCM) ... TPU
Turbo Resources Ltd. [*Toronto Stock Exchange symbol*] ... TBR
Turbo Sport Intercooler [*Automotive engineering*] ... TSI
Turbo Vapor Injector ... TVI
Turbo Vision [*Borland International*] [*Computer science*] (PCM) ... TV
Turboalternator ... T/A
Turboalternator (AAG) ... TURBOALT
Turboalternator Compressor ... TAC
Turboalternator Power System (IEEE) ... TAPS
Turbocharged [*Automotive engineering*] ... T
Turbocharged Generation 4 [*Automotive engine identification*] ... TCIV
Turbocharged Generation One [*Automotive engine identification*] ... TCI
Turbocharger [*Automotive engineering*] ... TC
Turbocharger [*Automotive engineering*] ... TURBO
Turbocharger Management System [*Automotive electronics*] ... TCMS
Turbochef, Inc. [*NASDAQ symbol*] (SAG) ... TRBO
Turbochef, Inc. [*Associated Press*] (SAG) ... Turbochf
Turbodiesel [*Automotive engineering*] ... TD
Turbo-Electric Tanker ... TET
Turbo-Electric Vessel ... TEV
Turbofan [*Engine*] ... TF
Turbofan Engine ... TFE
Turbogenerator ... TG
Turbogenerator (AAG) ... TURBOGEN
Turbojet ... TJ
Turbojet Aircraft ... TJA
Turbojet Engine ... TJE
Turbojet Propulsion ... TJP
Turbopool Ltd. [*British ICAO designator*] (FAAC) ... TPL
Turbopower Unit ... TPU
Turboprop (AAG) ... TP
Turboprop Aircraft ... TPA
Turbopropeller Engine ... TPE
Turbopump (AAG) ... TP
Turbopump Assembly (KSC) ... TPA
Turbopump Control ... TPC
Turbopump Oxidizer Cavity Purge (SAA) ... TPOCP
Turboshaft Engine (IEEE) ... ts
Turboshaft Engine ... TSE
Turbosynchro Transmitter (IAA) ... TS
Turbulence [*Aviation*] (FAAC) ... TB
Turbulence ... TURB
Turbulence Amplifier ... TA
Turbulence Measuring System ... TMS
Turbulence-Generating Pot [*Automotive engineering*] ... TGP
Turbulent [*NWS*] (FAAC) ... TURBT

Turbulent Air Jet .... TAJ
Turbulent Air Pilot Environment Research [*NASA-FAA project*] .... TAPER
Turbulent Bed Contactor [*Chemical engineering*] .... TBC
Turbulent Boundary Layer .... TBL
Turbulent Bounded Jet .... TBJ
Turbulent Confined Jet .... TCJ
Turbulent Contacting Absorber .... TCA
Turbulent Far Wake .... TFW
Turbulent Kinetic Energy .... TKE
Tureia [*French Polynesia*] [*ICAO location identifier*] (ICLI) .... NTGY
Turf Course [*Horse racing*] .... TC
Turf Quality (OA) .... TQ
Turf Research Foundation [*Defunct*] (EA) .... TRF
Turfan Pahlavi (BJA) .... TPhl
Turfgrass Association of Australia .... TAA
Turin [*Italy*] [*Airport symbol*] (OAG) .... TRN
Turing Institute [*British*] (IRUK) .... TI
Turing Machine [*Mathematical model*] [*Computer science*] .... TM
Turismo Internationale [*Automobile model designation*] .... TI
Turk Haberler Ajansi [*Press agency*] [*Turkey*] .... THA
Turk Hava Tasimaciligi [*Turkish Air Transport*] [*ICAO designator*] (FAAC) .... THT
Turk Hava Yollari [*Turkish Airlines*] [*ICAO designator*] (FAAC) .... THY
Turk Hava Yollari [*ICAO designator*] (AD) .... TK
Turk Hava Yollari AO [*Turkish Airlines, Inc.*] .... THY
Turkestan .... Turkest
Turkey [*MARC geographic area code Library of Congress*] (LCCP) .... a-tu--
Turkey [*IYRU nationality code*] .... TK
Turkey [*ANSI two-letter standard code*] (CNC) .... TR
Turkey [*NATO*] .... TU
Turkey [*MARC country of publication code Library of Congress*] (LCCP) ...... tu
Turkey [*ANSI three-letter standard code*] (CNC) .... TUR
Turkey .... TURK
Turkey (VRA) .... Turk
Turkey Coryza [*Pathology*] .... TC
Turkey Creek [*Western Australia*] [*Airport symbol*] (AD) .... TKY
Turkey Embryo Fibroblast [*Biochemistry*] .... TEF
Turkey Gamma G [*Immunology*] .... TGG
Turkey Point Performance Enforcement Program [*Nuclear energy*]
  (NRCH) .... TPPEP
Turkey Point Station [*Nuclear energy*] (NRCH) .... TPS
Turkey Virus Hepatitis [*Medicine*] (DMAA) .... TVH
Turkish .... T
Turkish [*MARC language code Library of Congress*] (LCCP) .... tur
Turkish Air Force (NATG) .... TAF
Turkish Air Force .... TuAF
Turkish Airlines [*Airline flight code*] (ODBW) .... TK
Turkish American Friendship Society of the United States (EA) .... TAFSUS
Turkish American Physicians Association (EA) .... TAPA
Turkish Army (NATG) .... TA
Turkish Atomic Energy Commission .... TAEC
Turkish Children Foster Care (EA) .... TCFC
Turkish Communist Party - Marxist-Leninist [*Political party*] (PD) .... AKKO
Turkish Confederation of Trade Unions .... TCTU
Turkish Cypriot Aid Society of New York (EA) .... TCASNY
Turkish Cypriot Federated State .... TCFS
Turkish Federated State of Cyprus .... TFSC
Turkish General Staff (NATG) .... TGS
Turkish Investment Fund [*NYSE symbol*] (SPSG) .... TKF
Turkish Investment Fund [*Associated Press*] (SAG) .... Turksh
Turkish Investment Promotion and Information Center [*Subdivision of the
  Union of Chambers of Commerce, Industry, and Commodity Exchanges of
  Turkey*] .... TIPIC
Turkish Lira (BJA) .... TL
Turkish News Agency of Cyprus (EAIO) .... TNAC
Turkish People's Liberation Army (PD) .... TPLA
Turkish People's Liberation Party [*Political party*] (PD) .... TPLP
Turkish People's Liberation Party/Front .... TPLP/F
Turkish Radio & Television Corp. .... TRT
Turkish Reactor .... TR
Turkish Reactor Assembly (SAA) .... TRA
Turkish Republic of North Cyprus (BARN) .... TRNC
Turkish Revolutionary Communist Party [*Political party*] (PD) .... TDKP
Turkish Standards Institution .... TSI
Turkish Studies Association (EA) .... TSA
Turkish Women's League of America (EA) .... TWLA
Turkish Workers' and Peasants' Liberation Army .... TWPLA
Turkish-American Associations (EA) .... TAA
Turkish-United States Logistic Group .... TUSLOG
Turkish-United States Logistics Group Detachment (DNAB) .... TUSLOGDET
Turkiye Cumhuriyet Merkez Bankasi [*The Central Bank of the Republic of
  Turkey*] .... TCMB
Turkiye Emekci Partisi [*Workers' Party of Turkey*] [*Political party*] (PPW) .... TEP
Turkiye Halk Bankasi [*Bank*] [*Turkey*] .... H
Turkiye Isci Koylu Partisi [*Worker-Peasant Party of Turkey*] [*Political party*]
  (PD) .... TIKP
Turkiye Komunist Partisi .... TKP
Turkiye Ogretmenler Sendikasi .... TOS
Turkiye Tekstil ve Orme Sanayii Iscileri Sendikalari Federasyonu [*National
  Federation of Textile Unions*] [*Turkey*] .... TEKSIF
Turkmen [*MARC language code Library of Congress*] (LCCP) .... tuk
Turkmen Soviet Socialist Republic [*MARC geographic area code Library of
  Congress*] (LCCP) .... e-ur-tk
Turkmen Soviet Socialist Republic [*MARC country of publication code Library
  of Congress*] (LCCP) .... tkr
Turkmen Soviet Socialist Republic .... TurkmSSR

Turkmenistan [*ICAO designator*] (FAAC) .... TUA
Turko-Tataric [*MARC language code Library of Congress*] (LCCP) .... tut
Turks & Caicos Airways Ltd. [*ICAO designator Obsolete*] (OAG) .... BH
Turks and Caicos Canadian Association .... T & CCA
Turks and Caicos Islands [*MARC geographic area code Library of
  Congress*] (LCCP) .... nwtc--
Turks and Caicos Islands [*MARC country of publication code Library of
  Congress*] (LCCP) .... tc
Turks and Caicos Islands [*ANSI two-letter standard code*] (CNC) .... TC
Turks and Caicos Islands [*ANSI three-letter standard code*] (CNC) .... TCA
Turks and Caicos Islands [*International civil aircraft marking*] (ODBW) .... VQ-T
Turks & Caicos National Airlines [*ICAO designator*] (FAAC) .... TCI
Turks Islands [*West Indies*] [*Airport symbol*] (AD) .... TKI
Turku [*Finland ICAO location identifier*] (ICLI) .... EFTU
Turku [*Finland*] [*Airport symbol*] (OAG) .... TKU
Turlock, CA [*FM radio station call letters*] .... KBDG
Turlock, CA [*AM radio station call letters*] (RBYB) .... KCDR
Turlock, CA [*FM radio station call letters*] .... KCSS
Turlock, CA [*FM radio station call letters*] (RBYB) .... KWNN
Turlock City Library, Turlock, CA [*Library symbol Library of Congress*]
  (LCLS) .... CTur
Turmor-Associated Glycoprotein [*Biochemistry*] .... TAG
Turmor-Associated Rejection Antigen [*Immunology*] .... TARA
Turn [*or Turning*] .... T
Turn Altitude [*Aviation*] (FAAC) .... TNA
Turn Altitude/Height [*Aviation*] (DA) .... TA/H
Turn and Cough [*Medicine*] .... T & C
Turn Around [*Aviation*] (FAAC) .... TARND
Turn Buckle [*Automotive engineering*] .... T/BKL
Turn Coordination (MSA) .... TRN CRD
Turn, Cough, and Deep Breathe [*Medicine*] .... TC & DB
Turn, Cough, Deep Breathe [*Medicine*] (DMAA) .... TCDB
Turn, Cough, Hyperventilate [*Medicine*] .... TCH
Turn Height [*Aviation*] (FAAC) .... TNH
Turn In (DGA) .... T/In
Turn In a Pusher [*Organization combating drug traffic*] .... TIP
Turn Indicator Interference .... TII
Turn Left after Takeoff [*Aviation*] (FAAC) .... LT
Turn Off My Addiction [*Proposed clinic*] .... TOMA
Turn Off Television Saturday [*of Action for Children's Television
  organization*] .... TOTS
Turn Out Perfection [*US Air Force Southern Command's acronym for the Zero
  Defects Program*] .... TOP
[*A*] Turn Over [*A prospective customer who cannot be sold by one clerk and is
  turned over to another*] [*Merchandising slang*] .... TO
Turn Over, Please [*Correspondence*] (ROG) .... TOP
Turn per Second (IAA) .... TS
Turn Round Time (NITA) .... TRT
Turn Rule (WDMC) .... TR
Turn Signal [*Automotive engineering*] .... T/SIG
Turn toward Peace [*Later, WWWC*] [*An association*] (EA) .... TTP
Turn-and-Bank Indicators .... T & B
Turnaround (NASA) .... T/A
Turnaround Control [*Navy*] .... TURCO
Turnaround Fault Isolation [*Aviation*] .... TAFI
Turnaround Fault Isolation Manual .... TAFIM
Turnaround Index [*Computer science*] .... TAI
Turnaround Ranging Station [*Telecommunications*] (TEL) .... TARS
Turnaround Ratio .... TAR
Turnaround Requirements (MCD) .... TR
Turnaround Requirements Analysis [*NASA*] (NASA) .... TRA
Turnaround Time .... TAT
Turnaround Time, Repair Survival Rate and Cost Evaluation Report
  [*Navy*] (DNAB) .... TRACER
Turnaway Landing [*Navy*] (NVT) .... TWALNDG
Turnbuckle [*Aerospace*] (AAG) .... TRNBKL
Turnbuckle [*s*] [*Freight*] .... TURNBKLE
Turnbull & Asser [*Men's fashions*] .... T & A
Turnbull Associates [*British ICAO designator*] (FAAC) .... TNB
Turnbull Canyon [*California*] [*Seismograph station code, US Geological Survey
  Closed*] (SEIS) .... TCC
Turnbull's Practice [*New York*] [*A publication*] (DLA) .... Turn Pr
Turn-Cock (ROG) .... TC
Turndown Ratio .... TDR
Turned (AAG) .... TND
Turned (MSA) .... TRND
Turned and Bored .... T and B
Turned and Bored (IAA) .... TAB
Turned Out [*for Examination*] [*Tea trade*] (ROG) .... T/O
Turner [*Navy rating British*] .... T
Turner [*Maine*] [*Seismograph station code, US Geological Survey*] (SEIS) .... TRM
Turner and Phillips' English Chancery Reports [*A publication*] (DLA) .... T & P
Turner and Phillips' English Chancery Reports [*A publication*] (DLA) ..... Turn & P
Turner and Phillips' English Chancery Reports [*A publication*] (DLA) .... Turn & Ph
Turner and Russell's English Chancery Reports [*1822-25*] [*A publication*]
  (DLA) .... T & R
Turner and Russell's English Chancery Reports [*1822-24*] [*A publication*]
  (DLA) .... Tu & Rus
Turner and Russell's English Chancery Reports [*37 English Reprint*] [*1822-
  24*] [*A publication*] (DLA) .... Tur & R
Turner and Russell's English Chancery Reports [*37 English Reprint*] [*1822-
  24*] [*A publication*] (DLA) .... Tur & Ru
Turner and Russell's English Chancery Reports [*37 English Reprint*] [*1822-
  24*] [*A publication*] (DLA) .... Tur & Rus

Turner and Russell's English Chancery Reports [*37 English Reprint*] [*A publication*] (DLA) .... Turn & R
Turner and Russell's English Chancery Reports [*37 English Reprint*] [*A publication*] (DLA) .... Turn & R (Eng)
Turner and Russell's English Chancery Reports [*37 English Reprint*] [*A publication*] (DLA) .... Turn & Rus
Turner and Russell's English Chancery Reports [*37 English Reprint*] [*A publication*] (DLA) .... Turn & Russ
Turner Broadcast'A' [*AMEX symbol*] (TTSB) .... TBS.A
Turner Broadcast'B' [*AMEX symbol*] (TTSB) .... TBS.B
Turner Broadcasting System, Inc. [*AMEX symbol*] (SPSG) .... TBS
Turner Broadcasting System, Inc. [*Associated Press*] (SAG) .... TurnB
Turner Broadcasting Systems (NITA) .... TBS
Turner Classic Movies [*Television*] .... TCM
Turner, Collie & Braden, Inc., Houston, TX [*Library symbol Library of Congress*] (LCLS) .... TxHTu
Turner Corp. [*AMEX symbol*] (SPSG) .... TUR
Turner Corp. [*Associated Press*] (SAG) .... TurnrC
Turner Energy & Resources [*Vancouver Stock Exchange symbol*] .... TUN
Turner Network Television [*Cable-television system*] .... TNT
Turner on Copyright in Designs [*1849*] [*A publication*] (DLA) .... Turn Cop
Turner on Patents [*1851*] [*A publication*] (DLA) .... Turn Pat
Turner on Quieting Titles [*A publication*] (DLA) .... Turn Qui Tit
Turner Program Services [*Broadcasting*] .... TPS
Turner Society [*British*] (EAIO) .... TS
Turner Syndrome [*Medicine*] (DMAA) .... TS
Turner Teleport, Inc. [*Atlanta, GA*] [*Telecommunications service*] (TSSD) .... TTI
Turner Valley Public Library, Alberta [*Library symbol National Library of Canada*] (NLC) .... ATV
Turner-Fairbank Highway Research Center [*FHWA*] (TAG) .... TFHRC
Turners Falls, MA [*FM radio station call letters*] .... WPVQ
Turner's History of the Anglo Saxon [*A publication*] (DLA) .... Turn Anglo Sax
Turner's Practice of the Court of Chancery [*4th ed.*] [*1821*] [*A publication*] (DLA) .... Turn Ch Pr
Turner's Reports [*99-101 Kentucky*] [*A publication*] (DLA) .... Tur
Turner's Reports [*35-48 Arkansas*] [*A publication*] (DLA) .... Tur
Turner's Reports [*99-101 Kentucky*] [*A publication*] (DLA) .... Turn
Turner's Reports [*35-48 Arkansas*] [*A publication*] (DLA) .... Turn
Turner's Select Pleas of the Forest [*Selden Society Publication, Vol. 13*] [*A publication*] (DLA) .... Tur
Turner's Select Pleas of the Forest [*Selden Society Publication, Vol. 13*] [*A publication*] (DLA) .... Turn
Turner's Syndrome Society of the US (EA) .... TSS
Turn-In Document [*DoD*] .... TID
Turn-In Slip [*Military*] .... T/S
Turning Angle [*Automotive engineering*] .... TA
Turning Arbor .... TUAR
Turning Cam [*Tool*] (AAG) .... TUCA
Turning Circle [*Automotive engineering*] .... TC
Turning Diameter [*Automotive engineering*] .... TD
Turning Fixture .... TUFX
Turning Gear .... TRNGR
Turning Point .... TP
Turning Radius [*Automotive engineering*] .... TR
Turning Wrench [*Tool*] (AAG) .... TUWR
Turnip Crinkle Virus .... TC
Turnip Crinkle Virus .... TCV
Turnip Mosaic Virus .... TMV
Turnip Mosaic Virus .... TuMV
Turnip Mosaic Virus - Common .... TMV-C
Turnip Mosaic Virus - Legume .... TMV-L
Turnip Rosette Virus [*Plant pathology*] .... TROV
Turnip Yellow Mosaic Virus .... TYMV
Turnip Yellows Virus [*Plant pathology*] .... TYV
Turnkey [*Medicine*] (DMAA) .... T
Turnkey Systems Vendor [*Computer science*] (MHDI) .... TSV
Turn-Off Controlled Rectifier (PDAA) .... TOCR
Turn-On Command (KSC) .... TOC
Turn-On Rate (CAAL) .... TOR
Turn-On Time .... TOT
Turnout (AAG) .... TO
Turnover [*Number*] [*With reference to enzyme activity*] .... TO
Turnover (NTCM) .... TO
Turnover (NVT) .... TOVR
Turnover Device .... TOD
Turnover Frequency [*Chemical engineering*] .... TOF
Turnover Frequency .... TOF
Turnover Index [*Botany*] .... T
Turnover Number .... TON
Turnover Summary Report [*Military*] .... TSR
Turnpike .... TNPK
Turnpike .... TPK
Turnpike (MCD) .... TPKE
Turnpike .... TPKE
Turnpike [*Commonly used*] (OPSA) .... TRNPK
Turnpike [*Commonly used*] (OPSA) .... TRPK
Turnpike [*Commonly used*] (OPSA) .... TURNPIKE
Turnpike [*Commonly used*] (OPSA) .... TURNPK
Turns per Centimeter [*Yarn*] .... TPC
Turns per Inch .... TPI
Turns per Knot [*Navy*] (CAAL) .... TPK
Turns per Layer .... TPL
Turntable (MSA) .... TRNTBL
Turntable (ADA) .... TT
Turntable Desk (DEN) .... TD
Turntable Ladder .... TL
Turonian-Santonian [*Paleontology*] .... T-S
Turpentine [*Chemistry*] (DAVI) .... turp
Turqoise (VRA) .... turq
Turquoise (ROG) .... TURQ
Turret (AABC) .... TRT
Turret (MSA) .... TUR
Turret Captain [*Navy*] .... TC
Turret Director Trainer [*British military*] (DMA) .... TDT
Turret Drive Subsystem (DWSG) .... TDSS
Turret Electronics Unit [*Military*] (RDA) .... TEU
Turret Fire Control .... TFC
Turret Gun System [*Army*] .... TGS
Turret Head Limit Switch .... THLS
Turret Integrated Night Thermal Sight .... TINTS
Turret Integrated Xenon Illuminator .... TIXI
Turret Interaction Crew Simulator (MCD) .... TICS
Turret Lathe Stop Gauge .... TLSG
Turret Maintenance Trainer (MCD) .... TMT
Turret Mock-Up (MCD) .... TMU
Turret Trainer [*British military*] (DMA) .... TT
Turret-Anchored Production System [*Petroleum engineering*] .... TAPS
Turtle Airways [*ICAO designator*] (AD) .... KT
Turtle Airways Ltd. [*Fiji*] [*ICAO designator*] (FAAC) .... TLT
Turtle Excluder Device [*Fishing*] .... TEC
Turtle Excluder Device [*Marine science*] (OSRA) .... TED
Turtle Exclusion Device [*Tool attached to shrimp boats in the Gulf of Mexico which allows the endangered Kemp's ridley turtle to escape the shrimp nets*] [*Facetious translations: "Trawler Extinction Device," "Trawling Efficiency Device"*] .... TED
Turtle Hook Junior High School, Uniondale, NY [*Library symbol Library of Congress*] (LCLS) .... NUnTHJ
Turtle Island [*Fiji*] [*Airport symbol*] (OAG) .... TTL
Turtle Mountains [*California*] [*Seismograph station code, US Geological Survey*] (SEIS) .... TTM
Turun Yliopiston Kirjasto [*Turku School of Economics*], Turku, Finland [*Library symbol Library of Congress*] (LCLS) .... FiTK
Tusayan, AZ [*FM radio station call letters*] .... KSGC
Tuscaloosa [*Alabama*] [*Airport symbol*] (OAG) .... TCL
Tuscaloosa, AL [*AM radio station call letters*] .... WACT
Tuscaloosa, AL [*FM radio station call letters*] .... WACT-FM
Tuscaloosa, AL [*FM radio station call letters*] (RBYB) .... WBHJ-FM
Tuscaloosa, AL [*Television station call letters*] .... WCFT
Tuscaloosa, AL [*Television station call letters*] .... WDBB
Tuscaloosa, AL [*FM radio station call letters*] .... WFFX
Tuscaloosa, AL [*AM radio station call letters*] .... WSPZ
Tuscaloosa, AL [*AM radio station call letters*] .... WTNW
Tuscaloosa, AL [*AM radio station call letters*] .... WTSK
Tuscaloosa, AL [*FM radio station call letters*] .... WTUG
Tuscaloosa, AL [*FM radio station call letters*] .... WUAL
Tuscaloosa, AL [*FM radio station call letters*] .... WVUA
Tuscaloosa, AL [*AM radio station call letters*] .... WWPG
Tuscaloosa Oil & Gas [*Vancouver Stock Exchange symbol*] .... TSC
Tuscarora [*New York*] [*Seismograph station code, US Geological Survey Closed*] (SEIS) .... TUS
Tuscarora, Inc. [*NASDAQ symbol*] (NQ) .... TUSC
Tuscarora, Inc. [*Associated Press*] (SAG) .... Tuscln
Tuscola & Saginaw Bay Railway Co., Inc. [*AAR code*] .... TSBY
Tuscola, IL [*FM radio station call letters*] (RBYB) .... WEBX
Tuscola, MI [*FM radio station call letters*] .... WWBN
Tuscola Public Library, Tuscola, IL [*Library symbol Library of Congress*] (LCLS) .... ITu
Tusculanae Disputationes [*of Cicero*] [*Classical studies*] (OCD) .... Tusc
Tusculum College, Greeneville, TN [*Library symbol Library of Congress*] (LCLS) .... TGrT
Tusculum College, Greenville, TN [*Inactive*] [*OCLC symbol*] (OCLC) .... TCL
Tusculum, TN [*FM radio station call letters*] (RBYB) .... WSMG
Tuscumbia, AL [*AM radio station call letters*] .... WVNA
Tuscumbia, AL [*FM radio station call letters*] .... WVNA-FM
Tuscumbia, AL [*AM radio station call letters*] .... WZZA
Tushaun Resources, Inc. [*Vancouver Stock Exchange symbol*] .... TUS
Tuskegee Airmen, Inc. (EA) .... TAI
Tuskegee, AL [*Location identifier FAA*] (FAAL) .... MTZ
Tuskegee, AL [*Location identifier FAA*] (FAAL) .... TGE
Tuskegee, AL [*FM radio station call letters*] .... WACQ
Tuskegee, AL [*AM radio station call letters*] .... WBIL
Tuskegee, AL [*FM radio station call letters*] .... WBIL-FM
Tuskegee, AL [*FM radio station call letters*] (RBYB) .... WTGZ-FM
Tuskegee Institute, Tuskegee, AL [*Library symbol Library of Congress*] (LCLS) .... ATT
Tuskegee Institute, Tuskegee, AL [*OCLC symbol*] (OCLC) .... TUS
Tuskegee R. R. [*AAR code*] .... TK
Tuskegee University (GAGS) .... Tuskegee U
Tusra [*India*] [*ICAO location identifier*] (ICLI) .... VETS
Tussi Molesta [*When the Cough Is Troublesome*] [*Pharmacy*] .... TUSS MOL
Tussi Urgente [*When the Cough Is Troublesome*] [*Pharmacy*] .... TUSS URG
Tussilago [*Coltsfoot*] [*Pharmacology*] (ROG) .... TUSSIL
Tussis [*Cough*] [*Pharmacy*] .... TUS
Tussis [*Cough*] [*Latin*] (CPH) .... tuss
Tustin, CA [*Location identifier FAA*] (FAAL) .... NTK
Tustin Institute of Technology [*California*] .... TIT
Tustin Public Library, Tustin, MI [*Library symbol Library of Congress*] (LCLS) .... MiTu
Tut Enterprises, Inc. [*Toronto Stock Exchange symbol*] .... TTX
Tu-Tahl Petroleum, Inc. [*Vancouver Stock Exchange symbol*] .... TTP

Tutmonda Asocio pri Kibernetiko, Informatiko, kaj Sistemiko [*World Association of Cybernetics, Computer Science, and System Theory*] (EAIO) .... TAKIS
Tutmonda Esperantista Biblioteka Asocio [*International Association for Esperanto in Libraries - IAEL*] (EAIO) .... TEBA
Tutmonda Esperantista Junulara Organizo [*World Organization of Young Esperantists*] (EAIO) .... TEJO
Tutmonda Esperantista Jurnalista Asocio [*World Association of Esperanto Journalists - WAEJ*] (EAIO) .... TEJA
Tutmonda Esperantista Vegetara Asocio [*World Esperantist Vegetarian Association - WEVA*] (EAIO) .... TEVA
Tutmonda Parolspuro-Asocio [*Universal Association for Speech Tracing - UAST*] (EAIO) .... TPA
Tutor Support Scheme [*Australia*] .... TSS
Tutored Videotape Instruction .... TVI
Tutorial Computer-Assisted Instruction (IEEE) .... TCAI
[*A*] Tutorial System [*1971*] [*Computer science*] (CSR) .... ATS
Tutoring Adults through Literacy Councils (EDAC) .... TALC
Tutti [*Sing or Play Together*] [*Music*] .... T
Tuttle and Carpenter's Reports [*52 California*] [*A publication*] (DLA) .... Tutt & C
Tuttle and Carpenter's Reports [*52 California*] [*A publication*] (DLA) .... Tutt & Carp
Tuttle and Carpenter's Reports [*52 California*] [*A publication*] (DLA) .... Tuttle
Tuttle and Carpenter's Reports [*52 California*] [*A publication*] (DLA) .... Tuttle & Carpenter
Tutto Solo [*All by Itself*] [*Music*] .... TS
Tutuka [*South Africa*] [*ICAO location identifier*] (ICLI) .... FATT
Tuula Vauhkonen [*Regional Institute of Occupational Health*], Oulv, Finland [*Library symbol*] [*Library of Congress*] (LCLS) .... FiOTV
Tuvalu [*International civil aircraft marking*] (ODBW) T2
Tuvalu [*ANSI three-letter standard code*] (CNC) .... TUV
Tuvalu [*ANSI two-letter standard code*] (CNC) .... TV
Tuvalu and Kiribati Philatelic Society (EA) .... TKPS
Tuvalu Philatelic Society (EA) .... TPS
Tuxedo (DSUE) .... TUX
Tuxedo Park Library, Tuxedo Park, NY [*Library symbol Library of Congress*] (LCLS) .... NTuxp
Tuxpan [*Mexico ICAO location identifier*] (ICLI) .... MMTX
Tuxpan [*Mexico*] [*Airport symbol*] (AD) .... TUX
Tuxpeno [*Race of maize*] .... TUX
Tuxtla Gutierrez [*Mexico ICAO location identifier*] (ICLI) .... MMTB
Tuxtla Gutierrez [*Mexico ICAO location identifier*] (ICLI) .... MMTG
Tuxtla Gutierrez [*Mexico*] [*Airport symbol*] (AD) .... TGS
Tuxtla Gutierrez [*Mexico*] [*Airport symbol*] (OAG) .... TGZ
Tuy Hoa [*South Vietnam*] [*Airport symbol*] (AD) .... TBB
Tuzigoot National Monument .... TUZI
TV Filme, Inc. [*NASDAQ symbol*] (SAG) .... PYTV
TV Filme, Inc. [*Associated Press*] (SAG) .... TV Flme
TV Guide Entertainment Network .... TVGEN
TVG Technologies [*Associated Press*] (SAG) .... TVG
TVG Technologies [*Associated Press*] (SAG) .... TVG Tch
TVG Technologies [*NASDAQ symbol*] (SAG) .... TVGLF
TVG Technologies [*NASDAQ symbol*] (SAG) .... TVGTF
TVG Technologies [*NASDAQ symbol*] (SAG) .... TVGUF
TVG Technologies [*NASDAQ symbol*] (SAG) .... TVGWF
TVG Technologies [*NASDAQ symbol*] (SAG) .... TVGZF
TVOntario, Toronto, Ontario [*Library symbol National Library of Canada*] (NLC) .... OTET
TVR Car Club [*Later, TVRCCNA*] (EA) .... TVRCC
TVX Gold [*NYSE symbol*] (TTSB) .... TVX
TVX Gold, Inc. [*NYSE symbol*] (SAG) .... TVX
TVX Gold, Inc. [*Associated Press*] (SAG) .... TVX Gld
TVX Mining Corp. [*Formerly, Treasure Valley Explorations Ltd.*] [*Toronto Stock Exchange symbol*] .... TVX
Twaddell [*Specific gravity scale*] [*Physics*] .... TW
Twaddell [*Physics*] .... Twad
Twain Harte, CA [*FM radio station call letters*] .... KKBN
T-wave Atrial [*Found on electrocardiograms*] (DAVI) .... Ta
Tweed Public Library, Ontario [*Library symbol National Library of Canada*] (BIB) .... OTWE
Tween Deck [*on a ship*] (DS) .... TWD
Twelfth Air Defense Group Headquarters, Vancouver, British Columbia, Canada .... CANAIRVAN
Twelfth Night [*Shakespearean work*] .... TN
Twelfth Night [*Shakespearean work*] (BARN) .... Twel N
Twelve English Statesmen [*A publication*] .... TES
Twente Airlines [*Netherlands*] [*FAA designator*] (FAAC) .... TWO
Twente University of Technology (NITA) .... TUT
Twentieth Anniversary Mobilization (EA) .... TAM
Twentieth Century Fund (EA) .... TCF
Twentieth Century Industries [*Associated Press*] (SAG) 20CenInd
Twentieth Century Industries [*NYSE symbol*] (SPSG) .... TW
[*The*] Twentieth Century New Testament [*A publication*] (BJA) .... TC
Twentieth Century Spanish Association of America (EA) .... TCSAA
Twentieth Century Young Adult Writers [*A publication*] .... TCYAW
Twentieth Century-Fox Film Corp., Beverly Hills, CA [*Library symbol Library of Congress*] (LCLS) .... CBevT
Twentieth Century-Fox Film Corp., Research Library, Los Angeles, CA [*Library symbol Library of Congress*] (LCLS) .... CLTC
Twentieth of a Point [*Computer science*] (CDE) .... TWIP
Twentieth-Century Literary Criticism [*A publication*] .... TCLC
Twenty (ADA) .... TWY
Twenty Committee [*British espionage unit named after a "double-cross" operation it conducted during World War II*] XX
Twenty Statements Test .... TST
Twenty-First Century Foundation (EA) .... TFCF

Twenty-first Century Land Warrior [*Army*] (INF) 21CLW
Twenty-Foot Container Equivalent Unit [*MARAD*] (TAG) .... TEU
Twenty-Foot Equivalent [*Shipping*] .... TEQ
Twenty-Foot Equivalent Unit [*Used to compare capacity of containerships*] .... TEU
[*The*] Twenty-Four Books of the Holy Scriptures (1853) [*I. Leeser*] (BJA) .... Le
Twenty-Four Hour [*Continuous*] Operation [*Aviation*] H24
Twenty-Four-Hour Automatic Teller [*Trademark for self-service banking display panel*] .... THAT
Twenty-Four-Hour Urine [*Urology*] (DAVI) U24H
Twentyfourmo [*Book up to 15 centimeters in height*] .... T
Twentynine Palms [*California*] [*Airport symbol*] (OAG) .... TNP
Twentynine Palms [*California*] [*Seismograph station code, US Geological Survey*] (SEIS) .... TPC
Twentynine Palms, CA [*FM radio station call letters*] .... KCDZ
Twentynine Palms, CA [*FM radio station call letters*] .... KDHI
Twentynine Palms, CA [*FM radio station call letters*] .... KQYN
Twentynine Palms, CA [*TV station call letters*] (RBYB) .... KVMD-TV
Twentynine Palms, CA [*Location identifier FAA*] (FAAL) .... NXP
Twentynine Palms, CA [*Location identifier FAA*] (FAAL) .... TNP
Twi [*MARC language code Library of Congress*] (LCCP) .... twi
Twice a Week [*Advertising frequency*] .... TAW
Twice a Week [*Pharmacy*] (DAVI) .... TIW
Twickenham [*Postcode*] (ODBW) .... TW
Twilight .... TWLT
Twilight All Night .... TAN
Twilight Colony School, Valleyview, Alberta [*Library symbol National Library of Canada*] (BIB) .... AVVTS
Twilight Sentinel Amplifier [*Automotive engineering*] .... TSA
Twilight Zone [*Aviation*] .... TWIZN
[*The*] Twilight Zone [*Television program created by Rod Serling*] .... TZ
Twilight-Zoner [*Undecided voter*] [*Political slang*] .... TZ
Twillingate Public Library, Newfoundland [*Library symbol National Library of Canada*] (NLC) .... NFTW
Twillingate Public Library, Twillingate, NF, Canada [*Library symbol Library of Congress*] (LCLS) .... CaNfTw
Twin .... TW
Twin Accelerator Ring Transfer (IEEE) .... TART
Twin Agent Unit [*Fire fighting*] (NVT) .... TAU
Twin and Add (SAA) .... TAD
Twin and Multiply (IAA) .... TMU
Twin and Subtract (SAA) .... TSU
Twin Bonanza Association (EA) .... TBA
Twin Boundary Diffusion .... TBD
Twin Branch Railroad Co. [*AAR code*] .... TB
Twin Camshaft [*Automotive engineering*] .... TC
Twin Carburetor [*Automotive engineering*] .... TC
Twin Channel Substrate Mesa (NITA) .... TCSM
Twin Cities Army Ammunition Plant (AABC) .... TCAAP
Twin Cities Biomedical Consortium [*Library network*] .... TCBC
Twin City Bancorp [*NASDAQ symbol*] (TTSB) .... TWIN
Twin City Bancorp, Inc. [*NASDAQ symbol*] (SAG) .... TWIN
Twin City Bancorp, Inc. [*Associated Press*] (SAG) .... TwinCtyB
Twin Disc [*NYSE symbol*] (TTSB) .... TDI
Twin Disc, Inc. [*NYSE symbol*] (SPSG) .... TDI
Twin Disc, Inc. [*Associated Press*] (SAG) .... TwinDs
Twin Eagles Resources, Inc. [*Vancouver Stock Exchange symbol*] .... TWN
Twin Engine .... TE
Twin Exchangeable Disc Storage (NITA) .... TEDS
Twin Falls [*Idaho*] [*Airport symbol*] (OAG) .... TWF
Twin Falls, ID [*FM radio station call letters*] .... KAWZ
Twin Falls, ID [*FM radio station call letters*] .... KBSW
Twin Falls, ID [*FM radio station call letters*] .... KCIR
Twin Falls, ID [*AM radio station call letters*] .... KEZJ
Twin Falls, ID [*FM radio station call letters*] .... KEZJ-FM
Twin Falls, ID [*Television station call letters*] .... KIPT
Twin Falls, ID [*Television station call letters*] .... KKVI
Twin Falls, ID [*AM radio station call letters*] .... KLIX
Twin Falls, ID [*FM radio station call letters*] .... KLIX-FM
Twin Falls, ID [*Television station call letters*] .... KMVT
Twin Falls, ID [*AM radio station call letters*] .... KTFI
Twin Falls Public Library, Twin Falls, ID [*Library symbol Library of Congress*] (LCLS) .... IdTf
Twin Falls Victory [*Tracking ship*] [*NASA*] .... TFV
Twin I-Beam [*Ford Motor Co.*] [*Truck front suspension*] .... TIB
Twin Jet Nebulizer [*Pharmacology*] (DAVI) .... TJN
Twin Lake, MI [*FM radio station call letters*] .... WBLV
Twin Lakes [*California*] [*Seismograph station code, US Geological Survey*] (SEIS) .... TWL
Twin Lakes, IA [*FM radio station call letters*] .... KTLB
Twin Lens [*Photography*] (DGA) .... TL
Twin Lens Reflex [*Camera*] (MCD) .... TLR
Twin Linear Loop Exciter (IAA) .... TLLE
Twin Otter [*Airplane code*] .... Dht
Twin Peaks [*California*] [*Seismograph station code, US Geological Survey*] (SEIS) .... TWN
Twin Richfield Oils Ltd. [*Toronto Stock Exchange symbol*] .... TWR
Twin Ridge Substrate (NITA) .... TRS
Twin Rivers Correctional Center, Monroe, WA [*Library symbol Library of Congress*] (LCLS) .... WaMonT
Twin Screw [*Shipping*] (DS) .... T
Twin Screw (ADA) .... TS
Twin Screw (DS) .... TW
Twin Screw .... TWSC
Twin Sideband .... TSB
Twin Sideband (IAA) .... TSEB

Twin Sideband ... TWSB
Twin Springs [*Nevada*] [*Seismograph station code, US Geological Survey Closed*] (SEIS) ... TSV
Twin Tandem Wheel Loading [*Aviation*] ... TTWL
Twin Traction-Beam [*Ford Motor Co.*] [*Truck four-wheel drive front suspension*] ... TTB
Twin Trapezoidal Links [*Mazda*] [*Automotive engineering*] ... TTL
Twin Unit Pack [*for vehicles*] ... TUP
Twin Valley Elementary School, Twin Valley, MN [*Library symbol*] [*Library of Congress*] (LCLS) ... MnTwvE
Twin Valley High School, Twin Valley, MN [*Library symbol*] [*Library of Congress*] (LCLS) ... MnTwvH
Twin Wheel Loading [*Aviation*] ... TWL
Twin with Bath [*Tourist accommodations*] (WDAA) ... TWB
Twin-Ball Fire Fighting Unit [*Military*] (PDAA) ... TBFFU
Twin-Ball Fire Fighting Unit [*Navy*] (DNAB) ... TBFU
Twin-Cartridge Machine ... TCM
Twin-Cushion Surface Effect Vehicle (PDAA) ... TCSEV
Twin-Engined Helicopter (MCD) ... TEH
Twi-Night [*or Twilight-Night*] [*Doubleheader in baseball*] ... TWI-N
Twinless Twins Support Group (EA) ... TTSG
Twin-Row High-Density [*Trees*] (DICI) ... TRHD
Twins and Multiple Births Association [*British*] (DBA) ... TAMBA
Twins Foundation (EA) ... TF
Twin-Screw Steamer [*Nautical*] ... TSS
Twin-Wheel Stripper ... TWS
Twinwire Pulp Board (DGA) ... TPB
Twirly Birds (EA) ... TB
Twisp, WA [*FM radio station call letters*] ... KVLR
Twiss. Black Book of the Admiralty [*A publication*] (DLA) ... Bl B Adm
Twiss. Black Book of the Admiralty [*A publication*] (DLA) ... Black Bk Adm
Twiss. Law of Nations in Time of Peace [*2nd ed.*] [*1884*] [*A publication*] (DLA) ... Tw Nat P
Twiss. Law of Nations in Time of War [*2nd ed.*] [*1875*] [*A publication*] (DLA) ... Tw Nat W
Twist and Turn [*Barbie doll collector term*] ... TNT
Twist Drill and Reamer Association [*British*] (DBA) ... TD & RA
Twist Drill Gauge ... TDG
Twisted (IAA) ... TW
Twisted Bonded Pair ... TBP
Twisted Double Shielded (MCD) ... TWD
Twisted Intramolecular Charge Transfer [*Biochemistry*] ... TICT
Twisted Jute Packing and Oakum Institute [*Defunct*] (EA) ... TJPOI
Twisted Nematic [*Telecommunications*] (TEL) ... TN
Twisted Nematic Liquid [*Telecommunications*] (IAA) ... TNC
Twisted Nematic Liquid Crystal Display [*Telecommunications*] (IAA) ... TNLCD
Twisted Nematic Mode [*Telecommunications*] (IAA) ... TNM
Twisted Nemetic Field Effect [*Telecommunications*] (IAA) ... TNFE
Twisted Pair-Physical Medium Dependent [*Telecommunications*] (CDE) ... TP-PMD
Twisted Racetrack ... TRT
Twisted Shielded Pairs [*Cables*] (NASA) ... TSP
Twisted Sister Fan Club (EA) ... TSFC
Twisted Tape Boiling Water Reactor (IEEE) ... TTBWR
Twisted Telephone Radio, Shielded, Armored ... TTRSA
Twisted Wire Pair ... TWP
Twisted-Pair Cable ... TPC
Twisted-Pair Ethernet [*Intel Corp.*] ... TPE
Twisted-Pair Medium Attachment Unit (PCM) ... TP-MAU
Twisted-Pair Shielded ... TPS
Twisted-Pair, Telephone, Heat and Flame Resistant, Armored [*Wire technology*] (IAA) ... TTHFA
Twister (AAG) ... TW
Twist-Grain-Boundary [*Liquid crystal science*] ... TGB
Twisting Moment ... TM
Twitch Tension [*Neurology*] (DAVI) ... TT
Twitchell-Allen Three-Dimensional Personality Test [*Psychology*] ... TA3DPT
Two Cycle [*Mechanics*] ... TC
Two Degrees of Freedom ... TDF
Two Dimensional Elliptic, Parabolic and Eigenvalue Problems (MHDI) ... TWODEPEP
Two Eagle School, Pablo, MT [*Library symbol*] [*Library of Congress*] (LCLS) ... MtPaTS
Two Element Synthesis Telescope (ADA) ... TEST
Two Gentlemen of Verona [*Shakespearean work*] ... TGV
Two Gentlemen of Verona [*Shakesperean work*] (BARN) ... Two Gent
Two Hands ... TH
Two Harbors High School, Two Harbors, MN [*Library symbol*] [*Library of Congress*] (LCLS) ... MnThHS
Two Harbors, MN [*FM radio station call letters*] ... WRSR
Two Harbors Public Library, Two Harbors, MN [*Library symbol*] [*Library of Congress*] (LCLS) ... MnTh
Two Hills Public Library, Alberta [*Library symbol National Library of Canada*] (NLC) ... ATHI
Two Hills Public Library, Two Hills, AB, Canada [*Library symbol*] [*Library of Congress*] (LCLS) ... CaAThi
Two Hundred Contemporary Authors [*A publication*] ... TCA
Two Incomes, Kids [*Lifestyle classification*] ... TICKS
Two Incomes, No Kids [*Lifestyle classification*] ... Tink
Two Main Orbiting Spacecraft (SAA) ... TMOS
Two Mixed Layer (IAA) ... TML
[*The*] **Two Noble Kinsmen** [*Shakespearean work*] ... TNK
Two Phase Vacuum Extraction [*Engineering*] ... TPVE
Two Photon Fluorescence [*Electronics*] (OA) ... TPF
Two Photon Laser Scanning Microscope ... TPLSM
Two Pion Exchange [*Nuclear physics*] (OA) ... TPE
Two Pole (MSA) ... DP
Two Rivers, WI [*AM radio station call letters*] ... WCUB
Two Rivers, WI [*AM radio station call letters*] ... WTRW
Two Sides (WDMC) ... 2S
Two Stripper in Series Permeater [*Chemical engineering*] ... TSSP
Two Subcarrier (IAA) ... TSC
Two/Ten Foundation (EA) ... TTF
Two/Ten National Foundation [*Later, TTF*] (EA) ... TTNF
Two Terminal Series Parallel Networks ... TTSPN
Two Thousand Two Target Term Trust, Inc. [*Associated Press*] (SAG) ... 2002TT
Two Thousand Two Target Term Trust, Inc. [*NYSE symbol*] (SAG) ... TTR
Two Way Logic Circuit (PDAA) ... TWLC
Two Wheeled [*Freight*] ... TO WHD
Two-Arm Spectrometer Solenoid (MCD) ... TASSO
Two-Axis Free Gyro (AAG) ... TAFG
Two-Axis Optical Pickoff (PDAA) ... TOP
Two-Axis Pneumatic Pickup (IEEE) ... TAPP
Two-Axis Rate (SAA) ... TAR
Two-Axis Tracking ... TAT
Two-Axis Tracking Pedestal ... TATP
Two-Base Hit [*Baseball*] ... 2B
Two-Base Hit [*Baseball*] ... 2BH
Two-Body Force ... TBF
Two-Body Problem ... TBP
Two-Box [*Oceanography*] ... 2B
Two-Carrier Space-Charge-Limited Current ... TCSCLC
Two-Cavity Klystron ... TCK
Two-Channel Scan Camera (NOAA) ... TCSC
Two-Color Radiometer ... TCR
Two-Component TOKAMAK ... TCT
Two-Conductor [*Wire or cable*] ... 2/C
Two-Conductor Cables [*JETDS nomenclature*] [*Military*] (CET) ... WD
Two-Dimensional ... 2-D
Two-Dimensional Deflection System (IAA) ... TDDS
Two-Dimensional Echocardiogram [*Medicine*] (CPH) ... 2-DE
Two-Dimensional Electron System [*Physics*] ... 2DES
Two-Dimensional Equilibrium ... TDE
Two-Dimensional Finite Cylinder (IAA) ... TDC
Two-Dimensional Probabilistic Image (PDAA) ... TDPI
Two-Dimensional Transesophageal Echocardiography [*Cardiology*] (DAVI) ... 2-D TEE
Two-dimensional Transthoracic ... TTE
Two-Flow Electronic [*Automotive engineering*] ... TFE
Two-Fluid Manometer ... TFM
Two-Fraction Fast Exchange [*Biophysics*] ... TFE
Two-Gas Regenerative Lift Support System ... TGRLSS
Two-Hour Pregnancy Test [*Obstetrics*] (DAVI) ... 2HR
Two-Impinging-Stream Reactor [*Chemical engineering*] ... TIS
Two-Level Fluctuation [*Physics*] ... TLF
Two-Level System [*Physics*] ... TLS
Two-Loop Test Apparatus [*Nuclear energy*] (NRCH) ... TLTA
Two-Lung Ventilation [*Medicine*] ... TLV
Two-Phase ... 2PH
Two-Phase Flow ... TPF
Two-Phase Principle ... TPP
Two-Phase Thermosyphon [*Heat exchanger*] ... TPTS
Two-Photon Absorption (PDAA) ... TPA
Two-Photon Coherent States (MCD) ... TCS
Two-Photon Excitation [*Fluorescence spectrometry*] ... TPE
Two-Photon Laser Scanning Microscopy ... TPLSM
Two-Photon Photoemission Spectroscopy ... TPPE
Two-Point Boundary Value (PDAA) ... TPBV
Two-Point Boundary Value Equation [*Mathematics*] ... TBVE
Two-Point Boundary Value Problem ... TPBVP
Two-Position Nozzle (MCD) ... TPN
Two-Post Signal Flow Graph (PDAA) ... TPSFG
Two-Pulse Photon Echo [*Spectroscopy*] ... 2PE
Two-Region Physics Critical Experiment (NRCH) ... TRX
Two-Seater Fighter [*Air Force British*] ... TSF
Two-Seater Fighter Aircraft [*Navy*] ... 2F
Two-Speed Destroyer Sweeper [*Military*] ... TSDS
Two-Stage Command [*NASA*] (GFGA) ... TSC
Two-Stage Hydrocracker [*Chemical engineering*] ... TSHC
Two-Stage Least Squares [*Statistics*] ... TS
Two-Stage Least Squares [*Statistics*] ... TSLS
Two-Stage Liquefaction [*Chemical engineering*] ... TSL
Two-Stage Reverse Osmosis [*Chemical engineering*] ... TSRO
Two-Stage-to-Orbit [*Aerospace technology*] (PS) ... TSTO
Two-Station Training ... TST
Two-Step Antenna ... TSA
Two-Step Formal Advertising (MCD) ... TSFA
Two-Step Sealed Bidding (AAGC) ... TSSB
Two-Step,Two-Frequency ... TSTF
Two-Tone Keying ... TTK
Two-Tone Modulation ... TTM
Two-Way Air Data Link [*Tactical Air Command*] ... TWADL
Two-Way Alternate (IAA) ... TWA
Two-Way Data Messaging ... TWDM
Two-Way/Delay Dial [*Telecommunications*] (TEL) ... TWDD
Two-Way Finite Automata ... TFA
Two-Way/Immediate Dial [*Telecommunications*] (TEL) ... TWID
Two-Way Mirror ... TWM
Two-Way Radio Link (LAIN) ... TWRL
Two-Way Simultaneous (IAA) ... TWS

Two-Way Time [*Seismology*] .... TWT
Two-Way Travel Time [*Seismology*] .... TWTT
Two-Way/Wink Start [*Telecommunications*] (TEL) .... TWWS
Two-Way-Traffic-in-Ideas Conference [*of Labor Party*] [*British*] .... TWT
Two-Wheel Drive [*Automotive engineering*] 2WD
Two-Wheel Steering [*Automotive engineering*] 2WS
Two-Wire Direct Interface (MHDB) .... TDI
Two-Wire Vertical [*Grape culture*] .... TWV
Two-Year[*-Old*] **Course** [*Horse racing*] .... TYC
Two-Year-Old [*Horse racing*] (ROG) .... TYO
TWX Interlibrary Loan Network [*Library network*] .... TWXIL
Twyford Plant Laboratories Ltd. [*British*] (IRUK) .... TPL
Tychon's Assembler (MCD) .... TAS
Tyco International [*NYSE symbol*] (SPSG) .... TYC
Tyco International [*Associated Press*] (SAG) .... TycoInt
Tyco Toys [*NYSE symbol*] (TTSB) .... TTI
Tyco Toys [*Associated Press*] (SAG) .... TycoT
Tyco Toys, Inc. [*NYSE symbol*] (SPSG) .... TTI
Tyco Toys, Inc. [*Associated Press*] (SAG) .... TycoToy
Tye Explorations, Inc. [*Vancouver Stock Exchange symbol*] .... TYE
Tye, TX [*FM radio station call letters*] .... KBCY
Tyee [*Alaska*] [*Airport symbol*] (AD) .... TEE
Tyee Airways Ltd. [*Canada ICAO designator*] (FAAC) .... TYE
Tygas Resources Corp. [*Vancouver Stock Exchange symbol*] .... TYA
Tying Goals [*Sports*] .... TG
Tylan General [*NASDAQ symbol*] (TTSB) .... TYGN
Tylan General, Inc. [*NASDAQ symbol*] (SAG) .... TYGN
Tylan General, Inc. [*Associated Press*] (SAG) .... TylanG
Tylenol [*McNeil Consumer Products Co.*] (DAVI) .... TYCO
Tylenol [*McNeil Consumer Products Co.*] (DAVI) .... tyl
Tylenol and Codeine [*Pharmacy*] .... TYCO
Tyler [*Diocesan abbreviation*] [*Texas*] (TOCD) .... TYL
Tyler [*Texas*] [*Airport symbol*] (OAG) .... TYR
Tyler Arboretum, Lima, PA [*Library symbol Library of Congress*] (LCLS) .... PLimT
Tyler Carnegie Public Library, Tyler, TX [*Library symbol Library of Congress*] (LCLS) .... TxTy
Tyler Corp. [*NYSE symbol*] (SPSG) .... TYL
Tyler Corp. [*Associated Press*] (SAG) .... Tyler
Tyler Junior College [*Texas*] .... TJC
Tyler on Boundaries, Fences, Etc. [*A publication*] (DLA) .... Tyl Boun
Tyler on Ejectment and Adverse Enjoyment [*A publication*] (DLA) .... Tyl Eject
Tyler on Ejectment and Adverse Enjoyment [*A publication*] (DLA) .... Tyler Ej
Tyler on Fixtures [*A publication*] (DLA) .... Tyl Fix
Tyler on Infancy and Coverture [*A publication*] (DLA) .... Tyl Inf
Tyler on Partnership [*A publication*] (DLA) .... Tyl Part
Tyler on Usury, Pawns, and Loans [*A publication*] (DLA) .... Tyl Us
Tyler/Pounds Field [*Texas*] [*ICAO location identifier*] (ICLI) .... KTYR
Tyler Public Library, Tyler, MN [*Library symbol*] [*Library of Congress*] (LCLS) .... MnTy
Tyler Resources, Inc. [*Toronto Stock Exchange symbol*] .... TYS
Tyler, TX [*FM radio station call letters*] .... KDOK
Tyler, TX [*AM radio station call letters*] .... KGLD
Tyler, TX [*FM radio station call letters*] .... KGLY
Tyler, TX [*FM radio station call letters*] .... KKUS
Tyler, TX [*Television station call letters*] .... KLTV
Tyler, TX [*FM radio station call letters*] .... KNUE
Tyler, TX [*AM radio station call letters*] .... KTBB
Tyler, TX [*FM radio station call letters*] .... KTYL
Tyler, TX [*FM radio station call letters*] .... KVNE
Tyler, TX [*AM radio station call letters*] .... KYZS
Tyler, TX [*AM radio station call letters*] .... KZEY
Tyler Vocational Card Sort [*Guidance*] .... TVCS
Tylerdale Connecting [*AAR code*] .... TYC
Tyler's American Ecclesiastical Law [*A publication*] (DLA) .... Tyl Eccl L
Tyler's Edition of Mitford's Equity Pleading [*A publication*] (DLA) .... Mitf & Ty Eq Pl
Tyler's Edition of Stephen on Principles of Pleading [*A publication*] (DLA) .... Tyler Steph Pl
Tyler's Edition of Stephen on the Principles of Pleading [*A publication*] (DLA) .... Tyl St Pl
Tyler's Vermont Reports [*1800-03*] [*A publication*] (DLA) .... Tyler
Tyler's Vermont Supreme Court Reports [*1800-03*] [*A publication*] (DLA) .... Tyl
Tylertown, MS [*AM radio station call letters*] .... WTYL
Tylertown, MS [*FM radio station call letters*] .... WTYL-FM
Tyloma [*Also called a callus*] [*Orthopedics*] (DAVI) .... Tyl
Tylox Resources Corp. [*Vancouver Stock Exchange symbol*] .... TYX
Tymnet DTS, Inc. [*San Jose, CA*] [*Telecommunications*] (TSSD) .... TDI
Tymnet Telegram (NITA) .... TYME-GRAM
Tympanic Membrane [*Anatomy*] .... TM
Tympanic Membrane [*Anatomy*] (CPH) .... Tymp Mem
Tympanic Membrane [*Otorhinolaryngology*] (DAVI) .... tymp memb
Tympanicity [*Referring to auscultation of the chest*] [*Medicine*] (DAVI) .... Tymp
Tympanium (VRA) .... tymp
Tympanostomy [*Otorhinolaryngology*] (DAVI) .... tymp
Tympanostomy with Tube Placement [*Otorhinolaryngology*] (DAVI) .... T & T
Tympanostomy with Tube Placement [*Otorhinolaryngology*] (DAVI) .... TcT
Tympany .... tymp
Tyndale House Bulletin [*Cambridge*] [*A publication*] (BJA) .... TyndHB
Tyndale New Testament Commentaries [*A publication*] (BJA) .... Ty
Tyndale New Testament Commentary [*A publication*] (BJA) .... TNTC
Tyndale Paper [*A publication*] (APTA) .... TP
Tyndall Air Force Base [*Florida*] .... TAFB
Tyne and Tees [*50th Northumbrian Division*] [*British military*] (DMA) .... TT
Tyne and Wear Development Corp. [*British*] (ECON) .... TWDC
Tyne Division [*British military*] (DMA) .... TD
Tyne Tees Television [*British*] (DI) .... TTT
Tyneside Scottish [*British military*] (DMA) .... TS
Tyng's Reports [*2-17 Massachusetts*] [*A publication*] (DLA) .... Tyng
Tyoevaeen ja Pienviljelijaein Sosialidemokraattinen Liitto [*Social Democratic League of Workers and Smallholders*] [*Finland Political party*] (PPE) .... TPSL
Tyonek, AK [*Location identifier FAA*] (FAAL) .... TYE
Type .... T
Type (NASA) .... TP
Type .... TY
Type A Behavior Pattern [*Medicine*] (DMAA) .... TABP
Type Address Code .... TAC
Type Americain [*World War I troop train in France made according to US specifications*] .... TA
Type and Crossmatch [*Clinical chemistry*] .... T & X
Type and Crossmatch [*of blood*] .... TC
Type and Learn Concept [*Minolta Corp. office system*] .... TLC
Type and Screen .... T & S
Type Approval .... TA
Type [*Command*] **Automated Data System** [*Navy*] .... TADS
Type Availability .... TA
Type Certificate .... TC
Type Classification .... TC
Type Classification [*Military*] (AABC) .... TCLAS
Type Classification - Contingency .... TC-CON
Type Classification Date [*Army*] .... TCD
Type Classification, Limited Procurement .... TCLP
Type Classification - Limited Production .... TC-LP
Type Classification - Limited Production Urgent .... TC-LPU
Type Classification - Obsolete (MCD) .... TCOBS
Type Classification - Standard (MCD) .... TC STD
Type Classified - Limited Producation Test .... TC-LPT
Type Commander .... TYCOM
Type Commander Amphibious Training (DOMA) .... TCAT
Type Commander Core Training (DOMA) .... TCCT
Type Commands, Atlantic (DNAB) .... TYCOMSLANT
Type Commands, Pacific (DNAB) .... TYCOMSPAC
Type Designators (MSA) .... TYDE
Type Designer [*MARC relator code*] [*Library of Congress*] (LCCP) .... tyd
Type Directors Club (EA) .... TDC
Type Equipment (MCD) .... TE
Type Equipment Code (MCD) .... TEC
Type Finish Specification (MCD) .... TFS
Type Genus .... TG
Type Issue/Defuel Codes (AAGC) .... TID
Type Item [*Military*] .... TI
Type Length and Value (TNIG) .... TLV
Type Maintenance Code (MCD) .... TMC
Type Metal [*Printing*] (DGA) .... TM
Type, Model, and Series .... TMS
Type of Activity Code [*Military*] .... TAC
Type of Address (TNIG) .... TOA
Type of Agent .... TOA
Type of Blast .... TOB
Type of Changed Code [*Army*] .... TCC
Type of Flight (SAA) .... TF
Type of Foundation [*IRS*] .... TF
Type of Leaf Serration [*Botany*] .... TSERR
Type of Legal Organization .... TOLO
Type of Organization Code [*IRS*] .... TO
Type of Professional Activity .... TPA
Type of Service (TNIG) .... TOS
Type of Shift (IAA) .... TS
Type of Shipment .... TOS
Type of Transport [*Shipping*] (DS) .... TOT
Type Rating Examiner [*Aviation*] (DA) .... TRE
Type Requisition Code [*Military*] .... TRC
Type, Series, and Model (MCD) .... TSM
Type Specification .... TS
Type Training [*Navy*] (NVT) .... TYT
Type Training in Port [*Navy*] (NVT) .... TYTIPT
Type Unique [*French standard troop train, World War I*] .... TU
Type Unit Characteristics .... TUCHA
Type Unit Code (CINC) .... TUC
Type-1 Spinocerebellar Ataxia [*Medicine*] (ECON) SCA-1
Type-Approval Model .... TAM
Type-Approval Test .... TAT
Type-Approval Test Review Committee .... TATRC
Typed [*Manuscript descriptions*] .... T
Typed (BJA) .... Typ
Typed Letter Signed .... TLS
Typefounding (ADA) .... TFG
Type-Plate .... TYPL
Types of Assistance Code [*Army*] .... TAC
Typescript .... TS
Typescripts [*Typography*] (WDAA) .... TSS
Typesetting .... TYPSG
Typesetting (MSA) .... TYPSTG
Typesetting Lead (MSA) .... TSL
Typesetting Run Off (DGA) .... TROFF
Typesetting System for Scientific Document [*Computer science*] (PDAA) .... TSSD
Type-Specific [*Antibodies*] [*Microbiology*] (DAVI) .... TS
Type-Specific Antibody [*Immunology*] .... TSA
Type-Specific M (Protein) [*Immunology*] .... TSM
Type-Token Ratio [*Education of the hearing-impaired*] .... TTR
Typewriter (AAG) .... TW

Typewriter (ADA) .... TYPW
Typewriter .... TYPWRT
Typewriter .... TYPWRTR
Typewriter .... TYPWRTR
Typewriter Adapter (MHDB) .... TWA
Typewriter Buffer .... TWB
Typewriter Keyboard .... TWK
Typewriter Manufacturers Export Association [Defunct] .... TMEA
Typewriter Output .... TYPOUT
Typewriter Trade and Allied Workers' Association [A union] [British] .... TTAWA
Typewriter-Oriented Documentation-Aid System .... TODAS
Typhlosole [Biology] .... T
Typhoid .... T
Typhoid Dysentery (AAMN) .... TD
Typhoid Fever (DSUE) .... TY
Typhoid H [Infectious diseases] (DAVI) .... TYP-H
Typhoid, Paratyphoid A and B [Vaccine] .... TAB
Typhoid, Paratyphoid A, and Paratyphoid B, and Tetanus Toxoid
   Combined [A vaccine] (DAVI) .... TABT
Typhoid, Paratyphoid A, and Paratyphoid B, Tetanus Toxoid, and Diptheria
   Toxoid Combined [A vaccine] (DAVI) .... TABTD
Typhoid-Paratyphoid [Medicine] .... TPT
Typhoid-Paratyphoid A, B and C [Vaccine] [Medicine] (BABM) ..... TABC
Typhoon .... TYPH
Typhoon Operation Experiment (EERA) .... TOPEX
Typhoon Operational Experiment [Meteorology] .... TOPEX
Typical (AAG) .... TYP
Typical Address Access (NITA) .... TAA
Typical Airland Resupply Profile (MCD) .... TARP
Typical Army Ball-Up [Slang for a military muddle] .... TABU
Typical Coastal Command Foul Up [RAF slang] [World War II] ..... TCCFU
Typical Digital Automatic Computer .... TYDAC
Typical Egg Mass .... TEM
Typical Ocean Model [Oceanography] .... TOM
Typical System Acquisition Flow .... TSAF
Typing Test for Business .... TTB
Typographed [Philately] .... Typo
Typographer [MARC relator code] [Library of Congress] (LCCP) ...... tyg
Typographer [or Typography] .... TYPOG
Typographers Association of New York (EA) .... TANY
Typographers International Association (EA) .... TIA
Typographic Adviser (DGA) .... TA
Typographic Communications Association (EA) .... TCA
Typographic Council for Spelling Reform (EA) .... TCSR
Typographic Draftsman [Navy] .... TD
Typographic Support System (MCD) .... TSS
Typographical .... TYPO
Typographical Error (AAG) .... TYPER
Typographical Error (NTCM) .... TYPO
Typography [or Typographer] (AAG) .... TYP
Typography (VRA) .... typogr
Typtone Soy Broth [Cell growth medium] (DAVI) .... TSB
Typus Conservandus [Conserved Type] [Latin] .... typ cons
Tyranni Triginta [of Scriptores Historiae Augustae] [Classical studies]
   (OCD) .... Tyr Trig
Tyrannosaurus Rex [A dinosaur] .... Trex
Tyrex Oil [NASDAQ symbol] (TTSB) .... TYRX
Tyrex Oil Co. [Associated Press] (SAG) .... Tyrex
Tyrex Oil Co. [NASDAQ symbol] (NQ) .... TYRX
Tyrolean [or Tirolean] [Reference to a state in western Austria] [Reference to
   an alpine region that is divided between Austria and Italy] (BARN) .... Tyrol

Tyrolean Airways [Austria ICAO designator] (ICDA) .... TQ
Tyrolean Airways [Austria ICAO designator] (FAAC) .... TYR
Tyrolean Airways [ICAO designator] (AD) .... VO
Tyrolean Jet Service [Austria ICAO designator] (FAAC) .... TYJ
Tyrone [County in Ireland] (ROG) .... TYR
Tyrone County [Ireland] (BARN) .... Tyr
Tyrone Energy Park (NRCH) .... TEP
Tyrone, PA [Location identifier FAA] (FAAL) .... TON
Tyrone, PA [FM radio station call letters] .... WGMR
Tyrone, PA [AM radio station call letters] .... WTRN
Tyrosine [An amino acid] .... tyr
Tyrosine [Also, Y] [An amino acid] .... Tyr
Tyrosine [One-letter symbol; see Tyr] .... Y
Tyrosine Activation Motif [Biochemistry] .... TAM
Tyrosine Aminotransferase [An enzyme] .... TAT
Tyrosine Aminotransferase Regulator .... TATr
Tyrosine Decarboxylase [An enzyme] .... TDC
Tyrosine Ethyl Ester [Organic chemistry] (MAE) .... TEE
Tyrosine Hydroxylase [An enzyme] .... TH
Tyrosine Hydroxylase [An enzyme] .... TOH
Tyrosine Hydroxylase-Immunoreactivity [Physiology] .... TH-IR
Tyrosine Kinase Domain [Genetics] .... TK
Tyrosine Oxidase [An enzyme] .... TO
Tyrosine-D-Arginine [Biochemistry] .... TDA
Tyrosine-Rich Amelogenin Polypeptide [Biochemistry of dental enamel] ...... TRAP
Tyrosyl-tRNA [Transfer Ribonucleic Acid] Synthetase .... TyrRS
Tyrrell County Public Library, Columbia, NC [Library symbol Library of
   Congress] (LCLS) .... NcCola
Tyrrell Museum of Palaeontology, Drumheller, Alberta [Library symbol
   National Library of Canada] (NLC) .... ADTMP
Tyrrell Public Library, Beaumont, TX [Library symbol Library of Congress]
   (LCLS) .... TxBea
Tyrwhitt and Granger's English Exchequer Reports [1835-36]
   [A publication] (DLA) .... T & G
Tyrwhitt and Granger's English Exchequer Reports [1830-35]
   [A publication] (DLA) .... Tyr
Tyrwhitt and Granger's English Exchequer Reports [1830-35]
   [A publication] (DLA) .... Tyr & Gr
Tyrwhitt and Granger's English Exchequer Reports [1830-35]
   [A publication] (DLA) .... Tyrw
Tyrwhitt and Granger's English Exchequer Reports [1835-36]
   [A publication] (DLA) .... Tyrw & G
Tyrwhitt and Granger's English Exchequer Reports [1835-36]
   [A publication] (DLA) .... Tyrw & G (Eng)
Tyseley [British depot code] .... TYS
Tyson Foods CI'A' [NASDAQ symbol] (TTSB) .... TYSNA
Tyson Foods, Inc. [NASDAQ symbol] (NQ) .... TYSN
Tyson Foods, Inc. [Associated Press] (SAG) .... Tyson
Tyson Valley [Missouri] [Seismograph station code, US Geological Survey]
   (SEIS) .... TYS
Tysons Financial [NASDAQ symbol] (TTSB) .... TYFC
Tytler on Military Law and Courts-Martial [3rd ed.] [1812] [A publication]
   (DLA) .... Tyt Mil L
Tytler on Military Law and Courts-Martial [A publication] (DLA) .... Tytler Mil Law
Tyumen Airlines [Russian Federation] [ICAO designator] (FAAC) ..... TYM
Tyumen Commodity Exchange [Russian Federation] (EY) .... TCE
Tyuratam [Satellite launch complex] [Former USSR] .... TYU
Tzaneen [South Africa] [ICAO location identifier] (ICLI) .... FATZ
Tzaneen [South Africa] [Airport symbol] (OAG) .... LTA
Tzivos Hashem (EA) .... TH

U
By Meaning

U Interface Circuit (NITA) .... UIC
U. S. Geological Survey .... USGS
U S WEST Communic Grp [*NYSE symbol*] (TTSB) .... USW
Ua Huka [*French Polynesia*] [*ICAO location identifier*] (ICLI) .... NTMU
Ua Huka [*Marquesas Islands*] [*Airport symbol*] (OAG) .... UAH
Ua Pou [*French Polynesia*] [*ICAO location identifier*] (ICLI) .... NTMP
Ua Pou [*Marquesas Islands*] [*Airport symbol*] (OAG) .... UAP
Uafhaengige Parti [*Independent Party*] [*Denmark Political party*] (PPE) .... U
UAITC/CIT/Audio Visual Services, Anchorage, AK [*Library symbol Library of
 Congress*] (LCLS) .... AkAAVS
UAL Corp. [*NYSE symbol*] (SPSG) .... UAL
UAL Corp. 12.25% Dep'B'Pfd [*NYSE symbol*] (TTSB) .... UALPrB
UAP, Inc. [*Toronto Stock Exchange symbol*] .... UAP
UARCO, Inc. [*Formerly, United Autographic Register Co.*] .... UARCO
Uas-Four [*British ICAO designator*] (FAAC) .... UAS
Uas-One [*British ICAO designator*] (FAAC) .... UAA
Uas-Three [*British ICAO designator*] (FAAC) .... UAJ
Uas-Two [*British ICAO designator*] (FAAC) .... UAG
Uaupes [*Brazil*] [*Airport symbol*] (AD) .... UUP
Ubaldus [*Authority cited in pre-1607 legal work*] (DSA) .... Ubal
Ubatuba [*Brazil*] [*Airport symbol Obsolete*] (OAG) .... UBT
Ube [*Japan*] [*Airport symbol*] (OAG) .... UBJ
Uberaba [*Brazil ICAO location identifier*] (ICLI) .... SBUR
Uberaba [*Brazil*] [*Airport symbol*] (OAG) .... UBA
Uberlandia [*Brazil ICAO location identifier*] (ICLI) .... SBUL
Uberlandia [*Brazil*] [*Airport symbol*] (OAG) .... UDI
Ubertus de Bobio [*Flourished, 1214-37*] [*Authority cited in pre-1607 legal
 work*] (DSA) .... Ub
Ubertus de Bobio [*Flourished, 1214-37*] (DSA) .... Ub Bo
Ubertus de Bobio [*Flourished, 1214-37*] [*Authority cited in pre-1607 legal
 work*] (DSA) .... Ub de Bo
Ubi Supra [*In the Place Mentioned Above*] [*Latin*] .... US
Ubichromanol-9 (DAVI) .... Q₉
Ubichromenol-9 (DAVI) .... Q₉
Ubihydroquinone [*Ubiquinol*] [*Laboratory science*] (DAVI) .... Q-H₂
Ubiquinone [*Coenzyme Q*] [*Also, CoQ, Q, UQ*] [*Biochemistry*] ..... U
Ubiquinone [*Also, CoQ, Q, U*] [*Biochemistry*] .... UQ
Ubiquitin-Conjugating [*Protein*] .... UBC
Ubiquitous Crystallization Process [*Photovoltaic energy systems*] .... UCP
Ubiquitous Immunopoietic Polypeptide [*Immunochemistry*] .... UBIP
Ubombo [*Swaziland*] [*ICAO location identifier*] (ICLI) .... FDUB
Ubon Ratchathani [*Thailand*] [*Airport symbol*] (OAG) .... UBP
Ubon Ratchathani [*Thailand*] [*ICAO location identifier*] (ICLI) ...... VTUU
Ubon Ratchathani/Loeng Nok Tha [*Thailand*] [*ICAO location identifier*]
 (ICLI) .... VTUT
Ubrub [*Indonesia*] [*ICAO location identifier*] (ICLI) .... WAJU
Ubundu [*Zaire*] [*ICAO location identifier*] (ICLI) .... FZIF
UC Television Network Corp. [*Associated Press*] (SAG) .... UC
UC Television Network Corp. [*Associated Press*] (SAG) .... UC TVNet
UC Television Network Corp. [*NASDAQ symbol*] (SAG) .... UCTN
UCar International [*Associated Press*] (SAG) .... UCar
UCar International [*NYSE symbol*] (SAG) .... UCR
UCB [*Belgium*] [*Research code symbol*] .... UCB
UCB Chemie [*Germany*] [*Research code symbol*] .... UCB
Uccle [*Belgium*] [*Seismograph station code, US Geological Survey*] (SEIS) ...... UCC
Uchiza [*Peru*] [*ICAO location identifier*] (ICLI) .... SPIZ
UCI Medical Affiliates [*NASDAQ symbol*] (TTSB) .... UCIA
UCI Medical Affiliates, Inc. [*NASDAQ symbol*] (SAG) .... UCIA
UCI Medical Affiliates, Inc. [*Associated Press*] (SAG) ...... UCIMed
UCLA [*University of California, Los Angeles*]-Alaska Law Review
 [*A publication*] (DLA) .... UCLA-Alaska L Rev
UCLA Business Forecasting Project [*Information service or system*] (IID) ...... BFP
UCLA [*University of California, Los Angeles*] Intramural Law Review
 [*A publication*] (DLA) .... UCLA Intra L Rev
UCLA [*University of California, Los Angeles*] Journal of Environmental Law
 and Policy [*A publication*] (DLA) .... UCLA J Envt'l L & Pol'y
UCLA [*University of California at Los Angeles*] Pacific Basin Law Journal
 [*A publication*] (DLA) .... UCLA Pac Basin LJ
Ud Dictum [*As directed*] [*Pharmacy*] (DAVI) .... UD
Udaipur [*India*] [*Airport symbol*] (OAG) .... UDR
Udaipur [*India*] [*ICAO location identifier*] (ICLI) .... VIUD
Udaipur Solar Observatory [*India*] .... USO
Udal's Fiji Law Reports [*A publication*] (DLA) .... Udal
UDAM [*Universal Digital Avionics Module*] Microprocessor Software Support
 System (MCD) .... UMSSS

Uddeholm [*Sweden*] [*Seismograph station code, US Geological Survey*]
 (SEIS) .... UDD
Udine [*Italy*] [*Seismograph station code, US Geological Survey*] (SEIS) .... UDI
Udine/Campoformido [*Italy ICAO location identifier*] (ICLI) .... LIPD
Udmurt Commodity Universal Exchange [*Russian Federation*] (EY) .... UCUE
Udon Thani [*Thailand*] [*Airport symbol*] (OAG) .... UTH
Udon Thani [*Thailand*] [*ICAO location identifier*] (ICLI) .... VTUD
Udruzena Metalna Industrija [*Belgrade, Yugoslavia*] .... UMI
Uebereinkommen [*Agreement*] [*German*] (ILCA) .... Ueb
Ueberlieferungsgeschichte des Pentateuch (M. Noth) [*A publication*]
 (BJA) .... UP (Noth)
Ueberlieferungsgeschichtliche Studien (M. Noth) [*A publication*]
 (BJA) .... US (Noth)
Uebersetzen [*Translate*] [*German*] .... u
Uelzen [*Germany ICAO location identifier*] (ICLI) .... EDVU
Uetersen [*Germany ICAO location identifier*] (ICLI) .... EDHE
UF-6 Chemical Feed Station [*Nuclear energy*] (NRCH) .... UFCS
UF-6 Recovery Room [*Nuclear energy*] (NRCH) .... UFR
Ufficiale [*Official, Officer*] (EY) .... UFF
Ufficio Informazioni Militare [*Office of Military Information*] [*Italian*] ...... UIM
UFO [*Unidentified Flying Object*] Catalog [*Center for Unidentified Flying Object
 Studies*] .... UFOCAT
UFO Investigators Network [*British*] .... UFOIN
UFP Technologies [*Commercial firm Associated Press*] (SAG) .... UFP Tch
UFP Technologies [*Commercial firm NASDAQ symbol*] (SAG) .... UFPT
UFS, Inc. [*ICAO designator*] (FAAC) .... UFS
Ugana Revenue Authority .... URA
Uganda [*International vehicle registration*] (ODBW) .... EAU
Uganda [*MARC geographic area code Library of Congress*] (LCCP) .... f-ug--
Uganda [*ANSI two-letter standard code*] (CNC) .... UG
Uganda [*MARC country of publication code Library of Congress*] (LCCP) .... ug
Uganda [*ANSI three-letter standard code*] (CNC) .... UGA
Uganda (VRA) .... UGAN
Uganda (VRA) .... Ugan
Uganda Air Force (PDAA) .... UAF
Uganda Airlines [*ICAO designator*] (AD) .... QU
Uganda Airlines Corp. [*ICAO designator*] (FAAC) .... UGA
Uganda Freedom Movement (PD) .... UFM
Uganda Investment Authority .... UIA
Uganda Investment Authority .... UIA
Uganda Journal [*A publication*] .... UgJ
Uganda Law Focus [*A publication*] (DLA) .... Ug LF
Uganda Law Focus [*A publication*] (DLA) .... Uganda LF
Uganda Law Reports [*Africa*] [*A publication*] (DLA) .... Ug LR
Uganda Law Reports [*A publication*] (DLA) .... ULR
Uganda Legal Focus [*A publication*] (DLA) .... Uganda Leg Focus
Uganda National Liberation Army [*Political party*] (AF) .... UNLA
Uganda National Rescue Front (PD) .... UNRF
Uganda Patriotic Movement (PD) .... UPM
Uganda People's Congress [*Suspended*] .... UPC
Uganda Popular Front [*Political party*] (PD) .... UPF
Uganda Protectorate Law Reports [*Africa*] [*A publication*] (DLA) .... Ug Pr LR
Uganda Protectorate Law Reports [*1904-51*] [*A publication*] (DLA) .... Uganda LR
Uganda Protectorate Law Reports [*1904-51*] [*A publication*] (DLA) .... ULR
Uganda Protectorate Law Reports [*1904-51*] [*A publication*] (DLA) .... UPLR
Uganda Public Employees' Union .... UPEU
Uganda Railways Corp. (DCTA) .... URC
Uganda Rifles [*British military*] (DMA) .... UR
Uganda Trades' Union Congress .... UTUC
Uganda Vernacular, Primary and Junior Secondary Teachers' Union ...... UVPJU
Ugandan National Liberation Front [*Political party*] (PD) ...... UNLF
Uganik [*Alaska*] [*Airport symbol*] (OAG) .... UGI
Ugaritic [*MARC language code Library of Congress*] (LCCP) .... uga
Ugaritic Handbook [*C. H. Gordon*] [*A publication*] (BJA) ...... UH
Ugaritic Literature [*C. H. Gordon*] [*A publication*] (BJA) ...... UL
Ugaritic Manual [*A publication*] (BJA) .... UgM
Ugaritic Manual [*C. H. Gordon*] [*A publication*] (BJA) ...... UM
Ugaritic Textbook [*A publication*] (BJA) .... UgT
Ugaritic-Hebrew Philology [*Rome*] [*M. Dahood*] [*A publication*] (BJA) ...... UHP
Ugashik [*Alaska*] [*Airport symbol*] (OAG) .... UGA
Ugashik, AK [*Location identifier FAA*] (FAAL) .... UGA
Uggscombe [*England*] .... UGGSC
UGI Corp. [*Formerly, United Gas Improvement Co.*] [*NYSE symbol*] (SPSG) .... UGI
Ugland Air AS [*Norway ICAO designator*] (FAAC) .... UGG
Uglegorsk [*Former USSR Seismograph station code, US Geological Survey*]
 (SEIS) .... UGL

Uglies Unlimited (EA) ... UU
Ugly Duckling Corp. [*NASDAQ symbol*] (SAG) ... UGLY
Ugly Duckling Corp. [*Associated Press*] (SAG) ... UglyDck
Ugly Man on Campus [*Contest*] ... UMOC
Ugly Sky [*Navigation*] ... U
Ugly Threatening Weather [*Meteorology*] ... U
Ugric [*Finno-Ugric Linguistic Family*] (BARN) ... Ug
U-Groove Power Metal-Oxide Semiconductor Field Effect Transistor (IAA) ... UMOST
U-Grooved Metal Oxide Semiconductors (MCD) ... UMOS
Ugurusu [*Japan*] [*Seismograph station code, US Geological Survey*] (SEIS) ... URS
Ugutio [*Huguccio*] [*Deceased, 1210*] [*Authority cited in pre-1607 legal work*] (DSA) ... U
Ugutio [*Huguccio*] [*Deceased, 1210*] [*Authority cited in pre-1607 legal work*] (DSA) ... Ug
Uherske Hradiste [*Former Czechoslovakia*] [*Airport symbol Obsolete*] (OAG) ... UHE
UHF [*Ultrahigh Frequency*] **Doppler System** ... UDOP
Uhr [*Clock*] [*German*] ... U
Uhrichsville, OH [*AM radio station call letters*] ... WBTC
Uhrichsville, OH [*FM radio station call letters*] ... WTUZ
Uhrzuender [*Clockwork fuze*] [*German military - World War II*] ... UZ
UICI [*Associated Press*] (SAG) ... UICI
Uige [*Angola*] [*Airport symbol Obsolete*] (OAG) ... UGO
Uige/Vige [*Angola*] [*ICAO location identifier*] (ICLI) ... FNUG
Uigur [*MARC language code Library of Congress*] (LCCP) ... uig
Uijeongbu [*South Korea ICAO location identifier*] (ICLI) ... RKSB
Uiju [*North Korea ICAO location identifier*] (ICLI) ... ZKUJ
Uinta Basin Array [*Utah*] [*Seismograph station code, US Geological Survey Closed*] (SEIS) ... UBO
Uinta Basin Observatory ... UBO
Uinta Basin Seismological Observatory ... UBSO
Uis [*Namibia*] [*ICAO location identifier*] (ICLI) ... FAUS
Uitenhage [*South Africa*] [*ICAO location identifier*] (ICLI) ... FAUH
Uitenhage Volunteer Rifles [*British military*] (DMA) ... UVR
Uitgave [*Edition*] [*Netherlands*] (ILCA) ... Uitg
UJB Financial Corp. [*Formerly, United Jersey Banks*] [*NYSE symbol*] (SPSG) ... UJB
UJB Financial Corp. [*Formerly, United Jersey Banks*] [*Associated Press*] (SAG) ... UJB Fn
Ujjain [*India*] [*Geomagnetic observatory code*] ... UJJ
Ujung Pandang [*Indonesia*] [*Airport symbol*] (OAG) ... UPG
Ujung Pandang [*Indonesia*] [*ICAO location identifier*] (ICLI) ... WAAZ
Ujung Pandang/Hasanuddin [*Indonesia*] [*ICAO location identifier*] (ICLI) ... WAAA
UK Catalogue Training (NITA) ... UKCTRAIN
UK Centre for Communication Standards in the Manufacturing and Process Industries (ACII) ... ComCentre
UK Home Office [*British ICAO designator*] (FAAC) ... UKP
UK Library Database System (NITA) ... UKLDS
UK [*British Library*] **Machine Readable Catalogue** [*Bibliographic database*] ... UK MARC
UK MARC [*United Kingdom Machine-Readable Cataloging*] [*Source file*] [*UTLAS symbol*] ... UKM
UK Retrospective (NITA) ... UKR
UK [*United Kingdom*] **Trade Marks** [*The Patent Office*] [*British Information service or system*] (IID) ... UKTM
Uke Resources [*Vancouver Stock Exchange symbol*] ... UKE
Ukelele (DSUE) ... UKE
Ukhta Airenterprise [*Former USSR*] [*FAA designator*] (FAAC) ... UKH
Ukiah [*California*] [*Airport symbol*] (AD) ... UKI
Ukiah [*California*] [*Seismograph station code, US Geological Survey*] (SEIS) ... UKI
Ukiah, CA [*FM radio station call letters*] ... KPRA
Ukiah, CA [*FM radio station call letters*] ... KQPM
Ukiah, CA [*AM radio station call letters*] ... KUKI
Ukiah, CA [*FM radio station call letters*] ... KUKI-FM
Ukiah, CA [*FM radio station call letters*] ... KWNE
Ukiah, CA [*Location identifier FAA*] (FAAL) ... UKI
Ukiah Public Library, Ukiah, CA [*Library symbol Library of Congress*] (LCLS) ... CUk
Ukiah Public Library, Ukiah, OR [*Library symbol*] [*Library of Congress*] (LCLS) ... OrUk
Ukiyo-E Society of America (EA) ... USA
Ukraine ... UKR
Ukraine [*International civil aircraft marking*] (ODBW) ... UR
Ukraine Air Service [*FAA designator*] (FAAC) ... ASG
Ukraine Airalliance [*FAA designator*] (FAAC) ... UKL
Ukraine Airtrack [*FAA designator*] (FAAC) ... UAP
Ukraine-Aviatrans [*FAA designator*] (FAAC) ... UKU
Ukrainian [*MARC language code Library of Congress*] (LCCP) ... ukr
Ukrainian Academy of Arts and Science, Winnipeg, Manitoba [*Library symbol National Library of Canada*] (NLC) ... MWUA
Ukrainian Academy of Arts and Sciences in the United States, New York, NY [*Library symbol Library of Congress*] (LCLS) ... NNUVAN
Ukrainian Academy of Arts and Sciences in the US (EA) ... UAAS
Ukrainian Academy of Arts and Sciences of Canada ... UVAN
Ukrainian Academy of Medical Sciences (EA) ... UAMS
Ukrainian American League (EA) ... UAL
Ukrainian American Veterans (EA) ... UAV
Ukrainian Artists Association in USA (EA) ... UAAUSA
Ukrainian Canadian Archives and Museum, Edmonton, Alberta [*Library symbol National Library of Canada*] (BIB) ... AEUCA
Ukrainian Canadian Servicemen's Association ... UCSA
Ukrainian Catholic Soyuz of Brotherhoods and Sisterhoods (EA) ... UCSBS
Ukrainian Catholic Students of the United States [*Defunct*] (EA) ... UCSUS
Ukrainian Center for Social Research (EA) ... UCSR
Ukrainian Congress Committee of America (EA) ... UCCA
Ukrainian Cultural and Educational Centre, Winnipeg, Manitoba [*Library symbol National Library of Canada*] (NLC) ... MWUCE
Ukrainian Engineers' Society of America (EA) ... UESA
Ukrainian Fraternal Association (EA) ... UFA
Ukrainian Free Society of America (EA) ... UFSA
Ukrainian Gold Cross (EA) ... UGC
Ukrainian Gold Cross (EA) ... UKC
Ukrainian Institute of America (EA) ... UIA
Ukrainian Library Association of America (EA) ... ULAA
Ukrainian Life Cooperative Association [*Defunct*] (EA) ... ULCA
Ukrainian Medical Association of North America (EA) ... UMANA
Ukrainian Museum of Canada [*UTLAS symbol*] ... UMC
Ukrainian Museum of Canada, Saskatoon, Saskatchewan [*Library symbol National Library of Canada*] (NLC) ... SSUMC
Ukrainian Museum of Canada, Saskatoon, SK, Canada [*Library symbol*] [*Library of Congress*] (LCLS) ... CaSSUMC
Ukrainian Music Institute in America ... UMI
Ukrainian National Academy of Sciences ... UNAS
Ukrainian National Aid Association of America (EA) ... UNAAA
Ukrainian National Association (EA) ... UNA
Ukrainian National Democratic Organization ... UNDO
Ukrainian National Information Service (EA) ... UNIS
Ukrainian National Women's League of America (EA) ... UNWLA
Ukrainian National Youth Federation of America [*Later, Ukrainian Youth Association of America*] (EA) ... UNYFA
Ukrainian Patriarchal World Federation (EA) ... UPWF
Ukrainian Philatelic and Numismatic Society (EA) ... UPNS
Ukrainian Political Science Association in the United States (EA) ... UPSA
Ukrainian Professional Society of America (EA) ... UPSA
Ukrainian Research and Information Institute [*Defunct*] (EA) ... URII
Ukrainian Research Foundation [*Defunct*] (EA) ... URF
Ukrainian Soviet Socialist Republic [*MARC geographic area code Library of Congress*] (LCCP) ... e-ur-un
Ukrainian Soviet Socialist Republic [*ISO two-letter standard code*] (CNC) ... UA
Ukrainian Soviet Socialist Republic [*ISO three-letter standard code*] (CNC) ... UKR
Ukrainian Soviet Socialist Republic [*MARC country of publication code Library of Congress*] (LCCP) ... unr
Ukrainian Women's Association of Canada ... UWAC
Ukrainian Workingmen's Association [*Later, UFA*] (EA) ... UWA
Ukrainian Youth League of North America [*Defunct*] (EA) ... UYLNA
Ukrains'ka Halyts'ka Armiia ... UHA
Ukrains'ka Kooperativna Rada Kanadi ... UKRK
Ukrains'ka Natsional'na Rada ... UNR
Ukrainska Partiia Samostiinykiv-Sotsiialistiv [*Ukrainian Party of Socialist-Independentists*] [*Russian Political party*] (PPE) ... UPSS
Ukrainska Partiia Sotsialistov Revolyutsionerov [*Ukrainian Socialist Revolutionary Party*] [*Russian Political party*] (PPE) ... USR
Ukrainska Partiia Sotsialistov Revolyutsionerov-Borotbists [*Ukrainian Socialist Revolutionary Party-Fighters*] [*Russian Political party*] (PPE) ... USR-Borotbists
Ukrains'ka Povstans'ka Armiia ... UPA
Ukrains'ka Revoliutsiino-Demokratychna Partiia ... URDP
Ukrainska Sotsial Demokraticheskaia Truda Partiia [*Ukrainian Social Democratic Labor Party*] [*Russian Political party*] (PPE) ... USDTP
Ukranian Soviet Socialist Republic ... UkrSSR
'Ukzin (BJA) ... 'Uk
'Ukzin (BJA) ... 'Ukz
Ulamona Field Station [*New Britain*] [*Seismograph station code, US Geological Survey*] (SEIS) ... ULA
Ulan Bator [*Mongolia*] [*Seismograph station code, US Geological Survey Closed*] (SEIS) ... OBM
Ulan Bator [*Mongolia*] [*Geomagnetic observatory code*] ... UBA
Ulan Bator [*Mongolia*] [*Airport symbol*] (OAG) ... ULN
U-Landshjaelp fra Folk til Folk [*Development Aid From People to People*] [*Denmark*] (EAIO) ... UFF
Ulanhot [*China*] [*Airport symbol*] (OAG) ... HLH
Ulan-Ude/Mukhino [*Former USSR ICAO location identifier*] (ICLI) ... UIUU
Ulcerative Colitis [*Medicine*] ... UC
Ulcerative Dermal Necrosis [*Medicine*] ... UDN
Ulcerative Dermatitis [*Dermatology*] (DAVI) ... UD
Ulco [*South Africa*] [*ICAO location identifier*] (ICLI) ... FAUC
Uldall Catheter [*Medicine*] (MEDA) ... UC
Uldericus de Bamberg [*Flourished, 12th century*] [*Authority cited in pre-1607 legal work*] (DSA) ... Ul
Ulei [*Vanuatu*] [*ICAO location identifier*] (ICLI) ... NVSU
Ulen-Hitteral High School, Ulen, MN [*Library symbol*] [*Library of Congress*] (LCLS) ... MnUlH
Ulen-Hitterdal Elementary School, Hitterdal, MN [*Library symbol*] [*Library of Congress*] (LCLS) ... MnHitE
Ulex Europaeus Agglutinin I ... UEAI
Ulex europeus Agglutinin [*Immunology*] ... UEA
ULI - the Urban Land Institute (EA) ... ULI
Ulitsa [*Street*] (EY) ... UL
Ullage (AAG) ... U
Ullage [*NASA*] (KSC) ... ULL
Ullage Rocket (KSC) ... UR
Ullage Simulation Assembly (MCD) ... USA
Ullrich-Turner Syndrome [*Genetics*] ... UTS
Ullucus Virus C [*Plant pathology*] ... UVC
Ulm [*Germany ICAO location identifier*] (ICLI) ... EDOE
Ulm [*Germany ICAO location identifier*] (ICLI) ... EDZD
Ulman's Law Record [*New York*] [*A publication*] (DLA) ... Ulm L Rec
Ulnar Anconeal Process ... UAP

Ulnar Collateral Ligament [Anatomy]	UCL
Ulnar Deviation [Medicine]	UD
Ulnar Nerve [Anatomy] (DAVI)	UN
Ulongwe [Mozambique] [ICAO location identifier] (ICLI)	FQUG
Ulrich's International Periodicals Directory [A publication]	UIPD
ULS Capital Corp. [Toronto Stock Exchange symbol]	ULS
Ulsan [South Korea ICAO location identifier] (ICLI)	RKPU
Ulster Archaeological Society	UAS
Ulster Architectural Heritage Society	UAHS
Ulster Cancer Foundation [Northern Ireland] (EAIO)	UCF
Ulster Constitution Defence Committee [Northern Ireland]	UCDC
Ulster County Community College, Stone Ridge, NY [Library symbol Library of Congress] (LCLS)	NSrU
Ulster Defence Association	UDA
Ulster Defence Force	UDF
Ulster Defence Regiment [Military unit] [British]	UDR
Ulster Democratic Unionist Party [Northern Ireland] [Political party] (PPW)	DUP
Ulster Diploma in Dairying	UDD
Ulster Diploma in Poultry Husbandry	UDP
Ulster Folklife Society (EA)	UFS
Ulster Freedom Fighters	UFF
Ulster Historical Foundation (EA)	UHF
Ulster King-at-Arms	UKA
Ulster Loyalist Central Coordinating Committee [Ireland]	ULCC
Ulster Loyalist Democratic Party [Northern Ireland] [Political party] (PPW)	ULDP
Ulster Parliament (DAS)	UP
Ulster Petroleums Ltd. [Toronto Stock Exchange symbol]	ULP
Ulster Popular Unionist Party [Northern Ireland] [Political party] (PPW)	UPUP
Ulster Progressive Unionist Party [Northern Ireland] [Political party] (PPW)	UPUP
Ulster Special Service Force [British military] (DMA)	USSF
Ulster Teacher's Union [Ireland] (AIE)	UTU
Ulster Television [Ireland] (DI)	UTV
Ulster Unionist Party	UU
Ulster Unionist Party [British Political party]	UUP
Ulster University College (ACII)	UUC
Ulster Volunteer Force	UVF
Ulster Workers' Council	UWC
Ulster-Irish Society (EA)	UIS
Ultimate (AAG)	ULT
Ultimate Asbestos Fibril	UAF
Ultimate Assignment	ULTSIGN
Ultimate Collider [Particle accelerator]	UC
Ultimate Dependability [Automotive designation]	UD
Ultimate Destination [Army] (AABC)	ULDEST
Ultimate Elastic Wall Stress [Mechanical engineering]	UEWS
Ultimate Electronics [Commercial firm NASDAQ symbol] (SAG)	ULTE
Ultimate Electronics [Commercial firm Associated Press] (SAG)	UltElct
Ultimate Factor of Safety	UFS
Ultimate Heat Sink [Nuclear energy] (NRCH)	UHS
Ultimate Holding Company	UHC
Ultimate Hour Estimate (MCD)	UHE
[The] Ultimate in Foul Ups [Military slang] [Bowdlerized version]	TUIFU
[The] Ultimate Musical Experience [Rock music group]	TUME
Ultimate Network of Intelligent Tire Technology	UNIT
Ultimate Operating Capability	UOC
Ultimate Operational Configuration (AAG)	UOC
Ultimate Oxygen Demand [Water conservation] (WDAA)	UOD
Ultimate Plant Protection System [Nuclear energy] (NRCH)	UPPS
Ultimate Players Association (EA)	UPA
Ultimate Range Ballistic Missile [Air Force]	URBM
Ultimate Sampling Unit (GFGA)	USU
Ultimate Strength Design (IEEE)	USD
Ultimate Tensile Strength [or Stress]	UTS
Ultimate User [Nuclear energy]	UU
Ultimate Weapon (AAG)	UW
Ultimatist Life Society (EA)	ULS
Ultimatist Religious Bodies on Earth (EA)	URBOE
Ultime [Lastly] [Pharmacy]	ULT
Ultimo [In the Month Preceding the Present] [Latin] (WGA)	ult
Ultimo [In the Month Preceding the Present] [Latin]	ULTO
Ultimo Praescriptus [The Last Ordered] [Pharmacy] (ROG)	ULT PRAESCR
Ultimobranchial [Bodies] [Medicine]	UB
Ultimobranchial Glands [Endocrinology]	UBG
Ultimum Praescriptus [Last Prescribed] [Latin] [Pharmacy] (DAVI)	ult praes
Ultra Clean Coal (ERG)	UCC
Ultra Electronics Components Ltd. (IAA)	UECL
Ultra Electronics Ltd. (IAA)	UEL
Ultra Glow Cosmetics [Vancouver Stock Exchange symbol]	GLO
Ultra High Bypass [Aviation] (DA)	UHB
Ultra High Frequency [Also, UHF] (DOAD)	U
Ultra High Luminance Vacuum Fluorescent Display [Automotive engineering]	UHLVFD
Ultra High Molecular Weight Polythene	UHMWPE
Ultra High Performance [Automotive engineering]	UHP
Ultra High Reduction (NITA)	UHR
Ultra High Resolution Facsimile (NITA)	UHRF
Ultra High Viscosity Index	UHVI
Ultra Large Scale Integration (NTCM)	USLI
Ultra Light-Weight Camouflage Net System [Air Force] (RDA)	ULCANS
Ultra Linear Low-Density Polyethylene [Plastics technology]	ULLDPE
Ultra Long Range (DA)	ULR
Ultra Low Velocity Zone [Seismology]	ULVZ
Ultra Marathon Cycling Association (EA)	UMCA
Ultra Microfiche (EECA)	UMI

Ultra Pac [NASDAQ symbol] (TTSB)	UPAC
Ultra Pac, Inc. [Associated Press] (SAG)	UltPac
Ultra Pac, Inc. [NASDAQ symbol] (SAG)	UPAC
Ultra Presse [Press agency] [Colombia]	UP
Ultra Stable Oscillator [Instrumentation]	USO
Ultra Vans (EA)	UV
Ultra Violet Spectrometry Group [British] (DBA)	UVSG
Ultra-Audible	UA
Ultracentrifugal [Biochemistry] (MAE)	UC
Ultracold Neutron	UCN
Ultradata Corp. [NASDAQ symbol] (TTSB)	ULTD
Ultradata Corp. [NASDAQ symbol] (SAG)	ULTD
Ultradata Corp. [Associated Press] (SAG)	Ultrdta
Ultradata Sys Wrrt'A' [NASDAQ symbol] (TTSB)	ULTRW
UltraData Systems [NASDAQ symbol] (TTSB)	ULTR
UltraData Systems, Inc. [NASDAQ symbol] (SAG)	ULTR
UltraData Systems, Inc. [Associated Press] (SAG)	UltraD
UltraData Systems, Inc. [Associated Press] (SAG)	UltraDt
Ultradeep Water	UDW
Ultra-Doppler Sonography [Radiology] (DAVI)	UDS
Ultrafast Detection	UFD
Ultrafast Electron Diffraction [Physics]	UED
Ultrafast-Opening Parachute (NG)	UFOP
Ultrafem Inc. [NASDAQ symbol] (TTSB)	UFEM
Ultrafem, Inc. [NASDAQ symbol] (SAG)	UFEM
Ultrafem, Inc. [Associated Press] (SAG)	Ultrafem
Ultrafilter [or Ultrafiltration]	UF
Ultrafiltration Rate [Biomedicine]	UFR
Ultrafine	UF
Ultrafine Ammonium Perchlorate (MCD)	UFAP
Ultrafine Ground Calcium Carbonate [Inorganic chemistry]	UFGCC
Ultrafine Particle Inductively Coupled Plasma [Spectrometry]	UFP-ICP
Ultrafine Powder [Materials processing]	UFP
Ultraheat Tested [Milk] (CDAI)	UHT
Ultraheat Treated	UHT
Ultrahigh Altitude	UHA
Ultrahigh Capacity Storage	UHCS
Ultra-High Definition Television (DOM)	UDTV
Ultrahigh Doppler (NASA)	UDOP
Ultrahigh Efficiency [Arc lamp]	UHE
Ultrahigh Energy	UHE
Ultrahigh Frequency Radio Unit (MCD)	UHFRU
Ultrahigh Frequency Satellite Terminal System (MCD)	USTS
Ultrahigh Molecular Weight	UHMW
Ultrahigh Molecular Weight Polyethylene [Organic chemistry]	UHMW-PE
Ultra-High Performance [in UHP Imposer, a product of Opti-Copy, Inc.]	UHP
Ultra-High Porosity [Materials science]	UHP
Ultrahigh Power	UHP
Ultra-High Pressure [Water cutting tools]	UHP
Ultrahigh Purity	UHP
Ultrahigh Radio Navigation (NATG)	URN
Ultrahigh Resistance	UHR
Ultrahigh Resistance (IDOE)	uhr
Ultrahigh Resolution	UHR
Ultrahigh Speed	UHS
Ultrahigh Temperature	UHT
Ultrahigh Temperature (MAE)	ULT
Ultrahigh Vacuum	UHV
Ultrahigh Vacuum Chamber	UHVC
Ultrahigh Vacuum Chamber	UVC
Ultrahigh Vacuum Chemical Vapor Deposition [Coating technology] [Semiconductor technology]	UHV/CVD
Ultrahigh Vacuum Pump	UVP
Ultrahigh Vacuum Pumping Station	UVPS
Ultrahigh Vacuum System	UHVS
Ultrahigh Voltage	UHV
Ultrahigh-Frequency [Electricity of radio waves]	UHF
Ultrahigh-Frequency Direction Finder	UHFDF
Ultrahigh-Frequency Filter	UHFF
Ultrahigh-Frequency Generator	UHFG
Ultrahigh-Frequency/High-Frequency (MCD)	UHF/HF
Ultrahigh-Frequency Jammer	UHFJ
Ultrahigh-Frequency Multi-Platform Transceiver [Navy] (MCD)	UMPT
Ultrahigh-Frequency Oscillator	UHFO
Ultrahigh-Frequency Receiver	UHFR
Ultra-High-Level Container Airdrop System [Military] (MCD)	UHLCADS
Ultrahigh-Resolution Electron Spectrometer for Chemical Analysis	UHR-ESCA
Ultrahigh-Temperature Reactor Experiment [Nuclear energy]	UHTREX
Ultra-Intelligent Machine	UIM
UltrAir, Inc. [ICAO designator] (FAAC)	ULT
Ultrajectum [Utrecht] [Imprint] [Latin] (ROG)	ULTRAJ
Ultrak, Inc. [NASDAQ symbol] (NQ)	ULTK
Ultrak, Inc. [Associated Press] (SAG)	Ultrak
Ultrakurzwelle [Ultrashort wave] [German]	UKW
Ultrakurzwellenempfaenger [Very-High-Frequency Receiver] [German]	UKWE
Ultralarge Crude Carrier [Oil tanker]	ULCC
Ultra-Large Liquified Natural Gas Carrier (PDAA)	ULLNG
Ultralarge-Scale Integration [of circuits] [Semiconductor technology]	ULSI
Ultralente Insulin [Pharmacology] (DAVI)	U
ULtralife Batteries [NASDAQ symbol] (TTSB)	ULBI
Ultralife Batteries, Inc. [NASDAQ symbol] (SAG)	ULBI
Ultralife Batteries, Inc. [Associated Press] (SAG)	Ultralife
Ultra-Light Displacement Boat (PS)	ULDB
Ultra-Light Field Howitzer [British]	UFH
Ultralight Flight Organization (EA)	UFO

Ultralightweight Camouflage Net System [*Army*] ..... ULCANS
Ultra-Lightweight Coated [*Paper*] ..... ULWC
Ultra-Lightweight Panel (PDAA) ..... ULP
Ultralinear ..... UL
Ultralinear Rectifier ..... ULR
Ultralite Expendable Launch Vehicle [*NASA*] ..... UELV
Ultra-Long Range Guided Weapon (IAA) ..... ULRGW
Ultralow ..... UL
Ultralow Birth Weight [*Medicine*] (DMAA) ..... ULBW
Ultra-Low Carbon [*Metallurgical engineering*] ..... ULC
Ultralow Chamber Pressure (MCD) ..... ULP
Ultralow Distortion [*Electronics*] (ECII) ..... ULD
Ultra-Low Emissions Bus [*Automotive engineering*] ..... ULEB
Ultra-Low Emissions Engine [*Automotive engineering*] ..... ULEE
Ultra-Low Emissions Truck [*Automotive engineering*] ..... ULET
Ultra-Low Emissions Truck Engine ..... ULETE
Ultralow Energy Charge Analyzer [*Instrumentation*] ..... ULECA
Ultralow Expansion [*Trademark, Corning Glass Works*] ..... ULE
Ultralow Frequency ..... ULF
Ultra-Low Interstitial (PDAA) ..... ULI
Ultralow Sidelobe Antenna [*Air Force*] (MCD) ..... ULSA
Ultralow Tar [*Cigarettes*] [*Tobacco industry*] ..... ULT
Ultralow Temperature ..... ULT
Ultralow Volume ..... ULV
Ultralow-Cement Castable [*Ceramics*] ..... ULCC
Ultra-Low-Emission Vehicle ..... ULEV
Ultralow-Energy Wide-Angle Telescope ..... ULEWAT
Ultralow-Frequency Jammer ..... ULFJ
Ultralow-Frequency Oscillator ..... ULFO
Ultra-Low-Level Air-Drop [*British military*] (DMA) ..... ULLA
Ultralow-Pressure Rocket ..... ULPR
Ultralow-Temperature Isotropic [*Carbon*] ..... ULTI
Ultramar Capital Corp. [*Toronto Stock Exchange symbol*] ..... ULM
Ultramar Capital Corp. [*Associated Press*] (SAG) ..... Ultramr
Ultramar Corp. [*NYSE symbol*] (SPSG) ..... ULR
Ultramar Diamond Shamrock Corp. [*NYSE symbol*] (SAG) ..... UDS
Ultramar Diamond Shamrock Corp. [*Associated Press*] (SAG) ..... UltramDS
Ultramar Ltd. [*Toronto Stock Exchange symbol*] ..... ULT
Ultramarine [*Philately*] (ROG) ..... ULT
Ultramarine [*Philately*] (ROG) ..... ULTRA
Ultramicrobacteria ..... UMB
Ultramicroelectrode [*Electrochemical microscopy*] ..... UME
Ultramicrofiche ..... UMF
Ultramicrowaves ..... UMW
Ultrapherical Polynomial Filter (IAA) ..... UPF
Ultraphon & Supraphon [*Record label*] [*Former Czechoslovakia*] ..... U
Ultraportable RADAR (MCD) ..... UPR
Ultraprecise LASER Distance Measuring Instrument ..... ULDMI
Ultraprecision Parachute (NG) ..... UPP
Ultra-Precision Test Equipment (PDAA) ..... UPTE
Ultrapure Metal ..... UPM
Ultraquick [*Flashing*] **Light** [*Navigation signal*] ..... UQ
Ultra-Rapid Reader [*Computer science*] ..... URR
Ultrared (IAA) ..... UR
Ultrareliable RADAR (MCD) ..... URR
Ultrasensitive Enzymatic Radioimmunoassay [*Clinical chemistry*] ..... USERIA
Ultrasensitive Microwave Infrared Detector ..... USMID
Ultrasensitive Position (AFM) ..... USP
Ultrashort Takeoff and Landing [*Aviation*] (MCD) ..... USTOL
Ultrashort Wave ..... USW
Ultrashort Wave Propagation Panel (IAA) ..... USWP
Ultra-Small Electronics Research [*DoD*] ..... USER
Ultrasmall Structures Research Office [*University of Michigan*] [*Research center*] (RCD) ..... USRO
Ultrasoft X-Ray ..... USX
Ultrasoft X-Ray Fluroescence [*Spectroscopy*] ..... USXFS
Ultrasoft X-Ray Spectroscopy ..... USXRS
Ultrasonic (AAMN) ..... US
Ultrasonic Agitation ..... USA
Ultrasonic Bioassay Tank [*Aerospace*] ..... UBAT
Ultrasonic Bioassay Tank System [*Aerospace*] ..... UBATS
Ultrasonic Bonding Machine ..... UBM
Ultrasonic Cardiography [*Medicine*] (DMAA) ..... UCG
Ultrasonic Chemical Cleaning System ..... UCCS
Ultrasonic Computed Tomography [*For examining interiors of solids*] ..... UCT
Ultrasonic Contact Impedance [*Factory automation*] (BTTJ) ..... UCI
Ultrasonic Data Recording and Processing System (NRCH) ..... UDRPS
Ultrasonic Delay Line ..... UDL
Ultrasonic Detergent Action ..... UDA
Ultrasonic Dispersive Delay Line ..... UDDL
Ultrasonic Doppler Cardioscope [*Heartbeat monitor*] ..... UDC
Ultrasonic Echo Detection (PDAA) ..... UED
Ultrasonic Echo Ranging Equipment ..... UERE
Ultrasonic Engineering (MCD) ..... UE
Ultrasonic Epoxy Bonder ..... UEB
Ultrasonic Frequency (MSA) ..... UF
Ultrasonic Frequency Transformer [*or Translator*] ..... UFT
Ultrasonic Grain Refinement ..... UGR
Ultrasonic Grating Constant ..... UGC
Ultrasonic Hardness Tester ..... UHT
Ultrasonic Helmet Mounted Sight [*Army*] (MCD) ..... UHMS
Ultrasonic Industry (WDAA) ..... UI
Ultrasonic Industry Association (EA) ..... UIA
Ultrasonic Interferometer Manometer [*Instrumentation*] ..... UIM
Ultrasonic Journal Tester ..... UJT
Ultrasonic Kit ..... USK
Ultrasonic Leak Detector ..... ULD
Ultrasonic Light Diffraction ..... ULD
Ultrasonic Light Modulator ..... ULM
Ultrasonic Link Detector ..... USLD
Ultrasonic Liquid Level Sensor ..... ULLS
Ultrasonic Manufacturers Association [*Later, UIA*] (EA) ..... UMA
Ultrasonic Material Dispersion ..... UMD
Ultrasonic Material Testing ..... UMT
Ultrasonic Motion Sensor (MCD) ..... UMS
Ultrasonic Nebulizer ..... USN
Ultrasonic Parametric Resonance (IEEE) ..... UPR
Ultrasonic Radiation ..... USR
Ultrasonic Renal Scanning [*Nephrology*] (DAVI) ..... URS
Ultrasonic Resin Cleaner [*Nuclear energy*] (NRCH) ..... URC
Ultrasonic Ring Welder ..... URW
Ultrasonic Separation Detector ..... USD
Ultrasonic Soldering Equipment ..... USSE
Ultrasonic Soldering Iron ..... USSI
Ultrasonic Space Grating ..... USG
Ultrasonic Spectroscopy ..... US
Ultrasonic Storage Cell ..... USC
Ultrasonic System [*Vancouver Stock Exchange symbol*] ..... USI
Ultrasonic Test ..... UST
Ultrasonic Test ..... UT
Ultrasonic Test Unit ..... USTU
Ultrasonic Test Unit ..... UTU
Ultrasonic Thermal Action ..... UTA
Ultrasonic Transducer [*Crystal*] [*Used in measuring human cardiac output*] ..... UST
Ultrasonic Vapor Degresser ..... UVD
Ultrasonic Wave ..... UW
Ultrasonic Welding ..... USW
Ultrasonically Assisted Machining [*Manufacturing term*] ..... UAM
Ultrasonically Nebulized Distilled Water Challenge ..... UNDWC
Ultrasonically-Modulated Electron Resonance (PDAA) ..... UMER
Ultrasonography (DAVI) ..... US
Ultrasonography ..... USG
Ultrasound ..... US
Ultrasound [*Radiology*] (DAVI) ..... UTZ
Ultrasound Cardiogram (IAA) ..... UCG
Ultrasound in Medicine - Australia Society ..... UIMAS
Ultrasound Scanning ..... USS
Ultrasound Vibration Potential [*Determination of electrokinetic potential*] ..... UVP
Ultrasound-Guided Fine-Needle Aspiration Biopsy [*Medicine*] ..... UGFNAB
Ultrastable Arc Lamp ..... USA
Ultra-Stable Voltage Reference Unit (PDAA) ..... USVRU
Ultratech Stepper [*NASDAQ symbol*] (TTSB) ..... UTEK
Ultratech Stepper, Inc. [*Associated Press*] (SAG) ..... UltraStp
Ultratech Stepper, Inc. [*NASDAQ symbol*] (SAG) ..... UTEK
Ultrathin ..... UT
Ultrathin Window [*Spectroscopy*] ..... UTW
Ultratrace-Level [*Analytical chemistry*] ..... UTL
Ultravariable Resolution Single Interferometer Echelle Scanner (PDAA) ..... URSIES
Ultraviolet [*Electromagnetic spectrum range*] ..... UV
Ultraviolet (VRA) ..... uv
Ultraviolet A (Light) ..... UVA
Ultraviolet Absorption ..... UVA
Ultraviolet Acquisition Technique ..... UAT
Ultraviolet Amplification by Stimulated Emission of Radiation ..... UVASER
Ultraviolet Amplification by Stimulated Emission of Radiation System ..... UVASERS
Ultraviolet Argon LASER ..... UVAL
Ultraviolet Astronomical Satellite (PDAA) ..... UVAS
Ultraviolet B [*or Ultraviolet light, midrange sunbeam, spectrum*] [*Dermatology*] (DAVI) ..... UVB
Ultraviolet B (Light) ..... UVB
Ultraviolet Band ..... UV-B
Ultraviolet Blood Irradiation ..... UBI
Ultraviolet Communications ..... ULTRACOM
Ultraviolet Communications System ..... UVC
Ultraviolet Coronagraph Spectrometer [*Solar Physics*] ..... UVCS
Ultraviolet Detector ..... UVD
Ultraviolet Detector System ..... UDS
Ultraviolet Differential Absorption LIDAR [*Light Detection and Ranging*] (PDAA) ..... UVDIAL
Ultra-Violet Erasable Programmable Read Only Memory ..... UVEPROM
Ultraviolet Eraseable Read Only Memory (PDAA) ..... UVEROM
Ultraviolet Fiber Optics ..... UVFO
Ultraviolet Filter ..... UVF
Ultraviolet Floodlight (AAG) ..... UVF
Ultraviolet Floodlight ..... UVFLT
Ultraviolet Hydrogen Fire Detection System (DNAB) ..... UVHFDS
Ultraviolet Image Converter ..... UIC
Ultraviolet Image Converter (WGA) ..... UVICON
Ultraviolet Imaging Telescope ..... UIT
Ultraviolet Infrared Scene Generator ..... UVIRSG
Ultraviolet Inspection Light ..... UVIL
Ultraviolet Interference Filter ..... UIF
Ultraviolet Ion LASER ..... UVIL
Ultraviolet Irradiation ..... UVI
Ultraviolet Lamp ..... UVL
Ultraviolet LASER ..... UVL
Ultraviolet Light ..... UVL
Ultraviolet Light Cured ..... UVC

Ultraviolet Light, Long Wave ... UVA
Ultraviolet Light, Midrange Sunbeam Spectrum [*Ultraviolet B*] [*Dermatology*] (DAVI) ... UVB
Ultraviolet Light Stabilizer ... ULS
Ultraviolet Light Stabilizer ... UVLS
Ultraviolet Meter ... UVM
Ultraviolet Mitogenic Radiation ... UMR
Ultraviolet Nitric-Oxide Experiment ... UVNO
Ultraviolet Ozone Spectrometer (MCD) ... UOS
Ultraviolet Photoelectron Spectroscopy ... UPES
Ultraviolet Photoelectron Spectroscopy ... UVPES
Ultraviolet Photoemission Spectroscopy ... UPS
Ultraviolet Photometric and Polarimetric Explorer ... UPPE
Ultraviolet Photometry ... UVP
Ultraviolet Programmable Read Only Memory ... UVPROM
Ultraviolet Proton Radiation ... UPR
Ultraviolet Radiation ... UVR
Ultraviolet Radiometer (MCD) ... UVR
Ultraviolet Read Only Memory (IAA) ... UVROM
Ultraviolet Receiver ... UVR
Ultraviolet Resistant ... UVR
Ultraviolet Resonance Raman [*Spectroscopy*] ... UVRR
Ultraviolet Rocket ... UVR
Ultraviolet Scanning Spectrometer ... USS
Ultraviolet Solar Constant ... UVSC
Ultraviolet Spectral Analysis ... USA
Ultraviolet Spectral Photometer ... UVSP
Ultraviolet Spectroheliographic Instrument ... USI
Ultraviolet Spectrometer ... UVS
Ultraviolet Stratospheric Imaging Spectrometer (MCD) ... USIS
Ultraviolet Transmission ... UVT
Ultraviolet Tube ... UVT
Ultraviolet/Visible [*Spectroscopy*] ... UV-VIS
Ultraviolet-Biological (USDC) ... UV-B
Ultraviolet-Biological [*Marine science*] (OSRA) ... UV-R
Ultraviolet-Blue-Visible-Red [*Photometry*] ... UBVR
Ultraviolet-Blue-Visual [*Photometric system*] ... UBV
Ultraviolet-Erasable Programmable Read-Only Memories [*Computer science*] ... UV-EPROMS
Ultravisible ... UV
Ultra-Wide Band ... UWB
Ultriusque Juris Doctor [*Doctor of Either Law; i.e., Canon Law or Civil Law*] [*Latin*] ... UJD
Ultronic Data Systems (IAA) ... UDS
Ulu Bernam [*Malaysia*] [*ICAO location identifier*] (ICLI) ... WMBF
Ulundi [*South Africa*] [*ICAO location identifier*] (ICLI) ... FAUL
Uluru [*Ayers Rock - Mount Olga*] **National Park** (EERA) ... UNP
Ulusal Basin Ajansi [*News agency*] [*Turkey*] (MENA) ... UBA
Ulusal Birlik Partisi [*National Unity Party*] [*Turkish Cyprus*] [*Political party*] (EY) ... UBP
Ulyanovsk [*Former USSR Airport symbol*] (OAG) ... ULY
Ulyanovsk Higher Civil Aviation School [*Former USSR*] [*FAA designator*] (FAAC) ... UHS
Ulysses, KS [*AM radio station call letters*] ... KULY
Ulysses, KS [*Location identifier FAA*] ... ULS
Ulysses S. Grant Association (EA) ... USGA
Ulysses Simpson Grant [*US general and president, 1822-1885*] ... USG
Um Gefaellige Antwort Wird Gebeten [*The Favor of an Answer Is Requested*] [*Correspondence*] [*German*] ... U Gefl AWG
Umak [*Alaska*] [*Seismograph station code, US Geological Survey*] (SEIS) ... AD2
Umanak [*Greenland*] [*Airport symbol*] (AD) ... UMK
Umatilla Army Depot [*Oregon*] (AABC) ... UMAD
Umatilla County Library, Pendleton, OR [*Library symbol Library of Congress*] (LCLS) ... OrPeU
Umatilla Depot Activity [*Army*] ... UMDA
Umatilla Hospital, Umatilla, OR [*Library symbol*] [*Library of Congress*] (LCLS) ... OrUmaH
Umatilla Hospital, Umatilla, OR [*Library symbol Library of Congress*] (LCLS) ... OrUmH
Umatilla, OR [*AM radio station call letters*] ... KLWJ
Umatilla Public Library, Umatilla, OR [*Library symbol*] [*Library of Congress*] (LCLS) ... OrUma
UMB Financial [*NASDAQ symbol*] (TTSB) ... UMBF
UMB Financial Corp. [*Associated Press*] (SAG) ... UMB Fn
UMB Financial Corp. [*NASDAQ symbol*] (SAG) ... UMBF
Umbelliferyl [*Biochemistry*] ... Umb
Umberatana [*Australia Seismograph station code, US Geological Survey*] (SEIS) ... UMB
Umbertino's Restaurant [*Vancouver Stock Exchange symbol*] ... UMO
Umberto's Pasta Enterprises, Inc. [*Vancouver Stock Exchange symbol*] ... UMB
Umbilical (MCD) ... UMB
Umbilical (AAG) ... UMBL
Umbilical Artery [*Anatomy*] ... UA
Umbilical Artery Catheter [*Neonatology*] (DAVI) ... UAC
Umbilical Artery Line [*Neonatology*] (DAVI) ... UAL
Umbilical Cable [*or Connector*] ... UC
Umbilical Cable Unit Cooler [*Aerospace*] (AAG) ... UC
Umbilical Checkout Cable ... UCC
Umbilical Connector ... UC
Umbilical Cord [*Aerospace engineering*] ... UMBC
Umbilical Ejection Relay Assembly (AAG) ... UERA
Umbilical Handling Technician [*Computer science*] (IAA) ... UHT
Umbilical Junction Box ... UJB
Umbilical Mast [*NASA*] (KSC) ... UM
Umbilical Pin ... UP
Umbilical Test Set ... UTS
Umbilical Tower [*Aerospace*] ... UT
Umbilical Vein [*Anatomy*] ... UMB V
Umbilical Vein [*Anatomy*] (DAVI) ... umb ven
Umbilical Vein [*Medicine*] ... UV
Umbilical Vein Blood Flow ... UVBF
Umbilical Venous Catheter [*Medicine*] (MEDA) ... UVC
Umbrian [*Language, culture, etc.*] ... Umbr
Umbundu [*MARC language code Library of Congress*] (LCCP) ... umb
UMC Industries, Unidynamics Phoenix, Inc. Library, Goodyear, AZ [*Library symbol Library of Congress*] (LCLS) ... AzGoU
Umdrehung per Minuten [*Revolutions per Minute*] [*German*] ... UPM
Umdrehungen je Minute [*Revolutions per Minute*] [*German*] ... UG/M
Umea [*Sweden ICAO location identifier*] (ICLI) ... ESNU
Umea [*Sweden*] [*Seismograph station code, US Geological Survey*] (SEIS) ... UME
Umea [*Sweden*] [*Airport symbol*] (OAG) ... UME
Umea Universitetsbibliotek, Umea, Sweden [*Library symbol Library of Congress*] (LCLS) ... SwUmU
Umfreville's Office of Coroner [*A publication*] (DLA) ... Umfrev Off Cor
UMI [*University Microfilms International*] **Article Clearinghouse** [*Information service or system*] (IID) ... UMAC
Umiat, AK [*Location identifier FAA*] (FAAL) ... UMT
Umnak, AK [*Location identifier FAA*] (FAAL) ... UMB
Umnak, AK [*Location identifier FAA*] (FAAL) ... UNS
Umno Baru [*New Umno*] [*Malaysia*] [*Political party*] ... UB
Umot Me'uhadot [*United Nations*] [*Hebrew*] ... UM
Umpire [*Baseball*] ... U
Umpire (DSUE) ... UMP
Umpire Decisions, Benefit Claims [*England*] [*A publication*] (DLA) ... OUUID
Umpqua Community College, Roseburg, OR [*Library symbol Library of Congress*] (LCLS) ... OrRoU
UMTA [*Urban Mass Transit Administration*] **Transportation Planning System** ... UTPS
Umtali [*Zimbabwe*] [*Airport symbol*] (AD) ... UTA
Umtata [*South Africa*] [*Airport symbol*] (OAG) ... UTT
Umtata (K. D. Matanzima) [*South Africa*] [*ICAO location identifier*] (ICLI) ... FAUT
Umuarama [*Brazil*] [*Airport symbol*] (AD) ... UMU
Umweltforschungsdatenbank [*Data Bank for Environmental Research Projects*] [*Deutsches Umweltbundesamt*] [*Germany*] [*Information service or system*] (CRD) ... UFORDAT
Umweltliteraturedatenbank [*Data Bank for Environmental Literature*] [*Deutsches Umweltbundesamt*] [*Germany*] [*Information service or system*] (CRD) ... ULIDAT
UN Documents Index (NITA) ... UNDEX
Una Corda [*With one string or with the soft pedal*] [*Music*] ... UC
Unabhaengige Arbeiterpartei [*Independent Labor Party*] [*Germany Political party*] (PPE) ... UAP
Unabhaengige Demokratische Union [*Independent Democratic Union*] [*Austria Political party*] (PPE) ... UDU
Unabhaengige Sozialdemokratische Partei Deutschlands [*Independent Social Democratic Party of Germany*] [*Political party*] (PPE) ... USPD
Unabhaengige Volkspartei [*Independent People's Party*] [*Political party Germany*] (EAIO) ... UV
Unabkoemmlich [*Indispensable, irreplaceable*] [*German military - World War II*] ... UK
Unable [*ICAO designator*] (FAAC) ... UNA
Unable Higher Altitude [*Aviation*] (FAAC) ... UHA
Unable Higher Due Opposite Direction Traffic [*Aviation*] (FAAC) ... UHDODT
Unable Higher Due Same Direction Traffic [*Aviation*] (FAAC) ... UHDSDT
Unable Higher Due Traffic [*Aviation*] (FAAC) ... UHDT
Unable Lower Due Traffic [*Aviation*] (FAAC) ... ULDT
Unable to Approve [*ICAO designator*] (FAAC) ... UNAP
Unable to Approve Altitude Requested [*Aviation*] (FAAC) ... UNAR
Unable to Approve Arrival for the Time Specified [*Aviation*] (FAAC) ... UA
Unable to Approve Departure for the Time Specified [*Aviation*] (FAAC) ... UD
Unable to Contact Company Radio [*Aviation*] (FAAC) ... UNCC
Unable to Monitor (FAAC) ... UNMON
Unable to Read [*Laboratory science*] (DAVI) ... URED
Unabridged (ADA) ... UNAB
Unabridged ... UNABR
Unacceptable Face of Socialism (DSUE) ... UFOS
Unacceptable Quality Level ... UQL
Unaccompanied ... UNACC
Unaccompanied Baggage (MCD) ... UB
Unaccompanied Child [*Airline notation*] ... UC
Unaccompanied Enlisted Personnel Housing [*Navy*] (DNAB) ... UEPH
Unaccompanied Minor [*Airline passenger*] ... UM
Unaccompanied Officer Personnel Housing [*Navy*] ... UOPH
Unaccompanied Personnel Housing [*Military*] ... UPH
Unadilla, GA [*FM radio station call letters*] ... WAFI
Unadilla Valley Railroad (IIA) ... UV
Unadjusted Contractual Changes ... UCC
Unaggregated (MAE) ... UA
Unalakleet [*Alaska*] [*ICAO location identifier*] (ICLI) ... PAUN
Unalakleet [*Alaska*] [*Airport symbol*] (OAG) ... UNK
Unalakleet, AK [*Location identifier FAA*] (FAAL) ... JNR
Unalakleet, AK [*AM radio station call letters*] ... KNSA
Unalaska [*Alaska*] [*Seismograph station code, US Geological Survey Closed*] (SEIS) ... UNA
Unalaska, AK [*AM radio station call letters*] ... KIAL
Unallotted (AABC) ... UNALOT
Unallowable Items Program [*IRS*] ... UIP
Unaltered (ROG) ... UNALTD
Unanak [*Greenland*] [*ICAO location identifier*] (ICLI) ... BGUM
Unanesthetized [*Physiology*] ... UA

Unanimous ... UNAN
Unanswered (ROG) ... UNANSD
Unapix Enter Cl'B'Wrrt [*AMEX symbol*] (TTSB) ... UPX.WS.B
Unapix Entertainment [*AMEX symbol*] (TTSB) ... UPX
Unapix Entertainment, Inc. [*Associated Press*] (SAG) ... Unapix
Unapix Entertainment, Inc. [*Associated Press*] (SAG) ... Unpx
Unapix Entertainment, Inc. [*AMEX symbol*] (SAG) ... UPX
Unappointed (ROG) ... UNAPPD
Unassembled ... UNASSD
Unassigned [*Telecommunications*] (IAA) ... UA
Unassigned [*Telecommunications*] (TEL) ... UN
Unassigned (AABC) ... UNASGD
Unassigned [*Navy*] (NVT) ... UNASGN
Unassigned Direct Material [*Navy*] (DNAB) ... UDM
Unassigned Reading Frame [*Genetics*] ... URF
Unassorted (ROG) ... U/S
Unate Ringe Sum [*Logic expression*] (IEEE) ... URS
Unattached (ROG) ... UNATT
Unattached List, Indian Army ... ULIA
Unattached Officers' Association [*A union*] [*British*] ... UOA
Unattended [*Aviation*] (FAAC) ... UNATNDD
Unattended (ADA) ... UNATT
Unattended Answering Accessory (MHDB) ... UNA
Unattended Automatic Dial Back Up [*Telecommunications*] ... UADBU
Unattended Earth Terminal ... UET
Unattended Equipment Area ... UEA
Unattended/Expendable Electronic Countermeasure ... U/EECM
Unattended Expendable Jammer (MCD) ... UEJ
Unattended Ground Sensors ... UGS
Unattended Machinery Spaces (DS) ... UMS
Unattended Multipoint Communications Station (MHDI) ... UMCS
Unattended Repeater [*Telecommunications*] (OA) ... UR
Unattended Sensor Monitoring System ... USMS
Unattributed ... UNATTRIB
Unauthorized (DLA) ... Unauth
Unauthorized (AABC) ... UNAUTHD
Unauthorized Absence (MUGU) ... UA
Unauthorized Launch ... UL
Unauthorized Publication or Use of Communications ... UPUC
Unavailability Factor [*Electronics*] (IEEE) ... UF
Unavailable ... UA
Unavailable (FAAC) ... UNAVBL
Unavailable Hours [*Electronics*] (IEEE) ... UH
Unavailable, On Order [*Business term*] (NTCM) ... UOO
Unavoidable Delay ... UD
Unbalanced ... U
Unbalanced [*Telecommunications*] (TEL) ... UNBAL
Unbalanced Current Sensing (MCD) ... UCS
Unbewusste [*Unconscious Mind*] [*Psychology*] ... UBW
Unblanking (MSA) ... UNBLK
Unbleached (MSA) ... UBL
Unbleached [*Paper*] (DGA) ... unbld
Unbleached Arnold [*Paper*] (DGA) ... UA
Unbleached Kraft [*Pulp and paper processing*] ... UBK
Unbleached Muslin ... UMUS
Unblocked Serial Telemetry (MCD) ... UST
Unblocking [*Telecommunications*] (TEL) ... UBL
Unblocking Acknowledge [*Telecommunications*] (TEL) ... UBA
Unbonded Spool Type (DNAB) ... UBST
[*The*] **Unborn Book** [*A publication*] ... TUB
Unborrowed Reserves ... RU
Unbound (ROG) ... UNB
Unbound (WDMC) ... unb
Unbound (WDMC) ... Unbd
Unbound (WDAA) ... UNBD
Unbound Testosterone [*Endocrinology*] (DMAA) ... UT
Unbound Testosterone-Binding Globulin [*Immunology*] (DAVI) ... UTBG
Unbound Thyroxine Binding Globulin [*Endocrinology*] (AAMN) ... UTBG
Unbundled Stock Unit [*Investment term Obsolete*] ... USU
Unburned [*Ecology*] ... U
Unburned Carbon [*Fuel technology*] ... UBC
Unburned Hydrocarbon [*Also, UHC*] [*Fuel technology*] ... UBHC
Unburned Hydrocarbon [*Also, UBHC*] [*Fuel technology*] ... UHC
Unburned Hydrocarbons ... UHC
Unburned plus Ash [*Ecology*] ... UA
Unburned, Warmed [*Ecology*] ... UW
UNC, Inc. [*Formerly, United Nuclear Corporation*] [*NYSE symbol*] (SPSG) ... UNC
UNC, Inc. [*Formerly, United Nuclear Corp.*] [*Associated Press*] (SAG) ... UNCInc
Uncage ... UNCG
Uncatalogued (ADA) ... UNCAT
Uncertain (ADA) ... UNC
Uncertain About (DAVI) ... UA
Uncertain Etiology Upper Esophagus [*Medicine*] (DAVI) ... UE
Uncertain Glory: Folklore and the American Revolution [*A publication*] ... UG
Uncertain Inference System [*Logic*] ... UIS
Uncertainty [*Standard deviation*] [*Computer science*] ... UNCERT
Uncertainty Factor [*Toxicology*] ... UF
Uncertainty Phase Code (Alerting Service) [*Aviation*] (FAAC) ... INCERFA
Uncertainty Principle [*Quantum mechanics*] ... UP
Uncertified Patient [*British*] ... UP
Unchanged (MAE) ... UC
Unchanged Charge Distribution [*Fission*] ... UCD
Unchanged Conventional Treatment [*Medicine*] ... UCT
Uncia [*Bolivia*] [*ICAO location identifier*] (ICLI) ... SLUC
Uncirculated ... U
Uncirculated [*Numismatics*] ... UNC
Uncirculated (WDAA) ... UNCIR
Uncirculated Coins [*Numismatics*] ... UC
Uncircumcising Information Resources Center [*National Support Group*] ... UNCIRC
Unclad-Metal Breeder Reactor ... UMBR
Unclamp (IAA) ... UCL
Unclamp ... UNCLP
Unclassifiable [*Laboratory science*] (DAVI) ... UC
Unclassifiable Connective Tissue Disease [*Medicine*] (DMAA) ... UCTD
Unclassified ... U
Unclassified ... U/C
Unclassified (KSC) ... UNC
Unclassified (AABC) ... UNCLAS
Unclassified (BARN) ... unclass
Unclassified Controlled Nuclear Information [*Department of Energy*] ... UCNI
Unclassified Miscellaneous [*Navy ship symbol*] ... IX
Unclassified Miscellaneous Submarine [*Navy symbol*] (NVT) ... IXSS
Unclassified, Unlimited [*DoD*] ... U^2
Unclassified without Attachment ... UWOA
Uncle ... U
Uncle [*Phonetic alphabet*] [*Royal Navy World War I Pre-World War II*] [*World War II*] (DSUE) ... U
Uncle (DSUE) ... UNC
Uncle B Bakery, Inc. [*NASDAQ symbol*] (SAG) ... UNCB
Uncle B Bakery, Inc. [*Associated Press*] (SAG) ... UncleB
Uncle B's Bakery [*NASDAQ symbol*] (TTSB) ... UNCB
Uncle Remus Museum (EA) ... URM
Uncle Sam ... US
Uncle Sam Ain't Released Me Yet ... USARMY
Uncle Tom Cobley and All [*Refers to everyone*] [*Slang British*] (DSUE) ... UTCAA
Uncle Tom's Cabin [*Title of book by Harriet Beecher Stowe*] ... UTC
Unclear Pronoun Reference [*Used in correcting manuscripts, etc.*] ... REF
Unclipping [*Medicine*] ... UC
Unclosed Contract Status [*Military*] (AFIT) ... UCS
Uncoated ... UNCTD
Uncomfortable Loudness [*Audiometry*] ... UCL
Uncomfortable Loudness [*Sound level*] (DAVI) ... UCL
Uncomfortable Loudness Level (DAVI) ... ULL
Uncommitted Logic Array [*Semiconductor technology*] ... ULA
Uncommitted Logic Array [*Semiconductor technology*] (EECA) ... ULCA
Uncommon Species ... U
Uncompensated (MEDA) ... uncomp
Uncompensated Temperature Variation (TEL) ... UTV
Uncomplicated ... uncomp
Uncomplicated Urinary Tract Infection [*Medicine*] ... UUTI
Unconditional (IAA) ... UNC
Unconditional (ROG) ... UNCONDL
Unconditional Mean Square Error [*Statistics*] ... UMSE
Unconditional Selection ... US
Unconditional Stop (IAA) ... US
Unconditional Surrender ... US
Unconditioned ... uncond
Unconditioned Reflex [*or Response*] [*Psychometrics*] ... UCR
Unconditioned Reflex [*Psychometrics*] (AAMN) ... UNCOND REF
Unconditioned Reflex [*Neurology*] (DAVI) ... UR
Unconditioned Response [*Psychometrics*] ... UR
Unconditioned Stimulus [*Psychometrics*] ... UCS
Unconditioned Stimulus [*Psychometrics*] (AAMN) ... unCS
Unconditioned Stimulus [*Psychometrics*] (AAMN) ... UnS
Unconditioned Stimulus [*Psychometrics*] ... US
Unconfined Compressive Strength [*Rock mechanics*] ... UCS
Unconfined Vapor Cloud Explosion ... UVCE
Unconfirmed (ROG) ... UNCONFD
Unconjugated Bilirubin ... UCB
Unconjugated Bilirubin (MAE) ... UCBR
Unconscious [*Medicine*] ... UCS
Unconscious ... uncon
Unconsolidated Laws [*A publication*] (DLA) ... Unconsol Laws
Unconstitutional [*Legal shorthand*] (LWAP) ... UNCONSTAL
Unconstrained Requirements Report [*Army*] ... URR
Uncontainerable Goods [*Shipping*] (DS) ... UNCON
Uncontested Physical Searches [*CIA term for break-ins*] ... UPS
Uncontrollable Overtime ... UOT
Uncontrolled (DA) ... UNCTLD
Uncontrolled (index) Language (NITA) ... UL
Uncontrolled Stimulus (HGAA) ... UCS
Uncontrolled Term [*Online database field identifier*] ... UT
Uncontrolled Variable ... UCV
Unconventional Aerial Object ... UAO
Unconventional Military Operations (MCD) ... UMO
Unconventional Warfare [*Army*] ... UW
Unconventional Warfare Operations Area [*Army*] (AABC) ... UWOA
Uncooled Parametric Amplifier ... UPA
Uncorrected (WGA) ... UNCOR
Uncorrected ... uncorr
Uncorrected Data Processor ... UCDP
Uncorrected Stimulus [*Neurology*] (DAVI) ... UnCS
Uncorrelated Data Processor (IAA) ... UCDP
Uncoupled Hartree-Fock [*Physical chemistry*] ... UCHF
Uncoupling Protein [*Biochemistry*] ... UCP
Uncover ... Uncov
Uncovered Position (MHDW) ... UP
Uncrossed Olivocochlear Bundle [*Otology*] ... UOCB

UNCTAD [*United Nations Conference on Trade and Development*] **Reference UnitCatalogue** [*Information service or system*] (DUND) .... URUC
Unctus [*Smeared*] [*Pharmacy*] .... UNCT
Uncured Propellant End Burning Rocket (MCD) .... UPEBR
Uncut (ROG) .... UNCT
Uncut Edges [*Bookbinding*] .... UC
Und [*And*] [*German*] .... U
Und Andere [*And Others*] [*German*] .... UA
Und Andere Orte [*And Elsewhere*] [*German*] .... UAO
Und Anderes Mehr [*And So Forth*] [*German*] .... UAM
Und Oefters [*And Often*] [*German*] .... UO
Und So Fort [*And So Forth*] [*German*] .... USF
Und Zwar [*That Is*] [*German*] .... UZW
Undated .... UD
Undeb Bedyddwyr Cymru [*Baptist Union of Wales*] (EAIO) .... UBC
Undecaprenol [*Organic chemistry*] .... UND
Undecyl Dodecyl Phthalate .... UDP
Undeducted Contributions .... UC
Undeducted Purchase Price .... UPP
Undefined (IAA) .... U
Undefined .... UNDEF
Undefinitized Contractual Actions (DOMA) .... UCA
Undegraded Insulin Factor [*Medicine*] (MAE) .... UIF
Undelete [*Computer science*] [*Telecommunications*] .... u
Undeliverables [*Canadian*] [*Postal term*] (NFD) .... UDs
Undeliverables [*Fundraising*] .... UDs
Undelivered (FAAC) .... UNDLD
Undelivered Orders [*Army*] (AABC) .... UO
Undelivered Orders Cancelled [*Military*] .... UNDELORDCAN
Undelivered Orders Outstanding [*Military*] (AFM) .... UOO
Undelivered Orders Schedule [*Army*] .... UOS
Undenatured Bacterial Antigen .... UBA
Under .... U
Under (AAG) .... UND
Under Age [*i.e., entitled neither to a daily rum ration nor money instead*] [*See also G, T*] [*Obsolete*] [*Navy*] [*British*] .... UA
Under Agreement [*Legal term*] (DLA) .... U/A
Under Armor Auxiliary Power Unit [*US Army tanks*] (RDA) .... UAAPU
Under Armor Tow (MCD) .... UAT
Under Carriage (MCD) .... U/C
Under Charge .... UC
Under Color Addition [*Printing technology*] .... UCA
Under Construction .... UC
Under Conversion (NATG) .... U/C
Under Cover (ADA) .... U/C
Under Current (NASA) .... U/C
Under Deck (ADA) .... U/D
Under Deck Tank [*on a ship*] (DS) .... Un Dk
Under Direct Vision (DAVI) .... UD
Under Frequency (DNAB) .... UF
Under Frequency Protector (MCD) .... UFP
Under Frequency Relay .... UFR
Under Frequency Sensing (MCD) .... UFS
Under General Anesthesia (DAVI) .... UGA
Under Hatch Valve .... UHV
Under Honorable Conditions [*Military*] .... UHC
Under Instructions (ADA) .... U/I
Under Observation (DAVI) .... U/O
Under Other than Honorable Conditions [*Discharge*] [*Military*] .... UOHC
Under Other than Honorable Conditions [*Discharge*] [*Military*] .... UOTHC
Under PM Services [*Computer science*] (PCM) .... UPMS
Under Provisions Of [*Military*] .... UP
Under Provisions of Section [*Military*] .... UPS
Under Review (MHDB) .... UR
Under Seas Defense Exposition (ITD) .... USD
Under Secretaries Committee .... USC
Under Secretary .... US
Under Secretary for Civil Aviation .... USCA
Under Secretary of Defense [*DoD*] (RDA) .... USD
Under Secretary of Defense for Acquisition [*DoD*] (RDA) .... USD(A)
Under Secretary of State .... US of S
Under Secretary of State for the Royal Navy [*British*] .... USSRN
Under Secretary of the Air Force .... SAFUS
Under Secretary of the Air Force .... US of AF
Under Secretary of the Air Force (AAGC) .... USAF
Under Secretary of the Air Force .... USOFAF
Under Secretary of the Army .... US of A
Under Secretary of the Army .... USOFA
Under Secretary of the Navy .... UNDERSECNAV
Under Secretary of the Navy .... UNSECNAV
Under Secretary of the Navy .... USN
Under Secretary of the Navy's Office .... USO
Under Secretary of War [*Obsolete*] .... USecWar
Under Secretary of War [*Obsolete*] .... USW
Under Separate Cover .... USC
Under Sheriff .... UND SHER
Under Speed Relay (MCD) .... USR
Under the Circumstances [*Slang*] (ROG) .... CIRKS
Under the Rule [*Business term*] .... UR
Under the Tongue [*Pharmacy*] .... UT
Under the Wing [*Aircraft*] .... UTW
Under Thirty Group for Transit [*Defunct*] (EA) .... UTGT
Under Training [*British military*] (DMA) .... U/T
Under Trust [*Legal term*] (DLA) .... U/T
Under Usual Reserves .... UUR

Under Voltage .... UV
Under Voltage Relay .... UVR
Under Voltage Sensing (MCD) .... UVS
Under Will [*Legal term*] (DLA) .... U/W
Under-Color Removal [*Printing technology*] .... UCR
Undercurrent (IAA) .... UNC
Undercurrent .... UNDC
Undercut [*Technical drawings*] .... UC
Underdeck Tonnage .... UDT
Underdeveloped Countries .... UDC
Underdrive [*Automotive engineering*] .... U/DRV
Underdrive [*Automotive engineering*] .... UD
Undereducated .... UNDED
Underexposed [*Photography*] .... UEX
Underfashion Club (EA) .... UC
Underfashion Club of New York [*Formerly, CBWC*] (EA) .... UCNY
Underfeed Stoker Makers' Association [*British*] (BI) .... USMA
Underfloor (NASA) .... U
Underfrequency .... UNDF
Underfull Employment [*Economics*] .... UFL
Undergarment .... UG
Undergarment Accessories Association (EA) .... UAA
Underglaze (VRA) .... undglz
Undergoing (DNAB) .... UG
Undergoing (AABC) .... UNDG
Undergraduate .... UG
Undergraduate .... UNDGRAD
Undergraduate Computer Graphics Facility [*Stevens Institute of Technology*] [*Research center*] (RCD) .... UCGF
Undergraduate Engineering Program [*Air Force*] .... UGE
Undergraduate Grade-Point Average [*Higher education*] .... UGPA
Undergraduate Helicopter Pilot Training [*Army*] .... UGHP
Undergraduate Helicopter Pilot Training [*Army*] .... UHP
Undergraduate Helicopter Pilot Training (MCD) .... UHPT
Undergraduate Medical Education (HCT) .... UGME
Undergraduate Navigator Training [*Air Force*] (AFM) .... UNT
Undergraduate Navigator Training System [*Air Force*] .... UNTS
Undergraduate Pilot Training [*Air Force*] .... UPT
Undergraduate Pilot Training - Helicopter [*Air Force*] .... UPT-H
Undergraduate Pilot Training System (IAA) .... UPTS
Undergraduate Preparation of Educational Personnel [*Office of Education*] .... UPEP
Undergraduate Program [*Subject area tests*] .... UP
Undergraduate Record Examination [*Education*] .... UGRE
Undergraduate Record Examination [*Education*] .... URE
Undergraduate Research Opportunities Program [*Pronounced "your-op"*] [*Massachusetts Institute of Technology*] .... UROP
Undergraduate Research Participation [*National Science Foundation project*] [*Defunct*] (EA) .... URP
Undergraduate Research Participation Program [*Formerly, URP*] (EA) .... URPP
Undergraduate Science Engineering and Mathematics Education [*National Science Foundation*] (EGAO) .... USEME
Undergraduated Pre-Service Teacher Education Program [*National Science Foundation*] (EA) .... UPSTEP
Underground [*Technical drawings*] .... UG
Underground (AABC) .... UGND
Underground .... UNDGRD
Underground Baggage Facility [*Aviation*] (DA) .... UBF
Underground Building [*National Security Agency*] .... UBG
Underground Coal Gasification .... UCG
Underground Construction Research Council .... UCRC
Underground Distribution (MSA) .... UD
Underground Engineering Contractors Association [*Later, ECA*] (EA) .... UECA
Underground Excavation and Rock Properties Information Center (NITA) .... UERPIC
Underground Explosion Test (IAA) .... UET
Underground Facilities Protective Organization (EA) .... UFPO
Underground Feeder .... UF
Underground Hydro-Pumped Storage [*Room*] .... UHPS
Underground Injection [*of wastes*] .... UI
Underground Injection Control [*Environmental Protection Agency*] .... UIC
Underground Injection Practices Council (EA) .... UIPC
Underground Keybox Vault (NATG) .... UKV
Underground Mine Engineer .... UME
Underground Nuclear Explosion .... UNE
Underground Nuclear Explosion .... UNX
Underground Nuclear Test .... UNT
Underground Press Syndicate [*Later, APS*] (EA) .... UPS
Underground Pumped Hydro [*Energy storage*] .... UPH
Underground Railroad [*A smuggling system*] [*Criminal slang*] .... UGRR
Underground Residential Distribution [*Cable*] .... URD
Underground Rural Distribution (IAA) .... URD
Underground Security Storage Association [*Defunct*] .... USSA
Underground Service Entrance .... USE
Underground Sources of Drinking Water .... USDW
Underground Storage Tank [*Environmental Protection Agency*] .... UST
Underground Test (MCD) .... UGT
Underground Validation Facility [*Nuclear energy*] (NUCP) .... UVF
Underhatch .... UH
Underheat .... UHT
Underhill on Evidence [*A publication*] (DLA) .... Underhill Ev
Underhill on New Conveyancing [*1925*] [*A publication*] (DLA) .... Und Conv
Underhill on Parternship [*10th ed.*] [*1975*] [*A publication*] (DLA) .... Und Part
Underhill on Torts [*A publication*] (DLA) .... Und Torts
Underhill on Trusts and Trustees [*A publication*] (DLA) .... Und Tr

Underhill's Chancery Procedure [*1881*] [*A publication*] (DLA) ... Und Ch Pr
Underlay ... UL
Underlay Battle Manager ... ULBM
Underlever [*Rifles*] (DICI) ... U/L
Underload (NASA) ... UL
Underload ... UNDLD
Underlying Heart Rhythm [*Medicine*] (DMAA) ... UHR
Underlying Stock [*Finance*] ... US
Undermanned Tank Crew Test [*Military*] (MCD) ... UTCT
Under-Mentioned [*i.e., mentioned later in a document*] ... UM
Underpass [*Commonly used*] (OPSA) ... UNDERPASS
Underpass [*Postal Service standard*] (OPSA) ... UPAS
Underpass ... UPAS
Underpotential Deposition [*Electrochemistry*] ... UPD
Under-Proof [*Of spirituous liquors*] [*Distilling*] ... UP
Underrange (IEEE) ... U/R
Underreporter [*IRS*] ... UR
Underreporter Program [*IRS*] ... URP
Undersampling Ratio ... UDR
Undersea (AABC) ... USEA
Undersea and Hyperbaric Medical Society (EA) ... UHMS
Undersea Instrument Chamber [*Marine science*] (MSC) ... USIC
Undersea [*or Underwater*] **Long-Range Missile** [*Navy*] ... ULM
Undersea [*or Underwater*] **Long-Range Missile System** [*Redesignated "Trident"*] [*Navy*] ... ULMS
Undersea Medical Society, Inc. ... UMS
Undersea Multichannel Large-Scale Scattering Meter [*NASA*] (MCD) ... ULASM
Undersea Radioisotope Power Supply ... URIPS
Undersea Research Corp. ... URC
Undersea Research Vehicle [*or Vessel*] ... URV
Undersea Scientific Expedition ... USE
Undersea Surveillance System (MCD) ... USSS
Undersea Technology ... UST
Undersea Warfare ... USW
Undersea Warfare Development Division [*Navy*] (MCD) ... UWDD
Undersea Warfare Division [*Navy*] (DNAB) ... USWDIV
Undersea Weapon System ... UWS
Undersecretary of Defense for Policy (MCD) ... USD(P)
Underside ... U/S
Undersigned (ROG) ... UNDERSD
Undersigned (BARN) ... undsgd
Undersize (AAG) ... US
Underspeed (MSA) ... US
Understanding (ROG) ... UNDERSTG
Understanding Aging (EA) ... UA
Understanding British Industry [*An association*] (ODBW) ... UBI
Understanding Industry (AIE) ... UI
Understanding of the Problem (MCD) ... UOP
Understanding Personal and Racial Dignity [*Navy program*] ... UPWARD
Understanding Science in the Environment [*Australia*] ... USE
Understanding without Heavy Acronym Training (AIE) ... UWHAT
Undertaker (WGA) ... UNDTKR
Undertaking (ROG) ... UNDERTG
Undertakings for Collective Investment in Transferable Securities [*European Community*] ... UCITS
Undervoltage ... UNDV
Under-Voltage Circuit-Breaker [*Electronics*] (EECA) ... UVCB
Undervoltage Device ... UVD
Under-Voltage Protection [*Electronics*] (EECA) ... UVP
Underwater [*Missile launch environment symbol*] ... U
Underwater (KSC) ... UNDW
Underwater ... UW
Underwater (AABC) ... UWTR
Underwater [*JETDS nomenclature*] ... W
Underwater Acoustic Decoupler ... UAD
Underwater Acoustic Group [*British*] ... UAG
Underwater Acoustic Interference Coordinating Committee [*Military*] ... UAICC
Underwater Acoustic Receiving System [*Navy*] (MCD) ... UARS
Underwater Acoustic Resistance ... UAR
Underwater Acoustic Sound Source System ... UASSS
Underwater Actuator ... UA
Underwater Angle Receptacle ... UAR
Underwater Antivehicle Mine (MCD) ... UWAVM
Underwater Association for Scientific Research [*Margate, Kent, England*] [*Defunct*] (EAIO) ... UA
Underwater Battery [*Navy*] ... UB
Underwater Battery Director Indicator ... UBDI
Underwater Battery Fire Control [*Navy*] ... UBFC
Underwater Battery Fire Control System [*Navy*] ... UBFCS
Underwater Battery Plot [*Antisubmarine warfare*] ... UBP
Underwater Battery Plotting Room [*Navy*] (NVT) ... UBPLOT
Underwater Breathing Apparatus [*Navy*] (CAAL) ... UBA
Underwater Cable System ... UCS
Underwater Coded Command Release System ... UCCRS
Underwater Communications (MCD) ... UC
Underwater Communications [*Navy*] (CAAL) ... UWC
Underwater Communications System ... UCS
Underwater Conservation Society [*British*] (DI) ... UCS
Underwater Construction Team [*Navy*] (NVT) ... UCT
Underwater Control Rating 1st Class [*British military*] (DMA) ... UC1
Underwater Control Rating 2nd Class [*British military*] (DMA) ... UC2
Underwater Countermeasures and Weapons Establishment [*British*] ... UCWE
Underwater Countermeasures and Weapons Research Establishment [*British militar y*] (DMA) ... UCWRE
Underwater Crash Locator System (MCD) ... UCLS
Underwater Damage Assessment Television System (DNAB) ... UDATS
Underwater Data Link (MCD) ... UDL
Underwater Decompression Computer [*Navy*] (CAAL) ... UDC
Underwater Demolition [*Navy*] (NVT) ... UD
Underwater Demolition Team [*Navy*] ... UDT
Underwater Demolition Team Detachment [*Navy*] (NVT) ... UDTDET
Underwater Demolition Team/Explosive Ordnance Proposal [*Navy*] (MCD) ... UDT/EOD
Underwater Demolition Teams, Amphibious Forces, Pacific Fleet [*Navy*] ... UDTPHIBSPAC
Underwater Demolition Unit ... UDU
Underwater Detection and Classification System (IAA) ... UDACS
Underwater Detection Establishment [*British*] (MCD) ... UDE
Underwater Doppler Navigation ... UDN
Underwater Electric Potential ... UEP
Underwater Environmental Laboratory [*General Electric Co.*] ... UEL
Underwater Explorers' Club of Western Australia ... UECWA
Underwater Explorers Society (EA) ... UNEXSO
Underwater Explosion [*Navy*] ... UNDEX
Underwater Explosion Research and Development Center [*Navy*] (CAAL) ... UERDC
Underwater Explosives Research Division [*Navy*] ... UERD
Underwater Explosives Research Laboratory ... UERL
Underwater Fire Control [*Navy*] (CAAL) ... UWFC
Underwater Fire Control Computer [*Navy*] (CAAL) ... UFCC
Underwater Fire Control Group ... UFCG
Underwater Fire Control System ... UFCS
Underwater Fire Control System ... UWFCS
Underwater Guided Missile [*DoD*] (MCD) ... UGM
Underwater Habitat ... UWH
Underwater Integration Communication ... UNICOM
Underwater LASER Surveying System (MCD) ... ULSS
Underwater Launch ... UWL
Underwater Launch Control Energy Requirements ... ULCER
Underwater Launch Current and Energy Recorder ... ULCER
Underwater Locator Beacon (MCD) ... ULB
Underwater Locator Beacon ... ULR
Underwater Manifold Centre [*Shell Oil Co.*] [*British*] ... UMC
Underwater Mechanic [*Obsolete Navy*] ... ESM
Underwater Mechanic ... UM
Underwater Naturalist [*A publication*] (BRI) ... Under Nat
Underwater Naturalist [*A publication*] ... Underw Nat
Underwater Object Location and Search Operations [*Navy*] (NVT) ... UOLS
Underwater Object Locator ... UOL
Underwater Ordnance Development Group ... UODG
Underwater Ordnance Station [*Navy*] ... UOS
Underwater Ordnance Technician [*Navy*] (DNAB) ... UWORDTECH
Underwater Photographic Society (EA) ... UPS
Underwater Photography Instruction Association [*Defunct*] (EA) ... UPIA
Underwater Pipe Cutter ... UPC
Underwater Pump Jet ... UPJ
Underwater Range (MUGU) ... UWR
Underwater Research Group of New South Wales [*Australia*] ... URGNSW
Underwater Search, Detection, Classification (AAG) ... USDC
Underwater Security Advance Warnings [*Navy*] ... USAW
Underwater Society of America (EA) ... USA
Underwater Sound Advisory Group [*Navy*] ... USAG
Underwater Sound Explosive Devices Branch [*Naval Weapons Station*] [*Yorktown, VA*] ... USED
Underwater Sound Laboratory [*New London, CT*] [*Navy*] ... USL
Underwater Sound Projection ... USP
Underwater Sound Reference Detachment [*Orlando, FL*] [*Navy*] ... USRD
Underwater Sound Reference Division, Naval Research Laboratory ... USRD/NRL
Underwater Sound Reference Laboratory [*Navy*] ... USRL
Underwater Sound Source ... USS
Underwater Systems Group [*Range Commanders Council*] [*White Sands Missile Range, NM*] ... USG
Underwater Tactical Range, Pacific ... UTRP
Underwater Tank Facility ... UTF
Underwater Target-Activated Sensor (MCD) ... UTAS
Underwater Team (MSA) ... UWTM
Underwater Telephone [*Navy*] (CAAL) ... UQC
Underwater Telephone ... UWT
Underwater Telephone System ... UTS
Underwater Television ... UTV
Underwater Television and Inspection System ... UNIS
Underwater Terrain Navigation and Reconnaissance Simulator (MCD) ... UTNRS
Underwater Test Facility [*GE*] ... UTF
Underwater Tracking Equipment (MCD) ... UTE
Underwater Tracking Range ... UTR
Underwater Training Centre [*British*] ... UTC
Underwater Vehicle ... UV
Underwater Weapons [*British*] ... UW
Underwater Weapons and Countermeasures Establishment (BARN) ... UWCE
Underwater Weapons Control System ... UWCS
Underwater Weapons Department [*British military*] (DMA) ... UWD
Underwater Weapons System Design Disclosure Management Systems (KSC) ... UWSDDMS
Underwater Weapons Systems Engineering Center [*Navy*] (DNAB) ... UWSEC
Underwater Weapons Systems Reliability Data (KSC) ... UWSRD
Underwater Welding Habitat [*Deep-sea diving*] ... UWH
Underwater Wide-Angle Lens ... UWAL
Underwater-to-Air Missile [*Air Force*] ... UAM
Underwater-to-Air-to-Underwater (IAA) ... UAU
Underwater-to-Air-to-Underwater Missile [*Air Force*] ... UAUM

Underwater-to-Surface (IAA) .... US
Underwater-to-Surface Guided Weapon (MCD) .... USGW
Underwater-to-Surface Missile [Air Force] .... USM
Underwater-to-Underwater Missile [Air Force] .... UUM
Underway (NVT) .... U/W
Underway Acceptance Trials (MCD) .... UAT
Underway Material Inspection [Navy] (NVT) .... UMI
Underway Rearming [Navy] (NVT) .... REARM
Underway Replenishment [Military] .... UNREP
Underway Replenishment Group [Military] .... URG
Underway Replenishment Group [Military] .... URGR
Underway Training Unit .... UTU
Underway Training Unit .... UWATU
Underway Training Unit, Norfolk, Virginia (DNAB) .... UWAYTUNORVA
Underway Trial/Acceptance Trial [Navy] (NVT) .... UT/AT
Underway Trials [Shipbuilding] .... UT
Underway Trials and Material Inspection (MCD) .... UT/MI
Underwear .... UNDWR
Underwear Institute [Later, NKMA] (EA) .... UI
Underwear-Negligee Associates (EA) .... UNA
Underwood McLellan Ltd., Lethbridge, Alberta [Library symbol National
    Library of Canada] (NLC) .... ALUM
Underwood McLellan Ltd., Winnipeg, Manitoba [Library symbol National
    Library of Canada] (NLC) .... MWUML
Underwood McLellan Ltd., Winnipeg, MB, Canada [Library symbol Library of
    Congress] (LCLS) .... CaMWUML
Underwood on Art Copyright [A publication] (DLA) .... Und Art Cop
Underwood Public School, Underwood, MN [Library symbol] [Library of
    Congress] (LCLS) .... MnUnS
Underworld Nobility [Used by Walter Winchell to refer to mobsters in television
    series "The Untouchables"] .... UN
Underwriter [Insurance] .... U/W
Underwriter [Insurance] (DLA) .... U/Wr
Underwriter .... UNDERWRTR
Underwriter (DFIT) .... UW
Underwriters [Insurance] .... Urs
Underwriters Adjusting Company .... UAC
Underwriters Adjustment Bureau .... UAB
Underwriters Grain Association (EA) .... UGA
Underwriters Laboratories (EA) .... UL
Underwriters Laboratories, Inc. [Also, UL] .... ULI
Underwriters' Laboratories of Canada .... ULC
Underwriters Salvage Company .... USCo
Underwriters Service Association .... USA
Underwriters' Special Request .... US
Underwriting .... UNDERWRTNG
Underwriting Account [Insurance] .... U/A
Undesirable Discharge [Military] .... UD
Undesirable Discharge, Desertion without Trial [Navy] .... UDDE
Undesirable Discharge, Fraudulent Enlistment [Navy] .... UDFE
Undesirable Discharge, Trial by Civil Authorities [Navy] .... UDCA
Undesirable Discharge, Unfitness [Navy] .... UDUF
Undetected Defect .... UD
Undetermined [MARC language code Library of Congress] (LCCP) .... und
Undetermined .... UNDET
Undetermined (WGA) .... UNDETD
Undetermined (AABC) .... UNDETM
Undetermined .... UTD
Undetermined Aerodynamic Disturbance (MCD) .... UAD
Undetermined Brain Opacities [Magnetic Resonance Imaging] (CPH) .... UBO
Undetermined Etiology .... UDE
Undetermined Origin [Medicine] (AAMN) .... UDO
Undetermined Origin [Medicine] (DAVI) .... undet ori
Undetermined Origin [Medicine] (CPH) .... Undet Orig
UNDEX [Underwater Explosion] Test Facility [Navy] (RDA) .... UTF
Undifferentiated (BJA) .... UD
Undifferentiated B-Cell Lymphoma [Medicine] .... UBL
Undifferentiated Carcinoma [Oncology] .... UC
Undifferentiated Carcinoma of Nasopharyngeal Type [Oncology] .... UCNT
Undifferentiated Infiltrating [Tumor] [Oncology] .... UI
Undifferentiated Lymphoma [Medicine] (MAE) .... UL
Undiluted .... UD
Undistorted Power Output .... UPO
Undistorted Signal (IAA) .... US
Undistributed Budget (MCD) .... UB
Undistributed Net Income [Banking] .... UNI
Undistributed Personal Holding Company Income .... UPHCI
Undistributed Taxable Income .... UTI
Undivided (DLA) .... Und
Undivided Back [Deltiology] .... UNDBK
Undock [NASA] (KSC) .... UNDK
Unducted Fan [Type of prop engine developed by General Electric Co.] .... UDF
Undulating Beam Interaction Electron Tube .... UBITRON
Undulator Radiation [High-energy physics] .... UR
Unearned Income (MHDW) .... UI
Unearned Premium [Insurance] .... UP
Unearned Premiums Reserve [Finance] .... UPR
Unedged (DAC) .... U/E
Unemployed and Poverty Action Council (EA) .... UPAC
Unemployed Father (OICC) .... UF
Unemployed Full Pay [Military British] .... UFP
Unemployed Parent [Aid to Families with Dependent Children] (OICC) .... U
Unemployed Parent [Department of Health and Human Services] .... UP
Unemployed Peoples Union (NADA) .... OPU
Unemployed Supernumerary List [Military British] .... USL

Unemployed Time [Military British] .... UT
Unemployment .... U
Unemployment (GFGA) .... UE
Unemployment Assistance Board .... UAB
Unemployment Benefit Office [British] .... UBO
Unemployment Benefits [Unemployment insurance] (OICC) .... UB
Unemployment Compensation .... UC
Unemployment Compensation, Ex-Servicemen .... UCX
Unemployment Compensation, Federal Employees (DLA) .... UCFE
Unemployment Compensation Interpretation Service (DLA) .... UCIS
Unemployment Compensation News [James E. Frick, Inc.] [Information
    service or system] (CRD) .... UCN
Unemployment Insurance .... UI
Unemployment Insurance Act [Canada] .... UIA
Unemployment Insurance Code (OICC) .... UIC
Unemployment Insurance Code [A publication] (DLA) .... Un Ins Co
Unemployment Insurance Commission [Canada] .... UIC
Unemployment Insurance Commission, Ottawa, ON, Canada [Library symbol
    Library of Congress Obsolete] (LCLS) .... CaOOUI
Unemployment Insurance Department .... UID
Unemployment Insurance Reports [Commerce Clearing House]
    [A publication] (DLA) .... Unempl Ins Rep
Unemployment Insurance Reports (Commerce Clearing House)
    [A publication] (DLA) .... Unempl Ins Rep (CCH)
Unemployment Insurance Review [A publication] .... UNIR
Unemployment Insurance Service [Department of Labor] .... UIS
Unemployment Insurance Service Design Center [Department of Labor] .... UISDC
Unemployment Unit [An association British] .... UU
UNEP [United Nations Environment Program] Network for Latin America and
    the Carribean (EERA) .... UNEPNET-LAC
UNEP [United Nations Environmental Programme] Regional Office for Latin
    America (EAIO) .... UROLA
Unequal Error Protection (IEEE) .... UEP
Unequilibrated Ordinary Chondrites .... UOC
Unerupted (MAE) .... U
UNESCO Association/USA (EA) .... UA/USA
UNESCO Copyright Bulletin [A publication] (DLA) .... Copyright Bull
UNESCO Institute for Education .... UIE
UNESCO Publications and Periodicals .... UPP
UNESCO Publications Center (WDAA) .... UPC
UNESCO Regional Office for Education in Asia and Oceania [Thailand]
    (DLA) .... UROEA
UNESCO Relations Staff .... URS
UNESCO Statistical Yearbook [A publication] .... UN
Unesterified Fatty Acid [Biochemistry] .... UFA
Unevaluated (MCD) .... UNEV
Uneven [Quality of the bottom] [Nautical charts] .... unev
Unexecuted .... UNEX
Unexecuted Portion of Orders Cancelled .... UNORDCAN
Unexpected Home Attack [Medicine] .... UHA
Unexpected Real Incapacitation (DNAB) .... URI
Unexpected Wildlife Refuge (EA) .... UWR
Unexpired (ADA) .... UE
Unexpired Term [Real estate] [British] (ROG) .... UT
Unexplained .... UNEXPL
Unexplained Acute Respiratory Distress Syndrome .... UARDS
Unexplained Aerial Object .... UAO
Unexplained Infertility .... UI
Unexplained Respiratory Distress Syndrome [Medicine] .... URDS
Unexplained Standard Deviation [Statistics] .... USD
Unexploded .... UNEXPL
Unexploded (BARN) .... UX
Unexploded Antiaircraft [Shell] .... UXAA
Unexploded Antipersonnel Bomb .... UXAPB
Unexploded Bomb .... UEB
Unexploded Bomb .... UXB
Unexploded Bomb (SAA) .... UXPLD
Unexploded Booklet [Philately] .... UNB
Unexploded Gas Bomb .... UXGB
Unexploded Incendiary Bomb .... UXIB
Unexploded Ordnance .... UXO
Unexploded Ordnance Incident .... UXOI
Unexploded Parachuted Mine .... UXPM
Unexploded Shell [British military] (DMA) .... UXS
Unexploded Type G Mine .... UXTGM
Unexplored .... UNEXPL
Unfair Competition (MHDW) .... UC
Unfair Industrial Practice .... UIP
Unfair Labor Practice [Department of Labor] .... ULP
Unfair Labor Practices (WYGK) .... ULP
Unfavorable .... UNFAV
Unfavorable Balance of Trade (MHDW) .... UBOT
Unfavorable Information File [Military] .... UIF
Unfederated Malay States .... UMS
Unfinanced Requirement [Army] .... UFR
Unfinanced Requirement [Army] (AABC) .... UFR
Unfinished .... UFNSHD
Unfinished [Technical drawings] .... UNF
Unfinished .... UNFI
Unfinished .... UNFIN
Unfired Pressure Vessel .... UPV
Unfired Pressure Vessel Code (AAG) .... UPVC
Unfit for Broadcast (WDMC) .... UFB
Unflagged Order [Laboratory science] (DAVI) .... UFO
Unfractionated Heparin [Anticoagulant] .... uH

Unfractionated Reservoir [*Geology*] .... UR
Unfunded Requirement [*Military*] (AFIT) .... UR
Unfused (KSC) .... UNF
Ungava [*Canada*] .... UNG
Unge Hoyres Landsforbund [*Norway Political party*] (EAIO) .... UHL
Unglazed (VRA) .... unglz
Unglazed Ceramic Mosaic Tile [*Technical drawings*] .... UCMT
Unglazed Structural Facing Units [*Technical drawings*] .... USFU
Unglazed Structural Unit Base [*Technical drawings*] .... USUB
Unguentum [*Ointment*] [*Pharmacy*] .... UNG
Unguentum [*Ointment*] [*Pharmacy*] .... UNGT
Unguia [*Colombia*] [*Airport symbol*] (AD) .... UNC
Unhealthy to be Unpleasant [*Theatrical play*] (IIA) .... UTBU
Unheard (FAAC) .... UNHRD
Unheated Serum Reagin (Test) [*Clinical chemistry*] (AAMN) .... USR
Unholding Corp. [*NASDAQ symbol*] (TTSB) .... UHLD
Uni Air [*France ICAO designator*] (FAAC) .... UAR
Uni Air International [*France ICAO designator*] (ICDA) .... UF
Uni Air SA [*France ICAO designator*] (FAAC) .... UAI
Uni Holding Corp. [*NASDAQ symbol*] (SAG) .... UHLD
Uni Taschenbuecher GmbH [*German publishers cooperative*] .... UTB
Unia Socjaldemokratyczna Rzeczypospolitej Polskiej [*Social Democratic Union of the Republic of Poland*] [*Political party*] .... USDRP
Uniado do Centro Democrata Cristao [*Union of the Christian Democratic Center*] [*Portugal Political party*] (PPE) .... UCDC
Uniao Cultural Brasil-Estados Unidos [*Brazil-United States Cultural Union*] [*Brazil*] (EAIO) .... UCBEU
Uniao da Esquerda Socialista Democratica [*Union of the Socialist and Democratic Left*] [*Portugal Political party*] (PPW) .... UESD
Uniao da Vitoria [*Brazil*] [*Airport symbol*] (AD) .... UNI
Uniao das Populacoes de Angola [*Angolan People's Union*] [*Later, NFLA*] .... UPA
Uniao de Esquerda para a Democracia Socialista [*Left Union for Social Democracy*] [*Portugal Political party*] (PPE) .... UEDS
Uniao Democratica de Cabo Verde [*Democratic Union of Cape Verde*] .... UDC
Uniao Democratica de Cabo Verde [*Democratic Union of Cape Verde*] .... UDCV
Uniao Democratica Nacional [*National Democratic Union*] [*Brazil*] .... UDN
Uniao Democratica Nacional de Mocambique [*Mozambican National Democratic Union*] [*Later, FRELIMO*] [*Political party*] .... UDENAMO
Uniao Democratica Popular [*Popular Democratic Unity*] [*Portugal*] [*Political party*] .... UDP
Uniao do Povo para Independencia de Cabo Verde-Ressusitacao [*Cape Verde*] [*Political party*] (EY) .... UPICV-R
Uniao dos Povos das Ilhas do Cabo Verde [*Union of the Peoples of the Cape Verde Islands*] .... UPICV
Uniao Nacional Africana de Mocambique Independente [*Mozambique*] [*Political party*] .... UNAMI
Uniao Nacional para a Independencia Total de Angola [*National Union for the Complete Independence of Angola*] (AF) .... UNITA
Uniao Nacional Republicana [*National Republican Union*] [*Portugal Political party*] (PPE) .... UNR
Uniao Republicana [*Republican Union*] [*Portugal Political party*] (PPE) .... UR
Uniao Revolucionaria, Marxista-Leninista [*Marxist-Leninist Revolutionary Union*] [*Portugal Political party*] (PPE) .... UR M-L
Uniao Social Democratico [*Social Democratic Union*] [*Portugal Political party*] (PPE) .... USD
Uniaxial Gyrostabilizer .... UGS
Uniaxial Split-Sphere Apparatus [*Mineralogy*] .... USSA
Uniaxial Stress Field .... USF
Unibus Interface (IAA) .... UBI
Unibus Microchannel .... UMC
Unican Security Systems Ltd. [*Toronto Stock Exchange symbol*] .... UCS
Unicbank [*Unique Bank*] [*Hungary*] .... UB
Unichannel .... UC
Unico American [*NASDAQ symbol*] (TTSB) .... UNAM
Unico American Corp. [*NASDAQ symbol*] (NQ) .... UNAM
Unico American Corp. [*Associated Press*] (SAG) .... UnicoA
Unico Corp. [*Associated Press*] (SAG) .... Unico Cp
Unico Inc. [*NASDAQ symbol*] (TTSB) .... UNRC
UNICO, Inc. Delaware [*NASDAQ symbol*] (NQ) .... UICO
Unico, Inc. Delaware [*Associated Press*] (SAG) .... UniDE
Unico, Inc. New Mexico [*NASDAQ symbol*] (SAG) .... UNRC
Unico Inc. Oklahoma [*NASDAQ symbol*] (TTSB) .... UICO
Unico National (EA) .... UN
Unicom Corp. [*Formerly, Commonwealth Edison*] [*NYSE symbol*] (SAG) .... UCM
Unicom Corp. [*Formerly, Commonwealth Edison*] [*Associated Press*] (SAG) .... Unicom
UniComp, Inc. [*NASDAQ symbol*] (NQ) .... UCMP
UniComp, Inc. [*Associated Press*] (SAG) .... UniCmp
Unicorn [*Record label*] .... Uni
Unicorn Resources [*Vancouver Stock Exchange symbol*] .... UNO
Unicorns Unanimous [*An association*] (EA) .... UU
Unicorp Canada Corp. [*Toronto Stock Exchange symbol*] .... UNI
Unicorp Resources Ltd. [*Toronto Stock Exchange symbol*] .... UNR
Unicycling Society of America [*Later, USA, Inc.*] (EA) .... USA
Unicycling Society of America, Inc. (EA) .... USA Inc
Unidad Alavesa [*Spain Political party*] (EY) .... UA
Unidad de Izquierda Comunista [*Unity of the Communist Left*] [*Mexico Political party*] (PPW) .... UIC
Unidad Democratica Popular [*Popular Democratic Unity*] [*Peru*] [*Political party*] (PPW) .... UDP
Unidad Democratica Popular [*Popular Democratic Unity*] [*Bolivia*] [*Political party*] .... UDP
Unidad Informativa Computable [*Computerized Information Unit*] [*Mexico Information service or system*] (IID) .... UNICOM
Unidad Revolucionaria Nacional Guatemalteca [*Guatemalan National Revolutionary Unity*] [*Political party*] (PD) .... URNG
Unidensity Coherent Light Recording (IAA) .... UNICOH
Unidensity Coherent Light Recording (IEEE) .... UNICON
Unidentifiable (BJA) .... UD
Unidentified .... U/I
Unidentified (VRA) .... unid
Unidentified (DAVI) .... UNID
Unidentified .... UNIDENT
Unidentified [*Marketing surveys*] (NTCM) .... UUUU
Unidentified Atmospheric Noise (DNAB) .... UAN
Unidentified Atmospheric Phenomena .... UAP
Unidentified Bright Object .... UBO
Unidentified Endosteal Marrow Cell [*Hematology*] .... UEMC
Unidentified Flying Object [*"Flying saucers"*] [*Facetious translation: "Undue Fuss Over"*] .... UFO
Unidentified Flying Object Information Retrieval Center, Inc. (EA) .... UFOIRC
Unidentified Flying Object Research Queensland [*Australia*] .... UFORQ
Unidentified Foreign Object [*Medicine*] (DAVI) .... UFO
Unidentified Growth Factor .... UGF
Unidentified Infrared Band [*Astrophysics*] .... UIB
Unidentified Infrared Band [*Spectroscopy*] .... UIR
Unidentified Nonflying Objects .... UNFO
Unidentified Paleontological Object .... UPO
Unidentified Process Loss .... UPL
Unidentified Reading Frame [*Genetics*] .... URF
Unidentified Remittance [*IRS*] .... UR
Unidentified Remittance Amount File [*IRS*] .... URAF
Unidentified Remittance Control File [*IRS*] .... URCF
Unidentified Remittance File [*IRS*] .... URF
Unidentified Remittance Name File [*IRS*] .... URNF
Unidentified Submarine Object .... USO
Unidentified Submerged Illuminated Object (DNAB) .... USIO
Unidentified Superconducting Object (ECON) .... USO
Unidigital Inc. [*NASDAQ symbol*] (TTSB) .... UNDG
Unidigital, Inc. [*NASDAQ symbol*] (SAG) .... UNDG
Unidigital, Inc. [*Associated Press*] (SAG) .... Unidig
Unidimensional Drafting Manual .... UDM
Unidirectional .... UD
Unidirectional Categorical Grammar .... UCG
Unidirectional Composite (MCD) .... UDC
Unidirectional Current (IAA) .... UDC
Unidirectional Filamentary Composite .... UFC
Unidirectional Molding Compound (MCD) .... UMC
Unidirectional Transducer (IAA) .... UDT
Unifarm Association, Edmonton, AB, Canada [*Library symbol Library of Congress*] (LCLS) .... CaAEUN
Unifarm, Edmonton, Alberta [*Library symbol National Library of Canada*] (NLC) .... AEUN
Unifi, Inc. [*NYSE symbol*] (SPSG) .... UFI
Unifi, Inc. (MHDW) .... UNFI
Unifi, Inc. [*Associated Press*] (SAG) .... Unifi
Unificacion y Progreso [*Unification and Progress*] [*Mexico Political party*] (PPW) .... UPAC
Unification du Droit Prive .... UDP
Unification National Party [*South Korea Political party*] (EY) .... UNP
Unification of Law Yearbook [*A publication*] (DLA) .... Unific LYB
Unification of Units of Measurement Panel [*ICAO*] (DA) .... UUMP
Unified .... U
Unified (AAG) .... UN
Unified (DLA) .... Unif
Unified Action Armed Forces [*Military*] .... UNAAF
Unified and Specified [*or Strategic*] **Command** (MCD) .... U & S
Unified Arab Command (BJA) .... UAC
Unified Atomic Mass [*Physics*] (WDAA) .... U
Unified Atomic Mass Unit [*Nuclear energy*] (IAA) .... U
Unified Atomic Mass Unit (IDOE) .... u
Unified Automated Communication Network .... UACN
Unified Automatic Network [*Telecommunications*] (OA) .... UAN
Unified Classification Code (NITA) .... UCC
Unified Coarse [*Thread*] .... UNC
Unified Command [*DoD*] .... UCOM
Unified Command Plan [*Military*] (AFM) .... UCP
Unified Communications [*Radio station*] .... UNICOM
Unified Communications Navigation Identification .... UCNI
Unified Data Base .... UDB
Unified Data System [*Computer science*] .... UDS
Unified Direct Access Standards (IAA) .... UDAS
Unified Direct Access System (BUR) .... UDAS
Unified Electronic Computer System [*Air Force*] .... UECS
Unified Energy System [*Russia*] .... UES
Unified Extra Fine [*Thread*] .... UNEF
Unified Fine [*Thread*] .... UNF
Unified Fire Control (MCD) .... UFC
Unified Flexible Spacecraft Simulation .... UFSS
Unified Flight Analysis System [*NASA*] .... UFAS
Unified Forces [*Military*] .... UF
Unified Forces [*Military*] .... UNIFOR
Unified Industries, Inc. .... UII
Unified Information Access System .... UIAS
Unified Information Access System [*California State University*] .... UIAS
Unified Legal Services Program .... ULSP
Unified Life Cycle Engineering (MCD) .... ULCE
Unified Management Corp. Database [*Information service or system*] (CRD) .... UMC

Unified Memory Architecture [*Computer science*] (PCM) ... UMA
Unified Memory Architecture (PCM) ... UMA
Unified Miniature ... UNM
Unified Modular Plant [*Nuclear energy*] ... UNIMOD
Unified National Coarse Thread (IAA) ... UNC
Unified National Extra Fine Thread (IAA) ... UNEF
Unified National Fine (IAA) ... UNF
Unified National J Series Coarse [*Thread*] ... UNJC
Unified National J Series Extra Fine [*Thread*] ... UNJEF
Unified National J Series Fine [*Thread*] ... UNJF
Unified National J Series Special [*Thread*] ... UNJS
Unified Navy Field Test Program (MCD) ... UNFTP
Unified Network Management Architecture [*Computer science*] ... UNMA
Unified Network Management Architecture (TNIG) ... UNMA
Unified Network Planning Study ... UNPS
Unified Nimbus Observatory (MCD) ... UNO
Unified Numbering Systems [*for metals*] (MCD) ... UNS
Unified Numeric Representation Arithmetic Unit (PDAA) ... UNRAU
Unified Numerical Control Language (IAA) ... UNCL
Unified Parkinson's Disease Rating Scale ... UPDRS
Unified Pilot Publication System [*American Chemical Society*] ... UPPS
Unified Planning Work Program ... UPWP
Unified Prediction and Analysis Code (MCD) ... UNIPAC
Unified Programme [*Education*] (AIE) ... UP
Unified Radioactive Isodromic Regulator ... URIR
Unified S-Band (MCD) ... USB
Unified S-Band Communication and Navigation System [*NASA*] ... USCANS
Unified S-Band Equipment ... USBE
Unified S-Band Equipment ... USE
Unified S-Band System [*Radio*] ... USBS
Unified S-Band System [*Radio*] ... USS
Unified School District ... USD
Unified School District Number One, Mary D. Bradford High School, Kenosha, WI [*Library symbol Library of Congress*] (LCLS) ... WKenSD-B
Unified School District Number One, Media Center, Kenosha, WI [*Library symbol Library of Congress*] (LCLS) ... WKenSD
Unified School District Number One, Tremper High School, Kenosha, WI [*Library symbol Library of Congress*] (LCLS) ... WKenSD-T
Unified School District Number One, Walter Reuther High School, Kenosha, WI [*Library symbol Library of Congress*] (LCLS) ... WKenSD-R
Unified Science and Mathematics for Elementary Schools [*National Science Foundation*] ... USMES
Unified Soil Classification (GNE) ... USC
Unified Space Applications Mission (MCD) ... USAM
Unified Special [*Thread*] ... UNS
Unified Switching Equipment Practice (MCD) ... UNISWEP
Unified Test Plan ... UTP
Unified Theological Seminary, Barrytown, NY [*Library symbol*] [*Library of Congress*] (LCLS) ... NBaryU
Unified Transfer System [*Computer to translate Russian to English*] ... UTS
Unified Translation Lookaside Buffer [*Computer science*] (PCM) ... UTLB
Unified Transportation Assistance Program [*Proposed*] ... UTAP
Unified Vocational Preparation [*Manpower Services Commission*] [*British*] ... UVP
Unifirst Corp. [*NYSE symbol*] (SPSG) ... UNF
Unifirst Corp. [*Associated Press*] (SAG) ... UniFirst
Uniflex, Inc. [*AMEX symbol*] (SAG) ... UFX
Uniflex, Inc. [*Associated Press*] (SAG) ... Uniflex
Uniflow Diesel [*Nissan-designed engine*] ... UD
Unifly [*Italy ICAO designator*] (FAAC) ... BJA
Uniforce Services [*NASDAQ symbol*] (TTSB) ... UNFR
Uniforce Services, Inc. [*NASDAQ symbol*] (SAG) ... UNFR
Uniforce Services, Inc. [*Associated Press*] (SAG) ... Unifrce
Uniforce Temporary Personnel, Inc. [*New Hyde Park, NY*] [*NASDAQ symbol*] (NQ) ... UNFR
Uniforce Temporary Personnel, Inc. [*Associated Press*] (SAG) ... Unifrce
Uniform ... U
Uniform [*Phonetic alphabet*] [*International*] (DSUE) ... U
Uniform ... UNFRM
Uniform (DSUE) ... UNI
Uniform (AFM) ... UNIF
Uniform Accounting System (OICC) ... UAS
Uniform Adoption Act [*Proposed state law*] ... UAA
Uniform Air Quality Index [*Environmental Protection Agency*] (GFGA) ... UAQI
Uniform Aircraft Financial Responsibility Act [*National Conference of Commissioners on Uniform State Laws*] ... UAFRA
Uniform Airman Record ... UAR
Uniform Allowance [*Military*] ... UA
Uniform Ambulatory Medical Case Minimum Data Set [*Department of Health and Human Services*] (GFGA) ... UAMCMDS
Uniform Anatomical Gift Act [*For organ donation*] ... UAGA
Uniform Annual Cost ... UAC
Uniform Asymptotic Theory (IAA) ... UAT
Uniform Automated [*or Automatic*] **Data Processing** ... UADP
Uniform Automated [*or Automatic*] **Data Processing System** ... UADPS
Uniform Automated [*or Automatic*] **Data Processing System for Inventory Control Points** [*Navy*] ... UADPS-ICP
Uniform Automated [*or Automatic*] **Data Processing System for Stock Points** [*Navy*] ... UADPS-SP
Uniform Automated [*or Automatic*] **Data Processing System/Industrial Naval Air Station** ... UADPS/INAS
Uniform Automatic Data Processing System [*Navy*] ... USADPS
Uniform Bank Performance Report [*Federal Financial Institutions Examination Council*] ... UBPR
Uniform Bearing Stress ... UBS
Uniform Bill of Lading Act [*Legal shorthand*] (LWAP) ... UBLA
Uniform Billing ... UB
Uniform Biological Material Transfer Agreement [*National Institutes of Health*] ... UBMTA
Uniform Boiler and Pressure Vessel Laws Society (EA) ... UBPVLS
Uniform Brain Death Act [*National Conference of Commissioners on Uniform State Laws*] ... UBDA
Uniform Broadband Channel [*Telecommunications*] ... UBC
Uniform Building Code (NRCH) ... UBC
Uniform Business Rate [*Taxation*] [*British*] ... UBR
Uniform Call Distribution [*Telephone system*] ... UCD
Uniform Chart of Accounts [*DoD*] ... UCA
Uniform Child Custody Jurisdiction Act (EDAC) ... UCCJA
Uniform Chromaticity Scale [*Illuminant*] ... UCS
Uniform City Court Act [*A publication*] (DLA) ... Uniform City Ct Act
Uniform Classification Committee [*Later, NRFC*] (EA) ... UCC
Uniform Clinical Data Set ... UCDS
Uniform, Coarse-Grained [*Soil*] ... Uc
Uniform Code Council (EA) ... UCC
Uniform Code of Military Justice ... UCMJ
Uniform Commercial Code [*Also UCC*] (AAGC) ... CC
Uniform Commercial Code [*National Conference of Commissioners on Uniform State Laws*] ... UCC
Uniform Commercial Code Law Letter [*A publication*] (DLA) ... UCC Law Letter
Uniform Commercial Code Reporting Service [*A publication*] (DLA) ... UCC Rep Serv
Uniform Communications System ... UCS
Uniform Comparative Fault Act [*National Conference of Commissioners on Uniform State Laws*] ... UCFA
Uniform Conditional Sales Act [*Legal shorthand*] (LWAP) ... UCSA
Uniform Conservation Easement Act [*National Conference of Commissioners on Uniform State Laws*] ... UCEA
Uniform Consumer Credit Code [*National Conference of Commissioners on Uniform State Laws*] ... UCCC
Uniform Contract Format ... UCF
Uniform Contribution Among Tortfeasors Act [*National Conference of Commissioners on Uniform State Laws*] ... UCATA
Uniform Control Number (NASA) ... UCN
Uniform Controlled Substances Act [*National Conference of Commissioners on Uniform State Laws*] ... UCSA
Uniform Cost Accounting and Reporting System ... UCARS
Uniform Cost Accounting Standards (MCD) ... UCAS
Uniform Credit Code ... UCC
Uniform Crime Reporting Program [*FBI*] ... UCRP
Uniform Crime Reporting System (PDAA) ... UNICRIM
Uniform Crime Reports [*FBI*] ... UCR
Uniform Criminal Extradition Act [*National Conference of Commissioners on Uniform State Laws*] ... UCEA
Uniform Customs and Practice for Documentary Credits [*International Chamber of Commerce*] [*A publication*] (DS) ... UC & P
Uniform Customs and Practice for Documentary Credits [*International Chamber of Congress*] [*A publication*] ... UCP
Uniform Customs Practices (AAGC) ... UCP
Uniform Data Classification Code Structure [*Navy*] (NG) ... UDCCS
Uniform Data Language ... UDL
Uniform Data Link ... UDL
Uniform Datagram Protocol [*Telecommunications*] (OSI) ... UDP
Uniform Delivered Price [*Business term*] (MHDB) ... UDP
Uniform Determination of Death Act [*National Conference of Commissioners on Uniform State Laws*] ... UDDA
Uniform Disclaimer of Property Interests Act [*National Conference of Commissioners on Uniform State Laws*] ... UDPIA
Uniform Disclaimer of Transfers under Nontestamentary Instruments Act [*National Conference of Commissioners on Uniform State Laws*] ... UDTUNIA
Uniform Distribution of Unclaimed Property Act [*National Conference of Commissioners on Uniform State Laws*] ... UDUPA
Uniform District Court Act [*A publication*] (DLA) ... Uniform Dist Ct Act
Uniform Division of Income for Tax Purposes Act ... UDITPA
Uniform Divorce Recognition Act [*National Conference of Commissioners on Uniform State Laws*] ... UDRA
Uniform Effective Health Benefits ... UEHB
Uniform Electric Field ... UEF
Uniform Emission Standard (DCTA) ... UES
Uniform Enforcement of Foreign Judgments Act [*National Conference of Commissioners on Uniform State Laws*] ... UEFJA
Uniform Excess Reporting Procedures [*DoD*] ... UERPS
Uniform External Pressure ... UEP
Uniform Extradition and Rendition Act [*National Conference of Commissioners on Uniform State Laws*] ... UERA
Uniform Federal Accessibility Standards [*Department of Housing and Urban Development*] (GFGA) ... UFAS
Uniform Federal Procurement System (AAGC) ... UFPS
Uniform Federal Regional Council City ... UFRCC
Uniform Field Organization [*DoD*] ... UFO
Uniform Financial Accounting and Reporting Elements [*FTA*] (TAG) ... FARE
Uniform, Fine-Grained [*Soil*] ... Ug
Uniform Fire Incident Reporting System [*National Fire Protection Association*] ... UFIRS
Uniform Firearms Act ... UFA
Uniform Fraudulent Conveyance Act [*National Conference of Commissioners on Uniform State Laws*] ... UFCA
Uniform Fraudulent Transfer Act [*National Conference of Commissioners on Uniform State Laws*] ... UFTA
Uniform Freight Classification ... UFC
Uniform Freight Classification Committee ... UFCC
Uniform General Ledger Accounting Structure (NVT) ... UGLAS

Uniform Geometrical Theory of Diffraction (MCD) .... UGTD
Uniform Gifts to Minors Act [*National Conference of Commissioners on Uniform State Laws*] .... UGMA
Uniform Grain Storage Agreement (AAGC) .... UGSA
Uniform Grocery Product Code Council [*Later, UPCC*] (EA) .... UGPCC
Uniform Guidelines on Employee Selection Procedures [*Equal Employment Opportunity Commission*] (GFGA) .... UGESP
Uniform Heat Flux [*Engineering*] .... UHF
Uniform Hospital Discharge Data Set [*National Center for Health Statistics*] .... UHDDS
Uniform Individual Accident and Sickness Policy Provisions Act [*National Association of Insurance Commissioners*] .... UIASPPA
Uniform Inquiry Update and Edit (MHDI) .... UNIQUE
Uniform Inquiry Update Element .... UNIQUE
Uniform Inspection Guideline .... UIG
Uniform Inventory Control Point .... UICP
Uniform Inventory Control Points System [*Military*] .... UICP
Uniform Land Security Interest Act [*National Conference of Commissioners on Uniform State Laws*] .... ULSIA
Uniform Land Transactions Act [*National Conference of Commissioners on Uniform State Laws*] .... ULTA
Uniform Latex Particles .... ULP
Uniform Law Conference of Canada [*A publication*] (DLA) .... Unif L Conf Can
Uniform Law on the International Sale of Goods .... ULIS
Uniform Law Review [*A publication*] (DLA) .... ULR
Uniform Law Review [*A publication*] (DLA) .... Uniform L Rev
Uniform Laws, Annotated [*A publication*] (DLA) .... ULA
Uniform Lightness and Chromaticity Scale (PDAA) .... ULCS
Uniform Limited Partnership Act [*National Conference of Commissioners on Uniform State Laws*] .... ULPA
Uniform Loop Clock .... ULC
Uniform Low-Frequency Technique .... ULT
Uniform Machine Language Equipment Register [*RSPA*] (TAG) .... UMLER
Uniform Magnetic Field .... UMF
Uniform Management of Institutional Funds Act [*National Conference of Commissioners on Uniform State Laws*] .... UMIFA
Uniform Manufacturers Exchange (EA) .... UME
Uniform Marriage and Divorce Act [*National Conference of Commissioners on Uniform State Laws*] .... UMDA
Uniform Material Issue Priority [*Navy*] .... UMIP
Uniform Material Issue Priority System [*Navy*] (NG) .... UMIPS
Uniform Material Movement and Issue Priority System [*Navy*] (ANA) ...... UMMIS
Uniform Materiel Movement and Issue Priority System [*Military*] (AFM) .... UMMIPS
Uniform, Medium-Grained [*Soil*] .... Um
Uniform - Memory - Access [*Computer science*] .... UMA
Uniform Metric System Procedure Act [*National Conference of Commissioners on Uniform State Laws*] .... UMSPA
Uniform Military Material Issue Priority System (DNAB) .... UMMIPS
Uniform Military Material Movement and Issue Priority System (DNAB) .... UMMMIPS
Uniform Military Personnel Record (AFM) .... UMPR
Uniform Motion Coupling .... UMC
Uniform Moving Charge .... UMC
Uniform Narcotic Drug Act [*National Conference of Commissioners on Uniform State Laws*] .... UNDA
Uniform Officer Record .... UOR
Uniform Parole Reports [*Law Enforcement Assistance Administration*] .... UPR
Uniform Partnership Act .... UPA
Uniform Performance Assessment System [*Education*] .... UPAS
Uniform Perpetuation of Testimony Act [*National Conference of Commissioners on Uniform State Laws*] .... UPTA
Uniform Photographic Interpretation Report [*Military*] (AFM) .... UPIR
Uniform Planned Community Act [*National Conference of Commissioners on Uniform State Laws*] .... UPCA
Uniform Plumbing Code (DAC) .... UPC
Uniform Practice Code .... UPC
Uniform Principal and Income Act [*National Conference of Commissioners on Uniform State Laws*] .... UPIA
Uniform Printing and Supply .... UP & S
Uniform Probate Code .... UPC
Uniform Procurement Instrument Identification Numbering System (MCD) .... UPIINS
Uniform Procurement System .... UPS
Uniform Product Code Council [*Formerly, UGPCC*] (EA) .... UPCC
Uniform Program Salary Administration (MCD) .... UPSA
Uniform Quality Control Program .... UQCP
Uniform Quality Grading System [*Tires*] .... UQGS
Uniform Railroad Cost System [*BTS*] (TAG) .... URCS
Uniform Random Numerator [*Computer science*] .... URN
Uniform Ration Cost System (MCD) .... URCS
Uniform Reciprocal Enforcement of Support Act .... URESA
Uniform Reciprocal Licensing Act [*State law*] [*Insurance*] .... URLA
Uniform Reflectivity Mirror (PDAA) .... URM
Uniform Regulations .... UR
Uniform Relocation Assistance and Real Property Acquisition Act [*1970*] (OICC) .... URARPAA
Uniform Relocation Assistance and Real Property Acquisition Policies Act of 1970 .... URARPAPA
Uniform Rendition of Accused Persons Act [*National Conference of Commissioners on Uniform State Laws*] .... URAPA
Uniform Reporting System .... URS
Uniform Resistance Capacitance [*Electronics*] (IAA) .... URC
Uniform Resource Characteristic [*Computer science*] (EERA) .... URC
Uniform Resource Citations [*Computer science*] .... URC

Uniform Resource Identifier [*Computer science*] (EERA) .... URI
Uniform Resource Locator [*Telecommunications*] .... URL
Uniform Resource Name [*Computer science*] (EERA) .... URN
Uniform Resource Names [*Computer science*] .... URN
Uniform Retail Meat Identity Standard [*Pronounced "er-miss"*] .... URMIS
Uniform Retirement Date Act [*National Conference of Commissioners on Uniform State Laws*] .... URDA
Uniform Rights of the Terminally Ill Act [*National Conference of Commissioners on Uniform State Laws*] .... URTIA
Uniform Rules for Collections .... URC
Uniform Rules for Contract Guarantees .... URCG
Uniform Rules of Conduct for Interchange of Trade Data by Teletransmission [*ICC Publishing Co.*] [*A publication*] .... UNCID
Uniform Sales Act [*Legal shorthand*] (LWAP) .... USA
Uniform Securities Agent State Law Examination [*Investment term*] .... USASLE
Uniform Service Order Code [*Bell System*] (TEL) .... USOC
Uniform Services University of the Health Sciences, Bethesda, MD [*Library symbol Library of Congress*] (LCLS) .... MdBeU
Uniform Shipboard Automatic Data Processing .... USADP
Uniform Simplification of Land Transfers Act (DICI) .... USLTA
Uniform Simplification of Land Transfers Act [*National Conference of Commissioners on Uniform State Laws*] .... USOLTA
Uniform Simultaneous Death Act [*National Conference of Commissioners on Uniform State Laws*] .... USDA
Uniform Single Publication Act [*National Conference of Commissioners on Uniform State Laws*] .... USPA
Uniform Socio-Economic Reporting System [*Financial reporting system for voluntary health and welfare organizations*] .... USERS
Uniform Specification Program (AAG) .... USP
Uniform Specification Tree .... UST
Uniform Staffing Methodologies [*DoD*] .... USM
Uniform Standards for Professional Appraisal Practice .... USPAP
Uniform State Waterway Marking System (DICI) .... USWMS
Uniform System .... US
Uniform System of Accounts [*Telecommunications*] (TEL) .... USOA
Uniform System of Accounts Prescribed for Natural Gas Companies .... USPG
Uniform System of Accounts, Public Utilities, and Licensees [*Federal Power Commission*] .... USPL
Uniform System of Citation [*Legal term*] (DLA) .... Unif Sys Citation
Uniform Systems of Accounts and Reports for Certified Air Carriers [*Civil Aeronautics Board*] .... USAR
Uniform Testamentary Additions to Trusts Act [*National Conference of Commissioners on Uniform State Laws*] .... UTATA
Uniform Theory of Diffraction (IAA) .... UTD
Uniform Tire Quality Grade .... UTQG
Uniform Tire Quality Grading Standards [*Department of Transportation*] (GFGA) .... UTQGS
Uniform Transfers to Minors Act [*National Conference of Commissioners on Uniform State Laws*] .... UTMA
Uniform Trust Receipts Act [*Legal shorthand*] (LWAP) .... utra
Uniform Trustees' Powers Act [*National Conference of Commissioners on Uniform State Laws*] .... UTPA
Uniform Vehicle Code .... UVC
Uniform Vehicle Code Annotated .... UVCA
Uniform Warehouse Receipts Act (LWAP) .... UWRA
Uniform Wave Motion .... UWM
Uniform Wave Train .... UWT
Uniform Work Breakdown Structure .... UWBS
Uniformed Firefighters Association .... UFA
Uniformed Services Academy of Family Physicians (EA) .... USAFP
Uniformed Services Contingency Act .... USCA
Uniformed Services Contingency Option Act .... USCOA
Uniformed Services Employment and Re-employment Rights Act [*Military*] .... USERRA
Uniformed Services Family Health Plan [*DoD*] .... USFHP
Uniformed Services Former Spouse Protection Act [*Military*] .... USFSPA
Uniformed Services Health Benefits .... USHB
Uniformed Services Health Benefits Program .... USHBP
Uniformed Services Identification and Privilege Card (AFM) .... USIPC
Uniformed Services Journal [*A publication*] .... USJ
Uniformed Services Pay Act .... USPA
Uniformed Services Savings Deposits Program (AABC) .... USSDP
Uniformed Services Special Pay Act (DNAB) .... USSPA
Uniformed Services Treatment Facility [*DoD*] .... USTF
Uniformed Services University of the Health Sciences [*Bethesda, MD*] [*DoD*] (EGAO) .... USUHS
Uniformed Services University of the Health Sciences Library, Bethesda, MD [*OCLC symbol*] (OCLC) .... USU
Uniformed Services Voluntary Insurance Program .... USVIP
Uniformity .... UNIF
Uniformly Labeled [*Also, UL*] [*Compound, with radioisotope*] .... U
Uniformly Labeled [*Compound, with radioisotope*] [*Also, U*] .... UL
Uniformly Minimum Variance Unbiased Estimator (PDAA) .... UMVUE
Uniformly Most Powerful Test [*Statistics*] .... UMP
Uniformly Redundant Array .... URA
Uniformly Reflexive Structure (IAA) .... URS
Uniformly-Sampled-Autoregressive Moving Average (PDAA) .... USAM
Unify Corp. [*NASDAQ symbol*] (SAG) .... UNFY
Unify Corp. [*Associated Press*] (SAG) .... UnifyCp
Unigene Laboratories [*NASDAQ symbol*] (TTSB) .... UGNE
Unigene Laboratories, Inc. [*NASDAQ symbol*] (NQ) .... UGNE
Unigene Labs, Inc. [*Associated Press*] (SAG) .... Unigen
Unigene Labs, Inc. [*Associated Press*] (SAG) .... Unign
Unigene Labs Wrrt'B' [*NASDAQ symbol*] (TTSB) .... UGNEZ
Unigesco, Inc. [*Toronto Stock Exchange symbol*] .... UGO

Uniglobe International Energy Corp. [*Vancouver Stock Exchange symbol*] ..... UIG
UniHolding Corp. [*Associated Press*] (SAG) ..... UniHoldg
Unijunction Transistor ..... UJT
Unijunction Transistor Oscillator (IAA) ..... UJTO
Unilab Corp. [*NASDAQ symbol*] (NQ) ..... ULAB
Unilab Corp. [*Associated Press*] (SAG) ..... Unilab
Unilabo [*France*] [*Research code symbol*] ..... SPE
Unilateral (DAVI) ..... unil
Unilateral ..... unilat
Unilateral Absence of Excretion [*Medicine*] ..... UAE
Unilateral Administrative Order ..... UAO
Unilateral Arms Control ..... UNICORN
Unilateral Cleft of Lip and Palate [*Medicine*] (DMAA) ..... UCLP
Unilateral Declaration of Independence [*of Southern Rhodesia*] ..... UDI
Unilateral Neglect [*Neurology*] (DAVI) ..... UN
Unilateral Nevoid Telangiectasia [*Medicine*] (DMAA) ..... UNTS
Unilateral Ovariectomy [*Gynecology*] ..... ULO
Unilateral Renovascular Disease [*Nephrology*] (DAVI) ..... URVD
Unilateral Salpingo-Oophorectomy [*Gynecology*] (MAE) ..... USO
Unilens Optical [*Vancouver Stock Exchange symbol*] ..... UOC
Unilever ADR [*NYSE symbol*] (TTSB) ..... UL
Unilever Computer Services Ltd. (NITA) ..... UCSL
Unilever Ltd. [*NYSE symbol*] (SPSG) ..... UL
Unilever Ltd. [*Associated Press*] (SAG) ..... Unilevr
Unilever NV [*NYSE symbol*] (SPSG) ..... UN
Unilever NV [*Associated Press*] (SAG) ..... UnlNV
Unimar Co. [*Associated Press*] (SAG) ..... Unimar
Unimar Indonesian Participating Units [*AMEX symbol*] (SPSG) ..... UMR
Unimar Indonesian Ptc Units [*AMEX symbol*] (TTSB) ..... UMR
[*The*] **Unimark Group** [*Associated Press*] (SAG) ..... Unimark
[*The*] **Unimark Group** [*NASDAQ symbol*] (SAG) ..... UNMG
Uni-Marts, Inc. [*AMEX symbol*] (SPSG) ..... UNI
Uni-Marts, Inc. [*Associated Press*] (SAG) ..... UniMrt
Unimed, Inc. [*NASDAQ symbol*] (NQ) ..... UMED
Unimed, Inc. [*Associated Press*] (SAG) ..... Unimed
Unimed Pharmaceuticals [*NASDAQ symbol*] (TTSB) ..... UMED
Unimplemented User Operation [*Computer science*] (EECA) ..... UUO
Unimproved Capital Value [*Business term*] (ADA) ..... UCV
Uninet Japan Ltd. [*Telecommunications*] ..... UJL
Uninfected Red Blood Cells [*Hematology*] ..... URBC
Uninflated Movement Party [*Australia Political party*] (ADA) ..... UMP
Uninhabited Combat Air Vehicle ..... UCAV
Uninsured Motorists [*Insurance*] ..... UM
Uninsured Motorists Coverage [*Insurance*] ..... UMC
Unintegrated Viral DNA [*Deoxyribonucleic Acid*] [*Pathology*] ..... UVD
Unintentional Frequency Modulation on Pulse (MCD) ..... UFMOP
Unintentional RADAR Interference (IAA) ..... URI
Unintentional Radiation Exploitation (AFM) ..... URE
Unintentional Radiation Intelligence (MCD) ..... URINT
Uninterruptable Computer Power ..... UCP
Uninterruptable Power Source (DAVI) ..... UPS
Uninterruptable Power Supply (EERA) ..... UPS
Uninterruptable Power Supply (ACII) ..... UPS
Uninterruptable Voltage Source [*Electric power supply*] ..... UVS
Uninterrupted Automatic Control ..... UAC
Uninterrupted Sustained Silent Reading ..... USSR
Uninterruptible AC [*Alternating Current*] **Electric Power System** (IAA) ..... UPS
Uninterruptible Application Error [*Computer science*] (CDE) ..... UAE
Uninterruptible Power Supply [*or System*] ..... UPS
Unio Mallorquina [*Majorcan Union*] [*Political party*] (PPW) ..... UM
Union [*or Unionist*] ..... U
Union (MSA) ..... UN
Union ..... UN
Union [*Commonly used*] (OPSA) ..... UNION
Union Academique Internationale [*International Academic Union - IAU*] (EAIO) ..... UAI
Union Acceptance Corp. Class A [*NASDAQ symbol*] (SAG) ..... UACA
Union Acceptance Corp. Class A [*Associated Press*] (SAG) ..... UnionA
Union Acceptance'A' [*NASDAQ symbol*] (TTSB) ..... UACA
Union Aeromaritime de Transport [*Privately-owned French airline*] ..... UAT
Union Africaine de Management de Banques pour le Developpement [*African Union of Development Bank Management*] [*Benin*] (EAIO) ..... UAMBD
Union Africaine de Physique [*African Union of Physics - AUP*] (EAIO) ..... UAP
Union Africaine des Artistes de Spectacle [*Union of African Performing Artists - UAPA*] (EAIO) ..... UAAS
Union Africaine et Malagache [*African and Malagasy Union*] [*Later, Common Afro-Malagasy Organization*] ..... UAM
Union Africaine et Mauricienne de Banques pour le Developpement [*African and Mauritian Union of Banks for Development*] [*Benin*] (AF) ..... UAMBD
Union and League of Romanian Societies of America (EA) ..... ULRSA
Union Arabe de Ciment et des Materiaux de Construction [*Arab Union for Cement and Building Materials - AUCBM*] (EAIO) ..... UACMC
Union Army of Commemoration ..... UAC
Union Association [*Major league in baseball, 1884*] ..... U
Union Association [*Major league in baseball, 1884*] ..... UA
Union Astronomique Internationale [*International Astronomical Union - IAU*] ..... UAI
Union Bank [*British*] (ROG) ..... UB
Union Bank [*NASDAQ symbol*] (SPSG) ..... UBNK
Union Bank [*Associated Press*] (SAG) ..... UnBnk
Union Bank of Bavaria ..... UBB
Union Bank of Finland ..... UBF
Union Bank of Switzerland ..... UBS
Union Bankshares [*NASDAQ symbol*] (TTSB) ..... UBSH
Union Bankshares Corp. [*NASDAQ symbol*] (SAG) ..... UBSH
Union Bankshares Corp. [*Associated Press*] (SAG) ..... UnBkCp
Union Bankshares Ltd. [*NASDAQ symbol*] (SAG) ..... UBSC
Union Bankshares Ltd. [*Associated Press*] (SAG) ..... UnionBsh
Union Belge et Luxembourgeoise de Droit Penal [*Belgian and Luxembourg Association of Penal Law*] (EAIO) ..... UBLDP
Union Bouddhique d'Europe [*Buddhist Union of Europe - BUE*] (EAIO) ..... UBE
Union Broadcasting System [*Fictitious broadcasting organization in film "Network"*] ..... UBS
Union Caledonienne [*Caledonian Union*] [*Political party*] (PPW) ..... UC
Union Camerounaise [*Cameroonese Union*] [*Political party*] ..... UC
Union Camerounaise des Travailleurs Croyants [*Cameroonese Union of Believing Workers*] ..... UCTC
Union Camp [*NYSE symbol*] (TTSB) ..... UCC
Union Camp Corp. [*NYSE symbol*] (SPSG) ..... UCC
Union Camp Corp. [*Associated Press*] (SAG) ..... UnCmp
Union Canadienne des Etudiants ..... UCE
Union Canadienne des Religieuses Contemplatives ..... UCRC
Union Canadienne des Travailleurs Unis des Brasseries, Farines, Cereales, Liqueurs Douces, et Distilleries [*International Union of United Brewery, Flour, Cereal, Soft Drink, and Distillery Workers of America - BFCSD*] ..... BFCLD
Union Carbide [*NYSE symbol*] (TTSB) ..... UK
Union Carbide Agricultural Products Co., Inc., Research Triangle Park, Durham, NC [*Library symbol Library of Congress*] (LCLS) ..... NcDurUC
Union Carbide and Carbon/Electric Metallurgical Co. (AAG) ..... UCC/EMC
Union Carbide and Carbon Research Laboratories (AAG) ..... UCCRL
Union Carbide Biocide [*Trademark*] [*Union Carbide Corp.*] ..... UCARCIDE
Union Carbide Canada Equipment Trust Units [*Toronto Stock Exchange symbol*] ..... UCT
Union Carbide Canada Ltd. [*Toronto Stock Exchange symbol*] ..... UCC
Union Carbide Canada Ltd., Pointe-Aux-Trembles, PQ, Canada [*Library symbol Library of Congress*] (LCLS) ..... CaQMUC
Union Carbide Canada Ltd., Pointe-Aux-Trembles, Quebec [*Library symbol National Library of Canada*] (NLC) ..... QMUC
Union Carbide Canada Ltd., Toronto, ON, Canada [*Library symbol*] [*Library of Congress*] (LCLS) ..... CaOTUNC
Union Carbide Canada Ltd., Toronto, Ontario [*Library symbol National Library of Canada*] (NLC) ..... OTUNC
Union Carbide Corp. [*Associated Press*] (SAG) ..... UCarb
Union Carbide Corp. (KSC) ..... UCC
Union Carbide Corp. [*Wall Street slang name: "Ukelele"*] [*NYSE symbol*] (SPSG) ..... UK
Union Carbide Corp., Chemicals and Plastics Division, Texas City, TX [*Library symbol Library of Congress*] (LCLS) ..... TxTUC
Union Carbide Corp., Chemicals and Plastics Library, Brownsville, TX [*Library symbol Library of Congress*] (LCLS) ..... TxBUC
Union Carbide Corp., Film-Packaging Division, Chicago, IL [*Library symbol Library of Congress*] (LCLS) ..... ICUC
Union Carbide Corp., Grand Junction, CO [*Library symbol Library of Congress*] (LCLS) ..... CoGjUC
Union Carbide Corp., Houston, TX [*Library symbol Library of Congress*] (LCLS) ..... TxHUC
Union Carbide Corp., Library, Indianapolis, IN [*OCLC symbol*] (OCLC) ..... IMK
Union Carbide Corp., Linde Division, Tonawanda, NY [*Library symbol Library of Congress*] (LCLS) ..... NTonL
Union Carbide Corp., Niagara Falls, NY [*Library symbol Library of Congress*] (LCLS) ..... NNiaUC
Union Carbide Corp. - Nuclear Division (MCD) ..... UCC-ND
Union Carbide Corp., South Charleston, WV [*Library symbol Library of Congress*] (LCLS) ..... WvScU
Union Carbide Corp., Tarrytown Technical Center, Tarrytown, NY [*Library symbol Library of Congress*] (LCLS) ..... NTaUC
Union Carbide Electronics (IAA) ..... UCE
Union Carbide Nuclear Co., Oak Ridge National Laboratories, Biology Library, OakRidge, TN [*Library symbol Library of Congress*] (LCLS) ..... TONL-B
Union Carbide Nuclear Co., Oak Ridge National Laboratories, Gaseous Diffusi, Oak Ridge, TN [*Library symbol*] [*Library of Congress*] (LCLS) ..... TONL-G
Union Carbide Nuclear Co., Oak Ridge National Laboratories, Oak Ridge, TN [*Library symbol*] [*Library of Congress*] (LCLS) ..... TONL
Union Carbide Nuclear Co., Oak Ridge National Laboratories, Thermal-Nuclear Library, Oak Ridge, TN [*Library symbol Library of Congress*] (LCLS) ..... TONL-T
Union Carbide Nuclear Co., Oak Ridge National Laboratories, Y-12 Technical Library, Oak Ridge, TN [*Library symbol Library of Congress*] (LCLS) ..... TONL-Y
Union Carbide Nuclear Corp. ..... UCNC
Union Carbide Plastics Co., Bound Brook, NJ [*Library symbol Library of Congress*] (LCLS) ..... NjBbU
Union Carbide Research Institute (KSC) ..... UCRI
Union Catalog of Medical Monographs and Multimedia [*Medical Library Center of New York*] [*No longer available online*] [*Information service or system*] (CRD) ..... UCOM
Union Catalog of the Atlanta-Athens Area, Atlanta, GA [*OCLC symbol*] (OCLC) ..... GUC
Union Catalogue of Books, National Library of Canada [*Catalogue Collectif desLivres, Bibliotheque Nationale du Canada*] **Ottawa, Ontario** [*Library symbol National Library of Canada*] (NLC) ..... OONLB
Union Catalogue of British Columbia Newspapers, Victoria, British Columbia [*Library symbol National Library of Canada*] (NLC) ..... BViUCN
Union Catalogue of British Columbia's Newspapers, Victoria, BC, Canada [*Library symbol*] [*Library of Congress*] (LCLS) ..... CaBViUCN
Union Catalogue of Serials, National Library of Canada [*Catalogue Collectif des Periodiques, Bibliotheque Nationale du Canada*] **Ottawa, Ontario** [*Library symbol National Library of Canada*] (NLC) ..... OONLS

Union Catholique Internationale de la Presse [*International Catholic Union of the Press*] (EAIO) .... UCIP
Union Catholique Internationale de Service Social [*Catholic International Union for Social Service*] [*Brussels, Belgium*] (EAIO) .... UCISS
Union Centrafricaine de la Fraternite Chretienne des Malades et Handicapes (EAIO) .... UCFCMHPH
Union Centriste et Radicale [*France Political party*] (EY) .... UCR
Union Centro y Democratica Cristiana de Catalunya [*Union of the Center and Christian Democrats of Catalonia*] [*Spain Political party*] (PPE) .... UCDCC
Union Chimique Belge [*Belgium*] .... UCB
Union Chimique Elf-Aquitaine [*France*] .... UCEA
Union Chretienne Democrate d'Europe Centrale [*Christian Democratic Union of Central Europe - CDUCE*] (EAIO) .... UCDEC
Union Chretienne Democrate Libanaise [*Lebanese Christian Democratic Union*] [*Political party*] (PPW) .... UCDL
Union City Free Public Library, Union City, NJ [*Library symbol Library of Congress*] (LCLS) .... NjUc
Union City, IN [*FM radio station call letters*] .... WBNN
Union City, IN [*FM radio station call letters*] .... WOEI
Union City, OH [*FM radio station call letters*] .... WTGR
Union City, PA [*FM radio station call letters*] .... WCTL
Union City Public Library, Union City, IN [*Library symbol Library of Congress*] (LCLS) .... InUc
Union City, TN [*Location identifier FAA*] (FAAL) .... OQZ
Union City, TN [*Location identifier FAA*] (FAAL) .... UCY
Union City, TN [*AM radio station call letters*] .... WENK
Union City, TN [*FM radio station call letters*] .... WKWT
Union City, TN [*FM radio station call letters*] .... WWUC
Union Civica Nacional [*National Civic Union*] [*Dominican Republic*] [*Political party*] (PPW) .... UCN
Union Civica Radical [*Radical Civic Union*] [*Argentina*] (PD) .... UCR
Union Civica Radical del Pueblo [*Moderate radical political party*] [*Argentina*] .... UCRP
Union Civica Radical Intransigente [*Left-wing radical political party*] [*Argentina*] .... UCRI
Union Club, New York, NY [*Library symbol Library of Congress*] (LCLS) .... NNUnionC
Union College, Barbourville, KY [*Library symbol Library of Congress*] (LCLS) .... KyBvU
Union College Character Research Project (EA) .... UCCRP
Union College, Cranford, NJ [*Library symbol Library of Congress*] (LCLS) .... NjCrU
Union College (Kentucky) (GAGS) .... Union C (Ky)
Union College, Lincoln, NE [*Library symbol Library of Congress*] (LCLS) .... NbLU
Union College, Lincoln, NE [*OCLC symbol*] (OCLC) .... NCU
Union College (New York) (GAGS) .... Union C (NY)
Union College, Schenectady, NY [*Library symbol Library of Congress*] (LCLS) .... NSchU
Union College, Schenectady, NY [*OCLC symbol*] (OCLC) .... ZWU
Union Comorienne pour le Progres [*Comorian Union for Progress*] (PD) .... UCP
Union Congolaise des Syndicats Libres [*Congolese Union of Free Syndicates*] [*Leopoldville*] .... UCSL
Union Constitutionelle [*Constitutional Union*] [*Morocco*] [*Political party*] (PPW) .... UC
Union Continentale Africaine des Villes Jumelees [*Continental African Union of Twin Cities*] .... UCAVJ
Union Corp. [*NYSE symbol*] (SPSG) .... UCO
Union Corp. [*Associated Press*] (SAG) .... UnionC
Union County Clerk, Elizabeth, NJ [*Library symbol Library of Congress*] (LCLS) .... NjEliCoC
Union County Library, Union, SC [*Library symbol*] [*Library of Congress*] (LCLS) .... ScUn
Union County Public Library, Liberty, IN [*Library symbol Library of Congress*] (LCLS) .... InLib
Union County Public Library, Monroe, NC [*Library symbol Library of Congress*] (LCLS) .... NcMon
Union Culturelle et Technique de Langue Francaise [*French-Language Cultural and Technical Union*] [*Paris, France*] (EA) .... UCTF
Union Culturelle Francais [*French Cultural Union*] .... UCF
Union Culturelle Katangaise [*Katangan Cultural Union*] .... UCK
Union Cycliste Internationale [*International Cycling Union*] [*Switzerland*] (EA) .... UCI
Union d'Action des Jeunes de Guinee [*Guinean Union of Youth Action*] .... UAJG
Union d'Assistance Technique pour l'Automobile et la Circulation Routiere [*Union of Technical Assistance for Motor Vehicle and Road Traffic*] [*Geneva, Switzerland*] (EAIO) .... UNATAC
Union de Asociaciones Tecnicas Internacionales [*Union of International Engineering Organizations - UIEO*] [*Spanish*] (ASF) .... UATI
Union de Campesinos Salvadorcenos [*Peasant Union*] [*El Salvador*] .... UCS
Union de Centro Democratico [*Union of the Democratic Center*] [*Spain Political party*] (PPE) .... UCD
Union de Fribourg: Institut International des Sciences Sociales et Politiques [*Union de Fribourg: International Institute of Social and Political Sciences*] [*Fribourg/Pensier, Switzerland*] (EAIO) .... UF
Union de Guerreros Blancos [*White Warriors' Union*] [*El Salvador*] [*Political party*] (PD) .... UGB
Union de Izquierda Revolucionaria [*Union of the Revolutionary Left*] [*Peru*] [*Political party*] (PPW) .... UNIR
Union de la Gauche Socialiste .... UGS
Union de la Jeunesse Communiste du Canada (Marxiste-Leniniste) .... UJCC(M-L)
Union de la Jeunesse Congolaise [*Congolese Youth Union*] .... UJC
Union de la Jeunesse Congolaise [*Congolese Youth Union*] .... UJEKO
Union de la Jeunesse de la Cote d'Ivoire [*Ivory Coast Youth Union*] .... UJCD
Union de la Jeunesse Democratique du Kongo [*Union of Democratic Youth of the Congo*] .... UJDK
Union de la Jeunesse Democratique Gabonaise [*Union of Democratic Youth of Gabon*] .... UJDG
Union de la Lutte Communiste [*Burkina Faso*] [*Political party*] (EY) .... ULC
Union de l'Europe Occidentale [*Western European Union - WEU*] (EAIO) .... UEO
Union de l'Ouest Cameroun [*Union of West Cameroon*] .... UOC
Union de Melillenses Independientes [*Spanish North Africa*] [*Political party*] (MENA) .... UMI
Union de Mouvements Democratiques [*Djibouti*] [*Political party*] (EY) .... UMD
Union de Mujeres Americanas [*United Women of the Americas*] .... UMA
Union de Obreros Estivadores de Filipinos [*Union of Longshoremen of the Philippines*] .... UOEF
Union de Paises Exportadores de Banano [*Union of Banana-Exporting Countries - UBEC*] (EAIO) .... UPEB
Union de Patriotas Espanoles [*Union of Patriots*] [*Spanish*] .... UPE
Union de Rassemblement et du Centre [*France Political party*] (ECON) .... URC
Union de Transports Aeriens [*Air Transport Union*] [*Private airline*] [*France*] (EY) .... UTA
Union de Universidades de America Latina [*Union of Latin American Universities*] [*Mexico*] .... UDUAL
Union Defence Force [*British*] .... UDF
Union del Centro Democratico [*Union of the Democratic Center*] [*Argentina Political party*] (EY) .... UCeDe
Union del Centro Nacional [*Union of the National Center*] [*Guatemala*] [*Political party*] .... UCN
Union del Pueblo [*Union of the People*] [*Mexico*] (PD) .... UP
Union del Pueblo Canario [*Union of the Canarian People*] [*Spain Political party*] (PPE) .... UPC
Union del Pueblo de Melilla [*Spanish North Africa*] [*Political party*] (MENA).... UPM
Union del Pueblo Navarrese [*Union of the Navarrese People*] [*Spain Political party*] (PPW) .... UPN
Union del Pueblo Patriotico [*Ecuador*] [*Political party*] (EY) .... UPP
Union Delegates Committee [*Air carrier designation symbol*] .... UDC
Union Democrata Foral [*Spain Political party*] (EY) .... UDF
Union Democrata Nacional [*National Democratic Union*] [*El Salvador*] [*Political party*] (PPW) .... UDN
Union Democratica Cristiana [*Christian Democratic Union*] [*Bolivia*] [*Political party*] (PPW) .... UDC
Union Democratica Independiente [*Independent Democratic Union*] [*Chile*] [*Political party*] (PPW) .... UDI
Union Democratica Nicaraguense [*Nicaraguan Democratic Union*] [*Political party*] (PD) .... UDN
Union Democratique [*New Caledonia*] [*Political party*] (EY) .... UD
Union Democratique Bretonne - Unvaniezh Demokratel Breizh [*Breton Democratic Union*] [*France Political party*] (PPW) .... UDB
Union Democratique Centrafricaine [*Central African Democratic Union*] [*Political party*] (PPW) .... UDC
Union Democratique Dahomeenne [*Benin*] [*Political party*] .... UDD
Union Democratique de la Jeunesse Marocaine [*Democratic Union of Moroccan Youth*] .... UDJM
Union Democratique de la Jeunesse Voltaique [*Voltaic Democratic Youth Union*] .... UDJV
Union Democratique des Femmes Camerounaises [*Cameroonese Democratic Women's Union*] .... UDEFEC
Union Democratique des Femmes Tunisiennes [*Democratic Union of Tunisian Women*] .... UDFT
Union Democratique des Forces du Progres [*Benin*] [*Political party*] (EY) .... UDFP
Union Democratique des Independants [*Democratic Union of Independents*] [*France Political party*] (PPE) .... UDI
Union Democratique des Populations Togolaises [*Democratic Union of Togolese People*] .... UDPT
Union Democratique du Cameroun [*Political party*] (EY) .... UDC
Union Democratique du Centre [*Democratic Union of the Center*] [*Switzerland Political party*] (PPE) .... UDC
Union Democratique du Peuple Malien [*Mali People's Democratic Union*] [*Political party*] (PPW) .... UDPM
Union Democratique et Sociale Gabonaise [*Gabonese Democratic and Social Union*] .... UDSG
Union Democratique et Socialiste de la Resistance [*Democratic and Socialist Union of the Resistance*] [*France Political party*] (PPE) .... UDSR
Union Democratique Mauritanienne [*Mauritanian Democratic Union*] [*Political party*] (PD) .... UDM
Union Democratique pour la Cinquieme Republique [*Democratic Union for the Fifth Republic*] [*France Political party*] (PPE) .... UD-Ve
Union Democratique pour la Defense des Interets Africains [*Democratic Union to Defend African Interests*] .... UDDIA
Union Democratique pour le Renouveau Social [*Benin*] [*Political party*] (EY) .... UDRS
Union Democratique pour le Respect du Travail - Respect voor Arbeid en Democratie [*Democratic Union for the Respect of Labor*] [*Belgium Political party*] (PPW) .... UDRT/RAD
Union Democratique Senegalaise [*Senegalese Democratic Union*] .... UDS
Union Democratique Togolaise [*Togolese Democratic Union*] .... UDETO
Union Democratique Unioniste [*Tunisia*] [*Political party*] (EY) .... UDU
Union Democratique Voltaique [*Voltaic Democratic Union*] [*Banned, 1974*] .... UDV
Union Departemental de Syndicats du Mungo [*Departmental Union of the Trade Unions of Mungo*] [*Cameroon*] .... UDSM
Union des Artistes [*Union of Artists*] [*Canada*] .... UA
Union des Associations des Distributeurs d'Eau de Pays Membres des Communautes Europeennes [*Union of the Water Supply Associations from Countries of the European Communities*] (EAIO) .... EUREAU
Union des Associations des Etablissements Thermaux de la CE [*Union of Associations of Thermal Baths Establishments in the EC*] (ECED) .... UTHE

Union des Associations des Fabricants de Pates Alimentaires de la Communaute Economique Europeenne [*Union of Organizations of Manufacturers of Pasta Products in the European Economic Community*] ... UNAFPA
Union des Associations des Producteurs Europeens de Farine de Viande [*Union of Associations of European Meat Meal Producers UAEM*] [*Later, European Renderers Association - EURA*] (EAIO) ... UAPEFV
Union des Associations des Riziers de la CEE [*Union of Rice Associations of the EEC*] (ECED) ... UARCEE
Union des Associations Europeennes des Distributeurs d'Eau [*Union of European Associations of Water Suppliers*] [*Belgium*] (EAIO) ... UAEDE
Union des Associations Europeennes d'Etudiants [*Union of European Student Associations*] ... UAEE
Union des Associations Internationales [*Union of International Associations - UIA*] (EAIO) ... UAI
Union des Associations Techniques Internationales [*Union of International Technical Associations - UITA*] (EAIO) ... UATI
Union des Associations Traditionelles du Cameroun [*Union of Traditional Associations of Cameroon*] ... UNATRACAM
Union des Avocats Arabes [*Arab Lawyers Union - ALU*] (EAIO) ... UAA
Union des Banques Arabes et Francaises [*Union of Arab and French Banks*] [*France*] ... UBAF
Union des Capitales de la Communaute Europeenne [*Union of Capitals of the European Community*] ... UCCE
Union des Chefs et des Populations du Nord [*Union of Chiefs and Peoples of the North*] [*Togo*] ... UCPN
Union des Clubs pour le Renouveau de la Gauche [*Union of Clubs for the Renovation of the Left*] [*France Political party*] (PPE) ... UCRG
Union des Colons Agricoles du Kivu [*Union of Agricultural Settlers of Kivu*] [*Congo - Leopoldville*] ... UNAKI
Union des Colons de la Province Orientale [*Union of Settlers in Orientale Province*] ... UNICOL
Union des Colons du Katanga [*Settlers' Union of Katanga*] ... UCOL
Union des Communistes de France Marxiste-Leniniste [*Marxist-Leninist Union of Communists of France*] [*Political party*] (PPW) ... UCFML
Union des Confederations Sportives Africaines [*Association of African Sports Confederations - AASC*] [*Yaounde, Cameroon*] (EAIO) ... UCSA
Union des Croyants Malagaches [*Malagasy Christian Union*] ... UCM
Union des Democrates et Patriotes Burkinabe [*Burkino Faso*] [*Political party*] (EY) ... UDPB
Union des Democrates Sociaux de Madagascar [*Union of Social Democrats of Madagascar*] ... UDSM
Union des Distributeurs de Papiers et Cartons [*European Union of Paper, Board, and Packaging Wholesalers*] (PDAA) ... EUROGROPA
Union des Ecrivains du Monde Noir [*World Union of Black Writers - WUBW*] (EAIO) ... UEMN
Union des Editeurs de Langue Francaise (EAIO) ... UELF
Union des Etudiants Communistes [*France*] ... UEC
Union des Etudiants et Anciens des Instituts Sociaux de Congo [*Congolese Union of Students and Former Students of Social Institutes*] ... UNEASICO
Union des Etudiants Ouest Africains [*Union of West African Students*] ... UEOA
Union des Exploitations Electriques en Belgique ... UEEB
Union des Fabricants Europeens de Compteurs de Gaz [*Union of European Manufacturers of Gas Meters*] (EAIO) ... FACOGAZ
Union des Fabricants Europeens de Regulateurs de Pression du Gaz [*Union of European Manufacturers of Gas Pressure Controllers*] (EAIO) ... FAREGAZ
Union des Facteurs du Canada [*Letter Carriers' Union of Canada - LCUC*] ... UFC
Union des Feculeries de Pommes de Terre de la CE [*EC*] (ECED) ... UFE
Union des Federalistes et Republicains Independants [*Zaire*] [*Political party*] (EY) ... UFERI
Union des Femmes d'Algerie [*Union of Algerian Women*] ... UFA
Union des Femmes de l'Ouest Africain [*West African Women's Union*] ... UFOA
Union des Femmes Democratiques du Canada ... UFDC
Union des Femmes du Togo [*Togolese Women's Union*] ... UFEMTO
Union des Foires Internationales [*Union of International Fairs*] (EAIO) ... UFI
Union des Forces Democratiques [*Union of Democratic Forces*] [*Mali*] [*Political party*] (EY) ... UFD
Union des Forces Democratiques [*Union of Democratic Forces*] [*France Political party*] (PPE) ... UFD
Union des Forces Democratiques du Cameroun [*Union of Democratic Forces of Cameron*] [*Political party*] (EY) ... UFDC
Union des Forces Populaires pour la Democratie et le Progres [*Niger*] [*Political party*] (EY) ... UFPDP
Union des Francais a l'Etranger [*Union of French Citizens Abroad*] [*Political party*] (PPW) ... UFE
Union des Francais de Bon Sens [*Union of Frenchmen of Good Sense*] [*Political party*] (PPW) ... UFBS
Union des Gaullistes de Progres [*Union of Progressive Gaullists*] [*France Political party*] (PPE) ... UGP
Union des Groupements d'Achat Cooperatifs de Detaillants de l'Europe [*Association of Cooperative Retailer-Owned Wholesalers of Europe - ACROWE*] (EAIO) ... UGAL
Union des Groupements Professionnels de l'Industrie de le Feculerie de Pommes deTerre [*Union of Professional Groups of the Potato Starch Industry*] ... UFE
Union des Guineens au Senegal [*Union of Guineans in Senegal*] [*Political party*] (PD) ... UGS
Union des Independants de Tananarive [*Union of Independents of Tananarive*] ... UIT
Union des Independants du Dahomey [*Independents Union of Dahomey*] ... UNIDAHO
Union des Industries de la Communaute Europeenne [*Union of Industries of the European Community*] [*Belgium*] ... UNICE
Union des Industries Ferroviaires Europeennes [*Union of European Railway Industries*] (EA) ... UNIFE
Union des Interets Sociaux Congolais [*Congolese Union of Social Interests*] ... UNISCO
Union des Jeunesses Communistes Marxistes-Leninistes [*Union of Young Marxist-Leninist Communists*] [*France Political party*] (PPE) ... UJCML
Union des Musiciens Nordiques [*Nordic Musicians' Union - NMU*] (EAIO) ... UMN
Union des Opposants Malgaches Exterieurs [*Madagascar*] [*Political party*] (EY) ... UOME
Union des Originaires de Mauritanie du Sud [*Union of Natives of South Mauritania*] ... UOMS
Union des Patriotes Democrates et Progressistes [*Niger*] [*Political party*] (EY) ... UPDP
Union des Patriotes Democratiques [*Haiti*] [*Political party*] (EY) ... UPD
Union des Paysans Ruraux et Progressistes [*Union of Rural and Progressive Farmers*] [*Congo-Kasai*] ... UPRP
Union des Pilotes Professionels Internationaux [*International Professio nal Drivers Union*] [*French*] ... UPPI
Union des Populations Camerounaises [*Union of Cameroonian Peoples*] (PD) ... UPC
Union des Populations de Guinee [*Guinea People's Union*] (PD) ... UPG
Union des Populations Rurales [*Union of Rural People*] [*Lomela-Kasai*] ... UPR
Union des Populations Rurales du Congo [*Union of Rural People of the Congo*] ... UNIPOCONGO
Union des Producteurs de Levure-Aliment de la CEE [*Union of Dried Yeast Producers of the Common Market*] ... UPLAC
Union des Producteurs, Transporteurs, et Distributeurs d'Energie Electrique d'Afrique [*Union of Producers, Conveyors, and Distributors of Electric Power in Africa - UPDEA*] (EAIO) ... UPDEA
Union des Radio-Televisions Nationales Africaines [*African National Radio-Television Union*] (AF) ... URTNA
Union des Republicains d'Action Sociale [*Union of Republicans of Social Action*] [*France Political party*] (PPE) ... URAS
Union des Republicains du Cameroun [*Political party*] (EY) ... URC
Union des Republiques de l'Afrique Centrale [*Union of Central African Republics*] ... URAC
Union des Republiques Socialistes Sovietiques [*Union of Socialist Soviet Republics; USSR*] ... URSS
Union des Resistants pour une Europe Unie [*Union of Resistance Veterans for a United Europe*] ... URPE
Union des Ressortissants du Congo pour la Defense et la Promotion du Congo [*Union of Congolese for the Defense and Promotion of the Congo*] ... URCO
Union des Scolaires Nigeriens [*Union of Nigerian Scholars*] ... USN
Union des Services Routiers des Chemins de Fer Europeens [*Union of European Railways Road Services*] ... URF
Union des Sociaux-Democrates [*Burkina Faso*] [*Political party*] (EY) ... USD
Union des Societes de Pediatrie du Moyen-Orient et de la Mediterranee [*Union of Middle Eastern and Mediterranean Pediatric Societies - UMEMPS*] [*Athens, Greece*] (EAIO) ... USPMOM
Union des Syndicats Autonomes Camerounais [*Federation of Cameroonese Autonomous Unions*] ... USAC
Union des Syndicats Autonomes de Madagascar [*Federation of Malagasy Autonomous Unions*] ... USAM
Union des Syndicats Autonomes des Travailleurs Tchadiens [*Federation of Autonomous Workers Unions of Chad*] ... USATT
Union des Syndicats Confederes du Togo [*Federation of Confederated Unions of Togo*] ... USCT
Union des Syndicats Croyants du Cameroun [*Federation of Cameroonese Believers' Unions*] ... USCC
Union des Syndicats des Services Publics Europeens et Internationaux [*European and International Public Services Union*] [*Later, EUROFEDOP*] (EAIO) ... USSPEI
Union des Syndicats des Travailleurs Algeriens [*Federation of Unions of Algerian Workers*] ... USTA
Union des Syndicats des Travailleurs du Dahomey [*Federation of Workers' Unions of Dahomey*] ... USTD
Union des Syndicats Libres du Dahomey [*Federation of Free Unions of Dahomey*] ... USLD
Union des Syndicats Professionels du Cameroun [*Federation of Professional Trade Unions of Cameroon*] ... USPC
Union des Transports Aeriens [*France ICAO designator*] (FAAC) ... UTA
Union des Travailleurs Communistes Libertaires [*Union of Libertarian Communist Workers*] [*France Political party*] (PPW) ... UTCL
Union des Travailleurs de la Moyenne Cote d'Ivoire [*Union of Middle Ivory Coast Workers*] ... UTMCI
Union des Travailleurs de Mauritanie [*Union of Workers of Mauritania*] ... UTM
Union des Travailleurs de Mayotte [*Comoros*] (PD) ... UTM
Union des Travailleurs du Senegal [*Senegalese Workers Union*] ... UTS
Union des Verts pour le Developpement du Burkina [*Burkina Faso*] [*Political party*] (EY) ... UVDB
Union Dominions Trust [*Commercial firm*] ... UDT
Union Douaniere des Etats de l'Afrique et l'Ouest [*Customs Union of West African States*] [*Later, CEAO*] ... UDEAO
Union Douaniere Equatoriale [*Equatorial Customs Union*] ... UDE
Union Douaniere et Economique de l'Afrique Centrale [*Central African Customs and Economic Union*] (EAIO) ... UDEAC
Union du Centre [*Mayotte*] [*Political party*] (EY) ... UDC
Union du Commerce des Engrais des Pays de la Communaute Economique Europeenne [*Union of the Fertilizer Trade of Countries of the EEC*] [*Hasselt, Belgium*] (EAIO) ... UCEPCEE
Union du Moyen-Congo [*Union of the Middle Congo*] ... UMC
Union du Peuple Gabonais [*Political party*] (EY) ... UPG
Union du Peuple Malgache [*Malagasy People's Union*] ... UPM
Union du Rassemblement du Centre [*Mayotte*] [*Political party*] (EY) ... URC

Union Economique BENELUX .... UEB
Union Economique du Congo [*Economic Union of the Congo*] [*Usumbura*] .... UNECO
Union Economique France, Italie, Benelux .... FRITALUX
Union Electric [*NYSE symbol*] (TTSB) .... UEP
Union Electric, $3.50 Pfd [*NYSE symbol*] (TTSB) .... UEPPrA
Union Electric, $4.00 Pfd [*NYSE symbol*] (TTSB) .... UEPPrC
Union Electric, $4.50 Pfd [*NYSE symbol*] (TTSB) .... UEPPrD
Union Electric, $4.56 Pfd [*NYSE symbol*] (TTSB) .... UEPPrE
Union Electric, $6.40 Pfd [*NYSE symbol*] (TTSB) .... UEPPrG
Union Electric, $7.44 Pfd [*NYSE symbol*] (TTSB) .... UEPPrI
Union Electric Co. .... UEC
Union Electric Co. [*NYSE symbol*] (SPSG) .... UEP
Union Electric Co. [*Associated Press*] (SAG) .... UnE
Union Electric Co. [*Associated Press*] (SAG) .... UnEl
Union Electric Co. [*Associated Press*] (SAG) .... UnElec
Union Electric Co., St. Louis, MO [*Library symbol Library of Congress*] (LCLS) .... MoSUE
Union Electrica Madrilena [*Spain*] .... UEM
Union Energy [*Toronto Stock Exchange symbol*] (SPSG) .... UEI
Union Espanola Benefica de California (EA) .... UEBC
Union et Fraternite Francaise [*French Union and Fraternity*] [*Political party*] (PPE) .... UFF
Union Europaeischer Forstberufsverbaende [*Union of European Foresters*] [*Teningen-Heimbach, Federal Republic of Germany*] (EAIO) .... UEF
Union Europeenne de la Carrosserie [*European Union of Coachbuilders - EUC*] [*Belgium*] .... UEC
Union Europeenne de la Presse Sportive [*European Sports Press Union*] (EAIO) .... UEPS
Union Europeenne de l'Ameublement [*European Furniture Manufacturers Federation*] (EAIO) .... UEA
Union Europeenne de l'Artisanat et des Petites et Moyennes Entreprises [*European Association of Craft, Small and Medium-Sized Enterprises*] [*EC*] (ECED) .... UEAPME
Union Europeenne de Malacologie [*European Malacological Union*] .... UEM
Union Europeenne de Pedopsychiatres [*European Union for Child Psychiatry*] .... UEP
Union Europeenne de Radiodiffusion [*European Broadcasting Union - EBU*] (EAIO) .... UER
Union Europeenne Democrate Chretienne [*European Christian Democratic Union*] .... UEDC
Union Europeenne des Alcools, Eaux de Vie et Spiritueux [*European Union of Alcohol, Brandies and Spirits*] [*EC*] (ECED) .... UEAES
Union Europeenne des Arabisants et des Islamisants [*European Union of Arab and Islamic Studies - EUAIS*] [*Spain*] (EAIO) .... UEAI
Union Europeenne des Aveugles [*European Blind Union - EBU*] (EAIO) .... UEA
Union Europeenne des Commerces du Betail .... UECB
Union Europeenne des Conseillers Techniques et Scientifiques [*European Union of Technical and Scientific Advisers*] [*EC*] (ECED) .... UNECTES
Union Europeenne des Constructeurs de Logements [*European Union of Independent Building Contractors*] .... UECL
Union Europeenne des Etudiants Juifs [*European Union of Jewish Students - EUJS*] (EA) .... UEEJ
Union Europeenne des Experts Comptables Economiques et Financiers [*European Union of Public Accountants*] .... UEC
Union Europeenne des Exploitants d'Abbatoirs [*European Abbattoirs Union*] [*EC*] (ECED) .... UEEA
Union Europeenne des Fabricants de Bijouterie Fantaisie [*Union of European Fashion Jewelry Manufacturers*] [*Italy*] (EAIO) .... UNEBIF
Union Europeenne des Federalistes .... UEF
Union Europeenne des Fondeurs et Fabricants de Corps Gras Animaux [*European Union of Animal Fat Producers*] (EA) .... UNEGA
Union Europeenne des Independants en Lubrifiants [*European Union of Independent Lubricant Manufacturers*] [*EC*] (ECED) .... UEIL
Union Europeenne des Industries de Transformation de Pomme de Terre [*European Union of the Potato Processing Industries*] .... UEITP
Union Europeenne des Jeunes Democrates-Chretiens [*European Union of Young Christian Democrats*] .... UEJDC
Union Europeenne des Medecins Omnipraticiens [*European Union of General Practitioners*] (EA) .... UEMO
Union Europeenne des Medecins Specialistes [*European Society of Medical Specialists*] [*Belgium*] (SLS) .... UEMS
Union Europeenne des Negociants Detaillants en Combustibles [*European Union of Merchant Dealers in Combustibles*] [*Switzerland*] .... UENDC
Union Europeenne des Negociants en Combustibles [*European Fuel Merchants Union*] .... EUROCOM
Union Europeenne des Negociants en Cuirs et Peaux Bruts [*European Association of Traders in Leather and Raw Hides*] [*EC*] (ECED) .... UENCPB
Union Europeenne des Pharmacies Sociales [*European Union of the Social Pharmacies*] [*EC*] (ECED) .... UEPS
Union Europeenne des Practiciens en Medecine Dentaire [*European Union of Dental Medicine Practitioners*] (EAIO) .... UEPMD
Union Europeenne des Promoteurs Constructeurs [*European Union of Developers and House Builders*] [*Belgium*] (EAIO) .... UEPC
Union Europeenne des Sources d'Eaux Minerales du Marche Commun [*European Union of Natural Mineral Water Sources of the Common Market*] (EAIO) .... UNESEM
Union Europeenne des Veterinaires Practiciens [*European Union of Practising Veterinary Surgeons*] (EAIO) .... UEVP
Union Europeenne du Commerce Ambulant [*European Union of Door-to-Door Trade*] [*EC*] (ECED) .... UECA
Union Europeenne du Commerce de Gros des Pommes de Terre [*European Union of the Wholesale Potato Trade*] [*Common Market*] .... UCOPOM
Union Europeenne du Commerce de Gros en Fruits et Legumes [*European Union of the Fruit and Vegetable Wholesale, Import, and Export Trade*] [*Brussels, Belgium*] (EAIO) .... EUCOFEL
Union Europeenne du Commerce des Produits Laitiers et Derives [*European Union of Importers, Exporters, and Dealers in Dairy Products*] (EAIO) .... EUCOLAIT
Union Europeenne du Commerce du Betail et de la Viande [*European Livestock and Meat Trading Union*] (EAIO) .... UECBV
Union Europeenne du Commerce Laitier [*European Milk Trade Union*] [*Common Market*] .... UNECOLAIT
Union Europeenne Feminine [*European Union of Women*] .... UEF
Union Europeenne pour l'Agrement Technique dans la Construction [*European Union of Agrement*] (EAIO) .... UEAtc
Union Evangelique Mondiale [*World Evangelical Fellowship*] .... UEM
Union Explosivos-Rio Tinto [*Spain*] .... UERT
Union Federaliste des Communautes Ethniques Europeennes [*Federal Union of European Nationalities*] .... UFCE
Union Federazioni Italiane Bocce [*Italian lawn bowling, or boccie, organization*] .... UFIB
Union Financiere Internationale pour le Developpement de l'Afrique [*International Financial Union for the Development of Africa*] .... UFIDA
Union Flag [*Navy British*] .... UN
Union Fleuve de Mano [*Mano River Union - MRU*] (EAIO) .... UFM
Union Flight [*ICAO designator*] (FAAC) .... UNF
Union for Democratic Action .... UDA
Union for Democratic Communications (EA) .... UDC
Union for Experimenting Colleges and Universities [*Later, UI*] (EA) .... UECU
Union for Liberation and Democracy [*Suriname*] [*Political party*] (EY) .... UBD
Union for National Draft Opposition .... UNDO
Union for Radical Political Economics (EA) .... URPE
Union for Radical Review of Radical Political Economics [*A publication*] (EAAP) .... RRPE
Union for Research and Experimentation in Higher Education [*Later, UECU*] .... UREHE
Union for the Protection of the Human Person by International, Social, and Economic Cooperation [*Defunct*] (EA) .... UPHPISEC
Union for the Total Liberation of Angola .... UNITA
Union for Traditional Judaism (EA) .... UTJ
Union Francaise des Annuaires Professionels [*French Union for Professional Yearbooks*] [*Trappes*] [*Information service or system*] (IID) .... UFAP
Union Francaise des Organismes de Documentation (NITA) .... UFOD
Union Franco-Iberique pour la Coordination de la Production et du Transport de l'Electricite [*Franco-Iberian Union for Coordinating the Production and Transmission of Electricity*] (EAIO) .... UFIPTE
Union Franco-Nigerienne [*French-Nigerian Union*] .... UFN
Union Free School District (BARN) .... UFSD
Union Freight R. R. [*AAR code*] .... UNF
Union Frontier Police [*European Economic Community*] (ECON) .... UFP
Union Gas Ltd., Chatham, ON, Canada [*Library symbol*] [*Library of Congress*] (LCLS) .... CaOChaUG
Union Gas Ltd., Chatham, Ontario [*Library symbol National Library of Canada*] (NLC) .... OCUG
Union General de Trabajadores de Espana [*General Union of Spanish Workers*] [*In exile*] .... UGT
Union Generale de Travailleurs Tunisiens [*General Federation of Tunisian Workers*] .... UGTT
Union Generale des Cooperatives Agricoles d'Approvisionnement .... UGCAA
Union Generale des Etudiants Congolais [*General Union of Congolese Students*] .... UGEC
Union Generale des Etudiants d'Afrique Occidentale [*General Union of West African Students*] .... UGEAO
Union Generale des Etudiants du Maroc [*General Union of Moroccan Students*] .... UGEM
Union Generale des Etudiants et Eleves Dahomeens .... UGEED
Union Generale des Etudiants Guineens [*General Union of Guinean Students*] .... UGEG
Union Generale des Etudiants Musulmans d'Algerie [*General Union of Moslem Students of Algeria*] .... UGEMA
Union Generale des Etudiants Tunisiens [*General Union of Tunisian Students*] .... UGET
Union Generale des Syndicats Algeriens [*General Federation of Algerian Trade Unions*] .... UGSA
Union Generale des Travailleurs Algeriens [*General Union of Algerian Workers*] .... UGTA
Union Generale des Travailleurs Centrafricains [*General Union of Central African Workers*] .... UGTC
Union Generale des Travailleurs d'Afrique Noire [*General Union of Workers of Black Africa*] .... UGTAN
Union Generale des Travailleurs de la Cote D'Ivoire [*General Union of Workers of the Ivory Coast*] .... UGTCI
Union Generale des Travailleurs de Mauritanie [*General Union of Workers of Mauritania*] .... UGTM
Union Generale des Travailleurs du Cameroun [*General Union of Workers of Cameroon*] .... UGTC
Union Generale des Travailleurs du Dahomey [*General Union of Workers of Dahomey*] .... UGTD
Union Generale des Travailleurs du Kamerun [*General Union of Workers of the Cameroon*] .... UGTK
Union Generale des Travailleurs du Maroc [*General Union of Workers of Morocco*] .... UGTM
Union Generale des Travailleurs du Senegal [*General Union of Workers of Senegal*] .... UGTS
Union Geodesique et Geophysique Internationale [*International Union of Geodesy and Geophysics*] .... UGGI
Union Geographique Internationale [*International Geographical Union*] .... UGI

Union Giovantu Benadir [*Benadir Youth Union*] [*Somalia*] ... UGB
Union Graduate School [*Yellow Springs, Ohio*] ... UGS
Union Graduate School, Cincinnati, OH [*Library symbol Library of Congress*] (LCLS) ... OCUG
Union Guide (IAA) ... UG
Union Guineene de Transports [*Guinea*] [*ICAO designator*] (FAAC) ... GIU
Union House of Assembly [*South Africa*] (DAS) ... UHA
Union Institute (EA) ... UI
Union Internacional de Proteccion a la Infancia [*International Union for Child Welfare*] ... UIPI
Union Internacional de Sindicatos de Trabajadores de la Agricultura, de los Bosques, y de las Plantaciones [*Trade Unions International of Agricultural, Forestry, and Plantation Workers*] ... UISTABP
Union Internationale Catholique des Classes Moyennes [*International Catholic Union of the Middle Classes*] ... UICM
Union Internationale Contre la Tuberculose [*International Union Against Tuberculosis - IUAT*] (EAIO) ... UICT
Union Internationale Contre la Tuberculose et les Maladies Respiratoires [*International Union Against Tuberculosis and Lung Disease - IUATLD*] (EAIO) ... UICTMR
Union Internationale Contre l'Alcoolisme ... UIA
Union Internationale Contre le Cancer [*International Union Against Cancer*] [*Switzerland*] ... UICC
Union Internationale Contre le Peril Venerien et la Treponematose [*International Union Against the Venereal Diseases and the Treponematoses*] ... UIPVT
Union Internationale Contre les Maladies Veneriennes et les Treponematoses [*International Union Against the Venereal Diseases and the Treponematoses - IUVDT*] ... UIMVT
Union Internationale d'Action Morale et Sociale [*International Union for Moral and Social Action*] ... UIAMS
Union Internationale d'Associations de Proprietaires de Wagons Particuliers [*International Union of Private Railway Truck Owners' Associations*] (EAIO) ... UIP
Union Internationale de Banque en Guinee (EY) ... UIBG
Union Internationale de Chimie Pure et Appliquee [*International Union of Pure and Applied Chemistry*] ... UICPA
Union Internationale de Cristallographie [*International Union of Crystallography*] (EAIO) ... UIC
Union Internationale de Ferrecarriles [*International Union of Railways*] ... UIF
Union Internationale de Grands Magasins [*International Union of Department Stores*] ... UNIMA
Union Internationale de Jeunesse Democrate Chretienne [*International Union of Young Christian Democrats*] ... UIJDC
Union Internationale de la Couverture et Plomberie (EA) ... UICP
Union Internationale de la Jeunesse Socialiste [*International Union of Socialist Youth*] ... UIJS
Union Internationale de la Marionnette [*International Puppeteers Union*] [*France*] ... UNIMA
Union Internationale de la Navigation Fluviale [*International Union for Inland Navigation - IUIN*] (EAIO) ... UINF
Union Internationale de la Patisserie, Confiserie, Glacerie [*International Union of Bakers and Confectioners*] ... UIPCG
Union Internationale de la Press Catholique [*International Union of the Catholic Press*] [*France*] ... UIPC
Union Internationale de la Presse Catholique [*International Catholic Press Union*] ... UIPC
Union Internationale de la Presse Medicale [*International Union of the Medical Press*] ... UIPM
Union Internationale de la Presse Radiotechnique et Electronique [*Freiburg, Federal Republic of Germany*] (EAIO) ... UIPRE
Union Internationale de la Propriete Fonciere Batie [*International Union of Landed Property Owners*] ... UIPFB
Union Internationale de la Propriete Immobiliere [*International Union of Property Owners*] [*Paris, France*] (EAIO) ... UIPI
Union Internationale de la Resistance et de la Deportation [*International Union of Resistance and Deportee Movements*] ... UIRD
Union Internationale de l'Artisanat et des Petites et Moyennes Entreprises [*International Association of Crafts and Small and Medium-Sized Enterprises*] ... UIAPME
Union Internationale de l'Exploitation Cinematographique [*International Union of Cinematographic Exhibitors*] (EAIO) ... UIEC
Union Internationale de l'Humanisme et de l'Ethique ... UIHE
Union Internationale de l'Industrie du Gaz [*International Gas Union - IGU*] [*Paris, France*] (EAIO) ... UIIG
Union Internationale de Mecanique Theorique et Appliquee [*International Union of Theoretical and Applied Mechanics*] ... UITAM
Union Internationale de Patinage [*International Skating Union - ISU*] [*Davos-Platz, Switzerland*] (EAIO) ... UIP
Union Internationale de Pentathlon Moderne et Biathlon [*International Union for Modern Pentathlon and Biathlon*] (EAIO) ... UIPMB
Union Internationale de Physique Pure et Appliquee [*International Union of Pure and Applied Physics*] ... UIP
Union Internationale de Physique Pure et Appliquee [*International Union of Pure and Applied Physics*] ... UIPPA
Union Internationale de Producteurs et Distributeurs d'Energie Electrique [*International Union of Producers and Distributors of Electrical Energy*] [*France*] ... UNIPEDE
Union Internationale de Protection de l'Enfance [*International Union for Child Welfare - IUCW*] [*Geneva, Switzerland*] [*Defunct*] (EA) ... UIPE
Union Internationale de Radiodiffusion [*International Broadcasting Union*] [*Also, IBU*] (NTCM) ... UIR
Union Internationale de Secours [*International Relief Union*] ... UIS
Union Internationale de Secours aux Enfants ... UISE
Union Internationale de Speleologie [*International Union of Speleology - IUS*] (EAIO) ... UIS
Union Internationale de Tir [*International Shooting Union*] [*See also IS*] [*Germany*] (EAIO) ... UIT
Union Internationale d'Editeurs [*International Publishers Association - IPA*] (EAIO) ... UIE
Union Internationale d'Education pour la Sante [*International Union of Health Education - IUHE*] [*Paris, France*] (EAIO) ... UIES
Union Internationale d'Electrothermie [*International Union for Electroheat*] (EAIO) ... UIE
Union Internationale des Architectes [*International Union of Architects*] (EAIO) ... UIA
Union Internationale des Associations d'Alpinisme [*International Union of Alpine Associations*] [*Switzerland*] ... UIAA
Union Internationale des Associations d'Annonceurs [*International Union of Advertisers Associations*] ... UIAA
Union Internationale des Associations de Diplomes Universitaires en Sciences Economiques et Commerciales ... UNIADUSEC
Union Internationale des Associations de Prevention de la Pollution Atmospherique [*International Union of Air Pollution Prevention Associations*] (EAIO) ... UIAPPA
Union Internationale des Associations Techniques Cinematographiques [*International Union of Technical Cinematograph Associations - IUTCA*] (EAIO) ... UNIATEC
Union Internationale des Assureurs Aeronautiques ... UIAA
Union Internationale des Automobile-Clubs Medicaux [*International Union of Associations of Doctor-Motorists*] ... UIACM
Union Internationale des Avocats [*International Union of Lawyers*] ... UIA
Union Internationale des Centres du Batiment [*International Union of Building Centers*] [*British*] ... UICB
Union Internationale des Chauffeurs Routiers [*International Union of Lorry Drivers - IULD*] (EAIO) ... UICR
Union Internationale des Chemins de Fer [*International Union of Railways*] (EAIO) ... UIC
Union Internationale des Chemins de Fer (EERA) ... UIC
Union Internationale des Cinemas [*International Union of Cinemas*] (EAIO) ... UNIC
Union Internationale des Constructeurs d'Ascenseurs [*International Union of Elevator Constructors - IUEC*] ... UICA
Union Internationale des Distributeurs de Chaleur [*International Union of Heat Distributors*] (EAIO) ... UNICHAL
Union Internationale des Editeurs [*International Union of Publishers*] (NTCM) ... UIE
Union Internationale des Entrepreneurs de Peinture ... UIEP
Union Internationale des Entrepreneurs de Peinture [*International Union of Master Painters - IUMP*] (EAIO) ... UNIEP
Union Internationale des Etudiants [*International Union of Students - IUS*] (EAIO) ... UIE
Union Internationale des Etudiants en Architecture [*International Union of Students in Architecture*] ... UIEA
Union Internationale des Fabricants d'Impermeables ... UIFI
Union Internationale des Federations de Detaillants en Produits Laitiers ... UIFL
Union Internationale des Femmes Architectes [*International Union of Women Architects - IUWA*] (EAIO) ... UIFA
Union Internationale des Femmes Liberales Chretiennes [*International Union of Liberal Christian Women*] ... UFLC
Union Internationale des Guides et Scouts d'Europe [*International Union of European Guides and Scouts - IUEGS*] [*Chateau Landon, France*] (EAIO) ... UIGSE
Union Internationale des Infirmieres Diplomees d'Etat [*International Union of Registered Nurses*] [*France*] (EAIO) ... UIIDE
Union Internationale des Journalistes Agricoles [*International Union of Agricultural Journalists*] ... UIJA
Union Internationale des Journalistes et de la Presse de Langue Francaise [*International Union of French-Language Journalists and Press - IUFLJP*] (EAIO) ... UIJPLF
Union Internationale des Laboratoires Independents [*International Union of Independent Laboratories*] [*Elstree, Hertfordshire, England*] (EAIO) ... UILI
Union Internationale des Magistrats [*International Association of Judges - IAJ*] (EAIO) ... UIM
Union Internationale des Maisons de Jeunesse [*Service de la FIJC*] ... UIMJ
Union Internationale des Maitres Boulangers [*International Union of Master Bakers*] ... UIB
Union Internationale des Metis [*International Union of Individuals of Mixed Parentage*] ... UIM
Union Internationale des Organisations de Detaillants de la Branche Alimentaire [*International Federation of Grocers' Associations*] ... UIDA
Union Internationale des Organismes Familiaux [*International Union of Family Organizations - IUFO*] [*France*] ... UIOF
Union Internationale des Organismes Officiels de Tourisme [*International Union of Official Travel Organizations*] ... UIOOT
Union Internationale des Organismes Touristiques et Culturels des Postes et des Telecommunications [*International Union of Tourist and Cultural Associations in the Postal and Telecommunications Services*] ... UTCPTT
Union Internationale des Orientalistes [*International Union of Orientalists*] ... UIO
Union Internationale des Ouvriers du Vetement pour Dames [*International Ladies' Garment Workers' Union - ILGW*] ... UIOVD
Union Internationale des Publicitaires ... UIP
Union Internationale des Radioecologistes [*International Union of Radioecologists - IUR*] (EAIO) ... UIR
Union Internationale des Rembourreurs de l'Amerique du Nord [*Upholsterers' International Union of North America - UIU*] [*Canada*] ... UIR
Union Internationale des Sciences Anthropologiques et Ethnologiques [*International Union of Anthropological and Ethnological Sciences - IUAES*] (EAIO) ... UISAE

Union Internationale des Sciences Biologiques [*International Union of Biological Sciences*] ..... UISB
Union Internationale des Sciences de la Nutrition [*International Union of Nutritional Sciences - IUNS*] [*Wageningen, Netherlands*] (EA) ..... UISN
Union Internationale des Sciences Prehistoriques et Protohistoriques [*International Union of Prehistoric and Protohistoric Sciences*] ..... UISPP
Union Internationale des Services Medicaux des Chemins de Fer [*International Union of Railway Medical Services*] ..... UIMC
Union Internationale des Societes de la Paix [*International Union of Peace Societies*] ..... UISP
Union Internationale des Societies d'Ingenieurs Forestiers [*International Union of Societies of Foresters - IUSF*] [*Ottawa, ON*] (EAIO) ..... UISIF
Union Internationale des Superieures Majeures [*International Union of Superiors General*] [*Rome, Italy*] (EAIO) ..... UISG
Union Internationale des Syndicats de Police [*International Union of Police Syndicates*] (EAIO) ..... UISP
Union Internationale des Syndicats des Industries Alimentaires ..... UIA
Union Internationale des Syndicats des Industries de l'Alimentation et des Tabacs ..... UIAT
Union Internationale des Syndicats des Industries Metallurgiques et Mecaniques ..... UISMM
Union Internationale des Syndicats des Mineurs [*Miners' Trade Unions International*] ..... UISM
Union Internationale des Syndicats des Mineurs et des Travailleurs de l'Energie [*Trade Unions International of Miners and Workers in Energy - TUIMWE*] (EAIO) ..... UISMTE
Union Internationale des Syndicats des Travailleurs Agricoles et Forestiers et des Organisations des Paysans Travailleurs ..... UISTAF
Union Internationale des Syndicats des Travailleurs de l'Agriculture, des Forets, et des Plantations [*Trade Unions International of Agriculture, Forestry, and Plantation Workers - TUIAFPW*] [*Prague, Czechoslovakia*] (EAIO) ..... UISTAFP
Union Internationale des Syndicats des Travailleurs des Industries Chimiques du Petrole et Similaires ..... UISTICPS
Union Internationale des Syndicats des Travailleurs des Transports [*Trade Unions International of Transport Workers*] (EAIO) ..... UIS
Union Internationale des Syndicats des Travailleurs des Transports [*Trade Unions International of Transport Workers*] [*Hungary*] (EAIO) ..... UIS Transport
Union Internationale des Syndicats des Travailleurs du Batiment, du Bois, et desMateriaux de Construction [*Trade Unions International of Workers of the Building, Wood, and Building Materials Industries*] ..... UITBB
Union Internationale des Syndicats des Travailleurs du Commerce [*Trade Unions International of Workers in Commerce*] ..... UISTC
Union Internationale des Techniciens Orthopedistes [*International Association of Orthotist and Prosthetists*] (EA) ..... INTERBOR
Union Internationale des Telecommunications [*International Telecommunication Union*] [*French United Nations*] (DUND) ..... UIT
Union Internationale des Transports Publics [*International Union of Public Transport*] (EAIO) ..... UITP
Union Internationale des Travailleurs de l'Alimentation et des Branches Connexes [*International Union of Food and Allied Workers Associations*] ..... UITA
Union Internationale des Travailleurs Unis de l'Alimentation et du Commerce [*United Food and Commercial Workers Union*] [*Canada*] ..... TUAC
Union Internationale des Typographes [*International Typographical Union - ITU*] ..... UIT
Union Internationale des Villes et Pouvoirs Locaux [*International Union of Local Authorities*] ..... UIV
Union Internationale d'Etudes Sociales [*International Union for Social Studies*] ..... UIES
Union Internationale d'Histoire et de Philosophie des Sciences ..... UIHPS
Union Internationale d'Hygiene et de Medecine Scolaires et Universitaires [*International Union of School and University Health and Medicine - IUSUHM*] [*Brussels, Belgium*] (EAIO) ..... UIHMSU
Union Internationale du Cinema Non Professionnel [*International Union of Amateur Cinema*] (EAIO) ..... UNICA
Union Internationale du Commerce de Gros en Fleurs [*International Union of the Wholesale Flower Trade*] ..... UNION FLEURS
Union Internationale du Commerce en Gros de la Fleur [*International Union for the Wholesale Flower Trade*] ..... UICGF
Union Internationale du Commerce et de la Reparation du Cycle et du Motocycle [*International Union of Cycle and Motocycle Trade and Repair*] [*Germany*] ..... UNICOCYM
Union Internationale du Notariat Latin [*International Union of Latin Notaries*] ..... UINL
Union Internationale Monarchiste [*Weinsberg, Federal Republic of Germany*] (EAIO) ..... UIM
Union Internationale Motonautique [*Union of International Motorboating*] (EAIO) ..... UIM
Union Internationale pour la Conservation de la Nature et de ses Resources [*International Union for Conservation of Nature and Natural Resources*] [*Switzerland*] (EAIO) ..... UICNR
Union Internationale pour la Cooperation Culturelle [*International Union for Cultural Co-operation*] ..... UNO-CARA-PEN
Union Internationale pour la Liberte d'Enseignement [*International Union for the Liberty of Education*] ..... UILE
Union Internationale pour la Protection de la Nature [*International Union for the Protection of Nature - IUPN*] [*Later, IUCN*] ..... UIPN
Union Internationale pour la Protection de la Propriete Industrielle [*International Union for the Protection of Industrial Property*] ..... UIPPI
Union Internationale pour la Protection des Obtentions Vegetales [*International Union for the Protection of New Varieties of Plants*] (EAIO) ..... UPOV
Union Internationale pour la Science, la Technique, et les Applications du Vide [*International Union for Vacuum Science, Technique, and Applications - IUVSTA*] (EAIO) ..... UISTAV
Union Internationale pour le Protection de la Moralite Publique [*International Union for the Protection of Public Morale*] [*France*] ..... UIMP
Union Internationale pour l'Etude des Insectes Sociaux [*International Union for the Study of Social Insects - IUSSI*] [*Netherlands*] ..... UIEIS
Union Internationale Sportive des Postes, des Telephones, et des Telecommunications [*International Sports Union of Post, Telephone, and Telecommunications Services - ISUPTTS*] [*Switzerland*] ..... UISPTT
Union Internationale Universitaire Socialiste et Democratique [*International Union of Social Democratic Teachers*] ..... UIUSD
Union Interparlementaire [*Inter-Parliamentary Union*] (EAIO) ..... UI
Union Interparlementaire ..... UIP
Union Interprofessionnelle du Gabon [*Inter-Trade Union of Gabon*] ..... UNIGABON
Union Involved Racketeering [*FBI undercover investigation*] ..... UNIRAC
Union Island [*Windward Islands*] [*Airport symbol*] (OAG) ..... UNI
Union Jack ..... UJ
Union Jack Club [*British military*] (DMA) ..... UJC
Union Joint (MSA) ..... UJ
Union Junior College [*New Jersey*] ..... UJC
Union Katangaise [*Katanga Union*] ..... UK
Union Label and Service Trades Department (of AFL-CIO) [*American Federation of Labor and Congress of Industrial Organizations*] (EA) ..... ULSTD
Union Labor Report [*Bureau of National Affairs*] [*Information service or system*] (CRD) ..... ULR
Union Latino Americana de Sociedades de Tisiologia [*Latin American Union of Societies of Phthisiology*] ..... ULAST
Union Latino-Americaine de la Presse Catholique ..... ULAPC
Union Latino-Americaine des Jeunesses Evangeliques [*Union of Latin American Evangelical Youth*] ..... ULAJE
Union Latinoamericana de Ciegos [*Latin American Blind Union - LABU*] [*Montevideo, Uruguay*] (EAIO) ..... ULAC
Union Latinoamericana de Juventudes Ecumenicas [*Union of Latin American Ecumenical Youth - ULAEY*] (EAIO) ..... ULAJE
Union Law Review [*South Africa*] [*A publication*] (DLA) ..... ULR
Union League Club, New York, NY [*Library symbol Library of Congress*] (LCLS) ..... NNUnionL
Union Liberal [*Liberal Union*] [*Spain Political party*] (PPW) ..... UL
Union Liberale-Democratique Suisse [*Liberal Democratic Union of Switzerland*] [*Political party*] (PPE) ..... ULDS
Union Library Catalogue ..... ULC
Union Library Catalogue of Pennsylvania, Philadelphia, PA [*Library symbol Library of Congress*] (LCLS) ..... PPULC
Union Library Co., Hatboro, PA [*Library symbol Library of Congress Obsolete*] (LCLS) ..... PHatU
Union List ..... UL
Union List of Higher Degree Theses in Australian Libraries [*University of Tasmania Library*] [*Australia Information service or system*] (CRD) ..... HDEG
Union List of Montana Serials [*Library network*] ..... ULMS
Union List of Montana Serials, Bozeman, MT [*Library symbol Library of Congress*] (LCLS) ..... MtBULM
Union List of Scientific Serials in Canadian Libraries, Ottawa, ON, Canada [*Library symbol Library of Congress*] (LCLS) ..... CaOONUL
Union List of Scientific Serials in Canadian Libraries [*Catalogue Collectif des Publications Scientifiques dans les Bibliotheques Canadiennes*] **Ottawa, Ontario** [*Library symbol National Library of Canada*] (NLC) ..... OONUL
Union List of Selected Serials of Michigan [*Wayne State University Libraries*] [*Ceased*] [*Information service or system*] (IID) ..... ULOSSOM
Union List of Serials in the Social Sciences and Humanities Held by Canadian Libraries ..... CANUCS
Union List of Serials in the Social Sciences and Humanities Held by Canadian Libraries [*National Library of Canada*] [*Information service or system*] (CRD) ..... ULSSSHCL
Union Marocaine du Travail [*Moroccan Labor Union*] ..... UMT
Union Mathematique Africaine [*African Mathematical Union - AMU*] (EA) ..... UMA
Union Mathematique Internationale [*International Mathematical Union - IMU*] (EAIO) ..... UMI
Union Medicale Arabe [*Arab Medical Union*] (EAIO) ..... UMA
Union Medicale Balkanique [*Balkan Medical Union*] (EAIO) ..... UMB
Union Membership Agreement (DCTA) ..... UMA
Union Memorial Hospital, Finney Medical Library, Baltimore, MD [*Library symbol Library of Congress*] (LCLS) ..... MdBUM
Union Miniere du Haut Katanga [*Mining Company of Upper Katanga*] ..... UMHK
Union, MO [*AM radio station call letters*] ..... KLPW
Union, MO [*FM radio station call letters*] ..... KLPW-FM
Union Mondiale d'Avancee Humaine [*World Union for Human Progress*] ..... UMAH
Union Mondiale de Billard [*World Billiards Union - WBU*] [*Switzerland*] ..... UMB
Union Mondiale de Ski Nautique [*World Water Ski Union - WWSU*] [*Montreaux, Switzerland*] (EAIO) ..... UMSN
Union Mondiale Democrate Chretienne [*Christian Democratic World Union*] ..... UMDC
Union Mondiale des Aveugles [*World Blind Union - WBU*] (EA) ..... UMA
Union Mondiale des Enseignants Catholiques [*World Union of Catholic Teachers*] [*Rome, Italy*] ..... UMEC
Union Mondiale des Etudiants Juifs [*World Union of Jewish Students - WUJS*] (EAIO) ..... UMEJ
Union Mondiale des Organisations Feminines Catholiques [*World Union of Catholic Women's Organizations - WUCWO*] [*Canada*] ..... UMOFC
Union Mondiale des Organisations Syndicales sur Base Economique et Sociale Liberale [*World Union of Liberal Trade Union Organizations*] ..... UMOSBESL
Union Mondiale des Pioniers de Stockholm [*World Union of Stockholm Pioneers*] (EAIO) ..... UMPS

Union Mondiale des Romains Libres [World Union of Free Romanians - WUFR] [Creteil, France] (EAIO) .... UMRL

Union Mondiale des Societes d'Histoire Pharmaceutique [World Organization of Societies of Pharmaceutical History] .... UMHP

Union Mondiale des Voix Francaises [World Union of French-Speakers - WUFS] (EAIO) .... UMVF

Union Mondiale du Mapam [World Union of Mapam - WUM] (EAIO) .... UMM

Union Mondiale Pour la Nature (EERA) .... UICN

Union Mondiale pour la Protection de la Sante des Populations Juives et Oeuvres de Secours aux Enfants .... OSE

Union Mondiale pour la Sauvegarde de l'Enfance et de l'Adolescence [World Union for the Safeguard of Youth] .... UMOSEA

Union Mondiale pour un Judaisme Liberal .... UMJL

Union Movement Party [British] .... UM

Union, MS [FM radio station call letters] (RBYB) .... WZKS

Union Mundial de Mujeres Democrata Cristianas [World Union of Christian Democratic Women] [Venezuela Political party] (EAIO) .... UMFDC

Union Mundial pro Interlingua (EA) .... UMI

Union Nacional [National Union] [Spain Political party] (PPE) .... UN

Union Nacional de Campesinas Autenticos de Honduras [National Union of Authentic Peasants of Honduras] (PD) .... UNCAH

Union Nacional Democratica [National Democratic Union] [Ecuador] [Political party] (PPW) .... UNADE

Union Nacional Democratica [El Salvador] [Political party] (EY) .... UND

Union Nacional Odriista [Peruvian political party] .... UNO

Union Nacional Opositora [Electoral alliance] [Nicaragua] (EY) .... UNO

Union Nacional Paraguaya [Paraguayan political party] .... UNP

Union Nationale [National Union] [Canada Political party] .... UN

Union Nationale Africaine du Ruanda-Urundi [African National Union of Ruanda-Urundi] .... UNARU

Union Nationale Camerounaise [Cameroon National Union] .... UNC

Union Nationale de la Jeunesse Algerienne [Algeria] [Political party] (EY) .... UNJA

Union Nationale des Agriculteurs Tunisiens [National Union of Tunisian Farmers] .... UNAT

Union Nationale des Associations de Parents et Amis de Personnes Handicapees Mentales [Formerly, Union Nationale des Associations de Parents d'Enfants Inadeptes] [France] (EAIO) .... UNAPEI

Union Nationale des Associations de Soins et Service a Domicile [Also, National Organisation for Home Care] [France] (EAIO) .... UNASSAD

Union Nationale des Cheminots du Cameroun [National Union of Railway Workers of Cameroon] .... UNCC

Union Nationale des Eleves et Etudiants de la Guadeloupe [National Union of Pupils and Students of Guadeloupe] (PD) .... UNEEG

Union Nationale des Eleves et Etudiants du Mali [National Union of Pupils and Students of Mali] (PD) .... UNEEM

Union Nationale des Etudiants Camerounais [National Union of Cameroonese Students] .... UNEC

Union Nationale des Etudiants du Maroc [National Union of Moroccan Students] (PD) .... UNEM

Union Nationale des Femmes Algeriennes [Algeria] [Political party] (EY) .... UNFA

Union Nationale des Femmes de Tunisie [National Union of Tunisian Women] .... UNFT

Union Nationale des Forces Populaires [National Union of Popular Forces] [Political party Morocco] .... UNFP

Union Nationale des Independants [National Union of Independents] [Monaco] (PPE) .... UNI

Union Nationale des Intellectuels et Universitaires Malgaches [National Union of Intellectuals and University People of Madagascar] .... UNIUM

Union Nationale des Ouvriers Congolais [National Union of Congolese Workers] .... UNOC

Union Nationale des Syndicats Agricoles Forestiers, des Bois, de l'Elevage, et de la Peche du Cameroun [National Union of Farmers, Fishermen, Forest Guards, and Timber Workers of Cameroon] .... UNASABEC

Union Nationale des Syndicats des Travailleurs de la Haute Volta [National Federation of Workers' Unions of the Upper Volta] .... UNSTHV

Union Nationale des Syndicats des Travailleurs du Dahomey [National Federation of Workers' Unions of Dahomey] .... UNSTD

Union Nationale des Travailleurs Angolais [National Union of Angolan Workers] .... UNTA

Union Nationale des Travailleurs Congolais [National Union of Congolese Workers] .... UNTC

Union Nationale des Travailleurs de Cote d'Ivoire [National Union of Ivory Coast Workers] .... UNTCI

Union Nationale des Travailleurs du Congo [National Union of Workers of the Congo] .... UNATRACO

Union Nationale des Travailleurs du Mali [National Union of Malian Workers] .... UNTM

Union Nationale des Travailleurs du Senegal [National Union of Workers of Senegal] .... UNTS

Union Nationale des Travailleurs du Togo [National Union of Togolese Workers] .... UNTT

Union Nationale des Travailleurs Nigeriens [National Union of Nigerian Workers] .... UNTN

Union Nationale et Democratique [National Democratic Union] [Monaco] [Political party] (PPW) .... UND

Union Nationale pour la Democratie aux Comoros [Political party] (EY) .... UNDC

Union Nationale pour la Democratie et le Developpement [Madagascar] [Political party] (EY) .... UNDD

Union Nationale pour la Democratie et le Progres [The Congo] [Political party] (EY) .... UNDP

Union Nationale pour la Democratie et le Progres [Cameroon] [Political party] (EY) .... UNDP

Union Nationale pour la Democratie et le Progres [Benin] [Political party] (EY) .... UNDP

Union Nationale pour la Solidarite et le Progres [Benin] [Political party] (EY) .... UNSP

Union Nationale pour l'Independence [National Union for Independence] [Djibouti] (PPW) .... UNI

Union Nationale pour l'Initiative et la Responsabilite [National Union for Initiative and Responsibility] [France Political party] (PPW) .... UNIR

Union Nationale Progressite [National Progressive Union] [Burundi] .... UNAP

Union Nationale Ruandaise [Ruanda National Union] .... UNAR

Union Nationals Democracy Party [Myanmar] [Political party] (EY) .... UNDP

Union Nigerienne Democratique [Political party] (EY) .... UND

Union Nordique pour la Sante et le Travail [Nordic Union for Health and Work] (EAIO) .... UNST

Union Nouvelle Caledonienne [New Caledonia] [Political party] (FEA) .... UNC

Union of African Performing Artists [See also UAAS] (EAIO) .... UAPA

Union of African States .... UAS

Union of Air Pollution Prevention Associations (EAIO) .... UAPPA

Union of American Biological Societies (BARN) .... UABS

Union of American Hebrew Congregations (EA) .... UAHC

Union of American Physicians [Later, UAPD] (EA) .... UAP

Union of American Physicians and Dentists (EA) .... UAPD

Union of Anarchist Groups [British] .... UAG

Union of Arab Football Associations (EAIO) .... UAFA

Union of Arab Historians (EA) .... UAH

Union of Arab Jurists [Baghdad, Iraq] .... UAJ

Union of Arab Stock Exchanges .... UASE

Union of Associations of European Meat Meal Producers [See also UAPEFV] [Later, Eurpoean Renderers Association - EURA] (EAIO) .... UAEM

Union of Associations of Fish Meal Manufacturers in the EEC (EAIO) .... UAFMMEEC

Union of Australian College Academics Northern Territory .... UACANT

Union of Australian College Academics South Australia .... UACASA

Union of Australian Women National Office .... UAWNO

Union of Automobile, Motorcycle, and Cycle Technology .... UAMCT

Union of Black Clergy and Laity of the Episcopal Church [Later, UBE] (EA) .... UBCL

Union of Black Episcopalians [Defunct] (EA) .... UBE

Union of Burma Airways .... UBA

Union of Burma Applied Research Institute .... UBARI

Union of Burma Atomic Energy Centre .... UBAEC

Union of Burma Bank (DS) .... UBB

Union of Cafe Owners and Soft Drink Dealers of the European Economic Community [Paris, France] .... UCOSDDEEC

Union of Catholic Asian News [Kwun Tong, Hong Kong] (EAIO) .... UCAN

Union of Catholic Institutions for the Mentally Handicapped and Persons with Learning Disabilities [Germany] (EAIO) .... UCIMHPLD

Union of Catholic Mothers [British] (DI) .... UCM

Union of Catholic Students [British] (AEBS) .... UCS

Union of Central African States (EY) .... UCAS

Union of Central African States .... UEAC

Union of Coffee Planters [Madagascar] (EAIO) .... UCP

Union of Communications Workers [British] (ECON) .... UCW

Union of Concerned Scientists (EA) .... UCS

Union of Construction, Allied Trades, and Technicians [British] .... UCATT

Union of Councils for Soviet Jews (EA) .... UCSJ

Union of Democratic Control [British] .... UDC

Union of Democratic Forces [Bulgaria] [Political party] .... UDF

Union of Democratic Forces [Mauritania] [Political party] (EY) .... UDF

Union of Democratic Mineworkers [British] .... UDM

Union of Democratic Thais in the US (EA) .... UDT

Union of Educational Institutions [British] .... UEI

Union of EEC Soft Drinks Associations (EAIO) .... UNESDA

Union of Electrical Operatives [British] .... UEO

Union of European Abattoirs [Belgium] (EAIO) .... UEA

Union of European Associations of Water Suppliers [Belgium] (EAIO) ..... UEAWS

Union of European Fashion Jewellery Manufacturers [Italy] (EAIO) .... UEFJM

Union of European Football Associations [Switzerland] (EAIO) .... UEFA

Union of European Practitioners in Industrial Property [EC] (ECED) .... UPEPI

Union of Evangelical Baptists (EAIO) .... UEB

Union of Flight Attendants (EA) .... UFA

Union of Girls' Schools for Social Service [British] (BI) .... UGSS

Union of Independent Colleges of Art (EA) .... UICA

Union of Independent Companies [British] (DBA) .... UIC

Union of Industrial and Employers' Confederations of Europe (EAIO) .... UNICE

Union of International Associations [See also UAI] [Brussels, Belgium] (EAIO) .... UIA

Union of International Conventions .... UIC

Union of International Engineering Organizations (EAIO) .... UIEO

Union of International Motorboating (EA) .... UIM

Union of International Technical Associations [See also UATI] [ICSU] [Paris, France] (EAIO) .... UITA

Union of Jewish Women [Zimbabwe] (EA) .... UJW

Union of Latin American Ecumenical Youth (EA) .... ULAEY

Union of Latin American Universities (EA) .... ALAU

Union of Latin Writers and Artists [Paris, France] (EAIO) .... ULWA

Union of Middle Eastern and Mediterranean Pediatric Societies [Greece] (EAIO) .... UMEMPA

Union of Middle Eastern and Mediterranean Pediatric Societies [See also USPMOM] [Athens, Greece] (EAIO) .... UMEMPS

Union of Moderate Parties [Vanuatu] [Political party] (PPW) .... UMP

Union of Operative Card Makers and Wire Drawers [British] .... UOCMWD

Union of Orthodox Jewish Congregations of America (EA) .... UOJC

Union of Orthodox Jewish Congregations of America (EA) .... UOJCA

Union of Orthodox Rabbis of the US and Canada (EA) .... UORUSC

Union of Palestinian Women's Association in North America (EA) .... UPWA

Union of People's Youth [Bulgaria] .... UPY

Union of Platers Helpers [*British*] ... UPH
Union of Poles in America (EA) ... UPA
Union of Polish Women in America (EA) ... UPWA
Union of Post Office Workers [*British*] (DCTA) ... UPW
Union of Rail Canada Traffic Controllers [*See also CCFC*] ... RCTC
Union of Railway Signalmen [*British*] ... URS
Union of Saddlers and General Leather Workers [*British*] ... USGLW
Union of Salt, Chemical, and Industrial General Workers [*British*] (BI) ... USCIGW
Union of Scientific Leisure Clubs [*France*] (EAIO) ... UDSL
Union of Sephardic Congregations (EA) ... USC
Union of Sets (IDOE) ... U
Union of Ship Distributive and Allied Workers [*British*] (DCTA) ... USDAW
Union of Shop, Distributive, and Allied Workers [*British*] (ODBW) ... Usdaw
Union of South Africa ... USA
Union of South Africa ... USAFR
Union of South Africa Water Courts Decisions [*A publication*] (DLA) ... W Ct SA
Union of Soviet Socialist Republics [*Initialism represents Russian phrase, Soyuz Sotsialistiches Kikh Respublik*] ... CCCP
Union of Soviet Socialist Republics [*Formerly, SX*] [*License plate code assigned to foreign diplomats in the US*] ... FC
Union of Soviet Socialist Republics [*IYRU nationality code*] (IYR) ... SR
Union of Soviet Socialist Republics [*ANSI two-letter standard code*] (CNC) ... SU
Union of Soviet Socialist Republics [*ANSI three-letter standard code*] (CNC) ... SUN
Union of Soviet Socialist Republics [*Later, FC*] [*License plate code assigned to foreign diplomats in the US*] ... SX
Union of Soviet Socialist Republics [*See also SSSR, CCCP*] ... USSR
Union of Students in Ireland (AIE) ... USI
Union of Superiors General (EA) ... USG
Union of Textile Workers [*British*] (EAIO) ... UTW
Union of the Corsican People [*France*] ... UPC
Union of the Democratic Centre [*Sahara*] [*Political party*] (PPW) ... UDC
Union of the Finance-Personnel in Europe [*EC*] (ECED) ... UFE
Union of the Gas Industries of the Common Market Countries [*Defunct*] (EAIO) ... MARCOGAZ
Union of the Sisters of the Presentation of the Blessed Virgin Mary (TOCD) ... PBVM
Union of Voluntary Organisations for the Handicapped [*British*] (DBA) ... UVOH
Union of Watch, Clock, and Clock Case Makers [*British*] ... UWCCCM
Union of West African Voluntary Workcamps Associations [*Ghana*] (EAIO) ... UWAVWA
Union of Women Teachers [*British*] (DI) ... UWT
Union Office (ROG) ... UO
Union Oil Co. ... UOCO
Union Oil Co. of California, Brea, CA [*Library symbol Library of Congress*] (LCLS) ... CBreU
Union Oil Co. of Canada Ltd., Calgary, Alberta [*Library symbol National Library of Canada*] (NLC) ... ACUNO
Union Oil of Canada Ltd., Calgary, AB, Canada [*Library symbol Library of Congress*] (LCLS) ... CaACUNO
Union Ouvriere du Viet-Nam [*Vietnam Labor Union*] [*South Vietnam*] ... UOV
Union Ouvriere et Paysanne pour la Democratie Proletarienne [*Peasant and Worker Union for Proletarian Democracy*] [*France Political party*] (PPE) ... UOPDP
Union Pacific [*NYSE symbol*] (TTSB) ... UNP
Union Pacific Corp. [*NYSE symbol*] (SPSG) ... UNP
Union Pacific Corp. [*Associated Press*] (SAG) ... UnPac
Union Pacific Corp. ... UP
Union Pacific Law Department. Bulletin [*A publication*] (DLA) ... Union Pac LDB
Union Pacific Railroad Co. ... UNPAC
Union Pacific Railroad Co. ... UPRR
Union Pacific Resources Group [*NYSE symbol*] (TTSB) ... UPR
Union Pacific Resources Group, Inc. [*Associated Press*] (SAG) ... UPacRs
Union Pacific Resources Group, Inc. [*NYSE symbol*] (SAG) ... UPR
Union Pan Africaine des Postes [*Pan African Postal Union - PAPU*] (EAIO) ... UPAP
Union Panafricaine des Etudiants [*All Africa Students Union - AASU*] (EAIO) ... UPE
Union Panafricaine des Journalistes ... UPAJ
Union Panafricaine des Telecommunications [*Pan African Telecommunications Union - PATU*] (EAIO) ... UPAT
Union Panafricaine des Travailleurs Croyants [*Pan-African Union of Believing Workers*] ... UPTC
Union Panamericana [*Pan-American Union*] [*Washington, DC*] ... UPA
Union Pan-Americana de Asociaciones de Igenieros [*Pan American Federation of Engineering Societies*] [*Uruguay*] (EAIO) ... UPADI
Union para la Democracia y el Desarrollo Social [*Equatorial Guinea*] [*Political party*] (EY) ... UDDS
Union Parish Library, Farmerville, LA [*Library symbol Library of Congress*] (LCLS) ... LFaU
Union Park, FL [*FM radio station call letters*] (RBYB) ... WEAZ
Union Patriotica [*Patriotic Union*] [*Spain Political party*] (PPE) ... UP
Union Patriotica [*Patriotic Union*] [*Colombia*] [*Political party*] ... UP
Union Patriotica Bonairiana [*Bonaire Patriotic Union*] [*Netherlands Antilles*] [*Political party*] (PPW) ... UPB
Union Patriotique Haitienne [*Haitian Patriotic Union*] (EA) ... UPH
Union Petroliere Europeenne Independante [*Independent European Petroleum Union*] (EAIO) ... UPEI
Union Planters [*NYSE symbol*] (TTSB) ... UPC
Union Planters [*NASDAQ symbol*] (SAG) ... UPCP
Union Planters [*Associated Press*] (SAG) ... UPlntr
Union Planters 8% Cv'E'Pfd [*NASDAQ symbol*] (TTSB) ... UPCPO
Union Planters Corp. [*NYSE symbol*] (CTT) ... UPC
Union Planters Corp. [*Associated Press*] (SAG) ... UPlnt
Union Planters National Bank, Memphis, TN [*Library symbol Library of Congress*] (LCLS) ... TMUP
Union Pontificale Missionnaire [*Pontifical Missionary Union - PMU*] [*Later, PMUPR*] ... UPM
Union Populaire Locale [*Wallis and Futuna Islands*] [*Political party*] (FEA) ... UPL
Union Populaire pour la Liberation de la Guadeloupe [*Popular Union for the Liberation of Guadeloupe*] (PD) ... UPLG
Union Popular [*Popular Union*] [*Uruguay*] (PD) ... UP
Union Postal de las Americas, Espana, y Portugal [*Postal Union of the Americas, Spain, and Portugal*] [*Uruguay*] (EAIO) ... UPAEP
Union Postal de las Americas y Espana [*Postal Union of the Americas and Spain - PUAS*] (EAIO) ... UPAE
Union Postale Arabe [*Arab Postal Union*] ... UPA
Union Postale des Pays du Nord [*Nordic Postal Union - NPU*] (EAIO) ... UPPN
Union Postale Universelle [*Universal Postal Union*] [*Switzerland Also, an information service or system*] (IID) ... UPU
Union pour Construire l'Independence [*New Caledonia*] [*Political party*] (EY) ... UPCI
Union pour la Communaute Franco-Africaine [*Union for the Franco-African Community*] [*Niger*] ... UCFA
Union pour la Coordination de la Production et du Transport de l'Electricite [*Union for the Coordination of the Production and Transport of Electric Power - UCPTE*] (EAIO) ... UCPTE
Union pour la Defense de la Republique [*Union for the Defense of the Republic*] [*France Political party*] (PPE) ... UDR
Union pour la Defense des Commercants et des Artisans [*Union for the Defense of Traders and Artisans*] [*France Political party*] (PPE) ... UDCA
Union pour la Defense des Interets du Tchad [*Union for the Defense of Chadian Interests*] ... UDIT
Union pour la Democratie Congolaise [*Political party*] (EY) ... UDC
Union pour la Democratie et la Reconstruction Nationale [*Benin*] [*Political party*] (EY) ... UDRN
Union pour la Democratie et la Solidarite Nationale [*Benin*] [*Political party*] (EY) ... UDS
Union pour la Democratie et le Developpement [*Mali*] [*Political party*] (EY) ... UDD
Union pour la Democratie et le Developpement Mayumba [*Gabon*] [*Political party*] (EY) ... UDD
Union pour la Democratie et le Progres Social [*Democratic Union of Social Progress*] [*Zaire*] [*Political party*] ... UDPS
Union pour la Democratie Francaise [*Union for French Democracy*] [*France Political party*] (PPW) ... UDF
Union pour la Democratie Francaise [*Union for French Democracy*] [*Wallis and Futuna Islands*] [*Political party*] (EY) ... UDF
Union pour la Democratie Francaise [*Union for French Democracy*] [*Mayotte*] [*Political party*] (EY) ... UDF
Union pour la Democratie Francaise [*Union for French Democracy*] [*New Caledonia*] [*Political party*] (PPW) ... UDF
Union pour la Democratie Francaise [*Union for French Democracy*] [*Reunion*] [*Political party*] (PPW) ... UDF
Union pour la Democratie Francaise [*Union for French Democracy*] [*French Guiana*] [*Political party*] (PPW) ... UDF
Union pour la Democratie Francaise [*Union for French Democracy*] [*Martinique*] [*Political party*] (PPW) ... UDR
Union pour la Democratie Populaire [*Union for People's Democracy*] [*Senegal*] [*Political party*] (PPW) ... UDP
Union pour la France [*France Political party*] ... UPF
Union pour la Langue Internationale Ido [*Union for the International Language Ido*] ... ULI
Union pour la Liberte et le Developpement [*Benin*] [*Political party*] (EY) ... ULD
Union pour la Majorite Nouvelle [*Union for the New Majority*] [*France Political party*] (PPE) ... UMN
Union pour la Nouvelle Republique Senegalaise [*Union for the New Senegalese Republic*] [*Political party*] ... UNRS
Union pour la Reconciliation Nationale [*Haiti*] [*Political party*] (EY) ... URN
Union pour le Commerce des Bois Tropicaux dans la CEE [*Association for Trade in Tropical Woods in the EEC*] (ECED) ... UCBT
Union pour le Developpement et le Progres Social [*The Congo*] [*Political party*] (EY) ... UDPS
Union pour le Progres Comorien [*Union for Comorian Progress*] [*Political party*] (PPW) ... UPC
Union pour le Progres National [*Union for National Progress*] [*Burundi*] [*Political party*] (PPW) ... UPRONA
Union pour le Progres Social et le Democratie [*The Congo*] [*Political party*] (EY) ... UPSD
Union pour les Interets du Peuple Congolais [*Union for the Interests of the Congolese People*] ... UNICO
Union Professionnelle des Stockeurs de Cereales dans la CEE [*Organization of Cereal Storage Firms in the European Economic Community*] ... UNISTOCK
Union Professionnelle Internationale des Gynecologues et Obstetriciens [*International Union of Professional Gynecologists and Obstetricians*] ... UPIGO
Union Progressiste Congolaise [*Congolese Progressive Union*] ... UPC
Union Progressiste Congolaise [*Congolese Progressive Union*] ... UPCO
Union Progressiste Congolaise [*Congolese Progressive Union*] ... UPECO
Union Progressiste de l'Equateur [*Progressive Union of Equateur Province*] [*Congo - Leopoldville*] ... UPEQUA
Union Progressiste du Congo [*Progressive Union of the Congo*] [*Niangara*] ... UPROCO
Union Progressiste Guineenne [*Guinean Progressive Union*] ... UPG
Union Progressiste Mauritanienne [*Mauritanian Progressive Union*] ... UPM
Union Progressiste Melanesienne [*New Caledonia*] [*Political party*] (FEA) ... UPM
Union Progressiste Melanesienne [*Progressive Melanesian Union*] [*New Caledonia*] [*Political party*] (PPW) ... UPMI

Union Progressiste Senegalaise [*Senegalese Progressive Union*] [*Political party*] (AF) ... UPS
Union Progressive des Femmes Marocaines [*Progressive Union of Moroccan Women*] ... UPFM
Union Property Investors, Inc. [*Associated Press*] (SAG) ... UnProp
Union Property Investors, Inc. [*NASDAQ symbol*] (SAG) ... UPIC
Union Radio Scientifique Internationale [*International Union of Radio Science*] [*Also, ISRU*] [*Belgium*] ... URSI
Union Radio Scientifique Internationale (EERA) ... URSI
Union Railroad Co. [*Pittsburgh, PA*] [*AAR code*] ... URR
Union Railroad of Oregon [*AAR code*] ... UO
Union Railway of Memphis [*AAR code*] ... URY
Union Regionale de Bamileke [*Regional Union of Bamileke*] [*Cameroon*] ... URB
Union Regionale des Syndicats du Nyong-et-Sanaga ... URSNSC
Union Regionale des Syndicats du Wouri [*Regional Union of Wouri Unions*] ... URSW
Union Reporter, Camden, NJ [*Library symbol Library of Congress*] (LCLS) ... NjCaUR
Union Republicaine du Peuple [*Benin*] [*Political party*] (EY) ... URP
Union Republicana Democratica [*Democratic Republican Union*] [*Puerto Rico, Venezuela*] ... URD
Union Research Institute, Kowloon, Hong Kong [*Library symbol Library of Congress*] (LCLS) ... URI
Union Restaurants Collectifs Europeens [*European Catering Association*] (EAIO) ... RCE
Union Restaurants Collectifs Europeens [*European Catering Association*] [*Germany*] (EAIO) ... URCE
Union Revolucionaria Popular Ecuatoriana [*Ecuadorean Popular Revolutionary Union*] [*Political party*] (PPW) ... URPE
Union Revolutionnaire des Banques [*Burkina Faso*] (EY) ... UREBA
Union Rheinische Braunkohlen Kraftstoff [*West Germany*] ... URBK
Union Saint-Jean-Baptiste (EA) ... USJB
Union Saint-Jean-Baptiste d'Amerique, Woonsocket, RI [*Library symbol Library of Congress*] (LCLS) ... RWoU
Union, SC [*Location identifier FAA*] (FAAL) ... UOT
Union, SC [*AM radio station call letters*] ... WBCU
Union Scientifique Continentale de Verre [*European Union for the Scientific Study of Glass - EUSSG*] (EAIO) ... USCV
Union Senegalaise du Travail [*Senegalese Labor Union*] ... UST
Union Settlement Association (EA) ... US
Union Social-Democrate [*Social Democratic Union*] [*The Ivory Coast*] [*Political party*] (EY) ... USD
Union Sociale Camerounaise [*Cameroonese Social Union*] ... USC
Union Sociale Democratique [*Cameroon*] [*Political party*] (EY) ... USD
Union Socialiste des Forces Populaires [*Socialist Union of Popular Forces*] [*Morocco*] [*Political party*] (PPW) ... USFP
Union Socialiste des Musulmans Mauritaniens [*Socialist Union of Mauritanian Moslems*] ... USMM
Union Socialiste Tchadienne [*Chadian Socialist Union*] ... UST
Union Soudanaise - Rassemblement Democratique Africain [*Mali*] [*Political party*] (EY) ... US-RDA
Union Sportive Interuniversitaire Canadienne ... USIC
Union Sportive Interuniversitaire Canadienne Feminine ... USICF
Union Springs, AL [*FM radio station call letters*] (RBYB) ... WSFU-FM
Union Suisse des Syndicats Autonomes [*Swiss Association of Autonomous Unions*] ... USSA
Union Switch & Signal [*NASDAQ symbol*] (TTSB) ... UNSW
Union Switch & Signal, Inc. [*NASDAQ symbol*] (SAG) ... UNSW
Union Switch & Signal, Inc. [*Associated Press*] (SAG) ... UnSwtch
Union Syndicale de l'Agriculture [*Union of Agricultural Workers*] [*Morocco*] ... USA
Union Syndicale de Travail Centrafricaine [*Union of Central African Workers*] (EY) ... USTC
Union Syndicale des Artistes Lyriques [*French*] (ROG) ... US des AL
Union Syndicale des Bases Americaines [*Union of American Base Workers*] [*Morocco*] ... USBA
Union Syndicale des Travailleurs de Guinee [*Guinean Federation of Workers*] ... USTG
Union Syndicale des Travailleurs du Soudan [*Federation of Sudanese Workers*] [*Mali*] ... USTS
Union Syndicale Suisse [*Swiss Federation of Trade Unions*] ... USS
Union Technique de l'Electricite [*France*] ... UTE
Union Technique des Ingenieurs Conseils [*French*] ... UTICI
Union Telegraphique Internationale (MSC) ... UTI
Union Terminal Railway Co. [*AAR code*] ... UT
Union Territoriale des Syndicats de Cadres, Agents de Maitrise, Techniciens, et Assimiles du Senegal [*Territorial Union of Leaders, Supervising Personnel, and Related Workers of Senegal*] ... UNISCAMTA
Union Territoriale des Syndicats - Force Ouvrieres [*Territorial Federation of Trade Unions - Workers' Force*] [*French Somaliland*] ... UTS-FO
Union Territoriale du Senegal des Travailleurs [*Senegalese Workers Union*] ... UTTS
Union Territory [*India*] (BARN) ... UT
Union Texas Petroleum [*Associated Press*] (SAG) ... UnTex
Union Texas Petroleum [*NYSE symbol*] (TTSB) ... UTH
Union Texas Petroleum Co., Houston, TX [*Library symbol Library of Congress*] (LCLS) ... TxHUTP
Union Texas Petroleum Holdings, Inc. [*NYSE symbol*] (SPSG) ... UTH
Union Theological Seminary ... UTS
Union Theological Seminary in Virginia ... UTSV
Union Theological Seminary Library, Richmond, VA [*OCLC symbol*] (OCLC) ... VUT
Union Theological Seminary, McAlpin Collection, New York, NY [*Library symbol Library of Congress*] (LCLS) ... NNUT-Mc
Union Theological Seminary, New York, NY [*Library symbol Library of Congress*] (LCLS) ... NNUT
Union Theological Seminary, New York, NY [*OCLC symbol*] (OCLC) ... VYN
Union Theological Seminary, Richmond, VA [*Library symbol Library of Congress*] (LCLS) ... ViRUT
Union Township, NJ [*FM radio station call letters*] ... WKNJ
Union Township Public Library, Union, NJ [*Library symbol Library of Congress*] (LCLS) ... NjU
Union Transportation [*AAR code*] ... UTR
Union Tunisienne de l'Artisanat et du Commerce [*Tunisian Union of Artisans and Merchants*] ... UTAC
Union University [*Tennessee*] ... UU
Union University, Jackson, TN [*Library symbol Library of Congress*] (LCLS) ... TJaU
Union Valdotaine [*Valdotaine Union*] [*Italy Political party*] (EAIO) ... UV
Union Valenciana [*Spain Political party*] (EY) ... UV
Union Wallisienne et Futunienne pour la Caledonie [*Wallisian and Futunian Union for Caledonia*] [*Political party*] (PPW) ... UWFPC
Union Women's Alliance to Gain Equality [*Defunct*] (EA) ... UWAGE
Union Women's Alliance to Gain Equality [*Defunct*] (EA) ... WAGE
Unionamerica Hldgs ADS [*NYSE symbol*] (TTSB) ... UA
Unionamerica Holdings PLC [*NYSE symbol*] (SAG) ... UA
Unionamerica Holdings PLC [*Associated Press*] (SAG) ... Unionam
UnionBanCal 8.375% Dep 'A' Pfd [*NASDAQ symbol*] (TTSB) ... UBNKZ
UnionBanCal Corp. [*Associated Press*] (SAG) ... UnBanCal
UnionBanCal Corp. [*NASDAQ symbol*] (SAG) ... UNBC
UnionBanCal Corp. [*NASDAQ symbol*] (TTSB) ... UNBC
UnionBanCal Corp. [*Associated Press*] (SAG) ... UnBCal
UnionBancorp, Inc. [*NASDAQ symbol*] (SAG) ... UBCD
UnionBancorp, Inc. [*Associated Press*] (SAG) ... UnionBc
Uniondale High School, Uniondale, NY [*Library symbol Library of Congress*] (LCLS) ... NUnH
Uniondale Public Library, Uniondale, NY [*Library symbol Library of Congress*] (LCLS) ... NUn
Unione Cattolica Italiana Insegnanti Medi ... UCIIM
Unione di u Populu Corsu [*Union of the Corsican People*] [*France Political party*] (PPE) ... UPC
Unione Europea di Medicina Sociale [*European Union of Social Medicine - EUSM*] (EAIO) ... UEMS
Unione Europea di Relazioni Pubbliche [*European Union of Public Relations - International Service Organization - EURPISO*] (EAIO) ... UERP
Unione Internazionale des Giovani Democratici Cristiana [*International Union of Young Christian Democrats*] ... UIGDC
Unione Italiana Agenti Rappresentati Viaggiatori e Piazzisti [*Italian Union of Agents and Travelers*] ... UIARVEP
Unione Italiana Bancari [*Italian Union of Bank Employees*] ... UIB
Unione Italiana del Lavoro [*Italian Union of Labor*] ... UIL
Unione Italiana Dipendenti Aziende Commerciali ed Affini [*Italian Union of Commerical and Allied Workers*] ... UIDAC
Unione Italiana Lavoratori Albergo e Mensa [*Italian Union of Hotel and Restaurant Workers*] ... UILAM
Unione Italiana Lavoratori Assicurazioni [*Italian Union of Insurance Workers*] ... UILA
Unione Italiana Lavoratori Aziende Gas [*Italian Union of Gas Workers*] ... UIL-GAS
Unione Italiana Pescatori [*Italian Union of Fishermen*] ... UIP
Unione Maniferro [*Somalia*] ... UM
Unione Medicale Mediterranea Latina [*Latin Mediterranean Medical Union - LMMU*] [*Mantua, Italy*] (EAIO) ... UMML
Unione Nazionale dell'Avicoltura [*Aviculture Union*] [*Italy*] (EY) ... UNA
Unione Nazionale Imprese di Meccanizzazione Agricola [*Agricultural Mechanization Enterprises Union*] [*Italy*] (EY) ... UNIMA
Unione Nazionale Protezione Antiaere [*Italy*] ... UNPA
Unione per la Lotta alla Tubercolosi [*Union of Anti-Tuberculosis Association Workers*] [*Italy*] ... ULT
Unione Politica Maltese [*Maltese Political Union*] [*Political party*] (PPE) ... UPM
Unione Progressista della Gioventu Somala [*Progressive Union of Somali Youth*] ... UPGS
Unione Sindacale Ferrovieri Italiani [*National Union of Italian Railway Workers*] ... USFI
Unione Stampa Periodica Italiana [*Press association*] (EY) ... USPI
Unione Tipografico-Editrice Torinese [*Publisher*] [*Italy*] ... UTET
Unione Valdostana-Partito Sardo d'Azione [*Italy*] [*Political party*] (ECED) ... UV-PSdA
Union-Intersection [*Statistics*] ... UI
Unionist Committee for Social Reform [*British*] ... UCSR
Unionist Liberal [*British*] (ROG) ... UL
Unionist Party [*Northern Ireland*] [*Political party*] ... U
Unionist Party of Northern Ireland [*Political party*] (PPW) ... UPNI
Unionist Progressive Party [*Egypt*] [*Political party*] ... UPP
Uniono por la Linguo Internaciona Ido [*International Language Union*] (EA) ... ULI
Unions [*Commonly used*] (OPSA) ... UNIONS
Unions [*Postal Service standard*] (OPSA) ... UNS
Unions ... UNS
Unions' Nation-Wide Coordinating Council for Oil and Allied Industries [*Defunct*] (EA) ... UNWCC
Uniontown, AL [*FM radio station call letters*] ... WVFG
Uniontown, PA [*AM radio station call letters*] ... WMBS
Uniontown, PA [*FM radio station call letters*] ... WPQR
Unionville [*Nevada*] [*Seismograph station code, US Geological Survey Closed*] (SEIS) ... UVN
Unipara [*Having borne one child*] [*Gynecology and obstetrics*] (DAVI) ... Para 1
Uniphase Corp. [*Associated Press*] (SAG) ... Uniphase
Uniphase Corp. [*NASDAQ symbol*] (SAG) ... UNPH
Unipolar Bipolar (IAA) ... UNIBI
Unipolar Field-Effect Transistor (IAA) ... UFET
Unipolar Field-Effect Transistor ... UNIFET
Unipolar Magnetic Regions ... UMR

Unipolar Straight Binary Code (IAA) ... USBCODE
Uniprocessor ... UP
Unipub, Inc., New York, NY [*Library symbol Library of Congress*] (LCLS) ... NNUni
Unique (VRA) ... uniq
Unique ... UNQ
Unique Data Item (MCD) ... UDI
Unique Data Item Description (MCD) ... UDID
Unique Equipment Register (NASA) ... UER
Unique Indentifier [*Computer science*] ... UI
Unique Injector Concepts Development (MCD) ... UNICODE
Unique Jargon ... UJ
Unique Mobility [*AMEX symbol*] (TTSB) ... UQM
Unique Mobility, Inc. [*Associated Press*] (SAG) ... UniqMbl
Unique Mobility, Inc. [*AMEX symbol*] (SAG) ... UQM
Unique Product Advantage [*Advertising*] ... UPA
Unique Project Number (SSD) ... UPN
Unique Radiolytic Product [*Food technology*] ... URP
Unique Record Number [*Computer science*] (ADA) ... URN
Unique Reference Number [*Customs*] (DS) ... URN
Unique Resources Ltd. [*Vancouver Stock Exchange symbol*] ... UNQ
Unique Selling Point ... USP
Unique Selling Proposition [*Advertising*] ... USP
Unique Selling Proposition [*Finance*] ... USP
Unique Sequential Access Method ... USAM
Unique Signal Switch ... USS
Unique Suppliers List ... USL
Unique Word (IAA) ... UW
Unique-to-Site Equipment Review (SAA) ... USER
Uniroyal Chemical [*NASDAQ symbol*] (TTSB) ... UCHM
Uniroyal Chemical Corp. [*NASDAQ symbol*] (SAG) ... UCHM
Uniroyal Chemical Corp. [*Associated Press*] (SAG) ... UniroyC
Uniroyal, Dunlop, and Firestone [*Facetious translation of South African political party, United Democratic Front, which suppsedly executed dissenters with burning tires*] ... UDF
Uniroyal, Inc., Chemical Division, Information Center Library, Naugatuck, CT [*Library symbol Library of Congress*] (LCLS) ... CtNaUSR
Uniroyal Ltd., Guelph, ON, Canada [*Library symbol Library of Congress*] (LCLS) ... CaOGDR
Uniroyal Research Laboratories, Guelph, Ontario [*Library symbol National Library of Canada*] (NLC) ... OGDR
Uniroyal Technology [*NASDAQ symbol*] (TTSB) ... UTCI
Uniroyal Technology Corp. [*Associated Press*] (SAG) ... UnrylT
Uniroyal Technology Corp. [*Associated Press*] (SAG) ... UnrylTc
Uniroyal Technology Corp. [*NASDAQ symbol*] (SAG) ... UTCI
Uniroyal Technology Wrrt [*NASDAQ symbol*] (TTSB) ... UTCIW
Unisave Energy Ltd. [*Vancouver Stock Exchange symbol*] ... UEN
Uniscope Display System (NITA) ... UDS
Unisex ... UNSX
Unisex Edition of the American College Testing Program Interest Inventory (EDAC) ... UNIACT
UNISIST International Centre for Bibliographic Descriptions [*UNESCO*] [*Information service or system*] (IID) ... UNIBID
Unison ... UNIS
Unison HealthCare [*NASDAQ symbol*] (TTSB) ... UNHC
Unison HealthCare Corp. [*NASDAQ symbol*] (SAG) ... UNHC
Unison HealthCare Corp. [*Associated Press*] (SAG) ... UnisonH
Unison Software [*NASDAQ symbol*] (TTSB) ... UNSN
Unison Software, Inc. [*Associated Press*] (SAG) ... Unison
Unison Software, Inc. [*NASDAQ symbol*] (SAG) ... UNSN
Unisource Worldwide, Inc. [*Associated Press*] (SAG) ... Unisrce
Unisource Worldwide, Inc. [*NYSE symbol*] (SAG) ... UWW
Unisys $3.75cm Cv A Pfd [*NYSE symbol*] (TTSB) ... UISPrA
Unisys Corp. [*NYSE symbol*] (SPSG) ... UIS
Unisys Corp. [*Associated Press*] (SAG) ... Unisy
Unisys Corp. [*Associated Press*] (SAG) ... Unisys
Unit ... U
Unit (AAG) ... UN
Unit (MCD) ... UT
Unit Address Register ... UAR
Unit Allowance List (SAA) ... UAL
Unit Approval System [*for approval of aircraft materials, parts, and appliances*] [*FAA*] ... UAS
Unit Area Loading (AAG) ... UAL
Unit Assembly Drawing ... UAD
Unit Assets [*Army*] ... UA
Unit Assets by State [*Army*] ... UAS
Unit Authorization File ... UAF
Unit Authorization List ... UAL
Unit Authorization List Item ... UALI
Unit Automatic Exchange ... UAX
Unit Backspace Character [*Computer science*] ... UBS
Unit Basic Load [*Army*] ... UBL
Unit Beat Policing ... UBP
Unit Bill of Material (MHDW) ... UBM
Unit Bond (SAA) ... UB
Unit Call [*Also known as CCS*] [*Telecommunications*] ... UC
Unit Capability Measurement System (AFM) ... UCMS
Unit Card Reader ... UCR
Unit Chairman ... UC
Unit Check (ECII) ... UCK
Unit Check ... UK
Unit Checkout Equipment ... UCE
Unit Chemical Defense Study (MCD) ... UCDS
Unit Clerk ... UC
Unit Combat Fire Trainer [*Army*] ... UCOFT
Unit Committed Munitions List ... UCML
Unit Concept Indexing System ... UNICIS
Unit Conduct of Fire Trainer [*Army*] ... U-COFT
Unit Construction Index ... UCI
Unit Construction Practice (IAA) ... UCP
Unit Construction Principle (IAA) ... UCP
Unit Control Block (MCD) ... UCB
Unit Control Error (IAA) ... UCE
Unit Control File [*Air Force*] ... UCF
Unit Control Module [*Computer science*] (ECII) ... UCM
Unit Control Word [*Computer science*] (BUR) ... UCW
Unit Cooler ... UC
Unit Corp. [*Associated Press*] (SAG) ... Unit
Unit Corp. [*Associated Press*] (SAG) ... UnitC
Unit Corp. [*NYSE symbol*] (SPSG) ... UNT
Unit Corp. [*NASDAQ symbol*] (NQ) ... UNTE
Unit Corp. Wrrt [*NASDAQ symbol*] (TTSB) ... UNTEW
Unit Correction Entry ... UCE
Unit Cost ... UC
Unit Cost Exception Report [*Army*] ... UCER
Unit Cost of Production (MHDW) ... UCOP
Unit Cost of Sales ... UCS
Unit Cost Report [*Military*] (RDA) ... UCR
Unit Count (AFIT) ... UC
Unit Data and Control Diagram (IAA) ... UDCD
Unit Data Presentation Protocol Data Unit [*Telecommunications*] (OSI) ... UDPPDU
Unit Data System [*Military*] ... UDS
Unit Demand History Summary [*Military*] (AABC) ... UDHS
Unit Deployment of Containers (MCD) ... UDC
Unit Deployment Report (CINC) ... PLOYREP
Unit Derated Generation [*Electronics*] (IEEE) ... UDG
Unit Derated Hours [*Electronics*] (IEEE) ... UNDH
Unit Derating [*Electronics*] (IEEE) ... UND
Unit Derating Factor [*Electronics*] (IEEE) ... UDF
Unit Designation ... UD
Unit Designation List (DOMA) ... UDL
Unit Detail Listings [*Air Force*] ... UDL
Unit Development Folder (MCD) ... UDF
Unit Diary ... UD
Unit Dining Facilities ... UDF
Unit Director ... UD
Unit Document Listing (MCD) ... UDL
Unit Dose [*Medicine*] ... UD
Unit Dose Package [*Pharmacy*] (DAVI) ... UD
Unit Emergency Supply Kit ... UESK
Unit Emplaning Officer [*Military British*] ... UEO
Unit Endurance Chamber (MCD) ... UEC
Unit Entry ... UE
Unit Equipment [*as authorized to an Air Force unit*] ... UE
Unit Equipment Aircraft ... UEAC
Unit Equipment Report [*Marine Corps*] (DOMA) ... UER
Unit Equipment Table [*Military*] ... UET
Unit Essential Equipment [*Military*] (NATG) ... UEE
Unit Essential Spares Kit [*Military*] (AFM) ... UESK
Unit Establishment ... UE
Unit Evolutionary Period ... UEP
Unit Exception (CMD) ... UE
Unit Exception (ECII) ... UEX
Unit Exhausted [*Military*] (GFGA) ... UE
Unit Families Officer [*Military British*] ... UFO
Unit Fault Isolation (MCD) ... UFI
Unit First Appearance (SAA) ... UA
Unit for Research on Addictive Drugs [*University of Aberdeen*] [*British*] (IRUK) ... URAD
Unit Forecast Authorization Equipment Data (AFM) ... UFAED
Unit Functional Diagram (IAA) ... UFD
Unit Funded Costs (MCD) ... UFC
Unit Gas Noncommissioned Officer [*Army World War II*] ... UGNCO
Unit Gas Offices [*Army World War II*] ... UGO
Unit Handling System ... UHS
Unit Hardware Cost (MCD) ... UHC
Unit Head ... UH
Unit Heater [*Technical drawings*] ... UH
Unit Horizontal Tail ... UHT
Unit Hydrograph ... UH
Unit Identification Code [*Army*] (AABC) ... UIC
Unit Identification Code Information Officer [*Military*] (AABC) ... UICIO
Unit Identification System ... UIS
Unit Identifier Applications (MCD) ... UIA
Unit Impulse Train ... UIT
Unit Initial Range (MCD) ... UIR
Unit Instruments [*NASDAQ symbol*] (TTSB) ... UNII
Unit Instruments, Inc. [*California*] [*NASDAQ symbol*] (SAG) ... UNII
Unit Instruments, Inc. (California) [*Associated Press*] (SAG) ... Unit Inst
Unit Investment Trusts [*Standard and Poor's Corp.*] [*Information service or system*] ... UIT
Unit Kind Code [*Military*] (AFIT) ... UKC
Unit Ledger Card [*Computer science*] ... ULC
Unit Level Circuit Switch (CAAL) ... ULCS
Unit Level Code (AFM) ... ULC
Unit Level Computer Logistics System [*Army*] ... ULCS
Unit Level Computers [*Army*] ... ULC
Unit Level Learning Center ... ULLC
Unit Level Logistics System [*Army*] ... ULLS

Unit Level Message Switch ... ULMS
Unit Level Switchboard (MCD) ... ULS
Unit Line Number (DOMA) ... ULN
Unit Linked ... U/L
Unit Load ... UL
Unit Load Demand [*Nuclear energy*] (NRCH) ... ULD
Unit Load Device [*Shipping containers*] ... ULD
Unit Local Loading (AAG) ... ULL
Unit Location Equipment (MCD) ... ULE
Unit Logic Device ... ULD
Unit Mail Clerk ... UMC
Unit Mail Room [*Air Force*] (AFM) ... UMR
Unit Maintenance Aircraft Recovery Kit (MCD) ... UMARK
Unit Maintenance Collection Point [*Army*] (INF) ... UMCP
Unit Maintenance Management System ... UMMS
Unit Maintenance Support Equipment [*Army*] ... UMSE
Unit Manning Document [*DoD*] ... UMD
Unit Manning Report [*Army*] (ADDR) ... UMR
Unit Manning System [*Army*] (RDA) ... UMS
Unit Materiel Fielding Point [*Army*] (RDA) ... UMFP
Unit Ministry Team [*Military*] (INF) ... UMT
Unit Mission Equipment (AAG) ... UME
Unit Mobility Center [*Military*] (AFIT) ... UMC
Unit Mobility Equipment ... UME
Unit Mobilization Augmentation [*Army*] (DOMA) ... UMA
Unit Mobilization Personnel Assignment Report [*Navy*] (DNAB) ... UMPAR
Unit Monthly Equipment (MSA) ... UME
Unit Movement Data [*Military*] ... UMD
Unit Movement Identifier [*Army*] (AABC) ... UMI
Unit Movement Officer [*Army*] (INF) ... UMO
Unit of Acceleration [*Military*] ... G
Unit of Account [*European Monetary Agreement*] (EY) ... U/A
Unit of Activity (IDOE) ... U_a
Unit of Choice ... UOC
Unit of Coastal Sedimentation [*NERC*] [*British*] ... UCS
Unit of Comparative Plant Ecology [*Natural Environment Research Council*] [*British*] (IRUK) ... UCPE
Unit of Error (MCD) ... UOE
Unit of Fire [*Military*] (MUGU) ... UF
Unit of Grading (MHDW) ... UOG
Unit of Gravitational Force (NASA) ... G
Unit of Insect Neurophysiology and Pharmacology [*University of Cambridge*] [*British*] (IRUK) ... UINP
Unit of Instruction ... UOI
Unit of Issue (KSC) ... UI
Unit of Measure (IAA) ... U
Unit of Measure (MCD) ... UM
Unit of Medical Time [*Each 4-hour period after 40-hour work week*] [*British*] ... UMT
Unit of Packed Cells ... UPC
Unit of Processing Capacity ... UPC
Unit of Production (MHDW) ... UOP
Unit of Trading ... UOT
Unit of Value (MHDW) ... UOV
Unit Operating Procedure (NRCH) ... UOP
Unit Operator (NRCH) ... UO
Unit Owners' Association of Queensland [*Australia*] ... UOAQ
Unit Pack ... UP
Unit Packaging ... UNIPAC
Unit Personnel and Tonnage Table [*Military*] ... UP & T
Unit Personnel and Tonnage Table [*Military*] (AABC) ... UPTT
Unit Personnel List [*Army*] ... UPL
Unit Personnel Management Roster ... UPMR
Unit Personnel Office [*or Officer*] [*Military*] ... UPO
Unit Personnel Records Group [*Air Force*] (AFM) ... UPRG
Unit Personnel Records Group [*Air Force*] (AFM) ... UPRGp
Unit Personnel Section [*Military*] ... UPS
Unit Power Density [*Lighting*] ... UPD
Unit Price ... UP
Unit Price Standards (MCD) ... UPS
Unit Processing Code (AFM) ... UPC
Unit Production Cost ... UPC
Unit Production Manager [*Filmmaking*] ... UPM
Unit Proficiency Exercise ... UPE
Unit Proficiency System (AAG) ... UPS
Unit Proficiency System Requirements (AAG) ... UPSR
Unit Property Record and Equipment Authorization List ... UPREAL
Unit Property Record and Equipment List ... UPREL
Unit Pulmonary Toxicity Dose [*Deep-sea diving*] ... UPTD
Unit Readiness Report [*Army*] (AABC) ... URR
Unit Readiness System ... URS
Unit Real (IAA) ... UR
Unit Record [*Computer science*] ... UR
Unit Record Card ... URC
Unit Record Control ... URC
Unit Record Processor ... URP
Unit Recruit Training [*Army*] (AABC) ... URT
Unit Reference Designation [*Army*] ... URD
Unit Reference Sheet [*Military*] (AABC) ... URS
Unit Register ... UR
Unit Released by Blood Bank (DAVI) ... RLSO
Unit Replacement System Analysis [*Military*] ... URSA
Unit Representative [*Military*] (INF) ... UREP
Unit Review Group [*Nuclear energy*] (NRCH) ... URG
Unit Secretary (MEDA) ... US
Unit Security Officer (AAG) ... USO
Unit Security Technician ... UST
Unit Self-Sufficiency System (MCD) ... US3
Unit Separator [*Control character*] [*Computer science*] ... US
Unit Services Assistant [*Administration*] (DAVI) ... USA
Unit Share Investment Trust ... USIT
Unit Simulated Combat Mission (AAG) ... USCM
Unit Site Representative [*Army*] ... USR
Unit Spares List ... USL
Unit Status and Identity Report [*DoD*] ... UNITREP
Unit Status Report [*Army*] ... USR
Unit Stream Power [*Hydrology*] ... USP
Unit Support Equipment ... USE
Unit Support Plan (MCD) ... USP
Unit Territory Plan ... UTP
Unit Test Cases (NASA) ... UTC
Unit Test Folder [*Military*] ... UTF
Unit Test Plan ... UTP
Unit Tester (NASA) ... UT
Unit Time Coding ... UTC
Unit to Which Ordered Will Operate in an Overseas Area a Contemplated ContinuousPeriod of One Year or More [*Military*] ... UNITOPOS
Unit Total Cost ... UTC
Unit Training (NVT) ... UNITNG
Unit Training Assembly [*Military*] (AABC) ... UTA
Unit Training Center [*Military*] ... UTC
Unit Training Effectiveness Analysis [*Army*] ... UTEA
Unit Training Equipment Site [*Military*] (AABC) ... UTES
Unit Training Standard ... UTS
Unit Transmission Loss ... UTL
Unit Transmittal Letter [*Army*] ... UTL
Unit Trouble Shooting ... UTS
Unit Trust (ILCA) ... UT
Unit Trust Association [*British*] ... UTA
Unit Trust Portfolio Management Service [*Investment term British*] ... UTPMS
Unit Type Code (AFM) ... UTC
Unit under Test ... UUT
Unit Weight (MSA) ... UWT
Unit Years [*Electronics*] (IEEE) ... UY
Unita County Library, Evanston, WY [*Library symbol*] [*Library of Congress*] (LCLS) ... WyEV
Unitarian ... UNIT
Unitarian and Universalist Genealogical Society [*Defunct*] (EA) ... UUGS
Unitarian Church [*Australia*] ... UC
Unitarian Church of New South Wales [*Australia*] ... UCNSW
Unitarian Fellowship for Social Justice ... UFSJ
Unitarian Historical Society [*Later, UUHS*] (EA) ... UHS
Unitarian Laymen's League ... ULL
Unitarian Service Committee [*Later, UUSC*] [*Post-World War II*] ... USC
Unitarian Service Committee of Canada, Ottawa, Ontario [*Library symbol National Library of Canada*] (BIB) ... OOUSC
Unitarian Universalist Association Black Concerns Working Group (EA) ... UUABCWG
Unitarian Universalist Association of Congregations-Washington Office (EA) ... UUA/WO
Unitarian Universalist Association of Congregations-Washington Office for SocialJustice (EA) ... UUA/WOSJ
Unitarian Universalist Association-Washington Office for Social Concern [*Later,UUA/WOSJ*] (EA) ... UUA/WOSC
Unitarian Universalist Black Concerns Working Group (EA) ... UUBCWG
Unitarian Universalist Christian Fellowship (EA) ... UUCF
Unitarian Universalist Fellowship for Social Justice (EA) ... UUFSJ
Unitarian Universalist Historical Society (EA) ... UUHS
Unitarian Universalist Lesbian Gay Caucus (EA) ... UULGC
Unitarian Universalist Ministers Association (EA) ... UUMA
Unitarian Universalist Ministers' Partners Society (EA) ... UUMPS
Unitarian Universalist Musicians' Network (EA) ... UUMN
Unitarian Universalist Service Committee (EA) ... UUSC
Unitarian Universalist Society for Alcohol and Drug Education ... UUA
Unitarian Universalist Society for Alcohol Education [*Later, UUA*] (EA) ... UUSAE
Unitarian Universalist Women's Federation (EA) ... UUWF
Unitarian Universalists for Black and White Action (EA) ... BAWA
Unitary Development Plan (EERA) ... UDP
Unitary Irreducible Representation ... UIR
Unitary Launch Concept [*or Control*] (AAG) ... ULC
Unitary Payroll Benefit Accounting (MCD) ... UP/BA
Unitary Plan Wind Tunnel (KSC) ... UPWT
Unitary Pole Approximation ... UPA
Unitary Pole Expansion ... UPE
Unitary Symmetry (MCD) ... US
Unitas Malacologica [*An association Netherlands*] (EAIO) ... UM
Unitatis Redintegratio [*Decree on Ecumenism*] [*Vatican II document*] ... UR
Unit-Based Scheme (AIE) ... UBS
Unit-Count System ... UCS
Unite, Action, Liberation [*Guadeloupe*] [*Political party*] (EY) ... UAL
Unite Arithmetique et Logique [*Arithmetic and Logic Unit - ALU*] [*French*] ... UAL
Unite Australia Party [*Political party*] ... UAP
Unite Australia Party [*Australia Political party*] ... UNI
Unite Centrale de Traitement [*Central Processing Unit - CPU*] [*French*] ... UCT
Unite de Recherche et de Service en Technologie Minerale de l'Abitibi-Temiscamingue [*University of Quebec at Abitibi-Temiscamingue*] [*Canada Research center*] (RCD) ... URSTM
Unite d'Enseignement et de Recherche [*Units of Teaching and Research*] [*University of Paris*] ... UER
Unite Electromagnetique [*Electromagnetic Unit*] ... UEM

Unite et Progres du Burundi [*Unity and Progress of Burundi*] ... UNIPRO
Unite Guyanaise [*Guyanese Unity*] [*Political party*] (PPW) ... UG
Unitech (IAA) ... UT
Unitech Industries, Inc. [*Associated Press*] (SAG) ... Unitech
Unitech Industries, Inc. [*NASDAQ symbol*] (SAG) ... UTII
United ... U
United (GAVI) ... UA
United ... UN
United ... UNTD
United ... UTD
United 510 Owners (EA) ... UFO
United Abalone Divers' Association [*Australia*] ... UADA
United Action Armed Forces [*A publication*] ... UAAF
United Action for Animals (EA) ... UAA
United Activists for Animal Rights (EA) ... UAAR
United Africa Airline (Liberia), Inc. [*ICAO designator*] (FAAC) ... UFR
United African Airline [*Libya*] [*ICAO designator*] (ICDA) ... UQ
United African Appeal (EA) ... UAA
United African Co. ... UAC
United African National Congress ... UANC
United African National Council [*Zimbabwe*] [*Political party*] (PPW) ... UANC
United African Nationalist Movement (EA) ... UANM
United Against Cruelty to Animals [*British*] (DI) ... UACTA
United Air [*ICAO designator*] (AD) ... UE
United Air [*South Africa ICAO designator*] (FAAC) ... UTD
United Air Charters [*Zimbabwe*] [*ICAO designator*] (FAAC) ... UAC
United Air Lines, Inc. [*ICAO designator*] ... UA
United Air Lines, Inc. [*ICAO designator*] (FAAC) ... UAL
United Air Service [*Nigeria*] [*ICAO designator*] (FAAC) ... UHP
United Air Specialists [*NASDAQ symbol*] (TTSB) ... UASI
United Air Specialists, Inc. [*Associated Press*] (SAG) ... UAirSp
United Air Specialists, Inc. [*NASDAQ symbol*] (SAG) ... UASI
United Aircraft Corporate Systems Center (KSC) ... UACSC
United Aircraft Corp. [*Later, United Technologies Corp.*] ... UAC
United Aircraft Corp., East Hartford, CT [*Library symbol Library of Congress*] (LCLS) ... CtEhUA
United Aircraft Corp. Research Laboratory (KSC) ... UACRL
United Aircraft Information Management System ... UAIMS
United Aircraft of Canada Ltd. ... UACL
United Aircraft Research Laboratories ... UARL
United Allied Workers International Union (EA) ... UAWIU
United Amateur Press (EA) ... UAP
United Amateur Press Association [*Later, UAP*] (EA) ... UAPA
United Amer Healthcare [*NYSE symbol*] (TTSB) ... UAH
United American and Australasian Film Productions ... UAA
United American and Captive Nations Patriotic Movement (EA) ... UACNPM
United American Contractors Association (EA) ... UACA
United American Croats ... UAC
United American Healthcare Corp. [*NYSE symbol*] (SPSG) ... UAH
United American Healthcare Corp. [*Associated Press*] (SAG) ... UtdAHlt
United American Mechanics (EA) ... UAM
United American Progress Association (EA) ... UAPA
United American Ukrainian Organizations Committee (EA) ... UAUOC
United Ancient Order of Druids [*Freemasonry*] (ROG) ... UAOD
United Andean Indian Mission [*Superseded by Ecuador Concerns Committee*] ... UAIM
United Animal Nations (EAIO) ... UAN
United Arab Airlines ... UAA
United Arab Emirates [*Aircraft nationality and registration mark*] (FAAC) ... A6
United Arab Emirates [*ANSI two-letter standard code*] (CNC) ... AE
United Arab Emirates [*ANSI three-letter standard code*] (CNC) ... ARE
United Arab Emirates [*ICAO designator*] (FAAC) ... UAE
United Arab Emirates Air Force [*ICAO designator*] (FAAC) ... UAF
United Arab Muslim Association [*Australia*] ... UAMA
United Arab Republic [*Egypt*] [*MARC geographic area code Library of Congress*] (LCCP) ... f-ua--
United Arab Republic [*Egypt*] [*MARC country of publication code Library of Congress*] (LCCP) ... ua
United Arab Republic [*Egypt and Syria*] [*Obsolete*] ... UAR
United Arab Republic Broadcasting Corp. (IAA) ... UARBC
United Arab States ... UAS
United Artists Communications, Inc. ... UA
United Artists Theatre Circuit, Inc. ... UATC
United Asset Management Corp. [*NYSE symbol*] (SPSG) ... UAM
United Asset Mgmt [*NYSE symbol*] (TTSB) ... UAM
United Association for the Protection of Trade [*British*] ... UAPT
United Association of Christian Counselors International (EA) ... UACCI
United Association of Coremakers [*A union*] [*British*] ... UAC
United Association of Journeymen and Apprentices of the Plumbing and Pipe Fitting Industry of the United States and Canada ... PPF
United Association of Journeymen and Apprentices of the Plumbing and Pipe Fitting Industry of the United States and Canada (OICC) ... UA
United Association of Journeymen and Apprentices of the Plumbing and Pipe Fitting Industry of the U.S. and Canada (BARN) ... UAJAPPFI
United Association of Manufacturers' Representatives (EA) ... UAMR
United Australia Party [*Political party*] ... UAP
United Australian Television ... UATV
United Auto Group [*NYSE symbol*] (SAG) ... UAG
United Auto Group [*Associated Press*] (SAG) ... UtdAuto
United Auto Workers Community Action Program (EA) ... UAW-CAP
United Auto Workers, Family Auxiliary (EA) ... UAWFA
United Aviation Ltd. [*New Zealand*] [*ICAO designator*] (FAAC) ... UAV
United Aviation Services SA [*Spain ICAO designator*] (FAAC) ... SAU
United Bahamian Party [*Political party*] (PPW) ... UBP
United Baltic Appeal (EA) ... UBA
United Bancorp Ohio [*NASDAQ symbol*] (SAG) ... UBCP
United Bancorp Ohio [*Associated Press*] (SAG) ... UnBnOH
United Bank for Africa Ltd. ... UBA
United Bankshares [*NASDAQ symbol*] (TTSB) ... UBSI
United Bankshares, Inc. [*NASDAQ symbol*] (NQ) ... UBSI
United Bankshares, Inc. [*Associated Press*] (SAG) ... UBWV
United Bargemen and Watermen's Protective Society [*A union*] [*British*] ... UBWPS
United Beef Breeders' Association of Western Australia ... UBBAWA
United Bellows Tankage Module ... UBTM
United Benefice ... UB
United Bermuda Party [*Political party*] (PPW) ... UBP
United Better Dress Manufacturers Association (EA) ... UBDMA
United Beverages [*Vancouver Stock Exchange symbol*] ... UBL
United Bible Societies [*Stuttgart, Federal Republic of Germany*] (EA) ... UBS
United Bible Societies' Greek New Testament [*A publication*] (BJA) ... UGT
United Biscuits [*Commercial firm*] [*British*] ... UB
United Bison Resources [*Vancouver Stock Exchange symbol*] ... UBR
United Black Christians (EA) ... UBC
United Black Church Appeal (EA) ... UBCA
United Black Fund of America (EA) ... UBFA
United Board Chaplain [*British military*] (DMA) ... Un Bd Ch
United Board Chaplain [*British military*] ... UnBCh
United Board for Christian Higher Education in Asia (EA) ... UBCHEA
United Bowhunters of Connecticut ... UBC
United Boys' Brigades of America [*Later, BGBA*] (EA) ... UBBA
United Brands Co. (MHDW) ... UB
United Brethren in Christ ... UB
United Breweries of America (EA) ... UBA
United Brick and Clay Workers of America [*Later, ABCWIU*] (EA) ... UBCW
United Broadcasting System [*Network in TV series "America 2-Night"*] ... UBS
United Brotherhood [*Also written VC for secrecy*] [*Fenianism*] (ROG) ... UB
United Brotherhood of Carpenters and Joiners of America ... CJA
United Brotherhood of Carpenters and Joiners of America (EA) ... UBC
United Brotherhood of Carpenters and Joiners of America ... UBCJ
United Building Labourers' Union [*British*] ... UBLU
United Bus Owners of America (EA) ... UBOA
United Business Communications, Inc. [*Atlanta, GA*] [*Telecommunications*] (TSSD) ... UBC
United Business Education Association [*Later, NBEA*] ... UBEA
United Business Network [*United Business Communications, Inc.*] [*Atlanta, GA*] [*Telecommunications*] [*Defunct*] (TSSD) ... UBN
United Business Schools Association [*Later, AICS*] (EA) ... UBSA
United Cabinet and Chairmakers' Society [*A union*] [*British*] ... UCCS
United California Bank [*Los Angeles*] (IIA) ... UCB
United California Bank, Los Angeles, CA [*Library symbol Library of Congress*] (LCLS) ... CLUnB
United Cambridge Mines [*Vancouver Stock Exchange symbol*] ... UCB
United Campus Christian Fellowship [*Defunct*] ... UCCF
United Campuses to Prevent Nuclear War (EA) ... UCAM
United Canada Insurance Co. ... UC
United Canadian Shares Ltd. [*Toronto Stock Exchange symbol*] ... UCD
United Cancer Council (EA) ... UCC
United Canso Oil & Gas Ltd. [*Toronto Stock Exchange symbol*] ... UTC
United Capital Corp. [*AMEX symbol*] (SAG) ... AFP
United Capital Corp. [*Associated Press*] (SAG) ... UnCap
United Capital Funding Partnership LP [*Associated Press*] (SAG) ... UCapF
United Capital Funding Partnership LP [*NYSE symbol*] (SAG) ... UIL
United Caribbean Youth ... UCY
United Carolina Bancsh [*NASDAQ symbol*] (TTSB) ... UCAR
United Carolina Bancshares Corp. [*NASDAQ symbol*] (NQ) ... UCAR
United Carolina Bancshares Corp. [*Associated Press*] (SAG) ... UCarBk
United Carriers Systems, Inc. [*ICAO designator*] (FAAC) ... UCS
United Carters' and Motormen's Association of England [*A union*] ... UCMAE
United Carters' and Storemen's Union [*British*] ... UCSU
United Carters' Association [*A union*] [*British*] ... UCA
United Carters' Association of England [*A union*] ... UCAE
United Cat Federation (EA) ... UCF
United Cement, Lime, and Gypsum Workers International Union ... CLGW
United Cement, Lime, Gypsum, and Allied Workers International Union [*Formerly, CLGW*] (EA) ... UCLG
United Cerebral Palsy (DAVI) ... UCP
United Cerebral Palsy Associations (EA) ... UCPA
United Cerebral Palsy Research and Educational Foundation (EA) ... UCPREF
United Chain Makers' and Strikers' Union [*British*] ... UCMSU
United Chairmakers' Trade Society [*A union*] [*British*] ... UCTS
United Charity Institutions of Jerusalem (EA) ... UCI
United Chemists' Association Ltd. [*British*] (BI) ... UCA
United Chian Societies of America [*Later, CSA*] (EA) ... UCSA
United Christian Fellowship Ministry [*Australia*] ... UCFM
United Christian Missionary Society (EA) ... UCMS
United Christian Party [*Australia Political party*] ... UC
United Christian Party [*Australia Political party*] (ADA) ... UCP
United Christian Youth Movement [*Defunct*] (EA) ... UCYM
United Church Board for World Ministries (EA) ... UCBWM
United Church, British Columbia Conference, Archives, Vancouver, BC, Canada [*Library symbol Library of Congress*] (LCLS) ... CaBVaUBCA
United Church Coalition for Lesbian/Gay Concerns (EA) ... UCCL/GC
United Church of Canada Archives, Toronto, ON, Canada [*Library symbol Library of Congress*] (LCLS) ... CaOTCC
United Church of Canada Archives, Toronto, Ontario [*Library symbol National Library of Canada*] (NLC) ... OTCC
United Church of Christ ... UCC
United Church of Christ Commission for Racial Justice (EA) ... UCCCRJ

United Church of Christ Coordinating Center for Women in Church and Society (EA) .... CCW
United Church of Christ Coordinating Center for Women in Church and Society (EA) .... UCCCCWCS
United Church of Christ Ministers for Racial and Social Justice (EA) .... MRSJ
United Church Peace Fellowship [*Defunct*] (EA) .... UCPF
United Church Training School .... UCTS
United Church Women of the National Council of Churches (EA) .... UCW
United Cities Gas [*NASDAQ symbol*] (TTSB) .... UCIT
United Cities Gas Co. [*NASDAQ symbol*] (NQ) .... UCIT
United Cities Gas Co. [*Associated Press*] (SAG) .... UCitGs
United Citizens Coastal Protection League (EA) .... UCCPL
United City Bank [*Indonesia*] (EY) .... UNIBANK
United Civil Rights Committee .... UCRC
United Collision [*Vancouver Stock Exchange symbol*] .... UCA
United Commercial Bank [*India*] (EY) .... UCO
United Commercial Bank Ltd. [*Bangladesh*] .... UCB
United Commercial Travellers Association of Great Britain and Ireland, Inc. (BI) .... UCTA
United Commercial Travellers' Guild of Australia .... UCTGA
United Communist Party of Nepal [*Political party*] (EY) .... UCPN
United Community Funds and Councils of America [*Later, UWA*] (EA) .... UCFC
United Community Services .... UCS
United Companies Financial [*NYSE symbol*] (SAG) .... UC
United Companies Financial [*Associated Press*] (SAG) .... UCosF
United Companies Financial [*Associated Press*] (SAG) .... UtdCosF
United Companies Financial Corp. [*NASDAQ symbol*] (SAG) .... UCFC
United Computer Corporation (NITA) .... UCC
United Computing Systems, Inc. .... UCS
United Concerned Students (EA) .... UCS
United Confederate Veterans .... UCV
United Congressional Appeal (EA) .... UCA
United Construction Workers Association (OICC) .... UCWA
United Cooperative Farmers, Inc. .... UCF
United Coppersmiths Trade Protection Association [*A union*] [*British*] .... UCTPA
United Corporations Ltd. [*Toronto Stock Exchange symbol*] .... UNC
United Cos. Financial [*NASDAQ symbol*] (TTSB) .... UCFC
United Cos. Fin'l 6.75%'PRIDES' [*NASDAQ symbol*] (TTSB) .... UCFCP
United Council of Associations of Civil Employees of Pakistan .... UCACEP
United Council of Filipino Associations in Canada .... UCFAC
United Counties Trust Co. [*Associated Press*] (SAG) .... UCount
United Counties Trust Co. [*NASDAQ symbol*] (SAG) .... UCTC
United Country Party [*Australia Political party*] .... UCP
United Currency Options Market [*Philadelphia Stock Exchange*] (ECON) .... UCOM
United Dairy Industry Association (EA) .... UDIA
United Dance Merchants of America (EA) .... UDMA
United Data Collection System (MCD) .... UDCS
United Data Processing (BUR) .... UDP
United Dated Parts List [*Configuration listing*] (MCD) .... UDPL
United Daughters of the Confederacy (EA) .... UDC
United Defense Force [*Established by the Brussels Treaty*] (NATG) .... UNIFORCE
United Defense Limited Partnership (RDA) .... UDLP
United Democratic Alliance [*European political movement*] (ECON) .... UDA
United Democratic Front [*South Africa*] [*Political party*] (PPW) .... UDF
United Democratic Front [*India*] [*Political party*] (PPW) .... UDF
United Democratic Labour Party [*Trinidad and Tobago*] [*Political party*] (PPW) .... UDLP
United Democratic Party [*Belize*] [*Political party*] (PD) .... UDP
United Democratic Party [*Basotho*] [*Political party*] (PPW) .... UDP
United Democratic Party of Kurdistan [*Political party*] (BJA) .... UDPK
United Dental Care [*NASDAQ symbol*] (TTSB) .... UDCI
United Dental Care, Inc. [*NASDAQ symbol*] (SAG) .... UDCI
United Dental Care, Inc. [*Associated Press*] (SAG) .... UnDentC
United Detector Technology .... UDT
United Distillers (Australia) Ltd. [*Commercial firm*] .... UDAL
United Distillers (Guiness) [*Commercial firm*] .... UD(G)
United District Hospital, Staples, MN [*Library symbol*] [*Library of Congress*] (LCLS) .... MnStH
United Dominica Labour Party [*Political party*] (PPW) .... UDLP
United Dominion Indus [*NYSE symbol*] (TTSB) .... UDI
United Dominion Industries Ltd. [*NYSE symbol*] (SPSG) .... UDI
United Dominion Industries Ltd. [*Associated Press*] (SAG) .... UDomIn
United Dominion Realty Trust [*Associated Press*] (SAG) .... UDom
United Dominion Realty Trust, Inc. [*Associated Press*] (SAG) .... UDomR
United Dominion Realty Trust, Inc. [*NYSE symbol*] (SPSG) .... UDR
United Dominion Rlty Tr [*NYSE symbol*] (TTSB) .... UDR
United Drag Racers Association (EA) .... UDRA
United Duroc Swine Registry (EA) .... UDSR
United Earth Sciences Exploration Group [*British*] .... UESEG
United Earth Sciences Research Group [*British*] (NUCP) .... UESRG
United East India Co. .... UEIC
United Egg Association (EA) .... UEA
United Egg Producers (EA) .... UEP
United Electrical, Radio, and Machine Workers of America (EA) .... UE
United Electrical, Radio, and Machine Workers of America .... UERMWA
United Electrical, Radio, and Machine Workers of America [*Also, UERMWA*] (NTCM) .... UEW
United Electrical, Radio, and Machine Workers of Canada [*See also OUE*] .... UE
United Electrical Workers .... UEW
United Electro Dynamics (IAA) .... UED
United Electrodynamics (AAG) .... UE
United Elvis Presley Society (EAIO) .... UEPS
United Empire [*Canada*] .... UE
United Empire Loyalist .... UEL
United Engineering Center .... UEC
United Engineering Information System .... UEIS
United Engineering Societies (IAA) .... UES
United Engineering Steels [*Commercial firm British*] .... UES
United Engineering Trustees (EA) .... UET
United Engineers (Malaysia) Berhad (ECON) .... UEM
United Enginemen's Friendly Society [*A union*] [*British*] .... UEFS
United Epilepsy Association [*Later, EFA*] (EA) .... UEA
United European American Club .... UEAC
United European Power Grid (IAA) .... UEPG
United Families of America (EA) .... UFA
United Farm Workers of America (EA) .... UFW
United Farm Workers of America .... UFWA
United Farm Workers Organizing Committee [*Later, UFW*] .... UFWOC
United Farm Workers Union .... UFWU
United Farmers and Stockowners (EERA) .... UFS
United Farmers and Stockowners of South Australia .... UFSSA
United Fathers of America (EA) .... UFA
United Features Syndicate [*Commercial firm*] .... UFS
United Fed Svgs Bk Rocky Mt NC [*NASDAQ symbol*] (TTSB) .... UFRM
United Federal Party [*Northern Rhodesia*] .... UFP
United Federal Savings & Loan of Rocky Mount [*NASDAQ symbol*] (NQ) .... UFRM
United Federal Savings Bank [*Associated Press*] (SAG) .... UFedS
United Federation of Canadian Star Trekkers .... UFST
United Federation of College Teachers [*AFL-CIO*] .... UFCT
United Federation of Doll Clubs (EA) .... UFDC
United Federation of Planets (EA) .... UFP
United Federation of Postal Clerks [*Formerly, NFPOC*] [*Later, APWU*] (EA) .... UFPC
United Federation of Russian Workers' Organizations of USA and Canada (EA) .... UFRWO
United Federation of Teachers [*New York*] .... UFT
United Feeder Service [*ICAO designator*] (FAAC) .... UFS
United Fellowship for Christian Service [*Later, BMMFI*] (EA) .... UFCS
United Film Carriers Association [*Defunct*] (EA) .... UFCA
United Financial [*NASDAQ symbol*] (TTSB) .... UBMT
United Financial Management Ltd. [*Toronto Stock Exchange symbol*] .... UFM
United Fire & Casualty [*NASDAQ symbol*] (TTSB) .... UFCS
United Fire & Casualty Co. of Iowa [*NASDAQ symbol*] (NQ) .... UFCS
United Fire & Casualty Co. of Iowa [*Associated Press*] (SAG) .... UFireC
United Fire Equipment Service Association (EA) .... UFESA
United Firefighters Union of Australia .... UFUA
United Firefighters Union of South Australia .... UFUSA
United Firefighters Union of Western Australia .... UFUWA
United Fishermen and Allied Workers' Union [*Canada*] .... UFAWU
United Fishermen Union [*British*] .... UFU
United Flight Classification .... UFC
United Flowers-by-Wire Canada .... UFC
United Fly Tyers (EA) .... UFT
United Flying Octogenarians (EA) .... UFOs
United Focus [*Later, Omni Learning Institute*] (EA) .... UF
United Food and Commercial Workers International Union (EA) .... UFCW
United Food and Commercial Workers International Union (EA) .... UFCWIU
United Food Animal Association [*Defunct*] (EA) .... UFAA
United Foods Cl'A' [*AMEX symbol*] (TTSB) .... UFD.A
United Foods Cv Cl'B' [*AMEX symbol*] (TTSB) .... UFD.B
United Foods, Inc. [*AMEX symbol*] (SPSG) .... UFD
United Foods, Inc. [*Associated Press*] (SAG) .... UFood
United Force [*Guyana*] (PD) .... UF
United Foundation .... UF
United Four-Wheel Drive Associations (EA) .... UFWDA
United Free Church [*Scotland*] .... UFC
United Free Church of Scotland (DI) .... UFCS
United Freedom Front [*Defunct*] (EA) .... UFF
United Fresh Fruit and Vegetable Association (EA) .... UFFVA
United Friendly Boilermakers' Society [*A union*] [*British*] .... UFBS
United Front [*Sri Lanka*] [*Political party*] (FEA) .... UF
United Front of Political Movements [*Sierra Leone*] [*Political party*] (EY) .... UNIFOM
United Fruit Co. [*Railroad*] (MHDW) .... UFC
United Fruit Co., Boston, MA [*Library symbol Library of Congress*] (LCLS) .... MBUF
United Fund for Jewish Culture [*Defunct*] (EA) .... UFJC
United Fur Manufacturers Association (EA) .... UFMA
United Furnishing Trades Society [*A union*] [*British*] .... UFTS
United Furniture Workers of America (EA) .... UFW
United Furniture Workers of America .... UFWA
United Galaxy Sanitation Patrol [*In TV series "Quark"*] .... UGSP
United Galician Jews of America [*Defunct*] (EA) .... UGJA
United Garment Workers of America (EA) .... UGW
United Gas, Coke, and Chemical Workers of America [*Later, OCAW*] .... GCCW
United Gas Corp., Shreveport, LA [*Library symbol Library of Congress*] (LCLS) .... LShUG
United Gas Improvement Corp., Philadelphia, PA [*Library symbol Library of Congress Obsolete*] (LCLS) .... PPUG
United Gas Laboratories Internally Programmed Automatic Computer .... UGLIAC
United General Hospital, Medical Staff Library, Sedro Woolley, WA [*Library symbol*] [*Library of Congress*] (LCLS) .... WaSwH
United Givers Fund .... UGF
United Glass and Ceramic Workers of North America .... UGCW
United Global Petroleum, Inc. [*Vancouver Stock Exchange symbol*] .... UGP
United Gold Corp. [*Vancouver Stock Exchange symbol*] .... UGC
United Golfers' Association (EA) .... UGA
United Grain Growers, Winnipeg, Manitoba [*Library symbol National Library of Canada*] (NLC) .... MWUGG

United Grain Growers, Winnipeg, MB, Canada [*Library symbol Library of Congress*] (LCLS) .... CaMWUGG
United Grand Lodge of England [*Masonry*] .... UGLE
United Grand Lodge [*Masons*] **of New South Wales** [*Australia*] .... UGLNSW
United Graziers' Association of Queensland [*Australia*] .... UGAQ
United Graziers' Association of Queensland Union of Employees [*Australia*] .... UGAQUE
United Greek Orthodox Charities [*Defunct*] (EA) .... UGOC
United Greenwood [*Vancouver Stock Exchange symbol*] .... UGD
United Grounders' Society [*A union*] [*British*] .... UGS
United Guardian, Inc. [*AMEX symbol*] (SAG) .... UG
United Gulf Bank [*Middle East*] .... UGB
United Gunn Resources [*Vancouver Stock Exchange symbol*] .... UGR
United Halsingian Society of America [*Defunct*] (EA) .... UHSA
United Hatters, Cap, and Millinery Workers International Union (EA) .... HCMW
United Hatters, Cap, and Millinery Workers International Union .... UHCMWIU
United Health Foundations [*Defunct*] .... UHF
United Health Services, Wilson Hospital, Johnson City, NY [*Library symbol Library of Congress*] (LCLS) .... NJosnU
United Healthcare [*NYSE symbol*] (TTSB) .... UNH
United Healthcare Corp. [*Associated Press*] (SAG) .... UHlthCr
United Healthcare Corp. [*Minnetonka, MN*] [*NYSE symbol*] (NQ) .... UNH
United Healthcare Corp. (MHDW) .... UNIH
United Hearne Resources Ltd. [*Vancouver Stock Exchange symbol*] .... UHR
United Hebrew Trades of the State of New York (EA) .... UHT
United Hellenic American Congress (EA) .... UHAC
United Hellenic Voters of America (EA) .... UHVA
United Heritage Corp. [*NASDAQ symbol*] (NQ) .... UHCP
United Heritage Corp. [*Associated Press*] (SAG) .... UHrtg
United HIAS Service (EA) .... UHS
United Home Life Insurance Co. [*Greenwood, IN*] [*NASDAQ symbol*] (NQ) .... UHLI
United Home Life Insurance Co. [*Associated Press*] (SAG) .... UtdHmL
United Homeowners' Association (EA) .... UHA
United Homes, Inc. [*Vancouver Stock Exchange symbol*] .... UNH
United Horological Association of America [*Later, AWI*] .... UHAA
United Hospital Fund of New York, New York, NY [*Library symbol Library of Congress*] (LCLS) .... NNUH
United Hospital, Port Chester, NY [*Library symbol Library of Congress*] (LCLS) .... NPtcU
United Hospitals, Inc., St. Paul, MN [*Library symbol Library of Congress*] (LCLS) .... MnSUH
United Humanitarians (EA) .... UH
United Hungarian Jews of America (EA) .... UHJA
United Hunts Racing Association [*Later, NSHA*] .... UHRA
United Illuminating [*NYSE symbol*] (TTSB) .... UIL
United Illuminating Co. [*NYSE symbol*] (SPSG) .... UIL
United Illuminating Co. [*Associated Press*] (SAG) .... UIllum
United in Group Harmony Association (EA) .... UGHA
United Inches .... UI
United Independent Broadcasters (NTCM) .... UIB
United Indian Development Association (EA) .... UIDA
United Indian Missions, International (EA) .... UIMI
United Indian Planners Association [*Defunct*] (EA) .... UIPA
United Indian War Veterans, USA (EA) .... UIWV
United Indians of All Tribes Foundation (EA) .... UIATF
United Industrial [*NYSE symbol*] (TTSB) .... UIC
United Industrial Corp. [*NYSE symbol*] (SPSG) .... UIC
United Industrial Corp. [*Associated Press*] (SAG) .... UnitInd
United Inernational Holding, Inc. [*Associated Press*] (SAG) .... UtdIntH
United Infants' and Children's Wear Association (EA) .... UICWA
United Infertility Organization (EA) .... UIO
United Information Services, Inc. (IID) .... UIS
United Information Systems [*Burroughs Corp. and Sperry UNIVAC*] [*Formed by a merger of*] .... UNISYS
United Information Systems [*Marine science*] (OSRA) .... UNISYS
United Insulator Co. (IAA) .... UIC
United Insurance [*NASDAQ symbol*] (TTSB) .... UICI
United Insurance Companies, Inc. [*NASDAQ symbol*] (NQ) .... UICI
United Insurance Co., Inc. [*Associated Press*] (SAG) .... UtdIns
United International Antisubmarine Warfare .... UNITAS
United International Bureau for the Protection of Intellectual Property [*Superseded by WIPO*] .... UIBPIP
United International Club, Inc. .... UNIC
United International Holdings, Inc. [*NASDAQ symbol*] (SAG) .... UIHI
United International Research, Inc. .... UIR
United Intl Hldgs'A' [*NASDAQ symbol*] (TTSB) .... UIHIA
United Inventors and Scientists (IAA) .... UIS
United Inventors and Scientists of America (EA) .... UISA
United Ireland Party .... UIP
United Irish Counties Association of New York (EA) .... UICANY
United Iron Workers .... UIW
United Israel Appeal [*Australia*] .... UIA
United Israel World Union (EA) .... UIWU
United Italian American Labor Council (EA) .... UIALC
United Italian American League (EA) .... UIAL
United Jewish Appeal (EA) .... UJA
United Jewish Appeal - Federation of Jewish Philanthropies of New York (EA) .... UJAFJP
United Jewish Teachers Seminary [*Montreal*] [*A publication*] (BJA) .... UJTS
United Jewish Welfare Fund (IIA) .... UJWF
United Karate Federation (EA) .... UKF
United Kennel Club (EA) .... UKC
United Keno Hill Mines Ltd. [*Toronto Stock Exchange symbol*] .... UKH
United Kindgom Sugar Industry Association (DBA) .... UKSIA
United Kingdom [*MARC geographic area code Library of Congress*] (LCCP) .... e-uk--
United Kingdom [*ANSI two-letter standard code*] (CNC) .... GB
United Kingdom [*ANSI three-letter standard code*] (CNC) .... GBR
United Kingdom [*IYRU nationality code*] (IYR) .... K
United Kingdom [*MARC country of publication code Library of Congress*] (LCCP) .... uk
United Kingdom .... UK
United Kingdom Agricultural Production Committee .... UKAPC
United Kingdom Agricultural Research Council .... UKARC
United Kingdom Agricultural Supply Trade Association (DS) .... UKASTA
United Kingdom Air Defense Ground Environment .... UKADGE
United Kingdom Air Forces Command, Control, and Information System .... UKAIRCCIS
United Kingdom Airlines [*ICAO designator*] (AD) .... Air UK
United Kingdom Airways and Communication Region (IAA) .... UKAACREG
United Kingdom Alliance .... UKA
United Kingdom Alliance of Professional Teachers of Dancing (DBA) .... UKAPTD
United Kingdom Amalgamated Society of Shipwrights [*A union*] .... UKASS
United Kingdom and Havre, Antwerp, and Dunkirk [*Shipping*] (DS) .... UKHAD
United Kingdom and Havre-Hamburg [*Shipping*] (DS) .... UKHH
United Kingdom and Ireland Particleboard Association (EAIO) .... UKIPA
United Kingdom and Scandinavia (NATG) .... UNISCAN
United Kingdom Asian Women's Conference [*British*] .... UKAWG
United Kingdom Association for European Law [*British*] .... UKAEL
United Kingdom Association of Frozen Food Producers (DBA) .... UKAFFP
United Kingdom Association of Manufacturers of Bakers Yeast (DBA) .... UKAMBY
United Kingdom Association of Professional Engineers [*A union*] .... UKAPE
United Kingdom Association of Suggestion Schemes (DBA) .... UKASS
United Kingdom Association of Wood Packing Case Makers [*A union*] .... UKAWPCM
United Kingdom Atomic Energy Authority [*London, England*] [*Databank originator and operator*] [*Research center*] .... UKAEA
United Kingdom Atomic Energy Authority Office at Risley (IAA) .... UKR
United Kingdom Automatic Control Council (ACII) .... UKAC
United Kingdom Automation Council [*London, England*] .... UKAC
United Kingdom Band of Hope Union (EAIO) .... UKBHU
United Kingdom Bartenders' Guild (BI) .... UKBG
United Kingdom Base [*World War II*] .... UKB
United Kingdom Base Section [*World War II*] .... UKBS
United Kingdom Board Sailing Association (DBA) .... UKBSA
United Kingdom Bomber Command (NATG) .... UKBC
United Kingdom Central Council [*for Nursing, Midwifery, and Health Visiting*] .... UKCC
United Kingdom Chemical Information Service [*University of Nottingham*] [*Nottingham, England Information broker, databank originator, and host*] .... UKCIS
United Kingdom Coffee Association Ltd. (BI) .... UKCA
United Kingdom Combat Support Boat .... UKCSB
United Kingdom Commanders-in-Chiefs' Committee .... UKCICC
United Kingdom Commercial Corp. .... UKCC
United Kingdom Commercial Travellers Association (DI) .... UKCTA
United Kingdom Communication Region [*Air Force*] (MCD) .... UKCR
United Kingdom Continental Shelf .... UKCS
United Kingdom Council for Computing Development (NITA) .... UKCCD
United Kingdom Council for Music Education and Training (EAIO) .... UKCMET
United Kingdom Council for Overseas Student Affairs (DS) .... UKCOSA
United Kingdom Cutlery and Silverware Manufacturers Association (BI) .... UKCSMA
United Kingdom Dairy Association (DBA) .... UKDA
United Kingdom Dutch Rabbit Club (BI) .... UKDRC
United Kingdom Education and Research Networking Association (AIE) .... UKERNA
United Kingdom Energy [*Vancouver Stock Exchange symbol*] .... UKY
United Kingdom Energy Authority (DI) .... UKEA
United Kingdom Environmental Law Association (DBA) .... UKELA
United Kingdom Environmental Mutagen Society (EAIO) .... UKEMS
United Kingdom Federation of Business and Professional Women (DI) .... UKFBPW
United Kingdom Feline Register [*An association*] (DBA) .... UKFR
United Kingdom Fellmongers Association (BI) .... UKFA
United Kingdom for Orders [*Shipping*] .... UKFO
United Kingdom Fortifications Club (DBA) .... UKFC
United Kingdom Fund [*Associated Press*] (SAG) .... UKing
United Kingdom Fund [*NYSE symbol*] (SPSG) .... UKM
United Kingdom Glycerine Producers' Association (BI) .... UKGPA
United Kingdom Home Economics Federation [*British*] .... UKHEF
United Kingdom Housing Trust .... UKHT
United Kingdom Immigrants Advisory Service .... UKIAS
United Kingdom Import Plan .... UKIP
United Kingdom Industrial Space Committee (DBA) .... UKISC
United Kingdom Information Office, Toronto, ON, Canada [*Library symbol Library of Congress*] (LCLS) .... CaOTIO
United Kingdom Information Office, Toronto, Ontario [*Library symbol National Library of Canada*] (NLC) .... OTIO
United Kingdom Information Technology Organization .... UKITO
United Kingdom Infrared Telescope .... UKIRT
United Kingdom Insurance Brokers European Committee .... UKIBEK
United Kingdom International NOTAM Office [*ICAO location identifier*] (ICLI) .... EGGN
United Kingdom Joint Airborne Task Force [*British military*] (DMA) .... UKJATFOR
United Kingdom Jute Goods Association Ltd. (BI) .... UKJGA
United Kingdom Land Forces [*Military*] .... UKLF

United Kingdom Manufacturers and New Zealand Representatives Association (BI) ..... UKMANZRA
United Kingdom Medical Research Council ..... UKMRC
United Kingdom Meteorological Office ..... UKMO
United Kingdom Meteorological Office [*Marine science*] (OSRA) ..... UKMO
United Kingdom Ministry of Supply Staff ..... UKMOSS
United Kingdom Miscellaneous Islands [*MARC geographic area code Library of Congress*] (LCCP) ..... e-uk-ui
United Kingdom Miscellaneous Islands [*MARC country of publication code Library of Congress*] (LCCP) ..... ui
United Kingdom Mobile Force ..... UKMF
United Kingdom Mobile Force (Air) [*British military*] (DMA) ..... UKMF(A)
United Kingdom Mobile Force (Land) [*British military*] (DMA) ..... UKMF(L)
United Kingdom Module Constructors Association (DBA) ..... UKMCA
United Kingdom MOTNE Centre [*ICAO location identifier*] (ICLI) ..... EGGY
United Kingdom National Committee of the International Association on Water Pollution Research and Control (EAIO) ..... UKNCIAWPRC
United Kingdom National Nutrient Databank [*Ministry of Agriculture and Royal Society of Chemistry*] ..... UKNND
United Kingdom National Serials Data Centre [*Information service or system*] (IID) ..... UKNSDC
United Kingdom NATO Air Defense Region (NATG) ..... UKADR
United Kingdom/Netherlands (MCD) ..... UK/NL
United Kingdom Office for Library Networking ..... Ukoln
United Kingdom Official Publications [*Information service or system*] (IID) ..... UKOP
United Kingdom Offshore Operators' Association ..... UKOA
United Kingdom Offshore Operators' Association (DS) ..... UKOOA
United Kingdom On-Line User Group [*Information service or system*] (IID) ..... UKOLUG
United Kingdom Optical Sensors Collaborative Association (ACII) ..... UK OSCA
United Kingdom or Continent (Bordeaux-Hamburg) [*Shipping*] (DS) ..... UK/Cont (BH)
United Kingdom or Continent (Gibraltar-Hamburg) [*Shipping*] (DS) ..... UK/Cont (GH)
United Kingdom or Continent (Havre to Hamburg) (ROG) ..... UKCHH
United Kingdom or Continent (Havre-Hamburg) [*Shipping*] (DS) ..... UK/Cont (HH)
United Kingdom Outboard Boating Association (BI) ..... UKOBA
United Kingdom Paper and Packaging Directory [*A publication*] ..... UKPPD
United Kingdom Patternmakers' Association [*A union*] ..... UKPA
United Kingdom Permanent Representative [*EEC*] (DS) ..... UKREP
United Kingdom Petroleum Industry Association ..... UKPIA
United Kingdom Pilots Association (DS) ..... UKPA
United Kingdom Post Office [*Telecommunications*] (TEL) ..... UKPO
United Kingdom Postal Clerks' Association [*A union*] ..... UKPCA
United Kingdom Preserves Manufacturers Association (DBA) ..... UKPMA
United Kingdom Provident Institute [*Commercial firm*] ..... UKPI
United Kingdom Provision Trade Federation (DBA) ..... UKPTF
United Kingdom Reading Association [*British*] ..... UKRA
United Kingdom Renderers Association (DBA) ..... UKRA
United Kingdom Schmidt Telescope ..... UKST
United Kingdom Schmidt Telescope Unit ..... UKSTU
United Kingdom Science Park Association (DBA) ..... UKSPA
United Kingdom Serials Group ..... UKSG
United Kingdom Settlers' Association [*Australia*] ..... UKSA
United Kingdom Shipmakers' Association [*A union*] ..... UKSA
United Kingdom Society of Amalgamated Smiths and Strikers [*A union*] ..... UKSASS
United Kingdom Society of Coachmakers [*A union*] ..... UKSC
United Kingdom Society of Information Management (DBA) ..... UKSIM
United Kingdom Spoon Collectors Club (DBA) ..... UKSCC
United Kingdom Strike Command (NATG) ..... UKSTC
United Kingdom Subsatellite ..... UKS
United Kingdom Sugar Merchants' Association (BI) ..... UKSMA
United Kingdom Tariff (DS) ..... UKT
United Kingdom Tariff and Overseas Trade Classification (DS) ..... UKTOTC
United Kingdom Tea Association (DBA) ..... UKTA
United Kingdom Timber Trade Shipowners Mutual Association Ltd. (DS) ..... UKTTSMA
United Kingdom Trade Agency ..... UKTA
United Kingdom Treasury Delegation ..... UKTD
United Kingdom Treaty Series [*A publication*] ..... UKTS
United Kingdom Wool Growers Federation (DBA) ..... UKWGF
United Kingdom-South Africa Trade Association ..... UKSATA
United Kingdom-United States Agreement [*Intelligence*] [*1947*] ..... UKUSA
United Knitwear Manufacturers League (EA) ..... UKML
United Labor Congress [*Nigeria*] ..... ULC
United Labor Zionist Party [*Later, LZA*] (EA) ..... ULZP
United Laboratories Inc. [*Philippines*] ..... Unilab
United Labour Front [*Trinidad and Tobago*] (PD) ..... ULF
United Labour Organization [*Burma*] ..... ULO
United Latin Americans of America (EA) ..... ULAA
United Leader Resources, Inc. [*Vancouver Stock Exchange symbol*] ..... UNL
United Left [*Peru*] [*Political party*] ..... UL
United Left Democratic Front [*India*] [*Political party*] (PPW) ..... ULDF
United Left Front [*Nepal*] [*Political party*] (EY) ..... ULF
United Leisure Corp. [*NASDAQ symbol*] (SAG) ..... UTDL
United Leisure Corp. [*Associated Press*] (SAG) ..... UtdLeisr
United Leisure Wrrt'A' [*NASDAQ symbol*] (TTSB) ..... UTDLW
United Lesbian and Gay Christian Scientists (EA) ..... ULGCS
United Leukodystrophy Foundation (EA) ..... ULS
United Liberation Front of Assam [*India*] [*Political party*] (ECON) ..... ULFA
United Liberation Movement [*Liberia*] [*Political party*] (ECON) ..... ULIMO
United Liberty Resources Ltd. [*Vancouver Stock Exchange symbol*] ..... ULR
United Lightning Protection Association (EA) ..... ULPA
United Limited Sprints [*Auto racing*] ..... ULS
United Lincoln Resources, Inc. [*Vancouver Stock Exchange symbol*] ..... ULN
United Lithuanian Relief Fund of America (EA) ..... ULRA
United Lodge of Theosophists (EA) ..... ULT
United Lodge of Theosophists, London, ON, Canada [*Library symbol Library of Congress*] (LCLS) ..... CaOLT
United Lodge of Theosophists, London, Ontario [*Library symbol National Library of Canada*] (NLC) ..... OLT
United Lodge of Theosophists, Ottawa, ON, Canada [*Library symbol Library of Congress Obsolete*] (LCLS) ..... CaOOULT
United Lutheran Church Men [*Defunct*] (EA) ..... ULCM
United Lutheran Church of America (WDAA) ..... ULCA
United Lutheran Society (EA) ..... ULS
United Machine Workers' Association [*A union*] [*British*] ..... UMWA
United Malayan Banking Corp. ..... UMBC
United Malays National Organisation [*Malaysia*] [*Political party*] (ECON) ..... UNMO
United Malays National Organization [*Malaysia*] [*Political party*] ..... UMNO
United Male and Female Cardboard Box Makers' Association [*A union*] [*British*] ..... UMFCBMA
United Maritime Administration ..... UMA
United Maritime Authority ..... UMA
United Maritime Consultative Committee ..... UMCC
United Maritime Council ..... UMC
United Maritime Executive Board ..... UMEB
United Martial Arts Association (EA) ..... UMAA
United Mechanical Engineers' Society [*A union*] [*British*] ..... UMES
United Merchant Bar [*Commercial firm British*] ..... UMB
United Merchant Navy Christian Fellowship [*British*] ..... UMNCF
United Merchants & Manufacturers, Inc. [*NYSE symbol*] (SPSG) ..... UMM
United Merchants & Manufacturers, Inc. [*Associated Press*] (SAG) ..... UtdMM
United Merchants Research Center, Langley, SC [*Library symbol Library of Congress*] (LCLS) ..... ScLangU
United Meridian [*NYSE symbol*] (TTSB) ..... UNC
United Meridian Corp. [*NYSE symbol*] (SPSG) ..... UMC
United Meridian Corp. [*Associated Press*] (SAG) ..... UMeridn
United Methodist Association of Health and Welfare Ministries (EA) ..... UMA
United Methodist Associations of Preschools ..... UMAP
United Methodist Church ..... UMC
United Methodist Church, Commission on Archives and History, Dayton, OH [*Library symbol Library of Congress*] (LCLS) ..... ODaUM
United Methodist Church, Commission on Archives and History, Lake Junaluska, NC [*Library symbol Library of Congress*] (LCLS) ..... NcLjUM
United Methodist Committee on Relief (EA) ..... UMCOR
United Methodist Communications [*Information service or system*] (IID) ..... UMCOM
United Methodist Free Churches ..... UMFC
United Methodist Information [*Database*] [*United Methodist Communications*] [*Information service or system*] (CRD) ..... UMI
United Methodist Publishing House, Nashville, TN [*Library symbol Library of Congress*] (LCLS) ..... TNUM
United Methodist Voluntary Services ..... UMVS
United Methodist Women in Switzerland and in France (EAIO) ..... UMWSF
United Microelectronics Corp. (NITA) ..... UMC
United Micronesia Development Association ..... UMDA
United Mine Workers [*Also, UMWA*] (CDAI) ..... UMW
United Mineworker's Federation of Australia (EERA) ..... UMFA
United Mining Corp. [*Vancouver Stock Exchange symbol*] ..... UMC
United Mining Councils of America (EA) ..... UMCA
United Ministries in Education [*Later, HEMT/UMHE*] (EA) ..... UME
United Ministries in Higher Education [*Later, HEMT/UMHE*] (EA) ..... UMHE
United Missionary Society ..... UMS
United Mobile Homes [*AMEX symbol*] (TTSB) ..... UMH
United Mobile Homes, Inc. [*AMEX symbol*] (SAG) ..... UMH
United Mobile Homes, Inc. [*Associated Press*] (SAG) ..... UMobH
United Mortgage Bankers of America [*Philadelphia, PA*] (EA) ..... UMBA
United Motor Courts ..... UMC
United Movement for Democracy and Unification in Korea [*Defunct*] (EA) ..... UMDUK
United Movement for Democracy in Korea [*Later, UMDUK*] (EA) ..... UMDK
United Movement of Iranian National Forces [*Defunct*] (EA) ..... UMINF
United Mutual Fund Selector [*United Business Service Co.*] ..... UMFS
United National Association of Post Office Craftsmen [*Later, APWU*] ..... NAPO
United National Association of Post Office Craftsmen [*Later, APWU*] ..... UNAPOC
United National Bancorp [*NASDAQ symbol*] (NQ) ..... UNBJ
United National Bancorp [*Associated Press*] (SAG) ..... UNBNJ
United National Convention [*Ghana*] [*Political party*] (PPW) ..... UNC
United National Federal Party [*Zimbabwe*] [*Political party*] (PPW) ..... UNFP
United National Front [*Lebanon*] (BJA) ..... UNF
United National Independence Party [*Nigeria*] [*Political party*] ..... UNIP
United National Independence Party [*Trinidad and Tobago*] [*Political party*] (PPW) ..... UNIP
United National Independence Party [*Zambia*] [*Political party*] (PD) ..... UNIP
United National Independence Party of Zambia ..... UNIPZ
United National Indian Tribal Year (DICI) ..... UNITY
United National Indian Tribal Youth ..... UNITY
United National Life Insurance Society (EA) ..... UNLIS
United National Movement [*Saint Christopher and Nevis*] [*Political party*] (EY) ..... UNM
United National Party [*Sri Lanka*] [*Political party*] (PPW) ..... UNP
United Nations (EA) ..... UN
United Nations [*Marine science*] (OSRA) ..... UN
United Nations Action Program for Economic Cooperation ..... UNAPEC
United Nations Administrative Committee and Coordination (WDAA) ..... UNACC
United Nations Administrative Tribunal (EY) ..... UNAT
United Nations Advance Mission in Cambodia (ECON) ..... UNAMIC

United Nations Advisory Committee on the Application of Science and Technology to Development (ASF) .... UNCASTD
United Nations Africa Council .... UNAC
United Nations Angola Verification Mission .... UNAVEM
United Nations Appeal for Children .... UNAC
United Nations Asia and Far East Institute for the Prevention of Crime and Treatment of Offenders .... UNAFEI
United Nations Assistance Mission in Rwanda .... UNAMIR
United Nations Association .... UNA
United Nations Association in Canada (EAIO) .... UNAC
United Nations Association International Service [British] ... UNAIS
United Nations Association of Great Britain and Northern Ireland (EAIO) .... UNA-UK
United Nations Association of Hungary (EAIO) .... UNA-H
United Nations Association of Mauritius (EAIO) .... MUNA
United Nations Association of Mexico (EAIO) .... UNA-MEX
United Nations Association of Poland (EAIO) .... UNAP
United Nations Association of Sri Lanka (EAIO) .... UNASL
United Nations Association of Sweden (EAIO) .... UNAS
United Nations Association of the Congo (EAIO) .... UNAC
United Nations Association of the United States of America (AEBS) .... UNAUS
United Nations Association of the United States of America (EA) .... UNA-USA
United Nations Association of Turkey (EAIO) .... UNAT
United Nations Atomic Development Authority (NUCP) ...... UNADA
United Nations Atomic Energy Commission [Superseded by Disarmament Commission, 1952] .... UNAEC
United Nations Atomic Energy Control Commission .... UNAECC
United Nations Audiovisual Information Center .... UNAVIC
United Nations Beacon .... UNB
United Nations Bibliographic Information System [United Nations Headquarters] (IID) .... UNBIS
United Nations Border Relief Operation .... UNBRO
United Nations Bureau of Social Affairs .... UNBSA
United Nations Bureau of Technical Assistance Operations .... UNBTAO
United Nations Capital Development Fund .... UNCDF
United Nations Capital Development Fund (EERA) .... UNCDF
United Nations Cartographic Commission (BARN) .... UNCC
United Nations Censorship Network .... UNCN
United Nations Center for Human Settlement [Kenya] [Research center] (IRC) .... UNCHS
United Nations Center for Regional Development .... UNCRD
United Nations Center for Science and Technology for Development (EA) .... CSTD
United Nations Center for Science and Technology for Development (USDC) .... UNCSD
United Nations Center for Science and Technology for Development [Later, CSTD] (EAIO) .... UNCSTD
United Nations Centre Against Apartheid (EA) .... UNCAA
United Nations Centre for Human Rights [Switzerland] (EAIO) .... UNCHR
United Nations Centre for Regional Development (EERA) .... UNCRD
United Nations Centre for Science and Technology for Development (EA) .... UNCSTD
United Nations Centre on Transnational Corporations (ECON) .... UNCTC
United Nations Children's Fund [United Nations International Children's Emergency Fund] [Acronym is based on former name,] (EA) .... UNICEF
United Nations Childrens Fund, New York, NY [Library symbol Library of Congress] (LCLS) .... NNUN-CF
United Nations Civil Assistance Command, Korea .... UNCACK
United Nations Civilian Police [Peace-keeping force in Cyprus] .... UNCIVPOL
United Nations Command .... UNC
United Nations Command .... UNCMD
United Nations Command Military Armistice Commission ..... UNCMAC
United Nations Command (Rear) .... UNCR
United Nations Command Security Force [Military] (INF) .... UNCSF
United Nations Commission for Asia and the Far East .... UNCAFE
United Nations Commission for Europe .... UNCE
United Nations Commission for India and Pakistan .... UNCIP
United Nations Commission for Investigation of War Criminals .... UNCIWC
United Nations Commission for the Unification and Rehabilitation of Korea .... UNCURK
United Nations Commission of the USSR (EERA) .... UNEPCOM
United Nations Commission on Human Rights .... UNCHR
United Nations Commission on International Trade Law (PDAA) .... UNCITRAL
United Nations Commission on International Trade Law. Yearbook [A publication] (DLA) .... UN Comm Int'l Trade LYB
United Nations Committee on Information (EA) .... UNCI
United Nations Committee on Korea .... UNCOK
United Nations Committee on the Peaceful Uses of Outer Space (EA) .... COPUOS
United Nations Committee on the Peaceful Uses of Outer Space ...... UNCOPUOS
United Nations Compensation Commission (ECON) .... UNCC
United Nations Conciliation Commission for Palestine .... UNCCP
United Nations Conference of Plenipotentiaries .... UNCP
United Nations Conference on Applications of Science and Technology [1963] .... UNCAST
United Nations Conference on Desertification .... UNCOD
United Nations Conference on Environment and Development .... UNCED
United Nations Conference on Environment and Development (EERA)..... UNCED
United Nations Conference on International Organization [San Francisco, 1945] .... UNCIO
United Nations Conference on New and Renewable Sources of Energy [1981] .... UNERG
United Nations Conference on Science and Technology (BARN) .... UNCSAT
United Nations Conference on Science and Technology Education for Development (AIE) .... UNCSTD

United Nations Conference on the Exploration and Peaceful Uses of Outer Space .... UNISPACE
United Nations Conference on the Human Environment (MSC) .... UNCHE
United Nations Conference on the Law of the Sea .... UNCLOS
United Nations Conference on Trade and Development .... UNCTAD
United Nations Conference on Trade and Development, Trade and Development Board .... UNCTAD TDB
United Nations Confidence Restoration Operation (ECON) .... UNCRO
United Nations Confidence Restoration Operation in Croatia .... Uncro
United Nations Convention on the Law of the Sea (EERA) .... UNCLOS
United Nations Correspondents Association (EA) .... UNCA
United Nations Data Elements Directory [A publication] ...... UNTDED
United Nations Declaration of Human Rights (BJA) .... UNDHR
United Nations Department of Technical Cooperation for Development [United Nations] (GNE) .... UNDTCD
United Nations Development Advisory Team .... UNDAT
United Nations Development Cooperation Cycle .... UNDCC
United Nations Development Fund for Women (EA) .... UNIFEM
United Nations Development Program [Marine science] (OSRA) .... UNDP
United Nations Development Programme (EA) .... UNDP
United Nations Disarmament Commission [Also, DC, DC(UN)] .... UNDC
United Nations Disaster Relief Coordination .... UNDRC
United Nations Disaster Relief Office (EAIO) .... UNDRO
United Nations Disaster Relief Organization (EERA) .... UNDRO
United Nations Disengagement Observer Force [Damascus, Syria] .... UNDOF
United Nations Document Index .... UNDI
United Nations Documentation Information System (NITA) .... UNDIS
United Nations Economic and Social Commission for Asia and the Pacific [Bangkok, Thailand] (EAIO) .... ESCAP
United Nations Economic and Social Commission for Asia and the Pacific .... UNESCAP
United Nations Economic and Social Council. Official Record [A publication] (DLA) .... UNECOSOC
United Nations Economic and Social Council Official Record [A publication] (DLA) .... UNESCOR
United Nations Economic and Social Office in Beirut .... UNESOB
United Nations Economic Commission for Africa (EA) ...... UNECA
United Nations Economic Commission for Europe .... UNECE
United Nations Economic Commission for Europe (EERA) .... UN-ECE
United Nations Economic Commission for Latin America (BARN) .... UNECLA
United Nations Economic Development Administration .... UNEDA
United Nations Education Conference .... UNEC
United Nations Educational and Training Program for Southern Africa .... UNETPSA
United Nations Educational, Scientific, and Cultural Organization [Database originator and operator] [France Research center] .... UNESCO
United Nations Electoral Assistance Team .... UN/EAT
United Nations Emergency Force [to separate hostile forces of Israel and Egypt] .... UNEF
United Nations Emergency Force in the Middle East .... UNEF
United Nations Emergency Operation (PDAA) .... UNEO
United Nations Emergency Technical Aid Service .... UNETAS
United Nations Energy Planning [A publication] .... UNEP
United Nations Environment Fund .... UNEF
United Nations Environment Program [Marine science] (OSRA) .... UNEP
United Nations Environment Program Governing Council ..... UNEP GC
United Nations Environment Programme [Kenya] [Database originator] (EAIO) .... UNEP
United Nations Environment Programme/International Referral System .... UNEP/IRS
United Nations Environment Programme Participation Act of 1973 .... UNEPPA
United Nations European Headquarters [Geneva, Switzerland] .... UNE
United Nations Expanded Program of Technical Assistance .... UNEPTA
United Nations Film Board .... UNFB
United Nations Financing System for Science and Technology for Development (EY) .... UNFSSTD
United Nations Food and Agriculture Organization .... UNFAO
United Nations Food and Agriculture Organization Intergovernmental Committee [World Food Program] .... UGC
United Nations Food Conference (BARN) .... UNFC
United Nations Force in Somalia [Military] (INF) .... UNISOM
United Nations Forces in Cyprus (DMA) .... UNFICYP
United Nations Framework Convention on Climate Change .... UNFCCC
United Nations Fund for Drug Abuse Control .... UNFDAC
United Nations Fund for Namibia (EERA) .... UNFN
United Nations Fund for Population Activities .... UNFPA
United Nations Fund for Population Activities, New York, NY [Library symbol Library of Congress] (LCLS) .... NNUN-PA
United Nations Fund for Science and Technology Development (EERA) .... UNFSTD
United Nations General Assembly (MCD) .... UNGA
United Nations General Assembly Document (ILCA) .... A
United Nations General Assembly Official Record [A publication] (DLA) .... UNGAOR
United Nations Good Offices Mission in Afghanistan and Pakistan [Later, OSGAP] .... UNGOMAP
United Nations Group of Experts on Geographical Names .... UNGEGN
United Nations Guidelines for Trade Data Interchange .... UN-GTDI
United Nations Headquarters (DLA) .... UNHQ
United Nations Headquarters Nongovernmental Organizations Committee on Youth (EA) .... UNHNOCY
United Nations High Commission (BJA) .... UNHC
United Nations High Commission [or Commissioner] for Refugees .... UNHCR
United Nations High Commission for Refugees (EERA) ...... UNHCR
United Nations High Commissioner for Refugees (DLA) ...... UNCHR

United Nations Human Rights Commission (BJA) .... UNHRC
United Nations Index [*A publication*] .... UNDEX
United Nations India-Pakistan Observer Mission (BARN) .... UNIPON
United Nations Industrial Development Fund .... UNIDF
United Nations Industrial Development Organization [*Austria Also, an information service or system*] (IID) .... UNIDO
United Nations Information Center and Liaison Office (PDAA) ...... UNICLO
United Nations Information Centre .... UNIC
United Nations Information Centre and Liaison Office (PDAA) ...... UNICLO
United Nations Information for Teachers [*Information service or system*] (AEBS) .... UNIT
United Nations Information Organization .... UNIO
United Nations Information Service .... UNIS
United Nations Information System in Science and Technology (NITA) .... UNISIST
United Nations Ingergovernmental System of Information in Science and Technology [*UNESCO*] [*Zagreb, Yugoslavia*] .... UNISIST
United Nations Institute for Disarmament Research [*Research center Switzerland*] (IRC) .... UNIDIR
United Nations Institute for Training and Research [*New York*] [*ICSU*] [*Research center*] .... UNITAR
United Nations Interim Force in Lebanon .... UNIFIL
United Nations International Emergency Network [*Marine science*] (OSRA) .... UNIENET
United Nations International Force, Cyprus .... UNICYP
United Nations International School .... UNIS
United Nations International TOKAMAK Reactor [*Proposed experimental fusion power plant*] .... UNITOR
United Nations Iran-Iraq Military Observer Group .... UNIIMOG
United Nations Iraq/Kuwait Observer Mission .... UNIKOM
United Nations Joint Board of Strategy .... UNJBS
United Nations Joint Staff Pension Fund (ECON) .... UNJSPF
United Nations Juridical Year Book [*A publication*] (DLA) ...... UN Jur YB
United Nations Juridical Year Book [*A publication*] (DLA) ...... UN Juridical YB
United Nations Korean Reconstruction Agency .... UNKRA
United Nations Law of the Sea [*Conference*] .... UNLOS
United Nations Law Reports [*A publication*] (DLA) .... UNLR
United Nations League of Lawyers .... UNLL
United Nations Library, New York, NY [*Library symbol Library of Congress*] (LCLS) .... NNUN
United Nations Medal [*Military decoration*] .... UNM
United Nations Mediterranean Command (BJA) .... UNMC
United Nations Mediterranean Commission .... UNMC
United Nations Middle East Mission (EY) .... UNMEM
United Nations Military Observer Group for India and Pakistan (AABC) .... UNMOGIP
United Nations Military Observer Group in India and Pakistan [*1949*] .... Unmogip
United Nations Military Observers (BJA) .... UNMO's
United Nations Military Staff Committee (AABC) .... UNMSC
United Nations Mission in Bosnia and Herzegovina [*1995*] ...... Unmibh
United Nations Mission in Haiti [*1993*] .... Unmih
United Nations Mission in Haiti (ECON) .... UNMIH
United Nations Mission of Observers in Prevlaka [*Croatia, 1996*] ...... Unmop
United Nations Mixed Armistice Commission .... UNMAC
United Nations Multilateral Treaties [*A publication*] (DLA) ...... UNMT
United Nations Observer Corps (BJA) .... UNO
United Nations Observer Group in Lebanon .... UNOGIL
United Nations Observer Mission in Georgia [*1993*] .... Unomig
United Nations Oceanographic Organization .... UNOO
United Nations of the New Emerging Forces [*Indonesia*] .... UNNEFO
United Nations of Yoga [*Stockholm, Sweden*] (EAIO) .... UNY
United Nations Office Coordinating Humanitarian and Economic Aid to Afghanistan (ECON) .... UNOCA
United Nations Office for Emergency Operations in Africa [*Defunct*] (EA) .... UNOEOA
[*The*] United Nations Office for Project Services (ECON) .... UNOPS
United Nations Office for the Coordination of Humanitarian Assistance to Afghanistan (ECON) .... UNOCHA
United Nations Operation in Somalia (INF) .... UNOSOM
United Nations Operation in the Congo .... UNOC
United Nations Organization [*ICSU*] .... UNO
United Nations Organization - Geneva .... UNOG
United Nations Outer Space Affairs Division (EERA) .... UNOASD
United Nations Palestine Commission .... UNPC
United Nations Palestine Conciliation Commission (BJA) .... UNPCC
United Nations Participation Act of 1945 .... UNPA
United Nations Partisan Infantry Korea .... UNPIK
United Nations Peace Observation Commission .... UNPOC
United Nations Peacekeeping Force in Cyprus .... UNFICYP
United Nations Peacekeeping Force in Cyprus [*1964*] .... Unificyp
United Nations Philatelic Society [*Defunct*] (EA) .... UNPS
United Nations Philatelists (EA) .... UNP
United Nations Postal Administration .... UNPA
United Nations Preventive Deployment Force [*Macedonia*] .... Unpredep
United Nations Programme of Action for African Economic Recovery and Development [*1986-1990*] .... UN-PAAERD
United Nations Protection Force [*Former Yugoslavia*] (ECON) ...... UNPROFOR
United Nations Protection Force in the Former Yugoslavia .... UNPROFOR
United Nations Protective Forces .... UNPROFOR
United Nations Refugee Fund .... UNREF
United Nations Regional Cartographic Conferences on Asia and the Far East .... UNRCCFE
United Nations Regional Housing Center for ESCAP [*Economic and Social Commission for Asia and the Pacific*] [*India*] (EAIO) ...... UNRHCE

United Nations Regional Institute for Population Studies [*Legon, Ghana*] (EAIO) .... UNRIPS
United Nations Relief and Rehabilitation Administration [*"United Nations" derives from the wartime alliance of this name, not from any affiliation with the postwar international organization*] .... UNRRA
United Nations Relief and Rehabilitation Conference .... UNRRC
United Nations Relief and Works Agency for Palestine Refugees in the Near East [*Austria*] (PD) .... UNRWA
United Nations Relief and Works Agency for Palestine Refugees in the Near East [*Austria*] (DLA) .... UNRWAPR
United Nations Relief and Works Agency for Palestine Refugees in the Near East [*Pronounced: "Unwrap me"*] [*Austria*] .... UNRWAPRNE
United Nations Relief for Palestine Refugees .... UNRPR
United Nations Relief Operation in Dacca .... UNROD
United Nations Relief Works Agency (EERA) .... UNRWA
United Nations Reports of International Arbitral Awards [*A publication*] (DLA) .... R Int'l Arb Awards
United Nations Reports of International Arbitral Awards [*A publication*] (DLA) .... UNRIAA
United Nations Research Institute for Social Development (EA) ...... UNRISD
United Nations Resolutions [*A publication*] (DLA) .... UN Res
United Nations Resources and Transport Division .... UNRTD
United Nations Revolving Fund for Natural Resources Exploration (EERA) .... UNRFNRE
United Nations Rules for Electronic Data Interchange for Administration, Commerce, and Transport .... UN/EDIFACT
United Nations Sales Section [*for UN documents*] .... UNSS
United Nations Science and Technology Advisory Committee (AIE) ...... UNSTAC
United Nations Scientific Advisory Committee [*ICSU*] .... UNSAC
United Nations Scientific Committee on Effects of Atomic Radiation (EERA) .... UNSCEAR
United Nations Scientific Committee on the Effects of Atomic Radiation .... UNSCEAR
United Nations Scientific Conference on the Conservation and Utilization of Resources .... UNSCCUR
United Nations Secretariat Member [*License plate code assigned to foreign diplomats in the US*] .... A
United Nations Secretary General .... UNSG
United Nations Security Council .... UNSC
United Nations Security Forces, Hollandia (AABC) .... UNSFH
United Nations Service Medal [*Military decoration*] .... UNSM
United Nations Service Medal .... UNSVM
United Nations Social Commission .... UNSC
United Nations Social Defense Research Institute [*UN/Italy*] ...... UNSDRI
United Nations Social Development Division .... UNSDD
United Nations Space Registry (BARN) .... UNSR
United Nations Special Committee on Palestine .... UNSCOP
United Nations Special Committee on the Balkans [*Greece*] ...... UNSCOB
United Nations Special Fund .... UNSF
United Nations Special Session on Disarmament (PDAA) .... UNSSOD
United Nations Staff Union (EA) .... UNSU
United Nations Standards Co-Ordinating Committee .... UNSCC
United Nations Statistical Information System (DUND) .... UNSIS
United Nations Statistical Office (EERA) .... UNSO
United Nations Study Unit [*Philatelic organization*] (EA) .... UNSU
United Nations Subcommission on the Prevention of Discrimination and the Protection of Minorities [*Geneva, Switzerland*] (EAIO) ...... UNSPDPM
United Nations Sudano-Sahelian Office .... UNSO
United Nations Technical Assistance .... UNTA
United Nations Technical Assistance Administration .... UNTAA
United Nations Technical Assistance Fellowship .... UNTAF
United Nations Technical Assistance Mission (BARN) .... UNTAM
United Nations Temporary Committee on Korea .... UNTCOK
United Nations Temporary Executive Authority [*Supervised transfer of Netherlands New Guinea to Indonesia*] .... UNTEA
United Nations Theatre Group (EA) .... UNTG
United Nations Transition Assistance Group .... UNTAG
United Nations Transitional Authority in Cambodia (ECON) ...... UNTAC
United Nations Treaty Information System (DUND) .... UNTIS
United Nations Treaty Series [*Project*] [*University of Washington*] ...... UNTS
United Nations Truce Supervision Organization .... UNTSO
United Nations Trust Fund for Development Planning and Projections .... UNTFDPP
United Nations Trust Fund for Social Development .... UNTFSD
United Nations Trust Fund for Southern Africa (EERA) .... UNTSFA
United Nations Trust Territory .... UNTT
United Nations Trusteeship Council (BARN) .... UNTC
United Nations Trusteeship Council Official Record [*A publication*] (DLA) .... UNTCOR
United Nations University [*Tokyo*] .... UNU
United Nations University [*Marine science*] (OSRA) .... UNU
United Nations University/Institute of New Technologies .... UNU/INTECH
United Nations University International Institute for Software ...... UNUIIST
United Nations University / World Institute for Development Economics Research (DUND) .... UNU/WIDER
United Nations Volunteers (EAIO) .... UNV
United Nations War Crimes Commission [*"United Nations" derives from the wartime alliance of this name, not from any affiliation with the postwar international organization*] .... UNWCC
United Nations Women's Guild (EA) .... UNWG
United Nations, Woodrow Wilson Memorial Library, New York, NY [*Library symbol Library of Congress*] (LCLS) .... NNUN-W
United Nations Year Book [*A publication*] (DLA) .... UNYB
United Nations Yemen Observation Mission .... UNYOM
United Native Americans (EA) .... UNA

United Natl Bancorp [*NASDAQ symbol*] (TTSB) ... UNBJ
United Natural Foods, Inc. [*NASDAQ symbol*] (SAG) ... UNFI
United Natural Foods, Inc. [*Associated Press*] (SAG) ... UntdNat
United Negro College Fund (EA) ... UNCF
United Neighborhood Centers of America (EA) ... UNCA
United Network Command for Law and Enforcement [*Fictitious intelligence organization in various television series*] ... UNCLE
United Network Co. [*TV broadcasting network*] ... UNC
United Network for Organ Sharing [*Database*] (EA) ... UNOS
United New Conservationists (EA) ... UNC
United News & Media ADR [*NASDAQ symbol*] (TTSB) ... UNEWY
United News & Media PLC [*NASDAQ symbol*] (SAG) ... UNEWY
United News & Media PLC [*Associated Press*] (SAG) ... UtdNews
United News of India Ltd. [*News agency*] (FEA) ... UNI
United News Shops [*British*] ... UNS
United Newspapers Public Ltd. Co. (MHDW) ... UNEWY
United Nicaraguan Opposition ... UNO
United Northern Petroleum Corp. [*Vancouver Stock Exchange symbol*] ... UNP
United Nursing Homes, Seattle, WA [*Library symbol Library of Congress*] (LCLS) ... WaSUN
United Operative Bricklayers' Trade Protection Society [*A union*] [*British*] ... UOBTPS
United Operative Masons' and Granite Cutters' Union [*British*] ... UOMGCU
United Optical and Instrument Workers of America ... UOIW
United Order of Smiths [*A union*] [*British*] ... UOS
United Order of the Golden Cross [*Defunct*] (EA) ... UOGC
United Order of the Total Abstaining Sons of the Phoenix (ROG) ... UOTASP
United Order True Sisters (EA) ... UOTS
United Oromo People's Liberation Front [*Ethiopia*] [*Political party*] (EY) ... UOPLF
United Orpington Club (EA) ... UOC
United Orpington Club of America [*Later, UOC*] (EA) ... UOCA
United Orthodox Ministers and Cantors Association of America and Canada (EA) ... UOMCA
United Ostomy Association (EA) ... UOA
United Pacific Gold [*Vancouver Stock Exchange symbol*] ... UPG
United Packinghouse Food and Allied Workers [*Later, UFCWIU*] (EA) ... UPFAW
United Packinghouse Workers of America [*Later, UFCWIU*] ... UPWA
United Pants and Novelties Contractors Association [*Defunct*] (EA) ... UPNCA
United Papermakers and Paperworkers [*Later, UPIU*] (EA) ... UPP
United Paperworkers International Union (EA) ... UPIU
United Paramount Network [*Television*] ... UPN
United Paramount Network ... UPN
United Parcel Service ... UPS
United Parcel Service Co. [*ICAO designator*] (FAAC) ... UPS
United Parents of Absconded Children [*Defunct*] (EA) ... UPAC
United Parents under God (EA) ... UPG
United Parent-Teachers Association of Jewish Schools (EA) ... UPTA
United Park City Mines Co. [*NYSE symbol*] (SPSG) ... UPK
United Park City Mines Co. [*Associated Press*] (SAG) ... UPkMn
United Park City Mns [*NYSE symbol*] (TTSB) ... UPK
United Parkinson Foundation (EA) ... UPF
United Party [*Gambia*] [*Political party*] (PPW) ... UP
United Party [*Papua New Guinea*] [*Political party*] (PPW) ... UP
United Party of Haitian Communists ... UPHC
United Party of Nigeria ... UPN
United Pastrycooks' and Confectioners' Society [*British*] (BI) ... UPCS
United Patients Association for Pulmonary Hypertension (EA) ... UPAPH
United Patriotic Front [*Defunct*] (EA) ... UPF
United Patternmakers Association ... UPA
United Payors and United Providers, Inc. [*NASDAQ symbol*] (SAG) ... UPUP
United Payors and United Providers, Inc. [*Associated Press*] (SAG) ... UtdPay
United Peasants' Party [*Poland Political party*] (PD) ... UPP
United Pentecostal Church [*Australia*] ... UPC
United People's Association of Matabeleland [*Zimbabwe*] [*Political party*] (PPW) ... UPAM
United People's Front [*Singapore*] [*Political party*] (PPW) ... UPF
United People's Front [*Nepal*] [*Political party*] (EY) ... UPF
United People's Movement [*St. Vincent*] [*Political party*] (PPW) ... UPM
United People's Movement [*Antigua*] [*Political party*] (PPW) ... UPM
United People's Party [*Sierra Leone*] [*Political party*] ... UPP
United People's Party [*Grenada*] [*Political party*] (PPW) ... UPP
United People's Party of Arunachal [*India*] [*Political party*] (PPW) ... UPPA
United People's Party of Nigeria ... UPPN
United per Liter (DAVI) ... U/l
United Peregrine Society (EA) ... UPS
United Pest and Weed Control Association [*Australia*] ... UPWCA
United Pesticide Formulators and Distributors Association (EA) ... UPFD
United Pesticide Formulators and Distributors Association ... UPFDA
United Petroleum [*NASDAQ symbol*] (TTSB) ... UPET
United Petroleum Corp. [*NASDAQ symbol*] (SAG) ... UPET
United Petroleum Corp. [*Associated Press*] (SAG) ... UtdPetr
United Petroleum Corp. [*Associated Press*] (SAG) ... UtdPetrol
United Plant Guard Workers of America ... PGW
United Plastics Distributors Association [*Later, NAPD*] (EA) ... UPDA
United Poets Laureate International (EA) ... UPLI
United Polish Women of America (EA) ... UPWA
United Political Organization National Front [*Yeman*] (BARN) ... UPONF
United Popular Dress Manufacturers Association [*Later, LACA*] (EA) ... UPDMA
United Port District (WDAA) ... UPD
United Port Workers' Union [*Ceylon*] ... UPW
United Postal Service Network [*National mobile data network*] [*Proposed*] (ECON) ... UPSNET
United Postal Stationery Society (EA) ... UPSS
United Poultry Concerns [*An association*] (EA) ... UPC
United Power Association (IAA) ... UPA
United Power Co. [*British*] ... UPC
United Presbyterian ... UP
United Presbyterian Church ... UPC
United Presbyterian Health, Education, and Welfare Association [*Later, PHEWA*] (EA) ... UPHEWA
United Presbyterian Mission Library of the United Presbyterian Church in the USA, New York, NY [*Library symbol Library of Congress*] (LCLS) ... NNPRM
United Presbyterian Peace Fellowship (EA) ... UPPF
United Presbyterian Women (EA) ... UPW
United Press [*Merged with International News Service to form UPI*] ... UP
United Press International (EA) ... UPI
United Press International Audio (NTCM) ... UPIA
United Press International News-Features (NTCM) ... UPIN
United Press International Newspictures ... UPIN
United Press International Radio Network (NTCM) ... UPIRN
United Press International Television News (NTCM) ... UPITN
United Press of Bangladesh ... UPB
United Press of Pakistan ... UPP
United Producers of America [*Motion picture company*] ... UPA
United Professional Horsemen's Association (EA) ... UPHA
United Progressive Party [*Trinidad and Tobago*] [*Political party*] (PPW) ... UPP
United Progressive Party [*Zambia*] [*Political party*] ... UPP
United Protestant Association of New South Wales [*Australia*] ... UPANSW
United Provinces [*India*] ... UP
United Provinces Law Reports [*India*] [*A publication*] (DLA) ... UPLR
United Provinces Law Times [*India*] [*A publication*] (DLA) ... UPLT
[*The*] **United Provinces of North America** [*See also EFISGA*] [*Suggested early name for Canada*] ... TUPONA
United Public Library, Carlow, Dungannon, and Mayo Townships, Bancroft, Ontario [*Library symbol National Library of Canada*] (BIB) ... OBANU
United Public Utility Systems ... UPUS
United Public Workers of America ... UPW
United Racing Club [*Auto racing*] ... URC
United Racquetsports for Women (EA) ... URW
United Railroad Operating Crafts [*Defunct*] ... UROC
United Railroad Workers of America ... URWA
United Ratepayers' Campaign [*British*] (BI) ... URC
United Rayore Gas [*Vancouver Stock Exchange symbol*] ... URG
United Red Army [*Japan*] (PD) ... URA
United Redford Resources, Inc. [*Vancouver Stock Exchange symbol*] ... URR
United Reef Petroleums Ltd. [*Toronto Stock Exchange symbol*] ... URP
United Reform Church [*Australia*] ... URC
United Reform Church in England and Wales ... URC
United Religious Front [*Israel*] (BJA) ... URF
United Republic of Tanzania [*ANSI two-letter standard code*] (CNC) ... TZ
United Republic of Tanzania [*ANSI three-letter standard code*] (CNC) ... TZA
United Republican Fund ... URF
United Republicans of America ... URA
United Research, Inc. ... URI
United Research Service (MCD) ... URS
United Restaurants [*NASDAQ symbol*] (SAG) ... UNIR
United Restaurants, Inc. [*Associated Press*] (SAG) ... UtdR
United Restaurants, Inc. [*Associated Press*] (SAG) ... UtdRest
United Restaurants Wrrt'A' [*NASDAQ symbol*] (TTSB) ... UNIRW
United Restaurants Wrrt'B' [*NASDAQ symbol*] (TTSB) ... UNIRZ
United Restitution Organization ... URO
United Retail Fish Dealers Association of New York City (EA) ... URFDA-NYC
United Retail Group [*NASDAQ symbol*] (TTSB) ... URGI
United Retail Group, Inc. [*NASDAQ symbol*] (SAG) ... URGI
United Retail Group, Inc. [*Associated Press*] (SAG) ... UtRetail
United Rink Operators [*Defunct*] (EA) ... URO
United Road Transport Union [*British*] (DCTA) ... URTU
United Road Transport Workers' Association of England [*A union*] ... URTWAE
United Roumanian Jews of America (EA) ... URJA
United Rubber, Cork, Linoleum, and Plastic Workers of America (EA) ... URW
United Russia Societies Association [*London*] ... URSA
United Russian Orthodox Brotherhood of America (EA) ... UROBA
United Sabah National Organization [*Malaysia*] [*Political party*] (PPW) ... USNO
United Sabah People's Organization [*Pertubuhan Rakyat Sabah Bersatu*] [*Malaysia*] [*Political party*] (PPW) ... USPO
United Satellite Communications [*Cable TV programming service*] ... USC
United Satellite Communications Inc. ... USCI
United Satellites Ltd. [*London, England*] [*Telecommunications*] (TSSD) ... USL
United Saudi Commercial Bank ... USCB
United Savers Association (EA) ... USA
United Savings Bank FA [*Great Falls, MT*] [*NASDAQ symbol*] (NQ) ... UBMT
United Savings Bank FA [*Associated Press*] (SAG) ... USvBk
United Saw Service Association (EA) ... USSA
United Scenic Artists (EA) ... USA
United Scholarship Service [*Later, NCAIAE, NCAIE*] ... USS
United Schools International [*New Delhi, India*] (EAIO) ... USI
United Scientific Holdings [*Defense equipment manufacturer*] [*British*] ... USH
United Scientists for Environmental Responsibility and Protection (EERA) ... USERP
United Scleroderma Foundation (EA) ... USF
United Seamen's Service (EA) ... USS
United Sec Bancorp (WA) [*NASDAQ symbol*] (TTSB) ... USBN
United Secularists of America (EA) ... USA
United Securities Market [*British*] (CDAI) ... USM
United Security Bancorp (Washington) [*NASDAQ symbol*] (SAG) ... USBN
United Security Bancorp (Washington) [*Associated Press*] (SAG) ... USecBc
United Seniors Association, Inc. ... USA
United Serpents (EA) ... US
United Service ... US

United Service Club [*Charter jet service to Europe for servicemen and dependents*] ..... USC
United Service Institution (BARN) ..... USI
United Service Organizations, Inc. (EA) ..... USO
United Services Advisors, Inc. [*Associated Press*] (SAG) ..... USvAd
United Services Advisors, Inc. [*San Antonio, TX*] [*NASDAQ symbol*] (NQ) ..... USVS
United Services Automobile Association, San Antonio, TX [*Library symbol Library of Congress*] (LCLS) ..... TxSaUS
United Shareholders Association (EA) ..... USA
United Shareowners of America [*Defunct*] (EA) ..... USA
United Ship Scrapers' Protection League [*A union*] [*British*] ..... USSPL
United Shoe Workers of America [*Later, ACTWU*] (EA) ..... USWA
United Shoppers Association ..... USA
United Sidecar Association [*Later, USCA*] (EA) ..... USA
United Sidecar Association (EA) ..... USCA
United Single Women in Search of Men Who Aren't Gay, Married, or Hung-Up on Their Mothers [*Fictitious association*] ..... USWISOMWAGMOHOTM
United Siscoe Mines, Inc. [*Toronto Stock Exchange symbol*] ..... USO
United Sisters [*Defunct*] (EA) ..... US
United Sisters of Charity (EA) ..... USC
United Slate Tile and Composition Roofers, Damp and Waterproof Workers Association [*Later, UURWAW*] ..... RDWW
United Soccer Association [*Later, NASL*] ..... USA
United Soccer League (EA) ..... USL
United Social, Cultural, and Educational Foundation of India ..... USCEFI
United Socialist Alliance [*Sri Lanka*] [*Political party*] ..... USA
United Socialist Alliance of Greece (PPW) ..... ESPE
United Socialist Front [*Thailand*] [*Political party*] (PD) ..... USF
United Socialist Party [*South Korea Political party*] (PPW) ..... USP
United Societies of Physiotherapists (EA) ..... USPT
United Societies of the United States of America [*McKeesport, PA*] (EA) ..... USUSA
United Society for Christian Literature [*British*] ..... USCL
United Society for the Propagation of the Gospel [*Society for the Propaga tion of the Gospel in Foreign Parts and UMCA*] [*Formed by a merger of*] (EAIO) ..... USPG
United Society of Artists [*British*] (BI) ..... UA
United Society of Boilermakers and Iron and Steel Shipbuilders [*A union*] [*British*] ..... USBISS
United Society of Boilermakers, Shipbuilders, and Structural Workers [*A union*] [*British*] ..... USBSSW
United Society of Brushmakers [*A union*] [*British*] ..... USB
United Society of Carpenters and Joiners [*A union*] [*British*] ..... USCJ
United Society of Cork Cutters [*A union*] [*British*] ..... USCC
United Society of Drillers [*A union*] [*British*] ..... USD
United Society of Fitters and Smiths [*A union*] [*British*] ..... USFS
United Society of Mechanical Wood Workers [*A union*] [*British*] ..... USMWW
United Society of Pattern Makers [*A union*] [*British*] ..... USPM
United Society of Shakers, Shaker Library, Poland Spring, ME [*Library symbol Library of Congress*] (LCLS) ..... MePosS
United Soft Serve and Fast Food Association [*Later, NSSFFA*] (EA) ..... USSFFA
United Solomon Islands Party (PPW) ..... USIP
United Somali Congress [*Political party*] (EY) ..... USC
United Somali Front [*Political party*] (EY) ..... USF
United Sons of Israel (EA) ..... USI
United South African National Party ..... USANP
United South and Eastern Tribes (EA) ..... USET
United South West Africa Party [*Namibia*] [*Political party*] ..... USWAP
United Spanish War Veterans (EA) ..... USWV
United Specialty Agents Alliance [*Also known as USA Alliance*] (EA) ..... USAA
United Spoilers of America [*Later, MERCPAC*] (EA) ..... USA
United Sports Fans of America (EA) ..... USFA
United Sportsman Racers Association [*Defunct*] (EA) ..... USRA
United Sprint Association (EA) ..... USA
United Square Dancers of America (EA) ..... USDA
United Stamp Society for Shut-Ins (EA) ..... USSSI
United State Army School of Aviation Medicine (PDAA) ..... USASAM
United State Enrichment Corporation ..... USEC
United States [*MARC geographic area code Library of Congress*] (LCCP) ..... n-us--
United States ..... US
United States [*ANSI two-letter standard code*] ..... US
United States [*MARC country of publication code Library of Congress*] (LCCP) ..... us
United States [*ANSI three-letter standard code*] ..... USA
United States Academy of Arms [*Defunct*] (EA) ..... USAA
United States Accident Containment Team [*Government agency in 1985 movie "Warning Sign"*] ..... USACT
United States ACTION Library, Washington, DC [*Library symbol Library of Congress*] (LCLS) ..... DACT
United States Activities Board (IAA) ..... USAB
United States Activities Committee (IAA) ..... USAC
United States Adjutant General Publications Center ..... USAGPC
United States Adopted Name ..... USAN
United States Advanced Battery Consortium ..... USABC
United States Advanced Ceramics Association ..... USACA
United States Advisory Commission on Information ..... USACI
United States Advisory Commission on International Educational and Cultural Affairs ..... USACIECA
United States Advisory Committee on Antarctic Names [*1947-*] ..... US-ACAN
United States Aeronautical Reserve ..... USAR
United States Agency for Aviation Safety (MCD) ..... USAAVS
United States Agency for International Development [*Also, AID*] ..... USAID
United States Agency for International Development, Office of Population, Washington, DC [*Library symbol Library of Congress*] (LCLS) ..... DAID
United States Agency for International Development, Washington (PDAA) ..... USAID/W
United States Agricultural Information Network ..... USAIN
United States Aid Funds [*An association*] (PAZ) ..... USA FUNDS
United States Aikido Federation (EA) ..... USAF
United States Air Attache ..... USAIRA
United States Air Base (AAG) ..... USAB
United States Air Corps ..... USAC
United States Air Corps Specialist Reserve ..... USACSR
United States Air Force [*Washington, DC*] ..... USAF
United States Air Force Academy [*Colorado*] ..... USAFA
United States Air Force Academy, Colorado Springs, CO [*Library symbol Library of Congress*] (LCLS) ..... CoCA
United States Air Force Academy, Hospital Library, Colorado Springs, CO [*Library symbol Library of Congress*] (LCLS) ..... CoCA-H
United States Air Force Academy, USAF Academy, CO [*OCLC symbol*] (OCLC) ..... COH
United States Air Force Accounting and Finance Center, Denver, CO [*Library symbol Library of Congress*] (LCLS) ..... CoDAFA
United States Air Force, Aerospace Research Laboratories, Wright-Patterson Air Force Base, OH [*Library symbol Library of Congress*] (LCLS) ..... OWpAR
United States Air Force Air Crew School ..... USAFACS
United States Air Force Air Defense Weapons Center (MCD) ..... USAFADWC
United States Air Force Air Demonstration Squadron ..... USAFADS
United States Air Force, Air Force Logistics Command, Wright-Patterson Air ForceBase, OH [*Library symbol Library of Congress*] (LCLS) ..... OWpL
United States Air Force, Air Force Rocket Propulsion Laboratory, Edwards AFB, CA [*Library symbol Library of Congress*] (LCLS) ..... CEdA-R
United States Air Force Air Police School ..... USAFAPS
United States Air Force, Air University Library, Maxwell AFB, AL [*OCLC symbol*] (OCLC) ..... AAU
United States Air Force Airframe Production Contract ..... USAFAPC
United States Air Force Airlift Center ..... USAFALCENT
United States Air Force, Airlift Operations School, Scott Air Force Base, IL [*Library symbol Library of Congress*] (LCLS) ..... IScAF-A
United States Air Force Ammunition Control Point ..... USAFACP
United States Air Force, Armament Development and Test Center, Technical Library, Eglin Air Force Base, FL [*Library symbol Library of Congress*] (LCLS) ..... FEgAD
United States Air Force, Armament Laboratory, Technical Library, Eglin AFB, FL [*OCLC symbol*] (OCLC) ..... SCE
United States Air Force Art Program ..... USAFAP
United States Air Force Audiovisual Liaison Office ..... USAFAVLO
United States Air Force Auditor General ..... USAFAG
United States Air Force Ballistic Missile Division ..... USAFBMD
United States Air Force Bandsman School (AFM) ..... USAFBS
United States Air Force, Base Library, Eielson AFB, AK [*Library symbol Library of Congress*] (LCLS) ..... AkEiel
United States Air Force, Base Library, Ellington AFB, Houston, TX [*Library symbol Library of Congress*] (LCLS) ..... TxHE
United States Air Force, Base Library, Elmendorf AFB, AK [*Library symbol Library of Congress*] (LCLS) ..... AkElm
United States Air Force, Base Library, Griffiss Air Force Base, Rome, NY [*Library symbol Library of Congress*] (LCLS) ..... NRomAF
United States Air Force, Base Library, Lackland Air Force Base, TX [*Library symbol Library of Congress*] (LCLS) ..... TxLaH
United States Air Force, Base Library, McGuire Air Force Base, NJ [*Library symbol Library of Congress*] (LCLS) ..... NjMcUSAF
United States Air Force, Base Library, Minot AFB, ND [*Library symbol Library of Congress*] (LCLS) ..... NdMinAF
United States Air Force, Base Library, Peterson Field, CO [*Library symbol Library of Congress*] (LCLS) ..... CoPfAF
United States Air Force, Base Library, Scott AFB, IL [*Library symbol Library of Congress*] (LCLS) ..... IScAF
United States Air Force, Base Library, Vandenberg Air Force Base, CA [*Library symbol Library of Congress*] (LCLS) ..... CVanA
United States Air Force Basic Military School ..... USAFBMS
United States Air Force Bombardment School ..... USAFBS
United States Air Force, Cambridge Research Center, Bedford, MA [*Library symbol Library of Congress*] (LCLS) ..... MBdAF
United States Air Force Cambridge Research Laboratories ..... USAFCRL
United States Air Force, Cannon Air Force Base, Clovis, NM [*Library symbol Library of Congress*] (LCLS) ..... NmClA
United States Air Force, Castle Air Force Base Hospital, Merced, CA [*Library symbol Library of Congress*] (LCLS) ..... CMerUSAH
United States Air Force, Castle Grate Air Force Base Library, Merced, CA [*Library symbol Library of Congress*] (LCLS) ..... CMerUSAF
United States Air Force, Chanute Air Force Base Library, Chanute Air Force Base, IL [*Library symbol*] [*Library of Congress*] (LCLS) ..... IChaAF
United States Air Force Cockpit Procedures Trainer ..... USAF CPT
United States Air Force Communications Electronics Doctrine (IAA) ..... USAFCED
United States Air Force Court of Military Review (AFM) ..... USAF CMR
United States Air Force, Defense Institute of Security Administration Management, Wright-Patterson Air Force Base, OH [*Library symbol Library of Congress*] (LCLS) ..... OWpDI
United States Air Force, Defense Mapping Agency Aerospace Center, St. Louis, MO [*Library symbol Library of Congress*] (LCLS) ..... MoSDM
United States Air Force Dictionary [*A publication*] ..... USAFD
United States Air Force, Edwards Air Force Base, AFFTC Technical Library, Edwards AFB, CA [*OCLC symbol*] (OCLC) ..... CED
United States Air Force, Eglin Regional Hospital, Eglin Air Force Base, FL [*Library symbol Library of Congress*] (LCLS) ..... FEgRH
United States Air Force Environmental Health Laboratory ..... USAFEHL

United States Air Force Environmental Technical Application Center [*Scott Air Force Base, IL*] .... USAFETC

United States Air Force Environmental Technical Applications Center [*Scott Air Force Base, IL*] (AFM) .... USAFETAC

United States Air Force, Environmental Technical Applications Center, Air Weather Service Technical Library, Scott Air Force Base, IL [*Library symbol Library of Congress*] (LCLS) .... IScAF-E

United States Air Force Epidemiological Laboratory (AFM) .... USAFEL

United States Air Force European Postal and Courier Region (AFM) .... USAFEURPCR

United States Air Force Experimental Test Pilot School .... USAFETPS

United States Air Force Extension Course Institute .... USAFECI

United States Air Force Field Activity Group .... USAFFACG

United States Air Force Field Activity Squadron .... USAFFACS

United States Air Force Flexible Gunnery School .... USAFFGS

United States Air Force Flight Safety Research .... USAFFSR

United States Air Force, Flight Test Center Technical Library, Edwards AFB, CA [*Library symbol Library of Congress*] (LCLS) .... CEdA

United States Air Force Forces, Readiness Command .... USAFRED

United States Air Force, Francis E. Warren Air Force Base, Cheyenne, WY [*Library symbol Library of Congress*] (LCLS) .... WyFEW

[*The*] United States Air Force Group, American Mission for Aid to Turkey .... TUSAFG

United States Air Force, Hancock Air Base Library, Syracuse, NY [*Library symbol Library of Congress*] (LCLS) .... NSyAF

United States Air Force, Headquarters U.S. Air Force, Office of Air Force History, Bolling Air Force Base, Washington, DC [*Library symbol Library of Congress*] (LCLS) .... DAFH

United States Air Force Historical Division .... USAFHD

United States Air Force Historical Research Center .... USAFHRC

United States Air Force Honor Guard .... USAFHG

United States Air Force Hospital .... USAFH

United States Air Force, Hospital Medical Library/SGAL, Elmendorf Air Force Base, AK [*Library symbol Library of Congress*] (LCLS) .... AkElmM

United States Air Force, Human Resources Laboratory Library, Brooks Air Force Base, San Antonio, TX [*Library symbol Library of Congress*] (LCLS) .... TxSaBHR

United States Air Force in Europe .... USAFE

United States Air Force Institute of Technology .... USAFIT

United States Air Force Institute of Technology, Detachment 9, Francis E. WarrenAir Force Base, Cheyenne, WY [*Library symbol Library of Congress*] (LCLS) .... WyFEW-i

United States Air Force Institute of Technology, Grand Forks AFB, ND [*Library symbol Library of Congress*] (LCLS) .... NdGIT

United States Air Force Institute of Technology, Minot AFB, ND [*Library symbol Library of Congress*] (LCLS) .... NdMinIT

United States Air Force Institute of Technology, Wright-Patterson Air Force Base, OH [*Library symbol Library of Congress*] (LCLS) .... OWpIT

United States Air Force Instrument Flight Center (AFM) .... USAFIFC

United States Air Force Intelligence Publication .... USAFINTEL

United States Air Force Interceptor Weapons School .... USAFIWS

United States. Air Force Judge Advocate General. Law Review [*A publication*] (DLA) .... JAG L Rev

United States Air Force, Langley Air Force Base Library, Langley AFB, VA [*Library symbol Library of Congress*] (LCLS) .... ViLanAF

United States Air Force, Luke Air Force Base Library, Glendale, AZ [*Library symbol Library of Congress*] (LCLS) .... AzGAF

United States Air Force Manual [*A publication*] (AAGC) .... USAFM

United States Air Force Marksmanship Training Center .... USAFMTC

United States Air Force, Medical Center Library, SGEL, Wright Patterson AFB, OH [*Library symbol Library of Congress*] (LCLS) .... OWpM

United States Air Force Mideast Postal and Courier Region (AFM) .... USAFMEPCR

United States Air Force Mideast Postal and Courier Service (AFM) .... USAFMEPCS

United States Air Force Military Personnel Center .... USAFMPC

United States Air Force, Mountain Home Air Force Base Library, Mountain Home, ID [*Library symbol*] [*Library of Congress*] (LCLS) .... IdMhAF

United States Air Force, National Aerospace Education Library, Ellington AFB, Houston, TX [*Library symbol Library of Congress*] (LCLS) .... TxHE-NA

United States Air Force, National Range Division .... USAF/NRD

United States Air Force Navigation School .... USAFNS

United States Air Force, Norton Air Force Base, San Bernardino, CA [*Library symbol Library of Congress*] (LCLS) .... CSbUSAF

United States Air Force Occupational and Environmental Health Laboratory [*Brooks Air Force Base, TX*] .... USAFOEHL

United States Air Force, Office of Research Analyses, Technical Library, Holloman AFB, Albuquerque, NM [*Library symbol Library of Congress*] (LCLS) .... NmHORA

United States Air Force Office of Scientific Research .... USAFOSR

United States Air Force, Office of Scientific Research, Washington, DC [*Library symbol Library of Congress*] (LCLS) .... DAFOSR

United States Air Force Officer Candidate School .... USAFOCS

United States Air Force Pacific Postal and Courier Region .... USAFPACPCR

United States Air Force Personnel Development Center .... USAFPDC

United States Air Force Physical Evaluation Board (AFM) .... USAFPEB

United States Air Force Pilot School .... USAFPS

United States Air Force Plant Representative Office .... USAFPLREP

United States Air Force Plant Representative Office .... USAFPRO

United States Air Force, Pope Air Force Base, Base Library, Pope AFB, NC [*Library symbol Library of Congress*] (LCLS) .... NcPo

United States Air Force Postal and Courier Service .... USAFPCS

United States Air Force Postal and Courier Service, Europe-Mideast Region (AFM) .... USAFPCS Eur-Me Rgn

United States Air Force Postal and Courier Service, Latin American Region (AFM) .... USAFPCS LA Rgn

United States Air Force Postal and Courier Service, Pacific Region (AFM) .... USAFPCS Pac Rgn

United States Air Force Postal and Courier Service, United States Region (AFM) .... USAFPCS US Rgn

United States Air Force Radiological Health Laboratory .... USAFRHL

United States Air Force Recruiting Detachment .... USAFRD

United States Air Force Recruiting Group .... USAFRG

United States Air Force Recruiting Office .... USAFRO

United States Air Force Recruiting Service .... USAFRS

United States Air Force Recruiting Squadron .... USAFRSQ

United States Air Force, Regional Hospital, Medical Library, Sheppard AFB, TX [*Library symbol Library of Congress*] (LCLS) .... TxShpM

United States Air Force Representative (AFM) .... USAFR

United States Air Force Representative, UN Military Staff Committee .... USAIRMILCOMUN

United States Air Force Research Library, Hanscom Air Force Base, Hanscom, MA [*Library symbol Library of Congress*] (LCLS) .... MHansAF

United States Air Force Reserve .... USAFR

U.S. Air Force Reserve (440th Airlift Wing) [*FAA designator*] (FAAC) .... GQN

United States Air Force Reserve Officer Training Corps .... USAFROTC

United States Air Force Resident Representative (MCD) .... USAFRR

United States Air Force, Rome Air Development Center, Griffiss, NY [*Library symbol Library of Congress*] (LCLS) .... NRomAF-R

United States Air Force, Sacramento Peak Observatory, Sunspot, NM [*Library symbol Library of Congress*] (LCLS) .... NmSuAF

United States Air Force School of Aerospace Medicine .... USAFSAM

United States Air Force, School of Aerospace Medicine, Brooks Air Force Base, San Antonio, TX [*Library symbol Library of Congress*] (LCLS) .... TxSaBAM

United States Air Force School of Applied Aerospace Sciences (AFM) .... USAFSAAS

United States Air Force School of Applied Cryptologic Sciences (AFM) .... USAFSACS

United States Air Force School of Health Care Science .... USAFSCHCS

United States Air Force Security Policy Academy .... USAFSPA

United States Air Force Security Service [*Later, AFESC*] .... USAFSS

United States Air Force, Seymour Johnson Air Force Base, Base Library, Seymour Johnson AFB, NC [*Library symbol Library of Congress*] (LCLS) .... NcSj

United States Air Force Southern Air Division .... USAFSO

United States Air Force, Southern Command (MCD) .... USAFCO

United States Air Force Special Activities Group .... USAFSAG

United States Air Force Special Activities Squadron .... USAFSAS

United States Air Force Special Air Warfare Center (AFM) .... USAFSAWC

United States Air Force Special Operations Center (AFM) .... USAFSOC

United States Air Force Special Operations Force (AFM) .... USAFSOF

United States Air Force Special Operations School (AFM) .... USAFSOS

United States Air Force Special Reporting Agency .... USAFSRA

United States Air Force Special Treatment Center (AFM) .... USAFSTC

United States Air Force Standard Base Supply System .... USAFSBSS

United States Air Force Supervisory Examination (AFM) .... USAFSE

United States Air Force Tactical Air Reconnaissance Center (AFM) .... USAFTARC

United States Air Force Tactical Air Warfare Center (AFM) .... USAFTAWC

United States Air Force Tactical Airlift Center (AFM) .... USAFTALC

United States Air Force Tactical Fighter Weapons Center (AFM) .... USAFTFWC

United States Air Force Tactical Missile Control Point .... USAFTMCP

United States Air Force Technical Applications Center (MCD) .... USAFTAC

United States Air Force, Technical Library, Los Angeles, CA [*Library symbol Library of Congress*] (LCLS) .... CLUSAF

United States Air Force, Technical Library, Tyndall AFB, FL [*Library symbol Library of Congress*] (LCLS) .... FTyAF-T

United States Air Force Technical School .... USAFTS

United States Air Force Technical Training School .... USAFTTS

United States Air Force Test Pilot School .... USAF TESTPLTSCH

United States Air Force Test Pilot School (MCD) .... USAFTPS

United States Air Force - United States Postal Courier Region (AFM) .... USAF-USPCR

United States Air Force Water Port Liaison Office [*or Officer*] (AFM) .... USAFWPO

United States Air Force Water Port Logistics Office .... USAFWPLO

United States Air Force, Weapons Laboratory, Kirtland Air Force Base, Albuquerque, NM [*Library symbol Library of Congress*] (LCLS) .... NmAAF

United States Air Force, Whiteman Air Force Base Library, Whiteman AFB, MO [*Library symbol*] [*Library of Congress*] (LCLS) .... MoWhAF

United States Air Force, Wilford Hall Medical Center, Lackland AFB, TX [*Library symbol Library of Congress*] (LCLS) .... TxLaM

United States Air Force, Wright-Patterson Technical Library, Wright-Patterson Air Force Base, OH [*Library symbol Library of Congress*] (LCLS) .... OWpT

United States Air Force's Air-Ground Operations School .... USAFAGOS

United States Air Forces, Atlantic (AABC) .... USAFLANT

United States Air Forces in Europe Inspection and Safety Center .... USAFEISC

United States Air Forces in Europe Personnel Center .... USAFEPC

United States Air Forces in Europe - Turkey .... USAFE-T

United States Air Forces, Pacific .... USAFPAC

United States Air Forces Southern Command (AABC) .... USAFSO

United States Air Forces Strike Command (AABC) .... USAFSTRIKE

United States Air Group [*NYSE symbol*] (SAG) .... U

United States Air Group [*Associated Press*] (SAG) .... UsairG

United States Air Liaison Officer (CINC) .... USAIRLO

United States Air Racing Association [*Formerly, PRPA*] (EA) .... USARA

United States Air Service .... USAS

United States Air Target Chart .... USATC

U.S. Air Traffic Service Corporation [*FAA*] (TAG) .... USATS

United States Air University, Maxwell Air Force Base, Montgomery, AL [*Library symbol Library of Congress*] (LCLS) ... AMAU
United States Aircraft Insurance Group ... USAIG
United States Airspace System (NOAA) ... USAS
United States Allied Commission Austria ... USACA
United States Alpine Club [*Defunct*] ... USAC
United States Amateur Ballroom Dancers Association (EA) ... USABDA
United States Amateur Baseball Federation ... USABF
United States Amateur Confederation of Roller Skating (EA) ... USAC/RS
United States Amateur Dancers Association (EA) ... USADA
United States Amateur Jai Alai Players Association (EA) ... USAJAPA
United States Amateur Lacrosse Association ... USALA
United States Amateur Roller Skating Association [*Later, USAC/RS*] (EA) ... USARSA
United States Amateur Tug of War Association (EA) ... USATOWA
United States Amateur Wrestling Foundation (EA) ... USAWF
United States Amphibious Forces (AABC) ... USAMPHIBFOR
United States and Foreign Commercial Service (AAGC) ... US&FCS
United States Animal Health Association (EA) ... USAHA
United States Antarctic Program [*National Science Foundation*] ... USAP
United States Antarctic Projects Office ... USAPO
United States Antarctic Service [*1939-41*] [*Navy*] ... USAS
United States Antiaircraft Replacement Center ... USAARC
United States Apparel Council [*Defunct*] (EA) ... USAC
United States Appeals Reports [*A publication*] (DLA) ... US Ap
United States Appeals Reports [*A publication*] (DLA) ... US App
United States Arbitration Act [*A publication*] (DLA) ... USAA
United States Arbitration Act (AAGC) ... USAA
United States Archery Congress [*Defunct*] (EA) ... USAC
United States Armed Forces in Middle East ... USAFIME
United States Armed Forces Institute ... USAFI
United States Armed Forces Institute Test of General Educational Development (AEBS) ... USAFIGED
United States Armed Forces Staff College, Norfolk, VA [*Library symbol Library of Congress*] (LCLS) ... ViNSC
United States Armed Services Exploitation Center (AABC) ... USASEXC
United States Armor Association (EA) ... USAA
United States Arms Control and Disarmament Agency ... USACDA
U.S. Arms Control and Disarmament Agency Procurement Regulation [*A publication*] (AAGC) ... ACADPR
United States Army ... USA
United States Army Aberdeen Research and Development Center ... USAARDC
United States Army Adjutant General Combat Developments Agency (SAA) ... USAAGCDA
United States Army Adjutant General Data Processing Service Center (AABC) ... USAAGDPSC
United States Army Adjutant General Publications Center ... USAAGPC
United States Army Adjutant General's School (AABC) ... USAAGS
United States Army Administration Center [*Obsolete*] (AABC) ... USAAC
United States Army Administrative School Center and Fort Benjamin Harrison (AABC) ... USAASCFBH
United States Army Advance Command ... USAADVCOM
United States Army Advanced Ballistic Missile Defense Agency (AABC) ... USAABMDA
United States Army Advent Management Agency (MUGU) ... USAAMA
United States Army Advisor Group O - Army Reserve (AABC) ... USAAGAR
United States Army Advisory Group (National Guard) (AABC) ... USAAGNG
United States Army Aeromedical Center ... USAAMC
United States Army Aeromedical Research Laboratory [*Ft. Rucker, AL*] (AABC) ... USAARL
United States Army Aeromedical Research Unit ... USAARU
United States Army Aeronautical Depot Maintenance Center ... USAADMAC
United States Army Aeronautical Services Detachment ... USAASD
United States Army Aeronautical Services Detachment, Europe (AABC) ... USAASD-E
United States Army Aeronautical Services Detachment, Latin America (AABC) ... USAASD-LA
United States Army Aeronautical Services Detachment, Pacific (AABC) ... USAASD-PAC
United States Army Aeronautical Services Office (AABC) ... USAASO
United States Army Agency for Aviation Safety [*Formerly, USABAAR*] (AABC) ... USAAAVS
United States Army Air Corps ... USAAC
United States Army Air Defense Artillery Board ... USABD
United States Army Air Defense Artillery Board [*Fort Bliss, TX*] ... USARADABD
United States Army Air Defense Artillery School ... USAADASCH
United States Army Air Defense Board ... USAADB
United States Army Air Defense Board ... USARADBD
United States Army Air Defense Center ... USAADCEN
United States Army Air Defense Center and Fort Bliss (AABC) ... USAADCENFB
United States Army Air Defense Center and School ... USAADCS
United States Army Air Defense Command ... USARADCOM
United States Army Air Defense Engineering Agency [*Formerly, USASADEA*] [*AEC*] ... USAADEA
United States Army Air Defense School (AABC) ... USAADS
United States Army Air Defense School ... USARADSCH
United States Army, Air Defense School, Fort Bliss, TX [*Library symbol Library of Congress*] (LCLS) ... TxFbAD
United States Army Air Forces ... USAAF
United States Army Air Forces in the Middle East ... USAAFIME
United States Army Air Forces in the United Kingdom ... USAAFUK
United States Army Air Mobility Research and Development Center ... USAAMRDC
United States Army Air Mobility Research and Development Laboratory [*Also, AMR& DL, USAAMR & DL*] ... USAAMRDL
United States Army, Air Mobility Research and Development Laboratory, Fort Eustis, VA [*Library symbol Library of Congress*] (LCLS) ... ViFeAM
United States Army Air Service Command ... USAASC
United States Army Air Services [*World War II*] ... USAAS
United States Army Air Traffic Coordinating Officer ... USAATCO
United States Army Air Traffic Management System ... USAATMS
United States Army Airborne and Electronics Board [*Later, USAAESWBD*] ... USAABELCTBD
United States Army Airborne and Electronics Board (IAA) ... USAABNAELCTBD
United States Army Airborne and Special Operations Test Board (GFGA) ... USAABNSOTBD
United States Army Airborne Communications and Electronics Board ... USAACEBD
United States Army Airborne Communications and Electronics Board (AABC) ... USACEBD
United States Army Airborne, Electronics, and Special Warfare Board (AABC) ... USAAESWBD
United States Army Aircraft Base Maintenance Unit (AABC) ... USAABMU
United States Army Aircraft Development Test Activity ... USAADTA
United States Army, Alaska ... USARAL
United States Army Alaska Communications Center ... USARACS
United States Army Alcohol and Drug Abuse Team Training (MCD) ... USAADAT
United States Army Ambulance Service Association [*Defunct*] (EA) ... USSAC
United States Army Ammunition Procurement and Supply Agency ... USAAPSA
United States Army and Air Force Exchange Service, Dallas, TX [*Library symbol Library of Congress*] (LCLS) ... TxDaUSAF
United States Army Arctic Test Board ... USAATBD
United States Army Arctic Test Center ... USAATC
United States Army Armament Command ... USAARCOM
United States Army Armament Command ... USARMCOM
United States Army Armament, Munitions, and Chemical Command ... USAAMCCOM
United States Army Armament Research and Development Command (RDA) ... USARRADCOM
United States Army, Armament Research and Development Command, Science and Technical Library, Dover Site, Dover, NJ [*Library symbol Library of Congress*] (LCLS) ... NjDPA
United States Army Armament Research Development and Engineering Center ... USAARDEC
United States Army Armor and Desert Training Center ... USAADTC
United States Army Armor and Desert Training Center (AABC) ... USADTC
United States Army Armor and Engineer Board (AABC) ... USAARENBD
United States Army Armor and Engineer Board (RDA) ... USARENBD
United States Army Armor Board ... USAARMBD
United States Army Armor Center [*Fort Knox, KY*] ... USAARMC
United States Army Armor Center and School ... USAACS
United States Army Armor Human Research Unit [*Fort Knox, KY*] (AABC) ... USAARMHRU
United States Army Armor School ... USAARMS
United States Army Armor School, Fort Knox, KY [*Library symbol Library of Congress*] (LCLS) ... KyFkAS
United States Army Armor Signals (IAA) ... USAAS
United States Army, Army Engineering District, Office of Administrative Services, Galveston, TX [*Library symbol Library of Congress*] (LCLS) ... TxGA
United States Army, Army Language School Technical Library, Monterey, CA [*Library symbol Library of Congress*] (LCLS) ... CMontUSA
United States Army ARRADCOM - PLASTEC Division, Dover, NJ [*OCLC symbol*] (OCLC) ... ADP
United States Army ARRADCOM - STINFO Division, Dover, NJ [*OCLC symbol*] (OCLC) ... ADD
United States Army, Artillery and Guided Missile School, Fort Sill, OK [*Library symbol Library of Congress*] (LCLS) ... OkFsAGM
United States Army Artillery and Missile Center ... USAAMC
United States Army Artillery and Missile School [*Later, Field Artillery School*] ... USAAMS
United States Army Artillery Board ... USAARTYBD
United States Army Artillery Combat Developments (SAA) ... USAARTYCDA
United States Army Atmospheric Sciences Laboratory (RDA) ... USAASL
United States Army Attache ... USARMA
United States Army Audio-Visual Agency (AABC) ... USAAVA
United States Army Audit Agency ... USAAA
United States Army Audit Agency, Washington Region ... USAAAWR
United States Army Aviation Board ... USAAB
United States Army Aviation Board ... USAAVNBD
United States Army Aviation Center [*Fort Rucker*] ... USAAC
United States Army Aviation Center [*CONARC*] ... USAAVNC
United States Army Aviation Combat Developments Agency [*CDC*] ... USAACDA
United States Army Aviation Engineering Flight Activity [*Edwards Air Force Base, CA*] ... USAAEFA
United States Army Aviation Flight Information and Nav-Aids Office (AABC) ... USAAFINO
United States Army Aviation Flight Information Office ... USAAFIO
United States Army Aviation Human Research Unit [*Ft. Rucker, AL*] (AABC) ... USAAVNHRU
United States Army Aviation Logistics School (INF) ... USAALS
United States Army Aviation Materiel Command (AABC) ... USAAVCOM
United States Army Aviation Materiel Laboratories ... USAAML
United States Army Aviation Materiel Laboratories (AABC) ... USAAVLABS
United States Army Aviation Precision Demonstration Team (AABC) ... USAAPDT
United States Army Aviation Research and Development Command ... USAAVRADCOM
United States Army Aviation School [*CONARC*] ... USAAVNS
United States Army Aviation School, Fort Rucker, AL [*Library symbol Library of Congress*] (LCLS) ... AFrAS
United States Army Aviation Systems Command ... USAAVNSC

United States Army Aviation Systems Command [*Obsolete*] (AABC) ... USAAVSCOM
United States Army Aviation Systems Test Activity [*Also, AASTA*] ... USAASTA
United States Army Aviation Test Activity (AABC) ... USAAVNTA
United States Army Aviation Test Board ... USAAVNTBD
United States Army Avionics Field Office [*Formerly, USASAFO*] ... USAAFO
United States Army Ballistic Research Laboratories (AABC) ... USABRL
United States Army Ballistic Research Laboratories, Aberdeen Proving Grounds, MD [*OCLC symbol*] (OCLC) ... ADB
[*The*] **United States Army Band** (AABC) ... TUSAB
United States Army Base Command, Okinawa (AABC) ... USARBCO
United States Army, Berlin (AABC) ... USAB
United States Army Biological Laboratories (AABC) ... USABIOLABS
United States Army Biomedical Research and Development Laboratory [*Fort Detrick, MD*] ... USABRDL
United States Army Board for Aviation Accident Research [*Later, USAAAVS*] ... USABAAR
United States Army Broadcasting and Visual Activities, Pacific ... USABVAPAC
United States Army, Caribbean ... CAR
United States Army, Caribbean ... USARCARIB
United States Army, Carlisle Barracks Post Library, Carlisle Barracks, PA [*Library symbol Library of Congress*] (LCLS) ... PCarlPL
United States Army Catalog Data Agency (AABC) ... USACDA
United States Army Central Physical Evaluation Board (AABC) ... USACPEB
United States Army Chaplain Board ... USACHB
United States Army Chaplain School ... USACHS
United States Army Chemical Activity, Pacific (DOMA) ... USACAP
United States Army Chemical, Biological, and Radiological Weapons Orientation Course (AABC) ... USACBRWOC
United States Army Chemical, Biological, and Radiological Weapons Orientation Course Academic Advisory Board (AABC) ... USACBRWOCAAB
United States Army Chemical Center [*Later, United States Army Ordnance and Chemical Center and School*] ... USACMLC
United States Army Chemical Center and School [*Later, United States Army Ordnance and Chemical Center and School*] (AABC) ... USACMLCS
United States Army Chemical Corps Board ... USACMLCB
United States Army Chemical Corps Intelligence Agency ... USACCIA
United States Army Chemical Corps School ... USACMLCSCH
United States Army Chemical Corps Technical Committee ... USACCTC
United States Army Chemical Research and Development Laboratories ... USACMLRDL
United States Army Chemical School (AABC) ... USACMLS
United States Army, Chemical Systems Laboratory, Aberdeen Proving Ground, Aberdeen, MD [*Library symbol Library of Congress*] (LCLS) ... MdApgC
United States Army Chemical Warfare Laboratory ... USACWL
United States Army Chief of Support Services ... USACSS
[*The*] **United States Army Chorus** (AABC) ... TUSAC
United States Army CINPAC Support Group ... USACSG
United States Army Civil Affairs [*World War II*] ... USACA
United States Army Civil Affairs Combat Developments Agency (SAA) ... USACACDA
United States Army Civil Affairs School ... USACAS
United States Army, Civil Affairs School, Fort Gordon, GA [*Library symbol Library of Congress*] (LCLS) ... GFgC
United States Army Civilian Appellate Review Agency (GFGA) ... USACARA
United States Army Civilian Personnel Center (AABC) ... CIVPERCEN
United States Army Claims Service (AABC) ... USARCS
United States Army Claims Service Worldwide Information System (GFGA) ... USARCSWIS
United States Army Clothing and Textile Center ... USACTC
United States Army Clothing and Textile Materiel Center ... USACTMC
United States Army Club Management Agency (AABC) ... USACMA
United States Army Coating and Chemical Laboratory (AABC) ... USACCL
United States Army Cold Regions Research and Engineering Laboratory (AABC) ... USACRREL
United States Army, Cold Regions Research and Engineering Laboratory, Hanover, NH [*Library symbol Library of Congress*] (LCLS) ... NhHaCR
United States Army, Cold Regions Research and Engineering Laboratory Library, Hanover, NH [*OCLC symbol*] (OCLC) ... AFH
United States Army Cold Regions Test Center (INF) ... USACRTC
United States Army Combat Arms Training Board (AABC) ... USACATB
United States Army Combat Developments Command ... USACDC
United States Army Combat Developments Command Adjutant General Agency ... USACDCAGA
United States Army Combat Developments Command Air Defense Agency [*Fort Bliss, TX*] (AABC) ... USACDCADA
United States Army Combat Developments Command Armor Agency [*Fort Knox, KY*] (AABC) ... USACDCARMA
United States Army Combat Developments Command Artillery Agency (AABC) ... USACDCARTYA
United States Army Combat Developments Command Aviation Agency [*Fort Rucker, AL*] (AABC) ... USACDCAVNA
United States Army Combat Developments Command Chaplain Agency [*Fort Lee, VA*] (AABC) ... USACDCCHA
United States Army Combat Developments Command Chemical-Biological-Radiological Agency [*Fort McClellan, AL*] (AABC) ... USACDCCBRA
United States Army Combat Developments Command Civil Affairs Agency [*Fort Gordon, GA*] (AABC) ... USACDCCAA
United States Army Combat Developments Command Combat Arms Agency ... USACDCCARMSA
United States Army Combat Developments Command Combat Army Group [*Fort Le avenworth, KS*] [*Obsolete*] (AABC) ... USACDCCAG
United States Army Combat Developments Command Combat Service Support Group [*Fort Lee, VA*] [*Obsolete*] (AABC) ... USACDCCSSG
United States Army Combat Developments Command Combat Support Group [*Fort Belvoir, VA*] [*Obsolete*] (AABC) ... USACDCCSG
United States Army Combat Developments Command Combat Systems Group (AABC) ... USACDCCOMSG
United States Army Combat Developments Command Combined Arms Agency [*Fort Leavenworth, KS*] ... USACDCCA
United States Army Combat Developments Command Communications-Electronics Agency [*Fort Monmouth, NJ*] (AABC) ... USACDCCEA
United States Army Combat Developments Command Concept and Force Design Group (AABC) ... USACDCCONFG
United States Army Combat Developments Command Data Processing Field Office (AABC) ... USACDCDPFO
United States Army Combat Developments Command Engineer Agency [*Later, USACDCENA*] [*Fort Belvoir, VA*] (AABC) ... USACDCEA
United States Army Combat Developments Command Engineer Agency [*Formerly, USACDCEA*] (AABC) ... USACDCENA
United States Army Combat Developments Command Experimentation Center [*or Command*] [*Fort Ord, CA*] ... USACDCEC
United States Army Combat Developments Command Field Artillery Agency [*Fort Sill, OK*] (AABC) ... USACDCFAA
United States Army Combat Developments Command Finance Agency (AABC) ... USACDCFINA
United States Army Combat Developments Command Infantry Agency [*Later, USACDCINA*] [*Fort Benning, GA*] (AABC) ... USACDCIA
United States Army Combat Developments Command Infantry Agency [*Formerly, USACDCIA*] (AABC) ... USACDCINA
United States Army Combat Developments Command Institute of Advanced Studies [*Carlisle Barracks, PA*] [*Obsolete*] (AABC) ... USACDCIAS
United States Army Combat Developments Command Institute of Combined Arms and Support [*Fort Leavenworth, KS*] [*Obsolete*] (AABC) ... USACDCICAS
United States Army Combat Developments Command Institute of Land Combat [*Alexandria, VA*] [*Obsolete*] (AABC) ... USACDCILC
United States Army Combat Developments Command Institute of Nuclear Studies [*Fort Bliss, TX*] [*Obsolete*] (AABC) ... USACDCINS
United States Army Combat Developments Command Institute of Special Studies [*Fort Belvoir, VA*] [*Obsolete*] (AABC) ... USACDCISS
United States Army Combat Developments Command Institute of Strategic and Stability Operations [*Obsolete*] (AABC) ... USACDCISSO
United States Army Combat Developments Command Institute of Systems Analysis [*Fort Belvoir, VA*] [*Obsolete*] (AABC) ... USACDCISA
United States Army Combat Developments Command Intelligence Agency [*Fort Holabird, MD*] (MCD) ... USACDCINTA
United States Army Combat Developments Command Intelligence and Control Systems Group (AABC) ... USACDCINCSG
United States Army Combat Developments Command Internal Defense and Development Field Office (AABC) ... USACDCIDDFO
United States Army Combat Developments Command Judge Advocate Agency [*Charlottesville, VA*] (AABC) ... USACDCJAA
United States Army Combat Developments Command Maintenance Agency [*Aberdeen Proving Ground, MD*] (AABC) ... USACDCMA
United States Army Combat Developments Command Medical Service Agency [*Fort Sam Houston, TX*] (AABC) ... USACDCMSA
United States Army Combat Developments Command Nuclear Agency (AABC) ... USACDCNUA
United States Army Combat Developments Command Nuclear Group [*Fort Bliss, TX*] ... USACDCNG
United States Army Combat Developments Command Ordnance Agency [*Aberdeen Proving Ground, MD*] ... USACDCOA
United States Army Combat Developments Command Personnel and Administrative Services Agency [*Fort Benjamin Harrison, IN*] (AABC) ... USACDCPASA
United States Army Combat Developments Command Personnel and Logistics Systems Group (AABC) ... USACDCPALSG
United States Army Combat Developments Command Quartermaster Agency [*Fort Lee, VA*] ... USACDCQA
United States Army Combat Developments Command Special Operations Agency (AABC) ... USACDCSOA
United States Army Combat Developments Command Special Warfare Agency [*Fort Bragg, NC*] (AABC) ... USACDCSWA
United States Army Combat Developments Command Special Warfare and Civil AffairsGroup [*Fort Belvoir, VA*] ... USACDCSWCAG
United States Army Combat Developments Command Special Warfare Group ... USACDCSWG
United States Army Combat Developments Command Strategic Studies Institute (AABC) ... USACDCSSI
United States Army Combat Developments Command Supply Agency [*Later, USACDCSUA*] [*Fort Lee, VA*] (AABC) ... USACDCSA
United States Army Combat Developments Command Supply Agency [*Formerly, USACDCSA*] (AABC) ... USACDCSUA
United States Army Combat Developments Command Systems Analysis Group [*Fort Belvoir, VA*] (AABC) ... USACDCSAG
United States Army Combat Developments Command Transportation Agency [*Fort Eustis, VA*] (AABC) ... USACDCTA
United States Army Combat Developments Experimentation Command (GFGA) ... USACDEC
United States Army Combat Surveillance Agency (AAG) ... USACS
United States Army Combat Surveillance Agency ... USACSA
United States Army Combat Surveillance and Target Acquisition Training Command ... USACSTATC
United States Army Combat Surveillance School (AABC) ... USACSS
United States Army Combat Systems Test Activity [*Aberdeen Proving Ground, MD*] ... USACSTA
United States Army Combined Arms Center (AABC) ... USACAC

United States Army Combined Arms Combat Developments Agency ..... USACARMSCDA
United States Army Combined Arms Group (SAA) ..... USACAG
United States Army Command and Control Support Agency ..... USACCSA
United States Army Command and Control Support Detachment (AABC) ..... USACCSD
United States Army Command and General Staff College ..... USACGSC
United States Army, Command and General Staff College Library, Fort Leavenworth,KS [*Library symbol Library of Congress*] (LCLS) ..... KFIGS
United States Army Command Information Unit (AABC) ..... USACIU
United States Army Command Management School ..... USACMS
United States Army Command Reconnaissance Activities, Pacific Command ..... USACRAPAC
United States Army Commercial Communications Office ..... USACCO
United States Army Communications Agency ..... USACA
United States Army Communications and Electronics Command ..... USACECOM
United States Army Communications and Electronics Material and Readiness Command ..... USACERCOM
United States Army Communications Command (AABC) ..... USACC
United States Army Communications Command - Alaska (AABC) ..... USACC-A
United States Army Communications Command - Army Materiel Command (AABC) ..... USACC-AMC
United States Army Communications Command Communications Agency - Health Services Command (AABC) ..... USACC COMMAGCY-HSC
United States Army Communications Command Communications Agency - Military Traffic Management Command (AABC) ..... USACC COMMAGCY-MTMC
United States Army Communications Command Communications Agency - United States Army Criminal Investigation Command (AABC) ..... USACC COMMAGCY-USACIDC
United States Army Communications Command Communications Agency - United States Army Intelligence Center ..... USACC COMMAGCY-USAINTC
United States Army Communications Command - Continental United States (AABC) ..... USACC-CONUS
United States Army Communications Command - Europe (AABC) ..... USACC-EUR
United States Army Communications Command - Forces (AABC) ..... USACC-FORCES
United States Army Communications Command - Pacific (AABC) ..... USACC-PAC
United States Army Communications Command Radio and Frequency Management Division ..... USACC-R/FMD
United States Army Communications Command Safeguard Communications Agency ..... USACC-SAFCA
United States Army Communications Command Signal Group (AD) ..... USACC SIG GP (AD)
United States Army Communications Command - South (AABC) ..... USACC-SO
United States Army Communications Command - Thailand (AABC) ..... USACC-T
United States Army Communications Command - Training and Doctrine Command (AABC) ..... USACC-TRADOC
United States Army Communications Management Information Systems Activity ..... USACOMISA
United States Army Communications Research and Development Command ..... USACORADCOM
United States Army Communications Security Logistics Agency (AABC) ..... USACSLA
United States Army Communications Systems Agency (AABC) ..... USACSA
United States Army Communications Zone, Europe ..... USACOMZEUR
United States Army Communications-Electronics Combat Developments Agency [*Fort Huachuca, AZ*] ..... USACECDA
United States Army Communications-Electronics Engineering Installation Agency [*Fort Huachuca, AZ*] (AABC) ..... USACEEIA
United States Army Communications-Electronics Engineering Installation Agency - Western Hemisphere (AABC) ..... USACEEIA-WH
United States Army Communications-Electronics Engineering Installation Agency-Pacific (RDA) ..... USACEEIA-PAC
United States Army Communications-Electronics Installation Battalion (AABC) ..... USACEIBN
United States Army Community and Family Support (AAGC) ..... USACFSC
United States Army Community and Family Support Center (DOMA) ..... USACFSC
United States Army Computer Systems Command [*Fort Belvoir, VA*] ..... USACSC
United States Army Computer Systems Selection and Acquisition Agency (AABC) ..... USACSSAA
United States Army Computer Systems Support and Evaluation Agency (AABC) ..... USACSSEA
United States Army Computer Systems Support and Evaluation Command ..... USACESSEC
United States Army Computer Systems Support and Evaluation Command (IEEE) ..... USACSSC
United States Army Computer Systems Support and Evaluation Command ..... USACSSEC
United States Army Concepts Analysis Agency (AABC) ..... USACAA
United States Army, Concepts Analysis Agency, Bethesda, MD [*OCLC symbol*] (OCLC) ..... AFC
United States Army Congressional Correspondence Agency (AABC) ..... USACCA
United States Army Construction Agency, France ..... USACAF
United States Army Construction Agency, Korea ..... USACAK
United States Army Construction Engineering Research Laboratory, Champaign, IL [*Library symbol Library of Congress*] (LCLS) ..... IChamCE
United States Army Continental Army Command [*CONARC*] [*Superseded by FORSCOM*] ..... USACAC
United States Army Contracting Agency, Europe (AAGC) ..... USACAE
United States Army Contracting Command, Europe (AAGC) ..... USACCE
United States Army Contracting Support Agency (AAGC) ..... USACSA
United States Army Corps (AABC) ..... USAC
United States Army Corps of Engineers [*Merged with General Equipment Command*] ..... USACE
United States Army, Corps of Engineers, Baltimore, MD [*Library symbol Library of Congress*] (LCLS) ..... MdBAE
United States Army, Corps of Engineers, Buffalo District, Buffalo, NY [*OCLC symbol*] (OCLC) ..... AEF
United States Army, Corps of Engineers, Buffalo, NY [*Library symbol*] [*Library of Congress*] (LCLS) ..... NBuACE
United States Army, Corps of Engineers, Chicago, IL [*Library symbol Library of Congress*] (LCLS) ..... ICAE
United States Army, Corps of Engineers, Coastal Engineering Research Center, Fort Belvoir, VA [*OCLC symbol*] (OCLC) ..... AEB
United States Army, Corps of Engineers, Coastal Engineering Research Center, Fort Belvoir, VA [*Library symbol Library of Congress*] (LCLS) ..... DCER
United States Army, Corps of Engineers, Detroit District, Detroit, MI [*OCLC symbol*] (OCLC) ..... AEG
United States Army, Corps of Engineers, District Library St. Louis, St. Louis, MO [*Library symbol Library of Congress*] (LCLS) ..... MoSE
United States Army, Corps of Engineers, Fort Worth District, Fort Worth, TX [*OCLC symbol*] (OCLC) ..... AEW
United States Army, Corps of Engineers, Huntington District, Huntington, WV [*OCLC symbol*] (OCLC) ..... AEH
United States Army, Corps of Engineers, Huntington, WV [*Library symbol Library of Congress*] (LCLS) ..... WvHuE
United States Army, Corps of Engineers, Jacksonville District, Jacksonville, FL [*OCLC symbol*] (OCLC) ..... AEY
United States Army, Corps of Engineers, Los Angeles District, Los Angeles, CA [*OCLC symbol*] (OCLC) ..... AEC
United States Army, Corps of Engineers, Louisville District, Louisville, KY [*OCLC symbol*] (OCLC) ..... AEL
United States Army, Corps of Engineers, Lower Mississippi Valley Division, Vicksburg, MS [*OCLC symbol*] (OCLC) ..... AEM
United States Army, Corps of Engineers, Memphis District, Memphis, TN [*OCLC symbol*] (OCLC) ..... AEP
United States Army, Corps of Engineers, Mobile District, Mobile, AL [*OCLC symbol*] (OCLC) ..... AEI
United States Army Corps of Engineers National Civil Defense Computer Support Agency (AABC) ..... USACENCDCSA
United States Army, Corps of Engineers, New England Division, Waltham, MA [*OCLC symbol*] (OCLC) ..... AEE
United States Army, Corps of Engineers, New Orleans District, New Orleans, LA [*OCLC symbol*] (OCLC) ..... AEN
United States Army, Corps of Engineers, New York District, New York, NY [*OCLC symbol*] (OCLC) ..... AFN
United States Army, Corps of Engineers, North Atlantic Division, New York, NY [*OCLC symbol*] (OCLC) ..... AET
United States Army, Corps of Engineers, North Central Division, Chicago, IL [*OCLC symbol*] (OCLC) ..... AEX
United States Army, Corps of Engineers, North Pacific Division (NOAA) ..... USCE/NPD
United States Army, Corps of Engineers, Office of the Chief of Engineers Library, Washington, DC [*Library symbol Library of Congress*] (LCLS) ..... DACE
United States Army, Corps of Engineers, Office of the Chief of Engineers, Washington, DC [*OCLC symbol*] (OCLC) ..... AED
United States Army, Corps of Engineers, Ohio River District, Cincinnati, OH [*OCLC symbol*] (OCLC) ..... AEO
United States Army, Corps of Engineers, Omaha District, Omaha, NE [*OCLC symbol*] (OCLC) ..... AER
United States Army, Corps of Engineers, Philadelphia District Library, Custom House, Philadelphia, PA [*Library symbol Library of Congress*] (LCLS) ..... PPACE
United States Army, Corps of Engineers, Philadelphia District, Philadelphia, PA [*OCLC symbol*] (OCLC) ..... AFI
United States Army, Corps of Engineers, Portland District, Portland, OR [*OCLC symbol*] (OCLC) ..... AFP
United States Army, Corps of Engineers, Rock Island District, Rock Island, IL [*OCLC symbol*] (OCLC) ..... AEK
United States Army Corps of Engineers, Sacramento, Sacramento, CA [*OCLC symbol*] (OCLC) ..... UCS
United States Army, Corps of Engineers, St. Louis District, St. Louis, MO [*OCLC symbol*] (OCLC) ..... AEU
United States Army, Corps of Engineers, Savannah District, Savannah, GA [*OCLC symbol*] (OCLC) ..... AEV
United States Army, Corps of Engineers, Seattle District, Seattle, WA [*OCLC symbol*] (OCLC) ..... AFS
United States Army, Corps of Engineers, South Atlantic Division, Atlanta, GA [*OCLC symbol*] (OCLC) ..... AEA
United States Army, Corps of Engineers, Southwest Division, Dallas, TX [*OCLC symbol*] (OCLC) ..... AES
United States Army, Corps of Engineers, Tulsa District, Tulsa, OK [*OCLC symbol*] (OCLC) ..... AFT
United States Army, Corps of Engineers, Walla Walla District, Walla Walla, WA [*OCLC symbol*] (OCLC) ..... AFW
U.S. Army Corps of Engineers, Walla Walla District, Walla Walla, WA [*Library symbol*] [*Library of Congress*] (LCLS) ..... WaWAE
United States Army, Corps of Engineers, Waterways Experiment Station, Vicksburg,MS [*OCLC symbol*] (OCLC) ..... AFM
United States Army, Corps of Engineers, Waterways Experiment Station, Vicksburg,MS [*Library symbol Library of Congress*] (LCLS) ..... MsVE
United States Army, Corps of Engineers, Wilmington District, Wilmington, NC [*OCLC symbol*] (OCLC) ..... AFA
United States Army Counterinsurgency Support Office, Okinawa [*Obsolete*] (AABC) ..... USACISO
United States Army Counterintelligence Records Facility (MCD) ..... USACRF
United States Army Courier Service (AABC) ..... USACS
United States Army Courier Station (AABC) ..... USACSTA
United States Army Court of Military Review (AABC) ..... USACMR

United States Army Crime Records Center (AABC) .... USACRC
United States Army Criminal Investigation Command (BARN) .... USACIC
United States Army Criminal Investigation Command [*Formerly, USACIDA*] (AABC) .... USACICD
United States Army Criminal Investigation Division Agency [*Later, USACICD*] (AABC) .... USACIDA
United States Army Criminal Investigation Laboratory (AABC) .... USACIL
United States Army Criminal Investigation Repository .... USACIR
United States Army Data Processing Center .... USADPC
United States Army Data Services and Administrative Systems Command .... USADSC
United States Army Data Support Command .... USADATCOM
United States Army Data Support Command .... USADC
United States Army Davison Aviation Command (GFGA) .... USADAC
United States Army Defense Ammunition Center and School (AABC) .... USADACS
United States Army Dental Clinic .... USADC
United States Army Dependents' Education Group (AABC) .... USADEG
United States Army Depot Command, Japan (AABC) .... USADCJ
United States Army Depot, Japan (AABC) .... USADJ
United States Army Depot Support Command .... USADESCOM
United States Army Deserter Information Point (AABC) .... USADIP
United States Army Diamond Ordnance Fuze Laboratory [*Later, HDL*] .... USADOFL
United States Army Discharge Review Board (AABC) .... USADRB
United States Army Dispensary (AABC) .... USAD
United States Army Drug and Alcohol Operations Agency .... USADAOA
United States Army Electronic Intelligence and Security (AABC) .... USAEIS
United States Army Electronic Proving Ground (IAA) .... USAELCTPG
United States Army Electronic Proving Ground [*Fort Huachuca, AZ*] .... USAEPG
United States Army Electronic Proving Ground .... USAREPG
United States Army Electronic Research and Development Agency .... USAERDA
United States Army Electronic Systems Engineering Installation Agency (GFGA) .... USAESEIA
United States Army Electronics Command [*Obsolete*] .... USAEC
United States Army Electronics Command [*Obsolete*] .... USAECOM
United States Army Electronics Command [*Obsolete*] .... USECOM
United States Army Electronics Command Computation Agency [*Obsolete*] (AABC) .... USAECA
United States Army Electronics Command Financial Management Agency [*Obsolete*] (AABC) .... USAEFMA
United States Army Electronics Command Logistics Research Agency [*Obsolete*] (AABC) .... USAERA
United States Army Electronics Command Patent Agency [*Obsolete*] (AABC) .... USAEPA
United States Army, Electronics Command, Technical Documents Branch, Fort Monmouth, NJ [*Library symbol Library of Congress*] (LCLS) .... NjFmE-TD
United States Army Electronics Laboratories (IAA) .... USAEL
United States Army Electronics Logistics Research Office .... USAELRO
United States Army Electronics Materiel Agency [*Formerly, USASSA*] .... USAEMA
United States Army Electronics Materiel Agency, Fort Huachuca Procurement Office .... USAEMAFHPO
United States Army Electronics Materiel Agency, Fort Monmouth Procurement Office .... USAEMAFMPO
United States Army Electronics Materiel Agency, Plant Inventory Control Office .... USAEMAPICO
United States Army Electronics Materiel Agency, Washington Procurement Office .... USAEMAWPO
United States Army Electronics Materiel Support Agency [*Formerly, USASMSA*] .... USAEMSA
United States Army Electronics Regional Labor Office .... USAERLO
United States Army Electronics Research and Development Activity, White Sands [*New Mexico*] (AABC) .... USAERDAW
United States Army Electronics Research and Development Command (RDA) .... USAERADCOM
United States Army Electronics Research and Development Laboratory [*Formerly, USASRDL*] (MCD) .... USAERDL
United States Army Electronics Research Unit .... USAELRU
United States Army Electronics Support Command (AABC) .... USAESC
United States Army Electronics Technology and Devices Laboratory (Electronics Command) (AABC) .... USAET & DL (ECOM)
United States Army Engineer (AABC) .... USAE
United States Army Engineer Board .... USAEB
United States Army Engineer Center and Fort Belvoir (AABC) .... USAECFB
United States Army Engineer Center Brigade (AABC) .... USAECBDE
United States Army Engineer Center Regiment (AABC) .... USAECR
United States Army Engineer Combat Developments Agency (SAA) .... USAECDA
United States Army Engineer Command, Europe (AABC) .... USAENGCOMEUR
United States Army Engineer Command, Vietnam (Provisional) .... USAECV(P)
United States Army Engineer Construction Agency, Vietnam .... USAECAV
United States Army Engineer District .... USAED
United States Army Engineer District, Nashville, Nashville, TN [*OCLC symbol*] (OCLC) .... AEZ
United States Army Engineer District, Nashville, Nashville, TN [*Library symbol Library of Congress*] (LCLS) .... TNAE
United States Army Engineer Division, Europe (AABC) .... USAEDE
United States Army Engineer Division, Huntsville (AABC) .... USAEDH
United States Army Engineer Division, Lower Mississippi Valley (AABC) .... USAEDLMV
United States Army Engineer Division, Mediterranean (AABC) .... USAEDM
United States Army Engineer Division, Missouri River (AABC) .... USAEDMR
United States Army Engineer Division, New England (AABC) .... USAEDNE
United States Army Engineer Division, North Atlantic (AABC) .... USAEDNA
United States Army Engineer Division, North Central (AABC) .... USAEDNC
United States Army Engineer Division, North Pacific (AABC) .... USAEDNP
United States Army Engineer Division, Ohio River (AABC) .... USAEDOR
United States Army Engineer Division, Ohio River, Technical Library, Cincinnati,OH [*Library symbol Library of Congress*] (LCLS) .... OCAE
United States Army Engineer Division, Pacific Ocean (AABC) .... USAEDPO
United States Army Engineer Division, South Atlantic (AABC) .... USAEDSA
United States Army Engineer Division, South Pacific (AABC) .... USAEDSP
United States Army Engineer Division, Southwestern (AABC) .... USAEDSW
United States Army Engineer, Gulf District .... USAEGD
United States Army Engineer Maintenance Center (SAA) .... USAEMC
United States Army Engineer Mathematical Computation Agency (AABC) .... USAEMCA
United States Army, Engineer Museum, Fort Belvoir, VA [*Library symbol Library of Congress*] (LCLS) .... ViFbEM
United States Army Engineer Power Group (RDA) .... USAENPG
United States Army Engineer Power Group Engineering Division [*Fort Belvoir, VA*] .... USAENPG-ED
United States Army Engineer Procurement Office, Chicago .... USAEPOC
United States Army Engineer Reactor Group (AABC) .... USAERG
United States Army Engineer Research and Development Laboratories (IAA) .... USAERDL
United States Army Engineer Research and Development Laboratory, Technical Documents Center, Fort Belvoir, VA [*Library symbol Library of Congress*] (LCLS) .... DER
United States Army Engineer School .... USAES
United States Army Engineer School, Fort Belvoir, VA [*Library symbol Library of Congress*] (LCLS) .... ViFbE
United States Army Engineer Studies Center [*Fort Belvoir, VA*] .... USAESC
United States Army Engineer Topographic Laboratories [*Fort Belvoir, VA*] .... USAETL
United States Army Engineer Waterways Experiment Station .... USAEWES
United States Army Engineering and Housing Support Center (AAGC) .... EHSC
United States Army Engineers Library, Memphis, TN [*Library symbol Library of Congress*] (LCLS) .... TMUSAE
United States Army Enlisted Records and Evaluation Center (MCD) .... USAEREC
United States Army Enlisted Records and Evaluation Center .... USAREREC
United States Army Enlistment Eligibility Activity (AABC) .... USAEEA
United States Army Environmental Center (RDA) .... USAEC
United States Army Environmental Health Laboratory .... USAEHL
United States Army Environmental Hygiene Agency [*Aberdeen Proving Ground, MD*] (AABC) .... USAEHA
United States Army Environmental Hygiene Agency, Aberdeen Proving Grounds, MD [*OCLC symbol*] (OCLC) .... AHA
United States Army Equipment Authorization Review Activity (AABC) .... USAEARA
United States Army Equipment Authorizations Review Center (AABC) .... USAEARC
United States Army, Europe (MCD) .... USAEUR
United States Army, Europe .... USAREUR
United States Army, Europe, Adjutant General Liaison Office (AABC) .... USAREURAGLO
United States Army, Europe, Adjutant General Support Center (AABC) .... USAEAGSC
United States Army, Europe, Combat Support Training Center (AABC) .... USAREURCSTC
United States Army, Europe, Personnel Management and Replacement Activity (AABC) .... USAEPMARA
United States Army European Ordnance Command .... USAREURORDCOM
United States Army Exhibit Unit (AABC) .... USAEU
United States Army Facilities Engineering Support Agency (AABC) .... USAFESA
United States Army Facilities Engineering Support Agency Engineering Division .... USAFESA-ED
United States Army Facilities Engineering Support Agency Research and TechnologyDivision .... USAFESA-RT
United States Army Facilities Engineering Support Agency Research and TechnologyDivision .... USAFESA-RTD
United States Army Facilities Engineering Support Agency Technology Support Division [*Fort Belvoir, VA*] .... USAFESA-T
United States Army Facilities Engineering Support Agency - Technology Support Division .... USAFESA-TS
United States Army Facilities Engineering Support Agency - Technology Support Division .... USAFESA-TSD
United States Army Field Artillery Board [*Fort Sill, OK*] (AABC) .... USAFABD
United States Army Field Artillery Center and Fort Sill (AABC) .... USAFACFS
United States Army Field Artillery Center and School .... USAFACS
United States Army Field Artillery School [*Fort Sill, OK*] (AABC) .... USAFAS
United States Army Field Artillery School Morris Swett Technical Library Division [*Fort Sill, OK*] .... USAFAS/MSL
United States Army Field Band (AABC) .... USAFB
United States Army Field Forces Library, Fort Monroe, VA [*Library symbol Library of Congress*] (LCLS) .... ViFmUS
United States Army Field Office (RDA) .... USAFO
United States Army Field Operating Cost Agency (AABC) .... USAFOCA
United States Army Field Support Group (AABC) .... USAFSG
United States Army Finance and Accounting Center (AABC) .... USAFAC
United States Army Finance and Comptroller Information Systems Command (AABC) .... USAFINCISCOM
United States Army Finance School (AABC) .... USAFS
United States Army Flight Operations Facility (AABC) .... USAFOF
United States Army Food Service Center (AABC) .... USAFSC
United States Army Forces .... USAF
United States Army Forces, Antilles .... USARFANT
United States Army Forces, Atlantic (AABC) .... USARLANT
United States Army Forces, Central Command .... USARCENT
United States Army Forces, European Theater of Operations [*World War II*] .... USAFETO

United States Army Forces, Far East [*World War II*] .... USAFFE
United States Army Forces in Australia .... USAFIA
United States Army Forces in Central Africa [*World War II*] .... USAFICA
United States Army Forces in Central Canada [*World War II*] .... USAFCC
United States Army Forces in Central Pacific Area .... USAFICPA
United States Army Forces in Eastern Canada [*World War II*] .... USAFEC
United States Army Forces in Korea .... USAFIK
United States Army Forces in Liberia [*World War II*] .... USAFIL
United States Army Forces in New Zealand .... USAFINZ
United States Army Forces in South America .... USAFSA
United States Army Forces in the British Isles .... USAFBI
United States Army Forces in the Philippines (Northern Luzon) [*World War II*] .... USAFIP(NL)
United States Army Forces in the South Pacific Area .... USAFISPA
United States Army Forces (Korea), Eighth United States Army .... USAFEUSA
United States Army Forces, Mediterranean Theater of Operations [*World War II*] .... USAFMTO
United States Army Forces, Middle Pacific [*See AFMIDPAC*] [*World War II*] .... USAFMIDPAC
United States Army Forces, Pacific Ocean Areas [*World War II*] .... USAFPOA
United States Army Forces, Readiness Command .... USARRED
United States Army Forces, South Atlantic [*World War II*] .... USAFSA
United States Army Forces, Southern Command .... USARSO
United States Army Forces, Southern Command .... USARSOUTHCOM
United States Army Forces, Southern Command - Puerto Rico (AABC) .... USARSO-PR
United States Army Forces Strike Command (AABC) .... USARSTRIKE
United States Army Forces, Taiwan .... USARFT
United States Army, Foreign Science and Technical Center, Charlottesville, VA [*Library symbol Library of Congress*] (LCLS) .... ViCAF
United States Army Foreign Science and Technology Center (AABC) .... USAFSTC
United States Army FORSCOM, Fort Bragg Command Reference Center and Main Post, Fort Bragg, NC [*OCLC symbol*] (OCLC) .... APB
United States Army, Fort Campbell Post Library (R. F. Sink Memorial Library), Fort Campbell, KY [*Library symbol Library of Congress*] (LCLS) .... KyFc
United States Army, Fort George G. Meade Post Recreation Services Library, Fort George G. Meade, MD [*Library symbol Library of Congress*] (LCLS) .... MdFmA
United States Army, Fort Hamilton Post Library, Fort Hamilton, Brooklyn, NY [*Library symbol Library of Congress*] (LCLS) .... NBUSA
United States Army, Fort Irwin Post Library, Barstow, CA [*Library symbol Library of Congress*] (LCLS) .... CBarUSA
United States Army, Fort Lewis Library System, Grandstaff Library, Fort Lewis, WA [*Library symbol Library of Congress*] (LCLS) .... WaFtl
United States Army, Fort McPherson Post Library, Fort McPherson, GA [*Library symbol Library of Congress*] (LCLS) .... GFmA
United States Army, Fort Meyer Post Library, Fort Meyer, VA [*Library symbol Library of Congress*] (LCLS) .... ViFmyA
United States Army, Fort Ord Library System, Fort Ord, CA [*Library symbol Library of Congress*] (LCLS) .... CFoA
United States Army, Fort Stewart/Hunter AAF Library, Fort Stewart, GA [*Library symbol Library of Congress*] (LCLS) .... GFsH
United States Army, Frankford Arsenal Library, Philadelphia, PA [*Library symbol Library of Congress*] (LCLS) .... PPFA
United States Army Frequency Engineering Office (MCD) .... USARFEO
United States Army Frequency Management Directorate (MCD) .... USAFMD
United States Army Garrison (AABC) .... USAG
United States Army General Equipment Test Activity (AABC) .... USAGETA
United States Army [*Madigan*] **General Hospital, Tacoma, WA** [*Library symbol Library of Congress*] (LCLS) .... WaTAH
United States Army General Materiel and Parts Center (AABC) .... USAGMPC
United States Army General Materiel and Petroleum Activity .... USAGMPA
United States Army General Supplies Commodity Center .... USAGSC
United States Army Geodesy Intelligence and Mapping Research and Development Agency (AABC) .... USAGIMRADA
United States Army Ground Forces (MUGU) .... USAGF
United States Army Group, American Mission for Aid to Greece .... USAGG
United States Army, Hawaii .... USARHAW
United States Army Headquarters Area Command .... USAHAC
United States Army Health Clinic (AABC) .... USAHC
United States Army Health Service Command .... USAHSC
United States Army Health Services Data Systems Agency (AABC) .... USAHSDSA
United States Army History Institute (PDAA) .... USAHI
United States Army Homes [*Prefabricated houses, shipped overseas*] .... USAHOME
United States Army Hometown News Center (AABC) .... USAHTN
United States Army Hospital .... USAH
United States Army Hospital, Fort Leavenworth, KS [*Library symbol Library of Congress*] (LCLS) .... KFIAH
United States Army Hospital Ship .... USAHS
United States Army Human Engineering Laboratories (AABC) .... USAHEL
United States Army Imagery Interpretation Agency (AABC) .... USAIIA
United States Army Imagery Interpretation Center (AABC) .... USAIIC
United States Army in Greece .... USAG
United States Army Industrial and Personnel Security Group .... USAIPSG
United States Army Infantry Board .... USAIB
United States Army Infantry Center [*Fort Benning, GA*] .... USAIC
United States Army Infantry Human Research Unit [*Ft. Benning, GA*] (AABC) .... USAINFHRU
United States Army Infantry School .... USAIS
United States Army, Infantry School, Fort Benning, GA [*Library symbol Library of Congress*] (LCLS) .... GFbIS
United States Army Information and Data Systems Command .... USAIDSC
United States Army Information and Data Systems Command (AABC) .... USAIDSCOM
United States Army Information School [*Fort Slocum, New Rochelle, NY*] .... USARIS
United States Army, Information School, Fort Slocum, New Rochelle, NY [*Library symbol Library of Congress*] (LCLS) .... NNerAIS
United States Army Information Systems Command [*Fort Huachuca, AZ*] .... USAISC
United States Army Information Systems Command - 5th Signal Command (GFGA) .... USAISC-5th Sig Cmd
United States Army Information Systems Command - 7th Signal Command (GFGA) .... USAISC-7th Sig Cmd
United States Army Information Systems Command - Alaska (GFGA) .... USAISC-A
United States Army Information Systems Command - Army Materiel Command (GFGA) .... USAISC-AMC
United States Army Information Systems Command - Forces Command (GFGA) .... USAISC-FORSCOM
United States Army Information Systems Command - Health Services Command (GFGA) .... USAISC-HSC
United States Army Information Systems Command - Intelligence and Security Command (GFGA) .... USAISC-INSCOM
United States Army Information Systems Command - Military Traffic Management Command (GFGA) .... USAISC-MTMC
United States Army Information Systems Command - South (GFGA) .... USAISC-SO
United States Army Information Systems Command - Training and Doctrine Command (GFGA) .... USAISC-TRADOC
United States Army Information Systems Command - Western Command (GFGA) .... USAISC-WESTCOM
United States Army Information Systems Engineering Support Activity [*Fort Huachuca, AZ*] .... USAISESA
United States Army Information Systems Management Activity (GFGA) .... USAISMA
United States Army Information Systems Selection and Acquisition Activity (GFGA) .... USAISSAA
United States Army Information Systems Software Support Command (GFGA) .... USAISSSC
United States Army Institute for Military Assistance [*Fort Bragg, NC*] (AABC) .... USAIMA
United States Army, Institute for Military Assistance, Marquat Memorial Library,Fort Bragg, NC [*Library symbol Library of Congress*] (LCLS) .... NcFbIM
United States Army Institute for Military Systems (AABC) .... USAIMS
United States Army Institute of Administration (AABC) .... USAIA
United States Army Institute of Advanced Studies (SAA) .... USAIAS
United States Army Institute of Dental Research (AABC) .... USAIDR
United States Army Institute of Surgical Research [*Ft. Sam Houston, TX*] (AABC) .... USAISR
United States Army Intelligence Agency (GFGA) .... USAIA
United States Army Intelligence Agency (AABC) .... USAINTA
United States Army Intelligence and Security Board (MCD) .... USAINSBD
United States Army Intelligence and Security Command .... USAINSCOM
United States Army Intelligence and Threat Analysis Center (AABC) .... USAITAC
United States Army Intelligence Board .... USAINTB
United States Army Intelligence Center (IAA) .... USAIC
United States Army Intelligence Center .... USAINTC
United States Army Intelligence Center and School [*Fort Huachuca, AZ*] (AABC) .... USAICS
United States Army Intelligence Center and School Library, Fort Huachuca, AZ [*OCLC symbol*] (OCLC) .... TRZ
United States Army Intelligence Combat Developments (SAA) .... USAINTCDA
United States Army Intelligence Command .... USAIC
United States Army Intelligence Corps Agency .... USAINTCA
United States Army Intelligence Materiel Developments Agency (AABC) .... USAINTELMDA
United States Army Intelligence School .... USAINTS
United States Army Intelligence School, Fort Devens (GFGA) .... USAISD
United States Army Intelligence Security Board .... USAINSB
United States Army Intelligence Threat Analysis Detachment .... USAITAD
United States Army Intelligence Threat Analysis Group .... USAITAG
United States Army Intelligence Threats and Forecasts Group (AABC) .... USAITFG
United States Army Intelligence Training Center .... USAITC
United States Army Interagency Communications Agency (AABC) .... USAICA
United States Army International Logistics Center .... USAILC
United States Army International Logistics Command (AABC) .... USAILCOM
United States Army International Logistics Group (AABC) .... USAILG
United States Army Inventory Management Center (AABC) .... USAIMC
United States Army Inventory Research Office [*Philadelphia, PA*] .... USAIRO
United States Army Investigative Records Repository (AABC) .... USAIRR
United States Army Ionizing Radiation Center .... USAIRC
United States Army, Japan .... USARJ
United States Army Jefferson Proving Ground (PDAA) .... USAJPG
United States Army John Fitzgerald Kennedy Center for Military Assistance (AABC) .... USAJFKCENMA
United States Army John Fitzgerald Kennedy Center for Special Warfare [*Airborne*] (AABC) .... USAJFKCENSPWAR
United States Army Joint Household Goods Shipping Office of the Armed Forces .... USAJHGSOWA
United States Army Joint Support Command (AABC) .... USAJSC
United States Army, Korea (MCD) .... USARK
United States Army Korea Support Command (AABC) .... USAKORSCOM
United States Army Language School .... USALS
United States Army Leadership Human Research Unit [*Presidio of Monterey, CA*] (AABC) .... USALDRHRU
United States Army Legal Services Agency (AABC) .... USALSA
United States Army Liaison Group, Project Michigan .... USALGPM

United States Army Liaison Officer .... USARMLO
United States Army Library, Pentagon Building, Arlington, VA [*Library symbol Library of Congress*] (LCLS) .... DAL
United States Army Library, Washington, DC [*OCLC symbol*] (OCLC) .... ARL
United States Army Limited War Laboratory (AABC) .... USALWL
United States Army Logistic Control Activity (AABC) .... USALCA
United States Army Logistics Center .... USALC
United States Army Logistics Center (AABC) .... USALOGC
United States Army Logistics Center .... USALOGCTR
United States Army Logistics Center, Japan (AABC) .... USALCJ
United States Army Logistics Data Center .... USALDC
United States Army Logistics Depot, Japan .... USALDJ
United States Army Logistics Doctrine, Systems and Readiness Agency [*New Cumberland Army Depot, Harrisburg, PA*] (AABC) .... USALDSRA
United States Army Logistics Evaluation Agency (AABC) .... USALEA
United States Army Logistics Management Center [*Fort Lee, VA*] .... USALMC
United States Army Logistics Management Center, Fort Lee, VA [*Library symbol Library of Congress*] (LCLS) .... ViFIL
United States Army Los Angeles Procurement Agency (AABC) .... USALAPA
United States Army Maintenance Board (AABC) .... USAMB
United States Army Maintenance Data Processing Center .... USAMDPC
United States Army Maintenance Management Center (AABC) .... USAMMC
United States Army Maintenance Plant .... USAMP
United States Army Major Item Data Agency (AABC) .... USAMIDA
United States Army Management Engineering Training Activity [*Rock Island, IL*] (AABC) .... USAMETA
United States Army Management School .... USAMS
United States Army Management Systems Support Agency .... USAMSSA
United States Army Manpower Resources Research and Development Center (AABC) .... USAMANRRDC
United States Army Marksmanship Training Unit .... USAMTU
United States Army Marksmanship Unit [*Fort Benning, GA*] .... USAMU
United States Army Material and Mechanics Research Center, Watertown, MA [*OCLC symbol*] (OCLC) .... AMM
United States Army Material Command Headquarters, Technical Library, Alexandria,VA [*Library symbol Library of Congress*] (LCLS) .... ViAIA
United States Army Material Readiness Support Activity .... USAMRSA
United States Army Materiel Command [*Alexandria, VA*] .... USAMC
United States Army Materiel Command, Alexandria, VA [*OCLC symbol*] (OCLC) .... AXM
United States Army Materiel Command Automated Logistics Management Systems Agency (AABC) .... USAMCALMSA
United States Army Materiel Command Field Office (RDA) .... USAMCFO
United States Army Materiel Command Field Safety Agency (AABC) .... USAMCFSA
United States Army Materiel Command Installations and Service Agency (AABC) .... USAMCI & SA
United States Army Materiel Command Intern Training Center .... USAMC-ITC
United States Army Materiel Command Inventory Research Office .... USAMC-IRO
United States Army Materiel Command Logistic Systems Support Agency (AABC) .... USAMCLSSA
United States Army Materiel Command Logistics Data Center .... USAMCLDC
United States Army Materiel Command Surety Field Office .... USAMCSFO
United States Army Materiel Management Agency, Europe .... USAMMAE
United States Army Materiel Systems Analysis Agency .... USAMSAA
United States Army Mechanical and Technical Training Center [*Also called MECHTECH*] .... USAM & TTC
United States Army Medical Bioengineering Research and Development Laboratory [*Fort Detrick, MD*] [*Later, USABRDL*] (AABC) .... USAMBRDL
United States Army Medical Biomechanical Research Laboratory [*Walter Reed Army Medical Center*] (AABC) .... USAMBRL
United States Army Medical Center, Fort Gordon (AABC) .... USAMCFG
United States Army Medical Command, Europe (AABC) .... USAMEDCOMEUR
United States Army Medical Corps .... USAMC
United States Army Medical Department Board (RDA) .... USAMEDDBD
United States Army, Medical Department, Veterinary School, Chicago, IL [*Library symbol Library of Congress*] (LCLS) .... ICAVS
United States Army Medical Depot Activity, Ryukyu Islands (AABC) .... USAMDAR
United States Army Medical Environmental Engineering Research Unit .... USAMEERU
United States Army Medical Equipment and Optical School (AABC) ..... USAMEOS
United States Army Medical Equipment Research and Development Laboratory (AABC) .... USAMERDL
United States Army Medical Field Service School (AABC) .... USAMFSS
United States Army Medical Intelligence and Information Agency (AABC) .... USAMIIA
United States Army Medical Intelligence and Information Agency, Fort Detrick, MD [*Library symbol Library of Congress*] (LCLS) .... MdFdM
United States Army Medical Laboratory .... USAMEDLAB
United States Army Medical Laboratory (AABC) .... USAML
United States Army, Medical Library, Fort Gordon, GA [*Library symbol Library of Congress*] (LCLS) .... GFgML
United States Army, Medical Library, Sandia Base, Albuquerque, NM [*Library symbol Library of Congress*] (LCLS) .... NmAAM
United States Army Medical Materiel Agency (AABC) .... USAMMA
United States Army Medical Materiel Agency, Pacific (AABC) .... USAMMAPAC
United States Army Medical Optical and Maintenance Activity .... USAMOAMA
United States Army Medical Optical and Maintenance Agency (AABC) .... USAMOMA
United States Army Medical Research Acquisition Agency .... USAMRAA
United States Army Medical Research and Development Command [*Fort Detrick, MD*] .... USAMRDC
United States Army Medical Research and Nutrition (MCD) .... USAMRN
United States Army Medical Research and Nutrition Laboratory [*Denver, CO*] (AABC) .... USAMRNL
United States Army Medical Research Institute for Chemical Defense [*Aberdeen Proving Ground, MD*] (RDA) .... USAMRICD
United States Army Medical Research Institute of Infectious Diseases [*Fort Detrick, MD*] (AABC) .... USAMRIID
United States Army Medical Research Laboratory [*Fort Knox, KY*] (AABC) .... USAMRL
United States Army Medical Research Unit [*Malaysia, Panama*] (AABC) .... USAMRU
United States Army Medical Research Unit - Europe (INF) .... USAMRU-E
United States Army Medical Service .... USAMEDS
United States Army Medical Service Meat and Dairy Hygiene School .... USAMSMADHS
United States Army Medical Service Veterinary School (AABC) .... USAMEDSVS
United States Army Medical Training Center [*Ft. Sam Houston, TX*] (AABC) .... USAMEDTC
United States Army Medical Unit [*Frederick, MD*] .... USAMU
United States Army Medical Unit, Fort Detrick [*Maryland*] (AABC) .... USAMUFD
United States Army Memorial Affairs Agency (AABC) .... USAMAA
United States Army Metrology and Calibration Center (AABC) .... USAMCC
United States Army Middle East Air Forces [*World War II*] .... USAMEAF
United States Army Middle East Regional Communications Command .... USAMERCC
United States Army Military Academy Preparatory School .... USAMAPS
United States Army Military Assistance Program Logistics Agency .... USAMAPLA
United States Army Military District of Washington (BARN) .... USAMDW
United States Army Military Government in Korea .... USAMGIK
United States Army Military History Institute, Carlisle Barracks, PA [*OCLC symbol*] (OCLC) .... MHR
United States Army Military History Research Collection (AABC) .... USAMHRC
United States Army, Military History Research Collection, Carlisle Barracks, PA [*Library symbol Library of Congress*] (LCLS) .... PCarlMH
United States Army Military Mail Terminal .... USAMMT
United States Army Military Personnel and Transportation Assistance Office (AABC) .... USAMPTAO
United States Army Military Police and Chemical Schools/Training Center and FortMcClellan .... USAMP & CS/TCTFM
United States Army Military Police School (AABC) .... USAMPS
United States Army, Military Police School, Fort Gordon, GA [*Library symbol Library of Congress*] (LCLS) .... GFgMP
United States Army, Military Police School, Fort McClellan, AL [*Library symbol Library of Congress*] (LCLS) .... AFmMP
United States Army Mine Planter .... USAMP
United States Army Missile and Munitions Center School (AABC) .... USAMMCS
United States Army Missile Command [*Obsolete*] .... USAMC
United States Army Missile Command [*Obsolete*] (AABC) .... USAMICOM
United States Army Missile Detachment (AABC) .... USAMD
United States Army Mission .... USARMIS
United States Army Mobility Command [*Later, Troop Support Command*] .... USAMC
United States Army Mobility Command [*Later, Troop Support Command*] .... USAMOCOM
United States Army Mobility Equipment Command [*Obsolete*] .... USAMEC
United States Army Mobility Equipment Command [*Obsolete*] (AABC) .... USAMECOM
United States Army Mobility Equipment Research and Development Center (AABC) .... USAMERDC
United States Army, Morris Swett Library, Fort Sill, OK [*OCLC symbol*] (OCLC) .... OUO
United States Army Mothers, National [*Defunct*] (EA) .... USAMN
United States Army Mothers Organization, National (EA) .... USAM
United States Army Munitions Command [*Later, Armaments Command*] .... USAMC
United States Army Munitions Command [*Later, Armaments Command*] .... USAMUCOM
United States Army Natick Laboratories .... USA-NLABS
United States Army National Guard .... USANG
United States Army National Guard .... USARNG
United States Army, Navy, and Air Force Bandsmen's Association [*Defunct*] .... USANAFBA
United States Army Northern Ireland Base Command [*World War II*] ..... USANIBC
United States Army Northern Ireland Force [*World War II*] .... USANIF
United States Army Northern Warfare Training Center (AABC) .... USANWTC
United States Army Nuclear Agency (AABC) .... USANA
United States Army Nuclear and Chemical Surety Group [*Formerly, USANWSG*] (AABC) .... USANCSG
United States Army Nuclear Cratering Group (AABC) .... USANCG
United States Army Nuclear Defense Laboratory (AABC) .... USANDL
United States Army Nuclear Weapon Coordination Group .... USANWCG
United States Army Nuclear Weapon Surety Group [*Later, USANCSG*] .... USANWSG
United States Army Nurse Corps .... USANC
United States Army, Nye Library, Fort Sill, OK [*OCLC symbol*] (OCLC) .... OUQ
United States Army Officer Evaluation Center .... USAOEC
United States Army Operational Test and Evaluation Agency .... USAOTEA
United States Army Ordnance Ammunition Command [*Merged with Munitions Command, which later became Armaments Command*] .... USAOAC
United States Army, Ordnance Board, Aberdeen Proving Ground, Aberdeen, MD [*Library symbol Library of Congress*] (LCLS) .... MdApgOB
United States Army Ordnance Center and School [*Later, United States Army Ordnance and Chemical Center and School*] (AABC) .... USAOC & S
United States Army Ordnance Corps .... USAORDCORPS
United States Army Ordnance Corps Ballistic Research Laboratory .... USAOCBRL

United States Army Ordnance Corps Coating and Chemical Laboratory .... USAOCCCL

United States Army Ordnance Corps Development and Proof Services .... USAOCDPS

United States Army Ordnance District .... USAOD

United States Army Ordnance Guided Missile School .... USAOGMS

United States Army Ordnance Missile and Munitions Center and School .... USAOMMCS

United States Army Ordnance Missile Command [Later, Missile Command] .... USAOMC

United States Army Ordnance Missile Support Agency (AAG) .... USAOMSA

United States Army Ordnance Munitions and Missile Center and School .... USAORDMMCS

United States Army Ordnance Rocket Research Facility .... USAORRF

United States Army, Ordnance School, Aberdeen Proving Ground, Aberdeen, MD [Library symbol Library of Congress] (LCLS) .... MdApgO

United States Army Ordnance Special Weapons-Ammunition Command .... USAOSWAC

United States Army Ordnance Weapons Command [Merged with Missile Command] .... USAOWC

United States Army Ordnance-Chemical Center and School .... USAOCCS

United States Army Oversea Replacement Station .... USAOSREPLSTA

United States Army Oversea Research Program .... USAORP

United States Army Overseas Supply Agency (CINC) .... USAOSA

United States Army Overseas Supply Agency, New Orleans .... USAOSANO

United States Army Overseas Supply Agency, New York .... USAOSANY

United States Army Overseas Supply Agency, San Francisco .... USAOSASF

United States Army, Pacific .... USARPAC

United States Army Pacific Intelligence School (AABC) .... USARPACINTS

United States Army Parachute Team .... USAPT

United States Army Participation Group (AABC) .... USAPG

United States Army Personnel and Administration Combat Developments Activity (AABC) .... USAPACDA

United States Army Personnel Center .... USAPERSCEN

United States Army Personnel Coordination Center .... USAPCC

United States Army Personnel Data Support Center (AABC) .... USAPDSC

United States Army Personnel Information Activity (AABC) .... USAPIA

United States Army Personnel Research Office .... USAPRO

United States Army Personnel Security Group (AABC) .... USAPSG

United States Army Petroleum Center .... USAPC

United States Army Petroleum Distribution Command, Europe (AABC) .... USAPDCE

United States Army Petroleum Distribution System, Korea (AABC) .... USAPDSK

United States Army Photographic Agency [Obsolete] .... USAPA

United States Army Photointerpretation Center .... USAPIC

United States Army Physical Disability Agency .... USAPDA

United States Army Physical Evaluation Board (AABC) .... USAPEB

United States Army Physical Fitness School [Army] (INF) .... USAPFS

United States Army Physical Review Council (AABC) .... USAPRC

United States Army Pictorial Center .... USAPC

United States Army Polar Research and Development Center .... USAPRDC

United States Army Port Operations, Pusan (AABC) .... USAPOP

United States Army, Post Library, Aberdeen Proving Ground, Aberdeen, MD [Library symbol Library of Congress] (LCLS) .... MdApgP

United States Army, Post Library, Fort Benjamin Harrison, IN [Library symbol] [Library of Congress] (LCLS) .... InFtbh

United States Army, Post Library, Fort Benjamin Harrison, IN [Library symbol Library of Congress] (LCLS) .... InFtbhP

United States Army, Post Library, Vint Hill Farms Station, Warrenton, VA [Library symbol Library of Congress] (LCLS) .... ViWarUS

United States Army, Presidio of Monterey Library, Monterey, CA [Library symbol Library of Congress] (LCLS) .... CFoA-M

United States Army Primary Helicopter Center (AABC) .... USAPHC

United States Army Primary Helicopter School .... USAPHS

United States Army Procurement Agency, Europe (AABC) .... USAPAE

United States Army Procurement Agency, Vietnam .... USAPAV

United States Army Productions Equipment Agency .... USAPEQUA

United States Army Property Disposal Center [Merged with Defense Logistics Services Center] .... USAPDC

United States Army Publications Agency (GFGA) .... USARPA

United States Army Publications and Printing Agency .... USAPPA

United States Army Publications and Training Aids Center, Europe .... USAPATACE

United States Army Quartermaster Center and Fort Lee (AABC) .... USAQMCENFL

United States Army Quartermaster Center and School .... USAQMCS

United States Army Quartermaster Combat Developments Agency (SAA) .... USAQMCDA

United States Army Quartermaster Corps [Merged with Supply and Maintenance Command] .... USAQMC

United States Army Quartermaster School .... USAQMS

United States Army Quartermaster Training Command .... USAQMTC

United States Army Radio Propagation Agency (AABC) .... USARPA

United States Army Readiness Regions (AABC) .... USARR

United States Army Reception Station .... USARECSTA

United States Army Records Center .... USARCEN

United States Army, Recreational Services Post Library, Fort Greeley, AK [Library symbol Library of Congress] (LCLS) .... AkFg

United States Army, Recreational Services Post Library, Fort Richardson, AK [Library symbol Library of Congress] (LCLS) .... AkFr

United States Army, Recreational Services Post Library, Fort Wainwright, AK [Library symbol Library of Congress] (LCLS) .... AkFw

United States Army Recruiter Badge [Military decoration] (GFGA) .... RECBAD

United States Army Recruiter Badge [Military decoration] (AABC) .... USARctBad

United States Army Recruiting Command (AABC) .... USAREC

United States Army Regional Dental Activity (AABC) .... USARDA

United States Army Research and Development Laboratories .... USARDL

United States Army Research and Development Operational Research Advisory Group (AABC) .... USARDORAG

United States Army Research and Development School (AAG) .... USARADSCH

United States Army Research and Technical Labs (MCD) .... USARTL

United States Army Research, Development, and Acquisition Information Systems Agency (AABC) .... USARDAISA

United States Army Research, Development, and Standardization Group - Germany (RDA) .... USARDSG-GE

United States Army Research Institute for the Behavioral and Social Sciences (AABC) .... USARIBSS

United States Army Research Institute of Environmental Medicine [Natick, MA] (AABC) .... USARIEM

United States Army Research Office .... USARO

United States Army Research Office (Durham) .... USAROD

United States Army Research Program (IAA) .... USARP

United States Army Reserve .... USAR

United States Army Reserve Affairs, Europe (AABC) .... USARAE

United States Army Reserve Center (AABC) .... USARC

United States Army Reserve Components Personnel Center (AABC) .... USARCPC

United States Army Reserve Forces .... USARF

United States Army Reserve Losses Tally .... USARLT

United States Army Reserve Officer Training Corps .... USAROTC

United States Army Reserve Officers' Training Corps Region (AABC) .... USAROTCR

United States Army Reserve Personnel Center .... USARPERCEN

United States Army Reserve Report Activity Control List .... USARRACL

United States Army Reserve Troop List by State .... USARTLS

United States Army Reserve Unit Commander Unit .... USARUCU

United States Army Retraining Brigade (AABC) .... USARB

United States Army Returnee - Reassignment Station .... USARET-RSGSTA

United States Army Rock Island Arsenal .... USARIA

United States Army, Ryukyu Islands .... USARYIS

United States Army Safeguard Communications Agency (RDA) .... USASCA

United States Army Safeguard Logistics Command .... USASAFLOG

United States Army Safeguard System Command (AABC) .... USASAFSCOM

United States Army Safeguard Systems Office .... USARSSO

United States Army Safety Center .... USASC

United States Army Satellite Communications Agency (AABC) .... USASATCOMA

United States Army Satellite Communications Agency (IAA) .... USASCA

United States Army School, Europe [Obsolete] (AABC) .... USASCHEUR

United States Army School, Europe [Obsolete] .... USASEUR

United States Army School of the Americas [Fort Benning, AR] (INF) .... USARSA

United States Army Security Agency .... USASA

United States Army Security Agency Combat Development Activity (AABC) .... USASACDA

United States Army Security Agency Command Data Systems Activity (AABC) .... USASACDSA

United States Army Security Agency, Europe (AABC) .... USASAE

United States Army Security Agency Field Station .... USASAFS

United States Army Security Agency, Pacific (AABC) .... USASAPAC

United States Army Security Agency Signal Security Activity (AABC) .... USASASSA

United States Army Security Agency Systems Activity (AABC) .... USASASA

United States Army Security Agency Test and Evaluation Center (AABC) .... USASATEC

United States Army Security Agency Training Center and School (AABC) .... USASATC & S

United States Army Security Assistance Agency, Latin America (AABC) .... USASAALA

United States Army Security Assistance Center .... USASAC

United States Army Sergeant Major Academy (AABC) .... USASMA

United States Army Service Center for the Armed Forces (AABC) .... USASCAF

United States Army Services of Supply .... USASOS

United States Army Signal Air Defense Engineering Agency [Later, USAADEA] .... USASADEA

United States Army Signal Aviation Test Support Activity .... USASATSA

United States Army Signal Avionics Field Office [Later, USAAFO] .... USASAFO

United States Army Signal Center and Fort Gordon (AABC) .... USASC & FG

United States Army Signal Center and School .... USASCS

United States Army Signal Communications Security Agency .... USASCSA

United States Army Signal Corps [Merged with Communications and Electronics Command] .... USASC

United States Army Signal Corps [Merged with Communications and Electronics Command] .... USASIGC

United States Army Signal Corps School (IAA) .... USASCS

United States Army Signal Engineering Agency .... USASEA

United States Army Signal Engineering Laboratory (IAA) .... USASEL

United States Army Signal Engineering Laboratory (IAA) .... USASIGENGLAB

United States Army Signal Equipment Support Agency (MCD) .... USASESA

United States Army Signal Materiel Support Agency [Later, USAEMSA] .... USASIMSA

United States Army Signal Materiel Support Agency [Later, USAEMSA] .... USASMSA

United States Army Signal Missile Support Agency (IAA) .... USASMSA

United States Army Signal Missile Support Group .... USASMSG

United States Army Signal Research and Development Laboratory [Later, USAERDL] .... USASRDL

United States Army Signal Research Unit (IAA) .... USASIGRSCHUNIT

United States Army Signal School (AABC) .... USASIGS

United States Army Signal School and Center .... USASSC

United States Army, Signal School, Fort Monmouth, NJ [Library symbol Library of Congress] (LCLS) .... NjFmS

United States Army Signal Supply Agency [Later, USAEC] .... USASSA

United States Army Signal Supply Agency, Fort Monmouth Procurement Office ... USASSAFMPO
United States Army Signal Supply Agency, Midwestern Regional Office ... USASSAMRO
United States Army Signal Supply Agency, United States Army Electronic Proving Ground Procurement Office ... USASSAUSAEPGPO
United States Army Signal Supply Agency, Washington Procurement Office ... USASSAWPO
United States Army Signal Supply Agency, Western Regional Office ... USASSAWRO
United States Army Signal Training Center (IAA) ... USASIGTC
United States Army Signal Training Center [*Fort Gordon, GA*] ... USASTC
United States Army Signal Training Center (IAA) ... USASTCEN
United States Army Signal Training Command and Fort Monmouth ... USASTCFM
United States Army Signals Warfare Laboratory ... USASWL
United States Army, Sixth Army Command, Letterman General Hospital Libraries, San Francisco, CA [*Library symbol Library of Congress*] (LCLS) ... CSfUSA-L
United States Army, Sixth Army Command, Reference Center Library and Library Depot, San Francisco, CA [*Library symbol Library of Congress*] (LCLS) ... CSfUSA
United States Army Small Arms Systems Agency ... USASASA
United States Army Soldier Support Center and Fort Benjamin Harrison (AABC) ... USASSC & FBH
United States Army Southeastern Signal School (AABC) ... USASESS
United States Army, Southeastern Signal School, Fort Gordon, GA [*Library symbol Library of Congress*] (LCLS) ... GFgSS
United States Army Southern European Task Force ... USASETAF
United States Army Southern European Task Force ... USASTAF
United States Army Space and Strategic Defense Command ... USASSDC
United States Army Space Command ... USARSPACE
United States Army Special Forces (CINC) ... USASF
United States Army Special Forces Group ... USASFG
United States Army Special Forces Group, Vietnam ... USASFGV
United States Army Special Forces, Vietnam [*Obsolete*] ... USASFV
United States Army Special Security Detachment ... USASSD
United States Army Special Security Group (AABC) ... USASSG
United States Army Special Services Agency, Europe (AABC) ... USASPSAE
United States Army, Special Services Library, Fort Gordon, GA [*Library symbol Library of Congress*] (LCLS) ... GFgS
United States Army, Special Services Library System, Fort Bragg, NC [*Library symbol Library of Congress*] (LCLS) ... NcFb
United States Army, Special Services Post Library, Fort Dix, NJ [*Library symbol Library of Congress*] (LCLS) ... NjFdA
United States Army Special Warfare Combat Developments Agency (SAA) ... USASWCDA
United States Army Special Warfare School ... USASWS
United States Army Standardization Group ... USARSG
United States Army Standardization Group (Australia) ... USASG(Aus)
United States Army Standardization Group (Canada) (AABC) ... USASG(Ca)
United States Army Standardization Group (United Kingdom) (AABC) ... USASG(UK)
United States Army Strategic Air Forces in the Pacific ... USASTAF
United States Army Strategic Communications Command ... USASCC
United States Army Strategic Communications Command [*Later, USACC*] (AABC) ... USASTRATCOM
United States Army Strategic Communications Command - Alaska (AABC) ... USASTRATCOM-A
United States Army Strategic Communications Command - Continental United States (AABC) ... USASTRATCOM-CONUS
United States Army Strategic Communications Command - Europe (AABC) ... USASTRATCOM-EUR
United States Army Strategic Communications Command - Pacific (AABC) ... USASTRATCOM-PAC
United States Army Strategic Communications Command Signal Group - Thailand (AABC) ... USASTRATCOM-SIGGP-T
United States Army Strategic Communications Command - South (AABC) ... USASTRATCOM-SO
United States Army Strategic Communications Command - Vietnam [*Obsolete*] (AABC) ... USASTRATCOM-V
United States Army Strategic Defense Command ... USASDC
United States Army Strategic Intelligence School ... USASIS
United States Army Student Detachment (AABC) ... USASD
United States Army Subsistence Center ... USASC
United States Army Supply and Maintenance Command ... USASMC
United States Army Supply and Maintenance Command (MUGU) ... USASMCOM
United States Army Support Activity, Philadelphia (AABC) ... USASPTAP
United States Army Support Center ... USASC
United States Army Support Center (AABC) ... USASPTC
United States Army Support Center, Memphis (AABC) ... USASPTCM
United States Army Support Center, Philadelphia (AABC) ... USASPTCP
United States Army Support Center, Richmond (AABC) ... USASCR
United States Army Support Center, Richmond (AABC) ... USASPTCR
United States Army Support Command - Cam Ranh Bay [*Obsolete*] (AABC) ... USASUPCOM-CRB
United States Army Support Command, Chicago ... USASPTCC
United States Army Support Command, Hawaii (AABC) ... USASCH
United States Army Support Command - Qui Nhon [*Obsolete*] (AABC) ... USASUPCOM-QN
United States Army Support Command - Saigon [*Obsolete*] (AABC) ... USASUPCOM-SGN
United States Army Support Command, Vietnam [*Obsolete*] ... USARSCV
United States Army Support Command, Vietnam [*Obsolete*] ... USASCV
United States Army Support Group, Vietnam [*Obsolete*] ... USASGV
United States Army Support Office, Pacific (AABC) ... USASOPAC
United States Army Support, Thailand (AABC) ... USARSUPTHAI
United States Army Surgical Research Unit (AABC) ... USASRU
United States Army Tank-Automotive Command [*Obsolete*] ... USATACOM
United States Army Technical Library (DIT) ... USATL
United States Army, Technical Library, Aberdeen Proving Ground, Aberdeen, MD [*Library symbol Library of Congress*] (LCLS) ... MdApg
United States Army, Technical Library, Army Chemical Center, Edgewood, MD [*Library symbol Library of Congress*] (LCLS) ... MdEdgA
United States Army, Technical Reference Division Library, Fort Huachuca, AZ [*Library symbol Library of Congress*] (LCLS) ... AzFhA
United States Army Technical Support Activity (AABC) ... USATSA
United States Army Terminal Command, Atlantic ... USATCA
United States Army Terminal Command, Europe (AABC) ... USATCEUR
United States Army Terminal Command, Gulf (AABC) ... USATCG
United States Army Terminal Command, Pacific ... USATCP
United States Army Terminal Detachment, Great Lakes (AABC) ... USATDGL
United States Army Terminal Unit, Canaveral (AABC) ... USATUC
United States Army Terrain Analysis Center (MCD) ... USATAC
United States Army Terrestrial Sciences Center (AABC) ... USATSC
United States Army Test and Evaluation Command [*Obsolete*] ... USATEC
United States Army Test and Evaluation Command [*Obsolete*] ... USATECOM
United States Army, the Surgeon General ... USATSG
United States Army TMDE [*Test, Measurement, and Diagnostic Equipment*] **Support Group** ... USATSG
United States Army, Tobyhanna Army Depot Library, Tobyhanna, PA [*Library symbol Library of Congress*] (LCLS) ... PTobA
United States Army Topographic Command ... USATC
United States Army Topographic Command (AABC) ... USATOPOCOM
United States Army Topographic Command, Office of Geography, Washington, DC [*Library symbol Library of Congress*] (LCLS) ... DAM-Geog
United States Army Topographic Command, Washington, DC [*Library symbol Library of Congress*] (LCLS) ... DAM
United States Army Toxic and Hazardous Materials Agency (RDA) ... USATHAMA
United States Army TRADOC, Carlisle Barracks, Carlisle Barracks, PA [*OCLC symbol*] (OCLC) ... TSP
United States Army TRADOC, Defense Language Institute, Presidio of Monterey, CA [*OCLC symbol*] (OCLC) ... TSL
United States Army TRADOC, Engineering School Library and Learning Resource Center, Fort Belvoir, VA [*OCLC symbol*] (OCLC) ... TRB
United States Army, TRADOC, Fort Belvoir, Van Noy Post Library, Fort Belvoir, V A [*OCLC symbol*] (OCLC) ... BEL
United States Army TRADOC, Fort Benjamin Harrison Library System, Fort Benjamin Harrison, IN [*OCLC symbol*] (OCLC) ... TRH
United States Army TRADOC, Fort Benning Post and Infantry School Library, Fort Benning, GA [*OCLC symbol*] (OCLC) ... TRG
United States Army TRADOC, Fort Bliss, Fort Bliss, TX [*OCLC symbol*] (OCLC) ... TRT
United States Army TRADOC, Fort Devens, USAISD, Fort Devens, MA [*OCLC symbol*] (OCLC) ... TSD
United States Army TRADOC, Fort Dix Post Library, Fort Dix, NJ [*OCLC symbol*] (OCLC) ... TRD
United States Army TRADOC, Fort Eustis Post Library and Translation School Library, Fort Eustis, VA [*OCLC symbol*] (OCLC) ... TRE
United States Army TRADOC, Fort Gordon, United States Army Signal School and Fort Gordon, Fort Gordon, GA [*OCLC symbol*] (OCLC) ... TSG
United States Army TRADOC, Fort Hood, Fort Hood, TX [*OCLC symbol*] (OCLC) ... TRU
United States Army TRADOC, Fort Jackson, Fort Jackson, SC [*OCLC symbol*] (OCLC) ... TRJ
United States Army TRADOC, Fort Knox, Library Service Center, RSL Section, Fort Knox, KY [*OCLC symbol*] (OCLC) ... TRK
United States Army TRADOC, Fort Leavenworth Post Library, Commander, General Staff, Fort Leavenworth, KS [*OCLC symbol*] (OCLC) ... TRC
United States Army TRADOC, Fort Lee Post, Logistic Center, Logistic, Quartermaster, Fort Lee, VA [*OCLC symbol*] (OCLC) ... TRV
United States Army TRADOC, Fort Leonard Wood Post Library, Fort Leonard Wood, MO [*OCLC symbol*] (OCLC) ... TRW
United States Army TRADOC, Fort McClellan, Fort McClellan, AL [*OCLC symbol*] (OCLC) ... TRF
United States Army TRADOC, Fort Monroe Post Library and Headquarters Technical Library, Fort Monroe, VA [*OCLC symbol*] (OCLC) ... TRM
United States Army TRADOC, Fort Ord, CDEC Library, Fort Ord, CA [*OCLC symbol*] (OCLC) ... TRQ
United States Army TRADOC, Fort Rucker Post Library and Aviation School Library,Fort Rucker, AL [*OCLC symbol*] (OCLC) ... TRR
United States Army TRADOC, Fort Sill Post Library, Fort Sill, OK [*OCLC symbol*] (OCLC) ... TRO
United States Army TRADOC, Fort Story, Fort Story, VA [*OCLC symbol*] (OCLC) ... TSS
United States Army TRADOC, Fort Wadsworth, Chaplains Center Library, Fort Wadsworth, NY [*OCLC symbol*] (OCLC) ... TSN
United States Army TRADOC, Institute for Military Assistance, Library, Fort Bragg, NC [*OCLC symbol*] (OCLC) ... TRA
United States Army TRADOC, Ordnance and Chemical School Library, Aberdeen Proving Ground, MD [*OCLC symbol*] (OCLC) ... TRX
United States Army TRADOC, Redstone Arsenal, USAMMCS [*United States Army Missile and Munitions Center School*] **Technical Library, Redstone Arsenal, AL** [*OCLC symbol*] (OCLC) ... TSR
United States Army TRADOC Systems Analysis Activity (AABC) ... USATRASANA
United States Army TRADOC, TRADOC System Analysis [*TRASANA*], **White Sands Range, NM** [*OCLC symbol*] (OCLC) ... TRY
United States Army Traffic Management Agency, Central Europe (AABC) ... USATMACE
United States Army Training and Doctrine Command (BARN) ... USATDC

United States Army Training and Doctrine Command .... USATRADOC
United States Army, Training and Doctrine Command Library, Fort Monroe, VA [*Library symbol Library of Congress*] (LCLS) .... ViFmTD
United States Army Training Board .... USATB
United States Army Training Center .... USATC
United States Army Training Center, Air Defense .... USATCAD
United States Army Training Center, Air Defense .... USATCD
United States Army Training Center and Fort Leonard Wood (AABC) .... USATCFLW
United States Army Training Center, Armor [*Fort Knox, KY*] .... USATCARMOR
United States Army Training Center, Basic .... USATCBASIC
United States Army Training Center, Engineer [*Fort Leonard Wood, MO*] .... USATAC
United States Army Training Center, Engineer .... USATCENGR
United States Army Training Center, Engineer, Fort Leonard Wood [*Missouri*] (AABC) .... USATCEFLW
United States Army Training Center, Field Artillery [*Fort Sill, OK*] (AABC) .... USATC FA
United States Army Training Center, Infantry .... USATCINF
United States Army Training Device Agency .... USATDA
United States Army Training Support Center .... USATSC
United States Army TRALINET, Systems Center, ATPL-AOT, Fort Monroe, VA [*OCLC symbol*] (OCLC) .... TST
United States Army Tralinet Systems Center, Fort Monroe, VA [*Library symbol Library of Congress*] (LCLS) .... ViFmTS
United States Army Transfer Station .... USATRFSTA
United States Army Transport .... USAT
United States Army Transportation Agency (White House) (AABC) .... USATA(WH)
United States Army Transportation Aircraft Test and Support Activity .... USATATSA
United States Army Transportation and Aviation Logistics Schools (GFGA) .... USATALS
United States Army Transportation Aviation Field Office .... USATAFO
United States Army Transportation Center and Fort Eustis (AABC) .... USATCFE
United States Army Transportation Center and School .... USATC
United States Army Transportation Center and School .... USATCS
United States Army Transportation Corps Road Test Support Activity .... USATCRTSA
United States Army Transportation Engineering Agency (AABC) .... USATEA
United States Army Transportation Environmental Operations Group (AABC) .... USATREOG
United States Army Transportation Intelligence Agency .... USATIA
United States Army Transportation Materiel Command .... USATMC
United States Army Transportation Research and Engineering Command .... USATRECOM
United States Army Transportation Research Command .... USATRC
United States Army Transportation School .... USATSCH
United States Army Transportation School, Fort Eustis, VA [*Library symbol Library of Congress*] (LCLS) .... ViFeAT
United States Army Transportation Terminal, Brooklyn .... USATTB
United States Army Transportation Terminal Command, Arctic .... USATTCARC
United States Army Transportation Terminal Command, Atlantic .... USATTCA
United States Army Transportation Terminal Command, Gulf .... USATTCG
United States Army Transportation Terminal Command, Pacific .... USATTCP
United States Army Transportation Terminal Unit (AABC) .... USATTU
United States Army Transportation Test Activity, Yuma [*Arizona*] (AABC) .... USATTAY
United States Army Transportation Training Command .... USATTC
United States Army, Tripler Army Medical Center, Honolulu, HI [*Library symbol Library of Congress*] (LCLS) .... HHTM
United States Army Troop Medical Clinic (AABC) .... USATMC
United States Army Troop Support and Aviation Material Readiness Command, St. Louis, MO [*OCLC symbol*] (OCLC) .... ATS
United States Army Troop Support and Aviation Materiel Readiness Command [*St. Louis, MO*] .... USATSARCOM
United States Army Troop Support Command .... USATROSCOM
United States Army Tropic Test Center (AABC) .... USATTC
United States Army Tropical Research Medical Laboratory .... USATRML
United States Army, U.S. Army Center for Military History, Washington, DC [*Library symbol*] [*Library of Congress*] (LCLS) .... DAMH
United States Army, Vehicle (SAA) .... USARV
United States Army Vehicle Club [*British*] (DBA) .... USAVC
United States Army Veterinary School .... USAVETS
United States Army Vietnam [*Obsolete*] .... USARV
United States Army, Vietnam / Military Assistance Command, Vietnam (VNW) .... USARV/MACV
United States Army War College .... USAWC
United States Army War College, Carlisle Barracks, PA [*OCLC symbol*] (OCLC) .... AWC
United States Army War College, Carlisle Barracks, PA [*Library symbol Library of Congress*] (LCLS) .... PCarlA
United States Army Warrant Officers Association (EA) .... USAWOA
United States Army Waterways Experiment Station (AABC) .... USAWES
United States Army Weapons Command [*Later, Armaments Command*] .... USAWC
United States Army Weapons Command [*Later, Armaments Command*] (AABC) .... USAWECOM
United States Army, William Beaumont General Hospital, Medical and Technical Library, El Paso, TX [*Library symbol Library of Congress*] (LCLS) .... TxEWB
United States Army, Womack Army Hospital, Fort Bragg, NC [*Library symbol Library of Congress*] (LCLS) .... NcFbH
United States Assault Training Center [*World War II*] .... USATC
United States Assistant Army Attache .... USAARMA
United States Association of Evening Students (EA) .... USAES
United States Association of Firearm Instructors and Coaches (EA) .... USAFIC
United States Association of Former Members of Congress (EA) .... USAFMC
United States Association of Importers of Textiles and Apparel (EA) .... USA-ITA
United States Association of Independent Gymnastic Clubs (EA) .... USAIGC
United States Association of Museum Volunteers [*Later, AAMV*] (EA) .... USAMV
United States Athletes Association (EA) .... USAA
United States Atlantic Command [*DoD*] .... USACOM
United States Atlantic Subarea [*NATO*] .... USLANT
United States Atomic Energy Commission .... USAEC
United States Attorney (EPA) .... USA
United States Attorney's Office, Law Library, Newark, NJ [*Library symbol Library of Congress*] (LCLS) .... NjNA
United States Attorneys-General Reports [*A publication*] (DLA) .... Att'y Gen Rep
United States Auto Club (EA) .... USAC
United States Automated Mail Service [*Telecommunications*] (TSSD) .... USAM
United States Automobile Association, San Antonio, TX [*OCLC symbol*] (OCLC) .... USA
United States Auxiliary Naval Force .... USANF
United States Aviation Quarterly [*A publication*] (DLA) .... Aviation Q
United States Aviation Reports [*A publication*] (DLA) .... US Av
United States Aviation Reports [*A publication*] (DLA) .... US Av R
United States Aviation Reports [*A publication*] (DLA) .... US Avi Rep
United States Aviation Reports [*A publication*] (DLA) .... US Aviation Rep
United States Badminton Association (EA) .... USBA
United States Bancorp [*Associated Press*] (SAG) .... US BcOR
United States Bancorp [*Associated Press*] (SAG) .... US Bn
U.S. Bancorp 8.125%'A'Pfd [*NASDAQ symbol*] (TTSB) .... USBCP
United States Bank Note [*Printer of U.S. postage stamps*] (BARN) .... UBN
United States Bankruptcy Court (DLA) .... BR
United States Barrel Jumping Association (EA) .... USBJA
United States Bartenders Association (EA) .... USBA
United States Bartenders Guild [*Later, USBA*] (EA) .... USBG
United States Base Requirements Overseas [*Military*] (AABC) .... USBRO
United States Baseball Federation (EA) .... USBF
United States Bases [*British World War II*] .... USB
United States Basketball Writers Association (EA) .... USBWA
United States Beef Breeds Council (EA) .... USBBC
United States Beet Sugar Association (EA) .... USBSA
United States Behavioral Science Research Laboratory [*Obsolete*] (IEEE) .... USABESRL
United States Berlin Mission in Germany .... USBMG
United States Bicycle Polo Association (EA) .... USBPA
United States Biochemical Corp. [*Chemistry*] (DAVI) .... USB
United States Biological Survey [*US Government*] (EERA) .... UBS
U.S. Bioscience [*AMEX symbol*] (TTSB) .... UBS
United States Bioscience, Inc. [*Associated Press*] (SAG) .... US Bio
U.S. Bioscience Wrrt [*AMEX symbol*] (TTSB) .... UBS.WS
United States Blind Golfer's Association (EA) .... USBGA
United States Board of Tax Appeals [*Later, the Tax Court of the United States*] .... USBTA
United States Board of Tax Appeals Reports [*A publication*] (DLA) .... BTA
United States Boardsailing Association (EA) .... USBA
United States Boardsailing Association (EA) .... USBSA
United States Bocce Federation (EA) .... USBF
United States Book Exchange (SAA) .... USBE
United States Borax Research Corp., Anaheim, CA [*Library symbol Library of Congress*] (LCLS) .... CAnaU
United States Border Collie Club (EA) .... USBCC
United States Border Patrol [*Department of the Treasury*] .... USBP
United States Botanic Garden .... USBG
United States Bowling Instructors Association (EA) .... USBIA
United States Braille Chess Association (EA) .... USBCA
United States - Brazil Aviation Training Unit .... USBATU
United States Brewers Association [*Defunct*] (EA) .... USBA
United States Brewers Association, Washington, DC [*Library symbol Library of Congress*] (LCLS) .... DUSB
United States Brewers Foundation [*Later, USBA*] .... USBF
U.S. Bridge of N.Y. [*NASDAQ symbol*] (TTSB) .... USBR
United States Brookhaven National Laboratory, Medical Research Center Hospital, Upton, NY [*Library symbol Library of Congress*] (LCLS) .... NUpB-MH
United States Brookhaven National Laboratory, Upton, NY [*Library symbol Library of Congress*] (LCLS) .... NUpB
United States Bureau of Animal Industry. Monthly Record [*A publication*] (DLA) .... BAIMR
United States Bureau of Biological Survey [*Terminated, 1940; later, Fish and Wildlife Service*] .... USBBS
United States Bureau of Commercial Fisheries, Technological Laboratory Library, Ketchikan, AK [*Library symbol Library of Congress Obsolete*] (LCLS) .... AkKF
United States Bureau of Customs, Washington, DC [*Library symbol Library of Congress*] (LCLS) .... DCB
United States Bureau of Engraving and Printing .... USBEP
United States Bureau of Fisheries [*Terminated*] .... USBF
United States Bureau of Foreign and Domestic Commerce .... USBFDC
United States Bureau of Indian Affairs, Bethel Regional Library, Bethel, AK [*Library symbol Library of Congress*] (LCLS) .... AkBIA
United States Bureau of Insular Affairs .... USBIA
United States Bureau of Labor Statistics .... USBLS
United States Bureau of Land Management [*Department of the Interior*] .... USBLM
United States Bureau of Land Management, California Desert District, Riverside District Office, Riverside, CA [*Library symbol*] [*Library of Congress*] (LCLS) .... CRivLM
United States Bureau of Land Management, New Orleans Outer Continental Shelf Office, New Orleans, LA [*Library symbol Library of Congress*] (LCLS) .... LNLM
United States Bureau of Lighthouses .... USBL

United States Bureau of Marine Inspection and Navigation, Washington, DC [*Library symbol Library of Congress Obsolete*] (LCLS) .... DMIN
United States Bureau of Mines [*Department of the Interior*] .... USBM
United States Bureau of Mines, Alaska Field Operation Center, Juneau, AK [*Library symbol Library of Congress*] (LCLS) .... AkJBM
United States Bureau of Mines, Boulder City Metallurgy Research Laboratories, Boulder City, NV [*Library symbol Library of Congress*] (LCLS) .... NvBcBM
United States Bureau of Mines, College Park Research Center, College Park, MD [*Library symbol Library of Congress*] (LCLS) .... MdCpM
United States Bureau of Mines, Denver, CO [*Library symbol Library of Congress*] (LCLS) .... CoDBM
United States Bureau of Mines, Education and Training Center, Albany, OR [*Library symbol Library of Congress*] (LCLS) .... OrAlBM
United States Bureau of Mines, Fuels Technology Library, San Francisco, CA [*Library symbol Library of Congress*] (LCLS) .... CSfUM
United States Bureau of Mines, Laramie Petroleum Research Center, Laramie, WY [*Library symbol Library of Congress*] (LCLS) .... WyLarBM
United States Bureau of Mines, Mining Research Center, Spokane, WA [*Library symbol Library of Congress*] (LCLS) .... WaSpBM
United States Bureau of Mines, Morgantown, WV [*Library symbol Library of Congress*] (LCLS) .... WvMBM
United States Bureau of Mines, Petroleum Research Center, Bartlesville, OK [*Library symbol Library of Congress Obsolete*] (LCLS) .... OkBUSM
United States Bureau of Mines, Twin Cities, MN [*Library symbol Library of Congress*] (LCLS) .... MnTcM
United States Bureau of Mines, Western Field Operations Center, Spokane, WA [*Library symbol Library of Congress*] (LCLS) .... WaSpBMW
United States Bureau of Navigation .... USBN
United States Bureau of Navy Personnel [*Terminated*] .... USBNP
United States Bureau of Public Roads .... USBPR
United States Bureau of Reclamation [*Department of the Interior*] [*See also BOR*] .... USBR
United States Bureau of Reclamation, Denver, CO [*Library symbol Library of Congress*] (LCLS) .... CoDBR
United States Bureau of Reclamation, Sacramento, CA [*Library symbol Library of Congress*] (LCLS) .... CSBR
United States Bureau of Sport Fisheries and Wildlife, Wildlife Research Center, Denver, CO [*Library symbol Library of Congress*] (LCLS) .... CoDBW
United States Bureau of Standards .... USBS
United States Bureau of the Census (OICC) .... USBC
United States Bureau of the Census, Suitland, MD [*Library symbol Library of Congress*] (LCLS) .... DBC
United States Bureau on Geographical Names [*Terminated, 1947; later, Board on Geographical Names*] .... USBGN
United States Business and Industrial Council [*Washington, DC*] (EA) .... USBIC
United States Calorimetry Conference .... USCC
United States Camaro Club (EA) .... USCC
U.S. Can [*NYSE symbol*] (TTSB) .... USC
United States Canada [*Automobile content legislation*] .... USC
United States Cane Sugar Refiners' Association (EA) .... USCSRA
United States Canoe Association (EA) .... USCA
United States Cap Screw Service Bureau [*Later, Cap Screw and Special Threaded Products Bureau*] (EA) .... USCSSB
United States Capacitor Corp. (IAA) .... USCC
United States Capitol Historical Society (EA) .... USCHS
United States Capitol Police .... USCP
United States Catalog [*A bibliographic publication*] .... USC
United States Catheter Instrument [*Commercial firm*] (DAVI) .... USCI
United States Catholic Conference (EA) .... USCC
United States Catholic Conference, Washington, DC [*Library symbol Library of Congress*] (LCLS) .... DNCW
United States Catholic Mission Association (EA) .... USCMA
United States Catholic Mission Council (EA) .... USCMC
United States CB Radio Association (EA) .... USCBRA
U.S. Cellular [*AMEX symbol*] (TTSB) .... USM
United States Cellular Corp. [*Park Ridge, IL*] [*Telecommunications*] (TSSD) .... USCC
United States Central Command (INF) .... CENTCOM
United States Central Command .... USCENTCOM
United States Central Command - Air Forces .... USCENTAF
United States Central Intelligence Agency, McLean, VA [*OCLC symbol*] (OCLC) LCI
United States Cerebral Palsy Athletic Association (EA) .... USCPAA
United States Chamber of Commerce .... USCC
United States Cheese Makers Association (EA) .... USCMA
United States Chefs Ski Club (EA) .... USCSC
United States Chemical Warfare Committee .... USCWC
United States Chess Federation (EA) .... USCF
United States - China Educational Institute (EA) .... USCEI
United States Churchill Foundation [*Later, WCF*] .... USCF
United States Circuit Court .... USCC
United States Circuit Court of Appeals (AAGC) .... CCA
United States Circuit Court of Appeals .... USCCA
United States Circuit Court of Appeals, Fifth Circuit Law Library, New Orleans, LA [*Library symbol Library of Congress*] (LCLS) .... LNUCA
United States Circuit Court of Appeals, Fourth Circuit, Richmond, VA [*Library symbol Library of Congress*] (LCLS) .... ViRUCA
United States Circuit Court of Appeals Reports [*A publication*] (DLA) .... USCCA
United States Circuit Court of Appeals, Tenth Circuit, Denver, CO [*Library symbol Library of Congress*] (LCLS) .... CoDUCA
United States Citizen .... USC
United States Citizens' Congress [*Defunct*] .... USCC
United States Citizens' Rights Association (EA) .... USCRA
United States Civil Administration, Ryukyu Islands .... USCAR
United States Civil Aeronautics Board, Washington, DC [*Library symbol Library of Congress*] (LCLS) .... DCAB
United States Civil Aviation Mission (AFM) .... USCAM
United States Civil Defense Council (EA) .... USCDC
United States Civil Service Commission [*Later, MSPB*] .... USCSC
United States Civil Service Commission, Washington, DC [*Library symbol Library of Congress*] (LCLS) .... DCS
United States Civil Service Examination .... USCSE
United States Civilian Internee Information Center [*Army*] (AABC) .... USCIIC
United States Civilian Internee Information Center (Branch) [*Army*] (AABC) .... USCIIC(Br)
United States Claims Court (AAGC) .... USCC
United States Claims Court Rules [*A publication*] (DLA) .... Cl Ct R
United States Club Lacrosse Association (EA) .... USCLA
United States Coalition for Life (EA) .... USCL
United States Coast and Geodetic Survey [*Later, National Ocean Survey*] (MUGU) .... USC & G
United States Coast and Geodetic Survey (IAA) .... USCAGS
United States Coast and Geodetic Survey [*Later, National Ocean Survey*] .... USCGS
United States Coast Guard .... USCG
United States Coast Guard Academy [*New London, CT*] .... USCGA
United States Coast Guard Academy, New London, CT [*OCLC symbol*] (OCLC) .... CGA
United States Coast Guard Academy, New London, CT [*Library symbol Library of Congress*] (LCLS) .... CtNlCG
United States Coast Guard Air Detachment .... USCGAD
United States Coast Guard Air Station .... USCGAS
United States Coast Guard Aircraft and Supply Base .... USCGASB
United States Coast Guard Auxiliary .... USCGA
United States Coast Guard Auxiliary (EA) .... USCGAUX
United States Coast Guard Base .... USCGB
United States Coast Guard Chief Petty Officer Association (EA) .... CPOA
United States Coast Guard Cutter .... USCGC
United States Coast Guard Depot .... USCGD
United States Coast Guard Marine Fire and Safety Research Staff [*Groton, CT*] .... USCG-MFSRS
United States Coast Guard Naval Engineering Division .... USCG-E
United States Coast Guard Office of Boating Safety .... USCG-B
United States Coast Guard Office of Chief of Staff .... USCG-C
United States Coast Guard Office of Merchant Marine Safety .... USCG-M
United States Coast Guard Office of Navigation .... USCG-N
United States Coast Guard Receiving Center .... USCGRC
United States Coast Guard Research and Development Center Library, Groton, CT [*OCLC symbol*] (OCLC) .... CGR
United States Coast Guard Reserve .... USCGR
United States Coast Guard, Reserve (Temporary) .... USCGR(T)
United States Coast Guard, Reserve (Women) .... USCGR(W)
United States Coast Guard Shore Communication Facilities .... USCGSCF
United States Coast Guard Training Station .... USCGTS
United States Coast Survey .... USCS
United States Code [*Legal term*] .... USC
United States Code Annotated [*Law*] [*Based on official USC*] .... USCA
United States Code, Annotated, Appendix [*A publication*] (DLA) .... USCA App
United States Code Appendix [*A publication*] (DLA) .... USC App
United States Code Congressional and Administrative News [*A publication*] (DLA) .... US Code Cong & Ad News
United States Code Congressional and Administrative News [*A publication*] .... USCCAN
United States Code Service [*A publication*] (DLA) .... USCS
United States Code Supplement (BARN) .... usc sUPP
United States Collegiate Sports Council (EA) .... USCSC
United States Colored Troops [*Civil War*] .... USCT
United States Combat Developments Command Military Police Agency [*Fort Gordon, GA*] (AABC) .... USACDCMPA
United States Combined Training Association (EA) .... USCTA
United States Commander, Berlin .... USCOB
United States Commander, Eastern Atlantic (MCD) .... USCOMEAST
United States Commander in Chief, Space Command (DOMA) .... USCINCSPACE
United States Commander in Chief, Special Operations Command (DOMA) .... USCINCSOC
United States Commander in Chief, Special Operations Command (DOMA) .... USCINCSOCOM
United States Commander in Chief, Strategic Command (DOMA) .... USCINSTRAT
United States Commander in Chief, Transportation Command (DOMA) .... USCINCTRANSCOM
United States Commander, Naval Forces, Eastern Atlantic (NATG) .... USCOMEASTLANT
United States Commander, Submarines Group, Eastern Atlantic (NATG) .... USCOMSUBGRUEASTLANT
United States Commander-in-Chief, Air Force Forces, Readiness Command .... USCINCAFRED
United States Commander-in-Chief, Army Forces, Readiness Command .... USCINCARRED
United States Commander-in-Chief, Europe .... USCINCEUR
United States Commander-in-Chief Middle East, Africa South of the Sahara, and Southern Asia (GFGA) .... USCINCMEAFSA
United States Commander-in-Chief, Readiness Command .... USCINCRED
United States Commander-in-Chief, Southern Command (AFM) .... USCINCSO
United States Commander-in-Chief, Southern Command .... USCINCSOUTH
United States Commerce Court Opinions [*A publication*] (DLA) .... Com
United States Commercial Standard .... USCS
United States Commerical Co. [*World War II*] .... USCC
United States Commission of Maritime History (MSC) .... USCMH

United States Commission on Civil Rights, Washington, DC [*OCLC symbol*] (OCLC) ... CRN
United States Commission on Mathematical Instruction ... USCMI
United States Committee for Care of European Children [*Post-World War II*] ... USCCEC
United States Committee for Justice to Latin American Political Prisoners [*Defunct*] (EA) ... USLA
United States Committee for Refugees (EA) ... USCR
United States Committee for the Global Atmospheric Research Program [*Defunct*] (EA) ... USC-GARP
United States Committee for the Oceans (EA) ... USCO
United States Committee for the United Nations [*Later, UNA-USA*] ... USCUN
United States Committee for the United Nations Environment Program (EA) ... USUNEP
United States Committee for the World Health Organization (EA) ... USC-WHO
United States Committee of the International Association of Art (EA) ... USCIAA
United States Committee of the International Council on Monuments and Sites (EA) ... US/ICOMOS
United States Committee of the International Council on Social Welfare (EA) ... USCICSW
United States Committee on Large Dams of the International Commission on Large Dams (EA) ... USCOLD
United States Committee to Aid the National Liberation Front of South Vietnam ... CANLF
United States Committee to Promote Studies of the History of the Habsburg Monarchy [*Later, SAHH*] (EA) ... USCPSHHM
United States Committee-Sports for Israel (EA) ... USC-SFI
United States Communications Intelligence Board [*Later, National Security Agency*] ... USCIB
United States Communications Intelligence Board Intelligence Committee [*Obsolete*] ... USCIB/IC
United States Communications Security Board ... USCSB
United States Competitive Aerobics Federation ... USCAF
United States Compiled Statutes [*A publication*] (DLA) ... US Comp St
United States Components (IAA) ... USC
United States Conciliation Service [*Functions transferred to Federal Mediation and Conciliation Service, 1947*] ... USCS
United States Conference for the World Council of Churches (EA) ... USCWCC
United States Conference of City Health Officers (EA) ... USCCHO
United States Conference of City Human Service Officials (EA) ... USCCHSO
United States Conference of Local Health Officers (EA) ... USCLHO
United States Conference of Mayors (EA) ... USCM
United States Congress ... USC
United States Congressional Advisory Board (EA) ... USCAB
United States Constitution [*A publication*] (DLA) ... US Const
United States Consul General ... USCG
United States Continental Army Command [*Superseded by FORSCOM*] ... USCAC
United States Continental Army Command [*Superseded by FORSCOM*] ... USCONARC
United States Contract Awards (NITA) ... USCA
United States Copper Association [*Later, American Bureau of Metal Statistics*] (EA) ... USCA
United States Corporate Athletics Association (EA) ... USCAA
United States Cotton Commission ... USCC
United States Council for Automotive Research [*General Motors, Ford, and Chrysler*] (ECON) ... USCAR
United States Council for Automotive Research ... USCAR
United States Council for International Business (EA) ... USCIB
United States Council of the International Chamber of Commerce [*Later, USCIB*] (EA) ... USCICC
United States Council on International Banking (EA) ... USCIB
United States Council, World Veterans Federation (EA) ... WVF
United States Counterinsurgency Support Office ... USCISCO
United States Court of Appeals [*Formerly, United States Circuit Court of Appeals*] ... CA
United States Court of Appeals [*For the Circuit indicated*] (AAGC) ... Cir
United States Court of Appeals for the District of Columbia, Judges Library, Washington, DC [*OCLC symbol*] (OCLC) ... UCA
United States Court of Appeals for the District of Columbia, Washington, DC [*Library symbol Library of Congress*] (LCLS) ... DUCA
United States Court of Appeals, Portland, OR [*Library symbol*] [*Library of Congress*] (LCLS) ... OrPUCA
United States Court of Appeals, Syracuse, NY [*Library symbol Library of Congress*] (LCLS) ... NSyCA
United States Court of Claims (DLA) ... Ct Cls
United States Court of Claims (DLA) ... Ct of Cls
United States Court of Claims (DLA) ... US Ct Cl
United States Court of Claims [*Abolished, 1982*] ... USCC
United States Court of Claims Reports [*A publication*] (DLA) ... Court Cl
United States Court of Claims Reports [*A publication*] (DLA) ... Ct Cl
United States Court of Customs and Patent Appeals [*Now CAFC*] (AAGC) ... CCPA
United States Court of Customs and Patent Appeals [*Abolished, 1982*] ... USCCPA
United States Court of Military Appeals ... USCMA
United States Court of Military Appeals, Advance Opinions [*A publication*] (DLA) ... USCMA Adv Op
United States Courts of Appeals ... USCA
United States Criminal Code ... USCC
United States Criminal Court ... USCC
United States Croquet Association (EA) ... USCA
United States Cross Country Coaches Association (EA) ... USCCCA
United States Crutch Manufacturers Association (EA) ... USCMA
United States Cuban Sugar Council [*Defunct*] (EA) ... USCSC
United States Curling Association (EA) ... USCA
United States Custom Service, Washington, DC [*OCLC symbol*] (OCLC) ... USC
United States Customary System [*System of units used in the US*] ... USCS
United States Customs ... USC
United States Customs Appeals (DLA) ... Cust A
United States Customs Appeals (DLA) ... Cust App
United States Customs Bonded ... USCB
United States Customs Bureau, Digest of Customs and Related Laws [*A publication*] (DLA) ... CB Dig
United States Customs Court [*Later, United States Court of International Trade*] ... USCC
United States Customs Court Reports, Reappraisement Decision [*A publication*] (DLA) ... Reap Dec
United States Customs Court Reports, Reappraisement Decision [*A publication*] (DLA) ... Reapp Dec
United States Customs Inspectors' Association Port of New York (EA) ... USCIA
United States Customs Service [*A publication*] (DLA) ... Customs
United States Customs Service (MCD) ... USCS
United States Cycling Federation (EA) ... USCF
United States Data Corp. (NITA) ... USDATA
United States Deaf Skiers Association (EA) ... USDSA
United States Decisions in Martin's North Carolina Reports [*A publication*] (DLA) ... Mart Dec
United States Defense Atomic Support Agency, Sandia Base, Albuquerque, NM [*Library symbol Library of Congress*] (LCLS) ... NmADAS
United States Defense Attache Office [*or Officer*] (AABC) ... USDAO
United States Defense Committee (EA) ... USDC
United States Defense Communication Field Office (NATG) ... USDCFO
United States Defense Industrial Plant Equipment Center, Memphis, TN [*Library symbol Library of Congress*] (LCLS) ... TMDI
United States Defense Liaison Group, Indonesia [*Army*] (AABC) ... USDLGI
United States Delegate (NOAA) ... USDEL
United States Delegation, Inter-American Defense Board (AABC) ... USDELIADB
United States Delegation, United Nations Military Staff Committee ... USMILCOMUN
United States Dental Tennis Association (EA) ... USDTA
United States Department of Agriculture [*Washington, DC*] [*Database originator*] ... USDA
United States Department of Agriculture, Agricultural Research Service, Arthropod-Borne Animal Disease Research Laboratory, Denver, CO [*Library symbol Library of Congress*] (LCLS) ... CoDAD
United States Department of Agriculture, Agricultural Research Service, Eastern Utilization Research and Development Division, Philadelphia, PA [*Library symbol*] [*Library of Congress*] (LCLS) ... PPUSDA
United States Department of Agriculture, Agricultural Research Service, NationalAnimal Disease Laboratory, Ames, IA [*Library symbol Library of Congress*] (LCLS) ... IaAAR
United States Department of Agriculture, Agricultural Research Service, NorthernResearch Center Library, Peoria, IL [*Library symbol Library of Congress*] (LCLS) ... IPAR
United States Department of Agriculture, Animal and Plant Health Inspection Service, Plant Protection and Quarantine Programs (PDAA) ... USDA-APHIS-PP/Q
United States Department of Agriculture, APHIS [*Animal and Plant Health Inspection Service*], Plant Protection and Quarantine, Hyattsville, MD [*OCLC symbol*] (OCLC) ... AGH
United States Department of Agriculture, Cooperative Information System Agriculture Canada Library, Ontario, ON, Canada [*OCLC symbol*] (OCLC) ... AGV
United States Department of Agriculture, Eastern Regional Research Center, Philadelphia, PA [*OCLC symbol*] (OCLC) ... AGE
United States Department of Agriculture, Food and Nutrition Information Center, Beltsville, MD [*OCLC symbol*] (OCLC) ... AGB
United States Department of Agriculture, Food Safety and Quality Service Library- Agricultural South Building, Washington, DC [*OCLC symbol*] (OCLC) ... AGT
United States Department of Agriculture - Forest Service (PDAA) ... USDA-FS
United States Department of Agriculture, Forest Service, Engineering-TIC, Washington, DC [*OCLC symbol*] (OCLC) ... AGD
United States Department of Agriculture, Forest Service, Intermountain Forest and Range Experiment Station, Ogden, UT [*OCLC symbol*] (OCLC) ... AGI
United States Department of Agriculture, Forest Service, North Central Forest Experiment Station, St. Paul, MN [*OCLC symbol*] (OCLC) ... AGC
United States Department of Agriculture, Forest Service, Rocky Mountain Station,Fort Collins, CO [*OCLC symbol*] (OCLC) ... AGM
United States Department of Agriculture, Northern Regional Research Center, Peoria, IL [*OCLC symbol*] (OCLC) ... AGN
United States Department of Agriculture, Plum Island Animal Disease Center, Greenport, NY [*OCLC symbol*] (OCLC) ... AGG
United States Department of Agriculture, Plum Island Animal Disease Laboratory Library, Greenport, NY [*Library symbol Library of Congress*] (LCLS) ... NGrpAg
United States Department of Agriculture - Rural Electrification Administration (PDAA) ... USDA-REA
United States Department of Agriculture, Russell Agricultural Research Center, Athens, GA [*OCLC symbol*] (OCLC) ... AGR
United States Department of Agriculture, Russell Agriculture Research Center, Athens, GA [*Library symbol Library of Congress*] (LCLS) ... GAtAR
United States Department of Agriculture, Southern Forest Experiment Station, N ew Orleans, LA [*OCLC symbol*] (OCLC) ... AGQ
United States Department of Agriculture, Southern Regional Research Center, New Orleans, LA [*OCLC symbol*] (OCLC) ... AGS

United States Department of Agriculture, Southern Utilization and Development Division, Agricultural Research Service, New Orleans, LA [*Library symbol Library of Congress*] (LCLS) .... LNSU

United States Department of Agriculture, Water Conservation Laboratory Library, Phoenix, AZ [*Library symbol Library of Congress*] (LCLS) .... AzPhDA

United States Department of Agriculture, Western Regional Research Center, Berkeley, CA [*OCLC symbol*] (OCLC) .... AGW

United States Department of Agriculture, Western Regional Research Laboratory, Albany, CA [*Library symbol Library of Congress*] (LCLS) ...... CAlbA

United States Department of Commerce .... USDC

United States Department of Commerce .... USDOC

United States Department of Commerce, Houston Field Office Library, Houston, TX [*Library symbol Library of Congress*] (LCLS) .... TxHUSC

United States Department of Commerce, Memphis, TN [*Library symbol Library of Congress*] (LCLS) .... TMUSDC

United States Department of Commerce, National Marine Fisheries Service, Pascagoula, MS [*Library symbol Library of Congress*] (LCLS) .... MsPMF

United States Department of Commerce, National Oceanic and Atmospheric Administration, Atmospheric Sciences Library, Silver Spring, MD [*Library symbol Library of Congress*] (LCLS) .... DAS

United States Department of Commerce, National Oceanic and Atmospheric Administration, Gulf Coastal Fisheries Center, Panama City, FL [*Library symbol Library of Congress*] (LCLS) .... FPcG

United States Department of Commerce, National Oceanic and Atmospheric Administration, Marine and Earth Sciences Library, Rockville, MD [*Library symbol Library of Congress*] (LCLS) .... DME

United States Department of Commerce, National Oceanic and Atmospheric Administration, Miami Branch Library, Coral Gables, FL [*Library symbol Library of Congress*] (LCLS) .... FCgM

United States Department of Commerce, National Oceanic and Atmospheric Administration, Miami, FL [*Library symbol Library of Congress*] (LCLS) .... FMN

United States Department of Commerce, Washington, DC [*Library symbol Library of Congress*] (LCLS) .... DC

United States Department of Commerce, Washington, DC [*OCLC symbol*] (OCLC) .... DCL

United States Department of Defense .... USDD

United States Department of Defense .... USDOD

United States Department of Defense, Command and Control Technical Center, the Pentagon, Washington, DC [*Library symbol Library of Congress*] (LCLS) .... DCCTC

U.S. Department of Education .... ED

United States Department of Education .... USDE

United States Department of Energy (MCD) .... USDE

United States Department of Energy [*Also, an information service or system*] .... USDOE

United States Department of Energy Library, Washington, DC [*OCLC symbol*] (OCLC) .... DOE

United States Department of Energy, Morgantown Energy Technology Center, Morgantown, WV [*Library symbol*] [*Library of Congress*] (LCLS) .... WvMDOE

United States Department of Energy NEICA, Albuquerque, NM [*OCLC symbol*] (OCLC) .... DOF

United States Department of Energy, Office of Scientific and Technical Information, Oak Ridge, TN [*Library symbol*] [*Library of Congress*] (LCLS) .... TOE

United States Department of Energy, Regional Energy Information Center, Dallas, TX [*OCLC symbol*] (OCLC) .... DOD

United States Department of Energy, Washington, DC [*Library symbol Library of Congress*] (LCLS) .... DDOE

United States Department of Health and Human Services, Health Care Financial Administration, Baltimore, MD [*OCLC symbol*] (OCLC) .... HEC

United States Department of Health and Human Services, Health Care Financing Administration, Office of Research Demonstrations and Statistics, Baltimore, MD [*Library symbol Library of Congress*] (LCLS) .... MdBDH

United States Department of Health and Human Services, Washington, DC [*Library symbol Library of Congress*] (LCLS) .... DHHS

United States Department of Health, Education, and Welfare .... USDHE & W

United States Department of Health, Education, and Welfare, Washington, DC [*Library symbol Library of Congress*] (LCLS) .... DHEW

United States Department of Housing and Urban Development .... USDHUD

United States Department of Housing and Urban Development, Region I, Boston, MA [*OCLC symbol*] (OCLC) .... HOV

United States Department of Housing and Urban Development, Washington, DC [*Library symbol Library of Congress*] (LCLS) .... DHUD

United States Department of Housing and Urban Development, Washington, DC [*OCLC symbol*] (OCLC) .... HOU

United States Department of Interior, Office of Surface Mining, Denver, CO [*Library symbol Library of Congress*] (LCLS) .... CoDSM

United States Department of Justice .... USDJ

United States Department of Justice Library, Washington, DC [*OCLC symbol*] (OCLC) .... DOJ

United States Department of Justice, Washington, DC [*Library symbol Library of Congress*] (LCLS) .... DJ

United States Department of Labor .... USDL

United States Department of Labor Library, Washington, DC [*Library symbol Library of Congress*] (LCLS) .... DL

United States Department of Labor, Mine Safety and Health Administration, Denver, CO [*Library symbol Library of Congress*] (LCLS) .... CoDMSA

United States Department of Labor, Washington, DC [*OCLC symbol*] (OCLC) .... ULL

United States Department of State .... USDS

United States Department of State Library [*Division of Library and Reference Services*], Washington, DC [*Library symbol Library of Congress*] (LCLS) .... DS

United States Department of the Interior (DLA) .... US Dept Int

United States Department of the Interior .... USDI

United States Department of the Interior (MCD) .... USDOI

United States Department of the Interior, Alaska Pipeline Office, Anchorage, AK [*Library symbol Library of Congress*] (LCLS) .... AkAAP

United States Department of the Interior, Alaska Resources, Anchorage, AK [*OCLC symbol*] (OCLC) .... UDA

United States Department of the Interior, Alaska Resources Library, Anchorage, AK [*Library symbol Library of Congress*] (LCLS) .... AkAAR

United States Department of the Interior, Bureau of Land Management, Denver Service Center, Denver, CO [*Library symbol Library of Congress*] (LCLS) .... CoDBLM

United States Department of the Interior, Bureau of Mines, Pittsburgh Research Center, Pittsburgh, PA [*Library symbol Library of Congress*] (LCLS) .... PPiUSM

United States Department of the Interior, Bureau of Reclamation, Denver, CO [*OCLC symbol*] (OCLC) .... UDR

United States Department of the Interior, National Park Service, Midwest Archaeological Center, Lincoln, NE [*Library symbol Library of Congress*] (LCLS) .... NbLNP

United States Department of the Interior, Natural Resources Library, Washington,DC [*OCLC symbol*] (OCLC) .... UDI

United States Department of the Interior, Office of Surface Mining, Washington, DC [*Library symbol Library of Congress*] (LCLS) .... DSM

United States Department of the Interior, Patuxent Wildlife Research Center, Laurel, MD [*Library symbol Library of Congress*] (LCLS) .... MdLP

United States Department of the Interior, United States Geological Survey, Reston, VA [*OCLC symbol*] (OCLC) .... GIS

United States Department of the Interior, Washington, DC [*Library symbol Library of Congress*] (LCLS) .... DI

United States Department of the Interior, Western Archeological Center, Tucson, AZ [*OCLC symbol*] (OCLC) .... UDZ

United States Department of the Navy, Bureau of Naval Personnel, Washington, DC [*Library symbol Library of Congress*] (LCLS) .... DN-Pers

United States Department of the Navy, Department Library, Washington, DC [*Library symbol Library of Congress*] (LCLS) .... DN

United States Department of the Navy, Naval Air Systems Command, Arlington, VA [*Library symbol Library of Congress*] (LCLS) .... DN-Aer

United States Department of the Navy, Naval Facilities Engineering Command, Washington, DC [*Library symbol Library of Congress*] (LCLS) .... DN-YD

United States Department of the Navy, Naval Gun Factory, Washington, DC [*Library symbol Library of Congress Obsolete*] (LCLS) .... DN-GF

United States Department of the Navy, Naval Historical Center, Operational Archives, Washington, DC [*Library symbol Library of Congress*] (LCLS) .... DN-HC

United States Department of the Navy, Naval Intelligence Support Center, Washington, DC [*Library symbol Library of Congress*] (LCLS) .... DN-PIC

United States Department of the Navy, Naval Medical Research Institute, Bethesda, MD [*Library symbol Library of Congress*] (LCLS) .... DN-MRI

United States Department of the Navy, Naval Medical School, Bethesda, MD [*Library symbol Library of Congress*] (LCLS) .... DN-MS

United States Department of the Navy, Naval Observatory, Washington, DC [*Library symbol Library of Congress*] (LCLS) .... DN-Ob

United States Department of the Navy, Naval Oceanographic Office, Washington, DC [*Library symbol Library of Congress*] (LCLS) .... DN-HO

United States Department of the Navy, Naval Ordnance Laboratory, White Oak, MD [*Library symbol Library of Congress*] (LCLS) .... DN-OL

United States Department of the Navy, Naval Ordnance Station, Indian Head, MD [*Library symbol Library of Congress*] (LCLS) .... DN-PP

United States Department of the Navy, Naval Ordnance Systems Command, Arlington,VA [*Library symbol Library of Congress*] (LCLS) .... DN-Ord

United States Department of the Navy, Naval Photographic Center, Washington, DC [*Library symbol Library of Congress*] (LCLS) .... DN-PC

United States Department of the Navy, Naval Regional Medical Center, San Francisco, CA [*Library symbol Library of Congress*] (LCLS) .... DN-MRC

United States Department of the Navy, Naval Research Library, Arlington, VA [*Library symbol Library of Congress*] (LCLS) .... DN-RL

United States Department of the Navy, Naval Ship Research and Development Center, Carderock, MD [*Library symbol Library of Congress*] (LCLS) .... DN-TMB

United States Department of the Navy, Naval Ship Systems Command, Washington, DC [*Library symbol Library of Congress*] (LCLS) .... DN-Sh

United States Department of the Navy, Naval Supply Systems Command, Alexandria, VA [*Library symbol Library of Congress*] (LCLS) .... DN-SA

United States Department of the Navy, Naval Weapons Laboratory, Technical Library, Dahlgreen, VA [*Library symbol Library of Congress*] (LCLS) .... DN-NPG

United States Department of the Navy, Navy Training Publication Center, Pensacola, FL [*Library symbol Library of Congress*] (LCLS) .... DN-RTPC

United States Department of the Navy, Office of Naval Research, Arlington, VA [*Library symbol Library of Congress*] (LCLS) .... DN-ONR

United States Department of the Navy, Office of the General Counsel, Arlington, VA [*Library symbol Library of Congress*] (LCLS) .... DN-OGC

United States Department of the Navy, Office of the Judge Advocate General, Law Library, Washington, DC [*Library symbol Library of Congress*] (LCLS) .... DN-JAG

United States Department of the Navy, United States Marine Corps Historical Library, Washington, DC [*Library symbol Library of Congress*] (LCLS) .... DN-MHi

United States Department of the Treasury .... USDT

United States Department of the Treasury, Washington, DC [*Library symbol Library of Congress*] (LCLS) .... DT

United States Department of the Treasury, Washington, DC [*OCLC symbol*] (OCLC) .... DTL
United States Department of Transportation (MCD) .... USDOT
United States Department of Transportation .... USDT
United States Department of Transportation, Library, Washington, DC [*OCLC symbol*] (OCLC) .... TRL
United States Department of Transportation, Technical Information Center, Cambridge, MA [*Library symbol Library of Congress*] (LCLS) .... MCT
United States Department of Transportation, Transportation System Center, Cambridge, MA [*OCLC symbol*] (OCLC) .... TRS
United States Department of Transportation, Washington, DC [*Library symbol Library of Congress*] (LCLS) .... DDOT
United States Dependent Schools, European Area [*Army*] .... USDESEA
United States Dependent Schools, European Area [*Army*] (AABC) .... USDSEA
U.S. Diagnostic Labs [*NASDAQ symbol*] (TTSB) .... USDL
United States Digest [*A publication*] (DLA) .... US Dig
United States Direct Hire [*Military*] .... USDH
United States Disarmament Administration [*Transferred to US Arms Control and Disarmament Agency, 1961*] .... USDA
United States Disbursing Officer .... USDO
United States Disciplinary Barracks [*Military*] .... USDB
United States Dispensatory [*Pharmacology*] .... USD
United States Display Consortium (PCM) .... USDC
United States Distinguished International Shooter Badge [*Military decoration*] (AABC) .... USDISBad
United States District Court [*Used citation*] (AAGC) .... D
United States District Court (DLA) .... DC
United States District Court (BARN) .... U S Dist Ct
United States District Court .... USDC
United States District Court, Central Library, Portland, OR [*Library symbol*] [*Library of Congress*] (LCLS) .... OrPUDC
United States District Court, District of Hawaii (DLA) .... D Hawaii
United States District Court, District of Hawaii (DLA) .... H Dist Ct
United States District Court, District of Hawaii (DLA) .... Hawaii Dist
United States District Court District of Hawaii (DLA) .... US Dist Ct Haw
United States District Court, District of Hawaii (DLA) .... USDC Haw
United States District Court, District of Hawaii (DLA) .... USDC Hawaii
United States District Court, District of Hawaii, Reports [*A publication*] (DLA) .... USDC Haw
United States District Court, District of Hawaii, Reports [*A publication*] (DLA) .... USDC Hawaii
United States District Court for the Central District of California (DLA) .... CD Cal
United States District Court for the District of Alaska (DLA) .... D Alaska
United States District Court for the District of Arizona (DLA) .... D Ariz
United States District Court for the District of Colorado (DLA) .... D Colo
United States District Court for the District of Columbia (DLA) .... DC Dist Col
United States District Court for the District of Connecticut (DLA) .... D Conn
United States District Court for the District of Delaware (DLA) .... D Del
United States District Court for the District of Guam (DLA) .... D Guam
United States District Court for the District of Idaho (DLA) .... D Idaho
United States District Court for the District of Kansas (DLA) .... D Kan
United States District Court for the District of Maine (DLA) .... D ME
United States District Court for the District of Maryland (DLA) .... D MD
United States District Court for the District of Massachusetts (DLA) .... D Mass
United States District Court for the District of Minnesota (DLA) .... D Minn
United States District Court for the District of Montana (DLA) .... D Mont
United States District Court for the District of Nebraska (DLA) .... Neb
United States District Court for the District of Nevada (DLA) .... D Nev
United States District Court for the District of New Hampshire (DLA) .... D NH
United States District Court for the District of New Jersey (DLA) .... D NJ
United States District Court for the District of New Mexico (DLA) .... D NM
United States District Court for the District of North Dakota (DLA) .... D ND
United States District Court for the District of Oregon (DLA) .... D OR
United States District Court for the District of Puerto Rico (DLA) .... D PR
United States District Court for the District of Rhode Island (DLA) .... D RI
United States District Court for the District of South Carolina (DLA) .... D SC
United States District Court for the District of South Dakota (DLA) .... D SD
United States District Court for the District of the Virgin Islands (DLA) .... D VI
United States District Court for the District of Utah (DLA) .... D Utah
United States District Court for the District of Vermont (DLA) .... D VT
United States District Court for the District of Wyoming (DLA) .... D Wyo
United States District Court for the Eastern and Western Districts of Arkansas (DLA) .... ED Ark
United States District Court for the Eastern District of California (DLA) .... ED Cal
United States District Court for the Eastern District of Illinois (DLA) .... ED Ill
United States District Court for the Eastern District of Kentucky (DLA) .... ED KY
United States District Court for the Eastern District of Louisiana (DLA) .... ED LA
United States District Court for the Eastern District of Michigan (DLA) .... ED Mich
United States District Court for the Eastern District of Missouri (DLA) .... ED MO
United States District Court for the Eastern District of New York (DLA) .... EDNY
United States District Court for the Eastern District of North Carolina (DLA) .... EDNC
United States District Court for the Eastern District of Oklahoma (DLA) .... ED Okla
United States District Court for the Eastern District of Pennsylvania (DLA) .... ED PA
United States District Court for the Eastern District of Tennessee (DLA) .... ED Tenn
United States District Court for the Eastern District of Texas (DLA) .... ED Tex
United States District Court for the Eastern District of Virginia (DLA) .... ED VA
United States District Court for the Eastern District of Washington (DLA) .... ED Wash
United States District Court for the Eastern District of Wisconsin (DLA) .... ED Wis
United States District Court for the Middle District of Alabama (DLA) .... MD Ala
United States District Court for the Middle District of Florida (DLA) .... MD Fla
United States District Court for the Middle District of Georgia (DLA) .... MD GA
United States District Court for the Middle District of Louisiana (DLA) .... MD LA
United States District Court for the Middle District of North Carolina (DLA) .... MDNC
United States District Court for the Middle District of Pennsylvania (DLA) .... MD PA
United States District Court for the Middle District of Tennessee (DLA) .... MD Tenn
United States District Court for the Northern District of Alabama (DLA) .... ND Ala
United States District Court for the Northern District of California (DLA) .... ND Cal
United States District Court for the Northern District of Florida (DLA) .... ND Fla
United States District Court for the Northern District of Georgia (DLA) .... ND GA
United States District Court for the Northern District of Illinois (DLA) .... ND Ill
United States District Court for the Northern District of Indiana (DLA) .... ND Ind
United States District Court for the Northern District of Iowa (DLA) .... ND Iowa
United States District Court for the Northern District of Mississippi (DLA) .... ND Miss
United States District Court for the Northern District of New York (DLA) .... NDNY
United States District Court for the Northern District of Ohio (DLA) .... ND Ohio
United States District Court for the Northern District of Oklahoma (DLA) .... ND Okla
United States District Court for the Northern District of Texas (DLA) .... ND Tex
United States District Court for the Southern District of Alabama (DLA) .... SD Ala
United States District Court for the Southern District of California (DLA) .... SD Cal
United States District Court for the Southern District of Florida (DLA) .... SD Fla
United States District Court for the Southern District of Georgia (DLA) .... SD GA
United States District Court for the Southern District of Illinois (DLA) .... SD Ill
United States District Court for the Southern District of Indiana (DLA) .... SD Ind
United States District Court for the Southern District of Iowa (DLA) .... SD Iowa
United States District Court for the Southern District of Mississippi (DLA) .... SD Miss
United States District Court for the Southern District of New York (DLA) .... SDNY
United States District Court for the Southern District of Ohio (DLA) .... SD Ohio
United States District Court for the Southern District of Texas (DLA) .... SD Tex
United States District Court for the Southern District of West Virginia (DLA) .... SD W Va
United States District Court for the Western District of Kentucky (DLA) .... WD KY
United States District Court for the Western District of Louisiana (DLA) .... WD LA
United States District Court for the Western District of Michigan (DLA) .... WD Mich
United States District Court for the Western District of Missouri (DLA) .... WD MO
United States District Court for the Western District of New York (DLA) .... WDNY
United States District Court for the Western District of North Carolina (DLA) .... WDNC
United States District Court for the Western District of Oklahoma (DLA) .... WD Okla
United States District Court for the Western District of Pennsylvania (DLA) .... WD PA
United States District Court for the Western District of Tennessee (DLA) .... WD Tenn
United States District Court for the Western District of Texas (DLA) .... WD Tex
United States District Court for the Western District of Virginia (DLA) .... WD VA
United States District Court for the Western District of Washington (DLA) .... WD Wash
United States District Court for the Western District of Wisconsin (DLA) .... WD Wis
United States District Judge .... USDJ
United States District of Columbia (DLA) .... USDC
United States Diving, Inc. (EA) .... USD
United States Divorce Reform [*Defunct*] (EA) .... USDR
United States Document Office, Allied Land Forces, Southeastern Europe (AABC) .... USDOCOLANDSOUTHEAST
United States Documents Officer (AFM) .... USDOCO
United States Dollars .... USD
United States Dressage Federation (EA) .... USDF
United States Drone (SAA) .... USD
United States Duffers' Association [*Defunct*] (EA) .... USDA
United States Durum Growers Association (EA) .... USDGA
United States Eastern Amateur Ski Association [*Later, ESA*] .... USEASA
United States Economic Mission [*Foreign aid*] (VNW) .... USECOM
United States Economic Problems [*British World War II*] .... USE
United States Educational Foundation in Pakistan .... USEFP
United States Egg Marketers (EA) .... USEM
[*The*] **United States Electronic Mail Association** .... USEMA
United States Element Central Treaty Organization (AFM) .... USELMCENTO
United States Embassy .... USE
United States Embassy (MCD) .... USEMB
United States Embassy, Ottawa, ON, Canada [*Library symbol Library of Congress*] (LCLS) .... CaOOUSA
United States Employees' Compensation Commission [*Functions transferred to Federal Security Agency, 1946*] .... USECC
United States Employment Opportunities .... USEO
United States Employment Service [*Department of Labor*] .... USES

United States Endurance Cup [*Car racing*] .... USEC
U.S. Energy [*NASDAQ symbol*] (TTSB) .... USEG
United States Energy Corp. [*Associated Press*] (SAG) .... US Enr
United States Energy Research and Development Administration [*Superseded by Department of Energy, 1977*] .... USERDA
United States Energy Research and Development Administration, Boulder City Metallurgy Research Laboratories, Boulder City, NV [*Library symbol Library of Congress*] (LCLS) .... NvBcER
United States Energy Research and Development Administration, Washington, DC [*Library symbol Library of Congress*] (LCLS) .... DERDA
United States Energy Research Development Administration, Energy Research Center, Bartlesville, OK [*Library symbol Library of Congress*] (LCLS) .... OkBERDA
United States Energy Research Development Administration, Reno, NV [*Library symbol Library of Congress*] (LCLS) .... NvREr
United States Engineer Office .... USEO
United States Enrichment Corporation (DOGT) .... USEC
United States Envelope Co. .... USE
United States Environment and Resources Council [*Marine science*] (MSC) .... USREC
United States Environmental Protection Agency .... US EPA
U.S. Environmental Protection Agency .... US EPA
United States Environmental Protection Agency .... USEPA
United States Environmental Protection Agency, Annapolis Field Office, AnnapolisScience Center, Annapolis, MD [*Library symbol Library of Congress*] (LCLS) .... MdAEPA
United States Environmental Protection Agency, Cincinnati, OH [*Library symbol Library of Congress*] (LCLS) .... OCEPA
United States Environmental Protection Agency, Corvallis Environmental Research Laboratory, Corvallis, OR [*Library symbol Library of Congress*] (LCLS) .... OrCEPA
United States Environmental Protection Agency, Headquarters Library, Washington,DC [*Library symbol Library of Congress*] (LCLS) .... DEPA
United States Environmental Protection Agency, Kansas City, MO [*Library symbol Library of Congress*] (LCLS) .... MoKEP
United States Environmental Protection Agency, National Field Investigations Center Library, Denver, CO [*Library symbol Library of Congress*] (LCLS) .... CoDEPA
United States Environmental Protection Agency, National Marine Water Quality Laboratory, West Kingston, RI [*Library symbol Library of Congress*] (LCLS) .... RWkEPA
United States Environmental Protection Agency, National Water Quality Laboratory, Duluth, MN [*Library symbol Library of Congress*] (LCLS) .... MnDuEPA
United States Environmental Protection Agency, Office of Administration, LibraryServices Branch, Park, Durham, NC [*Library symbol Library of Congress*] (LCLS) .... NcDurEP
United States Environmental Protection Agency, Office of Noise Abatement and Control, Washington, DC [*Library symbol Library of Congress*] (LCLS) .... DEPA-NA
United States Environmental Protection Agency, Region I Library, Boston, MA [*Library symbol Library of Congress*] (LCLS) .... MBEPA
United States Environmental Protection Agency, Region X Library, Seattle, WA [*Library symbol*] [*Library of Congress*] (LCLS) .... WaSEPA
United States Environmental Protection Agency, Wheeling Field Office, Wheeling, WV [*Library symbol Library of Congress*] (LCLS) .... WvWEPA
United States Environmental Science Services Administration (AABC) .... USESSA
U.S. Environmental Solutions [*NASDAQ symbol*] (TTSB) .... USES
United States Equestrian Team (EA) .... USET
United States Equity Digest [*A publication*] (DLA) .... US Eq Dig
United States Escapee Program .... USEP
United States Establishment and Enterprise Microdata Base [*Brookings Institution*] .... USEEM
United States European Command .... USEUCOM
United States European Communications (SAA) .... USEUCOM
United States Exchange Stabilization Fund .... USESF
U.S. Exploration [*NASDAQ symbol*] (TTSB) .... USXP
United States Exploration, Inc. [*Associated Press*] (SAG) .... USExpInc
United States Exploration, Inc. [*NASDAQ symbol*] (SAG) .... USXP
United States Exploring Expedition [*1838-42*] [*Navy*] .... USEE
United States Facilities [*NYSE symbol*] (SAG) .... UF
United States Facilities [*Associated Press*] (SAG) .... US Facil
United States Facilities Corp. [*Associated Press*] (SAG) .... US Facl
United States Fastener Manufacturing Group [*Defunct*] (EA) .... USFMG
United States Federal Aviation Administration, Aeronautical Center Library, Oklahoma City, OK [*OCLC symbol*] (OCLC) .... OUR
United States Federal Aviation Administration, CAMI Library, Oklahoma City, OK [*OCLC symbol*] (OCLC) .... OUT
United States Federal Aviation Administration, Civil Aeromedical Institute, Oklahoma City, OK [*Library symbol Library of Congress*] (LCLS) .... OkOkFA
United States Federal Aviation Administration, Fort Worth, TX [*Library symbol Library of Congress*] (LCLS) .... TxFFAA
United States Federal Aviation Administration, National Aviation Facilities Experimental Center, Atlantic City, NJ [*Library symbol Library of Congress*] (LCLS) .... NjAcFA
United States Federal Aviation Administration, Washington, DC [*Library symbol Library of Congress*] (LCLS) .... DFAA
United States Federal Communications Commission, Washington, DC [*Library symbol Library of Congress*] (LCLS) .... DFCC
United States Federal Home Loan Bank Board, Research Library, Washington, DC [*Library symbol Library of Congress*] (LCLS) .... DFHL
United States Federal Power Commission Opinions and Decisions [*A publication*] (DLA) .... FPC
United States Federal Power Commission, Washington, DC [*Library symbol Library of Congress*] (LCLS) .... DFPC
United States Federal Trade Commission, Washington, DC [*Library symbol Library of Congress*] (LCLS) .... DFT
United States Federation of Amateur Roller Skaters [*Later, USAC-RS*] (EA) .... USFARS
United States Federation of Pelota (EA) .... USFP
United States Fencing Association (EA) .... USFA
United States Fencing Coaches Association (EA) .... USFCA
United States Fidelity & Guaranty Co. .... USF & G
United States Figure Skating Association (EA) .... USFSA
U.S. Filter [*NYSE symbol*] (TTSB) .... USF
United States Filter Corp. [*Associated Press*] (SAG) .... US Filter
United States Filter Corp. [*NYSE symbol*] (SAG) .... USF
United States Fire Administration [*Federal Emergency Management Agency*] (GFGA) .... USFA
United States Fire Companies Conference [*Defunct*] (EA) .... USFCC
United States Fish and Wildlife, Billings, MT [*Library symbol Library of Congress*] (LCLS) .... MtBilFW
United States Fish and Wildlife Service [*Department of the Interior*] .... USFWS
United States Fish and Wildlife Service, Alaska Area Office, Anchorage, AK [*OCLC symbol*] (OCLC) .... UDK
United States Fish and Wildlife Service, Atlanta, GA [*OCLC symbol*] (OCLC) .... FZZ
United States Fish and Wildlife Service, Atlanta, GA [*Library symbol Library of Congress*] (LCLS) .... GAFW
United States Fish and Wildlife Service, Billings, MT [*OCLC symbol*] (OCLC) .... UDO
United States Fish and Wildlife Service, Denver, CO [*OCLC symbol*] (OCLC) .... FZW
United States Fish and Wildlife Service, Fish Control Laboratory, La Crosse, WI [*Library symbol Library of Congress*] (LCLS) .... WLacFW
United States Fish and Wildlife Service, Laurel, MD [*OCLC symbol*] (OCLC) .... FZT
United States Fish and Wildlife Service, National Fishery Research Laboratory, La Crosse, WI [*OCLC symbol*] (OCLC) .... FZV
United States Fish and Wildlife Service, Portland, OR [*OCLC symbol*] (OCLC) .... FZY
United States Fish and Wildlife Service, Portland, OR [*Library symbol Library of Congress*] (LCLS) .... OrPFW
United States Fish and Wildlife Service, Region 2, Albuquerque, NM [*OCLC symbol*] (OCLC) .... UDE
United States Fish and Wildlife Service, Science Reference Library, Twin Cities,MN [*Library symbol Library of Congress*] (LCLS) .... MnTcFW
United States Fish and Wildlife Service, Science Reference Library, Twin Cities,MN [*OCLC symbol*] (OCLC) .... UDT
United States Fish and Wildlife Service, Sidell, LA [*Library symbol Library of Congress*] (LCLS) .... LSidFW
United States Fish and Wildlife Service, Slidell, LA [*OCLC symbol*] (OCLC) .... FZU
United States Fishmeal Importers Association [*Defunct*] (EA) .... USFMIA
United States Flag Football League (EA) .... USFFL
United States Flag Foundation (EA) .... USFF
United States Fleet .... USF
United States Fleet Air Defense Training Center .... USFADTC
United States Fleet Air Wing, Mediterranean (NATG) .... USFAIRWINGMED
United States Fleet Reserve .... USFR
United States Fleet Shore Radio Station .... USRAD
United States Fleet SONAR School .... USFSS
United States Floor Tennis Association [*Defunct*] (EA) .... USFTA
United States Foil Co. .... USFC
United States Food and Drug Administration, Atlanta, GA [*Library symbol Library of Congress*] (LCLS) .... GAFD
United States Food and Drug Administration, Bureau of Food, Washington, DC [*OCLC symbol*] (OCLC) .... BFL
United States Food and Drug Administration, Bureau of Food, Washington, DC [*Library symbol Library of Congress*] (LCLS) .... DFDA
United States Food and Drug Administration, Bureau of Medical Devices Library, Silver Spring, MD [*OCLC symbol*] (OCLC) .... BMD
United States Food and Drug Administration, Bureau of Medical Services, Silver Spring, MD [*Library symbol Library of Congress*] (LCLS) .... MdSsFD
United States Food and Drug Administration, Cincinnati, OH [*Library symbol Library of Congress*] (LCLS) .... OCFDA
United States Food and Drug Administration, Dallas, TX [*Library symbol Library of Congress*] (LCLS) .... TxDaUSFD
United States Food and Drug Administration. Notices of Judgment: Foods [*A publication*] (DLA) .... FNJ FDC
United States Food and Drug Administration, Rockville, MD [*Library symbol Library of Congress*] (LCLS) .... MdRFD
United States Forces (CINC) .... USF
United States Forces .... USFOR
United States Forces, British Isles [*World War II*] .... USFBI
United States Forces, China, Burma, India [*World War II*] .... USAFCBI
United States Forces, China, Burma, India Theater [*World War II*] .... USAFCBIT
United States Forces, China Theater .... USFCT
United States Forces, European Theater [*American headquarters for occupation of Germany after SHAEF was dissolved*] [*World War II*] .... USFET
United States Forces in Australia .... USFIA
United States Forces in Austria .... USFA
United States Forces in Azores .... USFORAZ
United States Forces in the Philippines .... USFIP
United States Forces, Japan (CINC) .... USFJ
United States Forces, Korea .... USFK
United States Forces, Korea .... USK
United States Forces Korea .... USKOREA

United States Forces, Occupation Austria [*World War II*] ... USFOA
United States Forces, Police ... USFP
United States Forces, Police Squadron ... USFPS
United States Forces, Taiwan Defense Command (CINC) ... USTDC
United States Forces, Vietnam ... USFV
United States Foreign Intelligence Surveillance Court ... USFISC
United States Foreign Medical Graduate (DHSM) ... USFMG
United States Foreign Service [*Department of State*] ... USFS
United States Forest Products Laboratory, Madison, WI [*Library symbol Library of Congress*] (LCLS) ... WMaF
United States Forest Service ... USFS
United States Forest Service, Atlanta, GA [*Library symbol Library of Congress*] (LCLS) ... GAFS
United States Forest Service, Intermountain Range and Experiment Station Library, Ogden, UT [*Library symbol Library of Congress*] (LCLS) ... UOFS
United States Forest Service, North Central Forest Experiment Station, St. Paul,MN [*Library symbol Library of Congress*] (LCLS) ... MnSUSF
United States Forest Service, Pacific Southwest Forest and Range Experiment Station, Berkeley, CA [*Library symbol Library of Congress*] (LCLS) ... CBUF
United States Forest Service, Range and Wildlife Habitat Laboratory, La Grande, OR [*Library symbol Library of Congress*] (LCLS) ... OrLgFS
United States Forest Service, Rocky Mountain Forest and Range Experiment Station, Fort Collins, CO [*Library symbol Library of Congress*] (LCLS) ... CoFFS
United States Foundation for International Scouting (EA) ... USFIS
United States Frequency Standard ... USFS
United States Fuel Administration [*Terminated*] ... USFA
United States Gallon (IAA) ... USG
United States Gallon (IAA) ... USGAL
United States Gauge ... USG
United States General Accounting Office, Seattle Regional Office, Seattle, WA [*Library symbol*] [*Library of Congress*] (LCLS) ... WaSGAO
United States General Accounting Office, Washington, DC [*Library symbol Library of Congress*] (LCLS) ... DGAO
United States Geological Survey [*Reston, VA*] [*Databank originator*] ... USGS
United States Geological Survey, Denver, CO [*Library symbol Library of Congress*] (LCLS) ... CoDGS
United States Geological Survey, Menlo Park, CA [*Library symbol Library of Congress*] (LCLS) ... CMenUG
United States Geological Survey, Metairie, LA [*OCLC symbol*] (OCLC) ... GIL
United States Geological Survey, Office of Marine Geology, Corpus Cristi, TX [*Library symbol*] [*Library of Congress*] (LCLS) ... TxCcG
United States Geological Survey, Resources/Appraisal Group, Denver, CO [*Library symbol Library of Congress*] (LCLS) ... CoDGS-R
United States Geological Survey, Reston, VA [*Library symbol Library of Congress*] (LCLS) ... DI-GS
United States Geological Survey, Spokane, WA [*Library symbol Library of Congress*] (LCLS) ... WaSpGS
United States Geological Survey, Water Resources Division, Helena, MT [*OCLC symbol*] (OCLC) ... GIH
United States Geological Survey, Water Resources Division, Helena, MT [*Library symbol*] [*Library of Congress*] (LCLS) ... MtHG
United States Geological Survey, Water Resources Division, Syosset, NY [*Library symbol Library of Congress*] (LCLS) ... NSyoG
United States Geological Survey, Water Resources Services, New York District, Albany, NY [*Library symbol Library of Congress*] (LCLS) ... NAIGS
United States Global Change Research Program [*Marine science*] (OSRA) ... US/GCRP
United States Global Change Research Program (BARN) ... USGCRP
United States Global Strategy Council (EA) ... USGSC
United States Global-Positioning-Satellite Industry Council ... USGIC
United States Gold Corp. [*Associated Press*] (SAG) ... US Gold
United States Gold Corp. [*NASDAQ symbol*] (SAG) ... USGL
U.S. Gold Corp. [*NASDAQ symbol*] (TTSB) ... USGL
United States Golf Association (EA) ... USGA
United States Golf Association, Far Hills, NJ [*Library symbol Library of Congress*] (LCLS) ... NjFhUGA
United States Government ... USG
United States Government Correspondence Manual ... USGCM
United States Government Life Insurance ... USGLI
United States Government Manual [*A publication*] (OICC) ... USGM
United States Government Printing Office ... USGPO
United States Government Printing Office, Alexandria, VA [*OCLC symbol*] (OCLC) ... GPO
United States Government Printing Office - Serials, Alexandria, VA [*OCLC symbol*] (OCLC) ... GPA
United States Government Printing Office, Serials Library, Alexandria, VA [*Library symbol Library of Congress*] (LCLS) ... DGPO-S
United States Government Printing Office, Washington, DC [*Library symbol Library of Congress*] (LCLS) ... DGPO
United States Government Purchasing Mission [*World War II*] ... USGPM
United States Government Report (IEEE) ... USGR
United States Government Report Announcements (IID) ... USGRA
United States Government Research and Development Reports [*Later, GRA*] ... USGRDR
United States Government Research and Development Reports Index [*Later, GRI*] ... USGRDR-I
United States Government Research Reports [*National Bureau of Standards publication*] ... USGRR
United States Government Standard Gage (IAA) ... USGSG
United States Grain Standards Act (GFGA) ... USGSA
United States Grand Prix [*Auto racing*] ... USGP
United States Grass Ski Association (EA) ... USGSA
United States Group Control Council/Austria [*World War II*] ... USGCC/A
United States Group Control Council/Germany [*World War II*] ... USGCC/G
United States Group of the Inter-Parliamentary Union (EA) ... USGIPU
United States Gymnastic Safety Association ... USGSA
United States Gymnastics Federation (EA) ... USGF
United States Gypsum Co., Chicago, IL [*Library symbol*] [*Library of Congress*] (LCLS) ... ICUG
United States Handball Association (EA) ... USHA
United States Handicap Tennis Association (EA) ... USHTA
United States Harness Writers' Association (EA) ... USHWA
United States Health Manpower Advisory Council ... USHMAC
U.S. Healthcare [*NASDAQ symbol*] (TTSB) ... USHC
United States Healthcare, Inc. [*Associated Press*] (SAG) ... US Hlth
United States Helium Plant [*Amarillo, TX*] ... USHP
United States Highland Dancing Association (EA) ... USHDA
United States Historical Documents Institute ... USHDI
United States Historical Documents Institute, Inc., Arlington, VA [*Library symbol Library of Congress*] (LCLS) ... ViArHD
United States Hockey League ... USHL
U.S. Home [*NYSE symbol*] (TTSB) ... UH
U.S. Home & Garden [*NASDAQ symbol*] (TTSB) ... USHG
U.S. Home Cv Pfd [*NYSE symbol*] (TTSB) ... UHPr
United States Home Guard ... USHG
U.S. Home Wrrt [*NYSE symbol*] (TTSB) ... UH.WS
U.S. HomeCare [*NASDAQ symbol*] (TTSB) ... USHO
United States Hop Growers Association ... USHGA
United States Hot Rod Association [*Auto racing*] ... USHRA
United States Housing Authority [*Functions transferred to Public Housing Commissioner, 1947*] ... USHA
United States Housing Corp. [*Terminated, 1952*] ... USHC
United States Hydrograph Laboratory ... USHL
United States Hydrographic Office [*Later, Naval Oceanographic Office*] ... USHO
United States Hygienic Laboratory ... USHL
United States Icelandic Defense Forces (MCD) ... USIDF
United States Immigration and Naturalization Service (BARN) ... USINS
United States Immigration and Naturalization Service, Monthly Review [*A publication*] (DLA) ... Immig & Naturalization Serv Mo Rev
United States Independent Telephone Association (EA) ... USITA
United States Indian Affairs Office, Digest of Decisions [*A publication*] (DLA) ... Ind A Dig
United States Indian International Travel Agency, Inc. ... USIITA
United States Industrial Chemical Co. (KSC) ... USICC
United States Industrial Chemicals Co., Research Center Library, Cincinnati, OH [*Library symbol Library of Congress*] (LCLS) ... OCUSI
United States Industrial College of the Armed Forces [*Fort McNair*], Washington, DC [*Library symbol Library of Congress*] (LCLS) ... DAIC
United States Industrial Council (EA) ... USIC
United States Industrial Outlook [*A publication*] ... USIO
United States Industries, Inc. [*Associated Press*] (SAG) ... US Inds
United States Industries, Inc. [*NYSE symbol*] (SAG) ... USI
United States Industries, Inc. [*NYSE symbol*] (SAG) ... USN
United States Industry ... USI
United States Information Agency [*Formerly called BECA, it later became known as ICA or USICA, then again as USIA*] ... USIA
United States Information Agency Acquisition Regulation [*A publication*] (AAGC) ... IAAR
United States Information Agency Procurement [*A publication*] (AAGC) ... USIAPR
United States Information Agency, Washington, DC [*OCLC symbol*] (OCLC) ... USI
United States Information Center [*Department of State*] (MCD) ... USIC
United States Information Service [*Name used abroad for USIA offices*] ... USIS
United States Information Service Library (DIT) ... USISL
United States Information Service, Ottawa, Ontario [*Library symbol National Library of Canada*] (NLC) ... OOUSA
United States Institute for Theatre Technology (EA) ... USITT
United States Institute of Oceanography (DNAB) ... USIO
United States Intelligence Board [*Later, NFIB*] [*National Security Council*] ... USIB
United States Inter-American Council [*Later, COA*] (EA) ... USIAC
United States Intercollegiate Lacrosse Association (EA) ... USILA
United States Interests Section [*Foreign Service*] ... USINT
United States Internal Revenue Bonded ... USIRB
United States Internal Revenue Bureau, Commissioner's Mimeographed Published Opinions [*A publication*] (DLA) ... Mim
United States International Air Travel Statistics Data Base [*I. P. Sharp Associates*] [*Canada*] (NITA) ... INS Data Base
United States International Airways ... UNI
United States International Book Association (NTCM) ... USIBA
United States International Communication Agency [*Also, ICA*] [*Formerly called BECA and USIA, it later became known again as USIA*] ... USICA
United States International Communications Agency, Ottawa, ON, Canada [*Library symbol Library of Congress*] (LCLS) ... CaOOUSI
United States International Marketing Center [*American Embassy, London*] (CB) ... USIMC
United States International Moth Class Association (EA) ... USIMCA
United States International Narcotics Control Commission ... USINCC
United States International Sailing Association (EA) ... USISA
United States International Skating Association ... USISA
United States International Speed Skating Association (EA) ... USISSA
United States International Tempest Association (EA) ... USITA
United States International Trade Commission ... USITC
United States International Trade Commission. Publication [*A publication*] (DLA) ... USITC Pub
United States International Trade Commission, Washington, DC [*OCLC symbol*] (OCLC) ... DTC
United States International Transportation Exposition (PDAA) ... USITE
United States International University [*San Diego, CA*] ... USIU

United States International University, Colorado Alpine Campus, Steamboat Springs, CO [*Library symbol Library of Congress*] (LCLS) ..... CoSsU
United States International University, San Diego, CA [*Library symbol Library of Congress*] (LCLS) .... CSdI
United States Inter-Parliamentary Union (EA) .... USIPU
United States Interstate Commerce Commission Reports [*A publication*] (DLA) .... USICC Rep
United States Interstate Commerce Commission Valuation Reports [*A publication*] (DLA) .... USICCVR
United States Interstate Commerce Commission, Washington, DC [*Library symbol Library of Congress*] (LCLS) .... DIC
United States/Japan Natural Resources Panel .... USJNRP
United States Jaycees (EA) .... USJ
United States Joint Chiefs of Staff (NATG) .... USJCS
United States Joint Communication Agency (NATG) .... USJCA
United States Joint Publications Research Service .... USJPRS
United States Joint Task Force (AABC) .... USJTF
United States Joint Unconventional Warfare Task Force (AABC) .... USJUWTF
United States Judo (EA) .... USJ
United States Judo Association (EA) .... USJA
United States Judo Federation (EA) .... USJF
United States Junior Chamber of Commerce [*Later, United States Jaycees*] (EA) .... US JAYCEE
United States Junior Chamber of Commerce [*Later, United States Jaycees*] (EA) .... USJCC
United States Jurist [*A publication*] (DLA) .... US Jur
United States Justice Foundation (EA) .... USJF
United States Kart Association [*Defunct*] (EA) .... USKA
United States Kerry Blue Terrier Club (EA) .... USKBTC
United States Korfball Federation (EA) .... USKF
United States Labor Party .... USLP
United States Lacrosse Coaches' Association (EA) .... USLCA
United States Lake Survey [*Marine science*] (MSC) .... USLS
United States Lakeland Terrier Club (EA) .... USLTC
United States Land Decisions (Proudfit) [*A publication*] (DLA) ...... Proudf Land Dec
United States Lanolin and Derivative Manufacturers Association [*Defunct*] (EA) .... USLDMA
United States Law Intelligencer and Review [*Providence and Philadelphia*] [*A publication*] (DLA) .... US Law Int
United States Law Journal [*A publication*] (DLA) ..... US Law Jour
United States Law Journal [*New Haven and New York*] [*A publication*] (DLA) .... USLJ
United States Law Magazine [*A publication*] (DLA) ..... US Law Mag
United States Law Magazine [*A publication*] (DLA) ..... USL Mag
United States Law Week [*A publication*] (NTCM) .... LW
United States Law Week [*Bureau of National Affairs*] [*A publication*] (DLA) .... USLW
United States Lawn Mower Racing Association .... USLMRA
United States Lawn Tennis Association [*Later, USTA*] (EA) .... USLTA
United States Laws (DLA) .... USL
United States League of Savings Associations [*Later, USLSI*] .... USLSA
United States League of Savings Associations, Chicago, IL [*Library symbol Library of Congress*] (LCLS) .... ICLSA
United States League of Savings Institutions [*Chicago, IL*] (EA) .... USLSI
United States Legation .... USL
United States Liaison Office [*or Officer*] .... USLO
United States Liaison Officer to Supreme Allied Commander, Atlantic (MUGU) .... USLO SACA
United States Library of Congress, Early State Records Collection, Washington, DC [*Library symbol Library of Congress*] (LCLS) .... DLC(ESR)
United States Library of Congress, Generalized Bibliography System, Washington, DC [*Library symbol*] [*Library of Congress*] (LCLS) ...... DLC-GB
United States Library of Congress, National Resources Program, Washington, DC [*Library symbol*] [*Library of Congress*] (LCLS) .... DLC-NR
United States Library of Congress, National Serials Data Program, Washington, DC [*Library symbol Library of Congress*] (LCLS) .... DLC-N
United States Library of Congress, National Translations Center, Washington, DC [*Library symbol Library of Congress*] (LCLS) .... DLC-NTC
United States Library of Congress, Priority Four Collection, Washington, DC [*Library symbol Library of Congress*] (LCLS) DLC-P4
United States Library of Congress, Regional and Cooperative Cataloging Division, Washington, DC [*Library symbol*] [*Library of Congress*] (LCLS) .... DLC-R
United States Library of Congress, Serial Record Division, Washington, DC [*Library symbol*] [*Library of Congress*] (LCLS) .... DLC-S
United States Library of Congress, Washington, DC [*Library symbol*] [*Library of Congress*] (LCLS) .... DLC
United States Library of Congress, Washington, DC [*OCLC symbol*] (OCLC) .... NSD
United States Lifesaving Association (EA) .... USLA
United States Lighthouse Society (EA) .... USLHS
United States Lighthouse Society (EA) .... USLS
United States Lime & Minerals Co. [*Associated Press*] (SAG) .... USLime
United States Livestock Sanitary Association [*Later, United States Animal Health Association*] (EA) .... USLSA
United States Locals Collectors (EA) .... USLC
[*The*] United States Logistics Group [*Military*] (AABC) ... TUSLOG
United States Logistics Support Office (AFM) .... USLSO
United States Long Distance [*Associated Press*] (SAG) ..... US LongD
United States Long Distance [*NASDAQ symbol*] (SAG) .... USLD
United States Longshoremen and Harborworkers Act ..... USL & H
United States Lowry Air Force Base, Denver, CO [*Library symbol Library of Congress*] (LCLS) .... CoDL
United States Luge Association (EA) .... USLA
United States Machine Screw Service Bureau [*Defunct*] (EA) .... USMSSB

United States Mail .... USM
United States Mallard Project [*Army*] .... USMP
United States Marine .... USM
United States Marine Air Corps .... USMAC
United States Marine Barracks .... USMB
United States Marine Corps .... USMC
United States Marine Corps Air Station .... USMCAS
United States Marine Corps, Air Station, Cherry Point, NC [*Library symbol Library of Congress*] (LCLS) .... NcCpM
United States Marine Corps Base (MCD) .... USMCB
United States Marine Corps Drill Instructors Association (EA) .... USMCDIA
United States Marine Corps, Marine Corps Air Station, Special Services for Station Library, New River Base, Jacksonville, NC [*Library symbol Library of Congress*] (LCLS) .... NcJaMC
United States Marine Corps, Marine Corps Base General Library, Camp Lejeune, NC [*Library symbol Library of Congress*] (LCLS) ...... NcCaLMC
United States Marine Corps Museum, Washington, DC [*Library symbol Library of Congress*] (LCLS) .... DMaM
United States Marine Corps Reserve .... USMCR
United States Marine Corps Reserve (Aviation Fleet) ..... USMCR(AF)
United States Marine Corps Reserve (Aviation, Organized) ... USMCR(AO)
United States Marine Corps Reserve (Aviation Specialist Transport Pilot, Volunteer) .... USMCR(NAVT)
United States Marine Corps Reserve (Aviation, Volunteer) ... USMCR(AV)
United States Marine Corps Reserve (Fleet) .... USMCR(F)
United States Marine Corps Reserve (Graduate Aviation Cadets, Volunteer) .... USMCR(NAVO)
United States Marine Corps Reserve (Limited Service) ... USMCR(LS)
United States Marine Corps Reserve (Naval Aviators) ..... USMCR(NAV)
United States Marine Corps Reserve (Organized) .... USMCR(O)
United States Marine Corps Reserve Training Center ..... USMCRTC
United States Marine Corps Reserve (Volunteer) .... USMCR(V)
United States Marine Corps Reserve (Volunteer Specialists) ..... USMCR(VS)
United States Marine Corps Reserve (Women) .... USMCR(W)
United States Marine Corps Schools, Educational Center, Quantico, VA [*Library symbol Library of Congress*] (LCLS) .... ViQM-E
United States Marine Corps Schools, Quantico, VA [*Library symbol Library of Congress*] (LCLS) .... ViQM
United States Marine Corps Selective Service Selectee ..... USMCSS
United States Marine Corps Selective Service Volunteer ..... USMCSSV
United States Marine Corps (Women) .... USMC(W)
United States Marine Corps Women's Reserve .... USMCWR
United States Marine Fisheries Service, Southeast Fisheries Center, Beaufort Laboratory, Beaufort, NC [*Library symbol Library of Congress*] (LCLS) .... NcBeaAE
United States Marine Hospital .... USMH
United States Marine Hospital Service .... USMHS
United States Marine Safety Association (EA) .... UMSA
United States Marine Safety Association (EA) .... USMSA
United States Maritime Administration .... USMA
United States Maritime Administration, Washington, DC [*Library symbol Library of Congress*] (LCLS) .... DMA
United States Maritime Commission [*Functions transferred to Department of Commerce, 1950*] .... USMC
United States Maritime Service .... USMS
United States Maritime Service Graduate Station .... USMSGS
United States Maritime Service Officers School .... USMSOS
United States Maritime Service Training School .... USMSTS
United States Maritime Service Training Ship .... USMSTS
United States Maritime Service Training Station .... USMSTS
United States Marshall Service [*Department of Justice*] ...... USMS
United States Marshals Office (BARN) .... USMO
United States Masters International Track Team [*Defunct*] ·(EA) .... USMITT
United States Masters Swimming (EA) .... USMS
United States Meat Export Federation (EA) .... USMEF
United States Medical Graduate .... USMG
United States Medical Intelligence and Information Agency, Frederick, MD [*OCLC symbol*] (OCLC) .... UAM
U.S. Medical Products [*NASDAQ symbol*] (TTSB) .... USMD
United States Members, United Nations Military Staff Committee .... USMEMILCOMUN
United States Men's Curling Association [*Later, USCA*] (EA) ...... USMCA
United States Merchant Marine .... USMM
United States Merchant Marine Academy [*Kings Point, NY*] ...... USMMA
United States Merchant Marine Academy, Kings Point, NY [*Library symbol Library of Congress*] (LCLS) .... NKipM
United States Merchant Marine Academy, Kings Point, NY [*OCLC symbol*] (OCLC) .... VYM
United States Merchant Marine Cadet Corps .... USMMCC
United States Merchant Marine Reserve .... USNRM
United States Merchant Marine Reserve Coastal Defense USNRM2
United States Merchant Marine Reserve Seagoing USNRM1
United States Message Text Formating .... USMTF
United States Metric Board [*Terminated*] .... USMB
United States Microgravity Laboratory [*NASA*] .... USML
United States Microgravity Payload [*NASA*] .... USMP
United States Military Academy (AAGC) .... MA
United States Military Academy [*West Point, NY*] .... USMA
United States Military Academy Department of Earth, Space, and Graphic Sciences [*West Point, NY*] .... USMA/ESGS
United States Military Academy Preparatory School ..... USMAPS
United States Military Academy Preparatory Unit .... USMAPU
United States Military Academy, West Point, NY [*Library symbol Library of Congress*] (LCLS) .... NWM
United States Military Academy, West Point, NY [*OCLC symbol*] (OCLC) .... YWM

United States Military Advisor's Representative (CINC) .... USMILADREP
United States Military Advisor's Representative, Southeast Asia Treaty Organization, Military Planning Office (CINC) .... USMILADREPSMPO
United States Military Advisory Group .... USMAG
United States Military Air Transport Service [Later, Military Airlift Command] .... USMATS
United States Military Assistance Command .... USMAC
United States Military Assistance Command, South Vietnam [Obsolete] .... USMACSV
United States Military Assistance Command, Thailand [Obsolete] (AFM) .... USMACTHAI
United States Military Assistance Command, Vietnam [Obsolete] .... USMACV
United States Military Attache .... USMA
United States Military Attache .... USMILATTACHE
United States Military Communications Electronics Board (NVT) .... USMCEB
United States Military Community Activity, Mannheim .... USMCAM
United States Military Construction Program (CINC) .... USMCP
United States Military Enlistment Processing Command .... USMEPC
United States Military Entrance Processing Command .... USMEPCOM
United States Military Information Control Committee (AFM) .... USMICC
United States Military Liaison Mission (MCD) .... USMLM
United States Military Liaison Mission to Commander-in-Chief, Group Soviet Forces, Germany (AABC) .... USMLMCINCGSFG
United States Military Liaison Office .... USMILLIAS
United States Military Liaison Office .... USMLO
United States Military Mission with the Iranian Army .... ARMISH
United States Military North African Mission [World War II] .... USMNAM
United States Military Specification Requirements (MCD) .... USMSR
United States Military Sports Association .... USMSA
United States Military Supply Mission to India (AFM) .... USMSMI
United States Military Technical Advisory Group (AFM) .... USMILTAG
United States Military Training Mission (MCD) .... USMTM
United States Military Training Mission to Saudi Arabia .... USMTMSA
United States Military Transport .... USMT
United States Minor Outlying Islands [ANSI two-letter standard code] (CNC) .... UM
United States Minor Outlying Islands [ANSI three-letter standard code] (CNC) .... UMI
United States Mint .... USM
United States Mint - Carson City (ROG) .... USMCC
United States Mint - San Francisco (ROG) .... USMS
United States Minutemen [Defunct] (EA) .... USM
United States Miscellaneous Caribbean Islands [MARC geographic area code Library of Congress] (LCCP) .... nwuc--
United States Miscellaneous Caribbean Islands [MARC country of publication code Library of Congress] (LCCP) .... uc
United States Miscellaneous Pacific Islands [MARC geographic area code Library of Congress] (LCCP) .... poup--
United States Miscellaneous Pacific Islands [MARC country of publication code Library of Congress] (LCCP) .... up
United States Mission, Berlin .... USBER
United States Mission to European Communities [Department of State] ..... USEC
United States Mission to NATO and European Regional Organizations .... USRO
United States Mission to the European Communities in Belgium and Luxembourg .... USMECBL
United States Mission to the European Office of the United Nations .... USMEOUN
United States Mission to the International Atomic Energy Agency .... USIAEA
United States Mission to the International Atomic Energy Agency in Austria .... USMIAEAA
United States Mission to the North Atlantic Treaty Organization [Department of State] (NATG) .... USNATO
United States Mission to the North Atlantic Treaty Organization and European Regional Organizations in France .... USNMATOEROF
United States Mission to the Organization for Economic Cooperation and Development [Department of State] .... USOECD
United States Mission to the Organization of American States [Department of State] .... USOAS
United States Mission Weekly Report [Military] .... USMWR
United States Modern Pentathlon and Biathlon Association [Later, USMPA] (EA) .... USMPBA
United States Modern Pentathlon Association (EA) .... USMPA
United States Modern Pentathlon Training Center [Military] (AABC) .... USMPTC
United States Monopoly Association (EA) .... USMA
United States Monthly Law Magazine [A publication] (DLA) ...... US Month Law Mag
United States Monthly Law Magazine [A publication] (DLA) .... USML Mag
United States Museum Librarian Society (EA) .... USMLS
United States National Aeronautics and Space Administration, Goddard Space Flight Center, Greenbelt, MD [Library symbol Library of Congress] (LCLS) .... DNASA-G
United States National Aeronautics and Space Administration, Technical Library, Wallops Island, VA [Library symbol Library of Congress] (LCLS) .... ViWiN
United States National Aeronautics and Space Administration, Washington, DC [Library symbol Library of Congress] (LCLS) .... DNASA
United States National Agricultural Library, Beltsville, MD [Library symbol Library of Congress] (LCLS) .... DNAL
United States National Arboretum, Washington, DC [OCLC symbol] (OCLC) .... AGA
United States National Arboretum, Washington, DC [Library symbol Library of Congress] (LCLS) .... DNAr
United States National Archives and Record Center, Fort Worth, TX [Library symbol Library of Congress] (LCLS) .... TxFNA
United States National Archives and Records Service (DIT) .... USNARS

United States National Archives and Records Service, National Archives Library, Washington, DC [Library symbol Library of Congress] (LCLS) ...... DNA
United States National Army .... USNA
United States National Bureau of Standards (IAA) .... USNBS
United States National Bureau of Standards, Gaithersburg, MD [Library symbol Library of Congress] (LCLS) .... DBS
United States National Central Bureau .... USNCB
United States National Commission for UNESCO [of the Department of State] .... USNC
United States National Committee [IEC] .... USNC
United States National Committee for Federation Internationale de Documentation .... USNCFID
United States National Committee for Solar-Terrestrial Research (MCD) .... USNC-STR
United States National Committee for the Decade for Natural Disaster Reduction .... USNC/DNDR
United States National Committee for the History of Geology (EA) .... USHIGEO
United States National Committee for the International Biological Program [Defunct] (EA) .... USNC/IBP
United States National Committee for the International Geophysical Year .... USNC-IGY
United States National Committee for the Preservation of Nubian Monuments [Defunct] (EA) .... USNCPNM
United States National Committee for the Union Radio Scientifique Internationale [International Union of Radio Science] (EA) .... USNC-URSI
United States National Committee, International Commission on Irrigation and Drainage .... USICID
United States National Committee/International Union of Radio Science (MCD) .... USNC/UPSI
United States National Committee of the International Electrotechnical Commission .... USNCIEC
United States National Committee of the International Peat Society (EA) .... USNCIPS
United States National Committee of the World Energy Conference (EA) .... USNCWEC
United States National Committee on Standardization .... USNS
United States National Council on Soil Mechanics and Foundation Engineering .... USNCSM & FE
United States National Environmental Health Sciences Center, Durham, NC [Library symbol Library of Congress] (LCLS) .... NcDurHS
United States National Guard .... USNG
United States National Institute of Dance (EA) .... USNID
United States National Institute of Health, Rocky Mountain Laboratory Library, Hamilton, MT [Library symbol Library of Congress] (LCLS) .... MtHamRL
United States National Institutes of Health, Bethesda, MD [Library symbol Library of Congress] (LCLS) .... DNIH
United States National Institutes of Health, Bureau of Health Manpower, Bethesda, MD [Library symbol Library of Congress] (LCLS) .... DNIH-HM
United States National Library of Medicine, Bethesda, MD [Library symbol Library of Congress] (LCLS) .... DNLM
United States National Marine Fisheries Service, Area Office, Anchorage, AK [Library symbol Library of Congress] (LCLS) .... AkAF
United States National Marine Fisheries Service, Auke Bay Fisheries Laboratory, Auke Bay, AK [Library symbol Library of Congress] (LCLS) .... AkAbF
United States National Marine Fisheries Service, Biological Laboratory, Galveston, TX [Library symbol Library of Congress] (LCLS) .... TxGUSFW
United States National Marine Fisheries Service, Northeast Fisheries Center, Woods Hole, MA [Library symbol Library of Congress] (LCLS) .... MWhN
United States National Marine Fisheries Service, Southwest Fisheries Center, La Jolla, CA [Library symbol Library of Congress] (LCLS) .... CLjFS
United States National Marine Fisheries Service, Southwest Fisheries Center, Tiburon Laboratory, Tiburon, CA [Library symbol Library of Congress] (LCLS) .... CTibF
United States National Military Representative .... USNMR
United States National Museum [Smithsonian Institution] .... USNM
United States National Oceanic and Atmospheric Administration, Environmental Research Laboratories Library, Boulder, CO [Library symbol Library of Congress] (LCLS) .... CoBBS
United States National Oceanic and Atmospheric Administration, National ClimaticCenter, Ashville, NC [Library symbol Library of Congress] (LCLS) .... NcANCC
United States National Oceanographic Data Center [Marine science] (OSRA) .... USNODC
United States National Ocean-Wide Survey Program (NOAA) .... USNOWSP
United States National Park Service, Cabrillo National Monument, San Diego, CA [Library symbol Library of Congress] (LCLS) .... CSdNPS
United States National Park Service, Denver, CO [Library symbol Library of Congress] (LCLS) .... CoDNPS
United States National Park Service, Everglades National Park, Homestead, FL [Library symbol Library of Congress] (LCLS) .... FHNP
United States National Park Service, Grand Canyon National Park Library, Grand Canyon, AZ [Library symbol Library of Congress] (LCLS) .... AzGrcN
United States National Park Service, Grand Portage Northern Minnesota Fur Trade Library, Grand Marais, MN [Library symbol] [Library of Congress] (LCLS) .... MnGmFT
United States National Park Service, Midwest Regional Office, Omaha, NE [Library symbol Library of Congress] (LCLS) .... NbONPS
United States National Park Service, National Capital Park Library, Washington, DC [Library symbol Library of Congress] (LCLS) .... DNPS
United States National Park Service, National Register Division, Washington, DC [Library symbol Library of Congress] (LCLS) .... DNPS-NR
United States National Park Service, Pacific Northwest Region, Seattle, WA [Library symbol] [Library of Congress] (LCLS) .... WaSNPS

United States National Parks Service [*USA*] (EERA) .... USNPS
United States National Railroad Adjustment Board Awards, First Division [*A publication*] (DLA) .... NRAB (1st D)
United States National Railroad Adjustment Board Awards, Fourth Division [*A publication*] (DLA) .... NRAB (4th D)
United States National Railroad Adjustment Board Awards, Second Division [*A publication*] (DLA) .... NRAB (2d D)
United States National Railroad Adjustment Board Awards, Third Division [*A publication*] (DLA) .... NRAB (3d D)
United States National Reference Preparation [*Centers for Disease Control*] .... USNRP
United States National Research Council [*Toxicology*] .... USNRC
United States National Stockpile Purchase Specification [*for metals*] ..... USNSPS
United States National Student Association [*Later, USSA*] ...... USNSA
United States National War College, Fort McNair, Washington, DC [*Library symbol Library of Congress*] (LCLS) .... DNW
United States NATO Hawk Liaison Office [*Missiles*] (NATG) ... USNAHALO
United States Natural Resources Conservation Service .... NRCS
United States Naval Academy [*Annapolis, MD*] .... USNA
United States Naval Academy Alumni Association .... USNAAA
United States Naval Academy, Annapolis [*Maryland*] ...... USNA ANNA
United States Naval Academy, Annapolis, MD [*Library symbol Library of Congress*] (LCLS) .... MdAN
United States Naval Academy, Annapolis, MD [*OCLC symbol*] (OCLC) .... UNA
United States Naval Academy Athletic Association .... USNAAA
United States Naval Academy Division of Engineering and Weapons .... USNA-EW
United States Naval Academy Energy-Environment Study Group and Development Team .... USNA-EPRD
United States Naval Administrative Command .... USNAC
United States Naval Advanced Base [*World War II*] .... USNAB
United States Naval Air Corps .... USNAC
United States Naval Air Development Center .... USNADC
United States Naval Air Development Center, Technical Information Library, Warminster, PA [*Library symbol*] [*Library of Congress*] (LCLS) .... PWarN
United States Naval Air Missile Test Center .... USNAMTC
United States Naval Air Service .... USNAS
United States Naval Air Station .... USNAS
United States Naval Air Station, Alameda, CA [*Library symbol Library of Congress*] (LCLS) .... CAlaUN
United States Naval Air Station Library, Millington, TN [*Library symbol Library of Congress*] (LCLS) .... TMiNA
United States Naval Air Station, Patuxent River, MD [*Library symbol Library of Congress*] (LCLS) .... MdPa
United States Naval Air Station, Pensacola, FL [*Library symbol Library of Congress*] (LCLS) .... FPeN
United States Naval Air Training Center .... USNATC
United States Naval Aircraft .... USNA
United States Naval Aircraft Factory, Philadelphia, PA [*Library symbol Library of Congress Obsolete*] (LCLS) .... PPUNA
United States Naval Amphibious Base .... USNAB
United States Naval Amphibious Base, Coronado, CA [*Library symbol Library of Congress*] (LCLS) .... CCoronUN
United States Naval Attache (GFGA) .... USNA
United States Naval Auxiliary Air Station .... USNAAS
United States Naval Avionics Facility .... USNAF
United States Naval Base (MUGU) .... USNB
United States Naval Civil Engineering Laboratory [*Port Hueneme, CA*] (SAA) .... USNCEL
United States Naval Civil Engineering Laboratory, Port Hueneme, CA [*Library symbol Library of Congress*] (LCLS) .... CPhCE
United States Naval Civil Engineering Research and Evaluation Laboratory .... USNCEREL
United States Naval Construction Battalion [*SEABEES*] [*BUDOCKS; later, FEC, NFEC*] .... USNCB
United States Naval Drydocks .... USNDD
United States Naval Electronics Laboratory .... USNEL
United States Naval Engineering Experiment Station [*Annapolis, MD*] ...... USEES
United States Naval Engineering Experiment Station [*Annapolis, MD*] (SAA) .... USNEES
United States Naval Fleet Reserve .... USNFR
United States Naval Forces, Continental Air Defense Command (DNAB) .... USNAVFORCONAD
United States Naval Forces, Eastern Atlantic and Mediterranean (MCD) .... USNELM
United States Naval Forces Europe (MCD) .... USNAVEUR
United States Naval Home, Philadelphia, PA [*Library symbol Library of Congress Obsolete*] (LCLS) .... PPUNH
United States Naval Hospital .... USNH
United States Naval Hospital, Medical Library, Oak Harbor, WA [*Library symbol*] [*Library of Congress*] (LCLS) .... WaOhNH
United States Naval Hospital, Millington, TN [*Library symbol Library of Congress*] (LCLS) .... TMiNH
United States Naval Hospital, Oakland, CA [*Library symbol Library of Congress*] (LCLS) .... CONH
United States Naval Hospital, San Diego, CA [*Library symbol Library of Congress*] (LCLS) .... CSdNH
United States Naval Institute (EA) .... USNI
United States Naval Liaison Officer .... USNLO
United States Naval Manpower Center (DNAB) .... USNMRC
United States Naval Medical Center, Bethesda, MD [*Library symbol Library of Congress*] (LCLS) .... DNMC
United States Naval Medical Field Research Laboratory, Camp Lejeune, NC [*Library symbol Library of Congress*] (LCLS) .... NcCaLM

United States Naval Member of the Allied Control Commission [*Germany*] .... USNACC
United States Naval Missile Facility .... USNMF
United States Naval Missile Test Center [*Point Mugu, CA*] (AAG) .... USNMTC
United States Naval Motion Picture Service (DNAB) .... USNMPS
United States Naval Observatory .... USNO
United States Naval Observatory Automated Data Service [*Database*] [*Information service or system*] (CRD) .... USNOADS
United States Naval Observatory Time Service Division [*Washington, DC*] .... USNO-TS
United States Naval Observatory, Time Service Sub-Station (DNAB) .... USNOBSYSUBSTA
United States Naval Observatory, Washington, DC [*OCLC symbol*] (OCLC) .... DNO
United States Naval Oceanographic Office [*Marine science*] (MSC) .... USNOO
United States Naval Oceanographic Office NSTL Station, Bay St. Louis, MS [*Library symbol*] [*Library of Congress*] (LCLS) .... MsBsNO
United States Naval Operating Bases System .... USNOBSY
United States Naval Ordnance Test Station .... USNOTS
United States Naval Ordnance Test Station, Pasadena, CA [*Library symbol Library of Congress*] (LCLS) .... CPUN
United States Naval Postgraduate School (GAGS) .... US Naval
United States Naval Postgraduate School (MUGU) .... USNPGS
United States Naval Postgraduate School .... USNPS
United States Naval Postgraduate School, Monterey, CA [*Library symbol Library of Congress*] (LCLS) .... CMontNP
United States Naval Prison .... USNP
United States Naval Proving Ground .... USNPG
United States Naval Radiological Defense Laboratory .... USNRDL
United States Naval Regional Dental Center (DNAB) .... USNAVREGDENCEN
United States Naval Regional Medical Center (DNAB) .... USNAVREGMEDCEN
United States Naval Repair Base .... USNRB
United States Naval Representative, United Nations Military Staff Committee .... USNAVYMILCOMUN
United States Naval Research Laboratory .... USNRL
United States Naval Reserve .... USNR
United States Naval Reserve Force .... USNRF
United States Naval Reserve - Retired (DNAB) .... USNR-R
United States Naval Reserve, Selective Volunteer .... USNRSV
United States Naval Reserve - Standby (DNAB) .... USNR-S
United States Naval Reserve Training Center .... USNRTC
United States Naval Reserve, Volunteer .... USNRV
United States Naval Reserve (Women's Reserve) .... USNR(W)
United States Naval Safety Code .... USNSC
United States Naval Ship [*Civilian manned*] .... USNS
United States Naval Shipyard, Technical Library, Mare Island, CA [*Library symbol Library of Congress*] (LCLS) .... CMiUN
United States Naval Shore Communication Facilities .... USNSCF
United States Naval Station .... USNS
United States Naval Station Library, Long Beach, CA [*Library symbol Library of Congress*] (LCLS) .... CLobUN
United States Naval Submarine Medical Center .... USNSMC
United States Naval Supply Activity (CINC) .... USNAVSUPACT
United States Naval Supply Research and Development Facility, Bayonne, NJ [*Library symbol Library of Congress*] (LCLS) .... NjBaNSRF
United States Naval Test Pilot School .... USNTPS
United States Naval Training .... USNATRA
United States Naval Training Center .... USNTC
United States Naval Training Center, Bainbridge, MD [*Library symbol Library of Congress*] (LCLS) .... MdBb
United States Naval Training Center, Great Lakes, IL [*Library symbol Library of Congress*] (LCLS) .... IGIN
United States Naval Training Device Center .... USNTDC
United States Naval Training School .... USNTS
United States Naval Vessel .... USS
United States Naval War College .... USNWC
United States Naval Weapons Center, China Lake, CA [*Library symbol Library of Congress*] (LCLS) .... CIN
United States Naval Weapons Station, Yorktown, VA [*Library symbol Library of Congress*] (LCLS) .... ViYNW
United States Naval Weather Service .... USNAVWEASERV
United States Navy .... USN
United States Navy and United States Marine Corps Reserve Center (DNAB) .... USN & USMCRC
United States Navy Astronautics Group (SAA) .... USNAG
United States Navy, Electronics Laboratory, San Diego, CA [*Library symbol Library of Congress*] (LCLS) .... CSdNEL
United States Navy, Environmental Prediction Research Facility, Monterey, CA [*Library symbol Library of Congress*] (LCLS) .... CMontUSN
United States Navy, Europe .... USANAVEUR
United States Navy Experimental Diving Station .... USNEDS
United States Navy Forces Southern Command (AFM) .... USNAVSO
United States Navy Hydrographic Office [*Later, NOO*] (NATG) .... USNHO
United States Navy (Inductee) (Special Assignment) .... USN(I)(SA)
United States Navy League .... USNL
United States Navy Medical Service Corps .... USNMSC
United States Navy Memorial Foundation (EA) .... USNMF
United States Navy Mine Defense Laboratory (MUGU) .... USNMDL
United States Navy, Mine Defense Laboratory, Technical Library, Panama City, FL [*Library symbol Library of Congress*] (LCLS) .... FPcNM
United States Navy, Naval Aerospace Medical Institute, Pensacola, FL [*Library symbol Library of Congress*] (LCLS) .... FPeN-M
United States Navy, Naval Arctic Research Laboratory, Barrow, AK [*Library symbol Library of Congress*] (LCLS) .... AkBarNA

United States Navy, Naval Missile Center, Point Mugu, CA [*Library symbol Library of Congress*] (LCLS) .... CPmuN
United States Navy, Naval Regional Medical Center, Bremerton, WA [*Library symbol Library of Congress*] (LCLS) .... WaBrNR
United States Navy, Naval Regional Medical Center, Library, Camp Lejeune, NC [*Library symbol Library of Congress*] (LCLS) .... NcCaLNM
United States Navy, Naval Regional Medical Center, Philadelphia, PA [*Library symbol Library of Congress*] (LCLS) .... PPNMC
United States Navy, Naval Ship Research and Development Laboratory, Annapolis, MD [*Library symbol Library of Congress*] (LCLS) .... MdANE
United States Navy, Naval Submarine Base, Bangor Library, Bremerton, WA [*Library symbol Library of Congress*] (LCLS) .... WaBrNS
United States Navy, Naval Training Equipment Center, Orlando, FL [*Library symbol Library of Congress*] (LCLS) .... FON
United States Navy, Naval Undersea Center, San Diego, CA [*Library symbol Library of Congress*] (LCLS) .... CSdNUC
United States Navy, Naval Underwater Systems Center, Technical Library, Newport,RI [*Library symbol Library of Congress*] (LCLS) .... RNNU
United States Navy Plan Representative Office .... USNAVPRO
United States Navy, Puget Sound Naval Shipyard, Engineering Library, Bremerton, WA [*Library symbol Library of Congress*] (LCLS) .... WaBrNP
United States Navy Radio and Sound Laboratory [*San Diego, CA*] .... USNR & SL
United States Navy Recruiting Station .... USNRS
United States Navy Regulations .... USNR
United States Navy Reporting Office [*or Officer*] .... USREPOF
United States Navy Representative, Military Staff Committee, United Nations (DNAB) .... USNAVMILCOMUN
United States Navy Research and Development Laboratory .... USNRDL
United States Navy - Reserve Officers Training Corps .... USN-ROTC
United States Navy - Retired (DNAB) .... USN-R
United States Navy (Retired) .... USN(Ret)
United States Navy Routing Office .... USRO
United States Navy Ship Missile System Engineering Station .... USNSMSES
United States Navy Southern Command .... USNAVSOUTHC
United States Navy Southern Command .... USNAVSOUTHCOM
United States Navy Southern Command .... USNSO
United States Navy Special Projects Office (DNAB) .... USNSPO
United States Navy Submarine Base, Naval Submarine Medical Research Laboratory, Groton, CT [*Library symbol Library of Congress*] (LCLS) .... CtGrN-M
United States Navy Submarine Base, Naval Submarine Medical Research Laboratory, Groton, CT [*Library symbol Library of Congress Obsolete*] (LCLS) .... CtGroN-M
United States Navy Travel Instructions .... USNTI
United States Navy Undersea Laboratory (IAA) .... USNUSL
United States Navy Underwater Sound Laboratory [*BUSHIPS; later, ESC, NESC*] .... USNUSL
United States Newspaper Program [*National Foundation on the Arts and the Humanities*] [*Information service or system*] (IID) .... USNP
United States, North of Cape Hatteras [*Shipping*] .... USNH
United States Northern Great Plains Research Center, Mandan, ND [*Library symbol Library of Congress*] (LCLS) .... NdManNG
United States Norton Owners' Association (EA) .... USNOA
United States NOTAM [*Notice to Airmen*] **System** [*Aviation*] (FAAC) .... USNS
United States Nuclear Data Committee [*Nuclear Regulatory Commission*] .... USNDC
United States Nuclear Regulatory Commission (NRCH) .... USNRC
United States Nuclear Regulatory Commission, Washington, DC [*Library symbol Library of Congress*] (LCLS) .... DNRC
United States Ocean Survey Plan (NOAA) .... USOSP
United States Oceanographic Office (PDAA) .... USOO
United States of ACORN [*Publication of the Association of Community Organizations for Reform Now*] .... USA
United States of America .... USA
United States of America .... USA
United States of America Confederation [*Later, USAC/RS*] (EA) .... USAC
United States of America Goju Association (DICI) .... USAGA
United States of America National Committee of the International Dairy Federation (EA) .... USNAC
United States of America Rugby Fives Association (EA) .... USARFA
United States of America Rugby Football Union (EA) .... USARFU
United States of America Standard (IEEE) .... USAS
United States of America Standard Character Set for Optical Character Recognition [*Computer science*] .... USASCOCR
United States of America Standard Character Set for Optical Character Recognition [*Computer science*] .... USASCSOCR
United States of America Standard Character Set for Optical Characters (IAA) .... USASCSOCR
United States of America Standard Code for Information Interchange (NOAA) .... USACII
United States of America Standard Code for Information Interchange .... USASCII
United States of America Standard Code for Information Interchange (IAA) .... USASII
United States of America Standards Institute [*Formerly, ASA*] [*Later, ANSI*] .... USASI
United States of Colombia .... USC
United States of Indonesia (BARN) .... USI
United States of North America [*Name of a cooperative community in Pleasantville, NY designed by Frank Lloyd Wright*] .... USONIA
United States of Poetry .... USOP
United States Office of Consumer Affairs .... USOCA
United States Office of Education [*Later, USDE*] .... USOE
United States Office of Management and Budget, Washington, DC [*Library symbol Library of Congress*] (LCLS) .... DBB
United States Office of Naval Research .... USONR
U.S. Office Products [*NASDAQ symbol*] (TTSB) .... OFIS
United States Olympic Association [*Later, USOC*] .... USOA
United States Olympic Committee (EA) .... USOC
United States Olympic Committee, Sports Medicine Division, Colorado Springs, CO [*Library symbol Library of Congress*] (LCLS) .... CoCOC-M
United States One-Design Class Council (EA) .... ODCC
United States Operations Mission [*Military*] .... USOM
United States Opinions Attorneys-General (Frith) [*Pt. 2., Vol. 21*] [*A publication*] (DLA) .... Frith
U.S. Opportunity Search [*NASDAQ symbol*] (TTSB) .... USOS
United States Ordnance Missile Command .... USOMC
United States Ordnance Producers Association [*Inactive*] (EA) .... USOPA
United States Organization for Disabled Athletes (EA) .... USODA
United States Organized Naval Reserve .... USNRO
United States Organized Naval Reserve Aviation USNRO2
United States Organized Naval Reserve Seagoing USNRO1
United States Orienteering Federation (EA) .... USOF
United States Othello Association (EA) .... USOA
United States Outdoor Volleyball Association (EA) .... USOVA
United States Outfitters .... USO
United States Outfitters .... USO
United States Oversea Internal Defense [*Army*] (AABC) .... USOID
United States Overseas [*Facetious translation of United Services Organization*] (VNW) .... USO
United States Overseas Airlines .... USOA
United States Overseas Tax Fairness Committee (EA) .... TFC
United States Pacific Command [*Military*] .... USPACOM
United States Pacific Issues Network [*Defunct*] (EA) .... USPIN
United States Pacifist Party [*Political party*] (EA) .... USPP
United States PanAsian American Chamber of Commerce (EAIO) .... USPAACC
United States Paper Exporters Council [*Defunct*] (EA) .... USPEC
United States Parachute Association (EA) .... USPA
United States Park Police [*Department of the Interior*] .... USPP
United States Park Service, Fort Vancouver National Historical Site, Vancouver, WA [*Library symbol Library of Congress*] (LCLS) .... WaVHS
United States Park Service, Harpers Ferry National Historical Park, Harpers Ferry, WV [*Library symbol Library of Congress*] (LCLS) .... WvHfP
United States Parole Commission [*Formerly, United States Parole Board*] .... USPC
United States Passport Agency [*Department of State*] .... USPA
United States Patent .... USP
United States Patent and Trademark Office .... USPTO
United States Patent Office [*Department of Commerce*] .... USPO
United States Patent Office, Arlington, VA [*Library symbol Library of Congress*] (LCLS) .... DP
United States Patent Office, Washington, DC [*OCLC symbol*] (OCLC) .... DCP
United States Patent Quarterly [*A publication*] (DLA) .... PQ
United States Patent Quarterly [*A publication*] (DLA) .... US Pat Q
United States Patent Quarterly [*A publication*] (DLA) .... US Pat Quar
United States Patent Quarterly [*A publication*] (DLA) .... US Pat Quart
United States Patents Quarterly .... USPQ
U.S. Pawn [*NASDAQ symbol*] (TTSB) .... USPN
United States Pawn, Inc. [*Associated Press*] (SAG) .... US Pawn
United States Pawn, Inc. [*NASDAQ symbol*] (SAG) .... USPN
United States Peace Corps (EA) .... USPC
United States Penitentiary .... USP
United States People for the United Nations [*Defunct*] (EA) .... US/PFUN
United States Pharmacopeia [*Following name of a substance, signifies substance meets standards set by USP*] .... USP
United States Pharmacopeia Dispensing Information .... USPDI
United States Pharmacopeial Convention [*Database producer*] (EA) .... USP
United States Pharmacopoeia .... USPh
United States Pharmacopoeial Convention .... USPC
U.S. Physical Therapy [*NASDAQ symbol*] (TTSB) .... USPH
United States Physical Therapy Association (EA) .... USPTA
United States Pigeon Shooting Federation [*Defunct*] (EA) .... USPSF
United States Pilots Association (EA) .... USPA
United States Police Canine Association (EA) .... USPCA
United States Political Science Information Service [*University of Pittsburgh*] (IID) .... UPSIS
United States Polo Association (EA) .... USPA
United States Pony Clubs (EA) .... USPC
United States Pony Trotting Association [*Defunct*] (EA) .... USPTA
United States Post Office [*Later, United States Postal Service*] .... USPO
United States Post Office Department. Official Opinions of the Solicitor [*A publication*] (DLA) .... Ops AAG POD
United States Postal History Society [*Defunct*] (EA) .... USPHS
United States Postal Service .... USPS
United States Postal Service Library, Washington, DC [*OCLC symbol*] (OCLC) .... USP
United States Postal Service, Washington, DC [*Library symbol Library of Congress*] (LCLS) .... DPO
United States Potash Co., Carlsbad, NM [*Library symbol Library of Congress*] (LCLS) .... NmCP
United States Potters' Association (EA) .... USPA
United States Poultry and Egg Producers Association (EA) .... USPEPA
United States Power Squadrons (EA) .... USPS
United States Precision Helicopter Team .... USPHT
United States Prisoner of War Information Center [*Army*] (AABC) .... USPWIC
United States Prisoner of War Information Center (Branch) [*Army*] (AABC) .... USPWIC(Br)
United States Privacy Council (EA) .... USPC
United States Private Security and Detective Association (EA) .... USPSDA
United States Procurement Committee .... USPC
United States Producer Price Index [*Database*] [*Department of Labor*] [*Information service or system*] (CRD) .... USPPI

United States Professional Development Institute ... USPDI

United States Professional Diving Coaches Association (EA) ... PDCA

United States Professional Diving Coaches Association (EA) ... USPDCA

United States Professional Lawn Tennis Association [*Later, USPTA*] (EA) ... USPLTA

United States Professional Tennis Association (EA) ... USPTA

United States Professional Tennis Registry (EA) ... USPTR

United States Property ... USP

United States Property and Disbursing Officer ... USPDO

United States Property and Fiscal Officer (AAGC) ... USP&FO

United States Property and Fiscal Officer [*Military*] ... USPFO

United States Public Health Service ... USPHS

United States Public Health Service, Arctic Health Research Center, Anchorage, AK [*Library symbol Library of Congress*] (LCLS) ... AkAH

United States Public Health Service, Court Decisions [*A publication*] (DLA) ... Pub Health

United States Public Health Service Hospital, Baltimore, MD [*Library symbol Library of Congress*] (LCLS) ... MdBPH

United States Public Health Service Hospital, Carville, LA [*Library symbol Library of Congress*] (LCLS) ... LCar

United States Public Health Service Hospital, Medical Service Library, Seattle, WA [*Library symbol Library of Congress*] (LCLS) ... WaSPH

United States Public Health Service, National Institute for Occupational Safety and Health, Appalachian Laboratory for Occupational Safety and Health Library, Morgantown, WV (LCLS) ... WvMNIO

United States Public Health Service Reserve ... USPHSR

United States Public-Land Surveys ... USPLS

United States Pulp Producers Association [*Later, API*] (EA) ... USPPA

United States Purchasing Commission ... USPC

United States Purchasing Exchange ... USPE

United States Quartermaster Corps ... USQMC

United States Quartermaster Corps, Food and Container Institute [*for the Armed Forces*], Chicago, IL [*Library symbol Library of Congress*] (LCLS) ... ICUSQ

United States Quartermaster Research and Development Center, Natick, MA [*Library symbol Library of Congress*] (LCLS) ... MNatQ

United States Racing Pigeon Association [*Defunct*] (EA) ... USRPA

United States Racquet Stringers Association (EA) ... USRSA

United States Racquetball Association (EA) ... USRA

United States Railroad Labor Board Decisions [*A publication*] (DLA) ... RLB

United States Railroad Retirement Board. Law Bulletin [*A publication*] (DLA) ... RRBLB

United States Railway Association [*In 1974, superseded United States Railroad Administration, which had been absorbed by the Department of Transportation in 1939*] [*Terminated in 1987*] ... USRA

United States Readiness Command ... USREDCOM

United States Reclamation Service ... USRS

United States Recreational Tennis Association (EA) ... USRTA

United States Red Cedar Shingle Industry ... USRCSI

United States Refugee Program ... USRP

United States Register [*Philadelphia*] [*A publication*] (DLA) ... US Reg

United States Regular Navy - Inductee ... USN-I

United States Regular Navy - Inductee - Construction Battalion ... USN-I-CB

United States Regular Navy Selective Volunteer ... USN-SV

United States Reports [*Vols. 42-65*] [*A publication*] (DLA) ... Howard SC

United States Reports [*A publication*] (NTCM) ... US

United States Reports [*A publication*] (DLA) ... US Rep

United States [*Supreme Court*] **Reports** ... USR

United States Representative, Military Staff Committee, United Nations ... USREPMILCOMUN

United States Representative, Standing Group [*Military*] (AABC) ... USRSG

United States Representative to NATO Military Committee (AABC) ... USRNMC

United States Representative to the Military Committee [*NATO*] ... USREPMC

United States Representative to the Military Committee Liaison Office [*NATO*] ... USREPMILCOMLO

United States Representative to the Military Committee Memorandum [*NATO*] ... USM

United States Reserve Components and Personnel Administration Center ... USRCPAC

United States Reserves ... USR

U.S. Restaurant Properties [*NASDAQ symbol*] (TTSB) ... USV

United States Revenue Cutter Service ... USRCS

United States Revenue Marine ... USRM

United States Revised Statutes [*A publication*] (DLA) ... US Rev St

United States Revised Statutes ... USRS

United States Revolver Association (EA) ... USRA

United States Rice Export Development Association [*Later, RCMD*] ... USREDA

United States Road Racing Championship ... USRRC

U.S. Robotics [*NASDAQ symbol*] (TTSB) ... USRX

United States Robotics Corp. [*NASDAQ symbol*] (SAG) ... USRX

United States Robotics, Inc. [*Associated Press*] (SAG) ... US Robt

United States Robotics Society (CSR) ... USRS

United States Rocket Society (EA) ... USRS

United States Rowing Association (EA) ... USRA

United States Rowing Society (EA) ... USRS

United States Salvage Association [*Defunct*] (EA) ... USSA

United States Satellite Broadcasting Co. [*Associated Press*] (SAG) ... USSatB

United States Satellite Broadcasting Co., Inc. [*Minneapolis, MN*] [*Telecommunications*] (TSSD) ... USSB

U.S. Satellite Broadcasting'A' [*NASDAQ symbol*] (TTSB) ... USSB

United States Satellite Systems, Inc. [*Defunct*] (TSSD) ... USSSI

United States Savings and Loan League [*Later, USLSI*] (EA) ... USSLL

United States Savings Bond (WDAA) ... USSB

United States Savings Bonds Division [*Department of the Treasury*] ... USSBD

United States Scientific Export Association ... USSEA

United States Secret Service [*Department of the Treasury*] ... USSS

United States Secret Service Uniformed Division ... USSS/UD

United States Security Authority [*for NATO affairs*] ... USSA

United States Security Authority for CENTO Affairs (AABC) ... USSAC

United States Security Authority for SEATO Affairs (AABC) ... USSAS

United States Security Authority, NATO ... USSAN

United States Sellers [*Standard threads*] (DEN) ... USS

United States Sellers Standard Thread ... USSST

United States Senate (AAGC) ... Sen

United States Senate ... USS

United States Senate Committee Report [*A publication*] (DLA) ... Sen Rep

United States Senate Press Photographers Gallery (EA) ... USSPG

United States Senate Press Photographers Gallery (EA) ... USSPPG

United States Senate Resolution [*A publication*] (DLA) ... S Res

United States Sending State Office [*Navy*] ... USSSO

United States Seniors Bowling Association [*Later, Seniors Division of the American Bowling Congress*] (EA) ... USSBA

United States Seniors Golf Association [*Defunct*] (EA) ... USSGA

United States Sentencing Commission ... USSC

United States Servas Committee (EA) ... USSC

United States Shellac Importers Association (EA) ... USSIA

United States Ship ... USS

United States Shipping Board [*Terminated, 1933*] ... USSB

United States Shipping Board Bureau Decisions [*A publication*] (DLA) ... USSBB

United States Shipping Board Decisions [*A publication*] (DLA) ... USSB

United States Signal Intelligence Directive (AABC) ... USSID

United States Signals Intelligence System (MCD) ... USSS

United States Signals Intellignce System (MCD) ... USSIS

United States Single Integrated Operational Plan (NATG) ... US-SIOP

United States Ski Association (EA) ... USSA

United States Ski Educational Foundation (EA) ... USSEF

United States Ski Writers Association [*Later, NASJA*] (EA) ... USSWA

United States Skibob Federation (EA) ... USSBF

United States Slo-Pitch Softball Association (EA) ... USSSA

United States Snowshoe Association (EA) ... USSA

United States Snowshoe Association (EA) ... USSSA

United States Soccer Federation (EA) ... USSF

United States Soccer Football Association [*Later, USSF*] (EA) ... USSFA

United States Social Security Administration, Baltimore, MD [*Library symbol Library of Congress*] (LCLS) ... MdBOAS

United States Social Security Board Unemployment Compensation Interpretation Service. Benefit Series [*A publication*] (DLA) ... Benefit Series UCIS

United States Society for Education through Art (EA) ... USSEA

United States Society for Esperantists Youth (EA) ... USEJ

United States Society of Esperanto Instructors [*Later, AATE*] ... USEI

United States Society of Esperanto Instructors [*Later, AATE*] (AEBS) ... USSEI

United States Softball Federation ... USSF

United States Soil Conservation Service (BARN) ... USSCS

United States Soldiers' and Airmen's Home (AABC) ... USSAH

United States Soldiers' Home ... USSH

United States Southern Command [*Air Force*] ... USSOUTHCOM

United States Space Administration (IAA) ... USSA

United States Space Command ... USSPACECOM

United States Space Education Association (EA) ... USSEA

United States Space Foundation (EA) ... USSF

United States Special Committee on Antarctic Names [*1943-47*] ... US-SCAN

United States Special Forces ... USSF

United States Special Forces Long Range Reconnaisance Patrol (VNW) ... USSF LRRP

United States Special Forces (Provisional) (CINC) ... USSF(P)

United States Special Operations Command [*DoD*] ... USSOC

United States Special Operations Command [*DoD*] ... USSOCOM

United States Sports Academy (EA) ... USSA

United States Sports Academy, Daphne, AL [*Library symbol*] [*Library of Congress*] (LCLS) ... ADaS

United States Sports Massage Federation (EA) ... USMF

United States Squash Racquets Association (EA) ... USSRA

United States Standard ... USS

United States Standard Atmosphere (KSC) ... USSA

United States Standard Gauge ... USSG

United States Standing Group Representative [*NATO*] ... USSGREP

United States State Department. Bulletin [*A publication*] (DLA) ... State Dept Bull

United States State Trials [*Wharton*] [*A publication*] (DLA) ... US St Tr

United States Statutes at Large [*A publication*] (DLA) ... St

United States Statutes at Large [*A publication*] (DLA) ... Stat at L

United States Statutes at Large [*A publication*] (DLA) ... US St at L

United States Statutes at Large [*A publication*] (DLA) ... US Stat

United States Steamer ... USS

United States Steamship ... USSS

United States Steel Corp., Pittsburgh, PA [*Library symbol Library of Congress*] (LCLS) ... PPiUS

United States Steel Corp., Research Center Library, Monroeville, PA [*Library symbol Library of Congress*] (LCLS) ... PMvS

United States Steel Foundation ... USSF

United States Stickball League (EA) ... USSBL

United States Stone and Bead Importers Association (EA) ... USSBIA

United States Strategic Air Force [*Later, Strategic Air Command*] ... USSAF

United States Strategic Air Force [*Later, Strategic Air Command*] ... USSTAF

United States Strategic Air Forces in Europe ... USSAFE

United States Strategic Bombing Survey [*Disbanded, 1946*] ... USSBS

United States Strategic Institute (EA) ... USSI

United States Strategic Tactical Air Force, Europe ... USSTAFE

United States Strike Command [*Military combined Tactical Air Command and Strategic Army Command Force*] ... USSC

United States Strike Command [*Military combined Tactical Air Command and Strategic Army Command Force*] ...... USSTRICOM
United States Student Association (EA) ...... USSA
United States Student Press Association [*Superseded by CPS*] ...... USSPA
United States Superintendent of Documents, Washington, DC [*Library symbol Library of Congress*] (LCLS) ...... DSD
United States Support Activities Group [*Military*] ...... USSAG
United States Support Activities / Seventh Air Force [*Vietnam*] (VNW) USSAG/7AF
United States Supreme Court ...... USSC
United States Supreme Court ...... USSCT
United States Supreme Court Bulletin (Commerce Clearing House) [*A publication*] (DLA) ...... S Ct Bull (CCH)
United States Supreme Court Library, Washington, DC [*OCLC symbol*] (OCLC) ...... LAW
United States Supreme Court Reporter [*A publication*] (DLA) ...... US Sup Ct
United States Supreme Court Reporter [*A publication*] (DLA) ...... US Sup Ct R
United States Supreme Court Reporter [*A publication*] (DLA) ...... US Sup Ct Rep
United States Supreme Court Reports [*A publication*] (DLA) ...... US
United States Supreme Court Reports [*A publication*] (AAGC) ...... US
United States Supreme Court Reports [*A publication*] (DLA) ...... USSC Rep
United States Supreme Court Reports, Lawyers' Edition [*A publication*] (DLA) ...... US Law Ed
United States Supreme Court Reports, Lawyers' Edition [*A publication*] (DLA) ...... US Rep (L Ed)
United States Supreme Court Reports, Lawyers' Edition [*A publication*] (DLA) ...... US Sup Ct (L Ed)
United States Supreme Court Reports, Lawyers' Edition, Advance Opinions [*A publication*] (DLA) ...... L Ed (Adv Ops)
United States Supreme Court Reports, Lawyers' Edition, Advance Opinions [*A publication*] (DLA) ...... Law Ed Adv Op
United States Supreme Court Reports, Lawyers' Edition, Second Series [*A publication*] (DLA) ...... Law Ed 2d
United States Supreme Court Reports, Photo Reproduction Set by Baldwin [*A publication*] (DLA) ...... Bald US Sup Ct Rep
United States Supreme Court Rule [*A publication*] (DLA) ...... Sup Ct R
United States Supreme Court, Washington, DC [*Library symbol Library of Congress*] (LCLS) ...... DUSC
United States Surfing Federation (EA) ...... USSF
U.S. Surgical [*NYSE symbol*] (TTSB) ...... USS
U.S. Surgical $2.20 Dep'DECS' [*NYSE symbol*] (TTSB) ...... USSPrA
United States Surgical Co. [*Associated Press*] (SAG) ...... US Srg
United States Surgical Corp. [*Associated Press*] (SAG) ...... US Surg
United States Surgical Corp. [*NYSE symbol*] (SPSG) ...... USS
United States Swimming Association (EA) ...... USSA
United States Swimming Foundation (EA) ...... USSF
United States Swimming, Inc. (EA) ...... USS
United States Synchronized Swimming, Inc. (EA) ...... USSSI
United States Table Tennis Association (EA) ...... USTTA
United States Tariff Commission [*Later, ITC*] ...... USTC
United States Tax Cases [*Commerce Clearing House*] [*A publication*] (DLA) ...... US Tax Cas
United States Tax Cases [*Commerce Clearing House*] [*A publication*] (DLA) ...... USTC
United States Tax Court Cases [*A publication*] (DLA) ...... TC
United States Tax Court, Library, Washington, DC [*OCLC symbol*] (OCLC) ...... UTC
United States Tax Court Reporters [*A publication*] (AAGC) ...... TC
United States Technical Advisory Group (IAA) ...... USTAG
United States Technical Industrial Intelligence Committee (MCD) ...... USTIIC
U.S. Technologies [*NASDAQ symbol*] (TTSB) ...... USXX
United States Technologies, Inc. [*Associated Press*] (SAG) ...... US Tech
United States Telephone Association (EA) ...... USTA
United States Tennessee Valley Authority ...... USTVA
United States Tennis Association, Inc. (EA) ...... USTA
United States Tenpin Bowling Federation (EA) ...... USTBF
United States Testing Co., Inc. (NASA) ...... UST
United States Testing Co., Inc. ...... USTC
United States/Thai Forces ...... USTAF
United States Time ...... UST
United States Time Standard [*National Institute of Standards and Technology*] ...... USTS
United States Touch and Flag Football Association (EA) ...... USTFFA
United States Tour Operators Association (EA) ...... USTOA
United States Touring Riders Association [*Defunct*] (EA) ...... USTRA
United States Tourist Council (EA) ...... USTC
United States Track and Field Federation [*Later, TFA/USA*] ...... USTFF
United States Track Coaches Association [*Later, TFA/USA*] ...... USTCA
United States Trade Representative [*Formerly, SRTN*] [*Executive Office of the President*] ...... USTR
United States Trade Secrets Act (AAGC) ...... USTSA
United States Trademark Association (EA) ...... USTA
United States Trademark Association (BARN) ...... USTMA
United States Training and Employment Service [*Abolished, 1971*] [*Department of Labor*] ...... USTES
United States Transmission Systems, Inc. [*Secaucus, NJ*] (TSSD) ...... USTS
United States Transportation Command [*MTMC*] (TAG) ...... TRANSCOM
United States Transportation Command ...... USTRANSCOM
United States Transportation Commission [*Proposed commission to consolidate CAB, ICC, and FMC*] ...... USTC
United States Transportation Research Command [*Army*] ...... USTRC
U.S. Transportation Sys [*NASDAQ symbol*] (TTSB) ...... USTS
United States Transportation Systems, Inc. [*Associated Press*] (SAG) ...... US Tran
United States Transportation Systems, Inc. [*Associated Press*] (SAG) ...... US Tran
United States Transportation Systems, Inc. [*Associated Press*] (SAG) ...... US Trn

United States Travel and Tourism Administration (USGC) ...... USTTA
United States Travel and Tourism Administration [*Formerly, US Travel Service*] [*Department of Commerce*] ...... USTTA
United States Travel Bureau ...... USTB
United States Travel Service [*Replaced by United States Travel and Tourism Administration*] [*Department of Commerce*] ...... USTS
United States Travelers' Overseas Personalized Service [*Also known as USTOPS*] ...... TOPS
United States Travelers' Overseas Personalized Service [*Also known as TOPS*] ...... USTOPS
United States Treasury Department (DLA) ...... US Treas Dept
United States Treasury Department ...... USTD
United States Treasury Regulations [*A publication*] (DLA) ...... Treas Regs
United States Treasury Regulations [*A publication*] (DLA) ...... US Treas Reg
United States Treaties and Other International Agreements [*A publication*] (DLA) ...... UST
United States Treaty Development [*A publication*] (DLA) ...... USTD
United States Treaty Series [*A publication*] (DLA) ...... TS
United States Treaty Series [*A publication*] (DLA) ...... US Treaty Ser
United States Trotting Association (EA) ...... USTA
United States Trout Farmers Association ...... TFA
United States Trout Farmers Association (EA) ...... USTFA
United States Truck Drivers Association ...... USTDA
U.S. Trust [*NASDAQ symbol*] (TTSB) ...... USTC
United States Tuna Foundation (EA) ...... USTF
United States Twirling Association (EA) ...... USTA
United States Ultralight Association (EA) ...... USUA
United States/United Kingdom ...... US/UK
United States United Nations Delegation (CINC) ...... USUN
United States Veteran's Administration Administrator's Decisions [*A publication*] (DLA) ...... USVAAD
United States Veterans Administration Center, Bay Pines, FL [*Library symbol Library of Congress*] (LCLS) ...... FBypV
United States Veterans Administration Center, Brentonwood Medical Library, Los Angeles, CA [*Library symbol Library of Congress*] (LCLS) ...... CLVA-B
United States Veterans Administration Center, Cheyenne, WY [*Library symbol Library of Congress*] (LCLS) ...... WyCV
United States Veterans Administration Center, Dublin, GA [*Library symbol Library of Congress*] (LCLS) ...... GDuV
United States Veterans Administration Center, Fort Harrison, MT [*Library symbol Library of Congress*] (LCLS) ...... MtFhV
United States Veterans Administration Center, Hot Springs, SD [*Library symbol Library of Congress*] (LCLS) ...... SdHsV
United States Veterans Administration Center, Johnson City, TN [*Library symbol Library of Congress*] (LCLS) ...... TJoV
United States Veterans Administration Center, Leavenworth, KS [*Library symbol Library of Congress*] (LCLS) ...... KLeVA
United States Veterans Administration Center, Library Services, Dayton, OH [*Library symbol Library of Congress*] (LCLS) ...... ODaV
United States Veterans Administration Center, Martinsburg, WV [*Library symbol Library of Congress*] (LCLS) ...... WvMaV
United States Veterans Administration Center, Medical Library, Hampton, VA [*Library symbol Library of Congress*] (LCLS) ...... ViHaV
United States Veterans Administration Center, Medical Library, Salisbury, NC [*Library symbol Library of Congress*] (LCLS) ...... NcSalVA
United States Veterans Administration Center, Medical Research Library, Los Angeles, CA [*Library symbol Library of Congress*] (LCLS) ...... CLVA
United States Veterans Administration Center, Prescott, AZ [*Library symbol Library of Congress*] (LCLS) ...... AzPrV
United States Veterans Administration Center, Sioux Falls, SD [*Library symbol Library of Congress*] (LCLS) ...... SdSifV
United States Veterans Administration Center, Togus, ME [*Library symbol Library of Congress*] (LCLS) ...... MeToV
United States Veterans Administration Center, Wilmington, DE [*Library symbol Library of Congress*] (LCLS) ...... DeWV
United States Veterans Administration Hospital, Albany, NY [*Library symbol Library of Congress*] (LCLS) ...... NAIVA
United States Veterans Administration Hospital, Albuquerque, NM [*Library symbol Library of Congress*] (LCLS) ...... NmAVA
United States Veterans Administration Hospital, Allen Park, MI [*Library symbol Library of Congress*] (LCLS) ...... MiApV
United States Veterans Administration Hospital, Amarillo, TX [*Library symbol Library of Congress*] (LCLS) ...... TxAmV
United States Veterans Administration Hospital, Ambulatory Care Service, Henderson, NV [*Library symbol Library of Congress*] (LCLS) ...... NvHV-A
United States Veterans Administration Hospital, American Lake, WA [*Library symbol Library of Congress*] (LCLS) ...... WaAlVA
United States Veterans Administration Hospital, Atlanta, GA [*Library symbol Library of Congress*] (LCLS) ...... GAVA
United States Veterans Administration Hospital, Baltimore, MD [*Library symbol Library of Congress*] (LCLS) ...... MdBV
United States Veterans Administration Hospital, Bath, NY [*Library symbol Library of Congress*] (LCLS) ...... NBaVA
United States Veterans Administration Hospital, Battle Creek, MI [*Library symbol Library of Congress*] (LCLS) ...... MiBatV
United States Veterans Administration Hospital, Beckley, WV [*Library symbol Library of Congress*] (LCLS) ...... WvBV
United States Veterans Administration Hospital, Bedford, MA [*Library symbol Library of Congress*] (LCLS) ...... MBdV
United States Veterans Administration Hospital, Big Spring, TX [*Library symbol Library of Congress*] (LCLS) ...... TxBsV
United States Veterans Administration Hospital, Birmingham, AL [*Library symbol Library of Congress*] (LCLS) ...... ABVA

United States Veterans Administration Hospital, Boston, MA [*Library symbol Library of Congress*] (LCLS) .... MBV
United States Veterans Administration Hospital, Brecksville, OH [*Library symbol Library of Congress*] (LCLS) .... OBrV
United States Veterans Administration Hospital, Brockton, MA [*Library symbol Library of Congress*] (LCLS) .... MBrockV
United States Veterans Administration Hospital, Bronx, NY [*Library symbol Library of Congress*] (LCLS) .... NNVAB
United States Veterans Administration Hospital, Brooklyn, NY [*Library symbol Library of Congress*] (LCLS) .... NBVA
United States Veterans Administration Hospital, Buffalo, NY [*Library symbol Library of Congress*] (LCLS) .... NBuVA
United States Veterans Administration Hospital, Butler, PA [*Library symbol Library of Congress*] (LCLS) .... PButV
United States Veterans Administration Hospital, Canandaigua, NY [*Library symbol Library of Congress*] (LCLS) .... NCanV
United States Veterans Administration Hospital, Charleston, SC [*Library symbol Library of Congress*] (LCLS) .... ScCV
United States Veterans Administration Hospital, Cincinnati, OH [*Library symbol Library of Congress*] (LCLS) .... OCV
United States Veterans Administration Hospital, Cleveland, OH [*Library symbol Library of Congress*] (LCLS) .... OClV
United States Veterans Administration Hospital, Columbia, SC [*Library symbol Library of Congress*] (LCLS) .... ScCoV
United States Veterans Administration Hospital, Dallas, TX [*Library symbol Library of Congress*] (LCLS) .... TxDaVA
United States Veterans Administration Hospital, Danville, IL [*Library symbol Library of Congress*] (LCLS) .... IDanviVA
United States Veterans Administration Hospital, Davis Park, Providence, RI [*Library symbol Library of Congress*] (LCLS) .... RPV
United States Veterans Administration Hospital, Denver, CO [*Library symbol Library of Congress*] (LCLS) .... CoDVA
United States Veterans Administration Hospital, Des Moines, IA [*Library symbol Library of Congress*] (LCLS) .... IaDmV
United States Veterans Administration Hospital, Downey, IL [*Library symbol Library of Congress*] (LCLS) .... IDoV
United States Veterans Administration Hospital, Durham, NC [*Library symbol Library of Congress*] (LCLS) .... NcDurV
United States Veterans Administration Hospital, East Orange, NJ [*Library symbol Library of Congress*] (LCLS) .... NjEoV
United States Veterans Administration Hospital, Erie, PA [*Library symbol Library of Congress*] (LCLS) .... PErV
United States Veterans Administration Hospital, Fargo, ND [*Library symbol Library of Congress*] (LCLS) .... NdFVA
United States Veterans Administration Hospital, Forest Hills Division, Augusta, GA [*Library symbol Library of Congress*] (LCLS) .... GAuV-F
United States Veterans Administration Hospital, Fort Howard, MD [*Library symbol Library of Congress*] (LCLS) .... MdFhV
United States Veterans Administration Hospital, Fort Lyon, CO [*Library symbol Library of Congress*] (LCLS) .... CoFtLVA
United States Veterans Administration Hospital, Fresno, CA [*Library symbol Library of Congress*] (LCLS) .... CFVA
United States Veterans Administration Hospital, Gainesville, FL [*Library symbol Library of Congress*] (LCLS) .... FGV
United States Veterans Administration Hospital, Hines, IL [*Library symbol Library of Congress*] (LCLS) .... IHineV
United States Veterans Administration Hospital, Houston, TX [*Library symbol Library of Congress*] (LCLS) .... TxHVA
United States Veterans Administration Hospital, Huntington, WV [*Library symbol Library of Congress*] (LCLS) .... WvHuV
United States Veterans Administration Hospital, Iron Mountain, MI [*Library symbol Library of Congress*] (LCLS) .... MiIrmV
United States Veterans Administration Hospital, Jackson, MS [*Library symbol Library of Congress*] (LCLS) .... MsJV
United States Veterans Administration Hospital, Kansas City, MO [*Library symbol Library of Congress*] (LCLS) .... MoKVA
United States Veterans Administration Hospital, Knoxville, IA [*Library symbol Library of Congress*] (LCLS) .... IaKnV
United States Veterans Administration Hospital, Lake City, FL [*Library symbol Library of Congress*] (LCLS) .... FLcV
United States Veterans Administration Hospital, Lebanon, PA [*Library symbol Library of Congress*] (LCLS) .... PLebV
United States Veterans Administration Hospital, Lenwood Division, Augusta, GA [*Library symbol Library of Congress*] (LCLS) .... GAuV-L
United States Veterans Administration Hospital, Lexington, KY [*Library symbol Library of Congress*] (LCLS) .... KyLxV
United States Veterans Administration, Hospital Library Service, Asheville, NC [*Library symbol Library of Congress*] (LCLS) .... NcAV
United States Veterans Administration Hospital, Library Service, Batavia, NY [*Library symbol Library of Congress*] (LCLS) .... NBatV
United States Veterans Administration, Hospital Library, Syracuse, NY [*OCLC symbol*] (OCLC) .... ZUK
United States Veterans Administration Hospital, Lincoln, NE [*Library symbol Library of Congress*] (LCLS) .... NbLVA
United States Veterans Administration Hospital, Little Rock, AR [*Library symbol Library of Congress*] (LCLS) .... ArLVA
United States Veterans Administration Hospital, Livermore, CA [*Library symbol Library of Congress*] (LCLS) CLivV
United States Veterans Administration Hospital, Long Beach, CA [*Library symbol Library of Congress*] (LCLS) .... CLobVA
United States Veterans Administration Hospital, Louisville, KY [*Library symbol Library of Congress*] (LCLS) .... KyLoV
United States Veterans Administration Hospital, Lyons, NJ [*Library symbol Library of Congress*] (LCLS) .... NjLyoV
United States Veterans Administration Hospital, Madison, WI [*Library symbol Library of Congress*] (LCLS) .... WMaVA
United States Veterans Administration Hospital, Manchester, NH [*Library symbol Library of Congress*] (LCLS) .... NhMV
United States Veterans Administration Hospital (Manhattan), New York, NY [*Library symbol Library of Congress*] (LCLS) .... NNVAM
United States Veterans Administration Hospital, Marion, IN [*Library symbol Library of Congress*] (LCLS) .... InMarV
United States Veterans Administration Hospital, Martinez, CA [*Library symbol Library of Congress*] (LCLS) .... CMartVA
United States Veterans Administration Hospital, Medical Library, Castle Point, NY [*Library symbol*] [*Library of Congress*] (LCLS) .... NCapV
United States Veterans Administration Hospital, Medical Library, Coatesville, PA [*Library symbol Library of Congress*] (LCLS) .... PCtvVA
United States Veterans Administration Hospital, Medical Library, Denver, CO [*Library symbol Library of Congress*] (LCLS) .... CoDVA-M
United States Veterans Administration Hospital, Medical Library, Poplar Bluff, MO [*Library symbol Library of Congress*] (LCLS) .... MoPobV
United States Veterans Administration Hospital, Memphis, TN [*Library symbol Library of Congress*] (LCLS) .... TMV
United States Veterans Administration Hospital, Miami, FL [*Library symbol Library of Congress*] (LCLS) .... FMV
United States Veterans Administration Hospital, Minneapolis, MN [*Library symbol Library of Congress*] (LCLS) .... MnMVA
United States Veterans Administration Hospital, Montgomery, AL [*Library symbol Library of Congress*] (LCLS) .... AMVA
United States Veterans Administration Hospital, Montrose, NY [*Library symbol Library of Congress*] (LCLS) .... NMontrVA
United States Veterans Administration Hospital, Muskogee, OK [*Library symbol Library of Congress*] (LCLS) .... OkMuV
United States Veterans Administration Hospital, New Orleans, LA [*Library symbol Library of Congress*] (LCLS) .... LNVA
United States Veterans Administration Hospital, Newington, CT [*Library symbol Library of Congress*] (LCLS) .... CtNeV
United States Veterans Administration Hospital, Northampton, MA [*Library symbol Library of Congress*] (LCLS) .... MNV
United States Veterans Administration Hospital, Northport, NY [*Library symbol Library of Congress*] (LCLS) .... NNopoVA
United States Veterans Administration Hospital, Oklahoma City, OK [*Library symbol Library of Congress*] (LCLS) .... OkOkV
United States Veterans Administration Hospital, Omaha, NE [*Library symbol Library of Congress*] (LCLS) .... NbOV
United States Veterans Administration Hospital, Oteen, NC [*Library symbol Library of Congress*] (LCLS) .... NcOtV
United States Veterans Administration Hospital, Outpatient Clinic, Brooklyn, NY [*Library symbol Library of Congress*] (LCLS) .... NBVA-O
United States Veterans Administration Hospital, Palo Alto, CA [*Library symbol Library of Congress*] (LCLS) .... CPaVA
United States Veterans Administration Hospital, Perry Point, MD [*Library symbol Library of Congress*] (LCLS) .... MdPpV
United States Veterans Administration Hospital, Philadelphia, PA [*Library symbol Library of Congress*] (LCLS) .... PPV
United States Veterans Administration Hospital, Portland, OR [*Library symbol Library of Congress*] (LCLS) .... OrPV
United States Veterans Administration Hospital, Richmond, VA [*Library symbol Library of Congress*] (LCLS) .... ViRV
United States Veterans Administration Hospital, Roseburg, OR [*Library symbol Library of Congress*] (LCLS) .... OrRoV
United States Veterans Administration Hospital, Saginaw, MI [*Library symbol Library of Congress*] (LCLS) .... MiSV
United States Veterans Administration Hospital, St. Cloud, MN [*Library symbol Library of Congress*] (LCLS) .... MnStclV
United States Veterans Administration Hospital, St. Louis, MO [*Library symbol Library of Congress*] (LCLS) .... MoSVA
United States Veterans Administration Hospital, Salem, VA [*Library symbol Library of Congress*] (LCLS) .... ViSaV
United States Veterans Administration Hospital, San Antonio, TX [*Library symbol Library of Congress*] (LCLS) .... TxSaV
United States Veterans Administration Hospital, San Diego, CA [*Library symbol Library of Congress*] (LCLS) .... CSdV
United States Veterans Administration Hospital, San Fernando, CA [*Library symbol Library of Congress*] (LCLS) .... CSfeVA
United States Veterans Administration Hospital, San Francisco, CA [*Library symbol Library of Congress*] (LCLS) .... CSfV
United States Veterans Administration Hospital, Seattle, WA [*Library symbol Library of Congress*] (LCLS) .... WaSVA
United States Veterans Administration Hospital, Sepulveda, CA [*Library symbol Library of Congress*] (LCLS) .... CSepVA
United States Veterans Administration Hospital, Sheridan, WY [*Library symbol Library of Congress*] (LCLS) .... WyShV
United States Veterans Administration Hospital, Spokane, WA [*Library symbol Library of Congress*] (LCLS) .... WaSpVA
United States Veterans Administration Hospital, Syracuse, NY [*Library symbol Library of Congress*] (LCLS) .... NSyVA
United States Veterans Administration Hospital, Tampa, FL [*Library symbol Library of Congress*] (LCLS) .... FTV
United States Veterans Administration Hospital, Tomah, WI [*Library symbol Library of Congress*] (LCLS) .... WToVA
United States Veterans Administration Hospital, Topeka, KS [*Library symbol Library of Congress*] (LCLS) .... KTVA
United States Veterans Administration Hospital, Tucson, AZ [*Library symbol Library of Congress*] (LCLS) .... AzTV
United States Veterans Administration Hospital, Tuscaloosa, AL [*Library symbol Library of Congress*] (LCLS) .... ATuV

United States Veterans Administration Hospital, Tuskegee, AL [*Library symbol Library of Congress*] (LCLS) .... ATV
United States Veterans Administration Hospital, Vancouver, WA [*Library symbol Library of Congress*] (LCLS) .... WaVVA
United States Veterans Administration Hospital, Waco, TX [*Library symbol Library of Congress*] (LCLS) .... TxWV
United States Veterans Administration Hospital, Walla Walla, WA [*Library symbol Library of Congress*] (LCLS) .... WaWV
United States Veterans Administration Hospital, West Haven, CT [*Library symbol Library of Congress*] (LCLS) .... CtWehavV
United States Veterans Administration Hospital, West Roxbury, MA [*Library symbol Library of Congress*] (LCLS) .... MWroxV
United States Veterans Administration Hospital, Wichita, KS [*Library symbol Library of Congress*] (LCLS) .... KWiVA
United States Veterans Administration Hospital, Wood, WI [*Library symbol Library of Congress*] (LCLS) .... WWoVA
United States Veterans Administration Medical Center, Fayetteville, NC [*Library symbol Library of Congress*] (LCLS) .... NcFayV
United States Veterans Administration Medical Center, Medical Library, Boise, ID [*Library symbol*] [*Library of Congress*] (LCLS) .... IdBV
United States Veterans Administration Medical Center, West Haven, CT [*Library symbol*] [*Library of Congress*] (LCLS) .... CtWhvV
United States Veterans Administration, Outpatients Clinic, Boston, MA [*Library symbol Library of Congress*] (LCLS) .... MBV-O
United States Veterans Administration Supply Depot, Somerville, NJ [*Library symbol Library of Congress*] (LCLS) .... NjSoVA
United States Veterans Administration, Washington, DC [*Library symbol Library of Congress*] (LCLS) .... DVA
United States Veterans Administration, West Side Hospital, Chicago, IL [*Library symbol Library of Congress*] (LCLS) ICV
United States Veterans' Assistance Center (OICC) .... USVAC
United States Veterans Bureau .... USVB
United States Veterans Bureau Director's Decisions [*A publication*] (DLA) .... USVBDD
United States Veterans Hospital .... USVH
United States Volleyball Association (BARN) .... USVA
United States Volleyball Association (EA) .... USVBA
United States Volunteers [*Civil War*] .... USV
United States Walter Reed Army Medical Center, Medical Library, Washington, DC [*Library symbol Library of Congress*] (LCLS) .... DWR-M
United States Walter Reed Army Medical Center, Post/Patient Library, Washington,DC [*Library symbol Library of Congress*] (LCLS) .... DWR
United States Walter Reed Army Medical Center, Research Institute, Washington, DC [*Library symbol Library of Congress*] (LCLS) .... DWR-I
United States War Ballot Commission [*World War II*] .... USWBC
United States War Department, Decisions of Board of Contract Adjustment [*A publication*] (DLA) .... War Dept BCA
United States Warehouse Act Bonded .... USWAB
United States Water Fitness Association (EA) .... USWFA
United States Water Polo (EA) .... USWP
United States Wayfarer Association (EA) .... USWA
United States Weather Bureau [*Later, National Weather Service*] .... USWB
United States Weightlifting Federation (EA) .... USWF
United States West Indies .... USWI
United States Wholesale Grocers' Association [*Later, NAWGA*] (EA) ...... USWGA
United States Women's Army Corps Center .... USWACC
United States Women's Army Corps School .... USWACS
United States Women's Curling Association (EA) .... USWCA
United States Women's Lacrosse Association (EA) .... USWLA
United States Women's Squash Racquets Association (EA) .... USWSRA
United States Women's Track Coaches Association (EA) .... USWTCA
United States Wood Screw Service Bureau [*Defunct*] (EA) .... USWSSB
United States Wrestling Federation (EA) .... USWF
U.S. Xpress Enterprises'A' [*NASDAQ symbol*] (TTSB) .... XPRSA
United States Youth Council [*Defunct*] (EA) .... USYC
United States Youth Soccer Association (EA) .... USYSA
United States Zone of the Interior .... USZI
U.S.-China Indl Exchange [*NASDAQ symbol*] (TTSB) .... CHDX
United States-German Committee on Learning and Remembrance [*Defunct*] (EA) .... USGCLR
United States-Japan Committee on Industry Related Policies and Their Trade Effects [*Acronym pronounced "use-jay-krip-tee"*] .... USJCIRPTE
United States-Japan Committee on Scientific Cooperation [*Department of State*] .... US-JCSC
United States-Japan Cooperative Program on Natural Resources .... UJNR
United States-Japan Science Program (MSC) .... UJSP
United States-Japan Trade Council (EA) .... US-JTC
United States-Mexico Chamber of Commerce [*See also CCMEU*] (EA) .... USMCOC
United States-New Zealand Council (EA) .... USNZC
United Stationers [*NASDAQ symbol*] (TTSB) .... USTR
United Stationers, Inc. [*Associated Press*] (SAG) .... UStatn
United Stationers, Inc. [*NASDAQ symbol*] (NQ) .... USTR
United Steam Engine Makers' Society [*A union*] [*British*] .... USEMS
United Steel Workers' Association of the Philippines .... USWAP
United Steel Workers' Union of Central Africa [*Rhodesia and Nyasaland*] .... USUCA
United Steelworkers [*Trade union*] [*British*] .... USW
United Steelworkers of America .... USA
United Steelworkers of America [*Also known as USW*] (EA) .... USWA
United Stets Automotive Materials Partnership .... USAMP
United Stevedores' Union [*British*] .... USU
United Stockcar Alliance [*Auto racing*] .... USA
United Stone and Allied Products Workers of America [*Later, USWA*] ...... SAPW

United Stone and Allied Products Workers of America [*Later, USWA*] (EA) .... USAPWA
United Strasser Club .... USC
United Street Machine Association (EA) .... USMA
United Street Rod Association [*Defunct*] (EA) .... USRA
United Strictly Kosher Butchers Association .... USKBA
United Student Aid Fund .... USAF
United Student Aid Funds (EA) .... USA
United Student Christian Council in United States .... USCC
United Students for America [*Defunct*] (EA) .... USA
United Students of America Foundation [*Defunct*] (EA) .... USAF
United Sugar Samplers' Association [*Defunct*] .... USSA
United Support of Artists [*In USA for Africa, the chorus of American pop stars who recorded "We Are the World" to benefit famine victims in Africa*] .... USA
United Survival Clubs (EA) .... USC
United Svcs Advisor(Pfd) [*NASDAQ symbol*] (TTSB) .... USVSP
United Swedish Societies (EA) .... USS
United Synagogue Commission on Jewish Education [*Later, USACJE*] (EA) .... USCJE
United Synagogue of America (EA) .... USA
United Synagogue of America Commission on Jewish Education (EA) .... USACJE
United Synagogue of America Commission on Jewish Education (EA) .... USACOJE
United Synagogue Youth (EA) .... USY
United System of Electronic Computers (IEEE) .... USEC
United Tank Makers' Association [*A union*] [*British*] .... UTMA
United Tanners' Society [*A union*] [*British*] .... UTS
United Tariff Bureau .... UTB
United Tariff Bureau, Inc., New York NY [*STAC*] .... UNT
United Tasmania Group [*Political party Australia*] .... UTG
United Teaching Profession (MCD) .... UTP
United Techniques Research Center [*Navy*] (DNAB) .... UTRC
United Technologies [*NYSE symbol*] (TTSB) .... UTX
United Technologies Automotive .... UTA
United Technologies Corp. [*Associated Press*] (SAG) .... UnTech
United Technologies Corp. .... UT
United Technologies Corp. [*Information service or system*] (IID) .... UTC
United Technologies Corp. [*NYSE symbol*] (SPSG) .... UTX
United Technologies Microelectronics Center (NITA) .... UTMC
United Technologies Online Catalog [*United Technologies Corp.*] [*Information service or system*] (IID) .... UTOC
United Technologies Research Centre .... UTRC
United Technology Center (IAA) .... UTC
United Technology Center, Sunnyvale, CA [*Library symbol Library of Congress*] (LCLS) .... CSvUT
United Telecommunications/U.S. Sprint, Westwood, KS [*Library symbol*] [*Library of Congress*] (LCLS) .... KWwUT
United Telegraph Workers [*Later, C/UBC*] (EA) .... UTW
United Telephone Cables (IAA) .... UTC
United Telephone Organizations .... UTO
United Television, Inc. [*Associated Press*] (SAG) .... UnTelev
United Television, Inc. [*NASDAQ symbol*] (NQ) .... UTVI
United Televison [*NASDAQ symbol*] (TTSB) .... UTVI
United Territory .... UT
United Textile Workers of America (EA) .... UTWA
United Theological Seminary, Dayton, OH [*Library symbol Library of Congress*] (LCLS) .... ODaTS
United Theological Seminary, Dayton, OH [*OCLC symbol*] (OCLC) .... UTS
United Theological Seminary of the Twin Cities, New Brighton, MN [*Library symbol Library of Congress*] (LCLS) .... MnNbU
United Thoroughbred Trainers of America (EA) .... UTTA
United Tiberias Institutions Relief Society (EA) .... UTIRS
United Tire & Rubber Co. Ltd. [*Toronto Stock Exchange symbol*] .... UDT
United Tobacco Growers Association [*Defunct*] (EA) .... UTGA
United Together [*An association Defunct*] (EA) .... UT
United Towns Organisation [*See also FMVJ*] [*Paris, France*] (EAIO) .... UTO
United Trade Press (Holdings) Ltd. [*Commercial firm British*] .... UTP
United Trades Union Congress [*India*] .... UTUC
United Transformer Corp. (IAA) .... UTC
United TransNet [*NYSE symbol*] (TTSB) .... UT
United Transport International [*Bennett's Transport*] [*British*] .... UTI
United Transport Service Employees [*Later, BRAC*] (EA) .... UTSE
United Transportation Union (EA) .... UTU
United Trekkers of Planet Earth [*An association*] (EA) .... UTPE
United Tri-Star Resources Ltd. [*Toronto Stock Exchange symbol*] .... UTS
United Truck Owners of America (EA) .... UTOA
United Trust [*NASDAQ symbol*] (TTSB) .... UTIN
United Trust & Credit [*Finance group*] [*British*] .... UTC
United Trust, Inc. [*Associated Press*] (SAG) .... UtdTst
United Trust, Inc. [*NASDAQ symbol*] (SAG) .... UTIN
United Turners', Machinists', and Athletic Woodworkers' Trade Union [*British*] .... UTMAWTU
United TVRO [*Television Receive Only*] Owners Association [*Defunct*] (EA) .... UTOA
United Typothetae of America [*Later, Printing Industries of America*] .... UTA
United Ukrainian American Relief Committee (EA) .... UUARC
United Ulster Unionist Coalition [*Northern Ireland*] .... UUUC
United Ulster Unionist Movement [*Northern Ireland*] .... UUUM
United Ulster Unionist Party [*Northern Ireland*] [*Political party*] (PPW) .... UUUP
United Underwear Contractors Association [*Defunct*] (EA) .... UUCA
United Union of Roofers, Waterproofers, and Allied Workers .... RWAW
United Union of Roofers, Waterproofers, and Allied Workers (EA) ...... UURWAW
United Unionist Action Council [*Northern Ireland*] .... UUAC
United Unions for Employees and Workers [*Lebanon*] .... UUEW

United University Club [*British*] ... UUC
United Video Satellite [*Associated Press*] (SAG) ... UtdVideo
United Video Satellite [*NASDAQ symbol*] (SAG) ... UVSG
United Video Satellite Gp'A' [*NASDAQ symbol*] (TTSB) ... UVSGA
United Vietnam Veterans Organization (EA) ... UVVO
United Virginia Bankshares, Inc., Richmond, VA [*Library symbol Library of Congress*] (LCLS) ... ViRUV
United Vision Group [*Associated Press*] (SAG) ... UtdVs
United Voluntary Motor Corps (EA) ... UVMC
United Voluntary Services (EA) ... UVS
United Waste Systems [*Associated Press*] (SAG) ... UtdWste
United Waste Systems [*NASDAQ symbol*] (SAG) ... UWST
United Water Res [*NYSE symbol*] (TTSB) ... UWR
United Water Resources [*Associated Press*] (SAG) ... UWR
United Water Resources, Inc. [*NYSE symbol*] (SPSG) ... UWR
United Way (OICC) ... UW
United Way International (EA) ... UWI
United Way of America (EA) ... UWA
United Way of America Services Identification System ... UWASIS
United Way of Greater Vancouver, Vancouver, BC, Canada [*Library symbol Library of Congress*] (LCLS) ... CaBVaUWGV
United Way of Greater Vancouver, Vancouver, British Columbia [*Library symbol National Library of Canada*] (NLC) ... BVAUWGV
United Way of Metropolitan Chicago, Chicago, IL [*Library symbol Library of Congress*] (LCLS) ... ICUnW
United Way of Metropolitan Chicago, Chicago, IL [*OCLC symbol*] (OCLC) ... IDN
United We Resist Additional Packaging [*Student legal action organization*] ... UNWRAP
United We Stand America ... USWA
United Weighers Association (EA) ... UWA
United Weldors International Union ... UW
United Westburne Industries Ltd. [*Toronto Stock Exchange symbol*] ... UWI
United Whiteruthenian [*Byelorussian*] **American Relief Committee** (EA) ... UWARC
United Wisconsin Services, Inc. [*Associated Press*] (SAG) ... UtdWis
United Wisconsin Services, Inc. [*NYSE symbol*] (SAG) ... UWZ
United Wisconsin Svcs [*NYSE symbol*] (TTSB) ... UWZ
United Women of the Americas (EA) ... UWA
United Women's Societies of the Adoration of the Most Blessed Sacrament [*Later,NUWSAMBS*] (EA) ... UWSAMBS
United Workers' Party [*St. Lucia*] [*Political party*] (PPW) ... UWP
United Workers' Party [*Guyana*] [*Political party*] (EY) ... UWP
United Workers' Party [*Hungary Political party*] (PPW) ... UWP
United World Atheists (EA) ... UWA
United World College of South East Asia [*Singapore*] (ECON) ... UWCSEA
United World Education and Research Trust (EAIO) ... UWERT
United World Education and Research Trust [*British*] (EAIO) ... UWT
United World Federalists [*Later, World Federalists Association*] (EA) ... UWF
United World Mission (EA) ... UWM
United World Press Cooperative [*Later, The Peoples Media Cooperative*] (EA) ... UWPC
United Zionist Revisionists of America [*Later, Herut - USA*] (EA) ... UZRA
United-Guardian, Inc. [*Associated Press*] (SAG) ... UGrdn
Unitel Video [*AMEX symbol*] (TTSB) ... UNV
Unitel Video, Inc. [*Associated Press*] (SAG) ... UnitelV
Unitel Video, Inc. [*AMEX symbol*] (SPSG) ... UNV
Uniterra Foundation (EA) ... UF
Unites States Joint Communication Board (IAA) ... USJCB
Unites States of America [*IYRU nationality code*] (IYR) ... US
UNITIL Corp. [*Associated Press*] (SAG) ... UNITIL
UNITIL Corp. [*AMEX symbol*] (SPSG) ... UTL
Uniting Church Historical Society [*Australia*] ... UCHS
Unitized Component Assembly [*Aerospace*] ... UCA
Unitized Digital Electronic Calculator (MCD) ... UDEC
Unitized Microwave Devices ... UMD
Unitog [*NASDAQ symbol*] (TTSB) ... UTOG
Unitog Co. [*Associated Press*] (SAG) ... Unitog
Unitog Co. [*NASDAQ symbol*] (NQ) ... UTOG
Unitrin, Inc. [*NASDAQ symbol*] (SAG) ... UNIT
Unitrin, Inc. [*Associated Press*] (SAG) ... Unitrin
Unitrode Corp. [*Associated Press*] (SAG) ... Unitrde
Unitrode Corp. [*NYSE symbol*] (SPSG) ... UTR
Unitrode Corp. [*NASDAQ symbol*] (SAG) ... UTRWW
Unitrode Corp. Wrrt [*NASDAQ symbol*] (TTSB) ... UTRWW
Units Compatibility Test ... UCT
Units Consistency Analyzer [*Computer science*] ... UCA
Units in Operation [*Business term*] ... UIO
Units of Variance ... UOV
Units per Application (DNAB) ... U/A
Units per Assembly [*Business term*] (MHDB) ... UPA
Units Position (IAA) ... UP
Units Tens (IAA) ... UT
Units to Round Out the Active Army ... UTROAA
Unity College [*London, England*] ... UC
Unity for Safe Airtravel [*Program of Air Line Pilots Association*] ... USA
Unity Gain Amplifier ... UGA
Unity Gain Bandwidth ... UGB
Unity Gain Bandwidth ... UGBW
Unity Gain Crossover ... UGC
Unity Hospital, Fridley, MN [*Library symbol Library of Congress*] (LCLS) ... MnFrUH
Unity Management System [*Bytex Corp.*] ... UMS
Unity of Czech Ladies and Men [*Later, CSA*] (EA) ... UCLM
Unity of Empire [*Award*] [*British*] ... UE
Unity Party [*Liberia*] [*Political party*] (EY) ... UP
Unity Party [*Sierra Leone*] [*Political party*] (EY) ... UP
Unity Railways Co. [*AAR code*] ... UNI
Unity School Library, Lee's Summit, MO [*Library symbol Library of Congress*] (LCLS) ... MoLeeU
Unity-and-Diversity Council [*Later, UD*] (EA) ... UDC
Unity-and-Diversity World Council (EA) ... UD
Unity-Displacement-Factor Frequency Changer (DICI) ... UDFFC
Uniunea Evreilor Romani (BJA) ... UER
UNIVAC Automated Documentation System [*Computer science*] ... UNADS
UNIVAC [*Universal Automatic Computer*] **Bill of Material Processor Random System** [*Computer science*] (IAA) ... UNIBORS
UNIVAC [*Universal Automatic Computer*] **Bill of Material Processor Sequential System** [*Computer science*] (IAA) ... UNIBOSS
UNIVAC Data Processing Center (HGAA) ... UDPC
UNIVAC Interactive Language [*Computer science*] (IEEE) ... UIL
UNIVAC Scientific Exchange [*Later, UI, USE, Inc.*] ... USE
UNIVAC Share Assembly Program [*Sperry UNIVAC*] [*Computer science*] (IEEE) ... UNISAP
UNIVAC Standard Airline System (HGAA) ... USAS
UNIVAC Storage and Retrieval System [*Sperry UNIVAC*] [*Computer science*] ... UNISTAR
UNIVAC Users Association [*Later, AUUA*] ... UUA
Univar Corp. [*Formerly, VWR United Corp.*] [*Associated Press*] (SAG) ... Univar
Univar Corp. [*Formerly, VWR United Corp.*] [*NYSE symbol*] (SPSG) ... UVX
Univax Biologies [*NASDAQ symbol*] (SAG) ... UNVX
Univax Biologies, Inc. [*Associated Press*] (SAG) ... Univax
UnivEd Technologies Ltd. [*British*] (IRUK) ... UTL
Univentricular Atrioventricular Connection [*Cardiology*] (DAVI) ... UAVC
Univentricular Heart [*Cardiology*] ... UVH
Universair [*Spain ICAO designator*] (FAAC) ... MDN
Universair [*Spain ICAO designator*] (FAAC) ... UNA
Universal ... U
Universal (AFM) ... UNIV
Universal ... UNIVRSL
Universal [*Former USSR*] [*FAA designator*] (FAAC) ... UVL
Universal Active Filter (IAA) ... UAF
Universal Aerial Refueling Receptacle Slipaway Installation (MCD) ... UARRSI
Universal African Nationalist Movement (EA) ... UANM
Universal Air Data Computer ... UADC
Universal Air Freight Corp. ... UAFC
Universal Air Transport [*British*] [*FAA designator*] (FAAC) ... UAT
Universal Air Travel Plan [*Commercial airlines credit system*] ... UATP
Universal Air Waybill [*Shipping*] (DS) ... UAWB
Universal Aircraft Flight Simulator/Trainer ... UAFS/T
Universal Airline Codes ... UAC
Universal Airline Codes (MCD) ... UAL
Universal Airlines, Inc. [*ICAO designator*] (FAAC) ... PNA
Universal Airlines, Inc. [*ICAO designator*] (FAAC) ... WEC
Universal Airways [*ICAO designator*] (AD) ... UV
Universal Airways, Inc. [*ICAO designator*] (FAAC) ... UVA
Universal Alliance of Diamond Workers [*See also AUOD*] [*Antwerp, Belgium*] (EAIO) ... UADW
Universal American Financial Corp. [*NASDAQ symbol*] (SAG) ... UHCO
Universal American Financial Corp. [*Associated Press*] (SAG) ... UnvAm
Universal American Financial Corp. [*Associated Press*] (SAG) ... UnvAmr
Universal Area Code [*Bureau of Census*] ... UAC
Universal Army Communication System ... UNACOM
Universal Assembly Language (IAA) ... UAL
Universal Association for Speech Tracing [*See also TPA*] (EAIO) ... UAST
Universal Asynchronous Receiver/Transmitter ... UART
Universal Auto Ind Wrrt [*NASDAQ symbol*] (TTSB) ... UVSLW
Universal Autograph Collectors Club (EA) ... UACC
Universal Automatic Computer [*Remington Rand Corp.*] [*Early computer*] ... UNIVAC
Universal Automatic Computer Scientific Exchange (IAA) ... USE
Universal Automatic Computer Users' Association (IAA) ... UUA
Universal Automatic Control and Test Equipment ... UACTE
Universal Automatic LASER Interferometer (DNAB) ... UALI
Universal Automatic Map Compilation Equipment ... UNAMACE
Universal Automatic Test Equipment ... UATE
Universal Automotive Inds [*NASDAQ symbol*] (TTSB) ... UVSL
Universal Automotive Inds, Inc. [*NASDAQ symbol*] (SAG) ... UVSL
Universal Automotive Industries, Inc. [*Associated Press*] (SAG) ... UAuto
Universal Automotive Industries, Inc. [*Associated Press*] (SAG) ... UnivAuto
Universal Availability of Publications [*International Federation of Library Associations*] ... UAP
Universal Availability of Publications ... UAP
Universal Azimuth Indicator ... UAI
Universal Ballet Academy [*Washington, DC*] ... UBA
Universal Battlefield Identification ... UBI
Universal Beer Agar [*Brewery bacteria culture medium*] ... UBA
Universal Bibliographic Control ... UBC
Universal Bibliographic Control and International MARC ... UBCIM
Universal Bibliographic Control and International MARC [*IFLA Core Program*] ... UBCIM
Universal Block Channel ... UBC
Universal Boattail Thor [*NASA*] ... UBT
Universal Book Code (NITA) ... UBC
Universal Book Tester [*Measures performance of binding*] ... UBT
Universal Boss Fitting ... UBF
Universal Broadband Network [*Telecommunications*] ... UBN
Universal Buddhist Fellowship (EA) ... UBF
Universal Buffer Controller ... UBC
Universal Builders Supply Co. ... UBS
Universal Building Block ... UBB
Universal Bus [*Digital Equipment Corp.*] ... UNIBUS

Universal Bus Exercisor (NASA) ... UBE
Universal Bus Interface Controller (NASA) ... UBIC
Universal Business Directory for the Pacific Islands [*A publication*] ... UBD
Universal Cable Adapter (IAA) ... UCAL
Universal Cable Circuit Analysis Program [*Bell System*] ... UNICCAP
Universal Cable Module (PCM) ... UCM
Universal Calibration Adapter ... UCA
Universal Call Sequence ... UCS
Universal Camera Control System ... UCCS
Universal Camera Site (KSC) ... UCS
Universal Card Read-In Program (IAA) ... UNCDRP
Universal Card Scanner [*Computer science*] (DIT) ... UCS
Universal Cargo Sling ... UCS
Universal Central Processor Unit [*Computer hardware*] ... UCPU
Universal Character Buffer ... UCB
Universal Character Set [*Computer science*] ... UCS
Universal Character Set Buffer [*Computer science*] (MHDB) ... UCSB
Universal Checkout Console (NASA) ... UCC
Universal Child Restraint Anchorage ... UCRA
Universal Christian Movement (EA) ... UCM
Universal Church of the Master (IIA) ... UCM
Universal Circuit Board Tester ... UCBT
Universal City, TX [*AM radio station call letters*] ... KSAH
Universal Classification Decimal (ECII) ... UCD
Universal Classification System ... UCS
Universal Clothing System [*Software package*] (NCC) ... UCS
Universal Code [*Used for giving transport aircraft meteorological information in wartime*] (NATG) ... UCO
Universal Code Synchronous Transmitter Receiver ... UCSTR
Universal Command System (KSC) ... UCS
Universal Commercial Paper [*Investment term*] ... UCP
Universal Communications Monitor ... UCM
Universal Communications Object (PCM) ... UCO
Universal Communications Subsystem (NITA) ... UCS
Universal Communications Switching Device ... UCSD
Universal Communications Switching System (MCD) ... UCSS
Universal Compiler (IEEE) ... UNICOMP
Universal Component System [*Computer science*] (PCM) ... UCS
Universal Components [*Construction*] ... UNICOM
Universal Computer Oriented Language [*Programming language*] [*Computer science*] ... UNCOL
Universal Computer-Oriented Language (IAA) ... UNICOL
Universal Computers Ltd. (NITA) ... UCL
Universal Connector Strip ... UCS
Universal Consolidated Ltd. [*British*] ... UCL
Universal Control System (NASA) ... UCS
Universal Cooperatives (EA) ... UNICO
Universal Coordinated Time ... UCT
Universal Copyright Convention ... UCC
Universal Corp. [*Associated Press*] (SAG) ... UnvslCp
Universal Corp. [*NYSE symbol*] (SPSG) ... UVV
[*The*] **Universal Coterie of Pipe Smokers** (EA) ... TUCOPS
Universal Craftsmen Council of Engineers (EA) ... UCCE
Universal Data Acquisition System ... UDAS
Universal Data Base (IAA) ... UDB
Universal Data Entry ... UDE
Universal Data Exchange [*Computer science*] (PCM) ... UDE
Universal Data Set (CMD) ... UDS
Universal Data System [*Army*] ... UDS
Universal Data Systems [*Hardware manufacturer*] ... UDS
Universal Data Transcriber [*Navy*] ... UDT
Universal Data Transfer Service [*ITT World Communications, Inc.*] [*Secaucus, NJ*] [*Telecommunications*] (TSSD) ... UDTS
Universal Data Transmission System [*For international access*] ... UDTS
Universal Database Access Service [*Telecommunications*] (TSSD) ... UDAS
Universal Dataflow and Telecommunication [*IFLA Core Program*] ... UDT
Universal Datagram Protocol [*Computer science*] (PCM) ... UDP
Universal Decimal Classification [*Online database field identifier*] ... UDC
Universal Decimal Code (IAA) ... UDC
Universal Decoder Memory Unit (DNAB) ... UDMU
Universal Detective Association [*Defunct*] (EA) ... UDA
Universal Development Laboratory [*Computer debugger*] [*Orion Instruments*] ... UDL
Universal Die Holder ... UDH
Universal Digital Adaptive Recognizer (IEEE) ... UDAR
Universal Digital Autopilot ... UDAP
Universal Digital Avionics Module (MCD) ... UDAM
Universal Digital Communications Network [*Computer science*] (PDAA) ... UDICON
Universal Digital Control ... UDC
Universal Digital Element Tester (MCD) ... UDET
Universal Digital Instrument (IAA) ... UDI
Universal Digital Operational Flight Trainer [*Navy*] ... UDOFT
Universal Digital Operational Flight Trainer Tool [*Navy*] (IAA) ... UDOFTT
Universal Digital Readout ... UDR
Universal Digital Switch (MCD) ... UDS
Universal Digital Test Set ... UDITS
Universal Digital Transducer Indicator ... UDTI
Universal Dipole (DEN) ... UD
Universal Disk Controller [*Central Point Software*] ... UDC
Universal Disk Format (PCM) ... UDF
Universal Display [*NASDAQ symbol*] (TTSB) ... PANL
Universal Display Corp. [*NASDAQ symbol*] (SAG) ... PANL
Universal Display Corp. [*Associated Press*] (SAG) ... UnDsp
Universal Display Corp. [*Associated Press*] (SAG) ... UnvDisp
Universal Display Wrrt [*NASDAQ symbol*] (TTSB) ... PANLW
Universal Distributed System [*UNIVAC*] ... UDS
Universal Document Reader (BUR) ... UDR
Universal Document Transport [*Computer science*] (OA) ... UDT
Universal Documentation System [*NASA*] ... UDS
Universal Documents Transfer [*Computer science*] (ECII) ... UDT
Universal Drafting Machine Corp. ... UDM
Universal Driver Rating System [*Harness racing*] ... UDRS
Universal Electron Microscope ... UEM
Universal Electronics, Inc. [*NASDAQ symbol*] (SAG) ... UEIC
Universal Electronics, Inc. [*Associated Press*] (SAG) ... UnvElc
Universal Emulating Terminal ... UET
Universal Emulating Terminal System [*Computer science*] (MHDB) ... UETS
Universal Engineer Tractor [*Later, BEST*] [*Army*] ... UET
Universal Engineer Tractor, Armored [*Army*] ... UETA
Universal Engineer Tractor, Rubber-Tired [*Army*] ... UERT
Universal Engineer Tractor, Rubber-Tired [*Army*] ... UETRT
Universal Environmental Shelter (KSC) ... UES
Universal Exhaust Gas Oxygen Sensor [*Fuel systems*] [*Automotive engineering*] ... UEGO
Universal Expenditure Tax [*British*] (DI) ... UET
Universal Extension Mechanism (KSC) ... UXM
Universal Far Infrared Sensor (MCD) ... UFIRS
Universal Federation of Travel Agents' Associations [*International Federation of Travel Agencies and Universal Organization of Travel Agents' Associations*] [*Formed by a merger of Australia*] (EAIO) ... UFTAA
Universal Feeder [*Medicine*] (DMAA) ... UF
Universal Fellowship of Metropolitan Community Churches (EA) ... UFMCC
Universal Fermi Interaction ... UFI
Universal Fiber Optic (MCD) ... UFO
Universal Field Element (MCD) ... UFE
Universal Field Multiplexer [*Computer science*] (ECII) ... UFM
Universal File Access Method ... UFAM
Universal Financial System (MHDW) ... UFS
Universal Fire Control System ... UFCS
Universal Firing Device [*Military*] (AABC) ... UFD
Universal Flight Computer ... UFC
Universal Flight Director Computer ... UFDC
Universal Flight Range and Endurance Data Indicator ... UNI-FREDI
Universal Flip-Flop [*Computer science*] ... UF-F
Universal Folded Plate [*Structural system*] (RDA) ... UFP
Universal Foods Corp. [*NYSE symbol*] (SPSG) ... UFC
Universal Foods Corp. [*Associated Press*] (SAG) ... UnvFd
Universal Foods Corp., Technical Information Services, Milwaukee, WI [*Library symbol Library of Congress*] (LCLS) ... WMUF
Universal Forest Products [*NASDAQ symbol*] (SAG) ... UFPI
Universal Forest Products [*Commercial firm Associated Press*] (SAG) ... UnivFor
Universal Frequency Counter ... UFC
Universal Functional Activity Coefficient [*Chemical engineering*] ... UNIFAC
Universal Gate for Logic Implementation [*Computer science*] (MCD) ... UGLI
Universal Generalization [*Rule of quantification*] [*Logic*] ... UG
Universal Government ... UG
Universal Graphic Recorder [*Raytheon Co.*] ... UGR
Universal Graphics Language Executive (MCD) ... UGLE
Universal Guided Column ... UGC
Universal Guided Missile Launcher [*Navy*] (MCD) ... UGML
Universal Hand Tool ... UHT
Universal Head-Down Display [*Computer science*] (PDAA) ... UNIHEDD
Universal Health Realty Income Trust [*NYSE symbol*] (SPSG) ... UHT
Universal Health Realty Income Trust [*Associated Press*] (SAG) ... UnvHR
Universal Health Services, Inc. [*NYSE symbol*] (NQ) ... UHS
Universal Health Services, Inc. [*Associated Press*] (SAG) ... UnvHlt
Universal Heights [*NASDAQ symbol*] (TTSB) ... UHTS
Universal Heights, Inc. [*NASDAQ symbol*] (SAG) ... UHTS
Universal Heights, Inc. [*Associated Press*] (SAG) ... UnvHgt
Universal Heights, Inc. [*Associated Press*] (SAG) ... UnvHt
Universal Heights Wrrt [*NASDAQ symbol*] (TTSB) ... UHTSW
Universal Hldg Wrrt [*NASDAQ symbol*] (TTSB) ... UHCOW
Universal Holding Corp. [*NASDAQ symbol*] (NQ) ... UHCO
Universal Holdings [*Associated Press*] (SAG) ... UnHd
Universal Holdings [*Associated Press*] (SAG) ... UnvHld
Universal Horizontal Tail [*Aviation*] (NG) ... UHT
Universal Hospital Services [*NASDAQ symbol*] (SAG) ... UHOS
Universal Hospital Services, Inc. [*Associated Press*] (SAG) ... UnvHsp
Universal Host Machine [*Computer science*] (MHDI) ... UHM
Universal Hypertrichosis Lanuginosa [*Medicine*] (MAE) ... UHL
Universal Identification Interface [*Allen-Bradley Co.*] ... UII
Universal Identifier (IAA) ... UID
Universal Imagery Exploitation Viewer (DNAB) ... UIEV
Universal Infrared Viewer (PDAA) ... UIRV
Universal Input/Output Controller (NITA) ... UIOC
Universal Input-Output [*Computer science*] (ECII) ... UIO
Universal Instantiation [*Rule of quantification*] [*Logic*] ... UI
Universal Integrated Communication System [*Military*] ... UNICOM
Universal Interactive Unit [*Telecommunications*] ... UIU
Universal Interline Reservations Code ... UIRC
Universal Intermolecular Force ... UIF
Universal International, Inc. [*NASDAQ symbol*] (SPSG) ... UNIV
Universal International, Inc. [*Associated Press*] (SAG) ... UnvInt
Universal Internet Number ... UIN
Universal Inverter and Register (MCD) ... UNIVER
Universal Isolation Switch ... UIS
Universal Jamming System ... UJS
Universal Japanese Coupe [*Automotive engineering*] ... UJC
Universal Japanese Custom [*Motorcycle design*] ... UJC

Universal Jet Air Start Unit (DWSG) ..... UJASU
Universal Jet Navigation Charts [*Air Force*] ..... JNU
Universal Jewish Encyclopedia [*New York*] [*1939-1943*] [*A publication*] (BJA) ..... UJE
Universal Job Control Language ..... UJCL
Universal Joint [*Automotive engineering*] ..... U/JNT
Universal Joint Task List ..... UJTL
Universal Keyboard [*Computer science*] (AABC) ..... UKB
Universal Language Description [*Computer science*] (IAA) ..... ULD
Universal Language for Typographic Reproduction Applications ..... ULTRA-X
Universal League (EAIO) ..... UL
Universal Library System (NITA) ..... ULISYS
Universal Life [*Insurance*] ..... UL
Universal Life Church ..... ULC
Universal Limited Art Editions ..... ULAE
Universal Line Multiplexer ..... ULM
Universal Linear Accelerator ..... UNILAC
Universal Load Cell ..... ULC
Universal Locator Airborne Integrated Data System (MCD) ..... ULAIDS
Universal Log Interpretation Computer Program (PDAA) ..... ULICP
Universal Logic Array [*Computer science*] (IAA) ..... ULA
Universal Logic Block (IEEE) ..... ULB
Universal Logic Circuit ..... ULC
Universal Logic Implementer ..... ULI
Universal Logic Module ..... ULM
Universal Logic Primitive (PDAA) ..... ULP
Universal Love and Brotherhood Association [*Kyoto, Japan*] (EAIO) ..... ULBA
Universal Machine Gun (MCD) ..... UM
Universal Machine Gun (MCD) ..... UMG
Universal Machine Language Equipment Register [*Association of American Railroads*] [*Information service or system*] (CRD) ..... UMLER
Universal Machine Readable Cataloging (ADA) ..... UNIMARC
Universal Maintenance Standards ..... UMS
Universal Manufacturing [*NASDAQ symbol*] (SAG) ..... UFMG
Universal Manufacturing Co. [*Associated Press*] (SAG) ..... UnvMfg
Universal Masonic Brotherhood (EA) ..... UMB
Universal Masonic Order of the Eastern Star (EA) ..... UMOES
Universal Match Corp. ..... UMC
Universal Measurement Assembly (MCD) ..... UMA
Universal Measuring Amplifier (KSC) ..... UMA
Universal Measuring Machine ..... UMM
Universal Measuring Microscope ..... UM
Universal Memory System [*Intel Corp.*] ..... UMS
Universal Mercator Grid (NVT) ..... UMG
Universal Microfilming Corporation, Salt Lake City, UT [*Library symbol Library of Congress Obsolete*] (LCLS) ..... UmC
Universal Microscope Spectro-Photometer ..... UMSP
Universal Microwave Trainer ..... UMT
Universal Military Pod (VNW) ..... UMP
Universal Military Service ..... UMS
Universal Military Training [*Participants known as Umtees*] [*Post World War II*] [*Army*] ..... UMT
Universal Military Training and Service Act ..... UMTSA
Universal Military Training Service [*or System*] (GPO) ..... UMTS
Universal Missile Building (MCD) ..... UMB
Universal Mission Load [*Military*] (AABC) ..... UML
Universal Mobile Telecommunications Services ..... UMTS
Universal MODEM [*Modulate/Demodulate*] **System** (DWSG) ..... UMS
Universal Monitor (MCD) ..... UM
Universal Movement for Scientific Responsibility [*See also MURS*] (EAIO) ..... UMSR
Universal Movement Theater Repertory [*Defunct*] ..... UMTR
Universal Multiline Controller ..... UMLC
Universal Multiple Bomb Rack (NG) ..... UMBR
Universal Multiprogramming System [*Computer science*] (MHDB) ..... UMS
Universal Multiprogramming System/Virtual Storage (NITA) ..... UMS/VS
Universal Naming Convention [*Computer science*] (PCM) ..... UNC
Universal National Fine (MCD) ..... UNF
Universal Naval Integrated Surface-to-Air Missile System (DOMA) ..... UNISAMS
Universal Navigation Beacon ..... UNB
Universal Navigation Computer ..... UNC
Universal Negro Improvement Association [*Organization led by Marcus Aurelius Garvey*] ..... UNIA
Universal Negro Improvement Association and African Communities League of the World (EA) ..... UNIA & ACLW
Universal Network Achitecture [*Telecommunications*] ..... UNA
Universal News Service [*British*] ..... UNS
Universal Night Answering [*Telecommunications*] (TEL) ..... UNA
Universal Night Sight ..... UNS
Universal Nonlinear Element ..... UNE
Universal Numeric Coding System [*Distilling industry*] ..... UNIMERC
Universal Numerical Interchange Terminal ..... UNIT
Universal Oil Products Co., Des Plaines, IL [*Library symbol Library of Congress*] (LCLS) ..... IDesU
Universal Operator Performance Analyzer and Recorder ..... UNOPAR
Universal Outdoor Holdings, Inc. [*Associated Press*] (SAG) ..... UnvsOut
Universal Outdoor Holdings, Inc. [*NASDAQ symbol*] (SAG) ..... UOUT
Universal Output Computer ..... UOC
Universal Package Test Panel ..... UPTP
Universal Parachute Support Tactical and Research Target (NG) ..... UPSTART
Universal Patents Bureau [*British*] (ROG) ..... UPB
Universal Payload Accommodation Capsule ..... UNIPAC
Universal Payload Fairing [*NASA*] (KSC) ..... UPLF
Universal Performance Assessment and Control System ..... UPACS
Universal Peripheral Controller ..... UPC
Universal Permissive Module [*Nuclear energy*] (IEEE) ..... UPM
Universal Personal Identification Code (MHDI) ..... UPIC
Universal Personal Identifier (NITA) ..... UPI
Universal Philatelic Cover Society ..... UPCS
Universal Pin Pack Connector ..... UPPC
Universal Plotting Sheet ..... UPS
Universal Polar Stereographic Grid ..... UPS
Universal Postal Congress (IAA) ..... UPC
Universal Postal Union [*United Nations*] (MENA) ..... UPU
Universal Postal Union Collectors (EA) ..... UPUC
Universal Postal Union Convention ..... UPUC
Universal Power Supply ..... UNPS
Universal Prefabricated Depot Automatic Test Equipment (DNAB) ..... UPDATE
Universal Presentation Interface [*Uniface Corp.*] ..... UPI
Universal Press Syndicate Co. ..... UPS
Universal Pre-Vent, Inc. [*Vancouver Stock Exchange symbol*] ..... UPV
Universal Problem-Oriented Language [*Computer science*] (MCD) ..... UNIPOL
Universal Procedure Pointer [*Computer science*] ..... UPP
Universal Procedure-Oriented Language ..... UNIPOL
Universal Processing System ..... UPS
Universal Processor [*Computer science*] ..... UNIPRO
Universal Processor [*TRW, Inc.-Motorola, Inc.*] [*Computer science*] ..... UP
Universal Product Code [*Inventory control*] ..... UPC
Universal Product Code ..... UPC
Universal Product Code-Europe (NITA) ..... UPC-E
Universal Programming Language [*Computer science*] (BUR) ..... UPL
Universal PROM Programmer ..... UPP
Universal Propulsion Stabilization, Retardation, and Separation [*Air Force*] ..... UPSTARS
Universal Proutist Farmers Federation (EA) ..... UPFF
Universal Proutist Intellectual Federation (EA) ..... UPIF
Universal Proutist Labour Federation (EA) ..... UPLF
Universal Proutist Student Federation (EA) ..... UPSF
Universal Proutist Youth Federation (EA) ..... UPYF
Universal Proximal Femoral Prosthesis [*Orthopedics*] (DAVI) ..... UPP
Universal Proximal Femur [*Prosthesis*] [*Orthopedics*] (DAVI) ..... UPF
Universal Publications, London [*British*] ..... UPL
Universal Quasichemical [*Chemical engineering*] ..... UNIQUAC
Universal RADAR Signal Processor ..... URSP
Universal RADAR Tracker ..... URT
Universal Radio Group ..... URG
Universal Radio Relay ..... UNIRAR
Universal Range, Endurance, Speed, and Time (NG) ..... U-REST
Universal Real-Time Information and Administration ..... URIA
Universal Real-Time Information Control and Administration (MCD) ..... URICA
Universal Receiver Clock ..... URCLK
Universal Reference Locator ..... URL
Universal Reference System ..... URS
Universal Regulating System ..... URS
Universal Relevance Group Enterprise in a National Theater [*Theater workshop*] ..... URGENT
Universal Reproducing Matrix System (PDAA) ..... URMS
Universal [*or Uniform*] **Resource Locator** [*Computer science*] ..... URL
Universal Resource Locator [*Telecommunication*] ..... URL
Universal Satellite Corp. [*New York, NY*] [*Telecommunications*] (TSSD) ..... USATCO
Universal Scheduling System (IAA) ..... USS
Universal Security Instruments, Inc. [*Associated Press*] (SAG) ..... UnvSc
Universal Security Instruments, Inc. [*Associated Press*] (SAG) ..... UnvSec
Universal Security Instruments, Inc. [*NASDAQ symbol*] (NQ) ..... USEC
Universal Seismic Associates [*Associated Press*] (SAG) ..... UnvSeis
Universal Seismic Associates [*NASDAQ symbol*] (SAG) ..... USAC
Universal Self Care [*NASDAQ symbol*] (TTSB) ..... USCI
Universal Self Care, Inc. [*Associated Press*] (SAG) ..... UnSlf
Universal Self Care, Inc. [*Associated Press*] (SAG) ..... UnvSelf
Universal Self Care, Inc. [*NASDAQ symbol*] (SAG) ..... USCI
Universal Self Care Wrrt'A' [*NASDAQ symbol*] (TTSB) ..... USCIW
Universal Self Care Wrrt'B' [*NASDAQ symbol*] (TTSB) ..... USCIZ
Universal Serial Bus [*Computer science*] (CDE) ..... USB
Universal Serials and Book Exchange, Inc. [*ACCORD*] [*UTLAS symbol*] ..... USB
Universal Serials and Book Exchange, Inc. [*Acronym now used as official name of association*] (EA) ..... USBE
Universal Series Regulator (IAA) ..... USR
Universal Service [*News agency*] ..... US
Universal Service Order [*Bell System*] (TEL) ..... USO
Universal Servicing Tool (NASA) ..... UST
Universal Set (IDOE) ..... U
Universal Ship Cancellation Society (EA) ..... USCS
Universal Sign Language (EERA) ..... USL
Universal Signal Processor ..... USP
Universal Software Interface [*MRI Systems Corp.*] ..... USI
Universal Software Market Identifier [*Technique Learning*] [*Information service or system*] (IID) ..... USMI
Universal Soil Loss Equation [*Agricultural engineering*] ..... USLE
Universal Specimen Chamber ..... USC
Universal Spectroscopy [*Trademark*] [*Kevex Corp.*] ..... UNISPEC
Universal Stabilized Night Sight ..... USNS
Universal Stainless & Alloy Products [*Associated Press*] (SAG) ..... UnvStain
Universal Stainless & Alloy Products [*NASDAQ symbol*] (SAG) ..... USAP
Universal Standard Book Code (PDAA) ..... USBC
Universal Standard Data ..... USD
Universal Standard Medical Labs [*NASDAQ symbol*] (SAG) ..... USML
Universal Standard Medical Labs, Inc. [*Associated Press*] (SAG) ..... UnvStdM
Universal Standard Time ..... UST
Universal Stray Voltage Tester ..... USVT
Universal Subject Access [*Librarianship*] ..... USA

Universal Subscriber Terminal (DNAB) .... UST
Universal Subscription Television .... USTV
Universal Symphony Orchestra and Music Institute (AEBS) .... UNISOMI
Universal Synchronous/Asynchronous Receiver and Transmitter [*Computer science*] .... USART
Universal Synchronous Receiver/Transmitter .... USRT
Universal Systems Patching [*Mod-Tap System, Inc.*] .... USP
Universal Systems Technologies Corp. .... USTC
Universal Tape Processor .... UTP
Universal Tape-to-Tape Converter .... UTTC
Universal Target Tracking Station (MCD) .... UTTS
Universal Teleservice [*Satellite information service*] .... UNITEL
Universal Terminal System [*Sperry UNIVAC*] [*Computer science*] .... UTS
Universal Terminalized Online Printing and Investigative Aid [*Bancroft-Parkman, Inc.*] [*Information service or system*] .... UTOPIA
Universal Test Console (KSC) .... UTC
Universal Test Equipment .... UTE
Universal Test Equipment Compiler (KSC) .... UTEC
Universal Test Message .... UTM
Universal Test Point (CAAL) .... UTP
Universal Test Station .... UTS
Universal Test Vehicle [*Military*] .... UTV
Universal Testing Machine .... UTM
Universal Text Interchange [*Computer science*] (PCM) .... UTI
Universal Threat System for Simulators .... UTSS
Universal Thrust Stand .... UTS
Universal Time [*Astronomy*] .... UT
Universal Time Code .... UTC
Universal Time Coordinated [*The universal time emitted by coordinated radio stations*] .... UTC
Universal Time Coordinated [*Marine science*] (OSRA) .... UTC
Universal Time Corrected (MCD) .... UTC
Universal Time Sharing [*Computer science*] (IEEE) .... UTS
Universal Time Standards (NG) .... UTS
Universal Timesharing System (NITA) .... UTS
Universal Timesharing System for Mainframes (HGAA) .... UTS-M
Universal Timesharing System for Superminis (HGAA) .... UTS-S
Universal Timesharing System/Virtual Storage (NITA) .... UTS/VS
Universal Torah Registry (EA) .... UTR
Universal Torpedo (MCD) .... UT
Universal Tracking Data Format (SSD) .... UTDF
Universal Tractor Transmission Oil [*Lubricants*] .... UTTO
Universal Trainer .... UT
Universal Training Reactor [*Nuclear energy*] (GFGA) .... UTR
Universal Trajector Compiler (IEEE) .... UNITRAC
Universal Transfer Device .... UTD
Universal Translator Oriented Language .... UTOL
Universal Transmitter Clock .... UTCLK
Universal Transporter Loader (MCD) .... UTL
Universal Transversal Mercator Converter [*Computer program*] .... MERCON
Universal Transverse Mercator [*Cartography*] .... UTM
Universal Transverse Mercator Map Projection (EERA) .... UTM
Universal Treatment Standard [*Environmental protection agency*] .... UTS
Universal Triangulation Program (IAA) .... UTRIP
Universal Trident Industries Ltd. [*Vancouver Stock Exchange symbol*] .... UTI
Universal Tube (IAA) .... UT
Universal Turing Machine [*Mathematical model*] [*Computer science*] (BYTE) .... UTM
Universal Turret (MCD) .... UT
Universal Underwater Mobile [*Robot*] .... UNUMO
Universal/Unrestricted [*Film certificate*] [*British*] .... U
Universal Valve Action Recorder .... UNIVAR
Universal Vendor Marking (WGA) .... UVM
Universal Versaplot Software (IAA) .... UVS
Universal VESA [*Video Electronics Standards Association*] **Bios Extension** (CDE) .... UniVBE
Universal Voltage Tester .... UVT
Universal Water Charts [*Air Force*] .... UWC
Universal Water-Activated Release System (DWSG) .... UWARS
Universal Weapon Control Stabilization System .... UWCSS
Universal Weapons Assembly Test Standard (MCD) .... UWATS
Universal Weather Landing Code .... UCO
Universal White Brotherhood [*An association France*] (EAIO) .... UWB
Universal Winding Co. (MCD) .... UWC
Universal Youth .... UY
Universala Artista Ligo de Esperantistoj [*Universal Artist League of Esperantists*] (EAIO) .... UALE
Universala Esperanto Asocio [*Universal Esperanto Association*] (EAIO) .... UEA
Universala Ligo [*Defunct*] (EA) .... UL
Universala Medicina Esperanto Asocio [*Universal Medical Esperanto Association*] (EAIO) .... UMEA
Universal-Fine Ammonium Perchlorate [*Organic chemistry*] (MCD) .... UFAP
Universal-International Studios (IIA) .... UI
Universalist .... UNIV
Universalist Historical Society [*Later, UUHS*] (EA) .... UHS
Universally Programmable Digitizer Update (IAA) .... UPD
Universally Unique Identifier [*Computer science*] .... UUID
Universe (MHDB) .... U
Universidad Autonoma Metropolitana [*Mexico*] (CROSS) .... UAM
Universidad de Barcelona, Biblioteca Universitaria y Provincal, Barcelona, Spain [*Library symbol Library of Congress*] (LCLS) .... SpBaU
Universidad de Barcelona, Facultad de Quimica y Fisica, Barcelona, Spain [*Library symbol*] [*Library of Congress*] (LCLS) .... SpBaU-SQ
Universidad de Buenos Aires, Buenos Aires, Argentina [*Library symbol Library of Congress*] (LCLS) .... AaBU
Universidad de Buenos Aires, Faculdad de Ciencias Exactas y Naturales, Buenos Aires, Argentina [*Library symbol Library of Congress*] (LCLS) .... AaBU-C
Universidad de Costa Rica, San Jose, Costa Rica [*Library symbol Library of Congress*] (LCLS) .... CrU
Universidad de las Naciones Unidas [*United Nations University*] [*Spanish*] (DUND) .... UNU
Universidad de San Carlos de Guatemala, Ciudad Universitaria, Guatemala City, Guatemala [*Library symbol Library of Congress*] (LCLS) .... GuGS
Universidad Iberoamericana, Mexico [*Library symbol Library of Congress*] (LCLS) .... MxMI
Universidad Iberoamericana, Mexico, DF, Mexico [*OCLC symbol*] (OCLC) .... UIA
Universidad Nacional Autonoma de Mexico (CROSS) .... UNAM
Universidad Nacional Autonoma de Mexico, Mexico City, Mexico [*Library symbol Library of Congress*] (LCLS) .... MxU
Universidad Nacional Autonoma, Tegucigalpa [*Honduras*] .... UNAH
Universidad Nacional de Cordoba, Cordoba, Argentina [*Library symbol Library of Congress*] (LCLS) .... AaCU
Universidad Nacional de La Plata, La Plata, Argentina [*Library symbol Library of Congress*] .... AaLU
Universidad Nacional de La Plata, La Plata, Argentina [*Library symbol*] [*Library of Congress*] (LCLS) .... AaLU
Universidad Nacional del Nordeste [*Argentina*] .... UNNE
Universidade Catolica de Pernambuco [*Brazil*] .... UNICAP
Universidade de Sao Paulo, Conjucto das Quimicas, Sao Paulo, Brazil [*Library symbol Library of Congress*] (LCLS) .... BrSU-Q
Universidade de Sao Paulo, Escola Politecnica, Sao Paulo, Brazil [*Library symbol Library of Congress*] (LCLS) .... BrSU-P
Universidade de Sao Paulo, Faculdade de Higiene e Saude Publica, Sao Paulo, Brazil [*Library symbol Library of Congress*] (LCLS) .... BrSU-H
Universidade de Sao Paulo, Faculdade de Medicina Veterinaria, Sao Paulo, Brazil [*Library symbol Library of Congress*] (LCLS) .... BrSU-MV
Universidade de Sao Paulo, Sao Paulo, Brazil [*Library symbol Library of Congress*] (LCLS) .... BrSU
Universita degli Studi, Biblioteca Alessandrina, Rome, Italy [*Library symbol Library of Congress*] (LCLS) .... ItRU
Universita degli Studi di Bari, Bari, Italy [*Library symbol Library of Congress*] (LCLS) .... ItBaU
Universita degli Studi, Pavia, Italy [*Library symbol Library of Congress*] (LCLS) .... ItPavU
Universita di Cagliari, Sardinia, Italy [*Library symbol Library of Congress*] (LCLS) .... ItCaU
Universita di Napoli, Istituto Chimico, Naples, Italy [*Library symbol Library of Congress*] (LCLS) .... ItNU-IC
Universita di Napoli, Naples, Italy [*Library symbol Library of Congress*] (LCLS) .... ItNU
Universita J. E. Purkyne [*Purkyne University*], Brno, Czechoslovakia [*Library symbol Library of Congress*] (LCLS) .... CzBrU
Universitaet Bremen, Bremen, Germany [*Library symbol Library of Congress*] (LCLS) .... GyBrU
Universitaetsbibliothek der Technischen Universitaet Hannover und Technische Informationsbibliothek, Hannover, Federal Republic of Germany [*Library symbol Library of Congress*] (LCLS) .... GyHTIB
Universitaetsbibliothek Karlsruhe [*Karlsruhe University Library*] [*Information retrieval*] .... UBKA
Universitaire Faculteiten Sint-Ignatius te Antwerpen, Antwerp, Belgium [*Library symbol Library of Congress*] (LCLS) .... BeAUSI
Universitaire Instelling Antwerpen, Wilrijk, Belgium [*Library symbol Library of Congress*] (LCLS) .... BeWiU
Universitas Negeri Padjadjaran [*Indonesia*] .... UNPAD
Universitas Viridis Montis [*University of the Green Mountains; i.e., University of Vermont*] .... UVM
Universitat Basel, Basel, Switzerland [*Library symbol Library of Congress*] (LCLS) .... SzBaU
Universitat Bielfeld, Kurt Schumacher, Bielfeld, Germany [*Library symbol Library of Congress*] (LCLS) .... GyBiU
Universitat des Saarlandes, Saarbrucken, Germany [*Library symbol Library of Congress*] (LCLS) .... GySaU
Universitat Dusseldorf, Grabbeplatz, Dusseldorf, Germany [*Library symbol Library of Congress*] (LCLS) .... GyDuU
Universitat Heidelberg Sinologisches Seminar de Universitat Heidelberg, Heidelberg, Germany [*Library symbol*] [*Library of Congress*] (LCLS) .... GyHeU-SS
Universitat Hohenheim (Landwirtschaftliche Hochschule), Stuttgart-Hohenheim, Germany [*Library symbol Library of Congress*] (LCLS) .... GyHoU
Universitat Regensburg, Regensburg, Germany [*Library symbol Library of Congress*] (LCLS) .... GyRU
Universitat Stuttgart, Stuttgart, Germany [*Library symbol Library of Congress*] (LCLS) .... GySU
Universitat Trier-Kaiserslautern, Kaiserslautern, Germany [*Library symbol Library of Congress*] (LCLS) .... GyKaU
Universitat Trier-Kaiserslautern, Schneidershof, Trier, Germany [*Library symbol Library of Congress*] (LCLS) .... GyTrU
Universitat Zurich, Universitatsspital-Bibliothek, Kantonsspital, Zurich, Switzerland [*Library symbol Library of Congress*] (LCLS) .... SzZU
Universitatsbibliothek Hannover und Technische Informationsbibliothek [*University Library of Hannover and Technical Information Library*] [*Information service or system*] (IID) .... UB/TIB
Universitats-Netz Austria [*Austrian University Network*] (TNIG) .... UNA
Universite Cooperative Internationale [*International Cooperative University*] .... UCI
Universite d'Alger, Algiers, Algeria [*Library symbol Library of Congress*] (LCLS) .... AlgAU
Universite de Grenoble, Bibliotheque Droit-Lettres, St.-Martin d'Heres, France [*Library symbol Library of Congress*] (LCLS) .... FrGrU

Universite de Liege, Liege, Belgium [*Library symbol Library of Congress*] (LCLS) .... BeLU
Universite de Lille, Bibliotheque de Section Droit-Lettres, Domaine Universitaire, Litteraire, et Juridique, Lille, France [*Library symbol Library of Congress*] (LCLS) .... FrLiU
Universite de Limoges, Bibliotheque des Lettres, Limoges, France [*Library symbol Library of Congress*] (LCLS) .... FrLimU-L
Universite de Limoges, Limoges, France [*Library symbol Library of Congress*] (LCLS) .... FrLimU
Universite de Lyon, Bibliotheque Centrale, Lyon, France [*Library symbol Library of Congress*] (LCLS) .... FrLyU
Universite de Moncton, Archives Acadiennes, Moncton, NB, Canada [*Library symbol Library of Congress*] (LCLS) .... CaNBMoUA
Universite de Moncton, Bibliotheque [*UTLAS symbol*] .... MON
Universite de Moncton, Bibliotheque de Droit, Moncton, NB, Canada [*Library symbol Library of Congress*] (LCLS) .... CaNBMoUD
Universite de Moncton, Law Library [*UTLAS symbol*] .... MOL
Universite de Moncton, Moncton, NB, Canada [*Library symbol Library of Congress*] (LCLS) .... CaNBMoU
Universite de Moncton, New Brunswick [*Library symbol National Library of Canada*] (NLC) .... NBMOU
Universite de Montreal, Bibliotheque [*UTLAS symbol*] .... MTR
Universite de Montreal, Bibliotheque des Sciences Humaines et Sociales, Section de Criminologie, Montreal, PQ, Canada [*Library symbol Library of Congress*] (LCLS) .... CaQMUSHS
Universite de Montreal, Bibliotheque des Sciences Sociales, Cartotheque, Montreal, PQ, Canada [*Library symbol Library of Congress*] (LCLS) .... CaQMUSC
Universite de Montreal, Bibliotheque d'Optometrie, Montreal, PQ, Canada [*Library symbol Library of Congress*] (LCLS) .... CaQMUO
Universite de Montreal, Bibliotheque Medicale, Montreal, PQ, Canada [*Library symbol Library of Congress Obsolete*] (LCLS) .... CaQMUM
Universite de Montreal, Bibliotheque Paramedicale, Montreal, PQ, Canada [*Library symbol Library of Congress*] (LCLS) .... CaQMUP
Universite de Montreal, Cartotheque de l'Institut de Geologie, Montreal, PQ, Canada [*Library symbol Library of Congress*] (LCLS) .... CaQMUGL
Universite de Montreal, Departement de Demographie, Montreal, PQ, Canada [*Library symbol Library of Congress*] (LCLS) .... CaQMUDD
Universite de Montreal, Departement de Geographie, Cartotheque, Montreal, PQ, Canada [*Library symbol Library of Congress*] (LCLS) .... CaQMUGC
Universite de Montreal, Departement de Geographie, Montreal, PQ, Canada [*Library symbol Library of Congress*] (LCLS) .... CaQMUG
Universite de Montreal, Ecole de Bibliotheconomie [*EDUCATSS*] [*UTLAS symbol*] .... EUE
Universite de Montreal, Ecole de Bibliotheconomie, Montreal, PQ, Canada [*Library symbol*] [*Library of Congress*] (LCLS) .... CaQMUEB
Universite de Montreal, l'Ecole de Criminologie, Montreal, PQ, Canada [*Library symbol Library of Congress*] (LCLS) .... CaQMUEC
Universite de Montreal, Montreal, PQ, Canada [*Library symbol Library of Congress*] (LCLS) .... CaQMU
Universite de Montreal, Quebec [*Library symbol National Library of Canada*] (NLC) .... QMU
Universite de Nancy, Bibliotheque Centrale, Nancy, France [*Library symbol Library of Congress*] (LCLS) .... FrNanU
Universite de Nancy, Bibliotheque des Lettres-Droit-Sciences, Nancy, France [*Library symbol Library of Congress*] (LCLS) .... FrNanU-L
Universite de Nantes, Section Droit-Lettres, Nantes, France [*Library symbol Library of Congress*] (LCLS) .... FrNU
Universite de Nantes, Section Medecine, Nantes, France [*Library symbol Library of Congress*] (LCLS) .... FrNU-M
Universite de Nantes, Section Sciences, Nantes, France [*Library symbol Library of Congress*] (LCLS) .... FrNU-S
Universite de Nice, Bibliotheque de Droit, Nice, France [*Library symbol Library of Congress*] (LCLS) .... FrNiU-D
Universite de Nice, Bibliotheque des Sciences, Nice, France [*Library symbol Library of Congress*] (LCLS) .... FrNiU-S
Universite de Paris a la Sorbonne, Bibliotheque de la Faculte des Lettres et de la Faculte des Sciences, Paris, France [*Library symbol Library of Congress*] (LCLS) .... FrPU
Universite de Paris a la Sorbonne, Faculte de Medecine, Paris, France [*Library symbol Library of Congress*] (LCLS) .... FrPU-M
Universite de Paris a la Sorbonne, Faculte des Sciences Pharmaceutiques et Biologiques de Paris-Luxembourg, Paris, France [*Library symbol Library of Congress*] (LCLS) .... FrPU-P
Universite de Paris, Faculte des Sciences, (Orsay), Orsay, France [*Library symbol Library of Congress*] (LCLS) .... FrPU-OS
Universite de Poitiers, Bibliotheque de Droit-Lettres, Poitiers, France [*Library symbol Library of Congress*] (LCLS) .... FrPoU
Universite de Quebec [*UTLAS symbol*] .... UQB
Universite de Quebec, Montreal, Quebec [*Library symbol National Library of Canada*] (NLC) .... QMUQ
Universite de Sherbrooke, Bibliotheque [*UTLAS symbol*] .... SBK
Universite de Sherbrooke, Centre Hospitalier Universitaire, Sherbrooke, PQ, Canada [*Library symbol Library of Congress*] (LCLS) .... CaQSherC
Universite de Sherbrooke, Departement de Geographie, Cartotheque, Sherbrooke, PQ, Canada [*Library symbol Library of Congress*] (LCLS) .... CaQSherUGC
Universite de Sherbrooke, Departement de Geographie, Sherbrooke, PQ, Canada [*Library symbol Library of Congress*] (LCLS) .... CaQSherUG
Universite de Sherbrooke, Faculte de Droit, Sherbrooke, PQ, Canada [*Library symbol Library of Congress*] (LCLS) .... CaQSherUD
Universite de Sherbrooke, Faculte des Sciences, Sherbrooke, PQ, Canada [*Library symbol*] [*Library of Congress*] (LCLS) .... CaQSherUS
Universite de Sherbrooke, Galerie d'Art et Centre Culturel, Sherbrooke, PQ, Canada [*Library symbol Library of Congress*] (LCLS) .... CaQSherUA
Universite de Sherbrooke, Programme de Recherche sur l'Amiante, Centre de Documentation, Sherbrooke, PQ, Canada [*Library symbol*] [*Library of Congress*] (LCLS) .... CaQSherURA
Universite de Sherbrooke, Publications Officielles [*UTLAS symbol*] .... SBG
Universite de Sherbrooke, Sherbrooke, PQ, Canada [*Library symbol Library of Congress*] (LCLS) .... CaQSherU
Universite des Nations Unies [*United Nations University*] [*French*] (DUND) .... UNU
Universite du Maine, Le Mans, France [*Library symbol Library of Congress*] (LCLS) .... FrLemU
Universite du Quebec a Chicoutimi [*Canada*] .... UQAC
Universite du Quebec a Hull [*Canada*] .... UQAH
Universite du Quebec a Montreal [*Canada*] .... UQAM
Universite du Quebec a Montreal, Cartotheque, Montreal, PQ, Canada [*Library symbol Library of Congress*] (LCLS) .... CaQMUQC
Universite du Quebec a Montreal, INRS-Urbanisation, Cartotheque, Montreal, PQ, Canada [*Library symbol Library of Congress*] (LCLS) .... CaQMUQIC
Universite du Quebec a Montreal, le Centre de Documentation des Sciences Juridiques, Montreal, PQ, Canada [*Library symbol Library of Congress*] (LCLS) .... CaQMUQDSJ
Universite du Quebec a Montreal, Montreal, PQ, Canada [*Library symbol Library of Congress*] (LCLS) .... CaQMUQ
Universite du Quebec a Montreal, Pavillon des Arts, Montreal, PQ, Canada [*Library symbol Library of Congress*] (LCLS) .... CaQMUQPA
Universite du Quebec a Quebec, Quebec, PQ, Canada [*Library symbol Library of Congress*] (LCLS) .... CaQQUQ
Universite du Quebec a Rimouski [*Canada*] .... UQAR
Universite du Quebec a Rimouski, Cartotheque, Rimouski, PQ, Canada [*Library symbol Library of Congress*] (LCLS) .... CaQRUC
Universite du Quebec a Rimouski, Rimouski, PQ, Canada [*Library symbol Library of Congress*] (LCLS) .... CaQRU
Universite du Quebec a Rouyn, Rouyn, PQ, Canada [*Library symbol Library of Congress*] (LCLS) .... CaQRUQR
Universite du Quebec a Trois-Rivieres, Archives Historiques, Trois-Rivieres, PQ,Canada [*Library symbol Library of Congress*] (LCLS) .... CaQTUAH
Universite du Quebec a Trois-Rivieres, Departement de Geographie, Cartotheque, Trois-Rivieres, PQ, Canada [*Library symbol Library of Congress*] (LCLS) .... CaQTUGC
Universite du Quebec a Trois-Rivieres, Imprimes Historiques, Trois-Rivieres, PQ , Canada [*Library symbol Library of Congress*] (LCLS) .... CaQTUIH
Universite du Quebec a Trois-Rivieres, Trois-Rivieres, PQ, Canada [*Library symbol Library of Congress*] (LCLS) .... CaQTU
Universite du Quebec, Bibliotheque des Sciences, Montreal, PQ, Canada [*Library symbol*] [*Library of Congress*] (LCLS) .... CaQMUQS
Universite du Quebec, Cartotheque, Chicoutimi, PQ, Canada [*Library symbol Library of Congress*] (LCLS) .... CaQCUGC
Universite du Quebec, Centre Quebecois des Sciences de l'Eau, Quebec, PQ, Canada [*Library symbol Library of Congress*] (LCLS) .... CaQQQE
Universite du Quebec, Chicoutimi, PQ, Canada [*Library symbol Library of Congress*] (LCLS) .... CaQCU
Universite du Quebec, Chicoutimi, Quebec [*Library symbol National Library of Canada*] (NLC) .... QCU
Universite du Quebec, Departement de Geographie, Chicoutimi, PQ, Canada [*Library symbol Library of Congress*] (LCLS) .... CaQCUG
Universite du Quebec, Ecole de Technologie Superieure, Montreal, PQ, Canada [*Library symbol Library of Congress*] (LCLS) .... CaQMUQET
Universite du Quebec, Ecole Nationale d'Administration Publique, Quebec, PQ, Canada [*Library symbol Library of Congress*] (LCLS) .... CaQQUQEN
Universite du Quebec, Ecole Nationale d'Aministration Publique, Montreal, PQ, Canada [*Library symbol*] [*Library of Congress*] (LCLS) .... CaQMUQEN
Universite du Quebec en Abitibi-Temiscamingue, Rouyn, Quebec [*Library symbol National Library of Canada*] (NLC) .... QRUQR
Universite du Quebec, Hull, Quebec [*Library symbol National Library of Canada*] (NLC) .... QHU
Universite du Quebec, INRS-Sante, Centre de Documentation, Montreal, PQ, Canada [*Library symbol*] [*Library of Congress*] (LCLS) .... CaQMUQIS
Universite du Quebec, Institut Armand-Frappier, Laval, PQ, Canada [*Library symbol Library of Congress*] (LCLS) .... CaQLAIAF
Universite du Quebec, Institut National de la Recherche Scientifique (Education), Quebec, PQ, Canada [*Library symbol Library of Congress*] (LCLS) .... CaQQUED
Universite du Quebec, Institut Nationale de la Recherche Scientifique (Eau), Quebec, PQ, Canada [*Library symbol Library of Congress*] (LCLS) .... CaQQUIE
Universite du Quebec, Quebec, Quebec [*Library symbol National Library of Canada*] (NLC) .... QQUQ
Universite du Quebec, Rimouski, Quebec [*Library symbol National Library of Canada*] (NLC) .... QRU
Universite du Quebec, Tele-Universite, Montreal, PQ, Canada [*Library symbol*] [*Library of Congress*] (LCLS) .... CaQMUQTM
Universite du Quebec, Tele-Universite, Ste.-Foy, Quebec, PQ, Canada [*Library symbol Library of Congress*] (LCLS) .... CaQQUQT
Universite du Quebec, Trois-Rivieres, Quebec [*Library symbol National Library of Canada*] (NLC) .... QTU
Universite du Quebec-Outaouais, Hull, PQ, Canada [*Library symbol Library of Congress*] (LCLS) .... CaQHU
Universite Laval, Bibliotheque [*UTLAS symbol*] LVL
Universite Laval, Cartotheque, Quebec, PQ, Canada [*Library symbol Library of Congress*] (LCLS) .... CaQQLaCa
Universite Laval, Centre International de Recherches sur le Bilinguisme, Quebec,PQ, Canada [*Library symbol Library of Congress*] (LCLS) .... CaQQLaCI
Universite Laval, Departement de Geologie et de Mineralogie, Quebec, PQ, Canada [*Library symbol Library of Congress*] (LCLS) .... CaQQLaGM

Universite Laval, Ecole des Arts Visuelles, Quebec, PQ, Canada [*Library symbol Library of Congress*] (LCLS) .... CaQQLaAV
Universite Laval, Faculte de Droit, Quebec, PQ, Canada [*Library symbol Library of Congress*] (LCLS) .... CaQQLaD
Universite Laval, Faculte de Foresterie et de Geodesie, Quebec, PQ, Canada [*Library symbol Library of Congress*] (LCLS) .... CaQQLaFG
Universite Laval, Faculte des Sciences de l'Agriculture et de l'Alimentation, Quebec, PQ, Canada [*Library symbol Library of Congress*] (LCLS) .... CaQQLaA
Universite Laval, Faculte des Sciences, Quebec, PQ, Canada [*Library symbol Library of Congress*] (LCLS) .... CaQQLaS
Universite Laval, Institut de Geographie, Quebec, PQ, Canada [*Library symbol Library of Congress*] (LCLS) .... CaQQLaG
Universite Laval, Quebec, PQ, Canada [*Library symbol Library of Congress*] (LCLS) .... CaQQLa
Universite Laval, Quebec, Quebec [*Library symbol National Library of Canada*] (NLC) .... QQLA
Universite Laval, Secteur Art et Architecture, Quebec, PQ, Canada [*Library symbol Library of Congress*] (LCLS) .... CaQQLaAA
Universite Laval, Societe Dante Aleghieri, Quebec, PQ, Canada [*Library symbol Library of Congress*] (LCLS) .... CaQQLaI
Universite Radiophonique et Televisuelle Internationale [*International Radio-Television University*] .... URTI
Universite Radiophonique Internationale [*International University of the Air*] (NTCM) .... URI
Universite Sainte Anne, Church Point, NS, Canada [*Library symbol Library of Congress*] (LCLS) .... CaNSCS
Universite Sainte-Anne, Church Point, Nova Scotia [*Library symbol National Library of Canada*] (NLC) .... NSCS
Universiteit van Amsterdam .... UvA
Universitet i Uppsala [*University of Uppsala*], Uppsala, Sweden [*Library symbol Library of Congress*] (LCLS) .... SwUU
Universitetet i Bergen [*University of Bergen*], Bergen, Norway [*Library symbol Library of Congress*] (LCLS) .... NoBeU
Universitetet i Oslo, Matematisk-Naturvitenskapelige Fakultet [*University of Oslo, Department of Mathematics and Natural Sciences*], Oslo, Norway [*Library symbol Library of Congress*] (LCLS) .... NoOU-M
Universitetet i Oslo [*University of Oslo*], Oslo, Norway [*Library symbol Library of Congress*] (LCLS) .... NoOU
Universitetet i Trondheim, Kongelige Norske Videnskabers Selskabs [*Universityof Trondheim, Royal Norwegian Society of Sciences and Letters*], Trondheim, N orway [*Library symbol Library of Congress*] (LCLS) .... NoTU-V
Universitetet i Trondheim, Norges Tekniske Hogskole [*University of Trondheim,Norwegian Institute of Technology*], Trondheim-NTH, Norway [*Library symbol Library of Congress*] (LCLS) .... NoTU-T
Universitetet i Trondheim [*University of Trondheim*], Trondheim, Norway [*Library symbol Library of Congress*] (LCLS) .... NoTU
Universitets- och Hogskoleambetet [*National Board of Universities and Colleges*] [*Ministry of Education and Cultural Affairs*] [*Information service or system*] [*Sweden*] (IID) .... UHA
Universiti Brunei Darussalam .... UBD
Universiti Sains Malaysia (University of Science, Malaysia), Minden, Penang, Malaysia [*Library symbol Library of Congress*] (LCLS) .... MlyPS
Universities Advisory Council .... UAC
Universities and Colleges Teaching, Learning, and Information Group [*Universities and Colleges Information Systems Association*] (AIE) .... UCTLIG
Universities and Public Schools Battalions [*Military units*] [*World War I*] [*British*] .... UPS
Universities and the Quest for Peace [*An association*] .... UQP
Universities Associated for Research and Education in Pathology (EA) .... UAREP
Universities Athletics Union [*British*] .... UAU
Universities Central Council on Admission [*British*] .... UCCA
Universities Committee for Non-Teaching Staff [*British*] .... UCNS
Universities Council for Adult Education [*British*] .... UCAE
Universities Council for the Education of Teachers (AIE) .... UCET
Universities Council on Water Resources (EA) .... UCOWR
Universities Council on Water Resources (MCD) .... UCWR
Universities Educational Fund for Palestinian Refugees [*British*] .... UNIPAL
Universities Expanded Ring and Satellite Experiment (NITA) .... UNIVERSE
Universities Federation for Animal Welfare [*British*] .... UFAW
Universities Field Staff International - Institute of World Affairs (EA) .... UFSI-IWA
Universities Funding Council [*British*] .... UF
Universities Funding Council [*British*] (ECON) .... UFC
Universities Mission to Central Africa [*Later, USPG*] [*British*] .... UMCA
Universities National Antiwar Fund .... UNAF
Universities Research Association (EA) .... URA
Universities Research Association, Inc. .... URAI
Universities Research Reactor [*British*] .... URR
Universities Space Research Association (EA) .... USRA
Universities Staff Association of South Australia .... USASA
Universities Superannuation Scheme .... USS
University .... U
University .... UN
University (ADA) .... UNI
University (AFM) .... UNIV
University (VRA) .... univ
University .... UNIV
University [*Mississippi*] [*Airport symbol*] (OAG) .... UOX
University [*British*] (ROG) .... VARSITY
University Academic Staff Association of New South Wales [*Australia*] .... UASANSW
University Affiliated Cincinnati Center for Developmental Disorders [*University of Cincinnati*] [*Research center*] (RCD) .... UACCDD
University Affiliated Research Centers (AAGC) .... UARC
University Air Squadrons .... UAS
University/Airline Bomber [*FBI investigation*] .... UNABOM
University Analytical Center [*University of Arizona*] [*Research center*] (RCD) .... UAC
University and College Designers Association (EA) .... UCDA
University and College Labor Education Association (EA) .... UCLEA
University and College Theatre Association (EA) .... UCTA
University Animal Care Program [*Arizona State University*] [*Research center*] (RCD) .... ACP
University Appointments Board [*British*] (DAS) .... UAB
University Association for Contemporary European Studies [*British*] .... UACES
University Association for Emergency Medicine (EA) .... UA/EM
University Association for Emergency Medicine .... UAEM
University Association for Professional Radio Education [*Broadcast Education Association*] (NTCM) .... UAPRE
University at the Corner of Lenox Avenue [*Nickname for "The Tree of Life," a Harlem bookstore*] .... UCLA
University Athletic Association (EA) .... UAA
University Aviation Association (EA) .... UAA
University Bancorp, Inc. [*NASDAQ symbol*] (SAG) .... UNIB
University Bancorp, Inc. [*Associated Press*] (SAG) .... UnivBcp
University Boat Race [*Cambridge and Oxford*] [*British*] (BARN) .... UBR
University Bookman [*A publication*] (BRI) .... Univ Bkmn
University Branch, Alberta Research Council, Edmonton, Alberta [*Library symbol National Library of Canada*] (NLC) .... AERU
University Bureaus of Business Research .... UBBR
University Center for Energy Research [*Oklahoma State University*] [*Research center*] (RCD) .... UCER
University Center for Environmental Studies [*Virginia Polytechnic Institute and State University*] [*Research center*] (RCD) .... UCES
University Center for Instructional Media and Technology [*University of Connecticut*] [*Research center*] (RCD) .... UCIMT
University Center for International Rehabilitation [*Michigan State University*] [*Research center*] (RCD) .... UCIR
University Center for International Studies [*University of Pittsburgh*] [*Research center*] (IID) .... UCIS
University Center for Social and Urban Research [*University of Pittsburgh*] [*Research center*] (RCD) .... UCSUR
University Center in Georgia, Inc. [*Library network*] .... UCGA
University Center, MI [*Television station call letters*] .... WUCM
University Christian Movement [*Formerly, NSCF*] [*Defunct*] .... UCM
University City Science Center [*Research center*] (RCD) .... UCSC
University Classification and Compensation System .... UCCS
University Clearing Office for Developing Countries .... UCOD
University Club, New York, NY [*Library symbol Library of Congress*] (LCLS) .... NNUnC
University Club of Chicago, Chicago, IL [*Library symbol Library of Congress*] (LCLS) .... ICUnC
University Club, Philadelphia, PA [*Library symbol Library of Congress Obsolete*] (LCLS) .... PPUnC
University Club, Washington, DC [*Library symbol Library of Congress*] (LCLS) .... DUC
University College .... UC
University College Buckingham [*British*] (AIE) .... UCB
University College, Cardiff [*Wales*] .... UCC
University College Cardiff English Centre for Overseas Students [*British*] (CB) .... CUECOS
University College Computer [*London, England*] (DEN) .... UCC
University College, Cork [*Ireland*] .... UCC
University College, Dublin [*Ireland*] .... UCD
University College Galway [*Ireland*] .... UCG
University College Hospital [*British*] (DI) .... UCH
University College, London, England [*OCLC symbol*] (OCLC) .... LON
University College of Cape Breton, Sydney, Nova Scotia [*Library symbol National Library of Canada*] (NLC) .... NSSX
University College of London (KSC) .... UCL
University College of North Wales .... UCNW
University College of Northern Victoria [*Australia*] .... UCNV
University College of Wales .... UCW
University College School [*British*] (BI) .... UCS
University College, University of Toronto, Ontario [*Library symbol National Library of Canada*] (NLC) .... OTUUC
University Colleges [*Public-performance tariff class*] [*British*] .... UC
University Community Hospital, Medical Library, Tampa, FL [*Library symbol*] [*Library of Congress*] (LCLS) .... FTUnH
University Computer Center [*University of Minnesota*] [*Research center*] (RCD) .... UCC
University Computer Center [*New Mexico State University*] [*Research center*] (RCD) .... UCC
University Computer Center [*San Diego State University*] [*Research center*] (RCD) .... UCC
University Computer Center [*Oklahoma State University*] [*Research center*] (RCD) .... UCC
University Computer Center [*North Dakota State University*] [*Research center*] (RCD) .... UCC
University Computer Services [*Ball State University*] [*Research center*] (RCD) .... UCS
University Computing and Information Services [*Villanova University*] [*Research center*] (RCD) .... UCIS
University Computing Co. [*International computer bureau*] .... UCC
University Computing Services [*University of Southern California*] [*Research center*] (RCD) .... UCS
University Computing Services [*State University of New York at Buffalo*] [*Research center*] (RCD) .... UCS
University Consortium for Geographic Information Science .... UCGIS

University Consortium for Instructional Development and Technology [EA] .... UCIDT
University Consortium in Educational Media and Technology [Later, UCIDT] .... UCEMT
University Corp. for Advanced Internet Development .... UCAID
University Corp. for Atmospheric Research [EA] .... UCAR
University Council for Educational Administration [EA] .... UCEA
University Counseling and Placement Association [AEBS] .... UCPA
University Department of Education [AIE] .... UDE
University Directors of Industrial Liaison [PDAA] .... UDIL
University Entrance Requirement [British] [DI] .... UER
University Extension .... UE
University Extension Manuals [A publication] .... UEM
University Extension Series [A publication] .... UES
University Film and Video Association [EA] .... UFVA
University Film and Video Foundation [EA] .... UFVF
University Film Association [Later, UFVA] [EA] .... UFA
University Film Foundation [EA] .... UFF
University Film Producers Association [Later, UFVA] [EA] .... UFPA
University for Man [Manhattan, KS] .... UFM
University Grants Commission [India] .... UGC
University Grants Committee [British] .... UGC
University Group Diabetes Program [Study group involving 12 medical schools] [Defunct] .... UGDP
University Health Services Clinic [DAVI] .... UHSC
University Heights, OH [FM radio station call letters] .... WUJC
University Hospital, Augusta, GA [Library symbol Library of Congress] (LCLS) .... GAuU
University Hospital Consortium .... UHC
University Hospital, London, ON, Canada [Library symbol Library of Congress] (LCLS) .... CaOLUH
University Hospital, London, Ontario [Library symbol National Library of Canada] (NLC) .... OLUH
University/Industry Cooperative Research Center for Communications and Signal Processing [North Carolina State University] [Research center] (RCD) .... CCSP
University Information Technology Corp. [MIT-Harvard] .... UNITEL
University Isotope Separator at Oak Ridge .... UNISOR
University Labor Education Association [Later, UCLEA] .... ULEA
University Laboratory Cooperative Program .... ULCP
University Laboratory Managers Association [Later, ALMA] [EA] .... ULMA
University Labour Federation [British] .... ULF
University Law College. Journal. Rajputana University [India] [A publication] (DLA) .... ULCJ
University Law College. Journal. Rajputana University [India] [A publication] (DLA) .... Univ L Coll J
University Law Review [United States] [A publication] (DLA) .... ULR
University Law Review [A publication] (DLA) .... Univ L Rev
University Law Review [A publication] (DLA) .... Univ LR
University Libraries Section [Association of College and Research Libraries] .... ULS
University Library [WDAA] .... UL
University Library and Information Services Committee [Committee of Vice Chancellors and Principals] [British] [AIE] .... ULISC
University Map Collection, Department of Geography, Sir George Williams Campus, Concordia University, Montreal, Quebec [Library symbol National Library of Canada] (NLC) .... QMGGM
University Map Collection, University of Alberta, Edmonton, Alberta [Library symbol National Library of Canada] (NLC) .... AEUM
University Marine Biological Station, Millport [UK] [Marine science] (OSRA) .... UMBSM
University Microfilms, Inc. [WDMC] .... UMI
University Microfilms International [Database producer] [IID] .... UMI
University Microfilms International, Ann Arbor, MI [OCLC symbol] (OCLC) .... EEU
University Microfilms International, Ann Arbor, MI [Library symbol Library of Congress] (LCLS) .... UnM
University Microfilms Ltd., Penn, Buckinghamshire, United Kingdom [Library symbol Library of Congress] (LCLS) .... UnM-L
University, MS [FM radio station call letters] .... WUMS
University Music Editions, New York, NY [Library symbol Library of Congress] (LCLS) .... UmE
University National Oceanographic Laboratory System [National Science Foundation] .... UNOLS
University National Oceanographic Laboratory System [Marine science] (OSRA) .... UNOLS
University Naval Training Division [Canada] .... UNTD
University NAVSTAR Consortium .... UNAVCO
[The] University Network [TNIG] .... UNINETT
University of Adelaide, Adelaide, SA, Australia [Library symbol Library of Congress] (LCLS) .... AuAU
University of Adelaide General Staff Association [Australia] .... UAGSA
University of Adelaide, Mawson Institute for Antartic Research, Adelaide, SA, Australia [Library symbol] [Library of Congress] (LCLS) .... AuAU-AR
University of Akron (GAGS) .... U Akron
University of Akron [Ohio] (PDAA) .... UA
University of Akron, Akron, OH [OCLC symbol] (OCLC) .... AKR
University of Akron, Akron, OH [Library symbol Library of Congress] (LCLS) .... OAkU
University of Akron, Law Library, Akron, OH [OCLC symbol] (OCLC) .... AKL
University of Akron, School of Law, Akron, Ohio [Library symbol Library of Congress] (LCLS) .... OAkU-L
University of Alabama (GAGS) .... U Ala
University of Alabama at Birmingham (GAGS) .... U Ala (Birm)
University of Alabama at Huntsville (GAGS) .... U Ala (Huntsville)

University of Alabama, Graduate School of Library Science, University, AL [OCLC symbol] (OCLC) .... ALG
University of Alabama Health Sciences Library, University, AL [Library symbol] [Library of Congress] (LCLS) .... AU-HS
University of Alabama in Birmingham .... UAB
University of Alabama in Birmingham, Birmingham, AL [Library symbol Library of Congress] (LCLS) .... ABAU
University of Alabama in Birmingham, Birmingham, AL [OCLC symbol] (OCLC) .... ABC
University of Alabama in Birmingham, Health Sciences Library, Birmingham, AL [OCLC symbol] (OCLC) .... ABH
University of Alabama in Birmingham, Lister Hill Library of the Health Sciences, Birmingham, AL [Library symbol Library of Congress] (LCLS) .... ABAU-M
University of Alabama in Huntsville .... UAH
University of Alabama in Huntsville, Huntsville, AL [Library symbol Library of Congress] (LCLS) .... AHAU
University of Alabama in Huntsville Research Institute .... UAHRI
University of Alabama, Law Library, University, AL [Library symbol Library of Congress] (LCLS) .... AU-L
University of Alabama, Library Sciences School, University, AL [Library symbol Library of Congress] (LCLS) .... AU-LS
University of Alabama, Medical Center, Birmingham, AL [Library symbol Library of Congress] (LCLS) .... AU-M
University of Alabama Research Institute (KSC) .... UARI
University of Alabama, University, AL [OCLC symbol] (OCLC) .... ALM
University of Alabama, University, AL [Library symbol Library of Congress] (LCLS) .... AU
University of Alaska (GAGS) .... U Alaska
University of Alaska [Anchorage, AK] .... U of A
University of Alaska [Anchorage, AK] .... UA
University of Alaska, Alaska Native Language Center, Fairbanks, AK [Library symbol] [Library of Congress] (LCLS) .... AkU-NL
University of Alaska, Anchorage .... UAA
University of Alaska, Anchorage, AK [Library symbol Library of Congress] (LCLS) .... AkAU
University of Alaska, Artic Environmental Information and Data Center, Anchorage, AK [Library symbol] [Library of Congress] (LCLS) .... AkU-AE
University of Alaska, Bio-Medical Library, Fairbanks, AK [Library symbol Library of Congress] (LCLS) .... AkU-M
University of Alaska Computer Network [Research center] (RCD) .... UACN
University of Alaska, Fairbanks .... UAF
University of Alaska, Fairbanks, AK [Library symbol Library of Congress] (LCLS) .... AkU
University of Alaska, Geophysical Institute Library, Fairbanks, AK [Library symbol] [Library of Congress] (LCLS) .... AkU-G
University of Alaska, Institute of Arctic Biology, Fairbanks, AK [Library symbol Library of Congress] (LCLS) .... AkU-AB
University of Alaska, Juneau Library, Juneau, AK [Library symbol Library of Congress] (LCLS) .... AkJU
University of Alaska, Juneau-Douglas Southeastern College, Auke Bay, AK [Library symbol Library of Congress] (LCLS) .... AkAbU
University of Alaska, Matanuska-Susitna Community College, Palmer, AK [Library symbol Library of Congress] (LCLS) .... AkPalU
University of Alaska Museum Library, Fairbanks, AK [Library symbol] [Library of Congress] (LCLS) .... AkU-Mu
University of Alaska, Wildlife Library, Fairbanks, AK [Library symbol] [Library of Congress] (LCLS) .... AkU-W
University of Alberta, Archives, Edmonton, AB, Canada [Library symbol Library of Congress] (LCLS) .... CaAEUA
University of Alberta Archives, Edmonton, Alberta [Library symbol National Library of Canada] (NLC) .... AEUA
University of Alberta Biotron [University of Alberta] [Research center] (RCD) .... UAB
University of Alberta, Boreal Institute for Northern Studies, Edmonton, AB, Canada [Library symbol Library of Congress] (LCLS) .... CaAEUB
University of Alberta, Department of Agricultural Engineering, Edmonton, AB, Canada [Library symbol] [Library of Congress] (LCLS) .... CaAEUAG
University of Alberta Devonian Botanic Garden [Canada] .... UADV
University of Alberta, Edmonton, AB, Canada [Library symbol Library of Congress] (LCLS) .... CaAEU
University of Alberta, Edmonton, Alberta [Library symbol National Library of Canada] (NLC) .... AEU
University of Alberta, Faculte Saint-Jean, Edmonton, AB, Canada [Library symbol Library of Congress] (LCLS) .... CaAEUSJ
University of Alberta, Faculty of Library Science, Edmonton, AB, Canada [Library symbol Library of Congress] (LCLS) .... CaAEULS
University of Alberta, Faculty of Library Science, Edmonton, AL, Canada [OCLC symbol] (OCLC) .... UAC
University of Alberta, Law Library, Edmonton, AB, Canada [Library symbol Library of Congress] (LCLS) .... CaAEUL
University of Alberta Library [UTLAS symbol] .... ALB
University of Alberta Microfungus Collection and Herbarium [Canada] .... UAMH
University of Alberta, Special Collections Department, Edmonton, AB, Canada [Library symbol Library of Congress] (LCLS) .... CaAEUS
University of Alberta, University Map Collection, Edmonton, AB, Canada [Library symbol Library of Congress] (LCLS) .... CaAEUM
University of Albuquerque, Albuquerque, NM [OCLC symbol] (OCLC) .... NMA
University of Albuquerque, Albuquerque, NM [Library symbol Library of Congress] (LCLS) .... NmAU
University of Amsterdam, Amsterdam, Netherlands [Library symbol Library of Congress] (LCLS) .... NeAU
[The] University of Arizona (GAGS) .... U Ariz
University of Arizona [Tucson, AZ] .... UA
University of Arizona (PDAA) .... UARZ

University of Arizona [*Seismograph station code, US Geological Survey Closed*] (SEIS) .... UOA

University of Arizona, Arid Lands Information Center, Tucson, AZ [*Library symbol*] [*Library of Congress*] (LCLS) .... AzU-A

University of Arizona College of Law, Library, Tucson, AZ [*OCLC symbol*] (OCLC) .... AZL

University of Arizona, College of Law, Tucson, AZ [*Library symbol Library of Congress*] (LCLS) .... AzU-L

University of Arizona College of Medicine [*Tucson*] .... UARZ/COM

University of Arizona, Graduate Library School, Tucson, AZ [*OCLC symbol*] (OCLC) .... LSA

University of Arizona, Health Sciences Center Library, Tucson, AZ [*OCLC symbol*] (OCLC) .... AZA

University of Arizona, Health Sciences Center, Tucson, AZ [*Library symbol Library of Congress*] (LCLS) .... AzU-M

University of Arizona, Tucson, AZ [*Library symbol Library of Congress OCLC symbol*] (LCLS) .... AzU

University of Arizona-Engineering Experiment Station (PDAA) .... UAZ-EES

University of Arkansas (GAGS) .... U Ark

University of Arkansas [*Fayetteville, AR*] .... U of A

University of Arkansas, Area Health Education Center, Jonesboro, AR [*Library symbol*] [*Library of Congress*] (LCLS) .... ArU-H

University of Arkansas at Little Rock, Law Library, Little Rock, AR [*OCLC symbol*] (OCLC) .... ALR

University of Arkansas at Little Rock, Law Library, Little Rock, AR [*Library symbol Library of Congress*] (LCLS) .... ArLUA-L

University of Arkansas at Little Rock, Little Rock, AR [*OCLC symbol*] (OCLC) .... AKU

University of Arkansas at Little Rock, Little Rock, AR [*Library symbol Library of Congress*] (LCLS) .... ArLUA

University of Arkansas at Monticello, Monticello, AR [*OCLC symbol*] (OCLC) .... AMK

University of Arkansas at Monticello, Monticello, AR [*Library symbol Library of Congress*] (LCLS) .... ArU-Mon

University of Arkansas at Pine Bluff, Pine Bluff, AR [*OCLC symbol*] (OCLC) .... AKB

University of Arkansas at Pine Bluff, Pine Bluff, AR [*Library symbol Library of Congress*] (LCLS) .... ArPbUA

University of Arkansas, Fayetteville, AR [*Library symbol Library of Congress*] (LCLS) .... ArU

University of Arkansas, Fayetteville, Fayetteville, AR [*OCLC symbol*] (OCLC) .... AFU

University of Arkansas for Medical Sciences, Area Health Education Center, Little Rock, AR [*OCLC symbol*] (OCLC) .... AHE

University of Arkansas Medical Center, Little Rock, AR [*Library symbol Library of Congress*] (LCLS) .... ArU-M

University of Arkansas Medical Science Campus, Little Rock, AR [*OCLC symbol*] (OCLC) .... AKM

University of Auckland [*New Zealand*] .... UA

University of Baltimore (GAGS) .... U Balt

University of Baltimore, Baltimore, MD [*OCLC symbol*] (OCLC) .... BAL

University of Baltimore, Baltimore, MD [*Library symbol Library of Congress*] (LCLS) .... MdBU

University of Baltimore, Law Library, Baltimore, MD [*Library symbol Library of Congress*] (LCLS) .... MdBU-L

University of Baltimore, Law Library, Baltimore, MD [*OCLC symbol*] (OCLC) .... MDL

University of Botswana, Lesotho, and Swaziland Law Journal [*A publication*] (DLA) .... UBLSLJ

University of Bradford .... ULB

University of Bridgeport (GAGS) .... U Bridgeport

University of Bridgeport, Bridgeport, CT [*Library symbol Library of Congress*] (LCLS) .... CtBU

University of Bridgeport, Bridgeport, CT [*OCLC symbol*] (OCLC) .... UBM

University of British Columbia [*Vancouver, BC*] .... UBC

University of British Columbia, Charles Crane Memorial Library, Vancouver, BC, Canada, [*Library symbol Library of Congress*] (LCLS) .... CaBVaUCC

University of British Columbia, Department of Geography, Vancouver, BC, Canada [*Library symbol Library of Congress*] (LCLS) .... CaBVaUG

University of British Columbia Institute of Oceanography [*Canada*] (MSC) .... UBCIO

University of British Columbia, Law Library, Vancouver, BC, Canada [*Library symbol Library of Congress*] (LCLS) .... CaBVaUL

University of British Columbia. Legal News [*A publication*] (DLA) .... UBCLN

University of British Columbia. Legal Notes [*A publication*] (DLA) .... UBC Notes

University of British Columbia Library [*UTLAS symbol*] .... UBC

University of British Columbia, Map Division, Vancouver, BC, Canada [*Library symbol Library of Congress*] (LCLS) .... CaBVaUM

University of British Columbia, Pulp and Paper Centre, Vancouver, BC, Canada [*Library symbol*] [*Library of Congress*] (LCLS) .... CaBVaPPC

University of British Columbia Retrospective Conversion [*UTLAS symbol*] .... UBR

University of British Columbia, School of Librarianship, Vancouver, BC, Canada [*OCLC symbol*] (OCLC) .... UBS

University of British Columbia, School of Library, Archival, and Information Studies, Vancouver, BC, Canada [*Library symbol*] [*Library of Congress*] (LCLS) .... CaBVaULS

University of British Columbia, Special Collections Division, Vancouver, BC, Canada [*Library symbol Library of Congress*] (LCLS) .... CaBVaUS

University of British Columbia, Vancouver, BC, Canada [*Library symbol Library of Congress*] (LCLS) .... CaBVaU

University of British Columbia, Vancouver, British Columbia [*Library symbol National Library of Canada*] (NLC) .... BVAU

University of British Columbia, Woodward Library, Vancouver, BC, Canada [*Library symbol Library of Congress*] (LCLS) .... CaBVaUW

University of Buffalo Foundation, Inc., Center for Tomorrow, State University of New York at Buffalo, Amherst, NY [*Library symbol*] [*Library of Congress*] (LCLS) .... NBuU-CT

University of Calcutta Medical Association of America .... UCMAA

University of Calgary, Alberta [*Library symbol National Library of Canada*] (NLC) .... ACU

University of Calgary Archives, Alberta [*Library symbol National Library of Canada*] (BIB) .... ACUA

University of Calgary, Arctic Institute of North America, Calgary, AB, Canada [*Library symbol Library of Congress*] (LCLS) .... CaACUAI

University of Calgary, Calgary, AB, Canada [*Library symbol Library of Congress*] (LCLS) .... CaACU

University of Calgary, Department of Education, Materials Centre Library, Calgary, AB, Canada [*Library symbol Library of Congress*] (LCLS) .... CaACUMC

University of Calgary, Faculty of Education, Calgary, AB, Canada [*Library symbol Library of Congress*] (LCLS) .... CaACUFE

University of Calgary Library [*UTLAS symbol*] .... UCL

University of Calgary, Maps Library, Calgary, AB, Canada [*Library symbol Library of Congress*] (LCLS) .... CaACUMA

University of Calgary, Medical Library, Calgary, AB, Canada [*Library symbol Library of Congress*] (LCLS) .... CaACUM

University of Calgary, Research Centre for Canadian Ethnic Studies, Calgary, AB,Canada [*Library symbol Library of Congress*] (LCLS) .... CaACUCES

University of Calgary, Rothney Astrophysical Observatory [*Canada*] (IRC) .... UCRAO

University of California .... UC

University of California at Berkeley (GAGS) .... U Cal (Berkeley)

University of California at Davis (GAGS) .... U Cal (Davis)

University of California at Davis. Law Review [*Davis, California*] [*A publication*] (DLA) .... Univ of Calif Davis L Rev

University of California at Davis, Medical Center (DAVI) .... UCDMC

University of California at Irvine (GAGS) .... U Cal (Irvine)

University of California at Irvine .... UCI

University of California at Irvine, Medical Center (DAVI) .... UCIMC

University of California at Los Angeles. Law Review [*A publication*] (DLA) .... CLA

University of California at Los Angeles. Law Review [*A publication*] (DLA) .... UCLA L Rev

University of California at Los Angeles. Law Review [*A publication*] (DLA) .... UCLA Law Rev

University of California at Los Angeles. Law Review [*Los Angeles, California*] [*A publication*] (DLA) .... Univ California Los Angeles L Rev

University of California at Riverside (GAGS) .... U Cal (Riverside)

University of California at San Diego (GAGS) .... U Cal (San Diego)

University of California at San Diego-p (NITA) .... UCSD-p

University of California at San Francisco (GAGS) .... U Cal (San Francisco)

University of California at Santa Barbara (GAGS) .... U Cal (Santa Barbara)

University of California at Santa Cruz (GAGS) .... U Cal (Santa Cruz)

University of California, Berkeley .... UCB

University of California, Berkeley, Agriculture Library, Berkeley, CA [*Library symbol Library of Congress*] (LCLS) .... CU-AGRI

University of California, Berkeley, Anthropology Library, Berkeley, CA [*Library symbol Library of Congress*] (LCLS) .... CU-ANTH

University of California, Berkeley, Archives Collection, Berkeley, CA [*Library symbol Library of Congress*] (LCLS) .... CU-UARC

University of California, Berkeley, Astronomy Library, Berkeley, CA [*Library symbol Library of Congress*] (LCLS) .... CU-ASTR

University of California, Berkeley, Bancroft Library, Berkeley, CA [*Library symbol Library of Congress*] (LCLS) .... CU-BANC

University of California, Berkeley, Berkeley, CA [*OCLC symbol*] (OCLC) .... CUY

University of California, Berkeley, Biochemistry Library, Berkeley, CA [*Library symbol Library of Congress*] (LCLS) .... CU-BIOC

University of California, Berkeley, Biology Library, Berkeley, CA [*Library symbol Library of Congress*] (LCLS) .... CU-BIOL

University of California, Berkeley, Center for Chinese Studies, Berkeley, CA [*Library symbol Library of Congress*] (LCLS) .... CU-CS

University of California, Berkeley, Chemistry Library, Berkeley, CA [*Library symbol Library of Congress*] (LCLS) .... CU-CHEM

University of California, Berkeley, Documents Department, Berkeley, CA [*Library symbol Library of Congress*] (LCLS) .... CU-DOCU

University of California, Berkeley, Earth Sciences Library, Berkeley, CA [*Library symbol Library of Congress*] (LCLS) .... CU-EART

University of California, Berkeley, Earthquake Engineering Research Center, Richmond, CA [*Library symbol*] [*Library of Congress*] (LCLS) .... CU-EERC

University of California, Berkeley, East Asiatic Library, Berkeley, CA [*Library symbol Library of Congress*] (LCLS) .... CU-EAST

University of California, Berkeley, Education-Psychology Library, Berkeley, CA [*Library symbol Library of Congress*] (LCLS) .... CU-EDUC

University of California, Berkeley Electronics Research Laboratory [*Research center*] (RCD) .... ERL-UCB

University of California, Berkeley, Engineering Library, Berkeley, CA [*Library symbol Library of Congress*] (LCLS) .... CU-ENGI

University of California, Berkeley, Entomology Library, Berkeley, CA [*Library symbol Library of Congress*] (LCLS) .... CU-ENTO

University of California, Berkeley, Environmental Design Library, Berkeley, CA [*Library symbol Library of Congress*] (LCLS) .... CU-ENVI

University of California, Berkeley, Forest Products Laboratory, Berkeley, CA [*Library symbol Library of Congress*] (LCLS) .... CU-FPRO

University of California, Berkeley, Forestry Library, Berkeley, CA [*Library symbol Library of Congress*] (LCLS) .... CU-FORE

University of California, Berkeley, Graduate Social Science Library, Berkeley, CA [*Library symbol Library of Congress*] (LCLS) .... CU-SOCS

University of California, Berkeley, Humanities Graduate Service, Berkeley, CA [Library symbol Library of Congress] (LCLS) .... CU-HUMA

University of California, Berkeley, Institute of Governmental Studies, Berkeley,CA [Library symbol Library of Congress] (LCLS) .... CU-IG

University of California, Berkeley, Institute of International Studies, Berkeley, CA [Library symbol Library of Congress] (LCLS) .... CU-IS

University of California, Berkeley, Institute of Transportation Studies, Berkeley, CA [Library symbol Library of Congress] (LCLS) .... CU-IT

University of California, Berkeley, Law Library, Berkeley, CA [Library symbol Library of Congress] (LCLS) .... CU-L

University of California, Berkeley, Library School Library, Berkeley, CA [Library symbol Library of Congress] (LCLS) .... CU-LIBR

University of California, Berkeley, Main Library, Berkeley, CA [Library symbol Library of Congress] (LCLS) .... CU

University of California, Berkeley, Maps Collection, Berkeley, CA [Library symbol Library of Congress] (LCLS) .... CU-MAPS

University of California, Berkeley, Mark Twain Collection, Berkeley, CA [Library symbol Library of Congress] (LCLS) .... CU-MARK

University of California, Berkeley, Mathematics/Statistics Library, Berkeley, CA [Library symbol Library of Congress] (LCLS) .... CU-MATH

University of California, Berkeley, Modern Authors Collection, Berkeley, CA [Library symbol Library of Congress] (LCLS) .... CU-MODE

University of California, Berkeley, Moffitt Undergraduate Library, Berkeley, CA [Library symbol Library of Congress] (LCLS) .... CU-UNDE

University of California, Berkeley, Morrison Collection, Berkeley, CA [Library symbol Library of Congress] (LCLS) .... CU-MORR

University of California, Berkeley, Music Library, Berkeley, CA [Library symbol Library of Congress] (LCLS) .... CU-MUSI

University of California, Berkeley, Newspaper and Microcopy Division, Berkeley, CA [Library symbol Library of Congress] (LCLS) .... CU-NEWS

University of California, Berkeley, Optometry Library, Berkeley, CA [Library symbol Library of Congress] (LCLS) .... CU-OPTO

University of California, Berkeley, Philosophy Library, Berkeley, CA [Library symbol Library of Congress] (LCLS) .... CU-PHIL

University of California, Berkeley, Physics Library, Berkeley, CA [Library symbol Library of Congress] (LCLS) .... CU-PHYS

University of California, Berkeley, Public Health Library, Berkeley, CA [Library symbol Library of Congress] (LCLS) .... CU-PUBL

University of California, Berkeley, Rare Books and Special Collections Department, Berkeley, CA [Library symbol Library of Congress] (LCLS) .... CU-RARE

University of California, Berkeley, Reference and Bibliography Collection, Berkeley, CA [Library symbol Library of Congress] (LCLS) .... CU-REFE

University of California, Berkeley School of Library and Information Science, Berkeley, CA [OCLC symbol] (OCLC) .... UCB

University of California, Berkeley, Social Welfare Library, Berkeley, CA [Library symbol Library of Congress] (LCLS) .... CU-SOCW

University of California, Berkeley, Sulfur Recovery Process .... UCBSRP

University of California, Berkeley, Water Resources Center Archives, Berkeley, CA [Library symbol Library of Congress] (LCLS) .... CU-WR

University of California, Davis .... UCD

University of California, Davis, Health Sciences Library, Davis, CA [Library symbol Library of Congress] (LCLS) .... CU-AM

University of California, Davis, Health Sciences Library, Davis, CA [OCLC symbol] (OCLC) .... CUX

University of California, Davis, Law Library, Davis, CA [Library symbol Library of Congress] (LCLS) .... CU-AL

University of California (Davis). Law Review [A publication] (DLA) .... UC Davis L Rev

University of California, Davis, Main Library, Davis, CA [Library symbol Library of Congress] (LCLS) .... CU-A

University of California, Davis, Shields Library, Davis, CA [OCLC symbol] (OCLC) .... CUV

University of California Division of War Research .... UCDWR

University of California Hastings College of Law (GAGS) .... Hastings C Law

University of California, Irvine, College of Medicine, Irvine, CA [Library symbol Library of Congress] (LCLS) .... CU-I-M

University of California, Irvine, General Library, Irvine, CA [Library symbol Library of Congress] (LCLS) .... CU-I

University of California, Irvine, Irvine, CA [OCLC symbol] (OCLC) .... CUI

University of California, Irvine, Medical Sciences Library, Irvine, CA [OCLC symbol] (OCLC) .... CIM

University of California, La Jolla .... UCLJ

University of California, Lawrence Berkeley Laboratory, Berkeley, CA [Library symbol Library of Congress] (LCLS) .... CU-Lbl

University of California Lawrence Livermore Laboratory (AAGC) .... UCLLL

University of California Lawrence Livermore Laboratory, Livermore, CA [Library symbol Library of Congress] (LCLS) .... CU-Lrl

University of California Lawrence Radiation Laboratory .... UCLRL

University of California, Los Angeles [Databank originator] .... UCLA

University of California, Los Angeles, Architecture and Urban Planning Library, Los Angeles, CA [Library symbol Library of Congress] (LCLS) .... CLU-AUP

University of California, Los Angeles, Art Library, Los Angeles, CA [Library symbol Library of Congress] (LCLS) .... CLU-ART

University of California, Los Angeles, Biomedical, Law, Physical Science, and Technology, Los Angeles, CA [OCLC symbol] (OCLC) .... CLU

University of California, Los Angeles, Biomedical Library, Los Angeles, CA [Library symbol Library of Congress] (LCLS) .... CLU-M

University of California, Los Angeles, Chemistry Library, Los Angeles, CA [Library symbol Library of Congress] (LCLS) .... CLU-CHM

University of California, Los Angeles, College Library, Los Angeles, CA [Library symbol Library of Congress] (LCLS) .... CLU-COL

University of California, Los Angeles, Department of Special Collections, Los Angeles, CA [Library symbol Library of Congress] (LCLS) .... CLU-S/C

University of California, Los Angeles, Education and Psychology Library, Los Angeles, CA [Library symbol Library of Congress] (LCLS) ... CLU-E/P

University of California, Los Angeles, Engineering and Mathematical Sciences Library, Los Angeles, CA [Library symbol Library of Congress] (LCLS) .... CLU-EMS

University of California, Los Angeles, Geology-Geophysics Library, Los Angeles, CA [Library symbol Library of Congress] (LCLS) .... CLU-G/G

University of California, Los Angeles, Graduate Reserve Service, Los Angeles, CA [Library symbol Library of Congress Obsolete] (LCLS) .... CLU-GRS

University of California, Los Angeles, Graduate School of Library and Information Science, Los Angeles, CA [OCLC symbol] (OCLC) .... CUG

University of California, Los Angeles, Law Library, Los Angeles, CA [Library symbol Library of Congress] (LCLS) .... CLU-L

University of California, Los Angeles, Main Library, Los Angeles, CA [Library symbol Library of Congress] (LCLS) .... CLU

University of California, Los Angeles, Management Library, Los Angeles, CA [Library symbol Library of Congress] (LCLS) .... CLU-MGT

University of California, Los Angeles, Map Library, Los Angeles, CA [Library symbol Library of Congress] (LCLS) .... CLU-MAP

University of California, Los Angeles, Music Library, Los Angeles, CA [Library symbol Library of Congress] (LCLS) .... CLU-MUS

University of California, Los Angeles, Non-Circulating Reading Center, Los Angeles, CA [Library symbol Library of Congress] (LCLS) .... CLU-N/C

University of California, Los Angeles, Oriental Library, Los Angeles, CA [Library symbol Library of Congress] (LCLS) .... CLU-O

University of California, Los Angeles, Physical Science and Technical Library, Los Angeles, CA [Library symbol Library of Congress] (LCLS) .... CLU-P

University of California, Los Angeles, Physics Library, Los Angeles, CA [Library symbol Library of Congress Obsolete] (LCLS) .... CLU-PHY

University of California, Los Angeles, Public Affairs Service, Los Angeles, CA [Library symbol Library of Congress] (LCLS) .... CLU-PAS

University of California, Los Angeles, Theater Arts Reading Room, Los Angeles, CA [Library symbol Library of Congress] (LCLS) .... CLU-T/A

University of California, Los Angeles, University Archives, Los Angeles, CA [Library symbol Library of Congress] (LCLS) .... CLU-U/A

University of California, Los Angeles, University Elementary School Library, LosAngeles, CA [Library symbol Library of Congress] (LCLS) .... CLU-UES

University of California, Los Angeles, University Research Library, Los Angeles,CA [Library symbol Library of Congress] (LCLS) .... CLU-URL

University of California, Los Angeles, URL-Reference Department, Los Angeles, CA [Library symbol Library of Congress] (LCLS) .... CLU-REF

University of California, Los Angeles, William Andrews Clark Memorial Library, Los Angeles, CA [Library symbol Library of Congress] (LCLS) .... CLU-C

University of California, Northern Regional Library Facility, Richmond, CA [Library symbol] [Library of Congress] (LCLS) .... CU-NL

University of California/Operations Research Center .... UCORC

University of California Radiation Laboratory (MCD) .... UCRL

University of California Research Laboratory (KSC) .... UCRL

University of California, Riverside (IID) .... UCR

University of California, Riverside, Bioagriculture Library, Riverside, CA [Library symbol Library of Congress] (LCLS) .... CU-RivA

University of California, Riverside, Main Library, Riverside, CA [Library symbol Library of Congress] (LCLS) .... CU-Riv

University of California, Riverside, Physical Sciences Library, Riverside, CA [Library symbol Library of Congress] (LCLS) .... CU-RivP

University of California, Riverside, Riverside, CA [OCLC symbol] (OCLC) .... CRU

University of California, San Diego .... UCSD

University of California, San Diego, Biomedical Library, San Diego, CA [Library symbol Library of Congress] (LCLS) .... CU-SM

University of California, San Diego, La Jolla, CA [OCLC symbol] (OCLC) ..... CUS

University of California, San Diego, Main Library, La Jolla, CA [Library symbol Library of Congress] (LCLS) .... CU-S

University of California, San Diego, Science and Engineering Library, San Diego,CA [Library symbol Library of Congress] (LCLS) .... CU-SSe

University of California, San Diego, Scripps Institute of Oceanography, San Diego, CA [Library symbol Library of Congress] (LCLS) .... CU-SSi

University of California, San Diego, Society-University Hospital, San Diego, CA [Library symbol Library of Congress] (LCLS) .... CU-SSh

University of California, San Francisco .... UCSF

University of California, San Francisco, CA [OCLC symbol] (OCLC) .... CUN

University of California, San Francisco, Hastings College of the Law, Library, San Francisco, CA [OCLC symbol] (OCLC) .... CUH

University of California, San Francisco, Hastings College of the Law, San Francisco, CA [Library symbol Library of Congress] (LCLS) .... CSfH

University of California, San Francisco, Medical Center, San Francisco, CA [Library symbol Library of Congress] (LCLS) .... CU-M

University of California, Santa Barbara .... UCSB

University of California, Santa Barbara, Main Library, Santa Barbara, CA [Library symbol Library of Congress] (LCLS) .... CU-SB

University of California, Santa Barbara, Santa Barbara, CA [OCLC symbol] (OCLC) .... CUT

University of California, Santa Cruz .... UCSC

University of California, Santa Cruz, Lick Observatory Library, Santa Cruz, CA [Library symbol Library of Congress] (LCLS) .... CMthL

University of California, Santa Cruz, Main Library, Santa Cruz, CA [Library symbol Library of Congress] (LCLS) .... CU-SC

University of California, Santa Cruz, Santa Cruz, CA [OCLC symbol] (OCLC) .... CUZ

University of California/Space Sciences Laboratory (KSC) .... UC/SSL

University of California Structural Engineering Laboratory (KSC) .... UCSEL

University of California, Union Catalog, Berkeley, CA [Library symbol Library of Congress] (LCLS) .... CU-UC

University of California Union List, Berkeley, CA [*OCLC symbol*] (OCLC) ..... UCU
University of Cambridge, Scott Polar Research Institute, Cambridge, England [*Library symbol*] [*Library of Congress*] (LCLS) ..... UkCU-P
University of Cape Town [*South Africa*] ..... UCT
University of Central Arkansas (GAGS) ..... U Cent Ark
University of Central Arkansas, Conway, AR [*OCLC symbol*] (OCLC) ..... AKC
University of Central Arkansas, Conway, AR [*Library symbol Library of Congress*] (LCLS) ..... ArCCA
University of Central England ..... UCE
University of Central Florida [*Orlando, FL*] ..... UCF
University of Central Florida, Orlando, FL [*OCLC symbol*] (OCLC) ..... FTU
University of Central Oklahoma (GAGS) ..... U Cent Okla
University of Central Queensland [*Australia*] ..... UCQ
University of Ceylon. Law Review [*A publication*] (DLA) ..... U Ceylon LR
University of Ceylon. Law Review [*A publication*] (DLA) ..... UCLR
[*The*] **University of Chicago** (GAGS) ..... U Chicago
University of Chicago [*Illinois*] (PDAA) ..... UC
University of Chicago, Bio-Medical Libraries, Chicago, IL [*Library symbol Library of Congress*] (LCLS) ..... ICU-M
University of Chicago Cancer Research Center [*Research center*] (RCD) ..... UCCRC
University of Chicago, Center for Health Administration Studies, Chicago, IL [*Library symbol Library of Congress*] (LCLS) ..... ICU-H
University of Chicago, Chicago, IL [*Library symbol Library of Congress*] (LCLS) ..... ICU
University of Chicago, Divinity School, Chicago, IL [*Library symbol Library of Congress*] (LCLS) ..... ICU-D
University of Chicago, Far Eastern Library, Chicago, IL [*Library symbol Library of Congress*] (LCLS) ..... ICU-FE
University of Chicago, Graduate Library School, Chicago, IL [*Library symbol Library of Congress*] (LCLS) ..... ICU-LS
University of Chicago, Graduate Library School, Chicago, IL [*OCLC symbol*] (OCLC) ..... IVE
University of Chicago, Law Library, Chicago, IL [*Library symbol Library of Congress*] (LCLS) ..... ICU-L
University of Chicago Law School (DLA) ..... UCHILS
University of Chicago School Mathematics Project (AEE) ..... UCSMP
University of Chicago, Yerkes Observatory, Williams Bay, WI [*Library symbol Library of Congress*] (LCLS) ..... ICU-Y
University of Chile, Valparaiso, Chile [*Library symbol Library of Congress*] (LCLS) ..... ChIU
University of Cincinnati (GAGS) ..... U Cincinnati
University of Cincinnati [*Ohio*] ..... UC
University of Cincinnati, Biology Library, Cincinnati, OH [*Library symbol Library of Congress*] (LCLS) ..... OCU-B
University of Cincinnati, Cincinnati, OH [*OCLC symbol*] (OCLC) ..... CIN
University of Cincinnati, Cincinnati, OH [*Library symbol Library of Congress*] (LCLS) ..... OCU
University of Cincinnati, College Conservatory of Music, Cincinnati, OH [*Library symbol Library of Congress*] (LCLS) ..... OCU-Mu
University of Cincinnati, College of Nursing, Cincinnati, OH [*Library symbol Library of Congress*] (LCLS) ..... OCU-N
University of Cincinnati, Design, Architecture, and Art Library, Cincinnati, OH [*Library symbol Library of Congress*] (LCLS) ..... OCU-DA
University of Cincinnati, Engineering Library, Cincinnati, OH [*Library symbol Library of Congress*] (LCLS) ..... OCU-E
University of Cincinnati, Geology-Geography Library, Cincinnati, OH [*Library symbol Library of Congress*] (LCLS) ..... OCU-Geo
University of Cincinnati, Law Library, Cincinnati, OH [*Library symbol Library of Congress*] (LCLS) ..... OCU-L
University of Cincinnati, Marx Law Library, Cincinnati, OH [*OCLC symbol*] (OCLC) ..... OML
University of Cincinnati, Mathematics Library, Cincinnati, OH [*Library symbol Library of Congress*] (LCLS) ..... OCU-Math
University of Cincinnati, Medical Center, Cincinnati, OH [*OCLC symbol*] (OCLC) ..... MXC
University of Cincinnati, Physics Library, Cincinnati, OH [*Library symbol Library of Congress*] (LCLS) ..... OCU-Ph
University of Cincinnati, School of Medicine, Cincinnati, OH [*Library symbol Library of Congress*] (LCLS) ..... OCU-M
University of Cincinnati Structural Dynamics Research Laboratory ..... UC-SDRL
University of Colorado (GAGS) ..... U Colo
University of Colorado at Boulder Long-Term Ecological Research Project [*Research center*] (RCD) ..... CULTER
University of Colorado at Colorado Springs, Colorado Springs, CO [*Library symbol Library of Congress*] (LCLS) ..... CoU-CS
University of Colorado at Colorado Springs, Colorado Springs, CO [*OCLC symbol*] (OCLC) ..... COX
University of Colorado at Denver, Auraria Libraries, Denver, CO [*OCLC symbol*] (OCLC) ..... COA
University of Colorado at Denver, Auraria Libraries, Denver, CO [*Library symbol Library of Congress*] (LCLS) ..... CoU-DA
University of Colorado, Boulder, CO [*OCLC symbol*] (OCLC) ..... COD
University of Colorado, Boulder, CO [*Library symbol Library of Congress*] (LCLS) ..... CoU
University of Colorado, Colorado General Hospital, Denver, CO [*Library symbol Library of Congress*] (LCLS) ..... CoU-GH
University of Colorado Health Sciences Center [*Denver*] ..... UCHSC
University of Colorado, Institute of Arctic and Alpine Research, World Data Center A for Glaciology, Boulder, CO [*Library symbol Library of Congress*] (LCLS) ..... CoU-IA
University of Colorado, Medical Center, Denver, CO [*OCLC symbol*] (OCLC) ..... COU
University of Colorado, Medical Center, Denver, CO [*Library symbol Library of Congress*] (LCLS) ..... CoU-M
University of Colorado School of Law (DLA) ..... UCOSL
University of Colorado, World Data Center A for Glaciology, Snow and Ice, Boulder, CO [*Library symbol*] [*Library of Congress*] (LCLS) ..... CoU-G
University of Connecticut ..... UCONN
University of Connecticut [*Storrs*] [*Seismograph station code, US Geological Survey*] (SEIS) ..... UCT
University of Connecticut, Hartford Branch, West Hartford, CT [*OCLC symbol*] (OCLC) UB2
University of Connecticut, Health Center Library, Farmington, CT [*OCLC symbol*] (OCLC) ..... UCH
University of Connecticut, Health Center Library, Hartford, CT [*Library symbol Library of Congress*] (LCLS) ..... CtU-H
University of Connecticut, Health Center Library, Processing Center, Farmington,CT [*OCLC symbol*] (OCLC) ..... UCP
University of Connecticut, Law Library, West Hartford, CT [*OCLC symbol*] (OCLC) ..... UCL
University of Connecticut, MBA Library, Hartford, CT [*Library symbol Library of Congress*] (LCLS) ..... CtHU
University of Connecticut, MBA Library, Hartford, CT [*OCLC symbol*] (OCLC) UB4
University of Connecticut Paleobotanical Collection ..... UCPC
University of Connecticut, School of Law, West Hartford, CT [*Library symbol Library of Congress*] (LCLS) ..... CtU-L
University of Connecticut, School of Social Work, West Hartford, CT [*Library symbol Library of Congress*] (LCLS) ..... CtU-SW
University of Connecticut, Southeastern Branch, Groton, CT [*Library symbol Library of Congress*] (LCLS) ..... CtGrU
University of Connecticut, Southeastern Branch, Groton, CT [*OCLC symbol*] (OCLC) UB3
University of Connecticut, Stamford Branch, Stamford, CT [*Library symbol Library of Congress*] (LCLS) ..... CtSU
University of Connecticut, Stamford Branch, Stamford, CT [*OCLC symbol*] (OCLC) UB1
University of Connecticut, Storrs, CT [*Library symbol Library of Congress*] (LCLS) ..... CtU
University of Connecticut, Storrs, CT [*OCLC symbol*] (OCLC) ..... UCW
University of Connecticut, Waterbury Branch, Waterbury, CT [*Library symbol Library of Congress*] (LCLS) ..... CtWatU
University of Connecticut, Waterbury Branch, Waterbury, CT [*OCLC symbol*] (OCLC) ..... UBW
University of Corpus Christi [*Texas*] [*Closed, 1973*] ..... UCC
University of Corpus Christi, Corpus Christi, TX [*Library symbol Library of Congress Obsolete*] (LCLS) ..... TxCcU
University of Crete, Crete, Greece [*Library symbol*] [*Library of Congress*] (LCLS) ..... GrCu
University of Dallas (GAGS) ..... U Dallas
University of Dallas, Irving, TX [*OCLC symbol*] (OCLC) ..... IVD
University of Dallas, Irving, TX [*Library symbol Library of Congress*] (LCLS) ..... TxDaU
University of Dayton (GAGS) ..... U Dayton
University of Dayton, Dayton, OH [*OCLC symbol*] (OCLC) ..... DAY
University of Dayton, Dayton, OH [*Library symbol Library of Congress*] (LCLS) ..... ODaU
University of Dayton. Intramural Law Review [*A publication*] (DLA) ..... Dayton
University of Dayton, Law Library, Dayton, OH [*Library symbol Library of Congress*] (LCLS) ..... ODaU-L
University of Dayton, Law Library, Dayton, OH [*OCLC symbol*] (OCLC) ..... ODL
University of Dayton, Marian Library, Dayton, OH [*Library symbol Library of Congress*] (LCLS) ..... ODaU-M
University of Dayton Research Institute [*Ohio*] ..... UDRI
University of Delaware (GAGS) ..... U Del
University of Delaware, Agricultural Experiment Station, Newark, DE [*Library symbol Library of Congress*] (LCLS) ..... DeU-Ag
University of Delaware Center for Composite Materials (RDA) ..... UD-CCM
University of Delaware, Newark, DE [*Library symbol Library of Congress*] (LCLS) ..... DeU
University of Delaware, Newark, DE [*OCLC symbol*] (OCLC) ..... DLM
University of Denver (GAGS) ..... U Denver
University of Denver [*Colorado*] ..... UD
University of Denver, Denver, CO [*Library symbol Library of Congress*] (LCLS) ..... CoDU
University of Denver, Denver, CO [*OCLC symbol*] (OCLC) ..... DVP
University of Denver, Graduate School of Librarianship, Denver, CO [*OCLC symbol*] (OCLC) ..... DGS
University of Detroit [*Michigan*] ..... U of D
University of Detroit, Colombiere Campus, Clarkston, MI [*Library symbol Library of Congress*] (LCLS) ..... MiDU-C
University of Detroit, Dental Library, Detroit, MI [*Library symbol Library of Congress*] (LCLS) ..... MiDU-D
University of Detroit, Detroit, MI [*OCLC symbol*] (OCLC) ..... EYU
University of Detroit, Detroit, MI [*Library symbol Library of Congress*] (LCLS) ..... MiDU
University of Detroit. Journal of Urban Law [*A publication*] (DLA) ..... Urban LJ
University of Detroit, Law Library, Detroit, MI [*Library symbol Library of Congress*] (LCLS) ..... MiDU-L
University of Detroit. Law Review [*A publication*] (DLA) ..... U Det L Rev
University of Detroit Mercy (GAGS) ..... U Detroit
University of District of Columbia, Van Ness Campus, Washington, DC [*OCLC symbol*] (OCLC) ..... DDU
University of Dublin [*Ireland*] ..... U of D
University of Dubuque (GAGS) ..... U Dubuque
University of Dubuque, Dubuque, IA [*Library symbol Library of Congress*] (LCLS) ..... IaDuU
University of Dubuque, Dubuque, IA [*OCLC symbol*] (OCLC) ..... IOV

University of Dubuque, Theological Seminary, Dubuque, IA [*Library symbol Library of Congress*] (LCLS) ... IaDuU-S
University of Durham Industrial Research Laboratories [*British*] ... UDIRL
University of East Anglia [*England*] ... UEA
University of East London (ECON) ... UeL
University of Edinburgh, Edinburgh, United Kingdom [*Library symbol Library of Congress*] (LCLS) ... UkEU
University of Essex Library, Colchester, England [*OCLC symbol*] (OCLC) ... EUE
University of Essex, Wivenhoe Park, Colchester, England [*Library symbol*] [*Library of Congress*] (LCLS) ... UkCoU
University of Evansville (GAGS) ... U Evansville
University of Evansville, Evansville, IN [*Library symbol Library of Congress*] (LCLS) ... InEU
University of Evansville, Evansville, IN [*OCLC symbol*] (OCLC) ... IUE
University of Florida (GAGS) ... U Fla
University of Florida [*Gainesville*] ... UF
University of Florida, Agricultural Experiment Station, Gainesville, FL [*Library symbol Library of Congress*] (LCLS) ... FU-A
University of Florida, Agricultural Library, Gainesville, FL [*OCLC symbol*] (OCLC) ... FUA
University of Florida, Chemistry-Pharmacy Library, Gainesville, FL [*Library symbol Library of Congress*] (LCLS) ... FU-CP
University of Florida, Gainesville, FL [*Library symbol Library of Congress*] (LCLS) ... FU
University of Florida, Gainesville, FL [*OCLC symbol*] (OCLC) ... FUG
University of Florida, Health Center Library, Gainesville, FL [*OCLC symbol*] (OCLC) ... FUH
University of Florida, Health Sciences, JHEP Processing Center, Gainesville, FL [*Library symbol*] [*Library of Congress*] (LCLS) ... FU-J
University of Florida, J. Hillis Miller Health Center Library, Gainesville, FL [*Library symbol Library of Congress*] (LCLS) ... FU-HC
University of Florida, Law Library, Gainesville, FL [*OCLC symbol*] (OCLC) ... FUB
University of Florida, Law Library, Gainesville, FL [*Library symbol Library of Congress*] (LCLS) ... FU-L
University of Florida Teaching Reactor ... UFTR
University of Florida Water Resources Research Center [*Research center*] (RCD) ... FWRRC
[*The*] **University of Georgia** (GAGS) ... U Georgia
University of Georgia (PDAA) ... UGA
University of Georgia, Athens, GA [*Library symbol Library of Congress*] (LCLS) ... GU
University of Georgia, Athens, GA [*OCLC symbol*] (OCLC) ... GUA
University of Georgia, DeRenne Georgia Library, Athens, GA [*Library symbol Library of Congress*] (LCLS) ... GU-De
University of Georgia, Experiment Station, Griffin, GA [*Library symbol Library of Congress*] (LCLS) ... GGriEx
University of Georgia, Law Library, Athens, GA [*Library symbol Library of Congress*] (LCLS) ... GU-L
University of Georgia, School of Pharmacy, Athens, GA [*Library symbol Library of Congress*] (LCLS) ... GU-P
University of Ghana. Law Journal [*A publication*] ... UGLJ
University of Ghana. Law Journal [*A publication*] (DLA) ... Un of Gh LJ
University of Ghana. Law Journal [*London, England*] [*A publication*] (DLA) ... Univ of Ghana LJ
University of Glasgow, Glasgow, United Kingdom [*Library symbol Library of Congress*] (LCLS) ... UkGU
University of Gottingen, Hannover, Germany [*Library symbol Library of Congress*] (LCLS) ... GyHGU
University of Guam, Agana, GU [*Library symbol Library of Congress*] (LCLS) ... GuaU
University of Guelph [*UTLAS symbol*] ... GUE
University of Guelph Document Holdings [*Database*] [*No longer available online*] ... GDOC
University of Guelph, Guelph, ON, Canada [*Library symbol Library of Congress*] (LCLS) ... CaOGU
University of Guelph, Ontario [*Library symbol National Library of Canada*] (NLC) ... OGU
University of Hard Knocks [*West Virginia*] [*"University" founded by Jim Comstock and based on the expression "school of hard knocks"*] ... UHK
University of Hartford (GAGS) ... U Hartford
University of Hartford, West Hartford, CT [*Library symbol Library of Congress*] (LCLS) ... CtWeharU
University of Hartford, West Hartford, CT [*OCLC symbol*] (OCLC) ... HRM
University of Hawaii (GAGS) ... U Hawaii
University of Hawaii [*Honolulu, HI*] ... UH
University of Hawaii [*Honolulu, HI*] (NOAA) ... UNIHI
University of Hawaii at Hilo, West Hawaii Library, Kealakekua, HI [*Library symbol*] [*Library of Congress*] (LCLS) ... HHIU-W
University of Hawaii, Hamilton Library, Honolulu, HI [*OCLC symbol*] (OCLC) ... HUH
University of Hawaii, Honolulu, HI [*Library symbol Library of Congress*] (LCLS) ... HU
University of Hawaii, Leahi Hospital, Hastings H. Walker Medical Library, Honolulu, HI [*Library symbol Library of Congress*] (LCLS) ... HU-M
University of Hawaii Press ... UHP
University of Health Science Chicago Medicine School (GAGS) ... U Health Sc (Chicago)
University of Health Sciences - Chicago Medical School ... UHS
University of Health Sciences - Chicago Medical School ... UHS-CMS
University of Health Sciences - Chicago Medical School, Chicago, IL [*Library symbol Library of Congress*] (LCLS) ... ICCM
University of Health Sciences, Kansas City, MO [*OCLC symbol*] (OCLC) ... MKC
University of Hong Kong, Hong Kong, Hong Kong [*UK*] [*Library symbol Library of Congress*] (LCLS) ... HkU
University of Houston (GAGS) ... U Houston
University of Houston at Clear Lake City, Houston, TX [*Library symbol Library of Congress*] (LCLS) ... TxClcU
University of Houston at Clear Lake City, Houston, TX [*OCLC symbol*] (OCLC) ... UHC
University of Houston Coastal Center [*Research center*] (RCD) ... UHCC
University of Houston, Downtown College, Houston, TX [*OCLC symbol*] (OCLC) ... THD
University of Houston, Downtown College, Houston, TX [*Library symbol Library of Congress*] (LCLS) ... TxHU-D
University of Houston, Houston, TX [*OCLC symbol*] (OCLC) ... TXH
University of Houston, Houston, TX [*Library symbol Library of Congress*] (LCLS) ... TxHU
University of Houston, Law Library, Main, Houston, TX [*OCLC symbol*] (OCLC) ... THL
University of Houston, Law School, Houston, TX [*Library symbol Library of Congress*] (LCLS) ... TxHU-L
University of Houston, Victoria Center, Victoria, TX [*OCLC symbol*] (OCLC) ... TXV
University of Houston, Victoria Center, Victoria, TX [*Library symbol Library of Congress*] (LCLS) ... TxViHU
University of Ibadan, Ibadan, Nigeria [*Library symbol Library of Congress*] (LCLS) ... NgIU
University of Icelands (Haskoli Islands), Reykjavik, Iceland [*Library symbol Library of Congress*] (LCLS) ... IcRU
University of Idaho (GAGS) ... U Idaho
University of Idaho, Law Library, Moscow, ID [*Library symbol Library of Congress*] (LCLS) ... IdU-L
University of Idaho, Moscow, ID [*Library symbol Library of Congress*] (LCLS) ... IdU
University of Illinois (GAGS) ... U Ill
University of Illinois [*Urbana, IL*] ... U of I
University of Illinois ... UIC
University of Illinois [*Record label*] ... UOI
University of Illinois, Archives, Urbana, IL [*Library symbol Library of Congress*] (LCLS) ... IU-Ar
University of Illinois at Chicago (GAGS) ... U Ill (Chicago)
University of Illinois at Chicago Circle ... UICC
University of Illinois at Chicago Circle, Chicago, IL [*OCLC symbol*] (OCLC) ... IAY
University of Illinois at Chicago Circle, Chicago, IL [*Library symbol Library of Congress*] (LCLS) ... ICIU
University of Illinois at Chicago Circle, Peoria School of Medicine, Peoria, IL [*Library symbol Library of Congress*] (LCLS) ... ICIU-PM
University of Illinois at Chicago Circle, Rockford School of Medicine, Rockford,IL [*Library symbol Library of Congress*] (LCLS) ... ICIU-RM
University of Illinois at Chicago Circle, Science Library, Chicago, IL [*Library symbol Library of Congress*] (LCLS) ... ICIU-S
University of Illinois at the Medical Center, Chicago, IL [*OCLC symbol*] (OCLC) ... IAX
University of Illinois at the Medical Center, Chicago, IL [*Library symbol Library of Congress*] (LCLS) ... IU-M
University of Illinois at Urbana-Champaign, University of Illinois Newspaper Library, Urbana-Champaign, IL [*Library symbol Library of Congress*] (LCLS) ... IU-Ne
University of Illinois, Biology Library, Urbana, IL [*Library symbol Library of Congress*] (LCLS) ... IU-B
University of Illinois Committee on School Mathematics ... UICSM
University of Illinois, Graduate School of Library Science, Urbana, IL [*OCLC symbol*] (OCLC) ... ILG
University of Illinois, Graduate School of Library Science, Urbana, IL [*Library symbol Library of Congress*] (LCLS) ... IU-LS
University of Illinois Hospital Eye and Ear Infirmary [*University of Illnois at Chicago*] [*Research center*] (RCD) ... IEEI
University of Illinois, Illinois Natural History Survey, Urbana, IL [*Library symbol Library of Congress*] (LCLS) ... IU-NH
University of Illinois, Illinois State Geological Survey, Urbana, IL [*Library symbol Library of Congress*] (LCLS) ... IU-GS
University of Illinois, Illinois State Water Survey, Champaign, IL [*Library symbol Library of Congress*] (LCLS) ... IU-WS
University of Illinois. Law Bulletin [*A publication*] (DLA) ... U Ill L Bull
University of Illinois. Law Bulletin [*A publication*] (DLA) ... U Ill LB
University of Illinois, Lincoln Room, Urbana, IL [*Library symbol Library of Congress*] (LCLS) ... IU-L
University of Illinois, Map and Geography Library, Urbana, IL [*Library symbol*] [*Library of Congress*] (LCLS) ... IU-MG
University of Illinois. Moot Court Bulletin [*A publication*] (DLA) ... Moot Ct Bull
University of Illinois, Music Library, Urbana, IL [*Library symbol Library of Congress*] (LCLS) ... IU-Mu
University of Illinois Press ... UIP
University of Illinois, Rare Book Room, Urbana, IL [*Library symbol Library of Congress*] (LCLS) ... IU-R
University of Illinois, School of Basic Medical Sciences, Library of Public Health Sciences, Urbana, IL [*Library symbol Library of Congress*] (LCLS) ... IU-H
University of Illinois Solid State Electronics Laboratory [*Research center*] (RCD) ... ISSEL
University of Illinois, Urbana ... UILU
University of Illinois, Urbana, IL [*Library symbol Library of Congress*] (LCLS) ... IU
University of Illinois, Urbana, IL [*OCLC symbol*] (OCLC) ... UIU
University of Illinois, Urbana-Champaign ... UIUC
University of Illinois, Veterinary Medicine Library, Urbana, IL [*Library symbol Library of Congress*] (LCLS) ... IU-V
University of Indianapolis (GAGS) ... U Indianapolis
[*The*] **University of Iowa** (GAGS) ... U Iowa
University of Iowa [*Iowa City, IA*] (OICC) ... U of I

University of Iowa, Botany-Chemistry Library, Iowa City, IA [Library symbol Library of Congress] (LCLS) .... IaU-B

University of Iowa, College of Law, Iowa City, IA [Library symbol Library of Congress] (LCLS) .... IaU-L

University of Iowa, Health Sciences Library, Iowa City, IA [Library symbol Library of Congress] (LCLS) .... IaU-M

University of Iowa Hospitals (DAVI) .... UIH

University of Iowa, Iowa City, IA [Library symbol Library of Congress] (LCLS) .... IaU

University of Iowa. Law Review [A publication] (DLA) .... U Iowa L Rev

University of Iowa, School of Library Science, Iowa City, IA [OCLC symbol] (OCLC) .... UIL

University of Judaism, Los Angeles, CA [Library symbol Library of Congress] (LCLS) .... CLJ

University of Kansas (GAGS) .... U Kans

University of Kansas [Lawrence, KS] .... UK

University of Kansas Automated Serials .... UKASE

University of Kansas Center for Research, Inc. [Research center] (RCD) .... CRINC

University of Kansas City [Later, University of Missouri at Kansas City] .... UKC

University of Kansas, Kenneth Spencer Research Library, Lawrence, KS [Library symbol Library of Congress] (LCLS) .... KU-S

University of Kansas, Law Library, Lawrence, KS [OCLC symbol] (OCLC) .... KFL

University of Kansas. Law Review [A publication] (DLA) .... U of Kansas L Rev

University of Kansas. Law Review [A publication] (DLA) .... UKLR

University of Kansas, Lawrence, KS [OCLC symbol] (OCLC) .... KKU

University of Kansas, Lawrence, KS [Library symbol Library of Congress] (LCLS) .... KU

University of Kansas, Medical Library, Kansas City, KS [OCLC symbol] (OCLC) .... KKP

University of Kansas Medicine Center (GAGS) .... U Kans Med Ctr

University of Kansas Nuclear Reactor .... UKNR

University of Kansas, School of Law, Lawrence, KS [Library symbol Library of Congress] (LCLS) .... KU-L

University of Kansas, School of Medicine, Kansas City, KS [Library symbol Library of Congress] (LCLS) .... KU-M

University of Kansas, School of Medicine-Witchita, Witchita, KS [Library symbol] [Library of Congress] (LCLS) .... KU-MW

University of Kansas, Spencer Library, Lawrence, KS [OCLC symbol] (OCLC) .... KFS

University of Kentucky (GAGS) .... U Ky

University of Kentucky (PDAA) .... UKY

University of Kentucky, Agricultural Science Center, Lexington, KY [Library symbol Library of Congress] (LCLS) .... KyU-ASC

University of Kentucky, Ashland Community College, Ashland, KY [Library symbol Library of Congress] (LCLS) .... KyU-A

University of Kentucky, Elizabethtown Community College, Elizabethtown, KY [Library symbol Library of Congress] (LCLS) .... KyU-E

University of Kentucky, Fort Knox Center, Fort Knox, KY [Library symbol Library of Congress] (LCLS) .... KyU-F

University of Kentucky, Law Library, Lexington, KY [Library symbol Library of Congress] (LCLS) .... KyU-L

University of Kentucky, Lexington, KY [OCLC symbol] (OCLC) .... KUK

University of Kentucky, Lexington, KY [Library symbol Library of Congress] (LCLS) .... KyU

University of Kentucky Medical Center [Lexington, KY] .... UKMC

University of Kentucky, Medical Center, Lexington, KY [OCLC symbol] (OCLC) .... KUM

University of Kentucky, Medical Center, Lexington, KY [Library symbol Library of Congress] (LCLS) .... KyU-M

University of Kentucky, Northern Center, Covington, KY [Library symbol Library of Congress] (LCLS) .... KyU-N

University of Kentucky, Northwest Center, Henderson, KY [Library symbol Library of Congress] (LCLS) .... KyU-H

University of Kentucky, Prestonburg Community College, Prestonburg, KY [OCLC symbol] (OCLC) .... KUP

University of Kentucky, Prestonburg Community College, Prestonburg, KY [Library symbol Library of Congress] (LCLS) .... KyU-P

University of Kentucky, Southeast Center, Cumberland, KY [OCLC symbol] (OCLC) .... KUS

University of Kentucky, Southeast Center, Cumberland, KY [Library symbol Library of Congress] (LCLS) .... KyU-C

University of King's College, Halifax, Nova Scotia [Library symbol National Library of Canada] (NLC) .... NSHK

University of King's College, Halifax, NS, Canada [Library symbol Library of Congress] (LCLS) .... CaNSHK

University of King's College, School of Journalism, Halifax, NS, Canada [Library symbol] [Library of Congress] (LCLS) .... CaNSHKJ

University of La Verne (GAGS) .... U La Verne

University of Lancaster Engineering Services [Research center British] (IRUK) .... ULES

University of Lapland, Lapland Artic Center, Rovaniemi, Lapland [Library symbol] [Library of Congress] (LCLS) .... FiRUL-A

University of Lethbridge, Alberta [Library symbol National Library of Canada] (NLC) .... ALU

University of Lethbridge, Department of Geography, Lethbridge, AB, Canada [Library symbol Library of Congress] (LCLS) .... CaALUG

University of Lethbridge, Lethbridge, AB, Canada [Library symbol Library of Congress] (LCLS) .... CaALU

University of Lethbridge Library [UTLAS symbol] .... ALU

University of Liverpool, Liverpool, United Kingdom [Library symbol Library of Congress] (LCLS) .... UkLiU

University of London and East Anglia Consortium [British] (AIE) .... ULEAC

University of London Computer Centre (NITA) .... ULCC

University of London, Kings College, London, United Kingdom [Library symbol Library of Congress] (LCLS) .... UkLU-K

University of London Library .... ULL

University of London, London, United Kingdom [Library symbol Library of Congress] (LCLS) .... UkLU

University of London Officer Training Corps [British military] (DMA) .... ULOTC

University of London Press (DGA) .... ULP

University of London Shared Cataloguing System (NITA) .... ULSCS

University of Louisville (GAGS) .... U Louisville

University of Louisville Archaeological Survey [Research center] (RCD) .... ULAS

University of Louisville, Dwight Anderson Music Library, Louisville, KY [Library symbol] [Library of Congress] (LCLS) .... KyLoU-Mu

University of Louisville, Health Sciences Library, Louisville, KY [Library symbol Library of Congress] (LCLS) .... KyLoU-HS

University of Louisville, Law Library, Louisville,KY [Library symbol] [Library of Congress] (LCLS) .... KyLoU-L

University of Louisville, Louisville, KY [OCLC symbol] (OCLC) .... KLG

University of Louisville, Louisville, KY [Library symbol Library of Congress] (LCLS) .... KyLoU

University of Louisville, School of Music Library, Louisville, KY [OCLC symbol] (OCLC) .... KLM

University of Louisville, University Archives and Records Center, Louisville, KY [Library symbol Library of Congress] (LCLS) .... KyLoU-Ar

University of Lowell, Lowell, MA [Library symbol Library of Congress] (LCLS) .... MLowU

University of Lowell - North Campus, Alumni/Lydon Memorial Library, Lowell, MA [Library symbol Library of Congress] (LCLS) .... MLowU-N

University of Lowell, North Campus, Lowell, MA [OCLC symbol] (OCLC) ..... ULN

University of Lowell, South Campus, Lowell, MA [OCLC symbol] (OCLC) ..... ULS

University of Maine (GAGS) .... U Maine

University of Maine at Augusta, Augusta, ME [OCLC symbol] (OCLC) .... AUG

University of Maine at Augusta, Augusta, ME [Library symbol Library of Congress] (LCLS) .... MeAU

University of Maine at Farmington, Farmington, ME [Library symbol Library of Congress] (LCLS) .... MeFarU

University of Maine at Farmington, Farmington, ME [OCLC symbol] (OCLC) .... UMF

University of Maine at Fort Kent, Fort Kent, ME [Library symbol Library of Congress] (LCLS) .... MeFtkU

University of Maine at Machias, Machias, ME [Library symbol Library of Congress] (LCLS) .... MeMacU

University of Maine at Portland/Gorham .... UMPG

University of Maine at Portland/Gorham, Gorham, ME [Library symbol Library of Congress] (LCLS) .... MeU-G

University of Maine at Portland/Gorham, Portland, ME [Library symbol Library of Congress] (LCLS) .... MeU-P

University of Maine at Portland-Gorham (GAGS) .... U Maine (Portland-Gorham)

University of Maine at Presque Isle, Presque Isle, ME [Library symbol Library of Congress] (LCLS) .... MePriU

University of Maine, Law Library, Portland, ME [Library symbol Library of Congress] (LCLS) .... MeU-L

University of Maine. Law Review [A publication] (DLA) .... ME L

University of Maine. Law Review [A publication] (DLA) .... U Maine L Rev

University of Maine, Orono .... UMO

University of Maine, Orono, ME [Library symbol Library of Congress] (LCLS) .... MeU

University of Malaya, Kuala Lumpur, Malaysia [Library symbol Library of Congress] (LCLS) .... MlyKU

University of Manchester Institute of Science and Technology [Databank or iginator and research institute] [British] .... UMIST

University of Manila. Law Gazette [Manila, Philippines] [A publication] (DLA) .... Univ of Manila L Gaz

University of Manitoba [Canada] .... UM

University of Manitoba, Architecture and Fine Arts Library, Winnipeg, MB, Canada [Library symbol Library of Congress] (LCLS) .... CaMWUAF

University of Manitoba, Dental Library, Winnipeg, MB, Canada [Library symbol Library of Congress] (LCLS) .... CaMWUD

University of Manitoba, Department of Geography, Winnipeg, MB, Canada [Library symbol Library of Congress] (LCLS) .... CaMWUG

University of Manitoba, Faculty of Law Library, Winnipeg, MB, Canada [Library symbol Library of Congress] (LCLS) .... CaMWLS

University of Manitoba Library [UTLAS symbol] .... MAN

University of Manitoba, Map and Atlas Collection, Winnipeg, MB, Canada [Library symbol Library of Congress] (LCLS) .... CaMWUM

University of Manitoba Medical Library [UTLAS symbol] .... UMM

University of Manitoba, Medical Library, Winnipeg, MB, Canada [Library symbol Library of Congress] (LCLS) .... CaMWM

University of Manitoba, Winnipeg, Manitoba [Library symbol National Library of Canada] (NLC) .... MWU

University of Manitoba, Winnipeg, MB, Canada [Library symbol Library of Congress] (LCLS) .... CaMWU

University of Maryland (GAGS) .... U Md

University of Maryland [College Park, MD] .... UMD

University of Maryland, Architecture Library, College Park, MD [Library symbol Library of Congress] (LCLS) .... MdU-Ar

University of Maryland, Art Library, College Park, MD [Library symbol Library of Congress] (LCLS) .... MdU-A

University of Maryland at Baltimore .... UMAB

University of Maryland, Baltimore (GAGS) .... U Md (Baltimore)

University of Maryland, Baltimore County .... UMBC

University of Maryland, Baltimore County Campus, Baltimore, MD [Library symbol Library of Congress] (LCLS) .... MdU-BC

University of Maryland, Baltimore County Campus, Catonsville, MD [OCLC symbol] (OCLC) .... MUB

University of Maryland, Baltimore, Health Sciences Library, Baltimore, MD [OCLC symbol] (OCLC) .... MDU

University of Maryland Biotechnology Institute .... UMBI

University of Maryland Center for Environmental and Estuarine Studies .... UMCEES

University of Maryland, Chemistry Library, College Park, MD [Library symbol Library of Congress] (LCLS) .... MdU-C

University of Maryland, College of Library and Information Services, College Park, MD [OCLC symbol] (OCLC) .... MDX

University of Maryland, College Park .... UMCP

University of Maryland, College Park, MD [Library symbol Library of Congress] (LCLS) .... MdU

University of Maryland, College Park, MD [OCLC symbol] (OCLC) .... UMC

University of Maryland, Eastern Shore .... UMES

University of Maryland, Eastern Shore, Princess Anne, MD [Library symbol Library of Congress] (LCLS) .... MdPM

University of Maryland, Eastern Shore, Princess Anne, MD [OCLC symbol] (OCLC) .... UME

University of Maryland, Engineering and Physical Sciences Library, College Park,MD [Library symbol Library of Congress] (LCLS) .... MdU-E

University of Maryland, Health Sciences Library, Baltimore, MD [Library symbol Library of Congress] (LCLS) .... MdU-H

University of Maryland Law Forum [A publication] (DLA) .... U Mary L Forum

University of Maryland Law Forum [A publication] (DLA) .... U Md LF

University of Maryland Mathematics Project .... UM-MaP

University of Maryland, School of Law, Baltimore, MD [OCLC symbol] (OCLC) .... LUM

University of Maryland, School of Law, Baltimore, MD [Library symbol Library of Congress] (LCLS) .... MdU-L

University of Maryland Teaching Reactor (NRCH) .... UMTR

University of Maryland, Undergraduate Library, College Park, MD [Library symbol Library of Congress] (LCLS) .... MdU-U

University of Massachusetts [Amherst, MA] .... UM

University of Massachusetts [Amherst, MA] .... UMASS

University of Massachusetts Amherst (GAGS) .... U Mass

University of Massachusetts, Amherst, MA [Library symbol Library of Congress] (LCLS) .... MU

University of Massachusetts Boston (GAGS) .... U Mass (Boston)

University of Massachusetts, Boston, Boston, MA [OCLC symbol] (OCLC) .... BMU

University of Massachusetts, Boston, MA [Library symbol Library of Congress] (LCLS) .... MBMU

University of Massachusetts Dartmouth (GAGS) .... U Mass (Dartmouth)

University of Massachusetts, Joseph P. Healy Library, Boston, MA [Library symbol] [Library of Congress] (LCLS) .... MBM

University of Massachusetts Lowell (GAGS) .... U Mass (Lowell)

University of Massachusetts, Medical Center, Worcester, MA [Library symbol Library of Congress] (LCLS) .... MWMU

University of Massachusetts, Medical Center, Worcester, MA [OCLC symbol] (OCLC) .... WQM

University of Massachusetts-Amherst, Amherst, MA [OCLC symbol] (OCLC) .... AUM

University of Mauritius, Reduit, Mauritius [Library symbol Library of Congress] (LCLS) .... MauU

University of Medicine and Dentistry of New Jersey (GAGS) .... U Med Dent NJ

University of Medicine and Dentistry of New Jersey .... UMD

University of Medicine and Dentistry of New Jersey [Newark] .... UMDNJ

University of Melbourne Alumni Association [Australia] ...... UMAA

University of Melbourne, Baillieu Library, Parkville, V, Australia [Library symbol Library of Congress] (LCLS) .... AuPaU

University of Melbourne, Melbourne, V, Australia [Library symbol Library of Congress] (LCLS) .... AuMU

University of Miami [Florida] .... UM

University of Miami, Coral Gables, FL [Library symbol Library of Congress] (LCLS) .... FMU

University of Miami, Coral Gables, FL [OCLC symbol] (OCLC) .... FQG

University of Miami (Florida) (GAGS) .... U Miami (Fla)

University of Miami, Florida [USA] [Marine science] (OSRA) .... UM

University of Miami Law Center (DLA) .... UMLC

University of Miami, Law Library, Coral Gables, FL [OCLC symbol] (OCLC) .... FML

University of Miami, Law Library, Coral Gables, FL [Library symbol Library of Congress] (LCLS) .... FMU-L

University of Miami Marine Laboratory [Florida] .... UMML

University of Miami, Medical Library, Miami, FL [Library symbol Library of Congress] (LCLS) .... FMU-M

University of Miami, Music Library, Coral Gables, FL [OCLC symbol] (OCLC) .... FMM

University of Miami, Music Library, Coral Gables, FL [Library symbol Library of Congress] (LCLS) .... FMU-Mu

University of Miami, Rosenstiel School of Marine and Atmospheric Sciences, Miami, FL [Library symbol Library of Congress] (LCLS) .... FMU-R

University of Miami, School of Medicine, Miami, FL [OCLC symbol] (OCLC) .... FQM

[The] University of Michigan (GAGS) .... U Mich

University of Michigan [Ann Arbor, MI] .... U of M

University of Michigan [Ann Arbor, MI] .... UMICH

University of Michigan, Ann Arbor, MI [OCLC symbol] (OCLC) .... EYM

University of Michigan, Ann Arbor, MI [Library symbol Library of Congress] (LCLS) .... MiU

University of Michigan, Asia Library, Ann Arbor, MI [Library symbol Library of Congress] (LCLS) .... MiU-A

University of Michigan Assembly Program .... UMAP

University of Michigan at Flint, and Charles Stewart Mott Community College, Flint, MI [Library symbol Library of Congress] (LCLS) .... MiFliC

University of Michigan, Avery and Julie Hopwood Room, Ann Arbor, MI [Library symbol Library of Congress] (LCLS) .... MiU-Ho

University of Michigan Biological Station [Research center] (RCD) .... UMBS

University of Michigan, Bureau of Government Library, Ann Arbor, MI [Library symbol Library of Congress] (LCLS) .... MiU-G

University of Michigan, Center for Research on Economic Development, Ann Arbor, MI [Library symbol Library of Congress] (LCLS) .... MiU-RE

University of Michigan, Dearborn Campus, Dearborn, MI [OCLC symbol] (OCLC) .... EYD

University of Michigan, Dearborn Campus, Dearborn, MI [Library symbol Library of Congress] (LCLS) .... MiDbU

University of Michigan, Graduate School of Business Administration, Ann Arbor, MI [Library symbol Library of Congress] (LCLS) .... MiU-BA

University of Michigan, Law Library, Ann Arbor, MI [Library symbol Library of Congress] (LCLS) .... MiU-L

University of Michigan Medical Center (BABM) .... UMMC

University of Michigan, Medical Center, Ann Arbor, MI [Library symbol Library of Congress] (LCLS) .... MiU-M

University of Michigan, Michigan Historical Collection, Ann Arbor, MI [Library symbol Library of Congress] (LCLS) .... MiU-H

University of Michigan Museum of Zoology .... UMMZ

University of Michigan, School of Library Science, Ann Arbor, MI [OCLC symbol] (OCLC) .... EER

University of Michigan, Transportation Library, Ann Arbor, MI [Library symbol Library of Congress] (LCLS) .... MiU-T

University of Michigan Transportation Research Institute [Research center] (RCD) .... UMTRI

University of Michigan, William L. Clements Library, Ann Arbor, MI [Library symbol Library of Congress] (LCLS) .... MiU-C

University of Mid-America [Consortium of six midwestern universities] .... UMA

University of Minesota Biocatalysis/Biodegradation Database .... UM-BBD

University of Minnesota (GAGS) .... U Minn

University of Minnesota, Archives, Minneapolis, MN [Library symbol Library of Congress] (LCLS) .... MnU-Ar

University of Minnesota, Biochemistry Library, St. Paul, MN [Library symbol Library of Congress] (LCLS) .... MnSU-Bc

University of Minnesota, Biomedical Library, Minneapolis, MN [Library symbol Library of Congress] (LCLS) .... MnU-B

University of Minnesota, Duluth, MN [Library symbol Library of Congress] (LCLS) .... MnDuU

University of Minnesota, Entomology Library, St. Paul, MN [Library symbol Library of Congress] (LCLS) .... MnSU-Et

University of Minnesota, Forestry Library, St. Paul, MN [Library symbol Library of Congress] (LCLS) .... MnSU-F

University of Minnesota, Freshwater Biological Institute, Navarre, MN [OCLC symbol] (OCLC) .... FWB

University of Minnesota, Freshwater Biological Institute, Navarre, MN [Library symbol Library of Congress] (LCLS) .... MnU-Fb

University of Minnesota, Immigration History Research Center, St. Paul, MN [Library symbol Library of Congress] (LCLS) .... MnU-IA

University of Minnesota, Kerlan Children's Books Collection, Minneapolis, MN [Library symbol Library of Congress] (LCLS) .... MnU-K

University of Minnesota, Law Library, Minneapolis, MN [OCLC symbol] (OCLC) .... MLL

University of Minnesota, Law Library, Minneapolis, MN [Library symbol Library of Congress] (LCLS) .... MnU-L

University of Minnesota, Manuscript Collection, Minneapolis, MN [Library symbol Library of Congress] (LCLS) .... MnU-MS

University of Minnesota, Minneapolis, MN [Library symbol Library of Congress] (LCLS) .... MnU

University of Minnesota, Minneapolis, MN [OCLC symbol] (OCLC) .... MNU

University of Minnesota, Morris, MN [Library symbol Library of Congress] (LCLS) .... MnMoU

University of Minnesota, Morris, Morris, MN [OCLC symbol] (OCLC) .... MNX

University of Minnesota, Pharmacy Library, Minneapolis, MN [Library symbol Library of Congress] (LCLS) .... MnU-Ph

University of Minnesota, Plant Pathology Library, St. Paul, MN [Library symbol Library of Congress] (LCLS) .... MnSU-PP

University of Minnesota, Rare Book Division, Minneapolis, MN [Library symbol Library of Congress] (LCLS) .... MnU-Rb

University of Minnesota Rosemont Aeronautical Laboratories (SAA) ...... UMRAL

University of Minnesota, St. Paul, MN [OCLC symbol] (OCLC) .... MNP

University of Minnesota, St. Paul, MN [Library symbol Library of Congress] (LCLS) .... MnSU

University of Minnesota, Social Welfare History Archives Center, St. Paul, MN [Library symbol Library of Congress] (LCLS) .... MnU-SW

University of Minnesota Technical College, Crookston, MN [OCLC symbol] (OCLC) .... MCR

University of Minnesota Technical College, Crookston, MN [Library symbol Library of Congress] (LCLS) .... MnCrU

University of Minnesota Technical College, Waseca, MN [Library symbol Library of Congress] (LCLS) .... MnWasU

University of Minnesota, the Hormel Institute, Austin, MN [OCLC symbol] (OCLC) .... HOR

University of Minnesota Union List of Serials, Minneapolis, MN [Library symbol Library of Congress] (LCLS) .... MnMULS

University of Minnesota, Veterinary Medicine Library, St. Paul, MN [Library symbol Library of Congress] (LCLS) .... MnSU-V

University of Minnesota, Waseca, Waseca, MN [OCLC symbol] (OCLC) .... MNQ

University of Minnesota-Duluth, Duluth, MN [OCLC symbol] (OCLC) .... MND

University of Minnesota-Duluth, Health Science Library, Duluth, MN [OCLC symbol] (OCLC) .... MNH

[The] University of Mississippi (GAGS) .... U Miss

University of Mississippi, Law School, University, MS [Library symbol Library of Congress] (LCLS) .... MsU-L

University of Mississippi, Medical Center, Jackson, MS [Library symbol Library of Congress] (LCLS) .... MsU-M
University of Mississippi Medicine Center (GAGS) .... U Miss (Med Cent)
University of Mississippi, School of Law Library, University, MS [OCLC symbol] (OCLC) .... MUW
University of Mississippi, School of Pharmacy, University, MS [Library symbol Library of Congress] (LCLS) .... MsU-P
University of Mississippi, University, MS [Library symbol Library of Congress] (LCLS) .... MsU
University of Mississippi, University, MS [OCLC symbol] (OCLC) .... MUM
University of Missouri at Columbia (GAGS) .... U Mo (Columbia)
University of Missouri at Kansas City (GAGS) .... U Mo (KC)
University of Missouri at Kansas City .... UMKC
University of Missouri at Kansas City, Dental School, Kansas City, MO [Library symbol Library of Congress] (LCLS) .... MoKU-D
University of Missouri at Kansas City, Instructional Materials Center, Kansas City, MO [Library symbol Library of Congress] (LCLS) .... MoKU-I
University of Missouri at Kansas City, Kansas City, MO [Library symbol Library of Congress] (LCLS) .... MoKU
University of Missouri at Kansas City, Kansas City, MO [OCLC symbol] (OCLC) .... UMK
University of Missouri at Kansas City, Law Library, Kansas City, MO [Library symbol] [Library of Congress] (LCLS) .... MoKu-L
University of Missouri at Kansas City, Medical Library, Kansas City, MO [Library symbol Library of Congress] (LCLS) .... MoKU-M
University of Missouri at Kansas City, Music Conservatory, Kansas City, MO [Library symbol Library of Congress] (LCLS) .... MoKU-Mus
University of Missouri at Rolla (GAGS) .... U Mo (Rolla)
University of Missouri at Rolla .... UMR
University of Missouri at Rolla, Library, Rolla, MO [OCLC symbol] (OCLC) .... UMR
University of Missouri at Rolla, Rolla, MO [Library symbol Library of Congress] (LCLS) .... MoRM
University of Missouri at St. Louis (GAGS) .... U Mo (St Louis)
University of Missouri at St. Louis, St. Louis, MO [Library symbol Library of Congress] (LCLS) .... MoU-St
University of Missouri at St. Louis, St. Louis, MO [OCLC symbol] (OCLC) .... UMS
University of Missouri. Bulletin. Law Series [A publication] (DLA) .... Law Ser MO Bull
University of Missouri. Bulletin. Law Series [A publication] (DLA) .... U MO B Law Ser
University of Missouri. Bulletin. Law Series [A publication] (DLA) .... U MO Bull L Ser
University of Missouri, Columbia, Columbia, MO [OCLC symbol] (OCLC) .... MUU
University of Missouri, Columbia, Health Sciences Library, Columbia, MO [OCLC symbol] (OCLC) .... MMU
University of Missouri, Columbia, MO [Library symbol Library of Congress] (LCLS) .... MoU
University of Missouri, Columbia School of Library and Information Science, Co lumbia, MO [OCLC symbol] (OCLC) .... UML
University of Missouri. Law Bulletin [A publication] (DLA) .... U MO L Bull
University of Missouri. Law Bulletin [A publication] (DLA) .... U of MLB
University of Missouri, Law School, Columbia, MO [OCLC symbol] (OCLC) .... LMU
University of Missouri, Medical Library, Kansas City, MO [Library symbol Library of Congress] (LCLS) .... MoU-M
University of Missouri Press .... UM
University of Missouri Research Reactor .... MURR
University of Missouri Research Reactor .... UMRR
University of Missouri, School of Dentistry, Kansas City, MO [Library symbol Library of Congress] (LCLS) .... MoU-D
University of Missouri, Veterinary Medicine Library, Columbia, MO [Library symbol Library of Congress] (LCLS) .... MoU-V
University of Montana (GAGS) .... U Mont
University of Montana at Missoula, Law School, Missoula, MT [Library symbol Library of Congress] (LCLS) .... MtU-L
University of Montana at Missoula, Missoula, MT [Library symbol Library of Congress] (LCLS) .... MtU
University of Montevallo (GAGS) .... U Montevallo
University of Montevallo, Montevallo, AL [Library symbol Library of Congress] (LCLS) .... AMonA
University of Nagpur, Nagpur, India [Library symbol Library of Congress] (LCLS) .... IiNaU
University of National Defense [Formerly, Industrial College of the Armed Forces and National War College] .... UND
University of Nebraska (GAGS) .... U Neb
University of Nebraska, Agriculture Library, Lincoln, NE [Library symbol Library of Congress] (LCLS) .... NbU-A
University of Nebraska at Kearney (GAGS) .... U Neb (Kearney)
University of Nebraska at Omaha (GAGS) .... U Neb (Omaha)
University of Nebraska at Omaha .... UNO
University of Nebraska at Omaha, Omaha, NE [Library symbol Library of Congress] (LCLS) .... NbOU
University of Nebraska at Omaha, Omaha, NE [OCLC symbol] (OCLC) .... NBU
University of Nebraska College of Law [Lincoln, NE] (DLA) .... UNBCL
University of Nebraska, College of Law, Lincoln, NE [Library symbol Library of Congress] (LCLS) .... NbU-L
University of Nebraska, College of Medicine, Omaha, NE [Library symbol Library of Congress] (LCLS) .... NbU-M
University of Nebraska - Lincoln .... UNL
University of Nebraska, Lincoln College of Law, Lincoln, NE [OCLC symbol] (OCLC) LLL
University of Nebraska, Lincoln, Lincoln, NE [OCLC symbol] (OCLC) .... LDL

University of Nebraska, Lincoln, NE [Library symbol Library of Congress] (LCLS) .... NbU
University of Nebraska Medical Center [Omaha, NB] .... UNMC
University of Nebraska, Medical Center, Omaha, NE [OCLC symbol] (OCLC) .... UNM
University of Nebraska Press (DGA) .... UNP
University of Nevada at Las Vegas (GAGS) .... U Nev (Las Vegas)
University of Nevada at Reno (GAGS) .... U Nev
University of Nevada, Las Vegas .... UNLV
University of Nevada, Las Vegas, NV [Library symbol Library of Congress] (LCLS) .... NvLN
University of Nevada, Reno, NV [Library symbol Library of Congress] (LCLS) .... NvU
University of Nevada System Computing Center [Research center] (RCD) .... UNSCC
University of New Brunswick [Canada] .... UNB
University of New Brunswick, Archives and Special Collections Department, Fredericton, NB, Canada [Library symbol Library of Congress] (LCLS) .... CaNBFUA
University of New Brunswick, Fredericton, NB, Canada [Library symbol Library of Congress] (LCLS) .... CaNBFU
University of New Brunswick, Fredericton, New Brunswick [Library symbol National Library of Canada] (NLC) .... NBFU
University of New Brunswick, Government Documents Department, Map Room, Fredericton, NB, Canada [Library symbol Library of Congress] (LCLS) .... CaNBFUM
University of New Brunswick in Saint John, Saint John, NB, Canada [Library symbol Library of Congress] (LCLS) .... CaNBSU
University of New Brunswick Law Library [UTLAS symbol] .... UNL
University of New Brunswick, Law Library, Fredericton, NB, Canada [Library symbol Library of Congress] (LCLS) .... CaNBFUL
University of New Brunswick. Law School. Journal [A publication] (DLA) .... UNBLSJ
University of New Brunswick Library [UTLAS symbol] .... UNB
University of New Brunswick, Saint John, New Brunswick [Library symbol National Library of Canada] (NLC) .... NBSU
University of New England [State] (EERA) .... UNE
University of New England - Armidale [Australia] .... UNE-A
University of New England, Armidale, NSW, Australia [Library symbol Library of Congress] (LCLS) .... AuArU
University of New England - Coffs Harbour Campus [Australia] .... UNE-CHC
University of New England Press [Australia] (ADA) .... UNEP
University of New Hampshire (GAGS) .... U NH
University of New Hampshire (PDAA) .... UNH
University of New Hampshire, Durham, NH [OCLC symbol] (OCLC) .... NHM
University of New Hampshire, Durham, NH [Library symbol Library of Congress] (LCLS) .... NhU
University of New Hampshire, Jackson Estuarine Laboratory, Durham, NH [OCLC symbol] (OCLC) .... EST
University of New Haven (GAGS) .... U New Haven
University of New Haven Computer Center [Research center] (RCD) .... UNHCC
University of New Haven, New Haven, CT [Library symbol Library of Congress] (LCLS) .... CtNhU
[The] University of New Mexico (GAGS) .... U NMex
University of New Mexico (PDAA) .... UNM
University of New Mexico, Albuquerque, NM [OCLC symbol] (OCLC) .... IQU
University of New Mexico, Albuquerque, NM [Library symbol Library of Congress] (LCLS) .... NmU
University of New Mexico, Law Library, Albuquerque, NM [Library symbol Library of Congress] (LCLS) .... NmU-L
University of New Mexico, Library of the Medical Sciences, School of Medicine and Bernalillo County Medical Society, Albuquerque, NM [Library symbol Library of Congress] (LCLS) .... NmU-M
University of New Mexico, Los Alamos, NM [Library symbol Library of Congress] (LCLS) .... NmLaU
University of New Mexico, Medical Center Library, Albuquerque, NM [OCLC symbol] (OCLC) .... MQM
University of New Mexico, School of Law, Albuquerque, NM [OCLC symbol] (OCLC) .... NML
University of New Orleans (GAGS) .... U N Orleans
University of New Orleans [Louisiana] .... UNO
University of New Orleans Medicine Center (GAGS) .... U N Orleans (Med Cent)
University of New Orleans, New Orleans, LA [Library symbol Library of Congress OCLC symbol] (LCLS) .... LNU
University of New South Wales [State] (EERA) .... UNSW
University of New South Wales Australia .... UNSW
University of New South Wales Institute of Languages [Australia] .... UNSWIL
University of New South Wales, Kensington, NSW, Australia [Library symbol Library of Congress] (LCLS) .... AuKU
University of New South Wales. Law Journal [A publication] .... Univ NSW Law J
University of New South Wales. Occasional Papers [A publication] .... Occ Pap Univ NSW
University of New York (ROG) .... UNY
University of Newark. Law Review [A publication] (DLA) .... Newark L Rev
University of Newark. Law Review [A publication] (DLA) .... U Newark L Rev
University of Newcastle, Newcastle, NSW, Australia [Library symbol Library of Congress] (LCLS) .... AuNcU
University of Newcastle, Newcastle-Upon-Tyne, England [OCLC symbol] (OCLC) .... EUN
University of Newcastle upon Tyne, Newcastle upon Tyne, United Kingdom [Library symbol] [Library of Congress] (LCLS) .... UkNcU
University of North Alabama (GAGS) .... U No Ala
University of North Alabama, Florence, AL [Library symbol Library of Congress] (LCLS) .... AFIT
University of North Alabama, Florence, AL [OCLC symbol] (OCLC) .... ANO

University of North Bengal, Darjeeling District, West Bengal, India [*Library symbol Library of Congress*] (LCLS) .... IiDaU

University of North Carolina [*Chapel Hill, NC*] .... UNC

University of North Carolina at Asheville, Asheville, NC [*Library symbol Library of Congress*] (LCLS) .... NcAU

University of North Carolina at Asheville, Asheville, NC [*OCLC symbol*] (OCLC) .... NIM

[*The*] University of North Carolina at Chapel Hill (GAGS) ..... U No Car (Chapel Hill)

University of North Carolina at Chapel Hill .... UNC-CH

University of North Carolina at Chapel Hill, Library School, Chapel Hill, NC [*Library symbol Library of Congress*] (LCLS) .... NcU-LS

University of North Carolina at Charlotte .... UNCC

University of North Carolina at Charlotte, Charlotte, NC [*Library symbol Library of Congress*] (LCLS) .... NcCU

University of North Carolina at Charlotte, Charlotte, NC [*OCLC symbol*] (OCLC) .... NKM

[*The*] University of North Carolina at Greensboro (GAGS) .... U No Car (Greensboro)

University of North Carolina at Greensboro, Greensboro, NC [*Library symbol Library of Congress*] (LCLS) .... NcGU

University of North Carolina at Wilmington, Wilmington, NC [*Library symbol Library of Congress*] (LCLS) .... NcWU

University of North Carolina, Bureau of Public Records, Collection and Research,Chapel Hill, NC [*Library symbol Library of Congress*] (LCLS) .... NcU-BPR

University of North Carolina, Carolina Population Center, Technical Information Service, Chapel Hill, NC [*Library symbol Library of Congress*] (LCLS) .... NcU-Pop

University of North Carolina, Chapel Hill, Chapel Hill, NC [*OCLC symbol*] (OCLC) .... NOC

University of North Carolina, Chapel Hill Library School, Chapel Hill, NC [*OCLC symbol*] (OCLC) .... NOA

University of North Carolina, Chapel Hill, NC [*Library symbol Library of Congress*] (LCLS) .... NcU

University of North Carolina, Division of Health Affairs, Chapel Hill, NC [*Library symbol Library of Congress*] (LCLS) .... NcU-H

University of North Carolina, Greensboro .... UNCG

University of North Carolina, Greensboro, Greensboro, NC [*OCLC symbol*] (OCLC) .... NGU

University of North Carolina, Health Science Library, Chapel Hill, NC [*OCLC symbol*] (OCLC) .... NOH

University of North Carolina, Institute of Government Library, Chapel Hill, NC [*Library symbol Library of Congress*] (LCLS) .... NcU-IG

University of North Carolina, Institute of Marine Sciences, Morehead City, NC [*Library symbol Library of Congress*] (LCLS) .... NcU-MS

University of North Carolina, Law Library, Chapel Hill, NC [*Library symbol Library of Congress*] (LCLS) .... NcU-L

University of North Carolina, Wilmington, Wilmington, NC [*OCLC symbol*] (OCLC) .... NXW

University of North Dakota (GAGS) .... U No Dak

University of North Dakota, Ellendale Branch, Ellendale, ND [*Library symbol Library of Congress Obsolete*] (LCLS) .... NdU-El

University of North Dakota Energy Research Center [*Grand Forks, ND*] [*Department of Energy*] (GRD) .... UNDERC

University of North Dakota, Grand Forks, ND [*Library symbol Library of Congress*] (LCLS) .... NdU

University of North Dakota, Grand Forks, ND [*OCLC symbol*] (OCLC) .... UND

University of North Dakota, Law Library, Grand Forks, ND [*Library symbol Library of Congress*] (LCLS) .... NdU-L

University of North Dakota, Law Library, Grand Forks, ND [*OCLC symbol*] (OCLC) .... UNE

University of North Dakota, Medical Library, Grand Forks, ND [*Library symbol Library of Congress*] (LCLS) .... NdU-M

University of North Dakota, Medical Library, Grand Forks, ND [*OCLC symbol*] (OCLC) .... UNF

University of North Dakota, Williston Branch, Williston, ND [*Library symbol Library of Congress*] (LCLS) .... NdWiU

University of North Florida (GAGS) .... U No Fla

University of North Florida, Jacksonville, FL [*Library symbol Library of Congress*] (LCLS) .... FJUNF

University of North Florida, Jacksonville, FL [*OCLC symbol*] (OCLC) .... FNP

University of North Texas (GAGS) .... U No Tex

University of Northern Colorado (GAGS) .... U No Colo

University of Northern Colorado [*Formerly, Colorado State College*] [*Greeley*] .... UNC

University of Northern Colorado, Greeley, CO [*Library symbol Library of Congress*] (LCLS) .... CoGrU

University of Northern Colorado, Greeley, CO [*OCLC symbol*] (OCLC) .... COV

University of Northern Iowa (GAGS) .... U No Iowa

University of Northern Iowa [*Cedar Falls, IA*] (OICC) .... UNI

University of Northern Iowa, Cedar Falls, IA [*Library symbol Library of Congress*] (LCLS) .... IaCfT

University of Northern Iowa, Cedar Falls, IA [*OCLC symbol*] (OCLC) .... NIU

University of Notre Dame [*Indiana*] .... ND

University of Notre Dame (GAGS) .... U Notre Dame

University of Notre Dame [*Indiana*] (KSC) .... UND

University of Notre Dame, Law School, Notre Dame, IN [*Library symbol Library of Congress*] (LCLS) .... InNd-L

University of Notre Dame, Life Sciences Research Library, Notre Dame, IN [*Library symbol Library of Congress*] (LCLS) .... InNd-LS

University of Notre Dame, Notre Dame, IN [*OCLC symbol*] (OCLC) .... IND

University of Notre Dame, Notre Dame, IN [*Library symbol Library of Congress*] (LCLS) .... InNd

University of Notre Dame Press .... UNDP

[*The*] University of Oklahoma (GAGS) .... U Okla

University of Oklahoma [*Record label*] .... UOK

University of Oklahoma, College of Pharmacy, Norman, OK [*Library symbol Library of Congress*] (LCLS) .... OkU-P

University of Oklahoma, Communication Department, Political Communications Center, Political Commercial Archives, Norman, OK [*Library symbol*] [*Library of Congress*] (LCLS) .... OkU-C

University of Oklahoma, Health Science Center Library, Oklahoma City, OK [*OCLC symbol*] (OCLC) .... OKH

University of Oklahoma, Health Sciences Center, Oklahoma City, OK [*Library symbol Library of Congress*] (LCLS) .... OkU-M

University of Oklahoma, Law Library, Norman, OK [*OCLC symbol*] (OCLC) .... OKL

University of Oklahoma, Law School, Norman, OK [*Library symbol Library of Congress*] (LCLS) .... OkU-L

University of Oklahoma, Library School, Norman, OK [*OCLC symbol*] (OCLC) .... OKV

University of Oklahoma, Norman (USDC) .... OU

University of Oklahoma, Norman [*USA*] [*Marine science*] (OSRA) .... OU

University of Oklahoma, Norman, OK [*Library symbol Library of Congress*] (LCLS) .... OkU

University of Oklahoma, Tulsa Medical College Library, Tulsa, OK [*OCLC symbol*] (OCLC) .... OUU

University of Oklahoma, Tulsa Medical College, Tulsa, OK [*Library symbol Library of Congress*] (LCLS) .... OkU-TM

University of Oklahoma, Western History Collections, Norman, OK [*Library symbol*] [*Library of Congress*] (LCLS) .... OkU-W

University of Oregon (GAGS) .... U Ore

University of Oregon, Computing Center, Eugene, OR [*Library symbol Library of Congress*] (LCLS) .... OrU-C

University of Oregon, Dental School, Portland, OR [*Library symbol Library of Congress*] (LCLS) .... OrU-D

University of Oregon, Eugene, OR [*Library symbol Library of Congress*] (LCLS) .... OrU

University of Oregon, Health Sciences Library, Portland, OR [*OCLC symbol*] (OCLC) .... OHS

University of Oregon, Law Library, Portland, OR [*Library symbol Library of Congress*] (LCLS) .... OrU-L

University of Oregon Library, Eugene, OR [*OCLC symbol*] (OCLC) .... ORU

University of Oregon, Medical School, Portland, OR [*Library symbol Library of Congress*] (LCLS) .... OrU-M

University of Oregon, Ocean and Coastal Law Center, Eugene, OR [*Library symbol*] [*Library of Congress*] (LCLS) .... OrU-O

University of Oregon, Oriental Museum, Portland, OR [*Library symbol Library of Congress*] (LCLS) .... OrU-Or

University of Oregon, School of Librarianship, Eugene, OR [*OCLC symbol*] (OCLC) .... OSL

University of Oregon, Science Division Library, Eugene, OR [*Library symbol Library of Congress*] (LCLS) .... OrU-S

University of Ottawa, Department of Criminology, Ottawa, ON, Canada [*Library symbol Library of Congress*] (LCLS) .... CaOOUC

University of Ottawa, Faculty of Law, Ottawa, ON, Canada [*Library symbol Library of Congress*] (LCLS) .... CaOOUD

University of Ottawa, Faculty of Psychology and Education, Ottawa, ON, Canada [*Library symbol Library of Congress Obsolete*] (LCLS) .... CaOOUP

University of Ottawa, Health Sciences Library, Ottawa, ON, Canada [*Library symbol Library of Congress*] (LCLS) .... CaOOUH

University of Ottawa, Institute of International Cooperation, Ottawa, ON, Canada [*Library symbol Library of Congress*] (LCLS) .... CaOOUIC

University of Ottawa Library [*UTLAS symbol*] .... OTT

University of Ottawa, Map Library, Ottawa, ON, Canada [*Library symbol Library of Congress*] (LCLS) .... CaOOUMA

University of Ottawa [*Universite d'Ottawa*] Ontario [*Library symbol National Library of Canada*] (NLC) .... OOU

University of Ottawa, Ottawa, ON, Canada [*Library symbol Library of Congress*] (LCLS) .... CaOOU

University of Ottawa, Vanier Library, Ottawa, ON, Canada [*Library symbol Library of Congress*] (LCLS) .... CaOOUM

University of Oxford (ROG) .... UO

University of Pennsylvania (GAGS) .... U Penn

University of Pennsylvania, Annenberg School of Communications, Philadelphia, PA [*Library symbol Library of Congress*] (LCLS) .... PU-AC

University of Pennsylvania Archives, Philadelphia, PA [*Library symbol*] [*Library of Congress*] (LCLS) .... PU-Ar

University of Pennsylvania, Biddle Law Library, Philadelphia, PA [*Library symbol Library of Congress*] (LCLS) .... PU-L

University of Pennsylvania, Biology Library, Philadelphia, PA [*Library symbol Library of Congress*] (LCLS) .... PU-BZ

University of Pennsylvania, Center for the Study of the History of Nursing, Philadelphia, PA [*Library symbol*] [*Library of Congress*] (LCLS) .... PU-N

University of Pennsylvania, Chemistry Library, Philadelphia, PA [*Library symbol Library of Congress*] (LCLS) .... PU-C

University of Pennsylvania, Edgar Fah Smith Memorial Library, Philadelphia, PA [*Library symbol Library of Congress*] (LCLS) .... PU-S

University of Pennsylvania, Evans Dental Library, Philadelphia, PA [*Library symbol Library of Congress*] (LCLS) .... PU-D

University of Pennsylvania, H. H. Furness Memorial Library, Philadelphia, PA [*Library symbol Library of Congress*] (LCLS) .... PU-F

University of Pennsylvania, Industrial Research Department, Philadelphia, PA [*Library symbol Library of Congress Obsolete*] (LCLS) .... PU-Ind

University of Pennsylvania, Mathematics-Physics Library, Philadelphia, PA [*Library symbol Library of Congress*] (LCLS) .... PU-Math

University of Pennsylvania, Medical School, Hospital Nurses Library, Philadelphia, PA [*Library symbol Library of Congress*] (LCLS) .... PU-Med-TS

University of Pennsylvania, Medical School, Philadelphia, PA [*Library symbol Library of Congress*] (LCLS) .... PU-Med

University of Pennsylvania, Moore School of Electrical Engineering, Philadelphia, PA [*Library symbol Library of Congress*] (LCLS) .... PU-EI

University of Pennsylvania, Morris Arboretum, Philadelphia, PA [*Library symbol Library of Congress*] (LCLS) .... PU-A

University of Pennsylvania, Penniman Library of Education, Philadelphia, PA [*Library symbol Library of Congress Obsolete*] (LCLS) .... PU-Penn

University of Pennsylvania, Pennsylvania School of Social Work, Philadelphia, PA [*Library symbol Library of Congress*] (LCLS) .... PU-PSW

University of Pennsylvania, Philadelphia, PA [*OCLC symbol*] (OCLC) .... PAU

University of Pennsylvania, Philadelphia, PA [*Library symbol Library of Congress*] (LCLS) .... PU

University of Pennsylvania Press (DGA) .... UPP

University of Pennsylvania, School of Fine Arts, Philadelphia, PA [*Library symbol Library of Congress*] (LCLS) .... PU-FA

University of Pennsylvania, School of Medicine, Philadelphia, PA [*OCLC symbol*] (OCLC) .... PAM

University of Pennsylvania, School of Music, Philadelphia, PA [*Library symbol Library of Congress*] (LCLS) .... PU-Music

University of Pennsylvania, School of Veterinary Medicine, Philadelphia, PA [*Library symbol Library of Congress*] (LCLS) .... PU-V

University of Pennsylvania, South Asia Regional Studies Library, Philadelphia, PA [*Library symbol Library of Congress*] (LCLS) .... PU-SRS

University of Pennsylvania, Towne Scientific School, Philadelphia, PA [*Library symbol Library of Congress*] (LCLS) .... PU-Sc

University of Pennsylvania, University Hospital, De Schweinitz Collection of Ophthalmology, Philadelphia, PA [*Library symbol Library of Congress*] (LCLS) .... PU-UH-DeS

University of Pennsylvania, University Hospital, Philadelphia, PA [*Library symbol Library of Congress*] (LCLS) .... PU-UH

University of Pennsylvania, University Museum, Philadelphia, PA [*Library symbol Library of Congress*] (LCLS) .... PU-Mu

University of Pennsylvania, Van Pelt Library, Special Collections, Philadelphia, PA [*Library symbol*] [*Library of Congress*] (LCLS) .... PU-Sp

University of Pennsylvania, Wharton School of Finance and Commerce, Philadelphia, PA [*Library symbol Library of Congress*] (LCLS) .... PU-W

University of Pittsburgh (GAGS) .... U Pitt

University of Pittsburgh Applied Research Center [*Research center*] (RCD) .... U-PARC

University of Pittsburgh, Archives of Industrial Society, Pittsburgh, PA [*Library symbol*] [*Library of Congress*] (LCLS) .... PPiU-IS

University of Pittsburgh at Greensburg, Greensburg, PA [*Library symbol Library of Congress*] (LCLS) .... PGbU

University of Pittsburgh at Johnstown, Johnstown, PA [*Library symbol Library of Congress*] (LCLS) .... PJoU

University of Pittsburgh, Blair-Lippincott Library, Eye and Ear Hospital of Pittsburgh, Pittsburgh, PA [*Library symbol Library of Congress*] (LCLS) .... PPiU-BL

University of Pittsburgh, Falk Library - Health Professions, Pittsburgh, PA [*OCLC symbol*] (OCLC) .... PFM

University of Pittsburgh Generalized Recording and Dissemination Experiment .... UPGRADE

University of Pittsburgh, Graduate School of Library and Information Sciences, Pittsburgh, PA [*Library symbol Library of Congress*] (LCLS) .... PPiU-LS

University of Pittsburgh, Graduate School of Public and International Affairs, Pittsburgh, PA [*Library symbol Library of Congress*] (LCLS).... PPiU-PIA

University of Pittsburgh, Graduate School of Public Health, Pittsburgh, PA [*Library symbol Library of Congress*] (LCLS) .... PPiU-PH

University of Pittsburgh, Henry Clay Frick Fine Arts Center, Pittsburgh, PA [*Library symbol Library of Congress*] (LCLS) .... PPiU-A

University of Pittsburgh, Johnstown, Johnstown, PA [*OCLC symbol*] (OCLC) .... PJC

University of Pittsburgh, Law School, Pittsburgh, PA [*OCLC symbol*] (OCLC) .... PLA

University of Pittsburgh, Law School, Pittsburgh, PA [*Library symbol Library of Congress*] (LCLS) .... PPiU-L

University of Pittsburgh, Maurice and Laura Falk Library of the Health Professions, Pittsburgh, PA [*Library symbol Library of Congress*] (LCLS) .... PPiU-H

University of Pittsburgh Medical Center .... UPMC

University of Pittsburgh, Natural Sciences Library, Pittsburgh, PA [*Library symbol Library of Congress*] (LCLS) .... PPiU-NS

University of Pittsburgh, Pittsburgh, PA [*OCLC symbol*] (OCLC) .... PIT

University of Pittsburgh, Pittsburgh, PA [*Library symbol Library of Congress*] (LCLS) .... PPiU

University of Pittsburgh Press (DGA) .... UPP

University of Pittsburgh Production Organization Exercise [*Simulation game*] .... UPPOE

University of Pittsburgh, School of Librarianship and Information Science, Pittsburgh, PA [*OCLC symbol*] (OCLC) .... DLS

University of Pittsburgh, Stephen Collins Foster Memorial [*Music*] Library,Pittsburgh, PA [*Library symbol Library of Congress*] (LCLS) ..... PPiU-SF

University of Portland (GAGS) .... U Portland

University of Portland, Portland, OR [*Library symbol Library of Congress*] (LCLS) .... OrPU

University of Portland, Portland, OR [*OCLC symbol*] (OCLC) .... OUP

University of Prince Edward Island [*Canada*] .... UPEI

University of Prince Edward Island, Charlottetown, PE, Canada [*Library symbol Library of Congress*] (LCLS) .... CaPCU

University of Prince Edward Island, Charlottetown, Prince Edward Island [*Library symbol National Library of Canada*] (NLC) .... PCU

University of Puerto Rico (GAGS) .... U Puerto Rico

University of Puerto Rico [*Mayaguez, PR*] .... UPR

University of Puerto Rico [*Mayaguez, PR*] .... UPRICO

University of Puerto Rico, Department of Marine Sciences, Mayaguez, PR [*Library symbol Library of Congress*] (LCLS) .... PrU-MS

University of Puerto Rico, Humacao Regional College, Humacao, PR [*Library symbol Library of Congress*] (LCLS) .... PrU-H

University of Puerto Rico, Law Library, San Juan, PR [*Library symbol Library of Congress*] (LCLS) .... PrU-L

University of Puerto Rico, Mayaguez (GAGS) .... U Puerto Rico, Mayaguez

University of Puerto Rico, Mayaguez Campus, Mayaguez, Puerto Rico [*Library symbol Library of Congress*] (LCLS) .... PrU-MA

University of Puerto Rico, Natural Science Library, Rio Piedras, PR [*Library symbol Library of Congress*] (LCLS) .... PrU-NS

University of Puerto Rico, Rio Piedras, PR [*Library symbol Library of Congress*] (LCLS) .... PrU

University of Puerto Rico, School of Medicine, San Juan, PR [*Library symbol Library of Congress*] (LCLS) .... PrU-M

University of Puget Sound (GAGS) .... U Puget Sound

University of Puget Sound School of Law (DLA) .... UPSSL

University of Puget Sound, Tacoma, WA [*Library symbol Library of Congress*] (LCLS) .... WaTU

University of Queensland [*State*] (EERA) .... UQ

University of Queensland Press [*Australia*] .... UQP

University of Queensland Press, Microform Division, St. Lucia, Brisbane, QLD, Australia [*Library symbol Library of Congress*] (LCLS) .... AuUqP

University of Queensland, St. Lucia, Brisbane, QLD, Australia [*Library symbol Library of Congress*] (LCLS) .... AuBrU

University of Redlands (GAGS) .... U Redlands

University of Redlands, Redlands, CA [*Library symbol Library of Congress*] (LCLS) .... CRedlU

University of Redlands, Redlands, CA [*OCLC symbol*] (OCLC) .... CUR

University of Regina, Department of Geography, Regina, SK, Canada [*Library symbol Library of Congress*] (LCLS) .... CaSRUG

University of Regina, Education Library, Regina, SK, Canada [*Library symbol*] [*Library of Congress*] (LCLS) .... CaSRUE

University of Regina, Faculty of Fine Arts, Regina, SK, Canada [*Library symbol Library of Congress*] (LCLS) .... CaSRUFA

University of Regina Library [*UTLAS symbol*] .... URL

University of Regina, Norman MacKenzie Art Gallery, Regina, SK, Canada [*Library symbol Library of Congress*] (LCLS) .... CaSRUNM

University of Regina, Regina, SK, Canada [*Library symbol Library of Congress*] (LCLS) .... CaSRU

University of Regina, Saskatchewan [*Library symbol National Library of Canada*] (NLC) .... SRU

University of Rhode Island (GAGS) .... U Rhode Island

University of Rhode Island .... URI

University of Rhode Island Computer Access [*University of Rhode Island Library*] (OLDSS) .... URICA

University of Rhode Island, Extension Division Library, Providence, RI [*OCLC symbol*] (OCLC) .... RIX

University of Rhode Island, Graduate Library School, Kingston, RI [*OCLC symbol*] (OCLC) .... RIL

University of Rhode Island, Kingston (USDC) .... URI

University of Rhode Island, Kingston, RI [*OCLC symbol*] (OCLC) .... RIU

University of Rhode Island, Kingston, RI [*Library symbol Library of Congress*] (LCLS) .... RU

University of Rhode Island, Kingston, RI [*Library symbol*] [*Library of Congress*] (LCLS) .... RUn

University of Richmond (GAGS) .... U Richmond

University of Richmond. Law Notes [*A publication*] (DLA) .... U Rich LN

University of Richmond. Law Notes [*Richmond, Virginia*] [*A publication*] (DLA) .... Univ of Richmond L Not

University of Richmond, Richmond, VA [*Library symbol Library of Congress*] (LCLS) .... ViRU

University of Richmond, Richmond, VA [*OCLC symbol*] (OCLC) .... VRU

University of Rochester (GAGS) .... U Rochester

University of Rochester [*New York*] (KSC) .... UR

University of Rochester Atomic Energy Project .... URAEP

University of Rochester Cancer Center [*Research center*] (RCD) .... URCC

University of Rochester, Department of Physics .... URP

University of Rochester, Eastman School of Music, Rochester, NY [*Library symbol Library of Congress*] (LCLS) .... NRU-Mus

University of Rochester, Memorial Art Gallery, Rochester, NY [*Library symbol Library of Congress*] (LCLS) .... NRU-A

University of Rochester, Miner Medical Library, Rochester, NY [*OCLC symbol*] (OCLC) .... RNM

University of Rochester, Rochester, NY [*Library symbol Library of Congress*] (LCLS) .... NRU

University of Rochester, Rochester, NY [*OCLC symbol*] (OCLC) .... RRR

University of Rochester, School of Medicine and Dentistry, Rochester, NY [*Library symbol Library of Congress*] (LCLS) .... NRU-M

University of Rochester, Women's College, Rochester, NY [*Library symbol Library of Congress*] (LCLS) .... NRU-W

University of Saint Michael's College, Toronto, ON, Canada [*Library symbol Library of Congress*] (LCLS) .... CaOTStM

University of Saint Michael's College, Toronto, Ontario [*Library symbol National Library of Canada*] (NLC) .... OTSTM

University of St. Thomas (GAGS) .... U St Thomas

University of Saint Thomas [*Texas*] .... UST

University of Saint Thomas, Houston, TX [*OCLC symbol*] (OCLC) .... TUT

University of Saint Thomas, Houston, TX [*Library symbol Library of Congress*] (LCLS) .... TxHST

University of San Diego (GAGS) .... U San Diego

University of San Diego .... USD

University of San Diego, James S. Copley Library, San Diego, CA [*OCLC symbol*] (OCLC) .... CDU

University of San Diego Law School, San Diego, CA [*Library symbol Library of Congress*] (LCLS) .... CSdU-L

University of San Diego Press (DGA) .... USDP

University of San Diego, San Diego, CA [*Library symbol Library of Congress*] (LCLS) .... CSdU

University of San Fernando Valley. Law Review [*A publication*] (DLA) .... U San Fernando Valley L Rev

University of San Fernando Valley. Law Review [*A publication*] (DLA) .... U San Fernando VL Rev

University of San Fernando Valley. Law Review [*Sepulveda, California*] [*A publication*] (DLA) .... Univ of San Fernando Valley L Rev

University of San Fernando Valley. Law Review [*A publication*] (DLA) .... USFVL Rev

University of San Francisco (GAGS) .... U San Fran

University of San Francisco [*California*] .... USF

University of San Francisco, Gleeson Library, San Francisco, CA [*OCLC symbol*] (OCLC) .... CUF

University of San Francisco, San Francisco, CA [*Library symbol Library of Congress*] (LCLS) .... CSfU

University of Santa Clara (GAGS) .... U Santa Clara

University of Santa Clara [*California*] .... USC

University of Santa Clara, Law Library, Santa Clara, CA [*Library symbol Library of Congress*] (LCLS) .... CStclU-L

University of Santa Clara, Orradre Library, Santa Clara, CA [*OCLC symbol*] (OCLC) .... STA

University of Santa Clara, Santa Clara, CA [*Library symbol Library of Congress*] (LCLS) .... CStclU

University of Santa Clara School of Law (DLA) .... SNCLAR

University of Saskatchewan, Government Publications, Saskatoon, SK, Canada [*Library symbol Library of Congress*] (LCLS) .... CaSSUGP

University of Saskatchewan, Law Library, Saskatoon, SK, Canada [*Library symbol Library of Congress*] (LCLS) .... CaSSUL

University of Saskatchewan Libraries [*UTLAS symbol*] .... SAK

University of Saskatchewan Libraries Machine-Assisted Reference Teleservices [*University of Saskatchewan Library*] [*Information service or system*] (IID) .... SMART

University of Saskatchewan, Medical Library, Saskatoon, SK, Canada [*Library symbol Library of Congress*] (LCLS) .... CaSSUM

University of Saskatchewan, Office of the Saskatchewan Archives, Saskatoon, SK, Canada [*Library symbol Library of Congress*] (LCLS) ..... CaSSA

University of Saskatchewan, Regina Campus, Campion College, Regina, SK, Canada [*Library symbol Library of Congress*] (LCLS) .... CaSRUC

University of Saskatchewan, Saskatoon, Saskatchewan [*Library symbol National Library of Canada*] (NLC) .... SSU

University of Saskatchewan, Saskatoon, SK, Canada [*Library symbol Library of Congress*] (LCLS) .... CaSSU

University of Saskatchewan, the Right Honourable John G. Diefenbaker Centre, Saskatoon, SK, Canada [*Library symbol Library of Congress*] (LCLS) .... CaSSUJD

University of Science and Arts of Oklahoma Libraries, Chickasha, OK [*OCLC symbol*] (OCLC) .... OUV

University of Science and Technology of China .... USTC

University of Scranton (GAGS) .... U Scranton

University of Scranton, Scranton, PA [*Library symbol Library of Congress*] (LCLS) .... PScU

University of Scranton, Scranton, PA [*OCLC symbol*] (OCLC) .... SRU

University of Sheffield, Postgraduate Librarianship, Sheffield, England [*OCLC symbol*] (OCLC) .... SHS

University of Sheffield, Postgraduate School of Librarianship, Sheffield, England [*OCLC symbol*] (OCLC) .... SHF

University of Sheffield, Sheffield, United Kingdom [*Library symbol Library of Congress*] (LCLS) .... UkShU

University of Singapore, Singapore, Singapore [*Library symbol Library of Congress*] (LCLS) .... SgpU

University of South Africa .... UNISA

University of South Alabama (GAGS) .... U So Ala

University of South Alabama, Biomedical Library, Mobile, AL [*OCLC symbol*] (OCLC) .... ACB

University of South Alabama, Biomedical Library, Mobile, AL [*Library symbol Library of Congress*] (LCLS) .... AMobU-M

University of South Alabama, Mobile, AL [*OCLC symbol*] (OCLC) .... ACM

University of South Alabama, Mobile, AL [*Library symbol Library of Congress*] (LCLS) .... AMobU

University of South Australia .... UniSA

University of South California, School of Library Science, Los Angeles, CA [*OCLC symbol*] (OCLC) .... SCS

University of South Carolina (GAGS) .... U So Car

University of South Carolina [*Columbia, SC*] .... USC

University of South Carolina at Sumter, Sumter, SC [*Library symbol Library of Congress*] (LCLS) .... ScU-Su

University of South Carolina, College of Librarianship, Columbia, SC [*OCLC symbol*] (OCLC) .... DCS

University of South Carolina, Columbia, SC [*Library symbol Library of Congress*] (LCLS) .... ScU

University of South Carolina, Columbia, SC [*OCLC symbol*] (OCLC) .... SUC

University of South Carolina. Governmental Review [*A publication*] (DLA) .... USC Gov't'l Rev

University of South Carolina Herbarium .... USCH

University of South Carolina, Law School, Columbia, SC [*Library symbol Library of Congress*] (LCLS) .... ScU-L

University of South Carolina Press (DGA) .... USCP

University of South Carolina, Regional Campus Processing Center, Columbia, SC [*OCLC symbol*] (OCLC) .... SZR

University of South Carolina, School of Medicine, Columbia, SC [*Library symbol Library of Congress*] (LCLS) .... ScU-M

University of South Carolina, School of Medicine, Columbia, SC [*OCLC symbol*] (OCLC) .... SUM

University of South Carolina, Science Library, Columbia, SC [*Library symbol Library of Congress*] (LCLS) .... ScU-S

University of South Carolina-Aiken, Aiken, SC [*Library symbol*] [*Library of Congress*] (LCLS) .... ScU-Ai

University of South Carolina-Beaufort, Beaufort, SC [*Library symbol*] [*Library of Congress*] (LCLS) .... ScU-B

University of South Carolina-Coastal Carolina, Conway, SC [*Library symbol*] [*Library of Congress*] (LCLS) .... ScU-C

University of South Carolina-Lancaster, Lancaster, SC [*Library symbol*] [*Library of Congress*] (LCLS) .... ScU-Lan

University of South Carolina-Salkehatchie, Allendale, SC [*Library symbol*] [*Library of Congress*] (LCLS) .... ScU-Sa

University of South Carolina-Spartanburg, Spartanburg, SC [*Library symbol*] [*Library of Congress*] (LCLS) .... ScU-Sp

University of South Carolina-Union, Union, SC [*Library symbol*] [*Library of Congress*] (LCLS) .... ScU-Un

University of South Dakota (GAGS) .... U So Dak

University of South Dakota at Springfield, Springfield, SD [*Library symbol Library of Congress*] (LCLS) .... SdSpU

University of South Dakota, Card Reproduction Project, Vermillion, SD [*OCLC symbol*] (OCLC) XXC

University of South Dakota, Law Library, Vermillion, SD [*Library symbol Library of Congress*] (LCLS) .... SdU-L

University of South Dakota, Law Library, Vermillion, SD [*OCLC symbol*] (OCLC) .... USE

University of South Dakota, Medical School, Vermillion, SD [*Library symbol Library of Congress*] (LCLS) .... SdU-M

University of South Dakota Press (DGA) .... USDP

University of South Dakota, Vermillion, SD [*Library symbol Library of Congress*] (LCLS) .... SdU

University of South Dakota, Vermillion, SD [*OCLC symbol*] (OCLC) .... USD

University of South Florida (GAGS) .... U So Fla

University of South Florida, College of Medicine, Tampa, FL [*Library symbol Library of Congress*] (LCLS) .... FTS-M

University of South Florida, Fort Myers Campus, Fort Myers, FL [*OCLC symbol*] (OCLC) .... FHF

University of South Florida, Media Center, Tampa, FL [*Library symbol Library of Congress*] (LCLS) .... FTS-MC

University of South Florida, St. Petersburg Campus, St. Petersburg, FL [*OCLC symbol*] (OCLC) .... FHS

University of South Florida, Sarasota Campus, Sarasota, FL [*OCLC symbol*] (OCLC) .... FHC

University of South Florida, Tampa, FL [*OCLC symbol*] (OCLC) .... FHM

University of South Florida, Tampa, FL [*Library symbol Library of Congress*] (LCLS) .... FTS

University of Southern California (GAGS) .... U So Cal

University of Southern California [*Los Angeles*] [*Seismograph station code, US Geological Survey*] (SEIS) .... USC

University of Southern California, Aeronautical Laboratory (MCD) .... USCAL

University of Southern California, Architecture and Fine Arts Department, Los Angeles, CA [*Library symbol Library of Congress*] (LCLS) .... CLSU-A

University of Southern California, Biochemical Library, Los Angeles, CA [*Library symbol Library of Congress*] (LCLS) .... CLSU-B

University of Southern California, Carl A. Richmond Collection, Los Angeles, CA [*Library symbol Library of Congress*] (LCLS) .... CLSU-Richm

University of Southern California, Education Department, Los Angeles, CA [*Library symbol Library of Congress*] (LCLS) .... CLSU-Ed

University of Southern California, Engineering Center (MCD) .... USCEC

University of Southern California, Farmington Plan Collection, Los Angeles, CA [*Library symbol Library of Congress*] (LCLS) .... CLSU-Farm

University of Southern California, Feuchtwanger Library, Los Angeles, CA [*Library symbol*] [*Library of Congress*] (LCLS) .... CLSU-Fe

University of Southern California, Feuchtwanger Memorial Collection, Los Angeles, CA [*Library symbol Library of Congress*] (LCLS) .... CLSU-Feucht

University of Southern California, Gordon Craig Collection, Los Angeles, CA [*Library symbol Library of Congress*] (LCLS) .... CLSU-Craig

University of Southern California, Gregg Lane College, Torchieu Collection, Los Angeles, CA [*Library symbol Library of Congress*] (LCLS) .... CLSU-LTorch

University of Southern California, H. G. Boddington Collection, Los Angeles, CA [*Library symbol Library of Congress*] (LCLS) .... CLSU-Bodd

University of Southern California, Hancock Library of Biology and Oceanography, Los Angeles, CA [*Library symbol Library of Congress*] (LCLS) .... CLSU-H

University of Southern California, Hoose Library of Philosophy, Los Angeles, CA [*Library symbol*] [*Library of Congress*] (LCLS) .... CLSU-Ho

University of Southern California, Hoose Library of Philosophy, Los Angeles, CA [*Library symbol Library of Congress*] (LCLS) .... CLSU-Hoose

University of Southern California, Kurt Lowenstein Collection, Los Angeles, CA [*Library symbol Library of Congress*] (LCLS) .... CLSU-Low

University of Southern California, Law Library, Los Angeles, CA [*Library symbol Library of Congress*] (LCLS) .... CLSU-L

University of Southern California, Lee Hefner Memorial Collection, Los Angeles, CA [*Library symbol Library of Congress*] (LCLS) .... CLSU-Hefner

University of Southern California, Los Angeles, CA [*Library symbol Library of Congress*] (LCLS) .... CLSU

University of Southern California, Los Angeles, CA [*OCLC symbol*] (OCLC) .... CSL

University of Southern California, Music Library, Los Angeles, CA [*Library symbol Library of Congress*] (LCLS) .... CLSU-Music

University of Southern California, Norris Medical Library, Los Angeles, CA [*OCLC symbol*] (OCLC) .... CSZ

University of Southern California Press (DGA) .... USCP

University of Southern California, Ruther Technology Library, Los Angeles, CA [Library symbol Library of Congress] (LCLS) .... CLSU-R
University of Southern California, School of Dentistry, Los Angeles, CA [Library symbol Library of Congress] (LCLS) .... CLSU-D
University of Southern California School of Law Tax Institute (DLA) .... So Calif Tax Inst
University of Southern California School of Law Tax Institute (DLA) .... US Cal Sch L Tax Inst
University of Southern California, School of Medicine Library, Los Angeles, CA [Library symbol Library of Congress] (LCLS) .... CLSU-M
University of Southern California Tax Institute (DLA) .... SCTI
University of Southern California Tax Institute (DLA) .... U So Cal Tax Inst
University of Southern California, Von KleinSmid Library of World Affairs, Los Angeles, CA [Library symbol] [Library of Congress] (LCLS) .... CLSU-Vo
University of Southern California, Von Kleinsmit Library of World Affairs, Los Angeles, CA [Library symbol Library of Congress] (LCLS) ...... CLSU-VKSmit
University of Southern Colorado, Pueblo, CO [OCLC symbol] (OCLC) .... COS
University of Southern Europe [Monaco] (ECON) .... USE
University of Southern Maine (GAGS) .... U So Maine
University of Southern Maine at Portland, Portland, ME [OCLC symbol] (OCLC) .... PGP
University of Southern Mississippi (GAGS) .... U So Miss
University of Southern Mississippi .... USM
University of Southern Mississippi, Gulf Park, Richard G. Cox Library, Long Beach, MS [Library symbol Library of Congress] (LCLS) .... MsLbU
University of Southern Mississippi, Hattiesburg, MS [Library symbol Library of Congress] (LCLS) .... MsHaU
University of Southern Mississippi, Hattiesburg, MS [OCLC symbol] (OCLC) .... MUS
[The] University of Southwestern Louisiana (GAGS) .... U Southwestern La
University of Southwestern Louisiana Herbarium .... USLH
University of Southwestern Louisiana, Lafayette, LA [Library symbol Library of Congress] (LCLS) .... LLafS
University of Southwestern Louisiana, Lafayette, LA [OCLC symbol] (OCLC) .... LWA
University of Steubenville, Steubenville, OH [OCLC symbol] (OCLC) .... STU
University of Stockholm, Department of Physical Geography, Trafala Glaciological Station, Stockholm, Sweden [Library symbol] [Library of Congress] (LCLS) .... SwSU-T
University of Stockholm Institute of Physics .... USIP
University of Strathclyde, Andersonian Library, Glasgow, Scotland [Library symbol] [Library of Congress] (LCLS) .... UkGUS
University of Subury [Universite de Sudbury] Ontario [Library symbol National Library of Canada] (NLC) .... OSUU
University of Sudbury, Sudbury, ON, Canada [Library symbol] [Library of Congress] (LCLS) .... CaOSuU
University of Surrey Satellite .... UOSAT
University of Sydney Faculty of Law. Proceedings of the Institute of Criminology [A publication] .... Syd Inst Crim Proc
University of Sydney. Institute of Criminology. Proceedings [A publication] .... Proc Inst Criminol Univ Sydney
University of Sydney. Institute of Criminology. Proceedings [Australia A publication] .... Univ S Inst of Crim Proceeding
University of Sydney, Sydney, NSW, Australia [Library symbol Library of Congress] (LCLS) .... AuSU
University of Tampa, Tampa, FL [Library symbol Library of Congress] (LCLS) .... FTU
University of Tampa, Tampa, FL [OCLC symbol] (OCLC) .... FUT
University of Tasmania [State] (EERA) .... UT
University of Tasmania Association [Australia] .... UTA
University of Tasmania Consultative Unit [State] (EERA) .... TASQUE
University of Tasmania - Hobart [Australia] .... UT-H
University of Tasmania, Hobart, TAS, Australia [Library symbol Library of Congress] (LCLS) .... AuHU
University of Tasmania - Launceston [Australia] .... UT-L
University of Tasmania. Law Review [A publication] (DLA) .... Tasmania LR
University of Tasmania Law Review [Australia A publication] .... Univ of Tas LR
University of Tasmania Law Review [Australia A publication] .... UTLR
University of Tasmania. News [A publication] .... Univ Tas News
University of Technology, Sydney [Australia] (ECON) .... UTS
University of Teheran Research Reactor .... UTRR
University of Tennessee (GAGS) .... U Tenn
University of Tennessee .... UT
University of Tennessee at Chattanooga (GAGS) .... U Tenn (Chattanooga)
University of Tennessee at Chattanooga .... UTC
University of Tennessee at Chattanooga, Chattanooga, TN [Library symbol Library of Congress] (LCLS) .... TCU
University of Tennessee at Chattanooga, Chattanooga, TN [OCLC symbol] (OCLC) .... TUC
University of Tennessee, at Knoxville .... UTK
University of Tennessee at Knoxville Computer Center [Research center] (RCD) .... UTCC
University of Tennessee at Knoxville Plasma Science Laboratory .... UTK/PSL
University of Tennessee at Martin (GAGS) .... U Tenn (Martin)
University of Tennessee at Martin .... UTM
University of Tennessee at Martin, Martin, TN [OCLC symbol] (OCLC) .... THM
University of Tennessee at Martin, Martin, TN [Library symbol Library of Congress] (LCLS) .... TMaU
University of Tennessee at Memphis (GAGS) .... U Tenn (Memphis)
University of Tennessee at Nashville .... UTN
University of Tennessee at Oak Ridge (GAGS) .... U Tenn (Oak Ridge)
University of Tennessee, Atomic Energy Commission (SAA) .... UTAEC
University of Tennessee Center for the Health Sciences/Knoxville, Preston Medical Library, Knoxville, TN [Library symbol Library of Congress] (LCLS) .... TU-H

University of Tennessee Center for the Health Sciences Library, Stollerman Library, Memphis, TN [Library symbol Library of Congress] (LCLS) .... TU-MS
University of Tennessee Center for the Health Sciences/Memphis Department of Family Medicine, Memphis, TN [Library symbol Library of Congress] (LCLS) .... TU-FM
University of Tennessee, Center for the Health Sciences, Memphis, TN [OCLC symbol] (OCLC) .... TUM
University of Tennessee College of Law (DLA) .... UTLC
University of Tennessee, Downtown Memphis Center, Memphis, TN [Library symbol Library of Congress] (LCLS) .... TU-MDC
University of Tennessee, Graduate School of Library and Information Sciences, Knoxville, TN [Library symbol] [Library of Congress] (LCLS) .... TU-LS
University of Tennessee, Knoxville, TN [OCLC symbol] (OCLC) .... TKN
University of Tennessee, Knoxville, TN [Library symbol Library of Congress] (LCLS) .... TU
University of Tennessee, Law Library, Knoxville, TN [OCLC symbol] (OCLC) .... TLK
University of Tennessee, Law Library, Knoxville, TN [Library symbol Library of Congress] (LCLS) .... TU-L
University of Tennessee Medical Center/Knoxville .... UTMC/K
University of Tennessee Medical Units, Memphis, TN [Library symbol Library of Congress] (LCLS) .... TU-M
University of Tennessee, Nashville, TN [Library symbol Library of Congress] (LCLS) .... TNTU
University of Tennessee Rehabilitation Engineering Program .... UTREP
University of Tennessee Space Institute .... UTSI
University of Tennessee, Space Institute Library, Tullahoma, TN [Library symbol Library of Congress] (LCLS) .... TU-SI
University of Texas .... UT
[The] University of Texas at Arlington (GAGS) .... U Tex (Arlington)
University of Texas at Arlington .... UTA
University of Texas at Arlington, Arlington, TX [OCLC symbol] (OCLC) .... IUA
University of Texas at Arlington, Arlington, TX [Library symbol Library of Congress] (LCLS) .... TxArU
[The] University of Texas at Austin (GAGS) .... U Tex (Austin)
University of Texas at Austin, Austin, TX [OCLC symbol] (OCLC) .... IXA
University of Texas at Austin, Graduate School of Library and Information Science, Austin, TX [Library symbol] [Library of Congress] (LCLS) .... TxU-LS
University of Texas at Austin Institute for Geophysics [Research center] (RCD) .... UT-IG
University of Texas at Austin School of Nursing .... UTASN
[The] University of Texas at Dallas (GAGS) .... U Tex (Dallas)
University of Texas at Dallas (MCD) .... UTD
University of Texas at Dallas, Richardson, TX [OCLC symbol] (OCLC) .... ITD
University of Texas at Dallas, Richardson, TX [Library symbol Library of Congress] (LCLS) .... TxU-Da
[The] University of Texas at El Paso (GAGS) .... U Tex (El Paso)
University of Texas at El Paso .... UTEP
University of Texas at El Paso, El Paso, TX [Library symbol Library of Congress] (LCLS) .... TxEU
University of Texas at El Paso, El Paso, TX [OCLC symbol] (OCLC) .... TXU
University of Texas at Permian Basin (GAGS) .... U Tex Perm Basin
University of Texas at San Antonio, San Antonio, TX [OCLC symbol] (OCLC) .... TXJ
University of Texas at San Antonio, San Antonio, TX [Library symbol Library of Congress] (LCLS) .... TxSaU
University of Texas at Tyler, Tyler, TX [OCLC symbol] (OCLC) .... TEX
University of Texas at Tyler, Tyler, TX [Library symbol] [Library of Congress] (LCLS) .... TxTyU
University of Texas, Austin, Institute of Geo-Physics, Austin, TX [Library symbol] [Library of Congress] (LCLS) .... TxU-GP
University of Texas, Austin, Law Library, Austin, TX [OCLC symbol] (OCLC) .... TXQ
University of Texas, Austin, TX [Library symbol Library of Congress] (LCLS) .... TxU
University of Texas, Business Administration and Economics Library, Austin, TX [Library symbol Library of Congress] (LCLS) .... TxU-B
University of Texas, Health Science Center at Dallas, Dallas, TX [OCLC symbol] (OCLC) .... IHS
University of Texas, Health Science Center at Dallas, Dallas, TX [Library symbol Library of Congress] (LCLS) .... TxDaS
University of Texas Health Science Center at Houston (GAGS) .... U Tex Health Sci Ctr (Houston)
University of Texas, Health Science Center at Houston, School Public Health, Houston, TX [OCLC symbol] (OCLC) .... TPH
University of Texas Health Science Center at San Antonio (GAGS) .... U Tex Health Sci Ctr (San Antonio)
University of Texas Health Science Center at San Antonio .... UTHSCSA
University of Texas, Health Science Center at San Antonio, San Antonio, TX [OCLC symbol] (OCLC) .... TSA
University of Texas Institute for Computer Science (NITA) .... UTICS
University of Texas, Law Library, Austin, TX [Library symbol Library of Congress] (LCLS) .... TxU-L
University of Texas, Lyndon Baines Johnson Presidential Library, Austin, TX [Library symbol Library of Congress] (LCLS) .... TxU-J
University of Texas, M. D. Anderson Hospital .... UTMDAH
University of Texas, M. D. Anderson Hospital and Tumor Institute, Houston, TX [Library symbol Library of Congress] (LCLS) .... TxU-A
University of Texas Medical Branch [Galveston] .... UTMB
University of Texas, Medical Branch Library, Galveston, TX [OCLC symbol] (OCLC) .... TMB
University of Texas Medical School at San Antonio, San Antonio, TX [Library symbol Library of Congress] (LCLS) .... TxU-STM

University of Texas, Medical School, Galveston, TX [Library symbol Library of Congress] (LCLS) .... TxU-M

University of Texas Medicine Branch at Galveston (GAGS) .... U Tex Med Br (Galveston)

University of Texas of the Permian Basin, Odessa, TX [OCLC symbol] (OCLC) .... TXO

University of Texas of the Permian Basin, Odessa, TX [Library symbol Library of Congress] (LCLS) .... TxU-O

University of Texas Pan American (GAGS) .... U Tex Pan Amer

University of Texas, School of Dentistry, Houston, TX [Library symbol Library of Congress] (LCLS) .... TxU-D

University of Texas School of Law (DLA) .... UTSL

University of Texas, School of Public Health, Houston, TX [Library symbol Library of Congress] (LCLS) .... TxU-PH

University of Texas Southwestern Medical School .... UTSMS

University of Texas System Cancer Center [Houston, TX] [Research center] .... UTSCC

University of the Andes [Merida] [Venezuela] [Seismograph station code, US Geological Survey] (SEIS) .... UAV

University of the Arts (GAGS) .... U Arts

University of the District of Columbia .... UDC

University of the District of Columbia, Washington, DC [Library symbol Library of Congress] (LCLS) .... DUDC

University of the East. Law Journal [Manila, Philippines] [A publication] (DLA) .... U East LJ

University of the East. Law Journal [Manila, Philippines] [A publication] (DLA) .... UE Law J

University of the Pacific (GAGS) .... U Pac

University of the Pacific [Stockton, CA] .... UOP

University of the Pacific, Pacific Marine Station, Dillon Beach, CA [Library symbol Library of Congress] (LCLS) .... CStoC-PM

University of the Pacific, Pacific Medical Center, Health Sciences Library, San Francisco, CA [Library symbol] [Library of Congress] (LCLS) .... CStoC-M

University of the Pacific, Science Library, Stockton, CA [Library symbol Library of Congress] (LCLS) .... CStoC-S

University of the Pacific, Stockton, CA [Library symbol Library of Congress] (LCLS) .... CStoC

University of the Philippines .... UP

University of the Philippines, Quezon City, Philippines [Library symbol Library of Congress] (LCLS) .... PiU

University of the South (GAGS) .... U of So

University of the South [Record label] .... UOS

University of the South, School of Theology, Sewanee, TN [Library symbol Library of Congress] (LCLS) .... TSewU-T

University of the South, Sewanee, TN [Library symbol Library of Congress] (LCLS) .... TSewU

University of the South, Sewanee, TN [OCLC symbol] (OCLC) ...... TWU

University of the West Indies [Jamaica] .... UWI

University of the West Indies, Cave Hill Campus, Bridgetown, Barbados [Library symbol Library of Congress] (LCLS) .... BarBu

University of the West Indies Centre for Environment and Development [Barbados] .... UWICED

University of the West Indies, Law Library, St. Michael, Barbados [Library symbol Library of Congress] (LCLS) .... BarBU-L

University of the West Indies, Mona, Kingston, Jamaica [Library symbol Library of Congress] (LCLS) .... JamKU

University of the Western Cape [South Africa] .... UWC

University of Tokyo (EDUCATSS) [UTLAS symbol] .... TUE

[The] University of Toledo (GAGS) .... U Toledo

University of Toledo College of Law (DLA) .... UTOLCL

University of Toledo, College of Law, Toledo, OH [OCLC symbol] (OCLC) .... UTL

University of Toledo. Intramural Law Review [A publication] (DLA) .... U Toledo Intra LR

University of Toledo, Law Library, Toledo, OH [Library symbol Library of Congress] (LCLS) .... OTU-L

University of Toledo, Toledo, OH [Library symbol Library of Congress] (LCLS) .... OTU

University of Toledo, Toledo, OH [OCLC symbol] (OCLC) .... TOL

University of Toronto [Ontario] .... U of T

University of Toronto [Ontario] .... UT

University of Toronto Archives, Ontario [Library symbol National Library of Canada] (NLC) .... OTUAR

University of Toronto, Archives, Toronto, ON, Canada [Library symbol Library of Congress] (LCLS) .... CaOTUAr

University of Toronto, Audiovisual Library, Toronto, ON, Canada [Library symbol Library of Congress] (LCLS) .... CaOTUAV

University of Toronto, Banting-Best Physiology Library, Toronto, ON, Canada [Library symbol Library of Congress] (LCLS) .... CaOTUBP

University of Toronto, Center for Industrial Relations, the Jean and Dorothy Newman Industrial Relations Library, Toronto, ON, Canada [Library symbol Library of Congress] (LCLS) .... CaOTUIRN

University of Toronto, Centre of Criminology, Toronto, ON, Canada [Library symbol Library of Congress] (LCLS) .... CaOTUCr

University of Toronto, Clarke Institute of Psychiatry, Toronto, ON, Canada [Library symbol Library of Congress] (LCLS) .... CaOTUDP

University of Toronto, David Dunlap Observatory, Toronto, ON, Canada [Library symbol Library of Congress] (LCLS) .... CaOTUD

University of Toronto, Department of Anatomy, Toronto, ON, Canada [Library symbol Library of Congress] (LCLS) .... CaOTUAn

University of Toronto, Department of Applied Physics, Toronto, ON, Canada [Library symbol Library of Congress] (LCLS) .... CaOTUAP

University of Toronto, Department of Biochemistry, Toronto, ON, Canada [Library symbol Library of Congress] (LCLS) .... CaOTUB

University of Toronto, Department of Botany, Toronto, ON, Canada [Library symbol Library of Congress] (LCLS) .... CaOTUDB

University of Toronto, Department of Chemical Engineering and Applied Chemistry, Toronto, ON, Canada [Library symbol Library of Congress] (LCLS) .... CaOTUCE

University of Toronto, Department of Chemistry, Toronto, ON, Canada [Library symbol Library of Congress] (LCLS) .... CaOTUC

University of Toronto, Department of Chemistry, Toronto, ON, Canada [Library symbol Library of Congress] (LCLS) .... COTUC

University of Toronto, Department of Civil Engineering, Toronto, ON, Canada [Library symbol Library of Congress] (LCLS) .... CaOTUCi

University of Toronto, Department of Electrical Engineering, Toronto, ON, Canada [Library symbol Library of Congress] (LCLS) .... CaOTUEE

University of Toronto, Department of Fine Arts, Toronto, ON, Canada [Library symbol Library of Congress] (LCLS) .... CaOTUFA

University of Toronto, Department of Geological Sciences, Toronto, ON, Canada [Library symbol Library of Congress] (LCLS) .... CaOTUG

University of Toronto, Department of Mathematics, Toronto, ON, Canada [Library symbol Library of Congress] (LCLS) .... CaOTUDM

University of Toronto, Department of Mechanical Engineering, Toronto, ON, Canada [Library symbol Library of Congress] (LCLS) .... CaOTUM

University of Toronto, Department of Metallurgical Engineering, Toronto, ON, Canada [Library symbol Library of Congress] (LCLS) .... CaOTUME

University of Toronto, Department of Mining Engineering, Toronto, ON, Canada [Library symbol Library of Congress] (LCLS) .... CaOTUMi

University of Toronto, Department of Pathology, Banting-Best Institute, Toronto, ON, Canada [Library symbol Library of Congress] (LCLS) ...... CaOTUPa

University of Toronto, Department of Physics, Toronto, ON, Canada [Library symbol Library of Congress] (LCLS) .... CaOTUP

University of Toronto, Department of Rare Books and Special Collections, Toronto, ON, Canada [Library symbol Library of Congress] (LCLS) .... CaOTURS

University of Toronto, Department of Zoology, Toronto, ON, Canada [Library symbol Library of Congress] (LCLS) .... CaOTUZ

University of Toronto, Environmental Sciences and Engineering, Toronto, ON, Canada [Library symbol Library of Congress] (LCLS) .... CaOTF

University of Toronto, Erindale College, Mississauga, ON, Canada [Library symbol Library of Congress] (LCLS) .... CaOME

University of Toronto, Faculty of Dentistry, Toronto, ON, Canada [Library symbol Library of Congress] (LCLS) .... CaOTUFD

University of Toronto, Faculty of Law, Toronto, ON, Canada [Library symbol Library of Congress] (LCLS) .... CaOTUL

University of Toronto, Faculty of Music, Toronto, ON, Canada [Library symbol Library of Congress] (LCLS) .... CaOTUFM

University of Toronto, Faculty of Pharmacy, Toronto, ON, Canada [Library symbol Library of Congress] (LCLS) .... CaOTUFP

University of Toronto, Geophysics Laboratory, Toronto, ON, Canada [Library symbol Library of Congress] (LCLS) .... CaOTUGL

University of Toronto, Innis College, Toronto, ON, Canada [Library symbol] [Library of Congress] (LCLS) .... CaOTUINC

University of Toronto, Institute for Aerospace Studies [Research center] (MCD) .... UTIAS

University of Toronto, Institute of Aerophysics (MCD) .... UTIA

University of Toronto, Institute of Aerophysics, Toronto, ON, Canada [Library symbol Library of Congress] (LCLS) .... CaOTUA

University of Toronto, Institute of Child Study, Toronto, ON, Canada [Library symbol Library of Congress] (LCLS) .... CaOTUCS

University of Toronto, Institute of Computer Science, Toronto, ON, Canada [Library symbol Library of Congress] (LCLS) .... CaOTUCC

University of Toronto Library [UTLAS symbol] .... UTL

University of Toronto, Library Automation Systems, Toronto, ON, Canada [Library symbol Library of Congress] (LCLS) .... CaOTULAS

University of Toronto Library, Brieflisted Records [UTLAS symbol] ...... UTB

University of Toronto Library, Government Documents [UTLAS symbol] ..... UTG

University of Toronto, Map Library, Toronto, ON, Canada [Library symbol Library of Congress] (LCLS) .... CaOTUMa

University of Toronto, New College, Toronto, ON, Canada [Library symbol] [Library of Congress] (LCLS) .... CaOTUNWC

University of Toronto, Ontario [Library symbol National Library of Canada] (NLC) .... OTU

University of Toronto Press, Ontario [Library symbol National Library of Canada] (NLC) .... OTUTP

University of Toronto Press, University of Toronto, Toronto, ON, Canada [Library symbol Library of Congress] (LCLS) .... CaOTUTP

University of Toronto, School of Architecture, Toronto, ON, Canada [Library symbol Library of Congress] (LCLS) .... CaOTUSA

University of Toronto, School of Hygiene, Toronto, ON, Canada [Library symbol Library of Congress] (LCLS) .... CaOTUH

University of Toronto. School of Law. Review [A publication] (DLA) .... U Tor L Rev

University of Toronto. School of Law. Review [A publication] (DLA) .... U Toronto Sch L Rev

University of Toronto, School of Library Science, Toronto, ON, Canada [Library symbol Library of Congress] (LCLS) .... CaOTULS

University of Toronto, School of Nursing, Toronto, ON, Canada [Library symbol Library of Congress] (LCLS) .... CaOTUN

University of Toronto, School of Physical and Health Education, Toronto, ON, Canada [Library symbol Library of Congress] (LCLS) .... CaOTUSP

University of Toronto, School of Social Work, Toronto, ON, Canada [Library symbol Library of Congress] (LCLS) .... CaOTUSW

University of Toronto, Science Medicine Library, Occupational and Environmental Health Unit, Toronto, ON, Canada [Library symbol] [Library of Congress] (LCLS) .... CaOTUHO

University of Toronto, Thomas Fisher Rare Book Library [UTLAS symbol] .... UTR

University of Toronto, Thomas Fisher Rare Book Library, Toronto, ON, Canada [Library symbol Library of Congress] (LCLS) .... CaOTUTF

University of Toronto, Toronto, ON, Canada [*Library symbol Library of Congress*] (LCLS) .... CaOTU

University of Toronto Union Catalogue Section [*UTLAS symbol*] .... KUT

University of Toronto, University College, Toronto, ON, Canada [*Library symbol*] [Library of Congress] (LCLS) .... CaOTUUC

University of Trinity College, Archives, Toronto, ON, Canada [*Library symbol Library of Congress*] (LCLS) .... CaOTTCA

University of Trinity College Archives, Toronto, Ontario [*Library symbol National Library of Canada*] (NLC) .... OTTCA

University of Trinity College, Toronto, ON, Canada [*Library symbol Library of Congress*] (LCLS) .... CaOTTC

University of Trinity College, Toronto, Ontario [*Library symbol National Library of Canada*] (NLC) .... OTTC

[*The*] University of Tulsa (GAGS) .... U Tulsa

University of Tulsa [*Oklahoma*] .... UT

University of Tulsa, College of Law, Tulsa, OK [*Library symbol Library of Congress*] (LCLS) .... OkTU-L

University of Tulsa, College of Law, Tulsa, OK [*OCLC symbol*] (OCLC) .... OKW

University of Tulsa. Law Journal [*Tulsa, Oklahoma*] [*A publication*] (DLA) .... Univ of Tulsa LJ

University of Tulsa, Tulsa, OK [*OCLC symbol*] (OCLC) .... OKT

University of Tulsa, Tulsa, OK [*Library symbol Library of Congress*] (LCLS) .... OkTU

University of Utah (GAGS) .... U Utah

University of Utah, Eccles Health Science Library, Salt Lake City, UT [*OCLC symbol*] (OCLC) .... UUE

University of Utah, Law Library, Salt Lake City, UT [*Library symbol Library of Congress*] (LCLS) .... UU-L

University of Utah, Library of Medical Sciences, Salt Lake City, UT [*Library symbol Library of Congress*] (LCLS) .... UU-M

University of Utah, Salt Lake City, UT [*Library symbol Library of Congress*] (LCLS) .... UU

University of Utah, Salt Lake City, UT [*OCLC symbol*] (OCLC) .... UUM

University of Utah Seismograph Stations [*Research center*] (RCD) .... UUSS

University of Vermont (GAGS) .... U Vt

University of Vermont (PDAA) .... UVM

University of Vermont and State Agricultural College, Wilbur Collection, Burlington, VT [*Library symbol Library of Congress*] (LCLS) .... VtU-W

University of Vermont, Bailey Library, Burlington, VT [*OCLC symbol*] (OCLC) .... VTU

University of Vermont, Burlington (USDC) .... UVM

University of Vermont, Burlington, VT [*Library symbol Library of Congress*] (LCLS) .... VtU

University of Vermont, College of Medicine, Burlington, VT [*Library symbol Library of Congress*] (LCLS) .... VtU-Med

University of Victoria [*British Columbia*] .... UVIC

University of Victoria, British Columbia [*Library symbol National Library of Canada*] (NLC) .... BVIV

University of Victoria, Department of History in Art, Victoria, BC, Canada [*Library symbol Library of Congress*] (LCLS) .... CaBViVA

University of Victoria, Geography Department, Victoria, BC, Canada [*Library symbol Library of Congress*] (LCLS) .... CaBViVG

University of Victoria Law Library [*UTLAS symbol*] VIL

University of Victoria, Law Library, Victoria, BC, Canada [*Library symbol Library of Congress*] (LCLS) .... CaBViVL

University of Victoria Library [*UTLAS symbol*] VIC

University of Victoria, Maltwood Art Museum, Victoria, BC, Canada [*Library symbol Library of Congress*] (LCLS) .... CaBViMH

University of Victoria, Victoria, BC, Canada [*Library symbol Library of Congress*] (LCLS) .... CaBViV

University of Virginia .... UVA

University of Virginia, C. Moore Health Sciences Library, Charlottesville, VA [*OCLC symbol*] (OCLC) .... VAM

University of Virginia, Charlottesville, VA [*OCLC symbol*] (OCLC) .... VA

University of Virginia, Charlottesville, VA [*Library symbol Library of Congress*] (LCLS) .... ViU

University of Virginia, Law Library, Charlottesville, VA [*OCLC symbol*] (OCLC) .... VAL

University of Virginia, Law Library, Charlottesville, VA [*Library symbol Library of Congress*] (LCLS) .... ViU-L

University of Virginia Medical Center, Health Sciences Library, Charlottesville, VA [*Library symbol Library of Congress*] (LCLS) .... ViU-H

University of Virginia, Music Library, Charlottesville, VA [*Library symbol Library of Congress*] (LCLS) .... ViU-Mu

University of Virginia Reactor .... UVAR

University of Virginia Reactor .... UVR

University of Virginia, School of General Studies, Eastern Shore Branch, WallopsIsland, VA [*Library symbol Library of Congress*] (LCLS) .... ViU-ES

University of Virginia, Science/Technology Information Center, Charlottesville, VA [*Library symbol Library of Congress*] (LCLS) .... ViU-ST

University of Wales Institute of Science and Technology [*British*] .... UWIST

University of Washington [*Seattle, WA*] .... U of W

University of Washington (GAGS) .... U Wash

University of Washington [*Seattle, WA*] .... UW

University of Washington Aeronautical Laboratory (MCD) .... UWAL

University of Washington, Drama Library, Seattle, WA [*Library symbol Library of Congress*] (LCLS) .... WaU-D

University of Washington, East Asia Library, Seattle, WA [*Library symbol Library of Congress*] (LCLS) .... WaU-EA

University of Washington, Far Eastern Library, Seattle, WA [*Library symbol Library of Congress Obsolete*] (LCLS) .... WaU-FE

University of Washington, Harborview Medical Center Library, Seattle, WA [*Library symbol Library of Congress*] (LCLS) .... WaU-MC

University of Washington, Health Sciences Library, Seattle, WA [*Library symbol Library of Congress*] (LCLS) .... WaU-HS

University of Washington, Law Library, Seattle, WA [*Library symbol Library of Congress*] (LCLS) .... WaU-L

University of Washington. Law Review [*A publication*] (DLA) .... U Wash L Rev

University of Washington, School of Librarianship, Seattle, WA [*OCLC symbol*] (OCLC) .... WAW

University of Washington, Seattle, WA [*Library symbol Library of Congress*] (LCLS) .... WaU

University of Washington Training Reactor .... UWTR

University of Waterloo, Environmental Studies Library, Waterloo, ON, Canada [*Library symbol Library of Congress*] (LCLS) .... CaOWtUE

University of Waterloo Library [*UTLAS symbol*] .... WAT

University of Waterloo, Ontario [*Library symbol National Library of Canada*] (NLC) .... OWTU

University of Waterloo, Waterloo, ON, Canada [*Library symbol Library of Congress*] (LCLS) .... CaOWtU

University of West Florida [*Pensacola*] .... UWF

University of West Florida, Pensacola, FL [*Library symbol Library of Congress*] (LCLS) .... FPeU

University of West Florida, Pensacola, FL [*OCLC symbol*] (OCLC) .... FWA

University of West Los Angeles. School of Law. Law Review [*A publication*] (DLA) .... UWLA Rev

University of Western Australia [*State*] (EERA) .... UWA

University of Western Australia, Nedlands, WA, Australia [*Library symbol Library of Congress*] (LCLS) .... AuNeU

University of Western Ontario (MCD) .... UWO

University of Western Ontario, Department of Geography, London, ON, Canada [*Library symbol Library of Congress*] (LCLS) .... CaOLUG

University of Western Ontario, Engineering Library, London, ON, Canada [*Library symbol*] [Library of Congress] (LCLS) .... CaOLUE

University of Western Ontario, Health Science Centre, London, ON, Canada [*Library symbol Library of Congress*] (LCLS) .... CaOLUM

University of Western Ontario, Law Library, London, ON, Canada [*Library symbol Library of Congress*] (LCLS) .... CaOLUL

University of Western Ontario Library [*UTLAS symbol*] .... UWO

University of Western Ontario, London, ON, Canada [*Library symbol Library of Congress*] (LCLS) .... CaOLU

University of Western Ontario, London, Ontario [*Library symbol National Library of Canada*] (NLC) .... OLU

University of Western Ontario, MacIntosh Gallery, London, ON, Canada [*Library symbol Library of Congress*] (LCLS) .... CaOLUMG

University of Western Ontario, School of Library and Information Science, Lond on, ON, Canada [*OCLC symbol*] (OCLC) .... UWO

University of Western Ontario, School of Library and Information Science, London, ON, Canada [*Library symbol Library of Congress*] (LCLS) .... CaOLUS

University of Western Ontario, Visual Arts Department, London, ON, Canada [*Library symbol Library of Congress*] (LCLS) .... CaOLUVA

University of Western Sydney [*State*] (EERA) .... UWS

University of Western Sydney - Macarthur [*Australia*] .... UWS-M

University of Western Sydney - Nepean [*Australia*] .... UWS-N

University of Windsor [*Ontario*] .... U of W

University of Windsor, Law Library, Windsor, ON, Canada [*Library symbol Library of Congress*] (LCLS) .... CaOWAL

University of Windsor. Law Review [*A publication*] (DLA) .... U Windsor L Rev

University of Windsor, Ontario [*Library symbol National Library of Canada*] (NLC) .... OWA

University of Windsor, Paul Martin Law Library [*UTLAS symbol*] .... PML

University of Windsor, Windsor, ON, Canada [*Library symbol Library of Congress*] (LCLS) .... CaOWA

University of Winnipeg Library [*UTLAS symbol*] .... UWL

University of Winnipeg, Manitoba [*Library symbol National Library of Canada*] (NLC) .... MWUC

University of Winnipeg, Winnipeg, MB, Canada [*Library symbol Library of Congress*] (LCLS) .... CaMWUC

University of Wisconsin (GAGS) .... U Wis

University of Wisconsin [*Madison, WI*] (MCD) .... UW

University of Wisconsin (PDAA) .... UWIS

University of Wisconsin, Agricultural Library, Madison, WI [*Library symbol Library of Congress*] (LCLS) .... WU-A

University of Wisconsin at Eau Claire (GAGS) .... U Wis (Eau Claire)

University of Wisconsin at Green Bay .... UWGB

University of Wisconsin at La Crosse (GAGS) .... U Wis (La Crosse)

University of Wisconsin at Milwaukee (GAGS) .... U Wis (Milwaukee)

University of Wisconsin at Milwaukee [*Seismograph station code, US Geological Survey*] (SEIS) .... UWM

University of Wisconsin at Oshkosh (GAGS) .... U Wis (Oshkosh)

University of Wisconsin at Platteville (GAGS) .... U Wis (Platteville)

University of Wisconsin at River Falls (GAGS) .... U Wis (River Falls)

University of Wisconsin at Stevens Point (GAGS) .... U Wis (Stevens Point)

University of Wisconsin at Stout (GAGS) .... U Wis (Stout)

University of Wisconsin at Superior (GAGS) .... U Wis (Superior)

University of Wisconsin at Whitewater (GAGS) .... U Wis (Whitewater)

University of Wisconsin, Center for Demography and Ecology, Madison, WI [*Library symbol Library of Congress*] (LCLS) .... WU-DE

University of Wisconsin Center-Sheboygan, Sheboygan, WI [*Library symbol Library of Congress*] (LCLS) .... WSheU

University of Wisconsin Center-Washington County, West Bend, WI [*Library symbol Library of Congress*] (LCLS) .... WWbU

University of Wisconsin Center-Waukesha County, Waukesha, WI [*Library symbol Library of Congress*] (LCLS) .... WWauU

University of Wisconsin, Engineering Library, Madison, WI [*Library symbol Library of Congress*] (LCLS) .... WU-E

University of Wisconsin, Land Tenure Center, Madison, WI [*Library symbol Library of Congress*] (LCLS) .... WU-LT

University of Wisconsin, Law Library, Madison, WI [*Library symbol Library of Congress*] (LCLS) .... WU-L

University of Wisconsin - Madison Bureau of Business Research [*Research center*] (RCD) .... UWBBR
University of Wisconsin, Madison Library School, Madison, WI [*OCLC symbol*] (OCLC) .... WID
University of Wisconsin - Madison Nuclear Reactor Laboratory [*Research center*] (RCD) .... UWNR
University of Wisconsin, Madison, WI [*Library symbol Library of Congress*] (LCLS) .... WU
University of Wisconsin, Primate Research Center, Primate Library, Madison, WI [*OCLC symbol*] (OCLC) .... WIY
University of Wisconsin, River Falls, River Falls, WI [*OCLC symbol*] (OCLC) .... WRF
University of Wisconsin, School of Medicine, Madison, WI [*Library symbol Library of Congress*] (LCLS) .... WU-M
University of Wisconsin, Stevens Point, Stevens Point, WI [*OCLC symbol*] (OCLC) .... WIS
University of Wisconsin TOKAMAK .... UWMAK
University of Wisconsin, Woodman Astronomical Library, Madison, WI [*Library symbol Library of Congress*] (LCLS) .... WU-WA
University of Wisconsin-Center System, Madison, WI [*Library symbol Library of Congress*] (LCLS) .... WMaUCS
University of Wisconsin-Eau Claire, Eau Claire, WI [*OCLC symbol*] (OCLC) .... GZE
University of Wisconsin-Eau Claire, Eau Claire, WI [*Library symbol Library of Congress*] (LCLS) .... WEU
University of Wisconsin-Extension, Madison, WI [*Library symbol Library of Congress*] (LCLS) .... WMaUEx
University of Wisconsin-Fond Du Lac, Fond Du Lac, WI [*Library symbol Library of Congress*] (LCLS) .... WFonU
University of Wisconsin-Green Bay, Fox Valley Campus, Menasha, WI [*Library symbol Library of Congress*] (LCLS) .... WMeU
University of Wisconsin-Green Bay, Green Bay, WI [*OCLC symbol*] (OCLC) .... GZW
University of Wisconsin-Green Bay, Green Bay, WI [*Library symbol Library of Congress*] (LCLS) .... WGrU
University of Wisconsin-La Crosse, La Crosse, WI [*OCLC symbol*] (OCLC) .... GZU
University of Wisconsin-La Crosse, La Crosse, WI [*Library symbol Library of Congress*] (LCLS) .... WLacU
University of Wisconsin-Madison, Health Sciences, Madison, WI [*OCLC symbol*] (OCLC) .... GZH
University of Wisconsin-Madison, Instructional Materials Center, Madison, WI [*OCLC symbol*] (OCLC) .... GZI
University of Wisconsin-Madison, Law Library, Madison, WI [*OCLC symbol*] (OCLC) .... GZL
University of Wisconsin-Madison, Madison, WI [*OCLC symbol*] (OCLC) .... GZM
University of Wisconsin-Milwaukee, Milwaukee, WI [*OCLC symbol*] (OCLC) .... GZN
University of Wisconsin-Milwaukee, Milwaukee, WI [*Library symbol Library of Congress*] (LCLS) .... WMUW
University of Wisconsin-Milwaukee, School of Library Science, Milwaukee, WI [*OCLC symbol*] (OCLC) .... GZJ
University of Wisconsin-Oshkosh, Oshkosh, WI [*OCLC symbol*] (OCLC) .... GZO
University of Wisconsin-Oshkosh, Oshkosh, WI [*Library symbol Library of Congress*] (LCLS) .... WOshU
University of Wisconsin-Parkside, Archives and Art Research Center, Kenosha, WI [*Library symbol Library of Congress*] (LCLS) .... WKenU-A
University of Wisconsin-Parkside, Kenosha, WI [*OCLC symbol*] (OCLC) .... GZP
University of Wisconsin-Parkside, Kenosha, WI [*Library symbol Library of Congress*] (LCLS) .... WKenU
University of Wisconsin-Platteville, Platteville, WI [*OCLC symbol*] (OCLC) .... GZV
University of Wisconsin-Platteville, Platteville, WI [*Library symbol Library of Congress*] (LCLS) .... WPlaU
University of Wisconsin-River Falls .... UW-RF
University of Wisconsin-River Falls, River Falls, WI [*Library symbol Library of Congress*] (LCLS) .... WRfU
University of Wisconsin-Stevens Point, Stevens Point, WI [*Library symbol Library of Congress*] (LCLS) .... WSpU
University of Wisconsin-Stout, Menomonie, WI [*OCLC symbol*] (OCLC) .... GZS
University of Wisconsin-Stout, Menomonie, WI [*Library symbol Library of Congress*] (LCLS) .... WMenU
University of Wisconsin-Superior, Jim Dan Hill Library, Superior, WI [*OCLC symbol*] (OCLC) .... WIE
University of Wisconsin-Superior, Superior, WI [*Library symbol Library of Congress*] (LCLS) .... WSU
University of Wisconsin-Whitewater, Whitewater, WI [*OCLC symbol*] (OCLC) .... GZT
University of Wisconsin-Whitewater, Whitewater, WI [*Library symbol Library of Congress*] (LCLS) .... WWhiwU
University of Wyoming (GAGS) .... U Wyo
University of Wyoming, Archive of Contemporary History, Laramie, WY [*Library symbol Library of Congress*] (LCLS) .... WyU-Ar
University of Wyoming, Laramie, WY [*Library symbol Library of Congress*] (LCLS) .... WyU
University of Wyoming, Library, Laramie, WY [*OCLC symbol*] (OCLC) .... WYU
University of Wyoming Research Reactor .... UWRR
University of Zambia. Law Bulletin [*A publication*] (DLA) .... U Zambia LB
University Officers Training Corps [*British military*] (DMA) .... UOTC
University Partnership [*Australia*] .... UP
University Peace Studies Network (EA) .... UPSN
University Photographers Association of America .... UPA
University Photographers Association of America (EA) .... UPAA
University Press of America .... UPA
University Press of New England .... UPNE
University Presses [*General term applied to presses of various universities*] .... UP

University Professors for Academic Order (EA) .... UPAO
University Program for the Comprehensive Handling and Utilization of Knowledge [*Humorous*] .... UPCHUK
University Publications of America [*Database producer*] (IID) .... UPA
University Reform Movement [*in Latin America*] .... URM
University Relations .... UR
University Research and Training [*Programs*] .... URT
University Research Centre [*British*] .... URC
University Research Expeditions Programs .... UREP
University Research Initiative [*DoD*] (RDA) .... URI
University Research Support [*Department of Energy*] .... URS
University Residence Environment Scale [*Student attitudes test*] .... URES
University Resident Theatre Association (EA) .... URTA
University Risk and Insurance Managers Association [*Later, URMIA*] (EA) .... URIMA
University Risk Management and Insurance Association [*Madison, WI*] (EA) .... URMIA
University Scholarships of Canada .... USC
University Science Development [*National Science Foundation*] .... USD
University Science Policy Planning [*Program*] [*National Science Foundation*] .... USPP
University Science Statistics Project [*Information service or system*] (IID) .... UNISTAT
University Seminary, Quebec, PQ, Canada [*Library symbol Library of Congress*] (LCLS) .... CaQQUS
University Space Experiments .... USE
University Space Physics Association .... USRA
University Statistics Center [*New Mexico State University*] [*Research center*] (RCD) .... USC
University Students for Law and Order .... USLO
University Studies in History and Economics [*A publication*] .... Univ Stud Hist Econ
University Studies in Western Australian History [*A publication*] .... Univ Stud W Aust Hist
University Systems, Inc. (AAGC) .... USI
University Teachers Certificate .... UTC
University Training Corps [*British*] .... UTC
University Training Reactor .... UTR
University Tutorial Series [*A publication*] .... UTS
University without Walls [*Twenty-one-university consortium*] .... UWW
University Women of Europe (EA) .... UWE
University Year for ACTION [*Refers to federal program, ACTION, which is not an acronym*] .... UYA
University-Affiliated Facility .... UAF
University-Affiliated Facility for the Mentally Retarded .... UAF-MR
University-Affiliated Program .... UAP
University-Enterprise Training Partnership [*European Community*] (AIE) .... UETP
University-Industry Research Program [*University of Wisconsin-Madison*] [*Information service or system*] (IID) .... UIR
University-Industry Research Relationship .... UIRR
University-Small Business Technology Consortium [*Defunct*] (EA) .... USBTC
Universitywide Energy Research Group [*University of California*] [*Research center*] (RCD) .... UERG
Universitywide Library Automation Program (NITA) .... ULAP
Universum Sokol Publishers, Perth Amboy, NJ [*Library symbol Library of Congress*] (LCLS) .... NjPeraSo
Universum-Film Aktien-Gesellschaft [*German motion picture company*] .... UFA
Univerzita Komenskeho Bratislava [*Comenius University of Bratislava*], Bratislava, Czechoslovakia [*Library symbol Library of Congress*] (LCLS) .... CzBU
Univex Mining Corp. [*Vancouver Stock Exchange symbol*] .... UNX
Univex SRL [*Italy ICAO designator*] (FAAC) .... UAD
Univl Corp. [*NYSE symbol*] (TTSB) .... UVV
Univl Electronics [*NASDAQ symbol*] (TTSB) .... UEIC
Univl Foods [*NYSE symbol*] (TTSB) .... UFC
Univl Forest Products [*NASDAQ symbol*] (TTSB) .... UFPI
Univl Health Realty [*NYSE symbol*] (TTSB) .... UHT
Univl Health Svs Cl'B' [*NYSE symbol*] (TTSB) .... UHS
Univl Holding Corp. [*NASDAQ symbol*] (TTSB) .... UHCO
Univl Hospital Svcs [*NASDAQ symbol*] (TTSB) .... UHOS
Univl International [*NASDAQ symbol*] (TTSB) .... UNIV
Univl Mfg [*NASDAQ symbol*] (TTSB) .... UFMG
Univl Security Instr [*NASDAQ symbol*] (TTSB) .... USEC
Univl Seismic Assoc [*NASDAQ symbol*] (TTSB) .... USAC
Univl Stainless/Alloy Prods [*NASDAQ symbol*] (TTSB) .... USAP
Univl Standard Medl Labs [*NASDAQ symbol*] (TTSB) .... USML
Uniwersytet Warszawski [*University of Warsaw*], Warsaw, Poland [*Library symbol Library of Congress*] (LCLS) .... PoWU
UNIX Europe Ltd. (NITA) .... UEL
Unix International [*Computer science*] (PCM) .... UI
Unix Sound File [*Computer science*] .... au
Unix Systems Association [*Defunct*] (EA) .... USA
Unix Systems Laboratory [*Computer science*] .... USL
Unix-to-Unix Call Procedure [*Telecommunications*] (OSI) .... UUCP
Unix-to-Unix Copy Program [*Computer science*] .... UUCP
UNIX-to-UNIX Copy Protocol (TNIG) .... UUCP
Unknown .... U
Unknown .... UK
Unknown (KSC) .... UKN
Unknown [*Telecommunications*] (TEL) .... UN
Unknown (AFM) .... UNK
Unknown (VRA) .... unk
Unknown .... UNKN
Unknown .... UNKWN
Unknown Amino Acid [*Laboratory science*] (DAVI) .... Xaa
Unknown Black Female (DAVI) .... UBF

Unknown Black Male (DAVI) ... UBM
Unknown Factor ... UF
Unknown Format (NITA) ... U format
Unknown or Variable Composition, Complex Reaction Products, and Biological Materials [*Chemical Abstracts Services*] ... UVCB
Unknown Precipitation [*ICAO*] (FAAC) ... UP
Unknown Quantity (IDOE) ... X
Unknown Quantity (IDOE) ... x
Unknown Resistance (IDOE) ... R_x
Unknown Respiratory Stress Syndrome [*Medicine*] ... URDS
Unknown Significance ... US
Unknown Subject [*FBI*] [*Acronym also used as title of television series*] ... UNSUB
Unknown Unknowns [*Design engineering*] ... UNK UNK
Unknown White Female (DAVI) ... UWF
Unknown White Male (DAVI) ... UWM
Unladen Weight (BARN) ... UW
Unlatch (MCD) ... UNLCH
Unlaunchable (IAA) ... ULN
Unlawful Detainer [*Legal term for an eviction proceeding*] ... UD
Unlawful Flight to Avoid Custody ... UFAC
Unlawful Flight to Avoid Prosecution ... UFAP
Unlawful Flight to Avoid Testimony ... UFAT
Unlawful Sexual Intercourse ... USI
Unlawfully Driving Away Auto ... UDAA
Unleaded Fuel [*Automotive engineering*] ... UNL
Unleaded Petrol [*British*] (ADA) ... ULP
Unless Caused by [*Insurance*] (BARN) ... ucb
Unless Otherwise Directed ... UNODIR
Unless Otherwise Indicated ... UNOINDC
Unless Otherwise Noted (OA) ... UON
Unless Otherwise Requested (NVT) ... UNOREQ
Unless Otherwise Specified (MSA) ... UOS
Unlicensed (DA) ... U
Unlicensed National Information Infrastructure (PCM) ... U-N11
Unlighted (FAAC) ... UNLGTD
Unlighted (DNAB) ... UNLTD
Unlighted Buoy [*USCG*] (TAG) ... ULB
Unlike-Sexed ... US
Unlimited [*Water depth*] ... u/l
Unlimited ... UNL
Unlimited ... UNLIM
Unlimited ... UNLTD
Unlimited Freak-Out [*Slang*] (DSUE) ... UFO
Unlimited Intermediate Storage [*Industrial engineering*] ... UIS
Unlimited Machine Access from Scattered Sites [*Computer science*] ... UMASS
Unlimited Potential Data through Automation Technology in Education (IEEE) ... UPDATE
Unlimited Register Machine ... URM
Unlimited Resources Ensure Keen Answers ... UREKA
Unlimited Sequential Input/Output ... USIO
Unlimited Time [*Broadcasting term*] ... U
Unliquidated ... UNLIQ
Unliquidated Dollar Balances (AAGC) ... UDB
Unliquidated Obligations (MCD) ... ULOS
Unlisted Securities Market [*London Stock Exchange*] ... USM
Unlisted Securities Trading Act [*1936*] ... USTA
Unlisted Trading Privileges ... UTP
Unlisten (IAA) ... UNL
Unload (IAA) ... UNLD
Unloaded Radial Tire Run-Out ... URTRO
Unloaded Radial Wheel Run-Out ... URWRO
Unloader Coil (IAA) ... UC
Unloading ... UNL
Unlock ... UNLK
Unlocking ... UNLKG
Unmanned (NASA) ... U/M
Unmanned (KSC) ... UNMD
Unmanned Aerial Reconnaissance System (DOMA) ... UARS
Unmanned Aerial [*or Aerospace*] **Surveillance** ... UAS
Unmanned Aerial Surveillance System (MCD) ... UASS
Unmanned Aerial [*or Air*] **Vehicle** (RDA) ... UAV
Unmanned Aerial Vehicle - Short Range (DWSG) ... UAV-SR
Unmanned Aerial Vehicle-Close Range [*Military*] ... UAV-CR
Unmanned Air Reconnaissance Vehicle (DOMA) ... UARV
Unmanned Airborne Position (MCD) ... UAP
Unmanned Aircraft [*Aviation*] ... UMA
Unmanned Arctic Research Submersible ... UARS
Unmanned Equipment Cabinet ... UEC
Unmanned Free Swimming Submersibles (DNAB) ... UFSS
Unmanned Geophysical Observatory [*National Science Foundation*] ... UGO
Unmanned Ground Vehicle [*Military robotics*] ... UGV
Unmanned Hypersonic Test Vehicle (MCD) ... UHTV
Unmanned Launch Operations [*NASA*] (KSC) ... ULO
Unmanned Launch Operations - Western Test Range [*NASA*] (KSC) ... ULOW
Unmanned Launch Space Vehicles [*NASA*] (KSC) ... ULSV
Unmanned Lunar Logistics Vehicle [*OMSF*] ... ULLV
Unmanned Lunar Orbiter [*NASA*] (MCD) ... ULO
Unmanned Multifunction Satellite ... UMS
Unmanned Orbital [*NASA*] (NASA) ... UMO
Unmanned Orbital Laboratory ... UMOL
Unmanned Orbital Multifunction Satellite ... UOMS
Unmanned Orbital Satellite ... UOS
Unmanned Recovery Platform [*Navy*] (NVT) ... URP
Unmanned Repeater Station [*Telecommunications*] (OA) ... URS
Unmanned Seismological Observatory ... USO
Unmanned Sensing Satellite System ... USSS
Unmanned Strike Vehicle ... USV
Unmanned Supersonic Test Vehicle (MCD) ... USTV
Unmanned Surveillance Equipment ... UMSE
Unmanned Surveillance Equipment ... USE
Unmanned Teleoperator Spacecraft (MCD) ... UTS
Unmanned Threat Emitter (DWSG) ... UMTE
Unmanned Undersea Vehicle [*Military robotics*] ... UUV
Unmanned Vehicle for Aerial Surveillance (MCD) ... UVAS
Unmanned Vehicle System ... UVS
Unmanned Vertical Flight [*NASA*] (NASA) ... UMVF
Unmanned Vertical Flight [*NASA*] (NASA) ... UVF
Unmanned Weather Station ... UWS
Unmannned Ground Vehicles/Systems Joint Project Office [*Army*] (RDA) ... UGV/SJPO
Unmarked ... UNMKD
Unmarried ... UM
Unmarried ... UNM
Unmarried Lady [*Citizens band radio slang*] ... XL
Unmarried-Catholics Correspondence Club (EA) ... UCCC
Unmounted ... UNMTD
Unna's Boot (MEDA) ... UB
Unnecessary (ROG) ... UNNECY
Unnecessary Repetition [*Used in correcting manuscripts, etc.*] ... REP
Unnilpentium [*Chemical element*] (CDAI) ... Unp
Unnilquadium [*Chemical element*] (CDAI) ... Unq
Unnormalized Aid Magnitude (SAA) ... UAM
Unnormalized Floating Multiply (SAA) ... UFM
Unnormalized Floating Subtract ... UFS
Unnumbered Acknowledge [*or Acknowledgement*] [*Telecommunications*] (IAA) ... U
Unnumbered Acknowledge [*or Acknowledgment*] [*Telecommunications*] (IEEE) ... UA
Unnumbered Information [*Telecommunications*] (OSI) ... UI
Uno [*Guinea-Bissau*] [*ICAO location identifier*] (ICLI) ... GGUN
Uno In Die [*Once daily*] [*Pharmacy*] (DAVI) ... UID
Uno Restaurant Corp. [*NYSE symbol*] (TTSB) ... UNO
Uno Restaurant Corp. [*Associated Press*] (SAG) ... UnoRst
Uno Restaurants, Inc. [*NYSE symbol*] (SAG) ... UNO
Unobserved (ROG) ... UNOBSD
Unocal Corp. [*NYSE symbol*] (SPSG) ... UCL
Unocal Corp. [*Associated Press*] (SAG) ... Unocal
Unoccupied ... U
Unofficial (DAVI) ... UNK
Unofficial (CPH) ... unoff
Unofficial (FAAC) ... UNOFFL
Unofficial Funds [*British*] ... UF
Unofficial Personnel Folder ... UPF
Unofficial Reports [*A publication*] (DLA) ... Unof
Unopened (ADA) ... UNOP
Unopened Edges [*Bookbinding*] (DGA) ... u/o/e
Unoperated Control ... UC
Unopposed ... UNOP
Unpacked (IAA) ... UNPKD
Unpaged ... UNP
Unpaid (AABC) ... UNPD
Unpaid (ADA) ... UPD
Unpaid Balance [*Business term*] (MHDB) ... UB
Unpaid Master ... UNPD-MSTR
Unpaved Surface [*Aviation*] (DA) ... u
Unpaying Guest [*In a rooming or boarding house*] ... UPG
Unperformed [*Music*] ... UNPERF
Unperformed (ROG) ... UNPERFD
Unplanned Derated Hours [*Electronics*] (IEEE) ... UDH
Unplanned Derating [*Electronics*] (IEEE) ... UD
Unplanned Event Pickup [*NASA*] (KSC) ... UEP
Unplanned Event Record [*NASA*] (KSC) ... UER
Unplanned Event Record Log [*NASA*] (KSC) ... UERL
Unplanned Loss Report [*Navy*] (DNAB) ... UPLR
Unplanned Outage Factor [*Electronics*] (IEEE) ... UOF
Unplanned Outage Hours [*Electronics*] (IEEE) ... UOH
Unplanned Outage Rate [*Electronics*] (IEEE) ... UOR
Unplasticized Polyvinyl Chloride ... UPVC
Unpleasant ... U
Unpopped Kernel [*Popcorn*] ... UPK
Unpopular Magnetic Fields ... UM
Unpostable [*Computer science*] ... UNP
Unpostable [*Computer science*] ... UP
Unpostable Code [*Computer science*] ... UPC
Unpredictable Main Event ... UME
Unpressurized Aerosol [*Therapy*] [*Pharmacology*] (DAVI) ... UPA
Unpriced Material ... UM
Unpriced Spare Parts List ... USPL
Unprogrammed Requirements (MCD) ... UR
Unprogrammed Transfer Register ... UTR
Unpublished ... UNPUB
Unpublished (AAGC) ... Unpub
Unpublished ... UNPUBD
Unpublished Research Information [*Conducted by National Science Foundation*] ... URI
Unpublished Scholarly Writings on World Religions (BJA) ... UWWR
Unqua Elementary School, Massapequa, NY [*Library symbol Library of Congress*] (LCLS) ... NMassUE
Unqualified (AABC) ... UNQUAL
Unquote ... UNQTE

Unquote (FAAC) ... UQOT
UNR Industries [*NASDAQ symbol*] (TTSB) ... UNRI
UNR Industries, Inc. [*Associated Press*] (SAG) ... UNR
UNR Industries, Inc. [*NASDAQ symbol*] (NQ) ... UNRI
Unreached Peoples Mission (EA) ... UPM
Unreadable (FAAC) ... UNRDBL
Unrealized Profit ... UP
Unrealized Profits (MHDW) ... UP
Unreasonable Risk to Health [*Drinking water standards*] [*Environmental Protection Agency*] ... URTH
Unrecoverable Application Error [*Computer science*] (PCM) ... UAE
Unreformed (ROG) ... UNREF
Unregistered Stock [*Finance*] ... US
Unregulated ... UNRGLTD
Unrelated (AAMN) ... UR
Unrelated (DAVI) ... uri
Unrelated Adult Man ... URAM
Unrelated Adult Woman ... URAW
Unrelated Business Income (DICI) ... UBI
Unrelated Business Income Tax ... UBIT
Unreleasable (MCD) ... UR
Unreliable ... UNREL
Unreliable (FAAC) ... UNRELBL
Unreliable ... UR
Unreliable Source of Intelligence [*Military*] ... E
Unreported Income [*IRS*] ... UI
Unreported Interstate Shipment of Cigarettes ... UISC
Unreported New York Estate Tax Cases [*Prentice-Hall, Inc.*] [*A publication*] (DLA) ... Unrep NY Est TC
Unreported Travancore Decisions [*A publication*] (DLA) ... Un Trav Dec
Unreported Wills Cases [*Prentice-Hall, Inc.*] [*A publication*] (DLA) ... Unrep Wills Cas
Unrepresented Nations and Peoples Organization ... UNPO
Unrequited Love [*Slang*] ... URL
Unresolved Complex Mixture ... UCM
Unresolved Safety Issue [*Nuclear energy*] (NRCH) ... USI
Unrestricted (FAAC) ... UNRSTD
Unrestricted Hartree-Fock [*Wave-Function*] ... UHF
Unrestricted Line Officer [*Navy*] (DNAB) ... ULO
Unrestricted Line Officer [*Navy*] ... URL
Unridable Bicycle ... URB
Unrotated Projectile [*Rocket*] ... UP
UNRWA [*United Nations Relief and Works Agency*] **International Staff Association** (EAIO) ... ISA
Unsafe Landing Warning ... ULW
Unsafe Lane Change (WDAA) ... ULC
Unsafe to Monitor (ACII) ... UTM
Unsaponifiable Matter [*Organic analytical chemistry*] ... USM
Unsatisfactory (MAE) ... uns
Unsatisfactory (AABC) ... UNSAT
Unsatisfactory ... UNSATFY
Unsatisfactory Condition (NASA) ... UC
Unsatisfactory Condition Report [*NASA*] ... UCR
Unsatisfactory Equipment Performance Report [*Military*] (AABC) ... UEPR
Unsatisfactory Equipment Report ... UER
Unsatisfactory Material/Condition Report (MCD) ... UM/CR
Unsatisfactory Material Notice (MSA) ... UMN
Unsatisfactory Material Report [*Military*] (AABC) ... UMR
Unsatisfactory Report ... UR
Unsatisfactory Report Questionnaire ... URQ
Unsatisfactory Specimen [*Laboratory science*] (DAVI) ... USPE
Unsatisfied Claim and Judgment [*State driver insurance*] ... UCJ
Unsatisfied Judgment Fund [*Insurance*] ... UJF
[*The*] **Unsatisfied Man** [*A publication*] ... TUM
Unsaturated [*Chemistry*] ... unsat
Unsaturated Fatty Acid [*Organic chemistry*] ... UFA
Unsaturated Hydroxyl-Terminated Polybutadiene [*Organic chemistry*] ... UHTPB
Unsaturated Iron-Binding Capacity [*Clinical chemistry*] ... UIBC
Unsaturated Polyester Resin [*Organic chemistry*] ... UPR
Unsaturated Polyethylene [*Organic chemistry*] ... UPE
Unsaturated Thermoset Polyester [*Organic chemistry*] ... UP
Unsaturated (Vitamin) B_{12} Binding Capacity ... UBBC
Unsaturated Zone Monitoring [*Environmental Protection Agency*] (ERG) ... UZM
Unscheduled (FAAC) ... UNSKED
Unscheduled DNA Synthesis [*Genetics*] ... UDS
Unscheduled Maintenance ... UM
Unscheduled Maintenance ... USM
Unscheduled Maintenance Action [*Military*] (AABC) ... UMA
Unscheduled Maintenance Manhours (MCD) ... UMMH
Unscheduled Maintenance Sample Data Collection (MCD) ... UMSDC
Unscheduled Not Mission Capable Both [*Maintenance and supply*] (MCD) ... UNMCB
Unscheduled Not Mission Capable Maintenance (MCD) ... UNMCM
Unscreened Granulated Aluminate [*Inorganic chemistry*] ... UGA
Unseasonable [*NWS*] (FAAC) ... UNSBL
Unseated Rider [*Horse racing*] ... U
Unsecured Loan Stock (DCTA) ... ULS
Unsegmented Storage Analyzer [*Instrumentation*] ... USA
Unsensitized ... USTZD
Unserviceable (IAA) ... UNSERV
Unserviceable (AABC) ... UNSVC
Unserviceable ... US
Unserviceable Generation Factor [*Military*] ... UGF
Unserviceable Items File ... UIF
Unserviceable Return Rate ... UNSVC-RT-R
Unshielded Twisted-Pair [*Computer science*] (PCM) ... UTP
Unsigned (WGA) ... UNSGD
Unsigned Division [*Computer science*] ... DIVU
Unsigned Integer [*Computer science*] ... UI
Unsigned Long Integer [*Computer science*] ... ULI
Unsigned Multiplication [*Computer science*] ... MULU
Unsigned Short Integer [*Computer science*] ... USI
Unsized Canvas (VRA) ... unsz c
Unsmoked Sheets (PDAA) ... USS
Unsolicited Commercial E-Mail [*Computer science*] ... UCE
Unsolicited Proposal (MCD) ... UP
Unsorted ... U/S
Unspecified Minor Construction Program [*Navy*] (DNAB) ... UMC
Unspecified Temperature ... UT
Unst [*Shetland Islands, Scotland*] [*Airport symbol*] (AD) ... UNE
Unst [*Scotland*] [*Airport symbol*] (OAG) ... UNT
Unst (Shetland Isles) [*British ICAO location identifier*] (ICLI) ... EGPW
Unstable (IDOE) ... uns
Unstable ... UNSTBL
Unstable Angina [*Medicine*] ... UA
Unstable Hemoglobin Disease [*Hematology*] (DAVI) ... UHD
Unstable Periodic Orbit ... UPO
Unstained Pollen [*Botany*] ... UP
Unsteady ... UNSTDY
Unsteady Heat Flux Sensor ... UHFS
Unsubscribe [*Computer science*] [*Telecommunications*] ... U
Unsuccessful Tenderers Fees ... UTF
Unsuppressed (MSA) ... UNSUPPR
Unsuppressed Selling Price ... USP
Unsuppressed Selling Price ... USSP
Unsweetened (ROG) ... UNSD
Unsymmetric Diethyltrianine (MCD) ... UDETA
Unsymmetrical ... U
Unsymmetrical ... UNS
Unsymmetrical (IDOE) ... uns
Unsymmetrical ... UNSYM
Unsymmetrical Dimethylhydrazine [*Rocket fuel base, convulsant poison*] ... UDMH
Unsymmetrical Dimethylhydrazine Hydrazine Blend (NASA) ... UDMH/H
Unsymmetrical Free Vibration ... UFV
Untempered (VRA) ... untemp
Unter [*Among*] [*German*] ... U
Untere Winkelgruppe [*Angles up to 45*] [*German military - World War II*] ... UW
Unterlafette [*Bottom carriage*] [*German military - World War II*] ... UL
Unterseeboot [*Submarine*] [*German*] ... U-BOOT
Untersuchungen zur Altorientalischen Geschichte [*H. Winckler*] [*A publication*] (BJA) ... UAG
Untersuchungen zur Geschichte und Altertumskunde Aegyptens [*K. Sethe*] [*A publication*] (BJA) ... UGAA
Untervaz [*Switzerland ICAO location identifier*] (ICLI) ... LSXU
Untested ... UT
Untethered Underwater Vehicle (DOMA) ... UUV
Unthreaded ... UNTHD
Until (DA) ... U
Until Advised (DA) ... UA
Until Advised by the Tower [*Aviation*] (FAAC) ... UAT
Until Cleared Down [*Aviation*] (FAAC) ... UCDWN
Until Cleared to Land by the Tower [*Aviation*] (FAAC) ... UCLT
Until Exhausted ... UE
Until Further Advised ... UFA
Until Further Notice ... UFN
Until Further Notice [*Military*] ... UNFURNOTE
Untitled (VRA) ... unt
Untouchable Force Organization [*Rap recording group*] ... UTFO
Untrained ... U/T
Untranslated Region [*Genetics*] ... UTR
Untreated [*Medicine*] ... U
Untreated [*Medicine*] ... UN
Untreated [*Medicine*] (DAVI) ... UT
Untreated ... UTRTD
Untreated Controls [*Medicine*] ... UC
Untreated Hard Pressed Fiberboard ... UHPFB
Untwist ... UNTW
UNUM Corp. [*NYSE symbol*] (SAG) ... UND
UNUM Corp. [*NYSE symbol*] (SPSG) ... UNM
UNUM Corp. [*Associated Press*] (SAG) ... UNUM
UNUM Corp. [*Associated Press*] (SAG) ... UNUM25
UNUM Corp. 8.80% 'MIDS' [*NYSE symbol*] (TTSB) ... UND
Unusable ... UNUSBL
Unused Undeducted Purchase Price ... UUPP
Unusual (ROG) ... UNUSL
Unusual Aerial Sighting (ADA) ... UAS
Unusual Appearing Child [*Medicine*] ... UAC
Unusual End of Program [*Computer science*] ... UEP
Unusual Event Recording System [*Jet transport*] ... UERS
Unusual Killing Device [*Counterintelligence*] ... UKD
Unusual Occurence Report (IAA) ... UORS
Unusual Occurrence Control ... UOC
Unusual Occurrence Report (NUCP) ... UOR
Unusual Order Form (MHDI) ... UOF
Unusual Position of Limbs (DAVI) ... UPL
Unusual Visibility ... V
Unvaniezh Kevredel Breizh [*Federalist Union of Brittany - FUB*] [*France*] (EAIO) ... UKB
Unverhofft Kommt Oft [*The Unexpected Often Happens*] [*Motto of Franz, Duke of Pomerania (1577-1620)*] ... UKO

Unverified .... Unverd
Unwanted Falling Objects (MCD) .... UFO
Unwatched [*With reference to a light*] [*Maps and charts*] .... U
Unwatermarked [*Philately*] .... UnwmK
Unwatermarked (WGA) .... UNWMKD
Unwed Parents Anonymous (EA) .... UPA
Unweighted Pair-Group Method with Arithmetic Means [*Phylogenetic analysis*] .... UPGMA
Unwilling, Led by the Unqualified, Doing the Unnecessary, for the Ungrateful [*Military slogan*] (VNW) .... UUUU
Unwritten (ROG) .... UNWR
Unzendake [*Japan*] [*Seismograph station code, US Geological Survey*] (SEIS) .... UNZ
UOL Publishing, Inc. [*Associated Press*] (SAG) .... UOL Pub
UOL Publishing, Inc. [*NASDAQ symbol*] (SAG) .... UOLP
Uonquen, Bolivar [*Venezuela ICAO location identifier*] (ICLI) .... SVUQ
Uoologisk Museum .... UZM
Up [*or Upper*] .... U
Up Ad Libitum [*Ambulatory*] [*Patient may walk*] (DAVI) .... up ad lib
Up and Down Drafts [*NWS*] (FAAC) .... UDDF
Up as Tolerated [*Medicine*] (DAVI) .... UAT
Up Center (WDMC) .... uc
Up Control [*Aerospace*] (AAG) .... UCTL
Up Converter .... UC
Up Converter (IDOE) .... upconv
Up/Down (KSC) .... U/D
Up Left [*The rear left portion of a stage*] [*A stage direction*] .... UL
Up Link [*Computer science*] .... UL
Up (quark) [*Atomic physics*] .... u
Up Range [*NASA*] (KSC) .... U/R
Up Right [*The rear right portion of a stage*] [*A stage direction*] .... UR
Up Stage [*Away from audience*] [*A stage direction*] .... US
Up Stage Center [*Away from audience*] [*A stage direction*] .... USC
Up Stage Left [*Away from audience*] [*A stage direction*] .... USL
Up Stage Right [*Away from audience*] [*A stage direction*] .... USR
Up Telecommunications Switch .... UTL
Up Telemetry (MCD) .... UTLM
Up Through [*Parapsychology*] .... UT
Up Time .... UT
Up Time Ratio .... UTR
Up to Date (MAE) .... UTD
Up with People (EA) .... UWP
Upala [*Costa Rica*] [*ICAO location identifier*] (ICLI) .... MRUP
Upala [*Costa Rica*] [*Airport symbol*] (AD) .... UPA
Upala [*Costa Rica*] [*Airport symbol Obsolete*] (OAG) .... UPL
Upavon [*British ICAO location identifier*] (ICLI) .... EGDJ
Upavon [*British ICAO location identifier*] (ICLI) .... EGRJ
Up-Data Buffer [*Computer science*] .... UDB
Up-Data Link [*Computer science*] .... UDL
Update [*Computer science*] .... U
Update [*Computer science*] (NASA) .... UD
Update [*Online database field identifier*] [*Computer science*] .... UP
Update .... UPD
Update [*National Weather Service*] (FAAC) .... UPDT
Update and Ephemeria (MUGU) .... UE
Update Control List .... UCL
Update Control Process [*Telecommunications*] (TEL) .... UCP
Update Report System (TEL) .... URS
Update Software Identity (MCD) .... USI
Update State [*Online database field identifier*] .... US
Update Training File [*IRS*] .... UTRF
Update Transaction System (TEL) .... UTS
Updated (VRA) .... nd
Updated (MSA) .... UDTD
Updated Coordinating Instructions (DOMA) .... UCI
Up-Down Counter .... UDC
Updraft (MSA) .... UPDFT
Upernavik [*Greenland*] [*ICAO location identifier*] (ICLI) .... BGUP
Upernavik [*Greenland*] [*Airport symbol*] (AD) .... UPV
Upflow Anaerobic Sludge Blanket (EERA) .... UASB
Upflow Sludge Blanket [*Reactor, wastewater treatment*] .... USB
Up-Front Control Panel (MCD) .... UFCP
Up-Front Control Set (MCD) .... UFCS
Upgrade [*Computer science*] .... UPG
Upgrade Pilot Training .... UPT
Upgrade Training [*Military*] (AFM) .... UGT
Upgraded Constellation (MCD) .... UPCON
Upgraded Data Terminal (MCD) .... UDT
Upgraded Early Warning RADAR [*Military*] .... UEWR
Upgraded Tactical Information Processing System [*Computer science*] .... UTIPS
Upgraded Third-Generation Enroute Software Program [*Computer science*] (MCD) .... UGT
Upgrading Training [*Job Training and Partnership Act*] (OICC) .... UG
Upham Memorial Library, Fredericksburg, IA [*Library symbol Library of Congress*] (LCLS) .... IaFre
Uphill Ski Club of Great Britain (EAIO) .... USCGB
Uphold [*Law*] (ROG) .... UPHD
Upholster .... UPHSTR
Upholstered .... UPHD
Upholstered Furniture Action Council (EA) .... UFAC
Upholstered Furniture Manufacturers Association (EA) .... UFMA
Upholsterer .... UPHLR
Upholsterers' International Union of North America [*USWA*] [*Absorbed by*] .... UIU
Upholstering .... UPHG
Upholstering (WGA) .... UPHLSTG
Upholstering .... UPHLSTRNG
Upholstery .... UPHLSTRY
Upholstery (WGA) .... UPHOL
Upholstery and Decorative Fabrics Association of America [*Defunct*] (EA) .... UDFAA
Upholstery and Drapery Fabric Manufacturers Association [*Later, UFMA*] .... UDFMA
Upholstery Fabric Manufacturers Association [*Defunct*] (EA) .... UFMA
Upholstery Leather Group [*Later, AG*] (EA) .... ULG
Upholstry (VRA) .... uphol
Upington [*South Africa*] [*Airport symbol*] (OAG) .... UTN
Upington/Pierre Van Ryneveld [*South Africa*] [*ICAO location identifier*] (ICLI) .... FAUP
Upjohn Co. [*Research code symbol*] .... PGA
Upjohn Co. [*Research code symbol*] .... U
Upjohn Co., Business Library, Kalamazoo, MI [*Library symbol*] [*Library of Congress*] (LCLS) .... MiKUp_B
Upjohn Co., Kalamazoo, MI [*Library symbol Library of Congress*] (LCLS) ..... MiKUp
Upjohn Co., Polymer Chemicals Division Library, La Porte, TX [*Library symbol Library of Congress*] (LCLS) .... TxLapU
Upjohn Co., Technical Library, Kalamazoo, MI [*OCLC symbol*] (OCLC) .... EXU
Upkeep Period [*Navy*] (NVT) .... UPK
Upland [*Plateau, highland*] [*Board on Geographic Names*] .... UPLD
Upland, CA [*Location identifier FAA*] (FAAL) .... CCB
Upland, CA [*Location identifier FAA*] (FAAL) .... JUP
Upland, IN [*FM radio station call letters*] (RBYB) .... WTUR
Upland Public Library, Upland, CA [*Library symbol Library of Congress*] (LCLS) .... CUpl
Uplands Library, Canada Institute for Scientific and Technical Information [*Bibliotheque d'Uplands, Institut Canadien de l'Information Scientifique et Technique*] **Ottawa, Ontario** [*Library symbol National Library of Canada*] (NLC) .... OONU
UpLink .... U/L
Uplink .... UPL
Uplink (NASA) .... UPLK
Uplink Command .... UC
Uplink Frequency .... UF
Uplink Logic Module .... UPLM
Uplink Multiplexer Unit (MCD) .... UMU
Up-Link Telemetry [*NASA*] (NASA) .... UPTLM
Uplink Text and Graphics System (NASA) .... UT & GS
Upolu Point [*Hawaii*] [*Airport symbol*] (OAG) .... UPP
Upon Completion of Course of Instruction, Detach [*Navy*] .... COMPCOURDET
Upon Completion of Duty, Hereby Designated Flight Surgeon [*Navy*] .... COMPDESFLTSURG
Upon Completion of Temporary Duty and When Directed, Detach [*Navy*] .... COMTEMDIRDET
Upon Completion of Temporary Duty, Detach [*Navy*] .... COMTEMDET
Upon Completion of Temporary Duty under Instruction [*Navy*] .... COMTEMINS
Upon Completion Return Duty Station and Resume Duties [*Navy*] ...... COMPRET
Upon Completion Thereof Will Return To [*Air Force*] .... UCWR
Upon Discharge Treatment [*Military*] .... DISTREAT
Upon Receipt .... UPREC
Upon Receipt of These Orders Communicate with Transportation Officer for Priority Designator via Government Air If Available to ____ .... RECOMMTRANSO
Upper (ROG) .... U
Upper (ADA) .... UP
Upper .... UPPR
Upper (AAG) .... UPR
Upper Acceptance Limit .... UAL
Upper Advisory Area [*Aviation*] (DA) .... UAA
Upper Advisory Route [*Aviation*] (DA) .... UAD
Upper Air Control (IAA) .... UAC
Upper Air Fallout [*Civil Defense*] .... UF
Upper Air Project .... UAP
Upper Air Route .... UAR
Upper Air Space (WDAA) .... UAS
Upper Airway [*Aviation*] (DA) .... UWY
Upper Airway Obstruction [*Medicine*] (DMAA) .... UAO
Upper and Lower (MSA) .... U & L
Upper and Lower Case (NITA) .... ULC
Upper Area Control Center [*Aviation*] .... UAC
Upper Area Control Center [*Aviation*] .... UACC
Upper Area Control Center [*ICAO designator*] (ICDA) .... ZU
Upper Area Control Centre [*FAA designator*] (FAAC) .... ZUZ
Upper Arlington, OH [*FM radio station call letters*] .... WLLD
Upper Arlington Public Library, Upper Arlington, OH [*Library symbol Library of Congress*] (LCLS) .... OUa
Upper Arlington Public Library, Upper Arlington, OH [*OCLC symbol*] (OCLC) .... UAP
Upper Arm .... UA
Upper Atmosphere Geophysics (KSC) .... UAG
Upper Atmosphere Mass Spectrometer .... UAMS
Upper Atmosphere Phenomena (IAA) .... UAP
Upper Atmosphere Research .... UAR
Upper Atmosphere Research Satellite (MCD) .... UARS
Upper Atmospheric Facilities Program [*Washington, DC National Science Foundation*] (GRD) .... UAF
Upper Atmospheric Research Program [*NASA*] (PDAA) .... UARP
Upper Atmospheric Research Program [*NASA*] [*Marine science*] (OSRA)..... UARP
Upper Atmospheric Sounder .... UAS
Upper Ball Joint Suspension [*Automotive engineering*] .... UBJ
Upper Bench [*Legal*] [*British*] (ROG) .... UB

Upper Bench Precedents Tempore Car. I [*A publication*] (DLA) .... UB Pr
Upper Bench Precedents Tempore Car. I [*England*] [*A publication*] (DLA) .... Up Ben Pr
Upper Bench Precedents Tempore Car. I [*A publication*] (DLA) .... Up Ben Pre
Upper Border Zone [*Geology*] .... UBZ
Upper Bound .... UB
Upper Bound .... UPB
Upper Bound of Information Translation Amount (MHDI) .... UBITA
Upper Bow [*Music*] (ROG) .... U
Upper Brace (MCD) .... UB
Upper Branchial Filament .... UBRF
Upper Burma Rulings [*India*] [*A publication*] (DLA) .... UBR
Upper Canada .... UC
Upper Canada Appeal Reports [*A publication*] (DLA) .... UC App
Upper Canada Appeal Reports [*A publication*] (DLA) .... UC App (Can)
Upper Canada Appeal Reports [*A publication*] (DLA) .... UC App Rep
Upper Canada Chambers Reports [*1846-52*] [*Ont.*] [*A publication*] (DLA) .... Chamb Rep
Upper Canada Chambers Reports [*A publication*] (DLA) .... UC Cham
Upper Canada Chambers Reports [*1846-52*] [*A publication*] (DLA) .... UC Cham (Can)
Upper Canada Chambers Reports [*1846-52*] [*A publication*] (DLA) .... UC Chamb
Upper Canada Chancery Chambers Reports [*A publication*] (DLA) .... Ch Ch
Upper Canada Chancery Chambers Reports [*A publication*] (DLA) .... Ch Cham
Upper Canada Chancery Chambers Reports [*A publication*] (DLA) .... Ch R
Upper Canada Chancery Chambers Reports [*1857-72*] [*Ontario*] [*A publication*] (DLA) .... Chamb R
Upper Canada Chancery Chambers Reports [*A publication*] (DLA) .... Chy Ch
Upper Canada Chancery Chambers Reports [*A publication*] (DLA) .... Chy Chrs
Upper Canada Chancery Chambers Reports [*1857-72*] [*A publication*] (DLA) .... Cooper
Upper Canada Chancery Reports [*1849-82*] [*A publication*] (DLA) .... UC Ch
Upper Canada Chancery Reports [*A publication*] (DLA) .... UC Ch (Can)
Upper Canada Chancery Reports [*1849-82*] [*A publication*] (DLA) .... UC Ch Rep
Upper Canada Chancery Reports [*A publication*] (DLA) .... UC Chan
Upper Canada College .... UCC
Upper Canada Common Pleas [*Legal term*] (DLA) .... CP
Upper Canada Common Pleas Division Reports [*Ontario*] [*A publication*] (DLA) .... UCCPD
Upper Canada Common Pleas Reports [*A publication*] (DLA) .... UCCP
Upper Canada Common Pleas Reports [*A publication*] (DLA) .... UCCP (Can)
Upper Canada Common Pleas Reports [*1864-71*] [*A publication*] (DLA) .... Van K & H
Upper Canada Court Records [*Report of Ontario Bureau of Archives*] [*A publication*] (DLA) .... UCCR
Upper Canada Error and Appeal Reports [*A publication*] (DLA) .... E & A
Upper Canada Error and Appeal Reports [*1846-66*] [*A publication*] (DLA) .... UC Err & App
Upper Canada Error and Appeal Reports [*1846-66*] [*A publication*] (DLA) .... UC Err & App (Can)
Upper Canada Error and Appeal Reports [*1846-66*] [*A publication*] (DLA) .... UCE & A
Upper Canada Jurist [*A publication*] (DLA) .... UC Jur
Upper Canada Jurist [*A publication*] (DLA) .... UC Jur (Can)
Upper Canada King's Bench Reports [*A publication*] (DLA) .... KBUC
Upper Canada King's Bench Reports, Old Series [*1831-44*] [*A publication*] (DLA) .... UCKB
Upper Canada King's Bench Reports, Old Series [*1831-44*] [*A publication*] (DLA) .... UCKB (Can)
Upper Canada King's Bench Reports, Old Series [*1831-44*] [*A publication*] (DLA) .... UCOS
Upper Canada Law Journal [*1855-1922*] [*A publication*] (DLA) .... UCLJ
Upper Canada Law Journal [*A publication*] (DLA) .... UCLJ (Can)
Upper Canada Law Journal, New Series [*A publication*] (DLA) .... UCLJ NS
Upper Canada Law Journal, New Series [*A publication*] (DLA) .... UCLJ NS (Can)
Upper Canada Practice Reports [*1850-1900*] [*Ontario*] [*A publication*] (DLA) .... PR
Upper Canada Practice Reports [*A publication*] (DLA) .... UC Pr (Can)
Upper Canada Practice Reports [*A publication*] (DLA) .... UC Pr R
Upper Canada Practice Reports [*1850-1900*] [*A publication*] (DLA) .... UC Pract
Upper Canada Practice Reports [*A publication*] (DLA) .... UCPR
Upper Canada Queen's Bench Reports [*A publication*] (DLA) .... UCQB
Upper Canada Queen's Bench Reports, Old Series [*A publication*] (DLA) .... UC QB OS
Upper Canada Queen's Bench Reports, Old Series [*A publication*] (DLA) .... UC QB OS (Can)
Upper Canada Reports [*A publication*] (DLA) .... UC Rep
Upper Canada Reports [*A publication*] (DLA) .... UCR
Upper Canada Village, Morrisburg, ON, Canada [*Library symbol Library of Congress*] (LCLS) .... CaOMorUC
Upper Canada Village, Morrisburg, Ontario [*Library symbol National Library of Canada*] (NLC) .... OMUC
Upper Characters (IAA) .... UC
Upper Circulating Reflux [*Chemical engineering*] .... UCR
Upper Circulating Reflux Bottom Section [*Chemical engineering*] .... UCRB
Upper Circulating Reflux Top Section [*Chemical engineering*] .... UCRT
Upper Class - Double [*or Dual*] **Income, No Kids** [*Lifestyle classification*] .... U-Dink
Upper Confidence Level [*Industrial engineering*] (IEEE) .... UCL
Upper Confidence Limit [*Statistics*] .... UCL
Upper Control (IAA) .... UC
Upper Control Area (NATG) .... UCA
Upper Control Center (NATG) .... UCC
Upper Control Limit [*Nuclear energy*] .... UCL
Upper Critical Depth [*Oceanography*] (WDAA) .... UCD
Upper Critical End Points [*Supercritical extraction*] .... UCEP
Upper Critical Ordering Transition [*Polymer physics*] .... UCOT
Upper Critical-Solution-Temperature .... UCST
Upper Cylinder .... UC
Upper Cylinder Lubricant [*Automotive engineering*] (WDAA) .... UCL
Upper Dead Center .... UDC
Upper Deck [*Naval*] .... UD
Upper Deck .... UDK
Upper Des Moines, Algona, IA [*Library symbol Library of Congress*] (LCLS) .... IaAlgUD
Upper Earnings Limit (PDAA) .... UEL
Upper Electrical Limit [*Nuclear energy*] (NRCH) .... UEL
Upper End Fitting [*Nuclear energy*] (NRCH) .... UEF
Upper Entrance [*Theater*] .... UE
Upper Epidermal Cell [*Botany*] .... UEC
Upper Epidermis [*Botany*] .... UE
Upper Equipment Bay [*NASA*] (KSC) .... UEB
Upper Esophageal Sphincter [*Anatomy*] .... UES
Upper Esophagus [*Medicine*] (DMAA) .... UE
Upper Explosive Limit .... UEL
Upper Extremity [*Orthopedics*] (DAVI) .... u/ext
Upper Extremity [*Medicine*] .... UE
Upper Facial Height [*Medicine*] .... UFH
Upper Figure of Merit .... UFM
Upper Flammable Limit .... UFL
Upper Gastrointestinal [*Medicine*] .... UGI
Upper Gastrointestinal Bleeding [*Medicine*] .... UGIB
Upper Gastrointestinal Series [*Medicine*] (DAVI) .... UGIS
Upper Gastrointestinal Tract Hemorrhage [*Medicine*] .... UGIH
Upper Great Lakes Regional Commission [*Department of Commerce*] .... UGLRC
Upper Group Stop [*Nuclear energy*] (NRCH) .... UGS
Upper Guard Band .... UGB
Upper Guide Structure [*Nuclear energy*] (NRCH) .... UGS
Upper Half .... UH
Upper Half Assembly .... UHA
Upper Head Injection [*Nuclear energy*] (NRCH) .... UHI
Upper Hemibody Irradiation [*Radiation Therapy*] (DAVI) .... UHBI
Upper Hemispherical (MCD) .... UH
Upper Heyford [*British ICAO location identifier*] (ICLI) .... EGUA
Upper Hudson Library Federation, Albany, NY [*Library symbol Library of Congress*] (LCLS) .... NAIUHL
Upper Hudson Library Federation, Albany, NY [*OCLC symbol*] (OCLC) .... VUE
Upper Hybrid Resonance [*Spectroscopy*] .... UHR
Upper Information Center [*Aviation*] .... UIC
Upper Information Region (NATG) .... UIR
Upper Information Service (DA) .... UIS
Upper Inner Quadrant [*Anatomy*] .... UIQ
Upper Internals Structure [*Nuclear energy*] (NRCH) .... UIS
Upper Internals Structure Jacking Mechanism [*Nuclear energy*] (NRCH) .... UISJM
Upper Ionized Layer of the Ionosphere (BARN) .... F
Upper Iowa University [*Fayette*] .... UIU
Upper Iowa University, Fayette, IA [*Library symbol Library of Congress*] (LCLS) .... IaFayU
Upper Iowa University, Fayette, IA [*OCLC symbol*] (OCLC) .... IOY
Upper Island Cove Public Library, Newfoundland [*Library symbol National Library of Canada*] (NLC) .... NFUI
Upper Island Cove Public Library, Upper Island Cove, NF, Canada [*Library symbol Library of Congress*] (LCLS) .... CaNfUI
Upper Lake Library District, Upper Lake, CA [*Library symbol Library of Congress*] (LCLS) .... CUpp
Upper Laterals [*Botany*] .... UL
Upper Layer Architecture [*Telecommunications*] (OSI) .... ULA
Upper Layer Protocol [*Telecommunications*] (OSI) .... ULP
Upper Layer Thickness [*Of ocean waters*] [*Oceanography*] .... ULT
Upper Left [*S-band antenna*] (NASA) .... UL
Upper Left Center [*The rear left center portion of a stage*] [*A stage direction*] .... ULC
Upper Left Quadrant (AAMN) .... ULQ
Upper Leg .... UL
Upper Leg Vein [*Anatomy*] .... UPLV
Upper Level [*Nuclear energy*] (NRCH) .... UL
Upper Level Deck [*Cargo containers*] .... ULD
Upper Level Management Advisor (IAA) .... ULMA
Upper Limb [*Upper edge of sun, moon, etc.*] [*Navigation*] .... UL
Upper Limen [*Psychology*] .... LU
Upper Limit .... UL
Upper Limiting Frequency (ADA) .... ULF
Upper Limits of Normal [*Medicine*] .... ULN
Upper Lip Length [*Medicine*] .... ULL
Upper List (NITA) .... UL
Upper Lobe [*Anatomy*] .... UL
Upper Magazine [*Typography*] .... UM
Upper Mantle Project .... UMP
Upper Mantle Project [*Marine science*] (OSRA) .... UMP
Upper Maximum Range .... UMR
Upper Medium [*Standard & Poor's bond rating*] [*Investment term*] .... A
Upper Memory Area [*Computer science*] .... UMA
Upper Memory Block [*Computer science*] (PCM) .... UMB
Upper Merion & Plymouth Railroad Co. [*AAR code*] .... UMP
Upper Midwest .... UMW
Upper Midwest Automated Clearing House Association (MHDW) .... UMACHA
Upper Midwest Regional Educational Laboratory, Inc. .... UMREL
Upper Mississippi River Basin .... UMRB
Upper Mississippi River Conservation Committee (EA) .... UMRCC
Upper Mississippi River Environmental Management Program [*Federal government*] .... UMREMP
Upper Montclair, NJ [*FM radio station call letters*] .... WMSC

Upper Motor [*Neurons*] [*Medicine*] ... UM
Upper Motor Neurogenic Bladder [*Neurology*] (DAVI) ... UMNB
Upper Motor Neuron [*Medicine*] ... UMN
Upper Motor Neuron Lesion [*Neurology*] ... UMNL
Upper Ottawa Valley Campus Resource Centre, Algonquin College, Pembroke, Ontario [*Library symbol National Library of Canada*] (NLC) ... OPEMAC
Upper Outer Quadrant [*Anatomy*] ... UOQ
Upper Outer Tube ... UOT
Upper Outer Zone [*Also called upper outer quadrant*] [*Anatomy*] (DAVI) ... UOZ
Upper Peninsula [*Michigan*] ... UP
Upper Peninsula Energy [*NASDAQ symbol*] (TTSB) ... UPEN
Upper Peninsula Energy Corp. [*NASDAQ symbol*] (NQ) ... UPEN
Upper Peninsula Energy Corp. [*Associated Press*] (SAG) ... UPenE
Upper Peninsula Off Road Vehicle Committee [*Michigan*] ... UPORVC
Upper Peninsula Sportsmen's Alliance ... UPSA
Upper Plenum Injection [*Nuclear energy*] (NRCH) ... UPI
Upper Plenum Test Facility [*Nuclear energy*] (NRCH) ... UPTF
Upper Proof (ROG) ... UP
Upper Quadrant [*Anatomy*] ... UQ
Upper Quadrile ... UQ
Upper Rail ... UR
Upper Reference Limit [*Analytical chemistry*] ... URL
Upper Respiratory [*Medicine*] ... UR
Upper Respiratory Allergy [*Medicine*] ... URA
Upper Respiratory Disease [*Medicine*] ... URD
Upper Respiratory Infection [*Medicine*] ... URI
Upper Respiratory Tract [*Medicine*] ... URT
Upper Respiratory Tract Infection [*Medicine*] ... URTI
Upper Rib Cage [*Anatomy*] ... URC
Upper Right (MCD) ... UR
Upper Right Center (WGA) ... URC
Upper Right Quadrant [*Medicine*] ... URQ
Upper Room Devotional Library and Museum, Nashville, TN [*Library symbol Library of Congress*] (LCLS) ... TNU
Upper Saddle River Historical Committee, Upper Saddle River, NJ [*Library symbol Library of Congress*] (LCLS) ... NjUsrHi
Upper Sandusky, OH [*FM radio station call letters*] ... WXML
Upper Sandusky, OH [*FM radio station call letters*] ... WYNT
Upper School [*British*] ... U
Upper Sequential Permissive [*Nuclear energy*] (NRCH) ... USP
Upper Sideband [*Telecommunications*] (EECA) ... UPS
Upper Sideband ... USB
Upper Sideband Upconverter (IAA) ... USBUC
Upper Solution Point ... USP
Upper Specified Limit ... USL
Upper Square Law Limit (IAA) ... USL
Upper Stage (MCD) ... US
Upper Sternal Border [*Anatomy*] (DAVI) ... USB
Upper Surface Blowing Technique [*Aviation*] (DA) ... USBT
Upper Surface Blown [*Jet flap*] [*Aviation*] ... USB
Upper Terminal Area (NATG) ... UTA
Upper Testing Area (IAA) ... UTA
Upper Thames Patrol [*British military*] (DMA) ... UTP
Upper Third [*Referring to long bones*] [*Medicine*] (DAVI) ... U/3
Upper Tibial Osteotomy [*Medicine*] (DMAA) ... UTO
Upper Torso ... UT
Upper Torso Restraint Assembly ... UTRA
Upper Tractor (ECII) ... UT
Upper Transition Altitude (SAA) ... UTAL
Upper Trip Point ... UTP
Upper Turning Point ... UTP
Upper Turret Half ... UTH
Upper Vas Deferens [*Anatomy*] ... UVD
Upper Vas Deferens-Seminal Vesicle Complex [*Anatomy*] ... UVD-SV
Upper Volta [*MARC geographic area code Library of Congress*] (LCCP) ... f-uv--
Upper Volta [*MARC country of publication code Library of Congress*] (LCCP) ... uv
Upper Winds [*Meteorology*] (FAAC) ... UWNDS
Upper Yarra Valley and Dandenong Regional Authority [*of Victoria*] [*State*] (EERA) ... UYVDRA
Upper Zone [*Geology*] ... UZ
Upper-Air Observation (SAA) ... UAO
Upper-Airway Disease (DAVI) ... UAD
Uppercase [*Typography*] (ADA) ... UC
Uppercase and Lowercase [*i.e., capital and small letters*] [*Typography*] ... U & LC
Upper-Class Speech [*"Non-U" designates the opposite*] ... U
Upper-Limb Disorder [*Medicine*] (ECON) ... ULD
Upper-Limit, Lower-Limit (SAA) ... UL-LL
Upper-Limit, Lower-Limit Comparator (SAA) ... UL-LLC
Upper-Respiratory-Tract Infection [*Medicine*] (DAVI) ... URI
Upper-Sideband, Suppressed-Carrier (IDOE) ... USSC
Upper-Stage Guidance Experiment ... UPSTAGE
Upper-Stage Reusable Payload ... URP
Upperville, VA [*Location identifier FAA*] (FAAL) ... GDX
Uppity Women [*An association*] (EA) ... UW
Uppsala [*Sweden ICAO location identifier*] (ICLI) ... ESCM
Uppsala [*Sweden*] [*Seismograph station code, US Geological Survey*] (SEIS) ... UPP
Uppsala/Akademiska [*Sweden ICAO location identifier*] (ICLI) ... ESHU
Uppsala University Institute of Physics [*Sweden*] ... UUIP
Uppsala Virus [*Medicine*] (MAE) ... Uv
Uprange Computer Input System ... UCIS
Uprange Computer Output System ... UCOS
Upravleniye Osobykh Otdelov [*Armed Forces Counterintelligence-Directorate*] [*Former USSR*] (LAIN) ... UOO
Upright (MSA) ... URT
Upright Drilling Machine ... UDM
Upright Perigee Stage [*Aerospace*] (MCD) ... UPS
Upright Posture (MAE) ... UP
Uprighting Subsystem [*NASA*] (KSC) ... US
Upsala College, East Orange, NJ [*Library symbol Library of Congress*] (LCLS) ... NjEoU
Upsala Elementary School, Upsala, MN [*Library symbol*] [*Library of Congress*] (LCLS) ... MnUpE
Upsala High School, Upsala, MN [*Library symbol*] [*Library of Congress*] (LCLS) ... MnUpH
Upsalquitch Lake, NB [*Television station call letters*] ... CKAM
Upset Price [*Business term*] (MHDB) ... UP
Upset Welding ... UW
Upset Welding-High Frequency ... UW-HF
Upset Welding-Induction ... UW-I
Upsher-Smith [*Commercial firm*] (DAVI) ... Upsher-S
Upshur's Review of Story on the Constitution [*A publication*] (DLA) ... Ups Sto
Upside-Down Flipper ... UDF
Upsilon [*Symbol*] [*Quantum physics*] ... Y
Upslope [*NWS*] (FAAC) ... UPSLP
Upstage (WDMC) ... U
Upstate Medical Center, Syracuse, NY [*OCLC symbol*] (OCLC) ... VYQ
Upstream [*Meteorology*] (FAAC) ... UPSTRM
Upstream (NTCM) ... US
Upstream Activating Sequence [*Genetics*] ... UAS
Upstream Activation Site [*Genetics*] ... UAS
Upstream Binding Factor [*Genetics*] ... UBF
Upstream Control Element [*Genetics*] ... UCE
Upstream Control Region [*Biochemistry*] ... UCR
Upstream Expression Sequence [*Genetics*] ... UES
Upstream Failure Indication (NITA) ... UFI
Upstream Heat Exchanger (AAG) ... USHE
Upstream Modulation Sequence [*Genetics*] ... UMS
Upstream Promoter Element [*Genetics*] ... UPE
Upstream Regulatory Region [*Genetics*] ... URR
Upstream Stimulatory Factor [*Genetics*] ... USF
Uptake Signal Sequence [*Genetics*] ... USS
Upton, KY [*FM radio station call letters*] (RBYB) ... WJCR-FM
Upton on Maritime Warfare and Prize [*A publication*] (DLA) ... Upt Mar W
Upton on Trade-Marks [*A publication*] (DLA) ... Upt Tr Mar
UPU [*Universal Postal Union*] **Staff Association** (EAIO) ... UPUSA
Upward (MSA) ... UPWD
Upward Bound Programs [*Department of Labor*] ... UBP
Upward Light Output Ratio (PDAA) ... ULOR
Upward Mobility Program ... UMP
Upward-Looking SONAR ... ULS
Upwind [*Aviation*] (FAAC) ... UW
'Uqsin (BJA) ... Uqs
Ur Excavations [*A publication*] (BJA) ... UEX
Ur Excavations: Texts [*London*] [*A publication*] (BJA) ... UET
Uraba, Medellin & Central Airways, Inc. ... UMCA
Uracil [*Biochemistry*] (MAE) ... U
Uracil [*Biochemistry*] ... Ura
Uracil Adenine Adenine [*Genetics*] ... UAA
Uracil Adenine Guanine [*Genetics*] ... UAG
Uracil Arabinoside [*Biochemistry*] ... ara-U
Uracil DNA [*Deoxyribonucleic acid*] ... UDG
Uracil DNA Glycosylase [*An enzyme*] ... UDG
Uracil Guanine Adenine [*Genetics*] ... UGA
Uracil Monophosphate [*Biochemistry*] (AAMN) ... UMP
Uracil Mustard [*Antineoplastic drug*] (AAMN) ... UM
Uraiavia [*Former USSR*] [*FAA designator*] (FAAC) ... URV
Urakawa [*Japan*] [*Seismograph station code, US Geological Survey*] (SEIS) ... URA
Ural [*Former USSR*] [*FAA designator*] (FAAC) ... URW
Ural Airlines [*Former USSR*] [*FAA designator*] (FAAC) ... SVR
Ural Commodity Exchange [*Russian Federation*] (EY) ... UCE
Ural Region, RSFSR [*MARC geographic area code Library of Congress*] (LCCP) ... e-uru-
Uralavialy [*Russian Federation*] [*ICAO designator*] (FAAC) ... URL
Uralic and Altaic Studies Department [*Indiana University*] [*Research center*] (RCD) ... DUAS
Uralinteravia [*Russian Federation*] [*ICAO designator*] (FAAC) ... URA
Urals Research Center for Radiation Medicine [*Russia*] ... URCRM
Uralsk [*Former USSR ICAO location identifier*] (ICLI) ... UARR
Urambo [*Tanzania*] [*ICAO location identifier*] (ICLI) ... HTUR
Uranerz Exploration & Mining Ltd., Saskatoon, Saskatchewan [*Library symbol National Library of Canada*] (NLC) ... SSUEM
Uranerz Exploration & Mining Ltd., Saskatoon, SK, Canada [*Library symbol Library of Congress*] (LCLS) ... CaSSUEM
Urania [*Record label*] [*USA, Europe, etc.*] ... Ura
Uranian Electrostatic Discharge [*Planetary science*] ... UED
Uranian Kilometric Radiation [*Planetary science*] ... UKR
Uranium [*Chemical element*] ... U
Uranium (ROG) ... UR
Uranium ... URNM
Uranium Canada Ltd. ... UC
Uranium Carbide [*Inorganic chemistry*] (OA) ... UC
Uranium City [*Canada*] [*Airport symbol*] (OAG) ... YBE
Uranium Dioxide ... UO2
Uranium Enrichment Associates [*Bechtel Corp., Union Carbide Corp., Westinghouse Electric Corp.*] ... UEA
Uranium Hexafluoride ... UF6
Uranium Institute [*British*] (EAIO) ... UI
Uranium Institute of America (EA) ... UIA

Uranium Mill Tailings (GAAI) .... UMT
Uranium Mill Tailings Radiation Control Act (GFGA) .... UMTRCA
Uranium Mill Trailings Remedial Action Program [*Department of Energy*] .... UMTRAP
Uranium Off-Gas Filter [*Nuclear energy*] (NRCH) .... UOGF
Uranium Ore Concentrate .... UOC
Uranium Ore Processing Association .... UOPA
Uranium Policy Review Committee [*Australia*] .... UPRC
Uranium Product Loadout [*Nuclear energy*] (NRCH) .... UPL
Uranium Production Reactor [*Nuclear energy*] .... UPR
Uranium Recycle Acid [*Nuclear energy*] (NRCH) .... URA
Uranium Resources [*NASDAQ symbol*] (TTSB) .... URIX
Uranium Resources, Inc. [*Associated Press*] (SAG) .... UranRes
Uranium Resources, Inc. [*Vancouver Stock Exchange symbol*] .... URI
Uranium Resources, Inc. [*NASDAQ symbol*] (NQ) .... URIX
Uranium Series Dating .... USD
Uranium Supply - Import Model [*Department of Energy*] (GFGA) .... USI
Uranium Tetrafluoride in Kiln [*Nuclear energy*] (NUCP) .... UTK
Uranium Ventilation Scrubber Cell [*Nuclear energy*] (NRCH) .... UVSC
Uranium-233 .... U-233
Uranium-234 .... U-234
Uranium-235 .... U-235
Uranium-236 .... U-236
Uranium-238 .... U-238
Uranium-Thorium Dating .... UTD
Uranus [*Astronomy*] (BARN) .... Uran
Uranyl Ammonium Phosphate [*Inorganic chemistry*] (SAA) .... UA
Uranyl Hexahydrate Nitrate (GFGA) .... UHN
Uranyl Nitrate Concentrate [*Nuclear energy*] .... UNC
Uranyl Nitrate Hexahydrate [*Inorganic chemistry*] .... UNH
Urasenke Tea Ceremony Society (EA) .... UTCS
Uravan Public Library, Uravan, CO [*Library symbol Library of Congress*] (LCLS) .... CoUr
Urban [*District Council*] [*British*] .... U
Urban .... URB
Urban Affairs Association (EA) .... UAA
Urban Affairs Institute (EA) .... UAI
Urban Affairs Reporter [*Commerce Clearing House*] [*A publication*] (DLA) .... Urb Aff Rep
Urban Airshed Model [*Environmental Protection Agency*] (GFGA) .... UAM
Urban and Economic Development Ltd. (AIE) .... URBED
Urban and Industrial Health (KSC) .... UIH
Urban and Regional Information System .... URIS
Urban and Regional Information Systems Association (EA) .... URISA
Urban and Regional Informations Systems Association .... URISA
Urban and Regional Planning Information Systems (EERA) .... URPIS
Urban and Rural Commuter Service [*MOCD*] (TAG) .... UCRS
Urban and Rural Systems Associates .... URSA
Urban Area (NTCM) .... UA
Urban Arts Theatre (EA) .... UAT
Urban Association [*Baseball*] .... U
Urban Bikeway Design Collaborative (EA) .... UBDC
Urban Combat Computer-Assisted Training System .... UCCATS
[*The*] **Urban Communications Game** .... URBCOM
Urban Comprehensive Health Care Information System (PDAA) .... UCHCIS
Urban Contemporary (WDMC) .... UC
Urban Council [*British*] (BARN) .... UC
Urban Crime Prevention Program [*Federal government*] .... UCPP
Urban Data Service [*International City Management Association*] (IID) .... UDS
Urban Decision Systems, Inc. [*Information service or system*] (IID) .... UDS
Urban Development Action Grant [*HUD*] .... UDAG
Urban Development Agency [*British*] .... UDA
Urban Development Bank .... URBANK
Urban Development Committee [*New South Wales, Australia*] .... UDC
Urban Development Corp. [*New York State agency*] .... UDC
Urban Development Institute [*Australia*] .... UDI
Urban Development Program [*University of Western Ontario*] [*Canada*] (IRC) .... UDP
Urban District .... UD
Urban District Council [*British*] .... UDC
Urban Dynamometer Driving Schedule [*EPA engine test*] .... UDDS
Urban Education [*Educational Resources Information Center (ERIC) Clearinghouse*] [*Columbia University*] (PAZ) .... UD
Urban Education [*A publication*] (BRI) .... Urban Ed
Urban Elderly Coalition (EA) .... UEC
Urban Environment Conference (EA) .... UEC
Urban Export Advisory Working Group [*Australia*] .... UEAWG
Urban Federation for Music Therapists [*Later, AAMT*] (EA) .... UFMT
Urban Fighting Weapon (MCD) .... UFW
Urban Forests [*A publication*] .... Urb For
Urban Gorillas (EA) .... UG
Urban Growth Boundary .... UGB
Urban History Group [*Defunct*] (EA) .... UHG
Urban Homesteading Assistance Board (EA) .... UHAB
Urban Homesteading Program Management Information System [*Department of Housing and Urban Development*] (GFGA) .... UHPMIS
Urban Impact Analysis (EG) .... UIA
Urban Information Center [*Milwaukee Urban Observatory*] [*Ceased operations*] [*Information service or system*] (IID) .... UIC
Urban Information Interpreters, Inc. (IID) .... UIII
Urban Information System (EERA) .... UIS
Urban Information Systems Inter-Agency Committee [*HUD Terminated*] (EGAO) .... USAC
Urban Initiatives (EA) .... UI
Urban Institute (EA) .... UI
Urban Institute, Washington, DC [*Library symbol Library of Congress*] (LCLS) .... DUrl
Urban Intelligence Reports (CINC) .... UIR
Urban Land (Ceiling and Regulation) Act [*India*] (ECON) .... ULCRA
[*The*] **Urban Land Institute** [*An association*] (EAAP) .... ULI
Urban Land Research Foundation (EA) .... ULRF
Urban Law and Policy [*A publication*] (ILCA) .... Urblaw
Urban Law Annual [*A publication*] (ILCA) .... Urban Law Ann
Urban Law Institute of Antioch School of Law [*Defunct*] (EA) .... ULI
Urban Law Review [*A publication*] (DLA) .... Urban L Rev
Urban League (MCD) .... UL
Urban Libraries Council (EA) .... ULC
Urban Library Trustees Council [*Later, ULC*] (EA) .... ULTC
Urban Management Information System .... UMIS
Urban Mass Transportation Act [*1964*] .... UMTA
Urban Mass Transportation Administration [*Department of Transportation*] .... UMTA
Urban Mass Transportation Research Information Service [*National Academy of Sciences*] [*Database*] (IID) .... UMTRIS
Urban Ministry Network [*Melbourne, Victoria, Australia*] .... UMN
Urban Outfitters, Inc. [*NASDAQ symbol*] (SAG) .... URBN
Urban Outfitters, Inc. [*Associated Press*] (SAG) .... UrbnOut
Urban Outfittlers [*NASDAQ symbol*] (TTSB) .... URBN
Urban Park and Recreation Recovery .... UPARR
Urban Planning Assistance Program .... UPAP
Urban Planning Directorate [*British*] .... UPD
Urban Planning Ministers Conference (EERA) .... UPMC
Urban Population File (MCD) .... URBPOP
Urban Programme Authority [*Education*] (AIE) .... UPA
Urban Rat [*Virus*] .... UR
Urban Redevelopment Authority .... URA
Urban Regeneration Grant [*British*] .... URG
Urban Regional Development Unit (EERA) .... URDU
Urban Renewal Administration [*of HHFA*] [*Terminated*] .... URA
Urban Renewal Handbook .... URHB
Urban Renewal Manual .... URM
Urban Renewal Project [*HUD*] (OICC) .... URP
Urban Research Centre on Office Technology [*Australia*] .... URCOT
Urban Resource Systems (EA) .... URS
Urban Resources Development Agency (OICC) .... URDA
Urban Sanitary Authority [*British*] .... USA
Urban Sanitary District [*British*] .... USD
Urban Scientific and Educational Research, Inc. [*Defunct*] (EA) .... USER INC
Urban Shopping Centers [*NYSE symbol*] (SPSG) .... URB
Urban Shopping Centers [*Associated Press*] (SAG) .... UrbnShp
Urban Studies Project .... USP
Urban Technology Conference .... UTC
Urban Telephone Network (OA) .... UTN
Urban Tracked Air-Cushion Vehicle [*Transit*] [*Department of Transportation*] .... UTACV
Urban Traffic Control System .... UTCS
Urban Training Center .... UTC
Urban Transport Planning System [*Australia*] .... UTPS
Urban Transportation Administration [*HUD*] .... UTA
Urban Transportation Assistance Program [*Canada*] .... UTAP
Urban Transportation Development Corp. [*Canada*] .... UTDC
Urban Transportation Development Corp., Kingston, ON, Canada [*Library symbol Library of Congress*] (LCLS) .... CaOKUTD
Urban Transportation Development Corp., Kingston, Ontario [*Library symbol National Library of Canada*] (NLC) .... OKUTD
Urban Transportation Development Corp., Toronto, ON, Canada [*Library symbol Library of Congress*] (LCLS) .... CaOTUTD
Urban Transportation Development Corp., Toronto, Ontario [*Library symbol National Library of Canada*] (NLC) .... OTUTD
Urban Transportation Modeling System [*TRB*] (TAG) .... UTMS
Urban Transportation Planning [*Department of Transportation*] (GFGA) .... UTP
Urban Transportation Planning Laboratory [*University of Pennsylvania*] [*Research center*] (RCD) .... UTPL
Urban Transportation Planning Package [*Bureau of the Census*] (GFGA) .... UTPP
Urban Vehicle Design Competition .... UVDC
Urban Water Research Association (EERA) .... UWRA
Urban Wildlife Research Center (EA) .... UWRC
Urbana College, Urbana, OH [*Library symbol Library of Congress*] (LCLS) .... OUrC
Urbana College, Urbana, OH [*OCLC symbol*] (OCLC) .... URB
Urbana Community Unit School District, Urbana, IL [*Library symbol*] [*Library of Congress*] (LCLS) .... IUrSD
Urbana Free Library, Urbana, IL [*Library symbol Library of Congress*] (LCLS) .... IUr
Urbana, IL [*AM radio station call letters*] .... WBCP
Urbana, IL [*Television station call letters*] .... WCCU
Urbana, IL [*AM radio station call letters*] .... WILL
Urbana, IL [*FM radio station call letters*] .... WILL-FM
Urbana, IL [*TV station call letters*] (RBYB) .... WILL-TV
Urbana, IL [*FM radio station call letters*] .... WKIO
Urbana, IL [*FM radio station call letters*] .... WPGU
Urbana Junior College [*Ohio*] .... UJC
Urbana, OH [*FM radio station call letters*] .... WKSW
Urbandale News, Urbandale, IA [*Library symbol*] [*Library of Congress*] (LCLS) .... IaUrN
Urbandale Public Library, Urbandale, IA [*Library symbol Library of Congress*] (LCLS) .... IaUr
Urbandale Public Library, Urbandale, IA [*Library symbol*] [*Library of Congress*] (LCLS) .... IaUrP
Urbanisme, Amenagement, Equipments, et Transports [*Reseau URBAMET*] [*France Information service or system*] (CRD) .... URBAMET

Urbanization ... URB
Urbanized Area (OICC) ... UA
Urbanized Area [*APTA*] [*FHWA*] (TAG) ... UZA
Urbis Conditae [*From the Foundation of the City; that is, of Rome*] [*Latin*] ... UC
Urdu [*Language*] (BARN) ... Ur
Urdu [*MARC language code Library of Congress*] (LCCP) ... urd
Urea Briquettes [*Agronomy*] ... UB
Urea Clearance [*Biochemistry*] (DAVI) ... C_u
Urea Clearance [*Clinical chemistry*] ... UC
Urea Clearance [*Test*] [*Medicine*] ... UCL
Urea Dialysance [*Medicine*] (MAE) ... Du
Urea Formaldehyde ... UF
Urea Inclusion Compound [*Chemistry*] ... UIC
Urea Kinetic Modeling [*Dialysis*] (CPH) ... UKM
Urea Nitrogen [*Laboratory science*] (DAVI) ... UREA
Urea Phosphate (OA) ... UP
Urea (Prilled) in Paper Packets [*Agronomy*] ... UPP
Urea Reduction Ratio ... URR
Urea-Ammonia Liquor ... UAL
Urea-Ammonium Nitrate [*Fertilizer*] ... UAN
Urea-Ammonium Nitrate Ammonium Sulfate [*Fertilizer*] ... UANAS
Urea-Ammonium Phosphate [*Organic chemistry*] ... UAP
Urea-Ammonium Sulfate [*Fertilizer*] ... UAS
Urea-Formaldehyde Foam Insulation ... UFFI
Urea-Nitrogen [*Medicine*] ... UN
Ureteral Back Pressure [*Medicine*] (MAE) ... UBP
Ureteral Orifice [*Anatomy*] (MAE) ... UO
Ureteral-Intestinal [*Medicine*] (DAVI) ... UI
Ureteropelvic [*Anatomy*] ... UP
Ureteropelvic Junction [*Anatomy*] ... UPJ
Ureterovesical [*Urology*] (DAVI) ... UV
Ureterovesical Angle [*Urology*] (DAVI) ... UVA
Ureterovesical Junction [*Anatomy*] (MAE) ... UVJ
Urethane Foam Contractors Association [*Defunct*] (EA) ... UFCA
Urethane Institute, Society of the Plastics Industry (EA) ... UISPI
Urethane Mixing Equipment ... UME
Urethane Technologies [*NASDAQ symbol*] (TTSB) ... UTEC
Urethane Technologies, Inc. [*Associated Press*] (SAG) ... Urethane
Urethane Technologies, Inc. [*NASDAQ symbol*] (SAG) ... UTEC
Urethra [*Anatomy*] ... ureth
Urethral and Cervical [*Medicine*] ... U & C
Urethral Catheter in [*Medicine*] (CPH) ... UCI
Urethral Catheter Out [*Medicine*] (MAE) ... UCO
Urethral Catheterization [*Medicine*] (MAE) ... UC
Urethral Discharge [*Medicine*] ... UD
Urethral Manipulation Syndrome [*Urology*] (DAVI) ... UMS
Urethral Pressure Profile [*Urology*] (DAVI) ... UPP
Urethral Profile at Rest [*Medicine*] ... UPR
Urethral Profile under Stress [*Medicine*] ... UPS
Urethrovesical [*Urology*] (DAVI) ... UV
Urethrovesical Angle [*Urology*] (DAVI) ... UVA
Urfa [*Turkey ICAO location identifier*] (ICLI) ... LTCH
Urfa [*Turkey*] [*Airport symbol*] (AD) ... URF
Urgench [*Former USSR Airport symbol*] (OAG) ... UGC
Urgency Justification Code [*Military*] (AFIT) ... UJC
Urgency of Need (MCD) ... UON
Urgency of Need Designator [*Military*] (AFM) ... UND
Urgent ... U
Urgent ... UGT
Urgent (AFM) ... URG
Urgent Action Service International [*British Library*] ... UAS
Urgent Amplified Failure of Unsatisfactory Report ... UAFUR
Urgent Care Center [*Medicine*] ... UCC
Urgent Data Request [*GIDEP*] ... UDR
Urgent Operation Requirement ... UOR
Urgent Postal Telegram ... UPT
Urgent Requirement (MCD) ... UR
Urgoon [*Afghanistan*] [*ICAO location identifier*] (ICLI) ... OAOG
Urheberrechtsgesetz [*German Copyright Act*] (DLA) ... URG
Urho Kekkonen [*President of Finland*] ... UKK
Uribe [*Colombia*] [*Airport symbol Obsolete*] (OAG) ... URI
Uric Acid ... UA
Uric Acid (DAVI) ... UAC
Uric Acid [*Laboratory science*] (DAVI) ... URC A
Uric Acid Nitrogen ... UAN
Uric Acid-Creatinine Ratio [*Physiology*] (MAH) ... UA/C
Uric Acid-Urine Spot [*test*] [*Laboratory science*] (DAVI) ... URC SP
Uridine [*One-letter symbol; see Urd*] ... U
Uridine [*Also, U*] [*A nucleoside*] ... Urd
Uridine Diphosphate [*Biochemistry*] (AAMN) ... UD
Uridine Diphosphate [*Biochemistry*] ... UDP
Uridine Diphosphate Galactose [*Biochemistry*] (MAH) ... UDPgal
Uridine Diphosphate Glucose [*Biochemistry*] ... UDPG
Uridine Diphosphate Glucose [*Biochemistry*] (DAVI) ... UDPglu
Uridine Diphosphate Glucuronic Acid [*Biochemistry*] ... UDPGA
Uridine Diphosphate Glucuronosyltransferase [*An enzyme Biochemistry*] ... UDPGT
Uridine Diphosphoglucose Pyrophosphorylase [*An enzyme*] ... UGPP
Uridine Diribose Phosphate [*Biochemistry*] ... UDRP
Uridine Monophosphate [*Biochemistry*] ... UMP
Uridine Phosphorylase [*An enzyme*] ... UP
Uridine Triphosphatase [*An enzyme*] ... UTP
Uridine Triphosphatase [*An enzyme*] ... UTPase
Uridine Triphosphate [*Biochemistry*] ... UTP
Uridine(diphospho)acetylglucosamine [*Biochemistry*] ... UDPAG
Uridinediphosphoglucose Dehydrogenase [*An enzyme*] ... UDPGDH
Uriman [*Venezuela*] [*Airport symbol*] (OAG) ... URM
Uriman, Bolivar [*Venezuela ICAO location identifier*] (ICLI) ... SVUM
Urin Glucose Spot [*Test*] [*Endocrinology*] (DAVI) ... GLUC-S
Urinal (ROG) ... U
Urinal (MSA) ... UR
Urinal Water Closet (MSA) ... URWC
Urinalysis [*Medicine*] (KSC) ... UA
Urinalysis-Routine and Microscopic [*Urology*] (DAVI) ... UR & M
Urinary Ammonium (DAVI) ... U_{NH4+}
Urinary Basement Membrane Antigen [*Immunology*] (DAVI) ... UA
Urinary Calcium Excretion [*Laboratory science*] (DAVI) ... $U_{Ca}V$
Urinary Catheter [*Medicine*] ... UC
Urinary Catheter In [*or Input*] [*Medicine*] ... UCI
Urinary Catheter Out [*or Output*] [*Medicine*] ... UCO
Urinary Chorionic Gonadotrophin [*Endocrinology*] ... UCG
Urinary Coproporphyrin [*Urology*] ... UCP
Urinary Coproporphyrin Test [*Urology*] ... UCPT
Urinary C-Peptide [*Urology*] ... UCP
Urinary Energy [*Nutrition*] ... UE
Urinary Follicle-Stimulating Hormone [*Medicine*] (DMAA) ... uFSH
Urinary Free Cortisol ... UFC
Urinary Immune Complex ... UIC
Urinary Infection [*Medicine*] ... UI
Urinary Kallikrein [*Medicine*] (DMAA) ... UK
Urinary Muramidase Activity [*Medicine*] (DMAA) ... UMA
Urinary Nitrogen [*Medicine*] (DAVI) ... UN
Urinary Nitrogen Appearance (DAVI) ... UNA
Urinary Osmolality Maximum [*Physiology*] (MAH) ... Umax
Urinary Osmolarity [*Medicine*] ... UOSM
Urinary Output [*Medicine*] ... UO
Urinary Stress Incontinence [*Urology*] (DAVI) ... USI
Urinary Titratable Acidity [*Laboratory science*] (DAVI) ... U_{TA}
Urinary Tract [*Medicine*] ... UT
Urinary Tract Infection [*Medicine*] ... UTI
Urinary Urea Nitrogen [*Clinical medicine*] ... UUN
Urinary Volume [*Physiology*] ... UV
Urinate [*or Urine*] [*Medicine*] ... U
Urine (DAVI) ... U
Urine ... UR
Urine (NASA) ... URN
Urine Analysis [*or Urinalysis*] [*Urology*] (DAVI) ... ur anal
Urine Cadmium Level ... UCd
Urine Collection and Pretreatment Unit (NASA) ... UCPU
Urine Collection Device [*NASA*] (MCD) ... UCD
Urine Collection System [*NASA*] (KSC) ... UCS
Urine Collection/Transfer Assembly [*Apollo*] [*NASA*] ... UCTA
Urine Culture [*Clinical chemistry*] (MAE) ... U/C
Urine Culture [*Urology*] (DAVI) ... UCX
Urine Culture Tube [*Clinical chemistry*] ... UCT
Urine Disposal Lock (DNAB) ... UDL
Urine Drug Screen [*Medicine*] ... UDS
Urine - Fasting [*Urology*] (DAVI) ... UR-FST
Urine Flow Rate ... UFR
Urine Glutamic-Oxaloacetic Transaminase [*An enzyme*] ... UGOT
Urine - Number of Hours/Glucose Tolerance [*The symbol is replaced with the correct numeral*] [*Endocrinology*] (DAVI) ... UR#HR
Urine Output [*Physiology*] ... UOP
Urine Pregnancy Test [*Gynecology*] (DAVI) ... UPT
Urine Protein Electrophoresis [*Biochemistry*] (DAVI) ... UPEP
Urine Receptacle Assembly [*NASA*] (MCD) ... URA
Urine Sample Volume Measurement System (MCD) ... USVMS
Urine Sampling and Collection System [*NASA*] ... USCS
Urine Sodium [*Nephrology*] (DAVI) ... UNa
Urine Sodium [*Medicine*] (DAVI) ... $U_{Na}V$
Urine Sodium Excretion [*Medicine*] (DAVI) ... $U_{Na}V$
Urine Specimen Volume Measuring Device ... USVMD
Urine Urobilin [*Clinical chemistry*] (DAVI) ... UU
Urine Urobilinogen [*Clinical chemistry*] ... UU
Urine Uroporphyrin [*Medicine*] (MAE) ... UUP
Urine Volume [*Urology*] (DAVI) ... UR VOL
Urine-Plasma Ratio [*Clinical chemistry*] ... U/P
Urine-Time [*Urology*] (DAVI) ... UR-TIM
Urine-Transfer System [*Apollo*] [*NASA*] ... UTS
Urkunde [*Document, Deed, Instrument*] [*German*] (ILCA) ... Urk
Urkunden der Ptolemaerzeit [*U. Wilcken*] [*A publication*] (BJA) ... UPz
Urkunden des Aegyptischen Altertums [*G. Steindorff*] [*Leipzig*] [*A publication*] (BJA) ... Urk
Urling on Foreign Patents [*A publication*] (DLA) ... Url For Pat
Urling on the Office of a Trustee [*A publication*] (DLA) ... Url Trust
Urling's Legal Guide for the Clergy [*A publication*] (DLA) ... Url Cl
Urner-Barry Publications, Jersey City, NJ [*Library symbol Library of Congress*] (LCLS) ... NjJUB
Urobilinogen [*Medicine*] (MAE) ... UBG
Urobilinogen [*Medicine*] (DAVI) ... UROBIL
Urobilinogen-2 Hour [*Gastroenterology*] (DAVI) ... URO-2H
Urocanic Acid [*Organic chemistry*] (AAMN) ... UA
UroCor Inc. [*NASDAQ symbol*] (TTSB) ... UCOR
UroCor, Inc. [*NASDAQ symbol*] (SAG) ... UCOR
UroCor, Inc. [*Associated Press*] (SAG) ... UroCor
Urocortin [*Neurochemistry*] ... UCN
Urogenital [*Medicine*] ... UG
Urogenital [*Medicine*] (CPH) ... uro-gen
Urogenital Mesenchyme [*Medicine*] ... UGM
Urogenital Sinus [*Anatomy*] ... UGS

Urogenital System [*Medicine*] ..... UGS
Urogenital Tract [*Medicine*] ..... UGT
UROHEALTH Sys Wrrt [*AMEX symbol*] (TTSB) ..... DVSWS
UROHEALTH Systems, Inc. [*AMEX symbol*] (SAG) ..... URO
UROHEALTH Systems, Inc. [*Associated Press*] (SAG) ..... Urohlt
UROHEALTH Systems, Inc. [*Associated Press*] (SAG) ..... Urohlth
UROHEALTH Systems'A'(New) [*AMEX symbol*] (TTSB) ..... URO
Urokeinase Plasminogen Activator [*Biochemistry*] ..... UPAR
Urokinase [*An enzyme*] ..... UK
Urokinase Plasminogen Activator [*An enzyme*] ..... UPA
Urokinase Pulmonary Embolism Trial ..... UPET
Urokinase-Type Plasminogen Activator Receptor [*Biochemistry*] ..... UPAR
Urological Rehabilitation and Research Center [*University of Alabama in Birmingham*] [*Research center*] (RCD) ..... URRC
Urological Surgery [*Medical specialty*] (DHSM) ..... U
Urologist (DAVI) ..... U
Urologix Inc. [*NASDAQ symbol*] (TTSB) ..... ULGX
Urologix, Inc. [*NASDAQ symbol*] (SAG) ..... ULGX
Urologix, Inc. [*Associated Press*] (SAG) ..... Urologix
Urology (DAVI) ..... U
Urology [*Medical Officer designation*] [*British*] ..... U
Urology ..... UR
Urology ..... URO
Urology ..... URO
Urology ..... UROL
Uromed Corp. [*NASDAQ symbol*] (SAG) ..... URMD
Uromed Corp. [*Associated Press*] (SAG) ..... Uromed
Uromiyeh [*Iran*] [*ICAO location identifier*] (ICLI) ..... OITR
Uromodulin ..... UM
Uroozgan [*Afghanistan*] [*Airport symbol Obsolete*] (OAG) ..... URZ
Uroporphyrin [*Biochemistry*] ..... UP
Uroporphyrin [*Biochemistry*] ..... URO
Uroporphyrin Isomerase [*An enzyme*] (AAMN) ..... UI
Uroporphyrinogen [*Biochemistry*] (MAE) ..... UPG
Uroporphyrinogen [*Biochemistry*] ..... URO
Uroporphyrinogen [*Biochemistry*] ..... UROGEN
Uroporphyrinogen Decarboxylase [*Also, UDase*] [*An enzyme*] ..... UD
Uroporphyrinogen Decarboxylase [*Also, UD*] [*An enzyme*] ..... UDase
Uroporphyrinogen I Synthase [*An enzyme*] ..... UROS
UroQuest Medical Corp. [*NASDAQ symbol*] (SAG) ..... UROQ
UroQuest Medical Corp. [*Associated Press*] (SAG) ..... UroQst
Urostomy Association [*British*] (DBA) ..... UA
Urrao [*Colombia*] [*Airport symbol*] (OAG) ..... URR
URS Corp. [*NYSE symbol*] (SPSG) ..... URS
Ursa Major [*Constellation*] ..... UMa
Ursa Major [*Constellation*] ..... UMaj
Ursa Minor [*Constellation*] ..... UMi
Ursa Minor [*Constellation*] ..... UMin
Urschrift [*Original, as of a document*] [*German military*] ..... U
Ursel [*Belgium ICAO location identifier*] (ICLI) ..... EBUL
Ursinus College, Collegeville, PA [*Library symbol Library of Congress*] (LCLS) ..... PClvU
Ursinus College, Collegeville, PA [*OCLC symbol*] (OCLC) ..... URS
Ursodeoxycholate [*Biochemistry*] ..... UDC
Ursodeoxycholic Acid ..... UDC
Ursodeoxycholic Acid [*Pharmacology*] ..... UDCA
Ursuline Academy, New Orleans, LA [*Library symbol Library of Congress*] (LCLS) ..... LNUrs
Ursuline College Library, Pepper Pike, OH [*OCLC symbol*] (OCLC) ..... URC
Ursuline College, Pepper Pike, OH [*Library symbol Library of Congress*] (LCLS) ..... OClUr
Ursuline Nuns of the Congregation of Paris (Cincinnati, OH) (TOCD) ..... OSU
Ursuline Nuns of the Congregation of Paris (Cleveland, OH) (TOCD) ..... OSU
Ursuline Nuns of the Congregation of Paris (Kansas City, KS) (TOCD) ..... OSU
Ursuline Nuns of the Congregation of Paris (Louisville, KY) (TOCD) ..... OSU
Ursuline Nuns of the Congregation of Paris (Owensboro, KY) (TOCD) ..... OSU
Ursuline Nuns of the Congregation of Paris (St. Martin, OH) (TOCD) ..... OSU
Ursuline Nuns of the Congregation of Paris (Toledo, OH) (TOCD) ..... OSU
Ursuline Nuns of the Congregation of Paris (Youngstown, OH) (TOCD) ..... OSU
Ursuline Nuns of the Congregation of Tildonk, Belgium [*Roman Catholic religious order*] ..... RU
Ursuline Sisters of Belleville (TOCD) ..... OSU
Ursuline Sisters of the Congregation of Tildonk, Belgium (TOCD) ..... OSU
Ursulines of Jesus [*Roman Catholic women's religious order*] ..... U de J
Urteil [*Judgment, Decision*] [*German*] (ILCA) ..... Urt
Urtica Dioica Agglutinin [*Biochemistry*] ..... UDA
Urticaria Pigmentosa [*Dermatology*] ..... UP
Urticarial Transfusion Reaction [*Medicine*] ..... UTR
Uruapan [*Mexico ICAO location identifier*] (ICLI) ..... MMPN
Uruapan [*Mexico*] [*Airport symbol*] (OAG) ..... UPN
Urubupunga [*Brazil*] [*Airport symbol*] (OAG) ..... URB
Uruguaiana [*Brazil*] [*Airport symbol*] (OAG) ..... URG
Uruguaiana/Rubem Berta [*Brazil ICAO location identifier*] (ICLI) ..... SBUG
Uruguay [*International civil aircraft marking*] (ODBW) CX
Uruguay [*International vehicle registration*] (ODBW) ..... ROU
Uruguay [*MARC geographic area code Library of Congress*] (LCCP) ..... s-uy--
Uruguay [*IYRU nationality code*] ..... U
Uruguay ..... Ur
Uruguay ..... URU
Uruguay (VRA) ..... Uru
Uruguay [*ANSI three-letter standard code*] (CNC) ..... URY
Uruguay [*ANSI two-letter standard code*] (CNC) ..... UY
Uruguay [*MARC country of publication code Library of Congress*] (LCCP) ..... uy
Uruguay Collectors Club (EA) ..... UCC
Urumqi [*China*] [*Airport symbol*] (OAG) ..... URC
Urumqi [*China*] [*ICAO location identifier*] (ICLI) ..... ZWUQ
Urumqi/Diwopu [*China*] [*ICAO location identifier*] (ICLI) ..... ZWWW
Uruzgan [*Afghanistan*] [*ICAO location identifier*] (ICLI) ..... OARG
US 1 Class Association (EA) ..... USOCA
US 1 Indus [*NYSE symbol*] (TTSB) ..... USO
US 1869 Pictorial Research Associates (EA) ..... PRA
US Activities Board [*IEEE*] ..... USAB
US A-Division Catamaran Association (EA) ..... USACA
[*The*] **US Agency for International Development's Regional Economic Development Services Office for West and Central Africa** (ECON) ..... USAID/REDSO/WCA
US Air [*ICAO designator*] (FAAC) ..... USA
US Air Force Occupational Measurement Center [*Randolph Air Force Base, TX*] (GRD) ..... USAFOMC
US Air Force Senior Noncommissioned Officer Academy (DOMA) ..... USAFSNCOA
US Air Traffic Controllers Organization [*Defunct*] (EA) ..... USATCO
US Albacore Association (EA) ..... USAA
US Alcohol Testing of America [*AMEX symbol*] (SPSG) ..... AAA
US Alcohol Testing of America, Inc. [*Associated Press*] (SAG) ..... US Al
US Alcohol Testing of America, Inc. [*Associated Press*] (SAG) ..... US Alc
US Ammunition Co. [*Vancouver Stock Exchange symbol*] ..... US
US Amputee Athletic Association (EA) ..... USAAA
US and Foreign Commercial Service [*Department of Commerce*] (CROSS) ..... US & FCS
US Animal Bank (EA) ..... USAB
US Antarctic Research Program (EA) ..... USARP
US Aquaculture Council [*Defunct*] (EA) ..... USAC
US Aquaculture Federation (EA) ..... USAF
US Aquatic Sports (EA) ..... USAS
US Armbrust Association (EA) ..... USAA
US Armor Association (EA) ..... USAA
US Army Aeronautical Services [*ICAO designator*] (FAAC) ..... GKA
US Army Armament, Munitions, and Chemical Command [*Pronounced "a-m-c-com"*] [*Rock Island, IL*] (RDA) ..... AMCCOM
US Army Aviation Development Test Activity [*Fort Rucker, AL*] (GRD) ..... USAAVNDTA
US Army Central TMDE [*Test, Measurement, and Diagnostic Equipment*] **Activity** (RDA) ..... USACTA
US Army Combat Identification System (RDA) ..... ACIS
US Army Construction Engineering Research Laboratory (RDA) ..... USACERL
US Army Engineer, Geodesy, Intelligence, and Mapping Research and Development Agency (NOAA) ..... USAEGIMRADA
US Army Force Integration Staff Agency (RDA) ..... USAFISA
US Army Forces, Middle Pacific [*Name commonly used for AFMIDPAC*] [*World War II*] ..... MIDPAC
US Army Health Professional Support Agency (DOMA) ..... USAHPSA
US Army John F. Kennedy Special Warfare Center and School (RDA) ..... USAJFKSWCS
US Army Kwajalein Atoll (DOMA) ..... USAKA
US Army Manpower Requirements and Documentation Agency ..... USAMARDA
US Army Medical Material Center-Europe (DOMA) ..... USAMMCE
US Army Medical Material Center-Saudi Arabia (DOMA) ..... USAMMCSA
US Army Medical Materiel Development Activity (RDA) ..... USA-MMDA
US Army Medical Research and Materiel Command (RDA) ..... USAMRMC
US Army Medical Research, Development, Acquisition, and Logistics Command (RDA) ..... USAMRDALC
US Army Missile Command (AAGC) ..... MICOM
US Army Nuclear and Chemical Agency (RDA) ..... USANCA
US Army Publications and Printing Command (DOMA) ..... USAPPC
US Army Ranger Association (EA) ..... USARA
US Army Readiness Command (MCD) ..... URARRED
US Army Regimental System (INF) ..... USARS
US Army Research, Development, and Standardization Group - United Kingdom (RDA) ..... USARDSG-UK
US Army Security Affairs Command (RDA) ..... USASAC
US Army Security Agency Group, Vietnam (VNW) ..... USASAGV
US Army Sergeants Major Course (INF) ..... USASMC
US Army Special Operations Command (INF) ..... USASOC
US Army Support Group (DOMA) ..... USASG
US Army Troop Support Agency (DOMA) ..... USATSA
US Association for Blind Athletes (EA) ..... USABA
US Association for Computational Mechanics (EA) ..... USACM
US Association for the Club of Rome (EA) ..... USACOR
US Association of Roller Canary Culturists (EA) ..... USARCC
US Atlantic and Gulf Ports/Eastern Mediterranean and North African Freight Conference [*New York, NY*] (EA) ..... USAGEM
US Atlantic Command [*Unified*] (DOMA) ..... USLANTCOM
US Atomic Energy Detection System (DOMA) ..... USAEDS
US Attorney's Manual [*A publication*] (DLA) ..... USAM
US Bancorp [*NASDAQ symbol*] (NQ) ..... USBC
US Base Association (EA) ..... USBA
US Bass [*An association Defunct*] (EA) ..... USB
US Bass Fishing Association [*Later, USB*] (EA) ..... USBFA
US Battery Trade Council ..... USBTC
US Biathlon Association (EA) ..... USBA
US Bioscience, Inc. [*AMEX symbol*] (SPSG) ..... UBS
US Bioscience, Inc. [*Associated Press*] (SAG) ..... US Biosci
US Board on Books for Young People (EA) ..... USBBY
US Bobsled and Skeleton Federation (EA) ..... USBF
US Bobsled and Skeleton Federation (EA) ..... USBSF
US Boomerang Association (EA) ..... USBA
US Branch of the International Committee for the Defense of the Breton Language (EA) ..... US ICDBL
US Bridge Corp. [*NASDAQ symbol*] (SAG) ..... USBG
US Bridge Corp. [*Associated Press*] (SAG) ..... USBrdge

US Bridge of New York [*Associated Press*] (SAG) .... USBrdgNY
US Bridge of NY Wrrt [*NASDAQ symbol*] (TTSB) .... USBRW
US Bridge on New York [*Associated Press*] (SAG) .... US Brg
US Bridge on New York [*NASDAQ symbol*] (SAG) .... USBR
US Business Committee on Jamaica [*Defunct*] (EA) .... USBCJ
US Campaign for the University of El Salvador (EA) .... US-CUES
US Can Corp. [*Associated Press*] (SAG) .... US Can
US Can Corp. [*NYSE symbol*] (SAG) .... USC
US Cancellation Club (EA) .... USCC
US Canola Association (EA) .... USCA
US Catholic Bishops' National Advisory Council (EA) .... NAC
US Catholic Historical Society (EA) .... USCHS
US Cellular Corp. [*Associated Press*] (SAG) .... US Cell
US Cellular Corp. [*AMEX symbol*] (SPSG) .... USM
US Census Report [*Database*] [*Business Publishers, Inc.*] [*Information service or system*] (CRD) .... USCR
US Check Airlines [*ICAO designator*] (FAAC) .... USC
US Classifications (NITA) .... USCLASS
US Commercial Office [*Department of Commerce, Department of State*] (IMH) .... USCO
US Commercial Service [*International Trade Administration*] .... USCS
US Commissioner of Internal Revenue (AAGC) .... Comm
US Committee Against Nuclear War [*Defunct*] (EA) .... USCANW
US Committee for Scientific Cooperation with Vietnam (EA) .... USCSCV
US Committee in Solidarity with the People of El Salvador (EA) .... CISPES
US Committee on Irrigation and Drainage [*Formerly, USCIDFC*] (EA) .... US/ICID
US Committee on Irrigation and Drainage (EA) .... USCID
US Committee on Irrigation, Drainage, and Flood Control [*Later, USCID*] (EA) .... USCIDFC
US Conference for the World Council of Churches (EA) .... WCC/US
US Corporate Council on South Africa (EA) .... USCCSA
US Council for Energy Awareness (EA) .... USCEA
US Council for Human Rights in the Balkans (EA) .... USCHRB
US Council for World Freedom (EA) .... USCWF
US Cultural Exchange and Sports Society (EA) .... USCESS
US Dairy Forage Research Center [*Research center*] (RCD) .... USDFRC
US Darting Association (EA) .... USDA
US Data Corp. [*Associated Press*] (SAG) .... USData
US Deaf Cycling Association (EA) .... UDCA
US Decade for Natural Disaster Reduction [*1990's*] .... USDNDR
US Defense Representative Office (DOMA) .... USDRO
US Delivery Systems, Inc. [*NYSE symbol*] (SAG) .... DLV
US Delivery Systems, Inc. [*Associated Press*] (SAG) .... USDeliv
US Department of Health and Human Services (GNE) .... HHS
US Department of Justice [*ICAO designator*] (FAAC) .... JUD
US Diagnostics [*NASDAQ symbol*] (SAG) .... USDL
US Diagnostics Co. [*Associated Press*] (SAG) .... US Diag
US Diagnostics Co. [*Associated Press*] (SAG) .... USDia
US Disc Sports Association (EA) .... USDA
US Disc Sports Association (EA) .... USDS
US Energy Corp. [*NASDAQ symbol*] (NQ) .... USEG
US Energy Systems, Inc. [*Associated Press*] (SAG) .... US ES
US Energy Systems, Inc. [*Associated Press*] (SAG) .... US ESys
US Energy Systems, Inc. [*NASDAQ symbol*] (SAG) .... USEY
US English [*An association*] (EA) .... USE
US Environment and Resources Council [*Defunct*] (EA) .... USERC
US Environmental Solutions, Inc. [*Associated Press*] (SAG) .... US EnvS
US Environmental Solutions, Inc. [*NASDAQ symbol*] (SAG) .... USES
US Express [*ICAO designator*] (FAAC) .... USX
US Facilities Corp. [*Costa Mesa, CA*] [*NASDAQ symbol*] (NQ) .... USRE
US Farm News, Hampton, IA [*Library symbol Library of Congress*] (LCLS) .... IaHampFN
US Farmers Association (EA) .... USFA
US Federation for Culture Collections (EA) .... USFCC
US Federation of Scholars and Scientists (EA) .... USFSS
US Feed Grains Council (EA) .... USFGC
US Filter Corp. [*NYSE symbol*] (SPSG) .... USF
US Flag and Touch Football League (EA) .... USFTL
US Flywheel Systems [*Research center*] (ECON) .... USFS
US Football League [*Defunct*] (EA) .... USFL
US Forces Command [*Specified*] (DOMA) .... USFORSCOM
US Franchise Systems, Inc. [*Associated Press*] (SAG) .... US Frch
US Franchise Systems, Inc. [*NASDAQ symbol*] (SAG) .... USFS
US Geodynamics Committee (EA) .... USGC
US Global Investors, Inc. [*NASDAQ symbol*] (SAG) .... GROW
US Global Investors, Inc. [*Associated Press*] (SAG) .... USGlobal
US Government Contract Awards (NITA) .... USGCA
US Grant Mining [*Vancouver Stock Exchange symbol*] .... USG
US Green Alliance (EA) .... USGA
US Hang Gliding Association (EA) .... USHGA
US Healthcare, Inc. [*NASDAQ symbol*] (NQ) .... USHC
US Helsinki Watch Committee (EA) .... USHWC
US Hide, Skin, and Leather Association (EA) .... USHSLA
US Hispanic Chamber of Commerce (EA) .... USHCC
US Holocaust Memorial Council (EA) .... USHMC
US Home & Garden, Inc. [*Associated Press*] (SAG) .... US HG
US Home & Garden, Inc. [*NASDAQ symbol*] (SAG) .... USHG
US Home & Garden, Inc. [*Associated Press*] (SAG) .... USHmGrd
US Home & Garden Wrrt'A' [*NASDAQ symbol*] (TTSB) .... USHGW
US Home Corp. [*NYSE symbol*] (SPSG) .... UH
US Home Corp. [*Associated Press*] (SAG) .... USHm
US Home Corp. [*Associated Press*] (SAG) .... USHme
US HomeCare Corp. [*Associated Press*] (SAG) .... USHmcr
US HomeCare Corp. [*NASDAQ symbol*] (SPSG) .... USHO
US Horse Cavalry Association (EA) .... USHCA
US Immigration and Naturalization Officers' Association (EA) .... USINOA
US, Inc. (EA) .... USI
US Industrial Coalition [*For finding commercial use of nuclear technology*] .... USIC
US Industries [*Subsidiary of the Hanson Group*] [*British*] (ECON) .... USI
US Inspection Agency (DOMA) .... USIA
US Institute of Human Rights (EA) .... USIHR
US Institute of Peace (EA) .... USIP
US International Fireball Association (EA) .... USIFA
US International Space Year Association (EA) .... US-ISY
US Islands 17 Class Association [*Defunct*] (EA) .... USISCA
US Jet, Inc. [*ICAO designator*] (FAAC) .... USJ
US Letter Carriers Mutual Benefit Association [*Washington, DC*] (EA) .... USLCMBA
US Liaison Office-Kuwait (DOMA) .... USLOK
US Liaison Office-Tunisia (DOMA) .... USLOT
US Lime & Minerals [*NASDAQ symbol*] (SPSG) .... USLM
US Long Distance [*Associated Press*] (SAG) .... US Long
US Long Distance [*Vancouver Stock Exchange symbol*] .... USL
US Long Distance [*NASDAQ symbol*] (SAG) .... USLD
US Marine Corps Combat Correspondents Association (EA) .... USMCCCA
US Mariner Class Association (EA) .... USMCA
US Maritime Academy (DOMA) .... USMA
US Marshal Service [*Department of Justice*] [*ICAO designator*] (FAAC) .... MSH
US Merchant Marine Veterans of World War II (EA) .... USMMVETS WW2
US Metric Association (EA) .... USMA
US Microfilm Corp., Jacksonville, FL [*Library symbol Library of Congress*] (LCLS) .... UsM
US Microgravity Payload [*NASA*] .... USMP
US Military Academy (DOMA) .... USMA
US Military Mission with the Iranian Gendarmerie .... GENMISH
US Mine Countermeasures Group (DOMA) .... USMCMG
US Mirror Class Association (EA) .... USMCA
US Munitions List (DOMA) .... USML
US National Committee for Byzantine Studies (EA) .... USNCBS
US National Committee for the Scientific Committee on Oceanic Research (EA) .... USNCSCOR
US National Committee for World Food Day (EA) .... USNCWFD
US National Committee of the Commission Internationale de l'Eclairage [*International Commission on Illumination*] (EA) .... USNC/CIE
US National Committee on Theoretical and Applied Mechanics (EA) .... USNC/TAM
US National Federation of Christian Life Communities (EA) .... USNFCLC
US National Fruit Export Council [*Defunct*] (EA) .... USNFEC
US National Ozone Expedition [*1986*] [*McMurdo Station, Antarctica*] .... NOZE
US National Society for the International Society of Soil Mechanics and Foundation Engineering (EA) .... USNSISSMFE
US Naval Forces, [*US*] **Central Command** (DOMA) .... USNAVCENT
US Naval Training Center, Bainbridge, MD [*Library symbol*] [*Library of Congress*] (LCLS) .... MdBbN
US Navy Pacific Missile Test Center .... USNPACMISTESCEN
US Navy Patrol Squadron (CINC) .... VPRON
US Navy Patrol Squadron (Land) (CINC) .... VP(L)
US Navy Patrol Squadron (Sea-Based) (CINC) .... VP(S)
US Nicaragua Friendship Project (EA) .... USNFP
US Nuclear Free Pacific Network (EA) .... USNFPN
US Office Products Co. [*NASDAQ symbol*] (SAG) .... OFIS
US Office Products Co. [*Associated Press*] (SAG) .... US OfcP
US Office - UTLAS Corp. [*UTLAS symbol*] .... USO
US One Industries, Inc. [*Formerly, Transcom, Inc.*] [*Associated Press*] (SAG) .... US 1 Inds
US One Industries, Inc. [*Formerly, Transcom, Inc.*] [*NYSE symbol*] (SAG) .... USO
US Opportunity Search, Inc. [*Associated Press*] (SAG) .... USOppS
US Opportunity Search, Inc. [*NASDAQ symbol*] (SAG) .... USOS
US Order, Inc. [*Associated Press*] (SAG) .... US Ord
US Order, Inc. [*NASDAQ symbol*] (SAG) .... USOR
US Out of Central America [*Defunct*] (EA) .... USOCA
US Overseas Cooperative Development Committee (EA) .... USOCDC
US Paddle Tennis Association (EA) .... USPTA
US Patent Data Base - Patent Technology Reports [*Patent and Trademark Office*] [*Database*] .... PAT-PTR
US Patent Model Foundation (EA) .... USPMF
US Patents (NITA) .... USPA
US Patents 70 (NITA) USP70
US Patents 77 (NITA) USP77
US Patents Alert [*Derwent, Inc.*] [*Database*] .... USPA
US Pawn, Inc. [*NASDAQ symbol*] (NQ) .... USPN
US Pay-Tel, Inc. [*Vancouver Stock Exchange symbol*] .... USY
US Peace Council (EA) .... USPC
US Philatelic Classics Society (EA) .... USPCS
US Physical Therapy, Inc. [*NASDAQ symbol*] (SAG) .... USPH
US Physical Therapy, Inc. [*Associated Press*] (SAG) .... USPhys
US Platinum [*Vancouver Stock Exchange symbol*] .... UPT
US Possessions Philatelic Society (EA) .... USPPS
US Postal Chess Union (EA) .... USPCU
US Postal Service (AAGC) .... PS
US Powerlifting Federation (EA) .... USPF
US Practical Shooting Association (EA) .... USPSA
US Precious Metals, Inc. [*Toronto Stock Exchange symbol Vancouver Stock Exchange symbol*] .... USP
US Professional Cycling Federation [*Later, USPRO*] (EA) .... USPCF
US Professional Cycling Federation (EA) .... USPRO
US Psychotronics Association (EA) .... USPA
US Public Interest Research Group (EA) .... USPIRG
US Publicity Director [*A publication*] .... USPD
US Real Property Holding Co. .... USRPHC

US Recommended Daily Allowance [*Nutrition*] ..... USRDA
US Region of Congregation of Mariannhill Missionaries (EA) ..... CMM
US Region of Congregation of Mariannhill Missionaries [*Later, CMM*] (EA) ..... USRCMM
US Relations Office of CLAT [*Central Latinoamericana de Trabajadores*] (EA) ..... USO-CLAT
US Repeating Arms Company ..... USRAC
US Requests for Proposals [*Washington Representative Service*] [*Information service or system Defunct*] (CRD) ..... USRFP
US Restaurant Properties Ltd. [*Formerly, Burger King Investors*] [*Associated Press*] (SAG) ..... US Rest
US Restaurant Properties Ltd. [*Formerly, Burger King Investors*] [*NYSE symbol*] (SAG) ..... USV
US Robotics, Inc. [*NASDAQ symbol*] (SPSG) ..... USRX
US Scottish Fiddling Revival (EA) ..... USSFR
US SerVis [*NASDAQ symbol*] (TTSB) ..... USRV
US SerVis, Inc. [*NASDAQ symbol*] (SAG) ..... USRV
US SerVis, Inc. [*Associated Press*] (SAG) ..... USSerVis
US Shake and Shingle Manufacturers Association (EA) ..... USSSMA
US Sheep Experiment Station [*University of Idaho*] [*Research center*] (RCD) ..... USSES
US Shoe Corp. [*NYSE symbol*] (SPSG) ..... USR
US Sidewinder Association (EA) ..... USSA
US Ski Coaches Association (EA) ..... USSCA
US Soling Association (EA) ..... USSA
US Spanish Merchants Association (EA) ..... USSMA
US Sports Acrobatic Federation (EA) ..... USSAF
US Steel Canada, Inc. [*Toronto Stock Exchange symbol*] ..... USS
US Steel Corp. [*Also, USSC*] [*Later, USX Corp.*] ..... USS
US Steel Corp. [*Also, USS*] [*Later, USX Corp.*] (MCD) ..... USSC
US Steel Corp. [*Formerly, USS, USSC*] ..... USX
US Student Pugwash Committee (EA) ..... USSPC
US Student Travel Service (EA) ..... USSTS
US Supreme Court Reporter [*West*] [*1882-present*] [*A publication*] (AAGC) ..... S Ct
US Supreme Court Reports (GPO) ..... US
US Sweetener Producers Group [*Later, ASA*] (EA) ..... USSPG
US Systems Corp. (EA) ..... USSC
US Taekwondo Union (EA) ..... USTU
US Targhee Sheep Association (EA) ..... USTSA
US Taxpayers Union (EA) ..... USTU
US Team Handball Federation (EA) ..... USTHF
US Technologies, Inc. [*NASDAQ symbol*] (NQ) ..... USXX
US Telecommunications Suppliers Association [*Later, TIA*] (EA) ..... USTSA
US Telecommunications Training Institute [*Washington, DC*] [*Telecommunications*] (TSSD) ..... USTTI
US Telephone, Inc. [*Dallas, TX*] [*Telecommunications*] (TSSD) ..... US TEL
US Tennis Court and Track Builders Association (EA) ..... USTC & TBA
US Tennis Writers Association (EA) ..... USTWA
US Tornado Association (EA) ..... USTA
US Trade Center [*Mexico*] (IMH) ..... USTC
US Transportation Systems, Inc. [*NASDAQ symbol*] (SAG) ..... USTS
US Travel Data Center (EA) ..... USTDC
US Triathlon Association [*Later, TRI-FED*] (EA) ..... USTA
US Trivia Association [*Defunct*] (EA) ..... USTA
US Trust Corp. [*Associated Press*] (SAG) ..... US Trst
US Trust Corp. [*NASDAQ symbol*] (NQ) ..... USTC
US Venetian Blind Association (EA) ..... USVBA
US WATS [*NASDAQ symbol*] (TTSB) ..... USWI
US Wats, Inc. [*Associated Press*] (SAG) ..... US Wats
US Wats, Inc. [*NASDAQ symbol*] (SAG) ..... USWI
US West [*NYSE symbol*] (SAG) ..... UMG
US West [*Associated Press*] (SAG) ..... USWest
US West [*Associated Press*] (SAG) ..... USWM
US West, Inc. [*NYSE symbol*] (SPSG) ..... USW
US West, Inc. [*Associated Press*] (SAG) ..... USWst
US West Media Group [*NYSE symbol*] (TTSB) ..... UMG
US Wheat Associates (EA) ..... USW
US Wireless Corp. [*Associated Press*] (SAG) ..... US WreCp
US Wireless Corp. [*NASDAQ symbol*] (SAG) ..... USWC
US Xpress Enterprises, Inc. [*Associated Press*] (SAG) ..... US Xprss
US Xpress Enterprises, Inc. [*NASDAQ symbol*] (SAG) ..... XPRS
US Yacht Racing Union (EA) ..... USYRU
US Yugoslav Economic Council (EA) ..... USYEC
USA Amateur Boxing Federation (EA) ..... USA/ABF
USA - Business and Industry Advisory Committee to the OECD [*Organization for Economic Cooperation and Development*] (EA) ..... USA-BIAC
USA Convertible Club [*Defunct*] (EA) ..... USACC
USA Detergents [*NASDAQ symbol*] (TTSB) ..... USAD
USA Detergents, Inc. [*Associated Press*] (SAG) ..... USA Det
USA Detergents, Inc. [*Associated Press*] (SAG) ..... USA Dt
USA Detergents, Inc. [*NASDAQ symbol*] (SAG) ..... USAD
USA Federation of Bocce (EA) ..... USAFOB
USA Field Hockey Association (EA) ..... USAFHA
USA Field Hockey Association (EA) ..... USFHA
USA Film Festival (EA) ..... USAFF
USA Finn Association (EA) ..... USAFA
USA Foundation (EA) ..... USAF
USA Harvest [*An association*] (EA) ..... USAH
USA Karate Federation (EA) ..... USAKF
USA Petites [*An association*] (EA) ..... USAP
USA Plowing Organization (EA) ..... USAPO
USA Toy Library Association (EA) ..... USATLA
USA Truck [*NASDAQ symbol*] (SAG) ..... USAK
USA Truck Co. [*Associated Press*] (SAG) ..... USA Trk
USA Victory Alliance (EA) ..... USAVA
USA Waste Service [*NYSE symbol*] (TTSB) ..... UW
USA Waste Services, Inc. [*Associated Press*] (SAG) ..... USA Wste
USA Waste Services, Inc. [*NYSE symbol*] (SPSG) ..... UW
USABancshares, Inc. [*NASDAQ symbol*] (SAG) ..... USAB
USABancshares, Inc. [*Associated Press*] (SAG) ..... USABnc
USABancShares'A' [*NASDAQ symbol*] (TTSB) ..... USAB
Usable Control ..... UC
Usable Depth (MCD) ..... UD
Usable Floor Area [*Classified advertising*] (ADA) ..... UFA
Usable in Place (MCD) ..... UIP
Usable Inside Area (MCD) ..... UIA
Usable Inside Depth (MCD) ..... UID
Usable Inside Width (MCD) ..... UIW
Usable Vector Table ..... UVT
Usable Width (MCD) ..... UW
USAF [*United States Air Force*] **Security Service** ..... USS
USAF [*United States Air Force*] **Specification Bulletin** (MCD) ..... BU
USAFE Command Intelligence Brief (MCD) ..... UCIB
Usage Based Requirements Determination [*Army*] (DOMA) ..... UBRD
Usage Block (MSA) ..... UB
Usage Data ..... UD
Usage Data Report ..... UDR
Usage Exception List (MCD) ..... UEL
Usage Frequency Indicator ..... UFI
Usage List (MSA) ..... UL
Usage Sensitive Pricing [*Telecommunications*] ..... USP
Usage Sensitive Service [*Telecommunications*] ..... USS
USair Express [*ICAO designator*] (AD) ..... US
USAIR Group [*NYSE symbol*] (SPSG) ..... U
USAir Group, Inc. [*Associated Press*] (SAG) ..... UsairG
USAir Grp $4.375 Cv Dep Pfd [*NYSE symbol*] (TTSB) ..... UPrB
Usak [*Turkey ICAO location identifier*] (ICLI) ..... LTBO
USA-Korean Karate Association (EA) ..... USA-KKA
Usakos [*Namibia*] [*ICAO location identifier*] (ICLI) ..... FAUK
US-Albania Friendship Association (EA) ..... USAFA
U.S.Alcohol Test'g 14% Cl'A'Pfd [*AMEX symbol*] (TTSB) ..... AAAPrA
USANA, Inc [*NASDAQ symbol*] (SAG) ..... USNA
USANA, Inc. [*Associated Press*] (SAG) ..... USANA
US-Arab Chamber of Commerce [*Defunct*] (EA) ..... USACC
USA-Republic of China Economic Council (EA) ..... USA-RCEC
USA-Republic of China Economic Council [*Crystal Lake, IL*] (EA) ..... USA-ROCEC
USAREUR [*United States Army, Europe*] **Command and Control Information System** ..... UCCIS
USAREUR Daily Intelligence Report (MCD) ..... UDIR
USAREUR [*United States Army, Europe*] **Support System** ..... USS
USAREUR Tactical Intelligence Center (MCD) ..... UTIC
US-Asia Institute (EA) ..... USAI
USA-USSR Citizens' Dialogue [*Defunct*] (EA) ..... UUCD
U-Save Foods Ltd. [*Vancouver Stock Exchange symbol*] ..... USV
Usbancorp, Inc. [*NASDAQ symbol*] (SAG) ..... UBAN
USbancorp, Inc. [*Associated Press*] (SAG) ..... USBPa
US-China Business Council (EA) ..... USCBC
US-China Education Foundation (EA) ..... USCEF
US-China Indl Exchange Wrrt'A' [*NASDAQ symbol*] (TTSB) ..... CHDXW
US-China Indl Exchange Wrrt'B' [*NASDAQ symbol*] (TTSB) ..... CHDXZ
US-China Industrial Exchange, Inc. [*Associated Press*] (SAG) ..... US Chlnd
US-China Industrial Exchange, Inc. [*Associated Press*] (SAG) ..... USCh
US-China Peoples Friendship Association (EA) ..... USCPFA
USCI, Inc. [*Associated Press*] (SAG) ..... USCI
USCI, Inc. [*NASDAQ symbol*] (SAG) ..... USCM
USCI Inc. [*NASDAQ symbol*] (TTSB) ..... USCM
USCS International, Inc. [*NASDAQ symbol*] (SAG) ..... USCS
USCS International, Inc. [*Associated Press*] (SAG) ..... USCS Int
USDA Current Research Information System (NITA) ..... USDA/CRIS
USDA [*United States Department of Agriculture*] **Human Nutrition Research Center on Aging at Tufts** [*Tufts University*] [*Research center*] (RCD) ..... HNRC
USDA [*United States Department of Agriculture*] **Regional Document Delivery** [*Library network*] ..... USDA RDD
USDA [*United States Department of Agriculture*] **Sedimentation Laboratory** [*Research center*] (RCD) ..... USDASL
USDA-Forest Service Volunteers Program (EA) ..... USDA-FSVP
USData Corp. [*Associated Press*] (SAG) ..... USData
USData Corp. [*NASDAQ symbol*] (SAG) ..... USDC
Use ..... U
Use and Occupancy [*Real estate*] ..... U & O
Use as Required (MSA) ..... UAR
Use Frequency Analysis ..... UFA
USE, Inc. [*Acronym is now organization's official name*] (EA) ..... UI
Use No Abbreviations (DNAB) ..... UNA
Use of Materials Bulletin [*Department of Housing and Urban Development*] [*A publication*] (GFGA) ..... UM
Use of Other Automobiles [*Insurance*] ..... UOA
Use Order [*Navy*] (NVT) ..... USEORD
Use the Source, Luke [*Computer hacker terminology, used to parody commands to Luke Skywalker in the movie "Star Wars"*] (NHD) ..... UTSL
Use until Exhausted ..... UUE
Useable on Code (MCD) ..... UOC
Used Beverage Can ..... UBC
Used Clothing Exporters Association of America (EA) ..... UCEA
Used For ..... UF
Used Fuel [*Nuclear energy*] (NUCP) ..... UF
Used Oil Recycling Coalition [*Automotive lubricants*] ..... UORC
Used On (MSA) ..... U/O
Used on Assembly ..... UOA
Used Truck Sales Network (EA) ..... UTSN

Used With .... U/W
Useful Life (SAA) .... UL
Useful Method .... UM
US-El Salvador Research and Information Center (EA) .... US-ESRIC
Useless .... US
Useless Loop [*Australia Airport symbol*] (OAG) .... USL
User Acceptance Test (MCD) .... UAT
User Action Analyzer .... UAA
User Adaptive Language .... UAL
User Advisory Committee [*Environmental Protection Agency*] (GFGA) .... UAC
User Advisory Group (RDA) .... UAG
User Advisory Group (EERA) .... UAG
User Agency .... UA
User Agent [*Telecommunications*] (PCM) .... UA
User Agent Entity [*Telecommunications*] (OSI) .... UAE
User Agent Layer [*Telecommunications*] (OSI) .... UAL
User Agent Protocol Data Unit [*Telecommunications*] (OSI) .... UAPDU
User Agent Sublayer [*Telecommunications*] (OSI) .... UASL
User Area [*Information storage*] .... UA
User Area Profile .... UAP
User Attribute Data Set [*Computer science*] (MDG) .... UADS
User Attribute Definition [*Computer science*] (IAA) .... UAD
User Block Handling Routine [*Computer science*] (IBMDP) .... UBHR
User Board (MHDB) .... UB
User Brain Damage [*Computer hacker terminology*] (NHD) .... UBD
User Class Identifier (NITA) .... UCI
User Cluster Language [*Computer science*] (MHDB) .... UCLAN
User Command [*Computer science*] (PCM) .... UCM
User Communications Manager [*Audio-video*] (NTCM) .... UCM
User Community [*Programming language*] [*Argonne National Laboratory Argonne, IL*] (CSR) .... DISSCO
User Computed Address [*Computer science*] (HGAA) .... UCA
User Control Block Table [*Computer science*] (MHDI) .... UCBTAB
User Control Interface Device [*Army*] .... UCID
User Control List [*Computer science*] (HGAA) .... UCL
User Control Routine (MCD) .... UCR
User Control Store .... UCS
User Datagram Protocol (BYTE) .... UDP
User Datagram Protocol/Internet Protocol [*Computer science*] .... UDP/IP
User Defined Key [*Computer science*] (HGAA) .... UDK
User Designation Codes [*Navy*] (NG) .... UDC
User Differential Range Error [*Navigation systems*] .... UDRE
User Digital Analog Controller .... UDAC
User Display Terminal .... UDT
User Dissemination Circuit [*Air Force Weather Center*] .... UDC
User Element [*Telecommunications*] (OSI) .... UE
User Equipment .... UE
User Equivalent Range Error .... UERE
User File Directory (NASA) .... UFD
User Files On-Line [*Computer science*] (MHDI) .... UFO
User Friendly Interface .... UFI
User Friendly Operating System [*UFO Systems, Inc.*] .... UFO
User Group [*Computer science*] .... UG
User Group Table [*Computer science*] (MHDB) .... UGT
User Header Label (CMD) .... UHL
User Identification [*Computer science*] .... USERID
User Identification Code .... UIC
User Input/Output Devices [*Computer science*] (RDA) .... UIOD
User Instruction Group .... UIG
User Instruction Register .... UIR
User Interface .... UI
User Interface Language (SSD) .... UIL
User Interface Management System [*Computer science*] .... UIMS
User Interface Requirement .... UIR
User Language [*Computer science*] (DIT) .... UL
User Language [*Computer science*] .... ULANG
User Level Remote Procedure Call [*Computer science*] .... URPC
User Maintenance Support Plan (MCD) .... UMSP
User Manual (MCD) .... UM
User Message Format .... UMF
User Need Date (KSC) .... UND
User Network (SSD) .... USENET
User Network Access Link Control .... UNALC
User Network Control Machine .... UNCM
User Network for Information Storage, Transfer Acquisition, and Retrieval (MCD) .... UNISTAR
User Network Interface [*Computer science*] .... UNI
User Network Interface to Everything [*A discussion list on the Internet*] (TNIG) .... UNITE
User On-Line Interaction [*Computer science*] .... UOI
User Operations Panel (SSD) .... UOP
User Operations Support (SSD) .... UOS
User Operations Support Group (SSD) .... UOSG
User Parameter Processing (NASA) .... UPP
User Process Table .... UPT
User Program (MCD) .... UP
User Program Sense Indicator .... UPSI
User Program Switch Indicator [*Computer science*] .... UPSI
User Programming Language [*Burroughs Corp.*] [*Computer science*] (IEEE) .... UPL
User Queue Table .... UQT
User Range Accuracy (SSD) .... URA
User Range Error .... URE
User Readout (MCD) .... URO
User Readout Simulator [*Army*] .... URS
User Requirements [*Nuclear energy*] (NRCH) .... UR
User Requirements Analysis .... URA
User Requirements Data Base (MHDB) .... URDS
User Requirements Document (MCD) .... URD
User Requirements Language [*Computer science*] .... URL
User Segment (SSD) .... US
User Selected and Required Schedule (SAA) .... USARS
User Service Center (MCD) .... USC
User Service Request .... USR
User Service Routine [*Digital Equipment Corp.*] .... USR
User Services Advisory Committee [*NERComP*] .... USAC
User Services Support (SSD) .... USS
User Software Integration Subsystem [*Space Flight Operations Facility, NASA*] .... USI
User Standards Forum for Information Technology (NITA) .... USFIT
User Status Reporting (MCD) .... USR
User Support Center (MCD) .... USC
User Support Environment (SSD) .... USE
User Support Group (NITA) .... USG
User Support System (MCD) .... USS
User Symbol Table [*Computer science*] (MHDB) .... UST
User System Evaluator [*Computer science*] (MHDB) .... USER
User/System Interface .... USI
User System Interface (NITA) .... USI
User Systems Ergonomics Research [*Computer science*] .... USER
User Systems Support Plan .... USSP
User Terminal and Display Subsystem [*Space Flight Operations Facility, NASA*] .... UTD
User Test .... UT
User Test and Evaluation [*Army*] (DOMA) .... UT & E
User Test Instrumentation [*Army*] .... UTI
User Test Program [*Army*] .... UTP
User to File Manager .... UFM
User Trailer Label (CMD) .... UTL
User Transfer Address .... UTA
User Unit (MCD) .... UU
User Visible Resources .... UVR
User Work Station (NASA) .... UWS
User Working Area .... UWA
User Written Application Test [*Computer science*] .... UWAT
User-Communication Interface [*Telecommunications*] .... UCI
User-Defined File Access Method [*Computer science*] (IT) .... UDFAM
User-Defined Function [*Computer science*] (PCM) .... UDF
User-Dependent-Type Code .... UDTC
User-Manufacturer Information Exchange .... UMIX
User-Oriented Data Display Language [*Computer science*] .... UODDL
User-Prompted Graphic Data Evaluation [*US Council on Environmental Quality*] .... UPGRADE
Users Files on Line (IAA) .... UFO
Users Master File (IAA) .... UMF
Users Network for Applied Modeling of Air Pollution [*Set of computer simulation models being developed by Battelle for EPA*] .... UNAMAP
Users of Automatic Information Display Equipment (EA) .... UAIDE
User's Terminal (MCD) .... UT
User-Supplied Data .... USD
User-to-User Signaling [*Telecommunications*] (DOM) .... UUS
USEUCOM [*United States European Command*] **Nuclear Interface Element Fastbreak** (MCD) .... UNIEF
USF & G Corp. [*NYSE symbol*] (SPSG) .... FG
USF & G Corp. [*Associated Press*] (SAG) .... USFG
USF & G Pacholder Fund, Inc. [*AMEX symbol*] (CTT) .... PHF
USF & G Pacholder Fund, Inc. [*Associated Press*] (SAG) .... USFGP
USF Constellation Foundation (EA) .... USFCF
USF&G $4.10cm Cv Exch A Pfd [*NYSE symbol*] (TTSB) .... PHFPrA
USF&G Pacholder Fd [*AMEX symbol*] (TTSB) .... PHF
USFreightways [*NASDAQ symbol*] (TTSB) .... USFC
USFreightways Corp. [*NASDAQ symbol*] (SAG) .... USFC
USFreightways Corp. [*Associated Press*] (SAG) .... USFreight
USG Corp. [*NYSE symbol*] (SPSG) .... USG
USG Corp. Wrrt [*NYSE symbol*] (TTSB) .... USG.WS
USGS [*United States Geological Survey*] **Water Resources Division, New York District, Albany, NY** [*OCLC symbol*] (OCLC) .... UDY
Usher of the Scarlet Rod (ROG) .... USR
Usher Syndrome Self-Help Network (EA) .... USSHN
U-Ship Inc. [*NASDAQ symbol*] (TTSB) .... USHP
Ushuaia [*Argentina ICAO location identifier*] (ICLI) .... SAWH
Ushuaia [*Argentina*] [*Airport symbol*] (OAG) .... USH
Using Command .... UC
Using Mails to Defraud .... UMTD
Using Reading in Creative Activities .... URICA
Using Television (WDMC) .... UT
US-Israel Binational Science Foundation (EA) .... BSF
US-Japan Business Council (EA) .... USJBC
US-Japan Culture Center (EA) .... USJAC
US-Japan Culture Center (EA) .... USJCC
US-Japan Trade Facilitation Committee (IMH) .... TFC
US-Korea Economic Council [*Later, KS*] (EA) .... USKEC
US-Korea Society [*Later, KS*] (EA) .... USKOS
USLIFE Corp. [*NYSE symbol*] (SPSG) .... USH
USLIFE Corp. [*Associated Press*] (SAG) .... USLIFE
USLIFE Income Fund [*NYSE symbol*] (TTSB) .... UIF
USLIFE Income Fund, Inc. [*NYSE symbol*] (SPSG) .... UIF
USLIFE Income Fund, Inc. [*Associated Press*] (SAG) .... UslfeF
US-Mexico Border Health Association (EA) .... USMBHA
US-Mexico Border Program (EA) .... USMBP

USMX, Inc. [*Formerly, US Minerals & Explorations Co.*] [*NASDAQ symbol*] (NQ) ... USMX
US-North Africa (Gibraltar) Convoy [*World War II*] ... UG
US-North Africa (Gibraltar) Convoy-Fast [*World War II*] ... UGF
US-North Africa (Gibraltar) Convoy-Slow [*World War II*] ... UGS
USO [*United Service Organizations*]-All Service Postal Chess Club [*Later, ASPCC*] (EA) ... USO-ASPCC
USP Real Est Inv Tr SBI [*NASDAQ symbol*] (TTSB) ... USPTS
USP Real Estate Investment Trust SBI [*Associated Press*] (SAG) ... USPRI
USP Real Estate Investment Trust SBI [*NASDAQ symbol*] (SPSG) ... USPTS
US-Pakistan Economic Council (EA) ... USPAK
Uspallata [*Argentina ICAO location identifier*] (ICLI) ... SAMU
Usque Ad [*As Far As*] [*Latin*] (ADA) ... UA
USREDCOM [*United States Readiness Command*] **Command and Control System** (AABC) ... RCACS
USS Engineers & Consultants, Inc. [*Information service or system*] (IID) ... UEC
USS Interphase (EA) ... USSI
USS Intrepid Association of Former Crew Members (EA) ... USSIAFCM
USS [*United States Ship*] **Liberty Veterans Association** (EA) ... ULVA
USS [*United States Ship*] **Natoma Bay Association** (EA) ... USSNBA
USS [*United States Ship*] **Oklahoma Association** (EA) ... USSOA
Ussel/Thalamy [*France ICAO location identifier*] (ICLI) ... LFCU
US-South Africa Leader Exchange Program (EA) ... USSALEP
USSR [*Union of Soviet Socialist Republics*] [*MARC geographic area code Library of Congress*] (LCCP) ... e-ur--
USSR [*Union of Soviet Socialist Republics*] [*MARC country of publication code Library of Congress*] (LCCP) ... ur
USSR State Committee for Foreign Tourism [*Defunct*] (EAIO) ... USSRCFT
UST Corp. [*Associated Press*] (SAG) ... UST Cp
UST Corp. [*NASDAQ symbol*] (NQ) ... USTB
UST, Inc. [*Formerly, US Tobacco*] [*NYSE symbol*] (SPSG) ... UST
USTA [*United States Tennis Association*] **National Junior Tennis League** (EA) ... USTA/NJTL
Ustav Vedeckych Lekarskych Informaci [*Institute for Medical Information*] [*Former Czechoslovakia Database operator*] [*Information service or system*] (IID) ... UVLI
UStel [*NASDAQ symbol*] (SAG) ... USTL
UStel Co. [*Associated Press*] (SAG) ... UStel
UStel Inc. [*NASDAQ symbol*] (TTSB) ... USTL
Ust-Elegest [*Former USSR Seismograph station code, US Geological Survey*] (SEIS) ... UER
US-Tibet Committee (EA) ... USTC
Ustica [*Italy ICAO location identifier*] (ICLI) ... LICU
Ustilago [*A fungus*] ... UST
Ust-Kulom [*Former USSR ICAO location identifier*] (ICLI) ... UUYT
Ust-Ordynsky [*Former USSR ICAO location identifier*] (ICLI) ... UIIO
Ustredi Vedeckych, Technickych, a Ekonomickych Informaci [*Former Czechoslovakia*] [*Information service or system*] (IID) ... UVTEI
Ustredna Kniznica Slovenskej Akademie Vied [*Central Library of the Slovak Academy of Science*], Bratislava, Czechoslovakia [*Library symbol Library of Congress*] (LCLS) ... CzBUK
Ustredni Rada Odboru [*Central Council of Trade Unions*] [*Czechoslovakia*] ... URO
Ustupo [*Panama*] [*Airport symbol*] (OAG) ... UTU
Ustus [*Burnt*] [*Pharmacy*] ... UST
Usual (ROG) ... USL
Usual and Customary ... U & C
Usual Childhood Diseases [*Medicine*] ... UCD
Usual Childhood Diseases [*Medicine*] ... UCHD
Usual Childhood Illnesses (DAVI) ... UCHI
Usual Childhood Illnesses (DAVI) ... UCI
Usual, Customary, and Reasonable (DAVI) ... UCR
Usual, Customary, and Reasonable Charges [*Medicine*] ... UCR
Usual, Customary, and Reasonable/Performance and Cost Efficiency [*Medicine*] (MEDA) ... UCR/PACE
Usual Diseases of Childhood [*Medicine*] ... UDC
Usual Health-Care [*Medicine*] ... UC
Usual Home Elsewhere [*Bureau of the Census*] (GFGA) ... UHE
Usual Interstitial Pneumonia [*Medicine*] ... UIP
Usual Marketing Requirement [*Business term*] ... UMR
Usual Place of Residence (MAE) ... UPOR
Usual Throat Flora [*Medicine*] (DAVI) ... UTF
Usually ... USU
Usually Reliable Source of Intelligence [*Military*] ... D
Usually Reliable Source of Intelligence Information [*Military*] ... B
Usurpandus [*To Be Used*] [*Pharmacy*] ... USURP
US-USSR Youth Exchange Program (EA) ... UUYEP
U.S.West Fin 7.96%'TOPrS' [*NYSE symbol*] (TTSB) ... USWPrA
USX Capital LLC [*Associated Press*] (SAG) ... USX Ca
USX Capital LLC [*NYSE symbol*] (SAG) ... XLC
USX Capital LLC 'MIPS' [*NYSE symbol*] (TTSB) ... XLCPr
USX CORP 6.50% CV Pfd [*NYSE symbol*] (TTSB) ... XPrA
USX Delhi Group [*NYSE symbol*] (SAG) ... DGP
USX Delhi Group [*Associated Press*] (SAG) ... USXDel
USX Marathon [*NYSE symbol*] (SAG) ... X
USX US Steel Group [*Formerly, US Steel Corp.*] [*Associated Press*] (SAG) ... USXUSS
USX US Steel Group [*Wall Street slang name: "Steel"*] [*NYSE symbol*] (SPSG) ... X
USX-Delhi Group [*NYSE symbol*] (SPSG) ... DGP
USX-Marathon Group [*NYSE symbol*] (SPSG) ... MRO
USX-Marathon Group [*Associated Press*] (SAG) ... USX
USX-Marathon Group [*Associated Press*] (SAG) ... USXMar
USX-Marathon Grp [*NYSE symbol*] (TTSB) ... MRO
USX-U.S. Steel Group [*NYSE symbol*] (TTSB) ... X
Ut Dictum [*As Directed*] [*Latin*] ... UD
Ut Dictum [*As Directed*] [*Latin*] ... UT DICT
Ut in Omnibus Glorificetur Deus [*That God May Be Glorified in All Things*] [*Latin*] ... UIOGD
Ut Infra [*As Below*] [*Latin*] ... UI
Ut Infra [*As Below*] [*Latin*] (ADA) ... UT INF
Ut Supra [*As Above*] [*Latin*] (WGA) ... us
Ut Supra [*As Above*] [*Latin*] ... UT SUP
Ut Supra [*As Above*] [*Latin*] ... UT SUPR
UT Technologies [*Vancouver Stock Exchange symbol*] ... UTT
Utah [*MARC geographic area code Library of Congress*] (LCCP) ... n-us-ut
Utah ... U
Utah [*Obsolete*] (ROG) ... UH
Utah [*Postal code*] ... UT
Utah (ODBW) ... Ut
Utah [*MARC country of publication code Library of Congress*] (LCCP) ... utu
Utah Administrative Code [*A publication*] (AAGC) ... UAC
Utah Administrative Code [*A publication*] (AAGC) ... Utah Admin Code
Utah Agricultural Experiment Station [*Utah State University*] [*Research center*] (RCD) ... UAES
Utah Army Depot (AABC) ... UTAD
Utah Coal Route [*AAR code*] ... UCR
Utah Code, Annotated [*A publication*] (DLA) ... UCA
Utah Code, Annotated [*A publication*] (DLA) ... Utah Code Ann
Utah College Library Council [*Library network*] ... UCLC
Utah Computer Retrieval Information Service [*Utah State Office of Education*] (OLDSS) ... U-CRIS
Utah Construction and Development Co., Inc. (AAGC) ... UCD
Utah Cooperative Fishery Research Unit [*Utah State University*] [*Research center*] (RCD) ... UCFRU
Utah Council for Computers in Education (EDAC) ... UCCE
Utah Industrial Commission. Bulletin [*A publication*] (DLA) ... Utah IC Bull
Utah Medical, Inc. [*Associated Press*] (SAG) ... UtahMed
Utah Medical, Inc. [*NASDAQ symbol*] (NQ) ... UTMD
Utah Medical Products [*NASDAQ symbol*] (TTSB) ... UTMD
Utah Mining and Minerals Resources Research Institute [*University of Utah*] [*Research center*] (RCD) ... MMRRI
Utah Oil Co. ... UTOCO
Utah Public Utilities Commission Report [*A publication*] (DLA) ... Utah PUC
Utah Railway Co. [*AAR code*] ... UTAH
Utah Reports [*A publication*] (DLA) ... U
Utah Reports [*A publication*] (DLA) ... UT
Utah Reports [*A publication*] (DLA) ... Utah R
Utah Reports, Second Series [*A publication*] (DLA) ... Utah 2d
Utah State Agricultural College ... USAC
Utah State Historical Society, Salt Lake City, UT [*Library symbol Library of Congress*] (LCLS) ... UHi
Utah State Library Commission, Division of the Blind and Physically Handicapped,Salt Lake City, UT [*Library symbol Library of Congress*] (LCLS) ... U-BPH
Utah State Library, Processing Center, Salt Lake City, UT [*OCLC symbol*] (OCLC) ... UUZ
Utah State Library, Salt Lake City, UT [*Library symbol Library of Congress*] (LCLS) ... U
Utah State Library, Salt Lake City, UT [*OCLC symbol*] (OCLC) ... ULC
Utah State University (PDAA) ... USU
Utah State University (GAGS) ... Utah St U
Utah State University, Logan, UT [*Library symbol Library of Congress*] (LCLS) ... ULA
Utah State University, Logan, UT [*OCLC symbol*] (OCLC) ... UUS
Utah Supreme Court Reports [*A publication*] (DLA) ... Utah
Utah Technical College at Salt Lake, Salt Lake City, UT [*Library symbol Library of Congress*] (LCLS) ... USIT
Utah Territory [*Prior to statehood*] ... UT
Utah Test and Training Range [*Air Force*] ... UTTR
Utah Test of Language Development [*Education*] ... UTLD
Utah University Engineering College ... UTEC
Utah Valley Community College, Orem, UT [*Library symbol*] [*Library of Congress*] (LCLS) ... UOrUC
Utah-Manhattan-Sundt & Associates (AAG) ... UMSA
Utapao [*Thailand*] [*Airport symbol Obsolete*] (OAG) ... UTP
Utashik Lake [*Alaska*] [*Seismograph station code, US Geological Survey*] (SEIS) ... UKL
Utd Cap Fd LP.9.625% CapSec'A' [*NYSE symbol*] (TTSB) ... UILPrA
Utd Dominion Rlty 9.25% 'A' Pfd [*NYSE symbol*] (TTSB) ... UDRPrA
Ute Public Library, Ute, IA [*Library symbol Library of Congress*] (LCLS) ... IaUte
Utendum [*To Be Used*] [*Pharmacy*] (ROG) ... UT
Utendus [*To Be Used*] [*Pharmacy*] ... U
Utendus [*To Be Used*] [*Pharmacy*] ... UTEND
Utendus More Solito [*To be Used in the Usual Manner*] [*Latin Pharmacy*] (MAE) ... utend mor sol
Utensil (MSA) ... UTN
Utensil (VRA) ... utnsl
Uterine Activity Interval [*Obstetrics*] ... UAI
Uterine Activity Unit [*Medicine*] (DMAA) ... UAU
Uterine Aspiration [*Medicine*] ... UA
Uterine Blood Flow [*Medicine*] (MAE) ... UBF
Uterine Contraction [*Obstetrics*] (AAMN) ... UC
Uterine Epithelium [*Medicine*] ... UE
Uterine Progesterone System [*Contraceptive device*] ... UPS
Uterine Stroma ... US
Uterine Vein [*Anatomy*] ... UV
Uterine Volume ... UV
Uterine-Relaxing Factor [*Endocrinology*] ... URF
Uteroglobin [*Physiology*] ... UG
Uteropedvic [*Gynecology*] (DAVI) ... UP
Uteropelvic Junction [*Anatomy*] (DAVI) ... UPJ

Uteroplacental Insufficiency [*Medicine*] .... UPI
Uteroplacental Ischemia [*Obstetrics*] (DAVI) .... UPI
Uteroplacental Respiratory Insufficiency [*Gynecology*] .... UPRI
Uterotubal Junction [*Medicine*] .... UTJ
Uterus [*Anatomy*] (DAVI) .... UT
UTI Energy [*AMEX symbol*] (TTSB) .... UTI
UTI Energy Corp. [*AMEX symbol*] (SPSG) .... UTI
UTI Energy Corp. [*Associated Press*] (SAG) .... UTI Eng
Uti Rogas [*Be It as You Desire*] [*Used by Romans to express assent to a proposition*] [*Latin*] .... UR
Utica [*New York*] [*Airport symbol*] (OAG) .... UCA
Utica College of Syracuse University, Utica, NY [*Library symbol Library of Congress*] (LCLS) .... NUtC
Utica College of Syracuse University, Utica, NY [*OCLC symbol*] (OCLC) VVV
Utica/Marcy Psychiatric Center, Marcy Campus Library, Utica, NY [*OCLC symbol*] (OCLC) .... ZUS
Utica/Marcy Psychiatric Center, Utica Campus Library, Utica, NY [*OCLC symbol*] (OCLC) .... ZUP
Utica, MI [*Location identifier FAA*] (FAAL) .... UIZ
Utica, MS [*FM radio station call letters*] .... WJXN
Utica Mutual Insurance Co., Library, New Hartford, NY [*OCLC symbol*] (OCLC) .... ZUO
Utica Mutual Insurance Co., Utica, NY [*Library symbol Library of Congress*] (LCLS) .... NUtMI
Utica, NY [*Location identifier FAA*] (FAAL) .... BKG
Utica, NY [*Location identifier FAA*] (FAAL) .... CJY
Utica, NY [*FM radio station call letters*] .... WFRG
Utica, NY [*Television station call letters*] .... WFXV
Utica, NY [*AM radio station call letters*] .... WIBX
Utica, NY [*Television station call letters*] .... WKTV
Utica, NY [*FM radio station call letters*] .... WLZW
Utica, NY [*FM radio station call letters*] .... WOUR
Utica, NY [*FM radio station call letters*] .... WPNR
Utica, NY [*FM radio station call letters*] .... WRCK
Utica, NY [*AM radio station call letters*] .... WRUN
Utica, NY [*AM radio station call letters*] .... WRVN
Utica, NY [*AM radio station call letters*] .... WTLB
Utica, NY [*FM radio station call letters*] .... WUNY
Utica, NY [*FM radio station call letters*] .... WUTQ
Utica, NY [*Television station call letters*] .... WUTR
Utica, NY [*FM radio station call letters*] .... WVVC
Utica Psychiatric Center, Utica, NY [*Library symbol Library of Congress*] (LCLS) .... NUtP
Utica Public Library, Utica, IL [*Library symbol Library of Congress*] (LCLS) .... IUt
Utica Public Library, Utica, MI [*Library symbol Library of Congress*] (LCLS) .... MiUt
Utica Public Library, Utica, NY [*Library symbol Library of Congress*] (LCLS) .... NUt
Utica Public Library, Utica, NY [*OCLC symbol*] (OCLC) .... ZVC
Utica-Bend (SAA) .... UB
Utila Island [*Honduras*] [*Airport symbol Obsolete*] (OAG) .... UII
Utila Island [*Honduras*] [*Airport symbol*] (AD) .... UTL
UtiliCorp Capital 8.875%'MIPS' [*NYSE symbol*] (TTSB) .... UCUPrC
Utilicorp Capital LP [*Associated Press*] (SAG) .... UtlCC
UtiliCorp United [*NYSE symbol*] (TTSB) .... UCU
UtiliCorp United $2.05 Pref [*NYSE symbol*] (TTSB) .... UCUPrA
Utilicorp United, Inc. [*NYSE symbol Toronto Stock Exchange symbol*] (SPSG) .... UCU
Utilicorp United, Inc. [*Associated Press*] (SAG) .... UtilC
Utilicorp United, Inc. [*Associated Press*] (SAG) .... UtiliCo
Utilitaire Logique Processor [*Programming language*] [*Computer science French*] .... ULP
Utilitarian (AAG) .... UTILN
Utilities Conservation Action Now [*Federal Energy Administration*] .... UCAN
Utilities Conservation Program [*Navy*] (NG) .... UCP
Utilities Control System [*NASA*] (KSC) .... UCS
Utilities Cost Analysis Report .... UCAR
Utilities Emergency Radio Network (IAA) .... UERN
Utilities Law Reporter [*A publication*] (DLA) .... ULR
Utilities Law Reporter [*Commerce Clearing House*] [*A publication*] (DLA) .... Util L Rep
Utilities Management Services (ACII) .... UMS
Utilities Telecommunications Council (EA) .... UTC
Utilities, Transportation, Communication .... UTC
Utilitiesman [*Navy rating*] .... UT
Utilitiesman, Boilerman [*Navy rating*] .... UTB
Utilitiesman, Chief [*Navy rating*] .... UTC
Utilitiesman, First Class [*Navy rating*] UT1
Utilitiesman, Master Chief [*Navy rating*] .... UTCM
Utilitiesman, Second Class [*Navy rating*] UT2
Utilitiesman, Senior Chief [*Navy rating*] .... UTCS
Utilitiesman, Third Class [*Navy rating*] UT3
Utilitiesman, Water and Sanitation [*Navy rating*] .... UTW
Utility [*Designation for all US military aircraft*] .... U
Utility (BUR) .... UT
Utility [*or Utilization*] (AFM) .... UTIL
Utility .... UTLTY
Utility (BUR) .... UTL
Utility Air Regulatory Group [*Environmental Protection Agency*] (GFGA) .... UARG
Utility Aircraft [*Lighter-than-Air*] [*Navy symbol*] (MUGU) .... ZU
Utility Aircraft Carrier [*Navy symbol Obsolete*] .... CVU
Utility Aircraft Requirements Study [*Army*] (DOMA) .... UTARS
Utility Airplane Company [*Army*] (VNW) .... UAC
Utility Airplane Council [*Defunct*] (EA) .... UAC
Utility Amphibian Plane [*Navy*] .... UAP
Utility and Data Flow (NASA) .... UDF
Utility and Support Programming Control Committee (SAA) .... USPCC

Utility Arborist Association (EA) .... UAA
Utility Assemble Communication Pool (IAA) .... UAC
Utility Assemble Compool .... UAC
Utility Assemble Master Communication (IAA) .... UAMC
Utility Assemble Master Compool .... UAMC
Utility Bill Performance Calculation (AAGC) .... UBPC
Utility Binary Dump [*Computer science*] .... UBD
Utility Boat .... UT
Utility Bridge (NASA) .... UB
Utility Car [*British*] .... UC
Utility Card Input .... UCI
Utility Cargo .... UC
Utility Commission Engineers Conference .... UCEC
Utility Communications Architecture [*Standardized computer program for utility companies*] (PS) .... UCA
Utility Communicators International (EA) .... UCI
Utility Compiler .... UCO
Utility Consulting Services [*Petroleum Information Corp.*] [*Information service or system*] (IID) .... UCS
Utility Consumers Action Network .... UCAN
Utility Control .... UCON
Utility Control Console .... UCC
Utility Control Facility .... UCF
Utility Control Program .... UCP
Utility Control Strategy Model [*Developed at Carnegie Mellon University for acid rain analysis*] .... UCSM
Utility Corridor .... UC
Utility Corridor (SAA) .... UTILIDOR
Utility Data Institute [*Information service or system*] (IID) .... UDI
Utility Data Reduction .... UDR
Utility Data Reduction Control (IAA) .... UDRC
Utility Data Reduction Output (IAA) .... UDRO
Utility Data Retrieval Control .... UDRC
Utility Data Retrieval Output .... UDRO
Utility Data Systems [*Information service or system*] (IID) .... UDS
Utility Dog [*Dog show term*] .... UD
Utility Dog [*Prefix*] .... U-UD
Utility Dog and Tracking Excellent [*Degree of obedience training*] .... UDTX
Utility Dog Excellent [*Dog show term*] [*Canada*] .... UDX
Utility Dog Title with a Tracking Dog Excellent Title .... UDTX
Utility Dog Title with a Tracking Dog Title .... UDT
Utility Dog Title with a Variable Surface Tracking Title .... UDVST
Utility Dog Tracker [*Degree of obedience training*] .... UDT
Utility Expenditure (MHDW) .... UE
Utility Facilities Program [*Computer science*] (IBMDP) .... UFP
Utility File .... UF
Utility Flight Unit [*Navy*] .... UFU
Utility General .... UGL
Utility Helicopter [*Military*] (AABC) .... UH
Utility Interim Table Simulation (SAA) .... UTS
Utility Interim Tape (SAA) .... UIT
Utility Iterative Operation .... UIO
Utility Jet Transport [*Air Force*] .... UCX
Utility Landplane [*Navy*] .... ULP
Utility, Lawn, and Garden Engines .... ULGE
Utility Lead [*Telecommunications*] (TEL) .... UL
Utility Library [*National Center for Atmospheric Research*] .... ULIB
Utility Motor Launch .... UTML
Utility Night Observer .... UNO
Utility Nuclear Waste Management Group (EA) .... UNWMG
Utility Octal Load .... UOL
Utility Path (IEEE) .... UP
Utility Plane [*Navy symbol*] .... VJ
Utility, Plant, and Reissue [*Patent applications*] .... UPR
Utility Player .... UT
Utility Practical Transport Aircraft System [*Army*] .... UPTAS
Utility Print Punch .... UPP
Utility Program (MCD) .... UP
Utility Program Operating System (IEEE) .... UPOS
Utility Radio Communication .... URC
Utility Radio Transmitter .... URT
Utility Read-In Program (IAA) .... URI
Utility Room (MSA) .... UR
Utility Satellite (IAA) .... US
Utility Seaplane [*Navy, Coast Guard*] .... USP
Utility Section Newsletter [*A publication*] (DLA) .... Util Sect Newl
Utility Shareholders Association (EA) .... USA
Utility Speed (GAVI) .... VU
Utility Squadron [*Navy*] .... UTRON
Utility Squadron [*Navy symbol*] (MCD) .... VU
Utility Squadron, Forward Area [*Navy*] .... UTRONFWDAREA
Utility Storage Print (SAA) .... USP
Utility Summary Program .... USP
Utility Support Structure (MCD) .... USS
Utility Tactical Support (SAA) .... UTS
Utility Tactical Transport (MCD) .... UTT
Utility Tactical Transport Aircraft System [*Helicopter*] [*Military*] .... UTTAS
Utility Tactical Transport Aviation Company [*US Army helicopters*] (VNW) .... UTT Avn
Utility Tactical Transport Company [*US Army helicopters*] (VNW) .... UTTCO
Utility Tape Copy (SAA) .... UTC
Utility Tape Processor .... UTP
Utility Transport Squadron (DNAB) .... UTRANSRON
Utility Value [*Psychology*] .... UV
Utility Water (AAG) .... UW

Utility Wing [*Navy*] (MUGU) .... UTWG
Utility Wing [*Navy*] .... UTWING
Utility Wing, Service Force, Atlantic [*Navy*] .... UTWINGSERVLANT
Utility Wing, Service Force, Pacific [*Navy*] .... UTWINGSERVPAC
Utility Workers Union of America .... UWU
Utility Workers Union of America (EA) .... UWUA
Utility-Oriented Language (MCD) .... UOL
Utilizable Protein [*Biochemistry*] (DICI) .... UP
Utilization .... UTLZTN
Utilization Air Force Specialty Code .... UAFSC
Utilization and Disposal Service [*Functions transferred to Property
  Management and Disposal Service*] [*General Services Administration*] .... UDS
Utilization Control .... UC
Utilization Factor .... UF
Utilization Management (WYGK) .... UM
Utilization of Enemy Electromagnetic Radiation (MSA) .... UTEELRAD
Utilization of Government Facilities Not Required as It Is Considered Such
  Utilization Would Adversely Affect Performance of Assigned
  Temporary Duty .... UTNOTREQ
Utilization of Theoretical Energy .... UTE
Utilization Reporting System (MCD) .... URS
Utilization Research Report .... URR
Utilization/Reutilization and Marketing [*DoD*] .... U & M
Utilization Review [*Preferred provider organization*] [*Medicine*] .... UR
Utilization Review Agency [*Insurance*] .... URA
Utilization Review Committee [*Medical records*] (DAVI) .... URC
Utilized Starch Equivalent (BARN) .... USE
Utilx Corp. [*Associated Press*] (SAG) .... Utilx
UTILX Corp. [*NASDAQ symbol*] (SPSG) .... UTLX
Utirik [*Marshall Islands*] [*Airport symbol*] (OAG) .... UTK
Utkela [*India*] [*ICAO location identifier*] (ICLI) .... VEUK
UTLAS International Canada [*Formerly, University of Toronto Library
  Automation System*] [*Library network*] .... UTLAS
UTLAS [*University of Toronto Library Automation System*] **International
  Canada, Toronto, Ontario** [*Library symbol National Library of Canada*]
  (NLC) .... OTULAS
Utne Reader [*A publication*] (BRI) .... Utne R
Utopia Creek [*Alaska*] [*Airport symbol*] (OAG) .... UTO
Utopian (WDAA) .... UTOP
Utowana Lake [*New York*] [*Seismograph station code, US Geological Survey*]
  (SEIS) .... UWL
Utsunomiya [*Japan ICAO location identifier*] (ICLI) .... RJTU
Utsunomiya [*Japan*] [*Seismograph station code, US Geological Survey*]
  (SEIS) .... UTS
Uttaradit [*Thailand*] [*Airport symbol*] (AD) .... UTI
Uttaradit [*Thailand*] [*ICAO location identifier*] (ICLI) .... VTPU
Uttaradit (West) [*Thailand*] [*ICAO location identifier*] (ICLI) .... VTCF
Uttering [*FBI standardized term*] .... UTT
Uttering and Publishing [*Legal term*] .... U & P
Utti [*Finland ICAO location identifier*] (ICLI) .... EFUT
Uttlesford [*England*] .... UTTL
Utuado, PR [*FM radio station call letters*] .... WERR
Utuado, PR [*AM radio station call letters*] .... WUPR

UTVA Aircraft Factory [*Former Yugoslavia*] [*ICAO aircraft manufacturer
  identifier*] (ICAO) .... U
UUB Financial [*Associated Press*] (SAG) .... UUB
UUNET Technologies [*NASDAQ symbol*] (TTSB) .... UUNT
UUnet Technologies, Inc. [*Associated Press*] (SAG) .... UUnet
UUnet Technologies, Inc. [*NASDAQ symbol*] (SAG) .... UUNT
UV [*Ultraviolet*] **Spectrometry Group** [*British*] .... UVG
Uvalde, TX [*FM radio station call letters*] (RBYB) .... KBNU-FM
Uvalde, TX [*FM radio station call letters*] .... KUVA
Uvalde, TX [*AM radio station call letters*] .... KVOU
Uvalde, TX [*FM radio station call letters*] .... KYUF
Uvalde, TX [*Location identifier FAA*] (FAAL) .... UVA
Uvas Verdes [*Bolivia*] [*ICAO location identifier*] (ICLI) .... SLUV
Uveitis, Glaucoma, and Hyphema Plus Vitreous Hemorrhage [*Syndrome*]
  [*Ophthalmology*] (DAVI) .... UGH
Uveitis-Glaucoma-Hyphema [*Ophthalmology*] .... UGH
Uvira [*Zaire*] [*Seismograph station code, US Geological Survey Closed*]
  (SEIS) .... UVI
Uvol [*Papua New Guinea*] [*Airport symbol*] (OAG) .... UVO
Uvulopalatopharyngoplasty [*Otorhinolaryngology*] (DAVI) .... UPP
Uvulo-Palato-Pharyngoplasty [*Surgical procedure*] [*Initials are derived from
  the name of the problem the procedure cures*] .... UPPP
Uvulopalatoplasty [*Otorhinolaryngology*] (DAVI) .... UPP
Uwajima [*Japan*] [*Seismograph station code, US Geological Survey*] (SEIS) ..... UWA
U-Wave [*on electrocardiogram*] [*Cardiology*] (DAVI) .... U
Uwekahuna [*Hawaii*] [*Seismograph station code, US Geological Survey*]
  (SEIS) .... UWE
Uxbridge [*British ICAO location identifier*] (ICLI) .... EGGF
Uxbridge [*British ICAO location identifier*] (ICLI) .... EGUU
Uxbridge Township Public Library, Uxbridge, ON, Canada [*Library symbol*]
  [*Library of Congress*] (LCLS) .... CaOUT
Uxbridge Township Public Library, Uxbridge, Ontario [*Library symbol
  National Library of Canada*] (NLC) .... OUT
Uxbridge Yeomanry Cavalry [*British military*] (DMA) .... UYC
Uxbridge-Scott Historical Society, Uxbridge, ON, Canada [*Library symbol*]
  [*Library of Congress*] (LCLS) .... CaOUSH
Uxbridge-Scott Historical Society, Uxbridge, Ontario [*Library symbol
  National Library of Canada*] (BIB) .... OUSH
Uxor [*Wife*] [*Latin*] (WGA) .... ux
Uyak [*Alaska*] [*Airport symbol*] (OAG) .... KUY
Uyak, AK [*Location identifier FAA*] (FAAL) .... KUY
Uyoku Jiten [*A publication*] .... UJ
Uyuni [*Bolivia*] [*ICAO location identifier*] (ICLI) .... SLUY
Uzbek (BARN) .... Uz
Uzbek [*MARC language code Library of Congress*] (LCCP) .... uzb
Uzbek Soviet Socialist Republic [*MARC geographic area code Library of
  Congress*] (LCCP) .... e-ur-uz
Uzbek Soviet Socialist Republic [*MARC country of publication code Library of
  Congress*] (LCCP) .... uzr
Uzbekistan Havo Jullary [*Uzbekistan Airways*] [*ICAO designator*] (FAAC) .... UZB
Uzes [*France ICAO location identifier*] (ICLI) .... LFNU
Uzhgorod [*Unuar*] [*Former USSR Seismograph station code, US Geological
  Survey*] (SEIS) .... UZH
Uzunagach [*Former USSR ICAO location identifier*] (ICLI) .... UAAN

V

By Meaning

V & L Enterprises [ACCORD] [UTLAS symbol] .... VLE
V & L Enterprises, Downsview, Ontario [Library symbol National Library of Canada] (NLC) .... OTVL
V Band Corp. [Associated Press] (SAG) .... V Band
V Band Corp. [NASDAQ symbol] (NQ) .... VBAN
V Channelled Substrate Inner Stripe (NITA) .... VSIS
"V" Device [Military decoration] (AABC) .... VDEV
V Fan Club (EA) .... VFC
V/STOL Approach System (MCD) .... VAPS
V/STOL Support Ship .... VSS
V. Zay Smith Associates Ltd., Calgary, AB, Canada [Library symbol Library of Congress] (LCLS) .... CaACVZS
V. Zay, Smith Associates Ltd., Calgary, Alberta [Library symbol National Library of Canada] (NLC) .... ACVZS
V3 London Gun [British military] (DMA) V
V-8 Juice Agar [Microbiology] .... VJA
Va Pwr Cap Tr 1 8.05% Pfd [NYSE symbol] (TTSB) .... VELPrT
Vaal Reefs Ex&Mng ADR [NASDAQ symbol] (TTSB) .... VAALY
Vaal Reefs Exploration [NASDAQ symbol] (NQ) .... VAAL
Vaal Reefs Exploration & Mining Co. Ltd. [Associated Press] (SAG) .... VaalRf
Vaala [Finland ICAO location identifier] (ICLI) .... EFVL
VAALCO Energy [NASDAQ symbol] (TTSB) .... VEIX
Vaasa [Finland ICAO location identifier] (ICLI) .... EFVA
Vaasa [Finland] [Airport symbol] (OAG) .... VAA
Vacancy [Real estate] (ADA) .... VAC
Vacancy Bit (IAA) .... VB
Vacant (AFM) .... VAC
Vacant Code Announcement (DNAB) .... VCA
Vacant National Number [Telecommunications] (TEL) .. VNN
Vacant Nozzle Shield Plug [Nuclear energy] (NRCH) ... VNSP
Vacant Property (ADA) .... VP
Vacarius [Flourished, 1144-70] [Authority cited in pre-1607 legal work] (DSA) .... Va
Vacate .... VAC
Vacated [Same case vacated] [Used in Shepard's Citations] [Legal term] (DLA) V
Vacation .... VAC
Vacation (ODBW) .... vac
Vacation and Senior Citizens Association (EA) .... VASCA
Vacation and Senior Citizens Association (EA) .... VSCA
Vacation Bible Schools (EA) .... VBS
Vacation Break U.S.A. [NASDAQ symbol] (TTSB) ..... VBRK
Vacation Break U.S.A., Inc. [NASDAQ symbol] (SAG) .. VBRK
Vacation Break U.S.A., Inc. [Associated Press] (SAG) .. VBUSA
Vacation Eligibility and Request Card [Military] ...... VERC
Vacation Exchange Club (EA) .... VEC
Vacationair, Inc. [Canada ICAO designator] (FAAC) ... VAC
Vacaville, CA [FM radio station call letters] .... KUIC
Vacaville, CA [Location identifier FAA] (FAAL) .... VQV
Vacaville District Library, Vacaville, CA [Library symbol Library of Congress] (LCLS) .... CVa
Vaccella [Flourished, 12th century] [Authority cited in pre-1607 legal work] (DSA) V
Vaccella [Flourished, 12th century] [Authority cited in pre-1607 legal work] (DSA) .... Va
Vaccella [Flourished, 12th century] [Authority cited in pre-1607 legal work] (DSA) .... Vac
Vaccella [Flourished, 12th century] [Authority cited in pre-1607 legal work] (DSA) .... Vacc
Vaccinate .... vacc
Vaccinated [Medicine] V
Vaccination [or Vaccine] [Medicine] .... VAC
Vaccination Scar [Medicine] .... VS
Vaccination Scar Upper Left Arm [Medicine] (MAE) ... VSULA
Vaccine [Medicine] .... VACCI
Vaccine Adverse Event Reporting System [Food and Drug Administration] .... VAERS
[National] Vaccine Injury Compensation Program [Established under the 1986 federal Childhood Vaccine Injury Act] (PAZ) ..... VICP
Vaccine Satellite Program (MCD) .... VACSAT
Vaccine-Associated Paralytic Poliomyelitis [Medicine] . VAPP
Vaccines for Children [Medicine] .... VPC
Vaccinia Early Transcription Factor [Genetics] .... VETF
Vaccinia Growth Factor [Biochemistry] .... VGF
Vaccinia Immune Globulin [Medicine] .... VIG
Vaccinia Virus VV
Vaccinia Virus: Wild Type [Virology] .... VV:WT

Vaccinia-Rabies Glycoprotein [Medicine] .... V-RG
Vache Follet [Mad Cow] [Deragatory term for French meat] .. VF
Vachel Lindsay Association (EA) .... VLA
Vachel Lindsay Association, Springfield, IL [Library symbol Library of Congress] (LCLS) .... ISVL
Vacu-Dry Co. [Associated Press] (SAG) .... VacDry
Vacu-Dry Co. [NASDAQ symbol] (NQ) .... VDRY
Vacuolar Apical Compartment [Cytology] .... VAC
Vacuolated Cell VC
Vacuole V
Vacuum (AAG) V
Vacuum (AABC) .... VAC
Vacuum (IDOE) .... vac
Vacuum .... VCM
Vacuum (AAG) .... VCM
Vacuum Actuated Control Switch (IAA) .... VCS
Vacuum and Vent Control Valve Distributor [Automotive engineering] ..... VACVVD
Vacuum and Vent Control Valve Thermactor [Automotive engineering] .... VACVVT
Vacuum Arc Degassing [Metal technology] .... VAD
Vacuum Arc Degassing .... VAD
Vacuum Arc Double-Electrode Remelting [Metallurgy] . VADER
Vacuum Arc Remelting [Steel alloy] .... VAR
Vacuum Arc Thrustor Program (MCD) .... VAT
Vacuum Aspiration [Medicine] .... VA
Vacuum Backing Pump .... VBP
Vacuum Bag Manufacturers Association [Defunct] (EA) .. VBMA
Vacuum Bell Jar .... VBJ
Vacuum Bottoms Recycle [Petroleum refining] .... VBR
Vacuum Brazed - Gas Quenched .... VBGQ
Vacuum Check Valve VCV
Vacuum Cleaner Manufacturers Association (EA) ..... VCMA
Vacuum Condensible Material [Astronomy] (OA) ...... VCM
Vacuum Condensing Point (IAA) .... VCP
Vacuum Contact Relay .... VCR
Vacuum Control Check Valve [Automotive engineering] . VCKV
Vacuum Control Switch .... VCS
Vacuum Control Switch - Cold Temperature [Automotive engineering] .... VCSCT
Vacuum Control Switch - Deceleration Idle [Automotive engineering] .... VCSDI
Vacuum Control Temperature Switch [Automotive engineering] .... VCTS
Vacuum Control Valve [Automotive engineering] VCV
Vacuum Dealers Trade Association (EA) .... VDTA
Vacuum Deposition Equipment .... VDE
Vacuum Differential Valve [Automotive engineering] .. VDV
Vacuum Diffusion Pump .... VDP
Vacuum Distillation (PDAA) .... VD
Vacuum Distillation/Overflow Sampler [Nuclear energy] (NRCH) ... VD/OS
Vacuum Distillation Unit [Petroleum technology] ...... VDU
Vacuum Distillation - Vapor Filtration .... VD-VF
Vacuum Distilled (WDAA) .... VAC DIST
Vacuum Electron Beam Welder .... VEBW
Vacuum Electronics Engineering Co. (MCD) .... VEECO
Vacuum Energy Diverter .... VED
Vacuum Enhanced Recovery [Computer science] ...... VER
Vacuum Erection Device [Medicine] .... VED
Vacuum Evaporator System .... VES
Vacuum Film Handling .... VFH
Vacuum Film Handling Technique .... VFHT
Vacuum Flash Pyrolysis .... VFP
Vacuum Fluorescent [Graphic arts] (DGA) .... VF
Vacuum Fluorescent Display [Computer science] ...... VFD
Vacuum Fore Pump .... VFP
Vacuum Form Tool (MCD) .... VFT
Vacuum Forming Machine .... VFM
Vacuum Freezing Ejector Absorption (PDAA) .... VFEA
Vacuum Freezing, Vapor Compression [Desalination] .. VFVC
Vacuum Friction Test .... VFT
Vacuum Gas Oil [Petroleum technology] .... VGO
Vacuum Gate Valve .... VGV
Vacuum Housing .... VH
Vacuum Hydrogen Furnace .... VHF
Vacuum Induction Melt, Vacuum Arc Remelt .... VIMVAR
Vacuum Induction Melting [Metallurgy] .... VIM
Vacuum Induction Melting .... VIM
Vacuum Insulated Evaporator (PDAA) .... VIE
Vacuum Leak Detector .... VLD
Vacuum Lens Blank .... VLB

Vacuum Lifting Unit .... VLU
Vacuum Loading System .... VLS
Vacuum Melting Furnace .... VMF
Vacuum Melting Module .... VMM
Vacuum Operation of Spacecraft Equipment (IAA) .... VOSE
Vacuum Optical Bench .... VOB
Vacuum Oven Sublimation [*Automotive exhaust emission testing*] .... VOS
Vacuum Oxygen Decarburization [*Stainless-steel processing*] .... VOD
Vacuum Pack Life Raft (DWSG) .... VPLR
Vacuum Packaged .... VP
Vacuum Penetration Unit .... VPU
Vacuum Pickup .... VP
Vacuum Pickup Pencil .... VPP
Vacuum Pickup System .... VPS
Vacuum Pipe Still [*Chemical engineering*] .... VPS
Vacuum Pipette Rig (PDAA) .... VPR
Vacuum Pressure Impregnation (IEEE) .... VPI
Vacuum Pump .... VP
Vacuum Pump Chamber .... VPC
Vacuum Pump Discharge Filter .... VPDF
Vacuum Pump Filter .... VPF
Vacuum Pump System .... VPS
Vacuum Pumping Module .... VPM
Vacuum Rectifying Tube .... VRT
Vacuum Regulator Solenoid [*Automotive engineering*] .... VRS
Vacuum Regulator Valve [*Automotive engineering*] .... VRV
Vacuum Relief System [*Nuclear energy*] (NRCH) .... VRS
Vacuum Reservoir [*Automotive engineering*] .... VRES
Vacuum Residuum Desulfurization [*Petroleum refining*] .... VRDS
Vacuum Restrictor [*Automotive engineering*] .... VREST
Vacuum Retard Delay Valve [*Automotive engineering*] .... VRDV
Vacuum Short Resid [*Petroleum technology*] .... VSR
Vacuum Society of Australia .... VSA
Vacuum Spark Advance Disconnect [*Auto air pollution control device*] .... VSAD
Vacuum Swing Adsorption [*Chemical engineering*] .... VSA
Vacuum Switch .... VS
Vacuum Switching Valve [*Automotive engineering*] .... VSV
Vacuum Telegraphy [*Telecommunications*] (IAA) .... VT
Vacuum Test Furnace .... VTF
Vacuum Thermal Chamber (IAA) .... VTC
Vacuum Thermal Stability Test (MCD) .... VTS
Vacuum Thermal Testing .... VTT
Vacuum Tower Bottoms [*Petroleum chemistry*] .... VTB
Vacuum Transmitting Valve [*Automotive engineering*] .... VTV
Vacuum Tube (IAA) V
Vacuum Tube [*Electronics*] .... VT
Vacuum Tube (IDOE) .... vt
Vacuum Tube Development Committee [*Columbia University*] (MCD) .... VTDC
Vacuum Tuberculin [*Medicine*] (MAE) .... VT
Vacuum Ultraviolet .... VUV
Vacuum Valve VV
Vacuum Valve Operating Handle .... VVOH
Vacuum Vent Valve [*Automotive engineering*] VVV
Vacuum Window Assembly .... VWA
Vacuum Wood Preservers Institute (EA) .... VWPI
Vacuum-Air-Nitrogen Distribution .... VAND
Vacuum-Assisted Molding [*Automotive technology*] .... VAM
Vacuum-Assisted Resin Infusion (RDA) .... VARI
Vacuum-Assisted Resin Injection .... VARI
Vacuum-Impregnated Inductor VII
Vacuum-Jacketed (KSC) .... VJ
Vacuum-Operated Throttle Modulator [*Automotive engineering*] .... VOTM
Vacuum-Processed Oxide Free .... VPOF
Vacuum-Tube Amplifier .... VTA
Vacuum-Tube Detector (IAA) .... VTD
Vacuum-Tube Launcher .... VTL
Vacuum-Tube Module .... VTM
Vacuum-Tube Oscillator (IAA) .... VO
Vacuum-Tube Oscillator (IAA) .... VTO
Vacuum-Tube Relay Driver .... VRD
Vacuum-Tube Transmitter .... VTT
Vacuum-Tube Transmitter .... VTX
Vacuum-Tube (Voltmeter) (DEN) .... VT(V)
Vacuum-Tube Voltmeter .... VTVM
Vadodara [*India*] [*Airport symbol*] (OAG) .... BDQ
Vadso [*Norway ICAO location identifier*] (ICLI) .... ENVD
Vadso [*Norway*] [*Airport symbol*] (AD) .... VDO
Vadso [*Norway*] [*Airport symbol*] (OAG) .... VDS
Vaengir [*ICAO designator*] (AD) .... QT
Vaerlose [*Denmark ICAO location identifier*] (ICLI) .... EKVL
Vaeroy [*Norway ICAO location identifier*] (ICLI) .... ENVY
Vaeroy [*Norway*] [*Airport symbol*] (OAG) .... VRY
VAFB [*Vandenberg Air Force Base*] **Operations and Maintenance Documentation** (NASA) .... VOMD
Vagabond V
Vagabond (DSUE) .... VAG
Vagabonds Removed [*Prison van nickname used during reign of VR, Victoria Regina*] [*British*] (DSUE) .... VR
Vagahova Ballet Academy [*Russia*] .... VBA
Vagal Stimulation [*Medicine*] (DAVI) .... VS
Vagar [*Faeroe Islands*] [*Airport symbol*] (AD) .... VAG
Vagar, Faroe Islands [*Denmark ICAO location identifier*] (ICLI) .... EKVG
Vagina [*Anatomy*] (DAVI) V
Vagina, Ectocervix, and Endocervix [*Medicine*] (DMAA) .... VCE
Vagina, Ectocervix, and Endocervix [*Cytopathology*] .... VEE
Vaginal [*Medicine*] .... VAG
Vaginal Acid Phosphatase [*An enzyme*] .... VAP
Vaginal Birth After Caesarean [*Obstetrics*] .... VBAC
Vaginal Contraceptive Film [*Medicine*] (BARN) .... VCF
Vaginal Delivery after Caesarean [*Obstetrics*] .... VDAC
Vaginal Epithelium [*Endocrinology*] .... VE
Vaginal Examination [*Medicine*] .... VE
Vaginal Hysterectomy [*Gynecology*] (DAVI) .... V Hyst
Vaginal Hysterectomy [*Gynecology*] (CPH) .... Vag Hyst
Vaginal Hysterectomy [*Gynecology*] .... VH
Vaginal Intraepithelial Dysplasia [*Gynecology*] (DAVI) .... VID
Vaginal Intraepithelial Neoplasia [*Medicine*] (DAVI) .... VAIN
Vaginal Intraepithelial Neoplasia [*Gynecology*] (DAVI) .... VIN
Vaginal Irrigation [*Medicine*] VI
Vaginal Irrigation Smear [*Medicine*] (MAE) .... VIS
Vaginal Stroma .... VS
Vaginitis [*Medicine*] .... VAG
Vagotomy and Pyloroplasty [*Medicine*] .... V & P
Vagrancy [*FBI standardized term*] .... VAG
Vagus Nerve Stimulation [*Physiology*] .... VNS
Vahitahi [*French Polynesia*] [*ICAO location identifier*] (ICLI) .... NTUV
Vaihoa [*Tuamotu Archipelago*] [*Seismograph station code, US Geological Survey*] (SEIS) .... VAH
Vail [*Colorado*] [*Airport symbol*] (OAG) .... WHR
Vail, CO [*FM radio station call letters*] (RBYB) .... KPRE
Vail, CO [*AM radio station call letters*] .... KSKE
Vail, CO [*FM radio station call letters*] .... KSKE-FM
Vail Observer, Vail, IA [*Library symbol*] [*Library of Congress*] (LCLS) .... IaVaO
Vail Public Library, Vail, CO [*Library symbol Library of Congress*] (LCLS) .... CoVa
Vaizey's Law of Settlements [*1887*] [*A publication*] (DLA) .... Vaizey
Vajont [*Belluno*] [*Italy*] [*Seismograph station code, US Geological Survey*] (SEIS) .... VAJ
Vak-Rosat [*Former USSR*] [*FAA designator*] (FAAC) .... VAK
Val D'Or [*Canada*] [*Airport symbol*] (OAG) .... YVO
Val d'Or Explorations [*Vancouver Stock Exchange symbol*] .... VAD
Val D'Or, PQ [*Television station call letters*] .... CFVS
Val D'Or, PQ [*FM radio station call letters*] .... CJMV
Val D'Or, PQ [*AM radio station call letters*] .... CKVD
Val D'Or, PQ [*ICAO location identifier*] (ICLI) .... CYVO
Val Joyeux [*France*] [*Later, CLF*] [*Geomagnetic observatory code*] .... VLJ
Val Rita-Harty Public Library, Val Rita, Ontario [*Library symbol National Library of Canada*] (BIB) .... OVRH
Valan Ltd. [*Moldova*] [*FAA designator*] (FAAC) .... VLN
Valandovo [*Yugoslavia*] [*Seismograph station code, US Geological Survey*] (SEIS) .... VAY
Valar Resources Ltd. [*Vancouver Stock Exchange symbol*] .... VLR
Valassis Communcations [*NYSE symbol*] (TTSB) VCI
Valassis Communications [*Associated Press*] (SAG) .... Valassis
Valassis Communications, Inc. [*NYSE symbol*] (SPSG) VCI
Valcausus [*Gualcosius*] [*Flourished, 11th-12th century*] [*Authority cited in pre-1607 legal work*] (DSA) .... Val
Valclair Resources Ltd. [*Vancouver Stock Exchange symbol*] .... VCR
Valda [*France*] [*Research code symbol*] LV
Valdese General Hospital, Valdese, NC [*Library symbol*] [*Library of Congress*] (LCLS) .... NcValH
Valdese, NC [*AM radio station call letters*] .... WSVM
Valdese Public Library, Valdese, NC [*Library symbol Library of Congress*] (LCLS) .... NcVal
Valdez [*Alaska*] [*ICAO location identifier*] (ICLI) .... PAVD
Valdez [*Ecuador*] [*ICAO location identifier*] (ICLI) .... SEVA
Valdez [*Alaska*] [*Airport symbol*] (OAG) .... VDZ
Valdez [*Alaska*] [*Seismograph station code, US Geological Survey Closed*] (SEIS) .... VLD
Valdez [*Alaska*] [*Seismograph station code, US Geological Survey*] (SEIS) .... VLZ
Valdez Airlines [*ICAO designator*] (AD) XX
Valdez, AK [*AM radio station call letters*] .... KCHU
Valdez, AK [*AM radio station call letters*] .... KVAK
Valdez, AK [*AM radio station call letters*] .... KVLD
Valdez, AK [*Location identifier FAA*] (FAAL) .... MNL
Valdez, AK [*Location identifier FAA*] (FAAL) .... VWS
Valdez Public Library, Valdez, AK [*Library symbol Library of Congress*] (LCLS) .... AkV
Valdez South [*Alaska*] [*Seismograph station code, US Geological Survey*] (SEIS) .... VZS
Valdez West [*Alaska*] [*Seismograph station code, US Geological Survey*] (SEIS) .... VZW
Valdivia [*Chile*] [*Seismograph station code, US Geological Survey*] (SEIS) VLV
Valdivia [*Chile*] [*Airport symbol*] (AD) .... ZAL
Valdivia/Pichoy [*Chile*] [*ICAO location identifier*] (ICLI) .... SCVD
Valdosta [*Georgia*] [*Airport symbol*] (OAG) .... VLD
Valdosta, GA [*Location identifier FAA*] (FAAL) .... MDG
Valdosta, GA [*Location identifier FAA*] (FAAL) .... VAD
Valdosta, GA [*FM radio station call letters*] .... WAAC
Valdosta, GA [*FM radio station call letters*] .... WAFT
Valdosta, GA [*AM radio station call letters*] .... WFVR
Valdosta, GA [*AM radio station call letters*] .... WGOV
Valdosta, GA [*Television station call letters*] .... WGVP
Valdosta, GA [*AM radio station call letters*] .... WJEM
Valdosta, GA [*FM radio station call letters*] .... WQPW
Valdosta, GA [*AM radio station call letters*] .... WVLD
Valdosta, GA [*FM radio station call letters*] .... WVVS
Valdosta, GA [*FM radio station call letters*] .... WWET
Valdosta, GA [*FM radio station call letters*] .... WWRQ
Valdosta, GA [*FM radio station call letters*] .... WYZK
Valdosta/Moody Air Force Base [*Georgia*] [*ICAO location identifier*] (ICLI) .... KVAD

Valdosta Moody Air Force Base, GA [*Location identifier FAA*] (FAAL) .... XDY
Valdosta Southern Railroad [*AAR code*] .... VSO
Valdosta State College (GAGS) .... Valdosta St C
Valdosta State College [*Georgia*] .... VSC
Valdosta State College, Valdosta, GA [*Library symbol Library of Congress*]
   (LCLS) .... GVaS
Valdosta State College, Valdosta, GA [*OCLC symbol*] (OCLC) .... GYG
Valdresfly, AS [*Norway*] [*FAA designator*] (FAAC) .... VLF
Vale (ROG) V
Vale of Rheidol Light Railway [*Wales*] .... V of R
Vale of Rheidol Light Railway [*Wales*] .... VR
Vale of Rheidol Light Railway [*Wales*] .... VRLTRY
Vale of White Horse [*Hounds*] .... VWH
Valemount Public Library, British Columbia [*Library symbol National Library of Canada*] (NLC) .... BVALE
Valence [*France*] [*Airport symbol*] (OAG) .... VAF
Valence Band Maximum [*Physics*] .... VBM
Valence Bond (DEN) .... VB
Valence Bond Maximum [*Physics*] .... VBM
Valence/Chabeuil [*France ICAO location identifier*] (ICLI) .... LFLU
Valence Effective Hamiltonian [*Physical chemistry*] .... VEH
Valence Electron Concentration (PDAA) .... VEC
Valence Force Field .... VFF
Valence Shell Electron Pair Repulsion [*Model for molecular structure*] .... VSEPR
Valence State Ionization Potentials [*of atoms*] .... VSIP
Valence Technology [*NASDAQ symbol*] (TTSB) .... VLNC
Valence Technology, Inc. [*Associated Press*] (SAG) .... ValTech
Valence Technology, Inc. [*NASDAQ symbol*] (SAG) .... VLNC
Valence-Alternation Pair [*Solid-state physics*] .... VAP
Valence-Bond Theory [*Physical chemistry*] .... VBT
Valence-Shell Electron Pair Repulsion [*Theory of molecular structure*] .... VSEPR
Valencia [*Spain ICAO location identifier*] (ICLI) .... LECL
Valencia [*Spain ICAO location identifier*] (ICLI) .... LEVC
Valencia [*Spain ICAO location identifier*] (ICLI) .... LEVM
Valencia [*Bolivia*] [*ICAO location identifier*] (ICLI) .... SLVN
Valencia [*Spain*] [*Airport symbol*] (OAG) VLC
Valencia [*Venezuela*] [*Airport symbol*] (OAG) .... VLN
Valencia Community College, Orlando, FL [*Library symbol Library of Congress*] (LCLS) .... FOV
Valencia Community College, Orlando, FL [*OCLC symbol*] (OCLC) ... FVC
Valencia/Internacional, Carabobo [*Venezuela ICAO location identifier*] (ICLI) .... SVVA
Valenciennes/Denain [*France ICAO location identifier*] (ICLI) .... LFAV
Valen's Commentaries [*A publication*] (DLA) .... Val Com
Valentia [*Ireland*] [*Seismograph station code, US Geological Survey*] (SEIS) .... VAL
Valentine (WGA) .... VA
Valentine (BARN) .... val
Valentine Gold [*Vancouver Stock Exchange symbol*] .... VGD
Valentine Meat Juice Co., Richmond, VA [*Library symbol Library of Congress*] (LCLS) .... ViRVM
Valentine Museum, Richmond, VA [*Library symbol Library of Congress*] (LCLS) .... ViRVal
Valentine, NE [*AM radio station call letters*] .... KVSH
Valentine, NE [*Location identifier FAA*] (FAAL) .... VTN
Valentine Public Library, Valentine, NE [*Library symbol Library of Congress*] (LCLS) .... NbV
Valera [*Venezuela*] [*Airport symbol*] (OAG) VLV
Valera/Dr. Antonio Nicolas Briceno, Trujillo [*Venezuela ICAO location identifier*] (ICLI) .... SVVL
Valerie Gold Resources [*Vancouver Stock Exchange symbol*] .... VLG
Valero Energy [*NYSE symbol*] (TTSB) .... VLO
Valero Energy $3.125 Cv Pfd [*NYSE symbol*] (TTSB) .... VLOPr
Valero Energy Corp. [*Associated Press*] (SAG) .... Valero
Valero Energy Corp. [*NYSE symbol*] (SPSG) .... VLO
Valery Giscard d'Estaing [*Former French President*] .... VGE
Valesdir [*Vanuatu*] [*ICAO location identifier*] (ICLI) .... NVSV
Valesdir [*Vanuata*] [*Airport symbol*] (OAG) .... VLS
Valet Air Services [*FAA designator*] (FAAC) .... VAR
Valett Inventory of Critical Thinking Abilities [*Child development test*] .... VICTA
Valetta [*Malta*] [*Airport symbol*] (AD) .... MLA
Valhalla Centre Municipal Library, Alberta [*Library symbol National Library of Canada*] (NLC) .... AVCM
Valhalla Energy Corp. [*Vancouver Stock Exchange symbol*] .... VLA
Valhalla Gold Group [*Vancouver Stock Exchange symbol*] .... VGG
Valhalla, NY [*FM radio station call letters*] .... WARY
Valhi, Inc. [*Associated Press*] (SAG) .... Valhi
Valhi, Inc. [*NYSE symbol*] (SPSG) .... VHI
Valid [*Decision or finding held valid for reasons given*] [*Used in Shepard's Citations*] [*Legal term*] (DLA) .... Va
Valid [*or Validation*] (KSC) .... VAL
Valid BIT [*Binary Digit*] Register [*Computer science*] (MHDB) .... VBP
Valid Memory Address [*Computer science*] .... VMA
Valid Target Presentation [*Military*] (CAAL) .... VTP
Valid Verifiable Defense [*Stamped on dismissed traffic tickets*] .... VVD
Validate (AABC) .... VALI
Validate Master Tape .... VMT
Validated Aircraft Logistics Utilization Evaluation [*Navy*] .... VALUE
Validated Data Record .... VDR
Validation .... VALDN
Validation (NASA) .... VALID
Validation (AAG) .... VLDTN
Validation Analysis Report [*Social Security Administration*] .... VAR
Validation and Recovery .... VR
Validation Control System .... VCS
Validation In-Process Review [*DoD*] .... VALIPR

Validation Master Plan [*Pharmaceutical processing*] .... VMP
Validation Material [*Social Security Administration*] .... VM
Validation of ASW [*Antisubmarine Warfare*] Subsystem Effectiveness Levels [*Navy*] (CAAL) .... VASSEL
Validation of Theoretical Automatic Checkout Techniques (MCD) .... VOTACT
Validation Parameter (DA) .... VP
Validation Plan [*Social Security Administration*] .... VP
Validation Procedures Library [*Social Security Administration*] .... PROCVAL
Validation Program Library [*Social Security Administration*] .... PROGVAL
Validation Reject Listing (MCD) .... VRL
Validation Report [*Army*] .... VR
Validation Summary Report .... VSR
Validation System (SSD) .... VAS
Validation Testing (MCD) .... VT
Validation Unit (AAG) .... VU
Validation/Verification (CAAL) .... V/V
Validity Check [*Data entry test program*] [*Computer science*] (IAA) VC
Validity Check and Readout (NITA) .... VCRO
Validity Generalization Testing (OICC) .... VG
Validity, Repeatability, and Reliability [*Examination*] .... VRR
Valine [*One-letter symbol; see Val*] V
Valine [*Also, V*] [*An amino acid*] .... Val
Valine [*An amino acid*] (DOG) .... val
Valine-Proline-Glycine-Glycine [*Biochemistry*] .... VPGG
Valine-Proline-Glycine-Valine-Glycine [*Biochemistry*] .... VPGVG
Valitocin [*Endocrinology*] .... VT
Valium [*A tranquilizer*] [*Roche Laboratories*] (DAVI) .... Val
Valium [*A tranquilizer*] [*Roche Laboratories*] (DAVI) .... Vals
Valium Anonymous (EA) .... VA
Valkenburg [*Netherlands ICAO location identifier*] (ICLI) .... EHVB
Valladolid [*Spain ICAO location identifier*] (ICLI) .... LEDM
Valladolid [*Spain ICAO location identifier*] (ICLI) .... LEVD
Valladolid [*Spain*] [*Airport symbol*] (OAG) VLL
Valle, AZ [*Location identifier FAA*] (FAAL) .... VLE
Valle de la Pascua [*Venezuela*] [*Airport symbol*] (AD) .... VDP
Valle De La Pascua, Guarico [*Venezuela ICAO location identifier*] (ICLI) ...... SVVP
Valle Grande [*Bolivia*] [*ICAO location identifier*] (ICLI) .... SLVG
Valle Hermoso [*Argentina ICAO location identifier*] (ICLI) .... SAMH
Vallecitos Boiling Water Reactor .... VBWR
Vallecitos Experimental Superheat Reactor .... VESR
Vallecitos Experimental Superheat Reactor (NRCH) .... VSR
Valledupar [*Colombia*] [*Airport symbol*] (OAG) .... VUP
Valledupar/Alfonso Lopez [*Colorado ICAO location identifier*] (ICLI) ...... SKVP
Vallejo, CA [*Television station call letters*] .... KPST
Vallejo, CA [*AM radio station call letters*] .... KXBT
Vallejo Junior College [*California*] .... VJC
Vallejo Naval and Historical Museum, Vallejo, CA [*Library symbol*] [*Library of Congress*] (LCLS) .... CVNM
Vallejo Public Library, Vallejo, CA [*Library symbol Library of Congress*] (LCLS) CV
Vallen Corp. [*Associated Press*] (SAG) .... Vallen
Vallen Corp. [*NASDAQ symbol*] (NQ) .... VALN
Vallenar [*Chile*] [*Airport symbol*] (AD) .... VLR
Vallenar/Vallenar [*Chile*] [*ICAO location identifier*] (ICLI) .... SCLL
Vallentine Peace Group [*Political party Australia*] .... VPG
Valles Marineris [*A filamentary mark on Mars*] .... VM
Valley [*British ICAO location identifier*] (ICLI) .... EGOV
Valley (ROG) V
Valley (MSA) .... VAL
Valley [*Commonly used*] (OPSA) .... VALLEY
Valley [*Commonly used*] (OPSA) .... VALLY
Valley [*Commonly used*] (OPSA) .... VLLY
Valley .... VLY
Valley (MCD) .... VLY
Valley (ADA) .... VY
Valley Air Services, Inc. [*ICAO designator*] (FAAC) .... VAR
Valley, Al [*FM radio station call letters*] (RBYB) .... WEBT
Valley, Al [*FM radio station call letters*] .... WRLD
Valley & Siletz Railroad Co. [*AAR code*] .... VS
Valley City, ND [*AM radio station call letters*] .... KOVC
Valley City, ND [*FM radio station call letters*] .... KOVC-FM
Valley City, ND [*FM radio station call letters*] (RBYB) .... KQDJ-FM
Valley City, ND [*Television station call letters*] .... KXJB
Valley City, ND [*Location identifier FAA*] (FAAL) .... VCY
Valley City Public Library, Valley City, ND [*Library symbol Library of Congress*] (LCLS) .... NdVc
Valley City State College, Valley City, ND [*OCLC symbol*] (OCLC) .... NDV
Valley City State College, Valley City, ND [*Library symbol Library of Congress*] (LCLS) .... NdVcT
Valley East Public Library, Val Caron, ON, Canada [*Library symbol Library of Congress*] (LCLS) .... CaOVc
Valley East Public Library, Val Caron, Ontario [*Library symbol National Library of Canada*] (NLC) .... OVC
Valley Elementary School, East Grand Forks, MN [*Library symbol*] [*Library of Congress*] (LCLS) .... MnEgfVE
Valley Elementary School, Pelham, AL [*Library symbol*] [*Library of Congress*] (LCLS) .... APeVE
Valley Fed Svgs Bk Sheffield [*NASDAQ symbol*] (TTSB) .... VAFD
Valley Federal Savings Bank [*NASDAQ symbol*] (NQ) .... VAFD
Valley Federal Savings Bank [*Associated Press*] (SAG) .... VlFdAla
Valley Fig Growers (EA) .... VFG
Valley Forge [*AMEX symbol*] (TTSB) .... VF
Valley Forge Corp. [*Associated Press*] (SAG) .... ValFrg
Valley Forge Corp. [*AMEX symbol*] (SPSG) .... VF
Valley Forge Historical Society (EA) .... VFHS

Valley Forge Historical Society, Valley Forge, PA [*Library symbol Library of Congress*] (LCLS) .... PVfHi

Valley Forge Research Center [*University of Pennsylvania*] [*Research center*] (RCD) .... VFRC

Valley Forge Scientific [*NASDAQ symbol*] (TTSB) .... VLFG

Valley Forge Scientific Corp. [*NASDAQ symbol*] (NQ) .... VLFG

Valley Forge Scientific Corp. [*Associated Press*] (SAG) .... VlyFrg

Valley FTU [*British ICAO designator*] (FAAC) .... VYT

Valley General Hospital, Renton, WA [*Library symbol Library of Congress*] (LCLS) .... WaReVG

Valley Girl [*Lifestyle classification*] .... Val

Valley Head, AL [*AM radio station call letters*] .... WQRX

Valley Health Services Association, Kentville, Nova Scotia [*Library symbol National Library of Canada*] (NLC) .... NSKVH

Valley Line Co. [*Steamship*] (MHDW) VLC

Valley Medical Center, Fresno, CA [*Library symbol Library of Congress*] (LCLS) .... CFVM

Valley Migrant League (EA) .... VML

Valley Mirror, Middleton, Nova Scotia [*Library symbol National Library of Canada*] (NLC) .... NSMV

Valley Mirror, Middleton, NS, Canada [*Library symbol*] [*Library of Congress*] (LCLS) .... CaNSMiV

Valley National Bancorp [*NYSE symbol*] (SPSG) .... VLY

Valley National Bancorp [*Associated Press*] (SAG) .... VlyBcp

Valley Natl Bancorp [*NYSE symbol*] (TTSB) .... VLY

Valley of Tetons District Library, Victor, ID [*Library symbol*] [*Library of Congress*] (LCLS) .... IdV

Valley Oil & Gas [*Vancouver Stock Exchange symbol*] .... VLY

Valley Railroad .... VRR

[*The*] **Valley Railroad Co.** [*AAR code*] .... VALE

Valley Resources [*AMEX symbol*] (TTSB) .... VR

Valley Resources, Inc. [*Associated Press*] (SAG) .... VallyRs

Valley Resources, Inc. [*AMEX symbol*] (SPSG) .... VR

Valley SAR Training Unit [*British ICAO designator*] (FAAC) VLL

Valley Station, KY [*FM radio station call letters*] (RBYB) .... WHTE-FM

Valley Station, KY [*FM radio station call letters*] (RBYB) .... WXNU

Valley Stream North High School, Valley Stream, NY [*Library symbol*] [*Library of Congress*] (LCLS) .... NVsNSH

Valley Systems [*NASDAQ symbol*] (TTSB) .... VALE

Valley Systems, Inc. [*NASDAQ symbol*] (SAG) .... VALE

Valley Systems, Inc. [*Associated Press*] (SAG) .... ValySy

[*The*] **Valley/Wall Blake** [*Anguilla Island*] [*ICAO location identifier*] (ICLI) .... TQPF

Valleyfield, PQ [*FM radio station call letters*] .... CKOD

Valleys [*Commonly used*] (OPSA) .... VALLEYS

Valleys [*Postal Service standard*] (OPSA) .... VLYS

Valleys .... VLYS

Valleyview Municipal Library, Alberta [*Library symbol National Library of Canada*] (NLC) .... AVVM

Valleyview Municipal Library, Valleyview, AB, Canada [*Library symbol*] [*Library of Congress*] (LCLS) .... CaAVvM

Vallicorp Holdings [*NASDAQ symbol*] (TTSB) .... VALY

ValliCorp Holdings, Inc. [*Associated Press*] (SAG) .... ValliCor

Vallicorp Holdings, Inc. [*NASDAQ symbol*] (NQ) .... VALY

Valmet Corp. ADS [*NYSE symbol*] (TTSB) .... VA

Valmet OY [*Finland ICAO aircraft manufacturer identifier*] (ICAO) VL

Valmeyer Community Unit School District 3, Valmeyer, IL [*Library symbol Library of Congress*] (LCLS) .... IValSD

Valmont Indus [*NASDAQ symbol*] (TTSB) .... VALM

Valmont Industries, Inc. [*NASDAQ symbol*] (NQ) .... VALM

Valmont Industries, Inc. [*Associated Press*] (SAG) .... Valmnt

Valorous Unit Award [*Military decoration*] .... VUA

Valosin-Containing Protein [*Biochemistry*] .... VCP

Valpar Resources [*Vancouver Stock Exchange symbol*] .... VLP

Valparaiso [*Chile*] [*Seismograph station code, US Geological Survey*] (SEIS) .... UTF

Valparaiso (DSUE) .... VALPO

Valparaiso [*Chile*] [*Seismograph station code, US Geological Survey*] (SEIS) .... VLP

Valparaiso [*Indiana*] [*Airport symbol*] (OAG) .... VPZ

Valparaiso/Eglin Air Force Base [*Florida*] [*ICAO location identifier*] (ICLI) .... KVPS

Valparaiso, FL [*Location identifier FAA*] (FAAL) .... CAH

Valparaiso, FL [*Location identifier FAA*] (FAAL) .... EGI

Valparaiso, FL [*Location identifier FAA*] (FAAL) .... HLY

Valparaiso, FL [*Location identifier FAA*] (FAAL) .... VPS

Valparaiso, IN [*Location identifier FAA*] (FAAL) .... VPZ

Valparaiso, IN [*AM radio station call letters*] .... WAKE

Valparaiso, IN [*FM radio station call letters*] .... WLJE

Valparaiso, IN [*AM radio station call letters*] .... WNWI

Valparaiso, IN [*FM radio station call letters*] .... WVUR

Valparaiso Technical Institute [*Indiana*] .... VTI

Valparaiso University (GAGS) .... Valparaiso U

Valparaiso University, Law Library, Valparaiso, IN [*OCLC symbol*] (OCLC) .... IVZ

Valparaiso University, Valparaiso, IN [*Library symbol Library of Congress*] (LCLS) .... InValU

Valparaiso University, Valparaiso, IN [*OCLC symbol*] (OCLC) .... IVU

Valparaiso Vidette-Messenger, Valparaiso, IN [*Library symbol Library of Congress*] (LCLS) .... InValVM

Valparaiso-Niceville, FL [*AM radio station call letters*] .... WFSH

Valparaiso-Porter County Public Library System, Valparaiso, IN [*Library symbol Library of Congress*] (LCLS) .... InVal

Valproic Acid [*Anticonvulsant compound*] .... VA

Valproic Acid [*Anticonvulsant compound*] .... VPA

Valreas-Visan [*France ICAO location identifier*] (ICLI) .... LFNV

Valsamata [*Kephallenia*] [*Greece*] [*Seismograph station code, US Geological Survey*] (SEIS) .... PVLS

Valspar Corp. [*NYSE symbol*] (SPSG) .... VAL

Valspar Corp. [*Associated Press*] (SAG) .... Valspar

Valstieciu Liaudininku Sajunga [*Peasant Populist Union*] [*Lithuania*] [*Political party*] (PPE) .... VLS

Valsts Biblioteka [*State Library of Latvia*], Riga, Latvia [*Library symbol Library of Congress*] (LCLS) .... Lat

Valtion Teknillinen Tutkimuskeskus [*Technical Research Center of Finland*] [*Espoo*] [*Information service or system*] (IID) .... VTT

Valtion Teknillinen Tutkimuskeskus, Helsinki, Finland [*Library symbol Library of Congress*] (LCLS) .... FiHT

Valtionrautatiet [*Finnish State Railways*] .... VR

Valuable and Attractive [*A marking used by RAF on such supplies as watches and cameras*] [*British*] .... V and A

Valuable and Effective Network Utility Services (BUR) .... VENUS

Valuable Cargo VC

Valuable-Items Policy [*Insurance*] (MHDI) .... VIP

Valuation .... VAL

Valuation .... VALN

Valuation .... VALUON

Valuation Board of Review [*Australia*] .... VBR

Valuation by Components Rule (ADA) .... VCR

Valuation Clause VC

Valuation Decisions [*A publication*] (DLA) .... VD

Valuation Officer (WDAA) .... VO

Valuation Reports, Interstate Commerce Commission [*A publication*] (DLA) .... Val Rep

Valuation Reports, Interstate Commerce Commission [*A publication*] (DLA) .... Val Rep ICC

Valuation Reports, Interstate Commerce Commission [*A publication*] (DLA) .... VR

Valuation Research Corp., Milwaukee, WI [*Library symbol Library of Congress*] (LCLS) .... WMV

Value V

Value (ECII) .... VA

Value (IDOE) .... val

Value .... VAL

Value .... VAL

Value Added (ADA) .... VA

Value Added and Data [*Communications network*] .... VAD

Value Added and Data Services .... VADS

Value Added by Advertising .... VABA

Value Added by Manufacturer [*Business term*] (MHDW) .... VABM

Value Added Manufacture [*Program*] .... VAM

Value Added Market (MHDB) .... VAM

Value Added Network [*Computer science Telecommunications*] .... VAN

Value Added Network Service [*Computer science Telecommunications*] .... VANS

Value Added Tax Tribunal Reports [*A publication*] .... VATTR

Value Added Utilisation System (EERA) .... VAUS

Value Aluminizing Machine .... VAM

Value Analysis .... VA

Value Analysis .... VA

Value Analysis of Management Practices (MCD) .... VAMP

Value and Lifestyle [*Classifications*] [*Marketing*] .... VALS

Value as Marine Policy [*Insurance*] (DS) .... VMP

Value City Department Stores [*Associated Press*] (SAG) .... ValueCty

Value City Department Stores [*NYSE symbol*] (SPSG) .... VCD

Value City Dept Stores [*NYSE symbol*] (TTSB) .... VCD

Value Creation Study Society (CINC) .... VCSS

Value Defined (MHDW) .... VALDEFD

Value Effectiveness .... VE

Value Engineered Indicator (NG) .... VEI

Value Engineering [*OMB Circular*] (AAGC) A-131

Value Engineering [*Military*] .... VE

Value Engineering .... VE

Value Engineering Audit .... VEA

Value Engineering Change .... VEC

Value Engineering Change Proposal [*Military*] .... VECP

Value Engineering Control Committee [*Military*] .... VECC

Value Engineering Design Review .... VEDR

Value Engineering Functional Cost Analysis .... VEFCA

Value Engineering Guideline .... VEG

Value Engineering Guideline .... VEGL

Value Engineering Incentive [*Office of Federal Procurement Policy*] .... VEI

Value Engineering Model (NG) .... VEM

Value Engineering Organization .... VEO

Value Engineering Program .... VEP

Value Engineering Program Guideline .... VEPG

Value Engineering Program Manager [*Military*] (AABC) .... VEPM

Value Engineering Program Requirement [*Office of Federal Procurement Policy*] (NG) .... VEPR

Value Engineering Proposal [*Army*] (RDA) .... VEP

Value Engineering Retrieval of Esoteric Administrative Data (PDAA) .... VEREAD

Value Engineering Staff Engineer .... VESE

Value Engineering Study Request (MCD) .... VESR

Value Engineering Supplier Program .... VESP

Value Engineering Task Force .... VETF

Value Engineering Training .... VET

Value Engineers Association (BARN) .... VEA

Value, Expertise, Client, Time, Attorney, Result [*Lawyer evaluation method*] .... VECTAR

Value for Duty [*Business term*] .... VFD

Value for Money [*Accounting*] .... VFM

Value Foundation (EA) .... VF

Value Health, Inc. [*Associated Press*] (SAG) .... ValHlth

Value Health, Inc. [*NYSE symbol*] (SAG) .... VH

Value Holdings [*NASDAQ symbol*] (SAG) .... VALH

Value Holdings [*Associated Press*] (SAG) .... ValHldg

Value Improving Products	VIP
Value in Performance	VIP
Value Incentive Clause [General Services Administration]	VIC
Value Included Entry [Business term]	VI
Value Investment Corp. [Toronto Stock Exchange symbol]	VAL
Value Leader [Automotive marketing]	VL
Value Line [NASDAQ symbol] (TTSB)	VALU
Value Line, Inc. [Associated Press] (SAG)	ValLn
Value Line, Inc. [NASDAQ symbol] (NQ)	VALU
Value Line, Inc. [Associated Press] (SAG)	ValueLn
Value Line Investment Survey [Finance]	VL
Value Management	VM
Value Not Obtained	VNO
Value of a Statistical Life [Mortality rating]	VSL
Value of Life Committee (EA)	VOLCOM
Value of Production	VOP
Value of Time Research [British]	VTR
Value Option Package [Automotive marketing]	VOP
Value Payable by Post	VPP
Value Pointer (MHDI)	VPTR
Value Property Trust [Associated Press] (SAG)	ValuePr
Value Property Trust [NYSE symbol] (SAG)	VLP
Value Purchase Agreement (HGAA)	VPA
Value Received Analysis (MHDW)	VRA
Value Task Force Team	VTFT
Value Television [Television program]	VTV
Value Truck Package	VTP
Value-Added Carrier [Telecommunications]	VAC
Value-Added Common Carrier [Telecommunications]	VACC
Value-Added Dealer [Business term]	VAD
Value-Added Distributor	VAD
Value-Added Driver [Computer science] (PCM)	VAD
Value-Added Process [Computer science] (PCM)	VAP
Value-Added Remarketer [or Reseller or Retailer] [Business term]	VAR
Value-Added Remarketers (NITA)	VARs
Value-Added Reseller	VAR
Value-Added Reseller / Value-Added Dealer (BTTJ)	VAR/VAD
Value-Added Service [Medical benefits]	VAS
Value-Added Service [Telecommunications] (TEL)	VAS
Value-Added Service Provider [Agreement] (IT)	VASP
Value-Added Statement (ADA)	VAS
Value-Added Supply Chain Optimization [Automotive industry cost management]	VASCO
Value-Added System Distributor (HGAA)	VASD
Value-Added Tax	VAT
Value-Based Self-Assessment [Model] (AAGC)	VBSA
Valued (ROG)	VALD
Valued as in Original Policy [Insurance]	VOP
Value-Operated Water Flash (DNAB)	VOWF
Value-Oriented Algorithmic Language [Computer science] (PDAA)	VAL
Valuer-General's Department [Australia]	VGD
Valuers' Qualification Board [Victoria, Australia]	VQB
Valuers' Registration Board of Queensland [Australia]	VRBQ
Valuers' Registration Board of Tasmania [Australia]	VRBT
Values and Lifestyles Program (WDMC)	VALS
Values Inventory [Management test]	VI
Values Inventory for Children [Attitude test]	VIC
ValueVision International, Inc. [Associated Press] (SAG)	ValVis
ValueVision International, Inc. [NASDAQ symbol] (SAG)	VVTV
ValueVision Intl'A' [NASDAQ symbol] (TTSB)	VVTV
ValuJet Airlines [NASDAQ symbol] (TTSB)	VJET
ValuJet Airlines, Inc. [Associated Press] (SAG)	ValuJet
ValuJet Airlines, Inc. [ICAO designator] (FAAC)	VJA
ValuJet Airlines, Inc. [NASDAQ symbol] (SAG)	VJET
Valve	V
Valve	VAL
Valve (AAG)	VLV
Valve Box	VB
Valve Control Amplifier (MDG)	VCA
Valve Drive Amplifier	VDA
Valve Driver Assembly (NASA)	VDA
Valve Engineer (WDAA)	VE
Valve Fuel Injection [Automotive engineering]	VFI
Valve in Receiver (DICI)	VIR
Valve Manufacturers Association of America (EA)	VMA
Valve Monitoring System (IAA)	VMS
Valve Mounting System	VMS
Valve Opening Time [Nuclear energy] (NRCH)	VOT
Valve Oscillator (DEN)	VO
Valve Pit (AAG)	VP
Valve Position Indicator (KSC)	VPI
Valve Positioner	VP
Valve Qualification Study	VQS
Valve Remanufacturers Council (EA)	VRC
Valve Replacement [Cardiology]	VR
Valve Seat (MSA)	VST
Valve Setpoint Tolerance [Nuclear energy] (NRCH)	VST
Valve Signal Light	VSL
Valve Solenoid Driver	VSD
Valve Stem (MSA)	VSTM
Valve Voltmeter (IAA)	VV
Valve Voltmeter (IAA)	VVM
Valveless Pulse Rocket	VPR
Valverde [Canary Islands] [Airport symbol] (OAG)	VDE

Valverde [Canary Islands] [Seismograph station code, US Geological Survey] (SEIS)	VVD
Valve-Regulated Battery [Energy source]	VRB
Valves Wide Open [Nuclear energy] (NRCH)	VWO
Valvular Disease of the Heart [Medicine]	VDH
Valvular Heart Disease	VHD
Valvular Pulmonic Stenosis [Cardiology] (DAVI)	VPS
Vamdrup [Denmark ICAO location identifier] (ICLI)	EKVD
Vamos [Greece] [Seismograph station code, US Geological Survey] (SEIS)	VAM
Vampire (BARN)	vamp
Vampire Information Exchange (EA)	VIE
Vampire Pen Pal Network [Defunct] (EA)	VPPN
Vampire Research Center (EA)	VRC
Vampire Studies Society [Defunct] (EA)	VSS
Van [Turkey ICAO location identifier] (ICLI)	LTCI
Van	V
Van [Turkey] [Airport symbol] (OAG)	VAN
Van Alen Simplified Scoring System [Tennis]	VASSS
Van Allen Belt Dosimeter	VABD
Van Allen Belts	VAB
Van Allen Simplified Scoring [Tennis] (IIA)	VASS
Van Buren [Catheter] [Surgery] (DAVI)	VB
Van Buren, AR [AM radio station call letters]	KAYR
Van Buren, AR [AM radio station call letters]	KFDF
Van Buren, AR [FM radio station call letters]	KLSZ
Van Buren County Leader, Farmington, IA [Library symbol Library of Congress] (LCLS)	IaFarmL
Van Buren County Library, Decatur, MI [Library symbol Library of Congress] (LCLS)	MiDec
Van Buren County Library, Webster Memorial Library Building, Decatur, MI [Library symbol Library of Congress] (LCLS)	MiDecV
Van Buren County Register, Keosauqua, IA [Library symbol Library of Congress] (LCLS)	IaKeVR
Van Buren, IN [FM radio station call letters]	WCJC
Van Buren Public Library, Van Buren, IN [Library symbol Library of Congress] (LCLS)	InVb
Van Container [Shipping] (DS)	V
Van Den Bergh [Liver function test]	VAND
Van Den Bergh [Liver function test]	VdB
Van Der Hout Associates Ltd. [Toronto Stock Exchange symbol]	VDH
Van der Stratten [Auto racing team]	VDS
Van der Waals Epitaxy [Physics]	VDWE
Van Deusen Post Library, Fort Monmouth, Fort Monmouth, NJ [OCLC symbol] (OCLC)	APV
Van Diemens Co. [NASDAQ symbol] (SAG)	VAND
Van Diemen's Land [Former name of Tasmania]	VDL
Van Doorne's Transmissie BV [Netherlands Automotive engineering]	VDT
Van Doorn's Automobile Fabrieken [Dutch automobile manufacturer; acronym used as name of its cars]	DAF
Van Fleet on Collateral Attack [A publication] (DLA)	Van Fleet Coll Attack
Van Halen Fan Club (EA)	VHFC
Van Heythuysen on Maritime Evidence [A publication] (DLA)	Van Hey Mar Ev
Van Heythuysen's Equity Draftsman [2nd ed.] [1828] [A publication] (DLA)	Van Hey Eq
Van Heythuysen's Equity Draftsman [2nd ed.] [1828] [A publication] (DLA)	VH Eq Dr
Van Heythuysen's Rudiments of English Law [A publication] (DLA)	Van Hey Rud
Van Horn, TX [Location identifier FAA] (FAAL)	VHN
Van Houten Associates [Information service or system] (IID)	VHA
Van Hove Singularities [Physics]	vHs
Van Kam Am Cap Adv Mun II [AMEX symbol] (TTSB)	VKI
Van Kam Am Cap Adv Muni [NYSE symbol] (TTSB)	VKA
Van Kam Am Cap Adv PA Mun [NYSE symbol] (TTSB)	VAP
Van Kam Am Cap Bd [NYSE symbol] (TTSB)	ACB
Van Kam Am Cap CA Muni [AMEX symbol] (TTSB)	VKC
Van Kam Am Cap CA Qual Mun [NYSE symbol] (TTSB)	VQC
Van Kam Am Cap CA Val Mun [NYSE symbol] (TTSB)	VCV
Van Kam Am Cap Cv Sec [NYSE symbol] (TTSB)	ACS
Van Kam Am Cap FL Mun Op [AMEX symbol] (TTSB)	VOF
Van Kam Am Cap FL Qual Mun [NYSE symbol] (TTSB)	VFM
Van Kam Am Cap Hi Inc. [NYSE symbol] (TTSB)	VLT
Van Kam Am Cap Inc.Tr [NYSE symbol] (TTSB)	ACD
Van Kam Am Cap Ins Muni [NYSE symbol] (TTSB)	VIM
Van Kam Am Cap Interm [NYSE symbol] (TTSB)	VIT
Van Kam Am Cap Inv Gr Mun [NYSE symbol] (TTSB)	VGM
Van Kam Am Cap Inv Grade [NYSE symbol] (TTSB)	VIG
Van Kam Am Cap InvGr CA Mun [NYSE symbol] (TTSB)	VIC
Van Kam Am Cap InvGr FL Mun [NYSE symbol] (TTSB)	VTF
Van Kam Am Cap InvGr NJ Mun [NYSE symbol] (TTSB)	VTJ
Van Kam Am Cap InvGr NY Mum [NYSE symbol] (TTSB)	VTN
Van Kam Am Cap InvGr PA Mun [NYSE symbol] (TTSB)	VTP
Van Kam Am Cap MA Val Mun [AMEX symbol] (TTSB)	VMV
Van Kam Am Cap Mun Inc. [NYSE symbol] (TTSB)	VMT
Van Kam Am Cap Mun Opp II [NYSE symbol] (TTSB)	VOT
Van Kam Am Cap Mun Tr [NYSE symbol] (TTSB)	VKQ
Van Kam Am Cap Muni Opp [NYSE symbol] (TTSB)	VMO
Van Kam Am Cap NJ Val Mun [AMEX symbol] (TTSB)	VJV
Van Kam Am Cap NY Qual Mun [NYSE symbol] (TTSB)	VNM
Van Kam Am Cap NY Val Mun [NYSE symbol] (TTBS)	VNV
Van Kam Am Cap OH Qual Mun [NYSE symbol] (TTSB)	VOQ
Van Kam Am Cap OH Val Mun [AMEX symbol] (TTSB)	VOV
Van Kam Am Cap PA Qual Mun [NYSE symbol] (TTSB)	VPQ
Van Kam Am Cap PA Val Mun [NYSE symbol] (TTSB)	VPV
Van Kam Am Cap Sel Sec Mun [AMEX symbol] (TTSB)	VKL

Van Kam Am Cap Str Sec Mun [*NYSE symbol*] (TTSB) ... VKS
Van Kam Am Cap Value Muni [*NYSE symbol*] (TTSB) ... VKV
Van Kampen Amer. Cap. Advantage Muni Income Trust [*NYSE symbol*] (SAG) ... VKA
Van Kampen Amer. Cap. Advantage Muni. Income Trust [*Associated Press*] (SAG) ... VKAdvM
Van Kampen Amer. Cap. Advantage Muni. Income Trust I [*Associated Press*] (SAG) ... VKAdM2
Van Kampen Amer. Cap. Advantage PA Muni. Income [*Associated Press*] (SAG) ... VKAdPA
Van Kampen Amer. Cap. Bond Fund [*Associated Press*] (SAG) ... VKACBd
Van Kampen Amer. Cap. Convertible Securities [*Associated Press*] (SAG) ... VKACCV
Van Kampen Amer. Cap. Income Trust [*Associated Press*] (SAG) ... VKACInc
Van Kampen Amer. Cap. Muni. Opportunity Trust [*Associated Press*] (SAG) ... VKMOT
Van Kampen Amer. Cap. Muni. Opportunity Trust 2 [*Associated Press*] (SAG) ... VKMOT2
Van Kampen Amer. Cap. Muni. Trust [*Associated Press*] (SAG) ... VKMuTr
Van Kampen Amer. Cap. Trust for Investment Grade FL [*Associated Press*] (SAG) ... VKTFL
Van Kampen Amer. Cap. Trust for Investment Grade NJ [*Associated Press*] (SAG) ... VKTNJ
Van Kampen Amer. Cap. Trust for Investment Grade NY [*Associated Press*] (SAG) ... VKTNY
Van Kampen Amer. Cap. Trust for Investment Grade PA [*Associated Press*] (SAG) ... VKTPA
Van Kampen Amer. Cap. Value Muni. Income Trust [*Associated Press*] (SAG) ... VKValMu
Van Kampen Merritt Advanced Muncipal Income Trust II [*AMEX symbol*] (SPSG) ... VKI
Van Kampen Merritt Advanced Municipal Income Trust [*NYSE symbol*] (SPSG) ... VKA
Van Kampen Merritt Advanced Municipal Income Trust [*Associated Press*] (SAG) ... VKMAd
Van Kampen Merritt Advantage Municipal Income Trust 2 [*Associated Press*] (SAG) ... VKMAd2
Van Kampen Merritt Advantage Pennsylvania Municipal Income Trust [*NYSE symbol*] (SPSG) ... VAP
Van Kampen Merritt Advantage Pennsylvania Municipal Income Trust [*Associated Press*] (SAG) ... VKMAPA
Van Kampen Merritt California Municipal Trust [*AMEX symbol*] (CTT) ... VKC
Van Kampen Merritt California Municipal Trust [*Associated Press*] (SAG) ... VKCal
Van Kampen Merritt California Quality Municipal Fund [*NYSE symbol*] (SAG) ... VQC
Van Kampen Merritt California Quality Municipal Trust [*Associated Press*] (SAG) ... VKCAQ
Van Kampen Merritt California Value Municipal Trust [*NYSE symbol*] (SPSG) ... VCV
Van Kampen Merritt California Value Municipal Trust [*Associated Press*] (SAG) ... VKCAV
Van Kampen Merritt Florida Municipal Opportunity [*Associated Press*] (SAG) ... VKFLO
Van Kampen Merritt Florida Municipal Opportunity Fund [*AMEX symbol*] (SPSG) ... VOF
Van Kampen Merritt Florida Quality Municipal [*NYSE symbol*] (SPSG) ... VFM
Van Kampen Merritt Florida Quality Municipal Trust [*Associated Press*] (SAG) ... VKFLQ
Van Kampen Merritt Intermediate Term High Income Trust [*NYSE symbol*] (SPSG) ... VIT
Van Kampen Merritt Intermediate Term High Income Trust [*Associated Press*] (SAG) ... VKITH
Van Kampen Merritt Investment Grade California Municipal [*NYSE symbol*] (SPSG) ... VIC
Van Kampen Merritt Investment Grade Florida Municipal [*NYSE symbol*] (SPSG) ... VTF
Van Kampen Merritt Investment Grade Municipal [*NYSE symbol*] (SPSG) ... VIG
Van Kampen Merritt Investment Grade Municipal Trust [*Associated Press*] (SAG) ... VKIGM
Van Kampen Merritt Investment Grade New Jersey Municipal [*NYSE symbol*] (SPSG) ... VTJ
Van Kampen Merritt Investment Grade New York Municipal [*NYSE symbol*] (SPSG) ... VTN
Van Kampen Merritt Investment Grade Pennsylvania Municipal [*NYSE symbol*] (SPSG) ... VTP
Van Kampen Merritt Limited Term High Income Trust [*Associated Press*] (SAG) ... VKLTH
Van Kampen Merritt Limited Term High Income Trust [*NYSE symbol*] (SPSG) ... VLT
Van Kampen Merritt Massachusetts Value Municipal [*Associated Press*] (SAG) ... VKMAV
Van Kampen Merritt Massachusetts Value Municipal Trust [*AMEX symbol*] (SPSG) ... VMV
Van Kampen Merritt Municipal Income Trust [*Associated Press*] (SAG) ... VKMIT
Van Kampen Merritt Municipal Income Trust [*NYSE symbol*] (CTT) ... VMT
Van Kampen Merritt Municipal Opportunity Trust [*Associated Press*] (SAG) ... VKMMO
Van Kampen Merritt Municipal Opportunity Trust [*NYSE symbol*] (SPSG) ... VMO
Van Kampen Merritt Municipal Opportunity Trust 2 [*Associated Press*] (SAG) ... VKMMO2
Van Kampen Merritt Municipal Opportunity Trust 2 [*NYSE symbol*] (SPSG) ... VOT
Van Kampen Merritt Municipal Trust [*Associated Press*] (SAG) ... VKMMT
Van Kampen Merritt Municipal Trust [*NYSE symbol*] (SPSG) ... VKQ
Van Kampen Merritt New Jersey Value Municipal Income [*Associated Press*] (SAG) ... VKNJV
Van Kampen Merritt New Jersey Value Municipal, Inc. [*AMEX symbol*] (SPSG) ... VJV
Van Kampen Merritt New York Quality Municipal [*Associated Press*] (SAG) ... VKNYQ
Van Kampen Merritt New York Quality Municipal [*NYSE symbol*] (SPSG) ... VNM
Van Kampen Merritt New York Value Municipal Income Trust [*Associated Press*] (SAG) ... VKNYV
Van Kampen Merritt New York Value Municipal Income Trust [*NYSE symbol*] (SPSG) ... VNV
Van Kampen Merritt Ohio Quality Municipal [*Associated Press*] (SAG) ... VKOHQ
Van Kampen Merritt Ohio Quality Municipal [*NYSE symbol*] (SPSG) ... VOQ
Van Kampen Merritt Ohio Value Municipal Income Trust [*Associated Press*] (SAG) ... VKOHV
Van Kampen Merritt Ohio Value Municipal Trust [*AMEX symbol*] (SPSG) ... VOV
Van Kampen Merritt Pennsylvania Quality Municipal [*NYSE symbol*] (SPSG) ... VPQ
Van Kampen Merritt Pennsylvania Quality Municipal Trust [*Associated Press*] (SAG) ... VKPAQ
Van Kampen Merritt Pennsylvania Value Municipal Income Trust [*NYSE symbol*] (SPSG) ... VPV
Van Kampen Merritt Pennsylvania Value Municipal Trust [*Associated Press*] (SAG) ... VKPAV
Van Kampen Merritt Select [*Associated Press*] (SAG) ... VKSelS
Van Kampen Merritt Select Securities Municipal Trust [*AMEX symbol*] (SPSG) ... VKL
Van Kampen Merritt Strategic Sector Municipal Trust [*NYSE symbol*] (SPSG) ... VKS
Van Kampen Merritt Strategic Sector Municipal Trust [*Associated Press*] (SAG) ... VKStrS
Van Kampen Merritt Trust for Insured Municipals [*NYSE symbol*] (SAG) ... VIM
Van Kampen Merritt Trust for Insured Municipals [*Associated Press*] (SAG) ... VKTIM
Van Kampen Merritt Trust for Investment Grade California [*Associated Press*] (SAG) ... VKTCA
Van Kampen Merritt Trust for Investment Grade Florida [*Associated Press*] (SAG) ... VKMTFL
Van Kampen Merritt Trust for Investment Grade Municipals [*NYSE symbol*] (SAG) ... VGM
Van Kampen Merritt Trust for Investment Grade Municipals [*Associated Press*] (SAG) ... VKTIG
Van Kampen Merritt Trust for Investment Grade New Jersey [*Associated Press*] (SAG) ... VKMTNJ
Van Kampen Merritt Trust for Investment Grade New York [*Associated Press*] (SAG) ... VKMTNY
Van Kampen Merritt Trust for Investment Grade Pennsylvania [*Associated Press*] (SAG) ... VKMTPA
Van Kampen Merritt Value Municipal Income Trust [*Associated Press*] (SAG) ... VKMVM
Van Kampen Merritt Value Municipal Income Trust [*NYSE symbol*] (SPSG) ... VKV
Van Koughnet's Reports [*15-21 Upper Canada Common Pleas*] [*1864-71*] [*A publication*] (DLA) ... Van K
Van Langenhoven [*Rifle*] ... V-L
Van Ness' Prize Cases [*United States*] [*A publication*] (DLA) ... VN
Van Ness' Prize Cases, United States District Court, District of New York [*A publication*] (DLA) ... Van N
Van Ness' Prize Cases, United States District Court, District of New York [*A publication*] (DLA) ... Van Ness Prize Cas
Van Norden Magazine [*New York*] [*A publication*] (ROG) ... VAN N
Van Nostrand Reinhold Co., Inc. [*Publisher*] ... VNR
Van Nuys Byzantine [*Diocesan abbreviation*] [*California*] (TOCD) ... VNN
Van Nuys, CA [*Location identifier FAA*] (FAAL) ... VNY
Van Ommeren [*AM symbol*] (TTSB) ... VOCCN
Van Riebeeck Decoration [*British military*] (DMA) ... DVR
Van Riebeeck Medal [*British military*] (DMA) ... VRM
Van Santvoord's Equity Practice [*A publication*] (DLA) ... Van Sant Eq Pr
Van Santvoord's Lives of the Chief Justices of the United States [*A publication*] (DLA) ... Van Sant Ch J
Van Santvoord's Pleadings [*A publication*] (DLA) ... Van Sant Pl
Van Santvoord's Precedents [*A publication*] (DLA) ... Van Sant Prec
Van Vleck [*Quantum mechanics*] ... VVK
Van Wert, OH [*Location identifier FAA*] (FAAL) ... VFU
Van Wert, OH [*Location identifier FAA*] (FAAL) ... VNW
Van Wert, OH [*FM radio station call letters*] ... WBYR
Van Wert, OH [*AM radio station call letters*] ... WERT
Vanadium [*Chemical element*] ... V
Vanadium [*Chemical*] (EERA) ... Va
Vanadium Carbide (PDAA) ... VC
Vanadium Phosphate [*Inorganic chemistry*] ... VPO
Vanadium Wire Equilibration [*Nuclear energy*] (NRCH) ... VWE
Vanadium Wire Equilibration Device [*Nuclear energy*] (NRCH) ... VWED
Vanadium-Phosphorus Oxide [*Inorganic chemistry*] ... VPO
Vanadocene Dichloride [*Antineoplastic drug*] ... VDC
Vanadyl Acetylacetonate [*Organic chemistry*] ... VAAC
Vananda Gold [*Vancouver Stock Exchange symbol*] ... VAG
Vanavara [*Former USSR ICAO location identifier*] (ICLI) ... UNKI
Vance County Technical Institute, Henderson, NC [*Library symbol Library of Congress*] (LCLS) ... NcHeV
Vance, SC [*Location identifier FAA*] (FAAL) ... VAN
Vance Township Library, Fairmount, IL [*Library symbol*] [*Library of Congress*] (LCLS) ... IFai
Vanceburg, KY [*AM radio station call letters*] ... WKKS
Vanceburg, KY [*FM radio station call letters*] ... WKKS-FM

Vancleve, KY [*AM radio station call letters*] .... WMTC
Vancleve, KY [*FM radio station call letters*] .... WMTC-FM
Vancomycin Hydrochloride, Colistimethate Sodium, Nystatin, [*Medium*] [*Microbiology*] (DAVI) .... VCN
Vancomycin Resistant Enterococcus .... VRE
Vancomycin-Colistin-Anisomycin [*Growth-inhibiting mixture*] [*Microbiology*] .... VCA
Vancomycin-Colistin-Nystatin [*Growth-inhibiting mixture*] [*Microbiology*] .... VCN
Vancouver [*Canada*] (WDAA) .... VANC
Vancouver [*Canada*] (BARN) .... Vcr
Vancouver [*Canada*] [*Airport symbol*] (OAG) .... YVR
Vancouver Art Gallery [*Canada*] .... VAG
Vancouver Art Gallery, British Columbia [*Library symbol National Library of Canada*] (NLC) .... BVAVA
Vancouver Art Gallery, Vancouver, BC, Canada [*Library symbol Library of Congress*] (LCLS) .... CaBVaVA
Vancouver, BC [*AM radio station call letters*] .... CBU
Vancouver, BC [*FM radio station call letters*] .... CBUF
Vancouver, BC [*FM radio station call letters*] .... CBU-FM
Vancouver, BC [*Television station call letters*] .... CBUFT
Vancouver, BC [*Television station call letters*] .... CBUT
Vancouver, BC [*FM radio station call letters*] .... CFOX
Vancouver, BC [*FM radio station call letters*] .... CFRO
Vancouver, BC [*AM radio station call letters*] .... CFUN
Vancouver, BC [*Television station call letters*] .... CHAN
Vancouver, BC [*AM radio station call letters*] (RBYB) .... CHMB
Vancouver, BC [*FM radio station call letters*] .... CHQM
Vancouver, BC [*FM radio station call letters*] .... CITR
Vancouver, BC [*FM radio station call letters*] .... CJJR
Vancouver, BC [*AM radio station call letters*] .... CJVB
Vancouver, BC [*AM radio station call letters*] .... CKBD
Vancouver, BC [*FM radio station call letters*] .... CKKS
Vancouver, BC [*AM radio station call letters*] .... CKLG
Vancouver, BC [*AM radio station call letters*] .... CKST
Vancouver, BC [*Television station call letters*] .... CKVU
Vancouver, BC [*AM radio station call letters*] .... CKWX
Vancouver, BC [*FM radio station call letters*] .... CKZZ
Vancouver, BC [*ICAO location identifier*] (ICLI) .... CWVR
Vancouver, BC [*ICAO location identifier*] (ICLI) .... CZVR
Vancouver Board of Trade Library, British Columbia [*Library symbol National Library of Canada*] (NLC) .... BVABOT
Vancouver City Archives, British Columbia [*Library symbol National Library of Canada*] (NLC) .... BVAA
Vancouver City Archives, Vancouver, BC, Canada [*Library symbol Library of Congress*] (LCLS) .... CaBVaA
Vancouver City College, Langara, Vancouver, BC, Canada [*Library symbol Library of Congress*] (LCLS) .... CaBVaVCL
Vancouver Community College, Langara Campus, Vancouver, British Columbia [*Library symbol National Library of Canada*] (NLC) .... BVAVCL
Vancouver Community College Library [*UTLAS symbol*] VCC
Vancouver Community College, Library Technician Program, Vancouver, BC, Canada [*Library symbol*] [*Library of Congress*] (LCLS) .... CaBVaVCLT
Vancouver General Hospital .... VGH
Vancouver Health Department, British Columbia [*Library symbol National Library of Canada*] (NLC) .... BVAHD
Vancouver Health Department, Vancouver, BC, Canada [*Library symbol*] [*Library of Congress*] (LCLS) .... CaBVaHD
Vancouver International Airport, Transport Canada [*Aeroport International de Vancouver, Transports Canada*], Richmond, British Columbia [*Library symbol National Library of Canada*] (NLC) .... BRTVIA
Vancouver International Amateur Film Festival [*Canada*] .... VIAFF
Vancouver/International, BC [*ICAO location identifier*] (ICLI) .... CYVR
Vancouver Island VI
Vancouver Island [*NWS*] (FAAC) .... VRISL
Vancouver Island Regional Library, Nanaimo, BC, Canada [*Library symbol Library of Congress*] (LCLS) .... CaBNVI
Vancouver Island Regional Library, Nanaimo, British Columbia [*Library symbol National Library of Canada*] (NLC) .... BNVI
Vancouver Laboratory, Fisheries and Oceans Canada [*Laboratoire de Vancouver, Peches et Oceans Canada*], British Columbia [*Library symbol Obsolete National Library of Canada*] (NLC) .... BVAF
Vancouver Laboratory, Pulp and Paper Research Institute of Canada, British Columbia [*Library symbol National Library of Canada*] (NLC) .... BVAPPR
Vancouver Memorial Hospital, Vancouver, WA [*Library symbol Library of Congress*] (LCLS) .... WaVMH
Vancouver Museums and Planetarium Association [*Canada*] .... VMPA
Vancouver Public Library, British Columbia [*Library symbol National Library of Canada*] (NLC) .... BVA
Vancouver Public Library, Fine Arts, Music, and Films Division, Vancouver, BC, Canada [*Library symbol Library of Congress*] (LCLS) .... CaBVaFA
Vancouver Public Library, Historic Photographic Collection, Vancouver, BC, Canada [*Library symbol Library of Congress*] (LCLS) .... CaBVaHP
Vancouver Public Library, Northwest History Collection, Vancouver, BC, Canada [*Library symbol Library of Congress*] (LCLS) .... CaBVaNHC
Vancouver Public Library, Vancouver, BC, Canada [*Library symbol Library of Congress*] (LCLS) .... CaBVa
Vancouver School of Art .... VSA
Vancouver School of Art, Vancouver, BC, Canada [*Library symbol Library of Congress*] (LCLS) .... CaBVaVSA
Vancouver School of Theology [*University of British Columbia*] .... VST
Vancouver School of Theology, British Columbia [*Library symbol National Library of Canada*] (NLC) .... BVAST
Vancouver School of Theology, Vancouver, BC, Canada [*Library symbol Library of Congress*] (LCLS) .... CaBVaST
Vancouver Stock Exchange [*Canada*] V
Vancouver Stock Exchange [*Canada*] .... VSE
Vancouver Ventures [*Vancouver Stock Exchange symbol*] .... VVR
Vancouver, WA [*AM radio station call letters*] .... KBMS
Vancouver, WA [*AM radio station call letters*] .... KKSN
Vancouver, WA [*Television station call letters*] .... KPDX
Vancouver, WA [*AM radio station call letters*] .... KVAN
Vancouver-Harbour Seaport [*Canada*] [*Airport symbol*] (OAG) .... CXH
Vancouver-Richmond Assoc. for Mentally Handicapped People .... VRAMHP
Vanda [*Antarctica*] [*Seismograph station code, US Geological Survey*] (SEIS) .... VND
Vandalia Community Unit, School District 203, Vandalia, IL [*Library symbol Library of Congress*] (LCLS) .... IVSD
Vandalia Correctional Center, Vandalia, IL [*Library symbol Library of Congress*] (LCLS) IVC
Vandalia, IL [*Location identifier FAA*] (FAAL) .... VLA
Vandalia, IL [*FM radio station call letters*] .... WKRV
Vandalia, IL [*AM radio station call letters*] .... WPMB
Vandalia Line [*Railroad*] VL
Vandalia, MO [*FM radio station call letters*] .... KLRK
Vandalism and Malicious Mischief [*Insurance*] .... V & MM
Vandel [*Denmark ICAO location identifier*] (ICLI) .... EKVA
Vandenberg Addendum Document [*Air Force*] (NASA) .... VAD
Vandenberg Air Force Base [*California*] .... VAFB
Vandenberg Atlas Modification Program [*Air Force*] (MCD) .... VAMP
Vandenberg Automatic Data Equipment [*Air Force*] .... VADE
Vandenberg Automatic Data Evaluation [*Air Force*] .... VADE
Vandenberg Automatic Test Equipment [*Air Force*] .... VATE
Vandenberg Engineering Test Program (SAA) .... VETP
Vandenberg Field Office [*Air Force*] (MCD) .... VFO
Vandenberg Field Office of Aerospace Research [*Air Force*] (PDAA) .... VFOAR
Vandenberg Ground Operations Requirement [*Air Force*] (NASA) .... VGOR
Vandenberg Launch Processing System [*Aerospace*] (MCD) .... VLPS
Vandenberg Launch Site [*Air Force*] .... VLS
Vandenberg Range Communications Control Center [*Air Force*] (MCD) .... VRCCC
Vandenberg Real Time Interface (MCD) .... V-RTIF
Vandenberg Shuttle Turnaround Analysis Group [*NASA*] (NASA) .... VSTAG
Vandenberg Test Center [*Air Force*] .... VTC
Vandenberg Test Program [*Air Force*] .... VTP
Vandenberg Tracking Station [*Air Force*] .... VTS
Vandenberge Junior High School, Elk River, MN [*Library symbol*] [*Library of Congress*] (LCLS) .... MnErVJ
Vandeno [*Race of maize*] .... VAN
Vander Linden's Practice [*Cape Colony*] [*A publication*] (DLA) .... Van L
Vanderbijlpark [*South Africa*] [*ICAO location identifier*] (ICLI) .... FAVP
Vanderbilt Gold [*PC symbol*] (TTSB) .... VGO
Vanderbilt Law Review [*A publication*] (DLA) .... Vanderbilt LR
Vanderbilt Medical Center, Nashville, TN [*OCLC symbol*] (OCLC) .... TJM
Vanderbilt, MI [*Television station call letters*] .... WGKU
Vanderbilt University (GAGS) .... Vanderbilt U
Vanderbilt University Library, Nashville, TN [*OCLC symbol*] (OCLC) .... TJC
Vanderbilt University Quarterly [*Tennessee*] [*A publication*] (ROG) .... VAND UNIV Q
Vanderbilt University School of Law (DLA) .... VANUSL
VanderCook College of Music, Chicago, IL [*Library symbol Library of Congress*] (LCLS) ICVC
Vandercook Elementary School, Rockford, IL [*Library symbol*] [*Library of Congress*] (LCLS) .... IRoVE
Vanderhoof, BC [*AM radio station call letters*] .... CIVH
Vanderhoof Public Library, British Columbia [*Library symbol National Library of Canada*] (NLC) .... BVDH
Vanderlinden's Laws of Holland [*A publication*] (DLA) .... Vander L
Vanderstraaten's Decisions in Appeal, Supreme Court [*1869-71*] [*Sri L.*] [*A publication*] (DLA) .... Vanderstraaten
Vanderstraaten's Reports [*1869-71*] [*Ceylon*] [*A publication*] (DLA) .... Vanderstr
V&L Enterprises, Downsview, ON, Canada [*Library symbol*] [*Library of Congress*] (LCLS) .... CaOTVL
Vandorex Energy [*Vancouver Stock Exchange symbol*] .... VDX
Vandyke [*Graphics*] .... VD
Vane Air Temperature [*Automotive engineering*] .... VAT
Vane Airflow Meter [*Automotive engineering*] .... VAF
Vane Axial .... VNXL
Vane Control System (MCD) .... VCS
Vane Kindergarten Test [*Child development test*] .... VKT
Vane Meter [*Automotive engineering*] .... VM
Vanex Resources Ltd. [*Vancouver Stock Exchange symbol*] VX
Vanga [*Zaire*] [*ICAO location identifier*] (ICLI) .... FZCD
Vangold Resources, Inc. [*Vancouver Stock Exchange symbol*] .... VN
Vangso [*Sweden ICAO location identifier*] (ICLI) .... ESSZ
Vanguard [*Record label*] .... Van
Vanguard Airlines [*NASDAQ symbol*] (TTSB) .... VNGD
Vanguard Airlines, Inc. [*Associated Press*] (SAG) .... VangAir
Vanguard Airlines, Inc. [*FAA designator*] (FAAC) .... VGD
Vanguard Airlines, Inc. [*NASDAQ symbol*] (SAG) .... VNGD
Vanguard Cellular Sys [*NASDAQ symbol*] (TTSB) .... VCELA
Vanguard Cellular Systems, Inc. [*NASDAQ symbol*] (NQ) .... VCEL
Vanguard Cellular Systems, Inc. [*Associated Press*] (SAG) .... VgrdCell
Vanguard Discount Brokerage Services [*Finance*] .... VDBS
Vanguard Launch Vehicle (SAA) VLV
Vanguard Operations Group .... VOG
Vanguard Party of the Malagasy Revolution .... VPMR
Vanguard Planning Summary [*Air Force*] .... VPS
Vanguard Real Estate Fd II [*AMEX symbol*] (TTSB) .... VRT
Vanguard Real Estate Fund I [*Associated Press*] (SAG) .... VREFI
Vanguard Real Estate Fund I [*AMEX symbol*] (SPSG) .... VRO
Vanguard Real Estate Fund II [*Associated Press*] (SAG) .... VREFII

Vanguard Real Estate Fund II [*AMEX symbol*] (SPSG) .... VRT
Vanguard Tracking Station [*NASA*] (NASA) .... VAN
Vanguard Unionist Loyalist Coalition [*Northern Ireland*] [*Political party*] .... VULC
Vanguard Unionist Progressive Party [*Northern Ireland*] [*Political party*] ...... VUPP
Vanguard Ventures [*Vancouver Stock Exchange symbol*] VV
Vanguarda de Comando de Caca aos Comunistas [*Vanguard of the Commando for Hunting Communists*] [*Brazil*] (PD) CCC
Vanguardia Comunista del Partido Obrero Revolucionario [*Bolivia*] [*Political party*] (PPW) .... VCPOR
Vanguardia Revolucionaria [*Revolutionary Vanguard*] [*Peru*] [*Political party*] (PPW) .... VR
Vanguardia Revolucionaria - Proletario Comunista [*Revolutionary Vanguard - Proletarian Communist*] [*Peru*] [*Political party*] (PPW) .... VR-PC
Vanier College [*UTLAS symbol*] .... VAN
Vanier College, Media Resources Centre, Montreal, PQ, Canada [*Library symbol Library of Congress*] (LCLS) .... CaQMVC
Vanier Institute of the Family [*Canada*] .... VIF
Vanier Institute of the Family, Ottawa, ON, Canada [*Library symbol Library of Congress*] (LCLS) .... CaOOVIF
Vanier Institute of the Family [*Institut Vanier de la Famille*] Ottawa, Ontario [*Library symbol National Library of Canada*] (NLC) .... OOVIF
Vanier Library, University of Ottawa [*Bibliotheque Vanier, Universite d'Ottawa*] Ontario [*Library symbol National Library of Canada*] (NLC) ...... OOUM
Vanier Public Library, Ontario [*Library symbol National Library of Canada*] (NLC) .... OVAN
Vanier Public Library, Vanier, ON, Canada [*Library symbol Library of Congress*] (LCLS) .... CaOVan
Vanier Reading Room, Place Vanier, Health Protection Branch, Health and Welfare Canada [*Salle de Lecture de Vanier, Place Vanier, Direction Generale de la Protection de la Sante, Sante et Bien-Etre Social Canada*], Ottawa, Ontario [*Library symbol National Library of Canada*] (NLC) .... OONHP
Vanilla (WDAA) .... VAN
Vanilla Bean Association of America (EA) .... VBAA
Vanilla Information Bureau (EA) .... VIB
Vanillin Thiosemicarbazone (IIA) .... VTS
Vanillylmandelic Acid [*Also, HMMA*] [*Biochemistry*] .... VMA
(Vanillyl)nonanamide [*Biochemistry*] .... VN
Vanimo [*Papua New Guinea*] [*Airport symbol*] (OAG) .... VAI
Vanished Children's Alliance (EA) .... VCA
Vanishing Point (VRA) .... van pt
Vanishing Point [*Term in art/drawing*] .... VP
Vanity Bar [*Classified advertising*] (ADA) .... VB
Vanity Fair [*A publication*] (WDMC) .... VF
Vanity Unit [*Classified advertising*] (ADA) .... VU
Vankleek Hill Public Library, Ontario [*Library symbol National Library of Canada*] (NLC) .... OVH
Vannes/Meucon [*France ICAO location identifier*] (ICLI) .... LFRV
Vannovskaya [*Former USSR Seismograph station code, US Geological Survey*] (SEIS) .... VAN
Vanrook [*Queensland*] [*Airport symbol*] (AD) .... VNR
Vans, Inc. [*NASDAQ symbol*] (SPSG) .... VANS
Vanstar Corp. [*NYSE symbol*] (TTSB) .... VST
Vanstates Resources Ltd. [*Vancouver Stock Exchange symbol*] .... VST
Vantage [*Washington*] [*Seismograph station code, US Geological Survey*] (SEIS) .... VTG
Vantage Information Consultants, Inc. [*Information service or system*] (IID) VICI
Vanterra Resources Ltd. [*Vancouver Stock Exchange symbol*] .... VRL
Vantive Corp. [*Associated Press*] (SAG) .... Vantive
Vantive Corp. [*NASDAQ symbol*] (SAG) .... VNTV
Vanuaaku Pati [*New Hebrides*] [*Political party*] (PD) .... VP
Vanuabalavu [*Fiji*] [*ICAO location identifier*] (ICLI) .... NFNN
Vanuabalavu [*Fiji*] [*Airport symbol*] (OAG) .... VBV
Vanua-Lava [*Sola*] [*New Hebrides*] [*Seismograph station code, US Geological Survey*] (SEIS) .... VLN
Vanuatu [*Aircraft nationality and registration mark*] (FAAC) .... YJ
Vanuatu Independent Alliance Party [*Political party*] (PPW) .... VIAP
Vanuatu Pati (PD) .... VP
Vanwin Resources Corp. [*Vancouver Stock Exchange symbol*] .... VAN
Vapor V
Vapor Axial Deposition [*Optical fiber technology*] .... VAD
Vapor Barrier [*Boots*] [*Army*] (INF) .... VB
Vapor Chamber Fin .... VCF
Vapor Cloud Explosion .... VCE
Vapor Coating System .... VCS
Vapor Compression Distillation .... VCD
Vapor Compression Distillation Subsystem (NASA) .... VCDS
Vapor Compression Evaporation .... VCE
Vapor Cooling System .... VCS
Vapor Crystal Facility [*Materal processing center*] (SSD) .... VCF
Vapor Crystal Growth [*Materials processing*] .... VCG
Vapor Crystal Growth System [*Materials processing*] .... VCGS
Vapor Density .... VD
Vapor Deposit Oxide (IAA) .... VAPOX
Vapor Deposited Silica [*Optical fiber technology*] .... VDS
Vapor Detection System .... VDS
Vapor Extraction System [*Engineering*] .... VES
Vapor Feed System .... VFS
Vapor Generation Accessory [*Instrumentation*] .... VGA
Vapor Growth Epitaxy [*Materials processing*] (IAA) .... VPE
Vapor Injection Curing [*Plastics technology*] VIC
Vapor Permeation Curing [*Plastics technology*] .... VPC
Vapor Phase Deposition [*Coating technology*] .... VPD
Vapor Phase Soldering (PDAA) .... VPS
Vapor Pressure .... VP

Vapor Pressure Correction Factor [*Nuclear energy*] (IAA) .... VPCF
Vapor Pressure Deficit [*Meteorology*] .... VPD
Vapor Pressure Osmometer [*or Osmometry*] [*Analytical chemistry*] .... VPO
Vapor Proof (IAA) .... VAPPRF
Vapor Reheat Process .... VRP
Vapor Return Line VL
Vapor Saver System [*Automobile*] .... VSS
Vapor Seal [*Technical drawings*] .... VS
Vapor Suppression [*Nuclear energy*] (NRCH) .... VS
Vapor Suppression System [*Nuclear energy*] (IAA) .... VSS
Vapor-Deposited Noncrystalline Solid (PDAA) .... VDNCS
Vaporization [*or Vaporizer*] (KSC) .... VAP
Vaporize (MSA) .... VPR
Vaporized Fuel Oil [*Process*] .... VFO
Vaporizer Concentrate [*Nuclear energy*] (NRCH) VC
Vaporizer Feed [*Nuclear energy*] (NRCH) .... VF
Vaporizing Liquid Plenum .... VLP
Vaporizing Oil .... VAPO
Vapor-Liquid Equilibrium .... VLE
Vapor-Liquid-Solid .... VLS
Vapor-Liquid-Solid Tracking [*Model*] (USDC) .... VLSTRACK
Vapor-Liquid-Solid Tracking [*Model*] [*Marine science*] (OSRA) .... VLSTRACK
Vapor-Phase Catalytic Exchange (MCD) .... VPCE
Vapor-Phase Chromatography [*Medicine*] (DMAA) .... VPC
Vapor-Phase Deacidification [*of books and documents*] .... VPD
Vapor-Phase Epitaxy .... VPE
Vapor-Phase Inhibitor [*See also VCI*] [*Chemical technology*] .... VPI
Vapor-Phase Oxidation [*Chemical processing*] .... VPO
Vapor-Phase-Grown Carbon Fiber .... VGCF
Vaportight (MSA) .... VT
Vapor-to-Liquid .... V/L
Vapour Levitation Epitaxy (NITA) .... VLE
Vapour Pressures and Vapour Liquid Equilibria (NITA) .... VP and VLE
Vapro Hazard Index [*Environmental science*] .... VHI
Varactor (MSA) .... VRCTR
Varactor Diode Test .... VDT
Varadero [*Cuba ICAO location identifier*] (ICLI) .... MUVR
Varadero [*Cuba*] [*Airport symbol*] (OAG) .... VRA
Varah [*L. A.*] Ltd. [*Toronto Stock Exchange symbol*] .... LAV
Varamin [*Iran*] [*ICAO location identifier*] (ICLI) .... OIIW
Varanasi [*India*] [*Seismograph station code, US Geological Survey*] (SEIS) .... VAR
Varanasi [*India*] [*ICAO location identifier*] (ICLI) .... VIBN
Varanasi [*India*] [*Airport symbol*] (OAG) .... VNS
Varberg [*Sweden ICAO location identifier*] (ICLI) .... ESGV
Varco International, Inc. [*Associated Press*] (SAG) .... Varco
Varco International, Inc. [*NYSE symbol*] (SPSG) .... VRC
Varco Int'l [*NYSE symbol*] (TTSB) .... VRC
Vardar Air [*Republic of Macedonia*] [*FAA designator*] (FAAC) .... BAA
Varela [*Guinea-Bissau*] [*ICAO location identifier*] (ICLI) .... GGVR
Varga Aircraft Corp. [*ICAO aircraft manufacturer identifier*] (ICAO) .... VG
Vargarda [*Sweden ICAO location identifier*] (ICLI) .... ESGO
Varginha [*Brazil*] [*Airport symbol*] (OAG) .... VAG
Varginha/Jam Brigadeiro Trompowsky [*Brazil ICAO location identifier*] (ICLI) .... SBVG
Var-Hour Meter [*Electricity*] .... VARHM
Var-Hour Meter [*Electricity*] .... VRH
Varia Historia [*of Aelianus*] [*Classical studies*] (OCD) .... VH
Varia Lectio [*Variant Reading*] [*Latin*] (ROG) .... VAR LECT
Varia Lectio [*Variant Reading*] [*Latin*] VL
Variable V
Variable (AFM) .... VAR
Variable .... VRB
Variable (BARN) .... vrbl
Variable Action Button (NVT) .... VAB
Variable Acuity Remote Viewing System (MCD) .... VARVS
Variable Air Capacitor .... VAC
Variable Air Volume .... VAV
Variable Alternatively Spliced Exon [*Genetics*] .... VASE
Variable Amplitude Correction Rack [*Telecommunications*] (OA) .... VACR
Variable [*or Visual*] Anamorphic Motion Picture [*Training device to provide realistic environment during simulated flight training*] (MCD) .... VAMP
Variable and Efficient Network Utility Service (IAA) .... VENUS
Variable Angle Launcher .... VAL
Variable Angle Monochromatic Fringe Observation [*Film thickness determination*] .... VAMFO
Variable Angle Sample Spinning [*Physics*] .... VASS
Variable Angle Scatterometer (MCD) .... VAS
Variable Angle Spectroscopic Ellipsometer .... VASE
Variable Angle, Variable Pitch .... VAVP
Variable Annuity .... VA
Variable Aperture Far Field .... VAFF
Variable Aperture Target Recognition (MCD) .... VATR
Variable Area Nozzle .... VAN
Variable Area Turbine .... VAT
Variable Attenuator Amplified .... VAA
Variable Attribute Raster Scan System (NITA) .... VARS
Variable, Attributes, Error Propagation (IEEE) .... VAEP
Variable Automatic Synthesis Program [*NASA*] .... VASP
Variable Autotransformer (IAA) .... VAT
Variable Axis Rotor Control System [*Telecommunications*] (TEL) .... VARC
Variable Ballast System .... VBS
Variable Bandpass Filter .... VBPF
Variable Bandwidth Filter .... VBF
Variable Bandwidth Tuning .... VBT
Variable BIT [*Binary Digit*] Rate [*Telecommunications*] .... VBR

Variable Block [Computer science]	VARBLK
Variable Body Armor (INF)	VBA
Variable Boost Control [System] [Automotive engineering]	VBC
Variable Cam Phaser [Automotive engineering]	VCP
Variable Cam Phasing [Automotive engineering]	VCP
Variable Capacitor (IAA)	VARCAP
Variable Capacitor (IAA)	VARIAC
Variable Capacitor	VARICAP
Variable Capacitor (DEN)	VC
Variable Center Distance [Computer science] (OA)	VCD
Variable Ceramic Capacitor	VCC
Variable Characteristic Car (ADA)	VCC
Variable Charge (DCTA)	VC
Variable Cockpit Training System (MCD)	VCTS
Variable Command Count (MCD)	VCC
Variable Compression Ratio	VCR
Variable Compression Vector (MHDI)	VCV
Variable Condenser [Radio]	Var Cond
Variable Conductance Heat Pipe	VCHP
Variable Contrast Resolution Test [Optics]	VCRT
Variable Control Block Area [Computer science]	VCBA
Variable Control Oil Pressure (MSA)	VCOP
Variable Correction Unit (IAA)	VCU
Variable Correlation Synchronization	VCS
Variable Cost (AAGC)	VC
Variable Crystal Filter (DEN)	VCF
Variable Crystal Oscillator (IAA)	VCO
Variable Crystal Oscillator	VXO
Variable Cycle Controller (IAA)	VCC
Variable Cycle Engine (MCD)	VCE
Variable Cycle Operation	VCO
Variable Cycle Technology	VCT
Variable Data Area (NASA)	VDA
Variable Data Table	VDT
Variable Deflection Thruster [Helicopter]	VDT
Variable Delay Line	VDL
Variable Delay Unit (IAA)	VDU
Variable Delivery	VDEL
Variable Density Tunnel	VDT
Variable Deposit Requirement [Business term] (ADA)	VDR
Variable Depth ASDIC (NATG)	VDA
Variable Depth Launch Facility (AAG)	VDLF
Variable Depth SONAR	VDS
Variable Depth SONAR System	VDSS
Variable Depth Transducer [Navy] (NVT)	VDT
Variable Diameter Rotor	VDR
Variable Differential Transformer	VDT
Variable Diode Circuit	VDC
Variable Diode Function Generator	VDFG
Variable Direction Microphone	VDM
Variable Displacement Compressor [Automotive engineering]	VDC
Variable Displacement Engine	VDE
Variable Display Equipment	VDE
Variable Display Training System	VDTS
Variable Drop Size [Color printing]	VDS
Variable Duration Impulse (IAA)	VDI
Variable Eddington Radiation Approximation (MCD)	VERA
Variable Elasticity of Substitution [Industrial production]	VES
Variable Electronic Filter	VEF
Variable Eletronegativity Self-Consistent Field [Physics]	VESCF
Variable Elevation Beam [RADAR]	VEB
Variable Emergence Electronically Rotated (MCD)	VEER
Variable Energy Absorber (MCD)	VEA
Variable Energy Content Curves (NOAA)	VECC
Variable Energy Cyclotron (IEEE)	VEC
Variable Exhaust Nozzle	VEN
Variable Explanation Sheet [Army]	VES
Variable Factor [Economics]	VF
Variable Field Length (MCD)	VFL
Variable File Channel	VFC
Variable/Fixed Wavelength [Electronics]	VFW
Variable Focal Length	VFL
Variable Format Message Entry Device [Computer science] (MCD)	VFMED
Variable Frequency [Electricity] (MSA)	VF
Variable Frequency Clock (IAA)	VFC
Variable Frequency Control	VFC
Variable Frequency Crystal (IAA)	VFC
Variable Frequency Drive [Instrumentation]	VFD
Variable Frequency Mixer (IAA)	VFX
Variable Frequency Monitor [Sony Corp.]	VFM
Variable Frequency Oscillator	VFO
Variable Frequency Selection System [Aviation] (DA)	VFSS
Variable Frequency Sine Wave	VFSW
Variable Frequency Synthesizer [Ariel Corp.] [Computer science]	VFS
Variable Fuel Flow Ducted Rocket (MCD)	VFFDR
Variable Fuel Vehicle [General Motors Corp.] [Automotive engineering]	VFV
Variable Function Key [Computer science] (ECII)	VFK
Variable Gain Amplifier	VGA
Variable Gas Capacitor	VGC
Variable Gear Ratio [Automotive steering systems]	VGR
Variable Generator of Unfamiliar Stimuli [Computer program]	VARGUS
Variable Geometry [Refers to an aircraft that is capable of altering the sweep of the wings while in flight] (NATG)	VG
Variable Geometry	VG
Variable Geometry Inlet	VGI
Variable Geometry Nozzle	VGN
Variable Geometry Rotor	VGR
Variable Geometry Structure	VGS
Variable Geometry Turbocharger [Automotive engineering]	VGT
Variable Geometry Wing [Aircraft]	VGW
Variable Geometry Wing Aircraft (AAG)	VGWA
Variable Grating Mode (PDAA)	VGM
Variable Heavy	VH
Variable Horsepower	VHP
Variable Housing Allowance (MCD)	VHA
Variable Impedance Tube	VIT
Variable Incentive Pay [Military] (NVT)	VIP
Variable Income Annuity	VIA
Variable Individual Protection [Insurance]	VIP
Variable Inductance Displacement Transducer (PDAA)	VIDT
Variable Inductance Pickup	VIP
Variable Induction Port System [Automotive engineering]	VIPS
Variable Induction System [Automotive engineering]	VIS
Variable Inductive Transducer [Automotive engineering]	VIT
Variable Inertia Charging System [Mazda Motor Co.] [Automotive engineering]	VICS
Variable Inflation System	VIS
Variable Information Processing [Naval Ordnance Laboratory] [Information retrieval]	VIP
Variable Information Processing Package	VIPP
Variable Injection Timing [Diesel engines]	VIT
Variable Inlet Guide Blades (MCD)	VIGB
Variable Inlet Vane [Nuclear energy] (NRCH)	VIV
Variable Input Phototypesetter	VIP
Variable Input-Output Code	VIOC
Variable Instruction Computer	VIC
Variable Intake and Mixture [Fuel systems] [Automotive engineering]	VIMIX
Variable Intake Manifold	VIM
Variable Integration Measurement System	VIMS
Variable Intensity Back Lighting (NITA)	VIBL
Variable Intensity Light [Aviation] (DA)	VI
Variable Interest Plus [Banking]	VIP
Variable Interest Rate	VIR
Variable Interlace System for Television Applications	VISTA
Variable Intermittent Duty (IAA)	VID
Variable Interval [Reinforcement schedule]	VI
Variable Item Processing System	VIPS
Variable Joining [Genetics]	VJ
Variable Length	VL
Variable Length (IAA)	VLN
Variable Length Cavity Resonance	VLCR
Variable Length Distinguishing Sequence (IAA)	VLDS
Variable Length Divide or Halt (SAA)	VDH
Variable Length Divide or Proceed (SAA)	VDP
Variable Length Field	VLF
Variable Length File Format (NITA)	V-format
Variable Length Multiply	VLM
Variable Length Shift Register [Computer science] (IAA)	VSR
Variable Length Text Processor (MHDI)	VLTP
Variable Length Word Symbolic Assembly System (IEEE)	VALSAS
Variable Level Access Method [Computer science]	VLAM
Variable Life Insurance	VLI
Variable Light [Immunology]	VL
Variable Loan Rate [Business term]	VLR
Variable Low-Frequency Standard	VLFS
Variable Magnetic Shunt [Electronics] (IAA)	VMS
Variable Major Protein [Genetics]	VMP
Variable Mass System	VMS
Variable Match Unit (IAA)	VMU
Variable Memory System [Computer science] (IAA)	VMS
Variable Message Cycle	VMC
Variable Message Formats (RDA)	VMF
Variable Message Sign	VMS
Variable Message System	VMS
Variable Mica Capacitor	VMC
Variable Microcycle Timing	VMT
Variable Moment of Inertia [Nuclear physics]	VMI
Variable Mu Tube [Electronics] (IAA)	VARIMU
Variable Mu Tube [Electronics]	VMT
Variable Navigation Ratio	VNR
Variable Neodymium LASER	VNL
Variable Neutralizing Capacitor	VNC
Variable Nozzle Slow Landing (MCD)	VNSL
Variable Number of Tandem Repeats [Genetics]	VNTR
Variable Number of Tandem Repeats Locus [Genetics] (DOG)	VNTR locus
Variable Oil Capacitor	VOC
Variable Omnirange Tactical (NASA)	VORTAC
Variable Operating and Safety Level (DNAB)	VOSL
Variable Operating Frequency (NATG)	VOF
Variable Orientation Launcher (AAG)	VOL
Variable Orifice Idle Spark Control [Automotive engineering]	VOISC
Variable Orifice Sound Attenuator [System] (DNAB)	VOSA
Variable Output Circuit (DEN)	VOC
Variable Padder Capacitor	VPC
Variable Parameter Record [Statistics] (IAA)	VPR
Variable Parameter Regression [Statistics]	VPR
Variable Parameter System	VPS
Variable Parameter Terrain-Avoidance RADAR	VPTAR
Variable Parts Feeder	VPF
Variable Performance Optimizing Controller (IAA)	VPOC

Variable Phase Filter	VPF
Variable Phase Function Generator	VPFG
Variable Pitch [*as, an aircraft propeller*]	VP
Variable Pitch Propeller	VPP
Variable Polarity Plasma [*Welding*]	VPP
Variable Power Drivetrain [*Automotive engineering*]	VPD
Variable Power Supply (MCD)	VPS
Variable Procedure (AAG)	VP
Variable Property	VP
Variable Pulse LASER	VPL
Variable Pulse Neodymium LASER	VPNL
Variable Pulse Repetition Frequency (IEEE)	VPRF
Variable Pulse Width [*Automotive engineering*]	VPW
Variable Quantization Level [*Algorithm developed by Aydin Monitor Corp.*] [*Telecommunications*]	VQL
Variable Quartz Capacitor	VQC
Variable Random Access Memory [*Computer science*]	VRAM
Variable Range Ballistic Missile [*DoD*] (MCD)	VRBM
Variable Range Delay Unit (PDAA)	VRDU
Variable Range Marker [*RADAR technology*]	VRM
Variable Range Reflector (IEEE)	VARR
Variable Rate [*Reinforcement*] [*Medicine*] (DAVI)	VR
Variable Rate Adaptive Multiplexing [*Telecommunications*] (TEL)	VRAM
Variable Rate Demand Obligation [*Finance*]	VRDO
Variable Ratio [*Reinforcement*]	VR
Variable Ratio Divider (IAA)	VRD
Variable Ratio Oiling	VRO
Variable Reach Rough Terrain Forklift [*Military*]	VRRTFL
Variable Reactor [*Electronics*] (EECA)	VARACTOR
Variable Reenlistment Bonus [*Military*] (AABC)	VRB
Variable Region [*Immunochemistry*]	V
Variable Relay Control Module [*Cooling systems*] [*Automotive engineering*]	VRCM
Variable Reluctance	VR
Variable Reluctance Cartridge	VRC
Variable Reluctance Microphone	VRM
Variable Reluctance Pickup	VRP
Variable Reluctance Transducer	VRT
Variable Resistance [*or Resistor*] (IAA)	VR
Variable Resistive Components Institute (EA)	VRCI
Variable Resistor	VARISTOR
Variable Retention of Diatomic Differential [*Physics*]	VRDDO
Variable Safety Level	VSL
Variable Scope Delta Modulation (NITA)	VSDM
Variable Search and Track Air Defense RADAR	VSTAR
Variable Separation Incentive [*DoD*]	VSI
Variable Size Parameter [*Thermodynamics*]	VSP
Variable Slit Set	VSS
Variable Slope Delta	VSD
Variable Slope Delta Modulation	VSDM
Variable SONAR System	VSS
Variable, Spanned, and Undefined Mode (IAA)	VSAM
Variable Specification List	VSL
Variable Speech Control [*Device that permits distortion-free rapid playback of speech recorded on tape*]	VSC
Variable Speed	V/SPD
Variable Speed (IEEE)	VS
Variable Speed Assembly [*Mechanical powertrain*]	VSA
Variable Speed Chopper	VSC
Variable Speed Constant Frequency	VSCF
Variable Speed Drive	VSD
Variable Speed Gear (DEN)	VSG
Variable Speed Tactical Trainer [*Air Force*] (MCD)	VSTT
Variable Speed Training Target	VSTT
Variable Stability Aircraft (NASA)	VSA
Variable (Stability) In-Flight Simulator Test Aircraft	VISTA
Variable Stability System [*Aviation*]	VSS
Variable Stability Trainer [*Aviation*]	VST
Variable Standing Wave Ratio (MCD)	VSWR
Variable Stream Control Engine [*NASA*] (MCD)	VSCE
Variable Stroke Engine	VSE
Variable [*or Variant*] Surface Glycoprotein [*Biochemistry*]	VSG
Variable Surface Tracking	VST
Variable Sweep (IEEE)	VS
Variable Sweep Wing	VSW
Variable Takeoff Rating (GAVI)	VTR
Variable Tandem Repetition [*Genetics*]	VTR
Variable Temperature Compensation Capacitor	VTCC
Variable Temperature Electrical Resistivity Measurement [*Physics*]	VTERM
Variable Thermal Control Surface	VTCS
Variable Threshold (IAA)	VT
Variable Threshold Digital Input	VTDI
Variable Threshold Logic	VTL
Variable Threshold Recently Used (MHDI)	VTRU
Variable Threshold Transistor	VTT
Variable Thrust	VT
Variable Thrust Engine	VTE
Variable Thrust Engine System	VTES
Variable Time [*Fuse*] [*Also known as a "proximity fuse"*]	VT
Variable Time (IDOE)	vt
Variable Time Delay	VTD
Variable Time, Fragmentation [*Military*] (CAAL)	VTF
Variable Time Non-Fragmenting [*Military*] (CAAL)	VTNF
Variable Time Step	VTS
Variable Timing Control [*Intake subsystem*] [*Automotive engineering*]	VTC
Variable Topology Random Access Memory [*Computer science*] (PDAA)	VTRAM
Variable Torque Distribution [*Automotive engineering*]	VTD
Variable Torque Distribution	VTD
Variable Tracking Strategy (MCD)	VTS
Variable Transfer Address	VTA
Variable Transformer	VT
Variable Transmission (ADA)	VT
Variable Transmission Window	VTW
Variable Trim Reentry Body (MCD)	VTRB
Variable Trimmer Capacitor	VTC
Variable Unblocked (MHDB)	VARUNB
Variable Underwater Experimental Community (PDAA)	VUEC
Variable Universal Life [*Insurance*]	VUL
Variable Vacuum Capacitor [*or Capacitance*]	VVC
Variable Valve Actuation [*Automotive engineering*]	VVA
Variable Valve Control [*Automotive*]	VVC
Variable Valve Timing [*Automotive*]	VVT
Variable Valve-Timing and Lift Electronic Control System - Economy [*Automotive technology*]	VTEC-E
Variable Venturi [*Automotive engineering*]	VV
Variable Voltage Capacitor (IAA)	VVC
Variable Voltage Rectifier	VVR
Variable Volume Piston Pump	VVPP
Variable Volume/Variable Temperature Sealed Housing for Evaporative Determination [*Automotive emissions testing*]	VV/VTSHED
Variable Width Pulse	VWP
Variable Word Length	VWL
Variable Word Size	VWS
Variable-Area Light-Reflecting Assembly [*Invented by T. C. Howard of Synergetics, Inc.*]	VALRA
Variable-Area Nozzle by Gas Injection (SAA)	VANGI
Variable-Capacitance Diode	VCD
Variable-Diversity-Joining [*Genetics*]	VDJ
Variable-Factor Programming	VFP
Variable-Flow Directed Rocket	VFDR
Variable-Grade Gravity Sewer	VGS
Variable-Interest-Rate Mortgage [*Real estate*]	VIRM
Variable-Length Coding [*Computer science*]	VLC
Variable-Length Indexed Sequential Access Method [*Computer science*] (MHDB)	VISAM
Variable-Mode Solid-Fueled Ramjet (MCD)	VMSFRJ
Variable-Nozzle Turbocharger [*Automotive engineering*]	VNT
Variable-Rate Mortgage [*Real estate*]	VRM
Variable-Rate Pulse Generator	VPG
Variable-Temperature Stepwise Desorption [*Chemical engineering*]	VTSD
Variable-Time [*Proximity Fuse*] (DOMA)	VT
Variable-Voltage Transformer (IEEE)	VARITRAN
Variably Initialized Translator for Algorithmic Languages [*Computer science*]	VITAL
Variae [*of Cassiodorus*] [*Classical studies*] (OCD)	Var
Variae Lectiones [*Variant Readings*] [*Latin*]	VV LL
Variamento [*In a Varied Style*] [*Music*] (ROG)	VARIA
Varian Associates [*NYSE symbol*] (SPSG)	VAR
Varian Associates [*Associated Press*] (SAG)	Varian
Varian Canada, Inc., Georgetown, ON, Canada [*Library symbol Library of Congress*] (LCLS)	CaOGeV
Varian Canada, Inc., Georgetown, Ontario [*Library symbol National Library of Canada*] (NLC)	OGEV
Varian Data Machines	VDM
Varian Omnitaste Real Time Executive [*Computer science*] (IAA)	VORTEX
Varian Telecommunication Access Method (IAA)	VTAM
Variance (WGA)	Va
Variance Analysis Report (MCD)	VAR
Variance at Completion (MCD)	VAC
Variance Frequency Processor (MCD)	VFP
Variance Index Score [*Statistics*]	VIS
Variance Inflation Factor [*Statistics*]	VIF
Variance Score [*Statistics*]	VS
Variance to Mean Rate	VMR
Variant [*Genetics*]	V
Variant [*Numismatics*]	VAR
Variant (DAVI)	VAR
Variant Angina Pectoris [*Cardiology*] (DAVI)	VAP
Variant Antigenic Type [*Genetics, immunology*]	VAT
Variant Frequency [*Biology*]	VF
Variant of Creutzfeldt-Jakob Disease [*Medicine*]	VCJD
Variant of Human Creutzfeldt-Jakob Disease [*Medicine*]	CJD
Variant Pinocytic [*Cell*] [*Medicine*]	VP
Variant Reading	VR
Variant Surface Glycoprotein [*Immunology*]	VSG
Variant-Specific Surface Antigen [*Genetics, immunology*]	VSA
Variation	V
Variation	VAR
Variation (ROG)	VARION
Variation (FAAC)	VARN
Variation Flow Analysis	VFA
Variation in Estimated Quantity (AAGC)	VEQ
Variation in Price (MHDB)	VIP
Variation per Day [*Navigation*]	VPD
Variation per Hour [*Navigation*]	VPH
Variation per Minute [*Navigation*]	VPM
Variation Simulation Analysis [*Automotive engineering*]	VSA
Variational Transition State Theory [*Physical chemistry*]	VTST
Variational Upper Bound	VUB

Varicella-Zoster [*Also, VZV*] [*A virus*] ... VZ
Varicella-Zoster [*Antibody*] [*Immunology*] (DAVI) ... V-Z
Varicella-Zoster Immune Globulin ... VZIG
Varicella-Zoster Virus [*Also, VZ*] ... VZV
Varicose Eczema [*Medicine*] ... VE
Varicose Ulcer [*Medicine*] ... VU
Varicose Vein (MAE) ... VV
Varied [*Quality of the bottom*] [*Nautical charts*] ... vard
Varied Intelligent System Target Acquisition ... VISTA
Variegate Porphyria [*Medicine*] ... VP
Variegated ... VAR
Varietas [*Variety*] [*Biology*] ... var
Varietas Nova [*New Variety*] [*Biology*] ... var nov
Variety (DAVI) ... va
Variety ... VAR
Variety (MSA) ... VRTY
Variety ... VRTY
Variety and Allied Entertainments Council [*British*] (BI) ... VAEC
Variety Artistes' Benevolent Fund [*British*] (ROG) ... VABF
Variety Artistes' Federation [*British*] (BI) ... VAF
Variety Clubs International (EA) ... VCI
Variety Reduction (WDAA) ... VR
Variety Theatres and Shows [*Public-performance tariff class*] [*British*] ... V
Variflex, Inc. [*Associated Press*] (SAG) ... Variflex
Variflex, Inc. [*NASDAQ symbol*] (SAG) ... VFLX
Varig Brazilian [*Airline flight code*] (ODBW) ... RG
Vari-L Co. [*Associated Press*] (SAG) ... Vari-L Co
Vari-L Co. [*NASDAQ symbol*] (SAG) ... VARL
Vari-L Company [*NASDAQ symbol*] (TTSB) ... VARL
Vario-Losser [*Electronics*] ... VL
Variometer (IAA) ... VA
Variometer (WGA) ... VAR
Various ... VAR
Various (VRA) ... vari
Various (ROG) ... VARS
Various Dates [*Bibliography*] ... VD
Various Dates (WDMC) ... vd
Various Dialects (WDAA) ... VAR DIAL
Various Editions and Translations (WDAA) ... VAR ED & TR
Various Paging [*Bibliography*] ... VP
Various Places [*MARC country of publication code Library of Congress*] (LCCP) ... vp
Various Publishers [*Bibliography*] ... VP
Various Years [*Bibliography*] ... VY
Various Years (WDMC) ... vy
Varipolarization Beacon Antenna ... VPBA
Varistor [*Telecommunications*] (IAA) ... VAR
Varistor [*Telecommunications*] (TEL) ... VRI
Varistor [*Electronics*] ... VRIS
Varitech Investors Corp. [*Toronto Stock Exchange symbol*] ... VRI
Varitech Resources [*Vancouver Stock Exchange symbol*] ... VAR
Varitronic Systems, Inc. [*Associated Press*] (SAG) ... Varitrn
Varitronic Systems, Inc. [*NASDAQ symbol*] (NQ) ... VRSY
Varity Corp. [*Associated Press*] (SAG) ... Varity
Varity Corp. [*NYSE symbol Toronto Stock Exchange symbol Vancouver Stock Exchange symbol*] (SPSG) ... VAT
Varityper ... VARI
Varkaus [*Finland ICAO location identifier*] (ICLI) ... EFVR
Varkaus [*Finland*] [*Airport symbol*] (OAG) ... VRK
Varlen Corp. [*Associated Press*] (SAG) ... Varlen
Varlen Corp. [*NASDAQ symbol*] (NQ) ... VRLN
Varmeter [*Engineering*] ... VARM
Varmlandsflyg AB [*Sweden ICAO designator*] (FAAC) ... SRL
Varna [*Bulgaria*] [*ICAO location identifier*] (ICLI) ... LBWN
Varna [*Bulgaria*] [*Airport symbol*] (OAG) ... VAR
Varnado, LA [*FM radio station call letters*] ... WBOX
Varnish (AAG) ... V
Varnish [*Technical drawings*] ... VAR
Varnish (VRA) ... var
Varnish ... VARN
Varnish Insulating Compound ... VIC
Varnish Makers' and Painters' Naphtha ... VM & P
Varnished Cambric [*Insulation*] ... VC
Varnished Cambric Insulation Material ... VCIM
Varnished Tube Association ... VTA
Varnishing Resistant [*Ink*] (DGA) ... VR
Varnish-Treated [*Insulation*] (MSA) ... V
Varnville [*South Carolina*] [*Seismograph station code, US Geological Survey*] (SEIS) ... VSC
Varo, Inc., Texas Division, Garland, TX [*Library symbol Library of Congress*] (LCLS) ... TxGarV
Varotsos Alexopoulos Nomicos [*Authors of a technique for predicting earthquakes*] ... VAN
Varrelbusch [*Germany ICAO location identifier*] (ICLI) ... EDWU
Varsity ... V
Varsity [*Record label*] ... Var
Varsity Spirit [*NASDAQ symbol*] (TTSB) ... VARS
Varsity Spirit Corp. [*NASDAQ symbol*] (SAG) ... VARS
Varsity Spirit Corp. [*Associated Press*] (SAG) ... VarSprt
Vars-Les-Crosses-Et-Les-Tronches [*France ICAO location identifier*] (ICLI) ... LFNK
Varudeklarationsnamnden [*Labeling system*] [*Sweden*] ... VDN
Varying (IAA) ... VAR
Varying ... VRYG
Varying Order [*British*] ... VO
Varying Radiation (IEEE) ... VARAD
VAS [*VISSR Atmospheric Sounder*] **Data Utilization Center** (USDC) ... VDUC
Vas Deferens [*Urology*] (DAVI) ... vas
Vas Vitreum [*A Glass Vessel*] [*Latin Pharmacy*] (MAE) ... vas vit
Vas Vitreum [*A Glass Vessel*] [*Pharmacy*] ... VAS VITR
Vasa Order of America [*Cranston, RI*] (EA) ... VOofA
Vascular [*Cardiology*] (DAVI) ... VAS
Vascular ... VASC
Vascular Access Device [*Cardiology*] (DAVI) ... VAD
Vascular Adhesion Protein [*Biochemistry*] ... VAP
Vascular Bundle [*Botany*] ... VB
Vascular Catheterization (CPH) ... VC
Vascular Cell Adhesion Molecule [*Cytology*] ... VCAM
Vascular Disease (CPH) ... Vas Dis
Vascular Disease [*Cardiology*] (DAVI) ... VD
Vascular Endothelial Growth Factor [*Biochemistry*] ... VEGF
Vascular Permeability Assay [*Clinical chemistry*] ... VPA
Vascular Permeability Mediator [*Hematology*] ... VPM
Vascular Radiology [*Medicine*] (DMAA) ... VAS RAD
Vascular Research Foundation ... VRF
Vascular Resistance [*Medicine*] (MAE) ... VR
Vascular Smooth Muscle [*Anatomy*] ... VSM
Vascular Smooth Muscle Cell [*Cytology*] ... VSMC
Vascular Strand [*Botany*] ... VS
Vascular Surgical Society [*British*] ... VSS
Vascular System (SAA) ... VS
Vascular Time ... VT
Vascular Tissue [*Botany*] ... V
Vascular Tracheoesophageal-Limb-Reduction [*Endocrinology*] ... VATER
Vascular-Permeability Factor [*Medicine*] ... VPF
Vasectomy (WDAA) ... VAS
Vasectomy Advancement Society of Great Britain ... VAS of GB
Vasenlisten zur Griechischen Heldensage [*A publication*] (OCD) ... Vasenlisten
Vasoactive Inhibitory Principle [*Biochemistry*] ... VIP
Vasoactive Intestinal Peptide [*or Polypeptide*] [*Biochemistry*] ... VIP
Vasoconstrictive [*Physiology*] ... VCR
Vasoconstrictor [*Medicine*] ... VC
Vasoconstrictor Center [*Physiology*] ... VCC
Vasoconstrictor Substance [*Physiology*] ... VCS
Vasodepressor Lipid [*Physiology*] ... VDL
Vasodepressor Material [*Physiology*] (MAE) ... VDEM
Vasodepressor Material [*Physiology*] ... VDM
Vasodilatation [*Physiology*] (AAMN) ... VASODIL
Vasodilation [*Cardiology*] (DAVI) ... VD
Vasodilator [*Cardiology*] (DAVI) ... VD
Vasodilator Center [*Physiology*] ... VDC
Vasodilator Substance [*Physiology*] ... VDS
Vasodilator-Stimulated Phosphoprotein [*Physiology*] ... VASP
Vasoexcitor Material [*Physiology*] ... VEM
Vasoinhibitory [*Medicine*] ... VI
Vasoinhibitory Center [*Physiology*] ... VIC
Vasoinhibitory Peptide [*Medicine*] (MAE) ... VIP
Vasomedical, Inc. [*NASDAQ symbol*] (SAG) ... VASO
Vasomedical, Inc. [*Associated Press*] (SAG) ... Vasomed
Vasomotor [*Physiology*] ... VM
Vasomotor Center [*Physiology*] ... VMC
Vasomotor Nervous System [*Physiology*] ... VNS
Vasomotor Rhinitis [*Medicine*] ... VMR
Vasopressin [*Endocrinology*] ... VP
Vasopressin-Like Peptide [*Biochemistry*] ... VLP
Vasotocin ... VT
Vassar Attitude Inventory [*Education*] ... VAI
Vassar College (GAGS) ... Vassar C
Vassar College, George Sherman Dickerson Music Library, Poughkeepsie, NY [*Library symbol*] [*Library of Congress*] (LCLS) ... NPV-Mu
Vassar College, Poughkeepsie, NY [*Library symbol Library of Congress*] (LCLS) ... NPV
Vassar College, Poughkeepsie, NY [*OCLC symbol*] (OCLC) ... VXW
Vassar, MI [*FM radio station call letters*] ... WOWE
Vassijaure [*Sweden*] [*Seismograph station code, US Geological Survey Closed*] (SEIS) ... VAS
Vassouras [*Brazil*] [*Geomagnetic observatory code*] ... VSS
VAST/IMA [*Versatile Avionics System Tester/Intermediate Maintenance Activity*] **Effectiveness by Workload Simulation** ... VIEWS
Vast Integrated Communications Environment [*Carnegie Mellon University*] [*Pittsburgh, PA*] ... VICE
VAST [*Versatile Avionics Shop Test*] **Interface Test Application Language** ... VITAL
VAST [*Versatile Avionics Shop Test*] **Operating System Code** ... VOSC
Vast Translator (KSC) ... VTRAN
Vastar Resources [*NYSE symbol*] (TTSB) ... VRI
Vastar Resources, Inc. [*Associated Press*] (SAG) ... Vastar
Vastar Resources, Inc. [*NYSE symbol*] (SAG) ... VRI
Vasteras [*Sweden*] [*Airport symbol*] (OAG) ... VST
Vasteras/Hasslo [*Sweden ICAO location identifier*] (ICLI) ... ESOW
Vasteras/Johannisberg [*Sweden ICAO location identifier*] (ICLI) ... ESSX
Vastervik [*Sweden ICAO location identifier*] (ICLI) ... ESSW
Vastervik [*Sweden*] [*Airport symbol*] (OAG) ... VVK
Vastervik Hospital [*Sweden ICAO location identifier*] (ICLI) ... ESHW
Vastus Intermedius [*Muscle*] (DAVI) ... VI
Vastus Medialis [*A muscle*] ... VM
Vastus Medialis Obliquus [*Muscle*] ... VMO
Vat Dye Institute [*Later, American Dye Manufacturers Institute*] (EA) ... VDI
Vat Petroleum [*Vancouver Stock Exchange symbol*] ... VT
Vatel Club (EA) ... VC

Vaterlaendische Union [*Patriotic Union*] [*Liechtenstein*] [*Political party*] (PPE) .... VU
Vatican [*International civil aircraft marking*] (ODBW) .... HV
Vatican (VRA) .... Vat
Vatican .... VAT
Vatican Advanced Technology Telescope [*At Mount Graham, AZ*] .... VATT
Vatican City [*MARC geographic area code Library of Congress*] (LCCP) .... e-vc--
Vatican City V
Vatican City [*ANSI two-letter standard code*] (CNC) .... VA
Vatican City [*ANSI three-letter standard code*] (CNC) .... VAT
Vatican City [*MARC country of publication code Library of Congress*] (LCCP) vc
Vatican Philatelic Society (EA) .... VPS
Vatican State (WDAA) .... VAT STA
Vatican's Sacred Congregation for the Doctrine of the Faith .... VSCDF
Vatomandry [*Madagascar*] [*ICAO location identifier*] (ICLI) .... FMMY
Vatomandry [*Madagascar*] [*Airport symbol*] (OAG) .... VAT
Vatomandry [*Malagasy*] [*Airport symbol*] (AD) .... VAT
Vatovaky [*Madagascar*] [*Seismograph station code, US Geological Survey*] (SEIS) .... VTY
Vattel's Law of Nations [*A publication*] (DLA) .... Vatt
Vattel's Law of Nations [*A publication*] (DLA) .... Vattel
Vattel's Law of Nations [*A publication*] (DLA) .... Vattel Law Nat
Vatukoula [*Fiji*] [*ICAO location identifier*] (ICLI) .... NFNV
Vaudeville .... VAUD
Vaughan Public Library, Maple, ON, Canada [*Library symbol Library of Congress*] (LCLS) .... CaOMap
Vaughan Public Library, Maple, Ontario [*Library symbol National Library of Canada*] (NLC) .... OMAP
Vaughan's English Common Pleas Reports [*124 English Reprint*] [*A publication*] (DLA) .... Vaug
Vaughan's English Common Pleas Reports [*124 English Reprint*] [*A publication*] (DLA) .... Vaugh
Vaughan's English Common Pleas Reports [*124 English Reprint*] [*A publication*] (DLA) .... Vaughan
Vaughan's English Common Pleas Reports [*124 English Reprint*] [*A publication*] (DLA) .... Vaughan (Eng)
Vaughan-Steffensrud Elementary School, Chisholm, MN [*Library symbol*] [*Library of Congress*] (LCLS) .... MnChiE
Vaughn Communications [*NASDAQ symbol*] (TTSB) .... VGHN
Vaughn Public Library, Ashland, WI [*Library symbol Library of Congress*] (LCLS) .... WAs
Vaughn Public Library, Ashland, WI [*Library symbol*] [*Library of Congress*] (LCLS) .... WAsL
Vaughn's, Inc. [*Associated Press*] (SAG) .... Vaughn
Vaughn's, Inc. [*NASDAQ symbol*] (NQ) .... VGHN
Vault .... VLT
Vault (VRA) .... vlt
Vault Door (AAG) .... VD
Vault Explorations, Inc. [*Vancouver Stock Exchange symbol*] .... VLT
Vauville [*France ICAO location identifier*] (ICLI) .... LFAU
Vauxhall [*Automobile*] (DSUE) .... VAUX
Vauxhall [*Automobile*] [*British*] VX
Vauxhall College of Building and Further Education [*London, England*] .... VCBFE
Vauxhall Public Library, Alberta [*Library symbol National Library of Canada*] (NLC) .... AVA
Vaux's Recorder's Decisions [*1841-45*] [*Philadelphia, PA*] [*A publication*] (DLA) .... Rec Dec
Vaux's Recorder's Decisions [*1841-45*] [*Philadelphia, PA*] [*A publication*] (DLA) .... Vaux
Vaux's Recorder's Decisions [*1841-45*] [*Philadelphia, PA*] [*A publication*] (DLA) .... Vaux (PA)
Vaux's Recorder's Decisions [*1841-45*] [*Philadelphia, PA*] [*A publication*] (DLA) .... Vaux Rec Dec
Vava'u [*Tonga*] [*ICAO location identifier*] (ICLI) .... NFTV
Vava'u [*Tonga Island*] [*Airport symbol*] (OAG) .... VAV
VAX Applicant Search System [*Science Applications International Corp.*] .... VASS
VAX OSI [*Virtual Address Extension Open Systems Interconnection*] **TransportService** (TNIG) .... VOTS
Vaxholm [*Sweden ICAO location identifier*] (ICLI) .... ESHV
Vaxjo [*Sweden*] [*Airport symbol*] (AD) .... VAV
Vaxjo [*Sweden*] [*Airport symbol*] (OAG) .... VXO
Vaxjo/Kronoberg [*Sweden ICAO location identifier*] (ICLI) .... ESMX
Vaxjo/Urasa [*Sweden ICAO location identifier*] (ICLI) .... ESFU
Vayikra Rabba (BJA) .... Vayr
Vayudoot [*India*] [*ICAO designator*] (FAAC) .... VDT
VB Anderson Co. [*BTAC*] (DAVI) .... VBA
VD [*Venereal Disease*] **National Hotline** [*Later, NSTDH*] (EA) .... VDNH
VDC Corp. [*NASDAQ symbol*] (TTSB) .... VDCLF
VDC Corp. Ltd. [*Associated Press*] (SAG) .... VDC
VDC Corp. Ltd. [*NASDAQ symbol*] (SAG) .... VDCLF
VDI-Nachrichten [*VDI-Verlag GmbH*] [*Database*] .... VDI-N
VDU Controller (NITA) .... VDUC
Veal Infusion Broth [*Immunology*] .... VIB
Veazey's Reports [*36-44 Vermont*] [*A publication*] (DLA) .... Veazey
VEB Deutsche Hydrierwerk, Rodleben [*East Germany*] [*Research code symbol*] .... HL
VEB Fahlberg-List [*East Germany*] [*Research code symbol*] .... J
VEB Fahlberg-List [*East Germany*] [*Research code symbol*] .... RG
VEB Fahlberg-List [*East Germany*] [*Research code symbol*] .... TA
VEB Farbenfabrik Wolfen [*East Germany*] [*Research code symbol*] .... SA
Vector [*Mathematics*] V
Vector (IDOE) v
Vector (NASA) .... VCTR
Vector (KSC) .... VEC
Vector Adaptive Predictive Coding [*Telecommunications*] .... VAPC
Vector Adaptive Transform Processing [*Computer science*] (PCM) .... VATP
Vector Addition System .... VAS
Vector Aeromotive [*NASDAQ symbol*] (TTSB) .... VCAR
Vector Aeromotive Corp. [*NASDAQ symbol*] (NQ) .... VCAR
Vector Aeromotive Corp. [*Associated Press*] (SAG) .... VctA
Vector Aeromotive Corp. [*Associated Press*] (SAG) .... VctAer
Vector Aeromotive Corp. [*Associated Press*] (SAG) .... VctAr
Vector Aeromotive Wrrt [*NASDAQ symbol*] (TTSB) .... VCARL
Vector Aeromotive Wrrt [*NASDAQ symbol*] (TTSB) .... VCARW
Vector Airborne Magnetometer (IEEE) .... VAM
Vector Analog Computer .... VAC
Vector Arithmetic Multiprocessor [*Computer science*] (IEEE) .... VAMP
Vector Autoregressive Model [*Mathematics*] .... VAR
Vector Averaging Current Meter [*Marine science*] (MSC) .... VACM
Vector Biology Laboratory [*University of Notre Dame*] [*Research center*] (RCD) .... VBL
Vector Character (NASA) VC
Vector Collecting Program [*Electronics design*] (IAA) .... VCP
Vector Control (KSC) .... V/C
Vector Control (MUGU) .... VEC
Vector Control Research Centre [*India*] .... VCRC
Vector Correction Program (SAA) .... VCP
Vector Data Buffer .... VDB
Vector Dominance Model [*Physics*] .... VDM
Vector Drawn Map .... VDM
Vector Electrocardiogram [*Cardiology*] (DAVI) .... VECG
Vector Electroencephalograph .... VEEG
Vector Element by Element Multiply (IAA) .... VEM
Vector Element by Element Sum (IAA) .... VES
Vector Equilibrium Principle [*Crystallography*] .... VEP
Vector Field .... VF
Vector Float-to-Fix (IAA) .... VFX
Vector Function Chainer (MHDB) .... VFC
Vector Generator [*Computer graphics*] .... VG
Vector Graphics Access Method .... VGAM
Vector Impedance Locus Plotter .... VILP
Vector Inner Product (IAA) .... VIP
Vector Instruction Processor .... VIP
Vector Instruction Set [*Computer science*] .... VIS
Vector International (EA) VI
Vector Length (MHDB) VL
Vector Magnetocardiogram [*Medicine*] (DMAA) .... VMCG
Vector Meson Dominance [*Particle physics*] (OA) .... VMD
Vector Message .... VM
Vector Miss Distance Indicator .... VMDI
Vector Move Convert (IAA) .... VMC
Vector Parallel Processor [*Computer science*] .... VPP
Vector Pressure Ratio Transducer .... VPRT
Vector Processing Facility (NITA) .... VPF
Vector Processing Subsystem .... VPSS
Vector Processing Subsystem/Vector Facility [*Computer science*] (HGAA) .... VPSS/VF
Vector Processor .... VP
Vector Product Format .... VPF
Vector Quantizer [*Computer science*] .... VQ
Vector Reaction Control System (SSD) .... VRCS
Vector Recurrent Iterated Function System [*Iterated Systems, Inc.*] [*Digital imaging*] .... VRIFS
Vector Scan [*Digital imaging*] (IAA) .... VS
Vector Scoring System [*Navy*] (MCD) .... VSS
Vector Voltmeter .... VVM
Vector-Borne Disease .... VBD
Vectorcardiogram [*Medicine*] .... VCG
Vectorcardiogram Electrode [*Cardiology*] (DAVI) .... H
Vectored Attack [*Navy*] (NVT) .... VECTAC
Vectored Lift Cannon Fighter [*Air Force*] (MCD) .... VLCF
Vectored Lift Fighter (MCD) .... VLF
Vectored Slipstream Principle .... VSP
Vectored Thrust Aircraft [*Aviation*] (DA) .... VAAC
Vectoring in Forward Flight (MCD) .... VIFF
Vectoring Service .... VS
Vector-Measuring Current Meter [*Instrumentation*] .... VMCM
Vectoroculogram .... VOG
Vectors Per Second (CDE) .... VPS
Vector-to-Raster Processor [*Computer graphics terminology*] .... VRP
Vectra Banking [*Associated Press*] (SAG) .... VectBk
Vectra Banking [*NASDAQ symbol*] (SAG) .... VTRA
Vectra Bkg 9.50%'A'Pfd [*NASDAQ symbol*] (TTSB) .... VTRAP
VECTRA Technologies [*NASDAQ symbol*] (SPSG) .... VCTR
Vectra Technologies [*Commercial firm Associated Press*] (SAG) .... VectraTc
Vecuronium [*A muscle relaxant*] Vc
Vedanta Society of Southern California (EA) .... VSSC
Vedanta Society of the City of New York (EA) .... VSCNY
Vedron Ltd. [*Toronto Stock Exchange symbol*] .... VDN
Vee Built [*Ship classification term*] (DS) .... V BLT
Vee One Side (DAC) V1S
Veeco Instruments [*NASDAQ symbol*] (TTSB) .... VECO
Veeco Instruments, Inc. [*NASDAQ symbol*] (SAG) .... VECO
Veeco Instruments, Inc. [*Associated Press*] (SAG) .... VeecoInst
Veedersburg, IN [*FM radio station call letters*] (RBYB) .... WKLR
Veen, Publishers [*Holland*] V
Veeneal [*ICAO designator*] (AD) .... TF
Veering (WGA) .... VRG
Vee-Twin [*Automotive engineering*] .... VT
Vega [*Record label*] [*France*] .... Veg

Vega Aircompany [*Russian Federation*] [*ICAO designator*] (FAAC) ... VEG
Vega Aircraft RADAR Enhancing System [*FAA*] ... VARES
Vega Baja, PR [*AM radio station call letters*] ... WEGA
Vega Target Control System [*Computer flight control of test vehicles*] ... VTCS
Vegan Society [*Oxford, England*] (EAIO) ... VS
Vegetable [*or Vegetation*] (KSC) ... VEG
Vegetable ... VEG
Vegetable Exchange [*Dietetics*] ... Veg Ex
Vegetable Growers' Association [*Australia*] ... VGA
Vegetable Growers Association of America [*Defunct*] (EA) ... VGAA
Vegetable Oil Export Corp. (EA) ... VOEC
Vegetable Parchment [*Paper*] (DGA) ... veg pcht
Vegetable Parchment [*Paper*] (DGA) ... VP
Vegetable Parchment Manufacturers Association [*Later, API*] (EA) ... VPMA
Vegetable Protein Association [*British*] (DBA) ... VPA
Vegetable Protein Products [*Food technology*] ... VPP
Vegetarian Association of America [*Defunct*] (EA) ... VAA
Vegetarian Awareness Network (EA) ... VEGANET
Vegetarian Brotherhood of America [*Defunct*] (EA) ... VBA
Vegetarian Catering Association [*British*] (BI) ... VCA
Vegetarian Education Network (EA) ... VENet
Vegetarian Information Service (EA) ... VIS
Vegetarian Meal [*Airline notation*] ... VGML
Vegetarian Nutritional Research Center (PDAA) ... VNRC
Vegetarian Resource Group (EA) ... VRG
Vegetarian Society of Australia ... VSA
Vegetarian Society of New York [*Defunct*] (EA) ... VSNY
Vegetarian Society of the United Kingdom (DBA) ... VSUK
Vegetation Condition Index [*for detecting and tracking droughts*] [*National Oceanic and Atmospheric Administration*] ... VCI
Vegetation Drought Index [*Agriculture*] (WDAA) ... VDI
Vegetation Index ... VI
Vegetation Management Program [*of the Northern Territory*] (EERA) ... VMP
Vegetation Protection Ordinance [*Brisbane*] (EERA) ... VPO
Vegetative Capability [*Biology*] ... VC
Vegetative Nucleus [*Botany*] ... VN
Vegreville Public Library, Alberta [*Library symbol National Library of Canada*] (NLC) ... AVE
Vegreville Public Library, Vegreville, AB, Canada [*Library symbol*] [*Library of Congress*] (LCLS) ... CaAVe
Vehicle (AFM) ... VEH
Vehicle (DAVI) ... vehic
Vehicle ... VEHIC
Vehicle Acquisition and Tracking System (SAA) ... VATS
Vehicle Activity Status Transmission (PDAA) ... VAST
Vehicle Analyst (MCD) ... VA
Vehicle and Equipment Maintenance System [*Software*] ... VEMS
Vehicle Antenna Position [*NASA*] ... VAP
Vehicle Anti-Theft System [*General Motors Corp.*] ... VATS
Vehicle Area Network [*Automotive engineering*] ... VAN
Vehicle Assembly and Checkout [*NASA*] (NASA) ... VAC
Vehicle Assembly Area [*NASA*] (MCD) ... VAA
Vehicle Assembly Building [*NASA*] (AFM) ... VAB
Vehicle Assembly Building Repeater [*NASA*] (KSC) ... VABR
Vehicle Austere Night Sight [*Army*] (MCD) ... VANS
Vehicle Authorization List [*Military*] (AFM) ... VAL
Vehicle Authorization Utilization Board [*Military*] ... VAUB
Vehicle Automatic State Transmitter (PDAA) ... VAST
Vehicle Automatic Test System ... VATS
Vehicle Builders and Repairers Association [*British*] (EAIO) ... VBRA
Vehicle Builders Employees Federation of Australia ... VBEFA
Vehicle Cargo Ship [*Navy symbol*] ... AKR
Vehicle Cargo Ship ... TAKR
Vehicle Charging and Potential Experiment (NASA) ... VCAP
Vehicle Check Point [*Military*] ... VCP
Vehicle Checkout Area ... VCA
Vehicle Checkout Laboratory ... VCL
Vehicle Checkout Set ... VECOS
Vehicle Collecting Point ... VCP
Vehicle Component Verification System [*Automotive engineering*] ... VCVS
Vehicle Condition Evaluation (MCD) ... VCE
Vehicle Condition Monitor [*Automotive engineering*] ... VCM
Vehicle Cone Index [*Engineering*] (OA) ... VCI
Vehicle Control and Operating System [*Army*] ... VCOS
Vehicle Control Group ... VCG
Vehicle Control Module [*Automotive engineering*] ... VCM
Vehicle Control Officer [*Air Force*] (AFM) ... VCO
Vehicle Cost Management System (NITA) ... VCMS
Vehicle Crew Chief [*NASA*] (KSC) ... VCC
Vehicle Data and Acquisition System [*Automotive engineering*] ... VDAS
Vehicle Data Bus [*Automotive engineering*] ... VDB
Vehicle Data Guide ... VDG
Vehicle Data Recorder ... VDR
Vehicle Data Table [*NASA*] (MCD) ... VDT
Vehicle Data Transmission System ... VDTS
Vehicle Deadlined for Maintenance (AFM) ... VDM
Vehicle Deadlined for Parts ... VDP
Vehicle Description Summary [*General Motors Corp.*] ... VDS
Vehicle Descriptor Section ... VDS
Vehicle Deselect Request [*NASA*] (KSC) ... VDR
Vehicle Detector and Cueing System ... VDECS
Vehicle Development Process [*Automotive project management*] ... VDP
Vehicle Direction and Position Indicator ... VDPI
Vehicle Discharge Lighting System ... VEDILIS
Vehicle Dynamics ... VEHDYN
Vehicle Dynamics Analysis [*Computer simulation*] [*Automotive engineering*] ... VDANL
Vehicle Dynamics Area ... VDA
Vehicle Dynamics Simulator [*NASA*] (NASA) ... VDS
Vehicle Ecological System (AAG) ... VES
Vehicle Effectiveness Remaining Converter ... VERC
Vehicle Elapsed Time (MCD) ... VET
Vehicle Electrical Engine Interface [*NASA*] (NASA) ... VEEI
Vehicle Electrical System Computer-Aided Design ... VESCAD
Vehicle Electrical Test System (ADA) ... VETS
Vehicle Electronics [*Program*] [*Army*] ... VETRONICS
Vehicle Electronics Engineering Institute ... VEEI
Vehicle Emergency Detection System [*NASA*] (KSC) ... VEDS
Vehicle Emission Control Information [*Automotive engineering*] ... VECI
Vehicle Emissions and Fuel Economy Laboratory [*Texas A & M University*] [*Research center*] (RCD) ... VEL
Vehicle End Item (NASA) ... VEI
Vehicle Energy and Biotechnology (MCD) ... VE & B
Vehicle Engagement Simulator (MCD) ... VES
Vehicle Engine Exhaust Smoke System [*Army*] (RDA) ... VEESS
Vehicle Engineering Analysis ... VEA
Vehicle Engineering Change Implementation Board (NASA) ... VECIB
Vehicle Environment Management System [*Automotive engineering*] ... VEMS
Vehicle Equipment and Government-Furnished Infrared Locator ... VEGIL
Vehicle Equipment Bay (MCD) ... VEB
Vehicle Equipment Safety Commission ... VESC
Vehicle Exhaust Smoke System (MCD) ... VESS
Vehicle Experimental (MCD) ... VE
Vehicle Flight Control System ... VFCS
Vehicle Flight Readiness (KSC) ... VFR
Vehicle for Initial Crawling [*Physical therapy*] (DAVI) ... VIC
Vehicle for the Investigation of Maintenance Control System (PDAA) ... VIMCOS
Vehicle Force Ratio (MCD) ... VFR
Vehicle Generating System ... VGS
Vehicle Ground Operation Requirements [*NASA*] (NASA) ... VGOR
Vehicle Ground Point [*NASA*] (NASA) ... VGP
Vehicle Ground Test [*NASA*] (NASA) ... VGT
Vehicle Heading Indicator ... VHI
Vehicle Headlight Aiming Device [*Automotive engineering*] ... VHAD
Vehicle Hit Indicator, Pyrotechnic ... VHIP
Vehicle Hours Traveled [*MOCD*] (TAG) ... VHT
Vehicle Ice-Breaking Air Cushion (PDAA) ... VIBAC
Vehicle Identification [*NASA*] (MCD) ... VEHID
Vehicle Identification Code (SSD) ... VIC
Vehicle Identification Number ... VIN
Vehicle in Use ... VIU
Vehicle Indicator Section ... VIS
Vehicle Inelastic Bending Response Analysis [*Computer program*] ... VIBRA
Vehicle Information and Communications System [*FHWA*] (TAG) ... VICS
Vehicle Information and Control System [*Highway traffic management*] ... VICS
Vehicle Information System [*Automotive engineering*] ... VIS
Vehicle Information Terminal ... VIT
Vehicle Inspection by System Parameter [*Automotive diagnostics*] ... VISP
Vehicle Inspection Program ... VIP
Vehicle Integrated Defense System [*Military*] ... VIDS
Vehicle Integrated Intelligence [*Army*] ... VINT^2
Vehicle Integrated Management System ... VIMS
Vehicle Integration Test Team [*NASA*] (MCD) ... VITT
Vehicle Intercommunications System (MCD) ... VIC
Vehicle Interface Subsystem [*Army*] (RDA) ... VIS
Vehicle Intrusion Detection Device ... VIDD
Vehicle Kilometers Traveled (GFGA) ... VKT
Vehicle Kit Test ... VKT
Vehicle Launch Center [*Automotive industry project management*] ... VLC
Vehicle Licensing and Traffic [*British*] ... VLT
Vehicle Location Unit [*FTA*] (TAG) ... VLU
Vehicle Magnetic Signature Duplicator (MCD) ... VEMASID
Vehicle Maintenance Area ... VMA
Vehicle Maintenance Monitor [*Automotive engineering*] ... VMM
Vehicle Maintenance Reporting Standard [*American Trucking Association*] ... VMRS
Vehicle Management and Mission Planning System [*NASA*] ... VMMPS
Vehicle Management System ... VMS
Vehicle Management Unit [*Powertrain*] [*Automotive engineering*] ... VMU
Vehicle Measuring Ground Support Equipment (KSC) ... VMGSE
Vehicle Model Movement ... VMM
Vehicle Monitoring System (RDA) ... VMS
Vehicle Monitoring System Electronics Assembly (RDA) ... VMSEA
Vehicle Motion Sensor ... VMS
Vehicle Mounted Explosive Container (MCD) ... VMEC
Vehicle Navigation Aid System ... VNAS
Vehicle Navigation Information System [*Automotive engineering*] ... VNIS
Vehicle Network Protocol [*Automotive engineering*] ... VNP
Vehicle Observer Corps [*Road Haulage Association*] [*British*] (DCTA) ... VOC
Vehicle Occupancy Rate [*MOCD*] (TAG) ... VOR
Vehicle off the Road [*British*] ... VOR
Vehicle on Stand (MCD) ... VOS
Vehicle On-Board Delivery ... VOD
Vehicle On-board RADAR Accident Avoidance [*Automotive safety*] ... VORAD
Vehicle Operations [*NASA*] (NASA) ... VO
Vehicle Ordnance Installation ... VOI
Vehicle Origin Survey [*R. L. Polk & Co.*] [*Information service or system*] (IID) ... VOS
Vehicle Out of Commission [*Army*] (AFIT) ... VOC
Vehicle Out of Commission for Maintenance [*Military*] ... VOCM

Vehicle Out of Commission for Parts [*Military*] .... VOCP
Vehicle Owner's Questionnaire [*Auto safety research*] .... VOQ
Vehicle Parking Protection Services [*British*] .... VPPS
Vehicle/Pedestrian Deviation [*FAA*] (TAG) .... VPD
Vehicle per Kilometer (AABC) .... VPK
Vehicle Performance Data .... VPD
Vehicle Performance Index [*Automobile technology*] .... VPI
Vehicle Personality Module [*Automotive engineering*] .... VPI
Vehicle Platform Center [*Automotive industry project management*] .... VPC
Vehicle Positioning Equipment (MCD) .... VPE
Vehicle Power Adapter .... VPA
Vehicle Power Supply [*Automotive engineering*] .... VPS
Vehicle Product Group .... VPG
Vehicle Project Manager [*NASA*] (NASA) .... VPM
Vehicle Propellant Loading Control Center .... VPLCC
Vehicle Propulsion Directorate [*Army and NASA joint operation*] (RDA) .... VPD
Vehicle Radio Remote Control .... VRRC
Vehicle Rapid-Fire Weapon System [*Army*] .... VRFWS
Vehicle Rapid-Fire Weapons System Successor (IEEE) .... VRFWSS
Vehicle Reaction Time .... VRT
Vehicle Reception Depot [*British military*] (DMA) .... VRD
Vehicle Recovery .... VR
Vehicle Recycling Partnership [*Agreement involving General Motors Corp., Ford Motor Co., and Chrysler Corp.*] .... VRP
Vehicle Recycling Partnership .... VRP
Vehicle Reference Controller [*Military*] .... VRC
Vehicle Reference Unit .... VRU
Vehicle Registration System [*Army*] .... VRS
Vehicle Research and Test Center [*National Highway Traffic Safety Administration*] (GRD) .... VRTC
Vehicle Research Corp. .... VRC
Vehicle Research Institute [*Society of Automotive Engineers*] .... VRI
Vehicle Retaining Board .... VRB
Vehicle, Road, and Traffic Intelligence Society .... VERTIS
Vehicle Roadside Communications .... VRC
Vehicle Safety Recall Campaign .... VSRC
Vehicle Scheduling Program [*Computer science*] .... VSP
Vehicle Scheduling Program Extended [*Computer science*] .... VSPX
Vehicle Sectoring Code .... VSC
Vehicle Security Association (EA) .... VSA
Vehicle Service Agreement [*Extended service contract*] .... VSA
Vehicle Service Assessment .... VSA
Vehicle Sizing and Performance (MCD) .... VESPER
Vehicle Sizing and Performance Evaluation Program (MCD) .... VSPEP
Vehicle Speed Activated Converter [*Automotive engineering*] .... V-SAC
Vehicle Speed Pulse Generator [*Automotive engineering*] .... VSPG
Vehicle Speed Sensor [*Automotive engineering*] .... VSS
Vehicle Stability System [*Truck engineering*] .... VSS
Vehicle State Monitor .... VSM
Vehicle Station [*NASA*] (KSC) .... VS
Vehicle Structure Analysis [*Automotive design*] .... VESTA
Vehicle Structures Directorate [*Army and NASA joint operation*] (RDA) .... VSD
Vehicle Surveillance System .... VSS
Vehicle Synthesis Program [*Aerospace*] .... VSP
Vehicle System Control .... VSC
Vehicle System Simulator .... VSS
Vehicle Systems Engineer (SAA) .... VSE
Vehicle Team Combat Exercise [*Army*] (INF) .... VTCE
Vehicle Team Subcaliber Exercise [*Army*] (INF) .... VTSE
Vehicle Technical Management Information System .... VETMIS
Vehicle Test Meter [*TACOM*] [*Army*] (RDA) .... VTM
Vehicle Test Plan [*NASA*] (NASA) .... VTP
Vehicle Test Specification .... VTS
Vehicle Theft .... VT
Vehicle Thermal Management System .... VTMS
Vehicle Time Reproducer (SAA) .... VTS
Vehicle to Roadside Communication System .... VRCS
Vehicle Track Recovery [*Military*] .... VTR
Vehicle Tracking Receiver .... VTR
Vehicle Tracking System [*Automotive engineering*] .... VTS
Vehicle Tracking Unit [*Automated traffic management*] .... VTU
Vehicle Unit (KSC) .... VU
Vehicle Utility (MCD) .... VU
Vehicle Vapor Recovery [*Automobile*] .... VVR
Vehicle Work Flow .... VWF
Vehicle-Miles Traveled .... VMT
Vehicle-Mounted Road Mine Detector System .... VMRMDS
Vehicle-Platform Center [*Ford Motor Co.*] (ECON) .... VPC
Vehicles (MCD) V
Vehicles per Day [*Military*] (AFM) .... VPD
Vehicles per Hour [*Traffic*] (AFM) .... VPH
Vehicles per Mile .... VPM
Vehicles to the Mile [*Military*] .... VTM
Vehicle-to-Roadside Communication [*Traffic management*] .... VRC
Vehicle-Tracked Retriever [*An armored recovery vehicle*] [*Army*] (VNW) .... VTR
Vehicular Accident [*British police*] .... VA
Vehicular Communications (MCD) VC
Vehicular Communications System .... VCS
Vehicular Disc Reproduction System (DICI) .... VDRS
Vehicular Electronics Laboratory .... VEL
Vehicular Equipment Complement Index (IEEE) .... VECI
Vehicular/Ground LASER Locator Designator (MCD) .... V/GLLD
Vehicular Infrared Alarm (MCD) .... VIRA
Vehicular Intercommunications System .... VIS

Vehicular LASER Locator Designator .... VLLD
Vehicular Leger Toot Terrain [*Light All-Terrain Vehicle*] [*French*] (MCD) .... VLTT
Vehicular Navigation System [*Military*] .... VNS
Vehicular On-Board RADAR [*Automotive engineering*] (PS) .... VORAD
Vehicular Planimetric Dead Reckoning Computer Operating Language .... VEPOL
Vehicular RADIAC [*Radioactivity Detection, Indication, and Computation*] System .... VRS
Vehicular Technology (MCD) .... VT
Vehicular Traffic Control .... VTC
Vehicular Traffic Control System (IEEE) .... VTCS
Vehicule Experimental de Recherches Aerothermodynamique et Structurale [*Glider*] [*France*] .... VERAS
Vehiculos Automotores Mexicanos [*Commercial firm*] .... VAM
Vehiculum [*Vehicle*] [*Latin*] (MAE) .... vehic
Veiling Glare Index [*Vision research*] .... VGI
Vein V
Vein Aortocoronary Artery Bypass Graft [*Cardiology*] (AAMN) .... VBG
Vein Graft [*Cardiology*] (DAVI) .... VG
Vein Ventures Ltd. [*Vancouver Stock Exchange symbol*] .... VVS
Veins [*Medicine*] VV
Vel [*Or*] [*Pharmacy*] V
Vel Similis [*Or Similar*] [*Latin*] (WGA) .... vel sim
Vela [*Constellation*] .... Vel
Vela Seismic Information Analysis Center (SAA) .... VESIAC
Vela Seismological Center [*Alexandria, VA*] .... VSC
Vela Uniform Platform .... VUP
Velar Lobe VL
Velban [*See VBL*] .... Ve
Velcro Indus NV [*NASDAQ symbol*] (TTSB) .... VELCF
Velcro Industries NV [*NASDAQ symbol*] (NQ) .... VELC
Velcro Industries NV [*Associated Press*] (SAG) .... Velcro
Velcro-Jumping while Intoxicated .... VJWI
Veliger Escape Aperture .... VEA
Velikiye Luki [*Former USSR ICAO location identifier*] (ICLI) .... ULOL
Velleius Paterculus [*First century AD*] [*Classical studies*] (OCD) .... Vell Pat
Vellore [*India*] [*ICAO location identifier*] (ICLI) .... VOVR
Vellum .... VEL
Vellum (VRA) .... vlm
Velma Teague Library, Glendale, AZ [*Library symbol Library of Congress*] (LCLS) .... AzG
Velocette Owners Club of North America (EA) .... VOCNA
Velocite [*Physics*] (DAVI) .... k
Velocity V
Velocity (IDOE) v
Velocity (IDOE) .... vel
Velocity (AFM) .... VEL
Velocity .... VELOC
Velocity [*NWS*] (FAAC) .... VLCTY
Velocity Acceleration Relationship .... VAR
Velocity Aid .... VA
Velocity along the X-Axis (NASA) VX
Velocity along the Y-Axis (NASA) .... VY
Velocity along the Z-Axis (NASA) .... VZ
Velocity Analysis Program .... VAP
Velocity and Steering Indicator (MCD) .... VSI
Velocity at Apogee (MCD) .... VA
Velocity Bin Commanded .... VBC
Velocity Change Indicator (NASA) VCI
Velocity Character (MCD) VC
Velocity, Closing VC
Velocity Compounded VC
Velocity Control Programmer .... VCP
Velocity Control Propulsion Subsystem [*NASA*] .... VCPS
Velocity Correction .... VELCOR
Velocity Counter VC
Velocity Cutoff System (KSC) .... VCS
Velocity Dealiasing Algorithm (USDC) .... VDA
Velocity Dealiasing Algorithm [*Marine science*] (OSRA) .... VDA
Velocity Equipment (MCD) .... VE
Velocity, Equivalent .... VE
Velocity Error .... VE
Velocity Failure .... VF
Velocity False Target [*Military*] (CAAL) .... VFT
Velocity Filter (IEEE) .... VELF
Velocity Gain (AAG) .... VELG
Velocity Gate Capture [*Military*] (CAAL) .... VGC
Velocity Gate Pulloff [*Military*] (CAAL) .... VGPO
Velocity Gate Stealer [*Military*] (CAAL) .... VGS
Velocity Gate Walkoff [*Military*] (CAAL) .... VGWO
Velocity Gravity .... VG
Velocity/Height .... V/H
Velocity Impact Hardening .... VIH
Velocity Indicating Coherent Integrator VICI
Velocity Inertia Navigation System .... VINS
Velocity Inertia RADAR Navigation System .... VIRNS
Velocity Integration, Detection, and Ranging (NG) .... VIDAR
Velocity Interferometer System for Any Reflector (MCD) .... VISAR
Velocity Interferometer System for any Reflector [*Instrumentation*] .... VISAR
Velocity, Internal VI
Velocity Limit VL
Velocity Made Good (WGA) .... Vmg
Velocity Max Operating (GAVI) .... VMO
Velocity Measurement System .... VMS
Velocity Measuring Unit (MCD) .... VMU
Velocity Meter .... VM

Velocity Minimum Control (AAG) .... VMC
Velocity Modulation .... VM
Velocity Never to Exceed .... VNE
Velocity, Normal Gravity, and Height .... VGH
Velocity of Circumferential Fiber Shortening [Cardiology] .... Vcf
Velocity of Contractile Element (DAVI) .... V$_{CE}$
Velocity of Detonation (IEEE) .... VOD
Velocity of Propagation (IAA) .... VP
Velocity of Sound [Symbol] [IUPAC] c
Velocity of Sound of Blood [on Doppler Study] [Cardiology] (DAVI) C
Velocity of Wireless Waves .... VWW
Velocity over Altitude Ratio Sensor (MCD) .... VOARS
Velocity per Performance .... VPP
Velocity Prediction Program .... VPP
Velocity Preset Module (MCD) .... VPM
Velocity Pressure .... VP
Velocity Reference Unit .... VRU
Velocity, Relative (MCD) .... VR
Velocity, Relative (GFGA) .... VREL
Velocity Response Shape (CET) .... VRS
Velocity, Rotation (MCD) .... VROT
Velocity Search (MCD) .... VS
Velocity Sensor Antenna .... VSA
Velocity Sensor, Oscillator, Multiplier (DNAB) .... VSOM
Velocity Sensor System .... VSS
Velocity, Staging .... VS
Velocity, Target .... VT
Velocity Test Barrel .... VTB
Velocity Time (MUGU) .... V-T
Velocity to Be Gained [Body X-Axis] [NASA] (NASA) .... VGX
Velocity to Be Gained [Body Y-Axis] [NASA] (NASA) .... VGY
Velocity to Be Gained [Body Z-Axis] [NASA] (NASA) .... VGZ
Velocity to Be Gained Related to IMU Orientation (MCD) .... VGIMU
Velocity Variation Tube .... VVT
Velocity Vector (AAG) VV
Velocity Vector Measurement .... VVM
Velocity Vector Measurement System .... VVMS
Velocity Vector Sensor Assembly .... VVSA
Velocity-Aligned Doppler Spectroscopy .... VADS
Velocity-Azimuth Display .... VAD
Velocity-Modulated Oscillator .... VMO
Velocity-Modulated Transistor [Solid-state physics] .... VMT
Velocity-Modulated Tube .... VMT
Velocity-Volume VV
Velopharyngeal Gap [Medicine] (DMAA) .... VPG
Velopharyngeal Insufficiency [Medicine] (MEDA) .... VPI
Velour and Crochet [Interlocking nylon tapes - one with tiny loops, the other with tiny hooks - invented as a reusable fastener by George de Mestral] .... VELCRO
Velvet (VRA) .... vel
Velvet Exploration Co. Ltd. [Vancouver Stock Exchange symbol] VLV
Velvet Tobacco Mottle Virus .... VTMoV
Velvet Underground [Musical group] .... VU
Vena Cava [Anatomy] VC
Venae [Veins] [Latin] [Anatomy] (DAVI) VV
Venae Sectio [Venesection] [Latin Medicine] (MAE) .... Vs
Venae Sectio Brachii [Bleeding in the Arm] [Pharmacy] (ROG) .... VSB
Vencor, Inc. [NYSE symbol] (SAG) VC
Vencor, Inc. [Associated Press] (SAG) .... Vencor
Venda Airways [South Africa ICAO designator] (FAAC) .... VAA
Venda Independent People's Party [Political party] (PPW) .... VIPP
Venda National Party [Political party] (PPW) .... VNP
Vendays-Montalivet [France ICAO location identifier] (ICLI) .... LFIV
Vendee [Legal shorthand] (LWAP) .... VEE
Vending .... VNDNG
Vending and Affixing Machine .... VAM
Venditione Exponas [Writ of Execution for Sheriff to Sell Goods] [Latin] (ROG) .... VEN EX
Vendome [Record label] [France] .... Ven
Vendor (AAG) V
Vendor (KSC) .... VEND
Vendor [Legal shorthand] (LWAP) .... VOR
Vendor and Purchaser [Sales] (ROG) .... V & P
Vendor Approval Form .... VAF
Vendor Approval Request (AAG) .... VAR
Vendor Automated Data System (MCD) .... VADS
Vendor Call (MCD) VC
Vendor Code (MCD) VC
Vendor Contact VC
Vendor Contract Notice .... VCN
Vendor Contract Technical Data .... VCTD
Vendor Data Article .... VDA
Vendor Data Article Control .... VDAC
Vendor Data Control (MCD) .... VDC
Vendor Data Control .... VENDAC
Vendor Data Information Engineering Order (MCD) .... VDIEO
Vendor Data Release Group (MCD) .... VDRG
Vendor Data Request .... VDR
Vendor Data Service .... VDS
Vendor Direct Shipment .... VDS
Vendor Documentation Inventory (NASA) .... VDI
Vendor Engineering Change Request [DoD] .... VECR
Vendor Engineering Memorandum (MCD) .... VEM
Vendor Engineering Procurement Liaison (MCD) .... VEPL
Vendor Identification Number [Sales] (MCD) .... VIN

Vendor Independent Messaging [Computer science] (PCM) .... VIM
Vendor Information Request [Sales] .... VIR
Vendor Information System for Innovative Treatment Technology [Database] [Environmental Protection Agency] .... VISITT
Vendor Initial Measurement [Sales] .... VIM
Vendor Item [Sales] (AAG) VI
Vendor Item List [Sales] (AAG) VIL
Vendor Item Release [Sales] .... VIR
Vendor List of Drawings .... VLD
Vendor Material Review Report [NASA] (KSC) .... VMRR
Vendor Part Modification (AAG) .... VPM
Vendor Parts Index [Sales] .... VPI
Vendor Parts List (AAG) .... VPL
Vendor Parts Number .... VPN
Vendor Provisioning Parts Breakdown (AAG) .... VPPB
Vendor Quality Assurance .... VQA
Vendor Quality Assurance Representative [Nuclear energy] (NRCH) .... VQAR
Vendor Quality Certification .... VQC
Vendor Quality Defect .... VQD
Vendor Quality Zero Defects .... VQZD
Vendor Rating [Sales] .... VR
Vendor Receiving Memorandum [Sales] .... VRM
Vendor Repairable Items List .... VRIL
Vendor Scan .... VSCAN
Vendor Shipping Configuration (AAG) .... VSC
Vendor Shipping Instruction .... VSI
Vendor Specification Microfilm File (DNAB) .... VSMF
Vendor Standard Settlement Program (AAG) .... VSSP
Vendor Supplier [Sales] (MCD) .... V/S
Vendor Test Procedure .... VTP
Vendor Trouble Report .... VTR
Vendor Working Authority .... VWA
Vendor Zero Defect .... VZD
Vendor-Furnished Equipment (NASA) .... VFE
Vendor-Furnished Material (MCD) .... VFM
Vendor's Item Engineering Order .... VIEO
Vendors per Block [Sales] .... VPB
Vendor's Shipping Document .... VSD
Vendor-Vendee Technical Committee .... VVTC
Venecia [Bolivia] [ICAO location identifier] (ICLI) .... SLVE
Veneer (WDAA) .... VEN
Veneer .... VENR
Veneer [Technical drawings] .... VNR
Veneer (VRA) .... vnr
Venera [Venus] and Gallei [Halley] [Russian spacecraft] .... VEGA
Venerabiles [Venerables] [Latin] (WGA) vv
Venerable V
Venerable (ODBW) .... Ven
Venerable Sage [Freemasonry] (ROG) .... VS
Venerated .... VEND
Venereal (WDAA) .... VEN
Venereal Case [Medical slang] VC
Venereal Disease .... VD
Venereal Disease Experimental Laboratory .... VDEL
Venereal Disease Gonorrhea .... VDG
Venereal Disease Reference Test [of Harris] .... VDRT
Venereal Disease Research Laboratory .... VDRL
Venereal Disease Syphilis .... VDS
Venereal Pamphlet [Navy] .... VP
Venereology [Medical Officer designation] [British] V
Venesection [Medicine] .... VS
Venetian .... VEN
Venetian (ROG) .... VENET
Venetian and Vertical Blind Association of America [Defunct] .... VVBAA
Venetian Blind Council [Formerly, VBI] .... VBC
Venetian Blind Institute [Later, VBC] (EA) .... VBI
Venetian Blind Manufacturers' Association of Australia .... VBMAA
Venetie [Alaska] [Airport symbol] (OAG) .... VEE
Venexcargo (Transporte Aereo de Carga SA) [Venezuela] [ICAO designator] (FAAC) .... VNX
Venezia/San Nicolo [Italy ICAO location identifier] (ICLI) .... LIPV
Venezia/Tessera [Italy ICAO location identifier] (ICLI) .... LIPZ
Venezolana Internacional de Aviacion Sociedad Anonima [Airline] [Venezuela] .... VIASA
Venezolana Internacional de Aviacion Sociedad Anonima (VIASA) [Venezuela ICAO designator] (ICDA) .... VA
Venezolana Servicios Expresos de Carga Internacional CA [Venezuela] [ICAO designator] (FAAC) .... VEC
Venezuela [MARC geographic area code Library of Congress] (LCCP) .... s-ve--
Venezuela [IYRU nationality code] (IYR) V
Venezuela [MARC country of publication code Library of Congress] (LCCP) .... ve
Venezuela [ANSI two-letter standard code] (CNC) .... VE
Venezuela [ANSI three-letter standard code] (CNC) .... VEN
Venezuela .... VENEZ
Venezuela (VRA) .... Venez
Venezuela [International vehicle registration and international civil aircraft marking] (ODBW) .... YV
Venezuela International Meteorological and Hydrological Experiment [Colorado State University project] .... VIMHEX
Venezuelan American Association of the United States (EA) .... VAA
Venezuelan American Association of the United States (EA) .... VAAUS
Venezuelan Chamber of Commerce of the United States .... VCCUS
Venezuelan Equine Encephalomyelitis [Virus] .... VEE
Venezuelan Trust Fund [Inter-American Development Bank] .... VTF

Venezuelan-American Chamber of Commerce and Industry (EA) ..... VenAmCham
Vengold, Inc. [*NASDAQ symbol*] (SAG) .... VENG
Vengold Inc. [*NASDAQ symbol*] (TTSB) .... VENGF
Vengold, Inc. [*Associated Press*] (SAG) .... Vengold
Venice [*Italy*] [*Airport symbol*] (OAG) .... VCE
Venice [*Italy*] [*Seismograph station code, US Geological Survey Closed*] (SEIS) .... VEN
Venice [*Diocesan abbreviation*] [*Florida*] (TOCD) .... VEN
Venice Committee (EA) VC
Venice Community Unit 3, Venice, IL [*Library symbol Library of Congress*] (LCLS) .... IVenCU
Venice, FL [*Location identifier FAA*] (FAAL) .... VNC
Venice, FL [*AM radio station call letters*] .... WAMR
Venice, FL [*Television station call letters*] .... WBSV
Venice, FL [*FM radio station call letters*] .... WCTQ
Venice, FL [*Location identifier FAA*] (FAAL) .... XVN
Venice Hospital [*Venice, FL*] .... VH
Venice Public Library, Venice, IL [*Library symbol Library of Congress*] (LCLS) .... IVen
Venice Simplon Orient-Express [*London-to-Venice train*] .... VSOE
Venipuncture [*Medicine*] (MAE) .... VP
Venire Facias [*Writ to Sheriff to Summon Jury*] [*Latin*] (ROG) .... VEN FA
Venite [*95th Psalm*] .... VEN
Venizelikon Phileleftheron Komma [*Venizelist Liberal Party*] [*Greek Political party*] (PPE) .... VenPK
Vennard College, University Park, IA [*Library symbol Library of Congress*] (LCLS) .... IaUpV
Vennootschap Onder Firma [*Limited Partnership*] [*Dutch*] (ILCA) .... VOF
Venoarterial [*Cardiology*] (DAVI) .... VA
Venom Immunotherapy [*Immunology*] [*Emergency medicine*] (DAVI) .... VIT
Venom Skin Test [*Immunology*] .... VST
Venomological Artifact Society (EA) .... VAS
Veno-Occlusive Disease [*of the liver*] .... VOD
Venous [*Medicine*] V
Venous Access Device [*Cardiology*] (DAVI) .... VAD
Venous Blood [*Medicine*] (DMAA) .... VB
Venous Capacitance [*Clinical chemistry*] (AAMN) VC
Venous Carbon Dioxide Pressure [*Medicine*] (MAE) .... PV_{CO_2}
Venous Clotting Time [*Clinical chemistry*] .... VCT
Venous Diameter Ratio [*Cancer detection*] .... VDR
Venous Digital Angiogram [*Cardiology*] (DAVI) .... VDA
Venous Emptying [*Cardiology*] (DAVI) .... VE
Venous Hematocrit [*Medicine*] (MAE) .... VH
Venous Impedance Plethysmography [*Medicine*] (DMAA) .... VIP
Venous in the Blood Phase [*Medicine*] (DAVI) v
Venous Occlusion Plethysmography [*Medicine*] (DMAA) .... VOP
Venous Pressure [*Medicine*] .... VP
Venous Pressure Gradient Support Stocking .... VPGS
Venous Reflux [*Medicine*] (DMAA) .... VR
Venous Return [*Medicine*] .... VR
Venous Stasis Retinopathy [*Medicine*] (MEDA) .... VSR
Venous Stop-Flow Pressure [*Medicine*] .... VSFP
Venous Thromboembolism [*Medicine*] (DAVI) .... VTE
Venous Thromboembolism [*Medicine*] .... VTE
Venous Thrombosis [*Cardiology*] (DAVI) .... VT
Venovenous [*Cardiology*] (DAVI) VV
Venraij/De Peel [*Netherlands ICAO location identifier*] (ICLI) .... EHDP
Venstre [*Liberal Party*] [*Norway Political party*] (PPE) V
Venstre (Liberale Parti) [*Liberal Party*] [*Denmark Political party*] (PPE) V
Venstresocialisterne [*Left Socialists Party*] [*Denmark Political party*] (PPE) .... VS
Vent V
Vent (NASA) .... VT
Vent and Supply Bay .... VSB
Vent Collection System [*Engineering*] .... VCS
Vent Gas Collection Header [*Nuclear energy*] (NRCH) .... VGCH
Vent Hole [*Technical drawings*] .... VH
Vent Isolation [*Nuclear energy*] (NRCH) VI
Vent Pipe [*Technical drawings*] .... VP
Vent Stack [*Technical drawings*] .... VS
Vent Valve VV
Ventanas [*Ecuador*] [*ICAO location identifier*] (ICLI) .... SEVT
Vent-Clearing Pressure [*Nuclear energy*] (NRCH) .... VP
Ventech Healthcare Corp., Inc. [*Toronto Stock Exchange symbol*] .... VHC
Vented Suppressive Shielding .... VSS
Ventersdorp [*South Africa*] [*ICAO location identifier*] (ICLI) .... FAVE
Ventex Energy [*Vancouver Stock Exchange symbol*] .... VTX
Ventilated Containers [*Shipping*] (DCTA) VC
Ventilated Flight Suit .... VFS
Ventilated Improved Pit [*Latrine*] .... VIP
Ventilated Wet Suit (DNAB) .... VWS
Ventilating .... VENT
Ventilating Deadlight [*Technical drawings*] .... VD
Ventilating Deadlight .... VDL
Ventilating Equipment (MSA) .... VE
Ventilation [*Medicine*] (DAVI) V
Ventilation [*Medicine*] (DAVI) .... VE
Ventilation (AFM) .... VENT
Ventilation Air Intake [*Hovercraft*] .... VAI
Ventilation Barrier Machine Room [*Nuclear energy*] (NRCH) .... VBMR
Ventilation/Circulation Ratio [*Medicine*] (MAE) .... V/C
Ventilation Control Module [*NASA*] .... VCM
Ventilation Control System [*NASA*] (KSC) .... VCS
Ventilation Duct Chase [*Nuclear energy*] (NRCH) .... VDC
Ventilation Management .... VM
Ventilation of the Alveolar Dead-space [*Medicine*] (DAVI) .... V_DA

Ventilation per Minute of the Anatomic Dead-space [*Medicine*] (DAVI) .... V_Dan
Ventilation/Perfusion [*Quotient*] [*Medicine*] .... V/Q
Ventilation/Perfusion Quotient [*Medicine*] (MAE) .... Va/Qc
Ventilation Rate .... VR
Ventilation Sampling Line (IEEE) .... VSL
Ventilation System [*NASA*] .... VS
Ventilation Umbilical Connector System .... VUCS
Ventilation Unit Condensate Drain Tank (IEEE) .... VUCDT
Ventilation-Perfusion [*Ratio*] [*Radiology*] (DAVI) .... VA/Q
Ventilation-Perfusion Scintigraphy .... V-P
Ventilator V
Ventilator .... VENT
Ventilator-Associated Pneumonia [*Medicine*] .... VAP
Ventilatory Capacity [*Physiology*] VC
Ventilatory Threshold [*Cardiology*] .... VeT
Venting Experiment [*Marine science*] (OSRA) .... VENTEX
Venting Experiment (USDC) .... VENTEX
Ventnor City Public Library, Ventnor City, NJ [*Library symbol*] [*Library of Congress*] (LCLS) .... NjVcP
Ventora Resources Ltd. [*Vancouver Stock Exchange symbol*] .... VNT
Ventral V
Ventral (WDAA) .... VEN
Ventral .... ventr
Ventral Area [*Anatomy*] .... VA
Ventral Funiculus [*Anatomy*] .... VF
Ventral Hyperstriatum Caudal Nucleus [*Neuroanatomy*] .... HVc
Ventral Intersegmental Muscles [*Anatomy*] .... VIM
Ventral Lateral Ventricular Nerve [*Anatomy*] .... v-LVN
Ventral Medial Hypothalamus [*Anatomy*] .... VMH
Ventral Midline Precursor [*Neuroanatomy*] .... vMP
Ventral Nerve [*Neuroanatomy*] .... VN
Ventral Nerve Cord [*Neuroanatomy*] .... VNC
Ventral Nervous System [*Neuroanatomy*] .... VNS
Ventral Nozzle .... VN
Ventral Nucleus of the Lateral Geniculate Body [*Medicine*] (DMAA) .... VLG
Ventral Pioneer [*Neuron*] .... VP
Ventral Posterior [*Anatomy*] .... VP
Ventral Posterior Thalamic [*Electrode for stimulation*] .... VPT
Ventral Posterolateral [*Anatomy*] .... VPL
Ventral Pressure Neurons [*of a leech*] .... Pv
Ventral Prostate Weight [*Medicine*] .... VPW
Ventral Root [*of a spinal nerve*] [*Anatomy*] .... VR
Ventral Root Potential [*Neurophysiology*] .... VRP
Ventral Root Reflex [*Medicine*] (DMAA) .... VRR
Ventral Septal Defect .... VSD
Ventral Spinal Cord [*Anatomy*] .... VSC
Ventral Striatum [*Neurology*] .... VSTR
Ventral Subiculum [*Brain anatomy*] .... VS
Ventral Surface, Nephridial Gland [*Anatomy*] .... VNG
Ventral Tegmental Area [*Anatomy*] .... VTA
Ventral Tegmental Nuclei [*Neuroanatomy*] .... VTN
Ventral Touch Neurons [*of a leech*] .... Tv
Ventral Wall, Kidney [*Anatomy*] .... VK
Ventralis Lateralis [*Brain anatomy*] VL
Ventricle (WDAA) .... VEN
Ventricle Brain Ratio [*Medicine*] .... VBR
Ventricle Pressure Response [*Cardiology*] .... VPR
Ventricle-Assist Device [*Cardiology*] .... VAD
Ventricular [*Cardiology*] .... VENT
Ventricular .... ventric
Ventricular Activation Time [*Cardiology*] .... VAT
Ventricular Activation Time (DAVI) .... VAT
Ventricular Aneurysm [*Cardiology*] .... VA
Ventricular Arrhythmia [*Cardiology*] .... VA
Ventricular Bigeminy [*Medicine*] .... V-BIG
Ventricular Complex [*Cardiology*] VC
Ventricular Conduction System [*Cardiology*] (CPH) .... VCS
Ventricular Coupling [*Cardiology*] VC
Ventricular Diastolic Fragmentation [*Medicine*] (DMAA) .... VDF
Ventricular Dilator [*Neuron*] [*Medicine*] .... VD
Ventricular Ectopic Activity [*Cardiology*] (MAE) .... VEA
Ventricular Ectopic Arrhythmia [*Cardiology*] (AAMN) .... VEA
Ventricular Ectopic Beats [*Cardiology*] .... VEB
Ventricular Ectopic Depolarization .... VED
Ventricular Ectopy .... V-ECT
Ventricular Ejection Fraction [*Cardiology*] (DAVI) .... VEF
Ventricular End-Diastolic Volume [*Medicine*] (MAE) .... VDV
Ventricular Extrasystole [*Cardiology*] (DAVI) .... VE
Ventricular Fibrillation [*Also, VF, VFIB*] [*Cardiology*] (AAMN) .... VENT FIB
Ventricular Fibrillation [*Also, vent fib, VFIB*] [*Cardiology*] .... VF
Ventricular Fibrillation [*Also, vent fib, VF*] [*Cardiology*] .... VFIB
Ventricular Fibrillation Threshold [*Cardiology*] .... VFT
Ventricular Filling Pressure [*Cardiology*] (DAVI) .... VFL
Ventricular Fluid [*Cardiology*] (MAE) .... VF
Ventricular Fluid Pressure [*Cardiology*] (MAE) .... VFP
Ventricular Flutter [*Cardiology*] (AAMN) .... VF
Ventricular Flutter [*Cardiology*] (DAVI) .... VFL
Ventricular Function Curve [*Cardiology*] (AAMN) .... VFC
Ventricular Gallop [*Cardiology*] .... VG
Ventricular Heart Disease [*Cardiology*] (DAVI) .... VHD
Ventricular Hypertrophy [*Cardiology*] (DAVI) .... VH
Ventricular Impulse Detector and Alarm [*Cardiology*] .... VIDA
Ventricular Inhibiting Synchronous with Atrium [*Cardiac pacemaker*] [*Trademark*] .... VISA
Ventricular Muscle [*Cardiology*] (MAE) .... VM

Ventricular Pacing, No Sensing, No Other Function [*Pacemaker*] [*Cardiology*] (MEDA) ... VOO
Ventricular Pacing, Ventricular Sensing, Inhibited Mode [*Pacemaker*] [*Cardiology*] (MEDA) ... VVI
Ventricular Pacing, Ventricular Sensing, Triggered Mode [*Pacemaker*] [*Cardiology*] (MEDA) ... VVT
Ventricular Premature [*beat*] [*Cardiology*] (DAVI) ... VP
Ventricular Premature Beat [*Cardiology*] ... VPB
Ventricular Premature Contraction [*Cardiology*] ... VPC
Ventricular Premature Depolarization [*Cardiology*] ... VPD
Ventricular Rate [*Cardiology*] ... VR
Ventricular Residual Volume [*Cardiology*] (MAE) ... VRV
Ventricular Septal Defect [*Cardiology*] ... VSD
Ventricular Septum [*Cardiology*] (DAVI) ... VS
Ventricular Stroke Work [*Cardiology*] (MAE) ... VSW
Ventricular Tachycardia [*Cardiology*] ... VT
Ventricular Tachycardia [*Cardiology*] ... V-TACH
Ventricular Wall Motion [*Cardiology*] (DAVI) ... VWM
Ventricular Zone [*Anatomy*] ... VZ
Ventriculoarterial Connections [*Cardiology*] (DAVI) ... VAC
Ventriculoatrial [*Cardiology*] (WGA) ... VA
Ventriculoatrial Conduction [*Cardiology*] (DAVI) ... VAC
Ventriculogram [*A roentgenogram*] ... VGM
Ventriculojugular [*Medicine*] ... VJ
Ventriculolumbar Perfusion [*Medicine*] (MEDA) ... VLP
Ventriculoperitoneal [*Medicine*] ... VP
Ventriculoperitoneal Shunt [*Neurology*] (DAVI) ... VPS
Ventriloquist ... VENT
Ventriloquist (WDMC) ... vent
Ventris' English Common Pleas Reports [*86 English Reprint*] [*A publication*] (DLA) ... Vent
Ventris' English Common Pleas Reports [*86 English Reprint*] [*A publication*] (DLA) ... Vent (Eng)
Ventris' English Common Pleas Reports [*86 English Reprint*] [*A publication*] (DLA) ... Ventr
Ventris' English King's Bench Reports [*A publication*] (DLA) ... Vent
Ventris' English King's Bench Reports [*A publication*] (DLA) ... Vent (Eng)
Ventritex, Inc. [*Associated Press*] (SAG) ... Ventritx
Ventritex, Inc. [*NASDAQ symbol*] (SPSG) ... VNTX
Ventrobasal Complex [*Brain anatomy*] ... VB
Ventrogluteal [*Anatomy*] (DAVI) ... VG
Ventrolateral [*Anatomy*] ... VL
Ventrolateral Marginal Zone [*Embryology*] ... VMZ
Ventrolateral Nucleus of the Hypothalamus [*Neurology*] (DAVI) ... VLH
Ventrolateral Preoptic ... VLPO
Ventromedial and Lateral Hypothalami [*Neuroanatomy*] ... VMLH
Ventromedial Nucleus [*Brain anatomy*] ... VMN
Ventspils [*Former USSR ICAO location identifier*] (ICLI) ... UMRW
Ventur [*Quality of carburetor barrel*] [*Automotive engineering*] ... V
Ventura, CA [*FM radio station call letters*] ... KAXX
Ventura, CA [*FM radio station call letters*] ... KBBY-FM
Ventura, CA [*FM radio station call letters*] ... KHAY
Ventura, CA [*Television station call letters*] ... KSTV
Ventura, CA [*AM radio station call letters*] ... KVEN
Ventura, CA [*FM radio station call letters*] (RBYB) ... KVYY-FM
Ventura, CA [*AM radio station call letters*] (RBYB) ... KXSP
Ventura Cnty Natl Bancorp [*NASDAQ symbol*] (TTSB) ... VCNB
Ventura College, Ventura, CA [*Library symbol Library of Congress*] (LCLS) ... CVtV
Ventura County Museum of History and Art, Ventura, CA [*Library symbol*] [*Library of Congress*] (LCLS) ... CVtMHA
Ventura County National Bancorp [*NASDAQ symbol*] (SAG) ... VCNB
Ventura County National Bancorp [*Associated Press*] (SAG) ... VenCty
Ventura County Railway Co. [*Army*] ... VCY
Ventura County-City Free Library, Ventura, CA [*Library symbol Library of Congress*] (LCLS) ... CVt
Ventura Publisher User's Group (EA) ... VPUG
Venture Capital [*or Capitalist*] [*Finance*] ... VC
Venture Capital Fund [*Finance*] ... VCF
Venture Capital/Special Situations [*Business term*] ... VS
Venture Clubs of the Americas (EA) ... VCA
Venture Database Publisher [*Computer science*] ... VDP
Venture Development Corp. [*Natick, MA*] [*Telecommunications*] (TSSD) ... VDC
Venture Evaluation and Review Technique ... VERT
Venture Gold Corp. [*Vancouver Stock Exchange symbol*] ... VEN
Venture Seismic Ltd. [*Associated Press*] (SAG) ... Venture
Venture Seismic Ltd. [*NASDAQ symbol*] (SAG) ... VSEIF
Venture Seismic Ltd. [*NASDAQ symbol*] (SAG) ... VSEWF
Venture Seismic Ltd Wrrt [*NASDAQ symbol*] (TTSB) ... VSEWF
Venture Stores [*NYSE symbol*] (TTSB) ... VEN
Venture Stores, Inc. [*NYSE symbol*] (SPSG) ... VEN
Venture Stores, Inc. [*Associated Press*] (SAG) ... VenSt
Venture Stores, Inc. [*Associated Press*] (SAG) ... VentSt
Venture Strs $3.25 Cv Dep Pfd [*NYSE symbol*] (TTSB) ... VENPr
Venture Touring Society ... VETS
Venture Touring Society (EA) ... VTS
Ventures in Community Improvement Demonstration Project (EDAC) ... VICI
Venturex Resources [*Vancouver Stock Exchange symbol*] ... VXX
Venturi [*Automotive engineering*] ... V
Venturi Vacuum Amplifier [*Automotive engineering*] ... VVA
Venturi Vacuum Transducer [*Engineering*] ... VVT
Venturian Corp. [*NASDAQ symbol*] (NQ) ... VENT
Venturian Corp. [*Associated Press*] (SAG) ... Venturn
Venue ... V
Venuleius Saturninus [*Flourished, 2nd century*] [*Authority cited in pre-1607 legal work*] (DSA) ... Venul
Venus (WDAA) ... VEN
Venus Air Services Ltd. [*Ghana*] [*ICAO designator*] (FAAC) ... VNS
Venus and Adonis [*Shakespearean work*] ... Ven
Venus and Adonis [*Shakespearean poem*] (BARN) ... Ven & Ad
Venus Departure Window [*NASA*] ... VDW
Venus Entry Body [*NASA*] ... VEB
Venus Environmental Satellite [*NASA, proposed*] ... VESAT
Venus Flyby Vehicle [*NASA*] ... VFV
Venus International Reference Atmosphere [*Meteorology*] ... VIRA
Venus Orbit Ejection [*NASA*] (MCD) ... VOE
Venus Orbiter Radiometric Temperature Experiment [*NASA*] ... VORTEX
Venus Orbiting and Imaging RADAR [*NASA*] ... VOIR
Venus RADAR Mapper [*Planetary exploration*] ... VRM
Venus, SA [*Greece*] [*FAA designator*] (FAAC) ... VER
Venus-Earth-Earth-Gravity-Assist [*Spacecraft trajectory*] ... VEEGA
Venus-Venus-Earth-Jupiter [*Trajectory*] ... VVEJ
VePesid, Carboplatin [*Antineoplastic drug*] (CDI) ... VC
Vepeside [*Etoposide*] [*Antineoplastic drug*] ... VP-16-213
Vera Institute of Justice (EA) ... VIJ
Veracruz [*Mexico*] [*Seismograph station code, US Geological Survey*] (SEIS) ... VCM
Veracruz [*Mexico*] [*Airport symbol*] (OAG) ... VER
Veracruz/General Heriberto Jara [*Mexico ICAO location identifier*] (ICLI) ... MMVR
Veractor Tuned Microwave Cavity ... VTC
Verae Historiae [*of Lucian*] [*Classical studies*] (OCD) ... Ver Hist
Verandah [*Classified advertising*] (ADA) ... VER
Verapamil [*A coronary vasodilator*] ... V
Verapamil [*A coronary vasodilator*] ... VER
Verapamil [*Antineoplastic drug*] (CDI) ... VPAM
Verapamil, Imipramine, Lidocaine, Tamoxifen, Chlorpromazine, Haloperidol [*Antineoplastic drug regimen*] ... VILTCH
Verb ... V
Verb (WDMC) ... v
Verb ... VB
Verb Active ... VA
Verb Active and Intransitive (ROG) ... VA & I
Verb Auxiliary [*Grammar*] (WDAA) ... V AUX
Verb Defective [*Grammer*] (WDAA) ... V DEF
Verb Deponent [*Grammer*] (WDAA) ... V DEP
Verb Imperative [*Grammar*] (WDAA) ... V IMPER
Verb Impersonal [*Grammar*] (WDAA) ... V IMP
Verb Intransitive ... VI
Verb Neuter ... VN
Verb Passive ... VP
Verb Phrase ... VP
Verb Reflexive [*Grammar*] (WDAA) ... V REFL
Verb Reflexive ... VR
Verb Transitive ... VT
Verbal ... V
Verbal ... VBL
Verbal Adjective ... VA
Verbal Adjective (WDAA) ... VBA
Verbal Auditory Screen for Children ... VASC
Verbal Communication Scales [*Educational testing*] ... VCS
Verbal Concrete Object ... VCO
Verbal Delay Announcement (NITA) ... VDA
Verbal Discrimination [*Psychology*] ... VD
Verbal Emotional (Stimuli) [*Psychology*] ... VE
Verbal Fluency Test [*Speech and language therapy*] (DAVI) ... VFT
Verbal Information Storage and Text Analysis [*in FORTRAN computer language*] ... VISTA
Verbal Instruction Programmed System ... VIPS
Verbal Intelligence Quotient (DAVI) ... VIO
Verbal Interaction Category System [*Student teacher test*] ... VICS
Verbal Language Development Scale [*Speech and language therapy*] (DAVI) ... VLDS
Verbal Nonemotional (Stimuli) [*Psychology*] ... VNE
Verbal Noun ... VBN
Verbal Noun ... VN
Verbal Order Purchase Agreement [*Sales*] ... VOPA
Verbal Orders ... VO
Verbal Orders by Direction of the President ... VODP
Verbal Orders of Commanding General ... VOCG
Verbal Orders of Commanding Officer ... VOCO
Verbal Orders of the Adjutant General ... VOTAG
Verbal Orders of the Chief of Staff ... VOCS
Verbal Orders of the Commander ... VOC
Verbal Orders of the Governor ... VOGOV
Verbal Orders of the Secretary of the Air Force ... VOSAF
Verbal Orders of the Secretary of the Army ... VOSA
Verbal Reprimand (DAVI) ... VR
Verbal Response Inventory ... VRI
Verbal Scale ... VS
Verbal Scale Intelligence Quotient (EDAC) ... VSIQ
Verbal Substantive (WDAA) ... VSB
Verbal Test ... VET
Verbal Underachievers [*Education*] ... VUA
Verbalize [*or Verbalization*] (DAVI) ... V
Verbal-Nonverbal Operation [*Psychometrics*] ... VNVO
Verband der Unabhaengigen [*League of Independents*] [*Dissolved, 1956*] [*Austria*] (PPE) ... VdU
Verband der Weiblichen Angestellten [*Association of Female Employees*] [*West Germany*] ... VWA
Verband Deutscher Elektrotechniker [*Association of German Electrical Engineers*] (EG) ... VDE

Verband Hannoverscher Warmblutzuchter [*Germany*] (EAIO) ..... VHW
Verbatim [*FAR clauses*] (AAGC) V
Verbatim (MSA) ..... VERB
Verbatim et Literatim [*Word for Word, An Exact Copy*] [*Latin*] (ROG) ..... VERB ET LIT
Verb-Consonant [*Education of the hearing-impaired*] VC
Verbessert [*Improved*] [*German*] ..... VERB
Verbi Causa [*For Example*] [*Latin*] VC
Verbi Dei Minister [*Minister, or Preacher, of the Word of God*] [*Latin*] ..... VDM
Verbi Gratia [*For Example*] [*Latin*] ..... VG
Verbindungsoffizier [*Liaison Officer*] [*German military - World War II*] ..... VO
Verbit & Co., Consultants to Management [*Bala Cynwyd, PA*] [*Telecommunications*] (TSSD) ..... VCO
Verb-Object [*Education of the hearing-impaired*] ..... VO
Verbs (ADA) VV
Verbum [*Verb*] [*Latin*] ..... verb
Verbum Dei Community (TOCD) ..... VDC
Verbum Domini [*Rome*] [*A publication*] (BJA) ..... VD
Verbum Domini Manet in Eternum [*The Word of the Lord Endureth Forever*] [*Latin*] ..... VDMIE
Verbum Sapienti Sat Est [*A Word to the Wise Is Sufficient*] [*Latin*] ..... Verb Sap
Verbundkatalog Maschinenlesbarer Katalogdaten Deutscher Bibliotheken [*Deutsches Bibliotheksinstitut*] [*Germany Information service or system*] (CRD) ..... VK
VERDAN [*Versatile Differential Analyzer*] **Checkout Panel** ..... VCP
Verdan Junction Box ..... VJB
Verden/Scharnhorst [*Germany ICAO location identifier*] (ICLI) ..... EDWV
Verdi Arcobaleno [*Italy*] [*Political party*] (ECED) ..... ARCOB
Verdi Peak [*California*] [*Seismograph station code, US Geological Survey*] (SEIS) ..... VPK
Verdi Public School, Verdi, MN [*Library symbol*] [*Library of Congress*] (LCLS) ..... MnVePS
Verdict [*Legal shorthand*] (LWAP) V
Verdict (ROG) ..... VERDT
Verdix ADA Development System (NITA) ..... VADS
Verdstone Gold Corp. [*Vancouver Stock Exchange symbol*] ..... VGC
Verdun Depression Rating Scale [*Medicine*] (MAE) ..... VDRS
Verdun, PQ [*FM radio station call letters*] ..... CKOI
Verdun, PQ [*AM radio station call letters*] ..... CKVL
Verdun/Rozelier [*France ICAO location identifier*] (ICLI) ..... LFGW
Verdun Target Symptom Rating Scale (MAE) ..... VTSRS
Verdun-Meuse-Argonne Veterans Association (EA) ..... VMAVA
Vereda ..... VER
Vereenigde Feministiche Partij [*Belgium Political party*] (EY) ..... VFP
Vereeniging [*South Africa*] [*ICAO location identifier*] (ICLI) ..... FAVV
Verein [*Association*] [*German*] ..... VER
Verein der Freunde Schloss Blutenburg [*Association of Friends of Schloss Blutenburg-AFSB*] [*Germany*] (EAIO) ..... VFSB
Verein Deutscher Eisenhuttenleute [*German Iron and Steel Engineers Association*] (IID) ..... VDEh
Verein Deutscher Ingenieure [*Society of German Engineers*] ..... VDI
Verein Deutscher Ingenieure-Commission on Air Pollution Prevention (EAIO) ..... VDICAPP
Verein Deutscher Ingenieure-Kommission Reinhaltung der Luft [*VDI - Commis sion on Air Pollution Prevention*] (EAIO) ..... VDIKRL
Verein fuer Raumschiffahrt [*Society for Space Travel*] [*Germany*] ..... VFR
Vereingung der Europaischen Verbande des Automatenwirtschaft [*Federation of European Coin-Machine Associations*] (EAIO) ..... VEVA
Vereinigte Arbeitnehmerpartei Deutschland [*United Employees' Party of Germany*] [*Political party*] (PPW) ..... VAD
Vereinigte Elektrizitaets und Bergwerks, AG [*Holding company*] [*Germany*] ..... VEBA
Vereinigte Energiewerke AG (ECON) ..... VEAG
Vereinigte Gruenen Oesterreich [*United Green Party of Austria*] [*Political party*] (EY) ..... VGO
Vereinigte Linke [*United Left*] [*Germany Political party*] (PPW) VL
Vereinigte Metallwerke Ranshofen-Berndorf [*AG*] ..... VMRB
Vereinigte Wirtschaftsdienste [*Press agency*] [*West Germany*] ..... VWD
Vereinigung der Gegenseitigen Bauernhilfe [*Mutual Farmers' Aid Society*] [*Germany*] ..... VdgB
Vereinigung van Arbeiders Radio Amateurs ..... VARA
Verenigde Democratische Partijen [*United Democratic Parties*] [*Surinam*] [*Political party*] (PPW) ..... VDP
Verenigde Nederlandse Uitgeversbedrijven [*Publishing group*] [*Netherlands*] ..... VNU
Vereniging [*Association*] [*Dutch*] (ILCA) ..... Ver
Vereniging Intercoop [*International Agricultural Society Intercoop*] [*Switzerland*] (EAIO) VI
Vereniging Lucht [*Clean Air Society in the Netherlands-CLAN*] (EAIO) VL
Vereniging van Luguaart Onderhoudbedrywe [*Association of Aviation Maintenance Organizations*] (EAIO) ..... VLO
Verfahrenstechnische Berichte [*Process Technology Reports*] [*A publication*] ..... VtB
Verfassung [*Constitution*] [*German*] (ILCA) V
Verfuegung [*Order, Decree*] [*German*] (ILCA) V
Verfuegungstruppen (BJA) ..... VT
Verge (ROG) ..... VER
Vergeltung [*Retaliation*] [*German*] V
Vergeltungswaffe 1 [*Pilotless flying bomb employed by the Germans*] [*World War II*] V-1
Vergeltungswaffe 2 [*Rocket bomb employed by the Germans during World War II*] [*Translation: Vengeance Weapon*] V-2
Vergeltungswaffe Bomb [*German "vengeance weapon"*] ..... V (Bomb)
Vergennes, VT [*FM radio station call letters*] ..... WIZN
Vergennes, VT [*FM radio station call letters*] ..... WWGT
Vergennes, VT [*FM radio station call letters*] (RBYB) ..... WXPS-FM
Vergil [*First century BC*] [*Classical studies*] (OCD) ..... Verg
Vergilian Society (EA) ..... VS
Vergleische [*Compare*] [*German*] (ROG) ..... VERGL
Verical Altitude and Take-Off and Landing (PDAA) ..... VATOL
Vericom Test Application System [*Vericom Ltd.*] [*Software package*] (NCC) ..... V-TAS
Verifax (VRA) ..... verfx
Verifiable Integrated Processor for Enhanced Reliability [*Computer science*] (BYTE) ..... VIPER
Verification (MSA) ..... VERIF
Verification Analysis Report (NASA) ..... VAR
Verification and Checkout Equipment ..... VACE
Verification and Evaluation Tests (MCD) ..... V & ET
Verification and Validation [*Computer science*] ..... V & V
Verification Code Counter (MCD) VCC
Verification Completion Notice (NASA) ..... VCN
Verification Condition VC
Verification Condition Generator ..... VCG
Verification Condition Generator (MHDB) ..... VCGEN
Verification Control Document (NASA) ..... VCD
Verification Control Sheet (NASA) ..... VCS
Verification Cross Reference Index ..... VCRI
Verification Description Document (NASA) ..... VDD
Verification Flight Instrumentation (NASA) ..... VFI
Verification Flight Test (MCD) ..... VFT
Verification Information Management System (DNAB) ..... VIMS
Verification Information System (NASA) ..... VIS
Verification Integration Plan (SSD) ..... VIP
Verification of Deposit [*Finance*] (EMRF) ..... VOD
Verification of Function ..... VF
Verification of Interceptor Tactics Logic (SAA) ..... VITAL
Verification of On-Chip Chip Array Logic (NITA) ..... VOCAL
Verification of the Origins of Rotation in Tornadoes Experiment ..... VORTEX
Verification Polarization (NASA) ..... VP
Verification Program [*Branch*] [*Forecast Systems Laboratory*] (USDC) ..... VP
Verification Program [*Branch*] [*Marine science*] (OSRA) ..... VP
Verification Readiness Review (NASA) ..... VRR
Verification Receiver ..... VR
Verification Site Approval [*NASA*] (MCD) ..... VSA
Verification Status Social Security Number (AABC) ..... VSSSN
Verification Technology Information Centre [*British*] (CB) ..... VERTIC
Verification Test Matrix ..... VTM
Verification Test Network [*NASA*] (MCD) ..... VTN
Verification Test Plan [*or Program*] (NASA) ..... VTP
Verification Test Report (NASA) ..... VTR
Verification Test Vehicle [*Military*] (CAAL) ..... VTV
Verification Traceability Matrix ..... VTM
Verification Unit Test Set (AFM) ..... VUTS
Verification, Validation, and Certification (MHDB) ..... VV & C
Verificationof Employement (EMRF) ..... VOE
Verified Additional Military Occupational Specialty ..... VAMOS
Verified Audit Circulation [*Newspaper auditing firm*] [*Advertising*] ..... VAC
Verified Audit Circulation Corp. (NTCM) ..... VAC
Verified Circulation Figure [*Advertising*] ..... VCF
Verified Encoded Logging (NTCM) ..... VEL
Verified Free Distribution [*British*] ..... VFD
Verified Primary Military Occupational Specialty ..... VPMOS
Verified Record Output [*Computer science*] ..... VRO
Verified Secondary Military Occupational Specialty ..... VSMOS
Verified, Validated, and Accredited (RDA) ..... VV & A
Verifone, Inc. [*Associated Press*] (SAG) ..... Verifne
Verifone, Inc. [*NYSE symbol*] (SAG) ..... VFI
Verify (AFM) ..... VER
Verify (AFM) ..... VFY
Verify (MSA) ..... VRFY
Verify Duplication (DNAB) ..... VERDUP
Verify Number If No Answer [*Telecommunications*] (TEL) ..... VN
Verifying Interpreting Punch (IAA) ..... VIP
Verifying Punch (CMD) ..... VP
Verifying the Installation of Products [*Military*] (SAA) ..... VIP
Verilink Corp. [*Associated Press*] (SAG) ..... Verilink
Verilink Corp. [*NASDAQ symbol*] (SAG) ..... VRLK
Veritable Master of Crewelwork ..... VMC
Veritas [*A publication*] ..... Ver
Veritas DGC, Inc. [*Associated Press*] (SAG) ..... VeritDGC
Veritas DGC, Inc. [*NYSE symbol*] (SAG) ..... VTS
Veritas Music Entertainment [*NASDAQ symbol*] (TTSB) ..... VMEI
Veritas Music Entertainment, Inc. [*Associated Press*] (SAG) ..... Veritas
Veritas Music Entertainment, Inc. [*NASDAQ symbol*] (SAG) ..... VMEI
Veritas Music Entmt Wrrt [*NASDAQ symbol*] (TTSB) ..... VMEIW
VERITAS Software [*NASDAQ symbol*] (TTSB) ..... VRTS
Veritas Software Corp. [*Associated Press*] (SAG) ..... VeritasSf
Veritas Software Corp. [*NASDAQ symbol*] (SAG) ..... VRTS
Veritatem in Caritate. Orgaan van de Protestanse Theologische Faculteit te Brussel [*A publication*] (BJA) ..... VeritCarit
Verity, Inc. [*Associated Press*] (SAG) ..... Verity
Verity, Inc. [*NASDAQ symbol*] (SAG) ..... VRTY
Verkehrswasserbaubibliothek [*Bundesanstalt fuer Wasserbau*] [*Database*] ..... VtB
Verlagsgruppe Georg von Holtzbrinck [*Commercial firm Germany*] ..... VGH
VERLORT [*Very-Long-Range Tracking*] **Azimuth** [*NASA*] ..... VA
VERLORT [*Very-Long-Range Tracking*] **Elevation** [*NASA*] ..... V-E
VERLORT [*Very-Long-Range Tracking*] **Range** [*NASA*] ..... V-R
Vermessung [*Survey*] [*German military*] V
Vermiculite V

Vermiculite [*Technical drawings*] ... VRM
Vermiculite Association (EA) ... VA
Vermiculite Institute [*Defunct*] ... VI
Vermifuge [*Destroying Worms*] [*Pharmacy*] (ROG) ... VER
Vermilion (ROG) ... VER
Vermilion (ROG) ... VERM
Vermilion, AB [*ICAO location identifier*] (ICLI) ... CYVG
Vermilion Community College, Ely, MN [*OCLC symbol*] (OCLC) ... VCC
Vermilion County Elementary Film Library, Hoopeston, IL [*Library symbol*] [*Library of Congress*] (LCLS) ... IHoF
Vermilion Parish Library, Abbeville, LA [*Library symbol Library of Congress*] (LCLS) ... LAbV
Vermilion Public Library, Alberta [*Library symbol National Library of Canada*] (NLC) ... AVER
Vermilion Public Library, Vermilion, AB, Canada [*Library symbol*] [*Library of Congress*] (LCLS) ... CaAVER
Vermillion Community College, Ely, MN [*Library symbol Library of Congress*] (LCLS) ... MnElyV
Vermillion Public Library, Vermillion, SD [*Library symbol Library of Congress*] (LCLS) ... SdV
Vermillion Resources [*Vancouver Stock Exchange symbol*] ... VER
Vermillion, SD [*FM radio station call letters*] ... KAOR
Vermillion, SD [*AM radio station call letters*] ... KOSZ
Vermillion, SD [*AM radio station call letters*] ... KUSD
Vermillion, SD [*FM radio station call letters*] ... KUSD-FM
Vermillion, SD [*Television station call letters*] ... KUSD-TV
Vermillion, SD [*FM radio station call letters*] ... KVHT
Vermon, BC [*Television station call letters*] (RBYB) ... CHKL-2
Vermont [*MARC geographic area code Library of Congress*] (LCCP) ... n-us-vt
Vermont (ROG) ... VER
Vermont ... VERM
Vermont [*Postal code*] ... VT
Vermont [*MARC country of publication code Library of Congress*] (LCCP) ... vtu
Vermont Academy of Arts and Sciences ... VAAS
Vermont Administrative Procedure Compilation [*A publication*] (DLA) ... VT Admin Comp
Vermont Bar Association Reports [*A publication*] (DLA) ... VT BA
Vermont Business Teachers Association (EDAC) ... VBTA
Vermont Department of Libraries, Southwest Regional Library, Rutland, VT [*Library symbol Library of Congress*] (LCLS) ... Vt-SWRL
Vermont Financial Services Corp. [*NASDAQ symbol*] (NQ) ... VFSC
Vermont Financial Services Corp. [*Associated Press*] (SAG) ... VtFin
Vermont Fin'l Svcs [*NASDAQ symbol*] (TTSB) ... VFSC
Vermont Government Register [*A publication*] (AAGC) ... VGR
Vermont Health Care Information, Consortium ... VHIC
Vermont Historical Society, Montpelier, VT [*Library symbol Library of Congress*] (LCLS) ... VtHi
Vermont Information Processes, Inc. [*Information service or system*] (IID) ... VIP
Vermont Junior College ... VJC
Vermont Law School (GAGS) ... Vt Law
Vermont Legislative Council, Montpelier, VT [*Library symbol Library of Congress*] (LCLS) ... Vt-LR
Vermont Maple Industry Council (EA) ... VMIC
Vermont Monitoring Cooperative (USDC) ... VMC
Vermont Monitoring Cooperative [*Marine science*] (OSRA) ... VMC
Vermont Motor Rate Bureau Inc., Barre VT [*STAC*] ... VMB
Vermont Natural Heritage Program [*Information service or system*] (IID) ... VNHP
Vermont Public Records Library, Montpelier, VT [*Library symbol Library of Congress*] (LCLS) ... Vt-PR
Vermont Pure Hldgs Ltd [*NASDAQ symbol*] (TTSB) ... VPUR
Vermont Pure Holdings [*Commercial firm Associated Press*] (SAG) ... VermPu
Vermont Pure Holdings [*NASDAQ symbol*] (SAG) ... VPUR
Vermont Railway, Inc. [*AAR code*] ... VTR
Vermont Reports [*A publication*] (DLA) ... V
Vermont Reports [*A publication*] (DLA) ... Ver
Vermont Reports [*A publication*] (DLA) ... Ver Rep
Vermont Reports [*A publication*] (DLA) ... Verm
Vermont Reports [*A publication*] (DLA) ... Vermont R
Vermont Reports [*A publication*] (DLA) ... Vermont Rep
Vermont Reports [*A publication*] (DLA) ... Vermt
Vermont Reports [*A publication*] (DLA) ... Vert
Vermont Reports [*A publication*] (DLA) ... VR
Vermont Reports [*A publication*] (DLA) ... VT
Vermont Reports [*A publication*] (AAGC) ... Vt
Vermont Reports [*A publication*] (DLA) ... VT R
Vermont Reports [*A publication*] (DLA) ... VT Rep
Vermont State College ... VSC
Vermont State Department of Libraries, Montpelier, VT [*OCLC symbol*] (OCLC) ... VSL
Vermont State Teachers College ... VSTC
Vermont Statutes [*A publication*] (DLA) ... VS
Vermont Statutes, Annotated [*A publication*] (DLA) ... VSA
Vermont Statutes, Annotated [*A publication*] (DLA) ... VT Stat Ann
Vermont Teddy Bear [*NASDAQ symbol*] (TTSB) ... BEAR
Vermont Teddy Bear Co. [*NASDAQ symbol*] (SAG) ... BEAR
Vermont Teddy Bear Co. [*Associated Press*] (SAG) ... VTTeddy
Vermont Telecommunications, Inc. [*Winooski, VT*] [*Telecommunications*] (TSSD) ... VTI
Vermont Yankee Generating Station [*Nuclear energy*] (NRCH) ... VYGS
Vermont Yankee Nuclear Plant (NRCH) ... VYNP
Vermont Yankee Nuclear Power Station (NRCH) ... VYNPS
Vermont-New Hampshire-New York Hospital Libraries [*Library network*] ... HLDS
Vermontville Public Library, Vermontville, MI [*Library symbol Library of Congress*] (LCLS) ... MiVer
Vern [*Nevada*] [*Seismograph station code, US Geological Survey Closed*] (SEIS) ... NYV
Vernacular (ADA) ... VERN
Vernacular Architecture Forum (EA) ... VAF
Vernacular Architecture Group [*British*] ... VAG
Vernacular Black English (WGA) ... VBE
Vernacular Society (EA) ... VS
Vernair Flying Services [*British ICAO designator*] (ICDA) ... VC
Vernal [*Utah*] [*Airport symbol*] (OAG) ... VEL
Vernal Conjunctivitis [*Ophthalmology*] ... VC
Vernal Equinox ... VE
Vernal Keratoconjunctivitis [*Ophthalmology*] (DAVI) ... VKC
Vernal, UT [*FM radio station call letters*] ... KLCY-FM
Vernal, UT [*AM radio station call letters*] ... KVEL
Verndale Public School, Verndale, MN [*Library symbol*] [*Library of Congress*] (LCLS) ... MnVerS
Vernehmungsoffizier [*Interrogation Officer*] [*German military - World War II*] ... VO
Vernier [*Engine*] (AAG) ... VER
Vernier [*Engineering*] ... VERN
Vernier [*Engine*] (AAG) ... VRN
Vernier [*Engine*] (NASA) ... VRNR
Vernier Auto Track (IAA) ... VAT
Vernier Control System ... VCS
Vernier Engine [*as a modifier*] (AAG) ... VE
Vernier Engine Cutoff [*Aerospace*] ... VCD
Vernier Engine Cutoff [*Aerospace*] ... VECO
Vernier Engine Vibration [*Aerospace*] ... VEV
Vernier Propulsion System [*Aerospace*] ... VPS
Vernier [*Engine*] **Reaction Control System** [*Aerospace*] (NASA) ... VRCS
Vernier Solo Accumulator [*Aerospace*] (AAG) ... VSA
Vernier Solo Hydraulic Power System [*Aerospace*] (AAG) ... VSHPS
Vernier Solo Power Supply [*Aerospace*] (AAG) ... VSPS
Vernier Step Gauge [*Aerospace*] ... VSG
Vernier Tracking by Automatic Correlation [*Aerospace*] ... VERNITRAC
Vernier Velocity Correction System [*Aerospace*] (KSC) ... VVCS
Vernitron $1.20 Exch Pfd [*NASDAQ symbol*] (TTSB) ... VRNTP
Vernitron Corp. [*Associated Press*] (SAG) ... Vernitrn
Vernitron Corp. [*Associated Press*] (SAG) ... Vernt
Vernitron Corp. [*NASDAQ symbol*] (SAG) ... VRNT
Vernon, AL [*FM radio station call letters*] ... WJEC
Vernon, AL [*AM radio station call letters*] ... WVSA
Vernon and Scriven's Irish King's Bench Reports [*1786-88*] [*A publication*] (DLA) ... V & S
Vernon and Scriven's Irish King's Bench Reports [*1786-88*] [*A publication*] (DLA) ... Vern & S
Vernon and Scriven's Irish King's Bench Reports [*1786-88*] [*A publication*] (DLA) ... Vern & S (Ir)
Vernon and Scriven's Irish King's Bench Reports [*1786-88*] [*A publication*] (DLA) ... Vern & Sc
Vernon and Scriven's Irish King's Bench Reports [*1786-88*] [*A publication*] (DLA) ... Vern & Scr
Vernon and Scriven's Irish King's Bench Reports [*1786-88*] [*A publication*] (DLA) ... Vern & Scriv
Vernon Area Library District, Prairie View, IL [*Library symbol*] [*Library of Congress*] (LCLS) ... IPra
Vernon, BC [*AM radio station call letters*] ... CICF
Vernon, BC [*AM radio station call letters*] ... CJIB
Vernon Branch, Osgoode Township Library, Ontario [*Library symbol National Library of Canada*] (NLC) ... OVOT
Vernon, CT [*AM radio station call letters*] ... WCTF
Vernon Hills, IL [*AM radio station call letters*] ... WNVR
Vernon Library, British Columbia [*Library symbol National Library of Canada*] (NLC) ... BV
Vernon Library, Vernon, BC, Canada [*Library symbol Library of Congress*] (LCLS) ... CaBV
Vernon Museum, Archives and Art Gallery, British Columbia [*Library symbol National Library of Canada*] (NLC) ... BVMA
Vernon Museum, Archives and Art Gallery, Vernon, BC, Canada [*Library symbol Library of Congress*] (LCLS) ... CaBVMA
Vernon Parish Library, Leesville, LA [*Library symbol Library of Congress*] (LCLS) ... LLeV
Vernon Public Library, Vernon, CA [*Library symbol Library of Congress*] (LCLS) ... CVer
Vernon Regional Junior College, Vernon, TX [*Library symbol Library of Congress*] (LCLS) ... TxVeC
Vernon, TX [*AM radio station call letters*] ... KVWC
Vernon, TX [*FM radio station call letters*] ... KVWC-FM
Vernon, TX [*Location identifier FAA*] (FAAL) ... VRT
Vernon's Annotated Missouri Rule [*A publication*] (DLA) ... VAMR
Vernon's Annotated Missouri Statutes [*A publication*] (DLA) ... MO Ann Stat (Vernon)
Vernon's Annotated Missouri Statutes [*A publication*] (DLA) ... VAMS
Vernon's Annotated Texas Civil Statutes [*A publication*] (DLA) ... Vernon's Ann Civ St
Vernon's Annotated Texas Code of Criminal Procedure [*A publication*] (DLA) ... Vernon's Ann CCP
Vernon's Annotated Texas Penal Code [*A publication*] (DLA) ... Vernon's Ann PC
Vernon's Annotated Texas Statutes [*A publication*] (DLA) ... VATS
Vernon's English Chancery Reports [*23 English Reprint*] [*A publication*] (DLA) ... Vern
Vernon's English Chancery Reports [*23 English Reprint*] [*A publication*] (DLA) ... Vern (Eng)
Vernon's Kansas Statutes, Annotated [*A publication*] (DLA) ... Kan Ann
Vernon's Kansas Statutes, Annotated [*A publication*] (DLA) ... Kan Subject Ann Vernon's

Vernon's Kansas Statutes, Annotated, Code of Civil Procedure [*A publication*] (DLA) ... Kan Civ Pro Stat Ann
Vernon's Kansas Statutes, Annotated, Code of Civil Procedure [*A publication*] (DLA) ... Kan Civ Pro Stat Ann (Vernon)
Vernon's Kansas Statutes, Annotated, Criminal Code and Code of Criminal Procedure [*A publication*] (DLA) ... Kan Crim Code & Code of Crim Proc (Vernon)
Vernon's Kansas Statutes, Annotated, Uniform Commercial Code [*A publication*] (DLA) ... Kan UCC Ann (Vernon)
Vernon's Texas Codes, Annotated [*A publication*] (DLA) ... VTCA
Vero Beach [*Florida*] [*Airport symbol*] (OAG) ... VRB
Vero Beach, FL [*Location identifier FAA*] (FAAL) ... VRB
Vero Beach, FL [*FM radio station call letters*] ... WAVW
Vero Beach, FL [*AM radio station call letters*] ... WAXE
Vero Beach, FL [*FM radio station call letters*] ... WGYL
Vero Beach, FL [*FM radio station call letters*] (RBYB) ... WPAW
Vero Beach, FL [*FM radio station call letters*] ... WQOL
Vero Beach, FL [*FM radio station call letters*] ... WSCF
Vero Beach, FL [*AM radio station call letters*] ... WTTB
Vero Beach/Vero Beach [*Florida*] [*ICAO location identifier*] (ICLI) ... KVRB
Verona [*Italy*] [*Airport symbol*] (OAG) ... VRN
Verona/Boscomantico [*Italy ICAO location identifier*] (ICLI) ... LIPN
Verona, WI [*FM radio station call letters*] (RBYB) ... WMMM-FM
Veronal-Buffered Diluent ... VBD
Veronal-Buffered Oxalated Saline ... VBOS
Veronal-Buffered Saline ... VBS
Veronal-Buffered Saline-Fetal Bovine Serum (MAE) ... VBS:FBS
Veronex Resources Ltd. [*Vancouver Stock Exchange symbol*] ... VEO
Veronex Resources Ltd. (MHDW) ... VEOXF
Veronis, Suhler & Associates, Inc. [*Telecommunications service*] (TSSD) ... VS & A
Verordnung [*Decree, Regulation, Ordinance*] [*German*] (ILCA) ... V
Verordnungsblatt [*Official Gazette*] [*German*] (ILCA) ... VBl
Verordnungsblatt fuer die Britische Zone [*Official Gazette of the Former British Zone of Occupation*] [*German*] (ILCA) ... VOBL BZ
Verotoxin [*Biochemistry*] ... VT
Verotoxin-Producing Escherichia Coli ... VTEC
Verpflegungsausgabestelle [*Rations distributing point*] [*German military - World War II*] ... VA
Verpflegungsoffizier [*Mess Officer*] [*German military - World War II*] ... VO
Verplanck on Contracts [*A publication*] (DLA) ... Verpl Cont
Verplanck on Evidence [*A publication*] (DLA) ... Verpl Ev
Versa Technologies [*NASDAQ symbol*] (TTSB) ... VRSA
Versa Technologies, Inc. [*Associated Press*] (SAG) ... Versa
Versa Technologies, Inc. [*NASDAQ symbol*] (NQ) ... VRSA
Versailles, IN [*FM radio station call letters*] ... WXCH
Versailles, KY [*FM radio station call letters*] ... WJMM
Versailles, MO [*FM radio station call letters*] ... KTKS
Versailles, OH [*Location identifier FAA*] (FAAL) ... VES
Versailles Project on Advanced Materials and Standards ... VAMAS
Versailles Republican, Versailles, IN [*Library symbol Library of Congress*] (LCLS) ... InVerR
Versar, Inc. [*Associated Press*] (SAG) ... Versar
Versar, Inc. [*AMEX symbol*] (SPSG) ... VSR
Versatile ... VERST
Versatile Aerial Simulation TOW [*Tube-Launched, Optically Tracked, Wire-Guided (Weapon)*] **Target** (MCD) ... VASTT
Versatile Automated Maintenance Information System (MCD) ... VAMIS
Versatile Automatic Data Exchange ... VADA
Versatile Automatic Data Exchange (MCD) ... VADE
Versatile Automatic Specification Tester ... VAST
Versatile Automatic Test Equipment [*Computers*] ... VATE
Versatile Automatic Test Equipment Assembly Program [*Computer science*] (IAA) ... VAP
Versatile Avionics Ship Test (IAA) ... VAST
Versatile Avionics Shop Test System (SAA) ... VAST
Versatile Avionics System Tester (GFGA) ... VAST
Versatile Avionics Test [*or Tester*] **Shop** [*NASA*] (DNAB) ... VATS
Versatile Base [*Bus*] **Connector** [*Electronics*] (BARN) ... VBC
Versatile Contour Measuring Machine (MCD) ... VERSACOMM
Versatile Corp. [*Vancouver Stock Exchange symbol*] ... CC
Versatile Corp. [*Toronto Stock Exchange symbol*] ... VCC
Versatile Differential Analyzer ... VERDAN
Versatile Drone Autopilot (MCD) ... VDA
Versatile Electro-Optical System (MCD) ... VEOS
Versatile Engine Tester ... VET
Versatile Exercise Mine [*Navy British*] ... VEM
Versatile Exercise Mine System [*Military*] (PDAA) ... VEMS
Versatile Exercise Mine System (DOMA) ... VENS
Versatile Experimental Reactor Assembly (DEN) ... VERA
Versatile High Speed [*Copier*] ... VHS
Versatile Information Processor [*Computer science*] ... VIP
Versatile Interface Adapter [*Telecommunications*] (IAA) ... VIA
Versatile Interior Multiplex System (PDAA) ... VIMS
Versatile Isotope Power System (MCD) ... VIPS
Versatile Message Transaction Protocol [*Computer science*] ... VMTP
Versatile Omnitask Real-Time Executive (NITA) ... VORTEX
Versatile Pacific Shipyards [*Shipbuilder*] [*Vancouver, Canada*] ... VPS
Versatile Packaging Machine ... VPM
Versatile Repair Facility ... VRF
Versatile Signal Device ... VSD
Versatile Signal [*or Symbol*] **Generator** ... VSG
Versatile Test Analysis RADAR (MCD) ... VERTAR
Versatile Tracking Mount (MCD) ... VTM
Versatile Training Systems (MCD) ... VTS
Versatile Upper Stage [*NASA*] ... VUS
Versatile Vickers Systems, Inc., Ottawa, ON, Canada [*Library symbol*] [*Library of Congress*] (LCLS) ... CaOOVV
Versatile Vickers Systems, Inc., Ottawa, Ontario [*Library symbol National Library of Canada*] (NLC) ... OOVV
Versatility Code ... VC
Verse ... V
Verse (WDMC) ... v
Verse ... VER
Verse ... VS
Versed Sine [*Engineering*] (KSC) ... VERS
Versed Sine (IDOE) ... vers
Verses ... VV
Versicherung [*Insurance*] [*German Business term*] ... VERS
Versicle ... V
Versicle ... VCLE
Versiculo [*In Such a Way*] [*Latin*] (ROG) ... V
Version ... V
Version (WDMC) ... v
Version (ROG) ... VER
Version (VRA) ... ver
Version (ROG) ... VERS
Version Control System [*Computer science*] ... VCS
Version Description Document (KSC) ... VDD
Versions (ROG) ... VSS
Verso [*Left-hand page*] [*Latin*] ... V
Verso (WDMC) ... v
Verso ... VO
Verso (BJA) ... VSO
Verstell Propeller (MCD) ... VP
Verstreute Boghazkoei-Texte [*A. Goetze*] [*A publication*] (BJA) ... VBot
Versus [*Against*] ... V
Versus (WDMC) ... v
Versus (WDMC) ... vs
Versus [*Against*] [*Latin*] ... VS
Vert [*Heraldry*] ... V
Vert [*Heraldry*] ... VER
Verte [*or Vertatur*] [*Turn Over*] [*Latin*] ... V
Vertebra [*or Vertebral*] [*Anatomy*] (DAVI) ... Vert
Vertebral, Anal, Cardiac, Tracheosophageal, Renal, and Limb [*Defects*] ... VACTERL
Vertebral, Anal, Tracheal, Esophageal, Renal ... VATER
Vertebral and/or Vascular Defects, Anorectal Malformation, Tracheoesophageal Fistula, Radial, Ray, or Renal Anomaly [*Syndrome*] [*Medicine*] (DAVI) ... VATER
Vertebral Artery [*Anatomy*] ... VA
Vertebral Body [*Anatomy*] (DAVI) ... VB
Vertebral Body Tenderness [*Medicine*] (DAVI) ... VBT
Vertebral Defects, Imperforate Anus, Tracheoesophageal Fistula, Radial and RenalDysplasia [*Syndrome*] [*Medicine*] (DAVI) ... VATER
Vertebral Defects, Imperforate Anus, Tracheoesophageal Fistula, Radial and RenalDysplasia, Limb Anomalies [*Syndrome*] [*Medicine*] (DAVI) ... VATERL
Vertebral or Vascular Defects, Anorectal Malformation, Cardiac Anomaly, Tracheoesophageal Fistula, Renal Anomaly, Limb Anomaly [*Syndrome*] (DAVI) ... VAD
Vertebral Vein [*Anatomy*] ... VV
Vertebral-Basilar Arteries [*Anatomy*] (CPH) ... VB
Vertebral-Basilar Insufficiency [*Medicine*] (CPH) ... VBI
Vertebral-Basilar System [*Medicine*] (CPH) ... VBS
Vertebrate ... VERT
Vertebrate ... VERTEB
Vertebrate Pest Program (EERA) ... VPP
Vertebrate Pests Committee (EERA) ... VPC
Vertebrobasilar Artery Insufficiency [*Medicine*] ... VBAI
Vertebrobasilar Dolichoectasia [*Medicine*] ... VBD
Vertex ... V
Vertex [*Obstetrics*] (DAVI) ... VE
Vertex (WGA) ... VER
Vertex ... VTX
Vertex [*Medicine*] ... VX
Vertex Adjacency Graph (MHDI) ... VAG
Vertex Communications Corp. [*Associated Press*] (SAG) ... VertexC
Vertex Communications Corp. [*Kilgore, TX*] [*NASDAQ symbol*] (NQ) ... VTEX
Vertex Communic'ns [*NASDAQ symbol*] (TTSB) ... VTEX
Vertex Industries [*NASDAQ symbol*] (TTSB) ... VETX
Vertex Industries, Inc. [*Associated Press*] (SAG) ... VertexI
Vertex Industries, Inc. [*Clifton, NJ*] [*NASDAQ symbol*] (NQ) ... VETX
Vertex Pharmaceuticals [*NASDAQ symbol*] (TTSB) ... VRTX
Vertex Pharmaceuticals, Inc. [*Associated Press*] (SAG) ... VertxPh
Vertex Pharmaceuticals, Inc. [*NASDAQ symbol*] (SPSG) ... VRTX
Vertex Processor ... VP
Vertex Resources Ltd. [*Vancouver Stock Exchange symbol*] ... VXR
Vertex Time of Arrival [*FAA*] (TAG) ... VTA
Vertical [*RADAR*] ... V
Vertical (WDMC) ... v
Vertical (KSC) ... VER
Vertical (MCD) ... VERT
Vertical (WDMC) ... vert
Vertical (IDOE) ... vert
Vertical Acceleration Ramp ... VAR
Vertical Accelerometer Unit ... VAU
Vertical Access Kit (NASA) ... VAK
Vertical Air Current ... VAC
Vertical Air Rocket (NATG) ... VAR

Vertical Alignment Design by the Nodal-Tangent and Undulation System (PDAA) .... VENUS
Vertical Amplifier (IAA) .... VA
Vertical and Direction Gyro .... VDG
Vertical and Horizontal [Telecommunications] (TSSD) .... V & H
Vertical and Horizontal Spread [Landfills] (EG) .... VHS
Vertical Angle Bench Mark .... VABM
Vertical Anisotropic Etch [Raytheon Co.] .... V-ATE
Vertical Approach Slope Indicator .... VASI
Vertical Arc Welder .... VAW
Vertical Arithmetic Unit .... VAU
Vertical Array Hydrophone .... VAH
Vertical Assault Lift .... VAL
Vertical Assault Medium Transport (MCD) .... VAMT
Vertical Assembly and Test Area (SSD) .... VATA
Vertical Assembly Building [NASA] .... VAB
Vertical Assembly Component Test Laboratory .... VACTL
Vertical Assembly Data Detector (NASA) .... VAK
Vertical Assembly Kit (NASA) .... VAK
Vertical Axis Bearing .... VAB
Vertical Axis Hydropower Turbine .... VAHT
Vertical Axis Pivots .... VAP
Vertical Axis Wind Turbine [Power generator] [See also VAWTG] .... VAWT
Vertical Axis Wind Turbine Generator [Also, VAWT] .... VAWTG
Vertical Azimuth Reference System (NATG) .... VARS
Vertical Banded Gastroplasty [Medicine] (MEDA) .... VBG
Vertical Beam [of light] .... VB
Vertical Blanking Interval [Telecommunications] .... VBI
Vertical Bomb [Air Force] .... VB
Vertical Camera (WDAA) .... VERTICAM
Vertical Carrier Onboard Delivery .... VCOD
Vertical Cask-Lifting Fixture [Nuclear energy] (NRCH) .... VCLF
Vertical Center (SAA) VC
Vertical Center Line VCL
Vertical Centering Control VCC
Vertical Centrifugal .... VCE
Vertical Channel Computer (SAA) VCC
Vertical Circle (IAA) VC
Vertical Clearance (DNAB) .... VERTCL
Vertical Contact Analog Display .... VCAD
Vertical Control Operator [Military] .... VCO
Vertical Crater Retreat [Mining technology] .... VCR
Vertical Current Meter .... VCM
Vertical Curve VC
Vertical Cutter Motion .... VCM
Vertical Danger Angle [Navigation] .... VDA
Vertical Data Processing .... VDP
Vertical Deflection [Symbol] (DEN) .... Y
Vertical Deflection Terminal (IAA) .... VDT
Vertical Deviation (DAVI) .... VD
Vertical Digital Analyzer (IAA) .... VERDAN
Vertical Dilution of Precision .... VDOP
Vertical Dipole (MCD) .... VDP
Vertical Direction Indicator (CAAL) .... VDI
Vertical Director Pointer (SAA) .... VDP
Vertical Display Generator (NG) .... VDG
Vertical Display Indicator (NG) .... VDI
Vertical Display Indicator Group .... VDIG
Vertical Display System [Navy] .... VDS
Vertical Double Diffused Metal Oxide Semiconductor (MCD) .... VDMOS
Vertical Double-Expansion [Engine] (DNAB) VERT-2-EXP
Vertical Drive .... VD
Vertical Earth Rate .... VER
Vertical Earth Scanning Test (SAA) .... VEST
Vertical Effective Radiated Power (MCD) .... VERP
Vertical Ejection Launch Aero-Reaction Control (MCD) .... VELARC
Vertical Ejector Rack (MCD) .... VER
Vertical Electrical Chase [Nuclear energy] (NRCH) .... VEC
Vertical Engine Test Stand .... VETS
Vertical Escape Collision Avoidance System [Aviation] .... VECAS
Vertical Exaggeration [Geology] .... VE
Vertical Extent of Mortality [Intertidal organisms] .... VEM
Vertical Extrusion Press .... VEP
Vertical Field Effect Transistor (IAA) .... VFET
Vertical File .... VF
Vertical Flight (NASA) .... VF
Vertical Flight Maneuver .... VFM
Vertical Flight Performance Criteria .... VFPC
Vertical Flight Test (MCD) .... VFT
Vertical Flow Horizontal .... VFH
Vertical Force Accounting System .... VFAS
Vertical Force Accounting System/Troop List (MCD) .... VFAS/TL
Vertical Force Development Management Information Systems .... VFDMIS
Vertical Format Buffer .... VFB
Vertical Format Control .... VFC
Vertical Format Unit (BUR) .... VFU
Vertical Forms Control (MHDB) .... VFC
Vertical Function Checkout .... VEFCO
Vertical Gradient Freeze [Crystal growing technique] .... VGF
Vertical Grain (NG) .... VG
Vertical Ground Vibration Test (MCD) .... VGVT
Vertical Gust (MCD) .... V-G
Vertical Gyro (MCD) .... VG
Vertical Gyro Alignment .... VGA
Vertical Gyro Indicator .... VGI
Vertical/Heads-Up Display [Aviation] (MCD) .... V/HUD

Vertical Hold Control .... VHC
Vertical Hook (IAA) .... VH
Vertical Impact Guidance System [Army] (MCD) .... VIGS
Vertical Improved Mail [Mail-delivery system for large buildings in which all tenants pick up their mail from lockboxes in a central mailroom] .... VIM
Vertical Impulse .... VIMP
Vertical in Line [Aircraft engine] V
Vertical Incidence (IAA) VI
Vertical Indicating Gyro Internally Lighted (MCD) .... VIGIL
Vertical Infrared Fuze (CAAL) .... VIF
Vertical Injection Logic [Computer science] VIL
Vertical Installation Automated Baseline [Army] .... VIABLE
Vertical Instruments Display System (MCD) .... VIDS
Vertical Integration Building [NASA] .... VIB
Vertical Internal Time Code [Electronic musical instruments] .... VITC
Vertical Interval [Mapmaking] VI
Vertical Interval Data Detector (NASA) .... VIDD
Vertical Interval Reference [Automatic color adjustment] [Television] .... VIR
Vertical Interval Reference Signal [Automatic color adjustment] [Television] (IAA) .... VIRS
Vertical Interval Test [Automatic color adjustment] [Television] (IAA) .... VIT
Vertical Interval Test Signal (IEEE) .... VITS
Vertical Interval Time Code (NTCM) .... VITC
Vertical Keel .... VK
Vertical Ladder [Technical drawings] VL
Vertical Landing (MCD) VL
Vertical Landing Aid [Military] (CAAL) .... VLA
Vertical Landing Point (AFM) .... VLP
Vertical Launch ASROC [Antisubmarine Rocket] .... VLA
Vertical Launch Facility .... VLF
Vertical Launch Modular Booster (MCD) .... VLMB
Vertical Launch SEAWOLF [Military British] .... VLSW
Vertical Launch System [Military] .... VLS
Vertical Launched Standard Missile (MCD) .... VLSM
Vertical Lift Aircraft Council (EA) .... VLAC
Vertical Lift Bridge (BARN) .... VLB
Vertical Lights [Navigation signal] .... Vert
Vertical Line Array .... VLA
Vertical Line Array DIFAR (MCD) .... VLAD
Vertical Line Array Directional .... VLAD
Vertical Line Through Center of Gravity (IAA) .... VCG
Vertical Liquid Spring .... VLS
Vertical Load Gun .... VLG
Vertical Loading Gun Mount (MCD) .... VLGM
Vertical Location of the Center of Buoyancy .... VCB
Vertical Location of the Center of Gravity .... VCG
Vertical Lockout .... VLO
Vertical Long Period .... VLP
Vertical Machining Center [Automotive manufacturing] .... VMC
Vertical Magnet .... VM
Vertical Magnetic Dipole (IEEE) .... VMD
Vertical Main Boiler [on a ship] (DS) .... VB
Vertical Main Distribution (IAA) .... VMD
Vertical Maintenance Facility (NASA) .... VMF
Vertical Market Structure (MHDB) .... VMS
Vertical Markets Information Database [Amidon/Litman Associates] [Information service or system] (CRD) .... VMI
Vertical Markets Information Index 1986 [Amidon/Litman Associates] [A publication] .... VMII 1986
Vertical Medium-Lead Burst [Neuron] .... VMLB
Vertical Meridian [Optics, Eye anatomy] .... VM
Vertical Metal-Oxide Semiconductor (IAA) .... VMOS
Vertical Metal-Oxide-Semiconductor Field-Effect Transistor (IDOE) .... VMOSFET
Vertical Milling Machine .... VMM
Vertical Motion [NWS] (FAAC) .... VRT MOTN
Vertical Motion Compensation (CAAL) .... VMC
Vertical Motion Index (PCM) .... VMI
Vertical Motion Simulator [NASA] .... VMS
Vertical Multijunction [Solar cell] .... VMJ
Vertical Navigation Mode (IEEE) .... VNAV
Vertical Navigation System .... VERNAV
Vertical Nutrient-Solution Transport System [i.e., plant stem] [Slang] .... VNTS
Vertical Obstacle SONAR (IAA) .... VOS
Vertical Oculus .... VO
Vertical Ommi-Range, Take-Off, Approach, and Landing System (PDAA) .... VORTAL
Vertical Omnidirectional Radio .... VOR
Vertical On-Board Delivery [Navy] (NVT) .... VOD
Vertical Output (IAA) .... VO
Vertical Ozone Distribution from the Absorption and Radiation of Ozone (AAG) .... VODARO
Vertical Ozone Profile .... VOP
Vertical Panel Mount .... VPM
Vertical Path (GAVI) .... VPATH
Vertical Path Computer (PDAA) .... VPC
Vertical Payload Handling Device [NASA] (MCD) .... VPHD
Vertical Photography (WDAA) .... V PH
Vertical Pinpoint (AFM) .... VPP
Vertical Planning (NG) .... VP
Vertical Plot Board [Navy] .... VPB
Vertical Point of Intersection [Transportation] .... VPI
Vertical Polarization (AFM) .... VERT
Vertical Polarization .... VP
Vertical Polarization Mode .... VPM
Vertical Pouch Packager .... VPP

Vertical Power Jump Test [*NASA*] (MCD) .... VPJT
Vertical Processing Facility [*NASA*] (MCD) .... VPF
Vertical Quadruple-Expansion [*Engine*] (DNAB) VERT-4-EXP
Vertical Radial (MSA) .... VTR
Vertical Random Format (NITA) .... VRF
Vertical Rate of Climb [*Aviation*] .... VROC
Vertical Receiving Array Hydrophone .... VRAH
Vertical Receiving Hydrophone .... VRH
Vertical Recovery Line [*NASA*] (NASA) .... VRL
Vertical Redundancy [*Telecommunications*] (IAA) .... VR
Vertical Redundancy Check [*Telecommunications*] (BUR) .... VRC
Vertical Redundancy Check Register [*Telecommunications*] (IAA) .... VRCR
Vertical Reference Attitude .... VRA
Vertical Reference Gyro (DA) .... VRG
Vertical Reference Line [*Technical drawings*] .... VRL
Vertical Reference Unit (MCD) .... VRU
Vertical Removal Fixture (NASA) .... VRF
Vertical Replenishment [*Navy*] (NVT) .... VERTREP
Vertical Resistance .... VR
Vertical Retort .... VR
Vertical Ride Control (OA) .... VRC
Vertical Rising Aircraft .... VRA
Vertical Rule (DGA) .... VR
Vertical Seismic Floor Response (IEEE) .... VSFR
Vertical Seismic Profile [*Geology*] .... VSP
Vertical [*Activity*] **Sensor** [*Physiology*] .... VS
Vertical Sensor Assembly .... VSA
Vertical/Short Takeoff [*and Landing*] (MCD) .... VSTO
Vertical/Short Takeoff and Landing [*Aircraft*] .... V/STOL
Vertical Side of Intermediate Distribution Frame [*Telecommunications*] (TEL) .... VIDF
Vertical Side of Main Distribution Frame [*Telecommunications*] (TEL) .... VMDF
Vertical Sideband [*Radio frequency*] [*Telecommunications*] (IAA) .... VSI
Vertical Signal [*or Situation*] **Indicator** [*Helicopters*] .... VSI
Vertical Situation Display .... VSD
Vertical Situation Display/Attitude Director Indicator (MCD) .... VSD/ADI
Vertical Size Ratio [*Ophthalmology*] .... VSR
Vertical Software [*AI Software*] [*Computer science*] .... VS
Vertical Sounding [*Telecommunications*] (OA) .... VS
Vertical Sounding System .... VSS
Vertical Spacing (IAA) VC
Vertical Speed [*Aviation*] .... VS
Vertical Speed Indicator [*Aviation*] .... VSI
Vertical Spike Soderberg [*Pot*] [*Aluminum processing*] .... VSS
Vertical Spread (MHDB) .... VS
Vertical Stereoscopic [*Photograph*] .... VS
Vertical Storage and Retrieval Systems .... VSR
Vertical Stripes [*Navigation markers*] .... VS
Vertical Support Structure .... VSS
Vertical Surface Emitting LASER .... VSEL
Vertical Sweep Generator [*Telecommunications*] (OA) .... VSG
Vertical Synchronization [*Computer science*] (IAA) .... VSYNCH
Vertical Synchronous [*Computer science*] .... VSYNC
Vertical System [*Government arrangement*] (OICC) .... VS
Vertical Tab [*Computer science*] (DOM) .... VT
Vertical Tabulate (NITA) .... VT
Vertical Tabulation [*or Tabulator*] [*Computer science*] .... VT
Vertical Tabulation Character [*Computer science*] .... VTAB
Vertical Tabulator (ECII) .... VT
Vertical Tail .... VT
Vertical Takeoff .... VTO
Vertical Takeoff and Horizontal Landing .... VTOHL
Vertical Takeoff and Landing [*Also, VTOL*] .... VERTOL
Vertical Takeoff and Landing [*Also, VERTOL*] [*Acronym used for a type of aircraft*] .... VTOL
Vertical Takeoff and Landing Jet [*Aircraft*] .... VERTIJET
Vertical Takeoff Gross Weight .... VTOGW
Vertical Takeoff Vertical Landing .... VTOVL
Vertical Tape Display (IAA) .... VTD
Vertical Technical Management Information System (MCD) .... VETMIS
Vertical Technology Insertion [*Business term Army*] (RDA) .... VTI
Vertical Temperature Profile [*or Profiling*] **Radiometer** .... VTPR
Vertical Test (SAA) .... VET
Vertical Test Facility [*NASA*] .... VTF
Vertical Test Fixture .... VTF
Vertical Test Flight (MCD) .... VTF
Vertical Test Range .... VTR
Vertical Test Site [*NASA*] (MCD) .... VTS
Vertical Test Stand [*NASA*] (KSC) .... VTS
Vertical Test System (NASA) .... VTS
Vertical the Army Authorization Document System .... VTAADS
Vertical Thrust Stand .... VTS
Vertical Track (GAVI) .... V/TRK
Vertical Track Distance (GAVI) .... VTK
Vertical Tracking Angle [*of a phonograph cartridge*] .... VTA
Vertical Tracking Force [*of a phonograph cartridge*] .... VTF
Vertical Transport and Exchange [*Oceanographic research program*] .... VERTEX
Vertical Trash Compactor (DWSG) .... VTC
Vertical Triple-Expansion [*Engine*] (DNAB) VERT-3-EXP
Vertical Tube Effects [*Desalination*] .... VTE
Vertical Tube Evaporation [*Desalination*] .... VTE
Vertical Tube Foam Evaporation [*Chemical engineering*] .... VTFE
Vertical Turbine Pump Association [*Defunct*] .... VTPA
Vertical Turret Lathe .... VTL
Vertical Unit Displacement [*Military*] (INF) .... VUD

Vertical Upward Force .... VUF
Vertical Velocity .... V/V
Vertical Velocity Console VVC
Vertical Velocity Indicator (MCD) VVI
Vertical Vertex Error (OA) .... VVE
Vertical Visibility [*Aviation*] (DA) .... VERVIS
Vertical Visibility (DA) VV
Vertical Volute Spring Suspension [*Technical drawings*] .... VVSS
Vertical Weld Head .... VWH
Vertical Weld Head Assembly .... VWHA
Vertical Wire Sky Screen (KSC) .... VWSS
Vertical-Blank [*Computer science*] (BYTE) .... VBL
Vertical-Cargo Integration Test Equipment [*NASA*] (MCD) .... V-CITE
Vertical-Cavity Surface Emitting LASER .... VCSEL
Vertical-Launched Antisubmarine Rocket (MCD) .... VLA
Vertical-Lift Airfield for Tactical Support (NVT) .... VATS
Vertical-Longitudinal Redundancy Check [*Electronics*] (ECII) .... VRC-LRC
Vertical-Looking RADAR .... VLR
Vertically Anchored Tire .... VAT
Vertically Integrated Liquid [*Marine science*] (OSRA) VIL
Vertically Integrated Liquid (USDC) VIL
Vertically Integrated Team [*Engineering*] .... VIT
Vertically Moored Platform [*Offshore drilling*] .... VMP
Vertically Polarized Dipole (MCD) .... VPD
Vertically Polarized Wave .... VPW
Vertically Referenced Attitude Display .... VRAD
Verticillium Wilt [*Plant pathology*] V
Verticillium Wilt, Fusarium Wilt, Nematode Resistance [*Tomato culture*] .... VFN
Verticilliuum albo-atrium [*A fungus*] .... VAA
Vertigo (WDAA) .... VERT
Vertolet Zhpa [*Ukraine*] [*FAA designator*] (FAAC) .... VTT
Vertrau Schau Wem [*Trust, but Be Careful Whom*] [*Motto of Johann Georg, Duke of Wohlau (1552-92)*] [*German*] .... VSW
Verturi Mask [*Medicine*] (MEDA) .... VM
Verumontanum [*Anatomy*] (DAVI) .... veru
Vervet [*African green monkey*] [*Medicine*] (DMAA) .... Verc
Vervet [*African green monkey*] [*Medicine*] (DMAA) .... VK
Verwaltungsamt fuer Wirtschaft [*Executive Committee for Economics*] [*Germany*] .... VFW
Verwaltungsgericht [*Administrative Court or Tribunal*] [*German*] (ILCA) .... VerwG
Verwaltungslexikon [*Administration Dictionary*] [*NOMOS Datapool*] [*Information service or system*] .... VLON
Very V
Very (WDMC) v
Very [*Automotive advertising*] .... VRY
Very (ROG) .... VY
Very Advanced Technology Light Twin (MCD) .... VATLIT
Very Big Accelerator (PDAA) .... VBA
Very Close in Defense .... VCID
Very Close-Up [*Cinematography*] (NTCM) .... VCU
Very Dear Brother [*Freemasonry*] .... VDB
Very Deep Water .... VDW
Very Difficult to Test [*Audiology*] .... VDTT
Very Early Smoke Detection Alarm .... VESDA
Very Early Warning System .... VEWS
Very Easy Rodent-Oriented Net-Wide Index of Computerized Archives .... VERONICA
Very Extreme Ultraviolet (MCD) .... VEU
Very Extreme Ultraviolet (MCD) .... VEUV
Very Fair .... VF
Very Fast Death Factor .... VFDF
Very Fast Train (EERA) .... VFT
Very Fine [*Condition*] [*Antiquarian book trade, numismatics, etc.*] .... VF
Very Fine Cognac .... VFC
Very Fine Soil [*Agronomy*] .... VF
Very General Algorithm (KSC) .... VGA
Very God-Damned Important Person .... VGDIP
Very Good [*Condition*] [*Antiquarian book trade, numismatics, etc.*] .... VG
Very Good Condition [*Doll collecting*] .... VGC
Very Good Condition (ODBW) .... vgc
Very Good Health [*Medicine*] .... VGH
Very Hard (IAA) .... VH
Very Heavy [*Cosmic ray nuclei*] .... VH
Very Heavy Bombardment [*Air Force*] .... VHB
Very Heavy Lift Helicopter .... VHLH
Very High .... VH
Very High Accuracy (NITA) .... VHA
Very High Achievement [*Tertiary entrance*] .... VHA
Very High Altitude .... VHA
Very High Altitude Abort [*NASA*] (KSC) .... VHAA
Very High Aluminum [*Rock composition*] .... VHA
Very High Bond Tape [*3M Co.*] .... VHB
Very High Burning Rate (MCD) .... VHBR
Very High Contrast [*Liquid crystal display*] .... VHC
Very High Current Configuration [*Magnetic field*] .... VHCC
Very High Density [*Computer science*] (CDE) .... VHD
Very High Dollar Value .... VHDV
Very High Frequency [*Also, VHF*] (DOAD) V
Very High Frequency Omnidirectional Radio Range [*FAA*] (TAG) .... VOR/VORTAC
Very High Output .... VHO
Very High Performance .... VHP
Very High Performance Computing and Communication [*Marine science*] (OSRA) .... VHPCC
Very High Performance Computing and Communication (USDC) .... VHPCC
Very High Polarization [*Raw sugar grade*] .... VHP

Very High Pressure ... VHP
Very High Reduction (NITA) ... VHR
Very High Resistance (IDOE) ... VHR
Very High Resolution Radiometer [NASA] ... VHRR
Very High Speed [Copier] ... VHS
Very High Speed Backbone Network System [Computer science] ... vBNS
Very High Speed Data (LAIN) ... VHSD
Very High Speed Radial Tire [Automotive engineering] ... VR
Very High Viscosity Index [Petroleum oils] ... VHVI
Very Highly Commended ... VHC
Very Important Cargo [Shipping] ... VIC
Very Important Contributors [Political] ... VIC
Very Important Customer ... VIC
Very Important Ladies ... VIL
Very Important Launch (MUGU) ... VIL
Very Important Object (DCTA) ... VIO
Very Important Passenger ... VIP
Very Important Patient (MAE) ... VIP
Very Important Person ... VIP
Very Important Person Indeed ... VIPI
Very Important Poor ... VIP
Very Important Pregnancy [In book title, "VIP Program"] ... VIP
Very Important Small Institution Travel Support ... VISITS
Very Important Traveler ... VIT
Very Informal Newsletter (NITA) ... VINE
Very Intelligent Surveillance and Target Acquisition [Army] (RDA) ... VISTA
Very Intelligent Terminal (IAA) ... VIT
Very Intense Neutron Source [Nuclear science] (OA) ... VINS
Very Large Airplane (PDAA) ... VLA
Very Large Antenna [Telecommunications] (IAA) ... VLA
Very Large Array [Radioscope] ... VLA
Very Large Array Telescope [NASA] ... VLAT
Very Large Bulk-Cargo Carrier (PDAA) ... VLBC
Very Large Cargo [or Crude] Carrier [Oil tanker] ... VLCC
Very Large Computerized Branch Exchange [Computer science] (MHDB) ... VLCBX
Very Large Floating Structure [Oceanography] ... VLFS
Very Large Herbivores ... VLH
Very Large Knowledge Base [Computer science] ... VLKB
Very Large Ore-Oil Carrier (PDAA) ... VLOOC
Very Large Scale Integrated Device (SSD) ... VLSID
Very Large Telescope [Proposed] [European Southern Observatory] ... VLT
Very Late Activation Antigen [Immunology] ... VLA
Very Lightly Hinged [Philately] ... VLH
Very Long Baseline ... VLB
Very Long Baseline Array ... VLBA
Very Long Baseline Interferometer [or Interferometry] ... VLBI
Very Long Baseline Interferometry [Used in a space orbiting project] ... VSOP
Very Long Endurance Acoustic Submarine Simulator ... VLEASS
Very Long Endurance Aircraft (PDAA) ... VLEA
Very Long Instruction Word [Computer architecture] [Multiflow Computer, Inc.] ... VLIW
Very Long Linear Collider [Proposed] [Former USSR] ... VLLC
Very Long Period Experiment [Geophysics] ... VLPE
Very Long Range ... VLR
Very Long Shot [A photograph or motion picture sequence taken from a considerable distance] ... VLS
Very Long-Burning Target Indicator [British military] (DMA) ... VLBTI
Very Long-Period Displacement [Volcanology] ... VLPD
Very Low Altitude ... VLA
Very Low Birth Rate ... VLBR
Very Low Birth Weight [Medicine] ... VLBW
Very Low Density [Biochemistry] (DAVI) ... VLD
Very Low Flow ... VLF
Very Low Nitrogen [Fuel technology] ... VLN
Very Low Pressure Pyrolysis ... VLPP
Very Low Range ... VLR
Very Low Resistance (IDOE) ... VLR
Very Low Speed ... VLS
Very Low Surface Brightness [Optics] ... VLSB
Very Low Titanium [Geology] ... VLT
Very Low-Level Waste (BARN) ... VLLW
Very Many Takeoffs and Landings (MCD) ... VMTOL
Very Many Thanks ... VMT
Very Massive Object [Astronomy] ... VMO
Very Narrow Aisle Truck (PDAA) ... VNA
Very North Shore [Women's Wear Daily] ... VNS
Very Old [Wines and spirits] ... VO
Very Old Pale [Designation on brandy labels] ... VOP
Very Old Scotch Whisky ... VOSW
Very Old Tawny [Wines and spirits] ... VOT
Very Old Version ... VOV
Very Promotable Item (WDMC) ... VPI
Very Public Person ... VPP
Very Quick [Flashing] Light [Navigation signal] ... VQ
Very Rare [Numismatics] ... RR
Very Reliable Product (AAMN) ... VRP
Very Respectfully [Letter closing] ... VR
Very Reverend ... V Rev
Very Serious List [Hospital administration] (DAVI) ... VSL
Very Seriously Ill [Army] (AABC) ... VSI
Very Severe Aplastic Anemia [Hematology] ... vSAA
Very Shallow Water (DOMA) ... VSW
Very Short Range (IDOE) ... vsr
Very Short Range ... VSR

Very Short Run [Printing technology] ... VSR
Very Short Time Constant (MCD) ... VSTC
Very Short Wave ... VSW
Very Short-Term Financing (MHDB) ... VSTF
Very Slightly Soluble ... VSLS
Very Small Aperture Terminal [Telecommunications] (TSSD) ... VSAT
Very Small Business System ... VSBS
Very Small Inclusions [Diamond clarity grade] ... VS
Very Small Local Exchange [Telecommunications] (TEL) ... VSLE
Very Small Quantity Generator [Environmental science] ... VSQG
Very Small Truck (DICI) ... VST
Very Soft (IAA) ... VS
Very Soluble ... VS
Very Special [Age of the Cognac] ... VS
Very Special Arts (EA) ... VSA
Very Special Old ... VSO
Very Special Quality ... VSQ
Very Special Reserve (ADA) ... VSR
Very Stable Oscillator ... VSO
Very Strong [Spectral] ... VS
Very Superior ... VS
Very Superior Extra Pale [Designation on brandy labels] (WGA) ... VSEP
Very Superior Old [Designation on brandy labels] ... VSO
Very Superior Old Pale [Designation on brandy labels. Facetious French translation is "Versez sans Oublier Personne," or "Pour without Forgetting Anyone"] ... VSOP
Very Susceptible [Plant pathology] ... VS
Very Ultraviolet (SSD) ... VUV
Very Urgent ... VU
Very Very Heavy [Cosmic ray nuclei] ... VVH
Very, Very Important Person ... VVIP
Very Very Old [Designation on brandy labels] ... VVO
Very Very Slightly Flawed [Gems] ... VVS
Very, Very Small Inclusions [Diamond clarity grade] ... VVS
Very Very Superior ... VVS
Very, Very Superior Old [Designation on brandy labels] ... VVSO
Very, Very Superior Old Pale [Designation on brandy labels] ... VVSOP
Very Virulent Marek Disease Virus [Medicine] (DMAA) ... vvMDV
Very Weak [Spectral] ... VW
Very Wide Area Mine (RDA) ... VWAM
Very Worshipful ... VW
Very-High Density Lipoprotein [Biochemistry] ... VHDL
Very-High Energy ... VHE
Very-High Frequency Radio Telephony (PDAA) ... VHFRT
Very-High Molecular Weight Polyethylene (PDAA) ... VHMWPE
Very-High Performance Integrated Circuit [Electronics] (PDAA) ... VHPIC
Very-High Voltage (IAA) ... VHV
Very-High-Frequency [Electronics] ... VHF
Very-High-Frequency, Amplitude Modulated (NASA) ... VHF/AM
Very-High-Frequency Direction-Finding ... VDF
Very-High-Frequency Direction-Finding ... VHF/DF
Very-High-Frequency Filter ... VHFF
Very-High-Frequency, Frequency Modulated (NOAA) ... VHF-FM
Very-High-Frequency Generator ... VHFG
Very-High-Frequency Indeed [Ultrahigh frequency] [British] ... VHFI
Very-High-Frequency Jammer ... VHFJ
Very-High-Frequency Omnidirectional Range ... VOR
Very-High-Frequency Omnirange (AFM) ... VHFOR
Very-High-Frequency Omnirange (IDOE) ... VOR
Very-High-Frequency Oscillator ... VHFO
Very-High-Frequency Receiver ... VHFR
Very-High-Frequency Termination ... VHFT
Very-High-Level Language ... VHLL
Very-High-Highly Repeated [Genetics] ... VHR
Very-High-Order Language ... VHOL
Very-High-Resistance Voltmeter (IDOE) ... VHRVM
Very-High-Speed Black and White [Photography] ... VHBW
Very-High-Speed Integrated [Electronics] ... VHSI
Very-High-Speed Integrated Circuit [Electronics] ... VHSIC
Very-High-Speed Optic Cable ... VHSOC
Very-High-Speed Transit ... VHST
Very-High-Temperature Reactor [Nuclear energy] ... VHTR
Very-Large Data Base (ADA) ... VLDB
Very-Large Data Base System ... VLDBS
Very-Large Low-Velocity Anomaly [Seismology] ... VLVA
Very-Large-Scale Immobilized Polymer Synthesis [Affymax Research Institute] [Organic chemistry] ... VLSIPS
Very-Large-Scale Integrated Circuit [Electronics] ... VLSIC
Very-Large-Scale Integration [of circuits] [Electronics] ... VLSI
Very-Lighweight Air Traffic Management Equipment (MCD) ... VLATME
Very-Long Delay Fuze [Military] (CAAL) ... VLDF
Very-Long-Chain Saturated Fatty Acid [Organic chemistry] ... VLCFA
Very-Long-Range Tracking [NASA] ... VERLORT
Very-Long-Range Tracking [NASA] (DNAB) ... VERLOT
Very-Low Fluence [Physics] ... VLF
Very-Low Impedance (IAA) ... VLI
Very-Low Inertia ... VLI
Very-Low Volume ... VLV
Very-Low-Calorie Diet ... VLCD
Very-Low-Cost Display (IAA) ... VLCD
Very-Low-Cost Harassment Vehicle (MCD) ... VLCHV
Very-Low-Density Lipoprotein [Biochemistry] ... VLDL
Very-Low-Density Lipoprotein [Biochemistry] (DAVI) ... VLDLP
Very-Low-Density Lipoprotein Triglyceride [Biochemistry] (AAMN) ... VLD-TG
Very-Low-Frequency [Electronics] ... VLF

Very-Low-Frequency Direct [*Electronics*] (IAA) ... VLFD
Very-Low-Frequency Jammer [*Electronics*] ... VLFJ
Very-Low-Frequency Receiver [*Electronics*] ... VLFR
Very-Quick Flashing Light ... V Qk Fl
Very-Short-Range Air Defense Weapon System (MCD) ... VSRADS
Very-Short-Range Air Defense Weapon System (NATG) ... VSRADWS
Very-Short-Range Ballistic Missile ... VSRBM
Very-Short-Range Ground Surveillance RADAR (MCD) ... VSRGSR
Very-Wide-Field Camera ... VWFC
Verzeichnis Lieferbarer Buecher [*List of Deliverable Books, i.e., books in print*] [*Germany*] ... VLB
VESA [*Video Electronics Standards Association*] **Advanced Feature Connector** ... VAFC
VESA [*Video Electronics Standards Association*] **BIOS Extension/Audio Interface** [*Basic Input-Output System*] (PCM) ... VBE/AI
VESA [*Video Electronics Standards Association*] **Local Bus** (PCM) ... VLB
VESA [*Video Electronics Standards Association*] **Media Channel** (PCM) ... VMC
Vesalius Trust (EA) ... VT
Veseco Vaginal Fistula [*Medicine*] ... VVF
Vesey and Beames' English Chancery Reports [*35 English Reprint*] [*A publication*] (DLA) ... V & B
Vesey and Beames' English Chancery Reports [*35 English Reprint*] [*A publication*] (DLA) ... Ve & B
Vesey and Beames' English Chancery Reports [*35 English Reprint*] [*A publication*] (DLA) ... Ves & B
Vesey and Beames' English Chancery Reports [*35 English Reprint*] [*A publication*] (DLA) ... Ves & B (Eng)
Vesey and Beames' English Chancery Reports [*35 English Reprint*] [*A publication*] (DLA) ... Ves & Bea
Vesey and Beames' English Chancery Reports [*35 English Reprint*] [*A publication*] (DLA) ... Ves & Beam
Vesey, Junior's, English Chancery Reports [*30-34 English Reprint*] [*A publication*] (DLA) ... Ves Jr
Vesey, Junior's, English Chancery Reports [*30-34 English Reprint*] [*A publication*] (DLA) ... Ves Jr (Eng)
Vesey, Junior's, English Chancery Reports [*30-34 English Reprint*] [*A publication*] (DLA) ... Ves Jun
Vesey, Junior's, English Chancery Reports, Edited by Ingraham [*A publication*] (ILCA) ... Ing Ves
Vesey, Senior's, English Chancery Reports [*27, 28 English Reprint*] [*A publication*] (ILCA) ... Ve
Vesey, Senior's, English Chancery Reports [*27, 28 English Reprint*] [*A publication*] (DLA) ... Ves
Vesey, Senior's, English Chancery Reports [*27, 28 English Reprint*] [*A publication*] (DLA) ... Ves Sen
Vesey, Senior's, English Chancery Reports [*27, 28 English Reprint*] [*A publication*] (DLA) ... Ves Sr
Vesey, Senior's, English Chancery Reports [*27, 28 English Reprint*] [*A publication*] (DLA) ... Ves Sr (Eng)
Vesica [*Bladder*] [*Latin*] (ADA) ... VES
Vesica Urinaria [*Urinary Bladder*] ... VES UR
Vesicle Attachment Sites [*Neurology*] ... VAS
Vesicle-Associated Membrane Protein [*Biochemistry*] ... VAMP
Vesicoureteral Reflex [*Nephrology*] ... VUR
Vesicoureteral Regurgitation [*Nephrology*] (MEDA) ... VUR
Vesicoureterogram [*Urology*] ... VCUG
Vesicovaginal [*Gynecology*] (DAVI) ... VV
Vesicovaginal Fistula Repair [*Gynecology*] (DAVI) ... VVFR
Vesicula [*Blister*] [*Latin*] (ADA) ... VES
Vesicula [*Blister*] [*Latin*] ... Vesic
Vesicular (AAMN) ... VES
Vesicular ... vesic
Vesicular Arbuscular Mycorrhizae [*Botany*] ... VAM
Vesicular Exanthema [*Virus*] ... VE
Vesicular Exanthema Swine Virus ... VESV
Vesicular Sound [*in auscultation of chest*] [*Medicine*] ... VS
Vesicular Stomatitis [*Also, VSV*] [*Virus*] ... VS
Vesicular Stomatitis Virus [*Also, VS*] ... VSV
Vesicular Stomatitis Virus Glycoprotein [*Biochemistry*] ... VSVG
Vesicular-Arbuscular [*Mycorrhiza*] [*Botany*] ... VA
Vesivehmaa [*Finland ICAO location identifier*] (ICLI) ... EFLA
Vesoul-Frotey [*France ICAO location identifier*] (ICLI) ... LFQW
Vespa Club of America (EA) ... VCA
Vespae [*Wasps*] [*of Aristophanes*] [*Classical studies*] (OCD) ... Vesp
Vespasian Warner Public Library, Clinton, IL [*Library symbol*] [*Library of Congress*] (LCLS) ... ICIP
Vespasian Warner Public Library, Clinton, IL [*Library symbol Library of Congress*] (LCLS) ... ICI
Vesper [*Evening*] [*Pharmacy*] ... VESP
Vespere [*In the Evening*] [*Latin*] (ADA) ... VES
Vespers ... V
Vess, Henry, Kansas City MO [*STAC*] ... VHY
Vessel (AABC) ... VES
Vessel (VRA) ... ves
Vessel Delivered in Partially-Completed Status [*Navy*] (DNAB) ... PR/COM
Vessel Leased to Brazil [*Navy*] ... LEA/BZ
Vessel Leased to China [*Navy*] ... LEA/CH
Vessel Leased to Ecuador [*Navy*] ... LEA/EC
Vessel Leased to France [*Navy*] ... LEA/FR
Vessel Leased to Greece [*Navy*] ... LEA/GR
Vessel Leased to Mexico [*Navy*] ... LEA/MX
Vessel Leased to Netherlands [*Navy*] ... LEA/NE
Vessel Leased to Norway [*Navy*] ... LEA/NO
Vessel Leased to Panama [*Navy*] ... LEA/PA
Vessel Leased to Paraguay [*Navy*] ... LEA/PG
Vessel Leased to Peru [*Navy*] ... LEA/PE
Vessel Leased to Russia [*Navy*] ... LEA/RU
Vessel Leased to United Kingdom [*Navy*] ... LEA/UK
Vessel Leased to Uruguay [*Navy*] ... LEA/UR
Vessel Movement Reporting System ... VMRS
Vessel of Opportunity [*Marine science*] (OSRA) ... VOS
Vessel Off-Gas [*Nuclear energy*] (NRCH) ... VOG
Vessel Ordnance Allowance List ... VOCAL
Vessel Patentcy Index [*Medicine*] ... VPI
Vessel Radiated Noise ... VRN
Vessel (Reactor) Steam Explosion [*Nuclear energy*] (IEEE) ... VSE
Vessel Support System (MCD) ... VSS
Vessel Traffic Management System (DS) ... VTMS
Vessel Traffic Service [*Harbor RADAR system*] [*Coast Guard*] ... VTS
Vessel Wall ... VW
Vessels and Cargo ... VESCA(S)
Vessels Disposed of by Sale through Navy Material Redistribution Agency [*Navy*] ... DI/SAL
Vessels Disposed of by Scrapping [*Navy*] ... DI/SCP
Vessels Disposed of by Sinking, Burning, Abandoning, or Other Means of Destruction [*Navy*] ... DI/DES
Vessels Disposed of by Using as Targets and Tests [*Navy*] ... DI/TES
Vessels in Forward Areas Transferred to State Department Foreign Liquidation Corporation [*Navy*] ... DI/FLC
Vessels Loaned to Army [*Navy*] ... LOAN/A
Vessels Loaned to Coast Guard [*Navy*] ... LOAN/C
Vessels Loaned to Miscellaneous Activities [*US Maritime Academy, etc.*] [*Navy*] ... LOAN/M
Vessels Loaned to States [*Navy*] ... LOAN/S
Vessels Loaned to War Shipping Administration [*Terminated, 1946*] [*Navy*] ... LOAN/W
Vessels Lost by Accident, Collision, or Similar Methods [*Navy*] ... LOST/A
Vessels Lost Due to Weather, Perils of the Sea, or Similar Reasons [*Navy*] ... LOST/P
Vessels Lost through Enemy Action [*Navy*] ... LOST/E
Vessels Transferred to Other Government Agencies and Miscellaneous Activities [*Navy*] ... DI/TRN
Vessels Transferred to War Shipping Administration - Maritime Commission for Disposition [*Navy*] ... DI/WSA
Vest [*H.D.*], Inc. [*NASDAQ symbol*] (SPSG) ... HDVS
Vest Individual Protective Reflective Adjustable [*System*] [*Military*] (INF) ... VIPRA
Vest Pocket ... VP
Vest Pocket Kodak [*Camera*] ... VPK
Vesta Airex [*Czechoslovakia*] [*ICAO designator*] (FAAC) ... VAX
Vesta Insurance Group [*Associated Press*] (SAG) ... VestaIns
Vesta Insurance Group [*NYSE symbol*] (SPSG) ... VTA
Vestaburg Public Library, Vestaburg, MI [*Library symbol Library of Congress*] (LCLS) ... MiVes
Vestal, NY [*FM radio station call letters*] ... WMXW
Vestal Public Library, Vestal, NY [*Library symbol Library of Congress*] (LCLS) ... NVe
Vestal Public Library, Vestal, NY [*Library symbol*] [*Library of Congress*] (LCLS) ... NVeL
Vestaur Securities [*NYSE symbol*] (TTSB) ... VES
Vestaur Securities, Inc. [*NYSE symbol*] (SPSG) ... VES
Vestaur Securities, Inc. [*Associated Press*] (SAG) ... VestSe
Vested Interest [*Business term*] (MHDW) ... VI
Vested Pension Plan (MHDB) ... VPP
Vested Right ... VR
Vesterheim Genealogical Center (EA) ... VGC
Vesthimmerland [*Denmark ICAO location identifier*] (ICLI) ... EKVH
Vestiarski Sisters (TOCD) ... VS
Vestibular [*Medicine*] (CPH) ... VEST
Vestibular Disorders Association (EA) ... VEDA
Vestibular Membrane [*Medicine*] ... VM
Vestibular Relay Neuron [*Neurology*] ... VRIV
Vestibule [*Classified advertising*] (ADA) ... VBULE
Vestibule (MSA) ... VEST
Vestibule (VRA) ... vstib
Vestibulo-Ocular Reflex [*Neurology*] ... VOR
Vestibulo-Ocular Reflex Suppression [*Ophthalmology*] ... VORS
Vestibuloocular Reflex with Fixation Light [*Ophthalmology*] ... VOR-FIX
Vestigial Sideband (NITA) ... VS
Vestigial Sideband [*Radio*] ... VSB
Vestigial Sideband - Amplitude Modulation ... VSB-AM
Vestigial Sideband Filter ... VSBF
Vestigial Sideband Filter ... VSF
Vestigial Sideband Modulation ... VSM
Vestigial Sideband Suppressed Carrier (NITA) ... VS-SC
Vestigial Testes [*Anatomy*] ... VET
Vestmannaeyjar [*Iceland*] [*ICAO location identifier*] (ICLI) ... BIVM
Vestmannaeyjar [*Iceland*] [*Airport symbol*] (OAG) ... VEY
Vestment (VRA) ... vstmt
Vestor Exploration [*Vancouver Stock Exchange symbol*] ... VRX
Vestra Reverendissima Paternitas [*Your Very Reverend Paternity*] [*Latin*] ... VRP
Vestre Landsret [*Western Court of Appeal*] [*Denmark*] (ILCA) ... VL
Vestro Foods, Inc. [*Associated Press*] (SAG) ... Vestro
Vestro Natural Foods [*NASDAQ symbol*] (TTSB) ... VEST
Vestro Natural Foods, Inc. [*NASDAQ symbol*] (NQ) ... VEST
Vestry [*Ecclesiastical*] (WGA) ... VES
Vestry [*Ecclesiastical*] (ROG) ... VEST
Veteran (AFM) ... VET
Veteran Air [*Ukraine*] [*FAA designator*] (FAAC) ... VPB
Veteran Air Pilots ... VAP

Veteran Car Club of Great Britain (BI) ... VCC
Veteran Corps of Artillery, State of New York, Constituting the Military Societyof the War of 1812 (EA) ... VCA
Veteran Motor Car Club of America (EA) ... VMCCA
Veteran Municipal Library, Alberta [*Library symbol National Library of Canada*] (NLC) ... AVM
Veteran Municipal Library, Veteran, AB, Canada [*Library symbol Library of Congress*] (LCLS) ... CaAVM
Veteran Vespa Club, US [*Defunct*] (EA) ... VVCUS
Veteran Wireless Operators Association (EA) ... VWOA
Veterana Esperantista Klubo [*Esperantist Club of Veterans - ECV*] (EAIO) ... VEK
Veterans Adjustment Scale (MEDA) ... VETS
Veterans Administration (TDOB) ... VA
Veterans Administration (WDAA) ... VET ADMIN
Veterans Administration Acquisition Regulation [*A publication*] (AAGC) ... VAAR
Veterans Administration Center ... VAC
Veterans Administration Construction Contract Appeals Board (AAGC) ... VACCAB
Veterans Administration Contract Appeals Board ... VACAB
Veterans Administration Cooperative Urological Research Group ... VACURG
Veterans Administration Hospital [*Later, VAMC*] ... VAH
Veterans Administration Hospital Representative [*Red Cross*] ... VAHR
Veterans Administration Libraries Online Resources ... VALOR
Veterans Administration Library Network [*Veterans Administration Washington, DC*] ... VALNET
Veterans Administration Matters [*FBI standardized term*] ... VAM
Veterans Administration Medical Center [*Formerly, VAH*] ... VAMC
Veterans Administration Nursing Home Care Program (GFGA) ... VANHC
Veterans Administration Office ... VAO
Veterans Administration Procurement [*or Purchase*] **Regulations** ... VAPR
Veterans Administration Prosthetics Center [*Later, VAREC*] ... VAPC
Veterans Administration Records Processing Center ... VARPC
Veterans Administration Regional Office (AFM) ... VARO
Veterans Administration Regulations ... VAR
Veterans Administration Rehabilitation Engineering Center [*Formerly, VAPC*] ... VAREC
Veterans Administration Schedule for Rating Disabilities (AABC) ... VASRD
Veterans Administration Seating Interface Orthosis for Paraplegics (DAVI) ... vasio-Para
Veterans Administration, Somerville, NJ [*OCLC symbol*] (OCLC) ... VET
Veterans Administration Surgical Oncology Group ... VASOG
Veterans Administration Voluntary Service ... VAVS
[*Department of*] **Veterans Affairs** ... VA
[*Department of*] **Veterans Affairs** (USGC) ... VA
Veterans Affairs Canada [*See also AACC*] ... VAC
Veterans Affairs, Canada [*Affaires des Anciens Combattants Canada*] **Charlottetown, Prince Edward Island** [*Library symbol National Library of Canada*] (NLC) ... PCV
Veterans Affairs Cooperative Study of Systemic Sepsis ... VACSSS
Veterans' Affairs Decisions, Appealed Pension and Civil Service Retirement Cases [*United States*] [*A publication*] (DLA) ... VAD
Veterans Affairs Learning Opportunities Residency Program ... VALOR
Veterans Affairs National Acquisition Center (AAGC) ... VANAC
Veterans Against Drugs ... VAD
Veterans Assistance Discharge System (MCD) ... VADS
Veteran's Association of the USS [*United States Ship*] **Iowa** (EA) ... VAUSSI
Veterans Bedside Network (EA) ... VBN
Veterans Benefit Counselor [*Veterans Administration*] (GFGA) ... VBC
Veterans Benefits Act, Public Law 345, 1944 ... GI (Bill)
Veterans Benefits Administration [*Department of Veterans Affairs*] ... VBA
Veterans Benefits Office ... VBO
Veterans Canteen Service [*Veterans Administration*] ... VCS
Veterans Canteen Service Field Office [*Veterans Administration*] ... VCSFO
Veterans Cost-of-Instruction ... VCOI
Veterans Cost-of-Instruction Program [*Higher Education Act*] ... VCIP
Veterans Council for American Rights and Equality (EA) ... VCARE
Veterans Cycle Racing Association [*British*] (DBA) ... VCRA
Veterans Division of the Non-Commissioned Officers Association of the USA (EA) ... VDNCOA
Veterans Education Outreach Program [*Department of Education*] (GFGA) ... VEOP
Veterans Education Project (EA) ... VEP
Veterans Educational Assistance [*Act*] ... VEA
Veterans Educational Assistance Program [*DoD*] ... VEAP
Veterans' Employment and Readjustment Act of 1972 ... VERA
Veterans' Employment and Training Service [*Department of Labor*] ... VETS
Veterans Employment Representative [*Department of Labor*] ... VER
Veterans Employment Service [*Later, VETS*] [*of USES*] ... VES
Veterans Federal Employment Representative [*Civil Service Commission*] ... VFER
Veterans for Peace (EA) ... VFP
Veterans Group Life Insurance ... VGLI
Veterans Health Care Act (AAGC) ... VHCA
Veterans Health Services and Research Administration [*Department of Veterans Affairs*] ... VHS & RA
Veterans Hospital ... VH
Veterans' Hospital Radio and Television Guild (EA) ... VHRTG
Veterans in Public Service Act ... VIPS
Veterans' Job Training Act ... VJTA
Veterans' Land Act [*Canada*] ... VLA
Veterans Memorial Medical Center ... VMMC
Veterans Memorial Public Library, Bismarck, ND [*OCLC symbol*] (OCLC) ... BPL
Veterans' Mortgage Indemnity Fund [*Department of Veterans Affairs*] ... VMIF
Veterans Mortgage Life Insurance ... VMLI
Veterans of Foreign Wars of the USA (EA) ... VFW
Veterans of Future Wars [*Facetious organization formed by Princeton students in 1930's*] ... VFW
Veterans of Pearl Harbor (EA) ... VPH
Veterans of Safety (EA) ... V of S
Veterans of Safety (EA) ... VOS
Veterans of the Abraham Lincoln Brigade (EA) ... VALB
Veterans of the Battle of the Bulge (EA) ... VBOB
Veterans of the US Posse Comitatus (EA) ... PC
Veterans of the Vietnam War (EA) ... VVnW
Veterans of Underage Military Service (EA) ... VUMS
Veterans of World War I of USA [*Defunct*] (EA) ... VWWI
Veterans Omnibus Health Care Act of 1976 ... VOHCA
Veterans Placement Service Board [*Post-World War II*] ... VPSB
Veterans Readjustment Appointment ... VRA
Veterans Readjustment Authority ... VRA
Veterans' Readjustment Benefits Act of 1966 (WYGK) ... VRBA
Veterans Reemployment Rights ... VRR
Veterans Reopened Insurance ... VRI
Veterans Special Life Insurance [*Veterans Administration*] ... VSLI
Veterans Time Trial Association [*Bicycling*] (DICI) ... VITA
Veterans Transition Franchise Initiative Program ... VETFR
Veterans Vigil of Honor (EA) ... VVH
Veteres Intrationes [*A publication*] (DLA) ... Vet Int
Veterinarian ... VETRN
Veterinary (AFM) ... VET
Veterinary ... VETRNRY
Veterinary Admissions Test (BARN) ... VAT
Veterinary and Remount Conducting Section [*British military*] (DMA) ... VRCS
Veterinary and Remount Service [*British military*] ... VR
Veterinary and Remount Service [*British military*] (DMA) ... VRS
Veterinary Aptitude Test ... VAT
Veterinary Assistant Surgeon [*British military*] (DMA) ... VAS
Veterinary Board [*Tasmania, Australia*] ... VB
Veterinary Board of Tasmania [*Australia*] ... VBT
Veterinary Board of Victoria [*Australia*] ... VBV
Veterinary Bulletin [*Database*] [*Commonwealth Bureau of Animal Health*] [*Information service or system*] (CRD) ... VB
Veterinary Cancer Society (EA) ... VCS
Veterinary Centers of America [*NASDAQ symbol*] (SAG) ... VCAI
Veterinary Centers of America, Inc. [*Associated Press*] (SAG) ... VetAm
Veterinary Centers of America, Inc. [*Associated Press*] (SAG) ... VetCtAm
Veterinary Collecting Post [*British military*] (DMA) ... VCP
Veterinary College Admission Test (PGP) ... VCAT
Veterinary Convalescent Hospital ... VCH
Veterinary Corps [*Military*] ... VC
Veterinary Creolin-Pearson ... VCP
Veterinary Ctrs of Amer [*NASDAQ symbol*] (TTSB) ... VCAI
Veterinary Documentation (NITA) ... VETDOC
Veterinary Evacuating Station [*British military*] (DMA) ... VES
Veterinary Evacuation Hospital ... VEH
Veterinary General Hospital ... VGH
Veterinary Hospital of the University of Pennsylvania ... VHUP
Veterinary Infectious Disease Organization [*University of Saskatchewan*] [*Canada Research center*] (RCD) ... VIDO
Veterinary Inspector (ADA) ... VI
Veterinary Investigation Centre [*Ministry of Agriculture, Fisheries, and Food*] [*British*] ... VIC
Veterinary Investigation Officer [*Ministry of Agriculture, Fisheries, and Food*] [*British*] ... VIO
Veterinary Investigation Service [*Ministry of Agriculture, Fisheries, and Food*] [*British*] ... VIS
Veterinary Laboratory, Alberta Agriculture, Fairview, Alberta [*Library symbol National Library of Canada*] (NLC) ... AFAAV
Veterinary Literature Documentation [*Derwent Publications Ltd.*] [*Bibliographic database London, England*] ... VETDOC
Veterinary Manufacturers' and Distributors' Association [*Australia*] ... VMDA
Veterinary Medical Association of Ireland (BI) ... VMAI
Veterinary Medical Data Program [*Association of Veterinary Medical Data Program Participants*] [*Information service or system*] (IID) ... VMDP
Veterinary Medical Libraries Section/Medical Library Association (EA) ... VMLS/MLA
Veterinary Medical Research Institute [*Iowa State University*] [*Research center*] (RCD) ... VMRI
Veterinary Medical Teaching Hospital [*University of California, Davis*] ... VMTH
Veterinary Medicine (DAVI) ... Vet Med
Veterinary Medicine Aptitude Test (GAGS) ... VMAT
Veterinary Medicine, Optometry, Podiatry, and Pharmacy [*HEW program*] ... VOPP
Veterinary Medicines Board [*Tasmania, Australia*] ... VMB
Veterinary Nurses' Association [*Australia*] ... VNA
Veterinary Officer [*British*] ... VO
Veterinary Orthopaedic Society (EA) ... VOS
Veterinary Products Committee [*British*] ... VPC
Veterinary Research Laboratory [*Montana State University*] [*Research center*] ... VRL
Veterinary Research Officer [*British*] ... VRO
Veterinary Science ... VetSci
Veterinary Specialists' Qualification Committee [*Victoria, Australia*] ... VSQC
Veterinary Surgeon ... VS
Veterinary Surgeons' Board of New South Wales [*Australia*] ... VSBNSW
Veterinary Surgeons' Board of Queensland [*Australia*] ... VSBQ
Veterinary Surgeons' Board of South Australia ... VSBSA
Veterinary Surgeons' Board of the Northern Territory [*Australia*] ... VSBNT
Veterinary Surgeons' Disciplinary Tribunal [*New South Wales, Australia*] ... VSDT

Veterinary Surgeon's Investigation Committee [*New South Wales, Australia*] ... VSIC
Veterinary Toxicology and Entomology Research Laboratory [*Department of Agriculture*] [*College Station, TX*] (GRD) ... VTERL
Veterinary Virus Research Institute [*New York State Veterinary College*] ... VVRI
Veto (OICC) ... V
Veto Resources Ltd. [*Vancouver Stock Exchange symbol*] ... VTR
VETRONICS [*Vehicle Electronics*] **Simulation Facility** [*Army*] (RDA) ... VSF
Vetus Itala (BJA) ... it
Vetus Natura Brevium [*A publication*] (DSA) ... V N B
Vetus Natura Brevium [*A publication*] (DSA) ... Vet N B
Vetus Testamentum [*Old Testament*] [*of the Bible*] [*Latin*] ... VT
Veut Dieu Saint Amour [*Knights Templar*] [*Freemasonry*] ... VDSA
Veuve [*Widow*] [*French*] (ROG) ... VE
Vevay, IN [*FM radio station call letters*] ... WKID
Vevay Reville-Enterprise, Vevay, IN [*Library symbol Library of Congress*] (LCLS) ... InVeRE
Vezey's [*or Vesey's*] **English Chancery Reports** [*A publication*] (DLA) ... Vez
VF Corp. [*Associated Press*] (SAG) ... VF Cp
VF Corp. [*NYSE symbol*] (SPSG) ... VFC
VF RADAR Intercept Officer (DNAB) ... VFI
VFW [*Vereinigte Flugtechnische Werke*]**-Fokker** [*Germany ICAO aircraft manufacturer identifier*] (ICAO) ... VF
VGM Capital Corp. [*Formerly, Vestgron Mines Ltd.*] [*Toronto Stock Exchange symbol*] ... VGM
V-Groove Metal-Oxide Semiconductor (MCD) ... VMOS
V-Groove on One Side [*Lumber*] ... KJS
V-Groove on Two Sides [*Lumber*] ... V2S
VHF [*Very-High-Frequency*] **Aural Omnirange** ... VAOR
VHF Digital Link [*FAA*] (TAG) ... VDL
VHF [*Very-High-Frequency*] **Omnidirectional Radio Beacon and Air Traffic Communications Station** (SAA) ... VOR/ATCS
VHF [*Very-High-Frequency*] **Omnidirectional Range and Distance Measuring Equipmentfor Average Coverage** (IAA) ... VORDAC
VHF [*Very-High-Frequency*] **Omnidirectional Range Collocated with TACAN** [*Tactical Air Navigation System*] (IAA) ... VORTAC
VHF [*Very-High-Frequency*] **Omnidirectional Range/Distance-Measuring Equipment** (CET) ... VORDME
VHF [*Very-High-Frequency*] **Omnidirectional Range/Distance-Measuring Equipment Compatible with TACAN** ... VOR/DMET
VHF [*Very-High-Frequency*] **Omnidirectional Range/Distance-Measuring for AirCoverage** ... VORDAC
VHF [*Very-High-Frequency*] **Omnidirectional Range Tactical Air Navigation** (IAA) ... VORTAC
VHF [*Very-High-Frequency*] **Omnirange Localizer** (CET) ... VORLOC
VHF [*Very-High-Frequency*] **Omnirange TACAN** ... VORTAC
VHF [*Very-High-Frequency*] **Omnitest** ... VOT
VHF [*Very-High-Frequency*] **Recovery Beacon** [*NASA*] (KSC) ... VRB
VHSIC [*Very-High-Speed Integrated Circuit*] **Hardware Description Language** [*Computer science*] ... VHDL
Via [*By Way Of*] [*Latin*] (ADA) ... V
Via Flight Planned Route [*Aviation*] (FAAC) ... VFPR
Via Low Frequency Direct [*Aviation*] (FAAC) ... VLFD
Via Net Loss [*Telecommunications*] ... VNL
Via Net Loss Factor (TEL) ... VNLF
Via Omni Direct [*Aviation*] (FAAC) ... VOD
Viable Birth [*Medicine*] ... VB
Viable but Not Culturable [*Microbiology*] ... VBNC
Viable Terrestrial Organism ... VTO
Viable Titanium Composite ... VTC
Viable Titanium Matrix Composite ... VTMC
Viacao Aerea Rio-Grandense SA [*Brazil*] [*ICAO designator*] (FAAC) ... VRG
Viacao Aerea Sao Paulo SA [*Airline*] [*Brazil*] ... VASP
Viacao Aerea Sao Paulo SA [*Brazil*] [*ICAO designator*] (FAAC) ... VSP
Viacom Inc Cl'A' [*AMEX symbol*] (TTSB) ... VIA
Viacom, Inc. [*AMEX symbol*] (SPSG) ... VIA
Viacom, Inc. [*Associated Press*] (SAG) ... Viac
Viacom, Inc. [*Associated Press*] (SAG) ... ViacB
Viacom, Inc. [*Associated Press*] (SAG) ... Viacom
Viacom Inc.'97 Wrrt [*AMEX symbol*] (TTSB) ... VIA WS.C
Viacom Inc.'99 Wrrt [*AMEX symbol*] (TTSB) ... VIA WIS.E
Viacom Inc. Cl'B' [*AMEX symbol*] (TTSB) ... VIA.B
Viaduct [*Commonly used*] (OPSA) ... VDCT
Viaduct ... VIA
Viaduct ... VIA
Viaduct [*Commonly used*] (OPSA) ... VIADCT
Viaduct [*Commonly used*] (OPSA) ... VIADUCT
Viajes Internacionales de Vacaciones SA [*Spain ICAO designator*] (FAAC) ... VIV
Viajes Internacionales de Vacaciones SA [*Spain ICAO designator*] (FAAC) ... VIVA
Vial ... VI
Viane Francaise [*French Meat*] ... VF
Vias Aereas Manabitas CIA Ltds. [*Ecuador*] [*FAA designator*] (FAAC) ... MBT
VIASA, Venezolana International de Aviacion SA [*Venezuela*] [*ICAO designator*] (FAAC) ... VIA
ViaSat, Inc. [*Associated Press*] (SAG) ... ViaSat
ViaSat, Inc. [*NASDAQ symbol*] (SAG) ... VSAT
Viasoft, Inc. [*NASDAQ symbol*] (SAG) ... VIAS
Viasoft, Inc. [*Associated Press*] (SAG) ... Viasoft
Viatel, Inc. [*Associated Press*] (SAG) ... Viatel
Viatel, Inc. [*NASDAQ symbol*] (SAG) ... VYTL
Vibo Valentia [*Italy ICAO location identifier*] (ICLI) ... LIBJ
Viborg [*Denmark ICAO location identifier*] (ICLI) ... EKVB
Vibraphone [*Music*] ... VIB
Vibrate (AAG) ... VIB
Vibrated Fluid Bed [*Chemical engineering*] ... VBF
Vibrating (AAG) ... VIBG
Vibrating Bag Unloader ... VBU
Vibrating Beam Accelerometer [*Inertial sensor*] (IEEE) ... VBA
Vibrating Coil Magnetometer ... VCM
Vibrating Dropping Mercury Electrode [*Electrochemistry*] ... VDME
Vibrating Head Magnetometer (IAA) ... VHM
Vibrating Plate Extractor [*Chemical engineering*] ... VBE
Vibrating Reed Capacitor ... VRC
Vibrating Reed Electrometer ... VRE
Vibrating Reed Relay ... VRR
Vibrating Sample Magnetometer ... VSM
Vibrating Screen Manufacturers Association (EA) ... VSMA
Vibrating String Accelerometer ... VSA
Vibrating Structure Gyroscope ... VSG
Vibrating Tie Under-Cutter (PDAA) ... VTU
Vibrating Wire Gauge (WDAA) ... VWG
Vibrating Wire Rate Sensor ... VWRS
Vibration (AAG) ... VB
Vibration (AAG) ... VIBN
Vibration ... VIBR
Vibration Acceptance Test ... VAT
Vibration Analysis and Detection Concept (DNAB) ... VIDEC
Vibration Analysis System ... VAS
Vibration Analysis Test Set (DWSG) ... VATS
Vibration and Acoustic Test Facility (NASA) ... VATF
Vibration and Acoustic Testing (IAA) ... VAAT
Vibration and Noise Tester (SAA) ... VANT
Vibration Conditioning Monitoring (ACII) ... VCM
Vibration Control Index ... VCI
Vibration Damping Fastener ... VDF
Vibration Damping Mount ... VDM
Vibration Data Accuracy Program ... VIDAP
Vibration Data Acquisition System (KSC) ... VDAS
Vibration Diagnostic Program ... VDP
Vibration Eliminator (OA) ... VE
Vibration Exciter Control ... VEC
Vibration Greatness ... VG
Vibration Indicator Early Warning System (MCD) ... VIEWS
Vibration Institute (EA) ... VI
Vibration Isolation Equipment (RDA) ... VIE
Vibration Isolation Module ... VIM
Vibration Isolation System ... VIS
Vibration Isolation Table ... VIT
Vibration Measurement Integrator ... VMI
Vibration Measuring System ... VMS
Vibration Open Test Assembly [*Nuclear energy*] (NRCH) ... VOTA
Vibration Pickup Amplifier ... VPA
Vibration Pickup Amplifier ... VPUA
Vibration Reducing Stiffener [*Automotive engineering*] ... VRS
Vibration Research Laboratory [*Stanford University*] (MCD) ... VRL
Vibration Safety Cutoff [*NASA*] (KSC) ... VSC
Vibration Seconds ... VS
Vibration Sensitive Relay ... VSR
Vibration Test Equipment ... VTE
Vibration Test Module (MCD) ... VTM
Vibration Test Plotting System ... VTPS
Vibration Test Specification ... VTS
Vibration Test System ... VTS
Vibration Testing ... VT
Vibration Transient Analysis (MCD) ... VITRAN
Vibration Velocity per Hour ... VVHR
Vibrational Circular Dichroism [*Spectrometry*] ... VCD
Vibrational Density of States [*Physics*] ... VDOS
Vibrational Energy Loss Electron Spectroscopy ... VELES
Vibrational Energy Transfer [*LASER*] (MCD) ... VET
Vibrational Microlamination (MCD) ... VIM
Vibrational Optical Activity [*Spectroscopy*] ... VOA
Vibrationally Adiabatic Potential [*Chemical physics*] ... VAP
Vibrational-Rotational [*Spectra*] [*Computer science*] ... VIBROT
Vibrational-Rotational [*Chemical kinetics*] ... V-R
Vibrational-to-Translational [*Energy transfer*] ... V-T
Vibrational-to-Vibrational [*Energy transfer*] ... V-V
Vibration-Dissociation Process ... VDP
Vibration-Induced White Finger [*Medicine*] ... VWF
Vibration-Recording Console (SAA) ... VIBRECON
Vibration-Rotation-Tunneling [*Spectroscopy*] ... VRT
Vibrations per Minute ... VPM
Vibrations per Second ... VPS
Vibrator (IAA) ... VB
Vibrator (IAA) ... VIB
Vibrator [*Printing*] (DGA) ... vib
Vibrator (IAA) ... VIBT
Vibrator Power Supply ... VPS
Vibrator Power Unit (MSA) ... VPU
Vibratory Bowl Feeder ... VBF
Vibratory Pan Feeder ... VPF
Vibratron Pressure Transducer ... VPT
Vibrio [*Microbiology*] ... V
Vibrio cholerae Neuraminidase [*An enzyme*] ... VCN
Vibrio Vulnificus [*A microorganism*] ... VV
Vibroacoustic (NASA) ... V-A
Vibroacoustic Test (NASA) ... VA
Vibroacoustic Test (NASA) ... VAT
Vibroacoustic Test Article (NASA) ... VATA

Vibroacoustic/Thermal/Vacuum Test Article (NASA) .... VA/TVTA
Vic [*Phonetic alphabet*] [*Pre-World War II*] (DSUE) V
Vical, Inc. [*Associated Press*] (SAG) .... Vical
Vical, Inc. [*NASDAQ symbol*] (SAG) VICL
Vicar [*or Vicarage*] V
Vicar [*or Vicarage*] VIC
Vicar Apostolic .... VA
Vicar Apostolic (BARN) .... Vic Ap
Vicar Choral VC
Vicar Choral .... VCHO
Vicar General and Vicar Foreign [*British*] (ROG) .... VG & VF
Vicar General's Office [*British*] (ROG) .... VGO
Vicar General's Office [*British*] .... VICGEN
Vicar Rural .... VR
Vicarious Interpolations Not Desired .... VIND
Vicarious Nucleophilic Substitution [*Organic chemistry*] .... VNS
Vicarious Trial and Error [*Psychology*] .... VTE
Vicarius Foraneus [*Vicar-Forane*] [*Latin*] .... VF
Vicarius Generalis [*Vicar-General*] [*Latin*] .... VG
Vicarm Arm Language .... VAL
Vice [*In a position or title*] V
Vice V
Vice .... VCE
Vice Admiral [*Navy*] O9
Vice Admiral [*Also, VADM, VADML*] .... VA
Vice Admiral [*Also, VA, VADML*] .... VADM
Vice Admiral British Pacific Fleet .... VABPF
Vice Chairman [*or Chairperson or Chairwoman*] VC
Vice Chairman, Joint Chiefs of Staff (DOMA) .... VCJCS
Vice Chancellor VC
Vice Chief of Defence Staff Personnel and Logistics [*British*] (RDA) .... VCDS(P & L)
Vice Chief of Naval Material Command .... VCNM
Vice Chief of Naval Operations .... VCNO
Vice Chief of Naval Operations .... VOPNAV
Vice Chief of Staff [*Air Force*] .... AFCVC
Vice Chief of Staff .... VC of S
Vice Chief of Staff .... VCS
Vice Chief of Staff [*Army*] (AAGC) .... VCSO
Vice Chief of Staff, Air Force .... VC/SAF
Vice Chief of Staff, Army [*Later, VCSA*] (AABC) .... VC of SA
Vice Chief of Staff, Army [*Formerly, VC of SA*] .... VCSA
Vice Chief of the General Staff [*in the field*] [*Military British*] (RDA) .... VCGS
Vice Commodore [*Navy*] (NVT) VC
Vice Consul VC
Vice Directorate for Production Office Procedure [*Defense Intelligence Agency*] (MCD) .... VPOP
Vice Grand [*Freemasonry*] (ROG) .... VG
Vice Grand Master (BJA) .... VGM
Vice Lieutenant [*British*] VL
Vice Minister of War (MCD) .... VMOW
Vice President .... VEEP
Vice President (AAG) .... VIP
Vice President .... VP
Vice President is Aboard Civil Aircraft (FAAC) EXEC-2
Vice President of the Faculty of Architects and Surveyors [*British*] (DBQ) .... VPFAS
Vice Presidential Protective Division [*US Secret Service*] .... VPPD
Vice President's Family is Aboard Aircraft (FAAC) EXEC-2F
Vice Versa (ODBW) vv
Vice Versa VV
Vice Versa (WDMC) vv
Vice Viewers International (EA) VVI
Vice-Admiralty Court [*British*] .... VAC
Vice-Chair of the Board (DD) .... v-chr
Vice-Chancellor's Courts [*England*] (DLA) VC
Vice-Chancellor's Courts (DLA) VCC
Vice-Chancellor's Reports [*English, Canadian*] [*A publication*] (DLA) .... VC Rep
Vice-Chief of Defence Staff [*British*] .... VCDS
Vice-Chief of the Air Staff [*British*] .... VCAS
Vice-Chief of the Imperial General Staff [*British*] .... VCIGS
Vice-Chief of the Naval Staff [*British*] .... VCNS
Vice-Chiefs of Staff [*British*] .... VCOS
Vice-Consul General [*British*] (ROG) .... VCG
Vicenza [*Italy ICAO location identifier*] (ICLI) .... LIPT
Vicenza [*Italy*] [*Airport symbol*] (AD) VIC
Vice-President (DD) .... v-p
Vice-President .... VPRES
Vice-President of the Geological Society [*British*] .... VPGS
Vice-President of the Linnaean Society [*British*] .... VPLS
Vice-President of the Royal Geographical Society [*British*] .... VPRGS
Vice-President of the Royal Institute [*British*] .... VPRI
Vice-President of the Royal Society [*British*] .... VPRS
Vice-President of the Society of Antiquaries [*British*] .... VPSA
Vice-President of the Zoological Society [*British*] .... VPZS
Vice-Presidential Service Badge [*Military decoration*] .... VPRESSVB
Vice-Principal [*British*] .... VP
Vice-Quartermaster-General .... VQMG
Viceroy Homes Ltd. [*Toronto Stock Exchange symbol*] .... VHL
Viceroy Resources Corp. [*Toronto Stock Exchange symbol Vancouver Stock Exchange symbol*] .... VOY
Viceroy-Designate [*British*] .... VD
Viceroy's Bodyguard [*British military*] (DMA) .... VRBG
Viceroy's Commissioned Officer [*British military*] (DMA) .... VCO
Vices [*Times*] [*Pharmacy*] VIC
Vice-Superintendent (DD) .... v-supt
Vichadero [*Uruguay*] [*Airport symbol Obsolete*] (OAG) .... VCH
Vichy [*France*] [*Airport symbol*] (AD) .... VHY
Vichy/Charmeil [*France ICAO location identifier*] (ICLI) .... LFLV
Vicia Cryptic Virus [*Plant pathology*] VCV
Vicinal [*Also, vic*] [*Chemistry*] v
Vicinal [*Also, v*] [*Chemistry*] vic
Vicinal Diketone [*Organic chemistry*] .... VDK
Vicinalis [*Neighboring*] [*Latin*] vic
Vicinity (AFM) .... VCNTY
Vicinity (NVT) .... VCTY
Vicinity [*Aviation*] (FAAC) .... VCY
Vicinity (AABC) VIC
Vicinity Map Series [*Bureau of the Census*] (GFGA) .... VMS
Vickers Diamond Hardness (IAA) .... VDH
Vickers Gas Operated [*British military*] (DMA) .... VGO
Vickers Hardness Number [*Also, VH, VHN*] .... HV
Vickers Hardness Number [*Also, HV, VHN*] (AAG) .... VH
Vickers Hardness Number [*Also, HV, VH*] .... VHN
Vickers Ltd. [*British ICAO designator*] (FAAC) .... VSB
Vickers Machine Gun [*British military*] (DMA) .... VMG
Vickers Pyramid Hardness Number (PDAA) .... VPH
Vickers Pyramid Number [*Hardness test*] .... VPN
Vickers Shipbuilding and Engineering Ltd. [*British*] .... VSEL
Vickers-Armstrong Gun .... VA
Vickers-Armstrong Ltd. .... V-A
Vicksburg [*Mississippi*] [*Airport symbol*] (AD) .... VKS
Vicksburg Community Library, Vicksburg, MI [*Library symbol Library of Congress*] (LCLS) .... MiVi
Vicksburg, MS [*Location identifier FAA*] (FAAL) .... VKS
Vicksburg, MS [*FM radio station call letters*] .... WBBV
Vicksburg, MS [*FM radio station call letters*] (RBYB) .... WJKK
Vicksburg, MS [*AM radio station call letters*] .... WQBC
Vicksburg, MS [*AM radio station call letters*] (RBYB) .... WRTM-AM
Vicksburg, MS [*FM radio station call letters*] .... WSTZ
Vicksburg, MS [*AM radio station call letters*] .... WVIX
Vicksburg National Military Park .... VICK
Vicksburg Public Library, Vicksburg, MS [*Library symbol Library of Congress*] (LCLS) .... MsV
Vicky and Sam [*Sebastiani*] [*Brand name of wines made by the Sebastianis*] .... Viansa
Vicon Indus [*AMEX symbol*] (TTSB) VII
Vicon Industries, Inc. [*Associated Press*] (SAG) .... Vicon
Vicon Industries, Inc. [*AMEX symbol*] (SPSG) VII
Vicor Corp. [*Associated Press*] (SAG) .... Vicor
Vicor Corp. [*NASDAQ symbol*] (SPSG) .... VICR
Vicor Corp. [*NASDAQ symbol*] (TTSB) .... VICR
VICORP Restaurants [*NASDAQ symbol*] (TTSB) .... VRES
Vicorp Restaurants, Inc. [*Associated Press*] (SAG) .... Vicorp
VICORP Restaurants, Inc. [*NASDAQ symbol*] (NQ) .... VRES
Victa Ltd. [*Aviation Division*] [*Australia ICAO aircraft manufacturer identifier*] (ICAO) .... VT
Victim Impact Statement .... VIS
Victim Support Scheme [*British*] (DI) .... VSS
Victims Anonymous (EA) .... VA
Victims for Victims [*Defunct*] (EA) VV
Victims of Child Abuse Laws (EA) .... VOCAL
Victims of Crime Act of 1984 .... VOCA
Victims of Crime and Leniency (EA) .... VOCAL
Victims of Crime Assistance Act .... VCA
Victims of Crime Association [*Australia*] .... VCA
Victims of Crime Association [*Australia*] .... VOCA
Victims of Incest Can Emerge (EA) .... VOICE
Victims of Institutionalised Cruelty, Exploitation and Supporters Inc. [*Australia*] .... VOICES
Victims of Terrorism Compensation Act .... VOTCA
Victor [*Phonetic alphabet*] [*International*] [*World War II*] (DSUE) V
Victor (WGA) .... VCT
Victor [*Record label*] Vic
Victor Airspeed Measuring System (MCD) .... VAMS
Victor Airways [*Aviation*] (FAAC) .... VA
Victor Analog Computer [*Computer science*] .... VAC
Victor D. Brenner [*Designer's mark, when appearing on US coins*] .... VDB
Victor Educational Services Institute [*Educational division of Victor Comptometer Corp.*] .... VESI
Victor Electrowriter Remote Blackboard [*Educational device of Victor Comptometer Corp.*] .... VERB
Victor Fly [*Italy ICAO designator*] (FAAC) .... VCF
Victor Public Library, Victor, CO [*Library symbol Library of Congress*] (LCLS) .... CoV
Victor Scoring System .... VSS
Victoria [*MARC geographic area code Library of Congress*] (LCCP) .... u-at-vi
Victoria V
Victoria [*State*] (EERA) V
Victoria [*Texas*] [*Airport symbol*] (OAG) .... VCT
Victoria [*British Columbia*] [*Seismograph station code, US Geological Survey*] (SEIS) VIC
Victoria [*Platen Press*] (DGA) vic
Victoria [*Diocesan abbreviation*] [*Texas*] (TOCD) VIC
Victoria [*Canada*] [*Airport symbol*] (OAG) .... YWH
Victoria [*Canada*] [*Airport symbol*] (OAG) .... YYJ
Victoria [*Chile*] [*Airport symbol*] (AD) .... ZIC
Victoria Acts of Parliament [*A publication*] (DLA) .... Vict Acts
Victoria and Albert Museum [*London, England*] .... V & A
Victoria and Albert Museum [*London*] (DSUE) .... VIC and ALB

Victoria and Albert Order [*British*] .... VA
Victoria Bankshares, Inc. [*NASDAQ symbol*] (NQ) .... VICT
Victoria Bankshares, Inc. [*Associated Press*] (SAG) .... VictBn
Victoria, BC [*AM radio station call letters*] .... CFAX
Victoria, BC [*FM radio station call letters*] .... CFMS
Victoria, BC [*FM radio station call letters*] .... CFUV
Victoria, BC [*Radio station call letters*] .... CFUV-FM
Victoria, BC [*Television station call letters*] .... CHEK
Victoria, BC [*FM radio station call letters*] (RBYB) .... CIOC-FM
Victoria, BC [*AM radio station call letters*] .... CJVI
Victoria, BC [*FM radio station call letters*] .... CKKQ
Victoria, BC [*FM radio station call letters*] (RBYB) .... CKMO-FM
Victoria, BC [*AM radio station call letters*] (RBYB) .... CKXM
Victoria Carriers [*Steamship*] (MHDB) VC
Victoria City Archives, British Columbia [*Library symbol National Library of Canada*] (NLC) .... BVICA
Victoria Civil Procedure Updater [*Australia A publication*] .... AVCP
Victoria College of Music [*London*] (ROG) .... VCM
Victoria College, Victoria, TX [*OCLC symbol*] (OCLC) .... TEV
Victoria College, Victoria, TX [*Library symbol Library of Congress*] (LCLS) .... TxViC
Victoria County Archives and Museum, Baddeck, Nova Scotia [*Library symbol National Library of Canada*] (NLC) .... NSBVCA
Victoria County Archives and Museum, Baddeck, NS, Canada [*Library symbol*] [*Library of Congress*] (LCLS) .... CaNSBadVCA
Victoria County History [*Classical studies*] (OCD) .... VCH
Victoria County Public Library, Bobcaygeon Branch, Bobcaygeon, ON, Canada [*Library symbol*] [*Library of Congress*] (LCLS) .... CaOBobV
Victoria County Public Library, Lindsay, ON, Canada [*Library symbol Library of Congress*] (LCLS) .... CaOLiV
Victoria County Public Library, Lindsay, Ontario [*Library symbol National Library of Canada*] (NLC) .... OLIV
Victoria Cross [*British*] VC
Victoria Cross (DSUE) .... VIC C
Victoria Cross and George Cross Association [*British*] (DBA) .... VC & GCAssn
Victoria Diego Resource Corp. [*Vancouver Stock Exchange symbol*] .... VCD
Victoria Docks [*British*] (ROG) .... VD
Victoria Falls [*Zimbabwe*] [*Airport symbol*] (OAG) .... VFA
Victoria Falls/Spray View [*Zimbabwe*] [*ICAO location identifier*] (ICLI) .... FVSV
Victoria Falls/Victoria Falls [*Zimbabwe*] [*ICAO location identifier*] (ICLI) .... FVFA
Victoria General Hospital, British Columbia [*Library symbol National Library of Canada*] (NLC) .... BVIGH
Victoria General Hospital, Health Sciences Library, Halifax, NS, Canada [*Library symbol Library of Congress*] (LCLS) .... CaNSHVGH
Victoria General Hospital, Winnipeg, Manitoba [*Library symbol National Library of Canada*] (NLC) .... MWVGH
Victoria General Hospital, Winnipeg, MB, Canada [*Library symbol Library of Congress*] (LCLS) .... CaMWVGH
Victoria Harness Racing Club [*Australia*] .... VHRC
Victoria Hospital, London, ON, Canada [*Library symbol Library of Congress*] (LCLS) .... CaOLVH
Victoria Imperatrix Regina [*Victoria Empress and Queen*] (ILCA) .... VIR
Victoria Institute [*British*] (DAS) VI
Victoria/International, BC [*ICAO location identifier*] (ICLI) .... CYYJ
Victoria Law Foundation [*Australia*] .... VLF
Victoria League for Commonwealth Fellowship [*British*] .... VLCF
Victoria League for Commonwealth Fellowship in Queensland [*Australia*] .... VLCFQ
Victoria League for Commonwealth Fellowship in South Australia .... VLCFSA
Victoria League for Commonwealth Fellowship in Victoria [*Australia*] .... VLCFV
Victoria Marine Radio, BC [*ICAO location identifier*] (ICLI) .... CWIR
Victoria Medal of Honour .... VMH
Victoria Medical and Hospital Libraries, Royal Jubilee Hospital Site, British Columbia [*Library symbol National Library of Canada*] (NLC) .... BVIRJ
Victoria Mounted Rifles [*British military*] (DMA) .... VMR
Victoria/New South Wales Border Anomalies Committee [*Australia*] .... VNSWBAC
Victoria Press Ltd., British Columbia [*Library symbol National Library of Canada*] (NLC) .... BVIPR
Victoria Press Ltd., Victoria, BC, Canada [*Library symbol Library of Congress*] (LCLS) .... CaBViPR
Victoria Public Library, Newfoundland [*Library symbol National Library of Canada*] (NLC) .... NFV
Victoria Public Library, Victoria, NF, Canada [*Library symbol Library of Congress*] (LCLS) .... CaNfV
Victoria Public Library, Victoria, TX [*OCLC symbol*] (OCLC) .... TVP
Victoria Public Library, Victoria, TX [*Library symbol Library of Congress*] (LCLS) .... TxVi
Victoria Regina [*Queen Victoria*] .... VR
Victoria Regina et Imperatrix [*Victoria, Queen and Empress*] .... VR et I
Victoria Regina et Imperatrix [*Victoria, Queen and Empress*] .... VRI
Victoria Reports, Admiralty [*A publication*] (DLA) .... VC Adm
Victoria Reports, Equity [*A publication*] (DLA) .... VC Eq
Victoria Resources [*Vancouver Stock Exchange symbol*] .... VIT
Victoria Rifles of Canada (DMA) .... VRC
Victoria River District [*Region*] (EERA) .... VRD
Victoria River District Conservation Association (EERA) .... VRDCA
Victoria River Downs [*Australia Airport symbol*] .... VCD
Victoria/South Australia Border Anomalies Committee .... V/SABAC
Victoria State Emergency Service [*Australia*] .... VSES
Victoria, TX [*AM radio station call letters*] .... KAMG
Victoria, TX [*Television station call letters*] .... KAVU
Victoria, TX [*FM radio station call letters*] .... KEPG
Victoria, TX [*FM radio station call letters*] .... KIXS
Victoria, TX [*AM radio station call letters*] .... KNAL
Victoria, TX [*FM radio station call letters*] .... KTXN
Victoria, TX [*Television station call letters*] .... KVCT

Victoria, TX [*FM radio station call letters*] .... KVIC
Victoria, TX [*FM radio station call letters*] .... KVLT
Victoria, TX [*FM radio station call letters*] (RBYB) .... KVRT
Victoria, TX [*FM radio station call letters*] .... KXBJ
Victoria, TX [*Location identifier FAA*] (FAAL) .... XFN
Victoria University. Law Review [*A publication*] (DLA) .... Vict UL Rev
Victoria University Library, University of Toronto [*UTLAS symbol*] .... KVU
Victoria University of Wellington [*New Zealand*] .... VUW
Victoria University, Toronto, ON, Canada [*Library symbol Library of Congress*] (LCLS) .... CaOTV
Victoria University, Toronto, Ontario [*Library symbol National Library of Canada*] (NLC) .... OTV
Victoria West [*South Africa*] [*ICAO location identifier*] (ICLI) .... FAVW
Victoria West [*South Africa*] [*Airport symbol*] (AD) .... VCW
Victoria-Carleton Courthouse, Woodstock, NB, Canada [*Library symbol Library of Congress*] (LCLS) .... CaNBWV
Victoria-Carleton Courthouse, Woodstock, New Brunswick [*Library symbol National Library of Canada*] (NLC) .... NBWV
Victorian Abalone Divers' Association [*Australia*] .... VADA
Victorian Abattoir and Meat Inspection Authority [*Australia*] .... VAMIA
Victorian Aboriginal Child Care Agency [*Australia*] .... VACCA
Victorian Aboriginal Community Services Association [*Australia*] .... VACSA
Victorian Aboriginal Legal Service [*Australia*] .... VALS
Victorian Aboriginal Mental Health Network [*Australia*] .... VAMHN
Victorian Academy for General Practice [*Australia*] .... VAGP
Victorian Accident Compensation Practice Guide [*Australia A publication*] .... AVW
Victorian Accident Compensation Reports [*Australia A publication*] .... Vic ACR
Victorian Administrative Reports [*Australia A publication*] .... VAR
Victorian Adoption Network for Information and Self Help [*Australia*] .... VANFISH
Victorian Advisory Council on Recreation for People with Disabilities [*Australia*] .... VACRPD
Victorian Agricultural Strategy [*State*] (EERA) .... VAS
Victorian Allied Health Professionals Association [*Australia*] .... VAHPA
Victorian Amateur Canoe Association [*Australia*] .... VACA
Victorian Amateur Football Association [*Australia*] .... VAFA
Victorian Amateur Football League [*Australia*] .... VAFL
Victorian Amateur Power Lifting Association [*Australia*] .... VAPLA
Victorian Ambulance Services Association [*Australia*] .... VASA
Victorian and Interstate Airways [*Australia*] .... V & IA
Victorian Animal Aid Trust [*Australia*] .... VAAT
Victorian Antique Dealers' Group [*Australia*] .... VADG
Victorian Apiarists' Association [*Australia*] .... VAA
Victorian Architectural Students' Society [*Australia*] .... VASS
Victorian Artificial Breeders [*Australia*] .... VAB
Victorian Arts and Entertainment Industry Training Board [*Australia*] .... VAEITB
Victorian Arts Council [*Australia*] .... VAC
Victorian Asbestos Removal Industry Consultative Committee [*Australia*] .... VARICC
Victorian Association for Deserted Children [*Australia*] .... VADC
Victorian Association for Drama in Education [*Australia*] .... VADE
Victorian Association for Multicultural Education [*Australia*] .... VAME
Victorian Association for Religious Education [*Australia*] .... VARE
Victorian Association of Bakers [*Australia*] .... VAB
Victorian Association of Day Nurseries [*Australia*] .... VADN
Victorian Association of Forest Industries [*Australia*] .... VAFI
Victorian Association of Occupational Therapists [*Australia*] .... VAOT
Victorian Association of Principals of Secondary Schools [*Australia*] .... VAPSS
Victorian Athletic League [*Australia*] .... VAL
Victorian Athletics Association [*Australia*] .... VAA
Victorian Autistic Childrens and Adults' Association [*Australia*] .... VACAA
Victorian Bar Association [*Australia*] .... VBA
Victorian Bar Council [*Australia*] .... VBC
Victorian Building and Construction Industry Training Council [*Australia*] .... VBCITC
Victorian Building Industries Disputes Board [*Australia*] .... VBIDB
Victorian Bush Nursing Association [*Australia*] .... VBNA
Victorian Business Migration Service [*Australia*] .... VBMS
Victorian Catholic Schools Association [*Australia*] .... VCSA
Victorian Centre for Photography [*Australia*] .... VCP
Victorian Centre for the Conservation of Cultural Material [*Australia*] .... VCCCM
Victorian Cervical Cytology Registry [*Australia*] .... VCCR
Victorian Chamber of Commerce and Industry [*Australia*] VCCI
Victorian Chamber of Mines [*Australia*] .... VCM
Victorian Children's Aid Society [*Australia*] .... VCAS
Victorian Clinical Genetics Services [*Australia*] .... VCGS
Victorian College of Optometry [*Australia*] .... VCO
Victorian Commercial Travellers' Association [*Australia*] .... VCTA
Victorian Community Services Employers' Association [*Australia*] .... VCSEA
Victorian Computer Society (IAA) .... VCS
Victorian Congress of Employer Associations [*Australia*] .... VCEA
Victorian Conservation Trust [*Australia*] .... VCT
Victorian Consolidated Statutes [*A publication*] (ILCA) .... Vict CS
Victorian Consumer Affairs Committee [*Australia*] .... VCAC
Victorian Conveyancing Cases [*Australia A publication*] .... V Conv R
Victorian Council for Children's Films and Television [*Australia*] .... VCCFT
Victorian Council for Sustainable Agriculture [*Australia*] .... VCSA
Victorian Council for the Mentally Retarded [*Australia*] .... VCMR
Victorian Council of Christian Education [*Australia*] .... VCCE
Victorian Council of Deaf People [*Australia*] .... VCDP
Victorian Council of Social Service [*Australia*] .... VCSS
Victorian Council of the Arts [*Australia*] .... VCA
Victorian Council on Fitness and General Health [*Australia*] .... VCFGH
Victorian Country Football League [*Australia*] .... VCFL
Victorian Country Press Association [*Australia*] .... VCPA

Victorian Credit Cooperative Association [*Australia*] .... VCCA
Victorian Cycling Federation [*Australia*] .... VCF
Victorian Dairy Products Association [*Australia*] .... VDPA
Victorian Deaf Society [*Australia*] .... VDS
Victorian Decoration [*British*] .... VD
Victorian Department of Conservation and Environment [*Australia*] .... VDCE
Victorian Department of Manufacturing and Industry Development [*Australia*] .... VDMID
Victorian Docklands Authority [*Australia*] .... VDA
Victorian Dried Fruits Board [*Australia*] .... VDFB
Victorian Drug Users' Advisory Committee [*Australia*] .... VDUAC
Victorian Education Foundation [*Australia*] .... VEF
Victorian Egg Marketing Board [*Australia*] .... VEMB
Victorian Electrical and Electronic Industry Training Committee [*Australia*] .... VEEITC
Victorian Environmental Education Council (EERA) .... VEEC
Victorian Era Series [*A publication*] .... VES
Victorian Exporters' Association [*Australia*] .... VEA
Victorian Family Almanac [*A publication*] .... Vic Fam Alm
Victorian Farmers Federation (EERA) .... VFF
Victorian Farmers' Federation Industrial Association [*Australia*] .... VFFIA
Victorian Federation of Catholic Parents' Clubs [*Australia*] .... VFCPC
Victorian Fellowship of Australian Writers [*Australia*] .... VFAW
Victorian Fishing Industry Training Committee [*Australia*] .... VFITC
Victorian Food and Nutrition Program [*Australia*] .... VFNP
Victorian Football Development Foundation [*Australia*] .... VFDF
Victorian Football League [*Receives television coverage in the US through the Entertainment and Sports Programming Network*] [*Australia*] .... VFL
Victorian Foundation for Survivors of Torture [*Australia*] .... VFST
Victorian Geographic Data Committee [*State*] (EERA) .... VGDC
Victorian Government Advertising Unit [*Australia*] .... VGAU
Victorian Government China Advisory Committee [*Australia*] .... VGCAC
Victorian Government Computing Centre [*Australia*] .... VGCC
Victorian Government Major Projects Unit [*Australia*] .... VGMPU
Victorian Government Printing Office [*Australia*] .... VGPO
Victorian Government Solicitor's Office [*Australia*] .... VGSO
Victorian Grants Commission [*Australia*] .... VGC
Victorian Green Alliance [*Political party Australia*] .... VGA
Victorian Gymnastic Association [*Australia*] .... VGA
Victorian Historical Journal [*A publication*] .... Vic His J
Victorian Historical Journal [*A publication*] .... Vic Hist J
Victorian House of Studies .... VHS
Victorian Immigration Advice and Rights Centre Inc. [*Australia Commercial firm*] .... VIARC
Victorian Importers' Association [*Australia*] .... VIA
Victorian Indo-Chinese Community Council [*Australia*] VICCC
Victorian Industrial Notes [*A publication*] .... VIN
Victorian Industrial Reports [*A publication*] .... VIR
Victorian Information Services Network [*Australia*] .... VISioN
Victorian Institute of Educational Research. Bulletin [*A publication*] .... Vic Inst Ed Res Bull
Victorian Institute of Marine Science [*State*] (EERA) .... VIMS
Victorian Institute of Marine Sciences Information System [*State*] (EERA) .... VIMSIS
Victorian Journal of History [*A publication*] .... VJH
Victorian Judgements Bulletin [*Australia A publication*] .... VJB
Victorian Law Journal [*A publication*] (DLA) .... Vict L
Victorian Medical Benevolent Association [*Australia*] .... VMBA
Victorian Medical Record Association [*Australia*] .... VMRA
Victorian Mental Illness Awareness Council [*Australia*] .... VMIAC
Victorian Military History Institute [*Defunct*] (EA) .... VMHI
Victorian Military Society (EAIO) .... VMS
Victorian Museum [*State*] (EERA) .... VM
Victorian Music Library [*Australia*] .... VML
Victorian National Parks Association [*Australia*] .... VNPA
Victorian Naturalists' Club (EERA) .... VNC
Victorian Office of Local Government [*Australia*] .... VOLG
Victorian Olympic Council [*Australia*] .... VOC
Victorian Order [*British*] (ROG) .... VO
Victorian Order of Nurses .... VON
Victorian Ornithological Research Group (EERA) .... VORG
Victorian Overseas Foundation [*Australia*] .... VOF
Victorian Parliamentary Debates [*A publication*] .... VPD
Victorian Planning and Environmental Law Association [*Australia*] .... VPELA
Victorian Police Force [*Australia*] .... VPF
Victorian Post-Secondary Accreditation Board [*Australia*] .... VPSAB
Victorian Prison Industries Commission [*Australia*] .... VICPIC
Victorian Prison Industries Commission [*Australia*] .... VPIC
Victorian Protestant Federation [*Australia*] .... VPF
Victorian Psychological Council [*Australia*] .... VPC
Victorian Psychologists' Association [*Australia*] .... VPA
Victorian Public Authorities Finance Agency [*Australia*] .... VPAFA
Victorian Public Library and Information Cooperative [*Australia*] .... VPLIC
[*The*] **Victorian Railways of Australia** (DCTA) .... VRA
Victorian Rare or Threatened Plants [*State*] (EERA) .... VROT
Victorian Relief Committee AT .... VRC
Victorian Reports (Australian) [*A publication*] (DLA) .... Vict R
Victorian Reports (Law)(Australia) [*A publication*] (ILCA) .... Vict L (Austr)
Victorian Road Transport Industry Training Committee [*Australia*] .... VRTITC
Victorian Rowing Association [*Australia*] .... VRA
Victorian Rugby League [*Australia*] .... VRL
Victorian Rugby League Referees' Association [*Australia*] .... VRLRA
Victorian Rugby Union [*Australia*] .... VRU
Victorian Safety Council [*Australia*] .... VSC
Victorian School of Languages [*Australia*] .... VSL
Victorian School of Massage and Physical Culture [*Australia*] .... VSMPC
Victorian Socialist Party [*Australia Political party*] .... VSP
Victorian Society (EA) .... VS
Victorian Society in America (EA) .... VSA
Victorian Solar Energy Research Council [*Australia*] .... VSERC
Victorian State Building Trades Union [*Australia*] .... VSTBU
Victorian Studies [*A publication*] (BRI) .... VS
Victorian Tapestry Workshop [*Australia*] .... VTW
Victorian Taxation Board of Review Case [*Australia A publication*] .... VTBR Case
Victorian Technology Centre [*Australia*] .... VTC
Victorian Temperance Alliance [*Australia*] .... VTA
Victorian Textile, Clothing and Footwear Industry Training Board [*Australia*] .... VTCFITB
Victorian Tobacco Leaf Marketing Board [*Australia*] .... VTLMB
Victorian Transport Accident Commission [*Australia*] .... VTAC
Victorian Union for Progressive Judaism [*Australia*] .... VUPJ
Victorian Vice-Chancellors' Committee [*Australia*] VVCC
Victorian Water Quality Monitoring Network [*State*] (EERA) .... VWQMN
Victorian Wheat Advisory Committee [*Australia*] .... VWAC
Victorian Wheat Research Foundation [*Australia*] .... VWRF
Victorian Wine Industry Association [*Australia*] .... VWIA
Victorian Women's Trust [*Australia*] .... VWT
Victorian Writers' Centre [*Australia*] .... VWC
Victorian Young Lawyers [*Australia*] .... VYL
Victorian Youth Advocacy Network [*Australia*] .... VYAN
Victoria's Resources [*A publication*] .... Vic's Res
Victoriaville Branch, Thunder Bay Public Library, Ontario [*Library symbol National Library of Canada*] (BIB) .... OTBV
Victoriaville, PQ [*AM radio station call letters*] .... CFDA
Victormaxx Technologies [*Associated Press*] (SAG) .... Victrm
Victormaxx Technologies [*NASDAQ symbol*] (SAG) .... VMAX
Victormaxx Technologies Wrrt [*NASDAQ symbol*] (TTSB) .... VMAXW
Victorville, CA [*FM radio station call letters*] .... KHMS
Victorville, CA [*AM radio station call letters*] (RBYB) .... KROY
Victorville, CA [*FM radio station call letters*] .... KVVQ
Victorville, CA [*FM radio station call letters*] .... KXRD
Victorville, CA [*Location identifier FAA*] (FAAL) VCV
Victorville/George Air Force Base [*California*] [*ICAO location identifier*] (ICLI) .... KVCV
Victory [*As in "the V campaign" in Europe, during World War II*] V
Victory .... VCTRY
Victory Disc [*Music*] (WDMC) .... V disc
Victory in Europe [*as in VE-Day*] .... VE
Victory in Europe Day [*World War II*] .... V-E (Day)
Victory in Vietnam Association .... VIVA
Victory Medal [*British*] .... VM
Victory Medal World War I [*British*] .... VMWWI
Victory Medal World War II [*British*] .... VMWWII
Victory over Japan [*Japanese surrender, World War II, 14 August 1945*] .... V-J (Day)
Victualling [*British military*] (DMA) V
Victualling Allowance [*British military*] (DMA) .... VA
Victualling Store Allowance [*British military*] (DMA) .... VSA
Victualling Stores Officer [*British military*] (DMA) .... VSO
Victualling Yard [*Obsolete Navy British*] (ROG) .... VY
Vidalia, GA [*Location identifier FAA*] (FAAL) .... VDI
Vidalia, GA [*FM radio station call letters*] .... WGPH
Vidalia, GA [*FM radio station call letters*] .... WTCQ
Vidalia, GA [*AM radio station call letters*] .... WVOP
Vidalia, LA [*AM radio station call letters*] .... KAIN
Vidalia, LA [*AM radio station call letters*] .... KVLA
VidaMed, Inc. [*NASDAQ symbol*] (SAG) .... VIDA
VidaMed, Inc. [*Associated Press*] (SAG) .... VidaMd
Vidarabine [*Also, ara-A*] [*Biochemistry*] .... Vira-A
Vidatron Enterprise Ltd. [*Vancouver Stock Exchange symbol*] .... VE
Vide [*See*] [*Latin*] (WGA) v
Vide [*or Videte*] [*See*] [*Latin*] .... VID
Vide Etiam [*See Also*] [*Latin*] (MAE) .... v et
Vide Infra [*See Below*] [*Latin*] (WGA) vi
Vide Locum [*See the Place Indicated*] [*Latin*] VL
Vide Supra [*See Above*] [*Latin*] .... VS
Videlicet [*Namely*] [*Latin*] .... VIZ
Videlicet [*Namely*] [*Latin*] VL
Video (SAA) V
Video (VRA) v
Video .... VID
Video (AAG) .... VID
Video Alliance for the Performing Arts (EA) .... VAPA
Video Amplifier .... VA
Video Amplifier .... VIDAMP
Video Amplifier Chain .... VAC
Video/Analog (NASA) .... V/A
Video Analog to Digital Converter .... VADC
Video and Cable Communications Section of the ALA (NITA) .... VCCS
Video and Data Acquisition (MCD) .... V & DA
Video and Data Processing Assembly (NASA) .... V & DA
Video and Synchronization [*Telecommunications*] (IAA) .... VS
Video Arts International, Inc. .... VAI
Video/Audio [*Telecommunications*] .... V/A
Video Audio Integrated Operation [*Computer science*] .... VAIO
Video/Audio Participative [*Education*] (OA) .... VAP
Video Bandwidth .... VBW
Video Bible Institute [*Defunct*] (EA) .... VBI
Video BIOS [*Basic Input-Output System*] **Extension** [*Computer science*] (PCM) .... VBE

Video Camera Kit .... VCK
Video Capture Adapter (PCM) .... VCA
Video Cartridge Recorder (IAA) .... VCR
Video Cassette Player .... VCP
Video Cassette Recorder .... VCR
Video Cassette System .... VCS
Video Channel [*Auckland, NZ*] VC
Video Clock [*Computer science*] .... VCLK
Video Clutter Suppression (CAAL) .... VCS
Video Coaxial Connector VCC
Video Combiner Unit (IAA) .... VCU
Video Command Generator (MCD) .... VCG
Video Communications System .... VCS
Video Compact Cassette [*Video recorder*] [*Philips*] VCC
Video Compression Sampler [*Computer science*] .... VCS
Video Computer System [*Atari, Inc.*] .... VCS
Video Concert Hall .... VCH
Video Console Indexing VICI
Video Contrast Seeker .... VCS
Video Contrast Tracker (PDAA) .... VCT
Video Control Unit (MCD) .... VCU
Video Copyright Protection Society [*British*] .... VCPS
Video Correlator VC
Video Data Acquisition System .... VDAS
Video Data Collection Program .... VDCP
Video Data Controller (NITA) .... VDC
Video Data Generator (NITA) .... VDG
Video Data Interrogator (SAA) .... VDI
Video Data Link (NVT) .... VDL
Video Data Processor .... VDP
Video Data Sequence (NTCM) .... VDSQ
Video Data Terminal [*Computer science*] .... VDT
Video Datagram Protocol [*Computer science*] .... VDP
Video Decoder .... VD
Video Delta Modulation .... VDM
Video Delta Modulation System .... VDMS
Video Detector Diode .... VDD
Video Device Interface [*Computer science*] (PCM) .... VDI
Video Digital Data Processing .... VDDP
Video Digitally Enhanced Compression (PCM) .... VIDEC
Video Digitizer System (MCD) .... VDS
Video Dimension Analysis [*Sports medicine*] .... VDA
Video Disc .... VISC
Video Disc Gunnery Simulator [*Army*] (INF) .... VIGS
Video Disc Recorder .... VDR
Video Disk (BUR) .... VD
Video Display (IAA) .... VD
Video Display [*NASDAQ symbol*] (TTSB) .... VIDE
Video Display Adapter with Digital Enhancement [*AT & T*] .... VDA/D
Video Display Board .... VDB
Video Display Controller (IAA) .... VDAC
Video Display Controller [*Computer science*] (MHDI) .... VDC
Video Display Corp. [*Associated Press*] (SAG) .... VidDsp
Video Display Corp. [*NASDAQ symbol*] (NQ) .... VIDE
Video Display Editor [*Computer science*] (CDE) .... VDE
Video Display Generator .... VDG
Video Display Information File (PCM) .... VDIF
Video Display Input .... VDI
Video Display Interface .... VDI
Video [*or Visual*] **Display Terminal** [*Computer science*] .... VDT
Video [*or Visual*] **Display Unit** [*Computer science*] .... VDU
Video Distribution Amplifier .... VDA
Video Distribution Unit .... VDU
Video Documentary (NTCM) .... VIDOC
Video Editing Terminal [*Computer science*] .... VET
Video Electronics Standards Association .... VESA
Video Electronics Standards Association (ACII) .... VESA
Video Enhanced Evaluation of Weathering [*Automotive paint durability*] .... VIEEW
Video Film Converter (OA) .... VFC
Video Fluorometric Detection Liquid Chromatograph .... VFLC
Video for Windows [*Microsoft Corp.*] (PCM) .... VFW
Video Frame Store (NITA) .... VFS
Video Free America (EA) .... VFA
Video Frequency .... VDF
Video Frequency .... VF
Video Frequency (IEEE) .... VIDF
Video Frequency Amplifier .... VFA
Video Frequency Carrier [*or Channel*] (CET) .... VFC
Video Generation Unit (NITA) .... VGU
Video Graphics Adapter [*Computer science*] .... VGA
Video Graphics Array [*Computer technology*] .... VGA
Video Graphics Controller [*Apple Computer, Inc.*] .... VGC
Video Graphics Generator .... VGG
Video Graphics Recorder (EECA) .... VGR
Video Guidance, Landing, and Imaging System [*NASA*] .... VGLIS
Video High Density [*Television*] .... VHD
Video Hits One [*Cable-television system*] [*Companion to MTV*] VH-1
Video Hits One [*Cable programming service*] (WDMC) VH1
Video Home System .... VHS
Video Home System - Compact .... VHS-C
Video Image Analysis .... VIA
Video Image Communication and Retrieval .... VICAR
Video Image Correlation VIC
Video Image Digitiser and Storage System [*Sirton Computer*] [*London, England*] .... VIDAS
Video Image Display Assembly [*Space Flight Operations Facility, NASA*] .... VID
Video Image Generator .... VIG
Video Image Processing System .... VIPS
Video Imaging System .... VIS
Video Imaging Technique for Assessing Exposure [*to pesticides*] .... VITAE
Video Inertial Pointing [*System*] [*NASA*] .... VIP
Video Information [*Winslow Associates*] [*No longer available*] [*Information service or system*] (IID) .... VIF
Video Information System [*Tandy Corp.*] (DOM) .... VIS
Video Input/Output .... VIO
Video Input to Automatic Computer (NITA) .... VIDIAC
Video Integrate (NVT) .... VINT
Video Integrating Group .... VIG
Video Integrator VI
Video Integrator and Processor .... VIP
Video Intensified Microscopy .... VIM
Video Interactive Gunnery System [*Military*] (INF) .... VIGS
Video Interactive Processing System .... VIPS
Video Interface Controller [*Computer science*] VIC
Video Interface Unit (MCD) .... VIU
Video Interface Unit Random Access Memory .... VIURAM
Video Interphone Communications System (SAA) .... VIDICODER
Video Isolation Channel Identifier (MCD) VICI
Video Jockey [*Television version of disc jockey; originated on all-rock-music cable station MTV*] .... VJ
Video Jukebox Network [*NASDAQ symbol*] (SAG) .... JUKE
Video Jukebox Network, Inc. [*Associated Press*] (SAG) .... VidJuke
Video Jukebox Ntwk [*NASDAQ symbol*] (TTSB) .... JUKE
Video Kinescope Recording (PDAA) .... VKR
Video Layout Terminal [*Computer science*] .... VLT
Video Load Impedance VLI
Video Logarithmic Amplifier .... VLA
Video Logic (IEEE) VL
Video Logic Unit (MCD) .... VLU
Video Long Player [*Video disk system*] [*Philips/MCA*] .... VLP
Video Lottery Tech [*NASDAQ symbol*] (TTSB) .... VLTS
Video Lottery Technologies, Inc. [*Associated Press*] (SAG) .... VideoL
Video Lottery Technologies, Inc. [*NASDAQ symbol*] (SPSG) .... VLTS
Video Lottery Terminal (ECON) .... VLT
Video Map Equipment .... VMAP
Video Map Module .... VMM
Video Mapping Group .... VMG
Video Matrix Terminal .... VMT
Video Micrographics (NITA) .... VMG
Video Mixer Group .... VMG
Video Modulation System .... VMS
Video Mosaic Imaging [*Computer science*] .... VMI
Video Movie System [*For video recording tapes*] .... VMS
Video Network Computer (PCM) .... VNC
Video News Release [*A news release in the form of video tape*] .... VNR
Video on Demand (ECON) .... VOD
Video on Line [*Computer science*] [*Italy*] .... VOL
Video Operator (NTCM) .... VO
Video Operator Distress Syndrome (HGAA) .... VODS
Video Output Impedance .... VOI
Video Output Voltage .... VOV
Video Plankton Recorder [*Oceanography*] .... VPR
Video Prelaunch Command Amplifier .... VPCA
Video Prelaunch Command Data System [*Air Force*] .... VPCDS
Video Processing and Electronic Reduction (IEEE) .... VIPER
Video Processing Equipment .... VPE
Video Processor (NVT) .... VP
Video Processor Control (MCD) .... VPC
Video Programme Service (NITA) .... VPS
Video Pulse Termination .... VPT
Video Random Access Memory .... VRAM
Video Reception System .... VRS
Video Recorder (NASA) .... VR
Video Recorder Kit .... VRK
Video Relay System .... VRS
Video Review Award .... VIRA
Video ROM (NITA) .... VROM
Video Round Table [*American Library Association*] .... VRT
Video Satellite Systems Inc. (NITA) .... VSS
Video Scanner Switch Matrix .... VSSM
Video Scroller Terminal [*Computer science*] .... VST
Video Select Switch (MCD) .... VSS
Video Selection .... VS
Video Sentry [*NASDAQ symbol*] (TTSB) .... VSEN
Video Sentry Corp. [*Associated Press*] (SAG) .... VideoSen
Video Sentry Corp. [*NASDAQ symbol*] (SAG) .... VSEN
Video Signal Processor .... VSP
Video Signal Simulator (NATG) .... VSS
Video Simulation Interface (NASA) .... VSI
Video Software Dealers Association (EA) .... VSDA
Video Source Book [*A publication*] .... VSB
Video Storage System [*or Subsystem*] .... VSS
Video Subcarrier Detector .... VSD
Video Supervisory Signal .... VSS
Video Sweep Integrator .... VSI
Video Switching Matrix (KSC) .... VSM
Video Switching Matrix System .... VSMS
Video Switching Network (MCD) .... VSN
Video Symbology Generator .... VSG
Video System Control Architecture [*Computer science*] (CDE) .... ViSCA

Video System Processor [*Telecommunications*] (TSSD) .... VSP
Video System Test .... VST
Video Systems Exposition and Conference (PDAA) .... VIDSEC
Video Tape Center [*Commercial firm British*] .... VTC
Video Tape Lecture .... VTL
Video Tape Network [*Defunct*] (EA) .... VTN
Video Tape Time-Code (NITA) .... VTTC
Video Teleconferencing .... VTC
Video Telemetering Camera Systems (AAG) .... VTCS
Video Telemetry (CPH) .... VT
Video Teletraining [*Military*] (INF) .... VTT
Video Terminal .... VT
Video Terminal Board [*Computer science*] (MHDB) .... VTB
Video Terminal Interface .... VTI
Video Timing and Control .... VTAC
Video Trade Association [*British*] (DBA) .... VTA
Video Transmission Engineering Advisory Committee [*Army*] (PDAA) ..... VITEAC
Video Update [*NASDAQ symbol*] (TTSB) .... VUPDA
Video Update Wrrt'A' [*NASDAQ symbol*] (TTSB) .... VUPDW
Video Update Wrrt'B' [*NASDAQ symbol*] (TTSB) .... VUPDZ
Video Updates, Inc. [*Associated Press*] (SAG) .... VideoU
Video Updates, Inc. [*Associated Press*] (SAG) .... VideoUpd
Video Updates, Inc. [*Associated Press*] (SAG) .... VidU
Video Updates, Inc. [*NASDAQ symbol*] (SAG) .... VUPD
Video User Interface [*Computer science*] (DOM) .... VUI
Video Verter Decision Storage .... VVDS
Video-Assisted Instruction .... VAI
Video-Assisted Thoracoscopic Surgery .... VATS
Video-Audio Range [*Radio*] .... VAR
Video-Augmented Tracking System (MCD) .... VATS
Video-Augmented Tracking System/Single Seat Night Attack Program (MCD) .... VATS/SNAP
Videocassette (DAVI) VC
Videocom Satellite Associates [*Dedham, MA*] [*Telecommunications*] (TSSD) .... VSA
Videoconferencing Systems, Inc. [*Norcross, GA*] [*Telecommunications service*] (TSSD) .... VSI
Videocystourethrography [*Medicine*] .... VCU
Video-Data [*Computer graphics*] (BYTE) .... VID
Videodensitometry [*Laboratory science*] (DAVI) .... VID
Videodisc Authoring System (NITA) .... VAS
Videodisc Controller VC
Videodisc Innovation Project (NITA) .... VIP
Videodisc Interpersonal Skills Training and Assessment (INF) .... VISTA
Videodisc Player [*RCA Corp.*] .... VDP
Videodisc-Mouse Interface .... VMI
Videodisk Recorder (WDMC) .... VDR
Video-Documentary Clearinghouse (EA) .... VDC
Video-Enhanced Contrast Polarization Microscopy .... VCPM
Video-Enhanced Contrast Technique [*Microscopy*] .... VEC
Video-Enhanced Differential Interference Contrast [*Microscopy*] .... VEDIC
Video-Enhanced User System [*Video conferencing*] .... VENUS
Videofile Microwave System .... VMS
Video-Game Epilepsy [*Neurology*] .... VGE
Videograph Display Control Unit .... VDCU
Videographic Systems of America, Inc. [*Ceased operation*] [*Information service or system*] (IID) .... VSA
Videographic Terminal .... VGT
Video-Intensified Fluorescence Microscopy .... VIFM
VideoLabs, Inc. [*Associated Press*] (SAG) .... VideoLab
VideoLabs, Inc. [*NASDAQ symbol*] (SAG) .... VLAB
VideoLan Tech [*NASDAQ symbol*] (TTSB) .... VLNT
VideoLan Technologies, Inc. [*Associated Press*] (SAG) .... VideoLan
VideoLan Technologies, Inc. [*Associated Press*] (SAG) .... VidLan
VideoLan Technologies, Inc. [*NASDAQ symbol*] (SAG) .... VLNT
Videolan Technologies Wrrt [*NASDAQ symbol*] (TTSB) .... VLNTW
Videonics, Inc. [*NASDAQ symbol*] (SAG) .... VDNX
Videonics, Inc. [*Associated Press*] (SAG) .... Videonics
Video-Pac Systems Ltd. [*Hollywood, CA*] [*Telecommunications service*] (TSSD) .... VPS
Videoplayer .... VP
Videos for Business and Training [*A publication*] .... VBT
VideoServer, Inc. [*Associated Press*] (SAG) .... VidServ
VideoServer, Inc. [*NASDAQ symbol*] (SAG) .... VSVR
Videotape .... VT
Videotape (VRA) .... vtp
Videotape Facilities Association (EA) .... VFA
Videotape Production Association (EA) .... VPA
Videotape Recorder (IAA) .... VDR
Videotape Recorder [*or Recording*] .... VTR
Video-Tape Recording (IDOE) .... VTR
Videotape Recording System .... VTRS
Videotape Response System .... VTRS
Videotex [*Telecommunications*] .... VTX
Videotex Access Point [*Computer science*] (IT) .... VAP
Videotex Editing Communications System (NITA) .... VECS
Videotex Industry Association (EA) .... VIA
Videotex Industry Association Ltd. (NITA) .... VIA
Videotex Information Service Providers Association of Canada [*Defunct*] (IID) .... VISPAC
Videotex Information System [*Radio Shack*] [*Information service or system*] (IID) .... VIS
Videotex Terminal Facility (NITA) .... VTF
Video-to-Hardcopy Recorder .... VHR
Videotron Groupe Ltee. SV [*Toronto Stock Exchange symbol*] .... VDO

Videotron Hldgs Plc 'ADS' [*NASDAQ symbol*] (TTSB) .... VRONY
Videotron Holdings PLC [*Associated Press*] (SAG) .... Videotr
Videotron Holdings PLC [*NASDAQ symbol*] (SAG) .... VRONY
Video-West Distributors Ltd. [*Vancouver Stock Exchange symbol*] .... VWD
Videsh Sanchar Nigam Ltd. [*India*] [*Telecommunications service*] (TSSD) ..... VSNL
Videtics International Corp. [*Vancouver Stock Exchange symbol*] VCI
Vidian's Exact Pleader [*1684*] [*A publication*] (DLA) .... VAC
Vidicon Alignment Coil .... VAC
Vidicon Camera System (MCD) .... VSC
Vidicon Camera Tube .... VCT
Vidicon Electron Tube .... VET
Vidicon Television Camera .... VTC
Vidin [*Bulgaria*] [*Airport symbol*] (OAG) .... VID
VIDION/International Association of Video (EA) .... IAV
Vidsel [*Sweden ICAO location identifier*] (ICLI) .... ESPE
Vidua [*Widow*] [*Latin*] (WGA) .... vid
Vie de France [*NASDAQ symbol*] (TTSB) .... VDEF
Vie de France Corp. [*McLean, VA*] [*NASDAQ symbol*] (NQ) .... VDEF
Vie de France Corp. [*Associated Press*] (SAG) .... Vie deFr
Vie Intellectuelle [*A publication*] (BJA) .... VInt
Viedma [*Argentina*] [*Airport symbol*] (OAG) .... VDM
Viedma/Gobernador Castello [*Argentina ICAO location identifier*] (ICLI) .... SAVV
Viel [*Coarse*] [*Latin*] (DAVI) V
Vienna [*Austria*] [*Airport symbol*] (OAG) .... VIE
Vienna [*Austria*] [*Seismograph station code, US Geological Survey*] (SEIS) ...... VIE
Vienna [*Austria*] (WDAA) .... VIEN
Vienna Allied Command [*British military*] (DMA) .... VIAC
Vienna Convention on Consular Relations (EERA) .... VCCR
Vienna Definition Language [*1960*] [*Computer science*] (CSR) .... VDL
Vienna Development Method [*Computer science*] .... VDM
Vienna, GA [*Location identifier FAA*] (FAAL) .... VNA
Vienna, GA [*AM radio station call letters*] .... WWWN
Vienna Institute for Development (EAIO) .... VID
Vienna International Centre [*United Nations*] VIC
Vienna International Centre Library [*Information service or system*] (IID) VICL
Vienna PeeDee Belemnite .... VPDB
Vienna Philharmonic Orchestra .... VPO
Vienna Standard Mean Ocean Water .... VSMOW
Vienna, WV [*FM radio station call letters*] .... WDMX
Viennair Luftfahrt GmbH [*Austria ICAO designator*] (FAAC) .... VNR
Vienna-Kobenzl [*Austria*] [*Seismograph station code, US Geological Survey*] (SEIS) .... VKA
Vienne/Reventin [*France ICAO location identifier*] (ICLI) .... LFHH
Viennola [*Record label*] [*Austria*] .... Vien
Vientiane [*Laos*] [*ICAO location identifier*] (ICLI) .... VLAO
Vientiane [*Laos*] [*Airport symbol*] (OAG) .... VTE
Vientiane/Wattay [*Laos*] [*ICAO location identifier*] (ICLI) .... VLVT
Vieques [*Puerto Rico*] [*ICAO location identifier*] (ICLI) .... TJVQ
Vieques [*Puerto Rico*] [*Seismograph station code, US Geological Survey Closed*] (SEIS) .... VQS
Vieques [*Puerto Rico*] [*Airport symbol*] (OAG) .... VQS
Vieques Air Link [*Caribbean airline*] .... VAL
Vieques Air Link, Inc. [*ICAO designator*] (FAAC) .... VES
Vieques Airlink [*ICAO designator*] (AD) VI
Vieques/Camp Garcia Airstrip [*Puerto Rico*] [*ICAO location identifier*] (ICLI) .... TJCG
Vieques, PR [*AM radio station call letters*] .... WIVV
Vieques, PR [*FM radio station call letters*] .... WSAN
Vierte Partei Deutschlands [*Fourth Party of Germany*] [*Political party*] (PPW) .... VPD
Vierteljahrschrift fuer Musikwissenschaft [*A publication*] .... VMW
Vierzon-Mereau [*France ICAO location identifier*] (ICLI) .... LFFV
Vieste [*Italy ICAO location identifier*] (ICLI) .... LIBI
Viet Cong Security Service (VNW) .... VSS
Viet Cong Suspect Confirmed (VNW) VCC
Viet Montagnard Cong .... VMC
Viet Nam Quoc Dan Dang [*Political party*] (VNW) .... VNQDD
Vietcong [*Vietnamese Communists*] VC
Vietcong Captured VCC
Vietcong Infrastructure VCI
Vietcong Infrastructure Neutralization System .... VCINS
Vietcong Killed .... VCK
Vietcong Killed in Action (Body Count) .... VC KIA(BC)
Vietcong Killed in Action (Possible) .... VC KIA(POSS)
Vietcong/North Vietnamese Army .... VC/NVA
Vietcong Prisoner of War .... VC PW
Vietcong Suspect .... VCS
Vierteljahresheft zur Statistik des Deutschen Reichs [*Germany*] .... VSDR
Vietminh (CINC) .... VM
Vietnam [*MARC geographic area code Library of Congress*] (LCCP) .... a-vt--
Vietnam [*License plate code assigned to foreign diplomats in the US*] .... LD
Vietnam .... Nam
Vietnam [*MARC country of publication code Library of Congress*] (LCCP) .... vm
Vietnam [*ANSI two-letter standard code*] (CNC) .... VN
Vietnam [*ANSI three-letter standard code*] (CNC) .... VNM
Vietnam (VRA) .... Vtnm
Vietnam Air Force .... VNAF
Vietnam Air Force Improvement and Modernization Program .... VNAF I & M
Vietnam Ammunition Program (AFM) .... VAMP
Vietnam Armed Forces .... VNAF
Vietnam Asset Reconciliation Procedure [*Military*] (AABC) .... VARP
Vietnam Campaign Medal [*Military decoration*] .... VNCM
Vietnam Christian Service [*Defunct*] (EA) .... VNCS
Vietnam Combat Veterans (EA) VCV
Vietnam Day Committee [*Antiwar group*] (VNW) .... VDC

Vietnam Demonstration [*FBI security file*] ..... VIDEM
Vietnam Educational Workers' Union [*North Vietnam*] ..... VEWU
Vietnam Era Veteran Recruitment Program ..... VEVERP
Vietnam Era Veterans (OICC) ..... VEV
Vietnam Era Veterans in Congress (EA) VVIC
Vietnam Era Veterans Inter-Tribal Association (EA) ..... VEITA
Vietnam Era Veterans Inter-Tribal Association (EA) ..... VEVITA
Vietnam Era Veterans Readjustment and Assistance Act of 1974 (WYGK) ..... VEVRA
Vietnam Expediting Task Force [*Military*] ..... VNETF
Vietnam Foundation (EA) ..... VNF
Vietnam General Confederation of Labor ..... VGCL
Vietnam General Federation of Trade Unions [*North Vietnam*] ..... VGFTU
Vietnam Head Injury Study ..... VHIS
Vietnam Helicopter Pilots Association (EA) ..... VHPA
Vietnam Individual Training Group [*Deactivated in December, 1972*] [*Military*] (VNW) ..... VITG
Vietnam Laboratory Assistance Program [*Naval Oceanographic Office*] ..... VLAP
Vietnam Laboratory Assistance Program, Army (RDA) ..... VLAPA
Vietnam Marine Corps ..... VNMC
Vietnam Nationalist Party [*Political party*] (VNW) ..... VNP
Vietnam Navy ..... VNN
Vietnam News Agency ..... VNA
Vietnam, North [*MARC geographic area code Library of Congress*] (LCCP) ..... a-vn--
Vietnam, North [*vm (Vietnam) used in records cataloged after January 1978*] [*MARC country of publication code Library of Congress*] (LCCP) ..... vn
Vietnam Press ..... VP
Vietnam Prisoners of War [*An association*] (AD) ..... NAMPMW
Vietnam Reactor ..... VNR
Vietnam Refugee and Information Services ..... VRIS
Vietnam Refugee Fund (EA) ..... VRF
Vietnam Service Medal [*Military decoration*] (AFM) ..... VSM
Vietnam, South [*MARC geographic area code Library of Congress*] (LCCP) ..... a-vs--
Vietnam, South [*vm (Vietnam) used in records cataloged after January 1978*] [*MARC country of publication code Library of Congress*] (LCCP) ..... vs
Vietnam Supply Rate [*Military*] (MCD) ..... VSR
Vietnam Veterans (OICC) VV
Vietnam Veterans Against the War (EA) ..... VVAW
Vietnam Veterans Agent Orange Victims (EA) ..... VVAOVI
Vietnam Veterans Arts Group [*Later, CTVWA*] (EA) ..... VVAG
Vietnam Veterans Association of Australia ..... VVAA
Vietnam Veterans, Inc. [*Defunct*] (EA) VVI
Vietnam Veterans Institute [*Research center*] (RCD) VVI
Vietnam Veterans Institute for Research and Advocacy (EA) ..... VVIRA
Vietnam Veterans Inter-Tribal Association (EA) ..... VVITA
Vietnam Veterans Leadership Program [*ACTION*] ..... VVLP
Vietnam Veterans Memorial (VNW) ..... VVM
Vietnam Veterans Memorial Fund [*Defunct*] (EA) ..... VVMF
Vietnam Veterans of America (EA) ..... VVA
Vietnam Women's Memorial Project (EA) ..... VWMP
Vietnam Workers' Party [*Political party*] (PPW) ..... VWP
Vietnam-Canada Foundation ..... VCF
Vietnam-Canada Foundation ..... VNCF
Vietnamese [*MARC language code Library of Congress*] (LCCP) ..... vie
Vietnamese ..... VNESE
Vietnamese Air Defense Force (MCD) ..... VADF
Vietnamese Air Force (MCD) ..... VAF
Vietnamese American Association ..... VAA
Vietnamese Catholic Federation in the USA (EA) ..... VCFUSA
Vietnamese Civilian (VNW) ..... VNC
Vietnamese Cross of Gallantry with Bronze Star [*Military decoration*] (AABC) ..... VCOFGWBS
Vietnamese Cross of Gallantry with Gold Star [*Military decoration*] (AABC) ..... VCOFGWGS
Vietnamese Cross of Gallantry with Palm [*Military decoration*] (AABC) ..... VCOFGWP
Vietnamese Cross of Gallantry with Silver Star [*Military decoration*] (AABC) ..... VCOFGWSS
Vietnamese Cultural Association of North America (EA) ..... VICANA
Vietnamese Government Information Department (VNW) ..... VDGI
Vietnamese Information Service ..... VIS
Vietnamese National Army ..... VNA
Vietnamese National Oceanographic Data Center [*Marine science*] (OSRA) ..... VNODC
Vietnamese National Railway System (CINC) ..... VNRS
Vietnamese Organization to Exterminate Communists and Restore the Nation (EA) ..... VOECRN
Vietnamese Senior Citizens Association (EA) ..... VSCA
Vietnamese Sisters Incarnational Consecration (TOCD) IC
Vietnamese Special Forces (CINC) ..... VNSF
Vietnamese Union Catalog Project, University of Michigan, Ann Arbor, MI [*Library symbol*] [*Library of Congress*] (LCLS) ..... VUCP
Vietnamese-American Children's Fund [*Defunct*] (EA) ..... VACF
VietNow (EA) ..... VN
Vieux Style [*Old Style*] [*French*] ..... VS
Vieux-Fort/Hewanorra International [*St. Lucia*] [*ICAO location identifier*] (ICLI) ..... TLPL
View [*Computer science*] [*Telecommunications*] v
View [*Commonly used*] (OPSA) ..... VIEW
View (MCD) ..... VW
View ..... VW
View (VRA) ..... vw
View Control System (HGAA) ..... VCS
View Factor ..... VF
View Loss VL
View Tech, Inc. [*Associated Press*] (SAG) ..... ViewT
View Tech, Inc. [*Associated Press*] (SAG) ..... ViewTc
View Tech, Inc. [*NASDAQ symbol*] (SAG) ..... VUTK
View Tech Wrrt [*NASDAQ symbol*] (TTSB) ..... VUTKW
Viewdata Corp. of America, Inc. [*Miami Beach, FL*] [*Telecommunications*] (TSSD) ..... VCA
VIEWDATA Terminal Program ..... VTP
Viewdata/Videotex Report [*Link Resources Corp.*] [*Information service or system*] (CRD) ..... VVR
Viewer Controlled Television (WDMC) ..... VCTV
Viewers for Quality Television (EA) ..... VQT
Viewers in Profile [*A. C. Nielsen Co. reports for television industry*] ..... VIP
Viewers Intent on Listing Violent Episodes on Nationwide Television [*Student legal action organization*] ..... VIOLENT
Viewers Per Household [*Television ratings*] (DOAD) ..... VPH
Viewers-per-Set [*Television ratings*] (WDMC) ..... VPS
Viewers-per-Viewing Household [*Television ratings*] (NTCM) ..... V/VH
Viewers-per-Viewing Household [*Television ratings*] (NTCM) ..... VPVH
Viewfinder [*Photography*] ..... VF
Viewfinder Tracking System ..... VTS
Viewfinder-Metering System (KSC) ..... VMS
Viewing Instantly Security Transactions Automatically [*Wall Street*] ..... VISTA
Viewing Window Deicing Unit ..... VWDU
Viewlogic Systems [*NASDAQ symbol*] (TTSB) ..... VIEW
Viewlogic Systems, Inc. [*NASDAQ symbol*] (SPSG) ..... VIEW
Viewlogic Systems, Inc. [*Associated Press*] (SAG) ..... Viewlg
Viewpoint (NASA) ..... VP
Viewpoint Adapter Assembly (NASA) ..... VAA
Views [*Commonly used*] (OPSA) ..... VIEWS
Views [*Postal Service standard*] (OPSA) ..... VWS
Viewscan Text System (NITA) ..... VTS
Vigan, Ilocos Sur [*Philippines*] [*ICAO location identifier*] (ICLI) ..... RPUQ
Vigente [*In Force*] [*Italian*] (ILCA) ..... Vig
Vigil (ROG) ..... VIG
Vigilance Committee VC
Vigilance, Initiative, Excellence [*Aerospace Defense Command's acronym for the Zero Defects Program*] ..... VIE
Vigilant Identification (MCD) ..... VIG
Viglius ab Ayta Zuichemus [*Deceased, 1577*] [*Authority cited in pre-1607 legal work*] (DSA) ..... Vigl
Vigna Di Valle [*Italy ICAO location identifier*] (ICLI) ..... LIRB
Vignette (VRA) ..... vgnt
Vignette (ADA) ..... VIG
Vignetted Halftone [*Graphic arts*] (DGA) ..... VHT
Vigo [*Spain ICAO location identifier*] (ICLI) ..... LEVX
Vigo [*Spain*] [*Airport symbol*] (OAG) ..... VGO
Vigo County Public Library, Terre Haute, IN [*Library symbol Library of Congress*] (LCLS) ..... InTV
Vigo County Public Library, Terre Haute, IN [*OCLC symbol*] (OCLC) IVC
Vigo County School Corp., Instructional Materials Center, Terre Haute, IN [*Library symbol Library of Congress*] (LCLS) ..... InTVS
Vigo County School Corp., Terre Haute, IN [*OCLC symbol*] (OCLC) ..... IVS
Vigorniensis [*Signature of the Bishops of Worcester*] [*Latin*] (ROG) ..... VIGORN
Vigoro Corp. [*NYSE symbol*] (SPSG) ..... VGR
Vigoro Corp. [*Associated Press*] (SAG) ..... Vigoro
Vigoroso [*With Vigor*] [*Music*] (ROG) ..... VIG
Vigorous (DAVI) ..... vig
Viisage Technology, Inc. [*Associated Press*] (SAG) ..... Viisage
Viisage Technology, Inc. [*NASDAQ symbol*] (SAG) ..... VISG
Viitasaari [*Finland ICAO location identifier*] (ICLI) ..... EFVI
Vijayawada [*India*] [*Airport symbol*] (OAG) ..... VGA
Vijayawada [*India*] [*ICAO location identifier*] (ICLI) ..... VOBZ
Vik [*Iceland*] [*Seismograph station code, US Geological Survey Closed*] (SEIS) ..... VIK
Vik Chandler Fan Club (EA) ..... VCFC
Vikarabad [*India*] [*ICAO location identifier*] (ICLI) ..... VOVB
Viking ..... VKG
Viking Air Lines ..... VIKA
Viking Change Status [*NASA*] ..... VCS
Viking Continuation Mission [*NASA*] ..... VCM
Viking Elementary School, Pelican Rapids, MN [*Library symbol*] [*Library of Congress*] (LCLS) ..... MnPerVE
Viking Error Analysis Monte Carlo Program [*Computer science*] ..... VEAMCOP
Viking Express, Inc. [*ICAO designator*] (FAAC) ..... WCY
Viking Flight Operations [*NASA*] ..... VFO
Viking Flight Team [*NASA*] ..... VFT
Viking Integrated Change [*NASA*] VIC
Viking International Airlines [*ICAO designator*] (FAAC) ..... VIK
Viking Lander [*NASA*] VL
Viking Lander Biological Instrument [*NASA*] ..... VLBI
Viking Lander Capsule [*NASA*] VLC
Viking Lander Imaging System [*NASA*] ..... VLIS
Viking Lander System [*NASA*] (KSC) ..... VLS
Viking Library System [*Library network*] ..... VLIS
Viking Library System, Fergus Falls, MN [*Library symbol*] [*Library of Congress*] (LCLS) ..... MnFfV
Viking Office Products [*Associated Press*] (SAG) ..... VkingOP
Viking Office Products [*NASDAQ symbol*] (SAG) ..... VKNG
Viking Office Products, Inc. [*Associated Press*] (SAG) ..... Viking OP
Viking Orbiter [*NASA*] ..... VO
Viking Orbiter Design Change [*NASA*] ..... VODC
Viking Orbiter System [*NASA*] ..... VOS
Viking Project Office [*NASA*] (KSC) ..... VPO

Viking Public Library, Alberta [*Library symbol National Library of Canada*] (NLC) .... AVIK
Viking Public Library, Viking, AB, Canada [*Library symbol*] [*Library of Congress*] (LCLS) .... CaVik
Viking RADAR Altimeter [*NASA*] .... VRA
Viking Society for Northern Research [*British*] .... VSNP
Viking Spacecraft [*NASA*] .... V-S/C
Viking Targeting Analysis Program [*NASA*] .... VITAP
Vikki's Special People (EA) .... VSP
Vila Cabral [*Mozambique*] [*Airport symbol*] (AD) VXC
Vila Coutinho [*Mozambique*] [*Airport symbol Obsolete*] (OAG) .... VHO
Vila Das Neves [*Sao Tome*] [*ICAO location identifier*] (ICLI) .... FPVN
Vila de Joao Belo [*Mozambique*] [*Airport symbol*] (AD) .... VJB
Vila Pery [*Mozambique*] [*Airport symbol*] (AD) .... VPY
Vila Real [*Portugal ICAO location identifier*] (ICLI) .... LPVR
Vila Real [*Portugal*] [*Airport symbol*] (OAG) .... VRL
Vilanculos [*Mozambique*] [*ICAO location identifier*] (ICLI) .... FQVL
Vilanculos [*Mozambique*] [*Airport symbol*] (AD) .... VNX
Vilas and Bryant's Edition of the Wisconsin Reports [*A publication*] (DLA) .... Vil & Br
Vilas' Criminal Reports [*1-5 New York*] [*A publication*] (DLA) .... Vilas
Vilhelmina [*Sweden ICAO location identifier*] (ICLI) .... ESNV
Vilhena [*Brazil*] [*Airport symbol*] (AD) .... BVH
Vilhena [*Brazil ICAO location identifier*] (ICLI) .... SBVH
Villa VIL
Villa Aroma [*Bolivia*] [*ICAO location identifier*] (ICLI) .... SLVA
Villa Cisneros [*Western Sahara*] [*ICAO location identifier*] (ICLI) .... GSVO
Villa Cisneros [*Spanish Sahara*] [*Airport symbol*] (AD) VIL
Villa De Soto [*Argentina ICAO location identifier*] (ICLI) .... SACS
Villa Dolores [*Argentina ICAO location identifier*] (ICLI) .... SAOD
Villa Dolores [*Argentina*] [*Airport symbol*] (AD) .... VDR
Villa Gesell [*Argentina ICAO location identifier*] (ICLI) .... SAZV
Villa Gesell [*Argentina*] [*Airport symbol*] (OAG) .... VLG
Villa Grajales [*Mexico*] [*Seismograph station code, US Geological Survey Closed*] (SEIS) .... VGM
Villa Gral, Mitre [*Argentina ICAO location identifier*] (ICLI) .... SACM
Villa Madonna College [*Kentucky*] .... VMC
Villa Maria College [*Erie, PA*] .... VMC
Villa Maria College, Erie, PA [*Library symbol Library of Congress*] (LCLS) .... PErVM
Villa Maria College of Buffalo, Buffalo, NY [*Library symbol Library of Congress*] (LCLS) .... NBuVM
Villa Maria Del Rio Seco [*Argentina ICAO location identifier*] (ICLI) .... SACV
Villa Mercedes [*Argentina*] [*Airport symbol*] (OAG) .... VME
Villa Mercy [*Maryland*] [*Seismograph station code, US Geological Survey Closed*] (SEIS) VIL
Villa Montes [*Bolivia*] [*ICAO location identifier*] (ICLI) .... SLVM
Villa Park Dam [*California*] [*Seismograph station code, US Geological Survey*] (SEIS) .... VPD
Villa Regional Library, Lakewood, CO [*Library symbol Library of Congress*] (LCLS) .... CoLw
Villa Reynolds [*Argentina ICAO location identifier*] (ICLI) .... SAOR
Villa Vista [*Bolivia*] [*ICAO location identifier*] (ICLI) .... SLBV
Villa Walsh College [*New Jersey*] .... VWC
Villacoublay [*France ICAO location identifier*] (ICLI) .... LFYO
Villacoublay/Velizy [*France ICAO location identifier*] (ICLI) .... LFPV
Villafranca [*Italy ICAO location identifier*] (ICLI) .... LIPX
Village V
Village VIL
Village VILL
Village [*Commonly used*] (OPSA) .... VILLAG
Village [*Commonly used*] (OPSA) .... VILLAGE
Village [*Commonly used*] (OPSA) .... VILLG
Village [*Commonly used*] (OPSA) .... VILLIAGE
Village (MCD) .... VLG
Village .... VLG
Village and Local Development .... VLD
Village & Marketing Corp. [*Jamaica*] .... VAMCO
Village Assistance [*or Action*] Team (DNAB) .... VAT
Village Aviation, Inc. [*ICAO designator*] (FAAC) .... CAM
Village Bancorp [*NASDAQ symbol*] (SAG) .... VBNK
Village Bancorp [*Associated Press*] (SAG) .... VilagBcp
Village Elementary School, Syosset, NY [*Library symbol Library of Congress*] (LCLS) .... NSyoVE
Village Green Bookstore [*NASDAQ symbol*] (TTSB) .... BOOK
Village Green Bookstore [*Associated Press*] (SAG) .... VillGrBk
[The] Village Green Bookstore, Inc. [*NASDAQ symbol*] (NQ) .... BOOK
Village Green Bookstore, Inc. [*Associated Press*] (SAG) .... VillGr
Village Green Bookstore, Inc. [*Associated Press*] (SAG) .... VillGrBk
Village Green Bookstore Wrrt [*NASDAQ symbol*] (TTSB) .... BOOKW
Village Level Workers [*India*] .... VLW
Village of Childhelp (EA) VC
Village Produce Association [*British*] (BI) .... VPA
Village Self-Development .... VSD
Village Self-Help .... VSH
Village Super Market, Inc. [*Associated Press*] (SAG) .... VilSpM
Village Super Market, Inc. [*NASDAQ symbol*] (NQ) .... VLGE
Village Super Market'A' [*NASDAQ symbol*] (TTSB) .... VLGEA
Village Voice [*A publication*] (BRI) VV
Village Voice Literary Supplement [*A publication*] (BRI) .... VLS
Villages [*Commonly used*] (OPSA) .... VILLAGES
Villages [*Commonly used*] (OPSA) .... VLGS
Villaguay [*Argentina ICAO location identifier*] (ICLI) .... SAAU
Villahermosa [*Mexico ICAO location identifier*] (ICLI) .... MMVA
Villahermosa [*Mexico*] [*Airport symbol*] (OAG) .... VSA
Villa-Lobos Music Society (EA) .... VLMS

Villandry Festival [*Record label*] [*France*] Vill
Villano [*Ecuador*] [*ICAO location identifier*] (ICLI) .... SEVI
Villanova, PA [*FM radio station call letters*] .... WXVU
Villanova University (GAGS) .... Villanova U
Villanova University, Business and Finance Library, Villanova, PA [*Library symbol Library of Congress*] (LCLS) .... PV-B
Villanova University, Law School, Villanova, PA [*Library symbol Library of Congress*] (LCLS) .... PV-L
Villanova University, Villanova, PA [*Library symbol Library of Congress*] (LCLS) .... PV
Villanova University, Villanova, PA [*OCLC symbol*] (OCLC) .... PVU
Villard Public School, Villard, MN [*Library symbol*] [*Library of Congress*] (LCLS) .... MnVilS
Villas .... VS
Villas, NJ [*FM radio station call letters*] .... WFNN
Villavicencio [*Colombia*] [*Airport symbol*] (OAG) VVC
Villavicencio/Vanguardia [*Colorado ICAO location identifier*] (ICLI) .... SKVV
Ville [*Commonly used*] (OPSA) .... VILLE
Ville VL
Ville VL
Ville de Laval, Archives des Freres des Ecoles Chretienne, Laval, PQ, Canada [*Library symbol*] [*Library of Congress*] (LCLS) .... CaQLFECA
Ville de Montreal, Bibliotheque de Documentation des Archives, Montreal, PQ, Canada [*Library symbol Library of Congress*] (LCLS) .... CaQMCih
Ville Marie [*Quebec*] [*Seismograph station code, US Geological Survey Closed*] (SEIS) .... VMC
Ville Platte, LA [*AM radio station call letters*] .... KVPI
Ville Platte, LA [*FM radio station call letters*] .... KVPI-FM
Villebon Resources Ltd. [*Vancouver Stock Exchange symbol*] .... VLN
Villefrance/Tarare [*France ICAO location identifier*] (ICLI) .... LFHV
Villefranche-De-Rouergue [*France ICAO location identifier*] (ICLI) .... LFCV
Ville-Marie, PQ [*AM radio station call letters*] .... CKVM
Villeneuve Resources [*Vancouver Stock Exchange symbol*] .... VIE
Villeneuve-Sur-Lot [*France ICAO location identifier*] (ICLI) .... LFCW
Villers Foundation [*Later, Families USA Foundation*] (EA) .... VF
Villerupt [*France ICAO location identifier*] (ICLI) .... LFAW
Villisca Review, Villisca, IA [*Library symbol*] [*Library of Congress*] (LCLS) .... IaVilR
Villonodular Synovitis [*Medicine*] (DAVI) .... VNS
Villonodular Synovitis [*Medicine*] (MAE) .... VS
Vilna Public Library, Alberta [*Library symbol National Library of Canada*] (NLC) .... AVI
Vilna Public Library, Vilna, AB, Canada [*Library symbol*] [*Library of Congress*] (LCLS) .... CaAVi
Vilnius [*Former USSR ICAO location identifier*] (ICLI) .... UMWW
Vilnius [*Former USSR Airport symbol*] (OAG) .... VNO
Vilnius Commodity Exchange [*Lithuania*] (EY) .... VICE
Vilocity [*Former USSR*] [*FAA designator*] (FAAC) .... VKT
Vilsbiburg [*Germany ICAO location identifier*] (ICLI) .... EDMP
Vilseck [*Germany ICAO location identifier*] (ICLI) .... EDOI
Vilshofen [*Germany ICAO location identifier*] (ICLI) .... EDMV
VIMRx Pharma Wrrt'B' [*NASDAQ symbol*] (TTSB) .... VMRXZ
VIMRx Pharmaceuticals [*NASDAQ symbol*] (TTSB) .... VMRX
VimRx Pharmaceuticals [*NASDAQ symbol*] (SAG) .... VMRX
VimRx Pharmaceuticals, Inc. [*Associated Press*] (SAG) .... Vimrx
Vimy Public Library, Alberta [*Library symbol National Library of Canada*] (NLC) .... AV
Vina Concha y Toro ADS [*NYSE symbol*] (TTSB) .... VCO
Vina Concha y Toro SA [*NYSE symbol*] (SAG) .... VCO
Vina Concha y Toro SA [*Associated Press*] (SAG) .... VinaConc
Vina Del Mar/Rodelillo [*Chile*] [*ICAO location identifier*] (ICLI) .... SCRD
Vinair-Helicopteros Ltda. [*Portugal ICAO designator*] (FAAC) .... VIN
Vinbarbital [*A hypnotic and sedative*] (DAVI) .... VIN
Vinblastine [*See VBL*] V
Vinblastine [*Velban, Vincaleukoblastine*] [*Also, V, Ve, VLB*] [*Antineoplastic drug*] .... VBL
Vinblastine, Actinomycin D, Bleomycin [*Antineoplastic drug regimen*] .... VAB
Vinblastine, Actinomycin D [*Dactinomycin*], Bleomycin [*Antineoplastic drug regimen*] .... VAB-I
Vinblastine, Actinomycin D [*Dactinomycin*], Bleomycin, Cisplatin [*Antineoplastic drug regimen*] .... VAB-II
Vinblastine, Actinomycin D [*Dactinomycin*], Bleomycin, Cisplatin, Chlorambucil, Cyclophosphamide [*Antineoplastic drug regimen*] .... VAB-III
Vinblastine, Actinomycin D [*Dactinomycin*] Bleomycin, Cisplatin, Cyclophosphamide, Chlorambucil, and Adriamycin [*Antineoplastic drug regimen*] (DAVI) .... VAB-IV
Vinblastine, Actinomycin D [*Dactinomycin*], Bloeomycin, Cisplatin, and Cyclophosphamide [*Antineoplastic drug regimen*] (DAVI) .... VAB-V
Vinblastine, Actinomycin D [*Dactinomycin*] Cisplatin (DAVI) .... VAP-II
Vinblastine, Actinomycin D [*Dactinomycin*], Platinol [*Cisplatin*] [*Antineoplastic drug regimen*] .... VAP
Vinblastine, Adriamycin, Bleomycin, CCNU [*Lomustine*], Dacarbazine [*Antineoplastic drug regimen*] .... VABCD
Vinblastine, Adriamycin, Thiotepa [*Antineoplastic drug regimen*] .... VATH
Vinblastine, Adriamycin, Thiotepa, Halotestin [*Fluoxymesterone*] [*Antineoplastic drug regimen*] .... VATH
Vinblastine, Bleomycin [*Antineoplastic drug regimen*] .... VB
Vinblastine, Bleomycin, and Platinol [*Antineoplastic drug regimen*] (MAE) .... VBP
Vinblastine, Bleomycin, Diamminedichloroplatinum [*Cisplatin*] [*Antineoplastic drug regimen*] .... VBD
Vinblastine, Bleomycin, Prednisone [*Antineoplastic drug*] (CDI) .... VBP
Vinblastine, Dacabazine, Cisplatin (CDI) .... VDP
Vinblastine, Platinol [*Cisplatin*], Bleomycin [*Antineoplastic drug regimen*] .... VPB
Vincaleukoblastine [*Also, V, VBL, Ve*] [*Antineoplastic drug*] .... VLB
Vincam Group [*NASDAQ symbol*] (TTSB) .... VCAM
Vince Smith Fan Club (EA) .... VSFC

Vincennes and Knox County Public Libraries, Vincennes, IN [*Library symbol Library of Congress*] (LCLS) .... InVi

Vincennes, IN [*Location identifier FAA*] (FAAL) .... OEA

Vincennes, IN [*AM radio station call letters*] .... WAOV

Vincennes, IN [*FM radio station call letters*] .... WFML

Vincennes, IN [*FM radio station call letters*] .... WVUB

Vincennes, IN [*Television station call letters*] .... WVUT

Vincennes, IN [*FM radio station call letters*] .... WZDM

Vincennes Sun Commercial, Vincennes, IN [*Library symbol Library of Congress*] (LCLS) .... InViSC

Vincennes University, Byron R. Lewis Historical Collections Library, Vincennes, IN [*Library symbol Library of Congress*] (LCLS) .... InViU-Hi

Vincennes University, Vincennes, IN [*Library symbol Library of Congress*] (LCLS) .... InViU

Vincennes University, Vincennes, IN [*OCLC symbol*] (OCLC) IVV

Vincent Massey Secondary School, Windsor, ON, Canada [*Library symbol Library of Congress*] (LCLS) .... CaOWVM

Vincent Massey Secondary School, Windsor, Ontario [*Library symbol National Library of Canada*] (NLC) .... OWVM

Vincent on Criticism and Libel [*A publication*] (DLA) .... Vinc Cr & Lib

Vincent Owners Club (EA) .... VOC

Vincent Van Gogh Foundation (EA) .... VVGF

Vincentian Congregation (TOCD) vc

Vincentian Congregation (India) (TOCD) VC

Vincentian Sisters of Charity [*Roman Catholic religious order*] .... VSC

Vincentius de Franchis [*Deceased, 1601*] [*Authority cited in pre-1607 legal work*] (DSA) .... Vincent de Franch

Vincentius Hispanus [*Deceased, 1248*] [*Authority cited in pre-1607 legal work*] (DSA) V

Vincentius Hispanus [*Deceased, 1248*] [*Authority cited in pre-1607 legal work*] (DSA) Vi

Vincentius Hispanus [*Deceased, 1248*] [*Authority cited in pre-1607 legal work*] (DSA) .... Vin

Vincentius Hispanus [*Deceased, 1248*] [*Authority cited in pre-1607 legal work*] (DSA) .... Vinc

Vincentius Palaeotus [*Deceased, 1498*] [*Authority cited in pre-1607 legal work*] (DSA) .... Vin Palaeot

Vincent's Angina [*Medicine*] .... VA

Vincent's Manual of Criminal Law [*A publication*] (DLA) .... Vinc Cr L

Vinces [*Ecuador*] [*ICAO location identifier*] (ICLI) .... SEVN

Vinchina [*Argentina*] [*Seismograph station code, US Geological Survey*] (SEIS) .... VCA

Vincit Sapientia Robur [*Wisdom Overcomes Strength*] [*Motto of Johann Ernst, Duke of Saxony-Eisenach (1566-1638)*] [*Latin*] .... VSR

Vincristine [*Also, LCR, O, V, VC, VCR*] [*Antineoplastic drug*] V

Vincristine [*Also, LCR, O, V, VCR*] [*Antineoplastic drug*] (AAMN) VC

Vincristine [*Also, LCR, O, V, VC*] [*Antineoplastic drug*] .... VCR

Vincristine, 5-Fluorouracil, Adriamycin, Mitomycin C [*Antineoplastic drug regimen*] (DAVI) .... VFAM

Vincristine, Actinomycin D, Cyclophosphamide [*Antineoplastic drug regimen*] .... VAC

Vincristine, Actinomycin, Methotrexate, Prednisone [*Antineoplastic drug regimen*] .... VAMP

Vincristine, Adriamycin, 6-Mercaptopurine, and Prednisone [*Antineoplastic drug regimen*] (DAVI) .... BOMB

Vincristine, Adriamycin, Cyclophosphamide [*Also, VACY*] [*Antineoplastic drug regimen*] .... VAC

Vincristine, Adriamycin, Cyclophosphamide [*Also, VAC*] [*Antineoplastic drug regimen*] .... VACY

Vincristine, Adriamycin, Cyclophosphamide [*Antineoplastic drug regimen*] (DAVI) .... VADRC

Vincristine, Adriamycin, Cyclophosphamide, Actinomycin D [*Dactinomycin*] [*Antineoplastic drug regimen*] (DAVI) .... VADA

Vincristine, Adriamycin, Cyclophosphamide, and Actinomycin D [*Dactinomycin*] (DAVI) .... VACAR

Vincristine, Adriamycin, Cyclophosphamide, Methotrexate [*Antineoplastic drug regimen*] .... VACM

Vincristine, Adriamycin, Decadron [*Antineoplastic drug*] (CDI) .... VAD

Vincristine, Adriamycin, Dexamethasone [*Antineoplastic drug regimen*] (MEDA) .... VAD

Vincristine, Adriamycin, DIC [*Dacarbazine*] [*Antineoplastic drug regimen*] .... VADIC

Vincristine, Adriamycin, Prednisolone, Cyclophosphamide [*Antineoplastic drug regimen*] .... VAP-Cyclo

Vincristine, Adriamycin, Prednisone [*Antineoplastic drug regimen*] .... VAP

Vincristine, Adriamycin, Procarbazine [*Antineoplastic drug regimen*] .... VAP

Vincristine Amethopterin [*Antitumor agent*] .... VAMP

Vincristine, Amethopterin [*Methotrexate*], **Fluorouracil, Adriamycin, Cyclophosphamide** [*Antineoplastic drug regimen*] .... VAFAC

Vincristine, Amethopterin [*Methotrexate*], **Mercaptopurine, Prednisone** [*Antineoplastic drug regimen*] .... VAMP

Vincristine and Prednisone [*Antineoplastic drug regimen*] .... VP

Vincristine, ara-C [*Cytarabine*], **Thioguanine, Daunorubicin** [*Antineoplastic drug regimen*] .... VATD

Vincristine, BCNU [*Carmustine*], **Adriamycin** [*Antineoplastic drug regimen*] .... VBA

Vincristine, BCNU [*Carmustine*], **Adriamycin, Prednisone** [*Antineoplastic drug regimen*] .... VBAP

Vincristine, Bleomycin, Cisplatin [*Antineoplastic drug regimen*] (DAVI) .... VBC

Vincristine, Bleomycin, Methotrexate [*Antineoplastic drug regimen*] .... VBM

Vincristine, Cyclophosphamide, Adriamycin, Prednisone [*Antineoplastic drug regimen*] .... VCAP

Vincristine, Cyclophosphamide, Fluorouracil [*Antineoplastic drug regimen*] .... VCF

Vincristine, Cyclophosphamide, Melphalan, Prednisone [*Antineoplastic drug regimen*] .... VCMP

Vincristine, Cyclophosphamide, Prednisone [*Antineoplastic drug regimen*] .... VCP

Vincristine, Cytosine Arabinoside, 6-Thioguanine, Daunomycin [*Antineoplastic drug regimen*] (DAVI) .... VAT

Vincristine, Daunorubicin, Prednisone [*Antineoplastic drug regimen*] .... VDP

Vincristine, Endoxan [*Cyclophosphamide*], **6-Mercaptopurine, Prednisone** [*Antineoplastic drug regimen*] (DAVI) .... VEMP

Vincristine, Endoxan [*Cyclophosphamide*], **Natulan , Prednisone** [*Procarbazine*] [*Antineoplastic drug regimen*] .... VENP

Vincristine, Endoxan [*Cyclophosphamide*], **Prednisone, Adriamycin** [*Antineoplastic drug regimen*] .... VEPA

Vincristine, L-Asparaginase, Prednisone [*Antineoplastic drug regimen*] .... VLP

Vincristine, Melphalan, Cyclophosphamide, Prednisone [*Antineoplastic drug regimen*] .... VMCP

Vincristine, Melphalan, Prednisone, Procarbazine [*Antineoplastic drug regimen*] .... VMPP

Vincristine, Methotrexate, Adriamycin, Actinomycin D [*Antineoplastic drug regimen*] .... VMAD

Vincristine, Methotrexate, VP-16 [*Etoposide*] [*Antineoplastic drug regimen*] (DAVI) .... VMV

Vincristine, Prednisone, Cyclophosphamide, Methotrexate, Fluorouracil [*Antineoplastic drug regimen*] .... VPCMF

Vincristine, Prednisone, Cytosine Arabinoside, Cyclophosphamide, and 6-Thioguanine [*Antineoplastic drug regimen*] (DAVI) .... T-COAP

Vincristine, Prednisone, Vinblastine, Chlorambucil, Procarbazine [*Antineoplastic drug regimen*] .... VPCPr

Vincristine, Prednisone, Vinblastine, Chlorambucil, Procarbazine [*Antineoplastic drug regimen*] .... VPVCPr

Vindesine [*Also, E*] [*Antineoplastic drug*] .... VDS

Vindication (ROG) .... VIND

Vine Grove, KY [*FM radio station call letters*] .... WRZI

Vinegar [*Phonetic alphabet*] [*Royal Navy World War I*] (DSUE) V

Vinegar Brewers Federation [*British*] (DBA) .... VBF

Vinegar Institute (EA) VI

Vineland Adaptive Behavior Scale [*Psychology*] (EDAC) .... VABS

Vineland Free Public Library, Vineland, NJ [*Library symbol Library of Congress*] (LCLS) .... NjV

Vineland Historical and Antiquarian Society, Vineland, NJ [*Library symbol Library of Congress*] (LCLS) .... NjVHi

Vineland Measurement of Social Competence [*Speech and language therapy*] (DAVI) .... VMSC

Vineland, NJ [*Television station call letters*] .... WHSP

Vineland, NJ [*AM radio station call letters*] .... WMIZ

Vineland, NJ [*FM radio station call letters*] .... WVLT

Vineland Social Maturity Scale [*Psychology*] .... VSMS

Viner [*E. A.*] **Holdings** [*Toronto Stock Exchange symbol*] .... EAV

Viner's Abridgment [*or Commentaries*] [*A publication*] (DLA) .... Vin Comm

Viner's Abridgment of Law and Equity [*1741-53*] [*A publication*] (DLA) .... Vin Abr (Eng)

Viner's Abridgment of Law and Equity [*1741-53*] [*A publication*] (DLA) .... Viner Abr

VINES [*Virtual Networking Software*] **Interprocess Communications Protocol** [*Computer science*] (PCM) .... VICP

Vinethene and Ether .... V & E

Vineyard [*California*] [*Seismograph station code, US Geological Survey Closed*] (SEIS) .... VIN

Vineyard Environmental Research Institute [*Research center*] (RCD) .... VERI

Vineyard Haven, MA [*Television station call letters*] .... WZBU

Vineyard Haven Public Library, Vineyard Haven, MA [*Library symbol Library of Congress*] (LCLS) .... MVh

Vineyard Telemeter [*California*] [*Seismograph station code, US Geological Survey Closed*] (SEIS) .... VIT

Vineyards Association of Tasmania [*Australia*] .... VAT

Vings [*Bulgaria*] [*ICAO designator*] (FAAC) .... VGS

Vinh [*Viet Nam*] [*ICAO location identifier*] (ICLI) .... VVVH

Viniculture (WDAA) .... VINI

Vinifera Wine Growers Association (EA) .... VWGA

Vinings Investment Properties Trust [*Associated Press*] (SAG) .... Vining

Vinings Investment Properties Trust [*NASDAQ symbol*] (SAG) .... VIPI

Vinings Invstmt Prop [*NASDAQ symbol*] (TTSB) .... VIPSC

Vinita, OK [*AM radio station call letters*] .... KITO

Vinita, OK [*FM radio station call letters*] .... KITO-FM

Vinland Property [*NASDAQ symbol*] (NQ) .... VIPT

Vinland Property Tr SBI [*NASDAQ symbol*] (TTSB) .... VIPTS

Vinland Property Trust [*Associated Press*] (SAG) .... Vinland

Vinnius' Commentary on the Institutes of Justinian [*A publication*] (DLA) .... Vinn ad Inst

Vinon [*France ICAO location identifier*] (ICLI) .... LFNF

Vins Delimites de Qualite Superieure [*Designation on French wine labels*] .... VDQS

Vinson, Elkins, Searls, Connally & Smith, Law Library, Houston, TX [*Library symbol Library of Congress*] (LCLS) .... TxHVE

Vint Hill Farms Station [*Army*] .... VHFS

Vinta Exploration Ltd. [*Vancouver Stock Exchange symbol*] .... VAE

Vintage and Classic Car Club [*Australia*] VCCC

Vintage and Classic Sailing Association [*British*] (DBA) .... VCSA

Vintage Austin Register [*Ashover, Derbyshire, England*] (EAIO) .... VAR

Vintage BMW [*Bavarian Motor Works*] **Motorcycle Owners** (EA) .... VBMWMO

Vintage Carriages Trust [*British*] (DBA) .... VCT

Vintage Chevrolet Club of America (EA) .... VCCA

Vintage Japanese Motorcycle Club (EA) .... VJMC

Vintage Light Music Society [*British*] .... VLMS

Vintage Motor Bike Club (EA) .... VMBC

Vintage Motor Cycle Club [*British*] (DBA) .... VMCC

Vintage Petroleum [*Associated Press*] (SAG) .... VintgPt

Vintage Petroleum [*NYSE symbol*] (SPSG) .... VPI

Vintage Racers of Old Motorcycles (EA) .... VROOM

Vintage Radio and Phonograph Society (EA) .... VRPS
Vintage Sailplane Association (EA) .... VSA
Vintage Sports Car Club [Australia] .... VSCC
Vintage Sports Car Club [British] (DBA) .... VSCC
Vintage Sports Car Club of America (EA) .... VSCCA
Vintage Sports Car Club of Australia .... VSCCA
Vintage Sports Car Club of South Australia .... VSCCSA
Vintage Thunderbird Club International (EA) .... VTCI
Vintage Thunderbird Club of America [Later, VTCI] (EA) .... VTCA
Vintage Triumph Register (EA) .... VTR
Vintage Volkswagen Club of America (EA) .... VVWCA
Vintage White Truck Association (EA) .... VWTA
Vintage Wireless Association [British] .... VWA
Vinton, IA [FM radio station call letters] .... KLLT
Vinton, IA [Location identifier FAA] (FAAL) .... VTI
Vinton Public Library, Vinton, IA [Library symbol Library of Congress]
(LCLS) .... IaVin
Vinton, VA [FM radio station call letters] .... WJJS
Vinton, VA [AM radio station call letters] .... WKBA
Vinton, VA [FM radio station call letters] (RBYB) .... WZZI-FM
Vinton's American Canon Law [A publication] (DLA) .... Vint Can Law
Vinum [Wine] [Pharmacy] (ROG) .... VIN
Vinyl V
Vinyl [Technical drawings] .... VIN
Vinyl (VRA) .... vn
Vinyl Acetate [Organic chemistry] (WDAA) .... VA
Vinyl Acetate - Ethylene [Organic chemistry] .... VAE
Vinyl Acetate - Ethylene - Vinyl Chloride [Organic chemistry] .... VAEVC
Vinyl Acetate Maleic Acid (DICI) .... VAMA
Vinyl Acetate Monomer [Organic chemistry] .... VAM
Vinyl Alcohol Acetate Resin [NASA] (KSC) .... VAAR
Vinyl Asbestos Tile [Technical drawings] .... VAT
Vinyl Bromide [Organic chemistry] .... VBR
Vinyl Chloride [Organic chemistry] VC
Vinyl Chloride Ethylene [Organic chemistry] .... VCE
Vinyl Chloride Ethylene Methyl Acrylate [Organic chemistry] .... VCEMA
Vinyl Chloride Methyl Acrylate [Organic chemistry] .... VCMA
Vinyl Chloride Monomer [Organic chemistry] .... VCM
Vinyl Chloride Monomer [Chemistry] (DAVI) .... VOM
Vinyl Chloride Vinyl Acetate [Organic chemistry] .... VCVAC
Vinyl Chloride Vinylidene Chloride [Organic chemistry] .... VCVDC
Vinyl Composition Tile .... VCT
Vinyl Cyanide [Organic chemistry] .... VCN
Vinyl (dimethyl) Oxazolinone [Organic chemistry] .... VDMO
Vinyl Ester .... VE
Vinyl Ester Sheet Molding Compound [Plastics] .... VESMC
Vinyl Fabric [Technical drawings] .... VF
Vinyl Fabrics Institute [Later, Chemical Fabrics and Film Association] (EA) .... VFI
Vinyl Insulation Material .... VIM
Vinyl Metal Industry Association [Defunct] (EA) .... VMIA
Vinyl Methyl Ether [Organic chemistry] .... VME
Vinyl Siding Institute (EA) .... VSI
Vinyl Sulfone [Organic chemistry] .... VS
Vinyl T-Butylstyrene [Organic chemistry] .... VTB
Vinyl Tile [Technical drawings] .... VT
Vinyl Window and Door Institute (EA) .... VWD
Vinylbenzyl Chloride [Organic chemistry] .... VBC
Vinylbenzyldimethylamine [Organic chemistry] .... VBDMA
Vinylcarbazole [Organic chemistry] .... VCZ
Vinylcyclohexene [Organic chemistry] .... VCH
Vinylene Carbonate [Organic chemistry] (WDAA) .... VCA
Vinylferrocene [Organic chemistry] .... VF
Vinylguaiacol [Biochemistry] .... VG
Vinylidene Fluoride [Organic chemistry] .... VDF
Vinylphenol [Biochemistry] .... VP
Vinylpolysilane [Organic chemistry] .... VPS
Vinylpyridine [Organic chemistry] .... VPY
Vinylpyrrolidinone [Organic chemistry] .... VP
(Vinylthiazolidinylidene)phenylamine [Organic chemistry] .... VTPA
Vinyltriethoxysilane [Organic chemistry] .... VTES
Vinyltrimethysilane [Organic chemistry] .... VTMS
Vinzolidine [Antineoplastic drug] .... VZL
Viola [Music] .... VA
Viola [Music] (ROG) .... VIOL
Viola [Music] .... VLA
Viola da Gamba Society [British] (DBA) .... VdGS
Viola da Gamba Society of America (EA) .... VdGSA
Viola d'Amore [Music] .... VDA
Viola d'Amore Society (EA) .... VDS
Viola d'Amore Society of America (EA) .... VASA
Viola Mottle Virus .... VMV
Violaceus [Purple] [Latin] (WGA) .... viol
Violating Local Option Law (WGA) .... VLOL
Violation Monitor and Remover [Bell System] .... VMR
Violation of Law of Road [Traffic offense charge] .... VLR
Violation of Lawful [Order] [Military] VL
Violation of Lawful Regulation Issued by the Secretary of the Navy .... VLRSN
Violation of [Local] Ordinance .... VO
Violent [NWS] (FAAC) .... VLNT
Violent Criminal Apprehension Program [Quantico, VA] [National Center for the Analysis of Violent Crime Department of Justice] .... VICAP
Violent Defectives [British] .... VD
Violet V
Violet VI
Violet (AAG) .... VIO

Violet, Indigo, Blue, Green, Yellow, Orange, Red [Mnemonic for the colors of the spectrum] .... VIBGYOR
Violet Red Bile [Microorganism growth medium] .... VRB
Violet Red Bile Agar [Microorganism growth medium] .... VRBA
Violet Tetrazolium (MAE) .... VT
Violetvale [Queensland] [Airport symbol] (AD) .... VIQ
Violin [Music] V
Violin [Music] (ROG) VL
Violin [Music] .... VLN
Violin [Music] .... VN
Violin Makers Association of Arizona International (EA) .... VMAAI
Violin Society of America (EA) .... VSA
Violincello [Music] VCL
Violini [Violins] [Music] .... VNI
Violini [Violins] [Music] VV
Violino [Violin] [Music] (ROG) .... VIO
Violino [Violin] [Music] (ROG) .... VIOLO
Violino [Violin] [Music] (ROG) .... VO
Violoncelli [Cellos] [Music] .... Celli
Violoncello [Music] .... CELLO
Violoncello [Music] VC
Violoncello [Music] .... VCLLO
Violoncello [Music] VLC
Violoncello [Music] .... VLLO
Violoncello Society (EA) .... VS
Violone [Double Bass] [Music] (ROG) .... VIOLE
Violone [Violins] [Music] .... VLE
Viomycin [Antibiotic compound] (AAMN) .... VM
Vion Pharmaceuticals [NASDAQ symbol] (TTSB) .... VION
Vion Pharmaceuticals, Inc. [NASDAQ symbol] (SAG) .... VION
Vion Pharmaceuticals, Inc. [Associated Press] (SAG) .... Vion
Vion Pharmaceuticals, Inc. [Associated Press] (SAG) .... VionPh
Vion Pharmaceuticals Unit [NASDAQ symbol] (TTSB) .... VIONU
Vion Pharmaceuticals Wrrt'A' [NASDAQ symbol] (TTSB) .... VIONW
Vion Pharmaceuticals Wrrt'B' [NASDAQ symbol] (TTSB) .... VIONZ
Vior Miniere d'Exploration Societe, Inc. [Toronto Stock Exchange symbol] .... VIO
VIP Air Charter, Inc. [FAA designator] (FAAC) .... FXF
VIP Dynasty International Marketing Corp. [Vancouver Stock Exchange symbol] .... VPI
VIP Global Capital [Associated Press] (SAG) .... VIP Glbl
VIP Global Capital [NASDAQ symbol] (SAG) .... VIPG
Viper Retrovirus .... VRV
Viper Rocket with Scanner (SAA) .... VIPERSCAN
Viper Venom (MAE) VV
Viper-Arrow (SAA) .... V-A
Viqueque [Timor] [Airport symbol] (AD) .... VLK
Viqueque [East Timor] [ICAO location identifier] (ICLI) .... WPVQ
Vir Bonus [A Good Man] [Latin] .... VB
Vir Clarissimus [A Most Illustrious Man] [Latin] VC
Vir Honestus [A Worthy Man] [Latin] .... VH
Vir Magnificus [A Great Man] [Latin] .... VM
Virac [Philippines] [Airport symbol] (OAG) .... VRC
Virac, Catanduanes [Philippines] [ICAO location identifier] (ICLI) .... RPUV
Viragen Europe Ltd. [NASDAQ symbol] (SAG) .... VERP
Viragen Europe Ltd. [Associated Press] (SAG) .... VirgErp
Viragen, Inc. [Associated Press] (SAG) .... Viragen
Viragen, Inc. [NASDAQ symbol] (SAG) .... VRGN
Virago Owners Club (EA) .... VOC
Viral Antibody, Acute [Immunology] (DAVI) .... VIR AC
Viral Antibody, Convalescent [Immunology] (DAVI) .... VR CON
Viral Antibody-Free [Environment] .... VAF
Viral Antigen [Medicine] (DMAA) .... VA
Viral Attachment Protein [Biochemistry] .... VAP
Viral Capsid Antibody [Hematology] .... VCA
Viral Capsular Antigen [Immunology] .... VCA
Viral Cell Surface Antigen [Medicine] (DMAA) .... VCSA
Viral Diarrhea [Medicine] (DMAA) .... VD
Viral Encephalitis [Neurology] (DAVI) .... VE
Viral Envelope Antigens [Immunology] .... VEA
Viral Glycoprotein [Medicine] (DMAA) .... VGP
Viral Haemorrhagic Disease .... VHD
Viral Hematodepressive Disease (MAE) .... VHD
Viral Hemorrhagic Septicemia [Medicine] .... VHS
Viral Hepatitis [Medicine] .... VH
Viral Hepatitis Panel [Hematology] (DAVI) .... VHP
Viral Interval Antigen [Virology] .... VIA
Viral Myocarditis [Medicine] .... VM
Viral Oncology Program [National Cancer Institute] .... VOP
Viral Particle [Medicine] .... VP
Viral Porcine Pneumonia [Veterinary medicine] .... VPP
Viral Protein [Biochemistry, genetics] .... VP
Viral Respiratory Infection [Medicine] .... VRI
Viral Respiratory Kit [Medicine] .... VRK
Viral Ribonucleic Acid [Medicine] (DMAA) .... VRNA
Viral Superantigen [Immunology] .... VSAG
Virally-Encoded Thymidine Kinase [Medicine] .... VTK
Virchow on Post Mortem Examinations [A publication] (DLA) .... Virch PM
Virchow-Pirquet Medical Society .... VPMS
Virco Manufacturing Co. [AMEX symbol] (SPSG) .... VIR
Virco Manufacturing Corp. [Associated Press] (SAG) .... Virco
Virco Mfg [AMEX symbol] (TTSB) .... VIR
Virden, IL [FM radio station call letters] .... WCVS
Virden Public Library, Virden, IL [Library symbol Library of Congress]
(LCLS) .... IVird

Virden-Elkhorn Regional Library, Virden, Manitoba [*Library symbol National Library of Canada*] (NLC) .... MVE
Virden-Elkhorn Regional Library, Virden, MB, Canada [*Library symbol Library of Congress*] (LCLS) .... CaMVE
Virgie, KY [*FM radio station call letters*] .... WZLK
Virgil C. Summer Nuclear Station (NRCH) .... VSNS
Virgil Partch [*Cartoonist*] .... VIP
Virgil Society (EA) .... VS
Virgin V
Virgin (WDAA) .... VG
Virgin .... VIRG
Virgin Air [*ICAO designator*] (AD) .... ZP
Virgin and Martyr [*Church calendars*] .... VM
Virgin Atlantic [*British ICAO designator*] (FAAC) .... VIR
Virgin Atlantic Airways [*ICAO designator*] (AD) .... VS
Virgin Gorda [*Virgin Islands*] [*ICAO location identifier*] (ICLI) .... TUPW
Virgin Gorda [*British Virgin Islands*] [*Airport symbol*] (AD) .... VGR
Virgin Gorda [*British Virgin Islands*] [*Airport symbol*] (OAG) .... VIJ
Virgin Islands [*MARC geographic area code Library of Congress*] (LCCP) .... nwvr
Virgin Islands (IAA) VI
Virgin Islands (WDAA) .... VIR IS
Virgin Islands [*International civil aircraft marking*] (ODBW) .... VP-LV
Virgin Islands Airways [*British*] [*FAA designator*] (FAAC) .... BVI
Virgin Islands, British [*MARC geographic area code Library of Congress*] (LCCP) .... nwvb--
Virgin Islands, British [*MARC country of publication code Library of Congress*] (LCCP) .... vb
Virgin Islands Code [*A publication*] (DLA) VIC
Virgin Islands Corp. [*Intended to promote VI economic development, dissolved 1966*] [*Department of the Interior*] VIC
Virgin Islands Department of Commerce (EA) .... VIDC
Virgin Islands Ecological Research Station .... VIERS
Virgin Islands National Park .... VIIS
Virgin Islands of the US [*MARC geographic area code Library of Congress*] (LCCP) .... nwvi--
Virgin Islands of the US [*ANSI two-letter standard code*] (CNC) VI
Virgin Islands of the US [*Postal code*] VI
Virgin Islands of the US [*IYRU nationality code*] [*MARC country of publication code Library of Congress*] (LCCP) vi
Virgin Islands of the US [*ANSI three-letter standard code*] (CNC) .... VIR
Virgin Islands Reports [*A publication*] (DLA) VI
Virgin Islands Rules and Regulations [*A publication*] (DLA) .... VIR & Regs
Virgin Islands Seaplane Shuttle, Inc. [*ICAO designator*] (FAAC) .... VSS
Virgin Islands Visitors Association .... VIVA
Virgin Mean Annual Discharge [*Of a river system*] .... VMAD
Virgini Immaculatae Bavaria Immaculata [*To the Immaculate Virgin Immaculate Bavaria*] [*Motto of the Order of St. George of Bavaria*] [*Latin*] .... VIBI
Virginia [*MARC geographic area code Library of Congress*] (LCCP) .... n-us-va
Virginia [*Postal code*] .... VA
Virginia [*MARC country of publication code Library of Congress*] (LCCP) .... vau
Virginia & Carolina Southern R. R. [*AAR code*] .... VCS
Virginia & Maryland Railroad [*AAR code*] .... VAMD
Virginia Appeals [*A publication*] (DLA) .... VA App
Virginia Associated Research Campus [*Later, Continuous Electron Beam Accelerator Facility*] [*Research center*] (RCD) .... VARC
Virginia Associated Research Center, Newport News, VA [*Library symbol Library of Congress*] (LCLS) .... ViNeV
Virginia Association for Institutional Research (EDAC) .... VAIR
Virginia Baptist Historical Society, University of Richmond, Richmond, VA [*Library symbol Library of Congress*] (LCLS) .... ViRVB
Virginia Bar News [*A publication*] (DLA) .... VA Bar News
Virginia Beach Fed Fini [*NASDAQ symbol*] (TTSB) .... VABF
Virginia Beach Federal Financial Corp. [*Associated Press*] (SAG) .... VaBch
Virginia Beach Federal Financial Corp. [*NASDAQ symbol*] (SAG) .... VABF
Virginia Beach/Oceana Naval Air Station [*Virginia*] [*ICAO location identifier*] (ICLI) .... KNTU
Virginia Beach Public Library System, Virginia Beach, VA [*OCLC symbol*] (OCLC) .... VPL
Virginia Beach, VA [*FM radio station call letters*] .... WJQI
Virginia Beach, VA [*FM radio station call letters*] .... WODC
Virginia Beach, VA [*FM radio station call letters*] (RBYB) .... WPTE-FM
Virginia Beach, VA [*AM radio station call letters*] .... WVAB
Virginia Beach, VA [*TV station call letters*] (RBYB) .... WVBT-TV
Virginia Blue Ridge Railway [*AAR code*] .... VBR
Virginia Capes [*Navy*] (CAAL) .... VACAPES
Virginia Cases (Brockenbrough and Holmes) [*A publication*] (DLA) .... VA Cas
Virginia Cases (Brockenbrough and Holmes) [*A publication*] (DLA) .... Vir
Virginia Cases (Brockenbrough and Holmes) [*A publication*] (DLA) .... Virg Cas
Virginia Central Railway [*AAR code*] VC
Virginia Chemicals, Inc., Portsmouth, VA [*Library symbol Library of Congress*] (LCLS) .... ViPoVC
Virginia Circuit Court Opinions [*A publication*] (DLA) .... VA Cir
Virginia Colonial Decisions (Randolph and Barrandall) [*A publication*] (DLA) .... VA Col Dec
Virginia Commonwealth University (GAGS) .... Va Commonwealth U
Virginia Commonwealth University .... VCU
Virginia Commonwealth University, Academic Division, Richmond, VA [*Library symbol Library of Congress*] .... ViRCU-A
Virginia Commonwealth University, Health Sciences Division, Richmond, VA [*Library symbol Library of Congress*] (LCLS) .... ViRCU-H
Virginia Commonwealth University, Richmond, VA [*Library symbol Library of Congress*] (LCLS) .... ViRCU
Virginia Commonwealth University, Richmond, VA [*OCLC symbol*] (OCLC) .... VRC

Virginia Community College System VCC
Virginia Crab Packers Association [*Defunct*] (EA) .... VCPA
Virginia Criminal Cases [*3-4 Virginia*] [*1789-1826*] [*A publication*] (DLA) .... VA Cas
Virginia Decisions [*A publication*] (DLA) .... VA Dec
Virginia Department of Environmental Quality .... VDEQ
Virginia Department of Environmental Quality (DOGT) .... VDEQ
Virginia El & Pwr $5 Pfd [*NYSE symbol*] (TTSB) .... VELPrE
Virginia Electric & Power Co. [*Associated Press*] (SAG) .... VaEP
Virginia Electric & Power Co. [*NYSE symbol*] (SPSG) .... VEL
Virginia Electric & Power Co. .... VEPCO
Virginia Electric & Power Co., Richmond, VA [*Library symbol Library of Congress*] (LCLS) .... ViREP
Virginia First Financial [*NASDAQ symbol*] (TTSB) .... VFFC
Virginia First Financial Corp. [*Associated Press*] (SAG) .... VaFst
Virginia First Financial Corp. [*Associated Press*] (SAG) .... VaFstSvg
Virginia First Financial Corp. [*NASDAQ symbol*] (SAG) .... VFFC
Virginia Gas Co. [*NASDAQ symbol*] (SAG) .... VGCO
Virginia Gas Co. [*Associated Press*] (SAG) .... VirgGas
Virginia Gas Co. [*Associated Press*] (SAG) .... VirgGs
Virginia Highlands Community College, Abingdon, VA [*Library symbol*] [*Library of Congress*] (LCLS) .... ViAbC
Virginia Highway Research Council, Charlottesville, VA [*Library symbol Library of Congress*] (LCLS) .... ViCVH
Virginia Historical Society, Richmond, VA [*Library symbol Library of Congress*] (LCLS) .... ViHi
Virginia, IL [*FM radio station call letters*] (RBYB) .... WVIL
Virginia Industrial Commission Opinions [*A publication*] (DLA) .... VA IC Ops
Virginia Institute for Scientific Research [*University of Richmond*] [*Research center*] (MCD) .... VISR
Virginia Institute for Scientific Research, Richmond, VA [*Library symbol Library of Congress*] (LCLS) .... ViRVI
Virginia Institute of Marine Science [*College of William and Mary*] [*Research center*] .... VIMS
Virginia Institute of Marine Science, Gloucester Point, VA [*Library symbol Library of Congress*] (LCLS) .... ViGpM
Virginia Intermont College VIC
Virginia Intermont College, Bristol, VA [*Library symbol Library of Congress*] (LCLS) .... ViBV
Virginia International Co. .... VICO
Virginia Journal of Natural Resources Law [*A publication*] (DLA) .... VJNRL
Virginia Junior College [*Minnesota*] [*Later, Mesabi Community College*] .... VJC
Virginia Junior-Senior High School, Virginia, MN [*Library symbol*] [*Library of Congress*] (LCLS) .... MnVHS
Virginia Law Digest [*A publication*] (DLA) .... VA L Dig
Virginia Law Journal [*Richmond*] [*A publication*] (DLA) .... VA Law J
Virginia Law Journal [*A publication*] (DLA) .... VA LJ
Virginia Law Journal [*A publication*] (DLA) .... Vir LJ
Virginia Law Journal [*Richmond*] [*A publication*] (DLA) .... Virg LJ
Virginia Law Register [*A publication*] (DLA) .... VA L Reg
Virginia Law Register, New Series [*A publication*] (DLA) .... VA L Reg NS
Virginia Law Weekly Dicta Compilation [*A publication*] (DLA) .... VA L Wk Dicta Comp
Virginia Mason Hospital, Medical Library, Seattle, WA [*Library symbol Library of Congress*] (LCLS) .... WaSH
Virginia Mason Hospital, Medical Library, Seattle, WA [*Library symbol*] [*Library of Congress*] (LCLS) .... WaSMH
Virginia Mason Research Center [*Virginia Mason Hospital and Mason Clinic*] [*Research center*] (RCD) .... VMRC
Virginia Medical College .... VMC
Virginia Medical Information System [*Library network*] .... VAMIS
Virginia Military Institute, Lexington, VA [*Library symbol Library of Congress*] (LCLS) ViLxV
Virginia Military Institute, Lexington, VA [*OCLC symbol*] (OCLC) .... VMI
Virginia, MN [*AM radio station call letters*] .... WHLB
Virginia, MN [*FM radio station call letters*] .... WUSZ
Virginia Museum of Fine Arts, Richmond, VA [*Library symbol Library of Congress*] (LCLS) .... ViRMu
Virginia Natural Heritage Program [*Virginia State Department of Conservation and Historic Resources*] [*Information service or system*] (IID) .... VANHP
Virginia Oak Tannery, Luray, VA [*Library symbol Library of Congress*] (LCLS) .... ViLuV
Virginia Panel Corp. (IAA) .... VPC
Virginia Polytechnic Institute and State University (GAGS) .... Va Poly Inst
Virginia Polytechnic Institute and State University [*Blacksburg*] .... VPI
Virginia Polytechnic Institute and State University, Blacksburg, VA [*Library symbol Library of Congress*] (LCLS) .... ViBlbV
Virginia Polytechnic Institute and State University, Blacksburg, VA [*OCLC symbol*] (OCLC) .... VPI
Virginia Poultry Breeders Association (EA) .... VPBA
Virginia Poultry Breeders Club [*Later, VPBA*] (EA) .... VPBC
Virginia Power Capital Trust I [*Associated Press*] (SAG) .... VaPw
Virginia Power Capital Trust I [*NYSE symbol*] (SAG) .... VEL
Virginia Public Library, Virginia, MN [*Library symbol Library of Congress*] (LCLS) .... MnV
Virginia Quarterly Review [*A publication*] (BRI) .... VQR
Virginia Regional Medical Center, Virginia, MN [*Library symbol*] [*Library of Congress*] (LCLS) .... MnVRM
Virginia Register of Regulations [*A publication*] (AAGC) .... Va Reg Regs
Virginia Register of Regulations [*A publication*] (AAGC) .... VAR
Virginia Register of Regulations [*A publication*] (AAGC) .... VR
Virginia Reports [*A publication*] (DLA) V
Virginia Reports [*A publication*] (DLA) .... VA
Virginia Reports [*A publication*] (AAGC) .... Va
Virginia Reports, Annotated [*A publication*] (DLA) .... VA R Ann
Virginia Reports, Annotated [*A publication*] (DLA) .... VA Rep Anno

Virginia Smelting Co., Portsmouth, VA [Library symbol Library of Congress] (LCLS) ..... ViPoVS
Virginia State Bar Association, Reports [A publication] (DLA) ..... VA SBA
Virginia State College [Petersburg] ..... VSC
Virginia State College, Petersburg, VA [Library symbol Library of Congress] (LCLS) ..... ViPetS
Virginia State College, Petersburg, VA [OCLC symbol] (OCLC) ..... VSC
Virginia State Law Library, Richmond, VA [Library symbol Library of Congress] (LCLS) ..... Vi-L
Virginia State Library for the Visually and Physically Handicapped, Richmond, VA [Library symbol Library of Congress] (LCLS) ..... Vi-BPH
Virginia State Library, Richmond, VA [Library symbol Library of Congress] (LCLS) Vi
Virginia State Library, Richmond, VA [OCLC symbol] (OCLC) VIC
Virginia State University (GAGS) ..... Va St U
Virginia State University Herbarium ..... VSUH
Virginia Supreme Court Reports [A publication] (DLA) ..... VA
Virginia Tax Review [A publication] (DLA) ..... Va Tax Rev
Virginia Technical Library System [Virginia Polytechnic Institute and State University Center for Library Automation] [Information service or system] ..... VTLS
Virginia Theological Seminary, Alexandria, VA [OCLC symbol] (OCLC) ..... VTS
Virginia Union List of Biomedical Serials [Library network] ..... VULBS
Virginia Union University [Richmond] ..... VUU
Virginia Union University, Richmond, VA [Library symbol Library of Congress] (LCLS) ..... ViRVU
Virginia Union University, Richmond, VA [OCLC symbol] (OCLC) ..... VUU
Virginia Water Resources Research Center [Virginia Polytechnic Institute and State University] [Research center] (RCD) ..... VWRRC
Virginia Wesleyan College, Norfolk, VA [Library symbol Library of Congress] (LCLS) ..... ViNWe
Virginia Western Community College, Brown Library, Roanoke, VA [Library symbol Library of Congress] (LCLS) ..... ViRoV
Virginia Woolf Society (EA) ..... VWS
Virginia-Carolina Peanut Association (EA) ..... VCPA
Virginia-Carolina Peanut Promotions [An association] (EA) ..... VCPP
Virginia-Hibbing, MN [FM radio station call letters] ..... WIRR
Virginian Railway Co. [AAR code] ..... VGN
Virginias Automated Clearing House Association ..... VACHA
Virginium (MAE) Vi
Virgin's Reports [52-60 Maine] [A publication] (DLA) ..... Vir
Virgin's Reports [52-60 Maine] [A publication] (DLA) ..... Virg
Virgin's Reports [52-60 Maine] [A publication] (DLA) ..... Virgin
Virgo [Constellation] ..... Vir
Virgo [Constellation] ..... Virg
Virgo Intacta [Medicine] VI
Viri Clarissimi [Most Illustrious Men] [Latin] VVCC
Viridian Inc. [TS symbol] (TTSB) V
Viridis [Green] [Pharmacy] ..... VIR
Virile Female Project [RJ Reynolds Tobacco Co. marketing strategy for proposed Dakota brand] ..... VF
Virilizing Adrenal Hyperplasia [Medicine] ..... VAH
Virion Infectivity Factor [Genetics] ..... VIF
Virogroup, Inc. [NASDAQ symbol] (SAG) ..... VIRO
Virogroup, Inc. [Associated Press] (SAG) ..... ViroGp
Virology ..... VIR
ViroPharma, Inc. [Associated Press] (SAG) ..... ViroPh
ViroPharma, Inc. [NASDAQ symbol] (SAG) ..... VPHM
Viroqua Public Library, Viroqua, WI [Library symbol Library of Congress] (LCLS) ..... WVi
Viroqua, WI [AM radio station call letters] ..... WVRQ
Viroqua, WI [FM radio station call letters] ..... WVRQ-FM
Virtual (HGAA) V
Virtual Access Control Unit ..... VACU
Virtual Access Method ..... VAM
Virtual Accounting Collecting System (MHDB) ..... VACS
Virtual Acoustic Synthesis [Electronics] (PS) ..... VAS
Virtual Address ..... VA
Virtual Address Extension [Computer science] ..... VAX
Virtual Address Extension/Virtual Memory System [Computer science] (DOM) ..... VAX/VMS
Virtual Address Translation ..... VAT
Virtual Address Translator (NITA) ..... VAT
Virtual Archival Storage Technology [Computer science] ..... VAST
Virtual Avionics Prototyping System [Virtual Prototypes, Inc.] ..... VAPS
Virtual Axial Dipole Moment [Geophysics] ..... VADM
Virtual Base Organization and Maintenance Processor ..... VBOMP
Virtual Block Processor ..... VBP
Virtual Bragg Scattering [Physics] ..... VBS
Virtual Channel Processor [Computer science] ..... VCP
Virtual Channel to Channel Adapter ..... VCTCA
Virtual Circuit VC
Virtual Circuit [Manager] (TNIG) VC
Virtual Circuit [Computer science] VC
Virtual Circuit Identifier VCI
Virtual Circuit [Call] Manager (TNIG) ..... VCM
Virtual City Associates Ltd. [London, England] [Telecommunications] (TSSD) ..... VCA
Virtual Classroom [Educational teleconferencing] VC
Virtual Communication Path [Computer science] (IAA) ..... VCP
Virtual Community of Tomorrow [Internet resource] [Computer science] ..... VCOT
Virtual Conference Center (PCM) VCC
Virtual Control Panel (NITA) ..... VCP
Virtual Control Processor [Computer science] (IAA) ..... VCP
Virtual Control Program (NITA) ..... VP
Virtual Control Program Interface [Computer science] (PCM) ..... VCPI

Virtual Coulomb Excitation (PDAA) ..... VCE
Virtual Counterpoise Procedure [Physical chemistry] ..... VCP
Virtual Crystal Approximation (WDAA) ..... VCA
Virtual Data ..... VD
Virtual Data Access Method (IEEE) ..... VDAM
Virtual Data Acquisition and Control [Computer science] (HGAA) ..... VIDAC
Virtual Data Description Language [Computer science] (MHDB) ..... VDDL
Virtual Device Driver [Computer science] (PCM) ..... VxD
Virtual Device Interface [Computer technology] ..... VDI
Virtual Device Metafile [Computer technology] (DGA) ..... VDM
Virtual Dipole Moment [Geodesy] ..... VDM
Virtual Disk [Computer science] ..... VDISK
Virtual Disk Library [Computer science] (MHDI) ..... VDLIB
Virtual Display Driver [Computer science] ..... VDD
Virtual DMA [Direct Memory Access] Service [Computer science] (PCM) ..... VDS
Virtual DOS [Disk Operating System] Machine [Computer science] (PCM) ..... VDM
Virtual Effective Address (NITA) ..... VEA
Virtual Electrode Model (OA) ..... VEM
Virtual Environment [Computer science] (ECII) ..... VE
Virtual Equal Real [Computer science] (MHDI) ..... V R
Virtual Equal Virtual [Computer science] (MHDI) ..... V V
Virtual Equals Real [Computer science] (IAA) ..... VR
Virtual File Allocation Table [Computer science] (CDE) ..... VFAT
Virtual File Server [Telecommunications] (OSI) ..... VFS
Virtual File Store [Telecommunications] (OSI) ..... VFS
Virtual Floppy [Computer science] (PCM) ..... VF
Virtual Geomagnetic Pole [Geophysics] ..... VGP
Virtual Grain Boundary Dislocation ..... VGBD
Virtual Hardware Monitor [Computer science] (IEEE) ..... VHM
Virtual High School ..... VHS
Virtual Home Space Builder ..... VHSB
Virtual Hospital [University of Iowa] [Online database] ..... VH
Virtual Image Display (MCD) ..... VID
Virtual Image Display System ..... VIDS
Virtual Image Processing [Optics] ..... VIP
Virtual Image Takeoff and Landing [Simulator] (MCD) ..... VITAL
Virtual Index Sequential Access Method (IAA) ..... VISAM
Virtual Information Environment [Computer science] (PCM) ..... VIE
Virtual Information Storage (BUR) ..... VIS
Virtual Input/Output [Computer science] (IBMDP) ..... VIO
Virtual Instruction Package (IAA) ..... VIP
Virtual Integrated Communications Access Method [Sperry UNIVAC] ..... VICAM
Virtual Interaction Controller VIC
Virtual Interactive Environment Workstation [NASA] (BYTE) ..... VIEWS
Virtual Interactive Machine Test Program Generator ..... VIMTPG
Virtual Interface Environment Workstation ..... VIEW
Virtual Line Switch ..... VLSW
Virtual Linkage System [or Subsystem] ..... VLS
Virtual Loadable Module [Computer science] ..... VLM
Virtual Machine [Computer science] ..... VM
Virtual Machine Assist [IBM Corp.] ..... VMA
Virtual Machine/Basic System Extension (NITA) ..... VM/BSE
Virtual Machine Communication Facility ..... VMCF
Virtual Machine Control Block [Computer science] (IBMDP) ..... VMBLOK
Virtual Machine Control Block ..... VMCB
Virtual Machine Control Program [Computer science] (IAA) ..... VP
Virtual Machine/Conversational Monitor System [Computer science] ..... VM/CMS
Virtual Machine Environment [International Computers Ltd.] ..... VME
Virtual Machine Experience ..... VEXP
Virtual Machine Identifier ..... VMID
Virtual Machine Manager [Computer science] (PCM) ..... VMM
Virtual Machine Monitor [Computer science] (IEEE) ..... VMM
Virtual Machine/Programming in Logic [Computer science] (HGAA) ..... VM/Prolog
Virtual Machine/System Extension (NITA) ..... VM/SE
Virtual Machine/System Product [Operating system for large IBM mainframe computers] ..... VM/SP
Virtual Machine Time-Sharing System [Computer science] (IEEE) ..... VMTSS
Virtual Manufacturing Device [Telecommunications] (OSI) ..... VMD
Virtual Memory [Computer science] (MCD) ..... VM
Virtual Memory Allocation ..... VMA
Virtual Memory Array Processing System ..... VMAPS
Virtual Memory File [Computer science] (PCM) ..... VMF
Virtual Memory Linking [Computer science] ..... VML
Virtual Memory Manager [Computer science] (BYTE) ..... VMM
Virtual Memory Operating System [Sperry UNIVAC] [Computer science] (IEEE) ..... VMOS
Virtual Memory Operating System [Computer science] ..... VMS
Virtual Memory Performance Enhancement [Computer science] (MHDI) ..... VMPE
Virtual Memory Technique [Computer science] (MDG) ..... VMT
Virtual Method Table [Computer science] (PCM) ..... VMT
Virtual Microsystems Ltd. (NITA) ..... VML
Virtual Multi-Access [Computer science] (IAA) ..... VM
Virtual Network Application [Computer science] ..... VNA
Virtual Network System Internet Control Protocol [Banyan Systems, Inc.] [Telecommunications] (PCM) ..... VICP
Virtual Network System Internet Protocol [Banyan Systems, Inc.] [Telecommunications] (PCM) ..... VIP
Virtual Networking Software [Banyan Systems] ..... VINES
Virtual Networks [Computer science] (HGAA) ..... VNET
Virtual Office ..... VO
Virtual Onsite Technology [Telecommunications] ..... VOT
Virtual Operating System ..... VOS
Virtual Page Number ..... VPN
Virtual Partitioned Access Method ..... VPAM
Virtual Pitch [Neurophysiology] ..... VP

Virtual Pivot Point [*Suspension*] [*Tandem bike*] ... VPP
Virtual Population Analysis ... VPA
Virtual PPI [*Plan-Position Indicator*] **Reflectoscope** [*RADAR*] ... VPR
Virtual PPI [*Plan-Position Indicator*] **Reflectoscope with Navigational Microfilm Projector** [*RADAR*] ... VPR-NMP
Virtual Printer Technology [*Dataproducts Corp.*] (PCM) ... VPT
Virtual Private Network [*US Sprint Communications Co.*] [*Atlanta, GA*] (TSSD) ... VPN
Virtual Processing Zero ... VPZ
Virtual Processor ... VP
Virtual Processor Complex [*Computer science*] (CDE) ... VPC
Virtual Processor Ratio [*Computer science*] ... VPR
Virtual Program/Conversation Software System (NITA) ... VP/CSS
Virtual Program Status Word ... VPSW
Virtual Programming System (NITA) ... VPS
Virtual Quantum ... VQ
Virtual RADAR Defense [*Army*] (MCD) ... VIRAD
Virtual Random Access Memory [*Computer science*] ... VRAM
Virtual Reality ... VR
Virtual Reality and Simulation ... VRS
Virtual Reality Markup [*or Modeling*] **Language** [*Software program*] ... VRML
Virtual Reality Modeling Language [*Computer science*] ... VRML
Virtual Reality Modeling Language ... VRML
Virtual Real-Time Executive ... VRTX
Virtual Real-Time Object-Oriented Memory Manager [*Computer science*] ... VROOMM
Virtual Redundancy Check [*Computer science*] ... VRC
Virtual Resource Executive [*Software*] [*NCR Corp.*] ... VRX
Virtual Resource Manager [*Computer science*] (IAA) ... VRM
Virtual Resource Unit (MCD) ... VRU
Virtual Resource Unit, Deferred ... VRD
Virtual Route [*Computer science*] ... VR
Virtual Screen Interface [*Computer science*] (HGAA) ... VSI
Virtual Sequential Access Method ... VSAM
Virtual Sprites [*Amiga computer hardware*] ... VSPRITES
Virtual Storage [*Computer science*] ... VS
Virtual Storage Access Method [*Computer science*] ... VSAM
Virtual Storage Exhibit/Advanced Function (NITA) ... VSE/AF
Virtual Storage Extension [*IBM Corp.*] [*Computer science*] ... VSE
Virtual Storage Interrupt (NITA) ... VSI
Virtual Storage Manager (BUR) ... VSM
Virtual Storage Memory [*Computer science*] (MCD) ... VSM
Virtual Storage One [*Computer science*] (HGAA) ... VS1
Virtual Storage Personal Computing [*IBM Corp.*] [*Computer science*] ... VSPC
Virtual Storage Productivity Aid [*Computer science*] (MHDB) ... VISPA
Virtual Storage System [*SEMIS*] ... VSS
Virtual Subscriber Computer ... VSC
Virtual Switching Point [*Telecommunications*] (TEL) ... VSP
Virtual System ... VS
Virtual System Access Method ... VSAM
Virtual Tape Library ... VTL
Virtual Telecommunications [*or Teleprocessing*] **Access Method** [*IBM Corp.*] [*Computer science*] ... VTAM
Virtual Telecommunications Access Method Entry ... VTAME
Virtual Terminal (BYTE) ... VT
Virtual Terminal (DOMA) ... VT
Virtual Terminal Access Method ... VTAM
Virtual Terminal Control [*Computer science*] (MHDB) ... VTC
Virtual Terminal Line Controller [*Computer science*] (MHDB) ... VTLC
Virtual Terminal Protocol ... VTP
Virtual Terminal Service (TNIG) ... VTS
Virtual Terminal Session/Multiple Access [*Computer science*] (HGAA) ... VTS/MA
Virtual Terminal Support [*Computer science*] (IAA) ... VTSU
Virtual Terminal System [*Computer science*] (MHDB) ... VTS
Virtual Tourist 2 ... VT2
Virtual Unit Address (BUR) ... VUA
Virtual Visual Environment Display [*Helmet equipped with liquid crystal display screens viewed through wide-angle lenses*] [*NASA*] ... VIVED
Virtual Zero ... VZ
Virtual-Egress Analysis and Simulation (ECON) ... VEGAS
Virtually (ILCA) ... Virt
Virtually Safe Dose [*Toxicology*] ... VSD
Virtually Safe Level [*Toxicology*] ... VSL
Virtually-Pivoted Beam LASER (IAA) ... VPB
Virtual-Memory Environment [*Computer science*] (EECA) ... VME
Virtual-Reality Machine [*Video technology*] (ECON) ... VR
Viru Viru [*Bolivia*] [*ICAO location identifier*] (ICLI) ... SLVR
Virulence [*Antigen*] [*Immunology*] ... Vi
Virulent ... V
Virulent ... VIR
Virulent Marek Disease Virus [*Medicine*] (DMAA) ... vMDV
Virus ... V
Virus Cancer Program [*National Cancer Institute*] ... VCP
Virus Growth Factor [*Biochemistry*] ... VGF
Virus Inactivating Agency [*Medicine*] ... VIA
Virus Infection Associated Antigen [*Immunology*] ... VIA
Virus Instructional Code Emulator [*Computer science*] ... VICE
Virus Isolated from Bovine Feces [*Medicine*] ... BF1
Virus Neutralization ... VN
Virus Neutralization Test [*Analytical biochemistry*] ... VNT
Virus Reference Laboratory ... VRL
Virus Reference Library (MAE) ... VRL
Virus Research Institute, Inc. [*Associated Press*] (SAG) ... VirusRes
Virus Research Institute, Inc. [*NASDAQ symbol*] (SAG) ... VRII
Virus Search and Destroy [*Computer science*] ... VSD
Virus Subcommittee of the International Nomenclature Committee [*Medicine*] (DMAA) ... VSINC
Virus-Antibody [*Immunology*] ... VA
Virus-Associated Hemophagocytic Syndrome [*Medicine*] ... VAHS
Virus-Induced Interferon [*Cell biology*] ... VIF
Virus-Like Infectious Agent [*Medicine*] ... VLIA
Virus-Like Particle ... VLP
Virusoid Lucerne Transient Streak Virus ... VLTSV
VirusScan Configuration [*Computer science*] ... VSC
Virus-Serum-Toxin Act ... VSTA
Visa for Travel to Australia (ADA) ... VFTTA
Visa Office [*Department of State*] ... VO
Visa Petition ... VP
Visalia [*California*] [*Airport symbol*] (OAG) ... VIS
Visalia, CA [*FM radio station call letters*] ... KARM
Visalia, CA [*FM radio station call letters*] ... KDUV
Visalia, CA [*FM radio station call letters*] ... KFSO
Visalia, CA [*Television station call letters*] ... KMPH
Visalia, CA [*Television station call letters*] ... KNXT
Visalia, CA [*FM radio station call letters*] ... KSEQ
Visalia, CA [*FM radio station call letters*] ... KSLK
Visalia, CA [*AM radio station call letters*] ... KTHX
Visalia Community Counseling Center, Visalia, CA [*Library symbol Library of Congress*] (LCLS) ... CViVC
Visalia Electric Railroad Co. [*AAR code*] ... VE
Visalia Public Library, Visalia, CA [*Library symbol Library of Congress*] (LCLS) ... CVi
Visbreaker [*Petroleum technology*] ... VB
Visby [*Sweden ICAO location identifier*] (ICLI) ... ESQV
Visby [*Sweden ICAO location identifier*] (ICLI) ... ESSV
Visby [*Sweden*] [*Airport symbol*] (OAG) ... VBY
Visceral ... visc
Visceral Larval Migrans [*Medicine*] ... VLM
Visceral Leishmaniasis [*Medicine*] ... VL
Visceral Leishmaniasis ... VL
Visceral Sinus ... VS
Visceral Yolk Sac [*Embryology*] ... VYS
Viscoelastic Damper ... VED
Viscoelastic Fiber ... VEF
Viscoelastic Flow ... VEF
Viscoelastic Stress Analysis ... VSA
Viscometer [*Engineering*] ... VISMR
Viscometer Recorder-Controller ... VRC
Viscomtesse [*Vicountess*] [*French*] (BARN) ... Vtesse
Viscoplastic Flow ... VPF
Viscosity [*Symbol*] [*Organic chemistry*] (DAVI) ... eta
Viscosity ... V
Viscosity ... VIS
Viscosity (AAG) ... VISC
Viscosity Control Agent ... VCA
Viscosity Factor (IAA) ... VF
Viscosity Grade [*Automotive engineering*] ... VG
Viscosity Gravity Constant ... VGC
Viscosity Improver [*Element in multigrade engine oil*] ... VI
Viscosity Index ... VI
Viscosity Index Improver [*for motor oil*] ... VII
Viscosity Modifier [*Lubricants*] ... VM
Viscosity Temperature Coefficient (IAA) ... VTC
Viscosity-Index Improver [*for motor oil*] ... VIP
Viscount [*or Viscountess*] ... V
Viscount [*or Viscountess*] ... VIS
Viscount [*or Viscountess*] ... VISC
Viscount [*or Viscountess*] ... VISCT
Viscount Air Services, Inc. [*ICAO designator*] (FAAC) ... VCT
Viscount Resources Ltd. [*Vancouver Stock Exchange symbol*] ... VIS
Viscous (USDC) ... VSG
Viscous Coupling [*Automotive engineering*] ... VC
Viscous Coupling Unit [*Automotive engineering*] ... VCU
Viscous Criterion ... VC
Viscous Limited-Slip Differential ... VLSD
Viscous Partial Thermoremanent Magnetization [*Geophysics*] ... VPTRM
Viscous Plastic Processing [*Materials science and technology*] ... VPP
Viscous Remanant Magnetization ... VRM
Viscous Response [*Medicine*] ... VR
Viscous Semi-Geostrophic [*Model*] [*Marine science*] (OSRA) ... VSG
Viscous Shock Layer ... VSL
Viscous Traction [*Automotive engineering*] (PS) ... VT
Viscous Transmission [*Automotive engineering*] ... VT
Viscous Transonic Equation ... VTE
Viscous Vortex Rate Sensor ... VVRS
Viscous-Damped Converter Clutch [*Automotive engineering*] ... VCC
Vise Break Distance [*Stress test for steel*] ... V
Vise Jaw [*Tool*] (AAG) ... VSJW
Viseu [*Portugal ICAO location identifier*] (ICLI) ... LPVZ
Vishakhapatnam [*India*] [*ICAO location identifier*] (ICLI) ... VEVZ
Vishakhapatnam [*Andhra, Waltair*] [*India*] [*Seismograph station code, US Geological Survey*] (SEIS) ... VIS
Vishakhapatnam [*India*] [*Airport symbol*] (OAG) ... VTZ
Vishay Intertechnolgy [*NYSE symbol*] (TTSB) ... VSH
Vishay Intertechnology, Inc. [*Associated Press*] (SAG) ... Vishay
Vishay Intertechnology, Inc. [*NYSE symbol*] (SPSG) ... VSH
Vishnu Resources [*Vancouver Stock Exchange symbol*] ... VSH
Visibility ... V
Visibility (BARN) ... VSBY
Visibility, Amount, Height of Cloud Top, Base [*Weather*] [*DoD*] ... VAT

Visibility and Management of Operating and Support Costs [*Army*] ...... VAMOSC
Visibility Decreasing Rapidly [*NWS*] (FAAC) ...... VSBYDR
Visibility Forecast (SAA) ...... VSFR
Visibility Impairment for Sulfur Transformation and Transport in the Atmosphere [*Environmental Protection Agency*] (GFGA) ...... VISTTA
Visibility Impariment [*Environmental Protection Agency*] VI
Visibility Increasing Rapidly [*NWS*] (FAAC) ...... VSBYIR
Visibility Laboratory [*Research center*] (RCD) ...... VIS LAB
Visibility of Intransit Cargo [*Shipping*] VIC
Visible [*or Visibility*] (AFM) ...... VIS
Visible (BARN) ...... VSB
Visible (MSA) ...... VSBL
Visible Achievement Liberates Unemployment [*DoD project for disadvantaged youth*] ...... VALUE
Visible [*or Visual*] **and Infrared Radiometer** [*NASA*] ...... VIR
Visible [*or Visual*] **and Infrared Radiometer** [*NASA*] ...... VIRR
Visible and Near Infrared (EERA) ...... VNIR
Visible and Near-Visible Frequency Intercept System [*Navy*] ...... VANFIS
Visible and Near-Visible Infrared (MCD) ...... VIS/NIR
Visible and Near-Visible Infrared (MCD) ...... VNIR
Visible Atmospheric Sounder (MCD) ...... VAS
Visible Caching Operating System [*AT & T*] ...... VCOS
Visible Calculation [*Electronic spreadsheet program brand*] ...... VisiCalc
Visible Energy Detection and Ranging ...... VEDAR
Visible Genetics, Inc. [*NASDAQ symbol*] (SAG) ...... VGIN
Visible Genetics, Inc. [*Associated Press*] (SAG) ...... VisGene
Visible Gold, Inc. [*Vancouver Stock Exchange symbol*] ...... VIG
Visible, Informative, Emotionally Appealing, Workable [*Package evaluation in marketing*] ...... VIEW
Visible/Infrared Intelligent Spectrometer ...... VIRIS
Visible Ink Press [*Publisher*] ...... VIP
Visible LASER Communication Experiment ...... VLCE
Visible Light Emission ...... VLE
Visible Light Generator ...... VLG
Visible Light Sensors (MCD) ...... VLS
Visible Light Transmittance ...... VLT
Visible Light-Emitting Diodes ...... VLED
Visible Panty Line [*In reference to clothing*] ...... VPL
Visible Record Computer (IAA) ...... VRC
Visible Record Machine (NITA) ...... VRM
Visible Speech Translator (IAA) ...... VST
Visible Supply ...... VS
Visible/Ultraviolet Experiment ...... VUE
Visible Ultraviolet Spectrometer (MCD) ...... VIS-UV
Visible-Infrared Mapping Spectrometer [*Instrumentation*] ...... VIMS
Visible-Infrared Spin Scan Radiometer [*NASA*] ...... VISSR
Visicalc (HGAA) VC
Visicalc Advanced Version (HGAA) ...... VAV
Visicoder Oscillograph System ...... VOS
Visigenic Software, Inc. [*Associated Press*] (SAG) ...... Visigenic
Visigenic Software, Inc. [*NASDAQ symbol*] (SAG) ...... VSGN
Visingso [*Sweden ICAO location identifier*] (ICLI) ...... ESSI
Visio Corp. [*Associated Press*] (SAG) ...... VisioCo
Visio Corp. [*NASDAQ symbol*] (SAG) ...... VSIO
Visio Oculus Dextra [*Vision, right eye*] [*Latin*] [*Ophthalmology*] (DAVI) ...... VOD
Visio Oculus Sinister [*Vision Left Eye*] [*Latin*] [*Ophthalmology*] (DAVI) ...... VOS
Visio Oculus Uterque [*Vision, Each Eye*] [*Ophthalmology*] [*Latin*] (MAE) ...... VOU
Vision V
Vision (AAMN) ...... VIS
Vision ...... VSN
Vision ...... VSN
Vision Airways Corp. [*Canada ICAO designator*] (FAAC) ...... VSN
Vision and Autonomous Systems Laboratory, Carnegie Mellon University [*Research center*] (RCD) ...... VASC
Vision Approach and Landing System [*Aviation*] ...... VSALS
Vision Business Systems Ltd. (NITA) ...... VBS
Vision Controllor [*Printer technology*] VC
Vision Distribution Amplifier (IAA) ...... VDA
Vision Educational Foundation (EA) ...... VEF
Vision Electric Recording Apparatus [*BBC*] ...... VERA
Vision Enhancement System ...... VES
Vision Field [*Ophthalmology*] (DAVI) ...... VF
Vision Foundation (EA) ...... VF
Vision Frequency ...... VF
Vision Industry Council of America (EA) ...... VICA
Vision Information Program (IID) ...... VIP
Vision Inspection Processor (NITA) ...... VIP
Vision Institute of America [*Later, VSP*] (EA) ...... VIA
Vision Intensified Microscopy ...... VIM
Vision Interfaith Satellite Network ...... VISN
Vision, Left Eye VL
Vision, Left Eye ...... VOS
Vision on Sound (IAA) ...... VOS
Vision, Right Eye ...... VOD
Vision, Right Eye ...... VR
Vision Sciences, Inc. [*Associated Press*] (SAG) ...... VisionSci
Vision Sciences, Inc. [*NASDAQ symbol*] (SAG) ...... VSCI
Vision Service Plan National [*Defunct*] (EA) ...... VSP
Vision Test [*Ophthalmology*] ...... VT
Vision Test Apparatus [*Ophthalmology*] ...... VTA
Vision Testing Device [*Ophthalmology*] ...... VTD
Visioneer, Inc. [*Associated Press*] (SAG) ...... Vision
Visioneer, Inc. [*NASDAQ symbol*] (SAG) ...... VSNR
Visioneer Inc. [*NASDAQ symbol*] (TTSB) ...... VSNR
Vision-Sciences Inc. [*NASDAQ symbol*] (TTSB) ...... VSCI
Visit V
Visit [*or Visitor*] ...... VIS
Visit (NVT) ...... VST
Visit, Board, Search, and Secure (DOMA) ...... VBSS
Visit Mexico [*Airline fares*] ...... VIMEX
Visit Request (AAG) ...... VR
Visit Ship in Port [*Navy*] (NVT) ...... VSTSP
Visit USA [*Airline fare*] ...... VUSA
Visitation Nuns [*Roman Catholic religious order*] ...... VHM
Visiting ...... VSTNG
Visiting Airmen's Quarters [*Air Force*] ...... VAQ
Visiting Card (BJA) ...... VCD
Visiting Committee [*British*] VC
Visiting Dignitary ...... VD
Visiting Enlisted Quarters [*Army*] (AABC) ...... VEQ
Visiting Friends [*An association*] (EA) ...... VF
Visiting Friends and Relatives [*Airlines*] ...... VFR
Visiting Judges [*British*] ...... VJ
Visiting Medical Officer (ADA) ...... VMO
Visiting Medical Practitioner ...... VMP
Visiting Nurse ...... VN
Visiting Nurse Association ...... VNA
Visiting Nurse Association of Chicago, Chicago, IL [*OCLC symbol*] (OCLC) ILX
Visiting Nurse Associations of America (EA) ...... VNAA
Visiting Nurse Service ...... VNS
Visiting Nurses Association, Chicago, IL [*Library symbol Library of Congress*] (LCLS) ...... ICVNA
Visiting Nursing Association of Buffalo, Buffalo, NY [*Library symbol Library of Congress*] (LCLS) ...... NBuVNA
Visiting Officers' Quarters [*Military*] ...... VOQ
Visiting Orchestra Consultative Association [*British*] (DI) ...... VOCA
Visiting Practice Only [*Chiropody*] [*British*] V
Visit-Investigate-Purchase [*Department of Commerce program*] ...... VIP
Visitor (DAVI) V
Visitor ...... VSTR
Visitor Experience and Resource Protection [*Park tourism management*] ...... VERP
Visitor Impact Management [*Park tourism management*] ...... VIM
Visitor Information Center [*Kennedy Space Center*] VIC
Visitor Information Centre [*Australian National Botanic Gardens*] (EERA) VIC
Visitor Information Publications [*Defunct*] (EA) ...... VIP
Visitor Program Service of Meridian House International (EA) ...... VPS
Visitor Services Project [*National Park Service*] ...... VSP
Visitor's Passport [*British*] ...... VP
Visna Lentivirus VLV
Visna Virus VV
V-Isolation with Polysilicon Backfill (IAA) ...... VIP
Visor ...... VR
Visor Rectical Helmet Mounted Unit [*Navy*] (MCD) ...... VRHMU
VISSR [*Visible-Infrared Spin Scan Radiometer*] **Atmospheric Sounder** [*NASA*] ...... VAS
VISSR [*Visible-Infrared Spin Scan Radiometer*] **Image Registration and Gridding System** (MCD) ...... VIRGS
Vista ...... VIS
Vista ...... VIS
Vista [*Commonly used*] (OPSA) ...... VIST
Vista [*Commonly used*] (OPSA) ...... VISTA
Vista [*Commonly used*] (OPSA) ...... VST
Vista [*Commonly used*] (OPSA) ...... VSTA
Vista 2000, Inc. [*NASDAQ symbol*] (SAG) ...... VIST
Vista 2000, Inc. [*Associated Press*] (SAG) Vista2000
Vista 2000 Inc. [*NASDAQ symbol*] (TTSB) ...... VISTE
Vista 2000 Wrrt'A' [*NASDAQ symbol*] (TTSB) ...... VISWE
Vista Bancorp [*NASDAQ symbol*] (SAG) ...... VBNJ
Vista Bancorp [*Associated Press*] (SAG) ...... VistaBcp
Vista Breau [*Peru*] [*ICAO location identifier*] (ICLI) ...... SPBU
Vista, CA [*AM radio station call letters*] ...... KCEO
Vista Gold Corp. [*AMEX symbol*] (SAG) ...... VGZ
Vista Gold Corp. [*Associated Press*] (SAG) ...... VistaG
Vista Hermosa [*Mexico*] [*Seismograph station code, US Geological Survey Closed*] (SEIS) ...... VHM
Vista Hermosa [*Mexico*] [*Seismograph station code, US Geological Survey*] (SEIS) ...... VHO
VISTA Info Solutions [*NASDAQ symbol*] (TTSB) ...... VINF
Vista Information Solutions, Inc. [*NASDAQ symbol*] (SAG) ...... VINF
Vista Information Solutions, Inc. [*Associated Press*] (SAG) ...... VistaInf
Vista Mines, Inc. [*Toronto Stock Exchange symbol*] ...... VAM
Vista Ventures [*Commercial firm*] [*British*] VV
Vistaril [*A central nervous system depressant*] (DAVI) ...... VISTAB
Visual V
Visual ...... VIS
Visual ...... VISL
Visual Acquisition Technique ...... VAT
Visual Action Time ...... VAT
Visual Acuity [*Also, VA*] [*Ophthalmology*] V
Visual Acuity [*Also, V*] [*Ophthalmology*] ...... VA
Visual Acuity by Optokinetic Nystagmus ...... VAOKN
Visual Acuity, Left Eye [*Ophthalmology*] (MAE) ...... VALE
Visual Acuity, Right Eye [*Ophthalmology*] (MAE) ...... VARE
Visual Acuity with Contact Lens Correction ...... VAcCL
Visual Acuity with Pin Hole ...... VAPH
Visual Acuity with Spectacle Correction ...... VAcC
Visual Acuity with Trial Frame ...... VAtf
Visual Acuity without Spectacle Correction [*Unaided*] ...... VAsC
Visual Aerial Reconnaissance and Surveillance [*Military*] (VNW) ...... VARS

Visual Aid	VA
Visual Aid Console	VAC
Visual Air Quality	VAQ
Visual Airborne Target Locator System [*Military*]	VATLS
Visual Airborne Target Locator System [*Military*] (PDAA)	VIATLS
Visual Aircraft Recognition (MCD)	VACR
Visual Alignment Indicators [*Tire maintenance*]	VAI
Visual Analog Mood Scale	VAMS
Visual Analog [*Pain*] Scale	VAS
Visual Analysis Subsystem [*Military*]	VASS
Visual Analysis System [*Military*]	VAS
Visual Anamorphic Motion Picture (AIA)	VAMP
Visual Apperception Test [*Psychology*]	VAT
Visual Approach and Landing Chart [*Aviation*]	VAL
Visual Approach Chart [*Aviation*] (FAAC)	VAC
Visual Approach for Management Planning (WDAA)	VAMP
Visual Approach Monitor [*Aviation*]	VAM
Visual Approach Monitor Chart (PDAA)	VAMC
Visual Approach Multiple Slope Indicator [*Aviation*]	VAMSI
Visual Approach Path Indicator [*Aviation*]	VAPI
Visual Approach Slope Indicator [*Aviation*]	VASI
Visual Approach Slope Indicator System [*Aviation*]	VASIS
Visual Artists and Galleries Association (EA)	VAGA
Visual Arts [*US Copyright Office class*]	VA
Visual Arts Department, University of Western Ontario, London, Ontario [*Library symbol National Library of Canada*] (NLC)	OLUVA
Visual Attack System	VAS
Visual Audio Kinetic Unit Multiples and Environments (PDAA)	VAKUME
Visual Audit Sheet (DNAB)	VAS
Visual Augmentation System	VAS
Visual Average Speed Computer and Recorder [*Speed trap*]	VASCAR
Visual Basic [*Computer science*] (PCM)	VB
Visual Basic, Applications Edition [*Microsoft Corp.*] [*Computer macro language*] (PCM)	VBA
Visual Basic Extension [*Computer science*]	VBX
Visual Call Sign [*Communications*]	VCS
Visual Capacity (AAMN)	V
Visual Capacity [*Acuity*]	VC
Visual Coincidence (SAA)	VC
Visual Comfort Factor	VCF
Visual Comfort Index	VCI
Visual Comfort Probability (IAA)	VCP
Visual Communication (WDAA)	VC
Visual Communication and Image Representation [*Computer science*]	VCIR
Visual Communications	VISCOM
Visual Communications Congress	VCC
Visual Communications Education	VICOED
Visual Communications Exhibition and Conference, United Kingdom (ITD)	VIS-COM-UK
Visual Communications Management	VICOM
Visual Communications Network, Inc. [*Cambridge, MA*]	VCN
Visual Component Library [*Computer science*]	VCL
Visual Conceptual Reading	VICORE
Visual Confirmation [*of voice takeoff clearing system*] [*Aviation*]	VICON
Visual Control Board	VCB
Visual Control Room	VCR
Visual Cortex	VC
Visual Countermeasure	VCM
Visual Course Adapter (MUGU)	VCA
Visual Data Acquisition	VIDAT
Visual Data Analysis	VDA
Visual Data Entry On-Line [*Computer science*]	VIDEO
Visual Descent Point [*FAA*] (TAG)	VDP
Visual Descent Point [*Aviation*] (FAAC)	VDP
Visual Detection Level (MAE)	VDL
Visual Development Environment [*Computer science*] (PCM)	VDE
Visual Difference [*Computer science*] (NHD)	VDIFF
Visual Discriminatory Acuity	VDA
Visual Display Data	VDD
Visual Display Input	VDI
Visual Display Module (EECA)	VDM
Visual Display of Quality	VDQ
Visual Display System	VDS
Visual Display Terminal (EECA)	VDT
Visual Display Unit (OA)	VDU
Visual Docking Guidance System [*Aviation*] (DA)	VDGS
Visual Docking Simulator	VDS
Visual Doppler Indicator (IAA)	VDI
Visual Edge Systems, Inc. [*NASDAQ symbol*] (SAG)	EDGE
Visual Edge Systems, Inc. [*Associated Press*] (SAG)	VisEd
Visual Edge Systems, Inc. [*Associated Press*] (SAG)	VisEdge
Visual Editing Terminal (NITA)	VET
Visual Education Consultants, Inc. (AEBS)	VEC
Visual Effects Simulator (MCD)	VES
Visual Efficiency	VE
Visual Efficiency Scale	VES
Visual Electronic Remote Blackboard (PDAA)	VERB
Visual Emission Observation [*Environmental Protection Agency*] (GFGA)	VEO
Visual Emissions [*Environmental Protection Agency*] (GFGA)	VE
Visual Environment Simulation System (MCD)	VESS
Visual Evoked Brain Response	VEBR
Visual Evoked Potential [*Electrophysiology*]	VEP
Visual Evoked Response	VER
Visual Examination (MEDA)	VE
Visual Exposure Indicator [*Advanced photo system*]	VEI

Visual Field	VF
Visual Field [*Ophthalmology*] (DAVI)	VF
Visual Field Control [*Aviation*]	VFC
Visual Field Information [*Aviation*]	VFI
Visual Field(s) Intact [*Ophthalmology*] (DAVI)	VFIT
Visual Flight Attachment [*Aviation*] (RDA)	VFA
Visual Flight Rules [*Aviation*]	VFR
Visual Flight Rules Control Tower Simulator [*Aviation*] (MCD)	VFRCTS
Visual Flight Simulator	VFS
Visual Form Builder [*Computer science*] (PCM)	VFB
Visual Functioning Assessment Tool [*Educational test*]	VFAT
Visual General Aviation Trainer	VGAT
Visual Glide Path Indicator	VGPI
Visual Glide Path Indicator [*Aviation*] (FAAC)	VSPI
Visual Glide Slope	VIGS
Visual Glide Slope Indicator	VGSI
Visual Gross Error	VGE
Visual Ground Position Indicator (NATG)	VGPI
Visual Half-Field	VHF
Visual Identification	VI
Visual Identification (CAAL)	VID
Visual Identification (MSA)	VISID
Visual Identification Point (AFM)	VIP
Visual Image Formula [*of psychotherapist Joseph Bird's self-help theory*]	VIF
Visual Image Processor (IAA)	VIP
Visual Image Projection	VIP
Visual Image Quality Indicator (PDAA)	VISQI
Visual Imagery System [*NASA*]	VIS
Visual Imaging Systems in Origination Network (DGA)	VISION
Visual Impairment	VI
Visual Indicating Equipment [*Telecommunications*] (IAA)	VIE
Visual Indicator Panel (IAA)	VIP
Visual Information	VI
Visual Information Center [*Oldsmobile*] [*Automotive engineering*]	VIC
Visual Information Control Console [*Telecommunications*] (IAA)	VICC
Visual Information Display and Control	VIDAC
Visual Information Display and Control (DGA)	VIDIAC
Visual Information Display and Retrieval System [*Computer science*] (PDAA)	VID-R
Visual Information Display System (MCD)	VIDS
Visual Information Display System/Maintenance Action Form (NVT)	VIDS/MAF
Visual Information Documentation [*Military*]	VIDOC
Visual Information for Satellite Telemetry Analysis	VISTA
Visual Information Processing	VIP
Visual Information Processing Interface Device (MCD)	VIPID
Visual Information Projection	VIP
Visual Information Storage	VIS
Visual Information System	VIS
Visual Information System Development Association (MHDB)	VISDA
Visual Information Systems for Image Transformation [*Air Force*]	VISIT
Visual Infrared Mapping Spectrometer	VIMS
Visual Input [*System*] [*AT & T*]	VIP
Visual Input Detection Instrumentation (MCD)	VIDI
Visual Inspection	VI
Visual Instruction Set [*Computer science*]	VIS
Visual Instrumentation Subsystem	VIS
Visual Interactive Programming [*Computer science*]	VIP
Visual Intercept Officer [*Navy*]	VIO
Visual Interface [*Computer science*] (NHD)	VI
Visual Landing Aid	VLA
Visual LASER Beam	VLB
Visual Laydown	VL
Visual Laydown Delivery (AFM)	VLD
Visual Low-Angle Drogue Delivery (AFM)	VLADD
Visual Lunacy Society (EA)	VLS
Visual Magnitude [*When followed by a two-digit number*]	V
Visual Management System (EERA)	VMS
Visual Maneuverability Aids (MCD)	VMA
Visual Maneuvering Height [*Aviation*] (DA)	VMH
Visual Maneuvering Indicator (MCD)	VMI
Visual Memory Scale [*Educational test*]	VMS
Visual Memory Task [*Neuropsychology test*]	VISMEM
Visual Meteorological Conditions [*Aviation*]	VMC
Visual Modifications [*Program*] [*Army*] (RDA)	VISMOD
Visual Motion Simulator (MCD)	VMS
Visual Motor Behavior Rehearsal [*Psychology*]	VMBR
Visual Navigation (MCD)	NAV
Visual Numerical Discrimination Pre-Test [*Medicine*] (DMAA)	VNDPT
Visual Observation Instrumentation Subsystem [*Lunar space program*]	VOIS
Visual Observation Integration Subsystem (AAG)	VOIS
Visual Omnidirectional Range (DNAB)	VOR
Visual Omnirange [*Directional Beacon*] [*Aviation*] (NG)	VOR
Visual Omnirange/Tactical Air Navigation (MCD)	VORTAN
Visual Omnirange Test [*Aviation*] (IAA)	VOT
Visual Order Error	VOE
Visual Packaging Association [*Defunct*] (EA)	VPA
Visual Pattern Discrimination (PDAA)	VPD
Visual Precision (WDAA)	VIPRE
Visual Precision Fire Control [*Navy*] (DNAB)	VIPRE FIRE
Visual Programmer [*Computer science*] (PCM)	ViP
Visual Programming Environment	VPE
Visual Programs Systems	VPS
Visual Punch Card	VPC
Visual Query Builder [*Computer science*] (PCM)	VQB
Visual Radio Range (IDOE)	vrr

Visual Radio Range	VRR
Visual Range Visibility [*Aviation*] (MCD)	VRV
Visual Rapid Reorder (MCD)	VRR
Visual Reaction Time (MHDB)	VRT
Visual Recognition Threshold	VRT
Visual Reconnaissance	VR
Visual Record Computer	VRC
Visual Record Printer	VRP
Visual Recording Facility (MCD)	VRF
Visual Reference Gate [*Aviation*] (FAAC)	VRG
Visual Reference System	VRS
Visual Report Builder [*Computer science*] (PCM)	VRB
Visual Reporting Point (DA)	VRP
Visual Reporting Post (MCD)	VRP
Visual Resource Management	VRM
Visual Resources [*A publication*]	VR
Visual Response System	VRS
Visual Route (DA)	VR
Visual Routine Processor [*Computer science*]	VRP
Visual Rule Instrument Landing (AAG)	VRI
Visual Satellite Tracking Program	VSTP
Visual Scan	VSCAN
Visual Science Information Center (ECII)	VISIC
Visual Search Microfilm File [*Trademark*] [*Computer science*]	VSMF
Visual Search on Microfilm (NITA)	VSMF
Visual Security Range (NATG)	VSR
Visual Sensor Set	VSS
Visual Signaling [*Military*]	VS
Visual Simulator Interface (MHDI)	VSI
Visual Site Inspection (GNE)	VSI
Visual Skills Appraisal [*Child development test*]	VSA
Visual Software Library [*Computer science*]	VSL
Visual Spectrophotometry	VIS
Visual Standing Wave Ratio (NASA)	VSWR
Visual Storage [*Computer science*]	VS
Visual Storage Administrator [*Windows*] [*Computer science*] (PCM)	VISTA
Visual Studies Workshop (EA)	VSW
Visual Systems Corp.	VISCO
Visual Systems Simulator [*FAA*]	VSS
Visual Table Builder [*Computer science*] (PCM)	VTB
Visual Talking [*Telecommunications*] (IAA)	VISTA
Visual Target Acquisition System [*Navy*] (MCD)	VITAS
Visual Target Acquisition System [*Navy*]	VTAS
Visual Target Identification Point (AFM)	VTIP
Visual Target RADAR Ranging	VTRR
Visual Target Reconnaissance and Acquisition (MCD)	VISTRAC
Visual Task Evaluation [*or Evaluator*] (MHDI)	VTE
Visual Technology Flight Simulator (MCD)	VTFS
Visual Technology Research Simulator (MCD)	VIRS
Visual Technology Research Simulator (CAAL)	VTRS
Visual Telegraphy	VT
Visual Time Code (WDMC)	viz-code
Visual Toss	VT
Visual Training Aid Specialist [*Navy*]	VA
Visual Training Officer [*Navy*]	VTO
Visual Transmitter Power	VTP
Visual Typing System (MCD)	VTS
Visual/Ultraviolet (SSD)	VIS/UV
Visual User Environment [*Military*]	VUE
Visual Workbench [*Computer science*] (PCM)	VWB
Visual-Acoustic-Magnetic Pressure (IEEE)	VAMP
Visual-Acoustic-Magnetic Program [*NOO*]	VAMP
VisualAge	VA
Visual-Auditory Screen Test for Children (DAVI)	VASC
Visual-Auditory-Kinesthetic-Tactile	VAKT
Visual-Aural Digit Span Test [*Educational test*]	VADS
Visual-Aural Radio Range (MSA)	VARR
Visual-Aural Range [*Radio*]	VAR
Visualization Application Steering Environment [*Computer science*]	VASE
Visualization in Scientific Computing [*Computer science*] (EERA)	ViSC
Visualizer-Verbalizer Questionnaire (EDAC)	VVQ
Visually Activated Switch System (MCD)	VASS
Visually Coupled Airborne Systems Simulator (IEEE)	VCASS
Visually Coupled Control System (MCD)	VCCS
Visually Coupled System (IEEE)	VCS
Visually Evoked Cortical Potential [*Neurophysiology*]	VECP
Visually Evoked Field [*Neurophysiology*]	VEF
Visually Evoked Potential [*Neurophysiology*]	VEP
Visually Handicapped [*Ophthalmology*] (DAVI)	VH
Visually Impaired Association (BARN)	VIA
Visually Impaired Data Processors International (EA)	VIDPI
Visually Impaired Piano Tuners International (EA)	VIPTI
Visually Impaired Secretarial/Transcribers Association [*Indianapolis, IN*] (EA)	VISTA
Visually Impaired Veterans of America (EA)	VIVA
[*Developmental Test of*] Visual-Motor Integration [*Also, Beery-Buktenica Test*] (PAZ)	VMI
Visual-Verbal Test [*Psychology*]	VVT
Visual-Vestibulo-Ocular Reflex [*Ophthalmology*] (DAVI)	VVOR
Visum Cultum [*Seen Cultivated*] [*Botany*] (ROG)	VC
Visum Siccum [*Seen in a Dried State*] [*Botany*] (ROG)	VS
Visum Sponanteum [*Seen Wild*] [*Botany*] (ROG)	V SP
Visum Sporadicum [*Seen Wild*] [*Botany*] (ROG)	V SP
Visum Vivum [*Seen Alive*] [*Botany*] (ROG)	VV
Visway Transport, Inc. [*Toronto Stock Exchange symbol*]	VWY

VISX, Inc. [*NASDAQ symbol*] (SAG)	VISX
Vita [*of Josephus*] [*Classical studies*] (OCD)	Vit
Vita Apollonii [*of Philostratus*] [*Classical studies*] (OCD)	VA
Vita Lucani [*of Suetonius*] [*Classical studies*] (OCD)	Vita Luc
Vita Plotini [*of Porphyry*] [*Classical studies*] (OCD)	Plot
Vitae Parallelae [*of Plutarch*] [*Classical studies*] (OCD)	Vit
Vitae Sophistarum [*of Philostratus*] [*Classical studies*] (OCD)	VS
Vital	VIT
Vital Area (NRCH)	VA
Vital Area Center (CAAL)	VAC
Vital Bus Inverter [*Computer science*] (IEEE)	VBI
Vital Capacity	VC
Vital Capacity (MAE)	vit cap
Vital Information for Education and Work (OICC)	VIEW
Vital Initial of Pregnancy [*In vitro fertilization*] (BABM)	VIP
Vital Initial of Pregnancy [*In vitro fertilization*] [*Obstetrics*] (DAVI)	VIP
Vital Load Center (MSA)	VLC
Vital National Objective (AAG)	VNO
Vital Pacific Resources Ltd. [*Vancouver Stock Exchange symbol*]	VPR
Vital Reaction [*on Autopsy*] [*Pathology*] (DAVI)	VB
Vital Records [*Medical records*] (DAVI)	VR
Vital Records [*Genealogy*]	VR
Vital Signs [*Medicine*]	VS
Vital Signs, Inc. [*Associated Press*] (SAG)	VitalSgn
Vital Signs, Inc. [*NASDAQ symbol*] (SAG)	VITL
Vital Signs Normal [*Medicine*] (MAE)	VSOK
Vital Signs Okay [*on Physical Examination*] (DAVI)	VSOK
Vital Signs Stable [*Medicine*]	VSS
Vital Statistics (BARN)	vit stat
Vital Statistics Cooperative Program [*Department of Health and Human Services*] (GFGA)	VSCP
Vital Wheat Gluten [*Vegetable protein*]	VWG
VitalCom Inc. [*NASDAQ symbol*] (TTSB)	VCOM
Vitale Bramani [*Inventor of rubber soles for boots used in mountain climbing*]	VIBRAM
Vitalink Pharmacy [*NASDAQ symbol*] (TTSB)	VTLK
Vitalink Pharmacy Services [*NASDAQ symbol*] (SAG)	VTLK
Vitalink Pharmacy Services, Inc. [*Associated Press*] (SAG)	Vitlnk
Vitalor Screening Pulmonary Function Test [*Medicine*] (DAVI)	VSPFT
Vita-Metall-Keramik [*German dental material for crowns and bridgework*]	VMK
Vitamin (MAE)	v
Vitamin	VIT
Vitamin A [*Used to indicate either dehydroretinol or retinol*] (DAVI)	VitA
Vitamin A Deficiency [*Medicine*] (DMAA)	VAD
Vitamin A$_1$ [*Also called retinol*] (DAVI)	VitA$_1$
Vitamin A$_2$ [*Also called dehydroretinal*] (DAVI)	VitA$_2$
Vitamin B [*A member of the vitamin B complex*] (DAVI)	VitB
Vitamin B$_1$ [*Also called thiamine*] (DAVI)	V-B1
Vitamin B$_1$ [*Also called thiamine*] (DAVI)	VitB$_1$
Vitamin B$_2$ [*Also called riboflavin*] (DAVI)	VitB$_2$
Vitamin B$_3$ [*Also called niacin and nicotinamide*] (DAVI)	VitB$_3$
Vitamin B$_5$ [*Also called calcium pantothenate and pantothenic acid*] (DAVI)	VitB$_5$
Vitamin B$_6$ [*Also called pyridoxine*] (DAVI)	V-B6
Vitamin B$_6$ [*Water-soluble substances including pyridoxine, pyridoxal, and pyridoxamine*] (DAVI)	VitB$_6$
Vitamin B$_{12}$ [*Also called Cyanocobolamine*] (DAVI)	V-B12
Vitamin B$_{12}$ [*Also called cobalamin and cyanocobalamin*] (DAVI)	VitB$_{12}$
Vitamin B$_c$ [*Also called folic acid*] (DAVI)	VitB$_c$
Vitamin C [*Also called ascorbic acid*] (DAVI)	VitC
Vitamin Capsule [*Pharmacy*] (DAVI)	VC
Vitamin D [*Also called calciferol a collective name for several fat-soluble compounds*] (DAVI)	VitD
Vitamin D Receptor [*Genetics*]	VDR
Vitamin D Receptor (DOG)	VDR
Vitamin D$_2$ [*Also called ergocalciferol*] (DAVI)	VitD$_2$
Vitamin D$_3$ [*Also called cholecalciferol and natural vitamin D*] (DAVI)	VitD$_3$
Vitamin D-Dependent Rickets [*Medicine*]	VDDR
Vitamin D-Resistant Rickets [*Medicine*] (DMAA)	VDRR
Vitamin D-Responsive Element [*Biochemistry*]	VDRE
Vitamin E [*Also called alpha-tocopherol*] (DAVI)	VitE
Vitamin E Research and Information Service (EA)	VERIS
Vitamin G [*Also called riboflavin*] (DAVI)	VitG
Vitamin H [*Also called biotin*] (DAVI)	VitH
Vitamin Information Bureau [*Defunct*] (EA)	VIB
Vitamin K [*A group of fat-soluble vitamins that promote clotting of the blood*] (DAVI)	VitK
Vitamin K$_1$ [*Also called phytonadione*] (DAVI)	VitK$_1$
Vitamin K$_2$ [*Also called menaquinone*] (DAVI)	VitK$_2$
Vitamin L [*A factor necessary for lactation in rats*] (DAVI)	VitL
Vitamin L$_1$ [*A factor necessary for lactation in rats and found in beef-liver extract*] (DAVI)	VitL$_1$
Vitamin M [*Also called folic acid*] (DAVI)	VitM
Vitamin PP [*Also called nicotinamide and nicotinic acid*] (DAVI)	VitPP
Vitamin U [*Also called antiulcer vitamin and cabagin vitamin*] (DAVI)	VitU
VitaminB$_{12b}$ [*Also called hydroxycobalamin*] (DAVI)	VitB$_{12b}$
Vitarum Auctio [*of Lucian*] [*Classical studies*] (OCD)	Vit Auct
Vitebsk [*Former USSR ICAO location identifier*] (ICLI)	UMII
Vitech America, Inc. [*Associated Press*] (SAG)	VitchAm
Vitech America, Inc. [*NASDAQ symbol*] (SAG)	VTCH
Vitek ImmunoDiagnostic Assay System	VIDAS
Vitellius [*of Suetonius*] [*Classical studies*] (OCD)	Vit
Vitello Ovi Solutus [*Dissolved in the Yolk of an Egg*] [*Pharmacy*]	Vit Ov Sol
Vitello Ovi Solutus [*Dissolved in the Yolk of an Egg*] [*Pharmacy*] (ROG)	VOS
Vitello Ovi Solutus [*Dissolved in yolk of egg*] [*Latin*] [*Pharmacology*] (DAVI)	VOS
Vitellogenin [*Biochemistry*]	VTG

Vitellus [*Yolk*] [*Latin Pharmacy*] (MAE) ... vit
Vitellus [*Yolk*] [*Pharmacy*] ... Vitel
Viterbo [*Italy ICAO location identifier*] (ICLI) ... LIRV
Viterbo College, La Crosse, WI [*Library symbol Library of Congress*] (LCLS) ... WLacVC
Vitesse Semiconductor [*NASDAQ symbol*] (TTSB) ... VTSS
Vitesse Semiconductor Corp. [*Associated Press*] (SAG) ... Vitesse
Vitesse Semiconductor Corp. [*NASDAQ symbol*] (SPSG) ... VTSS
Vitiated Air Heater ... VAH
Viticulture ... VITIC
Vitim [*Former USSR ICAO location identifier*] (ICLI) ... UIKW
VITIS-Viticulture and Enology Abstracts [*International Food Information Service*] [*Information service or system*] (IID) ... VITIS-VEA
Vitjaz [*Russian Federation*] [*ICAO designator*] (FAAC) ... VTZ
Vitkovice Air [*Czech Republic*] [*ICAO designator*] (FAAC) ... VTR
Vitor/San Isidro [*Peru*] [*ICAO location identifier*] (ICLI) ... SPVR
Vitoria [*Spain ICAO location identifier*] (ICLI) ... LEVT
Vitoria [*Spain*] [*Airport symbol*] (OAG) ... VIT
Vitoria [*Brazil*] [*Airport symbol*] (OAG) ... VIX
Vitoria Da Conquista [*Brazil ICAO location identifier*] (ICLI) ... SBQV
Vitoria/Goiabeira [*Brazil ICAO location identifier*] (ICLI) ... SBVT
Vitosha [*Bulgaria*] [*Seismograph station code, US Geological Survey*] (SEIS) ... VTS
Vitral Exhaustion and Depression (DAVI) ... VED
Vitramon Microwave Corp. (IAA) ... VMC
Vitran Corp. [*NASDAQ symbol*] (TTSB) ... VTNAF
Vitran Corp., Inc. [*Associated Press*] (SAG) ... VitranCo
Vitran Corp., Inc. [*Toronto Stock Exchange symbol*] ... VTN
Vitran Corp., Inc. [*NASDAQ symbol*] (SAG) ... VTNAF
Vitreoscilla Hemoglobin [*Genetics*] ... VHb
Vitreous (AAG) ... VIT
Vitreous [*Ophthalmology*] [*Latin*] (DAVI) ... vitr
Vitreous Carbon ... VC
Vitreous Enamel Development Council [*British*] (DI) ... VEDC
Vitreous Enamel Porcelain (IAA) ... VITROLAIN
Vitreous Environmental Group ... VEG
Vitreous Fluorophotometry [*Ophthalmology*] (DAVI) ... VFP
Vitreous Hemorrhage [*Ophthalmology*] (DAVI) ... VH
Vitreous Infusion Suction Cutter [*Ophthalmology*] ... VISC
Vitreous Silica Fabric ... VSF
Vitreum [*Glass*] [*Latin*] (ADA) ... VITR
Vitrified China Association [*Defunct*] ... VCA
Vitrified Clay [*Technical drawings*] ... VC
Vitrified Clay Tile [*Technical drawings*] ... VCT
Vitrified Stoneware ... VSW
Vitro Assistance Team ... VAT
Vitro Hanford Engineering Service [*Nuclear energy*] (NUCP) ... VHES
Vitro Laboratories, Silver Spring Laboratory Library, Silver Spring, MD [*Library symbol Library of Congress*] (LCLS) ... MdSsV
Vitro, Sociedad Anonima [*Associated Press*] (SAG) ... Vitro
Vitro, Sociedad Anonima ADS [*NYSE symbol*] (SPSG) ... VTO
Vitronectin Receptor [*Biochemistry*] ... VNR
Vitronics Corp. [*Associated Press*] (SAG) ... Vitronic
Vitronics Corp. [*Associated Press*] (SAG) ... Vitronic
Vitronics Corp. [*AMEX symbol*] (SPSG) ... VTC
Vitruvius [*First century BC*] [*Classical studies*] (OCD) ... Vitr
Vitry-En-Artois [*France ICAO location identifier*] (ICLI) ... LFQS
Vitry-Le-Francois/Vauclerc [*France ICAO location identifier*] (ICLI) ... LFSK
Vittel [*France*] [*Airport symbol*] (AD) ... VTL
Vittel/Champ De Courses [*France ICAO location identifier*] (ICLI) ... LFSZ
Viva Cristo Rey [*Long Live Christ the King*] [*Spanish*] ... VCR
Viva Voce [*Spoken Aloud*] [*Latin*] (ADA) ... VV
Vivace [*Lively*] [*Music*] ... VIV
Vivas, Care [*May You Live, Dear One*] [*Latin*] ... VX
Viven and Bassiere [*Rifle grenade*] ... VB
Vivian, LA [*AM radio station call letters*] ... KNCB
Vivian, LA [*FM radio station call letters*] ... KNCB-FM
Vivian, LA [*Location identifier FAA*] (FAAL) ... VIV
Vivian, Younger & Bond Ltd. ... VYB
Vivianus Tuscus [*Flourished, 13th century*] [*Authority cited in pre-1607 legal work*] (DSA) ... Vi
Vivianus Tuscus [*Flourished, 13th century*] [*Authority cited in pre-1607 legal work*] (DSA) ... Vivi
Vivianus Tuscus [*Flourished, 13th century*] [*Authority cited in pre-1607 legal work*] (DSA) ... Vivia
Vivid Technologies, Inc. [*Associated Press*] (SAG) ... VividTch
Vivid Technologies, Inc. [*NASDAQ symbol*] (SAG) ... VVID
Vivid-Inventive-Vital [*Spring fashions*] ... VIV
Vivigani [*Papua New Guinea*] [*Airport symbol*] (OAG) ... VIV
Vivisection [*Medicine*] (WDAA) ... VIVI
Vivisection ... VS
Vivisection Investigation League (EA) ... VIL
Vivra, Inc. [*NYSE symbol*] (SPSG) ... V
Vivra, Inc. [*Associated Press*] (SAG) ... Vivra
Vivre et Penser [*A publication*] (BJA) ... VP
Vivus, Inc. [*Associated Press*] (SAG) ... Vivus
Vivus, Inc. [*NASDAQ symbol*] (SAG) ... VVUS
Vixisti [*You Lived*] [*Latin*] ... V
Vixit [*He Lived*] [*Latin*] ... V
Vixit [*He Lived*] [*Latin*] ... VIX
Vixit Annos [*Lived a Certain Number of Years*] [*Latin*] (WDAA) ... VA
Vizardinus [*Guizzardinus*] [*Deceased, 1222*] [*Authority cited in pre-1607 legal work*] (DSA) ... Viz
Vizardinus [*Guizzardinus*] [*Deceased, 1222*] [*Authority cited in pre-1607 legal work*] (DSA) ... Vizar
Vizardinus [*Guizzardinus*] [*Deceased, 1222*] [*Authority cited in pre-1607 legal work*] (DSA) ... Vz
Vizardinus [*Guizzardinus*] [*Deceased, 1222*] [*Authority cited in pre-1607 legal work*] (DSA) ... Vzar
Vizard's Practice of the Court in Banc [*A publication*] (DLA) ... Viz Pr
Vizianagram [*India*] [*Seismograph station code, US Geological Survey*] (SEIS) ... VIZ
Vizmo [*Projection device*] (NTCM) ... VIZ
Vizmo (WDMC) ... viz
Vizsla Club of America (EA) ... VC of A
V-Joint [*Technical drawings*] ... VJ
V.L. Reishus High School, Biwabik, MN [*Library symbol*] [*Library of Congress*] (LCLS) ... MnBiwH
Vlaams Economisch Verbond ... VEV
Vlaamsch Nationaal Verbond [*Flemish National League*] [*Dissolved*] [*Belgium*] [*Political party*] (PPE) ... VNV
Vlaamsche Toeristenbond ... VTB
Vlaamse Ingenieurs-Vereinigung ... VIV
Vlaamse Luchtransportmaatschappij NV [*Belgium ICAO designator*] (FAAC) ... VLM
Vladimir Ilyich Lenin, Initiator of the October Revolution [*Given name popular in Russia after the Bolshevik Revolution*] ... VILIOR
Vladimir Nabokov [*In book title, "VN: The Life and Art of Vladimir Nabokov"*] ... VN
Vladimir Nabokov Society (EA) ... VNS
Vladivostok [*Russia*] [*Seismograph station code, US Geological Survey*] (SEIS) ... VLA
Vladivostok [*Russian port*] (BARN) ... Vlad
Vladivostok [*USSR*] [*Airport symbol*] (AD) ... VVO
Vlamertinghe [*City in Flanders*] [*World War I*] [*Army*] (DSUE) ... VLAM
VLBI [*Very Long Base-Line Interferometry*] **Space Observatory Program** [*Japan*] ... VSOP
VLBI [*Very Long BaselineInterferometry*] **Space Observatory Programme** ... VSOP
VLSI Implementation Centre [*Queen's University, Kingston*] [*Research center Canada*] ... VLSIIC
VLSI Technologies [*Associated Press*] (SAG) ... VLSI
VLSI Technology [*NASDAQ symbol*] (TTSB) ... VLSI
VLSI Technology, Inc. [*NASDAQ symbol*] (NQ) ... VLSI
VLSI Technology Inc. (NITA) ... VTI
VM-26 [*Teniposide*], Procarbazine, Prednisone [*Antineoplastic drug regimen*] ... VM-26PP
V-Mail Specialists [*Navy*] ... VM
VMARK Software [*NASDAQ symbol*] (TTSB) ... VMRK
Vmark Software, Inc. [*Associated Press*] (SAG) ... Vmark
Vmark Software, Inc. [*NASDAQ symbol*] (SAG) ... VMRK
VMEbus International Trade Association (EA) ... VITA
VMI [*Virginia Military Institute*] **Research Laboratories** [*Research center*] (RCD) ... VMIRL
VMS Hotel (SPSG) ... V
Vnatresna Makedonska Revolucionerna Organizacija [*Internal Macedonian Revolutionary Organization (Known popularly among English-speaking nations as the IMRO)*] [*Former Yugoslavia*] [*Political party*] (PPE) ... VMRO
Vnatresna Makedonska Revolucionerna Organizacija (Udruzena) [*Internal Macedonian Revolutionary Organization (United)*] [*Former Yugoslavia*] [*Political party*] (PPE) ... VMRO(U)
VNC Video Network [*Vancouver Stock Exchange symbol*] ... VNC
Vneshekonombank [*State Bank for Foreign Economic Affairs*] [*Former USSR*] ... VEB
VNR [*Van Nostrand Reinhold*] **Information Services** (IID) ... VIS
Vnukovo Airlines [*Former USSR*] [*FAA designator*] (FAAC) ... VKO
Voar Ltd. [*Angola*] [*FAA designator*] (FAAC) ... VRL
Vocabulaire de Theologie Biblique [*A publication*] (BJA) ... VThB
Vocabulary [*Linguistics*] ... VOC
Vocabulary ... VOCAB
Vocabulary Comprehension Scale [*Educational test*] ... VCS
Vocabulary Etymology ... VETY
Vocabulary File Utility ... VFU
Vocabulary Language (MHDI) ... VOCAL
Vocabulary of Intelligence Concept Expressions ... VOICE
Vocabulary Read-Only Memory [*Computer science*] ... VROM
Vocabulary Switching System [*Computer science*] ... VSS
Vocabulatory, Information, Block Design, Similarities [*Psychology*] ... VIBS
Vocal (AAG) ... VO
Vocal (ADA) ... VOC
Vocal Character Recognition ... VCR
Vocal Chords [*Musical slang*] ... VC's
Vocal Cord ... VC
Vocal Data Management System ... VDMS
Vocal Feedback Device [*Aid for stutterers developed at the University of Pittsburgh by Dr. George Shames*] ... VFD
Vocal Fremitus ... VF
Vocal Output and Input-Controlled Environment ... VOICE
Vocal Output for Industrial Systems (NITA) ... VOIS
Vocal Resonance ... VR
Vocal Students Practice Aid Records [*Record label*] ... VS
Vocal Synthesis ... VS
Vocal Tract Model (MHDI) ... VTM
Vocalization of the Egyptian Syllabic Orthography [*W. F. Albright*] [*A publication*] (BJA) ... VESO
VocalTec Ltd [*NASDAQ symbol*] (TTSB) ... VOCLF
Vocation ... VOCN
Vocational ... VOC
Vocational ... VOCAT
Vocational ... VOCNL
Vocational Adaptation Rating Scales [*Test*] ... VARS
Vocational Agriculture [*Education*] ... VO-AG

Vocational and Educational Services for Individuals with Disabilities .... VESID
Vocational and Rehabilitation Research Institute [University of Calgary] [Research center] (RCD) ..... VRRI
Vocational Apperception Test [Psychology] ..... VAT
Vocational Assistance Commission for Retired Servicemen (CINC) .... VACRS
Vocational Awards International [British] ..... VAI
Vocational Development Checklist (EDAC) ..... VDC
Vocational Development Inventory (EDAC) ..... VDI
Vocational Division, Selkirk College, Nelson, British Columbia [Library symbol National Library of Canada] (NLC) ..... BNSV
Vocational Education (OICC) ..... VE
Vocational Education (OICC) ..... VOC-ED
Vocational Education [Database] [Australia] ..... VOCED
Vocational Education Act [1963] ..... VEA
Vocational Education Board (OICC) ..... VEB
Vocational Education Committee (ACII) ..... VEC
Vocational Education Curriculum Materials Database [University of California, Berkeley] [Information service or system] (CRD) ..... VECM
Vocational Education Curriculum Specialists (OICC) ..... VECS
Vocational Education Data System ..... VEDS
Vocational Education Evaluation and Assessment Process [Pennsylvania] (EDAC) ..... VEEAP
Vocational Education Information System ..... VEIS
Vocational Education Planning Areas (OICC) ..... VEPA
Vocational Education Program Information System ..... VEPIS
Vocational Education Resources Information Center ..... VERIC
Vocational Education Services Grant (OICC) ..... VESG
Vocational Education Specialist (PGP) ..... V Ed S
Vocational Evaluation and Work Adjustment Association (EA) ..... VEWAA
Vocational Exploration Program [Office of Youth Programs] ..... VEP
Vocational Foundation, Inc. (EA) ..... VFI
Vocational Guidance (ADA) ..... VG
Vocational Industrial Clubs of America (EA) ..... VICA
Vocational Information and Evaluation Work Samples [Vocational guidance test] ..... VIEWS
Vocational Information for Education and Work (AEBS) ..... VIEW
Vocational Information through Computer Systems [Philadelphia School District] [Pennsylvania] [Information service or system] (IID) ..... VICS
Vocational Instructional Materials Section (EA) ..... VIM
Vocational Interest and Sophistication Assessment [Vocational guidance test] ..... VISA
Vocational Interest Blank [Psychology] (DAVI) ..... VIB
Vocational Interest, Experience, and Skill Assessment [Vocational guidance test] ..... VIESA
Vocational Interest Inventory [Vocational guidance test] VII
Vocational Interest, Temperament, and Aptitude System [Aptitude test] .... VITAS
Vocational Interests and Vocational Aptitudes [Psychology] ..... VIA
Vocational Interviewing and Placement (DNAB) ..... VIP
Vocational Nurse ..... VN
Vocational Office Education [NASA employment program] ..... VOE
Vocational Office Trainee ..... VOT
Vocational Opinion Index (OICC) ..... VOI
Vocational Preference Inventory [Psychology] ..... VPI
Vocational Preparation Programme (AIE) ..... VPP
Vocational Rehabilitation (OICC) ..... VocRehab
Vocational Rehabilitation ..... VR
Vocational Rehabilitation Act [1973] ..... VRA
Vocational Rehabilitation Administration [Later, Social and Rehabilitation Service] [HEW] ..... VRA
Vocational Rehabilitation and Counseling Service [Veterans Administration] ..... VR & C
Vocational Rehabilitation and Education (MAE) ..... VR & E
Vocational Rehabilitation Association ..... VRA
Vocational Rehabilitation Program (EDAC) ..... VRPSES
Vocational Rehabilitation Services ..... VRS
Vocational Rehabilitation Therapist ..... VRT
Vocational Skills Training [Funds] [Job Corps] ..... VST
Vocational Technical Education Consortium of States (OICC) ..... V-TECS
Vocational Training Authority [Australian Capital Territory] ..... VTA
Vocational Training Charitable Trust [British] ..... VTCT
Vocational Training Officer [Navy] ..... VTO
Vocational Training Scheme [British] ..... VTS
Vocational Training Service ..... VTS
Vocational Values Inventory [Guidance in education] VVI
Vocationally Oriented Adult Education and Literacy Program [Australia] ..... VOAEL
Vocationally Related Annual Goal ..... VRG
Vocational-Technical ..... VO-TECH
Vocational-Technical ..... VT
Vocationist Fathers (TOCD) ..... SDV
Vocationist Fathers, Society of the Divine Vocations (TOCD) ..... sdv
Vocationist Sisters (TOCD) ..... SDV
Vocations for Social Change [Employment clearinghouse] [Defunct] (EA) ..... VSC
Vocative V
Vocative ..... VOC
Vocative [Grammar] (ROG) ..... VOCAT
Voce [Voice] [Latin] V
Voce Italiana, Paterson, NJ [Library symbol Library of Congress] (LCLS) ..... NjPatV
Vodafone Group [NYSE symbol] (SPSG) ..... VOD
Vodafone Group [Associated Press] (SAG) ..... Vodafone
Vodafone Group ADR [NYSE symbol] (TTSB) ..... VOD
Vodavi Technology [Associated Press] (SAG) ..... Vodavi
Vodavi Technology [NASDAQ symbol] (SAG) ..... VTEK
Vodka and Tonic ..... V & T
Vodka Trade Association [British] (DBA) ..... VTA

Voelkischer Beobachter [A publication] ..... VB
Voenno-Vozdushnye Sily [Army Air Forces] [Part of the MO] [Former USSR] ..... VVS
Voenno-Vozdushnye Sily - Voenno-Morskogo Flota [Naval Air Force] [Former USSR] ..... VVS-VMF
Voeune Sai [Cambodia] [ICAO location identifier] (ICLI) ..... VDVS
Vogel: Johnson Agar [Microbiology] (DAVI) ..... VJ
Vogelback Computing Center [Northwestern University] [Research center] (RCD) VCC
Vogel-Bonner Citrate [Growth medium] ..... VBC
Vogel's Approximation Method ..... VAM
Voges-Proskauer [Bacteriology] ..... VP
Vogtareuth [Germany ICAO location identifier] (ICLI) ..... EDYV
Vogt-Koyanagi-Harada [Syndrome] [Ophthalmology] ..... VKH
Vogue [Record label] [France] ..... Vog
Voh [New Caledonia] [ICAO location identifier] (ICLI) ..... NWWF
Vohemar [Madagascar] [ICAO location identifier] (ICLI) ..... FMNV
Vohemar [Madagascar] [Airport symbol] (OAG) ..... VOH
Voi [Kenya] [ICAO location identifier] (ICLI) ..... HKVO
Voice V
Voice v
Voice (WDMC) ..... VCE
Voice (NASA) ..... VO
Voice (AAG) VX
Voice VX
Voice Access Arrangement ..... VAA
Voice Activation Technology (NITA) ..... VAT
Voice Actuated Address Mechanism (PDAA) ..... VAAM
Voice Actuation (MCD) ..... VA
Voice Analog to Digital Encoder ..... VADE
Voice Analyzer and Data Converter (MCD) ..... VADC
Voice Analyzer Data Converter ..... VADAC
Voice and Data Integrated System [Telecommunications] (TEL) ..... VADIS
Voice and Data Recording Auxiliary [NASA] (KSC) ..... VDRA
Voice & Data Resources, Inc. [Ashbury Park, NJ] [Information service or system Telecommunications] (TSSD) ..... VDR
Voice and Video Control and Editing Components (MCD) ..... VVCEC
Voice and Video Monitoring Component (MCD) ..... VVMC
Voice and Vision of the Iranian Revolution [Iranian television] ..... VVIR
Voice Answer Back ..... VAB
Voice Band [Telecommunications] ..... VB
Voice Band Compression (CET) ..... VOBANC
Voice Band Data (KSC) ..... VBD
Voice Bank [Telecommunications] (TEL) ..... VB
Voice Call Signs List ..... VCSL
Voice Call Signs Plan ..... VCSP
Voice Carry-Over [Hearing-impaired technolgoy] ..... VCO
Voice Ciphony (CET) VC
Voice Circuit (SSD) VC
Voice Circuit Reconfiguration Confirmation (SSD) ..... VCRC
Voice Code Translation (BUR) ..... VCT
Voice Coder [Telecommunications] (IAA) ..... VCO
Voice Coder (NITA) ..... VOCODER
Voice Coder ..... VODER
Voice Coil VC
Voice Coil of Speaker [Computer hardware] (IAA) VC
Voice Command System [Ground Communications Facility, NASA] ..... VCS
Voice Communication Panel ..... VCP
Voice Communication System ..... VCS
Voice Communications ..... VOCOM
Voice Communications Assembly [Ground Communications Facility, NASA] ..... VOCA
Voice Communications Laboratory VCL
Voice Communications Security System ..... VCSS
Voice Connecting Arrangement [Telecommunications] (TEL) ..... VCA
Voice Control Center [NASA] (KSC) VCC
Voice Control Switch [NASA] ..... VCS
Voice Control Systems [NASDAQ symbol] (TTSB) ..... VCSI
Voice Control Systems [Associated Press] (SAG) ..... VoiceC
Voice Control Systems [AMEX symbol] (SAG) ..... VPS
Voice Controlled Oscillator [Telecommunications] (TEL) ..... VCO
Voice Controlled Relay ..... VOX
Voice Data [NASA] V
Voice/Data (BUR) ..... V/D
Voice Data Communications ..... VODACOM
Voice Data Encoding System [Telecommunications] (IAA) ..... VDES
Voice Data Entry (NITA) ..... VDE
Voice Data Entry Terminal System ..... VDETS
Voice Data Fax [Telecommunications] ..... VDF
Voice Data Processor System ..... VDPS
Voice Data Switch ..... VDS
Voice Digital Display ..... VDD
Voice Digitization Rate ..... VDR
Voice Direct Line ..... VDL
Voice/Document Delivery System [Computer science] ..... VDDS
Voice E-Mail Messages [Computer science] ..... VEM
Voice Entry Terminal (NITA) ..... VET
Voice Equivalent Channel (MCD) ..... VEC
Voice Foundation (EA) ..... VF
Voice Frequency [Communications] ..... VF
Voice Frequency Carrier [or Channel] ..... VFC
Voice Frequency Carrier [or Channel] Telegraph [or Teletype] ..... VFCT
Voice Frequency Carrier Teletype (MSA) ..... VFCTT
Voice Frequency Equipment [Telecommunications] (IAA) ..... VFEQT
Voice Frequency Facility Terminal [Telecommunications] (TEL) ..... VFFT
Voice Frequency Filter ..... VFF

Voice Frequency Line [*Telecommunications*] (TEL) .... VFL
Voice Frequency Oscillator (NITA) .... VFO
Voice Frequency Signaling System .... VFSS
Voice Frequency Telegraph [*Telecommunications*] (OSI) .... VFCG
Voice Frequency Telegraphy (NATG) .... VFT
Voice Frequency Telegraphy .... VFTG
Voice Frequency Terminal .... VFT
Voice from the Silence [*An association*] (EA) .... VFS
Voice Gate Circuit Adaptors [*Computer science*] (MCD) .... VGCA
Voice Grade [*Telecommunications*] (TEL) .... VG
Voice Information Processing System [*UNISYS Corp.*] [*Blue Bell, PA*] [*Telecommunications service*] (TSSD) .... VIPS
Voice Information Processor .... VIP
Voice Information Service [*Telecommunications*] .... VIS
Voice Input Child Identicant [*Pronounced "Vicki"*] [*Young robot in television show "Small Wonder"*] VICI
Voice Input Code Identifier (MCD) VICI
Voice Input Module [*Cascade Graphics Development Ltd.*] [*Software package*] (NCC) .... VIM
Voice Integrated Presentations [*Telecommunications*] (RDA) .... VIP
Voice Intelligibility Processor [*Audio technology*] (ECON) .... VIP
Voice Interactive Avionics [*Army*] .... VIA
Voice Interactive Subsystem (MCD) .... VIS
Voice Interactive Technology .... VIT
Voice Intercom Subsystem (MCD) .... VIS
Voice Intercommunications Unit .... VIU
Voice Interface Frame [*Telecommunications*] (IAA) .... VIF
Voice Interface Unit [*Telecommunications*] (TEL) .... VIU
Voice Interference Analysis Set [*or System*] .... VIAS
Voice Internal Communications Equipment for Submarines (PDAA) .... VICES
Voice Interruption Priority System .... VIPS
Voice It Woldwide, Inc. [*Associated Press*] (SAG) .... Voice It
Voice It Worldwide [*NASDAQ symbol*] (TTSB) .... MEMO
Voice It Worldwide, Inc. [*NASDAQ symbol*] (SAG) .... MEMO
Voice Jamming Simulator, Weapons (SAA) .... VJSW
Voice Line Expansion [*Telecommunications*] (IAA) .... VLE
Voice Logging Recorder (DWSG) .... VLR
Voice Mail System [*Telecommunications*] (IAA) .... VMS
Voice Management Unit (DA) .... VMU
Voice Master Key .... VMKey
Voice Messaging System [*Telecommunications*] .... VMS
Voice Modulation .... VM
Voice Numerical Control .... VNC
Voice of America .... VA
Voice of America [*United States Information Agency*] .... VOA
Voice of Calvary [*An association*] .... VOC
Voice of China and Asia Missionary Society (EA) .... VOCA
[*The*] **Voice of Democratic Kampuchea** [*Radio station of the Red Khmers*] (PD) .... VODK
Voice of Informed Community Expression .... VOICE
Voice of Liberty Association (EA) .... VLA
Voice of Reason .... VOR
Voice of Reason [*Later, Americans for Religious Liberty*] (EA) .... VR
Voice of the Customer [*Business term*] .... VOC
Voice of the Listener [*British*] [*An association*] (DBA) .... VoL
Voice of the Mediterranean [*Broadcasting service jointly owned by Maltese and Libyan Governments*] (EY) .... VOM
Voice of the People of Burma [*Radio station of the Burma Communist Party*] (PD) .... VOPB
Voice of the People of Thailand [*Radio station of the Communist Party of Thailand*] (PD) .... VOPT
Voice of the Retarded [*An association*] (PAZ) .... VOR
Voice of United Nations Command .... VUNC
Voice of Vietnam [*Propaganda broadcast aimed at US POWs*] (VNW) .... VOV
Voice of Women .... VOW
Voice of Youth Advocates [*A publication*] (BRI) .... VOYA
Voice on the Net [*A consortium of internet users, vested interests, and software companies*] (PCM) .... VON
Voice Onset Time .... VOT
Voice Operated Database in Inquiry System (NITA) .... VODIS
Voice Operated Gain Adjustment Device (NITA) .... VOGAD
Voice Order Circuit (CET) .... VOC
Voice Order Wire .... VOW
Voice Output Communications Aid .... VOCA
Voice Output Exchange .... VOX
Voice Output Terminal [*Computer science*] (WDMC) .... VOT
Voice Over [*Commentary read over a program*] [*Television*] .... VO
Voice Pitch Analysis [*Consumer Response Corp.*] .... VOPAN
Voice, Plainfield, NJ [*Library symbol Library of Congress*] (LCLS) .... NjPlaV
Voice plus Telegraph [*Telecommunications*] (TEL) .... VPT
Voice plus Teleprinter Unit .... V + TU
Voice Position Report (DA) .... VPR
Voice Powered Tech International [*NASDAQ symbol*] (SAG) .... VPTI
Voice Powered Tech International, Inc. [*Associated Press*] (SAG) .... VcePw
Voice Powered Tech International, Inc. [*Associated Press*] (SAG) .... VoicePw
Voice Powered Tech Intl [*NASDAQ symbol*] (TTSB) .... VPTI
Voice Powered Tech Intl Wrrt [*NASDAQ symbol*] (TTSB) .... VPTIW
Voice Processing System [*Computer science*] (IT) .... VPS
Voice Read Out Unit [*Telecommunications*] (IAA) .... VRU
Voice Recognition and Synthesis System [*Aviation Navy*] .... VRASS
Voice Recognition Chip [*Electronics*] (EECA) .... VRC
Voice Recognition Control (MCD) .... VRC
Voice Recognition Module [*Computer science*] .... VRM
Voice Recognition System .... VRS
Voice Recognition Unit .... VRU
Voice Recording Assembly [*Ground Communications Facility, NASA*] .... VRCA
Voice Recording Subsystem .... VRS
Voice Reporting Fault Indicator .... VRFI
Voice Reporting Signal Assembly .... VRSA
Voice Reporting Signal System .... VRSS
Voice Response System (NITA) .... VRS
Voice Response Unit .... VRU
Voice Retrieval System (NITA) .... VRS
Voice Rotating Beacon .... VRB
Voice Signaling System .... VSS
Voice Storage System [*AT & T*] .... VSS
Voice Store and Forward [*Voice messaging*] .... VSF
Voice Store and Forward Messaging System [*Telecommunications*] (IAA) .... VSFS
Voice Stress (LAIN) .... VS
Voice Switch and Control System [*FAA*] .... VSCS
Voice Switch Monitor (MCD) .... VSM
Voice Switching [*Telecommunications*] (IAA) .... VS
Voice Telephone Conference .... VOICECON
Voice Terminal (NITA) .... VOTERM
Voice Tube [*Technical drawings*] .... VT
Voice Unit [*Signal amplitude measurement*] .... VU
Voice Verification System .... VVS
Voice Warning System .... VWS
Voice-Activated Encoding System .... VAES
Voice-Activated Transcription [*Machine*] (DAVI) .... VAT
Voice-Activated Typewriter .... VAT
Voice-Activated Word Processor [*Computer science*] .... VAWP
Voice-Analog-Digital Manual Switch (MCD) .... VADMS
Voiceband Subscriber Loop Emulator [*Telecom Analysis Systems, Inc.*] .... VSLE
Voice-Based Learning System (EDAC) .... VBLS
Voice-Controlled Carrier [*Telecommunications*] (IAA) VCC
Voice-Excitated Formant Vocoder (PDAA) .... VEFV
Voice-Excited VOCODER .... VEV
Voice-Initiated Cockpit Control and Integration [*Aviation*] (PDAA) VICCI
Voicemail International, Inc. [*Cupertina, CA*] [*Telecommunications*] (TSSD) .... VMI
Voice-Operated Carrier Switching Unit (IAA) .... VOCSU
Voice-Operated Changeover .... VOX
Voice-Operated Coder .... VOC
Voice-Operated Computerized Identification System (PDAA) .... VPCIS
Voice-Operated Control [*Telecommunications*] (IAA) .... VOC
Voice-Operated Control (IDOE) .... vox
Voice-Operated Demonstrator .... VODER
Voice-Operated Device Antising (CET) .... VODAS
Voice-Operated Device for Automatic Transmission .... VODAT
Voice-Operated Gain-Adjusting Amplifier [*NASA*] .... VOGAA
Voice-Operated Gain-Adjusting Device [*NASA*] .... VOGAD
Voice-Operated Identification Computer Entry System (PDAA) .... VOICES
Voice-Operated Inspection System [*Software*] .... VOIS
Voice-Operated Keying [*Computer science*] .... VOX
Voice-Operated Loss Control and Suppressor .... VOLCAS
Voice-Operated Relay .... VOPR
Voice-Operated Relay .... VOR
Voice-Operated Relay (IAA) .... VOY
Voice-Operated Relay Circuit (IAA) .... VOC
Voice-Operated Switch [*or System*] .... VOS
Voice-Operated Transmission .... VOX
Voice-Operated Typewriter Employing Morse [*Telecommunications*] (IAA) .... VOTEM
Voiceover/Sound on Tape [*Television*] (NTCM) .... VO/SOT
Voice-Processing Module [*Computer science*] .... VPM
Voice-Programming Language [*Computer science*] .... VPL
Voices [*Music*] VV
Voices in Vital America .... VIVA
Voices of Multicultural America [*A publication*] .... VMA
Voicespondence Club (EA) .... VS
VoiceStation System [*Sydis, Inc.*] [*San Jose, CA*] (TSSD) .... VSS
Voice-Stress Analyzer (ECII) .... VSA
Void [*Decision or finding held invalid for reasons given*] [*Used in Shepard's Citations*] [*Legal term*] (DLA) V
Void (AAG) .... VD
Void [*Urology*] (DAVI) .... VD
Void in Part [*Decision or finding held invalid in part for reasons given*] [*Used in Shepard's Citations*] [*Legal term*] (DLA) .... VP
Void Metallic Composite .... VMC
Void On Call to Operating Room (DAVI) .... VOCTOR
Voiding (MAE) .... vdg
Voiding Cystourethrogram [*Medicine*] .... VCU
Voiding Cystourethrogram [*Medicine*] .... VCUG
Voids [*Medicine*] (MAE) .... vs
Voids in Mineral Aggregate (DICI) .... VMA
Voinjama [*Liberia*] [*ICAO location identifier*] (ICLI) .... GLVA
Voinjama [*Liberia*] [*Airport symbol*] (OAG) .... VOI
Voiture sans Permis [*Car without license*] [*French*] .... VSP
Voix des Femmes Canadiennes pour la Paix [*Canadian Voice of Women for Peace*] [*See also VOW*] [*Canada*] (EAIO) .... VFCP
Voix des Notres [*Record label*] [*France*] .... VdN
Voix du Peuple Murundi [*Voice of the Murundi People*] .... VPM
Vojski Drzavne Varnosti [*Yugoslavia*] .... VDV
Volans [*Constellation*] .... Vol
Volans [*Constellation*] .... Voln
Volante [*Lightly and Rapidly*] [*Music*] (ROG) .... VOL
Volar [*Anatomy*] (WGA) .... Vol
Volar Intercalated Segment Instability [*Orthopedics*] .... VISI
Volare [*Russian Federation*] [*ICAO designator*] (FAAC) .... VLR
Volatile [*Chemistry*] (DAVI) .... vol

Volatile [*Chemistry*] (DAVI) .... volt
Volatile Combustible Material .... VCM
Volatile Condensable Material .... VCM
Volatile Corrosion Inhibitor [*See also VPI*] [*Metallurgy*] VCI
Volatile Dissolved Solids (MCD) .... VDS
Volatile Fatty Acid [*Organic chemistry*] .... VFA
Volatile Fission Product [*Nuclear energy*] (NUCP) .... VFP
Volatile Flavor Compound .... VFC
Volatile Halogenated Organic [*Analytical chemistry*] .... VHO
Volatile Halogenated Organic Compound [*Environmental chemistry*] .... VHOC
Volatile Hazardous Air Pollutant (EG) .... VHAP
Volatile Human Effluents .... VHE
Volatile Keying Assembly (AFM) .... VKA
Volatile Liquid Hydrocarbon .... VLH
Volatile Matter .... VM
Volatile Nitrogen (OA) .... VN
Volatile Nitrosamine [*Organic chemistry*] .... VNA
Volatile Oil .... VO
Volatile Organic Chemical .... VOC
Volatile Organic Compound [*Environmental chemistry*] .... VOC
Volatile Organic Fraction [*Automotive exhaust emission testing*] .... VOF
Volatile Organic Fractions .... VOF
Volatile Organic Hazardous Air Pollutant [*Environmental Protection Agency*] .... VOHAP
Volatile Organic Sampling Train [*For air analysis*] .... VOST
Volatile Profile Analysis [*Food chemistry*] .... VPA
Volatile Reducing Substance (OA) .... VRS
Volatile Solids [*Environmental science*] .... VS
Volatile Sulfur Compound [*Chemistry*] .... VSC
Volatile Suspended Solids [*Environmental science*] .... VSS
Volatilis [*Volatile*] [*Pharmacy*] .... VOL
Volcan Norte [*Costa Rica*] [*Seismograph station code, US Geological Survey*] (SEIS) AR9
Volcan Poas [*Costa Rica*] [*Seismograph station code, US Geological Survey*] (SEIS) .... VPS
Volcanic [*Quality of the bottom*] [*Nautical charts*] .... Vol
Volcanic (VRA) .... volc
Volcanic Ash [*ICAO*] (FAAC) .... VA
Volcanic Ash [*Quality of the bottom*] [*Nautical charts*] .... Vol Ash
Volcanic Ash Forecast Transport and Dispersion [*Model*] (USDC) .... VAFTAD
Volcanic Ash Forecast Transport and Dispersion [*Model*] [*Marine science*] (OSRA) .... VAFTAD
Volcanic Explosivity Index [*Measure of amounts of gas and ash that reach the atmosphere*] .... VEI
Volcanic Front [*Geology*] .... VF
Volcanic Origin (AAG) .... VO
Volcanic-Associated Massive Sulphide [*Geology*] .... VMS
Volcanics [*Lithology*] .... VOLC
Volcano (ROG) V
Volcano [*Maps and charts*] .... VOL
Volcano .... VOLC
Volcano Arenal [*Costa Rica*] [*Seismograph station code, US Geological Survey*] (SEIS) AR1
Volcano, HI [*FM radio station call letters*] .... KKOA
Volcano Resources Corp. [*Vancouver Stock Exchange symbol*] .... VOM
Volcano System Monitor [*Marine science*] (OSRA) .... VSM
Volcano Veterinary Center [*Rwanda*] VVC
Volcano-Tectonic [*Earthquake*] .... VT
Volga [*Former USSR*] [*FAA designator*] (FAAC) .... VLA
Volga Public Library, Volga, IA [*Library symbol Library of Congress*] (LCLS) .... IaVol
Volga, SD [*AM radio station call letters*] .... KJJQ
Volga, SD [*FM radio station call letters*] .... KKQQ
Volga-Dnepr [*Former USSR ICAO designator*] (FAAC) .... VDA
Volgens Bygaande Brief [*According to Accompanying Letter*] [*Correspondence*] [*Afrikaans*] .... vbb
Volgograd [*Former USSR Airport symbol*] (OAG) .... VOG
Volgo-Viatskii Region, RSFSR [*MARC geographic area code Library of Congress*] (LCCP) .... e-urv-
Volkel [*Netherlands ICAO location identifier*] (ICLI) .... EHVK
Volksbund fuer das Deutschtum im Ausland [*NAZI Germany*] .... VDA
Volksdeutsche Mittelstelle [*NAZI Germany*] .... VOMI
Volksgrenadier [*Title given to infantry divisions with distinguished combat records*] [*Germany*] [*World War II*] .... VG
Volksmarine .... VM
Volkspartie [*People's Party*] [*Liechtenstein*] [*Political party*] (PPE) .... VP
Volkspartij voor Vrijheid en Democratie [*People's Party for Freedom and Democracy*] [*Netherlands Political party*] (EAIO) .... VVD
Volkspolizei [*Also, VP*] .... VOPO
Volkspolizei [*Also, VOPO*] .... VP
Volkspolizeihelfer .... VPH
Volkspolizeikreisamt .... VPKA
Volksrust [*South Africa*] [*ICAO location identifier*] (ICLI) .... FAVU
Volksunie [*People's Union*] [*Belgium Political party*] .... VU
Volksunie-Europese Vrije Alliante [*Belgium*] [*Political party*] (ECED) .... VU-EVA
Volksunite [*United People's Party*] [*Belgium*] [*Political party*] .... VU
Volkswagen [*Automobile*] (DSUE) .... VOLKS
Volkswagen [*German automobile*] .... VW
Volkswagen Audi Group .... VAG
Volkswagen Caminhoes Limitada [*Brazil*] .... VWCL
Volkswagen Club of America (EA) .... VWCA
Volkswagen Convertible Owners of America [*Defunct*] (EA) .... VCOA
Volkswagen Insurance Co. .... VICO
Volkswagen of America .... VOA
Volkswagen of America (ECON) .... VWA
Volkswagen of America .... VWOA
Volkswagen Split Window Club of America (EA) .... VWSWCA
Volkswagen Toy Collectors of America [*Defunct*] (EA) .... VW-TCA
Volkswirtschaftsrat [*Political Economy Bureau*] [*German*] .... VWR
Volley (DA) .... VLY
Volleyball Association of Ireland (EAIO) .... VAI
Vologda [*Former USSR ICAO location identifier*] (ICLI) .... ULWW
Volos [*Greece*] [*ICAO location identifier*] (ICLI) .... LGVO
Volos [*Greece*] [*Airport symbol*] (AD) .... VOL
Volovan [*Malagasy*] [*Airport symbol*] (AD) .... WVV
Volpe National Transportation Systems Center (BARN) .... VNTSC
Volt [*Symbol*] [*SI unit of electric potential difference*] V
Volt (ROG) .... VO
Volt Frequency Monitor (DNAB) .... VFM
Volt Info Sciences [*NASDAQ symbol*] (TTSB) .... VOLT
Volt Information Sciences, Inc. [*NASDAQ symbol*] (NQ) .... VOLT
Volt Information Sciences, Inc. [*Associated Press*] (SAG) .... VoltInf
Volt Ohmmeter [*Electronics*] (IAA) .... VOM
Volt Peak-to-Peak (NASA) .... V P-P
Volt Second Transfer Ratio .... VSTR
Volta Aluminum Co. Ltd. .... VALCO
Volta Bureau for the Deaf, Washington, DC [*Library symbol Library of Congress*] (LCLS) .... DVB
Volta River and Basin [*MARC geographic area code Library of Congress*] (LCCP) .... fv----
Voltage (CET) .... E
Voltage V
Voltage (IDOE) v
Voltage (IAA) .... VE
Voltage (AAG) .... VLTG
Voltage Adjusting Rheostat .... VAR
Voltage Amperage Normalizer .... VOLTAN
Voltage Ampere Reactance [*AC electric motors*] .... VAR
Voltage Amplifier (IAA) .... VA
Voltage Amplifier Tube .... VAT
Voltage and Synchro Interface Module .... VASIM
Voltage Board (IAA) .... VB
Voltage Breakover (IAA) .... VBO
Voltage Calibration Set .... VCS
Voltage Changer (IAA) VC
Voltage Clock Trigger (IAA) .... VCT
Voltage Coefficient of Capacitance VCC
Voltage Coefficient of Resistance .... VCR
Voltage Comparator [*or Compensator*] (DEN) VC
Voltage Control of Amplification .... VCA
Voltage Control Resistor (IAA) .... VCR
Voltage Control Transfer .... VCT
Voltage Control Unit .... VCU
Voltage Crossing Detector .... VCD
Voltage Curve Tracer .... VCT
Voltage Detector .... VD
Voltage Detector (IEEE) .... VDET
Voltage Doubler Circuit .... VDC
Voltage Drop (MSA) .... VD
Voltage Efficiency [*Electrochemistry*] .... VE
Voltage Fault Detector [*Electronics*] (IAA) .... VFD
Voltage Gain .... VG
Voltage Impulse Protection (IAA) .... VIP
Voltage in Acceptable Range (MCD) .... VAR
Voltage Inner Gimbal .... EIG
Voltage Input (TEL) .... VIN
Voltage Inverter Switch (IAA) .... VIS
Voltage Limiter (IAA) .... VOLLIM
Voltage Monitor and Fault Indicating .... VMFI
Voltage Negative Immittance Converter .... VNIC
Voltage-[*Controlled Differential*] **Negative Resistance** [*Electronics*] (BARN) .... VNR
Voltage Negative-Impedance Converter [*Electronics*] (ECII) .... ENIC
Voltage Outer Gimbal .... EOG
Voltage Phasing Control (DEN) .... VPC
Voltage Readout Unit .... VRU
Voltage Reduction Technology (PCM) .... VRT
Voltage Reference (DEN) .... VR
Voltage Reference Amplifier .... VRA
Voltage Reference Tube .... VRT
Voltage Regulating Diode .... VRD
Voltage Regulator [*Automotive engineering*] .... V/REG
Voltage Regulator .... VR
Voltage Regulator Alarm .... VRA
Voltage Regulator Module .... VRM
Voltage Regulator Supervisory Panel (MCD) .... VRSP
Voltage Regulator Tube .... VRT
Voltage Regulator-Exciter .... VRE
Voltage Relay .... VR
Voltage Relay .... VRLY
Voltage Repair .... VR
Voltage Root Mean Square .... VRMS
Voltage Standing Wave .... VSW
Voltage Standing-Wave Frequency (DNAB) .... VSWF
Voltage Standing-Wave Ratio .... VSWR
Voltage Switching (IAA) .... VS
Voltage Time to Breakdown (DEN) .... VTB
Voltage to Digital Converter .... VDC
Voltage to Frequency [*Converter*] [*Computer science*] .... V/F
Voltage to Frequency Converter .... VFC
Voltage to Pulse Converter .... VPC

Voltage to Substrate and Sources [*Microelectronics*]	VSS
Voltage Transfer Function	VTF
Voltage Transformation Ratio [*Physics*]	VTR
Voltage Transformer (EECA)	VT
Voltage Tunable Magnetron	VTM
Voltage Tunable Microwave Oscillator	VTMO
Voltage Tunable Noise Source	VTNS
Voltage Tunable Oscillator	VTO
Voltage Variable Capacitance Diode	VVCD
Voltage Variable Capacitor	VVC
Voltage Variable Diode	VVD
Voltage Variation Indicator	VVI
Voltage-Alternating Current (NITA)	VAC
Voltage-Controlled Amplifier (NTCM)	VCA
Voltage-Controlled Capacitor	VCC
Voltage-Controlled Clock (IAA)	VCC
Voltage-Controlled Crystal Oscillator (IAA)	VCCO
Voltage-Controlled Crystal Oscillator	VCXO
Voltage-Controlled Current Source [*Electronics*]	VCCS
Voltage-Controlled Filter	VCF
Voltage-Controlled Frequency (IEEE)	VCF
Voltage-Controlled Generator	VCG
Voltage-Controlled Local Oscillator	VCLO
Voltage-Controlled Multivibrator	VCM
Voltage-Controlled Negative Capacitance (IAA)	VCNC
Voltage-Controlled Negative Resistance (IAA)	VCNR
Voltage-Controlled Oscillator	VCO
Voltage-Controlled Shift Register	VCSR
Voltage-Controlled Transfer (IAA)	VCT
Voltage-Controlled Voltage Source	VCVS
Voltage-Current Adapter (IAA)	VCA
Voltage-Current-Sequence (MCD)	VCS
Voltage-Dependent, Anion-Selective [*Proteins*] [*Biochemistry*]	VDAS
Voltage-Dependent, Anion-Selective Channels [*In the membrane of a mitochondrion*]	VDAC
Voltage-Dependent Calcium Channel [*Neurobiology*]	VDCC
Voltage-Dependent Resistor (DEN)	VDR
Voltage-Direct Current (NITA)	VDC
Voltage-Gated Calcium Channel [*Neurophysiology*]	VGCC
Voltage-Logic [*Electronics*] (IAA)	VL
Voltage-Logic-Current-Switching [*Electronics*]	VLCS
Voltage-Logic-Voltage-Switching [*Electronics*]	VLVS
Voltage-Modulated Transmission [*Electronics*]	VMT
Voltage-Regulated Plate Filament	VRPF
Voltage-Regulated Power Supply	VRPS
Voltage-Saturated Capacitor	VSC
Voltage-Sensing Relay	VSR
Voltage-Sensing Switch	VSS
Voltage-Sensitive Amplifier	VSA
Voltage-Sensitive Calcium Channel [*Physiology*]	VSCC
Voltage-Sensitive Oscillator (IAA)	VSO
Voltage-Stabilized Polyethylene (IAA)	VSP
Voltage-to-Frequency	VTOF
Voltage-Tuned Magnetron (IDOE)	vtm
Voltaire Alternative	VA
Voltaire Society (EA)	VS
Voltammeter (IAA)	VA
Voltammeter	VAM
Volt-Ampere (AAG)	V-A
Volt-Ampere (IDOE)	VA
Volt-Ampere Characteristics [*Microwave emission*]	VAC
Volt-Ampere Reactive	VAR
Volt-Ampere Reactive Hour (IAA)	VARH
Volt-Ampere Tester	VAT
Voltare [*Turn Over*] [*Latin*] (ROG)	V
Volt-Coulomb (DEN)	VC
Volterra [*Italy ICAO location identifier*] (ICLI)	LIQV
Volti [*Turn Over*] [*Music*]	V
Volti Subito [*Turn Over Quickly*] [*Music*]	VS
Voltmeter	V
Voltmeter	VM
Voltmeter Analog-to-Digital Converter	VAD
Voltmeter Calibrator	VOCA
Voltmeter Switch (MSA)	VS
Volt-Ohm Meter	VOM
Volt-Ohm-Ammeter (IDOE)	VOA
Volt-Ohm-Milliammeter	VOM
Volt-Ohm-Milliampere [*Electronics*] (IAA)	VOMA
Volt-Ohm-Milliampere Meter [*Electronics*] (IAA)	VOM
Volts	V
Volts AC (IDOE)	V_{ac}
Volts AC (IDOE)	vac
Volts AC (IDOE)	Vac
Volts Alternating Current	VAC
Volts DC (IDOE)	Vdc
Volts DC (IDOE)	V_{dc}
Volts Direct Current	VDC
Volts Peak (NASA)	VPK
Volts per Ampere (IDOE)	V/A
Volts per Meter (IDOE)	V/m
Volts per Meter [*Also, VPM*]	V/m
Volts per Meter [*Also, V/m*]	VPM
Volts per Mil (DEN)	V/M
Volts per Mil	V/mil
Volts per Mil	VPM

Volts per Mile (IAA)	VPM
Volts Working [*Electronics*] (ECII)	VW
Volt-Seconds [*Webers*] (IDOE)	Vs
Volt-Seconds per Ampere [*Henrys*] (IDOE)	Vs/A
Volume [*Bibliography*]	V
Volume [*Symbol*] [*IUPAC*]	V
Volume (WDMC)	V
Volume	VO
Volume (EY)	VOL
Volume (VRA)	vol
Volume	VOL
Volume (ODBW)	vol
Volume (IDOE)	vol
Volume (NTCM)	VV
Volume Accumulator Unit	VAU
Volume Air Flow [*Automotive engineering*]	VAF
Volume, American Stock Exchange [*Selection symbol*]	VOLA
Volume Analysis Information System Software	VANIS
Volume and Tension [*of pulse*]	V & T
Volume, Area, and Mass Properties (PDAA)	VAMP
Volume, Article [*or Chapter*], Paragraph, Sentence [*Numbers*] [*Indexing*]	VAPS
Volume Calculator (MHDI)	VOLCAL
Volume Catalog (IAA)	VOLCAT
Volume Control (DEN)	VC
Volume Control Tank [*Nuclear energy*] (NRCH)	VCT
Volume Dead Air Space (MAE)	Vd
Volume Deleted [*Finance*]	VD
Volume Discount [*Investment term*]	VD
Volume Ejection [*Medicine*]	VE
Volume Element (MAE)	voxel
Volume Folding and Limiting Amplifier	VFLA
Volume Footwear Retailers of America [*Later, FDRA*]	VFRA
Volume Fraction of Solids in a Slurry	VFS
Volume Identifier (MHDI)	VOLID
Volume Index [*Medicine*] (DHSM)	VI
Volume Indicator [*Radio equipment*]	VI
Volume Inverse Pricing [*Business term*]	VIP
Volume Investigation [*Three-dimensional imaging technology developed at The Toronto Hospital in Canada*]	VI
Volume Kill (WDAA)	VK
Volume Label (IAA)	VOL
Volume Limiting Amplifier	VLA
Volume Loadability Speed (IEEE)	VLS
Volume Median Diameter [*Particle size*]	VMD
Volume Merchandising Allowance (DOAD)	VMA
Volume, New York Stock Exchange [*Selection symbol*]	VOLN
Volume of Compartment [*Technical drawings*]	VC
Volume of Distribution	VD
Volume of Distribution at Steady State	VDSS
Volume of Distribution of Bilirubin [*Medicine*] (MAE)	VDBR
Volume of Expired Gas [*Medicine*] (DAVI)	V_E
Volume of Mechanical Dead Space [*Medicine*] (DAVI)	V_{DM}
Volume of Packed Red Cells [*Hematology*]	VPRC
Volume of Relaxation [*Medicine*] (DMAA)	Vr
Volume of Solute per Volume of Solution [*Pharmacology*] (DAVI)	v/v
Volume of the Anatomic Dead-space [*Medicine*] (DAVI)	V_{Dan}
Volume of the Sacred Law [*Freemasonry*]	VSL
Volume over Bark [*Forestry*]	VOB
Volume Oxygen Consumption [*Medicine*] (DAVI)	VO_2
Volume Packed Cells	VPC
Volume Percent (DAVI)	vol%
Volume Percent (MAE)	VPC
Volume Purchase Agreement [*Sales*]	VPA
Volume Rate [*Heat transmission symbol*]	Q
Volume Ratio [*Volume per Volume*] [*Pharmacology*] (DAVI)	vol/vol
Volume, Red Blood Cell [*Hematology*] (MAE)	VRBC
Volume Reduction [*Nuclear energy*] (NRCH)	VR
Volume Reduction and Solidification [*Hazardous waste disposal*]	VRS
Volume Review Exercise (DNAB)	VRE
Volume Sensitive Tariff [*Telecommunications*] (TEL)	VST
Volume/Serial	VOLSER
Volume Serial Number [*Computer science*] (IAA)	VSN
Volume Table of Contents [*Computer science*]	VOTC
Volume Table of Contents [*Computer science*]	VTOC
Volume Thickness Index	VTI
Volume Thoracic Gas [*Medicine*]	VTG
Volume Tidal Mechanical (MAE)	VTM
Volume, Toronto Stock Exchange [*Selection symbol*]	VOLT
Volume Unit [*Signal amplitude measurement*]	VU
Volume Unknown [*Medicine*]	VX
Volume/Volume	V/V
Volume-Pressure (MAE)	VP
Volume-Price Trend [*Finance*]	VPT
Volume-Pulse-Charge	VPC
Volume-Rendering Technique [*Computer graphics*] (BYTE)	VRT
Volumes (ODBW)	vv
Volumes per Million [*Measure of gas contamination*]	VPM
Volume-Sequence-Number [*Computer science*]	VSN
Volumetric	VLMTRC
Volumetric (WDAA)	VOLUM
Volumetric Energy Density [*of fuels*]	VED
Volumetric Indicating RADAR	VOLIR
Volumetric Mixing Ratio	VMR
Volumetric Redox Measurement [*Analytical chemistry*]	VRM
Volumetric Scanning RADAR	VOLSCAN

Volumetric Solution .... VS
Volume-Variety (PDAA) .... VOLVAR
Volume-Weighted Average [Statistics] .... VWA
Volume-Weighted Averages of Realized Prices .... VOLWARE
Volume-Weighted Mean [Statistical technique] .... VWM
Voluntary [or Volunteer] (AFM) .... VOL
Voluntary .... VOLNTRY
Voluntary .... VOLRY
Voluntary (ROG) .... VOLY
Voluntary Action Center .... VAC
Voluntary Action Indicated [FDA] .... VAI
Voluntary Admission [Psychiatry] (DAVI) .... vol adm
Voluntary Agency [Generic term for a charitable organization] ..... VOLAG
Voluntary Aid (ADA) .... VA
Voluntary Aid Detachment [British World War I nursing unit] ..... VAD
Voluntary Aided School [British] V
Voluntary Application Fill (DNAB) .... VAF
Voluntary Assistance Program .... VAP
Voluntary Auto Restraints [Import quotas on automobiles] ..... VAR
Voluntary Bankruptcy (MHDW) .... VB
Voluntary Census Committee (EA) VCC
Voluntary Closing [Prosthesis] [Medicine] VC
Voluntary College Letter [British] VCL
Voluntary Conservation Organisation (EERA) .... VCO
Voluntary Content Rating System [Solid Oak software] [Computer science]
    (PCM) .... VCR
Voluntary Cooperation Program [World Meteorological Organization] [United
    Nations] .... VCP
Voluntary Cooperative Information System [American Public Welfare
    Association] (EGAO) .... VCIS
Voluntary Data Inquiry .... VDI
Voluntary Early Release and Retirement Program [Army] ..... VERRP
Voluntary Early Retirement Authority [DoD] .... VERA
Voluntary Early Transition [Military] .... VET
Voluntary Effort [A cost containment program established by AHA, AMA, and
    FAH] .... VE
Voluntary Effort to Contain Health Care Costs (EA) .... VECHCC
Voluntary Employee Benefit Association [Type of trust established by a
    company, a union, or both to provide members with various insurance
    benefits] .... VEBA
Voluntary Environmental Organisation (EERA) .... VEO
Voluntary Euthanasia Society [British] (DBA) .... VES
Voluntary Export Restraints .... VER
Voluntary Fund for the United Nations Decade for Women (EA) ..... VFUNDW
Voluntary Home Mortgage Credit Program [of HHFA] [Terminated] ..... VHMCP
Voluntary Hospitals of America (EA) .... VHA
Voluntary Import Expansion [International trade] (ECON) ..... VIE
Voluntary Indefinite [Status] [Army] (INF) VI
Voluntary Insurance Association [Australia] .... VIA
Voluntary Interceptor [World War II British] VI
Voluntary International Service Assignments [of the Society of Friends] ..... KISA
Voluntary Interruption of Pregnancy [Obstetrics] (MAE) ..... VIP
Voluntary/Legal/Regulatory (IEEE) .... VOLERE
Voluntary Licensing Authority [Embryology] [British] ... VLA
Voluntary Loss Rate [of Air Force officers resigning before retirement] ..... VLR
Voluntary Movement Group (EAIO) .... VMG
Voluntary Observing Ship [Marine science] (OSRA) ..... VOS
Voluntary Observing Ships [Marine science] (MSC) ..... VOS
Voluntary Opening [Prosthesis] [Medicine] .... VO
Voluntary Organisations' Liaison Council for Under-Fives [British]
    (DI) .... VOLCUF
Voluntary Organisations of Communication and Language (DBA) ..... VOCAL
Voluntary Overseas Libraries Service .... VOLS
Voluntary Patient [British] .... VP
Voluntary Petroleum Allocation Program [Presidential] ..... VPAP
Voluntary Price Reduction (AABC) .... VPR
Voluntary Product Standard [National Bureau of Standards] ..... VPS
Voluntary Projects Programme [British] .... VPP
Voluntary Protection Program [OSHA] .... VPP
Voluntary Protection Programs Participants' Association ..... VPPPA
Voluntary Quit [Unemployment insurance] [Bureau of Labor Statistics]
    (OICC) .... VQ
Voluntary Reserve Training [British military] (DMA) .... VRT
Voluntary Restraint Arrangement [Import quotas] .... VRA
Voluntary Restriction Agreement [Pact between the US and Japan on
    automotive imports] .... VRA
Voluntary Returnees [Immigration Service] .... VR
Voluntary School (AIE) .... VS
Voluntary Separation Incentive [DoD] .... VSI
Voluntary Separation Incentive Program [DoD] .... VSIP
Voluntary Service International [British] (EAIO) .... VSI
Voluntary Service Overseas [Military] .... VSO
Voluntary Short-Term Disability Insurance .... VSDI
Voluntary Standards Bodies (IAA) .... VSBS
Voluntary Sterilization .... VS
Voluntary Surgical Opinion [Health insurance] (GHCT) ..... VSO
Voluntary Termination Incentive [Business term] .... VTI
Voluntary Termination of Pregnancy [Medicine] .... VTP
Voluntary Universal Marking Program (IAA) .... VUVM
[The] Voluntaryists (EA) .... TV
Volunteer [US Naval Reserve] V
Volunteer [British military] (DMA) .... Volr
Volunteer Adviser Corps (EA) .... VAC
Volunteer Air Reserve [Air Force] .... VAR
Volunteer Air Reserve Training [Air Force] .... VART

Volunteer Air Reserve Training Unit [Air Force] .... VARTU
Volunteer Air Units .... VAU
Volunteer Ambulance School of Instruction [Military British] (ROG) ..... VASI
Volunteer Army [Project, absorbed by MVA, 1972] .... VOLAR
Volunteer Army Ammunition Plant (AABC) .... VAAP
Volunteer Artillery [Military British] (ROG) .... VA
Volunteer Battalion [Military] .... VB
Volunteer Battalion Gordon Highlanders [British military] (DMA) ..... VBGH
Volunteer Cadet Corps [British] VCC
Volunteer Capital [NYSE symbol] (TTSB) VCC
Volunteer Capital Corp. [NYSE symbol] (SPSG) VCC
Volunteer Capital Corp. [Associated Press] (SAG) ..... VolCC
Volunteer Committees of Art Museums (EA) .... VCAM
Volunteer Committees of Art Museums of Canada and the United States
    (EA) .... VCAMCUS
Volunteer Conservation Officers .... VCO
Volunteer Consultant [Red Cross] VC
Volunteer Consultant for Office of Volunteers [Red Cross] ..... VCOV
Volunteer Corps VC
Volunteer Decoration [British] .... VD
Volunteer Defense Corps .... VDC
Volunteer Development Corps (EA) .... VDC
Volunteer Development Scotland (AIE) .... VDS
Volunteer Durham Medical Staff Corps [British military] (DMA) ..... VDMSC
Volunteer Engineers, Scientists, and Technicians [An association] ..... VEST
Volunteer Field Consultant [Red Cross] .... VFC
Volunteer Field Representative [Red Cross] .... VFR
Volunteer Fire Alarm (TEL) .... VFA
Volunteer Fire Department .... VFD
Volunteer Firefighter .... VFF
Volunteer Fireman .... VF
Volunteer Flight Officers Network .... VFON
Volunteer Gliding Schools [British] .... VGS
Volunteer Guards [British military] (DMA) .... VG
Volunteer Income Tax Assistance Program [Internal Revenue Service] ..... VITA
Volunteer Infantry Brigade [British military] (DMA) ..... VIB
Volunteer Informant Program [Navy] (DNAB) .... VIP
Volunteer Lawyers for the Arts (EA) .... VLA
Volunteer Lawyers for the Poor [An association] .... VLP
Volunteer Leadership Development Program [Canada] ..... VLDP
Volunteer Leadership Development Program [Canadian] (NFD) ..... VLDP
Volunteer Management Support Program [ACTION] ..... VMSP
Volunteer Marine Corps Reserve .... VMCR
Volunteer Military Rejectee (DNAB) .... VMR
Volunteer Missionary Movement [London Colney, Hertfordshire, England]
    (EAIO) .... VMM
Volunteer Observing Ship [Marine science] (OSRA) ..... VOS
Volunteer Observing Ship (EERA) .... VOS
Volunteer Observing Ship (USDC) .... VOS
Volunteer Officer Candidate [Army] .... VOC
Volunteer Oil Industry Communications Effort [Program] [Phillips Petroleum
    Co.] .... VOICE
Volunteer Optometric Services to Humanity/International (EA) ..... VOSH
Volunteer Political Party [Northern Ireland] .... VPP
Volunteer Prison League [Defunct] (EA) .... VPL
Volunteer Program Consultant [Red Cross] .... VPC
Volunteer Program of the Sisters, Servants of the Immaculate Heart of M
    ary (EA) .... VPSSIHM
Volunteer Reenlistment Bonus .... VRB
Volunteer Regiment [British military] (DMA) .... VR
Volunteer Reserve (BJA) .... VR
Volunteer Reserve Decoration [British] .... VRD
Volunteer Reserve Section .... VRS
Volunteer Reserve Training Unit [Coast Guard] .... VTU
Volunteer Reservists in Drill Pay Status [Navy] .... VDP
Volunteer Rifle Corps [Military British] (ROG) .... VRC
Volunteer Services for the Blind [Later, ASB] (EA) ..... VSB
Volunteer Staff Corps [British] (ROG) .... VSC
Volunteer State Community College, Gallatin, TN [OCLC symbol] (OCLC) .... TVS
Volunteer State Community College, Learning Resources Center, Gallatin,
    TN [Library symbol Library of Congress] (LCLS) ..... TGaV
Volunteer Talent Bank [American Association of Retired Persons] ..... VTB
Volunteer - The National Center [Later, NVC] (EA) ..... VNCCI
Volunteer Training Corps [An organization for home defense] [World War I]
    [British] .... VTC
Volunteer Training Unit .... VTU
Volunteer Training Unit (Merchant Marine Safety) .... VTU(MMS)
Volunteers for International Development [Later, Peaceworkers] (EA) ..... VID
Volunteers for International Technical Assistance (IAA) ..... VITA
Volunteers for Israel (EA) .... VFI
Volunteers for Israel (EA) VI
Volunteers for Peace (EA) .... VFP
Volunteers for Peaceful Change (EA) .... VPC
Volunteers for Vision [Defunct] (EA) .... V for V
Volunteers in Asia (EA) .... VIA
Volunteers in Education .... VIE
Volunteers in Overseas Cooperative Assistance (EA) ..... VOCA
Volunteers in Probation, Inc. [Later, VIP Division of National Council on Crime
    and Delinquency] (EA) .... VIPI
Volunteers in Service to America (EA) .... VISTA
Volunteers in Service to India's Oppressed and Neglected (EA) ..... VISION
Volunteers in Technical Assistance (EA) .... VITA
Volunteers in the National Forests Act [1972] .... VINFA
Volunteers in the Parks Act [1969] .... VIPA
Volunteers of America (EA) .... V of A

Volunteers of America (EA) ... VOA
Volusia County Public Libraries, Daytona Beach, FL [*Library symbol Library of Congress*] (LCLS) ... FDb
Volute ... VLT
Voluter Test [*Radiology*] (DAVI) ... V-test
Volve Marine Engines ... VME
Volvendus [*To be rolled*] [*Latin*] (DAVI) ... vol
Volvendus [*To Be Rolled*] [*Pharmacy*] (ADA) ... VOLV
Volvendus [*To Be Rolled*] [*Pharmacy*] ... VOLVEND
Volvo AB [*Sweden ICAO designator*] (FAAC) ... VOL
Volvo AB [*Sweden NASDAQ symbol*] ... VOLV
Volvo AB [*Associated Press*] (SAG) ... Volvo
Volvo AB 'B' ADR [*NASDAQ symbol*] (TTSB) ... VOLVY
Volvo Club of America (EA) ... VCoA
Volvo Concept Car [*Automotive engineering*] ... VCC
Volvo Engine Brake [*Volvo AB*] [*Diesel engines*] ... VEB
Volvo Mechanical Equipment [*Auto industry supplier*] ... VME
Volvo, Michigan, Euclid [*In company name VME Americas, Inc.*] ... VME
Volvo Sports America 1800 (EA) ... VSA/1800
Volvo Truck Corp. ... VTC
Vomeronasal [*Anatomy*] ... VN
Vomeronasal Organ [*Anatomy*] ... VNO
Vomited (DAVI) ... VOM
Vomiting [*Medicine*] ... V
Vomiting Gas [*US Chemical Corps symbol*] ... DM
Vomitione Urgente [*The Vomiting Being Troublesome*] [*Pharmacy*] (ROG) ... VOM URG
Von [*Of, From*] [*German*] ... V
Von Braun Astronomical Society (EA) ... VBAS
Von Hippel-Lindau Disease ... VHL
Von Holst's Constitutional History of the United States [*A publication*] (DLA) ... Von H Const Hist
Von Ihring's Struggle for Law [*A publication*] (DLA) ... Von Ihr Str for L
Von Karman Equation ... VKE
Von Karman Gas Dynamics Facility [*Arnold Air Force Base, TN*] [*Air Force*] ... VKF
Von Karman Institute (NATG) ... VKI
Von Karman Institute for Fluid Dynamics [*Belgium*] ... VKIFD
Von Mises Theory ... VMT
Von Neumann [*Procedure*] [*Statistics*] ... VN
Von Oben [*From the Top*] [*German*] ... VO
Von Recklinghausen Neurofibromatosis [*Medicine*] ... VRNF
Von Unten [*From the Bottom*] [*German*] ... VU
Von Willebrand [*disease and Factor*] [*Hematology*] (DAVI) ... VW
Von Willebrand factor [*Also, vWF, VWF*] [*Hematology*] ... vWf
Von Willebrand Syndrome [*Medicine*] (DMAA) ... vWS
Von Willebrand's Disease [*Medicine*] ... vWD
Von Willebrand's Factor VIII [*Hematology*] (DAVI) ... VIII-vwf
Von Zeipel Method ... VZM
Vons Companies [*NYSE symbol*] (SPSG) ... VON
Vons Companies [*Associated Press*] (SAG) ... Vons
Vons Cos. [*NYSE symbol*] (TTSB) ... VON
Voorhees College, Denmark, SC [*Library symbol Library of Congress*] (LCLS) ... ScDeV
Voorhees College, Denmark, SC [*OCLC symbol*] (OCLC) ... VCM
Voorheesville, NY [*FM radio station call letters*] (RBYB) ... WPTR-FM
Voorhies' Code [*New York*] [*A publication*] (DLA) ... Voorh Code
Voorhies' Criminal Jurisprudence of Louisiana [*A publication*] (DLA) ... Voorh Cr Jur
Voorhies' Louisiana Revised Statutes [*A publication*] (DLA) ... Voorh St
Voorschrift [*Rule, Order*] [*Dutch*] (ILCA) ... VS
Vooruitstrewende Hervormings Partij [*Progressive Reform Party*] [*Surinam*] [*Political party*] (PPW) ... VHP
Vopnafjordur [*Iceland*] [*ICAO location identifier*] (ICLI) ... BIVO
Vopnafjordur [*Iceland*] [*Airport symbol*] (OAG) ... VPN
VOR [*Very-High-Frequency Omnidirectional Range*] **Federal Airway** [*Followed by identification*] ... V
VOR [*Very-High-Frequency Omnidirectional Range*] **Test Signal** (CET) ... VOT
Vorausabteilung [*Advance detachment*] [*German military - World War II*] ... VA
Vorderasiatische Bibliothek [*H. Winckler and A. Jeremias*] [*Leipzig*] [*A publication*] (BJA) ... VAB
Vorderasien (BJA) ... VA
Vorgeschobener Beobachter [*Forward Observer*] [*German military*] ... VB
Vorheesville, NY [*FM radio station call letters*] ... WCDA
Vorigen Monats [*Of Last Month*] [*German*] ... VM
Vorlaeufige Arbeitsnormen ... VAN
Vormittags [*In the Morning*] [*German*] ... VORM
Vornado Realty Trust [*NYSE symbol*] (SPSG) ... VNO
Vornado Realty Trust, Inc. [*Associated Press*] (SAG) ... Vornado
Voronezh [*Former USSR ICAO location identifier*] (ICLI) ... UUOO
Voronezh [*USSR*] [*Airport symbol*] (AD) ... VRZ
Voronezhavia [*Former USSR*] [*FAA designator*] (FAAC) ... VRN
Vorposten [*Outpost*] [*German military*] ... VP
Vortex (AAG) ... VTX
Vortex Advisory System [*FAA*] ... VAS
Vortex Arc LASER ... VAL
Vortex Arc LASER Light ... VALL
Vortex Arc LASER Pump ... VALP
Vortex Breakdown Position ... VBP
Vortex Flow Control ... VFC
Vortex in Cell [*Fluid Mechanics*] ... VIC
VORTEX Interactive Data Entry Operation (NITA) ... VIDEO
Vortex Lattice Method ... VLM
Vortex Magnetic Separation [*Ore processing*] ... VMS
Vortex Rate Sensor ... VRS
VORTEX [*Varian Omnitask Real-Time Executive*] **Telecommunications Access Method** ... VTAM
Vortex Valve Rocket Motor (MCD) ... VVRM
Vortex Wake System [*Aviation*] (DA) ... VWS
Vorticity Area Index [*Meteorology*] ... VAI
Voskhod (BJA) ... Vos
Voslau [*Austria ICAO location identifier*] (ICLI) ... LOAV
Vossa Paternidade [*Yours Paternally*] [*Portuguese*] ... VP
Vossa Senhoria Ilustrissima [*Your Illustrious Lordship*] [*Portuguese*] ... VS Ilma
Vostok [*Former USSR Geomagnetic observatory code*] ... VOS
Vote America (EA) ... VA
Vote Profile Analysis ... VPA
Vote Tally System ... VTS
Votec [*ICAO designator*] (AD) ... WE
VOTEC, Servicos Aereos Regionais SA [*Brazil ICAO designator*] (ICDA) ... VO
Voter Education Project (EA) ... VEP
Voter Research & Surveys [*Commercial firm*] ... VRS
Voters for Choice [*Later, VFC*] (EA) ... VC
Voters for Choice/Friends of Family Planning (EA) ... VFC
Voters for Choice/Friends of Family Planning [*Later, VFC*] (EA) ... VFC/FFP
Voters Information Service [*Provides congressional voting records*] ... VIS
Voter-Switch-Disagreement Detector (PDAA) ... VSD
Votes National Committee (EA) ... VNC
Votic [*MARC language code Library of Congress*] (LCCP) ... vot
Voting [*Business term*] ... VTG
Voting Age Population ... VAP
Voting Assistance Officer ... VAO
Voting Pool [*Said of disposition of stocks*] ... VP
Voting Rights Act [*1965, 1970, 1975*] ... VRA
Voting Stock [*Investment term*] (MHDW) ... VS
Voting Trust [*Investment term*] ... VT
Voting Trust Certificate [*or Company*] [*Investment term*] ... VTC
Votre Altesse [*Your Highness*] [*French*] ... VA
Votre Altesse Electorale [*Your Electoral Highness*] [*French*] ... VAE
Votre Altesse Royale [*Your Royal Highness*] [*French*] ... VAR
Votre Eminence [*Your Eminence*] [*French*] ... VE
Votre Grace [*Your Grace*] [*French*] ... VG
Votre Grandeur [*Your Highness*] [*French*] ... VG
Votre Majeste [*Your Majesty*] [*French*] ... VM
Votre Seigneurie [*Your Lordship*] [*French*] ... VS
Voucher (MCD) ... VO
Voucher (AFM) ... VOU
Voucher Attached [*Banking*] ... V/A
Voucher Deduction [*Military*] (DNAB) ... VOU DED
Voucher Register and General Control [*Military*] (AABC) ... VRGC
Vought Aeronautics Division [*Ling-Temco-Vought*] ... VAD
Vouglans [*France*] [*Seismograph station code, US Geological Survey*] (SEIS) ... VOU
Vouka/Mandoro [*Congo*] [*ICAO location identifier*] (ICLI) ... FCMO
Vouka/Sidetra [*Congo*] [*ICAO location identifier*] (ICLI) ... FCMD
Vounda/Loubetsi [*Congo*] [*ICAO location identifier*] (ICLI) ... FCPI
Vous [*You*] [*French*] (ROG) ... V
Voussoirs (VRA) ... vsrs
Vowel ... V
Vowel (WDMC) ... v
Vowel Matching Test [*Education*] (EDAC) ... VMT
Vox Populi [*Voice of the People*] [*Latin*] ... VOX POP
Vox Reformata: Australasian Journal for Christian Scholarship [*A publication*] (APTA) ... VR
Voxel [*NASDAQ symbol*] (SAG) ... VOXL
Voxel Co. [*Associated Press*] (SAG) ... Voxel
Voxel Wrrt [*NASDAQ symbol*] (TTSB) ... VOXLW
Voxware, Inc. [*NASDAQ symbol*] (SAG) ... VOXW
Voxware, Inc. [*Associated Press*] (SAG) ... Voxware
Voyage (DS) ... voy
Voyage Alliance [*Later, IVA*] (EA) ... VA
Voyage Charter ... VC
Voyage Data Recorder ... VDR
Voyage Repairs [*Navy*] (NVT) ... VR
Voyager Biological Laboratory [*NASA*] ... VBL
Voyager Data Description Standards [*NASA*] (KSC) ... VDDS
Voyager Data Detailed Index [*NASA*] (KSC) ... VDDI
Voyager Data Distribution List [*NASA*] (KSC) ... VDDL
Voyager Data Processing Instructions [*NASA*] (KSC) ... VDPI
Voyager Information Flow Instructions [*NASA*] (KSC) ... VIFI
Voyager Mars [*NASA*] ... VM
Voyager Spacecraft Subsystem [*NASA*] ... VSS
Voyageur Airways Ltd. [*Canada ICAO designator*] (FAAC) ... VAL
Voyageur Arizona Muni Income [*AMEX symbol*] (TTSB) ... VAZ
Voyageur Arizona Municipal Income Fund [*AMEX symbol*] (SPSG) ... VAZ
Voyageur Arizona Municipal Income Fund [*Associated Press*] (SAG) ... VoyAZ
Voyageur CO Ins Muni Income [*AMEX symbol*] (TTSB) ... VCF
Voyageur Colorado Insured Municipal Income Fund [*AMEX symbol*] (SPSG) ... VCF
Voyageur Colorado Insured Municipal Income Fund [*Associated Press*] (SAG) ... VoyCO
Voyageur FL Insured Muni Inc. [*AMEX symbol*] (TTSB) ... VFL
Voyageur Florida Insured Municipal Income [*Associated Press*] (SAG) ... VoyFla
Voyageur Florida Insured Municipal Income Fund [*AMEX symbol*] (SPSG) ... VFL
Voyageur Minn Muni Income [*AMEX symbol*] (TTSB) ... VMN
Voyageur Minn Muni Income II [*AMEX symbol*] (TTSB) ... VMM
Voyageur Minn Muni Income III [*AMEX symbol*] (TTSB) ... VYM
Voyageur Minnesota Municipal Income [*AMEX symbol*] (SPSG) ... VYM
Voyageur Minnesota Municipal Income Fund [*AMEX symbol*] (SPSG) ... VMM

Voyageur Minnesota Municipal Income Fund 2, Inc. [*Associated Press*] (SAG) ... VoyMN2
Voyageur Minnesota Municipal Income Fund 3, Inc. [*Associated Press*] (SAG) ... VoyMN3
Voyageur Minnesota Municipal Income Fund, Inc. [*AMEX symbol*] (SPSG) ... VMN
Voyageur Minnesota Municipal Income Fund, Inc. [*Associated Press*] (SAG) ... VoyMN
Voyageur Missouri Municipal Income Fund [*Associated Press*] (SAG) ... VoyMO
Voyenno-promyshlennaya Komissiya [*Military Industrial Commission*] [*Former USSR*] (LAIN) ... VPK
Vozdushno-Desantnye Voiska [*Airborne Troops*] [*An autonomous command*] [*Former USSR*] ... VDV
VP-16[*Etoposide*], Cyclophosphamide, Adriamycin, Platinol [*Antineoplastic drug regimen*] (DAVI) ... VCAP-I
[*Cisplatin*] **VP-16**[*Etoposide*], Cycophosamide, Platinol [*Cisplatin*] [*Antineoplastic drug regimen*] (DAVI) ... VCP-1
VP-16 [*Etoposide*], Methotrexate, Citrovorum factor [*Antineoplastic drug regimen*] (DAVI) ... VMC
VP-16 [*Etoposide*] **Vincristine, Cyclophosphamide, Adriamycin** [*Antineoplastic drug regimen*] (DAVI) ... VOCA
VP-16-213 [*Etoposide*], Adriamycin, Methotrexate [*Antineoplastic drug regimen*] ... VAM
VP-16-213 [*Etoposide*], Adriamycin, Vincristine [*Antineoplastic drug regimen*]... VAV
VP-16-213 [*Etoposide*], Cyclophosphamide, Adriamycin, Platinol [*Cisplatin*] [*Antineoplastic drug regimen*] ... V-CAP III
Vraie Lumiere [*True Light*] [*Freemasonry*] [*French*] (ROG) ... VL
Vrede [*South Africa*] [*ICAO location identifier*] (ICLI) ... FAVD
Vredendal [*South Africa*] [*ICAO location identifier*] (ICLI) ... FAVR
Vrij Anti-Revolutionaire Partij [*Free Anti-Revolutionary Party*] [*Netherlands Political party*] (PPE) ... VAR
Vrije Universiteit Brussel [*Free University of Brussels*] [*Belgium*] [*Information service or system*] (IID) ... VUB
Vrijzinnige-Democratische Bond [*Radical Democratic League*] [*Netherlands Political party*] (PPE) ... VDB
Vrincioaia [*Romania*] [*Seismograph station code, US Geological Survey*] (SEIS) ... VRI
Vrnjacka Banja [*Yugoslavia*] [*Airport symbol*] (AD) ... VBN
Vroom's Law Reports [*30-85 New Jersey*] [*A publication*] (DLA) ... Vr
Vroom's Law Reports [*30-85 New Jersey*] [*A publication*] (DLA) ... Vroom
Vroom's Law Reports [*30-85 New Jersey*] [*A publication*] (DLA) ... Vroom (NJ)
Vrsac [*Former Yugoslavia*] [*ICAO location identifier*] (ICLI) ... LYVR
VRX-Multiprocessor (NITA) ... VRX-MP
Vry Langs Skip [*Free Alongside Ship*] [*Afrikaans*] ... VLS
Vry op Kaai [*Free on Quay*] [*Afrikaans*] ... VOK
Vryburg [*South Africa*] [*ICAO location identifier*] (ICLI) ... FAVB
Vryburg [*South Africa*] [*Airport symbol*] (OAG) ... VRU
Vryheid [*South Africa*] [*ICAO location identifier*] (ICLI) ... FAVY
Vryheid [*South Africa*] [*Airport symbol*] (OAG) ... VYD
VS Services Ltd. [*Toronto Stock Exchange symbol*] ... VSL
VSC Tech, Inc. [*Vancouver Stock Exchange symbol*] ... VIC
VSE Corp. [*Associated Press*] (SAG) ... VSE
VSE Corp. [*NASDAQ symbol*] (NQ) ... VSEC
Vsemirnaia Federatsiia Demokraticheskoi Molodezhi [*World Federation of Democratic Youth*] ... VFDM
Vsemirnaja Federacija Profsojuzov [*World Federation of Trade Unions*] ... VFP
Vserossiyskiy Tsentral'nyy Ispolnitel'nyy Komitet [*All-Russian Central Executive Committee of the Congress of Soviets*] [*Former USSR*] (LAIN) ... VTsIK
Vsesoiuznaia Gosudarstvennaia Biblioteka Inostrannoi Literatury [*All-Union State Library of Foreign Literature*], Moscow, Soviet Union [*Library symbol Library of Congress*] (LCLS) ... RuMLit
Vsesoiuznaia Knizhnaia Palata [*All-Union Book Chamber*], Ulitsa Oktiab r Skaia, Moscow, Soviet Union [*Library symbol*] [*Library of Congress*] (LCLS) ... RuMVKP
Vsesoiuznoe Obshchestvo Filatelistov [*or Fizioterapistov*] ... VOF
Vsesoiuznoe Obshchestvo Kul'turnoi Sviazi s Zagranitsei [*All-Union Society for Cultural Relations with Foreign Countries*] [*Former USSR*] ... VOKS
Vsesoiuznyi Nauchno-Issledovatel'skii Institut Miasnoi Promyshlennosti [*All-Union Scientific Research Institute of the Meat Industry*] ... VNIIMP
Vsesoyuznyy Institut Nauchnoy i Tekhnicheskoy Informatsii [*All-Union Institute of Scientific and Technical Information*] [*Former USSR*] ... VINITI
Vsesoyuznyy Tsentral'nyy Sovet Professional'nykh Soyuzov [*All-Union Central Council of Trade Unions*] [*Former USSR*] ... VTSPS
V-Shaped Isolation Regions Filled with Polycrystalline Silicon (IAA) ... VIP
VSI Enterprises [*Associated Press*] (SAG) ... VSI Ent
VSI Enterprises [*NASDAQ symbol*] (SAG) ... VSIN
VTAM Communications Network Application (NITA) ... VCNA
VTAM Telecommunications Network Architecture ... VTNA
Vtel Corp. [*NASDAQ symbol*] (SAG) ... VTEL
VTI Industries, Inc. [*Vancouver Stock Exchange symbol*] ... VIL
VTOL [*Vertical Takeoff and Landing*] [*or STOL - Short Takeoff and Landing when V is the second or only letter in a military aircraft designation*] ... V
VTOL [*Vertical Takeoff and Landing*] **Approach and Landing Technology** [*Program*] ... VALT
VTOL [*Vertical Takeoff and Landing*] **Integrated Flight Control** ... VIFC
VTOL [*Vertical Takeoff and Landing*] **Integrated Flight System Control** ... VIFSC
VTR Library, Canadian Broadcasting Corp. [*Videotheque, Societe Radio-Canada*], Vancouver, British Columbia [*Library symbol National Library of Canada*] (BIB) ... BVACBV
VTX Electronics [*AMEX symbol*] (SPSG) ... VTX
V-Type Metal Oxide Semiconductor (NITA) ... VMOS
Vuelos Asesorias y Representaciones SA de CV [*Mexico ICAO designator*] (FAAC) ... VSE
Vuelos Ejecutivos de Quertaro, SA de CV [*Mexico*] [*FAA designator*] (FAAC) ... VEQ
Vuelta de Correo [*Return Mail*] [*Spanish*] ... VC
Vuesenoria Ilustrisima [*Your Illustrious Ladyship (or Lordship)*] [*Spanish*] ... VSI
Vuilleumier Cycle Cooler ... VCC
Vuilleumier Cycle Cryogenic Cooler ... VCCC
Vulcain Experimental Nuclear Study [*Nuclear reactor*] [*Belgium*] ... VENUS
Vulcan [*Taviliu*] [*New Britain*] [*Seismograph station code, US Geological Survey*] (SEIS) ... VUL
Vulcan Air Defense (MCD) ... VAD
Vulcan Air Defense Systems (MCD) ... VADS
Vulcan Engagement Simulator (MCD) ... VES
Vulcan Gunner Monitor Unit (MCD) ... VGMU
Vulcan Gunner Tracking Evaluation (MCD) ... VGTE
Vulcan International Corp. [*AMEX symbol*] (SPSG) ... VUL
Vulcan International Corp. [*Associated Press*] (SAG) ... VulcCp
Vulcan Int'l Corp. [*AMEX symbol*] (TTSB) ... VUL
Vulcan Materials [*NYSE symbol*] (TTSB) ... VMC
Vulcan Materials Co. [*NYSE symbol*] (SPSG) ... VMC
Vulcan Materials Co. [*Associated Press*] (SAG) ... VulcM
Vulcan Packaging, Inc. [*Toronto Stock Exchange symbol*] ... VIP
Vulcan Public Library, Alberta [*Library symbol National Library of Canada*] (NLC) ... AVU
Vulcan Resources [*Vancouver Stock Exchange symbol*] ... VCN
Vulcan Society (EA) ... VS
Vulcan Training System (MCD) ... VTS
Vulcan Wheeled Carrier ... VWC
Vulcanization ... VULCN
Vulcanize (AAG) ... VUL
Vulcanize ... VULC
Vulcanized Fiber ... VF
Vulcanized India Rubber ... VIR
Vulcanized Interlinked Polyethylene [*Union Carbide Corp.*] ... VIP
Vulcanized Polyethylene (IAA) ... VPE
Vulcanized Rubber ... VR
Vulcanized Rubber Installation ... VRI
Vulcanizing ... VULC
Vulcano Piano [*Lipari Islands*] [*Seismograph station code, US Geological Survey*] (SEIS) ... VPL
Vulcan-Stinger Troop Proficiency Trainer [*Army*] ... VSTPT
Vulgar (WDAA) ... VUL
Vulgar ... VULG
Vulgar Latin ... VL
Vulgar Latin [*Language*] (BARN) ... VL
Vulgate [*Latin translation of the Bible*] [*A publication*] (BJA) ... V
Vulgate [*Latin translation of the Bible*] (BJA) ... Vg
Vulgate [*Version of the Bible*] (BARN) ... Vul
Vulgate [*Version of the Bible*] ... VULG
Vulgate Bible ... VB
Vulnerability Analysis of Nuclear Weapons in Allied Command, Europe [*Army*] (AABC) ... VANWACE
Vulnerability Analysis Team (MCD) ... VAT
Vulnerability and Hardening Working Group ... VHWG
Vulnerability and Lethality Test (System) (MCD) ... VALT(S)
Vulnerability and Survivability of the Armed Forces (MCD) ... V/SAF
Vulnerability Assessment ... VA
Vulnerability Assessment Laboratory [*White Sands Missile Range, NM*] [*Military*] (RDA) ... VAL
Vulnerability Assessment Modeling Program [*Air Force*] ... VAMP
Vulnerability Assessment Procedure (AAGC) ... VAP
Vulnerability/Hardness [*Refers to a weapon system's weakness and capabilities in withstanding adverse operating environments*] ... V/H
Vulnerability/Lethality Division [*Ballistic Research Laboratory*] (RDA) ... VLD
Vulnerability Number ... VN
Vulnerability Reduction [*Military*] (RDA) ... VR
Vulnerability Report [*Navy*] (NVT) ... VULREP
Vulnerable Area (NATG) ... VA
Vulnerable Period [*Physiology*] ... VP
Vulnerable Point ... VP
Vulnerary [*Medicine to heal wounds*] (ROG) ... VUL
Vulpecula [*Constellation*] ... Vul
Vulpecula [*Constellation*] ... Vulp
Vultee Owners and Pilots Association (EA) ... VOAPA
Vulture Study Group [*South Africa*] (EAIO) ... VSG
Vulva and Vagina [*Physiology*] ... VV
Vulval Precursor Cell [*Genetics*] ... VPC
Vungtau [*Viet Nam*] [*ICAO location identifier*] (ICLI) ... VVVT
Vunikawai [*Fiji*] [*Seismograph station code, US Geological Survey*] (SEIS) ... VUN
Vuotso [*Finland ICAO location identifier*] (ICLI) ... EFVU
Vutreshna Makidoniski Revoliutsionna Organizatsiia [*Internal Macedonian Revolutionary Organization*] [*Bulgaria*] [*Political party*] (PPE) ... VMRO
VWR Corp. [*Associated Press*] (SAG) ... VWRSci
VWR Corp. [*Seattle, WA*] [*NASDAQ symbol*] (NQ) ... VWRX
VWR Scientific Products [*NASDAQ symbol*] (TTSB) ... VWRX
Vyborg [*Former USSR Seismograph station code, US Geological Survey Closed*] (SEIS) ... VYB
Vyrex Corp. [*Associated Press*] (SAG) ... VyrexCp
Vyrex Corp. [*NASDAQ symbol*] (SAG) ... VYRX
Vyrex Corp. [*NASDAQ symbol*] (TTSB) ... VYRX
Vyrex Corp. [*Associated Press*] (SAG) ... VyrxCp
Vyrex Corp. Unit [*NASDAQ symbol*] (TTSB) ... VYRXU
Vyrex Corp. Wrrt [*NASDAQ symbol*] (TTSB) ... VYRXW
Vysshego Soveta Narodnogo Khozyaystva [*Supreme Council of National Economy*] [*Former USSR*] (LAIN) ... VSNKh

Vyzkumny Ustav Hutnictvi Zeleza, Dobra [*Dobra Iron and Steel Research Institute*] [*Information service or system*] (IID) .... VUHZ

Vyzkumny Ustav pro Matematickych Stroju [*Research Institute for Mathematical Machines*] [*Czechoslovakia*] .... VUMS

W
By Meaning

W. A. Rankin Memorial Library, Neodesha, KS [*Library symbol Library of Congress*] (LCLS) .... KNeo
W. A. Woodward Memorial Library, Cottage Grove, OR [*Library symbol Library of Congress*] (LCLS) .... OrCg
W. Alton Jones Cell Science Center, Inc. [*Research center*] (RCD) .... WAJCSC
W. Alton Jones Cell Science Center Library, Lake Placid, NY [*OCLC symbol*] (OCLC) .... VNG
W. & F. Pascoe Proprietory Ltd., Milsons Point, Australia [*Library symbol Library of Congress*] (LCLS) .... PpL
W. and F. Pascoe Proprietory Ltd., Milsons Point, NSW, Australia [*Library symbol*] [*Library of Congress*] (LCLS) .... PaPL
W. C. Bradley Memorial Library, Columbus, GA [*Library symbol Library of Congress*] (LCLS) .... GColu
W. E. Schulz & Associates, Inc. [*Telecommunications service*] (TSSD) .... WES
W. E. Upjohn Institute for Employment Research, Kalamazoo, MI [*Library symbol Library of Congress*] (LCLS) .... MiKWUp
W. E. Walter Memorial Library (Bremen Public Library), Bremen, IN [*Library symbol Library of Congress*] (LCLS) .... InBre
W. H. Allen [*Commercial firm British*] .... WHA
W. H. Smith Distributors [*British*] .... WHSD
W. I. Carr Sons & Co. Overseas [*Stockbroker*] [*Hong Kong*] .... WICO
W. K. Kellogg Health Sciences Library, Dalhousie University, Halifax, Nova Scotia [*Library symbol National Library of Canada*] (NLC) .... NSHDM
W. K. Lypynsky East European Research Institute (EA) .... WKLEERI
W. L. Wardrop & Associates, Winnipeg, Manitoba [*Library symbol National Library of Canada*] (NLC) .... MWWLW
W. L. Wardrop & Associates, Winnipeg, MB, Canada [*Library symbol Library of Congress*] (LCLS) .... CaMWWLW
W. M. Krogman Center for Research in Child Growth and Development [*University of Pennsylvania*] [*Research center*] (RCD) .... KGC
W. P. London & Associates, Niagara Falls, ON, Canada [*Library symbol Library of Congress*] (LCLS) .... CaONfWPL
W. P. London & Associates, Niagara Falls, Ontario [*Library symbol National Library of Canada*] (NLC) .... ONFWPL
W. P. Poythress Co., Richmond, VA [*Library symbol Library of Congress*] (LCLS) .... ViRPol
W. R. Carpenter Airlines [*Australia*] .... WRC
W. R. Carpenter Airlines [*Australia*] .... WRCA
W. R. Grace & Co., Agricultural Chemicals Group, Memphis, TN [*Library symbol Library of Congress*] (LCLS) .... TMGC
W. R. Grace & Co., Research Library, Columbia, MD [*Library symbol Library of Congress*] (LCLS) .... MdCoG
W. Ross MacDonald School, Brantford, ON, Canada [*Library symbol*] [*Library of Congress*] (LCLS) .... CaOBrtM
W. Ross MacDonald School, Brantford, Ontario [*Library symbol National Library of Canada*] (NLC) .... OBRM
W. T. Bandy Center for Baudelaire Studies (EA) .... CBS
W. T. Clarke Junior-Senior High School, East Meadow, NY [*Library symbol Library of Congress*] (LCLS) .... NEmCJS
W. Tresper Clarke Junior-Senior High School, Westbury, NY [*Library symbol*] [*Library of Congress*] (LCLS) .... NWeCJS
W. W. Harrington's Reports [*31-39 Delaware*] [*A publication*] (DLA) .... WWH
W. W. Holding Technical Institute, Raleigh, NC [*Library symbol Library of Congress*] (LCLS) .... NcRH
W. W. Woodbury School, Sandwich, IL [*Library symbol Library of Congress*] (LCLS) .... ISanW
Wa [*Ghana*] [*ICAO location identifier*] (ICLI) .... DGLW
Wa National Army [*Myanmar*] [*Political party*] (EY) .... WNA
Wa National Organization [*Myanmar*] [*Political party*] (EY) .... WNO
WAAC Ltd. - Nigeria Airways [*Nigeria*] [*ICAO designator*] (ICDA) .... WT
WAAC (Nigeria) Ltd. Nigeria Airways [*ICAO designator*] (FAAC) .... NGA
WAACC's [*Western Australian Automobile Chamber of Commerce*] **Motor Industry** [*A publication*] .... WAACC's Motor Ind
Waardenburg's Syndrome [*Medicine*] .... WS
Wabag [*Papua New Guinea*] [*Seismograph station code, US Geological Survey*] (SEIS) .... WAB
Wabag [*New Guinea*] [*Airport symbol*] (AD) .... WAB
Waban, Inc. [*Associated Press*] (SAG) .... Waban
Waban, Inc. [*NYSE symbol*] (SPSG) .... WBN
Wabash Carnegie Public Library, Wabash, IN [*Library symbol Library of Congress*] (LCLS) .... InWab
Wabash College, Crawfordsville, IN [*Library symbol Library of Congress*] (LCLS) .... InCW
Wabash College, Crawfordsville, IN [*OCLC symbol*] (OCLC) .... IWC
Wabash County Historical Museum, Wabash, IN [*Library symbol Library of Congress*] (LCLS) .... InWabHi
Wabash, Frisco, and Pacific Association (EA) .... WF & P
Wabash, IN [*Location identifier FAA*] (FAAL) .... IWH
Wabash, IN [*AM radio station call letters*] .... WAYT
Wabash, IN [*FM radio station call letters*] .... WKUZ
Wabash, IN [*FM radio station call letters*] .... WWIP
Wabash Motor Freight Tariff Association, Springfield IL [*STAC*] .... WAA
Wabash National [*NYSE symbol*] (TTSB) .... WNC
Wabash National Corp. [*Associated Press*] (SAG) .... Wabash
Wabash National Corp. [*NYSE symbol*] (SPSG) .... WNC
Wabash Plain Dealer, Wabash, IN [*Library symbol Library of Congress*] (LCLS) .... InWabPD
Wabash Railroad System [*AAR code Obsolete*] .... WAB
Wabash, St. Louis & Pacific Railway .... WStL & P
Wabash Valley Area Library Services Authority [*Library network*] .... WABASH VLY ALSA
Wabash Valley Historical Society, Terre Haute, IN [*Library symbol Library of Congress*] (LCLS) .... InTWHi
Wabash Valley Railroad Co. [*AAR code*] .... WVRC
Wabasha, MN [*AM radio station call letters*] .... KMFX
Wabash-Carnegie Public Library, Wabash, IN [*OCLC symbol*] (OCLC) .... XWC
Wabasso Elementary School, Wabasso, MN [*Library symbol*] [*Library of Congress*] (LCLS) .... MnWaES
Wabasso High School, Wabasso, MN [*Library symbol*] [*Library of Congress*] (LCLS) .... MnWaHS
Wabasso Public Library, Wabasso, MN [*Library symbol*] [*Library of Congress*] (LCLS) .... MnWa
Wabush [*Canada*] [*Airport symbol*] (OAG) .... YWK
Wabush, NF [*AM radio station call letters*] .... CFLW
Wabush, NF [*ICAO location identifier*] (ICLI) .... CYWK
Wabush Public Library, Newfoundland [*Library symbol National Library of Canada*] (NLC) .... NFWA
Wabush Public Library, Wabush, NF, Canada [*Library symbol Library of Congress*] (LCLS) .... CaNfWa
WAC [*Women's Army Corps*] **Officer Candidate Test** (AABC) .... WOCT
Waca [*Ethiopia*] [*Airport symbol*] (OAG) .... WAC
Wacca [*Ethiopia*] [*ICAO location identifier*] (ICLI) .... HAWC
Wachovia Corp. [*Associated Press*] (SAG) .... Wachovia
Wachovia Corp. [*NYSE symbol*] (SPSG) .... WB
Wackenhut Corp. [*Associated Press*] (SAG) .... WackhA
Wackenhut Corp. [*Associated Press*] (SAG) .... WackhB
Wackenhut Corp. [*NYSE symbol*] (SPSG) .... WAK
Wackenhut Corp. [*Associated Press*] (SAG) .... WckhB
Wackenhut Corp. 'B' [*NYSE symbol*] (TTSB) .... WAK B
Wackenhut Corp. Cl'A' [*NYSE symbol*] (TTSB) .... WAK
Wackenhut Corrections [*NYSE symbol*] (TTSB) .... WHC
Wackenhut Corrections Corp. [*Associated Press*] (SAG) .... WackCor
Wackenhut Corrections Corp. [*NASDAQ symbol*] (SAG) .... WCCX
Waco [*Texas*] [*Airport symbol*] (OAG) .... ACT
Waco, Beaumont, Trinity & Sabine Railway Co. [*AAR code*] .... WBTS
Waco/James Connally [*Texas*] [*ICAO location identifier*] (ICLI) .... KCNW
Waco Kungo [*Angola*] [*Airport symbol*] (OAG) .... CEO
Waco, TX [*Location identifier FAA*] (FAAL) .... CNW
Waco, TX [*AM radio station call letters*] .... KBBW
Waco, TX [*FM radio station call letters*] (RBYB) .... KBCT-FM
Waco, TX [*FM radio station call letters*] .... KCKR
Waco, TX [*Television station call letters*] .... KCTF
Waco, TX [*AM radio station call letters*] (RBYB) .... KKTK-AM
Waco, TX [*AM radio station call letters*] .... KRZI
Waco, TX [*FM radio station call letters*] .... KWBU
Waco, TX [*Television station call letters*] .... KWKT
Waco, TX [*AM radio station call letters*] .... KWTX
Waco, TX [*FM radio station call letters*] .... KWTX-FM
Waco, TX [*Television station call letters*] .... KWTX-TV
Waco, TX [*Television station call letters*] .... KXXV
Waco, TX [*Location identifier FAA*] (FAAL) .... ROB
Waco, TX [*AM radio station call letters*] .... WACO
Waco, TX [*FM radio station call letters*] .... WACO-FM
Waco/Waco Municipal [*Texas*] [*ICAO location identifier*] (ICLI) .... KACT
Wacoal Corp. [*Japan NASDAQ symbol*] .... WACL
Wacoal Corp. ADR [*Associated Press*] (SAG) .... Wacoal
Wacoal Corp. ADS [*NASDAQ symbol*] (TTSB) .... WACLY
Waco-McLennan County Library, Waco, TX [*Library symbol Library of Congress*] (LCLS) .... TxW
Wad Medani [*Sudan*] [*Airport symbol*] (AD) .... DNI
Wadati-Benioff Zone [*Geology*] .... WBZ
Waddilove on Marriage and Divorce [*1864*] [*A publication*] (DLA) .... Wad Mar & Div

Waddilove's Digest of Ecclesiastical Cases [*1849*] [*A publication*] (DLA) .... Wad Dig
Waddington [*British ICAO location identifier*] (ICLI) .... EGXW
Waddy Lake Resources, Inc. [*Toronto Stock Exchange symbol Vancouver Stock Exchange symbol*] .... WAD
Wade on American Mining Law [*A publication*] (DLA) .... Wade Am Mining Law
Wade on American Mining Law [*A publication*] (DLA) .... Wade Min
Wade on Attachment and Garnishment [*A publication*] (DLA) .... Wade Attachm
Wade on Retroactive Laws [*A publication*] (DLA) .... Wade Retro L
Wade on the Law of Notice [*A publication*] (DLA) .... Wade Not
Wadebridge [*England*] .... WADEBR
Wadena City Library, Wadena, MN [*Library symbol*] [*Library of Congress*] (LCLS) .... MnWad
Wadena Elementary School, Wadena, MN [*Library symbol*] [*Library of Congress*] (LCLS) .... MnWadE
Wadena High School, Wadena, MN [*Library symbol*] [*Library of Congress*] (LCLS) .... MnWadH
Wadena Junior High School, Wadena, MN [*Library symbol*] [*Library of Congress*] (LCLS) .... MnWadJ
Wadena, MN [*FM radio station call letters*] .... KKWS
Wadena, MN [*AM radio station call letters*] .... KWAD
Wadesboro, NC [*Location identifier FAA*] (FAAL) .... AFP
Wadesboro, NC [*AM radio station call letters*] .... WADE
Wadesboro, NC [*FM radio station call letters*] .... WRPL
Wadham College [*Oxford University*] (ROG) .... WADH
Wadhams Hall Seminary College, Library, Ogdensburg, NY [*OCLC symbol*] (OCLC) .... VNB
Wadhams Hall Seminary College, Ogdensburg, NY [*Library symbol Library of Congress*] (LCLS) .... NOgW
Wadi Ain [*South Arabia*] [*Airport symbol*] (AD) .... WDA
Wadi Halfa [*Sudan*] [*Airport symbol*] (AD) .... WHA
Wadi Halfa/Nuba Lake [*Sudan*] [*ICAO location identifier*] (ICLI) .... HSSW
Wadley Southern [*Railroad*] (MHDW) .... WS
Wadley Southern Railway Co. [*AAR code Obsolete*] .... WAS
Wadsworth Atheneum, Hartford, CT [*Library symbol Library of Congress*] (LCLS) .... CtHWa
Wadsworth Athneneum [*Hartford, CT*] .... WA
Wadsworth Library, Geneseo, NY [*Library symbol*] [*Library of Congress*] (LCLS) .... NGeno
Wafer (AAG) .... WAF
Wafer (MSA) .... WFR
Wafer Check Valve .... WCV
Wafer Parameter Identification System (IAA) .... WPIS
Wafer Scale Associative String Processor (NITA) .... WASP
Wafer Scale Systolic Processor (NITA) .... WASP
[*The*] **Waferboard Association** [*Later, SBA*] (EA) .... TWA
Waferboard Corp. Ltd. [*Toronto Stock Exchange symbol*] .... WFB
Wafer-Scale Integration [*Microelectronics*] .... WSI
WaferScale Integration, Inc. .... WSI
Waffenabwurfbehaelter [*Parachute Weapons Container*] [*German military - World War II*] .... WAB
Waffenkarren [*Weapons Cart*] [*German military - World War II*] .... WKA
Waffle [*Used in correcting manuscripts, etc.*] .... W
Wage Adjustment Board [*World War II*] .... WAB
Wage Analysis and Control (MHDB) .... WAC
Wage and Hour and Public Contracts Division [*Department of Labor*] [*Obsolete*] .... WHPC
Wage and Hour and Public Contracts Division [*Department of Labor*] [*Obsolete*] .... WHPCD
Wage and Hour Cases [*Bureau of National Affairs*] [*A publication*] (DLA) .... WH
Wage and Hour Cases [*Bureau of National Affairs*] [*A publication*] (DLA) .... WH Cas
Wage and Hour Cases [*A publication*] (AAGC) .... WHC
Wage and Hour Division [*Department of Labor*] (OICC) .... W & H
Wage and Hour Division [*Department of Labor*] (IAA) .... WAH
Wage and Hour Division [*Department of Labor*] .... WHD
Wage and Hour Management Information System [*Department of Labor*] (GFGA) .... WHMIS
Wage and Hour Reference Manual [*Bureau of National Affairs*] [*A publication*] (DLA) .... WH Man
Wage and Hour Reference Manual [*Bureau of National Affairs*] [*A publication*] (DLA) .... WHR Man
Wage and Hour Reporter [*Bureau of National Affairs*] [*A publication*] (DLA) .... Wage & Hour Rep
Wage and Hour Reporter [*Bureau of National Affairs*] [*A publication*] (DLA) .... WHR
Wage and Information Documents [*IRS*] .... WAID
Wage and Labor Standards Administration (OICC) .... WLSA
Wage and Manpower Process Utilizing Machine [*Bureau of Indian Affairs*] .... WAMPUM
Wage and Purchase Hire .... W & PH
Wage and Tax Statement [*IRS*] W-2
Wage Appeals Board [*Department of Labor*] .... WAB
Wage Board [*Civil Service classification*] .... WB
Wage Board Staff .... WBS
Wage Board, Supervisor [*Civil Service classification*] .... WB-S
Wage Change .... WC
Wage Class (MHDI) .... WC
Wage Earner [*Social Security Administration*] (OICC) .... WE
Wage Garnishment (MHDB) .... WG
Wage Grade [*Federal employee job classification*] .... WG
Wage Information Retrieval System [*IRS*] .... WIRS
Wage Pause Program [*Business term*] (ADA) .... WPP
Wage Record [*Social Security Administration*] (OICC) .... WA
Wage Stabilization Board [*Terminated, 1953*] .... WSB
Wage Withholding Form [*Revised version*] [*IRS*] W-4A
Wageningen [*Surinam*] [*ICAO location identifier*] (ICLI) .... SMWA
Wages [*Economics*] .... W
Wages Council [*British*] (DCTA) .... WC
Wages for Housework Committee (EA) .... WHC
Wagethe [*Indonesia*] [*Airport symbol*] (OAG) .... WET
Wagga Wagga [*Australia ICAO location identifier*] (ICLI) .... ASWG
Wagga Wagga [*Australia Airport symbol*] (OAG) .... WGA
Waghete [*Indonesia*] [*ICAO location identifier*] (ICLI) .... WABG
Wagin [*Australia Seismograph station code, US Geological Survey*] (SEIS) WA2
Waglisla Air, Inc. [*Canada ICAO designator*] (FAAC) .... SEH
Wagnalls Memorial Library, Lithopolis, OH [*Library symbol Library of Congress*] (LCLS) .... OLitW
Wagner Act of 1935 (WYGK) .... WA
Wagner College (GAGS) .... Wagner C
Wagner College, Staten Island, NY [*Library symbol Library of Congress*] (LCLS) .... NNWML
Wagner Computer (IAA) .... WAC
Wagner Earth Bridge .... WEB
Wagner Elementary School, Litchfield, MN [*Library symbol*] [*Library of Congress*] (LCLS) .... MnLitWES
Wagner Free Institute of Science, Philadelphia, PA [*Library symbol Library of Congress*] (LCLS) .... PPWa
Wagner Labor Relations Act (OICC) .... WLRA
Wagner Public Library, Wagner, SD [*Library symbol Library of Congress*] (LCLS) .... SdWa
Wagner Society of America (EA) .... WSA
Wagner Society of New York (EA) .... WSNY
Wagner-Peyser Act [*1933*] (OICC) .... WPA
Wagner's Missouri Statutes [*A publication*] (DLA) .... Wag St
Wagner's Missouri Statutes [*A publication*] (DLA) .... Wag Stat
Wagner's Missouri Statutes [*A publication*] (DLA) .... WS
Wagon (MSA) .... WAG
Wagon .... WGN
Wagon Box (MSA) .... WB
Wagoner, OK [*FM radio station call letters*] (RBYB) .... KRQZ-FM
Wagoner, OK [*AM radio station call letters*] .... KXTD
Wagons-Lits [*Railroad Sleeping or Pullman cars in Europe*] [*French*] .... WL
Wagons-Restaurants [*Railroad dining cars in Europe*] [*French*] .... WR
Waha Leaf [*British Honduras*] [*Airport symbol*] (AD) .... TZG
Wahaula [*Hawaii*] [*Seismograph station code, US Geological Survey*] (SEIS) .... WHA
Wahiawa, HI [*Location identifier FAA*] (FAAL) .... HHI
Wahlco Enviro Systems [*NYSE symbol*] (TTSB) .... WAL
Wahlco Environment Systems [*NYSE symbol*] (SPSG) .... WAL
Wahlco Environment Systems, Inc. [*Associated Press*] (SAG) .... Wahlco
Wahler Physical Symptoms Inventory [*Psychiatry*] (DAVI) .... WPSI
Wahlpartei der Unabhaengigen [*Electoral Party of Independents*] [*Austria Political party*] (PPE) .... WdU
Wahlstrom & Widstrand [*Publisher*] [*Sweden*] .... W & W
Wahluke [*Washington*] [*Seismograph station code, US Geological Survey*] (SEIS) .... WAH
Wahoo, NE [*Location identifier FAA*] (FAAL) .... AHQ
Wahpeton, ND [*Location identifier FAA*] (FAAL) .... BWP
Wahpeton, ND [*FM radio station call letters*] .... KGWB
Waikabubak/Tambolaka [*Indonesia*] [*ICAO location identifier*] (ICLI) .... WRRT
Waikato Aero Club, Inc. [*New Zealand*] [*ICAO designator*] (FAAC) .... WIK
Waikoloa [*Hawaii*] [*Airport symbol*] (OAG) .... WKL
Wailuku, HI [*Television station call letters*] .... KAII
Wailuku, HI [*FM radio station call letters*] .... KAOI-FM
Wailuku, HI [*Television station call letters*] .... KGMV
Wailuku, HI [*FM radio station call letters*] .... KKUA
Wailuku, HI [*Television station call letters*] .... KMAU
Wailuku, HI [*Television station call letters*] .... KMEB
Wailuku, HI [*AM radio station call letters*] .... KMVI
Wailuku, HI [*Television station call letters*] .... KOGG
Wailuku, HI [*Television station call letters*] .... KWHM
Waimanalo, HI [*Location identifier FAA*] (FAAL) .... BLW
Waimea-Kohala, Kamuela, Hawaii Island [*Hawaii*] [*ICAO location identifier*] (ICLI) .... PHMU
Wainfleet Township Library, Ontario [*Library symbol National Library of Canada*] (NLC) .... OWAT
Wainfleet Township Library, Wainfleet, ON, Canada [*Library symbol*] [*Library of Congress*] (LCLS) .... CaOWaT
Waingapu [*Indonesia*] [*Airport symbol*] (OAG) .... WGP
Waingapu [*Sumba Island*] [*Seismograph station code, US Geological Survey*] (SEIS) .... WSI
Waingapu/Mau Hau [*Indonesia*] [*ICAO location identifier*] (ICLI) .... WRRW
Wainoco Oil [*NYSE symbol*] (TTSB) .... WOL
Wainoco Oil Corp. [*Associated Press*] (SAG) .... Wainoc
Wainoco Oil Corp. [*NYSE symbol*] (SPSG) .... WOL
Wainscot .... WA
Wainscot (VRA) .... wnsct
Wainscot [*Technical drawings*] .... WSCT
Wainwright [*Alaska*] [*Airport symbol*] (OAG) .... AIN
Wainwright [*Alaska*] [*ICAO location identifier*] (ICLI) .... PAWT
Wainwright, AB [*AM radio station call letters*] .... CKKY
Wainwright Bank & Trust [*NYSE symbol*] (TTSB) .... WAIN
Wainwright Bank & Trust Co. [*NASDAQ symbol*] (CTT) .... WAIN
Wainwright Bank & Trust Co. [*Associated Press*] (SAG) .... WainBk
Wainwright Community Library, Alberta [*Library symbol National Library of Canada*] (NLC) .... AWAIC
Wainwright Community Library, Wainwright, AB, Canada [*Library symbol*] [*Library of Congress*] (LCLS) .... CaAWaiC
Wainwright House Center for Development of Human Potential [*Later, WH*] (EA) .... WHCDHP

Wainwright House Center for Development of Human Resources [*Later, WH*] (EA) ... WHCDHR
Waipahu, HI [*FM radio station call letters*] ... KDEO-FM
Waipahu, HI [*AM radio station call letters*] ... KJPN
Waipahu, HI [*FM radio station call letters*] ... KSSK
Waipapa Point [*New Zealand*] [*Seismograph station code, US Geological Survey Closed*] (SEIS) ... WPZ
Wairakei [*New Zealand*] [*Seismograph station code, US Geological Survey*] (SEIS) ... WNZ
Wairiri [*Glentunnel*] [*New Zealand*] [*Seismograph station code, US Geological Survey*] [*Closed*] (SEIS) ... WAI
Waist (ADA) ... W
Waist Tether [*NASA*] (KSC) ... WT
Wait Acknowledge ... WAK
Wait and Acknowledge (IAA) ... WACK
Wait before Transmitting Positive Acknowledgment ... WACK
Wait for Index (NASA) ... WIX
Wait for It (DI) ... WFI
Wait Order ... WO
Wait Time [*Computer science*] ... W
Wait Time [*Computer order entry*] ... WT
Wait-and-See Parsing [*Computer science*] (BYTE) ... WASP
Waite Park, MN [*FM radio station call letters*] ... KLZZ
Waite Park, MN [*AM radio station call letters*] ... KXSS
Waite Park Public Library, Waite Park, MN [*Library symbol*] [*Library of Congress*] (LCLS) ... MnWp
Waitemata Aero Club, Inc. [*New Zealand*] [*ICAO designator*] (FAAC) ... WTM
Waiter ... WTR
Waiting (MSA) ... WTG
Waiting Calls Indicator (NITA) ... WCI
Waiting List ... WL
Waiting on Cement ... WOC
Waiting on Orders ... WOO
Waiting on Weather [*Ocean storms*] ... WOW
Waiting Period (OICC) ... WP
Wait-on-User-Defined Event (MHDI) ... WOUDE
Waitress-Actress-Model [*Lifestyle classification*] ... WAM
Wait's Actions and Defences [*A publication*] (DLA) ... Wait Act & Def
Wait's Law and Practice in New York Justices' Courts [*A publication*] (DLA) ... Wait L & P
Wait's New York Annotated Code [*A publication*] (DLA) ... Wait Co
Wait's New York Digest [*A publication*] (DLA) ... Wait Dig
Wait's New York Practice [*A publication*] (DLA) ... Wait Pr
Wait's New York Practice [*A publication*] (DLA) ... Waits Prac
Wait's New York Table of Cases [*A publication*] (DLA) ... Wait Tab Ca
Wait's State Papers of the United States [*A publication*] (DLA) ... Wait St Pap
Waive Exchange If Necessary ... WEN
Waived (AABC) ... WVD
Waiver ... WA
Waiver of Coinsurance [*Fire contract clause*] ... W/C
Waiver of Notice [*Business term*] (MHDW) ... WON
Waiver of Premium [*Insurance*] (MHDW) ... WOP
Waiver of Premium [*Insurance*] ... WP
Wajax Ltd. [*Toronto Stock Exchange symbol*] ... WJX
Wajima [*Japan*] [*Seismograph station code, US Geological Survey*] (SEIS) ... WAJ
Wajir [*Kenya*] [*ICAO location identifier*] (ICLI) ... HKWJ
Wajir [*Kenya*] [*Airport symbol*] (OAG) ... WJR
Waka Waka [*Zambia*] [*ICAO location identifier*] (ICLI) ... FLWW
Wakamiya [*Japan*] [*Seismograph station code, US Geological Survey Closed*] (SEIS) ... WMY
Wakarusa Public Library, Wakarusa, IN [*Library symbol Library of Congress*] (LCLS) ... InWak
Wakashan [*MARC language code Library of Congress*] (LCCP) ... wak
Wakaura [*Wakayama Eri*] [*Japan*] [*Seismograph station code, US Geological Survey*] (SEIS) ... WKU
Wakaya [*Fiji*] [*Airport symbol Obsolete*] (OAG) ... KAY
Wakaya [*Fiji*] [*ICAO location identifier*] (ICLI) ... NFNW
Wakayama [*Japan*] [*Seismograph station code, US Geological Survey*] (SEIS) ... WKY
Wakde [*Indonesia*] [*ICAO location identifier*] (ICLI) ... WAJD
Wake [*Wake Island, Pacific Ocean*] [*Airport symbol*] (AD) ... AWK
Wake [*Wake Island*] [*Seismograph station code, US Geological Survey Closed*] (SEIS) ... WKE
Wake Analysis and Control (MCD) ... WAC
Wake County Health Department, Raleigh, NC [*Library symbol*] [*Library of Congress*] (LCLS) ... NcRWHD
Wake County Hospital System, Wake County Medical Center, Raleigh, NC [*Library symbol Library of Congress*] (LCLS) ... NcRWCM
Wake County Public Libraries, Cameron Village Regional Library, Raleigh, NC [*Library symbol*] [*Library of Congress*] (LCLS) ... NcR-C
Wake County Public Libraries, Fuquay-Varina Public Library, Fuquay-Varina, NC [*Library symbol*] [*Library of Congress*] (LCLS) ... NcR-F
Wake County Public Libraries, Raleigh, NC [*Library symbol Library of Congress*] (LCLS) ... NcR
Wake County Public Library, Raleigh, NC [*OCLC symbol*] (OCLC) ... NXA
Wake Forest College [*Later, WFU*] [*North Carolina*] ... WFC
Wake Forest Intramural Law Review [*A publication*] (DLA) ... Wake Forest Intra L Rev
Wake Forest, NC [*AM radio station call letters*] ... WFTK
Wake Forest University (GAGS) ... Wake Forest U
Wake Forest University [*North Carolina*] ... WF
Wake Forest University [*Winston-Salem, NC*] ... WFU
Wake Forest University, Babcock Graduate School of Management, Winston-Salem, NC [*Library symbol Library of Congress*] (LCLS) ... NcWsW-B
Wake Forest University, Bowman Gray School of Medicine, Wake Forest, NC [*Library symbol Library of Congress*] (LCLS) ... NcWsW-M
Wake Forest University, Law Library, Winston-Salem, NC [*OCLC symbol*] (OCLC) ... EWL
Wake Forest University, Law Library, Winston-Salem, NC [*Library symbol Library of Congress*] (LCLS) ... NcWsW-L
Wake Forest University, Winston-Salem, NC [*OCLC symbol*] (OCLC) ... EWF
Wake Forest University, Winston-Salem, NC [*Library symbol Library of Congress*] (LCLS) ... NcWsW
Wake Island [*MARC geographic area code Library of Congress*] (LCCP) ... powk--
Wake Island [*MARC country of publication code Library of Congress*] (LCCP) ... wk
Wake Island Air Force Base [*Wake Island*] [*ICAO location identifier*] (ICLI) ... PWAK
Wake Measurements RADAR [*Army*] (MCD) ... WMR
Wake Seeding and Quenching ... WSQ
Wake Shield Facility [*NASA*] ... WSF
Wake Vortex Avoidance System [*FAA*] ... WVAS
Wakefield [*Postcode*] (ODBW) ... WF
Wakefield Public Library, Wakefield, MI [*Library symbol Library of Congress*] (LCLS) ... MiWak
Wakefield, VA [*Location identifier FAA*] (FAAL) ... AKQ
Wakefield Volunteer Rifles [*British military*] (DMA) ... WVR
Wakefield-Peacedale, RI [*FM radio station call letters*] (RBYB) ... WDGE
Waking Imagined Analgesia [*Medicine*] ... WIA
Wakkanai [*Japan ICAO location identifier*] (ICLI) ... RJCW
Wakkanai [*Japan*] [*Seismograph station code, US Geological Survey*] (SEIS) ... WAK
Wakkanai [*Japan*] [*Airport symbol*] (OAG) ... WKJ
Wako-Kungo [*Angola*] [*ICAO location identifier*] (ICLI) ... FNWK
Waksman Institute of Microbiology [*Rutgers University*] [*Research center*] (RCD) ... WIM
Waksman Social Skills Rating Scale ... WSSRS
Wakunai [*Papua New Guinea*] [*Airport symbol*] (OAG) ... WKN
Walachian [*Romanian dialect*] (BARN) ... Walach
Walaha [*Vanuatu*] [*ICAO location identifier*] (ICLI) ... NVSW
Walaha [*Vanuatu*] [*Airport symbol*] (OAG) ... WLH
Walamo [*MARC language code Library of Congress*] (LCCP) ... wal
Walbro Corp. [*NASDAQ symbol*] (NQ) ... WALB
Walbro Corp. [*Associated Press*] (SAG) ... Walbro
Wald, Arnold, Goldberg, Rushton [*Test*] [*Statistics*] ... WAGR
Waldemar Medical Research Foundation, Woodbury, NY [*Library symbol Library of Congress*] (LCLS) ... NWbW
Walden [*Record label*] ... Wald
Walden Bancorp [*NASDAQ symbol*] (TTSB) ... WLDN
Walden Forever Wild (EA) ... WFW
Walden Forever Wild Committee (EA) ... WFWC
Walden Pond Advisory Committee (EA) ... WPAC
Walden Public Library, Lively, Ontario [*Library symbol National Library of Canada*] (BIB) ... OLIVW
Walden Public Library, Liverly, ON, Canada [*Library symbol*] [*Library of Congress*] (LCLS) ... CaOLivW
Walden Residential Prop [*NYSE symbol*] (TTSB) ... WDN
Walden Residential Properties [*Associated Press*] (SAG) ... Waldn
Walden Residential Properties [*Associated Press*] (SAG) ... WaldnRP
Walden Residential Properties [*NYSE symbol*] (SAG) ... WDN
Walden Woods Project [*An association*] (EA) ... WWP
Waldenstrom's Macroglobulinemia [*Medicine*] ... WM
Waldorf [*Record label*] ... Wal
Waldorf College, Forest City, IA [*Library symbol Library of Congress*] (LCLS) ... IaFcW
Waldorf, MD [*FM radio station call letters*] (RBYB) ... WWZZ-FM
Waldorf, MD [*FM radio station call letters*] ... WXTR
Waldport, OR [*AM radio station call letters*] ... KORC
Waldron, AR [*FM radio station call letters*] ... KRWA
Waldron District Library, Waldron, MI [*Library symbol Library of Congress*] (LCLS) ... MiWald
Waldron Ledge [*Hawaii*] [*Seismograph station code, US Geological Survey*] (SEIS) ... WLG
Wales [*MARC geographic area code Library of Congress*] (LCCP) ... e-uk-wl
Wales ... W
Wales [*Alaska*] [*Airport symbol*] (OAG) ... WAA
Wales [*MARC country of publication code Library of Congress*] (LCCP) ... wlk
Wales, AK [*Location identifier FAA*] (FAAL) ... WAA
Wales Council for Voluntary Action (DBA) ... WCVA
Wales Craft Council (DBA) ... WCC
Wales Tourist Board (DCTA) ... WTB
Walferdange [*Belgium*] [*Seismograph station code, US Geological Survey*] (SEIS) ... WLF
Walferstan and Bristowe's Election Cases [*1859-65*] [*A publication*] (DLA) ... W & B
Walford on Railways [*2nd ed.*] [*1846*] [*A publication*] (DLA) ... Walf Railw
Walford's Laws of the Customs [*1846*] [*A publication*] (DLA) ... Walf Cust
Walford's Parties to Actions [*1842*] [*A publication*] (DLA) ... Walf Part
Walgett [*Australia Airport symbol*] (OAG) ... WGE
Walgreen Co. [*NYSE symbol*] (SPSG) ... WAG
Walgreen Co. [*Associated Press*] (SAG) ... Walgrn
Walhalla, SC [*AM radio station call letters*] ... WGOG
Walhalla, SC [*FM radio station call letters*] ... WGOG-FM
Walk [*Baseball*] ... W
Walk [*Postal Service standard*] (OPSA) ... WALK
Walk ... WLK
Walk Around Inspection ... WAI
Walk In (ADA) ... WI
Walk In, Walk Out (ADA) ... WIWO
Walk on Floor [*Ataxia*] ... WOF

Walk with Aid of Cane (DAVI) .... WWAC
Walkaloosa Horse Association (EA) .... WHA
Walker Air Force Base (AAG) .... WAAFB
Walker and Elgood's Executors and Administrators [6th ed.] [1926]
   [A publication] (DLA) .... Walk Exec
Walker Art Center, Minneapolis, MN [Library symbol] [Library of Congress]
   (LCLS) .... MnMW
Walker Cay, Abaco Island [Bahamas] [ICAO location identifier] (ICLI) .... MYAW
Walker Elementary School, Rockford, IL [Library symbol] [Library of
   Congress] (LCLS) .... IRoWaE
Walker Interactive Sys [NASDAQ symbol] (TTSB) .... WALK
Walker Interactive Systems [NASDAQ symbol] (SAG) ...... WALK
Walker Interactive Systems, Inc. [Associated Press] (SAG) ...... WalkInt
Walker Manufacturing Co., Racine, WI [Library symbol Library of Congress]
   (LCLS) .... WRacWa
Walker Memorial Library, Westbrook, ME [Library symbol Library of
   Congress] (LCLS) .... MeWebr
Walker, MI [FM radio station call letters] .... WQFN
Walker, MN [Television station call letters] .... KCCW
Walker, MN [AM radio station call letters] .... KLLZ
Walker, MN [FM radio station call letters] .... KLLZ-FM
Walker on Patents [A publication] (DLA) .... Walk Pat
Walker on Wills [A publication] (DLA) .... Walk Wills
Walker Problem Behavior Identification Checklist [Education] .... WPBIC
Walker Public Library, Walker, MN [Library symbol] [Library of Congress]
   (LCLS) .... MnWal
Walker [Hiram] Resources Ltd. [Toronto Stock Exchange symbol Vancouver
   Stock Exchange symbol] (SPSG) .... HWR
Walker Ridge [California] [Seismograph station code, US Geological Survey]
   (SEIS) .... WKC
Walker Wingsail Systems [Shipbuilding] [British] .... WWS
Walker-Hackensack High School, Walker, MN [Library symbol] [Library of
   Congress] (LCLS) .... MnWalH
Walker-Lybarger Construction Co. [Colorado] .... WLCC
Walker's American Law [A publication] (DLA) .... Walk Am Law
Walker's Banking Law [2nd ed.] [1885] [A publication] (DLA) ...... Walk Bank L
Walker's Cay [Bahamas] [Airport symbol] (OAG) .... WKR
Walker's Cay Air Terminal [ICAO designator] (AD) .... XW
Walker's Equity Pleader's Assistant [A publication] (DLA) ...... Walk Eq Pl
Walker's Introduction to American Law [A publication] (DLA) ...... Walk Int
Walker's Louisiana Digest [A publication] (DLA) .... Walk LA Dig
Walker's Michigan Chancery Reports [A publication] (DLA) ...... Wal Ch
Walker's Michigan Chancery Reports [A publication] (DLA) ...... Walk
Walker's Michigan Chancery Reports [A publication] (DLA) ...... Walk Ch
Walker's Michigan Chancery Reports [A publication] (DLA) ...... Walk Ch Cas
Walker's Michigan Chancery Reports [A publication] (DLA) ...... Walk Ch Mich
Walker's Michigan Chancery Reports [A publication] (DLA) ...... Walk Chanc Rep
Walker's Michigan Chancery Reports [A publication] (DLA) ...... Walk (Mic) Ch
Walker's Michigan Chancery Reports [A publication] (DLA) ...... Walk Mich
Walker's Michigan Chancery Reports [A publication] (DLA) ...... Walk Michig Rep
Walker's Michigan Chancery Reports [A publication] (DLA) ...... Walker
Walker's Michigan Chancery Reports [A publication] (DLA) ...... Walker's Ch R
Walker's Pennsylvania Reports [1855-85] [A publication] (DLA) ...... Walk
Walker's Pennsylvania Reports [1855-85] [A publication] (DLA) ...... Walk PA
Walker's Pennsylvania Reports [1855-85] [A publication] (DLA) ...... Walker
Walker's Reports [96, 109 Alabama] [A publication] (DLA) ...... Walk
Walker's Reports [22-25, 38-51, 72-88 Texas] [1-10 Civil Appeals Texas]
   [A publication] (DLA) .... Walk
Walker's Reports [1 Mississippi] [A publication] (DLA) ...... Walk
Walker's Reports [1 Mississippi] [A publication] (DLA) ...... Walk Miss
Walker's Reports [22-25, 38-51, 72-88 Texas] [1-10 Civil Appeals Texas]
   [A publication] (DLA) .... Walk Tex
Walker's Reports [22-25, 38-51, 72-88 Texas] [1-10 Civil Appeals Texas]
   [A publication] (DLA) .... Walker
Walker's Reports [96, 109 Alabama] [A publication] (DLA) ...... Walker
Walker's Reports [1 Mississippi] [A publication] (DLA) ...... Walker
Walker's Theory of the Common Law [A publication] (DLA) ...... Walk Com L
Walkersville, MD [AM radio station call letters] .... WWTL
Walkerton Branch, Bruce County Public Library, Ontario [Library symbol
   National Library of Canada] (NLC) .... OWALK
Walkerton Independent-News, Walkerton, IN [Library symbol Library of
   Congress] (LCLS) .... InWalIN
Walkerton-Lincoln Township Public Library, Walkerton, IN [Library symbol
   Library of Congress] (LCLS) .... InWal
Walkerville Collegiate Institute, Windsor, ON, Canada [Library symbol Library
   of Congress] (LCLS) .... CaOWW
Walkerville Collegiate Institute, Windsor, Ontario [Library symbol National
   Library of Canada] (NLC) .... OWW
Walkerville Public Library, Walkerville, MI [Library symbol Library of
   Congress] (LCLS) .... MiWalv
Walkie-Talkie .... W/T
Walk-In Management Information System [Computer science] .... WIMIS
Walking and Dredging Self-Elevating Platform (PDAA) ...... WADSEP
Walking Association (EA) .... WA
Walking Beam Suspension (WDAA) .... WBS
Walking Hinge (KSC) .... WH
Walking Horse Owner's Association of America (EA) ...... WHOA
Walking Horse Owner's Association of America (EA) ...... WHOAA
Walking Horse Trainers Association (EA) .... WHTA
Walking Pattern (MHDI) .... WAKPAT
Walking Ventilation to Maximum Breathing Capacity Ratio [Medicine]
   (MAE) .... WV-MBC
Walking with Eyes Closed [Equilibrium test] .... WEC
Walking Wounded (ADA) .... WW
Walking Wounded Collecting Post [Military] .... WWCP

Walkover .... WO
Walks [Commonly used] (OPSA) .... WALKS
Walks plus Hits Divided by Innings Pitched [Baseball] ...... WHIP
Walkway (VRA) .... wlkwy
Walkway .... WLKWY
Walkways Center [Defunct] (EA) .... WC
Wall .... W
Wall [Postal Service standard] (OPSA) .... WALL
Wall & Redekop Corp. [Toronto Stock Exchange symbol Vancouver Stock
   Exchange symbol] .... WRK
Wall Box (ROG) .... WB
Wall Coated Open Tubular [Instrumentation] .... WCOT
Wall Data [NASDAQ symbol] (TTSB) .... WALL
Wall Data, Inc. [NASDAQ symbol] (SAG) .... WALL
Wall Data, Inc. [Associated Press] (SAG) .... WallData
Wall Distribution Frame (MUGU) .... WDF
Wall Effect Amplifier .... WEA
Wall Financial Co. [Vancouver Stock Exchange symbol] ...... WFC
Wall Financial Corp. [Toronto Stock Exchange symbol] ...... WFC
Wall Hung [Technical drawings] .... WH
Wall Hydrant [NFPA pre-fire planning symbol] (NFPA) ...... WH
Wall Lake Public Library, Wall Lake, IA [Library symbol Library of Congress]
   (LCLS) .... IaWall
Wall Motion (MEDA) .... WM
Wall Motion Abnormality [Cardiology] (DAVI) .... WMA
Wall Oven and Hot Plates [Classified advertising] (ADA) ...... WO & HPS
Wall Paper (VRA) .... wapa
Wall Paper Institute [Later, Wallcovering Manufacturers Association] (EA) ...... WPI
Wall Paper Merchants' Association of Great Britain (BI) ...... WPMA
Wall Plate Box .... WPB
Wall Receptacle (MUGU) .... WR
Wall Street .... WS
Wall Street Deli [Formerly, Sandwich Chef] [NASDAQ symbol] (SPSG) ...... WSDI
Wall Street Deli Co. [Associated Press] (SAG) .... WallSDI
Wall Street Journal [A publication] (DFIT) .... WSJ
Wall Street Journal (Eastern Edition) [A publication] (BRI) ...... WSJ
Wall Street Journal (Midwest Edition) [A publication] (BRI) ...... WSJ-MW
Wall Street Planning Group (EA) .... WSPG
Wall Street Ventures [Vancouver Stock Exchange symbol] ...... WSV
Wall Street Week [Television program] .... WSW
Wall Thickness [Nuclear energy] (NRCH) .... WT
Wall to Wall [Technical drawings] .... WTW
Wall Vent [Technical drawings] .... WV
Walla Walla [Washington] [Airport symbol] (OAG) .... ALW
Walla Walla College (GAGS) .... Walla Walla C
Walla Walla College [Washington] .... WWC
Walla Walla College, College Place, WA [Library symbol Library of
   Congress] (LCLS) .... WaWC
Walla Walla Community College, Walla Walla, WA [Library symbol Library of
   Congress] (LCLS) .... WaWWC
Walla Walla County Rural Library, Walla Walla, WA [Library symbol] [Library
   of Congress] (LCLS) .... WaWCL
Walla Walla High School, Walla Walla, WA [Library symbol] [Library of
   Congress] (LCLS) .... WAWHS
Walla Walla Public Library, Walla Walla, WA [Library symbol Library of
   Congress] (LCLS) .... WaW
Walla Walla Valley Railway Co. [AAR code] .... WWV
Walla Walla, WA [AM radio station call letters] (RBYB) ...... KGDC
Walla Walla, WA [FM radio station call letters] .... KHSS
Walla Walla, WA [FM radio station call letters] .... KNLT
Walla Walla, WA [AM radio station call letters] .... KTEL
Walla Walla, WA [FM radio station call letters] .... KTEL-FM
Walla Walla, WA [FM radio station call letters] (RBYB) ...... KTWY-FM
Walla Walla, WA [AM radio station call letters] .... KUJ
Walla Walla, WA [FM radio station call letters] .... KWCW
Walla Walla, WA [FM radio station call letters] (RBYB) ...... KWWS-FM
Walla Walla, WA [FM radio station call letters] .... KXRX
Wallace [Idaho] [Seismograph station code, US Geological Survey] (SEIS) ...... WAL
Wallace Barnes Co. .... WBCO
Wallace Barnes Steel [Wallace Barnes Co.] .... WBS
Wallace Communications Consultants [Tampa, FL] [Telecommunications]
   (TSSD) .... WCC
Wallace Computer Services, Inc. [Associated Press] (SAG) ...... WalCS
Wallace Computer Services, Inc. [NYSE symbol] (SPSG) ...... WCS
Wallace Computer Svc [NYSE symbol] (TTSB) .... WCS
Wallace Consolidated Community School District 195, Ottawa, IL [Library
   symbol Library of Congress] (LCLS) .... IOtWSD
Wallace Dam [Georgia] [Seismograph station code, US Geological Survey]
   (SEIS) .... WDG
Wallace, ID [FM radio station call letters] .... KSQA
Wallace, ID [AM radio station call letters] .... KWAL
Wallace Laboratories [Research code symbol] .... W
Wallace, NC [Location identifier FAA] (FAAL) .... ACZ
Wallace, NC [AM radio station call letters] .... WLSE
Wallace, NC [FM radio station call letters] .... WZKB
Wallace Public Library, Wallace, ID [Library symbol] [Library of Congress]
   (LCLS) .... IdW
Wallaceburg Public Library, Ontario [Library symbol National Library of
   Canada] (NLC) .... OWALL
Wallaceburg Public Library, Wallaceburg, ON, Canada [Library symbol
   Library of Congress] (LCLS) .... CaOWall
Wallace's Nova Scotia Reports [6 Nova Scotia Reports] [1884-1907]
   [A publication] (DLA) .... NSR Wall
Wallace's Nova Scotia Reports [A publication] (DLA) ...... Wall
Wallace's Principles of the Laws of Scotland [A publication] (DLA) ...... Wal Prin

Wallace's Principles of the Laws of Scotland [*A publication*] (DLA) .... Wall Pr
Wallace's Supreme Court Reports [*68-90 United States*] [*1863-74*] [*A publication*] (DLA) .... Wall
Wallace's Supreme Court Reports [*68-90 United States*] [*A publication*] (DLA) .... Wall Rep
Wallace's Supreme Court Reports [*68-90 United States*] [*A publication*] (DLA) .... Wall SC
Wallace's "The Reporters" [*A publication*] (DLA) .... Rep
Wallace's "The Reporters" [*A publication*] (DLA) .... Wall Rep
Wallace's United States Circuit Court Reports [*A publication*] (DLA) .... Wall
Wallace's United States Circuit Court Reports [*A publication*] (DLA) .... Wall CC
Wallace's United States Reports [*A publication*] (DLA) .... Wal US Rep
Wallace's United States Reports [*1863-74*] [*A publication*] (AAGC) .... Wall
Wallachian (ROG) .... WALL
Wallboard .... WB
Wallboard .... WBD
Wallboard .... WBRD
Wallboard (AAG) .... WLB
Wallcovering Distributors Association (EA) .... WDA
Wallcovering, Fabric, and Decor Retailers Association [*British*] (EAIO) .... WPWRA
Wallcovering Information Bureau (EA) .... WIB
Wallcovering Manufacturers Association (EA) .... WMA
Wallcovering Wholesalers Association [*Later, WDA*] (EA) .... WWA
Walled Lake, MI [*AM radio station call letters*] .... WPON
Wallenstein Laboratory [*Medium*] (BABM) .... WL
Wallerian Degeneration [*Medicine*] .... WD
Walleye Anglers Association of America [*Defunct*] (EA) .... WAAA
Walleye Filter Changer .... WFC
Walleye Measurements Program .... WAM
Wallila Gap [*Washington*] [*Seismograph station code, US Geological Survey*] (SEIS) .... WGW
Wallingford [*Municipal borough in England*] .... WALL
Wallingford, CT [*FM radio station call letters*] .... WWEB
Wallingford Storm Sewer Package [*Hydraulics Research*] [*Software package*] (NCC) .... WASSP
Wallis and Futuna [*MARC geographic area code Library of Congress*] (LCCP) .... powf--
Wallis and Futuna [*ANSI two-letter standard code*] (CNC) .... WF
Wallis and Futuna [*MARC country of publication code Library of Congress*] (LCCP) .... wf
Wallis and Futuna [*ANSI three-letter standard code*] (CNC) .... WLF
Wallis/Hififo [*Wallis and Futuna Islands*] [*ICAO location identifier*] (ICLI) .... NLWW
Wallis' Irish Chancery Reports [*A publication*] (DLA) .... Wall
Wallis' Irish Chancery Reports [*A publication*] (DLA) .... Wallis
Wallis' Irish Chancery Reports [*A publication*] (DLA) .... Wallis (Ir)
Wallis' Irish Chancery Reports, by Lyne [*A publication*] (DLA) .... Wal by L
Wallis' Irish Chancery Reports, by Lyne [*1776-91*] [*A publication*] (DLA) .... Wall Lyn
Wallis' Irish Chancery Reports, by Lyne [*1776-91*] [*A publication*] (DLA) .... Wallis by L
Wallis' Irish Chancery Reports, by Lyne [*1766-91*] [*A publication*] (DLA) .... Wallis by Lyne
Wallis Island [*Wallis and Futuna Islands*] [*Airport symbol*] (OAG) .... WLS
Wallis' Philadelphia Reports [*1855-85*] [*Pennsylvania*] [*A publication*] (DLA) .... Wall
Wallis' Select Cases, Edited by Lyne [*1766-91*] [*Ireland*] [*A publication*] (DLA) .... Lyne (Wall)
Wallisair Compagnie [*France ICAO designator*] (FAAC) .... WLR
Wallkill Public Library, Wallkill, NY [*Library symbol Library of Congress*] (LCLS) .... NWall
Wall-Motion Study (MEDA) .... WMS
Wall-Mounted Handling System [*AEC*] .... WMHS
Wall-Mounted Manipulator [*Nuclear energy*] (NRCH) .... WMM
Walloon (ROG) .... WAL
Walloon (ROG) .... WALL
Wallops Flight Center [*Formerly, WS*] [*NASA*] .... WFC
Wallops Island [*Off coast of Virginia*] .... WI
Wallops Island, NASA Center (MCD) .... WLP
Wallops Island/Wallops Station [*Virginia*] [*ICAO location identifier*] (ICLI) .... KWAL
Wallops Space Flight Center [*NASA*] (IAA) .... WSFC
Wallops Station [*Later, WFC*] [*NASA*] .... WAS
Wallops Station [*Later, WFC*] [*NASA*] .... WS
Wallowa County Library, Enterprise, OR [*Library symbol Library of Congress*] (LCLS) .... OrEnW
Wallowa Memorial Hospital, Burton Carlock Memorial Library, Enterprise, OR [*Library symbol Library of Congress*] (LCLS) .... OrEnWM
Wallpaper .... WLPAPER
Wall-to-Wall [*Carpeting*] [*Classified advertising*] .... WW
Wally Byam Caravan Club International (EA) .... WBCCI
Wal-Mart Stores [*NYSE symbol*] (TTSB) .... WMT
Wal-Mart Stores, Inc. [*Associated Press*] (SAG) .... WalMart
Wal-Mart Stores, Inc. [*NYSE symbol*] (SPSG) .... WMT
Walnut (VRA) .... wal
Walnut (WGA) .... WAL
Walnut, CA [*FM radio station call letters*] .... KSAK
Walnut Canyon National Monument .... WACA
Walnut Consolidated Community School District 285, Walnut, IL [*Library symbol Library of Congress*] (LCLS) .... IWalSD
Walnut Consolidated High School District 508, Walnut, IL [*Library symbol Library of Congress*] (LCLS) .... IWalHSD
Walnut Council (EA) .... WC
Walnut Cove Public Library, Walnut Cove, NC [*Library symbol Library of Congress*] (LCLS) .... NcWc
Walnut Cove Public Library, Walnut Cove, NC [*Library symbol*] [*Library of Congress*] (LCLS) .... NcWcL
Walnut Creek, CA [*FM radio station call letters*] .... KZWC
Walnut Elementary School, Uniondale, NY [*Library symbol Library of Congress*] (LCLS) .... NUnWE
Walnut Export Sales Co. (EA) .... WESCO
Walnut Financial Services [*NASDAQ symbol*] (TTSB) .... WNUT
Walnut Financial Services, Inc. [*Associated Press*] (SAG) .... WalnutF
Walnut Financial Services, Inc. [*NASDAQ symbol*] (SAG) .... WNUT
Walnut Marketing Board (EA) .... WMB
Walnut, MS [*AM radio station call letters*] .... WLRC
Walnut Public Library, Walnut, IA [*Library symbol Library of Congress*] (LCLS) .... IaWal
Walnut Ridge, AR [*Location identifier FAA*] (FAAL) .... ARG
Walnut Ridge, AR [*AM radio station call letters*] .... KRLW
Walnut Ridge, AR [*FM radio station call letters*] .... KRLW-FM
Walnut Ridge, AR [*Location identifier FAA*] (FAAL) .... LWQ
Walnut Township Library, Walnut, IL [*Library symbol Library of Congress*] (LCLS) .... IWal
Walpole Historical Society, Walpole, NH [*Library symbol Library of Congress*] (LCLS) .... NhWalHi
Walpole, MA [*FM radio station call letters*] .... WSRB
Walpole's Rubric of Common Law [*A publication*] (DLA) .... Walp Rub
Walrus (VRA) .... wlrs
Walseal .... WLSL
Walsenburg, CO [*FM radio station call letters*] .... KSPK
Walsh College, Canton, OH [*Library symbol Library of Congress*] (LCLS) .... OCanW
Walsh College, Canton, OH [*OCLC symbol*] (OCLC) .... WAL
Walsh Intl [*NASDAQ symbol*] (TTSB) .... WSHI
Walsh Public Library, Walsh, CO [*Library symbol Library of Congress*] (LCLS) .... CoWals
Walsh-Healey Act [*Labor*] .... W-H
Walsh-Healey Public Contracts Act (AAGC) .... WHA
Walsh-Healey Public Contracts Act [*1936*] [*Labor*] .... WHPCA
Walshire Assurance [*NASDAQ symbol*] (TTSB) .... WALS
Walshire Assurance Co. [*NASDAQ symbol*] (NQ) .... WALS
Walshire Assurance Co. [*Associated Press*] (SAG) .... Walshr
Walsh's Irish Registry Cases [*A publication*] (DLA) .... Walsh
Walsten Air Services [*Canada ICAO designator*] (FAAC) .... WAS
Walt Disney Comic Strip Maker [*Apple computer software*] .... WDCSM
Walt Disney Educational Media Co. .... WDEMCO
Walt Disney Hearing Rehabilitation Research Center [*Ear Research Institute*] .... HRRC
Walt Disney Memorial Cancer Institute .... WDMCC
Walt Disney Memorial Cancer Institute .... WDMCI
Walt Disney Productions, Burbank, CA [*Library symbol Library of Congress*] (LCLS) .... CBbWD
Walt Whitman Birthplace Association (EA) .... WWBA
Walt Whitman Birthplace Association, Huntington Station, NY [*Library symbol Library of Congress*] (LCLS) .... NHsW
Walt Whitman High School, Huntington Station, NY [*Library symbol*] [*Library of Congress*] (LCLS) .... NHsWH
Walt Whitman High School, Huntington Station, NY [*Library symbol Library of Congress*] (LCLS) .... NHusWH
Walt Whitman Society of America [*Defunct*] (EA) .... WWSA
Walter and Bates' Ohio Digest [*A publication*] (DLA) .... W & B Dig
Walter and Eliza Hall Institute of Medical Research [*Australia*] .... WEH
Walter Bagehot Research Council on National Sovereignty (EA) .... WBRC
Walter Bernard and Milton Glaser [*Founders of the magazine-design firm that bears their initials*] .... WBMG
Walter Cecil Rawls Library and Museum, Courtland, VA [*Library symbol Library of Congress*] (LCLS) .... ViCou
Walter Chiles Cox Memorial Foundation, Tucson, AZ [*Library symbol Library of Congress*] (LCLS) .... AzTCM
Walter Elias Disney [*These initials also identify the theme park division of Walt Disney Enterprises*] .... WED
Walter Hampden Memorial Library, New York, NY [*Library symbol Library of Congress*] (LCLS) .... NNWH
Walter Hinchman Associates, Inc. [*Telecommunications Defunct*] (TSSD) .... WHAI
Walter Industries [*NASDAQ symbol*] (TTSB) .... WLTR
Walter Industries, Inc. [*Associated Press*] (SAG) .... Walter
Walter Industries, Inc. [*NASDAQ symbol*] (SAG) .... WLTR
Walter Kidde Nuclear Laboratories, Inc. (MCD) .... WKNL
Walter Owen Bentley [*Automotive engineer*] [*British*] .... WO
Walter Owen Bentley [*Automotive engineer*] [*British*] .... WOB
Walter P. Chrysler Club (EA) .... WPC
Walter Reed Army Institute of Nursing (AABC) .... WRAIN
Walter Reed Army Institute of Research [*Washington, DC*] (MCD) .... WRAIR
Walter Reed Army Institute of Research, Washington, DC [*Library symbol Library of Congress*] (LCLS) .... DWRI
Walter Reed Army Medical Biomechanical Research Center, Forest Glen, MD [*Library symbol Library of Congress*] (LCLS) .... DWR-P
Walter Reed Army Medical Center .... WRAMC
Walter Reed Army Medical Center, Post/Patient Library, Washington, DC [*OCLC symbol*] (OCLC) .... WRB
Walter Reed Army Medical Center, Washington, DC [*OCLC symbol*] (OCLC) .... WRA
Walter Reed General Hospital (MCD) .... WRGH
Walter Reed Research Reactor [*Military*] .... WRRR
Walter Reed Society (EA) .... WRS
Walter S. Boardman Elementary School, Oceanside, NY [*Library symbol*] [*Library of Congress*] (LCLS) .... NocBE
Walter Winchell [*American journalist*] (IIA) .... WW
Walter Wright Pioneer Village, Dawson Creek, BC, Canada [*Library symbol*] [*Library of Congress*] (LCLS) .... CaBDCWW

Walter Wright Pioneer Village, Dawson Creek, British Columbia [*Library symbol National Library of Canada*] (NLC) .... BDCWW
Walterboro, SC [*Location identifier FAA*] (FAAL) .... RBW
Walterboro, SC [*AM radio station call letters*] .... WALD
Walterboro, SC [*FM radio station call letters*] (RBYB) .... WALI-FM
Walterboro, SC [*FM radio station call letters*] .... WONO
Walterboro, SC [*FM radio station call letters*] .... WPAL
Walters Art Gallery, Baltimore, MD [*Library symbol Library of Congress*] (LCLS) .... MdBWA
Walter's Code [*A publication*] (DLA) .... Walter C
Walter's Reports [*14-16 New Mexico*] [*A publication*] (DLA) .... Walter
Walters State Community College, Learning Resources Center, Morristown, TN [*Library symbol*] [*Library of Congress*] (LCLS) .... TMorW
Walter's Statute of Limitations [*4th ed.*] [*A publication*] (DLA) .... Walt Lim
Walthall County Library, Tylertown, MS [*Library symbol Library of Congress*] (LCLS) .... MsTy
Waltham, MA [*FM radio station call letters*] .... WBRS
Waltham, MA [*FM radio station call letters*] .... WCRB
Waltham, MA [*AM radio station call letters*] .... WRCA
Waltham, MA [*Location identifier FAA*] (FAAL) .... YFF
Waltham Public Library, Waltham MA [*Library symbol Library of Congress*] (LCLS) .... MWal
Walthamstow [*England*] .... WALTSTOW
Walthard's Cell Nest [*Gynecology*] (AAMN) .... WCN
Walthard's Cell Rests [*Medicine*] (MEDA) .... WCR
Walther League (EA) .... WL
Walton, IN [*FM radio station call letters*] (RBYB) .... WFRR-FM
Walton, NY [*AM radio station call letters*] .... WDLA
Walton, NY [*FM radio station call letters*] .... WDLA-FM
Walton on Husband and Wife [*Scotland*] [*A publication*] (DLA) .... Walt H & W
Waltonville Community Unit, School District 1, Waltonville, IL [*Library symbol Library of Congress*] (LCLS) .... IWaltSD
Waltz [*Music*] .... W
Walvis Bay [*Namibia*] [*Airport symbol*] (OAG) .... WVB
Walworth Barbour American International School in Israel (BJA) .... WBAIS
Walworth County Law Library, Elkhorn, WI [*Library symbol Library of Congress*] (LCLS) .... WEICL
Walworth Memorial Library, Walworth, WI [*Library symbol Library of Congress*] (LCLS) .... WWal
Walworth Public Schools, Walworth, WI [*Library symbol Library of Congress*] (LCLS) .... WWalPS
Walwyn, Inc. [*Toronto Stock Exchange symbol*] .... WYN
Wamba-Luadi [*Zaire*] [*ICAO location identifier*] (ICLI) .... FZDD
Wambrook [*Australia Seismograph station code, US Geological Survey*] (SEIS) .... WAM
Wamego, KS [*FM radio station call letters*] .... KHCA
Wamena [*Indonesia*] [*ICAO location identifier*] (ICLI) .... WAJW
Wamena [*Indonesia*] [*Airport symbol*] (OAG) .... WMX
Wana [*Pakistan*] [*ICAO location identifier*] (ICLI) .... OPWN
Wanatah Public Library, Wanatah, IN [*Library symbol Library of Congress*] (LCLS) .... InWan
Wanchese, NC [*AM radio station call letters*] .... WOBR
Wanchese, NC [*FM radio station call letters*] .... WOBR-FM
WAND [*Women's Action for Nuclear Disarmament*] **Education Fund** (EA) .... WAND EF
WAND [*Women's Action for Nuclear Disarmament*] **Education Fund** (EA) .... WEF
Wandel & Goltermann Tech [*NASDAQ symbol*] (TTSB) .... WGTI
Wandel & Goltermann Technologies [*Associated Press*] (SAG) .... WandGlt
Wandel & Goltermann Technologies [*NASDAQ symbol*] (SAG) .... WGTI
Wandell's New York Reports [*A publication*] (DLA) .... Wandell
Wander AG [*Research code symbol*] [*Switzerland*] .... AW
Wander AG [*Switzerland*] [*Research code symbol*] .... HF
Wander AG [*Switzerland*] [*Research code symbol*] .... W
Wanderer Books [*Publisher's imprint*] .... WFF
Wanderer Forum Foundation (EA) .... WAP
Wandering Atrial Pacemaker [*Cardiology*] .... WAP
[*The*] Wandering Hand Brigade [*Men who are likely to take liberties with women*] .... WHB
Wandering River Public Library, Alberta [*Library symbol National Library of Canada*] (NLC) .... AWR
Wandering River Public Library, Wandering River, AB, Canada [*Library symbol*] [*Library of Congress*] (LCLS) .... CaAWr
Wanderlust Interactive [*NASDAQ symbol*] (TTSB) .... LUST
Wanderlust Interactive, Inc. [*NASDAQ symbol*] (SAG) .... LUST
Wanderlust Interactive, Inc. [*Associated Press*] (SAG) .... Wandlst
Wanderlust Interactive, Inc. [*Associated Press*] (SAG) .... Wandlust
Wanderlust Interactive Wrrt [*NASDAQ symbol*] (TTSB) .... LUSTW
Wandsworth Borough News Co. Ltd., London, United Kingdom [*Library symbol Library of Congress*] .... UkLWa
Wandsworth's Legal Resource Project [*A publication*] (DLA) .... WLRP
Wane Aviation Ltd. [*Kenya*] [*FAA designator*] (FAAC) .... WAN
Wang Computer System .... WCS
Wang [*Laboratories, Inc.*] Image File Format [*Computer science*] (PCM) .... WIFF
Wang Information Services Corp. [*Telecommunications service*] (TSSD) .... WISC
Wang Institute of Graduate Studies, Tyngsboro, MA [*OCLC symbol*] (OCLC) .... WNI
Wang Integrated Image System .... WIIS
Wang Integrated Technology Show [*British*] .... WITS
Wang Interactive Learning System [*Computer science*] (HGAA) .... WILS
Wang International Standard Code for Information Interchange [*Pronounced "whiskey"*] [*Canada*] .... WISCII
Wang Intersystem Exchange .... WISE
Wang Laboratories [*NASDAQ symbol*] (TTSB) .... WANG
Wang Laboratories, Inc. [*NASDAQ symbol*] (SAG) .... WANG
Wang Laboratories, Inc. [*Associated Press*] (SAG) .... WangL

Wang Laboratories, Inc. [*Associated Press*] (SAG) .... WangLab
Wang Laboratories, Inc., Lowell, MA [*OCLC symbol*] (OCLC) .... WNG
Wang Labs Wrrt [*NASDAQ symbol*] (TTSB) .... WANGW
Wang Office Systems User Society (CSR) .... WOSUS
Wang Software Vendors' Association [*Defunct*] (EA) .... WSVA
Wang System Networking (HGAA) .... WSN
Wang Telephone Message Exchange [*Wang Laboratories, Inc.*] [*Telecommunications service*] (TSSD) .... WTMX
Wanganui [*New Zealand*] [*ICAO location identifier*] (ICLI) .... NZWU
Wanganui [*New Zealand*] [*Airport symbol*] (OAG) .... WAG
Wangen-Lachen [*Switzerland ICAO location identifier*] (ICLI) .... LSPV
Wangerooge [*Germany Airport symbol*] (OAG) .... AGE
Wangerooge [*Germany ICAO location identifier*] (ICLI) .... EDWG
Wanham Community Library, Alberta [*Library symbol National Library of Canada*] (NLC) .... AWC
Wanham Community Library, Wanham, AB, Canada [*Library symbol*] [*Library of Congress*] (LCLS) .... CaAWaC
Wanham School, Alberta [*Library symbol National Library of Canada*] (BIB) .... AWANS
Wanigan .... WAN
Wanigela [*Papua New Guinea*] [*Airport symbol*] (OAG) .... AGL
Wankie [*Zimbabwe*] [*Airport symbol*] (AD) .... WKI
Wankie Game Reserve [*Zimbabwe*] [*Airport symbol*] (AD) .... WKM
Wanliss Street [*New Britain*] [*Seismograph station code, US Geological Survey*] (SEIS) .... WAN
Wannaska School, Wannaska, MN [*Library symbol*] [*Library of Congress*] (LCLS) .... MnWanS
Wansee Elementary School, Lawrence, NY [*Library symbol Library of Congress*] (LCLS) .... NLawWE
Wanstead [*England*] .... WANST
Wantage [*Urban district in England*] .... WANT
Wantagh Elementary School, Wantagh, NY [*Library symbol Library of Congress*] (LCLS) .... NWanE
Wantagh Junior High School, Wantagh, NY [*Library symbol*] [*Library of Congress*] (LCLS) .... NWanJH
Wantagh Junior-Senior High, Wantagh, NY [*Library symbol Library of Congress*] (LCLS) .... NWanJS
Wantagh Public Library, Wantagh, NY [*Library symbol Library of Congress*] (LCLS) .... NWan
Wantagh Senior High School, Wantagh, NY [*Library symbol*] [*Library of Congress*] (LCLS) .... NWanSH
Wanted for Cash (MHDW) .... WFC
Wanting .... W
Wapakoneta, OH [*Location identifier FAA*] (FAAL) .... AXV
Wapakoneta, OH [*FM radio station call letters*] .... WZOQ
Wapato, WA [*FM radio station call letters*] .... KSOH
Wapello Public Library (Keck Memorial Library), Wapello, IA [*Library symbol Library of Congress*] (LCLS) .... IaWap
Wapello Republican, Wapello, IA [*Library symbol*] [*Library of Congress*] (LCLS) .... IaWapR
Wapenamanda [*Papua New Guinea*] [*Airport symbol*] (OAG) .... WBM
Wapentake [*Subdivision of some English shires*] .... WAP
Wapiti Aviation Ltd. [*Canada ICAO designator*] (FAAC) .... WPT
Wapiti Regional Library, Prince Albert, Saskatchewan [*Library symbol National Library of Canada*] (NLC) .... SPANC
Wapiti Regional Library, Prince Albert, SK, Canada [*Library symbol Library of Congress*] (LCLS) .... CaSPANC
Waples on Proceedings in Rem [*A publication*] (DLA) .... Wap Pr R
War .... W
War Agencies Employees Protective Association .... WAEPA
War Agricultural Executive Committee [*British*] (DAS) .... WAEC
War Aims [*British*] .... WA
War Air Service Program [*Department of Commerce*] .... WASP
War and Emergency Plan [*DoD*] .... WEP
War and Emergency Support Plan [*DoD*] .... WESP
War and Emergency Support Plan Exercise [*DoD*] .... WESPEX
War and Marine (DS) .... W & M
War and Mobilization Plan [*Air Force documents*] .... WMP
War and Peace Foundation (EA) .... WP
War and Peace Foundation (EA) .... WPF
War Artists' Advisory Committee [*British military*] (DMA) .... WAAC
War Assets Administration [*For disposal of US surplus war property*] [*Post-World War II*] .... WAA
War Assets Corp. [*Post-World War II*] [*Succeeded by War Assets Administration*] .... WAC
War at Sea (NVT) .... WAS
War at Sea Exercise [*Navy*] (DOMA) .... WASEX
War Cabinet [*World War II*] .... WC
War Cabinet Office [*World War II*] .... WCO
War Claims Commission [*Abolished, 1954*] .... WCC
War College .... WC
War Communications .... WC
War Communications Board [*World War II*] .... WCB
War Consumable Distribution Objective (AFM) .... WCDO
War Consumables Requirements Document [*Military*] (AFIT) .... WCRD
War Contracts Price Adjustment Board [*All functions dispersed, 1951*] .... WCPAB
War Control Data Processing Center (IAA) .... WCDPC
War Control Planners (EA) .... WCP
War Correspondent (DSUE) .... WARCO
War Cover Club (EA) .... WCC
War Crimes Commission (WDAA) .... WCC
War Crimes Group [*British*] .... WCG
War Crimes Tribunal [*Bertrand Russell*] [*Stockholm based pacifist organization founded during the Vietnam war*] (VNW) .... WCT
War Damage .... WD

War Damage Commission [*British*] ..... WDC
War Damage Corp. [*World War II*] ..... WDC
War Department [*Created, 1789; became Department of the Army, 1947*] ..... WD
War Department Board of Contract Appeals [*1942-50*] (AAGC) ..... WDBCA
War Department Chief of Staff, US Army [*World War II*] ..... WDCSA
War Department - Civil Affairs Division [*Obsolete*] ..... WARCAD
War Department Classified Message Center [*Obsolete World War II*] ..... WDCMC
War Department Constabulary [*British military*] (DMA) ..... WDC
War Department General Order [*Obsolete*] ..... WDGO
War Department General Staff [*Obsolete*] ..... WDGS
War Department Ground Forces [*Obsolete*] ..... WDGF
War Department Hardship Claims Board [*Obsolete*] ..... WDHCB
War Department Intelligence [*Obsolete*] ..... WDI
War Department Intelligence Collection Committee ..... WDICC
War Department Intelligence Collection Planning Committee ..... WDICPC
War Department Manpower Board [*Obsolete*] ..... WDMB
War Department, Operations Division, General Staff [*World War II*] ..... WDOPD
War Department Provost Marshal General, Investigation Division [*Obsolete*] ..... WDPMG-ID
War Department Special Staff [*Obsolete*] ..... WDSS
War Department Vehicle [*Obsolete*] ..... WDV
War Dog Training Unit [*British military*] (DMA) ..... WDTU
War Eagle Mining Co. [*Vancouver Stock Exchange symbol*] ..... WEM
War Economic Operation [*World War II*] ..... WEO
War Emergency Dose (DEN) ..... WED
War Emergency Formula ..... WEF
War Emergency Radio Service ..... WERS
War Engineering Board ..... WEB
War Establishment ..... WE
War Estate Tax Act [*1917*] ..... WETA
War Excess Profits Tax Act [*1917*] ..... WEPTA
War Finance Committee ..... WFC
War Food Administration [*Determined military, civilian, and foreign requirements for human and animal food, and for food used industrially*] [*Terminated, 1945*] [*World War II*] ..... WFA
War Frauds Unit ..... WFU
War Game Comparison (MCD) ..... WAGCOM
War Gaming and Simulation Center [*National Defense University*] ..... WGSC
War Guidance Requirements (AFM) ..... WGR
War Hazards Compensation Act ..... WHCA
War Headquarters (NATG) ..... WHQ
War Information Report [*British military*] (DMA) ..... WIR
War Insurance Corporation ..... WIC
War Legislation [*British World War II*] ..... WL
War Legislation, Civil Liabilities [*British World War II*] ..... WL(CL)
War Maintenance Reserve [*British*] ..... WMR
War Manpower Commission [*Within the Office of Emergency Management*] [*World War II*] ..... WMC
War Manpower Commission [*Within the Office of Emergency Management*] [*World War II*] ..... WMPC
War Manpower Commission Employment Stabilization (Plan) [*Terminated, 1945*] ..... WMPCES(P)
War Materials, Inc. ..... WMI
War Materiel Procurement Capability (AFIT) ..... WMPC
War Materiel Requirement (AFIT) ..... WMR
War Measures Act ..... WMA
War Memorial ..... WM
War Minerals Relief Commission [*Department of the Interior*] [*Abolished, 1940*] (EGAO) ..... WMRC
War Mobilization Board ..... WMB
War Munition Volunteers [*World War I*] [*British*] ..... WMV
War Office [*British*] ..... WO
War Office Casualty List [*British military*] (DMA) ..... WOCL
War Office Central Card Index [*British military*] (DMA) ..... WOCCI
War Office Selection Board [*British*] ..... WOSB
War on Community Ugliness [*Program*] [*Defunct*] (EA) ..... WOCU
War on Hunger [*Program*] (EA) ..... WOH
War on Hunger Office [*Department of State*] ..... WHO
War on Poverty (OICC) ..... WOP
War on Want [*An association*] (EAIO) ..... WOW
War on Waste [*Navy*] ..... WOW
War on Words ..... WOW
War Operation Plan Response [*Pronounced "whopper"*] [*Name of NORAD computer in film "WarGames"*] ..... WOPR
War Orientation [*Navy*] ..... WO
War Overtime Pay Act [*1943*] ..... WOPA
War Pensions Committee [*British military*] (DMA) ..... WPC
War Plan Division [*World War II*] ..... WPD
War Plan, Long-Range (CINC) ..... WPL
War Plan, Mid-Range ..... WPM
War Plan Naval Transportation Service ..... WPNTS
War Plan Orange [*World War II*] ..... WPO
War Plan, Short-Range ..... WPS
War Planning Memorandum (NATG) ..... WPM
War Planning Slate (CINC) ..... WPS
War Plans ..... WP
War Plans and Training ..... WP & T
War Powers Reporting System ..... WPRS
War Production Board [*World War II*] ..... WPB
War Production Fund [*World War II*] ..... WPF
War Readiness Materiel [*Air Force*] ..... WRM
War Readiness Materiel Rating [*Air Force*] ..... WRMRATE
War Readiness Materiel Status [*Air Force*] ..... WRMSTAT
War Readiness Spares Kit [*Air Force*] (AFM) ..... WRSK
War Records Office ..... WRO
War Refugee Board [*Terminated, 1945*] ..... WRB
War Relief Control Board [*President's*] ..... WRCB
War Relief for Nicaraguans (EA) ..... WRN
War Relocation Authority [*Within Office of Emergency Management*] [*To provide for the relocation of persons whose removal seemed necessary for national security, and for their maintenance and supervision*] [*World War II*] ..... WRA
War Reserve (AABC) ..... WR
War Reserve Allowance (CINC) ..... WRA
War Reserve Functional Coordinating Group [*DoD*] ..... WRFCG
War Reserve Materiel Rating System ..... WRMRS
War Reserve Materiel Requirement (AFIT) ..... WRMR
War Reserve Materiel Requirement Balance (AFIT) ..... WRMRB
War Reserve Materiel Requirement Protectable (AFIT) ..... WRMRP
War Reserve Materiel Stocks ..... WRMS
War Reserve Mobilization (CINC) ..... WRM
War Reserve Munitions ..... WRM
War Reserve Publication Shipment Memorandum ..... WRPSM
War Reserve Stockage List (MCD) ..... WARSL
War Reserve Stocks (AABC) ..... WRS
War Reserve Stocks for Allies (MCD) ..... WRSA
War Reserve (Weapon) ..... WR(W)
War Resisters International [*British*] ..... WRI
War Resisters League (EA) ..... WRL
War Resources Council [*Terminated*] ..... WRC
War Risk ..... WR
War Risk Insurance Decisions [*United States*] [*A publication*] (DLA) ..... WR
War Risks Insurance [*British*] ..... WRI
War Risks Only ..... WRO
War Safety Council ..... WASCO
War Savings Bond [*Allotment for purchase*] [*Navy*] ..... SAVBOND
War Savings Staff ..... WSS
War Scale (ADA) ..... WS
War Service ..... WS
War Service Indefinite ..... WSI
War Service Regulation ..... WSR
War Shipping Administration [*Within Office of Emergency Management*] [*World War II*] ..... WSA
War Shipping Administration Training Organization [*Terminated*] ..... WSATO
War, Strikes, Riots, and Civil Commotions [*Insurance*] (AIA) ..... WSRCC
War Substantive [*British military*] (DMA) ..... WS
War Substantive Lieutenant [*British*] ..... WSL
War Supplies Agency (NATG) ..... WSA
War Supporting Industries and Logistics (MCD) ..... WSI/L
War Tax ..... WT
War Tax Resistance [*An association Defunct*] (EA) ..... WTR
War Trade Board Rulings [*United States*] [*A publication*] (DLA) ..... WTBR
War Trade Department [*British World War II*] ..... WTD
War Training Service [*of the Civil Aeronautics Administration*] [*Formerly Civilian Pilot Training*] [*World War II*] ..... WTS
War Transport [*British military*] (DMA) ..... WT
War Transport Council [*Later, ITWC*] [*World War II*] ..... WTC
War Transportation Board [*World War II*] ..... WTB
War Veterans Administration [*Canada*] ..... WVA
War Veterans Allowance Board [*Canada*] ..... WVAB
War/Watch Foundation (EA) ..... WWF
War Widows Association [*British*] (DBA) ..... WWA
War Widows Guild of Australia ..... WWGA
War Will Never Happen [*Philosophy attributed to the Defense Department by former Deputy Assistant Secretary of Defense John F. Ahearne*] [*1987*] ..... WWNH
War Zone ..... WZ
Warangal [*India*] [*ICAO location identifier*] (ICLI) ..... VOWA
Warangal [*India*] [*Seismograph station code, US Geological Survey*] (SEIS) ..... WGL
Warba School, Warba, MN [*Library symbol*] [*Library of Congress*] (LCLS) ..... MnWbS
Warbelow's Air Ventures, Inc. [*ICAO designator*] (FAAC) ..... VNA
Warbirds of America [*Later, WB*] [*An association*] (EA) ..... WA
Warbirds of America (EA) ..... WB
Warbled Pure Tone [*Speech and language therapy*] (DAVI) ..... WPT
Warburg Investment Management International ..... WIMI
Warburg Public Library, Alberta [*Library symbol National Library of Canada*] (NLC) ..... AWA
Warburg-Keilin System [*Cytochrome-cytochrome oxidase system*] [*Named for Otto Warburg and D. Keilin*] ..... WK
Warburton Minerals [*Vancouver Stock Exchange symbol*] ..... WAM
Ward ..... WD
Ward Air [*ICAO designator*] (AD) ..... WD
Ward Atmosphere Scale [*Psychology*] ..... WAS
Ward Behavior Inventory [*Psychology*] ..... WBI
Ward Clerk [*Medicine*] ..... WC
Ward Foundation (EA) ..... WF
Ward Howell International Group [*British*] ..... WHIG
Ward Indicator Light ..... WIL
Ward Lock Educational [*Publisher*] [*British*] ..... WLE
Ward Manager [*Medicine*] ..... WM
Ward on Belligerent and Neutral Powers [*A publication*] (DLA) ..... War Bell
Ward on Legacies [*A publication*] (DLA) ..... Ward Leg
Ward Pound Ridge [*New York*] [*Seismograph station code, US Geological Survey*] (SEIS) ..... WPR
Ward Room Attendant [*British military*] (DMA) ..... WRA
Ward Secretary [*Medicine*] (MEDA) ..... WS
Wardair Canada Ltd. [*ICAO designator*] (FAAC) ..... WDA
Wardair, Inc. [*Toronto Stock Exchange symbol*] ..... WDI

Wardair International Ltd. [*Toronto Stock Exchange symbol Vancouver Stock Exchange symbol*] .... WDR
Warden [*South Africa*] [*ICAO location identifier*] (ICLI) .... FAWD
Warden .... W
Warden [*Washington*] [*Seismograph station code, US Geological Survey*] (SEIS) .... WRD
Warden .... WRDN
Warden and Smith's State Reports [*3 Ohio*] [*A publication*] (DLA) .... Ward & Sm
Warden and Smith's State Reports [*3 Ohio*] [*A publication*] (DLA) .... Warden & Smith
Warden's Association of America [*Later, NAAWS*] (EA) .... WAA
Wardens in the South East (AIE) .... WISE
Warden's State Reports [*2, 4 Ohio*] [*A publication*] (DLA) .... Ward
Warden's State Reports [*2, 4 Ohio*] [*A publication*] (DLA) .... Warden
Warden's Weekly Law and Bank Bulletin [*Ohio*] [*A publication*] (DLA) .... Warden's Law & Bk Bull
Warder Public Library of Springfield and Clark County, Springfield, OH [*Library symbol Library of Congress*] (LCLS) .... OS
Wardmaster [*British military*] (DMA) .... Wdr
Wardmaster Lieutenant [*British military*] (DMA) .... Wdr L
Wardrobe (WDMC) .... w
Wardrobe .... WR
Wardrobe (MSA) .... WRB
Wardroom [*Aerospace*] .... W
Wardroom [*Navy*] .... WR
Wardroom (WGA) .... WRM
Wardroom Window [*Aerospace*] (KSC) .... WW
Ward's Auto World [*A publication*] .... WAW
Ward's Business Directory [*A publication*] .... WBD
Ward's Engine Update [*A publication*] .... WEU
Ward's Justice of the Peace [*A publication*] (DLA) .... Ward Just
Ward's Law of Nations [*A publication*] (DLA) .... Ward Nat
Ward's Mechanical Tissue Pack [*Dentistry*] (BABM) .... WPk
Ward's Private Companies Profiles [*A publication*] .... WPCP
Ward's Sales Prospector [*A publication*] .... WSP
Wardship .... WARD
Ware (VRA) .... wr
Ware, MA [*Location identifier FAA*] (FAAL) .... UWA
Ware, MA [*AM radio station call letters*] .... WARE
Ware Resources Ltd. [*Vancouver Stock Exchange symbol*] .... WAS
Ware Shoals Railroad Co. [*AAR code*] .... WS
Wareham [*Municipal borough in England*] .... WAREH
Wareham Free Library, Wareham, MA [*Library symbol*] [*Library of Congress*] (LCLS) .... MWar
Warehouse .... W
Warehouse .... Whous
Warehouse (AABC) .... WHS
Warehouse (ODBW) .... whs
Warehouse (AAG) .... WHSE
Warehouse (VRA) .... wrhs
Warehouse .... WRHSE
Warehouse Book .... WB
Warehouse Distributor .... WD
Warehouse Distributors Association for Leisure and Mobile Products (EA) .... WDA
Warehouse Distributors Association for Leisure and Mobile Products (EA) .... WDALMP
Warehouse Economy Outlet [*A & P Co.*] .... WEO
Warehouse Industry National Standards Guidelines (ACRL) .... WINS
Warehouse Keeper [*British*] (ROG) .... WK
Warehouse Material Stores (AAG) .... WMS
Warehouse Receipt [*Often negotiable*] .... WR
Warehouse Warrant .... WW
Warehouseman [*Legal shorthand*] (LWAP) .... WHSMAN
Warehouseman (AABC) .... WHSMN
Warehousing .... WHSING
Warehousing .... WHSNG
Warehousing Education and Research Council (EA) .... WERC
Warehousing Gross Performance Measurement System (AFM) .... WGPMS
Waren [*Indonesia*] [*ICAO location identifier*] (ICLI) .... WABW
Warenzeichen [*Trademark*] [*German*] .... Wz
Ware's United States District Court Reports [*A publication*] (DLA) .... Ware
Ware's United States District Court Reports [*A publication*] (DLA) .... Ware's CC Rep
Ware's United States District Court Reports [*A publication*] (DLA) .... Ware's Rep
WARF [*Wartime Replacement Factors*] **Intermediate Materiel Processor** [*Military*] .... WIMP
Warfare (AFM) .... WARF
Warfare Analysis and Research System [*Navy*] .... WARS
Warfare Analysis Group [*Navy*] .... WAG
Warfare Analysis Laboratory [*Johns Hopkins University/Applied Physics Laboratory*] (DOMA) .... WAL
Warfare Commanders Course (DOMA) .... WCC
Warfare Mission Area (DOMA) .... WMA
Warfare Systems Directorate (MCD) .... WSD
Warfare Systems School [*Air Force*] (AFM) .... WSS
Warfare [*Commanders*] **Team Training** (DOMA) .... WTT
Warfare Vision Laboratory [*Army*] .... WVL
Warfarin [*Pharmacology*] (DAVI) .... WARF
Warfarin Dose Index .... WDI
Warfighter Information Network [*Army*] .... WIN
Warfighters' Simulation [*DoD*] .... WARSIM
Warfighting Rapid Acquisition Program .... WRAP
Warhead [*Nuclear*] (NG) .... W
Warhead (AAG) .... WARHD

Warhead .... WH
Warhead .... WHD
Warhead Attack Cruise Killer (MCD) .... WHACK
Warhead Detection Indicator (AAG) .... WDI
Warhead Electrical Connector .... WEC
Warhead Electrical System .... WES
Warhead Engagement Program [*Military*] .... WHEP
Warhead Interface Unit (MCD) .... WIU
Warhead Output Evaluation (MCD) .... WOE
Warhead Replacement Tactical Telemetry System (DWSG) .... WRTTM
Warhead Section [*Military*] (AABC) .... WHDS
Warhead Working Group [*Military*] .... WWG
Warheading Building (NATG) .... W/H
Warheads and Special Projects Laboratory [*Picatinny Arsenal*] .... W/SP
Warheads and Special Weapons Laboratory (MCD) .... WSWL
Waring Cox Law Firm, Memphis, TN [*Library symbol*] [*Library of Congress*] (LCLS) .... TMWC
Waris [*Papua New Guinea*] [*Seismograph station code, US Geological Survey*] (SEIS) .... WAA
Waris [*Indonesia*] [*ICAO location identifier*] (ICLI) .... WAJR
Warkworth Public Library, Ontario [*Library symbol National Library of Canada*] (NLC) .... OWAR
Warkworth Public Library, Warkworth, ON, Canada [*Library symbol Library of Congress*] (LCLS) .... CaOWar
Warland Creek [*Montana*] [*Seismograph station code, US Geological Survey Closed*] (SEIS) .... WCM
Warm .... W
Warm [*NWS*] (FAAC) .... WRM
Warm Air .... WA
Warm and Dry (MEDA) .... w/d
Warm Autoimmune Hemolytic Anemia [*Medicine*] .... WAIHA
Warm Core Ring [*Oceanography*] .... WCR
Warm Cranking Amperes [*Battery*] [*Automotive engineering*] .... WCA
Warm, Family Comedy [*Type of television show*] .... WARMEDY
Warm Fluctuating Temperatures .... WFT
Warm Fog Dispenser System (MCD) .... WFDS
Warm Front [*NWS*] (FAAC) .... WRMFNT
Warm Front Passage [*NWS*] (FAAC) .... WFP
Warm Gas Distribution System .... WGDS
Warm Gas Generator .... WGG
Warm Ionized Medium [*Astrophysics*] .... WIM
Warm Month Mean Temperature [*Climatology*] .... WMMT
Warm Neutral Medium [*Astrophysics*] .... WNM
Warm Pipe [*Nuclear energy*] (NRCH) .... WP
Warm Pool [*Oceanography*] .... WP
Warm Run Record .... WRR
Warm Shop [*Nuclear energy*] (NRCH) .... WS
Warm Springs [*Nevada*] [*Seismograph station code, US Geological Survey Closed*] (SEIS) .... WSN
Warm Springs, GA [*FM radio station call letters*] .... WJSP
Warm Springs, OR [*FM radio station call letters*] .... KTWI
Warm Springs, OR [*FM radio station call letters*] .... KWSO
Warm Springs Repeater [*Nevada*] [*Seismograph station code, US Geological Survey Closed*] (SEIS) .... WSR
Warm Tone [*Photography*] .... WT
Warm Up Time .... WUT
Warm White (DAC) .... WW
Warm White Deluxe (DAC) .... WWX
Warmbaths [*South Africa*] [*ICAO location identifier*] (ICLI) .... FAWA
Warm-Blood Cardioplegia [*Medicine*] .... WBC
Warmed-Over Flavor [*Food technology*] .... WOF
Warmifontaine [*Belgium*] [*Seismograph station code, US Geological Survey*] (SEIS) .... WRM
Warming .... WM
Warming Pan [*Refers to a clergyman holding a job under a bond of resignation*] [*Obsolete Slang British*] (DSUE) .... WP
Warminster, PA [*Location identifier FAA*] (FAAL) .... NJP
Warminster, PA [*FM radio station call letters*] .... WRDV
Warmley, SK [*Television station call letters*] .... CIEW
Warmth Detection Threshold .... WDT
Warm-Up Oxidation Catalyst [*Automotive engineering*] .... WUOC
Warm-Up Three-Way Catalyst [*Automotive engineering*] .... WUTWC
Warnaco Group [*NYSE symbol*] (SPSG) .... WAC
Warnaco Group, Inc. [*Associated Press*] (SAG) .... Warnaco
Warnaco Group'A' [*NYSE symbol*] (SPSG) .... WAC
Warnaco of Canada Ltd. [*Toronto Stock Exchange symbol*] .... WRN
Warner Amex Satellite Entertainment Co. [*Cable television*] .... WASEC
Warner & Swasey Co., Solon, OH [*OCLC symbol*] (OCLC) .... WAS
Warner Audio Publishing .... WAP
Warner Baird Library, Spring Lake, MI [*Library symbol Library of Congress*] (LCLS) .... MiSpl
Warner Brothers [*Television network*] .... WB
Warner Brothers, Inc., Research Library, Burbank, CA [*Library symbol Library of Congress*] (LCLS) .... CBbW
Warner Brothers Worldwide Publishing [*Commercial firm*] .... WBWP
Warner Insurance Services [*NYSE symbol*] (SPSG) .... WCP
Warner Insurance Services [*Associated Press*] (SAG) .... WrnIns
Warner Insurance Svcs [*NASDAQ symbol*] (TTSB) .... WISI
Warner Library, Tarrytown, NY [*Library symbol Library of Congress*] (LCLS) .... NTa
Warner Pacific College, Portland, OR [*Library symbol Library of Congress*] (LCLS) .... OrPWP
Warner Pacific College, Portland, OR [*OCLC symbol*] (OCLC) .... OWP
Warner Public Library, Alberta [*Library symbol National Library of Canada*] (NLC) .... AWAR
Warner Publishing Services .... WPS

Warner Robins Air Logistics Center [*Formerly, WRAMA*] (MCD) ... WRALC
Warner Robins Air Materiel Area [*Later, WRALC*] ... WRAMA
Warner Robins, GA [*Location identifier FAA*] (FAAL) ... RJM
Warner Robins, GA [*AM radio station call letters*] ... WCOP
Warner Robins, GA [*AM radio station call letters*] (RBYB) ... WITK
Warner Robins, GA [*FM radio station call letters*] (RBYB) ... WRBG
Warner Robins, GA [*FM radio station call letters*] ... WYIQ
Warner-Eddison Associates, Inc. [*Information service or system*] (IID) ... WEA
Warner-Lambert [*NYSE symbol*] (TTSB) ... WLA
Warner-Lambert Canada Ltd., Scarborough, Ontario [*Library symbol National Library of Canada*] (NLC) ... OTWLC
Warner-Lambert Canada Ltd., Sheridan Park, ON, Canada [*Library symbol Library of Congress*] (LCLS) ... CaOTWLC
Warner-Lambert Co. [*Associated Press*] (SAG) ... WarnL
Warner-Lambert Co. [*NYSE symbol*] (SPSG) ... WLA
Warner-Lambert/Parke-Davis [*Computer files of chemical and biological data*] ... WL/PD
Warner-Lambert Pharmaceutical Co. [*Research code symbol*] ... A
Warner-Lambert Pharmaceutical Co. [*Research code symbol*] ... NC
Warner-Lambert Pharmaceutical Co. [*Research code symbol*] ... P
Warner-Lambert Pharmaceutical Co. [*Research code symbol*] ... Pe
Warner-Lambert Pharmaceutical Co. [*Research code symbol*] ... W
Warner-Lambert Pharmaceutical Co. ... WL
Warner-Lambert Pharmaceutical Co. [*Research code symbol*] ... WR
Warner-Lambert Research Institute [*New Jersey*] ... WLRI
Warner-Lambert Research Institute, Morris Plains, NJ [*Library symbol Library of Congress*] (LCLS) ... NjMpW
Warning [*Railroad signal arm*] [*British*] ... W
Warning (NASA) ... WARN
Warning (AFM) ... WNG
Warning (MSA) ... WRN
Warning [*NWS*] (FAAC) ... WRNG
Warning (MUGU) ... WXG
Warning and Attack Assessment (MCD) ... WAAS
Warning and Caution Computer [*Aviation*] (MCD) ... WACC
Warning and Caution System [*Aviation*] (MCD) ... WACS
Warning and Indications in Europe (MCD) ... WINE
Warning and Report System (CET) ... WRS
Warning Area [*Followed by identification*] ... W
Warning Assessment Logic Terminal [*Air Force*] ... WALT
Warning Computer [*Aviation*] ... WC
Warning Decision Support System (USDC) ... WDSS
Warning Decision Support System [*Marine science*] (OSRA) ... WDSS
Warning Improvement Study Plan (MCD) ... WISP
Warning in Korea (MCD) ... WINK
Warning Indicators System Europe (MCD) ... WISE
Warning Information Correlation (MCD) ... WIC
Warning Light (SAA) ... WL
Warning Light Driver (IAA) ... WLD
Warning Light Monitor ... WLM
Warning Light Relay Driver ... WLRD
Warning Notice: Sensitive Intelligence Sources and Methods Involved (MCD) ... WNINTEL
Warning Order [*Military*] (INF) ... WARNORD
Warning Order ... WO
Warning Point Photocell ... WPPC
Warning Tag (AAG) ... WT
Warnkenhagen [*German Democratic Republic*] [*Geomagnetic observatory code*] ... WRH
Warnock Hersey Co. Ltd., Montreal, PQ, Canada [*Library symbol Library of Congress*] (LCLS) ... CaQMW
Warnock Hersey Co. Ltd., Montreal, Quebec [*Library symbol National Library of Canada*] (NLC) ... QMW
Warnock Hersey International Ltd., Vancouver, BC, Canada [*Library symbol Library of Congress*] (LCLS) ... CaBVaWH
Warnock Hersey International Ltd., Vancouver, British Columbia [*Library symbol National Library of Canada*] (NLC) ... BVAWH
War-Office Letter [*An order or an instruction*] [*British*] ... WOL
Warp 10 Technologies [*NASDAQ symbol*] (TTSB) ... WARPF
Warp 10 Technologies, Inc. [*NASDAQ symbol*] (SAG) ... WARP
Warp 10 Technologies, Inc. [*Associated Press*] (SAG) ... Warp10
Warping ... WRPG
Warracknabeal [*Victoria, Australia*] [*Airport symbol*] (AD) ... WKB
Warramunga Array [*Australia Seismograph station code, US Geological Survey*] (SEIS) ... WB2
Warramunga Array [*Australia Seismograph station code, US Geological Survey*] (SEIS) ... WB3
Warramunga Array [*Australia Seismograph station code, US Geological Survey*] (SEIS) ... WCB
Warramunga Array [*Australia Seismograph station code, US Geological Survey*] (SEIS) ... WR2
Warramunga Array [*Australia Seismograph station code, US Geological Survey*] (SEIS) ... WRA
Warramunga Array [*Australia Seismograph station code, US Geological Survey*] (SEIS) ... WRB
Warrant [*A document entitling holder to purchase a given issue of stock*] [*Investment term*] ... W
Warrant ... WAR
Warrant [*A document entitling holder to purchase a given issue of stock*] [*Investment term*] ... Warr
Warrant (ROG) ... WARRT
Warrant (AABC) ... WRNT
Warrant ... WRRNT
Warrant ... WT
Warrant Apprehension Narcotics Team [*In US Marshal Service's "Operation WANT"*] ... WANT
Warrant Claims Action [*Army*] ... WCA
Warrant Communication Officer [*British military*] (DMA) ... WCO
Warrant Issued for Extradite ... WAREX
Warrant Loss to Enlisted Status [*Revocation of appointment*] [*Navy*] ... WLTE
Warrant Master-at-Arms [*British military*] (DMA) ... WMAA
Warrant Mechanician [*British military*] (DMA) ... WM
Warrant of Arrest ... W/A
Warrant Office Entry Course, Reserve Component [*Army*] (INF) ... WOEC-RC
Warrant Officer [*Usually in combination with numbers to denote serviceman's grade*] [*Military*] ... WO
Warrant Officer Advanced Course [*Army*] (INF) ... WOAC
Warrant Officer Candidate Military Development Course ... WOCMDC
Warrant Officer Education System ... WOES
Warrant Officer Entry Course [*Military*] (INF) ... WOEC
Warrant Officer Flight Training [*Army*] (INF) ... WOFT
Warrant Officer Hospital Corps ... WOHC
Warrant Officer Junior Grade ... WOJG
Warrant Officer One [*Army*] ... WO1
Warrant Officer Personnel Management System [*Army*] ... WORMS
Warrant Officer Professional Development [*Military*] (MCD) ... WOPD
Warrant Officer Qualification Test [*Military*] ... WOQT
Warrant Officer, Royal Marines [*Navy British*] (ROG) ... RMWO
Warrant Officer Senior Course [*Army*] (DOMA) ... WOSC
Warrant Officer Service [*Army*] (DOMA) ... WOS
Warrant Officer Technical and Tactical Certification System [*Army*] ... WOTTCS
Warrant Officer Training System [*Military*] (INF) ... WOTS
Warrant Officers Association of the United States of America [*Defunct*] (EA) ... WOA
Warrant Ordnance Officer [*Navy British*] ... WOO
Warrant Stores Officer [*Navy British*] ... WSO
Warrant Telegraphist [*British military*] ... W Tel
Warrant Telegraphist [*British military*] (DMA) ... WT
Warrant to Pollute ... WTP
Warrant Wardmaster [*British military*] (DMA) ... W Wdr
Warrant Writer [*Navy British*] ... WW
Warrant Writer Officer [*British military*] (DMA) ... WWO
Warrantech Corp. [*Associated Press*] (SAG) ... Warntc
Warrantech Corp. [*New York, NY NASDAQ symbol*] (NQ) ... WTEC
Warranted (WGA) ... WARRTD
Warranted ... WD
Warranted Existing Class Maintained (DS) ... WECM
Warranty (MSA) ... WARR
Warranty Mean Time Between Failures [*Army*] ... WMTBF
Warranty [*Cost Effectiveness*] **Model** ... WARM
Warren Air Force Base [*Wyoming*] (AAG) ... WAFB
Warren & Ouachita Valley Railway Co. [*AAR code*] ... WOV
Warren & Saline River Railroad Co. [*AAR code*] ... WSR
Warren, AR [*AM radio station call letters*] ... KWRF
Warren, AR [*FM radio station call letters*] ... KWRF-FM
Warren Bancorp [*NASDAQ symbol*] (TTSB) ... WRNB
Warren Bancorp, Inc. [*Associated Press*] (SAG) ... Warren
Warren Bancorp, Inc. [*NASDAQ symbol*] (NQ) ... WRNB
Warren County Clerk, Belvidere, NJ [*Library symbol Library of Congress*] (LCLS) ... NjBelvCoC
Warren County Historical Society, Lebanon, OH [*Library symbol Library of Congress*] (LCLS) ... OLeWHi
Warren County Library, Belvidere, NJ [*Library symbol Library of Congress*] (LCLS) ... NjBelvW
Warren County Memorial Library, Warrenton, NC [*Library symbol Library of Congress*] (LCLS) ... NcWarW
Warren County Recorder's Office, Williamsport, IN [*Library symbol Library of Congress*] (LCLS) ... InWilCR
Warren Elementary School, Warren, MN [*Library symbol*] [*Library of Congress*] (LCLS) ... MnWarE
Warren Explorations Ltd. [*Toronto Stock Exchange symbol*] ... WEL
Warren Gamaliel Harding [*US president, 1865-1923*] ... WGH
Warren General Hospital, Warren, OH [*Library symbol*] [*Library of Congress*] (LCLS) ... OWH
Warren, Gorham & Lamont, Inc. [*Publisher*] ... WG & L
Warren, Gorham & Lamont, Inc. (DLA) ... WGLI
Warren Junior/Senior High School, Warren, MN [*Library symbol*] [*Library of Congress*] (LCLS) ... MnWarJS
Warren Library Association and County Division, Warren, PA [*Library symbol Library of Congress*] (LCLS) ... PWa
Warren Library Association and County Division, Warren, PA [*OCLC symbol*] (OCLC) ... WDL
Warren, MI [*FM radio station call letters*] ... WPHS
Warren. Moral, Social, and Professional Duties of Attorneys and Solicitors [*2nd ed.*] [*1851*] [*A publication*] (DLA) ... War Prof Dut
Warren, OH [*AM radio station call letters*] ... WANR
Warren, OH [*AM radio station call letters*] ... WRRO
Warren, PA [*AM radio station call letters*] ... WNAE
Warren, PA [*FM radio station call letters*] ... WRRN
Warren Public Library, Warren, MI [*Library symbol Library of Congress*] (LCLS) ... MiWar
Warren Public Library, Warren, OH [*Library symbol Library of Congress*] (LCLS) ... OW
Warren Public Library, Warren, OH [*OCLC symbol*] (OCLC) ... WPL
Warren Spring Laboratory [*Research center British*] (DCTA) ... WSL
Warren State Hospital, Warren, PA [*OCLC symbol*] (OCLC) ... PHW
Warren Township Public Library, Warren, NJ [*Library symbol Library of Congress*] (LCLS) ... NjWa
Warren, VT [*FM radio station call letters*] ... WDEV-FM

Warren Wilson College [*Swannan, NC*] ... WWC
Warren Wilson College, Swannanoa, NC [*Library symbol Library of Congress*] (LCLS) ... NcSwW
Warren-Newport Public Library District, Gurnee, IL [*OCLC symbol*] (OCLC) ... IHZ
Warren's Adventures of an Attorney in Search of Practice [*A publication*] (DLA) ... War Adv Att
Warren's Law Studies [*A publication*] (DLA) ... War L St
Warren's Ohio Criminal Law [*A publication*] (DLA) ... War Cr L
Warrensburg, MO [*FM radio station call letters*] ... KCMW
Warrensburg, MO [*AM radio station call letters*] ... KOKO
Warrensburg, NY [*FM radio station call letters*] ... WKBE
Warren-Teed [*Commercial firm*] (DAVI) ... Warren-T
Warren-Teed [*Commercial firm*] (DAVI) ... W-T
Warrenton, MO [*FM radio station call letters*] ... KFAV
Warrenton, MO [*AM radio station call letters*] ... KWRE
Warrenton, NC [*AM radio station call letters*] (RBYB) ... WARR
Warrenton, NC [*FM radio station call letters*] (RBYB) ... WXNC
Warrenton Railroad Co. [*AAR code*] ... WAR
Warrenton Railroad Co. [*Later, WAR*] [*AAR code*] ... WRNT
Warrenton, VA [*FM radio station call letters*] (RBYB) ... WINX-FM
Warrenton, VA [*AM radio station call letters*] ... WKCW
Warrenton, VA [*AM radio station call letters*] ... WPRZ
Warrenton, VA [*FM radio station call letters*] ... WQRA
Warrenton, VA [*FM radio station call letters*] ... WRCY
Warrick Enquirer, Boonville, IN [*Library symbol Library of Congress*] (LCLS) ... InBooE
Warrington, Inc. [*Toronto Stock Exchange symbol*] ... WRR
Warrington Wire Gauge (BARN) ... WWG
Warrior, AL [*FM radio station call letters*] (RBYB) ... WBHK-FM
Warrior, AL [*FM radio station call letters*] ... WLBI
Warrior Industry Ltd. [*Vancouver Stock Exchange symbol*] ... WAR
Warrior Preparation Center [*Kaiserslautern, Federal Republic of Germany*] [*USAREUR*] ... WPC
Warrior River Terminal Co. [*AAR code*] ... WRT
Warrnambool [*Australia Airport symbol*] (OAG) ... WMB
Warroad Elementary School, Warroad, MN [*Library symbol*] [*Library of Congress*] (LCLS) ... MnWarrE
Warroad High School, Warroad, MN [*Library symbol*] [*Library of Congress*] (LCLS) ... MnWarrH
Warroad, MN [*FM radio station call letters*] ... KKWQ
Warroad, MN [*Location identifier FAA*] (FAAL) ... RAD
Warroad Public Library, Warroad, MN [*Library symbol*] [*Library of Congress*] (LCLS) ... MnWarr
Wars [*Josephus*] (BJA) ... JosWars
Wars of the Jews [*of Josephus*] [*A publication*] (BJA) ... WJ
Warsak [*Pakistan*] [*Seismograph station code, US Geological Survey*] (SEIS) ... WRS
Warsaw [*Poland*] [*Seismograph station code, US Geological Survey*] (SEIS) ... WAR
Warsaw [*Poland*] [*Airport symbol*] (OAG) ... WAW
Warsaw Ghetto Resistance Organization (EA) ... WAGRO
Warsaw High School Library, Warsaw, NY [*OCLC symbol*] (OCLC) ... RXK
Warsaw, IL [*FM radio station call letters*] (RBYB) ... WIUW
Warsaw, IN [*Location identifier FAA*] (FAAL) ... ASW
Warsaw, IN [*Location identifier FAA*] (FAAL) ... TZY
Warsaw, IN [*AM radio station call letters*] ... WRSW
Warsaw, IN [*FM radio station call letters*] ... WRSW-FM
Warsaw, MO [*FM radio station call letters*] ... KAYQ
Warsaw, NY [*AM radio station call letters*] ... WCJW
Warsaw, NY [*FM radio station call letters*] ... WCOU
Warsaw Pact (NATG) ... WP
Warsaw Pact/Ballistic Research Laboratory (MCD) ... WPBRL
Warsaw Pact Countries (MCD) ... WPC
Warsaw Pact Member (WDAA) ... WP
Warsaw Pact Organization (MCD) ... WPO
Warsaw Public Library, Warsaw, IN [*Library symbol Library of Congress*] (LCLS) ... InWars
Warsaw Public Library, Warsaw, NC [*Library symbol Library of Congress*] (LCLS) ... NcWaw
Warsaw Times-Union, Warsaw, IN [*Library symbol Library of Congress*] (LCLS) ... InWarsTU
Warsaw Treaty Organization ... WTO
Warsaw, VA [*AM radio station call letters*] ... WNNT
Warsaw, VA [*FM radio station call letters*] ... WNNT-FM
Warstar Resources, Inc. [*Vancouver Stock Exchange symbol*] ... WTR
War-Supporting Industry ... WSI
Warszawa [*Poland ICAO location identifier*] (ICLI) ... EPRL
Warszawa/Okecie [*Poland ICAO location identifier*] (ICLI) ... EPWA
Wartburg College, Waverly, IA [*Library symbol Library of Congress*] (LCLS) ... IaWavW
Wartburg College, Waverly, IA [*OCLC symbol*] (OCLC) ... IOW
Wartburg Theological Seminary, Dubuque, IA [*Library symbol Library of Congress*] (LCLS) ... IaDuW
Wartburg, TN [*AM radio station call letters*] ... WECO
Wartburg, TN [*FM radio station call letters*] ... WECO-FM
Wartegg-Zeichentest [*Wartegg Symbol Test*] [*German Psychology*] ... WZT
Warthin-Starry [*Silver impregnation stain*] ... WS
Wartime ... WT
Wartime Active Replacement Factors (AABC) ... WARF
Wartime Aircraft Activity (AFM) ... WAA
Wartime Aircraft Activity Reporting [*System*] ... WAAR
Wartime Alignment of Reserve and Active Medical Systems ... WARAMS
Wartime Availability of Medical Personnel upon Mobilization ... WAMPUM
Wartime Basic Plan ... WBP
Wartime Capability Play, Short Range (SAA) ... WPS
Wartime Fuel Factors ... WAFF
Wartime Guidance [*Air Force*] (AFM) ... WG
Wartime Host Nation Support ... WHNS
Wartime Host Nation Support Information Management System (DOMA) ... WHNSIMS
Wartime Individual Augmentation Program [*Military*] ... WIAP
Wartime Information Board [*World War II Canada*] ... WIB
Wartime Information Security Program (MCD) ... WISP
Wartime Instruction Manual for Merchant Ships [*For deck officers of the United States Merchant Marine; popularly known as the "Convoy Bible"*] [*World War II*] ... WIMS
Wartime Intelligence Plan (NATG) ... WIP
Wartime Intelligence Plan, Allied Command Europe (NATG) ... WIPACE
Wartime Lines of Communication, Europe (AABC) ... WARLOCE
Wartime Logistics (AABC) ... WARLOG
Wartime Manpower and Personnel Readiness Team [*Military*] ... WMPRT
Wartime Manpower Planning System ... WARMAPS
Wartime Operational Availability [*DoD*] ... Aow
Wartime Order of Battle (NATG) ... WORBAT
Wartime Pacific Routing Instructions [*Navy*] ... WPRI
Wartime Personnel Replacement Operation [*Military*] ... WPRO
Wartime Personnel Requirements (NATG) ... WPR
Wartime Prices and Trade Board ... WPTB
Wartime Repair Parts Consumption (MCD) ... WARPAC
Wartime Replacement Factors [*DoD*] ... WARF
Wartime Report (MCD) ... WR
Wartime Requirements [*Air Force document*] (AFM) ... WR
Wartime Requirements for Ammunition, Materiel, and Personnel ... WARRAMP
Wartime Reserve Mode [*Military*] ... WARM
Wartime Standard Support System for Foreign Armed Forces (MCD) ... WSSSFAF
Wartime Support Capability ... WARSCAP
Wartime Traffic Priority List (NATG) ... WATPL
Wartime Unit Aircraft Activity (AFM) ... WUAA
Warton [*British ICAO location identifier*] (ICLI) ... EGNO
Warton BAE [*British ICAO designator*] (FAAC) ... WTN
Warvelle on Abstracts of Title [*A publication*] (DLA) ... Warv Abst
Warvelle's Elements of Real Property [*A publication*] (DLA) ... Warv El RP
Warvelle's Vendors and Purchasers of Real Property [*A publication*] (DLA) ... Warv V & P
Warwick China Collectors Club [*Defunct*] (EA) ... WCCC
Warwick, NY [*AM radio station call letters*] ... WTBQ
Warwick Public Library, Warwick, RI [*Library symbol Library of Congress*] (LCLS) ... RWar
Warwick Railway Co. [*AAR code*] ... WRWK
Warwick, RI [*AM radio station call letters*] ... WARV
Warwick's Opinions [*City Solicitor of Philadelphia, PA*] [*A publication*] (DLA) ... War Op
Warwick's Opinions [*City Solicitor of Philadelphia, PA*] [*A publication*] (DLA) ... Warwick's Op
Warwickshire (ROG) ... WAR
Warwickshire [*County in England*] ... WARKS
Warwickshire [*County in England*] ... WARW
Warwickshire [*County in England*] ... WARWICKS
Warwickshire [*County in England*] ... WARWS
Warwickshire Aerocentre Ltd. [*British*] [*FAA designator*] (FAAC) ... ATX
Warwickshire and Worcestershire Yeomanry [*British military*] (DMA) ... WWY
Warwickshire Yeomanry [*British military*] (DMA) ... WKY
Warwickshire Yeomanry [*British military*] (DMA) ... WY
Warwickshire Yeomanry Cavalry [*British military*] (DMA) ... WYC
Was Received ... W/R
Wasabi Resources Ltd. [*Toronto Stock Exchange symbol Vancouver Stock Exchange symbol*] ... WRS
Wasaga Beach Public Library, Ontario [*Library symbol National Library of Canada*] (BIB) ... OWAB
Wasatch Academy, Mount Pleasant, UT [*Library symbol Library of Congress*] (LCLS) ... UMpW
Wasawings AB [*Finland ICAO designator*] (FAAC) ... WWS
Wasaya Airways Ltd. [*Canada ICAO designator*] (FAAC) ... WSG
Wascana Campus, Saskatchewan Institute of Applied Science and Technology, R egina, Saskatchewan [*Library symbol National Library of Canada*] (NLC) ... SRRI
Wascana Hospital, Regina, Saskatchewan [*Library symbol National Library of Canada*] (NLC) ... SRSH
Wascana Hospital, Regina, SK, Canada [*Library symbol Library of Congress*] (LCLS) ... CaSRSH
Wascana Institute of Applied Arts and Sciences, Regina, SK, Canada [*Library symbol Library of Congress*] (LCLS) ... CaSRRI
Wasco, CA [*AM radio station call letters*] ... KERI
Wasco County Library, The Dalles, OR [*Library symbol Library of Congress*] (LCLS) ... OrTW
Waseca Inter-Library Resource Exchange [*Library network*] ... WIRE
Waseca, MN [*Location identifier FAA*] (FAAL) ... ACQ
Waseca, MN [*AM radio station call letters*] ... KOWO
Waseca, MN [*FM radio station call letters*] ... KRUE
Waseda University. Institute of Comparative Law. Bulletin [*Tokyo, Japan*] [*A publication*] (DLA) ... Bull Waseda Univ Inst of Comp Law
Wash (VRA) ... wa
Wash Basin ... WB
Wash Bucket ... WB
Wash Fountain (AAG) ... WF
Wash Frock Salesmen's Association (EA) ... WFSA
Wash Mutual $6 Cv Per'D'Pfd [*NASDAQ symbol*] (TTSB) ... WAMUN
Wash Nat'l Gas 7.45%Sr II Pfd [*NYSE symbol*] (TTSB) ... WNGPr
Wash Nat'l Gas 8.50%Sr III Pfd [*NYSE symbol*] (TTSB) ... WNGPrA

Wash Out [*Medicine*] .... WO
Wash Sale (MHDW) .... WS
Wash Trough .... WT
Wash Up [*Printing*] (DGA) .... WU
Washable Base (ADA) .... WB
Washable Suits, Novelties, and Sportswear Contractors Association (EA) .... WSNSCA
Washabo [*Surinam*] [*ICAO location identifier*] (ICLI) .... SMWS
Washabo [*Surinam*] [*Airport symbol*] (OAG) .... WSO
Washakie County Library, Ten Sleep Branch, Ten Sleep, WY [*Library symbol Library of Congress*] (LCLS) .... WyTs
Washakie County Library, Worland, WY [*Library symbol Library of Congress*] (LCLS) .... WyWo
Washboard [*Musical instrument used in some jazz bands*] .... WBD
Washburn and Moen [*Wire gauge*] .... W & M
Washburn and Moen Gauge (MSA) .... W & M GA
Washburn Elementary School, Duluth, MN [*Library symbol*] [*Library of Congress*] (LCLS) .... MnDuWE
Washburn on Criminal Law [*A publication*] (DLA) .... Wash Cr L
Washburn on Easements and Servitudes [*A publication*] (DLA) .... Wash Ease
Washburn on Easements and Servitudes [*A publication*] (DLA) .... Washb Easem
Washburn on Real Property [*A publication*] (DLA) .... Wash RP
Washburn on Real Property [*A publication*] (DLA) .... Washb Real Prop
Washburn University of Topeka (GAGS) .... Washburn U
Washburn University of Topeka [*Kansas*] .... WUT
Washburn University of Topeka, School of Law, Topeka, KS [*Library symbol Library of Congress*] (LCLS) .... KTW-L
Washburn University of Topeka, Topeka, KS [*OCLC symbol*] (OCLC) .... KKW
Washburn University of Topeka, Topeka, KS [*Library symbol Library of Congress*] (LCLS) .... KTW
Washburn University School of Law (DLA) .... WUSL
Washburn, WI [*FM radio station call letters*] .... WEGZ
Washburn's Reports [*18-23 Vermont*] [*A publication*] (DLA) .... Washburn
Washburn's Vermont Digest [*A publication*] (DLA) .... Wash Dig
Washburton and Hazard's Reports [*Prince Edward Island, Canada*] [*A publication*] (DLA) .... Wash & Haz PEI
Washed, Filtered Red Blood Cells [*Hematology*] .... WFRBC
Washed Overboard [*Shipping*] .... WOB
Washed Red Blood Cells [*Hematology*] (DAVI) .... WRBC
Washed Red Cells [*Medicine*] .... WRC
Washer .... WA
Washer (AAG) .... WASH
Washer (MSA) .... WSHR
Washer Visual Acuity Screening Technique [*Visual ability test*] .... WVAST
Washim [*India*] [*ICAO location identifier*] (ICLI) .... VAWM
Washine Chemical Corp. [*Research code symbol*] .... WS
Washing (MSA) .... WSHG
Washing .... WSHG
Washing Corrosion Control (MCD) .... WACC
Washing Machine [*Classified advertising*] (ADA) .... W/M
Washington [*District of Columbia*] [*ICAO location identifier*] (ICLI) .... KARF
Washington [*District of Columbia*] [*ICAO location identifier*] (ICLI) .... KDCC
Washington [*District of Columbia*] [*ICAO location identifier*] (ICLI) .... KRWA
Washington [*District of Columbia*] [*ICAO location identifier*] (ICLI) .... KWBC
Washington [*MARC geographic area code Library of Congress*] (LCCP) .... n-us-wa
Washington [*State*] [*Postal code*] .... WA
Washington [*District of Columbia*] [*Airport symbol*] (OAG) .... WAS
Washington [*District of Columbia*] [*Seismograph station code, US Geological Survey Closed*] (SEIS) .... WAS
Washington (AAG) .... WASH
Washington (ODBW) .... Wash
Washington [*MARC country of publication code Library of Congress*] (LCCP) .... wau
Washington [*Diocesan abbreviation*] [*District of Columbia*] (TOCD) .... WDC
Washington [*Obsolete*] (ROG) .... WN
Washington [*Pennsylvania*] [*Airport symbol*] (OAG) .... WSG
Washington Administrative Code [*A publication*] (AAGC) .... WAC
Washington Administrative Code [*A publication*] (DLA) .... Wash Admin Code
Washington Air Defense Sector [*ADC*] .... WAADS
Washington, Alaska, Montana, and Idaho [*Program for states without medical schools*] .... WAMI
Washington and Jefferson College [*Pennsylvania*] (IIA) .... W & J
Washington and Jefferson College [*Pennsylvania*] .... WJC
Washington and Jefferson College, Washington, PA [*Library symbol Library of Congress*] (LCLS) .... PWW
Washington and Lee University [*Lexington, VA*] .... W & L
Washington and Lee University (GAGS) .... Wash & Lee U
Washington and Lee University [*Virginia*] .... WLU
Washington and Lee University, Law Library, Lexington, VA [*Library symbol Library of Congress*] (LCLS) .... ViLxW-L
Washington and Lee University, Lexington, VA [*Library symbol Library of Congress*] (LCLS) .... ViLxW
Washington and Lee University, Lexington, VA [*OCLC symbol*] (OCLC) .... VLW
Washington & Old Dominion R. R. [*AAR code*] .... WOD
Washington Appellate Reports [*A publication*] (DLA) .... W Ap
Washington Appellate Reports [*A publication*] (DLA) .... Wa A
Washington Appellate Reports [*A publication*] (DLA) .... Wash App
Washington Aqueduct Division [*Army*] .... WAD
Washington Archaeological Research Center [*Washington State University*] [*Research center*] (RCD) .... WARC
Washington Area Girls Soccer League (TAG) .... WAGS
Washington, Baltimore & Annapolis Railroad [*Nickname: Wobble, Bump, and Amble*] .... WB & A
Washington Bar News [*A publication*] (DLA) .... Wash B News
Washington Bay [*Alaska*] [*Airport symbol*] (AD) .... WBA
Washington Beverage Insight [*Wells & Associates*] [*Information service or system*] (IID) .... WBI
Washington Bibliographic Service [*Information service or system*] (IID) .... WBS
Washington/Bolling Air Force Base [*District of Columbia*] [*ICAO location identifier*] (ICLI) .... KBOF
Washington Business Information, Inc. [*Information service or system*] (IID) .... WBII
Washington Calligraphers Guild (EA) .... WCG
Washington Capitals Fan Club (EA) .... WCFC
Washington Cathedral, Washington, DC [*Library symbol Library of Congress*] (LCLS) .... DNC
Washington Center of Foreign Policy Research (MCD) .... WCFPR
Washington Center, Rockford, IL [*Library symbol*] [*Library of Congress*] (LCLS) .... IRoWC
Washington Chinese Business Association .... WCBA
Washington Citizens for Recycling (EA) .... WCFR
Washington College (GAGS) .... Wash C
Washington College, Chestertown, MD [*Library symbol Library of Congress*] (LCLS) .... MdChW
Washington College of Law, Washington, DC [*OCLC symbol*] (OCLC) .... WCL
Washington Constr Grp [*NYSE symbol*] (TTSB) .... WAS
Washington Cooperative Fishery Research Unit [*University of Washington*] [*Research center*] (RCD) .... WCFRU
Washington Correction Center, Resident Library, Shelton, WA [*Library symbol Library of Congress*] (LCLS) .... WaShC-R
Washington Correction Center, Staff Library, Shelton, WA [*Library symbol Library of Congress*] (LCLS) .... WaShC
Washington County Cooperative Library Services [*Library network*] .... WCCLS
Washington County Cooperative Library Services, Aloha, OR [*Library symbol*] [*Library of Congress*] (LCLS) .... OrAh
Washington County Free Library, Hagerstown, MD [*Library symbol Library of Congress*] (LCLS) .... MdHag
Washington County Historical Society, Salem, IN [*Library symbol Library of Congress*] (LCLS) .... InSaWHi
Washington County Law Library, Hillsboro, OR [*Library symbol Library of Congress*] (LCLS) .... OrHilW
Washington County Library, Lake Elmo, MN [*Library symbol Library of Congress*] (LCLS) .... MnLeW
Washington County Library, Plymouth, NC [*Library symbol Library of Congress*] (LCLS) .... NcPly
Washington County Library, St. George, UT [*Library symbol Library of Congress*] (LCLS) .... UStgW
Washington County Library System, Greenville, MS [*Library symbol Library of Congress*] (LCLS) .... MsGW
Washington County Public Library, Abingdon, VA [*Library symbol Library of Congress*] (LCLS) .... ViAb
Washington County Recorder's Office, Salem, IN [*Library symbol Library of Congress*] (LCLS) .... InSaCR
Washington County Reports [*Pennsylvania*] [*A publication*] (DLA) .... Wash Co
Washington County Reports [*Pennsylvania*] [*A publication*] (DLA) .... Wash Co (PA)
Washington County Reports [*Pennsylvania*] [*A publication*] (DLA) .... Wash Co R
Washington County Reports [*Pennsylvania*] [*A publication*] (DLA) .... Wash Co Repr
Washington Court House, OH [*Location identifier FAA*] (FAAL) .... CSS
Washington Court House, OH [*FM radio station call letters*] .... WCHO
Washington Court House, OH [*AM radio station call letters*] .... WOFR
Washington, DC [*Location identifier FAA*] (FAAL) .... AJU
Washington, DC [*Location identifier FAA*] (FAAL) .... AML
Washington, DC [*Location identifier FAA*] (FAAL) .... ASO
Washington, DC [*Location identifier FAA*] (FAAL) .... BOF
Washington, DC [*Location identifier FAA*] (FAAL) .... DLX
Washington, DC [*Location identifier FAA*] (FAAL) .... DTD
Washington, DC [*Location identifier FAA*] (FAAL) .... GTN
Washington, DC [*Location identifier FAA*] (FAAL) .... JPN
Washington, DC [*Location identifier FAA*] (FAAL) .... NDV
Washington, DC [*Location identifier FAA*] (FAAL) .... OSZ
Washington, DC [*Location identifier FAA*] (FAAL) .... OWG
Washington, DC [*Location identifier FAA*] (FAAL) .... RXQ
Washington, DC [*Location identifier FAA*] (FAAL) .... SGC
Washington, DC [*FM radio station call letters*] .... WAMU
Washington, DC [*FM radio station call letters*] .... WASH
Washington, D.C. (VRA) .... Wash DC
Washington, DC [*Location identifier FAA*] (FAAL) .... WBC
Washington, DC [*Television station call letters*] (RBYB) .... WBDC-TV
Washington, DC [*FM radio station call letters*] .... WBIG
Washington, DC [*Television station call letters*] .... WDCA
Washington, DC [*FM radio station call letters*] .... WDCU
Washington, DC [*FM radio station call letters*] (RBYB) .... WEBR
Washington, DC [*FM radio station call letters*] .... WETA
Washington, DC [*Television station call letters*] .... WETA-TV
Washington, DC [*FM radio station call letters*] (RBYB) .... WGAY-FM
Washington, DC [*FM radio station call letters*] .... WGMS
Washington, DC [*Television station call letters*] .... WHMM
Washington, DC [*FM radio station call letters*] .... WHUR
Washington, DC [*Television station call letters*] .... WJLA
Washington, DC [*FM radio station call letters*] .... WKYS
Washington, DC [*AM radio station call letters*] .... WMAL
Washington, DC [*FM radio station call letters*] .... WMZQ
Washington, DC [*AM radio station call letters*] .... WOL
Washington, DC [*FM radio station call letters*] .... WPFW
Washington, DC [*Television station call letters*] .... WRC
Washington, DC [*FM radio station call letters*] .... WRQX
Washington, DC [*AM radio station call letters*] .... WTOP
Washington, DC [*Television station call letters*] .... WTTG
Washington, DC [*Television station call letters*] .... WUSA
Washington, DC [*AM radio station call letters*] .... WUST

Washington, DC [*AM radio station call letters*] .... WWDC
Washington, DC [*FM radio station call letters*] .... WWDC-FM
Washington, DC [*AM radio station call letters*] .... WWRC
Washington, DC [*AM radio station call letters*] .... WYCB
Washington, DC [*Location identifier FAA*] (FAAL) XII
Washington, DC [*Location identifier FAA*] (FAAL) .... ZDC
Washington Decisions [*A publication*] (DLA) .... Wash Dec
Washington Decisions [*A publication*] (DLA) .... WD
Washington Decisions, Second Series [*A publication*] (DLA) .... WD (2d)
Washington Department of Ecology .... WDOE
Washington Department of Ecology (DOGT) .... WDOE
Washington District Army Audit Agency (MUGU) .... WADAAA
Washington Document Center .... WDC
Washington Document Service [*Information service or system*] (IID) .... WDS
Washington [*District of Columbia*] **Dulles Airport** [*Airport symbol*] .... IAD
Washington/Dulles International [*District of Columbia*] [*ICAO location identifier*] (ICLI) .... KIAD
Washington Elementary School, Alexandria, MN [*Library symbol*] [*Library of Congress*] (LCLS) .... MnAleWE
Washington Elementary School, Cloquet, MN [*Library symbol*] [*Library of Congress*] (LCLS) .... MnClWE
Washington Elementary School, Crookston, MN [*Library symbol*] [*Library of Congress*] (LCLS) .... MnCrWE
Washington Elementary School, Detroit Lakes, MN [*Library symbol*] [*Library of Congress*] (LCLS) .... MnDlWE
Washington Elementary School, Ely, MN [*Library symbol*] [*Library of Congress*] (LCLS) .... MnElyWE
Washington Elementary School, Moorhead, MN [*Library symbol*] [*Library of Congress*] (LCLS) .... MnMohWE
Washington Elementary School, Willmar, MN [*Library symbol*] [*Library of Congress*] (LCLS) .... MnWilWES
Washington Energy [*NYSE symbol*] (TTSB) .... WEG
Washington Energy Co. [*Associated Press*] (SAG) .... WashEn
Washington Energy Co. [*NYSE symbol*] (SPSG) .... WEG
[*The*] **Washington Establishment** .... TWE
Washington Ethical Society (EA) .... WES
Washington Evening Journal, Washington, IA [*Library symbol Library of Congress*] (LCLS) .... IaWaJ
Washington Federal [*NASDAQ symbol*] (TTSB) .... WFSL
Washington Federal, Inc. (Seattle) [*Associated Press*] (SAG) .... WashFed
Washington Federal Savings & Loan Association of Seattle [*NASDAQ symbol*] (NQ) .... WFSL
Washington Federal Savings Bank [*NASDAQ symbol*] (NQ) .... WFSB
Washington Financial Reports (Bureau of National Affairs) [*A publication*] (DLA) .... Wash Fin Rep (BNA)
Washington Forest Protection Association (EA) .... WFPA
Washington Free Public Library, Washington, NJ [*Library symbol Library of Congress*] (LCLS) .... NjWas
Washington, GA [*AM radio station call letters*] .... WLOV
Washington, GA [*FM radio station call letters*] .... WLOV-FM
Washington Gallery of Modern Art .... WGMA
Washington Gas Light Co. [*Associated Press*] (SAG) .... WashGs
Washington Gas Light Co. [*NYSE symbol*] (SPSG) .... WGL
Washington Gas Lt [*NYSE symbol*] (TTSB) .... WGL
Washington Hall Junior College, Washington, DC [*Library symbol Library of Congress*] (LCLS) .... DWH
Washington Headquarters Association (EA) .... WHA
Washington Headquarters Services [*Military*] .... WHS
Washington Higher Education Telecommunications System [*Washington State University*] [*Pullman*] [*Telecommunications service*] (TSSD) .... WHETS
Washington Home Rule Committee [*Later, SDDC*] (EA) .... WHRC
Washington Homes [*NYSE symbol*] (TTSB) .... WHI
Washington Homes, Inc. [*Associated Press*] (SAG) .... WashHm
Washington Homes, Inc. [*NYSE symbol*] (SPSG) .... WHI
Washington Hospital Center, Medical Library, Washington, DC [*Library symbol Library of Congress*] (LCLS) .... DWHC
Washington Hospital Center, Medical Library, Washington, DC [*Library symbol Library of Congress*] (LCLS) .... DWHO
Washington Hospital Center, Washington, DC [*OCLC symbol*] (OCLC) .... WHC
Washington, IA [*Location identifier FAA*] (FAAL) .... AWG
Washington, IA [*AM radio station call letters*] .... KCII
Washington, IA [*FM radio station call letters*] .... KCII-FM
Washington, Idaho & Montana Railway Co. [*AAR code*] .... WIM
Washington, IN [*Location identifier FAA*] (FAAL) .... DCY
Washington, IN [*AM radio station call letters*] .... WAMW
Washington, IN [*FM radio station call letters*] .... WAMW-FM
Washington, IN [*FM radio station call letters*] .... WWBL
Washington Industrial Safety and Health Act (NUCP) .... WISHA
Washington Information Group, Ltd. [*Research center*] (TSSD) .... WIG
Washington Institute of Foreign Affairs (EA) .... WIFA
Washington Institute of Technology [*Washington, DC*] .... WIT
Washington Intelligence Data Processing System (SAA) .... WIPS
Washington Interagency Telecommunications System [*GSA*] .... WITS
Washington International Center (EA) .... WIC
Washington International College, Washington, DC [*Library symbol Library of Congress*] (LCLS) .... DWI
Washington International College, Washington, DC [*OCLC symbol*] (OCLC) .... WCI
Washington Inventory Service .... WIS
Washington Irving Home, Sleepy Hollow Restorations, Tarrytown, NY [*Library symbol Library of Congress Obsolete*] (LCLS) .... NTaI
Washington Irving Society [*Defunct*] (EA) .... WIS
Washington Journalism Center (EA) .... WJC
Washington Junior High School, Duluth, MN [*Library symbol*] [*Library of Congress*] (LCLS) .... MnDuWJ
Washington Jurist [*A publication*] (DLA) .... Wash Jur
Washington, LA [*AM radio station call letters*] .... KNEK
Washington, LA [*FM radio station call letters*] .... KNEK-FM
Washington Law Reporter [*District of Columbia*] [*A publication*] (DLA) .... Wash L Rep
Washington Law Reporter [*District of Columbia*] [*A publication*] (DLA) .... Wash Law Rep
Washington Law Reporter [*District of Columbia*] [*A publication*] (DLA) .... WLR
Washington Law Reporter (District of Columbia) [*A publication*] (DLA) .... Wash LR (Dist Col)
Washington, Leesburg [*Virginia*] [*ICAO location identifier*] (ICLI) .... KZDC
Washington Legal Foundation (EA) .... WLF
Washington Legislative Service (West) [*A publication*] (DLA) .... Wash Legis Serv
Washington Liaison Group (AFM) .... WLG
Washington Library Film Circuit [*Library network*] .... WLFC
Washington Library Network [*Washington State Library*] [*Olympia, WA*] [*Library network*] .... WLN
Washington Library Network, Olympia, WA [*Library symbol Library of Congress*] (LCLS) .... WaOLN
Washington Memorial Library, Middle Georgia Regional Library, Macon, GA [*Library symbol Library of Congress*] (LCLS) .... GM
Washington Metropolitan Area (AFM) .... WMA
Washington Metropolitan Area Transit Authority (BARN) .... WMATA
Washington Middle School, Brainerd, MN [*Library symbol*] [*Library of Congress*] (LCLS) .... MnBrWM
Washington Middle School, Princeton, IL [*Library symbol Library of Congress*] (LCLS) .... IPriWS
Washington Military Industrial Complex .... WASHMIC
Washington Missionary College, Tacoma Park, MD [*Library symbol Library of Congress Obsolete*] (LCLS) .... MdTW
Washington, MO [*FM radio station call letters*] .... KGNV
Washington, MO [*AM radio station call letters*] .... KSLQ
Washington, MO [*FM radio station call letters*] .... KSLQ-FM
Washington Monthly [*A publication*] (BRI) .... Wash M
Washington Music Institute .... WMI
Washington Mutual [*NASDAQ symbol*] (TTSB) .... WAMU
Washington Mutual $2.28'C'Pfd [*NASDAQ symbol*] (TTSB) .... WAMUO
Washington Mutual 7.60% 'E' Pfd' [*NASDAQ symbol*] (TTSB) .... WAMUM
Washington Mutual, Inc. [*Associated Press*] (SAG) .... WA Mutl
Washington Mutual, Inc. [*NASDAQ symbol*] (NQ) .... WAMU
Washington Mutual, Inc. [*Associated Press*] (SAG) .... WMut
Washington/National [*District of Columbia*] [*ICAO location identifier*] (ICLI) .... KDCA
Washington National [*NYSE symbol*] (TTSB) .... WNT
Washington [*DC*] **National Airport** [*Airport symbol*] .... DCA
Washington [*DC*] **National Airport** .... WANAP
Washington [*DC*] **National Airport** [*FAA*] .... WNA
Washington [*DC*] **National Airport** .... WNAP
Washington National Corp. [*Associated Press*] (SAG) .... WasN
Washington National Corp. [*NYSE symbol*] (SPSG) .... WNT
Washington National Corp. [*Associated Press*] (SAG) .... WshNat
Washington/National Flight Data Center [*District of Columbia*] [*ICAO location identifier*] (ICLI) .... KFDC
Washington National Insurance Co., Evanston, IL [*Library symbol Library of Congress*] (LCLS) .... IEWNI
Washington National Monument .... WNM
Washington National Monument Association (EA) .... WNMA
Washington National Records Center [*GSA*] (AABC) .... WNRC
Washington National Records Center [*GSA*] .... WNRCEN
Washington National Records Center, General Services Administration, Suitland, MD [*Library symbol Library of Congress*] (LCLS) .... MdSuFR
Washington Natl $2.50 Cv Pfd [*NYSE symbol*] (TTSB) .... WNTPr
Washington Natural Gas [*Associated Press*] (SAG) .... WashNt
Washington Natural Gas [*Associated Press*] (SAG) .... WashNt
Washington Natural Gas Co. [*NYSE symbol*] (SPSG) .... WNG
Washington Natural Gas Co. [*Associated Press*] (SAG) .... WshNt
Washington Natural Heritage Program [*Washington State Department of Natural Resources*] [*Olympia*] [*Information service or system*] (IID) .... WNHP
Washington Naval Air Facility [*District of Columbia*] [*ICAO location identifier*] (ICLI) .... KNSF
Washington [*DC*] **Naval Yard** .... WNY
Washington, NC [*Location identifier FAA*] (FAAL) .... OCW
Washington, NC [*FM radio station call letters*] .... WCZI
Washington, NC [*FM radio station call letters*] .... WDLX
Washington, NC [*FM radio station call letters*] (RBYB) .... WERO-FM
Washington, NC [*Television station call letters*] .... WITN
Washington, NC [*AM radio station call letters*] .... WRRF
Washington, NC [*AM radio station call letters*] .... WTOW
Washington Nuclear Plant (NRCH) .... WNP
Washington Office (FAAC) .... WO
Washington Office on Africa (EA) .... WOA
Washington Office on Haiti (EA) .... WOH
Washington Office on Latin America (EA) .... WOLA
Washington Operations Capabilities System .... WASHCAP
Washington Operations Research Council (MCD) .... WORC
Washington Opportunities for Women .... WOW
Washington, PA [*AM radio station call letters*] .... WJPA
Washington, PA [*FM radio station call letters*] .... WJPA-FM
Washington, PA [*AM radio station call letters*] .... WKZV
Washington, PA [*FM radio station call letters*] .... WXJX
Washington Parish Library, Franklinton, LA [*Library symbol Library of Congress*] (LCLS) .... LFrtW
Washington Post Co. [*Associated Press*] (SAG) .... WshPst
Washington Post Co. Class B [*NYSE symbol*] (SPSG) .... WPO
Washington Post'B' [*NYSE symbol*] (TTSB) .... WPO
Washington Press Club [*Formerly, WNPC*] .... WPC

Washington Public Library, Washington, IA [Library symbol Library of Congress] (LCLS) .... IaWa
Washington Public Power Supply System (DFIT) .... WHOOPS
Washington Public Power Supply System [Nicknamed "Whoops"] .... WPPSS
Washington Public Utility Commission Reports [A publication] (DLA) .... Wash PUR
Washington Real Estate Investment Trust [AMEX symbol] (SPSG) .... WRE
Washington Real Estate Investment Trust [Associated Press] (SAG) .... WRIT
Washington Reef Net Owners Association (EA) .... WRNOA
Washington Regional Engineers, Scientists, and Technicians .... WREST
Washington Regional Library for the Blind and Physically Handicapped, Seattle, WA [Library symbol Library of Congress] (LCLS) .... Wa-BPH
Washington REIT SBI [AMEX symbol] (TTSB) .... WRE
Washington Reports [1890-1939] [A publication] (DLA) .... W
Washington Reports [A publication] (DLA) .... Wa
Washington Reports [A publication] (DLA) .... Wash
Washington Reports [A publication] (DLA) .... Wn
Washington Reports, Second Series [A publication] (DLA) ...... Wash 2d
Washington Reports, Second Series [A publication] (DLA) .... Wn 2d
Washington Representative Services, Inc. [Information service or system] (IID) .... WRS
Washington Research Council [Research center] (RCD) .... WRC
Washington Revised Code, Annotated [A publication] (DLA) .... Wash Rev Code Ann
[The] Washington Savings Bank [AMEX symbol] (SPSG) .... WSB
Washington Savings Bank FSB (MD) [Associated Press] (SAG) ... WashSvg
Washington School, Hempstead, NY [Library symbol] [Library of Congress] (LCLS) .... NHemWE
Washington School of Psychiatry .... WSP
Washington School, Thief River Falls, MN [Library symbol] [Library of Congress] (LCLS) .... MnTW
Washington Science Center [Maryland] [Seismograph station code, US Geological Survey Closed] (SEIS) .... WSC
Washington Science Center, Building 5 (USDC) WSC-5
Washington Science Center, Building 5 [Marine science] (OSRA) WSC-5
Washington Scientific [NASDAQ symbol] (TTSB) .... WSCI
Washington Scientific Industries, Inc. [NASDAQ symbol] (NQ) .... WSCI
Washington Scientific Industries, Inc. [Associated Press] (SAG) .... WshSci
Washington Service Bureau [Publisher] (AAGC) .... WSB
Washington Soldiers' Home, Resident Library, Orting, WA [Library symbol Library of Congress] (LCLS) .... WaOrtS-R
Washington Soldiers' Home, Staff Library, Orting, WA [Library symbol Library of Congress] (LCLS) .... WaOrtS
Washington Special Action Group [National Security Council] .... WASAG
Washington Special Action Group [National Security Council] .... WSAG
Washington Square Press [Publisher's imprint] .... WSP
Washington Standardization Officers .... WSO
Washington Star, Washington, DC [Library symbol Library of Congress] (LCLS) .... DWS
Washington Star, Washington, NJ [Library symbol Library of Congress] (LCLS) .... NjWasW
Washington State Apple Commission (EA) .... WSAC
Washington State Bar Association. Proceedings [A publication] (DLA) .... Wash SBA
Washington State Center for Youth Services, Everett, WA [Library symbol Library of Congress] (LCLS) .... WaEYS
Washington State Center for Youth Services, Spokane, WA [Library symbol Library of Congress] (LCLS) .... WaSpYS
Washington State Center for Youth Services, Wenatchee, WA [Library symbol Library of Congress] (LCLS) .... WaWeYS
Washington State Center for Youth Services, Yakima, WA [Library symbol Library of Congress] (LCLS) .... WaYYS
Washington State Court of Appeals, Olympia, WA [Library symbol] [Library of Congress] (LCLS) .... WaOCA
Washington State Department of Education, Olympia, WA [Library symbol Library of Congress] (LCLS) .... WaOEd
Washington State Department of Natural Resources, Division of Geology and Earth Resources, Olympia, WA [Library symbol Library of Congress] (LCLS) .... WaONR
Washington State Department of Public Assistance, Ben Tidball Memorial Library, Olympia, WA [Library symbol Library of Congress] (LCLS) .... WaOB
Washington State Department of Transportation, Olympia, WA [Library symbol Library of Congress] (LCLS) .... WaOT
Washington State Electronics Council .... WSEC
Washington State Energy Office, Olympia, WA [Library symbol Library of Congress] (LCLS) .... WaOEng
Washington State Film Library, Olympia, WA [Library symbol Library of Congress] (LCLS) .... Wa-F
Washington State Historical Society, Tacoma, WA [Library symbol Library of Congress] (LCLS) .... WaHi
Washington State Holly Growers Association [Defunct] (EA) .... WSHGA
Washington State Institute of Technology (KSC) .... WSIT
Washington State Law Library, Olympia, WA [Library symbol Library of Congress] (LCLS) .... Wa-L
Washington State Library, Ecology Department, Olympia, WA [Library symbol Library of Congress] (LCLS) .... Wa-Ec
Washington State Library, Olympia, WA [Library symbol Library of Congress] (LCLS) .... Wa
Washington State Office for the Services for the Blind, Seattle, WA [Library symbol Library of Congress] (LCLS) .... WaSSB
Washington State Office of Adult Probation and Parole, Olympia, WA [Library symbol Library of Congress] (LCLS) .... WaOAP
Washington State Office of Adult Probation and Parole, Pasco, WA [Library symbol Library of Congress] (LCLS) .... WaPaAp
Washington State Office of Juvenile Parole Services, Everett, WA [Library symbol Library of Congress] (LCLS) .... WaEJP

Washington State Office of Juvenile Parole Services, Spokane, WA [Library symbol Library of Congress] (LCLS) .... WaSpJP
Washington State Office of Juvenile Parole Services, Tacoma, WA [Library symbol Library of Congress] (LCLS) .... WaTJP
Washington State Office of Juvenile Parole Services, Yakima, WA [Library symbol Library of Congress] (LCLS) .... WaYJP
Washington State Patrol, Olympia, WA [Library symbol] [Library of Congress] (LCLS) .... WaOP
Washington State Penitentiary, Walla Walla, WA [Library symbol Library of Congress] (LCLS) .... WaWP
Washington State Reformatory, Monroe, WA [Library symbol Library of Congress] (LCLS) .... WaMonR
Washington State Register [A publication] (DLA) .... Wash Admin Reg
Washington State Register [A publication] (AAGC) .... Wash St Reg
Washington State Reports [A publication] (DLA) .... Wash
Washington State Reports [A publication] (DLA) .... Wash St
Washington State Reports [A publication] (DLA) .... Wsh
Washington State Reports, Second Series [A publication] (DLA) .... W 2d
Washington State Reports, Second Series [A publication] (DLA) .... Wa 2d
Washington State School for the Blind, Vancouver, WA [Library symbol Library of Congress] (LCLS) .... WaVSB
Washington State School for the Deaf, Vancouver, WA [Library symbol Library of Congress] (LCLS) .... WaVSD
Washington State Teachers Retirement System (EDAC) .... WSTRS
Washington State Twin City Center for Youth Services, Chehalis, WA [Library symbol Library of Congress] (LCLS) .... WaChehYS
Washington State University (GAGS) .... Wash St U
Washington State University .... WSU
Washington State University, Open Pool Reactor .... WSUOPR
Washington State University, Pullman, WA [Library symbol Library of Congress] (LCLS) .... WaPS
Washington State University Shock Dynamics Laboratory [Pullman] .... WSU-SDL
Washington State University, Veterinary Medical Library, Pullman, WA [Library symbol Library of Congress] (LCLS) .... WaPS-V
Washington State University, Western Washington Research and Extension Center, Puyallup, WA [Library symbol Library of Congress] (LCLS) .... WaPuS
Washington Strategy Seminar (EA) .... WSS
Washington Street Elementary School, Franklin Square, NY [Library symbol] [Library of Congress] (LCLS) .... NFsWE
Washington Superindentent of Public Instruction, Olympia, WA [Library symbol] [Library of Congress] (LCLS) .... WaOPI
Washington Task Force on African Affairs [Defunct] (EA) .... WTFAA
Washington Technological Association (MCD) .... WTA
Washington Telecom Week [A publication] .... WTW
[The] Washington Terminal Co. [AAR code] .... WATC
Washington Territory .... W TER
Washington Territory (ROG) .... WASH T
Washington Territory [Prior to statehood] .... WT
Washington Territory Opinions [1854-64] [A publication] (DLA) .... Wash T
Washington Territory Opinions [1854-64] [A publication] (DLA) .... Wash Ter
Washington Territory Opinions [1854-64] [A publication] (DLA) .... Wash Terr
Washington Territory Opinions [1854-64] [A publication] (DLA) .... Wash Ty
Washington Territory Reports [1854-88] [A publication] (DLA) .... W Ty R
Washington Territory Reports [1854-88] [A publication] (DLA) .... Wash
Washington Territory Reports [1854-88] [A publication] (DLA) .... Wash T
Washington Territory Reports [1854-88] [A publication] (DLA) .... Wash Ter
Washington Territory Reports [1854-88] [A publication] (DLA) .... Wash Terr
Washington Territory Reports [1854-88] [A publication] (DLA) .... Wash Ty
Washington Territory Reports [1854-88] [A publication] (ILCA) .... Wn T
Washington Territory Reports [1854-88] [A publication] (DLA) .... WT
Washington Theological Coalition, Silver Spring, MD [Library symbol Library of Congress] (LCLS) .... MdSsW
Washington Times-Herald, Washington, IN [Library symbol Library of Congress] (LCLS) .... InWasTH
Washington Township Historical Society, Sewell, NJ [Library symbol Library of Congress] (LCLS) .... NjSewHi
Washington Township Library, Sunnyland Branch, Sunnyland, IL [Library symbol Library of Congress] (LCLS) .... IWas-Su
Washington Township Library, Washington, IL [OCLC symbol] (OCLC) .... IDW
Washington Township Library, Washington, IL [Library symbol Library of Congress] (LCLS) .... IWas
Washington Township, NJ [AM radio station call letters] .... WNJC
Washington Township Public Library, Lynn, IN [Library symbol Library of Congress] (LCLS) .... InLy
Washington Trust Bancorp [NASDAQ symbol] (TTSB) .... WASH
Washington Trust Bancorp, Inc. [NASDAQ symbol] (NQ) .... WASH
Washington Trust Bancorp, Inc. [Associated Press] (SAG) .... WashTrst
Washington University (PDAA) .... WU
Washington University Center for Composites Research [St. Louis, MO] .... WU/CCR
Washington University Center for Computational Mechanics [St. Louis, MO] .... WU/CCM
Washington University. Journal of Urban and Contemporary Law [A publication] (DLA) .... Wash UJ Urb & Contemp L
Washington University, Law Library, St. Louis, MO [OCLC symbol] (OCLC) .... WUL
Washington University. Law Review [A publication] (DLA) .... Wash UL Rev
Washington University, Medical School, St. Louis, MO [Library symbol Library of Congress] (LCLS) .... MoSW-M
Washington University (Missouri) (GAGS) .... Wash U (Mo)
Washington University Optoelectronics Laboratory [St. Louis, MO] .... WU/OEL
Washington University, St. Louis, MO [Library symbol Library of Congress] (LCLS) .... MoSW
Washington University, St. Louis, MO [OCLC symbol] (OCLC) ...... WTU

Washington University, School of Dentistry, St. Louis, MO [*Library symbol Library of Congress*] (LCLS) .... MoSW-D
Washington University, School of Fine Arts, St. Louis, MO [*Library symbol Library of Congress*] (LCLS) .... MoSW-F
Washington University, School of Law, St. Louis, MO [*Library symbol Library of Congress*] (LCLS) .... MoSW-L
Washington University, School of Medicine, St. Louis, MO [*OCLC symbol*] (OCLC) .... WUM
Washington University Semiconductor Research Laboratory [*St. Louis, MO*] .... WU/SRL
Washington University Technology Associates .... WUTA
Washington, UT [*AM radio station call letters*] .... KONY
Washington Utilities and Transportation Commission, Olympia, WA [*Library symbol*] [*Library of Congress*] (LCLS) .... WaOUT
Washington Veterans' Home, Medical Library, Retsil, WA [*Library symbol Library of Congress*] (LCLS) .... WaRetV
Washington Veterans' Home, Resident Library, Retsil, WA [*Library symbol Library of Congress*] (LCLS) .... WaRetV-R
Washington Water Power Co. [*Associated Press*] (SAG) .... WashWtr
Washington Water Power Co. [*NYSE symbol*] (SPSG) .... WWP
Washington Water Pwr [*NYSE symbol*] (TTSB) .... WWP
Washington Weekly Report [*Independent Bankers Association of America*] [*A publication*] .... WWR
Washington Western [*AAR code*] .... WWR
Washington Women's Network [*Defunct*] (EA) .... WWN
Washington Workshops Foundation (EA) .... WWF
Washington Yards [*Navy*] .... WY
Washington-Rose Elementary School, Roosevelt, NY [*Library symbol*] [*Library of Congress*] (LCLS) .... NRoosWE
Washingtons [*State*] **Department of Fish and Wildlife** .... WDFW
Washington's Headquarters Museum, Newburgh, NY [*Library symbol*] [*Library of Congress*] (LCLS) .... NNebgWM
Washington's Headquarters Museum, Newburgh, NY [*Library symbol Library of Congress*] (LCLS) .... NNegbWM
Washington's Reports [*1, 2 Virginia*] [*A publication*] (DLA) .... Wash
Washington's Reports [*16-23 Vermont*] [*A publication*] (DLA) .... Wash
Washington's Reports [*1, 2 Virginia*] [*A publication*] (DLA) .... Wash VA
Washington's United States Circuit Court Reports [*A publication*] (DLA) .... Wash
Washington's United States Circuit Court Reports [*A publication*] (DLA) .... Wash CC
Washington's United States Circuit Court Reports [*A publication*] (DLA) .... Wash CCR
Washington's United States Circuit Court Reports [*A publication*] (DLA) .... WCC
Washington's United States Circuit Court Reports [*A publication*] (DLA) .... WCCR
Washo [*MARC language code Library of Congress*] (LCCP) .... was
Washoe City [*Nevada*] [*Seismograph station code, US Geological Survey*] (SEIS) .... WCN
Washoe County Law Library, Reno, NV [*Library symbol Library of Congress*] (LCLS) .... NvRWL
Washoe County Library, Reno, NV [*Library symbol Library of Congress*] (LCLS) .... NvRW
Wash-Off Line Film (DGA) .... WOLF
Washout Rate .... WR
Washroom .... WR
Washta Library, Washta, IA [*Library symbol Library of Congress*] (LCLS) ..... IaWas
Washtenaw Community College, Ann Arbor, MI [*OCLC symbol*] (OCLC) .... EYA
Washtenaw Community College, Ann Arbor, MI [*Library symbol Library of Congress*] (LCLS) .... MiAaWC
Washtenaw County Library, Ann Arbor, MI [*Library symbol Library of Congress*] (LCLS) .... MiAaW
Wash-Water Recovery System [*in a spacecraft*] [*NASA*] .... WWRS
Wasilla, AK [*FM radio station call letters*] .... KMBQ
Wasilla Public Library, Wasilla, AK [*Library symbol Library of Congress*] (LCLS) .... AkWas
Wasior [*Indonesia*] [*ICAO location identifier*] (ICLI) .... WASW
Wasior [*West Irian, Indonesia*] [*Airport symbol*] (AD) .... WSR
Waskatenau Public Library, Alberta [*Library symbol National Library of Canada*] (NLC) .... AWAS
Waskatenau Public Library, Waskatenau, AB, Canada [*Library symbol*] [*Library of Congress*] (LCLS) .... CaAWas
Wasolo [*Zaire*] [*ICAO location identifier*] (ICLI) .... FZVL
WASP Funk [*1960's pop music*] .... Wunk
Waspam [*Nicaragua*] [*Airport symbol*] (AD) .... WSP
Wasser Gefahrdungsklasse [*Water hazard classification*] [*Germany*] .... WGK
Wassermann [*Test for syphilis*] .... Wass
Wassermann Antigen Reaction [*Test for syphilis*] [*Medicine*] .... WAR
Wassermann Reaction [*Test for syphilis*] [*Medicine*] .... WR
Wassmer Aviation [*France ICAO aircraft manufacturer identifier*] (ICAO) .... WA
Waste .... W
Waste .... WST
Waste Acceptance Criteria (GAAI) .... WAC
Waste Acid Detoxification and Reclamation [*Environmental science*] .... WADR
Waste Acid Release Reduction [*Environmental science*] .... WARR
Waste Analysis Plan [*Environmental Protection Agency*] (GFGA) .... WAP
Waste and Recycling Advisory Committee (EERA) .... WRAC
Waste Biochemical Oxygen Demand [*Oceanography*] .... WBOD
Waste Book (ROG) .... WB
Waste Calcination [*or Calcining*] **Facility** [*Nuclear energy*] .... WCF
Waste Channel and Containment Pressurization and Penetration System (IEEE) .... WCCPPS
Waste Collection Containers .... WCC
Waste Collection System [*NASA*] (MCD) .... WCS
Waste Collector Pump (IEEE) .... WCP
Waste Compaction Station [*Nuclear energy*] (NRCH) .... WCS
Waste Control System (SSD) .... WCS

Waste Crankcase Oils .... WCO
Waste Disposal [*Nuclear energy*] (NRCH) .... WD
Waste Disposal Authority [*British*] .... WDA
Waste Disposal Cask [*Nuclear energy*] (NRCH) .... WDC
Waste Disposal Code .... WDC
Waste Disposal (System) [*Nuclear energy*] (NRCH) .... WD(S)
Waste Encapsulation Storage Facility [*Nuclear energy*] (NRCH) .... WESF
Waste, Environment, and Technology [*Matrix*] [*Environmental Protection Agency*] .... WET
Waste Environmental Federation .... WEF
Waste Evaporator Condensate Storage Tank [*Nuclear energy*] (NRCH) .. WECST
Waste Extraction Test .... WET
Waste Gas [*Nuclear energy*] (NRCH) .... WG
Waste Gas Compressor [*Nuclear energy*] (NRCH) .... WGC
Waste Gas Decay Tank [*Nuclear energy*] (NRCH) .... WGDT
Waste Gas Disposal System [*Nuclear energy*] (NRCH) .... WGDS
Waste Gas Storage Tank [*Nuclear energy*] (IEEE) .... WGST
Waste Gas (System) [*Nuclear energy*] (NRCH) .... WG(S)
Waste Handling and Packaging Plant [*Department of Energy*] [*Oak Ridge National Laboratory*] (GAAI) .... WHPP
Waste Heat Boiler [*Nuclear energy*] (CAAL) .... WHB
Waste Heat Boiler Survey (DS) .... WHBS
Waste Heat Fire Tube Boiler (DS) .... WHFTB
Waste Heat Fire Tube Boiler Survey (DS) .... WHFTBS
Waste Heat Recovery Unit [*Chemical engineering*] .... WHRU
Waste Heat Removal .... WHR
Waste Heat Water Tube Boiler (DS) .... WHWTB
Waste Heat Water Tube Boiler Survey (DS) .... WHWTBS
Waste Isolation Pilot Plant [*Department of Energy*] .... WIPP
Waste Isolation Pilot Plant Technical Assistance Contractor [*Department of Energy*] (GAAI) .... WTAC
Waste Isolation Pilot Plant Transuranic Waste Baseline Inventory Report [*Department of Energy*] (GAAI) .... WTWBIR
Waste Isolation Pilot Project Integration Office [*Department of Energy*] [*Albuquerque, NM*] (GAAI) .... WPIO
Waste Isolation Safety Assessment Program .... WISAP
Waste Management (NASA) .... WM
Waste Management Advisory Council [*British*] (DCTA) .... WMAC
Waste Management and Economics Division [*Environmental Protection Agency*] (EPA) .... WMED
Waste Management and Personal Hygiene Facility [*NASA*] (KSC) ...... WM & PHF
Waste Management Area [*NASA*] .... WMA
Waste Management Association [*Australia*] .... WMA
Waste Management Authority [*New South Wales, Australia*] .... WMA
Waste Management Compartment [*NASA*] (KSC) .... WMC
Waste Management Database [*IAEA*] [*United Nations*] (DUND) .... WMDB
Waste Management Division [*Environmental Protection Agency*] (GFGA) .... WMD
Waste Management Education and Research Consortium [*New Mexico State University*] [*Research center*] (RCD) .... WERC
Waste Management Information Bureau [*Atomic Energy Authority*] [*British Information service or system*] (IID) .... WMIB
Waste Management Information System .... WMIS
Waste Management International [*Associated Press*] (SAG) .... WasteMI
Waste Management International Ltd. ADS [*NYSE symbol*] (SPSG) .... WME
Waste Management Paper [*British*] (DCTA) .... WMP
Waste Management Plan (EERA) .... WMP
Waste Management Research and Education Institute [*University of Tennessee*] .... WMREI
Waste Management System (MCD) .... WMS
Waste Management Technology Center [*Oak Ridge National Laboratory*].... WMTC
Waste Material [*Freight*] .... WSTE MAT
Waste Materials Management Act .... WMMA
Waste Mgmt Intl plc ADS [*NYSE symbol*] (TTSB) .... WME
Waste Minimization .... WM
Waste Minimization (GAAI) .... WMin
Waste Minimization and Containment Services, Inc. (ECON) .... WMC
Waste Minimization Opportunity Assessment [*Environmental science*] ...... WMOA
Waste Monitor Tank (IEEE) .... WMT
Waste Neutralization Tank [*Nuclear energy*] (NRCH) .... WNT
Waste of Money, Brains, and Time (NHD) .... WOMBAT
Waste Oil Heating Manufacturers Association (EA) .... WOHMA
Waste Oil to Energy Converter .... WOTEC
Waste Paper Recovery Association Ltd. [*British*] (BI) .... WPRA
Waste Pickle Liquor [*Industrial waste*] .... WPL
Waste Pipe [*Technical drawings*] .... WP
Waste Pollution Discharge Elimination System (IEEE) .... WPDES
Waste Processing Building [*Nuclear energy*] (NRCH) .... WPB
Waste Processing Building Chilled Water System [*Nuclear energy*] (NRCH) .... WPBCWS
Waste Processing System [*Nuclear energy*] (NRCH) .... WPS
Waste Product Costs [*Solid waste management*] .... WPC
Waste Reduction Always Pays [*Dow Chemical Co. antipollution program*].... WRAP
Waste Reduction Assessments Program [*Environmental Protection Agency*] .... WRAP
Waste Reduction Audit Protocol .... WRAP
Waste Reduction Evaluation at Federal Sites [*Environmental Protection Agency*] .... WREAFS
Waste Reduction Innovative Technology Evaluation [*Environmental Protection Agency*] .... WRITE
Waste Reduction Institute for Scientists and Engineers [*Environmental Protection Agency*] .... WRISE
Waste Reduction Institute for Training and Applications Research [*Environmental Protection Agency*] .... WRITAR
Waste Regulation Authority [*British*] .... WRA
Waste Sampling and Characterization Facility .... WSCF

Waste Shipping Facility [*Nuclear energy*] (NRCH) ... WSF
Waste Shipping Facility [*Nuclear energy*] (NUCP) ... WSH
Waste Solidification and Compaction Station [*Nuclear energy*] (NRCH) ... WSCS
Waste Solidification Engineering Prototype Plant [*Nuclear energy*] ... WSEP
Waste Stack [*Technical drawings*] ... WS
Waste System ... WS
Waste Tank ... WT
Waste Technology [*NASDAQ symbol*] (TTSB) ... WTEK
Waste Technology Corp. [*Associated Press*] (SAG) ... WasteTc
Waste Technology Corp. [*New York, NY NASDAQ symbol*] (NQ) ... WTEK
Waste Treatment Facility [*Nuclear energy*] (IEEE) ... WTF
Waste Watch [*Defunct*] (EA) ... WW
Waste Water Technology Centre [*Canada*] (ECON) ... WTC
Waste Water Treatment Facility [*Nuclear energy*] (NRCH) ... WTF
Waste Water Treatment Plant [*Also, WWTP*] ... WTP
Waste Water Treatment Plant [*Also, WTP*] ... WWTP
Waste Water Treatment System ... WWTS
Waste-Activated Sludge ... WAS
Wasteload Allocation [*Environmental science*] (FFDE) ... WLA
Wasteload Allocation / Total Maximum Daily Load [*Environmental Protection Agency*] (EPA) ... WLA/TMDL
Wastepaper ... WP
Wastepaper Basket [*or Bin*] ... WPB
Waste-Paper Utilization Council [*Defunct*] ... WPUC
Waste-to-Energy [*Resource recycling*] ... WTE
Wastewater ... WSTTWTR
Wastewater Coalition [*Environmental science*] ... WWC
Wastewater Sewage Treatment Plant (GNE) ... WSTP
Wastewater Treatment Facility ... WWTF
Wastewater Treatment Information Exchange [*National Small Flows Clearinghouse*] ... WTIE
Wasu [*Papua New Guinea*] [*Airport symbol*] (OAG) ... WSU
Watanabe Hereditary Hyperlipidemic [*Rabbits*] ... WHHL
Watauga County Library, Boone, NC [*Library symbol Library of Congress*] (LCLS) ... NcBo
Watch Check List Completed [*Aviation*] (FAAC) ... WCLC
Watch Commanders ... WC
Watch Committee [*British*] (ILCA) ... WC
Watch Condition (DOMA) ... WATCHCON
Watch Dog Timer ... WDT
Watch Error [*Navigation*] ... WE
Watch Material and Jewelry Distributors Association [*Formerly, WMDAA*] (EA) ... WMJDA
Watch Material Distributors Association of America [*Later, WMJDA*] (EA) ... WMDAA
Watch Station Trainer [*Military*] (DWSG) ... WST
Watch Time ... W
Watch Time ... WT
Watch Tower Bible and Tract Society ... WTB & TS
Watchable Wildlife Program ... WWP
Watchdog Timer (MCD) ... WT
Watchdog Title ... WH
Watchdogs of the Treasury (EA) ... WT
Watchdogs on Environment ... WOE
Watchers Against Television Commercial Harrassment [*Student legal action organization*] ... WATCH
Watchmakers of Switzerland Information Center (EA) ... WOSIC
Watchmakers of Switzerland Information Center (EA) ... WSIC
Watchman Service (LAIN) ... WS
Watchman-Examiner [*A publication*] (BJA) ... WE
Watcor Purification Systems, Inc. [*Vancouver Stock Exchange symbol*] ... WPF
Water (GNE) ... H_2O
Water [*Compound*] (RDA) ... H2O
Water ... W
Water [*Automotive engineering*] ... WAT
Water ... WTR
Water ... WTR
Water (VRA) ... wtr
Water Absorption Index [*Analytical chemistry*] ... WAI
Water Agar [*Microbiology*] ... WA
Water Alcohol Injection (MCD) ... WAI
Water Analyzer Kit ... WAK
Water and Energy Research Institute of the Western Pacific [*University of Guam*] [*Guam*] [*Research center*] (RCD) ... WERI
Water and Feed ... W & F
Water and Hazardous Waste Team (GNE) ... WHWT
Water and Land Division [*Environmental Protection Agency*] (GFGA) ... WLD
Water and Land Resource Utilization Simulation ... WALRUS
Water and Land Resources Use Simulation ... WALRUS
Water and Maritime Industry Union [*Australia*] ... WMIU
Water and Power Development Authority (IAA) ... WAPDA
Water and Power Development Consultancy Services ... WAPCOS
Water and Power Resources Service [*Formerly, Bureau of Reclamation*] [*Department of the Interior Name changed back to Bureau of Reclamation, 1981*] ... WPRS
Water and Rail [*Transportation*] ... WR
Water and Sewage Works Manufacturers Association [*Later, WWEMA*] (EA) ... WSWMA
Water and Sewer Distributors of America (EA) ... WSDA
Water and Steam Program [*NASA*] ... WASP
Water and Toxic Substances Health Research Division [*Environmental Protection Agency*] (GFGA) ... WTSHRD
Water and Waste Management Monitoring Research Division [*Environmental Protection Agency*] (EPA) ... WWMMRD
Water and Waste Management Staff [*Environmental Protection Agency*] (GFGA) ... WWMS
Water and Waste Management Subsystem [*NASA*] (KSC) ... WWMS
Water and Waste Subsystem [*Aerospace*] (MCD) ... WWS
Water and Waste Treatment ... W & WT
Water & Wastewater Division (ACII) ... WWID
Water and Wastewater Equipment Manufacturers Association (EA) ... WWEMA
Water Attenuation by Tritium Relaxation [*Physics*] ... WATR
Water Authorities Association [*British*] (ECON) ... WAA
Water Authorities Association (AIE) ... WAA
Water Authorities Superannuation Fund [*British*] ... WASF
Water Authority [*British*] (DCTA) ... WA
Water Authority of Western Australia ... WAWA
Water Awareness Training Education and Recruitment ... WATER
Water Ballast [*Shipping*] ... WB
Water Bank Program [*Department of Agriculture*] ... WBP
Water Barge [*Self-propelled*] [*Navy symbol*] ... YW
Water Barge [*Non-self-propelled*] [*Navy symbol*] ... YWN
Water Binding Capacity [*Also, WHC*] [*Food industry*] ... WBC
Water Binding Potential [*of protein*] ... WBP
Water Bird Conservation Group [*Australia*] ... WBCG
Water Board ... WB
Water Boiler (KSC) ... W/B
Water Boiler Neutron Source Reactor [*Nuclear energy*] ... WBNS
Water Boiler Reactor ... WBR
Water Bottle ... WB
Water Box ... WB
Water Chiller (DWSG) ... WC
Water Chiller ... WCHR
Water Closet [*A toilet*] [*Slang*] ... WC
Water Cock (ROG) ... WC
Water Column [*Mechanical engineering*] ... WC
Water Companies' Association [*British*] ... WCA
Water Conditioning Association International [*Later, WQA*] (EA) ... WCAI
Water Conditioning Foundation [*Later, WQA*] (EA) ... WCF
Water Conditioning Research Council [*Later, WQRC*] (EA) ... WCRC
Water Content ... WC
Water Control Board ... WCB
Water Control Module (KSC) ... WCM
Water Coolant Line (MCD) ... WCL
Water Coolant Loop (MCD) ... WCL
Water Cooler and Drinking Fountain Manufacturers Association ... WCDFMA
Water Cooler Unit (AAG) ... WCU
Water Damage (ADA) ... WD
Water Data Center [*Department of Agriculture*] [*Information service or system*] (IID) ... WDC
Water Data Sources Directory [*US Geological Survey*] [*Information service or system*] (CRD) ... WDSD
Water Data Unit (DCTA) ... WDU
Water Department (WDAA) ... WD
Water Desurger ... WD
Water Detection Response Team [*DoD*] ... WDRT
Water Dilution Volume [*Environmental chemistry*] (FFDE) ... WDV
Water Dispenser/Fire Extinguisher [*Apollo*] [*NASA*] ... WD/FE
Water Distilling Barge [*Non-self-propelled*] [*Navy symbol*] ... YWDN
Water Distribution Register of Organic Pollutants [*National Institutes of Health*] ... WDROP
Water Division [*Environmental Protection Agency*] (GFGA) ... WD
Water Electrolysis Plenum ... WEP
Water Electrolysis Rocket ... WER
Water Electrolysis System ... WES
Water Emersion Facility ... WEF
Water Enforcement Division [*Environmental Protection Agency*] (EPA) ... WED
Water Enforcement National Data Base (GNE) ... WENDB
Water Engineering Research Laboratory [*Cincinnati, OH*] [*Environmental Protection Agency*] (GRD) ... WERL
Water Entry Point [*Navy*] (CAAL) ... WEP
Water Environment Federation (EAIO) ... WEF
Water Equipment Wholesalers and Suppliers [*Formerly, WEWSA*] ... WEWAS
Water Equipment Wholesalers and Suppliers Association [*Later, WEWAS*] (EA) ... WEWSA
Water Equivalent (MCD) ... WE
Water Exercise Technique [*In book title "The W.E.T. Workout"*] ... WET
Water Export Control ... WEC
Water Extraction of Orange Solids [*Citrus processing*] ... WEOS
Water Facts Consortium [*Defunct*] (EA) ... WFC
Water Filter ... WF
Water Finish [*Paper*] ... WF
Water Flow Meter ... WFM
Water Fog ... WFG
Water for Injection [*Pharmacy*] ... WFI
Water for Peace Office [*Department of State*] ... WPO
Water for People [*An association*] (EA) ... WFP
Water Gas Shift [*Chemical reaction*] ... WGS
Water Gauge ... WG
Water Glycol (KSC) ... W/G
Water Glycol Service Unit (MCD) ... WGS
Water Graphite Reactor Experiment [*Nuclear energy*] ... WGR
Water Hammer ... WHAM
Water Hammer Eliminator ... WHE
Water Heater ... WH
Water Holding Capacity [*Also, WBC*] [*Food industry*] ... WHC
Water Horsepower ... WHP
Water Hydraulic Section ... WHS
Water Hydrogen Ammonia Methane ... WHAM

Water Immersion Facility [*NASA*] (KSC) ... WIF
Water Infiltration Course [*Army*] ... WIC
Water Injection ... WI
Water Injection Unit ... WIU
Water Inlet (DAC) ... WI
Water Insoluble Nonstarchy Polysaccharide [*Food composition*] ... WINP
Water Jacket (MSA) ... WJ
Water Jet Drilling (PDAA) ... WJD
Water Jet Propulsion Assembly (MCD) ... WPA
Water Jet Pump ... WJP
Water Landing Impact (SAA) ... WLI
Water LASER Heat Exchange ... WLHE
Water Level Recorder ... WLR
Water Lily Society (EA) ... WLS
Water Line ... WL
Water Line Zero (KSC) ... WL0
Water Literature (NITA) ... WATERLIT
Water Management Coordinating Committee [*Australia*] ... WMCC
Water Management Division [*Environmental Protection Agency*] (GFGA) ... WMD
Water Management Research Laboratory [*Fresno, CA*] [*Department of Agriculture*] (GRD) ... WMRL
Water Management Section [*Apollo*] [*NASA*] ... WMS
Water Meter ... WM
Water Meter ... WMR
Water Monitor (DS) ... WM
Water Operations Technical Support [*US Army Corps of Engineers*] ... WOTS
Water Outlet Gasket [*Automotive engineering*] ... WO
Water Packed ... WP
Water Phase Salt [*of smoked food*] ... WPS
Water Plane (MSA) ... WP
Water Planning Division [*Environmental Protection Agency*] (EPA) ... WPD
Water Point [*British Waterways Board sign*] ... W
Water Point ... WP
Water Point Systems [*Associated Press*] (SAG) ... WatrPnt
Water Pollution Control ... WPC
Water Pollution Control Administration [*Department of the Interior*] ... WPCA
Water Pollution Control Federation (EA) ... WPCF
Water Pollution Control Research [*Environmental Protection Agency*] ... WPCR
Water Pollution Research Laboratory [*British*] ... WPRL
Water Polution Control Plant [*Environmental science*] ... WPCP
Water Port Identifier Code ... WPIC
Water Port Liaison Office [*or Officer*] [*Air Force*] (AFM) ... WPLO
Water Port of Debarkation (AFM) ... WPOD
Water Port of Embarkation (AFM) ... WPOE
Water/Powder [*Ratio*] [*Pharmacology*] (DAVI) ... W/P
Water Pressure Integrity Test [*For testing water filters*] ... WPIT
Water Pressure Switch ... WPS
Water Programs Office [*Environmental Protection Agency*] ... WPO
Water Propeller (AAG) ... WP
Water Pump (AAG) ... WP
Water Pump Assembly ... WPA
Water Pump Package (NASA) ... WPP
Water Pump Propeller [*on a ship*] (DS) ... WTRPP
Water Purification System ... WPS
Water Quality Act (GFGA) ... WQA
Water Quality Analysis Unit - Purification [*Army*] ... WQAU-P
Water Quality Association (EA) ... WQA
Water Quality Based [*Environmental science*] ... WQB
Water Quality Certification [*Nuclear energy*] (NRCH) ... WQC
Water Quality Incentive Program [*Department of Agriculture*] ... WQIP
Water Quality Index ... WQI
Water Quality Indicator System [*Marine science*] (GFGA) ... WQIS
Water Quality Indicator System [*Marine science*] (MSC) ... WQUIS
Water Quality Instrument ... WQI
Water Quality Insurance Syndicate (EA) ... WQIS
Water Quality Management ... WQM
Water Quality Management Project ... WQMP
Water Quality Office [*Later, OWP*] [*Environmental Protection Agency*] ... WQO
Water Quality Research Council (EA) ... WQRC
Water Quality Research Program [*US Army Corps of Engineers*] ... WQRP
Water Quality-Based Effluent Limit [*Environmental Protection Agency*] ... WQBEL
Water Quantity Measuring Device ... WQMD
Water Quench Test ... WQT
Water Quenching (OA) ... WQ
Water Reactor Analysis Program [*Nuclear energy*] (NRCH) ... WRAP
Water Reactor Safety Research [*Nuclear energy*] (NRCH) ... WRSR
Water Recirculation System ... WRS
Water Recovery Subsystem [*NASA*] (KSC) ... WRS
Water Relief Valve ... WRV
Water Removal Mechanism ... WRM
Water Repellant [*Technical drawings*] ... WR
Water Research Association [*British*] (DCTA) ... WRA
Water Research Centre [*Research center British*] (IRC) ... WRC
Water Research Institute [*West Virginia University*] [*Research center*] (RCD) ... WRI
Water Resource Assessment Working Group [*Australia*] ... WRAWG
Water Resource Planning ... WRP
Water Resource Region [*Water Resources Council*] ... WRR
Water Resources Advisory Committee [*Australian Environment Council*] (EERA) ... WRAC
Water Resources Assessment Methodology [*Army Corps of Engineers*] ... WRAM
Water Resources Board [*British*] (DCTA) ... WRB
Water Resources Center [*University of Illinois*] ... WRC
Water Resources Congress (EA) ... WRC
Water Resources Council [*Inactive*] ... WRC
Water Resources Development Act (GFGA) ... WRDA
Water Resources Division [*US Geological Survey*] ... WRD
Water Resources Division, Manitoba Department of Natural Resources, Winnipeg, Manitoba [*Library symbol National Library of Canada*] (NLC) ... MWWR
Water Resources Document Reference Centre [*Canadian Department of Fisheries and the Environment*] [*Database*] (IID) ... WATDOC
Water Resources Document Reference System (NITA) ... WATDOC
Water Resources Forecasting System (USDC) ... WARFS
Water Resources Forecasting System [*Marine science*] (OSRA) ... WARFS
Water Resources Information File [*Terrain Analysis Center*] [*Army*] ... WRIF
Water Resources Information System [*New South Wales*] [*State*] (EERA) ... WARIS
Water Resources Information System (NOAA) ... WRIS
Water Resources Management Advisory Committee [*Australia*] ... WRMAC
Water Resources Planning Act [*1965*] ... WRPA
Water Resources Publications ... WRP
Water Resources Research [*A publication*] (NOAA) ... WRR
Water Resources Research Act [*1964*] ... WRRA
Water Resources Research Center [*University of Arizona*] (RCD) ... WRRC
Water Resources Research Center [*Purdue University*] (RCD) ... WRRC
Water Resources Research Center [*Indiana University*] (RCD) ... WRRC
Water Resources Research Center [*University of Minnesota of Minneapolis St. Paul*] (RCD) ... WRRC
Water Resources Research Center [*University of Massachusetts*] (RCD) ... WRRC
Water Resources Research Center [*University of Hawaii*] (RCD) ... WRRC
Water Resources Research Institute [*New Mexico State University*] [*Research center*] (RCD) ... WRRI
Water Resources Research Institute [*Oregon State University*] [*Research center*] (RCD) ... WRRI
Water Resources Research Institute [*Clemson University*] [*Research center*] ... WRRI
Water Resources Scientific Information Center [*US Geological Survey*] [*Reston, VA Database originator*] (IT) ... WARSIC
Water Resources Scientific Information Center [*US Geological Survey*] [*Reston, VA Database originator*] ... WRSIC
Water Retention (DAVI) ... WR
Water Rights Office [*Bureau of Indian Affairs*] ... WRO
Water Rinse [*Photography*] (DGA) ... WR
Water/Rock [*Ratio*] [*Geochemistry*] ... W/R
Water Round Torpedo (MSA) ... WRT
Water Safety ... WS
Water Safety Instructor [*Red Cross*] ... WSI
Water Safety Instructor Trainer [*Red Cross*] ... WSIT
Water/Sand Fillable ... WSF
Water Science Laboratories Proprietary Ltd. [*Australia*] ... WSL
Water Seal Drainage [*Medicine*] (MEDA) ... WSD
Water Separation Index, Modified ... WSIM
Water Service Operator (MCD) ... WSO
Water Servicer (NASA) ... WS
Water Servicing Unit (NASA) ... WSU
Water Ski Industry Association (EA) ... WSI
Water Ski Industry Association (EA) ... WSIA
Water Solenoid Valve ... WSV
Water Solubility Index [*Analytical chemistry*] ... WSI
Water Soluble ... WS
Water Soluble Carbodiimide [*Organic chemistry*] ... WSC
Water Soluble Gum Association (EA) ... WSGA
Water Space Amenity Commission [*British*] (DCTA) ... WSAC
Water Sports Australia ... WSA
Water Spray Boiler (NASA) ... WSB
Water Spray Protection [*Shipping*] (DS) ... WSP
Water Stability Index [*Agronomy*] ... WSI
Water Studies Centre [*Australia*] [*Chisholm Institute of Technology*] ... WSC
Water Supply ... WS
Water Supply and Destination ... WSD
Water Supply Forecast (NOAA) ... WSF
Water Supply Improvement Association [*Later, IDA*] (EA) ... WSIA
Water Supply Papers ... WSP
Water Supply Point ... WSP
Water Supply Research Laboratory [*National Environmental Research Center*] ... WSRL
Water Supply Tank ... WST
Water Surface [*Elevation*] ... WS
Water Surface Craft [*JETDS nomenclature*] ... S
Water Swallow [*Medicine*] (DMAA) ... WS
Water System ... WS
Water System (MCD) ... WTRSYS
Water Systems Council (EA) ... WSC
Water Tank ... WT
Water Tank Vessel [*Navy*] ... WTV
Water Tanker [*British*] ... WT
Water Tankers [*Navy symbol*] (MUGU) ... AWK
Water Technology Advisory Committee [*Australia*] ... WTAC
Water Tender [*Navy*] ... WT
Water Tender Construction Battalion [*Navy*] ... WTCB
Water Terminal Clearance Authority [*Army*] (AABC) ... WTCA
Water Thermal and Chemical Technology Center [*University of California*] [*Research center*] (RCD) ... WTC
Water Thermometer ... WT
Water, Toxics, and Pesticides Staff [*Environmental Protection Agency*] (GFGA) ... WTPS
Water Transport Association [*Defunct*] (EA) ... WTA
Water Treatment Plant [*Nuclear energy*] (NRCH) ... WTP
Water Turbine (MSA) ... WTURB

Water Turbine Closed Coupled (MSA) ...... WTCC
Water Turbine Direct (MSA) ...... WTD
Water Turnover Rate [Physiology] ...... WTR
Water Use Information System [Westinghouse Hanford Co.] (IID) ...... WUIS
Water Valley, MS [FM radio station call letters] (RBYB) ...... WLPX-FM
Water Valley, MS [FM radio station call letters] ...... WYCG
Water Valley Public Library, Alberta [Library symbol National Library of Canada] (NLC) ...... AWV
Water Valley Public Library, Water Valley, MS [Library symbol Library of Congress] (LCLS) ...... MsWv
Water Valve (ROG) ...... WV
Water Vapor Content ...... WVE
Water Vapor Electrolysis [Cell] ...... WVE
Water Vapor Electrolysis Module [NASA] ...... WVEM
Water Vapor Nitrogen [Nuclear energy] (NRCH) ...... WVN
Water Vapor Permeability [Physical chemistry] ...... WVP
Water Vapor Pressure ...... E
Water Vapor Sensor ...... WVS
Water Vapor Transmission ...... WVT
Water Vapor Transmission Rate ...... WVTR
Water Wall (Peripheral Jet) (AAG) ...... WWP
Water Wall (Side Skegs) (AAG) ...... WWS
Water Waste (NASA) ...... WW
Water/Wastewater Utilities [Environmental science] ...... WWU
Water Watch (Program) [Australia] ...... WW
Water-Activated Battery ...... WAB
Water-Alternating Gas [Petroleum engineering] ...... WAG
Water-Augmented Air Jet ...... WAA
Water-Augmented Air Jet ...... WAAJ
Water-Augmented Jet ...... WAJ
Water-Augmented Vehicle ...... WAVE
Water-Based Polishing Compound ...... WBPC
Waterbeach [British ICAO location identifier] (ICLI) ...... EGUK
Waterbed Manufacturers Association (EA) ...... WMA
Waterborne Commerce of the United States [DoD/COE] (TAG) ...... WCUS
Waterborne Guard Post (NVT) ...... WBGP
Waterborne Intrusion Detection System (MCD) ...... WIDS
Water-Borne Logistics Craft ...... WBLC
Waterbury [Connecticut] [Airport symbol] (AD) ...... OXC
Waterbury, CT [AM radio station call letters] ...... WATR
Waterbury, CT [FM radio station call letters] (RBYB) ...... WMRQ
Waterbury, CT [AM radio station call letters] (RBYB) ...... WQQW
Waterbury, CT [Television station call letters] ...... WTXX
Waterbury, CT [AM radio station call letters] ...... WWCO
Waterbury, CT [FM radio station call letters] ...... WWYZ
Waterbury, VT [AM radio station call letters] ...... WDEV
Waterbury, VT [FM radio station call letters] ...... WGLY
Watercolor (VRA) ...... wc
Watercolor on Paper (VRA) ...... wc/pa
Watercolor Spectrometer (PDAA) ...... WCS
Water-Cooled (DEN) ...... WC
Water-Cooled (AAG) ...... WCLD
Water-Cooled Copper ...... WCC
Water-Cooled Garment ...... WCG
Water-Cooled Reactor ...... WCR
Water-Cooled Rod ...... WCR
Water-Cooled Tube [Nuclear energy] (IAA) ...... WCT
Watercooler (AAG) ...... WCR
Watercraft Intensively Managed Items (AABC) ...... WIMI
Water-dispersed-in-Oil [emulsion] ...... W/O
Water-Dispersible Powder [Pesticide formulation] ...... WP
Water-Drop-Penetration Time [Agriculture] ...... WDPT
Watered Capital (MHDW) ...... WC
Watered Silk Cloth (DGA) ...... WSC
Watered Silk Paper (DGA) ...... WSP
Watered Stock ...... WS
Water-Extended Polyester ...... WEP
Water-Extracted Soluble Orange Solids [Citrus processing] ...... WESOS
Waterfall, AK [Location identifier FAA] (FAAL) ...... KWF
Waterfalls [Board on Geographic Names] ...... FLLS
Water-Flooded Helical Screw Low-Pressure Air Compressor [Navy] (CAAL) ...... WFHSLPAC
Waterford [Crystal glassware] (BARN) ...... Wat
Waterford [County in Ireland] (ROG) ...... WATERF
Waterford [County in Ireland] ...... WATERFD
Waterford [Glassware] (BARN) ...... Wtff
Waterford and Tranmore Railway [British] (ROG) ...... WTR
Waterford Generating Station [Nuclear energy] (NRCH) ...... WGS
Waterford Glass Group PLC (MHDW) ...... WATFY
Waterford Hospital, Health Services, St. John's, NF, Canada [Library symbol Library of Congress] (LCLS) ...... CaNfSWH
Waterford Public Library, Ontario [Library symbol National Library of Canada] (NLC) ...... OWAP
Waterford Public Library, Waterford, ON, Canada [Library symbol Library of Congress] (LCLS) ...... CaOWaP
Waterford Public Library, Waterford, WI [Library symbol Library of Congress] (LCLS) ...... WWatf
Waterford Steam Electric Station [Nuclear energy] (NRCH) ...... WSES
Waterford Wedgewood PLC ADR [Associated Press] (SAG) ...... WatfdW
Waterford Wedgwood Ltd. [NASDAQ symbol] (NQ) ...... WATF
Waterford Wedgwood plcADs [NASDAQ symbol] (TTSB) ...... WATFZ
Waterfowl USA (EA) ...... WUSA
Waterfront Center (EA) ...... WC
Watergate Special Prosecution Force [Terminated, 1977] [Department of Justice] ...... WSPF

Water-Glycol Cooling Unit Technician (SAA) ...... WGT
Water-Glycol Evaporator Control System (SAA) ...... WECS
Waterhouse Investor Service [NYSE symbol] (SPSG) ...... WHO
Waterhouse Investor Services, Inc. [Associated Press] (SAG) ...... Waterhse
Waterhouse Investor Svc [NYSE symbol] (TTSB) ...... WHO
Waterhouse-Friderichsen Syndrome [Medicine] ...... WFS
Water-in-Oil ...... W/O
Water-Insoluble Inorganic Residue (DICI) ...... WIIR
Water-Insoluble Nitrogen [Analytical chemistry] ...... WIN
Water-Jel Tech [NASDAQ symbol] (TTSB) ...... BURN
Water-Jel Technol Wrrt'A' [NASDAQ symbol] (TTSB) ...... BURNZ
Water-Jel Technologies [NASDAQ symbol] (SAG) ...... BURN
Water-Jel Technologies [Associated Press] (SAG) ...... WatrJ
Water-Jel Technologies [Associated Press] (SAG) ...... WatrJel
Water-Jel Technologies [NASDAQ symbol] (SAG) ...... XCED
Waterjet Machining [Factory automation] (BTTJ) ...... WJM
Waterkloof [South Africa] [ICAO location identifier] (ICLI) ...... FAWK
Waterless Electrical Data Generating Effortless ...... WEDGE
Waterline Length [Navy] ...... LWL
Waterload Test [Clinical chemistry] ...... WL
Waterload Test (DAVI) ...... WLT
Waterloo [Iowa] [Airport symbol] (OAG) ...... ALO
Waterloo [Army British] (ROG) ...... W
Waterloo and City Railway (ROG) ...... WCR
Waterloo Centre for Groundwater Research [University of Waterloo] [Canada] (IRC) ...... WCGR
Waterloo Centre for Integrated Manufacturing [University of Waterloo] [Canada Research center] (RCD) ...... WATCIM
Waterloo Centre for Process Development [University of Waterloo] [Research center] (RCD) ...... WCPD
Waterloo COBOL [Common Business-Oriented Language] [University of Waterloo] [Canada] ...... WATBOL
Waterloo Community School District 3, Waterloo, IL [Library symbol Library of Congress] (LCLS) ...... IWatISD
Waterloo Concordance (NITA) ...... WATCON
Waterloo County Board of Education [UTLAS symbol] ...... WBS
Waterloo County Board of Education, Kitchener, ON, Canada [Library symbol] [Library of Congress] (LCLS) ...... CaOKitWC
Waterloo County Board of Education, Kitchener, Ontario [Library symbol National Library of Canada] (NLC) ...... OKITWC
Waterloo County Board of Education, Professional Education Library [UTLAS symbol] ...... WBE
Waterloo, DE [Location identifier FAA] (FAAL) ...... ATR
Waterloo FORTRAN [University of Waterloo] [Canada] ...... WATFOR
Waterloo FORTRAN [Formula Translating System] IV [University of Waterloo] [Canada] (HGAA) ...... WATFIV
Waterloo, IA [FM radio station call letters] ...... KBBG
Waterloo, IA [FM radio station call letters] ...... KFMW
Waterloo, IA [AM radio station call letters] ...... KNWS
Waterloo, IA [FM radio station call letters] ...... KNWS-FM
Waterloo, IA [FM radio station call letters] ...... KOKZ
Waterloo, IA [Television station call letters] ...... KRIN
Waterloo, IA [AM radio station call letters] ...... KWLO
Waterloo, IA [AM radio station call letters] (RBYB) ...... KWOF
Waterloo, IA [Television station call letters] ...... KWWL
Waterloo, IA [AM radio station call letters] ...... KXEL
Waterloo Interactive Direct Job Entry Terminal System [IBM Corp.] ...... WIDJET
Waterloo, NY [FM radio station call letters] ...... WNYR
Waterloo, ON [FM radio station call letters] ...... CKMS
Waterloo Public Library, Ontario [Library symbol National Library of Canada] (NLC) ...... OWT
Waterloo Public Library, Quebec [Library symbol National Library of Canada] (NLC) ...... QW
Waterloo Public Library, Waterloo, IA [Library symbol Library of Congress] (LCLS) ...... IaW
Waterloo Public Library, Waterloo, IA [OCLC symbol] (OCLC) ...... IWV
Waterloo Public Library, Waterloo, ON, Canada [Library symbol Library of Congress] (LCLS) ...... CaOWt
Waterloo Public Library, Waterloo, PQ, Canada [Library symbol Library of Congress] (LCLS) ...... CaQW
Waterloo Railroad Co. [AAR code] ...... WLO
Waterloo Regional Library, Cambridge, ON, Canada [Library symbol Library of Congress] (LCLS) ...... CaOCaW
Waterloo Regional Library, Waterloo, Ontario [Library symbol National Library of Canada] (NLC) ...... OCW
Waterloo Research Institute [University of Waterloo] [Research center] (RCD) ...... WRI
Waterloo Resources, Inc. [Vancouver Stock Exchange symbol] ...... WAL
Waterloo-Grant Township Public Library, Waterloo, IN [Library symbol Library of Congress] (LCLS) ...... InWat
Waterloo-Wellington/Kitchener, ON [ICAO location identifier] (ICLI) ...... CYKF
Waterman on Set-Off [A publication] (DLA) ...... Wat Set-Off
Waterman on the Law of Trespass [A publication] (DLA) ...... Wat Tres
Waterman's Criminal Digest [United States] [A publication] (DLA) ...... Wat Cr Dig
Waterman's Criminal Procedure [A publication] (DLA) ...... Wat Cr Proc
Waterman's Justices' Manual [A publication] (DLA) ...... Wat Just
Watermarc Food Management Co. [NASDAQ symbol] (SAG) ...... WAMA
Watermarc Food Management Co. [Associated Press] (SAG) ...... Watermrc
Watermarc Food Management Co. [Associated Press] (SAG) ...... Watrm
Watermarc Food Mgmt [NASDAQ symbol] (TTSB) ...... WAMA
Watermarc Food Mgmt 9% Cv Pfd [NASDAQ symbol] (TTSB) ...... WAMAP
Watermarc Food Mgmt Wrrt'A' [NASDAQ symbol] (TTSB) ...... WAMAW
Watermark ...... WM
Watermark ...... WMK
Watermark Association of Artisans (EA) ...... WAA

Watermarked (WGA) ... WMKD
Watermelon Growers and Distributors Association ... WGDA
Watermelon Mosaic Virus ... WMV
Watermelon Mosaic Virus E ... WMV-E
Watermen and Lightermen's Protective Society [*A union*] [*British*] ... WLPS
Watermen and Riverside Labourers' Union [*British*] ... WRLU
Watermen, Lightermen, Tugmen, and Bargemen's Union [*British*] ... WLTBU
Watermen's Protective Society [*A union*] [*British*] ... WPS
Watermen's Trade Society [*A union*] [*British*] ... WTS
Watermeyer's Cape Of Good Hope Reports [*South Africa*] [*A publication*] (DLA) ... Wat CGH
Watermeyer's Cape Of Good Hope Reports [*South Africa*] [*A publication*] (DLA) ... Watermeyer
Watermeyer's Cape Of Good Hope Supreme Court Reports [*A publication*] (DLA) ... W
Watermeyer's Cape Of Good Hope Supreme Court Reports [*1857*] [*South Africa*] [*A publication*] (DLA) ... Wat
Water-Moderated Reactor ... WMR
Water-Oil Contact ... WOC
Water-Oil Ratio ... WOR
Water-Oil-Gas (AAG) ... WOG
Waterproof ... WP
Waterproof (MSA) ... WTRPRF
Waterproof Breathable [*Textile technology*] ... WB
Waterproof Fan Cooled (MSA) ... WPFC
Waterproof Membrane ... WPM
Waterproof Paper Manufacturers Association [*Later, API*] ... WPMA
Waterproof Paper Packing ... WPP
Waterproof Shroud ... WPS
Waterproofing (AAG) ... WPG
Waterproofing ... WTRPRFG
Water-Quality Biological [*Survey*] [*Army*] (RDA) ... WQB
Water-Repellent Wood Preservative (DICI) ... WRWP
Water-Retention Coefficient ... WRC
Water-Retention Value ... WRV
Waters Associates, Milford, MA [*OCLC symbol*] (OCLC) ... WTR
Waters Branch, Walden Public Library, Ontario [*Library symbol National Library of Canada*] (NLC) ... OWWA
Waters Computing Center [*Rose-Hulman Institute of Technology*] [*Research center*] (RCD) ... WCC
Waters Corp. [*NYSE symbol*] (SAG) ... WAT
Waters Corp. [*Associated Press*] (SAG) ... WatrsCp
Waters Instruments [*NASDAQ symbol*] (TTSB) ... WTRS
Waters Instruments, Inc. [*Associated Press*] (SAG) ... WatrIn
Waters Instruments, Inc. [*NASDAQ symbol*] (NQ) ... WTRS
Waters Intelligent Information Processor ... WIIP
Watershed ... WSTSHD
Watershed Foundation (EA) ... WF
Watershed Management Information System ... WAMIS
Watershed Modeling System ... WMS
Watershed Research Unit [*Columbia, MO*] [*Department of Agriculture*] (GRD) ... WRU
Waterside Workers' Federation of Australia ... WWFA
Watersmeet, MI [*Location identifier FAA*] (FAAL) ... RXW
Water-Soluble Adjuvant [*Immunology*] ... WSA
Water-Soluble Base ... WSB
Water-Soluble Dietary Fiber [*Medicine*] ... WSDF
Water-Soluble Fraction ... WSF
Water-Soluble Nitrogen [*Analytical chemistry*] ... WSN
Water-Soluble Nonstarchy Polysaccharide [*Food composition*] ... WSNP
Water-Soluble Vitamin ... WSV
Waterspout ... WTSPT
Water-Storage Cell [*Botany*] ... WS
Watertight ... WT
Watertight (MSA) ... WTRTT
Watertight Door ... WTD
Watertight Manhole (WDAA) ... WTMH
Waterton [*Colorado*] [*Seismograph station code, US Geological Survey Closed*] (SEIS) ... WTC
Watertown [*New York*] [*Airport symbol*] (OAG) ... ART
Watertown [*South Dakota*] [*Airport symbol*] (OAG) ... ATY
Watertown Arsenal [*Massachusetts*] [*Army*] ... WA
Watertown Arsenal Laboratory [*Massachusetts*] [*Army*] ... WAL
Watertown Arsenal Medical Laboratory [*Massachusetts*] [*Army*] ... WAML
Watertown, FL [*FM radio station call letters*] ... WQLC
Watertown Free Public Library, Watertown, MA [*Library symbol Library of Congress*] (LCLS) ... MWat
Watertown Free Public Library, Watertown, MA [*OCLC symbol*] (OCLC) ... WAT
Watertown Free Public Library, Watertown, WI [*Library symbol Library of Congress*] (LCLS) ... WWat
Watertown/International [*New York*] [*ICAO location identifier*] (ICLI) ... KART
Watertown Library, Watertown, CT [*Library symbol Library of Congress*] (LCLS) ... CtWat
Watertown, MN [*AM radio station call letters*] (RBYB) ... KWOM
Watertown, NY [*AM radio station call letters*] ... WATN
Watertown, NY [*FM radio station call letters*] ... WCIZ
Watertown, NY [*FM radio station call letters*] ... WJNY
Watertown, NY [*AM radio station call letters*] ... WNCQ
Watertown, NY [*Television station call letters*] ... WNPE
Watertown, NY [*FM radio station call letters*] ... WRVJ
Watertown, NY [*FM radio station call letters*] ... WSLJ
Watertown, NY [*AM radio station call letters*] ... WTNY
Watertown, NY [*FM radio station call letters*] ... WTNY-FM
Watertown, NY [*Television station call letters*] ... WWTI
Watertown Regional Library, Watertown, SD [*Library symbol Library of Congress*] (LCLS) ... SdW
Watertown, SD [*FM radio station call letters*] ... KDLO
Watertown, SD [*FM radio station call letters*] ... KIXX
Watertown, SD [*AM radio station call letters*] ... KSDR
Watertown, SD [*FM radio station call letters*] ... KSDR-FM
Watertown, SD [*AM radio station call letters*] ... KWAT
Watertown Township Library, Fostoria, MI [*Library symbol Library of Congress*] (LCLS) ... MiFos
Watertown, WI [*Location identifier FAA*] (FAAL) ... RYV
Watertown, WI [*FM radio station call letters*] ... WJJO
Watertown, WI [*AM radio station call letters*] ... WTTN
Water-Tube Auxiliary Boiler (DS) ... WT Aux B
Water-Tube Boiler [*Naval*] ... WT
Water-Tube Boiler [*Naval*] ... WTB
Water-Tube Boiler Survey (DS) ... WTBS
Water-Tube Boilermakers Association [*British*] (BI) ... WTBA
Water-Tube Domestic Boiler (DS) ... wtdb
Water-Use Efficiency [*Agriculture*] ... WUE
Water-Vapor-Saturated Air (PDAA) ... WVSA
Waterville [*AAR code*] ... WATR
Waterville [*Colby College*] [*Maine*] [*Seismograph station code, US Geological Survey*] (SEIS) ... WTR
Waterville [*Maine*] [*Airport symbol*] (OAG) ... WVL
Waterville, ME [*Location identifier FAA*] (FAAL) ... AVI
Waterville, ME [*Location identifier FAA*] (FAAL) ... RLU
Waterville, ME [*FM radio station call letters*] ... WEBB
Waterville, ME [*FM radio station call letters*] ... WMEW
Waterville, ME [*FM radio station call letters*] ... WMHB
Waterville, ME [*AM radio station call letters*] ... WTVL
Waterville, ME [*Location identifier FAA*] (FAAL) ... WVL
Waterville, OH [*Location identifier FAA*] (FAAL) ... VWV
Waterville Public Library, Waterville, ME [*Library symbol Library of Congress*] (LCLS) ... MeW
Watervliet Arsenal [*New York*] [*Army*] ... WVA
Watervliet Arsenal [*New York*] [*Army*] ... WVT
Watervliet Arsenal Library, Watervliet, NY [*Library symbol Library of Congress*] (LCLS) ... NWatvlA
Watervliet Public Library, Watervliet, MI [*Library symbol Library of Congress*] (LCLS) ... MiWatv
Waterwall (MSA) ... WW
Waterways Bulk Transportation Council (EA) ... WBTC
Waterways Commission [*Western Australia*] ... WC
Waterways Development, Transport Canada [*Developpement des vois Navigables, Transports Canada*] **Montreal, Quebec** [*Library symbol National Library of Canada*] (NLC) ... QMTR
Waterways Experiment Station [*Army Corps of Engineers*] [*Vicksburg, MS*] ... WES
Waterways Experiment Station Terrain Analyzer RADAR ... WESTAR
Waterways Freight Bureau [*Defunct*] (EA) ... WFB
Waterways Freight Bureau, Washington DC [*STAC*] ... WWB
Waterwheel ... WWHL
Water-White ... WW
Waterworks ... WW
Watery Diarrhea, Hypochlorhydria, Hypokalemia, and Alkalosis [*Medicine*] ... WDHHA
Watery Diarrhea, Hypokalemia [*Syndrome*] [*Medicine*] ... WDH
Watery Diarrhea, Hypokalemia, Achlorhydria [*Medicine*] ... WDHA
Watery Diarrhea, Hypokalemia, Hypochlorhydria [*Syndrome*] [*Medicine*] ... WDHH
Watford City, ND [*Location identifier FAA*] (FAAL) ... AFD
Watheroo [*Australia Seismograph station code, US Geological Survey Closed*] (SEIS) ... WAT
Watkins Glen, NY [*AM radio station call letters*] ... WGMF
Watkins on Conveyancing [*9th ed.*] [*1845*] [*A publication*] (DLA) ... Wat Con
Watkins on Conveyancing [*A publication*] (DLA) ... Watk Con
Watkins on Conveyancing [*A publication*] (DLA) ... Watk Conv
Watkins on Copyholds [*6th ed.*] [*1829*] [*A publication*] (DLA) ... Wat Cop
Watkins on Copyholds [*A publication*] (DLA) ... Watk Cop
Watkins on Copyholds [*A publication*] (DLA) ... Watk Copyh
Watkins on Descents [*A publication*] (DLA) ... Watk Des
Watkins-Johnson [*NYSE symbol*] (TTSB) ... WJ
Watkins-Johnson Co. [*Associated Press*] (SAG) ... WatkJn
Watkins-Johnson Co. [*NYSE symbol*] (SPSG) ... WJ
Watonga, OK [*FM radio station call letters*] ... KIMY
Watonwan County Library, St. James, MN [*Library symbol Library of Congress*] (LCLS) ... MnStj
Watsco, Inc. [*Associated Press*] (SAG) ... Watsc
Watsco, Inc. [*Associated Press*] (SAG) ... Watsco
Watsco, Inc. [*NYSE symbol*] (SAG) ... WSO
Watsco, Inc. [*AMEX symbol*] (SPSG) ... WSO
Watsco Inc. Cv Cl'B' [*AMEX symbol*] (TTSB) ... WSO.B
Watseka, IL [*AM radio station call letters*] ... WGFA
Watseka, IL [*FM radio station call letters*] ... WGFA-FM
Watseka Public Library, Watseka, IL [*Library symbol Library of Congress*] (LCLS) ... IWat
Watsha [*Zaire*] [*ICAO location identifier*] (ICLI) ... FZJI
Watson Collectors Club (EA) ... WCC
Watson General Corp. [*Associated Press*] (SAG) ... WatsGen
Watson General Corp. [*NASDAQ symbol*] (SPSG) ... WGEN
Watson Laboratories Air Materiel Command (SAA) ... WLAC
Watson Lake [*Canada*] [*Airport symbol*] (OAG) ... YQH
Watson Lake, YT [*ICAO location identifier*] (ICLI) ... CYQH
Watson on Arbitration [*A publication*] (DLA) ... Wats Arb
Watson on Partnership [*2nd ed.*] [*1807*] [*A publication*] (DLA) ... Wats Part
Watson Pharmaceuticals [*NASDAQ symbol*] (TTSB) ... WATS

Watson Pharmaceuticals, Inc. [*NASDAQ symbol*] (SAG) ... WATS
Watson Pharmaceuticals, Inc. [*Associated Press*] (SAG) ... WatsnPh
Watson Research Center [*IBM Corp.*] ... WRC
Watson Wyatt Worldwide [*Commercial firm*] (ECON) ... WW
Watson-Glaser Critical Thinking Appraisal (EDAC) ... WGCTA
Watson's Clergyman's Law [*A publication*] (DLA) ... Wats Cler Law
Watson's Compendium of Equity [*A publication*] (DLA) ... Wats Comp Eq
Watson's Compendium of Equity [*2 eds.*] [*1873, 1888*] [*A publication*] (DLA) ... Watson
Watson's Compendium of Equity [*A publication*] (DLA) ... Watson Eq
Watson's Constitutional History of Canada [*A publication*] (DLA) ... Wats Const Hist
Watson's Medical Jurisprudence [*A publication*] (DLA) ... Wats Med Jur
Watson's Office and Duty of Sheriff [*2nd ed.*] [*1848*] [*A publication*] (DLA) ... Wats Sher
Watson's United States Commissioners' Manual [*A publication*] (DLA) ... Wats Com Man
Watsonville, CA [*Location identifier FAA*] (FAAL) ... AYN
Watsonville, CA [*Television station call letters*] ... KCAH
Watsonville, CA [*Location identifier FAA*] (FAAL) ... WVI
Watsonville Public Library, Watsonville, CA [*Library symbol Library of Congress*] (LCLS) ... CWats
Watt [*Symbol*] [*SI unit of power*] (GPO) ... W
Watt (WDMC) ... w
Watt (IAA) ... WT
Watt Demand Meter (MSA) ... WD
Watt Electric ... We
Watt Meter (IAA) ... W
Watt Meter ... WM
Watt per Steradian Square Meter (WDAA) ... W/(SR-M^2)
Watt Second ... W S
Watt-Hour ... WH
Watt-Hour (AAG) ... W-HR
Watt-Hour Demand Meter ... WHDM
Watt-Hour Demand Meter, Thermal Type (IEEE) ... WHT
Watt-Hour Meter ... WHM
Watt-Hour Meter (IAA) ... WHRM
Watt-Hour Meter with Contact Device ... WHC
Watt-Hour Meter with Loss Compensator (MSA) ... WHL
Wattisham [*British ICAO location identifier*] (ICLI) ... EGUW
Wattle [*Ornithology*] ... W
Wattle Grove Press ... WGP
Wattle Tannin Equivalent [*Chemistry*] ... WTE
Wattle-Urea-Formaldehyde [*Adhesive component*] ... WUF
Watton [*British ICAO location identifier*] (ICLI) ... EGYR
Watt-per-Channel (IAA) ... WPC
Watts and Sergeant's Pennsylvania Reports [*1841-1845*] [*A publication*] (DLA) ... W & S
Watts and Sergeant's Pennsylvania Reports [*1841-45*] [*A publication*] (DLA) ... Watts & S
Watts and Sergeant's Pennsylvania Reports [*1841-45*] [*A publication*] (DLA) ... Watts & S (PA)
Watts and Sergeant's Pennsylvania Reports [*1841-45*] [*A publication*] (DLA) ... Watts & Serg
Watts Bar Dam [*TVA*] ... WBD
Watts Bar Nuclear Plant (NRCH) ... WBNP
Watts Industries [*Associated Press*] (SAG) ... WattsInd
Watts Industries [*NYSE symbol*] (SAG) ... WTS
Watts Industries'A' [*NYSE symbol*] (TTSB) ... WTS
Watts Labor Community Action Committee [*Los Angeles, CA*] ... WLCAC
Watt's Pennsylvania Reports [*A publication*] (DLA) ... W
Watts' Pennsylvania Reports [*1832-40*] [*A publication*] (DLA) ... Watts
Watts' Pennsylvania Reports [*1832-40*] [*A publication*] (DLA) ... Watts (PA)
Watts per Candle [*Electricity*] ... W/C
Watts per Candle (IDOE) ... W/c
Watts per Candle (IDOE) ... Wpc
Watts per Candle [*Electricity*] ... WPC
Watts per Meter Kelvin ... W/(M K)
Watts per Square Centimeter (CET) ... W/CM^2
Watts per Square Centimeter (IDOE) ... W/cm^2
Watts per Square Inch ... W/IN^2
Watts per Square Meter ... W/M^2
Watts per Square Meter Kelvin ... W/(M^2 K)
Watts per Square Meter Steradian ... W/(M^2 SR)
Watts per Steradian (NG) ... W/S
Watts per Steradian ... W/sr
Watts per Steradian (IDOE) ... W/wr
Watts per Steradian ... WPS
Watts' Reports [*1890-1939*] [*A publication*] (DLA) ... Wa
Watts' Reports [*16-24 West Virginia*] [*A publication*] (DLA) ... Watts
Watts Root-Mean-Square ... WRMS
Watt-Second (AAG) ... WSEC
Watt-Seconds ... w/s
Watusi International Association (EA) ... WIA
Wau [*Sudan*] [*ICAO location identifier*] (ICLI) ... HSWW
Wau [*Papua New Guinea*] [*Airport symbol*] (OAG) ... WUG
Wau [*Sudan*] [*Airport symbol*] (OAG) ... WUU
Waubay Public Library, Waubay, SD [*Library symbol Library of Congress*] (LCLS) ... SdWau
Waubon-Ogema-White Earth School, Waubon, MN [*Library symbol*] [*Library of Congress*] (LCLS) ... MnWauWE
Waubonsee Community College, Sugar Grove, IL [*Library symbol Library of Congress*] (LCLS) ... ISgW
Waubonsee Community College, Sugar Grove, IL [*OCLC symbol*] (OCLC) ... JAJ
Wauchula, FL [*AM radio station call letters*] ... WAUC
Waukee Public Library, Waukee, IA [*Library symbol Library of Congress*] (LCLS) ... IaWauke
Waukegan Avionics, Inc. [*ICAO designator*] (FAAC) ... SCP
Waukegan, IL [*Location identifier FAA*] (FAAL) ... UGN
Waukegan, IL [*AM radio station call letters*] ... WKRS
Waukegan, IL [*FM radio station call letters*] ... WXLC
Waukegan Public Library, Waukegan, IL [*Library symbol Library of Congress*] (LCLS) ... IWau
Waukesha County Historical Society, Waukesha, WI [*Library symbol Library of Congress*] (LCLS) ... WWauHi
Waukesha County Institute, Pewaukee, WI [*OCLC symbol*] (OCLC) ... WCT
Waukesha County Institution, Waukesha, WI [*Library symbol Library of Congress*] (LCLS) ... WWauI
Waukesha County Technical Institute, Pewaukee, WI [*Library symbol Library of Congress*] (LCLS) ... WPeW
Waukesha Memorial Hospital, Waukesha, WI [*Library symbol Library of Congress*] (LCLS) ... WWauH
Waukesha Public Library, Waukesha, WI [*OCLC symbol*] (OCLC) ... WIV
Waukesha Public Library, Waukesha, WI [*Library symbol Library of Congress*] (LCLS) ... WWau
Waukesha, WI [*Location identifier FAA*] (FAAL) ... SKC
Waukesha, WI [*Location identifier FAA*] (FAAL) ... UES
Waukesha, WI [*AM radio station call letters*] ... WAUK
Waukesha, WI [*FM radio station call letters*] ... WCCX
Waukesha, WI [*FM radio station call letters*] ... WMIL
Waukon Democrat, Waukon, IA [*Library symbol Library of Congress*] (LCLS) ... IaWaukD
Waukon, IA [*AM radio station call letters*] ... KNEI
Waukon, IA [*FM radio station call letters*] ... KNEI-FM
Waukon, IA [*Location identifier FAA*] (FAAL) ... UKN
Waukon Republican-Standard, Waukon, IA [*Library symbol Library of Congress*] (LCLS) ... IaWaukR
Waunakee, WI [*FM radio station call letters*] ... WYZM
Waupaca Free Public Library, Waupaca, WI [*Library symbol Library of Congress*] (LCLS) ... WWaupa
Waupaca, WI [*Location identifier FAA*] (FAAL) ... PCZ
Waupaca, WI [*AM radio station call letters*] ... WDUX
Waupaca, WI [*FM radio station call letters*] ... WDUX-FM
Waupun Public Library, Waupun, WI [*Library symbol*] [*Library of Congress*] (LCLS) ... WWaup
Waupun, WI [*AM radio station call letters*] ... WMRH
Wausau [*Wisconsin*] [*Airport symbol*] (OAG) ... AUW
Wausau [*Wisconsin*] **Central Wisconsin** [*Airport symbol*] (OAG) ... CWA
Wausau Hospitals, Inc., Wausau, WI [*Library symbol Library of Congress*] (LCLS) ... WWsW
Wausau Paper Mills [*Associated Press*] (SAG) ... WausauP
Wausau Paper Mills [*NASDAQ symbol*] (TTSB) ... WSAU
Wausau Paper Mills Co. [*NASDAQ symbol*] (NQ) ... WSAU
Wausau Public Library, Wausau, WI [*Library symbol Library of Congress*] (LCLS) ... WWs
Wausau, WI [*Television station call letters*] ... WAOW
Wausau, WI [*FM radio station call letters*] ... WCLQ
Wausau, WI [*FM radio station call letters*] ... WDEZ
Wausau, WI [*FM radio station call letters*] ... WHRM
Wausau, WI [*Television station call letters*] ... WHRM-TV
Wausau, WI [*FM radio station call letters*] ... WIFC
Wausau, WI [*FM radio station call letters*] (RBYB) ... WLBL-FM
Wausau, WI [*AM radio station call letters*] ... WSAU
Wausau, WI [*Television station call letters*] ... WSAW
Wausau, WI [*AM radio station call letters*] ... WXCO
Wausau, WI [*FM radio station call letters*] (RBYB) ... WXPW
Wausau, WI [*FM radio station call letters*] ... WYCO
Wauseon, OH [*Location identifier FAA*] (FAAL) ... USE
Wauseon, OH [*FM radio station call letters*] (RBYB) ... WYSA-FM
Wautoma, WI [*FM radio station call letters*] ... WAEI
Wauwatosa Public Library, Wauwatosa, WI [*Library symbol Library of Congress*] (LCLS) ... WWa
Wauwatosa-Milwaukee, WI [*FM radio station call letters*] (RBYB) ... WAMG
Wave Analyzer (IAA) ... WA
Wave and Current Advisory Service [*British*] ... WACAS
Wave Change ... W/C
Wave Data Analyzer [*Marine science*] (MSC) ... WDA
Wave Digital Filter (PDAA) ... WDF
Wave Dynamics Division [*US Army Corps of Engineers*] ... WDD
Wave Filters and Equalizers (MCD) ... WF & EQ
Wave Form Analyzer [*Instrumentation*] ... WFA
Wave Frequency [*Telecommunications*] (IAA) ... WF
Wave Height Correction ... W
Wave Height Indicator [*Oceanography*] ... WHI
Wave Information Studies Wave Model [*Computer science*] ... WISWAVE
Wave Information Study [*US Army Corps of Engineers*] ... WIS
Wave Meter ... WM
Wave Model (USDC) ... WAM
Wave Model [*Marine science*] (OSRA) ... WAM
Wave Momentum Flux Experiment [*National Science Foundation*] ... WAMFLEX
Wave Officers' Quarters ... WOQ
Wave Power Source ... WPS
Wave Propagation Laboratory [*Boulder, CO*] [*National Oceanic and Atmospheric Administration*] ... WPL
Wave Radiometer System ... WRS
Wave Retardation (DEN) ... WR
Wave Rider Information Processing System (USDC) ... WRIPS
Wave Rider Information Processing System [*Marine science*] (OSRA) ... WRIPS
Wave Run-Up ... WRU
Wave Soldering ... WS

Wave Soldering Fixture (MCD) ... WSF
Wave Superheater Hypersonic Tunnel (IAA) ... WSHT
Wave Systems Corp. [*Associated Press*] (SAG) ... WaveSys
Wave Systems Corp. [*NASDAQ symbol*] (SAG) ... WAVX
Wave Systems'A' [*NASDAQ symbol*] (TTSB) ... WAVX
Wave Technologies International, Inc. [*Associated Press*] (SAG) ... WaveTec
Wave Technologies Intl [*NASDAQ symbol*] (TTSB) ... WAVT
Wave Technologies Intl, Inc. [*NASDAQ symbol*] (SAG) ... WAVT
Wave Vector Filter ... WVF
Wave-Activated Turbine Generator (PDAA) ... WATG
Wave-Band (ADA) ... WB
Waveform [*Telecommunications*] (IAA) ... WF
Waveform Analysis for Nondestructive Evaluation [*Military computer software*] (RDA) ... WAND
Waveform Analyzer ... WA
Waveform Digitizer [*Telecommunications*] (IAA) ... WD
Waveform Distortion [*Telecommunications*] (IAA) ... WD
Waveform Distortion [*Telecommunications*] (TEL) ... WFD
Waveform Function Generator ... WFG
Waveform Generator ... WFG
Waveform Monitor ... WFM
Waveform Processing System ... WPS
Waveform Synthesizer (IAA) ... WS
Wavefront Analysis of Spatial Sampling [*Aircraft landing approach*] ... WASS
Wavefront Technologies, Inc. [*Associated Press*] (SAG) ... Wavefrnt
Waveguide (SAA) ... W
Waveguide ... WG
Waveguide Assembly ... WGA
Waveguide below Cutoff (IEEE) ... WBCO
Waveguide Delay Line ... WGDL
Waveguide Directional Coupler ... WGDC
Waveguide Directional Localizer ... WDL
Waveguide Filter ... WGF
Waveguide Frequency Meter ... WFM
Waveguide Glide Slope ... WGS
Waveguide Harmonic Filter ... WHF
Waveguide Impedance Measuring Set ... WIMS
Waveguide Isolator ... WGI
Waveguide Load ... WGL
Waveguide Meter ... WGM
Waveguide Moisture Indicator ... WMI
Waveguide Nitrogen Load ... WGNL
Waveguide Nitrogen Load ... WNL
Waveguide Operating below Cutoff (IEEE) ... WGBC
Waveguide Operating below Cutoff ... WOBC
Waveguide, Rectangular ... WR
Waveguide Shutter ... WGC
Waveguide Slot Array ... WSA
Waveguide Slot Array Antenna ... WSAA
Waveguide Standards (IAA) ... WAVEGD
Waveguide Transmission ... WT
Waveguide Window ... WGW
Waveguide-to-Coaxial [*Aerospace*] (AAG) ... WG-T-C
Waveland Public Library, Waveland, IN [*Library symbol Library of Congress*] (LCLS) ... InWav
Wavelength [*Electronics*] ... WL
Wavelength [*Electronics*] (IAA) ... WVL
Wavelength Dispersive [*Spectrometry*] ... WD
Wavelength Dispersive Spectrometer ... WDS
Wavelength Dispersive X-Ray [*Spectrometer*] ... WDX
Wave-Length Dispersive X-Ray Analysis ... WDXA
Wavelength Dispersive X-Ray Spectrometry ... WDXRS
Wavelength Division Multiplex [*or Multiplexing*] [*Telecommunications*] ... WDM
Wavelength-Dispersive X-Ray Fluorescence ... WDXRF
Wave-Modulated Oscilloscope ... WAMOSCOPE
Wave-Off Advisory System [*Aircraft carrier*] [*Navy*] ... WOAS
Wave-Off and Transition Control Unit ... WOTCU
Wave-Off Decision Device (MCD) ... WODD
WavePhore, Inc. [*NASDAQ symbol*] (SAG) ... WAVO
Waverly Democrat, Waverly, IA [*Library symbol Library of Congress*] (LCLS) ... IaWavD
Waverly Hills Tuberculosis Sanatorium, Waverly Hills, KY [*Library symbol Library of Congress*] (LCLS) ... KyWavH
Waverly House, Waverly, IA [*Library symbol Library of Congress*] (LCLS) ... IaWavH
Waverly, IA [*FM radio station call letters*] ... KWAR
Waverly, IA [*AM radio station call letters*] ... KWAY
Waverly, IA [*FM radio station call letters*] ... KWAY-FM
Waverly Inc. [*NASDAQ symbol*] (TTSB) ... WAVR
Waverly, NY [*FM radio station call letters*] ... WAVR
Waverly, OH [*AM radio station call letters*] ... WXIC
Waverly, OH [*FM radio station call letters*] ... WXIZ
Waverly Park Elementary School, East Rockaway, NY [*Library symbol*] [*Library of Congress*] (LCLS) ... NErWE
Waverly Park Elementary School, Lynbrook, NY [*Library symbol Library of Congress*] (LCLS) ... NLynWPE
Waverly Press, Inc. [*Associated Press*] (SAG) ... Waver
Waverly Press, Inc. [*NASDAQ symbol*] (NQ) ... WAVR
Waverly Resource Library, Thunder Bay Public Library, Ontario [*Library symbol National Library of Canada*] (NLC) ... OTB
Waverly, TN [*Location identifier FAA*] (FAAL) ... AEY
Waverly, TN [*AM radio station call letters*] ... WPHC
Waverly, TN [*FM radio station call letters*] ... WVRY
Waverney [*Queensland*] [*Airport symbol*] (AD) ... WAN
Waves in Space Plasma (SSD) ... WISP
WAVES [*Women Accepted for Volunteer Emergency Service*] **National** (EA) ... WN
WAVES National Corp. [*An association*] (EA) ... WNC
Waves on Magnetised Beams and Turbulence ... WOMBAT
Waves on Magnetized Beams and Turbulence [*Physics*] (ADA) ... WOMBAT
Wavetech Inc. [*NASDAQ symbol*] (TTSB) ... ITEL
Wavetech, Inc. [*Associated Press*] (SAG) ... Wavetech
Wavy Vortex Flow [*Fluid mechanics*] ... WFF
Wavy Walled Cylinder ... WWC
Wawa [*Canada*] [*Airport symbol*] (OAG) ... YXZ
Wawa, ON [*Television station call letters*] ... CBLAT-3
Wawa, ON [*AM radio station call letters*] ... CJWA
Wawa, ON [*FM radio station call letters*] (RBYB) ... CJWA-FM
Wax (VRA) ... wx
Wax ... WX
Wax Anti-Settling Additive [*Diesel fuel*] ... WASA
Wax Appearance Point [*Temperature at which waxy substances in fuel start to precipitate*] ... WAP
Wax Bean Agglutinin [*Biochemistry*] ... WBA
Wax Bite [*Dentistry*] ... WxB
Wax Insulating Compound ... WIC
Wax Pattern [*Dentistry*] ... WxP
Waxahachie, TX [*AM radio station call letters*] ... KBEC
Waxed ... WXD
Waxed Paper Institute [*Later, FPA*] (EA) ... WPI
Waxed Paper Merchandising Council [*Defunct*] ... WPMC
Waxhaw, NC [*FM radio station call letters*] (RBYB) ... WNMX-FM
Waxhaw, NC FM radio station call letters (RBYB) ... WIST-FM
Wax-Impregnated Graphite Electrode ... WIGE
Waxman Indus [*NYSE symbol*] (TTSB) ... WAX
Waxman Industries, Inc. [*NYSE symbol*] (SPSG) ... WAX
Waxman Industries, Inc. (MHDW) ... WAXM
Waxman Industries, Inc. [*Associated Press*] (SAG) ... Waxmn
Way [*Postal Service standard*] (OPSA) ... WAY
Way (ADA) ... WY
Way Control Block ... WCB
[*The*] **Way International** [*An association*] (EA) ... TWI
Way of Mountain Learning Center (EA) ... WMLC
Way Point (GAVI) ... WPT
Waybill [*Shipping*] ... WB
Waybo Resources Ltd. [*Vancouver Stock Exchange symbol*] ... WYR
Waycross [*Georgia*] [*Airport symbol*] (OAG) ... AYS
Waycross, GA [*Location identifier FAA*] (FAAL) ... AYS
Waycross, GA [*Location identifier FAA*] (FAAL) ... RNQ
Waycross, GA [*AM radio station call letters*] ... WACL
Waycross, GA [*AM radio station call letters*] ... WAYX
Waycross, GA [*FM radio station call letters*] ... WBGA
Waycross, GA [*FM radio station call letters*] (RBYB) ... WFGA-FM
Waycross, GA [*FM radio station call letters*] ... WHFX
Waycross, GA [*FM radio station call letters*] ... WWUF
Waycross, GA [*Television station call letters*] ... WXGA
Waycross, GA [*FM radio station call letters*] ... WXVS
Waycross Junior College, Waycross, GA [*Library symbol Library of Congress*] (LCLS) ... GWayC
Wayfarer International Committee [*Axminster, Devonshire, England*] (EAIO) ... WIC
Wayland Baptist College [*Texas*] ... WBC
Wayland Baptist College, Plainview, TX [*OCLC symbol*] (OCLC) ... TWB
Wayland Baptist College, Plainview, TX [*Library symbol Library of Congress*] (LCLS) ... TxPlW
Wayland News, Wayland, IA [*Library symbol Library of Congress*] (LCLS) ... IaWayN
Wayland Senior High School Library, Wayland, NY [*OCLC symbol*] (OCLC) ... RXL
Waylands Korongo [*Tanzania*] ... WK
Waylon Jennings Fan Club (EA) ... WJFC
Wayne Bancorp, Inc. [*Associated Press*] (SAG) ... WayneB
Wayne Bancorp, Inc. [*NASDAQ symbol*] (SAG) ... WNNB
Wayne Bancorp, Inc. [*NASDAQ symbol*] (SAG) ... WYNE
Wayne Bancorp, Inc. [*Associated Press*] (SAG) ... WyneB
Wayne City Community Unit, District 100, Wayne City, IL [*Library symbol Library of Congress*] (LCLS) ... IWaycCD
Wayne City Public Library, Wayne City, IL [*Library symbol Library of Congress*] (LCLS) ... IWayc
Wayne Community College, Goldsboro, NC [*Library symbol Library of Congress*] (LCLS) ... NcGoW
Wayne County Community College [*Detroit, MI*] ... WCCC
Wayne County Community College, Detroit, MI [*OCLC symbol*] (OCLC) ... EYV
Wayne County Community College, Detroit, MI [*Library symbol Library of Congress*] (LCLS) ... MiDWcC
Wayne County Courthouse, Corydon, IA [*Library symbol*] [*Library of Congress*] (LCLS) ... IaCoryWC
Wayne County Courthouse, Corydon, IA [*Library symbol Library of Congress*] (LCLS) ... IaCoryWCoC
Wayne County Federated Library System, Department for the Blind and Physically Handicapped, Wayne, MI [*Library symbol Library of Congress*] (LCLS) ... MiWaC-B
Wayne County Federated Library System, Wayne, MI [*Library symbol Library of Congress*] (LCLS) ... MiWaC
Wayne County Historical Society, Croydon, IA [*Library symbol*] [*Library of Congress*] (LCLS) ... IaCroyHi
Wayne County Historical Society, Promise City, IA [*Library symbol*] [*Library of Congress*] (LCLS) ... IaPrcWHi
Wayne County Historical Society, Promise City, IA [*Library symbol Library of Congress*] (LCLS) ... IaPreWHi

Wayne County Law Library, Wooster, OH [*Library symbol Library of Congress*] (LCLS) .... OWoWCL
Wayne County Public Library, Goldsboro, NC [*Library symbol Library of Congress*] (LCLS) .... NcGo
Wayne County Public Library, Wooster, OH [*Library symbol Library of Congress*] (LCLS) .... OWo
Wayne County Public Library, Wooster, OH [*OCLC symbol*] (OCLC) .... WCP
Wayne County Records, Court House, Wayne County, Detroit, MI [*Library symbol Library of Congress*] (LCLS) .... MiDWc
Wayne General and Technical College, Orrville, OH [*Library symbol Library of Congress*] (LCLS) .... OOrrW
Wayne General and Technical College, Orrville, OH [*Inactive*] [*OCLC symbol*] (OCLC) .... WGT
Wayne George Encoder Test Set .... WGETS
Wayne Hann Band Fan Club (EA) .... WHBFC
Wayne Horizontal Acceleration Mechanism .... WHAM
Wayne, NE [*AM radio station call letters*] .... KTCH
Wayne, NE [*FM radio station call letters*] .... KTCH-FM
Wayne, NE [*FM radio station call letters*] .... KWSC
Wayne, NE [*Location identifier FAA*] (FAAL) .... LCG
Wayne, NJ [*FM radio station call letters*] .... WPSC
Wayne Oakland Library Federation [*Library network*] .... WOLF
Wayne Public Library, Wayne, NJ [*Library symbol Library of Congress*] (LCLS) .... NjW
Wayne Savings & Loan Co. [*NASDAQ symbol*] (SAG) .... WAYN
Wayne Savings & Loan Co. [*Associated Press*] (SAG) .... WayneSv
Wayne State College (Nebraska) (GAGS) .... Wayne St C (Neb)
Wayne State College, Wayne, NE [*Library symbol Library of Congress*] (LCLS) .... NbWayS
Wayne State College, Wayne, NE [*OCLC symbol*] (OCLC) .... WAY
Wayne State University (GAGS) .... Wayne St U
Wayne State University [*Michigan*] .... WSU
Wayne State University, Detroit, MI [*OCLC symbol*] (OCLC) .... EYW
Wayne State University, Detroit, MI [*Library symbol Library of Congress*] (LCLS) .... MiDW
Wayne State University, Division of Library Science, Detroit, MI [*OCLC symbol*] (OCLC) .... EED
Wayne State University, Kresge-Hooker Science Library, Detroit, MI [*Library symbol Library of Congress*] (LCLS) .... MiDW-S
Wayne State University, Law Library, Detroit, MI [*Library symbol Library of Congress*] (LCLS) .... MiDW-L
Wayne State University, Medical Library, Detroit, MI [*Library symbol Library of Congress*] (LCLS) .... MiDW-M
Wayne State University, Miles Manuscript Collection, Detroit, MI [*Library symbol Library of Congress Obsolete*] (LCLS) .... MiDW-Mi
Wayne State University, School of Pharmacy, Detroit, MI [*Library symbol Library of Congress*] (LCLS) .... MiDW-P
Wayne State University, Walter P. Reuther Library of Labor and Urban Affairs, Archivesof Labor History and Urban Affairs, Detroit, MI [*Library symbol*] [*Library of Congress*] (LCLS) .... MiDW-AL
Wayne Svgs & Ln [*NASDAQ symbol*] (TTSB) .... WAYN
Wayne Township Library, Richmond, IN [*Library symbol*] [*Library of Congress*] (LCLS) .... InRM
Waynesboro, GA [*Location identifier FAA*] (FAAL) .... BXG
Waynesboro, GA [*FM radio station call letters*] .... WAEJ
Waynesboro, GA [*AM radio station call letters*] .... WBRO
Waynesboro, GA [*FM radio station call letters*] .... WYFA
Waynesboro, MS [*AM radio station call letters*] .... WABO
Waynesboro, MS [*FM radio station call letters*] .... WABO-FM
Waynesboro, PA [*FM radio station call letters*] .... WAYZ
Waynesboro, PA [*AM radio station call letters*] .... WHGT
Waynesboro Public Library, Waynesboro, VA [*Library symbol Library of Congress*] (LCLS) .... ViWb
Waynesboro, TN [*FM radio station call letters*] .... WFRQ
Waynesboro, TN [*AM radio station call letters*] .... WTNR
Waynesboro, VA [*AM radio station call letters*] .... WAYB
Waynesboro, VA [*FM radio station call letters*] .... WPVA
Waynesboro, VA [*AM radio station call letters*] .... WVAO
Waynesburg [*Pennsylvania*] [*Seismograph station code, US Geological Survey Closed*] (SEIS) .... WAY
Waynesburg & Washington Railroad Co. [*Absorbed into Consolidated Rail Corp.*] [*AAR code*] .... WAW
Waynesburg College, Waynesburg, PA [*OCLC symbol*] (OCLC) .... PWA
Waynesburg College, Waynesburg, PA [*Library symbol Library of Congress*] (LCLS) .... PWayC
Waynesburg, PA [*AM radio station call letters*] .... WANB
Waynesburg, PA [*FM radio station call letters*] .... WANB-FM
Waynesburg, PA [*Location identifier FAA*] (FAAL) .... WAY
Waynesburg, PA [*FM radio station call letters*] .... WCYJ
Waynesburg Southern [*AAR code*] .... WAS
Waynesville, MO [*FM radio station call letters*] .... KFBD
Waynesville, MO [*AM radio station call letters*] .... KJPW
Waynesville, MO [*FM radio station call letters*] .... KJPW-FM
Waynesville, MO [*AM radio station call letters*] .... KOZQ
Waynesville, NC [*AM radio station call letters*] .... WHCC
Waynesville, NC [*FM radio station call letters*] .... WQNS
Way-Point .... WP
Waypoint [*ICAO*] (FAAC) .... WPT
Waypoint Report [*Aviation*] (FAAC) .... WPRT
Ways [*Postal Service standard*] (OPSA) .... WAYS
Ways and Means (DLA) .... WM
Ways and Means Committee [*House of Representatives*] (WDAA) .... WMC
Ways of Looking at People Scale [*Psychology*] (AEBS) .... WLP
Ways plus Filling [*Textile testing*] .... W + F
Waysgoose [*Country fair*] (ROG) .... GOOSE
Wayside [*Minute Man National Historical Park*], Concord, MA [*Library symbol Library of Congress*] (LCLS) .... MCoW
Wazakhwa [*Afghanistan*] [*ICAO location identifier*] (ICLI) .... OADW
Wazirabad [*Afghanistan*] [*ICAO location identifier*] (ICLI) .... OAWZ
Wazo Hill [*Tanzania*] [*ICAO location identifier*] (ICLI) .... HTWH
WCI Canada Ltd. [*Toronto Stock Exchange symbol*] .... WCL
WCI Steel [*NYSE symbol*] (TTSB) .... WRN
WCI Steel, Inc. [*Associated Press*] (SAG) .... WCI Stl
WCI Steel, Inc. [*NYSE symbol*] (SAG) .... WRN
WCN Investment [*Vancouver Stock Exchange symbol*] .... WC
WCTU Railway Co. [*AAR code*] .... WCTR
WD-40 Co. [*Associated Press*] (SAG) .... WD 40
WD-40 Co. [*NASDAQ symbol*] (NQ) .... WDFC
WDL Flugdienst GmbH [*Germany ICAO designator*] (ICDA) .... WE
We Are Lost [*Army*] .... WAL
We Are Ridiculous [*Antiwar slogan*] .... WAR
We Can Do [*An association*] (EA) .... WCD
We Care (EA) .... WC
We Have, Ready with Called Party [*Telecommunications*] (TEL) .... WH
We Interrupt This Week [*Television program*] .... WITW
We May Be the Only Phone Company in Town, but We Try Not to Act Like It [*Slogan*] .... WMBTOPCITBWTNTALI
We Oppose Computers in Tournaments [*A chess players' group, formed in 1983*] .... WOCIT
We Remember Dean International (EA) .... WRDI
We Remember Elvis Fan Club (EA) .... WREFC
We the People [*Later, WPU*] (EA) .... WP
We the People, United (EA) .... WPU
We Turn in Pushers [*Organization combating drug traffic*] .... WE TIP
We Won't Write to Them until They Write to Us [*A servicemen's club*] .... WWWTTUTWTU
Weaco Resources Ltd. [*Vancouver Stock Exchange symbol*] .... WEO
Wead Library, Malone, NY [*Library symbol Library of Congress*] (LCLS) .... NMa
Weak [*Spectral*] .... W
Weak (DAVI) .... WK
Weak Affinity Chromatography [*Analytical chemistry*] .... WAC
Weak Anion Exchanger [*Chemistry*] .... WAX
Weak Anthropic Principle [*Term coined by authors John Barrow and Frank Tipler in their book, "The Anthropic Cosmological Principle"*] .... WAP
Weak Black Liquor [*Pulp and paper technology*] .... WBL
Weak Black Liquor Oxidation [*Pulp and paper technology*] .... WBLO
Weak Calf Syndrome [*Veterinary medicine*] .... WCS
Weak Cation Exchanger [*Chemistry*] .... WCX
Weak Disordered Magnetic Field .... WDMF
Weak Equity Axiom .... WEA
Weak Equivalence Principle [*Gravity*] .... WEP
Weak Exchange Degeneracy [*Particle physics*] (OA) .... WED
Weak External Reference [*Computer science*] (BUR) .... WXTRN
Weak Neutral Current [*Chemistry*] .... WNC
Weak Radial Field .... WRF
Weak Signal Reception .... WSR
Weak Signals [*Radio*] .... WS
Weaken .... WKN
Weakened Plane Joint .... WPJ
Weak-Lined T Tauri Stars [*Astronomy*] .... WTTS
Weakly Interacting Massive [*or Integrated Magnetic*] **Particle** [*Astrophysics*] .... WIMP
Weakly Positive [*Laboratory science*] (DAVI) .... W+
Weakly Positive (MAE) .... WP
Weakly Reactive (MAE) .... WR
Wealth of India [*A publication*] .... WOI
Wealth Resources Ltd. [*Vancouver Stock Exchange symbol*] .... WLH
Wealth Tax (PDAA) .... WT
Weam [*Papua New Guinea*] [*Airport symbol*] (OAG) .... WEP
Weapon .... WEP
Weapon (AAG) .... WPN
Weapon Accuracy and Results [*Model*] (MCD) .... WAR
Weapon Aiming and Mode Selector (MCD) .... WAMS
Weapon Aiming Error .... WAE
Weapon Allocation Model .... WAM
Weapon and/or Launcher .... W & L
Weapon and Tracked Combat Vehicle (MCD) .... WTCV
Weapon Arming Computer (MCD) .... WAC
Weapon Armourer [*British military*] (DMA) .... WA
Weapon Assignment and Target Extermination .... WAX
Weapon Assignment Display [*Air Force*] .... WAD
Weapon Assignment Unit [*Military*] (CAAL) .... WAU
Weapon Battery Terminal Equipment [*Air Force*] .... WBTE
Weapon Capability (SAA) .... WEACAP
Weapon Carrier .... WC
Weapon Control Area [*Military*] (CAAL) .... WCA
Weapon Control Computer (MCD) .... WCC
Weapon Control Computer Debug Program [*Military*] .... WCCDBP
Weapon Control Console [*Military*] (CAAL) .... WCC
Weapon Control Equipment .... WCE
Weapon Control Group [*Military*] (CAAL) .... WCG
Weapon Control Index [*Military*] (CAAL) .... WCI
Weapon Control Indicator Panel [*Military*] (CAAL) .... WCIP
Weapon Control Module (MCD) .... WCM
Weapon Control Panel [*Aviation*] .... WCP
Weapon Control Processor [*Military*] (CAAL) .... WCP
Weapon Control Station [*Military*] (CAAL) .... WCS
Weapon Control Status [*Military*] (INF) .... WCS
Weapon Control Switchboard [*Military*] (CAAL) .... WCSB
Weapon Control Switchboard (Gun) .... WCSB(G)

Weapon Control Switchboard (Missile)	WCSB(M)
Weapon Control Switchboard (Underwater Battery)	WCSB(UB)
Weapon Control System Console	WCSC
Weapon Control Systems Engineering [*Navy*] (NG)	WEPCOSE
Weapon Cost Test Site [*Military*] (CAAL)	WCTS
Weapon Data Index [*Navy*] (MCD)	WDI
Weapon Data Insert Panel (MCD)	WDIP
Weapon Data Link (MCD)	WDL
Weapon Defense Facility (AAG)	WDF
Weapon Delivery Computer (MCD)	WDC
Weapon Delivery Impairment (NVT)	WDI
Weapon Delivery Model (PDAA)	WDM
Weapon Delivery System	WDS
Weapon Description (MCD)	WD
Weapon Development Glide Entry	WEDGE
Weapon Direction Computer [*Military*] (CAAL)	WDC
Weapon Direction System Satellite Simulation [*Military*] (CAAL)	WDS SATSIM
Weapon Director [*SAGE*]	WD
Weapon Effectiveness Index (MCD)	WEI
Weapon Effects on D-Region Communications [*Computer code*]	WEDCOM
Weapon Effects Training Simulator (MCD)	WETS
Weapon Electrical System	WES
Weapon Engagement Console [*Military*] (CAAL)	WEC
Weapon Engagement Controller [*Military*] (CAAL)	WEC
Weapon Engagement Simulation Component (MCD)	WESC
Weapon Engagement Zone [*Army*] (ADDR)	WEZ
Weapon Engineering Station	WES
Weapon Engineering Station Representative (MCD)	WESREP
Weapon Evaluation System Photographic Analog Recorder (MCD)	WESPAR
Weapon Fire Simulator (MCD)	WFS
Weapon Fly-to-Point (NVT)	WPNFPT
Weapon Impact Scoring System [*Navy*] (MCD)	WISS
Weapon Index Number [*Military*] (CAAL)	WIN
Weapon Indicator Panel [*Military*] (CAAL)	WIP
Weapon Installation System Engineering	WISE
Weapon Interface Subsystem [*Army*] (INF)	WIS
Weapon Interface Subsystem [*Army*]	WIS
Weapon Iterface Subsystem Processor [*Military*] (INF)	WISP
Weapon Launch Console Switching Section (MCD)	WLCSS
Weapon Loading Director (NVT)	WLD
Weapon Mechanician [*British military*] (DMA)	WM
Weapon Monitor Panel (MCD)	WMP
Weapon Mounted Display	WMD
Weapon Optical Effects	WOE
Weapon Order Generation [*Military*] (CAAL)	WOG
Weapon Phenomenology (RDA)	WEPH
Weapon Position Preparation (MCD)	WPP
Weapon Radiation Effects on Communications Systems (MCD)	WRECS
Weapon Radius (NVT)	WR
Weapon Range (NATG)	WR
Weapon Research Establishment	WRE
Weapon Safety Trainer	WST
Weapon Selection (SAA)	WEASEL
Weapon Status and Approval Panel [*Military*] (CAAL)	WSAP
Weapon Status Digital Display	WSDD
Weapon Support Detachment (MCD)	WSD
Weapon Support Equipment [*Navy*] (NG)	WSE
Weapon Support Manager [*Air Force*]	WSM
Weapon Support Processor [*Military*] (CAAL)	WSP
Weapon Support Systems	WSS
Weapon System	WS
Weapon System Acceptance Schedule (AAG)	WSAS
Weapon System Acquisition Process (MCD)	WSAP
Weapon System Analysis Division [*Navy*]	WSAD
Weapon System Analysis Office [*Navy*] (MCD)	WSAO
Weapon System and Equipment Support Analysis	WSESA
Weapon System Base Supply Account [*Military*] (AFIT)	WSBSA
Weapon System Communications System (AAG)	WSCS
Weapon System Compatible Munition [*Military*]	WSCM
Weapon System Computer (MCD)	WSC
Weapon System Configuration Control [*Navy*] (AAG)	WSCC
Weapon System Configuration Control Manual [*Navy*] (NG)	WSCCM
Weapon System Configuration Management Board (MCD)	WSCMB
Weapon System Console [*Military*] (CAAL)	WSC
Weapon System Contractor	WSC
Weapon System Costing [*Navy*]	WSC
Weapon System Data Module	WSDM
Weapon System Demonstration Test Directive (AAG)	WSD/TD
Weapon System Design Criteria (AAG)	WSDC
Weapon System Designator	WSD
Weapon System Development [*Military*] (CAAL)	WSD
Weapon System Director	WSD
Weapon System Effectiveness Industry Advisory Committee	WSEIAC
Weapon System Electrical Diagrams	WSED
Weapon System Electromagnetic Environment Simulator (MCD)	WSEES
Weapon System Engineering [*Navy*] (NG)	WSE
Weapon System Engineering Laboratory	WSEL
Weapon System Equipment Component List	WSECL
Weapon System Evaluation Group [*DoD and Air Force*] (MCD)	WSEG
Weapon System Evaluation Missile [*Air Force*] (AFM)	WSEM
Weapon System Evaluation Program [*Air Force*]	WSEP
Weapon System Evaluation Test [*Navy*] (NG)	WSET
Weapon System File (MCD)	WSF
Weapon System Integration (MCD)	WSI
Weapon System Interface Trade Study [*Military*]	WSITS
Weapon System Logistic Reviews [*Navy*] (NG)	WSLR
Weapon System Logistics Officer [*Air Force*] (AFM)	WSLO
Weapon System Maintenance Action Center	WSMAC
Weapon System Management Team [*Army*] (RDA)	WSMaT
Weapon System Manager [*Air Force*] (AFM)	WSM
Weapon System Manual	WSM
Weapon System Materiel Officer [*Air Force*] (AFM)	WSMO
Weapon System Officer [*or Operator*] [*Air Force*] (AFM)	WSO
Weapon System Operability Test [*Military*] (CAAL)	WSOT
Weapon System Operational Concept (AAG)	WSOC
Weapon System Operator	WSO
Weapon System Phase-Out Procedure [*Air Force*] (AFM)	WSPOP
Weapon System Phasing Group	WSPG
Weapon System Planning Document (NVT)	WSPD
Weapon System Program (SAA)	WSP
Weapon System Program Guide List	WSPGL
Weapon System Program Review [*Army*]	WSPR
Weapon System Project Office [*Air Force*]	WSPO
Weapon System Purchasing Group	WSPG
Weapon System Readiness Test	WSRT
Weapon System Reliability [*Air Force*] (AFM)	WSR
Weapon System Replacement Operations (MCD)	WSRO
Weapon System Specification (AAG)	WSS
Weapon System Staff Manager [*Army*] (RDA)	WSSM
Weapon System Stock Control List (AAG)	WSSCL
Weapon System Stock Control Plan (SAA)	WSCP
Weapon System Stock List [*Army*]	WSSL
Weapon System Stock/Support List [*Air Force*] (AFIT)	WSSL
Weapon System Storage Site	WSSS
Weapon System Support Activities (AAG)	WSSA
Weapon System Support Center (AAG)	WSSC
Weapon System Support Code [*Navy*] (NG)	WSSC
Weapon System Support Development (MCD)	WSSD
Weapon System Support Group (MCD)	WSSG
Weapon System Support Manager (AAG)	WSSM
Weapon System Support Officer [*Army*] (RDA)	WSSO
Weapon System Tactical Handbook (MCD)	WSTH
Weapon System Tactical Tester	WESTT
Weapon System Task Analysis (AAG)	WSTA
Weapon System Test	WST
Weapon System Test Laboratory	WSTL
Weapon System Test Program	WSTP
Weapon System Total Complex	WSTC
Weapon System Trainer [*Navy*]	WST
Weapon System Training Effectiveness Analysis	WSTEA
Weapon System Training Set (AFM)	WSTS
Weapon Systems Accuracy [*formerly, Acceptance*] **Trials** [*Navy*] (NG)	WSAT
Weapon Systems Acquisition Management [*Navy*] (MCD)	WSAM
Weapon Systems Acquisition Manager Program Naval Officers (AAGC)	WSAM
Weapon Systems Management Information System [*Air Force*] (GFGA)	WSMIS
Weapon Systems Planning [*or Programming*] and Control System	WSPACS
Weapon Systems Pouch (AFM)	WSP
Weapon Systems Requirement (MCD)	WSR
Weapon Systems Support Program [*Defense Supply Agency*]	WSSP
Weapon Tactics Trainer (MCD)	WTT
Weapon Test	WT
Weapon Test Reports Committee [*AEC-DoD*]	WTRC
Weapon Training (MCD)	WT
Weapon Utility Analysis	WUA
Weaponization of Increased Speed Projectiles (MCD)	WISP
Weapon-Launching Console (MCD)	WLC
Weapons Alert Designator [*Army*] (ADDR)	WAD
Weapons Alert System [*NORAD*] (MCD)	WAS
Weapons Allocation and Desired Ground-Zero Optimizer [*Military*]	WALOPT
Weapons Allocation Branch (SAA)	WAB
Weapons Analyst [*British military*] (DMA)	WA
Weapons and Equipment Policy Committee [*British*] (RDA)	WEPC
Weapons and Equipment Policy Statement [*Australia*]	WEPS
Weapons and Facilities, Navy (NG)	WFN
Weapons and Integrated Navigation System (MCD)	WINS
Weapons and Mobility Command [*Army*]	WMC
Weapons and Tactics Analysis Center [*Navy*] (MCD)	WEPTAC
Weapons and Utilities Maintenance [*Military*] (GFGA)	WU
Weapons Application Study (SAA)	WAS
Weapons Assignment (NVT)	WA
Weapons Assignment Console	WAC
Weapons Assignment Linear Program	WALP
Weapons Assignment Officer [*Air Force*] (AFM)	WAO
Weapons Assignment Research Model [*Military*]	WARM
Weapons Assignment Technician (AFM)	WAT
Weapons Bay Door Drive Subsystem [*Military*]	WBDDS
Weapons Classification Defects [*Navy*] (NG)	WCD
Weapons Command [*Later, Armaments Command*] [*Army*]	WC
Weapons Command [*Later, Armaments Command*] [*Army*]	WECOM
Weapons Control [*or Controller*] (NVT)	WC
Weapons Control Check (NVT)	WCCK
Weapons Control Concept (MCD)	WCC
Weapons Control Officer	WCO
Weapons Control Order	WCO
Weapons Control Status	WCS
Weapons Control Subsystem (MCD)	WCSS
Weapons Control System	WCS
Weapons Control System Coordinator (NVT)	WCSC
Weapons Control System Simulator	WCSS

Weapons Control Unit (MCD)	WCU
Weapons Controller Training Squadron	WCTS
Weapons Crew Training Test [*TCATA*] (RDA)	WCTT
Weapons Data [*Navy*]	WD
Weapons Data Correlation System (MCD)	WDCS
Weapons Defended Area	WDA
Weapons Density List (AABC)	WDL
Weapons Development Effectiveness Laboratory (MCD)	WDEL
Weapons Directing Equipment (NVT)	WDE
Weapons Directing System [*Navy*]	WDS
Weapons Direction Evaluation (SAA)	WDE
Weapons Direction Program	WDP
Weapons Director Unit (MCD)	WDU
Weapons Display Generator (MCD)	WDG
Weapons Effect Display System [*AEC*]	WEDS
Weapons Effect Reporting Station [*Civil defense*]	WERS
Weapons Effect Signature Simulator	WESS
Weapons Effectiveness and System Test Environment [*Air Force*] (AFM)	WESTE
Weapons Effectiveness Buoy System	WEBS
Weapons Effectiveness Indices/Weighted Unit Values [*Military*]	WEI/WUV
Weapons Effectiveness Simulated Threat (MCD)	WEST
Weapons Effectiveness Systems Industry Advisory Committee (MCD)	WESIAC
Weapons Effectiveness Testing	WET
Weapons Effects Laboratory [*Army*] (RDA)	WEL
Weapons Effects Systems (MCD)	WES
Weapons Electrical [*Navy British*]	WE
Weapons Employment Handbook [*DASA*] (MCD)	WE-H
Weapons Engagement Scoring System	WESS
Weapons Engineer Officer [*British military*] (DMA)	WEO
Weapons Engineer Officer's Writer [*British military*] (DMA)	WEOW
Weapons Engineering [*Navy British*]	WE
Weapons Engineering Duty [*Navy*]	WED
Weapons Engineering Service Office [*DoD*]	WESO
Weapons/Equipment List	WEL
Weapons/Equipment System Designator Code	W/ESDC
Weapons Evaluation and Control Bureau [*USACDA*]	WECB
Weapons Evaluation Group [*Military*]	WEG
Weapons Exercise [*Navy*] (NVT)	WEPEX
Weapons Exhaust Study [*Military*] (MCD)	WEST
Weapons Fly-To Point [*Military*] (CAAL)	WFTP
Weapons Free Zone	WFZ
Weapons Guidance and Tracking (SAA)	WGT
Weapons Guidance Laboratory	WGL
Weapons Inspection Report [*Navy*] (NG)	WIR
Weapons Installation Interrupted for Parts (DNAB)	WSIIP
Weapons Installation Plan [*Navy*] (NG)	WIP
Weapons Integrated Materiel Manager [*Military*]	WIMM
Weapons Integration Facility (MCD)	WIF
Weapons Interception [*Military electronics*]	WIN
Weapons Interference Reduction Effort [*Navy*] (NG)	WIRE
Weapons Laboratory (MCD)	WL
Weapons Laboratory Civil Engineering Division [*Kirtland Air Force Base, NM*]	WLC
Weapons Liaison Officer (NVT)	WLO
Weapons Locating RADAR (AABC)	WLR
Weapons Logbook [*Military*] (AABC)	WLB
Weapons Management Improvement Program [*Military*] (AABC)	WMIP
Weapons Monitoring Center	WMC
Weapons Monitoring Console	WMC
Weapons Monitoring System	WMS
Weapons Neutron Research Facility [*Los Alamos*]	WNR
Weapons of Mass Destruction	WMD
Weapons Operational Systems Development [*NORAD*]	WOSD
Weapons Operations Research Office	WORO
Weapons Orientation Advanced (AFM)	WOA
Weapons Output Makeup	WOM
Weapons Power	WP
Weapons Procurement (DOMA)	WP
Weapons Procurement, Navy (NVT)	WPN
Weapons Production Engineering Center [*Navy*]	WPEC
Weapons Production Program	WPP
Weapons Program Section	WPS
Weapons Quality Engineering Center, Crane [*Indiana*]	WQEC/C
Weapons Readiness Achievement Program (MUGU)	WRAP
Weapons Readiness Analysis Program [*Navy*]	WRAP
Weapons Recommendation Sheet (MCD)	WRS
Weapons Release Computer [*or Controller*]	WRC
Weapons Release Computer Set [*or System*] (MCD)	WRCS
Weapons Release Programmer	WRP
Weapons Reliability Assurance Program [*Navy*] (DNAB)	WRAP
Weapons Replaceable [*or Replacement*] Assembly	WRA
Weapons Requirement [*DoD*]	WR
Weapons Research Establishment Camera Interception Single Shot	WRECISS
Weapons Research Establishment Digital Automatic Computer	WREDAC
Weapons Reserve Training Units [*Navy*]	WEPTU
Weapons Spares Report [*Navy*]	WSR
Weapons Specifications (NG)	WS
Weapons Spectrum Generator (PDAA)	WSG
Weapons Station	WPNSTA
Weapons Status Report [*Navy*] (NG)	WSR
Weapons Support Improvement Group [*DoD*] (DOMA)	WSIG
Weapons System	W/S
Weapons System [*Navy*]	WEPS

Weapons System Code	WSC
Weapons System Contract Status Report [*Navy*] (NG)	WSCSR
Weapons System Control Point	WSCP
[Weapons System Cost Model	WESCOM
Weapons System Demonstration (MCD)	WSD
Weapons System Designator Code (NVT)	WSDC
Weapons System Development Laboratory	WSDL
Weapons System Development Plan	WSDP
Weapons System Evaluation Division [*DoD*]	WESED
Weapons System Evaluation Facility (MCD)	WSEF
Weapons System Evaluation Facility Group Test (MCD)	WSEFGT
Weapons System Evaluation Group [*DoD*]	WESEG
Weapons System Evaluation Squadron	WSES
Weapons System Evaluator (MCD)	WSE
Weapons System Improvement Program (DWSG)	WSIP
Weapons System Maintenance Test (MCD)	WSMT
Weapons System Management Codes [*Navy*]	WSMC
Weapons System Master Plan [*Air Force*] (DOMA)	WSMP
Weapons System Partnerships Committee [*NATO*] (NATG)	WSPC
Weapons System Plan [*Navy*] (NG)	WESYP
Weapons System Planning Data [*Navy*]	WSPD
Weapons System Program Code [*Defense Supply Agency*]	WSPC
Weapons System Reliability Test (CINC)	WSRT
Weapons System Requisitioning Procedure [*Military*] (AABC)	WSRP
Weapons System Review (NVT)	WSR
Weapons System Security Flight [*Military*]	WSSF
Weapons System Status	WESS
Weapons System Support Program Manager (AFIT)	WSSPM
Weapons System Test Card (MCD)	WSTC
Weapons Systems Analysis [*Army*] (AABC)	WSA
Weapons Systems Data Link (MCD)	WSDL
Weapons Systems Effectiveness	WSE
Weapons Systems Effectiveness Factors	WSEF
Weapons Systems Evaluation Division [*DoD*] (WDAA)	WSED
Weapons Systems Integration Agent (MCD)	WSIA
Weapons Systems Personnel Planning Data (MCD)	WSPPD
Weapons Systems Progress Reporting Data	WSPRD
Weapons Technician [*Air Force*] (AFM)	WT
Weapons Testing Program (AAG)	WTP
Weapons Tight [*Weapons will engage only objects identified as hostile*]	WT
Weapons Training (NVT)	WPTNG
Weapons Training Detachment [*Military*]	WTD
Weapons Training Exercise (NVT)	WEPTRAEX
Weapons Training Instruction (MCD)	WTI
Weapons Training Site [*Military*]	WTS
Wear Durability Trial	WDT
Wear Resistant	WR
Wearable Artificial Kidney	WAK
Wearing (MSA)	WRG
Wearout Failure Period	WFP
Wearout Failure Period	WOFP
Wearout Rate (SAA)	WOR
Weather	W
Weather (AABC)	WEA
Weather	WTHR
Weather	WX
Weather Aircraft Equipped with Meteorological Gear [*Designation for all US military aircraft*]	W
Weather Almanac [*A publication*]	WA
Weather Almanac [*A publication*]	WAL
Weather Altimeter Voice Equipment	WAVE
Weather Amateur Radio Network (NOAA)	WARN
Weather Analysis Computer System [*Accu-Weather, Inc.*]	WACS
Weather and Air Movements (SAA)	WX-AM
Weather and Battle-Induced Contaminant (PDAA)	WBIC
Weather- and Boil-Proof (IEEE)	WBP
Weather and Fixed Map Unit [*FAA*]	WFMU
Weather and Radar Processor [*FAA*] (TAG)	WARP
Weather at Altitude [*Aviation*] (FAAC)	WX
Weather Atlas of the United States [*A publication*]	WA
Weather Bomber [*Air Force*]	WB
Weather, Briefing, Advisory, and Warning Service (AABC)	WBAWS
Weather Briefing Television (AFM)	WBTV
Weather Buoy Rocket	WEBROCK
Weather Bureau [*Later, National Weather Service*] (EA)	WB
Weather Bureau, Air Force, Navy [*Manuals*] [*Obsolete*]	WBAN
Weather Bureau Airport Station [*Obsolete*]	WBAS
Weather Bureau Central Office [*Obsolete*]	WBC
Weather Bureau Communications [*Obsolete*]	WBC
Weather Bureau Hurricane Forecast Office [*Obsolete*]	WBHO
Weather Bureau Meteorological Observation Station [*Obsolete*]	WBMO
Weather Bureau/National Weather Records Center [*Obsolete*] (KSC)	WB/NWRC
Weather Bureau Office [*Later, National Weather Service*]	WBO
Weather Bureau RADAR Remote [*Meteorology*]	WBRR
Weather Bureau Radiotheolite [*Meteorology*]	WBRT
Weather Bureau Regional Headquarters (FAAC)	WBRH
Weather Bureau Regional Office [*Obsolete*]	WBRO
Weather Bureau Signal Station [*Obsolete*]	WBSIGSTA
Weather Bureau Synoptic and Aviation Reporting Station [*Obsolete*]	WBSA
Weather Bureau Technical Memorandum: Hydrology [*Office of Hydrology*] [*Washington, DC*] [*A publication*]	WBTM HYDRO
Weather Card Data (IAA)	WCD
Weather Center [*Meteorology*] (DA)	WC
Weather Center [*Air Force*]	WECEN
[*The*] Weather Channel [*Cable TV programming service*]	TWC

Weather Condition [*Nuclear energy*] (NRCH) .... WC
Weather Control Research Association [*Later, Weather Modification Association*] .... WCRA
Weather Controlled Messages (NVT) .... WECON
Weather Data Facility .... WDF
Weather Deck [*of a ship*] (DS) .... W Dk
Weather Division [*Air Force*] (MCD) .... WD
Weather Emergency .... WE
Weather Facsimile (EERA) .... WEFAX
Weather Facsimile [*Environmental Science Services Administration*] (IAA) .... WEFC
Weather Facsimile Experiment [*Environmental Science Services Administration*] .... WEFAX
Weather Forecast Office (USDC) .... WFO
Weather Forecast Office [*Marine science*] (OSRA) .... WFO
Weather Group [*Air Force*] .... WG
Weather Group [*Air Force*] (AFM) .... WGp
Weather Group (4th) [*Washington, DC*] [*Air Force*] 4WG
Weather Information Branch [*Air Force*] (MCD) .... WIB
Weather Information Network and Display .... WIND
Weather Information Network and Display System [*NASA*] .... WINDS
Weather Information Remoting and Display System .... WIRDS
Weather Information Service [*Air Force*] (MCD) .... WIS
Weather Information Telemetry System [*Air Force*] (CET) .... WITS
Weather Integration with Tactical Intelligence System (MCD) .... WITIS
Weather Intelligence Unit [*Army*] (MCD) .... WIU
Weather Mapping System .... WMS
Weather Message Switching Center .... WMSC
Weather Message Switching Center Replacement (GAVI) .... WMSCR
Weather Modification Advisory Board .... WMAB
Weather Modification Association (EA) .... WMA
Weather Modification Program [*Boulder, CO*] [*Department of Commerce*] .... WMP
Weather Modification Program Office [*Marine science*] (MSC) .... WMPO
Weather Network Duty Officer [*Air Force*] (AFM) .... WNDO
Weather Network Management Center [*Air Force*] (AFM) .... WNMC
Weather Observation and Forecasting Control System .... WEARCON
Weather Observation Site Building (AABC) .... WOSB
Weather Observation Through Ambient Noise (USDC) .... WOTAN
Weather Observation Through Ambient Noise [*Marine science*] (OSRA) .... WOTAN
Weather Observing and Forecasting System [*Air Force*] (MCD) .... WOFS
Weather of US Cities [*A publication*] .... WUSC
Weather Permitting .... WP
Weather Processor (MCD) .... WEP
Weather Profile Facility .... WPF
Weather RADAR .... WXR
Weather RADAR Interface Unit (MCD) .... WRIU
Weather RADAR Set [*or System*] .... WRS
Weather Reconnaissance .... WR
Weather Reconnaissance Flight [*Navy*] (NVT) .... WXRECCO
Weather Reconnaissance Flight Pilot Report [*Aviation*] (FAAC) .... WXCON
Weather Reconnaissance Group [*Military*] .... WRG
Weather Reconnaissance Squadron [*Air Force*] (DNAB) .... WEARECONRON
Weather Reconnaissance Squadron [*Air Force*] (CINC) .... WRS
Weather Reconnaissance Squadron [*Air Force*] (AFM) .... WRSq
Weather Reconnaissance Squadron [*Air Force*] .... WXRCNSq
Weather Reconnaissance Wing [*Military*] .... WRW
Weather Reconnaissance Wing [*Air Force*] (AFM) .... WRWg
Weather Records Processing Centers .... WRPC
Weather Relay Broadcast Center .... WRBC
Weather Relay Center .... WRC
Weather Report (WDMC) .... WX
Weather Report Will Not be Filed for Transmission [*NWS*] (FAAC) .... FINO
Weather Research Facility [*Navy*] (GFGA) .... WEARESFAC
Weather Research Program [*Boulder, CO*] [*Department of Commerce*] (GRD) .... WRP
Weather Resistant (MSA) .... WR
Weather Review [*A publication*] .... W
Weather Scenario Test Tape (USDC) .... WSTT
Weather Scenario Test Tape [*Marine science*] (OSRA) .... WSTT
Weather Seal (AAG) .... WSL
Weather Search RADAR (MCD) .... WSR
Weather Service .... WS
Weather Service Airport (DA) .... WSAS
Weather Service Command [*Navy*] .... WEASERVCOMM
Weather Service Communications Center [*National Weather Service*] (NOAA) .... WSCC
Weather Service Communications Handbook [*National Weather Service*] (NOAA) .... WSCH
Weather Service Contract Meteorological Observatory (FAAC) .... WSCMO
Weather Service Cooperating Agencies [*National Weather Service*] (NOAA) .... WSCA
Weather Service Evaluation Officer [*National Weather Service*] .... WSEO
Weather Service Forecast Office [*National Weather Service*] .... WSFO
Weather Service Headquarters (NOAA) .... WSH
Weather Service Meteorological Observatory [*or Observations*] [*National Weather Service*] (NOAA) .... WSMO
Weather Service Office [*National Weather Service*] (NOAA) .... WSO
Weather Service Office for Agriculture [*National Weather Service*] (NOAA) .... WSO(AG)
Weather Service Office for Aviation [*National Weather Service*] (NOAA) .... WSO(AV)
Weather Service Office for Fire-Weather [*National Weather Service*] (NOAA) .... WSO(FW)
Weather Service Operations [*NWS*] (FAAC) .... WSOM
Weather Service Regional Headquarters [*National Weather Service*] (NOAA) .... WSRH
Weather Service Specialist [*National Weather Service*] .... WSS
Weather Services International Corp. [*Information service or system*] (IID) .... WSI
Weather Ship (NATG) .... W/S
Weather Squadron (MCD) .... WS
Weather Squadron [*Air Force*] (AFM) .... WSq
Weather Station .... WS
Weather Support Force [*Military*] (AFM) .... WSF
Weather Surveillance RADAR .... WSR
Weather Surveillance Radar (USDC) WSR-88D
Weather Surveillance Radar [*Marine science*] (OSRA) WSR-88D
Weather Surveillance RADAR Manual (NOAA) .... WSRM
Weather Task Force .... WETAF
Weather Team [*Air Force*] (AFM) .... WETM
Weather Underground (EA) .... WU
Weather Wing (MCD) .... WW
Weather Wing [*Air Force*] (AFM) .... WWg
Weather Wing (1st) [*California*] [*Air Force*] 1WW
Weather Wing (2nd) [*New York*] [*Air Force*] 2WW
Weather Wing (3rd) [*Nebraska*] [*Air Force*] 3WW
Weather Wing (4th) [*Colorado*] [*Air Force*] 4WW
Weather Wing (6th) [*Washington, DC*] [*Air Force*] 6WW
Weather Wing (7th) [*Illinois*] [*Air Force*] 7WW
Weather Wing Pamphlet [*Air Force*] (MCD) .... WWP
Weather Working .... WW
Weather Working Days [*Construction*] .... WWD
Weather Working Days, Fridays, and Holidays Excluded [*Shipping*] (DS) .... wwdFHEx
Weather Working Days, Sundays, and Holidays Excluded (DS) .... WWDSHEX
Weatherall Green Smith [*British*] (ECON) .... WGS
Weather-Atmospheric Sounding Projectile [*Research rocket*] .... WASP
Weatherboard (ADA) .... WB
Weatherford College, Weatherford, TX [*Library symbol Library of Congress*] (LCLS) .... TxWeaC
Weatherford Enterra [*NYSE symbol*] (SAG) .... WII
Weatherford Enterra [*Associated Press*] (SAG) .... WthfdEnt
[*The*] **Weatherford, Mineral Wells & Northwestern Railway Co.** [*AAR code*] .... WMWN
Weatherford, OK [*AM radio station call letters*] .... KWEY
Weatherford, OK [*FM radio station call letters*] .... KWEY-FM
Weatherford, OK [*Location identifier FAA*] (FAAL) .... OJA
Weatherford, TX [*FM radio station call letters*] (RBYB) .... KYQX
Weatherford, TX [*AM radio station call letters*] .... KZEE
Weatherford, TX [*Location identifier FAA*] (FAAL) .... WEA
Weather-Impacted Airspace (USDC) .... WIA
Weather-Impacted Airspace [*Marine science*] (OSRA) .... WIA
Weatherization Assistance Program (GNE) .... WAP
Weather-Modification Statistical Research Groups .... WMSRG
Weatherproof .... WP
Weatherproof (MSA) .... WTHPRF
Weatherproof Faience [*Tile*] (DICI) .... WF
Weatherproof Faience Mosaics (DICI) .... WFM
Weatherstrip Research Institute .... WRI
Weatherstripping (AAG) .... WS
Weathertight .... WEAT
Weave (VRA) .... wv
Weavelength-Scanning Polarization-Modulation Ellipsometry (PDAA) .... WSPME
Web .... W
Web (VRA) .... web
Web Action Time (MCD) .... WAT
Web Based Information Management System .... WIMS
Web Depth .... WD
Web Depth Index .... WDI
Web Depth Order .... WDO
Web Guide System .... WGS
Web Offset Association (EA) .... WOA
Web Offset Section [*Later, WOA*] (EA) .... WOS
Web Printing Press .... WPP
Web Sling and Tiedown Association (EA) .... WSTDA
Web Sling Association [*Later, WSTDA*] (EA) .... WSA
Webb and Duval's Reports [*1-3 Texas*] [*A publication*] (DLA) .... Webb & D
Webb and Duval's Reports [*1-3 Texas*] [*A publication*] (DLA) .... Webb & Duval
Webb & Knapp (Canada) Ltd. [*Vancouver Stock Exchange symbol*] .... WBK
Webb City, MO [*FM radio station call letters*] .... KIXQ
Webb City, MO [*AM radio station call letters*] .... KKLL
Webb City, MO [*FM radio station call letters*] .... KKLL-FM
Webb City, MO [*FM radio station call letters*] (RBYB) .... KXDG
Webb [*Del E.*] **Corp.** [*NYSE symbol*] (SPSG) .... WBB
Webb [*Del E.*] **Corp.** [*Associated Press*] (SAG) .... WebbD
Webb Institute of Naval Architecture [*Glen Cove, NY*] .... WINA
Webb Institute of Naval Architecture, Glen Cove, NY [*Library symbol Library of Congress*] (LCLS) .... NGlcW
Webb Institute of Naval Engineering .... WINE
Webb on the Judicature Act [*A publication*] (DLA) .... Webb Jud Act
Webb [*Del E.*] **Properties Corp.** (MHDW) .... DWP
Webbing .... WBG
Webbing (AAG) .... WEB
Webbing Equipment [*British military*] (DMA) .... WE
Webb-Pomerene Act [*1918*] .... WPA
Webb's Digest of Texas Criminal Cases [*A publication*] (DLA) .... Webb Cr Dig
Webb's English Supreme Court Practice [*A publication*] (DLA) .... Webb Supr Ct Pr
Webb's Kansas Pleading and Practice [*A publication*] (DLA) .... Webb Pl & Pr
Webb's Railroad Laws of Maine [*A publication*] (DLA) .... Webb RR
Webb's Reports [*6-20 Kansas*] [*A publication*] (DLA) .... Webb

Webb's Reports [*11-20 Texas Civil Appeals*] [*A publication*] (DLA) ... Webb
Webbwood Public Library, Ontario [*Library symbol National Library of Canada*] (NLC) ... OWEB
WebChat Broadcasting Station ... WBS
Webco Industries [*AMEX symbol*] (TTSB) ... WEB
Webco Industries, Inc. [*AMEX symbol*] (SAG) ... WEB
Webco Industries, Inc. [*Associated Press*] (SAG) ... WebcoInd
Weber [*Hearing test*] (MAE) ... W
Weber [*Symbol*] [*SI unit of magnetic flux*] ... Wb
Weber ... WBR
Weber Advanced Spatial Perception Test [*Vocational guidance test*] ... WASP
Weber Aircraft Co. ... WAC
Weber County Library, Ogden, UT [*Library symbol Library of Congress*] (LCLS) ... UO
Weber Fraction [*Psychology*] ... W
Weber Meter ... WB M
Weber Number [*IUPAC*] ... We
Weber per Square Meter [*Chemistry*] (DAVI) ... wb/m^2
Weber per Square Meter (IAA) ... WBSM
Weber State College [*Ogden, UT*] ... WSC
Weber State College [*Odgen, UT*] ... WSCO
Weber State College, Ogden, UT [*Library symbol Library of Congress*] (LCLS) ... UOW
Weber State College, Ogden, UT [*OCLC symbol*] (OCLC) ... UUO
WebSecure, Inc. [*NASDAQ symbol*] (SAG) ... WEBS
WebSecure, Inc. [*Associated Press*] (SAG) ... WebSec
WebSecure, Inc. [*Associated Press*] (SAG) ... WebSecr
Webster City Fed Svgs Bk [*NASDAQ symbol*] (TTSB) ... WCFB
Webster City Federal Savings Bank [*Associated Press*] (SAG) ... WbsCtyF
Webster City Federal Savings Bank [*NASDAQ symbol*] (SAG) ... WCFB
Webster City, IA [*Location identifier FAA*] (FAAL) ... EBS
Webster City, IA [*AM radio station call letters*] ... KQWC
Webster City, IA [*FM radio station call letters*] ... KQWC-FM
Webster City Junior College [*Iowa*] ... WCJC
Webster College, Eden Theological Seminary, Webster Groves, MO [*OCLC symbol*] (OCLC) ... ELW
Webster College, Webster Groves, MO [*Library symbol Library of Congress*] (LCLS) ... MoWgW
Webster Financial [*NASDAQ symbol*] (TTSB) ... WBST
Webster Financial Corp. [*Waterbury, CT*] [*NASDAQ symbol*] (NQ) ... WBST
Webster Financial Corp. [*Associated Press*] (SAG) ... WbstFn
Webster in Senate Documents [*A publication*] (DLA) ... Webster in Sen Doc
Webster Institute for Mathematics, Science, and Arts [*Webster College*] ... WIMSA
Webster, MA [*AM radio station call letters*] ... WGFP
Webster, MA [*FM radio station call letters*] ... WXXW
Webster, NY [*FM radio station call letters*] ... WDCZ
Webster, NY [*FM radio station call letters*] ... WFRW
Webster, NY [*FM radio station call letters*] ... WMHN
Webster Parish Library, Minden, LA [*Library symbol Library of Congress*] (LCLS) ... LMiW
Webster Public Library, Webster, SD [*Library symbol Library of Congress*] (LCLS) ... SdWe
Webster Springs, WV [*FM radio station call letters*] ... WAFD
Webster University (GAGS) ... Webster U
Webster's Biographical Dictionary [*A publication*] ... WBD
Webster's Dictionary [*A publication*] (DLA) ... Webst Dict
Webster's International Dictionary [*A publication*] (DLA) ... Webst Int Dict
Webster's New International Dictionary [*A publication*] (DLA) ... Webst New Int D
Webster's New Patent Law [*4th ed.*] [*1854*] [*A publication*] (DLA) ... Web Pat
Webster's Patent Cases [*1601-1855*] [*A publication*] (DLA) ... Web Pat Cas
Webster's Patent Cases [*1601-1855*] [*A publication*] (DLA) ... Web PC
Webster's Patent Cases [*England*] [*A publication*] (DLA) ... Webs
Webster's Patent Cases [*England*] [*A publication*] (DLA) ... Webs Pat Cas
Webster's Patent Cases [*1601-1855*] [*A publication*] (DLA) ... Webster Pat Cas
Webster's Patent Cases [*England*] [*A publication*] (DLA) ... Webster Pat Cas (Eng)
Webster's Patent Cases [*1601-1855*] [*A publication*] (DLA) ... WP Cas
Webster's Patent Cases [*1601-1855*] [*A publication*] (DLA) ... WPC
Webster's Patent Reports [*England*] [*A publication*] (DLA) ... WPR
Webster's Unabridged Dictionary [*A publication*] (DLA) ... Webst Dict Unab
WEC International (EA) ... WECI
Wechsler Adult Intelligence Scale [*Education*] ... WAIS
Wechsler Adult Intelligence Scale-Revised [*Test*] ... WAIS-R
Wechsler Intelligence Scale for Children [*Education*] ... WISC
Wechsler Intelligence Scale for Children - Revised [*Education*] ... WISC-R
Wechsler Memory Scale [*Neuropsychological test*] ... WMS
Wechsler Memory Scale, Form I [*Psychology*] (DAVI) ... WMS-I
Wechsler Objective Reading Dimensions [*Test*] ... WORD
Wechsler Preschool and Primary Scale of Intelligence [*Education*] ... WPPSI
Wechsler Preschool Primary Scale of Intelligence [*Education*] (DAVI) ... WPP
Wechsler-Bellevue [*Psychological test*] ... WB
Wechsler-Bellevue [*Test*] [*Psychiatry*] (DAVI) ... WB-I
Wechsler-Bellevue Intelligence Test [*Psychology*] (WDAA) ... WBIT
WED [*Walt E. Disney*] **Enterprises, Inc., Research Library, Glendale, CA** [*Library symbol Library of Congress*] (LCLS) ... CGlWD
Wedau [*Papua New Guinea*] [*Airport symbol*] (OAG) ... WED
Wedco Technologies [*NASDAQ symbol*] (SAG) ... WEDC
Wedco Technologies [*Associated Press*] (SAG) ... Wedco
Weddell Sea Bottom Water [*Oceanography*] ... WSBW
Wedding Photographers International (EA) ... WPI
Wedge (MSA) ... WG
Wedge Action [*British military*] (DMA) ... WA
Wedge Adjustable Cushioned Heel [*Orthopedics*] ... WACH
Wedge Biopsy [*Medicine*] ... WB
Wedge Nozzle Assembly ... WNA
Wedge Opening Load ... WOL
Wedge Power Clamp ... WPC
Wedge Type Jack ... WTJ
Wedged Hepatic Venous Pressure ... WHVP
Wedged Renal Venous Pressure [*Medicine*] (MAE) ... WRVP
Wedgefield, SC [*FM radio station call letters*] ... WIBZ
Wedgewood Resources [*Vancouver Stock Exchange symbol*] ... WGW
Wedgwood and Homan's Manual for Notaries and Bankers [*A publication*] (DLA) ... Wedg & Hom
Wedgwood Collectors Society [*Defunct*] (EA) ... WCS
Wedgwood International Seminar (EA) ... WIS
Wedgwood on American Government and Laws [*A publication*] (DLA) ... Wedg Gov & Laws
Wedgwood Society [*Defunct*] (EA) ... WS
Wedgwood Society of Australia ... WSA
Wedgwood's Dictionary of English Etymology [*A publication*] (DLA) ... Wedgw Dict Eng Etymology
Wedjh [*Saudi Arabia*] [*Airport symbol*] (OAG) ... EJH
Wednesday ... W
Wednesday ... WE
Wednesday (EY) ... WED
Wednesday (ODBW) ... Wed
Wednesday (ODBW) ... Weds
Wedron Consolidated Community School District 201, Wedron, IL [*Library symbol Library of Congress*] (LCLS) ... IWedSD
Wee Scots (EA) ... WS
We-Eat-This-Stuff-Up [*Mobile guerrilla force coded password*] [*Bowdlerized version*] (VNW) ... WETSU
Weed (WDAA) ... WD
Weed, CA [*FM radio station call letters*] ... KWHO
Weed Science Society of America (EA) ... WSSA
Weed Society of America [*Later, WSSA*] (EA) ... WSA
Weed Society of Australia (EERA) ... WSWA
Weed-Activated Spray Process [*Agriculture*] ... WASP
Week ... W
Week (WDMC) ... w
Week (WDMC) ... wk
Week (AFM) ... WK
Week Commencing (ADA) ... W/C
Week Ending ... W/E
Week Of (WDMC) ... w/o
Week Second Feet ... WSF
Weekday ... WKD
Weekday ... WKDAY
Weekend (ADA) ... WE
Weekend ... WKEND
Weekend ... WKND
Weekend Australian [*A publication*] ... Wk Aust
Weekend Executive Master of Business Administration (PGP) ... WEMBA
Weekend Pass (DAVI) ... WEP
Weekend Stress Syndrome [*Psychiatry*] ... WSS
Week-End Training Site [*Military*] (AABC) ... WETS
Weekend Travel [*Also, Z*] [*Airline fare code*] ... W
Weekend Travel [*Also, W*] [*Airline fare code*] ... Z
Weekly ... w
Weekly (WDMC) ... w
Weekly ... WKLY
Weekly Announcements ... WA
Weekly Arrival Schedule [*Military*] (AFIT) ... WAS
Weekly Audit Report File [*IRS*] ... WARF
Weekly Average Price ... WAP
Weekly Benefit Amount [*Unemployment insurance*] ... WBA
Weekly Boarding ... WB
Weekly Bulletin [*Army*] (AABC) ... WB
Weekly Cincinnati Law Bulletin [*Ohio*] [*A publication*] (DLA) ... Cin Law Bull
Weekly Cincinnati Law Bulletin [*A publication*] (DLA) ... Week Cin LB
Weekly Cincinnati Law Bulletin [*Ohio*] [*A publication*] (DLA) ... Wkly Cin Law Bul
Weekly Collection Report File [*IRS*] ... WCRF
Weekly Contact Hours ... WCH
Weekly Cost Ledger (MCD) ... WCL
Weekly Criminal Bulletin [*Canada Law Book, Inc.*] [*Information service or system*] ... WCB
Weekly Dose [*Medicine*] ... W
Weekly Government Abstracts [*National Technical Information Service*] ... WGA
Weekly Hospital Indemnity [*Insurance*] ... WHI
Weekly Induction Scheduling System [*Navy*] (NG) ... WISS
Weekly Intelligence Digest [*Military*] (CINC) ... WID
Weekly Intelligence Estimate Update [*Vietnam*] ... WIEU
Weekly Intelligence Review ... WIR
Weekly Jurist [*Bloomington, IL*] [*A publication*] (DLA) ... Week Jur
Weekly Law and Bank Bulletin [*Ohio*] [*A publication*] (DLA) ... Law & Bk Bull
Weekly Law and Bank Bulletin [*Ohio*] [*A publication*] (DLA) ... Week Law & Bk Bull
Weekly Law Bulletin [*Ohio*] [*A publication*] (DLA) ... B
Weekly Law Bulletin [*Ohio*] [*A publication*] (DLA) ... Bull O
Weekly Law Bulletin [*Ohio*] [*A publication*] (DLA) ... Law Bull
Weekly Law Bulletin [*Ohio*] [*A publication*] (DLA) ... Ohio Law Bull
Weekly Law Bulletin [*Ohio*] [*A publication*] (DLA) ... Ohio LB
Weekly Law Bulletin [*Ohio*] [*A publication*] (DLA) ... W Law Bul
Weekly Law Bulletin [*England*] [*A publication*] (DLA) ... Weekly L Bull
Weekly Law Bulletin [*Ohio*] [*A publication*] (DLA) ... Weekly Law B
Weekly Law Bulletin [*Ohio*] [*A publication*] (DLA) ... Wkly L Bul
Weekly Law Bulletin [*Ohio*] [*A publication*] (DLA) ... Wkly Law Bul
Weekly Law Bulletin [*Ohio*] [*A publication*] (DLA) ... WL Bull
Weekly Law Bulletin [*Ohio*] [*A publication*] (DLA) ... WL Bull (Ohio)
Weekly Law Bulletin [*Ohio*] [*A publication*] (DLA) ... WLB

Weekly Law Bulletin and Ohio Law Journal [A publication] (DLA).... Week Law Bull
Weekly Law Bulletin (Ohio) [A publication] (DLA) .... Bull (Ohio)
Weekly Law Gazette [Ohio] [A publication] (DLA) .... Gaz
Weekly Law Gazette [Ohio] [A publication] (DLA) .... Week L Gaz
Weekly Law Gazette [Ohio] [A publication] (DLA) .... Week Law Gaz
Weekly Law Gazette [Ohio] [A publication] (DLA) .... Wkly L Gaz
Weekly Law Gazette [Ohio] [A publication] (DLA) .... Wkly Law Gaz
Weekly Law Gazette [Ohio] [A publication] (ILCA) .... WLG
Weekly Law Gazette (Ohio) [A publication] (DLA) .... WL Gaz (Ohio)
Weekly Law Gazette (Reprint) [Ohio] [A publication] (DLA) .... WL Gaz
Weekly Law Magazine [1842-43] [A publication] (DLA) .... Week L Mag
Weekly Law Record [A publication] (DLA) .... Week L Rec
Weekly Law Record [A publication] (DLA) .... Week L Record
Weekly Law Reports [A publication] (DLA) .... Week LR
Weekly Law Reports [England] [A publication] (DLA) .... Weekly LR
Weekly Law Reports [British] .... WLR
Weekly Law Reports (England) [A publication] (DLA) .... Week LR (Eng)
Weekly Law Review [San Francisco] [A publication] (DLA) ...... Week L Rev
Weekly Newspaper Advertising Bureau [British] (BI) .... WNAB
Weekly Notes, Miscellaneous [A publication] (DLA) .... WN Misc
Weekly Notes of Cases [Pennsylvania] [A publication] (DLA) .... Week No
Weekly Notes of Cases [Pennsylvania] [A publication] (DLA) ..... Week No Cas
Weekly Notes of Cases [Pennsylvania] [A publication] (DLA) .... Weekly NC
Weekly Notes of Cases [Pennsylvania] [A publication] (DLA) .... Wk N
Weekly Notes of Cases [Pennsylvania] [A publication] (DLA) .... Wkly NC
Weekly Notes of Cases [Pennsylvania] [A publication] (DLA) ...... Wkly Notes Cas
Weekly Notes of Cases [Pennsylvania] [A publication] (DLA) .... Wkly Notes Cas (PA)
Weekly Notes of Cases [Pennsylvania] [A publication] (DLA) .... WN Cas
Weekly Notes of Cases [Pennsylvania] [A publication] (DLA) .... WN Cas (PA)
Weekly Notes of Cases [Pennsylvania] [A publication] (DLA) .... WNC
Weekly Notes of Cases [Pennsylvania] [A publication] (DLA) .... WNC (PA)
Weekly Notes of Cases (Law Reports) [England] [A publication] (DLA)..... Week No
Weekly Notes of Cases (Law Reports) [England] [A publication]
(DLA) .... Week No Cas
Weekly Notes of Cases (Law Reports) [England] [A publication]
(DLA) .... Week Notes Cas
Weekly Notes of English Law Reports [A publication] (DLA) .... WN
Weekly Notes of English Law Reports [A publication] (DLA) .... WN (Eng)
Weekly Notice to Airmen [FAA] .... WENOA
Weekly of Business Aviation [McGraw-Hill Information Services Co.]
[Information service or system] (CRD) .... WBA
Weekly Performance Status Report (MCD) .... WPSR
Weekly Premium [Insurance] .... WP
Weekly Readiness Check .... WRC
Weekly Record/American Book Publishing Record [A publication] .... WR/ABPR
Weekly Reporter [1853-1906] [A publication] (DLA) .... Week R
Weekly Reporter [England] [A publication] (DLA) .... Week Rep
Weekly Reporter [London] [A publication] (DLA) .... Week Reptr
Weekly Reporter [Bengal] [A publication] (DLA) .... Week Reptr
Weekly Reporter [London] [A publication] (DLA) .... Wkly Rep
Weekly Reporter [Bengal] [A publication] (DLA) .... WR
Weekly Reporter [England] [A publication] (DLA) .... WR
Weekly Reporter, Cape Provincial Division [South Africa] [A publication]
(DLA) .... WR
Weekly Reporter (England) [A publication] (DLA) .... Week R (Eng)
Weekly Significant Action Report (AFIT) .... WSAR
Weekly Statistical Bulletin [Database] [American Petroleum Institute]
[Information service or system] (CRD) .... WSB
Weekly Summary Report .... WSR
Weekly TIF [Taxpayer Information File] Update [IRS] .... WTU
Weekly Total-to-Date .... WTD
Weekly Transcript Reports [New York] [A publication] (DLA) .... Week Trans Rep
Weekly Transcript Reports [New York] [A publication] (DLA) .... Week Trans Repts
Weekly Transcript Reports [New York] [A publication] (DLA) .... WTR
Weekly Visitor, Audubon, NJ [Library symbol Library of Congress] (LCLS).... NjAuV
Weeks after Treatment .... WAT
Weeks Before Volume Production [Automotive project management] .... WBVP
Weeks Corp. [Associated Press] (SAG) .... Weeks
Weeks Corp. [NYSE symbol] (SAG) .... WKS
Weeks' Damnum Absque Injuria [A publication] (DLA) .... Weeks DA Inj
Weeks' Mining Legislation of Congress [A publication] (DLA) .... Weeks Min Leg
Weeks Old [Preceded by a number] [Neonatology] (DAVI) .... WO
Weeks Old [Medicine] (MEDA) .... wo
Weeks on Attorneys at Law [A publication] (DLA) .... Weeks Att at Law
Weeks on Depositions [A publication] (DLA) .... Weeks Dep
Weeks on Mines and Mineral Law [A publication] (DLA) .... Weeks Min
Weeksville, NC [Location identifier FAA] (FAAL) .... EKV
Weelde [Belgium ICAO location identifier] (ICLI) .... EBWE
Weeley [British ICAO location identifier] (ICLI) .... EGSW
Weeping [Shrub] .... W
Weeping Water, NE [Location identifier FAA] (FAAL) .... EPG
Weerakoon's Appeal Court Reports [Ceylon] [A publication] (DLA) .... Weer
Weert/Budel [Netherlands ICAO location identifier] (ICLI) .... EHBD
Wegener Corp. [Associated Press] (SAG) .... Wegenr
Wegener Corp. [NASDAQ symbol] (NQ) .... WGNR
Wegener's Granulomatosis [Medicine] .... WG
Wehnelt [A unit of roentgen ray hardness] (AAMN) .... W
Wehrmacht Graeberoffizier [Armed forces graves registration officer] [German
military - World War II] .... WGO
Wehrmachtfuehrungsstab [Armed Forces Operations Staff] [German military -
World War II] .... WFSt
Wehrmacht-Heer [Marking on Army vehicles] [German military - World War
II] .... WH
Wehrmacht-Luftwaffe [Marking on Air Force vehicles] [German military - World
War II] .... WL

Wehrmacht-Marine [Marking on Navy vehicles] [German military - World War
II] .... WM
Wehrmachtnachrichtenverbindungen [Armed Forces Signal Communications]
[German military - World War II] .... WNV
Wehrsportegruppe Hoffman Truppe [Hoffman Paramilitary Troop]
[Germany] .... WSG
Wehrstrafgesetz [Military Criminal Law] [German] (ILCA) .... WStG
Weibull Probability Paper [Statistics] .... WPP
Weibull Reliability Function [Statistics] .... WRF
Weibull Shape Parameter [Statistics] .... WSP
Weidels Auditory Processing Test [Speech and language therapy]
(DAVI) .... WAPT
Weidels Yes/No Reliability Test [Speech and language therapy] (DAVI)..... WY/NRT
Weiden [Germany ICAO location identifier] (ICLI) .... EDZY
Weiden, Oberpfalz [Germany ICAO location identifier] (ICLI) .... EDQW
Weidenfeld & Nicolson [Publisher] .... W & N
Weidingsvereniging van Suidelike Afrika [Grassland Society of Southern
Africa-GISSA] (EAIO) .... WVSA
Weigh in Motion .... WIM
Weighing (ROG) .... WG
Weighing .... WNG
Weighing and Inspection .... W & I
Weighing Less Than .... WLT
Weighing More Than .... WMT
Weighmaster (WGA) .... WHM
Weight [Symbol] [IUPAC] .... G
Weight .... W
Weight (WDMC) .... w
Weight .... WGHT
Weight [Shipping] (DS) .... WGT
Weight (DAVI) .... wgt
Weight (AAG) .... WT
Weight (ODBW) .... wt
Weight (IDOE) .... wt
Weight after Departure from Mars [NASA] .... WDM
Weight after Mars Arrival [NASA] .... WAMA
Weight after Melt [Metallurgy] .... WAM
Weight after Processing [Metallurgy] .... WAP
Weight, Alignment, and Mass Center Determination Equipment
(AAG) .... WAAMAC
Weight, Altitude, and Temperature (IEEE) .... WAT
Weight Analysis Data Report .... WADR
Weight and Balance .... W/B
Weight and Balance Computer (GAVI) .... WBC
Weight and Balance System (MCD) .... WBS
Weight and Value Engineering System [Computer science] .... WAVES
Weight Average Temperature [Chemical engineering] .... WAT
Weight Bearing .... WB
Weight before Departure from Mars Orbit [NASA] .... WDMO
Weight before Mars Capture [NASA] .... WBMC
Weight Data Transmitter (IAA) .... WDT
Weight Distribution Table .... WDT
Weight Estimating Relationship (KSC) .... WER
Weight Flow Rate (SAA) .... WFR
Weight Guaranteed .... WG
Weight Indicating Alarm [Engineering] .... WIA
Weight Note [Tea trade] (ROG) .... W/N
Weight of Authority [Legal shorthand] (LWAP) .... WOA
Weight of Fuel Flow (MCD) .... WOFF
Weight of Solute in Weight of Solvent [Chemistry] (DAVI) .... w/w
Weight of Solute per Weight of Total Solution [Chemistry] (DAVI) ...... w/w
Weight on Bit [Drilling technology] .... WOB
Weight on Nose Gear [Aviation] (MCD) .... WONG
Weight or Measurement .... W/M
Weight Part per Million .... WPPM
Weight Penalty .... WP
Weight per Foot (IAA) .... WTPFT
Weight per Volume [Ratio] [Chemistry] (DAVI) .... wt/vol
Weight per Weight [Ratio] [Chemistry] (DAVI) .... wt/wt
Weight Percent (SAA) .... W/O
Weight, Power, Fulcrum .... WPF
Weight Unit [Automobiles] .... WU
Weight/Volume [Concentration] [Chemistry] .... W/V
Weight Watchers [An association] .... WW
Weight Watchers International [Commercial firm] (EA) .... WWI
Weight/Weight .... W/W
Weight-Bearing (DAVI) .... WHB
Weight-Bearing as Tolerated [Orthopedics] (DAVI) .... WBAT
Weight-Bearing with Crutches [Orthopedics] (DAVI) .... WBC
Weighted Agreement Scores .... WAGS
Weighted Airman Promotion System [Air Force] .... WAPS
Weighted Average [Accounting] .... WA
Weighted Average Cost of Capital [Accounting] (ADA) .... WACC
Weighted Average Coupon [Finance] .... WAC
Weighted Average Inlet Temperature [Chemical engineering] ...... WAIT
Weighted Average Maturity [Finance] .... WAM
Weighted Average Remaining Term [Finance] .... WART
Weighted Common Examination Total (EDAC) .... WCET
Weighted Dilution of Precision .... WDOP
Weighted Effective Temperature (IAA) .... WET
Weighted Elementary Pupil Unit [Education] (AEE) .... WEPU
Weighted Equivalent Continuous Perceived Noise Level .... WECPNL
Weighted Guidelines [DoD] .... WGL
Weighted Guidelines Analysis [Air Force] (MCD) .... WGA
Weighted Guidelines Method [Navy] .... WGM

Weighted Guidelines System (AAGC) ... WGLS
Weighted Ion Concentration [*Air pollution measure*] ... WIC
Weighted Least Squares [*Statistics*] ... WLS
Weighted Linear Regression [*Mathematics*] ... WLR
Weighted Mean [*Psychology*] ... Mw
Weighted Nonlinear Regression [*Mathematics*] ... WNLR
Weighted Pair Group ... WPG
Weighted Sensitivity Analysis Program [*Environmental Protection Agency*] ... WSAP
Weighted Student Unit ... WSU
Weighted Sum of Deviation Squared [*Statistics*] ... WSDS
Weighted Total Demerits [*Lubricating oil test*] ... WTD
Weighted Unit Value (MCD) ... WUV
Weighter/Combiner (MCD) ... WGT/COMB
Weighter Record Analysis Program [*Computer science*] (MHDI) ... WRAP
Weight-for-Age (ADA) ... WFA
Weight-Hourly Space Velocity [*Fuel technology*] ... WHSV
Weighting (MSA) ... WTG
Weighting Factor (EG) ... WF
Weightless Analysis Sounding Probe [*NASA*] ... WASP
Weightless Environment Training Facility (SSD) ... WETF
Weightlessness Simulation Test ... WST
Weightlifting Federation of Africa (EAIO) ... WFA
Weightman's Marriage and Legitimacy [*1871*] [*A publication*] (DLA) ... Weight M & L
Weightman's Medico-Legal Gazette [*A publication*] (DLA) ... Weight Med Leg Gaz
Weight-on-Wheels (NASA) ... WOW
Weight-on-Wheels Lock-On [*NASA*] (NASA) ... WOWLON
Weights Analysis for Advanced Transportation Systems [*NASA*] ... WAATS
Weil-Felix [*Test*] [*Laboratory science*] (DAVI) ... WEIL
Weil-Felix Reaction [*Medicine*] (MAE) ... WF
Weil-Felix Reaction [*Medicine*] (MAE) ... WFR
Weil's Code of Wyoming Rules [*A publication*] (AAGC) ... WCWR
Weil's Wyoming Government Register [*A publication*] (AAGC) ... WWGR
Weimar Mercury, Weimar, TX [*Library symbol Library of Congress*] (LCLS) ... TxWeiM
Weimaraner Club of America (EA) ... WCA
Wein Zollordnung [*Wine Duty Order*] [*German*] ... WZO
Weiner Memorial Hospital, Marshall, MN [*Library symbol*] [*Library of Congress*] (LCLS) ... MnMarH
Weingarten Realty, Inc. [*Associated Press*] (SAG) ... WeinRl
Weingarten Realty Investors, Inc. [*NYSE symbol*] (SPSG) ... WRI
Weingarten Rlty SBI [*NYSE symbol*] (TTSB) ... WRI
Weipa [*Australia ICAO location identifier*] (ICLI) ... ABWP
Weipa [*Australia Airport symbol*] (OAG) ... WEI
Weippe Elementary School, Weippe, ID [*Library symbol*] [*Library of Congress*] (LCLS) ... IdWeES
Weippe Public Library, Weippe, ID [*Library symbol*] [*Library of Congress*] (LCLS) ... IdWe
Weir's Criminal Rulings [*India*] [*A publication*] (DLA) ... Weir
Weirton Steel [*NYSE symbol*] (TTSB) ... WS
Weirton Steel Corp. [*Associated Press*] (SAG) ... Weirt
Weirton Steel Corp. [*NYSE symbol*] (SPSG) ... WS
Weirton, WV [*AM radio station call letters*] ... WEIR
Weis Markets [*NYSE symbol*] (TTSB) ... WMK
Weis Markets, Inc. [*Associated Press*] (SAG) ... WeisMk
Weis Markets, Inc. [*NYSE symbol*] (SPSG) ... WMK
Weiser, ID [*AM radio station call letters*] ... KWEI
Weiser Public Library, Weiser, ID [*Library symbol*] [*Library of Congress*] (LCLS) ... IdWei
Weiss Comprehensive Articulation Test [*Education*] ... WCAT
Weitek Corp. [*Associated Press*] (SAG) ... Weitek
Weitek Corp. [*NASDAQ symbol*] (CTT) ... WWTK
Weitzer Homebuilders, Inc. [*Associated Press*] (SAG) ... WeitzrH
Weitzer Homebuilders, Inc. [*NASDAQ symbol*] (SAG) ... WTZRA
Weitzer Homebuilders'A' [*NASDAQ symbol*] (TTSB) ... WTZRA
Weizmann Institute of Science, Rehovot, Israel [*Library symbol Library of Congress*] (LCLS) ... IsRW
Weizmann Israel Archives [*Rehovoth*] (BJA) ... WA
Weizsaecker-Williams Method [*Physics*] ... WWM
Wejh [*Saudi Arabia*] [*ICAO location identifier*] (ICLI) ... OEWJ
Welch Aviation, Inc. [*ICAO designator*] (FAAC) ... TDB
Welch Fusiliers [*British military*] (DMA) ... WF
Welch, WV [*AM radio station call letters*] ... WELC
Welch, WV [*FM radio station call letters*] ... WELC-FM
Welch, WV [*AM radio station call letters*] ... WXEE
Welcome Home [*NASDAQ symbol*] (TTSB) ... WELC
Welcome Home, Inc. [*NASDAQ symbol*] (SAG) ... WELC
Welcome Home, Inc. [*Associated Press*] (SAG) ... WelcomH
Welcome North Mines [*Vancouver Stock Exchange symbol*] ... WLN
Welcome to Our Elvis World (EA) ... WTOEW
Weld (DAS) ... W
Weld County Library, Greeley, CO [*Library symbol Library of Congress*] (LCLS) ... CoGrW
Weld Fixture ... WF
Weld Flange Connection ... WFC
Weld Head Assembly ... WHA
Weld Quality Assurance ... WQA
Weld Timer Control Module ... WTCM
Weldable Printed Circuit ... WPC
Welded (VRA) ... wld
Welded (MSA) ... WLD
Welded Aluminum Alloy ... WAA
Welded Base (DAC) ... WB
Welded Cordwood Module ... WCM
Welded Electronic Packaging Association ... WEPA
Welded Joint Design ... WJD
Welded Modules for Electronic Assemblies [*NASA*] ... WMEA
Welded Ring Manufacturers Association [*Defunct*] ... WRMA
Welded Steel Tube Institute [*Later, STINA*] (EA) ... WSTI
Welded Wire Fabric [*Technical drawings*] ... WWF
Welded Wire Matrix ... WWM
Welder (MSA) ... WLDR
Welder Control Panel ... WCP
Welding ... WELD
Welding (IAA) ... WLDG
Welding and Testing Technology Energy Conference [*Acronym is used as name of association*] ... WATTec
Welding Equipment Maintenance and Repair [*UAW job classification*] ... WEMR
Welding Filler Material Control [*Nuclear energy*] (NRCH) ... WFMC
Welding Fixture (AAG) ... WLFX
[*The*] **Welding Institute** [*Information service or system*] (IID) ... TWI
Welding Institute [*Database originator and operator*] (EA) ... WI
Welding Institute of Canada (EAIO) ... WIC
Welding Institute of Canada, Oakville, Ontario [*Library symbol National Library of Canada*] (NLC) ... OTCWB
Welding Machine Arc ... WMA
Welding Manufacturers Association [*British*] (DBA) ... WMA
Welding Memorandum ... WM
Welding Procedure [*Nuclear energy*] (NRCH) ... WP
Welding Procedure Qualification Record [*Nuclear energy*] (NRCH) ... WPQR
Welding Procedure Specification [*Nuclear energy*] (NRCH) ... WPS
Welding Program [*Association of Independent Colleges and Schools specialization code*] ... W
Welding Research Council (EA) ... WRC
Welding Technology Institute of Australia ... WTIA
Weldless ... WLDS
Weldment (MSA) ... WLDMT
Weldon Memorial Library, Weldon, NC [*Library symbol Library of Congress*] (LCLS) ... NcWel
Weldon, NC [*AM radio station call letters*] ... WSMY
Weldon Spring Site Remedial Action Project [*Department of Energy*] [*Weldon Spring, MO*] (GAAI) ... WSSRAP
Weldotron Corp. [*Associated Press*] (SAG) ... Weldtrn
Weldotron Corp. [*AMEX symbol*] (SPSG) ... WLD
Weldwood of Canada Ltd. [*Toronto Stock Exchange symbol*] ... WLW
Weldwood Transportation Ltd. [*AAR code*] ... WT
Welen [*Former USSR Geomagnetic observatory code*] ... CWE
Welex Division, Haliburton Co., Houston, TX [*Library symbol Library of Congress*] (LCLS) ... TxHW
Welfare ... WEL
Welfare (AABC) ... WLF
Welfare Administration [*Became Social and Rehabilitation Service*] [*HEW*] ... WA
Welfare and Institutions Code (BARN) ... WIC
Welfare and Pension Plans Disclosure Act [*1958*] [*Department of Labor*] ... WPPDA
Welfare and Recreation [*Navy*] ... W & R
Welfare and Service Conditions Department [*British military*] (DMA) ... WSCD
Welfare Appointment Full Time [*Chiropody*] [*British*] ... WF
Welfare Entered Employment Rate [*Job Training and Partnership Act*] (OICC) ... WEER
Welfare Food Service [*British*] ... WFS
Welfare in Review [*A publication*] ... WIR
Welfare Law Bulletin [*A publication*] (DLA) ... Welfare L Bull
Welfare Law News [*A publication*] (DLA) ... Welfare L News
Welfare News [*A publication*] ... Welf News
Welfare of Animals Used for Research in Drugs and Therapy ... WARDS
Welfare of Enlisted Men [*Air Force*] ... WEM
Welfare of the Blind (EA) ... WOTB
Welfare Officer [*British military*] (DMA) ... WO
Welfare Planning Council, Los Angeles, CA [*Library symbol Library of Congress*] (LCLS) ... CLWelf
Welfare Recipient (OICC) ... WR
Welfare Research, Inc. (EA) ... WRI
Welfare State International [*Performance group*] [*British*] ... WSI
Welfare Worker [*British military*] (DMA) ... WW
Welford's Equity Pleadings [*1842*] [*A publication*] (DLA) ... Welf Eq
Welkom [*South Africa*] [*ICAO location identifier*] (ICLI) ... FAWM
Welkom [*South Africa*] [*Airport symbol*] (OAG) ... WEL
Well [*Commonly used*] (OPSA) ... WELL
Well [*Postal Service standard*] (OPSA) ... WL
Well ... WL
We'll Be Loyal Scouts [*Boy Scout slogan*] ... WEBELOS
Well Behaved Net ... WBN
Well Deck ... WD
Well Deck Debarkation Control [*Navy*] (CAAL) ... WDDC
Well Developed - Well Nourished [*Medicine*] ... WDWN
Well Differentiated [*Medicine*] ... WD
Well Drillers' Association [*British*] (DBA) ... WDA
Well Head Unit ... WHU
Well Healed [*Medicine*] (AAMN) ... WH
Well History Control System [*Later, Historical Well Data On-Line*] [*Petroleum Information Corp.*] [*Information service or system*] (IID) ... WHCS
Well Information Network [*Database*] ... WIN
Well Logging Cable ... WLC
Well Spouse Foundation (EA) ... WSF
Well to Right [*Aviation*] (FAAC) ... WTR
Well to Right of Course [*Aviation*] (FAAC) ... WRC
Well Water [*Nuclear energy*] (NRCH) ... WW
Well Water (System) [*Nuclear energy*] (NRCH) ... WW(S)

Welland, ON [*AM radio station call letters*] ... CHOW
Welland Public Library, Ontario [*Library symbol National Library of Canada*] (NLC) ... OWE
Welland Public Library, Welland, ON, Canada [*Library symbol Library of Congress*] (LCLS) ... CaOWe
Wellbeloved on Highways [*1829*] [*A publication*] (DLA) ... Well High
Wellborn Nursery [*Neonatology*] (DAVI) ... WBN
Wellcare Management Group [*NASDAQ symbol*] (SAG) ... WELL
WellCare Management Group [*NASDAQ symbol*] (TTSB) ... WELLE
Wellcare Management Group [*Associated Press*] (SAG) ... WellMgt
Wellco Enterprises [*AMEX symbol*] (TTSB) ... WLC
Wellco Enterprises, Inc. [*Associated Press*] (SAG) ... Wellco
Wellco Enterprises, Inc. [*AMEX symbol*] (SPSG) ... WLC
Wellcome Historical Medical Library [*Burroughs Wellcome Co.*] (DAVI) ... WHML
Wellcome Historical Medical Library, London, United Kingdom [*Library symbol Library of Congress*] (LCLS) ... UkLW
Wellcome Ltd. [*NYSE symbol*] (SPSG) ... WEL
Wellcome Ltd. [*Associated Press*] (SAG) ... Wellcome
Wellcome Research Laboratories [*Research center British*] (IRC) ... WRL
Wellcome Research Laboratories, Durham, NC [*Library symbol Library of Congress*] (LCLS) ... NcDurW
Well-Developed [*Medicine*] ... W-D
Well-Developed Collateral Circulation [*Medicine*] (DMAA) ... WDCC
Well-Developed Well-Nourished, Black Female (DAVI) ... WDWNBF
Well-Developed, Well-Nourished, Black Male (DAVI) ... WDWNBM
Well-Developed, Well-Nourished, White Female (DAVI) ... WDWNWF
Well-Developed, Well-Nourished, White Male (DAVI) ... WDWNWM
Well-Differentiated Lymphatic [*or Lymphocytic*] **Lymphoma** [*Oncology*] ... WDLL
Well-Differentiated Lymphocytic [*Lymphoma classification*] ... WDL
Well-Drained [*Soil*] ... WD
Weller Public Library, Waitsburg, WA [*Library symbol*] [*Library of Congress*] (LCLS) ... WaWaW
Weller-Strawser Scales of Adaptive Behavior [*Educational test*] ... WSSAB
Wellesbourne Mountford [*British ICAO location identifier*] (ICLI) ... EGBW
Wellesley College, Wellesley, MA [*Library symbol Library of Congress*] (LCLS) ... MWelC
Wellesley College, Wellesley, MA [*OCLC symbol*] (OCLC) ... WEL
Wellesley Hospital, Toronto [*UTLAS symbol*] ... WEL
[*The*] **Wellesley Hospital, Toronto, ON, Canada** [*Library symbol*] [*Library of Congress*] (LCLS) ... CaOTWH
Wellesley Hospital, Toronto, Ontario [*Library symbol National Library of Canada*] (NLC) ... OTWH
Wellesley Island [*New York*] [*Seismograph station code, US Geological Survey Closed*] (SEIS) ... WLI
Wellesley, MA [*FM radio station call letters*] ... WZLY
Well-Formed Formula [*Logic*] ... WFF
Well-Formed Net ... WFN
Wellhead Protection Area (GNE) ... WPA
Wellhead Tax [*Oil industry*] ... WT
Well-Healed Midline Scar [*Surgery*] (DAVI) ... WHMS
Wellington [*New Zealand*] [*ICAO location identifier*] (ICLI) ... NZHO
Wellington [*New Zealand*] [*ICAO location identifier*] (ICLI) ... NZWQ
Wellington [*New Zealand*] [*ICAO location identifier*] (ICLI) ... NZZW
Wellington [*New Zealand*] [*Seismograph station code, US Geological Survey*] (SEIS) ... WEL
Wellington [*New Zealand*] (BARN) ... Well
Wellington [*New Zealand*] [*Airport symbol*] (OAG) ... WLG
Wellington [*British depot code*] ... WLN
Wellington C. Mepham High School, Bellmore, NY [*Library symbol*] [*Library of Congress*] (LCLS) ... NBellmCM
Wellington, CO [*AM radio station call letters*] ... KIIX
Wellington County Board of Education [*UTLAS symbol*] ... WCB
Wellington County Board of Education, Education Library, Guelph, ON, Canada [*Library symbol*] [*Library of Congress*] (LCLS) ... CaOGWE
Wellington County Museum and Archives, Fergus, ON, Canada [*Library symbol*] [*Library of Congress*] (LCLS) ... CaOFerWM
Wellington County Museum and Archives, Fergus, Ontario [*Library symbol National Library of Canada*] (BIB) ... OFERWM
Wellington County Museum, Fergus, Ontario [*Library symbol National Library of Canada*] (BIB) ... OFEC
Wellington County Public Library, Fergus, ON, Canada [*Library symbol Library of Congress*] (LCLS) ... CaOFerW
Wellington County Public Library, Fergus, Ontario [*Library symbol National Library of Canada*] (NLC) ... OFERW
Wellington Hall Ltd. [*Associated Press*] (SAG) ... WellHall
Wellington Hall Ltd. [*NASDAQ symbol*] (NQ) ... WHAL
Wellington/International [*New Zealand*] [*ICAO location identifier*] (ICLI) ... NZWN
Wellington/Kelburn [*New Zealand*] [*ICAO location identifier*] (ICLI) ... NZKL
Wellington/Kilbirnie [*New Zealand*] [*ICAO location identifier*] (ICLI) ... NZKB
Wellington, KS [*Location identifier FAA*] (FAAL) ... EGT
Wellington, KS [*AM radio station call letters*] ... KLEY
Wellington, KS [*FM radio station call letters*] ... KWME
Wellington Properties Trust [*NASDAQ symbol*] (TTSB) ... WLPT
Wellington Public Library, Ontario [*Library symbol National Library of Canada*] (BIB) ... OWEL
Wellington Volunteer Rifles [*British military*] (DMA) ... WVR
Wellington, West Coast, and Taranaki Regiment [*British military*] (DMA) ... WWCT Regt
Well-Known ... WK
Well-Known Factor ... WKF
Wellman Advance, Wellman, IA [*Library symbol Library of Congress*] (LCLS) ... IaWelmA
Wellman, Inc. [*Associated Press*] (SAG) ... Wellmn
Wellman, Inc. [*NYSE symbol*] (CTT) ... WLM
Wellness and Health Activation Networks (EA) ... WHAN
Wellness Associates (EA) ... WA
[*A*] **Wellness Center, Inc.** (EA) ... AWCI
Well-Nourished [*Medicine*] ... W-N
Well-Nourished Female [*Medicine*] ... WNF
Well-Nourished Male [*Medicine*] ... WNM
Well-Off, Older Folks [*Lifestyle classification*] ... Woof
Well-Off Older Person [*Lifestyle classification*] ... Woopie
Well-Off, Over Fifty [*Lifestyle classification*] ... Woof
Wellore Energy, Inc. [*Toronto Stock Exchange symbol*] ... WLE
Wellpoint Health Networks [*Associated Press*] (SAG) ... WelptHlt
Wellpoint Health Networks [*NYSE symbol*] (SPSG) ... WLP
Wellpoint Hlth Networks [*NYSE symbol*] (TTBS) ... WLP
Wells [*Nevada*] [*Airport symbol Obsolete*] (OAG) ... LWL
Wells [*Commonly used*] (OPSA) ... WELLS
Wells ... WLS
Wells ... WLS
Wells College, Aurora, NY [*Library symbol Library of Congress*] (LCLS) ... NAurW
Wells Fargo [*NYSE symbol*] (TTSB) ... WFC
Wells Fargo 9% 'C' Dep Pfd [*NYSE symbol*] (TTSB) ... WFCPrC
Wells Fargo 9% Dep Pfd [*NYSE symbol*] (TTSB) ... WFCPrG
Wells Fargo 8.875% Dep Pfd [*NYSE symbol*] (TTSB) ... WFCPrD
Wells Fargo 9.875% Dep Pfd [*NYSE symbol*] (TTSB) ... WFCPrF
Wells Fargo Adj Rt B Pfd [*NYSE symbol*] (TTSB) ... WFCPrB
Wells Fargo & Co. [*Associated Press*] (SAG) ... WelF
Wells Fargo & Co. [*Associated Press*] (SAG) ... WellsF
Wells Fargo & Co. [*Associated Press*] (SAG) ... WF
Wells Fargo & Co. [*NYSE symbol*] (SPSG) ... WFC
Wells Fargo Bank, History Room Library, San Francisco, CA [*Library symbol Library of Congress*] (LCLS) ... CSfWF-H
Wells Fargo Bank, San Francisco, CA [*Library symbol Library of Congress*] (LCLS) ... CSfWF
Wells Fargo Investment Advisors (ECON) ... WFIA
Wells Financial [*NASDAQ symbol*] (TTSB) ... WEFC
Wells Financial Corp. [*NASDAQ symbol*] (SAG) ... WEFC
Wells Financial Corp. [*Associated Press*] (SAG) ... WellsFn
Wells Gold Ltd. [*Vancouver Stock Exchange symbol*] ... WSG
Wells Memorial Library, Lafayette, IN [*Library symbol Library of Congress*] (LCLS) ... InL
Wells Museum, British Columbia [*Library symbol National Library of Canada*] (NLC) ... BWM
Wells Museum, Wells, BC, Canada [*Library symbol*] [*Library of Congress*] (LCLS) ... CaBWM
Wells on Instruction to Juries and Bills of Exception [*A publication*] (DLA) ... Wells Inst Juries
Wells on Replevin [*A publication*] (DLA) ... Wells Rep
Wells on Replevin [*A publication*] (DLA) ... Wells Repl
Wells on the Jurisdiction of Courts [*A publication*] (DLA) ... Wells Jur
Wells on the Separate Property of Married Women [*A publication*] (DLA) ... Wells Mar Wom
Wells Public Library, Wells, ME [*Library symbol Library of Congress*] (LCLS) ... MeWe
Well's Questions of Law and Facts [*A publication*] (DLA) ... Wells L & F
Wells' Res Adjudicata and Stare Decisis [*A publication*] (DLA) ... Wells' Res Ad
Wells River, VT [*AM radio station call letters*] ... WYKR
Wellsboro, PA [*AM radio station call letters*] ... WNBT
Wellsboro, PA [*FM radio station call letters*] ... WNBT-FM
Wellsburg Public Library, Wellsburg, IA [*Library symbol Library of Congress*] (LCLS) ... IaWels
Wellsford Res Prop Tr 9.65% Pfd [*NYSE symbol*] (TTSB) ... WRPPrB
Wellsford Res Prop'A'Cv Pfd [*NYSE symbol*] (TTSB) ... WRPPr
Wellsford Residential Prop Tr [*NYSE symbol*] (TTSB) ... WRP
Wellsford Residential Property [*Associated Press*] (SAG) ... Welsf
Wellsford Residential Property [*Associated Press*] (SAG) ... Welsfd
Wellsford Residential Property Trust [*NYSE symbol*] (SPSG) ... WRP
Wells-Gardner Electr [*AMEX symbol*] (TTSB) ... WGA
Wells-Gardner Electronics Corp. [*Associated Press*] (SAG) ... WelGrd
Wells-Gardner Electronics Corp. [*AMEX symbol*] (SPSG) ... WGA
Wellsiania [*An association*] (EA) ... Wa
Well-Springs Foundation (EA) ... WSF
Wellston, OH [*FM radio station call letters*] ... WKOV
Wellston, OH [*AM radio station call letters*] ... WYPC
Wellsville, Addison & Galeton Railroad Corp. [*AAR code*] ... WAG
Wellsville, NY [*Location identifier FAA*] (FAAL) ... ELZ
Wellsville, NY [*FM radio station call letters*] ... WJQZ
Wellsville, NY [*AM radio station call letters*] ... WLSV
Well-Tempered Clavier [*Compositions of J. S. Bach*] ... WTC
Wellwood's Abridgment of Sea Laws [*A publication*] (DLA) ... Wellw Abr
Wels [*Austria ICAO location identifier*] (ICLI) ... LOLW
Welsby, Hurlstone, and Gordon's English Exchequer Reports [*1848-56*] [*A publication*] (DLA) ... Welsb H & G
Welsby, Hurlstone, and Gordon's English Exchequer Reports [*1848-56*] [*A publication*] (DLA) ... Welsb Hurl & G
Welsby, Hurlstone, and Gordon's English Exchequer Reports [*1848-56*] [*A publication*] (DLA) ... Welsby H & G
Welsby, Hurlstone, and Gordon's English Exchequer Reports [*1848-56*] [*A publication*] (DLA) ... Welsby H & G (Eng)
Welsby, Hurlstone, and Gordon's English Exchequer Reports [*1848-56*] [*A publication*] (DLA) ... WH & G
Welschbruch [*France*] [*Seismograph station code, US Geological Survey*] (SEIS) ... WLS
Welsh [*or Welch*] ... W
Welsh [*MARC language code Library of Congress*] (LCCP) ... wel
Welsh Agricultural Organisation Society (DBA) ... WAOS
Welsh Amateur Boxing Association [*British*] (DBA) ... WABA
Welsh Amateur Gymnastic Association (DBA) ... WAGA

Welsh Arts Council (EAIO) ..... WAC
Welsh Badminton Union (EAIO) ..... WBU
Welsh Baseball Union (DBA) ..... WBU
Welsh Bibliographical Society [*British*] ..... WBS
Welsh Black Cattle Association (EA) ..... WBCA
Welsh Black Cattle Society (DBA) ..... WBCA
Welsh Books Council ..... WBC
Welsh Bowling Association (DBA) ..... SBA
Welsh Centre for International Affairs [*British*] (CB) ..... WCIA
Welsh Chess Union (DBA) ..... WCU
Welsh Consumer Council [*British*] (ILCA) ..... WCC
Welsh Development Agency [*British*] (DS) ..... WDA
Welsh Dragon Aviation Ltd. [*British*] [*FAA designator*] (FAAC) ..... BNX
Welsh Elementary School, Rockford, IL [*Library symbol*] [*Library of Congress*] (LCLS) ..... IRoWeE
Welsh Engineers and Founders Association (DBA) ..... WE & FA
Welsh Figure Preference Test [*Psychology*] ..... WFPT
Welsh Folk Song Society [*British*] ..... WFSS
Welsh Grand Lodge of Wales [*Freemasonry*] ..... WGLW
Welsh Guards [*Military unit*] [*British*] ..... WG
Welsh Harp Society of North America (EA) ..... WHSNA
Welsh Health Common Services Authority ..... WHCSA
Welsh Hockey Association (DBA) ..... WHA
Welsh Horse [*British military*] (DMA) ..... WH
Welsh Hospitals and Health Services Association (DBA) ..... WH & HSA
Welsh Indoor Bowls Association (DBA) ..... WIBA
Welsh Industry and Commerce Trade Fair (ITD) ..... WI & CTF
Welsh Initiative for Specialised Employment ..... WISE
Welsh Joint Education Committee [*British*] ..... WJEC
Welsh Lacrosse Association (EAIO) ..... WLA
Welsh Language Society (EA) ..... WLS
Welsh Lawn Tennis Association (DBA) ..... WLTA
Welsh Liberal Democrats [*Political party*] (EAIO) ..... WLD
Welsh Music Information Centre - Canolfan Hysbysrwydd Cerddoriaeth Cymru [*University College*] (CB) ..... WMIC/CHCC
Welsh National Eisteddfod (DAS) ..... WNE
Welsh National Gymanfa Ganu Association (EA) ..... WNGGA
Welsh National Opera ..... WNO
Welsh Nationalist Party (DI) ..... WNP
Welsh Netball Association (DBA) ..... WNA
Welsh Office (DCTA) ..... WO
Welsh Pony and Cob Society (DBA) ..... WPCS
Welsh Pony and Cob Society of America (EA) ..... WPCSA
Welsh Pony Society of America [*Later, WPCSA*] (EA) ..... WPSA
Welsh Public Library, Welsh, LA [*Library symbol Library of Congress*] (LCLS) ..... LWeJ
Welsh Rugby Union [*British*] (DBA) ..... WRU
Welsh Secondary Schools Association [*British*] ..... WSSA
Welsh Society (EA) ..... WS
Welsh Springer Spaniel Club of America (EA) ..... WSSCA
Welsh Terrier Club of America (EA) ..... WTCA
Welsh Terrier Club of America Rescue Service (EA) ..... WTCARES
Welsh Venture Capital Funds ..... WVCF
Welsh Water Authority (DCTA) ..... WWA
Welsh Women's Hockey Association (DBA) ..... WWHA
Welshpool & Llanfair Light Railway [*Wales*] ..... W & L
Welshpool & Llanfair Light Railway [*Wales*] ..... W & LLR
Welsh's Irish Case at Siligo [*1838*] [*A publication*] (DLA) ..... Welsh
Welsh's Irish Case of James Feighny [*1838*] [*A publication*] (DLA) ..... Welsh
Welsh's Irish Registry Cases [*A publication*] (DLA) ..... Wel
Welsh's Irish Registry Cases [*A publication*] (DLA) ..... Welsh
Welsh's Irish Registry Cases [*A publication*] (DLA) ..... Welsh Reg Cas
Welt Organisation fur Schiffsmodellbau und Schiffsmodellsport [*World Organization for Modelship Building and Modelship Sport*] [*Austria*] (EAIO) ..... NAVIGA
Weltbund Freiheitlicher Arbeitnehmerverbande auf Liberaler Wirtschaftsgrundlage [*World Union of Liberal Trade Union Organisations - WULTUO*] [*Zurich, Switzerland*] (EAIO) ..... WFALW
Weltbund zum Schutze des Lebens [*World Union for the Protection of Life - WUPL-INT*] (EAIO) ..... WSL-INT
Welt-Eis-Lehre [*Cosmic Ice Theory*] [*German*] ..... WEL
Weltgewerkschaftsbund [*World Federation of Trade Unions*] ..... WGB
Welttierschutzbund [*Also known as WFPA, FMPA*] [*World Federation for the Protection of Animals*] ..... WTB
Welwyn Hall Research Association (PDAA) ..... WHRA
Wema [*Zaire*] [*ICAO location identifier*] (ICLI) ..... FZGH
Wembley Elementary School, Alberta [*Library symbol National Library of Canada*] (BIB) ..... AWEMS
Wembo-Nyama [*Zaire*] [*ICAO location identifier*] (ICLI) ..... FZVN
Wenatchee [*Washington*] [*Airport symbol*] (OAG) ..... EAT
Wenatchee [*Washington*] [*Seismograph station code, US Geological Survey*] (SEIS) ..... WNW
Wenatchee Valley College, Wenatchee, WA [*Library symbol Library of Congress*] (LCLS) ..... WaWeW
Wenatchee, WA [*Television station call letters*] ..... KCWT
Wenatchee, WA [*AM radio station call letters*] ..... KKRT
Wenatchee, WA [*FM radio station call letters*] ..... KKRV-FM
Wenatchee, WA [*FM radio station call letters*] (RBYB) ..... KPLW-FM
Wenatchee, WA [*AM radio station call letters*] ..... KPQ
Wenatchee, WA [*FM radio station call letters*] ..... KPQ-FM
Wenatchee, WA [*AM radio station call letters*] ..... KWWX
Wencarro Resources Ltd. [*Vancouver Stock Exchange symbol*] ..... WNC
Wenceslaus Anxiety Representation Taxonomy [*Satirical psychology term*] ..... WART
Wenchi [*Ghana*] [*ICAO location identifier*] (ICLI) ..... DGSW
Wendel Adkins Fan Club [*Defunct*] (EA) ..... WAFC
Wendell Public Library, Wendell, ID [*Library symbol*] [*Library of Congress*] (LCLS) ..... IdWen
Wendell School District, Wendell, ID [*Library symbol*] [*Library of Congress*] (LCLS) ..... IdWenSD
Wendell's Blackstone [*A publication*] (DLA) ..... Wend Bl
Wendell's Reports [*1826-41*] [*New York*] [*A publication*] (DLA) ..... W
Wendell's Reports [*New York*] [*A publication*] (DLA) ..... Wen
Wendell's Reports [*1826-41*] [*New York*] [*A publication*] (DLA) ..... Wend
Wendell's Reports [*1826-41*] [*New York*] [*A publication*] (DLA) ..... Wend (NY)
Wendell's Reports [*New York*] [*A publication*] (DLA) ..... Wend R
Wendell's Reports [*New York*] [*A publication*] (DLA) ..... Wend Rep
Wendell's Reports [*New York*] [*A publication*] (DLA) ..... Wendel
Wendell's Reports [*1826-41*] [*New York*] [*A publication*] (DLA) ..... Wendell
Wendell's Reports [*New York*] [*A publication*] (DLA) ..... Wendell Rep
Wendell's Reports [*New York*] [*A publication*] (DLA) ..... Wendell's Rep
Wendell's Reports [*1826-41*] [*New York*] [*A publication*] (DLA) ..... WR
Wendell-Zebulon, NC [*AM radio station call letters*] ..... WETC
Wendic [*MARC language code Library of Congress*] (LCCP) ..... wen
Wendover [*England*] ..... WEND
Wendover, NV [*FM radio station call letters*] ..... KYOU
Wendover, UT [*Location identifier FAA*] (FAAL) ..... ENV
Wendover/Wendover Auxiliary Air Base [*Utah*] [*ICAO location identifier*] (ICLI) ..... KENV
Wendt Bristol Health Service [*Associated Press*] (SAG) ..... WenBr
Wendt Bristol Health Service [*Associated Press*] (SAG) ..... WendtBr
Wendt Bristol Health Service [*AMEX symbol*] (SAG) ..... WMD
Wendt-Bristol Health Svcs [*AMEX symbol*] (TTSB) ..... WMD
Wendt-Bristol Health Wrrt [*AMEX symbol*] (TTSB) ..... WMDWS
Wendt's Maritime Legislation [*3rd ed.*] [*1888*] [*A publication*] (DLA) ..... Wendt Mar Leg
Wendt's Reports of Cases [*Ceylon*] [*A publication*] (DLA) ..... Wendt
Wendys International [*Associated Press*] (SAG) ..... Wendy
Wendy's International, Inc. [*NYSE symbol*] (SPSG) ..... WEN
Wendys International, Inc. [*Associated Press*] (SAG) ..... Wendys
Wendy's Intl [*NYSE symbol*] (TTSB) ..... WEN
Wenham Historical Society and Museum, Wenham, MA [*Library symbol Library of Congress*] (LCLS) ..... MWenhHi
Wenic Air Services [*Singapore*] [*ICAO designator*] (FAAC) ..... WNC
Wenig Fine [*Latin*] (DAVI) ..... W
Wenkite [*A zeolite*] ..... WEN
Wenner Difference Potentiometer ..... WDP
Wenner-Gren Foundation for Anthropological Research (EA) ..... WGFAR
Wenner-Gren Foundation for Anthropological Research, New York, NY [*Library symbol Library of Congress*] (LCLS) ..... NNWG
Wenona Community Unit, School District 1, Wenona, IL [*Library symbol Library of Congress*] (LCLS) ..... IWenSD
Wentworth Institute of Technical, Boston, MA [*Library symbol*] [*Library of Congress*] (LCLS) ..... MBWI
Wentworth Institute of Technology, Boston, MA [*OCLC symbol*] (OCLC) ..... WEN
Wentworth Library, Hamilton, ON, Canada [*Library symbol Library of Congress*] (LCLS) ..... CaOHWL
Wentworth Military Academy [*Lexington, MO*] ..... WMA
Wentworth Public Library [*UTLAS symbol*] ..... WEN
Wentworth Public Library, Hamilton, Ontario [*Library symbol National Library of Canada*] (NLC) ..... OHWL
Wentworth's Office of Executors [*A publication*] (DLA) ..... Off Ex
Wentworth's Office of Executors [*A publication*] (DLA) ..... Off Exec
Wentzel-Kramers-Brillouin Approximation [*Mathematics*] ..... WKB
Wentzel-Kramers-Brillouin-Jeffreys [*Approximation or Method*] [*Physics*] ..... WKBJ
Wenzell's Reports [*60 Minnesota*] [*A publication*] (DLA) ..... Wenz
Wepener [*South Africa*] [*ICAO location identifier*] (ICLI) ..... FAWP
Wepman Test of Auditory Discrimination [*Speech and language therapy*] (DAVI) ..... WTAD
Wer Informiert Woruber [*Who Advises about What*] [*Gesellschaft fuer Informationsmarkt-Forschung - GIF Detmold, Federal Republic of Germany*] [*Information service or system*] (IID) ..... WIW
Werdohl/Kuntrop [*Germany ICAO location identifier*] (ICLI) ..... EDKW
Wereldverband van Diamantbewerkers [*Worldwide Alliance of Diamond Workers*] (BARN) ..... WVD
Werewolf Research Center (EA) ..... WRC
Werke ohne Opuszahl [*Works without Opus Number*] [*Music*] ..... WOO
Werl [*Germany ICAO location identifier*] (ICLI) ..... EDCW
Werner Dahnz Co. Ltd. [*Toronto Stock Exchange symbol*] ..... WDZ
Werner Enterprises [*NASDAQ symbol*] (TTSB) ..... WERN
Werner Enterprises, Inc. [*Omaha, NE*] [*NASDAQ symbol*] (NQ) ..... WERN
Werner Enterprises, Inc. [*Associated Press*] (SAG) ..... Werner
Werner Memorial Public Library, Steamboat Springs, CO [*Library symbol Library of Congress*] (LCLS) ..... CoSs
Werner Oil & Gas Co. [*Vancouver Stock Exchange symbol*] ..... WOG
Werner Soederstroem Osakeyhtio [*Book printer*] [*Finland*] ..... WSOY
Werner's Syndrome [*Medicine*] ..... WS
Wernersville State Hospital, Wernersville, PA [*OCLC symbol*] (OCLC) ..... PHV
Wernicke-Korsakoff [*Syndrome*] [*Medicine*] ..... WK
Wernicke-Korsakoff Syndrome [*Chemical dependence*] (DAVI) ..... WKS
Wernicke-Korsakoff Syndrome Association [*Defunct*] (EA) ..... WKSA
Werombi [*Australia Seismograph station code, US Geological Survey*] (SEIS) ..... WER
Werthamar-Helfand-Hohenberg Theory [*Solid state physics*] ..... WHH
Wertheim [*Germany ICAO location identifier*] (ICLI) ..... EDOF
Wesbanco, Inc. [*Associated Press*] (SAG) ..... Wesbanc
Wesbanco, Inc. [*NASDAQ symbol*] (NQ) ..... WSBC
Wescal Resources, Inc. [*Vancouver Stock Exchange symbol*] ..... WEC
Wescan Energy Ltd. [*Vancouver Stock Exchange symbol*] ..... WCN
Wescap Enterprises Ltd. [*Vancouver Stock Exchange symbol*] ..... WE

Wescast Industries, Inc. [*NASDAQ symbol*] (SAG) .... WCST
Wescast Industries, Inc. [*Associated Press*] (SAG) .... Wescast
Wescast Industries'A' [*NASDAQ symbol*] (TTSB) .... WCSTF
Weschester County Archives, Elmsford, NY [*Library symbol*] [*Library of Congress*] (LCLS) .... NElmsAr
Wesco Financial [*AMEX symbol*] (TTSB) .... WSC
Wesco Financial Corp. [*Associated Press*] (SAG) .... Wesco
Wesco Financial Corp. [*AMEX symbol*] (SPSG) .... WSC
Wescosa Lumber Association [*Defunct*] (EA) .... WLA
Wesel/Romerwardt [*Germany ICAO location identifier*] (ICLI) .... EDLX
Weser-Wumme [*Germany ICAO location identifier*] (ICLI) .... EDWM
Weskett's Complete Digest of the Theory, Laws, and Practice of Insurance [*A publication*] (DLA) .... Wesk Ins
Weskett's Complete Digest of the Theory, Laws, and Practice of Insurance [*A publication*] (DLA) .... Weskett Ins
Weslaco, TX [*AM radio station call letters*] .... KRGE
Weslaco, TX [*Television station call letters*] .... KRGV
Wesley Biblical Seminary, Jackson, MS [*Library symbol Library of Congress*] (LCLS) .... MsJW
Wesley Bull & Associates, Inc. [*Seattle, WA*] [*Telecommunications*] (TSSD) .... WBAI
Wesley Central Mission [*Australia*] .... WCM
Wesley Long Community Hospital, Inc., Greensboro, NC [*Library symbol Library of Congress*] (LCLS) .... NcGCH
Wesley Medical Center, Wichita, KS [*Library symbol Library of Congress*] (LCLS) .... KWiWM
Wesley Theological Seminary, Washington, DC [*Library symbol Library of Congress OCLC symbol*] (LCLS) .... DWT
Wesleyan .... W
Wesleyan [*A publication*] .... WES
Wesleyan Calvinistic Methodists (ROG) .... WCM
Wesleyan Chapel (ROG) .... WC
Wesleyan College, Macon, GA [*Library symbol Library of Congress*] (LCLS) .... GMW
Wesleyan Free Church .... WFC
Wesleyan Historical Society [*British*] .... WHS
Wesleyan Mission [*Australia*] .... WM
Wesleyan Missionary Society .... WMS
Wesleyan Service Guild [*Defunct*] (EA) .... WSG
Wesleyan University (GAGS) .... Wesleyan U
Wesleyan University .... WU
Wesleyan University, Middletown, CT [*Library symboi Library of Congress*] (LCLS) .... CtW
Wesleyan University, Middletown, CT [*OCLC symbol*] (OCLC) .... WLU
Wesleyville Public Library, Newfoundland [*Library symbol National Library of Canada*] (NLC) .... NFWV
Wesleyville Public Library, Wesleyville, NF, Canada [*Library symbol Library of Congress*] (LCLS) .... CaNfWv
Weslin Junior-Senior High School, Trenton, IL [*Library symbol Library of Congress*] (LCLS) .... ITreWHS
Wesman Personnel Classification Test .... PCT
Wessex Air Services Ltd. [*British ICAO designator*] (FAAC) .... WSX
Wessex Regional Library and Information Service (NITA) .... WRLIS
Wessington Springs Carnegie Public Library, Wessington Springs, SD [*Library symbol Library of Congress*] (LCLS) .... SdWes
Wesson, MS [*FM radio station call letters*] .... WCLL
West [*or Western*] .... W
West [*or Western*] .... WES
West Africa .... W AFR
West Africa .... WA
West Africa Airlines Ltd. [*Ghana*] [*ICAO designator*] (FAAC) .... WCB
West Africa Command [*World War II*] .... WAC
West Africa Committee (EA) .... WAC
West Africa Rice Development Association .... WARDA
West Africa Supply Centre [*World War II*] .... WASC
West Africa War Council [*World War II*] .... WAWC
West Africa Wins Again [*A reminder that visitors to this region must exercise caution if they wish to avoid bureaucratic harrassment and overcharging*] .... WAWA
West African Airways [*ICAO designator*] (AD) .... QH
West African Airways Corp. .... WAAC
West African Archaeological Newsletter [*A publication*] .... WAAN
West African Clearing House [*Sierra Leone*] .... WACH
West African Cocoa Research Institution .... WACRI
West African College of Surgeons [*See also COAC*] [*Nigeria*] (EAIO) .... WACS
West African Consolidated Administrative Service Center [*Foreign Service*] .... WACASC
West African Court of Appeal Reports [*A publication*] (DLA) .... W Afr App
West African Court of Appeal, Selected Judgments [*A publication*] (DLA) .... WACA
West African Customs Union .... WACU
West African Development Bank [*Togo*] (EA) .... WADB
West African Economic Community [*Ivory Coast, Mali, Mauritania, Niger, Senegal, Upper Volta*] (ASF) .... WAEC
West African Federation of Associations for the Advancement of Handicapped Persons [*See also FOAPH*] [*Bamako, Mali*] (EAIO) .... WAFAH
West African Fisheries Commission .... WAFC
West African Forces [*British military*] (DMA) .... WAF
West African Frontier Force .... WAFF
West African Health Community (EA) .... WAHC
West African Journal of Archaeology [*A publication*] .... WAJA
West African Lands Committee. Report [*A publication*] (ILCA) .... WALC
West African Law Reports [*A publication*] (DLA) .... W Af LR
West African Law Reports [*Gambia, Ghana, and Sierra Leone*] [*A publication*] (DLA) .... WALR
West African Monsoon Experiment [*Marine science*] (OSRA) .... WAMEX
West African Pharmaceutical Federation [*Lagos, Nigeria*] (EAIO) .... WAPF
West African Produce Control Board [*World War II*] .... WAPCB
West African Regiment [*Military unit*] [*British*] .... WAR
West African Shippers Association [*British*] (DBA) .... WASA
West African Stored Products Research Unit .... WASPRU
West Air Sweden AB [*ICAO designator*] (FAAC) .... WEJ
West Allis Memorial Hospital, West Allis, WI [*Library symbol Library of Congress*] (LCLS) .... WWeaM
West Allis Public Library, West Allis, WI [*Library symbol Library of Congress*] (LCLS) .... WWea
West Antarctic Ice Sheet [*Geology*] .... WAIS
West Asia Blocking Ridge [*Meteorology*] .... WABR
West Australian [*A publication*] .... Wes Aust
West Australian Airways (ADA) .... WAA
West Australian Group of University Librarians .... WAGUL
West Australian Institute of Technology, South Bentley, WA, Australia [*Library symbol Library of Congress*] (LCLS) .... AuSbW
West Auxiliary Airborne Command Post (MCD) .... WAUXCP
West Aviation AS [*Norway ICAO designator*] (FAAC) .... WST
West Bablyon High School, West Babylon, NY [*Library symbol*] [*Library of Congress*] (LCLS) .... NWesbHS
West Babylon Junior High School, West Babylon, NY [*Library symbol*] [*Library of Congress*] (LCLS) .... NWesbJH
West Baden College, West Baden Springs, IN [*Library symbol Library of Congress*] (LCLS) .... InWebaC
West Bank of the Jordan River [*MARC country of publication code Library of Congress*] (LCCP) .... wj
West Barnstable, MA [*FM radio station call letters*] .... WKKL
West Baton Rouge Parish Library, Port Allen, LA [*Library symbol Library of Congress*] (LCLS) .... LPtaW
West Bay Public Library, Ontario [*Library symbol National Library of Canada*] (NLC) .... OWB
West Bend Journal, West Bend, IA [*Library symbol Library of Congress*] (LCLS) .... IaWbeJ
West Bend Public Library, West Bend, IA [*Library symbol Library of Congress*] (LCLS) .... IaWbe
West Bend Public Library, West Bend, WI [*Library symbol Library of Congress*] (LCLS) .... WWb
West Bend, WI [*Location identifier FAA*] (FAAL) .... ETB
West Bend, WI [*Location identifier FAA*] (FAAL) .... LLE
West Bend, WI [*AM radio station call letters*] .... WBKV
West Bend, WI [*FM radio station call letters*] .... WBWI
West Berlin [*MARC country of publication code Library of Congress*] (LCCP) .... wb
West Branch, MI [*Location identifier FAA*] (FAAL) .... BHW
West Branch, MI [*FM radio station call letters*] .... WBMI
West Branch Public Library, West Branch, MI [*Library symbol Library of Congress*] (LCLS) .... MiWe
West Branch Times, West Branch, IA [*Library symbol Library of Congress*] (LCLS) .... IaWbT
West Britain/East Ireland .... WB/EI
West Bromwich [*England*] [*Seismograph station code, US Geological Survey Closed*] (SEIS) .... WBE
West Bromwich Volunteer Rifle Corps [*British military*] (DMA) .... WBVRC
West by North .... WBN
West by North West [*Direction*] (EERA) .... WNW
West by South .... WBS
West by South West [*Direction*] (EERA) .... WSW
West Carleton Secondary School, Dunrobin, Ontario [*Library symbol National Library of Canada*] (BIB) .... ODWC
West Carleton Township Public Library, Carp, Ontario [*Library symbol National Library of Canada*] (BIB) .... OCWCT
West Carollton, OH [*FM radio station call letters*] .... WQRP
West Carroll Parish Library, Oak Grove, LA [*Library symbol Library of Congress*] (LCLS) .... LOgWC
West Carrollton, OH [*FM radio station call letters*] .... WROU
West Central [*Refers especially to London postal district*] .... WC
West Central Educational Cooperative Service Unit, Fergus Falls, MN [*Library symbol*] [*Library of Congress*] (LCLS) .... MnFfEC
West Central Elementary School, Elbow Lake, MN [*Library symbol*] [*Library of Congress*] (LCLS) .... MnElbE
West Central High School, Elbow Lake, MN [*Library symbol*] [*Library of Congress*] (LCLS) .... MnElbH
West Central Illinois Library Cooperative [*Library network*] .... WILC
West Chester, OH [*FM radio station call letters*] .... WLHS
West Chester, PA [*AM radio station call letters*] .... WCHE
West Chester State College, West Chester, PA [*Library symbol Library of Congress*] (LCLS) .... PWcS
West Chester State College, West Chester, PA [*OCLC symbol*] (OCLC) .... QWC
West Chester University of Pennsylvania (GAGS) .... West Chester U Pa
West Chicago/Du Page County [*Illinois*] [*ICAO location identifier*] (ICLI) .... KDPA
West Coast Air [*Gambia*] [*ICAO designator*] (FAAC) .... WBA
West Coast Air Corps Training Center .... WCACTC
West Coast Airlines, Inc. .... WC
West Coast Airlines, Inc. .... WCA
West Coast Airlines Ltd. [*Ghana*] .... WCA
West Coast Airlines Ltd. [*Ghana*] [*ICAO designator*] (FAAC) .... WCG
West Coast Amateur Radio Service (PDAA) .... WESCARS
West Coast Athletic Association (WDAA) .... WCAA
West Coast Bancorp [*NASDAQ symbol*] (SAG) .... WBAN
West Coast Bancorp Florida [*Associated Press*] (SAG) .... WstCstFL
West Coast Bancorp (OR) [*Associated Press*] (SAG) .... WCstB
West Coast Bancorp (Oregon) [*NASDAQ symbol*] (SAG) .... WCBO
West Coast Bancorp Oregon [*Associated Press*] (SAG) .... WstCstOR
West Coast Base Service Unit [*Navy*] .... WCBSU

West Coast Base Service Unit [*Navy*] ... WESCOBASESERVUNIT
West Coast Classified Military Operations Research Symposium ... WCCMORS
West Coast Commodity Exchange ... WCCE
West Coast Crossarm Association [*Defunct*] ... WCCA
West Coast [*Naval Publications*] **Distribution Center** ... WCDC
West Coast Electronic Manufacturers' Association [*Later, AEA*] ... WCEMA
West Coast Entertainment [*NASDAQ symbol*] (TTSB) ... WCEC
West Coast Entertainment Corp. [*NASDAQ symbol*] (SAG) ... WCEC
West Coast Entertainment Corp. [*Associated Press*] (SAG) ... WCstEnt
West Coast Formula Atlantic (Racing) ... WCAR
West Coast Freight Tariff Bureau ... WCFTB
West Coast Handling ... WCH
West Coast Hazardous Materials Management Conference (TSPED) ... HAZMACON
West Coast Lumber Inspection Bureau (EA) ... WCLIB
West Coast Lumbermen's Association [*Later, WWPA*] (EA) ... WCLA
West Coast Maritime Museum, Tofino, BC, Canada [*Library symbol*] [*Library of Congress*] (LCLS) ... CaBTOMM
West Coast Maritime Museum, Tofino, British Columbia [*Library symbol National Library of Canada*] (NLC) ... BTOMM
West Coast Metal Importers Association (EA) ... WCMIA
West Coast Mineral Association (EA) ... WCMA
West Coast Naval Publications Distribution Center (DNAB) ... WCDS
West Coast of Africa (ROG) ... WCA
West Coast of England [*Shipping*] ... WCE
West Coast of South America ... WCSA
West Coast of the United Kingdom ... WCUK
West Coast Off-Shore Tactical Control Surveillance System [*Navy*] (DNAB) ... WTCSS
West Coast Reporter [*A publication*] (DLA) ... W Coast Rep
West Coast Reporter [*A publication*] (DLA) ... West Co Rep
West Coast Reporter [*A publication*] (DLA) ... West Coast Rep
West Coast Shrimp Producers Association (EA) ... WCSPA
West Coast Sound School [*Navy*] ... WCSS
West Coast Sound School [*Navy*] ... WESCOSOUNDSCOL
West Coast Switching Center [*Jet Propulsion Laboratory, NASA*] ... WCSC
West Coast Transmission Ltd., Vancouver, BC, Canada [*Library symbol Library of Congress*] (LCLS) ... CaBVaWT
West Coast Transmission Ltd., Vancouver, British Columbia [*Library symbol National Library of Canada*] (NLC) ... BVAWCT
West Coast Travel [*Information service or system*] (IID) ... WCT
West Coast University [*Los Angeles, CA*] ... WCU
West Columbia, SC [*FM radio station call letters*] ... WSCQ
West Co. [*NYSE symbol*] (TTSB) ... WST
West Co., Inc. [*Associated Press*] (SAG) ... West
West Co., Inc. [*NYSE symbol*] (SPSG) ... WST
West Country Tourist Board [*British*] (DCTA) ... WCTB
West Covina, CA [*AM radio station call letters*] ... KGRB
West Covina, CA [*FM radio station call letters*] ... KMQA
West Covina, CA [*FM radio station call letters*] (RBYB) ... KRTO-FM
West Delta Resources Ltd. [*Vancouver Stock Exchange symbol*] ... WED
West Des Moines, IA [*FM radio station call letters*] ... KWDM
West Division (ROG) ... WD
West Drayton [*British ICAO location identifier*] (ICLI) ... EGWD
West Elementary School, Hendrum, MN [*Library symbol*] [*Library of Congress*] (LCLS) ... MnHenE
West Elementary School, Long Beach, NY [*Library symbol Library of Congress*] (LCLS) ... NLobWE
West Elementary School, Worthington, MN [*Library symbol*] [*Library of Congress*] (LCLS) ... MnWoWES
West End [*Grand Bahama Island, Bahamas*] [*Airport symbol*] (AD) ... WTD
West End, Grand Bahama Island [*Bahamas*] [*ICAO location identifier*] (ICLI) ... MYGW
West Essex Militia [*British*] ... WEM
West Essex Tribune, Livingston, NJ [*Library symbol Library of Congress*] (LCLS) ... NjLiW
West European Advisory Committee [*Radio Free Europe*] (NTCM) ... WEAC
West European Container Liners [*Shipping*] ... WEC
West Fargo, ND [*AM radio station call letters*] ... KFNW
West Feliciana Railroad (IIA) ... WF
West Ferris Secondary School, North Bay, ON, Canada [*Library symbol Library of Congress*] (LCLS) ... CaONBWF
West Ferris Secondary School, North Bay, Ontario [*Library symbol National Library of Canada*] (NLC) ... ONBWF
West Five [*Zambia*] [*ICAO location identifier*] (ICLI) ... FLWE
West Florida Coast ... WFC
West Florida Regional Library, Pensacola, FL [*Library symbol Library of Congress*] (LCLS) ... FPeW
West Florida Union List [*Library network*] ... WFUL
West Four [*Zambia*] [*ICAO location identifier*] (ICLI) ... FLWD
West Frankfort, IL [*AM radio station call letters*] ... WFRX
West Frankfort, IL [*FM radio station call letters*] ... WFRX-FM
West Frankfort, IL [*FM radio station call letters*] (RBYB) ... WQUL-FM
West Fraser Timber Co. Ltd. [*Toronto Stock Exchange symbol Vancouver Stock Exchange symbol*] ... WFT
West Freugh [*British ICAO location identifier*] (ICLI) ... EGOY
West Georgia College (GAGS) ... West Ga C
West Georgia College [*Carollton*] ... WGC
West Georgia College, Carrollton, GA [*Library symbol Library of Congress*] (LCLS) ... GCarrWG
West Georgia College, Carrollton, GA [*OCLC symbol*] (OCLC) ... GWC
West German ... WG
West Germanic [*Language, etc.*] ... WGMC
West Germany (WDAA) ... W GER
West Germany Air Force ... WGAF
West Glamorgan [*County in Wales*] ... W GLAM
West Gulf Maritime Association (EA) ... WGMA
West Hampton Beach/Suffolk County [*New York*] [*ICAO location identifier*] (ICLI) ... KFOK
West Hants Historical Society Museum, Windsor, Nova Scotia [*Library symbol National Library of Canada*] (NLC) ... NSWWH
West Hartford, CT [*FM radio station call letters*] ... WWUH
West Hartford Public Library, West Hartford, CT [*Library symbol Library of Congress*] (LCLS) ... CtWehar
West Hartford Public Library, West Hartford, CT [*OCLC symbol*] (OCLC) ... WHP
West Haven, CT [*FM radio station call letters*] ... WNHU
West Hazleton, PA [*AM radio station call letters*] (RBYB) ... WILP-AM
West Hazleton, PA [*AM radio station call letters*] ... WXPX
West Helena, AR [*FM radio station call letters*] ... KCLT
West Helena, AR [*AM radio station call letters*] ... KJIW
West Helena, AR [*FM radio station call letters*] ... KJIW-FM
West Hempstead High School, West Hempstead, NY [*Library symbol*] [*Library of Congress*] (LCLS) ... NWhHS
West Hempstead Middle School, West Hempstead, NY [*Library symbol*] [*Library of Congress*] (LCLS) ... NWhMS
West Hempstead Public Library, West Hempstead, NY [*Library symbol Library of Congress*] (LCLS) ... NWh
West High School, Rockford, IL [*Library symbol*] [*Library of Congress*] (LCLS) ... IRoWH
West Highland White Terrier Club of America (EA) ... WHWTCA
West Hills College, Coalinga, CA [*Library symbol Library of Congress*] (LCLS) ... CCoaJC
West India Committee [*British*] (EAIO) ... WIC
West India Dock ... WID
West India Fruit & Steamship [*AAR code*] ... WIF
West India Regiment ... WIR
West Indian Association for Commonwealth Literature and Language Studies [*Jamaica*] (EAIO) ... WIACLALS
West Indian Law Journal [*Jamaica*] [*A publication*] (DLA) ... WILJ
West Indian People's Movement [*Netherlands Antilles*] [*Political party*] (EY) ... WIPM
West Indian Reports [*A publication*] (DLA) ... WIR
West Indian Royal Garrison Artillery [*British military*] (DMA) ... WIRGA
West Indian Students Association (EA) ... WISA
West Indies [*MARC geographic area code Library of Congress*] (LCCP) ... nw----
West Indies (WDAA) ... W IND
West Indies (VRA) ... W Ind
West Indies [*Formerly, BWI*] ... WI
West Indies Associated State ... WIAS
West Indies Federation ... WIF
West Indies Sugar Association [*Later, SAC*] ... WISA
West Indies Trade Advisory Group [*British Overseas Trade Board*] (DS) ... WITAG
West Integrated Test Stand [*NASA*] ... WITS
West Iowa Technical Community College, Sioux City, IA [*Library symbol Library of Congress*] (LCLS) ... IaScWI
West Irian [*Aircraft nationality and registration mark*] (FAAC) ... PK
West Iron District Library, Iron River, MI [*Library symbol Library of Congress*] (LCLS) ... MiIrr
West Irondequoit High School Library, Rochester, NY [*OCLC symbol*] (OCLC) ... RXM
West Island College of Ontario, Ottawa [*Library symbol National Library of Canada*] (BIB) ... OOWIC
West Island College of Ontario, Ottawa, ON, Canada [*Library symbol*] [*Library of Congress*] (LCLS) ... CaOOWIC
West Isle Air, Inc. [*FAA designator*] (FAAC) ... WIL
West Islip Public Library, West Islip, NY [*Library symbol Library of Congress*] (LCLS) ... NWi
West Jefferson, NC [*Location identifier FAA*] (FAAL) ... FJB
West Jefferson, NC [*AM radio station call letters*] ... WKSK
West Jefferson School District No. 253, Terreton, ID [*Library symbol*] [*Library of Congress*] (LCLS) ... IdTerSD
West Jersey Bancshares [*NASDAQ symbol*] (TTSB) ... WJBS
West Jersey Bancshares, Inc. [*NASDAQ symbol*] (SAG) ... WJBS
West Jersey Bancshares, Inc. [*Associated Press*] (SAG) ... WJersB
West Jordan, UT [*AM radio station call letters*] ... KLLB
West Junior High School, Grand Junction, CO [*Library symbol Library of Congress*] (LCLS) ... CoGjWJ
West Kanaga [*Alaska*] [*Seismograph station code, US Geological Survey*] (SEIS) ... AK1
West Kanaga [*Alaska*] [*Seismograph station code, US Geological Survey Closed*] (SEIS) ... AT1
West Kent Imperial Yeomanry [*British military*] (DMA) ... WKIY
West Kent Volunteer Force [*British military*] (DMA) ... WKVF
West Kent Yeomanry [*British military*] (DMA) ... WKY
West Kildonan Public Library, Winnipeg, Manitoba [*Library symbol National Library of Canada*] (NLC) ... MWWK
West Klamath, OR [*AM radio station call letters*] ... KWSA
West Kootenay District Nursing Archives, Registered Nurses Association of British Columbia, Blueberry Creek, British Columbia [*Library symbol National Library of Canada*] (NLC) ... BBCRN
West Kuparuk, AK [*Location identifier FAA*] (FAAL) ... XPU
West Lafayette, IN [*AM radio station call letters*] ... WBAA
West Lafayette, IN [*FM radio station call letters*] ... WBAA-FM
West Lafayette, IN [*FM radio station call letters*] ... WGLM
West Lafayette, IN [*FM radio station call letters*] ... WHPL
West Lake Hills, TX [*AM radio station call letters*] ... KTXZ
West Lancashire Field Artillery [*Military unit*] [*British*] ... WLFA
West Lebanon Pike Township Public Library, West Lebanon, IN [*Library symbol Library of Congress*] (LCLS) ... InWele

West Liberty Index, West Liberty, IA [*Library symbol Library of Congress*] (LCLS) ... IaWll
West Liberty, KY [*AM radio station call letters*] ... WLKS
West Liberty, KY [*FM radio station call letters*] ... WLKS-FM
West Liberty State College [*West Virginia*] ... WLSC
West Liberty State College, West Liberty, WV [*Library symbol Library of Congress*] (LCLS) ... WvWelW
West Liberty, WV [*FM radio station call letters*] ... WGLZ
West Linn High School, West Linn, OR [*Library symbol Library of Congress*] (LCLS) ... OrWelH
West Linn Public Library, West Linn, OR [*Library symbol Library of Congress*] (LCLS) ... OrWel
West London Aero Services Ltd. [*British ICAO designator*] (FAAC) ... WLA
West London College [*England*] ... WLC
West London Railway (ROG) ... WLR
West Long Branch, NJ [*FM radio station call letters*] ... WMCX
West Longitude ... W Lon
West Longitude (BARN) ... W long
West Longitude (SSD) ... WL
West Longitude Date (AABC) ... WLD
West Lyon Herald, Inwood, IA [*Library symbol Library of Congress*] (LCLS) ... IaInwH
West Malling [*British ICAO location identifier*] (ICLI) ... EGKM
West Marine [*NASDAQ symbol*] (TTSB) ... WMAR
West Marine, Inc. [*NASDAQ symbol*] (SAG) ... WMAR
West Marine, Inc. [*Associated Press*] (SAG) ... WstMar
West Memphis, AR [*Location identifier FAA*] (FAAL) ... AWM
West Memphis, AR [*AM radio station call letters*] ... KSUD
West Merchant Bank (ECON) ... WMB
West Meridian Time ... WMT
West Mesa [*New Mexico*] [*Seismograph station code, US Geological Survey*] (SEIS) ... WMA
West Middle School [*South Carolina*] [*Seismograph station code, US Geological Survey*] (SEIS) ... WMS
West Midlands [*Metropolitan county in England*] ... WM
West Midlands Enterprise Board [*British*] (ECON) ... WMEB
West Milford, NJ [*Television station call letters*] ... WFME
West Monroe, LA [*Television station call letters*] ... KARD
West Monroe, LA [*AM radio station call letters*] ... KMBS
West Monroe, LA [*Television station call letters*] ... KMCT
West Monroe, LA [*FM radio station call letters*] ... KYEA
West Morris Star Journal, Ledgewood, NJ [*Library symbol Library of Congress*] (LCLS) ... NjLedW
West Mountain [*Utah*] [*Seismograph station code, US Geological Survey*] (SEIS) ... WMU
West New Guinea ... WNG
West New York Public Library, West New York, NJ [*Library symbol Library of Congress*] (LCLS) ... NjWesny
West New Yorker, Inc., Fairview, NJ [*Library symbol Library of Congress*] (LCLS) ... NjFvW
West Nile Encephalitis [*Medicine*] (DAVI) ... WNE
West Nile Virus ... WNV
West Nova Scotia Regiment (DMA) ... WNSR
West Of [*In outdoor advertising*] (WDMC) ... W/O
West of Scotland Agricultural College [*British*] (IRUK) ... WSAC
West on Extents [*1817*] [*A publication*] (DLA) ... West Ext
West on Patents [*A publication*] (DLA) ... West Pat
West One [*Zambia*] [*ICAO location identifier*] (ICLI) ... FLWA
West One Bancorp [*NASDAQ symbol*] (NQ) ... WEST
West One Bancorp [*Associated Press*] (SAG) ... WestOne
West Orange Free Public Library, West Orange, NJ [*Library symbol Library of Congress*] (LCLS) ... NjWo
West Pacific Ocean (SAA) ... WPO
West Pakistan Bank Employees' Federation ... WPBEF
West Pakistan Federation of Labor ... WPFL
West Pakistan Railway ... WPR
West Pakistan Research and Evaluation Center ... WEPREC
West Palm Beach [*Florida*] [*Airport symbol*] ... PBI
West Palm Beach, FL [*Location identifier FAA*] (FAAL) ... LNA
West Palm Beach, FL [*FM radio station call letters*] ... WAYF
West Palm Beach, FL [*AM radio station call letters*] ... WBZT
West Palm Beach, FL [*AM radio station call letters*] ... WEAT
West Palm Beach, FL [*FM radio station call letters*] ... WEAT-FM
West Palm Beach, FL [*Television station call letters*] ... WFLX
West Palm Beach, FL [*FM radio station call letters*] ... WIRK
West Palm Beach, FL [*AM radio station call letters*] ... WJNO
West Palm Beach, FL [*Television station call letters*] ... WPEC
West Palm Beach, FL [*Television station call letters*] ... WPTV
West Palm Beach, FL [*FM radio station call letters*] ... WRLX
West Palm Beach, FL [*FM radio station call letters*] ... WXEL
West Palm Beach, FL [*Television station call letters*] ... WXEL-TV
West Palm Beach Grand Prix [*Automobile racing event*] ... WPBGP
West Palm Beach/Palm Beach County Park [*Florida*] [*ICAO location identifier*] (ICLI) ... KLNA
West Palm Beach/Palm Beach International [*Florida*] [*ICAO location identifier*] (ICLI) ... KPBI
West Palm Beach Public Library, West Palm Beach, FL [*Library symbol Library of Congress*] (LCLS) ... FWpb
West Penn Power Co. [*Associated Press*] (SAG) ... WPen
West Penn Power Co. [*Associated Press*] (SAG) ... WPen25
West Penn Power Co. ... WPPC
West Penn Power Co. [*NYSE symbol*] (SAG) ... WQP
West Penn Power Co. [*NYSE symbol*] (SPSG) ... WSP
West Penn Pwr 4 1/2%cmPfd [*NYSE symbol*] (TTSB) ... WSPPr
West Penn Pwr 8.00% 'QUIDS' [*NYSE symbol*] (TTSB) ... WQP
West Pit [*Hawaii*] [*Seismograph station code, US Geological Survey Closed*] (SEIS) ... WPH
West Pittston-Exeter Railroad Co. [*AAR code*] ... WPE
West Plains, MO [*FM radio station call letters*] ... KKDY
West Plains, MO [*FM radio station call letters*] ... KSPQ
West Plains, MO [*AM radio station call letters*] ... KWPM
West Plains, MO [*Location identifier FAA*] (FAAL) ... PWN
West Plains Rural Library, Williston, ND [*Library symbol Library of Congress*] (LCLS) ... NdWiW
West Point [*Alaska*] [*Airport symbol*] (OAG) ... KWP
West Point ... WP
West Point, AK [*Location identifier FAA*] (FAAL) ... KWP
West Point Bee, West Point, IA [*Library symbol Library of Congress*] (LCLS) ... IaWpB
West Point Fellowship in Leader Development [*US Military Academy*] (INF) ... WPFILD
West Point, GA [*AM radio station call letters*] ... WCJM
West Point, GA [*FM radio station call letters*] ... WCJM-FM
West Point, GA [*AM radio station call letters*] (RBYB) ... WPLV-AM
West Point Graduate ... WPG
West Point, MS [*FM radio station call letters*] ... WKBB
West Point, MS [*Television station call letters*] ... WLOV
West Point, MS [*AM radio station call letters*] ... WROB
West Point, NE [*AM radio station call letters*] (RBYB) ... KTIC
West Point, NE [*FM radio station call letters*] ... KWPN-FM
West Point, NY [*Mint mark when appearing on US coins*] ... W
West Point Parents Club (EA) ... WPPC
West Point Protective Association [*Unofficial association of West Point graduates*] (VNW) ... WPPA
West Point Public Library, West Point, IA [*Library symbol Library of Congress*] (LCLS) ... IaWp
West Point, VA [*FM radio station call letters*] ... WPTG
West Point-Pepperell, Inc., West Point, GA [*Library symbol Library of Congress*] (LCLS) ... GWeP
West Pride Industry [*Vancouver Stock Exchange symbol*] ... WPI
West Publishing Co. (AAGC) ... West
West Publishing Company's Docket [*1909-41*] [*A publication*] (DLA) ... Dkt
West Publishing Company's Docket [*1909-41*] [*A publication*] (DLA) ... Docket
West Riding National Reserve [*British military*] (DMA) ... WRNR
West Riding Volunteers [*British military*] (DMA) ... WRV
West Rim Resources, Inc. [*Vancouver Stock Exchange symbol*] ... WRM
West Salem Public Library, West Salem, IL [*Library symbol Library of Congress*] (LCLS) ... IWes
West Salem, WI [*FM radio station call letters*] ... WQJY
West Saxon [*Dialect of Old English*] [*Language, etc.*] ... WS
West Saxon [*Dialect of Old English*] [*Language, etc.*] ... WSAX
West Sea Development [*Vancouver Stock Exchange symbol*] ... WSA
West Seattle General Hospital, Seattle, WA [*Library symbol Library of Congress*] (LCLS) ... WaSWG
West Semitic (BJA) ... WS
West Semitic (BJA) ... WSem
West Seneca State School, West Seneca, NY [*Library symbol Library of Congress*] (LCLS) ... NWsS
West Seven [*Zambia*] [*ICAO location identifier*] (ICLI) ... FLWG
West Shore Community College, Scottville, MI [*Library symbol Library of Congress*] (LCLS) ... MiScW
West Shore Railroad ... WSRR
West Siberian Region, RSFSR [*MARC geographic area code Library of Congress*] (LCCP) ... e-urw-
West Side [*In outdoor advertising*] (WDMC) ... W/S
West Side Elementary School, Marshall, MN [*Library symbol*] [*Library of Congress*] (LCLS) ... MnMarWES
West Side Story, Evansville, IN [*Library symbol Library of Congress*] (LCLS) ... InEWS
West Six [*Zambia*] [*ICAO location identifier*] (ICLI) ... FLWF
West Slope Community Library, Portland, OR [*Library symbol Library of Congress*] (LCLS) ... OrPWsC
West Somerset Imperial Yeomanry [*British military*] (DMA) ... WSIY
West Somerset Yeomanry [*British military*] (DMA) ... WSY
West Somerset Yeomanry Cavalry [*British military*] (DMA) ... WSYC
West Springfield, MA [*AM radio station call letters*] ... WACM
West Star (NITA) ... WESTAR
West Suburban Hospital, Oak Park, IL [*Library symbol Library of Congress*] (LCLS) ... IOaWH
West TeleServices Corp. [*Associated Press*] (SAG) ... WstTleS
West TeleServices Corp. [*NASDAQ symbol*] (SAG) ... WTSC
West Tennessee Experiment Station [*University of Tennessee at Knoxville*] [*Research center*] (RCD) ... WTES
West Terre Haute, IN [*FM radio station call letters*] ... WWVR
West Texas Intermediate [*Crude oil*] (ECON) ... WTI
West Texas Library System [*Library network*] ... WTLS
West Texas State College [*Later, WTSU*] ... WTSC
West Texas State University (GAGS) ... West Tex St U
West Texas State University [*Formerly, WTSC*] ... WTSU
West Texas State University, Canyon, TX [*OCLC symbol*] (OCLC) ... TWT
West Texas State University, Canyon, TX [*Library symbol Library of Congress*] (LCLS) ... TxCaW
West Three [*Zambia*] [*ICAO location identifier*] (ICLI) ... FLWC
West Thumb [*Wyoming*] [*Seismograph station code, US Geological Survey*] (SEIS) ... WTW
West Two [*Zambia*] [*ICAO location identifier*] (ICLI) ... FLWB
West Ulster Unionist Council [*Northern Ireland*] ... WUUC
West Union, IA [*Location identifier FAA*] (FAAL) ... XWY
West Union, OH [*Location identifier FAA*] (FAAL) ... AMT
West Union, OH [*FM radio station call letters*] ... WRAC

West Union, OH [*FM radio station call letters*] (RBYB) .... WVXW
West Valley City, UT [*AM radio station call letters*] .... KRGQ
West Valley College, Saratoga, CA [*Library symbol*] [*Library of Congress*] (LCLS) .... CSarW
West Valley Demonstration Project (DOGT) .... WVDP
West Valley Demonstration Project [*Department of Energy*] [*West Valley, NY*] (GAAI) .... WVDP
West Valley High School, Fairbanks, AK [*Library symbol*] [*Library of Congress*] (LCLS) .... AkFWHS
West Valley Medical Center, Medical Library, Caldwell, ID [*Library symbol*] [*Library of Congress*] (LCLS) .... IdCaH
West Valley, New York [*Commercial waste site from 1963-81*] (GAAI) .... WVNY
West Valley Nuclear Services Co. (GAAI) .... WVNS
West Valley Nuclear Services Co., West Valley, NY [*Library symbol Library of Congress*] (LCLS) .... NWevNS
West Vancouver Laboratory [*Department of Fisheries and Oceans*] [*Canada*] (IRC) .... WVL
West Vancouver Laboratory, Fisheries and Oceans Canada [*Laboratoire de West-Vancouver, Peches et Oceans Canada*] **British Columbia** [*Library symbol National Library of Canada*] (NLC) .... BVAPE
West Vancouver Memorial Library, British Columbia [*Library symbol National Library of Canada*] (NLC) .... BWV
West Vancouver Memorial Library, West Vancouver, BC, Canada [*Library symbol Library of Congress*] (LCLS) .... CaBWv
West View Elementary School, Rockford, IL [*Library symbol*] [*Library of Congress*] (LCLS) .... IRoWvE
West Virginia [*MARC geographic area code Library of Congress*] (LCCP) .... n-us-wv
West Virginia (AAG) .... W VA
West Virginia [*Postal code*] .... WV
West Virginia [*MARC country of publication code Library of Congress*] (LCCP) .... wvu
West Virginia Air Pollution Control Commission, Charleston, WV [*Library symbol Library of Congress*] (LCLS) .... WvCAP
West Virginia Assessment and Tracking System (EDAC) .... WVAATS
West Virginia Attorney General Reports [*A publication*] (DLA).... OAG West Virginia
West Virginia Baptist Historical Society Deposit, Department of Archives and History, Charleston, WV [*Library symbol Library of Congress*] (LCLS) .... WvCBHi
West Virginia Bowhunters Association .... WVBA
West Virginia Business Education Association (EDAC) .... WVBEA
West Virginia Code [*A publication*] (DLA) .... W Va Code
West Virginia Code [*1899*] [*A publication*] (DLA) .... Warth Code
West Virginia Code [*1899*] [*A publication*] (DLA) .... WVC
West Virginia College of Graduate Studies, Institute, WV [*Library symbol Library of Congress*] (LCLS) .... WvICG
West Virginia Constitution [*A publication*] (DLA) .... W Va Const
West Virginia Criminal Justice Review [*A publication*] (DLA) .... W Va Crim Just Rev
West Virginia Department of Agriculture, Charleston, WV [*Library symbol Library of Congress*] (LCLS) .... WvCA
West Virginia Department of Archives and History, Charleston, WV [*Library symbol Library of Congress*] (LCLS) .... Wv-Ar
West Virginia Department of Civil and Defense Mobilization, Charleston, WV [*Library symbol Library of Congress*] (LCLS) .... WvCCD
West Virginia Department of Health, Charleston, WV [*Library symbol Library of Congress*] (LCLS) .... WvCH
West Virginia Department of Highways, Charleston, WV [*Library symbol Library of Congress*] (LCLS) .... WvCHi
West Virginia Department of Mental Health, Charleston, WV [*Library symbol Library of Congress*] (LCLS) .... WvCMH
West Virginia Department of Mines, Charleston, WV [*Library symbol Library of Congress*] (LCLS) .... WvCMi
West Virginia Department of Natural Resources, Charleston, WV [*Library symbol Library of Congress*] (LCLS) .... WvCNR
West Virginia Department of Public Safety, Charleston, WV [*Library symbol Library of Congress*] (LCLS) .... WvCPS
West Virginia Division of Vocational Rehabilitation, Charleston, WV [*Library symbol Library of Congress*] (LCLS) .... WvCVR
West Virginia Graduate College (GAGS) .... West Va Col
West Virginia Institute of Technology .... WVIT
West Virginia Institute of Technology, Montgomery, WV [*Library symbol Library of Congress*] (LCLS) .... WvMonI
West Virginia Institute of Technology, Montgomery, WV [*OCLC symbol*] (OCLC) .... WVT
West Virginia Law Quarterly [*A publication*] (DLA) .... W Va LQ
West Virginia Law Quarterly [*A publication*] (DLA) .... WVLQ
West Virginia Library Commission, Book Express Unit, Charleston, WV [*Library symbol Library of Congress*] (LCLS) .... Wv-B
West Virginia Library Commission, Charleston, WV [*Library symbol Library of Congress*] (LCLS) .... Wv
West Virginia Library Commission, Library Science Department, Charleston, WV [*Library symbol Library of Congress*] (LCLS) .... Wv-LS
West Virginia Library Commission, Reference Department, WV [*Library symbol Library of Congress*] (LCLS) .... Wv-R
West Virginia Medical Center, Morgantown, WV [*Inactive*] [*OCLC symbol*] (OCLC) .... WVM
West Virginia Network for Educational Telecomputing [*Research center*] (RCD) .... WVNET
West Virginia Northern Railroad Co. [*AAR code*] .... WVN
West Virginia Public Service Commission Report [*A publication*] (DLA) .... W Va PSCR
West Virginia Public Utility Commission Reports [*A publication*] (DLA) .... W Va PUR
West Virginia Pulp & Paper Co., Covington, VA [*Library symbol Library of Congress*] (LCLS) .... ViCovW
West Virginia Register [*A publication*] (AAGC) .... W Va Reg
West Virginia Rehabilitation Research and Training Center [*West Virginia University*] [*Research center*] (RCD) .... WVRRTC
West Virginia Reports [*A publication*] (DLA) .... W Va Law Reports
West Virginia Reports [*A publication*] (DLA) .... W Va Rep
West Virginia Reports [*A publication*] (DLA) .... West Va
West Virginia Reports [*A publication*] (DLA) .... West Va Rep
West Virginia Reports [*A publication*] (DLA) .... WV
West Virginia Reports [*A publication*] (DLA) .... WV Rep
West Virginia Reports [*A publication*] (DLA) .... WVR
West Virginia School of Osteopathic Medicine .... WVSOM
West Virginia State College .... WVSC
West Virginia State College/College of Graduate Studies, Institute, WV [*OCLC symbol*] (OCLC) .... WVG
West Virginia State College, Institute, WV [*Library symbol Library of Congress*] (LCLS) .... WvIC
West Virginia State Fire Marshal's Department, Charleston, WV [*Library symbol Library of Congress*] (LCLS) .... WvCFM
West Virginia State Law Library, Charleston, WV [*Library symbol Library of Congress*] (LCLS) .... Wv-L
West Virginia State Technical Services, Charleston, WV [*Library symbol Library of Congress*] (LCLS) .... WvCTS
West Virginia Supreme Court Reports [*A publication*] (DLA) .... W Va
West Virginia Union Catalog Interlibrary Loan Network [*Library network*] .... WULC
West Virginia University (GAGS) .... West Va U
West Virginia University .... WVU
West Virginia University, Agricultural Engineering Library, Morgantown, WV [*Library symbol Library of Congress*] (LCLS) .... WvU-AE
West Virginia University, College of Law, Morgantown, WV [*Library symbol Library of Congress*] (LCLS) .... WvU-L
West Virginia University, Kanawha Valley Graduate Center, Nitro, WV [*Library symbol Library of Congress*] (LCLS) .... WvNiK
West Virginia University Library, Morgantown, WV [*OCLC symbol*] (OCLC) .... WVU
West Virginia University, Medical Center, Morgantown, WV [*Library symbol Library of Congress*] (LCLS) .... WvU-M
West Virginia University, Morgantown, WV [*Library symbol Library of Congress*] (LCLS) .... WvU
West Virginia University, Music Library, Morgantown, WV [*Library symbol Library of Congress*] (LCLS) .... WvU-Mu
West Virginia University, Physical Sciences Library, Morgantown, WV [*Library symbol Library of Congress*] (LCLS) .... WvU-P
West Virginia University, School of Journalism, Morgantown, WV [*Library symbol Library of Congress*] (LCLS) .... WvU-J
West Virginia Wesleyan College .... WVWC
West Virginia Wesleyan College, Buckhannon, WV [*Library symbol Library of Congress*] (LCLS) .... WvBuW
West Wales Field Society [*British*] .... WWFS
West Warwick, RI [*AM radio station call letters*] (RBYB) .... WHIM
West Washington County Community District 10, Okawville, IL [*Library symbol Library of Congress*] (LCLS) .... IOkCD
West Wind Aviation, Inc. [*Canada ICAO designator*] (FAAC) .... WEW
West Wyalong [*Australia Airport symbol*] (OAG) .... WWY
West Yarmouth, MA [*AM radio station call letters*] .... WUOK
West Yarmouth, MA [*FM radio station call letters*] .... WXTK
West Yellowstone, MT [*Location identifier FAA*] (FAAL) .... ESY
West Yellowstone, MT [*FM radio station call letters*] (RBYB) .... KWWF-FM
West Yellowstone, MT [*AM radio station call letters*] .... KWYS
West Yellowstone, MT [*Location identifier FAA*] (FAAL) .... LOW
West Yellowstone, MT [*Location identifier FAA*] (FAAL) .... WEY
West Yellowstone, MT [*Location identifier FAA*] (FAAL) .... WYS
[*The*] **West Yorkshire Regiment** [*Army British*] .... WYR
West Yorkshire Yeomanry Cavalry [*British military*] (DMA) .... WYYC
Westair Aviation, Inc. [*Canada ICAO designator*] (FAAC) .... NLF
Westair Aviation Ltd. [*Ireland*] [*ICAO designator*] (FAAC) .... EFF
Westair Commuter Airlines [*ICAO designator*] (AD) .... VB
Westair Commuter Airlines, Inc. [*ICAO designator*] (FAAC) .... SDU
WestAir Industries, Inc. [*ICAO designator*] (FAAC) .... PCM
Westam Oil Ltd. [*Vancouver Stock Exchange symbol*] .... WTO
WestAmerica Bancorp [*NASDAQ symbol*] (SAG) .... WABC
WestAmerica Bancorp [*Associated Press*] (SAG) .... WAmBc
Westamerica Bancorporation [*NASDAQ symbol*] (TTSB) .... WABC
WestAmerica Corp. [*NASDAQ symbol*] (SAG) .... WACC
WestAmerica Corp. [*Associated Press*] (SAG) .... WstAmer
Westar Group Ltd. [*Toronto Stock Exchange symbol Vancouver Stock Exchange symbol*] .... WGL
Westar Mining Ltd. [*Toronto Stock Exchange symbol Vancouver Stock Exchange symbol*] .... WML
Westark Community College, Fort Smith, AR [*Library symbol*] [*Library of Congress*] (LCLS) .... ArFsW
Westate Resources, Inc. [*Vancouver Stock Exchange symbol*] .... WTE
Westates Airlines [*ICAO designator*] (FAAC) .... WSA
West-Avin Oy [*Finland ICAO designator*] (FAAC) .... WAV
Westbank Corp. [*NASDAQ symbol*] (SAG) .... WBKC
Westbank Corp. [*Associated Press*] (SAG) .... Westbank
Westbank Museum, British Columbia [*Library symbol National Library of Canada*] (NLC) .... BWEM
Westbank Museum, Westbank, BC, Canada [*Library symbol*] [*Library of Congress*] (LCLS) .... CaBWEM
Westbank Resources, Inc. [*Vancouver Stock Exchange symbol*] .... WBR
Westbeth Corp. (EA) .... WC
Westbeth Playwrights Feminist Collective [*Defunct*] (EA) .... WPFC
Westbound .... WB
Westbound (FAAC) .... WBND

Westbridge Capital [*NYSE symbol*] (SAG) ... WBC
Westbridge Capital [*Associated Press*] (SAG) ... WstBrC
Westbridge Computer Corp. [*Toronto Stock Exchange symbol*] ... WB
Westbridge Resources Ltd. [*Vancouver Stock Exchange symbol*] ... WGR
Westbrook Christian School, Westbrook, MN [*Library symbol*] [*Library of Congress*] (LCLS) ... MnWeCS
Westbrook, ME [*AM radio station call letters*] ... WLPZ
Westbrook, ME [*FM radio station call letters*] ... WYNZ
Westbrook Public Library, Westbrook, MN [*Library symbol*] [*Library of Congress*] (LCLS) ... MnWeP
Westbrook Public School, Westbrook, MN [*Library symbol*] [*Library of Congress*] (LCLS) ... MnWePS
Westbrook-Walnut Grove Middle School, Walnut Grove, MN [*Library symbol*] [*Library of Congress*] (LCLS) ... MnWgMS
Westbury [*England*] ... WBURY
Westbury [*British depot code*] ... WES
Westbury Junior High School, Westbury, NY [*Library symbol*] [*Library of Congress*] (LCLS) ... NWeJH
Westbury Memorial Public Library, Westbury, NY [*Library symbol Library of Congress*] (LCLS) ... NWe
Westbury Senior High School, Houston, TX [*Library symbol Library of Congress*] (LCLS) ... TxHWH
Westbury Senior High School, Westbury, NY [*Library symbol*] [*Library of Congress*] (LCLS) ... NWeSH
Westbury's European Arbitration (Reilly) [*A publication*] (DLA) ... West
Westchester Academy of Medicine, Purchase, NY [*Library symbol Library of Congress*] (LCLS) ... NPurW
Westchester Community College [*Valhalla, NY*] ... WCC
Westchester Community College, Technical Services, Valhalla, NY [*OCLC symbol*] (OCLC) ... WCC
Westchester Community College, Valhalla, NY [*Library symbol Library of Congress*] (LCLS) ... NValhW
Westchester County Community Services Information System [*Westchester LibrarySystem*] [*Information service or system*] (IID) ... WCCSIS
Westchester County Courthouse, Harrison, NY [*Library symbol*] [*Library of Congress*] (LCLS) ... NHarnC
Westchester County Historical Society, Tuckahoe, NY [*Library symbol Library of Congress*] (LCLS) ... NTucW
Westchester County Medical Center ... WCMC
Westchester Library System [*Library network*] ... WLS
Westchester Library System, White Plains, NY [*Library symbol Library of Congress*] (LCLS) ... NWhpW
Westchester Library System, Yonkers, NY [*OCLC symbol*] (OCLC) ... VVW
Westchester Medical Center, Valhalla, NY [*Library symbol Library of Congress*] (LCLS) ... NValhM
Westchester Public Library [*UTLAS symbol*] ... WLS
Westchester Public Library, Chesterton, IN [*Library symbol Library of Congress*] (LCLS) ... InChe
Westchester Public Library, Westchester, IL [*Library symbol Library of Congress*] (LCLS) ... IWe
Westco Bancorp [*NASDAQ symbol*] (TTSB) ... WCBI
Westco Bancorp, Inc. [*NASDAQ symbol*] (SAG) ... WCBI
Westco Bancorp, Inc. [*Associated Press*] (SAG) ... WestcoB
Westcoast Energy [*Canada*] [*FAA designator*] (FAAC) ... BLK
Westcoast Energy [*NYSE symbol*] (TTSB) ... WE
Westcoast Energy, Inc. [*Vancouver Stock Exchange symbol*] ... W
Westcoast Energy, Inc. [*Toronto Stock Exchange symbol*] ... W
Westcoast Energy, Inc. [*NYSE symbol*] (SPSG) ... WE
Westcoast Energy, Inc. [*Associated Press*] (SAG) ... WstctEg
Westcorp, Inc. [*NYSE symbol*] (SPSG) ... WES
Westcorp, Inc. [*Associated Press*] (SAG) ... Westcp
Westcott & Laurance Line [*Steamship*] (MHDW) ... W & L
Westcott Communications [*NASDAQ symbol*] (SPSG) ... WCTV
Westcott Communications Co. [*Associated Press*] (SAG) ... WestcotC
Westdeutsche Landesbank [*West German bank*] ... WestLB
Westdeutsche Luftwerbung [*Airline*] [*Germany*] ... WDL
Westdeutsche Zeitschrift fuer Geschichte und Kunst [*A publication*] (OCD) ... Westd Zeit
Westdeutscher Rundfunk [*Radio network*] [*West Germany*] ... WDR
Westech Resources Ltd. [*Vancouver Stock Exchange symbol*] ... WSC
Westek Communications, Inc. [*Vancouver Stock Exchange symbol*] ... WCT
Westell Technologies, Inc. [*Associated Press*] (SAG) ... Westell
Westell Technologies, Inc. [*NASDAQ symbol*] (SAG) ... WSTL
Westell Technologies'A' [*NASDAQ symbol*] (TTSB) ... WSTL
Westerbeke Corp. [*Associated Press*] (SAG) ... Wstrbke
Westerbeke Corp. [*Avon, MA*] [*NASDAQ symbol*] (NQ) ... WTBK
Westerbork Synthesis Radio Telescope ... WSRT
WesterFed Financial [*NASDAQ symbol*] (TTSB) ... WSTR
Westerfed Financial Corp. [*Associated Press*] (SAG) ... Westerfed
Westerfed Financial Corp. [*NASDAQ symbol*] (SAG) ... WSTR
Westerhout [*Astronomy*] ... W
Westerland [*Germany Airport symbol*] (OAG) ... GWT
Westerland/Sylt [*Germany ICAO location identifier*] (ICLI) ... EDXW
Westerly [*A publication*] ... Westly
Westerly ... WLY
Westerly [*Rhode Island*] [*Airport symbol*] (OAG) ... WST
Westerly Public Library, Westerly, RI [*Library symbol Library of Congress*] (LCLS) ... RWe
Westerly, RI [*Location identifier FAA*] (FAAL) ... RLS
Westerly, RI [*AM radio station call letters*] ... WERI
Westerly, RI [*Location identifier FAA*] (FAAL) ... WST
Westerly, RI [*FM radio station call letters*] ... WWRX
Western ... WESTN
Western ... WRN
Western ... WSTN
Western ... WSTRN
Western Actuarial Bureau [*Later, ISO*] (EA) ... WAB
Western Administrative Support Center [*Marine science*] (OSRA) ... WASC
Western Administrative Support Center (USDC) ... WASC
Western Aerial Photography Laboratory [*Department of Agriculture*] ... WAPL
Western Aerospace Rescue and Recovery Center [*Air Force*] ... WARRC
Western Agricultural Chemicals Association (EA) ... WACA
Western Air Defense Command ... WADC
Western Air Defense Force ... WADF
Western Air Navigation Ltd. [*Australia*] ... WAN
Western Air Procurement District ... WAPD
Western Air Procurement District ... WEAPD
Western Airlines [*ICAO designator*] (AD) ... MB
Western Airlines (MHDW) ... W
Western Airlines, Inc. [*ICAO designator*] ... WA
Western Airlines, Inc. [*Facetious translation: What an Airline*] ... WAL
Western Airways and Air Communications Service (IAA) ... WAACS
Western Alaska [*Airlines*] (OAG) ... WK
Western Alaska Standard Time (IAA) ... WAST
Western Allegheny Railroad (IIA) ... WA
Western Allegheny Railroad Co. [*AAR code*] ... WAL
Western Allenbee Oil & Gas Co. Ltd. [*Vancouver Stock Exchange symbol*] ... WSE
Western Amateur Astronomers (EA) ... WAA
Western American Literature [*A publication*] (BRI) ... WAL
Western American Society for Italic Handwriting [*Formerly, WABSIH*] (EA) ... WASIH
Western and English Manufacturers Association [*Denver, CO*] (EA) ... WAEMA
Western Aphasia Battery [*Neuropsychology test*] ... WAB
Western Aphasia Battery Test [*Speech and language therapy*] (DAVI) ... WABT
Western Apicultural Society of North America (EA) ... WASNA
Western Apparel Manufacturers Show (ITD) ... WAM
Western Approaches [*to Great Britain and Ireland*] [*Obsolete*] ... WA
Western Approaches Convoy Instructions [*British military*] (DMA) ... WACI
Western Approaches Tactical Unit [*Navy*] ... WATU
Western Archeological Center [*Department of the Interior*] (GRD) ... WAC
Western Area ... WA
Western Area Frequency Coordinator ... WAFC
Western Area, Military Traffic Management and Terminal Service (AABC) ... WAMTMTS
Western Area Military Traffic Management Command (DICI) ... WAMTMC
Western Area Power Administration [*Department of Energy*] ... WAPA
Western Arid Resource Information System [*Queensland*] [*State*] (EERA) ... WARIS
Western Armenian Athletic Association (EA) ... WAAA
Western Artic Air Ltd. [*Canada ICAO designator*] (FAAC) ... WAL
Western Associated Modelers (EA) ... WAM
Western Associated Schools [*Australia*] ... WAS
Western Association for Art Conservation (EA) ... WAAC
Western Association of Broadcast Engineers [*Canada*] ... WABE
Western Association of Circuit Manufacturers ... WACM
Western Association of College and University Business Officers (AEBS) ... WACU
Western Association of Fish and Wildlife Agencies (EA) ... WAFWA
Western Association of Map Libraries (EA) ... WAML
Western Association of Minority Consulting Engineers (IAA) ... WAMCE
Western Association of Schools and Colleges (EA) ... WASC
Western Association of State Game and Fish Commissioners [*Later, Western Association of Fish and Wildlife Agencies*] (EA) ... WASGFC
Western Association of State Highway and Traffic Officials ... WASHTO
Western Association of State Highway Officials ... WASHO
Western Athletic Conference (EA) ... WAC
Western Atlantic Airlift Command Post [*Navy*] (DNAB) ... WAACP
Western Atlantic Area ... WESTLANT
Western Atlantic Ocean Experiment (USDC) ... WATOX
Western Atlantic Ocean Experiment [*Marine science*] (OSRA) ... WATOX
Western Atlas [*NYSE symbol*] (TTSB) ... WAI
Western Atlas, Inc. [*NYSE symbol*] (SAG) ... WAI
Western Atlas, Inc. [*Associated Press*] (SAG) ... WstAtlas
Western Atmospheric Deposition Task Force [*Environmental Protection Agency*] (GFGA) ... WADTF
Western Australia [*MARC geographic area code Library of Congress*] (LCCP) ... u-at-we
Western Australia [*State*] (EERA) ... WA
Western Australia Institute of Technology (NITA) ... WAIT
Western Australia Law Reform Commission. Bulletin [*A publication*] ... WALRC Bull
Western Australia Law Reports [*A publication*] (DLA) ... W Austl R
Western Australian Aboriginal Education Consultative Group ... WAAECG
Western Australian Academy of the Performing Arts ... WAAPA
Western Australian Agricultural Research Institute [*State*] (EERA) ... WARI
Western Australian Alcohol and Drug Authority ... WAADA
Western Australian Apple and Pear Council ... WAAPC
Western Australian Art Gallery ... WAAG
Western Australian Asparagus Growers' Association ... WAAGA
Western Australian Association for Mental Health ... WAAMH
Western Australian Association of Occupational Therapists ... WAAOT
Western Australian Ballet Company ... WABC
Western Australian Bar Association ... WABA
Western Australian Bible College ... WABC
Western Australian Biographical Index [*A publication*] (APTA) ... WABI
Western Australian Business Education College ... WABEC
Western Australian Catholic Education Office ... WACEO
Western Australian Centre for Remote and Rural Medicine ... WACRRM
Western Australian Centre for Self Esteem Education ... WACSEE
Western Australian Chamber of Commerce and Industry ... WACCI

Western Australian Club .... WAC
Western Australian Coastal Shipping Commission .... WACSC
Western Australian Council on the Ageing .... WACOTA
Western Australian Dairy Industry Liaison Committee ... WADILC
Western Australian Egg Marketing Board .... WAEMB
Western Australian Electoral Commission .... WAEC
Western Australian Environment Protection Authority (EERA) .... WAEPA
Western Australian Environmental Protection Agency ...... WAEPA
Western Australian Farmers' Association .... WAFA
Western Australian Farmers Federation (EERA) .... WAFF
Western Australian Federation of Rural Youth .... WAFRY
Western Australian Fire Brigade Board .... WAFBB
Western Australian Fishing Industry Council .... WAFIC
Western Australian Football Association .... WAFA
Western Australian Football Commission .... WAFC
Western Australian Forest Industry Training Council ...... WAFITC
Western Australian Fruit Advisory Council .... WAFAC
Western Australian Furniture Industry Council .... WAFIC
Western Australian Gould League .... WAGL
Western Australian Government Railways (PDAA) .... WAGR
Western Australian Government Railways Commission ..... WAGRC
Western Australian Government Railways Commission ... WESTRAIL
Western Australian Green Party [Political party] .... WAG
Western Australian Herbarium Plant Specimen Database [State]
  (EERA) .... WAHERE
Western Australian Heritage Committee .... WAHC
Western Australian Historical Society. Journal [A publication] ...... W Aust Hist Soc
Western Australian Industrial Court .... WAIC
Western Australian Institute of Applied Business Studies ...... WAIABS
Western Australian Institute of Applied Linguistics .... WAIAL
Western Australian Institute of Translators and Interpreters ...... WAITI
Western Australian International College .... WAIC
Western Australian Land Information Program [State] (EERA) ...... WALIP
Western Australian Land Information System [State] (EERA) ...... WALIS
Western Australian Law Libraries .... WALL
Western Australian Lawn Tennis Association .... WALTA
Western Australian Marine Research Laboratory .... WAMRL
Western Australian Meat Commission .... WAMC
Western Australian Meat Marketing Corp. [Commercial firm] ...... WAMMC
Western Australian Ministerial Advisory Council on Community
  Relations .... WAMACCR
Western Australian Mint .... WAM
Western Australian Museum .... WAM
Western Australian Nanny Training College .... WANTC
Western Australian Naturalists' Club (EERA) .... WANC
Western Australian Office of Higher Education .... WAOHE
Western Australian Olympic Council .... WAOC
Western Australian Opera .... WAO
Western Australian Opinion Polls .... WAOP
Western Australian Parliamentary Debates [A publication] ...... WAPD
Western Australian Potato Marketing Authority .... WAPMA
Western Australian Retail Industry Training Council ...... WARITC
Western Australian Road Transport Association .... WARTA
Western Australian Rugby League .... WARL
Western Australian Satellite Technology Applications Consortium [State]
  (EERA) .... WASTAC
Western Australian School of Nursing .... WASN
Western Australian School of Yoga .... WASY
Western Australian Science Teachers' Association .... WASTA
Western Australian Sewerage and Waste Quality Infrastructure Program
  [State] (EERA) .... WASAW
Western Australian Shippers' Council .... WASC
Western Australian Society for Computers and the Law ...... WASCL
Western Australian Society of Arts .... WASA
Western Australian Sports Federation .... WASF
Western Australian State Emergency Service .... WASES
Western Australian State Football League .... WASFL
Western Australian State Housing Commission .... HOMESWEST
Western Australian Survey and Mapping Advisory Council [State]
  (EERA) .... WASMAC
Western Australian Temperance Alliance .... WATA
Western Australian Tourism Commission .... WATC
Western Australian Tourist Centre .... WATC
Western Australian Treasury Corp. [Commercial firm] ...... WATC
Western Australian Tripartite Labour Consultative Council ...... WATLCC
Western Australian. Votes and Proceedings [A publication] ...... WAVP
Western Australian Water Resources Council (EERA) ...... WAWRC
Western Australian Week Council .... WAWC
Western Awning Association [Later, NPEA] (EA) .... WAA
Western Bank [Coos Bay, OR] [NASDAQ symbol] (NQ) ...... WSBK
Western Bank [Associated Press] (SAG) .... WtnBank
Western Baptist Bible College, El Cerrito, CA [Library symbol Library of
  Congress] (LCLS) .... CEcerB
Western Baptist Bible College, Salem, OR [Library symbol Library of
  Congress] (LCLS) .... OrSaWB
Western Base Section [England] [World War II] .... WBS
Western Beaufort Sea Ecological Cruise [Coast Guard] ...... WEBSEC
Western Beef [Associated Press] (SAG) .... WstBeef
Western Beef, Inc. [NASDAQ symbol] (SPSG) .... BEEF
Western Beet Sugar Producers [Defunct] .... WBSP
Western Behavioral Sciences Institute [Defunct] (EA) ...... WBSI
Western Biological Laboratories .... WBL
Western Bird Banding Association (EA) .... WBBA
Western Blot [Blood test] .... WB
Western Blot Assay [Analytical biochemistry] .... WBA

Western Bohemian Fraternal Association [Later, WFLA] (EA) ...... WBFA
Western Book Publishers Association (NTCM) .... WBPA
Western Boundary Current [Marine science] (MSC) .... WBC
Western Boundary Undercurrent [Atlantic Ocean] .... WBUC
Western Buddhist Order [British] (EAIO) .... WBO
Western Building Material Association (EA) .... WBMA
Western Business Education Association (AEBS) .... WBEA
Western Canada Concept [Political party] (PPW) .... WCC
Western Canada High School, Calgary, AB, Canada [Library symbol Library
  of Congress] (LCLS) .... CaACW
Western Canada High School, Calgary, Alberta [Library symbol National
  Library of Canada] (NLC) .... ACW
Western Canada Party [Separatist political party] .... WCP
Western Canadian Land [Vancouver Stock Exchange symbol] ...... WTL
Western Canadian Mining [Vancouver Stock Exchange symbol] ...... WCD
Western Canadian Universities Marine Biological Society ...... WCUMBS
Western Carolina Center, Staff Library, Morganton, NC [Library symbol
  Library of Congress] (LCLS) .... NcMoWC
Western Carolina College [Later, WCU] [North Carolina] ...... WCC
Western Carolina University (PDAA) .... WCARU
Western Carolina University [Cullowhee, NC] .... WCU
Western Carolina University (GAGS) .... West Car U
Western Carolina University, Cullowhee, NC [Library symbol Library of
  Congress] (LCLS) .... NcCuW
Western Carolina University, Cullowhee, NC [OCLC symbol] (OCLC) .... NMW
Western Carolina University Herbarium .... WCUH
Western Carolinas League [Baseball] .... WCL
Western Carolines [Navy] .... WESCAR
Western Carolines Subarea [Navy] .... WESCARSUBAREA
Western Carriers Tariff Bureau .... WCTB
Western Catholic Charismatic Renewal Services [A publication] ...... WCCRS
Western Catholic Union (EA) .... WCU
Western Cedar [Utility pole] [Telecommunications] (TEL) ...... WC
Western Center on Law and Poverty (EA) .... WCLP
Western Central .... WC
Western Central Atlantic Fisheries Commission [Food and Agriculture
  Organization of the UN] .... WECAF
Western Central Atlantic Fisheries Commission [Food and Agriculture
  Organization of the UN] (EAIO) .... WECAFC
Western Civilization .... WC
Western Classification .... WC
Western Coal Association [Australia] .... WCA
Western Coal Transportation Association (EA) .... WCTA
Western Collaborative Group Study [University of California]
  [Psychology] .... WCGS
Western College Association (EA) .... WCA
Western College for Women [Ohio] .... WCW
Western College for Women, Oxford, OH [Inactive] [OCLC symbol]
  (OCLC) .... WCW
Western College of Veterinary Medicine [Canada] .... WCVM
Western College Placement Association (AEBS) .... WCPA
Western College Reading and Learning Association (EA) ...... WCRLA
Western College Reading Association (EA) .... WCRA
Western Collegiate Hockey Association (EA) .... WCHA
Western Command .... WC
Western Command [Army] (AABC) .... WESCOM
Western Command [Army] .... WESTCOM
Western Communications Region [Air Force] .... WCOMMRGN
Western Communications Region [Air Force] (MCD) ..... WCR
Western Communications Region [Air Force] (AFM) ...... WESTCOMMRGN
Western Co. of North America [NYSE symbol] (SPSG) ...... WSN
Western Concrete Reinforcing Steel Institute [Later, CRSI] (EA) ...... WCRSI
Western Conference of Public Services Commissioners ...... WCPSC
Western Connecticut State College, Danbury, CT [Library symbol Library of
  Congress] (LCLS) .... CtDabN
Western Connecticut State College, Haas Library, Danbury, CT [OCLC
  symbol] (OCLC) .... CTD
Western Connecticut State University [Danbury] .... WCSU
Western Connecticut State University (GAGS) ...... West Conn St U
Western Conservative Baptist Theological Seminary, Portland, OR [Library
  symbol Library of Congress] (LCLS) .... OrPWB
Western Conservative Baptist Theological Seminary, Portland, OR [OCLC
  symbol] (OCLC) .... WBS
Western Contract Management Region [Air Force] .... WCMR
Western Coordination Office [Later, WOO] [NASA] .... WCO
Western Corporate Enterprises, Inc. [Toronto Stock Exchange symbol] ...... WCE
Western Correctional Center, Morganton, NC [Library symbol] [Library of
  Congress] (LCLS) .... NcMoWCC
Western Council on Higher Education for Nursing .... WCHEN
Western Counties Regional Library, Yarmouth, Nova Scotia [Library symbol
  National Library of Canada] (NLC) .... NSY
Western Counties Regional Library, Yarmouth, NS, Canada [Library symbol
  Library of Congress] (LCLS) .... CaNSY
Western Country Clubs [NASDAQ symbol] (TTSB) .... WCCI
Western Country Clubs, Inc. [NASDAQ symbol] (SAG) .... WCCI
Western Country Clubs, Inc. [Associated Press] (SAG) ...... WstnCC
Western Cover Society (EA) .... WCS
Western Dance Appreciation Society [British] (DBA) ...... WDAS
Western Data Processing Center [University of California, Los Angeles] ...... WDPC
Western Deep Levels ADR [NASDAQ symbol] (TTSB) ...... WDEPY
Western Deep Levels Ltd. [Associated Press] (SAG) ...... WDeep
Western Deep Levels Ltd. [NASDAQ symbol] (NQ) .... WDEP
Western Defense Command [Army] .... WDC
Western Defense Tactical Command (AAG) .... WDTC
Western d'Eldona Resources Ltd. [Toronto Stock Exchange symbol] ...... WDL

Western Desert Air Force ... WDAF
Western Desert Force [*World War II*] ... WDF
Western Design Engineering Exposition (PDAA) ... WESDEX
Western Development Division [*ARDC*] ... WDD
Western Development Laboratories ... WDL
Western Development Museum, Saskatoon, Saskatchewan [*Library symbol National Library of Canada*] (NLC) ... SSWD
Western Development Museum, Saskatoon, SK, Canada [*Library symbol Library of Congress*] (LCLS) ... CaSSWD
Western Digital [*NYSE symbol*] (TTSB) ... WDC
Western Digital Corp. [*NYSE symbol*] (SPSG) ... WDC
Western Digital Corp. [*Associated Press*] (SAG) ... WDigitl
Western District Area [*Air Force*] ... WDA
Western Diverging Volcanism [*Geology*] ... WDV
Western Diversification [*Diversification de l'Ouest*], Ottawa, Ontario [*Library symbol National Library of Canada*] (BIB) ... OOWD
Western Division Naval Facilities Engineering Command ... DIRWESTDOCKS
Western Division, Naval Facilities Engineering Command (DNAB) ... WESTDIVNAVFACENGCOM
Western Division, Naval Facilities Engineering Command ... WESTNAVFACENGCOM
Western Dredging Association (EA) ... WEDA
Western Earth Sciences Technologies [*Research center*] (RCD) ... WEST
Western Eastern Roadracers Association (EA) ... WERA
Western Economic Association International (EA) ... WEA
Western Economic Association International [*Later, WEA*] (EA) ... WEAI
Western Economic Union (DOMA) ... WEU
Western Education Development Group [*University of British Columbia*] [*Canada Research center*] ... WEDGE
Western Educational Society for Telecommunications [*Defunct*] (EA) ... WEST
Western Electric Air Defense Engineering Service (SAA) ... WEADES
Western Electric Co. (AAG) ... WE
Western Electric Co. (MCD) ... WECO
Western Electric Co., Inc., Baltimore, MD [*Library symbol Library of Congress*] (LCLS) ... MdBWesE
Western Electric Co., Inc., Engineering Research Center, Princeton, NJ [*Library symbol Library of Congress*] (LCLS) ... NjPW
Western Electric Co., Kearny, NJ [*Library symbol Library of Congress*] (LCLS) ... NjKWT
Western Electric Co., Legal Library, Greensboro, NC [*Library symbol Library of Congress*] (LCLS) ... NcGWE
Western Electric Co., Lexington Road Technical Library, Winston-Salem, NC [*Library symbol Library of Congress*] (LCLS) ... NcWsWE
Western Electric Co., Reynolda Road Technical Library, Winston-Salem, NC [*Library symbol Library of Congress*] (LCLS) ... NcWsWE-R
Western Electric Co., Springfield, NJ [*Library symbol Library of Congress*] (LCLS) ... NjSpW
Western Electric Co., Technical Library, Burlington, NC [*Library symbol Library of Congress*] (LCLS) ... NcBurWE
Western Electric Educational Fund ... WEEF
Western Electric Engineering Research Center (IAA) ... WEERC
Western Electronic Manufacturers Association [*Later, AEA*] (EA) ... WEMA
Western Electronic Week ... WEW
Western Electronics Maintenance Depot ... WEMD
Western Electronics Show and Convention [*IEEE*] ... WESCON
Western Encephalitis [*Medicine*] (MAE) ... WE
Western Encephalomyelitis [*Medicine*] (MAE) ... WE
Western Energy and Land Use Team, Fort Collins, CO [*OCLC symbol*] (OCLC) ... UDW
Western Energy Supply and Transmission Associates [*Utility antipollution group*] ... WEST
Western/English Retailers of America [*Defunct*] (EA) ... WERA
Western Environmental Technology Office (ACII) ... WETO
Western Equatorial Pacific Ocean Circulation Study (USDC) ... WEPOCS
Western Equatorial Pacific Ocean Climate Studies [*USA-Australia*] [*Marine science*] (OSRA) ... WEPOCS
Western Equestrian Socеity [*British*] (DBA) ... WES
Western Equine Encephalitis [*Virus*] (DAVI) ... WEE
Western Equine Encephalomyelitis [*Virus*] ... WEE
Western Europe and Others [*United Nations*] ... WEO
Western European Airport Authorities Conference (MCD) ... WEAAC
Western European and Others Group [*United Nations*] ... WEOG
Western European Association for Aviation Psychology (EA) ... WEAAP
Western European Basic Encyclopedia (MCD) ... WEBE
Western European Calibration Cooperation (ACII) ... WECC
Western European Geological Survey (EERA) ... WEGS
Western European Institute for Wood Preservation (EAIO) ... WEI
Western European Institute for Wood Preservation/Institut de l'Europe Occidentale pour l'Impregnation du Bois (EAIO) ... WEI/IEO
Western European Laboratory Accreditation Co-operation (ACII) ... WELAC
Western European Metal Trades Employers Organization [*Cologne, Federal Republic of Germany*] (EA) ... WEM
Western European Military Supply Board [*NATO*] (NATG) ... WEMSB
Western European Regional Planning Group [*NATO*] (NATG) ... WERPG
Western European Specialists Section [*Association of College and Research Libraries*] ... WESS
Western European Time (IAA) ... WET
Western European Union [*Also, WU*] [*See also UEO*] (EAIO) ... WEU
Western European Union [*Also, WEU*] (NATG) ... WU
Western European Union Chiefs of Staff (NATG) ... WUCOS
Western European Union Defense Organization (NATG) ... WUDO
Western European Union Finance and Economic Committee (NATG) ... WUFEC
Western European Vision ... WEV
Western Evangelical Seminary, Portland, OR [*Library symbol Library of Congress*] (LCLS) ... OrPW
Western Express Air Lines, Inc. [*Canada*] [*FAA designator*] (FAAC) ... WES
Western Fairs Association (EA) ... WFA
Western Falconry Association [*Defunct*] (EA) ... WFA
Western Federation of Miners ... WFM
Western Federation of Regional Construction Employers ... FORCE
Western Fidelity Funding [*NASDAQ symbol*] (TTSB) ... WFFI
Western Fidelity Funding, Inc. [*Associated Press*] (SAG) ... WestFidl
Western Fidelity Funding, Inc. [*NASDAQ symbol*] (SAG) ... WFFI
Western Field Operations Center [*Bureau of Mines*] [*Spokane, WA*] (GRD) ... WFOC
Western Fiordland Orthogneiss [*Geology*] ... WFO
Western Fish Toxicology Station [*Environmental Protection Agency*] ... WFTS
Western Fisheries Research Committee [*Australia*] ... WFRC
Western Flying Training Command [*AAFWFTC*] ... WFTC
Western Football Conference ... WFC
Western Forest Industries Association (EA) ... WFIA
Western Forestry and Conservation Association (EA) ... WFCA
Western Forestry Center (EA) ... WFC
Western Forestry Information Network [*Forest service*] [*Library network*] ... WESTFORNET
Western Fraternal Life Association (EA) ... WFLA
Western Front [*World War I*] ... WF
Western Frontier Force [*British military*] (DMA) ... WFF
Western Fruit Express ... WFEX
Western Gas Res $2.625 Cv Pfd [*NYSE symbol*] (TTSB) ... WGRPrA
Western Gas Res$2.28 cm Pfd [*NYSE symbol*] (TTSB) ... WGRPr
Western Gas Resources [*NYSE symbol*] (SPSG) ... WGR
Western Gas Resources [*Associated Press*] (SAG) ... WstGR
Western Gas Resources [*Associated Press*] (SAG) ... WstnGR
Western Gas Resources Co. [*Associated Press*] (SAG) ... WstG
Western Gear Corp. ... WGC
Western Geophysical Co., Houston, TX [*Library symbol Library of Congress*] (LCLS) ... TxHWG
Western Goals Foundation (EA) ... WGF
Western Goldfields, Inc. [*Toronto Stock Exchange symbol*] ... WGI
Western Golf Association (EA) ... WGA
Western Governors Conference ... WGC
Western Governors Policy Office ... WESTPO
Western Governors Regional Energy Policy Office ... WGREPO
Western Governors University ... WGU
Western Ground Electronics Engineering Installation Agency (AAG) ... WGEEIA
Western Growers Association (EA) ... WGA
Western Guidance Laboratory [*Wright Air Development Center*] (MUGU) ... WGL
Western Hardwood Association (EA) ... WHA
Western Harvest Sea [*Vancouver Stock Exchange symbol*] ... WHS
Western Hemisphere ... WH
Western Hemisphere Defense ... WHD
Western Hemisphere Friendship Association (EA) ... WHFA
Western Hemisphere Reserve ... WHR
Western Hemisphere Transmission System ... WHTS
Western Hemlock [*Utility pole*] [*Telecommunications*] (TEL) ... WH
Western Heraldry Organization (EA) ... WHO
Western Highway Institute (EA) ... WHI
Western Historical Quarterly [*A publication*] (BRI) ... WHQ
Western Historical Research Associates [*Defunct*] (EA) ... WHRA
Western History Association (EA) ... WHA
Western Hockey League ... WHL
Western Horsemen's Association [*British*] (DBA) ... WHA
Western Human Nutrition Research Center [*Department of Agriculture*] [*Research center*] (RCD) ... WHNRC
Western Humanities Review [*A publication*] (BRI) ... WHR
Western Illinois Library System [*Library network*] ... WILS
Western Illinois Library System, Monmouth, IL [*OCLC symbol*] (OCLC) ... IHX
Western Illinois Library System, Monmouth, IL [*Library symbol Library of Congress*] (LCLS) ... IMonW
Western Illinois University (GAGS) ... West Ill U
Western Illinois University [*Macomb*] ... WIU
Western Illinois University, Macomb, IL [*OCLC symbol*] (OCLC) ... IAZ
Western Illinois University, Macomb, IL [*Library symbol Library of Congress*] (LCLS) ... IMacoW
Western Indian States Agency Law Reports [*A publication*] (DLA) ... WISA Law Rep
Western Indian States Agency Law Reports [*A publication*] (DLA) ... WISALR
Western Information Network ... WIN
Western Information System for Energy Resources [*Dataline, Inc.*] [*Canada Information service or system*] ... WISER
Western Institute for Health Studies (EA) ... WIHS
Western International Trade Group [*Defunct*] (EA) ... WITG
Western International University, Phoenix, AZ [*OCLC symbol*] (OCLC) ... WIU
Western International Walking Horse Association (EA) ... WIWHA
Western Interpreters Association [*Later, NAI*] (EA) ... WIA
Western Interprovincial Football Union [*Canada*] ... WIFU
Western Interstate Commission for Higher Education (AEE) ... WICHE
Western Interstate Commission for Higher Education (GAGS) ... WICHE
Western Interstate Commission for Higher Education, Boulder, CO [*Library symbol Library of Congress*] (LCLS) ... CoBW
Western Interstate Energy Board/Western Interstate Nuclear Board (EA) ... WIEB/WINB
Western Interstate Library Coordinating Organization ... WILCO
Western Interstate Nuclear Board (NRCH) ... WINB
Western Interstate Nuclear Compact [*Later, WIEB/WINB*] ... WINC
Western Inv RE Tr SBI [*AMEX symbol*] (TTSB) ... WIR
Western Investment Real Estate Trust [*Associated Press*] (SAG) ... WIRET
Western Investment Real Estate Trust SBI [*AMEX symbol*] (SPSG) ... WIR

Western Iowa Technical Community College, Sioux City, IA [OCLC symbol] (OCLC) .... IWS
Western Jewish Institute, Los Angeles, CA [Library symbol Library of Congress] (LCLS) .... CLWJ
Western Joint Computer Conference .... WJCC
Western Journalism Center .... WJC
Western Jurist [Des Moines, Iowa] [A publication] (DLA) .... West Jur
Western Jurist [United States] [A publication] (DLA) .... WJ
Western Kentucky State College [Later, WKSU] .... WKSC
Western Kentucky State University [Formerly, WKSC] .... WKSU
Western Kentucky University (GAGS) .... West Ky U
Western Kentucky University [Formerly, WKSC] [Bowling Green] .... WKU
Western Kentucky University, Bowling Green, KY [Library symbol Library of Congress] (LCLS) .... KyBgW
Western Kentucky University, Kentucky Library, Bowling Green, KY [Library symbol Library of Congress] (LCLS) .... KyBgW-K
Western Kenya Aircharters Co. Ltd. [ICAO designator] (FAAC) .... WKC
Western King's Memorial Hospital, Berwick, Nova Scotia [Library symbol National Library of Canada] (NLC) .... NSBWK
Western Laboratory, National Research Council [Laboratoire de l'Ouest, Conseil National de Recherches] Vancouver, British Columbia [Library symbol National Library of Canada] (NLC) .... BVAN
Western Labour Arbitration Cases [A publication] (DLA) .... WLAC
Western Lacrosse Association [Canada] .... WLA
Western Larch [Utility pole] [Telecommunications] (TEL) .... WL
Western Launch Site [Military] .... WLS
Western Law Gazette [Cincinnati, OH] [A publication] (DLA) .... West L Gaz
Western Law Monthly [Ohio] [A publication] (DLA) .... West L Mo
Western Law Monthly [Ohio] [A publication] (DLA) .... West L Month
Western Law Monthly [Ohio] [A publication] (DLA) .... West Law M
Western Law Monthly [Ohio] [A publication] (DLA) .... West Law Month
Western Law Monthly [Ohio] [A publication] (DLA) .... West LM
Western Law Monthly [Cleveland, OH] [A publication] (DLA) .... WLM
Western Law Monthly (Reprint) [Ohio] [A publication] (DLA) .... Law Mo
Western Law Monthly (Reprint) [Ohio] [A publication] (DLA) .... West Law Mo
Western Law Reporter [Canada] [A publication] (DLA) .... West LR
Western Law Reporter [Canada] [A publication] (DLA) .... West LR (Can)
Western Law Reporter [Canada] [A publication] (DLA) .... WLR
Western Law Review [A publication] (DLA) .... West L Rev
Western Law Review [Canada] [A publication] (DLA) .... West Law Rev
Western Law Review [Canada] [A publication] (DLA) .... Western L Rev
Western Law Times [Canada] [A publication] (DLA) .... West LT
Western Law Times [1890-95] [A publication] (DLA) .... WLT
Western League [Baseball] .... WL
Western Legal Observer [A publication] (DLA) .... West Leg Obs
Western Legal Observer [A publication] (DLA) .... West Legal Obser
Western Legal Publications [Database] [Western Legal Publications Ltd.] [Information service or system] (CRD) .... WLP
Western Library Network [Formerly, Washington Library Network] [Olympia, WA] [Database] [Library of Congress] .... WLN
Western Literature Association (EA) .... WLA
Western Lumber Manufacturers [Later, Western Timber Association] [An association] (EA) .... WLM
Western Management Science Institute [University of California] (KSC) .... WMSI
Western Manitoba Regional Library, Brandon, Manitoba [Library symbol National Library of Canada] (NLC) .... MBW
Western Manitoba Regional Library, Brandon, MB, Canada [Library symbol Library of Congress] (LCLS) .... CaMBW
Western Manufacturing Technology Show and Conference (ITD) .... WMTS
Western Maquiladora Trade Association (CROSS) .... WMTA
Western Maryland College (GAGS) .... West Md C
Western Maryland College [Westminster] .... WMC
Western Maryland College, Westminster, MD [Library symbol Library of Congress] (LCLS) .... MdWemC
Western Maryland Public Libraries Regional Resource Center [Library network] .... WMPL
Western Massachusetts Electric Co. .... WMECO
Western Massachusetts Regional Library System, Springfield, MA [OCLC symbol] (OCLC) .... WRS
Western Massachusetts Regional Public Library System, Springfield, MA [Library symbol Library of Congress] (LCLS) .... MSW
Western Material Management, Machinery, and Welding Show [Canada] (ITD) .... WMM/MWS
Western Mediterranean Area [NATO] (NATG) .... MEDOC
Western Memorial Hospital, Corner Brook, Newfoundland [Library symbol National Library of Canada] (NLC) .... NFCBW
Western Memorial Hospital, Corner Brook, NF, Canada [Library symbol Library of Congress] (LCLS) .... CaNfCBrW
Western Mental Health Institute, Boliver, TN [Library symbol Library of Congress] (LCLS) .... TBolMH
Western Metal and Tool Exposition and Conference [American Society for Metals] (TSPED) .... WESTEC
Western Metropolitan Regional Aboriginal Land Council [Sydney, New South Wales, Australia] .... WMRALC
Western Michigan Genealogical Society, Grand Rapids, MI [Library symbol Library of Congress] (LCLS) .... MiGrW
Western Michigan University (GAGS) .... West Mich U
Western Michigan University [Kalamazoo] .... WMU
Western Michigan University, Kalamazoo, MI [OCLC symbol] (OCLC) .... EXW
Western Michigan University, Kalamazoo, MI [Library symbol Library of Congress] (LCLS) .... MiKW
Western Michigan University, School of Librarianship, Kalamazoo, MI [OCLC symbol] (OCLC) .... EXL
Western Micro Techn'gy [NASDAQ symbol] (TTSB) .... WSTM
Western Micro Technology, Inc. [Associated Press] (SAG) .... WMicTc

Western Micro Technology, Inc. [NASDAQ symbol] (NQ) .... WSTM
Western Microfilm Ltd., Edmonton, AB, Canada [Library symbol Library of Congress] (LCLS) .... WeM
Western Microwave, Inc. (IAA) .... WM
Western Microwave, Inc. [NASDAQ symbol] (NQ) .... WMIC
Western Microwave, Inc. [Associated Press] (SAG) .... WMicr
Western Military Electronics Center (KSC) .... WMEC
Western Mining Corp. [Commercial] (EERA) .... WMC
Western Mining Corp. [Associated Press] (SAG) .... WstMn
Western Mining Corp. Holdings ADS [NYSE symbol] (SPSG) .... WMC
Western Missouri Mental Health Center, Kansas City, MO [Library symbol Library of Congress] (LCLS) .... MoKW
Western Montana Clinic, Missoula, MT [Library symbol Library of Congress] (LCLS) .... MtMisW
Western Montana College, Dillon, MT [Library symbol Library of Congress] (LCLS) .... MtDiW
Western Motor Tariff Bureau .... WMTB
Western Motor Tariff Bureau, Los Angeles CA [STAC] .... WMT
Western National [NYSE symbol] (TTSB) .... WNH
Western National Corp. [NYSE symbol] (SAG) .... WNH
Western National Corp. [Associated Press] (SAG) .... WstnNat
Western Natural Gas Co., Houston, TX [Library symbol Library of Congress] (LCLS) .... TxHWN
Western Naval Task Force [Navy] .... WNTF
Western New England College (GAGS) .... West NE C
Western New England College [Springfield, MA] .... WNEC
Western New England College, Springfield, MA [OCLC symbol] (OCLC) .... WNE
Western New Mexico University (GAGS) .... West N Mex U
Western New Mexico University, Silver City, NM [OCLC symbol] (OCLC) .... IQW
Western New Mexico University, Silver City, NM [Library symbol Library of Congress] (LCLS) .... NmScW
Western New York Health Science Librarians [Library network] .... WNYHSL
Western New York Library Resources Council [Buffalo, NY] [Library network] .... WNYLRC
Western New York Library Resources Council, Buffalo, NY [OCLC symbol] (OCLC) .... VZX
Western New York Nuclear Research Center Reactor (NRCH) .... WNYNRC
Western Newspaper Union .... WNU
Western Nigeria Law Reports [A publication] (DLA) .... WNLR
Western Nigeria Legal Notice [A publication] (DLA) .... WNLN
Western NORAD Region .... WNR
Western Ocean Meeting Point .... WESTOMP
Western Ocean Meeting Point (DMA) .... WOMP
Western Offshore Drilling & Exploration Co. .... WODECO
Western Ohio Film Circuit [Library network] .... WOFC
Western Ohio Financial Corp. [NASDAQ symbol] (SAG) .... WOFC
Western Ohio Financial Corp. [Associated Press] (SAG) .... WstnOhF
Western Ohio Finl [NASDAQ symbol] (TTSB) .... WOFC
Western Ohio Railroad Co. [AAR code] .... WTOH
Western Ohio Regional Library Development System [Library network] .... WORLDS
Western Oil and Gas Association (EA) .... WOGA
Western Oil and Gas Association, Los Angeles, CA [Library symbol Library of Congress] (LCLS) .... CLWestO
Western Oklahoma Herbarium [Southwest Oklahoma State University] .... WOH
Western Oklahoma State College .... WOSC
Western Oklahoma State College, Library, Altus, OK [OCLC symbol] (OCLC) .... OUW
Western Operation .... WO
Western Operations Office [Later, WSO] [NASA] .... WOO
Western Oregon State College (GAGS) .... West Oregon St C
Western Oregon State College .... WOSC
Western Oregon State College, Monmouth, OR [Library symbol] [Library of Congress] (LCLS) .... OrMonW
Western Pacific [Military] (CINC) .... WESTPAC
Western Pacific Airlines [NASDAQ symbol] (TTSB) .... WPAC
Western Pacific Airlines, Inc. [FAA designator] (FAAC) .... KMR
Western Pacific Airlines, Inc. [Associated Press] (SAG) .... WestPac
Western Pacific Airlines, Inc. [NASDAQ symbol] (SAG) .... WPAC
Western Pacific Airservice [Solomon Islands] [ICAO designator] (FAAC) .... WPA
Western Pacific Base Command [Navy] .... WESTPACBACOM
Western Pacific Base Command [Marianas] [World War II] .... WPBC
Western Pacific Energy [Vancouver Stock Exchange symbol] .... WPE
Western Pacific Fisheries Consultative Committee [Marine science] (OSRA) .... WPECC
Western Pacific Fishery Management Council [National Oceanic and Atmospheric Administration] (GFGA) .... WPFMC
Western Pacific North [Navy] (CINC) .... WESTPACNORTH
Western Pacific Orthopaedic Association (EA) .... WPOA
[The] Western Pacific Railroad Co. [AAR code] .... WP
Western Pacific Railroad Co. (MHDW) .... WRS
Western Pacific Training Program for Midshipmen [Navy] (DNAB) .... WESTPACTRAMID
Western Pacific Warm Pod [Oceanography] .... WPWP
Western Pacific Warm Pool [Oceanography] .... WPWP
Western Packaging Exposition (TSPED) .... WEST PACK
Western Pennsylvania Advanced Technology Center [Research center] (RCD) .... WPATC
Western Pennsylvania Christian Broadcasting Co. [A cable TV station] .... WPCB
Western Pennsylvania Horological Institute .... WPHI
Western Pennsylvania School for the Deaf, Pittsburgh, PA [OCLC symbol] (OCLC) .... PIO
Western Personality Inventory [Psychology] .... WPI
Western Personnel Institute (AEBS) .... WPI

Western Personnel Institute, Pasadena, CA [*Library symbol Library of Congress*] (LCLS) .... CPW
Western Personnel Tests [*General intelligence test*] .... WPT
Western Piedmont Community College, Morganton, NC [*Library symbol Library of Congress*] (LCLS) .... NcMoW
Western Pine [*Utility pole*] [*Telecommunications*] (TEL) .... WP
Western Pine Association [*Later, WWPA*] (EA) .... WPA
Western Pistachio Association (EA) .... WPA
Western Plains Library System [*Library network*] .... WPLS
Western Plains Library System, Clinton, OK [*Library symbol Library of Congress*] (LCLS) .... OkClW
Western Plains Library System, Clinton, OK [*OCLC symbol*] (OCLC) .... OWE
Western Plains Zoo [*Dubbo, New South Wales, Australia*] .... WPZ
Western Plastics Exposition [*HBJ Expositions and Conferences*] (TSPED) .... WPE
Western Plateau [*NWS*] (FAAC) .... WPLTO
Western Power & Equip [*NASDAQ symbol*] (TTSB) .... WPEC
Western Power & Equipment Corp. [*NASDAQ symbol*] (SAG) .... WPEC
Western Power & Equipment Corp. [*Associated Press*] (SAG) .... WstnPw
Western Precipitation Corp., Los Angeles, CA [*Library symbol Library of Congress*] (LCLS) .... CLWP
Western Premium [*Vancouver Stock Exchange symbol*] .... WPM
Western Primary Standard Laboratory .... WPSL
Western Procurement Division [*Marine Corps*] .... WPD
Western Provident Association [*British*] (DI) .... WPA
Western Psychiatric Institute and Clinic [*University of Pittsburgh*] [*Research center*] (RCD) .... WPIC
Western Psychiatric Institute and Clinic, University of Pittsburgh, Pittsburgh, PA [*OCLC symbol*] (OCLC) .... PIP
Western Psychiatric Institute and Clinic, University of Pittsburgh, Pittsburgh, PA [*Library symbol Library of Congress*] (LCLS) .... PPiWP
Western Psychological Association (MCD) .... WPA
Western Publishing Co., Inc., Racine, WI [*Library symbol Library of Congress*] (LCLS) .... WRacWP
Western Publishing Group, Inc. [*New York, NY NASDAQ symbol*] (NQ) .... WPGI
Western Publishing Group, Inc. [*Associated Press*] (SAG) .... WstnPb
Western Rail Road Co. [*AAR code*] .... WRRC
Western Railroad Association (EA) .... WRA
Western Railroad Traffic Association (EA) .... WRTA
Western Railway Employees' Union [*India*] .... WREU
[*The*] **Western Railway of Alabama** .... W of A
[*The*] **Western Railway of Alabama** [*AAR code*] .... WA
Western Range Association (EA) .... WRA
Western Red and Northern White Cedar Association [*Later, WRCA*] (EA) .... WRNWCA
Western Red Cedar Association (EA) .... WRCA
Western Red Cedar Lumber Association (EA) .... WRCLA
Western Refrigerator Line Co. [*AAR code*] .... WRX
Western Region, Engineering and Architecture Library, Transport Canada [*Region de l'Ouest, Bibliotheque d'Ingenierie et d'Architecture, Transports Canada*], Edmonton, Alberta [*Library symbol National Library of Canada*] (NLC) .... AEMTC
Western Region Ethnic Disability Service [*Victoria, Australia*] .... WREDS
Western Region Library, Public Works Canada [*Bibliotheque de la Region de l'Ouest, Travaux Publics Canada*] **Edmonton, Alberta** [*Library symbol National Library of Canada*] (NLC) .... AEPWW
Western Region of Nigeria Law Reports [*A publication*] (DLA) .... WRNLR
Western Regional Consortium, Librarians' Networking Committee [*Library network*] .... WRCCHE
Western Regional Information Service Center [*University of California*] [*Information service or system Defunct*] (IID) .... WRISC
Western Regional Library, Transport Canada [*Bibliotheque Regionale de l'Ouest, Transports Canada*], North Vancouver, British Columbia [*Library symbol National Library of Canada*] (NLC) .... BNVTW
Western Regional Office .... WRO
Western Regional Office, Parks Canada [*Bureau Regional de l'Quest, Parcs Canada*] **Calgary, Alberta** [*Library symbol National Library of Canada*] (NLC) .... ACIA
Western Regional Public Library System [*Library network*] .... WRPLS
Western Regional Research Center [*Albany, CA*] [*Department of Agriculture*] (GRD) .... WRRC
Western Regional Resource Center [*University of Oregon*] [*Research center*] (RCD) .... WRRC
Western Reinforcing Steel Fabricators Association .... WRSFA
Western Reporter [*A publication*] (DLA) .... West R
Western Reporter [*A publication*] (DLA) .... West Rep
Western Res Cap 7.875%'QUIPS' [*NYSE symbol*] (TTSB) .... WRPrA
Western Research and Development Ltd., Calgary, AB, Canada [*Library symbol Library of Congress*] (LCLS) .... CaACWRD
Western Research & Development Ltd., Calgary, Alberta [*Library symbol National Library of Canada*] (NLC) .... ACWRD
Western Research Application Center [*University of Southern California*] .... WESRAC
Western Research Institute [*Laramie, WY*] [*Department of Energy*] (GRD) .... WRI
Western Reserve College .... West Res Coll
Western Reserve Historical Society, Cleveland, OH [*Library symbol Library of Congress*] (LCLS) .... OClWHi
Western Reserve Historical Society, Frederick C. Crawford Auto-Aviation Museum, Cleveland, OH [*Library symbol Library of Congress*] (LCLS) .... OClWHi-AM
Western Reserve Law Journal [*A publication*] (DLA) .... Wes Res Law Jo
Western Reserve Law Journal [*Ohio*] [*A publication*] (DLA) .... Wes Res Law Jrl
Western Reserve Law Notes [*A publication*] (DLA) .... Western Reserve LN
Western Reserve Law Review [*A publication*] (ILCA) .... WRL
Western Reserve University [*Later, Case Western Reserve University*] .... WRU
Western Reserve University Relay Searching Selector (SAA) .... WRUSS
Western Resources [*NYSE symbol*] (TTSB) .... WR
Western Resources [*Associated Press*] (SAG) .... WstnRs
Western Resources Capital I [*NYSE symbol*] (SAG) .... WR
Western Resources Capital I [*Associated Press*] (SAG) .... WtnRsC
Western Resources Capital II [*NYSE symbol*] (SAG) .... WR
Western Resources Capital II [*Associated Press*] (SAG) .... WstRes
Western Resources, Inc. [*Formerly, Kansas Power & Light Co.*] [*NYSE symbol*] (SPSG) .... WR
Western Resources, Inc. [*Associated Press*] (SAG) .... WstnRes
Western Resources Technology [*Vancouver Stock Exchange symbol*] .... WSN
Western Rift Zone [*Geology*] .... WRZ
Western River Guides Association (EA) .... WRGA
Western Rural Development Center [*Oregon State University*] [*Research center*] (RCD) .... WRDC
Western Sahara [*ANSI two-letter standard code*] (CNC) .... EH
Western Sahara [*ANSI three-letter standard code*] (CNC) .... ESH
Western Sahara Campaign for Human Rights and Humanitarian Relief (EA) .... WSC
Western Samoa [*MARC geographic area code Library of Congress*] (LCCP) .... pows--
Western Samoa (WDAA) .... W SAM
Western Samoa (VRA) .... W Sam
Western Samoa [*MARC country of publication code Library of Congress*] (LCCP) .... ws
Western Samoa [*ANSI two-letter standard code*] (CNC) .... WS
Western Samoa [*ANSI three-letter standard code*] (CNC) .... WSM
Western Satellite Research Network (PDAA) .... WSRN
Western School Law Review [*A publication*] (DLA) .... West School L Rev
Western Sea Frontier [*Navy*] .... WESSEAFRON
Western Sea Frontier [*Navy*] (MUGU) .... WESTSEAFRON
Western Sea Frontier [*Navy*] .... WSF
Western Secondary Standards Laboratory .... WSSL
Western Shelf Water [*Oceanography*] .... WSW
Western Simulation Council .... WSC
Western Single Side Band Association (EA) .... WSSBA
Western Slavonic Association [*Later, WSA Fraternal Life*] (EA) .... WSA
Western Snow Conference (EA) .... WSC
Western Social Science Association (EA) .... WSSA
Western Society of Business Publications [*Defunct*] (EA) .... WSBP
Western Society of Engineers .... WSE
Western Society of Engineers, Chicago, IL [*Library symbol Library of Congress*] (LCLS) .... ICW
Western Society of Gear Engineers (MCD) .... WSGE
Western Society of Malacologists (EA) .... WSM
Western Society of Naturalists (EA) .... WSN
Western Somali Liberation Front .... WSLF
Western Space and Missile Center [*Vandenberg Air Force Base, CA*] [*Air Force*] .... WSMC
Western Staff Services [*NASDAQ symbol*] (TTSB) .... WSTF
Western Star Trucks Hldg [*AMEX symbol*] (TTSB) .... WSH
Western Star Trucks Holdings Ltd. [*AMEX symbol*] (SAG) .... WSH
Western Star Trucks Holdings Ltd. [*Associated Press*] (SAG) .... WstStr
Western State College of Colorado [*Gunnison*] .... WSCC
Western State College of Colorado, Gunnison, CO [*Library symbol Library of Congress*] (LCLS) .... CoGuW
Western State College of Colorado, Gunnison, CO [*OCLC symbol*] (OCLC) .... COW
Western State Hospital, Resident Library, Tacoma, WA [*Library symbol Library of Congress*] (LCLS) .... WaTWH-R
Western State Hospital, Staff Library, Fort Steilacoom, WA [*Library symbol Library of Congress*] (LCLS) .... WaFsWS
Western State Hospital, Staff Library, Tacoma, WA [*Library symbol Library of Congress*] (LCLS) .... WaTWH
Western States Advertising Agencies Association (EA) .... WSAAA
Western States Angus Association (EA) .... WSAA
Western States Chiropractic College, Portland, OR [*Library symbol Library of Congress*] (LCLS) .... OrPWS
Western States Meat Association (EA) .... WSMA
Western States Meat Association (EA) .... WSMPA
Western States Movers Conference .... WSMC
Western States Small School Project .... WSSSP
Western States Weights and Measures Association .... WSWMA
Western Suburbs Development Disability Service [*Sydney, New South Wales, Australia*] .... WSDDS
Western Suburbs Greens [*Political party Australia*] .... WSG
Western Suburbs Regional Chamber of Commerce [*Sydney, New South Wales, Australia*] .... WSRCC
Western Support Office [*Formerly, WOO*] [*NASA*] .... WSO
Western Surfing Association (EA) .... WSA
Western Surgical Association (EA) .... WSA
Western Sydney Area Assistance Scheme [*Australia*] .... WSAAS
Western Sydney Information Technology Centre [*Australia*] .... WSITC
Western Sydney Planning and Development Committee [*Australia*] .... WSPDC
Western Systems Coordinating Council [*Regional power council*] .... WSCC
Western Tank Truck Carriers' Conference Inc., Denver CO [*STAC*] .... WTT
Western Tariff Service Inc., Oakland CA [*STAC*] .... WTS
Western Task Force [*Navy*] .... WTF
Western Tasmanian Wilderness National Parks World Heritage Area (EERA) .... TWHA
Western Teacher [*A publication*] .... W Teach
Western Technical Net [*Air Force*] .... WTN
Western Technical Training Command [*AAFWTTC*] .... WTTC
Western Telecommunications Consulting Co. [*Los Angeles, CA*] [*Telecommunications*] (TSSD) .... WTC

Western Telecommunications, Inc. [*Englewood, CO*] [*Telecommunications*] .... WTCI
Western Telematic, Inc. .... WTI
Western Test Range [*Formerly, Pacific Missile Range*] [*Air Force*] .... WTR
Western Test Range Manual [*Air Force*] (MCD) .... WTRM
Western Test Range Office of Safety [*Air Force*] (MCD) .... WTOS
Western Theological Seminary, Holland, MI [*OCLC symbol*] (OCLC) .... EXS
Western Theological Seminary, Holland, MI [*Library symbol Library of Congress*] (LCLS) .... MiHolW
Western Timber Association (EA) .... WTA
Western Tithe Cases [*England*] [*A publication*] (DLA) .... We
Western Transmedia [*NASDAQ symbol*] (TTSB) .... WTSM
Western Transmedia, Inc. [*Associated Press*] (SAG) .... WstTr
Western Transmedia, Inc. [*Associated Press*] (SAG) .... WstTrns
Western Transmedia, Inc. [*NASDAQ symbol*] (SAG) .... WTSM
Western Transmedia Wrrt [*NASDAQ symbol*] (TTSB) .... WTSMW
Western Transport Air Force .... WESTAF
Western Transportation Co. [*Later, WTCO*] [*AAR code*] .... WEST
Western Transportation Co. [*AAR code*] .... WTCO
Western Trinity Resource [*Vancouver Stock Exchange symbol*] .... WTZ
Western Tropical Atlantic Experiment (USDC) .... WESTRAX
Western Tropical Atlantic Experiment [*Marine science*] (OSRA) .... WESTRAX
Western Trunk Line Committee .... WTLC
Western Trunk Line Committee, Chicago IL [*STAC*] .... WTL
Western Underwriters Association [*Later, ISO*] .... WUA
Western Union (NITA) .... WU
Western Union Computer Utilities (IAA) .... WUCU
Western Union Corp. .... WUC
Western Union Electronic Mail, Inc. [*McLean, VA*] [*Telecommunications*] (TSSD) .... WUEMI
Western Union Exchange [*Teleprinter*] .... WUX
Western Union International [*Division of WUI, Inc.*] .... WUI
Western Union Long Distance Service [*Western Union Telegraph Co.*] [*Upper Saddle River, NJ*] [*Telecommunications*] (TSSD) .... WULDS
Western Union Space Communications, Inc. (MCD) .... WUSCI
Western Union Telegraph Co. (TSSD) .... WU
Western Union Telegraph Co. .... WUTC
Western Union Telegraph Co. .... WUTELCO
Western Union VideoConferencing, Inc. [*Defunct*] (TSSD) .... WUVCI
Western United Front [*Fiji*] [*Political party*] (PPW) .... WUF
Western Utilization Research Branch (MCD) .... WURB
Western Veterinary Conference (EA) .... WVC
Western Virginia Law Review [*A publication*] (DLA) .... West Va L Rev
Western Visayan Task Force [*World War II*] .... WVTF
Western Warner Oils [*Vancouver Stock Exchange symbol*] .... WWR
Western Washington Research and Extension Center [*Washington State University*] [*Research center*] (RCD) .... WWREC
Western Washington State College [*Later, WWU*], Bellingham, WA [*Library symbol Library of Congress*] (LCLS) .... WaBeW
Western Washington State University (GAGS) .... West Wash St U
Western Washington University .... WWU
Western Waste Industries [*Associated Press*] (SAG) .... WnWste
Western Waste Industries [*NYSE symbol*] (SPSG) .... WW
Western Water [*NASDAQ symbol*] (TTSB) .... WWTR
Western Water Co. [*Associated Press*] (SAG) .... WstWatr
Western Water Co. [*NASDAQ symbol*] (SAG) .... WWTR
Western Weekly, New Series [*Canada*] [*A publication*] (DLA) .... West Week NS
Western Weekly Notes [*Canada*] [*A publication*] (DLA) .... West Week N
Western Weekly Notes (Canada) [*A publication*] (DLA) .... West Week (Can)
Western Weekly Notes (Canada) [*A publication*] (DLA) .... West Week N (Can)
Western Weekly Notes (Canada) [*A publication*] (DLA) .... West Wkly
Western Weekly Reports [*Canada*] [*A publication*] (DLA) .... West Week Rep
Western Weekly Reports [*Carswell Co. Ltd.*] [*Canada Information service or system*] (CRD) .... WWR
Western Weekly Reports, New Series [*Canada*] [*A publication*] (DLA) .... WWR (NS)
Western Weighing and Inspection Bureau .... WW & IB
Western Winter Sports Representatives Association (EA) .... WWSRA
Western Wireless Corp. [*Associated Press*] (SAG) .... WstWire
Western Wireless Corp. [*NASDAQ symbol*] (SAG) .... WWCA
Western Wireless'A' [*NASDAQ symbol*] (TTSB) .... WWCA
Western Wisconsin Communications Cooperative [*Independence, WI*] [*Telecommunications*] (TSSD) .... WWCC
Western Wood Moulding and Millwork Producers [*Later, WMMPA*] (EA) .... WWMMP
Western Wood Moulding Producers [*Later, WMMPA*] (EA) .... WWMP
Western Wood Products Association [*Australia*] .... WWPA
Western Wooden Box Association (EA) .... WWBA
Western World Avon Club [*Defunct*] (EA) .... WWAC
Western World Haiku Society [*Defunct*] (EA) .... WWHS
Western World Pet Supply Association (EA) .... WWPSA
Western Writers of America (EA) .... WWA
Western Wyoming College, Rock Springs, WY [*Library symbol Library of Congress*] (LCLS) .... WyRsW
Western Yiddish (BJA) .... WY
Western Young Buddhist League (EA) .... WYBL
Western Youth Orchestra [*Australia*] .... WYO
Westernbank Puerto Rico [*NASDAQ symbol*] (SAG) .... WBPR
Westernbank Puerto Rico [*Associated Press*] (SAG) .... WstbPR
Westerners International (EA) .... WI
Westernized Oriental Gentleman [*Singapore term for native following Western fashions*] [*Other translations include "Wily Oriental Gentleman" and "Wonderful Oriental Gentleman"*] .... WOG
Westernport, MD [*FM radio station call letters*] .... WWPN
Western's Commentaries on the Laws of England [*A publication*] (DLA) .... West Com
Western's London Tithe Cases [*England*] [*A publication*] (DLA) .... West
Western's London Tithe Cases [*1535-1822*] [*A publication*] (DLA) .... West Ti Cas
Western's London Tithe Cases [*England*] [*A publication*] (DLA) .... West Tithe Cas
Westerra Resources Ltd. [*Vancouver Stock Exchange symbol*] .... WRT
Westerville, OH [*FM radio station call letters*] .... WOBN
Westerville Public Library, Westerville, OH [*Library symbol Library of Congress*] (LCLS) .... OWe
Westerville Public Library, Westerville, OH [*OCLC symbol*] (OCLC) .... OWL
Westeuropaeische Gesellschaft fuer Luftfahrtpsychologie [*Western European Association for Aviation Psychology - WEAAP*] (EA) .... WGL
Westfair Foods Ltd. [*Toronto Stock Exchange symbol*] .... WF
Westfalen Warmblood Association of America (EA) .... WWAA
Westfalische Wilhelms-Universitat Munster, Munster, Germany [*Library symbol Library of Congress*] (LCLS) .... GyMuW
Westfield Athenaeum, Westfield, MA [*Library symbol Library of Congress*] (LCLS) .... MWeA
Westfield, MA [*Location identifier FAA*] (FAAL) .... BAF
Westfield, MA [*Location identifier FAA*] (FAAL) .... SJB
Westfield, MA [*AM radio station call letters*] .... WNNZ
Westfield, MA [*FM radio station call letters*] .... WSKB
Westfield Memorial Hospital, Inc., Westfield, NY [*Library symbol Library of Congress*] (LCLS) .... NWefMH
Westfield Memorial Library, Westfield, NJ [*Library symbol Library of Congress*] (LCLS) .... NjWef
Westfield Minerals Ltd. [*Toronto Stock Exchange symbol Vancouver Stock Exchange symbol*] .... WFD
Westfield State College (GAGS) .... Westfield St C
Westfield State College, Westfield, MA [*Library symbol Library of Congress*] (LCLS) .... MWeT
Westford [*Massachusetts*] [*Seismograph station code, US Geological Survey*] (SEIS) .... WFM
Westfort Petroleums Ltd. [*Toronto Stock Exchange symbol*] .... WET
Westgrowth Petroleums Ltd. [*Toronto Stock Exchange symbol*] .... WGP
Westhampton Beach Junior High School, Westhampton Beach, NY [*Library symbol Library of Congress*] (LCLS) .... NWehbJH
Westhampton Beach, NY [*Location identifier FAA*] (FAAL) .... FOK
Westhampton Free Library, Westhampton Beach, NY [*Library symbol Library of Congress*] (LCLS) .... NWehb
Westhampton, NY [*FM radio station call letters*] (RBYB) .... WLRI-FM
Westhampton, NY [*FM radio station call letters*] .... WMRW
Westhill Resources [*Vancouver Stock Exchange symbol*] .... WHO
Westinghouse [*as in "Group W"*] .... W
Westinghouse Advanced Systems Planning Group .... WASP
Westinghouse Aerospace Electrical Division .... WAED
Westinghouse Air Arm Division .... WAAD
Westinghouse Air Brake [*NYSE symbol*] (TTSB) .... WAB
Westinghouse Air Brake Co. [*NYSE symbol*] (SAG) .... WAB
Westinghouse Air Brake Co. .... WABCO
Westinghouse Air Brake Co. [*Associated Press*] (SAG) .... WestAB
Westinghouse Alphanumeric Display (IAA) .... WAND
Westinghouse Audio Visual Electronics (IAA) .... WAVE
Westinghouse Broadcasting Co. .... WBC
Westinghouse Canada, Inc. [*Toronto Stock Exchange symbol*] .... WXC
Westinghouse Canada Inc., Atomic Tower Division, Port Hope, ON, Canada [*Library symbol Library of Congress*] (LCLS) .... CaOPhWA
Westinghouse Canada, Inc., Burlington, Ontario [*Library symbol National Library of Canada*] (NLC) .... OBWC
Westinghouse Commercial Atomic Power .... WCAP
Westinghouse Commercial Fuel Facility .... WCFF
Westinghouse Corp. .... WESCO
Westinghouse Defense and Space Center, Baltimore, MD [*Library symbol Library of Congress*] (LCLS) .... MdBWe
Westinghouse Defense Center .... WDC
Westinghouse Development Test Requirement Specification (IAA) .... WDTRS
Westinghouse Digital Airborne Computer .... WEDAC
Westinghouse Elec [*NYSE symbol*] (TTSB) .... WX
Westinghouse Electric Company .... WELCO
Westinghouse Electric Corp. .... WEC
Westinghouse Electric Corp. .... WECO
Westinghouse Electric Corp. [*Associated Press*] (SAG) .... WstgEl
Westinghouse Electric Corp. [*Wall Street slang name: "Wex"*] [*NYSE symbol*] (SPSG) .... WX
Westinghouse Electric Corp., East Pittsburgh, PA [*Library symbol Library of Congress*] (LCLS) .... PEpW
Westinghouse Electric Corp., Engineering Library, Horseheads, NY [*Library symbol Library of Congress*] (LCLS) .... NHorW
Westinghouse Electric Corp., Lamp Division, Bloomfield, NJ [*Library symbol Library of Congress*] (LCLS) .... NjBlW
Westinghouse Electric Corp., Nuclear Center Library, Pittsburgh, PA [*Library symbol Library of Congress*] (LCLS) .... PPiW-N
Westinghouse Electric Corp., Research and Development Center, Pittsburgh, PA [*Library symbol Library of Congress*] (LCLS) .... PPiW
Westinghouse Electric Corp., Waltz Mill Site Library, Madison, PA [*Library symbol Library of Congress*] (LCLS) .... PMadW
Westinghouse Electric International Co. (IAA) .... WEICO
Westinghouse Electronic Tubeless .... WET
Westinghouse Electronic Tubeless Analog Computer .... WETAC
Westinghouse Engineers Association National [*Defunct*] (EA) .... WEA-N
Westinghouse Hanford Co. (NRCH) .... WHC
Westinghouse Industrial Atomic Power (MCD) .... WIAP
Westinghouse Information Systems Laboratory (IAA) .... WISL
Westinghouse Integrated Compiling System (NITA) .... WICS
Westinghouse Microscan System (IAA) .... WMSS

Westinghouse Optimized Fuel Assembly [*Nuclear energy*] (NRCH) .... WOFA
Westinghouse Overall RADAR Tester and Calibrator .... WORTAC
Westinghouse Research and Development Center (MCD) .... WRDC
Westinghouse Research Laboratories (KSC) .... WRL
Westinghouse Resolver/Quantizer (IEEE) .... WRQ
Westinghouse Test Reactor .... WTR
Westinghouse Uninterruptible Power System (IAA) .... WUPS
Westinghouse-Astronuclear Laboratories .... W-AL
Westinghouse-Astronuclear Laboratories .... WANL
Westkuestenflug [*ICAO designator*] (AD) .... WK
Westlake Industry [*Vancouver Stock Exchange symbol*] .... WLK
Westlake's Conflict of Laws [*A publication*] (DLA) .... Westl Confl
Westlake's Private International Law [*7th ed.*] [*1925*] [*A publication*] (DLA) .... West Pr Int Law
Westlake's Private International Law [*A publication*] (DLA) .... Westl Priv Int Law
Westlake's Private International Law [*A publication*] (DLA) .... Westlake Int Private Law
Westland Helicopters Ltd. [*British ICAO designator*] (FAAC) .... WHE
Westland Helicopters Ltd. [*British*] (IRUK) .... WHL
Westland Helicopters Ltd. [*British ICAO aircraft manufacturer identifier*] (ICAO) .... WL
Westland New Post [*Terrorist organization*] [*Belgium*] (EY) .... WNP
Westley Mines Ltd. [*Toronto Stock Exchange symbol Vancouver Stock Exchange symbol*] .... WTY
Westlock, AB [*AM radio station call letters*] .... CFOK
Westlock Public Library, Alberta [*Library symbol National Library of Canada*] (NLC) .... AWES
Westmar College, Le Mars, IA [*Library symbol Library of Congress*] (LCLS) .... IaLemW
Westmar College, Le Mars, IA [*OCLC symbol*] (OCLC) .... IWW
West-Mar Resources Ltd. [*Vancouver Stock Exchange symbol*] .... WSM
Westmark Group Hldgs [*NASDAQ symbol*] (TTSB) .... WGHI
Westmark Group Holdings, Inc. [*Associated Press*] (SAG) .... Westmark
Westmark Group Holdings, Inc. [*Associated Press*] (SAG) .... Westmk
Westmark Group Holdings, Inc. [*NASDAQ symbol*] (SAG) .... WGHI
Westmeath [*County in Ireland*] (WGA) .... Westm
Westmeath [*County in Ireland*] (ROG) .... WMTH
Westmills Carpets Ltd. [*Toronto Stock Exchange symbol*] .... WES
Westmin Resources Ltd. [*Toronto Stock Exchange symbol Vancouver Stock Exchange symbol*] .... WMI
Westminister Theological Seminary, Philadelphia, PA [*OCLC symbol*] (OCLC) .... WTS
Westminster [*Record label*] .... West
Westminster [*London*] .... WESTM
Westminster [*England*] .... WMINST
Westminster Abbey [*London*] .... WA
Westminster Aquarium [*British music hall popular in the 1870s-80s*] (DSUE) .... AQ
Westminster Biographies [*A publication*] .... WB
Westminster Centre for Design and Technology [*British*] (AIE) .... WCDT
Westminster Choir College [*Princeton, NJ*] .... WCC
Westminster College [*London, England*] .... WC
Westminster College (GAGS) .... Westminster C
Westminster College, Fulton, MO [*Library symbol Library of Congress*] (LCLS) .... MoFuWC
Westminster College, Fulton, MO [*OCLC symbol*] (OCLC) .... MOW
Westminster College, New Wilmington, PA [*Library symbol Library of Congress*] (LCLS) .... PNwC
Westminster College, New Wilmington, PA [*OCLC symbol*] (OCLC) .... WFN
Westminster College, Salt Lake City, UT [*Library symbol Library of Congress*] (LCLS) .... USIW
Westminster College, Salt Lake City, UT [*OCLC symbol*] (OCLC) .... UUW
Westminster College, Tehuacana, TX [*Library symbol Library of Congress*] (LCLS) .... TxTehW
Westminster Commentaries [*Oxford*] [*A publication*] (BJA) .... WC
Westminster Dictionary of the Bible [*A publication*] (BJA) .... WDB
Westminster Dragoons [*British military*] (DMA) .... W Dgns
Westminster Dragoons [*British military*] (DMA) .... WD
Westminster Hall Chronicle and Legal Examiner [*1835-36*] [*A publication*] (DLA) .... Westm Hall Chron
Westminster Hall Chronicle and Legal Examiner [*1835-36*] [*A publication*] (DLA) .... WH Chron
Westminster Historical Atlas to the Bible [*A publication*] (BJA) .... WHAB
Westminster Kennel Club (EA) .... WKC
Westminster Library [*A publication*] .... WL
Westminster, MD [*Location identifier FAA*] (FAAL) .... EMI
Westminster, MD [*FM radio station call letters*] .... WGRX
Westminster, MD [*AM radio station call letters*] .... WTTR
Westminster Public Library, Westminster, CO [*Library symbol Library of Congress*] (LCLS) .... CoWm
Westminster School, Carlyle Fraser Library, Atlanta, GA [*Library symbol*] [*Library of Congress*] (LCLS) .... GAWS
Westminster Theological Seminary, Philadelphia, PA [*Library symbol Library of Congress*] (LCLS) .... PPWe
Westminster Version of the Bible [*A publication*] (BJA) .... WV
Westmont College, Santa Barbara, CA [*Library symbol*] [*Library of Congress*] (LCLS) .... CStbW
Westmont College, Santa Barbara, CA [*OCLC symbol*] (OCLC) .... CWS
Westmont Public Library, Westmont, IL [*Library symbol Library of Congress*] (LCLS) .... IWem
Westmoreland Coal [*NYSE symbol*] (TTSB) .... WCX
Westmoreland Coal [*Associated Press*] (SAG) .... WstmrC
Westmoreland Coal Co. [*NYSE symbol*] (SPSG) .... WCX
Westmoreland Coal Co. [*Associated Press*] (SAG) .... WmorC
Westmoreland Coal Co. [*Associated Press*] (SAG) .... WstmorC
Westmoreland County Community College, Youngwood, PA [*Library symbol Library of Congress*] (LCLS) .... PYoW
Westmoreland County Community College, Youngwood, PA [*OCLC symbol*] (OCLC) .... WJY
Westmoreland County Law Journal [*A publication*] (DLA) .... Wes CLJ
Westmoreland County Law Journal [*Pennsylvania*] [*A publication*] (DLA) .... West
Westmoreland County Law Journal [*Pennsylvania*] [*A publication*] (DLA) .... Westm
Westmoreland County Law Journal [*A publication*] (DLA) .... Westm LJ
Westmoreland County Law Journal [*Pennsylvania*] [*A publication*] (DLA) .... Westmore Co LJ (PA)
Westmoreland County Law Journal [*Pennsylvania*] [*A publication*] (DLA) .... Westmoreland
Westmoreland County Law Journal [*Pennsylvania*] [*A publication*] (DLA) .... Westmoreland Co LJ
Westmoreld Coal Cv Dep Ex Pfd [*NYSE symbol*] (TTSB) .... WCXPrA
Westmorland [*County in England*] .... WESTMD
Westmorland and Cumberland Imperial Yeomanry [*British military*] (DMA) .... WCIY
Westmorland and Cumberland Yeomanry [*British military*] (DMA) .... W & C
Westmorland and Cumberland Yeomanry Cavalry [*British military*] (DMA) .... WCYC
Westmount Public Library [*UTLAS symbol*] .... WMQ
Westmount Public Library, Quebec [*Library symbol National Library of Canada*] (NLC) .... QWSMM
Westmount Public Library, Westmount, PQ, Canada [*Library symbol Library of Congress*] (LCLS) .... CaQWsmM
Westmount Resources Ltd. [*Toronto Stock Exchange symbol*] .... WTT
West-Northwest .... WNW
West-Northwestward (FAAC) .... WNWWD
Weston [*Massachusetts*] [*Seismograph station code, US Geological Survey*] (SEIS) .... WES
Weston, Clevedon & Portishead Railway [*British*] .... WCPR
Weston County Public Library, Newcastle, WY [*Library symbol Library of Congress*] (LCLS) .... WyNe
Weston County Public Library, Upton Branch, Upton, WY [*Library symbol Library of Congress*] (LCLS) .... WyUp
Weston [*Roy F.*], **Inc.** [*Associated Press*] (SAG) .... Weston
Weston [*Roy F.*], **Inc.** [*West Chester, PA*] [*NASDAQ symbol*] (NQ) .... WSTN
Weston [*George*] **Ltd.** [*Toronto Stock Exchange symbol Vancouver Stock Exchange symbol*] .... WN
Weston Public Library, Weston, OR [*Library symbol*] [*Library of Congress*] (LCLS) .... OrWe
Weston Research Centre, Toronto, Ontario [*Library symbol National Library of Canada*] (NLC) .... OTWRC
Weston School of Theology, Cambridge, MA [*OCLC symbol*] (OCLC) .... BWE
Weston School of Theology, Cambridge, MA [*Library symbol Library of Congress*] (LCLS) .... MCW
Weston, WV [*Television station call letters*] .... WDTV
Weston, WV [*AM radio station call letters*] .... WHAW
Weston, WV [*FM radio station call letters*] .... WSSN
Weston(Roy F)'A' [*NASDAQ symbol*] (TTSB) .... WSTNA
Weston's Reports [*11-14 Vermont*] [*A publication*] (DLA) .... West
Weston's Reports [*11-14 Vermont*] [*A publication*] (DLA) .... Weston
Weston-Super-Mare [*British ICAO location identifier*] (ICLI) .... EGFI
Westover, WV [*FM radio station call letters*] .... WMQC
Westpac Banking ADS [*NYSE symbol*] (SPSG) .... WBK
Westpac Banking Corp. [*Australia Commercial firm*] .... WBC
Westpac Banking Corp. [*Associated Press*] (SAG) .... Wstpc
WESTPAC [*Western Pacific*] **Transportation Office** (CINC) .... WTO
Westpoint Stevens [*NASDAQ symbol*] (SAG) .... WPSN
Westpoint Stevens Co. [*Associated Press*] (SAG) .... WstptStv
Westport [*New Zealand*] [*ICAO location identifier*] (ICLI) .... NZWS
Westport [*New Zealand*] [*Airport symbol*] (OAG) .... WSZ
Westport Bancorp [*NASDAQ symbol*] (TTSB) .... WBAT
Westport Bancorp, Inc. [*Westport, CT*] [*NASDAQ symbol*] (NQ) .... WBAT
Westport Bancorp, Inc. [*Associated Press*] (SAG) .... WstpBc
Westport, CT [*FM radio station call letters*] .... WEBE
Westport, CT [*AM radio station call letters*] .... WMMM
Westport, CT [*FM radio station call letters*] .... WWPT
Westport Free Public Library, Westport, MA [*Library symbol*] [*Library of Congress*] (LCLS) .... MWpP
Westport, NY [*FM radio station call letters*] .... WADQ
Westport, NY [*FM radio station call letters*] (RBYB) .... WMEX-FM
Westport Public Library, Westport, CT [*Library symbol Library of Congress*] (LCLS) .... CtWep
Westport Public Library, Westport, CT [*OCLC symbol*] (OCLC) .... WES
Westport Research Group [*Information service or system*] (IID) .... WRG
Westport-North Crosby Public Library, Westport, ON, Canada [*Library symbol*] [*Library of Congress*] (LCLS) .... CaOWENC
Westport-North Crosby Public Library, Westport, Ontario [*Library symbol National Library of Canada*] (NLC) .... OWENC
Westra Preschool Assessment Questionnaire .... WPAQ
Westralian Forest Industries [*Australia Commercial firm*] .... WFI
Westray [*Scotland*] [*Airport symbol*] (OAG) .... WRY
Westrex Development Corp. [*Vancouver Stock Exchange symbol*] .... WXD
West's Annotated California Codes [*A publication*] (DLA) .... Ann Cal Codes
West's Annotated California Codes [*A publication*] (DLA) .... Cal (subject) Code (West)
West's Automatic Law Terminal .... WALT
West's Bankruptcy Reporter [*A publication*] (DLA) .... BR
West's Chancery Reports Tempore Hardwicke [*A publication*] (DLA) .... Cas T H
West's Chancery Reports Tempore Hardwicke [*England*] [*A publication*] (DLA) .... Cas T Hardw
West's English Chancery Cases [*25 English Reprint*] [*A publication*] (DLA) .... West Ch

West's English Chancery Cases [*25 English Reprint*] [*A publication*] (DLA) .... West Ch (Eng)
West's English Chancery Cases [*25 English Reprint*] [*A publication*] (DLA) .... West Chy
West's English Chancery Reports [*A publication*] (DLA) .... We
West's English Chancery Reports [*A publication*] (DLA) .... West
West's English Chancery Reports Tempore Hardwicke [*1736-39*] [*A publication*] (DLA) .... W Rep
West's English Chancery Reports Tempore Hardwicke [*1736-39*] [*A publication*] (DLA) .... West T H
West's English Chancery Reports Tempore Hardwicke [*1736-39*] [*A publication*] (DLA) .... West T Hard
West's English Chancery Reports Tempore Hardwicke [*1736-39*] [*A publication*] (DLA) .... West T Hardw
West's English Chancery Reports Tempore Hardwicke [*1736-39*] [*A publication*] (DLA) .... WR
West's Louisiana Code of Civil Procedure, Annotated [*A publication*] (DLA) .... LA Civ Code Ann (West)
West's Louisiana Code of Civil Procedure, Annotated [*A publication*] (DLA) .... LA Code Civ Pro Ann
West's Louisiana Code of Criminal Procedure, Annotated [*A publication*] (DLA) .... LA Code Crim Pro Ann
West's Louisiana Revised Statutes [*A publication*] (DLA) .... LSARS
West's Louisiana Revised Statutes, Annotated [*A publication*] (DLA) .... LA Rev Stat Ann (West)
West's Minnesota Statutes, Annotated [*A publication*] (DLA) .... Minn Stat Ann (West)
West's Opinions [*City Solicitor of Philadelphia, PA*] [*A publication*] (DLA) .... West's Op
West's Reports, English House of Lords [*A publication*] (DLA) .... We
West's Reports, English House of Lords [*A publication*] (DLA) .... West
West's Reports, English House of Lords [*A publication*] (DLA) .... West HL
West's Symboleographie [*Many eds.*] [*1590-1641*] [*A publication*] (DLA) .... West's Symb
West's Wisconsin Statutes, Annotated [*A publication*] (DLA) .... Wis Stat Ann (West)
Westside .... WSTSD
Westside Community Schools, Omaha, NE [*Library symbol*] [*Library of Congress*] (LCLS) .... NbOW
West-Southeast (ROG) .... WSE
West-Southwest .... WSW
West-Southwestern (FAAC) .... WSWRN
Westvaco Corp. [*NYSE symbol*] (SPSG) .... W
Westvaco Corp. [*Associated Press*] (SAG) .... Westvco
Westview High School, Media Center, Braham, MN [*Library symbol*] [*Library of Congress*] (LCLS) .... MnBhWH
Westview Resources [*Vancouver Stock Exchange symbol*] .... WVW
Westville Public Library, Westville, IL [*Library symbol Library of Congress*] (LCLS) .... IWev
Westwater Industries Ltd. [*Toronto Stock Exchange symbol*] .... WW
Westwood Corp. [*NASDAQ symbol*] (SAG) .... WNMP
Westwood Corp. [*Associated Press*] (SAG) .... Wstwd
Westwood Elementary School, St. Cloud, MN [*Library symbol*] [*Library of Congress*] (LCLS) .... MnStclW
Westwood Financial Corp. [*Associated Press*] (SAG) .... WstwdF
Westwood Financial Corp. [*NASDAQ symbol*] (SAG) .... WWFC
Westwood Free Public Library, Westwood, NJ [*Library symbol Library of Congress*] (LCLS) .... NjWew
Westwood Homestead Financial Corp. [*NASDAQ symbol*] (SAG) .... WEHO
Westwood Homestead Financial Corp. [*Associated Press*] (SAG) .... WstwdH
Westwood, KY [*FM radio station call letters*] .... WLUA
Westwood One [*NASDAQ symbol*] (TTSB) .... WONE
Westwood One, Inc. [*Culver City, CA*] [*NASDAQ symbol*] (NQ) .... WONE
Westwood One, Inc. [*Associated Press*] (SAG) .... WstwOn
Westwood Pharmaceuticals, Inc., Buffalo, NY [*Library symbol Library of Congress*] (LCLS) .... NBuWeP
Westwood Publications, Westwood, NJ [*Library symbol Library of Congress*] (LCLS) .... NjWewW
Westwork (VRA) .... wwk
Wet .... W
Wet Air Without Rain [*Meteorology*] (BARN) .... e
Wet Anode Tantalum .... WAT
Wet Bulb [*Thermometer, of a psychrometer*] [*Meteorology*] .... WB
Wet Bulb Globe Temperature .... WBGT
Wet Bulb Globe Temperature Index (RDA) .... WBGTI
Wet Bulb Globe Thermometer .... WBGT
Wet Bulb Temperature .... WBT
Wet Chemical Oxidation [*Chemistry*] .... WCD
Wet Chemical Oxidation [*Chemistry*] .... WCO
Wet Chemical System [*NFPA pre-fire planning symbol*] (NFPA) .... WC
Wet Crease Recovery Angle [*Textile technology*] .... WCRA
Wet Crude Handling Facilities [*Petroleum engineering*] .... WCHF
Wet Dew .... W
Wet Dog Shakes Syndrome [*Medicine*] (DMAA) .... WDS
Wet Dressing .... WD
Wet Environment Trainer [*Navy*] .... WET
Wet Film [*Radiology*] (DAVI) .... WF
Wet Globe Temperature (PDAA) .... WGT
Wet Ground Mica Association [*Defunct*] (EA) .... WGMA
Wet High Intensity Magnetic Separation (PDAA) .... WHIMS
Wet High-Intensity Magnet [*for mineral processing*] .... WHIM
Wet Lung Syndrome [*Medicine*] (DAVI) .... WLS
Wet Maximum Power Available (SAA) .... WMPA
Wet Metric Ton [*Waste management*] .... WMT
Wet Mock Simulated Launch [*NASA*] (KSC) .... WMSL
Wet Mount (MEDA) .... WM
Wet Oxidation Waste Treatment Technology (DOGT) .... DETOX
Wet Pack [*Medicine*] (AAMN) .... WP
Wet Pack [*Physical therapy*] (DAVI) .... WPk
Wet Peridotite Solidus [*Geology*] .... WPS
Wet Pick Up (IAA) .... WPU
Wet Process (MSA) .... WP
Wet Runway [*NWS*] (FAAC) .... WR
Wet Seal Cl'A' [*NASDAQ symbol*] (TTSB) .... WTSLA
Wet Seal, Inc. [*Associated Press*] (SAG) .... WetSeal
Wet Seal, Inc. [*NASDAQ symbol*] (SAG) .... WTSL
Wet Smoothed (BJA) .... WS
Wet Snow on Runway [*NWS*] (FAAC) .... WSR
Wet Tantalum Slug Capacitor (NASA) .... WTSC
Wet Tropics Community Consultative Committee [*Australia*] .... WTCCC
Wet Tropics Consultative Committee (EERA) .... WTCC
Wet Tropics Ministerial Council [*Australia*] .... WTMC
Wet Tropics Scientific Advisory Committee [*Australia*] .... WTSAC
Wet Tropics Structural Adjustment Package (EERA) .... WTSAP
Wet Weight Basis [*Drying*] (DICI) .... WWB
Wet-Air Oxidation (PDAA) .... WAO
Wetaskiwin, AB [*AM radio station call letters*] .... CKJR
Wetaskiwin City Archives, Alberta [*Library symbol National Library of Canada*] (BIB) .... AWCA
Wetaskiwin Municipal Library, Wetaskiwin, AB, Canada [*Library symbol Library of Congress*] (LCLS) .... CaAW
Wetaskiwin Public Library, Alberta [*Library symbol National Library of Canada*] (NLC) .... AW
Wetboek van Burgerlijke Regtsvordering [*Code of Civil Procedure*] [*Dutch*] (ILCA) .... WBR
Wetboek van Koophandel [*Commercial Code*] [*Dutch*] (ILCA) .... K
Wetboek van Koophandel [*Commercial Code*] [*Dutch*] (ILCA) .... WK
Wet-Bulb Potential Temperature (PDAA) .... WBPT
Wet-Fluorescence Magnetic Particle Technique [*Corrosion crack detection*] .... WFMPT
Wetherley [*England*] .... WETH
Wethersfield [*British ICAO location identifier*] (ICLI) .... EGVT
Wethersfield Historical Society, Wethersfield, CT [*Library symbol Library of Congress*] (LCLS) .... CtWetHi
Wethersfield Township, NY [*FM radio station call letters*] .... WNUC
Wethey's Reports [*Canada*] [*A publication*] (DLA) .... Weth
Wethey's Reports, Upper Canada Queen's Bench [*A publication*] (DLA) .... Weth UC
Wethey's Reports, Upper Canada Queen's Bench [*A publication*] (DLA) .... Wethey
Wetland Habitat Alliance of Texas .... WHAT
Wetlands Conservation Team .... WCT
Wet-Net Training [*Navy*] (NVT) .... WETNETNG
Wet-Process Phosphoric Acid [*Fertilizer*] .... WPA
Wettable Powder .... WP
Wetted Surface .... WS
Wetting-Drying and Temperature Fluctuation [*Geochemistry*] .... WDTF
Wettstein's Novum Testamentum Graecum [*A publication*] (BJA) .... Wett
Wettzell [*Federal Republic of Germany*] [*Seismograph station code, US Geological Survey*] (SEIS) .... WET
Wetumpka, AL [*AM radio station call letters*] .... WAPZ
Wet-Weather Parka and Trousers [*Army*] (INF) .... WWPT
Wewak [*Papua New Guinea*] [*ICAO location identifier*] (ICLI) .... AYWK
Wewak [*Papua New Guinea*] [*Seismograph station code, US Geological Survey*] (SEIS) .... WEK
Wewak [*Papua New Guinea*] [*Seismograph station code, US Geological Survey Closed*] (SEIS) .... WEW
Wewak [*Papua New Guinea*] [*Airport symbol*] (OAG) .... WWK
Wewoka, OK [*AM radio station call letters*] .... KWSH
Wexas International [*Commercial firm British*] (EAIO) .... WI
Wexford [*County in Ireland*] (ROG) .... WEX
Wexford [*County in Ireland*] (ROG) .... WEXF
Wexford [*County in Ireland*] .... WEXFD
Wexford Public Schools, Cadillac, MI [*Library symbol Library of Congress*] (LCLS) .... MiCadPS
Wey [*Unit of weight*] .... WY
Wey and Arun Canal Trust [*British*] (DBA) .... W & ACT
Weyburn, SK [*AM radio station call letters*] .... CFSL
Weyco Group [*NASDAQ symbol*] (TTSB) .... WEYS
Weyco Group, Inc. [*Associated Press*] (SAG) .... Weyco
Weyco Group, Inc. [*NASDAQ symbol*] (SAG) .... WEYS
Weyerhaeuser Co. [*Associated Press*] (SAG) .... Weyerh
Weyerhaeuser Co. [*NYSE symbol*] (SPSG) .... WY
Weyerhaeuser Co., Forestry Research Center, Centralia, WA [*Library symbol Library of Congress*] (LCLS) .... WaCeW
Weyerhaeuser Co., Tacoma, WA [*Library symbol Library of Congress*] (LCLS) .... WaTW
Weyerhaeuser Co., Technical Center, Tacoma, WA [*Library symbol Library of Congress*] (LCLS) .... WaTW-T
Weyerhauser Memorial Museum, Little Falls, MN [*Library symbol*] [*Library of Congress*] (LCLS) .... MnLfW
Weymouth [*Municipal borough in England*] .... WEYM
W.F. West High School, Chehalis, WA [*Library symbol*] [*Library of Congress*] (LCLS) .... WaChehHS
WFS Bancorp [*NASDAQ symbol*] (TTSB) .... WBCI
WFS Bancorp, Inc. [*NASDAQ symbol*] (SAG) .... WBCI
WFS Bancorp, Inc. [*Associated Press*] (SAG) .... WFS Bcp
WFS Financial [*NASDAQ symbol*] (TTSB) .... WFSI
WFS Financial, Inc. [*Associated Press*] (SAG) .... WFS Fn
WFS Financial, Inc. [*Associated Press*] (SAG) .... WFS Fncl
WFS Financial, Inc. [*NASDAQ symbol*] (SAG) .... WFSI
Whakatane [*New Zealand*] [*ICAO location identifier*] (ICLI) .... NZWK

Whakatane [*New Zealand*] [*Airport symbol*] (OAG) ... WHK
Whakatane [*New Zealand*] [*Seismograph station code, US Geological Survey*] (SEIS) ... WTZ
Whale (VRA) ... wha
Whale Adoption Project (EA) ... WAP
Whale and Dolphin Conservation Society [*British*] (DBA) ... WDCS
Whale Boat ... WB
Whale Center (EA) ... WC
Whale Cove, NT [*ICAO location identifier*] (ICLI) ... CYXN
Whale Protection Act 1980 [*Commonwealth Act*] (EERA) ... WPA
Whale Protection Fund (EA) ... WPF
Whale Rescue Centre [*Australia*] ... WRC
Whale Research and Conservation Fund [*Defunct*] (EA) ... WRCF
Whale Tumor Story [*Urban folklore term coined by Rodney Dale*] ... WTS
Whalehead [*Quebec*] [*Airport symbol*] (AD) ... YWH
Whaling Museum Society (EA) ... WMS
Whaling Museum Society, Inc., Cold Spring Harbor, NY [*Library symbol Library of Congress*] (LCLS) ... NCshWM
Whalsay [*Shetland Islands*] [*Airport symbol*] (OAG) ... WHS
Whangarei [*New Zealand*] [*ICAO location identifier*] (ICLI) ... NZWR
Whangarei [*New Zealand*] [*Airport symbol*] (OAG) ... WRE
Wharf ... WH
Wharf ... WHF
Wharf Owner's Liability [*Insurance*] ... WOL
Wharf Resources Ltd. [*Toronto Stock Exchange symbol*] ... WFR
Wharf Resources Ltd. [*NASDAQ symbol*] (NQ) ... WFRA
Wharf Resources Ltd. [*Associated Press*] (SAG) ... Wharf
Wharf Resources Ltd [*NASDAQ symbol*] (TTSB) ... WFRAF
Wharfage [*Shipping*] ... WHFG
Wharfage [*Shipping*] ... WHGE
Wharfage [*Shipping*] (WGA) ... WRFG
Wharfedale [*Printing*] (DGA) ... Wharfe
Wharfedale [*Printing*] (DGA) ... Whf
Wharfinger [*Shipping*] [*British*] (ROG) ... WHFR
Wharton & Northern [*Railroad*] (MHDB) ... W & N
Wharton & Northern Railroad Co. [*Absorbed into Consolidated Rail Corp.*] [*AAR code*] ... WHN
Wharton & Northern Railroad Co. [*Later, WHN*] [*AAR code*] ... WNO
Wharton and Stille's Medical Jurisprudence [*A publication*] (DLA) ... Whar & St Med Jur
Wharton and Stille's Medical Jurisprudence [*A publication*] (DLA) ... Whart & S Med Jur
Wharton Applied Research Center [*University of Pennsylvania*] [*Research center*] (RCD) ... WARC
Wharton County Junior College [*Texas*] ... WCJC
Wharton County Junior College, Wharton, TX [*Library symbol Library of Congress*] (LCLS) ... TxWhaC
Wharton County Library, Wharton, TX [*Library symbol Library of Congress*] (LCLS) ... TxWhaW
Wharton Econometric Forecasting Association [*FAA*] (TAG) ... WEFA
Wharton on Agency [*A publication*] (DLA) ... Whar Ag
Wharton on Agency [*A publication*] (DLA) ... Whart Ag
Wharton on Criminal Evidence [*A publication*] (DLA) ... Whar Cr Ev
Wharton on Criminal Evidence [*A publication*] (DLA) ... Whart Cr Ev
Wharton on Evidence in Civil Issues [*A publication*] (DLA) ... Whar Ev
Wharton on Evidence in Civil Issues [*A publication*] (DLA) ... Whart Ev
Wharton on Innkeepers [*1876*] [*A publication*] (DLA) ... Whar Innk
Wharton on Negligence [*A publication*] (DLA) ... Whart Neg
Wharton on Principles of Conveyancing [*1851*] [*A publication*] (DLA) ... Whar Conv
Wharton on the Law of Domicile [*A publication*] (DLA) ... Whar Dom
Wharton School, University of Pennsylvania (DLA) ... WHSUPA
Wharton, TX [*Location identifier FAA*] (FAAL) ... ARM
Wharton, TX [*AM radio station call letters*] ... KANI
Wharton's American Criminal Law [*A publication*] (DLA) ... Whar Am Cr L
Wharton's American Criminal Law [*A publication*] (DLA) ... Whar Cr Law
Wharton's American Criminal Law [*A publication*] (DLA) ... Whart Am Cr Law
Wharton's American Criminal Law [*A publication*] (DLA) ... Whart Cr Law
Wharton's American Criminal Law [*A publication*] (DLA) ... Whart Crim Law
Wharton's American Criminal Law [*A publication*] (DLA) ... Wharton
Wharton's Conflict of Laws [*A publication*] (DLA) ... Whar Con Law
Wharton's Conflict of Laws [*A publication*] (DLA) ... Whar Confl Law
Wharton's Conflict of Laws [*A publication*] (DLA) ... Whart Confl Laws
Wharton's Criminal Evidence [*A publication*] (DLA) ... Wharton Crim Evidence
Wharton's Criminal Law and Procedure [*A publication*] (DLA) ... Wharton Crim Proc
Wharton's Criminal Pleading and Practice [*A publication*] (DLA) ... Whar Cr Pl
Wharton's Criminal Pleading and Practice [*A publication*] (DLA) ... Whar Cri Pl
Wharton's Criminal Pleading and Practice [*A publication*] (DLA) ... Whart Cr Pl & Prac
Wharton's Law Dictionary [*or Lexicon*] [*A publication*] (DLA) ... Whart Law Dict
Wharton's Law Lexicon [*14th ed.*] [*1938*] [*A publication*] (DLA) ... Whar Law Dic
Wharton's Law Lexicon [*A publication*] (DLA) ... Whart Law Lexicon
Wharton's Law Lexicon [*A publication*] (DLA) ... Whart Lex
Wharton's Law Lexicon [*A publication*] (DLA) ... Wharton
Wharton's Law of Homicide [*A publication*] (DLA) ... Whar Hom
Wharton's Law of Homicide [*A publication*] (DLA) ... Whart Hom
Wharton's Law of Homicide [*A publication*] (DLA) ... Whart Homicide
Wharton's Law of Negligence [*A publication*] (DLA) ... Whar Neg
Wharton's Legal Maxims [*3rd ed.*] [*1903*] [*A publication*] (DLA) ... Whar Leg Max
Wharton's Pennsylvania Digest [*A publication*] (DLA) ... Whar Dig
Wharton's Pennsylvania Supreme Court Reports [*1835-41*] [*A publication*] (DLA) ... Wh
Wharton's Pennsylvania Supreme Court Reports [*1835-41*] [*A publication*] (DLA) ... Whar
Wharton's Pennsylvania Supreme Court Reports [*1835-41*] [*A publication*] (DLA) ... Whart
Wharton's Pennsylvania Supreme Court Reports [*1835-41*] [*A publication*] (DLA) ... Whart PA
Wharton's Pennsylvania Supreme Court Reports [*1835-41*] [*A publication*] (DLA) ... Wharton
Wharton's Precedents of Indictments and Pleas [*A publication*] (DLA) ... Whar Ind
Wharton's Precedents of Indictments and Pleas [*A publication*] (DLA) ... Whar Prec Ind
Wharton's United States State Trials [*A publication*] (DLA) ... Whar St Tr
Wharton's United States State Trials [*A publication*] (DLA) ... Whart St Tr
Wharton's United States State Trials [*A publication*] (DLA) ... Whart State Tr
Wharves (WGA) ... WHVS
What A World [*NASDAQ symbol*] (TTSB) ... WHAT
What A World, Inc. [*NASDAQ symbol*] (SAG) ... WHAT
What A World, Inc. [*Associated Press*] (SAG) ... WhatA
What A World, Inc. [*Associated Press*] (SAG) ... WhatAW
What A World Wrrt [*NASDAQ symbol*] (TTSB) ... WHATW
What Cheer Patriot-Chronicle, What Cheer, IA [*Library symbol Library of Congress*] (LCLS) ... IaWhaP
What Do I Read Next [*A publication*] ... WDIRN
What Do You Think ... WDYT
What Have You [*British*] (ADA) ... WHY
What Have You Done for the Fleet Today [*Navy*] ... WHYDFTFT
What I Like to Do [*Psychological testing*] ... WILD
What I Think and Feel (EDAC) ... WITF
What Is Going On [*Humorous definition of science*] ... WIGO
What Really Matters ... WRM
What the Heck [*Computer hacker terminology*] [*Bowdlerized version*] (NHD) ... WTH
What You Digitize Is What You Get ... WYDIWYG
What You Get Is No Surprise [*Pronounced "wiggins"*] [*Coined by Dave Tarrant, president of Lotus Development Corp.'s graphics products group*] ... WYGINS
What You See Before You Get It [*Computer science*] ... WYSBYGI
What You See Is All You Get ... WYSIAYG
What You See Is More or Less What You Get [*Pronounced "wizzi-mole-wig"*] ... WYSIMOLWYG
What You See Is What You Get [*Pronounced "wizziwig"*] [*Indicates that video display on word processor bears a high-quality resemblance to printed page that will result*] ... WYSIWYG
What You See Is What You Print [*Computer science*] ... WYSIWYP
Whatcom Community College, Ferndale, WA [*Library symbol Library of Congress*] (LCLS) ... WaFW
Whatcom County Law Library, Bellingham, WA [*Library symbol*] [*Library of Congress*] (LCLS) ... WaBeCoL
Whatcom County Public Library, Bellingham, WA [*Library symbol Library of Congress*] (LCLS) ... WaBeCo
What's Here and There [*Australia A publication*] ... WHAT
What's In It For Me [*Electronic mail language*] [*Computer science*] ... WIIFM
What's in It for Me? [*Fundraising*] ... WIIFM
What's New in Travel [*CompuServe Information Service*] [*Information service or system*] (CRD) ... WNT
What's Up? [*Internet language*] [*Computer science*] ... sup
Whatsoever ... WHATSR
Wheal and Flare Reaction [*Immunology*] ... WFR
Wheat Advisory Committee (Western Australia) ... WAC
Wheat Chlorotic Streak Virus [*Plant pathology*] ... WCSV
Wheat Curl Mite [*Entomology*] ... WCM
Wheat Dwarf Virus [*Plant pathology*] ... WDV
Wheat Flour Institute [*Miller's National Federation*] [*Absorbed by*] (EA) ... WFI
Wheat Foods Council (EA) ... WFC
Wheat Germ Agglutinin [*Biochemistry*] ... WGA
Wheat Gluten Industry Council (EA) ... WGIC
Wheat Gluten World [*A publication*] (EAAP) ... WGW
Wheat Industry Council (EA) ... WIC
Wheat Protein Concentrate [*Food technology*] ... WPC
Wheat Quality Council (EA) ... WQC
Wheat Research Committee for New South Wales [*Australia*] ... WRCNSW
Wheat Research Committee for Queensland [*Australia*] ... WRCQ
Wheat Research Committee for South Australia ... WRCSA
Wheat Research Committee for Victoria [*Australia*] ... WRCV
Wheat Research Committee for Western Australia ... WRCWA
Wheat Research Council [*Australia*] ... WRC
Wheat Ridge Foundation (EA) ... WRF
Wheat Rosette Stunt Virus [*Plant pathology*] ... WRSV
Wheat Soilborne Mosaic Virus ... WSBM
Wheat Soilborne Mosaic Virus ... WSBMV
Wheat Spindle Streak Mosaic Virus ... WSSMV
Wheat Straw ... WS
Wheat Streak Mosaic [*Plant pathology*] ... WSM
Wheat Streak Mosaic Virus ... WSMV
Wheat Yellow Leaf Virus [*Plant pathology*] ... WYLV
Wheat Yellow Mosaic Virus [*Plant pathology*] ... WYMV
Wheathampstead [*England*] ... WHEATH
Wheatland Regional Library, Saskatoon, Saskatchewan [*Library symbol National Library of Canada*] (NLC) ... SSW
Wheatland Regional Library, Saskatoon, SK, Canada [*Library symbol Library of Congress*] (LCLS) ... CaSSW
Wheatland Township Library, Remus, MI [*Library symbol Library of Congress*] (LCLS) ... MiRem
Wheatland, WY [*Location identifier FAA*] (FAAL) ... EAN
Wheatland, WY [*AM radio station call letters*] ... KYCN
Wheatland, WY [*FM radio station call letters*] ... KYCN-FM
Wheatland-Chili Junior/Senior High School Library, Scottsville, NY [*OCLC symbol*] (OCLC) ... RXN

Wheatley Junior-Senior High School, Old Westbury, NY [*Library symbol Library of Congress*] (LCLS) ... NOweWJ
Wheatley Junior-Senior High School, Old Westbury, NY [*Library symbol*] [*Library of Congress*] (LCLS) ... NOwWJ
Wheatley, ON [*Television station call letters*] ... CHWI
Wheaton College, Billy Graham Center, Wheaton, IL [*Library symbol*] [*Library of Congress*] (LCLS) ... IWW-G
Wheaton College, Norton, MA [*Library symbol Library of Congress*] (LCLS) ... MNoW
Wheaton College, Norton, MA [*OCLC symbol*] (OCLC) ... WHE
Wheaton College, Wheaton, IL [*OCLC symbol*] (OCLC) ... ICW
Wheaton College, Wheaton, IL [*Library symbol Library of Congress*] (LCLS) ... IWW
Wheaton Community Hospital, Wheaton, MN [*Library symbol*] [*Library of Congress*] (LCLS) ... MnWheH
Wheaton Community Library, Wheaton, MN [*Library symbol*] [*Library of Congress*] (LCLS) ... MnWhe
Wheaton Historical Association, Millville, NJ [*Library symbol Library of Congress*] (LCLS) ... NjMilvHi
Wheaton, IL [*FM radio station call letters*] ... WETN
Wheaton Information System for Education (IAA) ... WISE
Wheaton, MD [*AM radio station call letters*] ... WMDO
Wheaton, MN [*Location identifier FAA*] (FAAL) ... ETH
Wheaton on Maritime Captures and Prizes [*A publication*] (DLA) ... Wheat Cap
Wheaton Public Library, Wheaton, IL [*Library symbol Library of Congress*] (LCLS) ... IW
Wheaton Public Library, Wheaton, IL [*OCLC symbol*] (OCLC) ... JAD
Wheaton-Dumont High School, Wheaton, MN [*Library symbol*] [*Library of Congress*] (LCLS) ... MnWheHS
Wheaton's Elements of International Law [*A publication*] (DLA) ... Wheat El Int Law
Wheaton's Elements of International Law [*7th ed.*] [*1944*] [*A publication*] (DLA) ... Wheat Int Law
Wheaton's History of the Law of Nations [*A publication*] (DLA) ... Wheat Hist Law Nat
Wheaton's History of the Law of Nations [*A publication*] (DLA) ... Wheat Law of Nat
Wheaton's International Law [*A publication*] (DLA) ... Wh
Wheaton's International Law [*A publication*] (DLA) ... Wheat Int Law
Wheaton's Reports [*14-25 United States*] [*A publication*] (DLA) ... W
Wheaton's Reports [*14-25 United States*] [*A publication*] (DLA) ... Wh
Wheaton's Reports [*14-25 United States*] [*A publication*] (DLA) ... Wheat
Wheaton's Reports [*14-25 United States*] [*A publication*] (DLA) ... Wheaton
Wheaton's United States Supreme Court Reports [*1816-27*] [*A publication*] (AAGC) ... Wheat
Wheat-Sheep Zone [*Agriculture*] ... WSZ
Wheat-Soya Blend (EA) ... WSB
Wheden Cancer Detection Foundation, Sheridan, WY [*Library symbol Library of Congress*] (LCLS) ... WyShCD
Wheel ... WHL
Wheel (AAG) ... WHL
Wheel at Each Corner [*Automotive engineering*] ... WAEC
Wheel Bearing [*Automotive engineering*] ... W/BRG
Wheel Bumpers [*Technical drawings*] ... WHB
Wheel Center (MSA) ... WC
Wheel Chair [*Medicine*] (DMAA) ... wh ch
Wheel Control (MCD) ... WHECON
Wheel Drive [*Engineering*] ... WD
Wheel Drive Assembly ... WDA
Wheel Locks ... WL
Wheel of Progress (EA) ... WP
Wheel Slide Protection (PDAA) ... WSP
Wheel Speed Sensor [*Automotive engineering*] ... WSS
Wheel Vehicle (AABC) ... WVEH
Wheel Well (MCD) ... W/W
Wheelabrator Tech [*NYSE symbol*] (TTSB) ... WTI
Wheelabrator Technology [*Associated Press*] (SAG) ... WhlTech
Wheelabrator Technology [*NYSE symbol*] (SAG) ... WTI
Wheelbarrow (MSA) ... WB
Wheelbase ... WB
Wheelchair (DAVI) ... CH
Wheelchair ... WC
Wheelchair Motorcycle Association (EA) ... WMA
Wheelchair Pilots Association (EA) ... WPA
Wheelchair Sports Victoria [*Australia*] ... WSV
Wheelchair Tennis Players Association (EA) ... WTPA
Wheeled [*Vehicles*] (NATG) ... W
Wheeled ... WHLD
Wheeled Armoured Fighting Vehicle [*Military*] ... WAFV
Wheeled Fuel-Consuming Motor Vehicle ... WFCMV
Wheeled Mobility Test Rig [*Army*] (RDA) ... WMTR
Wheeled Vehicle Experimental Establishment [*British*] ... WVEE
Wheeled Vehicle Launched Bridge (MCD) ... WVLB
Wheeler AFB Range Communications Control Center (MCD) ... WRCCC
Wheeler Air Force Base, Oahu Island [*Hawaii*] [*ICAO location identifier*] (ICLI) ... PHHI
Wheeler Basin Regional Library, Decatur, AL [*Library symbol Library of Congress*] (LCLS) ... ADeW
Wheeler Dam [*TVA*] ... WHD
Wheeler Elementary School, Valley Stream, NY [*Library symbol Library of Congress*] (LCLS) ... NVsWhE
Wheeler Flying Service [*ICAO designator*] (AD) ... WR
Wheeler Laboratories, Inc. (MCD) ... WL
Wheeler on Slavery [*A publication*] (DLA) ... Wheel Slav
Wheeler, TX [*FM radio station call letters*] ... KPDR
Wheeler's Abridgment [*A publication*] (DLA) ... Wheeler Abr
Wheeler's Abridgment of American Common Law Cases [*A publication*] (DLA) ... Wheel Abr
Wheeler's Abridgment of American Common Law Cases [*A publication*] (DLA) ... Wheeler Am Cr Law
Wheeler's New York Criminal Cases [*3 vols.*] [*A publication*] (DLA) ... Wh Cr Cas
Wheeler's New York Criminal Cases [*A publication*] (DLA) ... Wh Crim Cas
Wheeler's New York Criminal Cases [*A publication*] (DLA) ... Wheel
Wheeler's New York Criminal Cases [*A publication*] (DLA) ... Wheel Cr C
Wheeler's New York Criminal Cases [*A publication*] (DLA) ... Wheel Cr Cas
Wheeler's New York Criminal Cases [*A publication*] (DLA) ... Wheel Cr Ch
Wheeler's New York Criminal Cases [*A publication*] (DLA) ... Wheeler CC
Wheeler's New York Criminal Cases [*A publication*] (DLA) ... Wheeler Cr Cas
Wheeler's New York Criminal Cases [*A publication*] (DLA) ... Wheeler Cr Cases
Wheeler's New York Criminal Cases [*A publication*] (DLA) ... Wheeler Crim Cas
Wheeler's New York Criminal Cases [*A publication*] (DLA) ... Wheeler's Cr Cases
Wheeler's New York Criminal Recorder [*1 Wheeler's Criminal Cases*] [*A publication*] (DLA) ... Wheel Cr Rec
Wheeler's New York Criminal Reports [*3 vols.*] [*A publication*] (DLA) ... Wh
Wheelhouse [*Automotive engineering*] ... W/HSE
Wheelhouse (MSA) ... WH
Wheeling [*West Virginia*] [*Airport symbol*] (AD) ... HLG
Wheeling Bridge Case [*A publication*] (DLA) ... Wheel Br Cas
Wheeling College, Wheeling, WV [*Library symbol Library of Congress*] (LCLS) ... WvWC
Wheeling College, Wheeling, WV [*OCLC symbol*] (OCLC) ... WWV
Wheeling Hospital, Medical Library, Wheeling, WV [*Library symbol Library of Congress*] (LCLS) ... WvWH
Wheeling Pittsburgh Corp. [*Later, WHX Corp.*] [*NYSE symbol*] (SPSG) ... WHX
Wheeling Railway ... WRY
Wheeling, WV [*Location identifier FAA*] (FAAL) ... HLG
Wheeling, WV [*AM radio station call letters*] (RBYB) ... WBBD-AM
Wheeling, WV [*FM radio station call letters*] ... WEGW
Wheeling, WV [*AM radio station call letters*] ... WKWK
Wheeling, WV [*FM radio station call letters*] ... WKWK-FM
Wheeling, WV [*AM radio station call letters*] (RBYB) ... WOHZ
Wheeling, WV [*FM radio station call letters*] ... WOVK
Wheeling, WV [*FM radio station call letters*] ... WPHP
Wheeling, WV [*Television station call letters*] ... WTRF
Wheeling, WV [*FM radio station call letters*] ... WVNP
Wheeling, WV [*AM radio station call letters*] ... WWVA
Wheeling-Charleston [*Diocesan abbreviation*] [*West Virginia*] (TOCD) ... WH
Wheel-Made (BJA) ... WM
Wheelock College (GAGS) ... Wheelock C
Wheelock College, Boston, MA [*Library symbol Library of Congress*] (LCLS) ... MBWS
Wheelock's Reports [*32-37 Texas*] [*A publication*] (DLA) ... Wheel
Wheelock's Reports [*32-37 Texas*] [*A publication*] (DLA) ... Wheel (Tex)
Wheels [*Automotive advertising*] ... WHLS
Wheelwrights and Coachmakers Operatives' Union [*British*] ... WCOU
Wheelwrights' and Smiths' Society [*A union*] [*British*] ... WSS
Wheezing Associated with Respiratory Injections ... WARI
Whelden Memorial Library, West Barnstable, MA [*Library symbol*] [*Library of Congress*] (LCLS) ... MWeba
When [*or While*] **Actually Employed** [*Government short jobs*] ... WAE
When [*or Where*] **Applicable** ... WHAP
When Authorized By ... WAB
When Authorized by the Oversea Commander [*Military*] ... WABTOC
When Available (KSC) ... WHAV
When Awake ... WA
When Directed ... WD
When Directed By ... DIRBY
When Directed, Detach Duty Indicated ... DIRDET
When Directed Proceed ... DIRPRO
When Discovered ... WD
When Distributed [*Stock exchange term*] (SPSG) ... WD
When Interrupt Block (NASA) ... WIB
When Issued [*Stock exchange term*] (SPSG) ... WI
When Push Comes to Shove ... WPCTS
When Relieved and When Directed Detached [*Duty Indicated*] ... RELDIRDET
When Relieved By [*Army*] ... RELBY
When Relieved Detached [*Duty Indicated*] ... RELDET
When Technology Fails [*A publication*] ... WTF
Whencesoever [*Legal*] [*British*] (ROG) ... WHENCESR
Whenever [*Legal*] [*British*] (ROG) ... WHENR
Whenever [*Legal*] [*British*] (ROG) ... WHNR
When-Issued-Basis [*Business term*] ... WIB
Whensoever [*Legal*] [*British*] (ROG) ... WHENSR
Whensoever [*Legal*] [*British*] (ROG) ... WHNSR
Whenuapai [*New Zealand*] [*ICAO location identifier*] (ICLI) ... NZWP
Where (AABC) ... WH
Where Are We Going ... WAWG
Where Economy Originates [*A & P Co. marketing slogan, now obsolete*] ... WEO
Where Used File [*Computer science*] (IAA) ... WUF
Where You Look Is What You Select ... WYLIWYS
Whereabouts [*Aviation*] (FAAC) ... WBTS
Whereabouts [*Legal*] [*British*] (ROG) ... WHRABTS
Whereafter [*Legal*] [*British*] (ROG) ... WHAR
Whereas ... WHAS
Whereas [*Legal*] [*British*] (ROG) ... WHRAS
Whereat [*Legal*] [*British*] (ROG) ... WHRAT
Whereby ... WHBY
Wherefore [*Legal*] [*British*] (ROG) ... WHFORE
Wherefrom [*Legal*] [*British*] (ROG) ... WHFM
Wherein [*Legal*] [*British*] (ROG) ... WHIN
Wherein ... WHRIN

Whereof [*Legal*] [*British*] (ROG) ... WHOF
Whereon [*Legal*] [*British*] (ROG) ... WHON
Where's the Beef [*Slogan created by the Dancer Fitzgerald Sample advertising agency for Wendy's International, Inc.*] ... WTB
Whereto [*Legal*] [*British*] (ROG) ... WHTO
Wherever [*Legal*] [*British*] (ROG) ... WHERER
Wherewith [*Legal*] [*British*] (ROG) ... WHWTH
Wherry (ROG) ... WY
Whether [*Legal*] [*British*] (ROG) ... WHER
Whether ... WHR
Whether Cleared Customs or Not [*Shipping*] (DS) ... WCCON
Whey Acidic Protein ... WAP
Whey Products Institute [*Later, ADPI*] (EA) ... WPI
Whey Protein Concentrate [*Food technology*] ... WPC
WHG Bancshares [*NASDAQ symbol*] (TTSB) ... WHGB
WHG Bancshares Corp. [*NASDAQ symbol*] (SAG) ... WHGB
WHG Bancshares Corp. [*Associated Press*] (SAG) ... WHGBcs
Which ... WH
Whidbey Island, WA [*Location identifier FAA*] (FAAL) ... NUW
Whidbey Island/Whidbey Island Naval Air Station [*Washington*] [*ICAO location identifier*] (ICLI) ... KNUW
Whiffle Tree [*Structural test*] (AAG) ... WT
While (AIA) ... Wh
While Awake (CPH) ... WA
While in Control Area [*Aviation*] (FAAC) ... WICA
While in Control Zone [*Aviation*] (FAAC) ... WICZ
Whim Creek Consolidated [*Toronto Stock Exchange symbol*] ... WCC
Whimbey Analytical Skills Inventory [*Educational test*] ... WASI
Whimsical Alternative Coalition Political Action Committee (EA) ... WACPAC
Whip ... W
Whip Inflation Now [*Slogan of President Gerald R. Ford's anti-inflation program, 1974*] [*Program discontinued March, 1975*] ... WIN
Whippanong Public Library, Whippany, NJ [*Library symbol Library of Congress*] (LCLS) ... NjWhi
Whipple Mountains Number 2 [*California*] [*Seismograph station code, US Geological Survey*] (SEIS) ... WH2
Whirlpool (MAE) ... whp
Whirlpool ... whpl
Whirlpool [*Medicine*] ... WP
Whirlpool Bath [*Medicine*] ... WPB
Whirlpool Bath Manufacturers Association [*Defunct*] (EA) ... WBMA
Whirlpool Corp. [*NYSE symbol*] (SPSG) ... WHR
Whirlpool Corp. [*Associated Press*] (SAG) ... Whrlpl
Whirlpool Corp., Research Library, St. Joseph, MI [*Library symbol Library of Congress*] (LCLS) ... MiStjW
Whirlpool Corp., Technical Information Center, Benton Harbor, MI [*OCLC symbol*] (OCLC) ... EXI
Whirlpool Corp., Technical Information Center, Benton Harbor, MI [*Library symbol Library of Congress*] (LCLS) ... MiBhW
Whirlpool, Massage, Exercise [*Medicine*] ... WMX
Whirlwind I ... WWI
Whirlwind I SAGE [*Semi-Automatic Ground Equipment*] **Evaluation** (SAA) ... WISE
Whirlwind II (SAA) ... WWII
Whishaw's Law Dictionary [*A publication*] (DLA) ... Whishaw
Whishaw's New Law Dictionary [*1829*] [*A publication*] (DLA) ... Whish LD
Whiskey [*Phonetic alphabet*] [*International*] (DSUE) ... W
Whiskey and Soda ... W & S
Whiskey Butte [*Idaho*] [*Seismograph station code, US Geological Survey Closed*] (SEIS) ... WBI
Whiskey Creek Resources [*Vancouver Stock Exchange symbol*] ... WCK
Whiskey Painters of America (EA) ... WPA
Whiskey-3 [*Shipboard radio*] ... AN-WSC-3
Whiskeytown Dam [*California*] [*Seismograph station code, US Geological Survey*] (SEIS) ... WDC
Whiskeytown-Shasta-Trinity National Recreation Area ... WHIS
Whispered (ADA) ... WH
Whispered Voice ... WV
Whistle [*Navigation*] ... WHIS
Whistle (MSA) ... WSTL
Whistleblower Protection Act of 1989 (WYGK) ... WPA
Whistle-Blowers Integrity in Science and Education [*An association*] ... WISE
Whistler, BC [*Television station call letters*] (RBYB) ... CHAN-7
Whistler, BC [*FM radio station call letters*] ... CISW
Whistletip [*Catheter*] [*Urology*] (DAVI) ... WT
Whitaker Index of Schizophrenic Thinking ... WIST
Whitaker on Liens [*A publication*] (DLA) ... Whitak Liens
Whitaker's Books in Print [*J. Whitaker & Sons Ltd.*] [*Information service or system*] (IID) ... WBIP
Whitaker's Rights of Lien and Stoppage in Transitu [*1812*] [*A publication*] (DLA) ... Whit Lien
Whitaker's Rights of Lien and Stoppage in Transitu [*1812*] [*A publication*] (DLA) ... Whit St Tr
Whitbourne Public Library, Newfoundland [*Library symbol National Library of Canada*] (NLC) ... NFWH
Whitbourne Public Library, Whitbourne, NF, Canada [*Library symbol Library of Congress*] (LCLS) ... CaNfWh
Whitbread Investment Co. [*British*] ... WIC
Whitbread Investment Trust [*British*] ... WIT
Whitby Psychiatric Hospital, Ontario [*Library symbol National Library of Canada*] (NLC) ... OWPH
Whitby Psychiatric Hospital, Whitby, ON, Canada [*Library symbol*] [*Library of Congress*] (LCLS) ... CaOWhPH
Whitby Public Library, Ontario [*Library symbol National Library of Canada*] (NLC) ... OWHP
Whitby Public Library, Whitby, ON, Canada [*Library symbol Library of Congress*] (LCLS) ... CaOWhP
Whitchurch [*England*] ... WHITCH
Whitchurch-Stouffville Public Library, Stouffville, Ontario [*Library symbol National Library of Canada*] (NLC) ... OSWS
White [*Light, buoy, beacon*] ... W
White (VRA) ... w
White (DAVI) ... W
White (WDMC) ... wh
White [*Thoroughbred racing*] ... WH
White ... WH
White (AAG) ... WHT
White (DAVI) ... WT
White Adipose Tissue [*Physiology*] ... WAT
White American Male (WDAA) ... W AM
White American Political Association (EA) ... WAPA
White and Orange [*Buoy*] ... WOR
White and Tudor's Leading Cases in Equity [*A publication*] (DLA) ... LC Eq
White and Tudor's Leading Cases in Equity [*9 eds.*] [*1849-1928*] [*A publication*] (DLA) ... W & T Eq Ca
White and Tudor's Leading Cases in Equity [*9 eds.*] [*1849-1928*] [*A publication*] (DLA) ... W & TLC
White and Tudor's Leading Cases in Equity [*9 eds.*] [*1849-1928*] [*A publication*] (DLA) ... Wh & TLC
White and Tudor's Leading Cases in Equity [*9th ed.*] [*1928*] [*A publication*] (DLA) ... Wh & Tud
White and Tudor's Leading Cases in Equity [*England*] [*A publication*] (DLA) ... White & T Lead Cas Eq
White and Tudor's Leading Cases in Equity [*England*] [*A publication*] (DLA) ... White & T Lead Cas in Eq (Eng)
White and Tudor's Leading Cases in Equity [*A publication*] (DLA) ... White & TL Cas
White and Tudor's Leading Cases in Equity [*9th ed.*] [*1928*] [*A publication*] (DLA) ... White & Tud LC
White and Tudor's Leading Cases in Equity [*A publication*] (DLA) ... White & Tudor
White and Willson's Civil Cases, Texas Court of Appeals [*A publication*] (DLA) ... White & Civ Cas Ct App
White and Willson's Civil Cases, Texas Court of Appeals [*A publication*] (DLA) ... Willson Civ Cas Ct App
White and Willson's Reports, Civil Cases, Texas Court of Appeals [*A publication*] (DLA) ... White & W
White and Willson's Reports, Civil Cases, Texas Court of Appeals [*A publication*] (DLA) ... White & W (Tex)
White and Wilson's [*or Willson's*] **Civil Cases, Texas Court of Appeals** [*A publication*] (DLA) ... Tex A Civ
White and Wilson's [*or Willson's*] **Civil Cases, Texas Court of Appeals** [*A publication*] (DLA) ... Tex A Civ Cas
White and Wilson's [*or Willson's*] **Civil Cases, Texas Court of Appeals** [*A publication*] (DLA) ... Tex App Civ Cas (Wilson)
White and Wilson's [*or Willson's*] **Civil Cases, Texas Court of Appeals** [*A publication*] (DLA) ... W & W
White and Wilson's [*or Willson's*] **Civil Cases, Texas Court of Appeals** [*A publication*] (DLA) ... W & W Civ Cases Court of Appeals
White and Wilson's [*or Willson's*] **Civil Cases, Texas Court of Appeals** [*A publication*] (DLA) ... W & W Con Cases
White and Wilson's [*or Willson's*] **Civil Cases, Texas Court of Appeals** [*A publication*] (DLA) ... W & W Con Rep
White and Wilson's [*or Willson's*] **Civil Cases, Texas Court of Appeals** [*A publication*] (DLA) ... W & WCC
White and Wilson's [*or Willson's*] **Civil Cases, Texas Court of Appeals** [*A publication*] (DLA) ... White & W Civ Cas Ct App
White Anglo-Saxon Catholic ... WASC
White Anglo-Saxon Male ... WASM
White Anglo-Saxon Protestant (DAVI) ... WAP
White Anglo-Saxon Protestant ... WASP
White Anglo-Saxon Protestant (ODBW) ... Wasp
White Anglo-Saxon Protestant Ambulatory [*Extension of WASP; indicates the necessity of being able-bodied as an additional requirement for success*] ... WASPA
White Anglo-Saxon Protestant Native Born of Native Parents ... WASP-NN
White Appalachian Southern Protestant [*Chicago slang*] ... WASP
White Aryan Resistance (EA) ... WAR
White Ashkenazi Sabra with Pull [*Israeli variation on White Anglo-Saxon Protestant*] ... WASP
White Bag Propellant [*Army*] (ADDR) ... WB
White Balance [*Television*] (NTCM) ... WB
White Beacon ... W Bn
White Blood Cell [*or Corpuscle*] [*Medicine*] ... WBC
White Blood Cell Count [*Medicine*] ... WBC
White Blood Cell Count [*Hematology*] (DAVI) ... WBCC
White Blood Cell Differential [*Hematology*] ... WBCD
White Blood Cells per High Power Field [*Hematology*] (MAE) ... WBC/HPF
White Bluff [*Washington*] [*Seismograph station code, US Geological Survey*] (SEIS) ... WBL
White Bluff, TN [*AM radio station call letters*] ... WQSE
White Border [*Deltiology*] ... W/BOR
White Cast Iron ... WCI
White Castle, LA [*AM radio station call letters*] ... KKAY
White Cathode Follower ... WCF
White Cell [*Medicine*] (AAMN) ... W
White Cell [*Medicine*] ... WC
White Cell Cast [*Hematology*] (MAE) ... WC
White Cell Count [*Hematology*] (MAE) ... WCC
White Child [*Medicine*] (DMAA) ... wh ch

White Citizens' Council (WDAA) ... WCC
White City, FL [*FM radio station call letters*] ... WFLM
White Clip Level [*Video technology*] ... WCL
White Clothing [*British military*] (DMA) ... W/C
White Cloud, MI [*Location identifier FAA*] (FAAL) ... HIC
White Clover Large Cryptic Virus [*Plant pathology*] ... WCLCV
White Clover Mosaic Virus [*Plant pathology*] ... WCLMV
White Clover Mosaic Virus ... WCMV
White Clover Small Cryptic Virus [*Plant pathology*] ... WCSCV
White Clover Temperate Virus [*Plant pathology*] ... WCTEV
White Collar [*Worker*] (DCTA) ... W/C
White Collar Productivity Improvement (MCD) ... WCPI
White Combination Potentiometer ... WCP
White Confederacy [*Defunct*] (EA) ... WC
White Count [*Hematology*] ... WC
White Cross League [*British*] ... WCL
White Crossover Vote [*Political science*] ... WCROS
White Dwarf [*Star*] (BARN) ... WD
White Dwarf [*Galactic science*] ... WD
White Edges (ADA) ... WE
White Edges [*Bookbinding*] (DGA) ... Wh e
White English Celtic Catholic ... WECC
White European Male [*Lifestyle classification*] (ECON) ... WEM
White Falcon [*A publication*] (DNAB) ... WF
White Fathers [*Roman Catholic men's religious order*] ... WF
White Female ... WF
White Fine Lustre Double Weight [*Photographic paper*] (DGA) ... WFLD
White Fir [*Botany*] ... WF
White Fish Authority [*MAFF*] [*British*] ... WFA
White Fuming Nitric Acid ... WFNA
White Gaussian Noise [*Random interference caused by movement of electricity in line*] [*Telecommunications*] (IAA) ... WGN
White Hall, AR [*FM radio station call letters*] ... KWDA
White Hall Township Library, White Hall, IL [*Library symbol Library of Congress*] (LCLS) ... IWhh
White Haven Center, White Haven, PA [*OCLC symbol*] (OCLC) ... PIA
White Hornet [*Immunology*] ... WH
White House ... WH
White House Army Signal Agency ... WHASA
White House Communications Agency (AABC) ... WHCA
White House Conference ... WHC
White House Conference on Aging ... WHCOA
White House Conference on Children and Youth (EA) ... WHCCY
White House Conference on Families [*June 5-July 3, 1980*] (EGAO) ... WHCF
White House Conference on Library and Information Services [*Washington, DC, 1979*] ... WHCLIS
White House Conference on Library and Information Services ... WHCOLIS
White House Conference on Library and Information Services Taskforce ... WHCLIST
White House Correspondents' Association (EA) ... WHCA
White House Historical Association (EA) ... WHHA
White House News Photographers Association (EA) ... WHNPA
[*The*] **White House Office** ... TWHO
[*The*] **White House Office** ... WHO
White House Personnel Office [*Terminated, 1974*] ... WHPO
White House Police [*Later, Executive Protective Service*] ... WHP
White House Science Council ... WHSC
White House Signal Support ... WHSS
White House Situation Room (MCD) ... WHSR
White [*David*], Inc. [*NASDAQ symbol*] (SAG) ... DAWH
White Incumbent ... WINC
White Indicating Light [*or lamp*] ... WIL
White Information [*Banking*] [*British*] ... WI
White Inhibited Fuming Nitric Acid (SAA) ... WIFNA
White Jewish Female [*Classified advertising*] ... WJF
White Laboratories, Inc. [*Research code symbol*] ... WL
White Lake, LA [*Location identifier FAA*] (FAAL) ... LLA
White Leghorn [*Poultry*] ... WL
White Letter [*or Line*] **Block** [*Typography*] (DGA) ... W/L/B
White Light (MSA) ... WL
White Light Coronagraph (KSC) ... WLC
White Light Coronagraph Experiment (KSC) ... WLCE
White Light Fringe Image Velocimeter (PDAA) ... WFIV
White Light Position ... WLP
White Lung Association (EA) ... WLA
White Male ... WM
White Male Candidate [*Politics*] ... WMC
White Memorial Medical Center, Los Angeles, CA [*Library symbol Library of Congress*] (LCLS) ... CLWM
White Metal ... WM
White Metal Casting Association [*British*] (DBA) ... WMCA
White Middle-Aged Female (MAE) ... WMF
White Middle-Aged Male (MAE) ... WMM
White Mountain [*Alaska*] [*Airport symbol*] (OAG) ... WMO
White Mountain, AK [*Location identifier FAA*] (FAAL) ... WMO
White Mountain Research Station [*Research center*] (RCD) ... WMRS
White Mountain Scenic Railroad [*AAR code*] ... WMSC
White Noise ... WN
White Noise Making [*Psychology*] ... WNM
White, Older Rich Man [*Lifestyle classification*] ... Worm
White on Black (DGA) ... WOB
White on Supplement and Revivor [*A publication*] (DLA) ... White Suppl
White Oval [*on Jupiter*] ... WO
White Owners Register (EA) ... WOR
White Painted (BJA) ... WP
White Paper (ADA) ... WP
White Park Cattle Association of America (EA) ... WPCAA
White Pass & Yukon Corp. Ltd. [*Toronto Stock Exchange symbol Vancouver Stock Exchange symbol AAR code*] ... WPY
White Pass & Yukon Railway [*Nickname: Wait Patiently and You'll Ride*] ... WP&YR
White Pennant [*Navy British*] ... WT
White Phosphorus [*Military*] ... WP
White Pigeon Township Library, White Pigeon, MI [*Library symbol Library of Congress*] (LCLS) ... MiWh
White Pine [*Michigan*] [*Seismograph station code, US Geological Survey*] (SEIS) ... WPM
White Pine Library System, Saginaw, MI [*OCLC symbol*] (OCLC) ... EZW
White Pine Library System, Saginaw, MI [*Library symbol Library of Congress*] (LCLS) ... MiSW
White Pine Software, Inc. [*Associated Press*] (SAG) ... WhtePne
White Pine Software, Inc. [*NASDAQ symbol*] (SAG) ... WPNE
White Plains [*New York*] [*Airport symbol*] (OAG) ... HPN
White Plains, NY [*Location identifier FAA*] (FAAL) ... OJZ
White Plains, NY [*AM radio station call letters*] ... WFAS
White Plains, NY [*FM radio station call letters*] ... WFAS-FM
White Plains Public Library, White Plains, NY [*Library symbol Library of Congress*] (LCLS) ... NWhp
White Plains Public Library, White Plains, NY [*OCLC symbol*] (OCLC) ... YPL
White Plains/Westchester [*New York*] [*ICAO location identifier*] (ICLI) ... KHPN
White Plate Flat Trackers Association (EA) ... WPFTA
White Port and Lemon Juice [*Title of both song and drink*] ... WPLJ
White Power Structure ... WPS
White Puerto Rican ... WPR
White Return [*Round trip fare for specified period*] [*British*] ... W
White River [*NASDAQ symbol*] (TTSB) ... WHRC
White River [*Alaska*] [*Seismograph station code, US Geological Survey*] (SEIS) ... WRG
White River Air Services Ltd. [*Canada ICAO designator*] (FAAC) ... WRA
White River Community Library, Ontario [*Library symbol National Library of Canada*] (NLC) ... OWRC
White River Corp. [*Associated Press*] (SAG) ... WhiteRvr
White River Corp. [*NASDAQ symbol*] (SAG) ... WHRC
White River Junction, VT [*FM radio station call letters*] ... WKXE
White River Junction, VT [*AM radio station call letters*] ... WNHV
White River News, Hazelton, IN [*Library symbol Library of Congress*] (LCLS) ... InHazN
White River, ON [*ICAO location identifier*] (ICLI) ... CYWR
White River Regional Library, Batesville, AR [*Library symbol*] [*Library of Congress*] (LCLS) ... ArBaWR
White Rock, NM [*FM radio station call letters*] ... KNLA
White Room [*NASA*] (KSC) ... W/R
White Rose Dollmakers Circle [*British*] [*An association*] (DBA) ... WRDC
White Russian Soviet Socialist Republic (IIA) ... WRSSR
White Sands Air Weather Detachment [*New Mexico*] ... WSAWD
White Sands/Condron Army Air Field [*New Mexico*] [*ICAO location identifier*] (ICLI) ... KWSD
White Sands Electromagnetic Pulse Systems Test Array [*New Mexico*] (RDA) ... WESTA
White Sands Field Center [*New Mexico*] ... WSFC
White Sands Ground Terminal [*NASA*] (MCD) ... WSGT
White Sands Integrated Range [*New Mexico*] (AAG) ... WSIR
White Sands Missile Range [*New Mexico*] [*Army*] ... WSMR
White Sands Missile Range Library, White Sands Missile Range, NM [*Library symbol Library of Congress*] (LCLS) ... NmWM
White Sands Missile Range Transverse Mercator [*Army*] (AABC) ... WSTM
White Sands Missile Test Center [*New Mexico*] ... WSMTC
White Sands NASA Ground Terminal (MCD) ... WSNGT
White Sands National Monument [*New Mexico*] ... WESA
White Sands, NM [*Location identifier FAA*] (FAAL) ... WSD
White Sands Operations [*New Mexico*] [*Formerly, White Sands Missile Operations*] [*NASA*] ... WSO
White Sands Proving Ground [*New Mexico*] [*Obsolete*] ... WSPG
White Sands Signal Agency [*New Mexico*] [*Military*] (MCD) ... WSSA
White Sands Signal Corps Agency [*New Mexico*] [*Military*] (AAG) ... WSSCA
White Sands Test Facility [*New Mexico*] [*Military*] ... WSTF
White Scale ... WHS
White Sidewall [*Tires*] ... WSW
White Single Male [*Classified advertising*] ... WSM
White Sisters [*Missionary Sisters of Our Lady of Africa*] [*Roman Catholic religious order*] ... WS
White Sisters of Charity of St. Vincent de Paul [*Roman Catholic religious order*] ... WSC
White Slave Traffic Act ... WSTA
White Smooth Glossy [*Photographic paper*] (DGA) ... WSG
White Smooth Glossy Double Weight [*Photographic paper*] (DGA) ... WSGD
White Smooth Glossy Single Weight [*Photographic paper*] (DGA) ... WSGS
White Smooth Lustre Double Weight [*Photographic paper*] (DGA) ... WSLD
White Squire (MHDW) ... WS
White Star Mobile Training Teams [*Military*] (CINC) ... WSMTT
White Star Parachute Flares [*Military*] (INF) ... WSP
White Stone, VA [*FM radio station call letters*] ... WNDJ
White Sucker [*Ichthyology*] ... WS
White Sulphur Springs & Yellowstone Park Railway Co. [*AAR code*] ... WSYP
White Sulphur Springs, WV [*Location identifier FAA*] (FAAL) ... SSU
White Sulphur Springs, WV [*AM radio station call letters*] ... WSLW
White Supercalendered Offset Paper [*Publishing*] ... WSOP
White Superficial Onychomycosis ... WSO
White Swan Elementary School, Rockford, IL [*Library symbol*] [*Library of Congress*] (LCLS) ... IRoWsE

White Turnout [Political science] .... WTURN
White, Urban, Middle Class, Protestant .... WUMP
White Waltham [British ICAO location identifier] (ICLI) .... EGLM
White Wolf-Kern Canyon [Geological fault] .... WWKC
White Wyandotte [Poultry] .... WW
White-Breasted Nuthatch [Ornithology] .... WN
Whitecourt, AB [Television station call letters] CFRN-3
Whitecourt, AB [ICAO location identifier] (ICLI) .... CYZU
Whitecourt Public Library, Alberta [Library symbol National Library of
  Canada] (NLC) .... AWH
White-Dwarf Luminosity Function [Galactic science] .... WDLF
Whiteface [New Hampshire] [Seismograph station code, US Geological
  Survey] (SEIS) .... WNH
Whitefield, NH [Location identifier FAA] (FAAL) .... GMA
Whitefield, NH [Location identifier FAA] (FAAL) .... HIE
Whitefish Branch, Walden Public Library, Ontario [Library symbol National
  Library of Canada] (NLC) .... OWWH
Whitefish Lake Band Public Library, Naughton, Ontario [Library symbol
  National Library of Canada] (NLC) .... ONWL
Whitefish, MT [AM radio station call letters] .... KJJR
Whitefish River Band Public Library, Birch Island, ON, Canada [Library
  symbol] [Library of Congress] (LCLS) .... CaOBIWR
Whitefish River Band Public Library, Birch Island, Ontario [Library symbol
  National Library of Canada] (NLC) .... OBIWR
Whitefish Senior High School, Whitefish, MT [Library symbol] [Library of
  Congress] (LCLS) .... MtWfSH
Whiteford on Charities [1878] [A publication] (DLA) ...... White Char
Whitehall Corp. [Associated Press] (SAG) .... Whitehl
Whitehall Corp. [NYSE symbol] (SPSG) .... WHT
Whitehall Free Library, Whitehall, NY [Library symbol] [Library of Congress]
  (LCLS) .... NWhh
Whitehall, MI [AM radio station call letters] .... WEFG
Whitehall, MI [FM radio station call letters] .... WEFG-FM
Whitehall, MI [FM radio station call letters] .... WKBZ
Whitehall, MT [Location identifier FAA] (FAAL) .... HIA
Whitehall, NY [FM radio station call letters] .... WNYV
Whitehall Township Public Library, Whitehall, PA [Library symbol Library of
  Congress] (LCLS) .... PWhi
Whitehall, WI [FM radio station call letters] .... WHTL
Whitehead Elementary School, Rockford, IL [Library symbol] [Library of
  Congress] (LCLS) .... IRoWhE
Whitehorse [Yukon Territory] [Seismograph station code, US Geological
  Survey] (SEIS) .... WHC
Whitehorse [Canada] [Airport symbol] (OAG) .... YXY
Whitehorse Historical Society, Whitehorse, YT, Canada [Library symbol
  Library of Congress] (LCLS) .... CaYWHS
Whitehorse Historical Society, Yukon [Library symbol National Library of
  Canada] (NLC) .... YWHS
Whitehorse Public Library, Whitehorse, YT, Canada [Library symbol] [Library
  of Congress] (LCLS) .... CaYW
Whitehorse Public Library, Yukon [Library symbol National Library of
  Canada] (NLC) .... YW
Whitehorse, YT [AM radio station call letters] .... CFWH
Whitehorse, YT [Television station call letters] .... CFWH-TV
Whitehorse, YT [FM radio station call letters] .... CHON
Whitehorse, YT [AM radio station call letters] .... CKRW
Whitehorse, YT [ICAO location identifier] (ICLI) .... CYXY
Whitehouse, FL [Location identifier FAA] (FAAL) .... NEN
Whitehouse, TX [FM radio station call letters] .... KISX
White-Indian-Negro .... WIN
Whitelaw School, Alberta [Library symbol National Library of Canada]
  (BIB) .... AWHS
Whiteley's Weights, Measures, and Weighing Machines [1879]
  [A publication] (DLA) .... White W & M
Whiteman Air Force Base (SAA) .... WAFB
Whitemore on Adoption of Children [A publication] (DLA) ... Whitm Adopt
Whiteriver, AZ [FM radio station call letters] .... KNNB
Whiteriver Public Library, Whiteriver, AZ [Library symbol Library of
  Congress] (LCLS) .... AzWhr
Whiteruthenian American Relief (EA) .... WAR
Whiteruthenian [Byelorussian] Congress Committee of America [Later,
  Byelorussian Congress Committee of America] (EA) .... WCCA
Whiteruthenian Institute of Arts and Science [Later, BIAS] (EA) ...... WIAS
White's Annotated Penal Code [Texas] [A publication]
  (DLA) .... White's Ann Pen Code
White's Justiciary Court Reports [3 vols.] [Scotland] [A publication]
  (DLA) .... White
White's Land Law of California [A publication] (DLA) ...... White LL
White's New Collection of the Laws, Etc., of Great Britain, France, and
  Spain [A publication] (DLA) .... White Coll
White's New Collection of the Laws, Etc. of Great Britain, France, and
  Spain [A publication] (DLA) .... White New Coll
White's Reports [10-15 West Virginia] [A publication] (DLA) ...... White
White's Reports [31-44 Texas Appeals] [A publication] (DLA) ...... White
White's Reports [10-15 West Virginia] [A publication] (DLA) ... White's Rep
White's Reports [31-44 Texas Appeals] [A publication] (DLA) ... White's Rep
Whitesboro, NY [FM radio station call letters] (RBYB) .... WOWZ
Whitesburg, KY [Location identifier FAA] (FAAL) .... BRG
Whitesburg, KY [FM radio station call letters] .... WMMT
Whitesburg, KY [AM radio station call letters] .... WTCW
Whitesburg, KY [FM radio station call letters] .... WXKQ
Whiteshell Nuclear Research Establishment [Atomic Energy of Canada Ltd.]
  [Research center] .... WNRE

Whiteshell Nuclear Research Establishment, Atomic Energy of Canada
  [Etablissement de Recherche Nucleaire Whiteshell, L'Energie Atomique du
  Canada] Pinawa,Manitoba [Library symbol National Library of Canada]
  (NLC) .... MPW
Whiteshell Reactor [Canada] .... WR
Whitetails Unlimited (EA) .... WTU
Whitetails Unlimited (EA) .... WU
White-Throated Sparrow [Ornithology] .... WS
Whiteville, NC [Location identifier FAA] (FAAL) .... CPC
Whiteville, NC [AM radio station call letters] .... WENC
Whiteville, NC [AM radio station call letters] .... WTXY
Whiteville, NC [FM radio station call letters] .... WZFX
Whitewall Tire [Automotive accessory] .... WW
Whiteware Research Association [Defunct] (EA) .... WRA
Whitewater Unified School District, Joint Number One, Whitewater, WI
  [Library symbol Library of Congress] (LCLS) .... WWhiwSD
Whitewater Valley Area Library Services Authority [Library network] ...... WVALSA
Whitewater, WI [FM radio station call letters] .... WISQ
Whitewater, WI [FM radio station call letters] (RBYB) ..... WKCH-FM
Whitewater, WI [FM radio station call letters] .... WSLD
Whitewater, WI [FM radio station call letters] .... WSUW
Whitewing Labs [NASDAQ symbol] (TTSB) .... WWLI
Whitewing Labs, Inc. [Associated Press] (SAG) .... Whtewg
Whitewing Labs, Inc. [Associated Press] (SAG) .... Whtewng
Whitewing Labs, Inc. [NASDAQ symbol] (SAG) .... WWLI
Whitewing Labs Wrrt [NASDAQ symbol] (TTSB) .... WWLIW
Whitgift Scholar [British] .... Whit Schol
Whiting Field [Milton] [Florida] [Seismograph station code, US Geological
  Survey] [Closed] (SEIS) .... WFF
Whiting Public Library, Whiting, IN [Library symbol Library of Congress]
  (LCLS) .... InWh
Whiting, WI [FM radio station call letters] .... WYTE
Whiting-Robertsdale Historical Society, Whiting, IN [Library symbol Library
  of Congress] (LCLS) .... InWhHi
Whitland [British depot code] .... WTD
Whitley City, KY [FM radio station call letters] .... WHAY
Whitley County Recorder's Office, Columbia City, IN [Library symbol Library
  of Congress] (LCLS) .... InColcCR
Whitman College, Walla Walla, WA [Library symbol Library of Congress]
  (LCLS) .... WaWW
Whitman Co. [NYSE symbol] (SPSG) .... WH
Whitman Corp. [NYSE symbol] (TTSB) .... WH
Whitman Corp. [Associated Press] (SAG) .... Whitmn
Whitman County Library, Colfax, WA [Library symbol Library of Congress]
  (LCLS) .... WaCol
Whitman Education Group [Associated Press] (SAG) .... WhitmE
Whitman Education Group [AMEX symbol] (SAG) .... WIX
Whitman Education Group [AMEX symbol] (TTSB) .... WIX
Whitman Elementary School, Syosset, NY [Library symbol Library of
  Congress] (LCLS) .... NSyoWhE
Whitman, MA [Location identifier FAA] (FAAL) .... HTM
Whitman Medical Corp. [Associated Press] (SAG) .... WhitmM
Whitman Medical Corp. [AMEX symbol] (SAG) .... WIX
Whitman Mission National Historic Site .... WHMI
Whitman's Massachusetts Libel Cases [A publication] (DLA) ... Whitm Lib Cas
Whitman's Patent Cases [United States] [A publication] (DLA) ... Whit Pat Cas
Whitman's Patent Cases [United States] [A publication] (DLA) ... Whitm Pat Cas
Whitman's Patent Cases [United States] [A publication]
  (DLA) .... Whitman Pat Cas (US)
Whitman's Patent Law Review [Washington, DC] [A publication]
  (DLA) .... Whitm Pat Law Rev
Whitman's Patent Laws of All Countries [A publication] (DLA) ... Whit Pat
Whitman's Patent Laws of All Countries [A publication] (DLA) ... Whitm Pat Law
Whitmarsh's Bankrupt Law [2nd ed.] [1817] [A publication] (DLA) ... Whitm BL
Whitney [Hawaii] [Seismograph station code, US Geological Survey Closed]
  (SEIS) .... WHI
Whitney Communications Corp. [New York, NY] .... WCC
Whitney Damon Dextrose [Agar] (BABM) .... WD
Whitney Holding [NASDAQ symbol] (TTSB) .... WTNY
Whitney Holding Corp. [Associated Press] (SAG) .... WhitnyH
Whitney Holding Corp. [NASDAQ symbol] (SAG) .... WTNY
Whitney Museum of American Art [New York, NY] .... WMAA
Whitney Museum of American Art, New York, NY [Library symbol Library of
  Congress] (LCLS) .... NNWhit
Whitney Public Library, Porcupine, Ontario [Library symbol National Library
  of Canada] (NLC) .... OPW
Whitney's Land Laws [Tennessee] [A publication] (DLA) ...... Whitney
Whitneyville, PA [FM radio station call letters] .... WLIH
Whitstone [England] .... WHITS
Whitsunday Resort (Long Island) [Australia Airport symbol] ... HAP
Whittaker Corp. [Associated Press] (SAG) .... Whittakr
Whittaker Corp. [NYSE symbol] (SPSG) .... WKR
Whitten's Medium [for cell incubation] .... WM
Whittier College (GAGS) .... Whittier C
Whittier College, School of Law, Whittier, CA [Library symbol Library of
  Congress] (LCLS) .... CWhC-L
Whittier College, Whittier, CA [OCLC symbol] (OCLC) .... CWC
Whittier College, Whittier, CA [Library symbol Library of Congress]
  (LCLS) .... CWhC
Whittier Elementary School, Brainerd,MN [Library symbol] [Library of
  Congress] (LCLS) .... MnBrWE
Whittier Historical Society, Whittier, CA [Library symbol] [Library of
  Congress] (LCLS) .... CWhHi
Whittier Home Association, Amesbury, MA [Library symbol Library of
  Congress] (LCLS) .... MAmW

Whittier Public Library, Whittier, CA [*Library symbol Library of Congress*] (LCLS) .... CWh
Whittle Communications Corp., Knoxville, TN [*Library symbol*] [*Library of Congress*] (LCLS) .... TKWC
Whittlesey [*Urban district in England*] .... WHITTL
Whittlesey's Reports [*32-41 Missouri*] [*A publication*] (DLA) .... Whitt
Whittlesey's Reports [*32-41 Missouri*] [*A publication*] (DLA) .... Whittlesey
Whittman-Hart Inc. [*NASDAQ symbol*] (TTSB) .... WHIT
Whittmore Champion, Whittmore, IA [*Library symbol Library of Congress*] (LCLS) .... IaWhitC
Whitworth College (GAGS) .... Whitworth C
Whitworth College, Spokane, WA [*Library symbol Library of Congress*] (LCLS) .... WaSpW
Whitworth. Equity Precedents [*A publication*] (ILCA) .... Whit Eq Pr
Whitworth Scholar [*British*] .... WHSCH
Whitworth's Equity Precedents [*A publication*] (DLA) .... Whit Eq Pr
Who .... WH
Who Are You [*Communication*] .... WRU
Who Cares, Anyway .... WCA
Who is Calling [*Amateur Radio*] (BARN) .... QRZ
Who Is Publishing in Science [*An Institute for Scientific Information publication*] [*Trademark*] .... WIPIS
Who Owns Corporate America [*A publication*] .... WOCA
Who Was Who [*A publication*] .... WWW
WHO [*World Health Organization*] **Western Pacific Regional Centre for the Promotion of Environmental Planning and Applied Studies** (EAIO) .... PEPAS
[*The*] **Who, What, or Where Game** [*Also, WWW*] [*Television show*] .... 3W's
[*The*] **Who, What, or Where Game** [*Also, 3W's*] [*Television show*] .... WWW
Who, What, When, Where, Why [*Journalism*] .... 5W's
Whoever [*Legal*] [*British*] (ROG) .... WHOER
Whok Seumawe/Malikus Saleh [*Indonesia*] [*ICAO location identifier*] (ICLI) .... WITM
Whole [*Response*] [*Medicine*] .... W
Whole Animal Cell Sorting .... WACS
Whole Blood [*Hematology*] (DAVI) .... QB
Whole Blood .... WB
Whole Blood [*Hematology*] (DAVI) .... WhB
Whole Blood Activated Partial Thromboplastin Time [*Hematology*] (DAVI) .... WBAPTT
Whole Blood Cell Count [*Hematology*] (DAVI) .... WBC
Whole Blood Folate [*Hematology*] (MAE) .... WBF
Whole Blood Hematocrit [*Hematology*] (MAE) .... WBH
Whole Blood Partial Thromboplastin Time [*Hematology*] .... WBPTT
Whole Blood Serotonin [*Biochemistry*] .... WBS
Whole Blood Serum of a Patient with Obstructive Jaundice [*Hematology*] (DAVI) .... WSOJ
Whole Blood Volume [*Hematology*] (DAVI) .... QBV
Whole Body [*Medicine*] .... WB
Whole Body [*Nuclear energy*] (NRCH) .... WB
Whole Body Activity (DAVI) .... WBA
Whole Body Hyperthermia [*Emergency medicine*] (DAVI) .... WBH
Whole Body Radiation .... WBR
Whole Body Scan [*Medicine*] (DMAA) .... WBS
Whole Body Shower .... WBS
Whole Bow [*Music*] (ROG) .... WB
Whole Colds [*Medicine*] .... W (Colds)
Whole Complement (MAE) .... WC
Whole Core Accident [*Nuclear energy*] (NRCH) .... WCA
Whole Cow's Milk .... WCM
Whole Depth .... WD
Whole Earth Decision Support System (EERA) .... WEDSS
Whole Earth Lectronic Link [*Telecommunications*] .... WELL
Whole Earth Review [*A publication*] (BRI) .... WER
Whole Earth Software Catalog [*A publication*] .... WESC
Whole Earth Telescope [*Global network of telescopes*] .... WET
Whole Economy [*Department of Employment*] [*British*] .... WE
Whole Effluent Toxicity [*Environmental Protection Agency*] .... WET
Whole Farm Plan Incentives Scheme [*of Victoria*] (EERA) .... WFPIS
Whole Farm Planning Program [*of Tasmania*] (EERA) .... WFPP
Whole Foods Market [*NASDAQ symbol*] (TTSB) .... WFMI
Whole Foods Market, Inc. [*NASDAQ symbol*] (SAG) .... WFMI
Whole Foods Market, Inc. [*Associated Press*] (SAG) .... WholeFd
Whole Human Embryo [*Type of cell line*] .... WHE
Whole Lithosphere Failure [*Geology*] .... WLF
Whole Milk (MAE) .... WM
Whole Mononuclear Cell [*Biochemistry*] .... WMNC
Whole Mount (AAMN) .... WM
Whole Ragweed Extract (MAE) .... WRE
Whole Rock [*Geology*] .... WR
Whole Rumen Digesta [*Dairy science*] (OA) .... WRD
Whole System Replacement Operation [*Army*] (INF) .... WSRO
Whole Tree Chips (PDAA) .... WTC
Whole Virus Vaccine [*Immunology*] .... WVV
Whole Wheat Flour (OA) .... WWF
Whole Word Designator [*Computer science*] .... W
Whole-Blood Clotting Time [*Hematology*] .... WBCT
Whole-Blood Recalcification Time [*Hematology*] .... WBRT
Whole-Body Extract [*Immunology*] .... WBE
Whole-Life Insurance (MHDB) .... WLI
Whole-Powder-Pattern Decomposition [*Crystallography*] .... WPPD
Wholesale (MHDB) .... whl
Wholesale (WGA) .... WHOL
Wholesale .... WHOL
Wholesale .... WHSLE
Wholesale Applications Management System (MHDB) .... WAMS
Wholesale Beer Association Executives of America (EA) .... WBAEA
Wholesale Buyers' Gifts Fair [*British*] (ITD) .... WBGF
Wholesale Commission Florists of America [*Later, WF & FSA*] .... WCFA
Wholesale Commodity Line (GFGA) .... WCL
Wholesale Confectioners Alliance Ltd. [*British*] (BI) .... WCA
Wholesale Confectionery and Tobacco Trade Alliance [*British*] (DBA) .... WCTA
Wholesale Dealer in Wines .... WDW
Wholesale Demand Deposit Accounting (DICI) .... WDDA
Wholesale Distributors Association (EA) .... WDA
Wholesale Druggists Merchandising Association (EA) .... WDMA
Wholesale Dry Goods Institute [*Later, NATAD*] .... WDGI
Wholesale Egg Distributors' Association [*British*] (BI) .... WEDA
Wholesale Floorcovering Distributors' Association [*British*] (BI) .... WFDA
Wholesale Florists and Florist Suppliers of America (EA) .... WF & FSA
Wholesale Footwear Distributors' Association [*British*] (BI) .... WFDA
Wholesale Grocers' Association of Scotland (DBA) .... WGAS
Wholesale Interservice Supply Agreement [*Military*] (NG) .... WISA
Wholesale Interservice Supply Support Agreements [*Military*] .... WISSA
Wholesale Interservices Support Agreement [*DoD*] .... WISA
Wholesale Inventory Management System (MHDB) .... WIMS
Wholesale Leather Distributors Association [*British*] (BI) .... WLDA
Wholesale Milk Buyers and Distributors' Association [*Australia*] .... WMBDA
Wholesale Nursery Growers of America (EA) .... WNGA
Wholesale Photo Finishers' Association [*British*] (BI) .... WPFA
Wholesale Price Index [*Economics*] .... WPI
Wholesale Price Index [*Data File*] .... WPINDEX
Wholesale Sales Tax .... WST
Wholesale School, Art, and Stationery Supplies Association [*Later, WSA*] (EA) .... WSASSA
Wholesale Stationers' Association (EA) .... WSA
Wholesale Stationery and Office Equipment Association [*Later, WSA*] (EA) .... WSOEA
Wholesale Storage Site (DNAB) .... WSS
Wholesale Tobacco Trade Association of Great Britain and Northern Ireland (BI) .... WTTA
Wholesale Traders' Association [*British*] (DBA) .... WTA
Wholesale Variety Bakers Association (EA) .... WVBA
Wholesale Wine [*License*] .... WW
Wholesaler .... WHSLR
Wholesalers Institutional Service Extension [*Division of National American Wholesale Grocers Association*] .... WISE
Wholesome & Hearty Foods [*NASDAQ symbol*] (TTSB) .... WHFI
Wholesome & Hearty Foods [*Associated Press*] (SAG) .... WholHty
Wholesome & Hearty Foods, Inc. [*NASDAQ symbol*] (SAG) .... WHFI
Whole-Time Consultants' Association [*British*] (BI) .... WTCA
Wholly-Owned Subsidiary [*Business term*] (MHDW) .... WOS
Whom It May Concern .... WIMC
Whonnock Industries Ltd. [*Toronto Stock Exchange symbol Vancouver Stock Exchange symbol*] .... WHN
Whooping Cough [*Medicine*] .... WC
Whooping Crane Conservation Association (EA) .... WCCA
Whore (DSUE) .... WH
Whorls and Compounds [*Fingerprint description*] .... W
Who's Inventing What [*A publication*] .... WIW
Who's Wealthy in America [*A publication*] .... WWA
Who's Who [*A publication*] .... WW
Who's Who Among Asian Americans [*A publication*] .... WWAA
Who's Who among Black Americans [*A publication*] .... WWBA
Who's Who among Hispanic Americans [*A publication*] .... WWHA
Who's Who in America [*A publication*] .... WWA
Who's Who in Art [*A publication*] .... WWA
Who's Who in Australia [*A publication*] .... WWA
Who's Who in Consulting [*A publication*] .... WWC
Who's Who in Saudi Arabia [*A publication*] .... WWSA
Who's Who in Technology [*A publication*] .... WWT
Who's Who in the Theatre [*A publication*] .... WWIT
Who's Who in the World of Women [*Australia A publication*] .... WWWW
Who's Who in World Jewry [*A publication*] (BJA) .... WWWJ
Who's Who Resource File [*Minority Business Development Agency*] [*Database*] .... WWRF
Whosoever [*Legal*] [*British*] (ROG) .... WHOSOR
WHX Corp. [*NYSE symbol*] (TTSB) .... WHX
WHX Corp.'A'Cv Pfd [*NYSE symbol*] (TTSB) .... WHXPr
WHX Corp.'B'Cv Pfd [*NYSE symbol*] (TTSB) .... WHXPrB
WHX Corp. Holding Co. [*Associated Press*] (SAG) .... WHX
WHX Corp. Holding Co. [*Associated Press*] (SAG) .... WHX Cp
Why Don't You Take Your Change In War Savings Stamps [*Cashier's sign*] [*World War II*] .... WDYTYCIWSS
Why Have Overages Afterwards [*DoD*] .... WHOA
Why Have You Forsaken Us [*Informal fundraising term*] (NFD) .... WHYFU
Why Have You Forsaken Us? [*Fundraising*] .... WHYFU
Why Have You Forsaken Us Letter [*Fundraising*] .... YFU
Whyalla [*Australia Airport symbol*] (OAG) .... WYA
Whyte & Hirschboeck, Law Library, Milwaukee, WI [*Library symbol Library of Congress*] (LCLS) .... WMW
Whyte Museum of the Canadian Rockies (Archives), Banff, Alberta [*Library symbol National Library of Canada*] (NLC) .... ABA
Whyte Museum of the Canadian Rockies (Gallery), Banff, Alberta [*Library symbol National Library of Canada*] (NLC) .... ABPWG
WI Wheels International [*Vancouver Stock Exchange symbol*] .... WIW
Wiarton Branch, Bruce County Public Library, Ontario [*Library symbol National Library of Canada*] (NLC) .... OWI
Wiarton, ON [*Television station call letters*] CKCO-2
Wiarton, ON [*ICAO location identifier*] (ICLI) .... CYVV

Wibaux Public Library, Wibaux, MT [*Library symbol*] [*Library of Congress*] (LCLS) ... MtW
WIC [*Women, Infants, and Children*] **Income Verification Survey** [*Food and Nutrition Service*] [*Department of Agriculture*] (GFGA) ... WIV
WIC Western International Communications Ltd. [*Toronto Stock Exchange symbol Vancouver Stock Exchange symbol*] ... WIC
Wicat Interactive System for Education (NITA) ... WISE
Wicat Interactive Terminal (NITA) ... WIT
Wichabai [*Guyana*] [*ICAO location identifier*] (ICLI) ... SYWI
Wichabai [*Guyana*] [*Airport symbol*] (AD) ... WBG
Wichita [*Kansas*] [*Airport symbol*] (OAG) ... ICT
Wichita [*Diocesan abbreviation*] [*Kansas*] (TOCD) ... WCH
Wichita Auditory Fusion Test ... WAFT
Wichita Auditory Processing Test [*Child development test*] ... WAPT
Wichita Automatic Linear Data Output ... WALDO
Wichita Board of Trade [*Defunct*] (EA) ... WBT
Wichita Clinic, Wichita, KS [*Library symbol Library of Congress*] (LCLS) ... KWiWC
Wichita Falls [*Texas*] [*Airport symbol*] (OAG) ... SPS
Wichita Falls & Southern Railroad (IIA) ... WF & S
Wichita Falls/Sheppard Air Force Base and Municipal [*Texas*] [*ICAO location identifier*] (ICLI) ... KSPS
Wichita Falls, TX [*Television station call letters*] ... KAUZ
Wichita Falls, TX [*Television station call letters*] ... KFDX
Wichita Falls, TX [*Television station call letters*] ... KJTL
Wichita Falls, TX [*AM radio station call letters*] ... KLLF
Wichita Falls, TX [*FM radio station call letters*] ... KLUR
Wichita Falls, TX [*FM radio station call letters*] ... KMOC
Wichita Falls, TX [*FM radio station call letters*] ... KNIN-FM
Wichita Falls, TX [*FM radio station call letters*] ... KQXC
Wichita Falls, TX [*FM radio station call letters*] ... KTEO
Wichita Falls, TX [*FM radio station call letters*] ... KTLT
Wichita Falls, TX [*FM radio station call letters*] ... KWFS
Wichita Falls, TX [*FM radio station call letters*] (RBYB) ... KWFS-FM
Wichita Falls, TX [*AM radio station call letters*] ... KWFT
Wichita Falls, TX [*Location identifier FAA*] (FAAL) ... SHP
Wichita Falls, TX [*Location identifier FAA*] (FAAL) ... SKB
Wichita, KS [*Location identifier FAA*] (FAAL) ... BEC
Wichita, KS [*Location identifier FAA*] (FAAL) ... CEA
Wichita, KS [*Location identifier FAA*] (FAAL) ... HOV
Wichita, KS [*Location identifier FAA*] (FAAL) ... HZW
Wichita, KS [*Location identifier FAA*] (FAAL) ... IAB
Wichita, KS [*Television station call letters*] ... KAKE
Wichita, KS [*FM radio station call letters*] ... KCFN
Wichita, KS [*FM radio station call letters*] ... KEYN
Wichita, KS [*AM radio station call letters*] ... KFDI
Wichita, KS [*FM radio station call letters*] ... KFDI-FM
Wichita, KS [*AM radio station call letters*] ... KFH
Wichita, KS [*FM radio station call letters*] ... KIBN
Wichita, KS [*FM radio station call letters*] ... KICT
Wichita, KS [*FM radio station call letters*] ... KKRD
Wichita, KS [*FM radio station call letters*] ... KMUW
Wichita, KS [*AM radio station call letters*] ... KNSS
Wichita, KS [*AM radio station call letters*] ... KQAM
Wichita, KS [*FM radio station call letters*] ... KRBB
Wichita, KS [*Television station call letters*] ... KSAS
Wichita, KS [*AM radio station call letters*] ... KSGL
Wichita, KS [*Television station call letters*] ... KSNW
Wichita, KS [*Television station call letters*] ... KWCV
Wichita, KS [*FM radio station call letters*] ... KYFW
Wichita, KS [*AM radio station call letters*] ... KZSN
Wichita, KS [*Location identifier FAA*] (FAAL) ... TWI
Wichita/McConnell Air Force Base [*Kansas*] [*ICAO location identifier*] (ICLI) ... KIAB
Wichita/Mid-Continent [*Kansas*] [*ICAO location identifier*] (ICLI) ... KICT
Wichita Mountains Array [*Oklahoma*] [*Seismograph station code, US Geological Survey Closed*] (SEIS) ... WMO
Wichita Mountains Seismological Laboratory ... WMSL
Wichita Mountains Seismological Observatory ... WMSO
Wichita Public Library, Wichita, KS [*OCLC symbol*] (OCLC) ... KFW
Wichita Public Library, Wichita, KS [*Library symbol Library of Congress*] (LCLS) ... KWi
Wichita River Oil Corp. [*Associated Press*] (SAG) ... WichRO
Wichita River Oil Corp. [*AMEX symbol*] (SPSG) ... WRO
Wichita State University (GAGS) ... Wichita St U
Wichita State University [*Kansas*] (PDAA) ... WSU
Wichita State University, Wichita, KS [*OCLC symbol*] (OCLC) ... KSW
Wichita State University, Wichita, KS [*Library symbol Library of Congress*] (LCLS) ... KWiU
Wick [*British ICAO location identifier*] (ICLI) ... EGPC
Wick [*Scotland*] [*Airport symbol*] (OAG) ... WIC
Wicked (DAS) ... W
Wickenburg, AZ [*FM radio station call letters*] (RBYB) ... KBSZ
Wickenburg, AZ [*FM radio station call letters*] ... KRDS
Wickenburg, AZ [*FM radio station call letters*] (RBYB) ... KSWG-FM
Wickenburg, AZ [*AM radio station call letters*] ... KTIM
Wickenburg Public Library, Wickenburg, AZ [*Library symbol Library of Congress*] (LCLS) ... AzWic
Wickenby [*British ICAO location identifier*] (ICLI) ... EGNW
Wicker (VRA) ... wkr
Wickes Lumber [*NASDAQ symbol*] (TTSB) ... WIKS
Wickes Lumber Co. [*Associated Press*] (SAG) ... WickLu
Wickes Lumber Co. [*NASDAQ symbol*] (SAG) ... WIKS
Wicket ... W
Wicket (ODBW) ... w
Wicket ... WKT
Wickford [*England*] ... WICKF
Wickford, RI [*AM radio station call letters*] (RBYB) ... WKFD
Wickham [*Australia Airport symbol*] ... WHM
Wickliffe, KY [*AM radio station call letters*] ... WBCE
Wickliffe, KY [*FM radio station call letters*] ... WGKY
Wicklow [*County in Ireland*] (ROG) ... WICK
Wicklow [*County in Ireland*] ... WICKL
Wicklow [*County in Ireland*] (ROG) ... WLOW
Wicomico County Free Library, Salisbury, MD [*Library symbol Library of Congress*] (LCLS) ... MdSalW
WICOR, Inc. [*NYSE symbol*] (SPSG) ... WIC
WICOR, Inc. [*Associated Press*] (SAG) ... WICOR
Wide [*Women's shoe width*] ... D
Wide (ODBW) ... w
Wide (WDMC) ... w
Wide ... W
Wide (VRA) ... wd
Wide Analysis Sheet ... WAS
Wide Angle (WDMC) ... WA
Wide Angle [*Photography*] ... WA
Wide Angle Collimated Display System [*Aviation*] (DA) ... WACS
Wide Angle Visual System (MCD) ... WAVS
Wide Antiarmor Minimissile (MCD) ... WASP
Wide Application System Adapter ... WASAR
Wide Area Antipersonnel Munition Cluster Bomb Unit (VNW) ... WAAPM-CBU
Wide Area Information Server [*Computer science*] ... WAIS
Wide Area Information Service [*or Server*] [*Telecommunications*] ... WAIS
Wide Area Information Transfer System [*Computer science*] (PCM) ... WAITS
Wide Area Mine Clearance [*Army*] (DOMA) ... WAMC
Wide Area Network [*Telecommunications*] ... WAN
Wide Area Network Interface Co-Processor [*Communications adapter*] (PCM) ... WNIC
Wide Area Side Penetrator Mine [*Army*] (ADDR) ... WASPM
Wide Area Surveillance [*Military*] ... WAS
Wide Area Telecommunications Service (NITA) ... WAT
Wide Area Telephone Service ... WATS
Wide Area Transmission Service [*or System*] ... WATS
Wide Band Beam [*Physics*] ... WBB
Wide Band Cable Systems Committee (NITA) ... WBCSC
Wide Band Noise (DAVI) ... WBN
Wide Bay Burnett Conservation Council (EERA) ... WBBCC
Wide Beam Special LASER (MCD) ... WBSL
Wide Body STOL [*Short Takeoff and Landing*] [*Aviation*] (IAA) ... WBS
Wide Character String Length [*Computer science*] (PCM) ... WCSLEN
Wide Deadband [*NASA*] ... WDB
Wide Dynamic Range ... WDR
Wide Field Camera ... WFC
Wide Field of View ... WFOV
Wide Field Optical Filter ... WFOF
Wide Field Optics ... WFO
Wide Field/Planetary Camera ... WFPC
Wide Flange (DAC) ... WF
Wide Flange Beam [*Metal industry*] ... WFB
Wide Gap Spark Chamber [*Electronics*] (OA) ... WGSC
Wide Information Network Data Online [*Government Printing Office*] ... WINDO
Wide, Notched P Wave [*Cardiology*] ... WNPW
Wide Pore [*Chromatography*] ... WP
Wide Pulse Blanking (MCD) ... WPB
Wide Pulse Width Modulation ... WPWM
Wide Range [*Nuclear energy*] (NRCH) ... WR
Wide Range Achievement Test-Revised ... Wrat-R
Wide Range Analog Input Subsystem ... WRAIS
Wide Range Employability Sample Test ... WREST
Wide Range Intelligence-Personality Test [*Personality development test*] [*Psychology*] ... WRIPT
Wide Range Interest and Opinion Test ... WRIOT
Wide Range (Monitor) [*Nuclear energy*] (NRCH) ... WR(M)
Wide Ratio [*Automotive engineering*] ... WR
Wide Receiver [*Football*] ... WR
Wide Sense Cyclo-Stationary [*Telecommunications*] ... WSCS
Wide Sense Stationary [*Telecommunications*] (IAA) ... WSS
Wide Sense Stationary Uncorrelated Scattering [*Telecommunications*] (IAA) ... WSSUS
Wide Shot [*Photography*] ... WS
Wide Whitewall Tire [*Automotive accessory*] ... WWW
Wide World of Entertainment [*TV program*] ... WWE
Wide Zone Alpha (MAE) ... WZa
Wide-Angle Display System ... WADS
Wide-Angle Fixed-Field Locating Equipment ... WAFFLE
Wide-Angle High Aperture (MCD) ... WAHA
Wide-Angle Impedance Matching (PDAA) ... WAIM
Wide-Angle Infinity Display Equipment ... WIDE
Wide-Angle Lens ... WAL
Wide-Angle Michelson Interferometer (PDAA) ... WAMI
Wide-Angle, Michelson-Doppler Imaging Interferometer (SSD) ... WAMDII
Wide-Angle Optical System ... WAOS
Wide-Angle Optics Weapon Assignment Display [*DoD*] ... WAD
Wide-Angle Panorama [*Photography*] [*NASA*] ... WAP
Wide-Angle Raster Head-Up Display (MCD) ... WARHUD
Wide-Angle Scanning Array Lens Antenna ... WASCAL
Wide-Angle Self-Destruct (MCD) ... WASD
Wide-Angle Sensor ... WAS
Wide-Angle Sun Seekers (SAA) ... WASS
Wide-Angle Tail [*Galactic radio source*] ... WAT
Wide-Angle [*Galilean*] **Telescopes** ... WAT's

Wide-Angle X-Ray Diffraction	WAXD
Wide-Angle X-Ray Scattering	WAXS
Wide-Aperture Array (MCD)	WAA
Wide-Aperture Radio Location Array	WARLA
Wide-Aperture Research Facility [For hurricane detection]	WARF
Wide-Area Active Surveillance [Military] (MCD)	WAAS
Wide-Area Active Surveillance System [Military] (MCD)	WASS
Wide-Area Antiarmor Munitions [Military] (MCD)	WAAM
Wide-Area Antipersonnel Mine [Military]	WAAPM
Wide-Area AppleTalk Network [Telecommunications]	WAAN
Wide-Area Augmentation System [Navigation systems]	WAAS
Wide-Area Data Service [Data transmission service]	WADS
Wide-Area Defense Missile (MCD)	WADM
Wide-Area Differential Global Positioning Satellite	WADGPS
Wide-Area Display (MCD)	WAD
Wide-Area Military Traffic Management and Terminal Service	WATS
Wide-Area Mine [Military] (MCD)	WAM
Wide-Area Mine Seismic Target Acquisition Sensor [Military] (MCD)	WAMSTAS
Wide-Area Remote Sensors	WARS
Wide-Area Telecommunications [formerly, Telephone] Service [American Telephone & Telegraph Co. contract billing system]	WATS
Wide-Area Telephone Service [Telecommunications] (IAA)	WATS
Wide-Area Traffic Control (PDAA)	WATC
Wide-Area-Network Module [Telecommunications]	WNIM
Wideawake [Ascension Island] [ICAO location identifier] (ICLI)	FHAW
Wideband [Radio transmission]	WB
Wideband [Radio] (MCD)	WDB
Wideband Acoustical Processor (CAAL)	WAP
Wideband Adapter Transformer	WAT
Wideband Adapter Transformer	WBAT
Wideband Amplifier	WA
Wideband Amplifier	WBA
Wideband Antenna System	WAS
Wideband Cassegrain Antenna	WCA
Wideband Cassegrain Antenna Feed System	WCAFS
Wideband Channel [Telecommunications]	WBC
Wideband Coherent Video (IEEE)	WBCV
Wideband Communications Line	WMCL
Wideband Communications Subsystem	WBCS
Wideband Coupler	WBC
Wideband Current Transformer	WBCT
Wideband Data	WBD
Wideband Data Assembly [Ground Communications Facility, NASA]	WBDA
Wideband Data Interleaver (MCD)	WBDI
Wideband Data Line [or Link]	WBDL
Wideband Data Recorder	WBR
Wideband Data Switch	WBDX
Wideband Dicke-Fix (CET)	WBDF
Wideband Dicke-Fix (MSA)	WBDFX
Wideband Directional Coupler	WDC
Wideband Electronics	WBE
Wideband Frequency Modulation	WBFM
Wideband High Intercept Probability	WHIP
Wideband High-Density Data Acquisition (MCD)	WHIDDA
Wideband Information Network Services [Computer science]	WINS
Wideband Intermediate Frequency (MCD)	WBIF
Wideband LASER	WBL
Wideband Limiter	WL
Wideband Limiting (IEEE)	WBL
Wideband Multichannel Receiver	WBMCR
Wideband Multichannel Receiver	WMR
Wideband Noise Limiting	WBNL
Wideband Noise Voltage	WBNV
Wideband Optical Modulation	WOM
Wideband Oscilloscope	WBO
Wideband Overlap	WBO
Wideband Patch Bay [Telecommunications] (IAA)	WBPB
Wideband Receiver	WBR
Wideband Remote Switch (IEEE)	WBRS
Wideband Signal Conditioner (NASA)	WBSC
Wideband Signal Conditioner (MCD)	WSC
Wideband Signal Processor	WSP
Wide-band Spread Spectrum Signal Generator	WSSSG
Wideband System [Ground Communications Facility, NASA]	WBS
Wideband System for Acquiring and Recording Data	WISARD
Wideband Terminal (MCD)	WBT
Wideband Transformer [or Transmitter]	WBT
Wideband Transmission Relay Acoustic Communications (MCD)	WIDETRACK
Wideband Transmission System (KSC)	WBTS
Wideband Video Tape Recorder	WBVTR
Wideband Voltage	WBV
Wideband Voltage-Controlled Crystal Oscillator	WBVCXO
Wideband Voltage-Controlled Oscillator	WBVCO
Wideband-Limiter-Heterodyne-Narrowband (PDAA)	WLHN
Widebeam (NATG)	WB
Widebeam High-Density Pulsed Source (MCD)	WHIPS
WideCom Group [NASDAQ symbol] (SAG)	WIDE
WideCom Group [Associated Press] (SAG)	WideC
WideCom Group [Associated Press] (SAG)	WideCm
WideCom Group [NASDAQ symbol] (TTSB)	WIDEF
WideCom Group [NASDAQ symbol] (SAG)	WIDW
WideCom Group Wrrt [NASDAQ symbol] (TTSB)	WIDWF
Widefield, CO [FM radio station call letters]	KKLI
Wide-Field Infrared Explorer [Satellite]	WIDE
Wide-Finding RADAR (MCD)	WFR

Wide-Frequency Antenna	WFA
Widely (FAAC)	WDLY
Widener College, Chester, PA [Library symbol Library of Congress] (LCLS)	PCW
Widener College, Chester, PA [OCLC symbol] (OCLC)	UWC
Widener University (GAGS)	Widener U
Widening Occupational Roles Kit (EDAC)	WORK
Wide-Open Throttle	WOT
Wide-Open Throttle Air-Conditioning Cut-Off Switch [Automotive engineering]	WAC
Wide-Open Throttle Switch [Automotive engineering]	WOTS
Wider (WGA)	WDR
Wider Opportunities for Women (EA)	WOW
Wider Quaker Fellowship (EA)	WQF
Wider Share Ownership Council [British] (DBA)	WSOC
Wider Television Access [British]	WTVA
Wide-Range Achievement Test	WRAT
Wide-Range Burner (DNAB)	WRB
Wide-Range Imaging Spectrophotometer [Naval Oceanographic Office]	WISP
Wide-Range Neutron Indicator (IEEE)	WRNI
Wide-Range Nuclear Instrument (IEEE)	WRNI
Wide-Range Recording and Monitoring [System] [Radiation]	WRAM
Wide-Range Sensor	WRS
Wideroe's Flyveselskap AS [Norway ICAO designator] (FAAC)	WIF
Wideros Flyveselskap [ICAO designator] (AD)	WF
Widescope Resources Ltd. [Vancouver Stock Exchange symbol]	WPR
Widespan Zoom Stereoscope (SAA)	WZS
Widespread	WDSPR
Widespread (FAAC)	WDSPRD
Widespread Depression Orchestra	WDO
Widow [or Widower]	W
Widow	WD
Widow [or Widower]	WID
Widow [Genealogy]	WW
Widow Of [Genealogy]	WW/O
Widowed (DAVI)	W
Widowed Jewish Female [Classified advertising]	WJF
Widowed Jewish Male [Classified advertising]	WJM
Widowed Oriental Female [Classified advertising]	WOF
Widowed Oriental Male [Classified advertising]	WOM
Widowed Persons Service (EA)	WPS
Widowed White Female [Classified advertising]	WWF
Widowed White Male [Classified advertising]	WWM
Widower [Legal shorthand] (LWAP)	WIDR
Widower [Genealogy]	WWR
Widows', Children's, and Dependents' Pension [British]	WCDP
Widows Consultation Center [Defunct] (EA)	WCC
Widows of World War I (EA)	WWWI
Widows' War Pensions and Gratuities [British]	WWPG
Width (WDMC)	w
Width	W
Width (MSA)	WD
Width (VRA)	wd
Width	WDT
Width	WID
Width (WGA)	WTH
Width across Flats (MSA)	WAF
Width Codes (AAG)	WC
Width-to-Diameter [Ratio] (KSC)	W/D
Width-to-Length [Ratio] (MDG)	W/e
Width-to-Length [Ratio] (IAA)	WL
Wiedemann Developed Template (MCD)	WDT
Wiederaufbaugesellschaft fuer die Juedische Bevoelkerung der Bucovina [A publication] (BJA)	WAG
Wiederwerbgesetz (BJA)	WWG
Wien [Austria ICAO location identifier] (ICLI)	LOVV
Wien [Austria ICAO location identifier] (ICLI)	LOWM
Wien Air Alaska [Air carrier designation symbol]	WAA
Wien Air Alaska [ICAO designator] (AD)	WC
Wien Automatic Systems Planning [Nuclear energy] (NUCP)	WASP
Wien Bridge Circuit [Physics]	WBC
Wien Bridge Oscillator [Physics]	WBO
Wien Displacement Law [Physics]	WDL
Wien Radiation Law [Physics]	WRL
Wien/Schwechat [Austria ICAO location identifier] (ICLI)	LOWW
Wien-Auhof [Austria] [Geomagnetic observatory code]	WIA
Wiener Canonical Expansion [Mathematics]	WCE
Wiener Institut fuer Internationale Wirtschaftsvergleiche [Vienna Institute for Comparative Economic Studies] [Information service or system] (IID)	WIIW
Wiener Library [London] (BJA)	WL
Wiener Mapping Procedure	WMP
Wiener Neustadt [Austria ICAO location identifier] (ICLI)	LOXN
Wiener Oeffentlicher Kueche [Viennese Open Kitchen] [Nonprofit temperance restaurant chain] [Austria]	WOK
Wiener Random Process [Mathematics]	WRP
Wiener Studien [A publication] (OCD)	Wien Stud
Wien-Kobenzl [Austria] [Geomagnetic observatory code]	WIK
Wier-in-Tube Sensor (PDAA)	WIT
Wiesbaden [Germany ICAO location identifier] (ICLI)	EDAW
Wiesbaden [Germany ICAO location identifier] (ICLI)	EDOU
Wiest Lake [California] [Seismograph station code, US Geological Survey] (SEIS)	WLK
Wife (WDMC)	w
Wife	W
Wife [Citizens band radio slang]	YF
Wife (Ex-Young-Lady) [Amateur radio slang]	YF(XYL)

Wife Of [*Genealogy*] .... WF/O
Wife's Divorce (ROG) .... WD
Wife's Judicial Separation [*Legal*] [*British*] (ROG) .... WJS
Wife's Restitution of Conjugal Rights [*Law suit*] [*British*] (ROG) .... WRCR
Wiggins Airways [*ICAO designator*] (FAAC) .... WIG
Wiggins, MS [*FM radio station call letters*] (RBYB) .... WCPR-FM
Wiggins, MS [*AM radio station call letters*] .... WIGG
Wiggins Teape Paper [*Commercial firm British*] .... WTP
Wight's Scottish Election Cases [*1784-96*] [*A publication*] (DLA) .... Wight El Cas
Wightwick's English Exchequer Reports [*145 English Reprint*] [*A publication*] (DLA) .... Wight
Wightwick's English Exchequer Reports [*145 English Reprint*] [*A publication*] (DLA) .... Wightw
Wightwick's English Exchequer Reports [*145 English Reprint*] [*A publication*] (DLA) .... Wightw (Eng)
Wigmore on Evidence [*A publication*] (DLA) .... Wigm Ev
Wigmore on Wills [*A publication*] (DLA) .... Wig Wills
Wigner-Seitz [*Construction cell*] [*Solid state physics*] .... W-S
Wigner-Seitz Method [*Solid state physics*] .... WSM
Wigorniensis [*Signature of Bishop of Worcester*] [*British*] (ROG) .... WIGORN
Wigram [*New Zealand*] [*ICAO location identifier*] (ICLI) .... NZWG
Wigram on Discovery [*2nd ed.*] [*1840*] [*A publication*] (DLA) .... Wig Disc
Wigram on Extrinsic Evidence [*A publication*] (DLA) .... Wig Ev
Wigram on Loills [*A publication*] (DLA) .... Wig
Wikalat Al-Maghreb Al-Arabi [*News agency*] [*Morocco*] (MENA) .... WMA
Wikwemikong Band Public Library, Ontario [*Library symbol National Library of Canada*] (NLC) .... OWIB
Wilanour Resources Ltd. [*Toronto Stock Exchange symbol*] .... WLR
Wilberforce, OH [*FM radio station call letters*] .... WCSU
Wilberforce on Construction and Operation of Statutes [*1881*] [*A publication*] (DLA) .... Wilb Stat
Wilberforce on Statute Law [*A publication*] (DLA) .... Wilberforce
Wilberforce University, Wilberforce, OH [*Library symbol Library of Congress*] (LCLS) .... OWibfU
Wilberforce University, Wilberforce, OH [*OCLC symbol*] (OCLC) .... WBU
Wilbur Hot Springs Health Sanctuary (EA) .... WHSHS
Wilbur Public Schools System, Wilbur, WA [*Library symbol Library of Congress*] (LCLS) .... WaWiS
Wilbur Wright Community College, Chicago, IL [*Library symbol Library of Congress*] (LCLS) .... ICWC
Wilbur's, Inc. [*ICAO designator*] (FAAC) .... WFO
Wilcannia [*Australia Airport symbol*] (OAG) .... WIO
Wilco Mining Co. Ltd. [*Toronto Stock Exchange symbol*] .... WIL
Wilcox, AZ [*FM radio station call letters*] .... KWCX
Wilcox on Municipal Corporations [*Ohio*] [*A publication*] (DLA) .... Wilc Mun Corp
Wilcox Solar Observatory .... WSO
Wilcox's Condensed Ohio Reports [*A publication*] (DLA) .... Ohio Cond
Wilcox's Condensed Ohio Reports [*A publication*] (DLA) .... Ohio Cond R
Wilcox's Condensed Ohio Reports [*A publication*] (DLA) .... Wilcox Cond
Wilcox's Condensed Ohio Reports (Reprint) [*1-7 Ohio*] [*A publication*] (DLA) .... Wilc Cond
Wilcox's Condensed Ohio Reports (Reprint) [*1-7 Ohio*] [*A publication*] (DLA) .... Wilc Cond Rep
Wilcox's Lackawanna Reports [*Pennsylvania*] [*A publication*] (DLA) .... Wilcox
Wilcox's Reports [*10 Ohio*] [*A publication*] (DLA) .... Wilcox
Wild Aim Guess [*Bowdlerized version*] .... WAG
Wild and Scenic Rivers Act .... WSR
Wild and Scenic Rivers Act .... WSRA
Wild Animal Propagation Trust [*Defunct*] .... WAPT
Wild Bird Feeding Institute (EA) .... WBFI
Wild Blueberry Association of North America (EA) .... WBANA
Wild Canid Survival and Research Center - Wolf Sanctuary (EA) .... WCSRC
Wild Caught Animal [*Medicine*] (DMAA) .... WC
Wild Cucumber Mosaic Virus [*Plant pathology*] .... WCMV
Wild Dog Destruction Board [*New South Wales, Australia*] .... WDDB
Wild Flower Preservation Society (EA) .... WFPS
Wild Goose Association (EA) .... WGA
Wild Horse [*Utah*] [*Seismograph station code, US Geological Survey*] (SEIS) .... WHU
Wild Horse Industry [*Vancouver Stock Exchange symbol*] .... WHI
Wild Horse Organized Assistance (EA) .... WHOA
Wild Horse Parks [*Montana*] [*Seismograph station code, US Geological Survey Closed*] (SEIS) .... WHM
Wild Horses of America Registry (EA) .... WHAR
Wild Oats Markets, Inc. [*NASDAQ symbol*] (SAG) .... OATS
Wild Oats Markets, Inc. [*Associated Press*] (SAG) .... WildOats
Wild Pitch [*Baseball*] .... WP
Wild Rose Resources [*Vancouver Stock Exchange symbol*] .... WR
Wild Track [*Cinematography*] .... WT
Wild Type [*of a species*] [*Genetics*] .... WT
Wild Weasel [*Aerospace*] .... W/W
Wild Weasel Squadron [*Air Force*] .... WWS
Wild-Assed-Guess Principle [*Military slang*] (VNW) .... WAG
Wild-Ass-Guess [*Aviation*] .... WAG
Wildcat .... WLC
Wildcat Service Corp. (EA) .... WSC
Wildenrath [*Germany ICAO location identifier*] (ICLI) .... EDUW
Wilder District Library, Wilder, ID [*Library symbol*] [*Library of Congress*] (LCLS) .... IdWi
Wilder Memorial Library, Weston, VT [*Library symbol Library of Congress*] (LCLS) .... VtWeo
Wilderness [*State*] (EERA) .... W
Wilderness Airline (1975) Ltd. [*Canada ICAO designator*] (FAAC) .... WLD
Wilderness Education Association (EA) .... WEA
Wilderness Inquiry [*An association*] (EA) .... WI
Wilderness Leadership International (EA) .... WLI
Wilderness Medical Society (EA) .... WMS
[*The*] **Wilderness Society** (EERA) .... TWS
Wilderness Society (EA) .... WS
Wilderness Study Area [*Department of the Interior*] .... WSA
Wilderness Trail Bike .... WTB
Wilderness Watch (EA) .... WW
Wilde's Supplement to Barton's Conveyancing [*A publication*] (DLA) .... Wilde Conv
Wilde's Supplement to Barton's Conveyancing [*A publication*] (DLA) .... Wilde Sup
Wildfire Coordinating Committee (EA) .... WCC
Wildfire Resources Ltd. [*Vancouver Stock Exchange symbol*] .... WIF
Wildflecken [*Germany ICAO location identifier*] (ICLI) .... EDOW
Wildfowl Foundation (EA) .... WF
Wildfowl Trust [*British*] .... WFT
Wildfowl Trust of North America (GNE) .... WTNA
Wildfowlers' Association of Great Britain .... WAGB
Wildfowlers' Association of Great Britain and Ireland (BI) .... WAGBI
Wildland .... WLDND
Wildland Resources Center [*University of California*] [*Research center*] (RCD) .... WRC
Wildlife .... WLDLF
Wildlife Advisory Committee [*Tasmania, Australia*] .... WAC
[*CSIRO Division of*] **Wildlife and Ecology** [*Commonwealth*] (EERA) .... W&E
Wildlife and Inland Waters Library, Environment Canada [*Bibliotheque de la Faune et des Eaux Interieures, Environement Canada*] **Ste-Foy, Quebec** [*Library symbol National Library of Canada*] (NLC) .... QQE
Wildlife Conservation Fund of America (EA) .... WCFA
Wildlife Conservation International (EA) .... WCI
Wildlife Disease Association (EA) .... WDA
Wildlife Disease Association, Ames, IA [*Library symbol Library of Congress*] (LCLS) .... IaAWD
Wildlife Division, Nova Scotia Department of Lands and Forests, Kentville, Nova Scotia [*Library symbol National Library of Canada*] (NLC) .... NSKL
Wildlife Foundation Australian Capital Territory .... WFACT
Wildlife Habitat Enhancement Council (EA) .... WHEC
Wildlife in Australia [*A publication*] .... Wildl A
Wildlife Information Center (EA) .... WIC
Wildlife Legislative Fund of America (EA) .... WLFA
Wildlife Management Institute (EA) .... WMI
Wildlife Preservation Society of Australia .... WLPSA
Wildlife Preservation Society of Australia (EERA) .... WPSA
Wildlife Preservation Society of Queensland (EERA) .... WPSQ
Wildlife Preservation Trust International (EA) .... WPTI
Wildlife Protection (Regulations and Exports and Imports) [*Act 1982*] (EERA) .... WP (REI)
Wildlife Refuge Reform Coalition (EA) .... WRRC
Wildlife Rehabilitation Council (EA) .... WRC
Wildlife Research Project .... WRP
Wildlife Reserve [*State*] (EERA) .... WR
[*The*] **Wildlife Society** (EA) .... TWS
[*The*] **Wildlife Society** .... WS
Wildlife Sound Recording Society [*British*] .... WSRS
Wildlife Trade Monitoring Unit (GNE) .... WTMU
Wildman, Harrold, Allen & Dixon, Chicago, IL [*Library symbol*] [*Library of Congress*] (LCLS) .... ICWHA
Wildman. Search, Capture, and Prize [*A publication*] (ILCA) .... Wildm Search
Wildman's International Law [*A publication*] (ILCA) .... Wildm Int L
Wildman's International Law [*A publication*] (DLA) .... Wildm Int Law
Wildrose Petroleum Ltd. [*Vancouver Stock Exchange symbol*] .... WIR
Wildwood [*Alaska*] [*ICAO location identifier*] (ICLI) .... PAWW
Wildwood/Cape May County [*New Jersey*] [*ICAO location identifier*] (ICLI) .... KWWD
Wildwood Crest, NJ [*FM radio station call letters*] .... WDOX
Wildwood Crest Public Library, Wildwood, NJ [*Library symbol*] [*Library of Congress*] (LCLS) .... NjWw
Wildwood, FL [*AM radio station call letters*] .... WHOF
Wildwood Historical Commission, Wildwood, NJ [*Library symbol Library of Congress*] (LCLS) .... NjWwHi
Wildwood House [*Publisher*] [*British*] .... WH
Wildwood Leader, Wildwood, NJ [*Library symbol Library of Congress*] (LCLS) .... NjWwL
Wildwood, NJ [*Location identifier FAA*] (FAAL) .... CEJ
Wildwood, NJ [*AM radio station call letters*] .... WCMC
Wildwood, NJ [*Television station call letters*] .... WMGM
Wildwood, NJ [*Location identifier FAA*] (FAAL) .... WWD
Wildwood, NJ [*FM radio station call letters*] .... WZXL
Wildwood Public Library, Alberta [*Library symbol National Library of Canada*] (NLC) .... AWILD
Wiley [*John*] **& Sons** [*NYSE symbol*] (SAG) .... JW
Wiley [*John*] **& Sons** [*Associated Press*] (SAG) .... WileyJA
Wiley College, Marshall, TX [*Library symbol Library of Congress*] (LCLS) .... TxMaW
Wiley College, Marshall, TX [*Inactive*] [*OCLC symbol*] (OCLC) .... WYC
Wiley, John & Sons class A [*Associated Press*] (SAG) .... WileyJB
Wilford Hall United States Air Force Medical Center [*Lackland Air Force Base, TX*] (GRD) .... WHMC
Wilfrid Laurier University [*Canada*] .... WLU
Wilfrid Laurier University, Waterloo, ON, Canada [*Library symbol Library of Congress*] (LCLS) .... CaOWtL
Wilfrid Laurier University [*Formerly, Waterloo Lutheran University*] **Waterloo, Ontario** [*Library symbol National Library of Canada*] (NLC) .... OWTL
Wilgram and O'Hara on Wills [*A publication*] (DLA) .... W & O Wills
Wilhelm Furtwangler Society of America (EA) .... WFSA
Wilhelmshaven [*Federal Republic of Germany*] [*Geomagnetic observatory code*] .... WLH

Wilhelmshaven/Mariensiel [*Germany ICAO location identifier*] (ICLI) ... EDWI
Wilkerson/Wilkinson Clearinghouse (EA) ... WWC
Wilkes [*Antarctica*] [*Seismograph station code, US Geological Survey Closed*] (SEIS) ... WIL
Wilkes College (GAGS) ... Wilkes C
Wilkes College Library, Wilkes-Barre, PA [*OCLC symbol*] (OCLC) ... WBC
Wilkes College, Wilkes-Barre, PA [*Library symbol Library of Congress*] (LCLS) ... PWbW
Wilkes Community College, Wilkesboro, NC [*Library symbol Library of Congress*] (LCLS) ... NcWiW
Wilkes County Public Library, North Wilkesboro, NC [*Library symbol Library of Congress*] (LCLS) ... NcNw
Wilkes-Barre Connecting Railroad [*AAR code*] ... WBC
Wilkes-Barre Connecting Railroad (MHDB) ... WBCRR
Wilkes-Barre, PA [*Location identifier FAA*] (FAAL) ... CYE
Wilkes-Barre, PA [*Location identifier FAA*] (FAAL) ... LHY
Wilkes-Barre, PA [*AM radio station call letters*] ... WBAX
Wilkes-Barre, PA [*Television station call letters*] ... WBRE
Wilkes-Barre, PA [*Location identifier FAA*] (FAAL) ... WBW
Wilkes-Barre, PA [*FM radio station call letters*] ... WCLH
Wilkes-Barre, PA [*AM radio station call letters*] ... WILK
Wilkes-Barre, PA [*FM radio station call letters*] ... WKRZ
Wilkes-Barre, PA [*FM radio station call letters*] ... WMGS
Wilkes-Barre, PA [*FM radio station call letters*] ... WRKC
Wilkes-Barre, PA [*AM radio station call letters*] ... WYCK
Wilkes-Barre/Scranton [*Pennsylvania*] [*Derived from location of airport: Avoca, Pennsylvania*] [*Airport symbol*] ... AVP
Wilkes-Barre/Scranton, PA [*Location identifier FAA*] (FAAL) ... IZK
Wilkesboro, NC [*Location identifier FAA*] (FAAL) ... IKB
Wilkesboro, NC [*FM radio station call letters*] ... WSIF
Wilkesboro, NC [*AM radio station call letters*] ... WWWC
Wilkie Collins Society [*British*] (DBA) ... WCS
Wilkie, Farr & Gallagher, New York, NY [*Library symbol Library of Congress*] (LCLS) ... NNWFG
Wilkins' Leges Anglo-Saxonicae Ecclesiasticae et Civiles [*A publication*] (DLA) ... Wilk Leg Ang Sax
Wilkinson County Library System, Woodville, MS [*Library symbol Library of Congress*] (LCLS) ... MsWov
Wilkinson. Limitation of Actions [*A publication*] (ILCA) ... Wilk Lim
Wilkinson on Precedents in Conveyancing [*4th ed.*] [*1890*] [*A publication*] (DLA) ... Wilk Prec
Wilkinson on Public Funds [*1839*] [*A publication*] (DLA) ... Wilk Funds
Wilkinson on Replevin [*1825*] [*A publication*] (DLA) ... Wilk Repl
Wilkinson on Shipping [*1843*] [*A publication*] (DLA) ... Wilk Ship
Wilkinson, Owen, Paterson, and Murray's New South Wales Reports [*1862-65*] [*A publication*] (DLA) ... Wilk
Wilkinson, Owen, Paterson, and Murray's New South Wales Reports [*1862-65*] [*A publication*] (DLA) ... Wilk & Mur
Wilkinson, Owen, Paterson, and Murray's New South Wales Reports [*1862-65*] [*A publication*] (DLA) ... Wilk & Ow
Wilkinson, Owen, Paterson, and Murray's New South Wales Reports [*1862-65*] [*A publication*] (DLA) ... Wilk & Pat
Wilkinson, Paterson, and Murray's New South Wales Reports [*1862-65*] [*A publication*] (DLA) ... Wilk P & M
Wilkinson Sword Company [*British military*] (DMA) ... WSC
Wilkinson. Texas Court of Appeals and Civil Appeals [*A publication*] (DLA) ... Wilk
Wilkinson's Office of Sheriff [*A publication*] (DLA) ... Wilk Sh
Will Accept, If Offered, the Position [*Aviation*] (FAAC) ... WAIOP
Will Adjust (AABC) ... WA
Will Advise [*Business term*] ... W
Will Advise (HGAA) ... wa
Will Advise (FAAC) ... WLAV
Will Be (AABC) ... WB
Will Be Forwarded (NOAA) ... WIBFD
Will Be In (DAVI) ... WBI
Will Be Issued ... WBI
Will Be Issued (NOAA) ... WIBIS
Will Call ... WC
Will Call Back ... WCB
Will Comply (ODBW) ... wilco
Will Comply [*Used after "Roger"*] [*Radio term*] ... WILCO
Will Dated [*Genealogy*] (ROG) ... WD
Will Factor [*Psychology*] ... w
Will Not ... WN
Will Not Be ... WNB
Will Not Depart This Station [*Army*] (AABC) ... NODESTA
Will Not Proceed ... WNP
Will Not Process ... WNP
Will Proceed To ... WP
Will Proceed Without Delay ... WPWOD
Will Proved [*Legal*] [*British*] (ROG) ... WP
Will Rogers Library, Claremore, OH [*Library symbol Library of Congress*] (LCLS) ... OkClaW
Will Rogers Memorial Fund, Saranac Lake, NY [*Library symbol Library of Congress*] (LCLS) ... NSIW
Will Rogers State Historic Park, Pacific Palisades, CA [*Library symbol Library of Congress*] (LCLS) ... CPpR
Will Rogers World Airport [*FAA*] (TAG) ... OKC
Will Send Boat ... WSB
Will Ship (MCD) ... WS
Will Talk [*Telecommunications*] (TEL) ... WT
Will to Fire ... WTF
Will You Accept, If Offered, the Position Of [*Aviation*] (FAAC) ... WYAIO
Willa Cather Pioneer Memorial and Educational Foundation (EA) ... WCPMEF
Willa Cather Pioneer Memorial, Red Cloud, NE [*Library symbol Library of Congress*] (LCLS) ... NbRcW
Willamette Falls Community Hospital, Oregon City, OR [*Library symbol Library of Congress*] (LCLS) ... OrOWH
Willamette Indus [*NASDAQ symbol*] (TTSB) ... WMTT
Willamette Industries, Inc. [*Associated Press*] (SAG) ... Willamt
Willamette Industries, Inc. [*NASDAQ symbol*] (NQ) ... WMTT
Willamette Law Journal [*A publication*] (ILCA) ... WLJ
Willamette Tariff Bureau Inc., Portland OR [*STAC*] ... WTB
Willamette University (GAGS) ... Willamette U
Willamette University College of Law (DLA) ... WILUCL
Willamette University, Law Library, Salem, OR [*Library symbol Library of Congress*] (LCLS) ... OrSaW-L
Willamette University, Law Library, Salem, OR [*OCLC symbol*] (OCLC) ... OWT
Willamette University, Salem, OR [*Library symbol Library of Congress*] (LCLS) ... OrSaW
Willamette University, Salem, OR [*OCLC symbol*] (OCLC) ... OWS
Willamette Valley Vineyards, Inc. [*Associated Press*] (SAG) ... WillmVV
Willamette Valley Vineyards, Inc. [*NASDAQ symbol*] (SAG) ... WVVI
Willamina Public Library, Willamina, OR [*Library symbol Library of Congress*] (LCLS) ... OrWi
Willams-Sonoma, Inc. [*Associated Press*] (SAG) ... WmsSon
Willan's Criminal Law of Canada [*A publication*] (DLA) ... Will Cr L
Willard Library, Battle Creek, MI [*OCLC symbol*] (OCLC) ... EEW
Willard Library, Evansville, IN [*Library symbol Library of Congress*] (LCLS) ... InEW
Willard Library, Evansville, IN [*OCLC symbol*] (OCLC) ... IWL
Willard Memorial Library, Willard, OH [*Library symbol Library of Congress*] (LCLS) ... OWil
Willard, MO [*FM radio station call letters*] ... KOSP
Willard on Real Estate and Conveyancing [*A publication*] (DLA) ... Will Real Est
Willard Pease Oil & Gas Co. [*NASDAQ symbol*] (NQ) ... WPOG
Willard Psychiatric Center, Willard, NY [*Library symbol Library of Congress*] (LCLS) ... NWilP
Willard Public Library, Battle Creek, MI [*Library symbol Library of Congress*] (LCLS) ... MiBatW
Willard's Equity Jurisprudence [*A publication*] (DLA) ... Will Eq Jur
Willcock's Medical Profession [*1830*] [*A publication*] (DLA) ... Willc Med Pr
Willcock's Municipal Corp. [*A publication*] (ILCA) ... Willc Mun Corp
Willcock's Municipal Corp. [*A publication*] (DLA) ... Willcock Mun Corp
Willcock's The Office of Constable [*A publication*] (DLA) ... Willc Const
Willcox, AZ [*AM radio station call letters*] ... KHIL
Willcrest Resources Ltd. [*Vancouver Stock Exchange symbol*] ... WCR
Wille [*Will Factor*] [*Psychology*] ... W
Willelmus Rex [*King William*] ... WR
Willem Mengelberg Society (EA) ... WMS
Willemstad/Hato, Curacao Island [*Netherlands Antilles*] [*ICAO location identifier*] (ICLI) ... TNCC
Willes' English Common Pleas Reports [*125 English Reprint*] [*A publication*] (DLA) ... Will
Willes' English Common Pleas Reports [*125 English Reprint*] [*A publication*] (DLA) ... Willes
Willes' English Common Pleas Reports [*125 English Reprint*] [*A publication*] (DLA) ... Willes (Eng)
Willet Elementary School, Hicksville, NY [*Library symbol Library of Congress*] (LCLS) ... NHickWE
Willets Road Intermediate School, Roslyn Heights, NY [*Library symbol Library of Congress*] (LCLS) ... NRoslhWI
William [*Phonetic alphabet*] [*Royal Navy World War I Pre-World War II*] [*World War II*] (DSUE) ... W
William Addison Dwiggins [*American type designer and illustrator, 1880-1956*] ... WAD
William Alexander Percy Memorial Library, Greenville, MS [*Library symbol Library of Congress*] (LCLS) ... MsG
William Allen White Foundation (EA) ... WAWF
William and Mary [*King and Queen of England*] (ROG) ... W & M
William and Mary College. Bulletin [*A publication*] (DLA) ... Bull Coll Wm & Mary
William and Mary (King and Queen of England) (DLA) ... Wm & M
William and Mary Quarterly [*A publication*] (BRI) ... W&M Q
William and Mary Review of Virginia Law [*A publication*] (DLA) ... Wm & Mary Rev VA L
William and Mary Review of Virginia Law [*A publication*] (DLA) ... WMR
William Ave. Branch, Winnipeg Public Library, Manitoba [*Library symbol National Library of Canada*] (NLC) ... MWW
William B. McGuire Nuclear Station (NRCH) ... WMNS
William B. Stephens Memorial Library, Philadelphia, PA [*Library symbol Library of Congress Obsolete*] (LCLS) ... PPSteph
William Beaumont Army Medical Center (AABC) ... WBAMC
William Beaumont Hospital, Royal Oak, MI [*Library symbol Library of Congress*] (LCLS) ... MiRoyWB
William Beaumont Hospital, Troy, MI [*Library symbol Library of Congress*] (LCLS) ... MiTrWB
William C. Brown Publishers ... WCB
William Carey College (GAGS) ... Wm Carey C
William Carey College, Hattiesburg, MS [*Library symbol Library of Congress*] (LCLS) ... MsHaW
William Cobbett Society (EAIO) ... WCS
William Controls, Inc. [*Associated Press*] (SAG) ... WilmCtr
William Controls, Inc. [*NASDAQ symbol*] (NQ) ... WMCO
William Douglas McAdams, Inc., Medical Library, New York, NY [*Library symbol Library of Congress*] (LCLS) ... NNWM
William E. De Luca Jr. Elementary School, North Babylon, NY [*Library symbol*] [*Library of Congress*] (LCLS) ... NNbLE
William F. Laman Public Library, North Little Rock, AR [*Library symbol*] [*Library of Congress*] (LCLS) ... ArNlr

William Faulkner Foundation [Defunct] (EA) .... WFF
William Fogg Memorial Library, Eliot, ME [Library symbol Library of Congress] (LCLS) .... MeEl
William Grand Prix Racing Ltd. [Cayman Islands] [ICAO designator] (FAAC) .... WGP
William H. Rorer [Research code symbol] .... WHR
William H. Rorer, Inc., Fort Washington, PA [Library symbol Library of Congress] (LCLS) .... PFwR
William H. Zimmer Nuclear Power Station [Also, ZPS] (NRCH) .... WZNPS
William Heinemann [Publisher] [British] .... WH
William Henry Harrison [US president, 1773-1841] .... WHH
William Herschel Telescope .... WHT
William Howard Taft [US president, 1857-1930] .... WHT
William Hunter Society (EA) .... WHS
William II [German emperor and king of Prussia, 1888-1918] (DSUE) W2
William Jennings Bryan University [Tennessee] .... WJBU
William Jennings Bryan University, Dayton, TN [Library symbol Library of Congress] (LCLS) .... TDaB
William Jewell College [Liberty, MO] .... WJC
William Jewell College, Liberty, MO [OCLC symbol] (OCLC) .... MOI
William Jewell College, Liberty, MO [Library symbol Library of Congress] (LCLS) .... MoLiWJ
William (King of England) (DLA) .... W
William (King of England) (DLA) .... Will
William (King of England) (DLA) .... Wm
William L. Buck School, Valley Stream, NY [Library symbol] [Library of Congress] (LCLS) .... NVsBE
William L. Patterson Foundation [Defunct] (EA) .... WLPF
William Lake Museum, British Columbia [Library symbol National Library of Canada] (NLC) .... BWLM
William Lyon MacKenzie Collegiate Institute, Downsview, ON, Canada [Library symbol Library of Congress] (LCLS) .... CaOTWL
William Lyon Mackenzie Collegiate Institute, Downsview, Ontario [Library symbol National Library of Canada] (NLC) .... OTWL
William M. Mercer Ltd., Toronto, ON, Canada [Library symbol Library of Congress] (LCLS) .... CaOTWM
William M. Mercer Ltd., Toronto, Ontario [Library symbol National Library of Canada] (NLC) .... OTWM
William M. Mercer, Montreal, PQ, Canada [Library symbol Library of Congress] (LCLS) .... CaQMWM
William M. Mercer, Montreal, Quebec [Library symbol National Library of Canada] (NLC) .... QMWM
William McKinley [US president, 1843-1901] .... WMcK
William Mitchell College of Law (GAGS) .... Wm Mitchell C Law
William Mitchell College of Law [St. Paul, MN] .... WMCL
William Mitchell College of Law Library, St. Paul, MN [OCLC symbol] (OCLC) .... WMM
William Mitchell College of Law, St. Paul, MN [Library symbol Library of Congress] (LCLS) .... MnSWM
William Morris Society [Later, WMS/AB] (EA) .... WMS
William Morris Society, American Branch (EA) .... WMS/AB
William Morris Society and Kelmscott Fellowship [Kelmscott Fellowship and William Morris Society] [Formed by a merger of] (EAIO) .... WMSKF
William Paterson College [Wayne, NJ] .... WPC
William Paterson College of New Jersey (GAGS) .... Wm Paterson C NJ
William Paterson College of New Jersey, Wayne, NJ [Library symbol Library of Congress] (LCLS) .... NjWP
William Patterson College of New Jersey, Wayne, NJ [OCLC symbol] (OCLC) .... NJP
William Penn Association [Pittsburgh, PA] (EA) .... WPA
William Penn College [Oskaloosa, IA] .... WPC
William Penn College, Oskaloosa, IA [Library symbol Library of Congress] (LCLS) .... IaOskW
William Penn College, Oskaloosa, IA [OCLC symbol] (OCLC) .... IOX
William Penn Fraternal Association [Later, WPA] (EA) .... WPFA
William Penn House (EA) .... WPH
William Perry Fan Club [Defunct] (EA) .... WPFC
William Peterson College of New Jersey .... WPC
William Rainey Harper College, Palatine, IL [Library symbol Library of Congress] (LCLS) .... IPalH
William Randolph Hearst [American newspaper publisher, 1863-1951] .... WRH
William Richard Morris [Automobile industrialist] [British] .... WRM
William Robinson's English Admiralty Reports [1838-52] [A publication] (DLA) .... Rob Jun
William Robinson's English Admiralty Reports [1838-52] [A publication] (DLA) .... Wm Rob
William Robinson's English Admiralty Reports [1838-52] [A publication] (DLA) .... Wm Rob Adm
William Roper Hull Home, Calgary, AB, Canada [Library symbol] [Library of Congress] (LCLS) .... CaACWR
William Roper Hull Home, Calgary, Alberta [Library symbol National Library of Canada] (NLC) .... ACWR
William S. Covert School, Hempstead, NY [Library symbol] [Library of Congress] (LCLS) .... NHemCE
William S. Hein and Co., Inc. [Publisher] (DLA) .... Hein
William S. Hein & Co., Inc., Buffalo, NY [Library symbol Library of Congress] (LCLS) .... WsH
William Shatner Connection (EA) .... WSC
William Shatner Fellowship [Defunct] (EA) .... WSF
William Tell Gunnery Mate .... WT
William W. Story's United States Circuit Court Reports [A publication] (DLA) .... William W Story's Rept
William Woods College [Fulton, MO] .... WWC
Williams' Abridgment of Cases [1798-1803] [A publication] (DLA) .... Will Abr
Williams Act [1968] .... WA

Williams Aerial Systems Platform [One-man flying platform] .... WASP
Williams Air, Inc. [ICAO designator] (FAAC) .... WLS
Williams and Bruce's Admiralty Practice [3 eds.] [1869-1902] [A publication] (DLA) .... Williams & B Adm Jur
Williams and Bruce's Admiralty Practice [3 eds.] [1869-1902] [A publication] (DLA) .... Williams & Bruce Ad Pr
Williams & Wilkins [Publishing company] .... W & W
Williams' Annual Register [New York] [A publication] (DLA) .... Will Ann Reg
Williams' Annual Register [New York] [A publication] (DLA) .... Wms Ann Reg
Williams' Auctions [5th ed.] [1829] [A publication] (DLA) .... Will Auct
Williams Awareness Sentence Completion [Personality development test] [Psychology] .... WASC
Williams, AZ [FM radio station call letters] .... KVTF
Williams, AZ [AM radio station call letters] .... KYET
Williams' Bankruptcy Practice [17 eds.] [1870-1958] [A publication] (DLA) .... Williams B Pr
Williams Brothers Canada Ltd., Calgary, AB, Canada [Library symbol Library of Congress] (LCLS) .... CaACWB
Williams Brothers Canada Ltd., Calgary, Alberta [Library symbol National Library of Canada] (NLC) .... ACWB
Williams, CA [Location identifier FAA] (FAAL) .... ILA
Williams Coal Seam Gas Realty [NYSE symbol] (SPSG) .... WTU
Williams Coal Seam Gas Rlty [NYSE symbol] (TTSB) .... WTU
Williams Coal Seam Royalty Trust [Associated Press] (SAG) .... WilmCS
Williams College (GAGS) .... Williams C
Williams College, Chapin Library, Williamstown, MA [Library symbol Library of Congress] (LCLS) .... MWiW-C
Williams College, Williamstown, MA [Library symbol Library of Congress] (LCLS) .... MWiW
[The] Williams Companies [Associated Press] (SAG) .... Williams
Williams Companies [Associated Press] (SAG) .... Willm
Williams Companies [Associated Press] (SAG) Willm25
Williams Companies [Associated Press] (SAG) Willms25
[The] Williams Companies [NYSE symbol] (SPSG) .... WMB
Williams Companies [NYSE symbol] (SAG) .... WMZ
Williams Controls [NASDAQ symbol] (TTSB) .... WMCO
Williams Cos. [NYSE symbol] (TTSB) .... WMB
Williams Cos. $2.21 cm Pfd [NYSE symbol] (TTSB) .... WMBPrA
Williams Cos. 9.60%'QUICS' [NYSE symbol] (TTSB) .... WMZ
Williams Domain [Computer science] (IAA) .... WD
Williams Elementary School, Pasadena, TX [Library symbol] [Library of Congress] (LCLS) .... TxPWE
Williams Flexion Exercises [Orthopedics] (DAVI) .... WFE
Williams flexion exercises [Orthopedics] (DAVI) .... Wms flex ex
Williams Grove Old Timers [An association] (EA) .... WGOT
Williams' Justice [A publication] (DLA) .... Will Just
Williams, Kastner, Gibbs, Law Library, Seattle, WA [Library symbol] [Library of Congress] (LCLS) .... WaSWK
Williams Lake [Canada] [Airport symbol] (OAG) .... YWL
Williams Lake, BC [FM radio station call letters] .... CFFM
Williams Lake, BC [Television station call letters] (RBYB) CITM-1
Williams Lake, BC [AM radio station call letters] .... CKWL
Williams Lake, BC [ICAO location identifier] (ICLI) .... CYWL
Williams Lake Museum, Williams Lake, BC, Canada [Library symbol] [Library of Congress] (LCLS) .... CaBWLM
Williams' Law and Practice of Bankruptcy [19th ed.] [1977] [A publication] (DLA) .... Will Bankt
Williams' Law Dictionary [A publication] (DLA) .... Will LD
Williams' Massachusetts Citations [A publication] (DLA) .... Will Mass Cit
Williams' Massachusetts Reports [1 Massachusetts] [1804-05] [A publication] (DLA) .... Will
Williams' Notes to Saunders' Reports [A publication] (DLA) .... Will Saund
Williams' Notes to Saunders' Reports [A publication] (DLA) .... Williams Saund
Williams' Notes to Saunders' Reports [England] [A publication] (DLA) .... Wms Notes
Williams on Executors [15th ed.] [1970] [A publication] (DLA) .... Will Ex
Williams on Executors [A publication] (DLA) .... Williams Ex'rs
Williams on Executors [15th ed.] [1970] [A publication] (DLA) .... Wms Ex
Williams on Executors, Randolph and Talcott Edition [A publication] (DLA) .... Williams Ex'rs R & T Ed
Williams on Personal Property [A publication] (DLA) .... Williams Pers Prop
Williams on Real Property [A publication] (DLA) .... Will Real Pr
Williams on Real Property [A publication] (DLA) .... Williams Real Prop
Williams on Rights of Common [A publication] (DLA) .... Will Com
Williams on Rights of Common [A publication] (DLA) .... Williams Common
Williams on Seisin [A publication] (DLA) .... Williams Seis
Williams on Seisin of the Freehold [1878] [A publication] (DLA) .... Will Seis
Williams on the Settlement of Real Estates [A publication] (DLA) .... Will Sett
Williams on the Study of the Law [A publication] (DLA) .... Will St L
Williams' Petitions in Chancery [1880] [A publication] (DLA) .... Will Pet Ch
Williams Public Library, Williams, AZ [Library symbol Library of Congress] (LCLS) .... AzWi
Williams Ranch [California] [Seismograph station code, US Geological Survey Closed] (SEIS) .... WRC
Williams' Real Assets [1861] [A publication] (DLA) .... Will Real Ass
Williams' Reports [1 Massachusetts] [A publication] (DLA) .... Will Mass
Williams' Reports [1 Massachusetts] [A publication] (DLA) .... Williams
Williams' Reports [10-12 Utah] [A publication] (DLA) .... Williams
Williams' Reports [1 Massachusetts] [A publication] (DLA) .... Wms Mass
Williams Research Corp. .... WRC
Williams Syndrome [Medicine] .... WS
Williams Syndrome Association (EA) .... WSA
Williams Telecommunications Co. [Tulsa, OK] [Telecommunications service] (TSSD) .... WilTel

Williams Telecommunications Group [*Telecommunications service*] (TSSD) .... WTG
Williams' Vermont Reports [*27-29 Vermont*] [*A publication*] (DLA) .... Will
Williams' Vermont Reports [*27-29 Vermont*] [*A publication*] (DLA) .... Will VT
Williams' Vermont Reports [*27-29 Vermont*] [*A publication*] (DLA) .... Williams
Williams' Vermont Reports [*27-29 Vermont*] [*A publication*] (DLA) .... Wms VT
Williamsburg County Library, Kingstree, SC [*Library symbol*] [*Library of Congress*] (LCLS) .... ScK
Williamsburg Jounal-Tribune, Williamsburg, IA [*Library symbol Library of Congress*] (LCLS) .... IaWmbgJT
Williamsburg, KY [*AM radio station call letters*] .... WEKC
Williamsburg, KY [*AM radio station call letters*] .... WEZJ
Williamsburg, KY [*FM radio station call letters*] .... WEZJ-FM
Williamsburg Regional Library, Williamsburg, VA [*Library symbol*] [*Library of Congress*] (LCLS) .... ViWR
Williamsburg Technical College, Kingstree, SC [*Library symbol Library of Congress*] (LCLS) .... ScKW
Williamsburg Technical College, Kingstree, SC [*OCLC symbol*] (OCLC) .... WMB
Williamsburg, VA [*FM radio station call letters*] .... WCWM
Williamsburg, VA [*FM radio station call letters*] (RBYB) .... WLEE-FM
Williamsburg, VA [*AM radio station call letters*] .... WMBG
Williams-Landel-Ferry [*Polymer physics*] .... WLF
Williamson, WV [*AM radio station call letters*] .... WBTH
Williamson, WV [*FM radio station call letters*] .... WXCC
Williamsport [*Pennsylvania*] [*Airport symbol*] (OAG) .... IPT
Williamsport District Library Center [*Library network*] .... NCLD
Williamsport, MD [*FM radio station call letters*] .... WCRH
Williamsport, MD [*FM radio station call letters*] .... WYII
Williamsport, PA [*Location identifier FAA*] (FAAL) .... IPT
Williamsport, PA [*Television station call letters*] .... WILF
Williamsport, PA [*FM radio station call letters*] .... WILQ
Williamsport, PA [*FM radio station call letters*] .... WKSB
Williamsport, PA [*AM radio station call letters*] .... WLYC
Williamsport, PA [*FM radio station call letters*] (RBYB) .... WPGY
Williamsport, PA [*AM radio station call letters*] .... WRAK
Williamsport, PA [*FM radio station call letters*] .... WRLC
Williamsport, PA [*FM radio station call letters*] .... WWAS
Williamsport, PA [*AM radio station call letters*] .... WWPA
Williamsport Review-Republican, Williamsport, IN [*Library symbol Library of Congress*] (LCLS) .... InWilR
Williamsport-Washington Township Public Library, Williamsport, IN [*Library symbol Library of Congress*] (LCLS) .... InWil
Williams-Sonoma [*NASDAQ symbol*] (TTSB) .... WSGC
Williams-Sonoma, Inc. [*NASDAQ symbol*] (NQ) .... WSGC
Williams-Steiger Act of 1970 (WYGK) .... WSA
Williamston, NC [*Location identifier FAA*] (FAAL) .... MCZ
Williamston, NC [*FM radio station call letters*] .... WCBZ
Williamston, NC [*AM radio station call letters*] .... WIAM
Williamstown [*Massachusetts*] [*Seismograph station code, US Geological Survey Closed*] (SEIS) .... WLL
Williamstown Branch, Stormount, Dundas, and Glengarry County Library, Ontario [*Library symbol National Library of Canada*] (NLC) .... OWISDG
Williamstown High School, Williamstown, NJ [*Library symbol Library of Congress*] (LCLS) .... NjWilH
Williamstown, KY [*FM radio station call letters*] .... WNKR
Williamtown [*Australia ICAO location identifier*] (ICLI) .... ASWM
Willie Nelson Fan Club (EA) .... WNFC
Willimantic, CT [*FM radio station call letters*] .... WECS
Willimantic, CT [*AM radio station call letters*] .... WILI
Willimantic, CT [*FM radio station call letters*] .... WILI-FM
Willimantic State Teachers College [*Connecticut*] .... WSTC
Willing Workers for Organic Farms [*Australia*] .... WWOF
Willingboro Public Library, Willingboro, NJ [*Library symbol Library of Congress*] (LCLS) .... NjWi
Willingdon Public Library, Alberta [*Library symbol National Library of Canada*] (NLC) .... AWIL
Willingdon Public Library, Willingdon, AB, Canada [*Library symbol*] [*Library of Congress*] (LCLS) .... CaAWil
Willingness to Avoid (EERA) .... WTA
Willingness-to-Accept [*Market research*] .... WTA
Willingness-to-Pay [*Market research*] .... WTP
Willis Corroon Group ADS [*NYSE symbol*] (SPSG) .... WCG
Willis Corroon Ltd. [*Associated Press*] (SAG) .... WillCor
Willis, Joyce, McMinnville OR [*STAC*] .... WJE
Willis on Equity Pleading [*1820*] [*A publication*] (DLA) .... Will Eq Pl
Willis on Equity Pleading [*1820*] [*A publication*] (DLA) .... Willis Eq
Willis on Interrogatories [*A publication*] (DLA) .... Willis Int
Willis on Trustees [*A publication*] (DLA) .... Willis Trust
Willis-Bund's Cases from State Trials [*A publication*] (DLA) .... Will-Bund St Tr
Williston [*South Africa*] [*ICAO location identifier*] (ICLI) .... FAWL
Williston [*North Dakota*] [*Airport symbol*] (OAG) .... ISN
Williston, FL [*FM radio station call letters*] .... WFEZ
Williston/International [*North Dakota*] [*ICAO location identifier*] (ICLI) .... KISN
Williston, ND [*Location identifier FAA*] (FAAL) .... ISN
Williston, ND [*FM radio station call letters*] .... KDSR
Williston, ND [*AM radio station call letters*] .... KEYZ
Williston, ND [*FM radio station call letters*] .... KPPR
Williston, ND [*Television station call letters*] .... KUMV
Williston, ND [*Television station call letters*] .... KWSE
Williston, ND [*Television station call letters*] .... KXMD
Williston, ND [*FM radio station call letters*] .... KYYZ
Williston, ND [*Location identifier FAA*] (FAAL) .... SFW
Williston on Contracts [*A publication*] (DLA) .... Williston
Williston on Sales [*A publication*] (DLA) .... Williston
Williston Park Public Library, Williston Park, NY [*Library symbol Library of Congress*] (LCLS) .... NWp
Williston, SC [*FM radio station call letters*] .... WAAW
Willits, CA [*AM radio station call letters*] .... KLLK
Willits, CA [*FM radio station call letters*] (RBYB) .... KZYZ
Willits Elementary School, Syosset, NY [*Library symbol Library of Congress*] (LCLS) .... NSyoWE
Willits Public Library, Willits, CA [*Library symbol Library of Congress*] (LCLS) .... CWit
Willmar Junior High School, Willmar, MN [*Library symbol*] [*Library of Congress*] (LCLS) .... MnWilJS
Willmar, MN [*Location identifier FAA*] (FAAL) ILL
Willmar, MN [*FM radio station call letters*] (RBYB) .... KBHZ-FM
Willmar, MN [*AM radio station call letters*] .... KDJS
Willmar, MN [*FM radio station call letters*] .... KDJS-FM
Willmar, MN [*FM radio station call letters*] .... KQIC
Willmar, MN [*AM radio station call letters*] .... KWLM
Willmar Public Schools, Willmar, MN [*Library symbol*] [*Library of Congress*] (LCLS) .... MnWilPS
Willmar Regional Treatment Center, Staff Library, Willmar, MN [*Library symbol*] [*Library of Congress*] (LCLS) .... MnWilRC
Willmar Senior High School, Willmar, MN [*Library symbol*] [*Library of Congress*] (LCLS) .... MnWilSH
Willmar State Junior College, Willmar, MN [*Library symbol Library of Congress*] (LCLS) .... MnWilS
Willmar Technical Center, Willmar, MN [*Library symbol*] [*Library of Congress*] (LCLS) .... MnWilTC
Willmore, Wollaston, and Davison's English Queen's Bench Reports [*1837*] [*A publication*] (DLA) .... Will Woll & D
Willmore, Wollaston, and Davison's English Queen's Bench Reports [*1837*] [*A publication*] (DLA) .... Will Woll & Dav
Willmore, Wollaston, and Davison's English Queen's Bench Reports [*1837*] [*A publication*] (DLA) .... Willm W & D
Willmore, Wollaston, and Davison's English Queen's Bench Reports [*A publication*] (DLA) .... Wilm W & D
Willmore, Wollaston, and Davison's English Queen's Bench Reports [*1837*] [*A publication*] (DLA) .... WW & D
Willmore, Wollaston, and Hodges' English Queen's Bench Reports [*1838-39*] [*A publication*] (DLA) .... Will Woll & H
Willmore, Wollaston, and Hodges' English Queen's Bench Reports [*1838-39*] [*A publication*] (DLA) .... Will Woll & Hodg
Willmore, Wollaston, and Hodges' English Queen's Bench Reports [*1838-39*] [*A publication*] (DLA) .... Willm W & H
Willmore, Wollaston, and Hodges' English Queen's Bench Reports [*1838-39*] [*A publication*] (DLA) .... WW & H
Willmore, Wollaston, and Hodges' English Queen's Bench Reports [*1838-39*] [*A publication*] (DLA) .... WW & H (Eng)
Willoughby Historical Museum, Niagara Falls, Ontario [*Library symbol National Library of Canada*] (BIB) .... ONFWM
Willoughby, OH [*Location identifier FAA*] (FAAL) .... LNN
Willoughby, OH [*Location identifier FAA*] (FAAL) .... LQL
Willoughby-Eastlake, OH [*AM radio station call letters*] .... WELW
Willoughby-Eastlake Public Library, Willowick, OH [*Library symbol Library of Congress*] (LCLS) .... OWillo
Willow Branch Library, Cisco, IL [*Library symbol Library of Congress*] (LCLS) .... ICis
Willow Bunch, SK [*Television station call letters*] CBKT-2
Willow Bunch, SK [*Television station call letters*] CKCK-2
Willow Elementary School, Valley Stream, NY [*Library symbol Library of Congress*] (LCLS) .... NVsWE
Willow Grove, PA [*Location identifier FAA*] (FAAL) .... NMZ
Willow Grove, PA [*Location identifier FAA*] (FAAL) .... NXX
Willow Grove/Willow Grove Naval Air Station [*Pennsylvania*] [*ICAO location identifier*] (ICLI) .... KNXX
Willow Mixed Media (EA) .... WMM
Willow Mountain [*Alaska*] [*Seismograph station code, US Geological Survey Closed*] (SEIS) .... WLM
Willow Public Library, Willow, AK [*Library symbol Library of Congress*] (LCLS) .... AkWill
Willow Resources Ltd. [*Vancouver Stock Exchange symbol*] .... WWZ
Willow River Camp Library, Willow River, MN [*Library symbol*] [*Library of Congress*] (LCLS) .... MnWrC
Willow River School, Willow River, MN [*Library symbol*] [*Library of Congress*] (LCLS) .... MnWrS
Willow Road School, Franklin Square, NY [*Library symbol*] [*Library of Congress*] (LCLS) .... NFsWS
Willow Run Aeronautical Center [*Michigan*] (MCD) .... WRAC
Willow Run Airport [*Michigan*] [*Airport symbol*] .... YIP
Willow Run Laboratory [*NASA*] (KSC) .... WRL
Willow Run Research Center [*Air Force*] .... WRRC
Willow Society (EA) .... WS
Willow Springs, MO [*AM radio station call letters*] .... KUKU
Willow Springs, MO [*FM radio station call letters*] .... KUKU-FM
Willowair Ltd. [*British ICAO designator*] (FAAC) .... WLO
Willowbrook [*Virus*] (MAE) .... WB
Willowmore [*South Africa*] [*ICAO location identifier*] (ICLI) .... FAWO
Willows, CA [*AM radio station call letters*] .... KIQS
Willows, CA [*FM radio station call letters*] .... KQSC
Willows, CA [*Location identifier FAA*] (FAAL) .... WLW
Willows Public Library, Willows, CA [*Library symbol Library of Congress*] (LCLS) .... CWiW
Wills and Administration of Estates [*Law*] .... WAE
Wills Club (EA) .... WC
Wills, Estates, and Trusts (Prentice-Hall, Inc.) [*A publication*] (DLA) .... Wills Est & Tr (P-H)

Wills, Estates, Trusts [*Prentice-Hall, Inc.*] [*A publication*] (DLA) .... Wills Est Tr
Wills Eye Hospital, Philadelphia, PA [*Library symbol Library of Congress*] (LCLS) .... PPWiH
Wills Eye Society of Ex-Residents (EA) .... WESE
Wills on Circumstantial Evidence [*A publication*] (DLA) .... Wills Cir Ev
Wills on Circumstantial Evidence [*A publication*] (DLA) .... Wills Circ Ev
Wills Sainte Claire Owners Club (EA) .... WSCOC
Willson's Reports [*29-30 Texas Appeals*] [*1, 2, Texas Civil Appeals*] [*A publication*] (DLA) .... Will
Willson's Reports, Civil Cases [*29-30 Texas Appeals*] [*1, 2 Texas Court of Appeals*] [*A publication*] (DLA) .... Willson
Willson's Revised Penal Code, Code of Criminal Procedure, and Penal Laws of Texas [*A publication*] (DLA) .... Willson Tex Cr Law
Willys Air Cooled [*Automotive engineering*] .... WAC
Willys Club (EA) .... WC
Willys Club of America [*Later, WC*] (EA) .... WCA
Willys Overland Jeepster Club (EA) .... WOJC
Willys-Overland-Knight Registry (EA) .... WOKR
Wilmar Industries [*NASDAQ symbol*] (TTSB) .... WLMR
Wilmington [*Delaware*] [*Airport symbol*] (OAG) .... ILG
Wilmington [*North Carolina*] [*Airport symbol*] (OAG) .... ILM
Wilmington [*California*] [*Airport symbol*] (AD) .... WGM
Wilmington [*Diocesan abbreviation*] [*Delaware*] (TOCD) .... WIL
Wilmington [*Delaware*] (BARN) .... Wmg
Wilmington [*North Carolina*] [*Seismograph station code, US Geological Survey*] (SEIS) .... WNC
Wilmington [*New York*] [*Seismograph station code, US Geological Survey*] (SEIS) .... WNY
Wilmington Area Biomedical Libraries [*Library network*] .... WABLC
Wilmington Area Health Education Center Medical Library, Wilmington, NC [*Library symbol*] [*Library of Congress*] (LCLS) .... NcWHE
Wilmington College, Wilmington, OH [*Library symbol Library of Congress*] (LCLS) .... OWilmC
Wilmington College, Wilmington, OH [*OCLC symbol*] (OCLC) .... WMC
Wilmington, DE [*Location identifier FAA*] (FAAL) .... DQO
Wilmington, DE [*AM radio station call letters*] .... WDEL
Wilmington, DE [*Television station call letters*] .... WHYY
Wilmington, DE [*AM radio station call letters*] .... WILM
Wilmington, DE [*AM radio station call letters*] .... WJBR
Wilmington, DE [*FM radio station call letters*] .... WJBR-FM
Wilmington, DE [*FM radio station call letters*] .... WMPH
Wilmington, DE [*FM radio station call letters*] .... WSTW
Wilmington, DE [*Television station call letters*] .... WTGI
Wilmington/Greater Wilmington [*Delaware*] [*ICAO location identifier*] (ICLI) .... KILG
Wilmington, IL [*FM radio station call letters*] (RBYB) .... WYKT
Wilmington Institute Free Library and the New Castle County Free Library, Wilmington, DE [*Library symbol Library of Congress*] (LCLS) .... DeWI
Wilmington Institute Free Library and the New Castle County Free Library, Wilmington, DE [*OCLC symbol*] (OCLC) .... DWW
Wilmington Marine Geological Laboratory [*North Carolina*] (NOAA) .... WMGL
Wilmington Medical Center, Wilmington, DE [*OCLC symbol*] (OCLC) .... DLG
Wilmington, NC [*Location identifier FAA*] (FAAL) .... CLB
Wilmington, NC [*Location identifier FAA*] (FAAL) .... ILM
Wilmington, NC [*AM radio station call letters*] (RBYB) .... WAHH-AM
Wilmington, NC [*AM radio station call letters*] .... WBMS
Wilmington, NC [*Television station call letters*] .... WECT
Wilmington, NC [*FM radio station call letters*] .... WGNI
Wilmington, NC [*FM radio station call letters*] .... WHQR
Wilmington, NC [*AM radio station call letters*] .... WMFD
Wilmington, NC [*FM radio station call letters*] .... WMNX
Wilmington, NC [*Television station call letters*] .... WSFX
Wilmington, NC [*Television station call letters*] .... WUNJ
Wilmington, NC [*FM radio station call letters*] .... WUOY
Wilmington, NC [*Television station call letters*] .... WWAY
Wilmington, NC [*AM radio station call letters*] .... WWIL
Wilmington, NC [*FM radio station call letters*] (RBYB) .... WWIL-FM
Wilmington, NC [*FM radio station call letters*] .... WWQQ
Wilmington/New Hannover County [*North Carolina*] [*ICAO location identifier*] (ICLI) .... KILM
Wilmington, OH [*Location identifier FAA*] (FAAL) .... ILN
Wilmington, OH [*Location identifier FAA*] (FAAL) .... MXQ
Wilmington, OH [*AM radio station call letters*] .... WKFI
Wilmington, OH [*FM radio station call letters*] .... WSWO
Wilmington Public Library, College Square Branch, Wilmington, NC [*Library symbol Library of Congress*] (LCLS) .... NcW-C
Wilmington Public Library, College Square Branch, Wilmington, NC [*Library symbol*] [*Library of Congress*] (LCLS) .... NcWC
Wilmington Public Library, Wilmington, NC [*Library symbol Library of Congress*] (LCLS) .... NcW
Wilmington Public Library, Wilmington, OH [*Library symbol Library of Congress*] (LCLS) .... OWilm
Wilmington Trust Co. [*NASDAQ symbol*] (NQ) .... WILM
Wilmington Trust Corp. [*NASDAQ symbol*] (TTSB) .... WILM
Wilmington Trust Corp. [*Associated Press*] (SAG) .... WilmTr
Wilmington, VT [*FM radio station call letters*] .... WVAY
Wilmore, KY [*FM radio station call letters*] (RBYB) .... WVRB
Wilmot on Mortgages [*A publication*] (DLA) .... Wilm Mort
Wilmot's Digest of the Law of Burglary [*A publication*] (DLA) .... Wilm Burg
Wilmot's Notes and Opinions, King's Bench [*97 English Reprint*] [*A publication*] (DLA) .... Wilm
Wilmot's Notes and Opinions, King's Bench [*97 English Reprint*] [*A publication*] (DLA) .... Wilm Judg
Wilmot's Notes and Opinions, King's Bench [*97 English Reprint*] [*A publication*] (DLA) .... Wilm Op
Wilmot's Notes and Opinions, King's Bench [*97 English Reprint*] [*A publication*] (DLA) .... Wilmot's Notes
Wilmot's Notes and Opinions, King's Bench [*97 English Reprint*] [*A publication*] (DLA) .... Wilmot's Notes (Eng)
Wilmot's Notes of Opinions and Judgments [*A publication*] (DLA) .... Not Op
Wilms' Tumor [*Oncology*] .... WT
Wilms Tumor, Aniridia, Genitourinary Abnormalities, and Mental Retardation [*Syndrome*] [*Medicine*] .... WAGR
Wilms' Tumor Locus [*Genetics*] [*Oncology*] .... WTL
Wilshire Club [*Defunct*] (EA) .... WC
Wilshire Energy Resources, Inc. [*Toronto Stock Exchange symbol*] .... WSH
Wilshire Financial Services Group, Inc. [*NASDAQ symbol*] (SAG) .... WFSG
Wilshire Financial Services Group, Inc. [*Associated Press*] (SAG) .... Wilshire
Wilshire Oil Co. of Texas [*Associated Press*] (SAG) .... WilshrO
Wilshire Oil Co. of Texas [*NYSE symbol*] (SPSG) .... WOC
Wilshire Oil Texas [*NYSE symbol*] (TTSB) .... WOC
Wilshire Technologies [*AMEX symbol*] (TTSB) .... WIL
Wilshire Technologies, Inc. [*AMEX symbol*] (SPSG) .... WIL
Wilshire Technologies, Inc. [*Associated Press*] (SAG) .... WilshTc
Wilson [*Oklahoma*] [*Seismograph station code, US Geological Survey*] (SEIS) .... WLO
Wilson and Courtenay's Scotch Appeal Cases [*A publication*] (DLA) .... W & C
Wilson and Courtenay's Scotch Appeal Cases [*A publication*] (DLA) .... Wils & Court
Wilson & McLane, Inc. [*Information service or system*] (IID) .... W & M
Wilson and Shaw's Scotch Appeal Cases, English House of Lords [*A publication*] (DLA) .... W & S
Wilson and Shaw's Scotch Appeal Cases, English House of Lords [*A publication*] (DLA) .... W & S App
Wilson and Shaw's Scottish Appeal Cases [*1825-35*] [*A publication*] (DLA) .... Wils & S
Wilson and Shaw's Scottish Appeal Cases [*1825-35*] [*A publication*] (DLA) .... Wils & S (Scot)
Wilson and Shaw's Scottish Appeal Cases [*1825-35*] [*A publication*] (DLA) .... Wils & Sh
Wilson and Shaw's Scottish Appeal Cases [*1825-35*] [*A publication*] (DLA) .... Wilson & Shaw
Wilson, AR [*FM radio station call letters*] (RBYB) .... KAFW
Wilson Blair [*Agar*] [*Microbiology*] (DAVI) .... WB
Wilson Blair [*Agar*] (BABM) .... WB
Wilson Butte [*Washington*] [*Seismograph station code, US Geological Survey*] (SEIS) .... WBW
Wilson Cloud Chamber [*Physics*] .... WCC
Wilson College, Chambersburg, PA [*Library symbol Library of Congress*] (LCLS) .... PChW
Wilson College, Chambersburg, PA [*OCLC symbol*] (OCLC) .... PVW
Wilson County Public Library, Wilson, NC [*Library symbol Library of Congress*] (LCLS) .... NcWil
Wilson County Technical Institute, Wilson, NC [*Library symbol Library of Congress*] (LCLS) .... NcWilW
Wilson Creek [*Kentucky*] [*Seismograph station code, US Geological Survey*] (SEIS) .... WCK
Wilson Creek, NV [*Location identifier FAA*] (FAAL) ILC
Wilson Creek, WA [*FM radio station call letters*] .... KVYF
Wilson Dam [*TVA*] .... WD
Wilson Elementary School, Rockville Centre, NY [*Library symbol Library of Congress*] (LCLS) .... NRockWE
Wilson Free Library, Wilson, NY [*Library symbol Library of Congress*] (LCLS) .... NWils
Wilson Historical Society, Wilson, NY [*Library symbol Library of Congress*] (LCLS) .... NWilsHi
Wilson Knight Interdiscipline Society (EA) .... WKIS
Wilson Knight Interdiscipline Society and Foundation (EA) .... WKISF
Wilson Library Bulletin [*A publication*] (BRI) .... WLB
Wilson Memorial Hospital, Wilson, NC [*Library symbol*] [*Library of Congress*] (LCLS) .... NcWilH
Wilson Middle School, Rockford, IL [*Library symbol*] [*Library of Congress*] (LCLS) .... IRoWMS
Wilson, NC [*FM radio station call letters*] .... WAHD
Wilson, NC [*AM radio station call letters*] .... WGTM
Wilson, NC [*AM radio station call letters*] .... WLLY
Wilson, NC [*Television station call letters*] (RBYB) .... WRAY-TV
Wilson, NC [*FM radio station call letters*] .... WRDU
Wilson, NC [*AM radio station call letters*] .... WVOT
Wilson on Arbitrations [*A publication*] (DLA) .... Wils Arb
Wilson on Fines and Recoveries [*A publication*] (DLA) .... Wils Fines
Wilson on Springing Uses [*A publication*] (DLA) .... Wils Uses
Wilson on the Judicature Acts, Etc. [*A publication*] (DLA) .... Wils Jud Acts
Wilson Ornithological Society (EA) .... WOS
Wilson Pharmaceutical & Chemical Corp. .... WPCC
Wilson Quarterly [*A publication*] (BRI) .... Wil Q
Wilson Repeater (IEEE) .... WR
Wilson-Kimmelstiel [*Disease*] (MAE) .... WK
Wilson-Kimmelstiel Disease [*Medicine*] (DMAA) .... WKD
Wilson's Creek Battlefield National Park .... WICR
Wilson's Disease [*Medicine*] .... WD
Wilson's Disease Association (EA) .... WDA
Wilson's English Chancery Reports [*37 English Reprint*] [*A publication*] (DLA) .... Wils
Wilson's English Chancery Reports [*37 English Reprint*] [*A publication*] (DLA) .... Wils Ch
Wilson's English Chancery Reports [*37 English Reprint*] [*A publication*] (DLA) .... Wils Ch (Eng)
Wilson's English Chancery Reports [*37 English Reprint*] [*A publication*] (DLA) .... Wilson

Wilson's English Common Pleas [*A publication*] (DLA) .... Wils CP
Wilson's English Common Pleas Reports, 3 [*95 English Reprint*] [*A publication*] (DLA) .... Wils
Wilson's English Common Pleas Reports, 3 [*95 English Reprint*] [*A publication*] (DLA) .... Wils (Eng)
Wilson's English Exchequer Reports [*159 English Reprint*] [*1805-17*] [*A publication*] (DLA) .... Wils Ex
Wilson's English Exchequer Reports [*159 English Reprint*] [*A publication*] (DLA) .... Wils Exch
Wilson's English Exchequer Reports [*159 English Reprint*] [*A publication*] (DLA) .... Wils Exch (Eng)
Wilson's English King's Bench and Common Pleas Reports [*A publication*] (DLA) .... Wilson
Wilson's English King's Bench Reports [*95 English Reprint*] [*1742-74*] [*A publication*] (DLA) .... Wils
Wilson's English Privy Council Reports [*A publication*] (DLA) .... Wils PC
Wilson's Entries and Pleading [*3 Lord Raymond's King's Bench and Common PleasReports*] [*England*] [*A publication*] (DLA) .... Wils Ent
Wilson's Exchequer in Equity Reports [*England*] [*A publication*] (DLA) .... Wilson
Wilson's Glossary of Indian Terms [*A publication*] (DLA) .... Wils Ind Gloss
Wilson's History of Modern English Law [*A publication*] (DLA) .... Wils Mod Eng Law
Wilson's Indiana Superior Court Reports [*A publication*] (DLA) .... Ind Super
Wilson's Indiana Superior Court Reports [*A publication*] (DLA) .... Wils Ind
Wilson's Indiana Superior Court Reports [*A publication*] (DLA) .... Wils Super (Ind)
Wilson's Indiana Superior Court Reports [*A publication*] (DLA) .... Wilson
Wilson's Indiana Superior Court Reports [*A publication*] (DLA) .... Wilson Super Ct (Ind)
Wilson's Indiana Superior Court Reports [*A publication*] (DLA) .... Wilson's R
Wilson's Parliamentary Law [*A publication*] (DLA) .... Wils Parl L
Wilson's [*or Willson's*] **Reports** [*Texas Civil Cases, Court of Appeals*] [*A publication*] (DLA) .... W
Wilson's Reports [*48-59 Minnesota*] [*A publication*] (DLA) .... Wils Minn
Wilson's Reports [*1-3 Oregon*] [*A publication*] (DLA) .... Wils Oreg
Wilson's Reports [*1-3 Oregon*] [*A publication*] (DLA) .... Wilson
Wilson's Reports [*48-59 Minnesota*] [*A publication*] (DLA) .... Wilson
Wilson's Revised and Annotated Statutes [*Oklahoma*] [*A publication*] (DLA) .... Wilson's Rev & Ann St
Wilt-Inducing Factor [*Plant pathology*] .... WIF
Wilton Manors, FL [*AM radio station call letters*] .... WEXY
Wilton Public Library, Wilton Junction, IA [*Library symbol Library of Congress*] (LCLS) .... IaWij
Wiltshire [*County in England*] (ODBW) .... Wilts
Wiltshire [*County in England*] .... WILTS
Wiltshire Libraries in Cooperation (NITA) .... WILCO
Wiluna [*Australia Airport symbol*] (OAG) .... WUN
Wimberly Resources [*Vancouver Stock Exchange symbol*] .... WBY
Wimbledon Lawn Tennis Championship [*British*] .... WLTC
Wimborne Minster [*Urban district in England*] .... WIMB
Wimpy International [*Commercial firm British*] .... WI
Win [*Sports*] .... W
Win Over Communism [*A fund-raising subsidiary of the Unification Church*] .... WOC
Winamac, IN [*Location identifier FAA*] (FAAL) .... RWN
Winant and Clayton Volunteers (EA) .... WCV
Winch (DS) .... W
Winch (AAG) .... WN
Winchcombe [*England*] .... WINCH
Winchendon, MA [*FM radio station call letters*] .... WINQ
Winchester [*Borough in South England*] (ROG) .... W'CHESTER
Winchester [*City in England*] (ROG) .... WINCH
Winchester & Western Railroad Co. [*AAR code*] .... WW
Winchester Arms Collectors Association (EA) .... WACA
Winchester Branch, Stormount, Dundas, and Glengarry County Public Library, Ontario [*Library symbol National Library of Canada*] (NLC) .... OWSDG
Winchester Capital [*Vancouver Stock Exchange symbol*] .... WHC
Winchester Center Fire [*Rifles*] (DICI) .... WCF
Winchester City Museum [*British*] .... WCM
Winchester Diversified [*Vancouver Stock Exchange symbol*] .... WIS
Winchester Engineering and Analytical Center [*Food and Drug Administration*] [*Winchester, MA*] (GRD) .... WEAC
Winchester Financial [*Vancouver Stock Exchange symbol*] .... WOS
Winchester, IN [*Location identifier FAA*] (FAAL) .... AWW
Winchester, IN [*FM radio station call letters*] .... WZZY
Winchester, KY [*AM radio station call letters*] (RBYB) .... WINH-AM
Winchester, KY [*AM radio station call letters*] .... WLNT
Winchester, KY [*FM radio station call letters*] .... WWYC
Winchester Magnum (INF) .... WMG
Winchester, NH [*FM radio station call letters*] .... WXOD
Winchester, NV [*AM radio station call letters*] .... KZTY
Winchester, TN [*Location identifier FAA*] (FAAL) .... BGF
Winchester, TN [*AM radio station call letters*] .... WCDT
Winchester, VA [*Location identifier FAA*] (FAAL) .... EEY
Winchester, VA [*AM radio station call letters*] .... WINC
Winchester, VA [*FM radio station call letters*] .... WINC-FM
Winchester, VA [*AM radio station call letters*] .... WNTW
Winchester, VA [*FM radio station call letters*] .... WTRM
Winchester, VA [*FM radio station call letters*] .... WUSQ
Winchester Word Book [*A publication*] .... WB
Winchester-Western Co., New Haven, CT [*Library symbol Library of Congress*] (LCLS) .... CtNhW
Winch's Book of Entries [*A publication*] (DLA) .... W Ent
Winch's Book of Entries [*A publication*] (DLA) .... Win Ent
Winch's English Common Pleas Reports [*124 English Reprint*] [*A publication*] (DLA) .... Win
Winch's English Common Pleas Reports [*124 English Reprint*] [*A publication*] (DLA) .... Winch
Winch's English Common Pleas Reports [*124 English Reprint*] [*A publication*] (DLA) .... Winch (Eng)
Wind [*In reference to wind velocity*] .... W
Wind (MSA) .... WD
Wind (KSC) .... WND
Wind Amplified Rotor Platform .... WARP
Wind Amplifier Rotor Platform .... WARP
Wind and Watermill Section [*of the Society for the Protection of Ancient Buildings*] (EA) .... WWS
Wind Cave National Park .... WICA
Wind Correction Angle [*Aviation*] (DA) .... WCA
Wind Deflection [*Ballistics*] .... WD
Wind Direction .... WD
Wind Direction .... WDIR
Wind Direction (GAVI) .... WINDR
Wind Direction and Velocity Indicator [*Aviation*] .... WINDAV
Wind Direction Indicator [*ICAO*] (FAAC) .... WDI
Wind Electric System [*Telecommunications*] (TEL) .... WES
Wind Energy Conversion .... WEC
Wind Energy Conversion System .... WECS
Wind Energy Generator .... WEG
Wind Energy Society of America [*Inactive*] .... WESA
Wind Energy Systems Act of 1980 .... WESA
Wind Erosion Equation (EERA) .... WEE
Wind Erosion Equation .... WEQ
Wind Finding RADAR (IAA) .... WF
Wind Force (WGA) .... WF
Wind Imaging Interferometer .... WINDII
[*The*] **Wind in the Willows** [*Book by Kenneth Grahame*] .... TWITW
Wind Indicating Systems for Navigation Aircraft in Missile Support .... WINSNAMS
Wind Load .... WL
Wind Magnitude (GAVI) .... WINDMG
Wind Measuring Device .... WMD
Wind Measuring System .... WMS
Wind Offset .... WO
Wind Oriented Rapid [*or Rocket*] **Deployment** (MCD) .... WORD
Wind over Deck (MCD) .... WOD
Wind Power System .... WPS
Wind Profiler Demonstration Network (USDC) .... WPDN
Wind Profiler Demonstration Network [*Marine science*] (OSRA) .... WPDN
Wind Restraint Area (SAA) .... WRA
Wind River Resources [*Vancouver Stock Exchange symbol*] .... WID
Wind River Systems [*NASDAQ symbol*] (TTSB) .... WIND
Wind River Systems, Inc. [*NASDAQ symbol*] (SAG) .... WIND
Wind River Systems, Inc. [*Associated Press*] (SAG) .... WindRivr
Wind River Systems, Inc. [*Associated Press*] (SAG) .... WindRvr
Wind Satellite .... Windsat
Wind Satellite (SSD) .... WS
Wind Shear [*Aviation*] (FAAC) .... WS
Wind Shear Spike (SAA) .... WSS
Wind Shear Warning / Recovery Guidance System (DA) .... WW/RGS
Wind Shield (NASA) .... WS
Wind Shift [*NWS*] (FAAC) .... WSHFT
Wind Sounding Capability .... WSC
Wind Speed .... WS
Wind Speed Detector .... WSD
Wind Speed Indicator .... WSI
Wind Spirit Air, Inc. [*FAA designator*] (FAAC) .... WSI
Wind Tape Generation .... WTG
Wind Temperature Correction .... WTC
Wind Tunnel .... WT
Wind Tunnel Data .... WTD
Wind Tunnel Data Encoding and Evaluation [*System*] [*Boeing Co.*] .... WINDEE
Wind Tunnel Memorandum .... WTM
Wind Tunnel Model .... WTM
Wind Tunnel Note .... WTN
Wind Tunnel Study .... WTS
Wind Tunnel Test .... WTT
Wind Turbine Generator .... WTG
Wind Vector [*or Velocity*] [*Navigation*] .... W/V
Wind Velocity East (MCD) .... WVE
Wind Velocity North (MCD) .... WVN
Windarra Minerals Ltd. [*Vancouver Stock Exchange symbol Toronto Stock Exchange symbol*] .... WRA
Wind-Assisted Ship Propulsion (DS) .... WASP
Windber, PA [*AM radio station call letters*] .... WBEM
Winder .... WNDR
Winder, GA [*Location identifier FAA*] (FAAL) .... IDR
Winder, GA [*Location identifier FAA*] (FAAL) .... WDR
Winder, GA [*AM radio station call letters*] .... WIMO
Winder, GA [*FM radio station call letters*] .... WYFW
Windfall Elimination Provision (GFGA) .... WEP
Windfall Profit .... WP
Windfall Profit Tax .... WPT
Windflower Mining Ltd. [*Vancouver Stock Exchange symbol*] .... WFL
Windham [*New York*] [*Seismograph station code, US Geological Survey*] (SEIS) .... WND
Windham College, Putney, VT [*Library symbol Library of Congress*] (LCLS) .... VtPuW
Windham Free Public Library, Windham, CT [*Library symbol*] [*Library of Congress*] (LCLS) .... CtWih

Windham Public Library, Windham, NY [*Library symbol Library of Congress*] (LCLS) ... NWin
Windhoek [*South Africa*] [*ICAO location identifier*] (ICLI) ... FAWW
Windhoek [*Namibia*] [*Airport symbol*] (OAG) ... WDH
Windhoek [*Namibia*] [*Seismograph station code, US Geological Survey*] (SEIS) ... WIN
Windhoek/Eros [*Namibia*] [*ICAO location identifier*] (ICLI) ... FAWE
Windhoek/J. G. Strijdom [*Namibia*] [*ICAO location identifier*] (ICLI) ... FAWH
Windhoek-Eros [*Namibia*] [*Airport symbol*] (OAG) ... ERS
Winding (MSA) ... WDG
Winding Engine Manufacturers' Association [*British*] (BI) ... WEMA
Winding Specification (IAA) ... WS
Winding to Winding (MSA) ... W/W
Windkracht Nederland Information Centre [*Netherlands Wind Energy Information Centre*] [*Nethergy Ltd.*] [*Database producer*] (IID) ... WNI
Windlass ... WNDLS
Windmere Corp. [*Associated Press*] (SAG) ... Windmr
Windmere Corp. [*NYSE symbol*] (SPSG) ... WND
Windmill Class Association (EA) ... WCA
Windmill Study Unit [*American Topical Association*] (EA) ... WSU
Windom Area High School, Windom, MN [*Library symbol*] [*Library of Congress*] (LCLS) ... MnWinHS
Windom Area Hospital, Windom, MN [*Library symbol*] [*Library of Congress*] (LCLS) ... MnWinH
Windom, MN [*AM radio station call letters*] ... KDOM
Windom, MN [*FM radio station call letters*] ... KDOM-FM
Windom, MN [*Location identifier FAA*] (FAAL) ... MWM
Windom Public Library, Windom, MN [*Library symbol*] [*Library of Congress*] (LCLS) ... MnWin
Windorah [*Australia Airport symbol*] (OAG) ... WNR
Window (NASA) ... W
Window (MSA) ... WDO
Window ... WDW
Window [*Technical drawings*] ... WIN
Window (VRA) ... wndw
Window ... WNDW
Window Atmosphere Sounding Projectile [*NASA*] ... WASP
Window Contamination Control Number ... WCCS
Window Coverings Association of America (EA) ... WCAA
Window Definition Record [*Computer science*] ... WDR
Window Deicing Unit ... WDU
Window Detector ... WD
Window Dimension [*Technical drawings*] ... WD
Window Glass Cutters League of America [*Later, GBBA*] (EA) ... WGCL
Window Guard (AAG) ... WG
Window Heat Control Unit ... WHCU
Window Identifier [*Computer science*] ... WID
Window Meteoroid Experiment [*NASA*] (KSC) ... WME
Window Regulator [*Automotive engineering*] ... W/REG
Window Rock, AZ [*Location identifier FAA*] (FAAL) ... AWR
Window Rock, AZ [*AM radio station call letters*] ... KTNN
Window Rock, AZ [*FM radio station call letters*] ... KWIM
Window Rock, AZ [*FM radio station call letters*] ... KWRK
Window Rock Public Library, Window Rock, AZ [*Library symbol Library of Congress*] (LCLS) ... AzWr
Window Sash Glaziers' Union [*British*] ... WSGU
Window Shade Manufacturers Association (EA) ... WSMA
Window Test Apparatus ... WTA
Window Unit (MSA) ... WU
Window-Frame ... WF
Windowing System Manager [*Computer science*] (PCM) ... WSM
Windows 95 [*Computer science*] (WDMC) ... Win 95
Windows Application Binary Interactive [*Computer science*] ... WABI
Windows Application Programming Environment [*Computer science*] (BTTJ) ... WAPE
[*A*] **Windows Command** [*Computer science*] (PCM) ... WINCMD
Windows Compact Edition [*Computer science*] (PCM) ... Win CE
Windows Entertainment Pack [*Computer science*] ... WEP
Windows for Workgroups [*Microsoft Corp.*] ... WFW
Windows for Workgroups [*Microsoft Corp.*] ... WFWG
Windows Hardware Engineering Conference ... WinHEC
Windows Hardware Engineering Conference ... WinHEC
Windows Hardware Engineering Conference [*Microsoft Corp.*] [*Computer science*] ... WinHEC
Windows Help Authoring Guide [*Computer software*] [*Microsoft Corp.*] (PCM) ... WHAG
Windows Help Authoring Tools [*Computer software*] [*Microsoft Corp.*] (PCM) ... WHAT
Windows Help Project Editor [*Microsoft Corp.*] (PCM) ... WHPE
Windows, Icons, Mice, and Pointer [*Computer science*] (OSI) ... WIMP
Windows, Icons, Mice, and Pucks [*Computer science*] (DGA) ... WIMP
windows, icons, mouse and pull-down menus [*computers*] ... WIMP
Windows/Icons/Mouse/Pull-Down-Menus [*Computer science*] (BYTE) ... WIMP
Windows Information Exchange [*Information service or system*] (IID) ... WIX
Windows Interface Language [*Computer science*] (PCM) ... WIL
Windows - Internet Naming Service ... WINS
Windows Metafile [*Vector file format*] [*Computer science*] (PCM) ... WMF
Windows Metafile Format [*Computer science*] ... WMF
Windows on Windows [*Computer software*] (CDE) ... WOW
Windows Open Services Architecture [*Microsoft Corp.*] (PCM) ... WOSA
Windows Open Systems Architecture [*Computer science*] ... WOSA
Windows Personal Librarian [*Computer software*] ... WPL
Windows Portability Libraries [*Computer science*] ... WPL
Windows/Presentation Manager Association (EA) ... WPMA
Windows Printing System [*Microsoft Corp.*] (PCM) ... WPS
Windows Random Access Memory (PCM) ... WRAM
Windows Scripting Host [*Computer science*] ... WSH
Windows Sockets [*Internet*] ... Winsock
Windows Sound File [*Computer science*] ... wav
Windows Visual Keyboard [*Computer science*] (ECON) ... WiVik
Windows-Based Terminal [*Computer science*] ... WBT
Windows-Based Terminal Server [*Microsoft Corp.*] ... WTS
Winds and Temperatures Aloft Forecast [*Symbol*] [*National Weather Service*] ... FD
Winds, Heights, and Temperatures ... WHAT
Windscale ... WSL
Windscale Advanced Gas-Cooled Reactor ... WAGR
Windscale Nuclear Laboratories [*British*] (NUCP) ... WNL
Windscale Nuclear Power Development Laboratories [*British*] (NUCP) ... WNPDL
Windscale Vitrification Plant [*British*] (NUCP) ... WVP
Windshear Air Data Loader [*Aviation*] ... WADL
Windshield (AAG) ... WSHLD
Windshield Flight Environment Simulator (PDAA) ... WFES
Windshield Guidance Display ... WGD
Windshield Temperature Control Systems ... WTCS
Windshield Wiper [*Automotive engineering*] ... W/WPR
Windsonde (KSC) ... WS
Windsor [*Municipal borough in England*] ... WIND
Windsor [*Canada*] [*Airport symbol*] (OAG) ... YQG
Windsor Board of Education [*UTLAS symbol*] ... WIN
Windsor Board of Education, Ontario [*Library symbol National Library of Canada*] (NLC) ... OWBE
Windsor Board of Education, Windwor, ON, Canada [*Library symbol*] [*Library of Congress*] (LCLS) ... CaOWBE
Windsor, CA [*AM radio station call letters*] ... KEZD
Windsor Castle, Royal Archives, Windsor, Berkshire, United Kingdom [*Library symbol*] [*Library of Congress*] (LCLS) ... UkWC-A
Windsor, CO [*FM radio station call letters*] ... KUAD
Windsor, CO [*AM radio station call letters*] ... KVVS
Windsor, CT [*AM radio station call letters*] ... WKND
Windsor Historical Society, Fyler House, Windsor, CT [*Library symbol*] [*Library of Congress*] (LCLS) ... CtWisHi
Windsor Institute of Complementology [*Later, ICS*] (EA) ... WIC
Windsor Locks/Bradley International [*Connecticut*] [*ICAO location identifier*] (ICLI) ... KBDL
Windsor Locks, CT [*Location identifier FAA*] (FAAL) ... BDL
Windsor Locks, CT [*Location identifier FAA*] (FAAL) ... IKX
Windsor Locks, CT [*Location identifier FAA*] (FAAL) ... MYQ
Windsor Memorial Public Library, Newfoundland [*Library symbol National Library of Canada*] (NLC) ... NFWI
Windsor Memorial Public Library, Windsor, NF, Canada [*Library symbol Library of Congress*] (LCLS) ... CaNfWi
Windsor Microfilming Co., Windsor, ON, Canada [*Library symbol Library of Congress*] (LCLS) ... WmC
Windsor, NC [*AM radio station call letters*] ... WBTE
Windsor, NC [*FM radio station call letters*] ... WDRP
Windsor, NC [*FM radio station call letters*] ... WURB
Windsor, NS [*AM radio station call letters*] ... CFAB
Windsor, ON [*AM radio station call letters*] ... CBE
Windsor, ON [*AM radio station call letters*] ... CBEF
Windsor, ON [*FM radio station call letters*] ... CBE-FM
Windsor, ON [*Television station call letters*] ... CBEFT
Windsor, ON [*Television station call letters*] ... CBET
Windsor, ON [*Television station call letters*] ... CICO-32
Windsor, ON [*FM radio station call letters*] ... CIDR
Windsor, ON [*Television station call letters*] ... CIII-1
Windsor, ON [*FM radio station call letters*] ... CIMX
Windsor, ON [*FM radio station call letters*] ... CJAM
Windsor, ON [*AM radio station call letters*] ... CKLW
Windsor, ON [*AM radio station call letters*] ... CKWW
Windsor, ON [*ICAO location identifier*] (ICLI) ... CYQG
Windsor Public Library, Ontario [*Library symbol National Library of Canada*] (NLC) ... OW
Windsor Public Library, Windsor, CO [*Library symbol Library of Congress*] (LCLS) ... CoWi
Windsor Public Library, Windsor, ON, Canada [*Library symbol Library of Congress*] (LCLS) ... CaOW
Windsor Resources, Inc. [*Vancouver Stock Exchange symbol*] ... WSR
Windsor Township Library, Dimondale, MI [*Library symbol Library of Congress*] (LCLS) ... MiDi
Windsor, VA [*FM radio station call letters*] ... WSVY
Windsor, VT [*FM radio station call letters*] ... WVPR
Windsor, VT [*Television station call letters*] ... WVTA
Windstar Foundation (EA) ... WF
Wind-Time Analyzer ... WITAN
Windward [*Botany*] ... W
Windward (KSC) ... WWD
Windward Island Passages Monitoring Program (USDC) ... WIMP
Windward Island Passages Monitoring Program [*Marine science*] (OSRA) ... WIMP
Windward Islands [*MARC geographic area code Library of Congress*] (LCCP) ... nwwi--
Windward Islands (WDAA) ... WI
Windward Islands (WDAA) ... WIND I
Windward Islands Airways International NV [*Netherlands ICAO designator*] (FAAC) ... WIA
Windward Islands Airways International NV [*Netherlands ICAO designator*] (ICDA) ... WM
Windward Islands' Banana Association ... WINBAN
Windward Passage Patrol [*Navy*] (NVT) ... WPP

Wine Advisory Board [*Later, WAG*] (EA) .... WAB
Wine and Brandy Producers' Association of Australia .... WBPAA
Wine and Brandy Producers' Association of South Australia .... WBPASA
Wine and Brandy Producers' Cooperative Association of South
    Australia .... WBPCASA
Wine and Food Society of New South Wales [*Australia*] .... WFSNSW
Wine and Spirits Guild of America (EA) .... WSGA
Wine and Spirits Shippers Association (EA) .... WSSA
Wine and Spirits Wholesalers of America (EA) .... WSWA
Wine Appreciation Guild (EA) .... WAG
Wine Conference of America [*Defunct*] (EA) .... WCA
Wine Exchange [*Computer network*] .... WEX
Wine Gallon .... WG
Wine Grape Industry Negotiating Committee [*Victoria, Australia*] .... WGINC
Wine Information Bureau [*Australia*] .... WIB
Wine Institute (EA) .... WI
Wine Institute, San Francisco, CA [*Library symbol Library of Congress*]
    (LCLS) .... CSfW
Wine Label Circle (EA) .... WLC
Winegrape Growers' Council of Australia .... WGCA
Win-Eldrich Mines Ltd. [*Toronto Stock Exchange symbol*] .... WEX
Winemakers' Federation of Australia .... WFA
Winer's Unreported Opinions, New York Supreme Court [*A publication*]
    (DLA) .... Win
Wines of Westhorpe [*Commercial firm British*] .... WW
Winex Resources, Inc. [*Vancouver Stock Exchange symbol*] .... WIX
Winfair Elementary School, Windom, MN [*Library symbol*] [*Library of Congress*] (LCLS) .... MnWinWES
Winfield, AL [*AM radio station call letters*] .... WKXM
Winfield, AL [*FM radio station call letters*] .... WKXM-FM
Winfield/Arkansas City, KS [*Location identifier FAA*] (FAAL) .... SOR
Winfield/Arkansas City, KS [*Location identifier FAA*] (FAAL) .... WLD
Winfield Capital [*NASDAQ symbol*] (TTSB) .... WCAP
Winfield Capital Corp. [*NASDAQ symbol*] (SAG) .... WCAP
Winfield Capital Corp. [*Associated Press*] (SAG) ...... Winfield
Winfield Capital Corp. [*Associated Press*] (SAG) ...... Winfld
Winfield Capital Wrrt [*NASDAQ symbol*] (TTSB) .... WCAPW
Winfield, KS [*FM radio station call letters*] (RBYB) .... KAZY-FM
Winfield, KS [*AM radio station call letters*] .... KKLE
Winfield, KS [*FM radio station call letters*] .... KKWM
Winfield, KS [*FM radio station call letters*] (RBYB) .... KSOK-FM
Winfield, KS [*FM radio station call letters*] .... KSWC
Winfield Public Library, Alberta [*Library symbol National Library of Canada*]
    (NLC) .... AWI
[*The*] Winfield Railroad Co. [*AAR code*] .... WNF
Winfield, TX [*FM radio station call letters*] .... KALK
Winfield's Adjudged Words and Phrases, with Notes [*A publication*]
    (DLA) .... Winfield Words & Phrases
Winfrith [*England*] .... WINF
Winfrith Improved Multi-Group Scheme [*Nuclear energy*] (NUCP) .... WIMS
Wing .... WG
Wing [*of a ship*] (DS) .... WNG
Wing Airways (Pty) Ltd. [*South Africa ICAO designator*] (FAAC) .... WNG
Wing Attack [*Netball*] .... WA
Wing Bar Lights [*Aviation*] .... WBAR
Wing Battle Manager [*Air Force*] .... WBM
Wing Chord Plane [*Aviation*] .... WCP
Wing Command Post (MCD) .... WCP
Wing Commander [*British military*] .... W/Cdr
Wing Commander [*British military*] (DMA) .... W Comm
Wing Commander [*British military*] .... WC
Wing Commander [*British military*] (NATG) .... WG/CDR
Wing Commander [*British military*] (DMA) .... Wg Cmdr
Wing Commander [*British military*] (DMA) .... Wg Cr
Wing Control During Boost .... WCDB
Wing Defence [*Netball*] .... WD
Wing Design Optimization with Aerolastic Constraints [*Computer program*] .... WIDOWAC
Wing Director of Intelligence .... DOI
Wing Elevon (MCD) .... WE
Wing Engineer Squadron Detachment (DNAB) .... WESDET
Wing Equipment Repair Squadron .... WERS
Wing Forward (WGA) .... WF
Wing Half (WDAA) .... WH
Wing in Ground .... WIG
Wing Main [*Airfield*] (NATG) .... W/M
Wing Main Airfield (NATG) .... WMA
Wing Maintenance Officer .... WMO
Wing Officer [*British military*] (DMA) .... Wg O
Wing Officer [*British military*] (DMA) .... Wg Offr
Wing Operations Center (CINC) .... WOC
Wing Outer Panel [*Aviation*] .... WOP
Wing Reference Line [*Aviation*] .... WRL
Wing Reference Plan [*Aviation*] .... WRP
Wing Security Control [*Air Force*] (AFM) .... WSC
Wing Station [*Aviation*] .... WS
Wing Tank Structure .... WTS
Wing Transportation Squadron Detachment [*Navy*] (DNAB) .... WTSDET
Wing Warrant Officer [*RAF*] [*British*] .... WWO
Wingate College, Wingate, NC [*Library symbol Library of Congress*]
    (LCLS) .... NcWin
Wingate College, Wingate, NC [*OCLC symbol*] (OCLC) .... NWC
Wingate Computer Center (HGAA) .... WCC
Wingate Elementary School Library, Grand Junction, CO [*Library symbol Library of Congress*] (LCLS) .... CoGjWE

Wingate, NC [*FM radio station call letters*] .... WRCM
Wingate's Maxims [*A publication*] (DLA) .... Wing
Wingate's Maxims [*A publication*] (DLA) .... Wing Max
Wingback [*Football*] .... WB
Winged Reentry Vehicle (IAA) .... WRV
Winged Russia [*Russian Federation*] [*ICAO designator*] (FAAC) .... WDR
Winged Surface Effect Vehicle (PDAA) .... WSEV
Winged Warriors/National B-Body Owners Association (EA) .... WW
Wingfold .... WF
Wingfoot Lighter-Than-Air Society [*Later, Lighter-Than-Air Society*]
    (EA) .... WLTAS
Wingham, ON [*AM radio station call letters*] .... CKNX
Wingham, ON [*FM radio station call letters*] .... CKNX-FM
Wingham, ON [*Television station call letters*] .... CKNX-TV
Wing-in-Ground Effect (PDAA) .... WIGE
Wing-Level Bombing System (SAA) .... WLBM
Wings Air Transport Co. [*Sudan*] [*ICAO designator*] (FAAC) .... WAT
Wings Airways [*ICAO designator*] (FAAC) .... WAW
Wings Airways [*ICAO designator*] (AD) .... WQ
Wings Aviation Ltd. [*Guyana*] [*FAA designator*] (FAAC) .... WOL
Wings Club (EA) .... WC
Wings, Engines, Fuselage, Tail [*System for identifying aircraft*] .... WEFT
Wings Express, Inc. [*ICAO designator*] (FAAC) .... WEX
Wings, Nonstraight-Taper Analysis (MCD) .... WINSTAN
Wings of Alaska [*ICAO designator*] (AD) .... SE
Wings of Hope [*An association*] (EA) .... WH
Wings of Hope [*An association*] (EA) .... WOH
Wings West [*ICAO designator*] (AD) .... RM
Wingspread (WGA) .... WS
Wingst [*Federal Republic of Germany*] [*Geomagnetic observatory code*] .... WNG
Wingwork Aviation [*British ICAO designator*] (FAAC) .... WNW
Winifrede Railroad Co. [*AAR code*] .... WNFR
Winisk [*Canada*] [*Airport symbol*] (OAG) .... YWN
Wink, TX [*Location identifier FAA*] (FAAL) .... INK
Wink/Winkler County [*Texas*] [*ICAO location identifier*] (ICLI) .... KINK
Winkelmann Countermeasures, Inc. [*Vancouver Stock Exchange symbol*] .... WCM
Winkelmann-Dibley Ford [*Race car*] .... WDF
Winkelmann-Dibley Formula B [*Race car*] .... WDB
Winkelmann-Dibley Hillclimb [*Race car*] .... WDH
Winkelmann-Dibley Volkswagen [*Race car*] .... WDV
Winkleigh [*England*] .... WINK
Winkler-Morden, MB [*AM radio station call letters*] .... CKMW
Winland Electronics [*NASDAQ symbol*] (TTSB) .... WLET
Winland Electronics, Inc. [*Associated Press*] (SAG) .... Winlnd
Winland Electronics, Inc. [*NASDAQ symbol*] (SAG) .... WLET
Winlink (St. Lucia) Ltd. [*ICAO designator*] (FAAC) .... WIN
Winlock, WA [*FM radio station call letters*] (RBYB) .... KITI
Winn Parish Library, Winnfield, LA [*Library symbol Library of Congress*]
    (LCLS) .... LWiW
Winn-Dixie Stores [*NYSE symbol*] (TTSB) .... WIN
Winn-Dixie Stores, Inc. [*NYSE symbol*] (SPSG) .... WIN
Winn-Dixie Stores, Inc. [*Associated Press*] (SAG) .... WinDix
Winnebago County Hospital, Winnebago, WI [*Library symbol Library of Congress*] (LCLS) .... WWiC
Winnebago County Medical Society, Rockford, IL [*Library symbol Library of Congress*] (LCLS) .... IRoWM
Winnebago, IL [*FM radio station call letters*] .... WKMQ
Winnebago Indus [*NYSE symbol*] (TTSB) .... WGO
Winnebago Industries, Inc. [*NYSE symbol*] (SPSG) .... WGO
Winnebago Industries, Inc. [*Associated Press*] (SAG) .... Winnbg
Winnebago International Travelers (EA) .... WIT
Winnebago, NE [*FM radio station call letters*] .... KSUX
Winnebago State Hospital, Winnebago, WI [*Library symbol Library of Congress*] (LCLS) .... WWiS
Winnefox Library System [*Library network*] .... WLS
Winnemucca [*Nevada*] [*Seismograph station code, US Geological Survey Closed*] (SEIS) .... WMN
Winnemucca, NV [*Location identifier FAA*] (FAAL) .... EMC
Winnemucca, NV [*Television station call letters*] (RBYB) .... KANM
Winnemucca, NV [*AM radio station call letters*] .... KWNA
Winnemucca, NV [*FM radio station call letters*] .... KWNA-FM
Winnemucca, NV [*TV station call letters*] (RBYB) .... KWNV-TV
Winnemucca, NV [*Location identifier FAA*] (FAAL) .... WMC
Winner, SD [*Location identifier FAA*] (FAAL) .... ISD
Winner, SD [*FM radio station call letters*] (RBYB) .... KGGK-FM
Winner, SD [*AM radio station call letters*] .... KWYR
Winner, SD [*FM radio station call letters*] .... KWYR-FM
Winner, SD [*FM radio station call letters*] (RBYB) .... KZZP
Winner's Bitch [*Dog show term*] .... WB
Winner's Dog [*Dog show term*] .... WD
Winners Entertainment [*Commercial firm Associated Press*] (SAG) .... WinrEnt
Winners Entertainment [*Commercial firm NASDAQ symbol*] (SAG) .... WINS
Winners on Wheels [*An association*] (PAZ) .... WOW
Winnetka, IL [*FM radio station call letters*] .... WNTH
Winnetka Public Library District, Northfield Branch, Northfield, IL [*Library symbol Library of Congress*] (LCLS) .... IWin-N
Winnetka Public Library, Winnetka, IL [*OCLC symbol*] (OCLC) .... IWE
Winnetka Public Library, Winnetka, IL [*Library symbol Library of Congress*]
    (LCLS) .... IWin
Winnfield, LA [*Location identifier FAA*] (FAAL) .... IFJ
Winnfield, LA [*AM radio station call letters*] .... KVCL
Winnfield, LA [*FM radio station call letters*] .... KVCL-FM
Winning Pitcher [*Baseball*] .... WP
Winning the Hearts and Minds [*of the people*] [*Vietnam pacification program*] .... WHAM

Winnipeg [*Canada*] (BARN) ... Winn
Winnipeg [*Canada*] [*Airport symbol*] (OAG) ... YWG
Winnipeg Art Gallery, Manitoba [*Library symbol National Library of Canada*] (NLC) ... MWWA
Winnipeg Art Gallery, Winnipeg, MB, Canada [*Library symbol Library of Congress*] (LCLS) ... CaMWWA
Winnipeg Bible College, Otterburne, Manitoba [*Library symbol National Library of Canada*] (NLC) ... MOWBC
Winnipeg Bible College, Otterburne, MB, Canada [*Library symbol Library of Congress*] (LCLS) ... CaMOWBC
Winnipeg Centennial Library, Manitoba [*Library symbol National Library of Canada*] (NLC) ... MW
Winnipeg Clinic, Manitoba [*Library symbol National Library of Canada*] (NLC) ... MWWC
Winnipeg Clinic, Winnipeg, MB, Canada [*Library symbol Library of Congress*] (LCLS) ... CaMWWC
Winnipeg Free Press Co. Ltd., Manitoba [*Library symbol National Library of Canada*] (NLC) ... MWFP
Winnipeg Free Press Co. Ltd., Winnipeg, MB, Canada [*Library symbol Library of Congress*] (LCLS) ... CaMWFP
Winnipeg/International, MB [*ICAO location identifier*] (ICLI) ... CYWG
Winnipeg Jets Booster Club (EA) ... WJBC
Winnipeg, MB [*AM radio station call letters*] ... CBW
Winnipeg, MB [*FM radio station call letters*] ... CBW-FM
Winnipeg, MB [*Television station call letters*] ... CBWFT
Winnipeg, MB [*Television station call letters*] ... CBWT
Winnipeg, MB [*FM radio station call letters*] (RBYB) ... CFWM-FM
Winnipeg, MB [*FM radio station call letters*] ... CHIQ
Winnipeg, MB [*AM radio station call letters*] ... CIFX
Winnipeg, MB [*FM radio station call letters*] ... CITI
Winnipeg, MB [*FM radio station call letters*] ... CJKR
Winnipeg, MB [*AM radio station call letters*] ... CJOB
Winnipeg, MB [*AM radio station call letters*] ... CKJS
Winnipeg, MB [*FM radio station call letters*] ... CKMM
Winnipeg, MB [*Television station call letters*] ... CKND
Winnipeg, MB [*AM radio station call letters*] ... CKRC
Winnipeg, MB [*Television station call letters*] ... CKY
Winnipeg, MB [*Television station call letters*] ... CKY-TV
Winnipeg, MB [*ICAO location identifier*] (ICLI) ... CWWG
Winnipeg, MB [*ICAO location identifier*] (ICLI) ... CZWG
Winnipeg Municipal Hospital, Manitoba [*Library symbol National Library of Canada*] (NLC) ... MWMH
Winnipeg Municipal Hospital, Winnipeg, MB, Canada [*Library symbol Library of Congress*] (LCLS) ... CaMWMH
Winnipeg Public Library [*UTLAS symbol*] ... WPL
Winnipeg Public Library, William Avenue Branch, Winnipeg, MB, Canada [*Library symbol*] [*Library of Congress*] (LCLS) ... CaMWW
Winnipeg Public Library, Winnipeg, MB, Canada [*Library symbol Library of Congress*] (LCLS) ... CaMW
Winnipeg/St. Andrews, MB [*ICAO location identifier*] (ICLI) ... CYAV
Winnipeg School Division No. 1, Teachers' Library and Resource Centre, Winnipeg,MB, Canada [*Library symbol Library of Congress*] (LCLS) ... CaMWSD
Winnipeg School of Nursing, Health Science Centre, Winnipeg, MB, Canada [*Library symbol Library of Congress*] (LCLS) ... CaMWSN
Winnipeg Stock Exchange (HGAA) ... WSE
Winnipeg Tribune, Manitoba [*Library symbol National Library of Canada*] (NLC) ... MWT
Winnipeg Tribune, Winnipeg, MB, Canada [*Library symbol Library of Congress*] (LCLS) ... CaMWT
Winnsboro, LA [*AM radio station call letters*] ... KMAR
Winnsboro, LA [*FM radio station call letters*] ... KMAR-FM
Winnsboro, SC [*Location identifier FAA*] (FAAL) ... FDW
Winnsboro, TX [*FM radio station call letters*] ... KWNS
Winograd Fourier Transform Algorithm (MCD) ... WFTA
Winona [*Minnesota*] [*Airport symbol*] (AD) ... ONA
Winona [*Diocesan abbreviation*] [*Minnesota*] (TOCD) ... WIN
Winona & St. Peter Railroad ... W & StP
Winona, MN [*AM radio station call letters*] ... KAGE
Winona, MN [*FM radio station call letters*] ... KAGE-FM
Winona, MN [*FM radio station call letters*] ... KHME
Winona, MN [*FM radio station call letters*] ... KQAL
Winona, MN [*FM radio station call letters*] ... KSMR
Winona, MN [*AM radio station call letters*] ... KWNO
Winona, MN [*Location identifier FAA*] (FAAL) ... ONA
Winona, MS [*AM radio station call letters*] ... WONA
Winona, MS [*FM radio station call letters*] ... WONA-FM
Winona Public Library, Winona, MN [*Library symbol Library of Congress*] (LCLS) ... MnWino
Winona State College [*Later, Winona State University*] [*Minnesota*] ... WSC
Winona State College [*Later, Winona State University*], Winona, MN [*Library symbol Library of Congress*] (LCLS) ... MnWinoS
Winona State University (GAGS) ... Winona St U
Winona State University, Winona, MN [*OCLC symbol*] (OCLC) ... MNI
Winona Tri College University Library Network [*Library network*] ... WALDO
Winpak Ltd. [*Toronto Stock Exchange symbol*] ... WPK
Winrock International Institute for Agricultural Development (EA) ... WIIAD
Winrock International Library, Petit Jean Mountain, Morrilton, AR [*Library symbol*] [*Library of Congress*] (LCLS) ... ArMoW
Wins [*Sports*] ... W
WinsLoew Furniture [*NASDAQ symbol*] (TTSB) ... WLFI
WinsLoew Furniture, Inc. [*Associated Press*] (SAG) ... WinsLoew
WinsLoew Furniture, Inc. [*NASDAQ symbol*] (SAG) ... WLFI
Winslow [*Arizona*] [*Airport symbol*] (OAG) ... INW
Winslow [*England*] ... WINS
Winslow, AZ [*Location identifier FAA*] (FAAL) ... INW
Winslow, AZ [*FM radio station call letters*] (RBYB) ... KFMR-FM
Winslow, AZ [*AM radio station call letters*] ... KINO
Winslow Furniture, Inc. [*NASDAQ symbol*] (SAG) ... WLFI
Winslow Gold Corp. [*Vancouver Stock Exchange symbol*] ... WGC
Winspear Resources [*Vancouver Stock Exchange symbol*] ... WSP
Winstar Communications [*NASDAQ symbol*] (SAG) ... WCII
Winstar Communications [*Commercial firm Associated Press*] (SAG) ... Winstar
Winsted Public Library, Winsted, MN [*Library symbol*] [*Library of Congress*] (LCLS) ... MnWs
Winsted Public School, Winsted, MN [*Library symbol*] [*Library of Congress*] (LCLS) ... MnWsPS
Winston & Strawn, Chicago, IL [*Library symbol Library of Congress*] (LCLS) ... ICWS
Winston Churchill Foundation (EA) ... WCF
Winston Cup ... WC
Winston Hotels [*NASDAQ symbol*] (TTSB) ... WINN
Winston Hotels, Inc. [*NASDAQ symbol*] (SAG) ... WINN
Winston Hotels, Inc. [*Associated Press*] (SAG) ... WinstonH
Winston, OR [*AM radio station call letters*] ... KGRV
Winston Resources [*AMEX symbol*] (TTSB) ... WRS
Winston Resources Ltd. [*Associated Press*] (SAG) ... WinstRs
Winston Resources Ltd. [*Vancouver Stock Exchange symbol*] ... WRE
Winston Resources Ltd. [*AMEX symbol*] (SPSG) ... WRS
Winston S. Churchill Association [*Defunct*] (EA) ... WCA
Winston Salem/Smith-Reynolds [*North Carolina*] [*ICAO location identifier*] (ICLI) ... KINT
Winston Spencer Churchill [*1874-1965*] [*British statesman and prime minister*] ... WSC
Winston's North Carolina Equity Reports [*A publication*] (DLA) ... Win Eq
Winston's North Carolina Equity Reports [*A publication*] (DLA) ... Winst
Winston's North Carolina Equity Reports [*A publication*] (DLA) ... Winst Eq
Winston's North Carolina Equity Reports [*A publication*] (DLA) ... Winst Eq (NC)
Winston's North Carolina Law Reports [*A publication*] (DLA) ... Winst
Winston's North Carolina Law Reports [*A publication*] (DLA) ... Winst L (NC)
Winston's North Carolina Reports [*1863-64*] [*A publication*] (DLA) ... Win
Winston-Salem [*North Carolina*] [*Airport symbol*] (AD) ... INT
Winston-Salem, NC [*Location identifier FAA*] (FAAL) ... INT
Winston-Salem, NC [*AM radio station call letters*] ... WAAA
Winston-Salem, NC [*AM radio station call letters*] ... WBFJ
Winston-Salem, NC [*FM radio station call letters*] ... WBFJ-FM
Winston-Salem, NC [*FM radio station call letters*] ... WFDD
Winston-Salem, NC [*FM radio station call letters*] ... WKZL
Winston-Salem, NC [*FM radio station call letters*] ... WMQX-FM
Winston-Salem, NC [*AM radio station call letters*] ... WPIP
Winston-Salem, NC [*AM radio station call letters*] (RBYB) ... WPOL
Winston-Salem, NC [*AM radio station call letters*] ... WSJS
Winston-Salem, NC [*AM radio station call letters*] ... WSMX
Winston-Salem, NC [*FM radio station call letters*] ... WSNC
Winston-Salem, NC [*AM radio station call letters*] ... WTOB
Winston-Salem, NC [*FM radio station call letters*] ... WTQR
Winston-Salem, NC [*Television station call letters*] ... WUNL
Winston-Salem, NC [*Television station call letters*] ... WXII
Winston-Salem, NC [*Television station call letters*] (RBYB) ... WXLV-TV
Winston-Salem, NC [*FM radio station call letters*] ... WXRI
Winston-Salem Southbound Railway Co. [*AAR code*] ... WSS
Winston-Salem State University, Winston-Salem, NC [*OCLC symbol*] (OCLC) ... ESM
Winston-Salem State University, Winston-Salem, NC [*Library symbol Library of Congress*] (LCLS) ... NcWsU
Winstree [*England*] ... WINST
Winter [*Vessel load line mark*] ... W
Winter [*Germany ICAO aircraft manufacturer identifier*] (ICAO) ... WI
Winter ... WIN
Winter ... WTR
Winter Advanced Course for Immunology and Infectious Diseases [*Japan International Friendship and Welfare Foundation*] ... WACIID
Winter Exercise (MCD) ... WINTEX
Winter Garden, FL [*AM radio station call letters*] ... WOKB
Winter Harbor, ME [*FM radio station call letters*] (RBYB) ... WAKN
Winter Haven, FL [*Location identifier FAA*] (FAAL) ... GIF
Winter Haven, FL [*FM radio station call letters*] ... WPCV
Winter Haven, FL [*AM radio station call letters*] ... WSIR
Winter Icing and Storms Project (USDC) ... WISP
Winter Icing and Storms Project [*Marine science*] (OSRA) ... WISP
Winter Navigation Board ... WNB
Winter, North Atlantic [*Vessel load line mark*] ... WNA
Winter Park, FL [*FM radio station call letters*] ... WLOQ
Winter Park, FL [*AM radio station call letters*] ... WPRD
Winter Park, FL [*FM radio station call letters*] ... WPRK
Winter Park Public Library, Winter Park, FL [*Library symbol Library of Congress*] (LCLS) ... FWp
Winter Soldier Archive [*Defunct*] (EA) ... WSA
Winter Sports [*NASDAQ symbol*] (TTSB) ... WSKI
Winter Sports, Inc. [*Associated Press*] (SAG) ... WinterSpt
Winter Sports, Inc. [*NASDAQ symbol*] (SAG) ... WSKI
Winter Study Group ... WSG
Winter Weddell Sea Project [*Marine science*] (OSRA) ... WWSP
Winter Wheat (Russian) Mosaic Virus [*Plant pathology*] ... WWMV
Winterization (AAG) ... WTRZN
Winterization Test (AAG) ... WT
Winterize (AAG) ... WTRZ
Winterquist Elementary School, Esko, MN [*Library symbol*] [*Library of Congress*] (LCLS) ... MnEskWE
[*The*] **Winter's Tale** [*Shakespearean work*] (BARN) ... Wint T
[*The*] **Winter's Tale** [*Shakespearean work*] ... WT

Winters, TX [*Location identifier FAA*] (FAAL) .... IEW
Winters, TX [*FM radio station call letters*] (RBYB) .... KAJL
Winterset, IA [*FM radio station call letters*] (RBYB) .... KZZQ
Winterset Madisonian, Winterset, IA [*Library symbol Library of Congress*] (LCLS) .... IaWintM
Winterset Public Library, Winterset, IA [*Library symbol Library of Congress*] (LCLS) .... IaWint
Winterswijk [*Netherlands*] [*Seismograph station code, US Geological Survey*] (SEIS) .... WTS
Winterthur [*Switzerland ICAO location identifier*] (ICLI) .... LSPH
Winterton Public Library, Newfoundland [*Library symbol National Library of Canada*] (NLC) .... NFWIN
Winterton Public Library, Winterton, NF, Canada [*Library symbol Library of Congress*] (LCLS) .... CaNfWin
Winthrop Avenue Elementary School, Bellmore, NY [*Library symbol*] [*Library of Congress*] (LCLS) .... NBellmWE
Winthrop College (GAGS) .... Winthrop C
Winthrop College, Rock Hill, SC [*Library symbol Library of Congress*] (LCLS) .... ScRhW
Winthrop College, Rock Hill, SC [*OCLC symbol*] (OCLC) .... SWW
Winthrop Laboratories [*Research code symbol*] .... WIN
Winthrop News, Winthrop, IA [*Library symbol Library of Congress*] (LCLS) .... IaWinN
Winthrop Resources [*NASDAQ symbol*] (TTSB) .... WINR
Winthrop Resources Corp. [*NASDAQ symbol*] (SAG) .... WINR
Winthrop Resources Corp. [*Associated Press*] (SAG) .... WinthpRs
Winton [*Australia Airport symbol*] (OAG) .... WIN
Winton, CA [*FM radio station call letters*] .... KFMK
Winton, CA [*FM radio station call letters*] (RBYB) .... KLOQ-FM
Winton Financial [*NASDAQ symbol*] (TTSB) .... WFCO
Winton Financial Corp. [*NASDAQ symbol*] (SAG) .... WFCO
Winton Financial Corp. [*Associated Press*] (SAG) .... Winton
Winward Islands Airways International [*Netherlands Antilles*] (EY) .... WIA
WinWhatWhere (PCM) W3
Winzen International, Inc. [*Vancouver Stock Exchange symbol*] .... WZI
Winzen Research, Inc. .... WRI
Wipe Out (MSA) .... WO
Wiped Film Evaporation .... WFE
Wipim [*Papua New Guinea*] [*Airport symbol*] (OAG) .... WPM
Wiping (MSA) .... WPG
Wiping Form (AAG) .... WPFM
Wiping Reflex [*Physiology*] .... WR
Wipperfurth/Neye [*Germany ICAO location identifier*] (ICLI) .... EDKN
Wirawila [*Sri Lanka*] [*ICAO location identifier*] (ICLI) .... VCCW
Wire .... W
Wire .... WI
Wire (VRA) .... wi
Wire Adhesion Promoter .... WAP
Wire and Cable (NASA) .... W & C
Wire and Wire-Like Object Detection System [*Helicopter*] (MCD) .... WWLODS
Wire Antenna Modeling Program (PDAA) .... WAMP
Wire Arc Seismic Section Profiler .... WASSP
Wire Armored [*Cables*] .... WA
Wire Assembly (MSA) .... WA
Wire Association [*Later, WAI*] .... WA
Wire Association International (EA) .... WAI
Wire Automated Check System (MCD) .... WACS
Wire Bound (IEEE) .... WBD
Wire Bound .... WRBND
Wire Bridge Circuit .... WBC
Wire Bundle Assembly (MCD) .... WBA
Wire Bundles (MCD) .... W/B
Wire Chief [*Test clerk*] [*Telecommunications*] (TEL) .... WC
Wire Chief Test Panel [*Telecommunications*] (TEL) .... WCTP
Wire Contact Relay .... WCR
Wire Data Service .... WDS
Wire Fabricators Association [*Naperville, IL*] (EA) .... WFA
Wire Foundation (EA) .... WF
Wire Gauge .... WG
Wire Glass (AAG) .... WGL
Wire Grid Lens .... WGL
Wire Grid Polarizer .... WGP
Wire Harness Board (MCD) .... WHB
Wire Installation Tester for Negating Errors by Sequencing and Standardization .... WITNESS
Wire Jig Board (MCD) .... WJB
Wire Line Adapter (MCD) .... WLA
Wire Line Antenna .... WLA
Wire Line MODEMS .... WLM
Wire Line Timing .... WLT
Wire Machinery Builders Association [*Later, WISA*] (EA) .... WMBA
Wire Mattress Federation .... WMF
Wire Measure Gauge .... WMG
Wire Mesh .... WM
Wire Mesh Screen (OA) .... WMS
Wire Metallizing Gun .... WMG
Wire Nonpayment .... WNP
Wire Obstacle Warning System (IEEE) .... WOWS
Wire Payment .... WP
Wire Products Association [*British*] (BI) .... WPA
Wire Recorder (DEN) .... WR
Wire Reinforcement Institute (EA) .... WRI
Wire Relay Radio System .... WRRS
Wire Rope (AAG) .... WR
Wire Rope Export Conference [*British*] (DBA) .... WREC
Wire Rope Institute .... WRI
Wire Rope Technical Board (EA) .... WRTB
Wire Routing Guide (MCD) .... WRG
Wire Send [*Telecommunications*] (TEL) .... WS
Wire Shift Register .... WSR
Wire Sound .... WS
Wire Strain Gauge .... WSG
Wire Strike Protection System (MCD) .... WSPS
Wire Test Chamber .... WTC
Wire Ticket [*NASA*] (NASA) .... WT
Wire Traceability and Accountability [*NASA*] (NASA) .... WTA
Wire Transfer [*Banking*] .... WT
Wire Way [*Technical drawings*] .... WW
Wire Wheel [*Automotive accessory*] .... WW
Wire Wrap (NASA) .... WW
Wire Wrap Fixture .... WWF
Wire Wrap Machine .... WWM
Wire Wrap Panels (MCD) .... WWP
Wirebar [*Metal industry*] .... WB
Wirebound Box Manufacturers Association (EA) .... WBMA
Wired Discrete (NASA) .... WD
Wired Glass [*Technical drawings*] .... WG
Wired Program Computer .... WPC
Wired Shelf Group [*Telecommunications*] (TEL) .... WSG
Wired-Core Matrix .... WCM
Wired-Core Memory .... WCM
Wire-Explosion-Spray Coating (PDAA) .... WESC
Wireless [*Communication*] (IAA) .... W
Wireless [*Telecommunications*] (IAA) .... WRLS
Wireless [*Communications*] .... WX
Wireless Air Gunner [*British military*] (DMA) .... WAG
Wireless Air Gunners School [*British military*] (DMA) .... WAGS
Wireless and Electrical Mechanic [*British*] (DSUE) .... WEM
Wireless Application Protocol [*Computer science*] .... WAP
Wireless Auxiliary Station [*Telecommunications*] (IAA) .... WASTN
Wireless Cable Association (TSSD) .... WCA
Wireless Cable Atlanta [*NASDAQ symbol*] (TTSB) .... WCAI
Wireless Cable of Atlanta, Inc. [*NASDAQ symbol*] (SAG) .... WCAI
Wireless Cable of Atlanta, Inc. [*Associated Press*] (SAG) .... Wireless
Wireless Communication (IAA) .... WC
Wireless Crew Communications System (LAIN) .... WCCS
Wireless Data Link .... WDL
Wireless Development Unit .... WDU
Wireless In-Building Network [*Motorola, Inc.*] [*Computer science*] .... WIN
Wireless Intelligence and Development Unit [*British military*] (DMA) .... WIDU
Wireless Interphone System (MCD) .... WIS
Wireless Manager (ACRL) .... WM
Wireless Network Access .... WNA
Wireless One [*NASDAQ symbol*] (TTSB) .... WIRL
Wireless One, Inc. [*Associated Press*] (SAG) .... WireOne
Wireless One, Inc. [*NASDAQ symbol*] (SAG) .... WIRL
Wireless Operationally Linked Electronic and Video Exploration System .... WOLVES
Wireless Operator .... WO
Wireless Operator [*RAF slang*] [*World War II*] .... WOP
Wireless Operator [*British military*] (IAA) .... WOPTR
Wireless Operator and Air Gunner [*British military*] (IAA) .... WOPAG
Wireless Operator Mechanic [*British*] (DSUE) .... WOM
Wireless Preservation Society [*British*] .... WPS
Wireless Set (MCD) .... WS
Wireless Station (IAA) .... WS
Wireless Telecom [*AMEX symbol*] (TTSB) .... WTT
Wireless Telecom Group [*Formerly, Noise Com, Inc.*] [*Associated Press*] (SAG) .... Wirelesst
Wireless Telecom Group [*Associated Press*] (SAG) .... WirelssT
Wireless Telecom Group [*Formerly, Noise Com, Inc.*] [*AMEX symbol*] (SAG) .... WTT
Wireless Telegraph Direction Finder (IAA) .... WTDF
Wireless Telegraphy [*or Telephony*] .... WT
Wireless Telegraphy Direction (IAA) .... WTDR
Wireless Telegraphy Message (IAA) .... WTMGE
Wireless Telegraphy Officer [*British military*] (DMA) .... WTO
Wireless Telegraphy Station [*Telecommunications*] (IAA) .... WTS
Wireless Transceiver (ACRL) .... WT
Wireless Transmitter .... WT
Wireless Truck [*British*] .... WT
Wireless Van [*British*] .... WV
Wireman (AABC) .... WRMN
Wiretap, Investigation Monitoring, and Eavesdrop Activities (MCD) .... WIMEA
Wiretap Online Library [*Online database*] .... WOL
Wire-Wound .... WW
Wirewound (IDOE) .... ww
Wire-Wound Porous Material .... WPM
Wire-Wound Resistor .... WWR
Wire-Wound Variable Resistor .... WWVR
Wire-Wrapped Breadboard .... WWBB
Wiring .... WIRG
Wiring (IAA) .... WNG
Wiring .... WRG
Wiring and Connective Device, Semiautomatic (DNAB) .... WICOMATIC
Wiring Around Frame (MSA) .... WAF
Wiring Data Handbook .... WDH
Wiring Diagram (IAA) .... WD
Wiring Diagram Maintenance List .... WDML
Wiring Integration Design (IEEE) .... WIDE

Wiring Interface Tester (MCD) ... WIT
Wiring List ... WL
Wirlwind Resources Ltd. [*Vancouver Stock Exchange symbol*] ... WHD
Wirral Railway [*British*] (ROG) ... WR
Wirtschaft [*Economy, Industry*] [*German*] ... WIRTSCH
Wirtschaft und Statistik [*Germany*] ... WS
Wirtschaftliche Aufbau Vereinigung [*Economic Reconstruction Union*] [*Germany Political party*] (PPE) ... WAV
Wirtschaftsverwaltungshauptamt (BJA) ... WVHA
Wirtschaftswoche-Datenbank [*Economic Week Data Bank*] [*Society for Public Economics*] [*Germany*] [*Information service or system*] (IID) ... WW
Wisbech [*Municipal borough in England*] ... WISB
Wisc Pwr/Lt 4 1/2cm Pfd vtg [*AMEX symbol*] (TTSB) ... WISPr
Wiscair [*ICAO designator*] (AD) ... FD
Wiscasset, ME [*Location identifier FAA*] (FAAL) ... ISS
Wisco of Canada Ltd. [*Vancouver Stock Exchange symbol*] ... WCA
Wisconsin [*MARC geographic area code Library of Congress*] (LCCP) ... n-us-wi
Wisconsin [*Postal code*] ... WI
Wisconsin (ODBW) ... Wis
Wisconsin (AAG) ... WIS
Wisconsin (AFM) ... WISC
Wisconsin [*MARC country of publication code Library of Congress*] (LCCP) ... wiu
Wisconsin [*Obsolete*] (ROG) ... WN
Wisconsin Academy of Sciences, Arts, and Letters ... WASAL
Wisconsin Administrative Code [*A publication*] (DLA) ... Wis Admin Code
Wisconsin Alumni Research Foundation Institute, Inc., Madison, WI [*Library symbol Library of Congress*] (LCLS) ... WMaW
Wisconsin Alumni Research Foundation, Madison, WI [*Library symbol Library of Congress*] (LCLS) ... WMaAR
Wisconsin Attorney General Reports [*A publication*] (DLA) ... Ops Atty Gen Wisc
Wisconsin Automated Clearing House Association ... WACHA
Wisconsin Automatic Test Apparatus ... WATA
Wisconsin Baptist State Convention, Milwaukee, WI [*Library symbol Library of Congress*] (LCLS) ... WMBC
Wisconsin Bar Bulletin [*A publication*] (LWAP) ... WIS B BULL
Wisconsin Board of Tax Appeals Decisions [*A publication*] (DLA) ... WBTA
Wisconsin Board of Tax Appeals Decisions (Commerce Clearing House) [*A publication*] (DLA) ... WBTA-CCH Tax Reporter
Wisconsin Board of Tax Appeals Reports [*A publication*] (DLA) ... Wis BTA
Wisconsin Card Sorting Test [*Neuropsychology test*] ... WCST
Wisconsin Career Information System [*Information service or system*] ... WCIS
Wisconsin Center for Applied Microelectronics [*University of Wisconsin - Madison*] [*Research center*] (RCD) ... WCAM
Wisconsin Center for Education Research [*Madison*] ... WCER
Wisconsin Central Trans [*NASDAQ symbol*] (TTSB) ... WCLX
Wisconsin Central Transportation Corp. [*NASDAQ symbol*] (SPSG) ... WCLX
Wisconsin Central Transportation Corp. [*Associated Press*] (SAG) ... WiscCt
Wisconsin Cheese and Sausage Promotions (EA) ... WCSP
Wisconsin Cheese and Specialty Food Merchants Association (EA) ... WCSFMA
Wisconsin Cheese Makers' Association (EA) ... WCMA
Wisconsin Clinical Cancer Center [*University of Wisconsin*] [*Research center*] (RCD) ... WCCC
Wisconsin Dairy Products Association (EA) ... WDPA
Wisconsin Dells, WI [*AM radio station call letters*] ... WNNO
Wisconsin Dells, WI [*FM radio station call letters*] ... WNNO-FM
Wisconsin Department of Health and Social Services, Bureau of Research, Madison,WI [*Library symbol Library of Congress*] (LCLS) ... WMaBR
Wisconsin Department of Health and Social Services, Community Health Service, Madison, WI [*Library symbol Library of Congress*] (LCLS) ... WMaCH
Wisconsin Department of Natural Resources ... WDNR
Wisconsin Department of Public Instruction, Reference and Loan Library, Madison,WI [*OCLC symbol*] (OCLC) ... GZR
Wisconsin Division for Library Services, Bureau for Reference and Local Services, Madison, WI [*Library symbol Library of Congress*] (LCLS) ... WMaLS
Wisconsin Division of Health Policy and Planning Library, Madison, WI [*Library symbol Library of Congress*] (LCLS) ... WMaH
Wisconsin Elementary and Secondary School Accounting System (EDAC) ... WESSAS
Wisconsin Energy Corp. [*NYSE symbol*] (SPSG) ... WEC
Wisconsin Energy Corp. [*Associated Press*] (SAG) ... WiscEn
Wisconsin Evangelical Lutheran Synod ... WELS
Wisconsin Experiment Package [*NASA*] (MCD) ... WEP
Wisconsin Gas Co., Milwaukee, WI [*Library symbol Library of Congress*] (LCLS) ... WMGa
Wisconsin General Test Apparatus [*Psychology*] ... WGTA
Wisconsin Gift Cheese Association (EA) ... WGCA
Wisconsin H-Alpha Mapper [*Astrophysics*] ... WHAM
Wisconsin Hydrologic Transport Model ... WHTM
Wisconsin Industrial Commission Workmen's Compensation Reports [*A publication*] (DLA) ... Wis IC
Wisconsin Information Resources for Education (EDAC) ... WIRE
Wisconsin Information Science and Communications Consortium [*University of Wisconsin - Madison*] [*Research center*] (RCD) ... WISCOM
Wisconsin Institute of Technology ... WIT
Wisconsin Instructional Computing Consortium (EDAC) ... WICC
Wisconsin Interlibrary Loan Service ... WILS
Wisconsin Interlibrary Loan Service, Madison, WI [*OCLC symbol*] (OCLC) ... GZY
Wisconsin Interlibrary Loan Service - Wisconsin Library Consortium [*Library network*] ... WILS/WLC
Wisconsin International Law Journal [*A publication*] (DLA) ... Wis Int'l LJ
Wisconsin Legal News [*Milwaukee*] [*A publication*] (DLA) ... Wis Leg N
Wisconsin Legal News [*Milwaukee*] [*A publication*] (DLA) ... Wis LN
Wisconsin Legislative Service (West) [*A publication*] (DLA) ... Wis Legis Serv
Wisconsin Library Consortium (NITA) ... WLC
Wisconsin Library Consortium, Madison, WI [*OCLC symbol*] (OCLC) ... TQY
Wisconsin Library Consortium, Madison, WI [*OCLC symbol*] (OCLC) ... TQZ
Wisconsin Lutheran Seminary, Mequon, WI [*Library symbol Library of Congress*] (LCLS) ... WMeqW
Wisconsin Motor Carriers Association Inc., Madison WI [*STAC*] ... WMC
[*The*] **Wisconsin Network** [*Telecommunications service*] (TNIG) ... WISCNET
Wisconsin Pharmacal Co., Inc. [*AMEX symbol*] (SAG) ... FHC
Wisconsin Pharmacal Company, Inc. [*Associated Press*] (SAG) ... WisPhrm
Wisconsin Physicians Service [*Army*] ... WPS
Wisconsin Power & Light Co. [*AMEX symbol*] (SAG) ... WIS
Wisconsin Power & Light Co. [*Associated Press*] (SAG) ... WisP
Wisconsin Procedure for Appraisal of Clinical Competence (EDAC) ... W-PACC
Wisconsin Program for the Renewal and Improvement of Secondary Education (EDAC) ... WRISE
Wisconsin Public Service Commission Opinions and Decisions [*A publication*] (DLA) ... Wis PSC Ops
Wisconsin Public Service Commission Reports [*A publication*] (DLA) ... Wis PSC
Wisconsin Railroad Commission Opinions and Decisions [*A publication*] (DLA) ... Wis RC Ops
Wisconsin Railroad Commission Reports [*A publication*] (DLA) ... Wis RCR
Wisconsin Railroad Commission Reports [*A publication*] (DLA) ... WRCR
Wisconsin Rapids [*Wisconsin*] [*Airport symbol*] (OAG) ... ISW
Wisconsin Rapids, McMillan Library, Wisconsin Rapids, WI [*OCLC symbol*] (OCLC) ... WWR
Wisconsin Rapids, WI [*Location identifier FAA*] (FAAL) ... EKP
Wisconsin Rapids, WI [*Location identifier FAA*] (FAAL) ... ISW
Wisconsin Rapids, WI [*AM radio station call letters*] ... WFHR
Wisconsin Rapids, WI [*FM radio station call letters*] ... WGLX
Wisconsin Regional Primate Research Center, Madison, WI [*Library symbol Library of Congress*] (LCLS) ... WMaPR
Wisconsin Reports [*A publication*] (DLA) ... W
Wisconsin Reports [*A publication*] (DLA) ... Wis
Wisconsin Reports [*A publication*] (DLA) ... Wis R
Wisconsin Reports [*A publication*] (DLA) ... Wis Rep
Wisconsin Reports [*A publication*] (DLA) ... Wisc
Wisconsin Reports [*A publication*] (DLA) ... WR
Wisconsin Reports, Second Series [*A publication*] (DLA) ... Wis 2d
Wisconsin School for the Deaf, Delavan, WI [*Library symbol Library of Congress*] (LCLS) ... WDSD
Wisconsin Scottish Rite Bodies AASR, Milwaukee, WI [*Library symbol Library of Congress*] (LCLS) ... WMFM
Wisconsin State Bar Association. Bulletin [*A publication*] (DLA) ... Wis BA Bull
Wisconsin State Bar Association. Bulletin [*A publication*] (DLA) ... Wis Bar Bull
Wisconsin State Bar Association. Bulletin [*A publication*] (DLA) ... Wis SBA Bull
Wisconsin State College [*Later, University of Wisconsin*] ... WSC
Wisconsin State Data Center [*Wisconsin State Department of Administration*] [*Madison*] [*Information service or system*] (IID) ... WSDC
Wisconsin State Law Library [*Wisconsin State Library*], Madison, WI [*Library symbol Library of Congress*] (LCLS) ... W-L
Wisconsin State Library, Processing Center, Madison, WI [*OCLC symbol*] (OCLC) ... WIG
Wisconsin Statutes [*A publication*] (DLA) ... Wis Stat
Wisconsin Statutes Annotated [*A publication*] (DLA) ... WSA
Wisconsin Student Bar Journal [*A publication*] (DLA) ... Wisc Stud BJ
Wisconsin Survey Research Laboratory [*University of Wisconsin*] [*Research center*] (RCD) ... WSRL
Wisconsin Tandem Mirror ... WITAMIR
Wisconsin Tax Appeals Commission Reports [*A publication*] (DLA) ... Wis Tax App C
Wisconsin Test Facility [*Navy*] ... WTF
Wisconsin Ultraviolet Photo-Polarimeter Experiment ... WUPPE
Wisconsin Valley Library Service, Wausau, WI [*Library symbol Library of Congress*] (LCLS) ... WWsWV
Wisdom [*Old Testament book*] ... Wis
Wisdom [*Old Testament book*] ... WISD
Wisdom [*Old Testament Book*] (BJA) ... Ws
Wisdom, Acclaim, and Status through Expenditures [*Fictional government agency in book "Alice in Blunderland"*] ... WASTE
Wisdom Middle School, Levittown, NY [*Library symbol*] [*Library of Congress*] (LCLS) ... NLevWM
Wisdom of Solomon [*Old Testament book*] ... Wisd of Sol
Wisdom of the East Series [*A publication*] ... WES
Wise Old Men [*Term used to refer to group of US statesmen including Dean Acheson, Charles Bohlen, Averell Harriman, George Kennan, Robert Lovett, and John McCloy*] ... WOM
Wise, VA [*Location identifier FAA*] (FAAL) ... LNP
Wise, VA [*Location identifier FAA*] (FAAL) ... OWN
Wiseman [*Alaska*] [*Airport symbol*] (OAG) ... WSM
Wiseman, AK [*Location identifier FAA*] (FAAL) ... WSM
Wiser Oil [*NYSE symbol*] (TTSB) ... WZR
[*The*] **Wiser Oil Co.** [*Associated Press*] (SAG) ... WiserO
Wiser Oil Co. [*NYSE symbol*] (SAG) ... WZR
Wishard Memorial Hospital, Indianapolis, IN [*Library symbol Library of Congress*] (LCLS) ... InIWis
Wishard Memorial Hospital, Indianapolis, IN [*OCLC symbol*] (OCLC) ... IWI
Wishek, ND [*AM radio station call letters*] ... KDRQ
Wishes and Fears Inventory [*Psychology*] ... WFI
Wishing Well [*An association*] (EA) ... WW
Wiskott-Aldrich Syndrome [*Immunology*] ... WAS
Wisman Aviation [*ICAO designator*] (FAAC) ... WSM
WISP [*Winter Icing and Storms Project*] **Instrument Test** (USDC) ... WISPIT
WISP [*Winter Icing and Storms Project*] **Instrument Test** [*Marine science*] (OSRA) ... WISPIT
Wiss, Janney, Elstner, & Associates, Northbrook, IL [*Library symbol Library of Congress*] (LCLS) ... INbW

Wissahickon Valley Public Library, Ambler, PA [*Library symbol Library of Congress*] (LCLS) .... PAm

Wissenschaft des Judentums [*A publication*] (BJA) .... WdJ

Wissenschaftliche Gesellschaft fuer Luft- und Raumfahrt [*Scientific Association for Air and Space Travel*] [*German*] .... WGLR

Wissenschaftliche Monographien zum Alten und Neuen Testament [*A publication*] (BJA) .... WMANT

Wissenschaftliche Untersuchungen zum Neuen Testament [*Tuebingen*] [*A publication*] (BJA) .... WissUnNT

Wissenschaftliche Untersuchungen zum Neuen Testament [*Tuebingen*] [*A publication*] (BJA) .... WUNT

Wissenschaftliche Zeitschrift [*A publication*] .... WZ

Wissenschaftliche Zeitschrift fuer Juedische Geschichte [*A publication*] (BJA) .... WZG

Wissenschaftliche Zeitschrift fuer Juedische Theologie [*A publication*] (BJA) .... WZJT

Wissenschaftliche Zeitschrift fuer Juedische Theologie [*A publication*] (BJA) .... WZJTh

Wissenschaftlich-Technischer Arbeitskreis fuer Denkmalpflege und Bauwerksanierung [*International Association for the Protection of Monuments and Restoration of Buildings*] (EAIO) .... WTA

Wissenschaftsgemeinschaft Blaue Liste .... WBL

Wissenschaftsrat [*Science Council*] [*Germany*] .... WR

Wistar Institute of Anatomy and Biology, Philadelphia, PA [*Library symbol Library of Congress*] (LCLS) .... PPWI

Wistar-Furth [*Rat strain*] .... WF

Wistar-Kyoto [*Rat variety*] .... WKY

Wisteria Vein Mosaic Virus .... WVMV

Wiswesser Line Notation [*Chemical structure*] .... WLN

Wit Kommando [*White Commando*] [*South Africa*] .... WK

Wit of the Jews [*A publication*] .... WIJ

Witbank [*South Africa*] [*ICAO location identifier*] (ICLI) .... FAWI

Witches International Craft Association (EA) .... WICA

Witco Corp. [*NYSE symbol*] (SPSG) .... WIT

Witco Corp. [*Associated Press*] (SAG) .... Witco

With (VRA) .... w/

With (WDMC) .... w

With .... W

With Added [*Freight*] .... W ADD

With All Faults [*i.e., to be sold as is*] .... WAF

With All Faults (WDMC) .... waf

With All Risks [*Insurance*] .... WAR

With Answers .... WA

With Average [*Insurance*] .... WA

With Binder [*Freight*] .... W BNDR

With Blowout (MSA) .... W/BO

With Certificate [*Philately*] .... Crt

With Corrections [*Publishing*] .... WC

With Dependents (MCD) .... WD

With Disease (MAE) .... WD

With Due Bills [*Stocks*] (MHDW) .... WDB

With Effect From .... WEF

With Enclosure (DNAB) .... W/ENCL

With Equipment (AABC) .... WE

With Equipment and Spare Parts .... W/E & SP

With Fittings [*Freight*] .... W FTTNGS

With Food Element .... WFE

With Grain .... WG

With Modification of Vertical Profile (GAVI) .... W/MOD

With Much Pleasure [*Meaning, "We accept the invitation"*] .... WMP

With No Down Payment [*Business term*] (WDAA) .... WNDP

With Other Goods [*Business term*] .... WOG

With Other Goods (ODBW) .... wog

With Other Natural Flavors [*Food science*] .... WONF

With Other Property (BARN) .... WOP

With Particular Average .... WPA

With Partition [*Freight*] .... W PAR

With Power Unit (NATG) .... WPU

With Prior Service .... WPS

With Promotion To (NOAA) .... WPT

With Reference To (WDAA) .... W REF

With Reference To .... WRT

With Regard To (WDAA) .... W REG

With Regard To (NHD) .... WRT

With Respect To (KSC) .... WRT

With Restrictive Language (MCD) .... WL

With Rights [*Securities*] .... WR

With Snow Tires [*Automotive advertising*] .... W/SNWS

With Step Change in Altitude (GAVI) .... W/STEP

With Stock [*Business term*] .... W/S

With Tape .... WT

With the Rule Astigmatism [*Ophthalmology*] .... WRA

With the Will Annexed .... WWA

With Title [*Bibliography*] .... WT

With/Warhead [*Nuclear*] .... W/WH

With Warrants [*Stock exchange term*] (SPSG) .... WW

With Winch .... WW

With Winch .... WWN

Withdrawal .... W

Withdrawal (DLA) .... W/D

Withdrawal .... WDR

Withdrawal (ROG) .... WITHDRL

Withdrawal Body Shakes [*Medicine*] (DMAA) .... WBS

Withdrawal of Availability [*Military*] (AFM) .... WDA

Withdrawal of Enthusiasm [*Airline pilots objection to "Welcome aboard" talks*] .... WOE

Withdrawal Seizure-Prone [*Mouse strain*] .... WSP

Withdrawal Seizure-Resistant [*Mouse strain*] .... WSR

Withdrawn (AFM) .... WD

Withdrawn Failing [*Education*] (WGA) .... WF

Withdrawn Passing [*Education*] (WGA) .... WP

Witheridge [*England*] .... WITH

Withers Public Library, Bloomington, IL [*Library symbol Library of Congress*] (LCLS) .... IBlo

Withholding (AFM) .... WH

Withholding Agent (DLA) .... WA

Withholding Exemptions [*Army*] (AABC) .... WE

Withholding Statement (AAG) .... WS

Withholding Tax [*IRS*] (AAG) .... W/TAX

Withholding Tax (DFIT) .... W/Tax

Withholding Tax [*IRS*] .... WT

Within (WGA) .... W

Within .... WI

Within (ROG) .... WN

Within Functional Limits [*Physical therapy*] (DAVI) .... WFL

Within Normal Limits [*Medicine*] .... WNL

Within Visual Range [*Missile*] (MCD) .... WVR

Within Visual Range Air-to-Air Missile .... WVRAAM

Within-Grade Increase .... WGI

Without (NITA) .... W/O

Without (IDOE) .... w/o

Without (ROG) .... WITHT

Without (AFM) .... WO

Without .... WT

Without Benefit of Salvage .... WBS

Without Binder [*Freight*] .... W O BNDR

Without Blowout (MSA) .... W/OBO

Without Charge (ODBW) .... wc

Without Charge .... WC

Without Chest Pain [*Medicine*] .... sCP

Without Compensation (ODBW) .... woc

Without Compensation (ADA) .... WOC

Without Dependents [*Military*] (AFM) .... WOD

Without Enclosure (MCD) .... WOE

Without Equipment .... WOE

Without Equipment and Spare Parts .... W/OE & SP

Without Film [*Bacteriology*] (DAVI) .... O

Without Fittings [*Freight*] .... W O FTTNGS

Without Glasses [*Ophthalmology*] (DAVI) .... VS

Without Margin .... WM

Without Optical Brightener [*Biochemistry*] .... WOB

Without Pain (DAVI) .... WOP

Without Partition [*Freight*] .... W O PAR

Without Passport [*Immigration terminology*] [*Acronym often referred to early 20th century Italian immigrants*] .... WOP

Without Payment .... WOP

Without Penalty .... W/O/P

Without Personnel .... WOP

Without Personnel and Equipment .... WOPE

Without Preference [*Rating*] .... WOP

Without Prejudice .... WP

Without Priorities .... WOP

Without Securities or Warrants [*Business term*] XX

Without Voice Facilities on Range or Radiobeacon Frequency .... W

Without Whiskers (IAA) .... WOW

Without Winch .... WOWN

Withrow's American Corporation Cases [*A publication*] (DLA) .... With Corp Cas

Withrow's American Corporation Cases [*A publication*] (DLA) .... Withrow

Withrow's Reports [*9-21 Iowa*] [*A publication*] (DLA) .... Withrow

Witkin's Summary of California Law [*A publication*] (DLA) .... Witkin Cal Summary

Witness (AABC) .... WIT

Witness [*Legal*] [*British*] (ROG) .... WITNS

Witness .... WTN

Witness .... WTNS

Witness for Peace (EA) .... WFP

Witness Protection and Relocation [*Government agency in film "F/X"*] .... WPR

Witness Protection Program (BARN) .... WPP

Witness Security Program [*US government program for protection of witnesses whose lives are endangered by their testimony*] .... WITSEC

Witness Terms (NITA) .... WT

Witnessed .... WITNED

Witnesses [*Legal*] [*British*] (ROG) .... WITSS

Witnesseth [*Legal*] [*British*] (ROG) .... WITNETH

Witnesseth [*Legal*] [*British*] (ROG) .... WTNSTH

Witnessing [*Legal*] [*British*] (ROG) .... WTSNG

Witt Community Unit, School District 66, Witt, IL [*Library symbol Library of Congress*] (LCLS) .... IWiSD

Witt Memorial Library, Witt, IL [*Library symbol Library of Congress*] (LCLS) .... IWi

Wittenberg University, Springfield, OH [*Library symbol Library of Congress*] (LCLS) .... OSW

Wittenberg University, Springfield, OH [*OCLC symbol*] (OCLC) .... WIT

Wittenborn [*Psychiatric rating scale*] (DMAA) .... WITT

Wittenborn Psychiatric Rating Scale .... WPRS

Wittenoom Gorge [*Western Australia*] [*Airport symbol*] (AD) .... ITT

Wittering [*British ICAO location identifier*] (ICLI) .... EGXT

Wittering FTU [*British ICAO designator*] (FAAC) .... WIT

Witterungseinfluesse und Zeitunterschied [*Weather factors and time difference*] [*German military - World War II*] .... WEZU

Witteveen [*Netherlands*] [*Seismograph station code, US Geological Survey*] (SEIS) .... WIT
Witthaus and Becker's Medical Jurisprudence [*A publication*] (DLA) .... Witthaus & Becker's Med Jur
Wittlesford [*England*] .... WITTL
Wittman, AZ [*Location identifier FAA*] (FAAL) .... BRZ
Wittmundhafen [*Germany ICAO location identifier*] (ICLI) .... EDNT
Witton Network Analyzer .... WINA
Wittsburg Lake [*Arkansas*] [*Seismograph station code, US Geological Survey Closed*] (SEIS) .... WLA
Witu [*Papua New Guinea*] [*Airport symbol*] (OAG) .... WIU
Witwatersrand Local Division Reports [*South Africa*] [*A publication*] (DLA) .... W
Witwatersrand Native Labour Association [*Nyasaland*] .... WENELA
Witwatersrand Native Labour Association [*Nyasaland*] .... WNLA
Wives of Older Men [*An association*] (EA) .... WOOM
Wives of the Armed Forces, Emeritus [*Defunct*] (EA) .... WAFE
Wives Self-Help Foundation (EA) .... WSHF
Wix, Inc. [*Toronto Stock Exchange symbol*] .... WXL
Wixamtree [*England*] .... WIXAMT
Wiz Technology [*ECM symbol*] (TTSB) .... WIZ EC
Wiz Technology, Inc. [*AMEX symbol*] (SAG) .... WIZ
Wiz Technology, Inc. [*Associated Press*] (SAG) .... WizTch
Wiztec Solutions [*NASDAQ symbol*] (TTSB) .... WIZTF
Wiztec Solutions Ltd. [*NASDAQ symbol*] (SAG) .... WIZT
Wiztec Solutions Ltd. [*Associated Press*] (SAG) .... WiztecS
Wkay Resources [*Vancouver Stock Exchange symbol*] .... WKA
W.L. Gore Associates, Medical Products Division, Flagstaff, AZ [*Library symbol*] [*Library of Congress*] (LCLS) .... AzFGM
Wliams Companies [*NYSE symbol*] (SAG) .... WMZ
WLR Foods [*Associated Press*] (SAG) .... WLR Fds
WLR Foods, Inc. [*Associated Press*] (SAG) .... WLR Fd
WLR Foods, Inc. [*NASDAQ symbol*] (NQ) .... WLRF
WM Helijet [*Vancouver Stock Exchange symbol*] .... WMH
Wm. Kelley High School, Silver Bay, MN [*Library symbol*] [*Library of Congress*] (LCLS) .... MnSibHS
WMC Ltd ADS [*NYSE symbol*] (TTSB) .... WMC
WMS Airways BV [*Netherlands ICAO designator*] (FAAC) .... WMS
WMS Industries [*Associated Press*] (SAG) .... WMS
WMS Industries, Inc. [*Formerly, Williams Electronics*] [*NYSE symbol*] (SPSG) .... WMS
WMX Technologies [*NYSE symbol*] (SPSG) .... WMX
WMX Technologies, Inc. [*Associated Press*] (SAG) .... WMX Tc
WNED-TV, Buffalo, NY [*Library symbol Library of Congress*] (LCLS) .... NBuWNED
Woburn [*Parish in England*] .... WOB
Woburn Public Library, Woburn, MA [*Library symbol Library of Congress*] (LCLS) .... MWo
WOCE [*World Ocean Circulation Experiment*] **Hydrographic Experiment** (USDC) .... WHP
WOCE [*World Ocean Circulation Experiment*] **Hydrographic Program** [*Marine science*] (OSRA) .... WHP
WOCE [*World Ocean Circulation Experiment*] **Hydrologic Program Office** [*Marine science*] (OSRA) .... WHPO
WOCE [*World Ocean Circulation Experiment*] **International Project Office** [*Marine science*] (OSRA) .... WOCE-IPO
WOCE [*World Ocean Circulation Experiment*] **Numerical Experimentation Group** [*Marine science*] (OSRA) .... WOCE-NEG
WOCE [*World Ocean Circulation Experiment*] **Scientific Steering Group** [*Marine science*] (OSRA) .... WOCE-SSG
WOCE [*World Ocean Circulation Experiment*] **Scientific Steering Group** [*Marine science*] (OSRA) .... WSSG
WOCE [*World Ocean Circulation Experiment*] **Sea Level Center** [*Marine science*] (OSRA) .... WSLC
WOCE [*World Ocean Circulation Experiment*] **Sea Level Center** (USDC) .... WSLC
Woden's Coven [*Germany Defunct*] (EAIO) .... WC
Woensdrecht [*Netherlands ICAO location identifier*] (ICLI) .... EHWO
Woerner's Treatise on the American Law of Administration [*A publication*] (DLA) .... Woerner Adm'n
Woerterbuch [*Dictionary*] [*German*] (ROG) .... WTB
Woerterbuch der Aegyptischen Sprache [*A publication*] (BJA) .... WB
Woerterbuch der Aegyptischen Sprache [*A publication*] (BJA) .... WBAS
Woerterbuch der Mythologie [*A publication*] (BJA) .... WBM
Woerterbuch der Mythologie [*A publication*] (BJA) .... WbMyth
Woerterbuch der Ugaritischen Sprache [*A publication*] (BJA) .... WUS
Woerterbuch ueber die Talmudim und Midraschim [*J. Levy*] [*A publication*] (BJA) .... Levy WTM
Wofford College, Spartanburg, SC [*Library symbol Library of Congress*] (LCLS) .... ScSpW
Wofford College, Spartanburg, SC [*OCLC symbol*] (OCLC) .... SPW
Wohl Associates [*Bala Cynwyd, PA*] [*Telecommunications*] (TSSD) .... WA
Woitape [*Papua New Guinea*] [*Airport symbol*] (OAG) .... WTP
Woking School, Alberta [*Library symbol National Library of Canada*] (BIB) .... AWOS
Wokingham [*Municipal borough in England*] .... WOK
Wolbach, NE [*Location identifier FAA*] (FAAL) .... OBH
Wolcott Public Library, Wolcott, IN [*Library symbol Library of Congress*] (LCLS) .... InWol
Wolcott's Chancery Reports [*7 Delaware*] [*A publication*] (DLA) .... Wol
Wold Farm Foods [*Commercial firm British*] .... WFF
Wolf Creek Generating Station [*Nuclear energy*] (NRCH) .... WCGS
Wolf First Class [*A philanderer*] [*Slang*] .... WFC
Wolf [*Howard B.*], Inc. [*AMEX symbol*] (SPSG) .... HBW
Wolf [*Howard B.*], Inc. [*Associated Press*] (SAG) .... WolfHB
Wolf Lake, IN [*Location identifier FAA*] (FAAL) .... OLK
[*A*] **Wolf on the Loose** [*Slang*] .... AWOL
Wolf Point [*Montana*] [*Airport symbol*] (OAG) .... OLF
Wolf Point, MT [*AM radio station call letters*] .... KVCK
Wolf Point, MT [*FM radio station call letters*] .... KVCK-FM
Wolf Point, MT [*Location identifier FAA*] (FAAL) .... OLF
Wolf River Resources Ltd. [*Vancouver Stock Exchange symbol*] .... WLF
Wolf Trap Farm Park [*National Park Service designation*] .... WOTR
Wolf Trap Foundation for the Performing Arts (EA) .... WTFPA
Wolfe Angel Committee [*Defunct*] (EA) .... WAC
Wolfe Computer Operator Aptitude Test .... WCOAT
Wolfe Data Entry Operator Aptitude Test .... WDEOAT
Wolfe Island Branch, Frontenac County Public Library, Ontario [*Library symbol National Library of Canada*] (NLC) .... OWIFC
Wolfe Pack (EA) .... WP
Wolfe Programming Aptitude Test .... WPAT
Wolfe Programming Language Test: COBOL .... WCOBL
Wolfe Screening Test for Programming Aptitude .... WPT
Wolfeboro, NH [*AM radio station call letters*] .... WASR
Wolfeboro, NH [*FM radio station call letters*] .... WLKZ
Wolfeboro Railroad Co., Inc. [*AAR code*] .... WLFB
Wolferstan and Bristow's English Election Cases [*1859-65*] [*A publication*] (DLA) .... Wolf & B
Wolferstan and Dew's English Election Cases [*1856-58*] [*A publication*] (DLA) .... W & D
Wolferstan and Dew's English Election Cases [*1856-58*] [*A publication*] (DLA) .... Wolf & D
Wolfe-Spence Programming Aptitude Test .... WSPAT
Wolfe-Winrow CICS/VS Command Level Proficiency Test [*Computer science*] .... WWCICS
Wolff-Parkinson-White [*Syndrome*] [*Cardiology*] .... WPW
Wolfhagen/Granerberg [*Germany ICAO location identifier*] (ICLI) .... EDGW
Wolf-Hirschorn Syndrome [*Medicine*] .... WHS
Wolfram [*Tungsten*] [*Chemical element*] .... W
Wolfram Inert Gas (MCD) .... WIG
Wolf-Raye [*Star classification*] .... WR
Wolfson Centre for Electrochemical Science [*British*] (CB) .... WCES
Wolfson Microelectronics Institute (NITA) .... WMI
Wolfsonian Foundation, Miami Beach, FL [*Library symbol*] [*Library of Congress*] (LCLS) .... FMbW
Wolfville Historical Museum, Nova Scotia [*Library symbol National Library of Canada*] (NLC) .... NSWH
Wolfville Historical Museum, Wolfville, NS, Canada [*Library symbol Library of Congress*] (LCLS) .... CaNSWH
Wollaston and Limerick Public Library, Coe Hill, Ontario [*Library symbol National Library of Canada*] (BIB) .... OCHWL
Wollaston Lake [*Canada*] [*Airport symbol*] (OAG) .... ZWL
Wollastonite [*CIPW classification*] [*Geology*] .... wo
Wollaston's English Bail Court Reports [*A publication*] (DLA) .... Wol
Wollaston's English Bail Court Reports [*A publication*] (DLA) .... Woll BC
Wollaston's English Bail Court Reports, Practice Cases [*1840-41*] [*A publication*] (DLA) .... Woll
Wollaston's English Bail Court Reports, Practice Cases [*A publication*] (DLA) .... WP Cas
Wollaston's English Bail Court Reports, Practice Cases [*A publication*] (DLA) .... WPC
Wollongong [*Australia Airport symbol*] .... WOL
Wollongong Integrated Network (HGAA) .... WIN
Wollongong Public Library, Wollongong, NSW, Australia [*Library symbol Library of Congress*] (LCLS) .... AuWol
Wolof [*MARC language code Library of Congress*] (LCCP) .... wol
Wolohan Lumber [*NASDAQ symbol*] (TTSB) .... WLHN
Wolohan Lumber Co. [*NASDAQ symbol*] (NQ) .... WLHN
Wolohan Lumber Co. [*Associated Press*] (SAG) .... Wolohn
Wolseley [*South Africa*] [*ICAO location identifier*] (ICLI) .... FAWY
Wolseley Pattern [*British military*] (DMA) .... WP
Wolseley Register (EA) .... WR
Wolstenholme and Cherry's Conveyancing Statutes [*13th ed.*] [*1972*] [*A publication*] (DLA) .... W & C Conv
Wolters Kluwer Nv [*AM symbol*] (TTSB) .... WOSIN
Wolverhampton [*British depot code*] .... WPN
Wolverhampton Volunteer Defence Force [*British military*] (DMA) .... WVDF
Wolverhampton Volunteer Rifle Corps [*British military*] (DMA) .... WVRC
Wolverine Community Library, Wolverine, MI [*Library symbol Library of Congress*] (LCLS) .... MiWol
Wolverine Society of America (EA) .... WSA
Wolverine Tube [*NYSE symbol*] (TTSB) .... WLV
Wolverine Tube, Inc. [*NYSE symbol*] (SPSG) .... WLV
Wolverine Tube, Inc. [*Associated Press*] (SAG) .... WolvTub
Wolverine World Wide [*NYSE symbol*] (TTSB) .... WWW
Wolverine World Wide, Inc. [*NYSE symbol*] (SPSG) .... WWW
Wolverine World-Wide, Inc. [*Associated Press*] (SAG) .... WolvWW
Wolverton [*England*] [*Seismograph station code, US Geological Survey*] (SEIS) .... WOL
Wolverton [*Urban district in England*] .... WOLV
Wolves on the Track [*A group of philanderers looking for girls*] [*Slang*] .... WOTT
Womack Army Hospital Medical Library, Fort Bragg, NC [*OCLC symbol*] (OCLC) .... WAH
Woman (ADA) .... W
Woman (DAVI) .... WM
[*The*] **Woman Activist** (EA) .... TWA
Woman Activist Fund (EA) .... WAF
Woman Citizen Series [*A publication*] .... WCS
Woman Health International [*Defunct*] (EA) .... WHI
[*A*] **Woman in Jeopardy** [*Screenwriter's lexicon*] .... WOMJEP
Woman in Rock .... WIR

[*The*] **Woman Is Requested to Pay** [*Some claim that this acronym, originally a designation for certain school dances, evolved into a slang term denoting any male unable to afford a date*] ... TWIRP
Woman Marine (SAA) ... WM
Woman Offender Report [*A publication*] (DLA) ... Woman Offend Rep
Woman Ordnance Worker ... WOW
Woman Police Constable [*Scotland Yard*] ... WPC
Woman Using Television (WDMC) ... WUT
Woman Who Has Everything ... WWHE
Woman's Auxiliary (DAVI) ... WA
Woman's Auxiliary to the American Medical Association [*Later, AMAA*] (EA) ... WAAMA
Woman's Auxiliary to the Student American Medical Association (DAVI) ... WASAMA
Woman's Benefit Association [*Later, NABA*] ... WBA
Woman's Christian Association Hospital, Jamestown, NY [*Library symbol Library of Congress*] (LCLS) ... NJamW
Woman's Education and Leadership Forum (EA) ... WELF
Woman's Freedom League ... WFL
Woman's Home and Foreign Mission Society (EA) ... WHFMS
Woman's Journal [*A publication*] ... Woman's J
Woman's Medical College of Pennsylvania ... WMCP
Woman's Missionary Union (EA) ... WMU
Woman's National Auxiliary Convention of Free Will Baptists (EA) ... WNACFWB
Woman's National Democratic Club (EA) ... WNDC
Woman's National Farm and Garden Association (EA) ... WNFGA
Woman's National Sabbath Alliance [*Defunct*] ... WNSA
Woman's Organization of the National Association of Retail Druggists (EA) ... WONARD
Woman's Study Club & Library, Dundee, NY [*Library symbol*] [*Library of Congress*] (LCLS) ... NDd
Woman's Union Missionary Society of America [*Later, UFCS*] (EA) ... WUMS
Woman's Workshop [*Defunct*] (EA) ... WWS
Woman's Year ... WY
Womanspeak [*A publication*] ... Womspk
Women ... WMN
Women ... WO
Women Accepted for Volunteer Emergency Service [*US Navy Women's Reserve*] [*World War II and later*] ... WAVES
Women Against Military Madness (EA) ... WAMM
Women Against Pornography (EA) ... WAP
Women Against Rape [*An association*] (EA) ... WAR
Women Against the Ordination of Women [*Australia*] ... WAOW
Women Against Violence Against Women (EA) ... WAVAW
Women Against Violence in Pornography and Media (EA) ... WAVPM
Women Airforce Service Pilots WWII (EA) ... WASPWWII
Women and Development Unit (EA) ... WAND
Women and Employment [*An association*] (EA) ... WE
Women and Food Information Network [*Defunct*] (EA) ... WFIN
Women and Foundations/Corporate Philanthropy (EA) ... WAF/CP
Women and Health Roundtable (EA) ... WHR
Women and Labour Conference. Papers [*A publication*] ... Women Labour Conf Pap
Women and Manual Trades [*British*] [*An association*] (DBA) ... WAMT
Women and Mathematics Education (EA) ... WME
Women and Priests Involved (EA) ... WPI
Women and the Australian Church ... WATAC
Women and the Military Project [*An association*] (EA) ... WMP
Women and Vocational Education [*Australia*] ... WAVE
Women Appointed Volunteer Emergency Services [*British World War II*] ... WAVES
Women Associated with Crossdressers Communication Network (EA) ... WACS
Women Band Directors National Association (EA) ... WBDNA
Women Educators (EA) ... WE
Women Employed [*Chicago, IL*] (EA) ... WE
Women Employed Advocates (EA) ... WEA
Women Employed Institute (EA) ... WEI
Women Entrepreneurs [*Defunct*] (EA) ... WE
Women Executives in Public Relations [*New York, NY*] (EA) ... WEPR
Women Executives in State Government (EA) ... WESG
Women Executives International Tourism Association [*Defunct*] (EA) ... WEXITA
Women Exploited (EA) ... WE
Women Exploited by Abortion (EA) ... WEBA
Women for a Meaningful Summit (EA) ... WMS
Women for a Secure Future (EA) ... WSF
Women for Guatemala (EA) ... WG
Women for Peace in the Middle East (EA) ... WPME
Women for Racial and Economic Equality (EA) ... WREE
Women for Sobriety (EA) ... WFS
Women Grocers of America (EA) ... WGA
Women Happy in Minis [*Boise, Idaho, group opposing below-the-knee fashions introduced in 1970*] ... WHIM
Women Helping Women (EA) ... WHW
Women, Heritage, and Museums [*British*] [*An association*] (DBA) ... WHAM
Women in Advertising and Marketing (EA) ... WAM
Women in Aerospace (EA) ... WIA
Women in Agribusiness [*An association*] (EA) ... WIA
Women in Broadcast Technology (EA) ... WBT
Women in Cable (EA) ... WIC
Women in Cell Biology (EA) ... WICB
Women in Chemistry Network [*Australia*] ... WICN
Women in Communications (EA) ... WC
Women in Communications ... WIC
Women in Communications, Inc. (EA) ... WICI
Women in Community Service (EA) ... WICS
Women in Crisis (EA) ... WIC
Women in Data Processing (EA) ... WDP
Women in Design International [*Later, DI*] (EA) ... WIDI
Women in Development [*Peace Corps*] ... WID
Women in Development [*Bureau of the Census*] [*A publication*] (GFGA) ... WID
Women in Distribution [*Commercial firm*] ... WIND
Women in Education [*Australia*] ... WIE
Women in Energy (EA) ... WE
Women in Engineering Centre (EAIO) ... WIE
Women in Enterprise [*British*] [*An association*] (DBA) ... WE
Women in Entertainment [*British*] ... WIE
Women in Film (EA) ... WIF
Women in Financial Development (NFD) ... WFD
Women in Fire Service (EA) ... WFS
Women in Flavor & Fragrance Commerce Inc. ... WFFC
Women in Government Relations (EA) ... WGR
Women in Housing and Finance (EA) ... WHF
Women in Information Processing (EA) ... WIP
Women in International Security (EA) ... WIIS
Women in Leadership [*Project*] ... WIL
Women in Management [*Chicago, IL*] (EA) ... WIM
Women in Medicine [*British*] [*An association*] (DBA) ... WIM
Women in Military Service for America Memorial Foundation ... WIMSA
Women in Mining National (EA) ... WIM
Women in Mining National (EA) ... WIMN
Women in Municipal Government (EA) ... WIMG
Women in National Service [*Name given by Ladies' Home Journal to American housewives and their teen-age daughters, "the greatest reserve strength of America"*] [*World War II*] ... WINS
Women in Natural Resources Management Program (EERA) ... WNRM
Women in Naval Service ... WINS
Women in Numerous Kitchens [*World War II*] ... WINKS
Women in Political and Public Life [*British*] (DI) ... WIPPL
Women in Production (EA) ... WIP
Women in Production Service [*A voluntary, semimilitary organization of women employees, primarily at the E. I. du Pont de Nemours & Co., at Richmond, Va.*] [*World War II*] ... WIPS
Women in Public Service (EA) ... WPS
Women in Radio and Electrical Service [*World War II*] ... WIRES
Women in RMIT [*Royal Melbourne Institute of Technology*] **Group** [*Australia*] ... WIRMIT
Women in Sales Association (EA) ... WIS
Women in Scholarly Publishing (EA) ... WISP
Women in Show Business (EA) ... WiSB
Women in Soccer (EA) ... WIS
Women in Space Earliest (SAA) ... WISE
Women in Sport Foundation [*Australia*] ... WISF
Women in Technical Service [*World War II*] ... WITS
Women in Technology International ... WITI
Women in Telecommunications [*Defunct*] (EA) ... WIT
Women in the Air Force ... WAF
Women in the Army (MCD) ... WITA
Women in the Arts [*Defunct*] (EA) ... WITA
Women in the Arts Foundation (EA) ... WIA
Women in the Mainstream [*Defunct*] (EA) ... WM
Women in the Medical Service [*Army*] ... WMS
Women in the National Rifle Association ... WINRA
Women in the Senate and House [*Political fund-raising group*] ... WISH
Women in the Wind [*An association*] (EA) ... WW
Women in Transition (EA) ... WIT
Women Incensed over Traditional Coed Hoopla [*Feminist group*] ... WITCH
Women, Infants, and Children [*Supplemental food program*] [*Department of Agriculture*] ... WIC
Women into Science and Engineering [*1984 campaign sponsored by the Equal Opportunities Commission and the Engineering Council*] [*British*] ... WISE
Women Involved in Farm Economics (EA) ... WIFE
Women Judges' Fund for Justice (EA) ... WJFJ
Women Lawyers' Association of New South Wales [*Australia*] ... WLANSW
Women Lawyers' Association of Tasmania [*Australia*] ... WLAT
Women Liberal Democrat [*British Political party*] (EAIO) ... WLD
Women Library Workers [*Defunct*] (EA) ... WLW
Women Life Underwriters Conference (EA) ... WLUC
Women Make Movies (EA) ... WMM
Women Marines ... WM
Women Marines Association (EA) ... WMA
Women of All Red Nations (EA) ... WARN
Women of Color Partnership Program (EA) ... WCPP
Women of the American Press Service [*Accredited American women war correspondents*] [*World War II*] ... WAPS
Women of the Church Coalition (EA) ... WCC
Women of the Church of God (EA) ... WCG
Women of the Motion Picture Industry, International [*Dallas, TX*] ... WMPI
Women of the Motion Picture Industry, International (EA) ... WOMPI
Women of the National Agricultural Aviation Association (EA) ... WNAAA
Women of the Year Luncheon [*British*] (DI) ... WOYL
Women on Stamps Study Unit [*American Topical Association*] [*Defunct*] (EA) ... WOSSU
Women on Stamps Unit [*American Topical Association*] (EA) ... WSU
Women on Their Own [*An association*] (EA) ... WOTO
Women on Wheels (EA) ... WOW
Women on Wine (EA) ... WOW
Women on Words and Images (EA) ... WOWI
Women Ordnance Workers [*A national voluntary organization*] [*World War II*] ... WOWS
Women Organised Against Sexual Harassment [*British*] (DI) ... WOASH
Women Organized Against Rape ... WOAR

Women Organized to Respond to Life-Threatening Diseases (EA) .... WORLD
Women Our Wonders [*Antifeminist men's group*] .... WOW
Women Outdoors (EA) .... WO
Women Professional Bowlers Association (EA) .... WPBA
Women Public Health Officer's Association [*British*] .... WPHOA
Women Refusing to Accept Tenant Harassment (EA) .... WRATH
Women Returners Network (AIE) .... WRN
Women Strike for Peace (EA) .... WSP
Women Teachers' Franchise Union (AIE) .... WTFU
Women to the World [*An association*] (EA) .... WW
Women Umpires [*World War II*] .... WUMPS
Women United Against Rape .... WUAR
Women United for United Nations (EA) .... WUUN
Women Using Television (WDMC) .... WUT
Women Who Love Too Much [*Title of book by Robin Norwood*] WWL2M
Women Who Love Too Much [*Title of book by Robin Norwood*] .... WWLTM
Women Who Want to be Women [*An association*] (NTCM) .... WWWW
Women Working Home [*A publication*] .... WWH
Women World War Veterans (EA) .... WWWV
Women-Church: an Australian Journal of Feminist Studies in Religion [*A publication*] (APTA) .... W-C
Women's Access Grant Program [*Australia*] .... WAGP
Women's Action Alliance (EA) .... WAA
Women's Action Alliance (Australia) .... WAA(A)
Women's Action for New Directions [*An association*] .... WAND
Women's Action for Nuclear Disarmament (EA) .... WAND
Women's Action Group on Excision and Infibulation [*British Defunct*] (EAIO) .... WAGFEI
Women's Action Movement .... WAM
Women's Action Program [*HEW*] .... WAP
Women's Addiction Service [*National Institute of Mental Health*] .... WAS
Women's Advisory Committee [*Trades Union Congress*] [*British*] (DCTA) .... WAC
Women's Advisory Unit [*South Australia*] .... WAU
Women's Aerobic Circuit [*Exercise regimen at some health spas*] .... WAC
Women's Africa Committee of the African-American Institute (EA) .... WACAAI
Women's Aglow Fellowship (EA) .... WAF
Women's Agricultural Security Production Service [*British military*] (DMA) .... WASPS
Women's Air Force Services [*British military*] (DMA) .... WAFS
Women's Air Training Corps .... WATC
Women's Airforce Service Pilots [*World War II*] .... WASP
Women's Alliance for Theology, Ethics, and Ritual (EA) .... WATER
Women's All-Star Association (EA) .... WASA
Women's Alternative Economics Network [*An association*] (CROSS) .... WAEN
Women's Amateur Athletic Association [*British*] (DBA) .... WAAA
Women's Ambulance and Transportation Corps .... WATC
Women's American Basketball Association [*Defunct*] (EA) .... WABA
Women's American ORT (EA) .... WAO
Women's Apparel Chains Associations [*Defunct*] (EA) .... WACA
Women's Aquatic Network (EA) .... WAN
Women's Armed Services Integration Act of 1948 .... WASIA
Women's Army Auxiliary Corps [*Name later changed to WAC*] [*World War II*] .... WAAC
Women's Army Classification Battery (AABC) .... WACB
Women's Army Corps [*Formerly, WAAC*] [*Abolished, 1978*] (GPO) .... WAC
Women's Army Corps of India [*British military*] (DMA) .... WACI
Women's Army Corps Reserve .... WACRES
Women's Army Corps Service Medal [*Military decoration*] .... WACSM
Women's Army Corps Veterans Association (EA) .... WACVA
Women's Art Association of Canada [*1887, Lyceum Club and Women's Art Association from 1930*] (NGC) .... WAAC
Women's Association for Symphony Orchestras [*Later, AMSO*] (EA) .... WASO
Women's Association for the Defense of Four Freedoms for Ukraine (EA) .... WADFFU
Women's Association of the African Independent Churches .... WAAIC
Women's Automotive Maintenance Staff .... WAMS
Women's Auxiliary Air Force [*Functioned under direct command of RAF*] [*World War II British*] .... WAAF
Women's Auxiliary Army Service [*British*] .... WAAS
Women's Auxiliary Army Service Corps [*British*] .... WAASC
Women's Auxiliary Corps [*British*] (DAS) .... WAC
Women's Auxiliary Ferrying Squadron [*Part of Air Transport Command*] [*World War II*] .... WAFS
Women's Auxiliary Fire Service [*British World War II*] .... WAFS
Women's Auxiliary Force [*World War I*] [*Later, Victory Corps*] [*British*] .... WAF
Women's Auxiliary of the American Merchant Marine [*World War II*] .... WAAMMS
Women's Auxiliary of the ICA [*International Chiropractors Association*] (EA) .... WAICA
Women's Auxiliary Police Corps [*British World War II*] .... WAPC
Women's Auxiliary Service Platoon .... WASPS
Women's Auxiliary Territorial Service [*British military*] (DMA) .... WATS
Women's Auxiliary to the Military Order of the Cootie (EA) .... WAMOC
Women's Auxiliary Training Service .... WATS
Women's Basketball Coaches Association (EA) .... WBCA
Women's Basketball League [*Defunct*] (EA) .... WBL
Women's Board of Missions .... WBM
Women's Board of Missions of the Interior .... WBMI
Women's Broadcasting Corp. .... WBC
Women's Budget Program [*Australia*] .... WBP
Women's Budget Statement [*Australia*] .... WBS
Women's Bureau [*Department of Labor*] .... WB
Women's Bureau, Labour Canada [*Bureau de la Main-d'Oeuvre Feminine, Travail Canada*] **Ottawa, Ontario** [*Library symbol National Library of Canada*] (NLC) .... OOLWB
Women's Business Enterprise .... WBE
Women's Campaign Fund (EA) .... WCF
Women's Career Center Library, Rochester, NY [*OCLC symbol*] (OCLC) .... RVN
Women's Catholic Order of Foresters [*Later, NCSF*] (EA) .... WCOF
Women's Caucus for Art (EA) .... WCA
Women's Caucus for Political Science (EA) .... WCPS
Women's Caucus for the Modern Languages (EA) .... WCML
Women's Caucus of the Endocrine Society (EA) .... WCES
Women's Caucus: Religious Studies [*Defunct*] (EA) .... WC:RS
Women's Christian Association .... WCA
Women's Civic Club Library, Holly, CO [*Library symbol Library of Congress*] (LCLS) .... CoHol
Women's Classical Caucus (EA) .... WCC
Women's Coalition to Stop US Intervention in Central America [*Later, WCSUICAC*] [*Defunct*] (EA) .... WCSUICA
Women's Coalition to Stop US Intervention in Central America and the Caribbean (EA) .... WCSUICAC
Women's College [*University of Sydney*] [*Australia*] .... WC
Women's College Coalition (EA) .... WCC
Women's Commission of the Iranian Students Association (EA) .... WC-ISA
Women's Computer Literacy Project [*Commercial firm*] (EA) .... WCLP
Women's Connubial Temperance Union [*Satirical*] .... WCTU
Women's Consultative Committee [*Ministry of Labour*] [*British World War II*] .... WCC
Women's Council for the Histadrut in Israel (EA) .... WCHI
Women's Council of Realtors [*of the National Association of Realtors*] (EA) .... WCR
Women's Council on Energy and the Environment (EA) .... WCEE
Women's Cricket Association [*British*] .... WCA
Women's Defence Relief Corps [*World War I*] [*British*] .... WDRC
Women's Democratic International Federation (NATG) .... WDIF
Women's Diocesan Association [*British*] .... WDA
Women's Distance Committee (EA) .... WDC
Women's Division of Christian Service [*of the Board of Missions, The Methodist Church*] .... WDCS
Women's Drug Research Project (EA) .... WDR
Women's Economic Agenda Project [*An association*] .... WEAP
Women's Economic Rights Project (EA) .... WERP
Women's Economic Round Table (EA) .... WERT
Women's Education Group (AIE) .... WEDG
Women's Education Resource Centre [*Women's Education Group*] [*British*] (CB) .... WERC
Women's Educational and Industrial Union (EA) .... WEIU
Women's Educational Equity Act [*1974*] .... WEEA
Women's Educational Equity Communications Network [*Defunct*] .... WEECN
Women's Educational Equity Program (EA) .... WEEP
Women's Emergency Corps [*World War I*] [*British*] .... WEC
Women's Emergency Shelter and Training Scheme [*New South Wales, Australia*] .... WESTS
Women's Employment, Education, and Training Advisory Group (EERA) .... WEETAG
Women's Employment Federation [*British*] (BI) .... WEF
Women's Engineering Society (IAA) .... WES
Womens Engineering Society (ACII) .... WES
Women's Enlistment Screening Test [*Military*] .... WEST
Women's Enterprise Development Agency [*Established in 1987*] [*British*] .... WEDA
Women's Environment and Development Organization .... WEDO
Women's Equity Action League [*Defunct*] (EA) .... WEAL
Women's Equity Program [*Defunct*] (EA) .... WEP
Women's Extra [*Size*] .... WX
Women's Farm and Garden Association [*British*] (BI) .... WFGA
Women's Fashion Fabrics Association [*Defunct*] (EA) .... WFFA
Women's Film, Television, and Video Network (EAIO) .... WFTVN
Women's Financial Advisory Service [*Australia*] .... WFAS
Women's Financial Information Program [*American Association of Retired Persons*] (BARN) .... WFIP
Women's Firsts [*A publication*] .... WF
Women's Flying Training Detachment [*World War II*] .... WFTD
Women's Football Association [*British*] .... WFA
Women's Forage Corps [*World War I*] [*British*] .... WFC
Women's Forum on National Security [*Defunct*] (EA) .... WFNS
Women's Funding Assistance Project (EA) .... WFAP
Women's Gas Federation [*British*] (BI) .... WGF
Women's Global Network on Reproductive Rights [*Formerly, International Contraception, Abortion, and Sterilisation Campaign*] (EA) .... WGNRR
Women's Hall of Fame [*Later, NWHF*] (EA) .... WHF
Women's Health Action and Mobilization (EA) .... WHAM
Women's Health Advisory Service [*Australia*] .... WHAS
Women's Health and Abortion Project (EA) .... WHAP
Women's Health Care Association [*Australia*] .... WHCA
Women's Health in Industry [*Australia*] .... WHII
Women's Health Information Centre [*British*] (CB) .... WHIC
Women's Health Initiative [*National Institutes of Health*] .... WHI
Women's Health Research Institute .... WHRI
Women's Health Study .... WHS
Women's Health Trial [*Department of Health and Human Services*] (GFGA) .... WHT
Women's Heathy Eating and Living [*Medicine*] .... WHEI
Women's History Network (EA) .... WHN
Women's History Research Center, Inc., Berkeley, CA [*Library symbol Library of Congress*] (LCLS) .... CBW
Women's Hockey Association [*Australia*] .... WHA
Women's Home Mission Association .... WHMA
Women's Independent Cinema House [*British*] .... WITCH
Women's Independent Film Exchange [*Defunct*] (EA) .... WIFE
Women's Independent Label Distribution Network (EA) .... WILD
Women's Industrial and National Service Corps [*World War II British*] .... WINS

Women's Information and Referral Centre [*Australia*] .... WIRC
Women's Information and Study Centre .... WISC
Women's Information Bank (EA) .... WIB
Women's Information Exchange (EA) .... WIE
Women's Information Network for Asia and the Pacific [*ESCAP*] [*United Nations*] (DUND) .... WINAP
Women's Information Service, Inc. .... WISE
[*The*] **Women's Institute** (EA) .... TWI
Women's Institute [*British*] .... WI
Women's Institute for Freedom of the Press (EA) .... WIFP
Women's Interagency HIV [*Human Immuno Deficiency Virus*] **Study** [*Medicine*] .... WIHS
Women's Interart Center (EA) .... WIC
Women's Inter-Church Council of Canada .... WICC
Women's Interest Division [*Australia*] .... WID
Women's International Art Club .... WIAC
Women's International Art Club, London [*1899*] (NGC) .... WIAC
Women's International Association of Aeronautics (IAA) .... WIAA
Women's International Bowling Congress (EA) .... WIBC
Women's International Cultural Federation [*See also FICF*] (EAIO) .... WICF
Women's International Democratic Federation [*See also FDIF*] [*Berlin, German Democratic Republic*] (EAIO) .... WIDF
Women's International Information and Communication Service [*Italy and Switzerland*] .... ISIS
Women's International League for Peace and Freedom [*Switzerland*] (EAIO) .... WILPF
Women's International League for Peace and Freedom, US Section (EA) .... WILPF-US
Women's International Motorcycle Association (EA) .... WIMA
Women's International Network (EA) .... WIN
Women's International Non-Government Organisation [*British*] (DI) .... WINGO
Women's International ORT .... WIO
Women's International Professional Tennis Council (EA) .... WIPTC
Women's International Religious Fellowship (EA) .... WIRF
Women's International Resource Centre [*British*] (EAIO) .... WIRC
Women's International Resource Exchange (EA) .... WIRE
Women's International Surfing Association (EA) .... WISA
Women's International Tennis Association (EA) .... WITA
Women's International Tennis Federation .... WITF
Women's International Terrorist Conspiracy from Hell [*Feminist group*] .... WITCH
Women's International Zionist Organization [*Tel Aviv, Israel*] (EA) .... WIZO
Women's Inter-University Athletic Board [*British*] (BI) .... WIUAB
Women's Inter-Varsity Athletics Board [*British*] (DI) .... WIVAB
Women's Interview Study of Health .... WISH
Women's Issues Coordinator [*Australia*] .... WIC
Women's Issues Plan [*Australia*] .... WIP
Women's Issues, Status, and Education (EA) .... WISE
Women's Jazz Festival [*Defunct*] (EA) .... WJFI
Women's Jewelry Association (EA) .... WJA
Women's Joint Congressional Committee (EA) .... WJCC
Women's Joint Legislative Committee for Equal Rights [*Defunct*] (EA) .... WJLCER
Women's Labor History Film Project (EA) .... WLHFP
Women's Land Army [*Part of the United States Crop Corps*] [*World War II*] .... WLA
Women's Law Fund (EA) .... WLF
Women's Law Journal [*A publication*] (DLA) .... Women L Jour
Women's Law Journal [*A publication*] (DLA) .... Women's LJ
Women's Law Project (EA) .... WLP
Women's Law Reporter [*A publication*] (DLA) .... Women's L Rptr
Women's League for Israel (EA) .... WLI
Women's League of Health and Beauty (EAIO) .... WLHB
Women's Legal Defense Fund (EA) .... WLDF
Women's Legal Education and Action Fund [*Canada*] .... LEAF
Women's Legal Resource Centre [*Sydney, New South Wales, Australia*] .... WLRC
Women's Legion [*World War I*] [*British*] .... WL
Women's Liberation (ADA) .... WL
Women's Lobby [*Defunct*] (EA) .... WL
Women's Market Handbook [*A publication*] .... WMH
Women's Martial Arts Union [*Defunct*] (EA) .... WMAU
Women's Media Workshop [*Defunct*] (EA) .... WMW
Women's Medical Specialist .... WMS
Women's Medical Specialists Corps .... WMSC
Women's Military Pilots Association (EA) .... WMPA
Women's Missionary and Service Commission of the Mennonite Church (EA) .... WMSCMC
Women's Missionary Council of the Christian Methodist Episcopal Church (EA) .... WMCCMEC
Women's Missionary Society, AME [*African Methodist Episcopal*] **Church** (EA) .... WMS
Women's Missionary Union, SBC Library, Birmingham, AL [*Library symbol*] [*Library of Congress*] (LCLS) .... ABWM
Women's Motorcyclist Foundation (EA) .... WMF
Women's National Abortion Action Coalition [*Defunct*] .... WONAAC
Women's National Aquatic Forum (EA) .... WNAF
Women's National Basketball Association [*Defunct*] (EA) .... WNBA
Women's National Book Association (EA) .... WNBA
Women's National Cancer Control Campaign [*British*] .... WNCCC
Women's National Commission [*British*] (EAIO) .... WNC
Women's National Institute [*Defunct*] (EA) .... WNI
Women's National Land Service Corps [*World War I*] [*British*] .... WNLSC
Women's National Press Club [*Later, WPC*] (EA) .... WNPC
Women's National Republican Club (EA) .... WNRC
Women's Network of the Council for Adult Education in Latin America [*See also RM-CEAAL*] [*Quito, Ecuador*] (EAIO) .... WN-CAELA
Women's News Service .... WNS
Women's Occupational Health Resource Center (EA) .... WOHRC
Women's Olympic Distance Committee [*Later, WDC*] (EA) .... WODC
Women's Ordination Conference (EA) .... WOC
Women's Organization for Mentoring, Education and Networking Unlimited, Inc. .... WOMEN
Women's Organization of Hapoel Hamizrachi [*Later, EWA*] (EA) .... WOHH
Women's Outpatient Unit (AAMN) .... WOU
Women's Overseas Service League (EA) .... WOSL
Women's Patriotic Conference on National Defense (EA) .... WPCND
Women's Pavilion, Royal Victoria Hospital, Montreal, Quebec [*Library symbol National Library of Canada*] (NLC) .... QMRVW
Women's Peace Initiative (EA) .... WPI
Women's Political Caucus .... WPC
Women's Press Association (NTCM) .... WPA
Women's Prison Association (EA) .... WPA
Women's Professional Basketball League [*Defunct*] (EA) .... WPBL
Women's Professional Billiard Alliance (EA) .... WPBA
Women's Professional Racquetball Association (EA) .... WPRA
Women's Professional Rodeo Association (EA) .... WPRA
Women's Project Officer .... WPO
Women's Protestant Union [*British*] .... WPU
Women's Rabbinic Alliance [*Later, WSA*] (EA) .... WRA
Women's Radical Action Project [*Feminist group*] .... WRAP
Women's Relief Corps .... WRC
Women's Repetition Injury Support Team [*Australia*] .... WRIST
Women's Research and Education Institute (EA) .... WREI
Women's Research and Resources Centre (EAIO) .... WRRC
Women's Reserve [*Navy*] .... WR
Women's Reserve Ambulance Society [*World War I*] [*British*] .... WRAS
Women's Reserve, Aviation Nonflying Duties [*USNR officer designation*] .... WA
Women's Reserve, Civil Engineering Corps Duties [*USNR commissioned officer designation*] .... W-V(S) (CEC)
Women's Reserve, Communications Duties [*USNR officer designation*] .... WC
Women's Reserve, Dental Corps Duties [*USNR commissioned officer designation*] .... W-V(S) (DC)
Women's Reserve, Emergency Duties [*USNR commissioned officer designation*] .... W-V(S)
Women's Reserve, Engineering Duties [*USNR officer designation*] .... WE
Women's Reserve, Hospital Corps Duties [*USNR commissioned officer designation*] .... W-V(S) (H)
Women's Reserve, Intelligence Duties [*USNR officer designation*] .... WI
Women's Reserve, Legal Specialist Duties [*USNR officer designation*] .... WL
Women's Reserve, Medical Corps Duties [*USNR commissioned officer designation*] .... W-V(S) (MC)
Women's Reserve of the Coast Guard Reserve .... WRCGR
Women's Reserve, Ordnance Duties [*USNR officer designation*] .... WO
Women's Reserve, Supply Corps Duties [*USNR commissioned officer designation*] .... W-V(S) (SC)
Women's Reserve, Unlimited Service [*USNR officer designation*] .... W
Women's Review of Books [*A publication*] (BRI) .... Wom R Bks
Women's Rights Committee (EA) .... WRC
Women's Rights Law Reporter [*A publication*] (ILCA) .... Women's Rights L Reptr
Women's Rights Project (EA) .... WRP
Women's Roundtable (EA) .... WR
Women's Royal Air Force [*British*] .... WRAF
Women's Royal Air Force Volunteer Reserve [*British military*] (DMA) .... WRAFVR
Women's Royal Army Corps [*British*] .... WRAC
Women's Royal Australian Naval Service [*World War II*] (DSUE) .... WAN
Women's Royal Canadian Naval Service [*World War II*] .... WRCNS
Women's Royal English Navy (IIA) .... WREN
Women's Royal Indian Naval Service [*British military*] (DMA) .... WRINS
Women's Royal Naval Reserve [*British military*] (DMA) .... WRNR
Women's Royal Naval Service [*Acronym is a phonetic reference to members of this British service branch*] [*Also, WRNS*] .... WRENS
Women's Royal Naval Service [*Also, WRENS*] [*A member is familiarly called a "Wren"*] [*British*] .... WRNS
Women's Royal Naval Service Reserve [*British military*] (DMA) .... WRNSR
Women's Royal Naval Volunteer Reserve [*British military*] (DMA) .... WRNVR
Women's Royal Voluntary Service [*Formerly, WVS*] [*British*] .... WRVS
Women's Services [*Military British*] .... WS
Women's Services Branch, Saskatchewan Department of Advanced Education and Manpower, Regina, Saskatchewan [*Library symbol National Library of Canada*] (NLC) .... SRAEW
Women's Shelter [*Australia*] .... WS
Women's Size .... WS
Women's Social and Political Union [*British*] .... WSPU
Women's Social Service for Israel (EA) .... WSSI
Women's Social Services [*Salvation Army*] .... WSS
Women's Solid Fuel Council [*British*] (DI) .... WSFC
Women's Sports Foundation (EA) .... WSF
Women's Squash Rackets Association [*British*] (BI) .... WSRA
Women's Student Association (EA) .... WSA
Women's Studies Section [*Association of College and Research Libraries*] .... WSS
Women's Suffrage (ROG) .... WS
Women's Suffrage Movement (ROG) .... WSM
Women's Talent Corps [*Later, CHS*] (EA) .... WTC
Women's Tennis Association [*Later, WITA*] (EA) .... WTA
Women's Theater Council .... WTC
Women's Trade Society of Fancy Leather Workers [*A union*] [*British*] .... WTSFLW
Women's Training and Resources Corp. .... WTRC
Women's Transport Service [*British*] .... WTS
Women's Transportation Seminar [*Later, WTSN*] (EA) .... WTS
Women's Transportation Seminar-National (EA) .... WTSN
Women's Travelers Center and Information Bank [*Later, WIB*] (EA) .... WTCIB
Women's Tricycle Association [*British*] (BI) .... WTA

Women's United Service League [*British*] .... WUSL
Women's Universal Movement [*Defunct*] (EA) .... WUM
Women's Veterinary Medical Association [*Later, AWV*] .... WVMA
Women's Voluntary Services [*Coordinated work of women for national service*] [*Later, WRVS*] [*British*] [*World War II*] .... WVS
Women's Volunteer Reserve [*World War I*] [*British*] .... WVR
Women's Vote Project [*Defunct*] (EA) .... WVP
Women's War Savings Division .... WWSD
Women's War Service Auxiliary [*British military*] (DMA) .... WWSA
Women's Wear Daily [*A publication*] (WDMC) .... WWD
Women's Welfare Service [*Defunct*] (EA) .... WWS
Women's Welsh Clubs of America (EA) .... WWCA
Women's World Banking [*Financial organization*] .... WWB
Women's Zionist Organization of America .... WZOA
Womens's National Loyal League [*Established by Elizabeth Cady Stanton and Susan B. Anthony*] .... WNLL
Womenwealth Ambika [*An association British*] (EAIO) .... WA
Wometco Home Theatre [*Subscription television service*] .... WHT
Won [*Sports statistics*] .... W
Won [*Monetary unit*] [*South Korea*] .... W
Won on Foul [*Boxing*] .... WF
Wonder Marine Resources [*Vancouver Stock Exchange symbol*] .... WMR
Wonder Woman Foundation [*Defunct*] (EA) .... WWF
Wonderware Corp. [*NASDAQ symbol*] (SAG) .... WNDR
Wonderware Corp. [*Associated Press*] (SAG) .... Wondwre
Wondoola [*Queensland*] [*Airport symbol*] (AD) .... WON
Wonford [*England*] .... WONF
Wongan Hills [*Australia Seismograph station code, US Geological Survey*] (SEIS) WA1
Wonga-Wongue [*Gabon*] [*ICAO location identifier*] (ICLI) .... FOGW
Wonju [*South Korea ICAO location identifier*] (ICLI) .... RKNW
Wonken [*Venezuela*] [*Airport symbol*] (OAG) .... WOK
Wontner's Land Registry Practice [*12th ed.*] [*1975*] [*A publication*] (DLA) .... Wont Land Reg
Wood .... W
Wood (VRA) .... wd
Wood (AAG) .... WD
Wood and Iron [*Freight*] .... WDI
Wood and Long's Digest [*Illinois*] [*A publication*] (DLA) .... W & L Dig
Wood and Solid Fuel Association of Retailers and Manufacturers (EA) .... WARM
Wood and Synthetic Flooring Institute (EA) .... WSFI
Wood and Wire [*Freight*] .... WDW
Wood Awning Type Window .... WATW
Wood Bancorp [*NASDAQ symbol*] (TTSB) .... FFWD
Wood Bancorp [*Associated Press*] (SAG) .... WoodBcp
Wood Base [*Technical drawings*] .... WB
Wood Block Floor [*Technical drawings*] .... WBF
Wood Blocking .... WBL
Wood Boring .... WDBOR
Wood Buffalo National Park, Parks Canada [*Parc National Wood Buffalo, Parcs Canada*] **Fort Smith, Northwest Territories** [*Library symbol National Library of Canada*] (NLC) .... NWFSPCW
Wood Burning [*Fireplace*] [*Classified advertising*] .... WB
Wood Carver's Association [*British*] (DBA) .... WCA
Wood Casement Window [*Technical drawings*] .... WCW
Wood Casing .... WC
Wood County District Public Library, Bowling Green, OH [*OCLC symbol*] (OCLC) .... OWC
Wood County Hospital, Marshfield, WI [*Library symbol Library of Congress*] (LCLS) .... WMarW
Wood Covers (DS) .... WC
Wood Door [*Technical drawings*] .... WD
Wood Door and Frame [*Technical drawings*] .... WDF
Wood Dye Stain .... WDS
Wood Energy Institute [*Later, WHA*] (EA) .... WEI
Wood Fiber Blanket Institute [*Defunct*] .... WFBI
Wood Flooring Institute of America [*Later, WSFI*] (EA) .... WFI
Wood Foundation Institute [*Defunct*] (EA) .... WFI
Wood Furring Strips [*Technical drawings*] .... WFS
Wood Hat Block Manufacturers Association (EA) .... WHBMA
Wood Heating Alliance (EA) .... WHA
Wood Heating Education and Research Foundation (EA) .... WHERF
Wood Jalousie .... WJ
Wood Junior College [*Mathison, MS*] .... WJC
Wood Machinery Manufacturers of America (EA) .... WMMA
Wood Moulding and Millwork Producers [*Later, WMMPA*] (EA) .... WMMP
Wood Moulding and Millwork Producers Association (EA) .... WMMPA
Wood Naval Stores Export Association .... WNSEA
Wood Office Furniture Institute (EA) .... WOFI
Wood on Conveyancing [*A publication*] (DLA) .... Wood Conv
Wood on Fire Insurance [*A publication*] (DLA) .... Woods Ins
Wood on Landlord and Tenant [*A publication*] (DLA) .... Wood Land & T
Wood on Landlord and Tenant [*A publication*] (DLA) .... Wood Landl & Ten
Wood on Limitation of Actions [*A publication*] (DLA) .... Wood Lim
Wood on Mandamus [*A publication*] (DLA) .... Wood Man
Wood on Master and Servant [*A publication*] (DLA) .... Wood Mast & Serv
Wood on Mercantile Agreements [*A publication*] (DLA) .... Wood
Wood on Nuisances [*A publication*] (DLA) .... Wood Nuis
Wood on Trade Marks [*1876*] [*A publication*] (DLA) .... Wood Tr M
Wood or Steel [*Freight*] .... WD STL
Wood Panel (AAG) .... WDP
Wood Park Elementary School, Commack, NY [*Library symbol*] [*Library of Congress*] (LCLS) .... NCoWE
Wood Pattern (MSA) .... WP
Wood Plastic Material .... WPM
Wood Products Manufacturers Association (EA) .... WPMA
Wood Products Purchasing Office [*Defense Construction Supply Center*] [*Defense Supply Agency*] .... WPPO
Wood Raw Material Equivalent (EERA) .... WRME
Wood Ridge Memorial Library, Wood Ridge, NJ [*Library symbol Library of Congress*] (LCLS) .... NjWor
Wood River, IL [*AM radio station call letters*] .... KFNS
Wood River Public Library, Wood River, IL [*Library symbol Library of Congress*] (LCLS) .... IWor
Wood River Township Hospital, Medical Library, Wood River, IL [*Library symbol Library of Congress*] (LCLS) .... IWorH
Wood Stove [*Freight*] .... WD STV
Wood Strength [*Botany*] .... WOODST
Wood Supply Zone (EERA) .... WSZ
Wood Tank Manufacturers Association (EA) .... WTMA
Wood Threshold (MSA) .... WT
Wood Truss Council of America (EA) .... WTCA
Wood Turners and Shapers Association [*Later, WPMA*] (EA) .... WTSA
Wood Turners Service Bureau [*Later, WPMA*] .... WTSB
Wood Weight [*Botany*] .... WOODWT
Wood, Wire, and Metal Lathers' International Union [*Later, UBC*] .... LIU
Wood, Wire, and Metal Lathers' International Union [*Later, UBC*] (EA) .... WWML
Wood Wool Slab Manufacturers Association [*British*] (DBA) .... WWSMA
Woodbine, GA [*AM radio station call letters*] .... WCGA
Woodbine Public Library, Woodbine, IA [*Library symbol Library of Congress*] (LCLS) .... IaWob
Woodbine Twiner, Woodbine, IA [*Library symbol Library of Congress*] (LCLS) .... IaWobT
Woodblock (VRA) .... wdbl
Woodbourne [*New Zealand*] [*ICAO location identifier*] (ICLI) .... NZWB
Woodbridge [*British ICAO location identifier*] (ICLI) .... EGVG
Woodbridge, VA [*Location identifier FAA*] (FAAL) .... BQG
Woodbridge, VA [*FM radio station call letters*] .... WJZW
Woodburn, OR [*AM radio station call letters*] .... KWBY
Woodburn Public Library, Woodburn, OR [*Library symbol Library of Congress*] (LCLS) .... OrWo
Wood-Burning Fireplace [*Classified advertising*] (WGA) .... WBF
Wood-Burning Fireplace [*Classified advertising*] .... WBFP
Woodbury and Minot's United States Circuit Court Reports [*3 vols.*] [*A publication*] (DLA) .... W & M
Woodbury and Minot's United States Circuit Court Reports [*A publication*] (DLA) .... Wood & M
Woodbury and Minot's United States Circuit Court Reports [*A publication*] (DLA) .... Wood & Minot
Woodbury and Minot's United States Circuit Court Reports [*A publication*] (DLA) .... Woodb & M
Woodbury and Minot's United States Circuit Court Reports, First Circuit [*A publication*] (DLA) .... Woodb & Min (CC)
Woodbury Daily Times, Woodbury, NJ [*Library symbol Library of Congress*] (LCLS) .... NjWdT
Woodbury, TN [*FM radio station call letters*] .... WBOZ
Woodbury, TN [*AM radio station call letters*] .... WBRY
Woodchip Research Committee [*Australia*] .... WRC
Woodchopper, AK [*Location identifier FAA*] (FAAL) .... WOO
Woodchuck Hepatitis Virus .... WHV
Woodcock Language Proficiency Battery [*Achievement test*] .... WLPB
Woodcock Reading Mastery Tests [*Educational test*] .... WRMT
Woodcock-Johnson Psychoeducational Battery [*Psychology*] (DAVI) .... WJPB
Woodcock-Johnson Psychoeducational Battery [*Educational test*] .... WJPEB
Woodcut (VRA) .... wdct
Woodcut (ROG) .... WDCT
Woodcutting (MSA) .... WCTG
Wooddesson's Elements of Jurisprudence [*A publication*] (DLA) .... Wood El Jur
Wooddesson's Lecture [*A publication*] (DLA) .... Wooddesson Lect
Wooddesson's Lectures on the Laws of England [*A publication*] (DLA) .... Wood Lect
Wooddesson's Lectures on the Laws of England [*A publication*] (DLA) .... Woodd Lect
Wooded Island [*Washington*] [*Seismograph station code, US Geological Survey*] (SEIS) .... WIW
Wooden [*Shipping*] (ROG) .... W
Wooden .... WDN
Wooden Box (MSA) .... WBX
Wooden Box Institute [*Defunct*] (EA) .... WBI
Wooden Canoe Heritage Association (EA) .... WCHA
Wooden Pail and Tub Association .... WPTA
Wooden Ships & Iron Men (PCM) .... WSIM
Wooden Ware [*Freight*] .... WDNOWRE
Wood-Engraver [*MARC relator code*] [*Library of Congress*] (LCCP) .... wde
Woodenville Group Home, Woodenville, WA [*Library symbol Library of Congress*] (LCLS) .... WaWnvGH
Woodfall on Landlord and Tenant [*25 eds.*] [*1802-1958*] [*A publication*] (DLA) .... Woodf
Woodfall on Landlord and Tenant [*28th ed.*] [*1978*] [*A publication*] (DLA) .... Woodf L & T
Woodfall on Landlord and Tenant [*25 eds.*] [*1802-1958*] [*A publication*] (DLA) .... Woodf Landl & T
Woodfall on Landlord and Tenant [*25 eds.*] [*1802-1958*] [*A publication*] (DLA) .... Woodf Landl & Ten
Woodfall's Celebrated Trials [*A publication*] (DLA) .... Woodf Cel Tr
Woodfall's Parliamentary Debates [*A publication*] (DLA) .... Woodf Parl Deb
Woodfield Road School, Rockville Centre, NY [*Library symbol*] [*Library of Congress*] (LCLS) .... NRockWR
Woodford [*British ICAO location identifier*] (ICLI) .... EGCD

Woodford [*England*] ... WOODF
Woodford BAE [*British ICAO designator*] (FAAC) ... WFD
Woodford Flight Test Center [*British ICAO designator*] (FAAC) ... WTC
Woodfree [*Paper*] (DGA) ... W
Woodfree Antique [*Paper*] (DGA) ... WA
Woodfree Bank and Bond [*Paper*] (DGA) ... WBB
Woodfree Bank and Bond [*Paper*] (DGA) ... WFBB
Woodfree Coated [*Paper*] (DGA) ... WC
Woodfree Machine-Coated Paper (DGA) ... WMC
Woodfree Machine-Finished Paper (DGA) ... WMF
Woodfree Off-Machine Coated Board Paper (DGA) ... WOMCB
Woodfree Off-Machine Coated Paper (DGA) ... WOC
Woodfree Off-Machine Coated Paper (DGA) ... WOMC
Woodfree Off-Machine Paper (DGA) ... WO
Woodfree Offset Cartridge Paper (DGA) ... WOC
Woodfree Printing Paper (DGA) ... WP
Woodfree Pulp Board (DGA) ... WP
Woodfree Pulp Board (DGA) ... WPB
Woodfree Uncoated Boars [*Paper*] (DGA) ... WUB
Woodgate Air Services [*British ICAO designator*] (FAAC) ... WOD
Woodgate Air Services Ltd. [*Zambia*] [*FAA designator*] (FAAC) ... WHL
Woodhaven Center, Philadelphia, PA [*OCLC symbol*] (OCLC) ... PIW
Woodhead Indus [*NASDAQ symbol*] (TTSB) ... WDHD
Woodhead Industries, Inc. [*NASDAQ symbol*] (NQ) ... WDHD
Woodhead Industries, Inc. [*Associated Press*] (SAG) ... Woodhd
Woodill Wildfire Registry (EA) ... WWR
Woodlake, CA [*FM radio station call letters*] ... KFRR
Woodland Avenue Elementary School, Hicksville, NY [*Library symbol*] [*Library of Congress*] (LCLS) ... NHickWoE
Woodland, CA [*FM radio station call letters*] ... KSFM
Woodland Free Public Library, Woodland, CA [*Library symbol Library of Congress*] (LCLS) ... CWo
Woodland Indian Cultural Educational Centre, Brantford, ON, Canada [*Library symbol Library of Congress*] (LCLS) ... CaOBrtWI
[*The*] **Woodland Indian Cultural Educational Centre, Brantford, Ontario** [*Library symbol National Library of Canada*] (NLC) ... OBRWI
Woodland Junior High School, Duluth, MN [*Library symbol*] [*Library of Congress*] (LCLS) ... MnDuWJH
Woodland Junior High School, East Meadow, NY [*Library symbol*] [*Library of Congress*] (LCLS) ... NEmWJ
Woodland Park Public Library, Woodland Park, CO [*Library symbol Library of Congress*] (LCLS) ... CoWp
Woodland Resource Analysis Program [*Tennessee Valley Authority*] ... WRAP
Woodlands Library Cooperative, Albion, MI [*Library symbol Library of Congress*] (LCLS) ... MiAlbW
Woodlands Mountain Institute (EA) ... WMI
Woodlawn, IL [*FM radio station call letters*] ... WDML
Woodleigh [*England*] ... WOODL
Woodman and Tidy on Forensic Medicine [*A publication*] (DLA) ... Woodm & T For Med
Woodman's Reports of Thacher's Criminal Cases [*Massachusetts*] [*A publication*] (DLA) ... Woodman Cr Cas
Woodmen of the World (EA) ... WOW
Woodmen of the World Life Insurance Society (EA) ... WWLIS
Woodmen Rangers (EA) ... WR
Woodmen Rangers and Rangerettes (EA) ... WRR
Woodmere Academy, Woodmere, NY [*Library symbol*] [*Library of Congress*] (LCLS) ... NWdmA
Woodmere Middle School, Hewlett, NY [*Library symbol*] [*Library of Congress*] (LCLS) ... NHewWM
Woodpecker Repellent [*In company name, WPR Co.*] ... WPR
Wood-Plastic Combination [*or Composite*] ... WPC
Woodridge Public Library, Woodridge, IL [*Library symbol Library of Congress*] (LCLS) ... IWori
Woodroast Sys Wrrt [*NASDAQ symbol*] (TTSB) ... WRSIW
Woodroast Systems [*NASDAQ symbol*] (TTSB) ... WRSI
Woodroast Systems, Inc. [*Associated Press*] (SAG) ... Wdrst
Woodroast Systems, Inc. [*Associated Press*] (SAG) ... Woodr
Woodroast Systems, Inc. [*NASDAQ symbol*] (SAG) ... WRSI
Woodroast Systems, Inc. [*NASDAQ symbol*] (SAG) ... WRSUC
Woodrow Wilson Birthplace Foundation (EA) ... WWBF
Woodrow Wilson College of Law, Atlanta, GA [*Library symbol Library of Congress*] (LCLS) ... GAWW
Woodrow Wilson International Center for Scholars (EA) ... WWICS
Woodrow Wilson International Center for Scholars, Washington, DC [*Library symbol Library of Congress*] (LCLS) ... DWW
Woodrow Wilson National Fellowship Foundation (EA) ... WWNFF
Woodrow Wilson Rehabilitation Center, Fishersville, VA [*Library symbol*] [*Library of Congress*] (LCLS) ... ViFvW
Woodruff ... WDF
Woodruff Memorial Library, La Junta, CO [*Library symbol Library of Congress*] (LCLS) ... CoLj
Woodruff, SC [*AM radio station call letters*] ... WJKI
Woods and Forests Department [*South Australia*] ... WFD
Wood's Digest of Laws [*California*] [*A publication*] (DLA) ... Wood's Dig
Wood's English Tithe Cases, Exchequer [*4 vols.*] [*A publication*] (DLA) ... Wood
Woods Hole Database, Inc. [*Information service or system*] (IID) ... WHDB
Woods Hole In-Situ Pump [*Marine biology*] [*Instrumentation*] ... WHISP
Woods Hole, Martha's Vineyard & Nantucket Steamship Authority (MHDB) ... WHMV & NSSA
Woods Hole Oceanographic Institution [*Woods Hole, MA*] [*Research center*] ... WHOI
Wood's Institutes of English Law [*A publication*] (DLA) ... Wood Inst
Wood's Institutes of English Law [*A publication*] (DLA) ... Wood Inst Eng L
Wood's Institutes of English Law [*A publication*] (DLA) ... Woods Ins
Wood's Institutes of the Civil Law of England [*A publication*] (DLA) ... Wood Civ L
Wood's Institutes of the Civil Law of England [*A publication*] (DLA) ... Wood's Civ Law
Wood's Institutes of the Civil Law of England [*A publication*] (DLA) ... Wood's Inst Civ L
Wood's Institutes of the Common Law [*A publication*] (DLA) ... Wood Com L
Wood's Institutes of the Common Law [*A publication*] (DLA) ... Wood Inst Com Law
Wood's Institutes of the Common Law [*A publication*] (DLA) ... Wood's Inst Com L
Wood's Law of Railroads [*A publication*] (DLA) ... Wood Ry Law
Wood's Manitoba Reports [*1875-83*] [*A publication*] (DLA) ... Wood's R
Wood's Mayne on Damages [*A publication*] (DLA) ... Wood Mayne Dam
Woods Memorial Hospital, Etowah, TN [*Library symbol*] [*Library of Congress*] (LCLS) ... TEtWH
Woods Memorial Library, Falls City, NE [*Library symbol Library of Congress*] (LCLS) ... NbFc
Woods Memorial Library, Falls City, NE [*Library symbol*] [*Library of Congress*] (LCLS) ... NbFcP
Wood's Oriental Cases [*Malaya*] [*A publication*] (DLA) ... WOC
Woods Road Elementary School, North Babylon, NY [*Library symbol*] [*Library of Congress*] (LCLS) ... NNbWE
Wood's Tithe Cases [*England*] [*A publication*] (DLA) ... Wood Decr
Wood's Tithe Cases [*1650-1798*] [*A publication*] (DLA) ... Wood Ti Cas
Wood's Tithe Cases [*1650-1798*] [*A publication*] (DLA) ... Wood Tit Cas
Wood's Treatise on the Statutes of Frauds [*A publication*] (DLA) ... Woods St Frauds
Woods' United States Circuit Court Reports [*A publication*] (DLA) ... Wood
Woods' United States Circuit Court Reports [*A publication*] (DLA) ... Woods
Woods' United States Circuit Court Reports [*A publication*] (DLA) ... Woods CC
Wood-Sheathed Deck [*of a ship*] (DS) ... WS
Wood-Shingle Roof [*Technical drawings*] ... WSR
Woodside [*California*] [*Seismograph station code, US Geological Survey*] (SEIS) ... WDS
Woodside, CA [*Location identifier FAA*] (FAAL) ... OSI
Woodstock [*Maryland*] [*Seismograph station code, US Geological Survey Closed*] (SEIS) ... WOO
Woodstock, IL [*FM radio station call letters*] ... WZSR
Woodstock Museum, Ontario [*Library symbol National Library of Canada*] (BIB) ... OWOM
Woodstock Museum, Woodstock, ON, Canada [*Library symbol*] [*Library of Congress*] (LCLS) ... CaOWoM
Woodstock, NB [*AM radio station call letters*] ... CJCJ
Woodstock, NY [*FM radio station call letters*] ... WDST
Woodstock, ON [*FM radio station call letters*] ... CKDK
Woodstock Public (Fisher Memorial) Library, Woodstock, NB, Canada [*Library symbol Library of Congress*] (LCLS) ... CaNBW
Woodstock Public Library, Ontario [*Library symbol National Library of Canada*] (NLC) ... OWO
Woodstock Public Library, Woodstock, ON, Canada [*Library symbol Library of Congress*] (LCLS) ... CaOWo
Woodstock, VA [*AM radio station call letters*] ... WAMM
Woodstock, VA [*FM radio station call letters*] ... WAZR
Woodstock, VT [*FM radio station call letters*] ... WMXR
Woodstown, NJ [*Location identifier FAA*] (FAAL) ... OOD
Woodvale [*British ICAO location identifier*] (ICLI) ... EGOW
Woodvale Aviation Co. Ltd. [*British ICAO designator*] (FAAC) ... WVL
Woodville State Hospital, Carnegie, PA [*OCLC symbol*] (OCLC) ... PHX
Woodville, TX [*AM radio station call letters*] ... KVLL
Woodville, TX [*FM radio station call letters*] ... KVLL-FM
Woodward Biomedical Library, University of British Columbia, Vancouver, British Columbia [*Library symbol National Library of Canada*] (NLC) ... BVAUW
Woodward Carnegie Library, Woodward, OK [*Library symbol Library of Congress*] (LCLS) ... OkWo
Woodward Memorial Library, LeRoy, NY [*Library symbol Library of Congress*] (LCLS) ... NLer
Woodward, OK [*FM radio station call letters*] (RBYB) ... KJOV-FM
Woodward, OK [*FM radio station call letters*] ... KMZE
Woodward, OK [*AM radio station call letters*] ... KSIW
Woodward, OK [*FM radio station call letters*] ... KWDQ
Woodward, OK [*FM radio station call letters*] ... KWFX
Woodward, OK [*FM radio station call letters*] ... KWOX
Woodward, OK [*Location identifier FAA*] (FAAL) ... OWU
Woodward, OK [*Location identifier FAA*] (FAAL) ... WWR
Woodward Parkway School, Farmingdale, NY [*Library symbol*] [*Library of Congress*] (LCLS) ... NFarWP
Woodward Public Library, Woodward, IA [*Library symbol Library of Congress*] (LCLS) ... IaWow
Woodward-Clyde Consultants, Clifton, NJ [*Library symbol Library of Congress*] (LCLS) ... NjClifW
Woodward-Clyde Consultants, Pasadena [*California*] ... WCCP
Woodward's Decisions [*Pennsylvania*] [*A publication*] (DLA) ... Woodw
Woodward's Decisions [*1861-74*] [*Pennsylvania*] [*A publication*] (DLA) ... Woodw Dec
Woodward's Decisions [*1861-74*] [*Pennsylvania*] [*A publication*] (DLA) ... Woodw Dec PA
Woodward's Ltd. [*Toronto Stock Exchange symbol Vancouver Stock Exchange symbol*] ... WDS
Woodwind [*Instrument*] [*Music*] ... WW
Woodwork (BARN) ... wdwk
Woodwork [*Freight*] ... WDWRK
Woodwork ... WOODWK
Woodworking ... WOODWKG
Woodworking Association of North America (EA) ... WANA
Woodworking Machinery Distributors Association (EA) ... WMDA
Woodworking Machinery Importers Association of America (EA) ... WMIA

Woodworking Machinery Suppliers Association [*British*] (DBA) ... WMSA
Woody [*California*] [*Seismograph station code, US Geological Survey Closed*] (SEIS) ... WDY
Woody Allen's Fall Picture [*Designation reflecting the filmmaker's reluctance to provide information about his movies in advance of their commercial release*] [*See also WASP*] ... WAFP
Woody Allen's Spring Picture [*Designation reflecting the filmmaker's reluctance to provide information about his movies in advance of their commercial release*] [*See also WAFP*] ... WASP
Woody Plant [*Botany*] ... W
Woody Point [*Australia Seismograph station code, US Geological Survey Closed*] (SEIS) ... WPA
Woody's Office Power Pack [*Pinecliffe International*] [*Computer science*] (PCM) ... WOPR
Wool ... WL
Wool (VRA) ... wl
Wool Back [*Knitting*] ... WB
Wool Bureau (EA) ... WB
Wool Forward [*Knitting*] ... WFD
Wool Hat Manufacturers Association of America (EA) ... WHMAA
Wool Industry Bureau of Statistics [*British*] (CB) ... WIBS
Wool Industry Policy Council [*Australia*] ... WIPC
Wool Industry Research Association [*British*] (DI) ... WIRA
Wool Manufacturers Council (EA) ... WMC
Wool over Needle [*Knitting*] ... WON
Wool Pullers Council of America (EA) ... WPCA
Wool Research and Development Corp. [*Commonwealth*] (EERA) ... WRDC
Wool Round Needle [*Knitting*] ... WRN
Wool Textile Manufacturers of Australia ... WTMA
Wool Textiles Production Board of Control [*World War I*] [*British*] ... WTPBC
Wool Valuers Association [*Australia*] ... WVA
Wool Yarn Jobbers Credit Association [*Defunct*] (EA) ... WYJCA
Woolclassers' Association of Australia ... WAA
Woolen ... WOOL
Woolen and Silk Textiles Industries Board [*New Deal*] ... WSTIB
Woolen Hosiery Institute of America [*Defunct*] (EA) ... WHIA
Woolen Jobbers Association (EA) ... WJA
Woolens and Worsteds of America [*Defunct*] (EA) ... WAWA
Woolens and Worsteds of America [*Defunct*] ... WWA
Woolf on Adulterations [*1874*] [*A publication*] (DLA) ... Woolf Adult
Woolknit Associates (EA) ... WA
Woollen and Worsted Trades Association [*British*] (BI) ... WWTA
Woolrych's Certificates [*1826*] [*A publication*] (DLA) ... Woolr Cert
Woolrych's Criminal Law [*1862*] [*A publication*] (DLA) ... Woolr Cr L
Woolrych's Law of Waters [*2nd ed.*] [*1851*] [*A publication*] (DLA) ... Woolr LW
Woolrych's Law of Waters [*A publication*] (DLA) ... Woolr Waters
Woolrych's Law of Ways [*2nd ed.*] [*1847*] [*A publication*] (DLA) ... Woolr Ways
Woolrych's Party Walls [*1845*] [*A publication*] (DLA) ... Woolr PW
Woolrych's Rights of Common [*2nd ed.*] [*1850*] [*A publication*] (DLA) ... Woolr Com
Woolrych's Sewert [*3rd ed.*] [*1864*] [*A publication*] (DLA) ... Woolr Sew
Woolrych's Window Lights [*2nd ed.*] [*1864*] [*A publication*] (DLA) ... Woolr Wind L
Woolsey, GA [*Location identifier FAA*] (FAAL) ... VWO
Woolsey's Introduction to Study of International Law [*6th ed.*] [*1888*] [*A publication*] (DLA) ... Wool Int
Woolsey's Introduction to Study of International Law [*6th ed.*] [*1888*] [*A publication*] (DLA) ... Wools Int L
Woolsey's Political Science [*A publication*] (DLA) ... Wools Pol Science
Woolsey's Political Science [*A publication*] (DLA) ... Woolsey Polit Science
Woolwich Armstrong Gun ... WA
Woolwich College [*London, England*] ... WC
Woolworth [*F.W.*] **Corp.** [*Wall Street slang name: "Five & Dime"*] [*Associated Press*] (SAG) ... Wolw
Woolworth [*F.W.*] **Corp.** [*Wall Street slang name: "Five & Dime"*] [*Associated Press*] (SAG) ... Wolwth
Woolworth Corp. [*Wall Street slang name: "Five & Dime"*] [*NYSE symbol Toronto Stock Exchange symbol*] (SPSG) ... Z
Woolworth Corp. $2.20 Cv Pfd [*NYSE symbol*] (TTSB) ... ZPrA
Woolworth's Reports [*1 Nebraska*] [*A publication*] (DLA) ... Woolw
Woolworth's Reports [*1 Nebraska*] [*A publication*] (DLA) ... Woolw Rep
Woolworth's United States Circuit Court Reports [*A publication*] (DLA) ... Wool
Woolworth's United States Circuit Court Reports [*A publication*] (DLA) ... Woolw
Woolworth's United States Circuit Court Reports [*A publication*] (DLA) ... Woolw Rep
Woolworth's United States Circuit Court Reports [*A publication*] (DLA) ... Woolworth
Woolworth's United States Circuit Court Reports [*A publication*] (DLA) ... Woolworth's Cir Ct R
Woolworth's United States Circuit Court Reports (Miller's Decisions) [*A publication*] (DLA) ... Wool CC
Wooly-Monkey Sarcoma Virus [*Medicine*] (PDAA) ... WSV
Woomera [*Australia ICAO location identifier*] (ICLI) ... AAWR
Woomera [*Australia ICAO location identifier*] (ICLI) ... APWR
Woomera [*Australia Airport symbol*] (OAG) ... UMR
Woomera [*Australia*] (BARN) ... WOM
Woonsocket, RI [*AM radio station call letters*] ... WNRI
Woonsocket, RI [*AM radio station call letters*] ... WOON
Woonsocket, RI [*FM radio station call letters*] ... WWKX
Wooroona [*Queensland*] [*Airport symbol*] (AD) ... WOQ
Wooster Community Hospital, Wooster, OH [*Library symbol*] [*Library of Congress*] (LCLS) ... OWoH
Wooster, OH [*Location identifier FAA*] (FAAL) ... BJJ
Wooster, OH [*Location identifier FAA*] (FAAL) ... SLW
Wooster, OH [*FM radio station call letters*] ... WCWS
Wooster, OH [*FM radio station call letters*] ... WKRW
Wooster, OH [*AM radio station call letters*] ... WKVX
Wooster, OH [*FM radio station call letters*] ... WQKT
Wooton Desk Owners Society (EA) ... WDOS
Worcester [*South Africa*] [*ICAO location identifier*] (ICLI) ... FAWC
Worcester [*Massachusetts*] [*Airport symbol*] (OAG) ... ORH
Worcester [*Massachusetts*] [*Seismograph station code, US Geological Survey Closed*] (SEIS) ... WOR
Worcester [*British depot code*] ... WOS
Worcester Area Cooperating Libraries [*Worcester, MA*] [*Library network*] ... WACL
Worcester Art Museum, Worcester, MA [*Library symbol Library of Congress*] (LCLS) ... MWM
Worcester Art Museum, Worcester, MA [*OCLC symbol*] (OCLC) ... WXM
Worcester County Law Library Association, Worcester, MA [*Library symbol Library of Congress*] (LCLS) ... MWCL
Worcester County Public Library, Snow Hill, MD [*Library symbol*] [*Library of Congress*] (LCLS) ... MdSnW
Worcester Foundation for Experimental Biology ... WFEB
Worcester Historical Society, Worcester, MA [*Library symbol Library of Congress*] (LCLS) ... MWHi
Worcester Junior College [*Massachusetts*] ... WJC
Worcester, MA [*Location identifier FAA*] (FAAL) ... CLY
Worcester, MA [*Location identifier FAA*] (FAAL) ... EKW
Worcester, MA [*Location identifier FAA*] (FAAL) ... RSR
Worcester, MA [*FM radio station call letters*] ... WAAF
Worcester, MA [*FM radio station call letters*] ... WBPR
Worcester, MA [*FM radio station call letters*] ... WCHC
Worcester, MA [*AM radio station call letters*] ... WCRN
Worcester, MA [*FM radio station call letters*] ... WCUW
Worcester, MA [*FM radio station call letters*] ... WICN
Worcester, MA [*AM radio station call letters*] ... WNEB
Worcester, MA [*AM radio station call letters*] ... WORC
Worcester, MA [*FM radio station call letters*] ... WSRS
Worcester, MA [*AM radio station call letters*] ... WTAG
Worcester, MA [*AM radio station call letters*] ... WWTM
Worcester, MA [*Television station call letters*] ... WYDN
Worcester Polytechnic Institute (GAGS) ... Worcester Poly Inst
Worcester Polytechnic Institute [*Massachusetts*] ... WPI
Worcester Polytechnic Institute, Worcester, MA [*Library symbol Library of Congress*] (LCLS) ... MWP
Worcester Polytechnic Institute, Worcester, MA [*OCLC symbol*] (OCLC) ... WPG
Worcester Public Library and Central Massachusetts Regional Library System Headquarters, Worcester, MA [*Library symbol Library of Congress*] (LCLS) ... MW
Worcester Public Library, Worcester, MA [*OCLC symbol*] (OCLC) ... WZW
Worcester State College (GAGS) ... Worcester St C
Worcester State College, Worcester, MA [*Library symbol Library of Congress*] (LCLS) ... MWW
Worcester State College, Worcester, MA [*OCLC symbol*] (OCLC) ... WRM
Worcester State Hospital, Worcester, MA [*Library symbol Library of Congress*] (LCLS) ... MWSH
Worcester's Dictionary [*A publication*] (DLA) ... Wor Dict
Worcester's Dictionary [*A publication*] (DLA) ... Worcest Dict
Worcester's Dictionary of the English Language [*A publication*] (DLA) ... Worcester
Worcestershire [*County in England*] ... WORC
Worcestershire [*County in England*] ... WORCS
Worcestershire and Sherwood Foresters Regiment [*Military unit*] [*British*] ... WFR
Word ... W
Word ... WD
Word Add ... WA
Word Address Format ... WAF
Word After [*Message handling*] ... WA
Word and Number Assessment Inventory [*Aptitude test*] ... WNAI
Word Association Test [*Psychology*] ... WAT
Word Before [*Message handling*] ... WB
Word Buffer Register (MSA) ... WBR
Word Combine and Multiplexer ... WCM
Word Control Logic ... WCL
Word Control [*or Count*] **Register** ... WCR
Word Count [*Computer science*] ... WC
Word Description Drawing (SAA) ... WDD
Word Discrimination Score ... WDS
Word Display ... WD
Word Driver and Gate [*Computer science*] (IAA) ... WDAG
Word Driver BIT [*Binary Digit*] [*Computer science*] (MHDI) ... WDB
Word Fluency (DAVI) ... W
Word Fluency [*Psychology*] ... WF
Word for Windows [*Computer science*] ... WFW
Word for Windows Office Power Pack [*Computer program disk*] (PCM) ... WOPR
Word Image Processing System [*Datacopy Corp.*] ... WIPS
Word in Life: Journal of Religious Education [*A publication*] (APTA) ... WL
Word Intelligibility ... WI
Word Intelligibility by Picture Identification [*Artificial intelligence*] ... WIPI
Word Length (IAA) ... WL
Word Line ... WL
Word Mark (BUR) ... WM
Word of God Institute [*Later, NIWG*] (EA) ... WGI
Word of Life Fellowship (EA) ... WLF
Word on the Way ... WOW
Word Processing [*Computer science*] (DCTA) ... WORP
Word Processing [*Movement to improve secretarial/clerical function through a managed system of people, procedures, and modern office equipment*] ... WP
Word Processing/Administrative Support [*Extension of Word Processing*] ... WP/AS

Word Processing and Administrative Support System [*Computer science*] (HGAA) ..... WPAAS
Word Processing and Office Equipment (MHDI) ..... WPOE
Word Processing Aptitude Battery [*Test*] ..... WPAB
Word Processing Center ..... WPC
Word Processing/Data Processing System (HGAA) ..... WP/DP
Word Processing Document Exchange Program ..... WPDX
Word Processing/Office Systems (HGAA) ..... WP/OS
Word Processing Society ..... WPS
Word Processing Society, Inc. (EA) ..... WPSI
Word Processing System (BUR) ..... WPS
Word Processing Test ..... WPT
Word Processing Users' Group ..... W/PUG
Word Processor (ADA) ..... WP
Word Processor (ODBW) ..... wp
Word Processor Assessment Battery [*Selection and placement test*] ..... WPAB
Word Punch ..... WP
Word Recognition System ..... WRS
Word Restoration ..... WR
Word Selection (WDAA) ..... WORSE
Word Sync ..... WS
Word Synchronizing Track (NITA) ..... WST
Word Target [*Psychology*] ..... WT
Word Terminal ..... WT
Word Terminal Synchronous ..... WTS
Word Type ..... WT
Word Underscore Character [*Computer science*] ..... WUS
Wordbook (ROG) ..... WDBK
Wordcount, Creative Writing Services, Inc., Ottawa, Ontario [*Library symbol National Library of Canada*] (NLC) ..... OOWC
Worden Community Unit, School District 16, Worden, IL [*Library symbol Library of Congress*] (LCLS) ..... IWordSD
Worden Reading Center, Worden, IL [*Library symbol Library of Congress*] (LCLS) ..... IWordR
Wording (WGA) ..... WDG
Wording to Be Agreed [*Insurance*] (AIA) ..... WDG TBA
Word-of-Mouth (WDMC) ..... WOM
Word-Oriented Random Access Memory [*Computer science*] (MCD) ..... WORAM
WordPerfect for Disk Operating System [*Computer science*] ..... WPDOS
WordPerfect for Windows [*Computer science*] ..... WPWIN
WordPerfect Graphic [*Novell, Inc.*] [*File format*] ..... WPG
WordPerfect Information System Environment [*Computer science*] ..... WISE
WordPerfect Presentations [*WordPerfect Corp.*] [*Computer science*] (PCM) ..... WPP
Words a Minute ..... WAM
Words and Authors Index [*Computer-produced index*] ..... WADEX
[*The*] **Words of Moses from Qumran. Cave One** (BJA) 1QDM
Words Out of Ordinary Language (WDAA) ..... WOOOL
Words per Minute (KSC) ..... W/M
Words per Minute (IAA) ..... WMIN
Words per Minute (IDOE) ..... wpm
Words per Minute (WDMC) ..... wpm
Words per Minute ..... WPM
Words per Second ..... WPS
WordStar [*Computer program*] ..... WS
Wordsworth's Election Cases [*England*] [*A publication*] (DLA) ..... Words Elect Cas
Wordsworth's Law of Elections [*6th ed.*] [*1868*] [*A publication*] (DLA) ..... Words Elect
Wordsworth's Law of Joint-Stock Companies [*A publication*] (DLA) ..... Words JS
Wordsworth's Law of Mining [*A publication*] (DLA) ..... Words Min
Wordsworth's Law of Patents [*A publication*] (DLA) ..... Words Pat
Wordsworth's Railway and Canal Companies [*A publication*] (DLA) ..... Words Ry & C
Wordy [*Used in correcting manuscripts, etc.*] ..... WDY
Work [*Physics*] (BARN) ..... A
Work [*or w*] [*Symbol IUPAC*] ..... W
Work ..... WK
Work Accomplishment Code [*Military*] (AFIT) ..... WAC
Work Accomplishment Code [*Navy*] (NG) ..... WKACC
Work Acquisition Routine ..... WAR
Work Activities Center ..... WAC
Work Activity Program ..... WAP
Work Activity Sampling Plan ..... WASP
Work Adjustment Program [*Education*] ..... WAD
Work Allotment Board [*New Deal*] ..... WAB
Work Analysis and Measurement (WDAA) ..... WAM
Work Analysis Program [*Computer science*] (BUR) ..... WAP
Work and Flop (WDMC) ..... W & F
Work and Flop [*Printing*] (WDMC) ..... W & F
Work and Inspection Record (SAA) ..... W & IR
Work and Occupations [*A publication*] (BRI) ..... WOC
Work and People [*A publication*] ..... Wo Peo
Work and Turn (WDMC) ..... W&T
Work Aptitude Profile and Practice Set [*Test*] ..... WAPPS
Work Area Pointer Table [*Computer science*] ..... WAPT
Work Assessment Course (AIE) ..... WAC
Work Assignment (MCD) ..... WA
Work Assignment Card (MCD) ..... WAC
Work Assignment Procedure ..... WAP
Work Authorization (MCD) ..... WA
Work Authorization and Delegation ..... WAD
Work Authorization Document [*NASA*] ..... WAD
Work Authorization Document/Shop Order (NASA) ..... WAD/SO
Work Authorization Material List (DNAB) ..... WAML
Work Authorization Number (NASA) ..... WAN
Work Authorization/Program Status Factor ..... WA/PSF
Work Authorization Report [*or Request*] [*NASA*] (MCD) ..... WAR
Work Based Learning (AIE) ..... WBL
Work Book ..... WB
Work Breakdown Sheets [*Army*] ..... WBS
Work Breakdown Structure [*Computer science*] ..... WBS
Work Breakdown Structure Code (MCD) ..... WBSC
Work Breakdown Structure Control Board [*Army*] (AABC) ..... WBSCB
Work Capacity (MAE) ..... WC
Work Card (AAG) ..... WC
Work Center (AFM) ..... WC
Work Center Code ..... WCC
Work Center Description (AFM) ..... WCD
Work Circle (AAG) ..... WC
Work Control (AAG) ..... WC
Work Control Center (AAG) ..... WCC
Work Control Data Base (NASA) ..... WCDB
Work Control Plan (AAG) ..... WCP
Work Control Station ..... WCS
Work Control Status ..... WCS
Work Control Supervisor [*Air Force*] ..... WKCONSUPVR
Work Control System (NASA) ..... WCS
Work Core Storage ..... WCS
Work [*or Working*] **Day** (AFM) ..... WD
Work Description (MCD) ..... WD
Work Directive (MCD) ..... WD
Work Distribution Policy (AAG) ..... WDP
Work Element Timer and Recorder for Automatic Computing ..... WETARFAC
Work Environment Scale [*Test*] ..... WES
Work Experience ..... WE
Work Experience and Training ..... WET
Work Experience Education (DNAB) ..... WEE
Work Experience Instructor (OICC) ..... WEI
Work Experience on Employer's Premises [*Manpower Services Commission*] [*British*] (DI) ..... WEEP
Work Experience Program [*Department of Labor*] ..... WEP
Work Experience Training Program (OICC) ..... WETP
Work/Family Life Database [*Database*] ..... WFLD
Work Flow Language [*Computer science*] (BUR) ..... WFL
Work Force Effectiveness and Development Group [*Office of Personnel Management*] (GRD) ..... WED
Work Function [*Physics*] ..... WF
Work Function Difference [*Physics*] (IAA) ..... WFD
Work Function Surface ..... WFS
Work Glove Institute [*Later, WGMA*] (EA) ..... WGI
Work Glove Manufacturers Association (EA) ..... WGMA
Work Group System [*Computer hardware*] (PCM) ..... WGS
Work Handling and Maintenance [*Navy*] (NG) ..... WHAM
Work Health Authority [*Northern Territory, Australia*] ..... WHA
Work, Health, Love [*Camp Fire Girls slogan*] ..... WOHELO
Work Hour (KSC) ..... WH
Work Hours Act of 1962 (WYGK) ..... WHA
Work in America Institute (EA) ..... WAI
Work in Hand (ILCA) ..... WIH
Work in Place (AABC) ..... WIP
Work in Process ..... WIP
Work in Process Measurement (MCD) ..... WIPM
Work in Progress (AFM) ..... WIP
Work Incentive Program [*Later, ETSC*] (EA) ..... WIN
Work Incentive Program [*Department of Health, Education, and Welfare; Department of Labor*] (DLA) ..... WIP
Work Injury Followback Survey [*Bureau of Labor Statistics and National Center for Health Statistics*] (GFGA) ..... WIFS
Work Injury Reports [*Human Resources*] (WYGK) ..... WIR
Work Inspection Characteristics List ..... WICL
Work Isolation Pilot Project [*NASA*] ..... WIPP
Work Item Tracking System [*Nuclear energy*] (NRCH) ..... WITS
Work Learning Guide (AIE) ..... WLG
Work Light ..... WL
Work Line (MSA) ..... WL
Work Measurement [*Army*] (AABC) ..... WM
Work Measurement System [*Postal Service*] ..... WMS
Work Metabolic Rate (MAE) ..... WMR
Work Methods and Standards ..... WM & S
Work Motivation Inventory [*Test*] ..... WMI
Work Notice (AAG) ..... WN
Work of Breathing [*Medicine*] (DAVI) ..... WOB
Work of Fracture [*Ceramic property*] ..... WOF
Work of Mary [*An association*] (EAIO) ..... WM
Work on Hand [*Insurance*] ..... WOH
Work Opportunities Unlimited ..... WOU
Work Order ..... WO
Work Order and Work Accomplishment Record ..... WOWAR
Work Order Authorization (MCD) ..... WOA
Work Order Bin (MCD) ..... WOB
Work Order Control (MCD) ..... WOC
Work Order Control System (MCD) ..... WOCS
Work Order Generator [*Military*] ..... WOG
Work Order Load Forecast (MCD) ..... WOLF
Work Order Number (MCD) ..... WON
Work Order Register (MCD) ..... WOR
Work Order Release (MCD) ..... WOR
Work Order Request ..... WOR
Work Order Status File (MCD) ..... WOSF
Work Ordering and Reporting Communication System [*Army*] ..... WORCS

Work Ordering and Reporting Communications System [*Army*] (MCD) ..... WRCS
Work Order-Work Authorization (SSD) ..... WO-WA
Work Outline Retrieval (MCD) ..... WOR
Work Package (NASA) ..... WP
Work Package Action (MCD) ..... WPA
Work Package Address (MCD) ..... WPA
Work Package Concept (MCD) ..... WPC
Work Package Description [*NASA*] (NASA) ..... WPD
Work Package Grouping [*NASA*] (NASA) ..... WPG
Work Package Management (MCD) ..... WPM
Work Package Manpower and Cost Plan [*NASA*] (NASA) ..... WPMCP
Work Package Milestone Progress Report (MCD) ..... WPMRR
Work Package Plan [*NASA*] (NASA) ..... WPP
Work Package Planning Sheet [*NASA*] (NASA) ..... WPPS
Work Picture [*or Print*] [*Cinematography*] ..... W/P
Work Plan Analysis and Scheduling Technique (MHDB) ..... WOPAST
Work Planning and Control [*Computer science*] ..... WP + C
Work Preparation (AIE) ..... WP
Work Procedure [*Nuclear energy*] (NRCH) ..... WP
Work Process Flow [*NASA*] (NASA) ..... WPF
Work Process Indicator (NASA) ..... WPI
Work Program (NATG) ..... WP
Work Progress Indicator [*NASA*] (NASA) ..... WPI
Work Queue Directory ..... WKQDR
Work Ranch [*California*] [*Seismograph station code, US Geological Survey*] (SEIS) ..... WKR
Work Rate (AAMN) ..... WR
Work Release Order (MCD) ..... WRO
Work Request (MCD) ..... WR
Work Requirement (CAAL) ..... WR
Work Safety Analysis [*Engineering*] ..... WSA
Work Sciences Association [*British*] (DBA) ..... WSA
Work Shop [*Military*] ..... WS
Work Shop Equipment (SAA) ..... WSE
Work Simplification Program [*Military*] ..... WSP
Work Stand (MCD) ..... WS
Work Statement (AAG) ..... WS
Work Station [*NASA*] (NASA) ..... W/S
Work Station Control Center [*NASA*] (NASA) ..... WSCC
Work Station Facility ..... WSF
Work Station Utility ..... WSU
Work Stoppage (AAG) ..... WS
Work Study Program (OICC) ..... WSP
Work Summarization System (MCD) ..... WSS
Work Systems Package [*Navy underwater salvage operation*] (DICI) ..... WSP
Work to Be Done (ADA) ..... WTBD
Work Track [*Cinematography*] ..... W/T
Work Training in Industry ..... WTI
Work Transfer Record (KSC) ..... WTR
Work Transfer Request ..... WTR
Work Type (NITA) ..... WT
Work Unit [*Air Force*] (AFM) ..... WU
Work Unit Assignment [*Navy*] (NG) ..... WUA
Work Unit Code ..... WUC
Work Unit Code File (NASA) ..... WUCF
Work Unit Code Manual ..... WUCM
Work Unit Data Bank ..... WUDB
Work Unit Engineer ..... WUE
Work Unit Information System [*Database*] [*DTIC*] ..... WUIS
Work Unit Manager ..... WUM
Work Unit Plan [*Navy*] (NG) ..... WUP
Work Unit Time Standard [*Air Force*] (AFM) ..... WUTS
Work Unit Tracking Subsystem (MCD) ..... WUTS
Work Values Inventory [*Psychometrics*] ..... WVI
Work without Opus Number (WGA) ..... WoO
Workable Hatch [*Shipping*] (DS) ..... WH
Work-and-Turn [*Printing*] (WDMC) ..... W & T
Workbench (AAG) ..... WB
Workbench Rack (MCD) ..... WBR
WorkCare Appeals Board [*Victoria, Australia*] ..... WCAB
Workcover Authority of New South Wales [*Australia*] ..... WCANSW
Worked All America [*Amateur radio*] [*Contacted at least one station in all counties*] (IAA) ..... WAA
Worked All Continents [*Contacted at least one station on all continents*] [*Amateur radio*] ..... WAC
Worked All Countries [*Contacted at least one station in all countries*] [*Amateur radio*] (IAA) ..... WAC
Worked All Europe [*Contacted at least one station in all European countries*] [*Amateur radio*] (IAA) ..... WAE
Worked All Goose (IAA) ..... WAG
Worked All Italian Provinces [*Amateur radio*] (IAA) ..... WAIP
Worked All Italy [*Amateur radio*] (IAA) ..... WAI
Worked All Prefixes [*Amateur radio*] (IAA) ..... WPX
Worked All States [*Contacted at least one station in all states*] [*Amateur radio*] ..... WAS
Worked All Yokosuka [*Amateur radio*] (IAA) ..... WAY
Worked All Zones [*Contacted at least one station in all zones*] [*Amateur radio*] (IAA) ..... WAZ
Worked Off (DGA) ..... W/O
Worked Republic of India Award [*Amateur radio*] (IAA) ..... WRIA
Worked Three Oceans [*Amateur radio*] (IAA) ..... WTO
Worker ..... WKR
Worker ..... WRKR
Worker Adjustment and Retraining Notification (AAGC) ..... WARN
Worker Adjustment and Retraining Notification Act [*1988*] ..... WARN
Worker Adjustment and Retraining Notification Act [*1988*] ..... WARNA
Worker Adjustment Assistance ..... WAA
Worker and Visitor Entrance System [*Secret Service*] (GFGA) ..... WAVES
Worker Readjustment Program [*Department of Labor*] ..... WRAP
Worker Trait Group ..... WTG
Worker-Machine Interface ..... WMI
Workers Anonymous [*Mythical organization created by columnist Arthur Hoppe that helps hard working individuals*] ..... WA
Workers' Christian Fellowship [*British*] (BI) ..... WCF
Workers' Compensation and Employers' Liability [*Insurance*] ..... WC & EL
Workers' Compensation and Rehabilitation Commission [*Western Australia*] ..... WCRC
Workers' Compensation Board [*Australia*] ..... WCB
Workers Compensation Board of British Columbia, Vancouver, BC, Canada [*Library symbol Library of Congress*] (LCLS) ..... CaBVaWC
Workers Compensation Board of British Columbia, Vancouver, British Columbia [*Library symbol National Library of Canada*] (NLC) ..... BVAWC
Worker's Compensation Board, Vocatioal Rehabilitation Library, Toronto, ON, Canada [*Library symbol*] [*Library of Congress*] (LCLS) ..... CaOTWCV
Workers' Compensation Cases (New Zealand) [*A publication*] (DLA) ..... WCC (NZ)
Worker's Compensation (Dust Diseases) Board [*Australia*] ..... WC(DD)B
Workers' Compensation Legislation in Australia [*A publication*] ..... WCLA
Workers' Defence Committee [*Ghana*] [*Political party*] (PPW) ..... WDC
Workers' Defence Union [*British*] ..... WDU
Workers' Defense Committee [*Poland*] (PD) ..... WDC
Workers' Defense League (EA) ..... WDL
Workers Education Association (EERA) ..... WEA
Workers' Educational Association ..... WEA
Workers' Educational Association of New South Wales [*Australia*] ..... WEANSW
Workers' Educational Association of South Australia ..... WEASA
Workers Health and Safety Centre, Don Mills, Ontario [*Library symbol National Library of Canada*] (BIB) ..... ODW
Worker's International Industrial Union ..... WIIU
Workers' Music Association [*British*] ..... WMA
Workers' Organization for Socialist Action [*South Africa Political party*] (EY) ..... WOSA
Worker's Party [*Ireland*] [*Political party*] ..... WP
Workers Party of Canada ..... WPC
Workers' Party of Jamaica [*Political party*] (EY) ..... WPJ
Workers' Party of Turkey ..... WPT
Workers'/People's Defence Committee [*Ghana*] [*Political party*] ..... W/PDC
Workers' Rehabilitation and Compensation Corp. [*South Australia*] ..... WRCC
Workers' Revolutionary Party [*British*] (PPW) ..... WRP
Workers Solidarity Alliance (EA) ..... WSA
Workers' Union of Ireland (BI) ..... WUI
Workers Unity League [*Canada*] ..... WUL
Workers World Party [*Political party*] (EA) ..... WWP
Workers-Peasants Red Guards [*North Korea*] ..... WPRG
Workflow Innovation Toolkit (PCM) ..... WIT
Workforce Management Staff [*Environmental Protection Agency*] (GFGA) ..... WMS
Workgroup for Indians in South America [*Netherlands*] ..... WIZA
Workgroup for Indians of North America [*Acronym is based on foreign phrase Netherlands*] ..... KIVA
Workgroup Indian Project [*Netherlands*] ..... WIP
Workgroup Technology [*NASDAQ symbol*] (TTSB) ..... WKGP
Workhouse [*British*] (ROG) ..... WORKHO
Working (MSA) ..... WKG
Working ..... WKG
Working Alternating Current (DEN) ..... WAC
Working Ampere Alternating Current (IAA) ..... WAAC
Working Association of Mothers [*British*] (DI) ..... WAM
Working Capital ..... WC
Working Capital Fund ..... WCF
Working Capital Management Account [*Merrill Lynch & Co.*] ..... WCMA
Working Circle [*Technical drawings*] ..... WC
Working Class Hero (EA) ..... WCH
Working Committee of the Aeronautical Board ..... WCAB
Working Committee of the Scientific Institutes for Crafts in the EEC Countries [*Munich, Federal Republic of Germany*] (EAIO) ..... WCSICEC
Working Committee on Weather Operations ..... WC/WO
Working Community of the European Gypsum Industry (EAIO) ..... EUROGYPSUM
Working Current (IAA) ..... WC
Working Data Base (MHDI) ..... WDB
Working Direct Current (DEN) ..... WDC
Working Directory (MHDI) ..... WDIR
Working Distance [*Microscopy*] ..... WD
Working Draft (OSI) ..... WD
Working Group ..... WG
Working Group against Racism in Children's Resources (AIE) ..... WGARCR
Working Group Agenda Item (SAA) ..... WGAI
Working Group Director ..... WGD
Working Group for Community Development Reform [*Defunct*] (EA) ..... WGCDR
Working Group for Democracy in Chile (EA) ..... WGDC
Working Group for Space Physics Research ..... WGSPR
Working Group Indigenous Peoples [*Netherlands*] (EAIO) ..... WIP
Working Group of Agriculture (EERA) ..... WGA
Working Group of the Army Study Advisory Committee (AABC) ..... WASAC
Working Group of US Overseas Educational Advisers in South America [*Defunct*] (EA) ..... WGUSEASA
Working Group on Antarctic Meteorology [*Marine science*] (OSRA) ..... WGAM
Working Group on Climate Change Detection [*Marine science*] (OSRA) ..... WGCCD
Working Group on Data [*Marine science*] (OSRA) ..... WGD
Working Group on Data (USDC) ..... WGD
Working Group on Domestic Hunger and Poverty (EA) ..... WGDHP
Working Group on Extraterrestrial Resources [*Defunct NASA*] ..... WGER

Working Group on Geodesy and Geographic Information (EERA) .... WG-GGI
Working Group on Internal Instrumentation [*NASA*] .... WGII
Working Group on International Shipping Legislation [*UNCTAD*] (DS) .... ISLWG
Working Group on Marine Sediments [*Marine science*] (OSRA) .... WGMS
Working Group on Multilateral Assistance [*Department of the Treasury*] .... WGMA
Working Group on Numerical Experimentation [*Marine science*] (OSRA) .... WGNE
Working Group on Radiation Fluxes [*Marine science*] (OSRA) .... WGRF
Working Group on Rural Development [*Department of Agriculture*] (EGAO) .... WGRD
Working Group on Satellite Ionospheric Measurements [*NASA*] .... WGSIM
Working Group on Satellites [*Marine science*] (OSRA) .... WGSAT
Working Group on Sea Ice [*Marine science*] (OSRA) .... WGSI
Working Group on Sustainable Agriculture [*Australia*] .... WGSA
Working Group on the Assessment of Toxic Chemicals [*British*] .... WATCH
Working Group on Tracking and Computation [*NASA*] .... WGTC
Working Group on Untouchables (EA) .... WGU
Working Group on Waterborne Cryptosporidiosis [*Medicine*] .... WGWC
Working Group on Weather Communications [*NATO*] (NATG) .... WGWC
Working Group on Weather Plans [*NATO*] (NATG) .... WGWP
Working Group Report .... WGR
Working Heart Rate [*Cardiology*] .... WHR
Working Layout (SAA) .... WLO
Working Level .... WL
Working Level Month [*Nuclear energy*] .... WLM
Working Mathematics Group (AIE) .... WMG
Working Memory [*Psychology*] .... WM
Working Men's Club [*British*] (BARN) .... WMC
Working Mothers Association [*British*] (DBA) .... WMA
Working Overseer (ADA) .... WO
Working Paper .... WP
Working Papers (AAGC) .... W/P
Working Papers Exhibits and Rate Schedules (AAGC) .... WPEARS
Working Party .... WP
Working Party on Aquaculture [*Australia*] .... WPA
Working Party on Feral Animals [*Australia*] .... WPFA
Working Party on Library and Book Trade Relations [*British*] .... LIBSTAD
Working Party on Rationing [*Allied German Occupation Forces*] .... WPR
Working Party Three [*Economic Policy Committee of the Organization for Economic Cooperation and Development*] WP3
Working People's Alliance [*Guyana*] (PD) .... WPA
Working Point .... WP
Working Point [*Technical drawings*] .... WPT
Working Pressure .... WP
Working Pressure .... WPR
Working Program Advisory Committee [*DoD*] .... WPAC
Working Reference Material [*Nuclear energy*] (NRCH) .... WRM
Working Reference of Livestock Regulatory Establishments, Stations, and Officials [*A publication*] .... WRLS
Working Reference Telephone Circuit [*Telecommunications*] (TEL) .... WRTC
Working Register .... WR
Working Security Committee [*Navy*] .... WSC
Working Space .... WS
Working Steam Pressure .... WSP
Working Storage [*Computer science*] (MDG) .... WS
Working Stress Design [*Nuclear energy*] (NRCH) .... WSD
Working Timetable (DCTA) .... WTT
Working Tools [*Freemasonry*] .... WT's
Working Transmission Reference System [*Telecommunications*] (TEL) .... WRS
Working Voltage (IAA) .... WKGV
Working Voltage (MSA) .... WV
Working Voltage, Alternating Current (DEN) .... WVAC
Working Voltage, Direct Current .... WVDC
Working Water Pressure .... WWP
Working Weekends on Organic Farms [*British*] [*An association*] (DBA) .... WWOOF
Working with Shortages (MCD) .... WWS
Working Women (NTCM) .... WW
Working Women Education Fund (EA) .... WWEF
Working Women, National Association of Officeworkers (EA) .... WW
Working Women's Institute [*Defunct*] (EA) .... WWI
Working Women's United Institute [*Later, WWI*] (EA) .... WWUI
Working-Capital Account (MHDW) .... WCA
Workingmens Cap Hldgs [*NASDAQ symbol*] (TTSB) .... WCHI
Workingmens Capital Holdings, Inc. [*NASDAQ symbol*] (SAG) .... WCHI
Workingmens Capital Holdings, Inc. [*Associated Press*] (SAG) .... WorkCap
Workingmen's Institute, New Harmony, IN [*Library symbol Library of Congress*] (LCLS) .... InHhW
Workingmen's Institute, New Harmony, IN [*Library symbol*] [*Library of Congress*] (LCLS) .... InNhW
Workload (AABC) .... WL
Workload and Cost Schedule [*Military*] (AABC) .... WLCS
Workload and Productivity Analysis (MCD) .... WAPALS
Workload and Repair Activity Process Simulator (PDAA) .... WRAPS
Workload and Resources Correlation Analysis Technique [*Army*] .... WARCAT
Workload and Resources Evaluation System [*Navy*] .... WARES
Workload Control File .... WCF
Workload Control Number (MCD) .... WCN
Workload Factor (AFM) .... WLF
Workload Transaction Code [*Navy*] (NG) .... WTC
Workmanship Assurance .... WA
Workmen's Benefit Fund of the USA [*Carle Place, NY*] (EA) .... WBF
Workmen's Circle [*New York, NY*] (EA) .... WC
Workmen's Compensation [*Insurance*] .... W
Workmen's Compensation [*Department of Health and Human Services*] .... WC
Workmen's Compensation Act .... WCA
Workmen's Compensation and Insurance Reports [*1912-33*] [*A publication*] (DLA) .... WC & I Rep
Workmen's Compensation and Insurance Reports [*1912-33*] [*England*] [*A publication*] (DLA) .... WC & Ins (Eng)
Workmen's Compensation and Insurance Reports [*1912-33*] [*England*] [*A publication*] (DLA) .... WC & Ins Rep
Workmen's Compensation and Insurance Reports [*1912-33*] [*England*] [*A publication*] (DLA) .... WC & IR
Workmen's Compensation and Insurance Reports [*1912-33*] [*A publication*] (DLA) .... WC Ins Rep
Workmen's Compensation Board .... WCB
Workmen's Compensation Board, Toronto, ON, Canada [*Library symbol Library of Congress*] (LCLS) .... CaOTWC
Workmen's Compensation Cases [*Legal*] [*British*] .... WCC
Workmen's Compensation Law Journal [*A publication*] (DLA) .... WCLJ
Workmen's Compensation Law Reporter [*Commerce Clearing House*] [*A publication*] (DLA) .... Workmen's Comp L Rep
Workmen's Compensation Law Review [*A publication*] (DLA) .... WCLR
Workmen's Compensation Law Review [*A publication*] (DLA) .... Workmen's Comp L Rev
Workmen's Compensation Opinions, United States Department of Commerce [*A publication*] (DLA) .... WC Ops
Workmen's Compensation Reports [*A publication*] (DLA) .... WC Rep
Workmen's Compensation Supplement to Department Reports of Pennsylvania [*A publication*] (DLA) .... PA WC Bd (Dep Rep Sup)
Workout from Starting Gate [*Horse racing*] .... G
Workout Handily from Gate [*Horse racing*] .... HG
Workpack Scheduling System [*Industrial engineering*] .... WSS
Workpackage Risk Analysis Procedure (AAGC) .... WRAP
Workpackage Risk Assessment Procedure (AAGC) .... WRAP
Workplace Basic Education Project [*Australia*] .... WBEP
Workplace Environmental Exposure Level [*A guide series published by the AIHA - American Industrial Hygiene Association*] [*A publication*] .... WEEL
Workplace Hazardous Materials Information System [*Canada*] .... WHMIS
Workplace Industrial Relations Survey [*British*] .... WIRS
Workplace Information Centre [*New South Wales, Australia*] .... WIC
Workplace Optimization and Layout Planning (MHDB) .... WOLAP
Workplace Shell [*IBM Corp.*] [*Computer science*] (PCM) .... WPS
Workplace Standards Administration [*Department of Labor*] .... WSA
Workprint [*Cinematography*] (NTCM) .... WP
Work-Related Education and Training (AIE) .... WRET
Works .... WKS
Works and Building, High Priority [*British World War II*] .... WBA
Works and Building, Low Priority [*British World War II*] .... WBZ
Works and Building Services [*British military*] (DMA) .... W & B
Works Department .... WD
Works Information and Management System [*M & E White Consultants Ltd.*] [*Software package*] (NCC) .... WIMS
Works on Courts and Their Jurisdiction [*A publication*] (DLA) .... Works Courts
Works' Practice, Pleading, and Forms [*A publication*] (DLA) .... Works Pr
Works Progress Administration [*Later, Work Projects Administration*] [*Part of President Franklin D. Roosevelt's New Deal*] .... WPA
Works Technical New Policy (EERA) .... WTNP
Worksafe Australia .... WA
Worksheet [*Data format*] .... WK
Worksheet (AAG) .... WS
Worksheet File [*Computer science*] .... WKS
Worksheet Global Recalculation Automatic [*Computer science*] .... WGRA
Worksheet Inspection Card .... WIC
[*The*] **WorkSheet Optimizer** [*Laptop tool*] [*Brubaker Software*] (PCM) .... WSO
Workshop (AAG) .... WKS
Workshop .... WKSP
Workshop .... WRKSHP
Workshop (NATG) .... WSP
Workshop Analysis and Scheduling Programming .... WASP
Workshop Assembly [*Torpedo*] .... WA
Workshop Attitude Control System (MCD) .... WACS
Workshop Computer Interface .... WCI
Workshop Computer Interface Unit (MCD) .... WCIU
Workshop Control (IAA) .... WS
Workshop for Cultural Democracy (EA) .... WCD
Workshop In Library Leadership [*Canada*] .... WILL
Workshop in Nonviolence (EA) .... WIN
Workshop Institute for Living-Learning (EA) .... WILL
Workshop Library on World Humour (EA) .... WLWH
Workshop of the Players Art [*New York City*] .... WPA
Workshop on Alternative Energy Strategies .... WAES
Workshop on the Determination of Anti-Epileptic Drugs in Body Fluids .... WODADIBOF
Workshop Reporting (IAA) .... WR
Workshop Test and Handling Equipment [*Military*] (CAAL) .... WTHE
Workshop Trains [*British*] .... WT
Workshop Unit (MSA) .... WU
Workshops in Emergency Management [*RSPA*] (TAG) .... WEM
Workspace Pointer (MHDB) .... WP
Workspace Register Pointer [*Computer science*] (IAA) .... WP
Workstation Automatic Script Processor (NITA) .... WASP
Workstation Laboratory (PCM) .... WSL
Workstation Publishing Software .... WPS
Work-Up .... w/u
Worland [*Wyoming*] [*Airport symbol*] (OAG) .... WRL
Worland, WY [*FM radio station call letters*] .... KKLX
Worland, WY [*AM radio station call letters*] .... KWOR
Worland, WY [*Location identifier FAA*] (FAAL) .... RLY
Worland, WY [*Location identifier FAA*] (FAAL) .... WRL

World ... W
World ... WLD
World Academy of Art and Science [*Solna, Sweden*] (EA) ... WAAS
World Academy of Arts and Culture (EA) ... WAAC
World Acceptance [*NASDAQ symbol*] (TTSB) ... WRLD
World Acceptance Corp. [*Associated Press*] (SAG) ... WldAccep
World Acceptance Corp. [*Associated Press*] (SAG) ... WldAcp
World Acceptance Corp. [*NASDAQ symbol*] (SPSG) ... WRLD
World Access, Inc. [*NASDAQ symbol*] (SAG) ... WAXS
World Access, Inc. [*Associated Press*] (SAG) ... WrldAcc
World Action for Recycled Material and Energy from Rubbish (EERA) ... WARMER
World Administrative Radio Conference [*International Telecommunication Union*] (NTCM) ... WARC
World Administrative Radio Conference for Broadcast Satellite Service [*International Telecommunication Union*] (NTCM) ... WARC-BS
World Administrative Radio Conference for Maritime Mobile Telecommunications ... WARC-MAR
World Administrative Radio Conference for Space Communication ... WAR
World Administrative Radio Conference for Space Telecommunications ... WARC-ST
World Adoption International Fund ... WAIF
World Aerial Photographic Index [*Meteorology*] ... WAPI
World Aeronautical Chart (FAAC) ... WAC
World Affairs Center for the United States [*Later, FPA*] ... WAC
World Affairs Council of Northern California, San Francisco, CA [*Library symbol Library of Congress*] (LCLS) ... CSfWA
World Affairs Report [*Database*] [*California Institute of International Studies*] [*Information service or system*] (CRD) ... WAR
World Africa Chamber of Commerce (EA) ... WACC
World Against Toys Causing Harm ... WATCH
World Agricultural Outlook Board [*Department of Agriculture*] (GFGA) ... WAOB
World AIDS Foundation ... WAF
World Air Cargo Organisation (PDAA) ... WACO
World Air Network Co. Ltd. [*Japan ICAO designator*] (FAAC) ... WAC
World Aircraft Flight Operation, Inc. [*ICAO designator*] (FAAC) ... PEX
World Airline Entertainment Association ... WAEA
World Airline (Gambia) Ltd. [*ICAO designator*] (FAAC) ... WAG
World Airline Historical Society (EA) ... WAHS
World Airlines Clubs Association [*Montreal, PQ*] (EAIO) ... WACA
World Airlines Hobby Club (EA) ... WAHC
World Airways [*NASDAQ symbol*] (TTSB) ... WLDA
World Airways (GAVI) ... WO
World Airways [*ICAO designator*] (AD) ... WO
World Airways, Inc. [*NASDAQ symbol*] (SAG) ... WLDA
World Airways, Inc. [*Associated Press*] (SAG) ... WldAir
World Airways, Inc. [*ICAO designator*] (FAAC) ... WOA
World Airways, Inc. [*Air carrier designation symbol*] ... WRLX
World Alliance of Reformed Churches [*Alliance of the Reformed Churches th roughout the World Holding the Presbyterian System and International Congregational Council*] [*Formed by a merger of*] (EAIO) ... WARC
World Alliance of Young Men's Christian Associations [*Geneva, Switzerland*] (EAIO) ... WAYMCA
World Aluminum Abstracts [*Aluminum Association*] [*Information service or system A publication*] (IID) ... WAA
World Amateur Golf Council (EA) ... WAGC
World & I [*A publication*] (BRI) ... W&I
World Anti-Communist League [*South Korea*] (EAIO) ... WACL
World Apostolate of Fatima [*The Blue Army*] (EAIO) ... WAF
World Aquaculture Society (EA) ... WAS
World Aquathemes Ltd. [*Vancouver Stock Exchange symbol*] ... WDA
World Arabian Horse Organization [*Windermere, England*] (EAIO) ... WAHO
World Archaeological Society (EA) ... WAS
World Archeological Congress ... WAC
World Area Code (MCD) ... WAC
World Area Forecast Center [*Aviation*] (FAAC) ... WAFC
World Area Forecast System [*Meteorology*] ... WAFS
World Area Forecast System [*Marine science*] (OSRA) ... WAFS
World Area Grid (MCD) ... WAG
World Arm Wrestling Federation (EA) ... WAWF
World Around Songs (EA) ... WAS
World Artifex Society (EAIO) ... WAS
World Assembly of Muslim Youth [*Riyadh, Saudi Arabia*] (EAIO) ... WAMY
World Assembly of Small and Medium Enterprises [*See also AMPME*] [*India*] (EAIO) ... WASME
World Assembly of Youth [*Bronshoj, Denmark*] (EAIO) ... WAY
World Assistance Corps [*Paris, France*] (EAIO) ... WAC
World Association for Adult Education ... WAAE
World Association for Animal Production [*Rome, Italy*] (EAIO) ... WAAP
World Association for Buiatrics [*Hanover, Federal Republic of Germany*] (EAIO) ... WAB
World Association for Case Method Research and Application ... WACRA
World Association for Celebrating the Year 2000 [*British*] ... WACY 2000
World Association for Chinese Church Music (EAIO) ... WACCM
World Association for Christian Broadcasting (IAA) ... WACB
World Association for Christian Communication ... WACC
World Association for Dynamic Psychiatry (EAIO) ... WADP
World Association for Educational Research [*See also AMSE*] [*Ghent, Belgium*] (EAIO) ... WAER
World Association for Element Building and Prefabrication [*Hamburg, Federal Republic of Germany*] (EAIO) ... WAEP
World Association for Emergency and Disaster Medicine [*Bristol, England*] (EAIO) ... WAEDM
World Association for Hebrew Language and Culture (EAIO) ... WAHLC
World Association for Infant Psychiatry [*Later, WAIPAD*] (EA) ... WAIP
World Association for Infant Psychiatry and Allied Disciplines (EA) ... WAIPAD
World Association for Medical Informatics (IAA) ... WAMI
World Association for Psychosocial Rehabilitation (EAIO) ... WAPR
World Association for Psychosocial Rehabilitation - US Branch (EA) ... WAPR
World Association for Public Opinion Research (EA) ... WAPOR
World Association for Sexology (EA) ... WAS
World Association for Solid Waste Transfer and Exchange ... WASTE
World Association for the Advancement of Veterinary Parasitology [*Thessaloniki, Greece*] (EAIO) ... WAAVP
World Association for the History of Veterinary Medicine [*Hanover, Federal Republic of Germany*] (EAIO) ... WAHVM
World Association for World Federation [*Netherlands*] ... WAWF
World Association of Center Associates (EA) ... WACA
World Association of Christian Radio Amateurs and Listeners [*Hull, England*] (EAIO) ... WACRAL
World Association of Commercial and Special Vehicle Editors ... ACE
World Association of Cooks Societies (EA) ... WACS
World Association of Daily Vacation Bible Schools [*Later, VBS*] (EA) ... WADVBS
World Association of Detectives (EA) ... WAD
World Association of Document Examiners (EA) ... WADE
World Association of Esperanto Journalists [*See also TEJA*] [*Cittadella, Italy*] (EAIO) ... WAEJ
World Association of Girl Guides and Girl Scouts [*See also AMGE*] [*British*] (EAIO) ... WAGGGS
World Association of Industrial and Technological Research Organizations [*Arhus, Denmark*] ... WAITRO
World Association of Judges (EA) ... WAJ
World Association of Law Professors (EA) ... WALP
World Association of Law Students (EA) ... WALS
World Association of Lawyers (EA) ... WAL
World Association of Manufacturers and Distributors of Educational Materials (EAIO) ... WORLDDIDAC
World Association of Methodist Radio Amateurs and Clubs ... WAMRAC
World Association of Nuclear Operators (ECON) ... WANO
World Association of Pathology Societies ... WAPS
World Association of Societies of Pathology - Anatomic and Clinical (EA) ... WASP
World Association of Soil and Water Conservation (EA) ... WASWC
World Association of Travel Agencies (EAIO) ... WATA
World Association of Upper Silesians (EA) ... WAUS
World Association of Veteran Athletes (EAIO) ... WAVA
World Association of Veterinary Anatomists (EA) ... WAVA
World Association of Veterinary Food-Hygienists [*See also AMVHA*] [*Berlin, Federal Republic of Germany*] (EAIO) ... WAVFH
World Association of Veterinary Laboratory Diagnosticians (EAIO) ... WAVLD
World Association of Veterinary Microbiologists, Immunologists, and Specialists in Infectious Diseases [*See also AMVMI*] [*Maisons-Alfort, France*] (EAIO) ... WAVMI
World Association of Veterinary Pathologists (EAIO) ... WAVP
World Association on Sarcoidosis and Other Granulomatous Disorders (EAIO) ... WASOG
World Association to Remove Prejudice Against the Handicapped ... WARPATH
World Associations for Social Psychiatry (EA) ... WASP
World Atlatl Association (EA) ... WAA
World Bank ... WB
World Bank (EERA) ... WB
World Bank Atlas [*Monetary conversion rate*] (ECON) ... WA
World Bank Bond (MHDW) ... WBB
World Batch Forum (ACII) ... WBF
World Bicycle Polo Federation (EA) ... WBPF
World Billiards Union (EAIO) ... WBU
World Bird Sanctuary (EA) ... WBS
World Black and African Festival of Arts and Culture ... FESTAC
World Blind Union (EA) ... WBU
World Book - Childcraft International, Inc., Research Library, Chicago, IL [*OCLC symbol*] (OCLC) ... IPZ
World Book Congress ... WBC
World Book Encyclopaedia Science Service, Inc., Houston, TX [*Library symbol Library of Congress*] (LCLS) ... TxHWB
World Book-Childcraft International, Inc., Chicago, IL [*Library symbol Library of Congress*] (LCLS) ... ICWB
World Bottle [*Ecology*] ... WOBO
World Bowling Writers (EA) ... WBW
World Boxing Association [*Later, WBO*] (EA) ... WBA
World Boxing Council [*Information service or system*] (IID) ... WBC
World Boxing Organization (EA) ... WBO
World Bridge Federation ... WBF
World Broadcasting System (NTCM) ... WBS
World Brotherhood ... WB
World Buffalo Association Ltd. Agricultural Association (EA) ... WBA
World Bureau of Metal Statistics [*British*] (EAIO) ... WBMS
World Business Council [*Washington, DC*] (EA) ... WBC
World Business Directory [*A publication*] ... WBD
World Campus Afloat [*Cruise ship educational program*] (EA) ... WCA
World Cancer Research Fund ... WCRF
World Candlepin Bowling Council ... WCBC
World Catalog of International Chemical Equipment [*A publication*] ... WOICE
World Catholic Federation for the Biblical Apostolate [*Stuttgart, Federal Republic of Germany*] (EAIO) ... WCFBA
World Cement Industries [*Vancouver Stock Exchange symbol*] ... WDT
World Center for Islamic Education (EA) ... WCIE
World Centre for Scientific Information ... WCSI
World Centre for the Performing Arts ... WCPA
World Chamber of Commerce Service (EA) ... WCCS
World Champion (BARN) ... Wld Ch

World Championship Cutter and Chariot Racing Association (EA) ..... WCC&CRA
World Championship Tennis, Inc. ..... WCT
World Championship Wrestling ..... WCW
World Cheerleader Council (EA) ..... WCC
World Children's Day Foundation (EA) ..... WCDF
World Christian Action [*Australia*] ..... WCA
World Christian Encyclopedia [*A publication*] ..... WCE
World Christian Life Community [*Italy*] (EAIO) ..... WCLC
World Citizens Assembly [*Later, AWC*] (EA) ..... WCA
World Climate and Data Monitoring Program [*Marine science*] (OSRA) ..... WCDMP
World Climate Applications and Services Program (EERA) ..... WCASP
World Climate Applications Program [*WMO*] [*ICSU*] ..... WCAP
World Climate Data and Monitoring Program (EERA) ..... WCDMP
World Climate Data Information Referral Service [*World Meteorological Organization*] [*Information service or system*] (IID) ..... INFOCLIMA
World Climate Data Program [*WMO*] [*ICSU*] ..... WCDP
World Climate Impact Assessment and Response Strategies Program (EERA) ..... WCIRP
World Climate Impact Studies Program [*Marine science*] (OSRA) ..... WCIP
World Climate Impact Studies Program (EERA) ..... WCISP
World Climate Impacts Program [*WMO*] [*ICSU*] ..... WCIP
World Climate Program [*WMO*] [*ICSU*] ..... WCP
World Climate Research Program (EERA) ..... WCRP
World Climate Research Programme [*WMO*] [*ICSU*] ..... WCRP
World Climate System Monitoring Program [*Marine science*] (OSRA) ..... WCSMP
World Color Press [*NYSE symbol*] (TTSB) ..... WRC
World Commission on Environment and Development (EA) ..... WCED
World Committee for the United Nations Decade of Disabled Persons (EA) ..... WCUNDDP
World Committee for Trade Action [*See also CMAP*] [*Brussels, Belgium*] (EAIO) ..... WCTA
World Communication Association (EA) ..... WCA
World Communication Report [*Database*] [*UNESCO*] (DUND) ..... WCR
World Communications Year [*1983*] ..... WCY
[*The*] **World Community of Al-Islam in the West** ..... WCIW
World Community Projects (EA) ..... WCP
World Computer Graphics Association (EA) ..... WCGA
World Concern (EA) ..... WC
World Confederation for Physical Therapy [*British*] (EA) ..... WCPT
World Confederation of Billiards Sports [*Malaysia*] (EAIO) ..... WCBS
World Confederation of General Zionists [*Later, WCUZ*] (EA) ..... WCGZ
World Confederation of Jewish Community Centers (EA) ..... WCJCC
World Confederation of Labour [*See also CMT*] [*Brussels, Belgium*] (EAIO) ..... WCL
World Confederation of Organizations of the Teaching Profession [*Internat ional Federation of Secondary Teachers and IFTA*] [*Formed by a merger of*] (EAIO) ..... WCOTP
World Confederation of Productivity Science (EAIO) ..... WCPS
World Confederation of Teachers [*See also CSME*] [*Brussels, Belgium*] (EAIO) ..... WCT
World Confederation of United Zionists (EA) ..... WCUZ
World Conference of Animal Health Industries [*Australia*] ..... WCAHI
World Conference of Ashkenazi and Sephardi Synagogues ..... WCASS
World Conference of Jewish Communal Service (EA) ..... WCJCS
World Conference on Computers in Education ..... WCCE
World Conference on Missionary Radio [*Later, ICB*] (NTCM) ..... WCMR
World Conference on Non-Destructive Testing (PDAA) ..... WCNDT
World Conference on Religion and Peace (EAIO) ..... WCRP
World Conference on Religion and Peace, USA Section (EA) ..... WCRP/USA
World Congress Centre [*Melbourne, Australia*] ..... WCC
World Congress of Faiths - The Inter-Faith Fellowship [*British*] (EAIO) ..... WCF
World Congress of Flight ..... WCF
World Congress of Gay and Lesbian Jewish Organizations (EA) ..... WCGLJO
World Congress of Poets (EA) ..... WCP
World Congress of Professional Hypnotists (EA) ..... WCPH
World Congress of Sports Medicine ..... WCSM
World Congress of Teachers of Dancing (EA) ..... WCTD
World Congress on Computing [*Trade show*] ..... WCC
World Congress on Metal Finishing (PDAA) ..... WCMF
World Congress on Superconductivity [*An association*] ..... WCS
World Conservation Monitoring Centre [*Information service or system*] (IID) ..... WCMC
World Conservation Strategy (GNE) ..... WCS
World Conservation Union ..... IUCN
World Constitution and Parliament Association (EA) ..... WCPA
World Convention of Churches of Christ (EA) ..... WCCC
World Coordinate ..... WC
World Corp. [*Associated Press*] (SAG) ..... WrldCp
World Correctional Service Center (EA) ..... WCSC
World Council for Curriculum and Instruction (EA) ..... WCCI
World Council for Gifted and Talented Children (EA) ..... WCGTC
World Council for the Welfare of the Blind [*Later, WBU*] (EAIO) ..... WCWB
World Council of Blind Lions [*Later, ACBL*] (EA) ..... WCBL
World Council of Christian Education [*Later absorbed into Office of Education of World Council of Churches*] ..... WCCE
World Council of Christian Education and Sunday School Association [*Later, WCCE*] (EA) ..... WCCESSA
World Council of Christians [*Defunct*] (EA) ..... WCC
World Council of Churches [*Geneva, Switzerland*] ..... WCC
World Council of Churches Ecumenical Youth Service (EA) ..... EYS
World Council of Clergy [*Defunct*] (EA) ..... WCC
World Council of Comparative Education Societies (EA) ..... WCCES
World Council of Credit Unions [*Madison, WI*] (EA) ..... WOCCU
World Council of Indigenous Peoples [*Ottawa, ON*] (EAIO) ..... WCIP
World Council of Jewish Archives (EAIO) ..... WCJA
World Council of Peace (NATG) ..... WCP
World Council of Service Clubs [*New Zealand*] (EAIO) ..... WOCO
World Council of Synagogues (EA) ..... WCS
World Council of Young Men's Service Clubs (EA) ..... WOCO
World Council on Jewish Education ..... WCJE
World Court Clubs Association [*Defunct*] (EA) ..... WCCA
World Crafts Council (EA) ..... WCC
World Curling Federation [*British*] (EAIO) ..... WCF
World Dance Alliance ..... WDA
World Darts Federation (EAIO) ..... WDF
World Data Bank (NITA) WDB-1
World Data Center [*National Academy of Sciences*] [*Data collection and exchange center*] ..... WDC
World Data Center A [*National Academy of Sciences*] ..... WDC-A
World Data Center B [*National Academy of Sciences*] ..... WDC-B
World Data Center for Greenhouse Gases [*Marine science*] (OSRA) ..... WDCGG
World Data Centre on Micro-Organisms (EERA) ..... WDC
World Data Centre on Microorganisms (EERA) ..... WDCM
World Data Centres (EERA) ..... WDC
World Day for Peace (EA) ..... WDFP
World Deist Society (EA) ..... WDS
World Development Action [*An association British*] ..... WDA
World Development Corp. ..... WDC
World Development Movement [*British*] ..... WDM
World Dictionary of Awards and Prizes [*A publication*] ..... WDAP
World Digital Data for the Environmental Sciences (EERA) ..... WDDES
World Digital Database for Environmental Sciences [*Marine science*] (OSRA) ..... WDDES
World Diplomatic Guide [*A publication*] ..... WDG
World Disarmament Campaign (EAIO) ..... WDC
World Disarmament Conference (NATG) ..... WDC
World Diving Coaches Association (EA) ..... WDCA
World Draughts (Checkers) Federation [*See also FMJD*] [*Dordrecht, Netherlands*] (EAIO) ..... WDF
World Dredging Association (MSC) ..... WDA
World Dredging Conference ..... WODCON
World Druze Congress (EA) ..... WDC
World Ecologists Foundation [*Philippines*] (EAIO) ..... WE
World Economic Forum (EAIO) ..... WEF
World Economic Prospects (NITA) ..... WEP
World Economic Summit ..... WES
World Education (EA) ..... WEI
World Education Fellowship (EA) ..... WEF
World Education, Inc. ..... WE
World Electroless Nickel Society [*Defunct*] (EA) ..... WENS
World Electrotechnical Congress (PDAA) ..... WELC
World Employment Program [*of the International Labour Organization*] [*Geneva, Switzerland*] [*United Nations*] ..... WEP
World Encyclopedia of Recorded Music, 1925-55 [*A publication*] ..... WERM
World Endurance Championship [*Auto racing*] ..... WEC
World Energy Conference [*See also CME*] [*London, England*] (EAIO) ..... WEC
World Energy Council ..... WEC
World Energy Data System [*Department of Energy*] [*Information service or system*] (IID) ..... WENDS
World Energy Outlook [*International Energy Agency*] ..... WEO
World Energy Research Authority ..... WERA
World Environment Action Plan (EERA) ..... WEAP
World Environment and Resources Council [*Louvain, Belgium*] (EAIO) ..... WERC
World Environment Center (EA) ..... WEC
World Environment Centre (EERA) ..... WEC
World Environment Day ..... WED
World Environment Institute ..... WEI
World Equity Benchmark Shares [*AMEX symbol*] (SAG) ..... EWA
World Equity Benchmark Shares [*AMEX symbol*] (SAG) ..... EWC
World Equity Benchmark Shares [*AMEX symbol*] (SAG) ..... EWD
World Equity Benchmark Shares [*AMEX symbol*] (SAG) ..... EWG
World Equity Benchmark Shares [*AMEX symbol*] (SAG) ..... EWH
World Equity Benchmark Shares [*AMEX symbol*] (SAG) ..... EWI
World Equity Benchmark Shares [*AMEX symbol*] (SAG) ..... EWJ
World Equity Benchmark Shares [*AMEX symbol*] (SAG) ..... EWK
World Equity Benchmark Shares [*AMEX symbol*] (SAG) ..... EWL
World Equity Benchmark Shares [*AMEX symbol*] (SAG) ..... EWM
World Equity Benchmark Shares [*AMEX symbol*] (SAG) ..... EWN
World Equity Benchmark Shares [*AMEX symbol*] (SAG) ..... EWO
World Equity Benchmark Shares [*AMEX symbol*] (SAG) ..... EWP
World Equity Benchmark Shares [*AMEX symbol*] (SAG) ..... EWQ
World Equity Benchmark Shares [*AMEX symbol*] (SAG) ..... EWS
World Equity Benchmark Shares [*AMEX symbol*] (SAG) ..... EWU
World Equity Benchmark Shares [*AMEX symbol*] (SAG) ..... EWW
World Equity Benchmark Shares [*Associated Press*] (SAG) ..... WEB Bel
World Equity Benchmark Shares [*Associated Press*] (SAG) ..... WEB HK
World Equity Benchmark Shares [*Associated Press*] (SAG) ..... WEB Ita
World Equity Benchmark Shares [*Associated Press*] (SAG) ..... WEB Jpn
World Equity Benchmark Shares [*Associated Press*] (SAG) ..... WEB Mal
World Equity Benchmark Shares [*Associated Press*] (SAG) ..... WEB Mex
World Equity Benchmark Shares [*Associated Press*] (SAG) ..... WEB Net
World Equity Benchmark Shares [*Associated Press*] (SAG) ..... WEB Sing
World Equity Benchmark Shares [*Associated Press*] (SAG) ..... WEB Spn
World Equity Benchmark Shares [*Associated Press*] (SAG) ..... WEB Swd
World Equity Benchmark Shares [*Associated Press*] (SAG) ..... WEB Swz
World Equity Benchmark Shares [*Associated Press*] (SAG) ..... WEB UK
World Equity Benchmark Shares [*Associated Press*] (SAG) ..... WEBAstla
World Equity Benchmark Shares [*Associated Press*] (SAG) ..... WEBAstr
World Equity Benchmark Shares [*Associated Press*] (SAG) ..... WEBCan
World Equity Benchmark Shares [*Associated Press*] (SAG) ..... WEBFra

World Equity Benchmark Shares [*Associated Press*] (SAG) .... WEBGer
World Equity Benchmark Shares [*Investment term*] .... WEBS
World Esperantist Association for Education, Science, and Culture [*Germany*] (EAIO) .... WEADSC
World Esperantist Vegetarian Association [*See also TEVA*] [*Dublin, Republic of Ireland*] (EAIO) .... WEVA
World Evangelical Fellowship (EA) .... WEF
World Evangelism (EA) .... WE
World Event/Interaction Survey (DNAB) .... WEIS
World Export Processing Zones Association [*Flagstaff, AZ*] (EA) .... WEPZA
World Fast-Draw Association (EA) .... WFDA
World Fax Directory [*Information service or system*] (IID) .... WFD
World Federal Authority Committee [*Dundas, ON*] (EAIO) .... WFAC
World Federalist Association (EA) .... WFA
World Federalist Movement [*Netherlands*] (EAIO) .... WFM
World Federalist Youth [*Netherlands*] .... WFY
World Federalist Youth - United States of America [*Later, Action for World Community: World Federalist Youth in the USA*] (EA) .... WFY-USA
World Federalist Youth - Youth Movement for a New International Order [*Amsterdam, Netherlands*] (EAIO) .... WFY/NIO
World Federation for Culture Collections (EAIO) .... WFCC
World Federation for Medical Education (EA) .... WFME
World Federation for Mental Health (EA) .... WFMH
World Federation for Physical Therapy .... WFPT
World Federation for the Protection of Animals [*Also known as FMPA, WTB*] [*Later, WSPA*] .... WFPA
World Federation of Advertisers [*See also FMA*] [*Brussels, Belgium*] (EAIO) .... WFA
World Federation of Agricultural Workers [*See also FMTA*] (EAIO) .... WFAW
World Federation of Agriculture and Food Workers (EA) .... WFAFW
World Federation of Americans Abroad [*France*] (EAIO) .... WFAA
World Federation of Associations of Pediatric Surgeons [*Barcelona, Spain*] (EAIO) .... WFAPS
World Federation of Associations of YMCA Secretaries [*Nigeria*] (EAIO) .... WFAOS
World Federation of Baton Twirling and Majorette Associations (EA) .... WFBTMA
World Federation of Bergen-Belsen Associations (EA) .... WFBBA
World Federation of Building Service Contractors (EA) .... WFBSC
World Federation of Catholic Young Women and Girls [*Later, WFCY*] .... WFCYWG
World Federation of Catholic Youth .... WFCY
World Federation of Christian Life Communities [*See also FMCVC*] [*Rome, Italy*] (EAIO) .... WFCLC
World Federation of Czechoslovak Exile (EA) .... WFCE
World Federation of Dark Shadows Clubs (EA) .... WFDSC
World Federation of Democratic Women .... WFDW
World Federation of Democratic Youth [*See also FMJD*] [*Budapest, Hungary*] (EAIO) .... WFDY
World Federation of Development Financing Institutions [*See also FEMIDE*] [*Madrid, Spain*] (EAIO) .... WFDFI
World Federation of Diaconal Associations and Sisterhoods [*Germany*] (EAIO) .... DIAKONIA
World Federation of Direct Selling Associations [*Washington, DC*] (EA) .... WFDSA
World Federation of Doctors Who Respect Human Life [*Ostend, Belgium*] (EAIO) .... WFDWRHL
World Federation of Doctors Who Respect Human Life (United States Section) (EA) .... WFDRHL
World Federation of Educational Associations [*Later, WCOTP*] (EA) .... WFEA
World Federation of Engineering Organizations [*Paris, France*] .... WFEO
World Federation of Estonian Women's Clubs (EA) .... WFEWC
World Federation of Europeans (By Birth or Descent) (EA) .... WFE
World Federation of Free Latvians (EA) .... WFFL
World Federation of Friends of Museums [*See also FMAM*] [*Paris, France*] (EAIO) .... WFFM
World Federation of Health Agencies for the Advancement of Voluntary Surgical Contraception (EA) .... WFHAAVSC
World Federation of Hemophilia [*Montreal, PQ*] (EA) .... WFH
World Federation of Hungarian Artists (EA) .... WFHA
World Federation of Hungarian Freedom Fighters (EA) .... WFHFF
World Federation of Hungarian Jews (EA) .... WFHJ
World Federation of Industrial Workers' Unions .... WOFIWU
World Federation of International Music Competitions [*Switzerland*] (EAIO) .... WFICM
World Federation of International Music Competitions [*See also FMCIM*] (EAIO) .... WFIMC
World Federation of Investors (EAIO) .... WFI
World Federation of Iranian Students .... WFIS
World Federation of Islamic Missions [*Karachi, Pakistan*] (EAIO) .... WFIM
World Federation of Jewish Journalists [*Tel Aviv, Israel*] (EAIO) .... WFJJ
World Federation of Liberal and Radical Youth [*Later, IFLRY*] .... WFLRY
World Federation of Merino Breeders [*Australia*] .... WFMB
World Federation of Methodist Women [*Seoul, Republic of Korea*] (EAIO) .... WFMW
World Federation of Methodist Women, North America Area (EA) .... WFMWNAA
World Federation of Modern Language Teachers' Association (EA) .... WFMLTA
World Federation of Neurology (EA) .... WFN
World Federation of Neurosurgical Societies [*Nijmegen, Netherlands*] (EA) .... WFNS
World Federation of Nuclear Medicine and Biology (NUCP) .... WFNMB
World Federation of Occupational Therapists [*London, ON*] (EAIO) .... WFOT
World Federation of Parasitologists [*Bilthoven, Netherlands*] (EAIO) .... WFP
World Federation of Personnel Management Associations [*Alexandria, VA*] (EA) .... WFPMA
World Federation of Pipe Line Contractors Association (EA) .... WFPLCA
World Federation of Proprietary Medicine Manufacturers .... WFPMM
World Federation of Public Health Associations (EA) .... WFPHA
World Federation of Rose Societies [*Hurlingham, Argentina*] (EAIO) .... WFRS
World Federation of Scientific Workers [*See also FMTS*] [*ICSU*] [*British*] (EAIO) .... WFSW
World Federation of Societies of Anaesthesiologists [*Bristol, England*] (EAIO) .... WFSA
World Federation of Societies of Intensive and Critical Care Medicine (EAIO) .... WFSICCM
World Federation of Taiwanese Associations (EA) .... WFTA
World Federation of the Cossack National Liberation Movement [*Later, WFCNLMC*] (EA) .... WFCNLM
World Federation of the Cossack National Liberation Movement of Cossackia (EA) .... WFCNLMC
World Federation of the Deaf [*Rome, Italy*] .... WFD
World Federation of the Societies of Biological Psychiatry (EA) .... WFSBP
World Federation of the Sporting Goods Industry (EAIO) .... WFSGI
World Federation of Trade Unions [*See also FSM*] [*Prague, Czechoslovakia*] (EAIO) .... WFTU
World Federation of Trade Unions of Non-Manual Workers [*See also FMTNM*] [*Antwerp, Belguim*] (EAIO) .... WFNMW
World Federation of Trade Unions of Non-Manual Workers [*Belgium*] (EY) .... WFTUNMW
World Federation of Travel Journalists and Writers (EA) .... WFTJW
World Federation of Ukrainian Patriarchal Associations (EA) .... WFUPA
World Federation of Ukrainian Women's Organizations [*Toronto, ON*] (EA) .... WFUWO
World Federation of UNESCO Clubs and Associations .... WFUCA
World Federation of United Nations Associations (EA) .... WFUNA
World Federation of Workers in Food, Tobacco, and Hotel Industries [*See also FMATH*] (EAIO) .... WFFTH
World Fellowship of Buddhist Youth [*Bangkok, Thailand*] (EAIO) .... WFBY
World Fellowship of Buddhists [*Bangkok, Tahiland*] (EAIO) .... WFB
World Fellowship of Slavic Evangelical Christians (EA) .... WFSEC
World Fertility Survey [*Program*] .... WFS
World Flying Disc Federation (EAIO) .... WFDF
World Folk Music Association (EA) .... WFMA
World Food and Agricultural Outlook and Situation Board [*Department of Agriculture*] .... WFAOSB
World Food Council [*United Nations*] (EAIO) .... WFC
World Food Day [*October 16*] .... WFD
World Food Programme [*Rome, Italy*] [*United Nations*] .... WFP
World Food Programs (EERA) .... WFP
World Food Security [*FAO program*] [*United Nations*] .... WFS
World Footbag Association (EA) .... WFA
World Football League [*Dissolved, 1975*] .... WFL
World for Christ Crusade (EA) .... WCC
World Forest Institute (GNE) .... WFI
World Forestry Center (EA) .... WFC
World Friendship Association .... WFA
World Friendship Centre (EA) .... WFC
World Friendship Federation .... WFF
World Fuel Services [*NYSE symbol*] (TTSB) .... INT
World Fuel Services Corp. [*NYSE symbol*] (SAG) .... INT
World Fuel Services Corp. [*Associated Press*] (SAG) .... WldFuel
World Fundraising Council (NFD) .... WFC
World Future Society (EA) .... WFS
World Futures Studies Federation (EA) .... WFSF
World Games Coordination Committee [*Karsruhe, Federal Republic of Germany*] (EAIO) .... WGCC
World Games Council (EAIO) .... WGC
World Geodetic Spheroid 1984 (EERA) WGS84
World Geodetic System (MUGU) .... WGS
World Geophysical Interval .... WGI
World Glacier Inventory (EERA) .... WGI
World Glacier Monitoring Service [*of the International Union of Geodesy and Geophysics*] (EA) .... WGMS
World Goodwill (EA) .... WG
World Gospel Crusades (EA) .... WGC
World Gospel Mission (EA) .... WGM
World Government of the Age of Enlightenment - US (EA) .... WGAE-US
World Government Organization Coalition (EAIO) .... WGOC
World Government Organization Coordinating Council [*Later, WGOC*] (EA) .... WGOCC
World Government Sponsors .... WGS
World GRID Association (EA) .... WGRIDA
World Guide to Abbreviations of Organizations [*A publication*] .... WGAO
World Guide to Environmental Issues [*A publication*] .... WGEIO
World Guide to Libraries [*A publication*] .... WGL
World Health Foundation, United States of America [*Defunct*] (EA) .... WHF-USA
World Health Organization [*The pronunciation "who" is not acceptable*] [*United Nations affiliate Databank originator*] [*Switzerland*] .... WHO
World Health Organization International Reference Preparation (DAVI) .... WHOIRP
World Health Organization Library Information System (IID) .... WHOLIS
World Health Organization/Panafrican Centre for Emergency Preparedness and Response [*United Nations*] .... WHO/EPR
World Health Research Center .... WHRC
World Health Statistics Data Base [*World Health Organization*] [*Information service or system*] (IID) .... WHS
World Health Workers for Peace and NonIntervention in Latin America (EAIO) .... WHWPNLA
World Heart Corp. [*NASDAQ symbol*] (SAG) .... WHRT
World Heart Corp. [*Associated Press*] (SAG) .... WrldHrt

World Hemophilia AIDS [*Acquired Immune Deficiency Syndrome*] **Center** (EA) ... WHAC
World Hereford Council (EAIO) ... WHC
World Heritage (EERA) ... WH
World Heritage Area [*Commonwealth*] (EERA) ... WHA
World Heritage Committee [*See also CPM*] (EAIO) ... WHC
World Heritage Fund [*UNESCO*] ... WHF
World Heritage List [*UNESCO*] ... WHL
World Heritage Listing ... WHL
World Hobie Class Association [*Later, IHCA*] (EA) ... WHCA
World Hockey Association ... WHA
World Home Bible League [*Later, BL*] (EA) ... WHBL
World Housing Organization ... WHO
World Hunger Education Service (EA) ... WHES
World Hunger/Global Development Program [*Defunct*] (EA) ... WHGDP
World Hunger Year (EA) ... WHY
World Hydrocarbon Program (NITA) ... WHP
World Hydrological Cycle Observing System [*Marine science*] (OSRA) ... WHYCOS
World Ice Theory [*Hans Horbiger*] ... WIT
World Impact (EA) ... WI
World Impact Services (EA) ... WIS
World Index of Space Imagery [*Meteorology*] ... WISI
World Industry Conference on Environmental Management ... WICEM
World Industry Council for the Environment ... WICE
World Information Centre for Bilingual Education [*See also CMIEB*] [*Paris, France*] (EAIO) ... WICBE
World Information Management System [*Air Force*] (GFGA) ... WIMS
World Information Network [*Information service or system*] (IID) ... WIN
World Information Service on Energy (EA) ... WISE
World Information Synthesis and Encyclopaedia [*Project of American Association for the Advancement of Science and American Society for Information Science*] ... WISE
World Information System in Informatics (NITA) ... WISI
World Information Systems Exchange [*Defunct*] (EA) ... WISE
World Institute Council (EA) ... WIC
World Institute for Computer-Assisted Teaching (NITA) ... WICAT
World Institute for Development Economics Research [*United Nations*] ... WIDER
World Institute for Scientific Humanism [*Defunct*] (EA) ... WISH
World Institute for World Peace ... WIWP
World Institute of Black Communications (EA) ... WIBC
World Institute of Buddhist Culture ... IBC
World Institute of Ecology and Cancer [*See also IMEC*] (EAIO) ... WIEC
World Institute of Sephardic Studies (BJA) ... WISS
World Institute on Disability (EA) ... WID
World Insulation and Acoustic Congress Organization (EA) ... WIACO
World Integrated Nuclear Evaluation System [*Department of Energy*] (GFGA) ... WINES
World Intellectual Property Organisation [*of United Nations*] (EERA) ... WIPO
World Intellectual Property Organization [*Switzerland*] (IID) ... WIPO
World International Medical Association (EA) ... WIMA
World International Nail and Beauty Association (EA) ... WINBA
World Invitation Club Basketball Championships [*British*] ... WICBC
World Jazz Association [*Defunct*] (EA) ... WJA
World Jersey Cattle Bureau [*Jersey, Channel Islands, England*] ... WJCB
World Jewish Congress, American Section (EA) ... WJC
World Jewish Genealogy Organization (EA) ... WJGO
World Jewish Register [*A publication*] (BJA) ... WJR
World Journal, Ackley, IA [*Library symbol Library of Congress*] (LCLS) ... IaAcW
World Journal Tribune [*Defunct New York City afternoon newspaper*] ... WJT
World Jurist Association (EAIO) ... WJA
World Koala Research [*Australia*] ... WKR
World Laboratory Animal Liberation Week ... WLALW
World Land Use Survey [*International Geographical Union*] (BARN) ... WLUS
World Law Fund (EA) ... WLF
World Law Review [*A publication*] (DLA) ... WLR
World Law Review [*A publication*] (DLA) ... World L Rev
World League for Freedom and Democracy [*South Korea*] (EAIO) ... WLFD
World League for the Protection of Animals ... WLFPA
World League of American Football [*1991*] ... WLAF
World Leisure and Recreation Association [*Formerly, IRA*] (EA) ... WLRA
World List of Future International Meetings [*A publication*] ... WL
World List of Scientific Periodicals [*A publication*] (DIT) ... WLSP
World Listening Service (EA) ... WLS
World Literacy of Canada (EAIO) ... WLC
World Literary Academy (EAIO) ... WLA
World Literature Today [*A publication*] (BRI) ... WLT
World Magnetic Survey [*Defunct*] ... WMS
World Manufacturer Identifier ... WMI
World Manx Association ... WMA
World Mariculture Society (EA) ... WMS
World Maritime Administrative Radio Conference (DS) ... WMARC
World Maritime University [*Sweden*] (DCTA) ... WMU
World Markets [*British investment firm*] [*Formerly, Wood Mackenzie*] ... WM
World Markets for US Exports [*A publication*] ... WMUSE
World Martial Arts Association (EA) ... WMAA
World Masters Cross-Country Ski Association (EA) ... WMCCSA
World Medical Association [*Ferney-Voltaire, France*] ... WMA
World Medical Association for Perfect Health [*Also known as United States Association of Physicians*] (EA) ... WMAFPH
World Medical Mission (EA) ... WMM
World Medical Relief (EA) ... WMR
World Meeting Planners Congress and Exposition [*Defunct*] (EA) ... WMPCE
World Mental Health Year [*1960*] ... WMHY
World Mercy Fund (EA) ... WMF
World Metal Index [*Sheffield City Libraries*] [*British Information service or system*] (IID) ... WMI
World Meteorological Center [*World Meteorological Organization*] ... WMC
World Meteorological Intervals ... WMI
World Meteorological Office (NITA) ... WMO
World Meteorological Organization [*See also OMM*] [*Geneva, Switzerland*] [*United Nations*] (EAIO) ... WMO
World Methodist Council (EA) ... WMC
World Methodist Historical Society (EA) ... WMHS
World Microfilms Division, Oyez Equipment Ltd., London, United Kingdom [*Library symbol Library of Congress*] (LCLS) ... WmS
World Microfilms Publications, London, United Kingdom [*Library symbol Library of Congress*] (LCLS) ... WmP
World Ministries Commission (EA) ... WMC
World Mission Prayer League (EA) ... WMPL
World Missions Fellowship (EA) ... WMF
World Missions to Children [*Later, WMF*] (EA) ... WMC
World Modeling Association (EA) ... WMA
World Monetary Organization ... WMO
World Monitor [*Television program*] ... WM
World Monuments Fund (EA) ... WMF
World Movement of Christian Workers [*See also MMTC*] [*Brussels, Belgium*] (EAIO) ... WMCW
World Movement of Mothers [*See also MMM*] [*Paris, France*] (EAIO) ... WMM
World Muslim Congress (BJA) ... WMC
World Nature Association (EA) ... WNA
World Neighbors (EA) ... WN
World New Religion [*An association*] (EA) ... WNR
World News Network [*In Muriel Dobbin's novel "Going Live"*] ... WNN
World News Tonight [*Television program*] ... WNT
World Ninepin Bowling Association [*Germany*] (EAIO) ... WNBA
World Nuclear Fuel Market (NRCH) ... WNFM
World Ocean and Cruise Liner Society (EA) ... WOCLS
World Ocean Circulation Experiment [*World Climate Research Programme*] ... WOCE
World Ocean Watch [*Marine science*] (OSRA) ... WOW
World Oceanographic Center (MSC) ... WOC
World Oceanographic Data Display ... WODD
World Oceanographic Data Processing and Services Center (MSC) ... WOPC
World Oceanographic Organization ... WOO
[*The*] **World of Dark Shadows** (EA) ... TWODS
World of Invention [*A publication*] ... WOI
World of Learning [*A publication*] ... WL
World of Michael Jackson (EA) ... WMJ
World of Music, Arts, and Dance [*Festival*] (PCM) ... WOMAD
World of Outlaws [*Auto racing*] ... WOO
World of Scientific Discovery [*A publication*] ... WSD
World of Winners [*A publication*] ... WOW
World of Work [*Career-oriented course of study*] ... WOW
World Offshore Accident Data ... WOAD
World Oil Project [*Massachusetts Institute of Technology*] [*National Science Foundation*] (IID) ... WOP
World Opportunities International (EA) ... WOI
World Order Models Project ... WOMP
World Order Research Institute ... WORI
World Organisation of General Systems and Cybernetics [*Lytham St. Annes, Lancashire, England*] (EAIO) ... WOGSC
World Organisation of Systems and Cybernetics (EAIO) ... WOSC
World Organization for Human Potential (EA) ... WOHP
World Organization for Jews from Arab Countries (EA) ... WOJAC
World Organization of Automotive Hobbyists ... WOAH
World Organization of Building Officials (EA) ... WOBO
World Organization of China Painters (EA) ... WOCP
World Organization of Dredging Associations (EA) ... WODA
World Organization of Dredging Associations Proceedings of World Dredging Congress [*A publication*] (EAAP) ... WODCON
World Organization of Gastroenterology [*See also OMGE*] [*Edinburgh, Scotland*] (EAIO) ... WOG
World Organization of Jewish Deaf [*Tel Aviv, Israel*] (EAIO) ... WOJD
World Organization of Mothers of All Nations ... WOMAN
World Organization of National Colleges, Academies, and Academic Associations ofGeneral Practitioners/Family Physicians [*Australia*] (EAIO) ... WONCA
World Organization of the Ovulation Method - Billings, USA [*Later, Families of the Americas Foundation*] ... WOOMB
World Organization of the Teaching Professions [*Switzerland*] ... WOTP
World Organization to Restore Male Supremacy (EA) ... WORMS
World Outside Centrally Planned Economic Area [*Nuclear energy*] (NUCP) ... WOCA
World Outside Communist Areas ... WOCA
World Ozone Data Center [*Marine science*] (OSRA) ... WO3DC
World Ozone Data Center [*Marine science*] (OSRA) ... WODC
World Ozone Data Centre (EERA) ... WODC
World Packaging Organization [*See also OME*] [*Paris, France*] (EAIO) ... WPO
World Paper Currency Collectors (EA) ... WPCC
World Parliament Association ... WPA
World Patents Index [*Derwent Publications Ltd.*] [*Database*] ... WPI
World Peace Brigade (EA) ... WPB
World Peace Congress ... WPC
World Peace Council [*See also CMP*] (EAIO) ... WPC
World Peace Foundation (EA) ... WPF
World Peace One [*An association*] (EA) ... WPI
World Peace through Law Center (EA) ... WPTLC
World Peacemakers (EA) ... WP
World Pen Pals (EA) ... WPP

World Petroleum Congresses - a Forum for Petroleum Science, Technology, Economics, and Management (EAIO) .... WPC
World Pharmaceuticals Directory [A publication] .... WPD
World Pheasant Association [Reading, Berkshire, England] (EAIO) .... WPA
World Pheasant Association of the USA (EA) .... WPA-USA
World Philatelic Congress of Holy Land, Israel, and Judaica Societies (EA) .... WPC
World Philatelic Congress of Holy Land, Israel, and Judaica Societies (EA) .... WPCHLIJS
World Photography Society (EA) .... WPS
World Plan Executive Council [Later, WGAE-US] (EA) .... WPEC
World Planning Chart [Aviation] .... WPC
World Ploughing Organisation [Carlisle, Cumbria, England] (EAIO) .... WPO
World Poetry Society Intercontinental (EA) .... WPSI
World Policy Institute .... WPI
World Politics [A publication] (BRI) .... WP
World Politics Simulation .... WPS
World Pooling Committee (MCD) .... WPC
World Population Society (EA) .... WPS
World Population Year [1974] [United Nations] .... WPY
World Power Conference [Later, WEC] .... WPC
World Presbyterian Alliance .... WPA
World Presbyterian Missions (EA) .... WPM
World Press Freedom Committee (EA) .... WPFC
World Press Institute (EA) .... WPI
World Print Council (EA) .... WPC
World Priorities (EA) .... WP
World Pro Skiing-Racers Association [Defunct] (EA) .... WPS-RA
World Professional Armwrestling Association [Defunct] (EA) .... WPAWA
World Professional Billiards and Snooker Association (BARN) .... WPBSA
World Professional Karate Organization (DICI) .... WPKO
World Professional Squash Association (EA) .... WPSA
World Prohibition Federation .... WPF
World Proof Numismatic Association (EA) .... WPNA
World Psychiatric Association [Copenhagen, Denmark] (EAIO) .... WPA
World Pumpkin Confederation (EA) .... WPC
World Rabbinic Committee for the Preservation of Ancient Tombs in Tiberias (EA) .... WRCPATT
World Rabbit Science Association [Cheltenham, Gloucestershire, England] (EAIO) .... WRSA
World Radio Handbook .... WRH
World Radio Missionary Fellowship (EA) .... WRMF
World Radio TV Handbook [A publication] .... WRTH
World Rainforest Movement [Penang, Malaysia] (EAIO) .... WRM
World Rally Championship .... WRC
World Refugee Year .... WRY
World Register of Scientific Periodicals .... WRSP
World Rehabilitation Association for the Psycho-Socially Disabled (EA) .... WRASPD
World Rehabilitation Fund (EA) .... WRF
World Relief Canada .... WRC
World Relief Corp. (EA) .... WRC
World Reporter [World Council of Credit Unions] [A publication] .... WR
World Research Foundation (EA) .... WRF
World Research, Inc. [San Diego, CA] (EA) .... WRI
World Resources Institute (EA) .... WRI
World Risk Analysis Package [S. J. Rundt & Associates] [Information service or system] (IID) .... WRAP
World River [Geology] .... WR
World Road Association [Finland] (EAIO) .... WRA
World Robotic Boxing Association (EA) .... WRBA
World Roller Hockey League .... WRHL
World Romani Congress .... WRC
World Safety and Accident Prevention Congress (PDAA) .... WOSAPCON
World Safety Organization [United Nations] .... WSO
World Safety Research Institute .... WSRI
World Salt Foundation (EA) .... WSF
World Satellite Terminal [Telecommunications] (IAA) .... WST
World Science Fiction [France] (EAIO) .... WSF
World Science Fiction Society (EA) .... WSFS
World Scout Bureau [Geneva, Switzerland] (EA) .... WSB
World Scout Foundation [Geneva, Switzerland] (EA) .... WSF
World Secret Service Association [Later, WAD] (EA) .... WSSA
World Semiconductor Trade Statistics [Semiconductor Industry Association] [Information service or system] (IID) .... WSTS
World Sephardi Federation [See also FSM] [Geneva, Switzerland] (EAIO) ..... WSF
World Series Cricket .... WSC
World Service Authority, District 5: Orient-Mediterranean Sea Coast [Israel] .... WSA
World Service Authority of the World Government of World Citizens (EAIO) .... WGWC
World Service Authority of the World Government of World Citizens (EA) .... WSA-WGWC
World Service Television [BBC] (ECON) .... WSTV
World SF [Science Fiction] (EA) .... WSF
World Ship Society [Haywards Heath, West Sussex, England] .... WSS
World Ship Trust [Cambridge, England] .... WST
World Shortwave Listeners Club (EA) .... WSLC
World Showcase Fellowship Program [Walt Disney World] .... WSFP
World Sign Associates (EA) .... WSA
World Simulation Organization .... WSO
World Small Animal Veterinary Association [See also AMVPA] [Hatfield, Hertfordshire, England] (EAIO) .... WSAVA
World Socialist Party - Ireland [Political party] (EAIO) .... WSP-I
World Socialist Party of New Zealand [Political party] (EAIO) .... WSPNZ

World Socialist Party of the United States (EA) .... WSPUS
World Society for Stereotactic and Functional Neurosurgery (EA) .... WSSFN
World Society for the Protection of Animals [WFPA and ISPA] [Formed by a merger of] (EA) .... WSPA
World Solidarity [Belgium] (EAIO) .... WS
World Space Directory [A publication] .... WSD
World Space Foundation (EA) .... WSF
World Spanish Congress (EA) .... WSC
World Spiritual Council (EA) .... WSC
World Sports Medicine Association of Registered Therapists ..... WORLD SMART
World Sports Prototype Championship [Auto racing] .... WSPC
World Sportscar Championship [Auto racing] .... WSC
World Straw Conference .... WSC
World Strengthlifting Federation [India] (EAIO) .... WSF
World Student Christian Federation (EA) .... WSCF
World Students Relief .... WSR
World Studies Data Bank (IID) .... WSDB
World Sugar Research Organisation (EAIO) .... WSRO
World Synoptic Interval .... WSI
World System Teletext (NTCM) .... WST
World Systems Division [of Communications Satellite Corp.] [Telecommunications] (TEL) .... WSD
World Taekwondo Federation [Seoul, Republic of Korea] (EAIO) .... WTF
World Tape Pals (EA) .... WTP
World Tapes for Education [Defunct] .... WTE
World Tasar Class Association (EAIO) .... WTCA
World Team Tennis [League] .... WTT
World Technology Industry [Vancouver Stock Exchange symbol] .... WLD
World Teleport Association [New York, NY] [Telecommunications] (TSSD)..... WTA
World Terminal Synchronous (IAA) .... WTS
World Theosophical Youth Federation [Porto Alegre, Brazil] (EAIO) .... WTYF
World Timecapsule Fund (EA) .... WTF
World Tourism Organization [Madrid, Spain] .... WTO
World Trade (IAA) .... WT
World Trade Center [New York City] .... WTC
World Trade Center Arhus [Denmark] (EAIO) .... WTCA
World Trade Center Club Chongqing [China] .... WTCCQ
World Trade Center Geneva [Switzerland] (EAIO) .... WTCGV
World Trade Center Istanbul [Turkey] (EAIO) .... WTCIS
World Trade Center Korea .... WTCK
World Trade Center Libraries, San Francisco, CA [Library symbol Library of Congress] (LCLS) .... CSfWT
World Trade Center Metro Manila [Philippines] (EAIO) .... WTCMM
World Trade Center of Abidjan [Ivory Coast] (EAIO) .... WTCAJ
World Trade Center of New Orleans [New Orleans, LA] (EA) .... WTC
World Trade Center of Nigeria (EAIO) .... WTCN
World Trade Center Oslo [Norway] (EAIO) .... WTCO
World Trade Centers Association (EA) .... WTCA
World Trade Centre - Cyprus (EAIO) .... WTCCY
World Trade Centre Nanjing [China] (EAIO) .... WTCNJ
World Trade Directory [Department of Commerce] [A publication] .... WTD
World Trade Directory Reports [A publication Department of Commerce] .... WTDR
World Trade in Minerals Data Base System [Computer science] .... WTMS
World Trade Information Center (NITA) .... WTIC
World Trade Institute .... WTI
World Trade Law Journal [A publication] (DLA) .... World Trade LJ
World Trade Organisation (EERA) .... WTO
World Trade Organization [Trade and tariff regulation] (ECON) .... WTO
World Trade Resources Guide [A publication] .... WTRG
World Trade Statistics Database [Data-Star] [British Information service or system] (IID) .... TRADSTAT
World Trade Telegraph (IAA) .... WTTELE
World Trade Writers Association [New York, NY] (EA) .... WTWA
World Traders Data Report (AAGC) .... WTDR
World Translations Index [International Translations Centre] [Information service or system] .... WTI
World Travel Information Directory [A publication] .... WTID
World Travel Market [Trade show] [British] (ITD) .... WTM
World Underwater Federation (ASF) .... WUF
World Union [Pondicherry, India] (EA) .... WU
World Union for a Universal Alphabet (EA) .... WUUA
World Union for Progressive Judaism (EA) .... WUPJ
World Union for the Protection of Life [See also WSL-INT] (EAIO) .... WUPL-INT
World Union for the Safeguard of Youth .... WUSY
World Union of Black Writers [See also UEMN] (EAIO) .... WUBW
World Union of Catholic Philosophical Societies (EA) .... WUCPS
World Union of Catholic Teachers .... WUCT
World Union of Catholic Women's Organizations [Rosemere, PQ] (EAIO) .... WUCWO
World Union of Christian Democratic Women [Venezuela Political party] (EAIO) .... WUCDU
World Union of Free Romanians [See also UMRL] [Creteil, France] (EAIO) .... WUFR
World Union of Free Thinkers .... WUF
World Union of Free Trade Unions .... WUFTU
World Union of French-Speakers [See also UMVF] (EAIO) .... WUFS
World Union of Jewish Students [Jerusalem, Israel] .... WUJS
World Union of Karatedo Organizations [Solna, Sweden] (EAIO) .... WUKO
World Union of Liberal Trade Union Organisations [See also WFALW] [Zurich, Switzerland] (EAIO) .... WULTUO
World Union of Mapam [See also UMM] (EAIO) .... WUM
World Union of Martyred Towns, Peace Towns (EAIO) .... WUMTPT
World Union of National Socialists (EA) .... WUNS
World Union of Nigerians .... WUN

World Union of Organizations for the Safeguard of Youth [*Later, UMOSEA*] ..... WUOSY
World Union of Process Servers ..... WUPS
World Union of Pythagorean Organizations [*Ivybridge, Devonshire, England*] (EAIO) ..... WUPO
World Union of Stockholm Pioneers (EAIO) ..... WUSP
World Union of Tnuat Haherut Hatzorar [*Tel Aviv, Israel*] (EAIO) ..... WUTHH
World Union Saint Gabriel [*Esher, Surrey, England*] (EAIO) ..... WUSG
World United Formosans for Independence [*Political party*] (EY) ..... WUFI
World University, International Institute of the Americas, Barbosa Esq. Guayama,San Juan, PR [*Library symbol Library of Congress*] (LCLS) ..... PrSW-I
World University, Miami Learning Resource Center, Miami, FL [*OCLC symbol*] (OCLC) ..... WUF
World University Roundtable ..... WUR
World University, San Juan, PR [*Library symbol Library of Congress*] (LCLS) ..... PrSW
World University, San Juan, PR [*OCLC symbol*] (OCLC) ..... PRW
World University Service [*See also EUM*] [*Geneva, Switzerland*] (EAIO) ..... WUS
World University Service of Canada [*See also EUMC*] ..... WUSC
World University Service (United Kingdom) (DI) ..... WUS(UK)
World University Service/USA (EA) ..... WUS-US
World University-Miami, Miami, FL [*Library symbol Library of Congress*] (LCLS) ..... FMW
World Veterans Federation [*See also FMAC*] [*Paris, France*] (EAIO) ..... WVF
World Veterans Fund [*Defunct*] (EA) ..... WVF
World Veterinary Association [*See also AMV*] [*Madrid, Spain*] (EAIO) ..... WVA
World Veterinary Poultry Association [*See also AMVA*] [*Huntingdon, Cambridgeshire, England*] (EAIO) ..... WVPA
World Vision [*An association*] (EA) ..... WV
World Vision Australia ..... WVA
World Vision International ..... WVI
World War ..... WW
World War I ..... WWI
World War I Aeroplanes (EA) ..... WWI AERO
World War I Victory Medal [*Military decoration*] ..... WWIVM
World War II ..... WWII
World War II Equivalent [*Three-year and eight-month unit of time measurement proposed by former Under Secretary of the Navy R. James Woolsey*] ..... WOWATE
World War II Honorable Service Lapel Button (AFM) ..... WWIIHSLB
World War II Victory Medal [*Military decoration*] ..... WWIIVM
World War III ..... WWIII
World War Tank Corps Association (EA) ..... WWTCA
World Warning Agency (MCD) ..... WWA
World Watch Institute (EERA) ..... WWI
World Water Ski Union [*See also UMSN*] [*Montreux, Switzerland*] (EAIO) ..... WWSU
World Waterpark Association (EA) ..... WWA
World Watusi Association (EA) ..... WWA
World Weather Program [*National Science Foundation*] ..... WWP
World Weather System ..... WWS
World Weather Watch [*World Meteorological Organization*] [*Databank*] (IID) ..... WWW
World Weatherwatch [*Canada ICAO designator*] (FAAC) ..... XWW
World Wide Air Services [*Australia*] ..... WWAS
World Wide Airlines, Inc. ..... WWA
World Wide Avon Bottle Collectors Club (EA) ..... WWABCC
World Wide Baraca-Philathea Union (EA) ..... WWBPU
World Wide Company (MHDW) ..... WWC
World Wide Exchange [*Commercial firm*] (EA) ..... WWX
World Wide Fund for Nature [*Australia*] (EERA) ..... WWFA
World Wide Fund for Nature [*Australia*] ..... WWFN
World Wide Fund for Nature Australia ..... WWFNA
World Wide Horse Registry for the American White and the American Creme (EA) ..... WWHRAWAC
World Wide Military Command Control System Automated Data Processing ..... WAD
World Wide Minerals Ltd. [*Toronto Stock Exchange symbol Vancouver Stock Exchange symbol*] ..... WWS
World Wide Navigational Weather Warning Service ..... WWNWS
World Wide News Service (BJA) ..... WWNS
World Wide Pet Lovers Society [*Defunct*] (EA) ..... WWPLS
World Wide Time [*National Bureau of Standards call letters*] (MUGU) ..... WWV
World Wide Time Hawaii [*National Bureau of Standards call letters*] (MUGU) ..... WWVH
World Wide Vermiculture [*An association*] (EA) ..... WWV
World Wide Wait [*Computer science*] ..... WWW
World Wide Web [*Software*] [*Computer science*] (EERA) ..... WWW
World Wide Web Consortium [*Internet*] W3C
World Wide White and Creme Horse Registry (EA) ..... WWWCR
World Wildlife Fund (EA) ..... WWF
World Wildlife Fund International [*Later, Worldwide Fund for Nature*] (EAIO) ..... WWFI
World Wildlife Fund - United States (EA) ..... WWF-US
World without War Council (EA) ..... WWWC
World Women in the Environment [*Formerly, World Women in Defense of the Environment*] (EA) ..... WorldWIDE
World Young Women's Christian Association (DI) ..... WYWCA
World Young Women's Christian Association (EAIO) ..... YWCA
World Youth Congress on Food and Development (EAIO) ..... WYCFD
World Youth Crusade for Freedom (EA) ..... WYCF
World Youth Forum [*Defunct*] (EA) ..... WYF
World Zionist Organization [*Israel*] ..... WZO
World-Class Manufacturing [*Management technique*] ..... WCM
WorldCom, Inc. [*NASDAQ symbol*] (SAG) ..... WCOM
WorldCom, Inc. [*Associated Press*] (SAG) ..... WorldC
WorldCom, Inc. [*Associated Press*] (SAG) ..... WorldCm
WorldCorp., Inc. [*NYSE symbol*] (SPSG) ..... WOA
Worldloppet (EA) ..... WL
Worldmark Encyclopedia of the Nations [*A publication*] ..... WEN
Worldmark Encyclopedia of the States [*A publication*] ..... WES
World's Christian Endeavor Union (EA) ..... WCEU
World's Classics [*A publication*] ..... WC
World's Epoch Makers [*A publication*] ..... WEM
World's Fair Collectors Society (EA) ..... WFCS
World's Great Explorers [*A publication*] ..... WGE
World's Greatest Environment Statement (EERA) ..... WGES
World's Greatest Jazz Band ..... WGJB
World's Greatest Newspaper [*Sometimes used in reference to Chicago Tribune*] ..... WGN
Worlds of Wonder [*Electronic toy manufacturer*] ..... WOW
World's Oldest Socketed Tool [*Refers to archeological discovery of a tool dated 2500 BC*] ..... WOST
World's Poultry Science Association [*See also AVI*] [*Celle, Federal Republic of Germany*] (EAIO) ..... WPSA
World's Poultry Science Association, USA Branch (EA) ..... WPSA
World's Press News [*A publication*] (DGA) ..... WPN
World's Woman's Christian Temperance Union [*Australia*] (EAIO) ..... WWCTU
World's Wristwrestling Championship (EA) ..... WWC
WORLDSCALE [*Worldwide Tanker Nominal Freight Scale*] (DS) ..... w
Worldscale ..... WS
Worldtalk Communication Corp. [*Associated Press*] (SAG) ..... Wrldtalk
Worldtalk Communication Corp. [*NASDAQ symbol*] (SAG) ..... WTLK
Worldtalk Communications [*NASDAQ symbol*] (TTSB) ..... WTLK
Worldteam (EA) ..... WT
Worldtex, Inc. [*Associated Press*] (SAG) ..... Wldtex
Worldtex, Inc. [*NYSE symbol*] (SPSG) ..... WTX
Worldview International Foundation (EAIO) ..... WIF
WorldViews: A Quarterly Review of Resources for Education and Action [*A publication*] (BRI) ..... WorldV
Worldwatch Institute (EA) ..... WI
Worldways Canada Ltd. [*ICAO designator*] (FAAC) ..... WWC
Worldwide ..... WRLDWD
Worldwide ..... WW
World-Wide Academy of Scholars [*Defunct*] (EA) ..... WWAS
Worldwide Air Cargo Commodity Classification (DS) ..... WACCC
Worldwide Air Charter Systems [*Canada ICAO designator*] (FAAC) ..... CSW
Worldwide Airborne Command Post [*Air Force*] (AFM) ..... WWABNCP
Worldwide Airline Services, Inc. [*ICAO designator*] (FAAC) ..... LWD
Worldwide Ammunition Reporting Program (NG) ..... WARP
Worldwide Ammunition Reporting System [*Military*] ..... WARS
Worldwide Asset Position [*Military*] (AABC) ..... WWAP
Worldwide Assurance for Employees of Public Agencies [*Falls Church, VA*] (EA) ..... WAEPA
Worldwide Atmospheric Gravity Wave Study [*Ionospheric physics*] ..... WAGS
Worldwide AUTODIN [*Automatic Digital Information Network*] **Restoral Plan** (CET) ..... WARP
Worldwide Aviation Logistics Conference (RDA) ..... WALC
Worldwide Aviation Services Ltd. [*Venezuela*] [*ICAO designator*] (FAAC) ..... WWA
Worldwide Branch Locations of Multinational Companies [*A publication*] ..... WBLMC
Worldwide Church of God ..... WCG
Worldwide Collectors Club [*Later, ISWSC*] (EA) ..... WCC
World-Wide Command and Control Information System (MCD) ..... WWCCIS
Worldwide Creme Horse Registry (EA) ..... WCHR
Worldwide Crisis Alerting Network (MCD) ..... WCAN
Worldwide Data Management System ..... WWDMS
World-Wide Dave Clark Fan Club [*Defunct*] (EAIO) ..... WWDCFC
Worldwide Dental Health Service (EA) ..... WDHS
Worldwide Digital System Architecture ..... WWDSA
Worldwide Dollarvest Fund [*NYSE symbol*] (SAG) ..... WDV
Worldwide Dollarvest Fund [*Associated Press*] (SAG) ..... WldwDlr
World-Wide Education Service [*Parents' National Educational Union*] [*British*] ..... WES
Worldwide Energy Corp. [*Toronto Stock Exchange symbol*] (SPSG) ..... WWE
World-Wide Engineering Logistics Support [*Military*] ..... WELS
Worldwide Entertainment & Sports Cp. [*Associated Press*] (SAG) ..... WwE & S un
Worldwide Entertainment & Sports Cp. [*Associated Press*] (SAG) ..... WwE & Sp
Worldwide Entertainment & Sports Cp. [*NASDAQ symbol*] (SAG) ..... WWES
Worldwide Equities Ltd. [*Toronto Stock Exchange symbol*] ..... WOW
Worldwide Equities Ltd. [*Toronto Stock Exchange symbol*] ..... WW
Worldwide Evangelization Crusade (EA) ..... WEC
Worldwide Fair Play for Frogs Committee (EA) ..... WFPFC
Worldwide Fair Play for Frogs Committee ..... WWFC
Worldwide Fast for Peace [*An association Defunct*] (EA) ..... WFP
Worldwide Fiero Club (EA) ..... WFC
Worldwide Franchise Directory [*A publication*] ..... WFD
Worldwide Friendship International (EA) ..... WFI
WorldWide Fund for Nature (EA) ..... WWF
Worldwide Government Directory [*A publication*] ..... WGD
Worldwide Household Goods Information System for Traffic Management [*Army*] (AABC) ..... WHIST
Worldwide Improved Technical Control (MCD) ..... WWITC
Worldwide Indicators and Monitoring System (DOMA) ..... WWIMS
Worldwide Information and Trade System ..... WITS
World-Wide Information Service [*Information service or system*] (IID) ..... WISE
Worldwide Information Services ..... WWIS
Worldwide Information System [*Navy*] ..... WIS
Worldwide Integrated Communications [*Mohawk Data Sciences Corp.*] [*Parsippany, NJ*] [*Telecommunications*] (TSSD) ..... WINC
Worldwide Integrated Management of Subsistence ..... WIMS

Worldwide Integrated Management of Subsistence [*Military*] (NVT) .... WWIMS
Worldwide Intelligence Communication (MCD) .... INTELCOM
Worldwide Intelligence Communications System (MCD) .... WICS
Worldwide Interactive Trading System [*Information service or system*] (IT) .... WITS
Worldwide Inventory Objective (AABC) .... WWIO
Worldwide John Fogerty Fanclub (EAIO) .... WJFFC
Worldwide Joint Coordinator Center [*NATO*] (NATG) .... WWJCC
Worldwide Logistics Management Office [*Army*] .... WLMO
Worldwide Marriage Encounter (EA) .... WME
Worldwide Marriage Encounter (EA) .... WWME
Worldwide Military Command and Communications System [*Pronounced "wimex"*] .... WWMCCS
Worldwide Military Command and Control Information Systems, Joint Program Office .... WISJMPO
Worldwide Military Command and Control System [*DoD*] (MCD) .... WMCCS
Worldwide Military Command and Control System [*DoD*] .... WWMCCS
World-Wide Missions (EA) .... WWM
Worldwide Mobile Communications Routing Index (DNAB) .... WWRI
Worldwide Monitor [*Vancouver Stock Exchange symbol*] .... WWM
World-Wide Navigational Warning Service [*Marine science*] (OSRA) .... WWNWS
Worldwide Network of Standard Seismograph [*Stations*] .... WWNSS
Worldwide Network of Standard Seismograph Stations (PDAA) .... WWNSS
Worldwide News Service. Jewish Telegraphic Agency (BJA) .... WNS
Worldwide On-Line Data and Document Intelligence System .... WODDIN
Worldwide Operations Control Center [*United States Information Agency*] .... WOCC
Worldwide Organizational Structure for Army Medical Support (AABC) .... WORSAMS
Worldwide Pen Friends (EA) .... WPF
World-Wide Plantation Walker Registry (EA) .... WPWR
Worldwide Plug and Socket [*Proposed standard electrical plug for international use*] [*Pronounced "whoops"*] .... WPS
Worldwide Port System [*Army*] (RDA) .... WPS
World-Wide Prayer and Missionary Union (EA) .... WWPMU
Worldwide Radio Navigation Warning System [*Intergovernmental Maritime Consultative Organization*] (GFGA) .... WRNWS
Worldwide Satellite Observing Network (MCD) .... WSON
Worldwide Searches (EA) .... WS
Worldwide Secure Voice Architecture (MCD) .... WWSVA
World-Wide Secure Voice Communications System (MCD) .... WWSVCS
World-Wide Secure Voice Conference System (MCD) .... WWSVCS
Worldwide Seismology Net [*National Bureau of Standards*] .... WWSN
Worldwide Service Project .... WSP
World-Wide Software Support Branch (MCD) .... WWSSB
Worldwide Standard Data Management System (MCD) .... WWDMS
World-Wide Standard Seismograph Network [*Earthquake detection*] .... WWSSN
Worldwide Standardized Seismograph Network [*US Geological Survey*] .... WWSSN
World-Wide Stroke Foundation (EA) .... WWSF
Worldwide Surveillance Program [*Military*] (NG) .... WWSP
Worldwide Synchronization of Atomic Clocks .... WOSAC
Worldwide Tapetalk [*An association*] (EA) .... WWTT
Worldwide Technical Control Improvement Program (MCD) .... WWTCIP
Worldwide Television News Corp. (WDMC) .... WTN
Worldwide Television-FM DX Association (EA) .... WTFDA
Worldwide Travel Information Contact Book [*A publication*] .... WTICB
Worldwide Value Fund [*NYSE symbol*] (SPSG) .... VLU
Worldwide Value Fund [*Associated Press*] (SAG) .... WrldVl
Worldwide Warranty [*Canon USA, Inc.*] .... WWW
Worldwide Water Resources Database .... WRDB
World-Wide Web [*Information service*] [*European Organization for Nuclear Research*] (ECON) W3
World-Wide Web [*Telecommunications*] (PCM) .... WWW
Worldwide Women Professional Bowlers (EA) .... WWPB
Worldwide Wrestling Federation [*Later, WWF*] .... WWWF
Worm Community System [*Neurology database*] .... WCS
Worm Gear [*Mechanical engineering*] .... WMGR
Worm Gear Jack .... WGJ
Worm Gear Screw Jack .... WGSJ
Worm Runner's Digest [*A satirical publication*] .... WRD
Worm Screw Jack .... WSJ
Wormald International Sensory Aids (NITA) .... WISA
Worms [*Germany ICAO location identifier*] (ICLI) .... EDFV
Worms [*Germany ICAO location identifier*] (ICLI) .... EDOM
Wormshaft .... WMSFT
Wormwheel .... WMWHL
Worn by Astronaut [*NASA*] (KSC) .... WBA
Worn Out in Service [*Military*] .... WOIS
Worn-Out Wolf [*An aging philanderer*] [*Slang*] .... WOW
Worrall Publications, Inc., Orange, NJ [*Library symbol Library of Congress*] (LCLS) .... NjOW
Worrall Publishing Co., Maplewood, NJ [*Library symbol Library of Congress*] (LCLS) .... NjMapW
Worrall's Bibliotheca Legum [*A publication*] (DLA) .... Wor Bib Leg
Worry, Want, and Wickedness [*Causes of insanity, according to Victorian medical theory*] .... 3W's
Worse (FAAC) .... WRS
Worse Case Difference (IAA) .... WCD
Worse than Expected [*Politics*] .... WTE
Worship .... WP
Worship Arts Clearing House (EA) .... WACH
Worship Resources Office [*An association*] (EA) .... WRO
Worshipful [*Freemasonry*] .... W
Worshipful [*Freemasonry*] (ROG) .... WFL
Worshipful .... WOR
Worshipful (ROG) .... WPFL
Worshipful .... WPFUL
Worshipful .... WPL
Worshipful Brother [*Freemasonry*] .... W BRO
Worshipful Master [*Freemasonry*] .... WM
Worsley and District Library Society, Alberta [*Library symbol National Library of Canada*] (BIB) .... AWD
Worsley School, Alberta [*Library symbol National Library of Canada*] (BIB) .... AWORS
Worst Case Analysis .... WCA
Worst Case Circuit Analysis .... WCCA
Worst Cycle Quantity Level (PDAA) .... WCQL
Worst Injection Timing (PDAA) .... WIT
Worst Path Loss .... WPL
Worst Pattern (IAA) .... WP
Worst Possible Accident [*Nuclear safety*] .... WPA
Worst-on-Worst .... WOW
Worth Analysis Model (IEEE) .... WAM
Worth County Courthouse, Northwood, IA [*Library symbol Library of Congress*] (LCLS) .... IaNowdCoC
Worth County Courthouse, Northwood, IA [*Library symbol*] [*Library of Congress*] (LCLS) .... IaNowdWC
Worth Four-Dot Test [*Ophthalmology*] W4D
Worth Public Library District, Worth, IL [*Library symbol Library of Congress*] (LCLS) .... IWo
Worthiest Soldier in the Group .... WSG
Worthing [*City in England*] .... WRTHG
Worthington [*Minnesota*] [*Airport symbol*] (OAG) .... OTG
Worthington Biochemical Corp. [*Research code symbol*] .... EC
Worthington Christian School, Worthington, MN [*Library symbol*] [*Library of Congress*] (LCLS) .... MnWoWCS
Worthington Compressor & Engine International, Buffalo, NY [*Library symbol Library of Congress*] (LCLS) .... NBuW
Worthington Foods [*NASDAQ symbol*] (SAG) .... WFDS
Worthington Foods [*Associated Press*] (SAG) .... WorthFd
Worthington Foods, Inc. [*Associated Press*] (SAG) .... WortFds
Worthington Indus [*NASDAQ symbol*] (TTSB) .... WTHG
Worthington Industries [*Associated Press*] (SAG) .... Worthgtn
Worthington Industries, Inc. [*NASDAQ symbol*] (NQ) .... WTHG
Worthington Jefferson Township Public Library, Worthington, IN [*Library symbol Library of Congress*] (LCLS) .... InWo
Worthington Junior College [*Minnesota*] [*Later, Worthington Community College*] .... WJC
Worthington Junior High, Worthington, MN [*Library symbol*] [*Library of Congress*] (LCLS) .... MnWoJH
Worthington, MN [*FM radio station call letters*] (RBYB) .... KITN
Worthington, MN [*Television station call letters*] (RBYB) .... KSMN
Worthington, MN [*AM radio station call letters*] .... KWOA
Worthington, MN [*FM radio station call letters*] .... KWOA-FM
Worthington Public Library, Worthington, OH [*Library symbol*] [*Library of Congress*] (LCLS) .... OWor
Worthington Public Library, Worthington, OH [*OCLC symbol*] (OCLC) .... OWR
Worthington Regional Hospital, Worthington, MN [*Library symbol*] [*Library of Congress*] (LCLS) .... MnWoH
Worthington Register [*Defunct*] (EA) .... WR
Worthington Senior High School, Worthington, MN [*Library symbol*] [*Library of Congress*] (LCLS) .... MnWoSH
Worthington State Junior College [*Later, Worthington Community College*], Worthington, MN [*Library symbol Library of Congress*] (LCLS) .... MnWoS
Worthington Times, Worthington, IN [*Library symbol Library of Congress*] (LCLS) .... InWoT
Worthington-Marshall, MN [*FM radio station call letters*] .... KRSW
Worthington's General Precedent for Wills [*5th ed.*] [*1852*] [*A publication*] (DLA) .... Worth Prec Wills
Worthington's Power of Juries [*1825*] [*A publication*] (DLA) .... Worth Jur
Worthy Chief Templar .... WCT
Worthy Grand Chaplain [*Freemasonry*] .... WGC
Worthy Grand Conductor [*Freemasonry*] (ROG) .... WGC
Worthy Grand Guardian [*Freemasonry*] .... WGG
Worthy Grand Guide [*Freemasonry*] .... WGG
Worthy Grand Herald [*Freemasonry*] .... WGH
Worthy Grand Marshal [*or Master*] [*Freemasonry*] .... WGM
Worthy Grand Sentinel [*Freemasonry*] .... WGS
Worthy Patriarch .... WP
Worthy Sister (BJA) .... WS
Worton, MD [*FM radio station call letters*] .... WKHS
Wotho [*Marshall Islands*] [*Airport symbol*] (OAG) .... WTO
Wotje [*Marshall Islands*] [*Airport symbol*] (OAG) .... WTE
Wotquenne Catalog [*Used to catalog music of C.P.E Bach*] (BARN) .... WQ
Wotton. Leges Wallicae [*A publication*] (DLA) .... Wott Leg Wal
Would .... WD
Wouldn't It Be Nice If [*Computer hacker terminology*] (NHD) .... WIBNI
Wound (AAMN) .... WD
Wound (MSA) .... WND
Wound Angiogensis Factor [*Biochemistry*] .... WAF
Wound Data Munitions Effectiveness Team (MCD) .... WDMET
Wound Elastomeric Insulation (MCD) .... WEI
Wound Fluid [*Emergency Medicine*] (DAVI) .... WOFL
Wound Glass Fiber .... WGF
Wound Healing Society .... WHS
Wound, Missile [*Military*] (DAVI) .... W/M
Wound of Entry [*Medicine*] .... WOE
Wound, Skin, Enteric [*Isolation*] [*Medicine*] .... WSE
Wound Tumor Virus [*Plant pathology*] .... WTV

Wound Width [*Forestry*] ... WW
Wounded [*Military*] ... WDED
Wounded by Hostile Action ... WHA
Wounded in Action [*Military*] ... WIA
Wounds ... WDS
Wounds Received in Action [*Incurred in*] **Combat with the Enemy or in Line of Duty** [*Army*] (AABC) ... WRACELD
Woven (VRA) ... wv
Woven ... WVN
Woven Elastic Manufacturers Association [*Later, EFMCNTA*] (MSA) ... WEM
Woven Elastic Manufacturers Association [*Later, EFMCNTA*] (EA) ... WEMA
Woven Fabric Belting Manufacturers Association (EA) ... WFBMA
Woven Integrated Structure Laminates [*Army*] ... WISL
Woven Wire Cloth ... WWC
Woven Wire Products Association (EA) ... WWPA
Wow and Flutter ... W/F
WPC [*Walter P. Chrysler*] **Club** (EA) ... WPCC
WPI Group [*NASDAQ symbol*] (TTSB) ... WPIC
WPI Group, Inc. [*Associated Press*] (SAG) ... WPI Grp
WPI Group, Inc. [*NASDAQ symbol*] (SAG) ... WPIC
WPL Holdings [*NYSE symbol*] (SPSG) ... WPH
WPL Holdings [*Associated Press*] (SAG) ... WPL H
WPP Group ADS [*NASDAQ symbol*] (TTSB) ... WPPGY
WPP Group PLC [*NASDAQ symbol*] (SAG) ... WPGDY
WPP Group PLC [*Associated Press*] (SAG) ... WPP Gp
WPP Group PLC [*Associated Press*] (SAG) ... WPP Grp
WPP Group PLC [*NASDAQ symbol*] (SAG) ... WPPG
WPS Resources [*NYSE symbol*] (TTSB) ... WPS
WPS Resources Corp. [*NYSE symbol*] (SAG) ... WPS
WPS Resources Corp. [*Associated Press*] (SAG) ... WPS Res
W.R. Grace & Co., Cryovac Division Technical Library, Duncan, SC [*Library symbol*] [*Library of Congress*] (LCLS) ... ScDunG
WRA, Inc. [*ICAO designator*] (FAAC) ... WRR
WRAF [*Women's Royal Naval Air Force*] **Staff Officer** [*British military*] (DMA) ... WSO
Wrangell [*Alaska*] [*Airport symbol*] (OAG) ... WRG
Wrangell, AK [*FM radio station call letters*] ... KSTK
Wrangell, AK [*Location identifier FAA*] (FAAL) ... RGL
Wrangell, AK [*Location identifier FAA*] (FAAL) ... WRG
Wrangell Public Library, Wrangell, AK [*Library symbol Library of Congress*] (LCLS) ... AkW
Wrangler (ROG) ... WRANG
Wrangler Aviation, Inc. [*FAA designator*] (FAAC) ... TDX
Wrangler Aviation, Inc. [*ICAO designator*] (FAAC) ... WRN
Wrap ... WR
Wrap-Around Fin Rocket (MCD) ... WAFR
Wrap-Around Folding Fin (MCD) ... WAFF
Wrap-Around Simulation Program [*Military*] (CAAL) ... WASP
Wrap-Around-Fin (PDAA) ... WAF
Wrapped ... WRPPD
Wrapper ... WRPR
Wrap-Spring Clutch ... WSC
Wrath of God [*Israeli counterterrorist group*] ... WOG
Wrath of God Syndrome ... WOGS
Wray, CO [*FM radio station call letters*] ... KATR
Wray, CO [*AM radio station call letters*] ... KRDZ
Wray Public Library, Wray, CO [*Library symbol Library of Congress*] (LCLS) ... CoWr
Wreath (WGA) ... WR
Wreck [*Nautical charts*] ... Wk
Wrecker (AAG) ... WKR
Wrecker ... WRCKR
Wrecker ... WRK
Wrecking ... WRCKG
Wredeby [*Finland ICAO location identifier*] (ICLI) ... EFWB
Wredemann-Frang Law ... WFL
Wreigie Memorial Library, Oxford Junction, IA [*Library symbol Library of Congress*] (LCLS) ... IaOxj
WREN [*Women's Royal Naval Service*] **Air Mechanic** [*British military*] (DMA) ... WRENAM
WREN [*Women's Royal Naval Service*] **Assistant Cook** [*British military*] (DMA) ... WRENACK
WREN [*Women's Royal Naval Service*] **Cinema Operator (Able)** [*British military*] (DMA) ... WRENCINE(AB)
WREN [*Women's Royal Naval Service*] **Cinema Operator (Ordinary)** [*British military*] (DMA) ... WRENCINE(ORD)
WREN [*Women's Royal Naval Service*] **Cook** [*British military*] (DMA) ... WRENCK
WREN [*Women's Royal Naval Service*] **Dental Hygienist** [*British military*] (DMA) ... WRENDHYG
WREN [*Women's Royal Naval Service*] **Dental Surgery Assistant** [*British military*] (DMA) ... WRENDSA
WREN [*Women's Royal Naval Service*] **Education Assistant** [*British military*] (DMA) ... WRENEDUC
WREN [*Women's Royal Naval Service*] **Meteorological Observer** [*British military*] (DMA) ... WRENMET
WREN [*Women's Royal Naval Service*] **Motor Transport Driver** [*British military*] (DMA) ... WRENMT
WREN [*Women's Royal Naval Service*] **Photographer** [*British military*] (DMA) ... WRENPHOT
WREN [*Women's Royal Naval Service*] **Quarters Assistant** [*British military*] (DMA) ... WRENQA
WREN [*Women's Royal Naval Service*] **(RADAR)** [*British military*] (DMA) ... WREN(R)
WREN [*Women's Royal Naval Service*] **Radio Electrical Mechanic** [*British military*] (DMA) ... WRENREM
WREN [*Women's Royal Naval Service*] **Radio Operator (Morse) 1st Class** [*British military*] (DMA) ... WRENRO(M)1
WREN [*Women's Royal Naval Service*] **Radio Operator (Morse) 2nd Class** [*British military*] (DMA) ... WRENRO(M)2
WREN [*Women's Royal Naval Service*] **Regulating** [*British military*] (DMA) ... WRENREG
Wren Resources Ltd. [*Vancouver Stock Exchange symbol*] ... WNS
WREN [*Women's Royal Naval Service*] **Steward** [*British military*] (DMA) ... WRENSTD
WREN [*Women's Royal Naval Service*] **Stores Accountant** [*British military*] (DMA) ... WRENSA
WREN [*Women's Royal Naval Service*] **Stores Assistant (Clothes)** [*British military*] (DMA) ... WRENS(C)
WREN [*Women's Royal Naval Service*] **Stores Assistant (Stores)** [*British military*] (DMA) ... WRENS(S)
WREN [*Women's Royal Naval Service*] **Stores Assistant (Victualling)** [*British military*] (DMA) ... WRENS(V)
WREN [*Women's Royal Naval Service*] **Telephonist** [*British military*] (DMA) ... WRENTEL
WREN [*Women's Royal Naval Service*] **Training Support Assistant** [*British military*] (DMA) ... WRENTSA
WREN [*Women's Royal Naval Service*] **Weapon Analyst** [*British military*] (DMA) ... WRENWA
WREN [*Women's Royal Naval Service*] **Writer (General)** [*British military*] (DMA) ... WRENWTR(G)
WREN [*Women's Royal Naval Service*] **Writer (Pay)** [*British military*] (DMA) ... WRENWTR(P)
WREN [*Women's Royal Naval Service*] **Writer (Shorthand)** [*British military*] (DMA) ... WRENWTR(S)
Wrench (MSA) ... WR
Wrens, GA [*FM radio station call letters*] ... WAKB
Wrens, GA [*Television station call letters*] ... WCES
Wren's Nest [*Joel Chandler Harris Home*], Atlanta, GA [*Library symbol Library of Congress*] (LCLS) ... GAH
Wrenshall Public School, Wrenshall, MN [*Library symbol*] [*Library of Congress*] (LCLS) ... MnWreS
Wrexham [*City in Wales*] ... WREX
Wrexham/Borras [*British ICAO location identifier*] (ICLI) ... EGCE
Wrexham Public Library, Wrexham, United Kingdom [*Library symbol Library of Congress*] (LCLS) ... UkWr
Wriezen [*Germany ICAO location identifier*] (ICLI) ... ETWN
Wright [*Blood group*] ... Wr
Wright Aero Medical Laboratory [*Air Force*] ... WAML
Wright Aeronautical Corp. (KSC) ... WA
Wright Aeronautical Corp. (MCD) ... WAC
Wright Aeronautical Division [*Curtiss-Wright Corp.*] ... WAD
Wright Aeronautical Laboratories (MCD) ... WAL
Wright Air Development Center [*Air Force*] ... WADC
Wright Air Development Division [*Air Force*] ... WADD
Wright Air Lines, Inc. [*ICAO designator*] (FAAC) ... WRT
Wright Brothers Memorial Wind Tunnel [*Massachusetts Institute of Technology*] [*Research center*] (RCD) ... WBWT
Wright Brothers National Memorial ... WRBR
Wright Center of Laboratories ... WCL
Wright County Historical Society, Buffalo, MN [*Library symbol*] [*Library of Congress*] (LCLS) ... MnBfHi
Wright County Monitor, Clarion, IA [*Library symbol Library of Congress*] (LCLS) ... IaClaM
Wright Dust Feed Mechanism (PDAA) ... WDFM
Wright Institute, Berkeley, CA [*Library symbol Library of Congress*] (LCLS) ... CBWI
Wright International Express, Inc. [*ICAO designator*] (FAAC) ... DWW
Wright Investors' Service [*Information service or system*] (IID) ... WIS
Wright on Tenures [*A publication*] (DLA) ... Wright Ten
Wright Peak Flow [*Medicine*] (DAVI) ... WPF
Wright Peak Flow [*Medicine*] (DAVI) ... WPK
Wright Peak Flow Meter [*Medicine*] (DAVI) ... WPFM
Wright Research and Development Center [*Wright-Patterson Air Force Base*] (GRD) ... WRDC
Wright State, Celina Branch, Celina, OH [*OCLC symbol*] (OCLC) ... WSC
Wright State University (GAGS) ... Wright St U
Wright State University, Dayton, OH [*Library symbol Library of Congress*] (LCLS) ... ODaWU
Wright State University, Dayton, OH [*OCLC symbol*] (OCLC) ... WSU
Wright State University, Health Sciences Library, Dayton, OH [*OCLC symbol*] (OCLC) ... WSM
Wright State University, Piqua Branch Campus, Piqua, OH [*Library symbol Library of Congress*] (LCLS) ... OPiWU
Wright State University, Piqua Branch Campus, Piqua, OH [*OCLC symbol*] (OCLC) ... WSP
Wright State University, School of Medicine, Fordham Library, Dayton, OH [*Library symbol Library of Congress*] (LCLS) ... ODaWU-H
Wright State University, Western Ohio Branch Campus, Celina, OH [*Library symbol Library of Congress*] (LCLS) ... ODaWU-W
Wright Vocational Coop Center, Buffalo, MN [*Library symbol*] [*Library of Congress*] (LCLS) ... MnBfW
Wright-Giemsa [*A stain*] [*Cytology*] ... WG
Wright-Hargreaves Mines Ltd. [*Toronto Stock Exchange symbol*] (SPSG) ... WRT
Wright-Patterson Air Force Base [*Ohio*] ... WPAFB
Wright-Patterson Contracting Center [*Ohio*] [*Air Force*] ... WPCC
Wright's Advice on the Study of the Law [*A publication*] (DLA) ... Wright St L
Wright's Criminal Conspiracies [*1873*] [*A publication*] (DLA) ... Wright Cr Cons
Wright's Introduction to the Law of Tenures [*A publication*] (DLA) ... W Ten
Wright's Ohio Nisi Prius Reports [*A publication*] (DLA) ... Wright NP
Wright's Ohio Reports [*1831-34*] [*A publication*] (DLA) ... W

Wright's Ohio Reports [*1831-34*] [*A publication*] (DLA) .... Wr Ch
Wright's Ohio Reports [*A publication*] (DLA) .... Wr Ohio
Wright's Ohio Reports [*1831-34*] [*A publication*] (DLA) .... Wright
Wright's Ohio Reports [*1831-34*] [*A publication*] (DLA) .... Wright Ch
Wright's Ohio Reports [*A publication*] (DLA) .... Wright (Ohio C)
Wright's Ohio Reports [*A publication*] (DLA) .... Wright R
Wright's Ohio Reports [*A publication*] (DLA) .... Wright's Rep
Wright's Reports [*37-50 Pennsylvania*] [*A publication*] (DLA) .... Wr
Wright's Reports [*37-50 Pennsylvania*] [*A publication*] (DLA) .... Wr PA
Wright's Reports [*37-50 Pennsylvania*] [*A publication*] (DLA) .... Wright
Wright's Tennessee Chancery Appeals Reports [*A publication*] (DLA) .... Chy App Rep
Wright's Tennessee Chancery Appeals Reports [*A publication*] (DLA) .... Tenn Ch Ap Reps
Wrightstown/McGuire Air Force Base [*New Jersey*] [*ICAO location identifier*] (ICLI) .... KWRI
Wrightstown, NJ [*Location identifier FAA*] (FAAL) .... GXU
Wrightstown, NJ [*Location identifier FAA*] (FAAL) .... JTQ
Wrightstown, NJ [*Location identifier FAA*] (FAAL) .... WRI
Wrightsville & Tennille R. R. [*AAR code*] .... WTR
Wrightsville & Tennille Railroad (IIA) .... W & T
Wrightsville, AR [*FM radio station call letters*] .... KYTN
Wrightsville Beach Test Facility [*Department of the Interior*] (NOAA) .... WBTF
Wrightsville, GA [*FM radio station call letters*] .... WDBN
Wrightsville Marine Biomedical Laboratory .... WMBL
Wrigley [*Canada*] [*Airport symbol*] (OAG) .... YWY
Wrigley [*Wm.*] **Jr. Co.** [*Associated Press*] (SAG) .... Wrigley
Wrigley [*Wm.*] **Jr. Co.** [*NYSE symbol*] (SPSG) .... WWY
Wrigley, NT [*ICAO location identifier*] (ICLI) .... CYWY
Wrigley,(Wm) Jr [*NYSE symbol*] (TTSB) .... WWY
Wrin, T. J., San Francisco CA [*STAC*] .... WTJ
Wringer .... WRGR
Wrinkle Recovery Angle (IAA) .... WRA
Wrinkled Paper (BARN) XX
Wrist [*Medicine*] .... WR
Wrist Disarticulation [*Medicine*] .... WD
Wrist Extension [*Sports medicine*] .... WEXT
Wrist Pin .... WSTPN
Wrist Pitch (MCD) .... WP
Wrist Roll (NASA) .... WR
Wrist Yaw (MCD) .... WY
Wrist-Hand Orthosis [*Medicine*] .... WHO
Writ of Assistance [*Legal term*] (DLA) .... Assist
Writ of Mandamus Will Issue [*Legal term*] (DLA) .... MI
Writable Character Generation Memory (NITA) .... WCGM
Writable Character Generation Module [*Computer science*] (BUR) .... WCGM
Writable Control Memory [*Computer science*] (BUR) .... WCM
Writable Control Storage [*Computer science*] .... WCS
Writable Diagnostic Control Store .... WDCS
Writable Instruction Set Computer [*Term coined by Phil Koopman, Jr.*] (BYTE) .... WISC
Write .... W
Write .... WR
Write Access Key .... WAK
Write Address Counter .... WAC
Write and Compute .... WC
Write Anywhere File Layout [*Network Appliance Corp.*] [*Computer science*] .... WAFL
Write Back and Invalidate Data [*Cache*] [*Computer instruction*] (PCM) .... WBINVD
Write Buffer .... WB
Write Check [*Computer science*] (IAA) .... WRCHK
Write Circuit for Queuing Messages [*Computer science*] (IAA) .... WOM
Write Control Character [*Computer science*] (IAA) .... WCC
Write Data .... WD
Write Data Check (CMD) .... WDC
Write Direct .... WD
Write Drum .... WDR
Write Enable [*Computer science*] (IEEE) .... WE
Write Enable [*Computer science*] (IAA) .... WEN
Write Enable/Program [*Computer science*] .... WE/PGM
Write End of File (SAA) .... WEF
Write Fault (MHDB) .... WF
Write Forward .... WF
Write Gate (MHDB) .... WG
Write Head Driver (SAA) .... WHD
Write Interface Unit .... WRIU
Write Machine-Specific Register [*Computer science*] .... WRMSR
Write Once [*Computer science*] (CDE) .... WO
Write Once Optical Disk (NITA) .... WOOD
Write Once, Read Mainly [*or Many Times, or Mostly*] [*Computer science*] .... WORM
Write Once, Read Many Compact Disk (EERA) .... WORM CD
Write Once, Read Never [*Computer science*] .... WORN
Write Once, Write Mostly [*Computer science*] (IAA) .... WOWM
Write Only .... WO
Write Optional Memory (IEEE) .... WOM
Write Out .... WO
Write Permit (NITA) .... WP
Write Permit Ring (NITA) .... WPR
Write Precompensation [*Computer science*] (CDE) .... WPcom
Write Printer Binary .... WPB
Write Printer Decimal .... WPD
Write Program Memory [*Computer science*] .... WPM
Write Protect .... WP
Write Protect [*Computer science*] (MHDB) .... WRPT
Write Protect Memory .... WPM
Write Punch [*Computer science*] (MCD) .... WPN
Write Punch [*Computer science*] .... WPU
Write Strobe .... WRS
Write Symbol Table .... WST
Write Tape Binary [*Computer science*] (IAA) .... WTB
Write Tape Decimal (IAA) .... WTD
[*The*] **Write Thing** [*An association*] (EA) .... TWT
Write Through [*Computer science*] (PCM) .... WT
Write Your Congressman Club (EA) .... WYCC
Write-After-Write [*Computer science*] .... WAW
Write-Back [*Computer science*] (PCM) .... WB
Write-Off [*Accounting*] .... W/O
Write-Once, Read-Many [*Computer science*] .... WORM
Write-One Read Memory .... WORM
Write-Only Memory [*Computer science*] .... WOM
Write-Only Read-Only Memory [*Computer science*] (MDG) .... WOROM
Writer (MSA) .... WR
Writer .... WRTR
Writer .... WTR
Writer/Editor (MCD) .... W/E
Writer of Accompanying Material [*MARC relator code*] [*Library of Congress*] (LCCP) .... wam
Writer Officer [*British military*] .... W
Writer Officer [*British military*] (DMA) .... WO
Writer to the Signet [*British*] .... WS
Writers' Action Group [*British*] .... WAG
Writers and Artists for Peace in the Middle East (EA) .... WAPME
Writers and Scholars Educational Trust [*British*] (EAIO) .... WSET
Writers and Scholars International [*British*] (EAIO) .... WSI
Writers and Their Work [*British Council*] .... WW
Writers' Development Trust [*Canada*] (EAIO) .... WDT
Writer's Digest [*A publication*] .... WD
Writer's Directory [*A publication*] .... WD
Writer's Electronic Bulletin Board [*Information service or system*] (IID) .... WEBB
Writers' Ever-Ready Textual Service [*Rent-A-Script*] [*Satirical*] .... WERTS
Writers Federation of Nova Scotia [*Canada*] (WWLA) .... WFNS
Writers for Animal Rights [*Defunct*] (EA) .... AnRts
Writers for Peace (EA) .... WP
Writers for Young Adults [*A publication*] .... WYA
Writers Guild of Alberta [*Canada*] (WWLA) .... WGA
Writers Guild of America, East (EA) .... WGAE
Writers Guild of America, West (EA) .... WGA
Writers Guild of America, West (EA) .... WGAW
Writers' Guild of Great Britain (DCTA) .... WGGB
Writers in Prison Committee of International PEN [*British*] (EAIO) .... WIPC
Writers of the Future [*Science fiction writing award*] .... WOTF
Writers' Sodality of America [*Defunct*] .... WSA
Writers Union of Canada .... WUC
Writers War Board .... WWB
Write-to-Operator [*Computer science*] (IBMDP) .... WTO
Write-to-Operator with Reply [*Computer science*] (IBMDP) .... WTOR
Write-Your-Own [*Insurance*] (MHDB) .... WYO
Write-Your-Own-Company [*Insurance*] (MHDB) .... WYOC
Writing [*Law*] (ROG) .... WG
Writing (ROG) .... WRITG
Writing Ability .... WA
Writing Academy (EA) .... WA
Writing Assistants' Association [*A union*] [*British*] .... WAA
Writing, Editing, and Publishing .... WEP
Writing Equipment Society [*British*] (DBA) .... WES
Writing Instrument Manufacturers Association (EA) .... WIMA
Writing on Back [*Deltiology*] .... W/B
Writing on Face [*Deltiology*] .... W/F
Writing Paper Manufacturers Association [*Later, API*] (EA) .... WPMA
Writing Parchment (DGA) .... Wtg P
Writing Proficiency Program [*Educational test*] .... WPP
Writing Proficiency Program/Intermediate System [*Educational test*] .... WPP/IS
Writing Push Down Acceptor (NITA) .... WPDA
Writing Pushdown Acceptor .... WPDA
Writing Services Center .... WSC
Writing-Aid and Author's Helper (EDAC) .... WANDAH
Written Advice of Contracting Officer [*Military*] .... WACO
Written Component [*Qualification test*] [*Military*] .... WC
Written Down Value [*Accounting*] .... WDV
Written Order [*Medicine*] .... W/O
Written Order of Withdrawal [*Banking*] .... WOW
Written Progress Report (HCT) .... WPR
Written Testimony (BJA) .... WT
Wroclaw [*Poland*] [*Airport symbol*] (OAG) .... WRO
Wrong .... W
Wrong .... wr
Wrong [*Telecommunications*] (TEL) .... WRG
Wrong Direction .... WRDIR
Wrong Font [*Publishing*] (WDMC) .... wf
Wrong Font [*Typesetting*] [*Proofreader's mark*] .... WF
Wrong Length Record [*Computer science*] .... WLR
Wrong Number [*Telecommunications*] (TEL) .... WN
Wrong Number [*Telecommunications*] (TEL) .... WNO
Wrong Signature Zero [*Nuclear science*] (OA) .... WSZ
Wrong Tense of Verb [*Used in correcting manuscripts, etc.*] .... T
Wrong Test Requested - Floor Error [*Medicine*] (DAVI) .... REQF
Wrong Test Requested - Laboratory Error [*Medicine*] (DAVI) .... REQL
Wrong Verb Form [*Used in correcting manuscripts, etc.*] V
Wrongful Death [*Legal shorthand*] (LWAP) .... WD
Wrongful Death Act (LWAP) .... WDA

Wrongful Detention [*British*] ..... WD
Wrotham Park [*Queensland*] [*Airport symbol*] (AD) ..... WKP
Wrought (VRA) ..... wrt
Wrought ..... WRT
Wrought Brass (MSA) ..... WBRS
Wrought Iron ..... WI
Wrought Steel (MSA) ..... WS
Wroughton [*British ICAO location identifier*] (ICLI) ..... EGDT
WRT Energy Corp. [*Associated Press*] (SAG) ..... WRT
WRT Energy Corp. [*Associated Press*] (SAG) ..... WRT En
WRT Energy Corp. [*NASDAQ symbol*] (SAG) ..... WRTE
WS and LB Robinson University College [*Australia*] ..... WSLBRUC
WSFS Financial [*NASDAQ symbol*] (TTSB) ..... WSFS
WSFS Financial Corp. [*NASDAQ symbol*] (SAG) ..... WSFS
WSI Corp. [*ICAO designator*] (FAAC) ..... XWS
WSMP, Inc. [*Formerly, Western Steer Mom 'n' Pop's, Inc.*] [*NASDAQ symbol*] (SPSG) ..... WSMP
WTD Industries [*NASDAQ symbol*] (TTSB) ..... WTDI
WTD Industries, Inc. [*Associated Press*] (SAG) ..... WTD
WTD Industries, Inc. [*Portland, OR*] [*NASDAQ symbol*] (NQ) ..... WTDI
Wuanco Engineering Technical Library, Pasadena, CA [*Library symbol Library of Congress*] (LCLS) ..... CPWi
Wuasa [*Indonesia*] [*ICAO location identifier*] (ICLI) ..... WAMU
Wuerttemberg Israelitische Religionsgemeinschaft [*A publication*] (BJA) ..... WIR
Wuerttembergische Landesbibliothek, Konrad Adenauer, Stuttgart, Germany [*Library symbol Library of Congress*] (LCLS) ..... GySW
Wuerzburg, Hospital [*Germany ICAO location identifier*] (ICLI) ..... EDIW
Wuerzburg-Schenkenturm [*Germany ICAO location identifier*] (ICLI) ..... EDFW
Wueste und Gelobtes Land [*A publication*] (BJA) ..... WGL
Wu-han [*Republic of China*] [*Seismograph station code, US Geological Survey*] (SEIS) ..... WUC
Wu-han [*Republic of China*] [*Seismograph station code, US Geological Survey*] (SEIS) ..... WUH
Wuhan [*China*] [*Airport symbol*] (OAG) ..... WUH
Wuhan [*China*] [*ICAO location identifier*] (ICLI) ..... ZHWH
Wuhan Airlines [*China*] [*ICAO designator*] (FAAC) ..... CWU
Wuhan/Nanhu [*China*] [*ICAO location identifier*] (ICLI) ..... ZHHH
Wulumuchi [*Republic of China*] [*Seismograph station code, US Geological Survey*] (SEIS) ..... WMQ
Wunnummin Lake Band Library, Ontario [*Library symbol National Library of Canada*] (BIB) ..... OWLB
Wunstorf [*Germany ICAO location identifier*] (ICLI) ..... EDNW
Wupatki National Monument ..... WUPA
Wurenlingen [*Switzerland ICAO location identifier*] (ICLI) ..... LSXW
Wurtach [*Afghanistan*] [*ICAO location identifier*] (ICLI) ..... OAWU
Wurtsboro, NY [*FM radio station call letters*] ..... WZAD
Wustite Magnetite [*Geology*] ..... WM
Wustum Museum of Fine Arts, Racine, WI [*Library symbol Library of Congress*] (LCLS) ..... WRacWM
Wuvulu Island [*Papua New Guinea*] [*Airport symbol*] (OAG) ..... WUV
Wu-wei [*Republic of China*] [*Seismograph station code, US Geological Survey*] (SEIS) ..... WUW
WVS Financial [*NASDAQ symbol*] (TTSB) ..... WVFC
WVS Financial Corp. [*NASDAQ symbol*] (SAG) ..... WVFC
WVS Financial Corp. [*Associated Press*] (SAG) ..... WVS Fn
WWMCCS [*Worldwide Military Command and Control System*] **Action Group** ..... WAG
WWMCCS [*Worldwide Military Command and Control System*] **ADP System SecurityManager** [*Automatic Data Processing*] (MCD) ..... WASSM
WWMCCS [*Worldwide Military Command and Control System*] **ADP System SecurityOfficer** [*Automatic Data Processing*] (MCD) ..... WASSO
WWMCCS [*Worldwide Military Command and Control System*] **Airborne Resources** (DOMA) ..... WWABNRES
WWMCCS [*Worldwide Military Command and Control System*] **Architecture Division** ..... WAD
WWMCCS [*Worldwide Military Command and Control System*] **Council Support Group** (MCD) ..... WCSG
WWMCCS [*Worldwide Military Command and Control System*] **Information Systems** ..... WIS
WWMCCS [*Worldwide Military Command and Control System*] **Intercomputer Network** [*DoD*] ..... WIN
WWMCCS [*Worldwide Military Command and Control System*] **Standard Graphics Terminal** (DOMA) ..... WSGT
WWMCCS [*Worldwide Military Command and Control System*] **Standard System Information Base** (MCD) ..... WSSIB
WWMCCS [*Worldwide Military Command and Control System*] **System Engineering Office** (MCD) ..... WSEO
WWMCCS [*Worldwide Military Command and Control System*] **Systems Engineer** (MCD) ..... WSE
WWMCCS [*Worldwide Military Command and Control System*] **Systems Specification** (MCD) ..... WSS
Wyandanch Memorial High School, Wyandanch, NY [*Library symbol*] [*Library of Congress*] (LCLS) ..... NwyaHS
Wyandanch Public Library, Wyandanch, NY [*Library symbol Library of Congress*] (LCLS) ..... NWya
Wyandotte [*Queensland*] [*Airport symbol*] (AD) ..... WYD
Wyandotte Bantam Club of America (EA) ..... WBCA
Wyandotte Southern Railroad Co. [*AAR code*] ..... WYS
Wyandotte Terminal Railroad Co. [*AAR code*] ..... WYT
Wyanet Consolidated High School District 510, Wyanet, IL [*Library symbol Library of Congress*] (LCLS) ..... IWyaSD
Wyangala [*Australia Seismograph station code, US Geological Survey Closed*] (SEIS) ..... WYA
Wyatt's Dickens' Chancery Reports [*A publication*] (DLA) ..... Wy Dic
Wyatt's Practical Register in Chancery [*England*] [*A publication*] (DLA) ..... Wy Pr R
Wyatt's Practical Register in Chancery [*1800*] [*A publication*] (DLA) ..... Wyatt Pr R
Wyatt's Practical Register in Chancery [*1800*] [*A publication*] (DLA) ..... Wyatt Prac Reg
Wyckoff Free Public Library, Wyckoff, NJ [*Library symbol Library of Congress*] (LCLS) ..... NjWy
Wyckoff News, Wyckoff, NJ [*Library symbol Library of Congress*] (LCLS) ..... NjWyN
Wyckoff Printing Co., Westfield, NJ [*Library symbol Library of Congress*] (LCLS) ..... NjWefW
Wycliffe [*English cleric, translated Bible into English, 1320-1384*] (BARN) ..... Wy
Wycliffe [*English cleric, translated Bible into English, 1320-1384*] (BARN) ..... Wycl
Wycliffe Bible Commentary [*A publication*] (BJA) ..... WBC
Wycliffe Bible Translators (EA) ..... WBT
Wycliffe College Library, University of Toronto [*UTLAS symbol*] ..... KWC
Wycliffe College, Toronto, ON, Canada [*Library symbol Library of Congress*] (LCLS) ..... CaOTW
Wycliffe College, Toronto, Ontario [*Library symbol National Library of Canada*] (NLC) ..... OTW
Wycombe [*England*] ..... WYC
Wycombe Air Centre [*British ICAO designator*] (FAAC) ..... WYC
Wycombe Air Park/Booker [*British ICAO location identifier*] (ICLI) ..... EGTB
Wyda Sysstems Canada Inc., Don Mills, ON, Canada [*Library symbol*] [*Library of Congress*] (LCLS) ..... CaODmWS
Wyda Systems Canada, Inc., Don Mills, Ontario [*Library symbol National Library of Canada*] (NLC) ..... ODMWS
Wydmar Developmental Corp. [*Vancouver Stock Exchange symbol*] ..... WD
Wye Junction Latching Circulator ..... WJLC
Wyeth Laboratories [*Research code symbol*] ..... S
Wyeth Laboratories [*Research code symbol*] ..... WL
Wyeth Laboratories [*Research code symbol*] ..... WY
Wyeth Laboratories - Human Diploid Cell Strain [*Rabies vaccine*] ..... W-HDCS
Wyeth Laboratories, Radnor, PA [*Library symbol Library of Congress*] (LCLS) ..... PRaW
Wyeth Ltd., Medical Library, Downsview, ON, Canada [*Library symbol*] [*Library of Congress*] (LCLS) ..... CaOTWY
Wyk Auf Fohr [*Germany ICAO location identifier*] (ICLI) ..... EDXY
Wyle Electronics [*NYSE symbol*] (TTSB) ..... WYL
Wyle Electronics Co. [*Formerly, Wyle Laboratories*] [*NYSE symbol*] (SAG) ..... WYL
Wyle Electronics Co. [*Formerly, Wyle Laboratories*] [*Associated Press*] (SAG) ..... WyleElec
Wyle Test Laboratories ..... WTL
Wyman-Gordon [*NASDAQ symbol*] (TTSB) ..... WYMN
Wyman-Gordon Co. [*Associated Press*] (SAG) ..... Wyman
Wyman-Gordon Co. [*NASDAQ symbol*] (NQ) ..... WYMN
Wyman's Reports [*India*] [*A publication*] (DLA) ..... Wyman
Wymoning Public Library, Wymoning, IL [*Library symbol Library of Congress*] (LCLS) ..... IWyo
Wyndham [*Australia Airport symbol*] ..... WYN
Wyndham Hotel [*NYSE symbol*] (TTSB) ..... WYN
Wynne, AR [*AM radio station call letters*] ..... KWYN
Wynne, AR [*FM radio station call letters*] ..... KWYN-FM
Wynne's Bovill's Patent Cases [*A publication*] (DLA) ..... Wynne Bov
Wynne's Eunomus [*A publication*] (DLA) ..... Eun
Wynne's Eunomus [*A publication*] (DLA) ..... Wynne Eun
Wynne's Life of Sir Leoline Jenkins [*1724*] [*A publication*] (DLA) ..... Sir L Jenk
Wynn's International, Inc. [*NYSE symbol*] (SPSG) ..... WN
Wynn's International, Inc. [*Associated Press*] (SAG) ..... Wynns
Wynn's Intl [*NYSE symbol*] (TTSB) ..... WN
Wynyard [*Australia ICAO location identifier*] (ICLI) ..... AMWY
Wynyard [*Australia Airport symbol*] (OAG) ..... WNY
Wynyard, SK [*Television station call letters*] ..... CHSS
Wynyard, SK [*Television station call letters*] CICC-1
Wynyard, SK [*ICAO location identifier*] (ICLI) ..... CYYO
Wyoming [*MARC geographic area code Library of Congress*] (LCCP) ..... n-us-wy
Wyoming [*Postal code*] ..... WY
Wyoming (AAG) ..... WYO
Wyoming (ODBW) ..... Wyo
Wyoming (ROG) ..... WYOM
Wyoming [*MARC country of publication code Library of Congress*] (LCCP) ..... wyu
Wyoming Airlines Ltd. [*ICAO designator*] (FAAC) ..... WYG
Wyoming Array [*Wyoming*] [*Seismograph station code, US Geological Survey*] (SEIS) ..... WYO
Wyoming Department of Agriculture, Cheyenne, WY [*Library symbol Library of Congress*] (LCLS) ..... WyCDA
Wyoming Department of Education, Cheyenne, WY [*Library symbol Library of Congress*] (LCLS) ..... WyCDE
Wyoming Department of Health and Social Services, Cheyenne, WY [*Library symbol Library of Congress*] (LCLS) ..... WyCHS
Wyoming Educational Computing Council (EDAC) ..... WECC
Wyoming Free Public Library, Wyoming, NY [*Library symbol Library of Congress*] (LCLS) ..... NWy
Wyoming Game and Fish Commission, Cheyenne, WY [*Library symbol Library of Congress*] (LCLS) ..... WyCGF
Wyoming Game and Fish Department ..... WGFD
Wyoming Girls' School, Sheridan, WY [*Library symbol Library of Congress*] (LCLS) ..... WyShGS
Wyoming Health Science Network, Laramie, WY [*OCLC symbol*] (OCLC) ..... WYM
Wyoming Health Science Network, University of Wyoming, Laramie, WY [*Library symbol Library of Congress*] (LCLS) ..... WyLarHN
Wyoming Highway Department, Cheyenne, WY [*Library symbol Library of Congress*] (LCLS) ..... WyCHD
Wyoming Historical and Geological Society, Wilkes-Barre, PA [*Library symbol Library of Congress*] (LCLS) ..... PWbH
Wyoming Industrial Institute, Worland, WY [*Library symbol Library of Congress*] (LCLS) ..... WyWoI
Wyoming Infant Stimulation Program (EDAC) ..... WISP

Wyoming Infrared Observatory .... WIRO
Wyoming, MI [*FM radio station call letters*] .... WYCE
Wyoming, MI [*AM radio station call letters*] .... WYGR
Wyoming Mining and Mineral Resource Research Institute [*University of Wyoming*] [*Research center*] (RCD) .... WMMRRI
Wyoming Natural Heritage Program [*Wyoming State Department of Environmental Quality*] [*Cheyenne*] [*Information service or system*] (IID) .... WNHP
Wyoming Pioneer Home, Thermopolis, WY [*Library symbol Library of Congress*] (LCLS) .... WyThP
Wyoming Public Library, Wyoming, IL [*OCLC symbol*] (OCLC) .... ISX
Wyoming Reports [*A publication*] (DLA) .... W
Wyoming Reports [*A publication*] (DLA) .... WY
Wyoming Reports [*A publication*] (DLA) .... Wyo
Wyoming Reports [*A publication*] (DLA) .... Wyom
Wyoming School for the Deaf, Casper, WY [*Library symbol Library of Congress*] (LCLS) .... WyCaD
Wyoming State Archives and Historical Department, Cheyenne, WY [*Library symbol Library of Congress*] (LCLS) .... Wy-Ar
Wyoming State Children's Home, Casper, WY [*Library symbol Library of Congress*] (LCLS) .... WyCaCH
Wyoming State Documents, Cheyenne, WY [*Library symbol Library of Congress*] (LCLS) .... Wy-D

Wyoming State Hospital, Evanston, WY [*Library symbol Library of Congress*] (LCLS) .... WyEvSH
Wyoming State Library, Cheyenne, WY [*Library symbol Library of Congress*] (LCLS) .... Wy
Wyoming State Library, Cheyenne, WY [*OCLC symbol*] (OCLC) .... WYZ
Wyoming State Training School, Lander, WY [*Library symbol Library of Congress*] (LCLS) .... WyLanT
Wyoming Territory .... WT
Wyoming Trucking Association, Casper WY [*STAC*] .... WTA
Wyoming Water Research Center [*University of Wyoming*] [*Research center*] (RCD) .... WWRC
Wythe's Virginia Chancery Reports [*1788-99*] [*A publication*] (DLA) ...... VA Ch Dec
Wythe's Virginia Chancery Reports [*1788-99*] [*A publication*] (DLA) .... Wy
Wythe's Virginia Chancery Reports [*1788-99*] [*A publication*] (DLA) .... Wythe
Wythe's Virginia Chancery Reports [*1788-99*] [*A publication*] (DLA) .... Wythe Ch (VA)
Wythe's Virginia Chancery Reports [*1788-99*] [*A publication*] (DLA) ..... Wythe (VA)
Wythe's Virginia Chancery Reports [*1788-99*] [*A publication*] (DLA) ...... Wythes CC
Wythe's Virginia Chancery Reports [*1788-99*] [*A publication*] (DLA) .... Wythe's R
Wythe's Virginia Chancery Reports [*1788-99*] [*A publication*] (DLA) .... Wythe's Rep
Wytheville Community College, Wytheville, VA [*Library symbol Library of Congress*] (LCLS) .... ViWyC
Wytheville, VA [*AM radio station call letters*] .... WYVE
Wyton [*British ICAO location identifier*] (ICLI) .... EGUY
Wyton FTU [*British ICAO designator*] (FAAC) .... WYT

X

By Meaning

X Automatic Code Translation (IEEE) .... XACT
X Protocol Data Unit (TNIG) .... XPDU
X Records [Division of RCA-Victor] [Record label] X
X Unit [A unit of wavelength] .... XU
X.400 Application Program Interface Association (EA) .... XAPIA
XACO, Inc., Buffalo, NY [Library symbol] [Library of Congress] (LCLS) .... NBuX
Xai-Xai [Mozambique] [ICAO location identifier] (ICLI) .... FQXA
Xangongo [Angola] [ICAO location identifier] (ICLI) .... FNXA
Xanthan Gum [Chemistry] .... XG
Xanthine [Biochemistry] .... Xa
Xanthine [Biochemistry] .... Xan
Xanthine Dehydrogenase [An enzyme] .... XDH
Xanthine Diphosphate [Biochemistry] (DAVI) .... XDP
Xanthine Oxidase [Also, XOD] [An enzyme] .... XO
Xanthine Oxidase [Also, XO] [An enzyme] .... XOD
Xanthine-Guanine Phosphoribosyltransferase [An enzyme] .... XGPRT
Xanthium strumarium [Cocklebur] .... XANST
Xanthochromic [Neurology] (DAVI) .... XANT
Xanthogranulomatous Pyelonephritis [Medicine] .... XGP
Xanthomatosis [Medicine] (DAVI) .... CTX
Xanthomatosis .... xanth
Xanthomonus Campestris [Bacteriology] XC
Xanthosine [One-letter symbol; see Xao] X
Xanthosine [Also, X] [A nucleoside] .... Xao
Xanthosine Diphosphate [Biochemistry] .... XDP
Xanthosine Monophosphate [Biochemistry] .... XMP
Xanthosine Triphosphate [Biochemistry] .... XTP
Xanthurenic Acid [Clinical chemistry] .... XA
Xapuri [Brazil] [Airport symbol] (AD) .... XAY
XATA Corp. [NASDAQ symbol] (TTSB) .... XATA
XATA Corp. [NASDAQ symbol] (SAG) .... XATA
XATA Corp. [Associated Press] (SAG) .... XATA
Xavantina [Brazil ICAO location identifier] (ICLI) .... SBXV
Xaverian College, Silver Spring, MD [Library symbol Library of Congress] (LCLS) .... MdSsX
Xaverian Missionary Fathers (TOCD) .... SX
Xaverian Missionary Fathers, St. Francis Xavier Mission Society (TOCD) .... sx
Xaverian Missionary Society of Mary, Inc. [Roman Catholic women's religious order] .... MM
Xaverian Missionary Society of Mary, Inc. (TOCD) .... XMM
Xavier Corp. [Associated Press] (SAG) .... XavrCp
Xavier Corp. [NASDAQ symbol] (SAG) .... XVRC
Xavier Mission Sisters [Catholic Mission Sisters of St. Francis Xavier] [Roman Catholic religious order] .... XMS
Xavier Society for the Blind (EA) .... XSB
Xavier University [Louisiana; Ohio] .... XU
Xavier University, Cincinnati, OH [Library symbol Library of Congress] (LCLS) .... OCX
Xavier University, Cincinnati, OH [OCLC symbol] (OCLC) .... XAV
Xavier University (Louisiana) (GAGS) .... Xavier U (La)
Xavier University, New Orleans, LA [Library symbol Library of Congress OCLC symbol] (LCLS) .... LNX
Xavier University (Ohio) (GAGS) .... Xavier U (Ohio)
Xaxaba [Botswana] [ICAO location identifier] (ICLI) .... FBXX
X-Axis X
X-Axis of External Tank [NASA] (NASA) .... XT
X-Axis of Orbiter [NASA] (NASA) .... XO
X-Axis of Payload [NASA] (NASA) .... XP
X-Axis of Solid Rocket Booster [NASA] (NASA) .... XS
X-Axis of Spacelab [NASA] (NASA) XL
X-Band Antenna Feed Horn .... XAFH
X-Band Antenna System .... XAS
X-Band Cassegrain Experimental .... XCE
X-Band Communications Transponder .... XCT
X-Band Diode Phase Shifter .... XDPS
X-Band Drive Amplifier .... XDA
X-Band Feed Horn .... XFH
X-Band Ferrite Modulator .... XFM
X-Band Frequency Converter .... XFC
X-Band Inteferometer Antenna .... XIA
X-Band Klystron .... XK
X-Band Limiter Attenuator .... XLA
X-Band Microwave Source .... XMS
X-Band Microwave Transmitter .... XMT
X-Band Navigation Beacon .... XNB
X-Band Parametric Amplifier .... XPA

X-Band Passive Array .... XPA
X-Band Phase Shifter .... XPS
X-Band Planar Array .... XPA
X-Band Planar Array Antenna .... XPAA
X-Band Power Amplifier .... XPA
X-Band Pseudopassive Array .... XPPA
X-Band Pulse Transmitter .... XPT
X-Band Pulsed Power Amplifier .... XPPA
X-Band RADAR Beacon .... XRB
X-Band Satellite Antenna .... XSA
X-Band Satellite Tracking Antenna .... XSTA
X-Band Scatterometer RADAR .... XSR
X-Band Stripline Tunnel Diode .... XSTD
X-Band Stripline Tunnel Diode Amplifier .... XSTDA
X-Band Tracking Antenna .... XTA
X-Band Transmitter .... XTX
X-Band Traveling Wave Amplifier .... XTWA
X-Band Traveling Wave MASER .... XTWM
X-Band Triode Oscillator .... XTO
X-Band Tunable Parametric Amplifier .... XTPA
Xband-Synthetic Aperture Radar (EERA) .... X-SAR
X-Body Axis Perpendicular to Orbit Plane [Aerospace] .... X-POP
X-Cal Resources Ltd. [Toronto Stock Exchange symbol] XCL
XcelleNet, Inc. [Associated Press] (SAG) .... XcelNet
XcelleNet, Inc. [NASDAQ symbol] (SAG) .... XNET
X-Chromosome XC
X-Chromosome Inactivation [Genetics] XCI
XCL Ltd. [Formerly, Exploration Company of Louisiana] [AMEX symbol] (SAG) XCL
XCL Ltd. [Formerly, Exploration Company of Louisiana] [Associated Press] (SAG) .... XCL Ltd.
Xebeck [Type of ship] (ROG) .... XBK
Xechem International [Associated Press] (SAG) .... Xechem
Xechem International [Associated Press] (SAG) .... Xechm
Xechem International [NASDAQ symbol] (SAG) .... ZKEM
Xechem Intl [NASDAQ symbol] (TTSB) .... ZKEM
Xechem Intl Wrrt [NASDAQ symbol] (TTSB) .... ZKEMW
Xeikon NV [NASDAQ symbol] (SAG) .... XEIK
Xeikon NV [Associated Press] (SAG) .... Xeikon
Xeikon N.V. ADR [NASDAQ symbol] (TTSB) .... XEIKY
Xenex Industries & Resources Ltd. [Vancouver Stock Exchange symbol] ...... XNX
Xenia, OH [AM radio station call letters] .... WBZI
Xenia, OH [FM radio station call letters] .... WZLR
Xenia, OH [Location identifier FAA] (FAAL) .... XEN
Xenium [Gift] (ROG) .... XUM
Xenium Resources, Inc. [Vancouver Stock Exchange symbol] ..... XRI
Xenogenic Fetal Skin [Medicine] .... XFS
Xenometrix, Inc. [Associated Press] (SAG) .... Xeno
Xenometrix, Inc. [Associated Press] (SAG) .... Xenomet
Xenometrix, Inc. [NASDAQ symbol] (SAG) .... XENOU
Xenometrix Inc. Wrrt [NASDAQ symbol] (TTSB) .... XENOW
Xenon [Chemical element] (IAA) X
Xenon [Chemical element] .... Xe
Xenon Arc Lamp .... XAL
Xenon Discharge Tube .... XDT
Xenon Flash Tube .... XFT
Xenon Fluoride (MCD) .... XEF
Xenon Infrared Searchlight .... XIRS
Xenon Infrared Searchlight .... XIS
Xenon Lamp Collimator XLC
Xenon Lamp Power Supply .... XLPS
Xenon LASER Discharge Tube .... XLDT
Xenon LASER Tube .... XLT
Xenon Light Source .... XLS
Xenon Light Source System .... XLSS
Xenon Optical Beacon .... XOB
Xenon Quartz Helix .... XQH
Xenon Short Arc Lamp .... XSAL
Xenon Solar Simulator .... XSS
Xenon-Filled Quartz Helix .... XFQH
Xenophon [428-354BC] [Classical studies] (OCD) .... Xen
Xenopsylla [A genus of fleas] (DAVI) X
Xenopus Vitellogenin .... xVit
Xenotech Systems, Inc., Kitchener, ON, Canada [Library symbol] [Library of Congress] (LCLS) .... CaOKitXS

Xenotech Systems, Inc., Kitchener, Ontario [*Library symbol National Library of Canada*] (NLC) .... OKXS
Xenotron Composer (DGA) XC
Xenotron Text Processing System (DGA) .... XTPS
Xenotron Video Composer (DGA) XVC
Xenova Group ADS [*NASDAQ symbol*] (TTSB) .... XNVAY
Xenova Group Ltd. [*Associated Press*] (SAG) .... Xenova
Xenova Group PLC [*NASDAQ symbol*] (SAG) .... XNVA
Xerces Society (EA) .... XS
Xeroderma Pigmentosum [*Inherited, disfiguring syndrome*] .... XDP
Xeroderma Pigmentosum [*Inherited, disfiguring syndrome*] .... XP
Xeromammography [*Radiology*] (DAVI) .... xero
Xeromammography [*Radiology*] (DAVI) .... XMM
Xerox 9700 Users' Association (EA) .... XPLOR
Xerox Canada, Inc. [*Toronto Stock Exchange symbol*] XXC
Xerox Computer Services [*Xerox Corp.*] .... XCS
Xerox Copy XC
Xerox Corp. [*Associated Press*] (SAG) .... Xerox
Xerox Corp. [*NYSE symbol*] (SPSG) .... XRX
Xerox Corp., El Segundo, CA [*OCLC symbol*] (OCLC) .... CXE
Xerox Corp., Research Center, Palo Alto, CA [*Library symbol Library of Congress*] (LCLS) .... CPaX
Xerox Corp., Rochester, NY [*Library symbol Library of Congress*] (LCLS) .... NRX
Xerox Corp., Xerox Library Services, Webster, NY [*OCLC symbol*] (OCLC) .... XER
Xerox Data Systems [*Formerly, SDS*] .... XDS
Xerox Dry Microfilm (NITA) .... XDM
Xerox Education Group .... XEG
Xerox Electro-Optical Systems .... XEOS
Xerox Family Education Services .... XFES
Xerox Graphic Printer [*Xerox Corp.*] .... XGP
Xerox Imaging System (PCM) .... XIS
Xerox Individualized Publishing .... XIP
Xerox Integrated Composition System [*Xerox Corp.*] [*Computer typesetting system*] .... XICS
Xerox International Center for Training and Management Development [*Leesburg, VA*] .... XICTMD
Xerox Learning Systems .... XLS
Xerox Memory System .... XMS
Xerox Network Services (NITA) .... XNS
Xerox Network Systems [*Telecommunications*] .... XNS
Xerox New Enterprises .... XNE
Xerox Operating System .... XOS
Xerox Planning Model [*A computerized representation of the Xerox Corp.'s operations*] .... XPM
Xerox Reproduction (AAG) .... XER
Xerox Research Centre of Canada Library [*UTLAS symbol*] .... XRC
Xerox Research Centre of Canada, Mississauga, Ontario [*Library symbol National Library of Canada*] (NLC) .... OMX
Xerox Team Vision [*Xerox Business Products and Systems Group*] [*El Segundo, CA*] (TSSD) .... XTV
Xerox Technology Ventures [*El Segundo, CA*] (ECON) .... XTV
Xerox Telecommunications Network [*Proposed*] (TSSD) .... XTEN
Xerox Virtual Printroom .... XVP
Xerxes [*Phonetic alphabet*] [*Royal Navy World War I*] (DSUE) X
Xeta Corp. [*NASDAQ symbol*] (NQ) .... XETA
XeTel Corp. [*NASDAQ symbol*] (TTSB) .... XTEL
X-Glucuronide .... X-Gluc
Xhosa [*MARC language code Library of Congress*] (LCCP) .... xho
Xi Psi Phi [*Fraternity*] .... XPP
Xi Sigma Pi [*Fraternity*] .... XSP
Xiamen [*China*] [*ICAO location identifier*] (ICLI) .... ZSAM
Xiamen Airlines [*China*] [*ICAO designator*] (FAAC) .... CXA
Xian [*China*] [*Airport symbol*] (OAG) .... SIA
Xian [*China*] [*ICAO location identifier*] (ICLI) .... ZLSN
Xiao Liu Qiu [*China*] [*ICAO location identifier*] (ICLI) .... RCLC
Xichang [*China*] [*Airport symbol*] (OAG) XIC
Xicor, Inc. [*NASDAQ symbol*] (NQ) .... XICO
Xicor, Inc. [*Associated Press*] (SAG) .... Xicor
Xieng Khouang [*Laos*] [*ICAO location identifier*] (ICLI) .... VLXG
Xieng Khouang [*Laos*] [*Airport symbol*] (AD) .... XIE
Xieng Khouang (Plaine Des Jarres) [*Laos*] [*ICAO location identifier*] (ICLI) .... VLXK
Xilinx, Inc. [*Associated Press*] (SAG) .... Xilinx
Xilinx, Inc. [*NASDAQ symbol*] (SAG) .... XLNX
X-Inactivation Centre [*Genetics*] XIC
Xinhua News Agency [*China*] .... XNA
Xining [*China*] [*Airport symbol*] (OAG) .... XNN
Xining [*China*] [*ICAO location identifier*] (ICLI) .... ZLXN
Xinshe [*China*] [*ICAO location identifier*] (ICLI) .... RCWK
Xinzhu [*China*] [*ICAO location identifier*] (ICLI) .... RCPO
Xionics Document Technologies, Inc. [*NASDAQ symbol*] (SAG) .... XION
Xionics Document Technologies, Inc. [*Associated Press*] (SAG) .... XionDoc
XIOS Research Corp., Ottawa, Ontario [*Library symbol National Library of Canada*] (BIB) .... OOX
Xiox Corp. [*NASDAQ symbol*] (NQ) .... XIOX
Xiphisternum [*Also called the xiphoid process*] [*Anatomy*] (DAVI) .... XS
Xiphoid Plus Number of Finger Breadths [*Height of fundus*] [*Obstetrics*] (DAVI) .... X+#
Xique-Xique [*Brazil*] [*Airport symbol*] (AD) .... XIQ
Xircom, Inc. [*NASDAQ symbol*] (SAG) .... XIRC
Xircom, Inc. [*Associated Press*] (SAG) .... Xircom
Xitron Portable Terminal (DGA) .... XPT
XL Food Systems Ltd. [*Toronto Stock Exchange symbol*] .... XLF
XL Operating System (NITA) .... XL/OS
XLConnect Solutions, Inc. [*Associated Press*] (SAG) .... XLCnnSl

XLConnect Solutions, Inc. [*NASDAQ symbol*] (SAG) .... XLCT
X-Linked Agammaglobulinaemia [*Medicine*] .... XLA
X-Linked Chronic Granulomatous Disease [*Medicine*] .... X-CGD
X-Linked Combined Immunodeficiency [*Immunology*] .... XCID
X-Linked Dominant (MEDA) .... XD
X-Linked Hupophosphatemia [*Medicine*] (DMAA) .... XLH
X-Linked, Lymphocyte-Regulated [*Genetics*] .... XLR
X-Linked Lymphoproliferative Syndrome [*Medicine*] .... XLP
X-Linked Lymphoproliferative Syndrome [*Medicine*] .... XLPS
X-Linked Mental Retardation [*Genetics*] .... XLMR
X-Linked Recessive Hypophosphataemic [*Rickets*] [*Medicine*] .... XLRH
X-Linked Recessive Nephrolithiasis [*Medicine*] .... XRN
X-Linked Server Combined Immunodeficiency [*"Bubble Boy" disease*] [*Medicine*] .... XSCID
Xograph (VRA) .... XOGP
XOMA Corp. [*NASDAQ symbol*] (SAG) .... XOMA
Xomed Surgical Products, Inc. [*NASDAQ symbol*] (SAG) .... XOMD
Xomen Surgical Products, Inc. [*Associated Press*] (SAG) .... XomedS
Xonics Electron Radiography [*Medical x-ray imaging equipment*] .... XERG
XOX Corp. [*Associated Press*] (SAG) .... XOX C
XOX Corp. [*NASDAQ symbol*] (SAG) .... XOXC
XP International BV [*Netherlands ICAO designator*] (FAAC) .... XPS
Xpedite Systems [*NASDAQ symbol*] (TTSB) .... XPED
Xpedite Systems, Inc. [*NASDAQ symbol*] (SAG) .... XPED
Xpedite Systems, Inc. [*Associated Press*] (SAG) .... Xpedite
Xplor Corp. [*Associated Press*] (SAG) .... Xplor
Xplor Corp. [*NASDAQ symbol*] (NQ) .... XPLR
Xplor Corp. [*NASDAQ symbol*] (TTSB) .... XPLR
XPRESS Information Services (IID) .... XIS
X-Ray (KSC) X
X-Ray [*Phonetic alphabet*] [*Pre-World War II International*] [*World War II*] (DSUE) X
X-Ray .... XR
X-Ray Absorption Fine Structure [*Organic chemistry*] .... XAFS
X-Ray Absorption Near-Edge Structure [*Spectroscopy*] .... XANES
X-Ray Absorption Spectroscopy .... XAS
X-Ray Analysis Trial .... XAT
X-Ray and Photofluorography Technician [*Navy*] .... XRP
X-Ray Assay Laboratories Ltd., Don Mills, Ontario [*Library symbol National Library of Canada*] (NLC) .... OTXRA
X-Ray Assay Laboratories Ltd., Don Mills, Toronto, ON, Canada [*Library symbol Library of Congress*] (LCLS) .... CaOTXRA
X-Ray Assistant [*British military*] X
X-Ray Assistant [*British military*] (DMA) .... XRA
X-Ray Attenuation Coefficient Information Center [*National Institute of Standards and Technology*] .... XACIC
X-Ray Background [*Cosmology*] .... XRB
X-Ray Bright Point [*Astronomy*] .... XBP
X-Ray Centroid .... XRC
X-Ray Crystal Density .... XRCD
X-Ray Density Measurement .... XDM
X-Ray Density Probe .... XDP
X-Ray Diffraction [*or Diffractometer*] .... XRD
X-Ray Diffraction Powder .... XDP
X-Ray Diffraction Powder Camera .... XDPC
X-Ray Diffraction System .... XDS
X-Ray Emission Gauge .... XEG
X-Ray Emission Spectra .... XES
X-Ray Energy Dispersive System [*Microparticle analysis*] .... XEDS
X-Ray Energy Spectrometry .... XES
X-Ray Events Analyzer (KSC) .... X-REA
X-Ray Exposure Study (NUCP) .... XES
X-Ray Flow Detection .... XFD
X-Ray Fluorescence [*Spectrometry*] .... XRF
X-Ray Fluorescence Absorption .... XFA
X-Ray Fluorescence Spectrometer .... XRFS
X-Ray Fluorescence Spectroscopy .... XFS
X-Ray Generator [*Instrumentation*] .... XRG
X-Ray Hazard Meter .... XHM
X-Ray Image Intensifier .... XRII
X-Ray Induced Auger Electron Spectroscopy .... XAES
X-Ray Intensity Meter .... XIM
X-Ray LASER .... XRL
X-Ray Luminosity Function [*Cosmology*] .... XLF
X-Ray Microanalyzer [*or Microscopy*] (IEEE) .... XRM
X-Ray Microdiffraction [*Surface analysis*] .... XRMD
X-Ray Multi-Mirror Mission [*Space observatory*] .... XMM
X-Ray Optical Interferometer .... XROI
X-Ray Out of Plaster [*Radiology*] (DAVI) .... XOP
X-Ray Photoelectron Diffraction .... XPD
X-Ray Photoelectron Diffraction .... XPED
X-Ray Photoelectron Spectroscopy (RDA) .... XPS
X-Ray Photoemission Spectroscopy .... XPS
X-Ray Polychromator .... XRP
X-Ray Projection Microscope (IEEE) .... XRPM
X-Ray Radial Distance Function [*Surface chemistry analysis*] .... XRDF
X-Ray Scattering Facility .... XSF
X-Ray Spectrometry .... XRS
X-Ray Spectropolarimetry Payload on Spacelab (MCD) .... EXPOS
X-Ray Standard Review Group [*Department of Health and Human Services*] (EGAO) .... XSRG
X-Ray Standing Wave [*Physics*] .... XSW
X-Ray Standing Wave Interference Spectroscopy .... XSWIS
X-Ray Stimulated Auger Electron Spectroscopy (MCD) .... XSAES
X-Ray Stress Measurement .... XSM

X-Ray Surface Forces Apparatus [*Imaging technique*]	X-SFA
X-Ray Technician [*Navy*]	XRT
X-Ray Telescope (MCD)	X-RT
X-Ray Therapy [*or Treatment*]	XRT
X-Ray Timing Explorer	XTE
X-Ray Tomographic Microscope	XTM
X-Ray Transition Radiation	XTR
X-Ray Tube	XT
X-Ray Unit [*Radiology*] (DAVI)	Xu
X-Ray Vidicon Analysis	XVA
X-Ray Vision	XV
X-Rite, Inc. [*NASDAQ symbol*] (NQ)	XRIT
X-Rite, Inc. [*Associated Press*] (SAG)	X-Rite
Xscribe Corp. [*NASDAQ symbol*] (NQ)	XSCR
Xscribe Corp. [*Associated Press*] (SAG)	Xscribe
XTRA Corp. [*NYSE symbol*] (SPSG)	XTR
XTRA Corp. [*Associated Press*] (SAG)	XTRA
XTree Tools for Networks [*XTree Co.*] [*Computer science*] (PCM)	XTN
Xugana [*Botswana*] [*ICAO location identifier*] (ICLI)	FBXG
X-Window Bitmap [*For images*]	XBM
Xxsys Technologies [*NASDAQ symbol*] (SAG)	XSYS
Xxsys Technologies [*Associated Press*] (SAG)	XsysTc
Xxsys Technologies [*Associated Press*] (SAG)	XxsysTc
XXsys Technology Wrrt [*NASDAQ symbol*] (TTSB)	XSYSW
X-Y Axis	XYA
X-Y Axis Table	XYAT
X-Y Plotter	XYP
X-Y Recorder	XYR
Xybernaut Corp. [*NASDAQ symbol*] (SAG)	XYBR
Xybernaut Corp. [*Associated Press*] (SAG)	Xybrnaut
Xybernaut Corp. [*Associated Press*] (SAG)	Xybrnt
Xylan Corp. [*Associated Press*] (SAG)	XylanCp
Xylan Corp. [*NASDAQ symbol*] (SAG)	XYLN
Xylan Corp. [*NASDAQ symbol*] (TTSB)	XYLN
Xylan Polyhydrogensulfate [*Antineoplastic drug*]	XPHS
Xylanolytic Enzyme Biodegradability [*Biochemistry*]	XEB
Xylem [*Botany*]	X
Xylem Disease [*Plant pathology*]	XD
Xylem Pressure Potential [*Botany*]	XPP
Xylem Sap Potential [*Botany*]	XSP
Xylem Sap Tension [*Botany*]	XST
Xylem-Limited Bacteria [*Plant pathology*]	XLB
Xylene Diisocyanate [*Organic chemistry*]	XDI
Xylene-Alcohol [*Mixture*] [*An insecticide*] (DAVI)	X-A mixture
Xylene-Dioxane-Cellosolve [*Scintillation solvent*]	XDC
Xylene-Dioxane-Ethanol [*Scintillation solvent*]	XDE
Xylenol Orange [*An indicator*] [*Chemistry*]	XO
Xylocaine [*Topical anesthetic*] [*Astra trademark for lidocaine*]	XYL
Xylogics, Inc. [*NASDAQ symbol*] (NQ)	XLGX
Xylogics, Inc. [*Associated Press*] (SAG)	Xylogic
Xylography [*Wood engraving*] (ROG)	XGRAPHY
Xylography [*Wood engraving*] (ROG)	XY
Xyloid [*Woody*] (ROG)	XOID
Xylophone [*Music*]	XYL
Xylophone [*Music*] (ADA)	XYLO
Xylose [*As substituent on nucleoside*] [*Biochemistry*]	x
Xylose [*Also, x*] [*A sugar*]	Xyl
Xylose-Lysine [*Agar base*] [*Microbiology*]	XL
Xylose-Lysine-Deoxycholate [*Growth medium*]	XLD
Xytronyx, Inc. [*Associated Press*] (SAG)	Xytron
Xytronyx, Inc. [*AMEX symbol*] (SPSG)	XYX
Xyvision Users Group (EA)	XUG

Y

By Meaning

Y Blaengwyr Cenedlaethol [*The National Resurgence Party of the Peoples of Britain*] ..... BC
Ya La [*Thailand*] [*ICAO location identifier*] (ICLI) ..... VTSY
Yaak [*Montana*] [*Seismograph station code, US Geological Survey*] (SEIS) ..... YKM
Yabucoa, PR [*AM radio station call letters*] ..... WXEW
Yacht (ADA) ..... Y
Yacht (ROG) ..... YCHT
Yacht (ROG) ..... YT
Yacht and Motor Boat Association [*British*] (BI) ..... YMBA
Yacht Architects and Brokers Association (EA) ..... YABA
Yacht Charter Association [*British*] (DBA) ..... YCA
Yacht Club ..... YC
Yacht Designers and Surveyors Association (EAIO) ..... YBDSA
Yacht Materially Prejudiced [*Yacht racing*] (IYR) ..... YMP
Yacht Measurement ..... YM
Yacht Racing Association [*British*] ..... YRA
Yacht Racing Associations Council (EA) ..... YRAC
Yacht Safety Bureau (EA) ..... YSB
Yacht Service [*British military*] (DMA) ..... YS
Yachting [*A publication*] (BRI) ..... Yacht
Yachting Club of America (EA) ..... YCA
Yachting Journalists' Association [*British*] (DBA) ..... YJA
Yachtsmen's Association of America (EA) ..... YAA
Yacimientos Arqueologicos [*Database*] [*Ministerio de Cultura*] [*Spanish*] [*Information service or system*] (CRD) ..... YAAR
Yacimientos Petroliferos Fiscales [*Argentinian oil company*] (ECON) ..... YPF
Yacuiba [*Bolivia*] [*Airport symbol*] (OAG) ..... BYC
Yacuiba [*Bolivia*] [*ICAO location identifier*] (ICLI) ..... SLYA
Yacuiba [*Bolivia*] [*Airport symbol*] (AD) ..... YAC
Yad La-Kore. La-Safran ule-Pe'ile Tarbut (BJA) ..... YL
Yad Tikvah Foundation (EA) ..... YTF
Yad Vashem [*An association Israel*] (EAIO) ..... YV
Yad Vashem Archives (BJA) ..... YVA
Yad V'Kidush Hashem, House of Martyrs (EA) ..... KH-M
Yadaim (BJA) ..... Yad
Yadkin County Public Library, Yadkinville, NC [*Library symbol Library of Congress*] (LCLS) ..... NcYad
YAG [*Yttrium Aluminum Garnet*] LASER Range-Finder ..... YLR
Yagi [*Kashiwara*] [*Japan*] [*Seismograph station code, US Geological Survey Closed*] (SEIS) ..... YAG
Yagoua [*Cameroon*] [*ICAO location identifier*] (ICLI) ..... FKKJ
Yahoo, Inc. [*Associated Press*] (SAG) ..... Yahoo
Yahoo, Inc. [*NASDAQ symbol*] (SAG) ..... YHOO
Yahoo Inc. [*NASDAQ symbol*] (TTSB) ..... YHOO
Yahoo Internet Life [*Computer science*] ..... YIL
Yahtse [*Alaska*] [*Seismograph station code, US Geological Survey*] (SEIS) ..... YAH
Yahweh [*Old Testament term for God*] ..... YHWH
Yahweh and the Gods of Canaan [*A publication*] (BJA) ..... YGC
Yahwist Source [*Biblical scholarship*] ..... J
Yaizu/Shizuhama [*Japan ICAO location identifier*] (ICLI) ..... RJNY
Yakak [*Alaska*] [*Seismograph station code, US Geological Survey*] (SEIS) AD5
Yakataga, AK [*Location identifier FAA*] (FAAL) ..... CYT
Yakim Nation Library, Toppenish, WA [*Library symbol*] [*Library of Congress*] (LCLS) ..... WaToY
Yakim Valley Genelogical Society, Yakima, WA [*Library symbol*] [*Library of Congress*] (LCLS) ..... WaYG
Yakima [*Diocesan abbreviation*] [*Washington*] (TOCD) ..... YAK
Yakima [*Washington*] [*Airport symbol*] (OAG) ..... YKM
Yakima Firing Center (MCD) ..... YFC
Yakima Valley College, Yakima, WA [*Library symbol Library of Congress*] (LCLS) ..... WaYY
Yakima Valley Memorial Hospital, Yakima, WA [*Library symbol Library of Congress*] (LCLS) ..... WaYM
Yakima Valley Museum and Historical Association, Yakima, WA [*Library symbol Library of Congress*] (LCLS) ..... WaYMHi
Yakima Valley Regional Library, Yakima, WA [*Library symbol Library of Congress*] (LCLS) ..... WaY
Yakima Valley School, Selah, WA [*Library symbol Library of Congress*] (LCLS) ..... WaSelY
Yakima Valley Transportation Co. [*AAR code*] ..... YVT
Yakima, WA [*Location identifier FAA*] (FAAL) ..... FCT
Yakima, WA [*Television station call letters*] ..... KAPP
Yakima, WA [*FM radio station call letters*] ..... KATS
Yakima, WA [*AM radio station call letters*] ..... KBBO
Yakima, WA [*FM radio station call letters*] ..... KDNA
Yakima, WA [*FM radio station call letters*] ..... KFFM

Yakima, WA [*Television station call letters*] ..... KIMA
Yakima, WA [*AM radio station call letters*] ..... KIT
Yakima, WA [*AM radio station call letters*] (RBYB) ..... KJOX-AM
Yakima, WA [*AM radio station call letters*] ..... KMWX
Yakima, WA [*Television station call letters*] ..... KNDO
Yakima, WA [*FM radio station call letters*] ..... KNWY
Yakima, WA [*FM radio station call letters*] ..... KRSE
Yakima, WA [*FM radio station call letters*] ..... KXDD
Yakima, WA [*FM radio station call letters*] (RBYB) ..... KYPL-FM
Yakima, WA [*FM radio station call letters*] ..... KYSC
Yakima, WA [*Television station call letters*] ..... KYVE
Yakima, WA [*AM radio station call letters*] ..... KZTA
Yakima, WA [*FM radio station call letters*] ..... KZTA-FM
Yakima, WA [*Location identifier FAA*] (FAAL) ..... XRY
Yako [*Burkina Faso*] [*ICAO location identifier*] (ICLI) ..... DHCY
Yakovlev [*Russian aircraft symbol; initialism taken from name of aircraft's designer*] ..... YAK
Yakovlev [*Former USSR ICAO aircraft manufacturer identifier*] (ICAO) ..... YK
YAK-Service [*Former USSR*] [*FAA designator*] (FAAC) ..... AKY
Yaku Shima [*Japan*] [*Airport symbol*] (OAG) ..... KUM
Yakushima [*Japan ICAO location identifier*] (ICLI) ..... RJFC
Yakushima [*Japan*] [*Seismograph station code, US Geological Survey Closed*] (SEIS) ..... YKS
Yakutat [*Alaska*] [*ICAO location identifier*] (ICLI) ..... PAYA
Yakutat [*Alaska*] [*Airport symbol*] (OAG) ..... YAK
Yakutat [*Alaska*] [*Seismograph station code, US Geological Survey Closed*] (SEIS) ..... YKT
Yakutat [*Alaska*] [*Seismograph station code, US Geological Survey*] (SEIS) ..... YKU
Yakutsk [*Former USSR Seismograph station code, US Geological Survey*] (SEIS) ..... YAK
Yaldymych [*Former USSR Seismograph station code, US Geological Survey Closed*] (SEIS) ..... YAT
Yale Arbovirus Research Unit [*Yale University*] [*Research center*] (RCD) ..... YARU
Yale Babylonian Collection (BJA) ..... YBC
Yale Club, New York, NY [*Library symbol Library of Congress*] (LCLS) ..... NNYC
Yale College (ROG) ..... YC
Yale Divinity School, New Haven, CT [*Inactive*] [*OCLC symbol*] (OCLC) ..... YU
Yale Judaica Series [*A publication*] (BJA) ..... YJS
Yale Law and Policy Review [*A publication*] (DLA) ..... Yale L & Pol'y Rev
Yale Law Journal [*A publication*] (BRI) ..... YLJ
Yale Medical School, New Haven, CT [*Inactive*] [*OCLC symbol*] (OCLC) ..... YUM
Yale Oriental Research [*A publication*] (BJA) ..... YOR
Yale Oriental Series. Babylonian Texts [*New Haven, CT*] [*A publication*] (BJA) ..... YBT
Yale Oriental Texts [*A publication*] (BJA) ..... YOT
Yale Peabody Museum ..... YPM
Yale Review [*A publication*] (BRI) ..... YR
Yale Review of Law and Social Action [*A publication*] (DLA) ..... Yale Rev Law & Soc Act'n
Yale Review of Law and Social Action [*A publication*] (DLA) ..... Yale Rev of L and Soc Action
Yale University (GAGS) ..... Yale U
Yale University ..... YU
Yale University, Babylonian Seminary, New Haven, CT [*Library symbol Library of Congress*] (LCLS) ..... CtY-BS
Yale University, Beinecke Rare Book and Manuscript Library, New Haven, CT [*Library symbol Library of Congress*] (LCLS) ..... CtY-BR
Yale University, Department of Economics, Economic Growth Center, New Haven, CT [*Library symbol Library of Congress*] (LCLS) ..... CtY-E
Yale University, Department of Epidemiology and Public Health, New Haven, CT [*Library symbol Library of Congress*] (LCLS) ..... CtY-EP
Yale University, Divinity School, New Haven, CT [*Library symbol Library of Congress*] (LCLS) ..... CtY-D
Yale University, Elizabethan Club, New Haven, CT [*Library symbol Library of Congress*] (LCLS) ..... CtY-EC
Yale University, Far Eastern Library, New Haven, CT [*Library symbol Library of Congress*] (LCLS) ..... CtY-FE
Yale University, Hammond Metallurgical Laboratories, New Haven, CT [*Library symbol Library of Congress*] (LCLS) ..... CtY-H
Yale University, Kirkland Hall, New Haven, CT [*Library symbol Library of Congress*] (LCLS) ..... CtY-K
Yale University, Kline Science Library, New Haven, CT [*Library symbol Library of Congress*] (LCLS) ..... CtY-KS
Yale University, Law Library, New Haven, CT [*Library symbol Library of Congress*] (LCLS) ..... CtY-L
Yale University Library ..... YUL

Yale University, Medical School, New Haven, CT [Library symbol Library of Congress] (LCLS) .... CtY-M
Yale University, New Haven, CT [Library symbol Library of Congress] (LCLS) .... CtY
Yale University, New Haven, CT [OCLC symbol] (OCLC) .... YUS
Yale University, Osborn Memorial Laboratories of Biological Sciences, New Haven, CT [Library symbol Library of Congress] (LCLS) .... CtY-B
Yale University, Peabody Museum of Natural History, New Haven, CT [Library symbol Library of Congress] (LCLS) .... CtY-P
Yale University Press (DGA) .... YUP
Yale University, School of Fine Arts, New Haven, CT [Library symbol Library of Congress] (LCLS) .... CtY-A
Yale University, School of Forestry, New Haven, CT [Library symbol Library of Congress] (LCLS) .... CtY-FS
Yale University, School of Music, New Haven, CT [Library symbol Library of Congress] (LCLS) .... CtY-Mus
Yale University, Social Sciences and Economic Growth Center, New Haven, CT [Library symbol Library of Congress] (LCLS) .... CtY-SSE
Yale University, Sterling Chemistry Laboratories, New Haven, CT [Library symbol Library of Congress] (LCLS) .... CtY-C
Yale University, Transportation Library, New Haven, CT [Library symbol Library of Congress] (LCLS) .... CtY-T
Yale University, Yale Center for British Art, New Haven, CT [Library symbol Library of Congress] (LCLS) .... CtY-BA
Yale-Brown Obsessive-Compulsive Scale [Psychology] .... Y-BOCS
Yale-China Association (EA) .... YCA
Yale-New Haven Hospital .... YNHH
Yalinga [Central African Republic] [ICAO location identifier] (ICLI) .... FEFY
Yalingimba [Zaire] [ICAO location identifier] (ICLI) .... FZGI
Yalkut Makhiri (BJA) .... YalMakh
Yalkut Shim'oni (BJA) .... Yal
Yalova [Turkey ICAO location identifier] (ICLI) .... LTBP
Yalova [Turkey] [Airport symbol] (AD) .... TYA
Yalta [Former USSR Seismograph station code, US Geological Survey Closed] (SEIS) .... YAL
Yalumet [Papua New Guinea] [Airport symbol] (OAG) .... KYX
Yam Internal Brown Spot Virus [Plant pathology] .... YIBSV
Yamagata [Japan] [Airport symbol] (OAG) .... GAJ
Yamagata [Japan ICAO location identifier] (ICLI) .... RJSC
Yamagata [Japan] [Seismograph station code, US Geological Survey] (SEIS) .... YAM
Yamaguchi-Ube, Honshu Island [Japan ICAO location identifier] (ICLI) .... RJDC
Yamaha Energy induction System .... YEIS
Yamaha Power Valve System .... YPVS
Yambio [Sudan] [ICAO location identifier] (ICLI) .... HSYA
Yamoussoukro [Ivory Coast] [Airport symbol] (OAG) .... ASK
Yamoussoukro [Ivory Coast] [ICAO location identifier] (ICLI) .... DIYO
Yampa Women's Club Library, Yampa, CO [Library symbol Library of Congress] (LCLS) .... CoYa
Yana Air Cargo (Kenya) Ltd. [ICAO designator] (FAAC) .... KYA
Yanan [China] [Airport symbol] (OAG) .... ENY
Yanan [China] [ICAO location identifier] (ICLI) .... ZLYA
Yanbu [Saudi Arabia] [Airport symbol] (OAG) .... YNB
Yancey County Public Library, Burnsville, NC [Library symbol Library of Congress] (LCLS) .... NcBv
Yancey Railroad Co. [AAR code] .... YAN
Yanceyville, NC [AM radio station call letters] .... WYNC
Yandina [Solomon Islands] [Airport symbol] (OAG) .... XYA
Yandina [Solomon Islands] [Airport symbol] (AD) .... YND
Yang Ming Line [Shipping] [Taiwan] .... YM
Yangambi [Zaire] [ICAO location identifier] (ICLI) .... FZIR
Yangi Qala [Afghanistan] [ICAO location identifier] (ICLI) .... OAYQ
Yangku [South Korea ICAO location identifier] (ICLI) .... RKNY
Yangoru [Papua New Guinea] [Seismograph station code, US Geological Survey] (SEIS) .... YAN
Yangtze Patrol, Asiatic Fleet [Navy] .... YANGPAT
Yangtze River and Basin [China, Mainland] [MARC geographic area code Library of Congress] (LCCP) .... a-ccg-
Yangtze Service Medal .... YSM
Yangzi Petrochemical Industrial Corp. [Commercial firm] [China] .... YPC
Yankee [Phonetic alphabet] [International] (DSUE) .... Y
Yankee (ROG) .... YANK
Yankee Atomic Electric Co. .... YAEC
Yankee Conference [College sports] .... YANCON
Yankee Conference [College sports] .... YC
Yankee Critical Facility [Nuclear energy] .... YCF
Yankee Energy System [NYSE symbol] (TTSB) .... YES
Yankee Energy System, Inc. [NYSE symbol] (SPSG) .... YES
Yankee Energy Systems, Inc. [Associated Press] (SAG) .... YankEnS
Yankee Group [Boston, MA] [Information service or system Telecommunications] (TSSD) .... YG
Yankee Nuclear Power Station (NRCH) .... YNPS
Yankee Power, Inc. [Vancouver Stock Exchange symbol] .... YKE
Yankee Team [Phase of the Indochina bombing operation during US military involvement in Vietnam] .... YT
Yankee Tractor Rocket Escape System (MCD) .... YTRES
Yanks Peak Resources [Vancouver Stock Exchange symbol] .... YPR
Yankton [South Dakota] [Airport symbol] (OAG) .... YKN
Yankton College, Yankton, SD [OCLC symbol] (OCLC) .... SDC
Yankton College, Yankton, SD [Library symbol Library of Congress] (LCLS) .... SdYC
Yankton Community Library, Yankton, SD [Library symbol Library of Congress] (LCLS) .... SdY
Yankton, SD [FM radio station call letters] .... KKYA
Yankton, SD [AM radio station call letters] .... KYNT

Yankton, SD [AM radio station call letters] .... WNAX
Yankton, SD [FM radio station call letters] .... WNAX-FM
Yanov [Later, LVV] [Former USSR Geomagnetic observatory code] .... YNV
Yao (Bantu) [MARC language code Library of Congress] (LCCP) .... yao
Yaounde [Cameroon] [ICAO location identifier] (ICLI) .... FKKY
Yaounde [Cameroon] [Airport symbol] (OAG) .... YAO
Yap [Caroline Islands] [ICAO location identifier] (ICLI) .... PTYA
Yap [Caroline Islands] [Airport symbol] (OAG) .... YAP
Yapacani [Bolivia] [ICAO location identifier] (ICLI) .... SLYI
Yapi-Kredi Bank [Turkey] (ECON) .... YK
Yapi-Kredi Bank [Turkey] (ECON) .... YKB
Yard [Measure] .... Y
Yard (IDOE) .... y
Yard [Navy] .... YD
Yard [Measure] .... YD
Yard [Measure] (ODBW) .... yd
Yard Activity Reporting and Decision System (PDAA) .... YARDS
Yard Bird [Confined to camp] [Military slang] .... YB
Yard Craft [Navy symbol] .... YC
Yard Drain Inlet (WDAA) .... YDI
Yard Floating Dry Dock [Non-self-propelled] [Navy symbol] .... YFD
Yard Freight Unit .... YFU
Yard Gully .... YG
Yard Oiler [Navy symbol] (DICI) .... YO
Yard Patrol .... YP
Yard Superintendent .... YS
Yard Tug [NYSE symbol] (DICI) .... YT
Yard Tug [Navy symbol] (DNAB) .... YWN
Yard Tug Big [Navy] .... YTB
Yarding (WGA) .... YDG
Yardley, PA [Location identifier FAA] (FAAL) .... ARD
Yards (MCD) .... YDS
Yards and Docks Supply Depot [Obsolete Navy] .... YDSD
Yards and Docks Supply Office [Navy] .... YDSO
Yards per Second .... YPS
Yardstick .... YS
Yardville National Bancorp [NASDAQ symbol] (SAG) .... YANB
Yardville National Bancorp [Associated Press] (SAG) .... YardvN
Yardville Natl Banc [NASDAQ symbol] (TTSB) .... YANB
Yard-Walk-Throughs [Navy] (NG) .... YWT
Yari [Colombia] [Airport symbol] (OAG) .... AYI
Yarinacocha [Peru] [ICAO location identifier] (ICLI) .... SPYC
Yarlung Zangbo Suture Zone [Geophysics] .... YZSZ
Yarmouth [Canada] [Airport symbol] (OAG) .... YQI
Yarmouth County Historical Society, Yarmouth, NS, Canada [Library symbol Library of Congress] (LCLS) .... CaNSYHM
Yarmouth, NS [Television station call letters] CBHFT-1
Yarmouth, NS [Television station call letters] CBHT-3
Yarmouth, NS [FM radio station call letters] .... CIFA
Yarmouth, NS [AM radio station call letters] .... CJLS
Yarmouth, NS [ICAO location identifier] (ICLI) .... CYQI
Yarn (VRA) .... ya
Yarn Merchants Association [Defunct] (EA) .... YMA
Yarn Over [Knitting] .... YO
Yarn to Back [Knitting] (ADA) .... YTB
Yarn to Front [Knitting] (BARN) .... yf
Yarn to Front [Knitting] (ADA) .... YTF
Yarns of Yesteryear Project (EA) .... YYP
Yarrow Admiralty Research Department [Navy British] .... Y-ARD
Yarsley Technical Centre Ltd. [Research center British] (IRC) .... YTEC
[The] Yarumal Foreign Mission Institute (Colombia) (TOCD) .... MXY
Yasa-Bonga [Zaire] [ICAO location identifier] (ICLI) .... FZDS
Yasodhara Ashram Society (EA) .... YAS
Yasouj [Iran] [ICAO location identifier] (ICLI) .... OISY
Yasyreta [Paraguay] [ICAO location identifier] (ICLI) .... SGYR
Yates Community Library, Lyndonville, NY [Library symbol Library of Congress] (LCLS) .... NLynd
Yate's Select Cases [1809] [New York] [A publication] (DLA) .... Sel Cas NY
Yates' Select Cases [1809] [New York] [A publication] (DLA) .... Yates Sel Cas
Yates' Select Cases [1809] [New York] [A publication] (DLA) .... Yates Sel Cas (NY)
Yates-Lee on Bankruptcy [3rd ed.] [1887] [A publication] (DLA) .... Yate-Lee
Yauca [Peru] [ICAO location identifier] (ICLI) .... SPYU
Yauco, PR [AM radio station call letters] .... WENA
Yauco, PR [Television station call letters] .... WIRS
Yauco, PR [AM radio station call letters] .... WKFE
Yaupi [Ecuador] [ICAO location identifier] (ICLI) .... SEYA
Yauri [Peru] [ICAO location identifier] (ICLI) .... SPIY
Yavapai College, Prescott, AZ [Library symbol Library of Congress] (LCLS) .... AzPrY
Yavapai College, Verde Campus, Clarkdale, AZ [Library symbol Library of Congress] (LCLS) .... AzPrY-V
Yavapai County Free Library District, Prescott, AZ [Library symbol] [Library of Congress] (LCLS) .... AzPrYC
Yaviza [Panama] [Airport symbol] (OAG) .... PYV
Yaw .... Y
Yaw Actuator Offset (KSC) .... YACTOFF
Yaw Analysis Methodology .... AM
Yaw and Pitch .... YAP
Yaw Attitude Sensor .... YAS
Yaw Axis .... YA
Yaw Axis (AAG) .... Y-Y
Yaw Channel .... YC
Yaw Control Axis [Symbol] .... R
Yaw Coupling .... YC
Yaw Coupling Parameter .... YCP

Yaw Damper [Aviation] (MCD) .... YD
Yaw Damper Computer .... YDC
Yaw Deviation .... YD
Yaw Error Amplifier .... YEA
Yaw Gimbal Command (KSC) .... YCMD
Yaw Integrated Flight Control Module (MCD) .... YIFCM
Yaw Microwave Sensor .... YMS
Yaw Phase Detector .... YPD
Yaw Precession Amplifier .... YPA
Yaw Ratio Controller (MCD) .... YRC
Yaw Ring .... YR
Yaw Steering Error .... YSE
Yaw Thrust Vector .... YTV
Yaw Trim (MCD) .... YT
Yaw Trim Angle .... YTA
Yaw Velocity Damping .... YVD
Yawing Moment (KSC) .... YM
Yawl (ROG) .... YL
Yawl .... YWL
Yawmiyyaet Filastiniyya (BJA) .... YF
Yaw-Roll (AAG) .... Y-R
Y-Axis .... Y
Y-Axis of External Tank [NASA] (NASA) .... YT
Y-Axis of Orbiter [NASA] (NASA) .... YO
Y-Axis of Payload [NASA] (NASA) .... YP
Y-Axis of Solid Rocket Booster [NASA] (NASA) .... YS
Y-Axis of Spacelab [NASA] (NASA) .... YL
Yazd [Iran] [Airport symbol] (OAG) .... AZD
Yazd [Iran] [ICAO location identifier] (ICLI) .... OIYT
Yazd [Iran] [ICAO location identifier] (ICLI) .... OIYY
Yazoo & Mississippi Valley Railroad Co. .... Y & MV
Yazoo City, MS [AM radio station call letters] .... WAZF
Yazoo City, MS [FM radio station call letters] .... WJNS
Yazoo-Sharkey Library System, Yazoo City, MS [Library symbol Library of Congress] (LCLS) .... MsY
Y-Body Axis Perpendicular to Orbit Plane [Aerospace] .... Y-POP
Y-Chromosome .... YC
Ye [Myanmar] [ICAO location identifier] (ICLI) .... VBYE
Ye Anciente and Secret Order of Quiet Birdmen (EA) .... YASOQB
Yea [Vote] .... Y
Year .... Y
Year (IDOE) .... y
Year (WDMC) .... y
Year (DAVI) .... yr
Year [Online database field identifier] (EY) .... YR
Year 2000 .... Y2K
Year Authorized (NITA) .... YA
Year Book 5 Henry V [England] [A publication] (DLA) .... Quinti Quinto
Year Book. Ames Foundation [A publication] (DLA) .... YB Ames
Year Book. Canadian Bar Association [A publication] (DLA) .... Can Bar Year Book
Year Book. European Convention on Human Rights [A publication] (DLA) .... YB Eur Conv on Human Rights
Year Book of Legal Studies [Madras, India] [A publication] (DLA) .... Yb of Leg Stud
Year Books of Edward I [A publication] (DLA) .... YB Ed I
Year Books, Part 1, Edward II [A publication] (DLA) .... YB P1 Edw II
Year Books, Part 7, Henry VI [A publication] (DLA) .... Yearb P7 Hen VI
Year Books, Part III [England] [A publication] (DLA) .... Secd Pt Edw III
Year Books, Part VIII [England] [A publication] (DLA) .... Secd Pt H VI
Year Books, Part X [5 Edw. 4, 1465] [A publication] (DLA) .... Long Quinto
Year Books, Rolls Series [1292-1546] [A publication] (DLA) .... YB (Rolls Ser)
Year Books, Rolls Series [1292-1546] [A publication] (DLA) .... YB (RS)
Year Books, Rolls Series, Edited by Horwood [1292-1307] [A publication] (DLA) .... YB (RS)
Year Books, Rolls Series, Edited by Horwood and Pike [1337-46] [A publication] (DLA) .... YB (RS)
Year Books, Selden Society [1307-19] [A publication] (DLA) .... YB (Sel Soc)
Year Books, Selden Society [1307-19] [A publication] (DLA) .... YB (SS)
Year Books, Selected Cases [A publication] (DLA) .... YBSC
Year End .... YE
Year Flown (MCD) .... YRFLN
Year Group .... YG
Year of Birth .... YOB
Year of Death .... YOD
Year of Energy Action .... YEA
Year of Entry (MHDB) .... YOE
Year of Grace Survey (DS) .... YGS
Year of Marriage .... YOM
Year of Publication (NITA) .... YP
Year of the Young Reader [1989] [Library of Congress campaign] .... YYR
Year Round Education (EDAC) .... YRE
Year to Date (MCD) .... YTD
Year to Date (EERA) .... YTD
Yearbook .... YB
Yearbook (BJA) .... Yr
Yearbook .... YRBK
Yearbook. Association of Attenders of Alumni of the Hague Academy of International Law [A publication] (DLA) .... YBAAA
Yearbook. European Convention on Human Rights [The Hague, Netherlands] [A publication] (DLA) .... YB Europ Conv HR
Yearbook. European Convention on Human Rights [The Hague, Netherlands] [A publication] (DLA) .... Yb of the Eur Conv on Human Rights
Yearbook. International Court of Justice [A publication] (DLA) .... YBICJ
Yearbook. International Law Commission [A publication] (DLA) .... YB Int'l L Comm'n
Yearbook. International Law Community [A publication] (DLA) .... YB Int L Comm

Yearbook. League of Nations [A publication] (DLA) .... YB League
Yearbook of Air and Space Law [A publication] (DLA) .... YB Air & Space L
Yearbook of Air and Space Law [A publication] (DLA) .... YBASL
Yearbook of Commercial Arbitration [A publication] (DLA) .... YBCA
Yearbook of Construction Articles [A publication] (AAGC) .... YCA
Yearbook of International Organizations [A publication] (DLA) .... YB Int'l Org
Yearbook of Procurement Articles [A publication] (AAGC) .... YPA
Yearbook of School Law [A publication] (DLA) .... YB Sch L
Yearbook of the United Nations [A publication] (DLA) .... YBUN
Yearbook of the United Nations [A publication] (DLA) .... YUN
Yearbook of World Polity [A publication] (DLA) .... YB World Pol
Yearbook on Human Rights [A publication] (DLA) .... YB Hum Rts
Yearbook on Human Rights [A publication] (DLA) .... YB Human Rights
Yearbook Printers Association (EA) .... YPA
Year-Class Strength Index [Pisciculture] .... YCI
Yearling .... yrl
Yearly (ROG) .... YRLY
Yearly Infrastructure Report (NATG) .... YIR
Yearly Meetings [Quakers] .... YM
Yearly Renewable Term [Insurance] .... YRT
Yearly Spares Cost (MCD) .... YSC
Year-Old .... YO
Year-Round Daylight Saving Time .... YRDST
Years before Present .... YBP
Year's Maximum Pensionable Earnings .... YMPE
Years of Extra Savings .... YES
Years of Potential Life Lost [Epidemiology] .... YPLL
Years of Service [Army] (INF) .... YOS
Years of Service Required .... YSR
Years of the North Atlantic Humpback [Collaborative study] .... YONAH
Years Old (DAVI) .... Y/O
Years Service for Severance Pay Purposes [Military] .... YSP
Yeast [cells] [Laboratory science] (DAVI) .... YST
Yeast Alcohol Dehydrogenase [An enzyme] .... YADH
Yeast Artificial Chromosome [Genetics] [Biochemistry] .... YAC
Yeast Carbon Base .... YCB
Yeast Centromere Plasmid [Genetics] .... YCp
Yeast Enolase [An enzyme] .... YE
Yeast Episomal Plasmid [Genetics] .... YEp
Yeast Estrogen System [Biochemistry] .... YES
Yeast Extract Agar [Microbiology] .... YEA
Yeast Extract - Dextrose Calcium Carbonate Agar [Microbiology] .... YDC
Yeast Extract - Glucose [Medium] .... YEG
Yeast Extract - Malt Extract [Medium] .... YM
Yeast Extract - Peptone Dextrose [Medium] .... YEPD
Yeast Extract Sucrose [Cell growth medium] .... YES
Yeast Extract-Casein Peptone [Medium] .... YECP
Yeast Extract-Peptones, Dextrose Medium [Microbiology] .... YPD
Yeast Integrating Plasmid [Genetics] .... YIp
Yeast Malt Broth .... YMB
Yeast Minimal Medium [Microorganism growth medium] .... YMM
Yeast Mold Count (OA) .... YMC
Yeast Morphology Agar (BABM) .... YMA
Yeast Nitrogen Base .... YNB
Yeast Peptone Broth [Microbiology] .... YPB
Yeast Phase (AAMN) .... YP
Yeates' Pennsylvania Reports [1791-1808] [A publication] (DLA) .... Y
Yeates' Pennsylvania Reports [1791-1808] [A publication] (DLA) .... Yea
Yeates' Pennsylvania Reports [1791-1808] [A publication] (DLA) .... Yeates
Yeates' Pennsylvania Reports [1791-1808] [A publication] (DLA) .... Yeates (PA)
Yebamoth (BJA) .... Yeb
Yechon [South Korea ICAO location identifier] (ICLI) .... RKTY
Yedi [Zaire] [ICAO location identifier] (ICLI) .... FZKI
Yedi'ot ha-Makhon le-Heker ha-Shirah ha-'Ivrit. Jerusalem (BJA) .... YMHSI
Yedi'ot ha-Makhon le-Mada'ei ha-Yahadut. Jerusalem (BJA) .... YMMY
Yedi'ot Numismatiyot be-Yisrael. Jerusalem (BJA) .... YedNum
Yedi'ot Yanai (BJA) .... YY
Yeelirie [Australia Airport symbol] (OAG) .... KYF
Yei [Sudan] [ICAO location identifier] (ICLI) .... HSYE
Yeldham [England] .... YELD
Yelimane [Mali] [ICAO location identifier] (ICLI) .... GAYE
Yellow [Symbol] (DAVI) .... j
Yellow [Phonetic alphabet] [Royal Navy World War I] (DSUE) .... Y
Yellow [Horticulture] .... Y
Yellow (AAG) .... YEL
Yellow (VRA) .... yel
Yellow (DAVI) .... YELL
Yellow [Maps and charts] .... YL
Yellow (ADA) .... YLW
Yellow .... YLW
Yellow Band Resources [Vancouver Stock Exchange symbol] .... YBD
Yellow Brick Road [Intelligence test] .... YBR
Yellow Caution Zone [Runway lighting] [Aviation] .... YCZ
Yellow Corp. [NASDAQ symbol] (SAG) .... YELL
Yellow Corp. [Associated Press] (SAG) .... YellowCp
Yellow Creek Bluff [Alaska] [Seismograph station code, US Geological Survey] (SEIS) .... YCB
Yellow Creek Nuclear Plant (NRCH) .... YCNP
Yellow, Cyan, and Magenta [Color model] (WDMC) .... YCM
Yellow Edges .... YE
Yellow Enzyme [Biochemistry] .... YE
Yellow Enzyme, Reduced [Biochemistry] .... YEH
Yellow Fever [Virus] (MAE) .... YF
Yellow Fever Virus [Virology] .... YFV
Yellow Indicating Light (IEEE) .... YIL

Yellow Jacket [*Immunology*] ... YJ
Yellow Jacket Venom [*Immunology*] ... YJV
Yellow Lamp (IAA) ... YL
Yellow Lamp Century Certificate (IAA) ... YLCC
Yellow Light (MSA) ... YLT
Yellow, Magenta, Cyan, Black (WDMC) ... YMCK
Yellow Magic Orchestra [*Musical group*] [*Japan*] ... YMO
Yellow Man ... YM
Yellow Metal ... YM
Yellow Page Rate Base Analysis Plan [*Bell System*] ... YRAP
Yellow Pages Datasystem [*National Planning Data Corp.*] [*Database*] ... YPD
Yellow Pages Service [*Telecommunications*] (TEL) ... YPS
Yellow Pine ... YP
Yellow Red Green Blue (IAA) ... YRGB
Yellow River and Basin [*China, Mainland*] [*MARC geographic area code Library of Congress*] (LCCP) ... a-ccy-
Yellow Sea and Area [*MARC geographic area code Library of Congress*] (LCCP) ... ay----
Yellow Sheet Price of Beef [*Business term*] ... YPBF
Yellow Sheet Price of Lamb [*Business term*] ... YPLB
Yellow Sheet Price of Pork [*Business term*] ... YPPK
Yellow Spot ... YS
Yellow Springs Institute for Contemporary Studies and the Arts (EA) ... YSICSA
Yellow Springs Instrument Co. ... YSI
Yellow Springs, OH [*FM radio station call letters*] ... WYSO
Yellow Varnish Cambric ... YVC
Yellow Wove [*Paper*] (DGA) ... YW
Yellow-Bellied Sapsucker [*Ornithology*] ... YS
Yellow-Dog Contract (MHDB) ... YDC
Yellow-Green ... YG
Yellow-Green Beacon [*Aviation*] ... YG
Yellowhead Museum, Clearwater, British Columbia [*Library symbol National Library of Canada*] (NLC) ... BCLYM
Yellowhead Regional Library, Spruce Grove, AB, Canada [*Library symbol Library of Congress*] (LCLS) ... CaASgY
Yellowhead Regional Library, Spruce Grove, Alberta [*Library symbol National Library of Canada*] (NLC) ... ASGY
Yellowish [*Philately*] ... yelsh
Yellowjack Resources [*Vancouver Stock Exchange symbol*] ... YJK
Yellowknife [*Northwest Territories*] [*Seismograph station code, US Geological Survey*] (SEIS) ... YKC
Yellowknife [*Canada*] [*Airport symbol*] (OAG) ... YZF
Yellowknife Array [*Northwest Territories*] [*Seismograph station code, US Geological Survey*] (SEIS) ... YKA
Yellowknife Bear Resources, Inc. [*Toronto Stock Exchange symbol*] ... YB
Yellowknife, NT [*AM radio station call letters*] ... CFYK
Yellowknife, NT [*Television station call letters*] ... CFYK-TV
Yellowknife, NT [*AM radio station call letters*] ... CJCD
Yellowknife, NT [*FM radio station call letters*] ... CKLB
Yellowknife, NT [*ICAO location identifier*] (ICLI) ... CYZF
Yellowknife Public Library, Northwest Territories [*Library symbol National Library of Canada*] (NLC) ... NWY
Yellowknife Public Library, Yellowknife, NT, Canada [*Library symbol*] [*Library of Congress*] (LCLS) ... CaNWY
Yellowroot Tea [*Folk remedy, extract of buttercup root*] ... YRT
Yellowstone (FAAC) ... YLSTN
Yellowstone City-County Helth Department, Billings, MT [*Library symbol*] [*Library of Congress*] (LCLS) ... MtBilYH
Yellowstone National Park ... YELL
Yellowstone National Travelers (EA) ... YNT
Yellowstone to Canada's Yukon Territory ... Y2Y
Yellowstone Treatment Center, Billings, MT [*Library symbol*] [*Library of Congress*] (LCLS) ... MtBilY
Yellowstone-Bighorn Research Association (EA) ... YBRA
Yellow-White ... YW
Yellville, AR [*FM radio station call letters*] ... KCTT
Yelverton's English King's Bench Reports [*1603-13*] [*A publication*] (DLA) ... Yel
Yelverton's English King's Bench Reports [*1603-13*] [*A publication*] (DLA) ... Yelv
Yelverton's English King's Bench Reports [*1603-13*] [*A publication*] (DLA) ... Yelv (Eng)
Yembe-Moke [*Zaire*] [*ICAO location identifier*] (ICLI) ... FZEM
Yemen Airlines [*Airline flight code*] (ODBW) ... IY
Yemen Airways [*ICAO designator*] (AD) ... IY
Yemen Arab Republic [*Aircraft nationality and registration mark*] (FAAC) ... 4W
Yemen Arab Republic ... YAR
Yemen Arab Republic [*ANSI two-letter standard code*] (CNC) ... YE
Yemen Arab Republic [*MARC country of publication code Library of Congress*] (LCCP) ... ye
Yemen Kuwait Bank for Trade & Investment ... YKB
Yemen (Sanaa) [*MARC geographic area code Library of Congress*] (LCCP) ... a-ye--
Yemen (Sanaa) [*ANSI three-letter standard code*] (CNC) ... YEM
Yemen Socialist Party [*South Yemen*] [*Political party*] (PD) ... YSP
Yemeni Riyal (BJA) ... YR
Yemenia, Yemen Airways [*ICAO designator*] (FAAC) ... IYE
Yemo [*Zaire*] [*ICAO location identifier*] (ICLI) ... FZGY
Yen [*Monetary unit in Japan*] ... Y
Yenbo [*Saudi Arabia*] [*ICAO location identifier*] (ICLI) ... OEYN
Yendi [*Ghana*] [*ICAO location identifier*] (ICLI) ... DGLY
Yengema [*Sierra Leone*] [*ICAO location identifier*] (ICLI) ... GFYE
Yengema [*Sierra Leone*] [*Airport symbol*] (OAG) ... WYE
Yeni Dogus Partisi [*New Dawn Party*] [*Turkish Cyprus*] [*Political party*] (EY) ... YDP
Yeni Kibris Partisi [*New Cypus Party*] [*Turkish Cyprus*] [*Political party*] (EY) ... YKP
Yenisehir [*Turkey ICAO location identifier*] (ICLI) ... LTBR
Yeniseysk [*Former USSR ICAO location identifier*] (ICLI) ... UNII
Yeoju [*South Korea ICAO location identifier*] (ICLI) ... RKSU
Yeoman ... Y
Yeoman [*Navy rating*] ... YN
Yeoman, Chief [*Navy rating*] ... YNC
Yeoman, First Class [*Navy rating*] ... YN1
Yeoman, Master Chief [*Navy rating*] ... YNCM
Yeoman, Second Class [*Navy rating*] ... YN2
Yeoman, Senior Chief [*Navy rating*] ... YNCS
Yeoman, Third Class [*Navy rating*] ... YN3
Yeomanry ... YEO
Yeomanry (WGA) ... YEOM
Yeomanry [*British military*] (DMA) ... Yeomy
Yeomanry Cavalry [*Military British*] ... YC
Yeongdongri [*South Korea ICAO location identifier*] (ICLI) ... RKSR
Yeosu [*South Korea ICAO location identifier*] (ICLI) ... RKJY
Yeovil [*British ICAO location identifier*] (ICLI) ... EGHG
Yeovil [*British depot code*] ... YEO
Yeovilton [*British ICAO location identifier*] (ICLI) ... EGDY
Yerevan/Zvartnots [*Former USSR ICAO location identifier*] (ICLI) ... UGEE
Yerger's Tennessee Reports [*9-18 Tennessee*] [*A publication*] (DLA) ... Yerg
Yerger's Tennessee Reports [*9-18 Tennessee*] [*A publication*] (DLA) ... Yerg (Tenn)
Yerger's Tennessee Supreme Court Reports [*A publication*] (DLA) ... Yer
Yerkesik [*Turkey*] [*Seismograph station code, US Geological Survey*] (SEIS) ... YER
Yermo, CA [*FM radio station call letters*] ... KRXV
Yermo, CA [*FM radio station call letters*] ... KYHT
Yersinea [*A genus of bacteria*] ... Y
Yersinia Arthritis [*Medicine*] (DMAA) ... YA
Yerushalmi [*Palestinian Talmud*] (BJA) ... Y
Yerushalmi [*Palestinian Talmud*] (BJA) ... Yer
Yerushalmi Fragments [*A publication*] (BJA) ... YF
Yes [*Citizens band radio slang*] ... YO
Yes Bay [*Alaska*] [*Airport symbol*] (AD) ... WYC
Yes Clothing [*NASDAQ symbol*] (TTSB) ... YSCO
Yes Clothing Co. [*Associated Press*] (SAG) ... YesClth
Yes Clothing Co. [*NASDAQ symbol*] (NQ) ... YSCO
Yes Entertainment [*NASDAQ symbol*] (TTSB) ... YESS
Yes Entertainment, Inc. [*Associated Press*] (SAG) ... YesEn
Yes Entertainment, Inc. [*Associated Press*] (SAG) ... YesEnt
Yes Entertainment, Inc. [*NASDAQ symbol*] (SAG) ... YESS
Yes/No (NITA) ... Y/N
Yeshiba Toledot Isaac. Tetuan (BJA) ... YTI
Yeshiva Benarroch. Tetuan (BJA) ... YB
Yeshiva University (GAGS) ... Yeshiva U
Yeshiva University [*New York*] ... YU
Yeshiva University, Albert Einstein College of Medicine, Bronx, NY [*Library symbol Library of Congress*] (LCLS) ... NNYU-M
Yeshiva University Cumulative Index of Films of Jewish Interest [*A publication*] (BJA) ... YUCI
Yeshiva University, Mendel Gottesman Library of Hebraica Judaica, New York, NY [*Library symbol Library of Congress*] (LCLS) ... NNYU-HJ
Yeshiva University, New York, NY [*Library symbol Library of Congress*] (LCLS) ... NNYU
Yeshiva University, New York, NY [*OCLC symbol*] (OCLC) ... YYP
Yeshiva University, Stern College, New York, NY [*Library symbol Library of Congress*] (LCLS) ... NNYU-S
Yeshivath Torah Hayim in Jerusalem (EA) ... YTHJ
Yes-No [*Response prompt*] ... YN
Yesterday [*Business term*] ... YDAY
Yesterday (DSUE) ... YEST
Yesterday ... YESTY
Yesterday's Authors of Books for Children [*A publication*] ... YABC
Yesterday's Children (EA) ... YC
Yet Another [*Computer hacker terminology*] (NHD) ... YA
Yet Another BASIC [*Beginner's All-Purpose Symbolic Instruction Code*] [*Computer science*] ... YAB
Yet Another Bloody Acronym [*Computer hacker terminology*] (NHD) ... YABA
Yet Another Compiler-Compiler (MHDB) ... YACC
Yet Another Compiler-Complier (HGAA) ... YACC
Yet Another Hierarchically Officious Oracle [*World Wide Web*] (DOM) ... Yahoo
Yet Another MODEM [*Modulator-Demodulator*] [*Communications program*] ... YAM
Yet Another Unix Nerd [*Computer hacker terminology*] (NHD) ... YAUN
Yet Another User Interface [*Computer science*] ... YAUI
Yet Another Word Processor (BYTE) ... YAWP
Yetminster [*England*] ... YETM
Yevamot (BJA) ... Yev
Yevreyskaya Entsiklopediya [*A publication*] (BJA) ... YE
Y-Force Operations Staff [*Army World War II*] ... Y-FOS
Yibal [*Oman*] [*ICAO location identifier*] (ICLI) ... OOYB
Yichang [*China*] [*Airport symbol*] (OAG) ... YIH
Yiddish [*MARC language code Library of Congress*] (LCCP) ... yid
Yiddish Dictionary Committee (EA) ... YDC
Yiddish Theatrical Alliance (EA) ... YTA
Yiddish Writers Union (EA) ... YWU
Yiddisher Kultur Farband (EA) ... YKUF
Yidishe Arbeter Froyen (BJA) ... YAF
Yidishe Landvirtshaftlekhe Gezelshaft [*A publication*] (BJA) ... YILAG
Yidisher Visnshaftlekher Institut [*Yiddish Scientific Institute*] ... YIVO
Yield [*Agriculture*] [*Stock exchange term*] ... Y
Yield [*Investment term*] ... YLD
Yield Analysis Pattern [*Computer science*] ... YAP
Yield Component Analysis [*Botany*] ... YCA
Yield Diffusion Bonding ... YDB
Yield Limit (WDAA) ... YL

Yield Measurement System .... YMS
Yield Point [*Ordinarily expressed in PSI*] .... YP
Yield Pressure (MAE) .... YP
Yield Safety Factor (IEEE) .... YSF
Yield Spread [*Investment term*] .... YS
Yield Strength [*Ordinarily expressed in PSI*] .... YS
Yield Strength Load Factor (IEEE) .... YSLF
Yield Strength to Elastic Modulus Ratio [*Dentistry*] .... YS/E
Yield Stress .... YS
Yield Stress Bonding .... YSB
Yield Stress Diffusion Bonding .... YSDB
Yield Threshold Test Ban Treaty [*1976*] .... YTTBT
Yield to Broker [*Investment term*] .... YTB
Yield to Call [*Investment term*] .... YTC
Yield to Maturity [*Investment term*] .... YTM
Yield to Total Elation .... YTTE
Yield Value (IAA) .... YV
Yielding (ROG) .... YLDG
YieldUp International Corp. [*NASDAQ symbol*] (SAG) .... YILD
YieldUP International Corp. [*Associated Press*] (SAG) .... YldUP
YieldUP Intl [*NASDAQ symbol*] (TTSB) .... YILD
YieldUP Intl Unit [*NASDAQ symbol*] (TTSB) .... YILDU
YieldUP Intl Wrrt'A' [*NASDAQ symbol*] (TTSB) .... YILDW
YieldUp Intl Wrrt'B' [*NASDAQ symbol*] (TTSB) .... YILDZ
Yinchuan [*China*] [*Airport symbol*] (OAG) .... INC
Yinchuan [*Republic of China*] [*Seismograph station code, US Geological Survey*] (SEIS) .... YNC
Yinchuan [*China*] [*ICAO location identifier*] (ICLI) .... ZLIC
Yingkow [*Republic of China*] [*Seismograph station code, US Geological Survey*] (SEIS) .... YIN
Yining [*China*] [*Airport symbol*] (OAG) .... YIN
Yining [*China*] [*ICAO location identifier*] (ICLI) .... ZWYN
Yirol [*Sudan*] [*ICAO location identifier*] (ICLI) .... HSYL
YIVO Institute for Jewish Research, New York, NY [*Library symbol Library of Congress*] (LCLS) .... NNYI
Ylivieska-Raudaskyla [*Finland ICAO location identifier*] (ICLI) .... EFYL
YM - YWHA, Montreal, Quebec [*Library symbol National Library of Canada*] (NLC) .... QMYH
Y-Matrix of Transistor (IDOE) .... yT
Y-Matrix of Vacuum Tube (IDOE) .... yV
YMCA Camp [*Montana*] [*Seismograph station code, US Geological Survey Closed*] (SEIS) .... YCM
YMCA [*Young Men's Christian Association*] **International Program Services** (EA) .... YMCAIPS
YMCA [*Young Men's Christian Association*] **International Student Service** (EA) .... ISS
Ymgyrch Diogelu Cymru Wledig [*Campaign for the Protection of Rural Wales*] [*See also CPRW*] (EAIO) .... YDCW
YM-YWHA Library, Montreal, PQ, Canada [*Library symbol Library of Congress*] (LCLS) .... CaQMYH
Yoakum, TX [*FM radio station call letters*] (RBYB) .... KYKM
Yoakum, TX [*Location identifier FAA*] (FAAL) .... OKT
Yoga Research Foundation (EA) .... YRF
Yogurt .... YGRT
Yogurt Extra Smooth [*Trademark of the Dannon Co., Inc.*] .... YES
Yogyakarta/Adi Sucipto [*Indonesia*] [*ICAO location identifier*] (ICLI) .... WIIJ
Yoho Pitch Extractor .... YPE
Yoke [*Phonetic alphabet*] [*World War II*] (DSUE) .... Y
Yokefellowship Prison Ministry (EA) .... YPM
Yoko [*Cameroon*] [*ICAO location identifier*] (ICLI) .... FKAY
Yokogawa Hewlett Packard Ltd. [*Japan*] .... YHP
Yokohama [*Japan*] [*Seismograph station code, US Geological Survey*] (SEIS) .... YOK
Yokohama Technical Research Center [*Mazda Motor Corp.*] .... YTRC
Yokosuka [*Japan*] [*Seismograph station code, US Geological Survey Closed*] (SEIS) .... YSK
Yokota [*Japan ICAO location identifier*] (ICLI) .... RJTY
Yola [*Nigeria*] [*ICAO location identifier*] (ICLI) .... DNYO
Yola [*Nigeria*] [*Airport symbol*] (OAG) .... YOL
Yola Clay Loam [*A soil type*] .... YC
Yolk Cytoplasmic Layer [*Embryology*] .... YCL
Yolk Sac (MAE) .... YS
Yolk Sac Carcinoma [*Oncology, pathology, and pediatrics*] (DAVI) .... YSC
Yolk Sac Tumor [*Oncology*] .... YST
Yolk Syncytial Layer [*Embryology*] .... YSL
Yolo County Free Library, Woodland, CA [*Library symbol Library of Congress*] (LCLS) .... CWoY
Yom Kippur (BJA) .... YK
Yom Kippur War (BJA) .... YKW
Yom Tov (BJA) .... YT
Yoma (BJA) .... Yo
Yoma (BJA) .... Yom
Yomitan [*Ryukyu Islands*] [*ICAO location identifier*] (ICLI) .... ROKW
Yonago [*Japan*] [*Airport symbol*] (OAG) .... YGJ
Yonago [*Japan*] [*Seismograph station code, US Geological Survey*] (SEIS) .... YON
Yonagunijima [*Japan*] [*Airport symbol*] (OAG) .... OGN
Yonagunijima [*Ryukyu Islands*] [*ICAO location identifier*] (ICLI) .... ROYN
Yonagunijima [*Ryukyu Islands*] [*Seismograph station code, US Geological Survey*] (SEIS) .... YOJ
Yonkers Financial [*NASDAQ symbol*] (TTSB) .... YFCB
Yonkers Public Library, Yonkers, NY [*Library symbol Library of Congress*] (LCLS) .... NY
Yonkers School System, Yonkers, NY [*Library symbol Library of Congress*] (LCLS) .... NYS
Yonkers School System, Yonkers, NY [*OCLC symbol*] (OCLC) .... YON
Yonsei University, Seoul, Korea [*Library symbol Library of Congress*] (LCLS) .... KoSYU
Yool on Waste, Nuisance, and Trespass [*1863*] [*A publication*] (DLA) .... Yool Waste
Yooralla Society of Victoria [*Australia*] .... YSV
Yopal/Yopal [*Colorado ICAO location identifier*] (ICLI) .... SKYP
Yorba Linda District Library, Yorba Linda, CA [*Library symbol Library of Congress*] (LCLS) .... CYI
Yorbeau Resources, Inc. [*Toronto Stock Exchange symbol*] .... YRB
Yoreh De'ah. Shulhan 'Arukh (BJA) .... YD
York, AL [*FM radio station call letters*] .... WSLY
York, AL [*AM radio station call letters*] .... WYLS
York and Lancaster Regiment [*Military unit*] [*British*] (DMA) .... Y & L
York and Lancaster Regiment [*Military unit*] [*British*] .... Y & LR
York Antibodies [*Immunology*] .... YK
York Borough Board of Education, Professional Education Library [*UTLAS symbol*] .... YBE
York Borough Board of Education, Toronto, ON, Canada [*Library symbol Library of Congress*] (LCLS) .... CaOTYBE
York Borough Board of Education, Toronto, Ontario [*Library symbol National Library of Canada*] (NLC) .... OTYBE
York Center, ME [*FM radio station call letters*] .... WCQL
York Center, ME [*FM radio station call letters*] (RBYB) .... WXHT-FM
York Centre [*Vancouver Stock Exchange symbol*] .... YCC
York College of Pennsylvania, York, PA [*Library symbol Library of Congress*] (LCLS) .... PYC
York College of Pennsylvania, York, PA [*OCLC symbol*] (OCLC) .... YCP
York College of the City University of New York, Jamaica, NY [*Library symbol Library of Congress*] (LCLS) .... NJY
York College of the City University of New York, Jamaica, NY [*OCLC symbol*] (OCLC) .... VMY
York College, York, NE [*Library symbol Library of Congress*] (LCLS) .... NbYC
York County Board of Education, Aurora, ON, Canada [*Library symbol Library of Congress*] (LCLS) .... CaOAuYCE
York County Board of Education, Aurora, Ontario [*Library symbol National Library of Canada*] (NLC) .... OAUYCE
York County Board of Education, Toronto, ON, Canada [*Library symbol Library of Congress*] (LCLS) .... CaOTYCE
York County Genealogical Society (EA) .... YCGS
York County Library, Rock Hill, SC [*Library symbol*] [*Library of Congress*] (LCLS) .... ScRh
York Financial [*NASDAQ symbol*] (TTSB) .... YFED
York Financial Corp. [*York, PA*] [*NASDAQ symbol*] (NQ) .... YFED
York Financial Corp. [*Associated Press*] (SAG) .... YorkFn
York Group [*NASDAQ symbol*] (TTSB) .... YRKG
York High School Library, Retsof, NY [*OCLC symbol*] (OCLC) .... RXO
York Hospital, York, PA [*Library symbol Library of Congress*] (LCLS) .... PYH
York International [*Associated Press*] (SAG) .... YorkIn
York International [*NYSE symbol*] (TTSB) .... YRK
York International Corp. [*NYSE symbol*] (SPSG) .... YRK
York, KY [*Location identifier FAA*] (FAAL) .... YRK
York Legal Record [*Pennsylvania*] [*A publication*] (DLA) .... YLR
York Legal Record [*Pennsylvania*] [*A publication*] (DLA) .... York
York Legal Record [*Pennsylvania*] [*A publication*] (DLA) .... York Leg Rec
York Legal Record [*Pennsylvania*] [*A publication*] (DLA) .... York Leg Rec (PA)
York Legal Record [*Pennsylvania*] [*A publication*] (DLA) .... York Leg Record
York, NE [*AM radio station call letters*] .... KAWL
York, NE [*FM radio station call letters*] .... KTMX
York, PA [*Location identifier FAA*] (FAAL) .... THV
York, PA [*FM radio station call letters*] .... WARM
York, PA [*AM radio station call letters*] .... WOYK
York, PA [*Television station call letters*] .... WPMT
York, PA [*AM radio station call letters*] .... WQXA
York, PA [*FM radio station call letters*] .... WQXA-FM
York, PA [*AM radio station call letters*] .... WSBA
York, PA [*FM radio station call letters*] .... WVYC
York Public Library [*UTLAS symbol*] .... YPL
York Public Library, Toronto, ON, Canada [*Library symbol Library of Congress*] (LCLS) .... CaOTYP
York Public Library, York, NE [*Library symbol Library of Congress*] (LCLS) .... NbY
York Region Board of Education [*UTLAS symbol*] .... AUR
York Regional Library, Fredericton, NB, Canada [*Library symbol Library of Congress*] (LCLS) .... CaNBFYR
York Regional Library, Fredericton, New Brunswick [*Library symbol National Library of Canada*] (NLC) .... NBFYR
York Regional Library Headquarters No. 2, Woodstock, NB, Canada [*Library symbol Library of Congress*] (LCLS) .... CaNBWY
York Regional Library, Headquarters No. 2, Woodstock, New Brunswick [*Library symbol National Library of Canada*] (NLC) .... NBWY
York Research [*NASDAQ symbol*] (TTSB) .... YORK
York Research Corp. [*NASDAQ symbol*] (NQ) .... YORK
York Research Corp. [*Associated Press*] (SAG) .... YorkRs
York, SC [*AM radio station call letters*] .... WBZK
York Technical College, Rock Hill, SC [*Library symbol*] [*Library of Congress*] (LCLS) .... ScRhY
York University Archives, Toronto, ON, Canada [*Library symbol*] [*Library of Congress*] (LCLS) .... CaOTYA
York University Archives, Toronto, Ontario [*Library symbol National Library of Canada*] (NLC) .... OTYA
York University Law Library [*UTLAS symbol*] .... YRL
York University, Law Library, Toronto, ON, Canada [*Library symbol Library of Congress*] (LCLS) .... CaOTYL
York University Library [*UTLAS symbol*] .... YRK
York University, Toronto, ON, Canada [*Library symbol Library of Congress*] (LCLS) .... CaOTY

York University, Toronto, Ontario [*Library symbol National Library of Canada*] (NLC) .... OTY
York-Antwerp Rules [*Marine insurance*] .... Y/A
York-Antwerp Rules [*Marine insurance*] .... YAR
Yorker [*Phonetic alphabet*] [*Pre-World War II*] (DSUE) .... Y
York-Hanover, PA [*FM radio station call letters*] .... WYCR
Yorkshire [*County in England*] .... YKS
Yorkshire [*County in England*] .... YORKS
Yorkshire [*County in England*] (ODBW) .... Yorks
Yorkshire and Humberside Council for Further and Higher Education [*British*] (AIE) .... YHCFE
Yorkshire Association of Power Loom Overlookers [*A union*] [*British*] (DCTA) .... YAPLO
Yorkshire Canary Club of America (EA) .... YCCA
Yorkshire Dialect Society [*British*] (DBA) .... YDS
Yorkshire Dragoons [*British military*] (DMA) .... YD
Yorkshire East Riding Regiment [*British military*] (DMA) .... Ye Et Rg Rt
Yorkshire European Airways Ltd. [*British ICAO designator*] (FAAC) .... JOR
Yorkshire European Airways Ltd. [*British ICAO designator*] (FAAC) .... SJT
Yorkshire Hussars [*British military*] (DMA) .... YH
Yorkshire Hussars Imperial Yeomanry [*British military*] (DMA) .... YHIY
[*The*] Yorkshire Light Infantry [*Military unit*] [*British*] .... YLI
Yorkshire, North Riding [*County in England*] (ROG) .... YNR
Yorkshire Society of Textile Craftsmen [*A union*] [*British*] (DCTA) .... YSTC
Yorkshire Television [*British*] .... YTV
Yorkshire Terrier Club of America (EA) .... YTCA
Yorkshire Trust Co. [*Toronto Stock Exchange symbol Vancouver Stock Exchange symbol*] .... YTC
Yorkshire, West Riding [*County in England*] (ROG) .... YWR
York-Sunbury Historical Society, Fredericton, NB, Canada [*Library symbol Library of Congress*] (LCLS) .... CaNBFY
York-Sunbury Historical Society, Fredericton, New Brunswick [*Library symbol National Library of Canada*] (NLC) .... NBFY
Yorkton [*Canada*] [*Airport symbol*] (OAG) .... YQV
Yorkton, SK [*Television station call letters*] CICC
Yorkton, SK [*AM radio station call letters*] .... CJGX
Yorkton, SK [*Television station call letters*] .... CKOS
Yorkton, SK [*ICAO location identifier*] (ICLI) .... CYQV
Yorktown Expert System for Multiple Virtual Storage Environments [*Computer science*] (HGAA) .... YES/MVS
Yorktown, VA [*Location identifier FAA*] (FAAL) .... NCY
Yorktown, VA [*FM radio station call letters*] .... WXEZ
Yorktown, VA [*FM radio station call letters*] .... WYCS
Yoro [*Honduras*] [*Airport symbol*] (AD) .... YOR
Yoron [*Ryukyu Islands*] [*ICAO location identifier*] (ICLI) .... RORY
Yoron-Jima [*Japan*] [*Airport symbol*] (OAG) .... RNJ
Yoruba [*MARC language code Library of Congress*] (LCCP) .... yor
Yosemite Airlines [*ICAO designator*] (AD) .... JE
Yosemite Association (EA) .... YA
Yosemite Museum, Nature Library, Yosemite, CA [*Library symbol Library of Congress*] (LCLS) .... CYoM
Yosemite National Park [*California*] [*Airport symbol Obsolete*] (OAG) .... OYS
Yosemite National Park .... YOSE
Yosemite Natural History Association (EA) .... YNHA
Yoshida Sarcoma [*Medicine*] .... YS
Yoshido Kogyo Kabushiki-Kaishi [*Yoshida Industries Ltd.*] [*Japan*] .... YKK
Yoshitomi Pharmaceutical Ind. Co. Ltd. [*Japan*] [*Research code symbol*] .... CLY
Yoshitomi Pharmaceutical Ind. Co. Ltd. [*Japan*] [*Research code symbol*] .... Y
Yosiwara [*Japan*] [*Seismograph station code, US Geological Survey Closed*] (SEIS) .... YOS
You .... Y
You Are Authorized (FAAC) .... URAUZ
You Be Darned [*Bowdlerized version*] (DSUE) .... UBDd
You Know You've Been Hacking Too Long When [*Computer science*] .... YKYBHTLW
You Won't Get Ahead Sitting on Your Afterdeck [*Slang Bowdlerized version*] .... YWGASOYA
Youcai Mosaic Virus [*Plant pathology*] .... YMV
Young [*Australia Airport symbol*] (OAG) .... NGA
Young (AAMN) .... Y
Young .... YNG
Young [*Australia Seismograph station code, US Geological Survey*] (SEIS) .... YOU
Young Achiever [*Australia*] .... YA
Young Actors Guild (EA) .... YAG
Young Adult [*Refers to books published for this market*] .... YA
Young Adult Book Review Index [*A publication*] .... YABRI
Young Adult Chronic Patient [*Medicine*] (MEDA) .... YACP
Young Adult Conservation Corps .... YACC
Young Adult Council of National Social Welfare Assembly (EA) .... YAC
Young Adult Institute and Workshop (EA) .... YAI
Young Adult Library Services Association [*American Library Association*] .... YALSA
Young Adult Services Division - of ALA [*American Library Association*] (EA) .... YASD
Young Adult Special Interest Group [*Canadian Library Association*] .... YASIG
Young American Bowling Alliance (EA) .... YABA
Young American Indian Council .... YAIC
Young Americans for Freedom (EA) .... YAF
Young Americans for Responsible Action .... YARA
Young Americans in Prague [*Expatriot Americans in the 1990's*] .... YAP
Young Americans of Polish Descent [*Defunct*] (EA) .... YAPD
Young America's Campaign Committee [*Later, FCM*] (EA) .... YACC
Young America's Foundation .... YAF
Young & Rubicam International [*Advertising agency*] .... Y & R
[*The*] Young and the Restless Fan Club (EA) .... YRFC

Young Artist Professional [*Lifestyle classification*] .... Yappie
Young Aspiring Professional [*In book title "YAP; the Official Young Aspiring Professional's Fast-Track Handbook"*] [*Lifestyle classification*] .... Yap
Young Astronaut Council (EA) .... YAC
Young, Attractive, Verbal, Intelligent, and Successful .... YAVIS
Young Audiences (EA) .... YA
Young Australian Male [*Lifestyle classification*] .... YAM
Young Black Programmers Coalition (EA) .... YBPC
Young British Designers .... YBD
Young Broadcasting, Inc. [*NASDAQ symbol*] (SAG) .... YBTV
Young Broadcasting, Inc. [*Associated Press*] (SAG) .... YoungBd
Young Broadcasting 'A' [*NASDAQ symbol*] (TTSB) .... YBTVA
Young Calvinist Federation (EA) .... YCF
Young Children: Priority One [*Kiwanis Club*] .... YCPO
Young Children's Social Desirability Scale (EDAC) .... YCSDS
Young Christian Movement [*Formerly, YCW*] [*Defunct*] .... YCM
Young Christian Student (AEBS) .... YCS
Young Christian Student Movement .... YCSM
Young Christian Workers [*Later, YCM*] (EA) .... YCW
Young Circle League of America [*Later, Workmen's Circle*] (EA) .... YCLA
Young Citizens Volunteers [*14th (Service) Battalion, Royal Irish Rifles*] [*British military*] (DMA) .... YCV
Young Collector Series [*A publication*] .... YCS
Young Communist International [*Dissolved, 1943*] .... YCI
Young Communist League of the United States of America (EA) .... YCL
Young Concert Artists (EA) .... YCA
Young Conservative Alliance of America [*Later, Campus Action Network*] (EA) .... YCA
Young Conservative Foundation [*Later, CAF*] (EA) .... YCF
Young Democratic Clubs of America [*Later, YDA*] (EA) .... YDCA
Young Democratic Progressive Party [*Macedonia*] [*Political party*] (EY) .... YDPP
Young Democrats of America (EA) .... YDA
Young Elementary School, Pasadena, TX [*Library symbol*] [*Library of Congress*] (LCLS) .... TxPYE
Young Engineers for Britain (ACII) .... YEB
Young England Library [*A publication*] .... YEL
Young Entomologists' Society (EA) .... YES
Young Entrepreneurs Organization [*Wichita, KS*] (EA) .... YEO
Young Eucalypt Program (EERA) .... YEP
Young Executive Society [*Automotive Warehouse Distributors Association*] .... YES
Young Executives Forum [*Automotive Service Industry Association*] .... YEF
Young Explorers Trust [*British*] (DBA) .... YET
Young Farmers' Club [*British*] .... YFC
Young Farmers Finance Council [*Australia*] .... YFFC
Young Filmakers Foundation (EA) .... YF
Young Filmakers/Video Arts [*Also known as Young Filmakers Foundation*] (EA) .... YF/VA
Young Flying Service [*ICAO designator*] (FAAC) .... YFS
Young Friends of North America (EA) .... YFNA
Young Grandmother .... YGM
Young Guard Society [*Later, GS*] (EA) .... YGS
Young Hard-of-Hearing Adults [*British*] (EAIO) .... YAHOH
Young Harris College, Young Harris, GA [*Library symbol Library of Congress*] (LCLS) .... GYC
Young Harris, GA [*AM radio station call letters*] .... WZCM
Young Indicted Professional [*Lifestyle classification*] .... Yippie
Young, Intact Animals [*Endocrinology*] .... YI
Young Interference Experiment [*Physics*] .... YIE
Young Israel Institute for Jewish Studies [*Defunct*] (EA) .... YIIJS
Young Kibbutz Movement [*Defunct*] (EA) .... YKM
Young Labour Council [*Australia*] .... YLC
Young Ladies Institute (EA) .... YLI
Young Ladies Radio League .... YLRL
Young Lady [*Amateur radio slang*] .... YL
Young Launderers' Movement [*British*] (BI) .... YLM
Young Lawyers Section Newsletter [*Australia A publication*] .... YLSN
Young Leadership Forum [*Multinational association based in Israel*] (EAIO) .... YLF
Young Liberal Movement of Australia .... YLMA
Young Life (EA) .... YL
Young Life Campaign (EA) .... YLC
Young Managing Printers [*British Printing Industries Federation*] .... YMP
Young Master Printer (DGA) .... YMP
Young Master Printers' Alliance (DGA) .... YMPA
Young Men's [*Christian Association*] .... YM
Young Men's and Young Women's Hebrew Association (EA) .... YM-YWHA
Young Men's and Young Women's Hebrew Association, Philadelphia, PA [*Library symbol Library of Congress Obsolete*] (LCLS) .... PPYH
Young Men's Catholic Association (BARN) .... UMCathA
Young Men's [*or Women's*] Christian Association [*Short form of reference, especially to the group's building or specific facility, as "the Y swimming pool"*] .... Y
Young Men's Christian Association (EA) .... YMCA
Young Men's Christian Association, Columbus, OH [*Library symbol Library of Congress*] (LCLS) .... OCoY
Young Men's Christian Association, Grand Central Branch Library, New York, NY [*Library symbol Library of Congress*] (LCLS) .... NNYMCA-GC
Young Men's Christian Association, National Council Historical Library, New York, NY [*Library symbol*] [*Library of Congress*] (LCLS) .... NNYMCA
Young Men's Christian Association, National Council Historical Library, New York, NY [*Library symbol Library of Congress*] (LCLS) .... NNYMCA-NC
Young Men's Christian Association of Australia .... YMCAA
Young Men's Christian Associations of the United States of America (EA) .... YMCA-USA
Young Men's Christian Union .... YMCU
Young Men's Division - Zeirei Agudath Israel (EA) .... YMDZAI

Young Men's Friendly Society [*British*] ... YMFS
Young Men's Hebrew Association [*Later, YM-YWHA*] ... YMHA
Young Men's Institute (EA) ... YMI
Young Men's Lyceum ... YML
Young Men's Mercantile Library Association, Cincinnati, OH [*Library symbol Library of Congress*] (LCLS) ... OCY
Young Mensa International Special Interest Group [*Defunct*] (EA) ... YMISIG
Young Menswear Association (EA) ... YMA
Young Musicians Foundation (EA) ... YMF
Young National Party [*Australia Political party*] ... YNP
Young National Party of Australia [*Political party*] (ADA) ... YNPA
Young National Party of Australia [*Political party*] ... YNPA
Young Newspapermen's Association [*British*] (BI) ... YNA
Young Officer [*British military*] (DMA) ... YO
Young Officers' Union [*Philippines*] ... YOU
Young, One Income, No Kids [*Lifestyle classification*] ... YOINK
Young People ... YP
Young People's Literature [*A publication*] ... YPL
Young People's LOGO Association (EA) ... YPLA
Young Peoples Socialist League [*Later, YSD*] (EA) ... YPSL
Young People's Society of Christian Endeavor ... YPSCE
Young Person (AIE) ... YP
Young Playwrights Festival [*Foundation of the Dramatists Guild*] ... YPF
Young Poalei Zion (BJA) ... YPZ
Young Presidents' Organization (EA) ... YPO
Young Printers' Conference (DGA) ... YPC
Young Printing Executives Club of New York (EA) ... YPEC
Young Radiator Co., Racine, WI [*Library symbol Library of Congress*] (LCLS) ... WRacY
Young Republican ... YR
Young Republican National Federation (EA) ... YRNF
Young Scientists of America Foundation [*Defunct*] (EA) ... YSAF
Young Social Democrats (EA) ... YSD
Young Socialist Alliance (EA) ... YSA
Young Socialist Movement ... YSM
Young Soldier ... YS
Young Solicitors' Group [*British*] ... YSG
Young Sowers' League [*British*] ... YSL
Young Stellar Object ... YSO
Young Tree Decline [*Plant pathology*] ... YTD
Young Ultimate Creative Kitscher [*Lifestyle classification*] ... Yuckie
Young Unescorted Single [*Lifestyle classification*] ... Yussie
Young Up-and-Coming Cuban American [*Lifestyle classification*] ... Yucca
Young Upward Professional Library Information Specialist [*Lifestyle classification*] ... Yuplis
Young Upwardly Mobile Cuban-American [*Lifestyle classification*] ... Yuca
Young Upwardly Mobile Marxist [*Lifestyle classification*] ... Yummie
Young Upwardly Mobile Mommy [*Lifestyle classification*] ... Yummy
Young Upwardly Mobile Mountains [*Rocky Mountains*] [*Geological take-off on the abbreviation, Yuppie*] [*Canada*] ... Yummie
Young Upwardly Mobile Papa [*Lifestyle classification*] ... Yumpy
Young Upwardly Mobile Professional [*Lifestyle classification*] ... Yumpie
Young Urban Baby [*Lifestyle classification*] ... Yubbie
Young Urban Breadwinner [*Lifestyle classification*] ... Yubbie
Young Urban Catholic [*Lifestyle classification*] ... Yuckie
Young Urban Failure [*Lifestyle classification*] ... Yuffie
Young Urban Laborer [*Lifestyle classification*] ... Yullie
Young Urban Minister [*Lifestyle classification*] ... Yummie
Young Urban Professional [*In book title "The Yuppie Handbook"*] [*Lifestyle classification*] ... Yuppie
Young, Urban Republican Professional [*Lifestyle classification*] ... Yurpie
Young Vic [*British theatrical company*] ... Y
Young Volunteers in ACTION ... YVA
Young Wales Society ... YWS
Young Women Committed to Action [*Feminist group*] ... YWCA
Young Women of the Church of Jesus Christ of Latter-Day Saints (EA) ... YW
Young Women of the Church of Jesus Christ of Latter-Day Saints [*Later, YW*] (EA) ... YWCJCLS
Young Women's [*Christian Association*] ... YW
Young Women's Christian Association of Australia ... YWCAA
Young Women's Christian Association of the United States of America (EA) ... YWCA-USA
Young Women's Christian Temperance Union ... YWCTU
Young Women's Hebrew Association [*Later, YM-YWHA*] ... YWHA
Young Women's Help Society [*British*] ... YWHS
Young Workers Liberation League ... YWLL
Young Workers Scheme [*British*] ... YWS
Young World Federalists [*Later, World Federalist Youth*] ... YWF
Young World Food and Development [*UN Food and Agriculture Organization*] ... YWFD
Young World Promotion Group [*UN Food and Agriculture Organization*] ... YWPG
Younge and Collyer's English Chancery Cases [*62-63 English Reprint*] [*1841-43*] [*A publication*] (DLA) ... Y & C Ch Cas
Younge and Collyer's English Chancery Cases [*62-63 English Reprint*] [*1841-43*] [*A publication*] (DLA) ... Y & CCC
Younge and Collyer's English Chancery Cases [*62-63 English Reprint*] [*A publication*] (DLA) ... Younge & C Ch Cas (Eng)
Younge and Collyer's English Chancery Cases [*62-63 English Reprint*] [*1841-43*] [*A publication*] (DLA) ... Younge & Ch Cas
Younge and Collyer's English Chancery Reports [*1841-43*] [*A publication*] (DLA) ... Y & C
Younge and Collyer's English Chancery Reports [*1841-43*] [*A publication*] (DLA) ... Y & C Ch
Younge and Collyer's English Chancery Reports [*1841-43*] [*A publication*] (DLA) ... Y & Coll
Younge and Collyer's English Chancery Reports [*1841-43*] [*A publication*] (DLA) ... You & Coll Ch
Younge and Collyer's English Chancery Reports [*62-63 English Reprint*] [*A publication*] (DLA) ... Younge & C Ch
Younge and Collyer's English Chancery Reports [*62-63 English Reprint*] [*A publication*] (DLA) ... Younge & Coll Ch
Younge and Collyer's English Exchequer Equity Reports [*1834-42*] [*A publication*] (DLA) ... Y & C
Younge and Collyer's English Exchequer Equity Reports [*1834-42*] [*A publication*] (DLA) ... Y & C Ex
Younge and Collyer's English Exchequer Equity Reports [*1834-42*] [*A publication*] (DLA) ... Y & C Exch
Younge and Collyer's English Exchequer Equity Reports [*1834-42*] [*A publication*] (DLA) ... Y & Coll
Younge and Collyer's English Exchequer Equity Reports [*1834-42*] [*A publication*] (DLA) ... You & Coll Ex
Younge and Collyer's English Exchequer Equity Reports [*160 English Reprint*] [*A publication*] (DLA) ... Younge & C Exch
Younge and Collyer's English Exchequer Equity Reports [*160 English Reprint*] [*A publication*] (DLA) ... Younge & C Exch (Eng)
Younge and Collyer's English Exchequer Equity Reports [*160 English Reprint*] [*A publication*] (DLA) ... Younge & Coll Ex
Younge and Jervis' English Exchequer Reports [*1826-30*] [*A publication*] (DLA) ... Y & J
Younge and Jervis' English Exchequer Reports [*A publication*] (DLA) ... You & Jerv
Younge and Jervis' English Exchequer Reports [*148 English Reprint*] [*A publication*] (DLA) ... Younge & J
Younge and Jervis' English Exchequer Reports [*148 English Reprint*] [*A publication*] (DLA) ... Younge & J (Eng)
Younge and Jervis' English Exchequer Reports [*148 English Reprint*] [*A publication*] (DLA) ... Younge & Je
Younge and Jervis' English Exchequer Reports [*148 English Reprint*] [*A publication*] (DLA) ... Younge & Jerv
Younger [*or Youngest*] ... Y
Younger (VRA) ... ygr
Younger (ODBW) ... yr
Younger ... YR
Younger American Playwright [*Slang*] ... YAP
Younger Brothers Band Fan Club [*Defunct*] (EA) ... YBBFC
Younger Chemists International Project [*American Chemical Society*] ... YOCHINPROJ
Younger Chemists Task Force [*American Chemical Society*] ... YCTF
Younger Dryas [*Geoscience*] ... YD
Younger Son (ROG) ... YS
Younger-Onset Rheumatoid Arthritis [*Medicine*] (DAVI) ... YORA
Younge's English Exchequer Equity Reports [*159 English Reprint*] [*A publication*] (DLA) ... Yo
Younge's English Exchequer Equity Reports [*159 English Reprint*] [*A publication*] (DLA) ... You
Younge's English Exchequer Equity Reports [*159 English Reprint*] [*A publication*] (DLA) ... Younge
Younge's English Exchequer Equity Reports [*159 English Reprint*] [*1830-32*] [*A publication*] (DLA) ... Younge Exch
Younge's English Exchequer Equity Reports [*159 English Reprint*] [*A publication*] (DLA) ... Younge Exch (Eng)
Younge's English Maritime Law Cases [*A publication*] (DLA) ... Younge ML Cas
Youngest ... YST
Youngest Empty Cell ... YEC
Youngest Living Child [*Medicine*] (DMAA) ... YLC
Young-Helmholtz Theory [*Physics*] ... YHT
Youngish Anglophone of Westmount and Notre-Dame-De-Grace [*Canadian Yuppie identified in Keith Harrison's novel "After Six Days"*] [*Lifestyle classification*] ... Yawnie
Youngman Oil & Gas [*Vancouver Stock Exchange symbol*] ... YOU
Young-of-the-Year [*Conservation*] ... YOY
Young's English Maritime Law Cases [*A publication*] (DLA) ... Young ML Cas
Young's Modulus of Elasticity [*Symbol*] [*See also E, YME*] ... Y
Young's Modulus of Elasticity [*See also E, Y*] ... YME
Young's Nautical Dictionary [*A publication*] (DLA) ... Young Naut Dict
Young's Nova Scotia Admiralty Cases [*A publication*] (DLA) ... Young Adm
Young's Nova Scotia Admiralty Decisions [*A publication*] (DLA) ... YAD
Young's Nova Scotia Vice-Admiralty Decisions [*A publication*] (DLA) ... Young Adm Dec
Young's Nova Scotia Vice-Admiralty Decisions [*A publication*] (DLA) ... Young Adm Dec (Nov Sc)
Young's Nova Scotia Vice-Admiralty Decisions [*A publication*] (DLA) ... Young VA Dec
Young's Nova Scotia Vice-Admiralty Decisions, Edited by Oxley [*A publication*] (DLA) ... Oxley
Young's Reports [*21-47 Minnesota*] [*A publication*] (DLA) ... Young
Youngstown [*Ohio*] [*ICAO location identifier*] (ICLI) ... KYNG
Youngstown [*Diocesan abbreviation*] [*Ohio*] (TOCD) ... Y
Youngstown [*Ohio*] [*Airport symbol*] (OAG) ... YNG
Youngstown and Mahoning County Public Library, Youngstown, OH [*OCLC symbol*] (OCLC) ... YMM
[*The*] **Youngstown & Northern Railroad Co.** [*AAR code*] ... YN
Youngstown & Southern Railway Co. [*AAR code*] ... YS
Youngstown Free Library, Youngstown, NY [*Library symbol Library of Congress*] (LCLS) ... NYo
Youngstown Municipal Library, Alberta [*Library symbol National Library of Canada*] (NLC) ... AYM
Youngstown Municipal Library, Youngstown, AB, Canada [*Library symbol Library of Congress*] (LCLS) ... CaAYM
Youngstown, NY [*AM radio station call letters*] (RBYB) ... WTOR-AM

Youngstown, OH [*Location identifier FAA*] (FAAL) ... MQK
Youngstown, OH [*FM radio station call letters*] ... WBBG
Youngstown, OH [*AM radio station call letters*] ... WBBW
Youngstown, OH [*Television station call letters*] ... WFMJ
Youngstown, OH [*AM radio station call letters*] ... WGFT
Youngstown, OH [*FM radio station call letters*] ... WHOT-FM
Youngstown, OH [*AM radio station call letters*] ... WKBN
Youngstown, OH [*FM radio station call letters*] ... WKBN-FM
Youngstown, OH [*Television station call letters*] ... WKBN-TV
Youngstown, OH [*AM radio station call letters*] (RBYB) ... WRTK
Youngstown, OH [*FM radio station call letters*] ... WYSU
Youngstown, OH [*FM radio station call letters*] ... WYTN
Youngstown, OH [*Television station call letters*] ... WYTV
Youngstown State University, Youngstown, OH [*Library symbol Library of Congress*] (LCLS) ... OYU
Youngstown State University, Youngstown, OH [*OCLC symbol*] (OCLC) ... YNG
Youngsville Public Library, Youngsville, NC [*Library symbol Library of Congress*] (LCLS) ... NcYo
Youngtown Public Library, Youngtown, AZ [*Library symbol Library of Congress*] (LCLS) ... AzYo
Younkers, Inc. [*NASDAQ symbol*] (SAG) ... YONK
Younkers, Inc. [*Associated Press*] (SAG) ... Younker
Yountville, CA [*AM radio station call letters*] ... KRKL
Your ... Y
Your (AAG) ... YR
Your (ODBW) ... yr
Your Activity ... URACTY
Your Business [*A publication*] (ADA) ... YB
Your Business [*A publication*] ... YB
Your Cable (DS) ... y/c
Your Curiosity Just Cost You a Quarter for the Jukebox [*Tavern sign*] ... YCJCYAQFTJB
Your Dispatch [*Military*] ... URDIS
Your Educational Plan (AEBS) ... YEP
Your Eyes Only (PCM) ... YEO
Your Heritage Protection Association (EA) ... YHPA
Your Improved Group Insurance Benefits ... YIGIB
Your Income Tax [*Computerized version of J. K. Lasser's book by the same name*] ... YIT
Your Marketing Consultant [*An electronic publication*] ... YMC
Your Message [*Aviation*] (FAAC) ... YMSG
Your Message Date [*Aviation*] (FAAC) ... YMSGD
Your Mileage May Vary [*E-Mail discussion*] ... YMMV
Your Own United Resources, Inc. (OICC) ... YOUR
Your Personal Network [*Information service or system*] ... YPN
Your Problem ... YP
Your Recommendation is Requested (FAAC) ... URIZR
You're on Your Own (DOMA) ... YOYO
Yours ... YRS
Yours in the Bond [*Motto of fraternity Tau Kappa Epsilon*] ... YITB
Yours Till Hell Freezes [*Slang British*] (DI) ... YTHF
Youssef Ben Tachfine [*Morocco*] [*Seismograph station code, US Geological Survey*] (SEIS) ... YBT
Youth ... YTH
Youth Accommodation Coalition of Victoria [*Australia*] ... YACV
Youth Action Policy Association [*Australia*] ... YAPA
Youth Affairs Council [*Australia*] ... YAC
Youth Affairs Lobby (AIE) ... YAL
Youth Against War and Fascism (EA) ... YAWF
Youth Ambassadors International (EA) ... YAI
Youth Ambassadors of America [*Later, YAI*] (EA) ... YAA
Youth and Christ Hang Together ... YACHT
Youth and Music Canada ... YMC
Youth and Performing Arts [*Australia*] ... YAPA
Youth Associated with the Restoration of Democracy [*Kenya*] [*Political party*] (EY) ... YARD
Youth Association of Synagogues in Great Britain (BI) ... YASGB
Youth Attitude Tracking Survey [*Navy*] ... YATS
Youth Basketball Association [*Joint program of NBA Players' Association and YMCA*] ... YBA
Youth Brigade [*Australia*] ... YB
Youth Bureau [*Australia*] ... YB
Youth Business Initiative Australia ... YBIA
Youth Campaign for Nuclear Disarmament [*British*] (BI) ... YCND
Youth Camping Association [*British*] (BI) ... YCA
Youth Challenge Program ... YCP
Youth Citizenship Fund (EA) ... YCF
Youth Civic Center ... YCC
Youth Clubs [*Public-performance tariff class*] [*British*] ... YC
Youth Clubs United ... YCU
Youth Committee Against Poverty ... YCAP
Youth Community Conservation and Improvement Projects [*Department of Labor*] ... YCCIP
Youth Community Service [*ACTION project*] ... YCS
Youth Conservation Corps (EA) ... YCC
Youth Conservative [*Political party*] [*British*] ... YC
Youth Correction Division [*Department of Justice*] ... YCD
Youth Cost per Entered Employment [*Job Training and Partnership Act*] (OICC) ... YCEE
Youth Counseling League (EA) ... YCL
Youth Development and Delinquency Prevention Administration [*Later, Youth D evelopment Bureau*] [*HEW*] ... YDDPA
Youth Development Association [*British*] (DBA) ... YDA
Youth Development Bureau [*Department of Health and Human Services*] ... YDB
Youth Development Center, Loysville, Loysville, PA [*OCLC symbol*] (OCLC) ... PIX
Youth Development Center, New Castle, New Castle, PA [*OCLC symbol*] (OCLC) ... PIY
Youth Development Center, Waynesburg, Waynesburg, PA [*OCLC symbol*] (OCLC) ... PIZ
Youth Development, Inc. (EA) ... YDI
Youth Education and Training Innovators (AIE) ... YETI
Youth Education Services [*Summer program*] ... YES
Youth Effectiveness Skills Program [*Australia*] ... YES
Youth Effectiveness Training [*A course of study*] ... YET
Youth Emergency Service ... YES
Youth Emotions Anonymous (EA) ... YEA
Youth Employment and Demonstration Projects Act of 1977 ... YEDPA
Youth Employment and Demonstration Training Act [*Department of the Interior*] ... YEDTA
Youth Employment and Training Programs [*Department of Labor*] ... YETP
Youth Employment Competency (OICC) ... YEC
Youth Employment Lobby [*Canada*] ... YEL
Youth Employment Officer [*British*] ... YEO
Youth Employment Service [*Department of Employment*] [*British*] (EA) ... YES
Youth Employment Support Volunteers Program [*ACTION*] ... YES
Youth Enquiry Service [*Australia*] ... YES
Youth Entered Employment Rate [*Job Training and Partnership Act*] (OICC) ... YEER
Youth Entering Service to America [*In YES Foundation, a volunteer organization proposed by the Bush administration*] ... YES
Youth Enterprise (AIE) ... YE
Youth Enterprise Scheme [*British*] (ODBW) ... YES
Youth Entry [*British military*] (DMA) ... YE
Youth Evangelism Association (EA) ... YEA
Youth Exchange Centre [*Seymour Mews House*] [*British*] (CB) ... YEC
Youth Exhibiting Stamps [*US Postal Service*] ... YES
Youth Female [*International Bowhunting Organization*] [*Class Equipment*] ... YF
Youth Film Distribution Center (EA) ... YFDC
Youth for Christ [*Australia*] ... YFC
Youth for Christ International [*See also JPC*] [*Singapore, Singapore*] (EAIO) ... YFCI
Youth for Christ/USA (EA) ... YFC/USA
Youth for Development and Cooperation (EAIO) ... YDC
Youth for Environmental Sanity ... YES
Youth for Understanding (EA) ... YFU
Youth for Understanding Australia ... YUA
Youth Forum Ltd. [*Australia Commercial firm*] ... YFL
Youth Forum of the European Communities [*See also FJCE*] (EAIO) ... YFEC
Youth Hostel ... YH
Youth Hostels Association ... YHA
Youth in Transition [*Australia*] ... YIT
Youth Incentive Entitlement Pilot Projects [*Department of Labor*] ... YIEPP
Youth Initiative Project (AIE) ... YIP
Youth Institute for Peace in the Middle East (EA) ... YIPME
Youth International Party [*Members known as "yippies"*] ... YIP
Youth International Party Line [*Superseded by Technological American Party*] ... YIPL
Youth Liberation Press (EA) ... YL
Youth Male Fingers [*International Bowhunting Organization*] [*Class Equipment*] ... YMF
Youth Male Release [*International Bowhunting Organization*] [*Class equipment*] ... YMR
Youth Mobility Program (OICC) ... YMP
Youth Music Australia ... YMA
Youth of All Nations (EA) ... YOAN
Youth of America Needs to Know ... YANK
Youth Opportunities Board ... YOB
Youth Opportunities Programme [*British*] (DCTA) ... YOP
Youth Opportunities Unlimited [*Project*] (EA) ... YOU
Youth Opportunity Campaign [*Civil Service Commission*] ... YOC
Youth Opportunity Centers ... YOC
Youth Opportunity Corps ... YOC
Youth Order United Toward Highway Safety (EA) ... YOUTHS
Youth Organizations United ... YOU
Youth Organizations USA (EA) ... YOUSA
Youth Parole Board and Youth Residential Board [*Victoria, Australia*] ... YPBYRB
Youth Policy Development Council [*Victoria, Australia*] ... YPDC
Youth Policy Institute (EA) ... YPI
Youth Population Ratio (OICC) ... YPR
Youth Pride, Inc. (EA) ... YPI
Youth Programs Office [*Bureau of Indian Affairs*] ... YPO
[*The*] **Youth Project** (EA) ... TYP
Youth Research Institute of New York (EA) ... YRINY
Youth Resources (EA) ... YR
Youth Risk Behavior Survey [*Medicine*] ... YRBS
Youth Section of the Democratic Socialists of America (EA) ... YSDSA
Youth Service America (EA) ... YSA
Youth Services International, Inc. [*Associated Press*] (SAG) ... YouthSv
Youth Services International, Inc. [*NASDAQ symbol*] (SAG) ... YSII
Youth Services Int'l [*NASDAQ symbol*] (TTSB) ... YSII
Youth Suicide National Center (EA) ... YSNC
Youth Tennis League (EA) ... YTL
Youth Training (AIE) ... YT
Youth Training and Employment Project ... YTEP
Youth Training Programme [*British*] (AIE) ... YTP
Youth Training Scheme [*British*] ... YTS
Youth Uncovering Krud [*Antipollution organization in Schenectady, New York*] ... YUK

Youth Unit of the Council for Environmental Education (EAIO) .... YUCEE
Youth Visiting Team [*British military*] (DMA) .... YVT
Youth with a Mission (EA) .... YWAM
Youth with a Mission [*Australia*] .... YWM
Youth Work Unit [*National Youth Bureau*] (AIE) .... YWU
Youthful Energetic Elderly Person Involved in Everything [*Aging yuppie*] [*Lifestyle classification*] .... Yeepie
Youths for Environment and Service [*Multinational association based in Turkey*] (EAIO) .... YES
Youth-to-Youth Committee International (EA) .... YYCI
Youth-to-Youth Sports Committee International [*Defunct*] (EA) .... YYSCI
Yo-Yo Stock [*Investment term*] .... YYS
Ypenburg [*Netherlands ICAO location identifier*] (ICLI) .... EHYB
YPF Sociedad Anonima [*NYSE symbol*] (SPSG) .... YPF
YPF Sociedad Anonima [*Associated Press*] (SAG) .... YPF Soc
YPF Sociedad Anonima ADS [*NYSE symbol*] (TTSB) .... YPF
Ypsilanti Area Public Library, Ypsilanti, MI [*Library symbol Library of Congress*] (LCLS) .... MiY
Ypsilanti, MI [*FM radio station call letters*] .... WEMU
Ypsilanti, MI [*AM radio station call letters*] .... WWCM
Y-Punch (IAA) .... Y
Yreka, CA [*AM radio station call letters*] .... KSYC
Yreka, CA [*FM radio station call letters*] (RBYB) .... KSYC-FM
Yreka Western Railroad Co. [*AAR code*] .... YW
Yri-York Ltd. [*Toronto Stock Exchange symbol*] .... YRI
Y-Stabilized Zirconia [*Physics*] .... YSZ
Ysterplaat [*South Africa*] [*ICAO location identifier*] (ICLI) .... FAYP
Ytterbium [*Chemical element*] .... Yb
Ytterbium 169 Pentetate Sodium [*Chemistry*] (DAVI) Yb-169-DTPA
Yttria-Stablized Zirconia [*Materials science*] .... YSZ
Yttrium [*Preferred form, but see also Yt*] [*Chemical element*] .... Y
Yttrium [*See also Y*] [*Chemical element*] .... Yt
Yttrium Aluminum Garnet LASER .... YAGL
Yttrium Aluminum LASER .... YAL
Yttrium Alumnium Iron Garnet [*LASER technology*] (IAA) .... YAIG
Yttrium Barium Copper Oxide [*Inorganic chemistry*] .... YBCO
Yttrium Garnet LASER .... YGL
Yttrium Iron Garnet .... YIG
Yttrium-Aluminum Garnet [*LASER technology*] .... YAG
Yttrium-Lithium-Fluoride [*Laser*] .... YLF
Yuba City, CA [*AM radio station call letters*] .... KOBO
Yuba City, CA [*AM radio station call letters*] .... KUBA
Yuba City, CA [*FM radio station call letters*] .... KXCL
Yuba College, Marysville, CA [*Library symbol Library of Congress*] (LCLS) .... CMaryY
Yucaipa, CA [*FM radio station call letters*] .... KLRD
Yucana Resources, Inc. [*Vancouver Stock Exchange symbol*] .... YUC
Yucatan .... YUC
Yucca (VRA) .... yuc
Yucca Flat, NV [*Location identifier FAA*] (FAAL) .... UCC
Yucca House National Monument .... YUBO
Yucca Mountain Site Characterization Office .... YMSCO
Yucca Valley, CA [*FM radio station call letters*] .... KNWZ-FM
Yucca Valley, CA [*FM radio station call letters*] (RBYB) .... KSES-FM
Yugawaralite [*A zeolite*] .... YUG
Yugntruf - Youth for Yiddish (EA) .... YYY
Yugoslav Airlines [*ICAO designator*] (AD) .... JU
Yugoslav Center for Technical and Scientific Documentation [*Information service or system*] (IID) .... YCTSD
Yugoslav Law [*A publication*] (DLA) .... Yugo L
Yugoslav National Tourist Office [*Defunct*] (EA) .... YNTO
Yugoslav People's Army .... JNA
Yugoslav Relief Society .... YRS
Yugoslavia [*MARC geographic area code Library of Congress*] (LCCP) .... e-yu--
Yugoslavia [*IYRU nationality code*] (IYR) .... Y
Yugoslavia .... Y-SLAV
Yugoslavia [*ANSI two-letter standard code*] (CNC) .... YU
Yugoslavia [*MARC country of publication code Library of Congress*] (LCCP) .... yu
Yugoslavia [*ANSI three-letter standard code*] (CNC) .... YUG
Yugoslavia (VRA) .... Yugo
Yugoslavia .... Yugos
Yugoslavia Federation of Trade Unions .... YFTU
Yugoslavian Air Force .... YAF
Yuguara [*Colombia*] [*Airport symbol*] (OAG) .... AYG
Yuki [*Zaire*] [*ICAO location identifier*] (ICLI) .... FZCY
Yukon Alpine Centennial Expedition .... YACE
Yukon Archives, Whitehorse, YT, Canada [*Library symbol Library of Congress*] (LCLS) .... CaYWA
Yukon Archives, Whitehorse, Yukon [*Library symbol National Library of Canada*] (NLC) .... YWA
Yukon Bibliography [*Boreal Institute for Northern Studies*] [*Canada Information service or system Information service or system*] (CRD) .... YKB
Yukon College, Whitehorse, Yukon [*Library symbol National Library of Canada*] (NLC) .... YWC
Yukon Law Library, Whitehorse, YT, Canada [*Library symbol Library of Congress*] (LCLS) .... CaYWL
Yukon Law Library, Whitehorse, Yukon [*Library symbol National Library of Canada*] (NLC) .... YWL
Yukon Ordinances [*Canada*] [*A publication*] (DLA) .... Yuk Ord
Yukon Public Service Staff Relations Board [*Canada*] .... YPSSRB
Yukon Regional Library, Whitehorse, YT, Canada [*Library symbol Library of Congress*] (LCLS) .... CaYWR
Yukon Reports [*Maritime Law Book Co. Ltd.*] [*Canada Information service or system*] (CRD) .... YR
Yukon Revenue Mines [*Vancouver Stock Exchange symbol*] .... YKR
Yukon Revised Ordinances [*Canada*] [*A publication*] (DLA) .... Yuk Rev Ord
Yukon Standard Time (IAA) .... YST
Yukon Territory [*MARC geographic area code Library of Congress*] (LCCP) .... n-cn-yk
Yukon Territory [*MARC country of publication code Library of Congress*] (LCCP) .... ykc
Yukon Territory [*Postal code*] [*Canada*] .... YT
Yukuharu Haiku Society [*Superseded by Yuki Teikei Haiku Society*] (EA) .... YHS
Yule Island [*Papua New Guinea*] [*Airport symbol*] (OAG) .... RKU
Yule Island [*New Guinea*] [*Airport symbol*] (AD) .... YLE
Yuli [*Republic of China*] [*Seismograph station code, US Geological Survey Closed*] (SEIS) .... TWF
Yuli [*Republic of China*] [*Seismograph station code, US Geological Survey*] (SEIS) TWF1
Yulin [*China*] [*Airport symbol*] (OAG) .... UYN
Yuma [*Arizona*] [*Airport symbol*] (OAG) .... YUM
Yuma, AZ [*Location identifier FAA*] (FAAL) .... BZA
Yuma, AZ [*Location identifier FAA*] (FAAL) .... DAC
Yuma, AZ [*AM radio station call letters*] .... KAWC
Yuma, AZ [*FM radio station call letters*] .... KAWC-FM
Yuma, AZ [*AM radio station call letters*] .... KBLU
Yuma, AZ [*FM radio station call letters*] .... KCFY
Yuma, AZ [*AM radio station call letters*] .... KEZC
Yuma, AZ [*FM radio station call letters*] .... KJOK
Yuma, AZ [*Television station call letters*] .... KSWT
Yuma, AZ [*FM radio station call letters*] .... KTTI
Yuma, AZ [*FM radio station call letters*] (RBYB) .... KYJT
Yuma, AZ [*Television station call letters*] .... KYMA
Yuma, AZ [*Location identifier FAA*] (FAAL) .... NYL
Yuma, AZ [*Location identifier FAA*] (FAAL) .... PCQ
Yuma City-County Public Library, Yuma, AZ [*Library symbol Library of Congress*] (LCLS) .... AzY
Yuma City-County Public Library, Yuma, AZ [*OCLC symbol*] (OCLC) .... YCC
Yuma Gold Mines Ltd. [*Vancouver Stock Exchange symbol*] .... YUM
Yuma Proving Ground [*Arizona*] [*Army*] (AABC) .... YPG
Yuma Public Library, Yuma, CO [*Library symbol Library of Congress*] (LCLS) .... CoY
Yuma Test Branch [*Yuma, AZ*] [*Army*] .... YTB
Yuma Test Station [*Missiles*] .... YTS
Yuma/Vincent Marine Corps Air Station [*Arizona*] [*ICAO location identifier*] (ICLI) .... KNYL
Yuma/Yuma Marine Corps Air Station, Yuma International [*Arizona*] [*ICAO location identifier*] (ICLI) .... KYUM
Yuma/Yuma Proving Ground, AZ [*Location identifier FAA*] (FAAL) .... LGF
Yumen [*Republic of China*] [*Seismograph station code, US Geological Survey*] (SEIS) .... YUM
Yunnan Airlines [*China*] [*ICAO designator*] (FAAC) .... CYH
Yunnan Province [*China, Mainland*] [*MARC geographic area code Library of Congress*] (LCCP) .... a-cc-yu
Yuojima [*Bonin Islands*] [*Seismograph station code, US Geological Survey Closed*] (SEIS) .... YUO
Yuppie [*As in Y-people*] .... Y
Yuppie Jeep .... YJ
Yuriko Resources [*Vancouver Stock Exchange symbol*] .... YUR
Yurimaguas [*Peru*] [*ICAO location identifier*] (ICLI) .... SPMS
Yurimaguas [*Peru*] [*Airport symbol*] (OAG) .... YMS
Yushan [*Mount Morrison*] [*Republic of China*] [*Seismograph station code, US Geological Survey*] (SEIS) .... YUS
Yushodo Booksellers Ltd., Tokyo, Japan [*Library symbol Library of Congress*] (LCLS) .... YoB
Yute Air Alaska, Inc. [*ICAO designator*] (FAAC) .... UYA
Yuzhno-Kurilsk [*Former USSR Seismograph station code, US Geological Survey*] (SEIS) .... YUK
Yuzhno-Sakhalinsk [*Russia*] [*Seismograph station code, US Geological Survey*] (SEIS) .... YSS
Yverdon [*Switzerland ICAO location identifier*] (ICLI) .... LSTY
Yves R. Simon Institute (EA) .... YRSI
Yves Saint Laurent [*French couturier*] .... YSL
Yvic Airlines [*Nigeria*] [*ICAO designator*] (FAAC) .... VYC
YWCA Library, Montreal, PQ, Canada [*Library symbol Library of Congress*] (LCLS) .... CaQMY
YWCA, Montreal, Quebec [*Library symbol National Library of Canada*] (NLC) .... QMY

Z
By Meaning

Z. Boskovic Air Charters Ltd. [*Kenya*] [*FAA designator*] (FAAC) .... ZBA
Z Club of America (EA) .... ZCA
Z. J. Loussac Public Library, Anchorage, AK [*Library symbol Library of Congress*] (LCLS) .... AkA
Z Seven Fund [*NASDAQ symbol*] (TTSB) .... ZSEV
Z Solar Inertial (MCD) .... ZSI
Z80A Processor Board [*North Star Computers*] (NITA) .... ZPB
Zaba Lee Enterprises [*Vancouver Stock Exchange symbol*] .... ZLE
Zabim (BJA) .... Zab
Zabol [*Iran*] [*ICAO location identifier*] (ICLI) .... OIZB
Zabolee [*Iran*] [*ICAO location identifier*] (ICLI) .... OIZL
Zabre [*Burkina Faso*] [*ICAO location identifier*] (ICLI) .... DHEZ
Zabriskie on the Public Land Laws of the United States [*A publication*] (DLA) .... Zab Land Laws
Zabriskie's Reports [*21-24 New Jersey*] [*A publication*] (DLA) .... Za
Zabriskie's Reports [*21-24 New Jersey*] [*A publication*] (DLA) .... Zab (NJ)
Zabrze [*Poland*] [*Seismograph station code, US Geological Survey*] (SEIS) .... ZAB
Zacatecas [*Mexico ICAO location identifier*] (ICLI) .... MMZC
Zacatecas [*Mexico*] [*Airport symbol*] (OAG) .... ZCL
Zachar Bay [*Alaska*] [*Airport symbol*] (OAG) .... KZB
Zachar Bay, AK [*Location identifier FAA*] (FAAL) .... KZB
Zacharias [*Old Testament book*] [*Douay version*] .... ZACH
Zachary Kurintner Books Ltd. [*British*] .... ZK
Zachary Taylor [*US president, 1784-1850*] .... ZT
Zacherley Fans at Large (EA) .... ZFAL
Zadar [*Former Yugoslavia*] [*ICAO location identifier*] (ICLI) .... LYZD
Zadar [*Former Yugoslavia*] [*Airport symbol*] (OAG) .... ZAD
Zadok Perspectives [*A publication*] (APTA) .... ZP
Zag Industries Ltd. [*NASDAQ symbol*] (SAG) .... ZAGI
Zag Industries Ltd. [*Associated Press*] (SAG) .... ZagIndus
Zaghouan [*Tunisia*] [*Seismograph station code, US Geological Survey*] (SEIS) .... ZGN
Zagora [*Morocco*] [*ICAO location identifier*] (ICLI) .... GMAZ
Zagreb [*Former Yugoslavia*] [*ICAO location identifier*] (ICLI) .... LYZA
Zagreb [*Former Yugoslavia*] [*ICAO location identifier*] (ICLI) .... LYZB
Zagreb [*Croatia*] [*Seismograph station code, US Geological Survey*] (SEIS) .... ZAG
Zagreb [*Croatia*] [*Airport symbol*] (OAG) .... ZAG
Zahedan [*Iran*] [*ICAO location identifier*] (ICLI) .... OIZH
Zahedan [*Iran*] [*ICAO location identifier*] (ICLI) .... OIZT
Zahedan [*Iran*] [*Airport symbol*] (OAG) .... ZAH
Zahnradfabrik Friedrichshafen AG [*West Germany*] .... ZF
Zaimische [*Later, KNS*] [*Former USSR Geomagnetic observatory code*] .... KZN
Zaire [*Aircraft nationality and registration mark*] (FAAC) 9Q
Zaire [*Monetary unit in Zaire*] .... Z
Zaire [*ANSI three-letter standard code*] (CNC) .... ZAR
Zaire [*ANSI two-letter standard code*] (CNC) .... ZR
Zaire [*International vehicle registration*] (ODBW) .... ZRE
Zaire Aero Service [*ICAO designator*] (FAAC) .... ZAI
Zaire Aero Service [*ICAO designator*] (FAAC) .... ZAS
Zaire Fir [*Zaire*] [*ICAO location identifier*] (ICLI) .... FZZA
Zairean Airlines [*Zaire*] [*ICAO designator*] (FAAC) .... ZAR
Zakamensk [*Former USSR Seismograph station code, US Geological Survey*] (SEIS) .... ZAK
Zakinthos [*Greece*] [*ICAO location identifier*] (ICLI) .... LGZA
Zakinthos [*Greece*] [*Airport symbol*] (OAG) .... ZTH
Zale Corp. [*NASDAQ symbol*] (SAG) .... ZALE
Zale Corp. [*Associated Press*] (SAG) .... ZaleCp
Zale Corp. Wrrt'A' [*NASDAQ symbol*] (TTSB) .... ZALEW
Zaleski, OH [*Location identifier FAA*] (FAAL) .... ZLK
Zalingei [*Sudan*] [*ICAO location identifier*] (ICLI) .... HSZA
Zama [*Japan ICAO location identifier*] (ICLI) .... RJTW
Zama City Community Library, Alberta [*Library symbol National Library of Canada*] (NLC) .... AZCC
Zama City Community Library, Zama City, AB, Canada [*Library symbol*] [*Library of Congress*] (LCLS) .... CaAZcC
Zama City School, High Level, Alberta [*Library symbol National Library of Canada*] (BIB) .... AHLZS
Zama/Rankin [*Japan ICAO location identifier*] (ICLI) .... RJTR
Zamak Zinc Alloy .... ZZA
Zambezi [*Zambia*] [*Airport symbol*] (OAG) .... BBZ
Zambezi [*Zambia*] [*ICAO location identifier*] (ICLI) .... FLZB
Zambezi River and Basin [*MARC geographic area code Library of Congress*] (LCCP) .... fz----
Zambia [*Aircraft nationality and registration mark*] (FAAC) 9J
Zambia [*MARC geographic area code Library of Congress*] (LCCP) .... f-za--
Zambia [*MARC country of publication code Library of Congress*] (LCCP) .... za
Zambia (WDAA) .... ZAM
Zambia (VRA) .... Zam
Zambia [*ANSI two-letter standard code*] (CNC) .... ZM
Zambia [*ANSI three-letter standard code*] (CNC) .... ZMB
Zambia Airways [*ICAO designator*] (AD) .... QZ
Zambia Airways [*Airline flight code*] (ODBW) .... QZ
Zambia Airways [*ICAO designator*] (FAAC) .... ZAC
Zambia Law Journal [*A publication*] (DLA) .... Zam LJ
Zambia Law Journal [*A publication*] (DLA) .... Zambia LJ
Zambia Law Journal [*A publication*] (DLA) .... ZLJ
Zambia National Congress - Southern Rhodesia .... ZANC
Zambia News Agency .... ZANA
Zamboanga [*Philippines*] [*Airport symbol*] (OAG) .... ZAM
Zamboanga/International [*Philippines*] [*ICAO location identifier*] (ICLI) .... RPMZ
Zambon [*Italy*] [*Research code symbol*] .... Z
Zamora [*Mexico ICAO location identifier*] (ICLI) .... MMZM
Zamora [*Ecuador*] [*ICAO location identifier*] (ICLI) .... SEZA
Zanaga [*Congo*] [*Airport symbol*] (OAG) .... ANJ
Zanaga [*Congo*] [*ICAO location identifier*] (ICLI) .... FCBZ
Zanart Entertainment [*NASDAQ symbol*] (SAG) .... ZANA
Zanart Entertainment [*Associated Press*] (SAG) .... Zanart
Zanart Entmt [*NASDAQ symbol*] (TTSB) .... ZANA
Zanart Entmt Unit [*NASDAQ symbol*] (TTSB) .... ZANAU
Zanart Entmt Wrrt'A' [*NASDAQ symbol*] (TTSB) .... ZANAW
Zanderij [*Surinam*] [*Airport symbol*] (AD) .... ZAN
Zane Grey's West Society (EA) .... ZGWS
Zane's Reports [*4-9 Utah*] [*A publication*] (DLA) .... Zane
Zanesville [*Ohio*] [*Airport symbol*] (AD) .... ZZV
Zanesville, OH [*FM radio station call letters*] .... WCVZ
Zanesville, OH [*AM radio station call letters*] .... WHIZ
Zanesville, OH [*FM radio station call letters*] .... WHIZ-FM
Zanesville, OH [*Television station call letters*] .... WHIZ-TV
Zanesville, OH [*FM radio station call letters*] .... WOUZ
Zanesville, OH [*Location identifier FAA*] (FAAL) .... ZZV
Zangri, S. J., Chicago IL [*STAC*] .... ZSJ
Zanjan [*Iran*] [*ICAO location identifier*] (ICLI) .... OITZ
Zante [*Greece*] [*Seismograph station code, US Geological Survey*] (SEIS) .... ZAN
Zantop Airways, Inc. .... ZAT
Zantop International Airlines, Inc. [*ICAO designator*] (FAAC) .... ZAN
Zantop International Airlines, Inc. [*Air carrier designation symbol*] .... ZIAX
Zanzibar [*Tanzania*] [*ICAO location identifier*] (ICLI) .... HTZA
Zanzibar (BARN) .... Zan
Zanzibar .... ZANZ
Zanzibar (VRA) .... Zanz
Zanzibar [*Tanzania*] [*Airport symbol*] (OAG) .... ZNZ
Zanzibar [*Tanzania*] .... ZZB
Zanzibar and Pemba Federation of Labour .... ZPFL
Zanzibar and Pemba People's Party .... ZPPP
Zanzibar Law Reports [*1919-50*] [*A publication*] (DLA) .... ZLR
Zanzibar Nationalist Party .... ZNP
Zanzibar Protectorate Law Reports [*Africa*] [*A publication*] (DLA) .... Zanzib Prot LR
Zanzibar Protectorate Law Reports [*1868-1950*] [*A publication*] (DLA) .... ZLR
Zap Gun .... ZG
Zapala [*Argentina*] [*Airport symbol*] (OAG) .... APZ
Zapalote-Chico [*Race of maize*] .... Z-C
Zapalote-Grande [*Race of maize*] .... Z-G
Zapata Corp. [*NYSE symbol*] (TTSB) .... ZAP
Zapata Corp. [*NYSE symbol*] (SAG) .... ZAP
Zapata Corp. [*Associated Press*] (SAG) .... Zapata
Zapata Corp. [*NYSE symbol Toronto Stock Exchange symbol*] .... ZOS
Zapopan [*Mexico ICAO location identifier*] (ICLI) .... MMZP
Zaporozhe [*USSR*] [*Airport symbol*] (AD) .... ZAP
Zaporozh'ye [*Former USSR Airport symbol Obsolete*] (OAG) .... OZH
Zapotal De Guanacaste [*Costa Rica*] [*ICAO location identifier*] (ICLI) .... MRZP
Zapotec [*MARC language code Library of Congress*] (LCCP) .... zap
Zaragoza [*Spain ICAO location identifier*] (ICLI) .... LEZA
Zaragoza [*Spain ICAO location identifier*] (ICLI) .... LEZG
Zaragoza [*Cuba ICAO location identifier*] (ICLI) .... MUZG
Zaragoza [*Spain*] [*Airport symbol*] (OAG) .... ZAZ
Zarand [*Iran*] [*ICAO location identifier*] (ICLI) .... OIKZ
Zaranj [*Afghanistan*] [*ICAO location identifier*] (ICLI) .... OAZG
Zarephath, NJ [*FM radio station call letters*] .... WAWZ
Zaria [*Nigeria*] [*ICAO location identifier*] (ICLI) .... DNZA
Zaria [*Nigeria*] [*Geomagnetic observatory code*] .... ZAR
Zaria [*Nigeria*] [*Airport symbol*] (AD) .... ZAR
Zaring Homes [*NASDAQ symbol*] (TTSB) .... ZHOM

Zaring Homes, Inc. [*Associated Press*] (SAG) .... Zaring
Zaring Homes, Inc. [*NASDAQ symbol*] (SAG) .... ZHOM
Zarkani Air Services [*Egypt*] (EY) .... ZAS
Zartman Association of America (EA) .... ZAA
Zarzaitine/In Amenas [*Algeria*] [*ICAO location identifier*] (ICLI) .... DAUZ
Zas Airlines of Egypt [*FAA designator*] (FAAC) .... ZAS
Zastron [*South Africa*] [*ICAO location identifier*] (ICLI) .... FAZA
Zavalla [*Texas*] [*Seismograph station code, US Geological Survey Closed*] (SEIS) .... ZAV
Zavim (BJA) .... Zav
Zavitz Technology, Inc. [*Toronto Stock Exchange symbol*] .... ZVZ
Z-Axis .... Z
Z-Axis along Local Vertical (MCD) .... Z-LV
Z-Axis Modulation .... ZAM
Z-Axis of External Tank [*NASA*] (NASA) .... ZT
Z-Axis of Orbiter [*NASA*] (NASA) .... ZO
Z-Axis of Payload [*NASA*] (NASA) .... ZP
Z-Axis of Solid Rocket Booster [*NASA*] (NASA) .... ZS
Z-Axis of Spacelab [*NASA*] (NASA) .... ZL
Zeatin-O-Glucoside [*Biochemistry*] .... ZOG
Zebahim (BJA) .... Zeb
Zebak [*Afghanistan*] [*ICAO location identifier*] (ICLI) .... OAZB
Zebec Resources [*Vancouver Stock Exchange symbol*] .... ZBC
Zebra [*Phonetic alphabet*] [*Royal Navy World War I Pre-World War II*] [*World War II*] (DSUE) .... Z
Zebra (ROG) .... ZEB
Zebra Body [*Medicine*] (DMAA) .... ZB
Zebra Energy Breeder Assembly .... ZEBRA
Zebra Stripe Display .... ZSD
Zebra Technologies Corp. [*NASDAQ symbol*] (SPSG) .... ZBRA
Zebra Technologies Corp. [*Associated Press*] (SAG) .... Zebra
Zebra Technologies'A' [*NASDAQ symbol*] (TTSB) .... ZBRA
Zebulon, GA [*FM radio station call letters*] .... WEKS
Zebulon Pike Detention Center, Colorado Springs, CO [*Library symbol Library of Congress*] (LCLS) .... CoCZ
Zebulun Israel Seafaring Society (EA) .... ZISS
Zechariah (BJA) .... Zc
Zechariah [*Old Testament book*] .... Zec
Zechariah [*Old Testament book*] .... Zech
Zeeland, MI [*FM radio station call letters*] .... WGNB
Zeeland, MI [*FM radio station call letters*] .... WJQK
Zeeland, MI [*AM radio station call letters*] (RBYB) .... WMFN
Zeeland, MI [*AM radio station call letters*] .... WWJQ
Zeeland Public Library, Zeeland, MI [*Library symbol Library of Congress*] (LCLS) .... MiZ
Zeeland Steamship Co. (MHDW) .... ZSC
Zeeman-Effect Atomic Absorption [*Spectrometry*] .... ZAA
Zeerust [*South Africa*] [*ICAO location identifier*] (ICLI) .... FAZR
Zefkrome Yarn Program [*Dow Chemical Co.*] .... ZYP
Zeigler Coal Holding [*NYSE symbol*] (TTSB) .... ZEI
Zeigler Coal Holding Co. [*NYSE symbol*] (SAG) .... ZEI
Zeigler Coal Holding Co. [*Associated Press*] (SAG) .... ZeigCoal
Zeirei Agudath Israel (EA) .... ZAI
Zeiss Historica Society of America (EA) .... ZHSA
Zeiss Light Section Microscope .... ZLSM
Zeitgeist, Enhancement, and Nonglare [*Camera lens finish developed by Sigma*] .... ZEN
Zeitlich Untauglich [*Temporarily Unfit*] [*German military - World War II*] .... ZU
Zeitschrift [*Review*] [*German*] .... ZTSCHR
Zeitschrift der Savigny-Stiftung fuer Rechtsgeschichte. Romanistische Abteilung [*A publication*] (OCD) .... Sav Zeitschr
Zeitschrift fuer Auslaendisches und Internationales Privatrecht [*Berlin and Tubingen, Germany*] [*A publication*] (DLA) .... Zschft f Ausl u Intl Privatr
Zeitschrift fuer das Gesamte Familienrecht [*German A publication*] (DLA) .... Fam RZ
Zeitschrift fuer die Evangelischen Religionsunterricht [*A publication*] (BJA) .... ZEvR
Zeitschrift fuer die Oesterreichischen Gymnasien [*A publication*] (OCD) .... Z fur die Ost Gym
Zeitschrift fuer die Wissenschaft des Judentums [*Leopold Zunz*] [*A publication*] (BJA) .... ZZ
Zeitschrift fuer Evangelische Ethik. Gutersloh [*A publication*] (BJA) .... ZevE
Zeitschrift fuer Geschichtswissenschaft [*A publication*] (DLA) .... ZfG
Zeitschrift fuer Luftrecht- und Weltraumrechtsfragen [*German A publication*] (DLA) .... ZFL
Zeitschrift fuer Luftrecht- und Weltraumrechtsfragen [*A publication*] (DLA) .... Zschft Luft- u Weltr-Recht
Zeitschrift fuer Papyrologie und Epigraphik [*A publication*] (BJA) .... ZPapEpigr
Zeitschrift fuer Rechtsvergleichung [*Vienna, Austria*] [*A publication*] (DLA) .... Zschft Rechtsvergl
Zeitschrift fuer Rundfunk und Fernsehen [*Journal for Radio and Television*] [*NOMOS Datapool*] [*Information service or system*] .... RUFE
Zeitschrift fuer Schweizerisches Recht/Revue de Droit Suisse/Revista di Diritto Svizzero [*Basel, Switzerland*] [*A publication*] (DLA) .... Z f Schweiz Recht
Zeitschrift fuer Urheber und Medienrecht [*Journal for Copyright and Communication*] [*NOMOS Datapool*] [*Database producer*] .... ZUM
Zeitschrift fuer Versicherungswesen [*German A publication*] (DLA) .... ZfV
Zeitschriftendatenbank [*German Union Catalog of Serials*] [*Deutsches Bibliotheksinstitut*] [*Germany*] [*Information service or system*] (CRD) .... ZDB
Zeitschriftenkatalog der Bayerischen Staatsbibliothek, Munchen [*Serials Catalogue of the Bavarian State Library, Munich*] [*Deutsches Bibliotheksinstitut*] [*Germany*] [*Information service or system*] (CRD) .... ZBSB
Zeitung [*Newspaper, Review*] [*German*] (ILCA) .... Z
Zelena Slovenije [*Greens of Slovenia*] [*Political party*] (EY) .... ZS
Zell Am See [*Austria ICAO location identifier*] (ICLI) .... LOWZ
Zella 74 [*Libya*] [*ICAO location identifier*] (ICLI) .... HLZA
Zellweger Syndrome [*Also, ZWS*] [*Medicine*] .... ZS
Zellweger Syndrome [*Medicine*] .... ZWS
Zelovo [*Enthusiastically*] [*Music*] (ROG) .... ZEL
Zeltweg [*Austria ICAO location identifier*] (ICLI) .... LOXZ
Zemex Corp. [*Associated Press*] (SAG) .... Zemex
Zemex Corp. [*NYSE symbol*] (SPSG) .... ZMX
Zemio [*Central African Republic*] [*ICAO location identifier*] (ICLI) .... FEFZ
Zen and the Art of Motorcycle Maintenance [*A novel*] .... ZAMM
Zen Buddhism (BARN) .... ZB
Zen Studies Society (EA) .... ZSS
Zenaga [*MARC language code Library of Congress*] (LCCP) .... zen
Zenana Bible and Medical Mission [*British*] (DI) .... ZBMM
Zenco Resources, Inc. [*Vancouver Stock Exchange symbol*] .... ZNO
Zen-Do Kai Martial Arts Association, International (EA) .... ZDK
Zeneca Group [*NYSE symbol*] (SPSG) .... ZEN
Zeneca Group [*Associated Press*] (SAG) .... Zeneca
Zeneca Group ADR [*NYSE symbol*] (TTSB) .... ZEN
Zener Diode .... ZD
Zener Voltage [*Electronics*] (OA) .... Vz
Zener Voltage Regulator .... ZVR
Zener Voltage Regulator Diode .... ZVRD
Zenit [*Former USSR*] [*FAA designator*] (FAAC) .... EZT
Zenith .... Z
Zenith (WDAA) .... ZEN
Zenith .... ZN
Zenith Angle [*Geophysics*] .... ZA
Zenith Angle Distribution .... ZAD
Zenith Data Systems .... ZDS
Zenith Description (WDAA) .... ZD
Zenith Distance [*Navigation*] .... Z
Zenith Distance [*Navigation*] .... ZD
Zenith Electronics [*NYSE symbol*] (TTSB) .... ZE
Zenith Electronics Corp. [*NYSE symbol*] (SPSG) .... ZE
Zenith Electronics Corp. [*Associated Press*] (SAG) .... ZenithE
Zenith Energetic Particle Spectrometer (SSD) .... ZEPS
Zenith National Insurance Corp. [*Associated Press*] (SAG) .... ZenNtl
Zenith National Insurance Corp. [*NYSE symbol*] (SPSG) .... ZNT
Zenith Natl Insurance [*NYSE symbol*] (TTSB) .... ZNT
Zenith Radio Corp. .... ZRC
Zenix Income Fund [*Associated Press*] (SAG) .... Zenix
Zenix Income Fund [*NYSE symbol*] (SPSG) .... ZIF
Zenon Park, SK [*Television station call letters*] CBKFT-5
Zentralabteilung Strahlenschutz [*Central Department for Radiation Protection*] [*Germany*] .... ZST
Zentralarchiv fuer Empirische Sozialforschung [*Central Archives for Empirical Social Research*] [*University of Cologne*] [*Information service or system*] (IID) .... ZA
Zentralbibliothek Zurich, Zurich, Switzerland [*Library symbol Library of Congress*] (LCLS) .... SzZ
Zentralblatt [*Official Gazette*] [*German*] (ILCA) .... Z
Zentralblatt [*Official Gazette*] [*German*] .... Ztbl
Zentralblatt der Deutschen Demokratischen Republik [*A publication*] (DLA) .... Zbl DDR
Zentralblatt fuer Sozialversicherung und Versorgung [*German A publication*] (DLA) .... Zbl Soz Vers
Zentraldeutsche Rundfunk [*Central German Radio*] .... ZDR
Zentrale Dokumentationsstelle der Freien Wohlfahrtspflege fuer Fluechtlinge eV [*Germany*] .... ZDWF
Zentralinstitut fuer Information und Dokumentation [*Central Institute for Information and Documentation*] [*Germany Information service or system*] (IID) .... ZIID
Zentralinstitut Physik der Erde [*Potsdam*] .... ZIPE
Zentralkommittee [*Central Committee*] [*of the Socialist Union Party of the German Democratic Republic*] .... ZK
Zentralrat [*Central Board*] [*German*] .... ZR
Zentral-Sparkasse [*Banking Austria*] (ECON) .... Z
Zentralstelle Dokumentation Elektrotechnik [*Electrical Engineering Documentation Center*] [*Originator and database*] [*Germany Information service or system*] (IID) .... ZDE
Zentralstelle fuer Agrardokumentation und -Information [*Center for Agricultural Documentation and Information*] [*Databank originator*] [*Information service or system*] [*Germany*] (IID) .... ZADI
Zentralstelle fuer Atomkernenergie-Dokumentation beim Gmelin-Institut [*Central Agency for Atomic Energy Documentation of the Gmelin Institute*] [*Germany Database originator Also, AED*] .... ZAED
Zentralstelle fuer Luft- Raumfahrtdokumentation und Information [*Center for Documentation and Information in Aeronautics and Astronautics*] [*West Germany*] [*Information service or system*] .... ZLDI
Zentralstelle fuer Psychologische Information und Dokumentation [*Center for Psychological Information and Documentation*] [*Database operator*] [*Germany Information service or system*] (IID) .... ZPID
Zentralverband der Elektrotechnischen Industrie [*Electrical Equipment Industry Association*] [*Germany*] (EY) .... ZVEI
Zentralwohlfahrtsstelle der Juden in Deutschland [*A publication*] (BJA) .... ZWS
Zentralwohlfahrtsstelle der Juden in Deutschland [*A publication*] (BJA) .... ZWSt
Zentrum fur Moleculare Biologie Heidelberg [*Center for Molecular Biology Heidelberg*] .... ZMBH
Zentrumspartei [*Center Party*] [*German Political party*] (PPE) .... Z
Zenzelinus de Cassanis [*Deceased, 1334*] [*Authority cited in pre-1607 legal work*] (DSA) .... Zen
Zenzelinus de Cassanis [*Deceased, 1334*] [*Authority cited in pre-1607 legal work*] (DSA) .... Zenz
Zeolite [*Chemistry*] .... ZEO
Zeos International Ltd. [*NASDAQ symbol*] (NQ) .... ZEOS

Zep Energy [*Vancouver Stock Exchange symbol*]	ZP
Zephaniah [*Old Testament book*]	Zep
Zephaniah [*Old Testament book*]	Zeph
Zephaniah (BJA)	Zp
Zephiran-Trisodium Phosphate [*Medicine*] (DMAA)	Z-TSP
Zephyr Aviation Services, Inc. [*ICAO designator*] (FAAC)	RZR
Zephyrhills, FL [*AM radio station call letters*]	WZHR
Zephyrhills, FL [*Location identifier FAA*] (FAAL)	ZPH
Zeppelin (DSUE)	ZEP
Zeppelin Collectors Club (EA)	ZCC
Zera' Kodesh (BJA)	ZK
Zera'im (BJA)	Zer
Zerex Saab Pro Series [*Auto racing*]	ZSPS
Zermatt [*Switzerland ICAO location identifier*] (ICLI)	LSEZ
Zermelo-Fraenkel [*Set theory*] [*Mathematics*]	ZF
Zero [*India*] [*ICAO location identifier*] (ICLI)	VEZO
Zero (WDMC)	z
Zero	Z
Zero (IDOE)	z
Zero Ability to Pay [*Real estate*]	ZAP
Zero Access Storage	ZAS
Zero Address Instruction	ZAI
Zero Adjuster (MSA)	ZA
Zero Administration for Windows [*Microsoft Corp.*] [*Computer science*]	ZAW
Zero Administration Initiative for Windows [*Microsoft Corp.*] [*Computer science*]	ZAW
Zero Administration Kit [*Computer science*]	ZAK
Zero Alignment Fixture	ZAF
Zero and Add	ZA
Zero and Add Packed	ZAP
Zero and Subtract	ZS
Zero Angle of Attack	ZAA
Zero Antiaircraft Potential [*Missile*]	ZAAP
Zero Antiaircraft Potential [*Missile*] (MCD)	ZAP
Zero Assignment Parallel Processor (NITA)	ZAPP
Zero Balance Accounts (TDOB)	ZBA
Zero Balance Entry [*Banking*]	ZE
Zero Balance, Reimbursable Account [*Year-end reclassification of taxable income*]	ZEBRA
Zero Based Analysis	ZBA
Zero Beat [*Radio*]	ZB
Zero Beat Reception [*Radio*]	ZBR
Zero Bend Radius	ZBR
Zero Bias Anomaly	ZBA
Zero Bit Insertion/Deletion (NITA)	ZBID
Zero Bracket Amount [*IRS*]	ZBA
Zero Byte Time Slot Interchange (ACRL)	ZBTSI
Zero Calibration (MCD)	Z/CAL
Zero Code Suppression (ACRL)	ZCS
Zero Corp. [*Associated Press*] (SAG)	Zero
Zero Corp. [*NYSE symbol*] (SPSG)	ZRO
Zero Cost Ration Option (TDOB)	ZCRO
Zero Count Table (IAA)	ZCT
Zero Coupon Eurosterling Bearer or Registered Accruing Certificates (TDOB)	ZEBRA
Zero Coupon Issue (Security) [*In bond listings of newspapers*]	ZR
Zero Crossing Constant False Alarm Rate (IAA)	ZCCFAR
Zero Crossing Constant False Alarm Rate (MSA)	ZXCFAR
Zero Crossing Detector	ZCD
Zero Crossing Rate	ZCR
Zero Crossover (MHDB)	ZCO
Zero Day [*The date fixed for any important military operation*] [*British*]	Z (Day)
Zero Dead Volume [*Chromatography*]	ZDV
Zero Defects	ZD
Zero Defects Council	ZDC
Zero Defects Program	ZDP
Zero Defects Program Audit	ZDPA
Zero Defects Program Guideline	ZDPG
Zero Defects Program Objective	ZDPO
Zero Defects Program Responsibility	ZDPR
Zero Defects Proposal	ZDP
Zero Delay Device	ZDD
Zero Deletion Data Link	ZDDL
Zero Delivery Pressure (IEEE)	ZDP
Zero Differential Overlap (DMAA)	ZDO
Zero Discharge (DAVI)	ZD
Zero Economic Growth	ZEG
Zero Effort Networking [*Novell*] [*Computer science*]	ZEN
Zero Effusion	ZE
Zero Electrophoretic Mobility [*Analytical chemistry*]	ZEM
Zero Emissions Vehicle	ZEV
Zero End Expiratory Pressure [*Medicine*]	ZEEP
Zero Energy (BARN)	ZE
Zero Energy	ZOE
Zero Energy Assembly [*Nuclear energy*]	ZEA
Zero Energy Breeder Reactor Assembly [*British*]	ZEBRA
Zero Energy Coefficient	ZEC
Zero Energy Critical Assemblies Reactor [*British*] (DEN)	ZERA
Zero Energy Deuterium [*Type of nuclear reactor*]	ZED
Zero Energy Experimental Pile [*Nuclear reactor*] [*Canada*]	ZEEP
Zero Energy Growth	ZEG
Zero Energy Nitrogen-Heated Thermal Reactor [*British*] (MCD)	ZENITH
Zero Energy Plutonium-Fueled Fast Reactor [*British*] (DEN)	ZEPHYR
Zero Energy Reactor for Lattice Investigation and New Assemblies [*India*]	ZERLINA

Zero Energy Reflection	ZER
Zero Energy Reflection Coefficient	ZERC
Zero Energy System [*Nuclear energy*]	ZES
Zero Energy Thermal Reactor [*British*]	ZETR
Zero Energy Thermonuclear Apparatus [*or Assembly*] [*AEC*]	ZETA
Zero Energy Uranium System [*British*]	ZEUS
Zero Entropy Automorphism	ZEA
Zero Environmental Impact	ZEI
Zero Excess Propellants Line	ZEPL
Zero Express Dialing	ZED
Zero Extraction Force (EECA)	ZEF
Zero Failure Criteria (IEEE)	ZFC
Zero Field Splitting	ZFS
Zero Frequency	ZF
Zero Fuel Weight [*Aviation*]	ZFW
Zero Grade Air	ZGA
Zero Gradient Synchrotron [*AEC*]	ZGS
Zero Gravity	OG
Zero Gravity (IEEE)	ZG
Zero Gravity Facility [*NASA*]	ZGF
Zero Headspace Extractor [*Environmental Protection Agency*] (ERG)	ZHE
Zero Hour (WDAA)	Z HR
Zero Immune Globulin (WDAA)	ZIG
Zero Income, No Kids [*Lifestyle classification*]	Zink
Zero Input	ZI
Zero Insertion Force [*Electronics*]	ZIF
Zero Interest Payment [*Banking*]	ZIP
Zero Internal Resistance	ZIR
Zero Intersymbol Interference - Zero Derivative (PDAA)	ZII-ZD
Zero Inventory [*Industrial engineering*]	OI
Zero Kilowatt (IEEE)	zkW
Zero Kinetic Energy [*Physics*]	ZEKE
Zero Level Drift	ZLD
Zero Level Sparing (MCD)	ZLS
Zero Lift	ZL
Zero Lift Cord	ZLC
Zero Lift Drag	ZLD
Zero Line Gap	ZLG
Zero Lot Line [*Real estate*]	ZLL
Zero Marker (MCD)	ZM
Zero Memory Non-Linear (IAA)	ZNL
Zero Moisture Basis [*Chemical analysis*]	ZMB
Zero Net Growth Isocline [*Ecological graph*]	ZNGI
Zero Offset Rapid Reaction Ordnance	ZORRO
Zero on Originality (WDMC)	ZOO
Zero Order Detector (MCD)	ZOD
Zero Order Hold [*Telescope*]	ZOH
Zero Order Interpolar (IAA)	ZOI
Zero Order Polynomial Interpolator	ZOPI
Zero Order Polynomial Predictor	ZOPP
Zero Order Predictor	ZOP
Zero Order Variable Aperture Nonredundant Point Transmitted [*Compression algorithm*] (MCD)	ZVA
Zero Output	ZO
Zero Path Difference	ZPD
Zero Period Acceleration [*Nuclear energy*] (NRCH)	ZPA
Zero Point Energy	ZPE
Zero Point of Charge	ZPC
Zero Population Growth (EA)	ZPG
Zero Power Physics Reactor	ZPPR
Zero Power Plutonium Reactor [*Nuclear energy*]	ZPPR
Zero Power Reactor [*Nuclear energy*]	ZPR
Zero Power Reactor Facility [*AEC*]	ZPRF
Zero Power Test	ZPT
Zero Print Control (IAA)	ZPC
Zero Quality Control	ZQC
Zero Quantum Transition [*Physics*]	ZQT
Zero Radial Play	ZRP
Zero Range Approximation [*Nuclear science*] (OA)	ZRA
Zero Rate [*Valued added tax*]	Z
Zero Rate Error (MCD)	ZRE
Zero Reaction Tool	ZERT
Zero Reaction Tool	ZRT
Zero Resistance Ammeter [*Instrumentation*]	ZRA
Zero Risk Level (GFGA)	ZRL
Zero Shift	ZS
Zero Sight Line (DNAB)	ZSL
Zero Size Image	ZSI
Zero Skip Frequency (IAA)	ZSF
Zero State (IAA)	ZS
Zero Subcarrier Chromaticity	ZSC
Zero Sum [*Genetics*]	ZS
Zero Suppress	ZS
Zero Suppress (IAA)	ZSUP
Zero Time Outage [*Nuclear energy*] (NRCH)	ZTO
Zero Transmission Level Point (IEEE)	OTLP
Zero Transmission Power	ZXMP
Zero Turn-Around Time [*Microcomputer*] [*Hitachi Ltd.*]	ZTAT
Zero Voltage Switch	ZVS
Zero Wait [*Industrial engineering*]	ZW
Zero Wave Velocity	ZWV
Zero Wavelength	ZWL
Zero Wear	ZW
Zero Word Count	ZWC
Zero-Age Main Sequence [*Astronomy*]	ZAMS

Zero-Base Budgeting .... ZBB
Zero-Base Media Planning .... ZBMP
Zero-Base Operational Planning and Budgeting (MHDB) .... ZBOP
Zero-Base Programming [Military] .... ZBP
Zero-Base Review .... ZBR
Zero-Based (IAA) .... ZB
Zero-Based Analysis (ADA) .... ZBA
Zero-Based Linearity .... ZBL
Zero-Based Tactical Quality Management [Army] .... ZBTQM
Zero-Ductility Transition (IEEE) .... ZDT
Zero-Emission Vehicle [Automotive engineering] (PS) .... ZEV
Zero-Emissions Bus .... ZEB
Zero-Emissions Truck .... ZET
Zero-Field Cooled [Physics] .... ZFC
Zero-Field Deuterium Nuclear Magnetic Resonance .... ZFDNMR
Zero-Field Nuclear Magnetic Resonance .... ZFNMR
Zero-Field Splitting Constant [Physics] .... ZFSC
Zero-G Antenna Range (SSD) .... ZAR
Zero-Gravity Effect .... ZGE
Zero-Gravity Environment .... ZGE
Zero-Gravity Expulsion .... ZGE
Zero-Gravity Expulsion Technique .... ZET
Zero-Gravity Expulsion Technique .... ZGET
Zero-Gravity Generator .... ZGG
Zero-Gravity Locomotion Simulator [NASA] (PS) .... ZLS
Zero-Gravity Shower .... ZGS
Zero-Gravity Simulator .... ZGS
Zero-Gravity Trainer [NASA] (NASA) .... ZGT
Zero-Gravity Whole Body Shower .... ZGWBS
Zero-Length Launch [Missiles] .... ZEL
Zero-Length Launch [Missiles] (MCD) .... ZELL
Zero-Length Launch [Missiles] .... ZLL
Zero-Length Launch and Mat Landing [Missiles] (MCD) .... ZELMAL
Zero-Length Takeoff (MCD) .... ZLTO
Zero-Length Vector .... ZLV
Zero-Level Emissions Vehicle .... Z-LEV
Zero-Magnetostrictive Composition (PDAA) .... ZMC
Zero-Phonon Hole [Spectroscopy] .... ZPH
Zero-Phonon Line [Physics] .... ZPL
Zero-Point Vibration .... ZPV
Zero-Point-Motion [Physics] .... ZPM
Zero-Relative Velocity .... ZRV
Zeros Extended (IAA) .... ZE
Zero-Set Amplifier (MSA) .... ZSA
ZEROSLOTLAN [Avatar Technologies, Inc.] [In Alliance ZSL, a PC network] .... ZSL
Zero-Speed Generator .... ZSG
Zero-Speed Pulse Generator .... ZSPG
Zero-Temperature Coefficient (MSA) .... ZTC
Zero-Temperature Coefficient Resistor .... ZCR
Zero-Temperature Plasma .... ZTP
Zeroth Order Logarithmic Distribution .... ZOLD
Zero-Velocity Fading [Aviation] (AIA) .... ZVF
Zero-Zero Condition .... ZZC
Zero-Zero Visibility .... ZZV
Zero-Zero Weather .... ZZW
Zerstoerergeschwader [Twin-engine fighter wing] [German military - World War II] .... ZG
Zerubbabel [Freemasonry] (ROG) .... Z
Zeta (NUCP) .... Z
Zeta Beta Tau [Fraternity] .... ZBT
Zeta Erythrocyte Sedimentation Rate [Medicine] (DMAA) .... Z-ERS
Zeta Erythrocyte Sedimentation Rate [Hematology] (DAVI) .... Z-ESR
Zeta Phi Eta .... ZPE
Zeta Sedimentation Rate [Medicine] (CPH) .... ZSR
Zeta Tau Alpha [Sorority] .... ZTA
Zeus Acquisition RADAR [Missile defense] .... ZAR
Zeus Defense Center [Missile defense] .... ZDC
Zeus Defense Center Tape and Buffer System [Missiles] (IEEE) .... ZDCTBS
Zeus Discrimination RADAR [Missile defense] .... ZDR
Zeus Early Missile Test RADAR [Missile defense] (AABC) .... ZEMTR
Zeus Malfunction Array RADAR [Missile defense] (IAA) .... ZMAR
Zeus Multifunction Array RADAR [Missile defense] .... ZMAR
Zeus Multifunction Array RADAR / Multifunction Array RADAR [Missile defense] (SAA) .... ZMAR/MAR
Zeus Multiple Array RADAR [Missile defense] (IAA) .... ZMAR
Zeus Phased Array RADAR [Missile defense] .... ZPAR
Zeus Production Evaluation Program [Missiles] (MCD) .... ZPED
Zeus Program Analysis [Missiles] .... ZPA
Zeus Project Engineer Network [Missiles] .... ZPEN
Zeus Project Office [Missiles] .... ZPO
Zeus Target Joint Working Group [Missiles] (AAG) .... ZTJWG
Zeus Up-Range Facility [Missiles] (AAG) .... ZURF
Zeus-Nike X Program Office [Missiles] (MCD) .... ZNXPO
Zevahim (BJA) .... Zev
Zhangjiang [China] [Airport symbol] (OAG) .... ZHA
Zhanjiang [China] [ICAO location identifier] (ICLI) .... ZGZJ
Zhaotong [China] [Airport symbol] (OAG) .... ZAT
Zhejiang Airlines [China] [ICAO designator] (FAAC) .... CJG
Zhengzhou [China] [Airport symbol] (OAG) .... CGO
Zhengzhou [China] [ICAO location identifier] (ICLI) .... ZHCC
Zhob [Pakistan] [ICAO location identifier] (ICLI) .... OPZB
Zhob [Pakistan] [Airport symbol] (OAG) .... PZH
Zhongfei General Aviation Co. [China] [FAA designator] (FAAC) .... CFZ
Zhongyuan Aviation Co. [China] [ICAO designator] (FAAC) .... CYN
Zi Mischari [Merchant fleet] [Israel] .... ZIM

Zia Airlines [ICAO designator] (AD) .... ZU
Zidovudine [Antiviral] .... ZDV
Ziegfeld Club (EA) .... ZC
Ziegfeld Follies .... ZF
Ziegler Company, Inc. [AMEX symbol] (SAG) .... ZCO
Ziegler Co., Inc. [Associated Press] (SAG) .... Ziegler
Ziegler Cos. [AMEX symbol] (TTSB) .... ZCO
Ziehl-Neelsen [A biological stain] .... ZN
Zielona Gora [Poland] [Airport symbol] (OAG) .... IEG
Ziff Desktop Information [Commercial firm] (PCM) .... ZDI
Ziff-Davis .... ZD
Ziff-Davis Benchmark Operation (PCM) .... ZDBOp
Ziff-Davis Benchmark Operation [Computer utility tool] (PCM) .... ZDBOP
Ziff-Davis Interactive Co. [Computer science] (PCM) .... ZDI
Ziggurat (VRA) .... zig
Ziguinchor [Senegal] [ICAO location identifier] (ICLI) .... GOGG
Ziguinchor [Senegal] [Airport symbol] (OAG) .... ZIG
Zig-Zag .... ZZ
Zig-Zag Diagram .... ZZD
Zigzag in Line [Electronics] (EECA) .... ZIL
Zigzag In-Line Package [Wells American] [Computer science] .... ZIP
Zig-Zag Rectifier .... ZZR
Zigzag Riveting (MSA) .... ZZR
Zihuatanejo [Mexico ICAO location identifier] (ICLI) .... MMZH
Zihuatanejo [Mexico] [Airport symbol] (OAG) .... ZIH
Zi-ka-wei [Republic of China] [Seismograph station code, US Geological Survey] (SEIS) .... ZKW
Zil Elwannyen Sesel [Formerly, Zil Eliogne Sesel, then Zil Elwagne Sesel] .... ZES
Zila, Inc. [NASDAQ symbol] (NQ) .... ZILA
Ziliolus de Cremona [Authority cited in pre-1607 legal work] (DSA) .... Zi de Cmo
Zilla Court Decisions, Bengal, Madras, Northwest Provinces [India] [A publication] (DLA) .... Zilla CD
Zilog Development System (NITA) .... ZDS
Zilog Eight Bit Microprocessor (HGAA) Z80
Zilog Eight Bit One-Chip Microcomputer (HGAA) Z8
Zilog, Inc. [Associated Press] (SAG) .... Zilog
Zilog, Inc. [NYSE symbol] (SAG) .... ZLG
Zilog List Processor [Programming language] [1979] (CSR) .... ZLISP
Zilog Sixteen Bit Microprocessor (HGAA) Z8000
Zim Passenger Line (MHDB) .... ZPL
Zimbabwe [Aircraft nationality and registration mark] (FAAC) .... Z
Zimbabwe [IYRU nationality code] (IYR) .... ZB
Zimbabwe .... Zim
Zimbabwe (WDAA) .... ZIMB
Zimbabwe [ANSI two-letter standard code] (CNC) .... ZW
Zimbabwe [ANSI three-letter standard code] (CNC) .... ZWE
Zimbabwe African National Liberation Army (PD) .... ZANLA
Zimbabwe African National Union [Political party] (PPW) .... ZANU
Zimbabwe African National Union - Patriotic Front [Political party] (PD) .... ZANU-PF
Zimbabwe African People's Organization .... ZAPO
Zimbabwe African People's Union .... ZAPU
Zimbabwe Banking Corp. Ltd. .... ZB
Zimbabwe Banking Corp. Ltd. .... ZIMBANK
Zimbabwe Democratic Party [Political party] (PPW) .... ZDP
Zimbabwe Independent People's Revolutionary Army (PD) .... ZIPRA
Zimbabwe International Trade Fair (ECON) .... ZITF
Zimbabwe People's Army .... ZIPA
Zimbabwe Professional Hunters & Guides Association .... ZPHGA
Zimbabwe Progressive Party [Political party] (PPW) .... ZPP
Zimbabwe Rhodesian Information Office [An association] (EA) .... ZRIO
Zimbabwe United People's Organization [Political party] (PPW) .... ZUPO
Zimbabwe Unity Movement [Political party] (ECON) .... ZUM
Zimchurud [Former USSR Seismograph station code, US Geological Survey Closed] (SEIS) .... ZIM
Zimex Aviation Ltd. [Switzerland ICAO designator] (FAAC) .... IMX
Zimmerman [Used with a number in cataloging music of Henry Purcell] (BARN) .... Z
Zimmerman Elementary School, Zimmerman, MN [Library symbol] [Library of Congress] (LCLS) .... MnZE
Zimmerman Preschool Language Scale (DAVI) .... ZPLS
Zimmerman Registry [An association] (EA) .... ZR
Zinc [Chemical symbol is Zn] .... Z
Zinc (VRA) .... zi
Zinc [Chemical element] .... Zn
Zinc Alloy Die Casters' Association [British] (BI) .... ZADCA
Zinc Aluminium Coater [Metallurgy] .... ZAC
Zinc, Aluminium, Magnesium (PDAA) .... ZAM
Zinc Ammonium Chloride [Organic chemistry] (WDAA) .... ZAC
Zinc and Lead International Service .... ZALIS
Zinc Atmospheric Tracer .... ZAT
Zinc Battery Electrode .... ZBE
Zinc Borate [Trademark for a flame retardant compound] [Humphrey Chemical Co.] .... ZB
Zinc Chloride Poisoning (DMAA) .... ZCP
Zinc Chromate Primer .... ZCP
Zinc Deficiency (DMAA) .... ZD
Zinc Depletion Syndrome [Medicine] (DMAA) .... ZDS
Zinc Detection System .... ZDS
Zinc Development Association [British] (EAIO) .... ZDA
Zinc Development Association/Lead Development Association/Cadmium Association [Information service or system] (IID) .... ZDA/LDA/CA
Zinc Dialklydithiophosphate [Automotive lubricants] .... ZDP
Zinc Dialklydithiophosphate [Automotive lubricants] .... ZDTP
Zinc Dialkyldithiophosphate [Organic chemistry] .... ZDDP

Zinc Dibenzyldithiocarbamate [*Organic chemistry*] (DICI) ... ZDBT

Zinc Dibenzyldithiocarbamate [*Rubber accelerator*] ... ZDC

Zinc Dibutyldithiocarbamate [*Organic chemistry*] ... ZBDC

Zinc Die Casting ... ZDC

Zinc Diethyldithiocarbamate [*Organic chemistry*] ... ZDEC

Zinc Dimethyldithiocarbamate [*Organic chemistry*] ... ZMDC

Zinc Dimetylacrylate [*Plastics technology*] ... ZDMA

Zinc Ethylenebis(dithiocarbamate) [*Agricultural fungicide*] ... ZinEB

Zinc, E-Vitamin, Siberian Ginseng, Turnera [*Health product*] [*British*] ... ZEST

Zinc Finger [*Protein*] (DMAA) ... ZF

Zinc Finger Protein (DMAA) ... ZFP

Zinc Flocculation [*Medical test*] (MAE) ... Zn Fl

Zinc Gluconate [*Organic chemistry*] ... ZG

Zinc Gluconate [*Organic chemistry*] ... ZnG

Zinc Glycinate Marker [*Immunochemistry*] ... ZGM

Zinc Heads [*Freight*] ... ZH

Zinc Impurity Photodetector ... ZIP

Zinc Institute [*Defunct*] (EA) ... ZI

Zinc Iodide-Osmium [*Biological staining procedure*] ... ZIO

Zinc, Lead, and Cadmium Abstracts [*Zinc Development Association/Lead Development Association/Codmium Association*] [*British Defunct Information service or system*] (CRD) ... ZLC

Zinc Mercaptobenzimidazole [*Organic chemistry*] ... ZMB

Zinc Mercaptobenzothiazole [*Organic chemistry*] ... ZMBT

Zinc Metaarsenite [*Insecticide, wood preservative*] ... ZMA

Zinc Metals Research Institute ... ZMRI

Zinc Oxide [*Also, called white zinc*] [*Pharmacology*] (DAVI) ... ZnO

Zinc Oxide Non-Linear Resistance (IAA) ... ZNR

Zinc Oxide Pigment ... ZOP

Zinc Oxide Producers' Association [*European Council of Chemical Manufacturers Federations*] [*Belgium*] (EAIO) ... ZOPA

Zinc Oxide Resistor ... ZOR

Zinc Oxide-Eugenol [*Dental cement*] ... ZNOE

Zinc Oxide-Eugenol [*Dental cement*] ... ZOE

Zinc Oxide-Eugenol Cement [*Dentistry*] (DAVI) ... F_2

Zinc Peroxide [*Pharmacology*] ... ZPO

Zinc Pigment Development Association [*British*] (BI) ... ZPDA

Zinc Primary Battery ... ZPB

Zinc Protophorphyrin [*Biochemistry*] ... ZPP

Zinc Protoporphyrin [*Biochemistry*] ... ZnP

Zinc Pyrithione [*Antibacterial*] ... ZNP

Zinc Resistor ... ZNR

Zinc Sedimentation Rate (MEDA) ... ZSR

Zinc Silicate Coat ... ZSC

Zinc Storage Battery ... ZSB

Zinc Sulfide (BYTE) ... ZnS

Zinc Sulfide Atmospheric Tracer ... ZSAT

Zinc Sulfide Detection System ... ZSDS

Zinc Sulfide Detector ... ZSD

Zinc Sulfide System ... ZSS

Zinc Sulfide Tracer ... ZST

Zinc Tannate of Naloxone [*Opiate antagonist*] ... ZTN

Zinc-Air Battery ... ZAB

Zinc-Air Primary Battery ... ZAPB

Zinc-Aluminum [*An alloy*] ... ZA

Zinc-Coated Bolt ... ZCB

Zinc-Coated Nut ... ZCN

Zinc-Coated Screw ... ZCS

Zinc-Coated Washer ... ZCW

Zinc-Doped Germanium ... ZDG

Zinc-Electrochemical Cell ... ZEC

Zinc-Electrochemical Cell ... ZECC

Zincograph (DGA) ... zinco

Zinc-Phosphate Coating ... ZPC

Zinc-Silver-Oxide Battery (RDA) ... ZSOB

Zinder [*Niger*] [*ICAO location identifier*] (ICLI) ... DRZR

Zinder [*Niger*] [*Airport symbol*] (OAG) ... ZND

Zinfandel Club [*British*] (EAIO) ... ZC

Zing Technologies [*NASDAQ symbol*] (TTSB) ... ZING

Zing Technologies, Inc. [*NASDAQ symbol*] (SAG) ... ZING

Zinn's Select Cases in the Law of Trusts [*A publication*] (DLA) ... Zinn Ca Tr

Zinsser-Engman-Cole [*Syndrome*] [*Medicine*] (DMAA) ... ZEC

Zinziber [*Ginger*] [*Pharmacology*] (ROG) ... ZZ

Zion Bemishpat Tipadeh (Isaiah 1:27) (BJA) ... ZBT

Zion, IL [*AM radio station call letters*] ... WKGA

Zion, IL [*FM radio station call letters*] ... WNIZ

Zion, IL [*AM radio station call letters*] (RBYB) ... WTAU-AM

Zion Lutheran School, Sanborn, MN [*Library symbol*] [*Library of Congress*] (LCLS) ... MnSanLS

Zion Nuclear Plant (NRCH) ... ZNP

Zion Probabilistic Safety Study [*Nuclear energy*] (NRCH) ... ZPSS

Zion Research Library, Brookline, Boston, MA [*Library symbol*] [*Library of Congress*] (LCLS) ... MBrZ

Zion-Benton Library District, Zion, IL [*OCLC symbol*] (OCLC) ... JAR

Zion-Benton Public Library District, Zion, IL [*Library symbol Library of Congress*] (LCLS) ... IZ

Zionic Research and Development Institute [*Defunct*] (EA) ... ZRDI

Zionism (BJA) ... Zion

Zionist ... Z

Zionist Archives and Library (BJA) ... ZAL

Zionist Archives and Library, New York, NY [*Library symbol Library of Congress*] (LCLS) ... NNZi

Zionist Congress [*Australia*] ... ZC

Zionist Federation [*British*] (DBA) ... ZF

Zionist Federation Educational Trust [*British*] (DI) ... ZFET

Zionist Federation of Great Britain and Ireland (DI) ... ZFGBI

Zionist Occupational Government ... ZOG

Zionist Organization of America (EA) ... ZOA

Zionist Year Book [*A publication*] (BJA) ... ZYB

Zionistische Vereinigung fuer Deutschaland [*Zionist Federation of Germany*] ... ZVfD

Zions Bancorp [*NASDAQ symbol*] (TTSB) ... ZION

Zion's Cooperative Mercantile Institution [*Department store in Salt Lake City, UT*] ... ZCMI

Zions Utah Bancorp [*NASDAQ symbol*] (SAG) ... ZION

Zions Utah Bancorp [*Associated Press*] (SAG) ... ZionBcP

Zionsville, IN [*Location identifier FAA*] (FAAL) ... HZP

Zip Code Attachment Program [*Computer science*] (WDMC) ... ZAP

Zip Code Demographic Data Base [*Demographic Research Co., Inc.*] [*Information service or system*] (CRD) ... ZDDB

ZIP Code Distribution ... ZD

Zip Fastener Manufacturers Association [*British*] (BI) ... ZFMA

Zip Fastener Manufacturers Association [*British*] (DBA) ... ZFMA

ZIP [*Zone Improvement Plan*] **Mail Translator** [*Postal Service*] ... ZMT

Zipper Jacket ... ZJ

Zipper Tubing ... ZT

Zipp-Forming Cells [*Immunology*] ... ZFC

Zippy Collectors Club [*Defunct*] (EA) ... ZCCI

Zircon [*CIPW classification*] [*Geology*] ... Z

Zirconia Fuel Cell ... ZFC

Zirconia Grain Stabilized [*Metal alloys*] ... ZGS

Zirconia-Coated Crucible ... ZCC

Zirconia-Coated Iridium Crucible ... ZCIC

Zirconia-Iridium Crucible ... ZIC

Zirconium [*Symbol is Zr*] [*Chemical element*] (ROG) ... Z

Zirconium [*Chemical element*] ... Zr

Zirconium, Barium, Lanthanum, Aluminum, Sodium Fluoride [*Molar composition of glass*] [*Chemistry*] ... ZBLAN

Zirconium Boride Silicon Carbide (PDAA) ... ZRBSC

Zirconium Hydride Reactor ... ZHR

Zirconium-Water Oxidation Kinetics (NRCH) ... ZWOK

Zirku [*United Arab Emirates*] [*ICAO location identifier*] (ICLI) ... OMAZ

Zisco [*Zimbabwe*] [*ICAO location identifier*] (ICLI) ... FVZC

Zitel Corp. [*Associated Press*] (SAG) ... Zitel

Zitel Corp. [*NASDAQ symbol*] (NQ) ... ZITL

Zivena Beneficial Society (EA) ... ZBS

Zizit (BJA) ... Ziz

Zjednoczenie Chrzescijansko-Narodowe [*Christian National Union*] [*Poland Political party*] (EY) ... ZChN

Zjednoczone Stronnictwo Ludowe [*United Peasants' Party*] [*Poland Political party*] (PPW) ... ZSL

Zloty [*Monetary unit*] [*Poland*] ... Z

Zloty [*Monetary unit*] [*Poland*] (EY) ... ZL

Zmiesana Komisia Medzinarodnej Dohody o Rybolove vo Vodach Dunaja [*International Commission for Agreement on the Danube Fishing*] [*Former Czechoslovakia*] (EAIO) ... ZKMDRVD

Zmiesana Komisia o Rybolove vo Vodach Dunaja [*Joint Danube Fishery Commission - JDFC*] [*Zilina, Czechoslovakia*] (EAIO) ... ZKRVD

Zmotoryzowane Oddzialy Milicji Obywatelskiej [*Motorized Units of People's Militia*] [*Poland's riot police*] ... ZOMO

Znamenity Amerikansky Pisatel [*Famous American Writer*] [*Russian*] ... ZAP

Zodiac (ROG) ... ZOD

Zodiac Air [*Bulgaria*] [*ICAO designator*] (FAAC) ... AZV

Zodiac Records [*Record label*] ... Zod

Zodiacal Light Device ... ZLD

Zodiacal Microparticle Multiparameter Analysis System [*NASA*] ... ZMMAS

Zoen Tencararius [*Flourished, 13th century*] [*Authority cited in pre-1607 legal work*] (DSA) ... Z

Zoen Tencararius [*Flourished, 13th century*] [*Authority cited in pre-1607 legal work*] (DSA) ... Zo

Zoersel [*Belgium ICAO location identifier*] (ICLI) ... EBZR

Zoladex [*Antineoplastic drug*] (CDI) ... ZDX

Zoladex (DMAA) ... ZOL

Zolfo Springs, FL [*FM radio station call letters*] ... WZZS

Zoll [*Customs Duty*] [*German*] ... Z

Zoll Medical [*NASDAQ symbol*] (TTSB) ... ZOLL

Zoll Medical Corp. [*NASDAQ symbol*] (SAG) ... ZOLL

Zoll Medical Corp. [*Associated Press*] (SAG) ... ZollMed

Zollgesetz [*Tariff Law*] [*German*] ... ZG

Zollinger-Ellison [*Syndrome*] [*Medicine*] ... ZE

Zollinger-Ellison Syndrome [*Medicine*] ... ZES

Zoltek Companies [*NASDAQ symbol*] (SAG) ... ZOLT

Zoltek Co. [*NASDAQ symbol*] (TTSB) ... ZOLT

Zoltek Cos. [*Associated Press*] (SAG) ... Zoltek

Zomax Optical Media [*NASDAQ symbol*] (TTSB) ... ZOMX

Zomax Optical Media, Inc. [*NASDAQ symbol*] (SAG) ... ZOMX

Zomax Optical Media, Inc. [*Associated Press*] (SAG) ... ZomxOpt

Zomba [*Malawi*] [*Airport symbol*] (AD) ... ZOM

Zona Fasciculata [*Of adrenal cortex*] [*Anatomy*] ... ZF

Zona Glomerulosa [*Of adrenal cortex*] [*Anatomy*] ... ZG

Zona Pellucida [*Embryology*] ... ZP

Zona Receptor Kinase [*An enzyme*] ... ZRK

Zona Reticularis [*Of adrenal cortex*] [*Anatomy*] ... ZR

Zonagen, Inc. [*NASDAQ symbol*] (SAG) ... ZONA

Zonagen, Inc. [*Associated Press*] (SAG) ... Zonagen

Zonal Echo Planar Imaging (DMAA) ... ZEPI

Zonal Electric Comfort Council [*Defunct*] (EA) ... ZECC

Zonal Elementary Circulative Mechanism ... ZECM

Zonal Gravity Harmonic ... ZGH

Zonal Harmonic ... ZH

Zonal Index ... ZI
Zonal Interdiction Missile (NVT) ... ZIM
Zonal Westerly Wind [*Climatology*] ... ZWW
Zonal Wind Stress [*Meteorology*] ... ZWS
Zonaras [*Twelfth century AD*] [*Classical studies*] (OCD) ... Zonar
Zonda [*Argentina*] [*Seismograph station code, US Geological Survey*] (SEIS) ... ZON
Zone ... Z
Zone (IDOE) ... z
Zone (WDMC) ... z
Zone ... ZN
Zone (IAA) ... ZO
Zone a Urbaniser en Priorite [*Priority Urbanization Zone*] [*French*] ... ZUP
Zone Air Defense Control Center (NATG) ... ZADCC
Zone Axis Pattern (MCD) ... ZAP
Zone Capacity ... ZC
Zone Code (IAA) ... Z
Zone Constant Angular Velocity [*Computer science*] ... ZCAV
Zone Controlled Deposition (IAA) ... ZCD
Zone Defense Integrated Active Capability (IEEE) ... ZODIAC
Zone Description ... ZD
Zone Effect ... ZE
Zone Electrophoresis [*Analytical biochemistry*] ... ZE
Zone Electrophoresis System ... ZES
Zone Field Selection [*Physics*] (IAA) ... ZFS
Zone Finder [*Telecommunications*] (OA) ... ZF
Zone Gradient Synchrotron [*Nickname: Ziggy*] ... ZGS
Zone Heat Flux ... ZHF
Zone Heater ... ZH
Zone Immunoelectrophoresis [*Analytical biochemistry*] ... ZIE
Zone Improvement Plan [*Postal Service code*] ... ZIP
Zone Information Protocol (BYTE) ... ZIP
Zone Information Socket (ACRL) ... ZIS
Zone Information Table [*Computer science*] (PCM) ... ZIT
Zone Marker ... Z
Zone Marker ... ZMKR
Zone Melting Model ... ZMM
Zone Meridian [*Lower or upper branch*] ... Z
Zone of Action ... ZA
Zone of Avoidance [*Astronomy*] ... ZOA
Zone of British Occupation [*Military*] ... ZBO
Zone of Convenience (ADA) ... ZOC
Zone of Convergence [*Aviation*] (DA) ... ZOC
Zone of Correct Reading (IAA) ... ZCR
Zone of Entry [*Military*] (AABC) ... ZOE
Zone of Exclusion (MCD) ... ZOE
Zone of Fire [*Military*] (AAG) ... ZF
Zone of Fire [*Military*] ... ZOF
Zone of Flow Establishment ... ZFE
Zone of Incorporation [*Environmental Protection Agency*] (ERG) ... ZOI
Zone of Inhibited Phage Plaques [*Immunology*] ... Zipp
Zone of Initial Dilution [*Effluents*] (EG) ... ZID
Zone of Interior [*Military*] ... Z of I
Zone of Interior [*Military*] ... ZI
Zone of Interior Armies ... ZIA
Zone of Nonproliferating Cells [*Cytology*] ... ZNC
Zone of Peace, Freedom and Neutrality [*ASEAN*] ... ZOPFAN
Zone of Peace, Freedom and Neutrality Declaration (EERA) ... ZOPFAN
Zone of Polarizing Activity [*Embryology, genetics*] ... ZPA
Zone of Reconnaissance ... ZOR
Zone of Responsibility ... ZR
Zone of Separation [*United Nations*] (INF) ... ZOS
Zone of the Interior Consumers Network (MCD) ... ZICON
Zone Petroleum Corp. [*Vancouver Stock Exchange symbol*] ... ZON
Zone Position Indicator (IAA) ... ZPI
Zone Project Officer ... ZPO
Zone Punch [*Computer science*] (IAA) ... ZP
Zone Refined ... ZR
Zone Reserved for Memory (NITA) ... ZRM
Zone Standard Time ... ZST
Zone Telephony Box [*Telecommunications*] (ACRL) ... ZTB
Zone Time [*Navigation*] ... ZT
Zone Transportation Officer [*Military*] ... ZTO
Zone Usage Measurement (WDAA) ... ZUM
Zone Wind Computer ... ZWC
Zone Wind Plotter ... ZWP
Zone-BIT [*Binary Digit*] **Recording** [*Computer science*] ... ZBR
Zoned Lens Lamp ... ZLL
Zone-Melting Recrystallization [*Crystallography*] ... ZMR
Zones of Communications [*Military*] ... Z of C
Zongo [*La Paz*] [*Bolivia*] [*Seismograph station code, US Geological Survey*] (SEIS) ... ZLP
Zongo [*La Paz*] [*Bolivia*] [*Seismograph station code, US Geological Survey*] (SEIS) ... ZOBO
Zonguldak [*Turkey ICAO location identifier*] (ICLI) ... LTAS
Zonguldak [*Turkey*] [*Airport symbol*] (AD) ... ZDK
Zoning [*Legal shorthand*] (LWAP) ... ZNG
Zoning Board of Approval [*Generic term*] (WGA) ... ZBA
Zonta Club [*Australia*] ... ZC
Zonta Club of Perth [*Western Australia*] ... ZCP
Zonta International (EA) ... ZI
Zonta International Districts (Australia) ... ZID(A)
Zoo Education Service [*South Australia*] ... ZES
Zoochemistry (ROG) ... ZOOCHEM
Zoogeography (ROG) ... ZOOGEOG
Zoological [*or Zoology*] ... ZOOL
Zoological Action Committee [*Defunct*] (EA) ... ZOOACT
Zoological Action Program [*Defunct*] (EA) ... ZAP
Zoological Board of Victoria [*Australia*] ... ZBV
Zoological Gardens ... ZG
Zoological Gardens Board [*Western Australia*] ... ZGB
Zoological Origin ... ZO
Zoological Record Online [*Bio Sciences Information Service*] [*Information service or system*] (IID) ... ZR
Zoological Record Outline ... ZRO
Zoological Records [*BioSciences Information Service*] ... ZREC
Zoological Society [*British*] ... ZS
Zoological Society of London [*British*] ... ZSL
Zoological Society of Philadelphia, PA [*Library symbol Library of Congress Obsolete*] (LCLS) ... PPZ
Zoological Society of Southern Africa [*See also DUSA*] [*Port Elizabeth, South Africa*] (EAIO) ... ZSSA
Zoological Station of Naples ... ZSN
Zoologische Staatssammlung Muenchen ... ZSM
Zoologisk Museum, University of Copenhagen [*Denmark*] ... ZMUC
Zoom Back [*Cinematography*] (WDMC) ... ZB
Zoom In [*Cinematography and Video*] ... Z/I
Zoom In [*Photography*] (NITA) ... ZI
Zoom/MODEM [*ZOOM Telephonics, Inc.*] ... ZM
Zoom Optical System ... ZOS
Zoom Optical Target Simulator (OA) ... ZOTS
Zoom Out [*Cinematography*] ... Z/O
Zoom Telephonics [*Vancouver Stock Exchange symbol*] ... ZMT
Zoom Telephonics [*NASDAQ symbol*] (TTSB) ... ZOOM
Zoom Telephonics, Inc. [*NASDAQ symbol*] (SAG) ... ZOOM
Zoom Telephonics, Inc. [*Associated Press*] (SAG) ... ZoomTl
Zoom Transfer Scope (OA) ... ZTS
Zoomed Video [*Toshiba*] (PCM) ... ZV
Zoomed Video Port (PCM) ... ZV Port
Zoomorphism (VRA) ... zmphm
Zoopathology (BARN) ... zoopath
Zoophytology (ROG) ... ZOOPH
Zoosporangia [*Botany*] ... ZS
Zorah Media Corp. [*Vancouver Stock Exchange symbol*] ... ZOR
Zoran Corp. [*Associated Press*] (SAG) ... Zoran
Zoran Corp. [*NASDAQ symbol*] (TTSB) ... ZRAN
Zoran Corp. [*NASDAQ symbol*] (SAG) ... ZRAN
Zorgo [*Burkina Faso*] [*ICAO location identifier*] (ICLI) ... DHEO
Zork Interactive Language [*Computer science*] ... ZIL
Zorrillos [*Peru*] [*ICAO location identifier*] (ICLI) ... SPLS
Zorritos [*Peru*] [*ICAO location identifier*] (ICLI) ... SPOS
Zose [*Republic of China*] [*Seismograph station code, US Geological Survey*] (SEIS) ... ZSC
Zoster Immune Globulin [*Immunology*] (MAH) ... Z/G
Zoster Immune Globulin [*Immunology*] ... ZIG
Zoster Immune Plasma [*Immunology*] ... ZIP
Zouar [*Chad*] [*ICAO location identifier*] (ICLI) ... FTTR
Zouche's Admiralty Jurisdiction [*A publication*] (DLA) ... Zouch Adm
Zouerate [*Mauritania*] [*ICAO location identifier*] (ICLI) ... GQPZ
Zouerate [*Mauritania*] [*Airport symbol*] (OAG) ... OUZ
Zouying [*China*] [*ICAO location identifier*] (ICLI) ... RCRA
Zoxazolamine Paralysis Time [*In experimental animals*] ... ZPT
Z-Seven Fund, Inc. [*Associated Press*] (SAG) ... Z Sevn
Z-Seven Fund, Inc. [*NASDAQ symbol*] (NQ) ... ZSEV
Zu Gott Mein Trost [*In God My Comfort*] [*Motto of Ernst, Duke of Braunschweig-Luneburg (1564-1611)*] [*German*] ... ZGMT
Zu Haenden [*Attention Of, Care Of, To Be Delivered To*] [*German*] (GPO) ... zH
Zu Haenden [*Attention Of, Care Of, To Be Delivered To*] [*German*] ... zHd
Zu Verfuegung [*At Disposal*] [*German*] [*Business term*] ... ZV
Zu [*or Zur*] **Zeit** [*At This Time*] [*German*] ... ZZ
Zu Zu [*Tennessee*] [*Seismograph station code, US Geological Survey Closed*] (SEIS) ... ZZT
Zucchini Yellow Fleck Virus [*Plant pathology*] ... ZYFV
Zucchini Yellow Mosaic Virus ... ZYMV
Zucker Diabetic Fatty [*Rat strain*] ... ZDF
Zuckerman-Moloff [*Sewage treatment method*] ... Z-M
Zuckung [*Contraction or spasm*] [*German Medicine*] ... Z
Zuender [*Fuze*] [*German military*] ... Z
Zuercher Bibel (BJA) ... Z
Zuercher Bibel (BJA) ... ZB
Zug und Zerschneidezuender [*Pull-and-Cut Igniter*] [*German military - World War II*] ... ZUZZ
Zugdidi [*Former USSR Seismograph station code, US Geological Survey Closed*] (SEIS) ... ZUG
Zugzuender [*Pull Igniter*] [*German military - World War II*] ... ZZ
Zugzwang Postal Chess Association (EA) ... ZPCA
Zuid Afrikaansche Republick Politie [*South African Republic Police*] (DSUE) ... ZARP
Zuiver Wentenschappelijk Orderzock [*Netherlands*] ... ZWO
Zuliana de Aviacion [*Venezuela*] [*ICAO designator*] (FAAC) ... ULA
Zulu [*Phonetic alphabet*] [*International*] (DSUE) ... Z
Zulu [*MARC language code Library of Congress*] (LCCP) ... zul
Zulu Time [*Greenwich Mean Time*] (AFM) ... Z
Zum Beispiel [*For Example*] [*German*] ... ZB
Zumba-Pucupamba [*Ecuador*] [*ICAO location identifier*] (ICLI) ... SEZP
Zung Depression Scale [*Psychiatry*] (DAVI) ... ZDS
Zung Measurement of Depression [*Scale*] ... ZMD
Zung Self-Rating Depression Scale [*Psychology*] ... ZS-RDS
Zung Self-Rating Scale [*For depression*] ... ZSRS
Zuni [*MARC language code Library of Congress*] (LCCP) ... zun

Zuni Energy [*Vancouver Stock Exchange symbol*] .... ZUE
Zuni, NM [*FM radio station call letters*] .... KSHI
Zuni Pueblo/Blackrock [*New Mexico*] [*ICAO location identifier*] (ICLI) .... KZUN
Zuni Pueblo, NM [*Location identifier FAA*] (FAAL) .... ZUN
Zurfund International Ltd. [*Vancouver Stock Exchange symbol*] .... ZUR
Zurich [*Switzerland ICAO location identifier*] (ICLI) .... LSAZ
Zurich [*Switzerland ICAO location identifier*] (ICLI) .... LSSW
Zurich [*Switzerland ICAO location identifier*] (ICLI) .... LSZH
Zurich [*Switzerland*] [*Airport symbol*] (OAG) .... ZRH
Zurich [*Switzerland*] [*Seismograph station code, US Geological Survey*]
(SEIS) .... ZUR
Zurich Energy Corp. [*Vancouver Stock Exchange symbol*] .... ZEC
Zurich, Mainz, Munich, Darmstadt [*A joint European university effort on ALGOL processors*] .... ZMMD
Zurich Provisional Relative Sunspot Number [*NASA*] .... ZPRSN
Zurich Reinsurance Centre [*NYSE symbol*] (TTSB) .... ZRC
Zurich Reinsurance Centre Holdings [*NYSE symbol*] (SPSG) .... ZRC
Zurich Reinsurance Centre Holdings [*Associated Press*] (SAG) .... ZurichR
Zurich Sunspot Number [*Astrophysics*] .... ZSN
Zurich-Lageren [*Switzerland*] [*Seismograph station code, US Geological Survey*] (SEIS) .... ZUL
Zurn Indus [*NYSE symbol*] (TTSB) .... ZRN
Zurn Industries, Inc. [*NYSE symbol*] (SPSG) .... ZRN
Zurn Industries, Inc. [*Associated Press*] (SAG) .... ZurnIn
Zusammen [*Together*] [*Chemistry*] .... (Z)
Zusammen [*Together*] [*Music*] .... ZUS
Zuse [*Calculator*] (HGAA) .... Z
Zusters van Liefe Jezus en Maria [*Sisters of Charity of Jesus and Mary - SCJM*] [*Belgium*] (EAIO) .... ZLJM
Zutendaal [*Belgium ICAO location identifier*] (ICLI) .... EBSL
Z'va Hagana Le'Israel [*Israel Defense Forces*] [*Hebrew*] .... ZAHAL
Zvishavane [*Zimbabwe*] [*ICAO location identifier*] (ICLI) .... FVSH
Zweeppartij [*Whipping Party*] [*Political party Belgium*] .... ZP
Zweibrucken [*Germany ICAO location identifier*] (ICLI) .... EDAM
Zweibrucken [*Germany ICAO location identifier*] (ICLI) .... EDEY
Zweig Fund [*NYSE symbol*] (SPSG) .... ZF
Zweig Fund [*Associated Press*] (SAG) .... Zweig
Zweig Total Return Fd [*NYSE symbol*] (TTSB) .... ZTR
Zweig Total Return Fund, Inc. [*NYSE symbol*] (CTT) .... ZTR
Zweig Total Return Fund, Inc. [*Associated Press*] (SAG) .... ZweigTl
Zweites Deutsches Fernsehen [*Television network*] [*West Germany*] .... ZDF

Zwiazek Ludowo-Narodowy [*Populist-Nationalist Alliance*] [*Poland Political party*] (PPE) .... ZLN
Zwischensatz [*Interpolation*] [*Music*] .... Zw
Zwischenscheibe [*Disk*] [*Also, called intermediate disk, Z band, and Z line*] [*Laboratory science*] (DAVI) .... Z
Zycad Corp. [*NASDAQ symbol*] (NQ) .... ZCAD
Zycad Corp. [*Associated Press*] (SAG) .... Zycad
Zycon Corp. [*NASDAQ symbol*] (SAG) .... ZCON
Zycon Corp. [*NASDAQ symbol*] (TTSB) .... ZCON
Zycon Corp. [*Associated Press*] (SAG) .... Zycon
Zydeco Energy [*NASDAQ symbol*] (TTSB) .... ZNRG
Zydeco Energy, Inc. [*NASDAQ symbol*] (SAG) .... ZNRG
Zydeco Energy, Inc. [*Associated Press*] (SAG) .... ZydcoE
Zydeco Energy, Inc. [*Associated Press*] (SAG) .... ZydecoE
Zydeco Energy Wrrt [*NASDAQ symbol*] (TTSB) .... ZNRGW
Zydowska Agencja Telegraficzna (BJA) .... ZAT
Zygion (DMAA) .... Zy
Zyglo-Fluorescent Penetrant .... ZFP
Zyglo-Fluorescent Penetrant Testing .... ZFPT
Zygo Corp. [*NASDAQ symbol*] (NQ) .... ZIGO
Zygo Corp. [*Associated Press*] (SAG) .... Zygo
Zygocactus Virus X [*Plant pathology*] .... ZVX
Zygomatic [*Otorhinolaryngology*] (DAVI) .... ZMC
Zygomaticomaxillary Complex [*Otorhinolaryngology*] (DAVI) .... ZMC
Zygote Intrafallopian Transfer [*Obstetrics*] .... ZIFT
Zygote Intrafallopian Tube Transfer [*Medicine*] (DMAA) .... ZIFT
Zygote Resources [*Vancouver Stock Exchange symbol*] .... ZYG
Zygotene (DMAA) .... zyg
Zygotene [*Deoxyribonucleic Acid*] [*Genetics*] (DOG) .... zyg
Zyloprim [*Burroughs Wellcome Co.*] [*Pharmacology*] (DAVI) .... Zylo
Zyma AG [*Switzerland*] [*Research code symbol*] .... Z
Zymbal Gland [*Anatomy*] .... ZG
Zymosan-Activated Serum [*Immunology*] .... ZAS
Zymosan-Activated Plasma Rabbit [*Medicine*] (DMAA) .... ZAP
Zymosan-Treated Serum [*Medicine*] (DMAA) .... ZTS
Zynaxis, Inc. [*NASDAQ symbol*] (SAG) .... ZNXS
Zynaxis, Inc. [*Associated Press*] (SAG) .... Zynaxis
Zytec Corp. [*NASDAQ symbol*] (SAG) .... ZTEC
Zytec Corp. [*Associated Press*] (SAG) .... Zytec
Zytec Systems, Inc. [*Toronto Stock Exchange symbol Vancouver Stock Exchange symbol*] .... ZSI
ZZ Top Fan Club (EA) .... ZZTFC